# 2003 Standard Catalog of WORLD COINS

by Chester L. Krause and Clifford Mishler ▪ Colin R. Bruce II, Senior Editor

## 1901-Present

**Randy Thern**
Numismatic Catalog
Supervisor

**l J. Borgmann**
v Issues Editor

**George Cuhaj**
Managing Editor

**Joel T. Edler**
U.S. Market Analyst

Ron Guth, Dr. Dennis G. Rainey, Dr. R. A. Rodgers

**UNCIRCULATED VALUATIONS**

The uncirculated valuations represented in this edition are for typical quality specimens, for some of the more popularly collected series. Brilliant uncirculated (BU), or superior quality examples may easily command 10% to 50% premiums, or even greater where particularly popular or rare types or dates are concerned.

**BULLION VALUE (BV) MARKET VALUATIONS**

Valuations for all platinum, gold, palladium or silver coins of the more common, basically bullion types, or those possessing only modest numismatic premiums are presented in this edition based on market levels of $460 per ounce for platinum, $278 for gold, $380 for palladium and $4.25 per ounce for silver. Wherever the letters "BV" - Bullion Value - appear in a value column, that particular issue in the condition indicated generally trades at or near the bullion value of its precious metal content. Further information on using this catalog to evaluate platinum, gold, palladium or silver coins amid fluctuating precious metal market conditions is presented in the introduction.

*"Perfection is immutable, but for things imperfect,*
*to change is the way to perfect them."*

*- Owen Feltham (1602-1668)*

## 2003 Standard Catalog of®

# WORLD COINS

by Chester L. Krause and Clifford Mishler ▪ Colin R. Bruce II, Senior Editor

Published in the United States by

krause publications
700 East State Street • Iola, WI 54990-0001
715/445-2214 • FAX: 715/445-4087 www.krause.com


Library of Congress Catalog Card Number: 79-940940
International Standard Book Number: 0-87349-401-6

Printed in the United States of America

# TABLE OF CONTENTS



# ADVERTISING INDEX

# 30 YEARS OF KNOWLEDGE

Welcome to the 30th Edition of the *Standard Catalog of World Coins*. What began in 1972 as a single-volume chronicle of world coinage from the mid-1800's to the first issues of the 1970's has grown into a century-specific, four-volume set that catalogs a wealth of numismatic history spanning over four centuries, from 1601 to the dawn of the 21st century. What you hold in your hands is the oldest sibling in that family of numismatic reference materials.

Through the years, research conducted by contributors and staff editors gradually expanded the parameters of the individual coin listings, introducing earlier eras and sometimes somewhat esoteric issues. As a result, the database from which annual editions of the *Standard Catalog of World Coins* developed had proliferated to include the first half of the 19th century, then the 18th and 17th centuries, on a selective basis as useful and reliable listings could be utilized.

Eventually supplementing the circulating coin listings were such specialized categories as Patterns, Piefonts, Trial Strikes, Medallic and Pretender issues, related Token coinage, NCLT's, and Collector and Presentation Sets - any "coins" individuals pursuing an interest in a given country might logically expect to encounter.

Annual editions of the Standard Catalog gradually developed growing pains, becoming heavy and unwieldy. In an effort to manage the swelling tome, lighter-weight paper was introduced, listings were condensed, photos were overlaid, and coverage of the more esoteric realms were selectively removed from edition to edition. By the mid-1990's, coverage was, for all intents and purposes, devoted exclusively to regular issue and commemorative coinages of the 19th and 20th centuries. A wealth of available, desirable information on world coinages had been placed on hold. The demand for the return of this excised data to the listings mounted as editions passed. Effective with the 24th edition of the *Standard Catalog of World Coins,* we resolved that the logical solution to the content vs. capacity dilemma was to dedicate individual volumes to the numismatic evolution of each century.

With the explosion of world commemorative programs and the steady accumulation of data, the resulting mass of the 20th Century *Standard Catalog of World Coins* earned the nicknames the "telephone book" and the "bible" of world numismatics. The astounding 2,304-page 30th Edition maintains this reputation, representing a third of the nearly 7,000-page Standard Catalog database.

The volume before you embraces within the confines of the 20th and now 21st centuries comprehensive, detailed coverage that is complete with detailed treatments of the aforementioned specialized categories. But again, with the advent of a new century and the continuing march of new issues, the 20th century catalog is pressing its boundaries.

If your collecting interests pull you back to earlier eras, we refer you to the sister volumes, which explore coverage by century. The 19th Century (1801-1900), 18th Century (1701-1800) and 17th Century (1601-1700) editions provide similar comprehensive and detailed representation. These three volumes, plus the present 20th century volume, provide collectors and dealers with a comprehensive, nearly 7,000-page source - a veritable library of international numismatic history with the user-friendly convenience of century-specific data.

We are pleased to offer the numismatic enthusiast this living and breathing reference set, which authoritatively embraces exhaustive and definitive treatments of the diverse and sometimes challenging scopes of coverage spanning a rich, four-century run of world coinage. This resource presents a body of knowledge that will augment and stimulate your future interests. In the presentation of successor editions of each as the marketplace demands, the set becomes a dynamic, scholarly effort to the measure of what you, the user, contribute to make them something more than what they presently are. Toward that end, you are invited - make that encouraged - as were those who became users of the first *Standard Catalog of World Coins* 30 years ago, to suggest revisions and enhancements.

## New Style and Function for the 21st Century

The present edition features thousands of changes and enhancements to previous listings. Tens of thousands of revised and updated valuations, as well as hundreds of fully illustrated listings of new regular-issue and commemorative coins released by world mints over the past couple of years represent only a fraction of the improvements offered in this edition. A completely revised format has been employed for this 30th edition, which features an easier-to-use alphabetical organization, full composition details and denominations included with each type listing, a renewed emphasis on Political breakdowns and more distinct separation by coinage types. The perceptive user of the Standard Catalog of World Coins will also appreciate myriad revisions and improvements of the descriptive text incorporated in the listings. These major rearrangements have been designed to make the catalog more useful to those of us who love the study of coins.

Welcome to the complete, one-volume reference for 20th and 21st century world coins collecting — "basically a compilation of the digested knowledge," as stated in the introduction to the first edition, "which students of the numismatic science have contributed to the coin collecting hobby through the years," enhanced through the incorporation of original contributions that have substantially enriched the scope of awareness...humble still, but hopefully a worthy successor to the ideals embodied in the publication of the first *Standard Catalog of World Coins* in 1972.

- Clifford Mishler

# STANDARD INTERNATIONAL NUMERAL SYSTEMS



| WESTERN | 0 | ½ | 1 | 2 | 3 | 4 | 5 | 6 | 7 | 8 | 9 | 10 | 50 | 100 | 500 | 1000 |
|---|---|---|---|---|---|---|---|---|---|---|---|---|---|---|---|---|
| ROMAN | | | I | II | III | IV | V | VI | VII | VIII | IX | X | L | C | D | M |
| ARABIC-TURKISH | ٠ | ١/٢ | ١ | ٢ | ٣ | ٤ | ٥ | ٦ | ٧ | ٨ | ٩ | ١٠ | ٥٠ | ١٠٠ | ٥٠٠ | ١٠٠٠ |
| MALAY—PERSIAN | ٠ | ١/٢ | ١ | ٢ | ٣ | ۴ | ۵ | ٦ or ۶ | ٧ | ٨ | ٩ | ١٠ | ۵٠ | ١٠٠ | ۵٠٠ | ١٠٠٠ |
| EASTERN ARABIC | ۰ | ½ | ۱ | ۲ | ۳ | ۴ | ۵ | ۶ | ۷ | ۸ | ۹ | ۱۰ | ۵۰ | ۱۰۰ | ۵۰۰ | ۱۰۰۰ |
| HYDERABAD ARABIC | ۰ | ١/٢ | ١ | ٢ | ٣ | ۴ | ۵ | ۶ | ۷ | ۸ | ۹ | ۱۰ | ۵۰ | ۱۰۰ | ۵۰۰ | ۱۰۰۰ |
| INDIAN (Sanskrit) | ० | १/२ | १ | २ | ३ | ४ | ५ | ६ | ७ | ८ | ९ | १० | ५० | १०० | ५०० | १००० |
| ASSAMESE | ০ | ১/২ | ১ | ২ | ৩ | ৪ | ৫ | ৬ | ৭ | ৮ | ৯ | ১০ | ৫০ | ১০০ | ৫০০ | ১০০০ |
| BENGALI | ০ | ১/২ | ১ | ২ | ৩ | ৪ | ৫ | ৬ | ৭ | ৮ | ৯ | ১০ | ৫০ | ১০০ | ৫০০ | ১০০০ |
| GUJARATI | ૦ | ૧/૨ | ૧ | ૨ | ૩ | ૪ | ૫ | ૬ | ૭ | ૮ | ૯ | ૧૦ | ૫૦ | ૧૦૦ | ૫૦૦ | ૧૦૦૦ |
| KUTCH | ० | १/२ | १ | २ | ३ | ४ | ५ | ६ | ७ | ८ | ९ | १० | ५० | १०० | ५०० | १००० |
| DEVAVNAGRI | ० | १/२ | १ | २ | ३ | ४ | ५ | ६ or ६ | ७ | ८ | ९ or ९ | १० | ५० | १०० | ५०० | १००० |
| NEPALESE | ० | १/२ | १ or १ | २ | ३ | ४ | ५ or ५ | ६ | ७ | ८ or ८ | ९ or ९ | १० | ५० | १०० | ५०० | १००० |
| TIBETAN | ༠ | ༡/༢ | ༡ | ༢ | ༣ | ༤ | ༥ | ༦ | ༧ | ༨ | ༩ | ༡༠ | ༥༠ | ༡༠༠ | ༥༠༠ | ༡༠༠༠ |
| MONGOLIAN | ᠐ | ᠑/᠒ | ᠑ | ᠒ | ᠓ | ᠔ | ᠕ | ᠖ | ᠗ | ᠘ | ᠙ | ᠑᠐ | ᠕᠐ | ᠑᠐᠐ | ᠕᠐᠐ | ᠑᠐᠐᠐ |
| BURMESE | ၀ | ၁/၂ | ၁ | ၂ | ၃ | ၄ | ၅ | ၆ | ၇ | ၈ | ၉ | ၁၀ | ၅၀ | ၁၀၀ | ၅၀၀ | ၁၀၀၀ |
| THAI-LAO | ๐ | ๑/๒ | ๑ | ๒ | ๓ | ๔ | ๕ | ๖ | ๗ | ๘ | ๙ | ๑๐ | ๕๐ | ๑๐๐ | ๕๐๐ | ๑๐๐๐ |
| JAVANESE | ꧐ | | ꧑ | ꧒ | ꧓ | ꧔ | ꧕ | ꧖ | ꧗ | ꧘ | ꧙ | ꧑꧐ | ꧕꧐ | ꧑꧐꧐ | ꧕꧐꧐ | ꧑꧐꧐꧐ |
| ORDINARY CHINESE JAPANESE-KOREAN | 零 | 半 | 一 | 二 | 三 | 四 | 五 | 六 | 七 | 八 | 九 | 十 | 十五 | 百 | 百五 | 千 |
| OFFICIAL CHINESE | | | 壹 | 貳 | 叁 | 肆 | 伍 | 陸 | 柒 | 捌 | 玖 | 拾 | 拾伍 | 佰 | 佰伍 | 仟 |
| COMMERCIAL CHINESE | | | 〡 | 〢 | 〣 | 〤 | 〥 | 〦 | 〧 | 〨 | 〩 | 十 | 〥十 | 〡百 | 〥百 | 〡千 |
| KOREAN | | 반 | 일 | 이 | 삼 | 사 | 오 | 육 | 칠 | 팔 | 구 | 십 | 오십 | 백 | 오백 | 천 |
| GEORGIAN | | | ა | ბ | გ | დ | ე | ვ | ზ | ჱ | თ | ი | ნ | რ | ფ | ჩ |
| | | | ლ (11) | კ (20) | ლ (30) | მ (40) | ნ (50) | ჲ (60) | ო (70) | პ (80) | ჟ (90) | რ (100) | ს (200) ტ (300) | უ (400) | ქ (600) ღ (700) | ყ (800) |
| ETHIOPIAN | ◆ | | ፩ | ፪ | ፫ | ፬ | ፭ | ፮ | ፯ | ፰ | ፱ | ፲ | ፶ | ፻ | ፭፻ | ፲፻ |
| | | | | ፳ (20) | ፴ (30) | ፵ (40) | | ፷ (60) | ፸ (70) | ፹ (80) | ፺ (90) | | | | | |
| HEBREW | | | א | ב | ג | ד | ה | ו | ז | ח | ט | י | נ | ק | תק | |
| | | | | כ (20) | ל (30) | מ (40) | | ס (60) | ע (70) | פ (80) | צ (90) | | ר (200) ש (300) | ת (400) | תר (600) תש (700) | תת (800) |
| GREEK | | | Α | Β | Γ | Δ | Ε | ΣΤ | Ζ | Η | Θ | Ι | Ν | Ρ | Φ | Α |
| | | | | Κ (20) | Λ (30) | Μ (40) | Ξ (60) | Ο (70) | Π (80) | | Σ (200) | Τ (300) | Υ (400) | Χ (600) | Ψ (700) | Ω (800) |

# ACKNOWLEDGMENTS

Many individuals have contributed countless changes, which have been incorporated into previous and now this thirtieth edition. While all may not be acknowledged, special appreciation is extended to the following who have exhibited a special enthusiasm for this edition.

## SPECIAL CONTRIBUTORS

Ron Guth, Dr. Dennis G. Rainey, Dr. K. A. Rodgers

Dr. Lawrence A. Adams
Esko Ahlroth
Stephen Album
Antonio Alessandrini
Don Bailey
Paul Baker
Yuri Barshay
Mitchell A. Battino
Albert Beck
Dr. Anton Belcev
Richard Benson
Peter N. Berger
Allen G. Berman
Wolfgang Bertsch
Jack Beymer
Joseph Boling
Larry Briggs
Klaus Bronny
Chris Budesa
Doru Calin
Peter A. Chase
Jay Cline
Scott E. Cordry
Joao Cosme
Jerry Crain
Lee Crane
Vincent Craven-Bartle
Raymond E. Czahor
Howard A. Daniel III
Eric G. Dawson, M.D.
Jean-Paul Divo
Yossi Dotan
James R. Douglas
Richard G. Doty
Sheridan Downey
Kevin L. Doyle
Dr. Jan M. Dyroff
Graham P. Dyer
Stephen Eccles
Wilhelm Eglseer
Esko Ekman
Jack Erb
Michael Findlay
George A. Fisher, Jr.
Horace P. Flatt
Joe Flores
Luis H. Flores
Donald T. Fox
Wayne Freese
Arthur Friedberg
K. M. Froseth
Vladimir Gamboa
Eng. Lajos Gergely
Dennis Gill
Lawrence S. Goldberg
Mark Goldberg
David R. Gotkin
Brian Greer
Mario Guiterrez Minera
Ron Guth
Marcel Häberling
Ray Hackett
Flemming L. Hansen
Brian Hannon
David Harrison
Martin Rodney Hayter
Istvan Hegedus
James H. Higby
Wade Hinderling
Joe Hollingsworth
Anton Holt
Nicolae Hridan
Serge Huard
Charles L. Huff
Dr. Norman Jacobs
Ton Jacobs
David Jen
Roberto Jovel
William M. Judd
Robert W. Julian
Borge R. Juul
Alex Kaglyan
Craig Keplinger
E. James Kindrake
Peter Kraneveld
Peter Krix
Russell Kruzell
Thomas Lautz
Lee Shin Song
Nirat Lertchitvikul
Richard Lobel
Jim Long
Richard A. Long
Rudi Lotter
Alan Luedeking
Ma Tak Wo
Enrico Manara
Virg Marshall
Jeff Means
Jürgen Mikeska
Harry Miller
Juozas Minikevicius
Robert Mish
Ernie Mix
Ing. Benjamin M. Mizrachi R.
Dr. Richard Montrey
Paul Montz
Steve Musil
Hitoshi Nagai
Vladimir Nastich
Oen E. Nelson
N. Douglas Nicol
Andrew Oberbillig
Jim O'Donnell
Wayne N. Palmer
Gus A. Pappas
Dick Parker
Marc Pelletier
Juan Pena
Kirsten F. Petersen
Jens Pilegaard
Richard Ponterio
Kent Ponterio
Mircea Raicopol
Dr. Dennis G. Rainey
Kavan Ratnatunga
Tony Raymond
Nick Rhodes
Dana Roberts

Dr. K. A. Rodgers
William M. Rosenblum
Clinton P. Rusaw
Arnaldo Russo
John Sacher
Erwin Schaffer
Gerhard Schön
Dr. Wolfgang Schuster
Michael Sedgwick
Ladislav Sin
Evzen Sknouril
Bruce W. Smith
Jørgen Sømod
William F. Spengler
Bob Steinberg
Benjamin Swagerty
Alim A. Sumana
M. Louis Teller
Tonin Thaci
Rick Tomaska
Anthony Tumonis
Robert van Bebber
J. L. Van der Schueren
J. J. Van Grover
Erik J. Van Loon
Igor Victorov-Orlov (deceased)
Helen Wallace
R.W. Walter
Justin C. Wang
John Wells
Paul Welz
Stewart Westdal
J. Hugh Witherow
Joseph Zaffern
Roger Zago

## AUCTION HOUSES AND DISTRIBUTORS

David Akers Numismatics
Bowers & Merena, Inc.
Educational Coin Company
Heritage Numismatic Auctions
Hess-Divo Ltd.
Gerhard Hirsch
Thomas Høiland Møntauktion
Fritz Rudolf Künker
Leu Numismatik AG
Münzenhandlung Harald Möller, GmbH
Noble Numismatics, Pty. Ltd.
Omni Trading B. V.
Ponterio & Associates
Laurens Schulman, b.v.
Sotheby's
Stack's
Superior Galleries
UBS, AG
World Wide Coins of California

## SOCIETIES, INSTITUTIONS AND INTERNATIONAL MINTS

American Numismatic Association
American Numismatic Society
Austrian Mint
British Museum
British Royal Mint
Central Bank of The Russian Federation
Johns Hopkins University
Mint of Finland
Norwegian Mint
Numismatics International
Pobjoy Mint
Royal Canadian Mint
Royal Dutch Mint
Singapore Mint
Smithsonian Institution
U.S. Mint
Vatican City Government Numismatic Office

## PUBLICATIONS

*The Statesman's Yearbook, 2001*.
137th Edition
by Barry Turner, editor, The Statesman's Yearbook Office, The Macmillan Press Ltd., 25 Eccleston, Place, London SW1W 9NF, United Kingdom
(Statistical and Historical Annual of the States of the World)

### A special thanks to these members of the Krause Publications production team:

Bonnie Tetzlaff - Database Publishing Specialist
Sandra Morrison
Deb McCue
Suzanne Olkowski
Cari Ullom
Cheryl Hayburn - Pre-Press Operations Manager
Gordon Ullom
Sherry Dopp
Kay Sanders
Ethel Thulien
Sally Olson
Stacy Bloch

# COUNTRY INDEX

## A



## B



## C



## D

# "The I.A.P.N. dealer, your guide to the world of numismatics"

More than one hundred of the world's most respected coin dealers are members of the I.A.P.N. (International Association of Professional Numismatists). I.A.P.N. members offer the collector an exceptional selection of quality material, expert cataloguing, outstanding service and realistic pricing.
The I.A.P.N. also maintains the International Bureau for the Suppression of Counterfeit Coins (I.B.S.C.C.) which for a fee can provide expert opinions on the authenticity of coins submitted to it.
A booklet listing the names, addresses and specialities of all I.A.P.N. members is available without charge by writing to the I.A.P.N. General Secretary, Jean-Luc Van der Schueren, 14 rue de la Bourse, B-1000 BRUXELLES, Belgium. Tel: +32-2-513 3400; Fax: +32-2-512 2528; E-mail: iapnsecret@compuserve.com; Web site: http://www.iapn.ch.

**ARGENTINA**

DERMAN, Alberto José
Señor Alberto José Derman
Avenida Corrientes 368
BUENOS AIRES

**AUSTRALIA**

NOBLE NUMISMATICS Pty Ltd.
Mr. Jim Noble
169 Macquarie Street, SYDNEY, NSW 2000

**AUSTRIA**

HERINEK, Gerhard
Josefstadterstrasse, 27, 1082 WIEN VIII
MOZELT, Erich
Herr Erich Mozelt
Postfach 19, 1043 WIEN

**BELGIUM**

FRANCESCHI & FILS. B.
M. Druso Franceschi
Rue de la Croix-de-Fer, 10 B - 1000 BRUXELLES
M. Jean Elsen s.a.
Avenue de Tervueren, 65, B - 1040 BRUXELLES
VAN DER SCHUEREN, Jean-Luc
Rue de la Bourse, 14, B - 1000 BRUXELLES

**CANADA**

RANDY WEIR NUMISMATICS Ltd.
P.O. Box 64577, UNIONVILLE, ONT.L3R OM9

**EGYPT**

BAJOCCHI JEWELLERS
Cav. Pietro Bajocchi
Abdel Khalek Sarwat Street, 45, 11511 CAIRO

**ENGLAND**

A.H. BALDWIN & SONS Ltd.
Mr. A.H.E. Baldwin
Adelphi Terrace, 11, GB - LONDON, WC2N 6BJ
DAVIES Ltd
Mr. Paul Davies
P.O. Box 17, GB - ILKLEY, W.Yorksh., LS29 8TZ
EIMER, Christopher
Mr. Christopher Eimer
P.O. Box 352, GB - LONDON, NW11 7RF
FORMAT OF BIRMINGHAM Ltd.
Mr. Garry Charman
Bennetts Hill, 18, GB - BIRMINGHAM, B2 5QJ
KNIGHTSBRIDGE COINS
Mr. Stephen C. Fenton
Duke Street, 43, St. James's, GB - LONDON, SW1Y 6DD
LUBBOCK & SON Ltd.
Mr. Richard M. Lubbock
Regent Street, 315, GB - LONDON, W1B 2HR
RUDD Chris
Mr. Chris Rudd
P.O. Box 222, GB - AYLSHAM, Norfolk, NR11 6TY
SPINK & SON Ltd.
Mr. John Pett
69 Southampton Row, Bloomsbury,
GB - LONDON WC1B 4ET

**FRANCE**

BOURGEY, Sabine
Rue Drouot, 7, F - 75009 PARIS
BURGAN, Claude - Maison FLORANGE
Rue du 4 Septembre, 8, F - 75002 PARIS
MAISON PLATT S.A.
M. Gerard Barre
B.P. 2612
F - 75026 Cedex 01 PARIS
NUMISMATIQUE & CHANGE DE PARIS
Mme Annette Vinchon
Rue de la Bourse, 3, F - 75002 PARIS
O.G.N.
M. Pierre Crinon
Rue de Richelieu, 64, F - 75002 PARIS
POINSIGNON-NUMISMATIQUE (A.)
M. Alain Poinsignon
Rue des Francs Bourgeois, 4, F - 67000 STRASBOURG
SILBERSTEIN, Claude, COMPTOIR de NUMISMATIQUE
M. Claude Silberstein
Rue Vivienne, 39, F - 75002 PARIS
SPES NUMISMATIQUE
M. Alain Weil
Rue de Richelieu, 54, F - 75001 PARIS
VINCHON-NUMISMATIQUE
M. Jean Vinchon
Rue de Richelieu, 77, F - 75002 PARIS

**GERMANY**

DILLER, Johannes
Herr Johannes Diller
Postfach 70 04 29, D - 81304 MUNCHEN
FRITZ RUDOLF KUNKER MUNZENHANDLUNG
Gutenbergstrasse, 23, D - 49076 OSNABRUCK
GARLICH, Kurt B.
Herr Kurt B. Garlich
Albert Schweizer Strasse, 24A, D - 63303 DREIEICH-GOTZENHAIN
GIESSENER MUNZHANDLUNG DIETER GORNY GmbH
Herr Dieter Gorny
Maximihansplatz, 20, D - 80333 MUNCHEN
HIRSCH NACHF, (Gerhard)
Frau Dr. Francisca Bernheimer
Promenadeplatz, 10/II, D - 80333 MUNCHEN
JACQUIER, Paul-Frances
Honsellstrasse, 8, D - 77694 KEHL am RHEIN
KAISER MUNZFACHGESCHAFT (Rudiger)
Herr Rudiger Kaiser
Mittelweg, 54, D - 60318 FRANKFURT
KRICHELDORF NACHF, (H.H.)
Herr Volker Kricheldorf
Gunterstalstrasse, 16, D - 79102 FREIBURG i. Br.
KURPFALZISCHE MUNZHANDLUNG - KPM
Herr H. Gehrig
Augusta-Anlage, 52, D - 68165 MANNHEIM
LANZ NUMISMATIK
Dr. Hubert Lanz
Luitpoldblock - Maximiliansplatz, 10, D - 80333 MUNCHEN
MENZEL, Niels
Dachsteinweg 12, D - 12107 BERLIN-MARIENDORF
MUNZEN- UND MEDAILLENHANDLUNG STUTGART
Herr Stefan Sonntag
Charlottenstrasse, 4, D - 70182 STUTTGART
MUNZENETAGE - ANTIKE NUMISMATIK
Herr Dr. Michael Brandt
Marktplatz 14, D - 70173 STUTTGART
NEUMANN GmbH (Ernst)
Herr Ernst Neumann
Watteplatz, 6, D - 89312 GUNZBURG
MANFRED OLDING MUNZENHANDLUNG
Herr Manfred Olding
Goldbreede 14, D - 49078 OSNABRUCK
PEUS NACHF, (Dr. Busso)
Herr Dieter Raab
Bornwiesenweg, 34, D - 60322 FRANKFURT/M
RITTER MUNZHANDLUNG GmbH
Herr J. Ritter
Postfach 24 01 26, D - 40090 DUSSELDORF
TIETJEN & Co.
Herr Detlef Tietjen
Spitalerstrasse, 30, D - 20095 HAMBURG
WESTFALISCHE AUKTIONSGESELLSCHAFT
Herr Udo Gans Nordring 22, D - 59821 ARNSBERG

**ISRAEL**

EIDELSTEIN, Adolfo
P.O. Box 5135, 31051 HAIFA
QEDAR, Shraga, NUMISMATIST
Mr. Shraga Qedar
P.O. Box 520, 91004 JERUSALEM

**ITALY**

BARANOWSKY s.a.s.
Dott. Vincenzo FILONARDI
Via del Corso, 184, I - 00187 ROMA
BERNARDI, Giulio S.R.L.
Sign. Gianni Paoletti
Casella Postale 560, I - 34121 TRIESTE
CRIPPA NUMISMATICA S.A.S.
Sign. Paòlo Crippa
Via degli-Omenoni, 2, I - 20121 MILANO
DE FALCO, Alberto
Corso Umberto, 24, I - 80138 NAPOLI
FALLANI, Carlo-Maria
Via del Babuino, 58a, I - 00187 ROMA
MARCHESI GINO & FIGLIO
Sign. Giuseppe Marchesi
Viale Pietramellara, 35, I - 40121 BOLOGNA

PAOLUCCI, Raffaele
Via San Francesco, 154, I - 35121 PADOVA
RATTO, Marco
Via A. Manzoni, 14 (Palazzo Trivulzio), I - 20121 MILANO
RINALDI, Marco
Via Cappello, 23 (Casa di Giulietta), I - 37121 VERONA

**JAPAN**

DARUMA INTERNATIONAL GALLERIES
Mr. Yuji Otani
2-16-32-701, Takanawa, Minato-ku, TOKYO 108-0074
TAISEI COINS CORPORATION
Mr. Masahiro Oka
Nishino Kinryoo Bldg., 4 F, 4-9-4
Hacchobori, Chuo-Ku, TOKYO 104-0032
WORLD COINS JAPAN
Mr. Eiichi Ishii
1-15-5, Hamamatsu-cho, Minato-ku, TOKYO 105-0013

**LUXEMBOURG**

PROBST, Romain
M. Romain Probst
20, rue J.P. Kommes, L - 6988 HOSTERT

**MONACO**

EDITIONS VICTOR GADOURY
M. Francesco Pastrone
57 rue Grimaldi, "Le Panorama", MC - 98000 MONACO
LE LOUIS D'OR
M. Romolo Vescovi
Avenue des Papalins, 9, MC - 98000 MONACO

**NETHERLANDS**

MEVIUS NUMISBOOKS INTERNATIONAL BV
Mr. Johan Mevius
Oosteinde, 97, NL - 7671 AT VRIEZENVEEN
SCHULMAN BV, Laurens
Brinklaan, 84a, NL - 1404 GM BUSSUM
WESTERHOF, Jille Binne
Mr. Jille Binne Westerhof
Trekpad, 38-40, NL - 8742 KP BURGWERD

**NORWAY**

OSLO MYNTHANDEL AS
Mr. Jan Olav Aamlid
Postboks 355 Sentrum, N - 0101 OSLO
NUMISPORTO LDA
Mr. Ferreira Leite
Av. Combatentes Grande Guerra 610 Lj6,
P - 4200-186 PORTO

**SINGAPORE**

TAISEI STAMPS & COINS (S) PTE LTD.
Mr B.H. Lim
116 Middle Rd.#09-02, ICB Enterpr.House, 188972
SINGAPORE

**SPAIN**

CALICO, X. & F.
Senor Don Xavier Calico
Plaza del Angel, 2, E - 08002 BARCELONA
JANO S.L.
Mr. Juan R. Cayon
Alcala, 35, E - 28014 MADRID
SEGARRA, Fernando P. Senor Don Fernando P. Segarra
Plaza Mayor 26, E - 28012 MADRID
VICO, S.A. (Jesus)
Mr. Jesus Vico
Jorge Juan n 83 Duplicado, E - 28009 MADRID

**SWEDEN**

B. AHLSTROM MYNTHANDEL AB
Mr. Bjarne Ahlstrom
P.O. Box 7662, S - 103 94 STOCKHOLM
NORDLINDS MYNTHANDEL AB
Mr. Hans Hirsch
P.O. Box 5132, S - 102 43 STOCKHOLM

**SWITZERLAND**

ADOLPH HESS AG
Herr H.J. Schramm
Postfach 7070, CH - 8023 ZURICH
HESS-DIVO AG
M. Jean-Paul Divo
Postfach 7070, CH - 8023 ZURICH
LEU NUMISMATIK AG
Herr Heiner Stolz
Postfach 4738, CH - 8022 ZURICH
MUNZEN UND MEDAILLEN AG
Dr. Hans Voegtli
Postfach 3647, CH - 4002 BASEL
NUMISMATICA ARS CLASSICA AG
M. Roberto Russo
Postfach 745, CH - 8025 ZURICH
STERNBERG AG (Frank)
Mrs. Claudia Sternberg
Schanzengasse, 10 (Bhf. Stadelhofen), CH - 8001 ZURICH

**UNITED STATES OF AMERICA**

BASOK, Alexander
Mr. Alexander Basok
1954 First Street #186, HIGHLAND PARK, IL 60035
BERK Ltd (Harlan J.)
North Clark Street, 31, CHICAGO, IL 60602
BOWERS AND MERENA GALLERIES, INC.
P.O. Box 1224, WOLFEBORO, NH 03894
BULLOWA, C. E. - COINHUNTER
Mrs. C.E. Bullowa (Mrs. Earl E. Moore)
1616 Walnut Street, Suite 2112,
PHILADELPHIA, PA 19103
COIN AND CURRENCY INSTITUTE INC.
Mr. Arthur Friedberg
P.O. Box 1057, CLIFTON, NJ 07014
COIN GALLERIES
Mr. Jan Eric Blamberg
123 West 57th Street, NEW YORK, NY 10019
CRAIG, Freeman
P.O. Box 4176, SAN RAFAEL, CA 94913
DAVISSON'S LTD.
Dr. Allan Davisson, COLD SPRING, MN 56320-1050
DUNIGAN, Mike
5332 Birchman, FORT WORTH, TX 76107
FORD, John J. Jr.
Mr. John J. Ford Jr.
P.O. Box 10317, PHOENIX, AZ 85064
FREEMAN & SEAR
Mr. Robert D. Freeman
P.O. Box 641352, LOS ANGELES, CA 90064-6352
FROSETH INC. (K.M.)
P.O. Box 23116, MINNEAPOLIS, MN 55423
GILLIO INC. (Ronald J.) - GOLDMUNZEN INTERNATIONAL
State Street, 1103, SANTA BARBARA, CA 93101
HARVEY, Stephen
Mr. Stephen Harvey
P.O. Box 3778, BEVERLY HILLS, CA 90212
HINDERLING, Wade
P.O. Box 606, MANHASSET, N.Y. 11030
JONATHAN K. KERN Co.
441 South Ashland Avenue, LEXINGTON, KY 40502-2114
KOVACS, Frank L.
P.O. Box 25300, SAN MATEO, CA 94402
KREINDLER, B. & H.
White Birch Drive, 15, Dix Hills, NY 11746
MALTER & Co INC.. (Joel L.)
Mr. Joel Malter
17005 Ventura Boulevard, ENCINO, CA 91316
MARGOLIS, Richard
P.O. Box 2054, TEANECK, NJ 07666
MARKOV, Dmitry, COINS & MEDALS
Mr. Dmitry Markov
P.O. Box 950, NEW YORK, NY 10272
MILCAREK, Dr. Ron
P.O. Box 1028, GREENFIELD, MA 01302
PONTERIO & ASSOCIATES, INC.
1818 Robinson Avenue, SAN DIEGO, CA 92103
RARCOA, INC.
Mr. E. Milas
6262 South Route, 83, WILLOWBROOK, IL 60514
RARE COIN GALLERIES
Mr. Robert van Bebber
P.O. Box 569, GLENDALE, CA 91209
ROSENBLUM William M./RARE COINS
P.O. Box 355, EVERGREEN, CO 80437-0355
RYNEARSON, Dr. Paul
P.O. Box 4009, MALIBU, CA 90264
SINGER, Dr. Gordon Andreas
P.O. Box 235 GREENBELT, MD 20768-0235
STACK'S
Mr. Harvey Stack
123 West 57th Street, NEW YORK, NY 10019
STEPHENS INC., (Karl)
Mr. Karl Stephens
P.O. Box 3038, FALLBROOK, CA 92088
STREINER, Eric Inc.
119 West 57th Street, Suite 1218, NEW YORK, NY 10019
SUBAK INC.
Mr. Carl Subak
22 West Monroe Street, Room 1506, CHICAGO, IL 60603
TELLER NUMISMATIC ENTERPRISES
Mr. M. Louis Teller
16027 Ventura Boulevard, Suite 606, ENCINO, CA 91436
WADDELL, Edward J. Ltd.
Mr. Edward J. Waddell Jr.
P.O. Box 3759, FREDERICK, MD 21705-3759
WORLD-WIDE COINS OF CALIFORNIA
Mr. James F. Elmen
P.O. Box 3684, SANTA ROSA, CA 95402

**VENEZUELA**

NUMISMATICA GLOBUS
Senor Antonio ALESSANDRINI
Apartado de Correos 50418, 1050-A CARACAS

## E



## F



## G



## H



## I



## J



## K

# Foreign Exchange Table

The latest foreign exchange rates below apply to trade with banks in the country of origin. The left column shows the number of units per U.S. dollar at the official rate. The right column shows the number of units per dollar at the free market rate.

| Country | Official #/$ | Market #/$ |
|---|---|---|
| Afghanistan (Afghan) | 4,750 | 28,700 |
| Albania (Lek) | 143 | – |
| Algeria (Dinar) | 80 | – |
| Andorra uses Euro | | |
| Angola (Readjust Kwanza) | 37.4 | – |
| Anguilla uses E.C. Dollar | 2.67 | – |
| Antigua uses E.C. Dollar | 2.67 | – |
| Argentina (Peso) | 2.77 | – |
| Armenia (Dram) | 575 | – |
| Aruba (Florin) | 1.79 | – |
| Australia (Dollar) | 1.89 | – |
| Austria (Euro) | 1.138 | – |
| Azerbaijan (Manat) | 4,775 | – |
| Bahamas (Dollar) | 1.00 | – |
| Bahrain Is.(Dinar) | .377 | – |
| Bangladesh (Taka) | 57 | – |
| Barbados (Dollar) | 1.99 | – |
| Belarus (Ruble) | 1,725 | – |
| Belgium (Euro) | 1.138 | – |
| Belize (Dollar) | 1.97 | – |
| Benin uses CFA Franc West | 746 | – |
| Bermuda (Dollar) | .99 | – |
| Bhutan (Ngultrum) | 49 | – |
| Bolivia (Boliviano) | 7.05 | – |
| Bosnia-Herzegovina (Deutschmark) | 2.22 | – |
| Botswana (Pula) | 6.65 | – |
| British Virgin Islands uses U.S. Dollar | 1.00 | – |
| Brazil (Real) | 2.28 | – |
| Brunei (Dollar) | 1.84 | – |
| Bulgaria (Lev) | 2.22 | – |
| Burkina Faso uses CFA Fr.West | 746 | – |
| Burma (Kyat) | 6.79 | – |
| Burundi (Franc) | 870 | – |
| Cambodia (Riel) | 3,835 | – |
| Cameron uses CFA Franc Central | 746 | – |
| Canada (Dollar) | 1.589 | – |
| Cape Verde (Escudo) | 120 | – |
| Cayman Is.(Dollar) | 0.82 | – |
| Central African Rep. | 746 | – |
| CFA Franc Central | 746 | – |
| CFA Franc West | 746 | – |
| CFP Franc | 136.5 | – |
| Chad uses CFA Franc Central | 746 | – |
| Chile (Peso) | 550 | – |
| China, P.R. (Renminbi Yuan) | 8.277 | – |
| Colombia (Peso) | 2,260 | – |
| Comoros (Franc) | 560 | – |
| Congo uses CFA Franc Central | 746 | – |
| Congo-Dem.Rep. (Congolese Franc) | 325 | – |
| Cook Islands (Dollar) | 1.73 | – |
| Costa Rica (Colon) | 350 | – |
| Croatia (Kuna) | 8.4 | – |
| Cuba (Peso) | 22.00 | 37.00 |
| Cyprus (Pound) | .65 | – |
| Czech Republic (Koruna) | 35 | – |
| Denmark (Danish Krone) | 8.5 | – |
| Djibouti (Franc) | 170 | – |
| Dominica uses E.C. Dollar | 2.67 | – |
| Dominican Republic (Peso) | 17.4 | – |
| East Caribbean (Dollar) | 2.67 | – |
| Ecuador uses U.S. Dollar | | |
| Egypt (Pound) | 4.61 | – |
| El Salvador (Colon) | 8.75 | – |
| England (Sterling Pound) | .698 | – |
| Equatorial Guinea uses CFA Franc Central | 746 | – |
| Eritrea (Nafka) | 7.67 | – |
| Estonia (Kroon) | 17.8 | – |
| Ethiopia (Birr) | 8.4 | – |
| Euro | 1.138 | – |
| Falkland Is. (Pound) | .70 | – |
| Faroe Islands (Krona) | 8.45 | – |
| Fiji Islands (Dollar) | 2.25 | – |
| Finland (Euro) | 1.138 | – |
| France (Euro) | 1.138 | – |
| French Polynesia uses CFP Franc | 136.5 | – |
| Gabon (CFA Franc) | 746 | – |
| Gambia (Dalasi) | 18.4 | – |
| Georgia (Lari) | 1.97 | – |
| Germany (Euro) | 1.138 | – |
| Ghana (Cedi) | 7,750 | – |
| Gibraltar (Pound) | .697 | – |
| Greece (Euro) | 1.138 | – |
| Greenland uses Danish Krone | | |
| Grenada uses E.C. Dollar | 2.67 | – |
| Guatemala (Quetzal) | 7.89 | – |
| Guernsey uses Sterling Pound | .698 | – |
| Guinea Bissau (CFA Franc) | 746 | – |
| Guinea Conakry (Franc) | 1,980 | – |
| Guyana (Dollar) | 180 | – |
| Haiti (Gourde) | 27 | – |
| Honduras (Lempira) | 16.2 | – |
| Hong Kong (Dollar) | 7.8 | – |
| Hungary (Forint) | 280 | – |
| Iceland (Krona) | 100 | – |
| India (Rupee) | 48.8 | – |
| Indonesia (Rupiah) | 9,500 | – |
| Iran (Rial) | 1,750 | 8,100 |
| Iraq (Dinar) | .31 | 1,800 |
| Ireland (Euro) | 1.138 | – |
| Isle of Man uses Sterling Pound | .698 | – |
| Israel (New Sheqalim) | 4.75 | – |
| Italy (Euro) | 1.138 | – |
| Ivory Coast uses CFA Franc West | 746 | – |
| Jamaica (Dollar) | 47.6 | – |
| Japan (Yen) | 130 | – |
| Jersey uses Sterling Pound | .698 | – |
| Jordan (Dinar) | .71 | – |
| Kazakhstan (Tenge) | 150 | – |
| Kenya (Shilling) | 78 | – |
| Kiribati uses Australian Dollar | | |
| Korea-PDR (Won) | 2.20 | 170.0 |
| Korea-Rep. (Won) | 1,325 | – |
| Kuwait (Dinar) | .307 | – |
| Kyrgyzstan (Som) | 48.3 | – |
| Laos (Kip) | 7,600 | – |
| Latvia (Lat) | .63 | – |
| Lebanon (Pound) | 1,500 | – |
| Lesotho (Maloti) | 11.1 | – |
| Liberia (Dollar) "JJ" | 1.00 | 20.00 |
| "Liberty" | – | 40.00 |
| Libya (Dinar) | 1.32 | – |
| Liechtenstein uses Swiss Franc | | |
| Lithuania (Litas) | 3.93 | – |
| Luxembourg (Euro) | 1.138 | – |
| Macao (Pataca) | 8.03 | – |
| Macedonia (New Denar) | 70.5 | – |
| Madagascar (Franc) | 6,500 | – |
| Malawi (Kwacha) | 75 | – |
| Malaysia (Ringgit) | 3.8 | – |
| Maldives (Rufiya) | 11.77 | – |
| Mali uses CFA Franc West | 746 | – |
| Malta (Lira) | .45 | – |
| Marshall Islands uses U.S.Dollar | | |
| Mauritania (Ouguiya) | 280 | – |
| Mauritius (Rupee) | 30.4 | – |
| Mexico (Peso) | 9.01 | – |
| Moldova (Leu) | 13.5 | – |
| Monaco uses Euro | | |
| Mongolia (Tugrik) | 1,100 | – |
| Montenegro uses Yugo New Dinar | | |
| Montserrat uses E.C. Dollar | 2.67 | – |
| Morocco (Dirham) | 11.6 | – |
| Mozambique (Metical) | 23,100 | – |
| Myanmar (Burma) (Kyat) | 6.79 | – |
| Namibia (Rand) | 11.16 | – |
| Nauru uses Australian Dollar | | |
| Nepal (Rupee) | 77 | – |
| Netherlands (Euro) | 1.138 | – |
| Netherlands Antilles (Gulden) | 1.78 | – |
| New Caledonia uses CFP Franc | 136.5 | – |
| New Zealand (Dollar) | 2.283 | – |
| Nicaragua (Cordoba Oro) | 14.03 | – |
| Niger uses CFA Franc West | 746 | – |
| Nigeria (Naira) | 116 | – |
| Northern Ireland uses Sterling Pound | .698 | – |
| Norway (Krone) | 8.7 | – |
| Oman (Rial) | .385 | – |
| Pakistan (Rupee) | 60 | – |
| Palau uses U.S.Dollar | | |
| Panama (Balboa) uses U.S.Dollar | | |
| Papua New Guinea (Kina) | 3.72 | – |
| Paraguay (Guarani) | 4,900 | – |
| Peru (Nuevo Sol) | 3.45 | – |
| Philippines (Peso) | 51 | – |
| Poland (Zloty) | 4.08 | – |
| Portugal (Euro) | 1.138 | – |
| Qatar (Riyal) | 3.64 | – |
| Romania (Leu) | 33,000 | – |
| Russia (New Ruble) | 31.25 | – |
| Rwanda (Franc) | 450 | – |
| St. Helena (Pound) | .697 | – |
| St. Kitts uses E.C. Dollar | 2.67 | – |
| St. Lucia uses E.C. Dollar | 2.67 | – |
| St. Vincent uses E.C. Dollar | 2.67 | – |
| San Marino uses Euro | | |
| Sao Tome e Principe (Dobra) | 9,020 | – |
| Saudi Arabia (Riyal) | 3.75 | – |
| Scotland uses Sterling Pound | .698 | – |
| Senegal uses CFA Franc West | 746 | – |
| Seychelles (Rupee) | 5.62 | 6.50 |
| Sierra Leone (Leone) | 2,025 | 2,500 |
| Singapore (Dollar) | 1.83 | – |
| Slovakia (Sk.Koruna) | 47.5 | – |
| Slovenia (Tolar) | 255 | – |
| Solomon Is.(Dollar) | 6.13 | – |
| Somalia (Shilling) | 2,600 | – |
| Somaliland (Somali Shilling) | 1,800 | 4,000 |
| South Africa (Rand) | 11.07 | – |
| Spain (Euro) | 1.138 | – |
| Sri Lanka (Rupee) | 96 | – |
| Sudan (Dinar) | 259 | 300 |
| Surinam (Guilder) | 2,180 | – |
| Swaziland (Lilangeni) | 11.2 | – |
| Sweden (Krona) | 10.25 | – |
| Switzerland (Franc) | 1.67 | – |
| Syria (Pound) | 52 | – |
| Taiwan (NT Dollar) | 35 | – |
| Tajikistan (Ruble) | 746 | – |
| Tanzania (Shilling) | 980 | – |
| Thailand (Baht) | 43.5 | – |
| Togo uses CFA Franc West | 746 | – |
| Tonga (Pa'anga) | 2.16 | – |
| Transdniestra (New Ruble) | 3,500,000 | 4,500,000 |
| Trinidad & Tobago (Dollar) | 6.12 | – |
| Tunisia (Dinar) | 1.49 | – |
| Turkey (Lira) | 1,310,000 | – |
| Turkmenistan (Manat) | 33.8 | – |
| Turks & Caicos uses U.S. Dollar | | |
| Tuvalu uses Australian Dollar | | |
| Uganda (Shilling) | 1,800 | – |
| Ukraine (Hryvnia) | 5.3 | – |
| United Arab Emirates (Dirham) | 3.673 | – |
| Uruguay (Peso Uruguayo) | 15.5 | – |
| Uzbekistan (Som) | 775 | – |
| Vanuatu (Vatu) | 145 | – |
| Vatican City uses Euro | | |
| Venezuela (Bolivar) | 900 | – |
| Vietnam (Dong) | 15,200 | – |
| Western Samoa (Tala) | 3.45 | – |
| Yemen (Rial) | 174 | – |
| Yugoslavia (Novih Dinar) | 67 | – |
| Zambia (Kwacha) | 4,400 | – |
| Zimbabwe (Dollar) | 55.5 | 120 |

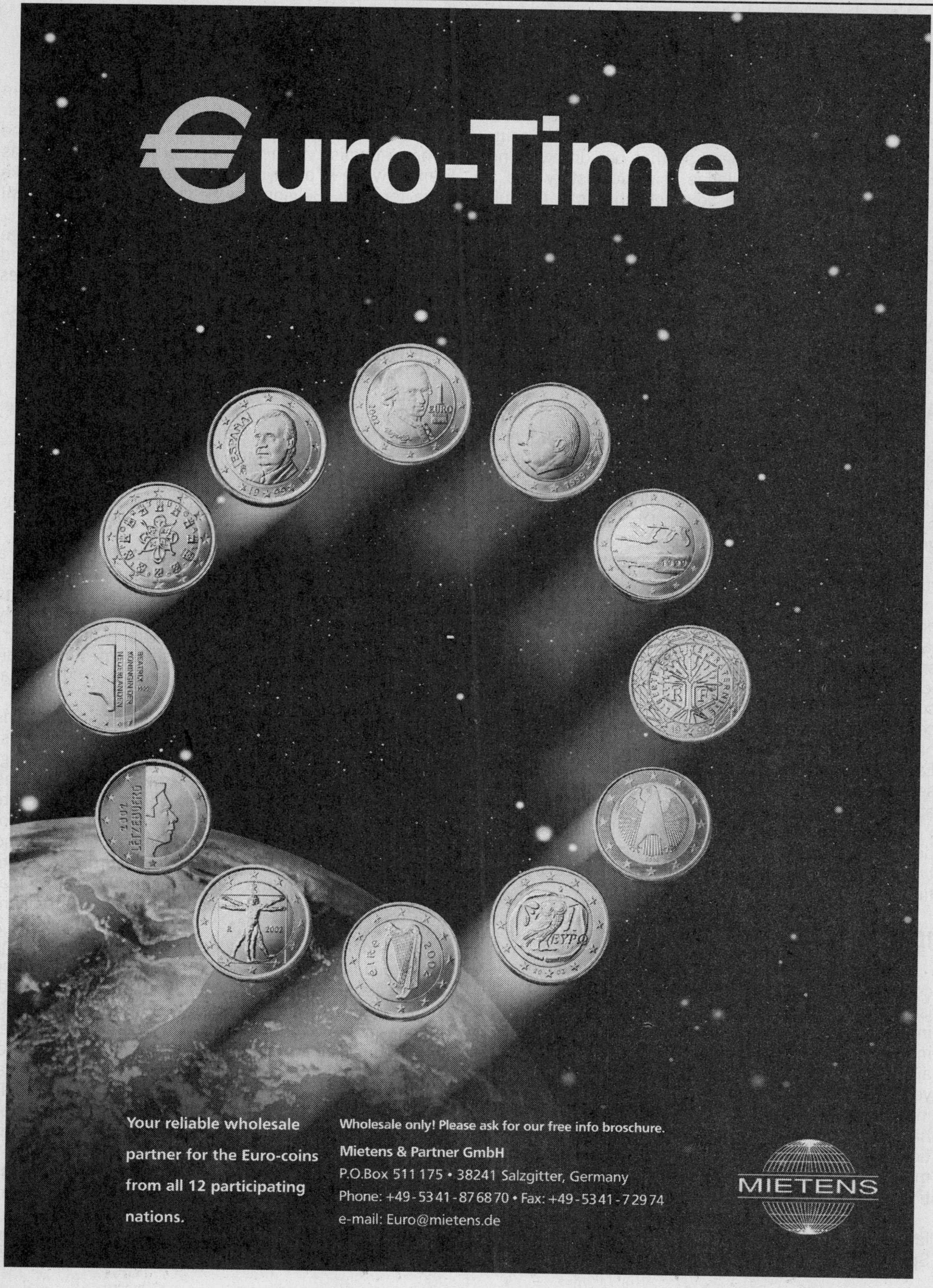

# HOW TO USE THIS CATALOG

This catalog series is designed to serve the needs of both the novice and advanced collectors. It provides a comprehensive guide to over 400 years of world coinage. It is generally arranged so that persons with no more than a basic knowledge of world history and a casual acquaintance with coin collecting can consult it with confidence and ease. The following explanations summarize the general practices used in preparing this catalog's listings. However, because of specialized requirements, which may vary by country and era, these must not be considered ironclad. Where these standards have been set aside, appropriate notations of the variations are incorporated in that particular listing.

## ARRANGEMENT

Countries are arranged alphabetically. Political changes within a country are arranged chronologically. In countries where Rulers are the single most significant political entity a chronological arrangement by Ruler has been employed. Distinctive sub-geographic regions are listed alphabetically following the countries main listings. A few exceptions to these rules may exist. Refer to the Country Index.

Diverse coinage types relating to fabrication methods, revaluations, denomination systems, non-circulating categories and such have been identified, separated and arranged in logical fashion. Chronological arrangement is employed for most circulating coinage, i.e., Hammered coinage will normally precede Milled coinage, monetary reforms will flow in order of their institution. Non-circulating types such as Essais, Pieforts, Patterns, Trial Strikes, Mint and Proof sets will follow the main listings, as will Medallic coinage and Token coinage.

Within a coinage type coins will be listed by denomination, from smallest to largest. Numbered types within a denomination will be ordered by their first date of issue.

## IDENTIFICATION

The most important step in the identification of a coin is the determination of the nation of origin. This is generally easily accomplished where English-speaking lands are concerned, however, use of the country index is sometimes required. The coins of Great Britain provide an interesting challenge. For hundreds of years the only indication of the country of origin was in the abbreviated Latin legends. In recent times there have been occasions when there has been no indication of origin. Only through the familiarity of the monarchical portraits, symbols and legends or indication of currency system are they identifiable.

The coins of many countries beyond the English-language realm, such as those of French, Italian or Spanish heritage, are also quite easy to identify through reference to their legends, which appear in the national languages based on Western alphabets. In many instances the name is spelled exactly the same in English as in the national language, such as France; while in other cases it varies only slightly, like Italia for Italy, Belgique or Belgie for Belgium, Brasil for Brazil and Danmark for Denmark.

This is not always the case, however, as in Norge for Norway, Espana for Spain, Sverige for Sweden and Helvetia for Switzerland. Some other examples include:

DEUTSCHES REICH - Germany 1873-1945
BUNDESREPUBLIC DEUTSCHLAND - Federal Republic of Germany.
DEUTSCHE DEMOKRATISCHE REPUBLIK - German Democratic Republic.
EMPIRE CHERIFIEN MAROC - Morocco.
ESTADOS UNIDOS MEXICANOS - United Mexican States (Mexico).
ETAT DU GRAND LIBAN - State of Great Lebanon (Lebanon).

Thus it can be seen there are instances in which a little schooling in the rudiments of foreign languages can be most helpful. In general, colonial possessions of countries using the Western alphabet are similarly identifiable as they often carry portraits of their current rulers, the familiar lettering, sometimes in combination with a companion designation in the local language.

Collectors have the greatest difficulty with coins that do not bear legends or dates in the Western systems. These include coins bearing Cyrillic lettering, attributable to Bulgaria, Russia, the Slavic states and Mongolia, the Greek script peculiar to Greece, Crete and the Ionian Islands; The Amharic characters of Ethiopia, or Hebrew in the case of Israel. Dragons and sunbursts along with the distinctive word characters attribute a coin to the Oriental countries of China, Japan, Korea, Tibet, Viet Nam and their component parts.

The most difficult coins to identify are those bearing only Persian or Arabic script and its derivatives, found on the issues of nations stretching in a wide swath across North Africa and East Asia, from Morocco to Indonesia, and the Indian subcontinent coinages which surely are more confusing in their vast array of Nagari, Sanskrit, Ahom, Assamese and other local dialects found on the local issues of the Indian Princely States. Although the task of identification on the more modern issues of these lands is often eased by the added presence of Western alphabet legends, a feature sometimes adopted as early as the late 19th Century, for the earlier pieces it is often necessary for the uninitiated to laboriously seek and find.

Except for the cruder issues, however, it will be found that certain characteristics and symbols fea-

tured in addition to the predominant legends are typical on coins from a given country or group of countries. The toughra monogram, for instance, occurs on some of the coins of Afghanistan, Egypt, the Sudan, Pakistan, Turkey and other areas of the late Ottoman Empire. A predominant design feature on the coins of Nepal is the trident; while neighboring Tibet features a lotus blossom or lion on many of their issues.

To assist in identification of the more difficult coins, we have assembled the *Instant Identifier* and *Monogram* sections presented on the following pages. They are designed to provide a point of beginning for collectors by allowing them to compare unidentified coins with photographic details from typical issues.

We also suggest reference to the *Index of Coin Denominations* presented here and also the comprehensive Country Index, where the inscription will be found listed just as it appears on the coin for nations using the Western alphabet.

## DATING

Coin dating is the final basic attribution consideration. Here, the problem can be more difficult because the reading of a coin date is subject not only to the vagaries of numeric styling, but to calendar variations caused by the observance of various religious eras or regal periods from country to country, or even within a country. Here again with the exception of the sphere from North Africa through the Orient, it will be found that most countries rely on Western date numerals and Christian (AD) era reckoning, although in a few instances, coin dating has been tied to the year of a reign or government. The Vatican, for example dates its coinage according to the year of reign of the current pope, in addition to the Christian-era date.

Countries in the Arabic sphere generally date their coins to the Muslim era (AH), which commenced on July 16, 622 AD (Julian calendar), when the prophet Mohammed fled from Mecca to Medina. As their calendar is reckoned by the lunar year of 354 days, which is about three percent (precisely 2.98%) shorter than the Christian year, a formula is required to convert AH dating to its Western equivalent. To convert an AH date to the approximate AD date, subtract three percent of the AH date (round to the closest whole number) from the AH date and add 622. A chart converting all AH years from 1010 (July 2, 1601) to 1421 (May 25, 2028) is presented as the Heijra Chart on page 35.

The Muslim calendar is not always based on the lunar year (AH), however, causing some confusion, particularly in Afghanistan and Iran, where a calendar based on the solar year (SH) was introduced around 1920. These dates can be converted to AD by simply adding 621. In 1976 the government of Iran implemented a new solar calendar based on the foundation of the Iranian monarchy in 559 BC. The first year observed on the new calendar was 2535 (MS), which commenced March 20, 1976. A reversion to the traditional SH dating standard occurred a few years later.

Several different eras of reckoning, including Christian and Muslim (AH), have been used to date coins of the Indian subcontinent. The two basic systems are the Vikrama Samvat (VS), which dates from Oct. 18, 58 BC, and the Saka era, the origin of which is reckoned from March 3, 78 AD. Dating according to both eras appears on various coins of the area.

Coins of Thailand (Siam) are found dated by three different eras. The most predominant is the Buddhist era (BE), which originated in 543 BC. Next is the Bangkok or Ratanakosindsok (RS) era, dating from 1781 AD; followed by the Chula-Sakarat (CS) era, dating from 638 AD. The latter era originated in Burma and is used on that country's coins.

Other calendars include that of the Ethiopian era (EE), which commenced seven years, eight months after AD dating; and that of the Jewish people, which commenced on Oct. 7, 3761 BC. Korea claims a legendary dating from 2333 BC, which is acknowledged in some of its coin dating. Some coin issues of the Indonesian area carry dates determined by the Javanese Aji Saka era (AS), a calendar of 354 days (100 Javanese years equal 97 Christian or Gregorian calendar years), which can be matched to AD dating by comparing it to AH dating.

The following table indicates the year dating for the various eras, which correspond to 2002 in Christian calendar reckoning, but it must be remembered that there are overlaps between the eras in some instances.

|  | |  |
|---|---|---|
| Christian era (AD) | - | 2002 |
| Muslim era (AH) | - | AH1423 |
| Solar year (SH) | - | SH1380 |
| Monarchic Solar era (MS) | - | MS2561 |
| Vikrama Samvat (VS) | - | VS2059 |
| Saka era (SE) | - | SE1924 |
| Buddhist era (BE) | - | BE2545 |
| Bangkok era (RS) | - | RS221 |
| Chula-Sakarat era (CS) | - | CS1364 |
| Ethiopian era (EE) | - | EE1996 |
| Jewish era | - | 5762 |
| Korean era | - | 4335 |
| Javanese Aji Saka era (AS) | - | AS1935 |
| Fasli era (FE) | - | FE1412 |

Coins of Asian origin - principally Japan, Korea, China, Turkestan and Tibet and some modern gold issues of Turkey - are generally dated to the year of the government, dynasty, reign or cyclic eras, with the dates indicated in Asian characters which usually read from right to left. In recent years, however, some dating has been according to the Christian calendar and in Western numerals. In Japan, Asian character dating was reversed to read from left to right in Showa year 23 (1948 AD).

More detailed guides to less prevalent coin dating systems, which are strictly local in nature, are presented with the appropriate listings.

Some coins carry dates according to both locally observed and Christian eras. This is particularly true in the Arabic world, where the Hejira date may be

indicated in Arabic numerals and the Christian date in Western numerals, or both dates in either form.

The date actually carried on a given coin is generally cataloged here in the first column (Date) to the right of the catalog number. If this date is by a non-christian dating system, such as 'AH'(Muslim), the Christian equivalent date will appear in parentheses(), for example AH1336(1917). Dates listed alone in the date column which do not actually appear on a given coin, or dates which are known, but do not appear on the coin, are generally enclosed by parentheses with 'ND' at the left, for example ND(1926).

Timing differentials between some era of reckoning, particularly the 354-day Mohammedan and 365-day Christian years, cause situations whereby coins which carry dates for both eras exist bearing two year dates from one calendar combined with a single date from another.

Countermarked Coinage is presented with both 'Countermark Date' and 'Host Coin' date for each type. Actual date representation follows the rules outlined above.

## NUMBERING SYSTEM

Some catalog numbers assigned in this volume are based on established references. This practice has been observed for two reasons: First, when world coins are listed chronologically they are basically self-cataloging; second, there was no need to confuse collectors with totally new numeric designations where appropriate systems already existed. As time progressed we found many of these established systems incomplete and inadequate and have now replaced many with new KM numbers. When numbers change appropriate cross-referencing has been provided.

Some of the coins listed in this catalog are identified or cross-referenced by numbers assigned by R.S. Yeoman (Y#), or slight adaptations thereof, in his *Modern World Coins*, and *Current Coins of the World*. For the pre-Yeoman dated issues, the numbers assigned by William D. Craig (C#) in his Coins of the World (1750-1850 period), 3rd edition, have generally been applied.

In some countries, listings are cross-referenced to Robert Friedberg's (FR#) *Gold Coins of the World* or *Coins of the British World*. Major Fred Pridmore's (P#) studies of British colonial coinage are also referenced, as are W.H. Valentine's (V#) references on the *Modern Copper Coins of the Muhammadan States*. Coins issued under the Chinese sphere of influence are assigned numbers from E. Kann's (K#) *Illustrated Catalog of Chinese Coins* and T.K. Hsu's (Su) work of similar title. In most cases, these cross-reference numbers are presented in the descriptive text for each type.

## DENOMINATIONS

The second basic consideration to be met in the attribution of a coin is the determination of denomination. Since denominations are usually expressed in numeric, rather than word form on a coin, this is usually quite easily accomplished on coins from nations, which use Western numerals, except in those instances where issues are devoid of any mention of face value, and denomination must be attributed by size, metallic composition or weight. Coins listed in this volume are generally illustrated in actual size. Where size is critical to proper attribution, the coin's millimeter size is indicated.

The sphere of countries stretching from North Africa through the Orient, on which numeric symbols generally unfamiliar to Westerners are employed, often provide the collector with a much greater challenge. This is particularly true on nearly all pre-20th Century issues. On some of the more modern issues and increasingly so as the years progress, Western-style numerals usually presented in combination with the local numeric system are becoming more commonplace on these coins.

Determination of a coin's currency system can also be valuable in attributing the issue to its country of origin. A comprehensive alphabetical index of currency names, applicable to the countries as cataloged in this volume, with all individual nations of use for each, is presented in this section.

The included table of *Standard International Numeral Systems* presents charts of the basic numeric designations found on coins of non-Western origin. Although denomination numerals are generally prominently displayed on coins, it must be remembered that these are general representations of characters, which individual coin engravers may have rendered in widely varying styles. Where numeric or script denominations designation forms peculiar to a given coin or country apply, such as the script used on some Persian (Iranian) issues. They are so indicated or illustrated in conjunction with the appropriate listings.

## MINTAGES

Quantities minted of each date are indicated where that information is available, generally stated in millions, and usually rounded off to the nearest 10,000 pieces. On quantities of a few thousand or less, actual mintages are generally indicated. For combined mintage figures the abbreviation "Inc. Above" means Included Above, while "Inc. Below" means Included Below. "Est." beside a mintage figure indicates the number given is an estimate or mintage limit.

## MINT AND PRIVY MARKS

The presence of distinctive, but frequently inconspicuously placed, mintmarks indicates the mint of issue for many of the coins listed in this catalog. An appropriate designation in the date listings notes the presence, if any, of a mint mark on a particular coin type by incorporating the letter or letters of the mint mark adjoining the date, i.e., 1950D or 1927R.

The presence of mint and/or mintmaster's privy marks on a coin in non-letter form is indicated by

## Sending Scanned Images by Email

Over the past 2 years or so, we have been receiving an ever-increasing flow of scanned images from sources worldwide. Unfortunately, many of these scans could not be used due to the type of scan, or simple incompatability with our systems. We appreciate the effort it takes to produce these images and accuracy they add to the catalog listings.

Here are a few simple instructions to follow when producing these scans. We encourage you to continue sending new images or upgrades to those currently illustrated and please do not hesitate to ask questions about this process.

— Scan all images within a resolution range of 200 dpi to 300 dpi

— Size setting should be at 100%

— Scan in true 4-color

— Save images as 'jpeg' or 'tiff' and name in such a way, which clearly identifies the country of origin of the note

— Please email with a request to confirm receipt of the attachment

— Please send images to thernr@krause.com

incorporating the mint letter in lower case within parentheses adjoining the date; i.e. 1927(a). The corresponding mark is illustrated or identified in the introduction of the country.

In countries such as France and Mexico, where many mints may be producing like coinage in the same denomination during the same time period, divisions by mint have been employed. In these cases the mint mark may appear next to the individual date listings and/or the mint name or mint mark may be listed in the Note field of the type description.

Where listings incorporate mintmaster initials, they are always presented in capital letters separated from the date by one character space; i.e., 1850 MF. The different mintmark and mintmaster letters found on the coins of any country, state or city of issue are always shown at the beginning of listings.

## METALS

Each numbered type listing will contain a description of the coins metallic content. The traditional coinage metals and their symbolic chemical abbreviations sometimes used in this catalog are:

| | |
|---|---|
| Platinum - (PT) | Copper - (Cu) |
| Gold - (Au) | Brass - |
| Silver - (Ag) | Copper-nickel - (CN) |
| Billion - | Lead - (Pb) |
| Nickel - (Ni) | Steel - |
| Zinc - (Zn) | Tin - (Sn) |
| Bronze - (Ae) | Aluminum - (Al) |

During the 18th and 19th centuries, most of the world's coins were struck of copper or bronze, silver and gold. Commencing in the early years of the 20th century, however, numerous new coinage metals, primarily non-precious metal alloys, were introduced. Gold has not been widely used for circulation coinages since World War I, although silver remained a popular coinage metal in most parts of the world until after World War II. With the disappearance of silver for circulation coinage, numerous additional compositions were introduced to coinage applications.

Most recent is the development of clad or plated planchets in order to maintain circulation life and extend the life of a set of production dies as used in the production of the copper-nickel clad copper 50 centesimos of Panama or in the latter case to reduce production costs of the planchets and yet provide a coin quite similar in appearance to its predecessor as in the case of the copper plated zinc core United States 1983 cent.

Modern commemorative coins have employed still more unusual methods such as bimetallic coins, color applications and precious metal or gem inlays.

## OFF-METAL STRIKES

Off-metal strikes previously designated by "(OMS)" which also included the wide range of error coinage struck in other than their officially authorized compositions have been incorporated into Pattern listings along with special issues, which were struck for presentation or other reasons.

Collectors of Germanic coinage may be familiar with the term "Abschlag" which quickly identifies similar types of coinage.

## PRECIOUS METAL WEIGHTS

Listings of weight, fineness and actual silver (ASW), gold (AGW), platinum or palladium (APW) content of most machine-struck silver, gold, platinum and palladium coins are provided in this edition. This information will be found incorporated in each separate type listing, along with other data related to the coin.

The ASW, AGW and APW figures were determined by multiplying the gross weight of a given coin by its known or tested fineness and converting the resulting gram or grain weight to troy ounces, rounded to the nearest ten-thousandth of an ounce. A silver coin with a 24.25-gram weight and .875 fineness for example, would have a fine weight of approximately 21.2188 grams, or a .6822 ASW, a factor that can be used to accurately determine the intrinsic value for multiple examples.

The ASW, AGW or APW figure can be multiplied by the spot price of each precious metal to determine the current intrinsic value of any coin accompanied by these designations.

## WEIGHTS AND FINENESSES

Coin weights are indicated in grams (abbreviated "g") along with fineness where the information is of value in differentiating between types. These weights are based on 31.103 grams per troy (scientific) ounce, as opposed to the avoirdupois (commercial) standard of 28.35 grams. Actual coin weights are generally shown in hundredths or thousands of a gram; i.e., 0.500 SILVER 2.9200g.

As the silver and gold bullion markets have advanced and declined sharply in recent years, the fineness and total precious metal content of coins has become especially significant where bullion coins - issues which trade on the basis of their intrinsic metallic content rather than numismatic value - are concerned. In many instances, such issues have become worth more in bullion form than their nominal collector values or denominations indicate.

Establishing the weight of a coin can also be valuable for determining its denomination. Actual weight is also necessary to ascertain the specific gravity of the coin's metallic content, an important factor in determining authenticity.

### TROY WEIGHT STANDARDS

24 Grains = 1 Pennyweight
480 Grains = 1 Ounce
31.103 Grams = 1 Ounce

### UNIFORM WEIGHTS

15.432 Grains = 1 Gram
0.0648 Gram = 1 Grain

**AVOIRDUPOIS STANDARDS**

27-11/32 Grains = 11 Dram
437-1/2 Grains = 1 Ounce
28.350 Grams = 1 Ounce

## BULLION VALUE CHARTS

Universal silver, gold, and platinum bullion value charts are provided for use in combination with the ASW, AGW and APW factors to determine approximate intrinsic values of listed coins. By adding the component weights as shown in troy ounces on each chart, the approximate intrinsic value of any silver, gold or platinum coin's precious metal content can be determined.

Again referring to the examples presented in the above section, the intrinsic value of a silver coin with a .6822 ASW would be indicated as $4.43 + based on the application of the silver bullion chart. This result is obtained by moving across the top to the $6.50 column, then moving down to the line indicated .680 in the far left hand corner which reveals a bullion value of $4.420. To determine the value of the remaining .0022 of ASW, return up the same column to the .002 line, the closest factor available, where a $ .0130 value is indicted. The two factors total $4.433, which would be slightly less than actual value.

The silver bullion chart provides silver values in thousandths from .001 to .009 troy ounce, and in hundredths from .01 to 1.00 in 50¢ value increments from $3.00 to $10.50. If the market value of silver exceeds $10.50, doubling the increments presented will provide valuations in $1 steps from $6.00 to $21.00.

The gold/platinum bullion chart is similarly arranged in $10 increments from $350 to $490, and by doubling the increments presented, $20 steps from $700 to $980 can be determined.

Valuations for most of the silver, gold, platinum and palladium coins listed in this edition are based on assumed market values of $4.25 per troy ounce for silver, $278 for gold, $460 for platinum, and $380 for palladium. To arrive at accurate current market indications for these issues, increase or decrease the valuations appropriately based on any variations in these indicated levels.

## HOMELAND TYPES

Homeland types are coins which colonial powers used in a colony, but do not bear that location's name. In some cases they were legal tender in the homeland, in others not. They are listed under the homeland and cross-referenced at the colony listing.

## COUNTERMARKS/COUNTERSTAMPS

There is some confusion among collectors over the terms "countermark" and "counterstamp" when applied to a coin bearing an additional mark or change of design and/or denomination.

To clarify, a countermark might be considered similar to the "hall mark" applied to a piece of silverware, by which a silversmith assured the quality of the piece. In the same way, a countermark assures the quality of the coin on which it is placed, as, for example, when the royal crown of England was countermarked (punched into) on segmented Spanish reales, allowing them to circulate in commerce in the British West Indies. An additional countermark indicating the

**Coin Alignment**

**Medal Alignment**

## COIN vs MEDAL ALIGNMENT

Coins are traditionally struck with obverse and reverse aligned at a rotation of 180 degrees from each other. When a coin is held for vertical viewing with the obverse design aligned upright and the index finger and thumb at the top and bottom, upon rotation from left to right for viewing the reverse, the latter will be upside down. Such alignment is called "coin rotation." Some coins are struck with the obverse and reverse designs mated on an alignment of zero or 360 degrees. If such an example is held and rotated as described, the reverse will appear upright. This is the alignment, which is generally observed in the striking of medals, and for that reason coins produced in this manner are considered struck in "medal rotation". In some instances, usually through error, certain coin issues have been struck to both alignment standards, creating interesting collectible varieties, which will be found noted in some listing.

new denomination may also be encountered on these coins.

Countermarks are generally applied singularly and in most cases indiscriminately on either side of the "host" coin.

Counterstamped coins are more extensively altered. The counterstamping is done with a set of dies, rather than a hand punch. The coin being counterstamped is placed between the new dies and struck as if it were a blank planchet as found with the Manila 8 reales issue of the Philippines. A more unusual application where the counterstamp dies were smaller than the host coin in the revalidated 50 centimos and 1 colon of Costa Rica issued in 1923.

## PHOTOGRAPHS

To assist the reader in coin identification, every effort has been made to present actual size photographs of every coinage type listed. Obverse and reverse are illustrated, except when a change in design is restricted to one side, and the coin has a diameter of 39mm or larger, in which case only the side required for identification of the type is generally illustrated. All coins up to 60mm are illustrated actual size, to the nearest 1/2mm up to 25mm, and to the nearest 1mm thereafter. Coins larger than 60mm diameter are illustrated in reduced size, with the actual size noted in the descriptive text block. Where slight change in size is important to coin type identification, actual millimeter measurements are stated.

## TRADE COINS

From approximately 1750-1940, a number of nations, particularly European colonial powers and commercial traders, minted trade coins to facilitate commerce with the local populace of Africa, the Arab countries, the Indian subcontinental, Southeast Asia and the Far East. Such coins generally circulated at a value based on the weight and fineness of their silver or gold content, rather than their stated denomination. Examples include the sovereigns of Great Britain and the gold ducat issues of Austria, Hungary and the Netherlands. Trade coinage will sometimes be found listed at the end of the domestic issues.

## VALUATIONS

Values quoted in this catalog represent the current market and are compiled from recommendations provided and verified through various source documents and specialized consultants. **It should be stressed, however, that this book is intended to serve only as an aid for evaluating coins, actual market conditions are constantly changing and additional influences, such as particularly strong local demand for certain coin series, fluctuation of international exchange rates and worldwide collection patterns must also be considered. Publication of this catalog is not intended as a solicitation by the publisher, editors or contributors to buy or sell the coins listed at the prices indicated.**

All valuations are stated in U.S. dollars, based on careful assessment of the varied international collector market. Valuations for coins priced below $100.00 are generally stated in full amounts - i.e. 37.50 or 95.00 - while valuations at or above that figure are rounded off in even dollars - i.e. $125.00 is expressed 125. A comma is added to indicate thousands of dollars in value.

For the convenience of overseas collectors and for U.S. collectors doing business with overseas dealers, the base exchange rate for the national currencies of approximately 180 countries are presented in the Foreign Exchange Table.

**It should be noted that when particularly select uncirculated or proof-like examples of uncirculated coins become available they can be expected to command proportionately high premiums.** Such examples in reference to choice Germanic Thalers are referred to as "erst schlage" or first strikes.

## TOKEN COINAGE

At times local economic conditions have forced regular coinage from circulation or found mints unable to cope with the demand for coinage, giving rise to privately issued token coinage substitutes. British tokens of the late 1700s and early 1880s, and the German and French and French Colonial emergency emissions of the World War I era are examples of such tokens being freely accepted in monetary transactions over wide areas. Tokens were likewise introduced to satisfy specific restricted needs, such as the leper colony issues of Brazil, Colombia and the Philippines.

This catalog includes introductory or detailed listings with "Tn" prefixes of many token coinage issues, particularly those which enjoyed wide circulation and where the series was limited in diversity. More complex series, and those more restricted in scope of circulation are generally not listed, although a representative sample may be illustrated and a specialty reference provided.

## MEDALLIC ISSUES

Medallic issues are segregated following the regular issue listings. Grouped there are coin-type issues, which can generally be identified as commemoratives produced to the country's established coinage standards but without the usual indicator of denomination. These pieces may or may not feature designs adapted from the country's regular issue or commemorative coinage, and may or may not have been issued in conjunction with related coinage issues.

## RESTRIKES, COUNTERFEITS

Deceptive restrike and counterfeit (both contemporary and modern) examples exist of some coin issues. Where possible, the existence of restrikes is noted. Warnings are also incorporated in instances where particularly deceptive counterfeits are known to exist. Collectors who are uncertain about the authenticity of a coin held in their collection, or being offered for sale, should take the precaution of having it authenticated by the American Numismatic Association Authentication Bureau, 818 N. Cascade, Colorado Springs, CO 80903. Their reasonably priced certification tests are widely accepted by collectors and dealers alike.

## NON-CIRCULATING LEGAL TENDER COINS

Coins of non-circulating legal tender (NCLT) origin are individually listed and integrated by denomination into the regular listings for each country. These coins fall outside the customary definitions of coin-of-the-realm issues, but where created and sold by, or under authorization of, agencies of sovereign governments expressly for collectors. These are primarily individual coins and sets of a commemorative nature, marketed at prices substantially in excess of face value, and usually do not have counterparts released for circulation.

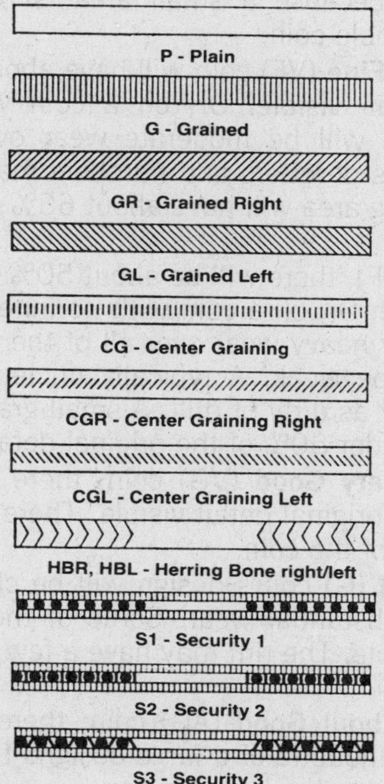


## NEW ISSUES

All newly released coins that have been physically observed by our staff and those that have been confirmed by press time have been incorporated in this edition. Exceptions exist in some countries where current date coin production lags far behind and other countries whose fiscal year actually begins in the latter half of the current year.

Collectors and dealers alike are kept up to date with worldwide new issues having newly assigned catalog reference numbers in the monthly feature *"World Coin Roundup"* in *World Coin News*. A free sample copy will be sent upon request. Overseas requests should include 1 international postal reply coupon for surface mail or 2 international postal reply coupons for air mail dispatch: Write to *World Coin News*, 700 East State St., Iola, WI 54990 USA.

## SETS

Listings in this catalog for specimen, proof and mint sets are for official, government-produced sets. In many instances privately packaged sets also exist.

**Mint Sets/Fleur de Coin Sets:** Specially prepared by worldwide mints to provide banks, collectors and government dignitaries with examples of current coinage. Usually subjected to rigorous inspection to insure that top quality specimens of selected business strikes are provided. One of the most popular mint set is that given out by the monarch of Great Britain each year on Maunday Thursday. This set contains four special coins in denominations of 1, 2, 3 and 4 pence, struck in silver and contained in a little pouch. They have been given away in a special ceremony for the poor for more than two centuries.

The Paris Mint introduced polyvinyl plastic cases packed within a cardboard box for homeland and colonial Fleur de Coin sets of the 1960s. British colonial sets were issued in velvet-lined metal cases similar to those used for proof sets. For its client nations, the Franklin Mint introduced a sealed composition of cardboard and specially molded hard clear plastic protective container inserted in a soft plastic wallet. Recent discovery that soft polyvinyl packaging has proved hazardous to coins has resulted in a change to the use of hard, inert plastics for virtually all mint sets.

Some of the highest quality mint sets ever produced were those struck by the Franklin Mint during 1972-74. In many cases matte finish dies were used to strike a polished proof planchet. Later on, from 1975, sets contained highly polished, glassy-looking coins (similar to those struck by the Bombay Mint) for collectors over a period of 12 years.

**Specimen Sets:** Forerunners of today's proof sets. In most cases the coins were specially struck, perhaps even double struck, to produce a very soft or matte finish on the effigies and fields, along with high, sharp, "wire" rims. The finish is rather dull to the naked eye.

The original purpose of these sets was to provide VIPs, monarchs and mintmasters around the world with samples of the highest quality workmanship of a particular mint. These were usually housed in elaborate velvet-lined leather and metal cases.

**Proof-like Sets** are relatively new to the field of numismatics. During the mid 1950s the Royal Canadian Mint furnished the hobby with specially selected early business strike coins that exhibited some qualities similar to proof coinage. However, the "proof-like" fields are generally flawed and the edges are rounded. These pieces are not double struck. These are commonly encountered in cardboard holders, later in soft plastic or pliofilm packaging. Of late, the Royal Canadian Mint packages such sets in rigid plastic cases.

Many worldwide officially issued proof sets would in reality fall into this category upon careful examination of the quality of the coin's finish.

Another term encountered in this category is "Special Select," used to describe the crowns of the Union of South Africa and 100-schilling coins produced for collectors in the late 1970s by the Austrian Mint.

**Proof Sets:** This is undoubtedly among the most misused terms in the hobby, not only by collectors and dealers, but also by many of the world mints.

A true proof set must be at least double-struck on specially prepared polished planchets and struck using dies (often themselves polished) of the highest quality.

Modern-day proof quality consists of frosted effigies surrounded by absolute mirror-like fields.

Listings for proof sets in this catalog are for officially issued proof sets so designated by the issuing authority, and may or may not possess what are considered modern proof quality standards.

It is necessary for collectors to acquire the knowledge to allow them to differentiate true proof sets from would-be proof sets and proof-like sets which may be encountered.

## CONDITIONS/GRADING

Wherever possible, coin valuations are given in four or five grades of preservation. For modern commemoratives, which do not circulate, only uncirculated values are usually sufficient. Proof issues are indicated by the word "Proof" next to the date, with valuation proceeded by the word "value" following the mintage. For very recent circulating coins and coins of limited value, one, two or three grade values are presented.

There are almost no grading guides for world coins. What follows is an attempt to help bridge that gap until a detailed, illustrated guide becomes available.

In grading world coins, there are two elements to look for: 1) Overall wear, and 2) loss of design details, such as strands of hair, feathers on eagles, designs on coats of arms, etc.

The age, rarity or type of a coin should not be a consideration in grading.

Grade each coin by the weaker of the two sides. This method appears to give results most nearly consistent with conservative American Numismatic Association standards for U.S. coins. Split grades, i.e., F/VF for obverse and reverse, respectively, are normally no more than one grade apart. If the two sides are more than one grade apart, the series of coins probably wears differently on each side and should then be graded by the weaker side alone.

Grade by the amount of overall wear and loss of design detail evident on each side of the coin. On coins with a moderately small design element, which is prone to early wear, grade by that design alone. For example, the 5-ore (KM#554) of Sweden has a crown above the monogram on which the beads on the arches show wear most clearly. So, grade by the crown alone.

For **Brilliant Uncirculated** (BU) grades there will be no visible signs of wear or handling, even under a 30-power microscope. Full mint luster will be present. Ideally no bags marks will be evident.

For **Uncirculated** (Unc.) grades there will be no visible signs of wear or handling, even under a 30-power microscope. Bag marks may be present.

For Almost Uncirculated (AU), all detail will be visible. There will be wear only on the highest point of the coin. There will often be half or more of the original mint luster present.

On the **Extremely Fine** (XF or EF) coin, there will be about 95% of the original detail visible. Or, on a coin with a design with no inner detail to wear down, there will be a light wear over nearly all the coin. If a small design is used as the grading area, about 90% of the original detail will be visible. This latter rule stems from the logic that a smaller amount of detail needs to be present because a small area is being used to grade the whole coin.

The **Very Fine** (VF) coin will have about 75% of the original detail visible. Or, on a coin with no inner detail, there will be moderate wear over the entire coin. Corners of letters and numbers may be weak. A small grading area will have about 66% of the original detail.

For **Fine** (F), there will be about 50% of the original detail visible. Or, on a coin with no inner detail, there will be fairly heavy wear over all of the coin. Sides of letters will be weak. A typically uncleaned coin will often appear as dirty or dull. A small grading area will have just under 50% of the original detail.

On the **Very Good** (VG) coin, there will be about 25% of the original detail visible. There will be heavy wear on all of the coin.

The **Good** (G) coin's design will be clearly outlined but with substantial wear. Some of the larger detail may be visible. The rim may have a few weak spots of wear.

On the **About Good** (AG) coin, there will typically be only a silhouette of a large design. The rim will be worn down into the letters if any.

## STANDARD INTERNATIONAL GRADING TERMINOLOGY AND ABBREVIATIONS

| | PROOF | UNCIRCULATED | EXTREMELY FINE | VERY FINE | FINE | VERY GOOD | GOOD | POOR |
|---|---|---|---|---|---|---|---|---|
| **U.S. and ENGLISH SPEAKING LANDS** | PRF | UNC | EF or XF | VF | F | VG | G | PR |
| **BRAZIL** | — | (1)FDC or FC | (3) S | (5) MBC | (7) BC | (8) BC/R | (9) R | UT GeG |
| **DENMARK** | M | 0 | 01 | 1 + | 1 | 1 ÷ | 2 | 3 |
| **FINLAND** | 00 | 0 | 01 | 1 + | 1 | 1? | 2 | 3 |
| **FRANCE** | FB Flan Bruni | FDC Fleur de Coin | SUP Superbe | TTB Très très beau | TB Très beau | B Beau | TBC Très Bien Conservée | BC Bien Conservée |
| **GERMANY** | PP Polierte Platte | STG Stempelglanz | VZ Vorzüglich | SS Sehr schön | S Schön | S.G.E. Sehr gut erhalten | G.E. Gut erhalten | Gering erhalten |
| **ITALY** | FS Fondo Specchio | FDC Fior di Conio | SPL Splendido | BB Bellissimo | MB Molto Bello | B Bello | M | — |
| **JAPAN** | — | 未使用 | 極美品 | 美品 | 並品 | — | — | — |
| **NETHERLANDS** | — Proef | FDC Fleur de Coin | Pr. Prachtig | Z.f. Zeer fraai | Fr. Fraai | Z.g. Zeer goed | G | — |
| **NORWAY** | M | 0 | 01 | 1 + | 1 | 1 ÷ | 2 | 3 |
| **PORTUGAL** | — | Soberba | Bela | MBC | BC | MREG | REG | MC |
| **SPAIN** | Prueba | SC | EBC | MBC | BC + | BC | RC | MC |
| **SWEDEN** | Polerad | 0 | 01 | 1 + | 1 | 1? | 2 | — |

Strong or weak strikes, partially weak strikes, damage, corrosion, attractive or unattractive toning, dipping or cleaning should be described along with the above grades. These factors affect the quality of the coin just as do wear and loss of detail, but are easier to describe.

In the case of countermarked/counterstamped coins, the condition of the host coin will have a bearing on the end valuation. The important factor in determining the grade is the condition, clarity and completeness of the countermark itself. This is in reference to countermarks/counterstamps having raised design while being struck in a depression.

Incuse countermarks cannot be graded for wear. They are graded by the clarity and completeness including the condition of the host coin which will also have more bearing on the final grade/valuation determined.

## Sending Scanned Images by Email

Over the past 2 years or so, we have been receiving an ever-increasing flow of scanned images from sources worldwide. Unfortunately, many of these scans could not be used due to the type of scan, or simple incompatability with our systems. We appreciate the effort it takes to produce these images and accuracy they add to the catalog listings.

Here are a few simple instructions to follow when producing these scans. We encourage you to continue sending new images or upgrades to those currently illustrated and please do not hesitate to ask questions about this process.

— Scan all images within a resolution range of 200 dpi to 300 dpi
— Size setting should be at 100%
— Scan in true 4-color
— Save images as 'jpeg' or 'tiff' and name in such a way, which clearly identifies the country of origin of the note
— Please email with a request to confirm receipt of the attachment
— Please send images to thernr@krause.com

# A GUIDE TO INTERNATIONAL NUMERICS

| | ENGLISH | CZECH | DANISH | DUTCH | ESPERANTO | FRENCH |
|---|---|---|---|---|---|---|
| 1/4 | one-quarter | jeden-ctvrt | én kvart | een-kwart | unu-kvar'ono | un-quart |
| 1/2 | one-half | jeden-polovieni or pul | én halve | een-half | unu-du'one | un-demi |
| 1 | one | jeden | én | een | unu | un |
| 2 | two | dve | to | twee | du | duex |
| 3 | three | tri | trre | drie | tri | trois |
| 4 | four | ctyri | fire | vier | kvar | quatre |
| 5 | five | pet | fem | vijf | kvin | cinq |
| 6 | six | sest | seks | zes | ses | six |
| 7 | seven | sedm | syv | zeven | sep | sept |
| 8 | eight | osm | otte | acht | ok | huit |
| 9 | nine | devet | ni | negen | nau | neuf |
| 10 | ten | deset | ti | tien | dek | dix |
| 12 | twelve | dvaná ct | tolv | twaalf | dek du | douze |
| 15 | fifteen | patná ct | femten | vijiftien | dek kvin | quinze |
| 20 | twenty | dvacet | tyve | twintig | du'dek | vingt |
| 24 | twenty-four | dvacet-ctyri | fireog tyve | twintig-vier | du'dek kvar | vingt-quatre |
| 25 | twenty-five | dvacet-pet | fem og tyve | twintig-vijf | du'dek kvin | vingt-cinq |
| 30 | thirty | tricet | tredive | dertig | tri'dek | trente |
| 40 | forty | ctyricet | fyrre | veertig | kvar'dek | quarante |
| 50 | fifty | padesát | halytreds | vijftig | kvin'dek | cinquante |
| 60 | sixty | sedesát | tres | zestig | ses'dek | soizante |
| 70 | seventy | sedmdesát | halvfjerds | zeventig | sep'dek | soizante |
| 80 | eighty | osemdesát | firs | tachtig | ok'dek | quatre-vingt |
| 90 | ninety | devadesát | halvfjerds | negentig | nau'dek | quatre-vingt-dix |
| 100 | one hundred | jedno sto | et hundrede | ee-honderd | unu-cento | un-cent |
| 1000 | thousand | tisí c | tusind | duizend | mil | mille |

| | GERMAN | HUNGARIAN | INDONESIAN | ITALIAN | NORWEGIAN | POLISH |
|---|---|---|---|---|---|---|
| 1/4 | einvertel | egy-negyed | satu-suku | uno-guarto | en-fjeerdedel | jeden-c weirc |
| 1/2 | einhalb | egy-fél | satu-setengah | uno-mezzo | en-halv | jeden-polowa |
| 1 | ein | egy | satu | uno | en | jeden |
| 2 | zwei | kettö | dud | due | to | dwa |
| 3 | drei | három | tiga | tre | tre | trzy |
| 4 | vier | négy | empot | quattro | fire | cztery |
| 5 | fünf | öt | lima | cinque | fem | piec' |
| 6 | sechs | hat | enam | sei | seks | szes'c' |
| 7 | sieben | hét | tudjuh | sette | sju | siedem |
| 8 | acht | nyolc | delapan | otto | atte | osiem |
| 9 | neum | kilenc | sembilan | nove | ni | dziewiec' |
| 10 | zehn | tí z | sepuluh | dieci | ti | dziesiec' |
| 12 | zwolf | tizenketto | duabelas | dodici | tolv | dwanas' cie |
| 15 | fünfzehn | tizenöt | lima belas | quindici | femten | pietnas'cie |
| 20 | zwanzig | húsz | dua pulah | venti | tjue or tyve | dwadzies'cia |
| 24 | vierundzwanzig | húsz-négy | dua pulah-empot | venti-quattro | tjue-fire or tyve-fire | dwadzies'cia-cztery |
| 25 | fünfundzwanzig | húsz-öt | dua-pulah-lima | venti-cinque | tjue-fem or tyve-fem | dwadzies'cia-piec |
| 30 | dreissig | harminc | tigapulah | trenta | tredve | trydzies'ci |
| 40 | vierzig | negyven | empat pulah | quaranta | forti | czterdries'ci |
| 50 | fünfzig | otven | lima pulah | cinquanta | femti | piec'dziesiat |
| 60 | sechzig | hatvan | enam pulah | sessanta | seksti | szes'c'dziesiat |
| 70 | siebzig | hetven | tudjuh pulu | settanta | sytti | siedemdziesiat |
| 80 | achtzig | nyolvan | delapan puluh | ottonta | atti | osiemdziesiat |
| 90 | neuzig | kilencven | sembilan puluh | novanta | nitty | dziewiec'dziesiat |
| 100 | ein hundert | egy-száz | satu-seratus | uno-cento | en-hundre | jeden-sto |
| 1000 | tausend | ezer | seribu | mille | tusen | tysiac |

| | PORTUGUESE | ROMANIAN | SERBO-CROATIAN | SPANISH | SWEDEN | TURKISH |
|---|---|---|---|---|---|---|
| 1/4 | um-quarto | un-sfert | jedan-ceturtina | uno-cuarto | en-fjärdedel | bir-ceyrek |
| 1/2 | un-meio | o-jumatate | jedan-polovina | uno-medio | en-hälft | bir-yarim |
| 1 | um | un | jedan | uno | en | bir |
| 2 | dois | doi | dva | dos | tva | iki |
| 3 | trés | trei | tri | tres | tre | üc |
| 4 | quatro | patru | cetiri | cuatro | fyra | dört |
| 5 | cinco | cinci | pet | cinco | fem | bes |
| 6 | seis | sase | sest | seis | sex | alti |
| 7 | sete | sapte | sedam | siete | sju | yedi |
| 8 | oito | opt | osam | ocho | atta | sekiz |
| 9 | nove | noua | devet | nueve | io | dokuz |
| 10 | dez | zece | deset | diez | tio | on |
| 12 | doze | doisprezece | dvanaest | doce | tolv | on iki |
| 15 | quinze | cincisprezece | petnaest | quince | femton | on bes |
| 20 | vinte | douazeci | dvadset | veinte | tjugu | yirmi |
| 24 | vinte-quatro | douazeci-patru | dvadesel-citiri | veinte-cuarto | tjugu-fyra | yirmi-dört |
| 25 | vinte-cinco | douazeci-cinci | dvadeset-pet | veinte-cinco | tjugu-fem | yirmi-bes |
| 30 | trinta | treizeci | trideset | treinta | trettio | otuz |
| 40 | quarenta | patruzeci | cetrdeset | cuarenta | fyrtio | kirk |
| 50 | cinqüenta | cincizeci | padeset | cincuenta | femtio | elli |
| 60 | sessenta | saizeci | sezdeset | sesenta | sextio | altmis |
| 70 | setenta | saptezeci | sedamdeset | setenta | sjuttio | yetmis |
| 80 | oitenta | optzeci | osamdeset | ochenta | attio | seksen |
| 90 | noventa | novazeci | devedeset | noventa | nittio | doksan |
| 100 | un-cem | o-suta | jedan-sto | uno-ciente | en-hundra | bir-yüz |
| 1000 | mil | mie | hiljada | mil | tusen | bin |

# INSTANT IDENTIFIER

Aachen
(German States)

Albania

Austria

Baden
(German States)

Bradenburg
Ansbach
(German States)

Finland

Jever
(German States)

Frankfurt
(German States)

Furstenberg
(German States)

Geneva
(Swiss Cantons)

German Empire

Montenegro
(Yugoslavia)

Nurnberg
(German States)

Milan
(Italian States)

Prussia
(German States)

Russia (Czarist)
Russian Poland

Schwarzburg-
Rudolstadt
(German States)

Schwarzburg-
Sondershausen
(German States)

Serbia
(Yugoslavia)

Teutonic Order
(German States)

Genoa
(Italian States)

Syrian Arab
Republic

United Arab
Republic
(Egypt, Syria)

Arab Republic
of Egypt
Libya

Yemen
Arab Republic

Bulgaria

Burma
(Myanmar)

Ethiopia

Finland

Norway

Gorizia
(Italian States)

Hannover
(German States)

Hesse-
Darmstadt
(German States)

Hohenlohe-
Neuenstein-
Oehringen
(German States)

Iran
(Persia)

Morocco

Siberia

Tibet
(China)

Nepal

Morocco
(AH1371 = 1951AD)

Manchukuo
(China)

Japan

# INSTANT IDENTIFIER

Hanau-Munzenberg (German States)

Nassau (German States)

Hesse-Cassel (German States)

Sri Lanka (Ceylon)

Tibet (China)

Utrecht (Netherlands)

Venice (Italian States)

Neuchatel (Swiss Cantons)

China (Empire-Provincial)

China (Empire-Provincial)

Japan

Japan

African States

Bretzenheim (German States)

Hall in Swabia (German States)

Greenland

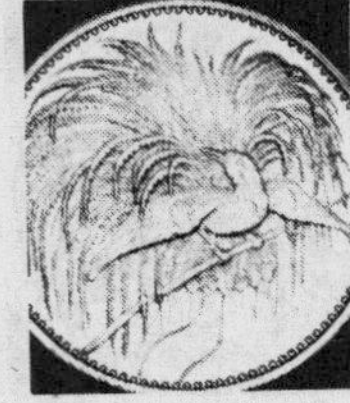
German New Guinea (Papua New Guinea)

Lithuania

Mongolia

Sudan

Algeria

Lowenstein-Wertheim (German States)

Maldive Islands

Afghanistan

Ireland

Israel

Lebanon

Papal States (Vatican)

Regensburg (German States)

Sweden

North Korea

CCCP-Russia

CCCP-Russia

Yugoslavia

Taiwan (Rep. of China))

Mainz (German States)

Solms-Laubach (German States)

Ticino (Swiss Cantons)

Fugger (German States)

Naples & Sicily (Italian States)

Saxe-Saalfeld (German States)

Stolberg-Stolberg (German States)

# INSTANT IDENTIFIER

French Colonial

French Colonial

French Colonial

Bangladesh

Isle Of Man
Sicily

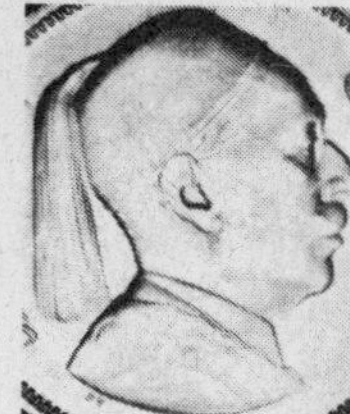
Libya

Anhalt-Bernburg
(German States)

Aargau
(Swiss Cantons)

Augsburg
(German States)

Basel
(Swiss Cantons)

Bavaria
(German States)

Brazil

Bremen
(German States)

Luzern
(Swiss Cantons)

Chur Pfalz
(German States)

Fulda
(German States)

Glarus
(Swiss Cantons)

Grand Duchy
Of Warsaw
(Poland)

Graubunden
(Swiss Cantons)

Hamburg
(German States)

Lucca
(Italian States)

Hesse-Cassel
(German States)

Hesse-Homburg
(German States)

Hildesheim
(German States)

Hohenzollern-
Hechingen
(German States)

Hungary

Julich-Berg
(German States)

Gelderland
(Netherlands)

Lippe-Detmold
(German States)

Lubeck
(German States)

Mecklenburg-
Strelitz
(German States)

Oldenburg
(German States)

Passau
(German States)

Portugal

Vaud
(Swiss Cantons)

Anhalt
(Joint Coinage)
(German States)

Oldenburg
(German States)

Schwarzenberg
(German States)

Schaffhausen
(Swiss Cantons)

Paderborn
(German States)

Thurgau
(Swiss Cantons)

Westfrisia
(Netherlands)

# INSTANT IDENTIFIER

Arenberg (German States)

Rhenish Confederation (German States)

Reuss-Greiz (German States)

Sardinia (Italian States)

Saxony (German States)

Schaumburg-Lippe (German States)

Schleswig-Holstein (German States)

St. Gall (Swiss Cantons)

Slovakia

Solothurn (Swiss Cantons)

Unterwalden (Nidwalden) (Swiss Cantons)

Wurttemberg (German States)

Wurzburg (German States)

Zurich (Swiss Cantons)

Waldeck-Pyrmont (German States)

Iraq

Pakistan

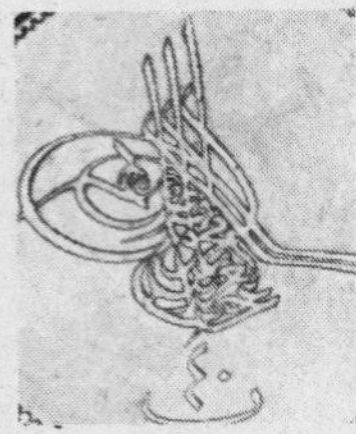
Turkey-Egypt Sudan, Algeria (Ottoman Empire)

Muscat & Oman, Oman

Saudi Arabia

Tunisia

Wismar (German States)

Order of Malta

Bamberg (German States)

Brunswick-Wolfenbuttel (German States)

Brunswick-Luneburg (German States)

Erfurt Mainz (German States)

Hannover (German States)

Eichastatt (German States)

Greece

Serbia

Switzerland

Albania

Israel

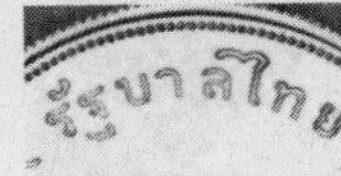
Thailand (Siam)

Japan (Dai Nippon)

South Korea

Sitten (Swiss Cantons)

Rostock (German States)

Saint Alban (German States)

English East India Co. (Sumatra)

China, Japan, Annam, Korea
(All holed 'cash' coins look quite similar.)

Japan

Korea

# HEJIRA DATE CONVERSION CHART

## HEJIRA DATE CHART

HEJIRA (Hijra, Hegira), the name of the Muslim era (A.H. = Anno Hegirae) dates back to the Christian year 622 when Mohammed "fled" from Mecca, escaping to Medina to avoid persecution from the Koreish tribemen. Based on a lunar year the Muslim year is 11 days shorter.

*= Leap Year (Christian Calendar)

| AH Hejira | AD Christian Date |
|---|---|
| 1010 | 1601, July 2 |
| 1011 | 1602, June 21 |
| 1012 | 1603, June 11 |
| 1013 | 1604, May 30 |
| 1014 | 1605, May 19 |
| 1015 | 1606, May 19 |
| 1016 | 1607, May 9 |
| 1017 | 1608, April 28 |
| 1018 | 1609, April 6 |
| 1019 | 1610, March 26 |
| 1020 | 1611, March 16 |
| 1021 | 1612, March 4 |
| 1022 | 1613, February 21 |
| 1023 | 1614, February 11 |
| 1024 | 1615, January 31 |
| 1025 | 1616, January 20 |
| 1026 | 1617, January 9 |
| 1027 | 1617, December 29 |
| 1028 | 1618, December 19 |
| 1029 | 1619, December 8 |
| 1030 | 1620, November 26 |
| 1031 | 1621, November 16 |
| 1032 | 1622, November 5 |
| 1033 | 1623, October 25 |
| 1034 | 1624, October 14 |
| 1035 | 1625, October 3 |
| 1036 | 1626, September 22 |
| 1037 | 1627, September 12 |
| 1038 | 1628, August 31 |
| 1039 | 1629, August 21 |
| 1040 | 1630, July 10 |
| 1041 | 1631, July 30 |
| 1042 | 1632, July 19 |
| 1043 | 1633, July 8 |
| 1044 | 1634, June 27 |
| 1045 | 1635, June 17 |
| 1046 | 1636, June 5 |
| 1047 | 1637, May 26 |
| 1048 | 1638, May 15 |
| 1049 | 1639, May 4 |
| 1050 | 1640, April 23 |
| 1051 | 1641, April 12 |
| 1052 | 1642, April 1 |
| 1053 | 1643, March 22 |
| 1054 | 1644, March 10 |
| 1055 | 1645, February 27 |
| 1056 | 1646, February 17 |
| 1057 | 1647, February 6 |
| 1058 | 1648, January 27 |
| 1059 | 1649, January 15 |
| 1060 | 1650, January 4 |
| 1061 | 1650, December 25 |
| 1062 | 1651, December 14 |
| 1063 | 1652, December 2 |
| 1064 | 1653, November 22 |
| 1065 | 1654, November 11 |
| 1066 | 1655, October 31 |
| 1067 | 1656, October 20 |
| 1068 | 1657, October 9 |
| 1069 | 1658, September 29 |
| 1070 | 1659, September 18 |
| 1071 | 1660, September 6 |
| 1072 | 1661, August 27 |
| 1073 | 1662, August 16 |
| 1074 | 1663, August 5 |
| 1075 | 1664, July 25 |
| 1076 | 1665, July 14 |
| 1077 | 1666, July 4 |
| 1078 | 1667, June 23 |
| 1079 | 1668, June 11 |
| 1080 | 1669, June 1 |
| 1081 | 1670, May 21 |
| 1082 | 1671, May 10 |
| 1083 | 1672, April 29 |
| 1084 | 1673, April 18 |
| 1085 | 1674, April 7 |
| 1086 | 1675, March 28 |

| AH Hejira | AD Christian Date |
|---|---|
| 1087 | 1676, March 16* |
| 1088 | 1677, March 6 |
| 1089 | 1678, February 23 |
| 1090 | 1679, February 12 |
| 1091 | 1680, February 2* |
| 1092 | 1681, January 21 |
| 1093 | 1682, January 10 |
| 1094 | 1682, December 31 |
| 1095 | 1683, December 20 |
| 1096 | 1684, December 8* |
| 1097 | 1685, November 28 |
| 1098 | 1686, November 17 |
| 1099 | 1687, November 7 |
| 1100 | 1688, October 26* |
| 1101 | 1689, October 15 |
| 1102 | 1690, October 5 |
| 1103 | 1691, September 24 |
| 1104 | 1692, September 12* |
| 1105 | 1693, September 2 |
| 1106 | 1694, August 22 |
| 1107 | 1695, August 12 |
| 1108 | 1696, July 31* |
| 1109 | 1697, July 20 |
| 1110 | 1698, July 10 |
| 1111 | 1699, June 29 |
| 1112 | 1700, June 18 |
| 1113 | 1701, June 8 |
| 1114 | 1702, May 28 |
| 1115 | 1703, May 17 |
| 1116 | 1704, May 6* |
| 1117 | 1705, April 25 |
| 1118 | 1706, April 15 |
| 1119 | 1707, April 4 |
| 1120 | 1708, March 23* |
| 1121 | 1709, March 18 |
| 1122 | 1710, March 2 |
| 1123 | 1711, February 19 |
| 1124 | 1712, February 9* |
| 1125 | 1713, January 28 |
| 1126 | 1714, January 17 |
| 1127 | 1715, January 7 |
| 1128 | 1715, December 27 |
| 1129 | 1716, December 16* |
| 1130 | 1717, December 5 |
| 1131 | 1718, November 24 |
| 1132 | 1719, November 14 |
| 1133 | 1720, November 2* |
| 1134 | 1721, October 22 |
| 1135 | 1722, October 12 |
| 1136 | 1723, October 1 |
| 1137 | 1724, September 29* |
| 1138 | 1725, September 9 |
| 1139 | 1726, August 29 |
| 1140 | 1727, August 19 |
| 1141 | 1728, August 7* |
| 1142 | 1729, July 27 |
| 1143 | 1730, July 17 |
| 1144 | 1731, July 6 |
| 1145 | 1732, June 24* |
| 1146 | 1733, June 14 |
| 1147 | 1734, June 3 |
| 1148 | 1735, May 24 |
| 1149 | 1736, May 12* |
| 1150 | 1737, May 1 |
| 1151 | 1738, April 21 |
| 1152 | 1739, April 10 |
| 1153 | 1740, March 29* |
| 1154 | 1741, March 19 |
| 1155 | 1742, March 8 |
| 1156 | 1743, February 25 |
| 1157 | 1744, February 15* |
| 1158 | 1745, February 3 |
| 1159 | 1746, January 24 |
| 1160 | 1747, January 13 |
| 1161 | 1748, January 2 |
| 1162 | 1748, December 22* |
| 1163 | 1749, December 11 |
| 1164 | 1750, November 30 |
| 1165 | 1751, November 20 |
| 1166 | 1752, November 8* |
| 1167 | 1753, October 29 |
| 1168 | 1754, October 18 |
| 1169 | 1755, October 7 |
| 1170 | 1756, September 26* |
| 1171 | 1757, September 15 |
| 1172 | 1758, September 4 |
| 1173 | 1759, August 25 |
| 1174 | 1760, August 13* |
| 1175 | 1761, August 2 |
| 1176 | 1762, July 28 |
| 1177 | 1763, July 12 |

| AH Hejira | AD Christian Date |
|---|---|
| 1178 | 1764, July 1* |
| 1179 | 1765, June 20 |
| 1180 | 1766, June 9 |
| 1181 | 1767, May 30 |
| 1182 | 1768, May 18* |
| 1183 | 1769, May 7 |
| 1184 | 1770, April 27 |
| 1185 | 1771, April 16 |
| 1186 | 1772, April 4* |
| 1187 | 1773, March 25 |
| 1188 | 1774, March 14 |
| 1189 | 1775, March 4 |
| 1190 | 1776, February 21* |
| 1191 | 1777, February 9 |
| 1192 | 1778, January 30 |
| 1193 | 1779, January 19 |
| 1194 | 1780, January 8* |
| 1195 | 1780, December 28* |
| 1196 | 1781, December 17 |
| 1197 | 1782, December 7 |
| 1198 | 1783, November 26 |
| 1199 | 1784, November 14* |
| 1200 | 1785, November 4 |
| 1201 | 1786, October 24 |
| 1202 | 1787, October 13 |
| 1203 | 1788, October 2* |
| 1204 | 1789, September 21 |
| 1205 | 1790, September 10 |
| 1206 | 1791, August 31 |
| 1207 | 1792, August 19* |
| 1208 | 1793, August 9 |
| 1209 | 1794, July 29 |
| 1210 | 1795, July 18 |
| 1211 | 1796, July 7* |
| 1212 | 1797, June 26 |
| 1213 | 1798, June 15 |
| 1214 | 1799, June 5 |
| 1215 | 1800, May 25 |
| 1216 | 1801, May 14 |
| 1217 | 1802, May 4 |
| 1218 | 1803, April 23 |
| 1219 | 1804, April 12* |
| 1220 | 1805, April 1 |
| 1221 | 1806, March 21 |
| 1222 | 1807, March 11 |
| 1223 | 1808, February 28* |
| 1224 | 1809, February 16 |
| 1225 | 1810, February 6 |
| 1226 | 1811, January 26 |
| 1227 | 1812, January 16* |
| 1228 | 1813, January 4 |
| 1229 | 1813, December 24 |
| 1230 | 1814, December 14 |
| 1231 | 1815, December 3 |
| 1232 | 1816, November 21* |
| 1233 | 1817, November 11 |
| 1234 | 1818, October 31 |
| 1235 | 1819, October 20 |
| 1236 | 1820, October 9* |
| 1237 | 1821, September 28 |
| 1238 | 1822, September 18 |
| 1239 | 1823, September 7 |
| 1240 | 1824, August 26* |
| 1241 | 1825, August 16 |
| 1242 | 1826, August 5 |
| 1243 | 1827, July 25 |
| 1244 | 1828, July 14* |
| 1245 | 1829, July 3 |
| 1246 | 1830, June 22 |
| 1247 | 1831, June 12 |
| 1248 | 1832, May 31* |
| 1249 | 1833, May 21 |
| 1250 | 1834, May 10 |
| 1251 | 1835, April 29 |
| 1252 | 1836, April 18* |
| 1253 | 1837, April 7 |
| 1254 | 1838, March 27 |
| 1255 | 1839, March 17 |
| 1256 | 1840, March 5* |
| 1257 | 1841, February 23 |
| 1258 | 1842, February 12 |
| 1259 | 1843, February 1 |
| 1260 | 1844, January 22* |
| 1261 | 1845, January 10 |
| 1262 | 1845, December 30 |
| 1263 | 1846, December 20 |
| 1264 | 1847, December 9 |
| 1265 | 1848, November 27* |
| 1266 | 1849, November 17 |
| 1267 | 1850, November 6 |
| 1268 | 1851, October 27 |

| AH Hejira | AD Christian Date |
|---|---|
| 1269 | 1852, October 15* |
| 1270 | 1853, October 4 |
| 1271 | 1854, September 24 |
| 1272 | 1855, September 13 |
| 1273 | 1856, September 1* |
| 1274 | 1857, August 22 |
| 1275 | 1858, August 11 |
| 1276 | 1859, July 31 |
| 1277 | 1860, July 20* |
| 1278 | 1861, July 9 |
| 1279 | 1862, June 29 |
| 1280 | 1863, June 18 |
| 1281 | 1864, June 6* |
| 1282 | 1865, May 27 |
| 1283 | 1866, May 16 |
| 1284 | 1867, May 5 |
| 1285 | 1868, April 24* |
| 1286 | 1869, April 13 |
| 1287 | 1870, April 3 |
| 1288 | 1871, March 23 |
| 1289 | 1872, March 11* |
| 1290 | 1873, March 1 |
| 1291 | 1874, February 18 |
| 1292 | 1875, February 7 |
| 1293 | 1876, January 28* |
| 1294 | 1877, January 16 |
| 1295 | 1878, January 5 |
| 1296 | 1878, December 26 |
| 1297 | 1879, December 15 |
| 1298 | 1880, December 4* |
| 1299 | 1881, November 23 |
| 1300 | 1882, November 12 |
| 1301 | 1883, November 2 |
| 1302 | 1884, October 21* |
| 1303 | 1885, October 10 |
| 1304 | 1886, September 30 |
| 1305 | 1887, September 19 |
| 1306 | 1888, September 7* |
| 1307 | 1889, August 28 |
| 1308 | 1890, August 17 |
| 1309 | 1891, August 7 |
| 1310 | 1892, July 26* |
| 1311 | 1893, July 15 |
| 1312 | 1894, July 5 |
| 1313 | 1895, June 24 |
| 1314 | 1896, June 12* |
| 1315 | 1897, June 2 |
| 1316 | 1898, May 22 |
| 1317 | 1899, May 12 |
| 1318 | 1900, May 1 |
| 1319 | 1901, April 20 |
| 1320 | 1902, April 10 |
| 1321 | 1903, March 30 |
| 1322 | 1904, March 18* |
| 1323 | 1905, March 8 |
| 1324 | 1906, February 25 |
| 1325 | 1907, February 14 |
| 1326 | 1908, February 4* |
| 1327 | 1909, January 23 |
| 1328 | 1910, January 13 |
| 1329 | 1911, January 2 |
| 1330 | 1911, December 22 |
| 1331 | 1912, December 11* |
| 1332 | 1913, November 30 |
| 1333 | 1914, November 19 |
| 1334 | 1915, November 9 |
| 1335 | 1916, October 28* |
| 1336 | 1917, October 17 |
| 1337 | 1918, October 7 |
| 1338 | 1919, September 26 |
| 1339 | 1920, September 15* |
| 1340 | 1921, September 4 |
| 1341 | 1922, August 24 |
| 1342 | 1923, August 14 |
| 1343 | 1924, August 2* |
| 1344 | 1925, July 22 |
| 1345 | 1926, July 12 |
| 1346 | 1927, July 1 |
| 1347 | 1928, June 20* |
| 1348 | 1929, June 9 |
| 1349 | 1930, May 29 |
| 1350 | 1931, May 19 |
| 1351 | 1932, May 7* |
| 1352 | 1933, April 26 |
| 1353 | 1934, April 16 |
| 1354 | 1935, April 5 |
| 1355 | 1936, March 24* |
| 1356 | 1937, March 14 |
| 1357 | 1938, March 3 |
| 1358 | 1939, February 21 |
| 1359 | 1940, February 10* |

| AH Hejira | AD Christian Date |
|---|---|
| 1360 | 1941, January 29 |
| 1361 | 1942, January 19 |
| 1362 | 1943, January 8 |
| 1363 | 1943, December 28 |
| 1364 | 1944, December 17* |
| 1365 | 1945, December 6 |
| 1366 | 1946, November 25 |
| 1367 | 1947, November 15 |
| 1368 | 1948, November 3* |
| 1369 | 1949, October 24 |
| 1370 | 1950, October 13 |
| 1371 | 1951, October 2 |
| 1372 | 1952, September 21* |
| 1373 | 1953, September 10 |
| 1374 | 1954, August 30 |
| 1375 | 1955, August 20 |
| 1376 | 1956, August 8* |
| 1377 | 1957, July 29 |
| 1378 | 1958, July 18 |
| 1379 | 1959, July 7 |
| 1380 | 1960, June 25* |
| 1381 | 1961, June 14 |
| 1382 | 1962, June 4 |
| 1383 | 1963, May 25 |
| 1384 | 1964, May 13* |
| 1385 | 1965, May 2 |
| 1386 | 1966, April 22 |
| 1387 | 1967, April 11 |
| 1388 | 1968, March 31* |
| 1389 | 1969, March 20 |
| 1390 | 1970, March 9 |
| 1391 | 1971, February 27 |
| 1392 | 1972, February 16* |
| 1393 | 1973, February 4 |
| 1394 | 1974, January 25 |
| 1395 | 1975, January 14 |
| 1396 | 1976, January 3* |
| 1397 | 1976, December 23* |
| 1398 | 1977, December 12 |
| 1399 | 1978, December 2 |
| 1400 | 1979, November 21 |
| 1401 | 1980, November 9* |
| 1402 | 1981, October 30 |
| 1403 | 1982, October 19 |
| 1404 | 1983, October 8 |
| 1405 | 1984, September 27* |
| 1406 | 1985, September 16 |
| 1407 | 1986, September 6 |
| 1408 | 1987, August 26 |
| 1409 | 1988, August 14* |
| 1410 | 1989, August 3 |
| 1411 | 1990, July 24 |
| 1412 | 1991, July 13 |
| 1413 | 1992, July 2* |
| 1414 | 1993, June 21 |
| 1415 | 1994, June 10 |
| 1416 | 1995, May 31 |
| 1417 | 1996, May 19* |
| 1418 | 1997, May 9 |
| 1419 | 1998, April 28 |
| 1420 | 1999, April 17 |
| 1421 | 2000, April 6* |
| 1422 | 2001, March 26 |
| 1423 | 2002, March 15 |
| 1424 | 2003, March 5 |
| 1425 | 2004, February 22* |
| 1426 | 2005, February 10 |
| 1427 | 2006, January 31 |
| 1428 | 2007, January 20 |
| 1429 | 2008, January 10* |
| 1430 | 2008, December 29 |
| 1431 | 2009, December 18 |
| 1432 | 2010, December 8 |
| 1433 | 2011, November 27* |
| 1434 | 2012, November 15 |
| 1435 | 2013, November 5 |
| 1436 | 2014, October 25 |
| 1437 | 2015, October 15* |
| 1438 | 2016, October 3 |
| 1439 | 2017, September 22 |
| 1440 | 2018, September 12 |
| 1441 | 2019, September 11* |
| 1442 | 2020, August 20 |
| 1443 | 2021, August 10 |
| 1444 | 2022, July 30 |
| 1445 | 2023, July 19* |
| 1446 | 2024, July 8 |
| 1447 | 2025, June 27 |
| 1448 | 2026, June 17 |
| 1449 | 2027, June 6* |
| 1450 | 2028, May 25 |

# Coin Denomination Index

**ESCUDO** - Angola
Azores
Cape Verde
Chile
Guinea-Bissau
India-Portugese
Madeira Islands
Mozambique
Portugal
Saint Thomas & Prince Island
Timor
**EURO** - Bosnia-Herzegovina
Finland
France
Germany - Federal Republic
Isle of Man
Netherlands
Turkey
**EYRIR** - Iceland

## F

**FALUS** - Uzbekistan
**FANAM** - India - Princely States
**FARTHING** - Great Britain
Ireland Republic
Jamaica
**FEN** - China
China, Japanese Puppet States
China, People's Republic
China, Republic of
**FENIG** - Poland
**FENIGOW** - Poland
**FENINGA** - Bosnia-Herzegovina
**FIL** - Bahrain
Al Fujairah
Iraq
Jordan
Kuwait
Mutawakkilite
South Arabia
United Arab Emirates
Yemen Arab Republic
Yemen, Democratic Republic of
**FILLER** - Hungary
**FLORIN** - Aruba
Australia
East Africa
Fiji
Great Britain
Ireland Republic
Malawi
New Zealand
South Africa
**FLORINI** - Italy
**FLORINO** - Italy
**FORINT** - Hungary
**FRANC** - Algeria
Belgian Congo
Belgium
Benin
Burundi
Cambodia
Cameroon
Central African Republic
Central African States
Chad
Comoros
Congo Republic
Congo, Democratic Republic
Dahomey
Danish West Indies
Djibouti
Equatorial African States
Equatorial Guinea
France
French Afars & Issas
French Equitorial Africa
French Oceana
French Polynesia
French Somaliland
French West Africa
Gabon
Guadeloupe
Guinea
Ivory Coast
Katanga
Luxembourg
Madagascar
Mali
Martinique
Monaco
Morocco
New Caledonia
New Hebrides
Niger
Reunion
Rwanda
Rwanda & Burundi
Saint Pierre & Miquelon
Senegal
Switzerland
Togo
Tunisia
West African States
**FRANCO** - Equatorial Guinea
**FRANG AR** - Albania
**FRANK** - Liechtenstein
**FRANKEN** - Belgium
Liechtenstein
Saarland
**FUANG** - Thailand-Siam
**FUN** - Korea

## G

**GAUCHO** - Uruguay
**GERSH** - Ethiopia
**GHIRSH** - Hejaz
Hejaz & Nejd
Saudi Arabia
Sudan
**GOLDE** - Sierra Leone
**GOURDE** - Haiti
**GRAMO** - Bolivia
**GRAMS** - Afghanistan
**GRANI** - Malta, Order of
**GROATS** - Great Britain
**GROSCHEN** - Austria
**GROSZ** - Poland
**GROSZE** - Poland
**GROSZY** - Poland
**GUARANI** - Paraguay
**GUILDER** - Suriname
**GUINEA** - Saudi Arabia
**GULDEN** - Curacao
German States
Netherlands
Netherlands Antilles
Netherlands East Indies
Poland
Suriname
**GUTSCHRIFTSMARKE** - German States

## H

**HABIBI** - Afghanistan
**HALALA** - Mutawakkilite
Saudi Arabia
**HALER** - Czechoslovakia
**HALERE** - Czechoslovakia
**HALERU** - Bohemia & Moravia
Czech Republic
Czechoslovakia
**HALIEROV** - Slovakia
**HAO** - Viet Nam
**HARF** - Mutawakkilite
**HAU** - Tonga
**HELLER** - Austria
German East Africa
Hungary
**HRYVEN** - Ukraine
**HRYVNI** - Ukraine
**HRYVNIA** - Ukraine
**HWAN** - Korea-South

## I

**IMADI RIYAL** - Mutawakkilite
**INTI** - Peru
**INTIS** - Peru

## J

**JIAO** - China, People'S Republic
**KABIR** - Mutawakkilite

## K

**KARBOVANET** - Ukraine
**KARBOVANTSIV** - Ukraine
**KEPING** - Malay Peninsula
**KHUMSI** - Quaiti State of Hadhramaut
**KILO** - Tatarstan
**KINA** - Papua New Guinea
**KIP** - Laos
**KOBO** - Nigeria
**KOPEEK** - Transnistria
**KOPEJEK** - Tannu Tuva
**KOPEK** - Germany-Empire
Russia
Spitzbergen
**KOPIYKA** - Ukraine
**KOPIYKY** - Ukraine
**KOPIYOK** - Ukraine
**KORI** - India - Independent Kingdoms
India - Princely States
**KORONA** - Hungary
**KORUN** - Czech Republic
Czechoslovakia
Slovakia
**KORUNA** - Bohemia & Moravia
Czech Republic
Czechoslovakia
Slovakia
**KOULA** - Tonga
**KRAN** - Iran
**KRONA** - Iceland
Sweden
**KRONE** - Austria
Denmark
Greenland
Liechtenstein
Norway
**KRONEN** - Austria
Liechtenstein
**KRONER** - Denmark
Greenland
Norway
**KRONOR** - Sweden
**KRONUR** - Iceland
**KROONI** - Estonia
**KRUGERRAND** - South Africa
**KUNA** - Croatia
**KURUS** - Turkey
**KURUSH** - Turkey
**KWACHA** - Malawi
Zambia
**KWANZA** - Angola
**KYAT** - Myanmar
**KYATS** - Myanmar

## L

**LAARI** - Maldive Islands
**LANG** - Annam
**LARI** - Georgia
**LARIAT** - Maldive Islands
**LARIN** - Maldive Islands
**LATI** - Latvia
**LATS** - Latvia
**LATU** - Latvia
**LEI** - Moldova
Romania
**LEK** - Albania
**LEKE** - Albania
**LEKU** - Albania
**LEMPIRA** - Honduras
**LEONE** - Sierra Leone
**LEPTA** - Crete
Greece
**LEPTON** - Crete
**LEU** - Moldova
Romania
**LEV** - Bulgaria
**LEVA** - Bulgaria
**LI** - China
China, Japanese Puppet States
**LIANG** - China
**LIBRA** - Peru
**LICENTE** - Lesotho
**LIKUTA** - Congo, Democratic Republic
**LILANGENI** - Swaziland
**LIP** - Slovenia
**LIPA** - Croatia
Slovenia
**LIPE** - Croatia
Slovenia
**LIRA** - Italy
Malta
Mutawakkilite
San Marino
Syria
Turkey
Vatican City
**LIRAH** - Israel
**LIRE** - Italian Somaliland
Italy
San Marino
Vatican City
**LIRI** - Malta
**LIROT** - Israel
**LISENTE** - Lesotho
**LITAI** - Lithuania
**LITAS** - Lithuania
**LITRES** - Tatarstan
**LITU** - Lithuania
**LIVRE** - Lebanon
**LOTI** - Lesotho
**LOWE** - Bophuthatswana
**LUHLANGA** - Swaziland
**LUMA** - Armenia
**LWEI** - Angola

## M

**MACE** - China
**MAKUTA** - Congo, Democratic Republic
Zaire
**MALOTI** - Lesotho
**MANAT** - Azerbaijan
Turkmenistan
**MAREK** - Poland
**MARK** - Estonia
German States
German-Democratic Republic
Germany - Federal Republic
Germany, Third Reich
Germany, Weimar Republic
Germany-Empire
Poland
**MARKA** - Bosnia-Herzegovina
Estonia
**MARKKA** - Finland
**MARKKAA** - Finland
**MATONA** - Ethiopia
**MATONAS** - Ethiopia
**MAZUNA** - Morocco
**MAZUNAS** - Morocco
**MEI** - China, Republic of
**METICA** - Mozambique
**METICAIS** - Mozambique
**METICAL** - Mozambique
**METICAS** - Mozambique
**MIL** - Cyprus
Israel
Malta
**MILLIEME** - Egypt
Libya
**MILLIM** - Sudan
Tunisia
**MISCAL** - China
**MOHAR** - Nepal
**MOHUR** - India - Independent Kingdoms
India - Princely States
**MOMME** - Japan
**MONGO** - Mongolia
**MU** - Myanmar

## N

**NAIRA** - Nigeria
**NGULTRUM** - Bhutan
**NGWEE** - Zambia
**NKWE** - Bophuthatswana
**NOBLE** - Isle of Man

## O

**OCTORINO** - Great Britain
**ONZA** - Chile
Cuba
Mexico
**ORE** - Denmark
Faeroe Islands
Greenland
Iceland
Norway
Sweden
**OUGUIYA** - Mauritania
**OUNCE** - China, People's Republic
South Africa

## P

**PA'ANGA** - Tonga
**PAGODA** - India - Princely States
**PAHLAVI** - Iran
**PAI** - India - Princely States
**PAISA** - Afghanistan
Bhutan
India - Princely States
India-Republic
Nepal
Pakistan
**PAISE** - Afghanistan
India-Republic
**PARA** - Hejaz
Montenegro
Serbia
Turkey
Yugoslavia
**PARE** - Montenegro
Serbia
**PATACA** - Macao
**PAYALO** - India - Independent Kingdoms
**PE** - Myanmar
**PENCE** - Ascension Island
Australia
Biafra
British West Africa
Falkland Islands
Fiji
Gambia, The
Ghana
Gibraltar
Great Britain
Guernsey

Guyana
Ireland Republic
Isle of Man
Jersey
Malawi
New Guinea
New Zealand
Nigeria
Rhodesia
Rhodesia and Nyasaland
Saint Helena
Saint Helena & Ascension
South Africa
Southern Rhodesia
Tristan Da Cunha
Zambia
**PENGO** - Hungary
**PENNIA** - Finland
**PENNY** - Australia
British West Africa
Falkland Islands
Fiji
Gambia, The
Ghana
Gibraltar
Great Britain
Guernsey
Ireland Republic
Isle of Man
Jamaica
Jersey
Malawi
New Guinea
New Zealand
Nigeria
Rhodesia and Nyasaland
Saint Helena & Ascension
South Africa
Southern Rhodesia
Zambia
**PERPER** - Montenegro
**PERPERA** - Montenegro
**PESETA** - Equatorial Guinea
Saharawi Arab Democratic Republic
Spain
Spain Civil War
**PESEWA** - Ghana
**PESO** - Argentina
Bolivia
Chile
Colombia
Cuba
Dominican Republic
El Salvador
Guatemala
Guinea-Bissau
Honduras
Mexico
Mexico-Revolutionary
Nicaragua
Paraguay
Philippines
Uruguay
**PFENNIG** - German East Africa
German States
German-Democratic Republic
Germany - Federal Republic
Germany, Third Reich
Germany, Weimar Republic
Germany-Empire
Poland
**PFENNING** - Germany-Empire
**PHAN** - Annam
Ireland Republic
**PIASTRE** - Cyprus
Egypt
Ethiopia
French Indo-China
Hejaz
Jordan
Lebanon
Libya
Nejd
Sudan
Syria
Viet Nam
**PICE** - Bhutan
India - Princely States
India-British
India-Republic
Pakistan
**PIE** - India - Princely States
India-British
Pakistan
**PISA** - Philippines
**PISO** - Philippines
**PITIS** - Malay Peninsula
**PLATINA** - Isle of Man
**POISHA** - Bangladesh
**POLUSHKA** - Russia
**POND** - South Africa
**POUND** - Alderney
Ascension Island
Australia
Biafra
Cyprus
Egypt
Falkland Islands
Ghana
Gibraltar
Great Britain
Guernsey
Isle of Man
Jersey
Malta
Rhodesia
Saint Helena
Saint Helena & Ascension
Saudi Arabia
South Africa
South Georgia and the South Sandwich Islands
Sudan
Syria
Tristan Da Cunha
**PROTEA** - South Africa
**PRUTA** - Israel
**PRUTAH** - Israel
**PUL** - Afghanistan
**PULA** - Botswana
**PYA** - Myanmar

## Q

**QAPIK** - Azerbaijan
**QINDAR AR** - Albania
**QINDAR ARI** - Albania
**QINDARKA** - Albania
**QIRSH** - Egypt
Jordan
**QUETZAL** - Guatemala
**QUINDAR LEKU** - Albania

## R

**RAND** - South Africa
**RAPPEN** - Switzerland
**REAIS** - Brazil
**REAL** - Brazil
El Salvador
Guatemala
**REALES** - Mexico
**REICHSMARK** - Germany, Third Reich
Germany, Weimar Republic
**REICHSPFENNIG** - Germany, Third Reich
Germany, Weimar Republic
**REIS** - Azores
Brazil
Portugal
**RENTENPFENNIG** - Germany, Weimar Republic
**RIAL** - Iran
Morocco
Muscat & Oman
Mutawakkilite
Oman
Ras Al-Khaimah
Yemen Arab Republic
**RIEL** - Cambodia
**RIN** - Japan
**RINGGIT** - Malaysia
**RIYAL** - Ajman
Al Fujairah
Hejaz & Nejd
Iraq
Mutawakkilite
Qatar
Ras Al-Khaimah
Saudi Arabia
Sharjah
Umm Al Qaiwain
Yemen Arab Republic
Yemen Republic
**RIYALS** - Mutawakkilite
Yemen Arab Republic
**ROUBLE** - Belarus
Russia
Russian Caucasia
Spitzbergen
Tajikistan
Uzbekistan
**ROYAL** - Gibraltar
**RUBLE** - Russia
**RUFIYAA** - Maldive Islands
**RUPEE** - Afghanistan
Bhutan
Ceylon
Djibouti
India - Independent Kingdoms
India - Princely States
India-British
India-Republic
Keeling Cocos Islands
Mauritius
Nejd
Nepal
Pakistan
Seychelles
Sharjah
Sri Lanka
Tibet
**RUPIA** - India-Portugese
Indonesia
Italian Somaliland
**RUPIAH** - Indonesia
**RUPIE** - German East Africa
**RUPIEN** - German East Africa
**RYAL** - Oman

## S

**S.M.** - German States
**SALUNG** - Thailand-Siam
**SANAR** - Afghanistan
**SANTIM** - Morocco
**SANTIMAT** - Morocco
**SANTIMI** - Latvia
**SANTIMS** - Latvia
**SANTIMU** - Latvia
**SAPEQUE** - French Indo-China
**SAR** - China
**SATANG** - Thailand-Siam
**SCELLINO** - Somalia
**SCHILLING** - Austria
Malawi
**SCUDI** - Malta, Order of
San Marino
**SCUDO** - Malta, Order of
San Marino
**SEN** - Brunei
Cambodia
Indonesia
Japan
Malaysia
Netherlands East Indies
Thailand-Siam
**SENE** - Western Samoa
**SENGI** - Congo, Democratic Republic
**SENITI** - Tonga
**SENT** - Estonia
**SENTE** - Lesotho
**SENTI** - Estonia
Somalia
Tanzania
**SENTIMO** - Philippines
**SERTRUMS** - Bhutan
**SERTUM** - Bhutan
**SHAHI** - Afghanistan
Iran
**SHEQALIM** - Israel
**SHEQEL** - Israel
**SHILINGI** - Tanzania
**SHILLING** - Australia
Biafra
British West Africa
Cyprus
East Africa
Fiji
Gambia, The
Ghana
Great Britain
Guernsey
Ireland Republic
Jamaica
Jersey
Kenya
New Guinea
New Zealand
Nigeria
Rhodesia
Rhodesia and Nyasaland
Somalia
Somaliland
South Africa
Southern Rhodesia
Uganda
Zambia
**SHO** - Tibet
**SHOKANG** - Tibet
**SKAR** - Tibet
**SOL** - Peru
**SOLDE** - India-Portugese
**SOLE** - Peru
**SOM** - Kyrgystan
Uzbekistan
**SOMALO** - Somalia
**SOVEREIGN** - Andorra
Australia
Canada
Cyprus
Gibraltar
Great Britain
India-British
Isle of Man
Jersey
Saudi Arabia
South Africa
**SOVRANO** - Malta, Order of
**SRANG** - Tibet
**STOTINKA** - Bulgaria
**STOTINKI** - Bulgaria
**STOTINOV** - Slovenia
**SU** - Viet Nam
**SUCRE** - Ecuador
**SUVERENA** - Bosnia-Herzegovina
**SYLI** - Guinea

## T

**TAEL** - China
China, Japanese Puppet States
French Indo-China
**TAKA** - Bangladesh
**TAKKA** - Bangladesh
**TALA** - Tokelau Islands
Western Samoa
**TALLERO** - Eritrea
**TAM** - Tibet
**TAMBALA** - Malawi
**TANGA** - India-Portugese
**TANGKA** - Tibet
**TARI** - Malta, Order of
**TENE** - Cook Islands
**TENGA** - Uzbekistan
**TENGE** - Kazakhstan
**TENNESI** - Turkmenistan
**THEBE** - Botswana
**THETRI** - Georgia
**TIEN** - Annam
**TILLA** - Afghanistan
Uzbekistan
**TIYIN** - Uzbekistan
**TOEA** - Papua New Guinea
**TOLA** - India-British
Nepal
**TOLAR** - Slovenia
**TOLARJA** - Slovenia
**TOLARJEV** - Slovenia
**TOMAN** - Iran
Russian Caucasia
**TRAMBIYO** - India - Independent Kingdoms
**TUGRIK** - Mongolia
**TYIN** - Kazakhstan

## U

**URUGUAYAN PESOS** - Uruguay

## V

**VAN** - Annam
**VATU** - Vanuatu
**VERRECHNUNGSMARK** - German States
**VERRECHNUNGSMARKE** - German States
**VINAR** - Slovenia

## W

**WEN** - China, Republic of
**WERK** - Ethiopia
**WON** - Korea
Korea-North
Korea-South

## X

**XU** - Viet Nam

## Y

**YANG** - Korea
**YEN** - Japan
**YUAN** - China, People's Republic
China, Republic of

## Z

**ZAIRE** - Congo, Democratic Republic
Zaire
**ZALAT** - Mutawakkilite
**ZLOTE** - Poland
**ZLOTY** - Poland
**ZLOTYCH** - Poland
**ZOLOTNIK** - Russia

# MINT INDEX

## A

**A** - Augsburg, Hohenlohe-Neuenstein-Neuenstein (German States)
**A** - Austria (Vienna), Hungary, Liechtenstein, Venice (Italian States)
**A** - Berlin, East Friesland (German States)
**A** - Medellin (Colombia)
**A** - Paris (France)
**AA** - Metz (France)
**A-B** - Abrud (Transylvania)
**ABERYSTWYTH** - Great Britain
**ABRUD** - Transylvania
**A-C** - Klausenberg (Transylvania)
**A-F** - Fogarasch (Transylvania)
**AI** - Karlsburg (Transylvania)
**AIX** - France
**AL-IV** - Karlsburg (Transylvania)
**ALGIERS** - Algeria
**ALTONA** - Denmark
**AMBERG** - Pfalz (German States)
**AMIENS** - France
**AMSTERDAM** - Holland (Netherlands)
**ANGERS** - France
**AR** - Arras (France)
**ARBOGA** - Sweden
**ARRAS** - France, Artois (Spanish Netherlands)
**AUGSBURG** - Austria, Hohenlohe-Neuenstein-Neuenstein (German States)
**AURICH** - East Friesland (German States)
**AVESTA** - Sweden
**AVIGNON** - Vatican Papal City States
**AZ**Zlatna (Transylvania)

## B

**B** - Bacain (India-Portuguese)
**B** - Bahia (Brazil)
**B** - Bamberg, Bayersdorf, Bayreuth, Brandenburg-Bayreuth (German States)
**B** - Barcelona, Burgos (Spain)
**B** - Bologna (Italy)
**B** - Breslau, Posen (Poland); East Friesland (German States)
**B** - Dieppe, Rouen (France)
**B** - Kormoczbanya, Kremnitz, (Hungary)
**B** - Nuevo Reino (Bogota)
**Ba** - Barcelona (Spain-Local)
**BA** - Barcelona (Spain)
**BACAIN** - India-Portuguese
**BADENWEILER** - Lorraine (France)
**BAHIA** - Brazil
**BARCELONA** - Spain
**BAYONNE** - France
**BB** - Strasbourg (France)
**BD** - Pau (France)
**BE** - Bistrice (Romania)
**BERGA** - Spain
**BERLIN** - Brandenburg, East Friesland, Reuss, Sayn-Wittgenstein-Berleburg, Sayn-Wittgenstein-Wittgenstein (German States)
**BERNE** - Liechtenstein
**BESCANON** - France
**BE - V** - Bistrice (Romania)
**BEZ** - Bistrice (Romania)
**BILBAO** - Spain
**BISTRICE** - Romania, Transylvania
**BN** - Nagybanya (Hungary)
**BOGOTA** - Colombia
**BOIZENBURG** - Mecklenburg-Gustrow (German States)
**BOLOGNA** - Bozzolo, Sardinia (Italian States); Vatican Papal City States
**BORDEAUX** - France
**BOUILLON** - Belgium
**BOURGES** - France
**BP** - Budapest (Hungary)
**BRESLAU** - Austria, East Friesland (German States), Posen (Poland)
**BRIEG** - Austria
**BRISTOL** - Great Britain
**BROMBERG** - Poland, Riga
**BRUNN** - Austria
**BRUSSELS** - Spain
**B.T.** - Bistrice (Romania)
**BUCHSWEILER** - Hanau-Lichtenburg (German States)
**BUDAPEST** - Hungary
**BUDWEIS** - Austria
**BUREAU OF ROYAL TRANSPORTATION** - Korea
**BURGOS** - Spain

## C

**C** - Cadiz, Cuenca (Spain)
**C** - Caen (France)
**C** - Cartagena (Colombia)
**C** - Catalonia, Zaragoza (Spain-Local)
**C** - Christophstal (German States)
**C** - Civitas (Transylvania)
**C** - Cleves (German States)
**C** - Kulmbach-Brandenburg-Bayreuth (German States)
**C** - Prague (Bohemia)
**C** - Saint Lo (France)
**C-A** - Karlsburg (Transylvania)
**CA** - Cuenca, Zaragoza (Spain)
**CA** - Vienna (Hungary)
**CADIZ** - Spain
**CAEN** - France
**CARLISLE** - Great Britain
**CARTAGENA** - Colombia
**CASSEL** - Hesse-Cassel (German States)
**CASSOVIA** - Transylvania
**CATALONIA** - Spain, Spain-Local
**C-B** - Cibiniu-Sibiu (Transylvania)
**CB** - Claudiopolis, Kronstadt, Hermannstadt (Transylvania)
**CC** - Cassovia (Transylvania)
**CELLE** - Brunswick-Luneburg-Calenberg-Hannover (German States)
**CF** - Fagaras (Transylvania)
**CH** - Chalons (France)
**CH** - Pressburg (Hungary)
**CHAMBERY** - Sardinia (Italian States)
**CHESTER** - Great Britain
**CHOLLA MILITARY FORT** - Korea
**CHOLLA LEFT NAVAL BASE** - Korea
**CHOLLA PROVINCIAL OFFICE** - Korea
**CHOLLA RIGHT NAVAL BASE** - Korea
**CHRISTOPHSTAL** - Wurttemberg (German States)
**CI** - Hermannstadt (Transylvania)
**CI-BI** - Hermannstadt (Transylvania)
**CIBIN** - Hermannstadt (Transylvania)
**CLAUSTHAL** - Brunswick-Luneburg-Calenberg Hannover (German States)
**CLEVES** - German States
**CM** - Hermannstadt (Transylvania)
**CM** - Kaschau (Hungary)
**COBLENZ** - Trier (German States)
**COLCHESTER** - Great Britain
**COLOMBO** - Ceylon (Shri Lanka)
**COMMANDO MILITARY UNIT** - Korea
**COPENHAGEN** - Denmark
**COR.** - Kronstadt (Transylvania)
**CORUNA** - Spain
**CRAILSHEIM** - Brandenburg-Ansbach (German States)
**CREUSSEN** - Brandenburg-Bayreuth (German States)
**CROSSEN** - Brandenburg (German States)
**CT** - Christophstal (German States)
**CUENCA** - Spain
**CUGNON** - Lowenstein-Wertheim-Rochefort (German States)
**CUZ or CUZO plain** - Cuzco (Peru)
**CUZCO** - Peru
**CUZO monogram** - Cuzco (Peru)
**CV** - Klausenburg (Transylvania)
**CW** - Hermannstadt (Transylvania)

## D

**D** - Aurich, Dusseldorf, East Friesland Julich-Berg (German States)
**D** - Graz (Styria)
**D** - Lyon (France)
**D** - Salzburg (Austria)
**DACHSBACH** - Brandenburg-Ansbach, Brandenburg-Bayreuth (German States)
**DARMSTADT** - Hanau-Lichtenberg (German States)
**DIEPPE** - France
**DIJON** - France
**DOMITZ** - Mecklenburg-Schwerin (German States)
**DORDRECHT** - Holland (Netherlands)
**DRESDEN** - East Friesland, Saxony (German States)
**DRIESEN** - Brandenburg (German States)
**DUSSELDORF** - Julich-Berg (German States)

## E

**E** - Evora (Portugal)
**E** - Karlsburg (Transylvania)
**E** - Tours (France)
**EL** - Ellrich, Sayn-Wittgenstein-Wittgenstein (German States)
**ELLRICH** - Hohnstein (German States)
**ENSISHEIM** - Alsace (French States), Austria
**ERLANGEN** - Brandenburg-Bayreuth (German States)
**EVORA** - Portugal
**EXETER** - Great Britain

## F

**F** - Angers (France)
**F** - East Friesland, Frankfurt am Main, Freudenstadt-Wurttemburg, Furth; Bamberg, Brandenburg-Ansbach, Magdeburg (German States)
**F** - Hall (Austria), Venice (Italian States)
**F** - Nuevo Reino (Colombia)
**FAGARAS** - Transylvania
**FB** - Felso Banya (Transylvania)
**FELSO BANYA** - Transylvania
**FERRARA** - Vatican Papal City States
**FEURS** - France
**FLANDERS** - Spanish Netherlands
**FLORENCE** - Lorraine (France), Sardinia, Tuscany (Italian States), Italy
**FOG.** - Fogarasch (Transylvania)
**FOGARASCH** - Transylvania
**FOOD SUPPLY OFFICE** - Korea
**FRANKFURT** - Frankfurt am Main (German States)
**FREDERIKSBORG** - Denmark
**FRIEDBERG** - Hohenlohe-Waldenburg-Schilllingsfurst (German States)
**FRIEDEWALDE** - Sayn-Altenkirchen (German States)
**FS** - Nuevo Reino (Colombia)
**FT** - Klausenburg; Hermannstadt (Transylvania)
**FURTH** - Austria, Bamburg, Brandenburg-Ansbach, Brandenburg-Bayreuth, Franconian Circle (German States)

## G

**G** - Gera (German States)
**G** - Glatz, Glogau (Silesia)
**G** - Graz (Styria)
**G** - Gunzburg (Austria)
**G** - Nagybanya (Hungary)
**G** - Poitiers (France)
**GA** - Karlsburg (Transylvania)
**GADEBUSCH** - Mecklenburg-Gustrow, Mecklenburg Schwerin (German States)
**GENERAL MILITARY OFFICE** - Korea
**GENGE** - Azerbaijan
**GENOA** - Bozzolo, Sardinia (Italian States)
**GERA** - Reuss (German States)
**GITSCHIN** - Austrian States
**GLATZ** - Austria
**GLOGAU** - Austria
**GLUCKSTADT** - Mecklenburg-Gustrow (German States), Denmark
**GM** - Mantua (Italian States)
**GN** - Nagybanya (Hungary)
**GOTHENBURG** - Sweden
**GR** - Graz (Styria)
**GRAZ** - Austria
**GRENADA** - Spain
**GROIEN** - Mecklenburg-Gustrow (German States)
**GUBBIO** - Vatican Papal City States
**GUNZBURG** - Austria
**GUSTROW** - Mecklenburg-Gustrow (German States)
**GYF** - Karlsburg (Hungary)
**GYULAFEHERVAR** - Hungary

## H

**H** - Gunzburg (Austria)
**H** - Hermannstadt (Transylvania)
**H** - La Rochelle (France)
**HA** - Hall (Austria), Hungary
**HALBERSTADT** - Brandenberg (German States)
**HALL** - Austria, Venice (Italian States)
**HANAU** - Hanau-Lichtenberg (German States)
**HANNOVER** - Reuss (German States)
**HASSELT** - Belgium
**HEIDELBERG** - Hanau-Lichtenberg, Pfalz (German States)
**HELSINGER** - Denmark
**HERMANNSTADT** - Austria; Transylvania
**HILDESHEIM** - Hildesheim (German States)
**HS** - Hermannstadt (Transylvania)

## I

**I** - Limoges (France)

## J

**JAFNA** - Ceylon (Shri Lanka)
**JOACHIMSTAL** - Austria

## K

**K** - Bordeaux (France)
**K** - Hohenlohe-Langenburg, Kirchberg (German States)
**K** - Kormoczbanya, Kremnitz (Hungary)
**KAESONG TOWNSHIP MILITARY OFFICE** - Korea
**KALMAR** - Sweden
**KARLSBURG** - Hungary, Transylvania
**KASCHAU** - Austria, Hungary
**KASSA** - Hungary
**KB** - Kormoczbanya (Hungary)
**K-B or K.B.** - Kremnitz (Hungary)
**KENGIS** - Sweden
**KING'S NORTON** - Angola
**KIRCHBERG** - Hohenlohe-Langenburg (German States)
**KIS SELYK** - Transylvania
**KITZINGEN** - Brandenburg-Ansbach (German States)
**KLAGENFURT** - Austria
**KLAUSENBURG** - Austria, Transylvania
**KLETTENBERG** - Sayn-Wittgenstein-Wittgenstein (German States)
**KN** - King's Norton (Great Britain)
**KO** - Klausenberg (Transylvania)
**KOLLN ANDER SPREE** - Brandenburg (German States)
**KONGSBERG** - Norway
**KONIGSEGG** - Brandenburg (German States), East Prussia (Poland)
**KORMOCZBANYA** - Hungary
**KRAIN** - Austria
**KRAKOW** - Poland
**KREMNITZ** - Austria, Hungary, Transylvania
**KRONSTADT** - Transylvania
**KS** - Kis Selyk (Transylvania)
**KULMBACH** - Brandenburg-Bayreuth (German States)
**KUTTENBERG** - Austria
**KV** - Klausenburg (Transylvania)
**KYONGSANG LEFT NAVAL BASE** - Korea
**KYONGSANG NAVAL STATION** - Korea
**KYONGSANG PROVINCIAL OFFICE** - Korea
**KYONGSANG RIGHT NAVAL BASE** - Korea

## L

**L** - Bayonne (France)
**L** - Hesse-Cassel, Langenburg-Hohenlohe-Langenburg, Leipzig, Lippoldsberg, Saxony (German States)
**L** - Lima (Peru)
**L** - Lisbon (Portugal)
**L** - Lobsenz (Poland)
**LANDSKRONA** - Sweden
**LANGENBURG** - German States
**LA PLATA** - Bolivia
**LA ROCHELLE** - France
**LAY** - France
**LEIPZIG** - Saxony (German States), Poland
**LEMBERG** - Poland
**LENINGRAD** - Russia
**LIEGE** - Belgium
**LIEGNITZ** - Austria
**LILLE** - France
**LIMA** - Peru
**LIMAE** - Lima (Peru)
**LIMOGES** - France
**LIPPOLDSBERG** - Hesse-Cassel (German States)
**LINARES** - Spain

**LISBON** - Portugal
**LIVORNO** - Tuscany (Italian States)
**LMK** - Vilna
**LOBSENZ** - Poland
**LONDON** - Great Britain
**LUNDY** - Great Britain
**LUNEN** - Brandenburg (German States)
**LYNGBY** - Denmark
**LYON** - France

## M

**M** - Lombardy, Toulouse (France)
**M** - Madrid (Spain)
**M.** - Mainz (Austria)
**M** - Medellin (Colombia)
**M** - Mediasch (Transylvania)
**M** - Milan, Sardinia (Italy)
**M** - Monaco
**MACON** - France
**MADRID** - Spain
**MAESEYCK** - Belgium
**MAGDEBURG** - Brandenburg, East Friesland (German States)
**MAHLE - (MALE)** Maldive Islands
**MAINZ** - Austria
**MANNHEIM** - Pfalz (German States)
**MANTUA** - Austria
**MAROMME** - France
**MARIENEHE** - Mecklenburg-Gustrow (German States)
**MB** - Brieg (Silesia)
**MC** - Hermannstadt, Kaschau (Transylvania)
**MEDELLIN** - Antioquia, Colombia
**MEDIASCH** - Transylvania
**METZ** - France
**MEXICO CITY** - Mexico
**MIDDELBURG** - Zeeland (Netherlands)
**MILAN** - Austria, Bozzolo, Sardinia (Italian States)
**MILITARY TRAINING COMMAND** - Korea
**MINDEN** - Brandenburg, Sayn-Wittgenstein-Wittgenstein
**MINISTRY OF INDUSTRY** - Korea
**MM** - Mukachiv (Transylvania)
**Mo** - Mexico City (Mexico)
**MO - COM - N-E** - Nagy-Enyed (Transylvania)
**MODENA** - Bozzolo (Italian States)
**MONACO** - Monaco
**MONETA WSCHOVENSIS** - Poland
**MONTPELLIER** - France
**MORLASS** - France
**MORITZBERG** - Hildesheim (German States)
**MOSCOW** - Russia
**MR** - Hermannstadt (Transylvania)
**MUKACHIV** - Transylvania
**MUNICH** - Bavaria (German States)
**MW** - Moneta Wschovensis (Poland)
**Mxo** - Mexico City (Mexico)

## N

**N** - Montpellier (France)
**N - NIENBURG** - Brunswick-Luneburg-Celle, (German States)
**N - NIDDA** - Hesse-Darmstadt (German States)
**N** - Nuevo Reino (Colombia)
**N - NUREMBERG** - Franconian Circle (German States)
**NACKHCHAWAN** - Azerbaijan
**NAGYBANYA** - Austria, Hungary, Transylvania
**NAGY-ENYED** - Transylvania
**NAMUR** - Spanish Netherlands
**NANCY** - Lorraine (France)
**NANTES** - France
**N-B or NB** - Nagybanya (Hungary)
**NE** - Nagy-Enyed (Transylvania)
**NEGAPATNAM** - Ceylon (Shri Lanka)
**NEISSE** - Austria
**NER** - Cartagena (Colombia)
**NEUBURG am INN** - Austria
**NEUENSTEIN** - Hohelohe (German States)
**NEWARK** - Great Britain
**NIDDA** - Hesse-Darmstadt (German States)
**NIENBURG** - Brunswick-Luneburg-Celle (German States)
**NIKOLSBURG** - Austria
**NORWICH** - Great Britain
**NR** - Cartagena, Nuevo Reino (Colombia)
**NRE** - Cartagena (Colombia)
**NUEVO REINO (Bogota)** - Colombia
**NUREMBERG** - Franconian Circle, Hohenlohe Neuenstein-Weikersheim (German States)
**NYKOPING** - Sweden

## O

**O** - Clermont (France)
**O** - Olmutz (Austria)
**O** - Onolzbach (Ansbach), Brandenburg-Ansbach (German States)
**O** - Oravicza (Hungary)
**O** - Riom (France)
**OELS** - Austria
**OFFENBACH** - Pfalz (German States)
**OHLAU** - Austria
**OLMUTZ** - Austria
**OPPELN** - Austria
**ORASTIE** - Transylvania
**ORAVICZA** - Austria
**OXFORD** - Great Britain

## P

**P** - Dijon (France)
**P** - Pamplona (Spain-Local)
**P** - Pernambuco (Brazil)
**P** - Popayan (Colombia)
**P** - Porto (Portugal)
**P** - Potosi (Mexico)
**P** - Prague (Bohemia)
**PAMPLONA** - Spain-Local
**PARIS** - France, Monaco
**PARIS - Privy Marks Only** - France, Monaco
**PARMA** - Bozzolo (Italian States)
**PAU** - France
**PERNAMBUCO** - Brazil
**PHILIPSBURG** - Trier (German States)
**PISIA** - Tuscany (Italian States)
**PISIS** - Tuscany (Italian States)
**PM** - Prague (Austria)
**PN or Pn** - Popayan (Colombia)
**POITTERS** - France
**PONTEFRACT** - Great Britain
**POPAYAN** - Colombia
**PORTO** - Portugal
**POSEN** - Poland
**POTOSI** - Bolivia
**POZSONY** - Hungary
**PP** - Pamplona (Spain), Pressburg (Hungary)
**P-R** - Gunzburg (Austria)
**PRAGUE** - Austria
**PRESSBURG** - Austria, Hungary
**PTA monogram** - La Plata (Bolivia)
**PTS monogram** - Potosi (Bolivia)
**P'YONGAN PROVINCIAL OFFICE** - Korea

## Q

## R

**R** - Rio de Janeiro (Brazil)
**R - ROTH** - Brandenburg-Ansbach (German States)
**RATIBOR** - Austria
**RATZEBURG** - Mecklenburg-Schwerin (German States)
**REGENSBURG** - Brandenburg (German States)
**REIMS** - France
**REMIREMONT** - Lorraine (France)
**RENNES** - France
**RINETEIN** - Schaumburg-Pinneberg (Denmark)
**RIO** - Brazil
**RIO DE JANEIRO** - Brazil
**RIOM** - France
**RN** - Cartagena (Colombia)
**ROMARTI (REMIREMONT)** - Lorraine (France)
**ROME** - Vatican Papal States
**ROQUEMAURE** - France
**ROSTOCK** - Mecklenburg-Gustrow (German States)
**ROUEN** - France
**Rs** - Rio de Janeiro (Brazil)

## S

**S** - Cartagena, Nuevo Reino (Colombia)
**S** - Reims (France)
**S** - Schmollnitz (Hungary)
**S** - Seville (Spain)
**S - SCHWABACH** - Brandenburg-Ansbach, Franconian Circle (German States)
**SAGAN** - Austria, Austrian States
**SAINT LO** - France
**SAINT PALAIS** - France
**SAINT POLTEN** - Austria
**SAINT VEIT** - Austria
**SALISBURY** - Great Britain
**SALZBURG** - Austria
**SANTHIA** - Sardinia (Italian States)
**SATER** - Sweden
**SB** - Schassburg (Transylvania)
**SCHASSBURG** - Transylvania
**SCHEMNITZ** - Hungary
**SCHLEUSINGEN** - Henneberg (German States)
**SCHMOLLNITZ** - Austria, Hungary, Italian States
**SCHWABACH** - Brandenburg-Ansbach, Franconian Circle (German States)
**SCHWAAN** - Mecklenburg-Gustrow (German States)
**SCHWERIN** - Mecklenburg-Schwerin (German States)
**SCHWARZENAU** - Sayn-Wittgenstein-Wittgenstein (German States)
**SCARBOROUGH** - Great Britain
**SEGOVIA** - Spain
**SEVILLE** - Spain
**SF** - Nuevo Reino (Colombia)
**SHREWSBURY** - Great Britain
**SL** - Seville (Spain)
**SODERKOPING** - Sweden
**SPECIAL ARMY UNIT** - Korea
**STARGARD** - Brandenburg (German States)
**STENAY** - Lorraine (France)
**STOCKHOLM** - Sweden
**STRASBOURG** - France
**STUTTGART** - Wurttemberg (German States)
**SV** - Hermannstadt, Orastie (Transylvania)
**SZOMOLNOK** - Hungary

## T

**T** - Nantes (France)
**T** - Toledo
**TESCHEN** - Austria
**TO** - Toledo (Spain)
**TOLEDO** - Spain
**TOWER** - London (Great Britain)
**TOULOUSE** - France
**TOURNAI** - Spanish Netherlands
**TOURS** - France
**TOWER OF LONDON** - Great Britain
**TREASURY DEPARTMENT** - Korea
**TRIER** - Trier (German States)
**TROPPAU** - Austria
**TROYES** - France
**TRUJILLO** - Spain
**TUBINGEN** Wurttemberg (German States)
**TRURO** - Great Britain
**TURIN** - Sardinia (Italian States)
**TUSCANY** - Bozzolo (Italian States)

## U

## V

**V** - Troyes (France)
**V** - Venice, Venetia (Italy)
**VADSTENA** - Sweden
**VALLADOLID** - Spain
**VALENCE** - France
**VENICE** - Austria, Venice (Italian States)
**VERCELLI** - Sardinia, Vercelli (Italian States)
**VI** - Vienna (Austria)
**VIENNA** - Austria, Italian States, Lobkowitz-Sternstein (German States)
**VIENNE** - France
**VILNA** - Lithuania
**VILNIUS** - Lithuania
**VM** - Sagan (Silesia)

## W

**W** - Breslau (Poland)
**W** - Lille (France)
**W** - Vienna (Austria)
**W** - Wschowa (Fraustadt)
**WEYMOUTH** - Great Britain
**WI** - Vienna (Austria), Hungary
**WISMAR** - Mecklenburg-Gustrow, Mecklenburg-Schwerin (German States)
**WITTGENSTEIN** - Sayn-Wittgenstein-Wittgenstein (German States)
**WONJU TOWNSHIP MILITARY OFFICE** - Korea
**WORCESTER** - Great Britain
**WORTH** - Hanau-Lichtenberg (German States)
**WSCHOWA** - Fraustadt (Poland)
**WURZBURG** - Austria

## X

**X** - Amiens (France)

## Y

**Y** - Bourges (France)
**YORK** - Great Britain

## Z

**Z** - Zaragoza (Spain-Local)
**ZB** - Zlatna (Transylvania)
**ZELLERFELD** - Brunswick-Luneburg-Calenberg Hannover, Brunswick-Luneburg-Celle (German States)
**ZLATNA** - Transylvania
**ZV** - Zecca Venezia (Venice, Italian States)

# SYMBOLS

**ANGEL FACE** - Brussels (Spanish Netherlands)
**AQUEDUCT** - Segovia (Spain)
**ARMS** - Amsterdam (Netherlands)
**BEE** - Dachsbach (German States)
**CLOVERLEAF** - Dachsbach, Denmark
**COW** - Pau (France)
**CROWNED M** - Metz (France)
**CROWNED ROOTS** - Cibiniu-Sibiu (Transylvania)
**CROSSED HAMMERS** - Kongsberg (Norway), Kuttenberg (Bohemia)
**CROSSED STAVES** - Denmark
**CROWN** - Copenhagen (Denmark)
**DOUBLE FLEUR-DE-LIS** - Oppeln (Silesia)
**EAGLE** - Hall (Austria)
**FLAG** - Sagan (Silesia)
**FLAGS** - Valladolid
**HALF MOON** - Erlangen (German States)
**HAND** - Antwerp (Spanish Netherlands)
**HEART** - Kulmbach (German States)
**LILLY** - Dachsbach (German States)
**LION RAMPANT** - Namur (Spanish Netherlands)
**LIS** - Flanders (Spanish Netherlands)
**ORB** - Altona (Denmark)
**POT HOOK** - Crailsheim (German States)
**RAT** - Arras (France)
**ROSE** - Dordrecht (Netherlands)
**ROSETTE** - Roth, Schwabach (German States)
**SCALLOPED SHELL** - Coruna (Spain)
**SHIELD** - Vienna (Austria)
**STAR** - Dresden, East Friesland (German States), Maastricht (Spanish Netherlands)
**TOWER** - Tournais (Spanish Netherlands)
**TOWER TOP (crenellated)** - Kitzingen
**TREE** - s'Hertogenbosch (Spanish Netherlands)
**TWO HORSESHOES** - Augsburg (German States)
**URN** - Creussen (German States)
**¢** - Aix (France)
**9** - Rennes (France)

# MINT DATA

**The mints, mint representatives and firms listed below provide numismatic services for acquring new issues.**

**Afghanistan:** (Cuban Mint) Numiversal Macco, Postfach 2565, D-6780 Pirmasons, W. Germany.

**Albania:** U.S.A.

**American Samoa:** MDM Deutsche Munze, Theodor-Huess Str. 7, 3300 Braunschweig, Germany.

**Andorra:** Servei D'Emissions Vegueria Episcopal, Prat de La Creu, 96.4t5a, Andorra La Vella, (Principat d'Andorra). FAX: 376-86-9099.

**Antigua-Barbuda:** British Royal Mint.

**Arabic Sahara, Democratic Republic:** See Afghanistan. Numiversal Postfach 2565, 6780 Pirmasens, Germany.

**Aruba:** See Netherlands.

**Austria:** Silver commemorative coins, special select sets and proof sets. Schoeller & Co., Bankaktiengesellschaft, Postfach 172, A-1011 Vienna, Austria. Universal Coins, 47 Clarence St., Suite 201, Ottawa, Ontario, K1N 9K1 Canada.

**Australia:** Mint sets, proof sets, gold and silver commemorative coins. Australian Coins: Universal Coins, 47 Rue Clarence, Suite 201, Ottawa, Ontario, K1N 9D1 Canada. Outside the U.S.: Royal Australian Mint, Controller of the Mint, Denison Street Deakin, Canberra, A.C.T. 2600, Australia. Perth Mint, 310 Hay St., East Perth, W.A. 6004, Australia. Bullion: MTB, 90 Broad St., New York, NY 10004-2290. Panda America, 3460 Torrance Blvd., Suite 100, Torrance, CA 90503.

**Bahamas:** British Royal Mint. For proof & mint sets, gold & silver commems: Paramount International, 4307 Vineland Rd. H-1, Orlando, FL 32811. (407) 841-0134, FAX: 407-423-2641.

**Bahrain:** Silver proof set. British Royal Mint.

**Bangladesh:** MDM (see American Samoa).

**Barbados:** Gold commemorative. Franklin Mint, Franklin Center, PA 19091. British Royal Mint, other commemoratives, Valcambi Mint, etc.

**Belarus:** Liberty Mint, 651 Columbia Lane, Provo, UT 84604.

**Belgium:** Monnaie Royale de Belgique, Boulevard Pacheco 32, B-1000 Bruxelles, Belgium, Omni-Trading b.v., Canadian 8a, 7316 BX Apeldoorn, Netherlands.

**Belize:** Gold coins. Franklin Mint, Franklin Center, PA 19091. British Royal Mint.

**Bermuda:** British Royal Mint. Bermuda Monetary Authority, P.O. Box HM2447, Hamilton HM JX, Bermuda.

**Bhutan:** MDM (see American Samoa).

**Botswana:** British Royal Mint.

**Brazil:** Casa Da Moeda Do Brasil, Rua Rene Bittencourt 371, 23565 Dist. Ind de Santa Cruz, Rio de Janeiro, Brazil.

**British Virgin Islands:** Franklin Mint, Franklin Center, PA 19091.

**Brunei:** Singapore Mint.

**Bulgaria:** Numismatika Shop, 29 Vitosha Blvd., Sofia, Bulgaria.

**Cambodia:** See Afghanistan.

**Canada:** Proof sets, specimen sets, uncirculated sets, proof and brilliant uncirculated silver dollars, gold commemoratives and bullion coins. Royal Canadian Mint, P.O. Box 457, Station A, Ottawa, Ontario K1N 8V5, Canada.

**Cayman Islands:** Currency Board, Government Administration Building, George Town, Grand Cayman, Cayman Islands, British West Indies.

**China, P.R.:** Pandas, MTB, One World Trade Center, Suite 3331, New York, NY 10048, also Panda America, 3460, Torrance Blvd., Suite 100, Torrance, CA 91436. (Pandas, sets and other commemorative & bullion coins).

**China, Rep.:** Circulation coinage. Bank of Taiwan, P.O. Box 8, 120, Chungking Road, South, Section 1, Taipei, Taiwan 100, Republic of China. Fred Weinberg, Inc., (see China, P.R.) lunar & panda issues.

**Congo:** See Afghanistan.

**Cook Islands:** Pobjoy Mint, (see Isle of Man), Singapore Mint & British Royal Mint, Franklin Mint (see British Virgin Islands), MDM (see American Samoa).

**Congo People's Rep.:** Numiversal (see Arab Sahara).

**Cuba:** Empresa Cubana de Acunaciones, Calle 44 #4302 esq. a. Ave. 43 Marianao, Ciudad de la Habana, Habana, Cuba. Also see Afghanistan.

**Czech Republic:** Ivo Cerny, P.O. Box 19, 69504 Hodonin, Czech Rep.

**Cyprus:** Silver commemorative coins, mint sets and proof sets. Central Bank of Cyprus, P.O. Box 5529, Nicosia, Cyrpus.

**Denmark:** Mint sets, 1981-84. Den Kongelige Moent, Solmarksvej5, DK-2605 Brondby, Denmark.

**Djibouti:** MDM (see American Samoa).

**Dominica:** British Royal Mint.

**Dominican Republic:** Banco Central De La Republica Dominicana, Apartado Postal 1347, Santo Domingo, Dominican Rep.

**Egypt:** U.S. distributor, Egyptian Coins Center, P.O. Box 77, Mohamed farid, Cairo, Egypt. Also Lauren Benson Inc., 215 Main St., Suite 603, Davenport, IA 52801, and Franklin Mint (see British Virgin Islands).

**Equatorial Guinea:** Infinsa Internationa, P.O. Box 8486, Madrid 28080 Spain.

**Estonia:** See Finland and British Royal Mint.

**Falkland Islands:** British Royal Mint.

**Fiji:** Pacific Sovereign Mint, Ltd., Ermington Mill, Ivybridge, Devon, England PL21 9NT. MDM (see American Samoa).

**Finland:** Mint of Finland, Box 13, SF-01671 Vantaa, Finland.

**France:** Fleur-de-coin sets, silver and gold pieforts, proof commemoratives. Le Directeur de Monnaies, 11, Quai de Conti, 75270 Paris, France, and Universal Coins, 47 Clarence St., Suite 201, Ottawa, Ontario, Canada K1N 9K1. Fred Weinberg, Inc., 16311 Ventura Blvd., #550, Encino, CA 91436. (Gold louvre series & others).

**Gambia:** British Royal Mint. MDM (see American Samoa).

**Germany:** Mint sets, proof sets and proof commemoratives. Verkaufsstelle fur Sammlemunzen der Bundersrepublik, Bahnhofstrasse 16-18, D-6380, Bad Homburg 1, Germany.

**Ghana:** British Royal Mint.

**Gibraltar:** Pobjoy Mint, (see Isle of Man).

**Great Britian:** Mint sets, proof sets and gold coinage. The British Royal Mint, P.O. Box 2570, Woodside, NY 11377-9864. Outside the U.S.: 7 Grosvenor Gardens, London SW1W 0BH, or Llantrisant, Pontyclun, Mid Glamoragan, Wales, CF7 8YT, United Kingdom and Australasians contact Australasian Numismatic Bureau of the Royal Mint of the United Kingdom, P.O. Box H114, Australia Square, New South Wales, 2000 Australia.

**British Royal Mint Commemorative & Collector Coins in U.S.A.:** Panda America, 3460 Torrance Blvd., Suite 100, Torrance, CA 90503.

**Greece:** Bank of, 341 Messogion Avenue, 15231 Halandri, Athens, Greece.

**Grenada:** British Royal Mint.

**Guernsey:** Commemoratives, proof sets and mint sets. British Royal Mint.

**Guinea:** MDM (see American Samoa).

**Guinea Bissau:** MDM (see American Samoa).

**Hong Kong:** Gold commemoratives. British Royal Mint.

**Hungary:** Commemoratives and circulation coins in uncirculated, proof and some restrikes. Magyar Nemzeti Bank, Szabadsagter H-1850, Budapest V, Hungary.

**HuttRiver Province:** Numismarketing Assoc., 5189 Jeffdale Ave., Woodland Hills, CA 91364. PH: 818-225-1348.

**Iceland:** Central Bank of Iceland, Kalkofnsvegi 1, 150 Reykjavik, Iceland.

**India:** Mint sets and proof sets. General Manager, India Government Mint, Shahid Bhagatsingh Road, Fort Bombay, 400023 India.

**Indonesia:** Indonesian Security Printing & Minting Co., Jalan Palatehan No. 4, Kebayoran Baru, Jakarta, Indonesia.

**Iraq:** Central Bank of, P.O. Box 64, Baghdad, Iraq.

**Ireland:** Central Bank of Ireland, Currency Centre, P.O. Box 61, Sandyford, Dublin 14, Rep. of Ireland.

**Isle of Man:** Mint sets, proof sets, commemoratives in various metals, bullion coins including platinum and gold. Pobjoy Mint Ltd., Mint House, Oldfields Rd., Sutton, Surrey, SM1 2NW, United Kingdom. U.S. distributor of platinum nobles and gold angels: Pobjoy Mint, P.O. Box 13826, Milwaukee, WI 53213. Canadian distribution: Graham Pobjoy, Box 37, St. Catherines, Ontario L2R 6R4, Canada. Cat Coins: MTB, 90 Broad St., New York, NY 10004-2290.

**Israel:** Commemorative coins and mint sets. Israel Government Coins and Medals Corp., 5 Ahad Ha'am St., Jerusalem 91022, Israel. Also J.J. Van Grover Ltd., 7 E. 35th St., Suite 10B, New York, NY 10016.

**Italy:** Edward A. Jencius, P.O. Box 41, Brooklyn, NY 11228-0041.

**Jamaica:** British Royal Mint.

**Japan:** Mint sets. Business section, Mint Bureau, Ministry of Finance, 1-79, Tenma 1-chome, Kita-ku, Osaka 530, Japan.

**Jersey:** Mint sets, proof sets and commemorative coinage. I.R. Monins, Homeland, St. John, Jersey, Channel Islands, JE3 4AB.

**Jordan:** Central Bank of Jordan, P.O. Box 37, Amman, Jordan.

**Kampuchea (Cambodia):** Havana (Cuba) Mint.

**Kazakhstan:** Universal Coins, 47 Clarence St., Suite 201, Ottawa, Ont. K1N 9K1 Canada.

**Kiribati:** Commemorative gold and silver proof coins. British Royal Mint. MDM (see American Samoa).

**Korea, North:** A.K. Jain, T.S.T., P.O. Box 96451, Tsimshatsui Post Office, Kowloon, Hong Kong.

**Korea, South:** Seoul Mint. Korea Mint Corp., 501-1, Daeheung-Dong, 300 Daejeon, Seoul, Republic of Korea. M & B Banking Corp., 90 Broad Street, New York, NY 10004.

**Kyrgyzstan:** Pobjoy Mint, Mint House Oldfields Road, Sutton, Surrey SM1 2NW England.

**Laos:** See Afghanistan. MDM (see American Samoa).

**Latvia:** Amerikas Latviesu Apvieniba, P.O. Box 4578, Rockville, MD 20849-4578.

**Lesotho:** Commemoratives-British Royal Mint. Circulation coins - Central Bank of Lesotho, Kingsway, P.O. Box 1184, Maseru 100, Lesotho.

**Lithuania:** Bank of Lithuania, Cash Dept., Gedimino Av. 6, 2001 Vilnuis, Lithuania.

**Luxembourg:** Caisse Generate de L'Etat, 5 Rue Goethe, Luxembourg and Institute Montetaire, 63 Avenue de La Liberte, L2983 Luxembourg.

**Macau:** Gold and silver commemoratives. See Isle of Man. Other: Instituto Emissor de Macau E.P., P.O. Box 494, Av. Da Republica 6, Macau. Pobjoy Mint (see Isle of Man).

**Malawi:** Brititsh Royal Mint.

**Malaysia:** Singapore Mint, Kilang Wang, Bank Negara Malaysia, P.O. Box 100, 40700 Shah Alam, Selangor, Malaysia.

**Maldives, Republic of:** Proof and mint sets. British Royal Mint. MDM (see American Samoa).

**Malta:** Mint sets, proof sets, gold and silver commemoratives. Said International, P.O. Box 345, Valletta, Malta. Also: British Royal Mint.

**Malta, Order of:** Proof commemorative coins and sets including gold and silver. Il Sovrano Militare Ordine di Malta, vai Bocca di Leone 68, Casella Postale 738, I-00100 Rome, Italy.

**Marshall Islands:** Marshall Islands Coin Fulfillment Center, 1 Unicover Center, Cheyenne, WY 82008.

**Mauritius:** British Royal Mint.

**Mexico:** Commemorative gold and silver coins. Libertads and proof sets are available from MTB Banking Corp., 90 Broad St., New York, NY 10004-2290. Also Banco de Mexico, Division de Coleccion Numismatica K312, Aptdo. 98 Bis Col. Centro Mexico, D.F., Mexico 06059.

**Mongolia:** MDM, B.H. Mayer's, Postfach 12 66, D-75112 Pforzheim, Germany. MDM (see American Samoa).

**Morocco:** Commemorative gold coins. British Royal Mint.

**Mozambique:** See Afghanistan.

**Nepal:** MDM (see American Samoa).

**Netherlands:** Fleur-de-coin sets, proof sets and commemorative coins. Royal Dutch Mint, P.O. Box 1057, Clifton, NJ 07014. Outside the U.S.: Dutch State Mint, Postbus 2407, NL-3500 GK, Utrecht, Netherlands.

**Netherlands Antilles:** See Netherlands.

**New Zealand:** Proof sets and commemoratives. Universal Coins, 47 Clarence St., Suite 201, Ottawa, Ontario, Canada K1N 9K1. Also Collector Currencey, Reserve Bank of New Zealand. MDM (see American Samoa).

**Nicaragua:** Infinsa International, P.O. Box 8486, Madrid 28080 Spain.

**Niue:** Pobjoy Mint, (see Isle of Man). Niue Coin Fulfillment Center, 7401 Cahill Road, Minneapolis, MN 55435. Also MDM (see American Samoa).

**Norway:** Mint sets. Norges Bank, Skillemyntkassen, P.O. Box 735, Sentrun, Oslo 1, Norway. Mint Address, (not for ordering coins): Royal Norwegian Mint, postboks 53, N-3601 Kongsberg, Norway.

**Oman:** British Royal Mint.

**Palau:** Panda America, 3460 Torrance Blvd., Suite 100, Torrance, CA 90503.

**Panama:** Emporium Hamburg, Lange Reihe 81, 2000 Hamburg 1, Germany.

**Papua New Guinea:** MDM (see American Samoa).

**Paraguay:** British Royal Mint.

**Phillippines:** Commemoratives, proof and mint sets. British Royal Mint.

**Pitcairn Islands:** British Royal Mint.

**Poland:** Banknotes & coins. Mint-Polsa, 56 Zelazna St., 00-958 Warsaw, Poland.

**Portugal:** Commemoratives. Portuguese State Mint (North American Office), P.O. Box 1071, Clifton, NJ 07014. Outside the U.S.: - Casada da Moeda, Av. Dr. Antonio Jose de Almeida, 1092 Lisbon, Codex, Portugal.

**Russia:** Current circulation and commemorative coinage. "Mezhnumizmatika", 9 Pushkinskaya St., Moscow 103009, Russia and MTB Banking Corp., 90 Broad St., New York, NY 10004. Fred Weinberg, Inc., 16311 Ventura Blvd., #550, Encino, CA 91436. Ballerina & proof coins 1988-. American Bullion & Coin, P.O. Box 283, Topanga, CA 90290.

**St. Christopher & Nevis:** British Royal Mint.

**St. Lucia:** British Royal Mint.

**St. Thomas & Prince:** British Royal Mint.

**St. Vincent:** British Royal Mint.

**San Marino:** Mint sets and gold coins. Dr. Marino Zanotti, Azienda Autonomado di Stato, Filatelica & Numismatica, Casella Postale 1, San Marino, 47031, Republic of San Marino. FAX: 378-88-2363.

**Sierra Leone:** Commemorative gold and silver coins. British Royal Mint.

**Seychelles:** See Gibralatar. MDM (see American Samoa).

**Singapore:** Proof sets and proof silver and uncirculated cupor-nickel commemorative coins. Singapore Mint, 249 Jalan Boon Lay, Singapore 2261, Rep. of Singapore. U.S. distributor: Panda America, 3460 Torrance Blvd., Suite 100, Torrance, CA 90503-5812. FAX: 65-264-0841.

**Slovakia:** Ivo Cerny, P.O. Box 19, 69504 Hodonin, Czech Rep.

**Slovenia:** Banka Slovenija, P.O. 440, Slovenska 35, 61001 Ljubljana, Slovenija.

**Solomon Islands:** MDM (see American Samoa).

**South Africa:** Mint sets, proof sets, gold bullion coins. Director, South African Mint, P.O. Box 464, Pretoria, Republic of South Africa.

**Spain:** Fabrica Nacional de Moneda Y Timbre, Jorge Juan 106, 28009 Jimenez, Madrid, Spain and D.E. Castano, Apdo. 71, Orihuela (Alicante) Spain.

**Surinam:** See Netherlands.

**Sweden:** Mint sets and commemoratives. Myntverklet, Box 401, S-631 06 Eskilstuna, Sweden.

**Switzerland:** Mint sets, proof sets and commemoratives. Banque Nationale Suisse, Bernastrasse 28, CH-3003, Berne, Switzerland.

**Tanzania:** British Royal Mint.

**Thailand:** Mint sets, gold coins and medallions. The Royal Decorations and Coins Division, Royal Grand Palace, Chakrapong Road, Bangkok 10200, Thailand.

**Tokelau:** Proof and uncirculated coins. MDM (see American Samoa). Pobjoy Mint (see Isle of Man).

**Tonga:** British Royal Mint and Pobjoy Mint. See Isle of Man. MDM (see American Samoa).

**Tuvalu:** MDM (see American Samoa).

**Uganda:** British Royal Mint.

**United Arab Emirates:** British Royal Mint.

**United States:** Mint sets, proof sets and commemoratives. Customer Service Center, U.S. Mint, 10001 Aerospace Dr., Lanham, MD 20706.

**Uzbekistan:** See Isle of Man.

**Vanuatu:** British Royal Mint. Also MDM (see American Samoa).

**Vatican City:** Commemoratives. Filatelico E Numismatico, I-00120 Vatican City, Italy. Universal Coins, 47 Clarence St., Suite 201, Ottawa, Ont., K1N 9K1 Canada.

**Vietnam:** See Afghanistan.

**Western Samoa:** Singapore Mint. Also MDM (see American Samoa).

**Other:**

**World Wildlife Fund:** Legal-tender gold and silver coins. Spink Modern Collections Ltd., 29-35 Gladstone Rd., Croydon, Surrey CR0 2BQ, England. Panda America, 3460 Torrance Blvd., Suite 100, Torrance, CA 90503.

**PLEASE NOTE:** Collectors wishing to make small or low cash value purchases will usually find it more advantageous to contact the New Issues Dealers Advertising in *World Coin News.*

# MONOGRAMS

MJ
Maximilian IV Joseph
Berg

CC99
Christian IX
Danish West Indies

V OC
Dutch East India
Co. (Indonesia)

CVII
Christian VII
Danish West Indies

CCX
Christian X
Danish West Indies

G
Georg
Mecklenburg-Strelitz

CWF
Carl Wilhelm
Ferdinand
Brunswick-
Wolfenbuttel

H7
Haakon VII
Norway

A
Albert I
Belgium

GRI
Georgius Rex
Imperator
New Guinea

L
Leopold II
Belgium

EAR
Ernest August Rex
Hannover

FRVI
Frederik VI Rex
Denmark

CX
Christian X
Denmark

A
Albert I
Belgium

AF
Adolph Friederich IV
Mecklenburg-Strelitz

B
Baudouin I
Belgium

C
Cayenne
French Guiana

CL
Carl & Louise
Saxe-Meiningen

CR
Christian VIII (Denmark)
Tranquebar

FW
Friedrich Wilhelm
Mecklenburg-Strelitz

C7
Christian VII
Tranquebar

C7
Christian VII
Denmark

CIX
Christian IX
Denmark

CCX
Christian X
Denmark

CCXIII
Charles XIII
Sweden

CLXIV
Carl XIV Johann
Norway

CXIV
Carl XIV Johann
Sweden

EP
Elizabeth-Philip
Great Britain

ERI
Edward Rex
Imperator
New Guinea

EIIR
Elizabeth II Regina
Cook Isl.

FA
Friedrich August
Lubeck Bishopric

FF
Friedrich Franz
Mecklenburg-
Schwerin

FJI
Franz Joseph I
Austria

O
Oscar I
Sweden

AFC
Alexius Friedrich
Christian
Anhalt-Bernburg

NII
Nicholas II
Russia

FRVII
Frederik VII Rex
Danish West Indies
Denmark

FC
Friedrich Christian
Brandenburg-
Bayreuth

AIII
Alexander III
Russia

W
William I
Netherlands

LLX
Ludwig X
Hesse-Darmstadt

# MONOGRAMS

MJ
Maximilian IV Joseph
Berg

FI
Frederick IX & Ingrid
Denmark

F VI R
Fred. VI Denmark
Tranquebar

FVII
Frederick VII
Denmark

FF8
Frederick VIII
Denmark

F IX R
Frederick IX
Denmark

FVII
Ferdinand VII
Mexico

PI
Paul I
Russia

FVII
Ferdinand VII
Mexico

FW
Friedrich Wilhelm III
Prussia

GA IV
Gustav Adolf IV
Sweden

HI
Nicholas I
Russia

HC
Henri Christophe
Haiti

HVII
Haakon VII
Norway

HN
Hieronymus
Napoleon
Westphalia

J
Joachim (Murat)
Berg

E(K)I II
Katherine II
Russia

L
Ludwig
Hesse-Darmstadt

L
Leopold
Belgium

LL III
Leopold III
Belgium

LL
Louis XVIII
Antwerp

C XIVJ
Carl XIV Johann
Norway

M
Morelos
Revolutionary
Mexico

M 2 R
Margrethe II Regina
Denmark

NII
Nicholas II
Russia

NI
Nicholas I
Russia

NFP
Nicholas Friedrich
Peter
Oldenburg

OII
Oscar II
Norway

E
Ernest I
Saxe-Coburg-Gotha

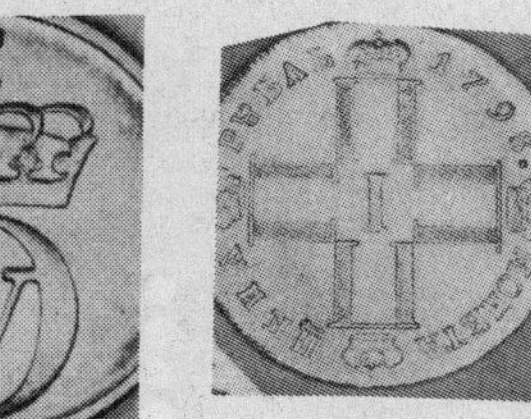
O V
Olav V
Norway

P I
Paul I
Russia

P III
Peter III
Russia

R
Rainier III
Monaco

WL
Wilhelm Landgraf
Hesse-Cassel

WR
William Rex
Hannover

PFA
Peter Friedrich
August
Oldenburg

OII
Oscar II
Sweden

GR
Georgius Rex
Hannover

FRVI
Frederik VI Rex
Tranquebar

PF
Paul Friedrich
Mecklenburg-
Schwerin

FII
Friedrich II
Wurttemberg

FER VII
Ferdinand VII
(Spain) Gerona

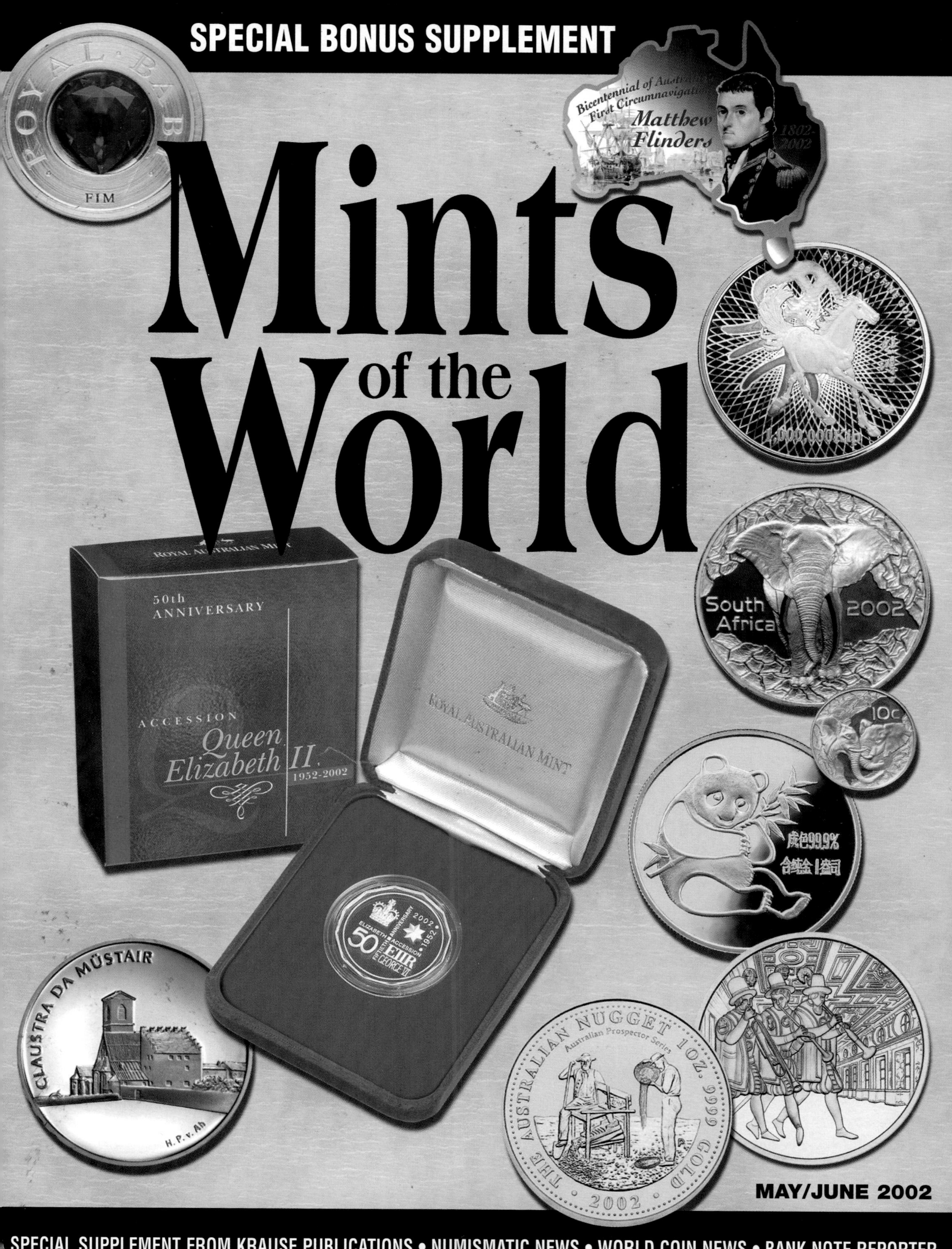
SPECIAL BONUS SUPPLEMENT
Mints of the World
MAY/JUNE 2002
SPECIAL SUPPLEMENT FROM KRAUSE PUBLICATIONS • NUMISMATIC NEWS • WORLD COIN NEWS • BANK NOTE REPORTER
ROYAL AUSTRALIAN MINT
50th ANNIVERSARY
ACCESSION Queen Elizabeth II 1952-2002
Bicentennial of Australia's First Circumnavigation
Matthew Flinders
1802-2002
South Africa 2002
CLAUSTRA DA MÜSTAIR
THE AUSTRALIAN NUGGET 1 OZ. 9999 GOLD
Australian Prospector Series
2002

FUJI International Mint Co.
•Company Overview•
Our company deals in several types of collectables, such as antique and modern Japanese coins, numismatic coins, overseas coins, swords, character goods and toys.
Our main line of business is retail sales advertised in a direct mail catalog sent out to customers on our house list.
In 1999, we also began acting as Japan's first private mint, starting creation, issuance and sales of officially sanctioned legal tender commemorative currencies in conjunction with overseas countries and central banks.
TRADE DOLLAR

### *The 2002 Krugerrand:*

The discovery of the main gold reef in 1886 in the Johannesburg area forever changed the history of South Africa – impacting specifically on the political and historical arenas.

And so it came to be that the beauty and warmth of shimmering gold that captivated the country eventually conquered the world.

The Krugerrand is one of the few South African brand names that appears on the top international branding list and is what most people associate with gold from South Africa.

Proof quality Krugerrands are available as limited editions that are individually packed and issued with a certificate of authenticity.

The Krugerrand is minted in the traditional 22 carat gold and is available in 1 oz, 1/2 oz, 1/4 oz and 1/10 oz. coins.

### *The 2002 Natura Series:*

Following the success of the international award winning Big Five (1994-1998) and Monarchs of Africa (1999-2001) themes, the 2002 Natura series will depict the first in the Wild Cats of Africa theme: The Cheetah.

The word "cheetah" is derived from a Hindi word meaning "the spotted one" which is an indication that this graceful predator once roamed beyond the confines of Africa.

The cheetah in motion is an extraordinary sight. Catlike, it will stalk its prey to a distance of 50 metres before starting the high-speed dash which has earned this beautiful animal the reputation of being the fastest mammal on earth.

The cheetah's profile reveals its small rounded head and short muzzle and high domed skull with unusually large nasal cavities that allows it to draw in large quantities of air after the extreme exertion of the hunt.

No two cheetahs are identical. Their spot patterns are as unique as a human fingerprint.

The Natura is minted in 24 carat (au 999.9) gold and is available in 1 oz. 1/2 oz, 1/4 oz and 1/10 oz. Coins.

### *The 2002 Wildlife Series:*

The Elephant: Strength of Africa, is the third theme in the popular Wildlife series. In 2000 this series featured The Lion: Predators of Africa, followed by The Buffalo: Power of Africa, in 2001.

The elephant is the largest living land mammal. It is estimated that this majestic animal has graced the earth for more that 1.6 million years. The last two remaining elephant species (African & Indian) now limited to tropical forest, savannas, deserts and river valleys.

The African elephant reaches a height of 4 meters and can, in spite of a weight of up to 7,000 kg, walk almost noiselessly. They are gregarious and keenly sensitive to each other's calls and movements. Elephants communicate not only by vocalization from their trunks, but also by touch, smell and posture.

This silver coin series consist of four coins: 50c (2oz), 20c (1oz), 10c (1/2 oz) and 5c (1/4 oz).

### *The 2002 Marine Life Series:*

The 2002 Marine Life series features Whales. It follows in the footsteps of the popular Knysna Sea Horse, Jackass Penguin, Great White Shark, Common Octopus and the Dolphin series.

A Brydes whale is depicted on the 2 1/2 c silver tickey, while the Southern Right whale is shown on the R2 silver crown. Both the Brydes and Southern Right whale belong to the Baleen family.
Whales have nostrils better known and blowholes, which open on the top of their heads in order to in- and exhale air while surfacing. These large aquatic mammals filter their food (mainly shrimp-like creatures called krill) from the seawater.

South Africa's coastline annually offers visitors the wonderful opportunity to watch these graceful giants of the oceans.

In preserving the images of these creatures of the deep, the South African Mint Company supports the conservation of whales and all other forms of valuable marine life, while adding to our impressive numismatic tradition.

# Austrian Mint
## New and Recent Issues

### 2002 Euro Mint Set

At the beginning of 2002, the euro replaced the schilling as the official currency of Austria. The 2002 BU mint set is thus the first Austrian set in euros. Order soon to avoid disappointment.

- the first annual euro set
- contains all 8 euro denominations
- available in BU finish only
- informative bilingual (English/German) folder

**$27.00 ea.***

### Ambrass Palace

- 1st issue in new series, "Palaces of Austria"
- 10 euros face value
- 37 mm in diameter
- 22.2g fine silver
- available in BU and proof
- BU is encapsulated
- Proof is encapsulated, with presentation case; numbered certificate of authenticity

**$27.00 ea.* (proof)**
**$20.00 ea.* (bu)**

### Christian Religious Orders

- 3rd issue in series, "2000 Years of Christianity"
- 50 euros face value
- 22 mm in diameter
- 10g fine gold
- available in proof only
- presentation case and numbered certificate of authenticity

**$163.00 ea.***

### Art Treasures of Austria - Illuminated Manuscripts

- 2nd issue in 4 coin series, "Art Treasures of Austria"
- 1000 schillings face value - <u>*the last schilling coin struck in Austria*</u>
- 30 mm in diameter
- 16g fine gold
- available in proof finish only
- encapsulated, presentation case, numbered certificate of authenticity

**$280.00 ea.***

---

**Euro Collections International, Inc.**
621 Discovery St., #727
Victoria, B.C.
CANADA V8W 2P9

**Three convenient ways to order:**
- **Toll free: 1-888-904-5544**
- **Fax: 250-658-1455**
- **on-line at www.eurocollections.com**

** plus shipping and handling*

# Austrian Mint

Precious metals in the form of minted coins have enjoyed a long tradition in Austria, and in fact, the history of the Austrian Mint which goes back to 1194. The date itself is of historical significance - for it was in this year that the ransom was paid for the release of King Richard the Lionheart of England which made possible the foundation of the Vienna's own Mint.

On January 1, 1989 the Austrian Mint passed from the Ministry of Finance into the hands of the Austrian National Bank, becoming one of the first major mints in the world to be "privatized". The Austrian National Bank is also the official Austrian banknote issuing authority.

For the over 800 year old Austrian Mint, the change meant a complete restructuring, and brought about the implementation of major investment and renovation programs. From a marketing point of view, it meant an exciting new flexibility in the areas of investment and collector coins. For the first time, the Vienna-based Mint began advertising and promotional campaigns for its coins on a national and international level.

The major success story of 1989 was the launching of the first European bullion coin to be struck in pure (999.9) gold. In order to ensure that the coin would be immediately recognized around the world as Austrian, it was dedicated to the world famous Vienna Philharmonic Orchestra. With its attractive design of musical instruments grouped to represent the orchestra, and the Golden Hall on the obverse where the Orchestra performs when in Vienna, the coin proved immediately popular and sold 419,000 ounces during the short three month launch period.

Since 1991, the Mint has been issuing commemorative coin series in gold and silver annually. Some of the coins already on the market have seen significant increases in their secondary market values.

In addition to minting sets of special uncirculated coins each year, the Austrian Mint restrikes gold coins struck by the Austrian Empire - Guldens, Crowns (Kronen) and Ducats. This year, 2002, the phenomenal changeover from schilling to Euro also successfully took place.

The most famous, however, is the restrike of the 1780 Maria Theresa Taler, a large silver coin. Known as the most famous silver coin of the world, it certainly has enjoyed a long minting history. The Taler is also known as the "Levantine Taler" because it was accepted as legal tender in parts of North Africa and Turkey, countries of the Levant, for many years.

Winner of many international awards for the coins of Austria and a leader of innovation such as color stamping, cutting stars through the edge of a coin and making one of the first legal tender titanium coins, the Austrian Mint's great tradition and consummate quality continues to excel.

The Austrian Mint has always believed that they are "minting Austria" and therefore has always devoted its coin products to the themes from Austria's rich history and the culture of this Alpine republic with its worldwide artistic and cultural standing.

AUSTRIAN MINT

A World First!
FREE
Huge Flinders Map with
Every Collection (approx 33 x 23.5 inches)
Official legal tender issues struck by
The Perth Mint exclusively for Downie's Ltd.
The Matthew Flinders Coin Collection
speaks volumes about the quality,
imagination and innovation of
Australia's precious metal specialists.
THE PERTH MINT
EST. 1899
HUGE
Colour Map
Bicentennial of Australia's
First Circumnavigation
Matthew
Flinders
1802-
2002
▲ This coin portrays the bustling
19th century metropolis of Port Jackson
(Sydney, Australia), where Flinders
finally docked the Investigator after
completing his voyage.
▼After boarding the French ship
Le Geographe for two meetings with
the Commander Nicholas Baudin,
Flinders dubbed the inlet
'Encounter Bay'.
1802
Meeting at
Encounter
Bay
Baudin
Flinders
Matthew
Flinders
H.M.S.
Investigator
►
Although rotting and increasingly dangerous, the
HMS Investigator carried Flinders and his crew
on their year long voyage around the Continent.
First Circumnavigation
of Terra Australis
1802
Matthew
Flinders
ONE DOLLAR
COOK ISLANDS
ELIZABETH II
2002
◄ Eye-catching, the
obverse of this official
legal
tender coin features the
Raphael Maklouf
portrait of Queen
Elizabeth II.
▲Illustrating the first circumnavigation
of the Great Southern Land, this superb
coin follows the path of Flinders epic
voyage around the Continent.
So many reasons why this set
should be part of your collection…
■ The first 'Map of Australia' coins!
■ Each 40.6 mm diameter coin comprises One Ounce of pure .999 silver.
■ A mere 2,500 of each coin has been struck by Perth Mint.
■ Each legal tender $1 coin is an official issue of the Cook Islands.
■ A 'treasure chest' timber case houses the collection.
■ An historical booklet with Certificate of Authenticity is provided.
■ A replica copy of Flinders' original map is included FREE.
■ Fantastic collector value for such innovative, beautiful coins.
Downie's Ltd
ESTABLISHED 1932
4533 MacArthur Blvd #888, Newport Beach CA 92660
Toll Free 1 800 6 DOWNIE (369643)
Phone: (949) 838 0250 Fax: (949) 838 0013
Email: DowniesUSA@downies.com
Order on our Website: www.downies.com

The Singapore Mint
proudly presents
Coins from Asia
1 OZ 999.9 GOLD
$50
Lion Gold Proof Coin
1 oz 999.9 Fine Gold
FOUR FACED BUDDHA
925 SILVER
CAMBODIA
Apsara Dance
925 SILVER
THE WONDERS OF THE WORLD ANGKOR WAT
999.9 GOLD 999 SILVER
Four-Faced Buddha
20gm 925 Silver Proof Coin
with diamond cut effect
Apsara Dance
20gm 925 Silver Proof Coin
with colour application
Angkor Wat
1 oz 925 Silver Proof Coin
with dynamic hologram on
999.9 Gold Insert
925 FINE SILVER
尼泊尔
NEPAL
Rs 1500
佛祖
LORD
BUDDHA
1/2 OZ 999.9 FINE GOLD
NEPAL 尼泊尔 ASARFI
The Smallest Nepal Buddha Gold Coin
999.9 gold, diameter of 7mm
Nepal Buddha
20gm 925 Silver Proof Coin
Nepal Buddha
1/2 oz 999.9 Gold Proof Coin
For more information www.mint.com.sg

The Singapore Mint
proudly presents
Coins from Asia
Singapore Lunar Horse
Gold Proof Coin
1 oz 999.9 Fine Gold
$250
1 TROY OZ 999.9 FINE GOLD
5 OZ 925 FINE SILVER
60,000Kip
1,000,000Kip
Laos Horse
5oz 999.9 Gold Proof Coin
with dynamic hologram
Laos Horse
5oz 925 Silver Proof Coin
with colour application
Vietnam Horse - Magnificent
1/2 oz 999.9 Gold Proof Coin
with dynamic hologram
YEAR OF THE HORSE
1/2 OZ FINE GOLD
2002
NGỰA VIỆT NAM
功 马 成 到
1st in the world
NGỰA VIỆT NAM
马
壬午
2002
YEAR OF THE HORSE
Vietnam Horse - Victorious
999 Silver Proof Coin
with 4-sided latent image
NGỰA VIỆT NAM
狀元馬
壬午
2002
999 FINE SILVER YEAR OF THE HORSE
Vietnam Horse - Success
999 Silver Proof Coin
with colour application
For more information
www.mint.com.sg

# Official Mint of the

## The Enterprise

*swissmint* is the official mint of the Swiss Confederation and is popularly known as the Federal Mint, or simply as the «Mint». Since 1st January 1998, this traditional institution has formed an independent unit of the Federal Finance Administration. Our new name signifies a new spirit: the entrepreneurial approach

of a modern company marketing its products and services both at home and abroad. *swissmint* employs a workforce of 21 men and women.

## Mastering the fine Art of Coining

Our main task is to mint Swiss coins for everyday circulation, and we produce large numbers of them both efficiently and cost-effectively. Nevertheless, quality is still our prime concern - after all, this is the world's hardest currency.

For numismatists and investors, there are *swissmint* memorial coins issued in special qualities: miniature works of art, minted with meticulous care and precision. Each coin represents an attractive investment.

## Swiss made

*swissmint* products incorporate fine artistry, time-honoured craftsmanship and technical perfection. This distinctive synthesis requires the know-how and experience of highly qualified minting experts, whose skills are placed at the entire disposal of all *swissmint* customers.

## A dynamic Company

Ongoing state-of-the-art modernisation and automatisation of machinery, attractive and superior products, exceptional specialist competence, as well as inventive marketing strategies all distinguish *swissmint* as an interesting partner.

## A selection of our products

| | Weight | Size | Alloy | Price BU | Price PP |
|---|---|---|---|---|---|
| 20-franc piece | 20 g | 33 mm | silver 0.835 | $ 14.00 | $ 34.00 |
| 50-franc piece | 11.29 g | 25 mm | gold 0.900 | – | $ 167.00 |
| Set of coins | – | – | unprecious metals | $ 17.00 | $ 44.00 |

### 2001
### Müstair Monastery 20-franc piece

Classified by the UNESCO as a World Heritage Site, the St. Johann monastery in Müstair, Canton of Grison, is among of the most striking legacies in the history of mankind. Its significance is based on many factors, but the best known among these are the frescoes dating from its foundation in about the year 800.

### 2001
### Heidi - Switzerland's best-known female personality 50-franc piece

Heidi is a phenomenon. A children's book which appeared in 1880 is still attractive to readers five generations later. The novel set in the Alps was successful from the very outset and has been translated into around fifty languages. Heidi is not only Switzerland's probably best-known children's heroine, but also the country's most famous female personality.

# Swiss Confederation

For more information visit our homepage www.swissmint.ch.

**2002**
**Expo.02 – Boy on the lake 20-franc piece**

Once every generation, Switzerland treats itself to a National Exhibition. To Expo.02, which takes place from 15th May to 20 October 2002, about 4.8 millions guests are expected. Expo.02 combines the multifaceted interests and energies of our country more effectively than any other project.

**2002**
**Expo.02 – Lakes region 50-franc piece**

An innovation of the sixth Swiss National Exhibition is that its site is not a city but an entire tourist region. Division of the Expo.02 into five arteplages, which are spread on the water and shores of the lakes, makes it easier to explore the treasures of the land of the Three Lakes.

**Set of coins 2001**

These sets contain, in addition to the year's Set of Swiss coins in circulation (1 rappen to 5 francs), a bi-metal coin on the theme «Zürcher Sechseläuten».

**Set of coins 2002**

These sets contain, in addition to the year's Set of Swiss coins in circulation (1 rappen to 5 francs), a bi-metal coin on the theme «Escalade de Genève».

2001

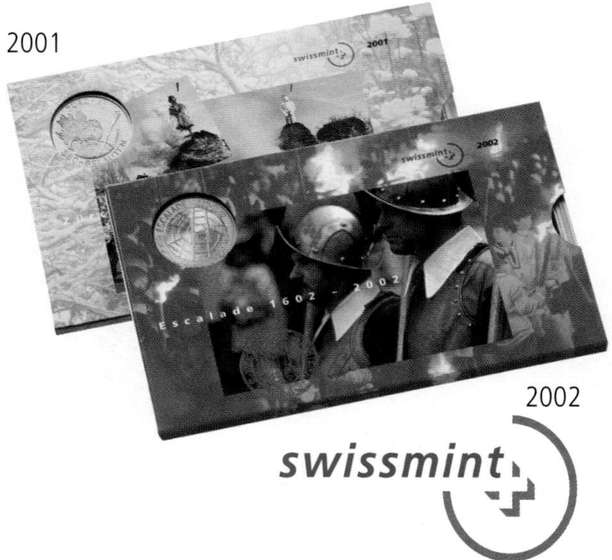


2002

swissmint

## I order the following items:

| Quantity | Description | Quality | Price |
|---|---|---|---|
| | Müstair Monastery | BU | $ 14.00 |
| | Müstair Monastery | PP | $ 34.00 |
| | Heidi | PP | $ 167.00 |
| | Set of coins 2001 | BU | $ 17.00 |
| | Set of coins 2001 | PP | $ 44.00 |
| | Expo.02 – Boy on the lake | BU | $ 14.00 |
| | Expo.02 – Boy on the lake | PP | $ 34.00 |
| | Expo.02 – Lakes region | PP | $ 167.00 |
| | Set of coins 2002 | BU | $ 17.00 |
| | Set of coins 2002 | PP | $ 44.00 |

Dispatching and mailing costs will be calculated separately.

☐ Please send me a Standing order form.

Name

First name

Postal address

Date of order Signature

Please send the order to ***swissmint***, Bernastrasse 28, CH-3003 Bern

# Krause Publications Coin Of The Year Program Nearly 20 Years Old

An awards program, the Coin of The Year, was launched in 1983 by WORLD COIN NEWS, a monthly periodical dedicated to collectors of world coins. The program is designed to enhance future design considerations, marketing techniques, aesthetic values and pride in workmanship in modern coinage. Each year a special worldwide blue-ribbon panel of experts selects the Coin of The Year and a winning coin in each of ten subsidiary classes:\

- *Most Artistic Coin
- *Most Popular Coin
- *Most Historically Significant Coin
- *Best Gold Coin (This category includes coins struck of gold, platinum, palladium, or other exotic precious metals.)
- *Best Silver Coin
- *Best Crown
- *Best Trade Coin
- *Most Innovative Coinage Concept
- *Most Inspirational Coin
- *Best Contemporary Event Coin

A distinguished panel of judges makes the selections. It consists of mint officials, engravers, officers of numismatic associations and coin dealer groups, world central bank and treasury officials, mass marketers of coins and independent experts from around the world, along with members of the Krause Publications' numismatic staff.

# A Wealth of Valuable Information at Your Fingertips

Standard Guide to Small-Size
U.S. Paper Money, 1928 to Date
4th Edition
by Dean Oakes & John Schwartz
Identify and evaluate small-size U.S. paper money with the most comprehensive listing available. More than 275 near-full-size photos provide detailed and positive identification to small-size paper money printed from 1928 to 2001. All values have been reviewed and updated and are listed in Very Good/Fine and Crisp Uncirculated condition. Serial number information is also updated.
Softcover • 6 x 9 • 360 pages
275+ b&w photos
**Item# HP06 • $24.95**

Standard Catalog of®
United States Paper Money
20th Edition
by Chester L. Krause and Robert F. Lemke, Joel T. Edler, Editor
The 20th anniversary edition of this respected guide includes the latest pricing information for U.S. paper money printed since 1813. With more than 5,500 listings and over 14,000 valuations, it features many items not listed in any other currency book. Along with large and small-size notes, national bank notes and fractional currency, you'll find error notes, military payment certificates and an extensive guide to authentication of United States currency.
Hardcover • 8-1/4 x 10-7/8 • 232 pages
600 b&w photos
**Item# SP20 • $29.95**

*To place an order call:*
*Call 800-258-0929* **Offer N12NS**
Monday–Friday, 7 am - 8 pm • Sat 8 am - 2 pm CST

**Satisfaction Guaranteed:** If for any reason you are not completely satisfied with your purchase, simply return it within 14 days and receive a full refund, less shipping charges.

**Sales tax:** CA, IA, IL, PA, TN, VA, WI residents please add appropriate sales tax.

**Shipping and Handling:** $4.00 1st book, $2.25 each additional. Non-US addresses $20.95 1st book, $5.95 each additional.

P.O. Box 5009, Iola, WI 54945-5009
*www.krausebooks.com*

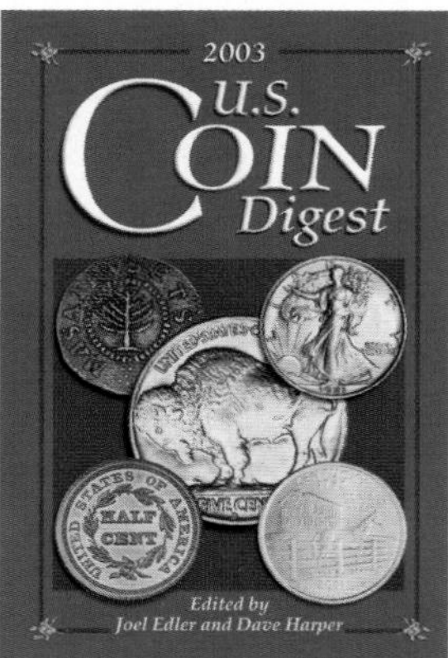


2003 U.S. Coin Digest
edited by Joel Edler and Dave Harper
You'll want to carry this portable guide with you to coin shows and club meetings. It's packed with more than 80,000 prices for U.S. coins from colonial times to present. Commemoratives, bullion coinage, mint and proof sets, and Hawaiian and Puerto Rican coins are also covered. You'll learn how money is made, how coins are graded, what's new at the largest coin show in America, and how to organize and care for your coin collection. The glossary will help you understand terms commonly used in the hobby, and the index makes it easy to find a specific coin listing.
Spiral • 6 x 9 • 256 pages
200 b&w photos • 900+ color photos
**Item# USCD • $11.95**

2002 Auction Prices Realized
21st Edition
edited by Randy Thern
Track U.S. coin auction sales with this annually updated reference that provides tens of thousands of listings with real market values in up to 10 grades of condition. Easily locate and research specific coins through the index. Includes a six-year trend analysis of prices paid at auction for the 100 top selling coins.
Softcover • 5-3/8 x 8-3/8 • 360 pages
**Item# AU21 • $75.00**

Collecting World Coins
A Century of Circulating Issues
1901 - Present, 9th Edition
by Chester L. Krause and Clifford Mishler, Colin R. Bruce II, Senior Editor
You will observe modern world history unfold through changes in governments, monetary reforms, inflationary periods, and wars as recorded in international coinage in this essential reference to circulating coins of the world from 1901 to date. Coins are classified according to country with more than 80,000 prices listed in up to four grades of preservation. Obverse and reverse photos of more than 20,000 coins make it easy for you to identify your coins.
Softcover • 8-1/2 x 11 • 768 pages
16,200 b&w photos
**Item# CC09 • $29.95**

Crime of 1873
The Comstock Connection
by Robert R. Van Ryzin
Award-winning author Robert Van Ryzin sheds new and illuminating light on the creation of the Morgan and Silver Trade dollars. From the mine to the mint, never-before-published information reveals wrongdoing at the highest levels of the U.S. Mint. If you collect U.S. coins, or have an interest in the Old West, the economy, or the mining industry this richly told and highly inclusive story will keep you spellbound. In addition to the historical content this is a complete price guide for Morgan and Trade Silver dollars.
Hardcover • 8-1/4 x 10-7/8 • 304 pages
300+ b&w photos
**Item# CRIM • $34.95**

**Specialized Issues**
**Volume One, 8th Edition**
by Colin R. Bruce II, Senior Editor/Neil Shafer, Editor
More than 51,000 updated prices for more than 17,000 notes are presented along with more than 8,000 photos of faces AND backs for easy identification. Helpful exchange and translation information lets you tour this special world with ease and accuracy.
Softcover • 8-1/2 x 11 • 1,184 pages
8,000 b&w photos
**Item# PS08 • $60.00**

**General Issues 1368-1960**
**Volume Two, 9th Edition**
edited by Neil Shafer & Colin R. Bruce II
This is the world's most comprehensive world paper money price guide and reference. The new 9th Edition includes 19,000+ listings of paper money circulating worldwide from 1368 through 1960 in three grades of condition and well over 50,000 up-to-date prices that reflect recent market activity. Introductory chapters are updated. An Exotic Language Photo Identification Guide is new to this edition and many photos are incorporated throughout.
Softcover • 8-1/2 x 11 • 1,184 pages
5,200+ b&w photos
**Item# PM09 • $65.00**

**Modern Issues 1961-2002**
**Volume Three, 8th Edition**
edited by Neil Shafer & George S. Cuhaj
The most comprehensive world paper money reference ever assembled now has updated pricing, several new and improved images, newly discovered issue dates, and an exciting new color photo gallery. More than 175 experts have priced more than 11,200 notes in three grades of condition. Additional references will teach you more about the paper money collecting hobby and make it easy for your to locate specific notes.
Softcover • 8-1/2 x 11 • 944 pages
7,300+ b&w photos • 8-page color section
**Item# WP08 • $42.95**

## Standard Catalog of® World Coins

by Chester L. Krause and Clifford Mishler, Colin R. Bruce II, Senior Editor

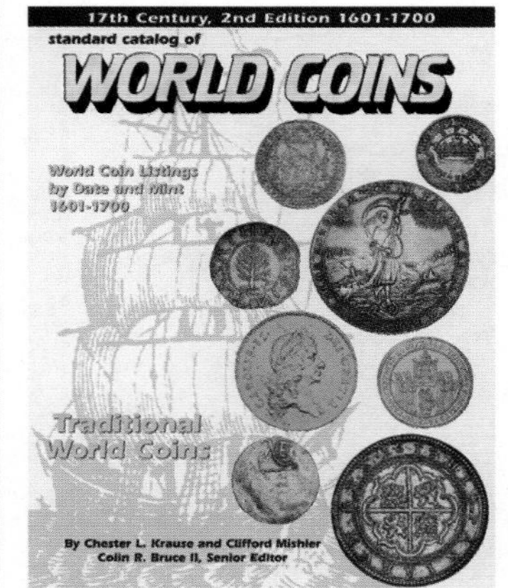


**1601-1700, 2nd Edition**
Every valuation has been reviewed and adjusted to reflect current market conditions. With illustrated instant identifiers, standard international numeral systems, global exchange rates and a cross-referenced country index, no collector will want to be without this completely updated edition.
Softcover • 8-1/2 x 11
1,272 pages
18,500 b&w photos
**Item# C402 • $65.00**

**1801-1900, 3rd Edition**
This prestigious guide is the only volume you need to identify and value 19th century world coins. Veteran coin experts have amassed coin denomination listings for every coin minted from 1801 to 1900 with tens of thousands of coins cataloged in up to four grades of condition. This third edition is heavily illustrated with new and improved photos and will appeal to all skill levels with helpful charts, glossaries and a user's guide.
Softcover • 8-1/4 x 10-7/8
1,200 pages
25,000 b&w photos
**Item# SCN03 • $50.00**

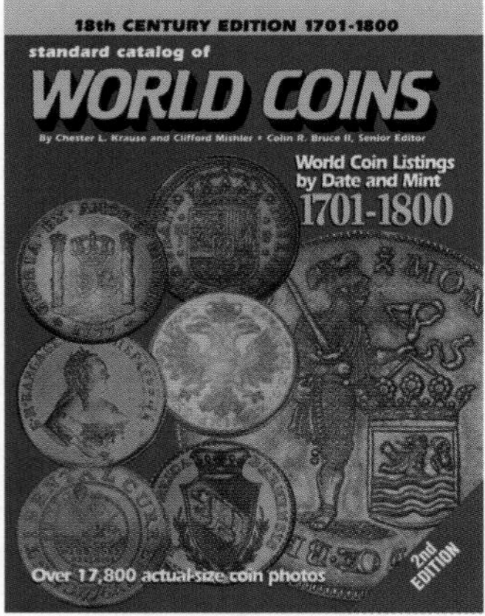


**1701-1800, 2nd Edition**
The latest values for coins from around the world dated 1701-1800 are conveniently listed by country and denomination in up to four grades of preservation. Includes more than 20,000 detailed photos for ease of identification. Companion volume to 17th, 19th, and 20th Century catalog/value guides.
Softcover • 8-1/2 x 11
1,248 pages
20,000 b&w photos
**Item# SE02 • $65.00**

NEW EDITION!

**1900-Present, 30th Edition**
More than one million world coin prices are listed in this 30th anniversary edition, covering every known coin minted since 1901. A new two-column format allows you to fully view obverse and reverse illustrations. Larger and more organized headers for each coin listing will help you easily differentiate similar listings. Essential reference information gives you a better understanding of the hobby, regardless of your collecting experience.
Softcover • 8-1/4 x 10-7/8
2,304 pages
48,000 b&w photos
**Item# SC30 • $52.95**

# ILLUSTRATED GUIDE TO EASTERN MINT NAMES

PREPARED ESPECIALLY FOR THE **STANDARD CATALOG OF WORLD COINS** © 2002 BY KRAUSE PUBLICATIONS

**Compiled by Harry S. Scherzer.**
**Scrip typeset by Ketab Corporation**

Eastern mint names are basically composed of the Arabic alphabet which in fact covers a number of languages — Arabic is Semitic: Persian is Indo-European; and Malayan is in the Malayo-Polynesian group. Differences are not just of dialect, they are of basic structure. However, Arabic itself is the really important one, bearing a relationship to other Oriental languages not unlike that of Latin to the languages of Europe. Just as medieval European coins are inscribed in Latin, so are the majority of the coins of North African, Turkish, Persian, and Indian origin inscribed until very recent times in Arabic. A limited knowledge of Persian will also be necessary for unravelling the Persian poetic couplets found on Indian and Persian coins particularly during the seventeenth and eighteenth centuries A.D.

(Courtesy of Richard J. Plant)

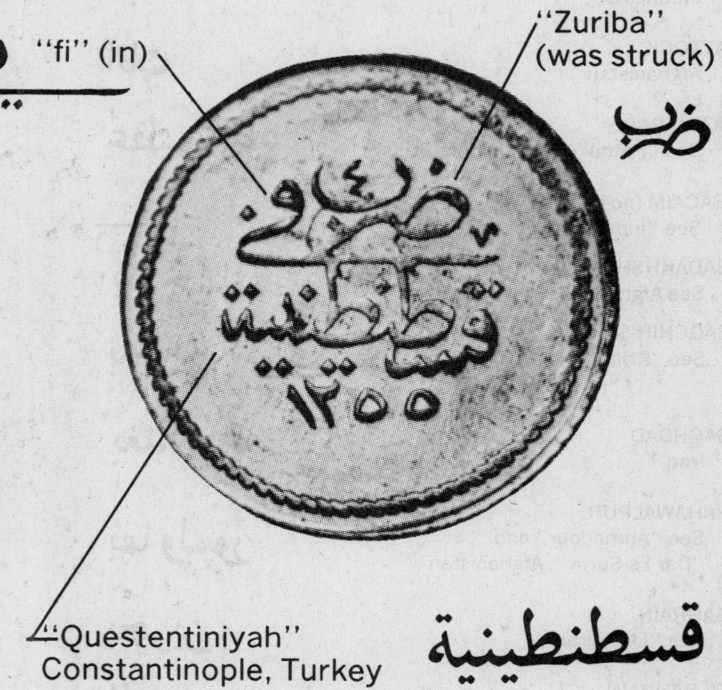


ANKARA
Turkey
انقره

AL-'ARAISH
"Larache", Morocco
العرايش

AL-'ARAISHAN
"Larache", Morocco
العرايشة

ABUSHAHR
"Bushire", Iran
ابو شهر

ADRANAH
"Edirne", Turkey
ادرنة

AFGHANISTAN
افغانستان

AHMADABAD
Bombay, India-British
احمد اباد

AHMADNAGAR-FARRUKHABAD
Afghanistan
احمدنكر فرخ اباد

AHMADPUR
See "Bahawalpur", Afghanistan
احمد پور

AHMADSHAHI
See "Ashraf Al-Bilad" and "Qandahar", Afghanistan
احمد شاهی

AJMAN
See "United Arab Emirates"
اجمان

AKSU
China-Sinkiang
اقصو

ALGERIA
See "Al-Jaza 'Iriyat"

BI-ANGLAND
"In England" (Birmingham)
For Morocco
بانكلند

BI-ANGLAND
"In England" (London)
For Morocco
بانكلند

DAULAT ANJAZANCHIYAH
"The State of Anjazanchiyah"
See Comoros
دولة انجزنجية

ANWALA
"Aonla," Afghanistan
انوله

AL-ARABIYAT AS-SA'UDIYAT
"Saudi-Arabian", Saudi Arabia
العربية السعودية

ARDEBIL
Iran
اردبيل

ARKAT
"Arcot", India-French
اركات

ASHRAF AL-BILAD
"Most Noble of Cities"
See "Ahmadshahi", Afghanistan
اشرف البلاد

# ILLUSTRATED GUIDE TO EASTERN MINT NAMES

ASTARABAD
Iran
استراباد

ATCHEH
Indonesia
اجه

ATTOCK
Afghanistan
اتك

AZIMABAD
See "Patna", Bengal, India-British
عظيم اباد

BACAIM (no legends)
See "India-Portuguese"
—

BADAKHSHAN
See Afghanistan
بد خشان

BAGCHIH-SERAI
See "Krim"
باغجه سراي

BAGHDAD
Iraq
بغداد

BAHAWALPUR
See "Ahmadpur" and "Dar Es-Surur", Afghanistan
بها ولپور

BAHRAIN
See "El-Bahrain"
بحرين

EL-BAHRAIN
"Of the Two Seas", Bahrain
البحرين

BALKH
See "Umm Al-Bilad", Afghanistan
بلخ

BANARAS
"Awadh", Bengal, India-British
بنارس

BANDAR ABBAS
Iran
بندر عباس

BANJARMASIN
Indonesia
بنجرمسن

BARELI
Afghanistan
بريلي

BI BARIZ
"In Paris"
For Morocco
بباريز

BEHBEHAN
Iran
بهبهان

BERLIN
For Morocco
برلين

BHAKHAR
Afghanistan
بهكر

BOMBAY
See "Munbai", Bombay, India-British
—

BORUJERD
Iran
بروجرد

NEGRI BRUNEI
"State of Brunei", Brunei
نكري بروني

BRUSAH
"Bursa", Turkey
بروسة

BUKHARA
See Russian Turkestan
بخارا

BUSHIRE
See "Abushahr", Iran
—

CALCUTTA
See "Kalkatah", Bengal, India-British
كلكته

COCHIN
See India-Dutch and "V.O.C.", India-Dutch
—

COMOROS
See "Anjazanchiyah", "The Largest of the Islands", Comoros
كموز

DACCA
See "Jahangirnagar", Bengal, India-British
—

DAMAO (no legends)
See India-Portuguese
—

DAR AL-AMAN
"Abode of Security" (honorific)
See "Multan"
دار الامان

DAR AL-ISLAM
See Bahawalpur, India Princely States
دار الالسلام

DAR AL-MULK
"Abode of the King" (honorific)
See "Kabul"
دارالملك

DAR AL-NUSRAT
"Abode of the New (Town?)" (honorific)
See "Herat"
دارالنصرت

DAR AL-KHILAFAT
"Abode of the Caliphate" (honorific)
See "Tehran" and "Yemen"
دار الخلافة

DAR AS-SALAM
"Abode of Peace" (honorific)
See "Ligkeh", Thailand
دار السلام

DAR AS-SULTANAT
"Abode of the Sultanate" (honorific)
See "Herat" and "Kabul", Afghanistan
دار السلطنة

DAR AS-SURUR
"Abode of Happiness" (honorific)
See "Bahawalpur", Afghanistan
دار السرور

DARBAND
Iran
دربند

# ILLUSTRATED GUIDE TO EASTERN MINT NAMES

DARFUR
See "Al-Fasher", Sudan — الفشير

DEHLI
See "Shajahanabad", Afghanistan — دهلي

DELI
Indonesia — دلي

DERA
"Dera Ghazi Khan", Afghanistan — ديره

DERAJAT
"Dera Ishmael Khan", Afghanistan — ديره جات

DEZFUL
Iran — دزفول

DIU (no legends)
See India-Portuguese — ——

DJIBOUTI
See "Jaibuti" — ——

EDIRNE
See "Adranah", Turkey — ——

EGYPT
See "Misr" and "Al-Misriyat" — ——

ERAVAN
Iran — ايروان

FARRUKHABAD
Bengal, India-British — فرخ اباد

AL-FASHER
See "Darfur", Sudan — الفشير

FES
"Fez", Morocco — فاس

FERGANA
See "Khoqand", Russian Turkestan — فرغانة

FILASTIN
"Palestine", Israel — فلسطين

AL-FUJAIRAH
See "United Arab Emirates" — الفجيره

GANJAH
Iran — كنجه

GERMAN EAST AFRICA
See "Sharakat Almaniyah", Tanzania — شراكة المانيا

GHAZNI
Afghanistan — غزني

GOA (no legends)
See India-Portuguese — ——

HAIDARABAD SIND MINT
Afghanistan — حيدرآباد سند

HALEB
"Allepo", Syria — حلب

HAMADAN
Iran — همدان

AL-HARAR
Ethiopia-Eritrea — الهرر

AL-HEJAZ
Saudi Arabia-Hejaz — الحجاز

HERAT
See "Dar Al-Nushat" and "Dar As-Sultanat", Afghanistan — هرات

HERAT
Iran — هرات

ILI
China-Sinkiang — الي

IRAN — ايران

AL-IRAQ
"Iraque" — العراق

AL-IRAQIYAT
"Iraqi," Iraq — العراقية

ISFAHAN
Iran — اصفهان

ISLAMBUL
Turkey — اسلامبول

ITALIAN SOMALILAND
See "Al-Somal Al-Italianiah", Somalia — الصومال الايطليانية

JAHANGIRNAGAR
See "Dacca", Bengal, India-British — جهانكيرنكر

BI-JAIBUTI
"In Djibouti", Djibouti — بجيبوتي

JAVA
Indonesia — جاوا

JAZA'IR
Algeria-Algiers — جزاير

AL-JAZA'IRIYAT
Algeria-Algiers — الجزايرة

JERING
"Jaring", Thailand — جريج

AL-JOMHURIYAT EL-IRAQIYAT
"The Iraqi Republic" Iraq — الجمهورية العرقية

AL-JOMHURIYAT EL-LUBNANIYAT
"The Lebanese Republic", Lebanon — الجمهورية البنانية

# ILLUSTRATED GUIDE TO EASTERN MINT NAMES

AL-JOMHURIYAT AL-MUTTAHIDAH AL-ARABIYAT
"United Arab Republic"
See "Egypt, Syria, Yemen"
الجمهورية المتحدة العربية

AL-JOMHURIYAT AS-SUDAN
"The Sudanese Republic", Sudan
الجمهورية السودان

AL-JOMHURIYAT AS-SURIYAT
"The Syrian Republic", Syria
الجمهورية السورية

AL-JOMHURIYAT AL-TUNISIAT
"The Tunisian Republic", Tunisia
الجمهورية التونسية

AL-JOMHURIYAT AL-TURKIYAH
"The Turkish Republic", Turkey
الجمهورية توركية

JORDAN
See "Al-Urduniyat" and "Al-Mamlakat, etc.," Jordan
——

KABUL
See "Dar Al-Mulk" > AH1163 and "Dar As-Sultanat" >AH1164, Afghanistan
كابل

KAFFA
Krim, Russian Caucasia
كفه

KALKATAH
"Calcutta", Bengal, India-British
كلكته

KASHAN
Iran
كاشان

KASHMIR
Afghanistan
كشمير

KASHQUAR
China-Sinkiang
كشقر

KEDAH
See "Bilad Kedah" and "Bilad Al-Perlis Kedah", Malaysia
كداه

KELANTAN
See "Khalifat Al-Mu'Minin" and "Negri Kelantin", Malaysia
كلنتن

KEMASIN
Malaysia
كماسن

KERMAN
Iran
كرمان

KERMANSHAHAN
See "Kermanshah", Iran
كرمانشاهان

KHALIFAT AL-MU'MININ
"Commander of the Faithful" (honorific)
See "Kelantin" and "Trengganu"
خليفة المؤمنين

KHALIFAT AL-KARAM
"Noble Caliph" (honorific)
See "Patani"
خليفة الكرم

KHANABAD
Afghanistan
خان اباد

KHOQAND
See Russian Turkestan
خوقند

KHUI
See "Khoy", Iran
خوى

AL-KHURFAH
See "Yemen"
الخرفاه

KHUTAN
China-Sinkiang
خوتن

KHWAREZM
Russian Turkestan-Khiva
خوارزم

KOSOVAH
Turkey
قوصوه

KOTSHA
China-Sinkiang
كوتشر

AL-KUWAIT
Kuwait
الكويت

LADAKH
Afghanistan
لداخ

LAHEJ
See "Yemen"
لحج

LAHIJAN
See "Gilan", Iran
لاهيجان

LAHORE
Afghanistan
لاهور

LEBANON
See "Al-Lubnaniyat" and "Jomhuriyat, etc."
——

AL-LIBIYAT
"Libyan", Libya
الليبية

LIBYA
See "Al-Libyat" and "Mamlakat, etc."
ليبيا

NEGRI LIGKEH
"State of Ligeh (or Ligor)"
See "Dar As-Salam", Thialand
نكري لغكه

# ILLUSTRATED GUIDE TO EASTERN MINT NAMES

AL-LUBNANIYAT
"Lebanese", Lebanon
النلنية

MACHHLIPATAN
See "Mazulipatam", India-French
"Masulipatam", India-Madras
مجهلي بتن

MACHHLIPATAN-BANDAR
See "Machhlipatan", India-Madras
مچهلي پتن بندر

AL-MAGHRIBIYAT
"Moroccan", Morocco
المغربية

TANAH MALAYU
"Land of the Malays"
See "Sumatra", Indonesia and
"Malacca", Malaysia
تانه ملايو

PULU MALAYU
"Island of the Malays"
See "Sumatra", Indonesia
فولو ملايو

MALUKA
Indonesia
ملوک

AL-MAMLAKAT AL-ARABIYAT
AL-SA'UDIYAT
"The Kingdom of Saudi Arabia"
المملكة
العربية السعودية

AL-MAMLAKAT AL-LIBIYAT
"The Kingdom of Libya"
المملكة الليبية

AL-MAMLAKAT AL-MAGHRIBIYAT
"The Kingdom of Morocco"
المملكة المغربية

AL-MAMLAKAT AL-MUTAWAKELIYAT
AL-YEMENIAT
"The Mutawakelite Kingdom of
Yemen"
المملكة
المتوكلية اليمنية

AL-MAMLAKAT AL-MISRIYAT
"The Kingdom of Egypt"
المملكة المصرية

AL-MAMLAKAT AL-URDUNIYAT
AL-HASHEMIYAT
"The Hashemite Kingdom of
Jordan"
المملكة
الاردنية الهاشمية

MANASTIR
Turkey
مناستر

MARAGHEH
Iran
مراغه

MARAKESH
"Marrakech", Morocco
مراكش

AL-MASCARA
Algeria-Algiers
المعسكر

MASH'HAD
Afghanistan
مشهد

MASH'HAD
Iran
مشهد

MASULIPATAM
See "Machhlipatan", India-Madras
—

MAZANDARAN
Iran
مازندران

MAZULIPATAM
See "Machhlipatan", India-French
—

MEDEA
Algeria-Algiers
مديه

MEKHA
"Mecca", Saudi-Arabia
مكة

MENANGKABAU
Indonesia
منفكابو

MIKNAS
"Meknes", Morocco
مكناس

MIKNASAH
"Meknes", Morocco
مكناسة

MISR
Egypt
مصر

AL-MISRIYAT
"Egptian", Egypt
المصرية

AL-MOHAMMEDIYAT ASH-SHERIFATE
"The Mohammedan Sherifate" or
"Empire Cherifien" (French), Morocco
المحمدية
الشريفة

MOMBASA
Kenya
ممباسه

MOROCCO
See "Al-Maghribyat" and
"Al-Mohammediyat Ash-Sherifate"
—

MOXOUDABAT
See "Murshidabad", India-French
—

MUBARAK
"Auspicious" (honorific)
See "Rikab"
مبارك

AL-MAKALA
"Mukalla"
See "Yemen"
المكلا

MULTAN
See "Dar Al-Aman", Afghanistan
ملتان

# ILLUSTRATED GUIDE TO EASTERN MINT NAMES

| | |
|---|---|
| MUNBAI<br>See "Bombay", India-British | منبي |
| MURADABAD<br>Afghanistan | مراد اباد |
| MURSHIDABAD<br>See "Moxoudabat", India-French | مرشد اباد |
| MURSHIDABAD<br>Bengal, India-British | مرشد اباد |
| MUSCAT<br>Oman | مسقط |
| NAJIBABAD<br>Afghanistan | نجيب اباد |
| NAKAPATTANAM (Tamil legends)<br>"Negapatnam", India-Dutch | நாகபட்டணம் |
| NAKHCHAWAN<br>Iran | نخجوان |
| NEGAPATNAM<br>See "Nakappattanam" | — |
| NEJD<br>Saudi Arabia | نجد |
| NIHAWAND<br>Iran | نهاوند |
| NUKHWI<br>"Sheki", Iran | نخوى |
| NUKHWI<br>See "Sheki",<br>Russian Caucasia | نخوي |
| OMAN | عمان |
| OMDURMAN<br>Sudan | ام درمان |
| PAHANG<br>"Pahang Company", Malaysia | فاحغ |
| PAKISTAN | پاكستان |
| PALEMBANG<br>Indonesia | فلمبغ |
| PALESTINE<br>See "Filastin", Israel | — |
| PANA'HABAD<br>"Shusha"<br>See "Karabagh",<br>Russian Caucasia | پناه باد |

| | |
|---|---|
| AL-PATANI<br>See "Khalifat Al-Karam",<br>"Khalifat Al-Mu'Minin" and<br>"Bilad Al-Patani", Thailand | الفطاني |
| PATNA<br>See "Azimabad", Bengal,<br>India-British | پتنه |
| PULU PENANG<br>"Prince of Wales Island", Malaysia | فولوفنيغ |
| NEGRI PERAQ<br>"State of Perak", Malaysia | نكري فيرق |
| PULU PERCHA<br>"Island of Sumatra", Indonesia | فولوفرج |
| PERLIS<br>See "Kedah", Malaysia | — |
| PESHAWAR<br>Afghanistan | پشاور |
| PHALICHERY<br>SEE "Pondichery", India-French | پهلجري |
| PONDICHERY<br>See "Phalichery", India-French | — |
| PONTIANAQ (no legends)<br>Indonesia | — |
| PULICAT (no legends)<br>See "India-Dutch" | — |
| QANDAHAR<br>See "Ashraf Al-Bilad" and<br>"Ahmadshahi", Afghanistan | قندهار |
| QATAR WA DUBAI<br>"Qatar and Dubai", Qatar | قطرودبي |
| DAULAT QATAR<br>"State of Qatar", Qatar | — |
| QAZWIN<br>Iran | قزوين |
| QUAITI<br>Yemen | قيطي |
| QUM<br>Iran | قم |
| QUSANTINAT<br>"Constantine", Algeria-Algiers | قسنطينة |
| QUSTINTINIYAH<br>"Constantinople", Turkey | قسطنطنية |
| RA'NASH<br>Iran | رعنش |

# ILLUSTRATED GUIDE TO EASTERN MINT NAMES

RABAT
See "Rabat Al-Fath", Morocco
رباط

RABAT AL-FATH
"Rabat", Morocco
رباط الفتح

RAS AL-KHAIMA
See "United Arab Emirates"
راس الخيمه

RASHT
Iran
رشت

REHMAN
Thailand
رحمن

REZA'IYEH
See "Urumi", Iran
رظاعيه

RIKAB
See "Mubarak", Afghanistan
ركاب

RIKAB
Iran
ركاب

SA'UJBALAQ
Iran
ساوج بلاق

SAGAR
Bengal, India-British
ساكر

SAHRIND
Afghanistan
شهرند

AL-SAIWI
See "Bilad Al-Saiwi", "Sai", "Saiburi" and "Teluban", Thailand
السيوي

SAN'A
See "Yemen", Yemen Republic
سنة

SARAKHS
Iran
سرخس

SARHIND
See "Sahrind", Afghanistan

SARI
Iran
ساري

SARI POL
Afghanistan
سربل

SAUDI ARABIA
"See "Al-Hejaz", "Nejd" and "Al-Arabiyat As-Sa'udiya", Saudi Arabia

NEGRI SELANGHUR
"State of Selangor", Malaysia
نكري سلاغور

SELANIK
"Salonika", Turkey
سلانيك

SHAJAHANABAD
See "Dehli", Afghanistan
شاجهان اباد

SHAMAKHI
Russian Caucasia
شماخ

SHAMAKHA
Russian Caucasia
شماخه

SHARAKAT ALMANIYAH
"German Company" or "German East Africa", Tanzania
شراكتة المانيا

ES-SHARJAH
See "United Arab Emirates"
الشارجة

SHIRAZ
Iran
شيراز

SHUSHTAR
Iran
شوشتر

NEGRI SIAK
"State of Siak", Indonesia
نكري سيك

SIMNAN
Iran
سمنان

SIND
Afghanistan
سند

AL-SOMAL AL-ITALIANIYAH
"Italian Somaliland", Somalia
الصومال الايطليانية

SULTANABAD
Iran
سلطاناباد

SUMENEP
Indonesia
سمنف

SURAT
See "Surate", India-French
سورت

SURAT
Bombay, India-British
سورت

AS-SURIYAT
"Syrian", Syria
السورية

AL-SUWAIR
"Essaouira Mogador", Morocco
الصوير

AL-SUWAIRAH
"Essaouira Mogador", Morocco
الصويرة

SYRIA
See "Haleb", As-Suriyat", "Jomhuriyat, etc.", Syria

TABARISTAN
Iran
طبرستان

TABRIZ
Iran
تبريز

# ILLUSTRATED GUIDE TO EASTERN MINT NAMES

TANGIER
See "Tanjah", Morocco

TANJAH
"Tangier", Morocco
طنجة

TAQIDEMT
Algeria-Algiers
تاقدمت

TARABALUS GHARB
"Tripoli West", Libya
طرابلس غرب

TARIM
See "Yemen"
تريم

NEGRI TARUMON
"State of Tarumon", Indonesia
نكري ترومن

TASHQURGHAN
Afghanistan
تاش قورغان

TATTA
Afghanistan
تته

TEGNAPATAM (no legends)
"Fort St. David", Madras, India-British

TEHRAN
See "Dar Al-Khilafat", Iran
طهران

TELLICHERY
Bombay, India-British
تلچري

TETUAN
Morocco
تطوان

TIFLIS
See Russia, Georgia
تفليس

TRANQUEBAR (no legends)
See "India-Danish"

TRENGKANU
See "Khalifat Al-Mu'Minin", Malaysia
ترغكانو

TUNIS
Tunisia
تونس

TUNISIA
See "Tunis", "Al-Tunisiyat", "Jomhuriyat, etc."

AL-TUNISIYAT
"Tunisian," Tunisia
التونسية

TURKEY
See "Turkiyah", "Jomhuriyat, etc."

AL-TURKIYAH
"Turkish", Turkey
التوركية

TUTICORIN (degenerate Nagari legends)
See "India-Dutch"

TUYSERKAN
Iran
توی سرکان

TANAH UGI
"Land of the Bugis", Indonesia
تانه اغيسى

UMM AL-BILAD
"Mother of Cities"
See "Balkh", Afghanistan
ام البلاد

UMM AL-QAIWAIN
See "United Arab Emirates"
ام القوين

UNITED ARAB EMIRATES
الامارات العربية المتحدة

UNITED ARAB REPUBLIC
See "Al-Jomhuriyat Al-Arabiyat AL-Muttahidah

AL-URDUNIYAT
"Jordanian", Jordan
الاردنية

URUMCHI
China-Sinkiang
ارومجي

URUMI
See "Reza'iyeh", Iran
ارومى

USHI
China-Sinkiang
اوش

WAN
"Van", Turkey
وان

YARKHAND
China-Sinkiang
يارقند

YARKHISSARMARAN
"Yanghissar"
China-Sinkiang
يارکسارمرن

YAZD
Iran
يزد

YEMEN
See "Sana", "Dar Al-Khilafat", Al-Yemeniyat", Mamlakat, etc."

AL-YEMENIYAT
"The Yemen"
اليمنية

ZANJAN
Iran
زنجان

ZANJIBARA
"Zanzibar", Tanzania
زنجباراه

# AFGHANISTAN

The Islamic State of Afghanistan, which occupies a mountainous region of Southwest Asia, has an area of 251,825 sq. mi. (652,090 sq. km.) and a population of 25.59 million. Presently, about a fifth of the total population lives in exile as refugees, (mostly in Pakistan). Capital: Kabul. It is bordered by Iran, Pakistan, Turkmenistan, Uzbekistan, Tajikistan, and China's Sinkiang Province. Agriculture and herding are the principal industries; textile mills and cement factories add to the industrial sector. Cotton, wool, fruits, nuts, oil, sheepskin coats and hand-woven carpets are normally exported but foreign trade has been interrupted since 1979.

Because of its strategic position astride the ancient land route to India, Afghanistan (formerly known as Aryana and Khorasan) was invaded by Darius I, Alexander the Great, various Scythian tribes, the White Huns, the Arabs, the Turks, Genghis Khan, Tamerlane, the Mughals, the Persians, and in more recent times by Great Britain. It was a powerful empire under the Kushans, Hephthalites, Ghaznavids and Ghorids. The name Afghanistan, "Land of the Afghans," came into use in the eighteenth and nineteenth centuries to describe the realm of the Afghan kings. For a short period, this mountainous region was the easternmost frontier of the Iranian world, with strong cultural influences from the Turks and Mongols to the north and India to the south.

Previous to 1747, Afghan Kings ruled not only in Afghanistan, but also in India, of which Sher Shah Suri was one. Ahmad Shah Abdali, founder of the Durrani dynasty, established his rule at Qandahar in 1747. His clan was known as Saddozai. He conquered large territories in India and eastern Iran, which were lost by his grandson Shah Zaman. A new family, the Barakzai, drove the Durrani king out of Kabul, the capital, in 1819, but the Durranis were not eliminated completely until 1858. Further conflicts among the Barakzai prevented full unity until the reign of Abdur Rahman in 1880. In 1929, King Amanullah, grandson of Abdul Rahman, was driven out of the country by a commoner known as Baccha-i-Saqao, "Son of the Water-Carrier", who ruled as Habibullah for less than a year before he was defeated by Muhammad Nadir Shah, a relative of the Barakzai. The last king, Muhammad Zahir Shah, became a constitutional though still autocratic monarch in 1964. In 1973 a coup d'etat displaced him and created the Republic of Afghanistan. A subsequent military coup established the pro-Soviet Democratic Republic of Afghanistan in 1978. Mounting resistance in the countryside and violence within the government led to the Soviet invasion of late 1979 and the installation of Babrak Karmal as prime minister. A brutal civil war ensued, which continues to the present, even after Soviet forces withdrew in 1989 and Karmal's government was defeated. An unstable coalition of former *Mujahideen* (Freedom Fighters) factions attempted to govern for several years but have been gradually overcome by the Taliban, a Muslim fundamentalist force supported from Pakistan.

On September 11, 2001, a terrorist attack on the United States, supported by the Taliban, led to retaliatory strikes by the U.S. Military and subsequent dismantling of the Taliban regime. During a UN-sponsored conference on Afghanistan that was held in Bonn, Germany, in early November 2001, an agreement was reached for an Interim Authority, under the leadership of Hamid Karzai, to be instated in Afghanistan on December 22, 2001 and to hold power for the following four to six months. During that time a "loya jirga" (Grand Council) is scheduled to decide on the follow-on Transitional Authority.

Afghanistan's traditional coinage was much like that of its neighbors Iran and India. There were four major mints: Kabul, Qandahar, Balkh and Herat. The early Durranis also controlled mints in Iran and India. On gold and silver coins, the inscriptions in Persian (called *Dari* in Afghanistan) included the name of the mint city and, normally, of the ruler recognized there, but some issues are anonymous. The arrangement of the inscriptions, and frequently the name of the ruler, was different at each mint. Copper coins were controlled locally and usually did not name any ruler. For these reasons the coinage of each mint is treated separately. The relative values of gold, silver, and copper coins were not fixed but were determined in the marketplace.

In 1890 Abdur Rahman had a modern mint set up in Kabul using British minting machinery and the help of British advisors. The other mints were closed down, except for the issue of local coppers. The new system had 60 paisa equal one rupee; intermediate denominations also had special names. In 1901 the name Afghanistan appeared on coins for the first time. A decimal system, 100 puls to the afghani, was introduced in 1925. The gold amani, rated at 20 afghanis, was a bullion coin.

The national symbol on most coins of the kingdom is a stylized mosque, within which is seen the *mihrab*, a niche indicating the direction of Mecca, and the *minbar*, the pulpit, with a flight of steps leading up to it. Inscriptions in Pashtu were first used under the rebel Habibullah, but did not become standard until 1950.

Until 1919, coins were dated by the lunar Islamic Hejira calendar (AH), often with the king's regnal year as a second date. The solar Hejira (SH) calendar was introduced in 1919 (1337 AH, 1298 SH). The rebel Habibullah reinstated lunar Hejira dating (AH 1347-50), but the solar calendar was used thereafter. The solar Hejira year begins on the first day of spring, about March 21. Adding 621 to the SH year yields the AD year in which it begins.

**RULERS**

Names of rulers are shown in Perso-Arabic script in the style usually found on their coins; they are not always in a straight line.

**BARAKZAI DYNASTY**

Abdur Rahman,

عبدالرحمن

AH1297-1319/1880-1901AD

Habibullah,

امان الله

AH1319-1337/1901-1919AD

Amanullah, AH1337,

حبيب الله
١٣٤٧(٥٣٨)

SH1298-1307/1919-1929AD

Habibullah (rebel, known as Baccha-i-Saqao),

حبيب الله

AH1347-1348/1929AD

Muhammed Nadir Shah, AH1348-1350,

محمد نادر شاه

SH1310-1312/1929-1933AD

Muhammad Zahir Shah,

محمد ظاهر شاه

SH1312-1352/1933-1973AD

Republic, SH1352-1358/1973-1979AD
Democratic Republic, SH1358-1373/1979-1994 AD
Islamic Republic, SH1373-1381/1994-2002AD

**MINTNAMES**

Coins were struck at numerous mints in Afghanistan and adjacent lands. These are listed below, together with their honorific titles, and shown in the style ordinarily found on the coins.

Afghanistan افغانستان

Ghazni غزني

Herat هرات

Kabul كابل

"Dar al-Mulk" Abode of the King Qandahar دار لملك

**MINT MARKS**

(k) – key Havana, Cuba

# KINGDOM OF AFGHANISTAN

## Habibullah
## AH1319-1337/1901-1919AD

### LOCAL COINAGE

**PAISA** **KM# 960.2** **Composition:** Copper **Note:** Counter-stamp on Iran 50 dinars, Y#4; Struck at Qandahar.

| Date | Mintage | Good | VG | F | VF | XF |
|---|---|---|---|---|---|---|
| AH1321 | — | 3.00 | 5.00 | 8.00 | 12.50 | — |
| AH1322 | — | 3.00 | 5.00 | 8.00 | 12.50 | — |

**PAISA** **KM# 960.1** **Composition:** Copper **Note:** Dump; Struck at Qandahar.

| Date | Mintage | Good | VG | F | VF | XF |
|---|---|---|---|---|---|---|
| AH1322 | — | 4.50 | 7.50 | 12.50 | 17.50 | — |

**PAISA** **KM# 956.1** **Composition:** Copper **Note:** Round or irregular flan; Struck at Herat.

| Date | Mintage | Good | VG | F | VF | XF |
|---|---|---|---|---|---|---|
| AH1322 | — | 2.50 | 4.00 | 7.50 | 12.50 | — |
| AH1328 | — | 2.50 | 4.00 | 7.50 | 12.50 | — |
| AH1329 | — | 2.50 | 4.00 | 7.50 | 12.50 | — |
| AH1330 | — | 2.50 | 4.00 | 7.50 | 12.50 | — |
| AH1331 | — | 2.50 | 4.00 | 7.50 | 12.50 | — |
| AH1332 | — | 2.50 | 4.00 | 7.50 | 12.50 | — |
| ND Date off flan | — | 1.50 | 2.50 | 5.00 | 8.00 | — |

**PAISA** **KM# 957** **Composition:** Copper **Note:** Struck over Iran, 50 Dinars, Y#4; Struck at Herat.

| Date | Mintage | Good | VG | F | VF | XF |
|---|---|---|---|---|---|---|
| AH1322 | — | 4.00 | 6.50 | 12.50 | 16.00 | — |
| AH1328 | — | 3.00 | 5.00 | 10.00 | 12.50 | — |

**PAISA** **KM# 963** **Composition:** Copper **Note:** Struck over British East India Co., 1/4 Anna; Struck at Ghazni.

| Date | Mintage | Good | VG | F | VF | XF |
|---|---|---|---|---|---|---|
| AH1322 | — | 10.00 | 20.00 | 35.00 | 75.00 | — |

**PAISA** **KM# 960.4** **Composition:** Copper **Note:** Counter-stamp on British East India Co., 1/4 Anna; Struck at Qandahar.

| Date | Mintage | Good | VG | F | VF | XF |
|---|---|---|---|---|---|---|
| AH1322 | — | 4.00 | 7.50 | 12.00 | 18.00 | — |
| AH1330 | — | 4.00 | 7.50 | 12.00 | 18.00 | — |

**PAISA** **KM# 960.3** **Composition:** Copper **Note:** Counter-stamp on Muscat and Oman, 1/4 Anna, KM#4; Struck at Qandahar.

| Date | Mintage | Good | VG | F | VF | XF |
|---|---|---|---|---|---|---|
| AH1322 | — | 3.75 | 6.50 | 10.00 | 15.00 | — |

**PAISA** **KM# 960.5** **Composition:** Copper **Note:** Overstruck on Oman, 1/4 Anna, KM#3.1; Struck at Qandahar.

| Date | Mintage | Good | VG | F | VF | XF |
|---|---|---|---|---|---|---|
| AH1322 | — | 3.75 | 6.50 | 10.00 | 15.00 | — |

**PAISA** KM# 956.3 **Composition:** Copper **Obverse:** Scroll symbol **Note:** Struck at Herat.

| Date | Mintage | Good | VG | F | VF | XF |
|---|---|---|---|---|---|---|
| AH1325 | — | 3.00 | 5.00 | 8.50 | 15.00 | — |

**PAISA** KM# 958.1 **Composition:** Copper **Obverse:** "Dar al-Nusrat" added above date **Note:** Struck at Herat.

| Date | Mintage | Good | VG | F | VF | XF |
|---|---|---|---|---|---|---|
| AH1331 | — | 2.50 | 4.00 | 7.50 | 12.50 | — |

**PAISA** KM# 958.2 **Composition:** Copper **Reverse:** Date below mosque **Note:** Struck at Herat.

| Date | Mintage | Good | VG | F | VF | XF |
|---|---|---|---|---|---|---|
| AH1331 | — | 3.50 | 5.00 | 8.50 | 15.00 | — |

**PAISA** KM# 956.2 **Composition:** Copper **Reverse:** In a rayed circle **Note:** Struck at Herat.

| Date | Mintage | Good | VG | F | VF | XF |
|---|---|---|---|---|---|---|
| AH1332 | — | 3.00 | 5.00 | 8.50 | 15.00 | — |

**PAISA** KM# 964 **Composition:** Copper **Note:** Struck at Qandahar.

| Date | Mintage | Good | VG | F | VF | XF |
|---|---|---|---|---|---|---|
| AH1333 | — | 2.00 | 3.50 | 6.00 | 10.00 | — |
| AH1334 | — | 2.00 | 3.50 | 6.00 | 10.00 | — |

**PAISA** KM# 973 **Composition:** Copper **Note:** Struck at Kabul.

| Date | Mintage | Good | VG | F | VF | XF |
|---|---|---|---|---|---|---|
| ND | — | — | — | — | — | — |

**2 PAISE** KM# 959 **Composition:** Copper **Note:** Similar to Paisa, KM#965 but inscribed "Do Paisa" below mosque.

| Date | Mintage | Good | VG | F | VF | XF |
|---|---|---|---|---|---|---|
| AH1329 | — | 3.00 | 5.00 | 8.50 | 13.50 | — |

## MILLED COINAGE

10 Dinar = 1 Paisa; 5 Paise = 1 Shahi; 2 Shahi = 1 Sanar; 2 Sanar = 1 Abbasi; 1-1/2 Abbasi = 1 Qiran; 2 Qiran = 1 Kabuli Rupee; 1 Tilla = 10 Rupees

**PAISA** KM# 848 **Composition:** Bronze Or Brass

| Date | Mintage | VG | F | VF | XF | Unc |
|---|---|---|---|---|---|---|
| AH1329 | — | 6.00 | 12.00 | 22.00 | 40.00 | — |
| AH1329/17 on KM#828 obverse die | — | 8.00 | 16.00 | 35.00 | 60.00 | — |

**PAISA** KM# 849 **Composition:** Bronze Or Brass **Size:** 21 mm.

| Date | Mintage | VG | F | VF | XF | Unc |
|---|---|---|---|---|---|---|
| AH1329 | — | 2.00 | 4.00 | 7.50 | 15.00 | — |
| AH1331 | — | 2.00 | 4.00 | 7.50 | 15.00 | — |
| AH1332 | — | 2.50 | 4.75 | 9.00 | 16.50 | — |
| AH1334 | — | 3.00 | 6.00 | 11.50 | 20.00 | — |

**PAISA** KM# 854 **Composition:** Bronze Or Brass **Size:** 19 mm. **Note:** Thick flan, reduced size.

| Date | Mintage | VG | F | VF | XF | Unc |
|---|---|---|---|---|---|---|
| AH1336 | — | 3.00 | 6.00 | 12.00 | 25.00 | — |

**PAISA** KM# 855 **Composition:** Bronze Or Brass **Note:** Thin flan.

| Date | Mintage | VG | F | VF | XF | Unc |
|---|---|---|---|---|---|---|
| AH1336 | — | 6.50 | 10.00 | 20.00 | 35.00 | — |
| AH1337 | — | 2.00 | 4.00 | 8.00 | 16.00 | — |

**PAISA** KM# 857 **Composition:** Bronze Or Brass **Size:** 20 mm. **Note:** Thin flan.

| Date | Mintage | VG | F | VF | XF | Unc |
|---|---|---|---|---|---|---|
| AH1337 | — | 6.50 | 10.00 | 20.00 | 35.00 | — |

**PAISA** KM# 858 **Composition:** Bronze Or Brass **Note:** Thin flan, 19-20 milimeters.

| Date | Mintage | VG | F | VF | XF | Unc |
|---|---|---|---|---|---|---|
| AH1337(1918) | — | 3.00 | 6.00 | 10.00 | 20.00 | — |
| SH1298(1919) | — | 4.50 | 8.00 | 15.00 | 32.50 | — |

**Note:** Three varieties are known dated AH1337.

**SANAR (10 Paisa)** KM# 846 **Weight:** 1.5500 g. **Composition:** 0.5000 Silver .0249 oz. ASW

| Date | Mintage | VG | F | VF | XF | Unc |
|---|---|---|---|---|---|---|
| AH1325 | — | 10.00 | 20.00 | 35.00 | 60.00 | — |
| AH1326 | — | 5.00 | 7.50 | 12.50 | 22.50 | — |
| AH1328 | — | 5.00 | 7.50 | 12.50 | 22.50 | — |
| AH1329 | — | 5.75 | 8.50 | 14.00 | 25.00 | — |

**SANAR (10 Paisa)** KM# 850 **Weight:** 1.5500 g. **Composition:** 0.5000 Silver .0249 oz. ASW **Note:** Coins dated AH1333 and 1337 are known in 2 varieties.

| Date | Mintage | VG | F | VF | XF | Unc |
|---|---|---|---|---|---|---|
| AH1329 | — | 4.00 | 7.00 | 12.00 | 22.00 | — |
| AH1330 | — | 3.00 | 6.00 | 10.00 | 20.00 | — |
| AH1331 | — | 3.00 | 6.00 | 10.00 | 20.00 | — |
| AH1332 | — | 3.00 | 6.00 | 10.00 | 20.00 | — |
| AH1333 | — | 3.00 | 5.00 | 9.00 | 16.00 | — |
| AH1335 | — | 3.00 | 5.00 | 9.00 | 16.00 | — |
| AH1337 | — | 3.00 | 6.00 | 10.00 | 20.00 | — |

**3 SHAHI (15 Paisa)** KM# 863 **Composition:** Copper **Obverse:** Without "Al-Ghazi" **Reverse:** Mosque in 8-pointed star **Note:** 32-33 milimeters.

| Date | Mintage | VG | F | VF | XF | Unc |
|---|---|---|---|---|---|---|
| AH1337(1918) | — | 5.00 | 12.00 | 20.00 | 35.00 | — |

**Note:** Three varieties are known.

**3 SHAHI (15 Paisa)** KM# 869 **Composition:** Copper **Obverse:** "Shamsi" left and below date

| Date | Mintage | VG | F | VF | XF | Unc |
|---|---|---|---|---|---|---|
| SH1298(1919) | — | 2.00 | 4.00 | 9.00 | 18.00 | — |

**Note:** Shamsi (Solar) is an additional word written on some of the coins dated SH1298, to show the change from a lunar to solar calendar.

**ABBASI (20 Paisa)** KM# 837 **Weight:** 3.1100 g. **Composition:** 0.5000 Silver .0499 oz. ASW

| Date | Mintage | VG | F | VF | XF | Unc |
|---|---|---|---|---|---|---|
| AH1320 | — | 30.00 | 60.00 | 100 | 225 | — |

**ABBASI (20 Paisa)** KM# 845 **Weight:** 3.1100 g. **Composition:** 0.5000 Silver .0499 oz. ASW

| Date | Mintage | VG | F | VF | XF | Unc |
|---|---|---|---|---|---|---|
| AH1324 | — | 35.00 | 70.00 | 125 | 250 | — |
| AH1328 | — | 35.00 | 70.00 | 125 | 250 | — |

**ABBASI (20 Paisa)** KM# 851 **Weight:** 3.1100 g. **Composition:** 0.5000 Silver .0499 oz. ASW

| Date | Mintage | VG | F | VF | XF | Unc |
|---|---|---|---|---|---|---|
| AH1329 | — | 6.00 | 11.00 | 16.00 | 24.00 | — |
| AH1330 | — | 6.00 | 11.00 | 16.00 | 24.00 | — |
| AH1333 | — | 5.00 | 10.00 | 15.00 | 22.50 | — |
| AH1334 | — | 5.00 | 10.00 | 15.00 | 22.50 | — |
| AH1335 | — | 5.00 | 10.00 | 15.00 | 22.50 | — |
| AH1337 | — | 5.00 | 10.00 | 15.00 | 22.50 | — |

**1/2 RUPEE (Qiran)** KM# 831 **Weight:** 4.6500 g. **Composition:** 0.5000 Silver .0747 oz. ASW **Obverse:** Toughra **Reverse:** Crossed cannons below mosque

| Date | Mintage | VG | F | VF | XF | Unc |
|---|---|---|---|---|---|---|
| AH1319 | — | 20.00 | 40.00 | 75.00 | 125 | — |

**1/2 RUPEE (Qiran)** KM# 838 **Weight:** 4.6500 g. **Composition:** 0.5000 Silver .0747 oz. ASW **Obverse:** Toughra divides date

| Date | Mintage | VG | F | VF | XF | Unc |
|---|---|---|---|---|---|---|
| AH1320 | — | 25.00 | 45.00 | 85.00 | 140 | — |
| AH1325 | — | 20.00 | 40.00 | 75.00 | 125 | — |

**1/2 RUPEE (Qiran)** KM# 841 **Weight:** 4.6500 g. **Composition:** 0.5000 Silver .0747 oz. ASW **Obverse:** Date at upper right of toughra **Reverse:** Dated AH1320

| Date | Mintage | VG | F | VF | XF | Unc |
|---|---|---|---|---|---|---|
| AH1321 | — | 25.00 | 45.00 | 85.00 | 140 | — |
| AH1323 | — | 30.00 | 55.00 | 100 | 170 | — |

**1/2 RUPEE (Qiran)** **KM# 844.1** (KM844) **Weight:** 4.6500 g. **Composition:** 0.5000 Silver .0747 oz. ASW **Obverse:** Inscription and date **Reverse:** Frozen date AH1320 split above mosque

| Date | Mintage | VG | F | VF | XF | Unc |
|---|---|---|---|---|---|---|
| AH1323 | — | 6.00 | 9.00 | 16.00 | 28.00 | — |
| AH1324 | — | 6.00 | 9.00 | 15.00 | 25.00 | — |
| AH1326 | — | 6.00 | 9.00 | 15.00 | 25.00 | — |
| AH1327/6 | — | 6.00 | 9.00 | 15.00 | 25.00 | — |
| AH1327 | — | 6.00 | 9.00 | 15.00 | 25.00 | — |
| AH1328 | — | 8.00 | 12.00 | 20.00 | 45.00 | — |
| AH1329 | — | 6.00 | 9.00 | 16.00 | 28.00 | — |

**1/2 RUPEE (Qiran)** **KM# 844.2** **Weight:** 4.6500 g. **Composition:** 0.5000 Silver .0747 oz. ASW **Obverse:** Inscription and date **Reverse:** Actual date at top

| Date | Mintage | VG | F | VF | XF | Unc |
|---|---|---|---|---|---|---|
| AH1326/3 | — | 25.00 | 45.00 | 75.00 | 135 | — |

**Note:** AH1326/0 for actual date on reverse

| Date | Mintage | VG | F | VF | XF | Unc |
|---|---|---|---|---|---|---|
| AH1329 | — | 25.00 | 45.00 | 75.00 | 135 | — |

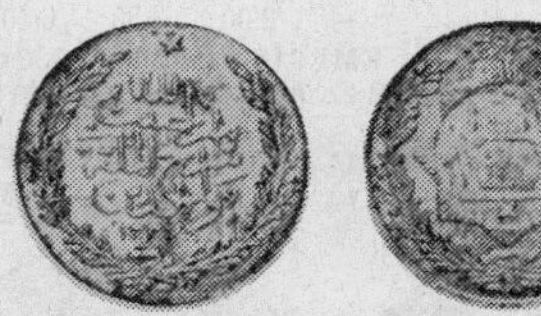

**1/2 RUPEE (Qiran)** **KM# 852** **Weight:** 4.6000 g. **Composition:** 0.5000 Silver .0739 oz. ASW

| Date | Mintage | VG | F | VF | XF | Unc |
|---|---|---|---|---|---|---|
| AH1329 | — | 3.50 | 5.50 | 8.50 | 16.00 | — |
| AH1333 | — | 3.50 | 5.50 | 8.50 | 16.00 | — |
| AH1334 | — | 4.50 | 7.50 | 12.50 | 22.50 | — |
| AH1335 | — | 4.50 | 7.50 | 12.50 | 22.50 | — |
| AH1337 | — | 3.50 | 5.50 | 8.50 | 16.00 | — |

**1/2 RUPEE (Qiran)** **KM# 864** **Weight:** 5.0000 g. **Composition:** Silver **Obv. Legend:** Name of "Habibullah" **Reverse:** Star of Solomon

| Date | Mintage | VG | F | VF | XF | Unc |
|---|---|---|---|---|---|---|
| AH1335 | — | — | 300 | 500 | — | — |

**1/2 RUPEE (Qiran)** **KM# 865** **Composition:** Silver **Obverse:** Uncircled inscription

| Date | Mintage | VG | F | VF | XF | Unc |
|---|---|---|---|---|---|---|
| AH1337(1918) | — | 4.00 | 9.00 | 15.00 | 25.00 | — |

**Note:** Five varieties are known.

**RUPEE** **KM# 832** **Weight:** 9.2000 g. **Composition:** 0.5000 Silver .0755 oz. ASW **Obverse:** Toughra of Habibullah in wreath, star above

| Date | Mintage | VG | F | VF | XF | Unc |
|---|---|---|---|---|---|---|
| AH1319 | — | 8.00 | 12.00 | 25.00 | 70.00 | — |

**Note:** Two varieties are known

**RUPEE** **KM# 833.1** **Weight:** 9.2000 g. **Composition:** 0.5000 Silver .0755 oz. ASW **Obverse:** "Afghanistan" above small toughra, star at right **Reverse:** Large inverted pyramid dome

| Date | Mintage | VG | F | VF | XF | Unc |
|---|---|---|---|---|---|---|
| AH1319 | — | 4.00 | 5.50 | 10.00 | 25.00 | — |
| AH1320 | — | 4.00 | 5.50 | 8.50 | 20.00 | — |
| AH1325 | — | 7.00 | 15.00 | 25.00 | 50.00 | — |

**RUPEE** **KM# 833.2** **Weight:** 9.2000 g. **Composition:** 0.5000 Silver .0755 oz. ASW **Obverse:** Without star

| Date | Mintage | VG | F | VF | XF | Unc |
|---|---|---|---|---|---|---|
| AH1319 | — | 4.00 | 5.50 | 10.00 | 25.00 | — |
| AH1325 | — | 7.00 | 15.00 | 25.00 | 50.00 | — |

**RUPEE** **KM# 839** **Weight:** 9.2000 g. **Composition:** 0.5000 Silver .0755 oz. ASW **Obverse:** "Afgahanistan" divided by a star above large toughra

| Date | Mintage | VG | F | VF | XF | Unc |
|---|---|---|---|---|---|---|
| AH1320 | — | 4.00 | 6.00 | 10.00 | 20.00 | — |

**RUPEE** **KM# 840.1** **Weight:** 9.2000 g. **Composition:** 0.5000 Silver .0755 oz. ASW **Reverse:** Small dome mosque

| Date | Mintage | VG | F | VF | XF | Unc |
|---|---|---|---|---|---|---|
| AH1320 | — | 5.00 | 8.00 | 15.00 | 35.00 | — |

**RUPEE** **KM# 840.2** **Weight:** 9.2000 g. **Composition:** 0.5000 Silver .0755 oz. ASW **Obverse:** Date in loop of toughra

| Date | Mintage | VG | F | VF | XF | Unc |
|---|---|---|---|---|---|---|
| AH1321 | — | 10.00 | 15.00 | 25.00 | 50.00 | — |

**RUPEE** **KM# 842.1** **Weight:** 9.2000 g. **Composition:** 0.5000 Silver .0755 oz. ASW **Reverse:** "Afghanistan" above mosque, crossed swords and cannons

| Date | Mintage | VG | F | VF | XF | Unc |
|---|---|---|---|---|---|---|
| AH1321 | — | 4.00 | 7.00 | 10.50 | 22.00 | — |

**Note:** Two varieties exist for AH1321 date

| Date | Mintage | VG | F | VF | XF | Unc |
|---|---|---|---|---|---|---|
| AH1322 | — | 4.00 | 7.00 | 10.50 | 22.00 | — |

**RUPEE** **KM# 842.2** **Weight:** 9.2000 g. **Composition:** 0.5000 Silver .0755 oz. ASW **Reverse:** Crossed cannons

| Date | Mintage | VG | F | VF | XF | Unc |
|---|---|---|---|---|---|---|
| AH1322 | — | 4.00 | 5.00 | 9.00 | 20.00 | — |
| AH1324 | — | 4.00 | 5.00 | 9.00 | 20.00 | — |
| AH1325 | — | 5.00 | 8.00 | 12.00 | 25.00 | — |
| AH1326 | — | 4.00 | 6.00 | 10.00 | 19.00 | — |
| AH1327/6 | — | 6.00 | 8.00 | 15.00 | 30.00 | — |
| AH1327 | — | 4.00 | 6.00 | 10.00 | 20.00 | — |
| AH1328 | — | 6.00 | 8.00 | 15.00 | 30.00 | — |

**Note:** Two varieties exist for AH1328 date.

| Date | Mintage | VG | F | VF | XF | Unc |
|---|---|---|---|---|---|---|
| AH1329 | — | 6.00 | 8.00 | 15.00 | 30.00 | — |

**RUPEE** **KM# 847.1** **Weight:** 9.2000 g. **Composition:** 0.5000 Silver .0755 oz. ASW **Obverse:** Date divided 13 Arabic "j" 28 **Reverse:** Large dome mosque without "Afghanistan"

| Date | Mintage | VG | F | VF | XF | Unc |
|---|---|---|---|---|---|---|
| AH1328 | — | 7.00 | 15.00 | 25.00 | 50.00 | — |

**RUPEE** **KM# 847.2** **Weight:** 9.2000 g. **Composition:** 0.5000 Silver .0755 oz. ASW **Obverse:** Date divided 132 Arabic "j" 8

| Date | Mintage | VG | F | VF | XF | Unc |
|---|---|---|---|---|---|---|
| AH1328 | — | 10.00 | 20.00 | 30.00 | 60.00 | — |

**RUPEE** **KM# 853** **Weight:** 9.2000 g. **Composition:** 0.5000 Silver .0755 oz. ASW **Obverse:** Name and titles of Habibullah in sprays **Reverse:** Mosque within sunburst **Note:** 25-26 milimeters; Two varieties exist for AH1330, 1331 and 1337 and three varieties exist for AH1333. Thickness of obverse inscription and size of mosque dome on reverse vary.

| Date | Mintage | VG | F | VF | XF | Unc |
|---|---|---|---|---|---|---|
| AH1329 | — | 4.00 | 6.00 | 10.00 | 20.00 | — |
| AH1330 | — | 4.00 | 6.00 | 9.00 | 18.50 | — |
| AH1331 | — | 4.00 | 6.00 | 9.00 | 18.50 | — |
| AH1332 | — | 4.00 | 6.00 | 9.00 | 18.50 | — |
| AH1333 | — | 4.00 | 6.00 | 9.00 | 18.50 | — |
| AH1334 | — | 4.00 | 6.00 | 9.00 | 18.50 | — |
| AH1335 | — | 4.00 | 6.00 | 9.00 | 18.50 | — |
| AH1337 | — | 4.00 | 6.00 | 10.00 | 20.00 | — |

**TILLA (10 Rupees)** **KM# 835** **Weight:** 4.6000 g. **Composition:** 0.9000 Gold .1331 oz. AGW **Obverse:** Star above toughra

| Date | Mintage | VG | F | VF | XF | Unc |
|---|---|---|---|---|---|---|
| AH1319 | — | 70.00 | 95.00 | 140 | 240 | — |

**TILLA (10 Rupees)** **KM# 836.1** **Weight:** 4.6000 g. **Composition:** 0.9000 Gold .1331 oz. AGW **Obverse:** Legend divided by star above toughra **Obv. Legend:** "Afghanistan"

| Date | Mintage | VG | F | VF | XF | Unc |
|---|---|---|---|---|---|---|
| AH1319 | — | 75.00 | 100 | 150 | 250 | — |

**TILLA (10 Rupees)** **KM# 836.2** **Weight:** 4.6000 g. **Composition:** 0.9000 Gold .1331 oz. AGW **Obverse:** Legend above toughra with star to right **Obv. Legend:** "Afghanistan"

| Date | Mintage | VG | F | VF | XF | Unc |
|---|---|---|---|---|---|---|
| AH1320 | — | 75.00 | 100 | 150 | 250 | — |

**TILLA (10 Rupees)** **KM# A856** **Weight:** 4.6000 g. **Composition:** 0.9000 Gold .1331 oz. AGW **Obverse:** Date divided

| Date | Mintage | VG | F | VF | XF | Unc |
|---|---|---|---|---|---|---|
| AH1325 | — | — | 450 | 650 | 900 | — |

**TILLA (10 Rupees)** **KM# 856** **Weight:** 4.6000 g. **Composition:** 0.9000 Gold .1331 oz. AGW **Obv. Legend:** Habibullah...

| Date | Mintage | VG | F | VF | XF | Unc |
|---|---|---|---|---|---|---|
| AH1335 | — | 170 | 200 | 260 | 330 | — |
| AH1336 | — | 100 | 120 | 175 | 240 | — |
| AH1337 | — | 110 | 130 | 180 | 220 | — |

**2 TILLAS (20 Rupees)** **KM# 879** **Weight:** 9.2000 g. **Composition:** 0.9000 Gold .2661 oz. AGW **Size:** 22 mm.

| Date | Mintage | F | VF | XF | Unc |
|---|---|---|---|---|---|
| SH1298(1919) | — | BV | 140 | 240 | 380 |

**4 TILLAS (40 Rupees)** **KM# 903** **Weight:** 18.5300 g. **Composition:** 0.9000 Gold .1997 oz. AGW

| Date | Mintage | VG | F | VF | XF | Unc |
|---|---|---|---|---|---|---|
| AH1337(1918) Rare | — | — | — | — | — | — |

**5 AMANI (50 Rupees)** **KM# 889** **Weight:** 23.0000 g. **Composition:** 0.9000 Gold .6656 oz. AGW **Obverse:** Persian "5" above toughra; "Al Ghazi" at right **Reverse:** Legend above mosque **Rev. Legend:** "Amaniya"

| Date | Mintage | VG | F | VF | XF | Unc |
|---|---|---|---|---|---|---|
| SH1299(1920) | — | BV | 400 | 675 | 1,500 | — |

**5 AMANI (50 Rupees)** **KM# 890** **Weight:** 23.0000 g. **Composition:** 0.9000 Gold .6656 oz. AGW **Obverse:** Star above toughta **Reverse:** Persian "5" above mosque

| Date | Mintage | VG | F | VF | XF | Unc |
|---|---|---|---|---|---|---|
| SH1299(1920) | — | BV | 400 | 675 | 1,500 | — |

# Amanullah
## AH1337, SH1298-1307/1919-1929AD

## LOCAL COINAGE

**PAISA** **KM# 965** **Composition:** Copper **Obverse:** Denomination "Yek Paisa" **Note:** Crudely struck; without mint name, believed to be struck at Kabul.

| Date | Mintage | Good | VG | F | VF | XF |
|---|---|---|---|---|---|---|
| SH1298(1919) | — | 4.50 | 7.50 | 12.50 | 20.00 | — |
| SH1299(1920) | — | 4.50 | 7.50 | 12.50 | 20.00 | — |

**PAISA** **KM# 966** **Composition:** Copper **Note:** Crudely struck; without mint name, believed to be struck at Kabul.

| Date | Mintage | Good | VG | F | VF | XF |
|---|---|---|---|---|---|---|
| SH1299(1920) | — | 6.00 | 10.00 | 16.50 | 24.00 | — |

**SHAHI (5 Paise)** **KM# 967** **Composition:** Copper **Reverse:** Both denominations **Note:** Crudely struck; without mint name, believed to be struck at Kabul.

| Date | Mintage | Good | VG | F | VF | XF |
|---|---|---|---|---|---|---|
| SH1298(1919) | — | 6.00 | 10.00 | 16.50 | 24.00 | — |
| SH1299(1920) | — | 7.50 | 12.50 | 20.00 | 30.00 | — |
| SH1299(1920) | — | 6.00 | 10.00 | 16.50 | 24.00 | — |

**10 PAISE** **KM# A846** **Composition:** Copper **Note:** Crudely struck; without mint name, believed to be struck at Kabul.

| Date | Mintage | Good | VG | F | VF | XF |
|---|---|---|---|---|---|---|
| SH1299(1920) | — | 7.50 | 12.50 | 20.00 | 30.00 | — |

## MILLED COINAGE

10 Dinar = 1 Paisa; 5 Paise = 1 Shahi; 2 Shahi = 1 Sanar; 2 Sanar = 1 Abbasi; 1-1/2 Abbasi = 1 Qiran; 2 Qiran = 1 Kabuli Rupee; 1 Tilla = 10 Rupees

**5 PUL** **KM# 906** **Weight:** 3.0000 g. **Composition:** Bronze Or Brass

| Date | Mintage | F | VF | XF | Unc |
|---|---|---|---|---|---|
| SH1304(1925) | — | 1.75 | 3.50 | 6.00 | 14.00 |
| SH1305(1926) | — | 1.50 | 3.00 | 5.50 | 14.00 |

**10 PUL** **KM# 907** **Weight:** 6.0000 g. **Composition:** Copper

| Date | Mintage | F | VF | XF | Unc |
|---|---|---|---|---|---|
| SH1304(1925) | — | 2.00 | 4.00 | 6.00 | 15.00 |
| SH1305(1926) | — | 2.50 | 4.50 | 7.00 | 20.00 |
| SH1306(1927) | — | 2.50 | 4.50 | 7.00 | 20.00 |

**20 PUL** **KM# 908** **Weight:** 2.0000 g. **Composition:** Billon **Note:** Varieties exist.

| Date | Mintage | F | VF | XF | Unc |
|---|---|---|---|---|---|
| SH1304(1925) | — | 50.00 | 75.00 | 100 | 170 |
| SH134(1925) Error | — | — | — | — | — |
| ND(ca.1926)(1926) | — | 35.00 | 60.00 | 90.00 | 160 |

**PAISA** **KM# 880** **Composition:** Bronze Or Brass

| Date | Mintage | VG | F | VF | XF | Unc |
|---|---|---|---|---|---|---|
| SH1299(1920) | — | 2.50 | 5.50 | 12.00 | 22.50 | — |
| SH1300(1921) | — | 3.50 | 7.00 | 15.00 | 25.00 | — |
| SH1301(1922) | — | 3.50 | 7.00 | 15.00 | 25.00 | — |
| **Note:** 2 varieties are known dated SH1301 | | | | | | |
| SH1302(1923) | — | 2.50 | 5.50 | 12.00 | 22.50 | — |
| SH1303(1924) | — | 2.50 | 5.50 | 12.00 | 22.50 | — |

**1/2 AFGHANI (50 Pul)** **KM# 909** **Weight:** 5.0000 g. **Composition:** 0.5000 Silver .0803 oz. ASW **Obverse:** Date below toughra

| Date | Mintage | F | VF | XF | Unc |
|---|---|---|---|---|---|
| SH1304/7(1925) | — | 2.00 | 3.50 | 6.50 | 18.50 |
| **Note:** Two varieties are known dated SH1304 | | | | | |
| SH1305/8(1926) | — | 2.00 | 3.50 | 6.50 | 18.50 |
| SH1306/9(1927) | — | 2.00 | 3.50 | 6.50 | 18.50 |

**1/2 AFGHANI (50 Pul)** **KM# 915** **Weight:** 5.0000 g. **Composition:** 0.5000 Silver .0803 oz. ASW **Obverse:** Date below mosque

| Date | Mintage | F | VF | XF | Unc |
|---|---|---|---|---|---|
| SH1307/10(1928) | — | 3.00 | 6.00 | 12.00 | 35.00 |

**AFGHANI (100 Pul)** **KM# 910** **Weight:** 10.0000 g. **Composition:** 0.9000 Silver .2893 oz. ASW **Obverse:** Date below toughra **Note:** Three varieties are known for date SH1304. Two varieties each are known for dates SH1305-06.

| Date | Mintage | F | VF | XF | Unc |
|---|---|---|---|---|---|
| SH1304/7(1925) | — | 3.00 | 6.00 | 12.00 | 28.00 |
| SH1305/8(1926) | — | 3.00 | 6.00 | 12.00 | 28.00 |
| SH1305/9(1926) | — | 3.00 | 6.00 | 12.00 | 28.00 |
| SH1306/9(1927) | — | 3.00 | 6.00 | 12.00 | 28.00 |

**SHAHI (5 Paise)** **KM# 859** **Composition:** Copper Or Brass **Note:** Thick flan.

| Date | Mintage | VG | F | VF | XF | Unc |
|---|---|---|---|---|---|---|
| AH1337 | — | 12.00 | 22.00 | 40.00 | 70.00 | — |

**SHAHI (5 Paise)** **KM# 860** **Composition:** Copper Or Brass **Note:** Thin flan.

| Date | Mintage | VG | F | VF | XF | Unc |
|---|---|---|---|---|---|---|
| AH1337 | — | 10.00 | 20.00 | 35.00 | 55.00 | — |

**SANAR (10 Paisa)** **KM# 861** **Composition:** Copper Or Brass **Note:** Thick flan.

| Date | Mintage | VG | F | VF | XF | Unc |
|---|---|---|---|---|---|---|
| AH1337 | — | 10.00 | 17.50 | 30.00 | 55.00 | — |

**SANAR (10 Paisa)** **KM# 862** **Composition:** Copper Or Brass **Note:** Thin flan.

| Date | Mintage | VG | F | VF | XF | Unc |
|---|---|---|---|---|---|---|
| AH1337 | — | 9.00 | 14.00 | 20.00 | 35.00 | — |

**3 SHAHI (15 Paisa)** KM# 872 **Composition:** Copper **Obverse:** "Shamsi" **Reverse:** Mosque in 7-pointed star

| Date | Mintage | VG | F | VF | XF | Unc |
|---|---|---|---|---|---|---|
| SH1298(1919) | — | 2.00 | 4.00 | 9.00 | 18.00 | — |

**3 SHAHI (15 Paisa)** KM# 870 **Composition:** Copper **Obverse:** "Al-Ghazi", without "Shamsi" by date **Reverse:** Mosque in 8-pointed star **Note:** 32-33 milimeters.

| Date | Mintage | VG | F | VF | XF | Unc |
|---|---|---|---|---|---|---|
| SH1298(1919) | — | 3.00 | 5.00 | 10.00 | 20.00 | — |
| SH1299(1920) | — | 3.00 | 5.00 | 10.00 | 20.00 | — |

**Note:** 2 varieties of SH1299 exist

**3 SHAHI (15 Paisa)** KM# 881 **Composition:** Copper **Obverse:** Without "Shamsi" **Note:** Four varieties for date SH1299 and three varieties for date SH1300 are known.

| Date | Mintage | VG | F | VF | XF | Unc |
|---|---|---|---|---|---|---|
| SH1298(1919) | — | 4.00 | 15.00 | 22.00 | 40.00 | — |
| AH1299(1920) | — | 1.50 | 3.50 | 8.00 | 17.00 | — |
| AH1300(1921) | — | 1.50 | 3.50 | 8.00 | 17.00 | — |

**3 SHAHI (15 Paisa)** KM# 871.1 **Weight:** 11.5000 g. **Composition:** Copper **Obverse:** "Al-Ghazi,"Shamsi" **Note:** Thick flan.

| Date | Mintage | VG | F | VF | XF | Unc |
|---|---|---|---|---|---|---|
| SH1298(1919) | — | 10.00 | 15.00 | 22.00 | 40.00 | — |

**3 SHAHI (15 Paisa)** KM# 871.2 **Weight:** 9.0000 g. **Composition:** Copper **Note:** Thin flan.

| Date | Mintage | VG | F | VF | XF | Unc |
|---|---|---|---|---|---|---|
| SH1298(1919) | — | 2.00 | 4.00 | 9.00 | 18.00 | — |

**Note:** 2 reverse varieties with 10 or 11 circular stars exist

**3 SHAHI (15 Paisa)** KM# 881a **Composition:** Brass **Note:** Previous KM#892.

| Date | Mintage | VG | F | VF | XF | Unc |
|---|---|---|---|---|---|---|
| SH1300(1921) | — | 4.00 | 8.00 | 15.00 | 30.00 | — |

**3 SHAHI (15 Paisa)** KM# 891 **Composition:** Brass **Obverse:** 8 stars around perimeter **Reverse:** 8 stars around perimeter

| Date | Mintage | VG | F | VF | XF | Unc |
|---|---|---|---|---|---|---|
| SH1300(1921) | — | — | — | — | — | — |

**3 SHAHI (15 Paisa)** KM# 893 **Composition:** Copper **Reverse:** Mosque in 7-pointed star

| Date | Mintage | VG | F | VF | XF | Unc |
|---|---|---|---|---|---|---|
| SH1300(1921) | — | 1.50 | 3.50 | 8.00 | 17.00 | — |
| SH1301(1922) | — | 1.50 | 3.50 | 8.00 | 17.00 | — |
| **Note:** 2 varieties of SH1301 exist | | | | | | |
| SH130x(1923) (error) | — | — | — | — | — | — |
| SH1303(1924) | — | 1.50 | 3.50 | 8.00 | 17.00 | — |

**ABBASI (20 Paisa)** KM# 874 **Composition:** Copper Or Billon

| Date | Mintage | VG | F | VF | XF | Unc |
|---|---|---|---|---|---|---|
| SH1298(1919) | — | 50.00 | 75.00 | 90.00 | 150 | — |

**ABBASI (20 Paisa)** KM# 882 **Composition:** Copper Or Billon **Size:** 25 mm.

| Date | Mintage | VG | F | VF | XF | Unc |
|---|---|---|---|---|---|---|
| SH1299(1920) | — | 15.00 | 30.00 | 50.00 | 75.00 | — |

**ABBASI (20 Paisa)** KM# 883 **Composition:** Copper Or Billon

| Date | Mintage | VG | F | VF | XF | Unc |
|---|---|---|---|---|---|---|
| SH1299(1920) | — | 2.00 | 6.00 | 15.00 | 30.00 | — |
| SH1300(1921) | — | 2.00 | 6.00 | 15.00 | 30.00 | — |
| SH1301(1922) | — | 2.00 | 6.00 | 15.00 | 30.00 | — |
| **Note:** Two varieties for date SH1301 exist. | | | | | | |
| SH1302(1923) | — | 2.00 | 6.00 | 15.00 | 30.00 | — |
| SH2031(1923) Error. | — | 7.00 | 15.00 | 30.00 | 50.00 | — |
| SH1303(1924) | — | 2.00 | 6.00 | 15.00 | 30.00 | — |

**1/2 RUPEE (Qiran)** KM# 866 **Composition:** Silver **Obverse:** Legend within circle and wreath

| Date | Mintage | VG | F | VF | XF | Unc |
|---|---|---|---|---|---|---|
| AH1337(1918) | — | 150 | 300 | 500 | 725 | — |

**1/2 RUPEE (Qiran)** KM# 875 **Weight:** 4.7500 g. **Composition:** 0.5000 Silver .0763 oz. ASW **Obverse:** Star above inscription, "Shamsi"

| Date | Mintage | VG | F | VF | XF | Unc |
|---|---|---|---|---|---|---|
| SH1298(1919) | — | 3.00 | 6.00 | 10.00 | 20.00 | — |

**Note:** Two varieties are known.

**1/2 RUPEE (Qiran)** KM# 876 **Weight:** 4.7500 g. **Composition:** 0.5000 Silver .0763 oz. ASW **Obverse:** "Al-Ghazi" above inscription, "Shamsi"

| Date | Mintage | VG | F | VF | XF | Unc |
|---|---|---|---|---|---|---|
| SH1298(1919) | — | 15.00 | 30.00 | 50.00 | 75.00 | — |

**1/2 RUPEE (Qiran)** KM# 884 **Weight:** 4.7500 g. **Composition:** 0.5000 Silver .0763 oz. ASW **Obverse:** Without "Shamsi"

| Date | Mintage | VG | F | VF | XF | Unc |
|---|---|---|---|---|---|---|
| SH1299(1920) | — | 3.00 | 4.00 | 7.00 | 15.00 | — |
| **Note:** Two varieties are known dated 1299 | | | | | | |
| SH1300(1921) | — | 3.00 | 4.00 | 7.00 | 15.00 | — |

**1/2 RUPEE (Qiran)** KM# 894 **Weight:** 4.7500 g. **Composition:** 0.5000 Silver .0763 oz. ASW

| Date | Mintage | VG | F | VF | XF | Unc |
|---|---|---|---|---|---|---|
| SH1300(1921) | — | 2.00 | 4.00 | 7.00 | 12.00 | — |
| SH1301(1922) | — | 2.00 | 4.00 | 7.00 | 12.00 | — |
| SH1302(1923) | — | 2.00 | 4.00 | 7.00 | 12.00 | — |
| SH1303(1924) | — | 2.00 | 4.00 | 7.00 | 12.00 | — |

**RUPEE** KM# 867 **Weight:** 9.2000 g. **Composition:** 0.5000 Silver .0755 oz. ASW **Obverse:** Name and titles of Amanullah, star above inscription

| Date | Mintage | VG | F | VF | XF | Unc |
|---|---|---|---|---|---|---|
| AH1337(1918) | — | 6.00 | 10.00 | 18.00 | 30.00 | — |

**Note:** Seven varieties are known.

**RUPEE** KM# 877 **Weight:** 9.0000 g. **Composition:** 0.9000 Silver .2604 oz. ASW **Obverse:** "Al-Ghazi" above inscription

| Date | Mintage | VG | F | VF | XF | Unc |
|---|---|---|---|---|---|---|
| SH1298(1919) | — | 4.50 | 6.50 | 10.00 | 18.50 | — |
| **Note:** Four varieties are known for date SH1298 | | | | | | |
| SH1299(1920) | — | 4.50 | 6.50 | 10.00 | 18.50 | — |
| **Note:** Two varieties are known for date SH1299 | | | | | | |

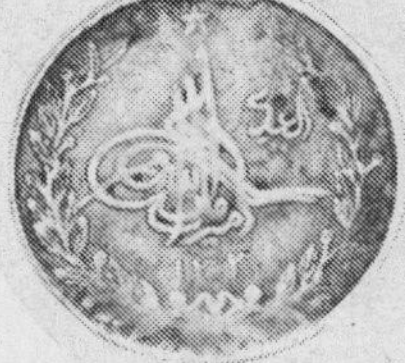

**RUPEE** KM# 885 **Weight:** 9.2500 g. **Composition:** 0.9000 Silver .2676 oz. ASW **Obverse:** Toughra of Amanullah

| Date | Mintage | VG | F | VF | XF | Unc |
|---|---|---|---|---|---|---|
| SH1299(1920) | — | 4.00 | 5.00 | 8.00 | 16.50 | — |
| SH1300(1921) | — | 4.00 | 5.00 | 8.00 | 16.50 | — |
| SH1301(1922) | — | 4.00 | 5.00 | 8.00 | 16.50 | — |
| SH1302/1(1923) | — | 4.00 | 5.00 | 8.00 | 16.50 | — |
| SH1302(1923) | — | 4.00 | 5.00 | 8.00 | 16.50 | — |
| SH1303(1924) | — | 4.00 | 5.00 | 8.00 | 16.50 | — |

**2-1/2 RUPEES** KM# 878 **Weight:** 22.9200 g. **Composition:** 0.9000 Silver .6632 oz. ASW **Note:** Two varieties each are known for dates SH 1298-1300.

| Date | Mintage | VG | F | VF | XF | Unc |
|---|---|---|---|---|---|---|
| SH1298(1919) | — | 12.50 | 16.50 | 20.00 | 45.00 | — |
| SH1299(1920) | — | 8.50 | 12.50 | 17.50 | 40.00 | — |
| SH1300(1921) | — | 8.50 | 12.50 | 17.50 | 40.00 | — |
| SH1301(1922) | — | 8.50 | 12.50 | 15.00 | 35.00 | — |
| SH1302(1923) | — | 8.50 | 12.50 | 15.00 | 35.00 | — |
| SH1303(1924) | — | 8.50 | 12.50 | 15.00 | 35.00 | — |

**5 RUPEES** **KM# 834.1** **Weight:** 45.6000 g. **Composition:** 0.9000 Silver 1.3194 oz. ASW **Reverse:** Similar to KM#826

| Date | Mintage | VG | F | VF | XF | Unc |
|---|---|---|---|---|---|---|
| AH1319 | — | 25.00 | 45.00 | 85.00 | 160 | — |

**5 RUPEES** **KM# 834.2** **Weight:** 45.6000 g. **Composition:** 0.9000 Silver 1.3194 oz. ASW **Obverse:** Date at left of toughra

| Date | Mintage | VG | F | VF | XF | Unc |
|---|---|---|---|---|---|---|
| AH1319 | — | 25.00 | 45.00 | 85.00 | 160 | — |

**5 RUPEES** **KM# 843** **Weight:** 45.6000 g. **Composition:** 0.9000 Silver 1.3194 oz. ASW **Note:** Most dates are recut dies. Two varieties are known for each date, AH1324 and 1327.

| Date | Mintage | VG | F | VF | XF | Unc |
|---|---|---|---|---|---|---|
| AH1322 | — | 20.00 | 25.00 | 45.00 | 90.00 | — |
| AH1324 | — | 15.00 | 20.00 | 45.00 | 85.00 | — |
| AH1326 | — | 15.00 | 20.00 | 45.00 | 85.00 | — |
| AH1327/6 | — | 15.00 | 20.00 | 45.00 | 85.00 | — |
| AH1328 | — | 22.50 | 30.00 | 55.00 | 110 | — |
| AH1329 | — | 25.00 | 40.00 | 70.00 | 135 | — |

**1/2 AMANI (5 Rupees)** **KM# 886** **Weight:** 2.3000 g. **Composition:** 0.9000 Gold .0665 oz. AGW

| Date | Mintage | VG | F | VF | XF | Unc |
|---|---|---|---|---|---|---|
| SH1299(1920) | — | BV | 35.00 | 55.00 | 85.00 | — |

**1/2 AMANI (5 Rupees)** **KM# 911** **Weight:** 3.0000 g. **Composition:** 0.9000 Gold .0868 oz. AGW

| Date | Mintage | F | VF | XF | Unc |
|---|---|---|---|---|---|
| SH1304/7(1925) | — | BV | 35.00 | 60.00 | 110 |
| SH1305/8(1926) | — | BV | 35.00 | 60.00 | 110 |
| SH1306/9(1927) | — | BV | 35.00 | 60.00 | 110 |

**TILLA (10 Rupees)** **KM# 868.1** **Weight:** 4.6000 g. **Composition:** 0.9000 Gold .1331 oz. AGW **Obv. Legend:** Amanullah... **Reverse:** Crossed swords below mosque

| Date | Mintage | VG | F | VF | XF | Unc |
|---|---|---|---|---|---|---|
| AH1337 | — | 100 | 125 | 160 | 225 | — |

**TILLA (10 Rupees)** **KM# 868.2** **Weight:** 4.6000 g. **Composition:** 0.9000 Gold .1331 oz. AGW **Reverse:** 6-pointed star below mosque

| Date | Mintage | VG | F | VF | XF | Unc |
|---|---|---|---|---|---|---|
| AH1337 | — | 100 | 135 | 175 | 250 | — |

**AMANI (10 Rupees)** **KM# 887** **Weight:** 4.6000 g. **Composition:** 0.9000 Gold .1331 oz. AGW

| Date | Mintage | VG | F | VF | XF | Unc |
|---|---|---|---|---|---|---|
| SH1299(1920) | — | BV | 55.00 | 75.00 | 135 | — |

**AMANI** **KM# 912** **Weight:** 6.0000 g. **Composition:** 0.9000 Gold .1736 oz. AGW

| Date | Mintage | F | VF | XF | Unc |
|---|---|---|---|---|---|
| SH1304/7(1925) | — | BV | 75.00 | 100 | 170 |
| SH1305/8(1926) | — | BV | 75.00 | 125 | 220 |
| SH1306/9(1927) | — | BV | 75.00 | 100 | 170 |

**2 AMANI (20 Rupees)** **KM# 888** **Weight:** 9.2000 g. **Composition:** 0.9000 Gold .2662 oz. AGW

| Date | Mintage | VG | F | VF | XF | Unc |
|---|---|---|---|---|---|---|
| SH1299(1920) | — | BV | 125 | 185 | 265 | — |
| SH1300(1921) | — | BV | 125 | 185 | 265 | — |
| SH1301(1922) | — | BV | 125 | 185 | 265 | — |
| SH1302(1923) | — | BV | 125 | 185 | 265 | — |
| SH1303(1924) | — | BV | 125 | 185 | 265 | — |

**2-1/2 AMANI** **KM# 914** **Weight:** 15.0000 g. **Composition:** 0.9000 Gold .4340 oz. AGW

| Date | Mintage | F | VF | XF | Unc |
|---|---|---|---|---|---|
| SH1306/9(1927) | — | — | — | 5,000 | 6,900 |

**HABIBI (30 Rupees)** **KM# 900** **Weight:** 4.6000 g. **Composition:** 0.9000 Gold .1331 oz. AGW **Obverse:** Small star replaces '30 Rupees' in legend

| Date | Mintage | VG | F | VF | XF | Unc |
|---|---|---|---|---|---|---|
| AH1347 | — | 75.00 | 125 | 200 | 325 | — |

## DECIMAL COINAGE

100 Pul = 1 Afghani; 20 Afghani = 1 Amani

**2 PUL** **KM# 905** **Weight:** 2.0000 g. **Composition:** Bronze Or Brass

| Date | Mintage | F | VF | XF | Unc |
|---|---|---|---|---|---|
| SH1304(1925) | — | 3.00 | 5.00 | 9.00 | 15.00 |
| SH1305(1926) | — | 3.00 | 5.00 | 9.00 | 15.00 |

**2-1/2 AFGHANIS** **KM# 913** **Weight:** 25.0000 g. **Composition:** 0.9000 Silver .7234 oz. ASW **Note:** Two varieties are known for each date.

| Date | Mintage | F | VF | XF | Unc |
|---|---|---|---|---|---|
| SH1305/8(1926) | — | 15.00 | 25.00 | 50.00 | 125 |
| SH1306/9(1927) | — | 15.00 | 20.00 | 40.00 | 80.00 |

## Habibullah

### Rebel known as Baccha - I - Saqao; AH1347-1348/1929AD

## LOCAL COINAGE

**5 PAISE** **KM# 969** **Composition:** Brass **Note:** Struck at Herat.

| Date | Mintage | Good | VG | F | VF | XF |
|---|---|---|---|---|---|---|
| AH1347 | — | 5.00 | 8.50 | 15.00 | 22.50 | — |

**10 PAISE** **KM# 970.1** **Composition:** Brass **Reverse:** Denomination "Dah" written above "Paisa" **Note:** Struck at Herat.

| Date | Mintage | Good | VG | F | VF | XF |
|---|---|---|---|---|---|---|
| AH1347 | — | 6.00 | 10.00 | 16.50 | 25.00 | — |

**10 PAISE** **KM# 970.2** **Composition:** Brass **Reverse:** Denomination "Dah" written at roght of "Paisa" **Note:** Struck at Herat.

| Date | Mintage | Good | VG | F | VF | XF |
|---|---|---|---|---|---|---|
| AH1347 | — | 7.50 | 12.50 | 20.00 | 30.00 | — |

**20 PAISE** **KM# 972** **Composition:** Brass **Note:** Struck at Herat.

| Date | Mintage | Good | VG | F | VF | XF |
|---|---|---|---|---|---|---|
| AH1347 | — | 7.50 | 12.50 | 20.00 | 30.00 | — |

## MILLED COINAGE

10 Dinar = 1 Paisa; 5 Paise = 1 Shahi; 2 Shahi = 1 Sanar; 2 Sanar = 1 Abbasi; 1-1/2 Abbasi = 1 Qiran; 2 Qiran = 1 Kabuli Rupee; 1 Tilla = 10 Rupees

**10 PAISE** **KM# 901** **Composition:** Copper

| Date | Mintage | VG | F | VF | XF | Unc |
|---|---|---|---|---|---|---|
| AH1348 | — | 6.00 | 12.00 | 20.00 | 40.00 | — |

**20 PAISE** **KM# 895** **Composition:** Bronze Or Brass

| Date | Mintage | VG | F | VF | XF | Unc |
|---|---|---|---|---|---|---|
| AH1347 | — | 3.00 | 5.00 | 7.50 | 17.50 | — |

**1/2 RUPEE (Qiran)** **KM# 896** **Weight:** 4.7000 g. **Composition:** 0.5000 Silver .0755 oz. ASW

| Date | Mintage | VG | F | VF | XF | Unc |
|---|---|---|---|---|---|---|
| AH1347 | — | 4.00 | 7.00 | 12.00 | 20.00 | — |

**1/2 RUPEE (Qiran)** **KM# 902** **Weight:** 4.7000 g. **Composition:** 0.5000 Silver .0755 oz. ASW

| Date | Mintage | VG | F | VF | XF | Unc |
|---|---|---|---|---|---|---|
| AH1348 | — | 12.00 | 20.00 | 32.00 | 50.00 | — |

**RUPEE** **KM# 897** **Weight:** 9.1000 g. **Composition:** 0.9000 Silver .2633 oz. ASW **Obverse:** Name and titles of Amir Habibullah (The Usurper)

| Date | Mintage | VG | F | VF | XF | Unc |
|---|---|---|---|---|---|---|
| AH1347 | — | 4.00 | 8.00 | 16.00 | 32.00 | — |

**RUPEE** **KM# 898** **Weight:** 9.1000 g. **Composition:** 0.9000 Silver .2633 oz. ASW **Obverse:** Title in circle

| Date | Mintage | VG | F | VF | XF | Unc |
|---|---|---|---|---|---|---|
| AH1347 | — | 25.00 | 35.00 | 55.00 | 90.00 | — |

**HABIBI (30 Rupees)** **KM# 899** **Weight:** 4.6000 g. **Composition:** 0.9000 Gold .1331 oz. AGW

| Date | Mintage | VG | F | VF | XF | Unc |
|---|---|---|---|---|---|---|
| AH1347 | — | 75.00 | 125 | 200 | 325 | — |

# Muhammed Nadir Shah

## AH1348-1350, SH1310-1312/1929-1933AD

## DECIMAL COINAGE

100 Pul = 1 Afghani; 20 Afghani = 1 Amani

**PUL** **KM# A922** **Composition:** Bronze Or Brass

| Date | Mintage | F | VF | XF | Unc |
|---|---|---|---|---|---|
| AH1349(1930) | — | 0.75 | 1.25 | 1.75 | 2.50 |

**PUL** **KM# 922** **Composition:** Bronze Or Brass **Obverse:** Toughra

| Date | Mintage | F | VF | XF | Unc |
|---|---|---|---|---|---|
| AH1349(1930) | — | 100 | 250 | 300 | 400 |

**2 PUL** **KM# 917** **Weight:** 2.0000 g. **Composition:** Bronze Or Brass

| Date | Mintage | F | VF | XF | Unc |
|---|---|---|---|---|---|
| AH1348(1929) | — | 1.25 | 2.50 | 3.50 | 8.00 |
| AH1349/8(1930) | — | 1.25 | 2.50 | 3.50 | 8.00 |

**5 PUL** **KM# 923** **Weight:** 3.0000 g. **Composition:** Bronze Or Brass

| Date | Mintage | F | VF | XF | Unc |
|---|---|---|---|---|---|
| AH1349(1930) | — | 1.75 | 2.75 | 4.50 | 12.50 |
| AH1350(1931) | — | 1.25 | 2.25 | 3.50 | 12.50 |

**Note:** Two varieties are known dated AH1350

**5 PUL** **KM# 929** **Weight:** 3.0000 g. **Composition:** Bronze Or Brass

| Date | Mintage | F | VF | XF | Unc |
|---|---|---|---|---|---|
| SH1311(1932) | — | 2.50 | 5.50 | 9.00 | 20.00 |
| SH1312(1933) | — | 2.50 | 5.50 | 9.00 | 20.00 |
| SH1313(1934) | — | 2.50 | 5.50 | 9.00 | 20.00 |
| SH1314(1935) | — | 2.50 | 5.50 | 9.00 | 20.00 |

**10 PUL** **KM# 918** **Composition:** Copper Or Brass **Note:** Illustration shows an example struck off-center; prices are for properly struck specimens.

| Date | Mintage | F | VF | XF | Unc |
|---|---|---|---|---|---|
| AH1348(1929) | — | 2.00 | 3.50 | 5.00 | 15.00 |
| AH1349(1930) 2 varieties | — | 2.25 | 4.00 | 5.50 | 15.00 |

**10 PUL** **KM# 930** **Composition:** Bronze Or Brass

| Date | Mintage | F | VF | XF | Unc |
|---|---|---|---|---|---|
| SH1311(1932) | — | 1.50 | 2.50 | 4.00 | 15.00 |
| SH1312(1933) | — | 1.50 | 2.50 | 4.00 | 15.00 |
| SH1313(1934) | — | 1.50 | 2.50 | 4.00 | 15.00 |
| SH1314(1935) | — | 1.50 | 2.50 | 4.00 | 15.00 |

**20 PUL** **KM# 919** **Composition:** Copper Or Brass

| Date | Mintage | F | VF | XF | Unc |
|---|---|---|---|---|---|
| AH1348(1929) | — | 2.00 | 4.00 | 10.00 | 22.00 |
| AH1349(1930) | — | 3.00 | 5.00 | 12.00 | 25.00 |

**25 PUL** **KM# 924** **Composition:** Copper Or Brass

| Date | Mintage | F | VF | XF | Unc |
|---|---|---|---|---|---|
| AH1349 | — | 2.50 | 5.00 | 10.00 | 20.00 |

**Note:** Two varieties are known dated AH1349.

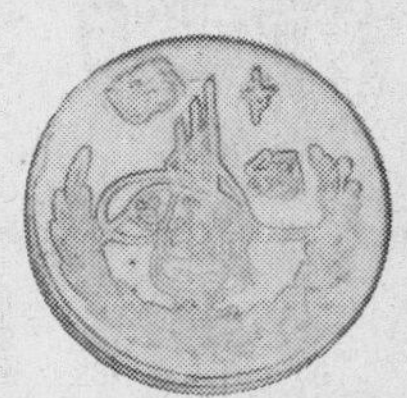

**1/2 AFGHANI (50 Pul)** **KM# 920** **Weight:** 5.0000 g. **Composition:** 0.5000 Silver .0803 oz. ASW **Obverse:** Date below mosque **Note:** Previous KM#919.

| Date | Mintage | F | VF | XF | Unc |
|---|---|---|---|---|---|
| AH1348/1(1929) | — | 1.50 | 2.50 | 5.50 | 14.00 |
| AH1349/2(1930) | — | 1.50 | 2.50 | 5.50 | 14.00 |
| AH1350/3(1931) | — | 1.50 | 2.50 | 5.50 | 14.00 |

**1/2 AFGHANI (50 Pul)** **KM# 926** **Weight:** 4.7500 g. **Composition:** 0.5000 Silver .0763 oz. ASW

| Date | Mintage | F | VF | XF | Unc |
|---|---|---|---|---|---|
| SH1310(1931) | — | 1.50 | 2.50 | 5.50 | 15.00 |
| SH1311(1932) | — | 1.50 | 2.50 | 5.50 | 15.00 |
| SH1312(1933) | — | 1.50 | 2.50 | 5.50 | 15.00 |

**AFGHANI (100 Pul)** **KM# 921** **Weight:** 9.9500 g. **Composition:** 0.9000 Silver .2879 oz. ASW

| Date | Mintage | F | VF | XF | Unc |
|---|---|---|---|---|---|
| AH1348(1929) | — | 3.00 | 5.00 | 9.00 | 16.50 |
| AH1349(1930) | — | 3.00 | 5.00 | 9.00 | 16.50 |
| AH1350(1931) | — | 3.00 | 5.00 | 9.00 | 16.50 |

**AFGHANI (100 Pul)** **KM# 927.1** **Weight:** 10.0000 g. **Composition:** 0.9000 Silver .2893 oz. ASW

| Date | Mintage | F | VF | XF | Unc |
|---|---|---|---|---|---|
| SH1310(1931) | — | 40.00 | 55.00 | 70.00 | 100 |
| SH1311(1932) | — | 110 | 160 | 180 | 260 |

**AFGHANI (100 Pul)** **KM# 927.2** **Weight:** 10.0000 g. **Composition:** 0.9000 Silver .2893 oz. ASW **Note:** Thick flan.

| Date | Mintage | F | VF | XF | Unc |
|---|---|---|---|---|---|
| SH1310(1931) | — | 250 | 375 | 500 | 700 |

**20 AFGHANIS** **KM# 925** **Weight:** 6.0000 g. **Composition:** 0.9000 Gold .1736 oz. AGW

| Date | Mintage | F | VF | XF | Unc |
|---|---|---|---|---|---|
| AH1348(1929) | — | 125 | 175 | 200 | 300 |
| AH1349(1930) | — | BV | 110 | 165 | 240 |
| AH1350(1931) | — | BV | 110 | 165 | 240 |

# Muhammed Zahir Shah

## SH1312-1352/1933-1973AD

## DECIMAL COINAGE

100 Pul = 1 Afghani; 20 Afghani = 1 Amani

**2 PUL** **KM# 928** **Weight:** 2.0000 g. **Composition:** Bronze Or Brass

| Date | Mintage | F | VF | XF | Unc |
|---|---|---|---|---|---|
| SH1311(1932) | — | 2.00 | 3.00 | 4.00 | 12.00 |
| SH1312(1933) | — | 1.50 | 2.25 | 3.00 | 10.00 |
| SH1313(1934) | — | 1.75 | 2.75 | 3.75 | 10.00 |
| SH1314(1935) | — | 2.00 | 3.00 | 4.00 | 12.00 |

**2 PUL** **KM# 936** **Composition:** Bronze

| Date | Mintage | F | VF | XF | Unc |
|---|---|---|---|---|---|
| SH1316(1937) | — | 0.15 | 0.20 | 0.35 | 1.00 |

**3 PUL** **KM# 937** **Composition:** Bronze

| Date | Mintage | F | VF | XF | Unc |
|---|---|---|---|---|---|
| SH1316(1937) | — | 0.35 | 0.50 | 0.75 | 2.00 |

**5 PUL** **KM# 938** **Composition:** Bronze

| Date | Mintage | F | VF | XF | Unc |
|---|---|---|---|---|---|
| SH1316(1937) | — | 0.35 | 0.50 | 0.75 | 2.00 |

**10 PUL** **KM# 939** **Composition:** Copper-Nickel

| Date | Mintage | F | VF | XF | Unc |
|---|---|---|---|---|---|
| SH1316(1937) | — | 0.40 | 0.65 | 1.00 | 3.00 |

**25 PUL** **KM# 931** **Composition:** Bronze Or Brass

| Date | Mintage | F | VF | XF | Unc |
|---|---|---|---|---|---|
| SH1312(1933) | — | 2.00 | 4.00 | 12.00 | 25.00 |
| SH1313(1934) | — | 2.00 | 4.00 | 12.00 | 25.00 |
| SH1314(1935) | — | 2.00 | 4.50 | 14.00 | 28.00 |
| SH1316(1937) | — | 2.00 | 4.50 | 14.00 | 28.00 |

**25 PUL** **KM# 940** **Composition:** Copper-Nickel

| Date | Mintage | F | VF | XF | Unc |
|---|---|---|---|---|---|
| SH1316(1937) | — | 0.60 | 0.75 | 1.50 | 3.50 |

**25 PUL** **KM# 941** **Composition:** Bronze

| Date | Mintage | F | VF | XF | Unc |
|---|---|---|---|---|---|
| SH1330(1951) | — | 0.15 | 0.25 | 0.50 | 1.00 |
| SH1331(1952) | — | 0.15 | 0.25 | 0.50 | 1.00 |
| SH1332(1953) | — | 0.15 | 0.25 | 0.50 | 1.00 |

**25 PUL** **KM# 943** **Composition:** Nickel Clad Steel **Edge:** Reeded

| Date | Mintage | F | VF | XF | Unc |
|---|---|---|---|---|---|
| SH1331(1952) | — | 1.00 | 2.00 | 3.50 | 7.00 |
| SH1332(1953) | — | 1.50 | 3.00 | 5.00 | 9.00 |

**25 PUL** **KM# 944** **Composition:** Nickel Clad Steel **Edge:** Plain

| Date | Mintage | F | VF | XF | Unc |
|---|---|---|---|---|---|
| SH1331(1952) | — | 0.30 | 0.50 | 0.60 | 1.00 |
| SH1332(1953) | — | 0.30 | 0.50 | 0.60 | 1.00 |
| SH1333(1954) | — | 0.30 | 0.50 | 0.60 | 1.00 |
| SH1334(1955) | — | 0.30 | 0.50 | 0.60 | 1.50 |

**25 PUL** **KM# 945** **Composition:** Aluminum **Note:** Struck on oversize 2 Afghani KM#949 planchets in 1970.

| Date | Mintage | F | VF | XF | Unc |
|---|---|---|---|---|---|
| SH1331(1952) | — | 0.50 | 1.00 | 3.00 | 10.00 |

**1/2 AFGHANI (50 Pul)** **KM# 932.1** **Weight:** 4.7500 g. **Composition:** 0.5000 Silver .0763 oz. ASW **Obverse:** Smaller dotted circle

| Date | Mintage | F | VF | XF | Unc |
|---|---|---|---|---|---|
| SH1312(1933) | — | 1.75 | 2.75 | 6.00 | 16.00 |

**1/2 AFGHANI (50 Pul)** **KM# 932.2** **Weight:** 4.7500 g. **Composition:** 0.5000 Silver .0763 oz. ASW **Obverse:** Larger dotted circle

| Date | Mintage | F | VF | XF | Unc |
|---|---|---|---|---|---|
| SH1313(1934) | — | 1.75 | 2.75 | 6.00 | 16.00 |
| SH1314(1935) | — | 1.75 | 2.75 | 6.00 | 16.00 |
| SH1315(1936) | — | 1.50 | 2.50 | 5.50 | 15.00 |
| SH1316(1937) | — | 1.50 | 2.50 | 5.50 | 15.00 |

**1/2 AFGHANI (50 Pul)** **KM# 942.1** **Composition:** Bronze **Obverse:** Denomination in numerals **Size:** 22.5 mm.

| Date | Mintage | F | VF | XF | Unc |
|---|---|---|---|---|---|
| SH1330(1951) | — | 0.35 | 0.65 | 1.00 | 3.00 |
| SH133x(1951) | — | 0.35 | 0.65 | 1.00 | 3.00 |

**1/2 AFGHANI (50 Pul)** **KM# 942.2** **Composition:** Bronze **Size:** 24 mm.

| Date | Mintage | F | VF | XF | Unc |
|---|---|---|---|---|---|
| SH1330(1951) | — | 20.00 | 30.00 | 40.00 | 50.00 |

**1/2 AFGHANI (50 Pul)** **KM# 946** **Composition:** Nickel Clad Steel

| Date | Mintage | F | VF | XF | Unc |
|---|---|---|---|---|---|
| SH1331(1952) | — | 0.20 | 0.35 | 0.65 | 2.00 |
| SH1332(1953) | — | 0.20 | 0.35 | 0.65 | 2.00 |
| SH1333(1954) | — | 0.35 | 0.55 | 1.00 | 3.00 |
| SH1334(1955) | — | 0.20 | 0.35 | 0.65 | 2.00 |

**1/2 AFGHANI (50 Pul)** **KM# 947** **Composition:** Nickel Clad Steel **Obverse:** Denomination in words

| Date | Mintage | F | VF | XF | Unc |
|---|---|---|---|---|---|
| SH1331(1952) | — | 0.40 | 0.65 | 0.85 | 2.50 |

**AFGHANI (100 Pul)** **KM# 953** **Composition:** Nickel Clad Steel

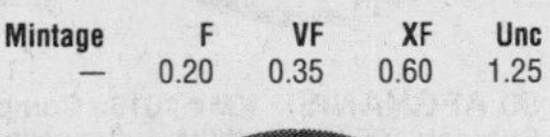

| Date | Mintage | F | VF | XF | Unc |
|---|---|---|---|---|---|
| SH1340(1961) | — | 0.20 | 0.35 | 0.60 | 1.25 |

**2 AFGHANIS** **KM# 949** **Composition:** Aluminum **Note:** This issue was withdrawn and demonetized due to extensive counterfeiting.

| Date | Mintage | F | VF | XF | Unc |
|---|---|---|---|---|---|
| SH1337(1958) | — | 0.60 | 1.00 | 1.50 | 2.50 |

**2 AFGHANIS** **KM# 954.1** **Composition:** Nickel Clad Steel **Note:** Coin type.

| Date | Mintage | F | VF | XF | Unc |
|---|---|---|---|---|---|
| SH1340(1961) | — | 0.25 | 0.45 | 0.85 | 2.00 |

**2 AFGHANIS** **KM# 954.2** **Composition:** Nickel Clad Steel **Note:** Medallic die orientation.

| Date | Mintage | F | VF | XF | Unc |
|---|---|---|---|---|---|
| SH1340(1961) | — | 0.25 | 0.45 | 0.85 | 2.00 |

**5 AFGHANIS** **KM# 955** **Composition:** Nickel Clad Steel **Note:** Mohammed Sahir Shah

| Date | Mintage | F | VF | XF | Unc |
|---|---|---|---|---|---|
| SH1340(1961)(1921) | — | 0.35 | 0.75 | 1.50 | 3.00 |

**5 AFGHANIS** **KM# 950** **Composition:** Aluminum **Note:** This issue was withdrawn and demonetized due to extensive counterfeiting.

| Date | Mintage | F | VF | XF | Unc |
|---|---|---|---|---|---|
| SH1337(1958) | — | 1.00 | 2.00 | 3.50 | 5.00 |

**10 AFGHANIS** **KM# 948** **Composition:** Aluminum

| Date | Mintage | F | VF | XF | Unc |
|---|---|---|---|---|---|
| SH1336(1957) | — | — | — | — | 900 |

**4 GRAMS** **KM# 935** **Weight:** 4.0000 g. **Composition:** 0.9000 Gold .1157 oz. AGW

| Date | Mintage | F | VF | XF | Unc |
|---|---|---|---|---|---|
| SH1315(1936) | — | BV | 65.00 | 90.00 | 165 |
| SH1317(1938) | — | BV | 65.00 | 90.00 | 165 |

**TILLA** **KM# 933** **Weight:** 6.0000 g. **Composition:** 0.9000 Gold .1736 oz. AGW

| Date | Mintage | F | VF | XF | Unc |
|---|---|---|---|---|---|
| SH1313(1934) | — | 125 | 150 | 185 | 275 |

**8 GRAMS** **KM# 934** **Weight:** 8.0000 g. **Composition:** 0.9000 Gold .2314 oz. AGW

| Date | Mintage | F | VF | XF | Unc |
|---|---|---|---|---|---|
| SH1314(1935) | — | BV | 120 | 160 | 250 |
| SH1315(1936) | — | BV | 120 | 160 | 250 |
| SH1317(1938) | — | BV | 120 | 160 | 250 |

**8 GRAMS** **KM# 952** **Weight:** 8.0000 g. **Composition:** 0.9000 Gold .2314 oz. AGW

| Date | Mintage | F | VF | XF | Unc |
|---|---|---|---|---|---|
| SH1339(1960) | 200 | — | — | 300 | 800 |

**Note:** Struck for royal presentation purposes. Specimens struck with the same dies (including the "8 grams", the "8" having been effaced after striking), but on thin planchets weighing 3.9-4 grams, exist. They are regarded as "mint sports". Market value $250.00 in Unc

# REPUBLIC

## SH1352-1357 / 1973-1978AD.

## STANDARD COINAGE

**25 PUL** **KM# 975** **Composition:** Brass Clad Steel

| Date | Mintage | F | VF | XF | Unc |
|---|---|---|---|---|---|
| SH1352(1973) | 45,950,000 | 0.25 | 0.50 | 1.00 | 2.00 |

**50 PUL** **KM# 976** **Composition:** Copper Clad Steel

| Date | Mintage | F | VF | XF | Unc |
|---|---|---|---|---|---|
| SH1352(1973) | 24,750,000 | 0.50 | 1.00 | 2.00 | 4.00 |

**5 AFGHANIS** **KM# 977** **Composition:** Copper-Nickel Clad Steel

| Date | Mintage | F | VF | XF | Unc |
|---|---|---|---|---|---|
| SH1352(1973) | 34,750,000 | 1.75 | 3.50 | 5.00 | 10.00 |

**250 AFGHANIS** **KM# 978** **Weight:** 28.5700 g. **Composition:** 0.9250 Silver .8496 oz. ASW **Series:** Conservation **Subject:** Snow Leopard

| Date | Mintage | F | VF | XF | Unc |
|---|---|---|---|---|---|
| 1978 | 4,370 | — | — | — | 28.00 |

**250 AFGHANIS** **KM# 979** **Weight:** 28.2800 g. **Composition:** 0.9250 Silver .8410 oz. ASW **Series:** Conservation **Subject:** Snow Leopard

| Date | Mintage | F | VF | XF | Unc |
|---|---|---|---|---|---|
| 1978 Proof | 4,387 | Value: 38.00 | | | |

**500 AFGHANIS** **KM# 980** **Weight:** 35.3000 g. **Composition:** 0.9250 Silver 1.0498 oz. ASW **Series:** Conservation **Subject:** Siberian Crane

| Date | Mintage | F | VF | XF | Unc |
|---|---|---|---|---|---|
| 1978 | 4,374 | — | — | — | 25.00 |

**500 AFGHANIS** **KM# 981** **Weight:** 35.0000 g. **Composition:** 0.9250 Silver 1.0408 oz. ASW **Series:** Conservation **Subject:** Siberian Crane

| Date | Mintage | F | VF | XF | Unc |
|---|---|---|---|---|---|
| 1978 Proof | 4,218 | Value: 35.00 | | | |

**10000 AFGHANIS** KM# 982 **Weight:** 33.4370 g. **Composition:** 0.9000 Gold .9676 oz. AGW **Series:** Conservation **Subject:** Marco Polo Sheep

| Date | Mintage | F | VF | XF | Unc |
|---|---|---|---|---|---|
| 1978 | 694 | — | — | — | 550 |
| 1978 Proof | 181 | Value: 950 | | | |

## DEMOCRATIC REPUBLIC
### SH1358-1371 / 1979-1992AD.

### STANDARD COINAGE

**25 PUL** KM# 990 **Composition:** Aluminum-Bronze

| Date | Mintage | F | VF | XF | Unc |
|---|---|---|---|---|---|
| SH1357(1978) | — | 0.25 | 0.50 | 1.00 | 2.00 |

**25 PUL** KM# 996 **Composition:** Aluminum-Bronze

| Date | Mintage | F | VF | XF | Unc |
|---|---|---|---|---|---|
| SH1359(1980) | — | 0.20 | 0.35 | 0.70 | 1.50 |

**50 PUL** KM# 992 **Weight:** 3.0000 g. **Composition:** Aluminum-Bronze

| Date | Mintage | F | VF | XF | Unc |
|---|---|---|---|---|---|
| SH1357(1978) | — | 0.50 | 0.80 | 1.50 | 2.50 |

**50 PUL** KM# 997 **Composition:** Aluminum-Bronze

| Date | Mintage | F | VF | XF | Unc |
|---|---|---|---|---|---|
| SH1359(1980) | — | 0.25 | 0.50 | 1.00 | 2.00 |

**AFGHANI** KM# 993 **Composition:** Copper-Nickel

| Date | Mintage | F | VF | XF | Unc |
|---|---|---|---|---|---|
| SH1357(1978) | — | 0.60 | 1.00 | 2.00 | 4.00 |

**AFGHANI** KM# 998 **Composition:** Copper-Nickel

| Date | Mintage | F | VF | XF | Unc |
|---|---|---|---|---|---|
| SH1359(1980) | — | 0.50 | 0.80 | 1.50 | 2.50 |

**2 AFGHANIS** KM# 994 **Composition:** Copper-Nickel

| Date | Mintage | F | VF | XF | Unc |
|---|---|---|---|---|---|
| SH1357(1978) | — | 1.00 | 1.50 | 2.00 | 4.00 |
| SH1358(1979) | — | 1.00 | 1.50 | 2.00 | 4.00 |

**2 AFGHANIS** KM# 999 **Composition:** Copper-Nickel **Obverse:** Similar to 1 Afghani, KM#998

| Date | Mintage | F | VF | XF | Unc |
|---|---|---|---|---|---|
| SH1359(1980) | — | 0.60 | 1.00 | 1.50 | 3.00 |

**5 AFGHANIS** KM# 995 **Weight:** 7.4000 g. **Composition:** Copper-Nickel

| Date | Mintage | F | VF | XF | Unc |
|---|---|---|---|---|---|
| SH1357(1978) | — | 1.00 | 2.00 | 4.00 | 6.50 |

**5 AFGHANIS** KM# 1000 **Weight:** 7.4000 g. **Composition:** Copper-Nickel

| Date | Mintage | F | VF | XF | Unc |
|---|---|---|---|---|---|
| SH1359(1980) | — | 1.00 | 1.50 | 2.00 | 4.00 |

**5 AFGHANIS** KM# 1001 **Composition:** Brass **Series:** F.A.O **Subject:** World Food Day

| Date | Mintage | F | VF | XF | Unc |
|---|---|---|---|---|---|
| SH1360(1981) | — | 0.25 | 0.50 | 1.00 | 1.75 |

**10 AFGHANIS** KM# 1015 **Composition:** Brass **Subject:** 70th Anniversary of Independence

| Date | Mintage | F | VF | XF | Unc |
|---|---|---|---|---|---|
| 1989 | — | — | — | — | 3.50 |

**50 AFGHANIS** KM# 1016 **Composition:** Copper-Nickel **Subject:** 100 Years of the Automobile

| Date | Mintage | F | VF | XF | Unc |
|---|---|---|---|---|---|
| ND | — | — | — | — | 14.00 |

**50 AFGHANIS** KM# 1006 **Composition:** Copper-Nickel **Series:** World Wildlife Fund **Subject:** Leopard

| Date | Mintage | F | VF | XF | Unc |
|---|---|---|---|---|---|
| 1987 | 28,000 | — | — | — | 14.00 |

**50 AFGHANIS** KM# 1024 **Composition:** Copper **Series:** Prehistoric Animals **Subject:** Deinotherium - Elephant

| Date | Mintage | F | VF | XF | Unc |
|---|---|---|---|---|---|
| 1993 | — | — | — | — | 15.00 |

**50 AFGHANIS** KM# 1032 **Composition:** Copper **Series:** Prehistoric Animals **Subject:** Ankylosaurus

| Date | Mintage | F | VF | XF | Unc |
|---|---|---|---|---|---|
| 1995 Proof | 100 | Value: 60.00 | | | |

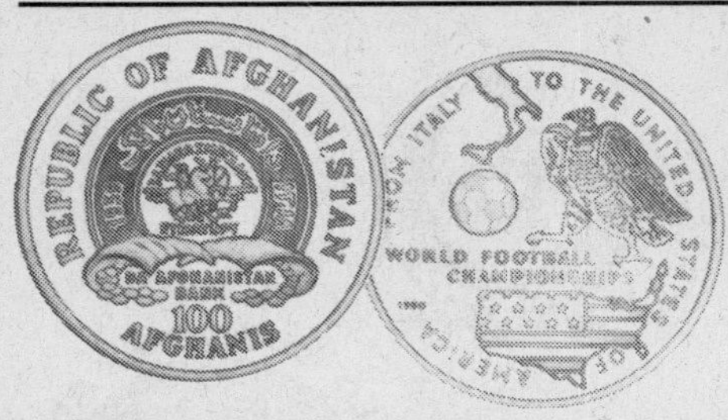

**100 AFGHANIS** **KM# 1014** **Composition:** Copper-Nickel **Series:** World Soccer Championship **Subject:** Italy to U.S.A.

| Date | Mintage | F | VF | XF | Unc |
|---|---|---|---|---|---|
| 1990 Proof | 10,000 | Value: 14.00 | | | |

**250 AFGHANIS** **KM# 1017** **Weight:** 20.3100 g. **Composition:** 0.9250 Silver .8716 oz. ASW **Series:** Conservation **Subject:** Snow Leopard

| Date | Mintage | F | VF | XF | Unc |
|---|---|---|---|---|---|
| 1978 | 4 | — | — | — | 500 |

**500 AFGHANIS** **KM# 1018** **Weight:** 35.4400 g. **Composition:** 0.9250 Silver 1.0539 oz. ASW **Series:** Conservation **Subject:** Siberian Crane

| Date | Mintage | F | VF | XF | Unc |
|---|---|---|---|---|---|
| 1978 4 pieces known | — | — | — | — | 500 |

**500 AFGHANIS** **KM# 1002** **Weight:** 9.0600 g. **Composition:** 0.9000 Silver .2622 oz. ASW **Series:** F.A.O. **Subject:** World Food Day

| Date | Mintage | F | VF | XF | Unc |
|---|---|---|---|---|---|
| SH1360(1981)(1981) Proof | — | Value: 25.00 | | | |

**500 AFGHANIS** **KM# 1003** **Weight:** 12.0000 g. **Composition:** 0.9990 Silver .3855 oz. ASW **Series:** 100th Anniversary of the Automobile

| Date | Mintage | F | VF | XF | Unc |
|---|---|---|---|---|---|
| ND | 2,000 | — | — | — | 40.00 |

**500 AFGHANIS** **KM# 1004** **Weight:** 12.0000 g. **Composition:** 0.9990 Silver .3855 oz. ASW **Series:** 1988 Winter Olympics **Subject:** Skaters

| Date | Mintage | F | VF | XF | Unc |
|---|---|---|---|---|---|
| ND | 10,000 | — | — | — | 35.00 |

**500 AFGHANIS** **KM# 1005** **Weight:** 12.0000 g. **Composition:** 0.9990 Silver .3855 oz. ASW **Series:** Wildlife Preservation **Subject:** Leopard

| Date | Mintage | F | VF | XF | Unc |
|---|---|---|---|---|---|
| 1986 | 5,000 | — | — | — | 35.00 |

**500 AFGHANIS** **KM# 1010** **Weight:** 12.0000 g. **Composition:** 0.9990 Silver .3855 oz. ASW **Series:** 1988 Summer Olympics **Subject:** Volleyball **Note:** Struck at Havana.

| Date | Mintage | F | VF | XF | Unc |
|---|---|---|---|---|---|
| 1987 (k) | 10,000 | — | — | — | 25.00 |

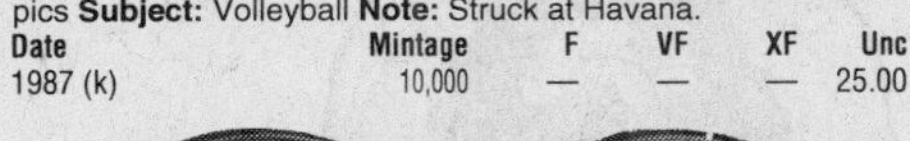

**500 AFGHANIS** **KM# 1007** **Weight:** 12.0000 g. **Composition:** 0.9990 Silver .3855 oz. ASW **Series:** European Soccer Championship **Subject:** West Germany **Note:** Struck at Havana.

| Date | Mintage | F | VF | XF | Unc |
|---|---|---|---|---|---|
| 1988 (k) | Est. 5,000 | — | — | — | 37.50 |

**500 AFGHANIS** **KM# 1009** **Weight:** 16.0000 g. **Composition:** 0.9990 Silver .5145 oz. ASW **Series:** 1986 World Soccer Championship - Mexico

| Date | Mintage | F | VF | XF | Unc |
|---|---|---|---|---|---|
| ND | 5,000 | — | — | — | 32.00 |

**500 AFGHANIS** **KM# 1011** **Weight:** 16.0000 g. **Composition:** 0.9990 Silver .5145 oz. ASW **Series:** 1990 World Soccer Championship **Subject:** Italy

| Date | Mintage | F | VF | XF | Unc |
|---|---|---|---|---|---|
| 1989 Proof | 10,000 | Value: 30.00 | | | |

**500 AFGHANIS** **KM# 1012** **Weight:** 16.0000 g. **Composition:** 0.9990 Silver .5145 oz. ASW **Series:** 1992 Summer Olympics **Subject:** Field Hockey

| Date | Mintage | F | VF | XF | Unc |
|---|---|---|---|---|---|
| 1989 Proof | 10,000 | Value: 30.00 | | | |

**500 AFGHANIS** KM# 1008.1 **Weight:** 16.0000 g. **Composition:** 0.9990 Silver .5145 oz. ASW **Series:** 1992 Winter Olympics **Subject:** Bobsledding **Obverse:** Short thick letters

| Date | Mintage | F | VF | XF | Unc |
|---|---|---|---|---|---|
| 1989 Proof | Est. 10,000 | Value: 30.00 | | | |

**500 AFGHANIS** KM# 1008.2 **Weight:** 16.0000 g. **Composition:** 0.9990 Silver .5145 oz. ASW **Series:** 1992 Winter Olympics **Subject:** Bobsledding **Obverse:** Tall thin letters

| Date | Mintage | F | VF | XF | Unc |
|---|---|---|---|---|---|
| 1989 Proof | Inc. above | Value: 35.00 | | | |

**500 AFGHANIS** KM# 1013 **Weight:** 12.0000 g. **Composition:** 0.9990 Silver .3855 oz. ASW **Series:** 1994 World Cup Soccer Games U.S.A.

| Date | Mintage | F | VF | XF | Unc |
|---|---|---|---|---|---|
| 1991 | — | — | — | — | 30.00 |

**500 AFGHANIS** KM# 1022 **Weight:** 20.0000 g. **Composition:** 0.9990 Silver .6430 oz. ASW **Series:** 1994 World Cup Soccer Games - U.S.A.

| Date | Mintage | F | VF | XF | Unc |
|---|---|---|---|---|---|
| 1992 Proof | — | Value: 45.00 | | | |

**500 AFGHANIS** KM# 1020 **Weight:** 16.0000 g. **Composition:** 0.9990 Silver .5145 oz. ASW **Series:** Prehistoric Animals **Subject:** Deinotherium - Elephant

| Date | Mintage | F | VF | XF | Unc |
|---|---|---|---|---|---|
| 1993 Proof | — | Value: 42.50 | | | |

**500 AFGHANIS** KM# 1021 **Weight:** 16.0000 g. **Composition:** 0.9990 Silver .5145 oz. ASW **Series:** Prehistoric Animals **Subject:** Styracosaurus

| Date | Mintage | F | VF | XF | Unc |
|---|---|---|---|---|---|
| 1994 Proof | — | Value: 45.00 | | | |

**500 AFGHANIS** KM# 1035 **Weight:** 16.0000 g. **Composition:** 0.9990 Silver .5145 oz. ASW **Series:** Prehistoric Animals **Subject:** Ankylosaurus

| Date | Mintage | F | VF | XF | Unc |
|---|---|---|---|---|---|
| 1995 Proof | — | Value: 50.00 | | | |

**Note:**

**500 AFGHANIS** KM# 1023 **Weight:** 20.0000 g. **Composition:** 0.9990 Silver .6430 oz. ASW **Series:** 1996 Olympics **Subject:** Three runners and building

| Date | Mintage | F | VF | XF | Unc |
|---|---|---|---|---|---|
| 1995 Proof | 15,000 | Value: 22.50 | | | |

**500 AFGHANIS** KM# 1039 **Weight:** 15.0000 g. **Composition:** 0.9990 Silver .4818 oz. ASW **Subject:** 16th World Cup - Soccer **Obverse:** National arms **Reverse:** Soccer player on ball background **Edge:** Plain

| Date | Mintage | F | VF | XF | Unc |
|---|---|---|---|---|---|
| 1997 Proof | — | Value: 37.50 | | | |

**10000 AFGHANIS** KM# 1019 **Weight:** 33.6600 g. **Composition:** 0.9000 Gold .9739 oz. AGW **Series:** Conservation **Subject:** Marco Polo Sheep

| Date | Mintage | F | VF | XF | Unc |
|---|---|---|---|---|---|
| 1978 | 4 | — | — | — | 2,000 |

## ISLAMIC STATE

### SH1373-1381 / 1994-2002AD.

### STANDARD COINAGE

**50 AFGHANIS** KM# 1026 **Composition:** Copper-Nickel **Series:** 50th Anniversary - United Nations **Obverse:** State emblem **Reverse:** Meditating figure with three doves

| Date | Mintage | F | VF | XF | Unc |
|---|---|---|---|---|---|
| ND | — | — | — | — | 8.50 |

**50 AFGHANIS** KM# 1030 **Composition:** Copper-Nickel **Series:** World Food Summit **Obverse:** State emblem **Reverse:** Gate of Zafar

| Date | Mintage | F | VF | XF | Unc |
|---|---|---|---|---|---|
| 1996 | — | — | — | — | 8.50 |

**50 AFGHANIS** KM# 1037 **Composition:** Copper-Nickel **Series:** Sydney Olympics 2000 **Obverse:** National emblem **Reverse:** Equestrian event

| Date | Mintage | F | VF | XF | Unc |
|---|---|---|---|---|---|
| 1999 | 10,000 | — | — | — | 7.50 |

**500 AFGHANIS** KM# 1031 **Weight:** 28.4300 g. **Composition:** 0.9250 Silver .8455 oz. ASW **Series:** 50th Anniversary United Nations **Obverse:** State emblem **Reverse:** Meditating figure with three doves

| Date | Mintage | F | VF | XF | Unc |
|---|---|---|---|---|---|
| ND Proof | — | Value: 40.00 | | | |

**500 AFGHANIS** KM# 1025 **Weight:** 20.0000 g. **Composition:** 0.9990 Silver .6430 oz. ASW **Subject:** Multicolor Lynx

| Date | Mintage | F | VF | XF | Unc |
|---|---|---|---|---|---|
| 1996 Proof | — | Value: 50.00 | | | |

**500 AFGHANIS** KM# 1027 **Weight:** 20.0000 g. **Composition:** 0.9990 Silver .6430 oz. ASW **Series:** XVI World Cup Soccer **Subject:** France **Obverse:** State emblem **Reverse:** Soccer player going for goal

| Date | Mintage | F | VF | XF | Unc |
|---|---|---|---|---|---|
| 1996 | 100 | — | — | — | 100 |
| 1996 Proof | — | Value: 45.00 | | | |

**500 AFGHANIS** KM# 1028 **Weight:** 20.1300 g. **Composition:** 0.9990 Silver .6465 oz. ASW **Series:** World Food Summit **Obverse:** State emblem **Reverse:** Zafar Gate, FAO logo, dates

| Date | Mintage | F | VF | XF | Unc |
|---|---|---|---|---|---|
| 1996 Proof | — | Value: 45.00 | | | |

**500 AFGHANIS** KM# 1029 **Weight:** 14.9500 g. **Composition:** 0.9990 Silver .4802 oz. ASW **Series:** World of Adventure **Obverse:** State emblem **Reverse:** Multicolor enamel airplane and statue, cameo portrait

| Date | Mintage | F | VF | XF | Unc |
|---|---|---|---|---|---|
| 1996 Proof | — | Value: 55.00 | | | |

**500 AFGHANIS** KM# 1036 **Weight:** 20.3100 g. **Composition:** 0.9990 Silver .6465 oz. ASW **Series:** Sydney Olympics 2000 **Obverse:** National emblem **Reverse:** Winged goddess bearing torch, Greek temples behind

| Date | Mintage | F | VF | XF | Unc |
|---|---|---|---|---|---|
| 1996 Proof | 500 | Value: 40.00 | | | |

**500 AFGHANIS** KM# 1036a **Weight:** 15.0000 g. **Composition:** 0.9990 Silver .4818 oz. ASW **Series:** Sydney Olympics 2000 **Reverse:** Winged Goddess bearing torch, Greek temples behind

| Date | Mintage | F | VF | XF | Unc |
|---|---|---|---|---|---|
| 1998 Proof | 7,500 | Value: 27.50 | | | |

**500 AFGHANIS** KM# 1033 **Weight:** 20.0000 g. **Composition:** 0.9990 Silver .6430 oz. ASW **Series:** Sydney Olympics 2000 **Obverse:** National emblem **Reverse:** Javelin thrower

| Date | Mintage | F | VF | XF | Unc |
|---|---|---|---|---|---|
| 1998 Proof | 5,000 | Value: 37.50 | | | |

**500 AFGHANIS** **KM# 1034** **Weight:** 20.0000 g. **Composition:** 0.9990 Silver .6430 oz. ASW **Subject:** Fauna of Asia **Obverse:** National emblem **Reverse:** Marco Polo Deer

| Date | Mintage | F | VF | XF | Unc |
|---|---|---|---|---|---|
| 1998 | 100 | — | — | — | 80.00 |

**500 AFGHANIS** **KM# 1038** **Weight:** 20.0000 g. **Composition:** 0.9990 Silver .6430 oz. ASW **Series:** Sydney Olympics 2000 **Obverse:** National emblem **Reverse:** Equestrian event

| Date | Mintage | F | VF | XF | Unc |
|---|---|---|---|---|---|
| 1999 Proof | 5,000 | Value: 30.00 | | | |

## PATTERNS

Including off metal strikes

| KM# | Date | Mintage | Identification | Mkt Val |
|---|---|---|---|---|
| Pn1 | 1310 | — | 1/2 Afghani. Silver. 4.7500 g. | — |
| Pn2 | 1336 | — | 5 Afghanis. Silver. Legend with off-center circle, denomination. National emblem with wreath, date | 350 |
| Pn3 | 1336 | — | 10 Afghanis. Silver. Toughra with off-center circle, denomination. National emblem with wreath, date | 350 |

## PIEFORTS

| KM# | Date | Mintage | Identification | Mkt Val |
|---|---|---|---|---|
| P1.1 | 1989 | 110 | 500 Afghanis. 0.9990 Silver. KM#1008.2 | 85.00 |
| P1.2 | 1989 | — | 500 Afghanis. 0.9990 Silver. KM#1008.2, pine tree without needles | 125 |
| P1.3 | 1989 | — | 500 Afghanis. 0.9990 Silver. KM#1008.2, pine tree with sagging branches | 85.00 |
| P1.4 | 1989 | — | 500 Afghanis. 0.9990 Silver. KM#1008.2, pine tree with uplifted branches | 85.00 |
| P2 | 1998 | — | 500 Afghanis. KM#1033 | 120 |
| P3 | 1999 | — | 500 Afghanis. KM#1038 | 80.00 |

# AJMAN

Ajman is the smallest and poorest of the emirates in the United Arab Emirates. It has an estimated area of 100sq. mi. (250 sq. km.) and a population of 6,000. Ajman's first act as an autonomous entity was entering into a treaty with Great Britain in 1820. On December 2, 1971 Ajman became one of the 6 original members of the United Arab Emirates.

**TITLES**

Ajman اجمان

**RULERS**

Abdul Aziz Bin Humaid al-Naimi, 1900-1908
Humaid Bin Abdul Aziz al-Naimi, 1908-1928
Rashid Bin Hamad al-Naimi, 1928-1981
Humaid Bin Rashid al-Naimi, 1981--

**MONETARY SYSTEM**

100 Dirhams = 1 Riyal

## UNITED ARAB EMIRAT

## NON-CIRCULATING LEGAL TENDER COINAGE

**RIYAL** **KM# 1.1** **Weight:** 3.9500 g. **Composition:** 0.6400 Silver .0812 oz. ASW **Reverse:** Two dates

| Date | Mintage | F | VF | XF | Unc | BU |
|---|---|---|---|---|---|---|
| AH1389(1969) | 20,000 | — | — | — | 7.50 | — |
| AH1389/1969 Proof | 1,200 | Value: 15.00 | | | | |

**RIYAL** **KM# 1.2** **Weight:** 3.9500 g. **Composition:** 0.6400 Silver .0812 oz. ASW **Reverse:** Three dates

| Date | Mintage | F | VF | XF | Unc | BU |
|---|---|---|---|---|---|---|
| AH1390(1970) | — | — | — | — | 20.00 | — |

**2 RIYALS** **KM# 2.1** **Weight:** 6.4500 g. **Composition:** 0.8350 Silver .1731 oz. ASW **Reverse:** Two dates

| Date | Mintage | F | VF | XF | Unc | BU |
|---|---|---|---|---|---|---|
| AH1389(1969) | 20,000 | — | — | — | 15.00 | — |
| AH1389 Proof | 1,200 | Value: 25.00 | | | | |

**2 RIYALS** **KM# 2.2** **Weight:** 6.4500 g. **Composition:** 0.8350 Silver .1731 oz. ASW **Reverse:** Three dates

| Date | Mintage | F | VF | XF | Unc | BU |
|---|---|---|---|---|---|---|
| AH1390(1970) | — | — | — | — | 30.00 | — |

**5 RIYALS** **KM# 3.1** **Weight:** 15.0000 g. **Composition:** 0.8350 Silver .4027 oz. ASW **Reverse:** Two dates

| Date | Mintage | F | VF | XF | Unc | BU |
|---|---|---|---|---|---|---|
| AH1389(1969) | 10,000 | — | — | — | 22.50 | — |
| AH1389/1969 Proof | 1,200 | Value: 40.00 | | | | |

**5 RIYALS** **KM# 3.2** **Weight:** 15.0000 g. **Composition:** 0.8350 Silver .4027 oz. ASW **Reverse:** Three dates

| Date | Mintage | F | VF | XF | Unc | BU |
|---|---|---|---|---|---|---|
| AH1390(1970) | — | — | — | — | 50.00 | — |
| AH1390 Proof | — | Value: 90.00 | | | | |

**5 RIYALS** **KM# 12** **Weight:** 15.0000 g. **Composition:** 0.9250 Silver .4460 oz. ASW **Subject:** Death of Gamal Abdel Nassar

| Date | Mintage | F | VF | XF | Unc | BU |
|---|---|---|---|---|---|---|
| AH1390/1970 Proof | 5,000 | Value: 27.50 | | | | |

**5 RIYALS** **KM# 17** **Weight:** 15.0000 g. **Composition:** 0.9250 Silver .4460 oz. ASW **Reverse:** Dag Hammarskjold

| Date | Mintage | F | VF | XF | Unc | BU |
|---|---|---|---|---|---|---|
| ND(1970) Proof | 1,175 | Value: 60.00 | | | | |

**5 RIYALS** **KM# 18** **Weight:** 15.0000 g. **Composition:** 0.9250 Silver .4460 oz. ASW **Reverse:** Mahatma Gandhi

| Date | Mintage | F | VF | XF | Unc | BU |
|---|---|---|---|---|---|---|
| ND(1970) Proof | 1,175 | Value: 60.00 | | | | |

**5 RIYALS** **KM# 19** **Weight:** 15.0000 g. **Composition:** 0.9250 Silver .4460 oz. ASW **Reverse:** Martin Luther King

| Date | Mintage | F | VF | XF | Unc | BU |
|---|---|---|---|---|---|---|
| ND(1970) Proof | 1,175 | Value: 60.00 | | | | |

**5 RIYALS** **KM# 20** **Weight:** 15.0000 g. **Composition:** 0.9250 Silver .4460 oz. ASW **Reverse:** George C. Marshall

| Date | Mintage | F | VF | XF | Unc | BU |
|---|---|---|---|---|---|---|
| ND(1970) Proof | 1,175 | Value: 60.00 | | | | |

**5 RIYALS** **KM# 21** **Weight:** 15.0000 g. **Composition:** 0.9250 Silver .4460 oz. ASW **Reverse:** Bertrand A. Russell

| Date | Mintage | F | VF | XF | Unc | BU |
|---|---|---|---|---|---|---|
| ND(1970) Proof | 1,175 | Value: 60.00 | | | | |

**5 RIYALS** **KM# 22** **Weight:** 15.0000 g. **Composition:** 0.9250 Silver .4460 oz. ASW **Reverse:** Albert Schweitzer

| Date | Mintage | F | VF | XF | Unc | BU |
|---|---|---|---|---|---|---|
| ND(1970) Proof | 1,175 | Value: 60.00 | | | | |

**5 RIYALS** **KM# 23** **Weight:** 15.0000 g. **Composition:** 0.9250 Silver .4460 oz. ASW **Reverse:** Jan Palach

| Date | Mintage | F | VF | XF | Unc | BU |
|---|---|---|---|---|---|---|
| ND(1970) Proof | 1,175 | Value: 60.00 | | | | |

**5 RIYALS** **KM# 24** **Weight:** 15.0000 g. **Composition:** 0.9250 Silver .4460 oz. ASW **Reverse:** Albert J. Luthuli

| Date | Mintage | F | VF | XF | Unc | BU |
|---|---|---|---|---|---|---|
| ND(1970) Proof | 1,175 | Value: 60.00 | | | | |

**5 RIYALS** **KM# 26** **Weight:** 15.0000 g. **Composition:** 0.9250 Silver .4460 oz. ASW **Series:** F.A.O.

| Date | Mintage | F | VF | XF | Unc | BU |
|---|---|---|---|---|---|---|
| AH1390 Proof | 2,000 | Value: 70.00 | | | | |

**Note:** This issue is not recognized by the FAO

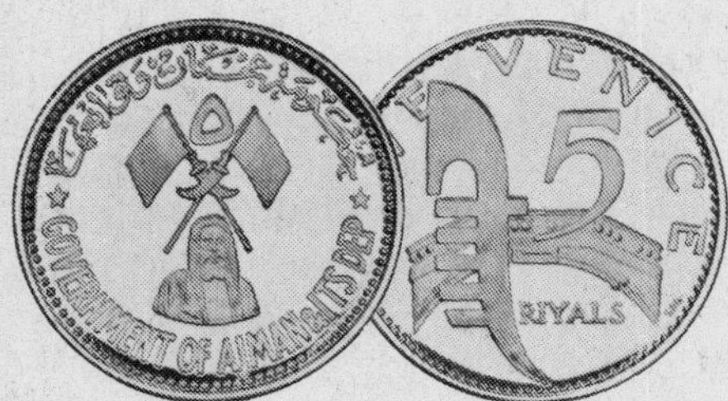


**5 RIYALS** **KM# 27** **Weight:** 15.0000 g. **Composition:** 0.9250 Silver .4460 oz. ASW **Subject:** Save Venice

| Date | Mintage | F | VF | XF | Unc | BU |
|---|---|---|---|---|---|---|
| ND(1971) Proof | 4,800 | Value: 100 | | | | |

**7-1/2 RIYALS** **KM# 5** **Weight:** 23.0000 g. **Composition:** 0.9250 Silver .6840 oz. ASW **Subject:** Rashid bin Humaid al-Naimi **Reverse:** Bonefish

| Date | Mintage | F | VF | XF | Unc | BU |
|---|---|---|---|---|---|---|
| AH1389(1970) | 4,350 | — | — | — | 55.00 | — |
| AH1389 Proof | 650 | Value: 85.00 | | | | |

**7-1/2 RIYALS** **KM# 6** **Weight:** 23.0000 g. **Composition:** 0.9250 Silver .6840 oz. ASW **Reverse:** Barbary Falcon

| Date | Mintage | F | VF | XF | Unc | BU |
|---|---|---|---|---|---|---|
| AH1389(1970) | 4,350 | — | — | — | 55.00 | — |
| AH1389 Proof | 650 | Value: 85.00 | | | | |

**7-1/2 RIYALS** **KM# 7** **Weight:** 23.0000 g. **Composition:** 0.9250 Silver .6840 oz. ASW **Reverse:** Gazelle

| Date | Mintage | F | VF | XF | Unc | BU |
|---|---|---|---|---|---|---|
| AH1389(1970) | 4,350 | — | — | — | 55.00 | — |
| AH1389 Proof | 650 | Value: 85.00 | | | | |

**7-1/2 RIYALS** **KM# 13** **Weight:** 23.0000 g. **Composition:** 0.8350 Silver .6175 oz. ASW **Subject:** Death of Gamal Abdel Nassar

| Date | Mintage | F | VF | XF | Unc | BU |
|---|---|---|---|---|---|---|
| AH1390/1970 Proof | 6,000 | Value: 45.00 | | | | |

**10 RIYALS** **KM# 9.1** **Weight:** 30.0000 g. **Composition:** 0.9250 Silver .8923 oz. ASW **Reverse:** Vladimir Lenin

| Date | Mintage | F | VF | XF | Unc | BU |
|---|---|---|---|---|---|---|
| ND(1970 Proof | — | Value: 55.00 | | | | |
| ND(1970) Matte | — | — | — | — | — | — |

**10 RIYALS** **KM# 9.2** **Weight:** 30.0000 g. **Composition:** 0.9250 Silver .8923 oz. ASW **Obverse:** PROOF added

| Date | Mintage | F | VF | XF | Unc | BU |
|---|---|---|---|---|---|---|
| ND(1970) Proof | 3,200 | Value: 45.00 | | | | |

**25 RIYALS** **KM# 15** **Weight:** 5.1750 g. **Composition:** 0.9000 Gold .1497 oz. AGW **Subject:** Death of Gamal Abdel Nassar

| Date | Mintage | F | VF | XF | Unc | BU |
|---|---|---|---|---|---|---|
| AH1390 Proof | 1,100 | Value: 125 | | | | |

**Note:** Some of these coins have a serial number on the obverse below the bust

**25 RIYALS** **KM# 28** **Weight:** 5.1750 g. **Composition:** 0.9000 Gold .1497 oz. AGW **Reverse:** Dag Hammarskjold

| Date | Mintage | F | VF | XF | Unc | BU |
|---|---|---|---|---|---|---|
| ND(1970) Proof | — | Value: 135 | | | | |

**25 RIYALS** **KM# 29** **Weight:** 5.1750 g. **Composition:** 0.9000 Gold .1497 oz. AGW **Reverse:** Mahatma Gandi

| Date | Mintage | F | VF | XF | Unc | BU |
|---|---|---|---|---|---|---|
| ND(1970) Proof | — | Value: 135 | | | | |

**25 RIYALS** **KM# 30** **Weight:** 5.1750 g. **Composition:** 0.9000 Gold .1497 oz. AGW **Reverse:** Martin Luther King

| Date | Mintage | F | VF | XF | Unc | BU |
|---|---|---|---|---|---|---|
| ND(1970) Proof | — | Value: 135 | | | | |

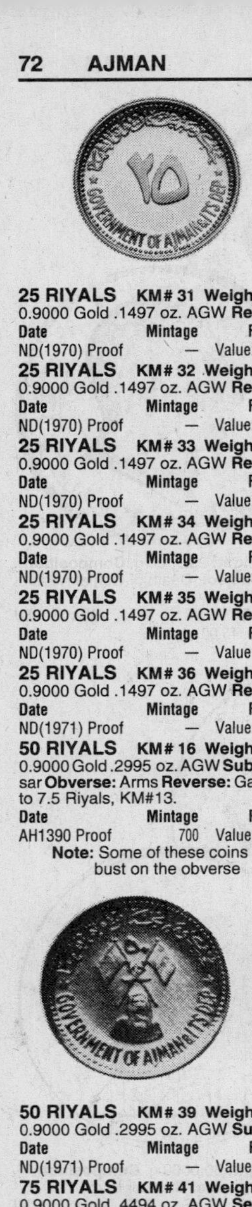

**25 RIYALS** **KM# 31** **Weight:** 5.1750 g. **Composition:** 0.9000 Gold .1497 oz. AGW **Reverse:** George C. Marshall

| Date | Mintage | F | VF | XF | Unc | BU |
|---|---|---|---|---|---|---|
| ND(1970) Proof | — | Value: 135 | | | | |

**25 RIYALS** **KM# 32** **Weight:** 5.1750 g. **Composition:** 0.9000 Gold .1497 oz. AGW **Reverse:** Bertrand A. Russell

| Date | Mintage | F | VF | XF | Unc | BU |
|---|---|---|---|---|---|---|
| ND(1970) Proof | — | Value: 135 | | | | |

**25 RIYALS** **KM# 33** **Weight:** 5.1750 g. **Composition:** 0.9000 Gold .1497 oz. AGW **Reverse:** Albert Schweitzer

| Date | Mintage | F | VF | XF | Unc | BU |
|---|---|---|---|---|---|---|
| ND(1970) Proof | — | Value: 135 | | | | |

**25 RIYALS** **KM# 34** **Weight:** 5.1750 g. **Composition:** 0.9000 Gold .1497 oz. AGW **Reverse:** Jan Palach

| Date | Mintage | F | VF | XF | Unc | BU |
|---|---|---|---|---|---|---|
| ND(1970) Proof | — | Value: 135 | | | | |

**25 RIYALS** **KM# 35** **Weight:** 5.1750 g. **Composition:** 0.9000 Gold .1497 oz. AGW **Reverse:** Albert J. Luthuli

| Date | Mintage | F | VF | XF | Unc | BU |
|---|---|---|---|---|---|---|
| ND(1970) Proof | — | Value: 135 | | | | |

**25 RIYALS** **KM# 36** **Weight:** 5.1750 g. **Composition:** 0.9000 Gold .1497 oz. AGW **Rev. Legend:** Save Venice

| Date | Mintage | F | VF | XF | Unc | BU |
|---|---|---|---|---|---|---|
| ND(1971) Proof | — | Value: 150 | | | | |

**50 RIYALS** **KM# 16** **Weight:** 10.3500 g. **Composition:** 0.9000 Gold .2995 oz. AGW **Subject:** Death of Gamal Abdel Nassar **Obverse:** Arms **Reverse:** Gamal Abdel Nassar **Note:** Similar to 7.5 Riyals, KM#13.

| Date | Mintage | F | VF | XF | Unc | BU |
|---|---|---|---|---|---|---|
| AH1390 Proof | 700 | Value: 245 | | | | |

**Note:** Some of these coins have a serial number below the bust on the obverse

**50 RIYALS** **KM# 39** **Weight:** 10.3500 g. **Composition:** 0.9000 Gold .2995 oz. AGW **Subject:** Save Venice

| Date | Mintage | F | VF | XF | Unc | BU |
|---|---|---|---|---|---|---|
| ND(1971) Proof | — | Value: 265 | | | | |

**75 RIYALS** **KM# 41** **Weight:** 15.5300 g. **Composition:** 0.9000 Gold .4494 oz. AGW **Series:** F.A.O **Obverse:** Fish

| Date | Mintage | F | VF | XF | Unc | BU |
|---|---|---|---|---|---|---|
| AH1389/1969 Proof | — | Value: 385 | | | | |

**100 RIYALS** **KM# 10** **Weight:** 20.7000 g. **Composition:** 0.9000 Gold .5990 oz. AGW **Reverse:** Vladimir Lenin

| Date | Mintage | F | VF | XF | Unc | BU |
|---|---|---|---|---|---|---|
| ND Proof | 1,000 | Value: 450 | | | | |

**100 RIYALS** **KM# 40** **Weight:** 20.7000 g. **Composition:** 0.9000 Gold .5990 oz. AGW **Subject:** Save Venice

| Date | Mintage | F | VF | XF | Unc | BU |
|---|---|---|---|---|---|---|
| ND(1971) Proof | — | Value: 465 | | | | |

## ESSAIS

With Assay or Proof

| KM# | Date | Mintage | Identification | Mkt Val |
|---|---|---|---|---|
| E1 | 1969 | 1,250 | Riyal. KM#1 | 15.00 |

| KM# | Date | Mintage | Identification | Mkt Val |
|---|---|---|---|---|
| E2 | 1969 | 1,250 | 2 Riyals. KM#2 | 20.00 |

| KM# | Date | Mintage | Identification | Mkt Val |
|---|---|---|---|---|
| E3 | 1969 | 1,250 | 5 Riyals. KM#3 | 30.00 |

| KM# | Date | Mintage | Identification | Mkt Val |
|---|---|---|---|---|
| E4 | 1970 | 100 | Riyal. | 35.00 |

| KM# | Date | Mintage | Identification | Mkt Val |
|---|---|---|---|---|
| E5 | 1970 | 100 | 2 Riyals. | 40.00 |

| KM# | Date | Mintage | Identification | Mkt Val |
|---|---|---|---|---|
| E6 | 1970 | 100 | 5 Riyals. | 75.00 |

| KM# | Date | Mintage | Identification | Mkt Val |
|---|---|---|---|---|
| E7 | 1970 | — | 5 Riyals. Aluminum. KM#12 | 40.00 |
| E8 | 1970 | — | 7-1/2 Riyals. KM#5 | 90.00 |
| E9 | 1970 | — | 7-1/2 Riyals. KM#6 | 90.00 |

| KM# | Date | Mintage | Identification | Mkt Val |
|---|---|---|---|---|
| E10 | 1970 | — | 7-1/2 Riyals. Aluminum. KM#13 | 55.00 |
| E11 | (1970) | 800 | 10 Riyals. | 75.00 |

## PATTERNS

Including off metal strikes

| KM# | Date | Mintage | Identification | Mkt Val |
|---|---|---|---|---|
| Pn1 | 1970 | — | 100 Dirhams. Copper-Nickel. | — |

## MINT SETS

| KM# | Date | Mintage | Identification | Issue Price | Mkt Val |
|---|---|---|---|---|---|
| MS1 | 1969 | — | KM#1.1-3.1 | — | 45.00 |
| MS2 | 1970 | 4,350 | KM#5-7 | — | 165 |

## PROOF SETS

| KM# | Date | Mintage | Identification | Issue Price | Mkt Val |
|---|---|---|---|---|---|
| PS1 | 1969 | 1,200 | KM#1.1-3.1 | 11.22 | 80.00 |
| PS10 | 1970 | — | KM#12, 13, 15 | — | 200 |
| PS11 | 1970 | — | KM#9.1, 9.2, 10 | — | 550 |
| PS2 | 1970 | 1,175 | KM#17-24 | — | 485 |
| PS3 | 1970 | — | KM#28-35 | — | 1,100 |
| PS4 | 1970 | — | KM#12, 13, 15, 16 | — | 415 |
| PS5 | 1970 | 100 | KM#E4-6 | — | 190 |
| PS6 | 1970 | 650 | KM#5-7 | 19.50 | 260 |
| PS7 | 1970 | — | KM#E9, E7, 10 | — | 580 |
| PS8 | 1970 | 800 | KM#E7, 10 | — | 500 |
| PS9 | 1970 | 5,000 | KM#12, 13 | 9.50 | 75.00 |
| PS12 | 1971 | — | KM#27, 36, 39, 40 | — | 980 |

The Republic of Albania, a Balkan republic bounded by Macedonia, Greece, Montenegro, and the Adriatic Sea, has an area of 11,100 sq. mi. (28,748 sq. km.) and a population of 3.49 million. Capital: Tirane. The country is predominantly agricultural, although recent progress has been made in the manufacturing and mining sectors. Petroleum, chrome, iron, copper, cotton textiles, tobacco and wood products are exported.

Since it had been part of the Greek and Roman empires little is known of the early history of Albania. After the disintegration of the Roman Empire Albania was overrun by Goths, Byzantines, Venetians and Turks. Skanderbeg, the national hero, resisted the Turks and established an independent Albania in 1443, but in 1468 the country again fell to the Turks and remained part of the Ottoman Empire for more than 400 years.

Independence was re-established by revolt in 1912, and the present borders established in 1913 by a conference of European powers, which, in 1914, placed Prince William of Wied on the throne; popular discontent forced his abdication within months. In 1920, following World War I occupancy by several nations, a republic was set up. Ahmed Zogu seized the presidency in 1925, and in 1928 he proclaimed himself king with the title of Zog I. King Zog fled when Italy occupied Albania in 1939 and enthroned King Victor Emanuel of Italy. Upon the surrender of Italy to the Allies in 1943, German troops occupied the country. They withdrew in 1944, and communist partisans seized power, naming Gen. Enver Hoxha provisional president. In 1946, following a victory by the communist front in the 1945 elections, a new constitution modeled on that of the USSR was adopted. In accordance with the constitution of Dec. 28, 1976, the official name of Albania was changed from the Peoples Republic of Albania to the Peoples Socialist Republic of Albania.

Albania's former Communists were routed in elections. March 1992, amid economic collapse and social unrest. Sali Berisha was elected as the first non-communist president since World War II. Rexhep Mejdani, elected president in 1997, succeeds him.

**RULERS**

Ahmed Bey Zogu - King Zog I, 1928-1939
Vittorio Emanuele III, 1939-1943

**MINT MARKS**

L – London
R - Rome
V – Vienna

**MONETARY SYSTEM**

100 Qindar Leku = 1 Lek
100 Qindar Ari = 1 Frang Ar = 5 Lek

## KINGDOM

**5 QINDAR LEKU** **KM# 1** **Composition:** Bronze

| Date | Mintage | F | VF | XF | Unc | BU |
|---|---|---|---|---|---|---|
| 1926R | 512,000 | 20.00 | 45.00 | 75.00 | 160 | — |

**10 QINDAR LEKU** **KM# 2** **Composition:** Bronze

| Date | Mintage | F | VF | XF | Unc | BU |
|---|---|---|---|---|---|---|
| 1926R | 511,000 | 14.00 | 30.00 | 65.00 | 140 | — |

**QINDAR AR** **KM# 14** **Composition:** Bronze

| Date | Mintage | F | VF | XF | Unc | BU |
|---|---|---|---|---|---|---|
| 1935R | 2,000,000 | 2.50 | 6.00 | 12.00 | 22.00 | — |

**2 QINDAR ARI** **KM# 15** **Composition:** Bronze

| Date | Mintage | F | VF | XF | Unc | BU |
|---|---|---|---|---|---|---|
| 1935R | 1,500,000 | 3.50 | 10.00 | 17.00 | 32.00 | — |

**1/4 LEKU** **KM# 3** **Composition:** Nickel

| Date | Mintage | F | VF | XF | Unc | BU |
|---|---|---|---|---|---|---|
| 1926R | 506,000 | 3.50 | 8.00 | 17.00 | 35.00 | — |
| 1927R | 756,000 | 3.50 | 8.00 | 15.00 | 30.00 | — |

**1/2 LEK** **KM# 4** **Composition:** Nickel

| Date | Mintage | F | VF | XF | Unc | BU |
|---|---|---|---|---|---|---|
| 1926R | 1,002,000 | 3.00 | 6.00 | 14.00 | 25.00 | — |

**1/2 LEK** **KM# 13** **Composition:** Nickel

| Date | Mintage | F | VF | XF | Unc | BU |
|---|---|---|---|---|---|---|
| 1930V | 500,000 | 3.00 | 5.50 | 11.00 | 20.00 | — |
| 1931L | 500,000 | 3.00 | 5.50 | 11.00 | 20.00 | — |
| 1931L Proof | — | — | — | — | — | — |

**LEK** **KM# 5** **Composition:** Nickel

| Date | Mintage | F | VF | XF | Unc | BU |
|---|---|---|---|---|---|---|
| 1926R | 1,004,000 | 2.00 | 4.00 | 10.00 | 25.00 | — |
| 1927R | 506,000 | 3.00 | 7.00 | 16.00 | 32.00 | — |
| 1930V | 1,250,000 | 1.50 | 3.00 | 7.00 | 22.00 | — |
| 1931L | 1,000,000 | 2.00 | 4.00 | 10.00 | 25.00 | — |
| 1931L Proof | — | — | — | — | — | — |

**FRANG AR** **KM# 6** **Weight:** 5.0000 g. **Composition:** 0.8350 Silver .1342 oz. ASW

| Date | Mintage | F | VF | XF | Unc | BU |
|---|---|---|---|---|---|---|
| 1927R | 100,000 | 60.00 | 100 | 160 | 320 | — |
| 1928R | 60,000 | 60.00 | 110 | 170 | 325 | — |

**FRANG AR** **KM# 16** **Weight:** 5.0000 g. **Composition:** 0.8350 Silver .1342 oz. ASW

| Date | Mintage | F | VF | XF | Unc | BU |
|---|---|---|---|---|---|---|
| 1935R | 700,000 | 5.00 | 10.00 | 22.00 | 60.00 | — |
| 1937R | 600,000 | 5.00 | 12.00 | 27.50 | 70.00 | — |

**FRANG AR** **KM# 18** **Weight:** 5.0000 g. **Composition:** 0.8350 Silver .1342 oz. ASW **Subject:** 25th Anniversary of Independence

| Date | Mintage | F | VF | XF | Unc | BU |
|---|---|---|---|---|---|---|
| 1937R | 50,000 | 8.00 | 16.00 | 35.00 | 80.00 | — |

**2 FRANGA ARI** **KM# 7** **Weight:** 10.0000 g. **Composition:** 0.8350 Silver .2684 oz. ASW

| Date | Mintage | F | VF | XF | Unc | BU |
|---|---|---|---|---|---|---|
| 1926R | 50,000 | 50.00 | 115 | 230 | 335 | — |
| 1927R | 50,000 | 60.00 | 140 | 250 | 365 | — |
| 1928R | 60,000 | 50.00 | 115 | 230 | 335 | — |

**2 FRANGA ARI** **KM# 17** **Weight:** 10.0000 g. **Composition:** 0.8350 Silver .2684 oz. ASW

| Date | Mintage | F | VF | XF | Unc | BU |
|---|---|---|---|---|---|---|
| 1935R | 150,000 | 10.00 | 30.00 | 70.00 | 120 | — |

**2 FRANGA ARI** **KM# 19** **Weight:** 10.0000 g. **Composition:** 0.8350 Silver .2684 oz. ASW **Subject:** 25th Anniversary of Independence

| Date | Mintage | F | VF | XF | Unc | BU |
|---|---|---|---|---|---|---|
| 1937R | 25,000 | 13.00 | 28.00 | 55.00 | 110 | — |

**5 FRANGA ARI** KM# 8.1 **Weight:** 25.0000 g. **Composition:** 0.9000 Silver .7234 oz. ASW

| Date | Mintage | F | VF | XF | Unc | BU |
|---|---|---|---|---|---|---|
| 1926R | 60,000 | 80.00 | 190 | 390 | 550 | — |
| 1927V | Est. 40,000 | — | — | — | — | — |

**Note:** Only exist as provas

**5 FRANGA ARI** KM# 8.2 **Weight:** 25.0000 g. **Composition:** 0.9000 Silver .7234 oz. ASW **Obverse:** Star below bust

| Date | Mintage | F | VF | XF | Unc | BU |
|---|---|---|---|---|---|---|
| 1926R | Inc. above | 120 | 290 | 470 | 650 | — |

**10 FRANGA ARI** KM# 9 **Weight:** 3.2258 g. **Composition:** 0.9000 Gold .933 oz. AGW

| Date | Mintage | F | VF | XF | Unc | BU |
|---|---|---|---|---|---|---|
| 1927R | 6,000 | 100 | 140 | 210 | 300 | — |

**20 FRANGA ARI** KM# 10 **Weight:** 6.4516 g. **Composition:** 0.9000 Gold .1867 oz. AGW

| Date | Mintage | F | VF | XF | Unc | BU |
|---|---|---|---|---|---|---|
| 1926R | — | 110 | 155 | 235 | 300 | — |
| 1927R | 6,000 | 110 | 150 | 225 | 295 | — |

**20 FRANGA ARI** KM# 12 **Weight:** 6.4516 g. **Composition:** 0.9000 Gold .1867 oz. AGW **Subject:** George Kastrioti "Skanderbeg"

| Date | Mintage | F | VF | XF | Unc | BU |
|---|---|---|---|---|---|---|
| 1926R | 5,900 | 120 | 160 | 275 | 385 | — |
| 1926 Fasces | 100 | — | — | 3,500 | 5,500 | — |
| **Note:** 90 pieces were reported melted | | | | | | |
| 1927V | 5,053 | — | 140 | 240 | 310 | — |

**20 FRANGA ARI** KM# 20 **Weight:** 6.4516 g. **Composition:** 0.9000 Gold .1867 oz. AGW **Subject:** 25th Anniversary of Independence

| Date | Mintage | F | VF | XF | Unc | BU |
|---|---|---|---|---|---|---|
| 1937R | 2,500 | — | 180 | 285 | 425 | — |

**20 FRANGA ARI** KM# 22 **Weight:** 6.4516 g. **Composition:** 0.9000 Gold .1867 oz. AGW **Subject:** Marriage of King Zog

| Date | Mintage | F | VF | XF | Unc | BU |
|---|---|---|---|---|---|---|
| 1938R | 2,500 | — | 180 | 285 | 425 | — |

**20 FRANGA ARI** KM# 24 **Weight:** 6.4516 g. **Composition:** 0.9000 Gold .1867 oz. AGW **Subject:** 10th Anniversary - Reign of King Zog

| Date | Mintage | F | VF | XF | Unc | BU |
|---|---|---|---|---|---|---|
| 1938R | 1,000 | — | 200 | 300 | 500 | — |

**Note:** Pieces struck in 1969 from new dies

**50 FRANGA ARI** KM# 25 **Weight:** 16.1290 g. **Composition:** 0.9000 Gold .4667 oz. AGW **Subject:** 10th Anniversary - Reign of King Zog

| Date | Mintage | F | VF | XF | Unc | BU |
|---|---|---|---|---|---|---|
| 1938R | 600 | — | 500 | 800 | 1,450 | — |

**Note:** Pieces struck in 1969 from new dies

**100 FRANGA ARI** KM# 11.1 **Weight:** 32.2580 g. **Composition:** 0.9000 Gold .9335 oz. AGW

| Date | Mintage | F | VF | XF | Unc | BU |
|---|---|---|---|---|---|---|
| 1926R | 6,614 | — | 550 | 750 | 1,150 | — |

**Note:** Mintage figures includes provas, Pr7-9

**100 FRANGA ARI** KM# 11.2 **Weight:** 32.2580 g. **Composition:** 0.9000 Gold .9335 oz. AGW **Obverse:** Star below bust

| Date | Mintage | F | VF | XF | Unc | BU |
|---|---|---|---|---|---|---|
| 1926R | Inc. above | — | 550 | 750 | 1,150 | — |

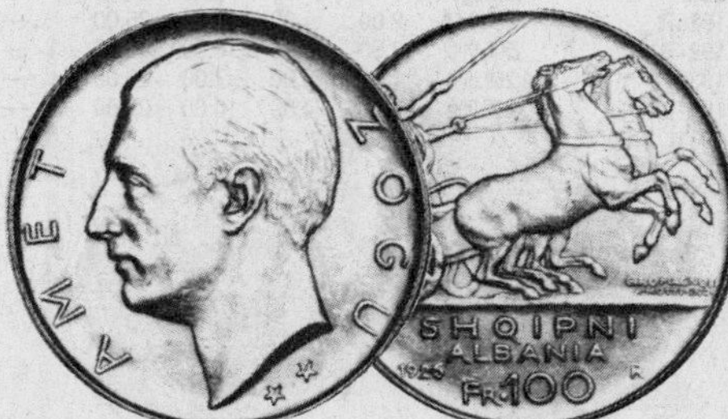

**100 FRANGA ARI** KM# 11.3 **Weight:** 32.2580 g. **Composition:** 0.9000 Gold .9335 oz. AGW **Obverse:** 2 stars below bust

| Date | Mintage | F | VF | XF | Unc | BU |
|---|---|---|---|---|---|---|
| 1926R | Inc. above | — | 550 | 750 | 1,150 | — |

**100 FRANGA ARI** KM# 11a.2 **Weight:** 32.2580 g. **Composition:** 0.9000 Gold .9335 oz. AGW **Obverse:** Star below bust

| Date | Mintage | F | VF | XF | Unc | BU |
|---|---|---|---|---|---|---|
| 1927R | Inc. above | — | 600 | 850 | 1,350 | — |

**100 FRANGA ARI** KM# 11a.3 **Weight:** 32.2580 g. **Composition:** 0.9000 Gold .9335 oz. AGW **Obverse:** 2 stars below bust

| Date | Mintage | F | VF | XF | Unc | BU |
|---|---|---|---|---|---|---|
| 1927R | Inc. above | — | 600 | 850 | 1,350 | — |

**100 FRANGA ARI** KM# 21 **Weight:** 32.2580 g. **Composition:** 0.9000 Gold .9335 oz. AGW **Subject:** 25th Anniversary of Independence

| Date | Mintage | F | VF | XF | Unc | BU |
|---|---|---|---|---|---|---|
| 1937R | 500 | — | 750 | 1,150 | 1,650 | — |

**100 FRANGA ARI** KM# 23 **Weight:** 32.2580 g. **Composition:** 0.9000 Gold .9335 oz. AGW **Subject:** Marriage of King Zog

| Date | Mintage | F | VF | XF | Unc | BU |
|---|---|---|---|---|---|---|
| 1938R | 500 | — | 700 | 1,100 | 1,600 | — |

**100 FRANGA ARI** KM# 26 **Weight:** 32.2580 g. **Composition:** 0.9000 Gold .9335 oz. AGW **Subject:** 10th Anniversary - Reign of King Zog

| Date | Mintage | F | VF | XF | Unc | BU |
|---|---|---|---|---|---|---|
| 1938R | 500 | — | 700 | 1,100 | 1,600 | — |

**Note:** Pieces restruck in 1969 from new dies

## ITALIAN OCCUPATION WWII

**0.05 LEK** KM# 27 **Composition:** Aluminum-Bronze

| Date | Mintage | F | VF | XF | Unc | BU |
|---|---|---|---|---|---|---|
| 1940R | 1,400,000 | 3.00 | 6.00 | 14.00 | 25.00 | — |
| 1941R Rare | 200,000 | — | — | — | — | — |

**0.10 LEK** **KM# 28** **Composition:** Aluminum-Bronze

| Date | Mintage | F | VF | XF | Unc | BU |
|---|---|---|---|---|---|---|
| 1940R | 550,000 | 4.00 | 8.00 | 18.00 | 30.00 | — |
| 1941R | 250,000 | 18.00 | 47.00 | 85.00 | 145 | — |

**0.20 LEK** **KM# 29** **Composition:** Stainless Steel

| Date | Mintage | F | VF | XF | Unc | BU |
|---|---|---|---|---|---|---|
| 1939R | 900,000 | 1.00 | 4.00 | 8.00 | 14.00 | — |
| **Note:** 1939 dated coins exist in 2 varieties, magnetic and non-magnetic | | | | | | |
| 1940R | 700,000 | 1.00 | 2.00 | 4.00 | 12.00 | — |
| 1941R | 1,400,000 | 1.00 | 2.00 | 4.00 | 12.00 | — |

**0.50 LEK** **KM# 30** **Composition:** Stainless Steel

| Date | Mintage | F | VF | XF | Unc | BU |
|---|---|---|---|---|---|---|
| 1939R | 100,000 | 1.50 | 4.00 | 8.00 | 20.00 | — |
| **Note:** 1939 dated coins exist in 2 varieties, magnetic and on-magnetic | | | | | | |
| 1940R | 500,000 | 1.50 | 3.00 | 6.00 | 16.00 | — |
| 1941R | — | 1.50 | 3.00 | 7.00 | 18.00 | — |

**LEK** **KM# 31** **Composition:** Stainless Steel **Note:** Coins dated after 1939 were not struck for circulation.

| Date | Mintage | F | VF | XF | Unc | BU |
|---|---|---|---|---|---|---|
| 1939R | 2,100,000 | 1.50 | 2.50 | 5.00 | 15.00 | — |
| **Note:** 1939 dated coins exist in 2 varieties, magnetic and on-magnetic | | | | | | |
| 1940R Rare | — | — | — | — | — | — |
| 1941R Rare | — | — | — | — | — | — |

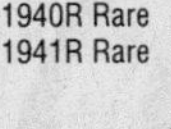

**2 LEK** **KM# 32** **Composition:** Stainless Steel **Note:** Coins dated after 1939 were not struck for circuation.

| Date | Mintage | F | VF | XF | Unc | BU |
|---|---|---|---|---|---|---|
| 1939R | 1,300,000 | 2.00 | 4.00 | 8.00 | 18.00 | — |
| **Note:** 1939 dated coins exist in 2 varieties, magnetic and non-magnetic | | | | | | |
| 1940R Rare | — | — | — | — | — | — |
| 1941R Rare | — | — | — | — | — | — |

**5 LEK** **KM# 33** **Weight:** 5.0000 g. **Composition:** 0.8350 Silver .1342 oz. ASW

| Date | Mintage | F | VF | XF | Unc | BU |
|---|---|---|---|---|---|---|
| 1939R | 1,350,000 | 6.00 | 12.00 | 30.00 | 70.00 | — |

**10 LEK** **KM# 34** **Weight:** 10.0000 g. **Composition:** 0.8350 Silver .2684 oz. ASW

| Date | Mintage | F | VF | XF | Unc | BU |
|---|---|---|---|---|---|---|
| 1939R | 175,000 | 40.00 | 70.00 | 115 | 210 | — |

# PEOPLES SOCIALIST REPUBLIC

**5 QINDARKA** **KM# 39** **Composition:** Aluminum

| Date | Mintage | F | VF | XF | Unc | BU |
|---|---|---|---|---|---|---|
| 1964 | — | 0.10 | 0.25 | 0.50 | 1.25 | — |

**5 QINDARKA** **KM# 44** **Composition:** Aluminum **Subject:** 25th Anniversary of Liberation

| Date | Mintage | F | VF | XF | Unc | BU |
|---|---|---|---|---|---|---|
| ND (1969) | — | 0.10 | 0.20 | 0.30 | 0.85 | — |

**5 QINDARKA** **KM# 71** **Composition:** Aluminum **Edge:** Plain

| Date | Mintage | F | VF | XF | Unc | BU |
|---|---|---|---|---|---|---|
| 1988 | — | — | — | — | 0.50 | — |

**10 QINDARKA** **KM# 40** **Composition:** Aluminum

| Date | Mintage | F | VF | XF | Unc | BU |
|---|---|---|---|---|---|---|
| 1964 | — | 0.15 | 0.30 | 0.60 | 1.50 | — |

**10 QINDARKA** **KM# 45** **Composition:** Aluminum **Subject:** 25th Anniversary of Liberation

| Date | Mintage | F | VF | XF | Unc | BU |
|---|---|---|---|---|---|---|
| ND (1969) | — | 0.10 | 0.20 | 0.35 | 1.00 | — |

**10 QINDARKA** **KM# 60** **Composition:** Aluminum

| Date | Mintage | F | VF | XF | Unc | BU |
|---|---|---|---|---|---|---|
| 1988 | — | — | — | — | 0.60 | — |

**20 QINDARKA** **KM# 41** **Composition:** Aluminum

| Date | Mintage | F | VF | XF | Unc | BU |
|---|---|---|---|---|---|---|
| 1964 | — | 0.20 | 0.40 | 0.60 | 1.75 | — |

**20 QINDARKA** **KM# 46** **Composition:** Aluminum **Subject:** 25th Anniversary of Liberation

| Date | Mintage | F | VF | XF | Unc | BU |
|---|---|---|---|---|---|---|
| ND (1969) | — | 0.15 | 0.30 | 0.50 | 1.25 | — |

**20 QINDARKA** **KM# 65** **Composition:** Aluminum

| Date | Mintage | F | VF | XF | Unc | BU |
|---|---|---|---|---|---|---|
| 1988 | — | — | — | — | 0.75 | — |

**50 QINDARKA** **KM# 42** **Composition:** Aluminum

| Date | Mintage | F | VF | XF | Unc | BU |
|---|---|---|---|---|---|---|
| 1964 | — | 0.50 | 0.75 | 2.00 | 4.00 | — |

**50 QINDARKA** **KM# 47** **Composition:** Aluminum **Subject:** 25th Anniversary of Liberation

| Date | Mintage | F | VF | XF | Unc | BU |
|---|---|---|---|---|---|---|
| ND (1969) | — | 0.30 | 0.50 | 1.00 | 2.00 | — |

**50 QINDARKA** **KM# 72** **Composition:** Aluminum **Edge:** Plain

| Date | Mintage | F | VF | XF | Unc | BU |
|---|---|---|---|---|---|---|
| 1988 | — | — | — | — | 1.25 | — |

**1/2 LEKU** **KM# 35** **Composition:** Zinc

| Date | Mintage | F | VF | XF | Unc | BU |
|---|---|---|---|---|---|---|
| 1947 | — | 0.40 | 0.80 | 1.50 | 3.00 | — |
| 1957 | — | 0.25 | 0.50 | 1.00 | 2.00 | — |

**LEK** **KM# 36** **Composition:** Zinc

| Date | Mintage | F | VF | XF | Unc | BU |
|---|---|---|---|---|---|---|
| 1947 | — | 0.60 | 1.00 | 2.00 | 4.50 | — |
| 1957 | — | 0.35 | 0.75 | 1.50 | 3.00 | — |

**LEK** **KM# 43** **Composition:** Aluminum

| Date | Mintage | F | VF | XF | Unc | BU |
|---|---|---|---|---|---|---|
| 1964 | — | 0.50 | 1.00 | 2.00 | 4.00 | — |

**LEK** **KM# 48** **Composition:** Aluminum **Subject:** 25th Anniversary of Liberation

| Date | Mintage | F | VF | XF | Unc | BU |
|---|---|---|---|---|---|---|
| ND (1969) | — | 0.35 | 0.75 | 1.25 | 2.50 | — |

**LEK** **KM# 66** **Composition:** Aluminum-Bronze

| Date | Mintage | F | VF | XF | Unc | BU |
|---|---|---|---|---|---|---|
| 1988 | — | — | — | — | 1.75 | — |

**LEK** **KM# 74** **Composition:** Aluminum

| Date | Mintage | F | VF | XF | Unc | BU |
|---|---|---|---|---|---|---|
| 1988 | — | — | — | — | 1.50 | — |

**LEK** **KM# 75** **Composition:** Bronze **Obverse:** Pelican **Reverse:** Denomination

| Date | Mintage | F | VF | XF | Unc | BU |
|---|---|---|---|---|---|---|
| 1996 | — | — | — | — | 1.25 | — |

**2 LEKE** **KM# 37** **Composition:** Zinc

| Date | Mintage | F | VF | XF | Unc | BU |
|---|---|---|---|---|---|---|
| 1947 | — | 0.50 | 1.25 | 2.25 | 5.00 | — |
| 1957 | — | 0.35 | 0.75 | 1.50 | 3.00 | — |

**2 LEKE** **KM# 67** **Composition:** Copper-Nickel **Subject:** 45th Anniversary - WWII

| Date | Mintage | F | VF | XF | Unc | BU |
|---|---|---|---|---|---|---|
| 1989 | — | — | — | — | 3.50 | — |

**2 LEKE** **KM# 73** **Composition:** Copper-Nickel

| Date | Mintage | F | VF | XF | Unc | BU |
|---|---|---|---|---|---|---|
| 1989 | — | — | — | — | 3.25 | — |

**5 LEKE** **KM# 38** **Composition:** Zinc

| Date | Mintage | F | VF | XF | Unc | BU |
|---|---|---|---|---|---|---|
| 1947 | — | 1.00 | 1.75 | 3.50 | 7.00 | — |
| 1957 | — | 0.50 | 1.00 | 2.00 | 3.50 | — |

**5 LEKE** **KM# 49.1** **Weight:** 16.6600 g. **Composition:** 0.9990 Silver .5165 oz. ASW **Subject:** 500th Anniversary - Liga Lissi Skanderbeg's Victory Over the Turks **Reverse:** Without date below arms, oval fineness countermark punched in

| Date | Mintage | F | VF | XF | Unc | BU |
|---|---|---|---|---|---|---|
| ND (1969) Proof | 8,540 | Value: 20.00 | | | | |

**Note:** Countermarks for 1968 and 1969 coins were hand positioned, then punched. The result is a variety of countermark positions, to the left and right of LEKE

**5 LEKE** **KM# 49.2** **Weight:** 16.6600 g. **Composition:** 0.9990 Silver .5165 oz. ASW **Reverse:** Date below arms

| Date | Mintage | F | VF | XF | Unc | BU |
|---|---|---|---|---|---|---|
| 1969 Proof | 1,500 | Value: 25.00 | | | | |

**Note:** Countermarks for 1968 and 1969 coins were hand positioned, then punched. The result is a variety of countermark positions, to the left and right of LEKE

**5 LEKE** **KM# 49.3** **Weight:** 16.6600 g. **Composition:** 0.9990 Silver .5165 oz. ASW **Reverse:** Date below arms, oval fineness in relief

| Date | Mintage | F | VF | XF | Unc | BU |
|---|---|---|---|---|---|---|
| 1970 Proof | 500 | Value: 30.00 | | | | |

**Note:** For the 1970 issue the fineness marking has been incorporated in the dies

**5 LEKE** **KM# 57** **Composition:** Copper-Nickel **Subject:** Seaport of Durazzo

| Date | Mintage | F | VF | XF | Unc | BU |
|---|---|---|---|---|---|---|
| 1987 | Est. 50,000 | — | — | — | 10.00 | — |

**5 LEKE** **KM# 57a** **Weight:** 50.0000 g. **Composition:** 0.9000 Gold 1.4470 oz. AGW **Subject:** Seaport of Durazzo

| Date | Mintage | F | VF | XF | Unc | BU |
|---|---|---|---|---|---|---|
| 1987 Proof | 5 | Value: 2,500 | | | | |

**5 LEKE** **KM# 61** **Composition:** Copper-Nickel **Subject:** 42nd Anniversary of First Railroad

| Date | Mintage | F | VF | XF | Unc | BU |
|---|---|---|---|---|---|---|
| 1988 | 20,000 | — | — | — | 15.00 | — |

**5 LEKE** **KM# 76** **Composition:** Steel **Obverse:** Imperial eagle **Reverse:** Olive branch, denomination

| Date | Mintage | F | VF | XF | Unc | BU |
|---|---|---|---|---|---|---|
| 1995 | — | — | — | — | 1.00 | — |

**10 LEKE** **KM# 50.1** **Weight:** 33.3300 g. **Composition:** 0.9990 Silver 1.0354 oz. ASW **Subject:** 500th Anniversary - Death of Prince Skanderbeg **Reverse:** Oval finess countermark punched in, no date below

| Date | Mintage | F | VF | XF | Unc | BU |
|---|---|---|---|---|---|---|
| ND Proof | 8,540 | Value: 35.00 | | | | |

**Note:** Countermark for 1968 and 1969 coins were hand positioned, then punched. The result is a variety of countermark positions, to the left and right of LEKE

**10 LEKE** **KM# 50.2** **Weight:** 33.3300 g. **Composition:** 0.9990 Silver 1.0354 oz. ASW **Reverse:** Date below arms

| Date | Mintage | F | VF | XF | Unc | BU |
|---|---|---|---|---|---|---|
| 1969 Proof | 1,500 | Value: 45.00 | | | | |

**Note:** Countermark for 1968 and 1969 coins were hand positioned, then punched. The result is a variety of countermark positions, to the left and right of LEKE

**10 LEKE** **KM# 50.3** **Weight:** 33.3300 g. **Composition:** 0.9990 Silver 1.0354 oz. ASW **Reverse:** Oval fineness is in relief, date below arms

| Date | Mintage | F | VF | XF | Unc | BU |
|---|---|---|---|---|---|---|
| 1970 Proof | 500 | Value: 50.00 | | | | |

**Note:** For the 1970 issues the fineness marking has been incorporated in the dies

**10 LEKE** **KM# 50.4** **Weight:** 33.3300 g. **Composition:** 0.9990 Silver 1.0354 oz. ASW **Reverse:** Hallmark countermark left of LEKE, oval fineness countermark in relief, date below arms

| Date | Mintage | F | VF | XF | Unc | BU |
|---|---|---|---|---|---|---|
| 1970 Proof | Inc. above | Value: 50.00 | | | | |

**Note:** For the 1970 issues the fineness marking has been incorporated in the dies

**10 LEKE** **KM# 68** **Weight:** 52.5000 g. **Composition:** 0.9250 Silver 1.5613 oz. ASW **Subject:** 1992 Summer Olympics - Equestrian **Reverse:** Horse and rider right, incuse design.

| Date | Mintage | F | VF | XF | Unc | BU |
|---|---|---|---|---|---|---|
| 1991 | 980 | — | — | — | 200 | — |

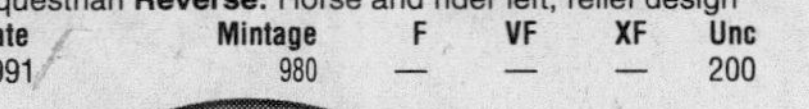

**10 LEKE** **KM# 69** **Weight:** 52.5000 g. **Composition:** 0.9250 Silver 1.5613 oz. ASW **Subject:** 1992 Summer Olympics - Equestrian **Reverse:** Horse and rider left, relief design

| Date | Mintage | F | VF | XF | Unc | BU |
|---|---|---|---|---|---|---|
| 1991 | 980 | — | — | — | 200 | — |

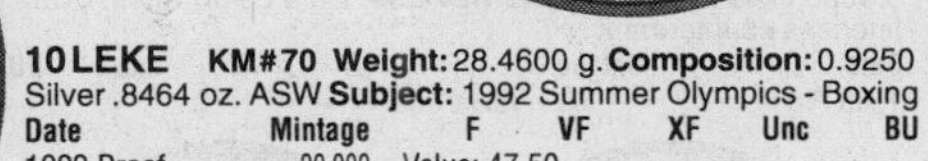

**10 LEKE** **KM# 70** **Weight:** 28.4600 g. **Composition:** 0.9250 Silver .8464 oz. ASW **Subject:** 1992 Summer Olympics - Boxing

| Date | Mintage | F | VF | XF | Unc | BU |
|---|---|---|---|---|---|---|
| 1992 Proof | 20,000 | Value: 47.50 | | | | |

**10 LEKE** **KM# 77** **Composition:** Brass **Obverse:** Fortress **Reverse:** Denomination, sprig with berries

| Date | Mintage | F | VF | XF | Unc | BU |
|---|---|---|---|---|---|---|
| 1996 | — | — | — | — | 1.25 | — |

**20 LEKE** **KM# 51.1** **Weight:** 3.9500 g. **Composition:** 0.9000 Gold .1143 oz. AGW **Subject:** 500th Anniversary - Death of Prince Skanderbeg **Obverse:** Date on ribbon **Reverse:** Oval fineness countermark punched in

| Date | Mintage | F | VF | XF | Unc | BU |
|---|---|---|---|---|---|---|
| 1968 | 2,920 | Value: 90.00 | | | | |

**Note:** Countermark for 1968 and 1969 coins were hand positioned, then punched. The result is a variety of countermark positions, to the left and right of LEKE

**20 LEKE** **KM# 51.2** **Weight:** 3.9500 g. **Composition:** 0.9000 Gold .1143 oz. AGW **Reverse:** Without fineness countermark (error)

| Date | Mintage | F | VF | XF | Unc | BU |
|---|---|---|---|---|---|---|
| 1968 Proof | Inc. above | Value: 90.00 | | | | |

**Note:** Countermark for 1968 and 1969 coins were hand positioned, then punched. The result is a variety of countermark positions, to the left and right of LEKE

**20 LEKE** **KM# 51.3** **Weight:** 3.9500 g. **Composition:** 0.9000 Gold .1143 oz. AGW **Reverse:** Cornucopia countermark at right of LEKE

| Date | Mintage | F | VF | XF | Unc | BU |
|---|---|---|---|---|---|---|
| 1968 Paris | 24 | — | — | — | 400 | — |

**Note:** Countermarks for 1968 and 1969 coins were hand positioned, then punched. The result is a variety of countermark positions, to the left and right of LEKE

**20 LEKE** **KM# 51.4** **Weight:** 3.9500 g. **Composition:** 0.9000 Gold .1143 oz. AGW **Reverse:** Date added below arms

| Date | Mintage | F | VF | XF | Unc | BU |
|---|---|---|---|---|---|---|
| 1969 Proof | 650 | Value: 125 | | | | |

**Note:** Countermarks for 1968 and 1969 coins were hand positioned, then punched. The result is a variety of countermark positions, to the left and right of LEKE

**20 LEKE** **KM# 51.5** **Weight:** 3.9500 g. **Composition:** 0.9000 Gold .1143 oz. AGW **Reverse:** Date below arms, oval fineness in relief

| Date | Mintage | F | VF | XF | Unc | BU |
|---|---|---|---|---|---|---|
| 1970 Proof | 500 | Value: 140 | | | | |

**Note:** For the 1970 issues the fineness marking has been incorporated in the dies

**20 LEKE** **KM# 51.6** **Weight:** 3.9500 g. **Composition:** 0.9000 Gold .1143 oz. AGW **Reverse:** Sunken countermark 1 AR left of LEKE and raised oval fineness countermark on right

| Date | Mintage | F | VF | XF | Unc | BU |
|---|---|---|---|---|---|---|
| 1970 Proof | — | — | — | — | — | — |

**Note:** For the 1970 issues the fineness marking has been incorporated in the dies

**20 LEKE** **KM# 78** **Composition:** Brass **Obverse:** Ancient sailing vessel **Reverse:** Denomination

| Date | Mintage | F | VF | XF | Unc | BU |
|---|---|---|---|---|---|---|
| 1996 | — | — | — | — | 1.50 | — |

**25 LEKE** **KM# 52.1** **Weight:** 83.3300 g. **Composition:** 0.9990 Silver 2.5887 oz. ASW **Obverse:** Dance with swords **Reverse:** Date below arms, oval fineness countermark

| Date | Mintage | F | VF | XF | Unc | BU |
|---|---|---|---|---|---|---|
| 1968 Proof | 8,540 | Value: 55.00 | | | | |

**Note:** Countermarks for 1968 and 1969 coins were hand positioned, then punched. The result is a variety of countermark positions, to the left and the right of LEKE

**25 LEKE** **KM# 52.2** **Weight:** 83.3300 g. **Composition:** 0.9990 Silver 2.5887 oz. ASW **Obverse:** Date below scene **Reverse:** Date below arms. Oval fineness countermark

| Date | Mintage | F | VF | XF | Unc | BU |
|---|---|---|---|---|---|---|
| 1969 Proof | — | Value: 65.00 | | | | |

**25 LEKE** **KM# 52.3** **Weight:** 83.3300 g. **Composition:** 0.9990 Silver 2.5887 oz. ASW **Obverse:** Without date **Reverse:** Oval fineness countermark in relief

| Date | Mintage | F | VF | XF | Unc | BU |
|---|---|---|---|---|---|---|
| 1970 Proof | 500 | Value: 90.00 | | | | |

**Note:** For the 1970 issue the fineness amrking has been incorporated in the dies

**50 LEKE** **KM# 53.1** **Weight:** 9.8700 g. **Composition:** 0.9000 Gold .2856 oz. AGW **Obverse:** Argirocastrum Ruins, date below **Reverse:** Oval fineness countermark

| Date | Mintage | F | VF | XF | Unc | BU |
|---|---|---|---|---|---|---|
| 1968 Proof | 3,120 | Value: 165 | | | | |

**50 LEKE** **KM# 53.2** **Weight:** 9.8700 g. **Composition:** 0.9000 Gold .2856 oz. AGW **Reverse:** Date below arms, oval fineness countermark

| Date | Mintage | F | VF | XF | Unc | BU |
|---|---|---|---|---|---|---|
| 1969 Proof | 500 | Value: 265 | | | | |

**50 LEKE** **KM# 53.3** **Weight:** 9.8700 g. **Composition:** 0.9000 Gold .2856 oz. AGW **Obverse:** Without date **Reverse:** Oval fineness countermark in relief

| Date | Mintage | F | VF | XF | Unc | BU |
|---|---|---|---|---|---|---|
| 1970 Proof | 100 | Value: 300 | | | | |

**Note:** For the 1970 issue the fineness marking has been incorporated in the dies.

**50 LEKE** **KM# 58a** **Weight:** 155.5000 g. **Composition:** 0.9990 Gold 4.9950 oz. AGW **Subject:** Seaport of Durazzo

| Date | Mintage | F | VF | XF | Unc | BU |
|---|---|---|---|---|---|---|
| 1987 Proof | 5 | Value: 5,300 | | | | |

**50 LEKE** **KM# 58** **Weight:** 168.1500 g. **Composition:** 0.9250 Silver 5.0012 oz. ASW **Subject:** Seaport of Durazzo **Obverse:** Similar to 5 Leke, KM#57 **Note:** Illustration reduced. Actual size 65 millimeters.

| Date | Mintage | F | VF | XF | Unc | BU |
|---|---|---|---|---|---|---|
| 1987 Proof | Est. 15,000 | Value: 120 | | | | |

**50 LEKE** **KM# 62** **Weight:** 168.1500 g. **Composition:** 0.9250 Silver 5.0012 oz. ASW **Subject:** 42nd Anniversary - First Railroad **Note:** Illustration reduced. Actual size 65 millimeters.

| Date | Mintage | F | VF | XF | Unc | BU |
|---|---|---|---|---|---|---|
| 1988 Proof | 7,500 | Value: 300 | | | | |

**50 LEKE** KM# 79 **Composition:** Copper-Nickel **Obverse:** Ancient equestrian **Reverse:** Denomination, tied oak sprigs

| Date | Mintage | F | VF | XF | Unc | BU |
|---|---|---|---|---|---|---|
| 1996 | — | — | — | — | 2.00 | — |

**100 LEKE** KM# 54.1 **Weight:** 19.7500 g. **Composition:** 0.9000 Gold .5715 oz. AGW **Obverse:** Peasant girl in national dress, date below **Reverse:** Oval fineness countermark

| Date | Mintage | F | VF | XF | Unc | BU |
|---|---|---|---|---|---|---|
| 1968 Proof | 3,470 | Value: 350 | | | | |

**Note:** Countermarks for 1968 and 1969 coins were hand positioned, then punched. The result is a variety of countermark positions, to the left and the right of LEKE

**100 LEKE** KM# 54.2 **Weight:** 19.7500 g. **Composition:** 0.9000 Gold .5715 oz. AGW **Obverse:** Date below scene **Reverse:** Date below arms, oval fineness countermark

| Date | Mintage | F | VF | XF | Unc | BU |
|---|---|---|---|---|---|---|
| 1969 Proof | 450 | Value: 450 | | | | |

**Note:** Countermarks for 1968 and 1969 coins were hand positioned, then punched. The result is a variety of countermark positions, to the left and the right of LEKE

**100 LEKE** KM# 54.3 **Weight:** 19.7500 g. **Composition:** 0.9000 Gold .5715 oz. AGW **Obverse:** Without date **Reverse:** Oval fineness countermark in relief

| Date | Mintage | F | VF | XF | Unc | BU |
|---|---|---|---|---|---|---|
| 1970 Proof | Inc. above | Value: 475 | | | | |

**100 LEKE** KM# 59 **Weight:** 6.4500 g. **Composition:** 0.9000 Gold .1866 oz. AGW **Subject:** Seaport of Durazzo **Obverse:** Arms **Reverse:** Ship in harbor **Note:** Similar to 5 Leke, KM#57.

| Date | Mintage | F | VF | XF | Unc | BU |
|---|---|---|---|---|---|---|
| 1987 Proof | 5,000 | Value: 180 | | | | |

**100 LEKE** KM# 63 **Weight:** 6.4500 g. **Composition:** 0.9000 Gold .1866 oz. AGW **Subject:** 42nd Anniversary - First Railroad **Obverse:** Train engine emerging from tunnel **Reverse:** Caboose leaving tunnel **Note:** Similar to 50 Leke, KM#62, but without hole in coin

| Date | Mintage | F | VF | XF | Unc | BU |
|---|---|---|---|---|---|---|
| 1988 Proof | 2,000 | Value: 280 | | | | |

**100 LEKE** KM# 80 **Ring Composition:** Copper-Nickel-**Center Weight:** 6.7000 g. **Center Composition:** Aluminum-Bronze **Obverse:** Allegorical figure, Teuta. **Reverse:** Denomination in wreath. **Edge:** Reeded

| Date | Mintage | F | VF | XF | Unc | BU |
|---|---|---|---|---|---|---|
| 2000 | — | — | — | — | 4.00 | — |

**200 LEKE** KM# 55.1 **Weight:** 39.4900 g. **Composition:** 0.9000 Gold 1.1427 oz. AGW **Subject:** Buthrotum Ruins **Reverse:** Similar to 100 Leke, KM#54.1

| Date | Mintage | F | VF | XF | Unc | BU |
|---|---|---|---|---|---|---|
| 1968 Proof | 2,170 | Value: 600 | | | | |

**Note:** Countermarks for 1968 and 1969 coins were hand positioned then punched. The result is a variety of countermark positions, to the left and right of LEKE

**200 LEKE** KM# 55.2 **Weight:** 39.4900 g. **Composition:** 0.9000 Gold 1.1427 oz. AGW **Reverse:** Date below arms, oval fineness countermark

| Date | Mintage | F | VF | XF | Unc | BU |
|---|---|---|---|---|---|---|
| 1969 Proof | 200 | Value: 775 | | | | |

**Note:** Countermarks for 1968 and 1969 coins were hand positioned then punched. The result is a variety of countermark positions, to the left and right of LEKE

**200 LEKE** KM# 55.3 **Weight:** 39.4900 g. **Composition:** 0.9000 Gold 1.1427 oz. AGW **Obverse:** Without date **Reverse:** Oval fineness countermark in relief

| Date | Mintage | F | VF | XF | Unc | BU |
|---|---|---|---|---|---|---|
| 1970 Proof | Inc. above | Value: 800 | | | | |

**500 LEKE** KM# 56.1 **Weight:** 98.7400 g. **Composition:** 0.9000 Gold 2.8574 oz. AGW **Subject:** 500th Anniversary - Death of Prince Skanderbeg **Reverse:** Similar to 100 Leke, KM#54.1

| Date | Mintage | F | VF | XF | Unc | BU |
|---|---|---|---|---|---|---|
| 1968 Proof | 1,520 | Value: 1,350 | | | | |

**Note:** Countermarks for 1968 and 1969 coins were hand positioned then punched. The result is a variety of countermark positions to the left and right of LEKE

**500 LEKE** KM# 56.2 **Weight:** 98.7400 g. **Composition:** 0.9000 Gold 2.8574 oz. AGW **Reverse:** Date below arms, oval fineness countermark

| Date | Mintage | F | VF | XF | Unc | BU |
|---|---|---|---|---|---|---|
| 1969 Proof | 200 | Value: 1,750 | | | | |

**Note:** Countermarks for 1968 and 1969 coins were hand positioned then punched. The result is a variety of countermark positions to the left and right of LEKE

**500 LEKE** KM# 56.3 **Weight:** 98.7400 g. **Composition:** 0.9000 Gold 2.8574 oz. AGW **Obverse:** Without date **Reverse:** Oval fineness countermark in relief

| Date | Mintage | F | VF | XF | Unc | BU |
|---|---|---|---|---|---|---|
| 1970 Proof | Inc. above | Value: 1,800 | | | | |

**7500 LEKE** KM# 64 **Weight:** 483.7500 g. **Composition:** 0.9000 Gold 13.9992 oz. AGW **Subject:** 42nd Anniversary - First Railroad **Obverse:** Train engine emerging from tunnel **Reverse:** Caboose leaving tunnel **Note:** Similar to 50 Leke, KM#62.

| Date | Mintage | F | VF | XF | Unc | BU |
|---|---|---|---|---|---|---|
| 1988 Proof | 50 | Value: 8,000 | | | | |

## TRIAL STRIKE

| KM# | Date | Mintage | Identification | Issue Price | Mkt Val |
|---|---|---|---|---|---|
| TS1 | 1969 | — | 500 Leke. Goldine-Brass. 56.3200 g. Blank with MET countermark.. Like KM56.2.Illustration reduced. Actual size: 55.1mm. | — | 200 |

## PATTERNS

Including off-metal strikes

| KM# | Date | Mintage | Identification | Mkt Val |
|---|---|---|---|---|
| Pn2 | 1927 | — | 5 Franga Ari. Copper. | — |
| Pn1 | 1927 | — | Frang Ar. Silver. Plain edge | 500 |
| Pn3 | 1928 | — | 2 Lek. Copper-Nickel. | — |

| KM# | Date | Mintage | Identification | Mkt Val |
|---|---|---|---|---|
| Pn4 | 1968 | — | 10 Leke. 0.9990 Silver. 31.6000 g. Like 10 Leke, KM#50.. Blank except for MET in rectangle at 6 o'clock.. Reeded edge | — |

## ESSAIS

| KM# | Date | Mintage | Identification | Mkt Val |
|---|---|---|---|---|
| E1 | 1926 | — | 5 Qindar Leku. Bronze. | — |
| E2 | 1926 | — | 10 Qindar Ari. Bronze. | — |
| E3 | 1926 | — | 1/2 Lek. Nickel. | — |
| E4 | 1926 | 50 | 2 Franga Ari. Silver. | 500 |
| E6 | 1927 | — | Frang Ar. Silver. | 500 |
| E7 | 1927 | 50 | 2 Franga Ari. Silver. | 650 |
| E5 | 1927 | — | Lek. Nickel. | — |
| E8 | 1927 | — | 100 Franga Ari. Silver. | — |
| E9 | 1928 | — | 2 Lek. Nickel. | — |
| E10 | 1928 | 50 | Frang Ar. Silver. | 500 |
| E11 | 1928 | 50 | 2 Franga Ari. Silver. | 650 |
| E12 | 1938 | — | 100 Franga Ari. Gold. without signature. | — |

| KM# | Date | Mintage | Identification | Mkt Val |
|---|---|---|---|---|
| E13 | 1986 | 10 | 5 Leke. Copper-Nickel. 27.7900 g. | 200 |

## PIEFORTS

| KM# | Date | Mintage | Identification | Mkt Val |
|---|---|---|---|---|
| P1 | 1988 | 250 | 50 Leke. 0.9250 Silver. KM#62 without tunnel hole. | 500 |

## PROVAS

Standard metals unless otherwise stated

| KM# | Date | Mintage | Identification | Issue Price | Mkt Val |
|---|---|---|---|---|---|
| Pr1 | 1926 | 50 | 5 Qindar Leku. Bronze. KM#1. | — | 400 |
| Pr2 | 1926 | 50 | 10 Qindar Leku. Bronze. KM#2. | — | 400 |

| KM# | Date | Mintage | Identification | Issue Price | Mkt Val |
|---|---|---|---|---|---|
| Pr3 | 1926 | 50 | 1/4 Leku. KM#3. | — | 500 |
| Pr4 | 1926 | — | 1/2 Lek. Nickel. | — | 400 |

| KM# | Date | Mintage | Identification | Issue Price | Mkt Val |
|---|---|---|---|---|---|
| Pr5 | 1926 | — | 1/2 Lek. Nickel. KM#4. | — | 400 |
| Pr6 | 1926 | 50 | Lek. KM#5. | — | 500 |
| Pr7 | 1926 | — | 2 Franga Ari. Silver. KM#7. | — | 500 |
| Pr8 | 1926 | — | 5 Franga Ari. KM#8. Modern copy of 5 Franga Ari exist in copper and bronze. | — | 750 |
| Pr9 | 1926 | — | 5 Franga Ari. Copper. KM#8. Modern copy of 5 Franga Ari exist in copper and bronze. | — | 450 |
| Pr10 | 1926 | — | 5 Franga Ari. KM#8. Modern copy of 5 Franga Ari exist in copper and bronze. | — | 500 |
| Pr11 | 1926 | — | 5 Franga Ari. Copper. KM#8. Modern copy of 5 Franga Ari exist in copper and bronze. | — | 450 |
| Pr12 | 1926 | 50 | 20 Franga Ari. KM#12. | — | 650 |
| Pr13 | 1926 | — | 20 Franga Ari. KM#12. | — | 5,000 |
| Pr14 | 1926 | — | 100 Franga Ari. Gold. KM#11.1. | — | 1,500 |
| Pr15 | 1926 | — | 100 Franga Ari. Star, KM#11.2. | — | 1,600 |
| Pr16 | 1926 | — | 100 Franga Ari. 2 stars, KM#11.3. | — | 1,600 |
| Pr17 | 1927 | — | 1/4 Leku. Nickel. KM#3. | — | 500 |
| Pr18 | 1927 | — | Lek. Nickel. KM#5. | — | 500 |
| Pr19 | 1927 | 50 | Frang Ar. KM#6. | — | 300 |
| Pr20 | 1927 | — | Frang Ar. KM#6. | — | 350 |
| Pr21 | 1927 | — | 2 Franga Ari. KM#7. | — | 300 |
| Pr22 | 1927 | — | 5 Franga Ari. Silver. | — | 450 |
| Pr24 | 1927 | — | 10 Franga Ari. Gold. KM#9. | — | 700 |
| Pr25 | 1927 | 50 | 10 Franga Ari. KM#9. | — | 700 |
| Pr26 | 1927 | — | 20 Franga Ari. Gold. KM#10. | — | 650 |
| Pr27 | 1927 | — | 20 Franga Ari. KM#12. | — | 600 |
| Pr28 | 1927 | 50 | 20 Franga Ari. KM#10. | — | 550 |
| Pr29 | 1927 | — | 100 Franga Ari. KM#11a. | — | 1,500 |
| Pr30 | 1927 | — | 100 Franga Ari. Star, KM#11a.1. | — | 1,600 |
| Pr31 | 1927 | — | 100 Franga Ari. 2 stars, KM#11a.2. | — | 1,600 |
| PrA32 | 1927 | — | 100 Franga Ari. Similar to 5 Franga Ari, KM#8.1. | — | 1,260 |
| Pr23 | 1927 | — | 5 Franga Ari. Silver. Matte proof. | — | — |
| PrA25 | 1927 | — | Frang Ar. Silver. similar to KM#9. | — | — |
| Pr33 | 1928 | — | 2 Lek. Nickel. KM#28. | — | — |
| Pr32 | 1928 | — | 2 Lek. Copper-Nickel. KM#28. | — | 200 |
| PrA34 | 1928 | — | 2 Lek. Nickel. 9.7800 g. Portrait. Double eagle | — | 300 |
| Pr34 | 1928 | — | Frang Ar. KM#6. | — | 200 |
| Pr35 | 1928 | — | 2 Franga Ari. KM#7. | — | 250 |
| PrA36 | 1928 | — | 2 Franga Ari. Silver. 10.0400 g. Portrait. Double eagle | — | 350 |
| Pr36 | 1928 | 50 | 100 Franga Ari. Gold. Bare head. | — | 2,750 |
| Pr37 | 1928 | 50 | 100 Franga Ari. Gold. Bare head, wreath. | — | 2,750 |
| Pr38 | 1928 | 50 | 100 Franga Ari. Gold. Uniformed bust. | — | 2,750 |
| Pr39 | 1929 | 50 | 100 Franga Ari. Gold. Bare head, wreath. | — | 2,750 |
| Pr40 | 1935 | 50 | Qindar Ar. KM#14. | — | 300 |
| Pr41 | 1935 | 50 | 2 Qindar Ari. KM#15. | — | 300 |
| Pr42 | 1935 | 50 | Frang Ar. Silver. | — | 400 |
| Pr43 | 1935 | 50 | 2 Franga Ari. Silver. | — | 500 |
| Pr44 | 1935 | — | 5 Franga Ari. Silver. Pattern. | — | — |
| Pr48 | 1937 | — | 10 Franga Ari. Gold. | — | — |
| Pr45 | 1937 | 50 | Frang Ar. KM#16. | — | 450 |
| Pr46 | 1937 | 50 | Frang Ar. Silver. | — | 500 |
| Pr47 | 1937 | 50 | 2 Franga Ari. Silver. | — | 525 |
| Pr49 | 1937 | 50 | 20 Franga Ari. Gold. KM#20. | — | 550 |
| Pr50 | 1937 | 50 | 100 Franga Ari. KM#21. | — | 1,800 |
| Pr51 | 1938 | 50 | 20 Franga Ari. KM#22. | — | 650 |
| Pr52 | 1938 | 50 | 20 Franga Ari. KM#24. | — | 650 |
| Pr53 | 1938 | 50 | 50 Franga Ari. | — | 1,750 |
| Pr54 | 1938 | 50 | 100 Franga Ari. KM#26. | — | 1,800 |
| Pr55 | 1938 | 50 | 100 Franga Ari. KM#23. | — | 1,800 |
| Pr56 | 1939 | — | 0.05 Lek. Proof. | — | 400 |
| Pr57 | 1939 | — | 0.10 Lek. Proof. | — | 400 |
| Pr58 | 1939 | — | 0.20 Lek. Proof | — | 500 |
| Pr59 | 1939 | — | 0.50 Lek. Proof. | — | 500 |
| Pr60 | 1939 | — | Lek. Proof. | — | 500 |
| Pr61 | 1939 | — | 2 Lek. Proof. | — | 525 |
| Pr62 | 1939 | — | 5 Lek. Proof. | — | 500 |
| Pr63 | 1939 | — | 10 Lek. Silver. Proof. | — | 625 |
| Pr64 | 1947 | — | 10 Qindar Leku. Aluminum. | — | — |
| Pr65 | 1947 | — | 5 Qindar Leku. Tombac. | — | — |
| Pr66 | 1947 | — | 10 Qindar Leku. Aluminum. | — | — |
| Pr67 | 1947 | — | 10 Qindar Leku. Tombac. | — | — |
| Pr68 | 1947 | — | 20 Quindar Leku. Aluminum. | — | — |
| Pr69 | 1947 | — | 20 Quindar Leku. Tombac. | — | — |
| Pr70 | 1947 | — | 50 Quindar Leku. Aluminum. | — | — |
| Pr71 | 1947 | — | 50 Quindar Leku. Tombac. | — | — |

## MINT SETS

| KM# | Date | Mintage | Identification | Issue Price | Mkt Val |
|---|---|---|---|---|---|
| MS1 | 1969 | — | KM#44-48 | 5.00 | 25.00 |

## PROOF SETS

| KM# | Date | Mintage | Identification | Issue Price | Mkt Val |
|---|---|---|---|---|---|
| PS1 | 1968 | 1,520 | KM#51, 53-56 | 470 | 2,550 |
| PS2 | 1968 | — | KM#49-56 | — | 2,650 |
| PSA2 | 1968 | 8,540 | KM#49, 50, 52 | 44.00 | 110 |
| PS3 | 1969 | — | KM#51, 53-56 | 470 | 3,385 |
| PS4 | 1969 | — | KM#49-56 | — | 3,520 |
| PSA4 | 1969 | 1,500 | KM#49, 50, 52 | 45.00 | 135 |
| PS5 | 1970 | — | KM#51.5, 53-56 | 516 | 3,515 |
| PS6 | 1970 | 500 | KM#49-50, 52 | 45.00 | 170 |
| PS7 | 1991 | 980 | KM#68-69 | — | 400 |

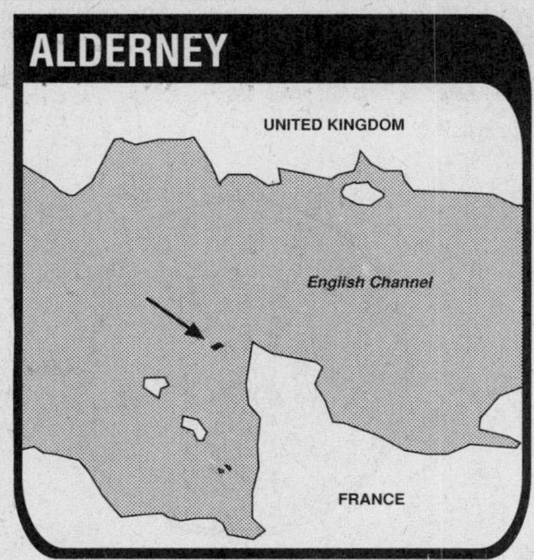


Alderney, the northernmost and third largest of the Channel Islands, separated from the coast of France by the dangerous 8-mile-wide tidal channel, has an area of 3 sq. mi. (8 km.) and a population of 1,686. It is a dependency of the British island of Guernsey, to the southwest. Capital: St. Anne. Principal industries are agriculture and raising cattle.

There is evidence of settlement in prehistoric times and Roman coins have been discovered on the island along with evidence of their buildings. Toward the close of the reign of Henry VIII, France began making plans to seize the Island of Sark. The English, realizing its strategic importance, began to build a defensive fort, which was abandoned some years later when Edward VI died. France constructed a large naval base at its northern tip, which incited the English into making Alderney the "Gibraltar of the Channel." Most of the Islanders were evacuated before the German occupation in 1940 but returned in 1945 when the Germans surrendered.

The Channel Islands have never been subject to the British Parliament and are self-governing units under the direct rule of the Crown acting through the Privy Council. Legislation was only recently introduced for the issue of its own coinage, a right it now shares with Jersey and Guernsey. Alderney is a dependency of the British island of Guernsey, to the southwest.

**RULERS**
British

**MONETARY SYSTEM**
5 Pence = 1 Shilling
25 Pence = 1 Crown
100 Pence = 1 Pound Sterling

**POUND** **KM# 4 Weight:** 9.5000 g. **Composition:** 0.9250 Silver .2826 oz. ASW **Ruler:** Queen Elizabeth II **Subject:** 40th Anniversary - Coronation

| Date | Mintage | F | VF | XF | Unc | BU |
|---|---|---|---|---|---|---|
| 1993 Proof | Est. 20,000 | Value: 35.00 | | | | |

**POUND** **KM# 12 Weight:** 9.5000 g. **Composition:** 0.9250 Silver .2826 oz. ASW **Ruler:** Queen Elizabeth II **Subject:** VE Day **Reverse:** VE Monogram and dove

| Date | Mintage | F | VF | XF | Unc | BU |
|---|---|---|---|---|---|---|
| ND(1995) Proof | Est. 20,000 | Value: 35.00 | | | | |

**POUND** **KM# 12a Weight:** 15.8000 g. **Composition:** 0.9160 Gold .4653 oz. AGW **Ruler:** Queen Elizabeth II **Subject:** VE Day **Reverse:** VE Monogram and dove

| Date | Mintage | F | VF | XF | Unc | BU |
|---|---|---|---|---|---|---|
| ND(1995) Proof | 500 | Value: 350 | | | | |

**2 POUNDS** **KM# 1 Composition:** Copper-Nickel **Ruler:** Queen Elizabeth II **Subject:** Royal Visit

| Date | Mintage | F | VF | XF | Unc | BU |
|---|---|---|---|---|---|---|
| 1989 | — | — | — | — | 10.00 | — |

**2 POUNDS** **KM# 1a Weight:** 28.2800 g. **Composition:** 0.9250 Silver .8411 oz. ASW **Ruler:** Queen Elizabeth II **Subject:** Royal Visit

| Date | Mintage | F | VF | XF | Unc | BU |
|---|---|---|---|---|---|---|
| 1989 Proof | 5,000 | Value: 50.00 | | | | |

**2 POUNDS** **KM# 1b Weight:** 47.5400 g. **Composition:** 0.9170 Gold 1.4011 oz. AGW **Ruler:** Queen Elizabeth II **Subject:** Royal Visit

| Date | Mintage | F | VF | XF | Unc | BU |
|---|---|---|---|---|---|---|
| 1989 Proof | 100 | Value: 850 | | | | |

**2 POUNDS** **KM# 2 Composition:** Copper-Nickel **Ruler:** Queen Elizabeth II **Subject:** Queen Mother's - 90th Birthday

| Date | Mintage | F | VF | XF | Unc | BU |
|---|---|---|---|---|---|---|
| 1990 | — | — | — | — | 8.50 | — |

**2 POUNDS** **KM# 2a Weight:** 28.2800 g. **Composition:** 0.9250 Silver .8411 oz. ASW **Ruler:** Queen Elizabeth II **Subject:** Royal Visit

| Date | Mintage | F | VF | XF | Unc | BU |
|---|---|---|---|---|---|---|
| 1990 Proof | 5,000 | Value: 50.00 | | | | |

**2 POUNDS** **KM# 2b Weight:** 47.5400 g. **Composition:** 0.9170 Gold 1.4011 oz. AGW **Ruler:** Queen Elizabeth II **Subject:** Queen Mother's - 90th Birthday

| Date | Mintage | F | VF | XF | Unc | BU |
|---|---|---|---|---|---|---|
| 1990 Proof | 90 | Value. 1,000 | | | | |

**2 POUNDS** **KM# 3 Composition:** Copper-Nickel **Ruler:** Queen Elizabeth II **Subject:** 40th Anniversary - Queen's Reign

| Date | Mintage | F | VF | XF | Unc | BU |
|---|---|---|---|---|---|---|
| 1992 | — | — | — | — | 8.50 | — |

**2 POUNDS** **KM# 3a Weight:** 28.2800 g. **Composition:** 0.9250 Silver .8411 oz. ASW **Ruler:** Queen Elizabeth II **Subject:** 40th Anniversary - Queen's Reign

| Date | Mintage | F | VF | XF | Unc | BU |
|---|---|---|---|---|---|---|
| 1992 Proof | 5,000 | Value: 50.00 | | | | |

**2 POUNDS** **KM# 3b Weight:** 47.5400 g. **Composition:** 0.9170 Gold 1.4011 oz. AGW **Ruler:** Queen Elizabeth II **Subject:** 40th Anniversary - Queen's Reign

| Date | Mintage | F | VF | XF | Unc | BU |
|---|---|---|---|---|---|---|
| 1992 Proof | 150 | Value: 850 | | | | |

**2 POUNDS** **KM# 5 Composition:** Copper-Nickel **Ruler:** Queen Elizabeth II **Subject:** 40th Anniversary - Coronation

| Date | Mintage | F | VF | XF | Unc | BU |
|---|---|---|---|---|---|---|
| 1993 | — | — | — | — | 8.00 | — |

**2 POUNDS** **KM# 5a Weight:** 28.2800 g. **Composition:** 0.9250 Silver .8411 oz. ASW **Ruler:** Queen Elizabeth II **Subject:** 40th Anniversary - Coronation

| Date | Mintage | F | VF | XF | Unc | BU |
|---|---|---|---|---|---|---|
| 1993 Proof | Est. 5,000 | Value: 50.00 | | | | |

**2 POUNDS** **KM# 7 Composition:** Copper-Nickel **Ruler:** Queen Elizabeth II **Subject:** Normandy Invasion **Reverse:** Normandy beach landing scene

| Date | Mintage | F | VF | XF | Unc | BU |
|---|---|---|---|---|---|---|
| 1994 | Est. 5,000,000 | — | — | — | 8.00 | — |

**2 POUNDS** **KM# 7a Weight:** 28.2800 g. **Composition:** 0.9250 Silver .8411 oz. ASW **Ruler:** Queen Elizabeth II **Subject:** Normandy Invasion **Reverse:** Normandy beach landing scene

| Date | Mintage | F | VF | XF | Unc | BU |
|---|---|---|---|---|---|---|
| 1994 Proof | — | Value: 50.00 | | | | |

**2 POUNDS** **KM# 13 Composition:** Copper-Nickel **Ruler:** Queen Elizabeth II **Subject:** Islander's Return **Reverse:** Steamship

| Date | Mintage | F | VF | XF | Unc | BU |
|---|---|---|---|---|---|---|
| ND(1995) | — | — | — | — | 10.00 | — |

**2 POUNDS** **KM# 13a Weight:** 28.2800 g. **Composition:** 0.9250 Silver .8411 oz. ASW **Ruler:** Queen Elizabeth II **Subject:** Isalnder's Return **Reverse:** Steamship

| Date | Mintage | F | VF | XF | Unc | BU |
|---|---|---|---|---|---|---|
| ND(1995) Proof | 10,000 | Value: 50.00 | | | | |

**2 POUNDS** **KM# 13b** **Weight:** 47.5400 g. **Composition:** 0.9160 Gold 1.4011 oz. AGW **Ruler:** Queen Elizabeth II **Subject:** Islander's Return **Reverse:** Steamship

| Date | Mintage | F | VF | XF | Unc | BU |
|---|---|---|---|---|---|---|
| ND(1995) Proof | 250 | Value: 850 | | | | |

**2 POUNDS** **KM# 16** **Composition:** Copper-Nickel **Ruler:** Queen Elizabeth II **Subject:** World Wildlife Fund **Obverse:** Queen's portrait **Reverse:** 2 Puffin birds

| Date | Mintage | F | VF | XF | Unc | BU |
|---|---|---|---|---|---|---|
| 1997 | — | — | — | — | 10.00 | — |

**2 POUNDS** **KM# 16a** **Weight:** 28.2800 g. **Composition:** 0.9250 Silver .8410 oz. ASW **Ruler:** Queen Elizabeth II **Subject:** World Wildlife Fund **Reverse:** 2 Puffin birds

| Date | Mintage | F | VF | XF | Unc | BU |
|---|---|---|---|---|---|---|
| 1997 Proof | — | Value: 47.50 | | | | |

**2 POUNDS** **KM# 17** **Weight:** 28.2800 g. **Composition:** 0.9250 Silver .8410 oz. ASW **Ruler:** Queen Elizabeth II **Subject:** Queen's Golden Wedding Anniversary **Obverse:** Queen's portrait **Reverse:** Queen crowning Prince Charles

| Date | Mintage | F | VF | XF | Unc | BU |
|---|---|---|---|---|---|---|
| ND(1997) | — | — | — | — | 8.50 | — |

**2 POUNDS** **KM# 18** **Weight:** 28.2800 g. **Composition:** 0.9250 Silver .8410 oz. ASW **Ruler:** Queen Elizabeth II **Subject:** Total Eclipse of the Sun **Obverse:** Queen's portrait **Reverse:** 2 sea birds and church

| Date | Mintage | F | VF | XF | Unc | BU |
|---|---|---|---|---|---|---|
| 1999 | — | — | — | — | 14.00 | — |

**2 POUNDS** **KM# 18a** **Weight:** 28.2800 g. **Composition:** 0.9250 Silver .8410 oz. ASW **Ruler:** Queen Elizabeth II **Subject:** Total Eclipse of the Sun **Obverse:** Queen's portrait **Reverse:** 2 sea birds and church

| Date | Mintage | F | VF | XF | Unc | BU |
|---|---|---|---|---|---|---|
| 1999 Proof | Est. 10,000 | Value: 47.50 | | | | |

**2 POUNDS** **KM# 18b** **Weight:** 47.5400 g. **Composition:** 0.9170 Gold 1.4011 oz. AGW **Ruler:** Queen Elizabeth II **Subject:** Total Eclipse of the Sun **Obverse:** Queen's portrait **Reverse:** 2 sea birds and church

| Date | Mintage | F | VF | XF | Unc | BU |
|---|---|---|---|---|---|---|
| 1999 Proof | Est. 100 | Value: 1,300 | | | | |

**5 POUNDS** **KM# 14** **Composition:** Copper-Nickel **Ruler:** Queen Elizabeth II **Subject:** Queen Mother - Children

| Date | Mintage | F | VF | XF | Unc | BU |
|---|---|---|---|---|---|---|
| 1995 | — | — | — | — | 15.00 | — |

**5 POUNDS** **KM# 14a** **Weight:** 28.2800 g. **Composition:** 0.9250 Silver .8411 oz. ASW **Ruler:** Queen Elizabeth II **Subject:** Queen Morther - Children

| Date | Mintage | F | VF | XF | Unc | BU |
|---|---|---|---|---|---|---|
| 1995 Proof | 10,000 | Value: 50.00 | | | | |

**5 POUNDS** **KM# 14b** **Weight:** 47.5400 g. **Composition:** 0.9160 Gold 1.4011 oz. AGW **Ruler:** Queen Elizabeth II **Subject:** Queen Mother - Children

| Date | Mintage | F | VF | XF | Unc | BU |
|---|---|---|---|---|---|---|
| 1995 Proof | 150 | Value: 850 | | | | |

**5 POUNDS** **KM# 15** **Composition:** Copper-Nickel **Ruler:** Queen Elizabeth II **Subject:** Queen Elizabeth's 70th Birthday - Flowers

| Date | Mintage | F | VF | XF | Unc | BU |
|---|---|---|---|---|---|---|
| 1996 | — | — | — | — | 16.00 | — |

**5 POUNDS** **KM# 15a** **Weight:** 28.2800 g. **Composition:** 0.9250 Silver .8411 oz. ASW **Ruler:** Queen Elizabeth II **Subject:** Queen Elizabeth's 70th Birthday - Flowers

| Date | Mintage | F | VF | XF | Unc | BU |
|---|---|---|---|---|---|---|
| 1996 Proof | Est. 10,000 | Value: 50.00 | | | | |

**5 POUNDS** **KM# 15b** **Weight:** 47.5400 g. **Composition:** 0.9170 Gold 1.4012 oz. AGW **Ruler:** Queen Elizabeth II **Subject:** Queen Elizabeth's 70th Birthday - Flowers

| Date | Mintage | F | VF | XF | Unc | BU |
|---|---|---|---|---|---|---|
| 1996 Proof | 250 | Value: 1,225 | | | | |

**5 POUNDS** **KM# 19** **Composition:** Copper-Nickel **Ruler:** Queen Elizabeth II **Subject:** Total Eclipse of the Sun **Obverse:** Portrait of Queen **Reverse:** Map of Alderney, pre, post and actual phases of eclipse

| Date | Mintage | F | VF | XF | Unc | BU |
|---|---|---|---|---|---|---|
| 1999 | — | — | — | — | 18.00 | — |

**5 POUNDS** **KM# 19a** **Weight:** 28.2800 g. **Composition:** 0.9250 Silver .8410 oz. ASW **Ruler:** Queen Elizabeth II

| Date | Mintage | F | VF | XF | Unc | BU |
|---|---|---|---|---|---|---|
| 1999 Proof | Est. 10,000 | Value: 55.00 | | | | |

**5 POUNDS** **KM# 20** **Weight:** 47.5400 g. **Composition:** 0.9166 Gold 1.4011 oz. AGW **Ruler:** Queen Elizabeth II **Subject:** Winston Churchill **Obverse:** Queen's portrait **Reverse:** Winston Churchill wearing hat **Edge:** Reeded **Note:** Struck at the British Royal mint.

| Date | Mintage | F | VF | XF | Unc | BU |
|---|---|---|---|---|---|---|
| 1999 Proof | 125,000 | Value: 865 | | | | |

**5 POUNDS** **KM# 21** **Weight:** 28.2800 g. **Composition:** Copper-Nickel **Ruler:** Queen Elizabeth II **Subject:** 60th Anniversary - Battle of Britain **Obverse:** Queen Elizabeth's head right. **Reverse:** Two spitfires in flight, pilot at bottom center. **Edge:** Reeded.

| Date | Mintage | F | VF | XF | Unc | BU |
|---|---|---|---|---|---|---|
| 2000 | — | — | — | — | 18.00 | — |

**5 POUNDS** **KM# 21a** **Weight:** 28.2800 g. **Composition:** 0.9250 Silver .8410 oz. ASW **Ruler:** Queen Elizabeth II **Subject:** 60th Anniversary - Battle of Britain **Obverse:** Queen Elizabeth's head right. **Reverse:** Two spitfires in flight, pilot at bottom center. **Edge:** Reeded.

| Date | Mintage | F | VF | XF | Unc | BU |
|---|---|---|---|---|---|---|
| 2000 Proof | — | Value: 55.00 | | | | |

**10 POUNDS** **KM# 8** **Weight:** 3.1300 g. **Composition:** 0.9990 Gold .1005 oz. AGW **Ruler:** Queen Elizabeth II **Subject:** Normandy Invasion **Reverse:** Paratroopers and Transport Plane

| Date | Mintage | F | VF | XF | Unc | BU |
|---|---|---|---|---|---|---|
| 1994 Proof | Est. 1,000 | Value: 80.00 | | | | |

**25 POUNDS** **KM# 6** **Weight:** 8.5130 g. **Composition:** 0.9170 Gold .2507 oz. AGW **Ruler:** Queen Elizabeth II **Subject:** 40th Anniversary - Coronation **Reverse:** Royal Carriage

| Date | Mintage | F | VF | XF | Unc | BU |
|---|---|---|---|---|---|---|
| 1993 Proof | Est. 1,000 | Value: 190 | | | | |

**25 POUNDS** **KM# 9** **Weight:** 7.8100 g. **Composition:** 0.9990 Gold .2509 oz. AGW **Ruler:** Queen Elizabeth II **Subject:** Normandy Invasion **Reverse:** Fighter Planes and Tank

| Date | Mintage | F | VF | XF | Unc | BU |
|---|---|---|---|---|---|---|
| 1994 Proof | Est. 1,000 | Value: 190 | | | | |

**25 POUNDS** KM# 23 **Weight:** 28.0000 g. **Composition:** Copper-Nickel **Ruler:** Queen Elizabeth II **Subject:** Golden Wedding Anniversary - Elizabeth and Philip **Obverse:** Queen Elizabeth's head right. **Reverse:** Queen Elizabeth crowning Charles as Prince of Wales, date (1947-1997) in legend.

| Date | Mintage | F | VF | XF | Unc | BU |
|---|---|---|---|---|---|---|
| ND(1997) | — | — | — | — | 18.00 | — |

**25 POUNDS** KM# 23a **Weight:** 28.2800 g. **Composition:** 0.9250 Silver **Ruler:** Queen Elizabeth II **Subject:** Golden Wedding Anniversary - Elizabeth and Philip **Obverse:** Queen Elizabeth's head right. **Reverse:** Queen Elizabeth crowning Charles as Prince of Wales, date (1947-1997) in legend.

| Date | Mintage | F | VF | XF | Unc | BU |
|---|---|---|---|---|---|---|
| ND(1997) Proof | — | Value: 19.50 | | | | |

**25 POUNDS** KM# 22 **Weight:** 7.8100 g. **Composition:** 0.9160 Gold .2302 oz. AGW **Ruler:** Queen Elizabeth II **Subject:** 60th Anniversary - Battle of Britain **Obverse:** Queen Elizabeth's head right. **Reverse:** Two spitfires in flight, pilot at bottom center. **Edge:** Reeded.

| Date | Mintage | F | VF | XF | Unc | BU |
|---|---|---|---|---|---|---|
| 2000 | — | Value: 275 | | | | |

**50 POUNDS** KM# 10 **Weight:** 15.6000 g. **Composition:** 0.9990 Gold .5014 oz. AGW **Ruler:** Queen Elizabeth II **Subject:** Normandy Invasion **Reverse:** British Gliders

| Date | Mintage | F | VF | XF | Unc | BU |
|---|---|---|---|---|---|---|
| 1994 In Proof sets only | Est. 1,000 | Value: 400 | | | | |

**100 POUNDS** KM# 11 **Weight:** 31.2100 g. **Composition:** 0.9990 Gold 1.0025 oz. AGW **Ruler:** Queen Elizabeth II **Subject:** Normandy Invasion **Reverse:** Normandy beach landing scene

| Date | Mintage | F | VF | XF | Unc | BU |
|---|---|---|---|---|---|---|
| 1994 Proof | Est. 500 | Value: 815 | | | | |

## PIEFORTS

| KM# | Date | Mintage | Identification | Mkt Val |
|---|---|---|---|---|
| P1 | 1989 | 500 | 2 Pounds. 0.9250 Silver. KM#1a. | 100 |
| P2 | 1990 | 500 | 2 Pounds. 0.9250 Silver. KM#2a. | 100 |
| P3 | 1992 | 750 | 2 Pounds. 0.9250 Silver. KM#3a. | 90.00 |
| P4 | 1993 | 500 | 2 Pounds. 0.9250 Silver. KM#5a. | 95.00 |
| P5 | 1994 | 500 | 2 Pounds. 0.9250 Silver. KM#7a. | 95.00 |
| P6 | ND(1995) | 500 | 2 Pounds. 0.9250 Silver. KM#13a. | 100 |
| P7 | 1995 | 500 | 5 Pounds. 0.9250 Silver. KM#14a. | 100 |
| P8 | 1996 | 500 | 5 Pounds. 0.9250 Silver. KM#15a. | 90.00 |

## PROOF SETS

| KM# | Date | Mintage | Identification | Issue Price | Mkt Val |
|---|---|---|---|---|---|
| PS1 | 1994 | 500 | KM#7a, 8-11 | — | 1,550 |
| PS2 | 1994 | I.A. | KM#8-11 | — | 1,500 |
| PS3 | 1994 | 500 | KM#7a, 8-10 | — | 735 |
| PS4 | 1994 | I.A. | KM#8-10 | — | 675 |

# ALGERIA

The Democratic and Popular Republic of Algeria, a North African country fronting on the Mediterranean Sea between Tunisia and Morocco, has an area of 919,595 sq. mi. (2,381,740 sq. km.) and a population of 31.6 million. Capital: Algiers (Alger). Most of the country's working population is engaged in agriculture although a recent industrial diversification, financed by oil revenues, is making steady progress. Wines, fruits, iron and zinc ores, phosphates, tobacco products, liquified natural gas, and petroleum are exported.

Algiers, the capital and chief seaport of Algeria, was the site of Phoenician and Roman settlements before the present Moslem city was founded about 950. Nominally part of the sultanate of Tilimsan, Algiers had a large measure of independence under the amirs of its own. In 1492 the Jews and Moors who had been expelled from Spain settled in Algiers and enjoyed an increasing influence until the imposition of Turkish control in 1518. For the following three centuries, Algiers was the headquarters of the notorious Barbary pirates as Turkish control became more and more nominal. The French took Algiers in 1830, and after a long and wearisome war completed the conquest of Algeria and annexed it to France, 1848. Following the armistice signed by France and Nazi Germany on June 22, 1940, Algeria fell under Vichy Government control until liberated by the Allied invasion forces under the command of Gen. D. D. Eisenhower on Nov. 8, 1942. The inability to obtain equal rights with Frenchmen led to an organized revolt, which began on Nov. 1, 1954 and lasted until a ceasefire was signed on July I, 1962. Independence was proclaimed on July 5, 1962, following a self-determination referendum, and the Republic was declared on September 25, 1962.

**MINT MARKS**
Paris – Privy marks only

**MONETARY SYSTEMS**
100 Centimes = 1 Franc

## FRENCH OCCUPATION

### COLONIAL COINAGE

**20 FRANCS** KM# 91 **Composition:** Copper-Nickel

| Date | Mintage | F | VF | XF | Unc | BU |
|---|---|---|---|---|---|---|
| 1949(a) | 25,556,000 | 1.00 | 2.00 | 5.00 | 10.00 | — |
| 1956(a) | 7,500,000 | 1.00 | 2.50 | 6.00 | 12.50 | — |

**50 FRANCS** KM# 92 **Composition:** Copper-Nickel

| Date | Mintage | F | VF | XF | Unc | BU |
|---|---|---|---|---|---|---|
| 1949(a) | 18,000,000 | 1.50 | 3.00 | 9.00 | 18.00 | — |

**100 FRANCS** KM# 93 **Composition:** Copper-Nickel **Note:** During World War II homeland coins were struck at the Paris Mint and the French 2 Francs, Y#89 were struck at the Philadelphia Mint for use in French African Territories.

| Date | Mintage | F | VF | XF | Unc | BU |
|---|---|---|---|---|---|---|
| 1950(a) | 22,189,000 | 1.50 | 3.00 | 10.00 | 20.00 | — |
| 1952(a) | 12,000,000 | 2.00 | 4.00 | 12.00 | 25.00 | — |

## TOKEN COINAGE

**5 CENTIMES** KM# TnB1 **Composition:** Aluminum **Issuer:** Bone Chamber of Commerce

| Date | Mintage | F | VF | XF | Unc | BU |
|---|---|---|---|---|---|---|
| 1915 | — | 6.00 | 10.00 | 15.00 | 30.00 | — |
| ND(1915) | — | 5.00 | 9.00 | 13.00 | 25.00 | — |

**5 CENTIMES** KM# TnC1 **Composition:** Aluminum **Issuer:** Bougie Chamber of Commerce

| Date | Mintage | F | VF | XF | Unc | BU |
|---|---|---|---|---|---|---|
| 1915 | — | 3.50 | 8.00 | 20.00 | 40.00 | — |

**5 CENTIMES** KM# TnB2 **Composition:** Brass **Issuer:** Bone Chamber of Commerce **Note:** Not a regular issue.

| Date | Mintage | F | VF | XF | Unc | BU |
|---|---|---|---|---|---|---|
| ND(1915) | — | — | 30.00 | 60.00 | 120 | — |

**5 CENTIMES** KM# TnA1 (KMTn1) **Composition:** Aluminum **Issuer:** Alger Chamber of Commerce **Reverse:** With J. Bory

| Date | Mintage | F | VF | XF | Unc | BU |
|---|---|---|---|---|---|---|
| 1916 | — | 5.00 | 10.00 | 18.00 | 35.00 | — |
| 1917 | — | — | 175 | 250 | 500 | — |
| **Note:** The year 1917 is not a regular issue | | | | | | |
| 1919 | — | 4.00 | 6.00 | 12.00 | 18.00 | — |
| 1921 | — | 5.00 | 10.00 | 18.00 | 35.00 | — |

**5 CENTIMES** KM# TnA2 (KMTn2) **Composition:** Iron **Issuer:** Alger Chamber of Commerce

| Date | Mintage | F | VF | XF | Unc | BU |
|---|---|---|---|---|---|---|
| 1916 | — | 30.00 | 50.00 | 100 | 200 | — |

**5 CENTIMES** KM# TnA3 (KMTn3) **Composition:** Zinc **Issuer:** Alger Chamber of Commerce

| Date | Mintage | F | VF | XF | Unc | BU |
|---|---|---|---|---|---|---|
| 1917 | — | 3.50 | 10.00 | 20.00 | 40.00 | — |
| 1919 | — | — | 35.00 | 70.00 | 150 | — |
| **Note:** The year 1919 is not a regular issue | | | | | | |

**5 CENTIMES** KM# TnA4 (KMTn4) **Composition:** Brass **Issuer:** Alger Chamber of Commerce

| Date | Mintage | F | VF | XF | Unc | BU |
|---|---|---|---|---|---|---|
| 1921 | — | — | 35.00 | 70.00 | 150 | — |
| **Note:** Not a regular issue | | | | | | |

**5 CENTIMES** KM# TnE1 **Composition:** Aluminum **Issuer:** Oran Chamber of Commerce

| Date | Mintage | F | VF | XF | Unc | BU |
|---|---|---|---|---|---|---|
| 1921 | — | 4.50 | 9.00 | 25.00 | 50.00 | — |

**5 CENTIMES** KM# TnD1 **Composition:** Aluminum **Issuer:** Constantine Chamber of Commerce

| Date | Mintage | F | VF | XF | Unc | BU |
|---|---|---|---|---|---|---|
| 1922 | — | 20.00 | 30.00 | 50.00 | 100 | — |

**10 CENTIMES** KM# TnB3 **Composition:** Aluminum **Issuer:** Bone Chamber of Commerce

| Date | Mintage | F | VF | XF | Unc | BU |
|---|---|---|---|---|---|---|
| 1915 | — | 4.00 | 10.00 | 22.00 | 40.00 | — |
| ND(1915) | — | 4.00 | 9.00 | 20.00 | 35.00 | — |

**10 CENTIMES** **KM# TnC2.1** **Composition:** Aluminum **Issuer:** Bougie Chamber of Commerce **Obverse:** Dots flank date

| Date | Mintage | F | VF | XF | Unc | BU |
|---|---|---|---|---|---|---|
| 1915 | — | 3.50 | 10.00 | 25.00 | 50.00 | — |

**10 CENTIMES** **KM# TnC2.2** **Composition:** Aluminum **Issuer:** Bougie Chamber of Commerce **Obverse:** Dot and triangle at right of date

| Date | Mintage | F | VF | XF | Unc | BU |
|---|---|---|---|---|---|---|
| 1915 | — | 3.00 | 6.00 | 15.00 | 30.00 | — |

**10 CENTIMES** **KM# TnC2a** **Composition:** Zinc **Issuer:** Bougie Chamber of Commerce

| Date | Mintage | F | VF | XF | Unc | BU |
|---|---|---|---|---|---|---|
| 1915 | — | 30.00 | 50.00 | 120 | 250 | — |

**10 CENTIMES** **KM# TnB4** **Composition:** Brass **Issuer:** Bone Chamber of Commerce **Note:** Not a regular issue.

| Date | Mintage | F | VF | XF | Unc | BU |
|---|---|---|---|---|---|---|
| ND(1915) | — | — | 32.50 | 65.00 | 130 | — |

**10 CENTIMES** **KM# TnA5 (KMTn5)** **Composition:** Aluminum **Issuer:** Alger Chamber of Commerce

| Date | Mintage | F | VF | XF | Unc | BU |
|---|---|---|---|---|---|---|
| 1916 Without J. Bory | — | 6.00 | 10.00 | 20.00 | 45.00 | — |
| 1918 Without J. BOry | — | 6.00 | 10.00 | 15.00 | 32.00 | — |
| 1919 With J. Bory | — | 4.00 | 6.00 | 12.00 | 25.00 | — |
| 1921 With J. BOry | — | 3.00 | 6.00 | 12.00 | 25.00 | — |
| 1921 Without J. Bory | — | 6.00 | 10.00 | 20.00 | 45.00 | — |

**10 CENTIMES** **KM# TnA6 (KMTn6)** **Composition:** Iron **Issuer:** Alger Chamber of Commerce **Reverse:** Without J. Bory

| Date | Mintage | F | VF | XF | Unc | BU |
|---|---|---|---|---|---|---|
| 1916 | — | 10.00 | 22.00 | 50.00 | 100 | — |

**10 CENTIMES** **KM# TnA7 (KMTn7)** **Composition:** Zinc **Issuer:** Alger Chamber of Commerce

| Date | Mintage | F | VF | XF | Unc | BU |
|---|---|---|---|---|---|---|
| 1917 | — | 5.00 | 12.50 | 30.00 | 60.00 | — |
| 1918 | — | — | 40.00 | 80.00 | 160 | — |
| **Note:** 1918 is not a regular issue | | | | | | |
| 1919 | — | — | 40.00 | 80.00 | 160 | — |
| **Note:** 1919 is not a regular issue | | | | | | |

**10 CENTIMES** **KM# TnA8 (KMTn8)** **Composition:** Brass **Issuer:** Alger Chamber of Commerce **Note:** Not a regular issue.

| Date | Mintage | F | VF | XF | Unc | BU |
|---|---|---|---|---|---|---|
| 1919 | — | — | 50.00 | 110 | 225 | — |
| 1921 | — | — | 65.00 | 125 | 245 | — |

**10 CENTIMES** **KM# TnE2** **Composition:** Aluminum **Issuer:** Oran Chamber of Commerce

| Date | Mintage | F | VF | XF | Unc | BU |
|---|---|---|---|---|---|---|
| 1921 | — | 3.50 | 8.00 | 22.00 | 45.00 | — |

**10 CENTIMES** **KM# TnE2a** **Composition:** Brass **Issuer:** Oran Chamber of Commerce

| Date | Mintage | F | VF | XF | Unc | BU |
|---|---|---|---|---|---|---|
| 1921 | — | — | 75.00 | 150 | 300 | — |

**10 CENTIMES** **KM# TnD2** **Composition:** Aluminum **Issuer:** Constantine Chamber of Commerce

| Date | Mintage | F | VF | XF | Unc | BU |
|---|---|---|---|---|---|---|
| 1922 | — | 15.00 | 25.00 | 45.00 | 90.00 | — |

**25 CENTIMES** **KM# TnE3** **Composition:** Aluminum **Issuer:** Oran Chamber of Commerce **Obverse:** Similar to 10 Centimes, KM#TnE2 **Reverse:** Similar to 25 Centimes, KM#TnE4

| Date | Mintage | F | VF | XF | Unc | BU |
|---|---|---|---|---|---|---|
| 1921 | — | 4.00 | 8.50 | 25.00 | 50.00 | — |

**25 CENTIMES** **KM# TnE4** **Composition:** Aluminum **Issuer:** Oran Chamber of Commerce **Obverse:** Small crowned shield, chains

| Date | Mintage | F | VF | XF | Unc | BU |
|---|---|---|---|---|---|---|
| 1921 | — | 5.00 | 10.00 | 30.00 | 60.00 | — |

**25 CENTIMES** **KM# TnE5** **Composition:** Aluminum **Issuer:** Oran Chamber of Commerce **Note:** For further listings of private token issues refer to the catalogue of French Emergency Tokens of 1914-1922 by Robert Lamb.

| Date | Mintage | F | VF | XF | Unc | BU |
|---|---|---|---|---|---|---|
| 1922 | — | 5.00 | 10.00 | 30.00 | 60.00 | — |

**50 CENTIMES** **KM# TnB5** **Composition:** Brass **Issuer:** Bone Chamber of Commerce

| Date | Mintage | F | VF | XF | Unc | BU |
|---|---|---|---|---|---|---|
| ND(1915) | — | 15.00 | 30.00 | 50.00 | 75.00 | — |

**50 CENTIMES** **KM# TnB6** **Composition:** Copper-Nickel **Issuer:** Bone Chamber of Commerce **Note:** Not a regular issue.

| Date | Mintage | F | VF | XF | Unc | BU |
|---|---|---|---|---|---|---|
| ND(1915) | — | — | 40.00 | 90.00 | 200 | — |

**FRANC** **KM# TnB7** **Composition:** Brass **Issuer:** Bone Chamber of Commerce

| Date | Mintage | F | VF | XF | Unc | BU |
|---|---|---|---|---|---|---|
| ND(1915) | — | 20.00 | 35.00 | 60.00 | 100 | — |

**FRANC** **KM# TnB8** **Composition:** Copper-Nickel **Issuer:** Bone Chamber of Commerce **Note:** Not a regular issue.

| Date | Mintage | F | VF | XF | Unc | BU |
|---|---|---|---|---|---|---|
| ND(1915) | — | — | 60.00 | 120 | 225 | — |

**FRANC** **KM# TnB9** **Composition:** Copper **Issuer:** Bone Chamber of Commerce **Note:** Not a regular issue.

| Date | Mintage | F | VF | XF | Unc | BU |
|---|---|---|---|---|---|---|
| ND(1915) | — | — | 90.00 | 150 | 300 | — |

# REPUBLIC

## STANDARD COINAGE

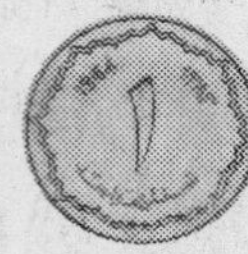

**CENTIME** **KM# 94** **Composition:** Aluminum

| Date | Mintage | F | VF | XF | Unc | BU |
|---|---|---|---|---|---|---|
| AH1383(1964) | 35,000,000 | — | 0.20 | 0.40 | 1.00 | — |

**2 CENTIMES** **KM# 95** **Composition:** Aluminum

| Date | Mintage | F | VF | XF | Unc | BU |
|---|---|---|---|---|---|---|
| AH1383(1964) | 50,000,000 | — | 0.20 | 0.40 | 1.00 | — |

**5 CENTIMES** **KM# 96** **Composition:** Aluminum

| Date | Mintage | F | VF | XF | Unc | BU |
|---|---|---|---|---|---|---|
| AH1383(1964) | 40,000,000 | — | 0.25 | 0.45 | 1.25 | — |

**5 CENTIMES** **KM# 101** **Composition:** Aluminum **Series:** F.A.O. **Subject:** 1st Four Year Plan **Note:** Varieties exist.

| Date | Mintage | F | VF | XF | Unc | BU |
|---|---|---|---|---|---|---|
| ND(1970) | 10,000,000 | — | 0.15 | 0.30 | 0.75 | — |

**5 CENTIMES** **KM# 106** **Composition:** Aluminum **Series:** F.A.O. **Subject:** 2nd Four Year Plan

| Date | Mintage | F | VF | XF | Unc | BU |
|---|---|---|---|---|---|---|
| ND(1974) | 10,000,000 | — | 0.15 | 0.30 | 0.75 | — |

**5 CENTIMES** **KM# 113** **Composition:** Aluminum **Series:** F.A.O. **Subject:** 1st Five Year Plan

| Date | Mintage | F | VF | XF | Unc | BU |
|---|---|---|---|---|---|---|
| ND(1980) | — | — | 0.20 | 0.50 | 1.50 | — |

**5 CENTIMES** **KM# 116** **Composition:** Aluminum **Series:** F.A.O. **Subject:** 2nd Five Year Plan **Note:** Varieties exist in planchet thickness.

| Date | Mintage | F | VF | XF | Unc | BU |
|---|---|---|---|---|---|---|
| ND(1985) | — | — | 0.10 | 0.25 | 0.70 | — |

**10 CENTIMES** **KM# 97** **Composition:** Aluminum-Bronze

| Date | Mintage | F | VF | XF | Unc | BU |
|---|---|---|---|---|---|---|
| AH1383(1964) | — | — | 0.25 | 0.50 | 1.50 | — |

**10 CENTIMES** **KM# 115** **Composition:** Aluminum **Note:** Varieties exist.

| Date | Mintage | F | VF | XF | Unc | BU |
|---|---|---|---|---|---|---|
| 1984 | — | — | 0.15 | 0.30 | 0.75 | — |

**20 CENTIMES** **KM# 98** **Composition:** Aluminum-Bronze

| Date | Mintage | F | VF | XF | Unc | BU |
|---|---|---|---|---|---|---|
| AH1383(1964) | — | — | 0.25 | 0.65 | 1.75 | — |

**20 CENTIMES** **KM# 103** **Composition:** Brass **Series:** F.A.O. **Subject:** Agricultural Revolution

| Date | Mintage | F | VF | XF | Unc | BU |
|---|---|---|---|---|---|---|
| 1972 | 20,000,000 | — | 0.10 | 0.25 | 0.75 | — |

**20 CENTIMES** **KM# 107.1** **Composition:** Aluminum-Bronze **Series:** F.A.O.

| Date | Mintage | F | VF | XF | Unc | BU |
|---|---|---|---|---|---|---|
| 1975 | 50,000,000 | — | 0.15 | 0.30 | 1.50 | — |

**20 CENTIMES** **KM# 107.2** **Composition:** Aluminum-Bronze **Series:** F.A.O. **Obverse:** Small flower above 20

| Date | Mintage | F | VF | XF | Unc | BU |
|---|---|---|---|---|---|---|
| 1975 | Inc. above | — | 0.15 | 0.30 | 1.50 | — |

**20 CENTIMES** **KM# 118** **Composition:** Aluminum-Bronze **Series:** F.A.O.

| Date | Mintage | F | VF | XF | Unc | BU |
|---|---|---|---|---|---|---|
| 1987 | 60,000,000 | — | 0.15 | 0.30 | 1.50 | — |

**50 CENTIMES** **KM# 99** **Composition:** Aluminum-Bronze

| Date | Mintage | F | VF | XF | Unc | BU |
|---|---|---|---|---|---|---|
| AH1383(1964) | — | — | 0.25 | 0.65 | 1.75 | — |

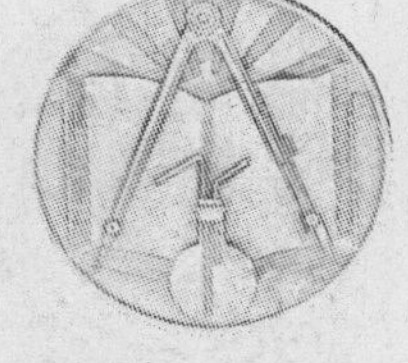

**50 CENTIMES** **KM# 102** **Composition:** Copper-Nickel-Zinc

| Date | Mintage | F | VF | XF | Unc | BU |
|---|---|---|---|---|---|---|
| AH1391(1971) | 10,000,000 | — | 0.15 | 0.30 | 1.00 | — |
| AH1393(1973) | — | — | 0.15 | 0.30 | 1.00 | — |

**50 CENTIMES** **KM# 109** **Composition:** Brass **Subject:** 30th Anniversary French-Algerian Clash

| Date | Mintage | F | VF | XF | Unc | BU |
|---|---|---|---|---|---|---|
| ND(1975) | 18,000,000 | — | 0.20 | 0.50 | 2.00 | — |

**50 CENTIMES** **KM# 111** **Composition:** Aluminum-Bronze **Subject:** 1400th Anniversary of Mohammad's Flight

| Date | Mintage | F | VF | XF | Unc | BU |
|---|---|---|---|---|---|---|
| AH1400(1980) | — | — | 0.20 | 0.50 | 2.50 | — |
| AH1401(1981) | — | — | 0.20 | 0.50 | 2.50 | — |

**50 CENTIMES** **KM# 119** **Composition:** Aluminum-Bronze **Subject:** 25th Anniversary of Constitution

| Date | Mintage | F | VF | XF | Unc | BU |
|---|---|---|---|---|---|---|
| 1988 | — | — | 0.15 | 0.35 | 2.00 | — |

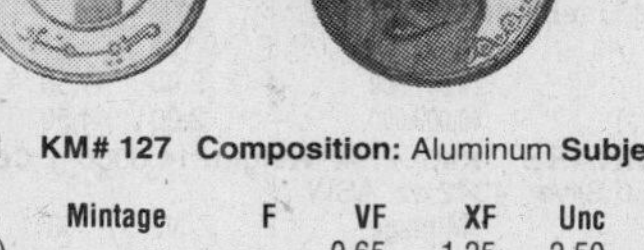

**1/4 DINAR** **KM# 127** **Composition:** Aluminum **Subject:** Fennec Fox

| Date | Mintage | F | VF | XF | Unc | BU |
|---|---|---|---|---|---|---|
| AH1413(1992) | — | — | 0.65 | 1.25 | 2.50 | — |
| AH1413 Proof | — | Value: 12.00 | | | | |
| AH1418(1998) | — | — | 0.65 | 1.25 | 2.50 | — |

**1/2 DINAR** **KM# 128** **Composition:** Steel **Subject:** Barbary Horse

| Date | Mintage | F | VF | XF | Unc | BU |
|---|---|---|---|---|---|---|
| AH1413(1992) | — | — | 0.65 | 1.25 | 2.50 | — |
| AH1413 Proof | — | Value: 12.00 | | | | |

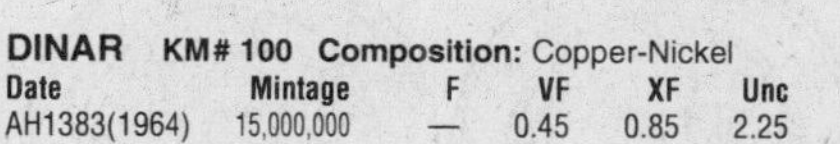

**DINAR** **KM# 100** **Composition:** Copper-Nickel

| Date | Mintage | F | VF | XF | Unc | BU |
|---|---|---|---|---|---|---|
| AH1383(1964) | 15,000,000 | — | 0.45 | 0.85 | 2.25 | — |

**DINAR** **KM# 104.1** **Composition:** Copper-Nickel **Series:** F.A.O.

| Date | Mintage | F | VF | XF | Unc | BU |
|---|---|---|---|---|---|---|
| 1972 | 20,000,000 | — | 0.45 | 0.85 | 2.00 | — |

**DINAR** **KM# 104.2** **Composition:** Copper-Nickel **Obverse:** Legend touches inner circle

| Date | Mintage | F | VF | XF | Unc | BU |
|---|---|---|---|---|---|---|
| 1972 | Inc. above | — | 0.45 | 0.85 | 2.00 | — |

**DINAR** **KM# 112** **Composition:** Copper-Nickel **Subject:** 20th Anniversary of Independence

| Date | Mintage | F | VF | XF | Unc | BU |
|---|---|---|---|---|---|---|
| ND(1983) | — | — | 0.75 | 1.50 | 4.50 | — |

**DINAR** **KM# 117** **Composition:** Copper-Nickel **Subject:** 25th Anniversary of Independence - Monument

| Date | Mintage | F | VF | XF | Unc | BU |
|---|---|---|---|---|---|---|
| 1987 | — | — | 0.65 | 1.25 | 3.50 | — |

**DINAR** **KM# 120** **Weight:** 3.2200 g. **Composition:** 0.9200 Gold .0953 oz. AGW **Subject:** Historical Coin - 5 Aspers of Abd-el-Kader

| Date | Mintage | F | VF | XF | Unc | BU |
|---|---|---|---|---|---|---|
| AH1411(1991) | — | — | — | — | 125 | — |

**DINAR** **KM# 129** **Composition:** Steel **Subject:** Prehistoric Buffalo

| Date | Mintage | F | VF | XF | Unc | BU |
|---|---|---|---|---|---|---|
| AH1413(1992) | — | — | 1.00 | 2.00 | 4.50 | — |
| AH1413 Proof | — | Value: 15.00 | | | | |
| AH1417(1997) | — | — | — | 2.00 | 4.50 | — |

**2 DINARS** **KM# 121** **Weight:** 6.4500 g. **Composition:** 0.9200 Gold .1908 oz. AGW **Subject:** Historical Coin - Dinar of 762 A.D. Rostomiden Dynasty

| Date | Mintage | F | VF | XF | Unc | BU |
|---|---|---|---|---|---|---|
| AH1411(1991) | — | — | — | — | 250 | — |

**2 DINARS** **KM# 130** **Composition:** Steel **Subject:** Camel's Head

| Date | Mintage | F | VF | XF | Unc | BU |
|---|---|---|---|---|---|---|
| AH1413(1992) | — | — | 1.00 | 2.50 | 5.50 | — |
| AH1413 Proof | — | Value: 18.00 | | | | |
| AH1417(1996) | — | — | 1.00 | 2.50 | 5.50 | — |

**2 DINARS** **KM# 133** **Composition:** Gold **Subject:** Historical Coin - 2 Dinar of Abd Al-Qadir, AH1222-1300

| Date | Mintage | F | VF | XF | Unc | BU |
|---|---|---|---|---|---|---|
| AH1417(1996) | — | — | 1.00 | 2.50 | 5.50 | — |

**5 DINARS** **KM# 105a.1** **Composition:** Nickel

| Date | Mintage | F | VF | XF | Unc | BU |
|---|---|---|---|---|---|---|
| ND(1972)(a) | — | — | 4.00 | 8.00 | 14.50 | — |

**5 DINARS** **KM# 105** **Weight:** 12.0000 g. **Composition:** 0.7500 Silver .2893 oz. ASW **Series:** F.A.O. **Subject:** 10th Anniversary **Note:** Privy mark owl.

| Date | Mintage | F | VF | XF | Unc | BU |
|---|---|---|---|---|---|---|
| ND(1972)(a) | — | — | 5.00 | 10.00 | 16.50 | — |

**5 DINARS** **KM# 108** **Composition:** Nickel **Subject:** 20th Anniversary of Revolution

| Date | Mintage | F | VF | XF | Unc | BU |
|---|---|---|---|---|---|---|
| ND(1974)(a) | — | — | 3.50 | 7.00 | 12.50 | — |

**5 DINARS** **KM# 105a.2** **Composition:** Nickel **Note:** Privy mark dolphin.

| Date | Mintage | F | VF | XF | Unc | BU |
|---|---|---|---|---|---|---|
| ND(1974)(a) | — | — | 4.00 | 8.00 | 14.50 | — |

**5 DINARS** **KM# 114** **Composition:** Nickel **Subject:** 30th Anniversary of Revolution

| Date | Mintage | F | VF | XF | Unc | BU |
|---|---|---|---|---|---|---|
| ND(1984) | — | — | 2.50 | 5.00 | 10.00 | — |

**5 DINARS** **KM# 122** **Weight:** 16.1200 g. **Composition:** 0.9200 Gold .4768 oz. AGW **Subject:** Historical Coin - Denar of Numidian King Massinissa, 238-148 B.C.

| Date | Mintage | F | VF | XF | Unc | BU |
|---|---|---|---|---|---|---|
| AH1411(1991) | — | — | — | — | 550 | — |

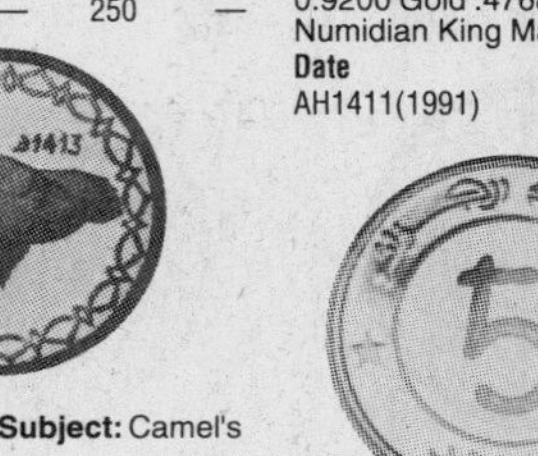

**5 DINARS** **KM# 123** **Composition:** Steel **Obverse:** Denomination **Reverse:** Elephant

| Date | Mintage | F | VF | XF | Unc | BU |
|---|---|---|---|---|---|---|
| AH1413(1992) | — | — | 1.50 | 3.50 | 7.00 | — |
| AH1413 Proof | — | Value: 20.00 | | | | |
| AH1414(1993) | — | — | 1.50 | 3.50 | 7.00 | — |
| AH1418(1997) | — | — | 1.50 | 3.50 | 7.00 | — |
| AH1417(1997) | — | — | 1.50 | 3.50 | 7.00 | — |
| AH1418(1998) | — | — | 1.50 | 3.50 | 7.00 | — |
| AH1419(1998) | — | — | 1.50 | 3.50 | 7.00 | — |

**10 DINARS** **KM# 110** **Weight:** 11.3700 g. **Composition:** Aluminum-Bronze

| Date | Mintage | F | VF | XF | Unc | BU |
|---|---|---|---|---|---|---|
| 1979 | 25,001,000 | — | 2.00 | 4.50 | 8.50 | — |
| 1981(a) | 40,000,000 | — | 2.00 | 4.50 | 8.50 | — |

**10 DINARS** **KM# 110a** **Weight:** 14.6000 g. **Composition:** 0.9250 Silver .4342 oz. ASW

| Date | Mintage | F | VF | XF | Unc | BU |
|---|---|---|---|---|---|---|
| 1979 | 1,000 | — | — | — | 35.00 | — |

**10 DINARS** **KM# 110b** **Weight:** 24.5000 g. **Composition:** 0.9000 Gold .7090 oz. AGW

| Date | Mintage | F | VF | XF | Unc | BU |
|---|---|---|---|---|---|---|
| 1979 | 100 | — | — | — | 1,250 | — |

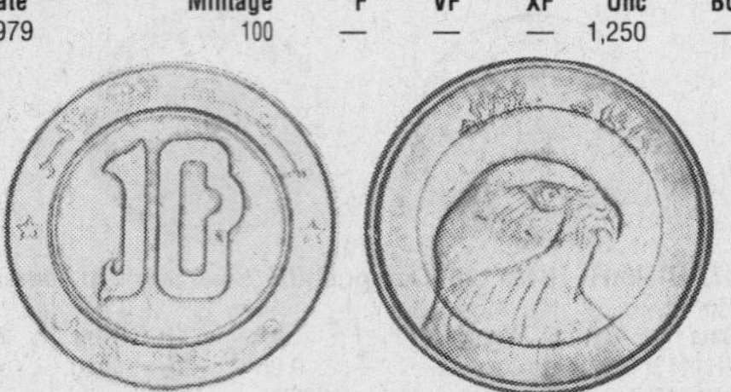

**10 DINARS** **KM# 124** **Ring Composition:** Steel **Center Composition:** Aluminum **Obverse:** Denomination **Reverse:** Falcon

| Date | Mintage | F | VF | XF | Unc | BU |
|---|---|---|---|---|---|---|
| AH1413(1992) | — | — | 2.00 | 6.00 | 12.00 | — |
| AH1413(1992) Proof | — | — | — | — | — | — |
| AH1414(1993) | — | — | 2.00 | 6.00 | 12.00 | — |
| AH1418(1997) | — | — | 2.00 | 6.00 | 12.00 | — |

**20 DINARS** **KM# 125** **Ring Composition:** Steel **Center Composition:** Brass **Obverse:** Denomination **Reverse:** Lion

| Date | Mintage | F | VF | XF | Unc | BU |
|---|---|---|---|---|---|---|
| AH1413(1992) | — | — | 3.00 | 7.00 | 15.00 | — |
| AH1413(1992) Proof | — | — | — | — | — | — |
| AH1414(1993) | — | — | 3.00 | 7.00 | 15.00 | — |
| AH1416(1996) | — | — | 3.00 | 7.00 | 15.00 | — |
| AH1417(1996) | — | — | 3.00 | 7.00 | 15.00 | — |
| AH1417(1997) | — | — | 3.00 | 7.00 | 15.00 | — |
| AH1418(1997) | — | — | 3.00 | 7.00 | 15.00 | — |
| AH1420(1999) | — | — | 3.00 | 7.00 | 15.00 | — |
| AH1427(2000) | — | — | 3.00 | 7.00 | 15.00 | — |

**50 DINARS** **KM# 126** **Ring Composition:** Brass **Center Composition:** Steel **Obverse:** Denomination **Reverse:** Gazelle

| Date | Mintage | F | VF | XF | Unc | BU |
|---|---|---|---|---|---|---|
| AH1413(1992) | — | — | 4.00 | 8.00 | 16.50 | — |
| AH1413 Proof | — | Value: 35.00 | | | | |
| AH1414(1993) | — | — | 4.00 | 8.00 | 16.50 | — |
| AH1416(1996) | — | — | 4.00 | 8.00 | 16.50 | — |
| AH1417(1996) | — | — | 4.00 | 8.00 | 16.50 | — |
| AH1414(1996) | — | — | 4.00 | 8.00 | 16.50 | — |
| AH1418(1998) | — | — | 4.00 | 8.00 | 16.50 | — |
| AH1419(1999) | — | — | 4.00 | 8.00 | 16.50 | — |

**50 DINARS** **KM# 131** **Ring Composition:** Brass **Center Composition:** Steel **Subject:** 40th Anniversary - Revolution

| Date | Mintage | F | VF | XF | Unc | BU |
|---|---|---|---|---|---|---|
| ND(1994)(1994) | — | — | 5.00 | 10.00 | 17.50 | — |
| ND(1994) Proof | — | Value: 37.50 | | | | |

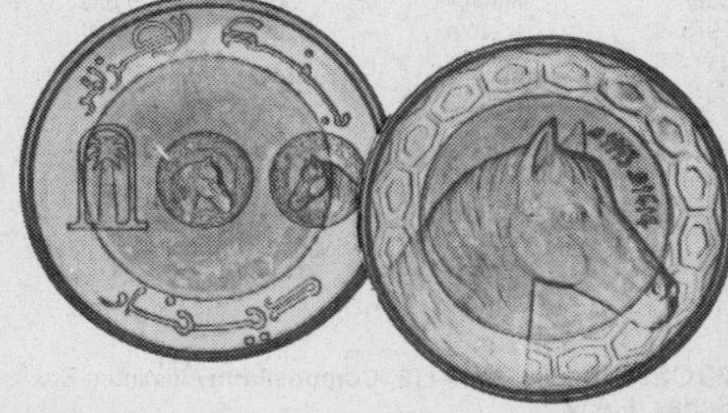

**100 DINARS** **KM# 132** **Center Composition:** Aluminum-Bronze **Obverse:** Denomination stylized with reverse design **Reverse:** Horse head

| Date | Mintage | F | VF | XF | Unc | BU |
|---|---|---|---|---|---|---|
| AH1413(1992) | — | — | 6.50 | 12.50 | 22.50 | — |
| AH1414(1993) | — | — | 6.50 | 12.50 | 22.50 | — |
| AH1415(1994) | — | — | 6.50 | 12.50 | 22.50 | — |
| AH1417(1997) | — | — | 6.50 | 12.50 | 22.50 | — |
| AH1418(1998) | — | — | 6.50 | 12.50 | 22.50 | — |

## ESSAIS

Standard metals unless otherwise noted

| KM# | Date | Mintage | Identification | Issue Price | Mkt Val |
|---|---|---|---|---|---|
| E1 | (1949) | 1,500 | 20 Francs. KM#91 | — | 25.00 |
| E2 | (1949) | 1,500 | 50 Francs. KM#92. | — | 30.00 |
| E3 | (1950) | 1,500 | 100 Francs. KM#93. | — | 35.00 |

| KM# | Date | Mintage | Identification | Issue Price | Mkt Val |
|---|---|---|---|---|---|
| E4 | (1972) | 2,250 | 5 Dinars. KM#105. | — | 20.00 |
| E5 | (1972) | 1,000 | 5 Dinars. KM#105a. | — | 25.00 |

| KM# | Date | Mintage | Identification | Issue Price | Mkt Val |
|---|---|---|---|---|---|

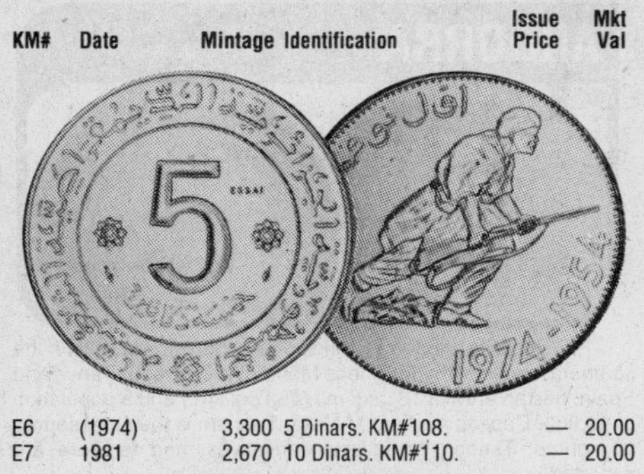

| KM# | Date | Mintage | Identification | Issue Price | Mkt Val |
|---|---|---|---|---|---|
| E6 | (1974) | 3,300 | 5 Dinars. KM#108. | — | 20.00 |
| E7 | 1981 | 2,670 | 10 Dinars. KM#110. | — | 20.00 |

## PIEFORTS WITH ESSAI

Double thickness - Standard metals unless otherwise noted

| KM# | Date | Mintage | Identification | Issue Price | Mkt Val |
|---|---|---|---|---|---|
| PE1 | 1949 | 104 | 20 Francs. KM#91. | — | 65.00 |
| PE2 | 1949 | 104 | 50 Francs. KM#92. | — | 65.00 |
| PE3 | 1950 | 104 | 100 Francs. KM#93. | — | 100 |

## PROOF SETS

| KM# | Date | Mintage | Identification | Issue Price | Mkt Val |
|---|---|---|---|---|---|
| PS1 | AH1314 (1992) | — | KM#123-130 | — | 160 |

# AMERICAN SAMOA

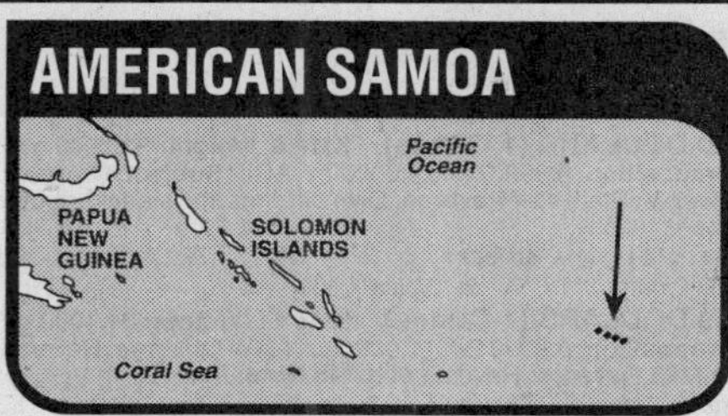


The Territory of American Samoa, with a population of 41,000, consists of seven major islands with a total land area of 76 sq. mi. (199 sq. km.) which are located about 2300 miles south-southwest of Hawaii. American Samoa was settled by the Polynesians around 600 BC. The capital is Pago Pago.

Samoa's long isolation from the western world ended in 1722 when the Dutch explorer, Jacob Roggeveen, came upon the islands. However, it wasn't until 1831 that European influence had any real impact. In that year, John Williams of the London Missionary Society arrived with eight Tahitian missionaries.

By 1900 the Samoan islands were being claimed by both Germany and the United States. Germany annexed several islands, which now comprise Western Samoa; the U.S. took Tutuila to use Pago Pago Bay as a coaling station for naval ships.

As Japan began emerging as an international power in the mid-1930's, the U.S. Naval station on Tutuila began to acquire new strategic importance; and in 1940 the Samoan Islands became a training and staging area for the U.S. Marine Corps.

A. P. Lutali, Governor of American Samoa, signed a historic proclamation on May 23, 1988 that authorized the minting of the first numismatic issue for this unincorporated territory administered by the United States Department of the Interior.

**MONETARY SYSTEM**

100 Cents = 1 Dollar

## U.S. TERRITORY

### NON-CIRCULATING NONLEGAL TENDER COINAGE

**DOLLAR** KM# 1 **Composition:** Bronze **Subject:** America's Cup

| Date | Mintage | F | VF | XF | Unc | BU |
|---|---|---|---|---|---|---|
| 1988 Proof | 2,000 | Value: 16.00 | | | | |

**5 DOLLARS** KM# 2 **Weight:** 31.1000 g. **Composition:** 0.9990 Silver 1.0000 oz. ASW **Subject:** America's Cup

| Date | Mintage | F | VF | XF | Unc | BU |
|---|---|---|---|---|---|---|
| 1988 Proof | 1,000 | Value: 40.00 | | | | |

**5 DOLLARS** KM# 6.1 **Weight:** 31.1000 g. **Composition:** 0.9990 Silver 1.0000 oz. ASW **Subject:** Olympics **Note:** Coin die alignment.

| Date | Mintage | F | VF | XF | Unc | BU |
|---|---|---|---|---|---|---|
| 1988 Proof | 1,000 | Value: 55.00 | | | | |

**5 DOLLARS** KM# 6.2 **Weight:** 31.1000 g. **Composition:** 0.9990 Silver 1.0000 oz. ASW **Note:** Medallic die alignment.

| Date | Mintage | F | VF | XF | Unc | BU |
|---|---|---|---|---|---|---|
| 1988 Proof | — | Value: 150 | | | | |

**25 DOLLARS** KM# 3 **Weight:** 155.5150 g. **Composition:** 0.9990 Silver 5.0000 oz. ASW **Subject:** America's Cup **Note:** Illustration reduced. Actual size 63mm.

| Date | Mintage | F | VF | XF | Unc | BU |
|---|---|---|---|---|---|---|
| 1988 Proof | 100 | Value: 200 | | | | |

**25 DOLLARS** **KM# 7** **Weight:** 155.5150 g. **Composition:** 0.9990 Silver 5.0000 oz. ASW **Subject:** Olympics **Obverse:** Gov. Lutali **Note:** Illustration reduced. Actual size 63mm.

| Date | Mintage | F | VF | XF | Unc | BU |
|---|---|---|---|---|---|---|
| ND(1988) Proof | 100 | Value: 385 | | | | |

**25 DOLLARS** **KM# 9** **Weight:** 155.5150 g. **Composition:** 0.9990 Silver 5.0000 oz. ASW **Subject:** Olympics **Reverse:** Symbols **Note:** Illustration reduced. Actual size 63mm.

| Date | Mintage | F | VF | XF | Unc | BU |
|---|---|---|---|---|---|---|
| 1988 Proof | 100 | Value: 165 | | | | |

**25 DOLLARS** **KM# 10** **Weight:** 155.5150 g. **Composition:** 0.9990 Silver 5.0000 oz. ASW **Subject:** Olympics **Note:** Similar to KM#7 but denomination: TWENTY-FIVE.

| Date | Mintage | F | VF | XF | Unc | BU |
|---|---|---|---|---|---|---|
| 1988 Proof | — | Value: 475 | | | | |

**50 DOLLARS (1/4 Ounce)** **KM# 4** **Weight:** 8.6397 g. **Composition:** 0.9000 Gold .2500 oz. AGW **Subject:** America's Cup

| Date | Mintage | F | VF | XF | Unc | BU |
|---|---|---|---|---|---|---|
| 1988 Proof | 100 | Value: 250 | | | | |

**100 DOLLARS (1 Ounce)** **KM# 5** **Weight:** 31.1000 g. **Composition:** 0.9990 Gold 1.0000 oz. AGW **Subject:** America's Cup **Obverse:** State seal **Reverse:** USA's yacht passing New Zealand's yacht

| Date | Mintage | F | VF | XF | Unc | BU |
|---|---|---|---|---|---|---|
| 1988 Proof | 50 | Value: 900 | | | | |

**100 DOLLARS (1 Ounce)** **KM# 8** **Weight:** 31.1000 g. **Composition:** 0.9990 Gold 1.0000 oz. AGW **Subject:** Olympics **Obverse:** State seal **Reverse:** Olympic rings and stadium above denomination

| Date | Mintage | F | VF | XF | Unc | BU |
|---|---|---|---|---|---|---|
| 1988 Proof | 50 | Value: 1,000 | | | | |

**100 DOLLARS (1 Ounce)** **KM# 11** **Weight:** 31.1000 g. **Composition:** 0.9990 Gold 1.0000 oz. AGW **Obverse:** Reverse of KM#5 **Reverse:** Reverse of KM#8 **Note:** Mule.

| Date | Mintage | F | VF | XF | Unc | BU |
|---|---|---|---|---|---|---|
| 1988 Proof | 5 | Value: 1,850 | | | | |

## PROOF SETS

| KM# | Date | Mintage | Identification | Issue Price | Mkt Val |
|---|---|---|---|---|---|
| PS1 | 1988 | — | KM#2-4 | 315 | 500 |

# ANDORRA

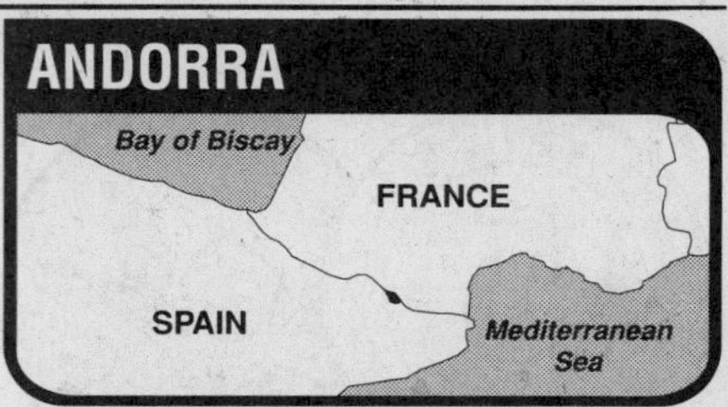


Principality of Andorra (Principat d'Andorra), situated on the southern slopes of the Pyrenees Mountains between France and Spain, has an area of 181 sq. mi. (453 sq. km.) and a population of 80,000. Capital: Andorra la Vella. Tourism is the chief source of income. Timber, cattle and derivatives, and furniture are exported.

According to tradition, the independence of Andorra derives from a charter Charlemagne granted the people of Andorra in 806 in recognition of their help in battling the Moors. An agreement between the Count of Foix (France) and the Bishop of Seo de Urgel (Spanish) in 1278 to recognize each other as Co-Princes of Andorra gave the state what has been its political form and territorial extent continuously to the present day. Over the years, the title on the French side passed to the Kings of Navarre, then to the Kings of France, and is now held by the President of France.

**RULERS**
Joan D.M. Bisbe D'Urgell I

**MONETARY SYSTEM**
100 Centims = 1 Diner
100 Pesetas = 1 Diner, 1983-85
125 Pesetas = 1 Diner, 1986-

**NOTE**: The Diners have been struck for collectors while French Francs and Spanish Pesetas are used in everyday commerce.

**MINT MARKS**
Crowned M = Madrid

## PRINCIPALITY

### STANDARD COINAGE

**CENTIM** **KM# 171** **Weight:** 1.2500 g. **Composition:** Aluminum **Subject:** F.A.O. **Obverse:** Denomination. **Reverse:** Winged figure carrying wheat. **Edge:** Plain.

| Date | Mintage | F | VF | XF | Unc | BU |
|---|---|---|---|---|---|---|
| 1999 | — | — | — | — | 1.50 | — |

**10 CENTIMS** **KM# 164** **Weight:** 6.8100 g. **Composition:** Brass **Obverse:** National arms **Reverse:** Building and arms **Edge:** Plain

| Date | Mintage | F | VF | XF | Unc | BU |
|---|---|---|---|---|---|---|
| 1997 | — | — | — | — | 4.00 | — |

**25 CENTIMS** **KM# 33** **Composition:** Bronze **Obverse:** Joan D.M. Bisbe D'Urgell I

| Date | Mintage | F | VF | XF | Unc | BU |
|---|---|---|---|---|---|---|
| 1986 | 10,000 | — | — | — | 5.00 | — |

**25 CENTIMS** **KM# 109** **Composition:** Copper-Nickel **Subject:** 50th Anniversary - F.A.O **Reverse:** People on globe adoring F.A.O. logo

| Date | Mintage | F | VF | XF | Unc | BU |
|---|---|---|---|---|---|---|
| 1995 | 50,000 | — | — | — | 7.00 | — |

**50 CENTIMS** **KM# 134** **Weight:** 0.6221 g. **Composition:** 0.9990 Gold .0100 oz. AGW **Obverse:** Fleury cross **Reverse:** Portrait of Queen Isabella I **Note:** Similar to 20 Diners, KM#137.

| Date | Mintage | F | VF | XF | Unc | BU |
|---|---|---|---|---|---|---|
| 1997 Proof | Est. 50,000 | Value: 30.00 | | | | |

**DINER** **KM# 14** **Composition:** Brass **Obverse:** Joan D.M. Bisbe D'Urgell I

| Date | Mintage | F | VF | XF | Unc | BU |
|---|---|---|---|---|---|---|
| 1983 | 28,000 | — | — | — | 8.00 | — |

**DINER** **KM# 15** **Composition:** Cast Copper

| Date | Mintage | F | VF | XF | Unc | BU |
|---|---|---|---|---|---|---|
| 1984 | 7,500 | — | — | — | 9.00 | — |

**DINER** **KM# 35** **Composition:** Brass

| Date | Mintage | F | VF | XF | Unc | BU |
|---|---|---|---|---|---|---|
| 1986 | 10,000 | — | — | — | 8.00 | — |

**DINER** **KM# 49** **Composition:** Copper-Nickel **Subject:** Pont de la Margineda

| Date | Mintage | F | VF | XF | Unc | BU |
|---|---|---|---|---|---|---|
| 1988 | 5,000 | — | — | — | 10.00 | — |

**DINER** **KM# 66** **Weight:** 10.3000 g. **Composition:** 0.9990 Silver .3312 oz. ASW

| Date | Mintage | F | VF | XF | Unc | BU |
|---|---|---|---|---|---|---|
| 1990 | 6,000 | — | — | — | 25.00 | — |

**DINER** **KM# 127** **Weight:** 10.0000 g. **Composition:** 0.5000 Silver .1607 oz. ASW **Subject:** Treaty of Rome **Obverse:** Crowned arms **Reverse:** Seated Europa placing laurel wreath on her head

| Date | Mintage | F | VF | XF | Unc | BU |
|---|---|---|---|---|---|---|
| 1997 Proof | 30,000 | Value: 20.00 | | | | |

**DINER** **KM# 135** **Weight:** 1.2441 g. **Composition:** 0.9990 Gold .0400 oz. AGW **Obverse:** Fleury cross **Reverse:** Portrait of Queen Isabella I **Note:** Similar to 20 Dinars, KM#137.

| Date | Mintage | F | VF | XF | Unc | BU |
|---|---|---|---|---|---|---|
| 1997 Proof | Est. 10,000 | Value: 50.00 | | | | |

**2 DINERS** **KM# 19** **Ring Composition:** Copper-Nickel **Center Composition:** Bronze **Subject:** Wildlife **Reverse:** Bear

| Date | Mintage | F | VF | XF | Unc | BU |
|---|---|---|---|---|---|---|
| 1984 | 5,000 | — | — | — | 27.50 | — |

**2 DINERS** **KM# 20** **Ring Composition:** Copper-Nickel **Center Composition:** Bronze **Subject:** Wildlife **Reverse:** Red squirrel

| Date | Mintage | F | VF | XF | Unc | BU |
|---|---|---|---|---|---|---|
| 1984 | 5,000 | — | — | — | 27.50 | — |

**2 DINERS** **KM# 21** **Ring Composition:** Copper-Nickel **Center Composition:** Bronze **Subject:** Wildlife **Reverse:** Ibex

| Date | Mintage | F | VF | XF | Unc | BU |
|---|---|---|---|---|---|---|
| 1984 | 5,000 | — | — | — | 27.50 | — |

**2 DINERS** **KM# 27** **Ring Composition:** Copper-Nickel **Center Composition:** Bronze **Subject:** 1988 Winter Olympics **Reverse:** Skier

| Date | Mintage | F | VF | XF | Unc | BU |
|---|---|---|---|---|---|---|
| 1985 | 11,000 | — | — | — | 22.50 | — |

**2 DINERS** **KM# 28** **Ring Composition:** Copper-Nickel **Subject:** 1988 Summer Olympics **Reverse:** High jumper

| Date | Mintage | F | VF | XF | Unc | BU |
|---|---|---|---|---|---|---|
| 1985 | 11,000 | — | — | — | 22.50 | — |

**2 DINERS** **KM# 36** **Composition:** Brass **Obverse:** Joan D.M. Bisbe D'Urgell I

| Date | Mintage | F | VF | XF | Unc | BU |
|---|---|---|---|---|---|---|
| 1986 | 10,000 | — | — | — | 12.50 | — |

**2 DINERS** **KM# 40** **Composition:** Copper-Nickel **Subject:** 1988 Summer Olympics **Reverse:** Tennis

| Date | Mintage | F | VF | XF | Unc | BU |
|---|---|---|---|---|---|---|
| 1987 | 20,000 | — | — | — | 14.50 | — |

**2 DINERS** **KM# 46** **Composition:** Copper-Nickel **Subject:** 1992 Winter & Summer Olympics **Reverse:** Kayaker and skier

| Date | Mintage | F | VF | XF | Unc | BU |
|---|---|---|---|---|---|---|
| 1987 | Est. 24,000 | — | — | — | 14.50 | — |

**2 DINERS** **KM# 50** **Composition:** Copper-Nickel **Obverse:** Church of Santa Coloma

| Date | Mintage | F | VF | XF | Unc | BU |
|---|---|---|---|---|---|---|
| 1988 | 5,000 | — | — | — | 15.00 | — |

**2 DINERS** **KM# 140** **Weight:** 20.0000 g. **Composition:** 0.9250 Silver .5948 oz. ASW **Subject:** 1988 Winter Olympics **Obverse:** Crowned arms, denomination **Reverse:** Bobsled

| Date | Mintage | F | VF | XF | Unc | BU |
|---|---|---|---|---|---|---|
| 1997 (1998) Proof | 30,000 | Value: 25.00 | | | | |

**5 DINERS** **KM# 16** **Composition:** Cast Copper **Obverse:** Joan D.M. Bisbe D'Urgell I

| Date | Mintage | F | VF | XF | Unc | BU |
|---|---|---|---|---|---|---|
| 1984 | 7,500 | — | — | — | 13.50 | — |

**5 DINERS** **KM# 29** **Composition:** Cast Copper **Subject:** 2nd Congress of the Catalan Language

| Date | Mintage | F | VF | XF | Unc | BU |
|---|---|---|---|---|---|---|
| 1986 | 6,000 | — | — | — | 15.00 | — |

**5 DINERS** **KM# 37** **Composition:** Bronze **Obverse:** Joan D.M. Bisbe D'Urgell I

| Date | Mintage | F | VF | XF | Unc | BU |
|---|---|---|---|---|---|---|
| 1986 | 10,000 | — | — | — | 17.50 | — |

**5 DINERS** **KM# 51** **Composition:** Copper-Nickel **Obverse:** Church of St. Climent de Pal

| Date | Mintage | F | VF | XF | Unc | BU |
|---|---|---|---|---|---|---|
| 1988 | 5,000 | — | — | — | 17.50 | — |

**5 DINERS** **KM# 80** **Weight:** 10.0000 g. **Composition:** 0.5000 Silver .1608 oz. ASW **Subject:** 1988 Winter Olympics **Reverse:** Cross-country skier

| Date | Mintage | F | VF | XF | Unc | BU |
|---|---|---|---|---|---|---|
| 1993 Proof | 50,000 | Value: 13.50 | | | | |

**5 DINERS** **KM# 102** **Weight:** 15.0000 g. **Composition:** 0.9250 Silver .4461 oz. ASW **Subject:** Andorran Circle of the Arts - 25th Anniversary

| Date | Mintage | F | VF | XF | Unc | BU |
|---|---|---|---|---|---|---|
| 1993 Proof | 3,000 | Value: 25.00 | | | | |

**5 DINERS** **KM# 111** **Weight:** 1.2500 g. **Composition:** 0.9990 Gold .0401 oz. AGW **Subject:** Wildlife **Obverse:** Crowned arms, denomination **Reverse:** Red squirrel

| Date | Mintage | F | VF | XF | Unc | BU |
|---|---|---|---|---|---|---|
| 1994 Proof | — | Value: 40.00 | | | | |

**5 DINERS** **KM# 112** **Weight:** 1.5552 g. **Composition:** 0.9990 Gold .0500 oz. AGW **Obverse:** Defiant eagle **Reverse:** Crowned denomination

| Date | Mintage | F | VF | XF | Unc | BU |
|---|---|---|---|---|---|---|
| 1995 Proof | — | Value: 50.00 | | | | |

**5 DINERS** **KM# 116** **Weight:** 15.0000 g. **Composition:** 0.9250 Silver .4461 oz. ASW **Subject:** XXIII Photographers Federation Congress

| Date | Mintage | F | VF | XF | Unc | BU |
|---|---|---|---|---|---|---|
| 1995 Proof | 3,000 | Value: 25.00 | | | | |

**5 DINERS** **KM# 117** **Weight:** 1.2441 g. **Composition:** 0.9990 Gold .0400 oz. AGW **Subject:** Wildlife **Reverse:** Chamois

| Date | Mintage | F | VF | XF | Unc | BU |
|---|---|---|---|---|---|---|
| 1996 Proof | Est. 100,000 | Value: 40.00 | | | | |

**5 DINERS** **KM# 118** **Weight:** 1.2441 g. **Composition:** 0.9990 Gold .0400 oz. AGW **Subject:** Wildlife **Reverse:** Brown bear and cub

| Date | Mintage | F | VF | XF | Unc | BU |
|---|---|---|---|---|---|---|
| 1996 Proof | Est. 100,000 | Value: 40.00 | | | | |

**5 DINERS** **KM# 141** **Weight:** 3.1103 g. **Composition:** 0.5850 Gold .0585 oz. AGW **Subject:** 1998 Winter Olympics **Obverse:** Crowned arms, denomination **Reverse:** Downhill skier

| Date | Mintage | F | VF | XF | Unc | BU |
|---|---|---|---|---|---|---|
| 1997 (1998) Proof | 5,000 | Value: 55.00 | | | | |

**5 DINERS** **KM# 155** **Ring Composition:** Brass**Center Weight:** 27.0000 g. **Center Composition:** Silver ASW **Obverse:** World globe amid stars **Reverse:** World globe with sun, planets and stars **Note:** Silver center and brass ring are within a silver ring.

| Date | Mintage | F | VF | XF | Unc | BU |
|---|---|---|---|---|---|---|
| 1999 Proof | — | Value: 30.00 | | | | |

**10 DINERS** **KM# 17** **Weight:** 8.0000 g. **Composition:** 0.9000 Cast Silver .2315 oz. ASW **Obverse:** Joan D.M. Bisbe D'Urgell I

| Date | Mintage | F | VF | XF | Unc | BU |
|---|---|---|---|---|---|---|
| 1984 | 7,500 | — | — | — | 22.50 | — |

**10 DINERS** **KM# 34** **Weight:** 8.0000 g. **Composition:** 0.9000 Cast Silver .2315 oz. ASW **Subject:** 1988 World Cup Soccer Games

| Date | Mintage | F | VF | XF | Unc | BU |
|---|---|---|---|---|---|---|
| 1986 Prooflike | 10,000 | — | — | — | 22.50 | — |

**10 DINERS** **KM# 38** **Weight:** 8.0000 g. **Composition:** 0.9250 Silver .2379 oz. ASW **Obverse:** Joan D.M. Bisbe D'Urgell I

| Date | Mintage | F | VF | XF | Unc | BU |
|---|---|---|---|---|---|---|
| 1986 | 10,000 | — | — | — | 22.50 | — |

**10 DINERS** **KM# 52** **Weight:** 8.0000 g. **Composition:** 0.9250 Silver .2379 oz. ASW **Obverse:** Church of St. Joan de Caselles

| Date | Mintage | F | VF | XF | Unc | BU |
|---|---|---|---|---|---|---|
| 1988 | 5,000 | — | — | — | 22.50 | — |

**10 DINERS** **KM# 53** **Weight:** 12.0000 g. **Composition:** 0.9250 Silver .3569 oz. ASW **Subject:** 1990 World Cup Soccer Games

| Date | Mintage | F | VF | XF | Unc | BU |
|---|---|---|---|---|---|---|
| 1989 Proof | 20,000 | Value: 13.50 | | | | |

**10 DINERS** **KM# 55** **Weight:** 12.0000 g. **Composition:** 0.9250 Silver .3569 oz. ASW **Subject:** 1992 Winter Olympics **Reverse:** Downhill skier

| Date | Mintage | F | VF | XF | Unc | BU |
|---|---|---|---|---|---|---|
| 1989 Proof | 15,000 | Value: 17.50 | | | | |

**10 DINERS** **KM# 56** **Weight:** 12.0000 g. **Composition:** 0.9250 Silver .3569 oz. ASW **Subject:** 1992 Summer Olympics **Reverse:** Soccer

| Date | Mintage | F | VF | XF | Unc | BU |
|---|---|---|---|---|---|---|
| 1989 Proof | 15,000 | Value: 17.50 | | | | |

**10 DINERS** **KM# 60** **Weight:** 12.0000 g. **Composition:** 0.9250 Silver .3569 oz. ASW **Subject:** 1990 World Cup Soccer Games **Reverse:** Map of Italy and soccer ball

| Date | Mintage | F | VF | XF | Unc | BU |
|---|---|---|---|---|---|---|
| 1989 Proof | 20,000 | Value: 17.50 | | | | |

**10 DINERS** **KM# 71** **Weight:** 12.0000 g. **Composition:** 0.9250 Silver .3569 oz. ASW **Subject:** ECU Customs Union **Reverse:** Charlemagne

| Date | Mintage | F | VF | XF | Unc | BU |
|---|---|---|---|---|---|---|
| ND(1992) Proof | 15,000 | Value: 40.00 | | | | |

**10 DINERS** **KM# 74** **Weight:** 31.1035 g. **Composition:** 0.9250 Silver .9250 oz. ASW **Subject:** Wildlife **Reverse:** Red squirrel

| Date | Mintage | F | VF | XF | Unc | BU |
|---|---|---|---|---|---|---|
| 1992 Proof | 15,000 | Value: 35.00 | | | | |

**10 DINERS** **KM# 75** **Weight:** 31.1035 g. **Composition:** 0.9250 Silver .9250 oz. ASW **Subject:** Wildlife **Reverse:** Chamois

| Date | Mintage | F | VF | XF | Unc | BU |
|---|---|---|---|---|---|---|
| 1992 Proof | 15,000 | Value: 35.00 | | | | |

**10 DINERS** **KM# 76** **Weight:** 31.1035 g. **Composition:** 0.9250 Silver .9250 oz. ASW **Subject:** Wildlife **Reverse:** Bears

| Date | Mintage | F | VF | XF | Unc | BU |
|---|---|---|---|---|---|---|
| 1992 Proof | 15,000 | Value: 35.00 | | | | |

**10 DINERS** **KM# 78** **Weight:** 31.1035 g. **Composition:** 0.9250 Silver .9250 oz. ASW **Subject:** Discovery of the New World **Reverse:** Stylized ship on globe

| Date | Mintage | F | VF | XF | Unc | BU |
|---|---|---|---|---|---|---|
| 1992 Proof | 15,000 | Value: 32.50 | | | | |

**10 DINERS** **KM# 84** **Weight:** 31.4700 g. **Composition:** 0.9250 Silver .9359 oz. ASW **Obverse:** Crowned arms above denomination and date **Reverse:** Stylized tree and birds

| Date | Mintage | F | VF | XF | Unc | BU |
|---|---|---|---|---|---|---|
| 1993 Proof | 15,000 | Value: 32.50 | | | | |

**10 DINERS** **KM# 85** **Weight:** 31.4700 g. **Composition:** 0.9250 Silver .9359 oz. ASW **Subject:** Space Exploration **Reverse:** Tethered space walker

| Date | Mintage | F | VF | XF | Unc | BU |
|---|---|---|---|---|---|---|
| 1993 Proof | 15,000 | Value: 35.00 | | | | |

**10 DINERS** **KM# 86** **Weight:** 31.4700 g. **Composition:** 0.9250 Silver .9359 oz. ASW **Subject:** 1994 World Cup Soccer **Reverse:** Player before world map

| Date | Mintage | F | VF | XF | Unc | BU |
|---|---|---|---|---|---|---|
| 1993 Proof | 20,000 | Value: 35.00 | | | | |

**10 DINERS** **KM# 87** **Weight:** 31.4700 g. **Composition:** 0.9250 Silver .9359 oz. ASW **Subject:** Pioneer Edward White

| Date | Mintage | F | VF | XF | Unc | BU |
|---|---|---|---|---|---|---|
| 1993 Proof | Est. 10,000 | Value: 50.00 | | | | |

**10 DINERS** **KM# 89** **Weight:** 31.4700 g. **Composition:** 0.9250 Silver .9359 oz. ASW **Subject:** ECU Customs Union **Reverse:** St. George

| Date | Mintage | F | VF | XF | Unc | BU |
|---|---|---|---|---|---|---|
| 1993 Proof | 25,000 | Value: 37.50 | | | | |

**10 DINERS** **KM# 95** **Weight:** 31.4700 g. **Composition:** 0.9250 Silver .9359 oz. ASW **Subject:** 1996 Summer Olympic Games **Reverse:** Cyclists

| Date | Mintage | F | VF | XF | Unc | BU |
|---|---|---|---|---|---|---|
| 1994 Proof | 50,000 | Value: 27.50 | | | | |

**10 DINERS** **KM# 97** **Weight:** 31.4700 g. **Composition:** 0.9250 Silver .9359 oz. ASW **Subject:** Andorra U.N. Membership **Obverse:** Arms above "ECU"

| Date | Mintage | F | VF | XF | Unc | BU |
|---|---|---|---|---|---|---|
| 1994 Proof | 25,000 | Value: 37.50 | | | | |

**10 DINERS** **KM# 98** **Weight:** 31.4700 g. **Composition:** 0.9250 Silver .9359 oz. ASW **Subject:** Discovery of the New World

| Date | Mintage | F | VF | XF | Unc | BU |
|---|---|---|---|---|---|---|
| 1994 Proof | 20,000 | Value: 42.50 | | | | |

**10 DINERS** **KM# 99** **Weight:** 31.4700 g. **Composition:** 0.9250 Silver .9359 oz. ASW **Subject:** ECU Customs Union **Reverse:** Peter III of Catalonia and Aragon

| Date | Mintage | F | VF | XF | Unc | BU |
|---|---|---|---|---|---|---|
| 1994 Proof | 25,000 | Value: 40.00 | | | | |

**10 DINERS** **KM# 105** **Weight:** 31.4700 g. **Composition:** 0.9250 Silver .9359 oz. ASW **Subject:** ECU Customs Union **Reverse:** Ramon Berenguer III

| Date | Mintage | F | VF | XF | Unc | BU |
|---|---|---|---|---|---|---|
| 1995 Proof | 30,000 | Value: 42.50 | | | | |

**10 DINERS** **KM# 108** **Weight:** 31.6000 g. **Composition:** 0.9250 Silver .9308 oz. ASW **Subject:** Admission to the Council of Europe **Obverse:** Arms above "ECU"

| Date | Mintage | F | VF | XF | Unc | BU |
|---|---|---|---|---|---|---|
| 1995 Proof | 35,000 | Value: 37.50 | | | | |

**10 DINERS** **KM# 110** **Weight:** 31.1035 g. **Composition:** 0.9250 Silver .9250 oz. ASW **Subject:** 50th Anniversary - F.A.O **Reverse:** Ceres holding grain

| Date | Mintage | F | VF | XF | Unc | BU |
|---|---|---|---|---|---|---|
| 1995 Proof | 10,000 | Value: 45.00 | | | | |

**10 DINERS** KM# 113 **Weight:** 31.1035 g. **Composition:** 0.9250 Silver .9250 oz. ASW **Subject:** Wildlife **Reverse:** Wolf

| Date | Mintage | F | VF | XF | Unc | BU |
|---|---|---|---|---|---|---|
| 1995 Proof | 20,000 | Value: 50.00 | | | | |

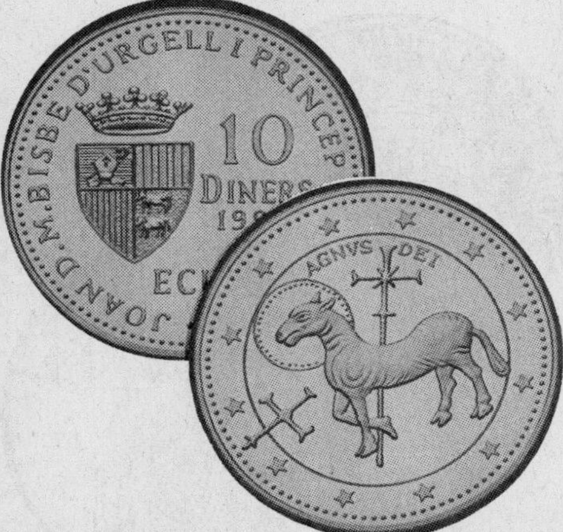


**10 DINERS** KM# 114 **Weight:** 31.1035 g. **Composition:** 0.9250 Silver .9250 oz. ASW **Subject:** Agnus Dei **Obverse:** Arms above "ECU"

| Date | Mintage | F | VF | XF | Unc | BU |
|---|---|---|---|---|---|---|
| 1995 Proof | Est. 35,000 | Value: 35.00 | | | | |

**10 DINERS** KM# 119 **Weight:** 31.4700 g. **Composition:** 0.9250 Silver .9359 oz. ASW **Obverse:** Arms above "ECU" **Reverse:** Frederic II on throne

| Date | Mintage | F | VF | XF | Unc | BU |
|---|---|---|---|---|---|---|
| 1996 Proof | Est. 30,000 | Value: 37.50 | | | | |

**10 DINERS** KM# 120 **Weight:** 31.4700 g. **Composition:** 0.9250 Silver .9359 oz. ASW **Reverse:** Sailing ship

| Date | Mintage | F | VF | XF | Unc | BU |
|---|---|---|---|---|---|---|
| 1996 Proof | Est. 20,000 | Value: 40.00 | | | | |

**10 DINERS** KM# 121 **Weight:** 31.4700 g. **Composition:** 0.9250 Silver .9359 oz. ASW **Obverse:** Arms above "ECU" **Reverse:** Pope crowning Charlemagne

| Date | Mintage | F | VF | XF | Unc | BU |
|---|---|---|---|---|---|---|
| 1996 Proof | Est. 30,000 | Value: 37.50 | | | | |

**10 DINERS** KM# 125 **Weight:** 31.4700 g. **Composition:** 0.9250 Silver .9359 oz. ASW **Subject:** 25th Anniversary - Msgr. Alanis, Co-prince and Bishop of Andorra **Obverse:** Crowned arms above "EURO" **Reverse:** Enthroned prince, date

| Date | Mintage | F | VF | XF | Unc | BU |
|---|---|---|---|---|---|---|
| 1996 Proof | 30,000 | Value: 40.00 | | | | |

**10 DINERS** KM# 130 **Weight:** 31.4700 g. **Composition:** 0.9250 Silver .9359 oz. ASW **Subject:** Treaty of Rome **Obverse:** Crowned arms above "EURO" **Reverse:** Seated Europa with olive branch and "EURO" shield, dates

| Date | Mintage | F | VF | XF | Unc | BU |
|---|---|---|---|---|---|---|
| 1997 Proof | 25,000 | Value: 40.00 | | | | |

**10 DINERS** KM# 166 **Weight:** 31.5500 g. **Composition:** 0.9250 Silver .9383 oz. ASW **Subject:** Palau del Princep **Obverse:** Crowned arms. **Reverse:** Crowned arms on house corner. **Edge:** Reeded.

| Date | Mintage | F | VF | XF | Unc | BU |
|---|---|---|---|---|---|---|
| 1997 Proof | — | Value: 35.00 | | | | |

**10 DINERS** KM# 131 **Weight:** 31.4700 g. **Composition:** 0.9250 Silver .9359 oz. ASW **Subject:** Wildlife **Obverse:** Crowned arms **Reverse:** Vixen with kit

| Date | Mintage | F | VF | XF | Unc | BU |
|---|---|---|---|---|---|---|
| 1997 Proof | 15,000 | Value: 45.00 | | | | |

**10 DINERS** **KM# 132** **Weight:** 31.4700 g. **Composition:** 0.9250 Silver .9359 oz. ASW **Obverse:** Crowned arms **Reverse:** Johan Sebastian Bach portrait

| Date | Mintage | F | VF | XF | Unc | BU |
|---|---|---|---|---|---|---|
| 1997 Proof | Est. 25,000 | Value: 37.50 | | | | |

**10 DINERS** **KM# 133** **Weight:** 31.4700 g. **Composition:** 0.9250 Silver .9359 oz. ASW **Obverse:** Crowned arms **Reverse:** Antonio Vivaldi portrait

| Date | Mintage | F | VF | XF | Unc | BU |
|---|---|---|---|---|---|---|
| 1997 Proof | Est. 25,000 | Value: 37.50 | | | | |

**10 DINERS** **KM# 136** **Weight:** 3.1103 g. **Composition:** 0.9990 Gold .1000 oz. AGW **Obverse:** Fleury cross **Reverse:** Portrait of Isabella I **Note:** Similar to 20 Diners, KM#137

| Date | Mintage | F | VF | XF | Unc | BU |
|---|---|---|---|---|---|---|
| 1997 Proof | Est. 5,000 | Value: 85.00 | | | | |

**10 DINERS** **KM# 142** **Weight:** 31.4700 g. **Composition:** 0.9250 Silver .9359 oz. ASW **Subject:** 1998 World Cup Soccer **Obverse:** Crowned arms and denomination **Reverse:** Eiffel Tower and soccer ball

| Date | Mintage | F | VF | XF | Unc | BU |
|---|---|---|---|---|---|---|
| 1997 Proof | 15,000 | Value: 45.00 | | | | |

**10 DINERS** **KM# 143** **Weight:** 31.4700 g. **Composition:** 0.9250 Silver .9359 oz. ASW **Subject:** Human Rights **Obverse:** Crowned arms **Reverse:** Allegorical figure of Justice

| Date | Mintage | F | VF | XF | Unc | BU |
|---|---|---|---|---|---|---|
| 1998 Proof | 25,000 | Value: 42.50 | | | | |

**10 DINERS** **KM# 165** **Weight:** 31.1100 g. **Composition:** 0.9990 Silver 1 oz. ASW **Subject:** Year of the Tiger **Obverse:** Multicolored cartoon tiger and Chinese legend **Reverse:** Denomination in crowned wreath **Edge:** Reeded

| Date | Mintage | F | VF | XF | Unc | BU |
|---|---|---|---|---|---|---|
| 1998 Proof | — | Value: 50.00 | | | | |

**10 DINERS** **KM# 146** **Weight:** 31.4700 g. **Composition:** 0.9250 Silver .9359 oz. ASW **Obverse:** Crowned arms **Reverse:** Portraitof Claudio Monteverdi, dates

| Date | Mintage | F | VF | XF | Unc | BU |
|---|---|---|---|---|---|---|
| 1998 Proof | 25,000 | Value: 37.50 | | | | |

**10 DINERS** **KM# 147** **Weight:** 31.4700 g. **Composition:** 0.9250 Silver .9359 oz. ASW **Subject:** George Friedrich Handel **Obverse:** Crowned arms **Reverse:** Portrait, dates

| Date | Mintage | F | VF | XF | Unc | BU |
|---|---|---|---|---|---|---|
| 1998 Proof | 25,000 | Value: 37.50 | | | | |

**10 DINERS** **KM# 150** **Weight:** 31.4700 g. **Composition:** 0.9250 Silver .9359 oz. ASW **Subject:** Europa **Obverse:** Crowned arms **Reverse:** Seated Europa

| Date | Mintage | F | VF | XF | Unc | BU |
|---|---|---|---|---|---|---|
| 1998 Proof | 25,000 | Value: 40.00 | | | | |

**10 DINERS** **KM# 151** **Weight:** 31.4700 g. **Composition:** 0.9250 Silver .9359 oz. ASW **Subject:** Europa **Obverse:** Crowned arms **Reverse:** Europa driving quadriga

| Date | Mintage | F | VF | XF | Unc | BU |
|---|---|---|---|---|---|---|
| 1998 Proof | 25,000 | Value: 40.00 | | | | |

**10 DINERS** **KM# 153** **Weight:** 31.4700 g. **Composition:** 0.9250 Silver .9359 oz. ASW **Subject:** 50th Anniversary - European Council **Obverse:** Crowned arms **Reverse:** Statue of Democracy

| Date | Mintage | F | VF | XF | Unc | BU |
|---|---|---|---|---|---|---|
| 1999 Proof | 15,000 | Value: 42.50 | | | | |

**10 DINERS** **KM# 156** **Weight:** 31.4700 g. **Composition:** 0.9250 Silver .9359 oz. ASW **Subject:** Jubilee 2000 **Obverse:** National arms **Reverse:** Birth of Jesus

| Date | Mintage | F | VF | XF | Unc | BU |
|---|---|---|---|---|---|---|
| 1999 Proof | 15,000 | Value: 40.00 | | | | |

**10 DINERS** **KM# 157** **Weight:** 31.4700 g. **Composition:** 0.9250 Silver .9359 oz. ASW **Subject:** Jubilee 2000 **Obverse:** National arms **Reverse:** Slaughter of the Innocents - Man with sword killing children

| Date | Mintage | F | VF | XF | Unc | BU |
|---|---|---|---|---|---|---|
| 1999 Proof | 15,000 | Value: 40.00 | | | | |

**10 DINERS** **KM# 158** **Weight:** 31.4700 g. **Composition:** 0.9250 Silver .9359 oz. ASW **Subject:** Jubilee 2000 **Obverse:** National arms **Reverse:** John the Baptist baptizing Jesus

| Date | Mintage | F | VF | XF | Unc | BU |
|---|---|---|---|---|---|---|
| 1999 Proof | 15,000 | Value: 40.00 | | | | |

**10 DINERS** **KM# 154** **Weight:** 31.4700 g. **Composition:** 0.9250 Silver .9359 oz. ASW **Subject:** 50th Anniversary - European Council **Obverse:** Crowned arms **Reverse:** Statue of Human Rights

| Date | Mintage | F | VF | XF | Unc | BU |
|---|---|---|---|---|---|---|
| 1999 Proof | 15,000 | Value: 42.50 | | | | |

**10 DINERS** **KM# 159** **Weight:** 31.4700 g. **Composition:** 0.9250 Silver .9359 oz. ASW **Subject:** Jubilee 2000 **Obverse:** National arms **Reverse:** Prodigal Son - Son kneeling before his father

| Date | Mintage | F | VF | XF | Unc | BU |
|---|---|---|---|---|---|---|
| 1999 Proof | 15,000 | Value: 40.00 | | | | |

**10 DINERS** **KM# 160** **Weight:** 31.4700 g. **Composition:** 0.9250 Silver .9359 oz. ASW **Subject:** Jubilee 2000 **Obverse:** National arms **Reverse:** Jesus' entry into Jerusalem

| Date | Mintage | F | VF | XF | Unc | BU |
|---|---|---|---|---|---|---|
| 1999 Proof | 15,000 | Value: 40.00 | | | | |

**10 DINERS** **KM# 161** **Weight:** 31.4700 g. **Composition:** 0.9250 Silver .9359 oz. ASW **Subject:** Jubilee 2000 **Obverse:** National arms **Reverse:** Last Supper scene

| Date | Mintage | F | VF | XF | Unc | BU |
|---|---|---|---|---|---|---|
| 1999 Proof | 15,000 | Value: 40.00 | | | | |

**10 DINERS** **KM# 162** **Weight:** 31.4700 g. **Composition:** 0.9250 Silver .9359 oz. ASW **Subject:** Jubilee 2000 **Obverse:** National arms **Reverse:** Jesus on the cross

| Date | Mintage | F | VF | XF | Unc | BU |
|---|---|---|---|---|---|---|
| 1999 Proof | 15,000 | Value: 40.00 | | | | |

**10 DINERS** **KM# 163** **Weight:** 31.4700 g. **Composition:** 0.9250 Silver .9359 oz. ASW **Subject:** Jubilee 2000 **Obverse:** National arms **Reverse:** Jesus standing in boat

| Date | Mintage | F | VF | XF | Unc | BU |
|---|---|---|---|---|---|---|
| 1999 Proof | 15,000 | Value: 40.00 | | | | |

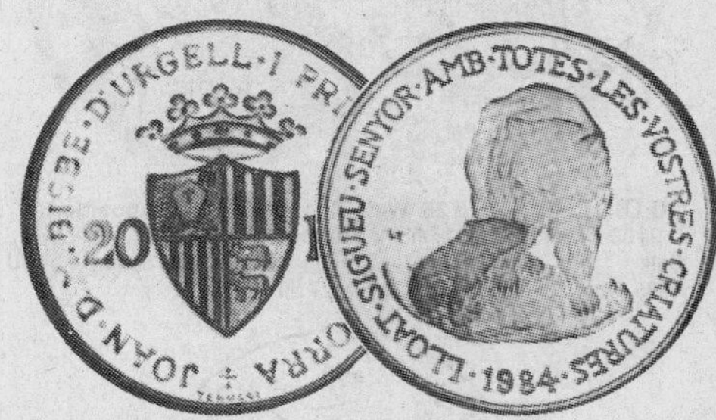

**20 DINERS** **KM# 22** **Weight:** 16.0000 g. **Composition:** 0.8350 Silver .4296 oz. ASW **Subject:** Wildlife **Reverse:** Bear

| Date | Mintage | F | VF | XF | Unc | BU |
|---|---|---|---|---|---|---|
| 1984 Proof | 5,000 | Value: 35.00 | | | | |

**20 DINERS** KM# 23 **Weight:** 16.0000 g. **Composition:** 0.8350 Silver .4296 oz. ASW **Subject:** Wildlife **Reverse:** Red squirrel

| Date | Mintage | F | VF | XF | Unc | BU |
|---|---|---|---|---|---|---|
| 1984 Proof | 5,000 | Value: 35.00 | | | | |

**20 DINERS** KM# 24 **Weight:** 16.0000 g. **Composition:** 0.8350 Silver .4296 oz. ASW **Subject:** Wildlife **Obverse:** Similar to KM#23 **Reverse:** Ibex

| Date | Mintage | F | VF | XF | Unc | BU |
|---|---|---|---|---|---|---|
| 1984 Proof | 5,000 | Value: 35.00 | | | | |

**20 DINERS** KM# 25 **Weight:** 16.0000 g. **Composition:** 0.9000 Silver .4630 oz. ASW **Subject:** 1984 Summer Olympics

| Date | Mintage | F | VF | XF | Unc | BU |
|---|---|---|---|---|---|---|
| 1984 Proof | 10,000 | Value: 35.00 | | | | |

**20 DINERS** KM# 26 **Weight:** 16.0000 g. **Composition:** 0.9000 Silver .4630 oz. ASW **Subject:** Christmas

| Date | Mintage | F | VF | XF | Unc | BU |
|---|---|---|---|---|---|---|
| 1985 Proof | 7,000 | Value: 27.50 | | | | |

**20 DINERS** KM# 39 **Weight:** 16.0000 g. **Composition:** 0.9000 Silver .4630 oz. ASW **Subject:** Olympic Tennis

| Date | Mintage | F | VF | XF | Unc | BU |
|---|---|---|---|---|---|---|
| 1987 | 10,000 | — | — | — | 50.00 | — |

**20 DINERS** KM# 43 **Weight:** 16.0000 g. **Composition:** 0.9000 Silver .4630 oz. ASW **Subject:** 1988 Summer Olympics **Reverse:** Stadium

| Date | Mintage | F | VF | XF | Unc | BU |
|---|---|---|---|---|---|---|
| 1988 | 12,000 | — | — | — | 50.00 | — |

**20 DINERS** KM# 47 **Weight:** 16.0000 g. **Composition:** 0.9250 Silver .4759 oz. ASW **Subject:** 1992 Winter Olympics **Reverse:** Pairs figure skating

| Date | Mintage | F | VF | XF | Unc | BU |
|---|---|---|---|---|---|---|
| 1988 Proof | 15,000 | Value: 35.00 | | | | |

**20 DINERS** KM# 48 **Weight:** 16.0000 g. **Composition:** 0.9250 Silver .4759 oz. ASW **Subject:** 1992 Summer Olympics **Reverse:** Gymnast on rings

| Date | Mintage | F | VF | XF | Unc | BU |
|---|---|---|---|---|---|---|
| 1988 Proof | 15,000 | Value: 35.00 | | | | |

**20 DINERS** KM# 54 **Weight:** 16.0000 g. **Composition:** 0.9250 Silver .4759 oz. ASW **Subject:** 1992 Summer Olympics **Reverse:** Wind surfer

| Date | Mintage | F | VF | XF | Unc | BU |
|---|---|---|---|---|---|---|
| 1989 Proof | 15,000 | Value: 35.00 | | | | |

**20 DINERS** KM# 57 **Weight:** 16.0000 g. **Composition:** 0.9250 Silver .4759 oz. ASW **Subject:** 1992 Summer Olympics **Obverse:** Similar to KM#47 **Reverse:** Kayaker

| Date | Mintage | F | VF | XF | Unc | BU |
|---|---|---|---|---|---|---|
| 1989 Proof | 15,000 | Value: 35.00 | | | | |

**20 DINERS** KM# 58 **Weight:** 16.0000 g. **Composition:** 0.9250 Silver .4759 oz. ASW **Subject:** 1992 Summer Olympics **Obverse:** Similar to KM#47 **Reverse:** Hurdler

| Date | Mintage | F | VF | XF | Unc | BU |
|---|---|---|---|---|---|---|
| 1990 Proof | 15,000 | Value: 35.00 | | | | |

**20 DINERS** KM# 59 **Weight:** 16.0000 g. **Composition:** 0.9250 Silver .4759 oz. ASW **Subject:** 1992 Summer Olympics **Obverse:** Similar to KM#47 **Reverse:** Equestrian

| Date | Mintage | F | VF | XF | Unc | BU |
|---|---|---|---|---|---|---|
| 1990 Proof | 15,000 | Value: 35.00 | | | | |

**20 DINERS** KM# 67 **Weight:** 21.0000 g. **Composition:** 0.9250 Silver .6246 oz. ASW **Subject:** European Small States Games **Reverse:** Equestrian

| Date | Mintage | F | VF | XF | Unc | BU |
|---|---|---|---|---|---|---|
| 1991 Proof | 5,000 | Value: 40.00 | | | | |

**20 DINERS** KM# 72 **Weight:** 26.5000 g. **Composition:** 0.9250 Silver .7435 oz. ASW **Subject:** ECU Customs Union **Obverse:** Similar to 10 Diners, KM#71 **Reverse:** Charlemagne **Note:** With 1.5 g. 0.917 gold inlay, 0.0442 oz. AGW.

| Date | Mintage | F | VF | XF | Unc | BU |
|---|---|---|---|---|---|---|
| ND(1992) | 5,000 | — | — | — | 100 | — |

**20 DINERS** **KM# 90** **Weight:** 26.5000 g. **Composition:** 0.9250 Silver .7435 oz. ASW **Subject:** ECU Customs Union **Reverse:** St. George **Note:** With 1.5 g. 0.917 gold inlay, 0.0442 oz. AGW.

| Date | Mintage | F | VF | XF | Unc | BU |
|---|---|---|---|---|---|---|
| 1993 Matte | 5,000 | — | — | — | 125 | — |

**20 DINERS** **KM# 100** **Weight:** 26.5000 g. **Composition:** 0.9250 Silver .7435 oz. ASW **Subject:** ECU Customs Union **Reverse:** Peter III of Catalonia and Aragon **Note:** With 1.5 g. 0.917 gold inlay, 0.0442 oz. AGW.

| Date | Mintage | F | VF | XF | Unc | BU |
|---|---|---|---|---|---|---|
| 1994 | 5,000 | — | — | — | 120 | — |

**20 DINERS** **KM# 106** **Weight:** 25.0000 g. **Composition:** 0.9250 Silver .7435 oz. ASW **Subject:** ECU Customs Union **Reverse:** Ramon Berenger III **Note:** With 1.6 g. 0.917 gold inlay, 0.0442 oz. AGW.

| Date | Mintage | F | VF | XF | Unc | BU |
|---|---|---|---|---|---|---|
| 1995 | 6,000 | — | — | — | 120 | — |

**20 DINERS** **KM# 122** **Weight:** 25.0000 g. **Composition:** 0.9250 Silver .7435 oz. ASW **Obverse:** Arms and "ECU" **Reverse:** Charlemagne being crowned **Note:** With 1.6 g. 0.917 gold inlay, 0.0442 oz. AGW.

| Date | Mintage | F | VF | XF | Unc | BU |
|---|---|---|---|---|---|---|
| 1996 | Est. 5,000 | — | — | — | 150 | — |

**20 DINERS** **KM# 128** **Weight:** 25.0000 g. **Composition:** 0.9250 Silver .7435 oz. ASW **Subject:** Treaty at Rome **Obverse:** Crowned arms above "EURO" **Reverse:** Seated Europa with child holding "EURO" shield **Note:** With 1.6 g. 0.917 gold inlay, 0.0442 oz. AGW.

| Date | Mintage | F | VF | XF | Unc | BU |
|---|---|---|---|---|---|---|
| 1997 | 5,000 | — | — | — | 90.00 | — |

**20 DINERS** **KM# 137** **Weight:** 6.2207 g. **Composition:** 0.9990 Gold .2000 oz. AGW **Obverse:** Fleury cross **Reverse:** Portrait of Isabella I

| Date | Mintage | F | VF | XF | Unc | BU |
|---|---|---|---|---|---|---|
| 1997 Proof | Est. 3,500 | Value: 165 | | | | |

**20 DINERS** **KM# 144** **Weight:** 25.0000 g. **Composition:** 0.9250 Silver .7435 oz. ASW **Subject:** Human Rights **Obverse:** Crowned arms **Reverse:** Young family and broken chain **Note:** With 1.5 g. 0.917 gold inlay, 0.0442 oz. AGW.

| Date | Mintage | F | VF | XF | Unc | BU |
|---|---|---|---|---|---|---|
| 1998 | 5,000 | — | — | — | 80.00 | — |

**20 DINERS** **KM# 148** **Weight:** 25.0000 g. **Composition:** 0.9250 Silver .7435 oz. ASW **Subject:** Olympics 2000 **Obverse:** Crowned arms **Reverse:** Javelin thrower **Note:** With 1.5 g. 0.917 gold inlay, 0.0442 oz. AGW.

| Date | Mintage | F | VF | XF | Unc | BU |
|---|---|---|---|---|---|---|
| 1998 | 5,000 | — | — | — | 75.00 | — |

**20 DINERS** **KM# 149** **Weight:** 25.0000 g. **Composition:** 0.9250 Silver .7435 oz. ASW **Subject:** Olympics 2000 **Obverse:** Crowned arms **Reverse:** Discus thrower

| Date | Mintage | F | VF | XF | Unc | BU |
|---|---|---|---|---|---|---|
| 1998 | 5,000 | — | — | — | 75.00 | — |

**20 DINERS** **KM# 167** **Weight:** 25.0000 g. **Composition:** 0.9250 Silver .7435 oz. ASW **Subject:** XXVII JOCS 2000 Olympics **Obverse:** Crowned arms, date and denomination. **Reverse:** Hurdler on gold inlay. **Edge:** Plain.

| Date | Mintage | F | VF | XF | Unc | BU |
|---|---|---|---|---|---|---|
| 2000 | 6,000 | — | — | — | 75.00 | — |

**20 DINERS** **KM# 168** **Weight:** 25.0000 g. **Composition:** 0.9250 Silver .7435 oz. ASW **Subject:** XXVII JOCS 2000 Olympics **Obverse:** Crowned arms, date and denomination. **Reverse:** Runner on gold inlay. **Edge:** Plain.

| Date | Mintage | F | VF | XF | Unc | BU |
|---|---|---|---|---|---|---|
| 2000 | 6,000 | — | — | — | 75.00 | — |

**20 DINERS** **KM# 169** **Weight:** 25.0000 g. **Composition:** 0.9250 Silver .7435 oz. ASW **Subject:** XXVII JOCS 2000 Olympics **Obverse:** Crowned arms, date and denomination. **Reverse:** Long jumper on gold inlay. **Edge:** Plain.

| Date | Mintage | F | VF | XF | Unc | BU |
|---|---|---|---|---|---|---|
| 2000 | 6,000 | — | — | — | 75.00 | — |

**20 DINERS** **KM# 170** **Weight:** 25.0000 g. **Composition:** 0.9250 Silver .7435 oz. ASW **Subject:** XXVII JOCS 2000 Olympics **Obverse:** Crowned arms, date and denomination. **Reverse:** Pole vaulter on gold inlay. **Edge:** Plain.

| Date | Mintage | F | VF | XF | Unc | BU |
|---|---|---|---|---|---|---|
| 2000 | 6,000 | — | — | — | 75.00 | — |

**25 DINERS** **KM# 18** **Weight:** 20.0000 g. **Composition:** 0.9000 Silver .5787 oz. ASW **Obverse:** Joan D.M. Bisbe D'Urgell I

| Date | Mintage | F | VF | XF | Unc | BU |
|---|---|---|---|---|---|---|
| 1984 | 4,450 | — | — | — | 45.00 | — |
| 1984 Proof | 550 | Value: 125 | | | | |

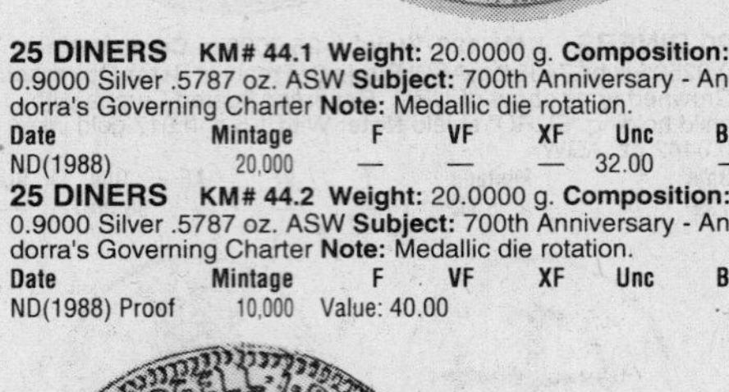


**25 DINERS** **KM# 44.1** **Weight:** 20.0000 g. **Composition:** 0.9000 Silver .5787 oz. ASW **Subject:** 700th Anniversary - Andorra's Governing Charter **Note:** Medallic die rotation.

| Date | Mintage | F | VF | XF | Unc | BU |
|---|---|---|---|---|---|---|
| ND(1988) | 20,000 | — | — | — | 32.00 | — |

**25 DINERS** **KM# 44.2** **Weight:** 20.0000 g. **Composition:** 0.9000 Silver .5787 oz. ASW **Subject:** 700th Anniversary - Andorra's Governing Charter **Note:** Medallic die rotation.

| Date | Mintage | F | VF | XF | Unc | BU |
|---|---|---|---|---|---|---|
| ND(1988) Proof | 10,000 | Value: 40.00 | | | | |

**25 DINERS** **KM# 61** **Weight:** 20.0000 g. **Composition:** 0.9000 Silver .5787 oz. ASW **Subject:** Millenary of the Bishop of Sala

| Date | Mintage | F | VF | XF | Unc | BU |
|---|---|---|---|---|---|---|
| 1989 | Est. 5,000 | — | — | — | 50.00 | — |

**25 DINERS** **KM# 65** **Weight:** 28.2800 g. **Composition:** 0.9250 Silver .8411 oz. ASW **Subject:** Red Cross

| Date | Mintage | F | VF | XF | Unc | BU |
|---|---|---|---|---|---|---|
| 1991 Proof | 3,000 | Value: 57.50 | | | | |

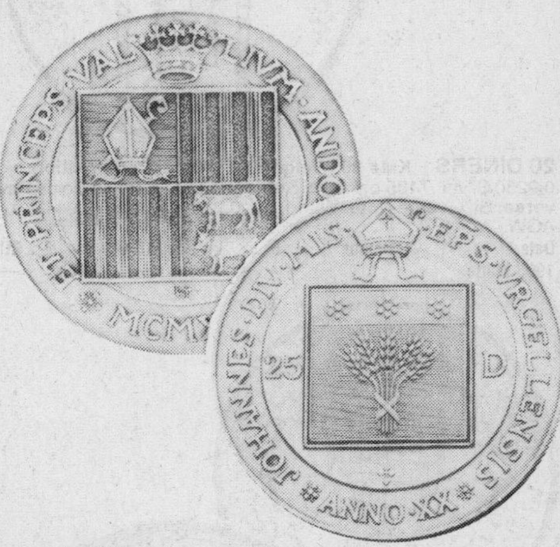


**25 DINERS** **KM# 69** **Weight:** 25.0000 g. **Composition:** 0.9250 Silver .7435 oz. ASW **Subject:** 20th Anniversary - Episcopal Co-prince **Note:** With 0.917 gold inlay, 0.0442 oz. AGW.

| Date | Mintage | F | VF | XF | Unc | BU |
|---|---|---|---|---|---|---|
| 1991 | 2,500 | — | — | — | 85.00 | — |

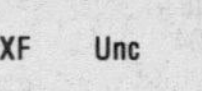

**25 DINERS** **KM# 73** **Weight:** 7.7700 g. **Composition:** 0.5830 Gold .1456 oz. AGW **Subject:** ECU Customs Union **Reverse:** St. Ermengol

| Date | Mintage | F | VF | XF | Unc | BU |
|---|---|---|---|---|---|---|
| 1992 Proof | 3,000 | Value: 100 | | | | |

**25 DINERS** **KM# 81** **Weight:** 7.7700 g. **Composition:** 0.5830 Gold .1456 oz. AGW **Subject:** 1994 Winter Olympic Games **Reverse:** Downhill skier

| Date | Mintage | F | VF | XF | Unc | BU |
|---|---|---|---|---|---|---|
| 1993 Proof | 6,000 | Value: 115 | | | | |

**25 DINERS** **KM# 91** **Weight:** 7.7700 g. **Composition:** 0.5830 Gold .1456 oz. AGW **Subject:** ECU Customs Union **Reverse:** Bishop riding a horse

| Date | Mintage | F | VF | XF | Unc | BU |
|---|---|---|---|---|---|---|
| 1993 Proof | 5,000 | Value: 115 | | | | |

**25 DINERS** **KM# 92** **Weight:** 7.7700 g. **Composition:** 0.5830 Gold .1456 oz. AGW **Subject:** 1994 World Cup Soccer

| Date | Mintage | F | VF | XF | Unc | BU |
|---|---|---|---|---|---|---|
| 1993 Proof | 5,000 | Value: 115 | | | | |

**25 DINERS** **KM# 96** **Weight:** 7.7700 g. **Composition:** 0.5830 Gold .1456 oz. AGW **Subject:** 1994 Summer Olympic Games **Reverse:** Tennis

| Date | Mintage | F | VF | XF | Unc | BU |
|---|---|---|---|---|---|---|
| 1994 Proof | 5,000 | Value: 115 | | | | |

**25 DINERS** **KM# 101** **Weight:** 7.7700 g. **Composition:** 0.5830 Gold .1456 oz. AGW **Subject:** ECU Customs Union **Obverse:** Coat of arms **Reverse:** Bishop Pere D'Urg standing

| Date | Mintage | F | VF | XF | Unc | BU |
|---|---|---|---|---|---|---|
| 1994 Proof | 5,000 | Value: 115 | | | | |

**25 DINERS** **KM# 107** **Weight:** 7.7700 g. **Composition:** 0.5830 Gold .1456 oz. AGW **Subject:** ECU Customs Union **Obverse:** Coat of arms **Reverse:** Bishop Pere D'Urg seated

| Date | Mintage | F | VF | XF | Unc | BU |
|---|---|---|---|---|---|---|
| 1995 Proof | 5,000 | Value: 115 | | | | |

**25 DINERS** **KM# 123** **Weight:** 7.7700 g. **Composition:** 0.5830 Gold .1456 oz. AGW **Obverse:** Arms and "ECU" **Reverse:** Seated Europa

| Date | Mintage | F | VF | XF | Unc | BU |
|---|---|---|---|---|---|---|
| 1996 Proof | Est. 5,000 | Value: 115 | | | | |

**25 DINERS** **KM# 129** **Weight:** 7.7700 g. **Composition:** 0.5830 Gold .1456 oz. AGW **Subject:** Treaty of Rome **Obverse:** Crowned arms **Reverse:** Europa on knee, holding large "EURO" shield

| Date | Mintage | F | VF | XF | Unc | BU |
|---|---|---|---|---|---|---|
| 1997 Proof | 5,000 | Value: 115 | | | | |

**25 DINERS** **KM# 139** **Ring Weight:** 3.1103 g. **Ring Composition:** 0.9995 Platinum .0999 oz. ASW AGW APW**Center Weight:** 3.1103 g. **Center Composition:** 0.9999 Gold .1000 oz. ASW AGW **Obverse:** Fleury cross **Reverse:** Swan in water

| Date | Mintage | F | VF | XF | Unc | BU |
|---|---|---|---|---|---|---|
| 1997 Proof | 10,000 | Value: 235 | | | | |

**25 DINERS** **KM# 145** **Weight:** 7.7700 g. **Composition:** 0.5850 Gold .1461 oz. AGW **Subject:** Human Rights **Obverse:** Crowned arms **Reverse:** Seated woman with quill

| Date | Mintage | F | VF | XF | Unc | BU |
|---|---|---|---|---|---|---|
| 1998 Proof | 5,000 | Value: 115 | | | | |

**50 DINERS** **KM# 63** **Weight:** 15.5500 g. **Composition:** 0.9990 Gold .5000 oz. AGW **Note:** There is a similar 1988 half-ounce without the denomination.

| Date | Mintage | F | VF | XF | Unc | BU |
|---|---|---|---|---|---|---|
| 1989 | 3,000 | — | — | — | 225 | — |
| 1989 Proof | — | Value: 250 | | | | |

**50 DINERS** **KM# 62** **Weight:** 17.0250 g. **Composition:** 0.9170 Gold .5000 oz. AGW **Reverse:** Antoni Gaudi

| Date | Mintage | F | VF | XF | Unc | BU |
|---|---|---|---|---|---|---|
| 1990 Proof | 3,000 | Value: 300 | | | | |

**50 DINERS** **KM# 64** **Weight:** 15.5500 g. **Composition:** 0.9990 Gold .5000 oz. AGW **Subject:** Wildlife **Reverse:** Red squirrel

| Date | Mintage | F | VF | XF | Unc | BU |
|---|---|---|---|---|---|---|
| 1990 Proof | 2,500 | Value: 275 | | | | |

**50 DINERS** **KM# 68** **Weight:** 15.5500 g. **Composition:** 0.9990 Gold .5000 oz. AGW **Subject:** Wildlife **Reverse:** Chamois

| Date | Mintage | F | VF | XF | Unc | BU |
|---|---|---|---|---|---|---|
| 1991 Proof | Est. 2,500 | Value: 275 | | | | |

**50 DINERS** **KM# 70** **Weight:** 13.3400 g. **Composition:** 0.5850 Gold .2509 oz. AGW **Subject:** 1992 Summer Olympic Games **Reverse:** Gymnast on rings

| Date | Mintage | F | VF | XF | Unc | BU |
|---|---|---|---|---|---|---|
| 1991 Proof | 3,000 | Value: 195 | | | | |

**50 DINERS** **KM# 93** **Weight:** 13.3400 g. **Composition:** 0.5850 Gold .2509 oz. AGW **Obverse:** Eagle

| Date | Mintage | F | VF | XF | Unc | BU |
|---|---|---|---|---|---|---|
| 1992 | — | — | — | — | 195 | — |

**50 DINERS** **KM# 77** **Weight:** 15.5520 g. **Composition:** 0.9999 Gold .4995 oz. AGW **Subject:** Wildlife **Reverse:** Bears

| Date | Mintage | F | VF | XF | Unc | BU |
|---|---|---|---|---|---|---|
| 1992 Proof | 2,500 | Value: 250 | | | | |

**50 DINERS** **KM# 82** **Weight:** 16.9650 g. **Composition:** 0.9160 Gold .4996 oz. AGW **Reverse:** Musician Pau Casals

| Date | Mintage | F | VF | XF | Unc | BU |
|---|---|---|---|---|---|---|
| 1993 Proof | 5,000 | Value: 250 | | | | |

**50 DINERS** **KM# 104** **Weight:** 155.5100 g. **Composition:** 0.9250 Silver 4.6253 oz. ASW **Subject:** 1st Anniversary - Andorran Constitution **Obverse:** Arms above "ECU" **Size:** 65 mm. **Note:** Illustration reduced.

| Date | Mintage | F | VF | XF | Unc | BU |
|---|---|---|---|---|---|---|
| 1994 | 5,000 | — | — | — | 185 | — |

**50 DINERS** **KM# 115** **Weight:** 155.5100 g. **Composition:** 0.9250 Silver 4.5058 oz. ASW **Subject:** 1996 Olympic Games **Obverse:** Arms above date **Reverse:** Angel lighting Olympic flame **Size:** 65.8 mm. **Note:** Illustration reduced.

| Date | Mintage | F | VF | XF | Unc | BU |
|---|---|---|---|---|---|---|
| 1995 | 5,000 | — | — | — | 185 | — |

**50 DINERS** **KM# 124** **Weight:** 155.5100 g. **Composition:** 0.9250 Silver 4.6253 oz. ASW **Subject:** Our Lady of Maritxell - Patroness of Andorra **Obverse:** Crowned arms in inner circle **Reverse:** Enthroned Madonna and child **Size:** 65 mm. **Note:** With insert of 2.5 g. 0.917 gold, 0.0737 AGW. Illustration reduced.

| Date | Mintage | F | VF | XF | Unc | BU |
|---|---|---|---|---|---|---|
| 1996 | 5,000 | — | — | — | 225 | — |

**50 DINERS** **KM# 152** **Weight:** 15.5520 g. **Composition:** 0.9160 Gold .4583 oz. AGW **Subject:** 250th Anniversary - Synod Constitution **Obverse:** Clerical arms **Reverse:** Madonna and child

| Date | Mintage | F | VF | XF | Unc | BU |
|---|---|---|---|---|---|---|
| 1998 Proof | 1,998 | Value: 300 | | | | |

**100 DINERS** **KM# 41** **Weight:** 5.0000 g. **Composition:** 0.9990 Gold .1607 oz. AGW

| Date | Mintage | F | VF | XF | Unc | BU |
|---|---|---|---|---|---|---|
| 1987 | 2,000 | — | — | — | 150 | — |

**100 DINERS** **KM# 42** **Weight:** 5.0000 g. **Composition:** 0.9990 Gold .1607 oz. AGW

| Date | Mintage | F | VF | XF | Unc | BU |
|---|---|---|---|---|---|---|
| 1988 | 2,000 | — | — | — | 225 | — |

**100 DINERS** **KM# 79** **Weight:** 31.1035 g. **Composition:** 0.9990 Gold 1 oz. AGW **Note:** There is a similar 1988 one-ounce without the denomination.

| Date | Mintage | F | VF | XF | Unc | BU |
|---|---|---|---|---|---|---|
| 1989 | 3,000 | — | — | — | 450 | — |

**100 DINERS** **KM# 94** **Weight:** 31.1035 g. **Composition:** 0.9990 Gold 1 oz. AGW **Obverse:** Eagle

| Date | Mintage | F | VF | XF | Unc | BU |
|---|---|---|---|---|---|---|
| 1992 | — | — | — | — | 450 | — |

**250 DINERS** **KM# 45** **Weight:** 12.0000 g. **Composition:** 0.9990 Gold .3858 oz. AGW **Subject:** 700th Anniversary - Andorra's Governing Charter

| Date | Mintage | F | VF | XF | Unc | BU |
|---|---|---|---|---|---|---|
| ND(1988) | 3,000 | — | — | — | 275 | — |

**SOVEREIGN** **KM# 30** **Weight:** 8.0000 g. **Composition:** 0.9180 Gold .2361 oz. AGW **Note:** Latin legend.

| Date | Mintage | F | VF | XF | Unc | BU |
|---|---|---|---|---|---|---|
| 1982 | 1,500 | — | — | — | 165 | — |

**SOVEREIGN** **KM# 31** **Weight:** 8.0000 g. **Composition:** 0.9180 Gold .2361 oz. AGW **Note:** Catalan legend.

| Date | Mintage | F | VF | XF | Unc | BU |
|---|---|---|---|---|---|---|
| 1982 | 1,500 | — | — | — | 165 | — |

**SOVEREIGN** **KM# 32** **Weight:** 8.0000 g. **Composition:** 0.9180 Gold .2361 oz. AGW **Note:** Latin legends.

| Date | Mintage | F | VF | XF | Unc | BU |
|---|---|---|---|---|---|---|
| 1983 | 1,500 | — | — | — | 165 | — |

## MEDALLIC COINAGE

**25 DINERS** **KM# M1** **Weight:** 14.0000 g. **Composition:** 0.9000 Silver .4051 oz. ASW **Obverse:** Charlemagne **Note:** Similar to 50 Diners, KM#M2.

| Date | Mintage | F | VF | XF | Unc | BU |
|---|---|---|---|---|---|---|
| 1960 Proof | 1,350 | Value: 35.00 | | | | |

**25 DINERS** **KM# M1a** **Composition:** Gold **Obverse:** Charlemagne **Note:** Similar to 50 Diners, KM#M2.

| Date | Mintage | F | VF | XF | Unc | BU |
|---|---|---|---|---|---|---|
| 1960 Proof | 8 | Value: 750 | | | | |

**25 DINERS** **KM# M1b** **Composition:** Platinum APW **Obverse:** Charlemagne **Note:** Similar to 50 Diners, KM#M2.

| Date | Mintage | F | VF | XF | Unc | BU |
|---|---|---|---|---|---|---|
| 1960 Proof | 3 | Value: 975 | | | | |

**25 DINERS** **KM# M3** **Weight:** 14.0000 g. **Composition:** 0.9000 Silver .4051 oz. ASW **Obverse:** Bishop Benlloch of Urgel

| Date | Mintage | F | VF | XF | Unc | BU |
|---|---|---|---|---|---|---|
| 1963 Proof | 1,350 | Value: 25.00 | | | | |

**25 DINERS** **KM# M3a** **Composition:** Gold **Obverse:** Bishop Benlloch of Urgel

| Date | Mintage | F | VF | XF | Unc | BU |
|---|---|---|---|---|---|---|
| 1963 Proof | 8 | Value: 600 | | | | |

**25 DINERS** **KM# M3b** **Composition:** Platinum APW **Obverse:** Bishop Benlloch of Urgel

| Date | Mintage | F | VF | XF | Unc | BU |
|---|---|---|---|---|---|---|
| 1963 Proof | 3 | Value: 775 | | | | |

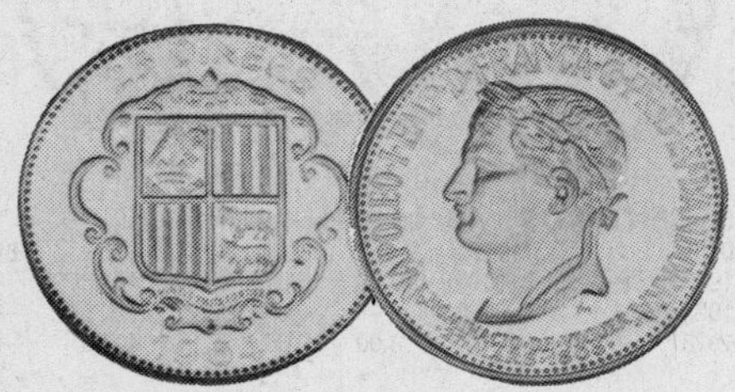

**25 DINERS** **KM# M5** **Weight:** 14.0000 g. **Composition:** 0.9000 Silver .4051 oz. ASW **Reverse:** Napoleon

| Date | Mintage | F | VF | XF | Unc | BU |
|---|---|---|---|---|---|---|
| 1964 Proof | 2,350 | Value: 25.00 | | | | |

**25 DINERS** **KM# M5a** **Composition:** Gold **Reverse:** Napoleon

| Date | Mintage | F | VF | XF | Unc | BU |
|---|---|---|---|---|---|---|
| 1964 Proof | 8 | Value: 600 | | | | |

**25 DINERS** **KM# M5b** **Composition:** Platinum APW **Reverse:** Napoleon

| Date | Mintage | F | VF | XF | Unc | BU |
|---|---|---|---|---|---|---|
| 1964 Proof | 3 | Value: 825 | | | | |

**25 DINERS** **KM# M7** **Weight:** 14.0000 g. **Composition:** 0.9000 Silver .4051 oz. ASW **Subject:** House of Council of Justice

| Date | Mintage | F | VF | XF | Unc | BU |
|---|---|---|---|---|---|---|
| 1965 Proof | 1,350 | Value: 35.00 | | | | |

**25 DINERS** **KM# M7a** **Composition:** Gold **Subject:** House of Council of Justice

| Date | Mintage | F | VF | XF | Unc | BU |
|---|---|---|---|---|---|---|
| 1965 Proof | 8 | Value: 550 | | | | |

**25 DINERS** **KM# M7b** **Composition:** Platinum APW **Subject:** House of Council of Justice

| Date | Mintage | F | VF | XF | Unc | BU |
|---|---|---|---|---|---|---|
| 1965 Proof | 3 | Value: 725 | | | | |

**50 DINERS** **KM# M2** **Weight:** 28.0000 g. **Composition:** 0.9000 Silver .8102 oz. ASW **Obverse:** Charlemagne

| Date | Mintage | F | VF | XF | Unc | BU |
|---|---|---|---|---|---|---|
| 1960 Proof | 3,100 | Value: 45.00 | | | | |

**50 DINERS** **KM# M2a** **Composition:** Gold **Obverse:** Charlemagne

| Date | Mintage | F | VF | XF | Unc | BU |
|---|---|---|---|---|---|---|
| 1960 Proof | 3 | Value: 1,750 | | | | |

**50 DINERS** **KM# M2b** **Composition:** Platinum APW **Obverse:** Charlemagne

| Date | Mintage | F | VF | XF | Unc | BU |
|---|---|---|---|---|---|---|
| 1960 Proof | 2 | Value: 2,500 | | | | |

**50 DINERS** **KM# M4** **Weight:** 28.0000 g. **Composition:** 0.9000 Silver .8102 oz. ASW **Obverse:** Bishop Benlloch of Urgel

| Date | Mintage | F | VF | XF | Unc | BU |
|---|---|---|---|---|---|---|
| 1963 Proof | 3,350 | Value: 35.00 | | | | |

**50 DINERS** **KM# M4a** **Composition:** Gold **Obverse:** Bishop Benlloch of Urgel

| Date | Mintage | F | VF | XF | Unc | BU |
|---|---|---|---|---|---|---|
| 1963 Proof | 8 | Value: 1,000 | | | | |

**50 DINERS** **KM# M4b** **Composition:** Platinum APW **Obverse:** Bishop Benlloch of Urgel

| Date | Mintage | F | VF | XF | Unc | BU |
|---|---|---|---|---|---|---|
| 1963 Proof | 3 | Value: 2,250 | | | | |

**50 DINERS** **KM# M6** **Weight:** 28.0000 g. **Composition:** 0.9000 Silver .8102 oz. ASW **Reverse:** Napoleon

| Date | Mintage | F | VF | XF | Unc | BU |
|---|---|---|---|---|---|---|
| 1964 Proof | 5,150 | Value: 35.00 | | | | |

**50 DINERS** **KM# M6a** **Composition:** Gold

| Date | Mintage | F | VF | XF | Unc | BU |
|---|---|---|---|---|---|---|
| 1964 Proof | 8 | Value: 1,000 | | | | |

**Note:**

**50 DINERS** **KM# M6b** **Composition:** Platinum APW

| Date | Mintage | F | VF | XF | Unc | BU |
|---|---|---|---|---|---|---|
| 1964 Proof | 3 | Value: 2,300 | | | | |

**50 DINERS** **KM# M8 (M7)** **Weight:** 28.0000 g. **Composition:** 0.9000 Silver .8102 oz. ASW **Subject:** House of Council of Justice

| Date | Mintage | Good | VG | F | VF | XF |
|---|---|---|---|---|---|---|
| 1965 Proof | 3,150 | Value: 50.00 | | | | |

**50 DINERS** **KM# M8a** **Composition:** Gold **Subject:** House of Council of Justice

| Date | Mintage | F | VF | XF | Unc | BU |
|---|---|---|---|---|---|---|
| 1965 Proof | 8 | Value: 1,000 | | | | |

**50 DINERS** **KM# M8b** **Composition:** Platinum APW **Subject:** House of Council of Justice

| Date | Mintage | F | VF | XF | Unc | BU |
|---|---|---|---|---|---|---|
| 1965 Proof | 3 | Value: 2,100 | | | | |

## PATTERNS

| KM# | Date | Mintage | Identification | Mkt Val |
|---|---|---|---|---|
| Pn1 | 1987 | — | 2 Diners. Nickel Plated Copper. KM#46. | — |

## MINT SETS

| KM# | Date | Mintage | Identification | Issue Price | Mkt Val |
|---|---|---|---|---|---|
| MS1 | 1986 | — | KM#33, 35-38 | 31.00 | 67.50 |

## PROOF SETS

| KM# | Date | Mintage | Identification | Issue Price | Mkt Val |
|---|---|---|---|---|---|
| PS1 | 1963 | 1,000 | KM#M3, M4 | 51.00 | 60.00 |
| PS2 | 1964 | — | M5, M6 | 51.00 | 60.00 |
| PS3 | 1964 | 4 | M5a, M6a | — | 1,600 |
| PS4 | 1965 | — | M7, M8 | 80.00 | 65.00 |
| PS5 | 1965 | — | M7a, M8a | — | 1,550 |

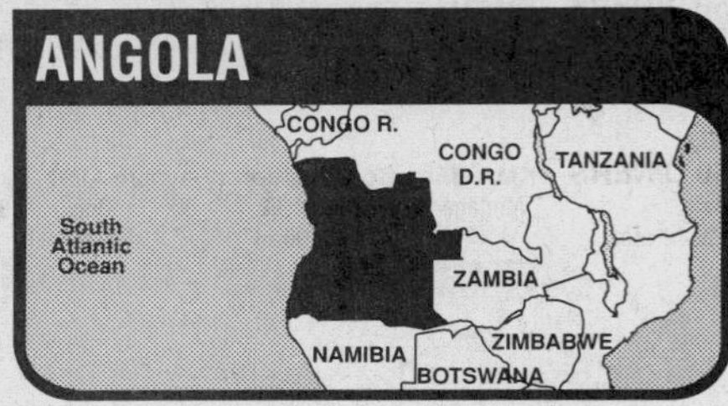


The Republic of Angola, a country on the west coast of southern Africa bounded by Zaire, Zambia, and Namibia (Southwest Africa), has an area of 481,351 sq. mi. (1,246,700 sq. km.) and a population of 12.78 million, predominantly Bantu in origin. Capital: Luanda. Most of the people are engaged in subsistence agriculture. However, important oil and mineral deposits make Angola potentially one of the richest countries in Africa. Iron and diamonds are exported.

The Portuguese navigator, Diogo Cao, discovered Angola in 1482 Angola. Portuguese settlers arrived in 1491, and established Angola as a major slaving center, which sent about 3 million slaves to the New World.

A revolt, characterized by guerrilla warfare, against Portuguese rule began in 1961 and continued until 1974, when a new regime in Portugal offered independence. The independence movement was actively supported by three groups; the National Front, based in Zaire, the Soviet-backed Popular Movement, and the moderate National Union. Independence was proclaimed on Nov. 11, 1975, and the Portuguese departed, leaving the Angolan people to work out their own political destiny. Within hours, each of the independence groups proclaimed itself Angola's sole ruler. A bloody intertribal civil war erupted in which the Communist Popular Movement, assisted by Soviet arms and Cuban mercenaries, was the eventual victor.

**RULERS**

Portuguese until 1975

**MINT MARKS**

KN - King's Norton

**MONETARY SYSTEM**

**(Until 1860)**

50 Reis = 1 Macuta (Commencing 1910)

100 Centavos = 20 Macutas = 1 Escudo

# PORTUGUESE COLONY

## DECIMAL COINAGE

Commencing 1910

100 Centavos = 20 Macutas = 1 Escudo

100 Centavos = 1 Escudo

**CENTAVO** **KM# 60** **Composition:** Bronze

| Date | Mintage | F | VF | XF | Unc | BU |
|---|---|---|---|---|---|---|
| 1921 | 1,360,000 | 7.50 | 12.50 | 30.00 | 65.00 | — |

**2 CENTAVOS** **KM# 61** **Composition:** Bronze

| Date | Mintage | F | VF | XF | Unc | BU |
|---|---|---|---|---|---|---|
| 1921 | 530,000 | 10.00 | 15.00 | 50.00 | 110 | — |

**5 CENTAVOS (1 Macuta)** **KM# 62** **Composition:** Bronze

| Date | Mintage | F | VF | XF | Unc | BU |
|---|---|---|---|---|---|---|
| 1921 | 720,000 | 5.00 | 18.00 | 45.00 | 80.00 | — |
| 1922 | 5,680,000 | 4.00 | 14.00 | 30.00 | 55.00 | — |
| 1923 | 5,840,000 | 4.00 | 14.00 | 30.00 | 55.00 | — |
| 1924 | — | 12.00 | 35.00 | 70.00 | 135 | — |

**5 CENTAVOS (1 Macuta)** **KM# 66** **Composition:** Nickel-Bronze

| Date | Mintage | F | VF | XF | Unc | BU |
|---|---|---|---|---|---|---|
| 1927 | 2,001,999 | 2.50 | 6.00 | 13.50 | 27.50 | — |

**10 CENTAVOS (2 Macutas)** **KM# 63** **Composition:** Copper-Nickel

| Date | Mintage | F | VF | XF | Unc | BU |
|---|---|---|---|---|---|---|
| 1921 | 160,000 | 10.00 | 30.00 | 65.00 | 120 | — |
| 1922 | 340,000 | 7.50 | 15.00 | 45.00 | 85.00 | — |
| 1923 | 2,960,000 | 3.50 | 8.00 | 20.00 | 45.00 | — |

**10 CENTAVOS (2 Macutas)** **KM# 67** **Composition:** Copper-Nickel

| Date | Mintage | F | VF | XF | Unc | BU |
|---|---|---|---|---|---|---|
| 1927 | 2,003,000 | 2.00 | 4.00 | 16.00 | 32.00 | — |
| 1928 | 1,000,000 | 2.00 | 4.00 | 16.00 | 32.00 | — |

**10 CENTAVOS (2 Macutas)** **KM# 70** **Composition:** Bronze **Subject:** 300th Anniversary - Revolution of 1648

| Date | Mintage | F | VF | XF | Unc | BU |
|---|---|---|---|---|---|---|
| 1948 | 10,000,000 | 0.50 | 1.00 | 3.50 | 7.50 | — |
| 1949 | 10,000,000 | 0.35 | 0.75 | 3.00 | 6.50 | — |

**10 CENTAVOS (2 Macutas)** **KM# 82** **Composition:** Aluminum

| Date | Mintage | F | VF | XF | Unc | BU |
|---|---|---|---|---|---|---|
| 1974 | 4,000,000 | — | — | — | 17.50 | — |

**Note:** Not released for circulation, but relatively available

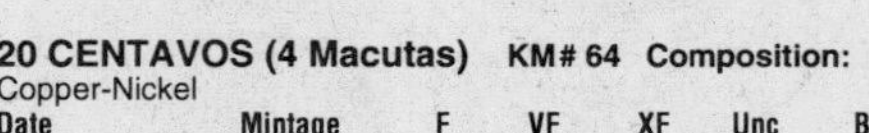

**20 CENTAVOS (4 Macutas)** **KM# 64** **Composition:** Copper-Nickel

| Date | Mintage | F | VF | XF | Unc | BU |
|---|---|---|---|---|---|---|
| 1921 | 2,115,000 | 4.00 | 9.00 | 22.00 | 40.00 | — |
| 1922 | 1,730,000 | 6.50 | 14.50 | 35.00 | 65.00 | — |

**20 CENTAVOS (4 Macutas)** **KM# 68** **Composition:** Copper-Nickel

| Date | Mintage | F | VF | XF | Unc | BU |
|---|---|---|---|---|---|---|
| 1927 | 2,001,000 | 2.50 | 4.00 | 8.00 | 20.00 | — |
| 1928 | 500,000 | 3.50 | 6.00 | 13.50 | 27.50 | — |

**20 CENTAVOS (4 Macutas)** **KM# 71** **Composition:** Bronze **Subject:** 300th Anniversary - Revolution of 1648

| Date | Mintage | F | VF | XF | Unc | BU |
|---|---|---|---|---|---|---|
| 1948 | 7,850,000 | 0.50 | 1.00 | 2.00 | 4.50 | — |
| 1949 | 2,150,000 | 4.00 | 7.50 | 12.50 | 22.50 | — |

**20 CENTAVOS (4 Macutas)** **KM# 78** **Composition:** Bronze

| Date | Mintage | F | VF | XF | Unc | BU |
|---|---|---|---|---|---|---|
| 1962 | 3,000,000 | — | 0.25 | 0.65 | 1.75 | — |

**50 CENTAVOS** **KM# 65** **Composition:** Nickel

| Date | Mintage | F | VF | XF | Unc | BU |
|---|---|---|---|---|---|---|
| 1922 | 6,000,000 | 3.00 | 10.00 | 20.00 | 40.00 | — |
| 1923 KN | 6,000,000 | — | — | 225 | 375 | — |
| 1923 | Inc. above | 3.00 | 10.00 | 20.00 | 40.00 | — |

**50 CENTAVOS** **KM# 69** **Composition:** Nickel-Bronze

| Date | Mintage | F | VF | XF | Unc | BU |
|---|---|---|---|---|---|---|
| 1927 | 1,608,000 | 5.00 | 18.00 | 35.00 | 70.00 | — |
| 1928/7 | 1,600,000 | 5.00 | 18.00 | 40.00 | 75.00 | — |
| 1928 | Inc. above | 3.50 | 12.50 | 30.00 | 65.00 | — |

**50 CENTAVOS** **KM# 72** **Composition:** Nickel-Bronze **Subject:** 300th Anniversary - Revolution of 1648

| Date | Mintage | F | VF | XF | Unc | BU |
|---|---|---|---|---|---|---|
| 1948 | 4,000,000 | 0.50 | 1.00 | 3.50 | 8.00 | — |
| 1950 | 4,000,000 | 0.50 | 1.00 | 3.50 | 8.00 | — |

**50 CENTAVOS** **KM# 75** **Composition:** Bronze

| Date | Mintage | F | VF | XF | Unc | BU |
|---|---|---|---|---|---|---|
| 1953 | 5,000,000 | — | 0.25 | 0.65 | 2.50 | — |
| 1954 | 11,731,000 | — | 0.20 | 0.40 | 1.75 | — |
| 1955 | 1,126,000 | — | 3.00 | 5.00 | 16.50 | — |
| 1957 | 8,873,000 | — | 0.20 | 0.45 | 2.00 | — |
| 1958 | 17,520,000 | — | 0.15 | 0.35 | 1.50 | — |
| 1961 | 8,750,000 | — | 0.20 | 0.45 | 2.00 | — |

**50 CENTAVOS** **KM# 75a** **Composition:** Copper-Nickel

| Date | Mintage | F | VF | XF | Unc | BU |
|---|---|---|---|---|---|---|
| 1974 | 150 | — | — | 125 | 250 | — |

**Note:** Not released for circulation

**ESCUDO** **KM# 76** **Composition:** Bronze

| Date | Mintage | F | VF | XF | Unc | BU |
|---|---|---|---|---|---|---|
| 1953 | 2,001,000 | — | 1.50 | 6.00 | 15.00 | — |
| 1956 | 2,989,000 | — | 1.00 | 4.00 | 10.00 | — |
| 1963 | 5,000,000 | — | 1.00 | 2.00 | 7.00 | — |
| 1965 | 5,000,000 | — | 1.00 | 2.00 | 7.00 | — |
| 1972 | 10,000,000 | — | 0.75 | 1.50 | 4.50 | — |
| 1974 | 6,214,000 | — | 0.75 | 1.50 | 4.50 | — |

**ESCUDO** **KM# 76a** **Composition:** Copper-Nickel **Note:** Not released for circulation.

| Date | Mintage | F | VF | XF | Unc | BU |
|---|---|---|---|---|---|---|
| 1972 Rare | — | — | — | — | — | — |
| 1974 Rare | — | — | — | — | — | — |

**2-1/2 ESCUDOS** **KM# 77** **Composition:** Copper-Nickel

| Date | Mintage | F | VF | XF | Unc | BU |
|---|---|---|---|---|---|---|
| 1953 | 6,008,000 | — | 1.00 | 2.50 | 10.00 | — |
| 1956 | 9,992,000 | — | 0.35 | 1.75 | 4.00 | — |
| 1967 | 6,000,000 | — | 0.35 | 1.75 | 4.00 | — |
| 1968 | 5,000,000 | — | 0.35 | 1.75 | 4.00 | — |
| 1969 | 5,000,000 | — | 0.35 | 1.75 | 4.00 | — |
| 1974 | 19,999,000 | — | 0.25 | 0.50 | 3.00 | — |

**5 ESCUDOS** **KM# 81** **Composition:** Copper-Nickel

| Date | Mintage | F | VF | XF | Unc | BU |
|---|---|---|---|---|---|---|
| 1972 | 8,000,000 | — | 10.00 | 20.00 | 45.00 | — |
| 1974 | Est. 3,343,000 | — | — | 100 | 200 | — |

**Note:** Not released for circulation

**10 ESCUDOS** **KM# 73** **Weight:** 5.0000 g. **Composition:** 0.7200 Silver .1157 oz. ASW

| Date | Mintage | F | VF | XF | Unc | BU |
|---|---|---|---|---|---|---|
| 1952 | 2,023,000 | — | 2.50 | 5.00 | 10.00 | — |
| 1955 | 1,977,000 | — | 2.50 | 5.00 | 10.00 | — |

**10 ESCUDOS** **KM# 79** **Composition:** Copper-Nickel

| Date | Mintage | F | VF | XF | Unc | BU |
|---|---|---|---|---|---|---|
| 1969 | 3,022,000 | — | 1.50 | 3.00 | 6.00 | — |
| 1970 | 978,000 | — | 2.00 | 4.00 | 7.00 | — |

**20 ESCUDOS** **KM# 74** **Weight:** 10.0000 g. **Composition:** 0.7200 Silver .2315 oz. ASW

| Date | Mintage | F | VF | XF | Unc | BU |
|---|---|---|---|---|---|---|
| 1952 | 1,002,999 | — | 2.50 | 6.00 | 13.50 | — |
| 1955 | 997,000 | — | 2.50 | 5.00 | 10.00 | — |

**20 ESCUDOS** **KM# 80** **Composition:** Nickel

| Date | Mintage | F | VF | XF | Unc | BU |
|---|---|---|---|---|---|---|
| 1971 | 1,572,000 | — | 0.75 | 2.00 | 4.00 | — |
| 1972 | 428,000 | — | 2.50 | 5.00 | 10.00 | — |

# PEOPLES REPUBLIC

## DECIMAL COINAGE

1975 -

100 Lwei = 1 Kwanza

**50 LWEI** **KM# 90** **Composition:** Copper-Nickel

| Date | Mintage | F | VF | XF | Unc | BU |
|---|---|---|---|---|---|---|
| 1979 | — | — | 0.10 | 0.30 | 1.00 | — |

**KWANZA** **KM# 83** **Composition:** Copper-Nickel

| Date | Mintage | F | VF | XF | Unc | BU |
|---|---|---|---|---|---|---|
| 1978 | — | — | 0.25 | 0.40 | 1.50 | — |
| 1979 | — | — | 0.25 | 0.40 | 1.50 | — |

**2 KWANZAS** **KM# 84** **Composition:** Copper-Nickel

| Date | Mintage | F | VF | XF | Unc | BU |
|---|---|---|---|---|---|---|
| ND(1978) | — | — | 0.40 | 0.60 | 1.75 | — |

**5 KWANZAS** **KM# 85** **Composition:** Copper-Nickel

| Date | Mintage | F | VF | XF | Unc | BU |
|---|---|---|---|---|---|---|
| ND(1978) | — | — | 0.65 | 1.25 | 2.50 | — |

**10 KWANZAS** **KM# 86.1** **Composition:** Copper-Nickel **Reverse:** Small date, dots near rim

| Date | Mintage | F | VF | XF | Unc | BU |
|---|---|---|---|---|---|---|
| 1978 | — | — | 1.50 | 2.50 | 4.50 | — |

**10 KWANZAS** **KM# 86.2** **Composition:** Copper-Nickel **Reverse:** Large date, dots away from rim

| Date | Mintage | F | VF | XF | Unc | BU |
|---|---|---|---|---|---|---|
| 1978 | — | — | 1.50 | 2.50 | 4.50 | — |

**20 KWANZAS** **KM# 87** **Composition:** Copper-Nickel

| Date | Mintage | F | VF | XF | Unc | BU |
|---|---|---|---|---|---|---|
| 1978 | — | — | 2.00 | 3.00 | 6.00 | — |

## REFORM COINAGE

**KWANZA** **KM# 97** **Weight:** 4.5000 g. **Composition:** Copper-Nickel **Obverse:** National arms, country name and date **Reverse:** Denomination **Edge:** Reeded

| Date | Mintage | F | VF | XF | Unc | BU |
|---|---|---|---|---|---|---|
| 1999 | — | — | — | — | 1.50 | — |

**2 KWANZAS** **KM# 98** **Weight:** 5.0000 g. **Composition:** Copper-Nickel **Obverse:** National arms, country name and date **Reverse:** Denomination **Edge:** Reeded

| Date | Mintage | F | VF | XF | Unc | BU |
|---|---|---|---|---|---|---|
| 1999 | — | — | — | — | 2.00 | — |

**5 KWANZAS** **KM# 99** **Weight:** 7.0000 g. **Composition:** Copper-Nickel **Obverse:** National arms, country name and date **Reverse:** Denomination **Edge:** Reeded

| Date | Mintage | F | VF | XF | Unc | BU |
|---|---|---|---|---|---|---|
| 1999 | — | — | — | — | 3.50 | — |

**10 KWANZAS** **KM# 93** **Weight:** 24.2250 g. **Composition:** Copper-Nickel **Subject:** Olympics **Obverse:** National arms **Reverse:** Olympic logo and allegory **Edge:** Reeded

| Date | Mintage | F | VF | XF | Unc | BU |
|---|---|---|---|---|---|---|
| 1999 Proof | — | Value: 15.00 | | | | |

**10 KWANZAS** KM# 100 **Weight:** 23.0500 g. **Composition:** Copper-Nickel **Subject:** Prince Henry the Navigator **Obverse:** Angolan arms. **Reverse:** Prince Henry in armour half facing left. **Edge:** Reeded.

| Date | Mintage | F | VF | XF | Unc | BU |
|---|---|---|---|---|---|---|
| 1999 Proof | — | Value: 15.00 | | | | |

**100 KWANZAS** KM# 94 **Weight:** 25.0000 g. **Composition:** 0.9250 Silver .7435 oz. ASW **Subject:** Olympics **Obverse:** National arms **Reverse:** Olympic logo and allegory

| Date | Mintage | F | VF | XF | Unc | BU |
|---|---|---|---|---|---|---|
| 1999 Proof | — | Value: 35.00 | | | | |

**10 CENTIMOS** KM# 95 **Weight:** 1.5000 g. **Composition:** Copper Plated Steel **Obverse:** National arms, country name and date **Reverse:** Denomination **Edge:** Reeded

| Date | Mintage | F | VF | XF | Unc | BU |
|---|---|---|---|---|---|---|
| 1999 | — | — | — | — | 0.50 | — |

**50 CENTIMOS** KM# 96 **Weight:** 3.0000 g. **Composition:** Copper Plated Steel **Obverse:** National arms, country name and date **Reverse:** Denomination **Edge:** Reeded

| Date | Mintage | F | VF | XF | Unc | BU |
|---|---|---|---|---|---|---|
| 1999 | — | — | — | — | 1.00 | — |

## PATTERNS

(Including off metal strikes)

| KM# | Date | Mintage | Identification | Mkt Val |
|---|---|---|---|---|
| Pn7 | 1972 | — | 50 Escudos. Silver. | 1,500 |

## PROVAS

| KM# | Date | Mintage | Identification | Issue Price | Mkt Val |
|---|---|---|---|---|---|
| Pr1 | 1921 | — | Centavo. KM#60. | — | 25.00 |
| Pr2 | 1921 | — | 2 Centavos. KM#61. | — | 25.00 |
| Pr3 | 1921 | — | 5 Centavos. KM#62. | — | 25.00 |
| Pr4 | 1921 | — | 10 Centavos. KM#63. | — | 35.00 |
| Pr5 | 1921 | — | 20 Centavos. KM#64. | — | 30.00 |
| Pr6 | 1922 | — | 5 Centavos. KM#62. | — | 25.00 |
| Pr7 | 1922 | — | 10 Centavos. KM#63. | — | 30.00 |
| Pr8 | 1922 | — | 20 Centavos. KM#64. | — | 30.00 |
| Pr9 | 1923 | — | 5 Centavos. KM#62. | — | 25.00 |
| Pr10 | 1923 | — | 10 Centavos. KM#63. | — | 30.00 |
| Pr11 | 1923 | — | 20 Centavos. KM#64. | — | 30.00 |
| Pr12 | 1924 | — | 5 Centavos. KM#62. | — | 100 |
| Pr13 | 1927 | — | 5 Centavos. KM#66. | — | 20.00 |
| Pr14 | 1927 | — | 10 Centavos. KM#67. | — | 20.00 |
| Pr15 | 1927 | — | 20 Centavos. KM#68. | — | 20.00 |
| Pr16 | 1927 | — | 50 Centavos. KM#69. | — | 20.00 |
| Pr17 | 1928 | — | 10 Centavos. KM#67. | — | 20.00 |
| Pr18 | 1928 | — | 20 Centavos. KM#68. | — | 20.00 |
| Pr19 | 1928 | — | 50 Centavos. KM#69. | — | 20.00 |
| Pr20 | 1948 | — | 10 Centavos. KM#70. | — | 20.00 |
| Pr21 | 1948 | — | 20 Centavos. KM#71. | — | 20.00 |
| Pr22 | 1948 | — | 50 Centavos. KM#72. | — | 20.00 |
| Pr23 | 1949 | — | 10 Centavos. KM#70. | — | 20.00 |
| Pr24 | 1949 | — | 20 Centavos. KM#71. | — | 20.00 |
| Pr25 | 1949 | — | 50 Centavos. KM#72. | — | 20.00 |
| Pr26 | 1950 | — | 50 Centavos. KM#72. | — | 15.00 |
| Pr27 | 1952 | — | 10 Escudos. KM#73. | — | 30.00 |
| Pr28 | 1952 | — | 20 Escudos. KM#74. | — | 42.00 |
| Pr29 | 1953 | — | 50 Centavos. KM#75. | — | 15.00 |
| Pr30 | 1953 | — | Escudo. KM#76. | — | 20.00 |
| Pr31 | 1953 | — | 2-1/2 Escudos. KM#77. | — | 30.00 |
| Pr32 | 1954 | — | 50 Centavos. KM#75. | — | 15.00 |
| Pr33 | 1954 | — | Escudo. KM#76. | — | 20.00 |
| Pr34 | 1954 | — | 2-1/2 Escudos. KM#77. | — | 30.00 |
| Pr35 | 1955 | — | 50 Centavos. KM#75. | — | 15.00 |
| Pr36 | 1955 | — | Escudo. KM#76. | — | 20.00 |
| Pr37 | 1955 | — | 2-1/2 Escudos. KM#77. | — | 30.00 |
| Pr38 | 1955 | — | 10 Escudos. KM#73. | — | 30.00 |
| Pr39 | 1955 | — | 20 Escudos. KM#74. | — | 42.00 |
| Pr40 | 1956 | — | 50 Centavos. KM#75. | — | 12.50 |
| Pr41 | 1956 | — | Escudo. KM#76. | — | 12.50 |
| Pr42 | 1956 | — | 2-1/2 Escudos. KM#77. | — | 12.50 |
| Pr43 | 1957 | — | 50 Centavos. KM#75. | — | 12.50 |
| Pr44 | 1957 | — | Escudo. KM#76. | — | 12.50 |
| Pr45 | 1957 | — | 2-1/2 Escudos. KM#77. | — | 12.50 |
| Pr46 | 1958 | — | 50 Centavos. KM#75. | — | 12.50 |
| Pr47 | 1958 | — | Escudo. KM#76. | — | 12.50 |
| Pr48 | 1958 | — | 2-1/2 Escudos. KM#77. | — | 12.50 |
| Pr49 | 1959 | — | 50 Centavos. KM#75. | — | 12.50 |
| Pr50 | 1959 | — | Escudo. KM#76. | — | 12.50 |
| Pr51 | 1959 | — | 2-1/2 Escudos. KM#77. | — | 12.50 |
| Pr52 | 1960 | — | 50 Centavos. KM#75. | — | 12.50 |
| Pr53 | 1960 | — | Escudo. KM#76. | — | 12.50 |
| Pr54 | 1960 | — | 2-1/2 Escudos. KM#77. | — | 12.50 |
| Pr55 | 1961 | — | 50 Centavos. KM#75. | — | 12.50 |
| Pr56 | 1961 | — | Escudo. KM#76. | — | 12.50 |
| Pr57 | 1961 | — | 2-1/2 Escudos. KM#77. | — | 12.50 |
| Pr58 | 1962 | — | 20 Centavos. KM#78. | — | 12.50 |
| Pr59 | 1962 | — | Escudo. KM#76. | — | 12.50 |
| Pr60 | 1962 | — | 2-1/2 Escudos. KM#77. | — | 12.50 |
| Pr61 | 1963 | — | Escudo. KM#76. | — | 12.50 |
| Pr62 | 1963 | — | 2-1/2 Escudos. KM#77. | — | 12.50 |
| Pr63 | 1964 | — | Escudo. KM#76. | — | 12.50 |
| Pr64 | 1964 | — | 2-1/2 Escudos. KM#77. | — | 12.50 |
| Pr65 | 1965 | — | Escudo. KM#76. | — | 12.50 |
| Pr66 | 1965 | — | 2-1/2 Escudos. KM#77. | — | 12.50 |
| Pr67 | 1966 | — | Escudo. KM#76. | — | 12.50 |
| Pr68 | 1966 | — | 2-1/2 Escudos. KM#77. | — | 12.50 |
| Pr69 | 1967 | — | Escudo. KM#76. | — | 12.50 |
| Pr70 | 1967 | — | 2-1/2 Escudos. KM#77. | — | 12.50 |
| Pr71 | 1968 | — | Escudo. KM#76. | — | 12.50 |
| Pr72 | 1968 | — | 2-1/2 Escudos. KM#77. | — | 12.50 |
| Pr73 | 1969 | — | Escudo. KM#76. | — | 12.50 |
| Pr74 | 1969 | — | 2-1/2 Escudos. KM#77. | — | 12.50 |
| Pr75 | 1969 | — | 10 Escudos. KM#79. | — | 12.50 |
| Pr76 | 1970 | — | Escudo. KM#76. | — | 12.50 |
| Pr77 | 1970 | — | 2-1/2 Escudos. KM#77. | — | 12.50 |
| Pr78 | 1970 | — | 10 Escudos. KM#79. | — | 12.50 |
| Pr79 | 1971 | — | Escudo. KM#76. | — | 12.50 |
| Pr80 | 1971 | — | 2-1/2 Escudos. KM#77. | — | 12.50 |
| Pr81 | 1971 | — | 20 Escudos. KM#80. | — | 12.50 |
| Pr82 | 1972 | — | Escudo. KM#76. | — | 12.50 |
| Pr83 | 1972 | — | 2-1/2 Escudos. KM#77. | — | 12.50 |
| Pr84 | 1972 | — | 5 Escudos. KM#81. | — | 12.50 |
| Pr85 | 1972 | — | 20 Escudos. KM#80. | — | 12.50 |
| Pr86 | 1974 | — | Escudo. KM#76. | — | 12.50 |

## MINT SETS

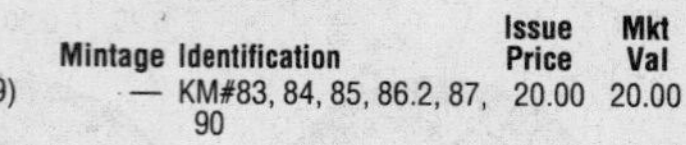

| KM# | Date | Mintage | Identification | Issue Price | Mkt Val |
|---|---|---|---|---|---|
| MS1 | ND (1979) | — | KM#83, 84, 85, 86.2, 87, 90 | 20.00 | 20.00 |

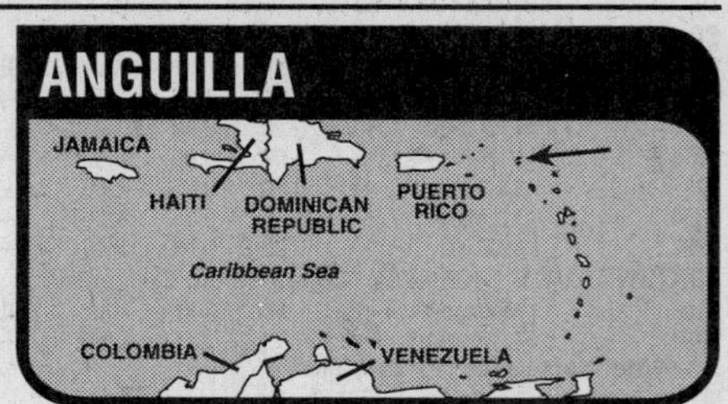


The British dependency of Anguilla, a self-governing British territory situated in the east Caribbean Sea about 60 miles (100 km.) northwest of St. Kitts, has an area of 35 sq. mi. (91 sq. km.) and an approximate population of 12,000. Capital: The Valley. In recent years, tourism has replaced the traditional fishing, stock raising and salt production as the main industry.

Anguilla was discovered by Columbus in 1493 and became a British colony in 1650. As the other British areas in the West Indies did, Anguilla officially adapted to sterling beginning in 1825. From 1950 to 1965, Anguilla was a member of the British Caribbean Territories (Eastern Group) Currency Board, whose coinage it used. In March 1967, Anguilla was joined politically with St. Christopher (St. Kitts), as it had been for much of its colonial history, and Nevis to form a British associated state.

On June 16, 1967, the Provisional Government of Anguilla unilaterally declared its independence and seceded from the Federation. Later, on July 11, 1967, a vote of confidence was taken and the results favored independence. Britain refused to accept the declaration (nor did any other country recognize it) and appointed a British administrator whom Anguilla accepted. However, in Feb. 1969 Anguilla ousted the British emissary, voted to sever all ties with Britain, and established the Republic of Anguilla. The following month Britain landed a force of paratroopers and policemen. This bloodless counteraction ended the self-proclaimed republic and resulted in the installation of a governing commissioner. The troops were withdrawn in Sept. 1969, and the Anguilla Act of July 1971 placed Anguilla directly under British control. A new constitution in 1976 established Anguilla as a self-governing British colony. Britain retains power over defense, police and civil service, and foreign affairs. Since 1981, Anguilla has employed the coinage of the East Caribbean States.

**NOTE**: There is no evidence that the issues of the self- proclaimed Provisional Government ever actually circulated. The c/s series most likely served as souvenirs of the "revolution".

**RULERS**

British

# BRITISH COLONY

## DECIMAL COINAGE

**1/2 DOLLAR** KM# 15 **Weight:** 3.6100 g. **Composition:** 0.9990 Silver .1160 oz. ASW **Obverse:** St. Mary's Church

| Date | Mintage | F | VF | XF | Unc | BU |
|---|---|---|---|---|---|---|
| ND Proof | 4,200 | Value: 15.00 | | | | |
| 1969 Proof | — | Value: 15.00 | | | | |
| 1970 Proof | Inc. above | Value: 15.00 | | | | |

**DOLLAR** KM# 16 **Weight:** 7.1800 g. **Composition:** 0.9990 Silver .2308 oz. ASW **Obverse:** Map - Flora and Fauna

| Date | Mintage | F | VF | XF | Unc | BU |
|---|---|---|---|---|---|---|
| ND Proof | 4,450 | Value: 18.00 | | | | |
| 1969 Proof | — | Value: 18.00 | | | | |
| 1970 Proof | Inc. above | Value: 18.00 | | | | |

**2 DOLLARS** KM# 17 **Weight:** 14.1400 g. **Composition:** 0.9990 Silver .4546 oz. ASW **Obverse:** National Flag and Map

| Date | Mintage | F | VF | XF | Unc | BU |
|---|---|---|---|---|---|---|
| ND Proof | 4,150 | Value: 25.00 | | | | |
| 1969 Proof | — | Value: 25.00 | | | | |
| 1970 Proof | Inc. above | Value: 25.00 | | | | |

**4 DOLLARS** KM# 18.1 **Weight:** 28.4800 g. **Composition:** 0.9990 Silver .9156 oz. ASW **Obverse:** Ship - Atlantic Star

| Date | Mintage | F | VF | XF | Unc | BU |
|---|---|---|---|---|---|---|
| ND Proof | 5,100 | Value: 50.00 | | | | |
| 1969 Proof | — | Value: 50.00 | | | | |
| 1970 Proof | Inc. above | Value: 50.00 | | | | |

**4 DOLLARS** KM# 18.2 **Weight:** 28.4800 g. **Composition:** 0.9990 Silver .9156 oz. ASW **Reverse:** 2 hallmarks at 4 o'clock

| Date | Mintage | F | VF | XF | Unc | BU |
|---|---|---|---|---|---|---|
| 1970 Proof | — | Value: 90.00 | | | | |

**5 DOLLARS** KM# 20 **Weight:** 2.4600 g. **Composition:** 0.9000 Gold .0711 oz. AGW **Obverse:** Methodist Church of West End

| Date | Mintage | F | VF | XF | Unc | BU |
|---|---|---|---|---|---|---|
| ND Proof | 1,925 | Value: 55.00 | | | | |
| 1969 Proof | — | Value: 55.00 | | | | |
| 1970 Proof | Inc. above | Value: 55.00 | | | | |

**10 DOLLARS** KM# 21 **Weight:** 4.9300 g. **Composition:** 0.9000 Gold .1426 oz. AGW **Obverse:** Dolphin and Sea Creatures

| Date | Mintage | F | VF | XF | Unc | BU |
|---|---|---|---|---|---|---|
| ND Proof | 1,615 | Value: 110 | | | | |
| 1969 Proof | — | Value: 110 | | | | |
| 1970 Proof | Inc. above | Value: 110 | | | | |

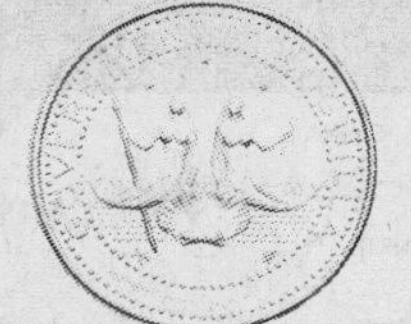

**20 DOLLARS** KM# 22 **Weight:** 9.8700 g. **Composition:** 0.9000 Gold .2856 oz. AGW **Obverse:** Mermaids

| Date | Mintage | F | VF | XF | Unc | BU |
|---|---|---|---|---|---|---|
| ND Proof | 1,395 | Value: 260 | | | | |
| 1969 Proof | — | Value: 260 | | | | |
| 1970 Proof | Inc. above | Value: 260 | | | | |

**100 DOLLARS** KM# 23 **Weight:** 49.3700 g. **Composition:** 0.9000 Gold 1.4287 oz. AGW **Subject:** Demonstrating Population

| Date | Mintage | F | VF | XF | Unc | BU |
|---|---|---|---|---|---|---|
| ND Proof | 710 | Value: 775 | | | | |
| 1969 Proof | — | Value: 775 | | | | |
| 1970 Proof | Inc. above | Value: 775 | | | | |

## PROVISIONAL GOVERNMENT COINAGE

Countermarked

| KM# | Date | Mintage | Identification | Issue Price | Mkt Val |
|---|---|---|---|---|---|
| 1 | 1951-1954 | 5,987 | Liberty Dollar. Countermark on Mexico 5 Pesos, KM#467. 54,000 of the below pieces were remelted. | 10.00 | 18.00 |
| 14 | 1921-1947 | 2 | 100 Liberty Dollars. Gold. Countermark on Mexico 50 Pesos, KM#481. | — | 3,000 |
| 2 | 1947-1948 | 1,530 | Liberty Dollar. Countermark on Mexico 5 Pesos, KM#465. | 10.00 | 27.50 |
| 3 | 1923-1926 | 1,531 | Liberty Dollar. Countermark on Peru Sol, KM#218.1. | 10.00 | 25.00 |

| KM# | Date | Mintage | Identification | Issue Price | Mkt Val |
|---|---|---|---|---|---|
| 3a | AH1382 | — | Liberty Dollar. Countermark on Yemen Riyal, Y#31. | 10.00 | 40.00 |
| 4 | AH1367-AH1381 | 494 | Liberty Dollar. Countermark on Yemen Ahmadi Riyal, Y#17. | 10.00 | 85.00 |
| 5 | 1907-1912 | 340 | Liberty Dollar. Countermark on Philippines Peso, KM#172. | 10.00 | 80.00 |

| KM# | Date | Mintage | Identification | Issue Price | Mkt Val |
|---|---|---|---|---|---|
| 6 | 1955-1956 | 250 | 100 Liberty Dollars. Countermark on Mexico 10 Pesos, KM#474. | 10.00 | 80.00 |
| 7.1 | 1931-1947 | 91 | 100 Liberty Dollars. Countermark on Panama Balboa, KM#13. | 10.00 | 115 |
| 7.2 | 1953 | I.A. | Liberty Dollar. Countermark on Panama Balboa, KM#21. | — | 115 |
| 8 | 1943-1944 | 21 | Liberty Dollar. Countermark on Ecuador Cinco Sucres, KM#79. | — | 175 |
| 9 | 1901-1905 | 15 | Liberty Dollar. Countermark on Mexico Peso, KM#409. | — | 220 |
| 10.1 | 1914 | 10 | Liberty Dollar. Countermark on China Republic Yuan Shih Kai Dollar, KM#329. | — | 250 |
| 10.2 | 1920-21 | 10 | Liberty Dollar. Countermark on China Republic Yuan Shih Kai Dollar, KM#329.6. | — | 250 |
| 11 | 1953 | 2 | Liberty Dollar. Countermark on Mexico 5 Pesos, KM#468. | — | 450 |
| 12 | 1901-1935 | 1 | Liberty Dollar. Countermark on Great Britain Trade Coinage, Y-T5. The countermark was done in San Francisco, California, on various crown-sized coins. | — | 500 |

## TRIAL STRIKES

| KM# | Date | Mintage | Identification | Mkt Val |
|---|---|---|---|---|
| TS1 | ND (1969) | — | 5 Dollars. Goldine-Brass. 1.5100 g. Design of KM-20.. Blank with MET countermark.. Reeded. edgeUniface. | 50.00 |

| KM# | Date | Mintage | Identification | Mkt Val |
|---|---|---|---|---|
| TS2 | 1969 | — | 100 Dollars. Goldine. | — |

| KM# | Date | Mintage | Identification | Mkt Val |
|---|---|---|---|---|

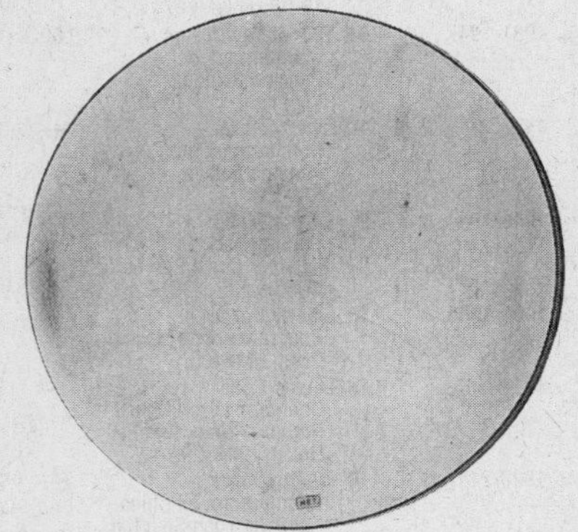

| KM# | Date | Mintage | Identification | Mkt Val |
|---|---|---|---|---|
| TS3 | ND (1969) | — | 100 Dollars. Goldine-Brass. 29.2100 g. Design of KM-23.. Blank with MET countermark.. Reeded. edge | 200 |

## PROOF SETS

| KM# | Date | Mintage | Identification | Issue Price | Mkt Val |
|---|---|---|---|---|---|
| PS1 | 1969 | — | KM#15-18, 20-23 | 225 | 1,310 |
| PS2 | 1969 | — | KM#15-18 | 25.50 | 110 |
| PS3 | 1969 | — | KM#20-23 | 200 | 1,200 |
| PS4 | 1970 | — | KM#15-18, 20-23 | 225 | 1,310 |
| PS5 | 1970 | — | KM#15-18 | 25.50 | 110 |
| PS6 | 1970 | — | KM#20-23 | 200 | 1,200 |

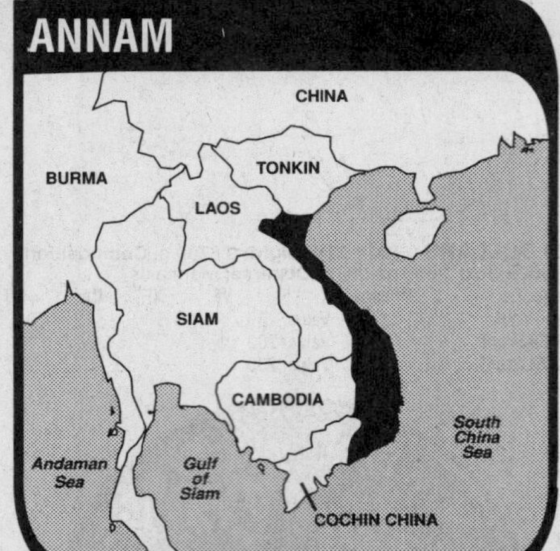


In 207 B.C. a Chinese general set up the Kingdom of Nam-Viet on the Red River. This kingdom was over-thrown by the Chinese under the Han Dynasty in 111 B.C., where upon the country became a Chinese province under the name of Giao-Chi, which was later changed to Annam or peaceful or pacified South. Chinese rule was maintained until 968, when the Vietnamese became independent until 1407 when China again invaded Viet Nam. The Chinese were driven out in 1428 and the country became independent and named Dai-Viet. Gia Long united the North and South as Dai Nam in 1802.

After the French conquered Dai Nam, they split the country into three parts. The South became the Colony of Cochin china; the North became the Protectorate of Tonkin; and the central became the Protectorate of Annam. The emperors were permitted to have their capital in Hue and to produce small quantities of their coins, presentation pieces, and bullion bars. Annam had an area of 57,840 sq. mi. (141,806 sq. km.) and a population of about 6 million. Chief products of the area are silk, cinnamon and rice. There are important mineral deposits in the mountainous inland.

## Protectorate of Annam

### EMPERORS

Thanh Thai, 1888-1907 成泰

Duy Tan, 1907-1916 維新

Khai Dinh, 1916-1925 啓定

Bao Dai, 1926-1945 保大

### IDENTIFICATION

Khai 

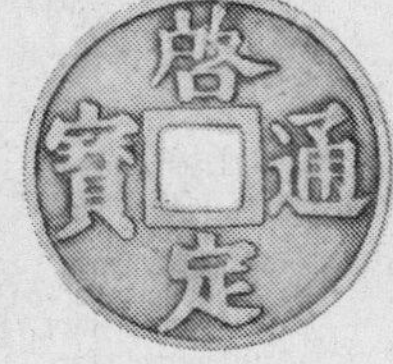


寶 Bao

Thong 

Dinh 定

Khai Dinh Thong Bao

## CYCLICAL DATES

| | 庚 | 辛 | 壬 | 癸 | 甲 | 乙 | 丙 | 丁 | 戊 | 己 |
|---|---|---|---|---|---|---|---|---|---|---|
| 戌 | 1850 1910 | | 1862 1922 | | 1874 1934 | | 1886 1946 | | 1838 1898 | |
| 亥 | | 1851 1911 | | 1863 1923 | | 1875 1935 | | 1887 1947 | | 1839 1899 |
| 子 | 1840 1900 | | 1852 1912 | | 1864 1924 | | 1876 1936 | | 1888 1948 | |
| 丑 | | 1841 1901 | | 1853 1913 | | 1865 1925 | | 1877 1937 | | 1889 1949 |
| 寅 | 1830 1890 | | 1842 1902 | | 1854 1914 | | 1866 1926 | | 1878 1938 | |
| 卯 | | 1831 1891 | | 1843 1903 | | 1855 1915 | | 1867 1927 | | 1879 1939 |
| 辰 | 1880 1940 | | 1832 1892 | | 1844 1904 | | 1856 1916 | | 1868 1928 | |
| 巳 | | 1881 1941 | | 1833 1893 | | 1845 1905 | | 1857 1917 | | 1869 1929 |
| 午 | 1870 1930 | | 1882 1942 | | 1834 1894 | | 1846 1906 | | 1858 1918 | |
| 未 | | 1871 1931 | | 1883 1943 | | 1835 1895 | | 1847 1907 | | 1859 1919 |
| 申 | 1860 1920 | | 1872 1932 | | 1884 1944 | | 1836 1896 | | 1848 1908 | |
| 酉 | | 1861 1921 | | 1873 1933 | | 1885 1945 | | 1837 1897 | | 1849 1909 |

**NOTE:** This table has been adapted from *Chinese Bank Notes* by Ward Smith and Brian Matravers.

Cyclical dates consist of a pair of characters one of which indicates the animal associated with that year. Every 60 years, this pair of characters is repeated. The first character of a cyclical date corresponds to a character in the first row of the chart above. The second character is taken from the column at left. In this catalog where a cyclical date is used, the abbreviation CD appears before the A.D. date.

Annamese silver and gold coins were sometimes dated according to the year of the emperor's reign. In this case, simply add the year of reign to the year in which the reign would be 1849 (1847 plus 3 = 1850 -1 = 1849 or 1847 = 1; 1848 = 2; 1849 = 3). In this catalog the A.D. date appears in parenthesis followed by the year of reign.

## NUMERALS

| NUMBER | CONVENTIONAL | FORMAL | COMMERCIAL |
|---|---|---|---|
| 1 | 一 元 | 壹 弌 | 〡 |
| 2 | 二 | 弍 貳 | 〢 |
| 3 | 三 | 叁 弎 | 〣 |
| 4 | 四 | 肆 | 〤 |
| 5 | 五 | 伍 | 〥 |
| 6 | 六 | 陸 | 〦 |
| 7 | 七 | 柒 | 〧 |
| 8 | 八 | 捌 | 〨 |
| 9 | 九 | 玖 | 〩 |
| 10 | 十 | 拾 什 | 十 |
| 20 | 十 二 or 廿 | 拾貳 | 〢十 |
| 25 | 五 十 二 or 五廿 | 伍拾貳 | 〢十〥 |
| 30 | 十 三 or 卅 | 拾叁 | 〣十 |
| 100 | 百 一 | 佰壹 | 〡百 |
| 1,000 | 千 一 | 仟壹 | 〡千 |
| 10,000 | 萬 一 | 萬壹 | 〡万 |
| 100,000 | 萬十 億 一 | 萬拾 億壹 | 十万 |
| 1,000,000 | 萬百一 | 萬佰壹 | 〡百万 |

**NOTE:** This table has been adapted from *Chinese Bank Notes* by Ward Smith and Brian Matravers.

### MONETARY SYSTEM

#### COPPER AND ZINC

10 Dong (zinc) = 1 Dong (copper)
600 Dong (zinc) = 1 Quan (string of cash)
Approx. 2600 Dong (zinc) = 1 Piastre

**NOTE:** Ratios between metals changed frequently, therefore the above is given as an approximate relationship.

#### SILVER AND GOLD

2-1/2 Quan = 1 Lang
10 Tien (Mace) = 1 Lang (Tael)
14 to 17 Piastres (silver) = 1 Piastre (gold)
14 to 17 Lang (silver) = 1 Lang (gold)

The real currency of Dai Nam and An Nam consisted of copper and zinc coins similar to Chinese cash-style coins and were called sapeques and dongs by the French.

The smaller gold pieces saw a limited circulation, mainly among the local merchants and foreign traders. The larger gold pieces were used mainly for hoarding, while

**NOTE:** Sch# are in reference to Albert Schroeder's *"Annam, Etudes Numismatiques"* or to the same numbering system used in *"Gold and Silver Coins of Annam"*, by Bernard Permar and John Novak.

### CHARACTER IDENTIFICATION

The Vietnamese used Chinese-style characters for official documents and coins and bars. Some were modified to their liking and will sometimes not match the Chinese character for the same word. The above identification and this table will translate most of the Vietnamese characters (Chinese-style) on their coins and bars described herein.

Chinese/French
Vietnamese/English

An Nam = name of the French protectorate
安南

Dai Nam = name of the country under Gia Long's Nguyen dynasty
大南

Viet Nam = name used briefly during Minh Mang's reign and became the modern name of the country
越南

河内 Ha Noi = city and province in north Dai Nam

内帑 Noi Thang = court treasury in the capital of Hue

年 Nien = year

造 Tao = made

銀 Ngan = silver

金 Kim = gold

錢 Tien = a weight of about 3.78 grams

兩 Lang = a weight of about 37.78 grams

貫 Quan = a string of cash style coins

分 Phan = a weight of about .38 grams

文 Van = cash-style coins

中平 Trung Binh = a name of weight standard

# FRENCH PROTECTORATE

## CAST COINAGE

Copper, brass, and zinc cash

**PHAN KM# 626 (Y1) Composition:** Cast Copper Alloys **Ruler:** Thanh Thai **Obverse:** Inscription: Than-thai Thong-bao **Reverse:** Plain

| Date | Mintage | Good | VG | F | VF | XF |
|---|---|---|---|---|---|---|
| ND(1888-1907) | — | 2.00 | 3.50 | 5.50 | 9.00 | — |

**PHAN KM# 654 (Y4) Composition:** Cast Copper Alloys **Ruler:** Khai Dinh **Obverse:** Inscription: Khai-dinh Thong-bao

| Date | Mintage | Good | VG | F | VF | XF |
|---|---|---|---|---|---|---|
| ND(1916-25) | — | 5.50 | 9.00 | 15.00 | 25.00 | — |

**PHAN KM# 661 (Y6a) Composition:** Cast Brass **Ruler:** Bao Dai **Obverse:** Inscription: Bao-dai Thong bao

| Date | Mintage | Good | VG | F | VF | XF |
|---|---|---|---|---|---|---|
| ND(1926-45) | — | 2.50 | 5.00 | 7.50 | 12.50 | — |

**10 VAN KM# 628 (Y2) Composition:** Cast Copper Alloys **Ruler:** Thanh Thai **Obverse:** Inscription: Thanh-thai Thong bao **Reverse:** "Thap Van"

| Date | Mintage | Good | VG | F | VF | XF |
|---|---|---|---|---|---|---|
| ND(1888-1907) | — | 0.50 | 0.75 | 1.25 | 2.50 | — |

**10 VAN KM# 652 (Y3) Composition:** Cast Brass **Ruler:** Duy Tan **Obverse:** Inscription: Duy-tan Thong bao

| Date | Mintage | Good | VG | F | VF | XF |
|---|---|---|---|---|---|---|
| ND(1907-16) | — | 0.50 | 0.75 | 1.25 | 2.50 | — |

**10 VAN KM# 664 (Y7) Composition:** Cast Brass **Ruler:** Bao Dai **Obverse:** Inscription: Bao-dai Thong bao

| Date | Mintage | Good | VG | F | VF | XF |
|---|---|---|---|---|---|---|
| ND(1926-45) | — | 2.00 | 3.50 | 7.50 | 12.50 | — |

## MILLED COINAGE

Brass

**PHAN KM# 656 (Y5.2) Composition:** Brass **Ruler:** Khai Dinh **Obverse:** Characters slightly different; inscription: Khai-dinh Thong bao

| Date | Mintage | Good | VG | F | VF | XF |
|---|---|---|---|---|---|---|
| ND(1916-25) | — | 2.00 | 3.50 | 6.00 | 10.00 | — |

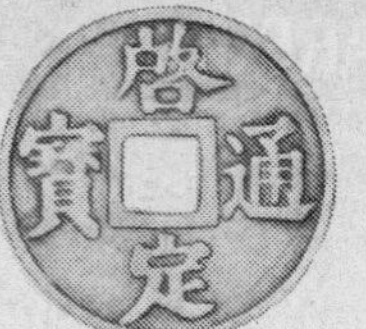
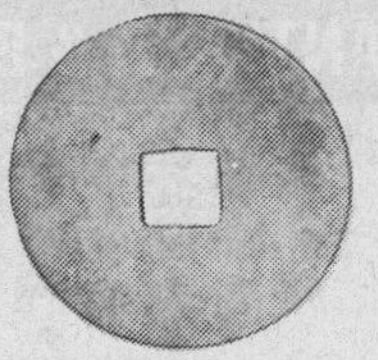

**PHAN KM# 655 (Y5.1) Composition:** Brass **Ruler:** Khai Dinh **Obverse:** Inscription: Khai-dinh Thong bao **Note:** Uniface.

| Date | Mintage | Good | VG | F | VF | XF |
|---|---|---|---|---|---|---|
| ND(1916-25) | — | 1.75 | 2.75 | 4.50 | 7.50 | — |

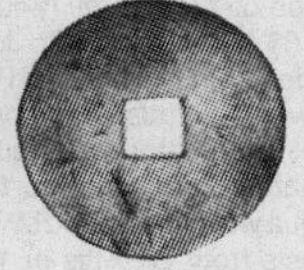

**PHAN KM# 662 (Y6) Composition:** Brass **Ruler:** Bao Dai **Obverse:** Inscription: Bao-dai Thong bao

| Date | Mintage | Good | VG | F | VF | XF |
|---|---|---|---|---|---|---|
| ND(1926-45) | — | 2.50 | 5.00 | 7.50 | 12.50 | — |

## SILVER MILLED COINAGE

**3 TIEN KM# 630 Composition:** Silver **Ruler:** Thanh Thai **Obverse:** Inscription: Thanh-thai Thong bao **Reverse:** Dragon **Note:** Cross-reference number Schroeder#428.

| Date | Mintage | VG | F | VF | XF | Unc |
|---|---|---|---|---|---|---|
| ND(1888-1907) | — | 70.00 | 140 | 240 | 400 | — |

## GOLD MILLED COINAGE

**TIEN KM# 634 Weight:** 3.9000 g. **Composition:** Gold **Ruler:** Thanh Thai **Obverse:** Inscription: Thanh-thai Thong bao **Reverse:** "Nhat Nguyen" **Note:** Cross-reference number Schroeder#432.

| Date | Mintage | VG | F | VF | XF | Unc |
|---|---|---|---|---|---|---|
| ND(1888-1907) | — | 325 | 600 | 950 | 1,450 | — |

**1-1/2 TIEN KM# 636 Weight:** 6.6000 g. **Composition:** Gold **Ruler:** Thanh Thai **Obverse:** Inscription: Thanh-thai Thong bao **Reverse:** Legend between moon and sun **Rev. Legend:** "Nhi Nghi" **Note:** Cross-reference number Schroeder#435.

| Date | Mintage | VG | F | VF | XF | Unc |
|---|---|---|---|---|---|---|
| ND(1888-1907) | — | 240 | 450 | 750 | 1,150 | — |

**3 TIEN KM# 638 Composition:** Gold **Ruler:** Thanh Thai **Obverse:** Inscription: "Thanh-thai Thong-bao" **Reverse:** Dragon **Note:** 10.50-12.40 grams. Cross-reference number Schroeder#433.

| Date | Mintage | VG | F | VF | XF | Unc |
|---|---|---|---|---|---|---|
| ND(1888-1907) | — | 1,000 | 2,000 | 3,250 | 5,000 | — |

**3 TIEN KM# 639 Composition:** Gold **Ruler:** Thanh Thai **Obverse:** Inscription: Thanh-thai Thong bao **Reverse:** "Tam Tho", dragon above Three Longevities **Note:** 10.00-10.50 grams. Cross-reference number Schroeder#436.

| Date | Mintage | VG | F | VF | XF | Unc |
|---|---|---|---|---|---|---|
| ND(1888-1907) | — | 550 | 1,000 | 1,700 | 2,600 | — |

**4 TIEN KM# 641 Weight:** 14.5000 g. **Composition:** Gold **Ruler:** Thanh Thai **Obverse:** Inscription: Thanh-thai Thong bao **Reverse:** "Tu My" between Four Perfections **Note:** Cross-reference number Schroeder#437.

| Date | Mintage | VG | F | VF | XF | Unc |
|---|---|---|---|---|---|---|
| ND(1888-1907) | — | 650 | 1,200 | 2,100 | 3,200 | — |

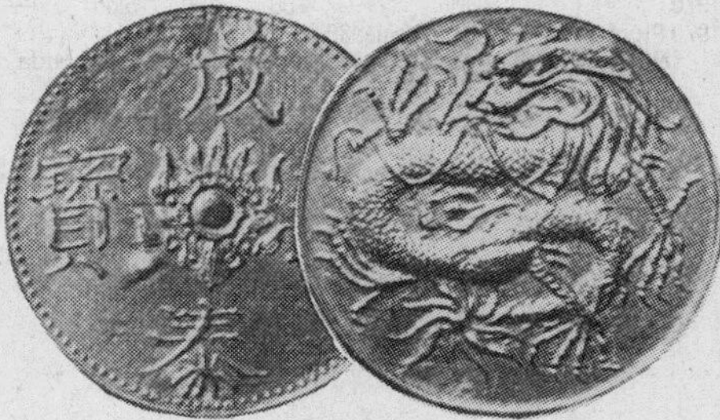

**6 TIEN KM# 645 Weight:** 23.0000 g. **Composition:** Gold **Ruler:** Thanh Thai **Obverse:** Inscription: Thanh-thai Thong bao **Reverse:** Large dragon **Note:** Cross-reference number Schroeder#382A.

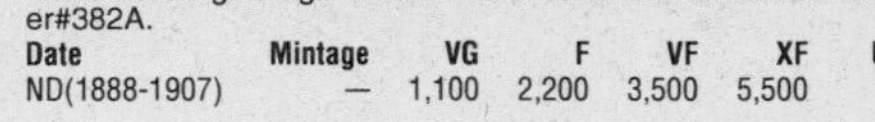

| Date | Mintage | VG | F | VF | XF | Unc |
|---|---|---|---|---|---|---|
| ND(1888-1907) | — | 1,100 | 2,200 | 3,500 | 5,500 | — |

# ANTIGUA & BARBUDA

JAMAICA
DOMINICAN REPUBLIC
HAITI
PUERTO RICO
Caribbean Sea
COLOMBIA
VENEZUELA

The Independent State of Antigua and Barbuda, located on the eastern edge of the Leeward Islands in the Caribbean Sea, has an area of 170 sq. mi. (440 sq. km.) and an estimated population of 68,000. Capital: St. John's. Prior to 1967, Antigua and its dependencies Barbuda and Redonda, comprised a presidency of the Leeward Islands. The mountainous island produces sugar, molasses, rum, cotton and fruit. Tourism is making an increasingly valuable contribution to the economy.

Antigua was discovered by Columbus in 1493, settled by British colonists from St. Kitts in 1632, occupied by the French in 1666, and ceded to Britain in 1667. It became an associated state with internal self-government on February 27, 1967. On November 1, 1981 it became independent as Antigua and Barbuda. As a constitutional monarchy, Elizabeth II is Queen of Antiqua and Barbuda and Head of State.

Spanish silver coinage and French colonial "Black Dogs" were used throughout the islands' early history; however, late in the seventeenth century the introduction of British tin farthings was attempted with complete lack of success. In 1822, British colonial Anchor Money was introduced.

From 1825 to 1955, Antigua was on the sterling standard and used British coins. Coins of the British Caribbean Territories (Eastern Group) and East Caribbean States circulated from 1955, and banknotes of East Caribbean Currency Authority are now used on the island. The early coinage was augmented by that of the East Caribbean States in 1981.

**RULERS**
British

## BRITISH ADMINISTRATION

### DECIMAL COINAGE

100 Cents = 1 Dollar

**4 DOLLARS** **KM# 1** **Composition:** Copper-Nickel **Ruler:** Elizabeth II **Series:** F.A.O.

| Date | Mintage | F | VF | XF | Unc | BU |
|---|---|---|---|---|---|---|
| 1970 | 14,000 | — | 4.00 | 7.00 | 15.00 | — |
| 1970 Proof | 2,000 | Value: 30.00 | | | | |

**Note:** For similar issues see Barbados, Dominica, Grenada, Montserrat, St. Kitts, St. Lucia and St. Vincent.

# ANTIGUA & BARBUDA

## BRITISH ADMINISTRATION

### DECIMAL COINAGE

**10 DOLLARS** **KM# 5** **Composition:** Copper-Nickel **Ruler:** Elizabeth II **Subject:** Royal Visit

| Date | Mintage | F | VF | XF | Unc | BU |
|---|---|---|---|---|---|---|
| 1985 | 100,000 | — | — | — | 9.00 | — |

**10 DOLLARS** **KM# 5a** **Weight:** 28.2800 g. **Composition:** 0.9250 Silver .8409 oz. ASW **Ruler:** Elizabeth II

| Date | Mintage | F | VF | XF | Unc | BU |
|---|---|---|---|---|---|---|
| 1985 Proof | 5,000 | Value: 40.00 | | | | |

**10 DOLLARS** **KM# 5b** **Weight:** 47.5400 g. **Composition:** 0.9170 Gold 1.4013 oz. AGW **Ruler:** Elizabeth II

| Date | Mintage | F | VF | XF | Unc | BU |
|---|---|---|---|---|---|---|
| 1985 Proof | 250 | Value: 1,200 | | | | |

**30 DOLLARS** **KM# 2** **Weight:** 31.1000 g. **Composition:** 0.5000 Silver .5 oz. ASW **Ruler:** Elizabeth II **Subject:** George Washington - Yorktown, 1781

| Date | Mintage | F | VF | XF | Unc | BU |
|---|---|---|---|---|---|---|
| 1982 Proof | 1,200 | Value: 37.50 | | | | |

**30 DOLLARS** **KM# 3** **Weight:** 31.1000 g. **Composition:** 0.5000 Silver .5 oz. ASW **Ruler:** Elizabeth II **Subject:** George Washington - Inauguration, 1789 **Obverse:** Similar to KM#2

| Date | Mintage | F | VF | XF | Unc | BU |
|---|---|---|---|---|---|---|
| 1982 Proof | 1,125 | Value: 40.00 | | | | |

**30 DOLLARS** **KM# 4** **Weight:** 31.3000 g. **Composition:** 0.5000 Silver .5 oz. ASW **Ruler:** Elizabeth II **Subject:** George Washington - Verplanck's Point, 1790 **Obverse:** Similar to KM#2

| Date | Mintage | F | VF | XF | Unc | BU |
|---|---|---|---|---|---|---|
| 1982 Proof | 675 | Value: 42.50 | | | | |

**100 DOLLARS** **KM# 6** **Ruler:** Elizabeth II **Subject:** Tropical Birds **Obverse:** Arms in circle, country name above, date below **Reverse:** Cattle Egret

| Date | Mintage | F | VF | XF | Unc | BU |
|---|---|---|---|---|---|---|
| 1988 Proof | 10,000 | Value: 110 | | | | |

The Argentine Republic, located in southern South America, has an area of 1,073,518 sq. mi. (3,761,274 sq. km.) and an estimated population of 37.03 million. Capital: Buenos Aires. Its varied topography ranges from the subtropical lowlands of the north to the towering Andean Mountains in the west and the wind-swept Patagonian steppe in the south. The rolling, fertile pampas of central Argentina are ideal for agriculture and grazing, and support most of the republic's population. Meatpacking, flour milling, textiles, sugar refining and dairy products are the principal industries. Oil is found in Patagonia, but most mineral requirements must be imported.

Argentina was discovered in 1516 by the Spanish navigator Juan de Solis. A permanent Spanish colony was established at Buenos Aires in 1580, but the colony developed slowly. When Napoleon conquered Spain, the Argentines set up their own government on May 25, 1810. Independence was formally declared on July 9, 1816. A strong tendency toward local autonomy, fostered by difficult transportation, resulted in a federalized union with much authority left to the states or provinces, which resulted in the coinage of 1817-1867.

Internal conflict through the first half century of Argentine independence resulted in a provisional national coinage, chiefly of crown-sized silver. Provincial issues mainly of minor denominations supplemented this.

**MINT MARKS**

A = Korea
B = Great Britain
BA = Buenos Aires
CORDOBA, CORDOVA
C = France
PTS = Potosi monogram (Bolivia)
R, RA, RIOJA, RIOXA
SE = Santiago del Estero
T, TM = Tucuman
TIERRA DEL FUEGO

**MONETARY SYSTEM**

8 Reales = 8 Soles = 1/2 Escudo
16 Reales or Soles = 1 Escudo
10 Decimos = 1 Real
100 Centavos = 1 Peso
10 Pesos = 1 Argentino

**(Commencing 1970)**

100 Old Pesos = 1 New Peso

**(Commencing June 1983)**

10,000 New Pesos = 1 Peso Argentino
1,000 Pesos Argentino = 1 Austral

**(Commencing 1985)**

1,000 Pesos Argentinos = 1 Austral
100 Centavos = 1 Austral

**(Commencing 1992)**

10,000 Australs = 1 Peso

# REPUBLIC

## DECIMAL COINAGE

**CENTAVO** **KM# 37** **Composition:** Bronze **Note:** Previous KM#12.

| Date | Mintage | F | VF | XF | Unc | BU |
|---|---|---|---|---|---|---|
| 1939 | 3,488,000 | 0.15 | 0.35 | 0.75 | 1.85 | — |
| 1940 | 3,140,000 | 0.15 | 0.35 | 0.75 | 1.85 | — |
| 1941 | 4,572,000 | 0.15 | 0.35 | 0.75 | 1.85 | — |
| 1942 | 496,000 | 0.30 | 0.75 | 1.50 | 7.50 | — |
| 1944 | 3,104,000 | 0.20 | 0.50 | 1.00 | 2.75 | — |
| 1973 | 1,294,000 | 0.10 | 0.25 | 0.55 | 1.50 | — |

**CENTAVO** **KM# 37a** **Composition:** Copper **Note:** Cruder diework. Previous KM#12a.

| Date | Mintage | F | VF | XF | Unc | BU |
|---|---|---|---|---|---|---|
| 1945 | 420,000 | 0.20 | 0.50 | 1.00 | 4.00 | — |
| 1946 | 4,450,000 | 0.15 | 0.35 | 0.50 | 1.25 | — |
| 1947 | 5,630,000 | 0.15 | 0.35 | 0.50 | 1.25 | — |
| 1948 | 4,420,000 | 0.15 | 0.35 | 0.50 | 1.25 | — |

**2 CENTAVOS** **KM# 38** **Composition:** Bronze **Note:** Previous KM#13.

| Date | Mintage | F | VF | XF | Unc | BU |
|---|---|---|---|---|---|---|
| 1939 | 5,490,000 | 0.15 | 0.35 | 0.75 | 2.00 | — |
| 1940 | 4,625,000 | 0.15 | 0.35 | 0.75 | 2.00 | — |
| 1941 | 4,567,000 | 0.15 | 0.35 | 0.75 | 2.00 | — |
| 1942 | 2,082,000 | 0.15 | 0.35 | 0.75 | 2.00 | — |
| 1944 | 387,000 | 0.25 | 0.50 | 1.00 | 6.50 | — |
| 1945 | 4,585,000 | 0.15 | 0.35 | 0.75 | 2.00 | — |
| 1946 | 3,395,000 | 0.15 | 0.35 | 0.75 | 2.00 | — |
| 1947 | 4,395,000 | 0.15 | 0.35 | 0.75 | 2.00 | — |

**2 CENTAVOS** **KM# 38a** **Composition:** Copper **Note:** Cruder diework. Previous KM#13a.

| Date | Mintage | F | VF | XF | Unc | BU |
|---|---|---|---|---|---|---|
| 1947 | Inc. above | 0.15 | 0.35 | 0.75 | 2.25 | — |
| 1948 | 3,645,000 | 0.15 | 0.35 | 0.75 | 2.25 | — |
| 1949 | 7,290,000 | 0.15 | 0.35 | 0.75 | 2.00 | — |
| 1950 | 903,000 | 0.25 | 0.65 | 1.25 | 3.75 | — |

**5 CENTAVOS** **KM# 34** **Composition:** Copper-Nickel **Note:** Previous KM#9.

| Date | Mintage | F | VF | XF | Unc | BU |
|---|---|---|---|---|---|---|
| 1903 | 2,502,000 | 0.25 | 0.50 | 3.00 | 12.00 | — |
| 1904 | 2,518,000 | 0.25 | 0.50 | 3.00 | 12.00 | — |
| 1905 | 4,359,000 | 0.25 | 0.50 | 3.00 | 12.00 | — |
| 1906 | 3,939,000 | 0.25 | 0.50 | 3.00 | 12.00 | — |
| 1907 | 1,682,000 | 0.50 | 1.00 | 5.00 | 20.00 | — |
| 1908 | 1,693,000 | 0.50 | 1.00 | 5.00 | 20.00 | — |
| 1909 | 4,650,000 | 0.25 | 0.50 | 3.00 | 12.00 | — |
| 1910 | 1,469,000 | 0.75 | 2.00 | 6.00 | 22.00 | — |
| 1911 | 1,431,000 | 0.25 | 0.75 | 4.00 | 15.00 | — |
| 1912 | 2,377,000 | 0.25 | 0.75 | 4.00 | 15.00 | — |
| 1913 | 1,477,000 | 0.25 | 0.75 | 4.00 | 15.00 | — |
| 1914 | 1,097,000 | 0.50 | 1.00 | 5.00 | 20.00 | — |
| 1915 | 1,310,000 | 0.30 | 0.75 | 3.50 | 15.00 | — |
| 1916 | 1,310,000 | 0.30 | 0.75 | 3.50 | 12.00 | — |
| 1917 | 1,009,000 | 0.75 | 1.50 | 4.00 | 15.00 | — |
| 1918 | 2,287,000 | 0.25 | 0.50 | 3.00 | 8.00 | — |
| 1919 | 2,476,000 | 0.25 | 0.50 | 3.00 | 8.00 | — |
| 1920 | 5,235,000 | 0.25 | 0.50 | 3.00 | 8.00 | — |
| 1921 | 7,040,000 | 0.20 | 0.35 | 2.00 | 7.00 | — |
| 1922 | 9,427,000 | 0.20 | 0.35 | 2.00 | 7.00 | — |
| 1923 | 6,256,000 | 0.20 | 0.35 | 2.00 | 7.00 | — |
| 1924 | 6,355,000 | 0.20 | 0.35 | 2.00 | 7.00 | — |
| 1925 | 3,955,000 | 0.20 | 0.35 | 2.00 | 7.00 | — |
| 1926 | 3,560,000 | 0.20 | 0.35 | 2.00 | 7.00 | — |
| 1927 | 5,650,000 | 0.20 | 0.35 | 2.00 | 7.00 | — |
| 1928 | 6,380,000 | 0.20 | 0.35 | 2.00 | 7.00 | — |
| 1929 | 11,831,000 | 0.20 | 0.35 | 2.00 | 7.00 | — |
| 1930 | 7,110,000 | 0.20 | 0.35 | 2.00 | 7.00 | — |
| 1931 | 506,000 | 2.00 | 4.00 | 8.00 | 20.00 | — |
| 1933 | 5,537,000 | 0.10 | 0.25 | 1.00 | 3.00 | — |
| 1934 | 1,288,000 | 0.25 | 0.50 | 3.00 | 7.00 | — |
| 1935 | 3,052,000 | 0.10 | 0.25 | 1.00 | 3.00 | — |
| 1936 | 7,175,000 | 0.10 | 0.25 | 1.00 | 3.00 | — |
| 1937 | 7,063,000 | 0.10 | 0.25 | 1.00 | 3.00 | — |
| 1938 | 10,252,000 | 0.10 | 0.25 | 1.00 | 3.00 | — |
| 1939 | 7,171,000 | 0.10 | 0.25 | 1.00 | 3.00 | — |
| 1940 | 10,191,000 | 0.10 | 0.25 | 1.00 | 3.00 | — |
| 1941 | 951,000 | 0.50 | 1.00 | 3.00 | 12.00 | — |
| 1942 | 8,692,000 | 0.10 | 0.25 | 1.00 | 3.00 | — |

**5 CENTAVOS** **KM# 40** **Composition:** Aluminum-Bronze **Note:** Previous KM#15.

| Date | Mintage | F | VF | XF | Unc | BU |
|---|---|---|---|---|---|---|
| 1942 | 2,130,000 | 0.15 | 0.35 | 1.00 | 3.00 | — |
| 1943 | 15,778,000 | 0.10 | 0.25 | 0.50 | 1.75 | — |
| 1944 | 21,081,000 | 0.10 | 0.25 | 0.50 | 1.75 | — |
| 1945 | 21,600,000 | 0.10 | 0.25 | 0.50 | 1.75 | — |
| 1946 | 20,460,000 | 0.10 | 0.25 | 0.50 | 1.75 | — |
| 1947 | 22,520,000 | 0.10 | 0.25 | 0.50 | 1.75 | — |
| 1948 | 42,790,000 | 0.10 | 0.25 | 0.50 | 1.75 | — |
| 1949 | 35,470,000 | 0.10 | 0.25 | 0.50 | 1.75 | — |
| 1950 | 13,500,000 | 0.10 | 0.25 | 0.50 | 1.75 | — |

**5 CENTAVOS** **KM# 43** **Composition:** Copper-Nickel **Reverse:** Jose de San Martin bust facing right **Edge:** Reeded **Note:** Previous KM#18.

| Date | Mintage | F | VF | XF | Unc | BU |
|---|---|---|---|---|---|---|
| 1950 | 3,460,000 | 0.20 | 0.40 | 0.60 | 2.00 | — |

**5 CENTAVOS** **KM# 46** **Composition:** Copper-Nickel **Reverse:** Jose de San Martin bust facing right **Edge:** Reeded **Note:** Previous KM#21.

| Date | Mintage | F | VF | XF | Unc | BU |
|---|---|---|---|---|---|---|
| 1951 | 34,994,000 | — | 0.20 | 0.30 | 0.50 | — |
| 1952 | 33,110,000 | — | 0.20 | 0.30 | 0.50 | — |
| 1953 | 20,129,000 | — | 0.20 | 0.30 | 0.50 | — |

**5 CENTAVOS** **KM# 46a** **Composition:** Copper-Nickel Clad Steel **Reverse:** Jose de San Martin bust facing right **Edge:** Plain **Note:** Previous KM#21a.

| Date | Mintage | F | VF | XF | Unc | BU |
|---|---|---|---|---|---|---|
| 1953 | 56,300,000 | — | 0.15 | 0.20 | 0.35 | — |

**5 CENTAVOS** **KM# 50** **Composition:** Copper-Nickel Clad Steel **Reverse:** Jose de San Martin bust facing right, smaller head **Edge:** Plain **Note:** Previous KM#25.

| Date | Mintage | F | VF | XF | Unc | BU |
|---|---|---|---|---|---|---|
| 1954 | 50,640,000 | — | 0.15 | 0.20 | 0.35 | — |
| 1955 | 42,200,000 | — | 0.15 | 0.20 | 0.35 | — |
| 1956 | 36,870,000 | — | 0.15 | 0.20 | 0.35 | — |

**5 CENTAVOS** **KM# 53** **Composition:** Copper-Nickel Clad Steel **Reverse:** Smaller head **Edge:** Plain **Note:** Jose de San Martin. Previous KM#28.

| Date | Mintage | F | VF | XF | Unc | BU |
|---|---|---|---|---|---|---|
| 1957 | 26,930,000 | — | 0.15 | 0.20 | 0.35 | — |
| 1958 | 13,108,000 | — | 0.15 | 0.20 | 0.35 | — |
| 1959 | 14,971,000 | — | 0.15 | 0.20 | 0.35 | — |

**10 CENTAVOS** **KM# 41** **Composition:** Aluminum-Bronze **Note:** Previous KM#16.

| Date | Mintage | F | VF | XF | Unc | BU |
|---|---|---|---|---|---|---|
| 1942 | 15,541,000 | 0.15 | 0.25 | 0.75 | 1.75 | — |
| 1943 | 13,916,000 | 0.15 | 0.25 | 0.75 | 1.75 | — |
| 1944 | 16,411,000 | 0.15 | 0.25 | 0.75 | 1.75 | — |
| 1945 | 12,500,000 | 0.15 | 0.25 | 0.75 | 1.75 | — |
| 1946 | 15,790,000 | 0.15 | 0.25 | 0.75 | 1.75 | — |
| 1947 | 36,430,000 | 0.15 | 0.25 | 0.75 | 1.75 | — |
| 1948 | 54,685,000 | 0.15 | 0.25 | 0.75 | 1.75 | — |
| 1949 | 57,740,000 | 0.15 | 0.25 | 0.75 | 1.75 | — |
| 1950 | 42,825,000 | 0.15 | 0.25 | 0.75 | 1.75 | — |

**10 CENTAVOS** **KM# 44** **Composition:** Copper-Nickel **Edge:** Reeded **Note:** Jose de San Martin. Previous KM#19.

| Date | Mintage | F | VF | XF | Unc | BU |
|---|---|---|---|---|---|---|
| 1950 | 17,505,000 | 0.20 | 0.40 | 0.60 | 1.75 | — |

**10 CENTAVOS** **KM# 47** **Composition:** Copper-Nickel **Edge:** Reeded **Note:** Jose de San Martin. Previous KM#22.

| Date | Mintage | F | VF | XF | Unc | BU |
|---|---|---|---|---|---|---|
| 1951 | 98,521,000 | — | 0.20 | 0.30 | 0.50 | — |
| 1952 | 67,328,000 | — | 0.20 | 0.30 | 0.50 | — |

**10 CENTAVOS** **KM# 47a** **Composition:** Nickel Clad Steel **Edge:** Plain **Note:** Previous KM#22a.

| Date | Mintage | F | VF | XF | Unc | BU |
|---|---|---|---|---|---|---|
| 1952 | 33,240,000 | — | 0.10 | 0.15 | 0.25 | — |
| 1953 | 106,685,000 | — | 0.10 | 0.15 | 0.25 | — |

**10 CENTAVOS** **KM# 51** **Composition:** Nickel Clad Steel **Obverse:** Smaller head **Edge:** Plain **Note:** Previous KM#26.

| Date | Mintage | F | VF | XF | Unc | BU |
|---|---|---|---|---|---|---|
| 1954 | 117,200,000 | — | 0.10 | 0.15 | 0.25 | — |
| 1955 | 97,045,000 | — | 0.10 | 0.15 | 0.25 | — |
| 1956 | 122,630,000 | — | 0.10 | 0.15 | 0.25 | — |

**10 CENTAVOS** **KM# 54** **Composition:** Nickel Clad Steel **Obverse:** Smaller head **Edge:** Plain **Note:** Previous KM#29.

| Date | Mintage | F | VF | XF | Unc | BU |
|---|---|---|---|---|---|---|
| 1957 | 52,810,000 | — | 0.10 | 0.15 | 0.25 | — |
| 1958 | 41,916,000 | — | 0.10 | 0.15 | 0.25 | — |
| 1959 | 29,183,000 | — | 0.10 | 0.15 | 0.25 | — |

**20 CENTAVOS** **KM# 36** **Composition:** Copper-Nickel **Note:** Previous KM#11.

| Date | Mintage | F | VF | XF | Unc | BU |
|---|---|---|---|---|---|---|
| 1905 | 4,455,000 | 0.75 | 2.00 | 5.00 | 20.00 | — |
| 1906 | 4,331,000 | 0.75 | 2.00 | 5.00 | 20.00 | — |
| 1907 | 3,730,000 | 1.00 | 3.00 | 7.00 | 25.00 | — |
| 1908 | 719,000 | 2.25 | 5.00 | 10.00 | 30.00 | — |
| 1909 | 1,329,000 | 0.50 | 1.50 | 4.00 | 15.00 | — |
| 1910 | 1,845,000 | 0.50 | 1.50 | 4.00 | 15.00 | — |
| 1911 | 1,110,000 | 0.50 | 1.50 | 4.00 | 15.00 | — |
| 1912 | 2,402,000 | 0.50 | 1.50 | 4.00 | 15.00 | — |
| 1913 | 1,579,000 | 0.50 | 1.00 | 2.50 | 10.00 | — |
| 1914 | 527,000 | 2.25 | 5.00 | 10.00 | 45.00 | — |
| 1915 | 1,921,000 | 0.50 | 1.00 | 2.50 | 7.50 | — |
| 1916 | 985,000 | 0.50 | 1.25 | 2.50 | 17.50 | — |
| 1918 | 1,638,000 | 0.40 | 0.75 | 2.00 | 7.50 | — |
| 1919 | 2,280,000 | 0.40 | 0.75 | 2.00 | 7.50 | — |
| 1920 | 7,572,000 | 0.40 | 0.75 | 2.00 | 6.25 | — |
| 1921 | 5,286,000 | 0.25 | 0.60 | 1.75 | 5.00 | — |
| 1922 | 2,324,000 | 0.25 | 0.60 | 1.75 | 5.00 | — |
| 1923 | 4,416,000 | 0.25 | 0.60 | 1.75 | 5.00 | — |
| 1924 | 3,676,000 | 0.25 | 0.60 | 1.75 | 5.00 | — |
| 1925 | 3,799,000 | 0.25 | 0.60 | 1.75 | 5.00 | — |
| 1926 | 3,250,000 | 0.25 | 0.50 | 1.25 | 3.75 | — |
| 1927 | 2,880,000 | 0.25 | 0.50 | 1.25 | 3.75 | — |
| 1928 | 2,886,000 | 0.25 | 0.50 | 1.25 | 3.75 | — |
| 1929 | 8,361,000 | 0.25 | 0.50 | 1.25 | 3.00 | — |
| 1930 | 8,281,000 | 0.25 | 0.50 | 1.25 | 3.00 | — |
| 1931 | 315,000 | 2.25 | 5.00 | 10.00 | 20.00 | — |
| 1935 | 1,127,000 | 0.25 | 0.60 | 1.75 | 5.00 | — |
| 1936 | 855,000 | 0.50 | 1.25 | 2.50 | 12.50 | — |
| 1937 | 3,314,000 | 0.25 | 0.50 | 1.50 | 3.75 | — |
| 1938 | 6,449,000 | 0.25 | 0.50 | 1.25 | 3.00 | — |
| 1939 | 3,555,000 | 0.25 | 0.50 | 1.25 | 3.00 | — |
| 1940 | 4,465,000 | 0.25 | 0.50 | 1.25 | 3.00 | — |
| 1941 | 600,000 | 0.50 | 1.00 | 2.00 | 10.00 | — |
| 1942 | 4,844,000 | 0.25 | 0.50 | 1.25 | 3.00 | — |

**20 CENTAVOS** **KM# 42** **Composition:** Aluminum-Bronze **Note:** Previous KM#17.

| Date | Mintage | F | VF | XF | Unc | BU |
|---|---|---|---|---|---|---|
| 1942 | 10,255,000 | 0.15 | 0.25 | 0.75 | 1.75 | — |
| 1943 | 13,775,000 | 0.15 | 0.25 | 0.75 | 1.75 | — |
| 1944 | 12,225,000 | 0.15 | 0.25 | 0.75 | 1.75 | — |
| 1945 | 13,340,000 | 0.15 | 0.25 | 0.75 | 1.75 | — |
| 1946 | 14,625,000 | 0.15 | 0.25 | 0.75 | 1.75 | — |
| 1947 | 23,165,000 | 0.15 | 0.25 | 0.75 | 1.75 | — |
| 1948 | 32,245,000 | 0.15 | 0.25 | 0.75 | 1.75 | — |
| 1949 | 67,115,000 | 0.15 | 0.25 | 0.75 | 1.75 | — |
| 1950 | 40,071,000 | 0.15 | 0.25 | 0.75 | 1.75 | — |

**20 CENTAVOS** **KM# 45** **Composition:** Copper-Nickel **Reverse:** Jose de San Martin portrait right **Edge:** Reeded **Note:** Previous KM#20.

| Date | Mintage | F | VF | XF | Unc | BU |
|---|---|---|---|---|---|---|
| 1950 | 86,770,000 | 0.15 | 0.25 | 0.60 | 1.50 | — |

**20 CENTAVOS** **KM# 48** **Composition:** Copper-Nickel **Reverse:** Jose de San Martin portrait right **Edge:** Reeded **Note:** Previous KM#23.

| Date | Mintage | F | VF | XF | Unc | BU |
|---|---|---|---|---|---|---|
| 1951 | 85,782,000 | 0.10 | 0.20 | 0.30 | 0.50 | — |
| 1952 | 69,796,000 | 0.10 | 0.20 | 0.30 | 0.50 | — |

**20 CENTAVOS** **KM# 48a** **Composition:** Nickel Clad Steel **Reverse:** Jose de San Martin portrait right **Edge:** Plain **Note:** Previous KM#23a.

| Date | Mintage | F | VF | XF | Unc | BU |
|---|---|---|---|---|---|---|
| 1952 | 12,863,000 | — | 0.15 | 0.25 | 0.50 | — |
| 1953 | 36,893,000 | — | 0.15 | 0.40 | 1.00 | — |

**20 CENTAVOS** **KM# 52** **Composition:** Nickel Clad Steel **Note:** Head size reduced slightly. Previous KM#27.

| Date | Mintage | F | VF | XF | Unc | BU |
|---|---|---|---|---|---|---|
| 1955 | 46,952,000 | — | 0.15 | 0.20 | 0.25 | — |
| 1956 | 35,995,000 | — | 0.15 | 0.20 | 0.25 | — |
| 1954 | 52,563,000 | — | 0.15 | 0.20 | 0.25 | — |

**20 CENTAVOS** **KM# 55** **Composition:** Nickel Clad Steel **Note:** Previous KM#30.

| Date | Mintage | F | VF | XF | Unc | BU |
|---|---|---|---|---|---|---|
| 1957 | 89,365,000 | — | 0.15 | 0.20 | 0.25 | — |
| 1958 | 52,710,000 | — | 0.15 | 0.20 | 0.25 | — |
| 1959 | 56,585,000 | — | 0.15 | 0.20 | 0.25 | — |
| 1960 | 21,254,000 | — | 0.15 | 0.20 | 0.25 | — |
| 1961 | 2,083,000 | — | 0.25 | 0.50 | 1.50 | — |

**50 CENTAVOS** **KM# 39** **Composition:** Nickel **Edge:** Reeded **Note:** Previous KM#14.

| Date | Mintage | F | VF | XF | Unc | BU |
|---|---|---|---|---|---|---|
| 1941 | 10,961 | 0.40 | 1.00 | 2.00 | 4.00 | — |

**50 CENTAVOS** **KM# 49** **Composition:** Nickel Clad Steel **Reverse:** Jose de San Martin portrait right **Edge:** Plain **Note:** Previous KM#24.

| Date | Mintage | F | VF | XF | Unc | BU |
|---|---|---|---|---|---|---|
| 1952 | 29,736,000 | 0.10 | 0.20 | 0.35 | 0.75 | — |
| 1953 | 62,814,000 | 0.10 | 0.20 | 0.35 | 0.75 | — |
| 1954 | 132,224,000 | 0.10 | 0.20 | 0.35 | 0.75 | — |
| 1955 | 75,490,000 | 0.10 | 0.20 | 0.35 | 0.75 | — |
| 1956 | 19,120,000 | 10.00 | 0.20 | 0.45 | 1.00 | — |

**50 CENTAVOS** **KM# 56** **Composition:** Nickel Clad Steel **Edge:** Plain **Note:** Previous KM#31.

| Date | Mintage | F | VF | XF | Unc | BU |
|---|---|---|---|---|---|---|
| 1957 | 18,139,000 | — | 0.10 | 0.25 | 0.30 | — |
| 1958 | 51,750,000 | 0.10 | 0.20 | 0.30 | 0.40 | — |
| 1959 | 13,997,000 | — | 0.10 | 0.20 | 0.30 | — |
| 1960 | 26,038,000 | 0.10 | 0.20 | 0.30 | 0.40 | — |
| 1961 | 11,106,000 | — | 0.10 | 0.20 | 0.35 | — |

**PESO** **KM# 57** **Composition:** Nickel Clad Steel **Note:** Previous KM#32.

| Date | Mintage | F | VF | XF | Unc | BU |
|---|---|---|---|---|---|---|
| 1957 | 118,118,000 | 0.10 | 0.20 | 0.40 | 0.85 | — |
| 1958 | 118,151,000 | 0.10 | 0.20 | 0.40 | 0.85 | — |
| 1959 | 237,733,000 | 0.10 | 0.20 | 0.30 | 0.60 | — |
| 1960 | 75,048,000 | 0.10 | 0.30 | 0.50 | 1.00 | — |
| 1961 | 76,897,000 | 0.10 | 0.30 | 0.50 | 1.00 | — |
| 1962 | 30,006,000 | 0.10 | 0.30 | 0.50 | 1.00 | — |

**PESO** **KM# 58** **Composition:** Nickel Clad Steel **Subject:** 150th Anniversary - Removal of Spanish Viceroy **Note:** Previous KM#33.

| Date | Mintage | F | VF | XF | Unc | BU |
|---|---|---|---|---|---|---|
| ND(1960) | 98,751,000 | 0.20 | 0.50 | 0.75 | 1.25 | — |

**5 PESOS** **KM# 59** **Composition:** Nickel Clad Steel **Reverse:** Sailing ship - Presidente Sarmiento **Note:** Previous KM#34.

| Date | Mintage | F | VF | XF | Unc | BU |
|---|---|---|---|---|---|---|
| 1961 | 37,423,000 | 0.10 | 0.20 | 0.30 | 0.60 | — |
| 1962 | 42,362,000 | 0.10 | 0.20 | 0.30 | 0.60 | — |
| 1963 | 71,769,000 | 0.10 | 0.20 | 0.30 | 0.60 | — |
| 1964 | 12,302,000 | 0.15 | 0.25 | 0.40 | 0.80 | — |
| 1965 | 19,450,000 | 0.10 | 0.20 | 0.30 | 0.60 | — |
| 1966 | 17,259,000 | 0.10 | 0.20 | 0.30 | 0.60 | — |
| 1967 | 17,806,000 | 0.10 | 0.20 | 0.30 | 0.60 | — |
| 1968 | 12,634,000 | 0.10 | 0.20 | 0.30 | 0.60 | — |

**10 PESOS** **KM# 60** **Composition:** Nickel Clad Steel **Obverse:** Gaucho **Note:** Previous KM#35.

| Date | Mintage | F | VF | XF | Unc | BU |
|---|---|---|---|---|---|---|
| 1962 | 57,401,000 | 0.10 | 0.20 | 0.30 | 0.65 | — |
| 1963 | 136,792,000 | 0.10 | 0.20 | 0.30 | 0.65 | — |
| 1964 | 46,576,000 | 0.10 | 0.20 | 0.30 | 0.65 | — |
| 1965 | 40,640,000 | — | 0.15 | 0.30 | 0.65 | — |
| 1966 | 50,733,000 | 0.10 | 0.20 | 0.30 | 0.65 | — |
| 1967 | 43,050,000 | 0.10 | 0.20 | 0.30 | 0.75 | — |
| 1968 | 36,588,000 | — | 0.15 | 0.30 | 0.65 | — |

**10 PESOS** **KM# 62** **Composition:** Nickel Clad Steel **Subject:** 150th Anniversary - Declaration of Independence. **Note:** Previous KM#37.

| Date | Mintage | F | VF | XF | Unc | BU |
|---|---|---|---|---|---|---|
| ND(1966) | 29,336,000 | 0.10 | 0.15 | 0.35 | 1.00 | — |

**25 PESOS** **KM# 61** **Composition:** Nickel Clad Steel **Subject:** 1st issue of National Coinage in 1813. **Note:** Previous KM#36.

| Date | Mintage | F | VF | XF | Unc | BU |
|---|---|---|---|---|---|---|
| 1964 | 20,485,000 | 0.10 | 0.25 | 0.50 | 1.35 | — |
| 1965 | 14,884,000 | 0.10 | 0.25 | 0.50 | 1.35 | — |
| 1966 | 16,426,000 | 0.10 | 0.25 | 0.50 | 1.35 | — |
| 1967 | 15,734,000 | 0.10 | 0.25 | 0.50 | 1.35 | — |
| 1968 | 4,446,000 | 0.10 | 0.25 | 0.75 | 1.75 | — |

**25 PESOS** **KM# 63** **Composition:** Nickel Clad Steel **Subject:** 80th Anniversary - Death of D. Faustino Sarmiento. **Note:** Previous KM#38.

| Date | Mintage | F | VF | XF | Unc | BU |
|---|---|---|---|---|---|---|
| 1968 | 15,804,000 | 0.25 | 0.60 | 0.85 | 1.65 | — |

## REFORM COINAGE

1970-1983; 100 Old Pesos = 1 New Peso

**CENTAVO** **KM# 64** **Composition:** Aluminum **Note:** Previous KM#39.

| Date | Mintage | F | VF | XF | Unc | BU |
|---|---|---|---|---|---|---|
| 1970 | 47,801,000 | — | — | 0.10 | 0.30 | — |
| 1971 | 44,644,000 | — | — | 0.10 | 0.30 | — |
| 1972 | 92,430,000 | — | — | 0.10 | 0.30 | — |
| 1973 | 29,515,000 | — | — | 0.10 | 0.30 | — |
| 1974 | 5,162,000 | — | — | 0.15 | 0.35 | — |
| 1975 | 3,840,000 | — | 0.10 | 0.20 | 0.50 | — |

**5 CENTAVOS** **KM# 65** **Composition:** Aluminum **Note:** Previous KM#40.

| Date | Mintage | F | VF | XF | Unc | BU |
|---|---|---|---|---|---|---|
| 1970 | 56,174,000 | — | 0.10 | 0.15 | 0.40 | — |
| 1971 | 3,798,000 | 0.10 | 0.20 | 0.35 | 0.65 | — |
| 1972 | 84,250,000 | — | 0.10 | 0.15 | 0.40 | — |
| 1973 | 113,912,000 | — | 0.10 | 0.15 | 0.40 | — |
| 1974 | 18,150,000 | — | 0.10 | 0.15 | 0.40 | — |
| 1975 | 6,940,000 | 0.10 | 0.20 | 0.35 | 0.65 | — |

**10 CENTAVOS** **KM# 66** **Composition:** Brass **Note:** Previous KM#41.

| Date | Mintage | F | VF | XF | Unc | BU |
|---|---|---|---|---|---|---|
| 1970 | 52,903,000 | — | 0.10 | 0.15 | 0.35 | — |
| 1971 | 135,623,000 | — | 0.10 | 0.15 | 0.35 | — |
| 1973 | 19,930,000 | — | 0.10 | 0.15 | 0.35 | — |
| 1974 | 79,156,000 | — | 0.10 | 0.15 | 0.35 | — |
| 1975 | 31,270,000 | — | 0.10 | 0.15 | 0.35 | — |
| 1976 | 730,000 | 0.10 | 0.20 | 0.35 | 1.00 | — |

**20 CENTAVOS** **KM# 67** **Composition:** Brass **Note:** Previous KM#42.

| Date | Mintage | F | VF | XF | Unc | BU |
|---|---|---|---|---|---|---|
| 1970 | 27,029,000 | — | 0.10 | 0.15 | 0.35 | — |
| 1971 | 32,211,000 | — | 0.10 | 0.15 | 0.35 | — |
| 1972 | 220,000 | 1.00 | 2.00 | 4.00 | 8.00 | — |
| 1973 | 9,676,000 | — | 0.10 | 0.15 | 0.35 | — |
| 1974 | 41,024,000 | — | 0.10 | 0.15 | 0.35 | — |
| 1975 | 26,540,000 | — | 0.10 | 0.15 | 0.35 | — |
| 1976 | 960,000 | — | 0.10 | 0.15 | 0.35 | — |

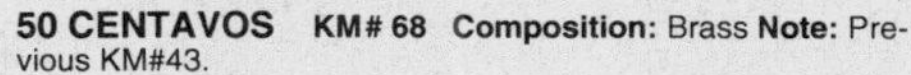

**50 CENTAVOS** **KM# 68** **Composition:** Brass **Note:** Previous KM#43.

| Date | Mintage | F | VF | XF | Unc | BU |
|---|---|---|---|---|---|---|
| 1970 | 44,748,000 | 0.10 | 0.15 | 0.30 | 0.60 | — |
| 1971 | 34,947,000 | 0.10 | 0.15 | 0.30 | 0.60 | — |
| 1972 | 40,960,000 | 0.10 | 0.15 | 0.30 | 0.60 | — |
| 1973 | 69,472,000 | 0.10 | 0.15 | 0.30 | 0.60 | — |
| 1974 | 63,063,000 | 0.10 | 0.15 | 0.30 | 0.60 | — |
| 1975 | 64,859,000 | 0.10 | 0.15 | 0.30 | 0.60 | — |
| 1976 | 9,768,000 | 0.10 | 0.15 | 0.30 | 0.60 | — |

**PESO** **KM# 69** **Composition:** Aluminum-Brass **Note:** Wide and narrow rim varieties exist. Previous KM#44.

| Date | Mintage | F | VF | XF | Unc | BU |
|---|---|---|---|---|---|---|
| 1974 | 77,292,000 | — | 0.10 | 0.25 | 0.75 | — |
| 1975 | 423,000,000 | — | 0.10 | 0.20 | 0.50 | — |
| 1976 | 100,075,000 | — | 0.10 | 0.20 | 0.50 | — |

**5 PESOS** **KM# 71** **Composition:** Aluminum-Bronze **Note:** Previous KM#46.

| Date | Mintage | F | VF | XF | Unc | BU |
|---|---|---|---|---|---|---|
| 1976 | 118,353,000 | — | 0.10 | 0.20 | 0.65 | — |
| 1977 | 64,738,000 | — | 0.10 | 0.20 | 0.65 | — |

**5 PESOS** **KM# 73** **Composition:** Aluminum-Bronze **Subject:** Admiral G. Brown Bicentennial **Note:** Previous KM#48.

| Date | Mintage | F | VF | XF | Unc | BU |
|---|---|---|---|---|---|---|
| 1977 | Inc. above | 0.10 | 0.15 | 0.30 | 0.75 | — |

**10 PESOS** **KM# 72** **Composition:** Aluminum-Bronze **Note:** Previous KM#47.

| Date | Mintage | F | VF | XF | Unc | BU |
|---|---|---|---|---|---|---|
| 1976 | 128,965,000 | 0.10 | 0.15 | 0.35 | 1.00 | — |
| 1977 | 113,400,000 | 0.10 | 0.15 | 0.35 | 1.00 | — |
| 1978 | 253,863,000 | 0.10 | 0.15 | 0.35 | 1.00 | — |

**10 PESOS** **KM# 74** **Composition:** Aluminum-Bronze **Subject:** Admiral G. Brown Bicentennial **Note:** Previous KM#49.

| Date | Mintage | F | VF | XF | Unc | BU |
|---|---|---|---|---|---|---|
| 1977 | Inc. above | 0.10 | 0.20 | 0.50 | 1.25 | — |

**20 PESOS** **KM# 75** **Composition:** Aluminum-Bronze **Subject:** 1978 World Soccer Championship **Note:** Previous KM#50.

| Date | Mintage | F | VF | XF | Unc | BU |
|---|---|---|---|---|---|---|
| 1977 | 1,506,000 | 0.10 | 0.20 | 0.40 | 1.00 | — |
| 1978 | 2,000,000 | 0.10 | 0.20 | 0.40 | 1.00 | — |

**50 PESOS** **KM# 76** **Composition:** Aluminum-Bronze **Subject:** 1978 World Soccer Championship **Note:** Previous KM#.51

| Date | Mintage | F | VF | XF | Unc | BU |
|---|---|---|---|---|---|---|
| 1977 | 1,506,000 | 0.10 | 0.20 | 0.40 | 1.00 | — |
| 1978 | 2,000,000 | 0.10 | 0.20 | 0.40 | 1.00 | — |

**50 PESOS** **KM# 81** **Composition:** Aluminum-Bronze **Subject:** 200th Anniversary - Birth of Jose de San Martin **Note:** Previous KM#56.

| Date | Mintage | F | VF | XF | Unc | BU |
|---|---|---|---|---|---|---|
| 1978 | 40,601,000 | 0.20 | 0.50 | 1.00 | 2.00 | — |

**50 PESOS** **KM# 83** **Composition:** Aluminum-Bronze **Reverse:** Jose de San Martin portrait right **Note:** Previous KM#58.

| Date | Mintage | F | VF | XF | Unc | BU |
|---|---|---|---|---|---|---|
| 1979 | 103,491,000 | 0.10 | 0.25 | 0.65 | 1.50 | — |
| 1980 | — | 0.10 | 0.25 | 0.65 | 1.50 | — |

**50 PESOS** **KM# 84** **Composition:** Aluminum-Bronze **Subject:** Conquest of Patagonia Centennial **Note:** Previous KM#59.

| Date | Mintage | F | VF | XF | Unc | BU |
|---|---|---|---|---|---|---|
| 1979 | Inc. above | 0.10 | 0.25 | 0.65 | 1.50 | — |

**50 PESOS** **KM# 83a** **Composition:** Brass Clad Steel **Reverse:** Jose de San Martin portrait right **Note:** Previous KM#58a.

| Date | Mintage | F | VF | XF | Unc | BU |
|---|---|---|---|---|---|---|
| 1980 | 94,730,000 | 0.10 | 0.25 | 0.65 | 1.25 | — |
| 1981 | 4,372,000 | 0.10 | 0.25 | 0.65 | 1.25 | — |

**100 PESOS** **KM# 77** **Composition:** Aluminum-Bronze **Subject:** 1978 World Soccer Championship **Note:** Previous KM#52.

| Date | Mintage | F | VF | XF | Unc | BU |
|---|---|---|---|---|---|---|
| 1977 | 1,506,000 | 0.15 | 0.30 | 0.75 | 1.50 | — |
| 1978 | 2,000,000 | 0.15 | 0.30 | 0.75 | 1.50 | — |

**100 PESOS** **KM# 82** **Composition:** Aluminum-Bronze **Subject:** 200th Anniversary - Birth of Jose de San Martin **Note:** Previous KM#57.

| Date | Mintage | F | VF | XF | Unc | BU |
|---|---|---|---|---|---|---|
| 1978 | 113,826,000 | — | 0.50 | 1.00 | 2.00 | — |

**100 PESOS** **KM# 85** **Composition:** Aluminum-Bronze **Reverse:** Jose de San Martin portrait right **Note:** Previous KM#60.

| Date | Mintage | F | VF | XF | Unc | BU |
|---|---|---|---|---|---|---|
| 1979 | 207,572,000 | 0.15 | 0.30 | 0.75 | 1.25 | — |
| 1980 | 154,260,000 | 0.15 | 0.30 | 0.75 | 1.25 | — |
| 1981 | 145,680,000 | 0.15 | 0.30 | 0.75 | 1.25 | — |

**100 PESOS** **KM# 86** **Composition:** Aluminum-Bronze **Subject:** Conquest of Patagonia Centennial **Note:** Previous KM#61.

| Date | Mintage | F | VF | XF | Unc | BU |
|---|---|---|---|---|---|---|
| 1979 | Inc. above | 0.15 | 0.30 | 0.75 | 1.50 | — |

**100 PESOS** **KM# 85a** **Composition:** Brass Clad Steel **Reverse:** Jose de San Martin portrait right **Note:** Previous KM#60a.

| Date | Mintage | F | VF | XF | Unc | BU |
|---|---|---|---|---|---|---|
| 1980 | Inc. above | 0.15 | 0.30 | 0.75 | 1.50 | — |
| 1981 | Inc. above | 0.15 | 0.30 | 0.75 | 1.50 | — |

**1000 PESOS** **KM# 78** **Weight:** 10.0000 g. **Composition:** 0.9000 Silver .2893 oz. ASW **Subject:** 1978 World Soccer Championship **Note:** Previous KM#53.

| Date | Mintage | F | VF | XF | Unc | BU |
|---|---|---|---|---|---|---|
| 1977 | 106,000 | — | — | 3.00 | 6.00 | — |
| 1977 Proof | 1,000 | Value: 17.50 | | | | |
| 1978 | 141,000 | — | — | 3.00 | 6.00 | — |
| 1978 Proof | 1,750 | Value: 17.50 | | | | |

**2000 PESOS** **KM# 79** **Weight:** 15.0000 g. **Composition:** 0.9000 Silver .4340 oz. ASW **Subject:** 1978 World Soccer Championship **Note:** Previous KM#54.

| Date | Mintage | F | VF | XF | Unc | BU |
|---|---|---|---|---|---|---|
| 1977 | 106,000 | — | — | 5.00 | 10.00 | — |
| 1977 Proof | 1,000 | Value: 22.50 | | | | |
| 1978 | 141,000 | — | — | 5.00 | 9.50 | — |
| 1978 Proof | 1,750 | Value: 22.50 | | | | |

**3000 PESOS** **KM# 80** **Weight:** 25.0000 g. **Composition:** 0.9000 Silver .7234 oz. ASW **Subject:** 1978 World Soccer Championship **Note:** Previous KM#55.

| Date | Mintage | F | VF | XF | Unc | BU |
|---|---|---|---|---|---|---|
| 1977 | 106,000 | — | — | 8.00 | 15.50 | — |
| 1977 Proof | 1,000 | Value: 35.00 | | | | |
| 1978 | 141,000 | — | — | 8.00 | 14.50 | — |
| 1978 Proof | 1,750 | Value: 35.00 | | | | |

## REFORM COINAGE

1983-1985; 10,000 Pesos = 1 Peso Argentino; 100 Centavos = 1 Peso Argentino

**CENTAVO** **KM# 87** **Composition:** Aluminum **Note:** Previous KM#62.

| Date | Mintage | F | VF | XF | Unc | BU |
|---|---|---|---|---|---|---|
| 1983 | 19,959,000 | — | — | — | 0.20 | — |

**5 CENTAVOS** **KM# 88** **Composition:** Aluminum **Note:** Previous KM#63.

| Date | Mintage | F | VF | XF | Unc | BU |
|---|---|---|---|---|---|---|
| 1983 | 59,870,000 | — | — | — | 0.25 | — |

**10 CENTAVOS** **KM# 89** **Composition:** Aluminum **Note:** Previous KM#64.

| Date | Mintage | F | VF | XF | Unc | BU |
|---|---|---|---|---|---|---|
| 1983 | 307,513,000 | — | — | — | 0.25 | — |

**50 CENTAVOS** **KM# 90** **Composition:** Aluminum **Note:** Previous KM#65.

| Date | Mintage | F | VF | XF | Unc | BU |
|---|---|---|---|---|---|---|
| 1983 | 243,909,000 | — | — | — | 0.45 | — |

**PESO** **KM# 91** **Composition:** Aluminum **Note:** National Congress. Previous KM#66.

| Date | Mintage | F | VF | XF | Unc | BU |
|---|---|---|---|---|---|---|
| 1984 | 785,791,000 | — | — | — | 0.50 | — |

**5 PESOS** **KM# 92** **Composition:** Brass **Obverse:** Buenos Aires City Hall **Note:** Previous KM#67.

| Date | Mintage | F | VF | XF | Unc | BU |
|---|---|---|---|---|---|---|
| 1984 | 11,206,000 | — | — | — | 0.65 | — |
| 1985 | 14,168,000 | — | — | — | 0.65 | — |

**10 PESOS** **KM# 93** **Composition:** Brass **Obverse:** Independence Hall at Tucuman **Note:** Previous KM#68.

| Date | Mintage | F | VF | XF | Unc | BU |
|---|---|---|---|---|---|---|
| 1984 | 16,528,000 | — | — | — | 0.85 | — |
| 1985 | 14,618,000 | — | — | — | 0.85 | — |

**50 PESOS** **KM# 94** **Composition:** Aluminum-Bronze **Subject:** 50th Anniversary of Central Bank **Note:** Previous KM#69.

| Date | Mintage | F | VF | XF | Unc | BU |
|---|---|---|---|---|---|---|
| 1985 | 26,400,000 | — | — | — | 1.00 | — |

## REFORM COINAGE

1985-1992; 1,000 Pesos Argentinos = 1 Austral; 100 Centavos = 1 Austral

**1/2 CENTAVO** **KM# 95** **Composition:** Brass **Note:** Rufous Hornero Bird. Previous KM#70.

| Date | Mintage | F | VF | XF | Unc | BU |
|---|---|---|---|---|---|---|
| 1985 | 7,490,000 | — | — | — | 0.35 | — |

**CENTAVO** **KM# 96.1** **Composition:** Brass **Obverse:** Common Rhea **Note:** Thick flan. Previous KM#71.1.

| Date | Mintage | F | VF | XF | Unc | BU |
|---|---|---|---|---|---|---|
| 1985 | 76,082,000 | — | — | — | 0.50 | — |

**CENTAVO** **KM# 96.2** **Composition:** Brass **Obverse:** Common Rhea **Note:** Thin flan. Previous KM#71.2.

| Date | Mintage | F | VF | XF | Unc | BU |
|---|---|---|---|---|---|---|
| 1986 | 18,934,000 | — | — | — | 0.50 | — |
| 1987 | 87,315,000 | — | — | — | 0.50 | — |

**5 CENTAVOS** **KM# 97.1** **Composition:** Brass **Obverse:** Pampas Cat **Note:** Thick flan. Previous KM#72.1

| Date | Mintage | F | VF | XF | Unc | BU |
|---|---|---|---|---|---|---|
| 1985 | 36,924,000 | — | — | — | 1.25 | — |

**5 CENTAVOS** **KM# 97.2** **Composition:** Brass **Obverse:** Pampas Cat **Note:** Thin flan. Previous KM#72.2.

| Date | Mintage | F | VF | XF | Unc | BU |
|---|---|---|---|---|---|---|
| 1986 | 66,414,000 | — | — | — | 1.25 | — |
| 1987 | 56,181,000 | — | — | — | 1.25 | — |
| 1988 | 23,895,000 | — | — | — | 1.25 | — |

**10 CENTAVOS** **KM# 98** **Composition:** Brass **Note:** Previous KM#73.

| Date | Mintage | F | VF | XF | Unc | BU |
|---|---|---|---|---|---|---|
| 1985 | 23,268,000 | — | — | — | 0.65 | — |
| 1986 | 158,427,000 | — | — | — | 0.65 | — |
| 1987 | 184,330,000 | — | — | — | 0.65 | — |
| 1988 | 174,003,000 | — | — | — | 0.65 | — |

**50 CENTAVOS** **KM# 99** **Composition:** Brass **Note:** Varieties exist. Previous KM#74.

| Date | Mintage | F | VF | XF | Unc | BU |
|---|---|---|---|---|---|---|
| 1985 | 13,884,000 | — | — | — | 1.50 | — |
| 1986 | 59,074,000 | — | — | — | 1.50 | — |
| 1987 | 64,525,000 | — | — | — | 1.50 | — |
| 1988 | 62,388,000 | — | — | — | 1.50 | — |

**AUSTRAL** **KM# 100** **Composition:** Aluminum **Obverse:** Buenos Aires City Hall **Note:** Previous KM#75.

| Date | Mintage | F | VF | XF | Unc | BU |
|---|---|---|---|---|---|---|
| 1989 | — | — | — | — | 0.15 | — |

**5 AUSTRALES** **KM# 101** **Composition:** Aluminum **Obverse:** Independence Hall at Tucuman **Note:** Previous KM#76.

| Date | Mintage | F | VF | XF | Unc | BU |
|---|---|---|---|---|---|---|
| 1989 | — | — | — | — | 0.25 | — |

**10 AUSTRALES** **KM# 102** **Composition:** Aluminum **Obverse:** Casa del Acuerdo **Note:** Previous KM#77.

| Date | Mintage | F | VF | XF | Unc | BU |
|---|---|---|---|---|---|---|
| 1989 | — | — | — | — | 0.35 | — |

**100 AUSTRALES** **KM# 103** **Composition:** Aluminum **Note:** Previous KM#78.

| Date | Mintage | F | VF | XF | Unc | BU |
|---|---|---|---|---|---|---|
| 1990 | — | — | — | — | 0.25 | — |
| 1991 | — | — | — | — | 0.25 | — |

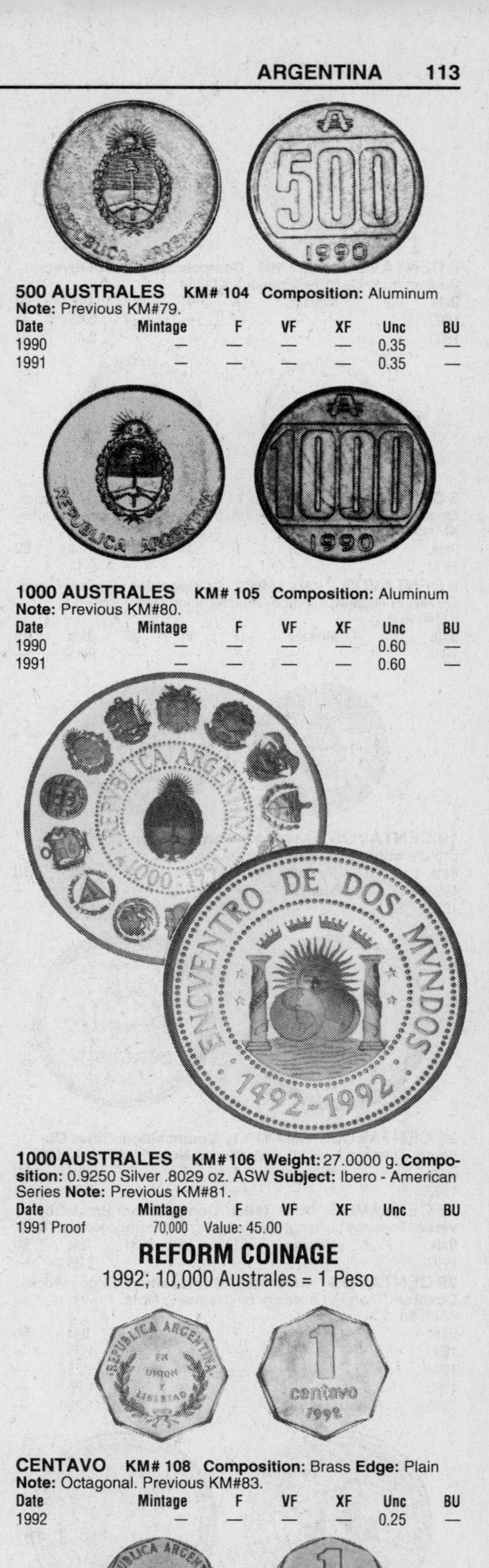

**500 AUSTRALES** **KM# 104** **Composition:** Aluminum **Note:** Previous KM#79.

| Date | Mintage | F | VF | XF | Unc | BU |
|---|---|---|---|---|---|---|
| 1990 | — | — | — | — | 0.35 | — |
| 1991 | — | — | — | — | 0.35 | — |

**1000 AUSTRALES** **KM# 105** **Composition:** Aluminum **Note:** Previous KM#80.

| Date | Mintage | F | VF | XF | Unc | BU |
|---|---|---|---|---|---|---|
| 1990 | — | — | — | — | 0.60 | — |
| 1991 | — | — | — | — | 0.60 | — |

**1000 AUSTRALES** **KM# 106** **Weight:** 27.0000 g. **Composition:** 0.9250 Silver .8029 oz. ASW **Subject:** Ibero - American Series **Note:** Previous KM#81.

| Date | Mintage | F | VF | XF | Unc | BU |
|---|---|---|---|---|---|---|
| 1991 Proof | 70,000 | Value: 45.00 | | | | |

## REFORM COINAGE

1992; 10,000 Australes = 1 Peso

**CENTAVO** **KM# 108** **Composition:** Brass **Edge:** Plain **Note:** Octagonal. Previous KM#83.

| Date | Mintage | F | VF | XF | Unc | BU |
|---|---|---|---|---|---|---|
| 1992 | — | — | — | — | 0.25 | — |

**CENTAVO** **KM# 113** **Composition:** Brass **Edge:** Reeded **Note:** Octagonal. Previous KM#88.

| Date | Mintage | F | VF | XF | Unc | BU |
|---|---|---|---|---|---|---|
| 1992 | — | — | — | — | 0.25 | — |
| 1993 | — | — | — | — | 0.25 | — |

**CENTAVO** **KM# 113a** **Composition:** Bronze **Edge:** Reeded **Note:** Octagonal. Previous KM#88a.

| Date | Mintage | F | VF | XF | Unc | BU |
|---|---|---|---|---|---|---|
| 1993 | — | — | — | — | 0.25 | — |
| 1997 | — | — | — | — | 0.25 | — |
| 1998 | — | — | — | — | 0.25 | — |
| 1999 | — | — | — | — | 0.25 | — |

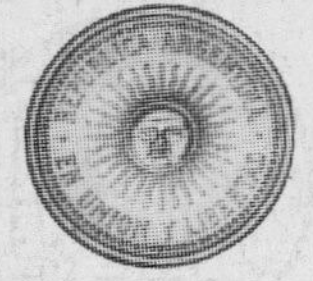

**5 CENTAVOS** **KM# 109** **Composition:** Brass **Obverse:** Radiant sunface **Note:** Previous KM#84.

| Date | Mintage | F | VF | XF | Unc | BU |
|---|---|---|---|---|---|---|
| 1992 | — | — | — | — | 0.45 | — |
| 1993 | — | — | — | — | 0.45 | — |

**5 CENTAVOS** **KM# 109a.1** **Composition:** Copper-Nickel **Obverse:** Radiant sunface. Fine, bold lettering **Note:** Previous KM#84a.1.

| Date | Mintage | F | VF | XF | Unc | BU |
|---|---|---|---|---|---|---|
| 1993 | — | — | — | — | 0.45 | — |

**5 CENTAVOS** **KM# 109a.2** **Composition:** Copper-Nickel **Obverse:** Radiant sunface. Bold lettering **Note:** Previous KM#84a.2.

| Date | Mintage | F | VF | XF | Unc | BU |
|---|---|---|---|---|---|---|
| 1994 | — | — | — | — | 0.45 | — |

**10 CENTAVOS** **KM# 107** **Composition:** Aluminum-Bronze **Edge:** Plain **Note:** Previous KM#82.

| Date | Mintage | F | VF | XF | Unc | BU |
|---|---|---|---|---|---|---|
| 1992 | 400,000,000 | — | — | — | 0.65 | — |
| 1993 | — | — | — | — | 0.65 | — |

**25 CENTAVOS** **KM# 110.1** **Composition:** Brass **Obverse:** Towered building, fine lettering **Note:** Previous KM#85.1.

| Date | Mintage | F | VF | XF | Unc | BU |
|---|---|---|---|---|---|---|
| 1992 | — | — | — | — | 1.25 | — |

**25 CENTAVOS** **KM# 110.2** **Composition:** Brass **Obverse:** Towered building, bold lettering **Note:** Previous KM#85.2.

| Date | Mintage | F | VF | XF | Unc | BU |
|---|---|---|---|---|---|---|
| 1993 | — | — | — | — | 1.25 | — |

**25 CENTAVOS** **KM# 110a** **Composition:** Copper-Nickel **Obverse:** Towered building, bold lettering **Note:** Previous KM#85a.

| Date | Mintage | F | VF | XF | Unc | BU |
|---|---|---|---|---|---|---|
| 1993 | — | — | — | — | 1.25 | — |
| 1994 | — | — | — | — | 1.25 | — |
| 1995 | — | — | — | — | 1.25 | — |
| 1996 | — | — | — | — | 1.25 | — |

**50 CENTAVOS** **KM# 111.1** **Composition:** Copper-Nickel **Obverse:** Tucuman Province Capital Building; fine lettering **Note:** Previous KM#86.1.

| Date | Mintage | F | VF | XF | Unc | BU |
|---|---|---|---|---|---|---|
| 1992 | — | — | — | — | 1.75 | — |

**50 CENTAVOS** **KM# 111.2** **Composition:** Copper-Nickel **Obverse:** Tucuman Province Capital Building; bold lettering. **Note:** Previous KM#86.2.

| Date | Mintage | F | VF | XF | Unc | BU |
|---|---|---|---|---|---|---|
| 1993 | — | — | — | — | 1.75 | — |
| 1994 | — | — | — | — | 1.75 | — |
| 1995 | — | — | — | — | 1.75 | — |

**50 CENTAVOS** **KM# 119** **Composition:** Copper-Nickel **Subject:** 50th Anniversary - UNICEF **Obverse:** Girl with rag doll **Reverse:** UNICEF logo above denomination **Note:** Previous KM#94.

| Date | Mintage | F | VF | XF | Unc | BU |
|---|---|---|---|---|---|---|
| 1996 | — | — | — | — | 2.00 | — |

**50 CENTAVOS** **KM# 121** **Composition:** Copper-Aluminum **Subject:** 50th Anniversary - Women's Right to Vote **Obverse:** Eva Paron portrait **Reverse:** Denomination **Note:** Previous KM#96.

| Date | Mintage | F | VF | XF | Unc | BU |
|---|---|---|---|---|---|---|
| 1997 | 2,000 | — | — | — | 2.25 | — |

**50 CENTAVOS** **KM# 124** **Composition:** Copper-Aluminum **Subject:** Mercosur **Obverse:** Southern Cross constellation **Reverse:** Denomination **Note:** Previous KM#99.

| Date | Mintage | F | VF | XF | Unc | BU |
|---|---|---|---|---|---|---|
| 1998 | — | — | — | — | 2.25 | — |

**PESO** **KM# 112.1** **Ring Composition:** Copper-Nickel **Center Composition:** Brass **Subject:** First Argentine Coin Design **Obverse:** Large legend **Reverse:** Large legend; pointed 9s **Note:** Previous KM#87.1.

| Date | Mintage | F | VF | XF | Unc | BU |
|---|---|---|---|---|---|---|
| 1994A | — | — | — | — | 3.75 | — |
| 1995A | — | — | — | — | 3.75 | — |
| 1995B | — | — | — | — | 3.75 | — |
| 1996A | — | — | — | — | 3.75 | — |
| 1996A | — | — | — | — | 3.75 | — |

**PESO** **KM# 112.2** **Ring Composition:** Copper-Nickel **Center Composition:** Brass **Subject:** First Argentine Coin Design **Obverse:** Small legend **Reverse:** Small legend; rounded 9s **Note:** Previous KM#87.2.

| Date | Mintage | F | VF | XF | Unc | BU |
|---|---|---|---|---|---|---|
| 1995C | — | — | — | — | 3.75 | — |

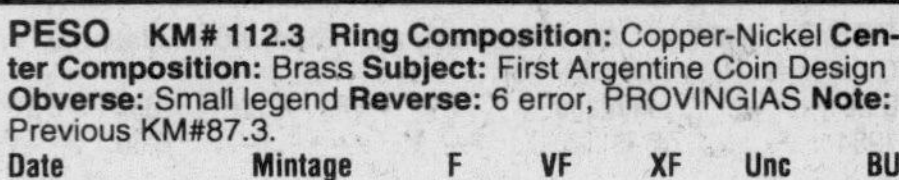

**PESO** **KM# 112.3** **Ring Composition:** Copper-Nickel **Center Composition:** Brass **Subject:** First Argentine Coin Design **Obverse:** Small legend **Reverse:** 6 error, PROVINGIAS **Note:** Previous KM#87.3.

| Date | Mintage | F | VF | XF | Unc | BU |
|---|---|---|---|---|---|---|
| 1995B | — | — | — | — | 7.50 | — |

**PESO** **KM# 126** **Weight:** 25.0000 g. **Composition:** 0.9000 Silver .7234 oz. ASW **Subject:** 50th Anniversary - United Nations **Obverse:** Dove over national arms **Reverse:** UN logo, denomination, dates **Note:** Previous KM#101.

| Date | Mintage | F | VF | XF | Unc | BU |
|---|---|---|---|---|---|---|
| 1995 Proof | 100,000 | Value: 35.00 | | | | |

**PESO** **KM# 120** **Ring Composition:** Copper-Nickel **Center Composition:** Brass **Subject:** 50th Anniversary - UNICEF **Obverse:** Girl with rag doll **Reverse:** UNICEF logo above denomination **Note:** Previous KM#95.

| Date | Mintage | F | VF | XF | Unc | BU |
|---|---|---|---|---|---|---|
| 1996 | 1,000,000 | — | — | — | 3.75 | — |

**PESO** **KM# 122** **Ring Composition:** Copper-Nickel **Center Composition:** Brass **Subject:** 50th Anniversary - Women's Right to Vote **Obverse:** Eva Peron portrait **Reverse:** Denomination **Note:** Previous KM#97.

| Date | Mintage | F | VF | XF | Unc | BU |
|---|---|---|---|---|---|---|
| 1997 | 1,000,000 | — | — | — | 3.75 | — |

**PESO** **KM# 125** **Ring Composition:** Copper-Nickel **Center Composition:** Brass **Subject:** Mercosur **Obverse:** Southern Cross constellation **Reverse:** Denomination **Note:** Previous KM#100.

| Date | Mintage | F | VF | XF | Unc | BU |
|---|---|---|---|---|---|---|
| 1998 | — | — | — | — | 3.75 | — |

**PESO** **KM# 127** **Weight:** 25.0000 g. **Composition:** 0.9000 Silver .7234 oz. ASW **Subject:** 100th Anniversary - Birth of Jorge Luis Borges **Obverse:** Profile portrait of Borges, dates **Reverse:** Labyrinth, sundial, denomination and date **Note:** Previous KM#102.

| Date | Mintage | F | VF | XF | Unc | BU |
|---|---|---|---|---|---|---|
| 1999 Proof | 5,000 | Value: 37.50 | | | | |

**2 PESOS** **KM# 114** **Composition:** Nickel **Subject:** National Constitution Convention **Note:** Previous KM#89.

| Date | Mintage | F | VF | XF | Unc | BU |
|---|---|---|---|---|---|---|
| ND(1994) | — | — | — | — | 8.00 | — |
| ND(1994) Proof | 5,500 | Value: 16.00 | | | | |

**2 PESOS** **KM# 114a** **Weight:** 12.4800 g. **Composition:** 0.9000 Silver .3612 oz. ASW **Subject:** National Constitution Convention **Note:** Previous KM#89a.

| Date | Mintage | F | VF | XF | Unc | BU |
|---|---|---|---|---|---|---|
| ND | — | — | — | — | 12.50 | — |
| ND Proof | 1,500 | Value: 25.00 | | | | |

**2 PESOS** **KM# 128** **Composition:** Copper-Nickel **Subject:** 100th Anniversary - Birth of Jorge Luis Borges **Obverse:** Profile portrait of Borges **Reverse:** Labyrinth, sundial, denomination and date **Note:** Previous KM#103.

| Date | Mintage | F | VF | XF | Unc | BU |
|---|---|---|---|---|---|---|
| 1999 | — | — | — | — | 8.00 | — |

**5 PESOS** **KM# 115** **Composition:** Nickel **Subject:** National Constitution Convention **Note:** Previous KM#90.

| Date | Mintage | F | VF | XF | Unc | BU |
|---|---|---|---|---|---|---|
| ND | — | — | — | — | 15.00 | — |
| ND Proof | 5,500 | Value: 25.00 | | | | |

**5 PESOS** **KM# 115a** **Weight:** 24.8000 g. **Composition:** 0.9000 Silver .7177 oz. ASW **Subject:** National Constitution Convention **Note:** Previous KM#90a.

| Date | Mintage | F | VF | XF | Unc | BU |
|---|---|---|---|---|---|---|
| ND(1994) | — | — | — | — | 25.00 | — |
| ND(1994) Proof | 1,500 | Value: 60.00 | | | | |

**25 PESOS** **KM# 116** **Weight:** 4.0320 g. **Composition:** 0.9000 Gold .1167 oz. AGW **Subject:** National Constitution Convention **Note:** Previous KM#91.

| Date | Mintage | F | VF | XF | Unc | BU |
|---|---|---|---|---|---|---|
| ND(1994) Proof | 1,500 | Value: 115 | | | | |

**25 PESOS** **KM# 118** **Weight:** 27.0000 g. **Composition:** 0.9250 Silver .8030 oz. ASW **Subject:** Environmental Protection **Reverse:** Giant Armadillo **Note:** Previous KM#93.

| Date | Mintage | F | VF | XF | Unc | BU |
|---|---|---|---|---|---|---|
| 1997 Proof | — | Value: 45.00 | | | | |

**25 PESOS** **KM# 123** **Weight:** 27.0000 g. **Composition:** 0.9250 Silver .8030 oz. ASW **Subject:** Ibero-American Series - LaZamba **Obverse:** Argentine arms in center **Reverse:** Zamba dancers **Note:** Previous KM#98.

| Date | Mintage | F | VF | XF | Unc | BU |
|---|---|---|---|---|---|---|
| 1997 | — | Value: 55.00 | | | | |

**50 PESOS** **KM# 117** **Weight:** 8.0640 g. **Composition:** 0.9000 Gold .2334 oz. AGW **Subject:** National Constitution Convention **Note:** Previous KM#92.

| Date | Mintage | F | VF | XF | Unc | BU |
|---|---|---|---|---|---|---|
| ND Proof | 1,500 | Value: 225 | | | | |

## PATTERNS

### Including off metal strikes

| KM# | Date | Mintage | Identification | Mkt Val |
|---|---|---|---|---|
| Pn35 | 19xx | — | Centavo. Copper. | — |
| Pn36 | 19xx | — | 2 Centavos. Copper. | — |
| Pn37 | 1925 | — | 2 Centavos. Copper. | — |
| Pn38 | 1925 | — | 2 Centavos. Bronze. | — |
| Pn39 | 1932 | — | Argentino. Copper. | — |
| Pn40 | 1932 | — | Argentino. Bronze. | — |
| Pn41 | 1933 | — | Argentino. Bronze. | — |
| Pn42 | 1934 | — | Argentino. Copper. | — |
| Pn43 | 1935 | — | Centavo. Copper. | — |
| Pn44 | 1935 | — | 2 Centavos. Copper. | — |
| Pn45 | 1936 | — | 50 Centavos. Bronze. | — |
| Pn46 | 1936 | — | 50 Centavos. Copper-Nickel. | — |
| Pn47 | 1936 | — | Peso. Bronze. | — |
| Pn48 | 1936 | — | Peso. Copper-Nickel. | — |

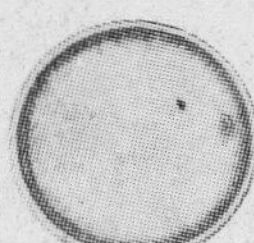

| KM# | Date | Mintage | Identification | Mkt Val |
|---|---|---|---|---|
| Pn49 | 1937 | — | Centavo. Copper. . Post horn mint mark | — |
| Pn50 | 1938 | — | Centavo. Copper. | — |
| Pn51 | 1938 | — | 2 Centavos. Copper. | — |
| Pn52 | 1940 | — | 50 Centavos. Bronze. | — |
| Pn53 | 1940 | — | 50 Centavos. Nickel. Head by Oudine | — |
| Pn54 | 1940 | — | 50 Centavos. Nickel. Head by L. Bazor | — |
| Pn55 | 1941 | — | 50 Centavos. Nickel. | — |
| Pn56 | 1943 | — | Peso. Bronze. | — |
| Pn57 | 1943 | — | Peso. Nickel. | — |
| Pn58 | 1943 | — | Peso. Bronze. . Condor | — |
| Pn59 | 1945 | — | Peso. Bronze. | — |
| Pn60 | 1945 | — | Peso. Copper-Nickel. | — |
| Pn61 | 1946 | — | Peso. Bronze. | — |
| Pn62 | 1946 | — | Peso. Copper-Nickel. | — |

| KM# | Date | Mintage | Identification | Mkt Val |
|---|---|---|---|---|
| Pn63 | 1971 | — | 50 Centavos. Silverish Aluminum. KM#43 | 75.00 |

| KM# | Date | Mintage | Identification | Mkt Val |
|---|---|---|---|---|
| Pn64 | 1975 | — | Peso. Aluminum-Brass. KM#45 | 125 |
| Pn65 | 1976 | — | 5 Pesos. Silverish Aluminum. KM#46 | — |

| KM# | Date | Mintage | Identification | Mkt Val |
|---|---|---|---|---|
| Pn66 | 1977 | — | 10 Pesos. Silverish Aluminum-Brass. KM#47 | — |

## MINT SETS

| KM# | Date | Mintage | Identification | Issue Price | Mkt Val |
|---|---|---|---|---|---|
| MS1 | 1879 | — | KM#Pn13-13b | — | 3,375 |
| MS2 | 1970 | — | KM#64-68 | — | 2.00 |
| MS3 | 1977 | — | KM#75-80 | — | 32.00 |
| MS4 | 1977 | — | KM#75-77 | — | 4.00 |
| MS5 | 1978 | — | KM#75-80 | — | 30.00 |
| MS6 | 1983 | — | KM#87-90 | — | 2.00 |

## PROOF SETS

| KM# | Date | Mintage | Identification | Issue Price | Mkt Val |
|---|---|---|---|---|---|
| PS1 | 1977 | 1,000 | KM#78-80 | — | 75.00 |
| PS2 | 1978 | 1,750 | KM#78-80 | 153 | 75.00 |
| PS5 | ND(1994) | 1,000 | KM#116, 117 | 375 | 345 |
| PS3 | ND(1994) | 5,500 | KM#114, 115 | — | 40.00 |
| PS4 | ND(1994) | 1,000 | KM#114a, 115a | 79.50 | 85.00 |

## CATAMARCA

## PROVINCE

### TOKEN COINAGE

Stabilization Currency Unit

**100000 AUSTRALES** **KM# Tn1** **Weight:** 15.0000 g. **Composition:** 0.9000 Silver .4341 oz. ASW **Subject:** Fray Mamerto Esquiu

| Date | Mintage | F | VF | XF | Unc | BU |
|---|---|---|---|---|---|---|
| 1990 | 200,000 | — | — | — | 28.50 | — |

**100000 AUSTRALES** **KM# Tn3** **Weight:** 14.8500 g. **Composition:** 0.9000 Silver .4297 oz. ASW **Subject:** 100th Anniversary - Coronation of Our Lady of the Valley

| Date | Mintage | F | VF | XF | Unc | BU |
|---|---|---|---|---|---|---|
| 1991 | — | — | — | — | 28.50 | — |

**4000000 AUSTRALES** **KM# Tn2** **Weight:** 20.0000 g. **Composition:** 0.7500 Gold .4823 oz. AGW **Subject:** Fray Mamerto Esquiu **Note:** Denomination determined upon release.

| Date | Mintage | F | VF | XF | Unc | BU |
|---|---|---|---|---|---|---|
| 1990 | 200 | — | — | — | 920 | — |

## LA RIOJA

## PROVINCE

### TOKEN COINAGE

Stabilization Currency Unit

**100000 AUSTRALES** **KM# Tn1** **Weight:** 15.0000 g. **Composition:** 0.9000 Silver .4341 oz. ASW **Subject:** 400th Anniversary - Foundation of La Rioja

| Date | Mintage | VG | F | VF | XF | Unc |
|---|---|---|---|---|---|---|
| 1991 | 200,000 | — | — | — | — | 28.50 |

**4000000 AUSTRALES** **KM# Tn2** **Weight:** 20.0000 g. **Composition:** 0.7500 Gold .4823 oz. AGW **Subject:** 400th Anniversary - Foundation of La Rioja

| Date | Mintage | VG | F | VF | XF | Unc |
|---|---|---|---|---|---|---|
| 1991 | 1,000 | — | — | — | 900 | — |

## ARMENIA

The Republic of Armenia, formerly Armenian S.S.R., is bordered to the north by Georgia, the east by Azerbaijan and the south and west by Turkey and Iran. It has an area of 11,506 sq. mi. (29,800 sq. km) and an estimated population of 3.66 million. Capital: Yerevan. Agriculture including cotton, vineyards and orchards, hydroelectricity, chemicals - primarily synthetic rubber and fertilizers, vast mineral deposits of copper, zinc and aluminum, and production of steel and paper are major industries.

Russia occupied Armenia in 1801 until the Russo-Turkish war of 1878. British intervention excluded either side from remaining although the Armenians remained more loyal to the Ottoman Turks, but in 1894 the Ottoman Turks sent in an expeditionary force of Kurds fearing a revolutionary movement. Large massacres were followed by retaliations, then amnesty was proclaimed which led right into WW I and once again occupation by Russian forces in 1916. After the Russian revolution the Georgians, Armenians and Azerbaijanis formed the short-lived Transcaucasian Federal Republic on Sept. 20, 1917, which broke up into three independent republics on May 26, 1918. Communism developed and in Sept. 1920 the Turks attacked the Armenian Republic; the Russians soon followed suit from Azerbaijan routing the Turks. On Nov. 29, 1920 Armenia was proclaimed a Soviet Socialist Republic. On March 12, 1922, Armenia, Georgia and Azerbaijan were combined to form the Transcaucasian Soviet Federated Socialist Republic, which on Dec. 30, 1922, became a part of U.S.S.R. On Dec. 5, 1936, the Transcaucasian federation was dissolved and Armenia became a constituent Republic of the U.S.S.R. A new constitution was adopted in April 1978. Elections took place on May 20, 1990. The Supreme Soviet adopted a declaration of sovereignty in Aug. 1991, voting to unite Armenia with Nagorno - Karabakh. This newly constituted "Republic of Armenia" became fully independent by popular vote in Sept. 1991. It became a member of the CIS in Dec. 1991.

Fighting between Christians in Armenia and Muslim forces of Azerbaijan escalated in 1992 and continued through early 1994. Each country claimed the Nagorno-Karabakh, an Armenian ethnic enclave, in Azerbaijan. A temporary cease-fire was announced in May 1994.

**MONETARY SYSTEM**

50 Luma = 1 Dram

**RULERS**

Persian, until 1724
Ottoman, 1724-1735
Russian, 1801-1878

**MINTNAMES**

Revan, (Erevan, now Yerevan)

## REPUBLIC

### STANDARD COINAGE

**10 LUMA** **KM# 51** **Composition:** Aluminum

| Date | Mintage | F | VF | XF | Unc | BU |
|---|---|---|---|---|---|---|
| 1994 | — | — | — | — | 0.25 | — |

**20 LUMA** **KM# 52** **Composition:** Aluminum

| Date | Mintage | F | VF | XF | Unc | BU |
|---|---|---|---|---|---|---|
| 1994 | — | — | — | — | 0.25 | — |

**50 LUMA** **KM# 53** **Composition:** Aluminum

| Date | Mintage | F | VF | XF | Unc | BU |
|---|---|---|---|---|---|---|
| 1994 | — | — | — | — | 0.45 | — |

**DRAM** **KM# 54** **Composition:** Aluminum

| Date | Mintage | F | VF | XF | Unc | BU |
|---|---|---|---|---|---|---|
| 1994 | — | — | — | — | 0.65 | — |

**3 DRAMS** **KM# 55** **Composition:** Aluminum

| Date | Mintage | F | VF | XF | Unc | BU |
|---|---|---|---|---|---|---|
| 1994 | — | — | — | — | 0.85 | — |

**5 DRAMS** **KM# 56** **Composition:** Aluminum

| Date | Mintage | F | VF | XF | Unc | BU |
|---|---|---|---|---|---|---|
| 1994 | — | — | — | — | 1.20 | — |

**5 DRAMS** **KM# 81** **Weight:** 31.3700 g. **Composition:** 0.9990 Silver 1.0076 oz. ASW **Subject:** 5th Anniversary - National Currency **Obverse:** National arms **Reverse:** 6 banknote designs

| Date | Mintage | F | VF | XF | Unc | BU |
|---|---|---|---|---|---|---|
| 1998 Proof | Est. 500 | Value: 70.00 | | | | |

**10 DRAMS** **KM# 58** **Composition:** Aluminum

| Date | Mintage | F | VF | XF | Unc | BU |
|---|---|---|---|---|---|---|
| 1994 | — | — | — | — | 2.00 | — |

**10 DRAMS** **KM# 82** **Weight:** 31.4500 g. **Composition:** 0.9990 Silver 1.0130 oz. ASW **Subject:** 10th Anniversary - Earthquake **Obverse:** National arms **Reverse:** Map and building

| Date | Mintage | F | VF | XF | Unc | BU |
|---|---|---|---|---|---|---|
| 1998 Proof | — | Value: 70.00 | | | | |

**25 DRAMS** **KM# 60** **Weight:** 31.1035 g. **Composition:** 0.9990 Silver 1.0000 oz. ASW **Subject:** David of Sasun **Obverse:** National arms above denomination **Reverse:** Monument

| Date | Mintage | F | VF | XF | Unc | BU |
|---|---|---|---|---|---|---|
| 1994 Proof | 5,000 | Value: 45.00 | | | | |

**100 DRAMS** **KM# 72** **Weight:** 28.2800 g. **Composition:** 0.9250 Silver .8411 oz. ASW **Subject:** 50th Anniversary - United Nations **Obverse:** National arms **Reverse:** Seated Madonna and child

| Date | Mintage | F | VF | XF | Unc | BU |
|---|---|---|---|---|---|---|
| 1995 Proof | 100,000 | Value: 40.00 | | | | |

**25 DRAMS** **KM# 57** **Weight:** 31.1035 g. **Composition:** 0.9990 Silver 1.0000 oz. ASW **Subject:** 1918 Battle of Sardarapat **Obverse:** National arms **Reverse:** Symbolic design

| Date | Mintage | F | VF | XF | Unc | BU |
|---|---|---|---|---|---|---|
| 1994 Proof | 3,000 | Value: 55.00 | | | | |

**25 DRAMS** **KM# 61** **Weight:** 31.1035 g. **Composition:** 0.9990 Silver 1.0000 oz. ASW **Subject:** Temple of Garni **Reverse:** Ancient building

| Date | Mintage | F | VF | XF | Unc | BU |
|---|---|---|---|---|---|---|
| 1994 Proof | 5,000 | Value: 40.00 | | | | |

**25 DRAMS** **KM# 62** **Weight:** 31.1035 g. **Composition:** 0.9990 Silver 1.0000 oz. ASW

| Date | Mintage | F | VF | XF | Unc | BU |
|---|---|---|---|---|---|---|
| 1994 Proof | — | Value: 42.50 | | | | |

**100 DRAMS** **KM# 64** **Weight:** 31.1035 g. **Composition:** 0.9990 Silver 1.0000 oz. ASW **Subject:** Chess Olympics

| Date | Mintage | F | VF | XF | Unc | BU |
|---|---|---|---|---|---|---|
| 1996 Proof | 2,000 | Value: 55.00 | | | | |

**100 DRAMS** **KM# 69** **Composition:** Copper-Nickel **Subject:** XXXII CHess Olympiad **Obverse:** Eagle and lion support arms **Reverse:** Stylized stork and chessboard in inner circle

| Date | Mintage | F | VF | XF | Unc | BU |
|---|---|---|---|---|---|---|
| 1996 | — | — | — | — | 7.00 | — |
| 1996 Proof | — | Value: 12.50 | | | | |

**25 DRAMS** **KM# 59** **Weight:** 28.2800 g. **Composition:** 0.9250 Silver .8411 oz. ASW **Reverse:** Apricot

| Date | Mintage | F | VF | XF | Unc | BU |
|---|---|---|---|---|---|---|
| 1994 Proof | Est. 10,000 | Value: 50.00 | | | | |

**25 DRAMS** **KM# 63** **Weight:** 31.1035 g. **Composition:** 0.9990 Silver 1.0000 oz. ASW **Subject:** Artsakh

| Date | Mintage | F | VF | XF | Unc | BU |
|---|---|---|---|---|---|---|
| 1994 Proof | — | Value: 40.00 | | | | |

**100 DRAMS** **KM# 70** **Weight:** 28.2800 g. **Composition:** 0.9250 Silver .8411 oz. ASW **Subject:** XXXII Chess Olympiad **Obverse:** Eagle and lion support arms **Reverse:** Stylized stork and chessboard

| Date | Mintage | F | VF | XF | Unc | BU |
|---|---|---|---|---|---|---|
| 1996 Proof | 10,000 | Value: 55.00 | | | | |

**100 DRAMS** **KM# 71** **Composition:** Copper-Nickel **Subject:** WWF Conserving Nature 1997 **Obverse:** National emblem **Reverse:** Caucasian otter

| Date | Mintage | F | VF | XF | Unc | BU |
|---|---|---|---|---|---|---|
| 1997 | — | — | — | — | 8.00 | — |

**100 DRAMS** **KM# 71a** **Weight:** 28.2800 g. **Composition:** 0.9250 Silver .8410 oz. ASW

| Date | Mintage | F | VF | XF | Unc | BU |
|---|---|---|---|---|---|---|
| 1997 Proof | 15,000 | Value: 50.00 | | | | |

**100 DRAMS** **KM# 76** **Composition:** Copper-Nickel **Subject:** Charents **Obverse:** National emblem **Reverse:** Facial portrait

| Date | Mintage | F | VF | XF | Unc | BU |
|---|---|---|---|---|---|---|
| 1997 | — | — | — | — | 4.00 | — |

**100 DRAMS** **KM# 77** **Weight:** 31.1500 g. **Composition:** 0.9990 Silver 1.0005 oz. ASW **Subject:** Marshal Bagramian **Obverse:** National arms **Reverse:** Uniformed portrait

| Date | Mintage | F | VF | XF | Unc | BU |
|---|---|---|---|---|---|---|
| 1997 Proof | — | Value: 45.00 | | | | |

**100 DRAMS** **KM# 78** **Composition:** Copper-Nickel **Subject:** WWF Conserving Nature **Obverse:** National arms **Reverse:** Armenian gull

| Date | Mintage | F | VF | XF | Unc | BU |
|---|---|---|---|---|---|---|
| 1998 | — | — | — | — | 8.00 | — |

**100 DRAMS** **KM# 79** **Weight:** 28.2800 g. **Composition:** 0.9250 Silver .8410 oz. ASW **Subject:** XVII Olympic Winter Games **Obverse:** Arms **Reverse:** Downhill skiers

| Date | Mintage | F | VF | XF | Unc | BU |
|---|---|---|---|---|---|---|
| 1998 Proof | — | Value: 40.00 | | | | |

**100 DRAMS** **KM# 80** **Weight:** 28.2800 g. **Composition:** 0.9250 Silver .8410 oz. ASW **Subject:** XVII Olympic Winter Games **Obverse:** Arms **Reverse:** Soccer players, map of France

| Date | Mintage | F | VF | XF | Unc | BU |
|---|---|---|---|---|---|---|
| 1998 Proof | — | Value: 50.00 | | | | |

**500 DRAMS** **KM# 73** **Weight:** 155.5175 g. **Composition:** 0.9990 Silver 5.000 oz. ASW **Subject:** Historical Armenian Coat of Arms - Lion **Obverse:** Similar to KM#74 **Edge:** WIth 5T0 .999 AG and serial number **Edge Lettering:** Plain

| Date | Mintage | F | VF | XF | Unc | BU |
|---|---|---|---|---|---|---|
| 1995 Proof | 300 | Value: 185 | | | | |

**500 DRAMS** **KM# 65** **Weight:** 155.5175 g. **Composition:** 0.9990 Silver 5.000 oz. ASW **Subject:** National Assembly Building **Edge:** 5TO .999 AG and serial number **Edge Lettering:** Plain **Note:**

| Date | Mintage | F | VF | XF | Unc | BU |
|---|---|---|---|---|---|---|
| 1995 Proof | 300 | Value: 185 | | | | |

**500 DRAMS** **KM# 66** **Weight:** 155.5175 g. **Composition:** 0.9990 Silver 5.000 oz. ASW **Subject:** Historical Armenian Coat of Arms Series **Obverse:** Similar to KM#74 **Reverse:** Crowned lion with staff, 11th century **Note:** Illustration reduced.

| Date | Mintage | F | VF | XF | Unc | BU |
|---|---|---|---|---|---|---|
| 1995 Proof | 300 | Value: 185 | | | | |

**500 DRAMS** **KM# 67** **Weight:** 155.5175 g. **Composition:** 0.9990 Silver 5.000 oz. ASW **Subject:** Historical Armenian Coat of Arms Series **Obverse:** Similar to KM#74 **Reverse:** Double eagle of the Arsacid Dynasty (63-428AD) **Note:** Illustration reduced.

| Date | Mintage | F | VF | XF | Unc | BU |
|---|---|---|---|---|---|---|
| 1995 Proof | 300 | Value: 185 | | | | |

**500 DRAMS** **KM# 74** **Weight:** 155.5175 g. **Composition:** 0.9990 Silver 5.000 oz. ASW **Subject:** Historical Armenian Coat of Arms - Double Eagle **Note:** Illustration reduced.

| Date | Mintage | F | VF | XF | Unc | BU |
|---|---|---|---|---|---|---|
| 1995 Proof | 300 | Value: 185 | | | | |

**1000 DRAMS** **KM# 68** **Weight:** 31.1035 g. **Composition:** 0.9990 Silver 1.0000 oz. ASW **Subject:** Armenian Money - Vignette from 100 Rouble Note

| Date | Mintage | F | VF | XF | Unc | BU |
|---|---|---|---|---|---|---|
| 1994 Proof | 5,000 | Value: 47.50 | | | | |

**1000 DRAMS** **KM# 83** **Weight:** 31.3100 g. **Composition:** 0.9990 Silver 1.0056 oz. ASW **Subject:** 300th Anniversary - Christian Armenia **Obverse:** National arms **Reverse:** Etchmiadzin church

| Date | Mintage | F | VF | XF | Unc | BU |
|---|---|---|---|---|---|---|
| 1998 Proof | — | Value: 65.00 | | | | |

**1000 DRAMS** **KM# 84** **Weight:** 31.3100 g. **Composition:** 0.9990 Silver 1.0056 oz. ASW **Subject:** 300th Anniversary - Christian Armenia **Obverse:** National arms **Reverse:** Ani church tower

| Date | Mintage | F | VF | XF | Unc | BU |
|---|---|---|---|---|---|---|
| 1998 Proof | — | Value: 65.00 | | | | |

**1000 DRAMS** **KM# 85** **Weight:** 31.3100 g. **Composition:** 0.9990 Silver 1.0056 oz. ASW **Subject:** 300th Anniversary - Christian Armenia **Obverse:** National arms **Reverse:** Haghpat carved stone cross

| Date | Mintage | F | VF | XF | Unc | BU |
|---|---|---|---|---|---|---|
| 1998 Proof | — | Value: 65.00 | | | | |

**25000 DRAMS** **KM# 75.1** **Weight:** 4.3000 g. **Composition:** 0.9000 Gold .1244 oz. AGW **Obverse:** National arms **Reverse:** Portrait of goddess Anahit **Edge:** Reeded

| Date | Mintage | F | VF | XF | Unc | BU |
|---|---|---|---|---|---|---|
| 1997 Proof | — | Value: 75.00 | | | | |

**25000 DRAMS** **KM# 75.2** **Weight:** 4.3000 g. **Composition:** 0.9000 Gold .1244 oz. AGW **Edge:** Plain

| Date | Mintage | F | VF | XF | Unc | BU |
|---|---|---|---|---|---|---|
| 1997 Proof | — | Value: 120 | | | | |

# ARUBA

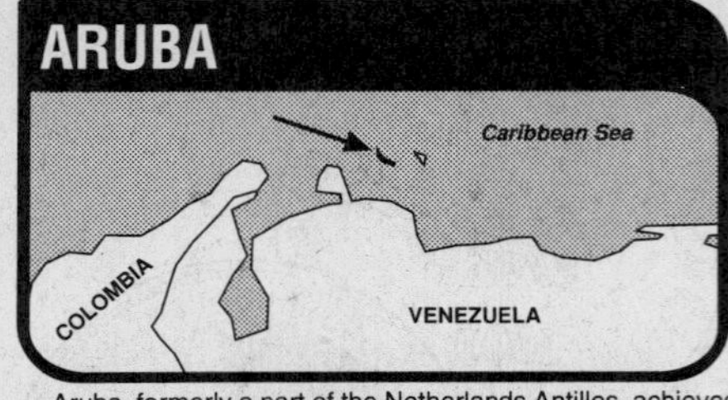


Aruba, formerly a part of the Netherlands Antilles, achieved on Jan. 1, 1986 a special status, "status aparte" as the third state under the Dutch crown, together with the Netherlands and the remaining five islands of the Netherlands Antilles. On Dec. 15, 1954 the Netherlands Antilles were given complete domestic autonomy and granted equality within the Kingdom of the Netherlands. The separate constitution put in place for Aruba in 1986 established it as an autonomous government within the Kingdom of the Netherlands. In 1990 Aruba opted to remain a part of the Kingdom without the promise of future independence.

The second largest island of the Netherlands Antilles, Aruba is situated near the Venezuelan coast. The island has an area of 74-1/2 sq. mi. (193 sq. km.) and a population of 65,974. Capital: Oranjestad, named after the Dutch royal family. Aruba was important in the processing and transportation of petroleum products in the first part of the twentieth century, but today the chief industry is tourism.

For earlier issues see Curacao and the Netherlands Antilles.

**RULERS**
Dutch

**MINT MARKS**
(u) Utrecht - Privy marks only
Anvil, 1986-1988
Bow and Arrow, 1989-1999
Bow and Arrow w/star, 2000
Winetendril with grapes, 2001-

**MONETARY SYSTEM**
100 Cents = 1 Florin

## DUTCH STATE
### "Status Aparte".

**5 CENTS** KM# 1 **Composition:** Nickel Bonded Steel

| Date | Mintage | F | VF | XF | Unc | BU |
|---|---|---|---|---|---|---|
| 1986(u) | 776,000 | — | 0.10 | 0.25 | 0.50 | — |
| 1987(u) | 462,000 | — | 0.10 | 0.25 | 0.50 | — |
| 1988(u) | 657,000 | — | — | — | 0.30 | — |
| 1989(u) | 770,000 | — | — | — | 0.30 | — |
| 1990(u) | 612,000 | — | — | — | 0.30 | — |
| 1991(u) | 412,000 | — | — | — | 0.30 | — |
| 1992(u) | 810,000 | — | — | — | 0.25 | — |
| 1993(u) | 709,000 | — | — | — | 0.25 | — |
| 1994(u) | 709,000 | — | — | — | 0.25 | — |
| 1995(u) | 809,000 | — | — | — | 0.25 | — |
| 1996(u) | 588,000 | — | — | — | 0.25 | — |
| 1997(u) | 536,000 | — | — | — | 0.25 | — |
| 1998(u) | 920,000 | — | — | — | 0.25 | — |
| 1999(u) | 824,000 | — | — | — | 0.25 | — |
| 2002(u) | — | — | — | — | 0.25 | — |

**10 CENTS** KM# 2 **Composition:** Nickel Bonded Steel

| Date | Mintage | F | VF | XF | Unc | BU |
|---|---|---|---|---|---|---|
| 1986(u) | 856,000 | — | 0.10 | 0.30 | 0.65 | — |
| 1987(u) | 372,000 | — | 0.10 | 0.30 | 0.65 | — |
| 1988(u) | 987,000 | — | — | 0.10 | 0.40 | — |
| 1989(u) | 610,000 | — | — | 0.10 | 0.40 | — |
| 1990(u) | 762,000 | — | — | 0.10 | 0.40 | — |
| 1991(u) | 512,000 | — | — | 0.10 | 0.40 | — |
| 1992(u) | 611,000 | — | — | 0.10 | 0.40 | — |
| 1993(u) | 1,008,999 | — | — | — | 0.35 | — |
| 1994(u) | 409,000 | — | — | — | 0.35 | — |
| 1995(u) | 919,000 | — | — | — | 0.35 | — |
| 1996(u) | 458,000 | — | — | — | 0.35 | — |
| 1997(u) | 424,000 | — | — | — | 0.35 | — |
| 1998(u) | 954,000 | — | — | — | 0.35 | — |
| 1999(u) | 1,005,000 | — | — | — | 0.35 | — |
| 2001(u) | 1,010,000 | — | — | — | 0.35 | — |
| 2002(u) | — | — | — | — | 0.35 | — |

**25 CENTS** KM# 3 **Composition:** Nickel Bonded Steel

| Date | Mintage | F | VF | XF | Unc | BU |
|---|---|---|---|---|---|---|
| 1986(u) | 856,000 | — | — | 0.35 | 0.75 | — |
| 1987(u) | 332,000 | — | — | 0.35 | 0.75 | — |
| 1988(u) | 117,000 | — | — | 0.35 | 0.75 | — |
| 1989(u) | 360,000 | — | — | — | 0.50 | — |
| 1990(u) | 512,000 | — | — | — | 0.50 | — |
| 1991(u) | 612,000 | — | — | — | 0.50 | — |
| 1992(u) | 461,000 | — | — | — | 0.50 | — |
| 1993(u) | 609,000 | — | — | — | 0.50 | — |
| 1994(u) | 109,000 | — | — | — | 0.50 | — |
| 1995(u) | 609,000 | — | — | — | 0.50 | — |
| 1996(u) | 289,000 | — | — | — | 0.50 | — |
| 1997(u) | 468,000 | — | — | — | 0.50 | — |
| 1998(u) | 641,000 | — | — | — | 0.50 | — |
| 1999(u) | 633,000 | — | — | — | 0.50 | — |
| 2001(u) | 720,000 | — | — | — | 0.50 | — |
| 2002(u) | — | — | — | — | 0.50 | — |

**50 CENTS** KM# 4 **Composition:** Nickel Bonded Steel

| Date | Mintage | F | VF | XF | Unc | BU |
|---|---|---|---|---|---|---|
| 1986(u) | 486,000 | — | — | 0.50 | 1.00 | — |
| 1987(u) | 122,000 | — | — | 0.50 | 1.00 | — |
| 1988(u) | 217,000 | — | — | 0.50 | 1.00 | — |
| 1989(u) | 110,000 | — | — | 0.50 | 1.00 | — |
| 1990(u) | 262,000 | — | — | 0.50 | 1.00 | — |
| 1991(u) | 312,000 | — | — | — | 0.75 | — |
| 1992(u) | 311,000 | — | — | — | 0.75 | — |
| 1993(u) | 459,000 | — | — | — | 0.75 | — |
| 1994(u) | 309,000 | — | — | — | 0.75 | — |
| 1995(u) | 259,000 | — | — | — | 0.75 | — |
| 1996(u) | 393,000 | — | — | — | 0.75 | — |
| 1997(u) | 28,000 | — | — | 0.60 | 1.25 | — |
| 1998(u) | 197,000 | — | — | — | 0.75 | — |
| 1999(u) | 446,000 | — | — | — | 0.75 | — |
| 2001(u) | 510,000 | — | — | — | 0.75 | — |
| 2002(u) | — | — | — | — | 0.75 | — |

**FLORIN** KM# 5 **Composition:** Nickel Bonded Steel

| Date | Mintage | F | VF | XF | Unc | BU |
|---|---|---|---|---|---|---|
| 1986(u) | 586,000 | — | — | 1.00 | 2.00 | — |
| 1987(u) | 272,000 | — | — | 1.00 | 2.00 | — |
| 1988(u) | 567,000 | — | — | 1.00 | 2.00 | — |
| 1989(u) | 410,000 | — | — | 1.00 | 2.00 | — |
| 1990(u) | 412,000 | — | — | 0.70 | 1.35 | — |
| 1991(u) | 162,000 | — | — | 0.70 | 1.35 | — |
| 1992(u) | 511,000 | — | — | 0.70 | 1.35 | — |
| 1993(u) | 409,000 | — | — | 0.70 | 1.35 | — |
| 1994(u) | 109,000 | — | — | 0.70 | 1.35 | — |
| 1995(u) | 209,000 | — | — | 0.70 | 1.35 | — |
| 1996(u) | 133,000 | — | — | 0.70 | 1.35 | — |
| 1997(u) | 416,000 | — | — | 0.70 | 1.35 | — |
| 1998(u) | 300,000 | — | — | 0.70 | 1.35 | — |
| 1999(u) | 431,000 | — | — | 0.70 | 1.35 | — |
| 2001(u) | 410,000 | — | — | 0.70 | 1.35 | — |
| 2002(u) | — | — | — | 0.70 | 1.35 | — |

**2-1/2 FLORIN** KM# 6 **Composition:** Nickel Bonded Steel

| Date | Mintage | F | VF | XF | Unc | BU |
|---|---|---|---|---|---|---|
| 1986(u) | 106,000 | — | — | 1.65 | 3.00 | — |
| 1987(u) | 32,000 | — | — | 1.65 | 3.00 | — |
| 1988(u) | 26,000 | — | — | 1.65 | 3.00 | — |
| 1989(u) | 15,000 | — | — | 1.65 | 3.00 | — |
| 1990(u) | 17,000 | — | — | — | 2.25 | — |
| 1991(u) | 17,000 | — | — | — | 2.25 | — |
| 1992(u) | 13,000 | — | — | — | 2.25 | — |
| 1993(u) | 11,000 | — | — | — | 2.25 | — |
| 1994(u) | 11,000 | — | — | — | 2.25 | — |
| 1995(u) | 11,000 | — | — | — | 2.25 | — |
| 1996(u) In set only | 8,000 | — | — | — | 3.50 | — |
| 1997(u) In set only | 8,000 | — | — | — | 3.50 | — |
| 1998(u) In set only | 8,000 | — | — | — | 3.50 | — |
| 1999(u) In set only | 8,000 | — | — | — | 2.25 | — |
| 2001(u) In set only | 10,000 | — | — | — | 2.25 | — |
| 2002(u) In set only | — | — | — | — | 2.25 | — |

**5 FLORIN** KM# 12 **Composition:** Nickel Bonded Steel

| Date | Mintage | F | VF | XF | Unc | BU |
|---|---|---|---|---|---|---|
| 1995(u) | 201,000 | — | — | — | 5.50 | — |
| 1996(u) | 350,000 | — | — | — | 5.50 | — |
| 1997(u) | 28,000 | — | — | — | 7.50 | — |
| 1998(u) | 162,000 | — | — | — | 5.50 | — |
| 1999(u) | 87,000 | — | — | — | 5.50 | — |
| 2001(u) In set only | 10,000 | — | — | — | 6.00 | — |
| 2002(u) | — | — | — | — | 5.50 | — |

**25 FLORIN** KM# 7 **Weight:** 25.0000 g. **Composition:** 0.9250 Silver .7435 oz. ASW **Subject:** Commonwealth of Aruba

| Date | Mintage | F | VF | XF | Unc | BU |
|---|---|---|---|---|---|---|
| 1986(u) | 5,000 | — | — | — | 20.00 | — |
| 1986(u) Proof | 10,000 | Value: 35.00 | | | | |

**25 FLORIN** **KM# 8** **Weight:** 25.0000 g. **Composition:** 0.9250 Silver .7435 oz. ASW **Subject:** Independence

| Date | Mintage | F | VF | XF | Unc | BU |
|---|---|---|---|---|---|---|
| 1991(u) | 2,500 | — | — | — | 25.00 | — |
| 1991(u) Proof | 4,600 | Value: 40.00 | | | | |

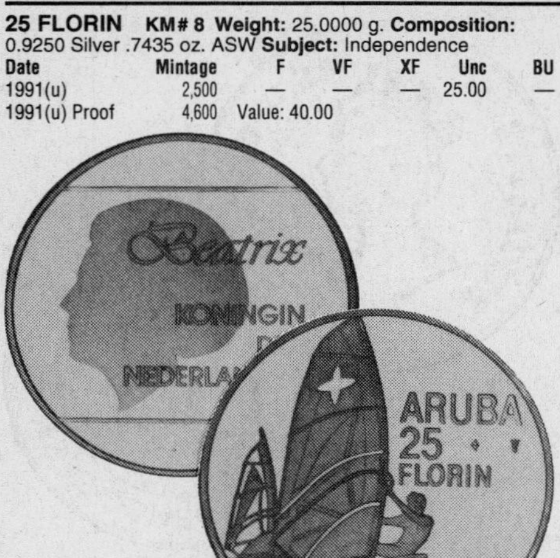


**25 FLORIN** **KM# 10** **Weight:** 25.0000 g. **Composition:** 0.9250 Silver .7435 oz. ASW **Subject:** Olympics - Windsurfing

| Date | Mintage | F | VF | XF | Unc | BU |
|---|---|---|---|---|---|---|
| 1992(u) | 2,000 | — | — | — | 27.50 | — |
| 1992(u) Proof | 15,000 | Value: 32.50 | | | | |

**25 FLORIN** **KM# 11** **Weight:** 25.0000 g. **Composition:** 0.9250 Silver .7435 oz. ASW **Reverse:** World War II Oil Tanker Convoys

| Date | Mintage | F | VF | XF | Unc | BU |
|---|---|---|---|---|---|---|
| 1994 | 1,500 | — | — | — | 27.50 | — |
| 1994 Proof | 4,000 | Value: 40.00 | | | | |

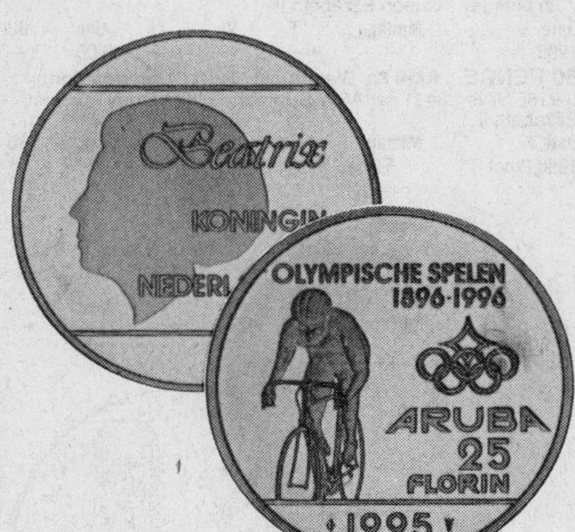


**25 FLORIN** **KM# 13** **Weight:** 25.0000 g. **Composition:** 0.9250 Silver .7435 oz. ASW **Reverse:** Olympic Games 1896-1996

| Date | Mintage | F | VF | XF | Unc | BU |
|---|---|---|---|---|---|---|
| 1995 | 1,000 | — | — | — | 35.00 | — |
| 1995 Proof | 2,100 | Value: 42.50 | | | | |

**25 FLORIN** **KM# 14** **Weight:** 25.0000 g. **Composition:** 0.9250 Silver .7435 oz. ASW **Reverse:** Olympic Games - Without Olympic Logo

| Date | Mintage | F | VF | XF | Unc | BU |
|---|---|---|---|---|---|---|
| 1995 Proof | 1,700 | Value: 47.50 | | | | |

**25 FLORIN** **KM# 15** **Weight:** 25.0000 g. **Composition:** 0.9250 Silver .7435 oz. ASW **Reverse:** Giant Sea Turtle

| Date | Mintage | F | VF | XF | Unc | BU |
|---|---|---|---|---|---|---|
| 1995 | 3,500 | — | — | — | 35.00 | — |
| 1995 Proof | 2,000 | Value: 45.00 | | | | |

**25 FLORIN** **KM# 18** **Weight:** 25.0000 g. **Composition:** 0.9250 Silver .7435 oz. ASW **Subject:** Tradition With Vision **Obverse:** Portrait of Vespucci, sailing vessel, map **Reverse:** Spanish fan and aboriginal design, dates

| Date | Mintage | F | VF | XF | Unc | BU |
|---|---|---|---|---|---|---|
| ND(1999) Proof | 1,850 | Value: 35.00 | | | | |

**50 FLORIN** **KM# 9** **Weight:** 6.7200 g. **Composition:** 0.9000 Gold .1945 oz. AGW **Subject:** Independence

| Date | Mintage | F | VF | XF | Unc | BU |
|---|---|---|---|---|---|---|
| 1991(u) Proof | 2,600 | Value: 140 | | | | |

**50 FLORIN** **KM# 16** **Weight:** 25.0000 g. **Composition:** 0.9250 Silver .7435 oz. ASW **Subject:** 10th Anniversary of Autonomy **Obverse:** Queen's silhoutte **Reverse:** Portions of national flag and anthem score **Note:** Similar to 100 Florin, KM#17

| Date | Mintage | F | VF | XF | Unc | BU |
|---|---|---|---|---|---|---|
| 1996 | 500 | — | — | — | 47.50 | — |
| 1996 Proof | 2,000 | Value: 42.50 | | | | |

**100 FLORIN** **KM# 17** **Weight:** 6.7200 g. **Composition:** 0.9000 Gold .1945 oz. AGW **Subject:** 10th Anniversary of Autonomy **Obverse:** Queen's silhoutte **Reverse:** Portions of national flag and anthem score

| Date | Mintage | F | VF | XF | Unc | BU |
|---|---|---|---|---|---|---|
| 1996 Proof | 2,600 | Value: 175 | | | | |

**100 FLORIN** **KM# 19** **Weight:** 6.7200 g. **Composition:** 0.9000 Gold .1945 oz. AGW **Subject:** Tradition With Vision **Obverse:** Portrait of Vespucci, sailing vessel, map **Reverse:** Spanish fan and aboriginal design, dates **Note:** Similar to 25 Florin, KM#19.

| Date | Mintage | F | VF | XF | Unc | BU |
|---|---|---|---|---|---|---|
| ND(1999) Proof | 1,100 | Value: 165 | | | | |

## MINT SETS

| KM# | Date | Mintage | Identification | Issue Price | Mkt Val |
|---|---|---|---|---|---|
| MS18 | 2001 | — | KM#1-6, 12, with medal | 15.00 | 14.50 |
| MS1 | 1986 | 36,200 | KM#1-6, with medal | 8.95 | 9.00 |
| MS2 | 1987 | 21,650 | KM#1-6, with medal | 9.95 | 12.50 |
| MS3 | 1988 | 16,500 | KM#1-6, with medal | 12.95 | 12.50 |
| MS4 | 1989 | 10,000 | KM#1-6, with medal | 12.00 | 12.50 |
| MS5 | 1990 | 12,000 | KM#1-6, with medal | — | 13.50 |
| MS6 | 1991 | 12,000 | KM#1-6, with medal | 14.50 | 13.50 |
| MS7 | 1992 | 10,500 | KM#1-6, with medal | — | 13.50 |
| MS8 | 1993 | 9,100 | KM#1-6, with medal | — | 16.00 |
| MS9 | 1994 | 9,100 | KM#1-6, with medal | 14.50 | 16.00 |
| MS10 | 1995 | 1,000 | KM#12 | — | 20.00 |
| MS11 | 1995 | 8,500 | KM#1-6, with medal | 17.50 | 14.50 |
| MS12 | 1995 | 2,500 | KM#15, 5 Florin banknote, with medal | 56.50 | 60.00 |
| MS13 | 1996 | 7,500 | KM#1-6, 12, with medal | 17.50 | 14.50 |
| MS14 | 1997 | 7,500 | KM#1-6, 12, with medal | 17.50 | 14.50 |
| MS15 | 1998 | 8,000 | KM#1-6, 12, with medal | 17.50 | 14.50 |
| MS16 | 1999 | 7,000 | KM#1-6, 12, with medal | 17.50 | 14.50 |
| MS17 | 2000 | 7,500 | KM#1-6, 12, with medal | 15.00 | 14.50 |

## PROOF SETS

| KM# | Date | Mintage | Identification | Issue Price | Mkt Val |
|---|---|---|---|---|---|
| PS1 | 1999 | — | KM#18-19, with Netherlands Antilles KM#45-47 | — | 600 |

# ASCENSION ISLAND

An island of volcanic origin, Ascension Island lies in the South Atlantic, 700 miles (1,100 km.) northwest of St. Helena. It has an area of 34 sq. mi. (88 sq. km.) on an island 9 miles (14 km.) long and 6 miles (10 km.) wide. Approximate population: 1,146. Although having little vegetation and scant rainfall, the island has a very healthy climate. The island is the nesting place for a large number of sea turtles and sooty terns. Phosphates and guano are the chief natural sources of income.

The island was discovered on Ascension Day, 1501, by Joao da Nova, a Portuguese navigator. It lay unoccupied until 1815, when occupied by the British. It was under Admiralty rule until 1922 when it was annexed as a dependency of St. Helena. During World War II an airfield was built that has been used as a fueling stop for Transatlantic flights to Southern Europe, North Africa and the Near-East.

**RULERS**
British

**MINT MARKS**
PM - Pobjoy Mint

## BRITISH ADMINISTRATION

### STANDARD COINAGE

**25 PENCE (Crown)** **KM# 1** **Composition:** Copper-Nickel **Subject:** 25th anniversary of coronation

| Date | Mintage | F | VF | XF | Unc | BU |
|---|---|---|---|---|---|---|
| 1978PM | — | — | — | — | 7.50 | — |

**25 PENCE (Crown)** **KM# 1a** **Weight:** 28.2800 g. **Composition:** 0.9250 Silver .8411 oz. ASW **Subject:** 25th anniversary of coronation

| Date | Mintage | F | VF | XF | Unc | BU |
|---|---|---|---|---|---|---|
| 1978PM | 70,000 | — | — | — | 15.00 | — |
| 1978PM Proof | 25,000 | Value: 22.50 | | | | |

**25 PENCE (Crown)** **KM# 2** **Weight:** 28.2800 g. **Composition:** 0.9250 Silver .8411 oz. ASW **Obverse:** Isle of Man crown **Reverse:** Ascension KM#1 **Note:** Error; mule.

| Date | Mintage | F | VF | XF | Unc | BU |
|---|---|---|---|---|---|---|
| ND(1978)PM | 367 | — | — | 150 | 200 | — |

**25 PENCE (Crown)** **KM# 3** **Composition:** Copper-Nickel **Subject:** Wedding of Prince Charles and Lady Diana

| Date | Mintage | F | VF | XF | Unc | BU |
|---|---|---|---|---|---|---|
| 1981PM | 50,000 | — | — | — | 4.50 | — |

**25 PENCE (Crown)** **KM# 3a** **Weight:** 28.2800 g. **Composition:** 0.5000 Silver .4546 oz. ASW **Subject:** Wedding of Prince Charles and Lady Diana

| Date | Mintage | F | VF | XF | Unc | BU |
|---|---|---|---|---|---|---|
| 1981 | 500 | — | — | — | 50.00 | — |

**25 PENCE (Crown)** **KM# 3b** **Weight:** 28.2800 g. **Composition:** 0.9250 Silver .8411 oz. ASW **Subject:** Wedding of Prince Charles and Lady Diana

| Date | Mintage | F | VF | XF | Unc | BU |
|---|---|---|---|---|---|---|
| 1981 Proof | 30,000 | Value: 25.00 | | | | |

**25 PENCE (Crown)** **KM# 4** **Weight:** 28.2800 g. **Composition:** 0.9250 Silver .8411 oz. ASW **Series:** International Year of the Scout

| Date | Mintage | F | VF | XF | Unc | BU |
|---|---|---|---|---|---|---|
| ND(1983) | 10,000 | — | — | — | 30.00 | — |
| ND(1983) Proof | 10,000 | Value: 40.00 | | | | |

**50 PENCE** **KM# 6** **Composition:** Copper-Nickel **Subject:** Royal visit of Prince Andrew

| Date | Mintage | F | VF | XF | Unc | BU |
|---|---|---|---|---|---|---|
| 1984 | 125,000 | — | — | — | 4.00 | — |

**50 PENCE** **KM# 6a** **Weight:** 28.2800 g. **Composition:** 0.9250 Silver .8411 oz. ASW **Subject:** Royal visit of Prince Andrew

| Date | Mintage | F | VF | XF | Unc | BU |
|---|---|---|---|---|---|---|
| 1984 Proof | 5,000 | Value: 22.50 | | | | |

**50 PENCE** **KM# 7** **Composition:** Copper-Nickel **Reverse:** Queen Mother fishing

| Date | Mintage | F | VF | XF | Unc | BU |
|---|---|---|---|---|---|---|
| 1995 | — | — | — | — | 4.00 | — |

**50 PENCE** **KM# 7a** **Weight:** 28.2800 g. **Composition:** 0.9250 Silver .841 oz. ASW **Reverse:** Queen Mother fishing

| Date | Mintage | F | VF | XF | Unc | BU |
|---|---|---|---|---|---|---|
| 1995 Proof | — | Value: 32.50 | | | | |

**50 PENCE** **KM# 7b** **Weight:** 47.5400 g. **Composition:** 0.9160 Gold 1.4001 oz. AGW **Reverse:** Queen Mother fishing

| Date | Mintage | F | VF | XF | Unc | BU |
|---|---|---|---|---|---|---|
| 1995 Proof | 150 | Value: 600 | | | | |

**50 PENCE** **KM# 8** **Composition:** Copper-Nickel **Subject:** 70th birthday - Queen Elizabeth II

| Date | Mintage | F | VF | XF | Unc | BU |
|---|---|---|---|---|---|---|
| 1996 | — | — | — | — | 6.00 | — |

**50 PENCE** **KM# 8a** **Weight:** 28.2800 g. **Composition:** 0.9250 Silver .8411 oz. ASW **Subject:** 70th birthday - Queen Elizabeth II

| Date | Mintage | F | VF | XF | Unc | BU |
|---|---|---|---|---|---|---|
| 1996 Proof | 5,000 | Value: 50.00 | | | | |

**50 PENCE** **KM# 11** **Composition:** Copper-Nickel **Series:** Montreal Olympics **Subject:** Queen's portrait **Reverse:** Royal couple behind horse and rider jumping British arms

| Date | Mintage | F | VF | XF | Unc | BU |
|---|---|---|---|---|---|---|
| 1997 | — | — | — | — | 8.00 | — |

**50 PENCE** **KM# 9** **Composition:** Copper-Nickel **Subject:** World Wildlife Fund - conserving nature **Reverse:** Frigate birds

| Date | Mintage | F | VF | XF | Unc | BU |
|---|---|---|---|---|---|---|
| 1998 | — | — | — | — | 7.50 | — |

**50 PENCE** **KM# 10** **Composition:** Copper-Nickel **Subject:** World Wildlife Fund - conserving nature **Reverse:** Long-tailed birds

| Date | Mintage | F | VF | XF | Unc | BU |
|---|---|---|---|---|---|---|
| 1998 | — | — | — | — | 7.50 | — |

**50 PENCE** **KM# 12** **Weight:** 28.7600 g. **Composition:** Copper-Nickel **Subject:** 100th Birthday of the Queen Mother **Obverse:** Queen's bust right. **Reverse:** Queen Mother's bust 3/4 facing half left. **Edge:** Reeded. **Size:** 38.5 mm.

| Date | Mintage | F | VF | XF | Unc | BU |
|---|---|---|---|---|---|---|
| ND (2000) | — | — | — | — | 8.50 | — |

**50 PENCE** **KM# 13** **Weight:** 28.6300 g. **Composition:** Copper-Nickel **Subject:** 75th Birthday of Queen Elizabeth **Obverse:** Queen's head right. **Reverse:** Crowned monogram above flowers. **Edge:** Reeded. **Size:** 38.6 mm.

| Date | Mintage | F | VF | XF | Unc | BU |
|---|---|---|---|---|---|---|
| 2001 | — | — | — | — | 8.00 | — |

**50 PENCE** **KM# 14** **Weight:** 28.6300 g. **Composition:** Copper-Nickel **Subject:** Centennial - Queen Victoria's Death **Obverse:** Queen's bust right. **Reverse:** Queen Victoria's 3/4 bust left. **Edge:** Reeded. **Size:** 38.6 mm.

| Date | Mintage | F | VF | XF | Unc | BU |
|---|---|---|---|---|---|---|
| 2001 | — | — | — | — | 8.00 | — |

**2 POUNDS** **KM# 5** **Weight:** 15.9800 g. **Composition:** 0.9170 Gold .4712 oz. AGW **Series:** International Year of the Scout **Reverse:** Boy Scout

| Date | Mintage | F | VF | XF | Unc | BU |
|---|---|---|---|---|---|---|
| 1983 | 2,000 | — | — | — | 450 | — |
| 1983 Proof | 2,000 | Value: 500 | | | | |

## PIEFORTS

| KM# | Date | Mintage | Identification | Mkt Val |
|---|---|---|---|---|
| P1 | 1995 | 500 | 50 Pence. KM7a. | 55.00 |

# AUSTRALIA

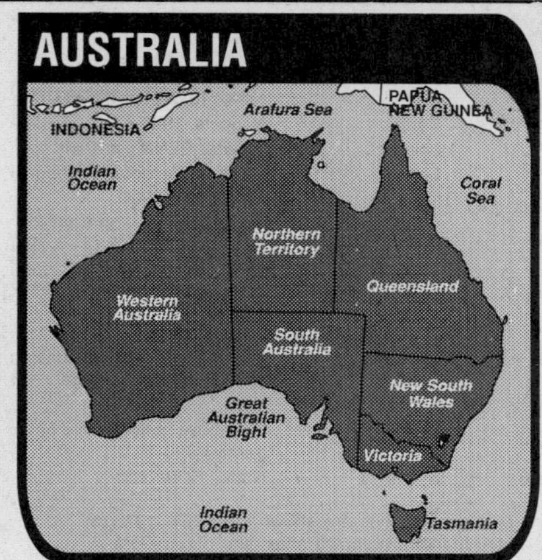


The Commonwealth of Australia, the smallest continent and largest island in the world, is located south of Indonesia between the Indian and Pacific oceans. It has an area of 2,967,893 sq. mi. (7,686,850 sq. km.) and an estimated population of 18.84 million. Capital: Canberra. Due to its early and sustained isolation, Australia is the habitat of such curious and unique fauna as the kangaroo, koala, platypus, wombat, echidna and frilled-necked lizard. The continent possesses extensive mineral deposits, the most important of which are iron ore, coal, gold, silver, nickel, uranium, lead and zinc. Raising Livestock, mining and manufacturing are the principal industries. Chief exports are wool, meat, wheat, iron ore, coal and nonferrous metals.

The first caucasians to see Australia probably were Portuguese and Spanish navigators of the late 16th century. In 1770, Captain James Cook explored the east coast and annexed it for Great Britain. New South Wales was founded as a penal colony, following the loss of British North America by Captain Arthur Phillip on January 26, 1788, a date now celebrated as Australia Day. Dates of creation of the six colonies that now comprise the states of the Australian Commonwealth are: New South Wales, 1823; Tasmania, 1825; Western Australia, 1838; South Australia, 1842; Victoria, 1851; Queensland, 1859. A constitution providing for the federation of the colonies was approved by the British Parliament in 1900. The Commonwealth of Australia came into being in 1901. Australia passed the Statute of Westminster Adoption Act on October 9, 1942, which officially established Australia's complete autonomy in external and internal affairs, thereby formalizing a situation that had existed for years. Australia is a member of the Commonwealth of Nations. Elizabeth II is Head of State as Queen of Australia.

Australia's currency system was changed from Pounds- Shillings-Pence to a decimal system of Dollars and Cents on Feb. 14, 1966.

**RULERS**

British

**MINT MARKS**

| Abbr. | Mint | Mint Marks |
|---|---|---|
| A | Adelaide | - |
| (b) | Bombay | I below bust; dots before and after HALF PENNY, 1942-43 |
| (b) | Bombay | I below bust dots before and after PENNY, 1942-43 |
| B | Brisbane | - |
| (c) | Calcutta | I above date, 1916-18 |
| (c) | Canberra | None, 1966 to date |
| C | Canberra | - |
| D | Denver | D above date 1/-& 2/-, below date on 3d |
| D | Denver | D below date on 6d |
| H | Heaton | H below date on silvere coins, 1914-15 |
| H | Heaton | H above date on bronze coins |
| (L) | London | 1910-1915 (no marks), 1966 |
| M | Melbourne | M below date on silver coins, 1916-20 |
| M | Melbourne | M above date on the ground on gold coins w/St. George |
| M | Melbourne | - |
| (m) | Melbourne | Dot below scroll on penny, 1919-20 |
| (m) | Melbourne | Two dots; below lower scroll and above upper, 1919-20 |
| (m) | Melbourne | None, 1921-1964, 1966 |
| P | Perth | P above date on the ground on gold coins w/St. George |
| (p) | Perth | Dot between KG (designer's initials), 1940-41 |
| (p) | Perth | Dot after PENNY, 1941-51, 1954-64 |

| | | |
|---|---|---|
| (p) | Perth | Dot after AUSTRALIA, 1952-53 |
| (p) | Perth | Dot before SHILLING, 1946 |
| (p) | Perth | None, 1922 penny, 1966 |
| P | Perth | Nuggets, 1986 |
| PL | London | PL after PENNY in 1951 |
| PL | London | PL on bottom folds of ribbon, 1951 threepence |
| PL | London | PL above date on sixpence |
| PL | | 1951 |
| S | San Francisco | S above or below date, 1942-44, mm exists w/ and w/o bulbous serifs |
| S | Sydney | S above date on the ground on gold coins w/St. George |
| S | Sydney | - |
| (sy) | Sydney | Dot above bottom scroll on penny 1920 |
| (sy) | Sydney | None, 1919-1926 |

Mint designations are shown in ( ). Ex. 1978(m).
Mint marks are shown after date. Ex. 1978M.

**PRIVY MARKS**

(ae) - American Eagle 

(aa) - Adelaide Assay 

(ba) - Basler Stab 

(bg) - Brandenburg Gate 

(d) – Ducat 

(dp) – Dump 

(e) – Emu 

(ev) - Edward V

(f) – Fok 

(f1) - Rev. 1 Florin, KM#31 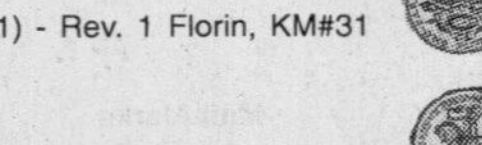

(f3) - Rev. 1 Florin, KM#33 

(f7) - Rev. 1 Florin, KM#47

(ge) - Golden Eagle 

(gv) - George V, small head 

(gV) - George V, large head

(h) – Hague 

(hd) - Holey Dollar 

(j) – Johanna 

(jw) - Japanese Royal Wedding 

(l) – Luk 

(lh) - Liberty Head 

(p) – Prospector 

(qv) - Queen Victoria 

(rv) - Royal Visit Florin, Rev. 1 Florin, KM#55

(s) – Shu 

(sg) - Spade Guinea 

(sm) - Sydney Mint Sovereign 

(so) - Sydney Opera House 

(sp) - Star Pagoda 

(sq) – State Quarter 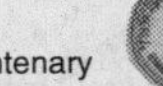

(sr) - Swan River/Rottnest Island Tercentenary 

(ta) - Team Australia (Commonwealth Games)

(w) – Whales  

(ww) - 50 Years Beyond WWII 

**MONETARY SYSTEM**

**(Until 1966)**
12 Pence = 1 Shilling
2 Shillings = 1 Florin
5 Shillings = 1 Crown
20 Shillings = 1 Pound

**Commencing 1966)**
100 Cents = 1 Dollar

# COMMONWEALTH OF AUSTRALIA

## POUND (SOVEREIGN) COINAGE

**1/2 PENNY KM# 22 Composition:** Bronze **Note:** Dies dated 1922 were used for the majority of the calendar year 1923, leaving only a small portion of this mintage figure as 1923 dated coins. Noble Numismatics sale No. 62, 11-99, nearly FDC proof realized $56,745.

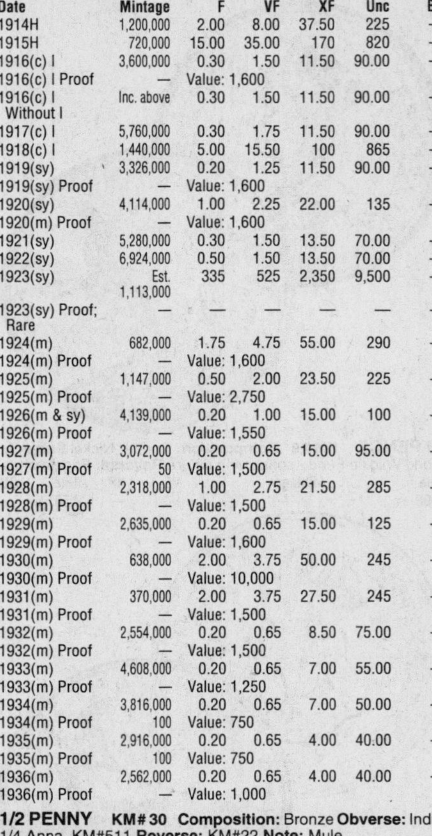

| Date | Mintage | F | VF | XF | Unc | BU |
|---|---|---|---|---|---|---|
| 1911(L) | 2,832,000 | 0.35 | 1.75 | 17.50 | 75.00 | — |
| 1911(L) Proof | — | Value: 1,600 | | | | |
| 1912H | 2,400,000 | 0.35 | 3.00 | 21.50 | 130 | — |
| 1912H Proof | — | Value: 1,600 | | | | |
| 1913(L) Wide date | 2,160,000 | 1.00 | 5.00 | 23.50 | 145 | — |
| 1913(L) Narrow date | Inc. above | 1.00 | 5.00 | 23.50 | 145 | — |
| 1914(L) | 1,440,000 | 1.75 | 7.50 | 35.00 | 225 | — |
| 1914H | 1,200,000 | 2.00 | 8.00 | 37.50 | 225 | — |
| 1915H | 720,000 | 15.00 | 35.00 | 170 | 820 | — |
| 1916(c) I | 3,600,000 | 0.30 | 1.50 | 11.50 | 90.00 | — |
| 1916(c) I Proof | — | Value: 1,600 | | | | |
| 1916(c) I Without I | Inc. above | 0.30 | 1.50 | 11.50 | 90.00 | — |
| 1917(c) I | 5,760,000 | 0.30 | 1.75 | 11.50 | 90.00 | — |
| 1918(c) I | 1,440,000 | 5.00 | 15.50 | 100 | 865 | — |
| 1919(sy) | 3,326,000 | 0.20 | 1.25 | 11.50 | 90.00 | — |
| 1919(sy) Proof | — | Value: 1,600 | | | | |
| 1920(sy) | 4,114,000 | 1.00 | 2.25 | 22.00 | 135 | — |
| 1920(m) Proof | — | Value: 1,600 | | | | |
| 1921(sy) | 5,280,000 | 0.30 | 1.50 | 13.50 | 70.00 | — |
| 1922(sy) | 6,924,000 | 0.50 | 1.50 | 13.50 | 70.00 | — |
| 1923(sy) | Est. 1,113,000 | 335 | 525 | 2,350 | 9,500 | — |
| 1923(sy) Proof; Rare | — | — | — | — | — | — |
| 1924(m) | 682,000 | 1.75 | 4.75 | 55.00 | 290 | — |
| 1924(m) Proof | — | Value: 1,600 | | | | |
| 1925(m) | 1,147,000 | 0.50 | 2.00 | 23.50 | 225 | — |
| 1925(m) Proof | — | Value: 2,750 | | | | |
| 1926(m & sy) | 4,139,000 | 0.20 | 1.00 | 15.00 | 100 | — |
| 1926(m) Proof | — | Value: 1,550 | | | | |
| 1927(m) | 3,072,000 | 0.20 | 0.65 | 15.00 | 95.00 | — |
| 1927(m) Proof | 50 | Value: 1,500 | | | | |
| 1928(m) | 2,318,000 | 1.00 | 2.75 | 21.50 | 285 | — |
| 1928(m) Proof | — | Value: 1,500 | | | | |
| 1929(m) | 2,635,000 | 0.20 | 0.65 | 15.00 | 125 | — |
| 1929(m) Proof | — | Value: 1,600 | | | | |
| 1930(m) | 638,000 | 2.00 | 3.75 | 50.00 | 245 | — |
| 1930(m) Proof | — | Value: 10,000 | | | | |
| 1931(m) | 370,000 | 2.00 | 3.75 | 27.50 | 245 | — |
| 1931(m) Proof | — | Value: 1,500 | | | | |
| 1932(m) | 2,554,000 | 0.20 | 0.65 | 8.50 | 75.00 | — |
| 1932(m) Proof | — | Value: 1,500 | | | | |
| 1933(m) | 4,608,000 | 0.20 | 0.65 | 7.00 | 55.00 | — |
| 1933(m) Proof | — | Value: 1,250 | | | | |
| 1934(m) | 3,816,000 | 0.20 | 0.65 | 7.00 | 50.00 | — |
| 1934(m) Proof | 100 | Value: 750 | | | | |
| 1935(m) | 2,916,000 | 0.20 | 0.65 | 4.00 | 40.00 | — |
| 1935(m) Proof | 100 | Value: 750 | | | | |
| 1936(m) | 2,562,000 | 0.20 | 0.65 | 4.00 | 40.00 | — |
| 1936(m) Proof | — | Value: 1,000 | | | | |

**1/2 PENNY KM# 30 Composition:** Bronze **Obverse:** India 1/4 Anna, KM#511 **Reverse:** KM#22 **Note:** Mule.

| Date | Mintage | F | VF | XF | Unc | BU |
|---|---|---|---|---|---|---|
| 1916(c) I | Est. 10 | 4,000 | 7,500 | — | — | — |

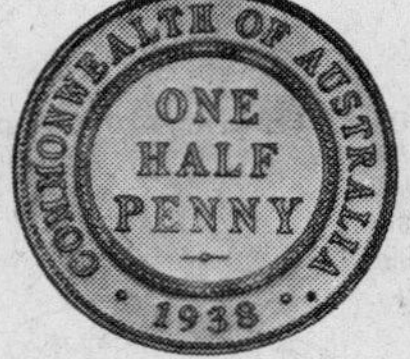

**1/2 PENNY KM# 35 Composition:** Bronze

| Date | Mintage | F | VF | XF | Unc | BU |
|---|---|---|---|---|---|---|
| 1938(m) | 3,014,000 | 0.20 | 0.50 | 1.75 | 17.50 | — |
| 1938(m) Proof | 250 | Value: 650 | | | | |
| 1939(m) | 4,382,000 | 0.20 | 0.50 | 3.50 | 25.00 | — |
| 1939(m) Proof | — | Value: 1,400 | | | | |

**1/2 PENNY KM# 41 Composition:** Bronze

| Date | Mintage | F | VF | XF | Unc | BU |
|---|---|---|---|---|---|---|
| 1939(m) | 504,000 | 3.75 | 6.50 | 42.50 | 270 | — |
| 1939(m) Proof | 100 | Value: 1,500 | | | | |
| 1940(m) | 2,294,000 | 0.20 | 0.75 | 5.00 | 35.00 | — |
| 1940(m) Proof | — | Value: 900 | | | | |
| 1941(m) | 5,011,000 | 0.20 | 0.65 | 3.00 | 20.00 | — |
| 1941(m) Proof | — | Value: 1,000 | | | | |
| 1941(p) Proof | — | Value: 1,000 | | | | |
| 1942(m) | 720,000 | 1.75 | 3.75 | 21.50 | 110 | — |
| 1942(m) Proof | — | Value: 900 | | | | |
| 1942(p) | 4,334,000 | 0.20 | 0.50 | 1.75 | 14.50 | — |
| 1942(p) Proof | — | Value: 1,000 | | | | |
| 1942(b) I | 6,000,000 | 0.15 | 0.25 | 1.75 | 18.00 | — |
| 1942(b) I Proof | — | Value: 800 | | | | |
| 1943(m) | 33,989,000 | 0.15 | 0.25 | 1.25 | 7.00 | — |
| 1943(p) Proof | — | Value: 1,000 | | | | |
| 1943(b) I | 6,000,000 | 0.20 | 0.35 | 2.75 | 14.50 | — |
| 1943(b) I Proof | — | Value: 800 | | | | |
| 1944(m) | 720,000 | 1.75 | 3.00 | 22.00 | 100 | — |
| 1944(m) Proof | — | Value: 1,200 | | | | |
| 1945(p) | 3,033,000 | 0.75 | 2.50 | 10.00 | 65.00 | — |
| 1945(p) Proof | — | Value: 850 | | | | |

| Date | Mintage | F | VF | XF | Unc | BU |
|---|---|---|---|---|---|---|
| 1945(p) Without dot | Inc. above | 1.25 | 2.50 | 12.50 | 55.00 | — |
| 1946(p) | 13,747,000 | 0.15 | 0.25 | 1.25 | 10.00 | — |
| 1946(p) Proof | — | Value: 850 | | | | |
| 1947(p) | 9,293,000 | 0.15 | 0.25 | 1.25 | 10.00 | — |
| 1947(p) Proof | — | Value: 850 | | | | |
| 1948(m) | 4,608,000 | 0.25 | 0.50 | 2.75 | 30.00 | — |
| 1948(m) Proof | — | Value: 1,000 | | | | |
| 1948(p) | 25,553,000 | 0.15 | 0.25 | 1.25 | 7.00 | — |
| 1948(p) Proof | — | Value: 850 | | | | |

**1/2 PENNY** KM# 42 **Composition:** Bronze **Obv. Legend:** IND: IMP: dropped

| Date | Mintage | F | VF | XF | Unc | BU |
|---|---|---|---|---|---|---|
| 1949(m) Proof | — | Value: 1,000 | | | | |
| 1949(p) | 22,310,000 | 0.15 | 0.25 | 2.00 | 10.00 | — |
| 1949(p) Proof | — | Value: 1,000 | | | | |
| 1950(p) | 12,014,000 | 0.15 | 0.50 | 3.50 | 13.50 | — |
| 1950(p) Proof | — | Value: 850 | | | | |
| 1951(p) with dot | — | 0.15 | 0.35 | 2.00 | 10.00 | — |
| 1951(p) with dot, Proof | — | Value: 850 | | | | |
| 1951(p) | 29,422,000 | 0.15 | 0.35 | 2.50 | 11.50 | — |
| 1951(p) Without dot; Proof | — | Value: 850 | | | | |
| 1951PL | 17,040,000 | 0.15 | 0.35 | 1.25 | 7.00 | — |

**Note:** 5.040 struck at the Birmingham Mint

| Date | Mintage | F | VF | XF | Unc | BU |
|---|---|---|---|---|---|---|
| 1951PL Proof | — | Value: 1,000 | | | | |
| 1952(p) | 1,832,000 | 0.50 | 2.25 | 7.00 | 25.00 | — |
| 1952(p) Proof | — | Value: 850 | | | | |

**1/2 PENNY** KM# 49 **Composition:** Bronze

| Date | Mintage | F | VF | XF | Unc | BU |
|---|---|---|---|---|---|---|
| 1953(p) | 23,967,000 | 0.15 | 0.25 | 0.50 | 5.00 | — |
| 1953(p) Proof | 16 | Value: 850 | | | | |
| 1954(p) | 21,963,000 | 0.15 | 0.25 | 0.50 | 6.00 | — |
| 1954(p) Proof | — | Value: 850 | | | | |
| 1955(p) Without dot | 9,343,000 | 0.15 | 0.25 | 0.50 | 6.00 | — |
| 1955(p) Without dot; Proof | 301 | Value: 600 | | | | |

**1/2 PENNY** KM# 61 **Composition:** Bronze **Obv. Legend:** F:D: added

| Date | Mintage | F | VF | XF | Unc | BU |
|---|---|---|---|---|---|---|
| 1959(m) | 10,166,000 | 0.10 | 0.15 | 0.25 | 0.85 | — |
| 1959(m) Proof | 1,506 | Value: 75.00 | | | | |
| 1960(p) | 17,812,000 | 0.10 | 0.15 | 0.25 | 0.85 | — |
| 1960(p) Proof | 1,030 | Value: 95.00 | | | | |
| 1961(p) | 20,183,000 | 0.10 | 0.15 | 0.25 | 0.85 | — |
| 1961(p) Proof | 1,040 | Value: 95.00 | | | | |
| 1962(p) | 10,259,000 | 0.10 | 0.15 | 0.25 | 2.00 | — |
| 1962(p) Proof | 1,064 | Value: 85.00 | | | | |
| 1963(p) | 16,410,000 | 0.10 | 0.15 | 0.25 | 0.85 | — |
| 1963(p) Proof | 1,060 | Value: 85.00 | | | | |
| 1964(p) | 18,230,000 | 0.10 | 0.15 | 0.25 | 0.85 | — |
| 1964(p) Proof; 1 known | — | Value: 3,000 | | | | |

**PENNY** KM# 23 **Composition:** Bronze

| Date | Mintage | F | VF | XF | Unc | BU |
|---|---|---|---|---|---|---|
| 1911(L) | 3,768,000 | 0.75 | 3.00 | 17.50 | 90.00 | — |
| 1911(L) Proof | — | Value: 1,800 | | | | |
| 1912H | 3,600,000 | 0.75 | 3.00 | 21.50 | 150 | — |
| 1912H Proof | — | Value: 1,800 | | | | |
| 1913(L) | 2,520,000 | 1.25 | 7.50 | 27.50 | 200 | — |
| 1914(L) | 720,000 | 3.00 | 8.50 | 60.00 | 425 | — |
| 1915(L) | 960,000 | 2.25 | 15.50 | 75.00 | 600 | — |
| 1915H | 1,320,000 | 1.75 | 8.50 | 55.00 | 500 | — |
| 1916(c) I | 3,324,000 | 0.50 | 1.50 | 15.00 | 100 | — |
| 1916(c) I Proof | — | Value: 1,800 | | | | |
| 1917(c) I | 6,240,000 | 0.40 | 1.00 | 12.50 | 125 | — |
| 1918(c) I | 1,200,000 | 3.75 | 15.50 | 70.00 | 550 | — |
| 1919(m) Without dots | 5,810,000 | 0.50 | 2.25 | 21.50 | 250 | — |
| 1919(m) Dot below bottom scroll | Inc. above | 1.00 | 3.75 | 35.00 | 200 | — |
| 1919(m) Dots below bottom scroll and above upper | — | 10.00 | 27.50 | 110 | — | |
| 1919(m) Proof | — | Value: 1,800 | | | | |
| 1920(m & sy) Without dots | — | 0.75 | 7.50 | 190 | 1,550 | — |
| 1920(m) Dot beow bottom scroll | Inc. above | 2.00 | 7.50 | 42.50 | 315 | — |
| 1920(m) Proof | — | Value: 1,800 | | | | |
| 1920(sy) Dot above bottom scroll | Inc. above | 3.00 | 7.50 | 42.50 | 470 | — |
| 1920 Dots below bottom scroll and above upper | Inc. above | 5.50 | 30.00 | 110 | — | — |
| 1921(m & sy) | 7,438,000 | 0.25 | 3.00 | 27.50 | 225 | — |
| 1922(m & p) | 12,697,000 | 0.25 | 2.50 | 27.50 | 225 | — |
| 1923(m) | 5,654,000 | 0.25 | 2.50 | 23.50 | 225 | — |
| 1923(m) Proof | — | Value: 1,600 | | | | |
| 1924(m & sy) | 4,656,000 | 0.25 | 1.50 | 18.50 | 210 | — |
| 1924(m) Proof | — | Value: 1,500 | | | | |
| 1925(m) | 1,639,000 | 12.50 | 50.00 | 190 | 3,750 | — |
| 1925(m) Proof | — | Value: 10,500 | | | | |
| 1926(m & sy) | 1,859,000 | 1.00 | 3.75 | 35.00 | 315 | — |
| 1926(m) Proof | — | Value: 1,800 | | | | |
| 1927(m) | 4,922,000 | 0.30 | 2.25 | 20.00 | 110 | — |
| 1927(m) Proof | 50 | Value: 1,200 | | | | |
| 1928(m) | 3,038,000 | 0.30 | 3.50 | 21.50 | 225 | — |
| 1928(m) Proof | — | Value: 1,800 | | | | |
| 1929(m) | 2,599,000 | 0.30 | 2.50 | 22.00 | 290 | — |
| 1929(m) Proof | — | Value: 1,750 | | | | |
| 1930(m) | Est. 3,000 | 4,250 | 7,200 | 20,000 | 40,000 | — |
| 1930(m) Proof; Rare | — | — | — | — | — | — |

**Note:** Noble Numismatics sale No. 52, 7-97, nearly FDC proof realized $126,500. Noble Numismatics sale No. 62, 11-99, FDC proof realized $162,665.

| Date | Mintage | F | VF | XF | Unc | BU |
|---|---|---|---|---|---|---|
| 1931(m) | 494,000 | 1.75 | 1.50 | 35.00 | 600 | — |
| 1931(m) Proof | — | Value: 1,750 | | | | |
| 1932(m) | 2,117,000 | 0.30 | 2.50 | 35.00 | 135 | — |
| 1933/2(m) | 5,818,000 | 3.00 | 11.50 | 47.50 | 270 | — |
| 1933(m) | Inc. above | 0.25 | 1.50 | 13.50 | 70.00 | — |
| 1933(m) Proof Sets | — | Value: 1,400 | | | | |
| 1934(m) | 5,808,000 | 0.25 | 0.85 | 13.50 | 60.00 | — |
| 1934(m) Proof | 100 | Value: 900 | | | | |
| 1935(m) | 3,725,000 | 0.25 | 0.75 | 12.50 | 55.00 | — |
| 1935(m) Proof | 100 | Value: 900 | | | | |
| 1936(m) | 9,890,000 | 0.25 | 0.75 | 10.00 | 45.00 | — |
| 1936(m) Proof | — | Value: 1,000 | | | | |

**PENNY** KM# 36 **Composition:** Bronze

| Date | Mintage | F | VF | XF | Unc | BU |
|---|---|---|---|---|---|---|
| 1938(m) | 5,552,000 | 0.25 | 0.50 | 3.75 | 22.50 | — |
| 1938(m) Proof | 250 | Value: 750 | | | | |
| 1939(m) | 6,240,000 | 0.25 | 0.50 | 3.75 | 27.50 | — |
| 1939(m) Proof | — | Value: 1,250 | | | | |
| 1940(m) | 4,075,000 | 0.30 | 1.00 | 6.50 | 45.00 | — |
| 1940(p) K.G. | 1,114,000 | 1.50 | 3.00 | 35.00 | 250 | — |
| 1941(m) | 1,588,000 | 0.30 | 1.00 | 8.50 | 45.00 | — |
| 1941(p) K.G. | 12,794,000 | 0.75 | 2.00 | 21.50 | 90.00 | — |
| 1941(p) Proof | — | Value: 1,600 | | | | |
| 1941(p) | Inc. above | 0.25 | 0.75 | 6.50 | 45.00 | — |
| 1941(p) K.G. high dot after Y | Inc. above | 0.50 | 1.25 | 8.50 | 42.50 | — |
| 1942(p) | 12,245,000 | 0.15 | 0.75 | 4.25 | 28.00 | — |
| 1942(p) Proof | — | Value: 1,200 | | | | |
| 1942(b) I | 9,000,000 | 0.15 | 0.50 | 3.50 | 22.50 | — |
| 1942(b) Without I | Inc. above | 1.75 | 3.75 | 10.00 | 55.00 | — |
| 1942(b) Proof | — | Value: 1,200 | | | | |
| 1943(m) | 11,112,000 | 0.20 | 0.50 | 5.00 | 22.50 | — |
| 1943(p) | 33,086,000 | 0.15 | 0.50 | 5.00 | 25.00 | — |
| 1943(p) Proof | — | Value: 1,000 | | | | |
| 1943(b) I | 9,000,000 | 0.20 | 0.50 | 4.25 | 20.00 | — |
| 1943(b) I Without I | Inc. above | 1.75 | 3.75 | 10.00 | 55.00 | — |
| 1943(b) Proof | — | Value: 800 | | | | |
| 1944(m) | 2,112,000 | 0.50 | 3.75 | 21.50 | 100 | — |
| 1944(p) | 27,830,000 | 0.15 | 0.50 | 3.50 | 25.00 | — |
| 1944(p) Proof | — | Value: 1,200 | | | | |
| 1945(p) | 15,173,000 | 0.20 | 0.75 | 4.75 | 32.00 | — |
| 1945(p) Proof | — | Value: 1,400 | | | | |
| 1945(b) I Rare | 6 | — | — | — | — | — |
| 1945(m) | — | — | — | — | 15,000 | — |
| 1946(m) | 240,000 | 5.50 | 15.50 | 42.50 | 470 | — |
| 1947(m) | 6,864,000 | 0.15 | 0.40 | 2.25 | 12.50 | — |
| 1947(p) | 4,490,000 | 0.50 | 1.25 | 6.50 | 45.00 | — |
| 1947(p) Proof | — | Value: 1,400 | | | | |
| 1948(m) | 26,616,000 | 0.15 | 0.40 | 2.25 | 12.50 | — |
| 1948(p) | 1,534,000 | 0.75 | 3.00 | 32.50 | 160 | — |
| 1948(p) Proof | — | Value: 1,500 | | | | |

**PENNY** KM# 43 **Composition:** Bronze **Obv. Legend:** IND: IMP. dropped

| Date | Mintage | F | VF | XF | Unc | BU |
|---|---|---|---|---|---|---|
| 1949M | 27,065,000 | 0.15 | 0.25 | 2.00 | 10.00 | — |
| 1949M Proof | — | Value: 2,000 | | | | |
| 1950M | 36,359,000 | 0.15 | 0.25 | 2.00 | 14.50 | — |
| 1950M Proof | — | Value: 2,000 | | | | |
| 1950P | 21,488,000 | 0.20 | 1.00 | 6.50 | 35.00 | — |
| 1950P Proof | — | Value: 1,200 | | | | |
| 1951M | 21,240,000 | 0.15 | 0.20 | 1.00 | 9.00 | — |
| 1951P | 12,888,000 | 0.20 | 0.40 | 4.00 | 22.50 | — |
| 1951P Proof | — | Value: 1,200 | | | | |
| 1951PL | 18,000,000 | 0.15 | 0.25 | 0.85 | 7.00 | — |
| 1951PL Proof | — | Value: 1,250 | | | | |
| 1952(m) | 12,408,000 | 0.15 | 0.30 | 1.00 | 7.00 | — |
| 1952(m) Proof | — | Value: 2,500 | | | | |
| 1952(p) | 45,514,000 | 0.15 | 0.30 | 1.00 | 6.50 | — |
| 1952(p) Proof | — | Value: 1,250 | | | | |

**PENNY** KM# 50 **Composition:** Bronze

| Date | Mintage | F | VF | XF | Unc | BU |
|---|---|---|---|---|---|---|
| 1953(m) | 6,936,000 | 0.20 | 0.75 | 3.00 | 14.50 | — |
| 1953(m) Proof | — | Value: 800 | | | | |
| 1953(p) | 6,203,000 | 0.20 | 0.65 | 1.50 | 16.50 | — |
| 1953(p) Proof | 16 | Value: 1,400 | | | | |

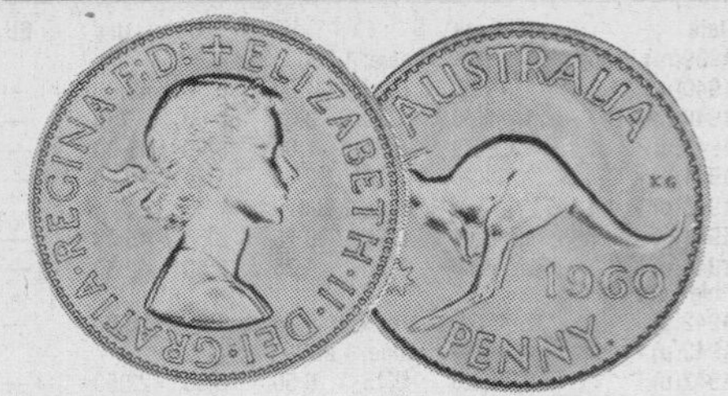

**PENNY** KM# 56 **Composition:** Bronze **Obv. Legend:** F:D: added

| Date | Mintage | F | VF | XF | Unc | BU |
|---|---|---|---|---|---|---|
| 1955(m) | 6,336,000 | 0.50 | 1.00 | 2.50 | 14.50 | — |
| 1955(m) Proof | 1,200 | Value: 100 | | | | |
| 1955(p) | 11,110,000 | 0.10 | 0.20 | 0.85 | 9.00 | — |
| 1955(p) Proof | 301 | Value: 900 | | | | |
| 1956(m) | 13,872,000 | 0.10 | 0.20 | 0.85 | 7.00 | — |
| 1956(m) Proof | 1,500 | Value: 75.00 | | | | |
| 1956(p) | 12,121,000 | 0.10 | 0.20 | 0.85 | 6.50 | — |
| 1956(p) Proof | 417 | Value: 750 | | | | |
| 1957(p) | 15,978,000 | 0.10 | 0.20 | 0.85 | 6.00 | — |
| 1957(p) Proof | 1,112 | Value: 150 | | | | |
| 1958(m) | 10,012,000 | 0.10 | 0.20 | 0.85 | 6.00 | — |
| 1958(m) Proof | 1,506 | Value: 75.00 | | | | |
| 1958(p) | 14,428,000 | 0.10 | 0.20 | 0.85 | 6.50 | — |
| 1958(p) Proof | 1,028 | Value: 125 | | | | |
| 1959(m) | 1,617,000 | 0.50 | 1.25 | 6.50 | 28.00 | — |
| 1959(m) Proof | 1,506 | Value: 75.00 | | | | |
| 1959(p) | 14,428,000 | 0.10 | 0.20 | 0.85 | 5.50 | — |
| 1959(p) Proof | 1,030 | Value: 125 | | | | |
| 1960(p) | 20,515,000 | 0.10 | 0.20 | 0.85 | 1.75 | — |
| 1960(p) Proof | 1,030 | Value: 100 | | | | |
| 1961(p) | 30,607,000 | 0.10 | 0.20 | 0.40 | 1.25 | — |
| 1961(p) Proof | 1,040 | Value: 100 | | | | |
| 1962(p) | 34,851,000 | 0.10 | 0.20 | 0.40 | 1.25 | — |
| 1962(p) Proof | 1,064 | Value: 95.00 | | | | |
| 1963(p) | 10,258,000 | 0.10 | 0.20 | 0.40 | 1.25 | — |
| 1963(p) Proof | 1,100 | Value: 95.00 | | | | |
| 1964(m) | 49,130,000 | 0.10 | 0.20 | 0.50 | 1.00 | — |
| 1964(p) | 54,590,000 | 0.10 | 0.20 | 0.50 | 1.00 | — |
| 1964(p) Proof; 1 known | — | Value: 4,000 | | | | |

**THREEPENCE** KM# 18 **Weight:** 1.4100 g. **Composition:** 0.9250 Silver .0419 oz. ASW

| Date | Mintage | F | VF | XF | Unc | BU |
|---|---|---|---|---|---|---|
| 1910(L) | 4,000,000 | 1.75 | 3.75 | 8.50 | 35.00 | — |
| 1910(L) Proof | — | Value: 700 | | | | |

**THREEPENCE** KM# 24 **Weight:** 1.4100 g. **Composition:** 0.9250 Silver .0419 oz. ASW

| Date | Mintage | F | VF | XF | Unc | BU |
|---|---|---|---|---|---|---|
| 1911(L) | 2,000,000 | 4.25 | 10.00 | 42.50 | 190 | — |
| 1911(L) Proof | — | Value: 2,000 | | | | |
| 1911(L) Reeded edge; Proof | — | Value: 10,000 | | | | |
| 1912(L) | 2,400,000 | 5.50 | 50.00 | 170 | 800 | — |
| 1914(L) | 1,600,000 | 8.50 | 27.50 | 100 | 580 | — |
| 1915(L) | 800,000 | 12.50 | 55.00 | 180 | 900 | — |
| 1916M | 1,913,000 | 5.00 | 11.50 | 55.00 | 385 | — |
| 1916M Proof | 25 | Value: 1,000 | | | | |
| 1917M | 3,808,000 | 1.75 | 5.50 | 18.50 | 135 | — |
| 1918M | 3,119,000 | 1.75 | 5.50 | 21.50 | 125 | — |
| 1919M | 3,201,000 | 2.50 | 8.50 | 27.50 | 145 | — |
| 1919M Proof | — | Value: 1,000 | | | | |
| 1920M | 4,196,000 | 6.50 | 15.00 | 55.00 | 380 | — |
| 1920M Proof | — | Value: 1,000 | | | | |
| 1921M | 7,378,000 | 1.75 | 4.25 | 17.50 | 95.00 | — |
| 1921(m) | Inc. above | 7.50 | 13.50 | 85.00 | 450 | — |
| 1922/1(m) | 5,531,000 | 2,125 | 4,750 | 9,500 | 17,500 | — |
| 1922(m) | Inc. above | 1.75 | 7.50 | 21.50 | 165 | — |
| 1922(m) Proof | — | Value: 1,000 | | | | |
| 1923(m) | 815,000 | 11.50 | 30.00 | 125 | 765 | — |
| 1924(m & sy) | 2,013,999 | 5.50 | 11.50 | 50.00 | 320 | — |
| 1924(m) Proof | — | Value: 900 | | | | |
| 1925(m & sy) Proof | 4,347,000 | 0.50 | 3.50 | 17.50 | 100 | — |
| 1925(m) Proof | — | Value: 900 | | | | |
| 1926(m & sy) | 6,158,000 | 0.50 | 2.00 | 16.50 | 90.00 | — |
| 1926(m) Proof | — | Value: 900 | | | | |
| 1927(m) | 6,720,000 | 0.50 | 2.00 | 13.50 | 80.00 | — |
| 1927(m) Proof | 50 | Value: 900 | | | | |
| 1928(m) | 5,000,000 | 0.50 | 2.00 | 16.50 | 85.00 | — |
| 1928(m) Proof | — | Value: 900 | | | | |
| 1934/3(m) | 1,616,000 | 20.00 | 38.50 | 150 | 600 | — |
| 1934(m) | Inc. above | 0.50 | 2.00 | 15.00 | 80.00 | — |
| 1934(m) Proof | 100 | Value: 750 | | | | |
| 1935(m) | 2,800,000 | 0.50 | 2.00 | 16.50 | 100 | — |
| 1935(m) Proof | — | Value: 550 | | | | |
| 1936(m) | 3,600,000 | 0.30 | 1.25 | 7.00 | 37.50 | — |
| 1936(m) Proof | — | Value: 650 | | | | |

**THREEPENCE** KM# 37 **Weight:** 1.4100 g. **Composition:** 0.9250 Silver .0419 oz. ASW

| Date | Mintage | F | VF | XF | Unc | BU |
|---|---|---|---|---|---|---|
| 1938(m) | 4,560,000 | 0.30 | 1.25 | 6.50 | 12.50 | — |
| 1938(m) Proof | 250 | Value: 300 | | | | |
| 1939(m) | 3,856,000 | 0.30 | 1.50 | 7.00 | 25.00 | — |
| 1939(m) Proof | — | Value: 450 | | | | |
| 1940(m) | 3,840,000 | 0.30 | 1.50 | 7.00 | 37.50 | — |
| 1941(m) | 7,584,000 | 0.30 | 1.00 | 3.75 | 20.00 | — |
| 1942(m) | 528,000 | 8.50 | 25.00 | 115 | 550 | — |
| 1942D | 16,000,000 | BV | 0.40 | 1.00 | 3.50 | — |
| 1942S | 8,000,000 | BV | 0.65 | 1.25 | 4.50 | — |
| 1943(m) | 24,912,000 | BV | 0.40 | 0.85 | 3.00 | — |
| 1943D | 16,000,000 | BV | 0.40 | 1.00 | 3.50 | — |
| 1943S | 8,000,000 | BV | 0.65 | 1.25 | 4.50 | — |
| 1944S | 32,000,000 | BV | 0.40 | 0.85 | 3.50 | — |

**THREEPENCE** KM# 37a **Weight:** 1.4100 g. **Composition:** 0.5000 Silver .0226 oz. ASW

| Date | Mintage | F | VF | XF | Unc | BU |
|---|---|---|---|---|---|---|
| 1947(m) | 4,176,000 | 0.85 | 2.00 | 7.00 | 25.00 | — |
| 1948(m) | 26,208,000 | — | BV | 1.75 | 5.00 | — |

**THREEPENCE** KM# 44 **Weight:** 1.4100 g. **Composition:** 0.5000 Silver .0226 oz. ASW **Obv. Legend:** IND: IMP. dropped

| Date | Mintage | F | VF | XF | Unc | BU |
|---|---|---|---|---|---|---|
| 1949(m) | 26,400,000 | — | BV | 1.75 | 5.50 | — |
| 1949(m) Proof | — | Value: 700 | | | | |
| 1950(m) | 35,456,000 | — | BV | 1.75 | 7.00 | — |
| 1951(m) | 15,856,000 | — | 0.50 | 2.50 | 10.00 | — |
| 1951PL | 40,000,000 | — | BV | 1.00 | 3.00 | — |
| 1951PL Proof | — | Value: 500 | | | | |
| 1952(m) | 21,560,000 | — | BV | 1.75 | 7.00 | — |

**THREEPENCE** KM# 51 **Weight:** 1.4100 g. **Composition:** 0.5000 Silver .0226 oz. ASW

| Date | Mintage | F | VF | XF | Unc | BU |
|---|---|---|---|---|---|---|
| 1953(m) | 7,664,000 | BV | 1.75 | 4.75 | 20.00 | — |
| 1953(m) Proof | — | Value: 500 | | | | |
| 1954(m) | 2,672,000 | 0.85 | 2.50 | 5.50 | 35.00 | — |
| 1954(m) Proof | — | Value: 600 | | | | |

**THREEPENCE** KM# 57 **Weight:** 1.4100 g. **Composition:** 0.5000 Silver .0226 oz. ASW **Obv. Legend:** F:D: added

| Date | Mintage | F | VF | XF | Unc | BU |
|---|---|---|---|---|---|---|
| 1955(m) | 27,088,000 | — | BV | 1.25 | 4.00 | — |
| 1955(m) Proof | 1,040 | Value: 45.00 | | | | |
| 1956(m) | 14,088,000 | — | BV | 1.25 | 4.50 | — |
| 1956(m) Proof | 1,500 | Value: 40.00 | | | | |
| 1957(m) | 26,704,000 | — | BV | 0.85 | 2.50 | — |
| 1957(m) Proof | 1,256 | Value: 40.00 | | | | |
| 1958(m) | 11,248,000 | — | BV | 1.75 | 4.50 | — |
| 1958(m) Proof | 1,506 | Value: 40.00 | | | | |
| 1959(m) | 19,888,000 | — | BV | 0.85 | 2.25 | — |
| 1959(m) Proof | 1,506 | Value: 40.00 | | | | |
| 1960(m) | 19,600,000 | — | BV | 0.60 | 1.00 | — |
| 1960(m) Proof | 1,509 | Value: 35.00 | | | | |
| 1961(m) | 33,840,000 | — | BV | 0.60 | 1.00 | — |
| 1961(m) Proof | 1,506 | Value: 35.00 | | | | |
| 1962(m) | 15,968,000 | — | BV | 0.60 | 1.00 | — |
| 1962(m) Proof | 2,016 | Value: 35.00 | | | | |
| 1963(m) | 44,016,000 | — | BV | 0.50 | 1.00 | — |
| 1963(m) Proof | 5,042 | Value: 25.00 | | | | |
| 1964(m) | 20,320,000 | — | BV | 0.50 | 1.25 | — |

**SIXPENCE** KM# 19 **Weight:** 2.8200 g. **Composition:** 0.9250 Silver .0838 oz. ASW

| Date | Mintage | F | VF | XF | Unc | BU |
|---|---|---|---|---|---|---|
| 1910(L) | 3,046,000 | 5.00 | 12.50 | 35.00 | 130 | — |
| 1910(L) Proof | — | Value: 800 | | | | |

**SIXPENCE** KM# 25 **Weight:** 2.8200 g. **Composition:** 0.9250 Silver .0838 oz. ASW

| Date | Mintage | F | VF | XF | Unc | BU |
|---|---|---|---|---|---|---|
| 1911(L) | 1,000,000 | 7.00 | 21.50 | 125 | 540 | — |
| 1911(L) Proof | — | Value: 2,000 | | | | |
| 1912(L) | 1,600,000 | 13.50 | 50.00 | 150 | 850 | — |
| 1914(L) | 1,800,000 | 5.50 | 12.50 | 70.00 | 400 | — |
| 1916M | 1,769,000 | 7.50 | 21.50 | 120 | 600 | — |
| 1916M Proof | 25 | Value: 1,750 | | | | |
| 1917M | 1,632,000 | 7.50 | 20.00 | 100 | 470 | — |
| 1918M | 915,000 | 20.00 | 65.00 | 235 | 1,125 | — |
| 1919M | 1,521,000 | 7.50 | 19.50 | 65.00 | 350 | — |
| 1919M Proof | — | Value: 1,600 | | | | |
| 1920M | 1,476,000 | 8.50 | 25.00 | 120 | 600 | — |
| 1920M Proof | — | Value: 2,500 | | | | |
| 1921(m) Proof | — | Value: 2,000 | | | | |
| 1921(m & sy) | 3,795,000 | 5.00 | 10.00 | 35.00 | 210 | — |
| 1922(sy) | 1,488,000 | 13.50 | 38.50 | 200 | 850 | — |
| 1922(sy) Proof | — | Value: 2,500 | | | | |
| 1923(m & sy) | 1,458,000 | 8.50 | 21.50 | 120 | 585 | — |
| 1924(m) Proof | — | Value: 2,000 | | | | |
| 1924(m & sy) | 1,038,000 | 8.50 | 21.50 | 150 | 800 | — |
| 1925(m) Proof | — | Value: 900 | | | | |
| 1925(m & sy) | 3,266,000 | 0.75 | 8.50 | 42.50 | 180 | — |
| 1926(m) Proof | — | Value: 900 | | | | |
| 1926(m & sy) | 3,609,000 | 0.75 | 7.00 | 27.50 | 100 | — |
| 1927(m) | 3,592,000 | 0.75 | 6.00 | 21.50 | 100 | — |
| 1927(m) Proof | 50 | Value: 900 | | | | |
| 1928(m) | 2,721,000 | 0.75 | 6.00 | 21.50 | 140 | — |
| 1928(m) Proof | — | Value: 900 | | | | |
| 1934(m) | 1,024,000 | 2.50 | 7.00 | 30.00 | 200 | — |
| 1934(m) Proof | 100 | Value: 700 | | | | |
| 1935(m) | 392,000 | 4.25 | 10.00 | 50.00 | 325 | — |
| 1935(m) Proof | — | Value: 1,000 | | | | |
| 1936(m) | 1,800,000 | 0.75 | 3.00 | 10.00 | 90.00 | — |
| 1936(m) Proof | — | Value: 900 | | | | |

**SIXPENCE** KM# 38 **Weight:** 2.8200 g. **Composition:** 0.9250 Silver .0838 oz. ASW

| Date | Mintage | F | VF | XF | Unc | BU |
|---|---|---|---|---|---|---|
| 1938(m) | 2,864,000 | 0.65 | 2.00 | 7.00 | 35.00 | — |
| 1938(m) Proof | 250 | Value: 400 | | | | |
| 1939(m) | 1,600,000 | 0.65 | 2.50 | 13.50 | 175 | — |
| 1939(m) Proof | — | Value: 900 | | | | |
| 1940(m) | 1,600,000 | 0.65 | 2.50 | 10.00 | 70.00 | — |
| 1941(m) | 2,912,000 | 0.65 | 2.00 | 5.50 | 30.00 | — |
| 1942(m) | 8,968,000 | BV | 1.25 | 3.50 | 20.00 | — |
| 1942D | 12,000,000 | BV | 0.75 | 2.00 | 8.50 | — |
| 1942S | 4,000,000 | BV | 0.75 | 2.00 | 14.50 | — |
| 1943D | 8,000,000 | BV | 0.75 | 2.00 | 8.50 | — |
| 1943S | 4,000,000 | BV | 0.75 | 2.00 | 12.00 | — |
| 1944S | 4,000,000 | BV | 1.00 | 2.50 | 10.00 | — |
| 1945(m) | 10,096,000 | BV | 1.00 | 2.50 | 8.50 | — |

**SIXPENCE** KM# 38a **Weight:** 2.8200 g. **Composition:** 0.5000 Silver .0453 oz. ASW

| Date | Mintage | F | VF | XF | Unc | BU |
|---|---|---|---|---|---|---|
| 1946(m) | 10,024,000 | BV | 0.85 | 3.50 | 18.50 | — |
| 1946(m) Prof | — | Value: 900 | | | | |
| 1948(m) | 1,584,000 | BV | 0.85 | 3.50 | 20.00 | — |

**SIXPENCE** KM# 45 **Weight:** 1.4100 g. **Composition:** 0.5000 Silver .0226 oz. ASW **Obv. Legend:** IND: IMP. dropped

| Date | Mintage | F | VF | XF | Unc | BU |
|---|---|---|---|---|---|---|
| 1950(m) | 10,272,000 | BV | 2.00 | 3.50 | 22.50 | — |
| 1950(m) Proof | — | Value: 1,500 | | | | |
| 1951(m) | 13,760,000 | BV | 1.50 | 2.75 | 16.50 | — |
| 1951PL | 20,024,000 | BV | 0.50 | 1.75 | 7.00 | — |
| 1951PL Proof | — | Value: 650 | | | | |
| 1952(m) | 2,112,000 | 0.75 | 4.25 | 21.50 | 150 | — |

**SIXPENCE** KM# 52 **Weight:** 1.4100 g. **Composition:** 0.5000 Silver .0226 oz. ASW

| Date | Mintage | F | VF | XF | Unc | BU |
|---|---|---|---|---|---|---|
| 1953(m) | 1,152,000 | 0.75 | 3.50 | 10.00 | 75.00 | — |
| 1953(m) Proof | — | Value: 700 | | | | |
| 1954(m) | 7,672,000 | BV | 0.85 | 1.50 | 5.00 | — |
| 1954(m) Proof | — | Value: 750 | | | | |

**SIXPENCE** KM# 58 **Weight:** 1.4100 g. **Composition:** 0.5000 Silver .0226 oz. ASW **Obv. Legend:** F:D: added

| Date | Mintage | F | VF | XF | Unc | BU |
|---|---|---|---|---|---|---|
| 1955M | 14,248,000 | BV | 0.75 | 1.75 | 8.00 | — |
| 1955(m) Proof | 1,200 | Value: 70.00 | | | | |
| 1956(m) | 7,904,000 | BV | 2.25 | 4.25 | 22.50 | — |
| 1956(m) Proof | 1,500 | Value: 55.00 | | | | |
| 1957(m) | 13,752,000 | BV | 0.50 | 0.85 | 3.50 | — |
| 1957(m) Proof | 1,256 | Value: 55.00 | | | | |
| 1958(m) | 17,944,000 | BV | 0.50 | 0.85 | 3.00 | — |
| 1958(m) Proof | 1,506 | Value: 50.00 | | | | |
| 1959(m) | 11,728,000 | BV | 0.50 | 1.00 | 5.00 | — |
| 1959(m) Proof | 1,506 | Value: 50.00 | | | | |
| 1960(m) | 18,592,000 | BV | 0.50 | 0.85 | 4.50 | — |
| 1960(m) Proof | 1,509 | Value: 45.00 | | | | |
| 1961(m) | 9,152,000 | BV | 0.50 | 0.85 | 2.75 | — |
| 1961(m) Proof | 1,506 | Value: 45.00 | | | | |
| 1962(m) | 44,816,000 | BV | 0.50 | 0.75 | 1.75 | — |
| 1962(m) Proof | 2,016 | Value: 45.00 | | | | |
| 1963(m) | 25,056,000 | BV | 0.50 | 0.75 | 1.75 | — |
| 1963(m) Proof | 5,042 | Value: 30.00 | | | | |

**SHILLING** KM# 20 **Weight:** 5.6500 g. **Composition:** 0.9250 Silver .1680 oz. ASW

| Date | Mintage | F | VF | XF | Unc | BU |
|---|---|---|---|---|---|---|
| 1910(L) | 2,536,000 | 3.75 | 15.00 | 65.00 | 135 | — |
| 1910(L) Proof | — | Value: 900 | | | | |

**SHILLING** KM# 26 **Weight:** 5.6500 g. **Composition:** 0.9250 Silver .1680 oz. ASW

| Date | Mintage | F | VF | XF | Unc | BU |
|---|---|---|---|---|---|---|
| 1911(L) | 1,700,000 | 9.50 | 27.50 | 85.00 | 525 | — |
| 1911(L) Proof | — | Value: 5,000 | | | | |
| 1912(L) | 1,000,000 | 20.00 | 95.00 | 185 | 1,850 | — |
| 1913(L) | 1,200,000 | 11.50 | 35.00 | 145 | 1,350 | — |
| 1914(L) | 3,300,000 | 6.50 | 17.50 | 65.00 | 350 | — |
| 1915(L) | 800,000 | 20.00 | 100 | 255 | 1,650 | — |
| 1915H | 500,000 | 30.00 | 115 | 375 | 3,400 | — |
| 1916M | 5,141,000 | 1.25 | 5.50 | 21.50 | 145 | — |
| 1916M Proof | 25 | Value: 1,750 | | | | |
| 1917M | 5,274,000 | 1.25 | 5.50 | 21.50 | 145 | — |
| 1918M | 3,761,000 | 3.75 | 13.50 | 42.50 | 165 | — |
| 1919M Proof | — | Value: 20,000 | | | | |
| 1920M | 520,000 | 5.50 | 21.50 | 100 | 900 | — |
| 1920M Proof | — | Value: 6,000 | | | | |
| 1921(sy) Star | 1,641,000 | 15.50 | 75.00 | 265 | 2,250 | — |

| Date | Mintage | F | VF | XF | Unc | BU |
|---|---|---|---|---|---|---|
| 1921(m) Star; Proof | — | Value: 7,500 | | | | |
| 1922(m) | 2,040,000 | 7.80 | 20.00 | 85.00 | 375 | — |
| 1922(m) Proof | — | Value: 2,700 | | | | |
| 1924(m & sy) | 674,000 | 15.50 | 45.00 | 220 | 1,000 | — |
| 1924(m) Proof | — | Value: 4,000 | | | | |
| 1925/3(m & sy) | 1,448,000 | 1.25 | 10.00 | 35.00 | 150 | — |
| 1925(m) Proof | — | Value: 1,500 | | | | |
| 1926(m & sy) | 2,352,000 | 1.25 | 10.00 | 42.50 | 160 | — |
| 1926(m) Proof | — | Value: 2,000 | | | | |
| 1927(m) | 1,146,000 | 3.75 | 10.00 | 30.00 | 135 | — |
| 1927(m) Proof | 50 | Value: 1,850 | | | | |
| 1928(m) | 664,000 | 10.00 | 22.50 | 135 | 765 | — |
| 1928(m) Proof | — | Value: 3,000 | | | | |
| 1931(m) | 1,000,000 | 3.75 | 10.00 | 42.50 | 170 | — |
| 1931(m) Proof | — | — | — | — | — | — |
| 1933(m) | 220,000 | 35.00 | 125 | 785 | 1,850 | — |
| 1933(m) Proof | — | Value: 10,000 | | | | |
| 1934(m) | 480,000 | 7.50 | 18.50 | 75.00 | 250 | — |
| 1934(m) Proof | 100 | Value: 900 | | | | |
| 1935(m) | 500,000 | 5.00 | 10.00 | 22.50 | 140 | — |
| 1935(m) Proof | — | Value: 1,000 | | | | |
| 1936(m) | 2,000,000 | 2.50 | 7.50 | 25.00 | 145 | — |
| 1936(m) Proof | — | Value: 1,250 | | | | |

**SHILLING** KM# 39 **Weight:** 5.6500 g. **Composition:** 0.9250 Silver .1680 oz. ASW

| Date | Mintage | F | VF | XF | Unc | BU |
|---|---|---|---|---|---|---|
| 1938(m) | 1,484,000 | 2.25 | 4.50 | 8.50 | 30.00 | — |
| 1938(m) Proof | 250 | Value: 500 | | | | |
| 1939(m) | 1,520,000 | 2.25 | 4.50 | 10.00 | 85.00 | — |
| 1939(m) Proof | — | Value: 2,000 | | | | |
| 1940(m) | 760,000 | 5.00 | 11.50 | 35.00 | 200 | — |
| 1941(m) | 3,040,000 | BV | 3.75 | 6.75 | 28.00 | — |
| 1942(m) | 1,380,000 | BV | 3.00 | 6.00 | 22.50 | — |
| 1942S | 4,000,000 | BV | 1.25 | 3.00 | 10.00 | — |
| 1943(m) | 2,720,000 | 2.25 | 5.00 | 13.50 | 65.00 | — |
| 1943S | 16,000,000 | BV | 1.25 | 2.50 | 8.00 | — |
| 1944(m) | 14,576,000 | BV | 2.50 | 6.00 | 24.00 | — |
| 1944S | 8,000,000 | BV | 1.25 | 2.50 | 10.00 | — |

**SHILLING** KM# 39a **Weight:** 5.6500 g. **Composition:** 0.5000 Silver .0908 oz. ASW

| Date | Mintage | F | VF | XF | Unc | BU |
|---|---|---|---|---|---|---|
| 1946(m) | 10,072,000 | BV | 2.50 | 4.50 | 15.00 | — |
| 1946(p) | 1,316,000 | 4.50 | 11.50 | 27.50 | 85.00 | — |
| 1948(m) | 4,131,999 | BV | 3.00 | 5.50 | 17.50 | — |

**SHILLING** KM# 46 **Weight:** 5.6500 g. **Composition:** 0.5000 Silver .0908 oz. ASW **Obv. Legend:** IND: IMP. dropped

| Date | Mintage | F | VF | XF | Unc | BU |
|---|---|---|---|---|---|---|
| 1950(m) | 7,188,000 | BV | 2.50 | 4.25 | 12.50 | — |
| 1952(m) | 19,644,000 | BV | 2.25 | 3.50 | 8.00 | — |

**SHILLING** KM# 53 **Weight:** 2.8200 g. **Composition:** 0.5000 Silver .0453 oz. ASW

| Date | Mintage | F | VF | XF | Unc | BU |
|---|---|---|---|---|---|---|
| 1953(m) | 12,204,000 | BV | 2.00 | 3.50 | 7.00 | — |
| 1953(m) Proof | — | Value: 700 | | | | |
| 1954(m) | 16,187,999 | BV | 2.00 | 3.50 | 8.00 | — |
| 1954(m) Proof | — | Value: 800 | | | | |

**SHILLING** KM# 59 **Weight:** 2.8200 g. **Composition:** 0.5000 Silver .0453 oz. ASW **Obv. Legend:** F:D: added

| Date | Mintage | F | VF | XF | Unc | BU |
|---|---|---|---|---|---|---|
| 1955(m) | 7,492,000 | BV | 1.50 | 3.50 | 12.50 | — |
| 1955(m) Proof | 1,200 | Value: 80.00 | | | | |
| 1956(m) | 6,064,000 | BV | 0.85 | 2.50 | 16.00 | — |
| 1956(m) Proof | 1,500 | Value: 70.00 | | | | |
| 1957(m) | 12,668,000 | BV | 0.65 | 1.25 | 5.00 | — |
| 1957(m) Proof | 1,256 | Value: 75.00 | | | | |
| 1958(m) | 7,412,000 | BV | 0.65 | 1.25 | 5.00 | — |
| 1958(m) Proof | 1,506 | Value: 55.00 | | | | |
| 1959(m) | 10,876,000 | BV | 0.65 | 1.00 | 4.50 | — |
| 1959(m) Proof | 1,506 | Value: 55.00 | | | | |
| 1960(m) | 14,512,000 | — | BV | 0.85 | 3.00 | — |
| 1960(m) Proof | 1,509 | Value: 50.00 | | | | |
| 1961(m) | 31,864,000 | — | BV | 0.65 | 1.75 | — |
| 1961(m) Proof | 1,506 | Value: 50.00 | | | | |
| 1962(m) | 6,592,000 | — | BV | 0.65 | 1.75 | — |
| 1962(m) Proof | 2,016 | Value: 50.00 | | | | |
| 1963(m) | 10,072,000 | — | BV | 0.65 | 1.75 | — |
| 1963(m) Proof | 5,042 | Value: 35.00 | | | | |

**FLORIN** KM# 21 **Weight:** 11.3100 g. **Composition:** 0.9250 Silver .3363 oz. ASW

| Date | Mintage | F | VF | XF | Unc | BU |
|---|---|---|---|---|---|---|
| 1910(L) | 1,259,000 | 25.00 | 115 | 275 | 675 | — |
| 1910(L) Proof | — | Value: 1,500 | | | | |

**FLORIN** KM# 27 **Weight:** 11.3100 g. **Composition:** 0.9250 Silver .3363 oz. ASW

| Date | Mintage | F | VF | XF | Unc | BU |
|---|---|---|---|---|---|---|
| 1911(L) | 950,000 | 25.00 | 115 | 365 | 2,000 | — |
| 1911(L) Proof | — | Value: 7,000 | | | | |
| 1912(L) | 1,000,000 | 20.00 | 125 | 425 | 2,600 | — |
| 1913(L) | 1,200,000 | 20.00 | 125 | 425 | 2,250 | — |
| 1914(L) | 2,300,000 | 10.00 | 30.00 | 100 | 585 | — |
| 1914H | 500,000 | 65.00 | 190 | 850 | 3,850 | — |
| 1914H Proof | — | Value: 9,500 | | | | |
| 1915(L) | 500,000 | 70.00 | 220 | 540 | 3,325 | — |
| 1915H | 750,000 | 42.50 | 135 | 300 | 1,800 | — |
| 1916M | 2,752,000 | 7.50 | 27.50 | 120 | 475 | — |
| 1916M Proof | 25 | Value: 2,250 | | | | |
| 1917M | 4,305,000 | 7.50 | 27.50 | 120 | 475 | — |
| 1918M | 2,095,000 | 8.50 | 37.50 | 125 | 550 | — |
| 1919M | 1,677,000 | 20.00 | 110 | 350 | 1,400 | — |
| 1920M Star; Proof | — | Value: 40,000 | | | | |
| 1921(m) | 1,247,000 | 20.00 | 120 | 385 | 1,575 | — |
| 1921(m) Proof | — | Value: 6,000 | | | | |
| 1922(m) | 2,057,999 | 15.50 | 100 | 240 | 1,300 | — |
| 1922(m) Proof | — | Value: 3,700 | | | | |
| 1923(m) | 1,038,000 | 11.50 | 75.00 | 190 | 900 | — |
| 1924(m) Proof | — | Value: 2,500 | | | | |
| 1924(m & sy) | 1,582,000 | 8.50 | 45.00 | 150 | 800 | — |
| 1925(m & sy) | 2,960,000 | 7.50 | 25.00 | 100 | 360 | — |
| 1925(m) Proof | — | Value: 2,300 | | | | |
| 1926(m & sy) | 2,487,000 | 7.50 | 25.00 | 110 | 500 | — |
| 1926(m) Proof | — | Value: 3,000 | | | | |
| 1927(m) | 3,420,000 | 6.00 | 15.50 | 75.00 | 300 | — |
| 1927(m) Proof | 50 | Value: 1,850 | | | | |
| 1928(m) | 1,962,000 | 7.00 | 21.50 | 100 | 335 | — |
| 1928(m) Proof | — | Value: 2,000 | | | | |
| 1931(m) | 3,129,000 | 3.75 | 11.50 | 60.00 | 175 | — |
| 1931(m) Proof | — | Value: 1,850 | | | | |
| 1932(m) | 188,000 | 100 | 270 | 820 | 3,650 | — |
| 1933(m) | 488,000 | 25.00 | 140 | 625 | 2,500 | — |

| Date | Mintage | F | VF | XF | Unc | BU |
|---|---|---|---|---|---|---|
| 1934(m) | 1,674,000 | 4.25 | 12.50 | 60.00 | 270 | — |
| 1934(m) Proof | 100 | Value: 1,250 | | | | |
| 1935(m) | 915,000 | 3.00 | 14.00 | 62.50 | 275 | — |
| 1935(m) Proof | — | Value: 1,250 | | | | |
| 1936(m) | 2,382,000 | 2.00 | 4.50 | 17.50 | 125 | — |
| 1936(m) Proof | — | Value: 1,350 | | | | |

**FLORIN** **KM# 31** **Weight:** 11.3100 g. **Composition:** 0.9250 Silver .3363 oz. ASW **Subject:** Opening of Parliament House, Canberra

| Date | Mintage | F | VF | XF | Unc | BU |
|---|---|---|---|---|---|---|
| 1927(m) | 2,000,000 | 1.75 | 5.50 | 10.00 | 35.00 | — |
| 1927(m) Proof | 400 | Value: 2,000 | | | | |

**FLORIN** **KM# 33** **Weight:** 11.3100 g. **Composition:** 0.9250 Silver .3363 oz. ASW **Subject:** Centennial of Victoria and Melbourne

| Date | Mintage | F | VF | XF | Unc | BU |
|---|---|---|---|---|---|---|
| 1934 | Est. 54,000 | 75.00 | 95.00 | 185 | 275 | — |
| **Note:** 21,000 pieces were melted | | | | | | |
| 1934 Proof | — | Value: 6,500 | | | | |

**FLORIN** **KM# 40** **Weight:** 11.3100 g. **Composition:** 0.9250 Silver .3363 oz. ASW

| Date | Mintage | F | VF | XF | Unc | BU |
|---|---|---|---|---|---|---|
| 1938(m) | 2,990,000 | 2.00 | 4.50 | 17.50 | 50.00 | — |
| 1938(m) Proof | — | Value: 800 | | | | |
| 1939(m) | 630,000 | 7.50 | 15.50 | 45.00 | 500 | — |
| 1939(m) Proof | — | Value: 2,500 | | | | |
| 1940(m) | 8,410,000 | BV | 3.75 | 8.50 | 28.00 | — |
| 1941(m) | 7,614,000 | BV | 3.75 | 6.00 | 25.00 | — |
| 1942(m) | 17,986,000 | BV | 3.50 | 5.00 | 22.50 | — |
| 1942S | 6,000,000 | BV | 3.75 | 6.00 | 25.00 | — |
| 1943(m) | 12,762,000 | BV | 3.00 | 4.25 | 20.00 | — |
| 1943S | 11,000,000 | BV | 3.00 | 4.25 | 18.00 | — |
| 1944(m) | 22,440,000 | BV | 3.00 | 4.25 | 22.50 | — |
| 1944S | 11,000,000 | BV | 3.00 | 4.25 | 18.00 | — |
| 1945(m) | 11,970,000 | BV | 3.75 | 7.50 | 35.00 | — |

**FLORIN** **KM# 40a** **Weight:** 11.3100 g. **Composition:** 0.5000 Silver .1818 oz. ASW

| Date | Mintage | F | VF | XF | Unc | BU |
|---|---|---|---|---|---|---|
| 1946(m) | 22,154,000 | BV | 1.75 | 3.50 | 13.50 | — |
| 1946(m) Proof | — | Value: 600 | | | | |
| 1947(m) | 39,292,000 | BV | 1.75 | 3.50 | 13.50 | — |
| 1947(m) Proof | — | Value: 600 | | | | |

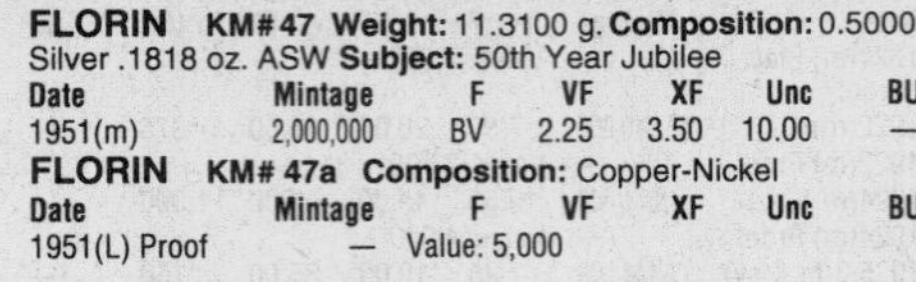

**FLORIN** **KM# 47** **Weight:** 11.3100 g. **Composition:** 0.5000 Silver .1818 oz. ASW **Subject:** 50th Year Jubilee

| Date | Mintage | F | VF | XF | Unc | BU |
|---|---|---|---|---|---|---|
| 1951(m) | 2,000,000 | BV | 2.25 | 3.50 | 10.00 | — |

**FLORIN** **KM# 47a** **Composition:** Copper-Nickel

| Date | Mintage | F | VF | XF | Unc | BU |
|---|---|---|---|---|---|---|
| 1951(L) Proof | — | Value: 5,000 | | | | |

**FLORIN** **KM# 48** **Weight:** 11.3100 g. **Composition:** 0.5000 Silver .1818 oz. ASW **Obv. Legend:** IND: IMP. dropped

| Date | Mintage | F | VF | XF | Unc | BU |
|---|---|---|---|---|---|---|
| 1951(m) | 10,068,000 | 2.25 | 5.00 | 10.00 | 30.00 | — |
| 1952(m) | 10,044,000 | 2.50 | 5.50 | 11.00 | 32.00 | — |

**FLORIN** **KM# 54** **Weight:** 11.3100 g. **Composition:** 0.5000 Silver .1818 oz. ASW

| Date | Mintage | F | VF | XF | Unc | BU |
|---|---|---|---|---|---|---|
| 1953(m) | 12,658,000 | BV | 3.00 | 5.00 | 11.00 | — |
| 1953(m) Proof | — | Value: 900 | | | | |
| 1954(m) | 15,366,000 | BV | 3.00 | 5.00 | 14.50 | — |
| 1954(m) Proof | — | Value: 1,000 | | | | |

**FLORIN** **KM# 55** **Weight:** 11.3100 g. **Composition:** 0.5000 Silver .1818 oz. ASW **Subject:** Royal Visit

| Date | Mintage | F | VF | XF | Unc | BU |
|---|---|---|---|---|---|---|
| 1954(m) | 4,000,000 | BV | 2.00 | 3.50 | 11.00 | — |

**FLORIN** **KM# 60** **Weight:** 11.3100 g. **Composition:** 0.5000 Silver .1818 oz. ASW **Obv. Legend:** F:D: added

| Date | Mintage | F | VF | XF | Unc | BU |
|---|---|---|---|---|---|---|
| 1956(m) | 8,090,000 | 2.25 | 3.75 | 10.00 | 32.00 | — |
| 1956(m) Proof | 1,500 | Value: 85.00 | | | | |
| 1957(m) | 9,278,000 | BV | 2.25 | 2.75 | 6.00 | — |
| 1957(m) Proof | 1,256 | Value: 55.00 | | | | |
| 1958(m) | 8,972,000 | BV | 2.25 | 2.75 | 5.85 | — |
| 1958(m) Proof | 1,506 | Value: 50.00 | | | | |
| 1959(m) | 3,500,000 | BV | 2.25 | 2.75 | 6.25 | — |
| 1959(m) Proof | 1,506 | Value: 45.00 | | | | |
| 1960(m) | 15,760,000 | BV | 2.00 | 2.35 | 4.00 | — |
| 1960(m) Proof | 1,509 | Value: 40.00 | | | | |
| 1961(m) | 9,452,000 | BV | 2.00 | 2.50 | 4.50 | — |
| 1961(m) Proof | 1,506 | Value: 40.00 | | | | |
| 1962(m) | 13,748,000 | BV | 2.00 | 2.35 | 4.00 | — |
| 1962(m) Proof | 2,016 | Value: 40.00 | | | | |
| 1963(m) | 12,002,000 | BV | 2.00 | 2.35 | 4.00 | — |
| 1963(m) Proof | 5,042 | Value: 30.00 | | | | |

**CROWN** **KM# 34** **Weight:** 28.2800 g. **Composition:** 0.9250 Silver .8411 oz. ASW

| Date | Mintage | F | VF | XF | Unc | BU |
|---|---|---|---|---|---|---|
| 1937(m) | 1,008,000 | 6.50 | 9.00 | 15.00 | 40.00 | — |
| 1937(m) Proof | 100 | Value: 4,000 | | | | |
| 1938(m) | 102,000 | 22.50 | 37.50 | 75.00 | 290 | — |
| 1938(m) Proof | 250 | Value: 4,500 | | | | |

## TRADE COINAGE

**1/2 SOVEREIGN** **KM# 12** **Weight:** 3.9940 g. **Composition:** 0.9170 Gold .1177 oz. AGW **Obverse:** Older veiled head **Reverse:** Mint mark above date

| Date | Mintage | F | VF | XF | Unc | BU |
|---|---|---|---|---|---|---|
| 1901M Proof | — | Value: 11,500 | | | | |
| 1901P Proof | — | Value: 20,000 | | | | |

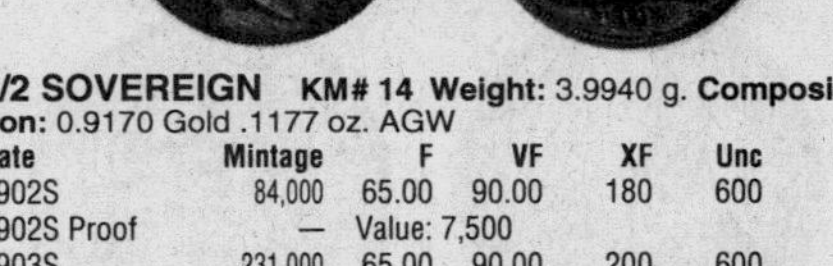

**1/2 SOVEREIGN** **KM# 14** **Weight:** 3.9940 g. **Composition:** 0.9170 Gold .1177 oz. AGW

| Date | Mintage | F | VF | XF | Unc | BU |
|---|---|---|---|---|---|---|
| 1902S | 84,000 | 65.00 | 90.00 | 180 | 600 | — |
| 1902S Proof | — | Value: 7,500 | | | | |
| 1903S | 231,000 | 65.00 | 90.00 | 200 | 600 | — |
| 1904P | 60,000 | 100 | 300 | 900 | 2,400 | — |
| 1906S | 308,000 | 60.00 | 75.00 | 100 | 400 | — |
| 1906M | 82,000 | 60.00 | 80.00 | 170 | 650 | — |
| 1907M | 400,000 | 60.00 | 75.00 | 100 | 500 | — |
| 1908S | 538,000 | 60.00 | 75.00 | 100 | 425 | — |
| 1908M | — | 60.00 | 75.00 | 100 | 400 | — |
| 1908P | 25,000 | 150 | 350 | 950 | 2,400 | — |
| 1909M | 186,000 | 60.00 | 75.00 | 140 | 550 | — |
| 1909P | 44,000 | 115 | 250 | 625 | 1,600 | — |
| 1910S | 474,000 | 60.00 | 75.00 | 100 | 300 | — |
| 1915P | 138,000 | 75.00 | 95.00 | 135 | 250 | — |
| 1916S | 448,000 | BV | 50.00 | 65.00 | 95.00 | — |
| 1918P 200-250 pieces | — | 250 | 450 | 650 | 1,200 | — |

**1/2 SOVEREIGN** **KM# 28** **Weight:** 3.9940 g. **Composition:** 0.9170 Gold .1177 oz. AGW

| Date | Mintage | F | VF | XF | Unc | BU |
|---|---|---|---|---|---|---|
| 1911S | 252,000 | BV | 55.00 | 75.00 | 95.00 | — |
| 1911S Matte Proof | — | — | — | — | 11,500 | — |
| 1911P | 130,000 | 75.00 | 95.00 | 135 | 270 | — |
| 1912S | 278,000 | BV | 55.00 | 75.00 | 95.00 | — |
| 1914S | 322,000 | BV | 55.00 | 75.00 | 95.00 | — |
| 1915S | 892,000 | BV | 40.00 | 65.00 | 90.00 | — |
| 1915M | 125,000 | BV | 55.00 | 75.00 | 110 | — |

**SOVEREIGN** **KM# 13** **Weight:** 7.9881 g. **Composition:** 0.9170 Gold .2354 oz. AGW **Obverse:** Older veiled head

| Date | Mintage | F | VF | XF | Unc | BU |
|---|---|---|---|---|---|---|
| 1901S | 3,012,000 | — | BV | 85.00 | 130 | — |
| 1901S | 3,012,000 | — | BV | 85.00 | 130 | — |
| 1901M | 3,987,000 | — | BV | 85.00 | 130 | — |
| 1901M Proof | — | Value: 10,000 | | | | |
| 1901P | 2,889,000 | — | BV | 110 | 220 | — |
| 1901P Proof | — | Value: 12,500 | | | | |

**SOVEREIGN** **KM# 15** **Weight:** 7.9881 g. **Composition:** 0.9170 Gold .2354 oz. AGW

| Date | Mintage | F | VF | XF | Unc | BU |
|---|---|---|---|---|---|---|
| 1902S | 2,813,000 | — | — | BV | 100 | — |
| 1902S Proof | — | Value: 12,500 | | | | |
| 1902M | 4,267,000 | — | — | BV | 100 | — |
| 1902P | 4,289,000 | — | — | BV | 100 | — |
| 1902P Proof | — | Value: 12,500 | | | | |
| 1903S | 2,806,000 | — | — | BV | 100 | — |
| 1903M | 3,521,000 | — | — | BV | 100 | — |
| 1903P | 4,674,000 | — | — | BV | 100 | — |
| 1904S | 2,986,000 | — | — | BV | 100 | — |
| 1904M | 3,743,000 | — | — | BV | 100 | — |
| 1904M Proof | — | Value: 12,500 | | | | |
| 1904P | 4,506,000 | — | — | BV | 100 | — |
| 1905S | 2,778,000 | — | — | BV | 100 | — |
| 1905M | 3,633,000 | — | — | BV | 100 | — |
| 1905P | 4,876,000 | — | — | BV | 100 | — |
| 1906S | 2,792,000 | — | — | BV | 100 | — |
| 1906M | 3,657,000 | — | — | BV | 100 | — |
| 1906P | 4,829,000 | — | — | BV | 100 | — |
| 1907S | 2,539,000 | — | — | BV | 100 | — |
| 1907M | 3,332,000 | — | — | BV | 100 | — |
| 1907P | 4,972,000 | — | — | BV | 100 | — |
| 1908S | 2,017,000 | — | — | BV | 100 | — |
| 1908M | 3,080,000 | — | — | BV | 100 | — |
| 1908P | 4,875,000 | — | — | BV | 100 | — |
| 1909S | 2,057,000 | — | — | BV | 100 | — |
| 1909M | 3,029,000 | — | — | BV | 100 | — |
| 1909P | 4,524,000 | — | — | BV | 100 | — |
| 1910S | 2,135,000 | — | — | BV | 100 | — |
| 1910M | 3,054,000 | — | — | BV | 100 | — |
| 1910M Proof | — | Value: 12,500 | | | | |
| 1910P | 4,690,000 | — | — | BV | 100 | — |

**SOVEREIGN** **KM# 29** **Weight:** 7.9881 g. **Composition:** 0.9170 Gold .2354 oz. AGW

| Date | Mintage | F | VF | XF | Unc | BU |
|---|---|---|---|---|---|---|
| 1911S | 2,519,000 | — | — | BV | 110 | — |
| 1911S Proof | — | Value: 12,500 | | | | |
| 1911M | 2,851,000 | — | — | BV | 110 | — |
| 1911M Proof | — | Value: 12,500 | | | | |
| 1911P | 4,373,000 | — | — | BV | 110 | — |
| 1912S | 2,227,000 | — | — | BV | 110 | — |
| 1912M | 2,467,000 | — | — | BV | 110 | — |
| 1912P | 4,278,000 | — | — | BV | 110 | — |
| 1913S | 2,249,000 | — | — | BV | 110 | — |
| 1913M | 2,323,000 | — | — | BV | 110 | — |
| 1913P | 4,635,000 | — | — | BV | 110 | — |
| 1914S | 1,774,000 | — | — | BV | 110 | — |
| 1914S Proof | — | Value: 11,500 | | | | |
| 1914M | 2,012,000 | — | — | BV | 110 | — |
| 1914P | 4,815,000 | — | — | BV | 110 | — |
| 1915S | 1,346,000 | — | — | BV | 110 | — |
| 1915M | 1,637,000 | — | — | BV | 110 | — |
| 1915P | 4,373,000 | — | — | BV | 110 | — |
| 1916S | 1,242,000 | — | — | BV | 110 | — |
| 1916M | 1,277,000 | — | — | BV | 110 | — |
| 1916P | 4,906,000 | — | — | BV | 110 | — |
| 1917S | 1,666,000 | — | — | BV | 110 | — |
| 1917M | 934,000 | — | — | BV | 110 | — |
| 1917P | 4,110,000 | — | — | BV | 110 | — |
| 1918S | 3,716,000 | — | — | BV | 110 | — |
| 1918M | 4,969,000 | — | — | BV | 110 | — |
| 1918P | 3,812,000 | — | — | BV | 110 | — |
| 1919S | 1,835,000 | — | — | BV | 110 | — |
| 1919M | 514,000 | — | BV | 90.00 | 145 | — |
| 1919P | 2,995,000 | — | — | BV | 100 | — |
| 1920S | 360,000 | 20,000 | 30,000 | 50,000 | 120,000 | — |
| 1920M | 530,000 | 1,000 | 1,500 | 2,150 | 4,550 | — |
| 1920P | 2,421,000 | — | — | BV | 120 | — |
| 1921S | 839,000 | 8,500 | 1,250 | 1,850 | 4,250 | — |
| 1921M | 240,000 | 1,500 | 3,500 | 5,750 | 9,500 | — |
| 1921P | 2,314,000 | — | — | BV | 110 | — |
| 1922S | 578,000 | 3,000 | 8,000 | 11,500 | 18,500 | — |
| 1922M | 608,000 | 1,000 | 3,000 | 5,250 | 9,500 | — |
| 1922P | 2,298,000 | — | — | BV | 125 | — |
| 1923S | 416,000 | 1,200 | 3,250 | 5,500 | 9,500 | — |
| 1923M | 510,000 | — | BV | 100 | 150 | — |
| 1923P | 2,124,000 | — | — | BV | 120 | — |
| 1924S | 394,000 | 150 | 600 | 1,000 | 1,800 | — |
| 1924M | 278,000 | — | BV | 100 | 150 | — |
| 1924P | 1,464,000 | BV | 135 | 185 | 285 | — |
| 1925S | 5,632,000 | — | — | BV | 110 | — |
| 1925M | 3,311,000 | — | — | BV | 110 | — |
| 1925P | 1,837,000 | BV | 165 | 200 | 350 | — |
| 1926S | 1,030,999 | 7,000 | 12,000 | 17,000 | 24,000 | — |
| 1926S Proof | — | Value: 27,000 | | | | |
| 1926M | 211,000 | — | BV | 100 | 140 | — |
| 1926P | 1,131,000 | 200 | 500 | 1,000 | 2,850 | — |
| 1927M | 310,000 | — | — | — | — | — |
| 1927P | 1,383,000 | BV | 165 | 200 | 350 | — |
| 1928M | 413,000 | 750 | 1,250 | 2,000 | 3,200 | — |
| 1928P | 1,333,000 | BV | 145 | 185 | 285 | — |

**SOVEREIGN** **KM# 32** **Weight:** 7.9881 g. **Composition:** 0.9170 Gold .2354 oz. AGW **Obverse:** Smaller head

| Date | Mintage | F | VF | XF | Unc | BU |
|---|---|---|---|---|---|---|
| 1929M | 436,000 | 600 | 1,000 | 1,750 | 3,150 | — |
| 1929M Proof | — | Value: 10,000 | | | | |
| 1929P | 1,606,000 | — | BV | 100 | 135 | — |
| 1930M | 77,000 | 90.00 | 120 | 185 | 250 | — |
| 1930M Proof | — | Value: 10,000 | | | | |
| 1930P | 1,915,000 | — | BV | 100 | 135 | — |
| 1931M | 57,000 | 120 | 220 | 400 | 575 | — |
| 1931M Proof | — | Value: 10,000 | | | | |
| 1931P | 1,173,000 | — | BV | 100 | 135 | — |

**2 POUNDS** **KM# 16** **Weight:** 15.9761 g. **Composition:** 0.9170 Gold .4707 oz. AGW **Note:** Gilt lead electrotypes exist.

| Date | Mintage | F | VF | XF | Unc | BU |
|---|---|---|---|---|---|---|
| 1902S Matte Proof | 4 | Value: 35,000 | | | | |

**5 POUNDS** **KM# 17** **Weight:** 39.9403 g. **Composition:** 0.9170 Gold 1.1771 oz. AGW **Note:** Gilt lead electrotypes exist.

| Date | Mintage | F | VF | XF | Unc | BU |
|---|---|---|---|---|---|---|
| 1902S Proof; Rare | Est. 3 | — | — | — | — | — |
| 1902S Matte Proof; Rare | Inc. above | — | — | — | — | — |

**Note:** Spink Australia Sale #30 11-89 nearly FDC realized $38,500

## DECIMAL COINAGE

**CENT** **KM# 62** **Composition:** Bronze **Reverse:** Ring-tailed opossum

| Date | Mintage | F | VF | XF | Unc | BU |
|---|---|---|---|---|---|---|
| 1966(c) | 146,457,000 | — | — | 0.15 | 0.45 | — |
| 1966(c) Proof | 18,000 | Value: 2.50 | | | | |
| 1966(m) Blunted whisker on right | 238,990,000 | — | 0.15 | 0.25 | 1.25 | — |
| 1966(p) Blunted 2nd whisker from right | 26,620,000 | 0.15 | 0.30 | 1.25 | 7.00 | — |
| 1967 | 110,055,000 | — | 0.15 | 0.25 | 1.75 | — |
| 1968 | 19,930,000 | — | 0.15 | 0.45 | 6.00 | — |
| 1969 | 87,680,000 | — | — | 0.15 | 0.50 | — |
| 1969 Proof | 13,000 | Value: 2.50 | | | | |
| 1970 | 72,560,000 | — | — | 0.15 | 0.50 | — |
| 1970 Proof | 15,000 | Value: 2.50 | | | | |
| 1971 | 102,455,000 | — | — | 0.15 | 0.45 | — |
| 1971 Proof | 10,000 | Value: 2.50 | | | | |
| 1972 | 82,400,000 | — | — | 0.10 | 0.45 | — |
| 1972 Proof | 10,000 | Value: 2.50 | | | | |
| 1973 | 140,710,000 | — | — | 0.10 | 0.25 | — |
| 1973 Proof | 10,000 | Value: 2.50 | | | | |
| 1974 | 131,720,000 | — | — | 0.10 | 0.25 | — |
| 1974 Proof | 11,000 | Value: 2.50 | | | | |
| 1975 | 134,775,000 | — | — | — | 0.20 | — |
| 1975 Proof | 23,000 | Value: 0.65 | | | | |
| 1976 | 172,935,000 | — | — | — | 0.20 | — |
| 1976 Proof | 21,000 | Value: 1.50 | | | | |
| 1977 | 153,430,000 | — | — | — | 0.20 | — |
| 1977 Proof | 55,000 | Value: 0.65 | | | | |
| 1978 | 97,253,000 | — | — | — | 0.15 | — |
| 1978 Proof | 39,000 | Value: 0.65 | | | | |
| 1979 | 130,339,000 | — | — | — | 0.15 | — |
| 1979 Proof | 36,000 | Value: 0.65 | | | | |
| 1980 | 137,892,000 | — | — | — | 0.15 | — |
| 1980 Proof | 68,000 | Value: 0.65 | | | | |
| 1981 | 223,900,000 | — | — | — | 0.15 | — |
| 1981 Proof | 86,000 | Value: 0.65 | | | | |
| 1982 | 134,290,000 | — | — | — | 0.15 | — |
| 1982 Proof | 100,000 | Value: 0.65 | | | | |
| 1983 | 205,625,000 | — | — | — | 0.15 | — |
| 1983 Proof | 80,000 | Value: 0.65 | | | | |
| 1984 | 74,735,000 | — | — | — | 0.15 | — |
| 1984 Proof | 61,000 | Value: 0.65 | | | | |

**CENT** **KM# 78** **Composition:** Bronze

| Date | Mintage | F | VF | XF | Unc | BU |
|---|---|---|---|---|---|---|
| 1985 | 38,300,000 | — | — | — | 0.10 | — |
| 1985 Proof | 75,000 | Value: 0.45 | | | | |
| 1986 In sets only | 180,000 | — | — | — | 2.25 | — |
| 1986 Proof | 67,000 | Value: 0.45 | | | | |
| 1987 | 127,000,000 | — | — | — | 0.10 | — |
| 1987 Proof | 70,000 | Value: 0.45 | | | | |
| 1988 | 56,910,000 | — | — | — | 0.10 | — |
| 1988 Proof | 106,000 | Value: 0.45 | | | | |
| 1989 | — | — | — | — | 0.10 | — |
| 1989 Proof | — | Value: 0.45 | | | | |
| 1990 | — | — | — | — | 0.10 | — |
| 1990 Proof | — | Value: 0.45 | | | | |
| 1991 | — | — | — | — | 0.10 | — |
| 1991 Proof | — | Value: 0.45 | | | | |

**CENT** **KM# 78a** **Weight:** 3.0100 g. **Composition:** 0.9250 Silver .0895 oz. ASW

| Date | Mintage | F | VF | XF | Unc | BU |
|---|---|---|---|---|---|---|
| 1991 Proof | 23,000 | Value: 10.00 | | | | |

**Note:** In Proof sets only

**2 CENTS** **KM# 63** **Composition:** Bronze **Reverse:** Frilled Lizard

| Date | Mintage | F | VF | XF | Unc | BU |
|---|---|---|---|---|---|---|
| 1966(c) | 145,226,000 | — | — | 0.10 | 0.45 | — |
| 1966(c) Proof | 18,000 | Value: 5.00 | | | | |
| 1966(m) Blunted 3rd left claw | 66,575,000 | — | 0.15 | 0.35 | 2.25 | — |
| 1966(p) Blunted 1st right claw | 217,735,000 | — | 0.15 | 0.25 | 1.25 | — |
| 1967 | 73,250,000 | — | 0.15 | 0.30 | 3.50 | — |
| 1968 | 17,000,000 | — | 0.15 | 0.55 | 4.25 | — |
| 1969 | 12,940,000 | — | 0.15 | 0.30 | 2.25 | — |
| 1969 Proof | 13,000 | Value: 4.75 | | | | |
| 1970 | 39,872,000 | — | — | 0.15 | 0.75 | — |
| 1970 Proof | 15,000 | Value: 4.75 | | | | |
| 1971 | 60,735,000 | — | — | 0.15 | 0.75 | — |
| 1971 Proof | 10,000 | Value: 4.75 | | | | |
| 1972 | 77,570,000 | — | — | 0.10 | 0.65 | — |
| 1972 Proof | 10,000 | Value: 4.25 | | | | |
| 1973 | 94,058,000 | — | — | 0.10 | 0.50 | — |
| 1973 Proof | 10,000 | Value: 4.25 | | | | |
| 1974 | 177,723,000 | — | — | 0.10 | 0.50 | — |
| 1974 Proof | 11,000 | Value: 4.25 | | | | |
| 1975 | 100,045,000 | — | — | 0.10 | 0.45 | — |
| 1975 Proof | 23,000 | Value: 0.75 | | | | |
| 1976 | 121,882,000 | — | — | 0.10 | 0.30 | — |
| 1976 Proof | 21,000 | Value: 2.25 | | | | |
| 1977 | 102,000,000 | — | — | 0.10 | 0.30 | — |
| 1977 Proof | 55,000 | Value: 0.75 | | | | |
| 1978 | 128,252,999 | — | — | 0.10 | 0.30 | — |
| 1978 Proof | 39,000 | Value: 0.75 | | | | |
| 1979 | 69,705,000 | — | — | 0.10 | 0.30 | — |
| 1979 Proof | 36,000 | Value: 0.75 | | | | |
| 1980 | 145,603,000 | — | — | 0.10 | 0.30 | — |
| 1980 Proof | 68,000 | Value: 0.75 | | | | |
| 1981 | 219,176,000 | — | — | 0.10 | 0.30 | — |
| 1981 Proof | 86,000 | Value: 0.75 | | | | |
| 1982 | 121,770,000 | — | — | 0.10 | 0.30 | — |
| 1982 Proof | 100,000 | Value: 0.75 | | | | |
| 1983 | 177,227,000 | — | — | 0.10 | 0.30 | — |
| 1983 Proof | 80,000 | Value: 0.75 | | | | |
| 1984 | 57,963,000 | — | — | 0.10 | 0.30 | — |
| 1984 Proof | 61,000 | Value: 0.75 | | | | |

**2 CENTS** **KM# 79** **Composition:** Bronze

| Date | Mintage | F | VF | XF | Unc | BU |
|---|---|---|---|---|---|---|
| 1985 | 34,500,000 | — | — | 0.10 | 0.25 | — |
| 1985 Prof | 75,000 | Value: 0.45 | | | | |
| 1986 In sets only | 180,000 | — | — | — | 0.75 | — |
| 1986 Proof | 67,000 | Value: 0.45 | | | | |
| 1987 In sets only | 200,000 | — | — | — | 0.75 | — |
| 1987 Proof | 70,000 | Value: 0.45 | | | | |
| 1988 | 28,905,000 | — | — | 0.10 | 0.25 | — |
| 1988 Proof | 106,000 | Value: 0.45 | | | | |
| 1989 | — | — | — | 0.10 | 0.25 | — |
| 1989 Proof | — | Value: 0.45 | | | | |
| 1990 | — | — | — | 0.10 | 0.25 | — |
| 1990 Proof | — | Value: 0.45 | | | | |
| 1991 | — | — | — | 0.10 | 0.25 | — |
| 1991 Proof | — | Value: 0.45 | | | | |

**2 CENTS** **KM# 79a** **Weight:** 6.0600 g. **Composition:** 0.9250 Silver .1802 oz. ASW

| Date | Mintage | F | VF | XF | Unc | BU |
|---|---|---|---|---|---|---|
| 1991 Proof | 23,000 | Value: 10.00 | | | | |

**Note:** In Proof sets only

**5 CENTS** **KM# 64** **Composition:** Copper-Nickel **Reverse:** Short-beaked Spiny Ant-eater **Note:** For 1966 dated examples, the length of the whisker next to the claw at left will indicate the mint: Canberra (less than .5mm) or London (greater than .6mm).

| Date | Mintage | F | VF | XF | Unc | BU |
|---|---|---|---|---|---|---|
| 1966(c) | 45,427,000 | — | 0.15 | 0.25 | 1.25 | — |
| 1966(c) Proof | 18,000 | Value: 7.50 | | | | |
| 1966(L) | 30,000,000 | — | 0.15 | 0.25 | 1.25 | — |
| 1966(L) Proof | — | Value: 12.50 | | | | |
| 1967 | 62,144,000 | — | 0.15 | 0.35 | 2.25 | — |
| 1968 | 67,336,000 | — | 0.15 | 0.40 | 3.00 | — |
| 1969 | 38,170,000 | — | 0.15 | 0.20 | 1.75 | — |
| 1969 Proof | 13,000 | Value: 10.00 | | | | |
| 1970 | 46,058,000 | — | — | 0.15 | 2.25 | — |
| 1970 Proof | 15,000 | Value: 10.00 | | | | |
| 1971 | 39,516,000 | — | 0.15 | 0.25 | 2.50 | — |
| 1971 Proof | 10,000 | Value: 10.00 | | | | |
| 1972 | 8,256,000 | 0.15 | 0.30 | 1.00 | 7.50 | — |
| 1972 Proof | 10,000 | Value: 8.50 | | | | |
| 1973 | 48,816,000 | — | 0.15 | 0.20 | 0.75 | — |
| 1973 Proof | 10,000 | Value: 8.50 | | | | |
| 1974 | 64,248,000 | — | 0.15 | 0.20 | 0.75 | — |
| 1974 Proof | 11,000 | Value: 8.50 | | | | |
| 1975 | 44,256,000 | — | — | 0.10 | 0.40 | — |
| 1975 Proof | 23,000 | Value: 1.75 | | | | |
| 1976 | 113,180,000 | — | — | 0.10 | 0.25 | — |
| 1976 Proof | 21,000 | Value: 3.75 | | | | |
| 1977 | 108,800,000 | — | — | 0.10 | 0.25 | — |
| 1977 Proof | 55,000 | Value: 1.75 | | | | |
| 1978 | 25,210,000 | — | — | 0.10 | 0.25 | — |
| 1978 Proof | 39,000 | Value: 1.75 | | | | |
| 1979 | 44,533,000 | — | — | 0.10 | 0.25 | — |
| 1979 Proof | 36,000 | Value: 1.75 | | | | |
| 1980 | 115,042,000 | — | — | 0.10 | 0.25 | — |
| 1980 Proof | 68,000 | Value: 1.25 | | | | |
| 1981 | 162,264,000 | — | — | 0.10 | 0.20 | — |
| 1981 Proof | 86,000 | Value: 1.25 | | | | |
| 1982 | 139,468,000 | — | — | 0.10 | 0.20 | — |
| 1982 Proof | 100,000 | Value: 1.25 | | | | |
| 1983 | 131,568,000 | — | — | 0.10 | 0.20 | — |
| 1983 Proof | 80,000 | Value: 1.75 | | | | |
| 1984 | 35,436,000 | — | — | 0.10 | 0.20 | — |
| 1984 Proof | 61,000 | Value: 1.75 | | | | |

**5 CENTS** **KM# 80** **Composition:** Copper-Nickel

| Date | Mintage | F | VF | XF | Unc | BU |
|---|---|---|---|---|---|---|
| 1985 In Mint sets only | 170,000 | — | — | — | 3.50 | — |
| 1985 Proof | 75,000 | Value: 2.50 | | | | |
| 1986 In Mint sets only | 180,000 | — | — | — | 0.75 | — |
| 1986 Proof | 67,000 | Value: 0.75 | | | | |
| 1987 | 73,500,000 | — | — | — | 0.20 | — |
| 1987 Proof | 70,000 | Value: 0.75 | | | | |
| 1988 | 65,424,000 | — | — | — | 0.20 | — |
| 1988 Proof | 106,000 | Value: 0.75 | | | | |
| 1989 | — | — | — | — | 0.20 | — |
| 1989 Proof | — | Value: 0.75 | | | | |
| 1990 | 1,446,000 | — | — | — | 0.20 | — |
| 1990 Proof | — | Value: 0.75 | | | | |
| 1991 | 29,889,000 | — | — | — | 0.20 | — |
| 1991 Proof | — | Value: 0.75 | | | | |
| 1992 | 3,000,000 | — | — | — | 0.20 | — |
| 1992 Proof | 47,000 | Value: 0.75 | | | | |
| 1993 | — | — | — | — | 0.20 | — |
| 1993 Proof | — | Value: 0.75 | | | | |
| 1994 | — | — | — | — | 0.20 | — |
| 1994 Proof | — | Value: 0.75 | | | | |
| 1995 | — | — | — | — | 0.20 | — |
| 1995 Proof | — | Value: 0.75 | | | | |
| 1996 | — | — | — | — | 0.20 | — |
| 1996 Proof | — | Value: 0.75 | | | | |
| 1997 | — | — | — | — | 0.20 | — |
| 1997 Proof | — | Value: 0.75 | | | | |
| 1998 | — | — | — | — | 0.20 | — |
| 1998 Proof | — | Value: 0.75 | | | | |

**5 CENTS** **KM# 80a** **Weight:** 3.2700 g. **Composition:** 0.9250 Silver .0972 oz. ASW

| Date | Mintage | F | VF | XF | Unc | BU |
|---|---|---|---|---|---|---|
| 1991 Proof | 23,000 | Value: 15.00 | | | | |

**Note:** In Proof sets only

**5 CENTS** **KM# 401** **Composition:** Copper-Nickel **Obverse:** Queen's portrait by Rank-Broadley

| Date | Mintage | F | VF | XF | Unc | BU |
|---|---|---|---|---|---|---|
| 1999 | — | — | — | — | 0.20 | — |
| 1999 Proof | — | Value: 0.75 | | | | |
| 2000 | — | — | — | — | 0.20 | — |
| 2000 Proof | — | Value: 0.75 | | | | |

**5 CENTS** **KM# 481** **Weight:** 5.5300 g. **Composition:** 0.9990 Silver .1776 oz. ASW **Series:** Masterpieces in Silver **Obverse:** Queen's head right. **Reverse:** Half penny reverse design of KM#41. **Edge:** Reeded. **Size:** 25 mm.

| Date | Mintage | F | VF | XF | Unc | BU |
|---|---|---|---|---|---|---|
| 1999 Proof | 15,000 | Value: 8.00 | | | | |

**10 CENTS** **KM# 65** **Composition:** Copper-Nickel **Reverse:** Superb Lyre-bird **Note:** For 1966 dated examples, 11 spikes on the left Lyre-bird indicates a strike from Canberra, 12 spikes indicate a London strike.

| Date | Mintage | F | VF | XF | Unc | BU |
|---|---|---|---|---|---|---|
| 1966(c) | 10,984,000 | — | 0.15 | 0.30 | 1.75 | — |
| 1966(c) Proof | 18,000 | Value: 8.00 | | | | |
| 1966(L) | 30,000,000 | — | 0.15 | 0.30 | 1.75 | — |
| 1966(L) Proof | — | Value: 12.00 | | | | |
| 1967 | 51,032,000 | — | 0.15 | 0.55 | 6.00 | — |
| 1968 | 57,194,000 | — | 0.15 | 0.45 | 4.25 | — |
| 1969 | 22,146,000 | — | 0.15 | 0.25 | 2.25 | — |
| 1969 Proof | 13,000 | Value: 8.50 | | | | |
| 1970 | 22,306,000 | — | 0.15 | 0.25 | 2.25 | — |
| 1970 Proof | 15,000 | Value: 8.50 | | | | |
| 1971 | 20,726,000 | — | 0.10 | 0.25 | 3.00 | — |
| 1971 Proof | 10,000 | Value: 8.00 | | | | |
| 1972 | 12,502,000 | — | 0.10 | 0.25 | 3.50 | — |
| 1972 Proof | 10,000 | Value: 7.00 | | | | |
| 1973 | 27,320,000 | — | 0.10 | 0.15 | 1.25 | — |
| 1973 Proof | 10,000 | Value: 7.00 | | | | |
| 1974 | 46,550,000 | — | 0.10 | 0.15 | 1.25 | — |
| 1974 Proof | 11,000 | Value: 7.00 | | | | |
| 1975 | 50,900,000 | — | 0.10 | 0.15 | 0.65 | — |
| 1975 Proof | 23,000 | Value: 1.75 | | | | |
| 1976 | 57,060,000 | — | 0.10 | 0.15 | 0.65 | — |
| 1976 Proof | 21,000 | Value: 3.75 | | | | |
| 1977 | 10,940,000 | — | 0.10 | 0.15 | 0.75 | — |
| 1977 Proof | 55,000 | Value: 1.75 | | | | |
| 1978 | 48,400,000 | — | 0.10 | 0.15 | 0.40 | — |
| 1978 Proof | 39,000 | Value: 1.75 | | | | |
| 1979 | 36,950,000 | — | 0.10 | 0.15 | 0.40 | — |
| 1979 Proof | 36,000 | Value: 1.75 | | | | |
| 1980 | 55,084,000 | — | 0.10 | 0.15 | 0.40 | — |
| 1980 Proof | 68,000 | Value: 1.50 | | | | |
| 1981 | 116,060,000 | — | 0.10 | 0.15 | 0.25 | — |

**Note:** One 1981 coin was struck on a Sri Lanka 50 cents planchet, KM#135.1. It carries an approximate value of $600

| Date | Mintage | F | VF | XF | Unc | BU |
|---|---|---|---|---|---|---|
| 1981 Proof | 86,000 | Value: 1.50 | | | | |
| 1982 | 61,492,000 | — | 0.10 | 0.15 | 0.25 | — |
| 1982 Proof | 100,000 | Value: 1.50 | | | | |
| 1983 | 82,318,000 | — | 0.10 | 0.15 | 0.25 | — |
| 1983 Proof | 80,000 | Value: 1.75 | | | | |
| 1984 | 25,728,000 | — | 0.10 | 0.15 | 0.25 | — |
| 1984 Proof | 61,000 | Value: 1.75 | | | | |

**10 CENTS** **KM# 81** **Composition:** Copper-Nickel

| Date | Mintage | F | VF | XF | Unc | BU |
|---|---|---|---|---|---|---|
| 1985 | 2,100,000 | — | — | 0.10 | 0.20 | — |
| 1985 Proof | 75,000 | Value: 1.00 | | | | |
| 1986 In sets only | 180,000 | — | — | — | 0.75 | — |
| 1986 Proof | 67,000 | Value: 1.00 | | | | |
| 1987 In sets only | 200,000 | — | — | — | 0.75 | — |
| 1987 Proof | 70,000 | Value: 1.00 | | | | |
| 1988 | 35,095,000 | — | — | — | 0.20 | — |
| 1988 Proof | 106,000 | Value: 1.00 | | | | |
| 1989 | — | — | — | — | 0.20 | — |
| 1989 Proof | — | Value: 1.00 | | | | |
| 1990 | 5,452,000 | — | — | — | 0.20 | — |
| 1990 Proof | — | Value: 1.00 | | | | |
| 1991 | 3,174,000 | — | — | — | 0.20 | — |
| 1991 Proof | — | Value: 1.00 | | | | |
| 1992 | 5,589,000 | — | — | — | 0.20 | — |
| 1992 Proof | 47,000 | Value: 1.00 | | | | |
| 1993 | — | — | — | — | 0.20 | — |
| 1993 Proof | — | Value: 1.00 | | | | |
| 1994 | — | — | — | — | 0.20 | — |
| 1994 Proof | — | Value: 1.00 | | | | |
| 1995 | — | — | — | — | 0.20 | — |
| 1995 Proof | — | Value: 1.00 | | | | |
| 1996 | — | — | — | — | 0.20 | — |
| 1996 Proof | — | Value: 1.00 | | | | |
| 1997 | — | — | — | — | 0.20 | — |
| 1997 Proof | — | Value: 2.00 | | | | |
| 1998 | — | — | — | — | 0.20 | — |
| 1998 Proof | — | Value: 2.00 | | | | |

**10 CENTS** **KM# 81a** **Weight:** 6.5200 g. **Composition:** 0.9250 Silver .1939 oz. ASW

| Date | Mintage | F | VF | XF | Unc | BU |
|---|---|---|---|---|---|---|
| 1991 Proof | 23,000 | Value: 15.00 | | | | |

**Note:** In Proof sets only

**10 CENTS** **KM# 402** **Composition:** Copper-Nickel **Obverse:** Queen's portrait by Rank-Broadley

| Date | Mintage | F | VF | XF | Unc | BU |
|---|---|---|---|---|---|---|
| 1999 | — | — | — | — | 0.30 | — |
| 1999 Proof | — | Value: 1.00 | | | | |
| 2000 | — | — | — | — | 0.30 | — |
| 2000 Proof | — | Value: 1.00 | | | | |

**10 CENTS** **KM# 482** **Weight:** 8.3600 g. **Composition:** 0.9990 Silver .2685 oz. ASW **Series:** Masterpieces in Silver **Ob-**

**verse:** Queen's head right. **Reverse:** Penny reverse design of KM#23. **Edge:** Reeded. **Size:** 30 mm.

| Date | Mintage | F | VF | XF | Unc | BU |
|---|---|---|---|---|---|---|
| 1999 Proof | 15,000 | Value: 12.00 | | | | |

**20 CENTS** **KM# 66** **Composition:** Copper-Nickel **Reverse:** Duckbill Platypus

| Date | Mintage | F | VF | XF | Unc | BU |
|---|---|---|---|---|---|---|
| 1966(c) | 28,223,000 | — | 0.20 | 0.75 | 8.50 | — |

**Note:** For 1966 dated examples, strikes from Canberra show a gap between sea line and right face of platypus

| Date | Mintage | F | VF | XF | Unc | BU |
|---|---|---|---|---|---|---|
| 1966(c) Proof | 18,000 | Value: 10.00 | | | | |

**Note:** For 1966 dated examples, strikes from Canberra show a gap between sea line and right face of platypus

| Date | Mintage | F | VF | XF | Unc | BU |
|---|---|---|---|---|---|---|
| 1966(L) Wave on base of 2 | — | — | — | — | 165 | — |
| 1966(L) | 30,000,000 | — | 0.20 | 0.65 | 7.00 | — |
| 1966(L) Proof | — | Value: 12.50 | | | | |
| 1967 | 83,848,000 | — | 0.20 | 1.15 | 12.50 | — |
| 1968 | 40,537,000 | — | 0.20 | 1.00 | 11.00 | — |
| 1969 | 16,501,999 | — | 0.20 | 1.00 | 11.00 | — |
| 1969 Proof | 13,000 | Value: 13.50 | | | | |
| 1970 | 23,271,000 | Value: 11.50 | | | | |
| 1970 Proof | 15,000 | Value: 13.50 | | | | |
| 1971 | 8,947,000 | Value: 11.50 | | | | |
| 1971 Proof | 10,000 | Value: 11.00 | | | | |
| 1972 | 16,643,000 | — | 0.15 | 0.50 | 6.00 | — |
| 1972 Proof | 10,000 | Value: 10.00 | | | | |
| 1973 | 23,356,000 | — | 0.15 | 0.45 | 7.00 | — |
| 1973 Proof | 10,000 | Value: 10.00 | | | | |
| 1974 | 33,548,000 | — | 0.15 | 0.45 | 6.50 | — |
| 1974 Proof | 11,000 | Value: 10.00 | | | | |
| 1975 | 53,300,000 | — | 0.15 | 0.20 | 1.75 | — |
| 1975 Proof | 23,000 | Value: 2.25 | | | | |
| 1976 | 59,774,000 | — | 0.15 | 0.20 | 0.75 | — |
| 1976 Proof | 21,000 | Value: 3.75 | | | | |
| 1977 | 41,272,000 | — | 0.15 | 0.20 | 0.65 | — |
| 1977 Proof | 55,000 | Value: 1.75 | | | | |
| 1978 | 38,781,000 | — | 0.15 | 0.20 | 0.65 | — |
| 1978 Proof | 39,000 | Value: 1.75 | | | | |
| 1979 | 22,300,000 | — | 0.15 | 0.20 | 0.85 | — |
| 1979 Proof | 36,000 | Value: 1.75 | | | | |
| 1980 | 77,673,000 | — | 0.15 | 0.20 | 0.40 | — |
| 1980 Proof | 68,000 | Value: 1.25 | | | | |
| 1981 | 164,500,000 | — | 0.15 | 0.20 | 0.40 | — |

**Note:** Some 1981 dated coins were struck on a Hong Kong 2 Dollar planchet, KM#37. 6 pieces are reported. Each carries an approximate value of $800

| Date | Mintage | F | VF | XF | Unc | BU |
|---|---|---|---|---|---|---|
| 1981 Proof | 86,000 | Value: 1.25 | | | | |
| 1982 | 76,600,000 | — | 0.15 | 0.20 | 0.40 | — |
| 1982 Proof | 100,000 | Value: 1.25 | | | | |
| 1983 | 55,113,000 | — | 0.15 | 0.20 | 0.40 | — |
| 1983 Proof | 80,000 | Value: 1.75 | | | | |
| 1984 | 27,820,000 | — | 0.15 | 0.20 | 0.35 | — |
| 1984 Proof | 61,000 | Value: 1.75 | | | | |

**20 CENTS** **KM# 82** **Composition:** Copper-Nickel

| Date | Mintage | F | VF | XF | Unc | BU |
|---|---|---|---|---|---|---|
| 1985 | 27,000,000 | — | 0.15 | 0.20 | 0.30 | — |
| 1985 Proof | 75,000 | Value: 1.75 | | | | |
| 1986 In sets only | 180,000 | — | — | — | 0.85 | — |
| 1986 Proof | 67,000 | Value: 2.50 | | | | |
| 1987 In sets only | 200,000 | — | — | — | 0.85 | — |
| 1987 Proof | 70,000 | Value: 1.25 | | | | |
| 1988 In sets only | 240,000 | — | — | — | 0.85 | — |
| 1988 Proof | 106,000 | Value: 1.25 | | | | |
| 1989 | — | — | — | — | 0.30 | — |
| 1989 Proof | — | Value: 1.25 | | | | |
| 1990 | — | — | — | — | 0.30 | — |
| 1990 Proof | — | Value: 1.25 | | | | |
| 1991 | — | — | — | — | 0.30 | — |
| 1991 Proof | — | Value: 1.25 | | | | |
| 1992 | — | — | — | — | 0.50 | — |
| 1992 Proof | 47,000 | Value: 1.25 | | | | |
| 1993 | — | — | — | — | 0.50 | — |
| 1993 Proof | — | Value: 1.25 | | | | |
| 1994 | — | — | — | — | 0.50 | — |
| 1994 Proof | — | Value: 1.25 | | | | |
| 1995 | — | — | — | — | 0.50 | — |
| 1995 Proof | — | Value: 1.25 | | | | |
| 1996 | — | — | — | — | 0.50 | — |
| 1996 Proof | — | Value: 1.25 | | | | |
| 1997 | — | — | — | — | 0.50 | — |
| 1997 Proof | — | Value: 1.25 | | | | |
| 1998 | — | — | — | — | 0.50 | — |
| 1998 Proof | — | Value: 1.25 | | | | |

**20 CENTS** **KM# 82a** **Weight:** 13.0900 g. **Composition:** 0.9250 Silver .3893 oz. ASW

| Date | Mintage | F | VF | XF | Unc | BU |
|---|---|---|---|---|---|---|
| 1991 Proof | 23,000 | Value: 20.00 | | | | |

**Note:** In Proof sets only

**20 CENTS** **KM# 295** **Weight:** 13.0900 g. **Composition:** 0.9250 Silver .3893 oz. ASW **Subject:** 50th Anniversary - United Nations

| Date | Mintage | F | VF | XF | Unc | BU |
|---|---|---|---|---|---|---|
| 1995 | — | — | — | — | 1.25 | — |

**20 CENTS** **KM# 410** **Weight:** 13.3600 g. **Composition:** 0.9990 Silver .4291 oz. ASW **Subject:** Masterpieces in Silver **Obverse:** Queen's portrait **Reverse:** 1927 florin design

| Date | Mintage | F | VF | XF | Unc | BU |
|---|---|---|---|---|---|---|
| 1998 Proof | — | Value: 20.00 | | | | |

**20 CENTS** **KM# 403** **Composition:** Copper-Nickel **Obverse:** Queen's portrait by Rank-Broadley **Reverse:** Similar to KM#82

| Date | Mintage | F | VF | XF | Unc | BU |
|---|---|---|---|---|---|---|
| 1999 | — | — | — | — | 0.50 | — |
| 1999 Proof | — | Value: 2.50 | | | | |
| 2000 | — | — | — | — | 0.50 | — |
| 2000 Proof | — | Value: 2.50 | | | | |

**20 CENTS** **KM# 483** **Weight:** 2.9900 g. **Composition:** 0.9990 Silver .0960 oz. ASW **Series:** Masterpieces in Silver **Obverse:** Queen's head right. **Reverse:** Threepence reverse design of KM#37. **Edge:** Reeded. **Size:** 17.5 mm.

| Date | Mintage | F | VF | XF | Unc | BU |
|---|---|---|---|---|---|---|
| 1999 Proof | 15,000 | Value: 8.00 | | | | |

**20 CENTS** **KM# 496** **Weight:** 13.3600 g. **Composition:** 0.9990 Silver .4291 oz. ASW **Series:** Masterpieces in Silver - 2000 Set **Obverse:** Queen's head right. **Reverse:** Edward VII bust right. **Edge:** Reeded. **Size:** 28.5 mm.

| Date | Mintage | F | VF | XF | Unc | BU |
|---|---|---|---|---|---|---|
| 2000 Proof | 15,000 | Value: 25.00 | | | | |

**20 CENTS** **KM# 497** **Weight:** 13.3600 g. **Composition:** 0.9990 Silver .4291 oz. ASW **Series:** Masterpieces in Silver - 2000 Set **Obverse:** Queen's head right. **Reverse:** George V bust left. **Edge:** Reeded. **Size:** 28.5 mm.

| Date | Mintage | F | VF | XF | Unc | BU |
|---|---|---|---|---|---|---|
| 2000 Proof | 15,000 | Value: 25.00 | | | | |

**20 CENTS** **KM# 498** **Weight:** 13.3600 g. **Composition:** 0.9990 Silver .4291 oz. ASW **Series:** Masterpieces in Silver - 2000 Set **Obverse:** Queen's head right. **Reverse:** Queen Elizabeth's first coin design. **Edge:** Reeded. **Size:** 28.5 mm.

| Date | Mintage | F | VF | XF | Unc | BU |
|---|---|---|---|---|---|---|
| 2000 Proof | 15,000 | Value: 25.00 | | | | |

**20 CENTS** **KM# 532** **Weight:** 11.3300 g. **Composition:** Copper-Nickel **Subject:** Centennial - Norfolk Island Federation **Obverse:** Queen's head right. **Reverse:** Plant on island map. **Size:** 28.5 mm.

| Date | Mintage | F | VF | XF | Unc | BU |
|---|---|---|---|---|---|---|
| 2001 | — | — | — | — | 1.75 | — |

**20 CENTS** **KM# 550** **Weight:** 11.3000 g. **Composition:** Copper-Nickel **Series:** Centenary of Federation - New South Wales **Obverse:** Queen's head right. **Reverse:** Flower on state map. **Edge:** Reeded. **Size:** 28.5 mm.

| Date | Mintage | F | VF | XF | Unc | BU |
|---|---|---|---|---|---|---|
| 2001 | — | — | — | — | 1.75 | — |
| 2001 Proof | — | Value: 2.50 | | | | |

**20 CENTS** **KM# 552** (KM551) **Weight:** 11.3000 g. **Composition:** Copper-Nickel **Series:** Centenary of Federation - Australian Capital Territory **Obverse:** Queen's head right. **Reverse:** Parliament house, map, flowers. **Edge:** Reeded. **Size:** 28.5 mm.

| Date | Mintage | F | VF | XF | Unc | BU |
|---|---|---|---|---|---|---|
| 2001 | — | — | — | — | 1.75 | — |
| 2001 Proof | — | Value: 2.50 | | | | |

**20 CENTS** **KM# 554** **Weight:** 11.3000 g. **Composition:** Copper-Nickel **Series:** Centenary of Federation - Queensland **Obverse:** Queen's head right. **Reverse:** Radiant design. **Edge:** Reeded. **Size:** 28.5 mm.

| Date | Mintage | F | VF | XF | Unc | BU |
|---|---|---|---|---|---|---|
| 2001 | — | — | — | — | 1.75 | — |
| 2001 Proof | — | Value: 2.50 | | | | |

**20 CENTS** KM# 556 **Weight:** 11.3000 g. **Composition:** Copper-Nickel **Series:** Centenary of Federation - Victoria **Obverse:** Queen's head right. **Reverse:** Capital building. **Edge:** Reeded. **Size:** 28.5 mm.

| Date | Mintage | F | VF | XF | Unc | BU |
|---|---|---|---|---|---|---|
| 2001 | — | — | — | — | 1.75 | — |
| 2001 Proof | — | Value: 2.50 | | | | |

**20 CENTS** KM# 558 **Weight:** 11.3000 g. **Composition:** Copper-Nickel **Series:** Centenary of Federation - Northern Territory **Obverse:** Queen's head right. **Reverse:** Two cranes in ritual dance. **Edge:** Reeded. **Size:** 28.5 mm.

| Date | Mintage | F | VF | XF | Unc | BU |
|---|---|---|---|---|---|---|
| 2001 | — | — | — | — | 1.75 | — |
| 2001 Proof | — | Value: 2.50 | | | | |

**20 CENTS** KM# 560 **Weight:** 11.3000 g. **Composition:** Copper-Nickel **Series:** Centenary of Federation - South Australia **Obverse:** Queen's head right. **Reverse:** Flower, landscape and stars. **Edge:** Reeded. **Size:** 28.5 mm.

| Date | Mintage | F | VF | XF | Unc | BU |
|---|---|---|---|---|---|---|
| 2001 | — | — | — | — | 1.75 | — |
| 2001 Proof | — | Value: 2.50 | | | | |

**20 CENTS** KM# 562 **Weight:** 11.3000 g. **Composition:** Copper-Nickel **Series:** Centenary of Federation - Western Australia **Obverse:** Queen's head right. **Reverse:** Rabbit-eared Bandicoot, plant and map. **Edge:** Reeded. **Size:** 28.5 mm.

| Date | Mintage | F | VF | XF | Unc | BU |
|---|---|---|---|---|---|---|
| 2001 | — | — | — | — | 1.75 | — |
| 2001 Proof | — | Value: 2.50 | | | | |

**20 CENTS** KM# 564 **Weight:** 11.3000 g. **Composition:** Copper-Nickel **Series:** Centenary of Federation - Tasmania **Obverse:** Queen's head right. **Reverse:** Tasmanian Devil on map. **Edge:** Reeded. **Size:** 28.5 mm.

| Date | Mintage | F | VF | XF | Unc | BU |
|---|---|---|---|---|---|---|
| 2001 | — | — | — | — | 1.75 | — |
| 2001 Proof | — | Value: 2.50 | | | | |

**25 CENTS (The Dump)** KM# 113 **Weight:** 7.7750 g. **Composition:** 0.9990 Silver .2500 oz. ASW **Reverse:** Aboriginal Culture

| Date | Mintage | F | VF | XF | Unc | BU |
|---|---|---|---|---|---|---|
| 1988 Proof | — | Value: 15.00 | | | | |

**25 CENTS (The Dump)** KM# 132 **Weight:** 7.7750 g. **Composition:** 0.9990 Silver .2500 oz. ASW **Reverse:** Wandjina of Aboriginal Mythology

| Date | Mintage | F | VF | XF | Unc | BU |
|---|---|---|---|---|---|---|
| 1989 Proof | 45,000 | Value: 15.00 | | | | |

**25 CENTS (The Dump)** KM# 155 **Weight:** 7.7750 g. **Composition:** 0.9990 Silver .2500 oz. ASW **Reverse:** 3 Mythological Creatures

| Date | Mintage | F | VF | XF | Unc | BU |
|---|---|---|---|---|---|---|
| 1990 Proof | 30,000 | Value: 15.00 | | | | |

**50 CENTS** KM# 67 **Weight:** 13.2800 g. **Composition:** 0.8000 Silver .3416 oz. ASW

| Date | Mintage | F | VF | XF | Unc | BU |
|---|---|---|---|---|---|---|
| 1966 | 36,454,000 | — | — | BV | 5.50 | — |
| 1966 Proof | 18,000 | Value: 70.00 | | | | |

**50 CENTS** KM# 68 **Composition:** Copper-Nickel

| Date | Mintage | F | VF | XF | Unc | BU |
|---|---|---|---|---|---|---|
| 1969 | 14,015,000 | — | 0.45 | 1.00 | 7.50 | — |
| 1969 Proof | 13,000 | Value: 55.00 | | | | |
| 1971 | 21,056,000 | — | 0.45 | 1.75 | 7.75 | — |
| 1971 Proof | 10,000 | Value: 35.00 | | | | |
| 1972 | 5,586,000 | — | 0.45 | 2.00 | 8.50 | — |
| 1972 Proof | 10,000 | Value: 35.00 | | | | |
| 1973 | 4,009,000 | — | 0.45 | 2.25 | 15.00 | — |
| 1973 Proof | 10,000 | Value: 35.00 | | | | |
| 1974 | 8,962,000 | — | 0.45 | 0.85 | 7.50 | — |
| 1974 Proof | 11,000 | Value: 30.00 | | | | |
| 1975 | 19,025,000 | — | 0.40 | 0.50 | 2.50 | — |
| 1975 Proof | 23,000 | Value: 10.00 | | | | |
| 1976 | 27,280,000 | — | 0.40 | 0.50 | 2.00 | — |
| 1976 Proof | 21,000 | Value: 20.00 | | | | |
| 1978 | 25,765,000 | — | 0.40 | 0.50 | 0.85 | — |
| 1978 Proof | 39,000 | Value: 6.75 | | | | |
| 1979 | 24,886,000 | — | 0.40 | 0.50 | 0.85 | — |
| 1979 Proof | 36,000 | Value: 7.75 | | | | |
| 1980 | 38,681,000 | — | 0.40 | 0.50 | 0.85 | — |
| 1980 Proof | 68,000 | Value: 5.50 | | | | |
| 1981 | 24,168,000 | — | 0.40 | 0.50 | 0.75 | — |
| 1981 Proof | 86,000 | Value: 5.50 | | | | |
| 1983 | 48,923,000 | — | — | 0.40 | 0.75 | — |
| 1983 Proof | 80,000 | Value: 7.75 | | | | |
| 1984 | 26,281,000 | — | — | 0.40 | 0.75 | — |
| 1984 Proof | 61,000 | Value: 7.75 | | | | |

**50 CENTS** KM# 69 **Composition:** Copper-Nickel **Subject:** 200th Anniversary - Cook's Australian Voyage

| Date | Mintage | F | VF | XF | Unc | BU |
|---|---|---|---|---|---|---|
| 1970 | 17,100,000 | — | 0.40 | 1.25 | 3.50 | — |
| 1970 Proof | 15,000 | Value: 50.00 | | | | |

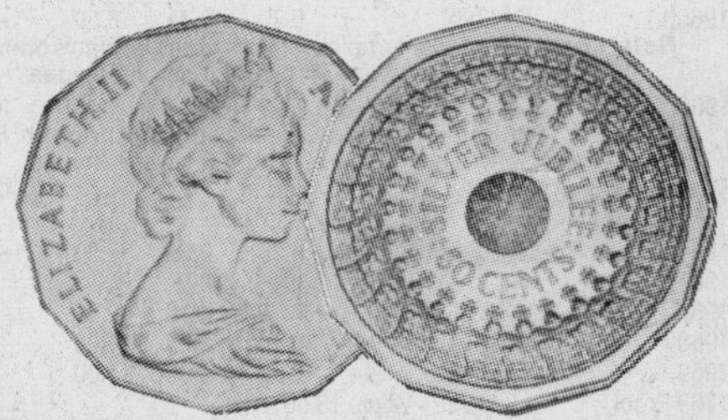

**50 CENTS** KM# 70 **Composition:** Copper-Nickel **Subject:** Queen's Silver Jubilee

| Date | Mintage | F | VF | XF | Unc | BU |
|---|---|---|---|---|---|---|
| 1977 | 25,076,000 | — | 0.40 | 0.50 | 1.25 | — |
| 1977 Proof | 55,000 | Value: 6.75 | | | | |

**50 CENTS** KM# A72 **Composition:** Copper-Nickel **Subject:** Mule **Obverse:** KM#70 **Reverse:** Fiji 50 Cent, KM#36

| Date | Mintage | F | VF | XF | Unc | BU |
|---|---|---|---|---|---|---|
| 1978 | — | — | — | — | — | — |

**50 CENTS** KM# 72 **Composition:** Copper-Nickel **Subject:** Wedding of Prince Charles and Lady Diana

| Date | Mintage | F | VF | XF | Unc | BU |
|---|---|---|---|---|---|---|
| 1981 | 44,100,000 | — | 0.40 | 0.50 | 1.25 | — |

**50 CENTS** KM# 74 **Composition:** Copper-Nickel **Subject:** XII Commonwealth Games - Birsbane

| Date | Mintage | F | VF | XF | Unc | BU |
|---|---|---|---|---|---|---|
| 1982 | 23,287,000 | — | 0.40 | 0.50 | 1.25 | — |
| 1982 Proof | 100,000 | Value: 5.50 | | | | |

**50 CENTS** KM# 83 **Composition:** Copper-Nickel

| Date | Mintage | F | VF | XF | Unc | BU |
|---|---|---|---|---|---|---|
| 1985 | 1,000,000 | — | — | 0.40 | 0.60 | — |
| 1985 Proof | 75,000 | Value: 3.50 | | | | |
| 1986 In sets only | 180,000 | — | — | — | 3.00 | — |
| 1986 Proof | 67,000 | Value: 3.50 | | | | |
| 1987 In sets only | 200,000 | — | — | — | 3.00 | — |
| 1987 Proof | 70,000 | Value: 3.50 | | | | |
| 1989 | — | — | — | — | 2.25 | — |
| 1989 Proof | — | Value: 3.50 | | | | |
| 1990 | — | — | — | — | 2.25 | — |
| 1990 Proof | — | Value: 3.50 | | | | |
| 1992 | — | — | — | — | 2.25 | — |
| 1992 Proof | 47,000 | Value: 3.50 | | | | |
| 1993 | — | — | — | — | 2.25 | — |
| 1993 Proof | — | Value: 3.50 | | | | |
| 1996 | — | — | — | — | 2.25 | — |
| 1996 Proof | — | Value: 3.50 | | | | |
| 1997 | — | — | — | — | 2.25 | — |
| 1997 Proof | — | Value: 3.50 | | | | |

**50 CENTS** KM# 99 **Composition:** Copper-Nickel **Subject:** Australian Bicentennial

| Date | Mintage | F | VF | XF | Unc | BU |
|---|---|---|---|---|---|---|
| 1988 | 2,793,000 | — | — | — | 2.25 | — |
| 1988 Proof | 106,000 | Value: 3.50 | | | | |

**50 CENTS** KM# 99a **Weight:** 18.0000 g. **Composition:** 0.9250 Silver .5353 oz. ASW

| Date | Mintage | F | VF | XF | Unc | BU |
|---|---|---|---|---|---|---|
| 1988 Proof | 25,000 | Value: 22.50 | | | | |
| 1989 Proof | 25,000 | Value: 22.50 | | | | |

**50 CENTS** KM# 127 **Weight:** 18.0000 g. **Composition:** 0.9250 Silver .5353 oz. ASW **Subject:** Cook Commemorative **Obverse:** Similar to KM#99 **Reverse:** Similar to KM#69

| Date | Mintage | F | VF | XF | Unc | BU |
|---|---|---|---|---|---|---|
| 1989 Proof | 25,000 | Value: 22.50 | | | | |

**50 CENTS** KM# 128 **Weight:** 18.0000 g. **Composition:** 0.9250 Silver .5353 oz. ASW **Subject:** Queen's Silver Jubilee **Obverse:** Similar to KM#99 **Reverse:** Similar to KM#70

| Date | Mintage | F | VF | XF | Unc | BU |
|---|---|---|---|---|---|---|
| 1989 Proof | 25,000 | Value: 22.50 | | | | |

**50 CENTS** KM# 129 **Weight:** 18.0000 g. **Composition:** 0.9250 Silver .5353 oz. ASW **Subject:** Wedding of Prince Charles and Lady Diana **Obverse:** Similar to KM#99 **Reverse:** Similar to KM#72

| Date | Mintage | F | VF | XF | Unc | BU |
|---|---|---|---|---|---|---|
| 1989 Proof | 25,000 | Value: 22.50 | | | | |

**50 CENTS** KM# 130 **Weight:** 18.0000 g. **Composition:** 0.9250 Silver .5353 oz. ASW **Subject:** XII Commonwealth Games - Brisbane **Obverse:** Similar to KM#99 **Reverse:** Similar to KM#74

| Date | Mintage | F | VF | XF | Unc | BU |
|---|---|---|---|---|---|---|
| 1989 Proof | 25,000 | Value: 22.50 | | | | |

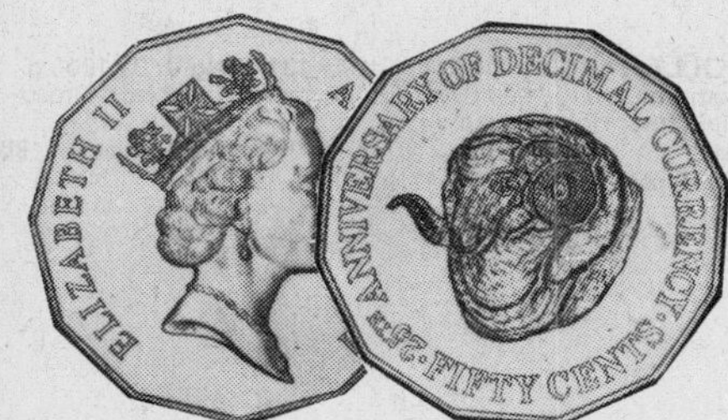


**50 CENTS** KM# 139 **Composition:** Copper-Nickel **Subject:** 25th Anniversary of Decimal Currency - Merino Ram

| Date | Mintage | F | VF | XF | Unc | BU |
|---|---|---|---|---|---|---|
| 1991 | 4,364,000 | — | — | 1.00 | 3.00 | — |
| 1991 Proof | — | Value: 11.50 | | | | |

**50 CENTS** KM# 139a **Weight:** 18.0000 g. **Composition:** 0.9250 Silver .5353 oz. ASW

| Date | Mintage | F | VF | XF | Unc | BU |
|---|---|---|---|---|---|---|
| 1991 Proof | 23,000 | Value: 18.00 | | | | |

**Note:** In Proof sets only

**50 CENTS** KM# 257 **Weight:** 18.0000 g. **Composition:** 0.9250 Silver .5353 oz. ASW **Subject:** International Year of the Family

| Date | Mintage | F | VF | XF | Unc | BU |
|---|---|---|---|---|---|---|
| 1994 | — | — | — | 1.00 | 3.00 | — |
| 1994 Proof | — | Value: 11.50 | | | | |

**50 CENTS** KM# 294 **Weight:** 18.0000 g. **Composition:** 0.9250 Silver .5353 oz. ASW **Subject:** Weary Dunlop

| Date | Mintage | F | VF | XF | Unc | BU |
|---|---|---|---|---|---|---|
| 1995 | — | — | — | 0.85 | 2.75 | — |
| 1995 Proof | — | Value: 11.50 | | | | |

**50 CENTS** KM# 364 **Weight:** 18.0000 g. **Composition:** 0.9250 Silver .5353 oz. ASW **Subject:** George Bass and Matthew Flinders **Obverse:** Queen's portrait **Reverse:** Portraits of Bass and Flinders

| Date | Mintage | F | VF | XF | Unc | BU |
|---|---|---|---|---|---|---|
| 1998 | — | — | — | 0.85 | 2.75 | — |
| 1998 Proof | — | Value: 11.50 | | | | |

**50 CENTS** KM# 411 **Weight:** 36.3100 g. **Composition:** 0.9990 Silver 1.1662 oz. ASW **Subject:** Masterpieces in Silver **Obverse:** Queen's portrait **Reverse:** 1937 crown design

| Date | Mintage | F | VF | XF | Unc | BU |
|---|---|---|---|---|---|---|
| 1998 Proof | 15,000 | Value: 25.00 | | | | |

**50 CENTS** KM# 404 **Composition:** Copper-Nickel **Obverse:** Queen's portrait by Rank-Broadley **Reverse:** Similar to KM#83

| Date | Mintage | F | VF | XF | Unc | BU |
|---|---|---|---|---|---|---|
| 1999 | — | — | — | 0.85 | 2.75 | — |
| 1999 Proof | — | Value: 6.50 | | | | |

**50 CENTS** KM# 484 **Weight:** 3.2400 g. **Composition:** 0.9990 Silver .1041 oz. ASW **Series:** Masterpieces in Silver **Obverse:** Queen's head right. **Reverse:** Sixpence reverse design of KM#25. **Edge:** Reeded. **Size:** 19.4 mm.

| Date | Mintage | F | VF | XF | Unc | BU |
|---|---|---|---|---|---|---|
| 1999 Proof | 15,000 | Value: 10.00 | | | | |

**50 CENTS** KM# 501 **Weight:** 16.8860 g. **Composition:** 0.9990 Silver .5424 oz. ASW **Subject:** Year of the Rabbit **Obverse:** Queen's head right. **Reverse:** Rabbit. **Edge:** Reeded. **Size:** 32.1 mm.

| Date | Mintage | F | VF | XF | Unc | BU |
|---|---|---|---|---|---|---|
| 1999 | — | — | — | — | 15.00 | — |
| 1999 Proof | 5,000 | Value: 25.00 | | | | |

**50 CENTS** KM# 437 **Composition:** Copper-Nickel **Subject:** Royal Visit **Obverse:** Queen's head right **Reverse:** Australian flag above Canberra Parliament House, British crown at right **Edge:** Plain 12 sided edge

| Date | Mintage | F | VF | XF | Unc | BU |
|---|---|---|---|---|---|---|
| 2000 Proof | 5,000 | Value: 2.50 | | | | |

**50 CENTS** KM# 437a **Weight:** 18.2400 g. **Composition:** 0.9990 Silver .5858 oz. ASW **Subject:** Royal Visit **Obverse:** Queen's head right **Reverse:** Australian flag above Canberra Parliament House, British crown at right

| Date | Mintage | F | VF | XF | Unc | BU |
|---|---|---|---|---|---|---|
| 2000 Proof | 25,000 | Value: 27.50 | | | | |

**50 CENTS** KM# 488 **Weight:** 15.5500 g. **Composition:** Copper-Nickel **Subject:** Millennium **Obverse:** Queen's head right. **Reverse:** Australian flag. **Edge:** Plain, 12-sided. **Size:** 31.5 mm.

| Date | Mintage | F | VF | XF | Unc | BU |
|---|---|---|---|---|---|---|
| 2000 | — | — | — | — | 3.00 | — |

**50 CENTS** KM# 488.1 **Weight:** 15.5500 g. **Composition:** Copper-Nickel **Subject:** Millennium **Obverse:** Queen's head right. **Reverse:** Multicolor Australian flag. **Edge:** Plain, 12-sided. **Size:** 31.5 mm.

| Date | Mintage | F | VF | XF | Unc | BU |
|---|---|---|---|---|---|---|
| 2000 Proof | — | Value: 12.50 | | | | |

**50 CENTS** KM# 522 **Weight:** 16.8860 g. **Composition:** 0.9990 Silver .5424 oz. ASW **Series:** Dragons **Obverse:** Queen's head right. **Reverse:** Dragon. **Edge:** Reeded. **Size:** 32.1 mm.

| Date | Mintage | F | VF | XF | Unc | BU |
|---|---|---|---|---|---|---|
| 2000 Proof | — | Value: 25.00 | | | | |

**50 CENTS** KM# 499 **Weight:** 36.3100 g. **Composition:** 0.9990 Silver 1.1662 oz. ASW **Series:** Masterpieces in Silver - 2000 Set **Obverse:** Queen's head right. **Reverse:** George VI's head left. **Edge:** Reeded. **Size:** 38.7 mm.

| Date | Mintage | F | VF | XF | Unc | BU |
|---|---|---|---|---|---|---|
| 2000 Proof | 15,000 | Value: 30.00 | | | | |

**50 CENTS** **KM# 491** **Composition:** Copper-Nickel **Subject:** Centenary of Federation, 1901-2001 **Obverse:** Queen's head right. **Reverse:** Commonwealth coat of arms. **Edge:** Plain 12-sided. **Size:** 31.5 mm.

| Date | Mintage | F | VF | XF | Unc | BU |
|---|---|---|---|---|---|---|
| 2001 | — | — | — | — | 2.50 | — |

**50 CENTS** **KM# 491a** **Weight:** 18.2400 g. **Composition:** 0.9990 Silver .5858 oz. ASW **Subject:** Centenary of Federation, 1901-2001 **Obverse:** Queen's head right. **Reverse:** Commonwealth coat of arms. **Edge:** Plain 12-sided. **Size:** 31.5 mm.

| Date | Mintage | F | VF | XF | Unc | BU |
|---|---|---|---|---|---|---|
| 2001 Proof | — | Value: 27.50 | | | | |

**50 CENTS** **KM# 533** **Weight:** 15.6000 g. **Composition:** Copper-Nickel **Subject:** Centennial - Norfolk Island Federation **Obverse:** Queen's head right. **Reverse:** Norfolk Island coat of arms. **Edge:** Plain 12-sided. **Size:** 31.4 mm.

| Date | Mintage | F | VF | XF | Unc | BU |
|---|---|---|---|---|---|---|
| 2001 | — | — | — | — | 2.50 | — |

**50 CENTS** **KM# 535** **Weight:** 16.8860 g. **Composition:** 0.9990 Silver .5424 oz. ASW **Subject:** Year of the Snake **Obverse:** Queen's head right. **Reverse:** Snake with eggs. **Edge:** Reeded. **Size:** 32.1 mm.

| Date | Mintage | F | VF | XF | Unc | BU |
|---|---|---|---|---|---|---|
| 2001 | 500,000 | — | — | — | 15.00 | — |

**50 CENTS** **KM# 549.1** **Weight:** 15.5500 g. **Composition:** Copper-Nickel **Series:** Centenary of Federation - Federation Arms **Obverse:** Queen's head right. **Reverse:** Arms above denomination. **Edge:** Plain, 12-sided. **Size:** 31.5 mm.

| Date | Mintage | F | VF | XF | Unc | BU |
|---|---|---|---|---|---|---|
| 2001 | — | — | — | — | 3.00 | — |

**50 CENTS** **KM# 549.2** **Weight:** 15.5500 g. **Composition:** Copper-Nickel **Series:** Centenary of Federation - Federation Arms **Obverse:** Queen's head right. **Reverse:** Multicolored arms. **Edge:** Plain, 12-sided. **Size:** 31.5 mm.

| Date | Mintage | F | VF | XF | Unc | BU |
|---|---|---|---|---|---|---|
| 2001 Proof | — | Value: 6.50 | | | | |

**50 CENTS** **KM# 551** **Weight:** 15.5500 g. **Composition:** Copper-Nickel **Series:** Centenary of Federation - New South Wales **Obverse:** Queen's head right. **Reverse:** State arms. **Edge:** Reeded, 12-sided. **Size:** 31.5 mm.

| Date | Mintage | F | VF | XF | Unc | BU |
|---|---|---|---|---|---|---|
| 2001 | — | — | — | — | 3.00 | — |
| 2001 Proof | — | Value: 6.50 | | | | |

**50 CENTS** **KM# 553** **Weight:** 15.5500 g. **Composition:** Copper-Nickel **Series:** Centenary of Federation - Australian Capital Territory **Obverse:** Queen's head right. **Reverse:** State arms. **Edge:** Reeded, 12-sided. **Size:** 31.5 mm.

| Date | Mintage | F | VF | XF | Unc | BU |
|---|---|---|---|---|---|---|
| 2001 | — | — | — | — | 3.00 | — |
| 2001 Proof | — | Value: 6.50 | | | | |

**50 CENTS** **KM# 555** **Weight:** 15.5500 g. **Composition:** Copper-Nickel **Series:** Centenary of Federation - Queensland **Obverse:** Queen's head right. **Reverse:** State arms. **Edge:** Reeded, 12-sided. **Size:** 31.5 mm.

| Date | Mintage | F | VF | XF | Unc | BU |
|---|---|---|---|---|---|---|
| 2001 | — | — | — | — | 3.00 | — |
| 2001 Proof | — | Value: 6.50 | | | | |

**50 CENTS** **KM# 557** **Weight:** 15.5500 g. **Composition:** Copper-Nickel **Series:** Centenary of Federation - Victoria **Obverse:** Queen's head right. **Reverse:** State arms. **Edge:** Reeded, 12-sided. **Size:** 31.5 mm.

| Date | Mintage | F | VF | XF | Unc | BU |
|---|---|---|---|---|---|---|
| 2001 | — | — | — | — | 3.00 | — |
| 2001 Proof | — | Value: 6.50 | | | | |

**50 CENTS** **KM# 559** **Weight:** 15.5500 g. **Composition:** Copper-Nickel **Series:** Centenary of Federation - Northern Territory **Obverse:** Queen's head right. **Reverse:** State arms. **Edge:** Reeded, 12-sided. **Size:** 31.5 mm.

| Date | Mintage | F | VF | XF | Unc | BU |
|---|---|---|---|---|---|---|
| 2001 | — | — | — | — | 3.00 | — |
| 2001 Proof | — | Value: 6.50 | | | | |

**50 CENTS** **KM# 561** **Weight:** 15.5500 g. **Composition:** Copper-Nickel **Series:** Centenary of Federation - South Australia **Obverse:** Queen's head right. **Reverse:** State arms. **Edge:** Reeded, 12-sided. **Size:** 31.5 mm.

| Date | Mintage | F | VF | XF | Unc | BU |
|---|---|---|---|---|---|---|
| 2001 | — | — | — | — | 3.00 | — |
| 2001 Proof | — | Value: 6.50 | | | | |

**50 CENTS** **KM# 563** **Weight:** 15.5500 g. **Composition:** Copper-Nickel **Series:** Centenary of Federation - Western Australia **Obverse:** Queen's head right. **Reverse:** State arms. **Edge:** Reeded, 12-sided. **Size:** 31.5 mm.

| Date | Mintage | F | VF | XF | Unc | BU |
|---|---|---|---|---|---|---|
| 2001 | — | — | — | — | 3.00 | — |
| 2001 Proof | — | Value: 6.50 | | | | |

**50 CENTS** **KM# 565** **Weight:** 15.5500 g. **Composition:** Copper-Nickel **Series:** Centenary of Federation - Tasmania **Obverse:** Queen's head right. **Reverse:** State arms. **Edge:** Reeded, 12-sided. **Size:** 31.5 mm.

| Date | Mintage | F | VF | XF | Unc | BU |
|---|---|---|---|---|---|---|
| 2001 | — | — | — | — | 3.00 | — |
| 2001 Proof | — | Value: 6.50 | | | | |

**DOLLAR (Holey Dollar)** **KM# 112** **Weight:** 31.1000 g. **Composition:** 0.9990 Silver 1.0000 oz. ASW **Subject:** Aboriginal Culture **Note:** Holey Dollar.

| Date | Mintage | F | VF | XF | Unc | BU |
|---|---|---|---|---|---|---|
| 1988 Proof | 100,000 | Value: 40.00 | | | | |

**DOLLAR (Holey Dollar)** **KM# 131** **Weight:** 31.1000 g. **Composition:** 0.9990 Silver 1.0000 oz. ASW **Subject:** Crocodiles **Note:** Holey Dollar.

| Date | Mintage | F | VF | XF | Unc | BU |
|---|---|---|---|---|---|---|
| 1989 Proof | 45,000 | Value: 40.00 | | | | |

**DOLLAR (Holey Dollar)** **KM# 154** **Weight:** 31.1000 g. **Composition:** 0.9990 Silver 1.0000 oz. ASW **Reverse:** Stylized Natives and Jungle **Note:** Holey Dollar.

| Date | Mintage | F | VF | XF | Unc | BU |
|---|---|---|---|---|---|---|
| 1990 Proof | 30,000 | Value: 40.00 | | | | |

**DOLLAR** **KM# 77** **Composition:** Nickel-Aluminum-Copper

| Date | Mintage | F | VF | XF | Unc | BU |
|---|---|---|---|---|---|---|
| 1984 | 185,985,000 | — | — | 1.00 | 4.00 | — |
| 1984 Proof | 159,000 | Value: 9.00 | | | | |

**DOLLAR** **KM# 84** **Composition:** Nickel-Aluminum-Copper

| Date | Mintage | F | VF | XF | Unc | BU |
|---|---|---|---|---|---|---|
| 1985 | 91,400,000 | — | — | 1.00 | 3.25 | — |
| 1985 Proof | 75,000 | Value: 9.00 | | | | |
| 1987 In sets only | 200,000 | — | — | — | 3.50 | — |
| 1987 Proof | 70,000 | Value: 9.00 | | | | |
| 1989 | — | — | — | 1.00 | 3.25 | — |
| 1989 Proof | — | Value: 9.00 | | | | |
| 1990 | — | — | — | 1.00 | 3.25 | — |
| 1990 Proof | — | Value: 9.00 | | | | |
| 1991 | — | — | — | 1.00 | 3.25 | — |
| 1991 Proof | — | Value: 9.00 | | | | |
| 1994 | — | — | — | 1.00 | 3.25 | — |
| 1994 Proof | — | Value: 9.00 | | | | |
| 1995 | — | — | — | 1.00 | 3.25 | — |
| 1995 Proof | — | Value: 9.00 | | | | |
| 1998 | — | — | — | 1.00 | 3.25 | — |
| 1998 Proof | — | Value: 9.00 | | | | |

**DOLLAR** **KM# 87** **Composition:** Aluminum-Bronze **Subject:** International Year of Peace

| Date | Mintage | F | VF | XF | Unc | BU |
|---|---|---|---|---|---|---|
| 1986 | 25,100,000 | — | — | 1.00 | 4.00 | — |
| 1986 Proof | 67,000 | Value: 20.00 | | | | |

**DOLLAR** **KM# 100** **Composition:** Aluminum-Bronze **Subject:** Aboriginal Art

| Date | Mintage | F | VF | XF | Unc | BU |
|---|---|---|---|---|---|---|
| 1988 | 1,564,000 | — | — | — | 4.00 | — |
| 1988 Proof | 106,000 | Value: 18.50 | | | | |

**DOLLAR** **KM# 100a** **Weight:** 11.4900 g. **Composition:** 0.9250 Silver .3417 oz. ASW **Subject:** Masterpieces in Silver

| Date | Mintage | F | VF | XF | Unc | BU |
|---|---|---|---|---|---|---|
| 1988 Proof | 25,000 | Value: 35.00 | | | | |
| 1990 Proof | 25,000 | Value: 35.00 | | | | |

**DOLLAR** **KM# 87a** **Weight:** 11.4900 g. **Composition:** 0.9250 Silver .3417 oz. ASW **Subject:** Masterpieces in Silver

| Date | Mintage | F | VF | XF | Unc | BU |
|---|---|---|---|---|---|---|
| 1990 Proof | 25,000 | Value: 35.00 | | | | |

**DOLLAR** **KM# 84a** **Weight:** 11.4900 g. **Composition:** 0.9250 Silver .3417 oz. ASW **Subject:** Masterpieces in Silver

| Date | Mintage | F | VF | XF | Unc | BU |
|---|---|---|---|---|---|---|
| 1990 Proof | 25,000 | Value: 35.00 | | | | |
| 1991 Proof | 23,000 | Value: 35.00 | | | | |

**Note:** In Proof sets only

**DOLLAR** **KM# 164** **Weight:** 31.1000 g. **Composition:** 0.9990 Silver 1.0000 oz. ASW **Reverse:** Australian Kookaburra

| Date | Mintage | F | VF | XF | Unc | BU |
|---|---|---|---|---|---|---|
| 1992 | 300,000 | — | — | — | 12.00 | — |
| 1993 | 300,000 | — | — | — | 12.00 | — |

**DOLLAR** **KM# 175** **Composition:** Aluminum-Bronze **Subject:** Olympics - Female Javelin Thrower **Edge:** Alternating reeded and plain sections

| Date | Mintage | F | VF | XF | Unc | BU |
|---|---|---|---|---|---|---|
| 1992 | 16,000 | — | — | — | 4.00 | — |
| 1992 Proof | 47,000 | Value: 20.00 | | | | |

**DOLLAR** **KM# 175a.1** **Weight:** 11.4900 g. **Composition:** 0.9250 Silver .3412 oz. ASW

| Date | Mintage | F | VF | XF | Unc | BU |
|---|---|---|---|---|---|---|
| 1992 Proof | 12,500 | Value: 85.00 | | | | |

**Note:** In Proof sets only

**DOLLAR** **KM# 175a.2** **Weight:** 11.4900 g. **Composition:** 0.9250 Silver .3412 oz. ASW **Edge:** Reeded

| Date | Mintage | F | VF | XF | Unc | BU |
|---|---|---|---|---|---|---|
| 1992 Proof | 2,500 | Value: 300 | | | | |

**DOLLAR** **KM# 209** **Weight:** 31.1000 g. **Composition:** 0.9990 Silver 1.0000 oz. ASW **Subject:** Australian Kookaburra

| Date | Mintage | F | VF | XF | Unc | BU |
|---|---|---|---|---|---|---|
| 1992 Proof | — | Value: 40.00 | | | | |
| 1992 (ae) Proof | 750 | Value: 185 | | | | |
| 1993 | Est. 300,000 | — | — | — | 12.00 | |

**DOLLAR** **KM# 211.1** **Weight:** 31.5700 g. **Composition:** 0.9990 Silver 1.0140 oz. ASW **Reverse:** Kangaroo **Edge:** Reeded

| Date | Mintage | F | VF | XF | Unc | BU |
|---|---|---|---|---|---|---|
| 1993C | 73,000 | — | — | — | 20.00 | — |

**DOLLAR** **KM# 211.2** **Weight:** 31.5700 g. **Composition:** 0.9990 Silver 1.0140 oz. ASW **Edge:** Reeded and plain sections

| Date | Mintage | F | VF | XF | Unc | BU |
|---|---|---|---|---|---|---|
| 1993C | 5,000 | — | — | — | 50.00 | — |

**DOLLAR** **KM# 212.1** **Weight:** 31.1035 g. **Composition:** 0.9990 Silver 1.0000 oz. ASW **Reverse:** Pair of Kookaburras

| Date | Mintage | F | VF | XF | Unc | BU |
|---|---|---|---|---|---|---|
| 1993 Proof | — | Value: 18.00 | | | | |
| 1993 (ge) Proof | 500 | Value: 65.00 | | | | |
| 1993 (so) Proof | 13,000 | Value: 45.00 | | | | |
| 1994 Proof | 2,500 | Value: 25.00 | | | | |
| 1994 (ta) Specimen | 15,000 | — | — | — | 22.50 | — |

**DOLLAR** **KM# 212.2 Weight:** 31.1035 g. **Composition:** 0.9990 Silver 1.0000 oz. ASW **Reverse:** American Eagle privy mark above date

| Date | Mintage | F | VF | XF | Unc | BU |
|---|---|---|---|---|---|---|
| 1993 Proof | 500 | Value: 65.00 | | | | |

**DOLLAR** **KM# 208a.1 Composition:** Silver **Edge:** Alternating reeded and plain sections

| Date | Mintage | F | VF | XF | Unc | BU |
|---|---|---|---|---|---|---|
| 1993 Proof | 20,000 | Value: 42.50 | | | | |

**DOLLAR** **KM# 208a.2 Composition:** Silver **Edge:** Reeded

| Date | Mintage | F | VF | XF | Unc | BU |
|---|---|---|---|---|---|---|
| 1993 Proof | 5,001 | Value: 120 | | | | |

**DOLLAR** **KM# 208 Composition:** Aluminum-Bronze **Note:** Visitors at mints and coin shows were allowed to strike a coin for a fee at the following C - Canberra, M - Hall of Manufacturers Pavilion Coin Show, Melbourne and S - Sydney International Coin Fair.

| Date | Mintage | F | VF | XF | Unc | BU |
|---|---|---|---|---|---|---|
| 1993 | 15,000,000 | — | — | — | 2.85 | — |
| 1993 Proof | — | Value: 16.50 | | | | |
| 1993C | 92,000 | — | — | — | 3.00 | — |
| 1993M | 60,000 | — | — | — | 3.00 | — |
| 1993S Proof | 88,000 | — | — | — | 3.00 | — |

**DOLLAR** **KM# 258 Composition:** Aluminum-Bronze **Subject:** 10th Anniversary - Introduction of Dollar Coin

| Date | Mintage | F | VF | XF | Unc | BU |
|---|---|---|---|---|---|---|
| 1994C | 123,000 | — | — | — | 3.00 | — |
| 1994M | 65,000 | — | — | — | 3.50 | — |
| 1994S | 74,000 | — | — | — | 3.50 | — |

**DOLLAR** **KM# 258a.1 Weight:** 14.4900 g. **Composition:** 0.9250 Silver .3417 oz. ASW **Edge:** Reeded and plain sections

| Date | Mintage | F | VF | XF | Unc | BU |
|---|---|---|---|---|---|---|
| 1994 Proof | 20,000 | Value: 42.50 | | | | |

**DOLLAR** **KM# 258a.2 Weight:** 14.4900 g. **Composition:** 0.9250 Silver .3417 oz. ASW **Edge:** Reeded

| Date | Mintage | F | VF | XF | Unc | BU |
|---|---|---|---|---|---|---|
| 1994 Proof | 5,000 | Value: 135 | | | | |

**DOLLAR** **KM# 260 Weight:** 31.1035 g. **Composition:** 0.9990 Silver 1.0000 oz. ASW **Reverse:** Kookaburra on branch

| Date | Mintage | F | VF | XF | Unc | BU |
|---|---|---|---|---|---|---|
| 1994 Proof | 2,500 | Value: 45.00 | | | | |
| 1995 Proof | 300,000 | Value: 12.50 | | | | |

**DOLLAR** **KM# 263.1 Weight:** 31.6350 g. **Composition:** 0.9990 Silver 1.0161 oz. ASW **Obverse:** Queen Elizabeth portrait **Reverse:** Kangaroo leaping **Edge:** Reeded

| Date | Mintage | F | VF | XF | Unc | BU |
|---|---|---|---|---|---|---|
| 1994C | 45,000 | — | — | — | 20.00 | — |

**DOLLAR** **KM# 263.2 Weight:** 31.6350 g. **Composition:** 0.9990 Silver 1.0161 oz. ASW **Edge:** Reeded and plain sections

| Date | Mintage | F | VF | XF | Unc | BU |
|---|---|---|---|---|---|---|
| 1994C | 2,500 | — | — | — | 120 | — |

**DOLLAR** **KM# 269 Composition:** Aluminum-Bronze **Subject:** A.B. Banjo Paterson - Waltzing Matilda

| Date | Mintage | F | VF | XF | Unc | BU |
|---|---|---|---|---|---|---|
| 1995B | 74,000 | — | — | — | 5.00 | — |
| 1995C | 156,000 | — | — | — | 4.50 | — |
| 1995M | 74,000 | — | — | — | 5.00 | — |
| 1995S | 83,000 | — | — | — | 5.00 | — |

**DOLLAR** **KM# 269a.1 Weight:** 14.4900 g. **Composition:** 0.9250 Silver .3417 oz. ASW **Edge:** Alternating reeded and plain sections

| Date | Mintage | F | VF | XF | Unc | BU |
|---|---|---|---|---|---|---|
| 1995 Proof | 20,000 | Value: 30.00 | | | | |

**DOLLAR** **KM# 269a.2 Weight:** 14.4900 g. **Composition:** 0.9250 Silver .3417 oz. ASW **Edge:** Reeded

| Date | Mintage | F | VF | XF | Unc | BU |
|---|---|---|---|---|---|---|
| 1995 Proof | Est. 2,500 | Value: 50.00 | | | | |

**DOLLAR** **KM# 289.1 Weight:** 31.6350 g. **Composition:** 0.9990 Silver 1.0161 oz. ASW **Reverse:** Kookaburra in flight

| Date | Mintage | F | VF | XF | Unc | BU |
|---|---|---|---|---|---|---|
| 1995P Proof | 4,900 | Value: 20.00 | | | | |
| 1996 | 300,000 | — | — | — | 18.00 | — |
| 1996 (bg) | 5,000 | — | — | — | 40.00 | — |
| 1996 (ba) | 2,500 | — | — | — | 42.00 | — |
| 1996 (sr) | 5,000 | — | — | — | 40.00 | — |

**DOLLAR** **KM# 293.1 Weight:** 31.6350 g. **Composition:** 0.9990 Silver 1.0161 oz. ASW **Reverse:** Kangaroo portrait **Edge:** Reeded

| Date | Mintage | F | VF | XF | Unc | BU |
|---|---|---|---|---|---|---|
| 1995C | 73,000 | — | — | — | 20.00 | — |

**DOLLAR** **KM# 293.2 Weight:** 31.6350 g. **Composition:** 0.9990 Silver 1.0161 oz. ASW **Edge:** Reeded and plain sections

| Date | Mintage | F | VF | XF | Unc | BU |
|---|---|---|---|---|---|---|
| 1995C | 2,500 | — | — | — | 110 | — |

**DOLLAR** **KM# 297 Weight:** 31.6350 g. **Composition:** 0.9990 Silver 1.0161 oz. ASW **Reverse:** Mother and Baby Kangaroo

| Date | Mintage | F | VF | XF | Unc | BU |
|---|---|---|---|---|---|---|
| 1996 | — | — | — | — | 22.50 | — |

**DOLLAR** **KM# 310 Composition:** Aluminum-Bronze **Subject:** Sir Henry Parks

| Date | Mintage | F | VF | XF | Unc | BU |
|---|---|---|---|---|---|---|
| 1996 | — | — | — | — | 4.00 | — |
| 1996 Proof | — | — | — | — | — | — |
| 1996A | — | — | — | — | 4.50 | — |
| 1996B | — | — | — | — | 4.50 | — |
| 1996C | 25,000 | — | — | — | 5.50 | — |
| 1996M | — | — | — | — | 4.50 | — |
| 1996S | 64,000 | — | — | — | 4.50 | — |

**DOLLAR** **KM# 310a Weight:** 11.4900 g. **Composition:** 0.9250 Silver .3417 oz. ASW

| Date | Mintage | F | VF | XF | Unc | BU |
|---|---|---|---|---|---|---|
| 1996 Proof | 20,000 | Value: 17.50 | | | | |

**DOLLAR** **KM# 326 Weight:** 31.1035 g. **Composition:** 0.9990 Silver 1.0000 oz. ASW **Subject:** 30th Anniversary - Decimal Coinage **Obverse:** Queen's portrait **Reverse:** Map and seven different coin designs

| Date | Mintage | F | VF | XF | Unc | BU |
|---|---|---|---|---|---|---|
| 1996 Proof | — | Value: 60.00 | | | | |

**DOLLAR** **KM# 289.2 Weight:** 31.1035 g. **Composition:** 0.9990 Silver 1.0000 oz. ASW **Edge:** Reeded and inscribed with date and serial

| Date | Mintage | F | VF | XF | Unc | BU |
|---|---|---|---|---|---|---|
| 1996 | 1,500 | — | — | — | 45.00 | — |

**DOLLAR** KM# 318 **Weight:** 31.1035 g. **Composition:** 0.9990 Silver 1.0000 oz. ASW **Reverse:** Kookaburra and Nestlings

| Date | Mintage | F | VF | XF | Unc | BU |
|---|---|---|---|---|---|---|
| 1997 | 300,000 | — | — | — | 13.50 | — |

**DOLLAR** KM# 325 **Weight:** 31.5600 g. **Composition:** 0.9990 Silver 1.0136 oz. ASW **Obverse:** Queen's portrait **Reverse:** Kangaroo drinking water, reflection

| Date | Mintage | F | VF | XF | Unc | BU |
|---|---|---|---|---|---|---|
| 1997C | — | — | — | — | 22.50 | — |

**DOLLAR** KM# 327 **Composition:** Aluminum-Bronze **Subject:** Sir Charles Kingsford Smith **Obverse:** Queen's portrait **Reverse:** Pilot above airplane, dates

| Date | Mintage | F | VF | XF | Unc | BU |
|---|---|---|---|---|---|---|
| 1997 | — | — | — | — | 4.00 | — |

**DOLLAR** KM# 355 **Composition:** Aluminum-Bronze **Subject:** Sir Charles Kingsford Smith **Obverse:** Queen's portrait **Reverse:** Portrait and airplane over map

| Date | Mintage | F | VF | XF | Unc | BU |
|---|---|---|---|---|---|---|
| 1997A | — | — | — | — | 3.00 | — |
| 1997B | — | — | — | — | 3.00 | — |
| 1997C | — | — | — | — | 3.00 | — |
| 1997M | — | — | — | — | 3.00 | — |
| 1997S | — | — | — | — | 3.00 | — |

**DOLLAR** KM# 355a **Weight:** 11.6600 g. **Composition:** 0.9990 Silver .3752 oz. ASW

| Date | Mintage | F | VF | XF | Unc | BU |
|---|---|---|---|---|---|---|
| 1997 Proof | 20,000 | Value: 17.50 | | | | |

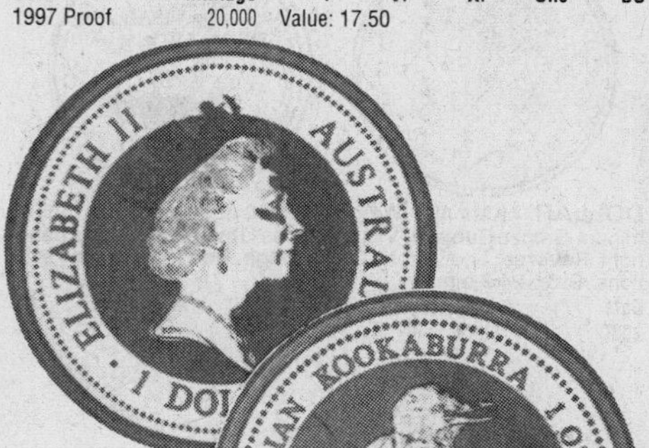


**DOLLAR** KM# 362 **Weight:** 31.1035 g. **Composition:** 0.9990 Silver 1.0000 oz. ASW **Subject:** Kookaburra **Obverse:** Queen's portrait **Reverse:** Bird on fence

| Date | Mintage | F | VF | XF | Unc | BU |
|---|---|---|---|---|---|---|
| 1997 Proof | 2,000 | Value: 30.00 | | | | |
| 1998 (1997) | — | — | — | — | 15.00 | — |

**DOLLAR** KM# 365 **Weight:** 32.0000 g. **Composition:** 0.9990 Silver 1.0278 oz. ASW **Obverse:** Queen's portrait **Reverse:** Kangaroo bounding left

| Date | Mintage | F | VF | XF | Unc | BU |
|---|---|---|---|---|---|---|
| 1998C | — | — | — | — | 20.00 | — |

**DOLLAR** KM# 366 **Composition:** Aluminum-Bronze **Subject:** Howard Florey **Obverse:** Queen's portrait **Reverse:** Portrait of Florey

| Date | Mintage | F | VF | XF | Unc | BU |
|---|---|---|---|---|---|---|
| 1998A | — | — | — | — | 4.25 | — |
| 1998B | — | — | — | — | 4.25 | — |
| 1998C | — | — | — | — | 4.25 | — |
| 1998M | — | — | — | — | 4.25 | — |
| 1998S | — | — | — | — | 4.25 | — |

**DOLLAR** KM# 366a **Weight:** 11.6600 g. **Composition:** 0.9990 Silver .3745 oz. ASW

| Date | Mintage | F | VF | XF | Unc | BU |
|---|---|---|---|---|---|---|
| 1998 Proof only | 20,000 | Value: 20.00 | | | | |

**DOLLAR** KM# 412 **Weight:** 31.1035 g. **Composition:** 0.9990 Silver 1.0000 oz. ASW **Subject:** 10th Anniversary - New Parliament House **Obverse:** Queen's portrait **Reverse:** Parliament building

| Date | Mintage | F | VF | XF | Unc | BU |
|---|---|---|---|---|---|---|
| 1998 Proof | 17,000 | Value: 60.00 | | | | |

**DOLLAR** KM# 398 **Weight:** 32.2500 g. **Composition:** 0.9990 Silver 1.0358 oz. ASW **Obverse:** Queen's portrait by Rank-Broadley **Reverse:** Pair of kangaroos

| Date | Mintage | F | VF | XF | Unc | BU |
|---|---|---|---|---|---|---|
| 1999 | — | — | — | — | 20.00 | — |
| 1999 Proof | — | Value: 30.00 | | | | |

**DOLLAR** KM# 399 **Weight:** 32.2500 g. **Composition:** 0.9990 Silver 1.0358 oz. ASW **Obverse:** Queen's portrait **Reverse:** Adult and chick kookaburras on branch

| Date | Mintage | F | VF | XF | Unc | BU |
|---|---|---|---|---|---|---|
| 1999 | — | — | — | — | 14.00 | — |

**DOLLAR** KM# 400 **Composition:** Aluminum-Bronze **Subject:** The Last of the Anzaca **Obverse:** Queen's portrait **Reverse:** Anzac soldier wearing bush hat

| Date | Mintage | F | VF | XF | Unc | BU |
|---|---|---|---|---|---|---|
| 1999C | — | — | — | — | 4.25 | — |
| 1999M | — | — | — | — | 4.25 | — |
| 1999S | — | — | — | — | 4.25 | — |
| 1999B | — | — | — | — | 4.25 | — |

**DOLLAR** KM# 400a **Weight:** 11.6600 g. **Composition:** 0.9990 Silver .3745 oz. ASW **Subject:** The Last of the Anzacs **Obverse:** Queen's head right **Reverse:** Anzac soldier wearing bush hat **Edge:** Reeded and plain sections on edge

| Date | Mintage | F | VF | XF | Unc | BU |
|---|---|---|---|---|---|---|
| 1999 Proof | 25,000 | Value: 25.00 | | | | |

**DOLLAR** KM# 405 **Composition:** Aluminum-Bronze **Subject:** International Year of Older People **Obverse:** Queen's portrait **Reverse:** IYPO logo **Size:** 25 mm.

| Date | Mintage | F | VF | XF | Unc | BU |
|---|---|---|---|---|---|---|
| 1999 | — | — | — | — | 4.25 | — |
| 1999 Proof | — | Value: 14.00 | | | | |

**DOLLAR** KM# 416 **Weight:** 31.7700 g. **Composition:** 0.9990 Silver 1.0204 oz. ASW **Obverse:** Queen's head right **Reverse:** Kookaburra on branch

| Date | Mintage | F | VF | XF | Unc | BU |
|---|---|---|---|---|---|---|
| 2000 (1999) | — | — | — | — | 16.00 | — |

**DOLLAR** KM# 476 **Weight:** 31.1035 g. **Composition:** 0.9990 Silver 1.0000 oz. ASW **Subject:** Majestic Images **Obverse:** Queen's head right **Reverse:** Queen's 3 previous portraits **Edge:** Reeded

| Date | Mintage | F | VF | XF | Unc | BU |
|---|---|---|---|---|---|---|
| 1999 Proof | 17,000 | Value: 65.00 | | | | |

**DOLLAR** KM# 502 **Weight:** 31.6350 g. **Composition:** 0.9990 Silver 1.0161 oz. ASW **Subject:** Year of the Rabbit **Obverse:** Queen's head right. **Edge:** Reeded. **Size:** 40.6 mm.

| Date | Mintage | F | VF | XF | Unc | BU |
|---|---|---|---|---|---|---|
| 1999 | — | — | — | — | 20.00 | — |
| 1999 Proof | 2,500 | Value: 45.00 | | | | |

**DOLLAR** KM# 485 **Weight:** 6.5700 g. **Composition:** 0.9990 Silver .2110 oz. ASW **Series:** Masterpieces in Silver **Obverse:** Queen's head right. **Reverse:** Shilling reverse design of KM#39. **Edge:** Reeded. **Size:** 23.6 mm.

| Date | Mintage | F | VF | XF | Unc | BU |
|---|---|---|---|---|---|---|
| 1999 Proof | 15,000 | Value: 18.00 | | | | |

**DOLLAR** KM# 489 **Weight:** 9.0000 g. **Composition:** Aluminum-Bronze **Subject:** Kangaroos **Obverse:** Queen's head by Rank-Broadly right. **Reverse:** Kangaroos. **Edge:** Reeded and plain sections. **Size:** 25 mm.

| Date | Mintage | F | VF | XF | Unc | BU |
|---|---|---|---|---|---|---|
| 2000 | — | — | — | — | 4.00 | — |
| 2000 Proof | — | Value: 10.00 | | | | |

**DOLLAR** KM# 490 **Weight:** 31.1035 g. **Composition:** 0.9990 Silver 1. oz. ASW **Subject:** Kangaroo Bullion **Obverse:** Queen's portrait by Rank-Broadly right. **Reverse:** Kangaroo with Australian map background. **Edge:** Reeded. **Size:** 40 mm.

| Date | Mintage | F | VF | XF | Unc | BU |
|---|---|---|---|---|---|---|
| 2000 | — | — | — | — | 11.50 | — |
| 2000 Proof | — | Value: 23.50 | | | | |

**DOLLAR** KM# 493 **Weight:** 9.0000 g. **Composition:** Aluminum-Bronze **Subject:** Victoria Cross **Obverse:** Queen's head right. **Reverse:** The Victoria Cross. **Edge:** Reeded and plain sections. **Size:** 24.9 mm.

| Date | Mintage | F | VF | XF | Unc | BU |
|---|---|---|---|---|---|---|
| 2000 | — | — | — | — | 4.50 | — |

**DOLLAR** KM# 509 **Weight:** 31.1035 g. **Composition:** 0.9990 Silver 1. oz. ASW **Subject:** Proclamation Coins of Australia **Obverse:** Queen's head right. **Reverse:** British penny of 1797. **Edge:** Reeded. **Size:** 40 mm.

| Date | Mintage | F | VF | XF | Unc | BU |
|---|---|---|---|---|---|---|
| 2000 Proof | — | Value: 65.00 | | | | |

**DOLLAR** KM# 514 **Weight:** 31.1035 g. **Composition:** 0.9990 Silver 1. oz. ASW **Subject:** Millenium **Obverse:** Queen's head right. **Reverse:** Gold inlay earth and radiant sun as seen from the moon's surface. **Edge:** Reeded. **Size:** 40.4 mm.

| Date | Mintage | F | VF | XF | Unc | BU |
|---|---|---|---|---|---|---|
| 2000 Prooflike | 30,000 | — | — | — | 35.00 | — |

**DOLLAR** KM# 529.1 **Weight:** 9.0000 g. **Composition:** Aluminum-Bronze **Subject:** Olymphilex Exhibition **Obverse:** Queen's head right. **Reverse:** Denomination and Olympic logo. **Edge:** Plain **Edge Lettering:** Incuse SYDNEY. **Size:** 24.9 mm.

| Date | Mintage | F | VF | XF | Unc | BU |
|---|---|---|---|---|---|---|
| 2000 | — | — | — | — | 4.00 | — |

**DOLLAR** KM# 529.2 **Weight:** 9.0000 g. **Composition:** Aluminum-Bronze **Obverse:** Queen's head right. **Reverse:** Denomination and Olympic logo. **Edge:** Plain. **Edge Lettering:** Incuse CANBERRA. **Size:** 24.9 mm.

| Date | Mintage | F | VF | XF | Unc | BU |
|---|---|---|---|---|---|---|
| 2000 | — | — | — | — | 4.50 | — |

**DOLLAR** KM# 422 **Composition:** Aluminum-Bronze **Subject:** HMAS Sydney II **Obverse:** Queen's head right **Reverse:** Ship above denomination **Edge:** Reeded

| Date | Mintage | F | VF | XF | Unc | BU |
|---|---|---|---|---|---|---|
| 2000 | — | — | — | — | 5.00 | — |

**DOLLAR** KM# 422a **Weight:** 11.6600 g. **Composition:** 0.9990 Silver .3754 oz. ASW **Obverse:** Queen's head right **Reverse:** HMAS Sydney II above denomination

| Date | Mintage | F | VF | XF | Unc | BU |
|---|---|---|---|---|---|---|
| 2000 Proof | 20,000 | Value: 30.00 | | | | |

**DOLLAR** KM# 424 **Weight:** 31.1035 g. **Composition:** 0.9990 Silver 1.0000 oz. ASW **Obverse:** Queen's portrait **Reverse:** Dragon

| Date | Mintage | F | VF | XF | Unc | BU |
|---|---|---|---|---|---|---|
| 2000 | — | — | — | — | 25.00 | — |

**DOLLAR** KM# 479 **Weight:** 31.9700 g. **Composition:** 0.9990 Silver 1.0268 oz. ASW **Obverse:** Queen's head right **Reverse:** 2 Kookaburras back to back on branch

| Date | Mintage | F | VF | XF | Unc | BU |
|---|---|---|---|---|---|---|
| 2001 | — | — | — | — | 17.50 | — |

**DOLLAR** KM# 530 **Weight:** 9.0000 g. **Composition:** Aluminum-Bronze **Subject:** Army Centennial **Obverse:** Queen's head right. **Reverse:** Army crest. **Edge:** Reeded and plain sections. **Size:** 24.9 mm.

| Date | Mintage | F | VF | XF | Unc | BU |
|---|---|---|---|---|---|---|
| 2001 | — | — | — | — | 4.00 | — |

**DOLLAR** KM# 530a **Weight:** 11.6600 g. **Composition:** 0.9990 Silver .3745 oz. ASW **Subject:** Army Centennial **Obverse:** Queen's head right. **Reverse:** Army crest. **Edge:** Reeded and plain sections. **Size:** 24.9 mm.

| Date | Mintage | F | VF | XF | Unc | BU |
|---|---|---|---|---|---|---|
| 2001 Proof | 20,000 | Value: 20.00 | | | | |

**DOLLAR** KM# 531 **Weight:** 9.0000 g. **Composition:** Aluminum-Bronze **Subject:** 50th Anniversary - Air Force **Obverse:** Queen's head right. **Reverse:** Air Force badge. **Edge:** Reeded and plain sections. **Size:** 24.9 mm.

| Date | Mintage | F | VF | XF | Unc | BU |
|---|---|---|---|---|---|---|
| 2001 | — | — | — | — | 4.00 | — |

**DOLLAR** KM# 534.1 (KM534) **Weight:** 9.5000 g. **Composition:** Brass **Subject:** Centennial - Norfolk Island Federation **Obverse:** Queen's head right. **Reverse:** Star and ribbon design. **Edge:** Plain and reeded sections. **Size:** 24.9 mm.

| Date | Mintage | F | VF | XF | Unc | BU |
|---|---|---|---|---|---|---|
| 2001 | — | — | — | — | 4.00 | — |

**DOLLAR** **KM# 536** **Weight:** 31.1035 g. **Composition:** 0.9990 Silver 1. oz. ASW **Subject:** Year of the Snake **Obverse:** Queen's head right. **Reverse:** Snake with eggs. **Edge:** Reeded. **Size:** 40 mm.

| Date | Mintage | F | VF | XF | Unc | BU |
|---|---|---|---|---|---|---|
| 2001 | 300,000 | — | — | — | 25.00 | — |

**DOLLAR** **KM# 534.2** **Weight:** 9.5000 g. **Composition:** Aluminum-Bronze **Subject:** Centenary of Norfolk Island Federation **Obverse:** Queen's head right. **Reverse:** Multicolor star and ribbon design. **Edge:** Plain and reeded sections. **Size:** 24.9 mm.

| Date | Mintage | F | VF | XF | Unc | BU |
|---|---|---|---|---|---|---|
| 2001 Proof | — | Value: 13.50 | | | | |

**DOLLAR** **KM# 492** **Weight:** 9.0000 g. **Composition:** Aluminum-Bronze **Subject:** Centenary of Federation, 1901-2001 **Obverse:** Queen's head right. **Reverse:** Centenary of Federation logo. **Edge:** Reeded. **Size:** 25 mm.

| Date | Mintage | F | VF | XF | Unc | BU |
|---|---|---|---|---|---|---|
| 2001 | — | — | — | — | 4.25 | — |
| 2001 Proof | — | Value: 14.00 | | | | |

**2 DOLLARS** **KM# 101** **Composition:** Aluminum-Bronze **Subject:** Aboriginal Man

| Date | Mintage | F | VF | XF | Unc | BU |
|---|---|---|---|---|---|---|
| 1988 | 59,679,000 | — | — | — | 4.25 | — |
| 1988 Proof | 106,000 | Value: 7.50 | | | | |
| 1989 | — | — | — | — | 4.25 | — |
| 1989 Proof | — | Value: 7.50 | | | | |
| 1990 | 339,000 | — | — | — | 4.25 | — |
| 1990 Proof | — | Value: 7.50 | | | | |
| 1991 | — | — | — | — | 4.25 | — |
| 1991 Proof | — | Value: 7.50 | | | | |
| 1992 | — | — | — | — | 4.25 | — |
| 1992 Proof | 47,000 | Value: 7.50 | | | | |
| 1993 | — | — | — | — | 4.25 | — |
| 1993 Proof | — | Value: 7.50 | | | | |
| 1994 | — | — | — | — | 4.25 | — |
| 1994 Proof | — | Value: 7.50 | | | | |
| 1995 | — | — | — | — | 4.25 | — |
| 1995 Proof | — | Value: 7.50 | | | | |
| 1996 | — | — | — | — | 4.25 | — |
| 1996 Proof | — | Value: 7.50 | | | | |
| 1997 | — | — | — | — | 4.25 | — |
| 1997 Proof | — | Value: 7.50 | | | | |
| 1998 | — | — | — | — | 4.25 | — |
| 1998 Proof | — | Value: 7.50 | | | | |

**2 DOLLARS** **KM# 101a** **Weight:** 8.4300 g. **Composition:** 0.9250 Silver .2507 oz. ASW

| Date | Mintage | F | VF | XF | Unc | BU |
|---|---|---|---|---|---|---|
| 1988 Proof | 25,000 | Value: 14.50 | | | | |
| 1991 Proof | 23,000 | Value: 14.50 | | | | |

**Note:** In Proof sets only

**2 DOLLARS** **KM# 179** **Weight:** 62.2070 g. **Composition:** 0.9990 Silver 2.0000 oz. ASW **Subject:** Australian Kookaburra - On Stump

| Date | Mintage | F | VF | XF | Unc | BU |
|---|---|---|---|---|---|---|
| 1992 | — | — | — | — | 25.00 | — |
| 1992 Proof | 5,000 | Value: 85.00 | | | | |
| 1992 (gv) Proof | 500 | Value: 160 | | | | |
| 1992 (hd) Specimen | 1,000 | — | — | — | 125 | — |
| 1993 (dp) Specimen | 1,000 | — | — | — | 125 | — |
| 1993 (w) Specimen | 1,000 | — | — | — | 135 | — |
| 1993 (e) Specimen | 1,000 | — | — | — | 115 | — |
| 1993 (ta) Specimen | 1,000 | — | — | — | 115 | — |

**2 DOLLARS** **KM# 227** **Weight:** 62.2070 g. **Composition:** 0.9990 Silver 2.0000 oz. ASW **Reverse:** Kookaburra feeding nestling

| Date | Mintage | F | VF | XF | Unc | BU |
|---|---|---|---|---|---|---|
| 1992 Proof | — | Value: 85.00 | | | | |
| 1992 (aa) Proof | 500 | Value: 375 | | | | |
| 1993 | — | — | — | — | 25.00 | — |
| 1993 Proof | — | Value: 85.00 | | | | |

**2 DOLLARS** **KM# 230** **Weight:** 62.2070 g. **Composition:** 0.9990 Silver 2.0000 oz. ASW **Reverse:** Pair of Kookaburras on branch

| Date | Mintage | F | VF | XF | Unc | BU |
|---|---|---|---|---|---|---|
| 1993 | — | — | — | — | 25.00 | — |
| 1993 Proof | — | Value: 85.00 | | | | |
| 1993 (sm) Proof | 750 | Value: 200 | | | | |
| 1993 (ae) Proof | 500 | Value: 300 | | | | |
| 1994 | — | — | — | — | 25.00 | — |
| 1994 Proof | — | Value: 85.00 | | | | |
| 1994 (gv) Specimen | 1,000 | — | — | — | 275 | — |
| 1994 (ev) Proof | 1,500 | Value: 200 | | | | |
| 1994 (gv) Specimen | 1,500 | — | — | — | 180 | — |

**2 DOLLARS** **KM# 261** **Weight:** 62.2070 g. **Composition:** 0.9990 Silver 2.0000 oz. ASW **Reverse:** Kookaburra on branch

| Date | Mintage | F | VF | XF | Unc | BU |
|---|---|---|---|---|---|---|
| 1995 | — | — | — | — | 28.00 | — |
| 1995 (f1) Proof | 1,500 | Value: 120 | | | | |
| 1995 (f3) Proof | 1,500 | Value: 135 | | | | |
| 1995 (f7) Proof | 1,500 | Value: 100 | | | | |
| 1995 (rv) Proof | 1,500 | Value: 90.00 | | | | |

**2 DOLLARS** **KM# 290** **Weight:** 62.2070 g. **Composition:** 0.9990 Silver 2.0000 oz. ASW **Reverse:** Kookaburra in flight

| Date | Mintage | F | VF | XF | Unc | BU |
|---|---|---|---|---|---|---|
| 1995P Proof | 650 | Value: 65.00 | | | | |
| 1995P (ww) Proof | 1,300 | Value: 135 | | | | |
| 1995 (ge) Proof | 800 | Value: 135 | | | | |

**Note:** Privy marks on gold insert

| Date | Mintage | F | VF | XF | Unc | BU |
|---|---|---|---|---|---|---|
| 1996 | — | — | — | — | 22.50 | — |
| 1996 (h) Proof | 1,500 | Value: 70.00 | | | | |
| 1996 (d) Proof | 1,500 | Value: 115 | | | | |

**Note:** Privy marks on gold insert

| Date | Mintage | F | VF | XF | Unc | BU |
|---|---|---|---|---|---|---|
| 1996 (j) Proof | 1,500 | Value: 120 | | | | |

**Note:** Privy marks on gold insert

| Date | Mintage | F | VF | XF | Unc | BU |
|---|---|---|---|---|---|---|
| 1996 (sg) Proof | 1,500 | Value: 130 | | | | |
| Note: Privy marks on gold insert | | | | | | |
| 1996 (sp) Proof | 1,500 | Value: 135 | | | | |
| Note: Privy marks on gold insert | | | | | | |

**2 DOLLARS** **KM# 319 Weight:** 62.2070 g. **Composition:** 0.9990 Silver 2.0000 oz. ASW **Reverse:** Kookaburra and nestling. Similar to 1 Dollar, KM#318

| Date | Mintage | F | VF | XF | Unc | BU |
|---|---|---|---|---|---|---|
| 1997 | — | — | — | — | 25.00 | — |

**2 DOLLARS** **KM# 363 Weight:** 62.2070 g. **Composition:** 0.9990 Silver 2.0000 oz. ASW **Subject:** Kookaburra **Obverse:** Queen's portrait **Reverse:** Bird on fence

| Date | Mintage | F | VF | XF | Unc | BU |
|---|---|---|---|---|---|---|
| 1998 (1997) | — | — | — | — | 25.00 | — |
| 1997 Proof | 2,000 | Value: 110 | | | | |

**2 DOLLARS** **KM# 406 Composition:** Aluminum-Bronze **Obverse:** Queen's portrait by Rank-Broadley **Reverse:** Similar to KM#101

| Date | Mintage | F | VF | XF | Unc | BU |
|---|---|---|---|---|---|---|
| 1999 | — | — | — | — | 4.50 | — |
| 1999 Proof | — | Value: 11.50 | | | | |
| 2000 | — | — | — | — | 4.50 | — |
| 2000 Proof | — | Value: 11.50 | | | | |

**2 DOLLARS** **KM# 445 Weight:** 62.7700 g. **Composition:** 0.9990 Silver 2.0000 oz. ASW **Obverse:** Queen's head right **Reverse:** 2 Kookaburras on branch **Edge:** Interrupted reeding on edge

| Date | Mintage | F | VF | XF | Unc | BU |
|---|---|---|---|---|---|---|
| 1999 | — | — | — | — | 25.00 | — |

**2 DOLLARS** **KM# 486 Weight:** 13.3600 g. **Composition:** 0.9990 Silver .4291 oz. ASW **Series:** Masterpieces in Silver **Obverse:** Queen's head right. **Reverse:** Gold sovereign reverse design of KM#29. **Edge:** Reeded. **Size:** 28.5 mm.

| Date | Mintage | F | VF | XF | Unc | BU |
|---|---|---|---|---|---|---|
| 1999 Proof | 15,000 | Value: 22.00 | | | | |

**2 DOLLARS** **KM# 503 Weight:** 62.7700 g. **Composition:** 0.9990 Silver 2.0161 oz. ASW **Subject:** Year of the Rabbit **Obverse:** Queen's head right. **Reverse:** Rabbit. **Edge:** Reeded and plain sections. **Size:** 49.9 mm.

| Date | Mintage | F | VF | XF | Unc | BU |
|---|---|---|---|---|---|---|
| 1999 | — | — | — | — | 25.00 | — |
| 1999 Proof | 2,500 | Value: 95.00 | | | | |

**2 DOLLARS** **KM# 523 Weight:** 62.2070 g. **Composition:** 0.9990 Silver 2. oz. ASW **Series:** Dragons **Obverse:** Queen's head right. **Reverse:** Dragon. **Edge:** Segmented reeding. **Size:** 50.3 mm.

| Date | Mintage | F | VF | XF | Unc | BU |
|---|---|---|---|---|---|---|
| 2000 Proof | — | Value: 100 | | | | |

**2 DOLLARS** **KM# 500 Weight:** 8.5500 g. **Composition:** 0.9990 Silver .2746 oz. ASW **Series:** Masterpieces in Silver - 2000 Set **Obverse:** Queen's head right. **Reverse:** Queen Victoria's bust left. **Edge:** Reeded. **Size:** 20.5 mm.

| Date | Mintage | F | VF | XF | Unc | BU |
|---|---|---|---|---|---|---|
| 2000 Proof | 15,000 | Value: 27.50 | | | | |

**2 DOLLARS** **KM# 417.1 Weight:** 62.8500 g. **Composition:** 0.9990 Silver 2.0187 oz. ASW **Obverse:** Queen's head right **Reverse:** Kookaburra on branch

| Date | Mintage | F | VF | XF | Unc | BU |
|---|---|---|---|---|---|---|
| 2000(1999) | — | — | — | — | 25.00 | — |

**2 DOLLARS** **KM# 417.2 (KM417) Weight:** 62.8500 g. **Composition:** 0.9990 Silver 2.0187 oz. ASW **Subject:** USA State Quarters - 2000 **Obverse:** Queen's head right. **Reverse:** Kookaburra on branch with five state quarter designs added below. **Edge:** Reeded and plain sections.

| Date | Mintage | F | VF | XF | Unc | BU |
|---|---|---|---|---|---|---|
| 2000 (1999) (sq) | — | — | — | — | 150 | — |

**2 DOLLARS** **KM# 537 Weight:** 62.2070 g. **Composition:** 0.9990 Silver 2. oz. ASW **Subject:** Year of the Snake **Obverse:** Queen's head right. **Reverse:** Snake with eggs. **Edge:** Segmented reeding. **Size:** 50.3 mm.

| Date | Mintage | F | VF | XF | Unc | BU |
|---|---|---|---|---|---|---|
| 2001 | — | — | — | — | 35.00 | — |

**5 DOLLARS** **KM# 102 Composition:** Aluminum-Bronze **Subject:** Parliament House

| Date | Mintage | F | VF | XF | Unc | BU |
|---|---|---|---|---|---|---|
| 1988 | — | — | — | — | 5.00 | — |
| 1988 Proof | 80,000 | Value: 15.00 | | | | |

**5 DOLLARS** **KM# 102a Weight:** 35.7900 g. **Composition:** 0.9250 Silver 1.0645 oz. ASW

| Date | Mintage | F | VF | XF | Unc | BU |
|---|---|---|---|---|---|---|
| 1988 Proof | 25,000 | Value: 18.50 | | | | |

**5 DOLLARS** **KM# 117 Weight:** 1.5710 g. **Composition:** 0.9990 Gold .0500 oz. AGW **Subject:** Red Kangaroo **Obverse:** Elizabeth II

| Date | Mintage | F | VF | XF | Unc | BU |
|---|---|---|---|---|---|---|
| 1989 Proof | 2,200 | Value: 30.00 | | | | |
| 1990 | Est. 200,000 | — | — | — | BV+ 35% | — |

**5 DOLLARS** **KM# 122 Weight:** 1.5710 g. **Composition:** 0.9990 Platinum .0500 oz. APW **Note:** Similar to 100 Dollars, KM#126.

| Date | Mintage | F | VF | XF | Unc | BU |
|---|---|---|---|---|---|---|
| 1989 Proof | 2,400 | Value: 38.00 | | | | |
| 1990 Proof | — | Value: 38.00 | | | | |

**5 DOLLARS** **KM# 138 Weight:** 31.1030 g. **Composition:** 0.9990 Silver 1.0000 oz. ASW **Reverse:** Australian Kookaburra **Note:** Special coin fair issues exist.

| Date | Mintage | F | VF | XF | Unc | BU |
|---|---|---|---|---|---|---|
| 1990 Proof | 22,000 | Value: 27.50 | | | | |
| 1991 | 300,000 | — | — | — | 11.50 | — |
| 1991 Proof | — | Value: 27.50 | | | | |

**5 DOLLARS** **KM# 134 Composition:** Aluminum-Bronze **Subject:** ANZAC Memorial

| Date | Mintage | F | VF | XF | Unc | BU |
|---|---|---|---|---|---|---|
| 1990 | — | — | — | — | 5.50 | — |
| 1990 Proof | — | Value: 32.50 | | | | |

**5 DOLLARS** **KM# 140 Weight:** 1.5710 g. **Composition:** 0.9990 Gold .0500 oz. AGW **Reverse:** Gray Kangaroo

| Date | Mintage | F | VF | XF | Unc | BU |
|---|---|---|---|---|---|---|
| 1990 Proof | 7,000 | Value: 28.00 | | | | |
| 1991 | 200,000 | — | — | — | BV+35% | — |

**5 DOLLARS** **KM# 145 Weight:** 1.5710 g. **Composition:** 0.9990 Platinum .0500 oz. APW **Obverse:** Similar to 100 Dollars, KM#149. **Reverse:** Koala

| Date | Mintage | F | VF | XF | Unc | BU |
|---|---|---|---|---|---|---|
| 1990 Proof | 2,500 | Value: 38.00 | | | | |
| 1991 | 20,000 | — | — | — | BV+ 35% | — |
| 1991 Proof | 1,000 | Value: 38.00 | | | | |

**5 DOLLARS** **KM# 189** **Weight:** 31.1030 g. **Composition:** 0.9990 Silver 1.0000 oz. ASW **Reverse:** Australian Kookaburra

| Date | Mintage | F | VF | XF | Unc | BU |
|---|---|---|---|---|---|---|
| 1990 | 300,000 | — | — | — | 15.00 | — |

**5 DOLLARS** **KM# 165** **Weight:** 1.5710 g. **Composition:** 0.9990 Gold .0500 oz. AGW **Subject:** Common Wallaroo **Obverse:** Elizabeth II **Reverse:** Similar to 100 Dollars, KM#169 **Note:** 1992 (ae) previously listed here is now KM#389.

| Date | Mintage | F | VF | XF | Unc | BU |
|---|---|---|---|---|---|---|
| 1991 Proof | 3,525 | Value: 30.00 | | | | |
| 1992 | 200,000 | — | — | — | BV+ 35% | — |

**5 DOLLARS** **KM# 389** **Weight:** 1.5710 g. **Composition:** 0.9990 Gold .0500 oz. AGW **Obverse:** Queen's portrait **Reverse:** Nail-tailed Wallaby **Note:** Similar to 25 Dollars, KM#391.

| Date | Mintage | F | VF | XF | Unc | BU |
|---|---|---|---|---|---|---|
| 1992 (ae) Proof | 500 | Value: 50.00 | | | | |

**5 DOLLARS** **KM# 170** **Weight:** 1.5710 g. **Composition:** 0.9990 Platinum .0500 oz. APW **Subject:** Koala **Obverse:** Elizabeth II **Reverse:** Similar to 100 Dollars, KM#174

| Date | Mintage | F | VF | XF | Unc | BU |
|---|---|---|---|---|---|---|
| 1992 | 20,000 | — | — | — | BV+ 35% | — |

**5 DOLLARS** **KM# 190** **Composition:** Aluminum-Bronze **Subject:** Australian Role in Space Industry

| Date | Mintage | F | VF | XF | Unc | BU |
|---|---|---|---|---|---|---|
| 1992 | 218,000 | — | — | — | 6.00 | — |
| 1992 Proof | 25,000 | Value: 20.00 | | | | |

**5 DOLLARS** **KM# 191** **Weight:** 1.5710 g. **Composition:** 0.9990 Platinum .0500 oz. APW **Obverse:** Similar to 100 Dollars, KM#195

| Date | Mintage | F | VF | XF | Unc | BU |
|---|---|---|---|---|---|---|
| 1993 | Est. 20,000 | — | — | — | BV+ 35% | — |

**5 DOLLARS** **KM# 213** **Weight:** 35.7900 g. **Composition:** 0.9250 Silver 1.0645 oz. ASW **Subject:** Aboriginal Exploration

| Date | Mintage | F | VF | XF | Unc | BU |
|---|---|---|---|---|---|---|
| 1993 Proof | 20,000 | Value: 22.50 | | | | |

**5 DOLLARS** **KM# 214** **Weight:** 35.7900 g. **Composition:** 0.9250 Silver 1.0645 oz. ASW **Subject:** Abel Tasman

| Date | Mintage | F | VF | XF | Unc | BU |
|---|---|---|---|---|---|---|
| 1993 Proof | 20,000 | Value: 22.50 | | | | |

**5 DOLLARS** **KM# 215** **Weight:** 35.7900 g. **Composition:** 0.9250 Silver 1.0645 oz. ASW **Subject:** Captain James Cook

| Date | Mintage | F | VF | XF | Unc | BU |
|---|---|---|---|---|---|---|
| 1993 Proof | 20,000 | Value: 22.50 | | | | |

**5 DOLLARS** **KM# 216** **Weight:** 35.7900 g. **Composition:** 0.9250 Silver 1.0645 oz. ASW **Subject:** Matthew Flinders

| Date | Mintage | F | VF | XF | Unc | BU |
|---|---|---|---|---|---|---|
| 1993 Proof | 20,000 | Value: 22.50 | | | | |

**5 DOLLARS** **KM# 217** **Weight:** 35.7900 g. **Composition:** 0.9250 Silver 1.0645 oz. ASW **Subject:** W. Lawson, G. Blayland and W.C. Wentworth

| Date | Mintage | F | VF | XF | Unc | BU |
|---|---|---|---|---|---|---|
| 1993 Proof | 20,000 | Value: 22.50 | | | | |

**5 DOLLARS** **KM# 233** **Weight:** 1.5710 g. **Composition:** 0.9990 Gold .0500 oz. AGW **Subject:** Whiptail Wallaby **Obverse:** Elizabeth II **Reverse:** Whiptail Wallaby

| Date | Mintage | F | VF | XF | Unc | BU |
|---|---|---|---|---|---|---|
| 1993 Proof | — | Value: 35.00 | | | | |
| 1994 | — | — | — | — | BV+ 35% | — |

**5 DOLLARS** **KM# 224** **Ring Composition:** Stainless Steel **Center Composition:** Aluminum-Bronze **Subject:** Women's Enfranchisement

| Date | Mintage | F | VF | XF | Unc | BU |
|---|---|---|---|---|---|---|
| 1994 | 250,000 | — | — | — | 9.00 | — |
| 1994 Proof | 23,000 | Value: 25.00 | | | | |

**5 DOLLARS** **KM# 224a** **Composition:** Aluminum-Bronze

| Date | Mintage | F | VF | XF | Unc | BU |
|---|---|---|---|---|---|---|
| 1994 Proof | 2,500 | Value: 35.00 | | | | |

**5 DOLLARS** **KM# 241** **Weight:** 1.5710 g. **Composition:** 0.9990 Gold .0500 oz. AGW **Reverse:** Red Kangaroo

| Date | Mintage | F | VF | XF | Unc | BU |
|---|---|---|---|---|---|---|
| 1994 Proof | — | Value: 35.00 | | | | |
| 1995 | 200,000 | — | — | — | BV+ 35% | — |

**5 DOLLARS** **KM# 249** **Weight:** 1.5710 g. **Composition:** 0.9990 Platinum .0500 oz. APW **Reverse:** Koala Mother and Baby

| Date | Mintage | F | VF | XF | Unc | BU |
|---|---|---|---|---|---|---|
| 1994 | 20,000 | — | — | — | BV+35% | — |

**5 DOLLARS** **KM# 264** **Weight:** 31.1040 g. **Composition:** 0.9250 Silver 1.0870 oz. ASW **Subject:** Explorer - Ludwig Leichhardt **Obverse:** Queen Elizabeth portrait

| Date | Mintage | F | VF | XF | Unc | BU |
|---|---|---|---|---|---|---|
| 1994 Proof | Est. 20,000 | Value: 18.50 | | | | |

**5 DOLLARS** **KM# 265** **Weight:** 31.1040 g. **Composition:** 0.9250 Silver 1.0870 oz. ASW **Subject:** Explorer - Charles Sturt

| Date | Mintage | F | VF | XF | Unc | BU |
|---|---|---|---|---|---|---|
| 1994 Proof | Est. 20,000 | Value: 18.50 | | | | |

**5 DOLLARS** KM# 266 **Weight:** 31.1040 g. **Composition:** 0.9250 Silver 1.0870 oz. ASW **Subject:** Explorer - Sir John Forrest

| Date | Mintage | F | VF | XF | Unc | BU |
|---|---|---|---|---|---|---|
| 1994 Proof | Est. 20,000 | Value: 18.50 | | | | |

**5 DOLLARS** KM# 267 **Weight:** 31.1040 g. **Composition:** 0.9250 Silver 1.0870 oz. ASW **Subject:** Explorer - John McDouall Stuart

| Date | Mintage | F | VF | XF | Unc | BU |
|---|---|---|---|---|---|---|
| 1994 Proof | Est. 20,000 | Value: 18.00 | | | | |

**5 DOLLARS** KM# 268 **Weight:** 31.1040 g. **Composition:** 0.9250 Silver 1.0870 oz. ASW **Subject:** Explorer - Sir Douglas Mawson

| Date | Mintage | F | VF | XF | Unc | BU |
|---|---|---|---|---|---|---|
| 1994 Proof | Est. 20,000 | Value: 18.00 | | | | |

**5 DOLLARS** KM# 278 **Weight:** 1.5710 g. **Composition:** 0.9990 Platinum .0500 oz. APW **Reverse:** Koala in fork of tree

| Date | Mintage | F | VF | XF | Unc | BU |
|---|---|---|---|---|---|---|
| 1994 Proof | — | Value: 40.00 | | | | |
| 1995 | — | — | — | — | BV+35% | — |

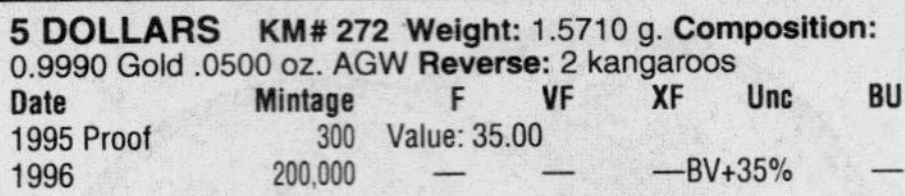

**5 DOLLARS** KM# 272 **Weight:** 1.5710 g. **Composition:** 0.9990 Gold .0500 oz. AGW **Reverse:** 2 kangaroos

| Date | Mintage | F | VF | XF | Unc | BU |
|---|---|---|---|---|---|---|
| 1995 Proof | 300 | Value: 35.00 | | | | |
| 1996 | 200,000 | — | — | — | BV+35% | — |

**5 DOLLARS** KM# 283 **Weight:** 1.5710 g. **Composition:** 0.9990 Platinum .0500 oz. APW **Reverse:** Baby koala on branch

| Date | Mintage | F | VF | XF | Unc | BU |
|---|---|---|---|---|---|---|
| 1995 Proof | 200 | Value: 40.00 | | | | |
| 1996 | 20,000 | — | — | — | BV+35% | — |

**5 DOLLARS** KM# 303 **Weight:** 35.7900 g. **Composition:** 0.9250 Silver 1.0645 oz. ASW **Subject:** The Gold Rush Era

| Date | Mintage | F | VF | XF | Unc | BU |
|---|---|---|---|---|---|---|
| 1995 Proof | 20,000 | Value: 17.50 | | | | |

**5 DOLLARS** KM# 304 **Weight:** 35.7900 g. **Composition:** 0.9250 Silver 1.0645 oz. ASW **Subject:** Cobb and Co. 1853, Stagecoach

| Date | Mintage | F | VF | XF | Unc | BU |
|---|---|---|---|---|---|---|
| 1995 Proof | 20,000 | Value: 17.50 | | | | |

**5 DOLLARS** KM# 305 **Weight:** 35.7900 g. **Composition:** 0.9250 Silver 1.0645 oz. ASW **Subject:** Elizabeth MacArthur, 1766-1850 - Sheep

| Date | Mintage | F | VF | XF | Unc | BU |
|---|---|---|---|---|---|---|
| 1995 Proof | 20,000 | Value: 17.50 | | | | |

**5 DOLLARS** KM# 306 **Weight:** 35.7900 g. **Composition:** 0.9250 Silver 1.0645 oz. ASW **Subject:** Col. William Light, 1786-1839 - City Plan

| Date | Mintage | F | VF | XF | Unc | BU |
|---|---|---|---|---|---|---|
| 1995 Proof | 20,000 | Value: 17.50 | | | | |

**5 DOLLARS** KM# 307 **Weight:** 35.7900 g. **Composition:** 0.9250 Silver 1.0645 oz. ASW **Subject:** Charles Todd, 1827-1910 - Telegraph Line

| Date | Mintage | F | VF | XF | Unc | BU |
|---|---|---|---|---|---|---|
| 1995 Proof | 20,000 | Value: 17.50 | | | | |

**5 DOLLARS** KM# 311 **Ring Composition:** Stainless Steel **Center Composition:** Aluminum-Bronze **Subject:** Sir Donald Bradman - Cricket Player

| Date | Mintage | F | VF | XF | Unc | BU |
|---|---|---|---|---|---|---|
| 1996 | 500,000 | — | — | — | 9.00 | — |
| 1997 | — | — | — | — | 9.00 | — |

**5 DOLLARS** KM# 312 **Composition:** Aluminum-Bronze **Subject:** Sir Donald Bradman Full Length Cricket Player

| Date | Mintage | F | VF | XF | Unc | BU |
|---|---|---|---|---|---|---|
| 1996 Proof | 23,000 | Value: 40.00 | | | | |

**5 DOLLARS** KM# 320 **Weight:** 1.5710 g. **Composition:** 0.9990 Gold .0500 oz. AGW **Obverse:** Queen's portrait **Reverse:** Kangaroo bounding right

| Date | Mintage | F | VF | XF | Unc | BU |
|---|---|---|---|---|---|---|
| 1996P Proof | — | Value: 50.00 | | | | |

**Note:** In proof sets only

**5 DOLLARS** **KM# 328** **Weight:** 35.7900 g. **Composition:** 0.9250 Silver 1.0645 oz. ASW **Subject:** Stockman **Obverse:** Queen's portrait **Reverse:** Cowboy with whip

| Date | Mintage | F | VF | XF | Unc | BU |
|---|---|---|---|---|---|---|
| 1996 Proof | 20,000 | Value: 17.50 | | | | |

**5 DOLLARS** **KM# 329** **Weight:** 35.7900 g. **Composition:** 0.9250 Silver 1.0645 oz. ASW **Subject:** Horse Racing **Obverse:** Queen's portrait **Reverse:** Horse racing scene

| Date | Mintage | F | VF | XF | Unc | BU |
|---|---|---|---|---|---|---|
| 1996 Proof | 20,000 | Value: 17.50 | | | | |

**5 DOLLARS** **KM# 330** **Weight:** 35.7900 g. **Composition:** 0.9250 Silver 1.0645 oz. ASW **Subject:** Dame Nellie Melba **Obverse:** Queen's portrait **Reverse:** Melba's portrait

| Date | Mintage | F | VF | XF | Unc | BU |
|---|---|---|---|---|---|---|
| 1996 Proof | 20,000 | Value: 17.50 | | | | |

**5 DOLLARS** **KM# 331** **Weight:** 35.7900 g. **Composition:** 0.9250 Silver 1.0645 oz. ASW **Subject:** Tom Roberts **Obverse:** Queen's portrait **Reverse:** Painter and painting

| Date | Mintage | F | VF | XF | Unc | BU |
|---|---|---|---|---|---|---|
| 1996 Proof | 20,000 | Value: 17.50 | | | | |

**5 DOLLARS** **KM# 332** **Weight:** 35.7900 g. **Composition:** 0.9250 Silver 1.0645 oz. ASW **Subject:** Henry Lawson **Obverse:** Queen's portrait **Reverse:** Author's portrait and letter to friends

| Date | Mintage | F | VF | XF | Unc | BU |
|---|---|---|---|---|---|---|
| 1996 Proof | 20,000 | Value: 17.50 | | | | |

**5 DOLLARS** **KM# 338** **Weight:** 1.5710 g. **Composition:** 0.9999 Gold .0500 oz. AGW **Subject:** Kangaroo **Obverse:** Queen's portrait **Reverse:** Kangaroo bounding right

| Date | Mintage | F | VF | XF | Unc | BU |
|---|---|---|---|---|---|---|
| 1997 | 200,000 | — | — | — | BV+ 35% | — |
| 1997 Proof | — | Value: 30.00 | | | | |

**5 DOLLARS** **KM# 344** **Weight:** 1.5710 g. **Composition:** 0.9995 Platinum .0500 oz. APW **Subject:** Koalas **Obverse:** Queen's portrait **Reverse:** Cudding koalas

| Date | Mintage | F | VF | XF | Unc | BU |
|---|---|---|---|---|---|---|
| 1997 | 20,000 | — | — | — | BV+ 35% | — |
| 1997 Proof | — | Value: 40.00 | | | | |

**5 DOLLARS** **KM# 356** **Composition:** Aluminum-Bronze **Subject:** Sydney 2000 **Obverse:** Queen's portrait **Reverse:** Runner

| Date | Mintage | F | VF | XF | Unc | BU |
|---|---|---|---|---|---|---|
| 2000 (1997) | — | — | — | — | 9.00 | — |

**5 DOLLARS** **KM# 357** **Composition:** Aluminum-Bronze **Series:** Sydney 2000 Olympics **Obverse:** Queen's portrait **Reverse:** Gymnast

| Date | Mintage | F | VF | XF | Unc | BU |
|---|---|---|---|---|---|---|
| 2000 (1997) | — | — | — | — | 8.00 | — |

**5 DOLLARS** **KM# 358** **Composition:** Aluminum-Bronze **Series:** Sydney 2000 Olympics **Obverse:** Queen's portrait **Reverse:** Sailors

| Date | Mintage | F | VF | XF | Unc | BU |
|---|---|---|---|---|---|---|
| 2000 (1997) | — | — | — | — | 9.00 | — |

**5 DOLLARS** **KM# 359** **Composition:** Aluminum-Bronze **Subject:** Sydney 2000 **Obverse:** Queen's portrait **Reverse:** Archer

| Date | Mintage | F | VF | XF | Unc | BU |
|---|---|---|---|---|---|---|
| 2000 (1997) | — | — | — | — | 9.00 | — |

**5 DOLLARS** **KM# 360** **Composition:** Aluminum-Bronze **Series:** Sydney 2000 Olympics **Obverse:** Queen's portrait **Reverse:** Field hockey player

| Date | Mintage | F | VF | XF | Unc | BU |
|---|---|---|---|---|---|---|
| 2000 (1997) | — | — | — | — | 8.00 | — |

**5 DOLLARS** **KM# 361** **Composition:** Aluminum-Bronze **Series:** Sydney 2000 Olympics **Obverse:** Queen's portrait **Reverse:** Power lifter

| Date | Mintage | F | VF | XF | Unc | BU |
|---|---|---|---|---|---|---|
| 2000 (1997) | — | — | — | — | 8.00 | — |

**5 DOLLARS** **KM# 544** **Weight:** 35.7900 g. **Composition:** 0.9250 Silver 1.0644 oz. ASW **Series:** Masterpieces of Transportation **Obverse:** Queen's head right. **Reverse:** Camel pack train. **Edge:** Reeded. **Size:** 38.9 mm.

| Date | Mintage | F | VF | XF | Unc | BU |
|---|---|---|---|---|---|---|
| 1997 Proof | 10,000 | Value: 25.00 | | | | |

**5 DOLLARS** **KM# 545** **Weight:** 35.7900 g. **Composition:** 0.9250 Silver 1.0644 oz. ASW **Series:** Masterpieces of Transportation **Obverse:** Queen's head right. **Reverse:** Riverboat. **Edge:** Reeded. **Size:** 38.9 mm.

| Date | Mintage | F | VF | XF | Unc | BU |
|---|---|---|---|---|---|---|
| 1997 Proof | 10,000 | Value: 25.00 | | | | |

**5 DOLLARS** **KM# 546** **Weight:** 35.7900 g. **Composition:** 0.9250 Silver 1.0644 oz. ASW **Series:** Masterpieces of Transportation **Obverse:** Queen's head right. **Reverse:** Steam locomotive. **Edge:** Reeded. **Size:** 38.9 mm.

| Date | Mintage | F | VF | XF | Unc | BU |
|---|---|---|---|---|---|---|
| 1997 Proof | 10,000 | Value: 25.00 | | | | |

**5 DOLLARS** **KM# 547** **Weight:** 35.7900 g. **Composition:** 0.9250 Silver 1.0644 oz. ASW **Series:** Masterpieces of Transportation **Obverse:** Queen's head right. **Reverse:** Ox drawn wagons. **Edge:** Reeded. **Size:** 38.9 mm.

| Date | Mintage | F | VF | XF | Unc | BU |
|---|---|---|---|---|---|---|
| 1997 Proof | 10,000 | Value: 25.00 | | | | |

**5 DOLLARS** **KM# 548** **Weight:** 35.7900 g. **Composition:** 0.9250 Silver 1.0644 oz. ASW **Series:** Masterpieces of Transportation **Obverse:** Queen's head right. **Reverse:** Steam tractor. **Edge:** Reeded. **Size:** 38.9 mm.

| Date | Mintage | F | VF | XF | Unc | BU |
|---|---|---|---|---|---|---|
| 1997 Proof | 10,000 | Value: 25.00 | | | | |

**5 DOLLARS** **KM# 386** **Composition:** Aluminum-Bronze **Subject:** 70th Anniversary - Royal Flying Doctor **Obverse:** Queen's portrait **Reverse:** Radio dispatcher and airplane

| Date | Mintage | F | VF | XF | Unc | BU |
|---|---|---|---|---|---|---|
| 1998 Proof | Est. 20,000 | Value: 18.50 | | | | |

**5 DOLLARS** **KM# 368** **Composition:** Aluminum-Bronze **Series:** Sydney 2000 Olympics **Obverse:** Queen's portrait **Reverse:** Cyclist

| Date | Mintage | F | VF | XF | Unc | BU |
|---|---|---|---|---|---|---|
| 2000 (1998) | — | — | — | — | 9.00 | — |

**5 DOLLARS** **KM# 369** **Composition:** Aluminum-Bronze **Series:** Sydney 2000 Olympics **Obverse:** Queen's portrait **Reverse:** Soccer player

| Date | Mintage | F | VF | XF | Unc | BU |
|---|---|---|---|---|---|---|
| 2000 (1998) | — | — | — | — | 9.00 | — |

**5 DOLLARS** **KM# 370** **Composition:** Aluminum-Bronze **Series:** Sydney 2000 Olympics **Obverse:** Queen's portrait **Reverse:** Triathalon swimmer

| Date | Mintage | F | VF | XF | Unc | BU |
|---|---|---|---|---|---|---|
| 2000 (1998) | — | — | — | — | 9.00 | — |

**5 DOLLARS** **KM# 371** **Weight:** 31.6350 g. **Composition:** 0.9990 Silver 1.0161 oz. ASW **Series:** Sydney 2000 Olympics **Obverse:** Queen's portrait **Reverse:** Australian map above multicolor logo

| Date | Mintage | F | VF | XF | Unc | BU |
|---|---|---|---|---|---|---|
| 2000 (1998) Proof | Est. 100,000 | Value: 40.00 | | | | |

**5 DOLLARS** **KM# 372** **Weight:** 31.6350 g. **Composition:** 0.9990 Silver 1.0161 oz. ASW **Series:** Sydney 2000 Olympics **Obverse:** Queen's portrait **Reverse:** 2 Great White sharks

| Date | Mintage | F | VF | XF | Unc | BU |
|---|---|---|---|---|---|---|
| 2000 (1998) Proof | Est. 100,000 | Value: 45.00 | | | | |

**5 DOLLARS** **KM# 374** **Ring Composition:** Stainless Steel **Center Composition:** Aluminum-Bronze **Subject:** 70 Years - Royal Flying Doctor Service **Obverse:** Queen's portrait **Reverse:** Insignia above bi-plane

| Date | Mintage | F | VF | XF | Unc | BU |
|---|---|---|---|---|---|---|
| 1998 | — | — | — | — | 10.00 | — |

**5 DOLLARS** **KM# 375** **Composition:** Aluminum-Bronze **Series:** Sydney 2000 Olympics **Obverse:** Queen's portrait **Reverse:** 2 handball players

| Date | Mintage | F | VF | XF | Unc | BU |
|---|---|---|---|---|---|---|
| 2000 (1998) | — | — | — | — | 9.00 | — |

**5 DOLLARS** **KM# 376** **Composition:** Aluminum-Bronze **Series:** Sydney 2000 Olympics **Obverse:** Queen's portrait **Reverse:** 2 wrrestlers

| Date | Mintage | F | VF | XF | Unc | BU |
|---|---|---|---|---|---|---|
| 2000 (1998) | — | — | — | — | 9.00 | — |

**5 DOLLARS** **KM# 377** **Composition:** Aluminum-Bronze **Series:** Sydney 2000 Olympics **Obverse:** Queen's portrait **Reverse:** Canoeing

| Date | Mintage | F | VF | XF | Unc | BU |
|---|---|---|---|---|---|---|
| 2000 (1998) | — | — | — | — | 9.00 | — |

**5 DOLLARS** **KM# 378** **Composition:** Aluminum-Bronze **Series:** Sydney 2000 Olympics **Obverse:** Queen's portrait **Reverse:** Softball player at bat

| Date | Mintage | F | VF | XF | Unc | BU |
|---|---|---|---|---|---|---|
| 2000 (1998) | — | — | — | — | 9.00 | — |

**5 DOLLARS** **KM# 379** **Weight:** 31.6350 g. **Composition:** 0.9990 Silver 1.0161 oz. ASW **Series:** Sydney 2000 Olympics **Obverse:** Queen's portrait **Reverse:** Frill-necked lizard

| Date | Mintage | F | VF | XF | Unc | BU |
|---|---|---|---|---|---|---|
| 2000 (1998) Proof | Est. 100,000 | Value: 42.50 | | | | |

**5 DOLLARS** **KM# 380** **Weight:** 31.6350 g. **Composition:** 0.9990 Silver 1.0161 oz. ASW **Series:** Sydney 2000 Olympics **Obverse:** Queen's portrait **Reverse:** 9 Australian faces of different races

| Date | Mintage | F | VF | XF | Unc | BU |
|---|---|---|---|---|---|---|
| 2000 (1998) Proof | Est. 100,000 | Value: 40.00 | | | | |

**5 DOLLARS** **KM# 381** **Weight:** 31.6350 g. **Composition:** 0.9990 Silver 1.0161 oz. ASW **Series:** Sydney 2000 Olympics **Obverse:** Queen's portrait **Reverse:** 2 dancing figures in dream circle, Olympic logo

| Date | Mintage | F | VF | XF | Unc | BU |
|---|---|---|---|---|---|---|
| 2000 (1998) Proof | Est. 100,000 | Value: 40.00 | | | | |

**5 DOLLARS** **KM# 382** **Weight:** 31.6350 g. **Composition:** 0.9990 Silver 1.0161 oz. ASW **Series:** Sydney 2000 Olympics **Obverse:** Queen's portrait **Reverse:** Kangaroo in circle of grass trees above games logo

| Date | Mintage | F | VF | XF | Unc | BU |
|---|---|---|---|---|---|---|
| 2000 (1998) Proof | Est. 100,000 | Value: 42.50 | | | | |

**5 DOLLARS** **KM# 407** **Composition:** Brass **Series:** Sydney 2000 Olympics **Obverse:** Queen's portrait **Reverse:** 2 basketball players

| Date | Mintage | F | VF | XF | Unc | BU |
|---|---|---|---|---|---|---|
| 2000 (1999) | — | — | — | — | 8.00 | — |

**5 DOLLARS** **KM# 408** **Composition:** Brass **Series:** Sydney 2000 Olympics **Obverse:** Queen's portrait **Reverse:** Tae Kwon Do competitor

| Date | Mintage | F | VF | XF | Unc | BU |
|---|---|---|---|---|---|---|
| 2000 (1999) | — | — | — | — | 8.00 | — |

**5 DOLLARS** **KM# 409** **Composition:** Brass **Series:** Sydney 2000 Olympics **Obverse:** Queen's portrait **Reverse:** Tennis player

| Date | Mintage | F | VF | XF | Unc | BU |
|---|---|---|---|---|---|---|
| 2000 (1999) | — | — | — | — | 8.00 | — |

**5 DOLLARS** **KM# 418** **Weight:** 20.0000 g. **Composition:** Brass **Series:** Sydney 2000 Olympics **Obverse:** Queen's head right **Reverse:** Shooter with shotgun

| Date | Mintage | F | VF | XF | Unc | BU |
|---|---|---|---|---|---|---|
| 2000 (1999) | — | — | — | — | 8.00 | — |

**5 DOLLARS** **KM# 419** **Weight:** 20.0000 g. **Composition:** Brass **Series:** Sydney 2000 Olympics **Obverse:** Queen's head right **Reverse:** Table tennis player

| Date | Mintage | F | VF | XF | Unc | BU |
|---|---|---|---|---|---|---|
| 2000 (1999) | — | — | — | — | 8.00 | — |

**5 DOLLARS** **KM# 420** **Weight:** 20.0000 g. **Composition:** Brass **Series:** Sydney 2000 Olympics **Obverse:** Queen's head right **Reverse:** Fencer in action

| Date | Mintage | F | VF | XF | Unc | BU |
|---|---|---|---|---|---|---|
| 2000 (1999) | — | — | — | — | 8.00 | — |

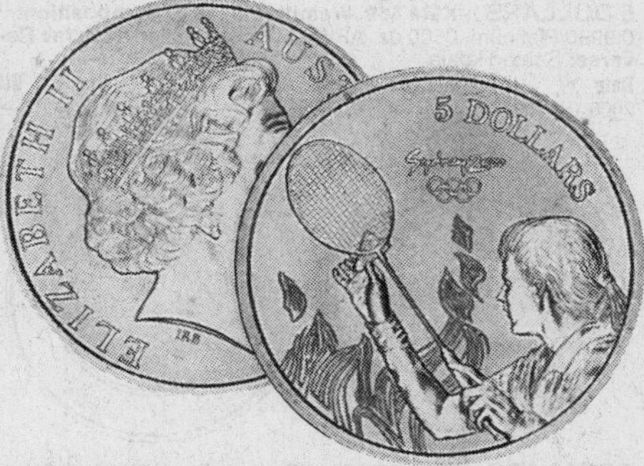


**5 DOLLARS** **KM# 421** **Weight:** 20.0000 g. **Composition:** Brass **Series:** Sydney 2000 Olympics **Obverse:** Queen's head right **Reverse:** Badminton player

| Date | Mintage | F | VF | XF | Unc | BU |
|---|---|---|---|---|---|---|
| 2000 (1999) | — | — | — | — | 9.00 | — |

**5 DOLLARS** **KM# 438** **Weight:** 31.6350 g. **Composition:** 0.9990 Silver 1.0161 oz. ASW **Series:** Sydney 2000 Olympics **Obverse:** Queen's head right **Reverse:** 2 emu's with eggs and chicks **Edge:** Reeded

| Date | Mintage | F | VF | XF | Unc | BU |
|---|---|---|---|---|---|---|
| 2000 (1999) Proof | 100,000 | Value: 40.00 | | | | |

**5 DOLLARS** **KM# 439** **Weight:** 31.6350 g. **Composition:** 0.9990 Silver 1.0161 oz. ASW **Series:** Sydney 2000 Olympics **Obverse:** Queen's head right **Reverse:** Koala in tree

| Date | Mintage | F | VF | XF | Unc | BU |
|---|---|---|---|---|---|---|
| 2000 (1999) Proof | 100,000 | Value: 40.00 | | | | |

**5 DOLLARS** **KM# 448** **Weight:** 1.5710 g. **Composition:** 0.9990 Gold .0505 oz. AGW **Obverse:** Queen's portrait right **Reverse:** Kangaroo facing left **Edge:** Reeded

| Date | Mintage | F | VF | XF | Unc | BU |
|---|---|---|---|---|---|---|
| 1999 | 200,000 | — | — | — | 30.00 | — |

**5 DOLLARS** **KM# 456** **Weight:** 1.5710 g. **Composition:** 0.9990 Platinum .0500 oz. APW **Obverse:** Queen's head right **Reverse:** Koala on log

| Date | Mintage | F | VF | XF | Unc | BU |
|---|---|---|---|---|---|---|
| 1999 | 20,000 | — | — | — | 40.00 | — |

**5 DOLLARS** **KM# 425** **Weight:** 1.5710 g. **Composition:** 0.9999 Gold .0500 oz. AGW **Subject:** Year of the Rabbit **Obverse:** Queen's portrait **Reverse:** Rabbit **Note:** Similar to 100 Dollars, KM#428.

| Date | Mintage | F | VF | XF | Unc | BU |
|---|---|---|---|---|---|---|
| 1999 | Est. 100,000 | — | — | — | 35.00 | — |

**5 DOLLARS** **KM# 464** **Weight:** 1.5710 g. **Composition:** 0.9990 Gold .0505 oz. AGW **Obverse:** Queen's head right **Reverse:** 2 kangaroos bounding left

| Date | Mintage | F | VF | XF | Unc | BU |
|---|---|---|---|---|---|---|
| 2000 | — | — | — | — | 30.00 | — |

**5 DOLLARS** **KM# 469** **Weight:** 1.5710 g. **Composition:** 0.9990 Platinum .0500 oz. APW **Obverse:** Queen's portrait **Reverse:** Seated koala

| Date | Mintage | F | VF | XF | Unc | BU |
|---|---|---|---|---|---|---|
| 2000 | — | — | — | — | 40.00 | — |

**5 DOLLARS** **KM# 478** **Ring Composition:** Stainless Steel **Center Weight:** 10.5200 g. **Center Composition:** Aluminum-Bronze **Subject:** Phar Lap **Obverse:** Queen's head right within ring **Reverse:** Jockey atop Phar Lap racing right **Edge:** Plain, 24-sided

| Date | Mintage | F | VF | XF | Unc | BU |
|---|---|---|---|---|---|---|
| 2000 | — | — | — | — | 8.50 | — |

**5 DOLLARS** **KM# 510** **Weight:** 28.0000 g. **Composition:** Aluminum-Bronze **Subject:** Phar Lap **Obverse:** Queen's head right. **Reverse:** Phar Lap and jockey. **Edge:** Reeded. **Size:** 38.7 mm.

| Date | Mintage | F | VF | XF | Unc | BU |
|---|---|---|---|---|---|---|
| 2000 Proof | 20,000 | Value: 25.00 | | | | |

**5 DOLLARS** **KM# 515** **Weight:** 31.6350 g. **Composition:** 0.9990 Silver 1.0161 oz. ASW **Series:** Olympics - Sydney Harbor Bridge **Obverse:** Queen's head right. **Reverse:** Sydney suspension bridge. **Edge Lettering:** GAMES OF THE XXVII OLYMPIAD twice. **Size:** 40.5 mm.

| Date | Mintage | F | VF | XF | Unc | BU |
|---|---|---|---|---|---|---|
| 2000 Prooflike | 100,000 | — | — | — | 40.00 | — |

**5 DOLLARS** **KM# 516** **Weight:** 31.6350 g. **Composition:** 0.9990 Silver 1.0161 oz. ASW **Series:** Olympics - Kookaburra **Obverse:** Queen's head right. **Reverse:** Kookaburra with Waratah leaves. **Size:** 40.5 mm.

| Date | Mintage | F | VF | XF | Unc | BU |
|---|---|---|---|---|---|---|
| 2000 Prooflike | 100,000 | — | — | — | 40.00 | — |

**5 DOLLARS** **KM# 517** **Composition:** Aluminum-Bronze **Subject:** Paralympics **Obverse:** Queen's head right. **Reverse:** Wheelchair racer and multicolor logo. **Edge:** Reeded. **Size:** 38.6 mm.

| Date | Mintage | F | VF | XF | Unc | BU |
|---|---|---|---|---|---|---|
| 2000 | Est. 30,000 | — | — | — | 12.50 | — |

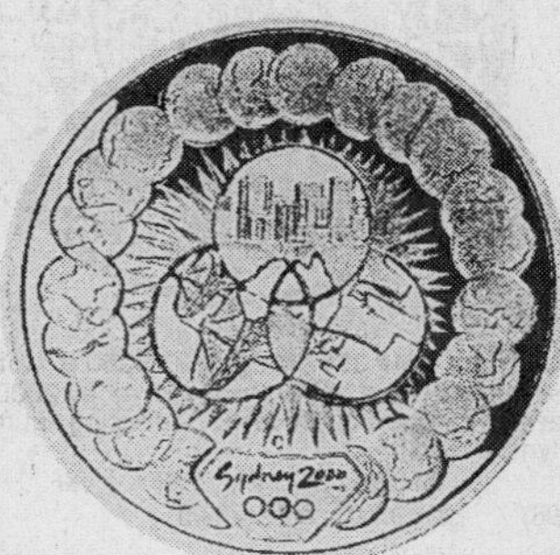


**5 DOLLARS** **KM# 440** **Weight:** 31.6350 g. **Composition:** 0.9990 Silver 1.0161 oz. ASW **Series:** Sydney 2000 Olympics **Obverse:** Queen's head right **Reverse:** 3 radint circular views within circle of round maps

| Date | Mintage | F | VF | XF | Unc | BU |
|---|---|---|---|---|---|---|
| 2000 Proof | 100,000 | Value: 37.50 | | | | |

**5 DOLLARS** **KM# 441** **Weight:** 31.6350 g. **Composition:** 0.9990 Silver 1.0161 oz. ASW **Series:** Sydney 2000 Olympics **Obverse:** Queen's head right **Reverse:** 7 figures like spokes in a wheel

| Date | Mintage | F | VF | XF | Unc | BU |
|---|---|---|---|---|---|---|
| 2000 Proof | 100,000 | Value: 37.50 | | | | |

**5 DOLLARS** **KM# 429** **Weight:** 20.0000 g. **Composition:** Brass **Series:** Sydney 2000 Olympics **Obverse:** Queen's head right **Reverse:** Pentathlon events portrayed by 5 participants

| Date | Mintage | F | VF | XF | Unc | BU |
|---|---|---|---|---|---|---|
| 2000 | — | — | — | — | 9.00 | — |

**5 DOLLARS** KM# 430 **Weight:** 20.0000 g. **Composition:** Brass **Obverse:** Queen's head right **Reverse:** Judo match

| Date | Mintage | F | VF | XF | Unc | BU |
|---|---|---|---|---|---|---|
| 2000 | — | — | — | — | 8.00 | — |

**5 DOLLARS** KM# 431 **Weight:** 20.0000 g. **Composition:** Brass **Series:** Sydney 2000 Olympics **Obverse:** Queen's head right **Reverse:** Rower

| Date | Mintage | F | VF | XF | Unc | BU |
|---|---|---|---|---|---|---|
| 2000 | — | — | — | — | 9.00 | — |

**5 DOLLARS** KM# 432 **Weight:** 20.0000 g. **Composition:** Brass **Series:** Sydney 2000 Olympics **Obverse:** Queen's head right **Reverse:** 2 men boxing

| Date | Mintage | F | VF | XF | Unc | BU |
|---|---|---|---|---|---|---|
| 2000 | — | — | — | — | 9.00 | — |

**5 DOLLARS** KM# 433 **Weight:** 20.0000 g. **Composition:** Brass **Series:** Sydney 2000 Olympics **Obverse:** Queen's head right **Reverse:** Volleyball player

| Date | Mintage | F | VF | XF | Unc | BU |
|---|---|---|---|---|---|---|
| 2000 | — | — | — | — | 9.00 | — |

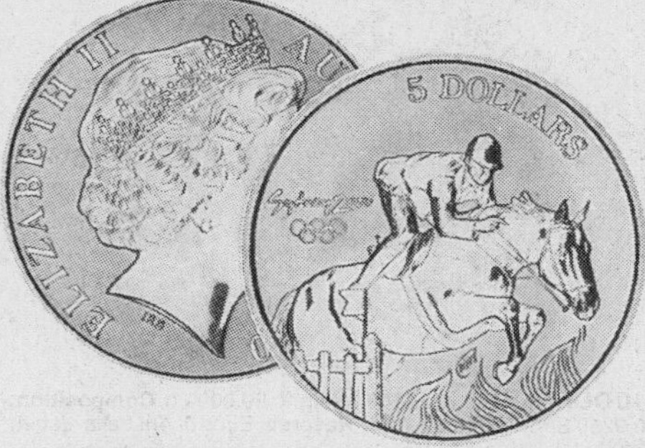

**5 DOLLARS** KM# 434 **Weight:** 1.5710 g. **Composition:** 0.9999 Gold .0500 oz. AGW **Series:** Sydney 2000 Olympics **Obverse:** Queen's head right **Reverse:** Equestrian putting horse through jumps

| Date | Mintage | F | VF | XF | Unc | BU |
|---|---|---|---|---|---|---|
| 2000 | — | — | — | — | 9.00 | — |

**5 DOLLARS** KM# 435 **Weight:** 1.5710 g. **Composition:** 0.9999 Gold .0500 oz. AGW **Series:** Sydney 2000 Olympics **Obverse:** Queen's head right **Reverse:** Pitcher winding up

| Date | Mintage | F | VF | XF | Unc | BU |
|---|---|---|---|---|---|---|
| 2000 | — | — | — | — | 9.00 | — |

**5 DOLLARS** KM# 436 **Weight:** 20.0000 g. **Composition:** Brass **Series:** Sydney 2000 Olympics **Obverse:** Queen's head right **Reverse:** Swimmer

| Date | Mintage | F | VF | XF | Unc | BU |
|---|---|---|---|---|---|---|
| 2000 | — | — | — | — | 9.00 | — |

**5 DOLLARS** KM# 538 **Weight:** 1.5710 g. **Composition:** 0.9990 Gold .0500 oz. AGW **Subject:** Year of the Snake **Obverse:** Queen's head right. **Reverse:** Snake in tree. **Edge:** Reeded. **Size:** 14.1 mm.

| Date | Mintage | F | VF | XF | Unc | BU |
|---|---|---|---|---|---|---|
| 2001 | 100,000 | — | — | — | 45.00 | — |

**10 DOLLARS** KM# 75 **Weight:** 20.0000 g. **Composition:** 0.9250 Silver .5949 oz. ASW **Subject:** XII Commonwealth Games - Brisbane

| Date | Mintage | F | VF | XF | Unc | BU |
|---|---|---|---|---|---|---|
| 1982 | 126,000 | — | — | — | 7.00 | — |
| 1982 Proof | 85,000 | Value: 10.00 | | | | |

**10 DOLLARS** KM# 85 **Weight:** 20.0000 g. **Composition:** 0.9250 Silver .5949 oz. ASW **Subject:** 150th Anniversary - State of Victoria

| Date | Mintage | F | VF | XF | Unc | BU |
|---|---|---|---|---|---|---|
| 1985 | 82,000 | — | — | — | 8.00 | — |
| 1985 Proof | 56,000 | Value: 16.00 | | | | |

**10 DOLLARS** KM# 88 **Weight:** 20.0000 g. **Composition:** 0.9250 Silver .5949 oz. ASW **Subject:** 150th Anniversary - South Australia

| Date | Mintage | F | VF | XF | Unc | BU |
|---|---|---|---|---|---|---|
| 1986 | 78,000 | — | — | — | 8.00 | — |
| 1986 Proof | 52,000 | Value: 16.00 | | | | |

**10 DOLLARS** KM# 93 **Weight:** 20.0000 g. **Composition:** 0.9250 Silver .5949 oz. ASW **Subject:** New South Wales

| Date | Mintage | F | VF | XF | Unc | BU |
|---|---|---|---|---|---|---|
| 1987 | 65,000 | — | — | — | 8.00 | — |
| 1987 Proof | 50,000 | Value: 16.00 | | | | |

**10 DOLLARS** KM# 103 **Weight:** 20.0000 g. **Composition:** 0.9250 Silver .5949 oz. ASW **Subject:** Landing of Governor Philip

| Date | Mintage | F | VF | XF | Unc | BU |
|---|---|---|---|---|---|---|
| 1988 | — | — | — | — | 10.00 | — |
| 1988 Proof | — | Value: 18.00 | | | | |

**10 DOLLARS** KM# 114 **Weight:** 20.0000 g. **Composition:** 0.9250 Silver .5949 oz. ASW **Subject:** Queensland

| Date | Mintage | F | VF | XF | Unc | BU |
|---|---|---|---|---|---|---|
| 1989 | — | — | — | — | 8.50 | — |
| 1989 Proof | — | Value: 16.50 | | | | |

**10 DOLLARS** KM# 133 **Weight:** 20.0000 g. **Composition:** 0.9250 Silver .5949 oz. ASW **Obverse:** Portrait of Queen Elizabeth II **Reverse:** Kookaburras

| Date | Mintage | F | VF | XF | Unc | BU |
|---|---|---|---|---|---|---|
| 1989 Proof | — | Value: 50.00 | | | | |

**10 DOLLARS** KM# 136 **Weight:** 20.0000 g. **Composition:** 0.9250 Silver .5949 oz. ASW **Obverse:** Portrait of Queen Elizabeth II **Reverse:** Sulpher-crested cockatoo

| Date | Mintage | F | VF | XF | Unc | BU |
|---|---|---|---|---|---|---|
| 1990 Proof | — | Value: 50.00 | | | | |

**10 DOLLARS** KM# 137 **Weight:** 20.0000 g. **Composition:** 0.9250 Silver .5949 oz. ASW **Subject:** Western Australia **Obverse:** Portrait of Queen Elizabeth II **Reverse:** Western Australia coat of arms

| Date | Mintage | F | VF | XF | Unc | BU |
|---|---|---|---|---|---|---|
| 1990 | — | — | — | — | 12.00 | — |
| 1990 Proof | — | Value: 22.50 | | | | |

**10 DOLLARS** KM# 153 **Weight:** 20.0000 g. **Composition:** 0.9250 Silver .5949 oz. ASW **Subject:** Tasmania

| Date | Mintage | F | VF | XF | Unc | BU |
|---|---|---|---|---|---|---|
| 1991 | 5,691 | — | — | — | 12.00 | — |
| 1991 Proof | 5,504 | Value: 30.00 | | | | |

**10 DOLLARS** KM# 156 **Weight:** 20.0000 g. **Composition:** 0.9250 Silver .5949 oz. ASW **Reverse:** Birds of Australia- Jabiru Stork

| Date | Mintage | F | VF | XF | Unc | BU |
|---|---|---|---|---|---|---|
| 1991 Proof | 50,000 | Value: 42.00 | | | | |

**10 DOLLARS** KM# 161 **Weight:** 62.2140 g. **Composition:** 0.9990 Silver 2.0000 oz. ASW **Reverse:** Australian Kookaburra

| Date | Mintage | F | VF | XF | Unc | BU |
|---|---|---|---|---|---|---|
| 1991 | — | — | — | — | 15.00 | — |
| 1991 Proof | 5,000 | Value: 55.00 | | | | |

**10 DOLLARS** KM# 180 **Weight:** 311.0670 g. **Composition:** 0.9990 Silver 10.0000 oz. ASW **Reverse:** Australian kookaburra on stump. Similar to 30 Dollars, KM#181

| Date | Mintage | F | VF | XF | Unc | BU |
|---|---|---|---|---|---|---|
| 1992 | — | — | — | — | 85.00 | — |
| 1992 Proof | 2,500 | Value: 325 | | | | |

**10 DOLLARS** KM# 188 **Weight:** 20.0000 g. **Composition:** 0.9250 Silver .5949 oz. ASW **Subject:** Northern Territory

| Date | Mintage | F | VF | XF | Unc | BU |
|---|---|---|---|---|---|---|
| 1992 | 23,000 | — | — | — | 10.00 | — |
| 1992 Proof | 18,000 | Value: 20.00 | | | | |

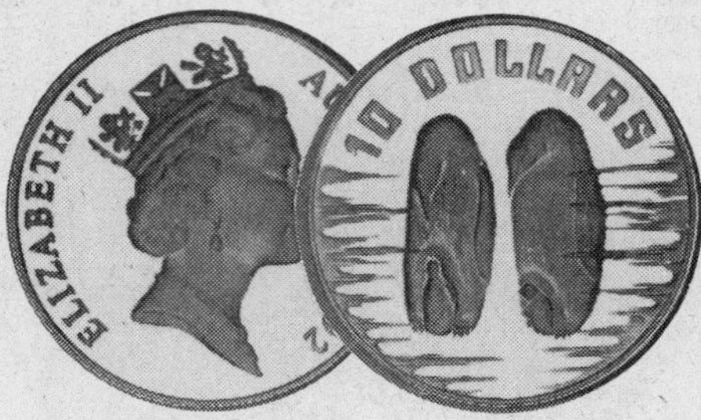


**10 DOLLARS** KM# 199 **Weight:** 20.0000 g. **Composition:** 0.9250 Silver .5949 oz. ASW **Reverse:** Emperor Penguin

| Date | Mintage | F | VF | XF | Unc | BU |
|---|---|---|---|---|---|---|
| 1992 Proof | Est. 35,000 | Value: 45.00 | | | | |

**10 DOLLARS** KM# 210 **Weight:** 20.0000 g. **Composition:** 0.9250 Silver .5949 oz. ASW **Reverse:** Australian Capital Territory

| Date | Mintage | F | VF | XF | Unc | BU |
|---|---|---|---|---|---|---|
| 1993 | — | — | — | — | 12.00 | — |
| 1993 Proof | — | Value: 20.00 | | | | |

**10 DOLLARS** KM# 221 **Weight:** 20.0000 g. **Composition:** 0.9250 Silver .5949 oz. ASW **Reverse:** Palm cockatoo

| Date | Mintage | F | VF | XF | Unc | BU |
|---|---|---|---|---|---|---|
| 1993 Proof | Est. 35,000 | Value: 45.00 | | | | |

**10 DOLLARS** KM# 317 **Weight:** 20.0000 g. **Composition:** 0.9250 Silver .5949 oz. ASW **Subject:** UNEP - Palm Cockatoo **Obverse:** Queen's portrait **Reverse:** Palm cockatoo with UNEP logo

| Date | Mintage | F | VF | XF | Unc | BU |
|---|---|---|---|---|---|---|
| 1993 Prof | Est. 55,000 | Value: 40.00 | | | | |

**10 DOLLARS** KM# 231 **Weight:** 311.0350 g. **Composition:** 0.9990 Silver 10.0000 oz. ASW **Subject:** The Australian Kookaburra **Obverse:** Queen's portrait **Reverse:** Pair of Kookaburras on branch **Note:** Illustration reduced. Actual size 75mm.

| Date | Mintage | F | VF | XF | Unc | BU |
|---|---|---|---|---|---|---|
| 1993 (ae) Proof | 500 | Value: 550 | | | | |
| 1994 | — | — | — | — | 75.00 | — |
| 1994 Proof | — | Value: 200 | | | | |

**10 DOLLARS** KM# 228 **Weight:** 311.0670 g. **Composition:** 0.9990 Silver 10.0000 oz. ASW **Reverse:** Kookaburra feeding nestling **Note:** Similar to 1 Dollar, KM#209.

| Date | Mintage | F | VF | XF | Unc | BU |
|---|---|---|---|---|---|---|
| 1993 | — | — | — | — | 75.00 | — |
| 1993 Proof | — | Value: 200 | | | | |

**10 DOLLARS** **KM# 223** **Weight:** 20.0000 g. **Composition:** 0.9250 Silver .5949 oz. ASW **Reverse:** Wedge-tailed eagle

| Date | Mintage | F | VF | XF | Unc | BU |
|---|---|---|---|---|---|---|
| 1994 Proof | 34,000 | Value: 45.00 | | | | |

**10 DOLLARS** **KM# 225** **Weight:** 20.7700 g. **Composition:** 0.9990 Silver .6678 oz. ASW **Series:** Olympic Gold Medalists - Edwin Flack 1896

| Date | Mintage | F | VF | XF | Unc | BU |
|---|---|---|---|---|---|---|
| 1994 Matte Proof | Est. 30,000 | Value: 20.00 | | | | |

**10 DOLLARS** **KM# 226** **Weight:** 20.7700 g. **Composition:** 0.9990 Silver .6678 oz. ASW **Series:** Olympic Gold Medalists - Sarah Durack 1912

| Date | Mintage | F | VF | XF | Unc | BU |
|---|---|---|---|---|---|---|
| 1994 Matte Proof | Est. 30,000 | Value: 20.00 | | | | |

**10 DOLLARS** **KM# 296** **Weight:** 20.7700 g. **Composition:** 0.9990 Silver .6678 oz. ASW **Reverse:** Numbat

| Date | Mintage | F | VF | XF | Unc | BU |
|---|---|---|---|---|---|---|
| 1995 Proof | 25,000 | Value: 32.50 | | | | |

**10 DOLLARS** **KM# 301** **Weight:** 20.7700 g. **Composition:** 0.9990 Silver .6678 oz. ASW **Series:** Olympic Gold Medalists - Dawn Fraser **Obverse:** Queen's portrait **Reverse:** Half-length portrait

| Date | Mintage | F | VF | XF | Unc | BU |
|---|---|---|---|---|---|---|
| 1995 Matte Proof | Est. 30,000 | Value: 25.00 | | | | |

**10 DOLLARS** **KM# 302** **Weight:** 20.7700 g. **Composition:** 0.9990 Silver .6678 oz. ASW **Series:** Olympic Gold Medalists - Murray Rose **Obverse:** Swimmer's portrait

| Date | Mintage | F | VF | XF | Unc | BU |
|---|---|---|---|---|---|---|
| 1995 Matte Proof | Est. 30,000 | Value: 25.00 | | | | |

**10 DOLLARS** **KM# 270** **Weight:** 311.0670 g. **Composition:** 0.9990 Silver 10.0000 oz. ASW **Reverse:** Kookaburra on branch **Note:** Similar to 1 Dollar, KM#260.

| Date | Mintage | F | VF | XF | Unc | BU |
|---|---|---|---|---|---|---|
| 1995 | — | — | — | — | 85.00 | — |
| 1995 Proof | — | Value: 300 | | | | |

**10 DOLLARS** **KM# 291** **Weight:** 311.0670 g. **Composition:** 0.9990 Silver 10.0000 oz. ASW **Reverse:** Kookaburra in flight **Note:** Illustration reduced. Actual size 75.5mm.

| Date | Mintage | F | VF | XF | Unc | BU |
|---|---|---|---|---|---|---|
| 1995P Proof | 1,300 | Value: 275 | | | | |
| 1995 (ge) Proof | 800 | Value: 300 | | | | |
| **Note:** Privy mark on gold insert | | | | | | |
| 1996 | — | — | — | — | 75.00 | — |

**10 DOLLARS** **KM# 314** **Weight:** 20.0000 g. **Composition:** 0.9250 Silver .5949 oz. ASW **Reverse:** Southern right whale with baby

| Date | Mintage | F | VF | XF | Unc | BU |
|---|---|---|---|---|---|---|
| 1996 Proof | 24,000 | Value: 35.00 | | | | |

**10 DOLLARS** **KM# 315** **Weight:** 20.7700 g. **Composition:** 0.9990 Silver .6678 oz. ASW **Series:** Australia's Greatest Olympics **Reverse:** Betty Cuthbert

| Date | Mintage | F | VF | XF | Unc | BU |
|---|---|---|---|---|---|---|
| 1996 Matte Unc | 30,000 | — | — | — | 22.50 | — |

**10 DOLLARS** **KM# 316** **Weight:** 20.7700 g. **Composition:** 0.9990 Silver .6678 oz. ASW **Series:** Australia's Greatest Olympics **Reverse:** Shirley Strickland

| Date | Mintage | F | VF | XF | Unc | BU |
|---|---|---|---|---|---|---|
| 1996 Matte Unc | 30,000 | — | — | — | 22.50 | — |

**10 DOLLARS** **KM# 353** **Weight:** 20.7700 g. **Composition:** 0.9990 Silver .6678 oz. ASW **Subject:** Sydney Opera House **Obverse:** Queen's portrait **Reverse:** Opera house and Sydney shoreline

| Date | Mintage | F | VF | XF | Unc | BU |
|---|---|---|---|---|---|---|
| 1997 Matte Proof | 20,000 | Value: 28.00 | | | | |

**10 DOLLARS** **KM# 354** **Weight:** 20.7700 g. **Composition:** 0.9990 Silver .6678 oz. ASW **Subject:** Sydney Harbour Bridge **Obverse:** Queen's portrait **Reverse:** Bridge over harbour

| Date | Mintage | F | VF | XF | Unc | BU |
|---|---|---|---|---|---|---|
| 1997 Matte Proof | 20,000 | Value: 28.00 | | | | |

**10 DOLLARS** **KM# 367.1** **Weight:** 20.0000 g. **Composition:** 0.9990 Silver .6678 oz. ASW **Subject:** Red-tailed Black Cockatoo **Obverse:** Queen's portrait **Reverse:** Cockatoo perched in dead tree

| Date | Mintage | F | VF | XF | Unc | BU |
|---|---|---|---|---|---|---|
| 1997 Proof | 24,000 | Value: 35.00 | | | | |

**10 DOLLARS** **KM# 367.2** **Weight:** 40.0000 g. **Composition:** 0.9250 Silver 1.1896 oz. ASW

| Date | Mintage | F | VF | XF | Unc | BU |
|---|---|---|---|---|---|---|
| 1997 Proof | 14,000 | Value: 50.00 | | | | |

**10 DOLLARS** **KM# 351** **Weight:** 311.0670 g. **Composition:** 0.9990 Silver 10.0000 oz. ASW **Subject:** Kookaburra and Nestling **Obverse:** Queen's portrait **Reverse:** Kookaburra looking right, nestling **Note:** Similar to 1 Dollar, KM#318.

| Date | Mintage | F | VF | XF | Unc | BU |
|---|---|---|---|---|---|---|
| 1997 | — | — | — | — | 75.00 | — |

**10 DOLLARS** KM# 494 **Weight:** 311.0350 g. **Composition:** 0.9990 Silver 10.0000 oz. ASW **Subject:** Kookaburra Bullion **Obverse:** Queen's head right. **Reverse:** Kookaburra on fence. **Edge:** Reeded and plain sections. **Size:** 75 mm. **Note:** Illustration reduced. Actual size: 75mm.

| Date | Mintage | F | VF | XF | Unc | BU |
|---|---|---|---|---|---|---|
| 1997P Proof | — | Value: 325 | | | | |

**10 DOLLARS** KM# 387 **Weight:** 20.7700 g. **Composition:** 0.9990 Silver .6671 oz. ASW **Subject:** Melbourne **Obverse:** Queen's portrait **Reverse:** Melbourne cricket grounds

| Date | Mintage | F | VF | XF | Unc | BU |
|---|---|---|---|---|---|---|
| 1998 Matte Proof | 20,000 | Value: 18.00 | | | | |

**10 DOLLARS** KM# 388 **Weight:** 20.7700 g. **Composition:** 0.9990 Silver .6671 oz. ASW **Subject:** Melbourne **Obverse:** Queen's portrait **Reverse:** Street car

| Date | Mintage | F | VF | XF | Unc | BU |
|---|---|---|---|---|---|---|
| 1998 Matte Proof | 20,000 | Value: 18.00 | | | | |

**10 DOLLARS** KM# 397 **Weight:** 20.0000 g. **Composition:** 0.9250 Silver .5948 oz. ASW **Subject:** Northern Hairy-Nosed Wombat **Obverse:** Queen's portrait **Reverse:** Wombat above denomination

| Date | Mintage | F | VF | XF | Unc | BU |
|---|---|---|---|---|---|---|
| 1998 Proof | 24,000 | Value: 32.50 | | | | |

**10 DOLLARS** KM# 414 **Weight:** 20.7700 g. **Composition:** 0.9990 Silver .6671 oz. ASW **Subject:** The Snowy Mountain Scheme **Obverse:** Queen's portrait **Reverse:** Tunnel building scene

| Date | Mintage | F | VF | XF | Unc | BU |
|---|---|---|---|---|---|---|
| 1999 | — | — | — | — | 18.00 | — |

**10 DOLLARS** KM# 415 **Weight:** 20.7700 g. **Composition:** 0.9990 Silver .6671 oz. ASW **Subject:** The Snowy Mountain Scheme **Obverse:** Queen's portrait **Reverse:** Dam building scene

| Date | Mintage | F | VF | XF | Unc | BU |
|---|---|---|---|---|---|---|
| 1999 | — | — | — | — | 18.00 | — |

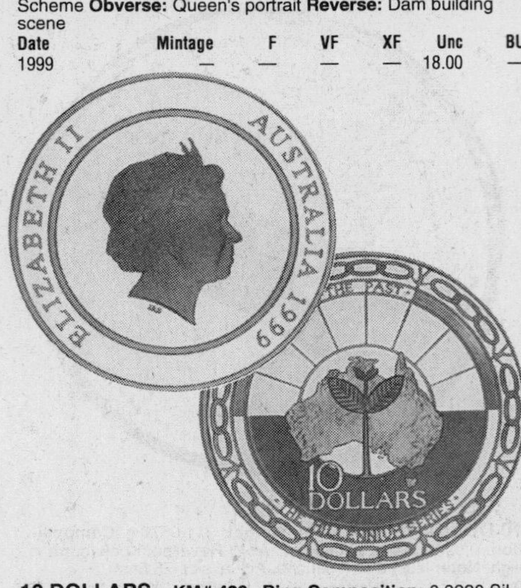

**10 DOLLARS** KM# 423 **Ring Composition:** 0.9990 SilverCenter **Weight:** 33.5300 g. **Center Composition:** Copper **Subject:** Millennium Series, The Past **Obverse:** Queen's head right **Reverse:** Seedling on Australian map above denomination with rising sun background **Edge:** Reeded

| Date | Mintage | F | VF | XF | Unc | BU |
|---|---|---|---|---|---|---|
| 1999 Proof | 20,000 | Value: 40.00 | | | | |

**10 DOLLARS** KM# 504 **Weight:** 312.3470 g. **Composition:** 0.9990 Silver 10.0321 oz. ASW **Subject:** Year of the Rabbit **Obverse:** Queen's head right. **Reverse:** Rabbit. **Edge:** Reeded and plain sections. **Size:** 75.5 mm.

| Date | Mintage | F | VF | XF | Unc | BU |
|---|---|---|---|---|---|---|
| 1999 | — | — | — | — | 80.00 | — |
| 1999 Proof | 2,500 | Value: 350 | | | | |

**10 DOLLARS** KM# 511 **Weight:** 36.0100 g. **Composition:** 0.9990 Silver 1.1566 oz. ASW **Series:** Millennium - The Present **Obverse:** Queen's head right. **Reverse:** Australian map behind young tree. **Edge:** Reeded. **Size:** 38.7 mm.

| Date | Mintage | F | VF | XF | Unc | BU |
|---|---|---|---|---|---|---|
| 2000 Proof | 20,000 | Value: 40.00 | | | | |

**10 DOLLARS** KM# 524 **Weight:** 311.0350 g. **Composition:** 0.9990 Silver 10.0000 oz. ASW **Series:** Dragons **Obverse:** Queen's head right **Reverse:** Dragon **Edge:** Segmented reeding **Size:** 75.5 mm.

| Date | Mintage | F | VF | XF | Unc | BU |
|---|---|---|---|---|---|---|
| 2000 Proof | — | Value: 275 | | | | |

**10 DOLLARS** KM# 518 **Weight:** 311.0350 g. **Composition:** 0.9990 Silver 10.0000 oz. ASW **Subject:** Paralympics **Obverse:** Queen's head right **Reverse:** Sydney Opera House and harbor bridge **Edge:** Lettering with logo **Edge Lettering:** GAMES OF THE XI PARALYMPIAD **Size:** 75 mm. **Note:** Illustration reduced. Actual size: 75mm.

| Date | Mintage | F | VF | XF | Unc | BU |
|---|---|---|---|---|---|---|
| 2000 Prooflike | 3,000 | — | — | — | 300 | — |

**10 DOLLARS** KM# 446 **Weight:** 312.3470 g. **Composition:** 0.9990 Silver 10.0000 oz. ASW **Obverse:** Queen's head right **Reverse:** 2 kookaburras on branch **Edge:** Interrupted reeding

| Date | Mintage | F | VF | XF | Unc | BU |
|---|---|---|---|---|---|---|
| 2000 | — | — | — | — | 75.00 | — |

**10 DOLLARS** KM# 539 **Weight:** 311.0350 g. **Composition:** 0.9990 Silver 10.0000 oz. ASW **Subject:** Year of the Snake **Obverse:** Queen's head right **Reverse:** Snake with eggs **Edge:** Segmented reeding **Size:** 75.5 mm.

| Date | Mintage | F | VF | XF | Unc | BU |
|---|---|---|---|---|---|---|
| 2001 | — | — | — | — | 150 | — |

**15 DOLLARS** KM# 89 **Weight:** 3.1103 g. **Composition:** 0.9990 Gold .1000 oz. AGW **Obverse:** Elizabeth II **Reverse:** Little Hero

| Date | Mintage | F | VF | XF | Unc | BU |
|---|---|---|---|---|---|---|
| 1986P Proof | 15,000 | Value: 60.00 | | | | |
| 1987 | 266,000 | — | — | — | BV+12% | — |
| 1988 | 104,000 | — | — | — | BV+12% | — |
| 1989 | — | — | — | — | BV+12% | — |

**15 DOLLARS** KM# 95 **Weight:** 3.1103 g. **Composition:** 0.9990 Gold .1000 oz. AGW **Reverse:** Golden Aussie

| Date | Mintage | F | VF | XF | Unc | BU |
|---|---|---|---|---|---|---|
| 1987P Proof | 15,000 | Value: 60.00 | | | | |

**15 DOLLARS** **KM# 104** **Weight:** 3.1103 g. **Composition:** 0.9990 Gold .1000 oz. AGW **Reverse:** Jubilee Nugget

| Date | Mintage | F | VF | XF | Unc | BU |
|---|---|---|---|---|---|---|
| 1988P Proof | Est. 10,000 | Value: 60.00 | | | | |

**15 DOLLARS** **KM# 108** **Weight:** 3.1370 g. **Composition:** 0.9990 Platinum .1000 oz. APW **Note:** Similar to 100 Dollars, KM#111.

| Date | Mintage | F | VF | XF | Unc | BU |
|---|---|---|---|---|---|---|
| 1988 | — | — | — | — | BV+15% | — |
| 1989 Proof | — | Value: 75.00 | | | | |

**15 DOLLARS** **KM# 123** **Weight:** 3.1370 g. **Composition:** 0.9990 Platinum .1000 oz. APW **Note:** Similar to 100 Dollars, KM#126.

| Date | Mintage | F | VF | XF | Unc | BU |
|---|---|---|---|---|---|---|
| 1989 Proof | 2,400 | Value: 75.00 | | | | |
| 1990 Proof | — | Value: 75.00 | | | | |

**15 DOLLARS** **KM# 118** **Weight:** 3.1103 g. **Composition:** 0.9990 Gold .1000 oz. AGW **Reverse:** Red kangaroo

| Date | Mintage | F | VF | XF | Unc | BU |
|---|---|---|---|---|---|---|
| 1989 Proof | 2,200 | Value: 60.00 | | | | |
| 1990 | 200,000 | — | — | — | BV+12% | — |

**15 DOLLARS** **KM# 141** **Weight:** 3.1103 g. **Composition:** 0.9990 Gold .1000 oz. AGW **Reverse:** Gray kangaroo

| Date | Mintage | F | VF | XF | Unc | BU |
|---|---|---|---|---|---|---|
| 1990 Proof | 7,000 | Value: 55.00 | | | | |
| 1991 | 150,000 | — | — | — | BV+12% | — |

**15 DOLLARS** **KM# 146** **Weight:** 3.1370 g. **Composition:** 0.9990 Platinum .1000 oz. APW **Subject:** Koala **Obverse:** Similar to 100 Dollars, KM#149

| Date | Mintage | F | VF | XF | Unc | BU |
|---|---|---|---|---|---|---|
| 1990 Proof | 2,500 | Value: 75.00 | | | | |
| 1991 | 20,000 | — | — | — | BV+15% | — |
| 1991 Proof | 1,000 | Value: 85.00 | | | | |

**15 DOLLARS** **KM# 166** **Weight:** 3.1103 g. **Composition:** 0.9990 Gold .1000 oz. AGW **Subject:** Common Wallaroo **Obverse:** Elizabeth II **Reverse:** Similar to 100 Dollars, KM#169

| Date | Mintage | F | VF | XF | Unc | BU |
|---|---|---|---|---|---|---|
| 1991 Proof | 1,975 | Value: 70.00 | | | | |
| 1992 | 150,000 | — | — | — | BV+12% | — |

**15 DOLLARS** **KM# 171** **Weight:** 3.1370 g. **Composition:** 0.9990 Platinum .1000 oz. APW **Subject:** Koala **Obverse:** Elizabeth II **Reverse:** Similar to 100 Dollars, KM#174

| Date | Mintage | F | VF | XF | Unc | BU |
|---|---|---|---|---|---|---|
| 1992 | 20,000 | — | — | — | BV+ 15% | — |

**15 DOLLARS** **KM# 390** **Weight:** 3.1103 g. **Composition:** 0.9990 Gold .1000 oz. AGW **Obverse:** Queen's portrait **Reverse:** Nail-tailed wallaby **Note:** Similar to 25 Dollars, KM#391.

| Date | Mintage | F | VF | XF | Unc | BU |
|---|---|---|---|---|---|---|
| 1992 (ae) Proof | 500 | Value: 100 | | | | |

**15 DOLLARS** **KM# 192** **Weight:** 3.1370 g. **Composition:** 0.9990 Platinum .1000 oz. APW **Obverse:** Similar to 100 Dollars, KM#195

| Date | Mintage | F | VF | XF | Unc | BU |
|---|---|---|---|---|---|---|
| 1993 | Est. 20,000 | — | — | — | BV+15% | — |

**15 DOLLARS** **KM# 234** **Weight:** 3.1103 g. **Composition:** 0.9990 Gold .1000 oz. AGW **Subject:** Whiptail Wallaby **Obverse:** Queen Elizabeth II **Reverse:** Whiptail wallaby

| Date | Mintage | F | VF | XF | Unc | BU |
|---|---|---|---|---|---|---|
| 1993 Proof | — | Value: 75.00 | | | | |
| 1994 | — | — | — | — | BV+12% | — |

**15 DOLLARS** **KM# 242** **Weight:** 3.1103 g. **Composition:** 0.9990 Gold .1000 oz. AGW **Reverse:** Red Kangaroo

| Date | Mintage | F | VF | XF | Unc | BU |
|---|---|---|---|---|---|---|
| 1994 Proof | — | Value: 75.00 | | | | |
| 1995 | 200,000 | — | — | — | BV+12% | — |

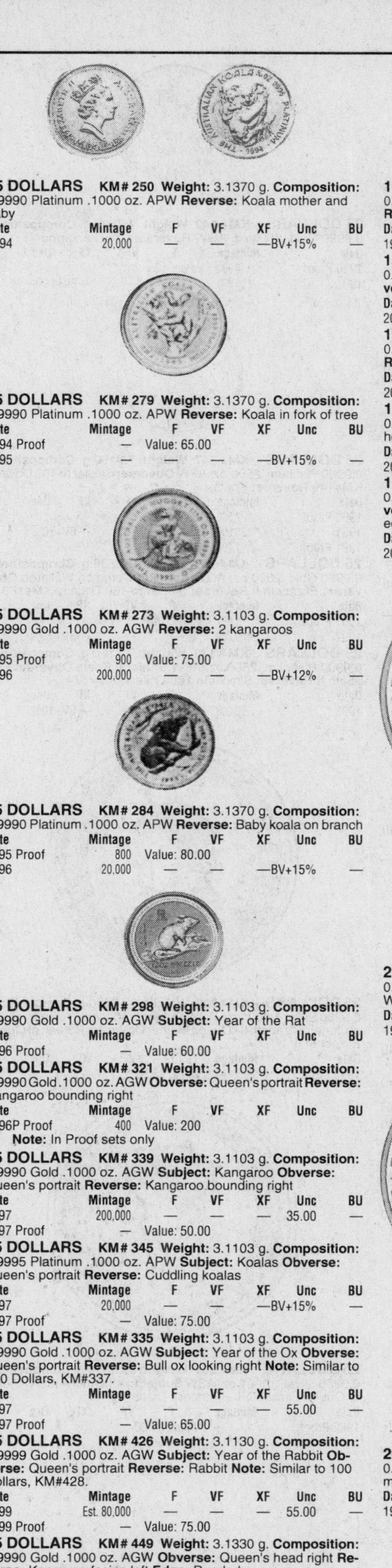

**15 DOLLARS** **KM# 250** **Weight:** 3.1370 g. **Composition:** 0.9990 Platinum .1000 oz. APW **Reverse:** Koala mother and baby

| Date | Mintage | F | VF | XF | Unc | BU |
|---|---|---|---|---|---|---|
| 1994 | 20,000 | — | — | — | BV+15% | — |

**15 DOLLARS** **KM# 279** **Weight:** 3.1370 g. **Composition:** 0.9990 Platinum .1000 oz. APW **Reverse:** Koala in fork of tree

| Date | Mintage | F | VF | XF | Unc | BU |
|---|---|---|---|---|---|---|
| 1994 Proof | — | Value: 65.00 | | | | |
| 1995 | — | — | — | — | BV+15% | — |

**15 DOLLARS** **KM# 273** **Weight:** 3.1103 g. **Composition:** 0.9990 Gold .1000 oz. AGW **Reverse:** 2 kangaroos

| Date | Mintage | F | VF | XF | Unc | BU |
|---|---|---|---|---|---|---|
| 1995 Proof | 900 | Value: 75.00 | | | | |
| 1996 | 200,000 | — | — | — | BV+12% | — |

**15 DOLLARS** **KM# 284** **Weight:** 3.1370 g. **Composition:** 0.9990 Platinum .1000 oz. APW **Reverse:** Baby koala on branch

| Date | Mintage | F | VF | XF | Unc | BU |
|---|---|---|---|---|---|---|
| 1995 Proof | 800 | Value: 80.00 | | | | |
| 1996 | 20,000 | — | — | — | BV+15% | — |

**15 DOLLARS** **KM# 298** **Weight:** 3.1103 g. **Composition:** 0.9990 Gold .1000 oz. AGW **Subject:** Year of the Rat

| Date | Mintage | F | VF | XF | Unc | BU |
|---|---|---|---|---|---|---|
| 1996 Proof | — | Value: 60.00 | | | | |

**15 DOLLARS** **KM# 321** **Weight:** 3.1103 g. **Composition:** 0.9990 Gold .1000 oz. AGW **Obverse:** Queen's portrait **Reverse:** Kangaroo bounding right

| Date | Mintage | F | VF | XF | Unc | BU |
|---|---|---|---|---|---|---|
| 1996P Proof | 400 | Value: 200 | | | | |

**Note:** In Proof sets only

**15 DOLLARS** **KM# 339** **Weight:** 3.1103 g. **Composition:** 0.9990 Gold .1000 oz. AGW **Subject:** Kangaroo **Obverse:** Queen's portrait **Reverse:** Kangaroo bounding right

| Date | Mintage | F | VF | XF | Unc | BU |
|---|---|---|---|---|---|---|
| 1997 | 200,000 | — | — | — | 35.00 | — |
| 1997 Proof | — | Value: 50.00 | | | | |

**15 DOLLARS** **KM# 345** **Weight:** 3.1103 g. **Composition:** 0.9995 Platinum .1000 oz. APW **Subject:** Koalas **Obverse:** Queen's portrait **Reverse:** Cuddling koalas

| Date | Mintage | F | VF | XF | Unc | BU |
|---|---|---|---|---|---|---|
| 1997 | 20,000 | — | — | — | BV+15% | — |
| 1997 Proof | — | Value: 75.00 | | | | |

**15 DOLLARS** **KM# 335** **Weight:** 3.1103 g. **Composition:** 0.9990 Gold .1000 oz. AGW **Subject:** Year of the Ox **Obverse:** Queen's portrait **Reverse:** Bull ox looking right **Note:** Similar to 100 Dollars, KM#337.

| Date | Mintage | F | VF | XF | Unc | BU |
|---|---|---|---|---|---|---|
| 1997 | — | — | — | — | 55.00 | — |
| 1997 Proof | — | Value: 65.00 | | | | |

**15 DOLLARS** **KM# 426** **Weight:** 3.1130 g. **Composition:** 0.9999 Gold .1000 oz. AGW **Subject:** Year of the Rabbit **Obverse:** Queen's portrait **Reverse:** Rabbit **Note:** Similar to 100 Dollars, KM#428.

| Date | Mintage | F | VF | XF | Unc | BU |
|---|---|---|---|---|---|---|
| 1999 | Est. 80,000 | — | — | — | 55.00 | — |
| 1999 Proof | — | Value: 75.00 | | | | |

**15 DOLLARS** **KM# 449** **Weight:** 3.1330 g. **Composition:** 0.9990 Gold .1000 oz. AGW **Obverse:** Queen's head right **Reverse:** Kangaroo facing left **Edge:** Reeded

| Date | Mintage | F | VF | XF | Unc | BU |
|---|---|---|---|---|---|---|
| 1999 | 200,000 | — | — | — | 40.00 | — |

**15 DOLLARS** **KM# 457** **Weight:** 3.1370 g. **Composition:** 0.9990 Platinum .1000 oz. APW **Obverse:** Queen's head right **Reverse:** Koala on log **Edge:** Reeded

| Date | Mintage | F | VF | XF | Unc | BU |
|---|---|---|---|---|---|---|
| 1999 | 20,000 | — | — | — | BV+15% | — |

**15 DOLLARS** **KM# 465** **Weight:** 3.1330 g. **Composition:** 0.9990 Gold .1000 oz. AGW **Obverse:** Queen's head right **Reverse:** 2 kangaroos bounding left **Edge:** Reeded

| Date | Mintage | F | VF | XF | Unc | BU |
|---|---|---|---|---|---|---|
| 2000 | — | — | — | — | 40.00 | — |

**15 DOLLARS** **KM# 470** **Weight:** 3.1370 g. **Composition:** 0.9990 Platinum .1000 oz. APW **Obverse:** Queen's head right **Reverse:** Seated koala **Edge:** Reeded

| Date | Mintage | F | VF | XF | Unc | BU |
|---|---|---|---|---|---|---|
| 2000 | — | — | — | — | BV+15% | — |

**15 DOLLARS** **KM# 526** **Weight:** 3.1103 g. **Composition:** 0.9990 Gold .1000 oz. AGW **Series:** Dragons **Obverse:** Queen's head right. **Reverse:** Dragon. **Edge:** Reeded. **Size:** 16.1 mm.

| Date | Mintage | F | VF | XF | Unc | BU |
|---|---|---|---|---|---|---|
| 2000 Proof | — | Value: 65.00 | | | | |

**15 DOLLARS** **KM# 540** **Weight:** 3.1103 g. **Composition:** 0.9990 Gold .1000 oz. AGW **Subject:** Year of the Snake **Obverse:** Queen's head right. **Reverse:** Snake in tree. **Edge:** Reeded. **Size:** 16.1 mm.

| Date | Mintage | F | VF | XF | Unc | BU |
|---|---|---|---|---|---|---|
| 2001 | 80,000 | — | — | — | 65.00 | — |

**20 DOLLARS** **KM#218** **Weight:** 33.6200 g. **Composition:** 0.9250 Silver 1.0000 oz. ASW **Series:** Olympics **Subject:** Track Winners

| Date | Mintage | F | VF | XF | Unc | BU |
|---|---|---|---|---|---|---|
| 1993 Proof | 100,000 | Value: 28.00 | | | | |

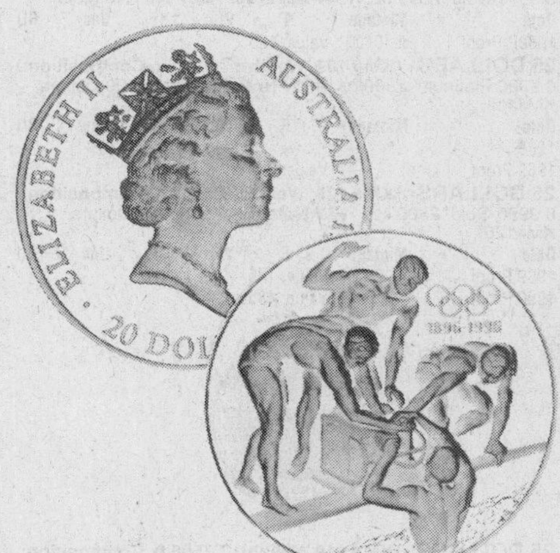

**20 DOLLARS** **KM#219** **Weight:** 33.6200 g. **Composition:** 0.9250 Silver 1.0000 oz. ASW **Series:** Olympics **Subject:** Swimmers

| Date | Mintage | F | VF | XF | Unc | BU |
|---|---|---|---|---|---|---|
| 1993 Proof | 100,000 | Value: 28.00 | | | | |

**20 DOLLARS** **KM# 519** **Ring Weight:** 5.0077 g. **Ring Composition:** 0.9990 Silver .1610 oz. ASW AGW**Center Weight:** 8.3979 g. **Center Composition:** 0.9990 Gold .6938 oz. ASW AGW **Subject:** Millennium **Obverse:** Queen's head right **Reverse:** Earth view from space **Edge:** Reeded **Size:** 32 mm.

| Date | Mintage | F | VF | XF | Unc | BU |
|---|---|---|---|---|---|---|
| 2000 Prooflike | Est. 7,500 | — | — | — | 200 | — |

**25 DOLLARS** **KM# 90** **Weight:** 7.7508 g. **Composition:** 0.9990 Gold .2500 oz. AGW **Obverse:** Elizabeth II **Reverse:** Gold Eagle

| Date | Mintage | F | VF | XF | Unc | BU |
|---|---|---|---|---|---|---|
| 1986P Proof | 15,000 | Value: 125 | | | | |
| 1987 | 233,000 | — | — | — | BV+10% | — |
| 1988 | 75,000 | — | — | — | BV+10% | — |
| 1989 | — | — | — | — | BV+10% | — |

**25 DOLLARS** **KM# 96** **Weight:** 7.7508 g. **Composition:** 0.9990 Gold .2500 oz. AGW **Reverse:** Father's Day

| Date | Mintage | F | VF | XF | Unc | BU |
|---|---|---|---|---|---|---|
| 1987P Proof | 15,000 | Value: 125 | | | | |

**25 DOLLARS** **KM# 105** **Weight:** 7.7508 g. **Composition:** 0.9990 Gold .2500 oz. AGW **Reverse:** Ruby Well Nugget

| Date | Mintage | F | VF | XF | Unc | BU |
|---|---|---|---|---|---|---|
| 1988P Proof | Est. 10,000 | Value: 125 | | | | |

**25 DOLLARS** **KM# 109** **Weight:** 7.8150 g. **Composition:** 0.9990 Platinum .2500 oz. APW **Note:** Similar to 100 Dollars, KM#111.

| Date | Mintage | F | VF | XF | Unc | BU |
|---|---|---|---|---|---|---|
| 1988 | — | — | — | — | BV+10% | — |
| 1989 Proof | — | Value: 200 | | | | |

**25 DOLLARS** **KM# 124** **Weight:** 7.7508 g. **Composition:** 0.9990 Gold .2500 oz. AGW **Note:** Similar to 100 Dollars, KM#126.

| Date | Mintage | F | VF | XF | Unc | BU |
|---|---|---|---|---|---|---|
| 1989 Proof | 2,400 | Value: 185 | | | | |
| 1990 Proof | — | Value: 185 | | | | |

**25 DOLLARS** **KM# 119** **Weight:** 7.7508 g. **Composition:** 0.9990 Gold .2500 oz. AGW **Reverse:** Red Kangaroo

| Date | Mintage | F | VF | XF | Unc | BU |
|---|---|---|---|---|---|---|
| 1989 Proof | 2,200 | Value: 145 | | | | |
| 1990 | Est. 200,000 | — | — | — | BV+10% | — |

**25 DOLLARS** **KM# 142** **Weight:** 7.7508 g. **Composition:** 0.9990 Gold .2500 oz. AGW **Reverse:** Gray kangaroo

| Date | Mintage | F | VF | XF | Unc | BU |
|---|---|---|---|---|---|---|
| 1990 Proof | 7,000 | Value: 125 | | | | |
| 1991 | 100,000 | — | — | — | BV+10% | — |

**25 DOLLARS** **KM# 147** **Weight:** 7.8150 g. **Composition:** 0.9990 Platinum .2500 oz. APW **Obverse:** Similar to 100 Dollars, KM#149 **Reverse:** Koala

| Date | Mintage | F | VF | XF | Unc | BU |
|---|---|---|---|---|---|---|
| 1990 Proof | 2,500 | Value: 200 | | | | |
| 1991 | 20,000 | — | — | — | BV+10% | — |
| 1991 Proof | 1,000 | Value: 210 | | | | |

**25 DOLLARS** **KM# 167** **Weight:** 7.7508 g. **Composition:** 0.9990 Gold .2500 oz. AGW **Subject:** Common Wallaroo **Obverse:** Elizabeth II **Reverse:** Similar to 100 Dollars, KM#169

| Date | Mintage | F | VF | XF | Unc | BU |
|---|---|---|---|---|---|---|
| 1991 Proof | 1,991 | Value: 140 | | | | |
| 1992 | 100,000 | — | — | — | BV+10% | — |

**25 DOLLARS** **KM# 172** **Weight:** 7.8150 g. **Composition:** 0.9990 Platinum .2500 oz. APW **Subject:** Koala **Obverse:** Elizabeth II **Reverse:** Similar to 100 Dollars, KM#174

| Date | Mintage | F | VF | XF | Unc | BU |
|---|---|---|---|---|---|---|
| 1992 | 20,000 | — | — | — | BV+10% | — |

**25 DOLLARS** **KM# 200** **Weight:** 33.6300 g. **Composition:** 0.9250 Silver 1.0001 oz. ASW **Subject:** 40th Anniversary - Reign of Queen Elizabeth II - Queen Mother **Obverse:** Portrait of Queen Elizabeth II

| Date | Mintage | F | VF | XF | Unc | BU |
|---|---|---|---|---|---|---|
| 1992 Proof | — | Value: 25.00 | | | | |

**25 DOLLARS** **KM# 201** **Weight:** 33.6300 g. **Composition:** 0.9250 Silver 1.0001 oz. ASW **Subject:** 40th Anniversary - Reign of Queen Elizabeth II - Princess Diana

| Date | Mintage | F | VF | XF | Unc | BU |
|---|---|---|---|---|---|---|
| 1992 Proof | — | Value: 25.00 | | | | |

**25 DOLLARS** **KM# 202** **Weight:** 33.6300 g. **Composition:** 0.9250 Silver 1.0001 oz. ASW **Subject:** 40th Anniversary - Reign of Queen Elizabeth II - Princess Anne

| Date | Mintage | F | VF | XF | Unc | BU |
|---|---|---|---|---|---|---|
| 1992 Proof | — | Value: 25.00 | | | | |

**25 DOLLARS** **KM# 203** **Weight:** 33.6300 g. **Composition:** 0.9250 Silver 1.0001 oz. ASW **Subject:** 40th Anniversary - Reign of Queen Elizabeth II - Prince Margaret

| Date | Mintage | F | VF | XF | Unc | BU |
|---|---|---|---|---|---|---|
| 1992 Proof | — | Value: 25.00 | | | | |

**25 DOLLARS** **KM# 391** **Weight:** 7.7508 g. **Composition:** 0.9990 Gold .2500 oz. AGW **Obverse:** Queen's portrait **Reverse:** Nail-tailed wallaby

| Date | Mintage | F | VF | XF | Unc | BU |
|---|---|---|---|---|---|---|
| 1992 (ae) Proof | 500 | Value: 215 | | | | |

**25 DOLLARS** **KM# 193** **Weight:** 7.8150 g. **Composition:** 0.9990 Platinum .2500 oz. APW **Obverse:** Similar to 100 Dollars, KM#195

| Date | Mintage | F | VF | XF | Unc | BU |
|---|---|---|---|---|---|---|
| 1992 (ae) Proof | 750 | Value: 220 | | | | |
| 1993 | Est. 20,000 | — | — | — | BV+10% | — |

**25 DOLLARS** **KM# 235** **Weight:** 7.7508 g. **Composition:** 0.9990 Gold .2500 oz. AGW **Subject:** Whiptail Wallaby **Obverse:** Queen Elizabeth II **Reverse:** Whiptail wallaby

| Date | Mintage | F | VF | XF | Unc | BU |
|---|---|---|---|---|---|---|
| 1993 (f) Proof | 200 | — | — | — | — | — |
| 1993 Proof | — | Value: 160 | | | | |
| 1994 | — | — | — | — | BV+10% | — |

**25 DOLLARS** **KM# 243** **Weight:** 7.7508 g. **Composition:** 0.9990 Gold .2500 oz. AGW **Reverse:** Red kangaroo

| Date | Mintage | F | VF | XF | Unc | BU |
|---|---|---|---|---|---|---|
| 1994 Proof | — | Value: 160 | | | | |
| 1995 | 150,000 | — | — | — | BV+10% | — |

**25 DOLLARS** **KM# 251** **Weight:** 7.8150 g. **Composition:** 0.9990 Platinum .2500 oz. APW **Subject:** Koala Mother and Baby **Obverse:** Queen Elizabeth II **Reverse:** Similar to 100 Dollars, KM#253

| Date | Mintage | F | VF | XF | Unc | BU |
|---|---|---|---|---|---|---|
| 1994 | 20,000 | — | — | — | BV+10% | — |

**25 DOLLARS** **KM# 280** **Weight:** 7.8150 g. **Composition:** 0.9990 Platinum .2500 oz. APW **Reverse:** Koala in fork of tree

| Date | Mintage | F | VF | XF | Unc | BU |
|---|---|---|---|---|---|---|
| 1994 Proof | — | Value: 225 | | | | |
| 1995 | — | — | — | — | BV+10% | — |

**25 DOLLARS** **KM# 274** **Weight:** 7.7508 g. **Composition:** 0.9990 Gold .2500 oz. AGW **Reverse:** 2 kangaroos

| Date | Mintage | F | VF | XF | Unc | BU |
|---|---|---|---|---|---|---|
| 1995 Proof | 650 | Value: 160 | | | | |
| 1996 | 150,000 | — | — | — | BV+10% | — |

**25 DOLLARS** **KM# 285** **Weight:** 7.8150 g. **Composition:** 0.9990 Platinum .2500 oz. APW **Reverse:** Baby koala on branch

| Date | Mintage | F | VF | XF | Unc | BU |
|---|---|---|---|---|---|---|
| 1995 Proof | 200 | Value: 225 | | | | |
| 1996 | 20,000 | — | — | — | BV+10% | — |

**25 DOLLARS** **KM# 299** **Weight:** 7.7508 g. **Composition:** 0.9990 Gold .2500 oz. AGW **Subject:** Year of the Rat

| Date | Mintage | F | VF | XF | Unc | BU |
|---|---|---|---|---|---|---|
| 1996 Proof | — | Value: 125 | | | | |

**25 DOLLARS** **KM# 322** **Weight:** 7.7508 g. **Composition:** 0.9990 Gold .2500 oz. AGW **Obverse:** Queen's portrait **Reverse:** Kangaroo bounding right

| Date | Mintage | F | VF | XF | Unc | BU |
|---|---|---|---|---|---|---|
| 1996(p) Proof | 400 | Value: 350 | | | | |

**Note:** In Proof sets only

**25 DOLLARS** **KM# 340** **Weight:** 7.7508 g. **Composition:** 0.9990 Gold .2500 oz. AGW **Subject:** Kangaroo **Obverse:** Queen's portrait **Reverse:** Kangaroo bounding right

| Date | Mintage | F | VF | XF | Unc | BU |
|---|---|---|---|---|---|---|
| 1997 | 200,000 | — | — | — | BV+10% | — |
| 1997 Proof | — | Value: 120 | | | | |

**25 DOLLARS** **KM# 346** **Weight:** 7.7508 g. **Composition:** 0.9995 Platinum .2500 oz. APW **Subject:** Koalas **Obverse:** Queen's portrait **Reverse:** Cuddling koalas

| Date | Mintage | F | VF | XF | Unc | BU |
|---|---|---|---|---|---|---|
| 1997 | 20,000 | — | — | — | BV+10% | — |
| 1997 Proof | — | Value: 210 | | | | |

**25 DOLLARS** **KM# 336** **Weight:** 7.7508 g. **Composition:** 0.9990 Gold .2500 oz. AGW **Subject:** Year of the Ox **Obverse:** Queen's portrait **Reverse:** Bull ox looking right **Note:** Similar to 100 Dollars, KM#337.

| Date | Mintage | F | VF | XF | Unc | BU |
|---|---|---|---|---|---|---|
| 1997 | — | — | — | — | 125 | — |
| 1997 Proof | 8,888 | Value: 160 | | | | |

**25 DOLLARS** **KM# 427** **Weight:** 7.8070 g. **Composition:** 0.9999 Gold .2510 oz. AGW **Subject:** Year of the Rabbit **Obverse:** Queen's portrait **Reverse:** Rabbit **Edge:** Reeded **Note:** Similar to 100 Dollars, KM#428.

| Date | Mintage | F | VF | XF | Unc | BU |
|---|---|---|---|---|---|---|
| 1999 | Est. 60,000 | — | — | — | 125 | — |
| 1999 Proof | — | Value: 200 | | | | |

**25 DOLLARS** **KM# 450** **Weight:** 7.8070 g. **Composition:** 0.9990 Gold .2500 oz. AGW **Obverse:** Queen's head right **Reverse:** Kangaroo facing left **Edge:** Reeded

| Date | Mintage | F | VF | XF | Unc | BU |
|---|---|---|---|---|---|---|
| 1999 | 150,000 | — | — | — | BV+10% | — |

**25 DOLLARS** **KM# 458** **Weight:** 7.8150 g. **Composition:** 0.9990 Platinum .2500 oz. APW **Obverse:** Queen's head right **Reverse:** Koala on log **Edge:** Reeded

| Date | Mintage | F | VF | XF | Unc | BU |
|---|---|---|---|---|---|---|
| 1999 | 20,000 | — | — | — | BV+10% | — |

**25 DOLLARS** **KM# 466** **Weight:** 7.8070 g. **Composition:** 0.9990 Gold .2500 oz. AGW **Obverse:** Queen's head right **Reverse:** 2 kangaroos bounding left **Edge:** Reeded

| Date | Mintage | F | VF | XF | Unc | BU |
|---|---|---|---|---|---|---|
| 2000 | — | — | — | — | BV+10% | — |

**25 DOLLARS** **KM# 471** **Weight:** 7.8150 g. **Composition:** 0.9990 Platinum .2500 oz. APW **Obverse:** Queen's head right **Reverse:** Seated koala **Edge:** Reeded

| Date | Mintage | F | VF | XF | Unc | BU |
|---|---|---|---|---|---|---|
| 2000 | — | — | — | — | BV+10% | — |

**25 DOLLARS** **KM# 527** **Weight:** 7.7508 g. **Composition:** 0.9990 Gold .2500 oz. AGW **Series:** Dragons **Obverse:** Queen's head right. **Reverse:** Dragon. **Edge:** Reeded. **Size:** 20.1 mm.

| Date | Mintage | F | VF | XF | Unc | BU |
|---|---|---|---|---|---|---|
| 2000 Proof | — | Value: 150 | | | | |

**25 DOLLARS** **KM# 541** **Weight:** 7.7508 g. **Composition:** 0.9990 Gold .2500 oz. AGW **Subject:** Year of the Snake **Obverse:** Queen's head right. **Reverse:** Snake in tree. **Edge:** Reeded. **Size:** 20.1 mm.

| Date | Mintage | F | VF | XF | Unc | BU |
|---|---|---|---|---|---|---|
| 2001 | 60,000 | — | — | — | 125 | — |

**30 DOLLARS** **KM# 181** **Weight:** 1100.1000 g. **Composition:** 0.9990 Silver 35.3376 oz. ASW **Subject:** Australian Kookaburra - On Stump **Note:** Illustration reduced. Actual size 100mm.

| Date | Mintage | F | VF | XF | Unc | BU |
|---|---|---|---|---|---|---|
| 1992 | — | — | — | — | 250 | — |
| 1992 Proof | 1,000 | Value: 600 | | | | |
| 1993 | — | — | — | — | 250 | — |
| 1993 (jw) Proof | 210 | Value: 400 | | | | |

**30 DOLLARS** **KM# 229** **Weight:** 1000.2108 g. **Composition:** 0.9990 Silver 32.1575 oz. ASW **Reverse:** Kookaburra feeding nestling **Note:** Similar to 1 Dollar, KM#209.

| Date | Mintage | F | VF | XF | Unc | BU |
|---|---|---|---|---|---|---|
| 1993 | — | — | — | — | 220 | — |
| 1993 Proof | — | Value: 350 | | | | |

**30 DOLLARS** **KM# 232** **Weight:** 1000.2108 g. **Composition:** 0.9990 Silver 32.1575 oz. ASW **Reverse:** Pair of kookaburras on branch **Note:** Illustration reduced. Actual size 100mm.

| Date | Mintage | F | VF | XF | Unc | BU |
|---|---|---|---|---|---|---|
| 1994 | — | — | — | — | 220 | — |
| 1994 Proof | — | Value: 350 | | | | |

**30 DOLLARS** **KM# 292** **Weight:** 1000.2108 g. **Composition:** 0.9990 Silver 32.1575 oz. ASW **Reverse:** Kookaburra in flight **Note:** Illustration reduced. Actual size 101mm.

| Date | Mintage | F | VF | XF | Unc | BU |
|---|---|---|---|---|---|---|
| 1995 (lh) Proof | 500 | Value: 375 | | | | |
| 1995P Proof | 1,000 | Value: 400 | | | | |
| 1996 | — | — | — | — | 200 | — |

**30 DOLLARS** **KM# 271** **Weight:** 1000.2108 g. **Composition:** 0.9990 Silver 32.1575 oz. ASW **Subject:** Kookaburra On Branch **Obverse:** Queen's portrait **Reverse:** Kookaburra on branch

| Date | Mintage | F | VF | XF | Unc | BU |
|---|---|---|---|---|---|---|
| 1995 | — | — | — | — | 250 | — |
| 1995 Proof | — | Value: 525 | | | | |

**30 DOLLARS** **KM# 495** **Weight:** 1100.1000 g. **Composition:** 0.9990 Silver 35.3376 oz. ASW **Subject:** Kookaburra Bullion **Obverse:** Queen's head right. **Reverse:** Kookaburra on fence. **Edge:** Reeded and plain sections with serial number. **Size:** 100 mm.

| Date | Mintage | F | VF | XF | Unc | BU |
|---|---|---|---|---|---|---|
| 1997P Proof | — | Value: 450 | | | | |

**30 DOLLARS** **KM# 505** **Weight:** 1002.5020 g. **Composition:** 0.9990 Silver 32.1989 oz. ASW **Subject:** Year of the Rabbit **Obverse:** Queen's head right. **Reverse:** Rabbit. **Edge:** Reeded and plain sections. **Size:** 101 mm.

| Date | Mintage | F | VF | XF | Unc | BU |
|---|---|---|---|---|---|---|
| 1999 | — | — | — | — | 225 | — |
| 1999 Proof | 2,500 | Value: 500 | | | | |

**30 DOLLARS** **KM# 447** **Weight:** 1002.5020 g. **Composition:** 0.9990 Silver 32.1989 oz. ASW **Obverse:** Queen's head right **Reverse:** 2 kookaburras on branch **Edge:** Reeded

| Date | Mintage | F | VF | XF | Unc | BU |
|---|---|---|---|---|---|---|
| 1999 | — | — | — | — | 250 | — |

**30 DOLLARS** **KM# 525.1 (KM525)** **Weight:** 1002.5020 g. **Composition:** 0.9990 Silver 32.2312 oz. ASW **Series:** Dragons **Obverse:** Queen's head right. **Reverse:** Dragon. **Edge:** Segmented reeding. **Size:** 101 mm.

| Date | Mintage | F | VF | XF | Unc | BU |
|---|---|---|---|---|---|---|
| 2000 Proof | — | Value: 350 | | | | |

**30 DOLLARS** **KM# 525.2** **Composition:** 0.9990 Silver **Series:** Dragons **Obverse:** Queen's head right. **Reverse:** Dragon with diamonds for eyes and multicolor ornamentation.

| Date | Mintage | F | VF | XF | Unc | BU |
|---|---|---|---|---|---|---|
| 2000 Proof | 5,000 | Value: 400 | | | | |

**30 DOLLARS** **KM# 520** **Weight:** 1002.5020 g. **Composition:** 0.9990 Silver 32.2312 oz. ASW **Series:** Olympics **Obverse:** Queen's head right. **Reverse:** Multicolor logo in center. **Rev. Legend:** 1 KILO .999 SILVER. **Edge Lettering:** GAMES OF THE XXVII OLYMPIAD **Size:** 100 mm. **Note:** Illustration reduced. Actual size: 100mm.

| Date | Mintage | F | VF | XF | Unc | BU |
|---|---|---|---|---|---|---|
| 2000 Proof | 20,000 | Value: 470 | | | | |

**30 DOLLARS** **KM# 542** **Weight:** 1002.5020 g. **Composition:** 0.9990 Silver 32.2312 oz. ASW **Subject:** Year of the Snake **Obverse:** Queen's head right. **Reverse:** Snake with eggs. **Edge:** Segmented reeding. **Size:** 101 mm.

| Date | Mintage | F | VF | XF | Unc | BU |
|---|---|---|---|---|---|---|
| 2001 | — | — | — | — | 335 | — |

**40 DOLLARS** **KM# 313** **Weight:** 31.1850 g. **Composition:** 0.9995 Palladium 1.0021 oz. **Reverse:** The Australian emu

| Date | Mintage | F | VF | XF | Unc | BU |
|---|---|---|---|---|---|---|
| 1995 | — | — | — | — | 600 | — |
| 1995 Proof | Est. 2,500 | Value: 650 | | | | |

**40 DOLLARS** **KM# 343** **Weight:** 31.1850 g. **Composition:** 0.9995 Palladium 1.0021 oz. **Obverse:** Queen's portrait **Reverse:** Emu and chicks

| Date | Mintage | F | VF | XF | Unc | BU |
|---|---|---|---|---|---|---|
| 1996 Proof | Est. 2,500 | Value: 650 | | | | |

**50 DOLLARS** **KM# 91** **Weight:** 15.5017 g. **Composition:** 0.9990 Gold .5000 oz. AGW **Obverse:** Elizabeth II **Reverse:** Hand of Faith

| Date | Mintage | F | VF | XF | Unc | BU |
|---|---|---|---|---|---|---|
| 1986P Proof | 15,000 | Value: 250 | | | | |
| 1987 | 188,000 | — | — | — | BV+7% | — |
| 1988 | 75,000 | — | — | — | BV+7% | — |
| 1989 | 100,000 | — | — | — | BV+7% | — |

**50 DOLLARS** **KM# 97** **Weight:** 15.5017 g. **Composition:** 0.9990 Gold .5000 oz. AGW **Reverse:** Bobby Dazzler

| Date | Mintage | F | VF | XF | Unc | BU |
|---|---|---|---|---|---|---|
| 1987P Proof | 15,000 | Value: 250 | | | | |

**50 DOLLARS** **KM# 106** **Weight:** 15.5017 g. **Composition:** 0.9990 Gold .5000 oz. AGW **Reverse:** Welcome nugget

| Date | Mintage | F | VF | XF | Unc | BU |
|---|---|---|---|---|---|---|
| 1988P Proof | Est. 10,000 | Value: 250 | | | | |

**50 DOLLARS** **KM# 110** **Weight:** 15.6050 g. **Composition:** 0.9990 Platinum .5000 oz. APW

| Date | Mintage | F | VF | XF | Unc | BU |
|---|---|---|---|---|---|---|
| 1988 | — | — | — | — | BV+7% | — |
| 1988 Proof | 12,000 | Value: 335 | | | | |
| 1989 Proof | — | Value: 320 | | | | |

**50 DOLLARS** **KM# 120** **Weight:** 15.5017 g. **Composition:** 0.9990 Gold .5000 oz. AGW **Reverse:** Red kangaroo

| Date | Mintage | F | VF | XF | Unc | BU |
|---|---|---|---|---|---|---|
| 1989 Proof | 2,200 | Value: 275 | | | | |
| 1990 | Est. 240,000 | — | — | — | BV+7% | — |

**50 DOLLARS** **KM# 125** **Weight:** 15.6050 g. **Composition:** 0.9990 Platinum .5000 oz. APW **Note:** Similar to 100 Dollars, KM#126.

| Date | Mintage | F | VF | XF | Unc | BU |
|---|---|---|---|---|---|---|
| 1989 Proof | 2,400 | Value: 365 | | | | |
| 1990 Proof | 8,000 | Value: 335 | | | | |

**50 DOLLARS** **KM# 143** **Weight:** 15.5017 g. **Composition:** 0.9990 Gold .5000 oz. AGW **Reverse:** Gray kangaroo

| Date | Mintage | F | VF | XF | Unc | BU |
|---|---|---|---|---|---|---|
| 1990 Proof | 5,000 | Value: 250 | | | | |
| 1991 | 100,000 | — | — | — | BV+7% | — |

**50 DOLLARS** **KM# 148** **Weight:** 15.6050 g. **Composition:** 0.9990 Platinum .5000 oz. APW **Reverse:** Koala

| Date | Mintage | F | VF | XF | Unc | BU |
|---|---|---|---|---|---|---|
| 1990 Proof | 5,500 | Value: 335 | | | | |
| 1991 | 20,000 | — | — | — | BV+7% | — |
| 1991 Proof | 2,000 | Value: 365 | | | | |

**50 DOLLARS** **KM# 162** **Weight:** 311.0670 g. **Composition:** 0.9990 Silver 10.0000 oz. ASW **Subject:** Australian Kookaburra **Obverse:** Queen Elizabeth II above denomination **Reverse:** Kookaburra bird

| Date | Mintage | F | VF | XF | Unc | BU |
|---|---|---|---|---|---|---|
| 1991 | — | — | — | — | 60.00 | — |
| 1991 Proof | 2,500 | Value: 250 | | | | |

**50 DOLLARS** **KM# 168** **Weight:** 15.5017 g. **Composition:** 0.9990 Gold .5000 oz. AGW **Subject:** Common Wallaroo **Obverse:** Elizabeth II **Reverse:** Similar to 100 Dollars, KM#169

| Date | Mintage | F | VF | XF | Unc | BU |
|---|---|---|---|---|---|---|
| 1991 Proof | 1,096 | Value: 300 | | | | |
| 1992 | 100,000 | — | — | — | BV+7% | — |

**50 DOLLARS** **KM# 173** **Weight:** 15.6050 g. **Composition:** 0.9990 Platinum .5000 oz. APW **Subject:** Koala **Obverse:** Queen Elizabeth II **Reverse:** Similar to 100 Dollars, KM#174

| Date | Mintage | F | VF | XF | Unc | BU |
|---|---|---|---|---|---|---|
| 1992 | 20,000 | — | — | — | BV+7% | — |

**50 DOLLARS** **KM# 392** **Weight:** 15.5017 g. **Composition:** 0.9990 Gold .5000 oz. AGW **Obverse:** Queen's portrait **Reverse:** Nail-tailed wallaby **Note:** Similar to 25 Dollars, KM#391.

| Date | Mintage | F | VF | XF | Unc | BU |
|---|---|---|---|---|---|---|
| 1992 (ae) Proof | 500 | Value: 500 | | | | |

**50 DOLLARS** **KM# 194** **Weight:** 15.6050 g. **Composition:** 0.9990 Platinum .5000 oz. APW **Obverse:** Similar to 100 Dollars, KM#195

| Date | Mintage | F | VF | XF | Unc | BU |
|---|---|---|---|---|---|---|
| 1993 | Est. 20,000 | — | — | — | BV+7% | — |

**50 DOLLARS** **KM# 236** **Weight:** 15.5017 g. **Composition:** 0.9990 Gold .5000 oz. AGW **Subject:** Whiptail Wallaby **Obverse:** Queen Elizabeth II **Reverse:** Whiptail wallaby

| Date | Mintage | F | VF | XF | Unc | BU |
|---|---|---|---|---|---|---|
| 1993 Proof | — | Value: 325 | | | | |
| 1994 | — | — | — | — | BV+7% | — |

**50 DOLLARS** **KM# 244** **Weight:** 15.5017 g. **Composition:** 0.9990 Gold .5000 oz. AGW **Reverse:** Red kangaroo

| Date | Mintage | F | VF | XF | Unc | BU |
|---|---|---|---|---|---|---|
| 1994 Proof | — | Value: 325 | | | | |
| 1995 | 30,000 | — | — | — | BV+10% | — |
| 1995 (f) Proof | 10,000 | Value: 225 | | | | |

**50 DOLLARS** **KM# 252** **Weight:** 15.6050 g. **Composition:** 0.9990 Platinum .5000 oz. APW **Reverse:** Koala mother and baby

| Date | Mintage | F | VF | XF | Unc | BU |
|---|---|---|---|---|---|---|
| 1994 | 5,000 | — | — | — | BV+7% | — |

**50 DOLLARS** KM# 281 **Weight:** 15.6050 g. **Composition:** 0.9990 Platinum .5000 oz. APW **Reverse:** Koala in fork of tree

| Date | Mintage | F | VF | XF | Unc | BU |
|---|---|---|---|---|---|---|
| 1994 Proof | — | Value: 375 | | | | |
| 1995 | — | — | — | — | BV+7% | — |

**50 DOLLARS** KM# 275.1 **Weight:** 15.5017 g. **Composition:** 0.9990 Gold .5000 oz. AGW **Reverse:** 2 kangaroos

| Date | Mintage | F | VF | XF | Unc | BU |
|---|---|---|---|---|---|---|
| 1995 Proof | 300 | Value: 325 | | | | |
| 1996 | 100,000 | — | — | — | BV+7% | — |
| 1996 (s) Proof | 13,000 | Value: 225 | | | | |
| 1996 (l) Proof | 3,000 | Value: 235 | | | | |

**Note:** In Proof sets only

| Date | Mintage | F | VF | XF | Unc | BU |
|---|---|---|---|---|---|---|
| 1996 (f) Proof | 13,000 | Value: 225 | | | | |

**50 DOLLARS** KM# 286 **Weight:** 15.6050 g. **Composition:** 0.9990 Platinum .5000 oz. APW **Reverse:** Baby koala on branch

| Date | Mintage | F | VF | XF | Unc | BU |
|---|---|---|---|---|---|---|
| 1995 Proof | 450 | Value: 375 | | | | |
| 1995 (ww) Proof | 300 | Value: 425 | | | | |

**Note:** In Proof sets only

| Date | Mintage | F | VF | XF | Unc | BU |
|---|---|---|---|---|---|---|
| 1996 | 5,000 | — | — | — | BV+7% | — |

**50 DOLLARS** KM# 341 **Weight:** 15.5017 g. **Composition:** 0.9990 Gold .5000 oz. AGW **Subject:** Kangaroo **Obverse:** Queen's portrait **Reverse:** Kangaroo bounding right

| Date | Mintage | F | VF | XF | Unc | BU |
|---|---|---|---|---|---|---|
| 1996 (p) Proof | 400 | Value: 600 | | | | |

**Note:** In Proof sets only

| Date | Mintage | F | VF | XF | Unc | BU |
|---|---|---|---|---|---|---|
| 1997 | 100,000 | — | — | — | 165 | — |
| 1997 Proof | — | Value: 185 | | | | |
| 1997 (f) Proof | 13,000 | Value: 225 | | | | |
| 1997 (l) Proof | 10,000 | Value: 225 | | | | |

**Note:** In Proof sets only

| Date | Mintage | F | VF | XF | Unc | BU |
|---|---|---|---|---|---|---|
| 1997 (s) Proof | 13,000 | Value: 225 | | | | |

**50 DOLLARS** KM# 275.2 **Weight:** 15.5017 g. **Composition:** 0.9990 Gold .5000 oz. AGW **Edge:** Reeded and inscribed with date and serial number

| Date | Mintage | F | VF | XF | Unc | BU |
|---|---|---|---|---|---|---|
| 1996 Proof | 500 | Value: 235 | | | | |

**50 DOLLARS** KM# 347 **Weight:** 15.5518 g. **Composition:** 0.9995 Platinum .5000 oz. APW **Subject:** Koalas **Obverse:** Queen's portrait **Reverse:** Cuddling koalas

| Date | Mintage | F | VF | XF | Unc | BU |
|---|---|---|---|---|---|---|
| 1997 | 5,000 | — | — | — | BV+7% | — |
| 1997 Proof | — | Value: 375 | | | | |

**50 DOLLARS** KM# 451 **Weight:** 15.5940 g. **Composition:** 0.9990 Gold .5000 oz. AGW **Obverse:** Queen's head right **Reverse:** Kangaroo facing left **Edge:** Reeded

| Date | Mintage | F | VF | XF | Unc | BU |
|---|---|---|---|---|---|---|
| 1999 | 100,000 | — | — | — | 165 | — |

**50 DOLLARS** KM# 459 **Weight:** 15.6050 g. **Composition:** 0.9990 Platinum .5000 oz. APW **Obverse:** Queen's head right **Reverse:** Koala on log **Edge:** Reeded

| Date | Mintage | F | VF | XF | Unc | BU |
|---|---|---|---|---|---|---|
| 1999 | 5,000 | — | — | — | 375 | — |

**50 DOLLARS** KM# 467 **Weight:** 15.5940 g. **Composition:** 0.9990 Gold .5000 oz. AGW **Obverse:** Queen's head right **Reverse:** 2 kangaroos bounding left **Edge:** Reeded

| Date | Mintage | F | VF | XF | Unc | BU |
|---|---|---|---|---|---|---|
| 2000 | — | — | — | — | 165 | — |

**50 DOLLARS** KM# 472 **Weight:** 15.6050 g. **Composition:** 0.9990 Platinum .5000 oz. APW **Obverse:** Queen's head right **Reverse:** Seated koala **Edge:** Reeded

| Date | Mintage | F | VF | XF | Unc | BU |
|---|---|---|---|---|---|---|
| 2000 | — | — | — | — | 375 | — |

**100 DOLLARS** KM# 92 **Weight:** 31.1035 g. **Composition:** 0.9990 Gold 1.0000 oz. AGW **Reverse:** Welcome Stranger

| Date | Mintage | F | VF | XF | Unc | BU |
|---|---|---|---|---|---|---|
| 1986P Proof | 15,000 | Value: 425 | | | | |
| 1987 | 259,000 | — | — | — | BV+4% | — |
| 1988 | 116,000 | — | — | — | BV+4% | — |
| 1989 | — | — | — | — | BV+4% | — |

**100 DOLLARS** KM# 98 **Weight:** 31.1035 g. **Composition:** 0.9990 Gold 1.0000 oz. AGW **Reverse:** Poseidon

| Date | Mintage | F | VF | XF | Unc | BU |
|---|---|---|---|---|---|---|
| 1987P Proof | 15,000 | Value: 425 | | | | |

**100 DOLLARS** KM# 107 **Weight:** 31.1035 g. **Composition:** 0.9990 Gold 1.0000 oz. AGW **Reverse:** Pride of Australia nugget

| Date | Mintage | F | VF | XF | Unc | BU |
|---|---|---|---|---|---|---|
| 1988P Proof | Est. 10,000 | Value: 425 | | | | |

**100 DOLLARS** KM# 111 **Weight:** 31.1850 g. **Composition:** 0.9990 Platinum 1.0000 oz. APW

| Date | Mintage | F | VF | XF | Unc | BU |
|---|---|---|---|---|---|---|
| 1988 | — | — | — | — | BV+4% | — |
| 1989 Proof | — | Value: 650 | | | | |

**100 DOLLARS** KM# 121 **Weight:** 31.1035 g. **Composition:** 0.9990 Gold 1.0000 oz. AGW **Reverse:** Red kangaroo

| Date | Mintage | F | VF | XF | Unc | BU |
|---|---|---|---|---|---|---|
| 1989 Proof | 2,200 | Value: 525 | | | | |
| 1990 | — | — | — | — | BV+4% | — |

**100 DOLLARS** KM# 126 **Weight:** 31.1850 g. **Composition:** 0.9990 Platinum 1.0000 oz. APW

| Date | Mintage | F | VF | XF | Unc | BU |
|---|---|---|---|---|---|---|
| 1989 Proof | 2,400 | Value: 650 | | | | |
| 1990 Proof | — | Value: 650 | | | | |

**100 DOLLARS** KM# 144 **Weight:** 31.1035 g. **Composition:** 0.9990 Gold 1.0000 oz. AGW **Reverse:** Gray kangaroo

| Date | Mintage | F | VF | XF | Unc | BU |
|---|---|---|---|---|---|---|
| 1990 Proof | 8,000 | Value: 425 | | | | |
| 1991 | 250,000 | — | — | — | BV+4% | — |

**100 DOLLARS** KM# 149 **Weight:** 31.1850 g. **Composition:** 0.9990 Platinum 1.0000 oz. APW **Reverse:** Koala

| Date | Mintage | F | VF | XF | Unc | BU |
|---|---|---|---|---|---|---|
| 1990 Proof | 3,500 | Value: 650 | | | | |
| 1991 | 75,000 | — | — | — | BV+4% | — |
| 1991 Proof | 1,000 | Value: 650 | | | | |

**100 DOLLARS** KM# 169 **Weight:** 31.1035 g. **Composition:** 0.9990 Gold 1.0000 oz. AGW **Reverse:** Common wallaroo

| Date | Mintage | F | VF | XF | Unc | BU |
|---|---|---|---|---|---|---|
| 1991 Proof | 3,000 | Value: 550 | | | | |
| 1992 | 250,000 | — | — | — | BV+4% | — |

**100 DOLLARS** KM# 174 **Weight:** 31.1850 g. **Composition:** 0.9990 Platinum 1.0000 oz. APW **Obverse:** Queen Elizabeth II **Reverse:** Koala

| Date | Mintage | F | VF | XF | Unc | BU |
|---|---|---|---|---|---|---|
| 1992 | 75,000 | — | — | — | BV+4% | — |

**100 DOLLARS** **KM# 393 Weight:** 31.1035 g. **Composition:** 0.9990 Gold 1.0000 oz. AGW **Obverse:** Queen's portrait **Reverse:** Nail-tailed wallaby **Note:** Similar to 25 Dollars, KM#391.

| Date | Mintage | F | VF | XF | Unc | BU |
|---|---|---|---|---|---|---|
| 1992 Proof | 784 | Value: 475 | | | | |
| 1993 | — | — | — | — | BV+4% | — |

**100 DOLLARS** **KM# 195 Weight:** 31.1850 g. **Composition:** 0.9990 Platinum 1.0000 oz. APW

| Date | Mintage | F | VF | XF | Unc | BU |
|---|---|---|---|---|---|---|
| 1993 | Est. 80,000 | — | — | — | BV+4% | — |

**100 DOLLARS** **KM# 237 Weight:** 31.1035 g. **Composition:** 0.9990 Gold 1.0000 oz. AGW **Subject:** Whiptail Wallaby **Obverse:** Queen Elizabeth II **Reverse:** Whiptail wallaby

| Date | Mintage | F | VF | XF | Unc | BU |
|---|---|---|---|---|---|---|
| 1993 Proof | — | Value: 600 | | | | |
| 1993 (f) Proof | 150 | Value: 650 | | | | |
| 1994 | — | — | — | — | BV+4% | — |

**100 DOLLARS** **KM# 245 Weight:** 31.1035 g. **Composition:** 0.9990 Gold 1.0000 oz. AGW **Reverse:** Red kangaroo

| Date | Mintage | F | VF | XF | Unc | BU |
|---|---|---|---|---|---|---|
| 1994 Proof | — | Value: 425 | | | | |
| 1995 | 350,000 | — | — | — | BV+4% | — |

**100 DOLLARS** **KM# 253 Weight:** 31.1850 g. **Composition:** 0.9990 Platinum 1.0000 oz. APW **Reverse:** Koala mother and baby

| Date | Mintage | F | VF | XF | Unc | BU |
|---|---|---|---|---|---|---|
| 1994 Prooflike | 100,000 | — | — | — | BV+4% | — |

**100 DOLLARS** **KM# 282 Weight:** 31.1850 g. **Composition:** 0.9990 Platinum 1.0000 oz. APW **Reverse:** Koala in fork of tree

| Date | Mintage | F | VF | XF | Unc | BU |
|---|---|---|---|---|---|---|
| 1994 Proof | — | Value: 675 | | | | |
| 1995 | — | — | — | — | BV+4% | — |

**100 DOLLARS** **KM# 276 Weight:** 31.1035 g. **Composition:** 0.9990 Gold 1.0000 oz. AGW **Reverse:** 2 kangaroos

| Date | Mintage | F | VF | XF | Unc | BU |
|---|---|---|---|---|---|---|
| 1995 Proof | 300 | Value: 600 | | | | |
| 1995 (ww) Proof | 600 | Value: 575 | | | | |
| 1996 | 350,000 | — | — | — | BV+4% | — |

**100 DOLLARS** **KM# 287 Weight:** 31.1850 g. **Composition:** 0.9990 Platinum 1.0000 oz. APW **Reverse:** Baby koala on branch

| Date | Mintage | F | VF | XF | Unc | BU |
|---|---|---|---|---|---|---|
| 1995 Proof | 200 | Value: 675 | | | | |
| 1996 | 100,000 | — | — | — | BV+4% | — |

**100 DOLLARS** **KM# 308 Weight:** 10.3678 g. **Composition:** 0.9160 Gold .3053 oz. AGW **Reverse:** The Waratah Flower

| Date | Mintage | F | VF | XF | Unc | BU |
|---|---|---|---|---|---|---|
| 1995 | 3,000 | — | — | — | 165 | — |

**100 DOLLARS** **KM# 308a Weight:** 10.3678 g. **Composition:** 0.9999 Gold .3333 oz. AGW

| Date | Mintage | F | VF | XF | Unc | BU |
|---|---|---|---|---|---|---|
| 1995 Proof | 2,500 | Value: 275 | | | | |

**100 DOLLARS** **KM# 300 Weight:** 31.1035 g. **Composition:** 0.9990 Gold 1.0000 oz. AGW **Subject:** Year of the Rat

| Date | Mintage | F | VF | XF | Unc | BU |
|---|---|---|---|---|---|---|
| 1996 Proof | — | Value: 425 | | | | |

**100 DOLLARS** **KM# 333a Weight:** 10.3678 g. **Composition:** 0.9999 Gold .3333 oz. AGW

| Date | Mintage | F | VF | XF | Unc | BU |
|---|---|---|---|---|---|---|
| 1996 Proof | — | Value: 275 | | | | |

**100 DOLLARS** **KM# 342 Weight:** 31.1035 g. **Composition:** 0.9990 Gold 1.0000 oz. AGW **Subject:** Kangaroo **Obverse:** Queen's portrait **Reverse:** Kangaroo bounding right

| Date | Mintage | F | VF | XF | Unc | BU |
|---|---|---|---|---|---|---|
| 1996 (p) Proof | — | Value: 550 | | | | |
| **Note:** In Proof sets only | | | | | | |
| 1997 | 350,000 | — | — | — | 300 | — |
| 1997 Proof | — | Value: 350 | | | | |

**100 DOLLARS** **KM# 333 Weight:** 10.3678 g. **Composition:** 0.9160 Gold .3053 oz. AGW **Subject:** Tasmanial Blue Gum Flower **Obverse:** Queen's portrait **Reverse:** Flowering plant with long, droopy leaves **Note:** Similar to 150 Dollars, KM#334.

| Date | Mintage | F | VF | XF | Unc | BU |
|---|---|---|---|---|---|---|
| 1996 | — | — | — | — | 165 | — |

**100 DOLLARS** **KM# 337 Weight:** 31.1035 g. **Composition:** 0.9990 Gold 1.0000 oz. AGW **Subject:** Year of the Ox **Obverse:** Queen's portrait **Reverse:** Ox looking right

| Date | Mintage | F | VF | XF | Unc | BU |
|---|---|---|---|---|---|---|
| 1997 | — | — | — | — | 400 | — |
| 1997 Proof | 8,888 | Value: 525 | | | | |

**100 DOLLARS** **KM# 348 Weight:** 31.1850 g. **Composition:** 0.9990 Platinum 1.0000 oz. APW **Subject:** Koalas **Obverse:** Queen's portrait **Reverse:** Cuddling koalas

| Date | Mintage | F | VF | XF | Unc | BU |
|---|---|---|---|---|---|---|
| 1997 | 100,000 | — | — | — | BV+4% | — |
| 1997 Proof | — | Value: 675 | | | | |

**100 DOLLARS** **KM# 384 Weight:** 10.3678 g. **Composition:** 0.9167 Gold .3053 oz. AGW **Subject:** Mangles' Kangaroo Paw Flower **Obverse:** Queens' portrait **Reverse:** Flower

| Date | Mintage | F | VF | XF | Unc | BU |
|---|---|---|---|---|---|---|
| 1997 | 3,000 | — | — | — | 165 | — |

**100 DOLLARS** **KM# 373 Weight:** 10.0210 g. **Composition:** 0.9999 Gold .3222 oz. AGW **Series:** Sydney Olympics 2000 **Obverse:** Queen's portrait **Reverse:** Runner training in rain

| Date | Mintage | F | VF | XF | Unc | BU |
|---|---|---|---|---|---|---|
| 2000 (1998) Proof | — | Value: 250 | | | | |

**100 DOLLARS** **KM# 383 Weight:** 10.0210 g. **Composition:** 0.9999 Gold .3222 oz. AGW **Series:** Sydney Olympics 2000 **Obverse:** Queen's portrait **Reverse:** Multicolor games logo

| Date | Mintage | F | VF | XF | Unc | BU |
|---|---|---|---|---|---|---|
| 2000 (1998) Proof | Est. 30,000 | Value: 250 | | | | |

**100 DOLLARS** **KM# 480 Weight:** 10.3678 g. **Composition:** 0.9160 Gold .3056 oz. AGW **Subject:** Stuart's Desert Pea **Obverse:** Queen's head right. **Reverse:** Plant with pods. **Edge:** Reeded. **Size:** 25 mm.

| Date | Mintage | F | VF | XF | Unc | BU |
|---|---|---|---|---|---|---|
| 1998 | 3,000 | — | — | — | 140 | — |

**100 DOLLARS** **KM# 480a Weight:** 10.3678 g. **Composition:** 0.9990 Gold .3333 oz. AGW **Subject:** Stuart's Desert Pea **Obverse:** Queen's head right. **Reverse:** Plant with pods. **Edge:** Reeded. **Size:** 25 mm.

| Date | Mintage | F | VF | XF | Unc | BU |
|---|---|---|---|---|---|---|
| 1998 Proof | 2,500 | Value: 190 | | | | |

**100 DOLLARS** **KM# 487** **Weight:** 10.3678 g. **Composition:** 0.9160 Gold .3056 oz. AGW **Obverse:** Queen's head right. **Reverse:** Common Heath flowers. **Edge:** Reeded. **Size:** 25 mm.

| Date | Mintage | F | VF | XF | Unc | BU |
|---|---|---|---|---|---|---|
| 1999 | 3,000 | — | — | — | 140 | — |

**100 DOLLARS** **KM# 487a** **Weight:** 10.3678 g. **Composition:** 0.9990 Gold .3333 oz. AGW **Obverse:** Queen's head right. **Reverse:** Common Heath flowers. **Edge:** Reeded. **Size:** 25 mm.

| Date | Mintage | F | VF | XF | Unc | BU |
|---|---|---|---|---|---|---|
| 1999 Proof | 2,500 | Value: 190 | | | | |

**100 DOLLARS** **KM# 428** **Weight:** 31.1620 g. **Composition:** 0.9999 Gold 1.0529 oz. AGW **Subject:** Year of the Rabbit **Obverse:** Queen's portrait. **Reverse:** Rabbit **Edge:** Reeded

| Date | Mintage | F | VF | XF | Unc | BU |
|---|---|---|---|---|---|---|
| 1999 | Est. 30,000 | — | — | — | 400 | — |
| 1999 Proof | — | Value: 600 | | | | |

**100 DOLLARS** **KM# 442** **Weight:** 10.0000 g. **Composition:** 0.9990 Gold .3215 oz. AGW **Series:** Sydney Olympics 2000 **Obverse:** Queen's head right **Reverse:** 3 athletic workout scenes **Edge:** Reeded

| Date | Mintage | F | VF | XF | Unc | BU |
|---|---|---|---|---|---|---|
| 2000 (1999) Proof | 30,000 | Value: 250 | | | | |

**100 DOLLARS** **KM# 443** **Weight:** 10.0000 g. **Composition:** 0.9990 Gold .3215 oz. AGW **Series:** Sydney Olympics 2000 **Obverse:** Queen's head right **Reverse:** Shot putter teaching seated children **Edge:** Reeded

| Date | Mintage | F | VF | XF | Unc | BU |
|---|---|---|---|---|---|---|
| 2000 (1999) Proof | 30,000 | Value: 250 | | | | |

**100 DOLLARS** **KM# 444** **Weight:** 10.0000 g. **Composition:** 0.9990 Gold .3215 oz. AGW **Series:** Sydney Olympics 2000 **Obverse:** Queen's head right **Reverse:** Sprinter being coached **Edge:** Reeded

| Date | Mintage | F | VF | XF | Unc | BU |
|---|---|---|---|---|---|---|
| 2000 (1999) Proof | 30,000 | Value: 250 | | | | |

**100 DOLLARS** **KM# 452** **Weight:** 31.1620 g. **Composition:** 0.9990 Gold 1.0000 oz. AGW **Obverse:** Queen's head right **Reverse:** Kangaroo facing left **Edge:** Reeded

| Date | Mintage | F | VF | XF | Unc | BU |
|---|---|---|---|---|---|---|
| 1999 | 350,000 | — | — | — | 400 | — |

**100 DOLLARS** **KM# 460** **Weight:** 31.1850 g. **Composition:** 0.9990 Platinum 1.0000 oz. APW **Obverse:** Queen's head right **Reverse:** Koala on log **Edge:** Reeded

| Date | Mintage | F | VF | XF | Unc | BU |
|---|---|---|---|---|---|---|
| 1999 | 100,000 | — | — | — | 675 | — |

**100 DOLLARS** **KM# 474 Ring Weight:** 5.0119 g. **Ring Composition:** 0.9990 Silver .1611 oz. ASW AGW**Center Weight:** 7.9881 g. **Center Composition:** 0.9170 Gold .2354 oz. ASW AGW **Subject:** Perth Mint Centennial Sovereign **Obverse:** Queen's head right **Reverse:** St. George slaying the dragon **Edge:** Reeded

| Date | Mintage | F | VF | XF | Unc | BU |
|---|---|---|---|---|---|---|
| ND(1999) Proof | 7,500 | Value: 500 | | | | |

**100 DOLLARS** **KM# 468** **Weight:** 31.1620 g. **Composition:** 0.9990 Gold 1.0000 oz. AGW **Obverse:** Queen's head right **Reverse:** 2 kangaroos bounding left **Edge:** Reeded

| Date | Mintage | F | VF | XF | Unc | BU |
|---|---|---|---|---|---|---|
| 2000 | — | — | — | — | 400 | — |

**100 DOLLARS** **KM# 473** **Weight:** 31.1850 g. **Composition:** 0.9990 Platinum 1.0000 oz. APW **Obverse:** Queen's head right **Reverse:** Seated koala **Edge:** Reeded

| Date | Mintage | F | VF | XF | Unc | BU |
|---|---|---|---|---|---|---|
| 2000 | — | — | — | — | 675 | — |

**100 DOLLARS** **KM# 512** **Weight:** 10.3678 g. **Composition:** 0.9160 Gold .3056 oz. AGW **Subject:** Cooktown Orchid **Obverse:** Queen's head right. **Reverse:** Orchid and denomination. **Edge:** Reeded. **Size:** 25 mm.

| Date | Mintage | F | VF | XF | Unc | BU |
|---|---|---|---|---|---|---|
| 2000 | 3,000 | — | — | — | 150 | — |

**100 DOLLARS** **KM# 512a** **Weight:** 10.3678 g. **Composition:** 0.9990 Gold .3333 oz. AGW **Subject:** Cooktown Orchid **Obverse:** Queen's head right. **Reverse:** Orchid and denomination. **Edge:** Reeded. **Size:** 25 mm.

| Date | Mintage | F | VF | XF | Unc | BU |
|---|---|---|---|---|---|---|
| 2000 Proof | 2,500 | Value: 200 | | | | |

**100 DOLLARS** **KM# 521** **Weight:** 10.0000 g. **Composition:** 0.9990 Gold .3215 oz. AGW **Series:** Olympics **Obverse:** Queen's head right. **Reverse:** Multicolor torch flames. **Edge:** Reeded. **Size:** 25 mm.

| Date | Mintage | F | VF | XF | Unc | BU |
|---|---|---|---|---|---|---|
| 2000 Proof | 20,000 | Value: 385 | | | | |

**100 DOLLARS** **KM# 528** **Weight:** 31.1035 g. **Composition:** 0.9990 Gold 1. oz. AGW **Series:** Dragons **Obverse:** Queen's head right. **Reverse:** Dragon. **Edge:** Reeded. **Size:** 32.1 mm.

| Date | Mintage | F | VF | XF | Unc | BU |
|---|---|---|---|---|---|---|
| 2000 Proof | — | Value: 460 | | | | |

**100 DOLLARS** **KM# 543** **Weight:** 31.1035 g. **Composition:** 0.9990 Gold 1. oz. AGW **Subject:** Year of the Snake **Obverse:** Queen's head right. **Reverse:** Snake in tree. **Edge:** Reeded. **Size:** 32.1 mm.

| Date | Mintage | F | VF | XF | Unc | BU |
|---|---|---|---|---|---|---|
| 2001 | 30,000 | — | — | — | 450 | — |

**150 DOLLARS** **KM# 163** **Weight:** 1000.1000 g. **Composition:** 0.9990 Silver 32.1575 oz. ASW **Subject:** Australian Kookaburra **Obverse:** Queen Elizabeth II above denomination **Reverse:** Kookaburra bird **Note:** Kilo

| Date | Mintage | F | VF | XF | Unc | BU |
|---|---|---|---|---|---|---|
| 1991 | — | — | — | — | 200 | — |
| 1991 Proof | 1,000 | Value: 600 | | | | |

**150 DOLLARS** **KM# 309** **Weight:** 15.5517 g. **Composition:** 0.9999 Gold .5000 oz. AGW **Reverse:** The Waratah Flower

| Date | Mintage | F | VF | XF | Unc | BU |
|---|---|---|---|---|---|---|
| 1995 Proof | 1,500 | Value: 400 | | | | |

**150 DOLLARS** **KM# 334** **Weight:** 15.5517 g. **Composition:** 0.9999 Gold .5000 oz. AGW **Subject:** Tasmanian Blue Gum Flower **Obverse:** Queen's portrait **Reverse:** Flowering plant with long, dropping leaves

| Date | Mintage | F | VF | XF | Unc | BU |
|---|---|---|---|---|---|---|
| 1996 Proof | — | Value: 400 | | | | |

**150 DOLLARS** **KM# 413** **Weight:** 15.5517 g. **Composition:** 0.9999 Gold .5000 oz. AGW **Obverse:** Queen's portrait **Reverse:** Stuart's desert pea

| Date | Mintage | F | VF | XF | Unc | BU |
|---|---|---|---|---|---|---|
| 1998 Proof | 1,500 | Value: 400 | | | | |

**150 DOLLARS** **KM# 475** **Weight:** 15.5517 g. **Composition:** 0.9999 Gold .5000 oz. AGW **Subject:** Common Heath Flower **Obverse:** Queen's head right **Reverse:** Flowers **Edge:** Reeded

| Date | Mintage | F | VF | XF | Unc | BU |
|---|---|---|---|---|---|---|
| 1999 Proof | 1,500 | Value: 400 | | | | |

**150 DOLLARS** **KM# 513 Weight:** 15.5518 g. **Composition:** 0.9990 Gold .5000 oz. AGW **Subject:** Cooktown Orchid **Obverse:** Queen's head right. **Reverse:** Orchid and denomination. **Edge:** Reeded. **Size:** 30 mm.

| Date | Mintage | F | VF | XF | Unc | BU |
|---|---|---|---|---|---|---|
| 2000 Proof | 1,500 | Value: 500 | | | | |

**200 DOLLARS** **KM#71 Weight:** 10.0000 g. **Composition:** 0.9170 Gold .2948 oz. AGW **Reverse:** Koala

| Date | Mintage | F | VF | XF | Unc | BU |
|---|---|---|---|---|---|---|
| 1980 | 208,000 | — | — | — | 125 | — |
| 1980 Proof | 50,000 | Value: 130 | | | | |
| 1983 | 88,000 | — | — | — | 125 | — |
| 1983 Proof | 16,000 | Value: 130 | | | | |
| 1984 | 49,000 | — | — | — | 125 | — |
| 1984 Proof | 13,000 | Value: 130 | | | | |

**200 DOLLARS** **KM#73 Weight:** 10.0000 g. **Composition:** 0.9170 Gold .2948 oz. AGW **Subject:** Wedding of Prince Charles and Lady Diana

| Date | Mintage | F | VF | XF | Unc | BU |
|---|---|---|---|---|---|---|
| 1981 | 78,000 | — | — | — | 125 | — |

**200 DOLLARS** **KM#76 Weight:** 10.0000 g. **Composition:** 0.9170 Gold .2948 oz. AGW **Subject:** XII Commonwealth Games-Brisbane

| Date | Mintage | F | VF | XF | Unc | BU |
|---|---|---|---|---|---|---|
| 1982 | 77,000 | — | — | — | 125 | — |
| 1982 Proof | 30,000 | Value: 125 | | | | |

**200 DOLLARS** **KM#86 Weight:** 10.0000 g. **Composition:** 0.9170 Gold .2948 oz. AGW **Reverse:** Koala

| Date | Mintage | F | VF | XF | Unc | BU |
|---|---|---|---|---|---|---|
| 1985 | 29,000 | — | — | — | 125 | — |
| 1985 Proof | 17,000 | Value: 130 | | | | |
| 1986 | 15,000 | — | — | — | 125 | — |
| 1986 Proof | 17,000 | Value: 130 | | | | |

**200 DOLLARS** **KM#94 Weight:** 10.0000 g. **Composition:** 0.9170 Gold .2948 oz. AGW **Subject:** Arthur Phillip

| Date | Mintage | F | VF | XF | Unc | BU |
|---|---|---|---|---|---|---|
| 1987 | 21,000 | — | — | — | 125 | — |
| 1987 Proof | 20,000 | Value: 130 | | | | |

**200 DOLLARS** **KM# 115 Weight:** 10.0000 g. **Composition:** 0.9170 Gold .2948 oz. AGW **Subject:** Bicentennial of Australia

| Date | Mintage | F | VF | XF | Unc | BU |
|---|---|---|---|---|---|---|
| 1988 | 11,000 | — | — | — | 125 | — |
| 1988 Proof | 20,000 | Value: 130 | | | | |

**200 DOLLARS** **KM# 116 Weight:** 10.0000 g. **Composition:** 0.9170 Gold .2948 oz. AGW **Subject:** Pride of Australia - Frilled-neck lizard **Obverse:** Similar to KM#115

| Date | Mintage | F | VF | XF | Unc | BU |
|---|---|---|---|---|---|---|
| 1989 | Est. 10,000 | — | — | — | 125 | — |
| 1989 Proof | Est. 25,000 | Value: 130 | | | | |

**200 DOLLARS** **KM# 135 Weight:** 10.0000 g. **Composition:** 0.9170 Gold .2948 oz. AGW **Subject:** Pride of Australia - Platypus

| Date | Mintage | F | VF | XF | Unc | BU |
|---|---|---|---|---|---|---|
| 1990 | — | — | — | — | 125 | — |
| 1990 Proof | — | Value: 130 | | | | |

**200 DOLLARS** **KM# 160 Weight:** 10.0000 g. **Composition:** 0.9170 Gold .2948 oz. AGW **Subject:** Pride of Australia - Emu

| Date | Mintage | F | VF | XF | Unc | BU |
|---|---|---|---|---|---|---|
| 1991 | — | — | — | — | 125 | — |
| 1991 Proof | — | Value: 130 | | | | |

**200 DOLLARS** **KM# 182 Weight:** 62.2140 g. **Composition:** 0.9990 Gold 2.0000 oz. AGW **Obverse:** Portrait of Queen Elizabeth II **Reverse:** Red kangaroo

| Date | Mintage | F | VF | XF | Unc | BU |
|---|---|---|---|---|---|---|
| 1992 | — | — | — | — | BV+4% | — |
| 1994 Prooflike | — | — | — | — | BV+4% | — |
| 1995 | — | — | — | — | BV+4% | — |
| 1996 | — | — | — | — | BV+4% | — |
| 1997 | — | — | — | — | BV+4% | — |

**200 DOLLARS** **KM# 185 Weight:** 62.2140 g. **Composition:** 0.9995 Platinum 2.0000 oz. APW **Obverse:** Portrait of Queen Elizabeth II **Reverse:** Koala

| Date | Mintage | F | VF | XF | Unc | BU |
|---|---|---|---|---|---|---|
| 1992 | — | — | — | — | BV+4% | — |
| 1992 Proof | — | Value: 1,500 | | | | |
| 1996 | — | — | — | — | BV+4% | — |

**200 DOLLARS** **KM# 259 Weight:** 10.0000 g. **Composition:** 0.9170 Gold .2948 oz. AGW **Subject:** Pride of Australia - Echidna

| Date | Mintage | F | VF | XF | Unc | BU |
|---|---|---|---|---|---|---|
| 1992 | — | — | — | — | 125 | — |
| 1992 Proof | — | Value: 130 | | | | |

**200 DOLLARS** **KM# 394 Weight:** 62.2140 g. **Composition:** 0.9990 Gold 2.0000 oz. AGW **Obverse:** Queen's portrait **Reverse:** Nail-tailed wallaby **Note:** Similar to 25 Dollars, KM#391.

| Date | Mintage | F | VF | XF | Unc | BU |
|---|---|---|---|---|---|---|
| 1992 Proof | 152 | Value: 1,000 | | | | |

**200 DOLLARS** **KM# 196 Weight:** 62.2140 g. **Composition:** 0.9995 Platinum 2.0000 oz. APW **Obverse:** Similar to 100 Dollars, KM#195

| Date | Mintage | F | VF | XF | Unc | BU |
|---|---|---|---|---|---|---|
| 1993 | — | — | — | — | BV+4% | — |
| 1994 | — | — | — | — | BV+4% | — |
| 1995 | — | — | — | — | BV+4% | — |
| 1997 | — | — | — | — | BV+4% | — |

**200 DOLLARS** **KM# 220 Weight:** 16.8200 g. **Composition:** 0.9170 Gold .4958 oz. AGW **Series:** Olympics **Reverse:** Gymnast in flight

| Date | Mintage | F | VF | XF | Unc | BU |
|---|---|---|---|---|---|---|
| 1993 Proof | 60,000 | Value: 200 | | | | |

**200 DOLLARS** **KM# 222** **Weight:** 10.0000 g. **Composition:** 0.9170 Gold .2948 oz. AGW **Reverse:** Squirrel glider possum

| Date | Mintage | F | VF | XF | Unc | BU |
|---|---|---|---|---|---|---|
| 1993 | 3,014 | — | — | — | 125 | — |
| 1993 Proof | 5,000 | Value: 130 | | | | |

**200 DOLLARS** **KM# 238** **Weight:** 62.2140 g. **Composition:** 0.9999 Gold 2.0000 oz. AGW **Subject:** Whiptail Wallaby **Obverse:** Queen Elizabeth I **Reverse:** Whiptail wallaby

| Date | Mintage | F | VF | XF | Unc | BU |
|---|---|---|---|---|---|---|
| 1993 Proof | — | Value: 1,450 | | | | |

**200 DOLLARS** **KM# 254** **Weight:** 62.2140 g. **Composition:** 0.9995 Platinum 2.0000 oz. APW **Subject:** Koala Mother and Baby **Obverse:** Queen Elizabeth II **Reverse:** Similar to 100 Dollars, KM#253

| Date | Mintage | F | VF | XF | Unc | BU |
|---|---|---|---|---|---|---|
| 1994 Proof | — | Value: 1,750 | | | | |

**200 DOLLARS** **KM# 262** **Weight:** 10.0000 g. **Composition:** 0.9170 Gold .2948 oz. AGW **Reverse:** Tasmanian devil

| Date | Mintage | F | VF | XF | Unc | BU |
|---|---|---|---|---|---|---|
| 1994 Proof | 5,000 | Value: 200 | | | | |

**200 DOLLARS** **KM# 246** **Weight:** 62.2140 g. **Composition:** 0.9999 Gold 2.0000 oz. AGW **Reverse:** Red kangaroo **Note:** Similar to 100 Dollars, KM#245.

| Date | Mintage | F | VF | XF | Unc | BU |
|---|---|---|---|---|---|---|
| 1994 Proof | 325 | Value: 1,500 | | | | |

**200 DOLLARS** **KM# 277** **Weight:** 62.2140 g. **Composition:** 0.9999 Gold 2.0000 oz. AGW **Reverse:** 2 kangaroos

| Date | Mintage | F | VF | XF | Unc | BU |
|---|---|---|---|---|---|---|
| 1995 Proof | 100 | Value: 1,600 | | | | |

**200 DOLLARS** **KM# 288** **Weight:** 62.2140 g. **Composition:** 0.9995 Platinum 2.0000 oz. APW **Reverse:** Baby koala on branch

| Date | Mintage | F | VF | XF | Unc | BU |
|---|---|---|---|---|---|---|
| 1995 Proof | 100 | Value: 1,650 | | | | |

**200 DOLLARS** **KM# 385** **Weight:** 15.5517 g. **Composition:** 0.9999 Gold .5000 oz. AGW **Subject:** Mangles' Kangaroo Paw Flower **Obverse:** Queen's portrait **Reverse:** Flower **Note:** Similar to 100 Dollars, KM#384.

| Date | Mintage | F | VF | XF | Unc | BU |
|---|---|---|---|---|---|---|
| 1997 Proof | — | Value: 400 | | | | |

**200 DOLLARS** **KM# 461** **Weight:** 62.3130 g. **Composition:** 0.9990 Platinum 2.0000 oz. APW **Obverse:** Queen's head right **Reverse:** Koala in tree **Edge:** Reeded

| Date | Mintage | F | VF | XF | Unc | BU |
|---|---|---|---|---|---|---|
| 1999 | — | — | — | — | 1,500 | — |

**250 DOLLARS** **KM# 204** **Weight:** 16.9500 g. **Composition:** 0.9170 Gold .4995 oz. AGW **Subject:** 40th Anniversary - Reign of Queen Elizabeth II - Queen Mother **Reverse:** Portrait of Queen Mother right in circle of crowns

| Date | Mintage | F | VF | XF | Unc | BU |
|---|---|---|---|---|---|---|
| 1992 Proof | Est. 5,000 | Value: 275 | | | | |

**250 DOLLARS** **KM# 205** **Weight:** 16.9500 g. **Composition:** 0.9170 Gold .4995 oz. AGW **Subject:** 40th Anniversary - Reign of Queen Elizabeth II - Princess Diana **Reverse:** Portrait of Princess Diana right in circle of crowns

| Date | Mintage | F | VF | XF | Unc | BU |
|---|---|---|---|---|---|---|
| 1992 Proof | Est. 5,000 | Value: 300 | | | | |

**250 DOLLARS** **KM# 206** **Weight:** 16.9500 g. **Composition:** 0.9170 Gold .4995 oz. AGW **Subject:** 40th Anniversary - Reign of Queen Elizabeth II - Princess Anne **Reverse:** Portrait of Princess Anne right in circle of crowns

| Date | Mintage | F | VF | XF | Unc | BU |
|---|---|---|---|---|---|---|
| 1992 Proof | Est. 5,000 | Value: 275 | | | | |

**250 DOLLARS** **KM# 207** **Weight:** 16.9500 g. **Composition:** 0.9170 Gold .4995 oz. AGW **Subject:** 40th Anniversary - Reign of Queen Elizabeth II - Princess Margaret **Reverse:** Portrait of Princess Margaret left in circle of crowns

| Date | Mintage | F | VF | XF | Unc | BU |
|---|---|---|---|---|---|---|
| 1992 Proof | Est. 5,000 | Value: 285 | | | | |

**500 DOLLARS** **KM# 157** **Weight:** 62.2140 g. **Composition:** 0.9990 Platinum 2.0000 oz. APW **Subject:** Koala **Obverse:** Queen Elizabeth II **Reverse:** Koala in tree

| Date | Mintage | F | VF | XF | Unc | BU |
|---|---|---|---|---|---|---|
| 1991 | — | — | — | — | BV+4% | — |
| 1991 Proof | 250 | Value: 1,650 | | | | |

**500 DOLLARS** **KM# 150** **Weight:** 62.2140 g. **Composition:** 0.9990 Gold 2.0000 oz. AGW **Reverse:** Red kangaroo **Note:** Similar to 100 Dollars, KM#121.

| Date | Mintage | F | VF | XF | Unc | BU |
|---|---|---|---|---|---|---|
| 1991 | — | — | — | — | BV+4% | — |
| 1991 Proof | 491 | Value: 1,450 | | | | |

**1000 DOLLARS** **KM# 183** **Weight:** 311.0670 g. **Composition:** 0.9999 Gold 10.0000 oz. AGW **Reverse:** Red kangaroo **Note:** Similar to 200 Dollars, KM#182.

| Date | Mintage | F | VF | XF | Unc | BU |
|---|---|---|---|---|---|---|
| 1992 | — | — | — | — | BV+3% | — |
| 1992 Proof | 40 | Value: 7,500 | | | | |
| 1995 | — | — | — | — | BV+3% | — |
| 1996 | — | — | — | — | BV+3% | — |
| 1997 | — | — | — | — | BV+3% | — |

**1000 DOLLARS** **KM# 186** **Weight:** 311.0670 g. **Composition:** 0.9995 Platinum 10.0000 oz. APW **Reverse:** Koala **Note:** Similar to 200 Dollars, KM#185.

| Date | Mintage | F | VF | XF | Unc | BU |
|---|---|---|---|---|---|---|
| 1992 | — | — | — | — | BV+4% | — |
| 1992 Proof | — | Value: 7,750 | | | | |
| 1996 | — | — | — | — | BV+4% | — |

**1000 DOLLARS** **KM# 395** **Weight:** 311.0670 g. **Composition:** 0.9990 Gold 10.0000 oz. AGW **Obverse:** Queen's portrait **Reverse:** Nail-tailed wallaby **Note:** Similar to 25 Dollars, KM#391.

| Date | Mintage | F | VF | XF | Unc | BU |
|---|---|---|---|---|---|---|
| 1992 Proof | 40 | Value: 6,500 | | | | |

**1000 DOLLARS** **KM# 197** **Weight:** 311.0670 g. **Composition:** 0.9995 Platinum 10.0000 oz. APW **Obverse:** Similar to 100 Dollars, KM#195 **Note:** Illustration reduced. Actual size 60.3mm.

| Date | Mintage | F | VF | XF | Unc | BU |
|---|---|---|---|---|---|---|
| 1993 | — | — | — | — | BV+4% | — |
| 1994 | — | — | — | — | BV+4% | — |
| 1995 | — | — | — | — | BV+4% | — |
| 1997 | — | — | — | — | BV+4% | — |

**1000 DOLLARS** **KM# 239** **Weight:** 311.0670 g. **Composition:** 0.9999 Gold 10.0000 oz. AGW **Obverse:** Queen Elizabeth II **Reverse:** Red kangaroo.

| Date | Mintage | F | VF | XF | Unc | BU |
|---|---|---|---|---|---|---|
| 1993 Proof | — | Value: 7,000 | | | | |

**1000 DOLLARS** **KM# 247** **Weight:** 311.0670 g. **Composition:** 0.9999 Gold 10.0000 oz. AGW **Subject:** Kangaroo **Reverse:** Kangaroo in diamond shape

| Date | Mintage | F | VF | XF | Unc | BU |
|---|---|---|---|---|---|---|
| 1994 Proof | — | Value: 7,000 | | | | |

**1000 DOLLARS** **KM# 255** **Weight:** 311.0670 g. **Composition:** 0.9995 Platinum 10.0000 oz. APW **Subject:** Koala Mother and Baby **Obverse:** Queen Elizabeth II **Reverse:** Similar to 100 Dollars, KM#253

| Date | Mintage | F | VF | XF | Unc | BU |
|---|---|---|---|---|---|---|
| 1994 | — | — | — | — | BV+4% | — |

**1000 DOLLARS** **KM# 454** **Weight:** 311.3170 g. **Composition:** 0.9990 Gold 10.0000 oz. AGW **Obverse:** Queen's head right **Reverse:** Red kangaroo bounding left **Edge:** Reeded

| Date | Mintage | F | VF | XF | Unc | BU |
|---|---|---|---|---|---|---|
| 1999 | — | — | — | — | 6,500 | — |

**1000 DOLLARS** **KM# 462** **Weight:** 311.6910 g. **Composition:** 0.9990 Platinum 10.0000 oz. APW **Obverse:** Queen's portrait right **Reverse:** Koala in tree **Edge:** Reeded

| Date | Mintage | F | VF | XF | Unc | BU |
|---|---|---|---|---|---|---|
| 1999 | — | — | — | — | BV+4% | — |

**2500 DOLLARS** **KM# 158** **Weight:** 311.0670 g. **Composition:** 0.9990 Platinum 10.0000 oz. APW **Subject:** Koala **Obverse:** Queen Elizabeth II **Reverse:** Koala in tree

| Date | Mintage | F | VF | XF | Unc | BU |
|---|---|---|---|---|---|---|
| 1991 | — | — | — | — | BV+4% | — |
| 1991 Proof | 100 | Value: 7,750 | | | | |

**2500 DOLLARS** KM# 151 **Weight:** 311.0670 g. **Composition:** 0.9990 Gold 10.0000 oz. AGW **Reverse:** Red kangaroo **Note:** Similar to 100 Dollars, KM#121.

| Date | Mintage | F | VF | XF | Unc | BU |
|---|---|---|---|---|---|---|
| 1991 | — | — | — | — | BV+3% | — |
| 1991 Proof | 124 | Value: 7,000 | | | | |

**3000 DOLLARS** KM# 184 **Weight:** 1000.1000 g. **Composition:** 0.9999 Gold 32.1575 oz. AGW **Reverse:** Red kangaroo **Note:** Similar to 200 Dollars, KM#182.

| Date | Mintage | F | VF | XF | Unc | BU |
|---|---|---|---|---|---|---|
| 1992 | — | — | — | — | BV+3% | — |
| 1992 Proof | 25 | Value: 24,500 | | | | |
| 1995 | — | — | — | — | BV+4% | — |
| 1996 | — | — | — | — | BV+3% | — |
| 1997 | — | — | — | — | BV+3% | — |

**3000 DOLLARS** KM# 187 **Weight:** 1000.1000 g. **Composition:** 0.9999 Platinum 32.1575 oz. APW **Reverse:** Koala **Note:** Similar to 200 Dollars, KM#185.

| Date | Mintage | F | VF | XF | Unc | BU |
|---|---|---|---|---|---|---|
| 1992 | — | — | — | — | BV+3.5% | — |
| 1992 Proof | — | Value: 21,500 | | | | |
| 1996 | — | — | — | — | BV+3.5% | — |

**3000 DOLLARS** KM# 396 **Weight:** 1000.1000 g. **Composition:** 0.9999 Platinum 32.1575 oz. APW **Obverse:** Queen's portrait **Reverse:** Nail-tailed wallaby **Note:** Similar to 25 Dollars, KM#391.

| Date | Mintage | F | VF | XF | Unc | BU |
|---|---|---|---|---|---|---|
| 1992 Proof | 25 | Value: 20,000 | | | | |

**3000 DOLLARS** KM# 198 **Weight:** 1000.1000 g. **Composition:** 0.9999 Platinum 32.1575 oz. APW **Obverse:** Similar to 100 Dollars, KM#195 **Note:** Illustration reduced. Actual size 75.3mm.

| Date | Mintage | F | VF | XF | Unc | BU |
|---|---|---|---|---|---|---|
| 1993 | — | — | — | — | BV+3.5% | — |
| 1994 | — | — | — | — | BV+3.5% | — |
| 1995 | — | — | — | — | BV+3.5% | — |
| 1997 | — | — | — | — | BV+3.5% | — |

**3000 DOLLARS** KM# 240 **Weight:** 1000.1000 g. **Composition:** 0.9999 Gold 32.1575 oz. AGW **Subject:** Whiptail wallaby **Obverse:** Queen Elizabeth II **Reverse:** Whiptail wallaby

| Date | Mintage | F | VF | XF | Unc | BU |
|---|---|---|---|---|---|---|
| 1993 Proof | — | Value: 21,500 | | | | |

**3000 DOLLARS** KM# 248 **Weight:** 1000.1000 g. **Composition:** 0.9999 Gold 32.1575 oz. AGW **Subject:** Kangaroo **Reverse:** Kangaroo in diamond shape

| Date | Mintage | F | VF | XF | Unc | BU |
|---|---|---|---|---|---|---|
| 1994 Proof | — | Value: 21,500 | | | | |

**3000 DOLLARS** KM# 256 **Weight:** 1000.1000 g. **Composition:** 0.9995 Platinum 32.1575 oz. APW **Subject:** Koala Mother and Baby **Obverse:** Queen Elizabeth II **Reverse:** Similar to 100 Dollars, KM#253

| Date | Mintage | F | VF | XF | Unc | BU |
|---|---|---|---|---|---|---|
| 1994 | — | — | — | — | BV+3.5% | — |

**3000 DOLLARS** KM# 455 **Weight:** 1000.3500 g. **Composition:** 0.9990 Gold 32.1588 oz. AGW **Obverse:** Queen's head right **Reverse:** Red Kangaroo bounding left **Edge:** Reeded

| Date | Mintage | F | VF | XF | Unc | BU |
|---|---|---|---|---|---|---|
| 1999 | — | — | — | — | 18,500 | — |

**3000 DOLLARS** KM# 463 **Weight:** 1001.0000 g. **Composition:** 0.9990 Platinum 32.1668 oz. APW **Obverse:** Queen's head right **Reverse:** Koala in tree **Edge:** Reeded

| Date | Mintage | F | VF | XF | Unc | BU |
|---|---|---|---|---|---|---|
| 1999 | — | — | — | — | BV+3.5% | — |

**10000 DOLLARS** KM# 159 **Weight:** 1000.1000 g. **Composition:** 0.9990 Platinum 32.1575 oz. APW **Subject:** Koala **Obverse:** Queen Elizabeth II **Reverse:** Red kangaroo

| Date | Mintage | F | VF | XF | Unc | BU |
|---|---|---|---|---|---|---|
| 1991 | — | — | — | — | BV+3.5% | — |
| 1991 Proof | 50 | Value: 25,000 | | | | |

**10000 DOLLARS** KM# 152 **Weight:** 1000.1000 g. **Composition:** 0.9990 Gold 32.1575 oz. AGW **Subject:** Koala **Reverse:** Red kangaroo **Note:** Similar to 100 Dollars, KM#121.

| Date | Mintage | F | VF | XF | Unc | BU |
|---|---|---|---|---|---|---|
| 1991 | — | — | — | — | BV+3% | — |
| 1991 Proof | 95 | Value: 21,500 | | | | |

## TOKEN COINAGE

P.O.W. — WWI Liverpool (NSW)

**THREEPENCE** KM# Tn-B1 **Composition:** Aluminum **Issuer:** WWI Liverpool (NSW) **Note:** Oval.

| Date | Mintage | F | VF | XF | Unc | BU |
|---|---|---|---|---|---|---|
| ND | — | — | 400 | 750 | 1,500 | — |

**THREEPENCE** KM# Tn-A1 **Composition:** Aluminum **Issuer:** WWI Liverpool (NSW) **Note:** Square.

| Date | Mintage | F | VF | XF | Unc | BU |
|---|---|---|---|---|---|---|
| ND | — | — | 100 | 150 | 250 | — |

## TOKEN COINAGE

P.O.W. — WWII Internment Camp

**PENNY** KM# Tn1.1 **Composition:** Brass **Issuer:** WWII Internment Camp

| Date | Mintage | F | VF | XF | Unc | BU |
|---|---|---|---|---|---|---|
| ND | — | 15.00 | 25.00 | 40.00 | 65.00 | — |

**PENNY** KM# Tn1.2 **Composition:** Brass **Issuer:** WWII Internment Camp **Note:** Center hole misplaced (error).

| Date | Mintage | F | VF | XF | Unc | BU |
|---|---|---|---|---|---|---|
| ND | — | 25.00 | 35.00 | 50.00 | — | — |

**PENNY** KM# Tn1.1a **Composition:** Copper-Nickel **Issuer:** WWII Internment Camp **Note:** Spink Australia Sale Nov. 1981. Lot 666A $600.

| Date | Mintage | F | VF | XF | Unc | BU |
|---|---|---|---|---|---|---|
| ND | — | — | — | — | — | — |

**THREEPENCE** KM# Tn2.1 **Composition:** Bronze **Issuer:** WWII Internment Camp **Obv. Legend:** INTERNMENT CAMPS

| Date | Mintage | F | VF | XF | Unc | BU |
|---|---|---|---|---|---|---|
| ND | — | 25.00 | 40.00 | 60.00 | 110 | — |

**THREEPENCE** KM# Tn2.2 **Composition:** Bronze **Issuer:** WWII Internment Camp **Obv. Legend:** INTERNMENT CAMP

| Date | Mintage | F | VF | XF | Unc | BU |
|---|---|---|---|---|---|---|
| ND | — | — | — | — | — | — |

**Note:** Reported, not confirmed

**SHILLING** KM# Tn3 **Composition:** Bronze **Issuer:** WWII Internment Camp

| Date | Mintage | F | VF | XF | Unc | BU |
|---|---|---|---|---|---|---|
| ND | — | 30.00 | 50.00 | 70.00 | 120 | — |

**5 SHILLING** KM# Tn5.1 **Composition:** Bronze

| Date | Mintage | F | VF | XF | Unc | BU |
|---|---|---|---|---|---|---|
| ND | — | — | 500 | 600 | 900 | — |

**5 SHILLING** KM# Tn5.3 **Composition:** Bronze **Note:** Center hole misplaced.

| Date | Mintage | F | VF | XF | Unc | BU |
|---|---|---|---|---|---|---|
| ND | — | — | 550 | 650 | 950 | — |

**5 SHILLING** KM# Tn5.2 **Composition:** Bronze **Note:** Without center hole.

| Date | Mintage | F | VF | XF | Unc | BU |
|---|---|---|---|---|---|---|
| ND | — | — | 550 | 650 | 950 | — |

**2 SHILLING** KM# Tn4.1 **Composition:** Bronze **Issuer:** WWII Internment Camp

| Date | Mintage | F | VF | XF | Unc | BU |
|---|---|---|---|---|---|---|
| ND | — | 65.00 | 100 | 150 | 200 | — |

**2 SHILLING** KM# Tn4.3 **Composition:** Bronze **Issuer:** WWII Internment Camp **Note:** Center hole misplaced.

| Date | Mintage | F | VF | XF | Unc | BU |
|---|---|---|---|---|---|---|
| ND | — | 65.00 | 110 | 165 | 225 | — |

**2 SHILLING** KM# Tn4.2 **Composition:** Bronze **Issuer:** WWII Internment Camp **Note:** Without center hole.

| Date | Mintage | F | VF | XF | Unc | BU |
|---|---|---|---|---|---|---|
| ND | — | 65.00 | 110 | 165 | 225 | — |

## PATTERNS

| KM# | Date | Mintage | Identification | Mkt Val |
|---|---|---|---|---|
| Pn7 | 1909 | — | Florin. | — |

| KM# | Date | Mintage | Identification | Mkt Val |
|---|---|---|---|---|
| Pn8 | 1919 | — | Penny. Copper-Nickel. 3.8900 g.T.3. | 4,500 |
| Pn8a | 1919 | — | Penny. Copper-Nickel. 4.2100 g.T.3. | 4,500 |
| Pn8b | 1919 | — | Penny. Copper-Nickel. 4.5400 g.T.3. | 4,500 |

| KM# | Date | Mintage | Identification | Mkt Val |
|---|---|---|---|---|
| Pn9 | 1919 | — | Penny. Copper-Nickel. 3.8900 g.T.4. | 4,500 |
| Pn9a | 1919 | — | Penny. 0.9170 Silver. 4.6700 g.T.4. | 12,500 |
| Pn10 | 1919 | — | Penny. Copper-Nickel. 3.8900 g.T.5. | 5,000 |
| Pn10a | 1919 | — | Penny. 0.9170 Silver. 4.6700 g.T.5. | 12,500 |
| Pn11 | 1919 | — | Penny. Copper-Nickel. 3.8900 g.T.6. | 4,500 |
| Pn11a | 1919 | — | Penny. 0.9170 Silver. 4.4100 g.T.6. | 12,500 |
| Pn12 | 1919 | — | Shilling. 0.6250 Silver. KM#26. | 50,000 |
| Pn13 | 1920 | — | 1/2 Penny. Copper-Nickel. 1.8100 g.T.1. | 4,000 |
| Pn13a | 1920 | — | 1/2 Penny. 0.9170 Silver. T.1. | 20,000 |
| Pn14 | 1920 | — | Penny. Copper-Nickel. 3.8900 g.T.7. | 4,000 |
| Pn14a | 1920 | — | Penny. Lead. T.7. | 3,500 |
| Pn15 | 1920 | — | Penny. Copper-Nickel. 3.8900 g.T.8. | 6,000 |
| Pn16 | 1920 | — | Penny. Copper-Nickel. 3.8900 g.T.9. | 6,500 |
| Pn17 | 1920 | — | Penny. Copper-Nickel. 3.8900 g.T.10. | 8,500 |
| PnA18 | 1920 | — | Shilling. Silver. KM#26, star above date. | 12,000 |
| Pn18 | 1920 | — | Florin. Silver. KM#27, star above date. | 15,000 |
| Pn19 | 1921 | — | 1/2 Penny. Copper-Nickel. 1.8100 g.T.2. | 6,000 |
| Pn20 | 1921 | — | Penny. Copper-Nickel. 3.8900 g.T.11. | 3,000 |
| Pn20a | 1921 | — | Penny. Copper-Nickel. 4.2100 g.T.11. | 3,000 |
| Pn20b | 1921 | — | Penny. Copper-Nickel. 4.5400 g.T.11. | 3,000 |
| Pn20c | 1921 | — | Penny. Nickel. T.11. | 3,000 |
| Pn21 | 1921 | — | Penny. Copper-Nickel. 3.8900 g.T.12. | 3,000 |
| Pn21a | 1921 | — | Penny. Copper-Nickel. 4.2100 g.T.12. | 3,000 |
| Pn21b | 1921 | — | Penny. Copper-Nickel. 4.5400 g.T.12. | 3,000 |
| Pn22 | 1921 | — | Penny. 4.5500 g.T.13. | — |
| Pn24 | 1937 | 12 | Penny. Bronze. | 28,000 |
| Pn25 | 1937 | 7 | Threepence. Silver. | 30,000 |
| Pn26 | 1937 | 6 | Shilling. Silver. | — |
| Pn28 | 1951 | — | 2 Shilling. Copper-Nickel. Jubilee. | 5,000 |
| Pn29 | 1967 | — | 50 Cents. Silver. KM#67. | — |
| Pn30 | 1968 | — | 50 Cents. Copper-Nickel. KM#68. | — |

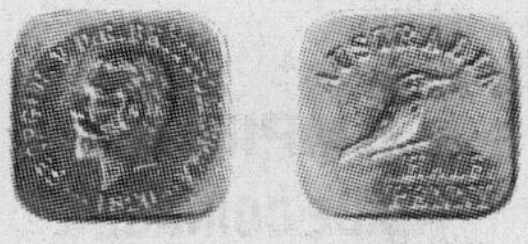

## PIEFORTS

| KM# | Date | Mintage | Identification | Mkt Val |
|---|---|---|---|---|
| P1 | 1989 | 15,000 | 10 Dollars. 0.9250 Silver. Kookaburra, KM#133. | 100 |
| P2 | 1990 | 15,000 | 10 Dollars. 0.9250 Silver. Cockatoo, KM#136. | 115 |
| P3 | 1991 | 17,000 | 10 Dollars. 0.9250 Silver. Jabiru Stork, Proof, KM#156. | 70.00 |
| P4 | 1992 | 15,000 | 10 Dollars. 0.9250 Silver. Penguins. | 85.00 |
| P5 | 1993 | — | 10 Dollars. 0.9250 Silver. Palm cockatoo, KM#221. | 100 |
| P6 | 1994 | 15,000 | 10 Dollars. 0.9250 Silver. Wedge tailed eagle, Proof, KM#223. | 75.00 |
| P7 | 1995 | 15,000 | 10 Dollars. 0.9250 Silver. Numbat, KM#296. | 75.00 |
| P8 | 1996 | 14,000 | 10 Dollars. 40.0000 g.Whales, Proof, KM#314. | 75.00 |
| P9 | 1997 | 14,000 | 10 Dollars. 40.0000 g.Cockatoo, Proof, KM#367. | 75.00 |
| P10 | 1998 | 14,000 | 10 Dollars. 40.0000 g.Wombat, Proof, KM#397. | 75.00 |

## TRIAL STRIKES

| KM# | Date | Mintage | Identification | Mkt Val |
|---|---|---|---|---|
| TS1 | (1927) | — | Shilling. Silver. Uniface. | 5,500 |
| TS2 | (1927) | — | Florin. Silver. Uniface. KM7. | 6,500 |
| TS3 | 1937 | 8 | Penny. Bronze. Uniface, reverse. | 9,000 |
| TS4 | 1937 | 15 | Threepence. Silver. Uniface, reverse. | 7,000 |
| TS5 | 1937 | 20 | Shilling. Silver. Uniface, reverse. | 5,500 |
| TS6 | 1937 | 15 | Florin. Silver. Uniface, reverse. | 7,500 |
| TSA5 | 1937 | — | Sixpence. Silver. Uniface, reverse. | — |

## MINT SETS

| KM# | Date | Mintage | Identification | Issue Price | Mkt Val |
|---|---|---|---|---|---|
| MS1 | 1966 | 16,359 | KM62-67 (Card) | 2.00 | 16.00 |
| MS2 | 1969 | 31,176 | KM62-66,68 | 2.50 | 20.00 |
| MS3 | 1970 | 40,230 | KM62-66, 69 | 2.50 | 10.00 |
| MS4 | 1971 | 28,572 | KM62-66,68 | 2.50 | 20.00 |
| MS5 | 1972 | 39,068 | KM62-66,68 | 2.75 | 20.00 |
| MS6 | 1973 | 30,928 | KM62-66,68 | 3.40 | 20.00 |
| MS7 | 1974 | 25,948 | KM62-66,68 | 3.60 | 17.00 |
| MS8 | 1975 | 30,121 | KM62-66,68 | 3.30 | 8.00 |
| MS9 | 1976 | 40,004 | KM62-66,68 | 3.80 | 8.00 |
| MS10 | 1977 | 128,000 | KM62-66, 70 | 4.20 | 5.00 |
| MS11 | 1978 | 70,000 | KM62-66,68 | 4.20 | 5.00 |
| MS12 | 1979 | 70,000 | KM62-66,68 | 4.50 | 4.00 |
| MS13 | 1980 | 100,000 | KM62-66,68 | 5.75 | 3.50 |
| MS14 | 1981 | 120,010 | KM62-66,68 | 6.50 | 5.00 |
| MS15 | 1982 | 195,950 | KM62-66,74 | 6.50 | 4.00 |
| MS16 | 1983 | 155,700 | KM62-66,68 | 5.00 | 5.00 |
| MS17 | 1984 | 150,014 | KM62-66,68 | 7.00 | 7.00 |
| MS18 | 1985 | 170,000 | KM78-84 | 4.00 | 6.00 |
| MS19 | 1986 | 180,000 | KM78-83,87 | 5.50 | 6.00 |
| MS20 | 1987 | 200,000 | KM78-84 | 8.00 | 5.00 |
| MS21 | 1988 | 240,000 | KM78-82,99-101 | 12.00 | 6.00 |
| MS22 | 1989 | — | KM78-84,101 | 12.00 | 6.00 |
| MS23 | 1990 | — | KM78-84, 101 | 12.00 | 45.00 |
| MS24 | 1991 | 25,000 | KM78-82,84,101,139 | 13.00 | 10.00 |
| MS25 | 1992 | 104,000 | KM80-83,101,175a.1 | 10.00 | 15.00 |
| MS26 | 1993 | — | KM80-83,101,208 | 10.00 | 7.00 |

| KM# | Date | Mintage | Identification | Issue Price | Mkt Val |
|---|---|---|---|---|---|
| MS27 | 1994 | 90,000 | KM80-82,84,101,257 | 11.25 | 7.00 |
| MS28 | 1994 | — | KM80-82,84,101,257 birth year holder | 11.25 | 20.00 |
| MS29 | 1995 | — | KM80-82,84,101,294 | — | 16.00 |
| MS30 | 1996 | — | KM80-83,101,310 Baby Set | 14.80 | 10.00 |
| MS31 | 1996 | — | KM80-83,101,310 plus Bronze Gumnut Baby medal | 19.35 | 22.00 |
| MS-A32 | 1997 | — | KM327, 355 | — | 7.00 |
| MS32 | 1997 | — | KM80-83,101,327 | — | 20.00 |
| MS33 | 1998 | — | KM80-82,83,101,364 | 12.75 | 12.75 |
| MS34 | 1998 | — | KM80-82,84,101,364 | 16.60 | 17.50 |
| MS37 | 1999 | — | KM400,405 | — | 10.00 |
| MS35 | 1999 | — | KM401-406 | 16.95 | 16.95 |
| MS36 | 1999 | — | KM401-406 plus Copper medal, Baby set | 20.50 | 20.50 |
| MS38 | 2000 | — | KM401-403, 406, 488-489 | 10.60 | 13.50 |
| MS39 | 2001 | — | KM532-533, 534.1 | 7.80 | 10.00 |
| MS40 | 2001 | — | KM534.1, 550-551 | 7.80 | 10.00 |
| MS41 | 2001 | — | KM534.1, 552-553 | 7.80 | 10.00 |
| MS42 | 2001 | — | KM534.1, 554-555 | 7.80 | 10.00 |
| MS43 | 2001 | — | KM534.1, 556-557 | 7.80 | 10.00 |
| MS44 | 2001 | — | KM534.1, 558-559 | 7.80 | 10.00 |
| MS45 | 2001 | — | KM534.1, 560-561 | 7.80 | 10.00 |
| MS46 | 2001 | — | KM534.1, 562-563 | 7.80 | 10.00 |
| MS47 | 2001 | — | KM534.1, 564-565 | 7.80 | 10.00 |
| MS48 | 2001 | — | KM532-533, 534.1, 549.1, 550-565 | 43.68 | 70.00 |

## PROOF SETS

| KM# | Date | Mintage | Identification | Issue Price | Mkt Val |
|---|---|---|---|---|---|
| PS25a | 1961(p) | 1,040 | KM56,61 | — | 225 |
| PS1 | 1902S | — | KM14-17; Rare | — | — |
| PS2 | 1911(L) | — | KM24-27 | — | 25,000 |
| PS3 | 1916M | 25 | KM24-27 | — | 7,000 |
| PS4 | 1925(m) | — | KM22-26 | — | 13,650 |
| PS5 | 1926(m) | — | KM22-27 | — | 9,400 |
| PS6 | 1927(m) | 50 | KM22-27 | — | 7,150 |
| PS7 | 1928(m) | — | KM22-27 | — | 9,550 |
| PS8 | 1929(m) | — | KM22-23 | — | 3,250 |
| PSA9 | 1930(m) | — | KM22-23 | — | 85.00 |
| PS9 | 1931(m) | — | KM22-27 | — | 7,000 |
| PS10 | 1933(m) | — | KM22-23 | — | 2,000 |
| PS11 | 1934(m) | 100 | KM22-27 | — | 7,500 |
| PS12 | 1935(m) | 100 | KM22-27 | — | 4,800 |
| PS13 | 1936(m) | — | KM22-27 | — | 6,350 |
| PS14 | 1938(m) | 250 | KM35-40 | — | 5,500 |
| PS15 | 1953(p) | — | KM49-50 | — | 3,500 |
| PS16 | 1955(m) | 1,200 | KM56-59 | — | 250 |
| PS17 | 1955(p) | 301 | KM49,56 | — | 2,000 |
| PS18 | 1956(m) | 1,500 | KM56-60 | — | 325 |
| PS19 | 1957(m) | 1,256 | KM57-60 | — | 225 |
| PS20 | 1958(m) | 1,506 | KM56-60 | — | 250 |
| PS21 | 1959(m) | 1,506 | KM56-61 | — | 325 |
| PS22 | 1960(m) | 1,509 | KM57-60 | — | 175 |
| PS23 | 1960(p) | 1,030 | KM56,61 | — | 225 |
| PS24 | 1961(m) | 1,506 | KM57-60 | — | 175 |
| PS25 | 1961(p) | 1,040 | KM56,61 | — | 225 |
| PS26 | 1962(m) | 2,016 | KM57-60 | — | 150 |
| PS27 | 1962(p) | 1,064 | KM56,61 | — | 200 |
| PS28 | 1963(m) | 5,042 | KM57-60 | — | 125 |
| PS29 | 1963(p) | 1,064 | KM56,61 | — | 225 |
| PS30 | 1966 | 18,110 | KM62-67 | 15.70 | 90.00 |
| PS31 | 1969 | 12,696 | KM62-66,68 | 11.25 | 90.00 |
| PS32 | 1970 | 15,112 | KM62-66,69 | 11.30 | 50.00 |
| PS33 | 1971 | 10,066 | KM62-66,68 | 11.30 | 45.00 |
| PS34 | 1972 | 10,272 | KM62-66,68 | 14.00 | 50.00 |
| PS35 | 1973 | 10,090 | KM62-66,68 | 15.50 | 70.00 |
| PS36 | 1974 | 11,103 | KM62-66,68 | 18.00 | 40.00 |
| PS37 | 1975 | 23,021 | KM62-66,68 | 17.00 | 12.00 |
| PS38 | 1976 | 21,200 | KM62-66,68 | 20.20 | 25.00 |
| PS39 | 1977 | 55,000 | KM62-66,70 | 20.20 | 8.00 |
| PS40 | 1978 | 38,513 | KM62-66,68 | — | 8.00 |
| PS41 | 1979 | 36,000 | KM62-66,68 | — | 12.00 |
| PS42 | 1980 | 68,000 | KM62-66,68 | — | 8.00 |
| PS43 | 1981 | 86,008 | KM62-66,68 | 48.00 | 8.00 |
| PS44 | 1982 | 100,000 | KM62-66,74 | 50.00 | 8.00 |
| PS45 | 1983 | 80,000 | KM62-66,68 | 39.00 | 9.00 |
| PS46 | 1984 | 61,398 | 62-66,68 | 39.00 | 9.00 |
| PS47 | 1985 | 74,809 | KM78-84 | 27.50 | 15.00 |
| PS49 | 1986P | 12,000 | KM89-92 | 1,445 | 1,200 |
| PS50 | 1986P | 3,000 | KM89,90 | 305 | 310 |
| PS48 | 1986 | 67,000 | KM78-83,87 | 40.00 | 20.00 |
| PS52 | 1987 | 12,000 | KM95-98 | 1,440 | 1,000 |
| PS53 | 1987 | 3,000 | KM95, 96 | 305 | 350 |
| PS51 | 1987 | 69,684 | KM78-84 | 40.00 | 10.00 |
| PS56 | 1988 | 25,000 | KM99a-102a | 85.00 | 130 |
| PS57 | 1988 | 9,000 | KM104-107 | — | 1,000 |
| PS58 | 1988 | 1,000 | KM104-105 | — | 200 |
| PS59 | 1988 | — | KM112-113 | 50.00 | 42.50 |
| PS54 | 1988 | 101,000 | KM78-82, 99-101 | — | 18.00 |
| PS55 | 1988 | 5,000 | KM78-82, 99-101, Coin Fair | — | 80.00 |
| PS62 | 1989 | 2,200 | KM117-121 | 1,595 | 1,100 |
| PS63 | 1989 | 2,400 | KM122-126 | 1,995 | 1,300 |
| PS64 | 1989 | 25,000 | KM99a,127-130 | — | 130 |
| PS65 | 1989 | — | KM131-132 | — | 42.50 |
| PS60 | 1989 | 2,500 | KM78-84,101 | — | 15.00 |
| PS61 | 1989 | — | KM78-84, 101 Coin Fair | — | 70.00 |
| PS-A72 | 1990 | — | KM154-155 | — | 42.50 |
| PS68 | 1990 | 5,000 | KM140-144 | — | 1,050 |
| PS69 | 1990 | 2,500 | KM145-149 | — | 1,300 |
| PS70 | 1990 | 2,000 | KM140-142 | 464 | 250 |
| PS71 | 1990 | 1,000 | KM138,144,149 | 1,900 | 1,200 |
| PS76 | 1990 | 25,000 | KM84a, 87a, 100a. Sydney Coin Fair. | 135 | 110 |
| PS66 | 1990 | — | KM78-84,101 | 55.00 | 20.00 |
| PS67 | 1990 | — | KM78-84, 101 Coin Fair | — | 80.00 |
| PS73 | 1991 | 1,000 | KM78-82,84,101a,139 | — | 70.00 |
| PS74 | 1991 | 2,000 | KM140-144 | — | 1,050 |
| PS77 | 1991 | 1,000 | KM140-142 | — | 250 |
| PSA-74 | 1991 | 23,000 | KM78a-82a,84a,101a,139a | — | 140 |
| PS72 | 1991 | 24,000 | KM78-82,84,101,139 | 55.00 | 30.00 |
| PS75 | 1991 | 1,000 | PS145-149 | — | 1,050 |
| PS-A79 | 1992 | 500 | KM165-168 | — | 1,000 |
| PS-A81 | 1992 | 264 | KM389-391 | 251 | 350 |
| PS-B81 | 1992 | 628 | KM389-393 | 1,058 | 1,350 |
| PS-C81 | 1992 | 500 | KM389-392 plus medal | 758 | 875 |
| PS-D81 | 1992(ae) | 750 | KM193, 209, 391 | — | 800 |
| PS78 | 1992 | 47,000 | KM80-83, 101, 175.1 | 40.00 | 20.00 |
| PS79 | 1992 | — | KM200-203, plus medal | 120 | 120 |
| PS80 | 1992 | 5,000 | KM204-207 plus medal | 1,520 | 1,520 |
| PS-E81 | 1993 | 500 | KM212, 230, 231 plus silver bar | — | 300 |
| PS82 | 1993 | 20,000 | KM213-217 | 94.50 | 100 |
| PS81 | 1993 | — | KM80-83, 101, 208 | — | 20.00 |
| PS84 | 1994 | 20,000 | KM264-268 | 101 | 125 |
| PS85 | 1994 | 20,000 | KM182, 232 (2), 253 | — | 2,000 |
| PS86 | 1994 | 25 | KM241, 260, 278 | 303 | 350 |
| PS83 | 1994 | 45,000 | KM80-82, 84, 101, 257 | — | 20.00 |
| PS-A89 | 1995 | 300 | KM276, 286, 290 | — | 1,150 |
| PS-A92 | 1995 | 800 | KM290-291 | — | 395 |
| PS87 | 1995 | 300 | KM272-276 | — | 1,000 |
| PS88 | 1995 | 200 | KM283-287 | — | 1,300 |
| PS89 | 1995 | 1,000 | KM289-292 | — | 1,290 |
| PS90 | 1995 | 300 | KM289-291 | — | 390 |
| PS91 | 1995 | 600 | KM289-290 | — | 42.00 |
| PSA87 | 1995 | — | KM80-82, 84, 101, 294 | — | 35.00 |
| PS-A95 | 1996 | 400 | KM321-322, 341 | 1,500 | 1,350 |
| PS-B95 | 1996 | — | KM80-83, 101, 310 | — | 20.00 |
| PS92 | 1996 | 3,000 | KM275, (f), (l), (s) privy marks | — | 800 |
| PS93 | 1996 | 45,000 | KM80-83, 101, 310. Baby set. | 47.40 | 18.00 |
| PS94 | 1996 | — | KM80-83, 101, 310, plus silver gumnut baby medal | 59.25 | 75.00 |
| PS95 | 1997 | 3,888 | KM335-337 | 914 | 925 |
| PS96 | 1997 | 3,000 | KM341 (f), (l), (s) privy marks | 782 | 800 |
| PS97 | 1998 | — | KM80-82, 84, 101, 364 | 40.60 | 30.00 |
| PS98 | 1998 | — | KM80-82, 84, 101, 364. Baby set. | 50.75 | 52.50 |
| MS-B36 | 1999 | 500 | KM501-505 | — | 1,050 |
| MS-C36 | 1999 | — | KM426-428 | — | 875 |
| PS-A10 | 1999 | 1,000 | KM501-503 | — | 170 |
| PS100 | 1999 | 15,000 | KM481-486 | 66.25 | 75.00 |
| PS99 | 1999 | — | KM401-406 | — | 35.00 |
| PS101 | 2000 | — | KM401-403, 406, 488.1, 489 | 34.35 | 40.00 |
| PS102 | 2000 | — | KM496-500 plus 20.5-gram silver ingot | — | 135 |
| PS103 | 2001 | — | KM532-533, 534.2 | 21.00 | 22.50 |
| PS104 | 2001 | — | KM534.2, 550-551 | 21.00 | 22.50 |
| PS105 | 2001 | — | KM534.2, 552-553 | 21.00 | 22.50 |
| PS106 | 2001 | — | KM534.2, 554-555 | 21.00 | 22.50 |
| PS107 | 2001 | — | KM534.2, 556-557 | 21.00 | 22.50 |
| PS108 | 2001 | — | KM534.2, 558-559 | 21.00 | 22.50 |
| PS109 | 2001 | — | KM534.2, 560-561 | 21.00 | 22.50 |
| PS110 | 2001 | — | KM534.2, 562-563 | 21.00 | 22.50 |
| PS111 | 2001 | — | KM534.2, 564-565 | 21.00 | 22.50 |
| PS112 | 2001 | — | KM532-533, 534.2, 549.2, 550-565 | 120 | 200 |

The Republic of Austria, a parliamentary democracy located in mountainous central Europe, has an area of 32,374 sq. mi. (83,850 sq. km.) and a population of 8.08 million. Capital: Wien (Vienna). Austria is primarily an industrial country. Machinery, iron, steel, textiles, yarns and timber are exported.

The territories later to be known as Austria were overrun in pre-Roman times by various tribes, including the Celts. Upon the fall of the Roman Empire, the country became a margravate of Charlemagne's Empire. Premysl II of Otaker, King of Bohemia, gained possession in 1252, only to lose the territory to Rudolf of Habsburg in 1276. Thereafter, until World War I, the story of Austria was conducted by the ruling Habsburgs.

During the 17th century, Austrian coinage reflected the geopolitical strife of three wars. From 1618-1648, the Thirty Years' War between northern Protestants and southern Catholics produced low quality, "kipperwhipper" strikes of 12, 24, 30, 60, 75 and 150 Kreuzer. Later, during the Austrian-Turkish War, 1660-1664, coinages used to maintain soldier's salaries also reported the steady division of Hungarian territories. Finally, between 1683 and 1699, during the second Austrian-Turkish conflict, new issues of 3, 6 and 15 Kreuzers were struck, being necessary to help defray mounting expenses of the war effort.

During World War I, the Austro-Hungarian Empire was one of the Central Powers with Germany, Bulgaria and Turkey. At the end of the war, the Empire was dismembered and Austria was established as an independent republic. In March 1938, Austria was incorporated into Hitler's short-lived Greater German Reich. Allied forces of both East and West occupied Austria in April 1945, and subsequently divided it into 4 zones of military occupation. On May 15, 1955, the 4 powers formally recognized Austria as a sovereign independent democratic state.

NOTE: During the **GERMAN OCCUPATION** (1938-1945), the German Reichsmark coins and banknotes were circulated.

150 Schillings = 100 Reichsmark

**RULERS**

Franz Joseph I, 1848-1916

Karl I, 1916-1918

# EMPIRE

## TRADE COINAGE

### Uniform

**DUCAT** **KM# 2267** **Weight:** 3.4909 g. **Composition:** 0.9860 Gold .1106 oz. AGW **Ruler:** Franz Joseph **Note:** 996,721 pieces were struck from 1920-1936.

| Date | Mintage | F | VF | XF | Unc | BU |
|---|---|---|---|---|---|---|
| 1901 | 349,000 | 60.00 | 100 | 125 | 175 | — |
| 1902 | 311,000 | 60.00 | 100 | 125 | 175 | — |
| 1903 | 380,000 | 60.00 | 100 | 125 | 175 | — |
| 1904 | 517,000 | 60.00 | 100 | 125 | 175 | — |
| 1905 | 392,000 | 60.00 | 125 | 150 | 200 | — |
| 1906 | 492,000 | 60.00 | 125 | 150 | 200 | — |
| 1907 | 554,000 | 60.00 | 125 | 175 | 250 | — |
| 1908 | 409,000 | 60.00 | 80.00 | 125 | 175 | — |
| 1909 | 366,000 | 60.00 | 80.00 | 100 | 150 | — |
| 1910 | 440,000 | 60.00 | 80.00 | 100 | 150 | — |
| 1911 | 591,000 | 60.00 | 80.00 | 100 | 125 | — |
| 1912 | 495,000 | 60.00 | 80.00 | 100 | 125 | — |
| 1913 | 320,000 | 60.00 | 80.00 | 100 | 125 | — |
| 1914 | 378,000 | 60.00 | 80.00 | 100 | 125 | — |
| 1915 Restrike | — | — | — | — | BV+ 10% | — |
| 1915 Restrike, Proof | — | Value: 50.00 | | | | |
| 1951 (Error for 1915) | — | 75.00 | 125 | 150 | 225 | — |

**4 DUCAT** KM# 2276 **Weight:** 13.9636 g. **Composition:** 0.9860 Gold .4430 oz. AGW **Ruler:** Franz Joseph **Obverse:** Similar to 4 Ducat, KM#2272, but without mint

| Date | Mintage | F | VF | XF | Unc | BU |
|---|---|---|---|---|---|---|
| 1900 | 47,000 | 225 | 250 | 500 | 600 | — |
| 1901 | 47,000 | 225 | 250 | 500 | 600 | — |
| 1901 | 52,000 | 225 | 250 | 450 | 600 | — |
| 1902 | 69,000 | 225 | 250 | 400 | 600 | — |
| 1903 | 73,000 | 225 | 250 | 400 | 600 | — |
| 1904 | 80,000 | 225 | 250 | 400 | 600 | — |
| 1905 | 91,000 | 225 | 250 | 400 | 550 | — |
| | 123,000 | | | | | |
| 1907 | 104,000 | 225 | 250 | 300 | 500 | — |
| 1908 | 80,000 | 225 | 250 | 450 | 600 | — |
| 1909 | 84,000 | 225 | 250 | 375 | 500 | — |
| 1910 | 101,000 | 225 | 250 | 275 | 400 | — |
| 1911 | 142,000 | 225 | 250 | 275 | 350 | — |
| 1912 | 151,000 | 225 | 250 | 275 | 350 | — |
| 1913 | 119,000 | 225 | 250 | 275 | 350 | — |
| 1914 | 102,000 | 225 | 250 | 275 | 350 | — |
| 1915 Restrike | — | — | — | — | BV+ 8% | |

**Note:** 496,501 pieces were struck from 1920-1936

## REFORM COINAGE

100 Heller = 1 Corona

**HELLER** KM# 2800 **Composition:** Bronze **Ruler:** Franz Joseph

| Date | Mintage | F | VF | XF | Unc | BU |
|---|---|---|---|---|---|---|
| 1900 | 26,981,000 | 0.20 | 0.50 | 1.50 | 4.00 | — |
| 1901 | 52,096,000 | 0.20 | 0.35 | 0.50 | 2.00 | — |
| 1902 | 20,553,000 | 0.20 | 0.50 | 1.25 | 3.00 | — |
| 1903 | 13,779,000 | 0.20 | 0.35 | 0.50 | 2.50 | — |
| 1909 | 12,668,000 | 0.20 | 0.35 | 0.50 | 2.50 | — |
| 1910 | 21,900,000 | 0.20 | 0.35 | 0.50 | 2.50 | — |
| 1911 | 18,387,000 | 0.20 | 0.35 | 0.50 | 2.50 | — |
| 1912 | 27,053,000 | 0.20 | 0.35 | 0.50 | 2.50 | — |
| 1913 | 8,782,000 | 0.20 | 0.35 | 0.50 | 2.50 | — |
| 1914 | 9,906,000 | 0.20 | 0.35 | 0.50 | 2.50 | — |
| 1915 | 5,670,000 | 0.20 | 0.35 | 0.75 | 2.50 | — |
| 1916 | 12,484,000 | 0.35 | 0.75 | 1.50 | 4.00 | — |

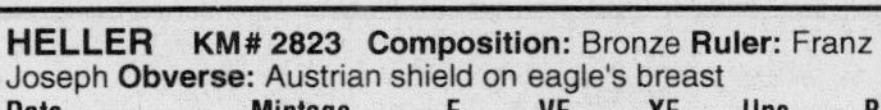

**HELLER** KM# 2823 **Composition:** Bronze **Ruler:** Franz Joseph **Obverse:** Austrian shield on eagle's breast

| Date | Mintage | F | VF | XF | Unc | BU |
|---|---|---|---|---|---|---|
| 1916 | Inc. above | 4.00 | 6.00 | 10.00 | 17.50 | — |

**2 HELLER** KM# 2801 **Composition:** Bronze **Ruler:** Franz Joseph

| Date | Mintage | F | VF | XF | Unc | BU |
|---|---|---|---|---|---|---|
| 1900 | 7,942,000 | 0.50 | 1.00 | 3.00 | 9.00 | — |
| 1901 | 12,157,000 | 2.00 | 3.00 | 6.00 | 25.00 | — |
| 1902 | 18,760,000 | 0.15 | 0.50 | 1.50 | 3.00 | — |
| 1903 | 26,983,000 | 0.50 | 1.50 | 3.00 | 8.00 | — |
| 1904 | 12,863,000 | 0.15 | 0.50 | 1.75 | 7.00 | — |
| 1905 | 6,679,000 | 0.75 | 2.75 | 5.50 | 15.00 | — |
| 1906 | 20,104,000 | 0.50 | 1.50 | 3.00 | 8.00 | — |
| 1907 | 23,804,000 | 0.15 | 0.25 | 0.75 | 3.00 | — |
| 1908 | 21,984,000 | 0.15 | 0.25 | 0.75 | 3.00 | — |
| 1909 | 25,975,000 | 0.15 | 0.25 | 0.75 | 3.00 | — |
| 1910 | 28,406,000 | 0.50 | 1.50 | 3.00 | 8.00 | — |
| 1911 | 50,007,000 | 0.15 | 0.25 | 0.50 | 2.00 | — |
| 1912 | 74,234,000 | 0.15 | 0.20 | 0.35 | 2.00 | — |
| 1913 | 27,432,000 | 0.35 | 0.75 | 2.25 | 6.00 | — |
| 1914 | 60,674,000 | 0.15 | 0.20 | 0.35 | 2.00 | — |
| 1915 | 7,870,000 | 0.15 | 0.20 | 0.35 | 2.00 | — |

**2 HELLER** KM# 2824 **Composition:** Iron **Ruler:** Karl I **Obverse:** Austrian shield on eagle's breast

| Date | Mintage | F | VF | XF | Unc | BU |
|---|---|---|---|---|---|---|
| 1916 | 61,909,000 | 0.50 | 1.00 | 2.00 | 7.50 | — |
| 1917 | 81,186,000 | 0.25 | 0.50 | 1.00 | 5.00 | — |
| 1918 | 66,352,999 | 0.25 | 0.50 | 1.00 | 4.00 | — |

**10 HELLER** KM# 2802 **Composition:** Nickel **Ruler:** Franz Joseph

| Date | Mintage | F | VF | XF | Unc | BU |
|---|---|---|---|---|---|---|
| 1907 | 8,662,000 | 0.25 | 0.50 | 1.00 | 4.00 | — |
| 1908 | 7,772,000 | 0.75 | 1.50 | 2.50 | 6.00 | — |
| 1909 | 20,462,000 | 0.15 | 0.25 | 0.75 | 2.50 | — |
| 1910 | 10,100,000 | 0.15 | 0.25 | 0.75 | 2.50 | — |
| 1911 | 3,634,000 | 1.00 | 2.00 | 3.50 | 8.00 | — |

**10 HELLER** KM# 2822 **Composition:** Copper-Nickel-Zinc **Ruler:** Franz Joseph

| Date | Mintage | F | VF | XF | Unc | BU |
|---|---|---|---|---|---|---|
| 1915 | 18,366,000 | 0.15 | 0.25 | 0.50 | 2.00 | — |
| 1916 | 27,487,000 | 0.15 | 0.25 | 0.50 | 2.00 | — |

**10 HELLER** KM# 2825 **Composition:** Copper-Nickel-Zinc **Ruler:** Franz Joseph **Obverse:** Austrian shield on eagle's breast

| Date | Mintage | F | VF | XF | Unc | BU |
|---|---|---|---|---|---|---|
| 1916 | 14,804,000 | 0.75 | 1.50 | 3.00 | 7.00 | — |

**20 HELLER** KM# 2803 **Composition:** Nickel **Ruler:** Franz Joseph

| Date | Mintage | F | VF | XF | Unc | BU |
|---|---|---|---|---|---|---|
| 1907 | 7,650,000 | 0.75 | 1.50 | 3.00 | 12.00 | — |
| 1908 | 7,469,000 | 0.75 | 1.25 | 2.50 | 9.00 | — |
| 1909 | 7,592,000 | 1.00 | 2.00 | 4.00 | 15.00 | — |
| 1911 | 19,560,000 | 0.25 | 0.35 | 1.00 | 5.00 | — |
| 1914 | 2,342,000 | 5.00 | 15.00 | 25.00 | 50.00 | — |

**20 HELLER** KM# 2826 **Composition:** Iron **Ruler:** Karl I **Obverse:** Austrian shield on eagle's breast

| Date | Mintage | F | VF | XF | Unc | BU |
|---|---|---|---|---|---|---|
| 1916 | 130,770,000 | 0.50 | 1.25 | 2.00 | 6.50 | — |
| 1917 | 127,420,000 | 0.50 | 1.25 | 2.00 | 5.50 | — |
| 1918 | 48,985,000 | 0.25 | 0.65 | 1.25 | 4.50 | — |

**CORONA** KM# 2804 **Weight:** 5.0000 g. **Composition:** 0.8350 Silver .1342 oz. ASW **Ruler:** Franz Joseph

| Date | Mintage | F | VF | XF | Unc | BU |
|---|---|---|---|---|---|---|
| 1901 | 10,387,000 | 1.75 | 2.75 | 5.00 | 10.00 | — |
| 1902 | 2,947,000 | 2.00 | 4.25 | 7.50 | 15.00 | — |
| 1903 | 2,198,000 | 2.00 | 4.25 | 8.00 | 25.00 | — |
| 1904 | 993,000 | 4.00 | 8.50 | 17.50 | 40.00 | — |
| 1905 | 505,000 | 10.00 | 25.00 | 45.00 | 85.00 | — |
| 1906 | 165,000 | 80.00 | 125 | 200 | 450 | — |
| 1907 | 244,000 | 30.00 | 60.00 | 100 | 300 | — |

**CORONA** KM# 2808 **Weight:** 5.0000 g. **Composition:** 0.8350 Silver .1342 oz. ASW **Ruler:** Franz Joseph **Subject:** 60th Anniversary of Reign

| Date | Mintage | F | VF | XF | Unc | BU |
|---|---|---|---|---|---|---|
| ND(1908) | 4,784,000 | 2.50 | 3.50 | 6.00 | 12.00 | — |

**CORONA** KM# 2820 **Weight:** 5.0000 g. **Composition:** 0.8350 Silver .1342 oz. ASW **Ruler:** Franz Joseph

| Date | Mintage | F | VF | XF | Unc | BU |
|---|---|---|---|---|---|---|
| 1912 | 8,457,000 | 1.50 | 2.00 | 3.00 | 8.00 | — |
| 1913 | 9,345,000 | 1.50 | 2.00 | 3.00 | 7.00 | — |
| 1914 | 37,897,000 | 1.50 | 2.00 | 3.00 | 6.00 | — |
| 1915 | 23,000,000 | 1.50 | 2.00 | 3.00 | 6.00 | — |
| 1916 | 12,415,000 | 1.50 | 2.00 | 3.00 | 6.00 | — |

**2 CORONA** KM# 2821 **Weight:** 10.0000 g. **Composition:** 0.8350 Silver .2684 oz. ASW **Ruler:** Franz Joseph

| Date | Mintage | F | VF | XF | Unc | BU |
|---|---|---|---|---|---|---|
| 1912 | 10,245,000 | 3.50 | 5.00 | 7.00 | 10.00 | — |
| 1913 | 7,256,000 | 3.50 | 5.00 | 7.00 | 10.00 | — |

**5 CORONA** **KM# 2807** **Weight:** 24.0000 g. **Composition:** 0.9000 Silver .6945 oz. ASW **Ruler:** Franz Joseph

| Date | Mintage | F | VF | XF | Unc | BU |
|---|---|---|---|---|---|---|
| 1900 | 8,525,000 | 8.00 | 12.50 | 30.00 | 75.00 | — |
| 1907 | 1,539,000 | 10.00 | 15.00 | 35.00 | 100 | — |
| 1907 Proof | — | Value: 650 | | | | |

**5 CORONA** **KM# 2809** **Weight:** 24.0000 g. **Composition:** 0.9000 Silver .6945 oz. ASW **Ruler:** Franz Joseph **Subject:** 60th Anniversary of Reign

| Date | Mintage | F | VF | XF | Unc | BU |
|---|---|---|---|---|---|---|
| ND(1908) | 5,090,000 | 7.50 | 12.50 | 27.50 | 65.00 | — |
| ND(1908) Proof | — | Value: 650 | | | | |

**5 CORONA** **KM# 2813** **Weight:** 24.0000 g. **Composition:** 0.9000 Silver .6945 oz. ASW **Ruler:** Franz Joseph **Obverse:** Large head without wreath, continuous legend

| Date | Mintage | F | VF | XF | Unc | BU |
|---|---|---|---|---|---|---|
| 1909 | 1,709,000 | 10.00 | 16.00 | 40.00 | 125 | — |

**5 CORONA** **KM# 2814** **Weight:** 24.0000 g. **Composition:** 0.9000 Silver .6945 oz. ASW **Ruler:** Franz Joseph **Obverse:** Similar to KM#2809, with smaller head **Reverse:** Similar to KM#2813

| Date | Mintage | F | VF | XF | Unc | BU |
|---|---|---|---|---|---|---|
| 1909 | 1,776,000 | 10.00 | 15.00 | 35.00 | 90.00 | — |

**10 CORONA** **KM# 2805** **Weight:** 3.3875 g. **Composition:** 0.9000 Gold .0980 oz. AGW **Ruler:** Franz Joseph **Obverse:** Laureate head of Franz Joseph I right **Reverse:** Eagle with value and date below

| Date | Mintage | F | VF | XF | Unc | BU |
|---|---|---|---|---|---|---|
| 1905 | 1,933,000 | BV | 50.00 | 60.00 | 85.00 | — |
| 1905 | 1,933,000 | BV | 50.00 | 60.00 | 85.00 | — |
| 1906 | 1,081,000 | BV | 50.00 | 60.00 | 85.00 | — |

**10 CORONA** **KM# 2810** **Weight:** 3.3875 g. **Composition:** 0.9000 Gold .0980 oz. AGW **Ruler:** Franz Joseph **Subject:** 60th Anniversary of Reign **Obverse:** Small plain head of Franz Joseph I right **Reverse:** Eagle, value below, 2 dates above

| Date | Mintage | F | VF | XF | Unc | BU |
|---|---|---|---|---|---|---|
| 1908 | 654,000 | BV | 55.00 | 65.00 | 100 | — |

**10 CORONA** **KM# 2815** **Weight:** 3.3875 g. **Composition:** 0.9000 Gold .0980 oz. AGW **Ruler:** Franz Joseph **Reverse:** Eagle, value and date below

| Date | Mintage | F | VF | XF | Unc | BU |
|---|---|---|---|---|---|---|
| 1909 | 2,320,000 | BV | 50.00 | 60.00 | 80.00 | — |

**10 CORONA** **KM# 2816** **Weight:** 3.3875 g. **Composition:** 0.9000 Gold .0980 oz. AGW **Ruler:** Franz Joseph **Obverse:** Large head

| Date | Mintage | F | VF | XF | Unc | BU |
|---|---|---|---|---|---|---|
| 1909 | 192,000 | 55.00 | 60.00 | 75.00 | 90.00 | — |
| 1910 | 1,004,999 | BV | 50.00 | 60.00 | 80.00 | — |
| 1911 | 1,286,000 | BV | 50.00 | 60.00 | 80.00 | — |
| 1912 Restrike | — | — | — | — | BV+ 10% | — |

**20 CORONA** **KM# 2806** **Weight:** 6.7751 g. **Composition:** 0.9000 Gold .1960 oz. AGW **Ruler:** Franz Joseph

| Date | Mintage | F | VF | XF | Unc | BU |
|---|---|---|---|---|---|---|
| 1900 | 27,000 | 200 | 400 | 600 | 800 | — |
| 1901 | 49,000 | 150 | 225 | 325 | 400 | — |
| 1901 | 49,000 | 150 | 225 | 325 | 400 | — |
| 1902 | 441,000 | BV | 100 | 125 | 150 | — |
| 1903 | 323,000 | BV | 100 | 125 | 150 | — |
| 1904 | 494,000 | BV | 100 | 125 | 150 | — |
| 1905 | 146,000 | 100 | 120 | 150 | 170 | — |

**20 CORONA** **KM# 2811** **Weight:** 6.7751 g. **Composition:** 0.9000 Gold .1960 oz. AGW **Ruler:** Franz Joseph **Subject:** 60th Anniversary of Reign **Reverse:** 2 dates above eagle

| Date | Mintage | F | VF | XF | Unc | BU |
|---|---|---|---|---|---|---|
| 1908 | 188,000 | 100 | 125 | 150 | 200 | — |

**20 CORONA** **KM# 2817** **Weight:** 6.7751 g. **Composition:** 0.9000 Gold .1960 oz. AGW **Ruler:** Franz Joseph

| Date | Mintage | F | VF | XF | Unc | BU |
|---|---|---|---|---|---|---|
| 1909 | 228,000 | 450 | 750 | 1,250 | 1,750 | — |

**20 CORONA** **KM# 2818** **Weight:** 6.7751 g. **Composition:** 0.9000 Gold .1960 oz. AGW **Ruler:** Franz Joseph

| Date | Mintage | F | VF | XF | Unc | BU |
|---|---|---|---|---|---|---|
| 1909 | 102,000 | 575 | 850 | 1,250 | 1,750 | — |
| 1910 | 386,000 | 110 | 150 | 250 | 350 | — |
| 1911 | 59,000 | 120 | 175 | 275 | 375 | — |
| 1912 | 4,460 | 250 | 325 | 400 | 500 | — |
| 1913 | 28,000 | 350 | 500 | 750 | 1,000 | — |
| 1914 | 82,000 | 125 | 225 | 300 | 500 | — |
| 1915 Restrike | — | — | — | — | BV+ 5% | — |
| 1916 | 72,000 | 2,500 | 3,500 | 5,500 | 7,500 | — |

**20 CORONA** **KM# 2827** **Weight:** 6.7751 g. **Composition:** 0.9000 Gold .1960 oz. AGW **Ruler:** Franz Joseph **Reverse:** Austrian shield on eaegle

| Date | Mintage | F | VF | XF | Unc | BU |
|---|---|---|---|---|---|---|
| 1916 | Inc. above | 450 | 550 | 900 | 1,200 | — |

**20 CORONA** **KM# 2828** **Weight:** 6.7751 g. **Composition:** 0.9000 Gold .1960 oz. AGW **Ruler:** Franz Joseph **Obverse:** Head of Kaiser Karl I **Reverse:** Similar to KM#2818 **Note:** All but one specimen were remelted.

| Date | Mintage | F | VF | XF | Unc | BU |
|---|---|---|---|---|---|---|
| 1918 Unique | Est. 2,000 | — | — | — | — | — |

**100 CORONA** **KM# 2812** **Weight:** 33.8753 g. **Composition:** 0.9000 Gold .9803 oz. AGW **Ruler:** Franz Joseph **Subject:** 60th Anniversary of Reign

| Date | Mintage | F | VF | XF | Unc | BU |
|---|---|---|---|---|---|---|
| 1908 | 16,000 | 500 | 600 | 900 | 1,400 | — |
| 1908 Proof | — | Value: 1,850 | | | | |

**100 CORONA** KM# 2819 **Weight:** 33.8753 g. **Composition:** 0.9000 Gold .9803 oz. AGW **Ruler:** Franz Joseph

| Date | Mintage | F | VF | XF | Unc | BU |
|---|---|---|---|---|---|---|
| 1909 | 3,203 | 500 | 650 | 950 | 1,500 | — |
| 1910 | 3,074 | 500 | 650 | 950 | 1,500 | — |
| 1911 | 11,165 | 500 | 650 | 950 | 1,500 | — |
| 1912 | 3,591 | 550 | 850 | 1,150 | 2,000 | — |
| 1913 | 2,696 | 500 | 800 | 1,200 | 1,700 | — |
| 1914 | 1,195 | 500 | 650 | 1,000 | 1,600 | — |
| 1915 Restrike | — | — | — | — | BV+ 2% | — |
| 1915 Restrike, Proof | — | — | — | — | — | — |

# REPUBLIC

## REFORM COINAGE

10,000 Kronen = 1 Schilling

**20 KRONEN** KM# 2830 **Weight:** 6.7751 g. **Composition:** 0.9000 Gold .1960 oz. AGW

| Date | Mintage | F | VF | XF | Unc | BU |
|---|---|---|---|---|---|---|
| 1923 | 6,988 | 650 | 1,400 | 1,850 | 2,500 | — |
| 1924 | 10,337 | 650 | 1,400 | 1,850 | 2,500 | — |

**100 KRONEN** KM# 2831 **Weight:** 33.8753 g. **Composition:** 0.9000 Gold .9802 oz. AGW

| Date | Mintage | F | VF | XF | Unc | BU |
|---|---|---|---|---|---|---|
| 1923 | 617 | 750 | 1,550 | 2,250 | 3,500 | — |
| 1923 Proof | — | Value: 4,000 | | | | |
| 1924 | 2,851 | 750 | 1,550 | 2,250 | 3,500 | — |

**100 KRONEN** KM# 2832 **Composition:** Bronze

| Date | Mintage | F | VF | XF | Unc | BU |
|---|---|---|---|---|---|---|
| 1923 | 6,404,000 | 4.00 | 8.00 | 15.00 | 30.00 | — |
| 1924 | 43,014,000 | 0.25 | 0.50 | 1.50 | 4.50 | — |

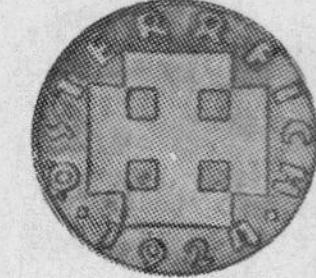

**200 KRONEN** KM# 2833 **Composition:** Bronze

| Date | Mintage | F | VF | XF | Unc | BU |
|---|---|---|---|---|---|---|
| 1924 | 57,160,000 | 0.50 | 1.00 | 2.00 | 6.50 | — |

**1000 KRONEN** KM# 2834 **Composition:** Copper-Nickel

| Date | Mintage | F | VF | XF | Unc | BU |
|---|---|---|---|---|---|---|
| 1924 | 72,353,000 | 0.75 | 1.50 | 3.00 | 8.00 | — |

## PRE WWII DECIMAL COINAGE

100 Groschen - 1 Schilling

**GROSCHEN** KM# 2836 **Composition:** Bronze

| Date | Mintage | F | VF | XF | Unc | BU |
|---|---|---|---|---|---|---|
| 1925 | 30,465,000 | 0.10 | 0.20 | 0.50 | 2.00 | — |
| 1926 | 15,487,000 | 0.10 | 0.30 | 0.75 | 2.00 | — |
| 1927 | 9,318,000 | 0.10 | 0.30 | 0.75 | 2.50 | — |
| 1928 | 17,189,000 | 0.10 | 0.30 | 0.75 | 2.50 | — |
| 1929 | 11,400,000 | 0.10 | 0.30 | 0.75 | 2.50 | — |
| 1930 | 8,893,000 | 0.10 | 0.30 | 0.75 | 2.50 | — |
| 1931 | 971,000 | 10.00 | 20.00 | 30.00 | 60.00 | — |
| 1932 | 3,040,000 | 1.00 | 2.50 | 5.00 | 7.50 | — |
| 1933 | 3,940,000 | 0.50 | 1.00 | 2.00 | 6.00 | — |
| 1934 | 4,232,000 | 0.15 | 0.50 | 1.00 | 4.00 | — |
| 1935 | 3,740,000 | 0.15 | 0.50 | 1.00 | 4.00 | — |
| 1936 | 6,020,000 | 0.50 | 1.00 | 3.00 | 9.00 | — |
| 1937 | 5,830,000 | 0.50 | 1.00 | 2.00 | 7.50 | — |
| 1938 | 1,650,000 | 2.00 | 3.00 | 6.00 | 15.00 | — |

**2 GROSCHEN** KM# 2837 **Composition:** Bronze

| Date | Mintage | F | VF | XF | Unc | BU |
|---|---|---|---|---|---|---|
| 1925 | 29,892,000 | 0.10 | 0.25 | 0.50 | 1.50 | — |
| 1926 | 17,700,000 | 0.10 | 0.30 | 0.75 | 2.00 | — |
| 1927 | 7,757,000 | 0.20 | 0.75 | 2.00 | 5.00 | — |
| 1928 | 19,478,000 | 0.10 | 0.30 | 0.75 | 2.00 | — |
| 1929 | 16,184,000 | 0.10 | 0.30 | 0.75 | 2.00 | — |
| 1930 | 5,709,000 | 0.20 | 0.60 | 1.50 | 4.00 | — |
| 1934 | 812,000 | 7.00 | 12.00 | 15.00 | 25.00 | — |
| 1935 | 3,148,000 | 0.20 | 0.60 | 1.50 | 4.00 | — |
| 1936 | 4,410,000 | 0.15 | 0.30 | 1.00 | 3.00 | — |
| 1937 | 3,790,000 | 0.20 | 0.40 | 1.25 | 3.50 | — |
| 1938 | 860,000 | 2.50 | 4.00 | 6.50 | 12.50 | — |

**5 GROSCHEN** KM# 2846 **Composition:** Copper-Nickel

| Date | Mintage | F | VF | XF | Unc | BU |
|---|---|---|---|---|---|---|
| 1931 | 16,631,000 | 0.15 | 0.40 | 0.80 | 2.00 | — |
| 1932 | 4,700,000 | 0.25 | 1.00 | 2.00 | 5.00 | — |
| 1934 | 3,210,000 | 0.30 | 1.00 | 2.50 | 6.00 | — |
| 1936 | 1,240,000 | 2.00 | 4.00 | 7.50 | 15.00 | — |
| 1937 | 1,540,000 | 20.00 | 30.00 | 45.00 | 80.00 | — |
| 1938 | 870,000 | 125 | 175 | 250 | 425 | — |

**10 GROSCHEN** KM# 2838 **Composition:** Copper-Nickel

| Date | Mintage | F | VF | XF | Unc | BU |
|---|---|---|---|---|---|---|
| 1925 | 66,199,000 | 0.10 | 0.25 | 0.50 | 3.00 | — |
| 1928 | 11,468,000 | 0.50 | 1.00 | 4.00 | 12.00 | — |
| 1929 | 12,000,000 | 0.40 | 0.75 | 1.50 | 4.50 | — |

**50 GROSCHEN** KM# 2850 **Composition:** Copper-Nickel

| Date | Mintage | F | VF | XF | Unc | BU |
|---|---|---|---|---|---|---|
| 1934 | 8,225,000 | 20.00 | 35.00 | 50.00 | 90.00 | — |
| 1934 Proof | Inc. above | Value: 125 | | | | |

**50 GROSCHEN** KM# 2854 **Composition:** Copper-Nickel

| Date | Mintage | F | VF | XF | Unc | BU |
|---|---|---|---|---|---|---|
| 1935 | 11,435,000 | 0.75 | 1.25 | 2.50 | 5.00 | — |
| 1935 Proof | Inc. above | Value: 80.00 | | | | |
| 1936 | 1,000,000 | 30.00 | 40.00 | 60.00 | 115 | — |
| 1936 Proof | Inc. above | Value: 140 | | | | |

**1/2 SCHILLING** KM# 2839 **Weight:** 3.0000 g. **Composition:** 0.6400 Silver .0617 oz. ASW

| Date | Mintage | F | VF | XF | Unc | BU |
|---|---|---|---|---|---|---|
| 1925 | 18,370,000 | 1.00 | 2.00 | 3.00 | 8.00 | — |
| 1926 | 12,943,000 | 2.00 | 4.00 | 6.00 | 12.00 | — |

**SCHILLING** KM# 2835 **Weight:** 7.0000 g. **Composition:** 0.8000 Silver .1800 oz. ASW **Reverse:** Coat of arms on spray of Edelweiss

| Date | Mintage | F | VF | XF | Unc | BU |
|---|---|---|---|---|---|---|
| 1924 | 11,086,000 | 1.50 | 2.50 | 4.50 | 10.00 | — |

**SCHILLING** KM# 2840 **Weight:** 6.0000 g. **Composition:** 0.6400 Silver .1235 oz. ASW

| Date | Mintage | F | VF | XF | Unc | BU |
|---|---|---|---|---|---|---|
| 1925 | 38,209,000 | 1.25 | 2.00 | 3.50 | 7.00 | — |
| 1926 | 20,157,000 | 1.25 | 2.00 | 4.00 | 8.00 | — |
| 1932 | 700,000 | 30.00 | 40.00 | 60.00 | 100 | — |

**SCHILLING** KM# 2851 **Composition:** Copper-Nickel

| Date | Mintage | F | VF | XF | Unc | BU |
|---|---|---|---|---|---|---|
| 1934 | 30,641,000 | 1.00 | 2.00 | 3.50 | 7.50 | — |
| 1934 Proof | — | Value: 150 | | | | |
| 1935 | 11,987,000 | 3.00 | 6.00 | 12.50 | 30.00 | — |

**2 SCHILLING** KM# 2843 **Weight:** 12.0000 g. **Composition:** 0.6400 Silver .2469 oz. ASW **Subject:** Centennial - Death of Franz Schubert

| Date | Mintage | F | VF | XF | Unc | BU |
|---|---|---|---|---|---|---|
| 1928 | 6,900,000 | 3.50 | 4.50 | 8.00 | 16.00 | — |
| 1928 | Inc. above | 3.50 | 4.50 | 8.00 | 16.00 | — |

**2 SCHILLING** KM# 2844 **Weight:** 12.0000 g. **Composition:** 0.6400 Silver .2469 oz. ASW **Subject:** 100th Anniversary - Birth of Dr. Theodor Billroth

| Date | Mintage | F | VF | XF | Unc | BU |
|---|---|---|---|---|---|---|
| 1929 | 2,000,000 | 5.00 | 8.00 | 16.00 | 32.50 | — |

**2 SCHILLING** KM# 2845 **Weight:** 12.0000 g. **Composition:** 0.6400 Silver .2469 oz. ASW **Subject:** 7th Centennial - Death of Walther von der Vogelweide

| Date | Mintage | F | VF | XF | Unc | BU |
|---|---|---|---|---|---|---|
| 1930 | 500,000 | 5.00 | 6.00 | 9.00 | 18.00 | — |
| 1930 Proof | Inc. above | Value: 125 | | | | |

**2 SCHILLING** KM# 2847 **Weight:** 12.0000 g. **Composition:** 0.6400 Silver .2469 oz. ASW **Subject:** 175th Anniversary - Birth of Wolfgang Mozart

| Date | Mintage | F | VF | XF | Unc | BU |
|---|---|---|---|---|---|---|
| 1931 | 500,000 | 7.00 | 14.00 | 22.00 | 50.00 | — |
| 1931 Proof | Inc. above | Value: 300 | | | | |

**2 SCHILLING** KM# 2848 **Weight:** 12.0000 g. **Composition:** 0.6400 Silver .2469 oz. ASW **Subject:** 200th Anniversary - Birth of Joseph Haydn

| Date | Mintage | F | VF | XF | Unc | BU |
|---|---|---|---|---|---|---|
| 1932 | 300,000 | 22.00 | 45.00 | 100 | 165 | — |
| 1932 Proof | Inc. above | Value: 500 | | | | |

**2 SCHILLING** KM# 2849 **Weight:** 12.0000 g. **Composition:** 0.6400 Silver .2469 oz. ASW **Subject:** Death of Dr. Ignaz Seipel

| Date | Mintage | F | VF | XF | Unc | BU |
|---|---|---|---|---|---|---|
| ND(1933) | 400,000 | 8.00 | 16.00 | 30.00 | 50.00 | — |
| ND(1933) Proof | Inc. above | Value: 400 | | | | |

**2 SCHILLING** KM# 2852 **Weight:** 12.0000 g. **Composition:** 0.6400 Silver .2469 oz. ASW **Subject:** Death of Dr. Engelbert Dollfuss

| Date | Mintage | F | VF | XF | Unc | BU |
|---|---|---|---|---|---|---|
| 1934 | 1,500,000 | 7.00 | 12.00 | 20.00 | 32.50 | — |
| 1934 Proof | Inc. above | Value: 275 | | | | |

**2 SCHILLING** KM# 2855 **Weight:** 12.0000 g. **Composition:** 0.6400 Silver .2469 oz. ASW **Subject:** 25th Anniversary - Death of Dr. Karl Lueger

| Date | Mintage | F | VF | XF | Unc | BU |
|---|---|---|---|---|---|---|
| 1935 | 500,000 | 8.00 | 16.00 | 25.00 | 45.00 | — |
| 1935 Proof | Inc. above | Value: 285 | | | | |

**2 SCHILLING** KM# 2858 **Weight:** 12.0000 g. **Composition:** 0.6400 Silver .2469 oz. ASW **Subject:** Bicentennial - Death of Prince Eugen of Savoy

| Date | Mintage | F | VF | XF | Unc | BU |
|---|---|---|---|---|---|---|
| 1936 | 500,000 | 6.00 | 9.00 | 18.00 | 30.00 | — |
| 1936 Proof | Inc. above | Value: 225 | | | | |

**2 SCHILLING** KM# 2859 **Weight:** 12.0000 g. **Composition:** 0.6400 Silver .2469 oz. ASW **Subject:** Bicentennial - Completeion of St. Charles Church

| Date | Mintage | F | VF | XF | Unc | BU |
|---|---|---|---|---|---|---|
| 1937 | 500,000 | 6.00 | 9.00 | 18.00 | 30.00 | — |
| 1937 Proof | Inc. above | Value: 185 | | | | |

**5 SCHILLING** KM# 2853 **Weight:** 15.0000 g. **Composition:** 0.8350 Silver .4027 oz. ASW **Reverse:** Madonna of Mariazell

| Date | Mintage | F | VF | XF | Unc | BU |
|---|---|---|---|---|---|---|
| 1934 | 3,066,000 | 11.50 | 17.50 | 30.00 | 55.00 | — |
| 1934 Proof | — | Value: 200 | | | | |
| 1935 | 5,377,000 | 11.50 | 17.50 | 30.00 | 55.00 | — |
| 1936 | 1,557,000 | 42.50 | 75.00 | 115 | 220 | — |

**25 SCHILLING** KM# 2841 **Weight:** 5.8810 g. **Composition:** 0.9000 Gold .1702 oz. AGW

| Date | Mintage | F | VF | XF | Unc | BU |
|---|---|---|---|---|---|---|
| 1926 Prooflike | 276,000 | — | — | — | 125 | — |
| 1927 Prooflike | 73,000 | — | — | — | 135 | — |
| 1928 Prooflike | 134,000 | — | — | — | 125 | — |
| 1929 Prooflike | 243,000 | — | — | — | 125 | — |
| 1930 Prooflike | 130,000 | — | — | — | 135 | — |
| 1931 Prooflike | 169,000 | — | — | — | 125 | — |
| 1933 Prooflike | 4,944 | — | — | — | 1,850 | — |
| 1934 Prooflike | 11,000 | — | — | — | 600 | — |

**25 SCHILLING** KM# 2856 **Weight:** 5.8810 g. **Composition:** 0.9000 Gold .1702 oz. AGW **Reverse:** St. Leopold

| Date | Mintage | F | VF | XF | Unc | BU |
|---|---|---|---|---|---|---|
| 1935 Prooflike | 2,880 | — | — | — | 1,000 | — |
| 1936 Prooflike | 7,260 | — | — | — | 850 | — |
| 1937 Prooflike | 7,660 | — | — | — | 850 | — |
| 1938 Prooflike | 1,360 | — | — | — | 25,000 | — |

**100 SCHILLING** KM# 2842 **Weight:** 23.5245 g. **Composition:** 0.9000 Gold .6806 oz. AGW

| Date | Mintage | F | VF | XF | Unc | BU |
|---|---|---|---|---|---|---|
| 1926 Prooflike | 64,000 | — | — | — | 450 | — |
| 1927 Prooflike | 69,000 | — | — | — | 450 | — |
| 1928 Prooflike | 40,000 | — | — | — | 550 | — |

| Date | Mintage | F | VF | XF | Unc | BU |
|---|---|---|---|---|---|---|
| 1929 Prooflike | 75,000 | — | — | — | 450 | — |
| 1930 Prooflike | 25,000 | — | — | — | 450 | — |
| 1931 Prooflike | 102,000 | — | — | — | 450 | — |
| 1933 Prooflike | 4,700 | — | — | — | 1,550 | — |
| 1934 Prooflike | 9,383 | — | — | — | 600 | — |

**100 SCHILLING** KM# 2857 **Weight:** 23.5245 g. **Composition:** 0.9000 Gold .6806 oz. AGW **Reverse:** Madonna of Mariazell

| Date | Mintage | F | VF | XF | Unc | BU |
|---|---|---|---|---|---|---|
| 1935 Prooflike | 951 | — | — | — | 5,500 | — |
| 1936 Prooflike | 12,000 | — | — | — | 1,650 | — |
| 1937 Prooflike | 2,900 | — | — | — | 2,250 | — |
| 1938 Prooflike | 1,400 | — | — | — | 25,000 | — |

## POST WWII DECIMAL COINAGE

100 Groschen - 1 Schilling

**GROSCHEN** KM# 2873 **Composition:** Zinc

| Date | Mintage | F | VF | XF | Unc | BU |
|---|---|---|---|---|---|---|
| 1947 | 23,758,000 | 0.15 | 0.25 | 0.75 | 2.50 | — |

**2 GROSCHEN** KM# 2876 **Composition:** Aluminum

| Date | Mintage | F | VF | XF | Unc | BU |
|---|---|---|---|---|---|---|
| 1950 | 21,600,000 | — | 0.15 | 0.60 | 4.00 | — |
| 1950 Proof | — | Value: 28.00 | | | | |
| 1951 | 7,370,000 | — | 0.25 | 1.00 | 4.50 | — |
| 1951 Proof | — | Value: 300 | | | | |
| 1952 | 37,851,000 | — | 0.15 | 0.50 | 2.50 | — |
| 1952 Proof | — | Value: 25.00 | | | | |
| 1954 | 49,879,000 | — | 0.15 | 0.50 | 2.50 | — |
| 1954 Proof | — | Value: 50.00 | | | | |
| 1957 | 23,211,000 | — | 0.15 | 0.50 | 3.00 | — |
| 1957 Proof | — | Value: 45.00 | | | | |
| 1962 | 6,692,000 | — | 0.15 | 0.50 | 2.50 | — |
| 1962 Proof | — | Value: 28.00 | | | | |
| 1964 Proof | 173,000 | Value: 6.50 | | | | |
| 1965 | 11,865,000 | — | 0.10 | 0.30 | 1.50 | — |
| 1965 Proof | — | Value: 2.50 | | | | |
| 1966 | 7,454,000 | — | 0.10 | 0.30 | 1.50 | — |
| 1966 Proof | — | Value: 7.50 | | | | |
| 1967 Proof | 13,000 | Value: 100 | | | | |
| 1968 | 176,000 | — | 0.10 | 0.30 | 1.50 | — |
| 1968 Proof | 22,000 | Value: 10.00 | | | | |
| 1969 Proof | 62,000 | Value: 6.00 | | | | |
| 1970 Proof | 277,000 | Value: 2.50 | | | | |
| 1971 Proof | 145,000 | Value: 2.50 | | | | |
| 1972 | 2,763,000 | — | — | 0.20 | 0.50 | — |
| 1972 Proof | 132,000 | Value: 1.00 | | | | |
| 1973 | 5,883,000 | — | — | 0.20 | 0.50 | — |
| 1973 Proof | 149,000 | Value: 1.00 | | | | |
| 1974 | 1,387,000 | — | — | 0.20 | 0.50 | — |
| 1974 Proof | 93,000 | Value: 1.00 | | | | |
| 1975 | 1,096,000 | — | — | 0.20 | 0.50 | — |
| 1975 Proof | 52,000 | Value: 1.00 | | | | |
| 1976 | 2,755,000 | — | — | 0.20 | 0.50 | — |
| 1976 Proof | 45,000 | Value: 1.00 | | | | |
| 1977 | 1,837,000 | — | — | 0.20 | 0.50 | — |
| 1977 Proof | 47,000 | Value: 1.00 | | | | |
| 1978 | 1,527,000 | — | — | 0.20 | 0.50 | — |
| 1978 Proof | 44,000 | Value: 1.00 | | | | |
| 1979 | 2,434,000 | — | — | 0.20 | 0.50 | — |
| 1979 Proof | 44,000 | Value: 1.00 | | | | |
| 1980 | 1,893,000 | — | — | 0.20 | 0.50 | — |
| 1980 Proof | 48,000 | Value: 10.00 | | | | |
| 1981 | 950,000 | — | — | 0.20 | 0.50 | — |
| 1981 Proof | 49,000 | Value: 10.00 | | | | |
| 1982 | 3,950,000 | — | — | 0.20 | 0.50 | — |
| 1982 Proof | 50,000 | Value: 3.00 | | | | |
| 1983 | 2,665,000 | — | — | 0.20 | 0.50 | — |
| 1983 Proof | 65,000 | Value: 2.00 | | | | |
| 1984 | 500,000 | — | — | 0.20 | 0.50 | — |
| 1984 Proof | 65,000 | Value: 2.00 | | | | |
| 1985 | 1,060,000 | — | — | 0.20 | 0.50 | — |
| 1985 Proof | 45,000 | Value: 5.00 | | | | |
| 1986 | 1,800,000 | — | — | 0.20 | 0.50 | — |
| 1986 Proof | 42,000 | Value: 10.00 | | | | |
| 1987 | 958,000 | — | — | 0.20 | 0.50 | — |
| 1987 Proof | 42,000 | Value: 6.00 | | | | |
| 1988 | 1,061,000 | — | — | 0.20 | 0.50 | — |
| 1988 Proof | 39,000 | Value: 2.00 | | | | |
| 1989 | 950,000 | — | — | 0.20 | 0.50 | — |
| 1989 Proof | 38,000 | Value: 2.00 | | | | |
| 1990 Proof | 35,000 | Value: 22.00 | | | | |
| 1991 | 2,600,000 | — | — | 0.20 | 0.50 | — |
| 1991 Proof | 27,000 | Value: 5.00 | | | | |
| 1992 In sets only | 25,000 | — | — | — | 20.00 | — |
| 1992 Proof | 25,000 | Value: 15.00 | | | | |
| 1993 In sets only | 35,000 | — | — | — | 20.00 | — |
| 1993 Proof | 28,000 | Value: 7.00 | | | | |
| 1994 In sets only | 25,000 | — | — | — | 25.00 | — |
| 1994 Proof | 25,000 | Value: 30.00 | | | | |

**5 GROSCHEN** KM# 2875 **Composition:** Zinc

| Date | Mintage | F | VF | XF | Unc | BU |
|---|---|---|---|---|---|---|
| 1948 | 17,200,000 | — | 0.20 | 0.75 | 12.00 | — |
| 1950 | 19,400,000 | — | 0.20 | 0.75 | 8.00 | — |
| 1950 Proof | — | Value: 200 | | | | |
| 1951 | 12,400,000 | — | 0.20 | 0.75 | 12.00 | — |
| 1951 Proof | — | Value: 35.00 | | | | |
| 1953 | 84,900,000 | — | 0.15 | 0.75 | 8.00 | — |
| 1955 | 17,000,000 | — | 0.15 | 0.75 | 12.00 | — |
| 1957 | 22,260,000 | — | 0.15 | 0.75 | 6.00 | — |
| 1957 Proof | — | Value: 50.00 | | | | |
| 1961 | 3,429,000 | — | 0.20 | 0.75 | 8.00 | — |
| 1961 Proof | — | Value: 25.00 | | | | |
| 1962 | 5,999,000 | — | 0.20 | 0.75 | 8.00 | — |
| 1963 | 13,295,000 | — | 0.15 | 0.75 | 8.00 | — |
| 1963 Proof | — | Value: 40.00 | | | | |
| 1964 | 4,659,000 | — | 0.15 | 0.75 | 4.00 | — |
| 1964 Proof | — | Value: 2.50 | | | | |
| 1965 | 9,481,000 | — | 0.10 | 0.50 | 3.00 | — |
| 1965 Proof | — | Value: 2.50 | | | | |
| 1966 | 9,348,000 | — | 0.10 | 0.50 | 3.00 | — |
| 1966 Proof | — | Value: 8.00 | | | | |
| 1967 | 4,404,000 | — | 0.10 | 0.50 | 3.00 | — |
| 1967 Proof | — | Value: 10.00 | | | | |
| 1968 | 7,372,000 | — | 0.10 | 0.50 | 3.00 | — |
| 1968 Proof | 16,000 | Value: 8.00 | | | | |
| 1969 | — | — | 0.10 | 0.50 | 3.00 | — |
| 1969 Proof | 44,000 | Value: 10.00 | | | | |
| 1970 | — | — | 0.10 | 0.50 | 3.00 | — |
| 1970 Proof | Est. 179,000 | Value: 2.50 | | | | |
| 1971 | Est. 66,000 | — | — | — | — | — |
| 1971 Proof | 125,000 | Value: 2.50 | | | | |
| 1972 | 10,979,000 | — | — | 0.20 | 0.75 | — |
| 1972 Proof | 116,000 | Value: 1.00 | | | | |
| 1973 | 10,336,000 | — | — | 0.20 | 0.75 | — |
| 1973 Proof | 120,000 | Value: 1.00 | | | | |
| 1974 | 2,911,000 | — | — | 0.20 | 0.75 | — |
| 1974 Proof | 87,000 | Value: 1.00 | | | | |
| 1975 | 7,102,000 | — | — | 0.20 | 0.75 | — |
| 1975 Proof | 51,000 | Value: 1.00 | | | | |
| 1976 | 8,079,000 | — | — | 0.20 | 0.75 | — |
| 1976 Proof | 45,000 | Value: 1.00 | | | | |
| 1977 | 1,600,000 | — | — | 0.20 | 0.75 | — |
| 1977 Proof | 45,000 | Value: 1.00 | | | | |
| 1978 | 2,657,000 | — | — | 0.20 | 0.75 | — |
| 1978 Proof | 44,000 | Value: 1.00 | | | | |
| 1979 | 4,927,000 | — | — | 0.20 | 0.75 | — |
| 1979 Proof | 44,000 | Value: 1.00 | | | | |
| 1980 | 3,100,000 | — | — | 0.20 | 0.75 | — |
| 1980 Proof | 48,000 | Value: 8.00 | | | | |
| 1981 | 450,000 | — | — | 0.20 | 0.75 | — |
| 1981 Proof | 49,000 | Value: 8.00 | | | | |
| 1982 | 3,950,000 | — | — | 0.20 | 0.75 | — |
| 1982 Proof | 50,000 | Value: 2.50 | | | | |
| 1983 | 501,000 | — | — | 0.20 | 0.75 | — |
| 1983 Proof | 65,000 | Value: 2.50 | | | | |
| 1984 | 988,000 | — | — | 0.20 | 0.75 | — |
| 1984 Proof | 65,000 | Value: 2.50 | | | | |
| 1985 | 1,915,000 | — | — | 0.20 | 0.75 | — |
| 1985 Proof | 45,000 | Value: 4.00 | | | | |
| 1986 | 1,008,000 | — | — | 0.20 | 0.75 | — |
| 1986 Proof | 42,000 | Value: 7.00 | | | | |
| 1987 | 1,048,000 | — | — | 0.20 | 0.75 | — |
| 1987 Proof | 42,000 | Value: 4.00 | | | | |
| 1988 | 1,261,000 | — | — | 0.20 | 0.75 | — |
| 1988 Proof | 39,000 | Value: 3.00 | | | | |
| 1989 | 2,604,000 | — | — | 0.20 | 0.75 | — |
| 1989 Proof | 38,000 | Value: 2.00 | | | | |
| 1990 | 2,608,000 | — | — | 0.20 | 0.75 | — |
| 1990 Proof | 35,000 | Value: 6.00 | | | | |
| 1991 | 2,400,000 | — | — | 0.20 | 0.75 | — |
| 1991 Proof | 27,000 | Value: 6.00 | | | | |
| 1992 | 670,000 | — | — | 0.20 | 0.75 | — |
| 1992 Proof | 25,000 | Value: 10.00 | | | | |
| 1993 In sets only | 35,000 | — | — | — | 12.00 | — |
| 1993 Proof | 28,000 | Value: 7.00 | | | | |
| 1994 In sets only | 25,000 | — | — | — | 15.00 | — |
| 1994 Proof | 25,000 | Value: 20.00 | | | | |

**10 GROSCHEN** KM# 2874 **Composition:** Zinc

| Date | Mintage | F | VF | XF | Unc | BU |
|---|---|---|---|---|---|---|
| 1947 | 6,845,000 | 0.75 | 2.00 | 4.00 | 22.00 | — |
| 1947 Proof | — | Value: 55.00 | | | | |
| 1948 | 66,205,000 | 0.20 | 0.50 | 1.00 | 3.50 | — |
| 1948 Proof | — | Value: 65.00 | | | | |
| 1949 | 51,202,000 | 0.20 | 0.50 | 1.00 | 3.50 | — |
| 1949 Proof | — | Value: 75.00 | | | | |

**10 GROSCHEN** KM# 2878 **Composition:** Aluminum

| Date | Mintage | F | VF | XF | Unc | BU |
|---|---|---|---|---|---|---|
| 1951 | 9,573,000 | — | 0.20 | 0.75 | 8.00 | — |
| 1951 Proof | — | Value: 85.00 | | | | |
| 1952 | 45,911,000 | — | 0.10 | 0.50 | 4.00 | — |
| 1952 Proof | — | Value: 50.00 | | | | |
| 1953 | 39,002,000 | — | 0.10 | 0.50 | 4.00 | — |
| 1953 Proof | — | Value: 175 | | | | |
| 1955 | 27,525,000 | — | 0.10 | 0.50 | 4.00 | — |
| 1955 Proof | — | Value: 28.00 | | | | |
| 1957 | 33,509,000 | — | 0.10 | 0.50 | 4.00 | — |
| 1957 Proof | — | Value: 150 | | | | |
| 1959 | 80,719,000 | — | 0.10 | 0.35 | 3.50 | — |
| 1959 Proof | — | Value: 45.00 | | | | |
| 1961 | 11,183,000 | — | 0.20 | 0.75 | 8.00 | — |
| 1961 Proof | — | — | — | — | — | — |
| 1962 | 24,635,000 | — | 0.10 | 0.35 | 3.50 | — |
| 1962 Proof | — | Value: 40.00 | | | | |
| 1963 | 38,062,000 | — | 0.10 | 0.35 | 3.50 | — |
| 1963 Proof | — | Value: 45.00 | | | | |
| 1964 | 34,928,000 | — | 0.10 | 0.20 | 2.00 | — |
| 1964 Proof | — | Value: 1.50 | | | | |
| 1965 | 37,025,000 | — | 0.10 | 0.20 | 2.00 | — |
| 1965 Proof | — | Value: 1.50 | | | | |
| 1966 | 24,991,000 | — | 0.10 | 0.20 | 2.00 | — |
| 1966 Proof | — | Value: 6.00 | | | | |
| 1967 | 32,552,999 | — | 0.10 | 0.20 | 2.00 | — |
| 1967 Proof | — | Value: 12.00 | | | | |
| 1968 | 42,412,000 | — | 0.10 | 0.20 | 2.00 | — |
| 1968 Proof | 16,000 | Value: 8.00 | | | | |
| 1969 | 19,953,000 | — | 0.10 | 0.20 | 2.00 | — |
| 1969 Proof | 27,000 | Value: 5.00 | | | | |
| 1970 | 36,998,000 | — | — | 0.10 | 0.45 | — |
| 1970 Proof | 102,000 | Value: 1.00 | | | | |
| 1971 | 57,450,000 | — | — | 0.10 | 0.45 | — |
| 1971 Proof | 82,000 | Value: 1.00 | | | | |
| 1972 | 75,661,000 | — | — | 0.10 | 0.45 | — |
| 1972 Proof | 81,000 | Value: 1.00 | | | | |
| 1973 | 60,244,000 | — | — | 0.10 | 0.45 | — |
| 1973 Proof | 97,000 | Value: 0.75 | | | | |
| 1974 | 55,924,000 | — | — | 0.10 | 0.45 | — |
| 1974 Proof | 78,000 | Value: 0.75 | | | | |
| 1975 | 60,576,000 | — | — | 0.10 | 0.45 | — |
| 1975 Proof | 49,000 | Value: 0.75 | | | | |
| 1976 | 39,367,000 | — | — | 0.10 | 0.45 | — |
| 1976 Proof | 44,000 | Value: 0.75 | | | | |
| 1977 | 53,610,000 | — | — | 0.10 | 0.45 | — |
| 1977 Proof | 44,000 | Value: 0.75 | | | | |
| 1978 | 57,857,000 | — | — | 0.10 | 0.45 | — |
| 1978 Proof | 43,000 | Value: 0.75 | | | | |
| 1979 | 103,686,000 | — | — | — | 0.45 | — |
| 1979 Proof | 44,000 | Value: 0.75 | | | | |
| 1980 | 79,848,000 | — | — | — | 0.45 | — |
| 1980 Proof | 48,000 | Value: 2.00 | | | | |
| 1981 | 92,268,000 | — | — | — | 0.45 | — |
| 1981 Proof | 49,000 | Value: 2.00 | | | | |
| 1982 | 99,950,000 | — | — | — | 0.45 | — |
| 1982 Proof | 50,000 | Value: 0.75 | | | | |
| 1983 | 93,768,000 | — | — | — | 0.45 | — |
| 1983 Proof | 65,000 | Value: 0.75 | | | | |
| 1984 | 86,603,000 | — | — | — | 0.45 | — |
| 1984 Proof | 65,000 | Value: 0.75 | | | | |
| 1985 | 86,304,000 | — | — | — | 0.45 | — |

| Date | Mintage | F | VF | XF | Unc | BU |
|---|---|---|---|---|---|---|
| 1985 Proof | 45,000 | Value: 0.75 | | | | |
| 1986 | 108,910,000 | — | — | — | 0.45 | — |
| 1986 Proof | 42,000 | Value: 1.50 | | | | |
| 1987 | 114,058,000 | — | — | — | 0.45 | — |
| 1987 Proof | 42,000 | Value: 0.75 | | | | |
| 1988 | 114,461,000 | — | — | — | 0.45 | — |
| 1988 Proof | 39,000 | Value: 0.75 | | | | |
| 1989 | 127,784,000 | — | — | — | 0.45 | — |
| 1989 Proof | 38,000 | Value: 0.75 | | | | |
| 1990 | 182,050,000 | — | — | — | 0.45 | — |
| 1990 Proof | 35,000 | Value: 1.50 | | | | |
| 1991 | 140,000,000 | — | — | — | 0.45 | — |
| 1991 Proof | 27,000 | Value: 1.50 | | | | |
| 1992 | 125,000,000 | — | — | — | 0.45 | — |
| 1992 Proof | 25,000 | Value: 1.50 | | | | |
| 1993 | 120,000,000 | — | — | — | 0.45 | — |
| 1993 Proof | 28,000 | Value: 1.50 | | | | |
| 1994 | 110,000,000 | — | — | — | 0.45 | — |
| 1994 Proof | 25,000 | Value: 2.00 | | | | |
| 1995 | 110,000,000 | — | — | — | 0.45 | — |
| 1995 Proof | 27,000 | Value: 1.50 | | | | |
| 1996 | 100,000,000 | — | — | — | 0.45 | — |
| 1996 Proof | 25,000 | Value: 2.50 | | | | |
| 1997 | — | — | — | — | 0.45 | — |
| 1997 Proof | 25,000 | Value: 2.50 | | | | |
| 1998 | — | — | — | — | 0.45 | — |
| 1998 Proof | 25,000 | Value: 3.00 | | | | |
| 1999 | — | — | — | — | 0.45 | — |
| 1999 Proof | 50,000 | Value: 1.50 | | | | |
| 2000 | — | — | — | — | 0.45 | — |
| 2000 Proof | — | Value: 1.50 | | | | |
| 2001 | — | — | — | — | 0.45 | — |
| 2001 Proof | — | Value: 1.50 | | | | |

**20 GROSCHEN** **KM# 2877** **Composition:** Aluminum-Bronze

| Date | Mintage | F | VF | XF | Unc | BU |
|---|---|---|---|---|---|---|
| 1950 | 1,610,000 | 0.20 | 0.50 | 2.00 | 13.50 | — |
| 1950 Proof | — | Value: 40.00 | | | | |
| 1951 | 7,781,000 | 0.10 | 0.25 | 0.75 | 2.75 | — |
| 1951 Proof | — | Value: 25.00 | | | | |
| 1954 | 5,343,000 | 0.10 | 0.25 | 0.75 | 2.75 | — |
| 1954 Proof | — | Value: 275 | | | | |

**50 GROSCHEN** **KM# 2870** **Composition:** Aluminum

| Date | Mintage | F | VF | XF | Unc | BU |
|---|---|---|---|---|---|---|
| 1946 | 13,058,000 | 0.20 | 0.50 | 1.75 | 10.00 | — |
| 1946 Proof | — | Value: 75.00 | | | | |
| 1947 | 26,990,000 | 0.15 | 0.35 | 1.25 | 6.50 | — |
| 1947 Proof | — | Value: 35.00 | | | | |
| 1952 | 7,455,000 | 0.40 | 1.00 | 2.50 | 8.50 | — |
| 1952 Proof | — | Value: 55.00 | | | | |
| 1955 | 16,919,000 | 0.20 | 0.40 | 1.25 | 4.50 | — |
| 1955 Proof | — | Value: 55.00 | | | | |

**50 GROSCHEN** **KM# 2885** **Composition:** Aluminum-Bronze

| Date | Mintage | F | VF | XF | Unc | BU |
|---|---|---|---|---|---|---|
| 1959 | 14,122,000 | — | 0.50 | 2.00 | 15.00 | — |
| 1959 Proof | — | Value: 25.00 | | | | |
| 1960 | 22,404,000 | — | 0.20 | 1.50 | 12.00 | — |
| 1960 Proof | — | Value: 100 | | | | |
| 1961 | 19,891,000 | — | 0.50 | 2.00 | 15.00 | — |
| 1961 Proof | — | Value: 75.00 | | | | |
| 1962 | 10,008,000 | — | 0.40 | 1.75 | 15.00 | — |
| 1962 Proof | — | Value: 40.00 | | | | |
| 1963 | 9,483,000 | — | 0.50 | 2.00 | 18.00 | — |
| 1963 Proof | — | Value: 40.00 | | | | |
| 1964 | 5,331,000 | — | 0.15 | 0.75 | 3.00 | — |
| 1964 Proof | — | Value: 1.50 | | | | |
| 1965 | 7,849,000 | — | 0.15 | 0.75 | 3.00 | — |
| 1965 Proof | — | Value: 1.50 | | | | |
| 1966 | 7,322,000 | — | 0.15 | 0.75 | 3.00 | — |
| 1966 Proof | — | Value: 10.00 | | | | |
| 1967 | 8,237,000 | — | 0.15 | 0.75 | 3.00 | — |
| 1967 Proof | — | Value: 15.00 | | | | |
| 1968 | 7,757,000 | — | 0.15 | 0.75 | 3.00 | — |
| 1968 Proof | 15,000 | Value: 10.00 | | | | |
| 1969 | 7,070,000 | — | 0.15 | 0.75 | 3.00 | — |
| 1969 Proof | 26,000 | Value: 5.00 | | | | |
| 1970 | 2,994,000 | — | 0.10 | 0.50 | 2.00 | — |
| 1970 Proof | 129,000 | Value: 3.00 | | | | |
| 1971 | 14,217,000 | — | — | 0.25 | 1.50 | — |
| 1971 Proof | 84,000 | Value: 2.50 | | | | |
| 1972 | 17,367,000 | — | — | 0.25 | 1.50 | — |
| 1972 Proof | 80,000 | Value: 2.00 | | | | |
| 1973 | 17,902,000 | — | — | 0.25 | 1.50 | — |
| 1973 Proof | 90,000 | Value: 2.00 | | | | |
| 1974 | 15,852,000 | — | — | 0.25 | 1.50 | — |
| 1974 Proof | 76,000 | Value: 2.00 | | | | |
| 1975 | 7,726,000 | — | — | 0.15 | 1.00 | — |
| 1975 Proof | 49,000 | Value: 1.50 | | | | |
| 1976 | 11,150,000 | — | — | 0.15 | 1.00 | — |
| 1976 Proof | 44,000 | Value: 1.50 | | | | |
| 1977 | 7,258,000 | — | — | 0.15 | 1.00 | — |
| 1977 Proof | 44,000 | Value: 1.50 | | | | |
| 1978 | 12,407,000 | — | — | 0.15 | 1.00 | — |
| 1978 Proof | 43,000 | Value: 1.50 | | | | |
| 1979 | 16,351,000 | — | — | 0.15 | 1.00 | — |
| 1979 Proof | 44,000 | Value: 1.50 | | | | |
| 1980 | 29,884,000 | — | — | 0.15 | 1.25 | — |
| 1980 Proof | 48,000 | Value: 3.50 | | | | |
| 1981 | 12,993,000 | — | — | 0.15 | 1.25 | — |
| 1981 Proof | 49,000 | Value: 3.50 | | | | |
| 1982 | 9,950,000 | — | — | 0.15 | 1.00 | — |
| 1982 Proof | 50,000 | Value: 1.50 | | | | |
| 1983 | 15,182,000 | — | — | 0.15 | 1.00 | — |
| 1983 Proof | 65,000 | Value: 1.50 | | | | |
| 1984 | 20,742,000 | — | — | 0.15 | 1.00 | — |
| 1984 Proof | 65,000 | Value: 2.00 | | | | |
| 1985 | 15,654,000 | — | — | 0.15 | 1.00 | — |
| 1985 Proof | 45,000 | Value: 2.00 | | | | |
| 1986 | 17,016,000 | — | — | 0.15 | 0.75 | — |
| 1986 Proof | 42,000 | Value: 2.00 | | | | |
| 1987 | 7,258,000 | — | — | 0.15 | 0.75 | — |
| 1987 Proof | 42,000 | Value: 2.00 | | | | |
| 1988 | 16,267,000 | — | — | 0.15 | 0.75 | — |
| 1988 Proof | 39,000 | Value: 2.00 | | | | |
| 1989 | 17,352,000 | — | — | 0.15 | 0.75 | — |
| 1989 Proof | 38,000 | Value: 2.00 | | | | |
| 1990 | 29,653,000 | — | — | 0.15 | 0.75 | — |
| 1990 Proof | 35,000 | Value: 2.00 | | | | |
| 1991 | 44,990,000 | — | — | 0.15 | 0.75 | — |
| 1991 Proof | 27,000 | Value: 2.00 | | | | |
| 1992 | 20,000,000 | — | — | — | 0.45 | — |
| 1992 Proof | 25,000 | Value: 2.00 | | | | |
| 1993 | 15,000,000 | — | — | — | 0.45 | — |
| 1993 Proof | 28,000 | Value: 2.00 | | | | |
| 1994 | 10,000,000 | — | — | — | 0.45 | — |
| 1994 Proof | 25,000 | Value: 2.50 | | | | |
| 1995 | 20,000,000 | — | — | — | 0.45 | — |
| 1995 Proof | 27,000 | Value: 2.00 | | | | |
| 1996 | 15,000,000 | — | — | — | 0.45 | — |
| 1996 Proof | 25,000 | Value: 2.50 | | | | |
| 1997 | — | — | — | — | 0.45 | — |
| 1997 Proof | 25,000 | Value: 2.50 | | | | |
| 1998 | — | — | — | — | 0.45 | — |
| 1998 Proof | 25,000 | Value: 3.00 | | | | |
| 1999 | — | — | — | — | 0.45 | — |
| 1999 Proof | 50,000 | Value: 2.00 | | | | |
| 2000 | — | — | — | — | 0.45 | — |
| 2000 Proof | — | Value: 2.00 | | | | |
| 2001 | — | — | — | — | 0.45 | — |
| 2001 Proof | — | Value: 2.00 | | | | |

**SCHILLING** **KM# 2871** **Composition:** Aluminum

| Date | Mintage | F | VF | XF | Unc | BU |
|---|---|---|---|---|---|---|
| 1946 | 27,336,000 | 0.30 | 1.00 | 2.50 | 20.00 | — |
| 1946 Proof | — | Value: 500 | | | | |
| 1947 | 35,838,000 | 0.20 | 0.50 | 1.50 | 6.00 | — |
| 1947 Proof | — | Value: 35.00 | | | | |
| 1952 | 23,231,000 | 0.25 | 0.75 | 1.65 | 7.00 | — |
| 1952 Proof | — | Value: 50.00 | | | | |
| 1957 | 28,649,000 | 0.25 | 0.75 | 1.65 | 7.00 | — |
| 1957 Proof | — | Value: 145 | | | | |

**SCHILLING** **KM# 2886** **Composition:** Aluminum-Bronze

| Date | Mintage | F | VF | XF | Unc | BU |
|---|---|---|---|---|---|---|
| 1959 | 46,726,000 | — | 0.25 | 0.75 | 12.00 | — |
| 1959 Proof | — | Value: 15.00 | | | | |
| 1960 | 46,111,000 | — | 0.25 | 1.50 | 20.00 | — |
| 1960 Proof | — | Value: 200 | | | | |
| 1961 | 51,115,000 | — | 0.25 | 1.50 | 15.00 | — |
| 1961 Proof | — | Value: 400 | | | | |
| 1962 | 9,303,000 | — | 0.25 | 1.50 | 15.00 | — |
| 1962 Proof | — | Value: 65.00 | | | | |
| 1963 | 20,863,000 | — | 0.25 | 1.50 | 20.00 | — |
| 1963 Proof | — | Value: 45.00 | | | | |
| 1964 | 15,651,000 | — | 0.25 | 1.25 | 3.50 | — |
| 1964 Proof | — | Value: 2.00 | | | | |
| 1965 | 21,290,000 | — | 0.25 | 0.75 | 3.50 | — |
| 1965 Proof | — | Value: 8.00 | | | | |
| 1966 | 18,688,000 | — | 0.25 | 0.75 | 3.50 | — |
| 1966 Proof | — | Value: 8.00 | | | | |
| 1967 | 22,214,000 | — | 0.25 | 0.75 | 3.50 | — |
| 1967 Proof | — | Value: 12.00 | | | | |
| 1968 | 30,860,000 | — | 0.25 | 0.75 | 3.50 | — |
| 1968 Proof | 17,000 | Value: 8.00 | | | | |
| 1969 | 10,285,000 | — | 0.25 | 0.75 | 3.50 | — |
| 1969 Proof | 28,000 | Value: 4.00 | | | | |
| 1970 | 10,679,000 | — | 0.20 | 0.50 | 2.50 | — |
| 1970 Proof | 100,000 | Value: 1.75 | | | | |
| 1971 | 27,974,000 | — | 0.20 | 0.50 | 2.50 | — |
| 1971 Proof | 82,000 | Value: 1.75 | | | | |
| 1972 | 54,577,000 | — | 0.15 | 0.30 | 1.50 | — |
| 1972 Proof | 78,000 | Value: 1.25 | | | | |
| 1973 | 41,332,000 | — | 0.15 | 0.30 | 1.50 | — |
| 1973 Proof | 90,000 | Value: 1.25 | | | | |
| 1974 | 43,712,000 | — | 0.15 | 0.30 | 1.50 | — |
| 1974 Proof | 77,000 | Value: 1.25 | | | | |
| 1975 | 13,989,000 | — | 0.15 | 0.30 | 1.50 | — |
| 1975 Proof | 49,000 | Value: 1.25 | | | | |
| 1976 | 28,748,000 | — | 0.15 | 0.30 | 1.50 | — |
| 1976 Proof | 44,000 | Value: 1.25 | | | | |
| 1977 | 19,584,000 | — | 0.15 | 0.30 | 1.50 | — |
| 1977 Proof | 44,000 | Value: 1.25 | | | | |
| 1978 | 35,632,000 | — | 0.15 | 0.30 | 1.50 | — |
| 1978 Proof | 43,000 | Value: 1.25 | | | | |
| 1979 | 64,802,000 | — | 0.15 | 0.30 | 1.50 | — |
| 1979 Proof | 44,000 | Value: 1.25 | | | | |
| 1980 | 49,855,000 | — | — | 0.15 | 0.75 | — |
| 1980 Proof | 48,000 | Value: 2.50 | | | | |
| 1981 | 37,502,000 | — | — | 0.15 | 0.75 | — |
| 1981 Proof | 49,000 | Value: 2.50 | | | | |
| 1982 | 29,950,000 | — | — | 0.15 | 0.75 | — |
| 1982 Proof | 50,000 | Value: 1.50 | | | | |
| 1983 | 38,186,000 | — | — | 0.15 | 0.75 | — |
| 1983 Proof | 65,000 | Value: 1.50 | | | | |
| 1984 | 31,891,000 | — | — | 0.15 | 0.75 | — |
| 1984 Proof | 65,000 | Value: 1.50 | | | | |
| 1985 | 49,150,000 | — | — | 0.15 | 0.75 | — |
| 1985 Proof | 45,000 | Value: 1.50 | | | | |
| 1986 | 57,618,000 | — | — | — | 0.65 | — |
| 1986 Proof | 42,000 | Value: 1.50 | | | | |
| 1987 | 44,158,000 | — | — | — | 0.65 | — |
| 1987 Proof | 42,000 | Value: 1.50 | | | | |
| 1988 | 51,561,000 | — | — | — | 0.65 | — |
| 1988 Proof | 39,000 | Value: 1.50 | | | | |
| 1989 | 62,821,000 | — | — | — | 0.65 | — |
| 1989 Proof | 38,000 | Value: 1.50 | | | | |
| 1990 | 103,710,000 | — | — | — | 0.50 | — |
| 1990 Proof | 35,000 | Value: 1.50 | | | | |
| 1991 | 117,700,000 | — | — | — | 0.50 | — |
| 1991 Proof | 27,000 | Value: 1.50 | | | | |
| 1992 | 55,000,000 | — | — | — | 1.25 | — |
| 1992 Proof | 25,000 | Value: 2.00 | | | | |
| 1993 | 60,000,000 | — | — | — | 1.25 | — |
| 1993 Proof | 28,000 | Value: 2.00 | | | | |
| 1994 | 50,000,000 | — | — | — | 1.25 | — |
| 1994 Proof | 25,000 | Value: 3.00 | | | | |
| 1995 | 70,000,000 | — | — | — | 1.25 | — |
| 1995 Proof | 27,000 | Value: 2.50 | | | | |
| 1996 | — | — | — | — | 1.25 | — |
| 1996 Proof | 25,000 | Value: 3.50 | | | | |
| 1997 | — | — | — | — | 1.25 | — |
| 1997 Proof | 25,000 | Value: 4.00 | | | | |
| 1998 | — | — | — | — | 1.25 | — |
| 1998 Proof | 25,000 | Value: 4.50 | | | | |
| 1999 | — | — | — | — | 1.25 | — |
| 1999 Proof | 50,000 | Value: 2.00 | | | | |
| 2000 | — | — | — | — | 1.25 | — |
| 2000 Proof | — | Value: 2.00 | | | | |
| 2001 | — | — | — | — | 1.25 | — |
| 2001 Proof | — | Value: 2.00 | | | | |

**2 SCHILLING** KM# 2872 **Composition:** Aluminum

| Date | Mintage | F | VF | XF | Unc | BU |
|---|---|---|---|---|---|---|
| 1946 | 10,082,000 | 0.45 | 1.25 | 2.75 | 25.00 | — |
| 1946 Proof | — | Value: 700 | | | | |
| 1947 | 20,140,000 | 0.45 | 1.25 | 2.50 | 20.00 | — |
| 1947 Proof | — | Value: 40.00 | | | | |
| 1952 | 149,000 | 55.00 | 100 | 200 | 350 | — |
| 1952 Proof | — | Value: 900 | | | | |

**5 SCHILLING** KM# 2879 **Composition:** Aluminum

| Date | Mintage | F | VF | XF | Unc | BU |
|---|---|---|---|---|---|---|
| 1952 | 29,873,000 | 1.00 | 2.00 | 5.00 | 12.50 | — |
| 1952 Proof | — | Value: 45.00 | | | | |
| 1957 | 240,000 | 100 | 200 | 300 | 500 | — |
| 1957 Proof | — | Value: 700 | | | | |

**5 SCHILLING** KM# 2889 **Weight:** 5.2000 g. **Composition:** 0.6400 Silver .1070 oz. ASW **Edge:** Reeded

| Date | Mintage | F | VF | XF | Unc | BU |
|---|---|---|---|---|---|---|
| 1960 | 12,618,000 | — | BV | 2.50 | 5.50 | — |
| 1960 Proof | 1,000 | Value: 65.00 | | | | |
| 1961 | 17,902,000 | — | BV | 2.50 | 4.50 | — |
| 1961 Proof | — | Value: 25.00 | | | | |
| 1962 | 6,771,000 | — | BV | 2.50 | 4.50 | — |
| 1962 Proof | — | Value: 50.00 | | | | |
| 1963 | 1,811,000 | BV | 2.00 | 4.00 | 14.50 | — |
| 1963 Proof | — | Value: 120 | | | | |
| 1964 | 4,030,000 | — | BV | 2.00 | 3.50 | — |
| 1964 Proof | — | Value: 3.50 | | | | |
| 1965 | 3,030,000 | — | BV | 2.00 | 3.50 | — |
| 1965 Proof | — | Value: 3.50 | | | | |
| 1966 | 4,481,000 | — | BV | 2.00 | 3.50 | — |
| 1966 Proof | — | Value: 8.00 | | | | |
| 1967 | 1,900,000 | BV | 2.00 | 4.00 | 6.00 | — |
| 1967 Proof | — | Value: 15.00 | | | | |
| 1968 | 4,792,000 | — | BV | 2.00 | 3.50 | — |
| 1968 Proof | 20,000 | Value: 8.00 | | | | |

**5 SCHILLING** KM# 2889a **Composition:** Copper-Nickel **Edge:** Plain

| Date | Mintage | F | VF | XF | Unc | BU |
|---|---|---|---|---|---|---|
| 1968 | 2,075,000 | — | 1.00 | 2.50 | 5.00 | — |
| 1969 | 41,222,000 | — | 0.75 | 1.50 | 4.00 | — |
| 1969 Proof | 21,000 | Value: 6.00 | | | | |
| 1970 | 15,771,000 | — | — | 1.00 | 4.00 | — |
| 1970 Proof | 92,000 | Value: 2.00 | | | | |
| 1971 | 14,408,000 | — | — | 1.00 | 4.00 | — |
| 1971 Proof | 84,000 | Value: 2.00 | | | | |
| 1972 | 12,444,000 | — | — | 1.00 | 4.00 | — |
| 1972 Proof | 75,000 | Value: 2.00 | | | | |
| 1973 | 8,259,000 | — | — | 1.00 | 4.00 | — |
| 1973 Proof | 87,000 | Value: 1.50 | | | | |
| 1974 | 17,956,000 | — | — | 1.00 | 4.00 | — |
| 1974 Proof | 76,000 | Value: 1.50 | | | | |
| 1975 | 6,849,000 | — | — | 0.75 | 4.00 | — |
| 1975 Proof | 49,000 | Value: 1.50 | | | | |
| 1976 | 1,458,000 | — | — | 1.00 | 5.00 | — |
| 1976 Proof | 44,000 | Value: 4.00 | | | | |
| 1977 | 6,423,000 | — | — | 0.65 | 2.00 | — |
| 1977 Proof | 44,000 | Value: 1.75 | | | | |
| 1978 | 9,907,000 | — | — | 0.65 | 2.00 | — |
| 1978 Proof | 43,000 | Value: 1.75 | | | | |
| 1979 | 11,607,000 | — | — | 0.65 | 2.00 | — |
| 1979 Proof | 44,000 | Value: 1.75 | | | | |
| 1980 | 14,448,000 | — | — | 0.65 | 2.00 | — |
| 1980 Proof | 48,000 | Value: 3.50 | | | | |
| 1981 | 13,837,000 | — | — | 0.65 | 2.00 | — |
| 1981 Proof | 49,000 | Value: 3.50 | | | | |
| 1982 | 4,950,000 | — | — | 0.65 | 1.50 | — |
| 1982 Proof | 50,000 | Value: 2.50 | | | | |
| 1983 | 9,268,000 | — | — | 0.65 | 1.50 | — |
| 1983 Proof | 65,000 | Value: 2.50 | | | | |
| 1984 | 13,763,000 | — | — | 0.65 | 1.50 | — |
| 1984 Proof | 65,000 | Value: 2.50 | | | | |
| 1985 | 12,750,000 | — | — | 0.60 | 1.25 | — |
| 1985 Proof | 45,000 | Value: 3.00 | | | | |
| 1986 | 16,559,999 | — | — | 0.60 | 1.25 | — |
| 1986 Proof | 42,000 | Value: 3.00 | | | | |
| 1987 | 9,758,000 | — | — | 0.60 | 1.25 | — |
| 1987 Proof | 42,000 | Value: 3.00 | | | | |
| 1988 | 10,161,000 | — | — | 0.60 | 1.25 | — |
| 1988 Proof | 39,000 | Value: 3.00 | | | | |
| 1989 | 24,043,000 | — | — | 0.60 | 1.25 | — |
| 1989 Proof | 38,000 | Value: 3.00 | | | | |
| 1990 | 36,512,000 | — | — | 0.60 | 1.25 | — |
| 1990 Proof | 35,000 | Value: 2.50 | | | | |
| 1991 | 24,000,000 | — | — | 0.60 | 1.25 | — |
| 1991 Proof | 27,000 | Value: 2.50 | | | | |
| 1992 | 20,000,000 | — | — | — | 1.25 | — |
| 1992 Proof | 25,000 | Value: 2.50 | | | | |
| 1993 | 20,000,000 | — | — | — | 1.25 | — |
| 1993 Proof | 28,000 | Value: 2.50 | | | | |
| 1994 | 10,000,000 | — | — | — | 1.25 | — |
| 1994 Proof | 25,000 | Value: 3.50 | | | | |
| 1995 | 20,000,000 | — | — | — | 1.25 | — |
| 1995 Proof | 27,000 | Value: 2.50 | | | | |
| 1996 | — | — | — | — | 1.25 | — |
| 1996 Proof | 25,000 | Value: 3.50 | | | | |
| 1997 | — | — | — | — | 1.25 | — |
| 1997 Proof | 25,000 | Value: 4.00 | | | | |
| 1998 | — | — | — | — | 1.25 | — |
| 1998 Proof | 25,000 | Value: 4.50 | | | | |
| 1999 | — | — | — | — | 1.25 | — |
| 1999 Proof | 50,000 | Value: 2.50 | | | | |
| 2000 | — | — | — | — | 1.25 | — |
| 2000 Proof | — | Value: 2.50 | | | | |
| 2001 | — | — | — | — | 1.25 | — |
| 2001 Proof | — | Value: 2.50 | | | | |

**10 SCHILLING** KM# 2882 **Weight:** 7.5000 g. **Composition:** 0.6400 Silver .1543 oz. ASW

| Date | Mintage | F | VF | XF | Unc | BU |
|---|---|---|---|---|---|---|
| 1957 | 15,636,000 | BV | 1.50 | 3.00 | 7.50 | — |
| 1957 Proof | — | Value: 80.00 | | | | |
| 1958 | 27,280,000 | BV | 1.50 | 3.00 | 7.50 | — |
| 1958 Proof | — | Value: 700 | | | | |
| 1959 | 3,923,000 | BV | 1.50 | 3.50 | 11.50 | — |
| 1959 Proof | — | Value: 40.00 | | | | |
| 1964 | 195,000 | 7.00 | 10.00 | 25.00 | 45.00 | — |
| 1964 Proof | 27,000 | Value: 15.00 | | | | |
| 1965 | 1,896,000 | BV | 1.50 | 3.50 | 11.50 | — |
| 1965 Proof | — | Value: 8.00 | | | | |
| 1966 | 3,392,000 | BV | 1.50 | 3.50 | 9.00 | — |
| 1966 Proof | — | Value: 12.00 | | | | |
| 1967 | 1,394,000 | BV | 1.50 | 3.50 | 11.50 | — |
| 1967 Proof | — | Value: 15.00 | | | | |
| 1968 | 1,525,000 | BV | 1.50 | 3.50 | 10.00 | — |
| 1968 Proof | 15,000 | Value: 9.00 | | | | |
| 1969 | 1,316,000 | BV | 1.50 | 3.50 | 11.50 | — |
| 1969 Proof | 20,000 | Value: 12.00 | | | | |
| 1970 | 4,493,000 | — | BV | 2.50 | 6.50 | — |
| 1970 Proof | 89,000 | Value: 5.00 | | | | |
| 1971 | 7,320,000 | — | BV | 2.50 | 5.50 | — |
| 1971 Proof | 80,000 | Value: 5.00 | | | | |
| 1972 | 14,210,000 | — | BV | 2.50 | 4.50 | — |
| 1972 Proof | 75,000 | Value: 5.00 | | | | |
| 1973 | 14,559,000 | — | BV | 2.50 | 4.50 | — |
| 1973 Proof | 80,000 | Value: 5.00 | | | | |

**10 SCHILLING** KM# 2918 **Composition:** Copper-Nickel Plated Nickel

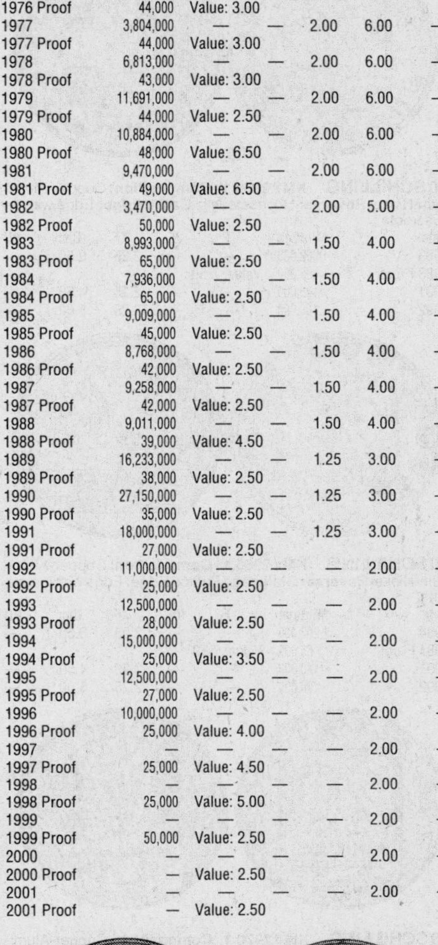

| Date | Mintage | F | VF | XF | Unc | BU |
|---|---|---|---|---|---|---|
| 1974 | 59,877,000 | — | — | 2.00 | 6.00 | — |
| 1974 Proof | 75,000 | Value: 4.00 | | | | |
| 1975 | 16,869,000 | — | — | 2.00 | 6.00 | — |
| 1975 Proof | 49,000 | Value: 3.00 | | | | |
| 1976 | 13,459,000 | — | — | 2.00 | 6.00 | — |
| 1976 Proof | 44,000 | Value: 3.00 | | | | |
| 1977 | 3,804,000 | — | — | 2.00 | 6.00 | — |
| 1977 Proof | 44,000 | Value: 3.00 | | | | |
| 1978 | 6,813,000 | — | — | 2.00 | 6.00 | — |
| 1978 Proof | 43,000 | Value: 3.00 | | | | |
| 1979 | 11,691,000 | — | — | 2.00 | 6.00 | — |
| 1979 Proof | 44,000 | Value: 2.50 | | | | |
| 1980 | 10,884,000 | — | — | 2.00 | 6.00 | — |
| 1980 Proof | 48,000 | Value: 6.50 | | | | |
| 1981 | 9,470,000 | — | — | 2.00 | 6.00 | — |
| 1981 Proof | 49,000 | Value: 6.50 | | | | |
| 1982 | 3,470,000 | — | — | 2.00 | 5.00 | — |
| 1982 Proof | 50,000 | Value: 2.50 | | | | |
| 1983 | 8,993,000 | — | — | 1.50 | 4.00 | — |
| 1983 Proof | 65,000 | Value: 2.50 | | | | |
| 1984 | 7,936,000 | — | — | 1.50 | 4.00 | — |
| 1984 Proof | 65,000 | Value: 2.50 | | | | |
| 1985 | 9,009,000 | — | — | 1.50 | 4.00 | — |
| 1985 Proof | 45,000 | Value: 2.50 | | | | |
| 1986 | 8,768,000 | — | — | 1.50 | 4.00 | — |
| 1986 Proof | 42,000 | Value: 2.50 | | | | |
| 1987 | 9,258,000 | — | — | 1.50 | 4.00 | — |
| 1987 Proof | 42,000 | Value: 2.50 | | | | |
| 1988 | 9,011,000 | — | — | 1.50 | 4.00 | — |
| 1988 Proof | 39,000 | Value: 4.50 | | | | |
| 1989 | 16,233,000 | — | — | 1.25 | 3.00 | — |
| 1989 Proof | 38,000 | Value: 2.50 | | | | |
| 1990 | 27,150,000 | — | — | 1.25 | 3.00 | — |
| 1990 Proof | 35,000 | Value: 2.50 | | | | |
| 1991 | 18,000,000 | — | — | 1.25 | 3.00 | — |
| 1991 Proof | 27,000 | Value: 2.50 | | | | |
| 1992 | 11,000,000 | — | — | — | 2.00 | — |
| 1992 Proof | 25,000 | Value: 2.50 | | | | |
| 1993 | 12,500,000 | — | — | — | 2.00 | — |
| 1993 Proof | 28,000 | Value: 2.50 | | | | |
| 1994 | 15,000,000 | — | — | — | 2.00 | — |
| 1994 Proof | 25,000 | Value: 3.50 | | | | |
| 1995 | 12,500,000 | — | — | — | 2.00 | — |
| 1995 Proof | 27,000 | Value: 2.50 | | | | |
| 1996 | 10,000,000 | — | — | — | 2.00 | — |
| 1996 Proof | 25,000 | Value: 4.00 | | | | |
| 1997 | — | — | — | — | 2.00 | — |
| 1997 Proof | 25,000 | Value: 4.50 | | | | |
| 1998 | — | — | — | — | 2.00 | — |
| 1998 Proof | 25,000 | Value: 5.00 | | | | |
| 1999 | — | — | — | — | 2.00 | — |
| 1999 Proof | 50,000 | Value: 2.50 | | | | |
| 2000 | — | — | — | — | 2.00 | — |
| 2000 Proof | — | Value: 2.50 | | | | |
| 2001 | — | — | — | — | 2.00 | — |
| 2001 Proof | — | Value: 2.50 | | | | |

**20 SCHILLING** KM# 2946.1 **Composition:** Copper-Aluminum-Nickel **Edge:** Edge with incuse dots

| Date | Mintage | F | VF | XF | Unc | BU |
|---|---|---|---|---|---|---|
| 1980 | 9,850,000 | — | — | 2.50 | 3.50 | — |
| 1980 Proof | 48,000 | Value: 20.00 | | | | |
| 1981 | 450,000 | — | — | 4.50 | 7.50 | — |
| 1981 Proof | 49,000 | Value: 22.50 | | | | |
| 1991 | 140,000 | — | — | 2.25 | 5.00 | — |
| 1992 | 100,000 | — | — | 2.25 | 6.00 | — |
| 1992 Proof | 25,000 | Value: 10.00 | | | | |

**20 SCHILLING** KM# 2955.1 **Composition:** Copper-Aluminum-Nickel **Subject:** 250th Anniversary - Birth of Joseph Haydn **Edge:** Edge with incuse dots

| Date | Mintage | F | VF | XF | Unc | BU |
|---|---|---|---|---|---|---|
| 1982 | 3,100,000 | — | — | 2.25 | 3.50 | — |
| 1982 Proof | 50,000 | Value: 9.00 | | | | |
| 1991 | 140,000 | — | — | 2.25 | 5.00 | — |
| 1992 | 100,000 | — | — | 2.25 | 6.00 | — |

**20 SCHILLING KM# 2960.1 Composition:** Copper-Aluminum-Nickel **Reverse:** Hochosterwitz Castle **Edge:** Edge with incuse dots

| Date | Mintage | F | VF | XF | Unc | BU |
|---|---|---|---|---|---|---|
| 1983 | 1,002,000 | — | — | 2.25 | 3.50 | — |
| 1983 Proof | 65,000 | Value: 7.50 | | | | |
| 1991 | 140,000 | — | — | 2.25 | 4.50 | — |
| 1992 | 100,000 | — | — | 2.25 | 5.00 | — |

**20 SCHILLING KM# 2965.1 Composition:** Copper-Aluminum-Nickel **Reverse:** Grafenegg Palace **Edge:** Edge with incuse dots

| Date | Mintage | F | VF | XF | Unc | BU |
|---|---|---|---|---|---|---|
| 1984 | 1,203,000 | — | — | 2.25 | 3.50 | — |
| 1984 Proof | 65,000 | Value: 7.50 | | | | |
| 1991 | 140,000 | — | — | 2.25 | 4.50 | — |
| 1992 | 100,000 | — | — | 2.25 | 5.00 | — |

**20 SCHILLING KM# 2970.1 Composition:** Copper-Aluminum-Nickel **Subject:** 200th Anniversary - Diocese of Linz **Edge:** Edge with incuse dots

| Date | Mintage | F | VF | XF | Unc | BU |
|---|---|---|---|---|---|---|
| 1985 | 814,000 | — | — | 2.25 | 4.50 | — |
| 1985 Proof | 45,000 | Value: 11.50 | | | | |
| 1991 | 140,000 | — | — | 2.25 | 4.50 | — |
| 1992 | 100,000 | — | — | 2.25 | 5.00 | — |

**20 SCHILLING KM# 2975.1 Composition:** Copper-Aluminum-Nickel **Subject:** 800th Anniversary - Georgenberger Treaty **Edge:** Edge with incuse dots

| Date | Mintage | F | VF | XF | Unc | BU |
|---|---|---|---|---|---|---|
| 1986 | 801,000 | — | — | 2.25 | 4.50 | — |
| 1986 Proof | 42,000 | Value: 16.50 | | | | |
| 1991 | 140,000 | — | — | 2.25 | 4.50 | — |
| 1992 | 100,000 | — | — | 2.25 | 5.00 | — |

**20 SCHILLING KM# 2980.1 Composition:** Copper-Aluminum-Nickel **Subject:** 300th Anniversary - Birth of Salzburg's Archbishop Thun **Edge:** Edge with incuse dots

| Date | Mintage | F | VF | XF | Unc | BU |
|---|---|---|---|---|---|---|
| 1987 | 508,000 | — | — | 2.25 | 4.50 | — |
| 1987 Proof | 42,000 | Value: 11.50 | | | | |

| Date | Mintage | F | VF | XF | Unc | BU |
|---|---|---|---|---|---|---|
| 1991 | 140,000 | — | — | 2.25 | 4.50 | — |
| 1992 | 100,000 | — | — | 2.25 | 5.00 | — |

**20 SCHILLING KM# 2988.1 Composition:** Copper-Aluminum-Nickel **Reverse:** Crowned eagle - Tyrol **Edge:** Edge with incuse dots

| Date | Mintage | F | VF | XF | Unc | BU |
|---|---|---|---|---|---|---|
| 1989 | 242,000 | — | — | 2.25 | 4.50 | — |
| 1989 Proof | 38,000 | Value: 8.00 | | | | |
| 1991 | 140,000 | — | — | 2.25 | 4.50 | — |
| 1992 | 100,000 | — | — | 2.25 | 5.00 | — |

**20 SCHILLING KM# 2993.1 Composition:** Copper-Aluminum-Nickel **Reverse:** Martinsturm in Bregenz **Edge:** Edge with incuse dots

| Date | Mintage | F | VF | XF | Unc | BU |
|---|---|---|---|---|---|---|
| 1990 | 250,000 | — | — | 2.25 | 4.50 | — |
| 1990 Proof | 35,000 | Value: 10.00 | | | | |
| 1991 | — | — | — | — | — | — |
| 1991 | 140,000 | — | — | 2.25 | 4.50 | — |
| 1992 | 100,000 | — | — | 2.25 | 6.50 | — |

**20 SCHILLING KM# 2995.1 Composition:** Copper-Aluminum-Nickel **Subject:** 200th Anniversary - Birth of Franz Grillparzer **Edge:** Edge wit incuse dots

| Date | Mintage | F | VF | XF | Unc | BU |
|---|---|---|---|---|---|---|
| 1991 | 610,000 | — | — | 2.25 | 4.50 | — |
| 1991 Proof | 27,000 | Value: 10.00 | | | | |
| 1992 | 100,000 | — | — | 2.25 | 5.00 | — |

**20 SCHILLING KM# 2995.2 Composition:** Copper-Aluminum-Nickel **Edge:** Plain

| Date | Mintage | F | VF | XF | Unc | BU |
|---|---|---|---|---|---|---|
| 1993 | 180,000 | — | — | 2.25 | 4.50 | — |

**20 SCHILLING KM# 2993.2 Composition:** Copper-Aluminum-Nickel **Edge:** Plain

| Date | Mintage | F | VF | XF | Unc | BU |
|---|---|---|---|---|---|---|
| 1993 | 180,000 | — | — | 2.25 | 4.50 | — |

**20 SCHILLING KM# 2960.2 Composition:** Copper-Aluminum-Nickel **Edge:** Plain

| Date | Mintage | F | VF | XF | Unc | BU |
|---|---|---|---|---|---|---|
| 1993 | 180,000 | — | — | 2.25 | 4.50 | — |

**20 SCHILLING KM# 2955.2 Composition:** Copper-Aluminum-Nickel **Edge:** Plain

| Date | Mintage | F | VF | XF | Unc | BU |
|---|---|---|---|---|---|---|
| 1993 | 180,000 | — | — | 2.25 | 5.00 | — |

**20 SCHILLING KM# 2946.2 Composition:** Copper-Aluminum-Nickel **Edge:** Plain

| Date | Mintage | F | VF | XF | Unc | BU |
|---|---|---|---|---|---|---|
| 1993 | 180,000 | — | — | 2.25 | 5.00 | — |
| 1993 Proof | 28,000 | Value: 10.00 | | | | |

**20 SCHILLING KM# 2980.2 Composition:** Copper-Aluminum-Nickel **Edge:** Plain

| Date | Mintage | F | VF | XF | Unc | BU |
|---|---|---|---|---|---|---|
| 1993 | 180,000 | — | — | 2.25 | 4.50 | — |

**20 SCHILLING KM# 2988.2 Composition:** Copper-Aluminum-Nickel **Edge:** Plain

| Date | Mintage | F | VF | XF | Unc | BU |
|---|---|---|---|---|---|---|
| 1993 | 180,000 | — | — | 2.25 | 4.50 | — |

**20 SCHILLING KM# 2975.2 Composition:** Copper-Aluminum-Nickel **Edge:** Plain

| Date | Mintage | F | VF | XF | Unc | BU |
|---|---|---|---|---|---|---|
| 1993 | 180,000 | — | — | 2.25 | 4.50 | — |

**20 SCHILLING KM# 2970.2 Composition:** Copper-Aluminum-Nickel **Edge:** Plain

| Date | Mintage | F | VF | XF | Unc | BU |
|---|---|---|---|---|---|---|
| 1993 | 180,000 | — | — | 2.25 | 4.50 | — |

**20 SCHILLING KM# 2965.2 Composition:** Copper-Aluminum-Nickel **Edge:** Plain

| Date | Mintage | F | VF | XF | Unc | BU |
|---|---|---|---|---|---|---|
| 1993 | 180,000 | — | — | 2.25 | 4.50 | — |

**20 SCHILLING KM# 2946.2 Composition:** Copper-Aluminum-Nickel **Edge:** Plain

| Date | Mintage | F | VF | XF | Unc | BU |
|---|---|---|---|---|---|---|
| 1993 | 180,000 | — | — | 2.25 | 5.00 | — |
| 1993 Proof | 28,000 | Value: 10.00 | | | | |

**20 SCHILLING KM# 3016 Composition:** Copper-Aluminum-Nickel **Subject:** 800th Anniversary - Vienna Mint

| Date | Mintage | F | VF | XF | Unc | BU |
|---|---|---|---|---|---|---|
| 1994 | 2,000,000 | — | — | — | 4.50 | — |
| 1994 Proof | 25,000 | Value: 12.50 | | | | |

**20 SCHILLING KM# 3022 Composition:** Copper-Aluminum-Nickel **Subject:** 1000th Anniversary - Krems

| Date | Mintage | F | VF | XF | Unc | BU |
|---|---|---|---|---|---|---|
| 1995 | 2,000,000 | — | — | — | 4.50 | — |
| 1995 Proof | 27,000 | Value: 10.00 | | | | |

**20 SCHILLING KM# 3033 Composition:** Copper-Aluminum-Nickel **Reverse:** Anton Bruckner

| Date | Mintage | F | VF | XF | Unc | BU |
|---|---|---|---|---|---|---|
| 1996 | — | — | — | — | 4.50 | — |
| 1996 Proof | 25,000 | Value: 15.00 | | | | |

**20 SCHILLING KM# 3041 Composition:** Copper-Aluminum-Nickel **Subject:** 850th Anniversary of St. Stephen's Cathedral **Obverse:** Denomination **Reverse:** Cathedral, dates

| Date | Mintage | F | VF | XF | Unc | BU |
|---|---|---|---|---|---|---|
| 1997 | — | — | — | — | 4.50 | — |
| 1997 Proof | 25,000 | Value: 16.50 | | | | |

**20 SCHILLING KM# 3048 Composition:** Copper-Aluminum-Nickel **Subject:** 500th Anniversary of Michael Pacher's Death **Obverse:** Denomination **Reverse:** Pacher's altar at St. Wolfgang

| Date | Mintage | F | VF | XF | Unc | BU |
|---|---|---|---|---|---|---|
| 1998 | — | — | — | — | 5.00 | — |
| 1998 Proof | 25,000 | Value: 17.50 | | | | |

**20 SCHILLING** **KM# 3056** **Composition:** Copper-Aluminum-Nickel **Obverse:** Denomination **Reverse:** Hugo Von Hofmannsthal

| Date | Mintage | F | VF | XF | Unc | BU |
|---|---|---|---|---|---|---|
| 1999 | — | — | — | — | 4.50 | — |
| 1999 Proof | — | Value: 12.50 | | | | |

**20 SCHILLING** **KM# 3064** **Composition:** Brass **Subject:** 150th Anniversary - First Austrian Postage Stamp **Obverse:** Denomination **Reverse:** Canceled stamp design **Edge:** Plain

| Date | Mintage | F | VF | XF | Unc | BU |
|---|---|---|---|---|---|---|
| 2000- | — | — | — | — | 4.50 | — |
| 2000- Proof | — | Value: 12.50 | | | | |

**20 SCHILLING** **KM# 3075** **Weight:** 8.1300 g. **Composition:** Brass **Subject:** Johann Nepomuk Nestroy **Obverse:** Denomination. **Reverse:** Bust of Nestroy half facing left. **Edge:** Plain. **Size:** 27.8 mm.

| Date | Mintage | F | VF | XF | Unc | BU |
|---|---|---|---|---|---|---|
| 2001- | 75,000 | — | — | — | 4.50 | — |

**25 SCHILLING** **KM# 2880** **Weight:** 13.0000 g. **Composition:** 0.8000 Silver .3344 oz. ASW **Subject:** Reopening of the National Theater in Vienna

| Date | Mintage | F | VF | XF | Unc | BU |
|---|---|---|---|---|---|---|
| 1955 | 1,499,000 | 3.50 | 7.50 | 10.00 | 20.00 | — |
| 1955 Proof | Est. 5,000 | Value: 100 | | | | |

**25 SCHILLING** **KM# 2881** **Weight:** 13.0000 g. **Composition:** 0.8000 Silver .3344 oz. ASW **Subject:** 200th Anniversary - Birth of Wolfgang Mozart

| Date | Mintage | F | VF | XF | Unc | BU |
|---|---|---|---|---|---|---|
| 1956 | 4,999,000 | — | — | 3.00 | 5.50 | — |
| 1956 Proof | Est. 1,500 | Value: 350 | | | | |

**25 SCHILLING** **KM# 2883** **Weight:** 13.0000 g. **Composition:** 0.8000 Silver .3344 oz. ASW **Subject:** 8th Centennial - Mariazell Basilica

| Date | Mintage | F | VF | XF | Unc | BU |
|---|---|---|---|---|---|---|
| 1957 | 4,999,000 | — | — | 3.00 | 5.50 | — |
| 1957 Proof | Est. 1,500 | Value: 300 | | | | |

**25 SCHILLING** **KM# 2884** **Weight:** 13.0000 g. **Composition:** 0.8000 Silver .3344 oz. ASW **Subject:** 100th Anniversary - Birth of Auer von Welsbach

| Date | Mintage | F | VF | XF | Unc | BU |
|---|---|---|---|---|---|---|
| 1958 | 4,999,000 | — | — | 3.00 | 5.50 | — |
| 1958 Proof | Est. 500 | Value: 1,500 | | | | |

**25 SCHILLING** **KM# 2887** **Weight:** 13.0000 g. **Composition:** 0.8000 Silver .3344 oz. ASW **Subject:** Centennial - Death of Archduke Johann

| Date | Mintage | F | VF | XF | Unc | BU |
|---|---|---|---|---|---|---|
| 1959 | 1,899,000 | — | — | 3.50 | 6.00 | — |
| 1959 Proof | Est. 1,000 | Value: 300 | | | | |

**25 SCHILLING** **KM# 2890** **Weight:** 13.0000 g. **Composition:** 0.8000 Silver .3344 oz. ASW **Subject:** 40th Anniversary - Carinthian Plebescite

| Date | Mintage | F | VF | XF | Unc | BU |
|---|---|---|---|---|---|---|
| 1960 | 1,599,000 | — | — | 3.50 | 6.00 | — |
| 1960 Proof | Est. 900 | Value: 350 | | | | |

**25 SCHILLING** **KM# 2891** **Weight:** 13.0000 g. **Composition:** 0.8000 Silver .3344 oz. ASW **Subject:** 40th Anniversary - Burgenland

| Date | Mintage | F | VF | XF | Unc | BU |
|---|---|---|---|---|---|---|
| 1961 | 1,399,000 | — | — | 3.50 | 6.00 | — |
| 1961 Proof | Est. 1,200 | Value: 200 | | | | |

**25 SCHILLING** **KM# 2892** **Weight:** 13.0000 g. **Composition:** 0.8000 Silver .3344 oz. ASW **Reverse:** Anton Bruckner

| Date | Mintage | F | VF | XF | Unc | BU |
|---|---|---|---|---|---|---|
| 1962 | 2,399,000 | — | — | 3.00 | 5.50 | — |
| 1962 Proof | Est. 3,000 | Value: 150 | | | | |

**25 SCHILLING** **KM# 2893** **Weight:** 13.0000 g. **Composition:** 0.8000 Silver .3344 oz. ASW **Subject:** 300th Anniversary - Birth of Prince Eugen

| Date | Mintage | F | VF | XF | Unc | BU |
|---|---|---|---|---|---|---|
| 1963 | 1,994,000 | — | — | 3.00 | 5.50 | — |
| 1963 Proof | 5,931 | Value: 80.00 | | | | |

**25 SCHILLING** **KM# 2895.1** **Weight:** 13.0000 g. **Composition:** 0.8000 Silver .3344 oz. ASW **Reverse:** Franz Grillparzer

| Date | Mintage | F | VF | XF | Unc | BU |
|---|---|---|---|---|---|---|
| 1964 | 1,664,000 | — | — | 3.50 | 6.00 | — |
| 1964 Proof | 36,000 | Value: 8.00 | | | | |

**25 SCHILLING** **KM# 2895.2** **Weight:** 13.0000 g. **Composition:** 0.8000 Silver .3344 oz. ASW **Obverse:** 9 shields (error)

| Date | Mintage | F | VF | XF | Unc | BU |
|---|---|---|---|---|---|---|
| 1964 Proof | 3,660 | Value: 300 | | | | |

**25 SCHILLING** **KM# 2897** **Weight:** 13.0000 g. **Composition:** 0.8000 Silver .3344 oz. ASW **Subject:** 150th Anniversary - Vienna Technical High School

| Date | Mintage | F | VF | XF | Unc | BU |
|---|---|---|---|---|---|---|
| 1965 | 1,563,000 | — | — | 3.50 | 6.00 | — |
| 1965 Proof | 37,000 | Value: 15.00 | | | | |

**25 SCHILLING** **KM# 2899** **Weight:** 13.0000 g. **Composition:** 0.8000 Silver .3344 oz. ASW **Subject:** 130th Anniversary - Death of Ferdinand Raimund

| Date | Mintage | F | VF | XF | Unc | BU |
|---|---|---|---|---|---|---|
| 1966 | 1,388,000 | — | — | 3.50 | 6.00 | — |
| 1966 Proof | 11,800 | Value: 50.00 | | | | |

**25 SCHILLING** **KM# 2901** **Weight:** 13.0000 g. **Composition:** 0.8000 Silver .3344 oz. ASW **Subject:** 250th Anniversary - Birth of Maria Theresa

| Date | Mintage | F | VF | XF | Unc | BU |
|---|---|---|---|---|---|---|
| 1967 | 2,472,000 | — | — | 3.00 | 5.50 | — |
| 1967 Proof | 28,000 | Value: 25.00 | | | | |

**25 SCHILLING** **KM# 2903** **Weight:** 13.0000 g. **Composition:** 0.8000 Silver .3344 oz. ASW **Subject:** 300th Anniversary - Birth of Von Hildebrandt

| Date | Mintage | F | VF | XF | Unc | BU |
|---|---|---|---|---|---|---|
| 1968 | 1,258,000 | BV | 2.50 | 4.00 | 8.50 | — |
| 1968 Proof | 42,000 | Value: 18.00 | | | | |

**25 SCHILLING** **KM# 2905** **Weight:** 13.0000 g. **Composition:** 0.8000 Silver .3344 oz. ASW **Reverse:** Peter Rosegger

| Date | Mintage | F | VF | XF | Unc | BU |
|---|---|---|---|---|---|---|
| 1969 | 1,356,000 | — | — | 3.50 | 5.50 | — |
| 1969 Proof | 44,000 | Value: 18.00 | | | | |

**25 SCHILLING** **KM# 2907** **Weight:** 13.0000 g. **Composition:** 0.8000 Silver .3344 oz. ASW **Subject:** 100th Anniversary - Birth of Franz Lehar

| Date | Mintage | F | VF | XF | Unc | BU |
|---|---|---|---|---|---|---|
| 1970 | 1,661,000 | — | — | 3.00 | 5.00 | — |
| 1970 Proof | 139,000 | Value: 7.50 | | | | |

**25 SCHILLING** **KM# 2910** **Weight:** 13.0000 g. **Composition:** 0.8000 Silver .3344 oz. ASW **Subject:** 200th Anniversary - Vienna Bourse

| Date | Mintage | F | VF | XF | Unc | BU |
|---|---|---|---|---|---|---|
| 1971 | 1,804,000 | — | — | 3.00 | 4.50 | — |
| 1971 Proof | 196,000 | Value: 5.50 | | | | |

**25 SCHILLING** **KM# 2912** **Weight:** 13.0000 g. **Composition:** 0.8000 Silver .3344 oz. ASW **Subject:** 50th Anniversary - Death of Carl M. Ziehrer

| Date | Mintage | F | VF | XF | Unc | BU |
|---|---|---|---|---|---|---|
| ND(1972) | 1,955,000 | — | — | 3.00 | 4.50 | — |
| ND(1972) Proof | 145,000 | Value: 5.50 | | | | |

**25 SCHILLING** **KM# 2915** **Weight:** 13.0000 g. **Composition:** 0.8000 Silver .3344 oz. ASW **Subject:** 100th Anniversary - Birth of Max Reinhardt

| Date | Mintage | F | VF | XF | Unc | BU |
|---|---|---|---|---|---|---|
| ND(1973) | 2,323,000 | — | — | 3.00 | 4.50 | — |
| ND(1973) Proof | 177,000 | Value: 5.50 | | | | |

**50 SCHILLING** **KM# 2888** **Weight:** 20.0000 g. **Composition:** 0.9000 Silver .5787 oz. ASW **Subject:** 150th Anniversary - Liberation of Tyrol

| Date | Mintage | F | VF | XF | Unc | BU |
|---|---|---|---|---|---|---|
| ND(1959) | 2,999,000 | — | 5.00 | 6.00 | 9.00 | — |
| ND(1959) Proof | Est. 800 | Value: 425 | | | | |

**50 SCHILLING** **KM# 2894** **Weight:** 20.0000 g. **Composition:** 0.9000 Silver .5787 oz. ASW **Subject:** 600th Anniversary - Union with Tirol

| Date | Mintage | F | VF | XF | Unc | BU |
|---|---|---|---|---|---|---|
| ND(1963) | 2,990,000 | — | 5.00 | 5.50 | 7.50 | — |
| ND(1963) Proof | 10,000 | Value: 75.00 | | | | |

**50 SCHILLING** **KM# 2896** **Weight:** 20.0000 g. **Composition:** 0.9000 Silver .5787 oz. ASW **Series:** Winter Olympics **Reverse:** Innsbruck - Ski jump

| Date | Mintage | F | VF | XF | Unc | BU |
|---|---|---|---|---|---|---|
| 1964 | 2,832,000 | — | 5.00 | 5.50 | 8.00 | — |
| 1964 Proof | 68,000 | Value: 20.00 | | | | |

**50 SCHILLING** **KM# 2898** **Weight:** 20.0000 g. **Composition:** 0.9000 Silver .5787 oz. ASW **Subject:** 600th Anniversary - Vienna University

| Date | Mintage | F | VF | XF | Unc | BU |
|---|---|---|---|---|---|---|
| ND(1965) | 2,163,000 | — | 5.00 | 5.50 | 7.50 | — |
| ND(1965) Proof | 37,000 | Value: 30.00 | | | | |

**50 SCHILLING** **KM# 2900** **Weight:** 20.0000 g. **Composition:** 0.9000 Silver .5787 oz. ASW **Subject:** 150th Anniversary - National Bank

| Date | Mintage | F | VF | XF | Unc | BU |
|---|---|---|---|---|---|---|
| ND(1966) | 1,782,000 | — | 5.00 | 5.50 | 7.50 | — |
| ND(1966) Proof | 17,000 | Value: 60.00 | | | | |

**50 SCHILLING** **KM# 2902** **Weight:** 20.0000 g. **Composition:** 0.9000 Silver .5787 oz. ASW **Subject:** Centennial of the Blue Danube Waltz

| Date | Mintage | F | VF | XF | Unc | BU |
|---|---|---|---|---|---|---|
| 1967 | 2,974,000 | — | 5.00 | 5.50 | 7.50 | — |
| 1967 Proof | 26,000 | Value: 60.00 | | | | |

**50 SCHILLING** **KM# 2904.1** **Weight:** 20.0000 g. **Composition:** 0.9000 Silver .5787 oz. ASW **Subject:** 50th Anniversary - The Republic **Reverse:** Matte surface between pillars

| Date | Mintage | F | VF | XF | Unc | BU |
|---|---|---|---|---|---|---|
| ND(1968) | 1,660,000 | — | 5.00 | 5.50 | 7.50 | — |
| ND(1968) Proof | 40,000 | Value: 22.50 | | | | |

**50 SCHILLING** **KM# 2904.2** **Weight:** 20.0000 g. **Composition:** 0.9000 Silver .5787 oz. ASW **Reverse:** Proof surface between pillars

| Date | Mintage | F | VF | XF | Unc | BU |
|---|---|---|---|---|---|---|
| 1968 Proof | — | Value: 150 | | | | |

**50 SCHILLING** **KM# 2906** **Weight:** 20.0000 g. **Composition:** 0.9000 Silver .5787 oz. ASW **Subject:** 450th Anniversary - Death of Maximilian I

| Date | Mintage | F | VF | XF | Unc | BU |
|---|---|---|---|---|---|---|
| 1969 | 2,045,000 | — | 5.00 | 5.50 | 7.50 | — |
| 1969 Proof | 55,000 | Value: 22.50 | | | | |

**50 SCHILLING** **KM# 2908** **Weight:** 20.0000 g. **Composition:** 0.9000 Silver .5787 oz. ASW **Subject:** 300th Anniversary - Innsbruck University

| Date | Mintage | F | VF | XF | Unc | BU |
|---|---|---|---|---|---|---|
| 1970 | 2,087,000 | — | 5.00 | 5.50 | 7.50 | — |
| 1970 Prof | 113,000 | Value: 9.00 | | | | |

**50 SCHILLING** **KM# 2909** **Weight:** 20.0000 g. **Composition:** 0.9000 Silver .5787 oz. ASW **Subject:** 100th Anniversary - Birth of Dr. Karl Renner

| Date | Mintage | F | VF | XF | Unc | BU |
|---|---|---|---|---|---|---|
| 1970 | 2,214,000 | — | 5.00 | 5.50 | 6.50 | — |
| 1970 Proof | 286,000 | Value: 8.00 | | | | |

**50 SCHILLING** **KM# 2911** **Weight:** 20.0000 g. **Composition:** 0.9000 Silver .5787 oz. ASW **Subject:** 80th Anniversary - Birth of Julius Raab

| Date | Mintage | F | VF | XF | Unc | BU |
|---|---|---|---|---|---|---|
| 1971 | 2,317,000 | — | 5.00 | 5.50 | 6.50 | — |
| 1971 Proof | 183,000 | Value: 8.00 | | | | |

**50 SCHILLING** **KM# 2913** **Weight:** 20.0000 g. **Composition:** 0.9000 Silver .5787 oz. ASW **Subject:** 350th Anniversary - Salzburg University

| Date | Mintage | F | VF | XF | Unc | BU |
|---|---|---|---|---|---|---|
| ND(1972) | 2,863,000 | — | 5.00 | 5.50 | 6.50 | — |
| ND(1972) Proof | 136,000 | Value: 8.00 | | | | |

**50 SCHILLING** **KM# 2914** **Weight:** 20.0000 g. **Composition:** 0.9000 Silver .5787 oz. ASW **Subject:** 100th Anniversary - Institute of Agriculture

| Date | Mintage | F | VF | XF | Unc | BU |
|---|---|---|---|---|---|---|
| ND(1972) | 1,891,000 | — | 5.00 | 5.50 | 6.50 | — |
| ND(1972) Proof | 109,000 | Value: 8.00 | | | | |

**50 SCHILLING** **KM# 2916** **Weight:** 20.0000 g. **Composition:** 0.9000 Silver .5787 oz. ASW **Subject:** 500th Anniversary - Bummerl House

| Date | Mintage | F | VF | XF | Unc | BU |
|---|---|---|---|---|---|---|
| 1973 | 2,842,000 | — | 5.00 | 5.50 | 6.50 | — |
| 1973 Proof | 158,000 | Value: 8.00 | | | | |

**50 SCHILLING** **KM# 2917** **Weight:** 20.0000 g. **Composition:** 0.9000 Silver .5787 oz. ASW **Subject:** 100th Anniversary - Birth of Dr. Theodor Korner

| Date | Mintage | F | VF | XF | Unc | BU |
|---|---|---|---|---|---|---|
| ND(1973) | 2,868,000 | — | 5.00 | 5.50 | 6.50 | — |
| ND(1973) Proof | 132,000 | Value: 8.00 | | | | |

**50 SCHILLING** **KM# 2919** **Weight:** 20.0000 g. **Composition:** 0.6400 Silver .4115 oz. ASW **Subject:** International Garden Exhibition

| Date | Mintage | F | VF | XF | Unc | BU |
|---|---|---|---|---|---|---|
| 1974 | 2,279,000 | — | — | 5.00 | 6.00 | — |
| 1974 Proof | 221,000 | Value: 7.00 | | | | |

**50 SCHILLING** **KM# 2920** **Weight:** 20.0000 g. **Composition:** 0.6400 Silver .4115 oz. ASW **Subject:** 125th Anniversary - Austrian Police Force

| Date | Mintage | F | VF | XF | Unc | BU |
|---|---|---|---|---|---|---|
| ND(1974) | 2,259,000 | — | — | 5.00 | 6.00 | — |
| ND(1974) Proof | 241,000 | Value: 7.00 | | | | |

**50 SCHILLING** **KM# 2921** **Weight:** 20.0000 g. **Composition:** 0.6400 Silver .4115 oz. ASW **Subject:** 1200th Anniversary - Salzburg Cathedral

| Date | Mintage | F | VF | XF | Unc | BU |
|---|---|---|---|---|---|---|
| 1974 | 2,293,000 | — | — | 5.00 | 6.00 | — |
| 1974 Proof | 207,000 | Value: 7.00 | | | | |

**50 SCHILLING** **KM# 2922** **Weight:** 20.0000 g. **Composition:** 0.6400 Silver 04115 oz. ASW **Subject:** 50th Year Austrian Broadcasting

| Date | Mintage | F | VF | XF | Unc | BU |
|---|---|---|---|---|---|---|
| 1974 | 2,290,000 | — | — | 5.00 | 6.00 | — |
| 1974 Proof | 210,000 | Value: 7.00 | | | | |

**50 SCHILLING** **KM# 2937** **Weight:** 20.0000 g. **Composition:** 0.6400 Silver 04115 oz. ASW **Subject:** 150th Anniversary - Death of Franz Schubert

| Date | Mintage | F | VF | XF | Unc | BU |
|---|---|---|---|---|---|---|
| 1978 | 1,868,000 | — | — | 5.00 | 6.00 | — |
| 1978 Proof | 132,000 | Value: 7.00 | | | | |

**50 SCHILLING** **KM# 3038** **Ring Composition:** Brass **Center Composition:** Copper-Nickel Plated Nickel **Subject:** Austrian Millenium **Obverse:** Circle of provincial arms around denomination **Reverse:** Arms below Heinrich I as knight on horse back

| Date | Mintage | F | VF | XF | Unc | BU |
|---|---|---|---|---|---|---|
| ND(1996) | 900,000 | — | — | — | 12.50 | — |
| ND(1996) BU | 100,000 | — | — | — | 25.00 | — |

**50 SCHILLING** **KM# 3044** **Ring Composition:** Brass **Center Composition:** Copper-Nickel Plated Nickel **Subject:** 100th Anniversary - Wiener Secession **Obverse:** Circle of provincial arms **Reverse:** Vienna secession building portal

| Date | Mintage | F | VF | XF | Unc | BU |
|---|---|---|---|---|---|---|
| ND(1997) | 1,400,000 | — | — | — | 7.50 | — |
| ND(1997) BU | 100,000 | — | — | — | 11.50 | — |

**50 SCHILLING** **KM# 3050** **Ring Composition:** Brass **Center Composition:** Copper-Nickel Plated Nickel **Subject:** Austrian Presidency of the European Union **Obverse:** Denomination **Reverse:** New Hofburg palace with logo

| Date | Mintage | F | VF | XF | Unc | BU |
|---|---|---|---|---|---|---|
| 1998 | 1,200,000 | — | — | — | 7.50 | — |
| 1998 BU | 100,000 | — | — | — | 11.50 | — |

**50 SCHILLING** **KM# 3053** **Ring Composition:** Brass **Center Composition:** Copper-Nickel Plated Nickel **Obverse:** Denomination in circle of shields **Reverse:** Konrad Lorenz with three Greylag geese

| Date | Mintage | F | VF | XF | Unc | BU |
|---|---|---|---|---|---|---|
| 1998 | 1,200,000 | — | — | — | 6.50 | — |
| 1998 Special Unc | 100,000 | — | — | — | 9.00 | — |

**50 SCHILLING** **KM# 3057** **Ring Composition:** Brass **Center Composition:** Copper-Nickel Plated Nickel **Subject:** Euro Currency **Obverse:** Denomination in circle of shields **Reverse:** Euro currency designs

| Date | Mintage | F | VF | XF | Unc | BU |
|---|---|---|---|---|---|---|
| 1999 | 1,200,000 | — | — | — | 6.50 | — |
| 1999 Special Unc | 100,000 | — | — | — | 9.00 | — |

**50 SCHILLING** **KM# 3061** **Ring Composition:** Brass **Center Composition:** Copper-Nickel Plated Nickel **Subject:** Centenary - Death of Johann Strauss **Obverse:** Circle of arms **Reverse:** Bust of Johann Strauss facing in right

| Date | Mintage | F | VF | XF | Unc | BU |
|---|---|---|---|---|---|---|
| ND(1999)- | 600,000 | — | — | — | 6.50 | — |
| ND(1999)- Special Unc | 100,000 | — | — | — | 9.00 | — |

**50 SCHILLING** **KM# 3066** **Ring Composition:** Brass **Center Composition:** Copper-Nickel Plated Nickel **Obverse:** Circle of arms **Reverse:** Bust of Sigmund Freud facing in right **Edge:** Plain

| Date | Mintage | F | VF | XF | Unc | BU |
|---|---|---|---|---|---|---|
| ND(2000)- | 600,000 | — | — | — | 6.50 | — |
| ND(2000)- Special Unc | 100,000 | — | — | — | 9.00 | — |

**50 SCHILLING** **KM# 3070** **Ring Composition:** Brass **Center Composition:** Copper-Nickel Plated Nickel **Obverse:** Circle of arms **Reverse:** Antique automobile and portrait of Ferdinand Porsche **Edge:** Plain **Note:** 100,000 of which are in blister-packs, with a value of $8.00 each.

| Date | Mintage | F | VF | XF | Unc | BU |
|---|---|---|---|---|---|---|
| 2000- | 700,000 | — | — | — | 6.50 | — |

**50 SCHILLING** **KM# 3076** **Ring Composition:** Brass-Center **Weight:** 8.1100 g. **Center Composition:** Copper-Nickel Plated Nickel **Subject:** The Schilling Era **Obverse:** Denomination and shields. **Reverse:** Four old coin designs. **Edge:** Plain. **Size:** 26.5 mm.

| Date | Mintage | F | VF | XF | Unc | BU |
|---|---|---|---|---|---|---|
| 2001- | 700,000 | — | — | — | 7.50 | — |

**100 SCHILLING** **KM# 2926** **Weight:** 23.9300 g. **Composition:** 0.6400 Silver .4924 oz. ASW **Series:** Winter Olympics - Innsbruck **Reverse:** Emblem

| Date | Mintage | F | VF | XF | Unc | BU |
|---|---|---|---|---|---|---|
| ND(1974) | 2,826,000 | — | — | — | 9.00 | — |
| ND(1974) Proof | 374,000 | Value: 10.00 | | | | |

**100 SCHILLING** **KM# 2927** **Weight:** 23.9300 g. **Composition:** 0.6400 Silver .4924 oz. ASW **Series:** Winter Olympics-Innsbruck **Reverse:** Buildings and Olympic Rings

| Date | Mintage | F | VF | XF | Unc | BU |
|---|---|---|---|---|---|---|
| ND(1974)(h) | 2,692,000 | — | — | — | 9.00 | — |
| ND(1974)(v) Select | Inc. above | — | — | — | 12.50 | — |
| ND(1974)(h) Proof | 223,000 | Value: 10.00 | | | | |
| ND(1974)(v) | 2,718,000 | — | — | — | 9.00 | — |
| ND(1974)(h) Select | Inc. above | — | — | — | 12.50 | — |
| ND(1974)(v) Proof | 232,000 | Value: 10.00 | | | | |

**100 SCHILLING** **KM# 2928** **Weight:** 23.9300 g. **Composition:** 0.6400 Silver .4924 oz. ASW **Series:** Winter Olympics-Innsbruck **Reverse:** Skier

| Date | Mintage | F | VF | XF | Unc | BU |
|---|---|---|---|---|---|---|
| ND(1974)(h) | 2,636,000 | — | — | — | 9.00 | — |
| ND(1974)(v) Select | Inc. above | — | — | — | 12.50 | — |
| ND(1974)(h) Proof | 179,000 | Value: 10.00 | | | | |
| ND(1974)(v) | 2,641,000 | — | — | — | 9.00 | — |

| Date | Mintage | F | VF | XF | Unc | BU |
|---|---|---|---|---|---|---|
| ND(1974)(h) Select | Inc. above | — | — | — | 12.50 | — |
| ND(1974)(v) Proof | 184,000 | Value: 10.00 | | | | |

**100 SCHILLING** **KM# 2929** **Weight:** 23.9300 g. **Composition:** 0.6400 Silver .4924 oz. ASW **Series:** Winter Olympics-Innsbruck **Reverse:** Ski Jump and Symbols

| Date | Mintage | F | VF | XF | Unc | BU |
|---|---|---|---|---|---|---|
| ND(1974)(h) | 2,611,000 | — | — | — | 9.00 | — |
| ND(1974)(h) Select | Inc. above | — | — | — | 12.50 | — |
| ND(1974)(h) Proof | 179,000 | Value: 10.00 | | | | |
| ND(1974)(v) | 2,627,000 | — | — | — | 9.00 | — |
| ND(1974)(v) Select | Inc. above | — | — | — | 12.50 | — |
| ND(1974)(v) Proof | 188,000 | Value: 10.00 | | | | |

**100 SCHILLING** **KM# 2923** **Weight:** 23.9300 g. **Composition:** 0.6400 Silver .4924 oz. ASW **Subject:** 150th Anniversary - Birth of Johann Strauss

| Date | Mintage | F | VF | XF | Unc | BU |
|---|---|---|---|---|---|---|
| 1975 | 2,646,000 | — | — | — | 9.00 | — |
| 1975 Select | Inc. above | — | — | — | 12.00 | — |
| 1975 Proof | 209,000 | Value: 10.00 | | | | |

**100 SCHILLING** **KM# 2924** **Weight:** 23.9300 g. **Composition:** 0.6400 Silver .4924 oz. ASW **Subject:** 20th Anniversary - State Treaty

| Date | Mintage | F | VF | XF | Unc | BU |
|---|---|---|---|---|---|---|
| 1975 | 3,215,000 | — | — | — | 9.00 | — |
| 1975 Select | Inc. above | — | — | — | 10.00 | — |
| 1975 Proof | 225,000 | Value: 10.00 | | | | |

**100 SCHILLING** **KM# 2925** **Weight:** 23.9300 g. **Composition:** 0.6400 Silver .4924 oz. ASW **Subject:** 50th Anniversary - Schilling

| Date | Mintage | F | VF | XF | Unc | BU |
|---|---|---|---|---|---|---|
| 1975 | 3,234,000 | — | — | — | 9.00 | — |
| 1975 Select | Inc. above | — | — | — | 10.00 | — |
| 1975 Proof | 201,000 | Value: 10.00 | | | | |

**100 SCHILLING** **KM# 2930** **Weight:** 23.9300 g. **Composition:** 0.6400 Silver .4924 oz. ASW **Subject:** 200th Anniversary - Burgtheater

| Date | Mintage | F | VF | XF | Unc | BU |
|---|---|---|---|---|---|---|
| ND(1976) | 1,630,000 | — | — | — | 9.50 | — |
| ND(1976) Select | Inc. above | — | — | — | 11.50 | — |
| ND(1976) Proof | 220,000 | Value: 11.50 | | | | |

**100 SCHILLING** **KM# 2931** **Weight:** 23.9300 g. **Composition:** 0.6400 Silver .4924 oz. ASW **Subject:** 1000th Anniversary - Carinthia

| Date | Mintage | F | VF | XF | Unc | BU |
|---|---|---|---|---|---|---|
| ND(1976) | 1,632,000 | — | — | — | 9.50 | — |
| ND(1976) Select | Inc. above | — | — | — | 11.50 | — |
| ND(1976) Proof | 168,000 | Value: 11.50 | | | | |

**100 SCHILLING** **KM# 2932** **Weight:** 23.9300 g. **Composition:** 0.6400 Silver .4924 oz. ASW **Subject:** 175th Anniversary - Birth of Johann Nestroy

| Date | Mintage | F | VF | XF | Unc | BU |
|---|---|---|---|---|---|---|
| 1976 | 1,761,000 | — | — | — | 9.50 | — |
| 1976 Select | — | — | — | — | 11.50 | — |
| 1976 Proof | 139,000 | Value: 11.50 | | | | |

**100 SCHILLING** **KM# 2934** **Weight:** 23.9300 g. **Composition:** 0.6400 Silver .4924 oz. ASW **Subject:** 1200th Anniversary - Kremsmunster Monastery

| Date | Mintage | F | VF | XF | Unc | BU |
|---|---|---|---|---|---|---|
| ND(1977) | 1,865,000 | — | — | — | 9.50 | — |
| ND(1977) Select | Inc. above | — | — | — | 11.50 | — |
| ND(1977) Proof | 135,000 | Value: 12.50 | | | | |

**100 SCHILLING** **KM# 2935** **Weight:** 23.9300 g. **Composition:** 0.6400 Silver .4924 oz. ASW **Subject:** 900th Anniversary - Hohensalzburg Fortress

| Date | Mintage | F | VF | XF | Unc | BU |
|---|---|---|---|---|---|---|
| 1977 | 1,878,000 | — | — | — | 9.50 | — |
| 1977 Select | Inc. above | — | — | — | 11.50 | — |
| 1977 Proof | 122,000 | Value: 12.50 | | | | |

**100 SCHILLING** **KM# 2936** **Weight:** 23.9300 g. **Composition:** 0.6400 Silver .4924 oz. ASW **Subject:** 500th Anniversary - Hall Mint

| Date | Mintage | F | VF | XF | Unc | BU |
|---|---|---|---|---|---|---|
| 1977 | 1,868,000 | — | — | — | 9.50 | — |
| 1977 Select | Inc. above | — | — | — | 11.50 | — |
| 1977 Proof | 132,000 | Value: 16.50 | | | | |

**100 SCHILLING** **KM# 2940** **Weight:** 23.9300 g. **Composition:** 0.6400 Silver .4924 oz. ASW **Subject:** 1100th Anniversary - Founding of Villach

| Date | Mintage | F | VF | XF | Unc | BU |
|---|---|---|---|---|---|---|
| ND(1978) | 1,569,000 | — | — | — | 9.50 | — |
| ND(1978) Select | Inc. above | — | — | — | 11.50 | — |
| ND(1978) Proof | 131,000 | Value: 12.50 | | | | |

**100 SCHILLING** **KM# 2943** **Weight:** 23.9300 g. **Composition:** 0.6400 Silver .4924 oz. ASW **Subject:** 200th Anniversary - Inn District

| Date | Mintage | F | VF | XF | Unc | BU |
|---|---|---|---|---|---|---|
| 1979 | 1,795,000 | — | — | — | 9.50 | — |
| 1979 Select | 75,000 | — | — | — | 11.50 | — |
| 1979 Proof | 130,000 | Value: 12.50 | | | | |

**100 SCHILLING** **KM# 2938** **Weight:** 23.9300 g. **Composition:** 0.6400 Silver .4924 oz. ASW **Subject:** 700th Anniversary - Gmunden

| Date | Mintage | F | VF | XF | Unc | BU |
|---|---|---|---|---|---|---|
| 1978 | 1,870,000 | — | — | — | 9.50 | — |
| 1978 Select | Inc. above | — | — | — | 11.50 | — |
| 1978 Proof | 130,000 | Value: 12.50 | | | | |

**100 SCHILLING** **KM# 2941** **Weight:** 23.9300 g. **Composition:** 0.6400 Silver .4924 oz. ASW **Subject:** Opening of Arlberg Tunnel

| Date | Mintage | F | VF | XF | Unc | BU |
|---|---|---|---|---|---|---|
| 1978 | 1,764,000 | — | — | — | 9.50 | — |
| 1978 Select | 80,000 | — | — | — | 11.50 | — |
| 1978 Proof | 156,000 | Value: 12.50 | | | | |

**100 SCHILLING** **KM# 2944** **Weight:** 23.9300 g. **Composition:** 0.6400 Silver .4924 oz. ASW **Reverse:** Vienna International Center

| Date | Mintage | F | VF | XF | Unc | BU |
|---|---|---|---|---|---|---|
| 1979 | 1,780,000 | — | — | — | 9.50 | — |
| 1979 Select | 75,000 | — | — | — | 11.50 | — |
| 1979 Proof | 145,000 | Value: 12.50 | | | | |

**100 SCHILLING** **KM# 2939** **Weight:** 23.9300 g. **Composition:** 0.6400 Silver .4924 oz. ASW **Subject:** 700th Anniversary - Battle of Durnkrut and Jedenspeigen

| Date | Mintage | F | VF | XF | Unc | BU |
|---|---|---|---|---|---|---|
| 1978 | 1,677,000 | — | — | — | 9.50 | — |
| 1978 Select | Inc. above | — | — | — | 11.50 | — |
| 1978 Proof | 123,000 | Value: 12.50 | | | | |

**100 SCHILLING** **KM# 2942** **Weight:** 23.9300 g. **Composition:** 0.6400 Silver .4924 oz. ASW **Subject:** 700th Anniversary - Cathedral of Wiener Neustadt

| Date | Mintage | F | VF | XF | Unc | BU |
|---|---|---|---|---|---|---|
| 1979 | 1,796,000 | — | — | — | 9.50 | — |
| 1979 Select | 70,000 | — | — | — | 11.50 | — |
| 1979 Proof | 134,000 | Value: 12.50 | | | | |

**100 SCHILLING** **KM# 2945** **Weight:** 23.9300 g. **Composition:** 0.6400 Silver .4924 oz. ASW **Reverse:** Festival and Congress Hall at Bregenz

| Date | Mintage | F | VF | XF | Unc | BU |
|---|---|---|---|---|---|---|
| 1979 | 1,498,000 | — | — | — | 9.50 | — |
| 1979 Select | 75,000 | — | — | — | 11.50 | — |
| 1979 Proof | 161,000 | Value: 12.50 | | | | |

**100 SCHILLING** **KM# 2996** **Weight:** 18.0000 g. **Composition:** 0.9000 Silver .5209 oz. ASW **Reverse:** Mozart - Salsburg

| Date | Mintage | F | VF | XF | Unc | BU |
|---|---|---|---|---|---|---|
| 1991 Proof | 99,000 | Value: 37.50 | | | | |

**100 SCHILLING** **KM# 2998** **Weight:** 18.0000 g. **Composition:** 0.9000 Silver .5209 oz. ASW **Reverse:** Mozart's Vienna Years - Burgtheater

| Date | Mintage | F | VF | XF | Unc | BU |
|---|---|---|---|---|---|---|
| 1991 Proof | 97,000 | Value: 37.50 | | | | |

**100 SCHILLING** **KM# 3001** **Weight:** 18.0000 g. **Composition:** 0.9000 Silver .5209 oz. ASW **Reverse:** Rudolph I

| Date | Mintage | F | VF | XF | Unc | BU |
|---|---|---|---|---|---|---|
| 1991 Proof | 75,000 | Value: 135 | | | | |

**100 SCHILLING** **KM# 3003** **Weight:** 18.0000 g. **Composition:** 0.9000 Silver .5209 oz. ASW **Reverse:** Maximilian I

| Date | Mintage | F | VF | XF | Unc | BU |
|---|---|---|---|---|---|---|
| 1992 Proof | 75,000 | Value: 75.00 | | | | |

**100 SCHILLING** **KM# 3005** **Weight:** 20.0000 g. **Composition:** 0.9000 Silver .5788 oz. ASW **Reverse:** Otto Nicolai

| Date | Mintage | F | VF | XF | Unc | BU |
|---|---|---|---|---|---|---|
| 1992 Proof | 68,000 | Value: 35.00 | | | | |

**100 SCHILLING** **KM# 3007** **Weight:** 18.0000 g. **Composition:** 0.9000 Silver .5209 oz. ASW **Reverse:** Karl V

| Date | Mintage | F | VF | XF | Unc | BU |
|---|---|---|---|---|---|---|
| 1992 Proof | 74,000 | Value: 50.00 | | | | |

**100 SCHILLING** **KM# 3009** **Weight:** 18.0000 g. **Composition:** 0.9000 Silver .5209 oz. ASW **Reverse:** Kaiser Leopold I

| Date | Mintage | F | VF | XF | Unc | BU |
|---|---|---|---|---|---|---|
| 1993 Proof | 73,000 | Value: 35.00 | | | | |

**100 SCHILLING** **KM# 3019** **Weight:** 18.0000 g. **Composition:** 0.9000 Silver .5209 oz. ASW **Reverse:** Franz Joseph I

| Date | Mintage | F | VF | XF | Unc | BU |
|---|---|---|---|---|---|---|
| 1994 Proof | 74,000 | Value: 35.00 | | | | |

**100 SCHILLING** **KM# 3020** **Weight:** 18.0000 g. **Composition:** 0.9000 Silver .5209 oz. ASW **Subject:** 1848 Revolution **Reverse:** Archduke Johann

| Date | Mintage | F | VF | XF | Unc | BU |
|---|---|---|---|---|---|---|
| 1994 Proof | 74,000 | Value: 35.00 | | | | |

**100 SCHILLING** **KM# 3034** **Weight:** 18.0000 g. **Composition:** 0.9000 Silver .5209 oz. ASW **Reverse:** First Republic - Coin, Buildings and Symbols

| Date | Mintage | F | VF | XF | Unc | BU |
|---|---|---|---|---|---|---|
| 1995 Proof | 68,000 | Value: 35.00 | | | | |

**100 SCHILLING** **KM# 3036** **Weight:** 18.0000 g. **Composition:** 0.9000 Silver .5209 oz. ASW **Reverse:** Leopold III

| Date | Mintage | F | VF | XF | Unc | BU |
|---|---|---|---|---|---|---|
| 1996 Proof | 69,000 | Value: 35.00 | | | | |

**100 SCHILLING** **KM# 3046** **Weight:** 18.0000 g. **Composition:** 0.9000 Silver .5209 oz. ASW **Series:** Habsburg Tragedies **Obverse:** Standing portrait in uniform of Emperor Maximilian of Mexico **Reverse:** Miramar palace and the SMS Novard

| Date | Mintage | F | VF | XF | Unc | BU |
|---|---|---|---|---|---|---|
| 1997 Proof | 65,000 | Value: 40.00 | | | | |

**100 SCHILLING** **KM# 3051** **Weight:** 18.0000 g. **Composition:** 0.9000 Silver .5209 oz. ASW **Series:** Habsburg Tragedies **Obverse:** Standing portrait in uniform of Crown Prince Rudolf **Reverse:** Hearse with military honor guard

| Date | Mintage | F | VF | XF | Unc | BU |
|---|---|---|---|---|---|---|
| 1998 Proof | Est. 50,000 | Value: 40.00 | | | | |

**100 SCHILLING** **KM# 3059** **Weight:** 18.0000 g. **Composition:** 0.9000 Silver .5209 oz. ASW **Series:** Habsburg Tragedies **Obverse:** Archduke Franz Ferdinand and Sophie **Reverse:** The couple getting into the car

| Date | Mintage | F | VF | XF | Unc | BU |
|---|---|---|---|---|---|---|
| 1999 Proof | Est. 50,000 | Value: 40.00 | | | | |

**100 SCHILLING** **KM# 3063** **Ring Composition:** 0.9000 Silver**Center Weight:** 9.0000 g. **Center Composition:** Titanium .2604 oz. ASW AGW **Subject:** Communications **Obverse:** Computer chip design **Reverse:** World map at center in ring **Edge:** Plain

| Date | Mintage | F | VF | XF | Unc | BU |
|---|---|---|---|---|---|---|
| 2000- Proof | 50,000 | Value: 45.00 | | | | |

**100 SCHILLING** **KM# 3068** **Weight:** 18.0000 g. **Composition:** 0.9000 Silver .5209 oz. ASW **Obverse:** Celtic salt miner **Reverse:** Celtic coin design with mounted warrior

| Date | Mintage | F | VF | XF | Unc | BU |
|---|---|---|---|---|---|---|
| 2000 Proof | 50,000 | Value: 40.00 | | | | |

**100 SCHILLING** **KM# 3069** **Weight:** 18.0000 g. **Composition:** 0.9000 Silver .5209 oz. ASW **Obverse:** Ancient Roman troops crossing pontoon bridge **Reverse:** Bust of Marcus Aurelius right **Edge:** Reeded

| Date | Mintage | F | VF | XF | Unc | BU |
|---|---|---|---|---|---|---|
| 2000- Proof | 50,000 | Value: 40.00 | | | | |

**100 SCHILLING** **KM# 3073** **Ring Weight:** 7.0000 g. **Ring Composition:** 0.9000 Silver .2604 oz. ASW AGW**Center Weight:** 3.7500 g. **Center Composition:** Titanium **Subject:** Transportation **Obverse:** Automobile engine. **Reverse:** Car, train, truck and plane. **Edge:** Plain. **Size:** 34 mm.

| Date | Mintage | F | VF | XF | Unc | BU |
|---|---|---|---|---|---|---|
| 2001- Proof | 50,000 | Value: 40.00 | | | | |

**100 SCHILLING** **KM# 3077** **Weight:** 18.0000 g. **Composition:** 0.9000 Silver .5209 oz. ASW **Subject:** Charlemagne **Obverse:** Holy Roman Emperor's crown above denomination. **Reverse:** Bust of Charlemagne facing half right holding sceptre. **Edge:** Reeded. **Size:** 34 mm.

| Date | Mintage | F | VF | XF | Unc | BU |
|---|---|---|---|---|---|---|
| 2001- Proof | 50,000 | Value: 40.00 | | | | |

**100 SCHILLING** **KM# 3079** **Weight:** 18.0000 g. **Composition:** 0.9000 Silver .5209 oz. ASW **Subject:** Duke Rudolf IV **Obverse:** University teaching scene. **Reverse:** Bust of Duke Rudolf IV at right facing half left, St. Stephen's cathedral at left. **Edge:** Reeded. **Size:** 34 mm.

| Date | Mintage | F | VF | XF | Unc | BU |
|---|---|---|---|---|---|---|
| 2001- Proof | 50,000 | Value: 40.00 | | | | |

**200 SCHILLING** **KM# 3004** **Weight:** 3.1100 g. **Composition:** 0.9999 Gold .1000 oz. AGW **Series:** Vienna Philharmonic Orchestra **Obverse:** Building **Reverse:** Instruments

| Date | Mintage | F | VF | XF | Unc | BU |
|---|---|---|---|---|---|---|
| 1991 | 83,000 | — | — | — | BV+13% | — |
| 1992 | 99,000 | — | — | — | BV+13% | — |
| 1993 | 10,000 | — | — | — | BV+13% | — |
| 1994 | 110,000 | — | — | — | BV+13% | — |
| 1995 | 151,000 | — | — | — | BV+13% | — |
| 1996 | 128,000 | — | — | — | BV+13% | — |
| 1997 | 12,000 | — | — | — | BV+13% | — |
| 1998 | — | — | — | — | BV+13% | — |
| 1999 | — | — | — | — | BV+13% | — |

**200 SCHILLING** **KM# 3026** **Weight:** 33.6300 g. **Composition:** 0.9250 Silver 1.0000 oz. ASW **Series:** Olympics **Reverse:** Ribbon Dancer **Edge Lettering:** CITIUS ALTIUS FORTIUS

| Date | Mintage | F | VF | XF | Unc | BU |
|---|---|---|---|---|---|---|
| 1995 Proof | Est. 100,000 | Value: 32.50 | | | | |

**200 SCHILLING** **KM# 3027** **Weight:** 33.6300 g. **Composition:** 0.9250 Silver 1.0000 oz. ASW **Series:** Olympics **Reverse:** Skier

| Date | Mintage | F | VF | XF | Unc | BU |
|---|---|---|---|---|---|---|
| 1995 Proof | Est. 100,000 | Value: 32.50 | | | | |

**500 SCHILLING** **KM# 2947** **Weight:** 23.9600 g. **Composition:** 0.6400 Silver .4930 oz. ASW **Subject:** Millennium **Reverse:** City of Steyr

| Date | Mintage | F | VF | XF | Unc | BU |
|---|---|---|---|---|---|---|
| 1980 | 825,000 | — | — | — | 50.00 | — |
| 1980 Select | 63,000 | — | — | — | 52.00 | — |
| 1980 Proof | 111,000 | Value: 58.00 | | | | |

**500 SCHILLING** **KM# 2948** **Weight:** 23.9600 g. **Composition:** 0.6400 Silver .4930 oz. ASW **Subject:** 25th Anniversary - State Treaty

| Date | Mintage | F | VF | XF | Unc | BU |
|---|---|---|---|---|---|---|
| ND(1980) | 787,000 | — | — | — | 50.00 | — |
| ND(1980) Select | 79,000 | — | — | — | 52.00 | — |
| ND(1980) Proof | 134,000 | Value: 58.00 | | | | |

**500 SCHILLING** **KM# 2949** **Weight:** 23.9600 g. **Composition:** 0.6400 Silver .4930 oz. ASW **Subject:** Bicentennial - Death of Maria Theresa

| Date | Mintage | F | VF | XF | Unc | BU |
|---|---|---|---|---|---|---|
| 1980 | 841,600 | — | — | — | 50.00 | — |
| 1980 Select | 86,400 | — | — | — | 50.00 | — |
| 1980 Proof | 172,000 | Value: 55.00 | | | | |

**500 SCHILLING** **KM# 2950** **Weight:** 23.9600 g. **Composition:** 0.6400 Silver .4930 oz. ASW **Subject:** Centennial - Austrian Red Cross

| Date | Mintage | F | VF | XF | Unc | BU |
|---|---|---|---|---|---|---|
| ND(1980) | 860,000 | — | — | — | 50.00 | — |
| ND(1980) Select | 90,000 | — | — | — | 50.00 | — |
| ND(1980) Proof | 200,000 | Value: 55.00 | | | | |

**500 SCHILLING** **KM# 2951** **Weight:** 23.9600 g. **Composition:** 0.6400 Silver .4930 oz. ASW **Subject:** 800th Anniversary - Verdun Altar

| Date | Mintage | F | VF | XF | Unc | BU |
|---|---|---|---|---|---|---|
| ND(1981) | 865,000 | — | — | — | 50.00 | — |
| ND(1981) Select | 85,000 | — | — | — | 50.00 | — |
| ND(1981) Proof | 200,000 | Value: 58.00 | | | | |

**500 SCHILLING** **KM# 2954** **Weight:** 23.9600 g. **Composition:** 0.6400 Silver .4930 oz. ASW **Subject:** 200th Anniversary - Religious Tolerance

| Date | Mintage | F | VF | XF | Unc | BU |
|---|---|---|---|---|---|---|
| ND(1981) | 792,000 | — | — | — | 50.00 | — |
| ND(1981) Select | 60,000 | — | — | — | 50.00 | — |
| ND(1981) Proof | 148,000 | Value: 55.00 | | | | |

**500 SCHILLING** **KM# 2958** **Weight:** 23.9600 g. **Composition:** 0.6400 Silver .4930 oz. ASW **Subject:** 825 Years of the Mariazell Shrine

| Date | Mintage | F | VF | XF | Unc | BU |
|---|---|---|---|---|---|---|
| 1982 | 590,400 | — | — | — | 50.00 | — |
| 1982 Select | 41,600 | — | — | — | 50.00 | — |
| 1982 Proof | 118,000 | Value: 55.00 | | | | |

**500 SCHILLING** **KM# 2952** **Weight:** 23.9600 g. **Composition:** 0.6400 Silver .4930 oz. ASW **Subject:** 100th Anniversary - Birth of Anton Wildgans

| Date | Mintage | F | VF | XF | Unc | BU |
|---|---|---|---|---|---|---|
| 1981 | 911,000 | — | — | — | 50.00 | — |
| 1981 Select | 72,000 | — | — | — | 50.00 | — |
| 1981 Proof | 167,000 | Value: 55.00 | | | | |

**500 SCHILLING** **KM# 2956** **Weight:** 23.9600 g. **Composition:** 0.6400 Silver .4930 oz. ASW **Subject:** 1500th Anniversary - Death of St. Severin

| Date | Mintage | F | VF | XF | Unc | BU |
|---|---|---|---|---|---|---|
| ND(1982) | 837,400 | — | — | — | 50.00 | — |
| ND(1982) Select | 42,600 | — | — | — | 50.00 | — |
| ND(1982) Proof | 120,000 | Value: 55.00 | | | | |

**500 SCHILLING** **KM# 2959** **Weight:** 23.9600 g. **Composition:** 0.6400 Silver .4930 oz. ASW **Subject:** 80th Anniversary - Birth of Leopold Figl

| Date | Mintage | F | VF | XF | Unc | BU |
|---|---|---|---|---|---|---|
| 1982 | 344,400 | — | — | — | 50.00 | — |
| 1982 Select | 39,600 | — | — | — | 50.00 | — |
| 1982 Proof | 116,000 | Value: 60.00 | | | | |

**500 SCHILLING** **KM# 2953** **Weight:** 23.9600 g. **Composition:** 0.6400 Silver .4930 oz. ASW **Subject:** 100th Anniversary - Birth of Otto Bauer

| Date | Mintage | F | VF | XF | Unc | BU |
|---|---|---|---|---|---|---|
| ND(1981) | 929,000 | — | — | — | 50.00 | — |
| ND(1981) Select | 65,000 | — | — | — | 50.00 | — |
| ND(1981) Proof | 156,000 | Value: 55.00 | | | | |

**500 SCHILLING** **KM# 2957** **Weight:** 23.9600 g. **Composition:** 0.6400 Silver .4930 oz. ASW **Subject:** 500 Years of Austrian Printing

| Date | Mintage | F | VF | XF | Unc | BU |
|---|---|---|---|---|---|---|
| 1982 | 589,800 | — | — | — | 50.00 | — |
| 1982 Select | 42,200 | — | — | — | 50.00 | — |
| 1982 Proof | 118,000 | Value: 55.00 | | | | |

**500 SCHILLING** **KM# 2961** **Weight:** 23.9600 g. **Composition:** 0.9250 Silver .7125 oz. ASW **Subject:** World Cup Horse Jumping Championship

| Date | Mintage | F | VF | XF | Unc | BU |
|---|---|---|---|---|---|---|
| 1983 | 368,000 | — | — | — | 50.00 | — |
| 1983 Proof | 132,000 | Value: 55.00 | | | | |

**500 SCHILLING** **KM# 2962** **Weight:** 23.9600 g. **Composition:** 0.9250 Silver .7125 oz. ASW **Subject:** Centennial - Vienna City Hall

| Date | Mintage | F | VF | XF | Unc | BU |
|---|---|---|---|---|---|---|
| ND(1983) | 466,000 | — | — | — | 50.00 | — |
| ND(1973) Proof | 134,000 | Value: 55.00 | | | | |

**500 SCHILLING** **KM# 2966** **Weight:** 23.9600 g. **Composition:** 0.9250 Silver .7125 oz. ASW **Subject:** 175th Anniversary - Tirolean Revolution

| Date | Mintage | F | VF | XF | Unc | BU |
|---|---|---|---|---|---|---|
| ND(1984) | 454,000 | — | — | — | 50.00 | — |
| ND(1984) Proof | 146,000 | Value: 55.00 | | | | |

**500 SCHILLING** **KM# 2969** **Weight:** 23.9600 g. **Composition:** 0.9250 Silver .7125 oz. ASW **Subject:** Centennial - Death of Fanny Elssler

| Date | Mintage | F | VF | XF | Unc | BU |
|---|---|---|---|---|---|---|
| 1984 | 465,000 | — | — | — | 50.00 | — |
| 1984 Proof | 135,000 | Value: 55.00 | | | | |

**500 SCHILLING** **KM# 2963** **Weight:** 23.9600 g. **Composition:** 0.9250 Silver .7125 oz. ASW **Subject:** Catholic Day - Pope's Visit

| Date | Mintage | F | VF | XF | Unc | BU |
|---|---|---|---|---|---|---|
| 1983 | 600,000 | — | — | — | 50.00 | — |
| 1983 Select | 60,000 | — | — | — | 50.00 | — |
| 1983 Proof | 140,000 | Value: 55.00 | | | | |

**500 SCHILLING** **KM# 2967** **Weight:** 23.9600 g. **Composition:** 0.9250 Silver .7125 oz. ASW **Subject:** 100th Anniversary - Commercial Shipping on Lake Constance

| Date | Mintage | F | VF | XF | Unc | BU |
|---|---|---|---|---|---|---|
| 1984 | 458,000 | — | — | — | 50.00 | — |
| 1984 Proof | 142,000 | Value: 55.00 | | | | |

**500 SCHILLING** **KM# 2971** **Weight:** 23.9600 g. **Composition:** 0.9250 Silver .7125 oz. ASW **Subject:** 400th Anniversary - Graz University

| Date | Mintage | F | VF | XF | Unc | BU |
|---|---|---|---|---|---|---|
| 1985 | 481,000 | — | — | — | 50.00 | — |
| 1985 Proof | 119,000 | Value: 55.00 | | | | |

**500 SCHILLING** **KM# 2964** **Weight:** 23.9600 g. **Composition:** 0.9250 Silver .7125 oz. ASW **Subject:** Centennial - Parliament Building

| Date | Mintage | F | VF | XF | Unc | BU |
|---|---|---|---|---|---|---|
| 1983 | 463,000 | — | — | — | 50.00 | — |
| 1983 Proof | 137,000 | Value: 55.00 | | | | |

**500 SCHILLING** **KM# 2968** **Weight:** 23.9600 g. **Composition:** 0.9250 Silver .7125 oz. ASW **Subject:** 700th Anniversary - Stams Stift in Tirol

| Date | Mintage | F | VF | XF | Unc | BU |
|---|---|---|---|---|---|---|
| 1984 | 462,000 | — | — | — | 50.00 | — |
| 1984 Proof | 138,000 | Value: 55.00 | | | | |

**500 SCHILLING** **KM# 2972** **Weight:** 23.9600 g. **Composition:** 0.9250 Silver .7125 oz. ASW **Subject:** 40 Years of Peace in Austria

| Date | Mintage | F | VF | XF | Unc | BU |
|---|---|---|---|---|---|---|
| ND(1985) | 384,000 | — | — | — | 50.00 | — |
| ND(1985) Proof | 116,000 | Value: 55.00 | | | | |

**500 SCHILLING** **KM# 2973** **Weight:** 23.9600 g. **Composition:** 0.9250 Silver .7125 oz. ASW **Subject:** 500th Anniversary - Canonization of Leopold III

| Date | Mintage | F | VF | XF | Unc | BU |
|---|---|---|---|---|---|---|
| ND(1985) | 388,000 | — | — | — | 50.00 | — |
| ND(1985) Proof | 112,000 | Value: 55.00 | | | | |

**500 SCHILLING** **KM# 2977** **Weight:** 23.9600 g. **Composition:** 0.9250 Silver .7125 oz. ASW **Subject:** 500th Anniversary - First Thaler Coin Struck at Hall Mint

| Date | Mintage | F | VF | XF | Unc | BU |
|---|---|---|---|---|---|---|
| ND(1986) | 401,000 | — | — | — | 50.00 | — |
| ND(1986) Proof | 99,000 | Value: 58.00 | | | | |

**500 SCHILLING** **KM# 2981** **Weight:** 23.9600 g. **Composition:** 0.9250 Silver .7125 oz. ASW **Subject:** 150th Anniversary - Austrian Railroad

| Date | Mintage | F | VF | XF | Unc | BU |
|---|---|---|---|---|---|---|
| ND(1987) | 205,000 | — | — | — | 50.00 | — |
| ND(1987) Proof | 95,000 | Value: 60.00 | | | | |

**500 SCHILLING** **KM# 2974** **Weight:** 23.9600 g. **Composition:** 0.9250 Silver .7125 oz. ASW **Subject:** 2000th Anniversary - Bregenz

| Date | Mintage | F | VF | XF | Unc | BU |
|---|---|---|---|---|---|---|
| 1985 | 388,000 | — | — | — | 50.00 | — |
| 1985 Proof | 112,000 | Value: 55.00 | | | | |

**500 SCHILLING** **KM# 2978** **Weight:** 23.9600 g. **Composition:** 0.9250 Silver .7125 oz. ASW **Subject:** 250th Anniversary - Birth of Prince Eugene of Savoy

| Date | Mintage | F | VF | XF | Unc | BU |
|---|---|---|---|---|---|---|
| 1986 | 400,000 | — | — | — | 50.00 | — |
| 1986 Proof | 100,000 | Value: 55.00 | | | | |

**500 SCHILLING** **KM# 2982** **Weight:** 23.9600 g. **Composition:** 0.9250 Silver .7125 oz. ASW **Subject:** 400th Anniversary - Birth of Salzburg's Archbishop von Raitenau

| Date | Mintage | F | VF | XF | Unc | BU |
|---|---|---|---|---|---|---|
| ND(1987) | 206,000 | — | — | — | 50.00 | — |
| ND(1987) Proof | 94,000 | Value: 55.00 | | | | |

**500 SCHILLING** **KM# 2976** **Weight:** 23.9600 g. **Composition:** 0.9250 Silver .7125 oz. ASW **Subject:** 300th Anniversary - St. Florian's Abbey

| Date | Mintage | F | VF | XF | Unc | BU |
|---|---|---|---|---|---|---|
| ND(1986) | 303,000 | — | — | — | 50.00 | — |
| ND(1986) Proof | 97,000 | Value: 55.00 | | | | |

**500 SCHILLING** **KM# 2979** **Weight:** 23.9600 g. **Composition:** 0.9250 Silver .7125 oz. ASW **Subject:** European Conference on Security and Cooperation

| Date | Mintage | F | VF | XF | Unc | BU |
|---|---|---|---|---|---|---|
| 1986 | 202,000 | — | — | — | 50.00 | — |
| 1986 Proof | 98,000 | Value: 55.00 | | | | |

**500 SCHILLING** **KM# 2983** **Weight:** 23.9600 g. **Composition:** 0.9250 Silver .7125 oz. ASW **Subject:** 800th Anniversary - Holy Cross Church

| Date | Mintage | F | VF | XF | Unc | BU |
|---|---|---|---|---|---|---|
| 1987 | 205,000 | — | — | — | 50.00 | — |
| 1987 Proof | 95,000 | Value: 55.00 | | | | |

**500 SCHILLING** **KM# 2984** **Weight:** 23.9600 g. **Composition:** 0.9250 Silver .7125 oz. ASW **Subject:** 850th Anniversary - St. Georgenberg Abbey

| Date | Mintage | F | VF | XF | Unc | BU |
|---|---|---|---|---|---|---|
| ND(1988) | 212,000 | — | — | — | 50.00 | — |
| ND(1988) Proof | 88,000 | Value: 58.00 | | | | |

**500 SCHILLING** **KM# 2985** **Weight:** 23.9600 g. **Composition:** 0.9250 Silver .7125 oz. ASW **Subject:** Pope's Visit to Austria

| Date | Mintage | F | VF | XF | Unc | BU |
|---|---|---|---|---|---|---|
| 1988 | 211,000 | — | — | — | 50.00 | — |
| 1988 Proof | 89,000 | Value: 58.00 | | | | |

**500 SCHILLING** **KM# 2986** **Weight:** 23.9600 g. **Composition:** 0.9250 Silver .7125 oz. ASW **Subject:** 100th Anniversary - Victor Adler and Christian Socialist Party

| Date | Mintage | F | VF | XF | Unc | BU |
|---|---|---|---|---|---|---|
| 1988 | 213,000 | — | — | — | 50.00 | — |
| 1988 Proof | 87,000 | Value: 58.00 | | | | |

**500 SCHILLING** **KM# 2987** **Weight:** 23.9600 g. **Composition:** 0.9250 Silver .7125 oz. ASW **Obverse:** Gustav Klimt **Reverse:** Art Nouveau

| Date | Mintage | F | VF | XF | Unc | BU |
|---|---|---|---|---|---|---|
| 1989 | 237,000 | — | — | — | 50.00 | — |
| 1989 Proof | 88,000 | Value: 58.00 | | | | |

**500 SCHILLING** **KM# 2989** **Weight:** 7.7760 g. **Composition:** 0.9999 Gold .2505 oz. AGW **Series:** Vienna Philharmonic Orchestra **Obverse:** Similar to 2000 Schilling, KM#2990

| Date | Mintage | F | VF | XF | Unc | BU |
|---|---|---|---|---|---|---|
| 1989 | 68,000 | — | — | — | BV+10% | — |
| 1990 | 41,000 | — | — | — | BV+10% | — |
| 1991 | 37,000 | — | — | — | BV+10% | — |
| 1992 | 44,000 | — | — | — | BV+10% | — |
| 1992 | 44,000 | — | — | — | BV+10% | — |
| 1994 | 30,000 | — | — | — | BV+10% | — |
| 1995 | 157,000 | — | — | — | BV+10% | — |
| 1996 | 138,000 | — | — | — | BV+10% | — |
| 1997 | 25,000 | — | — | — | BV+10% | — |
| 1998 | — | — | — | — | BV+10% | — |
| 1999 | — | — | — | — | BV+10% | — |

**500 SCHILLING** **KM# 2991** **Weight:** 23.9600 g. **Composition:** 0.9250 Silver .7125 oz. ASW **Obverse:** Koloman Moser **Reverse:** Stained Glass

| Date | Mintage | F | VF | XF | Unc | BU |
|---|---|---|---|---|---|---|
| 1989 | 228,000 | — | — | — | 50.00 | — |
| 1989 Proof | 83,000 | Value: 55.00 | | | | |

**500 SCHILLING** **KM# 2992** **Weight:** 23.9600 g. **Composition:** 0.9250 Silver .7125 oz. ASW **Obverse:** Egon Schiele **Reverse:** Expressionism

| Date | Mintage | F | VF | XF | Unc | BU |
|---|---|---|---|---|---|---|
| 1990 | 247,000 | — | — | — | 50.00 | — |
| 1990 Proof | 81,000 | Value: 55.00 | | | | |

**500 SCHILLING** **KM# 2994** **Weight:** 23.9600 g. **Composition:** 0.9250 Silver .7125 oz. ASW **Obverse:** Oskar Kokoschka **Reverse:** Expressionism

| Date | Mintage | F | VF | XF | Unc | BU |
|---|---|---|---|---|---|---|
| 1990 | 245,000 | — | — | — | 50.00 | — |
| 1990 Proof | 81,000 | Value: 55.00 | | | | |

**500 SCHILLING** **KM# 2997** **Weight:** 8.1130 g. **Composition:** 0.9860 Gold .2578 oz. AGW **Obverse:** Mozart **Reverse:** Don Giovanni

| Date | Mintage | F | VF | XF | Unc | BU |
|---|---|---|---|---|---|---|
| 1991 Proof | 50,000 | Value: 245 | | | | |

**500 SCHILLING KM# 3000 Weight:** 24.0000 g. **Composition:** 0.9250 Silver .7125 oz. ASW **Obverse:** Herbert von Karajan **Reverse:** Salzburg Festspielhaus

| Date | Mintage | F | VF | XF | Unc | BU |
|---|---|---|---|---|---|---|
| 1991 | 240,000 | — | — | — | 47.50 | — |
| 1991 Proof | 74,000 | Value: 55.00 | | | | |

**500 SCHILLING KM# 3002 Weight:** 24.0000 g. **Composition:** 0.9250 Silver .7125 oz. ASW **Obverse:** Karl Bohm

| Date | Mintage | F | VF | XF | Unc | BU |
|---|---|---|---|---|---|---|
| 1991 | 237,000 | — | — | — | 47.50 | — |
| 1991 Proof | 71,000 | Value: 55.00 | | | | |

**500 SCHILLING KM# 3006 Weight:** 8.1130 g. **Composition:** 0.9860 Gold .2578 oz. AGW **Subject:** 150th Anniversary - Vienna Philharmonic

| Date | Mintage | F | VF | XF | Unc | BU |
|---|---|---|---|---|---|---|
| 1992 Proof | 43,000 | Value: 185 | | | | |

**500 SCHILLING KM# 3010 Weight:** 24.0000 g. **Composition:** 0.9250 Silver .7125 oz. ASW **Obverse:** Gustav Mahler

| Date | Mintage | F | VF | XF | Unc | BU |
|---|---|---|---|---|---|---|
| 1992 | 256,000 | — | — | — | 47.50 | — |
| 1992 Proof | 64,000 | Value: 60.00 | | | | |

**500 SCHILLING KM# 3021 Weight:** 24.0000 g. **Composition:** 0.9250 Silver .7125 oz. ASW **Obverse:** Richard Strauss

| Date | Mintage | F | VF | XF | Unc | BU |
|---|---|---|---|---|---|---|
| 1992 | 236,000 | — | — | — | 47.50 | — |
| 1992 Proof | 63,000 | Value: 60.00 | | | | |

**500 SCHILLING KM# 3011 Weight:** 24.0000 g. **Composition:** 0.9250 Silver .7125 oz. ASW **Obverse:** Hallstatt and the Lakes Region

| Date | Mintage | F | VF | XF | Unc | BU |
|---|---|---|---|---|---|---|
| 1993 | 220,000 | — | — | — | 47.50 | — |
| 1993 Proof | 60,000 | Value: 60.00 | | | | |

**500 SCHILLING KM# 3012 Weight:** 8.1130 g. **Composition:** 0.9860 Gold .2578 oz. AGW **Reverse:** Emperors Rudolf II, Ferdinand II and Archduke Leopold Wilhelm

| Date | Mintage | F | VF | XF | Unc | BU |
|---|---|---|---|---|---|---|
| 1993 Proof | 50,000 | Value: 650 | | | | |

**500 SCHILLING KM# 3014 Weight:** 24.0000 g. **Composition:** 0.9250 Silver .7125 oz. ASW **Obverse:** Alpine Region

| Date | Mintage | F | VF | XF | Unc | BU |
|---|---|---|---|---|---|---|
| 1993 | 220,000 | — | — | — | 47.50 | — |
| 1993 Proof | 60,000 | Value: 60.00 | | | | |

**500 SCHILLING KM# 3015 Weight:** 8.1130 g. **Composition:** 0.9860 Gold .2578 oz. AGW **Obverse:** Congress of Vienna

| Date | Mintage | F | VF | XF | Unc | BU |
|---|---|---|---|---|---|---|
| 1994 Proof | 50,000 | Value: 225 | | | | |

**500 SCHILLING KM# 3017 Weight:** 24.0000 g. **Composition:** 0.9250 Silver .7125 oz. ASW **Obverse:** Pannonian Region **Reverse:** Dancers

| Date | Mintage | F | VF | XF | Unc | BU |
|---|---|---|---|---|---|---|
| 1994 | 190,000 | — | — | — | 47.50 | — |
| 1994 Proof | 60,000 | Value: 60.00 | | | | |

**500 SCHILLING KM# 3024 Weight:** 24.0000 g. **Composition:** 0.9250 Silver .7125 oz. ASW **Obverse:** River Region **Reverse:** Folk Paraders

| Date | Mintage | F | VF | XF | Unc | BU |
|---|---|---|---|---|---|---|
| 1994 | 190,000 | — | — | — | 47.50 | — |
| 1994 Proof | 60,000 | Value: 60.00 | | | | |

**500 SCHILLING** **KM# 3025** **Weight:** 24.0000 g. **Composition:** 0.9250 Silver .7125 oz. ASW **Obverse:** Austrian Hill Country **Reverse:** Farm Couple

| Date | Mintage | F | VF | XF | Unc | BU |
|---|---|---|---|---|---|---|
| 1995 | 190,000 | — | — | — | 47.50 | — |
| 1995 Proof | 60,000 | Value: 60.00 | | | | |

**500 SCHILLING** **KM# 3029** **Weight:** 24.0000 g. **Composition:** 0.9250 Silver .7125 oz. ASW **Obverse:** Alpine Foothills **Reverse:** Lumberjack

| Date | Mintage | F | VF | XF | Unc | BU |
|---|---|---|---|---|---|---|
| 1995 | Est. 190,000 | — | — | — | 47.50 | — |
| 1995 Proof | Est. 60,000 | Value: 60.00 | | | | |

**500 SCHILLING** **KM# 3023** **Ring Weight:** 8.1130 g. **Ring Composition:** 0.9860 Gold .2578 oz. ASW AGW**Center Weight:** 5.3330 g. **Center Composition:** 0.9000 Silver .1547 oz. ASW AGW **Subject:** European Union - Austrian Membership **Note:** Stars in outer ring are completely punched through.

| Date | Mintage | F | VF | XF | Unc | BU |
|---|---|---|---|---|---|---|
| 1995 Proof | 33,000 | Value: 185 | | | | |

**500 SCHILLING** **KM# 3032** **Weight:** 8.1130 g. **Composition:** 0.9860 Gold .2578 oz. AGW **Reverse:** Heinrich II Jasomirgott

| Date | Mintage | F | VF | XF | Unc | BU |
|---|---|---|---|---|---|---|
| 1996 Proof | Est. 50,000 | Value: 255 | | | | |

**500 SCHILLING** **KM# 3035** **Weight:** 24.0000 g. **Composition:** 0.9250 Silver .7125 oz. ASW **Obverse:** The Mill Region

| Date | Mintage | F | VF | XF | Unc | BU |
|---|---|---|---|---|---|---|
| 1996 | 190,000 | — | — | — | 47.50 | — |
| 1996 Proof | 60,000 | Value: 60.00 | | | | |

**500 SCHILLING** **KM# 3039** **Weight:** 24.0000 g. **Composition:** 0.9250 Silver .7125 oz. ASW **Series:** Towns Series - Innsbruck Square **Obverse:** View of town square **Reverse:** Outdoor market scene

| Date | Mintage | F | VF | XF | Unc | BU |
|---|---|---|---|---|---|---|
| 1996 | 160,000 | — | — | — | 47.50 | — |
| 1996 BU | 30,000 | — | — | — | 50.00 | — |
| 1996 Proof | 60,000 | Value: 60.00 | | | | |

**500 SCHILLING** **KM# 3040** **Weight:** 8.0400 g. **Composition:** 0.9950 Gold .2578 oz. AGW **Obverse:** People gathered at piano **Reverse:** Portrait, Franz Schubert dates, line of musical score

| Date | Mintage | F | VF | XF | Unc | BU |
|---|---|---|---|---|---|---|
| 1997 Proof | Est. 50,000 | Value: 240 | | | | |

**500 SCHILLING** **KM# 3042** **Weight:** 24.0000 g. **Composition:** 0.9250 Silver .7125 oz. ASW **Series:** Town Series - Bruck an der Mur **Obverse:** Ornate pavilion on cobblestone street **Reverse:** Ironsmith at work

| Date | Mintage | F | VF | XF | Unc | BU |
|---|---|---|---|---|---|---|
| 1997 | 125,000 | — | — | — | 42.00 | — |
| 1997 Special Unc | 25,000 | — | — | — | 50.00 | — |
| 1997 Proof | 50,000 | Value: 60.00 | | | | |

**500 SCHILLING** **KM# 3045** **Weight:** 24.0000 g. **Composition:** 0.9250 Silver .7125 oz. ASW **Obverse:** Stone pulpit of St. Stephen's cathedral **Reverse:** Stone mason at work

| Date | Mintage | F | VF | XF | Unc | BU |
|---|---|---|---|---|---|---|
| 1997 | 125,000 | — | — | — | 42.00 | — |
| 1997 Special Unc | 25,000 | — | — | — | 50.00 | — |
| 1997 Proof | 50,000 | Value: 60.00 | | | | |

**500 SCHILLING** **KM# 3047** **Weight:** 8.0000 g. **Composition:** 0.9950 Gold .2559 oz. AGW **Obverse:** New York and Kyoto views **Reverse:** Vienna boys choir

| Date | Mintage | F | VF | XF | Unc | BU |
|---|---|---|---|---|---|---|
| ND(1998) Proof | Est. 50,000 | Value: 250 | | | | |

**500 SCHILLING** **KM# 3049** **Weight:** 22.2000 g. **Composition:** 0.9250 Silver .6602 oz. ASW **Obverse:** Interior view of Admont Abbey Libary **Reverse:** Printers at work **Note:** Book printing.

| Date | Mintage | F | VF | XF | Unc | BU |
|---|---|---|---|---|---|---|
| 1998 | 125,000 | — | — | — | 42.00 | — |
| 1998 BU | 25,000 | — | — | — | 50.00 | — |
| 1998 Proof | 50,000 | Value: 60.00 | | | | |

**500 SCHILLING** **KM# 3054** **Weight:** 22.2000 g. **Composition:** 0.9250 Silver .6602 oz. ASW **Obverse:** Gold chalice and church **Reverse:** Goldsmith at work **Note:** Gold smithing.

| Date | Mintage | F | VF | XF | Unc | BU |
|---|---|---|---|---|---|---|
| 1998 | 125,000 | — | — | — | 42.00 | — |
| 1998 Special Unc | 25,000 | — | — | — | 50.00 | — |
| 1998 Proof | 50,000 | Value: 60.00 | | | | |

**500 SCHILLING** **KM# 3055** **Weight:** 8.0000 g. **Composition:** 0.9250 Gold .2559 oz. AGW **Obverse:** Waltzing couple and Strauss monument **Reverse:** Portrait of Johann Strauss and son, Johann

| Date | Mintage | F | VF | XF | Unc | BU |
|---|---|---|---|---|---|---|
| 1999 Proof | Est. 50,000 | Value: 250 | | | | |

**500 SCHILLING** **KM# 3058** **Weight:** 24.0000 g. **Composition:** 0.9250 Silver .7137 oz. ASW **Obverse:** Rosenburg Castle, falcon on perch in castle jousting court **Reverse:** Jousting knights

| Date | Mintage | F | VF | XF | Unc | BU |
|---|---|---|---|---|---|---|
| 1999 | Est. 125,000 | — | — | — | 42.00 | — |
| 1999 Special Unc | Est. 25,000 | — | — | — | 50.00 | — |
| 1999 Proof | Est. 50,000 | Value: 60.00 | | | | |

**500 SCHILLING** **KM# 3060** **Weight:** 24.0000 g. **Composition:** 0.9250 Silver .7137 oz. ASW **Obverse:** Burg Lockenhaus **Reverse:** Two Templar knights on horseback

| Date | Mintage | F | VF | XF | Unc | BU |
|---|---|---|---|---|---|---|
| 1999 | Est. 125,000 | — | — | — | 42.00 | — |
| 1999 Special Unc | Est. 25,000 | — | — | — | 50.00 | — |
| 1999 Proof | Est. 50,000 | Value: 60.00 | | | | |

**500 SCHILLING** **KM# 3065** **Weight:** 10.0000 g. **Composition:** 0.9860 Gold .3170 oz. AGW **Subject:** 2000th Birthday of Jesus Christ **Obverse:** 3 wise men presenting gifts **Reverse:** Portrait of Jesus

| Date | Mintage | F | VF | XF | Unc | BU |
|---|---|---|---|---|---|---|
| 2000 Proof | Est. 50,000 | Value: 250 | | | | |

**500 SCHILLING** **KM# 3067** **Weight:** 24.0000 g. **Composition:** 0.9250 Silver .7137 oz. ASW **Obverse:** Hochosterwitz Castle **Reverse:** Walter von der Vogelweide and royal couple **Edge:** Lettered

| Date | Mintage | F | VF | XF | Unc | BU |
|---|---|---|---|---|---|---|
| 2000- | 95,000 | — | — | — | 42.00 | — |
| 2000- Special Unc | 25,000 | — | — | — | 50.00 | — |
| 2000- Proof | 505,000 | Value: 55.00 | | | | |

**500 SCHILLING** **KM# 3071** **Weight:** 24.0000 g. **Composition:** 0.9250 Silver .7137 oz. ASW **Obverse:** Burg Hohenwerfen Castle **Reverse:** Medieval falcon training scene **Edge:** Lettered

| Date | Mintage | F | VF | XF | Unc | BU |
|---|---|---|---|---|---|---|
| 2000- | 95,000 | — | — | — | 42.00 | — |
| 2000- Special Unc | 25,000 | — | — | — | 50.00 | — |
| 2000- Proof | 50,000 | Value: 55.00 | | | | |

**500 SCHILLING** **KM# 3074** **Weight:** 10.0000 g. **Composition:** 0.9860 Gold .3170 oz. AGW **Subject:** 2000 Years of Christianity - Bible **Obverse:** Bible and symbols of the saints: Matthew, Luke, Mark and John. **Reverse:** St. Paul reading from a scroll to two listeners. **Edge:** Reeded. **Size:** 22 mm.

| Date | Mintage | F | VF | XF | Unc | BU |
|---|---|---|---|---|---|---|
| 2001- | 50,000 | — | — | — | 200 | — |

**500 SCHILLING** **KM# 3078** **Weight:** 24.0000 g. **Composition:** 0.9250 Silver .7137 oz. ASW **Subject:** Kufstein Castle **Obverse:** Castle view above denomination. **Reverse:** Emperor Maximilian being shown one of his new cannons. **Edge:** Lettered. **Size:** 37 mm.

| Date | Mintage | F | VF | XF | Unc | BU |
|---|---|---|---|---|---|---|
| 2001- | 120,000 | — | — | — | 45.00 | — |
| 2001- Proof | 50,000 | Value: 60.00 | | | | |

**500 SCHILLING** **KM# 3080** **Weight:** 24.0000 g. **Composition:** 0.9250 Silver .7137 oz. ASW **Subject:** Schattenburg Castle **Obverse:** Castle view. **Reverse:** Two medieval armourers at work. **Edge:** Lettered. **Size:** 37 mm.

| Date | Mintage | F | VF | XF | Unc | BU |
|---|---|---|---|---|---|---|
| 2001- | 95,000 | — | — | — | 42.00 | — |
| 2001- Special Unc | 25,000 | — | — | — | 50.00 | — |
| 2001- Proof | 50,000 | Value: 60.00 | | | | |

**1000 SCHILLING** **KM# 2933** **Weight:** 13.5000 g. **Composition:** 0.9000 Gold .3906 oz. AGW **Subject:** Babenberg Dynasty Millennium **Note:** Exists in shades of red to yellow gold.

| Date | Mintage | F | VF | XF | Unc | BU |
|---|---|---|---|---|---|---|
| ND (1976) | 1,800,000 | — | — | — | 175 | — |

**1000 SCHILLING** **KM# 2999** **Weight:** 16.2250 g. **Composition:** 0.9860 Gold .5155 oz. AGW **Obverse:** Mozart **Reverse:** The Magic Flute Opera

| Date | Mintage | F | VF | XF | Unc | BU |
|---|---|---|---|---|---|---|
| 1991 Proof | 30,000 | Value: 475 | | | | |

**1000 SCHILLING** **KM# 3008** **Weight:** 16.2250 g. **Composition:** 0.9860 Gold .5155 oz. AGW **Reverse:** Johann Strauss - Violinist

| Date | Mintage | F | VF | XF | Unc | BU |
|---|---|---|---|---|---|---|
| 1992 Proof | 42,000 | Value: 300 | | | | |

**1000 SCHILLING** **KM# 3013** **Weight:** 16.2250 g. **Composition:** 0.9860 Gold .5155 oz. AGW **Reverse:** Maria Theresia

| Date | Mintage | F | VF | XF | Unc | BU |
|---|---|---|---|---|---|---|
| 1993 Proof | 50,000 | Value: 345 | | | | |

**1000 SCHILLING** **KM# 3018** **Weight:** 26.6660 g. **Composition:** 0.9860 Silver .7733 oz. ASW **Subject:** 800th Anniversary of the Vienna Mint

| Date | Mintage | F | VF | XF | Unc | BU |
|---|---|---|---|---|---|---|
| ND (1994) Proof | 48,000 | Value: 300 | | | | |

**1000 SCHILLING** **KM# 3031** **Weight:** 15.5500 g. **Composition:** 0.9999 Gold .5000 oz. AGW **Series:** Vienna Philharmonic Orchestra

| Date | Mintage | F | VF | XF | Unc | BU |
|---|---|---|---|---|---|---|
| 1994 | 29,000 | — | — | — | BV+8% | — |
| 1995 | 95,000 | — | — | — | BV+8% | — |
| 1996 | 88,000 | — | — | — | BV+8% | — |
| 1997 | 34,000 | — | — | — | BV+8% | — |
| 1998 | — | — | — | — | BV+8% | — |
| 1999 | — | — | — | — | BV+8% | — |

**1000 SCHILLING** **KM# 3028** **Weight:** 16.9700 g. **Composition:** 0.9170 Gold .5014 oz. AGW **Series:** Olympics **Reverse:** Zeus **Edge Lettering:** CITIUS ALTIUS FORTIUS

| Date | Mintage | F | VF | XF | Unc | BU |
|---|---|---|---|---|---|---|
| 1995 Proof | Est. 60,000 | Value: 300 | | | | |

**1000 SCHILLING** **KM# 3030** **Weight:** 16.2250 g. **Composition:** 0.9860 Gold .5155 oz. AGW **Subject:** 50th Anniversary - Second Republic

| Date | Mintage | F | VF | XF | Unc | BU |
|---|---|---|---|---|---|---|
| 1995 Proof | 49,000 | Value: 345 | | | | |

**1000 SCHILLING** **KM# 3037** **Weight:** 16.2250 g. **Composition:** 0.9860 Gold .5155 oz. AGW **Subject:** Millennium of the Name Osterreich **Obverse:** Lang grant **Reverse:** Otto III

| Date | Mintage | F | VF | XF | Unc | BU |
|---|---|---|---|---|---|---|
| ND (1996) Proof | 50,000 | Value: 325 | | | | |

**1000 SCHILLING** **KM# 3043** **Weight:** 16.0000 g. **Composition:** 0.9950 Gold .5118 oz. AGW **Subject:** Habsburg Tragedies - Marie Antoinette **Obverse:** Marie holding flowers **Reverse:** Marie on trial

| Date | Mintage | F | VF | XF | Unc | BU |
|---|---|---|---|---|---|---|
| 1997 Proof | Est. 50,000 | Value: 325 | | | | |

**1000 SCHILLING** **KM# 3052** **Weight:** 16.2250 g. **Composition:** 0.9860 Gold .5155 oz. AGW **Obverse:** Empress Elizabeth bust right **Reverse:** Scene of Elizabeth's final moment

| Date | Mintage | F | VF | XF | Unc | BU |
|---|---|---|---|---|---|---|
| 1998 Proof | Est. 50,000 | Value: 325 | | | | |

**1000 SCHILLING** KM# 3062 **Weight:** 16.0000 g. **Composition:** 0.9950 Gold .5118 oz. AGW **Obverse:** Emperor Karl I bust facing **Reverse:** Interior view Habsburg crypt

| Date | Mintage | F | VF | XF | Unc | BU |
|---|---|---|---|---|---|---|
| 1999 Proof | Est. 50,000 | Value: 325 | | | | |

**1000 SCHILLING** KM# 3072 **Weight:** 16.0000 g. **Composition:** 0.9860 Gold .5027 oz. AGW **Obverse:** Heidentor ancient gate and statue **Reverse:** Constantius II portrait **Edge:** Reeded

| Date | Mintage | F | VF | XF | Unc | BU |
|---|---|---|---|---|---|---|
| 2000- | 30,000 | — | — | — | 325 | — |

**1000 SCHILLING** KM# 3081 **Weight:** 16.0000 g. **Composition:** 0.9860 Gold .5072 oz. AGW **Subject:** Austrian National Library **Obverse:** Archduke Maximilian as a student. **Reverse:** Library interior view. **Edge:** Reeded. **Size:** 30 mm.

| Date | Mintage | F | VF | XF | Unc | BU |
|---|---|---|---|---|---|---|
| 2001- | 30,000 | — | — | — | 325 | — |

**2000 SCHILLING** KM# 2990 **Weight:** 31.1035 g. **Composition:** 0.9999 Gold 1.0002 oz. AGW **Series:** Vienna Philharmonic Orchestra

| Date | Mintage | F | VF | XF | Unc | BU |
|---|---|---|---|---|---|---|
| 1989 | 351,000 | — | — | — | BV+4% | — |
| 1990 | 484,000 | — | — | — | BV+4% | — |
| 1991 | 233,000 | — | — | — | BV+4% | — |
| 1992 | 537,000 | — | — | — | BV+4% | — |
| 1993 | 235,000 | — | — | — | BV+4% | — |
| 1994 | 218,000 | — | — | — | BV+4% | — |
| 1995 | 645,000 | — | — | — | BV+4% | — |
| 1996 | 377,000 | — | — | — | BV+4% | — |
| 1997 | 408,000 | — | — | — | BV+4% | — |
| 1998 | — | — | — | — | BV+4% | — |
| 1999 | — | — | — | — | BV+4% | — |

## PATTERNS

Including off metal strikes

| KM# | Date | Mintage | Identification | Mkt Val |
|---|---|---|---|---|
| Pn68 | 1908 | — | 100 Kronen. Without mm. | — |
| Pn69 | 1909 | — | 100 Kronen. Without mm. | — |
| Pn70 | 1910 | — | 2 Kronen. Silver. . Similar to KM#2821 | 2,350 |
| Pn72 | 1913 | — | 2 Corona. Aluminum. KM#2821. | 200 |
| Pn73 | | — | 50 Heller. Iron. | 235 |
| Pn71 | 1913 | — | Krone. Aluminum. KM#2820. | — |
| Pn74 | 1914 | — | Heller. Copper. Privately produced by Karl Goetz in Munich, Germany. | 150 |
| Pn75 | 1914 | — | Heller. Silver. Privately produced by Karl Goetz in Munich, Germany. | 275 |
| Pn78 | 1915 | — | 20 Heller. Iron. KM#2826. | 450 |
| Pn80 | 1915 | — | Ducat. Aluminum. . Plain edge | 100 |
| Pn81 | 1915 | — | Ducat. Copper. . Reeded edge | 400 |
| Pn76 | 1915 | — | 2 Heller. Bronze. KM#2801. | — |
| Pn77 | 1915 | — | 2 Heller. Iron. KM#2801. | — |
| Pn79 | 1915 | — | 1/2 Krone. Silver. 2.5200 g. | — |
| Pn83 | 1916 | — | 2 Heller. Iron. | — |
| Pn82 | 1916 | — | Heller. Iron. KM#2823. | 275 |
| Pn84 | 1916 | — | 10 Heller. Aluminum. KM#2825. | 275 |
| Pn85 | 1916 | — | Krone. Aluminum. KM#2820. | 145 |
| Pn87 | 1917 | — | 10 Heller. Steel. . Plain edge10 in square, thin planchet. | 250 |
| Pn86 | 1917 | — | 10 Heller. Steel. . Plain edge10 in square, thick planchet. | — |
| Pn88 | 1917 | — | 10 Heller. Steel. . Milled edge | — |
| Pn89 | 1918 | — | 20 Heller. Aluminum. 20 in square. | — |
| Pn91 | 1918 | — | 5 Kronen. Brass. | — |
| Pn92 | 1918 | — | 20 Kronen. Copper. | — |
| Pn93 | 1918 | — | 20 Kronen. Gold. | — |
| Pn90 | 1918 | — | 20 Heller. Aluminum. KM#2826. | 250 |
| Pn94 | | — | 10 Schilling. Nickel. | 180 |
| Pn95 | | — | 20 Schilling. Nickel. | 400 |
| Pn96 | 1924 | — | 1/2 Schilling. KM#2839. | 1,250 |
| Pn97 | 1924 | — | Schilling. Silver. KM#2835 | 825 |
| Pn98 | 1924 | — | Schilling. Silver. KM#2835. KM#2835Octagonal planchets, 1 pair. | 700 |
| Pn99 | 1924 | — | 20 Kronen. Copper. . Reeded edgeKM#2830. | 1,500 |
| Pn100 | 1924 | — | 20 Kronen. Silver. . Reeded edgeUniface, KM#2830. | 700 |
| Pn101 | 1930 | — | 100 Schilling. Silver. . Plain edgeKM#2842. | 2,000 |
| Pn103 | 1931 | — | 5 Groschen. Gold. KM#2846. | 1,200 |
| Pn104 | 1931 | — | 100 Schilling. Copper. KM#2842. | 1,000 |
| Pn102 | 1931 | — | 5 Groschen. Copper-Nickel. | — |
| Pn105 | 1934 | — | 50 Groschen. Copper-Nickel. Uniface | — |
| Pn106 | 1934 | — | 50 Groschen. Copper-Nickel. . Uniface | — |
| Pn107 | 1934 | — | Schilling. Copper-Nickel. Uniface | 1,750 |
| Pn108 | 1934 | — | Schilling. Copper-Nickel. . Uniface | 1,750 |
| Pn109 | 1934 | — | 2 Schilling. Zinc. KM#2852. | 1,000 |
| Pn110 | 1934 | — | 2 Schilling. Zinc. One side struck on octagonal planchet, KM#2852. | 600 |
| Pn111 | 1935 | — | 25 Schilling. Gold. J. Prinz. | — |
| Pn112 | 1935 | — | 100 Schilling. Gold. J. Prinz. | — |
| Pn113 | 1937 | — | 2 Schilling. Copper. KM#2859. | 200 |
| Pn114 | 1938 | — | 5 Groschen. Gold. KM#2846. | 1,200 |
| Pn115 | 1947 | — | Schilling. Copper-Nickel. KM#2871. | 500 |
| Pn116 | 1959 | — | Schilling. Similar to KM#2886 | 850 |

## TRIAL STRIKES

| KM# | Date | Mintage | Identification | Mkt Val |
|---|---|---|---|---|
| TS1 | 1934 | — | 50 Groschen. Uniface | — |
| TS2 | 1934 | — | 50 Groschen. Uniface | — |
| TS3 | (1973) | — | 5 Schilling. Nickel. | 275 |
| TS4 | (1973) | — | 10 Schilling. Nickel. | 200 |
| TS5 | (1973) | — | 20 Schilling. Nickel. | 350 |
| TS6 | (1984) | — | 5 Groschen. Aluminum. . Plain edge | 175 |

## MINT SETS

| KM# | Date | Mintage | Identification | Issue Price | Mkt Val |
|---|---|---|---|---|---|
| MS1 | 1992 | 25,000 | KM#2875-2876, 2878, 2885-2886, 2889a, 2918, 2946.1 | — | 50.00 |
| MS2 | 1993 | 35,000 | KM#2875-2876, 2878, 2885-2886, 2889a, 2918, 2946.2 | — | 40.00 |
| MS9 | 2000 | — | KM#2878, 2885-2886, 2889a, 2918, 3064 | — | 22.50 |
| MS3 | 1994 | 25,000 | KM#2875-2876, 2878, 2885-2886, 2889a, 2918, 3016 | — | 70.00 |
| MS4 | 1995 | 27,000 | KM#2878, 2885-2886, 2889a, 2918, 3022 | — | 50.00 |
| MS5 | 1996 | 25,000 | KM#2878, 2885-2886, 2889a, 2918, 3033 | — | 35.00 |
| MS6 | 1997 | 25,000 | KM#2878, 2885-2886, 2889a, 2918, 3041 | — | 30.00 |
| MS7 | 1998 | — | KM#2878, 2885-2886, 2889a, 2918, 3048 | — | 22.50 |
| MS8 | 1999 | — | KM#2878, 2885-2886, 2889a, 2918, 3056 | 22.00 | 22.50 |
| MS10 | 2001 | 75,000 | KM#2878, 2885, 2886, 2889a, 2918, 3075 | 25.00 | 25.00 |

## PROOF SETS

| KM# | Date | Mintage | Identification | Issue Price | Mkt Val |
|---|---|---|---|---|---|
| PS1 | 1959 | 1,000 | KM#2887-2888 | — | 725 |
| PS2 | 1964 | 69,731 | KM#2875-2876, 2878, 2882, 2885-2886, 2889, 2895.1, 2896 | — | 55.00 |
| PS3 | 1964 | 2,700 | KM#2875-2876, 2878, 2882, 2885-2886, 2889, 2895.2, 2896 (error set) | — | 365 |
| PS4 | 1964 | — | KM#2875-2876, 2878, 2882, 2885-2886, 2889 | — | 22.50 |
| PS5 | 1965 | 83,000 | KM#2875-2876, 2878, 2882, 2885-2886, 2889 | — | 10.00 |
| PS6 | 1965 | 38,000 | KM#2882, 2889, 2897-2898 | 5.00 | 42.50 |
| PS7 | 1966 | 1,765 | KM#2875-2876, 2878, 2882, 2885-2886, 2889, 2899-2900 | — | 180 |
| PS8 | 1966 | — | KM#2875-2876, 2878, 2882, 2885-2886, 2889 | — | 60.00 |
| PS10 | 1967 | — | KM#2875-2876, 2878, 2882, 2885-2886, 2889 | — | 200 |
| PS9 | 1967 | 1,163 | KM#2875-2876, 2878, 2882, 2885-2886, 2889, 2901-2902 | 5.50 | 300 |
| PS11 | 1968 | 15,200 | KM#2875-2876, 2878, 2882, 2885-2886, 2889, 2903, 2904.1 | 5.75 | 110 |
| PS12 | 1968 | 20,000 | KM#2875-2876, 2878, 2882, 2885-2886, 2889 | — | 65.00 |
| PS13 | 1969 | 20,000 | KM#2875-2876, 2878, 2882, 2885-2886, 2889a, 2905-2906 | 7.50 | 90.00 |
| PS14 | 1969 | 21,000 | KM#2875-2876, 2878, 2882, 2885-2886, 2889a | — | 50.00 |
| PS15 | 1970 | — | KM#2875-2876, 2878, 2882, 2885-2886, 2889a, 2907-2908 | 8.25 | 35.00 |
| PS16 | 1970 | — | KM#2875-2876, 2878, 2882, 2885-2886, 2889a, 2907, 2909 | 8.25 | 35.00 |
| PS17 | 1970 | 92,000 | KM#2875-2876, 2878, 2882, 2885-2886, 2889a | — | 8.50 |
| PS18 | 1970 | — | KM#2907-2909 | 7.00 | 25.00 |
| PS19 | 1971 | — | KM#2875-2876, 2878, 2882, 2885-2886, 2889a, 2910-2911 | 8.25 | 28.00 |
| PS20 | 1971 | 84,000 | KM#2875-2876, 2878, 2882, 2885-2886, 2889a | — | 8.50 |
| PS21 | 1972 | — | KM#2875-2876, 2878, 2882, 2885-2886, 2889a, 2912-2913 | 8.50 | 25.00 |
| PS22 | 1972 | — | KM#2875-2876, 2878, 2882, 2885-2886, 2889a, 2912, 2914 | 8.50 | 25.00 |
| PS23 | 1972 | 75,000 | KM#2875-2876, 2878, 2882, 2885-2886, 2889a | — | 8.50 |
| PS24 | 1972 | — | KM#2912-2914 | 7.50 | 22.50 |
| PS27 | 1972 | — | KM#2912-2914 | — | 22.50 |
| PS25 | 1973 | — | KM#2875-2876, 2878, 2882, 2885-2886, 289a, 2915-2916 | — | 25.00 |
| PS26 | 1973 | 87,000 | KM#2875-2876, 2878, 2882, 2885-2886, 2889a | — | 10.00 |
| PS28 | 1974 | — | KM#2875-2876, 2878, 2885-2886, 2889a, 2918-2922, 2926 | 29.70 | 55.00 |
| PS29 | 1974 | — | KM#2875-2876, 2878, 2885-2886, 2889a, 2918, 2921 | — | 20.00 |
| PS30 | 1974 | 76,000 | KM#2875-2876, 2878, 2885-2886, 2889a, 2918 | — | 8.50 |
| PS31 | 1974 | — | KM#2919-2922, 2926 | 27.00 | 42.00 |
| PS32 | 1975 | — | KM#2875-2876, 2878, 2885-2886, 289a, 2918, 2923-2925 | 30.00 | 45.00 |
| PS34 | 1975 | — | KM#2923-2925 | 27.00 | 35.00 |
| PS33 | 1975 | 49,000 | KM#2875-2876, 2878, 2885-2886, 2889a, 2918 | — | 8.50 |

| KM# | Date | Mintage | Identification | Issue Price | Mkt Val |
|---|---|---|---|---|---|
| PS37 | 1976-1977 | — | KM#2930-2932, 2934-2936 | 27.00 | 85.00 |
| PS35 | 1976 | 44,000 | KM#2875-2876, 2878, 2885-2886, 2889a, 2918 | 3.00 | 9.50 |
| PS36 | 1977 | 44,000 | KM#2875-2876, 2878, 2885-2886, 2889a, 2918 | 3.15 | 8.50 |
| PS38 | 1978 | 43,000 | KM#2875-2876, 2878, 2885-2886, 2889a, 2918 | — | 9.50 |
| PS39 | 1979 | 44,000 | KM#2875-2876, 2878, 2885-2886, 2889a, 2918 | — | 9.50 |
| PS40 | 1980 | 48,000 | KM#2875-2876, 2878, 2885-2886, 2889a, 2918, 2946 | — | 28.00 |
| PS42 | 1981 | 49,000 | KM#2875-2876, 2878, 2885-2886, 2889a, 2918, 2946.1 | — | 28.00 |
| PS43 | 1982 | 50,000 | KM#2875-2876, 2878, 2885-2886, 2889a, 2918, 2955.1 | — | 14.00 |
| PS44 | 1983 | 65,000 | KM#2875-2876, 2878, 2885-2886, 2889a, 2918, 2960.1 | — | 12.50 |
| PS45 | 1984 | 65,000 | KM#2875-2876, 2878, 2885-2886, 2889a, 2918, 2965.1 | — | 12.50 |
| PS46 | 1985 | 45,000 | KM#2875-2876, 2878, 2885-2886, 2889a, 2918, 2970.1 | — | 20.00 |
| PS47 | 1986 | 42,000 | KM#2875-2876, 2878, 2885-2886, 2889a, 2918, 2975.1 | — | 30.00 |
| PS48 | 1987 | 42,000 | KM#2875-2876, 2878, 2885-2886, 2889a, 2918, 2980.1 | — | 22.00 |
| PS49 | 1988 | 39,000 | KM#2875-2876, 2878, 2885-2886, 2889a, 2918 | — | 12.50 |
| PS50 | 1989 | 38,000 | KM#2875-2876, 2878, 2885-2886, 2889a, 2918, 2988.1 | — | 17.50 |
| PS51 | 1990 | 35,000 | KM#2875-2876, 2878, 2885-2886, 2889a, 2918, 2993.1 | — | 42.50 |
| PS52 | 1991 | 27,000 | KM#2875-2876, 2878, 2885-2886, 2889a, 2918, 2995.1 | — | 22.00 |
| PS53 | 1992 | 25,000 | KM#2875-2876, 2878, 2885-2886, 2889a, 2918, 2946.1 | — | 45.00 |
| PS54 | 1993 | 28,000 | KM#2875-2876, 2878, 2885-2886, 2889a, 2918, 2946.2 | — | 35.00 |
| PS55 | 1994 | 25,000 | KM#2875-2876, 2878, 2885-2886, 2889a, 2918, 3016 | — | 75.00 |
| PS56 | 1995 | 27,000 | KM#2878, 2885, 2886, 2889a, 2918, 3022 | — | 37.50 |
| PS57 | 1996 | 25,000 | KM#2878, 2885, 2886, 2889a, 2918, 3033 | — | 45.00 |
| PS58 | 1997 | 25,000 | KM#2878, 2885, 2886, 2889a, 2918, 3041 | — | 50.00 |
| PS59 | 1998 | 25,000 | KM#2878, 2885, 2886, 2889a, 2918, 3048 | — | 60.00 |
| PS60 | 1999 | 25,000 | KM#2878, 2885, 2886, 2889a, 2918, 3056 | — | 27.50 |
| PS61 | 2000 | — | KM#2878, 2885, 2886, 2889a, 2918, 3064 | — | 27.50 |

# AZERBAIJAN

The Republic of Azerbaijan (formerly Azerbaijan S.S.R.) includes the Nakhichevan Autonomous Republic. Situated in the eastern area of Transcaucasia, it is bordered in the west by Armenia, in the north by Georgia and Dagestan, to the east by the Caspian Sea and to the south by Iran. It has an area of 33,430 sq. mi. (86,600 sq. km.) and a population of 7.8 million. Capital: Baku. The area is rich in mineral deposits of aluminum, copper, iron, lead, salt and zinc, with oil as its leading industry. Agriculture and livestock follow in importance.

Ancient home of Scythian tribes and known under the Romans as Albania and to the Arabs as Arran, the country of Azerbaijan was formed at the time of its invasion by Seliuk Turks and grew into a prosperous state under Persian suzerainty. From the 16th century the country was a theatre of fighting and political rivalry between Turkey, Persia and later Russia. Baku was first annexed to Russia by Czar Peter I in 1723 and remained under Russian rule for 12 years. After the Russian retreat the whole of Azerbaijan north of the Aras River became a khanate under Persian control. Czar Alexander I, after an eight-year war with Persia, annexed it in 1813 to the Russian empire.

Until the Russian Revolution of 1905, there was no political life in Azerbaijan. A Mussavat (Equality) party was formed in 1911 by Mohammed Emin, Rasulzade, a former Social Democrat. After the Russian Revolution of March 1917, the party started a campaign for independence. Baku, however, the capital with its mixed population, constituted an alien enclave in the country While a national Azerbaijani government was established at Gandzha (Elizavetpol), a Communist controlled council assumed power at Baku with Stepan Shaumian, an Armenian, at its head. The Gandzha government joined first, on Sept. 20, 1917, a Transcaucasian federal republic, but on May 28, 1918, proclaimed the independence of Azerbaijan. On June 4, 1918, at Batum, a peace treaty was signed with Turkey. Turko-Azerbaijani forces started an offensive against Baku, occupied since Aug. 17, 1918 by 1,400 British troops coming by sea from Anzali, Persia. On Sept. 14 the British evacuated Baku, returning to Anzali, and three days later the Azerbaijan government, headed by Fath Khoysky, established itself at Baku.

After the collapse of the Ottoman Empire, the British returned to Baku, at first ignoring the Azerbaijan government. A general election with universal suffrage for the Azerbaijan constituent assembly took place on Dec. 7, 1918 and out of 120 members there were 84 Mussavat supporters. On Jan. 15, 1920, the Allied powers recognized Azerbaijan de facto, but on April 27 of the same year the Red army invaded the country, and a Soviet republic of Azerbaijan was proclaimed the next day. Later it became a member of the Transcaucasian Federation joining the U.S.S.R. on Dec. 30, 1922, it became a self-constituent republic in 1936.

The Azerbaijan Communist party held its first congress at Baku in Feb. 1920. From 1921 to 1925 its first secretary was a Russian, S.M. Kirov, who directed a mass deportation to Siberia of about 120,000 Azerbaijani "nationalist deviationists," among them the country's first two premiers.

In 1990 it adopted a declaration of republican sovereignty and in Aug. 1991 declared itself formally independent. This action was approved by a vote of referendum in Jan. 1992. It announced its intention of joining the CIS in Dec. 1991, but a parliamentary resolution of Oct. 1992 declined to confirm its involvement. On Sept. 20, 1993, Azerbaijan became a member of the CIS. Communist President Mutaibov was relieved of his office in May 1992. On June 7, in the first democratic election in the country's history, a National Council replaced Mutaibov with Abulfez Elchibey. Surat Huseynov led a military coup against Elchibey and seized power on June 30, 1993. Huseynov became prime minister with former communist Geidar Aliyev, president.

Fighting commenced between Muslim forces of Azerbaijan and Christian forces of Armenia in 1992 and continued through early 1994. Each faction claimed the Nagorno-Karabakh, an Armenian ethnic enclave, in Azerbaijan. A cease-fire was declared in May 1994.

**MINTNAMES**

Genge (Elisabethpol, Kirovabad)
Nackhchawan
Shamakhi
Shirvan

**MONETARY SYSTEM**

100 Qapik = 1 Manat

## REPUBLIC

### DECIMAL COINAGE

**5 QAPIK** **KM# 31** **Composition:** Brass

| Date | Mintage | F | VF | XF | Unc | BU |
|---|---|---|---|---|---|---|
| 1992 | — | — | — | 2.00 | 4.00 | — |

**5 QAPIK** **KM# 31a** **Composition:** Aluminum

| Date | Mintage | F | VF | XF | Unc | BU |
|---|---|---|---|---|---|---|
| 1993 | — | — | — | — | 1.00 | — |

**10 QAPIK** **KM# 32** **Composition:** Aluminum

| Date | Mintage | F | VF | XF | Unc | BU |
|---|---|---|---|---|---|---|
| 1992 | — | — | — | — | 0.50 | — |

**20 QAPIK** **KM# 33** **Composition:** Brass

| Date | Mintage | F | VF | XF | Unc | BU |
|---|---|---|---|---|---|---|
| 1992 | — | — | — | 1.00 | 2.00 | — |
| 1993 | — | — | — | 1.00 | 2.00 | — |

**20 QAPIK** **KM# 33a** **Composition:** Aluminum **Note:** Varieties in spelling of Respublikas exist.

| Date | Mintage | F | VF | XF | Unc | BU |
|---|---|---|---|---|---|---|
| 1992 | — | — | — | — | 0.75 | — |
| 1993 | — | — | — | — | 0.75 | — |

**50 QAPIK** **KM# 34** **Composition:** Copper-Nickel **Obverse:** Maiden tower ruins

| Date | Mintage | F | VF | XF | Unc | BU |
|---|---|---|---|---|---|---|
| 1992 | — | — | — | 1.50 | 3.50 | — |
| 1994 | — | — | — | 1.50 | 3.50 | — |

**50 QAPIK** **KM# 34a** **Composition:** Aluminum

| Date | Mintage | F | VF | XF | Unc | BU |
|---|---|---|---|---|---|---|
| 1992 | — | — | — | — | 1.25 | — |
| 1993 | — | — | — | — | 0.75 | — |

**50 MANAT** **KM# A35** **Weight:** 28.2800 g. **Composition:** 0.9250 Silver .8411 oz. ASW **Subject:** 500th Anniversary Mehemmed Fuzuli **Obverse:** Deer by man comforting fallen comrade **Reverse:** Portrait of Fuzuli

| Date | Mintage | F | VF | XF | Unc | BU |
|---|---|---|---|---|---|---|
| 1996 Proof | 5,000 | Value: 65.00 | | | | |

**100 MANAT** **KM# A36** **Weight:** 7.9800 g. **Composition:** 0.9167 Gold .2354 oz. AGW **Subject:** 500th Anniversary Mehemmed Fuzuli **Obverse:** Deer by man comforting fallen comrade **Reverse:** Portrait of Fuzuli

| Date | Mintage | F | VF | XF | Unc | BU |
|---|---|---|---|---|---|---|
| 1996 Proof | 500 | Value: 325 | | | | |

## AZORES

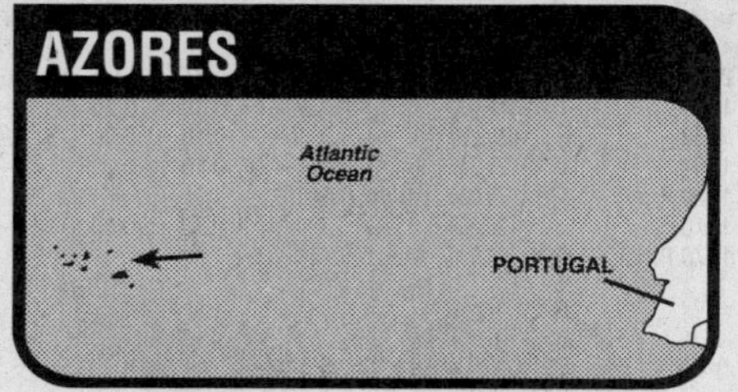


The Azores, an archipelago of nine islands of volcanic origin, are located in the Atlantic Ocean 740 miles (1,190 km.) west of Cape de Roca, Portugal. They are the westernmost region of Europe under the administration of Portugal and have an area of 902 sq. mi. (2,305 sq. km.) and a population of 236,000. Principal city: Ponta Delgada. The natives are mainly of Portuguese descent and earn their livelihood by fishing, wine making, basket weaving and the growing of fruit, grains and sugar cane. Pineapples are the chief item of export. The climate is particularly temperate, making the islands a favorite winter resort.

The Azores were discovered about 1427 by the Portuguese navigator Diogo de Sevill. Portugal secured the islands in the 15th century and established the first settlement on Santa Maria about 1439. From 1580 to 1640 the Azores were subject to Spain.

The Azores' first provincial coinage was ordered by law of August 19, 1750. Copper coins were struck for circulation in both the Azores and Madeira Islands. Keeping the same technical specifications but with different designs. In 1795 a second provincial coinage was introduced but the weight was reduced by 50 percent.

Angra on Terceira Island became the capital of the captaincy-general of the Azores in 1766 and it was here in 1826 that the constitutionalists set up a pro-Pedro government in opposition to King Miguel in Lisbon. The whole Portuguese fleet attacked Terceira and was repelled at Praia, after which Azoreans, Brazilians and British mercenaries defeated Miguel in Portugal. Maria de Gloria, Pedro's daughter, was proclaimed queen of Portugal on Terceira in 1828.

A U.S. naval base was established at Ponta Delgada in 1917.

After World War II, the islands acquired a renewed importance as a refueling stop for transatlantic air transport. The United States maintains defense bases in the Azores as part of the collective security program of NATO.

In 1976 the archipelago became the Autonomous Region of Azores.

**RULERS**
Portuguese

**MONETARY SYSTEM**
1000 Reis (Insulanos) = 1 Milreis

## PROVINCIAL COINAGE

**5 REIS** **KM# 16** **Composition:** Copper **Subject:** Carlos I

| Date | Mintage | F | VF | XF | Unc | BU |
|---|---|---|---|---|---|---|
| 1901 | 800,000 | 1.75 | 3.50 | 9.00 | 25.00 | — |

**10 REIS** **KM# 17** **Composition:** Copper **Subject:** Carlos I

| Date | Mintage | F | VF | XF | Unc | BU |
|---|---|---|---|---|---|---|
| 1901 | 600,000 | 2.00 | 4.00 | 10.00 | 28.00 | — |

## REPUBLIC

Portuguese 50 Centavos and 1 Escudo pieces dated 1935 were issued for circulation in Azores. These are found under the appropriate listing in Portugal.

## DECIMAL COINAGE

**25 ESCUDOS** **KM# 43** **Composition:** Copper-Nickel **Subject:** Regional Autonomy **Obverse:** Shields above denomination, stars below **Reverse:** Supported arms

| Date | Mintage | F | VF | XF | Unc | BU |
|---|---|---|---|---|---|---|
| 1980 | 770,000 | — | — | 2.50 | 5.00 | — |

**25 ESCUDOS** **KM# 43a** **Weight:** 11.0000 g. **Composition:** 0.9250 Silver .3272 oz. ASW **Subject:** Regional Autonomy **Obverse:** Shields above denomination, stars below **Reverse:** Supported arms

| Date | Mintage | F | VF | XF | Unc | BU |
|---|---|---|---|---|---|---|
| 1980 Proof | 12,000 | Value: 22.00 | | | | |

**100 ESCUDOS** **KM# 44** **Composition:** Copper-Nickel **Subject:** Regional Autonomy **Obverse:** Shields above denomination, stars below **Reverse:** Supported arms

| Date | Mintage | F | VF | XF | Unc | BU |
|---|---|---|---|---|---|---|
| 1980 | 270,000 | — | — | 4.50 | 10.00 | — |

**100 ESCUDOS** **KM# 44a** **Weight:** 16.5000 g. **Composition:** 0.9250 Silver .4908 oz. ASW **Subject:** Regional Autonomy **Obverse:** Shields above denomination, stars below **Reverse:** Supported arms

| Date | Mintage | F | VF | XF | Unc | BU |
|---|---|---|---|---|---|---|
| 1980 Proof | 12,000 | Value: 47.50 | | | | |

**100 ESCUDOS** **KM# 45** **Composition:** Copper-Nickel **Subject:** 10th Anniversary of Regional Autonomy **Obverse:** Supported arms **Reverse:** Flower

| Date | Mintage | F | VF | XF | Unc | BU |
|---|---|---|---|---|---|---|
| 1986 | 750,000 | — | — | — | 6.50 | — |

**100 ESCUDOS** **KM# 45a** **Weight:** 16.5000 g. **Composition:** 0.9250 Silver .4908 oz. ASW **Subject:** 10th Anniversary of Regional Autonomy **Obverse:** Supported arms **Reverse:** Flower

| Date | Mintage | F | VF | XF | Unc | BU |
|---|---|---|---|---|---|---|
| 1986 | 20,000 | — | — | — | 25.00 | — |
| 1986 Proof | 10,000 | Value: 37.50 | | | | |

**100 ESCUDOS** **KM# 46** **Composition:** Copper-Nickel **Subject:** 100th Anniversary - Death of Poet Antero de Quental **Obverse:** Offered hand with radiant sun behind, shield of arms below left **Reverse:** Bust of Antero de Quental facing

| Date | Mintage | F | VF | XF | Unc | BU |
|---|---|---|---|---|---|---|
| 1991 | 750,000 | — | — | — | 5.00 | — |

**100 ESCUDOS** **KM# 46a** **Weight:** 18.5000 g. **Composition:** 0.9250 Silver .5503 oz. ASW **Subject:** 100th Anniversary - Death of Poet Antero de Quental **Obverse:** Offered hand with radiant sun behind, shield of arms below left **Reverse:** Bust of Antero de Quental facing **Size:** 36 mm.

| Date | Mintage | F | VF | XF | Unc | BU |
|---|---|---|---|---|---|---|
| 1991 | 20,000 | — | — | — | 30.00 | — |

**100 ESCUDOS** **KM# 46b** **Weight:** 18.5000 g. **Composition:** 0.9250 Silver .5503 oz. ASW **Subject:** 100th Anniversary - Death of Poet Antero de Quental **Obverse:** Offered hand with radiant sun behind, shield of arms below left **Reverse:** Bust of Antero de Quental facing **Size:** 26 mm.

| Date | Mintage | F | VF | XF | Unc | BU |
|---|---|---|---|---|---|---|
| 1991 Proof | 30,000 | Value: 40.00 | | | | |

**100 ESCUDOS** **KM# 47** **Composition:** Copper-Nickel **Subject:** Centennial of Azorean Autonomy **Reverse:** Goshawk with wings spread below dates, 1895 above 1995

| Date | Mintage | F | VF | XF | Unc | BU |
|---|---|---|---|---|---|---|
| ND(1995) | 500,000 | — | — | — | 5.00 | — |

**100 ESCUDOS** **KM# 47a** **Weight:** 18.5000 g. **Composition:** 0.9250 Silver .5502 oz. ASW **Subject:** Centennial of Azorean Autonomy **Reverse:** Goshawk with wings spread below dates, 1895 over 1995

| Date | Mintage | F | VF | XF | Unc | BU |
|---|---|---|---|---|---|---|
| ND(1995) | 5,000 | — | — | — | 35.00 | — |
| ND(1995) Proof | 10,000 | Value: 50.00 | | | | |

## PATTERNS

(Including off metal strikes)

| KM# | Date | Mintage | Identification | Mkt Val |
|---|---|---|---|---|
| Pn5 | 1901 | — | 5 Reis. Aluminum. | 725 |
| Pn6 | 1901 | — | 10 Reis. Aluminum. | 725 |

## PROVAS

(Pr)

| KM# | Date | Mintage | Identification | Mkt Val |
|---|---|---|---|---|
| Pr1 | 1980 | — | 25 Escudos. Copper-Nickel. Incuse PROVA. | 150 |

| KM# | Date | Mintage | Identification | Mkt Val |
|---|---|---|---|---|
| Pr2 | 1980 | — | 100 Escudos. Copper-Nickel. Incuse PROVA. | 175 |
| Pr3 | 1986 | — | 100 Escudos. Copper-Nickel. Incuse PROVA. | 175 |

## PROOF SETS

| KM# | Date | Mintage | Identification | Issue Price | Mkt Val |
|---|---|---|---|---|---|
| PS1 | 1980 | 12,000 | KM43a-44a | 40.00 | 70.00 |

# BAHAMAS

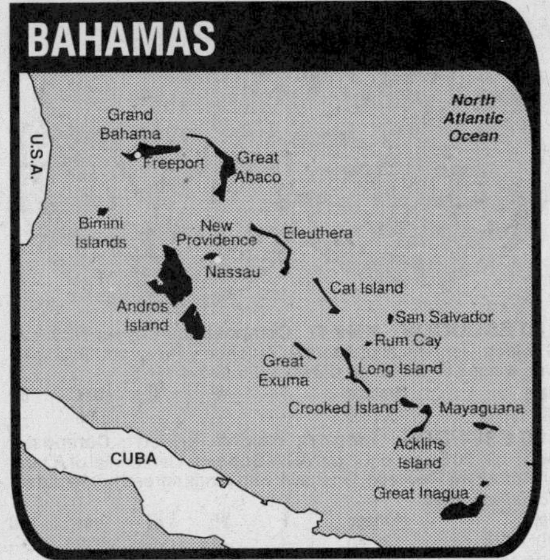


The Commonwealth of the Bahamas is an archipelago of about 3,000 islands, cays and rocks located in the Atlantic Ocean east of Florida and north of Cuba. The total land area of the 800 mile (1,287 km.) long chain of islands is 5,382 sq. mi. (13,935 sq. km.). They have a population of 302,000. Capital: Nassau. The Bahamas import most of their food and manufactured products and export cement, refined oil, pulpwood and lobsters. Tourism is the principal industry.

The Bahamas were discovered by Columbus October, 1492, upon his sighting of the island of San Salvador, but Spain made no attempt to settle them. British influence began in 1626 when Charles I granted them to the lord proprietors of Carolina, with settlements in 1629 at New Providence by colonists from the northern territory. Although the Bahamas were temporarily under Spanish control in 1641 and 1703, they continued under British proprietors until 1717, when, as the result of political and economic mismanagement, the civil and military governments were surrendered to the King and the islands designated a British Crown Colony. Full international agreement on British possession of the islands resulted from the Treaty of Versailles in 1783. The Bahamas obtained complete internal self-government under the constitution of Jan. 7, 1964. Full independence was achieved on July 10, 1973. The Bahamas is a member of the Commonwealth of Nations. Elizabeth II is Head of State, as Queen of the Bahamas.

The coinage of Great Britain was legal tender in the Bahamas from 1825 to the issuing of a definitive coinage in 1966.

**RULERS**

British

**MINT MARKS**

Through 1969 all decimal coinage of the Bahamas was executed at the Royal Mint in England. Since that time issues have been struck at both the Royal Mint and at the Franklin Mint (FM) in the U.S.A. While the mint mark of the latter appears on coins dated 1971 and subsequently, it is missing from the 1970 issues.

JP – John Pinches, London
None - Royal Mint
(t) - Tower of London
FM - Franklin Mint, U.S.A.

***NOTE**: From 1975-1985 the Franklin Mint produced coinage in up to 3 different qualities. Qualities of issue are designated in ( ) after each date and are defined as follows:

**(M) MATTE** - Normal circulation strike or a dull finish produced by sandblasting special uncirculated (polish finish) or proof quality dies.

**(U) SPECIAL UNCIRCULATED** - Polished or proof-like in appearance without any frosted features.

**(P) PROOF** - The highest quality obtainable having mirror-like fields and frosted features.

**MONETARY SYSTEM**

12 Pence = 1 Shilling

# COMMONWEALTH

## DECIMAL COINAGE

100 Cents = 1 Dollar

**CENT KM#2 Composition:** Nickel-Brass **Reverse:** Starfish

| Date | Mintage | F | VF | XF | Unc | BU |
|---|---|---|---|---|---|---|
| 1966 | 7,312,000 | — | — | 0.10 | 0.30 | — |
| 1968 | 800,000 | — | — | 0.25 | 0.75 | — |
| 1969 | 4,036,000 | — | — | 0.30 | 0.30 | — |
| 1969 Proof | 10,000 | Value: 0.50 | | | | |

**CENT KM# 15 Composition:** Bronze **Note:** Proof specimens of this date are struck in "special brass" which looks like a pale bronze.

| Date | Mintage | F | VF | XF | Unc | BU |
|---|---|---|---|---|---|---|
| 1970 | 125,000 | — | 0.10 | 0.25 | 0.50 | — |
| 1970 Proof | 23,000 | Value: 0.50 | | | | |

**CENT KM# 16 Composition:** Brass

| Date | Mintage | F | VF | XF | Unc | BU |
|---|---|---|---|---|---|---|
| 1971FM | 1,007,000 | — | — | 0.10 | 0.25 | — |
| 1971FM (P) | 31,000 | Value: 0.50 | | | | |
| 1972FM | 1,037,000 | — | — | 0.10 | 0.25 | — |
| 1972FM (P) | 35,000 | Value: 0.50 | | | | |
| 1973 | 7,000,000 | — | — | 0.10 | 0.25 | — |
| 1973FM | 35,000 | Value: 0.50 | | | | |
| 1973FM (P) | 1,040,000 | — | — | 0.10 | 0.25 | — |

**CENT KM# 59 Composition:** Brass

| Date | Mintage | F | VF | XF | Unc | BU |
|---|---|---|---|---|---|---|
| 1974 | 11,000 | — | — | 0.20 | 0.40 | — |
| 1974FM | 71,000 | — | — | 0.10 | 0.25 | — |
| 1974FM (P) | 94,000 | Value: 0.50 | | | | |
| 1975FM (M) | 60,000 | — | — | 0.10 | 0.25 | — |
| 1975FM (U) | 3,845 | — | — | 0.10 | 0.50 | — |
| 1975FM (P) | 29,000 | Value: 0.50 | | | | |
| 1976FM (M) | 60,000 | — | — | 0.10 | 0.25 | — |
| 1976FM (U) | 1,453 | — | — | 0.10 | 0.50 | — |
| 1976FM (P) | 23,000 | Value: 0.50 | | | | |
| 1977 | 3,000,000 | — | — | 0.10 | 0.25 | — |
| 1977FM (M) | 60,000 | — | — | 0.10 | 0.25 | — |
| 1977FM (U) | 713 | — | — | 0.50 | 1.50 | — |
| 1977FM (P) | 11,000 | Value: 0.50 | | | | |
| 1978FM (M) | 60,000 | — | — | 0.10 | 0.25 | — |
| 1978FM (U) | 767 | — | — | 0.50 | 1.50 | — |
| 1978FM (P) | 6,931 | Value: 0.75 | | | | |
| 1979 | — | — | — | 0.10 | 0.25 | — |
| 1979FM (P) | 2,053 | Value: 1.00 | | | | |
| 1980 | 4,000,000 | — | — | 0.10 | 0.25 | — |
| 1980FM (P) | 2,084 | Value: 1.00 | | | | |
| 1981 | 5,000,000 | — | — | 0.10 | 0.25 | — |
| 1981FM (M) | — | — | — | 0.10 | 0.25 | — |
| 1981FM (P) | 1,980 | Value: 1.00 | | | | |
| 1982 | 5,000,000 | — | — | 0.10 | 0.25 | — |
| 1982FM (M) | — | — | — | 0.10 | 0.25 | — |
| 1982FM (P) | 1,217 | Value: 1.00 | | | | |
| 1983 | 8,000,000 | — | — | 0.10 | 0.25 | — |
| 1983FM (P) | 1,020 | Value: 1.00 | | | | |
| 1984 | — | — | — | 0.10 | 0.25 | — |
| 1984FM (P) | 7,500 | Value: 0.75 | | | | |
| 1985 | 12,000,000 | — | — | 0.10 | 0.25 | — |
| 1985FM (P) | 7,500 | Value: 0.50 | | | | |

**CENT KM# 59a Composition:** Copper Plated Zinc

| Date | Mintage | F | VF | XF | Unc | BU |
|---|---|---|---|---|---|---|
| 1985 | — | — | — | 0.10 | 0.25 | — |
| 1987 | 12,000,000 | — | — | 0.10 | 0.25 | — |
| 1989 | 12,000,000 | — | — | 0.10 | 0.25 | — |
| 1989 Proof | — | Value: 0.75 | | | | |
| 1990 | — | — | — | 0.10 | 0.25 | — |
| 1991 | — | — | — | 0.10 | 0.25 | — |
| 1992 | — | — | — | 0.10 | 0.25 | — |
| 1995 | — | — | — | 0.10 | 0.25 | — |
| 1997 | — | — | — | 0.10 | 0.25 | — |
| 1998 | — | — | — | 0.10 | 0.25 | — |
| 1999 | — | — | — | 0.10 | 0.25 | — |

**5 CENTS KM# 3 Composition:** Copper-Nickel **Reverse:** Pineapple **Note:** The obverse of this coin also comes muled with the reverse of a New Zealand 2-cent piece, KM#32. The undated 1967 error is listed as New Zealand KM#33.

| Date | Mintage | F | VF | XF | Unc | BU |
|---|---|---|---|---|---|---|
| 1966 | 2,571,000 | — | — | 0.10 | 0.25 | — |
| 1968 | 600,000 | — | — | 0.10 | 0.30 | — |
| 1969 | 2,026,000 | — | — | 0.10 | 0.25 | — |
| 1969 Proof | 75,000 | Value: 0.50 | | | | |
| 1970 | 26,000 | — | — | 0.30 | 0.60 | — |
| 1970 Proof | 23,000 | Value: 0.75 | | | | |

**5 CENTS KM# 17 Composition:** Copper-Nickel

| Date | Mintage | F | VF | XF | Unc | BU |
|---|---|---|---|---|---|---|
| 1971FM | 13,000 | — | — | 0.15 | 0.40 | — |
| 1971FM (P) | 31,000 | Value: 0.50 | | | | |
| 1972FM | 11,000 | — | — | 0.15 | 0.40 | — |
| 1972FM (P) | 35,000 | Value: 0.50 | | | | |
| 1973FM | 21,000 | — | — | 0.15 | 0.40 | — |
| 1973FM (P) | 35,000 | Value: 0.50 | | | | |

**5 CENTS KM# 38 Composition:** Copper-Nickel
**Obv. Legend:** THE COMMONWEALTH OF THE BAHAMAS

| Date | Mintage | F | VF | XF | Unc | BU |
|---|---|---|---|---|---|---|
| 1973 | 1,000,000 | — | — | 0.10 | 0.65 | — |

**5 CENTS KM# 60 Composition:** Copper-Nickel

| Date | Mintage | F | VF | XF | Unc | BU |
|---|---|---|---|---|---|---|
| 1974FM | 23,000 | — | — | 0.10 | 0.25 | — |
| 1974FM (P) | 94,000 | Value: 0.50 | | | | |
| 1975 | — | — | — | 0.10 | 0.30 | — |
| 1975FM (M) | 12,000 | — | — | 0.10 | 0.25 | — |
| 1975FM (U) | 3,845 | — | — | 0.15 | 0.50 | — |
| 1975FM (P) | 29,000 | Value: 0.50 | | | | |
| 1976FM (M) | 12,000 | — | — | 0.10 | 0.25 | — |
| 1976FM (U) | 1,453 | — | — | 0.15 | 0.75 | — |
| 1976FM (P) | 23,000 | Value: 0.50 | | | | |
| 1977FM (M) | 12,000 | — | — | 0.10 | 0.35 | — |
| 1977FM (U) | 713 | — | — | 0.50 | 1.50 | — |
| 1977FM (P) | 11,000 | Value: 0.50 | | | | |
| 1978FM (M) | 12,000 | — | — | 0.10 | 0.35 | — |
| 1978FM (U) | 767 | — | — | 0.50 | 1.50 | — |
| 1978FM (P) | 6,931 | Value: 0.50 | | | | |
| 1979FM (P) | 2,053 | Value: 0.75 | | | | |
| 1980FM (P) | 2,084 | Value: 0.75 | | | | |
| 1981 | — | — | — | 0.10 | 0.25 | — |
| 1981FM (P) | 1,980 | Value: 0.75 | | | | |
| 1982FM (P) | 1,217 | Value: 0.75 | | | | |
| 1983 | 2,000,000 | — | — | 0.10 | 0.25 | — |
| 1983FM (P) | 1,020 | Value: 0.75 | | | | |
| 1984 | — | — | — | 0.10 | 0.25 | — |
| 1984FM (P) | 1,036 | Value: 0.75 | | | | |
| 1985FM (P) | 7,500 | Value: 0.75 | | | | |
| 1987 | 4,000,000 | — | — | 0.10 | 0.25 | — |
| 1989 | — | — | — | 0.10 | 0.25 | — |
| 1989 (P) | — | Value: 0.75 | | | | |
| 1991 | — | — | — | 0.10 | 0.25 | — |
| 1992 | — | — | — | 0.10 | 0.25 | — |
| 1998 | — | — | — | 0.10 | 0.25 | — |
| 1999 | — | — | — | 0.10 | 0.25 | — |

**10 CENTS** **KM# 4** **Composition:** Copper-Nickel **Reverse:** Bone Fish

| Date | Mintage | F | VF | XF | Unc | BU |
|---|---|---|---|---|---|---|
| 1966 | 2,198,000 | — | — | 0.10 | 0.30 | — |
| 1968 | 550,000 | — | — | 0.50 | 4.00 | — |
| 1969 | 2,026,000 | — | — | 0.10 | 0.30 | — |
| 1969 Proof | 10,000 | Value: 0.50 | | | | |
| 1970 | 27,000 | — | — | 0.15 | 0.40 | — |
| 1970 Proof | 23,000 | Value: 0.50 | | | | |

**10 CENTS** **KM# 18** **Composition:** Copper-Nickel

| Date | Mintage | F | VF | XF | Unc | BU |
|---|---|---|---|---|---|---|
| 1971FM | 13,000 | — | — | 0.15 | 0.50 | — |
| 1971FM (P) | 31,000 | Value: 0.50 | | | | |
| 1972FM | 11,000 | — | — | 0.15 | 0.50 | — |
| 1972FM (P) | 35,000 | Value: 0.50 | | | | |
| 1973FM | 15,000 | — | — | 0.15 | 0.50 | — |
| 1973FM (P) | 35,000 | Value: 0.50 | | | | |

**10 CENTS** **KM# 39** **Composition:** Copper-Nickel **Rev. Legend:** THE COMMONWEALTH OF THE BAHAMAS

| Date | Mintage | F | VF | XF | Unc | BU |
|---|---|---|---|---|---|---|
| 1973 | 1,000,000 | — | — | 0.15 | 0.85 | — |

**10 CENTS** **KM# 61** **Composition:** Copper-Nickel

| Date | Mintage | F | VF | XF | Unc | BU |
|---|---|---|---|---|---|---|
| 1974FM | 17,000 | — | — | 0.10 | 0.35 | — |
| 1974FM (P) | 94,000 | Value: 0.75 | | | | |
| 1975 | 3,000,000 | — | — | 0.10 | 0.25 | — |
| 1975FM (M) | 6,000 | — | — | 0.15 | 0.50 | — |
| 1975FM (U) | 3,845 | — | — | 0.15 | 0.50 | — |
| 1975FM (P) | 29,000 | Value: 0.75 | | | | |
| 1976FM (M) | 6,000 | — | — | 0.15 | 0.50 | — |
| 1976FM (U) | 1,453 | — | — | 0.25 | 1.00 | — |
| 1976FM (P) | 23,000 | Value: 0.75 | | | | |
| 1977FM (M) | 6,000 | — | — | 0.15 | 0.50 | — |
| 1977FM (U) | 713 | — | — | 0.50 | 1.50 | — |
| 1977FM (P) | 11,000 | Value: 0.75 | | | | |
| 1978FM (M) | 6,000 | — | — | 0.15 | 0.50 | — |
| 1978FM (U) | 767 | — | — | 0.50 | 1.50 | — |
| 1978FM (P) | 6,931 | Value: 1.00 | | | | |
| 1979FM (P) | 2,053 | Value: 1.25 | | | | |
| 1980 | 2,500,000 | — | — | 0.10 | 0.35 | — |
| 1980FM (P) | 2,084 | Value: 1.25 | | | | |
| 1981FM (P) | 1,980 | Value: 1.25 | | | | |
| 1982 | 2,000,000 | — | — | 0.10 | 0.35 | — |
| 1982FM (P) | 1,217 | Value: 1.25 | | | | |
| 1983FM (P) | 1,020 | Value: 1.25 | | | | |
| 1984FM (P) | 1,036 | Value: 1.25 | | | | |
| 1985 | 2,000,000 | — | — | 0.10 | 0.35 | — |
| 1985FM (M) | — | — | — | 0.15 | 0.50 | — |
| 1985FM (P) | 7,500 | Value: 1.00 | | | | |
| 1987 | 3,000,000 | — | — | 0.15 | 0.50 | — |
| 1989 | — | — | — | 0.15 | 0.50 | — |
| 1989 | — | Value: 1.00 | | | | |
| 1991 | — | — | — | 0.15 | 0.50 | — |
| 1992 | — | — | — | 0.15 | 0.50 | — |
| 1998 | — | — | — | 0.15 | 0.50 | — |

**15 CENTS** **KM# 5** **Composition:** Copper-Nickel **Reverse:** Hibiscus

| Date | Mintage | F | VF | XF | Unc | BU |
|---|---|---|---|---|---|---|
| 1966 | 930,000 | — | — | 0.20 | 0.75 | — |
| 1969 | 1,026,000 | — | — | 0.20 | 0.75 | — |
| 1969 Proof | 10,000 | Value: 1.00 | | | | |
| 1970 | 28,000 | — | — | 0.25 | 0.75 | — |
| 1970 Proof | 23,000 | Value: 0.75 | | | | |

**15 CENTS** **KM# 19** **Composition:** Copper-Nickel

| Date | Mintage | F | VF | XF | Unc | BU |
|---|---|---|---|---|---|---|
| 1971FM | 13,000 | — | — | 0.15 | 0.50 | — |
| 1971FM Proof | 31,000 | Value: 0.75 | | | | |
| 1972FM | 11,000 | — | — | 0.15 | 0.50 | — |
| 1972FM Proof | 35,000 | Value: 0.75 | | | | |
| 1973FM | 14,000 | — | — | 0.15 | 0.50 | — |
| 1973FM Proof | 35,000 | Value: 0.75 | | | | |

**15 CENTS** **KM# 62** **Composition:** Copper-Nickel

| Date | Mintage | F | VF | XF | Unc | BU |
|---|---|---|---|---|---|---|
| 1974FM | 15,000 | — | — | 0.20 | 0.50 | — |
| 1974FM (P) | 94,000 | Value: 0.50 | | | | |
| 1975FM (M) | 3,500 | — | — | 0.20 | 1.00 | — |
| 1975FM (U) | 3,845 | — | — | 0.20 | 1.00 | — |
| 1975FM (P) | 29,000 | Value: 0.50 | | | | |
| 1976FM (M) | 3,500 | — | — | 0.20 | 1.00 | — |
| 1976FM (U) | 1,453 | — | — | 0.25 | 1.50 | — |
| 1976FM (P) | 23,000 | Value: 0.50 | | | | |
| 1977FM (M) | 3,500 | — | — | 0.20 | 1.00 | — |
| 1977FM (U) | 713 | — | — | 0.50 | 2.00 | — |
| 1977FM (P) | 11,000 | Value: 0.50 | | | | |
| 1978FM (M) | 3,500 | — | — | 0.20 | 1.00 | — |
| 1978FM (U) | 767 | — | — | 0.50 | 2.00 | — |
| 1978FM (P) | 6,931 | Value: 0.75 | | | | |
| 1979FM (P) | 2,053 | Value: 1.00 | | | | |
| 1980FM (P) | 2,084 | Value: 1.00 | | | | |
| 1981FM (P) | 1,980 | Value: 1.00 | | | | |
| 1982FM (P) | 1,217 | Value: 1.25 | | | | |
| 1983FM (P) | 1,020 | Value: 1.25 | | | | |
| 1984FM (P) | 1,036 | Value: 1.25 | | | | |
| 1985FM (P) | 7,500 | Value: 0.75 | | | | |
| 1989 | — | — | — | 0.15 | 0.50 | — |
| 1989 (P) | — | Value: 1.00 | | | | |
| 1991 | — | — | — | 0.15 | 0.50 | — |
| 1992 | — | — | — | 0.15 | 0.50 | — |

**25 CENTS** **KM# 6** **Composition:** Nickel **Reverse:** Bahaminian sloop

| Date | Mintage | F | VF | XF | Unc | BU |
|---|---|---|---|---|---|---|
| 1966 | 3,685,000 | — | — | 0.25 | 0.50 | — |
| 1969 | 1,026,000 | — | — | 0.25 | 0.50 | — |
| 1969 | 10,000 | Value: 0.75 | | | | |
| 1970 | 26,000 | — | — | 0.35 | 0.75 | — |
| 1970FM (P) | 23,000 | Value: 1.00 | | | | |
| 1970FM (M) | — | — | — | — | — | — |

**25 CENTS** **KM# 20** **Composition:** Nickel

| Date | Mintage | F | VF | XF | Unc | BU |
|---|---|---|---|---|---|---|
| 1971FM | 13,000 | — | — | 0.25 | 0.50 | — |
| 1971FM (P) | 31,000 | Value: 0.75 | | | | |
| 1972FM | 11,000 | — | — | 0.25 | 0.50 | — |
| 1972FM (M) | — | — | — | 0.25 | 0.50 | — |
| 1972FM (P) | 35,000 | Value: 0.75 | | | | |
| 1973FM | 12,000 | — | — | 0.25 | 0.50 | — |
| 1973FM (P) | 35,000 | Value: 0.75 | | | | |

**25 CENTS** **KM# 63.1** **Weight:** 6.9000 g. **Composition:** Nickel

| Date | Mintage | F | VF | XF | Unc | BU |
|---|---|---|---|---|---|---|
| 1974FM | 13,000 | — | — | 0.25 | 0.50 | — |
| 1974FM (P) | 94,000 | Value: 0.75 | | | | |
| 1975FM (M) | 2,400 | — | — | 0.25 | 1.00 | — |
| 1975FM (U) | 3,845 | — | — | 0.25 | 1.00 | — |
| 1975FM (P) | 29,000 | Value: 0.75 | | | | |
| 1976FM (M) | 2,400 | — | — | 0.25 | 1.00 | — |
| 1976FM (U) | 1,453 | — | — | 0.30 | 1.25 | — |
| 1976FM (P) | 23,000 | Value: 0.75 | | | | |
| 1977 | — | — | — | 0.25 | 0.50 | — |
| 1977FM (M) | 2,400 | — | — | 0.25 | 1.00 | — |
| 1977FM (U) | 713 | — | — | 0.50 | 3.00 | — |
| 1977FM (P) | 11,000 | Value: 0.75 | | | | |
| 1978FM | 2,400 | — | — | 0.25 | 1.00 | — |
| 1978FM (U) | 767 | — | — | 0.50 | 3.00 | — |
| 1978FM (P) | 6,931 | Value: 1.00 | | | | |
| 1979 | — | — | — | 0.25 | 0.50 | — |
| 1979FM (P) | 2,053 | Value: 1.25 | | | | |
| 1980FM (P) | 2,084 | Value: 1.25 | | | | |
| 1981 | 1,600,000 | — | — | 0.25 | 0.50 | — |
| 1981FM (P) | 1,980 | Value: 1.25 | | | | |
| 1982FM (P) | 1,217 | Value: 1.50 | | | | |
| 1983FM (P) | 1,020 | Value: 1.50 | | | | |
| 1984FM (P) | 1,036 | Value: 1.50 | | | | |
| 1985 | 2,000,000 | — | — | 0.25 | 0.50 | — |
| 1985FM (P) | 7,500 | Value: 1.00 | | | | |
| 1987 | — | — | — | 0.25 | 0.50 | — |
| 1989 | — | — | — | 0.25 | 0.50 | — |
| 1989 (P) | — | Value: 1.25 | | | | |
| 1991 | — | — | — | 0.25 | 0.50 | — |
| 1992 | — | — | — | 0.25 | 0.50 | — |
| 1997 | — | — | — | 0.25 | 0.50 | — |
| 1998 | — | — | — | 0.25 | 0.50 | — |

**25 CENTS** **KM# 63.2** **Weight:** 5.7000 g. **Composition:** Nickel

| Date | Mintage | F | VF | XF | Unc | BU |
|---|---|---|---|---|---|---|
| 1998 | — | — | — | 0.25 | 0.50 | — |
| 2000 | — | — | — | 0.25 | 0.50 | — |

**50 CENTS** **KM# 7** **Weight:** 10.3700 g. **Composition:** 0.8000 Silver .2667 oz. ASW **Reverse:** Blue Marlin

| Date | Mintage | F | VF | XF | Unc | BU |
|---|---|---|---|---|---|---|
| 1966 | 701,000 | — | BV | 1.50 | 2.25 | — |
| 1969 | 26,000 | — | BV | 1.75 | 2.50 | — |
| 1969 Proof | 10,000 | Value: 3.00 | | | | |
| 1970 | 25,000 | — | BV | 1.75 | 2.50 | — |
| 1970 Proof | 23,000 | Value: 3.00 | | | | |

**50 CENTS** **KM# 21** **Weight:** 10.3700 g. **Composition:** 0.8000 Silver .2667 oz. ASW

| Date | Mintage | F | VF | XF | Unc | BU |
|---|---|---|---|---|---|---|
| 1971FM | 14,000 | — | BV | 1.75 | 2.50 | — |
| 1971FM (P) | 31,000 | Value: 3.00 | | | | |
| 1972FM | 12,000 | — | BV | 1.75 | 2.50 | — |
| 1972FM (P) | 35,000 | Value: 3.00 | | | | |

| Date | Mintage | F | VF | XF | Unc | BU |
|---|---|---|---|---|---|---|
| 1973FM | 11,000 | — | BV | 1.75 | 2.50 | — |
| 1973FM (P) | 35,000 | Value: 3.00 | | | | |

**50 CENTS** **KM# 64** **Composition:** Copper-Nickel

| Date | Mintage | F | VF | XF | Unc | BU |
|---|---|---|---|---|---|---|
| 1974FM | 12,000 | — | — | 0.50 | 2.00 | — |
| 1975FM (M) | 1,200 | — | — | 1.00 | 8.00 | — |
| 1975FM (U) | 3,828 | — | — | 0.65 | 4.00 | — |
| 1976FM (M) | 1,200 | — | — | 0.75 | 5.00 | — |
| 1976FM (U) | 1,453 | — | — | 0.65 | 4.00 | — |
| 1977FM (M) | 1,200 | — | — | 0.75 | 5.00 | — |
| 1977FM (U) | 713 | — | — | 1.25 | 10.00 | — |
| 1978FM (M) | 1,200 | — | — | 1.00 | 8.00 | — |
| 1978FM (U) | 767 | — | — | 1.25 | 10.00 | — |
| 1981FM (P) | 1,980 | Value: 3.00 | | | | |
| 1982FM (P) | 1,217 | Value: 3.50 | | | | |
| 1983FM (P) | 1,020 | Value: 3.50 | | | | |
| 1984FM (P) | 1,036 | Value: 3.50 | | | | |
| 1985FM (P) | 7,500 | Value: 2.50 | | | | |
| 1989 | — | — | — | 0.75 | 2.00 | — |
| 1989 Proof | — | Value: 2.50 | | | | |
| 1991 | — | — | — | 0.75 | 2.00 | — |
| 1992 | — | — | — | 0.75 | 2.00 | — |

**50 CENTS** **KM# 64a** **Weight:** 10.3700 g. **Composition:** 0.8000 Silver .2667 oz. ASW

| Date | Mintage | F | VF | XF | Unc | BU |
|---|---|---|---|---|---|---|
| 1974FM (P) | 94,000 | Value: 4.00 | | | | |
| 1975FM (P) | 29,000 | Value: 4.00 | | | | |
| 1976FM (P) | 23,000 | Value: 4.00 | | | | |
| 1977FM (P) | 11,000 | Value: 4.00 | | | | |
| 1978FM (P) | 6,931 | Value: 4.50 | | | | |
| 1979FM (P) | 2,053 | Value: 5.00 | | | | |
| 1980FM (P) | 2,084 | Value: 5.00 | | | | |

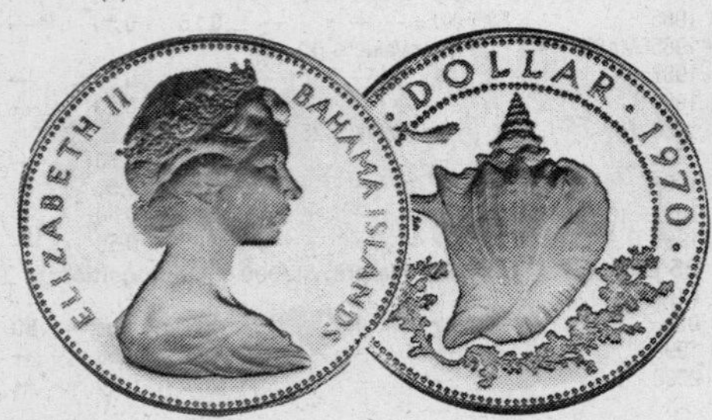


**DOLLAR** **KM# 8** **Weight:** 18.1400 g. **Composition:** 0.8000 Silver .4666 oz. ASW **Reverse:** Conch shell

| Date | Mintage | F | VF | XF | Unc | BU |
|---|---|---|---|---|---|---|
| 1966 | 406,000 | — | BV | 3.00 | 5.00 | — |
| 1969 | 26,000 | — | BV | 3.00 | 5.00 | — |
| 1969 Proof | 10,000 | Value: 6.00 | | | | |
| 1970 | 27,000 | — | BV | 3.00 | 5.00 | — |
| 1970 Proof | 23,000 | Value: 6.00 | | | | |

**DOLLAR** **KM# 22** **Weight:** 18.1400 g. **Composition:** 0.8000 Silver .4666 oz. ASW

| Date | Mintage | F | VF | XF | Unc | BU |
|---|---|---|---|---|---|---|
| 1971FM | 15,000 | — | BV | 3.00 | 5.00 | — |
| 1971FM (P) | 31,000 | Value: 6.00 | | | | |
| 1972FM | 18,000 | — | BV | 3.00 | 5.00 | — |
| 1972FM (P) | 35,000 | Value: 6.00 | | | | |
| 1973FM | 10,000 | — | BV | 3.00 | 5.00 | — |
| 1973FM (P) | 35,000 | Value: 6.00 | | | | |

**DOLLAR** **KM# 65** **Composition:** Copper-Nickel

| Date | Mintage | F | VF | XF | Unc | BU |
|---|---|---|---|---|---|---|
| 1974FM | 12,000 | — | — | 1.00 | 3.50 | — |
| 1975FM (M) | 600 | — | — | 7.50 | 25.00 | — |
| 1975FM (U) | 3,845 | — | — | 1.00 | 3.50 | — |
| 1976FM (M) | 600 | — | — | 7.50 | 25.00 | — |
| 1976FM (U) | 1,453 | — | — | 1.00 | 3.75 | — |
| 1977FM (M) | 600 | — | — | 7.50 | 25.00 | — |
| 1977FM (U) | 713 | — | — | 5.00 | 25.00 | — |
| 1978FM (U) | 1,367 | — | — | 2.00 | 10.00 | — |

**DOLLAR** **KM# 65a** **Weight:** 18.1400 g. **Composition:** 0.8000 Silver .4666 oz. ASW

| Date | Mintage | F | VF | XF | Unc | BU |
|---|---|---|---|---|---|---|
| 1974FM (P) | 94,000 | Value: 6.00 | | | | |
| 1975FM (P) | 29,000 | Value: 8.00 | | | | |
| 1976FM (P) | 23,000 | Value: 8.00 | | | | |
| 1977FM (P) | 11,000 | Value: 8.00 | | | | |
| 1978FM (P) | 6,931 | Value: 10.00 | | | | |
| 1979FM (P) | 2,053 | Value: 15.00 | | | | |
| 1980FM (P) | 2,084 | Value: 15.00 | | | | |

**DOLLAR** **KM# 65b** **Composition:** Copper-Nickel

| Date | Mintage | F | VF | XF | Unc | BU |
|---|---|---|---|---|---|---|
| 1981FM (P) | 1,980 | Value: 15.00 | | | | |
| 1989 | — | — | — | 1.50 | 3.50 | — |
| 1989 (P) | Est. 2,000 | Value: 15.00 | | | | |
| 1991 | — | — | — | 1.50 | 3.50 | — |
| 1992 | — | — | — | 1.50 | 3.50 | — |

**DOLLAR** **KM# 89** **Composition:** Copper-Nickel **Reverse:** Poinciana flower

| Date | Mintage | F | VF | XF | Unc | BU |
|---|---|---|---|---|---|---|
| 1982FM (P) | 1,217 | Value: 20.00 | | | | |

**DOLLAR** **KM# 93** **Composition:** Copper-Nickel **Subject:** 10th Anniversary of Independence **Reverse:** Allamanda flower

| Date | Mintage | F | VF | XF | Unc | BU |
|---|---|---|---|---|---|---|
| 1983FM (P) | 1,020 | Value: 20.00 | | | | |

**DOLLAR** **KM#104** **Composition:** Copper-Nickel **Reverse:** Bougainvillea flower

| Date | Mintage | F | VF | XF | Unc | BU |
|---|---|---|---|---|---|---|
| 1984FM (P) | 1,036 | Value: 20.00 | | | | |
| 1985FM (P) | 7,500 | Value: 10.00 | | | | |

**DOLLAR** **KM# 154** **Composition:** Copper-Nickel **Note:** Golf - Hole in One. Similar to 5 Dollars, KM#155.

| Date | Mintage | F | VF | XF | Unc | BU |
|---|---|---|---|---|---|---|
| 1994 | 20,000 | — | — | — | 15.00 | — |

**DOLLAR** **KM# 186** **Weight:** 1.2442 g. **Composition:** 0.9999 Gold .0400 oz. AGW **Reverse:** Two flamingos **Note:** Similar to 5 Dollars, KM#188.

| Date | Mintage | F | VF | XF | Unc | BU |
|---|---|---|---|---|---|---|
| 1995 Proof | — | Value: 50.00 | | | | |

**DOLLAR** **KM# 176** **Weight:** 31.1800 g. **Composition:** 0.9990 Silver 1.0015 oz. ASW **Subject:** Third Millennium - Year 2000

| Date | Mintage | F | VF | XF | Unc | BU |
|---|---|---|---|---|---|---|
| 1996 Proof | 50,000 | Value: 45.00 | | | | |

**2 DOLLARS** **KM# 9** **Weight:** 29.8000 g. **Composition:** 0.9250 Silver .8863 oz. ASW **Reverse:** National bird - two flamingos

| Date | Mintage | F | VF | XF | Unc | BU |
|---|---|---|---|---|---|---|
| 1966 | 104,000 | — | BV | 5.00 | 7.00 | — |
| 1969 | 26,000 | — | BV | 5.00 | 7.00 | — |
| 1969 Proof | 10,000 | Value: 8.00 | | | | |
| 1970 | 32,000 | — | BV | 5.00 | 7.00 | — |
| 1970 Proof | 23,000 | Value: 9.00 | | | | |

**2 DOLLARS** **KM# 23** **Weight:** 29.8000 g. **Composition:** 0.9250 Silver .8863 oz. ASW

| Date | Mintage | F | VF | XF | Unc | BU |
|---|---|---|---|---|---|---|
| 1971FM | 88,000 | — | BV | 5.00 | 8.00 | — |
| 1971FM (P) | 60,000 | Value: 10.00 | | | | |
| 1972FM | 65,000 | — | BV | 5.00 | 8.00 | — |
| 1972FM (P) | 59,000 | Value: 10.00 | | | | |
| 1973FM | 43,000 | — | BV | 5.00 | 8.00 | — |
| 1973FM (P) | 50,000 | Value: 10.00 | | | | |

**2 DOLLARS** **KM# 66** **Composition:** Copper-Nickel

| Date | Mintage | F | VF | XF | Unc | BU |
|---|---|---|---|---|---|---|
| 1974FM | 37,000 | — | — | 2.00 | 5.00 | — |
| 1975FM (M) | 300 | — | — | 9.00 | 25.00 | — |
| 1975FM (U) | 8,810 | — | — | 2.00 | 5.00 | — |
| 1976FM (M) | 300 | — | — | 9.00 | 25.00 | — |
| 1976FM (U) | 4,381 | — | — | 2.00 | 5.50 | — |
| 1977FM (M) | 300 | — | — | 9.00 | 25.00 | — |
| 1977FM (U) | 946 | — | — | 3.00 | 20.00 | — |
| 1978FM (U) | 1,067 | — | — | 3.00 | 15.00 | — |
| 1979FM (U) | 300 | — | — | 7.50 | 25.00 | — |
| 1980FM (U) | — | — | — | — | — | — |

**2 DOLLARS** **KM# 66a** **Weight:** 29.8000 g. **Composition:** 0.9250 Silver .8863 oz. ASW

| Date | Mintage | F | VF | XF | Unc | BU |
|---|---|---|---|---|---|---|
| 1974FM (P) | 129,000 | Value: 9.00 | | | | |
| 1975FM (P) | 45,000 | Value: 9.00 | | | | |
| 1976FM (P) | 35,000 | Value: 9.00 | | | | |
| 1977FM (P) | 15,000 | Value: 12.00 | | | | |
| 1978FM (P) | 11,000 | Value: 17.50 | | | | |
| 1979FM (P) | 2,053 | Value: 30.00 | | | | |
| 1980FM (P) | 2,084 | Value: 30.00 | | | | |

**2 DOLLARS** **KM# 66b** **Composition:** Copper-Nickel

| Date | Mintage | F | VF | XF | Unc | BU |
|---|---|---|---|---|---|---|
| 1981FM (P) | 1,980 | Value: 30.00 | | | | |
| 1989 | — | — | — | 2.00 | 6.00 | — |

**2 DOLLARS** **KM# 90** **Composition:** Copper-Nickel **Reverse:** Bahama swallows

| Date | Mintage | F | VF | XF | Unc | BU |
|---|---|---|---|---|---|---|
| 1982FM (P) | 1,217 | Value: 20.00 | | | | |

**2 DOLLARS** **KM# 94** **Composition:** Copper-Nickel **Subject:** 10th Anniversary of Independence **Reverse:** Honeycreepers

| Date | Mintage | F | VF | XF | Unc | BU |
|---|---|---|---|---|---|---|
| 1983FM (P) | 1,020 | Value: 20.00 | | | | |

**2 DOLLARS** **KM# 105** **Composition:** Copper-Nickel **Reverse:** Flamingos flying

| Date | Mintage | F | VF | XF | Unc | BU |
|---|---|---|---|---|---|---|
| 1984FM (P) | 1,036 | Value: 30.00 | | | | |
| 1985FM (P) | 7,500 | Value: 15.00 | | | | |

**2 DOLLARS** **KM# 66c** **Weight:** 16.8500 g. **Composition:** 0.9250 Silver .5012 oz. ASW

| Date | Mintage | F | VF | XF | Unc | BU |
|---|---|---|---|---|---|---|
| 1989 | Est. 4,000 | Value: 40.00 | | | | |
| 1991 | 600 | — | — | — | 100 | — |

**2 DOLLARS** **KM# 158** **Weight:** 28.2800 g. **Composition:** 0.9250 Silver .8411 oz. ASW **Subject:** Royal Visit **Reverse:** Portraits and yacht

| Date | Mintage | F | VF | XF | Unc | BU |
|---|---|---|---|---|---|---|
| 1994 Proof | 10,000 | Value: 40.00 | | | | |

**2 DOLLARS** **KM# 183.1** **Weight:** 23.3300 g. **Composition:** 0.9250 Silver .6938 oz. ASW **Series:** Olympics **Subject:** Catamaran Sailing **Rev. Legend:** OLIMPIC GAMES...

| Date | Mintage | F | VF | XF | Unc | BU |
|---|---|---|---|---|---|---|
| 1995 Proof | 30,000 | Value: 40.00 | | | | |

**2 DOLLARS** **KM# 183.2** **Weight:** 23.3300 g. **Composition:** 0.9250 Silver .6938 oz. ASW **Series:** Olympics **Subject:** Catamaran Sailing **Rev. Legend:** OLYMPIC GAMES...

| Date | Mintage | F | VF | XF | Unc | BU |
|---|---|---|---|---|---|---|
| 1995 | — | — | — | — | 150 | — |

**2 DOLLARS** **KM# 164** **Weight:** 30.0800 g. **Composition:** 0.9990 Silver .9982 oz. ASW **Series:** Flora and Fauna **Reverse:** Hibiscus flower **Note:** "Applique"

| Date | Mintage | F | VF | XF | Unc | BU |
|---|---|---|---|---|---|---|
| 1995 Proof | 25,000 | Value: 45.00 | | | | |

**2 DOLLARS** **KM# 165** **Weight:** 31.4000 g. **Composition:** 0.9990 Silver 1.0085 oz. ASW **Series:** Flora and Fauna **Reverse:** Bahama Amazon Parrot **Note:** "Applique"

| Date | Mintage | F | VF | XF | Unc | BU |
|---|---|---|---|---|---|---|
| 1995 Proof | 10,000 | Value: 55.00 | | | | |

**2 DOLLARS** **KM# 166** **Weight:** 31.4000 g. **Composition:** 0.9990 Silver 1.0085 oz. ASW **Series:** Flora and Fauna **Reverse:** Caribbean Monk Seal **Note:** "Applique"

| Date | Mintage | F | VF | XF | Unc | BU |
|---|---|---|---|---|---|---|
| 1995 Proof | 10,000 | Value: 55.00 | | | | |

**2 DOLLARS** **KM# 187** **Weight:** 3.1103 g. **Composition:** 0.9999 Gold .1000 oz. AGW **Reverse:** Two flamingos **Note:** Similar to 5 Dollars, KM#188.

| Date | Mintage | F | VF | XF | Unc | BU |
|---|---|---|---|---|---|---|
| 1995 Proof | — | Value: 100 | | | | |

**2 DOLLARS** **KM# 203** **Weight:** 23.3300 g. **Composition:** 0.9250 Silver .6938 oz. ASW **Subject:** Protect Our World **Obverse:** Queen's head right. **Reverse:** Flamingo and map. **Edge:** Reeded. **Size:** 38.6 mm.

| Date | Mintage | F | VF | XF | Unc | BU |
|---|---|---|---|---|---|---|
| 1996 Proof | — | Value: 50.00 | | | | |

**2 DOLLARS** **KM# 177** **Weight:** 3.1103 g. **Composition:** 0.9999 Gold .1000 oz. AGW **Subject:** Third Millennium - Year 2000 **Obverse:** Queen's portrait **Reverse:** Sea shell shaped map **Note:** Similar to 1 Dollar, KM#176.

| Date | Mintage | F | VF | XF | Unc | BU |
|---|---|---|---|---|---|---|
| 1996 Proof | 10,000 | Value: 80.00 | | | | |

**2 DOLLARS** **KM# 198** **Weight:** 28.2800 g. **Composition:** 0.9250 Silver .8410 oz. ASW **Subject:** WWF Conserving Nature **Obverse:** Queen's portrait **Reverse:** Spotfin Butterfly Fish and a Queen Angelfish

| Date | Mintage | F | VF | XF | Unc | BU |
|---|---|---|---|---|---|---|
| 1997 Proof | Est. 15,000 | Value: 45.00 | | | | |

**5 DOLLARS** **KM# 10** **Weight:** 42.1200 g. **Composition:** 0.9250 Silver 1.2527 oz. ASW

| Date | Mintage | F | VF | XF | Unc | BU |
|---|---|---|---|---|---|---|
| 1966 | 100,000 | — | BV | 6.00 | 12.00 | — |
| 1969 | 36,000 | — | BV | 6.00 | 12.00 | — |
| 1969 Proof | 10,000 | Value: 15.00 | | | | |
| 1970 | 43,000 | — | BV | 6.00 | 12.00 | — |
| 1970 Proof | 23,000 | Value: 15.00 | | | | |

**5 DOLLARS** **KM# 24** **Weight:** 42.1200 g. **Composition:** 0.9250 Silver 1.2527 oz. ASW

| Date | Mintage | F | VF | XF | Unc | BU |
|---|---|---|---|---|---|---|
| 1971FM | 29,000 | — | BV | 6.00 | 10.00 | — |
| 1971FM (P) | 31,000 | Value: 11.00 | | | | |

**5 DOLLARS** **KM# 33** **Weight:** 42.1200 g. **Composition:** 0.9250 Silver 1.2527 oz. ASW **Obverse:** Similar to KM#24

| Date | Mintage | F | VF | XF | Unc | BU |
|---|---|---|---|---|---|---|
| 1972FM | 32,000 | — | BV | 6.00 | 9.50 | — |
| 1972FM (P) | 35,000 | Value: 10.00 | | | | |
| 1973FM | 32,000 | — | BV | 6.00 | 9.50 | — |
| 1973FM (P) | 35,000 | Value: 10.00 | | | | |

**5 DOLLARS** **KM# 67** **Composition:** Copper-Nickel **Reverse:** National flag

| Date | Mintage | F | VF | XF | Unc | BU |
|---|---|---|---|---|---|---|
| 1974FM | 32,000 | — | — | — | 8.00 | — |
| 1975FM (M) | 200 | — | — | — | 40.00 | — |
| 1975FM (U) | 7,058 | — | — | — | 9.00 | — |
| 1976FM (M) | 200 | — | — | — | 40.00 | — |
| 1976FM (U) | 2,591 | — | — | — | 15.00 | — |
| 1977FM (M) | 200 | — | — | — | 40.00 | — |
| 1977FM (U) | 801 | — | — | — | 25.00 | — |
| 1978FM (U) | 1,244 | — | — | — | 15.00 | — |

**5 DOLLARS** **KM# 67a** **Weight:** 42.1200 g. **Composition:** 0.9250 Silver 1.2527 oz. ASW

| Date | Mintage | F | VF | XF | Unc | BU |
|---|---|---|---|---|---|---|
| 1974FM (P) | 94,000 | Value: 12.00 | | | | |
| 1975FM (P) | 29,000 | Value: 15.00 | | | | |
| 1976FM (P) | 23,000 | Value: 15.00 | | | | |
| 1977FM (P) | 11,000 | Value: 25.00 | | | | |
| 1978FM (P) | 6,931 | Value: 30.00 | | | | |
| 1979FM (P) | 2,053 | Value: 35.00 | | | | |
| 1980FM (P) | 2,084 | Value: 35.00 | | | | |

**5 DOLLARS** **KM# 67b** **Weight:** 42.1200 g. **Composition:** 0.5000 Silver .6771 oz. ASW **Note:** Reduced diameter.

| Date | Mintage | F | VF | XF | Unc | BU |
|---|---|---|---|---|---|---|
| 1981FM (P) | 1,980 | Value: 35.00 | | | | |

**5 DOLLARS** **KM# 91** **Weight:** 42.1200 g. **Composition:** 0.5000 Silver .6771 oz. ASW **Note:** Columbus Memorial

| Date | Mintage | F | VF | XF | Unc | BU |
|---|---|---|---|---|---|---|
| 1982FM (P) | 1,217 | Value: 35.00 | | | | |

**5 DOLLARS** **KM# 95** **Weight:** 42.1200 g. **Composition:** 0.5000 Silver .6771 oz. ASW **Subject:** 10th Anniversary of Independence **Reverse:** Flamingo

| Date | Mintage | F | VF | XF | Unc | BU |
|---|---|---|---|---|---|---|
| 1983FM (P) | 1,020 | Value: 40.00 | | | | |

**5 DOLLARS** **KM# 106** **Weight:** 42.1200 g. **Composition:** 0.5000 Silver .6771 oz. ASW **Note:** Historical map.

| Date | Mintage | F | VF | XF | Unc | BU |
|---|---|---|---|---|---|---|
| 1984FM (P) | 1,036 | Value: 45.00 | | | | |

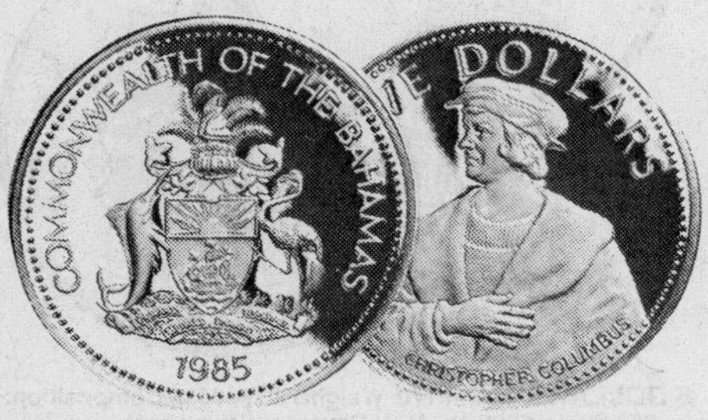


**5 DOLLARS** **KM# 107** **Weight:** 42.1200 g. **Composition:** 0.5000 Silver .6771 oz. ASW **Reverse:** Christopher Columbus

| Date | Mintage | F | VF | XF | Unc | BU |
|---|---|---|---|---|---|---|
| 1985FM (P) | 7,847 | Value: 30.00 | | | | |

**5 DOLLARS** **KM# 132** **Weight:** 19.4400 g. **Composition:** 0.9250 Silver .5782 oz. ASW **Reverse:** Christopher Columbus, sword, and flag

| Date | Mintage | F | VF | XF | Unc | BU |
|---|---|---|---|---|---|---|
| 1989 Proof | Est. 4,000 | Value: 40.00 | | | | |
| 1991 | 750 | — | — | — | — | 85.00 |
| 1991 Proof | 7,000 | Value: 50.00 | | | | |
| 1992 Proof | Est. 25,000 | Value: 35.00 | | | | |

**5 DOLLARS** **KM# 139** **Weight:** 19.4400 g. **Composition:** 0.9250 Silver .5782 oz. ASW **Series:** 500th Anniversary of the Americas **Reverse:** Columbus, along with Ferdinand and Isabella

| Date | Mintage | F | VF | XF | Unc | BU |
|---|---|---|---|---|---|---|
| 1991 Proof | Est. 25,000 | Value: 27.50 | | | | |

**5 DOLLARS** **KM# 140** **Weight:** 19.4400 g. **Composition:** 0.9250 Silver .5782 oz. ASW **Series:** 500th Anniversary of the Americas **Subject:** Columbus sighting land

| Date | Mintage | F | VF | XF | Unc | BU |
|---|---|---|---|---|---|---|
| 1991 Proof | Est. 25,000 | Value: 27.50 | | | | |

**5 DOLLARS** **KM# 141** **Weight:** 19.4400 g. **Composition:** 0.9250 Silver .5782 oz. ASW **Series:** 500th Anniversary of the Americas **Subject:** Columbus claiming the land

| Date | Mintage | F | VF | XF | Unc | BU |
|---|---|---|---|---|---|---|
| 1991 Proof | Est. 25,000 | Value: 27.50 | | | | |

**5 DOLLARS** **KM# 142** **Weight:** 19.4400 g. **Composition:** 0.9250 Silver .5782 oz. ASW **Series:** 500th Anniversary of the Americas **Reverse:** Jacques Carter and map

| Date | Mintage | F | VF | XF | Unc | BU |
|---|---|---|---|---|---|---|
| 1991 Proof | Est. 25,000 | Value: 27.50 | | | | |

**5 DOLLARS** **KM# 143** **Weight:** 19.4400 g. **Composition:** 0.9250 Silver .5782 oz. ASW **Series:** 500th Anniversary of the Americas **Reverse:** President Thomas Jefferson and Independence Hall

| Date | Mintage | F | VF | XF | Unc | BU |
|---|---|---|---|---|---|---|
| 1991 Proof | Est. 25,000 | Value: 27.50 | | | | |

**5 DOLLARS** **KM# 144** **Weight:** 19.4400 g. **Composition:** 0.9250 Silver .5782 oz. ASW **Series:** 500th Anniversary of the Americas **Reverse:** Simon Bolivar and Jose San Martin

| Date | Mintage | F | VF | XF | Unc | BU |
|---|---|---|---|---|---|---|
| 1991 Proof | Est. 25,000 | Value: 27.50 | | | | |

**5 DOLLARS** **KM# 146** **Weight:** 19.4400 g. **Composition:** 0.9250 Silver .5782 oz. ASW **Series:** 500th Anniversary of the Americas **Subject:** Electric light demonstration **Reverse:** Thomas Edison

| Date | Mintage | F | VF | XF | Unc | BU |
|---|---|---|---|---|---|---|
| 1991 Proof | Est. 25,000 | Value: 30.00 | | | | |

**5 DOLLARS** **KM# 145** **Weight:** 19.4400 g. **Composition:** 0.9250 Silver .5782 oz. ASW **Series:** 500th Anniversary of the Americas **Subject:** Abolition of slavery **Reverse:** President Abraham Lincoln

| Date | Mintage | F | VF | XF | Unc | BU |
|---|---|---|---|---|---|---|
| 1991 Proof | Est. 25,000 | Value: 30.00 | | | | |

**5 DOLLARS** **KM# 147** **Weight:** 19.4400 g. **Composition:** 0.9250 Silver .5782 oz. ASW **Series:** 500th Anniversary of the Americas **Subject:** Wright brothers' first airplane flight

| Date | Mintage | F | VF | XF | Unc | BU |
|---|---|---|---|---|---|---|
| 1991 Proof | Est. 25,000 | Value: 35.00 | | | | |

**5 DOLLARS** **KM# 148** **Weight:** 19.4400 g. **Composition:** 0.9250 Silver .5782 oz. ASW **Series:** 500th Anniversary of the Americas **Reverse:** Henry Ford and automobiles

| Date | Mintage | F | VF | XF | Unc | BU |
|---|---|---|---|---|---|---|
| 1991 Proof | Est. 25,000 | Value: 27.50 | | | | |

**5 DOLLARS** **KM# 149** **Weight:** 19.4400 g. **Composition:** 0.9250 Silver .5782 oz. ASW **Series:** 500th Anniversary of the Americas **Reverse:** President Teddy Roosevelt

| Date | Mintage | F | VF | XF | Unc | BU |
|---|---|---|---|---|---|---|
| 1991 Proof | Est. 25,000 | Value: 27.50 | | | | |

**5 DOLLARS** **KM# 150** **Weight:** 19.4400 g. **Composition:** 0.9250 Silver .5782 oz. ASW **Series:** 500th Anniversary of the Americas **Subject:** First manned moonlanding

| Date | Mintage | F | VF | XF | Unc | BU |
|---|---|---|---|---|---|---|
| 1991 Proof | Est. 25,000 | Value: 35.00 | | | | |

**5 DOLLARS** **KM# 138** **Weight:** 19.4400 g. **Composition:** 0.9250 Silver .5782 oz. ASW **Series:** Discovery of the New World **Obverse:** Coat of arms **Reverse:** Columbus' ships

| Date | Mintage | F | VF | XF | Unc | BU |
|---|---|---|---|---|---|---|
| 1992 Proof | Est. 25,000 | Value: 30.00 | | | | |

**5 DOLLARS** **KM# 192** **Weight:** 1.5550 g. **Composition:** 0.5000 Gold .0250 oz. AGW **Obverse:** Queen's portrait **Reverse:** Facing pair of flamingos

| Date | Mintage | F | VF | XF | Unc | BU |
|---|---|---|---|---|---|---|
| 1992 Proof | Est. 750 | Value: 70.00 | | | | |

**5 DOLLARS** **KM# 159** **Weight:** 23.3300 g. **Composition:** 0.9250 Silver .6939 oz. ASW **Reverse:** Pirate Captain Howell Davis

| Date | Mintage | F | VF | XF | Unc | BU |
|---|---|---|---|---|---|---|
| 1993 Proof | Est. 5,000 | Value: 47.50 | | | | |

**5 DOLLARS** **KM# 160** **Weight:** 23.3300 g. **Composition:** 0.9250 Silver .6939 oz. ASW **Reverse:** Pirate Captain Charles Vane

| Date | Mintage | F | VF | XF | Unc | BU |
|---|---|---|---|---|---|---|
| 1993 Proof | Est. 5,000 | Value: 47.50 | | | | |

**5 DOLLARS** **KM# 161** **Weight:** 23.3300 g. **Composition:** 0.9250 Silver .6939 oz. ASW **Reverse:** Pirate Captain Edward Teach

| Date | Mintage | F | VF | XF | Unc | BU |
|---|---|---|---|---|---|---|
| 1993 Proof | Est. 5,000 | Value: 47.50 | | | | |

**5 DOLLARS** **KM# 169** **Weight:** 23.3300 g. **Composition:** 0.9250 Silver .6939 oz. ASW **Subject:** World Soccer Championship

| Date | Mintage | F | VF | XF | Unc | BU |
|---|---|---|---|---|---|---|
| 1993 Proof | Est. 15,000 | Value: 40.00 | | | | |

**5 DOLLARS** **KM# 170** **Weight:** 23.3300 g. **Composition:** 0.9250 Silver .6939 oz. ASW **Reverse:** Sailing boat

| Date | Mintage | F | VF | XF | Unc | BU |
|---|---|---|---|---|---|---|
| 1993 Proof | Est. 20,000 | Value: 45.00 | | | | |

**5 DOLLARS** **KM# 155** **Weight:** 31.1035 g. **Composition:** 0.9990 Silver 1.0000 oz. ASW **Subject:** Golf - Hole in One

**Obverse:** National arms, legend around, date below **Obv. Legend:** COMMONWEALTH OF THE BAHAMAS **Reverse:** Golf ball rolling towards cup

| Date | Mintage | F | VF | XF | Unc | BU |
|---|---|---|---|---|---|---|
| 1994 Proof | Est. 50,000 | Value: 45.00 | | | | |

**5 DOLLARS** **KM# 201** **Weight:** 3.1103 g. **Composition:** 0.9990 Gold .1000 oz. AGW **Subject:** Golf - Hole in One **Obverse:** National arms, legend around, date below **Obv. Legend:**

COMMONWEALTH OF THE BAHAMAS **Reverse:** Golf ball rolling towards cup

| Date | Mintage | F | VF | XF | Unc | BU |
|---|---|---|---|---|---|---|
| 1994 Proof | 250,000 | Value: 125 | | | | |

**5 DOLLARS** KM# 171 **Weight:** 3.1103 g. **Composition:** 0.9990 Gold .1000 oz. AGW **Reverse:** Space shuttle and satellite

| Date | Mintage | F | VF | XF | Unc | BU |
|---|---|---|---|---|---|---|
| 1994 Proof | Est. 10,000 | Value: 50.00 | | | | |

**5 DOLLARS** KM# 172 **Weight:** 3.1103 g. **Composition:** 0.9990 Gold .1000 oz. AGW **Reverse:** Two Whistling Ducks in flight

| Date | Mintage | F | VF | XF | Unc | BU |
|---|---|---|---|---|---|---|
| 1994 Proof | Est. 15,000 | Value: 45.00 | | | | |

**5 DOLLARS** KM# 173 **Weight:** 31.4700 g. **Composition:** 0.9250 Silver .9359 oz. ASW **Reverse:** Ponce De Leon on horseback

| Date | Mintage | F | VF | XF | Unc | BU |
|---|---|---|---|---|---|---|
| 1994 Proof | Est. 10,000 | Value: 45.00 | | | | |

**5 DOLLARS** KM# 188 **Weight:** 6.2207 g. **Composition:** 0.9999 Gold .2000 oz. AGW **Obverse:** Queen's portrait **Reverse:** Two flamingos facing

| Date | Mintage | F | VF | XF | Unc | BU |
|---|---|---|---|---|---|---|
| 1995 Proof | — | Value: 175 | | | | |

**5 DOLLARS** KM# 178 **Weight:** 7.7758 g. **Composition:** 0.9999 Gold .2500 oz. AGW **Subject:** Third Millennium - Year 2000 **Obverse:** Queen's portrait **Reverse:** Sea shell-shaped world map

| Date | Mintage | F | VF | XF | Unc | BU |
|---|---|---|---|---|---|---|
| 1996 Proof | 5,000 | Value: 175 | | | | |

**10 DOLLARS** KM# 11 **Weight:** 3.9943 g. **Composition:** 0.9170 Gold .1177 oz. AGW **Subject:** Adoption of New Constitution **Reverse:** Fortress

| Date | Mintage | F | VF | XF | Unc | BU |
|---|---|---|---|---|---|---|
| 1967 | 6,200 | — | — | — | 55.00 | — |
| 1967 Proof | 850 | Value: 95.00 | | | | |

**10 DOLLARS** KM# 25 **Weight:** 3.9943 g. **Composition:** 0.9170 Gold .1177 oz. AGW

| Date | Mintage | F | VF | XF | Unc | BU |
|---|---|---|---|---|---|---|
| 1971 | 23,000 | — | — | — | 45.00 | — |
| 1971(t) Proof | 1,250 | Value: 70.00 | | | | |

**10 DOLLARS** KM# 26 **Weight:** 3.9943 g. **Composition:** 0.9170 Gold .1177 oz. AGW **Reverse:** Hallmark and fineness stamped near bottom **Note:** Struck by the Gori and Zucchi Mint, Italy.

| Date | Mintage | F | VF | XF | Unc | BU |
|---|---|---|---|---|---|---|
| 1971 | — | — | — | — | 45.00 | — |

**10 DOLLARS** KM# 34 **Weight:** 3.1950 g. **Composition:** 0.9170 Gold .0940 oz. AGW **Obverse:** Queen's portrait **Reverse:** Fortress

| Date | Mintage | F | VF | XF | Unc | BU |
|---|---|---|---|---|---|---|
| 1972 | 11,000 | — | — | — | 45.00 | — |
| 1972 Proof | 1,250 | Value: 70.00 | | | | |

**10 DOLLARS** KM# 40.1 **Weight:** 1.4500 g. **Composition:** 0.7500 Gold .0349 oz. AGW **Subject:** Independence Day - July 10 **Obverse:** Tobacco Dove **Reverse:** Without fineness and date

| Date | Mintage | F | VF | XF | Unc | BU |
|---|---|---|---|---|---|---|
| 1973 | — | — | — | — | 25.00 | — |
| 1973 Proof | — | Value: 30.00 | | | | |

**10 DOLLARS** KM# 40.2 **Weight:** 1.4500 g. **Composition:** 0.7500 Gold .0349 oz. AGW **Obverse:** Tobacco Dove **Reverse:** Date without fineness

| Date | Mintage | F | VF | XF | Unc | BU |
|---|---|---|---|---|---|---|
| 1973 | — | — | — | 25.00 | 30.00 | — |

**10 DOLLARS** KM# 41 **Weight:** 1.4500 g. **Composition:** 0.5850 Gold .0272 oz. AGW **Obverse:** Tobacco Dove **Reverse:** .585 fineness and date

| Date | Mintage | F | VF | XF | Unc | BU |
|---|---|---|---|---|---|---|
| 1973 | 9,960 | — | — | — | 25.00 | — |
| 1973 Proof | 1,260 | Value: 40.00 | | | | |

**10 DOLLARS** KM# 42 **Weight:** 49.7500 g. **Composition:** 0.9250 Silver 1.4795 oz. ASW **Subject:** Independence Day - July 10 **Obverse:** Legend around queen's portrait

| Date | Mintage | F | VF | XF | Unc | BU |
|---|---|---|---|---|---|---|
| 1973FM | 28,000 | — | — | — | 16.50 | — |
| 1973FM Proof | 63,000 | Value: 20.00 | | | | |

**10 DOLLARS** KM# 68 **Composition:** Copper-Nickel **Subject:** 1st Anniversary of Independence **Obverse:** National arms, date below **Reverse:** National flag

| Date | Mintage | F | VF | XF | Unc | BU |
|---|---|---|---|---|---|---|
| 1974FM Proof | 4,825 | — | — | — | 12.00 | — |

**10 DOLLARS** KM# 68a **Weight:** 50.4200 g. **Composition:** 0.9250 Silver 1.4994 oz. ASW

| Date | Mintage | F | VF | XF | Unc | BU |
|---|---|---|---|---|---|---|
| 1974FM Proof | 43,000 | Value: 15.00 | | | | |

**10 DOLLARS** **KM# 76** **Composition:** Copper-Nickel **Subject:** Anniversary of Independence **Obverse:** National arms **Reverse:** Yellow Elder

| Date | Mintage | F | VF | XF | Unc | BU |
|---|---|---|---|---|---|---|
| 1975FM (M) | 100 | — | — | — | 90.00 | — |
| 1975FM (U) | 5,325 | — | — | — | 12.50 | — |
| 1976FM (M) | 100 | — | — | — | 90.00 | — |
| 1976FM (U) | 100 | — | — | — | 90.00 | — |
| 1977FM (M) | 100 | — | — | — | 90.00 | — |
| 1977FM (U) | 369 | — | — | — | 60.00 | — |

**10 DOLLARS** **KM# 76a** **Weight:** 49.1000 g. **Composition:** 0.9250 Silver 1.4602 oz. ASW

| Date | Mintage | F | VF | XF | Unc | BU |
|---|---|---|---|---|---|---|
| 1975FM (P) | 63,000 | Value: 15.00 | | | | |
| 1976FM (P) | 10,000 | Value: 18.50 | | | | |
| 1977FM (P) | 4,424 | Value: 25.00 | | | | |

**10 DOLLARS** **KM# 78.1** **Weight:** 45.3600 g. **Composition:** 0.5000 Silver .7291 oz. ASW **Subject:** 5th Anniversary of Independence **Obverse:** National flag

| Date | Mintage | F | VF | XF | Unc | BU |
|---|---|---|---|---|---|---|
| 1978 Proof | 50,000 | Value: 25.00 | | | | |

**10 DOLLARS** **KM# 78.2** **Weight:** 45.3600 g. **Composition:** 0.5000 Silver .7291 oz. ASW **Reverse:** Tower mint mark after DOLLARS

| Date | Mintage | F | VF | XF | Unc | BU |
|---|---|---|---|---|---|---|
| 1978(t) Proof | — | Value: 25.00 | | | | |

**10 DOLLARS** **KM# 79** **Weight:** 45.3600 g. **Composition:** 0.5000 Silver .7291 oz. ASW **Subject:** 5th Anniversary of Independence **Obverse:** Arms

| Date | Mintage | F | VF | XF | Unc | BU |
|---|---|---|---|---|---|---|
| 1978 Proof | 50,000 | Value: 20.00 | | | | |

**10 DOLLARS** **KM# 84** **Weight:** 30.2800 g. **Composition:** 0.5000 Silver .4868 oz. ASW **Subject:** 10th Anniversary Caribbean Development Bank

| Date | Mintage | F | VF | XF | Unc | BU |
|---|---|---|---|---|---|---|
| 1980FM Proof | 1,001 | Value: 22.50 | | | | |

**10 DOLLARS** **KM# 85** **Weight:** 28.2800 g. **Composition:** 0.9250 Silver .8410 oz. ASW **Subject:** Wedding of Prince Charles and Lady Diana

| Date | Mintage | F | VF | XF | Unc | BU |
|---|---|---|---|---|---|---|
| 1981 Proof | 39,000 | Value: 30.00 | | | | |

**10 DOLLARS** **KM# 96** **Weight:** 30.2800 g. **Composition:** 0.5000 Silver .4867 oz. ASW **Subject:** 30th Anniversary - Coronation of Queen Elizabeth

| Date | Mintage | F | VF | XF | Unc | BU |
|---|---|---|---|---|---|---|
| 1983FM Proof | 3,374 | Value: 25.00 | | | | |

**10 DOLLARS** **KM# 97** **Weight:** 23.3300 g. **Composition:** 0.9250 Silver .6939 oz. ASW **Subject:** 10th Anniversary of Independence

| Date | Mintage | F | VF | XF | Unc | BU |
|---|---|---|---|---|---|---|
| 1983 Proof | 800 | Value: 37.50 | | | | |

**10 DOLLARS** **KM# 114** **Weight:** 23.3300 g. **Composition:** 0.9250 Silver .6939 oz. ASW **Subject:** Los Angeles Olypics **Obverse:** National arms **Reverse:** Sprinter

| Date | Mintage | F | VF | XF | Unc | BU |
|---|---|---|---|---|---|---|
| 1984 Proof | 2,100 | Value: 40.00 | | | | |

**10 DOLLARS** **KM# 127** **Weight:** 29.1700 g. **Composition:** 0.5000 Silver .4690 oz. ASW **Subject:** 10th Anniversary of Central Bank **Obverse:** National arms **Reverse:** Nummulite (Sand dollar)

| Date | Mintage | F | VF | XF | Unc | BU |
|---|---|---|---|---|---|---|
| 1984 Proof | 1,001 | Value: 50.00 | | | | |

**10 DOLLARS** **KM# 109** **Weight:** 28.2800 g. **Composition:** 0.9250 Silver .8411 oz. ASW **Subject:** Royal Visit

| Date | Mintage | F | VF | XF | Unc | BU |
|---|---|---|---|---|---|---|
| 1985 Proof | 1,060 | Value: 30.00 | | | | |

**10 DOLLARS** **KM# 109a** **Weight:** 47.5400 g. **Composition:** 0.9170 Gold 1.4013 oz. AGW **Subject:** Royal Visit

| Date | Mintage | F | VF | XF | Unc | BU |
|---|---|---|---|---|---|---|
| 1985 Proof | Est. 250 | Value: 800 | | | | |

**10 DOLLARS** **KM# 113** **Weight:** 28.2800 g. **Composition:** 0.5000 Silver .4546 oz. ASW **Subject:** Commonwealth Games

| Date | Mintage | F | VF | XF | Unc | BU |
|---|---|---|---|---|---|---|
| 1986 | 899 | — | — | — | 30.00 | — |

**10 DOLLARS** **KM# 113a** **Weight:** 28.2800 g. **Composition:** 0.9250 Silver .8411 oz. ASW

| Date | Mintage | F | VF | XF | Unc | BU |
|---|---|---|---|---|---|---|
| 1986 Proof | 1,343 | Value: 30.00 | | | | |

**10 DOLLARS** **KM# 120** **Weight:** 28.2800 g. **Composition:** 0.9250 Silver .8411 oz. ASW **Reverse:** Queen Isabella and Columbus

| Date | Mintage | F | VF | XF | Unc | BU |
|---|---|---|---|---|---|---|
| 1987 Proof | 1,800 | Value: 35.00 | | | | |

**10 DOLLARS** **KM# 123** **Weight:** 28.2800 g. **Composition:** 0.9250 Silver .8411 oz. ASW **Subject:** Columbus discovering America **Obverse:** Queen Elizabeth **Reverse:** Columbus sighting America

| Date | Mintage | F | VF | XF | Unc | BU |
|---|---|---|---|---|---|---|
| 1988 Proof | 1,704 | Value: 35.00 | | | | |

**10 DOLLARS** **KM# 128** **Weight:** 28.2800 g. **Composition:** 0.9250 Silver .8411 oz. ASW **Obverse:** Queen Elizabeth **Reverse:** Columbus with flag and sword

| Date | Mintage | F | VF | XF | Unc | BU |
|---|---|---|---|---|---|---|
| 1989 Proof | Est. 10,000 | Value: 30.00 | | | | |

**10 DOLLARS** **KM# 133** **Weight:** 28.2800 g. **Composition:** 0.9250 Silver .8411 oz. ASW **Series:** Discovery of the New World **Obverse:** Queen Elizabeth **Reverse:** Columbus

| Date | Mintage | F | VF | XF | Unc | BU |
|---|---|---|---|---|---|---|
| 1990 | 550 | — | — | — | 145 | — |
| 1990 Proof | 10,000 | Value: 30.00 | | | | |

**10 DOLLARS** **KM# 196** **Weight:** 28.2800 g. **Composition:** 0.9250 Silver .8411 oz. ASW **Series:** Discovery of the New World **Obverse:** Queen's portrait **Reverse:** 5-man rowboat, Columbus' ships in background

| Date | Mintage | F | VF | XF | Unc | BU |
|---|---|---|---|---|---|---|
| 1991 Proof | — | Value: 30.00 | | | | |

**10 DOLLARS** **KM# 193** **Weight:** 3.1450 g. **Composition:** 0.5000 Gold .0505 oz. AGW **Obverse:** Queen's portrait **Reverse:** Two flamingos facing

| Date | Mintage | F | VF | XF | Unc | BU |
|---|---|---|---|---|---|---|
| 1992 Proof | Est. 750 | Value: 100 | | | | |

**10 DOLLARS** **KM# 197** **Weight:** 28.2800 g. **Composition:** 0.9250 Silver .8411 oz. ASW **Series:** Discovery of the New World **Obverse:** Queen's portrait **Reverse:** Nina, Pinta, Santa Maria ships

| Date | Mintage | F | VF | XF | Unc | BU |
|---|---|---|---|---|---|---|
| 1992 Proof | — | Value: 30.00 | | | | |

**10 DOLLARS** **KM# 162** **Weight:** 136.0800 g. **Composition:** 0.9250 Silver 4.074 oz. ASW **Subject:** Expulsion of pirates **Obverse:** Queen's portrait, legend around, date below **Obv. Legend:** • COMMONWEALTH OF THE BAHAMAS • **Reverse:** Pirate ship **Rev. Legend:** • EXPULSIS PIRATIS • RESTITUTA COMMERCIA •

| Date | Mintage | F | VF | XF | Unc | BU |
|---|---|---|---|---|---|---|
| 1993 Proof | Est. 2,000 | Value: 120 | | | | |

**10 DOLLARS** **KM# 156** **Weight:** 7.7759 g. **Composition:** 0.9990 Gold .2500 oz. AGW **Subject:** Golf - Hole in One **Obverse:** National arms **Reverse:** Golfer making hole in one. **Note:** Actual hole in coin.

| Date | Mintage | F | VF | XF | Unc | BU |
|---|---|---|---|---|---|---|
| 1994 Proof | 2,500 | Value: 250 | | | | |

**10 DOLLARS** **KM# 167** **Weight:** 155.5175 g. **Composition:** 0.9990 Silver 5.0000 oz. ASW **Obverse:** National arms **Reverse:** Bahama Parrot

| Date | Mintage | F | VF | XF | Unc | BU |
|---|---|---|---|---|---|---|
| 1995 Proof | 2,500 | Value: 175 | | | | |

**10 DOLLARS** **KM# 168** **Weight:** 15.5518 g. **Composition:** 0.9990 Gold .5000 oz. AGW **Obverse:** Queen's portrait **Reverse:** Bahama Parrot

| Date | Mintage | F | VF | XF | Unc | BU |
|---|---|---|---|---|---|---|
| 1995 Proof | 2,000 | Value: 220 | | | | |

**10 DOLLARS** **KM# 174** **Weight:** 28.2800 g. **Composition:** 0.9250 Silver .8411 oz. ASW **Subject:** 25th Anniversary - Caribbean Development Bank **Obverse:** National arms

| Date | Mintage | F | VF | XF | Unc | BU |
|---|---|---|---|---|---|---|
| 1995 Proof | 1,000 | Value: 40.00 | | | | |

**10 DOLLARS** **KM# 189** **Weight:** 15.5517 g. **Composition:** 0.9999 Gold .5000 oz. AGW **Obverse:** Queen's portrait **Reverse:** Two flamingos facing

| Date | Mintage | F | VF | XF | Unc | BU |
|---|---|---|---|---|---|---|
| 1995 Proof | — | Value: 300 | | | | |

**10 DOLLARS** **KM# 179** **Weight:** 15.5517 g. **Composition:** 0.9999 Gold .5000 oz. AGW **Subject:** Third Millennium - Year 2000 **Obverse:** Queen's portrait **Reverse:** Sea shell-shaped world map

| Date | Mintage | F | VF | XF | Unc | BU |
|---|---|---|---|---|---|---|
| 1996 Proof | 5,000 | Value: 300 | | | | |

**10 DOLLARS** **KM# 200** **Weight:** 31.1035 g. **Composition:** 0.9990 Silver 1.0000 oz. ASW **Subject:** 50th Anniversary of the University of the West Indies **Obverse:** National arms **Reverse:** University arms, dates

| Date | Mintage | F | VF | XF | Unc | BU |
|---|---|---|---|---|---|---|
| 1998 Proof | 1,000 | Value: 55.00 | | | | |

**20 DOLLARS** **KM# 12** **Weight:** 7.9880 g. **Composition:** 0.9170 Gold .2355 oz. AGW **Subject:** Adoption of New Constitution **Reverse:** Lighthouse

| Date | Mintage | F | VF | XF | Unc | BU |
|---|---|---|---|---|---|---|
| 1967 | 6,200 | — | — | — | 110 | — |
| 1967 Proof | 850 | Value: 150 | | | | |

**20 DOLLARS** **KM# 27** **Weight:** 7.9880 g. **Composition:** 0.9170 Gold .2355 oz. AGW

| Date | Mintage | F | VF | XF | Unc | BU |
|---|---|---|---|---|---|---|
| 1971 | 22,000 | — | — | — | 95.00 | — |
| 1971(t) Proof | 1,250 | Value: 130 | | | | |

**20 DOLLARS** **KM# 28** **Weight:** 7.9880 g. **Composition:** 0.9170 Gold .2355 oz. AGW **Reverse:** Hallmark and fineness stamped at bottom **Note:** Struck by the Gori and Zucchi Mint, Italy.

| Date | Mintage | F | VF | XF | Unc | BU |
|---|---|---|---|---|---|---|
| 1971 Proof | — | — | — | — | 100 | — |

**20 DOLLARS** **KM# 35** **Weight:** 6.4800 g. **Composition:** 0.9170 Gold .1880 oz. AGW

| Date | Mintage | F | VF | XF | Unc | BU |
|---|---|---|---|---|---|---|
| 1972 | 10,000 | — | — | — | 90.00 | — |
| 1972 Proof | 1,250 | Value: 125 | | | | |

**20 DOLLARS** **KM# 43.1** **Weight:** 2.9000 g. **Composition:** 0.7500 Gold .0699 oz. AGW **Subject:** Independence Day - July 10 **Reverse:** Flamingos, without fineness and date

| Date | Mintage | F | VF | XF | Unc | BU |
|---|---|---|---|---|---|---|
| 1973 | — | — | — | — | 30.00 | — |
| 1973 Proof | — | Value: 40.00 | | | | |

**20 DOLLARS** **KM# 43.2** **Weight:** 2.9000 g. **Composition:** 0.7500 Gold .0699 oz. AGW **Subject:** Independence Day - July 10 **Reverse:** Flamingos, without fineness, high date

| Date | Mintage | F | VF | XF | Unc | BU |
|---|---|---|---|---|---|---|
| 1973 | — | — | — | — | 30.00 | — |
| 1973 Proof | — | Value: 40.00 | | | | |

**20 DOLLARS** **KM# 44** **Weight:** 2.9000 g. **Composition:** 0.5850 Gold .0545 oz. AGW **Reverse:** .585 fineness, low date

| Date | Mintage | F | VF | XF | Unc | BU |
|---|---|---|---|---|---|---|
| 1973 | 8,660 | — | — | — | 30.00 | — |
| 1973 Proof | 1,260 | Value: 40.00 | | | | |

**20 DOLLARS** **KM# 157** **Weight:** 15.5517 g. **Composition:** 0.9990 Gold .5000 oz. AGW **Obverse:** Arms **Reverse:** Golfer making hole in one **Note:** Actual hole in coin

| Date | Mintage | F | VF | XF | Unc | BU |
|---|---|---|---|---|---|---|
| 1994 Proof | 2,500 | Value: 350 | | | | |

**25 DOLLARS** **KM# 82** **Weight:** 37.3800 g. **Composition:** 0.9250 Silver 1.1117 oz. ASW **Subject:** 250th Anniversary of Parliament **Obverse:** Similar to 10 Dollars, KM#96

| Date | Mintage | F | VF | XF | Unc | BU |
|---|---|---|---|---|---|---|
| 1979 Proof | 3,002 | Value: 40.00 | | | | |

**25 DOLLARS** **KM# 110** **Weight:** 120.0000 g. **Composition:** 0.9250 Silver 3.5687 oz. ASW **Subject:** Columbus' Discovery of America **Obverse:** National arms

| Date | Mintage | F | VF | XF | Unc | BU |
|---|---|---|---|---|---|---|
| 1985 Proof | 1,950 | Value: 60.00 | | | | |

**25 DOLLARS** **KM# 115** **Weight:** 129.6000 g. **Composition:** 0.9250 Silver 3.8547 oz. ASW **Subject:** Bird Conservation **Obverse:** National arms **Reverse:** Flamingos

| Date | Mintage | F | VF | XF | Unc | BU |
|---|---|---|---|---|---|---|
| 1985 Proof | 1,060 | Value: 75.00 | | | | |

**25 DOLLARS** **KM# 118** **Weight:** 129.6000 g. **Composition:** 0.9250 Silver 3.8547 oz. ASW **Obverse:** Queen's portrait **Reverse:** Queen Isabella and Columbus

| Date | Mintage | F | VF | XF | Unc | BU |
|---|---|---|---|---|---|---|
| 1987 Proof | 1,750 | Value: 70.00 | | | | |

**25 DOLLARS** **KM# 124** **Weight:** 136.0000 g. **Composition:** 0.9250 Silver 4.0446 oz. ASW **Subject:** Columbus Discovering America **Obverse:** Queen's portrait **Reverse:** Columbus

| Date | Mintage | F | VF | XF | Unc | BU |
|---|---|---|---|---|---|---|
| 1988 Proof | 954 | Value: 110 | | | | |

**25 DOLLARS** **KM# 129** **Weight:** 136.0000 g. **Composition:** 0.9250 Silver 4.0446 oz. ASW **Obverse:** Queen Elizabeth **Reverse:** Christopher Columbus

| Date | Mintage | F | VF | XF | Unc | BU |
|---|---|---|---|---|---|---|
| 1989 Proof | 1,572 | Value: 70.00 | | | | |

**25 DOLLARS** **KM# 134** **Weight:** 136.0000 g. **Composition:** 0.9250 Silver 4.0446 oz. ASW **Series:** Discovery of the New World **Obverse:** Queen Elizabeth **Reverse:** Aborigine

| Date | Mintage | F | VF | XF | Unc | BU |
|---|---|---|---|---|---|---|
| 1990 Proof | 5,000 | Value: 65.00 | | | | |

**25 DOLLARS** **KM# 153** **Weight:** 136.0000 g. **Composition:** 0.9250 Silver 4.0446 oz. ASW **Series:** Discovery of the New World **Obverse:** Queen Elizabeth **Reverse:** Columbus

| Date | Mintage | F | VF | XF | Unc | BU |
|---|---|---|---|---|---|---|
| 1991 Proof | Est. 500 | Value: 175 | | | | |

**25 DOLLARS** **KM# 191** **Weight:** 136.0000 g. **Composition:** 0.9250 Silver 4.0446 oz. ASW **Reverse:** Columbus meeting native Americans

| Date | Mintage | F | VF | XF | Unc | BU |
|---|---|---|---|---|---|---|
| 1992 Proof | — | Value: 175 | | | | |

**25 DOLLARS** **KM# 194** **Weight:** 7.8300 g. **Composition:** 0.5000 Gold .1258 oz. AGW **Obverse:** Queen's portrait **Reverse:** Pair of flamingos

| Date | Mintage | F | VF | XF | Unc | BU |
|---|---|---|---|---|---|---|
| 1992 Proof | Est. 750 | Value: 200 | | | | |

**25 DOLLARS** **KM# 202** **Weight:** 31.1035 g. **Composition:** 0.9999 Gold 1.0000 oz. AGW **Subject:** Golf - Hole in One **Obverse:** National arms **Reverse:** Golf ball rolling towards hole

| Date | Mintage | F | VF | XF | Unc | BU |
|---|---|---|---|---|---|---|

**25 DOLLARS** **KM# 190** **Weight:** 31.1035 g. **Composition:** 0.9999 Gold 1.0000 oz. AGW **Obverse:** Queen's portrait **Reverse:** Two flamingos

| Date | Mintage | F | VF | XF | Unc | BU |
|---|---|---|---|---|---|---|
| 1995 Proof | — | Value: 500 | | | | |

**25 DOLLARS** **KM# 180** **Weight:** 31.1035 g. **Composition:** 0.9999 Gold 1.0000 oz. AGW **Subject:** Third Millennium - Year 2000 **Obverse:** Queen's portrait **Reverse:** Sea shell-shaped world map

| Date | Mintage | F | VF | XF | Unc | BU |
|---|---|---|---|---|---|---|
| 1996 Proof | 5,000 | Value: 500 | | | | |

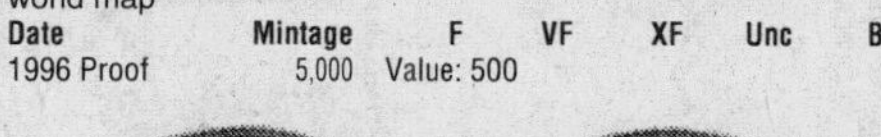

**50 DOLLARS** **KM# 13** **Weight:** 19.9710 g. **Composition:** 0.9170 Gold .5888 oz. AGW **Subject:** Adoption of New Constitution **Obverse:** Queen's portrait **Reverse:** Santa Maria

| Date | Mintage | F | VF | XF | Unc | BU |
|---|---|---|---|---|---|---|
| 1967 | 1,200 | — | — | — | 225 | — |
| 1967 Proof | 850 | Value: 300 | | | | |

**50 DOLLARS** **KM# 29** **Weight:** 19.9710 g. **Composition:** 0.9170 Gold .5888 oz. AGW

| Date | Mintage | F | VF | XF | Unc | BU |
|---|---|---|---|---|---|---|
| 1971 | 6,800 | — | — | — | 175 | — |
| 1971(t) Proof | 1,250 | Value: 225 | | | | |

**50 DOLLARS** **KM# 30** **Weight:** 19.9710 g. **Composition:** 0.9170 Gold .5888 oz. AGW **Reverse:** Hallmark and fineness stamped at bottom **Note:** Struck by the Gori and Zucchi Mint, Italy.

| Date | Mintage | F | VF | XF | Unc | BU |
|---|---|---|---|---|---|---|
| 1971 | — | — | — | — | 175 | — |

**50 DOLLARS** **KM# 36** **Weight:** 15.9700 g. **Composition:** 0.9170 Gold .4708 oz. AGW

| Date | Mintage | F | VF | XF | Unc | BU |
|---|---|---|---|---|---|---|
| 1972 | 2,250 | — | — | — | 175 | — |
| 1972 Proof | 1,250 | Value: 200 | | | | |

**50 DOLLARS** **KM# 45** **Weight:** 7.2700 g. **Composition:** 0.7500 Gold .1753 oz. AGW **Subject:** Independence Day - July 10 **Reverse:** Date below lobster; without fineness

| Date | Mintage | F | VF | XF | Unc | BU |
|---|---|---|---|---|---|---|
| 1973 | — | — | — | — | 60.00 | — |
| 1973 Proof | — | Value: 85.00 | | | | |

**50 DOLLARS** **KM# 46** **Weight:** 7.2700 g. **Composition:** 0.5850 Gold .1367 oz. AGW **Reverse:** .585 fineness to left, date to right

| Date | Mintage | F | VF | XF | Unc | BU |
|---|---|---|---|---|---|---|
| 1973 | 5,160 | — | — | — | 60.00 | — |
| 1973 Proof | 1,260 | Value: 85.00 | | | | |

**50 DOLLARS** **KM# 47** **Weight:** 7.3000 g. **Composition:** 0.7500 Gold .1760 oz. AGW **Reverse:** Without date or fineness

| Date | Mintage | F | VF | XF | Unc | BU |
|---|---|---|---|---|---|---|
| 1973 | — | — | — | — | 55.00 | — |

**50 DOLLARS** **KM# 48** **Weight:** 15.6448 g. **Composition:** 0.5000 Gold .2515 oz. AGW **Subject:** Independence Day - July 10

| Date | Mintage | F | VF | XF | Unc | BU |
|---|---|---|---|---|---|---|
| 1973JP | 23,000 | — | — | — | 100 | — |
| 1973JP | 18,000 | Value: 110 | | | | |

**50 DOLLARS** **KM# 69** **Weight:** 2.7300 g. **Composition:** 0.9170 Gold .0804 oz. AGW **Subject:** 1st Anniversary of Independence **Obverse:** Tobacco Dove **Reverse:** Without fineness

| Date | Mintage | F | VF | XF | Unc | BU |
|---|---|---|---|---|---|---|
| 1974 | 34,000 | — | — | — | 45.00 | — |
| 1974 Proof | 20,000 | Value: 50.00 | | | | |
| 1975 | 26,000 | — | — | — | 50.00 | — |
| 1975 Proof | 15,000 | Value: 55.00 | | | | |
| 1976 | 2,207 | — | — | — | 60.00 | — |
| 1976 Proof | Inc. above | Value: 55.00 | | | | |
| 1977 | 1,090 | — | — | — | 65.00 | — |
| 1977 Proof | — | Value: 85.00 | | | | |

**50 DOLLARS** **KM# 70** **Weight:** 2.7300 g. **Composition:** 0.9170 Gold .0804 oz. AGW **Reverse:** .917 fineness

| Date | Mintage | F | VF | XF | Unc | BU |
|---|---|---|---|---|---|---|
| 1974 | — | — | — | — | 50.00 | — |

**50 DOLLARS** **KM# 86** **Weight:** 2.6800 g. **Composition:** 0.5000 Gold .0430 oz. AGW **Obverse:** National arms **Reverse:** Flamingos in flight

| Date | Mintage | F | VF | XF | Unc | BU |
|---|---|---|---|---|---|---|
| 1981FM Proof | 2,050 | Value: 60.00 | | | | |

**50 DOLLARS** **KM# 92** **Weight:** 2.6800 g. **Composition:** 0.5000 Gold .0430 oz. AGW **Obverse:** National arms **Reverse:** Marlin (Swordfish)

| Date | Mintage | F | VF | XF | Unc | BU |
|---|---|---|---|---|---|---|
| 1982FM Proof | 841 | Value: 150 | | | | |

**50 DOLLARS** **KM# 98** **Weight:** 2.6800 g. **Composition:** 0.5000 Gold .0430 oz. AGW **Subject:** 10th Anniversary of Independence **Reverse:** Flamingo

| Date | Mintage | F | VF | XF | Unc | BU |
|---|---|---|---|---|---|---|
| 1983FM Proof | 962 | Value: 100 | | | | |

**50 DOLLARS** **KM# 103** **Weight:** 2.6800 g. **Composition:** 0.5000 Gold .0430 oz. AGW **Obverse:** National arms **Reverse:** Golden Allamanda

| Date | Mintage | F | VF | XF | Unc | BU |
|---|---|---|---|---|---|---|
| 1984FM Proof | 3,716 | Value: 50.00 | | | | |

**50 DOLLARS** **KM# 108** **Weight:** 2.6800 g. **Composition:** 0.5000 Gold .0430 oz. AGW **Obverse:** National arms **Reverse:** Santa Maria

| Date | Mintage | F | VF | XF | Unc | BU |
|---|---|---|---|---|---|---|
| 1985FM Proof | 1,575 | Value: 75.00 | | | | |

**50 DOLLARS** **KM# 199** **Weight:** 6.4800 g. **Composition:** 0.9167 Gold .1875 oz. AGW **Subject:** Jukando Festival **Obverse:** Queen's portrait **Reverse:** Three costumed magicians

| Date | Mintage | F | VF | XF | Unc | BU |
|---|---|---|---|---|---|---|
| 1994 Proof | — | Value: 150 | | | | |

**50 DOLLARS** **KM# 181** **Weight:** 2000.0000 g. **Composition:** 0.9990 Silver 64.2371 oz. ASW **Subject:** Third Millennium - Year 2000 **Obverse:** Queen's portrait **Reverse:** Sea shell-shaped world map

| Date | Mintage | F | VF | XF | Unc | BU |
|---|---|---|---|---|---|---|
| 1996 Proof | 2,000 | Value: 1,200 | | | | |

**100 DOLLARS** **KM# 14** **Weight:** 39.9400 g. **Composition:** 0.9170 Gold 1.1776 oz. AGW **Subject:** Adoption of New Constitution **Reverse:** Columbus

| Date | Mintage | F | VF | XF | Unc | BU |
|---|---|---|---|---|---|---|
| 1967 | 1,200 | — | — | — | 525 | — |
| 1967 Proof | 850 | Value: 600 | | | | |

**100 DOLLARS** **KM# 31** **Weight:** 39.9400 g. **Composition:** 0.9170 Gold 1.1776 oz. AGW

| Date | Mintage | F | VF | XF | Unc | BU |
|---|---|---|---|---|---|---|
| 1971 | 6,800 | — | — | — | 420 | — |
| 1971(t) Proof | 1,250 | Value: 575 | | | | |

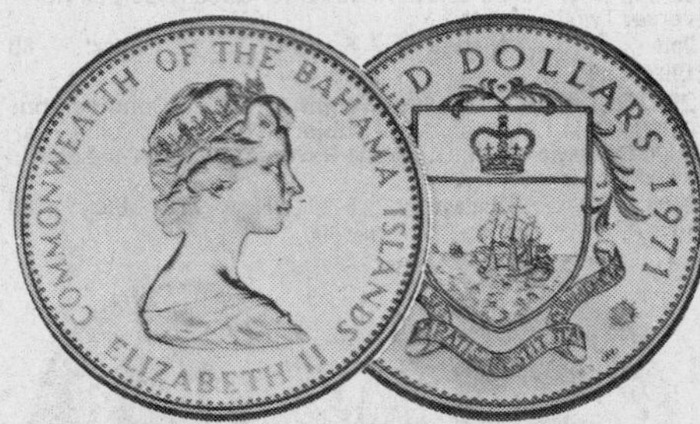


**100 DOLLARS** **KM# 32.1** **Weight:** 39.9400 g. **Composition:** 0.9170 Gold 1.1776 oz. AGW **Reverse:** Hallmark and fineness at bottom right

| Date | Mintage | F | VF | XF | Unc | BU |
|---|---|---|---|---|---|---|
| 1971 | — | — | — | — | 450 | — |

**100 DOLLARS** **KM# 32.2** **Weight:** 39.9400 g. **Composition:** 0.9170 Gold 1.1776 oz. AGW **Reverse:** Hallmark at bottom right, without fineness

| Date | Mintage | F | VF | XF | Unc | BU |
|---|---|---|---|---|---|---|
| 1971 | — | — | — | — | 450 | — |

**100 DOLLARS** **KM# 32.3** **Weight:** 39.9400 g. **Composition:** 0.9170 Gold 1.1776 oz. AGW **Reverse:** Fineness at bottom right without hallmark **Note:** Struck by the Gori and Zucchi Mint, Italy.

| Date | Mintage | F | VF | XF | Unc | BU |
|---|---|---|---|---|---|---|
| 1971 | — | — | — | — | 450 | — |

**100 DOLLARS** **KM# 37** **Weight:** 31.9500 g. **Composition:** 0.9170 Gold .9420 oz. AGW **Note:** The 1972 proof $100 is serially numbered on the edge.

| Date | Mintage | F | VF | XF | Unc | BU |
|---|---|---|---|---|---|---|
| 1972 | 2,250 | — | — | — | 375 | — |
| 1972 Proof | 1,250 | Value: 400 | | | | |

**100 DOLLARS** **KM# 49.1** **Weight:** 14.5400 g. **Composition:** 0.7500 Gold .3506 oz. AGW **Subject:** Independence Day - July 10 **Reverse:** Without fineness, date at bottom

| Date | Mintage | F | VF | XF | Unc | BU |
|---|---|---|---|---|---|---|
| 1973 | — | — | — | — | 120 | — |

**100 DOLLARS** **KM# 49.2** **Weight:** 14.5400 g. **Composition:** 0.7500 Gold .3506 oz. AGW **Subject:** Independence Day - July 10 **Reverse:** Without date or fineness

| Date | Mintage | F | VF | XF | Unc | BU |
|---|---|---|---|---|---|---|
| 1973 Proof | — | Value: 140 | | | | |

**100 DOLLARS** KM# 50.1 **Weight:** 14.5400 g. **Composition:** 0.5850 Gold .2735 oz. AGW **Reverse:** .585 fineness to left, date to right

| Date | Mintage | F | VF | XF | Unc | BU |
|---|---|---|---|---|---|---|
| 1973 | 4,660 | — | — | — | 115 | — |
| 1973 Proof | 1,260 | Value: 150 | | | | |

**Note:** Serial number on reverse

**100 DOLLARS** KM# 50.2 **Weight:** 14.5400 g. **Composition:** 0.5850 Gold .2735 oz. AGW **Reverse:** Date and fineness at right, serial number at left

| Date | Mintage | F | VF | XF | Unc | BU |
|---|---|---|---|---|---|---|
| 1973 | — | — | — | — | 140 | — |

**100 DOLLARS** KM# 50.3 **Weight:** 14.5400 g. **Composition:** 0.5850 Gold .2735 oz. AGW **Reverse:** Serial number at left, fineness below, date at right

| Date | Mintage | F | VF | XF | Unc | BU |
|---|---|---|---|---|---|---|
| 1973 | — | — | — | — | 150 | — |

**100 DOLLARS** KM# 71 **Weight:** 18.0145 g. **Composition:** 0.5000 Gold .2896 oz. AGW **Subject:** 1st Anniversary of Independence

| Date | Mintage | F | VF | XF | Unc | BU |
|---|---|---|---|---|---|---|
| 1974 | 4,486 | — | — | — | 110 | — |
| 1974 Proof | 4,153 | Value: 135 | | | | |

**100 DOLLARS** KM# 72 **Weight:** 5.4600 g. **Composition:** 0.9170 Gold .1609 oz. AGW **Reverse:** Broken waves behind flamingos' legs

| Date | Mintage | F | VF | XF | Unc | BU |
|---|---|---|---|---|---|---|
| 1974 | 29,000 | — | — | — | 65.00 | — |
| 1975 | — | — | — | — | 80.00 | — |

**100 DOLLARS** KM# 73 **Weight:** 5.4600 g. **Composition:** 0.9170 Gold .1609 oz. AGW **Reverse:** Unbroken waves behind flamingos' legs

| Date | Mintage | F | VF | XF | Unc | BU |
|---|---|---|---|---|---|---|
| 1974 Proof | 17,000 | Value: 75.00 | | | | |
| 1975 Proof | — | Value: 85.00 | | | | |
| 1976 | — | — | — | — | 90.00 | — |
| 1976 Proof | — | Value: 100 | | | | |
| 1977 | — | — | — | — | 110 | — |
| 1977 Proof | — | Value: 120 | | | | |

**100 DOLLARS** KM# 74 **Weight:** 5.4600 g. **Composition:** 0.9170 Gold .1609 oz. AGW **Reverse:** .917 fineness in oval

| Date | Mintage | F | VF | XF | Unc | BU |
|---|---|---|---|---|---|---|
| 1974 | — | — | — | — | 75.00 | — |

**100 DOLLARS** KM# 77 **Weight:** 18.0145 g. **Composition:** 0.5000 Gold .2896 oz. AGW **Subject:** 2nd Anniversary of Independence **Reverse:** Bahama Amazon Parrot

| Date | Mintage | F | VF | XF | Unc | BU |
|---|---|---|---|---|---|---|
| 1975 | 3,694 | — | — | — | 115 | — |
| 1975 Proof | 3,145 | Value: 125 | | | | |
| 1976 Proof | 761 | Value: 200 | | | | |
| 1977 Proof | 2,023 | Value: 150 | | | | |

**100 DOLLARS** KM# 80 **Weight:** 13.6000 g. **Composition:** 0.9630 Gold .4211 oz. AGW **Subject:** 5th Anniversary of Independence **Obverse:** Arms **Reverse:** H.R.H Prince Charles

| Date | Mintage | F | VF | XF | Unc | BU |
|---|---|---|---|---|---|---|
| 1978 Proof | 3,275 | Value: 200 | | | | |

**100 DOLLARS** KM# 81 **Weight:** 13.6000 g. **Composition:** 0.9630 Gold .4211 oz. AGW **Subject:** 5th Anniversary of Independence **Obverse:** Arms **Reverse:** Sir Milo B. Butler

| Date | Mintage | F | VF | XF | Unc | BU |
|---|---|---|---|---|---|---|
| 1978 Proof | 25,000 | Value: 200 | | | | |

**100 DOLLARS** KM# 87 **Weight:** 6.4800 g. **Composition:** 0.9000 Gold .1875 oz. AGW **Subject:** Wedding of Prince Charles and Lady Diana

| Date | Mintage | F | VF | XF | Unc | BU |
|---|---|---|---|---|---|---|
| 1981 Proof | 10,000 | Value: 150 | | | | |

**100 DOLLARS** KM# 99 **Weight:** 6.4800 g. **Composition:** 0.9000 Gold .1875 oz. AGW **Subject:** 10th Anniversary of Independence

| Date | Mintage | F | VF | XF | Unc | BU |
|---|---|---|---|---|---|---|
| 1983 Proof | 400 | Value: 185 | | | | |

**100 DOLLARS** KM# 111 **Weight:** 6.4800 g. **Composition:** 0.9000 Gold .1875 oz. AGW **Subject:** Columbus' Discovery of America

| Date | Mintage | F | VF | XF | Unc | BU |
|---|---|---|---|---|---|---|
| 1985 Proof | 450 | Value: 175 | | | | |

**100 DOLLARS** KM# 119 **Weight:** 6.4800 g. **Composition:** 0.9000 Gold .1875 oz. AGW **Obverse:** Queen's portrait **Reverse:** Queen Isabella and Christopher Columbus

| Date | Mintage | F | VF | XF | Unc | BU |
|---|---|---|---|---|---|---|
| 1987 Proof | 849 | Value: 175 | | | | |

**100 DOLLARS** KM# 125 **Weight:** 6.4800 g. **Composition:** 0.9000 Gold .1875 oz. AGW **Subject:** Columbus Discovering America **Obverse:** Queen Elizabeth **Reverse:** Columbus sighting America

| Date | Mintage | F | VF | XF | Unc | BU |
|---|---|---|---|---|---|---|
| 1988 Proof | 854 | Value: 175 | | | | |

**100 DOLLARS** KM# 130 **Weight:** 6.4800 g. **Composition:** 0.9000 Gold .1875 oz. AGW **Obverse:** Queen Elizabeth **Reverse:** Christopher Columbus

| Date | Mintage | F | VF | XF | Unc | BU |
|---|---|---|---|---|---|---|
| 1989 Proof | Est. 5,000 | Value: 150 | | | | |

**100 DOLLARS** KM# 135 **Weight:** 6.4800 g. **Composition:** 0.9000 Gold .1875 oz. AGW **Subject:** Discovery of New World **Obverse:** Queen Elizabeth II, date below **Reverse:** Columbus

| Date | Mintage | F | VF | XF | Unc | BU |
|---|---|---|---|---|---|---|
| 1990 | 500 | — | — | — | 250 | — |
| 1990 Proof | 5,000 | Value: 150 | | | | |

**100 DOLLARS** KM# 151 **Weight:** 6.4800 g. **Composition:** 0.9000 Gold .1875 oz. AGW **Subject:** Discovery of New World **Obverse:** Queen Elizabeth II, date below **Reverse:** 5-man rowboat

| Date | Mintage | F | VF | XF | Unc | BU |
|---|---|---|---|---|---|---|
| 1991 | 500 | — | — | — | — | — |

**100 DOLLARS** KM# 152 **Weight:** 6.4800 g. **Composition:** 0.9000 Gold .1875 oz. AGW **Subject:** Discovery of New World **Obverse:** Queen Elizabeth II, date below **Reverse:** Columbus' ships

| Date | Mintage | F | VF | XF | Unc | BU |
|---|---|---|---|---|---|---|
| 1992 Proof | Est. 5,000,000 | Value: 200 | | | | |
| 1992 Matte | — | Value: 250 | | | | |

**100 DOLLARS** **KM# 195** **Weight:** 999.9775 g. **Composition:** 0.9990 Silver 32.1500 oz. ASW **Subject:** Discovery of New World **Obverse:** Queen Elizabeth II, date below **Reverse:** Columbus' three ships

| Date | Mintage | F | VF | XF | Unc | BU |
|---|---|---|---|---|---|---|
| 1992 Proof | Est. 1,500 | Value: 700 | | | | |

**100 DOLLARS** **KM# 163** **Weight:** 999.9775 g. **Composition:** 0.9990 Silver 32.1500 oz. ASW **Series:** Whales of the World **Reverse:** Blue Whale

| Date | Mintage | F | VF | XF | Unc | BU |
|---|---|---|---|---|---|---|
| 1993 | 750 | — | — | — | — | — |

**100 DOLLARS** **KM# 184** **Weight:** 999.9775 g. **Composition:** 0.9990 Silver 32.1500 oz. ASW **Series:** Whales of the World **Reverse:** Killer Whale

| Date | Mintage | F | VF | XF | Unc | BU |
|---|---|---|---|---|---|---|
| 1994 Proof | 750 | Value: 750 | | | | |

**100 DOLLARS** **KM# 185** **Weight:** 999.9775 g. **Composition:** 0.9990 Silver 32.1500 oz. ASW **Series:** Whales of the World **Reverse:** Humpback Whale

| Date | Mintage | F | VF | XF | Unc | BU |
|---|---|---|---|---|---|---|
| 1995 Proof | 750 | Value: 750 | | | | |

**150 DOLLARS** **KM# 51** **Weight:** 8.1900 g. **Composition:** 0.9170 Gold .2414 oz. AGW **Subject:** Independence Day - July 10 **Reverse:** Lobster

| Date | Mintage | F | VF | XF | Unc | BU |
|---|---|---|---|---|---|---|
| 1973 | — | — | — | — | 90.00 | — |
| 1973 Proof | — | Value: 100 | | | | |
| 1974 | 7,128 | — | — | — | 115 | — |
| 1974 Proof | 4,787 | Value: 125 | | | | |
| 1975 | 3,141 | — | — | — | 150 | — |
| 1975 Proof | 2,770 | Value: 160 | | | | |
| 1976 Proof | 168 | Value: 250 | | | | |
| 1977 Proof | 327 | Value: 225 | | | | |

**150 DOLLARS** **KM# 52** **Weight:** 8.1900 g. **Composition:** 0.9170 Gold .2414 oz. AGW **Reverse:** Waves under lobster extend to its two front legs

| Date | Mintage | F | VF | XF | Unc | BU |
|---|---|---|---|---|---|---|
| 1974 Proof | — | Value: 125 | | | | |

**150 DOLLARS** **KM# 53** **Weight:** 8.1900 g. **Composition:** 0.9170 Gold .2414 oz. AGW **Reverse:** .917 fineness in oval

| Date | Mintage | F | VF | XF | Unc | BU |
|---|---|---|---|---|---|---|
| 1974 | — | — | — | — | 125 | — |

**200 DOLLARS** **KM# 54** **Weight:** 10.9200 g. **Composition:** 0.9170 Gold .3219 oz. AGW **Subject:** Independence Day - July 10

| Date | Mintage | F | VF | XF | Unc | BU |
|---|---|---|---|---|---|---|
| 1973 | — | — | — | — | 125 | — |
| 1973 Proof | — | Value: 135 | | | | |
| 1974 | 5,528 | — | — | — | 135 | — |
| 1974 Proof | 3,587 | Value: 140 | | | | |
| 1975 | 1,545 | — | — | — | 150 | — |
| 1975 Proof | 1,570 | Value: 150 | | | | |
| 1976 Proof | 168 | Value: 300 | | | | |
| 1977 Proof | 321 | Value: 280 | | | | |

**200 DOLLARS** **Weight:** 10.9200 g. **Composition:** 0.9170 Gold .3219 oz. AGW

| Date | Mintage | F | VF | XF | Unc | BU |
|---|---|---|---|---|---|---|
| 1974 Proof | — | Value: 135 | | | | |

**200 DOLLARS** **KM# 56** **Weight:** 10.9200 g. **Composition:** 0.9170 Gold .3219 oz. AGW **Reverse:** .917 fineness in oval

| Date | Mintage | F | VF | XF | Unc | BU |
|---|---|---|---|---|---|---|
| 1974 | — | — | — | — | 135 | — |

**200 DOLLARS** **KM# 57** **Weight:** 10.9200 g. **Composition:** 0.9170 Gold .3219 oz. AGW **Reverse:** .916 fineness at left, serial number stamped below arms

| Date | Mintage | F | VF | XF | Unc | BU |
|---|---|---|---|---|---|---|
| 1974 | — | — | — | — | 130 | — |

**200 DOLLARS** **Weight:** 10.9200 g. **Composition:** 0.9170 Gold .3219 oz. AGW **Reverse:** Without fineness, serial number to left

| Date | Mintage | F | VF | XF | Unc | BU |
|---|---|---|---|---|---|---|
| 1974 | — | — | — | — | 130 | — |

**250 DOLLARS** **KM# 83** **Weight:** 10.5800 g. **Composition:** 0.9000 Gold .3061 oz. AGW **Subject:** 250 Anniversary of Parliament

| Date | Mintage | F | VF | XF | Unc | BU |
|---|---|---|---|---|---|---|
| 1979 Proof | 1,835 | Value: 260 | | | | |

**250 DOLLARS** **KM# 137** **Weight:** 47.5400 g. **Composition:** 0.9170 Gold 1.4017 oz. AGW **Subject:** Royal Visit **Obverse:** Queen Elizabeth II **Reverse:** National arms

| Date | Mintage | F | VF | XF | Unc | BU |
|---|---|---|---|---|---|---|
| 1985 Proof | 100 | Value: 800 | | | | |

**250 DOLLARS** **KM# 117** **Weight:** 47.5400 g. **Composition:** 0.9170 Gold 1.4017 oz. AGW **Subject:** Commonwealth Games **Obverse:** National arms **Note:** Similar to 10 Dollars, KM#113.

| Date | Mintage | F | VF | XF | Unc | BU |
|---|---|---|---|---|---|---|
| 1985 Proof | 101 | Value: 800 | | | | |

**250 DOLLARS** **KM# 121** **Weight:** 47.5400 g. **Composition:** 0.9170 Gold 1.4017 oz. AGW **Obverse:** Queen Elizabeth II **Reverse:** Queen Isabella and Columbus

| Date | Mintage | F | VF | XF | Unc | BU |
|---|---|---|---|---|---|---|
| 1987 Proof | 100 | Value: 950 | | | | |

**250 DOLLARS** **KM# 126** **Weight:** 47.5400 g. **Composition:** 0.9170 Gold 1.4017 oz. AGW **Subject:** Columbus Discovering America **Obverse:** Queen Elizabeth **Reverse:** Columbus sighting America

| Date | Mintage | F | VF | XF | Unc | BU |
|---|---|---|---|---|---|---|
| 1988 Proof | 53 | Value: 1,200 | | | | |

**250 DOLLARS** **KM# 131** **Weight:** 47.5400 g. **Composition:** 0.9170 Gold 1.4017 oz. AGW **Obverse:** Queen Elizabeth **Reverse:** Christopher Columbus

| Date | Mintage | F | VF | XF | Unc | BU |
|---|---|---|---|---|---|---|
| 1989 Proof | Est. 250 | Value: 1,000 | | | | |

**250 DOLLARS** **KM# 136** **Weight:** 47.5400 g. **Composition:** 0.9170 Gold 1.4017 oz. AGW **Subject:** Discovery of New World **Obverse:** Queen Elizabeth II, date below **Reverse:** Native American

| Date | Mintage | F | VF | XF | Unc | BU |
|---|---|---|---|---|---|---|
| 1990 Proof | 500 | Value: 900 | | | | |

**250 DOLLARS** **KM# 175** **Weight:** 47.5400 g. **Composition:** 0.9170 Gold 1.4017 oz. AGW **Subject:** Discovery of New World

| Date | Mintage | F | VF | XF | Unc | BU |
|---|---|---|---|---|---|---|
| 1992 Proof | Est. 500 | Value: 900 | | | | |

**250 DOLLARS** **KM# 182** **Weight:** 47.5400 g. **Composition:** 0.9170 Gold 1.4017 oz. AGW **Subject:** Royal Visit **Note:** Similar to 2 Dollars, KM#158.

| Date | Mintage | F | VF | XF | Unc | BU |
|---|---|---|---|---|---|---|
| 1994 Proof | 100 | Value: 1,200 | | | | |

**500 DOLLARS** **KM# 88** **Weight:** 25.9200 g. **Composition:** 0.9000 Gold .7500 oz. AGW **Subject:** Wedding of Prince Charles and Lady Diana

| Date | Mintage | F | VF | XF | Unc | BU |
|---|---|---|---|---|---|---|
| 1981 Proof | 5,000 | Value: 550 | | | | |

**1000 DOLLARS** **KM# 100** **Weight:** 41.4700 g. **Composition:** 0.9000 Gold 1.2001 oz. AGW **Subject:** America's Cup Challenge

| Date | Mintage | F | VF | XF | Unc | BU |
|---|---|---|---|---|---|---|
| 1983 Proof | 300 | Value: 750 | | | | |

**2500 DOLLARS** **KM# 75** **Weight:** 407.2600 g. **Composition:** 0.9170 Gold 12.0082 oz. AGW **Note:** Similar to KM#66, Two Dollars.

| Date | Mintage | F | VF | XF | Unc | BU |
|---|---|---|---|---|---|---|
| 1974 Proof | 204 | Value: 6,000 | | | | |
| 1977 Proof | 168 | Value: 6,500 | | | | |

**2500 DOLLARS** **KM# 101** **Weight:** 407.2600 g. **Composition:** 0.9170 Gold 12.0082 oz. AGW **Subject:** 10th Anniversary of Independence

| Date | Mintage | F | VF | XF | Unc | BU |
|---|---|---|---|---|---|---|
| 1983 Proof | 55 | Value: 8,250 | | | | |

**2500 DOLLARS** **KM# 112** **Weight:** 407.2600 g. **Composition:** 0.9170 Gold 12.0082 oz. AGW **Subject:** Columbus' Discovery of America

| Date | Mintage | F | VF | XF | Unc | BU |
|---|---|---|---|---|---|---|
| 1985 Proof | 37 | Value: 8,250 | | | | |

**2500 DOLLARS** **KM# 116** **Weight:** 407.2600 g. **Composition:** 0.9170 Gold 12.0082 oz. AGW **Reverse:** Columbus and Isabella

| Date | Mintage | F | VF | XF | Unc | BU |
|---|---|---|---|---|---|---|
| 1987 Proof | 20 | Value: 10,000 | | | | |

**2500 DOLLARS** **KM# 122** **Weight:** 407.2600 g. **Composition:** 0.9170 Gold 12.0082 oz. AGW **Obverse:** Queen Elizabeth **Reverse:** Columbus sighting "New World"

| Date | Mintage | F | VF | XF | Unc | BU |
|---|---|---|---|---|---|---|
| 1988 Proof | 32 | Value: 10,000 | | | | |

## MINT SETS

| KM# | Date | Mintage | Identification | Issue Price | Mkt Val |
|---|---|---|---|---|---|
| MS1 | 1966 | 75,050 | KM#2-10 | 16.00 | 18.00 |
| MS2 | 1966 | 500,000 | KM#2-8 | 5.25 | 9.00 |
| MS3 | 1967 | 1,200 | KM#11-14 | 180 | 1,150 |
| MS4 | 1969 | 26,221 | KM#2-10 | 20.25 | 20.00 |
| MS5 | 1970 | 25,135 | KM#3-10, 15 | 20.25 | 20.00 |
| MS6 | 1971 | 12,895 | KM#16-24 | 20.25 | 20.00 |
| MS7 | 1971 | 6,800 | KM#25, 27, 29, 31 | 185 | 950 |
| MS8 | 1972 | 10,128 | KM#16-23, 33 | 22.75 | 19.00 |
| MS9 | 1972 | 2,250 | KM#34-37 | 185 | 700 |

| KM# | Date | Mintage | Identification | Issue Price | Mkt Val |
|---|---|---|---|---|---|
| MS10 | 1973 | 9,853 | KM#16-23, 33 | 23.75 | 19.00 |
| MS11 | 1973 | 4,660 | KM#40, 43, 47, 49.1 | — | 310 |
| MS12 | 1973 | — | KM#40, 43 | — | 85.00 |
| MS13 | 1974 | 11,004 | KM#59-67 | 22.50 | 16.00 |
| MS14 | 1974 | 5,528 | KM#51, 54, 69, 72 | — | 450 |
| MS15 | 1974 | — | KM#68, 71 | — | 170 |
| MS16 | 1975 | 3,845 | KM#59-67 | 27.00 | 18.00 |
| MS17 | 1975 | 1,545 | KM#51, 54, 69, 72 | — | 500 |
| MS18 | 1976 | 1,453 | KM#59-67 | 27.00 | 28.00 |
| MS19 | 1977 | 731 | KM#59-67 | 27.00 | 75.00 |
| MS20 | 1978 | 767 | KM#59-67 | 27.00 | 75.00 |
| MS21 | 1989 | — | KM#59a, 60-64, 65b | — | 30.00 |
| MS22 | 1991 | 5,000 | KM#59a, 60-64, 65b | — | 30.00 |
| MS23 | 1992 | — | KM#59a, 60-64, 65b | 24.00 | 30.00 |

## PROOF SETS

| KM# | Date | Mintage | Identification | Issue Price | Mkt Val |
|---|---|---|---|---|---|
| PS1 | 1967 | 850 | KM#11-14 | 252 | 1,245 |
| PS2 | 1969 | 10,381 | KM#2-10 | 35.00 | 25.00 |
| PS3 | 1970 | 22,827 | KM#3-10, 15 | 35.00 | 30.00 |
| PS5B | 1971 | — | KM#26, 28, 30, 32.1 | — | 800 |
| PS4 | 1971 | 30,507 | KM#16-24 | 35.00 | 25.00 |
| PS5A | 1971 | 1,250 | KM#25, 27, 29, 31 | 298 | 1,100 |
| PS6 | 1972 | 34,789 | KM#16-23, 33 | 35.00 | 25.00 |
| PS7 | 1972 | 1,250 | KM#34-37 | 565 | 1,000 |
| PS8 | 1973 | 34,815 | KM#16-23, 33 | 35.00 | 25.00 |
| PS9 | 1973 | 1,260 | KM#41, 44, 46, 50 | 402 | 375 |
| PS10 | 1974 | 93,776 | KM#59-63, 64a-67a | 45.00 | 25.00 |
| PS11 | 1974 | 3,587 | KM#51, 54, 69, 73 | 1,000 | 525 |
| PS12 | 1975 | 29,095 | KM#59-63, 64a-67a | 59.00 | 30.00 |
| PS13 | 1975 | 1,570 | KM#51, 54, 69, 73 | 1,000 | 525 |
| PS14 | 1976 | 22,570 | KM#59-63, 64a-67a | 59.00 | 28.00 |
| PS15 | 1976 | — | KM#51, 54, 69, 73 | 1,000 | 695 |
| PS16 | 1977 | 10,812 | KM#59-63, 64a-67a | 59.00 | 35.00 |
| PS17 | 1977 | — | KM#51, 54, 69, 73 | — | 625 |
| PS18 | 1978 | 6,931 | KM#59-63, 64a-67a | 59.00 | 45.00 |
| PS19 | 1979 | 2,053 | KM#59-63, 64a-67a | 115 | 65.00 |
| PS20 | 1979 | — | KM#82-83 | 445 | 300 |
| PS21 | 1980 | 2,084 | KM#59-63, 64a-67a | 145 | 65.00 |
| PS22 | 1981 | 1,980 | KM#59-64, 65b-67b | 62.00 | 60.00 |
| PS23 | 1982 | — | KM#59-64, 89-91 | 67.00 | 75.00 |
| PS24 | 1983 | 1,009 | KM#59-64, 93-95 | 67.00 | 75.00 |
| PS25 | 1984 | 7,500 | KM#59-64, 104-106 | 72.00 | 60.00 |
| PS26 | 1985 | 1,576 | KM#59-64, 104, 105, 107 | — | 65.00 |
| PS27 | 1989 | 2,000 | KM#59a, 60-64, 65b, 66c, 132 | 106 | 100 |
| PS28 | 1991 | 25,000 | KM#139-150 | 425 | 400 |
| PS29 | 1992 | 750 | KM#192-194 + gold-plated silver ingot | — | 400 |

# BAHRAIN

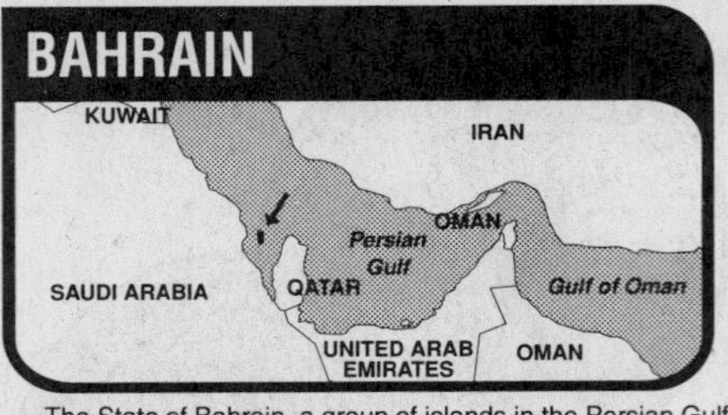


The State of Bahrain, a group of islands in the Persian Gulf off Saudi Arabia, has an area of 268 sq. mi. (622 sq. km.) and a population of 618,000. Capital: Manama. Prior to the depression of the 1930's, the economy was based on pearl fishing. Petroleum and aluminum industries and transit trade are the vital factors in the economy today.

The Portuguese occupied the islands in 1507 but were driven out in 1602 by Arab subjects of Persia. They in turn were ejected by Arabs of the Ataiba tribe from the Arabian mainland who have maintained possession up to the present time. The ruling sheikh of Bahrain entered into relations with Great Britain in 1805 and concluded a binding treaty of protection in 1861. In 1968 Great Britain decided to terminate treaty relations with the Persian Gulf sheikhdoms. Unable to agree on terms of union with the other sheikhdoms, Bahrain decided to seek independence as a separate entity and became fully independent on August 14, 1971.

Bahrain took part in the Arab oil embargo against the U.S. and other nations. The government bought controlling interest in the oil industry in 1975.

The coinage of the State of Bahrain was struck at the Royal Mint, London, England.

**RULERS**

**Al Khalifa Dynasty**
Isa Bin Ali, 1869-1932
Hamad Bin Isa, 1932-1942
Salman Bin Hamad, 1942-1961
Isa Bin Salman, 1961-1999
Hamed Bin Isa, 1999-

**MINT MARKS**

Bahrain بحرين

al-Bahrain = of the two seas البحرين

**MONETARY SYSTEM**

*Falus, Fulus* *Fals, Fils* *Falsan*

1000 Fils = 1 Dinar

**FILS KM# 1 Composition:** Bronze

| Date | Mintage | F | VF | XF | Unc | BU |
|---|---|---|---|---|---|---|
| AH1385(1965) | 1,500,000 | — | 0.10 | 0.20 | 0.40 | — |
| AH1385 Proof | 12,000 | Value: 1.00 | | | | |
| AH1386(1966) | 1,500,000 | — | 0.10 | 0.20 | 0.40 | — |
| AH1386 Proof | — | Value: 2.00 | | | | |

**FILS KM# 1a Weight:** 1.5000 g. **Composition:** 0.9250 Silver .0446 oz. ASW

| Date | Mintage | F | VF | XF | Unc | BU |
|---|---|---|---|---|---|---|
| AH1403 Proof | Est. 15,000 | Value: 3.00 | | | | |

**5 FILS KM# 2 Composition:** Bronze

| Date | Mintage | F | VF | XF | Unc | BU |
|---|---|---|---|---|---|---|
| AH1385(1965) | 8,000,000 | — | 0.10 | 0.20 | 0.40 | — |
| AH1385 Proof | 12,000 | Value: 1.00 | | | | |

**5 FILS KM# 2a Weight:** 2.0000 g. **Composition:** 0.9250 Silver .0595 oz. ASW

| Date | Mintage | F | VF | XF | Unc | BU |
|---|---|---|---|---|---|---|
| AH1403 Proof | Est. 15,000 | Value: 3.00 | | | | |

**5 FILS KM# 16 Composition:** Brass **Obverse:** Palm Tree

| Date | Mintage | F | VF | XF | Unc | BU |
|---|---|---|---|---|---|---|
| AH1412(1991) | — | — | — | — | 0.50 | — |

**10 FILS KM# 3 Composition:** Bronze

| Date | Mintage | F | VF | XF | Unc | BU |
|---|---|---|---|---|---|---|
| AH1385(1965) | 8,500,000 | — | 0.10 | 0.25 | 0.50 | — |
| AH1385 Proof | 12,000 | Value: 1.50 | | | | |

**10 FILS KM# 3a Weight:** 4.7500 g. **Composition:** 0.9250 Silver .1413 oz. ASW

| Date | Mintage | F | VF | XF | Unc | BU |
|---|---|---|---|---|---|---|
| AH1403 Proof | Est. 15,000 | Value: 4.00 | | | | |

**10 FILS KM# 17 Composition:** Brass **Obverse:** Palm Tree

| Date | Mintage | F | VF | XF | Unc | BU |
|---|---|---|---|---|---|---|
| AH1412(1991) | — | — | — | — | 0.75 | — |
| AH1420(2000) | — | — | — | — | 0.75 | — |

**25 FILS KM# 4 Composition:** Copper Nickel

| Date | Mintage | F | VF | XF | Unc | BU |
|---|---|---|---|---|---|---|
| AH1385(1965) | 11,250,000 | — | 0.20 | 0.35 | 0.75 | — |
| AH1385 Proof | 12,000 | Value: 2.00 | | | | |

**25 FILS KM# 4a Weight:** 1.7500 g. **Composition:** 0.9250 Silver .0521 oz. ASW

| Date | Mintage | F | VF | XF | Unc | BU |
|---|---|---|---|---|---|---|
| AH1403 Proof | Est. 15,000 | Value: 4.00 | | | | |

**25 FILS KM# 18 Composition:** Copper-Nickel **Obverse:** Ancient Painting

| Date | Mintage | F | VF | XF | Unc | BU |
|---|---|---|---|---|---|---|
| AH1412(1991) | — | — | — | — | 1.25 | — |

**50 FILS KM# 5 Composition:** Copper-Nickel

| Date | Mintage | F | VF | XF | Unc | BU |
|---|---|---|---|---|---|---|
| AH1385(1965) | 6,909,000 | — | 0.25 | 0.55 | 1.25 | — |
| AH1385 Proof | 12,000 | Value: 2.50 | | | | |

**50 FILS KM# 5a Weight:** 3.1000 g. **Composition:** 0.9250 Silver .0922 oz. ASW

| Date | Mintage | F | VF | XF | Unc | BU |
|---|---|---|---|---|---|---|
| AH1403 Proof | Est. 15,000 | Value: 5.00 | | | | |

**50 FILS** **KM# 19** **Composition:** Copper-Nickel **Obverse:** Stylized Sail Boats

| Date | Mintage | F | VF | XF | Unc | BU |
|---|---|---|---|---|---|---|
| AH1412(1991) | — | — | — | — | 1.50 | — |

**100 FILS** **KM# 6** **Composition:** Copper-Nickel

| Date | Mintage | F | VF | XF | Unc | BU |
|---|---|---|---|---|---|---|
| AH1385(1965) | 8,300,000 | — | 0.35 | 0.75 | 1.50 | — |
| AH1385 Proof | 12,000 | Value: 3.50 | | | | |

**100 FILS** **KM# 6a** **Weight:** 6.5000 g. **Composition:** 0.9250 Silver .1933 oz. ASW

| Date | Mintage | F | VF | XF | Unc | BU |
|---|---|---|---|---|---|---|
| AH1403 Proof | Est. 15,000 | Value: 6.00 | | | | |

**100 FILS** **KM# 20** **Ring Composition:** Brass **Center Composition:** Copper-Nickel **Obverse:** Coat of Arms

| Date | Mintage | F | VF | XF | Unc | BU |
|---|---|---|---|---|---|---|
| AH1412(1991) | — | — | — | — | 3.50 | — |
| AH1415(1994) | — | — | — | — | 3.50 | — |
| AH1417(1996) | — | — | — | — | 3.50 | — |

**250 FILS** **KM# 7** **Composition:** Copper-Nickel **Series:** F.A.O.

| Date | Mintage | F | VF | XF | Unc | BU |
|---|---|---|---|---|---|---|
| AH1389(1969) | 50,000 | — | 1.50 | 2.50 | 5.00 | — |
| AH1389 Proof | — | Value: 8.00 | | | | |
| AH1403(1982) | 3,000 | — | 1.75 | 3.50 | 10.00 | — |

**250 FILS** **KM# 7a** **Weight:** 15.0000 g. **Composition:** 0.9250 Silver .4461 oz. ASW

| Date | Mintage | F | VF | XF | Unc | BU |
|---|---|---|---|---|---|---|
| AH1403 Proof | Est. 15,000 | Value: 14.50 | | | | |

**500 FILS** **KM# 8** **Weight:** 18.3000 g. **Composition:** 0.8000 Silver .4707 oz. ASW **Reverse:** Opening of Isa Town

| Date | Mintage | F | VF | XF | Unc | BU |
|---|---|---|---|---|---|---|
| AH1385 Proof | 12,000 | Value: 17.50 | | | | |
| AH1388(1968) | 50,000 | — | 2.50 | 5.50 | 12.50 | — |
| AH1388 Proof | — | Value: 17.50 | | | | |

**500 FILS** **KM# 8a** **Weight:** 18.0600 g. **Composition:** 0.9250 Silver .5372 oz. ASW

| Date | Mintage | F | VF | XF | Unc | BU |
|---|---|---|---|---|---|---|
| AH1403 Proof | Est. 15,000 | Value: 35.00 | | | | |

**5 DINARS** **KM# 13** **Weight:** 19.4400 g. **Composition:** 0.9250 Silver .5782 oz. ASW **Reverse:** Gazelle **Edge Lettering:** World Wildlife Fund

| Date | Mintage | F | VF | XF | Unc | BU |
|---|---|---|---|---|---|---|
| AH1406 Proof | Est. 25,000 | Value: 35.00 | | | | |

**5 DINARS** **KM# 14** **Weight:** 19.4400 g. **Composition:** 0.9250 Silver .5782 oz. ASW **Reverse:** Save The Children

| Date | Mintage | F | VF | XF | Unc | BU |
|---|---|---|---|---|---|---|
| AH1410 Proof | Est. 20,000 | Value: 36.50 | | | | |

**5 DINARS** **KM# 21** **Weight:** 28.2300 g. **Composition:** 0.9250 Silver .8395 oz. ASW **Subject:** 50th Anniversary - United Nations **Obverse:** Portrait of Amir **Reverse:** UN building

| Date | Mintage | F | VF | XF | Unc | BU |
|---|---|---|---|---|---|---|
| AH1416 Proof | — | Value: 37.50 | | | | |

**50 DINARS** **KM# 11** **Weight:** 15.9800 g. **Composition:** 0.9170 Gold .4712 oz. AGW **Subject:** 50th Anniversary of Bahrain Monetary Agency

| Date | Mintage | F | VF | XF | Unc | BU |
|---|---|---|---|---|---|---|
| AH1398 Proof | 5,000 | Value: 300 | | | | |

**100 DINARS** **KM# 12** **Weight:** 31.9600 g. **Composition:** 0.9170 Gold .9424 oz. AGW **Subject:** 50th Anniversary of Bahrain Monetary Agency

| Date | Mintage | F | VF | XF | Unc | BU |
|---|---|---|---|---|---|---|
| AH1398 Proof | 5,000 | Value: 600 | | | | |

## MEDALLIC COINAGE

**10 DINARS** **KM# M1** **Weight:** 16.0000 g. **Composition:** 0.9170 Gold .4717 oz. AGW **Reverse:** Opening of Isa Town

| Date | Mintage | F | VF | XF | Unc | BU |
|---|---|---|---|---|---|---|
| AH1388(1968) | 3,000 | — | — | — | 350 | — |

**10 DINARS** **KM# M2** **Weight:** 16.0000 g. **Composition:** 0.9170 Gold .4717 oz. AGW **Reverse:** Independence Commemorative

| Date | Mintage | F | VF | XF | Unc | BU |
|---|---|---|---|---|---|---|
| AH1391(1971) | 3,000 | — | — | — | 350 | — |

**10 DINARS** **KM# M3** **Weight:** 16.0000 g. **Composition:** 0.9170 Gold .4717 oz. AGW **Reverse:** Opening of Hamad Town

| Date | Mintage | F | VF | XF | Unc | BU |
|---|---|---|---|---|---|---|
| AH1404 Proof | — | Value: 300 | | | | |

## MINT SETS

| KM# | Date | Mintage | Identification | Issue Price | Mkt Val |
|---|---|---|---|---|---|
| MS1 | 1992 | — | KM#16-20 | — | 10.00 |

## PROOF SETS

| KM# | Date | Mintage | Identification | Issue Price | Mkt Val |
|---|---|---|---|---|---|
| PS1 | Mixed | 20,000 | KM#1-6 1965; KM7 1969; KM8 1968 | 32.00 | 35.00 |
| PS2 | 1965 | 12,000 | KM#1-6, 8 | — | 30.00 |
| PS3 | 1983 | 15,000 | KM#1a-8a | 99.00 | 75.00 |

# BANGLADESH

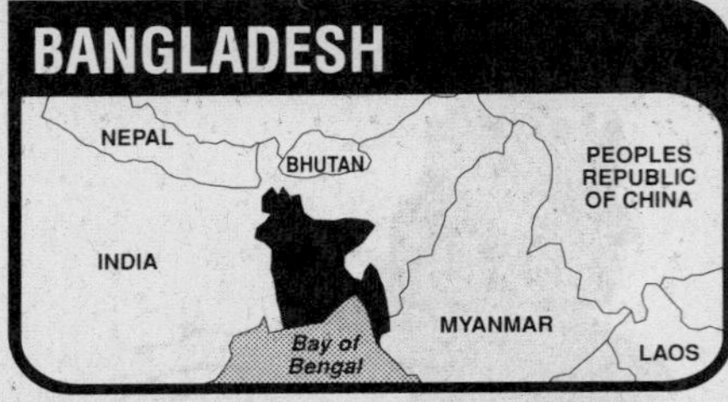


The Peoples Republic of Bangladesh (formerly East Pakistan), a parliamentary democracy located on the Bay of Bengal bordered by India and Burma, has an area of 55,598 sq. mi. (143,998 sq. km.) and a population of 128.1 million. Capital: Dhaka. The economy is predominantly agricultural. Jute products, jute and tea are exported.

British rule over the vast Indian sub-continent ended in 1947 when British India attained independence and was partitioned into the two successor states of India and Pakistan. Pakistan consisted of East and West Pakistan, two areas united by the Moslem religion but separated by culture and 1,000 miles of Indian territory. Restive under the de facto rule of the militant but fewer West Pakistanis, the East Pakistanis unsuccessfully demanded greater economic benefits and political reforms. The inability of the leaders of East and West Pakistan to resolve a political breakdown occasioned by the East Pakistan success in the general elections of 1970 precipitated massive civil disobedience in East Pakistan which West Pakistan sought to suppress militarily. East Pakistan seceded from Pakistan, March 26, 1971, and with the support of India declared an independent Peoples Republic of Bangladesh.

Bangladesh is a member of the Commonwealth of Nations. The president is the Head of State and the Government.

**MONETARY SYSTEM**

100 Poisha = 1 Taka

**DATING**

Christian era using Bengali numerals.

**POISHA** **KM# 5** **Composition:** Aluminum

| Date | Mintage | F | VF | XF | Unc | BU |
|---|---|---|---|---|---|---|
| 1974 | 300,000,000 | — | — | 0.10 | 0.15 | — |

**5 POISHA** **KM# 1** **Composition:** Aluminum

| Date | Mintage | F | VF | XF | Unc | BU |
|---|---|---|---|---|---|---|
| 1973 | Est. 47,088,000 | — | — | 0.10 | 0.20 | — |
| 1974 | — | — | — | 0.10 | 0.20 | — |

**5 POISHA** **KM# 6** **Composition:** Aluminum **Series:** F.A.O.

| Date | Mintage | F | VF | XF | Unc | BU |
|---|---|---|---|---|---|---|
| 1974 | 5,000,000 | — | — | 0.10 | 0.20 | — |
| 1975 | 3,000,000 | — | — | 0.10 | 0.20 | — |
| 1976 | 3,000,000 | — | — | 0.10 | 0.20 | — |
| 1977 | — | — | — | 0.10 | 0.20 | — |

**5 POISHA** **KM# 10** **Composition:** Aluminum **Series:** F.A.O.

| Date | Mintage | F | VF | XF | Unc | BU |
|---|---|---|---|---|---|---|
| 1977 | 90,000,000 | — | — | 0.10 | 0.15 | — |
| 1978 | 52,432,000 | — | — | 0.10 | 0.25 | — |
| 1979 | 120,096,000 | — | — | 0.10 | 0.15 | — |
| 1980 | 127,008,000 | — | — | 0.10 | 0.15 | — |
| 1981 | 72,992,000 | — | — | 0.10 | 0.15 | — |

**10 POISHA** **KM# 2** **Composition:** Aluminum

| Date | Mintage | F | VF | XF | Unc | BU |
|---|---|---|---|---|---|---|
| 1973 | Est. 21,500,000 | — | — | 0.10 | 0.35 | — |
| 1974 | — | — | — | 0.10 | 0.35 | — |

**10 POISHA** **KM# 7** **Composition:** Aluminum **Series:** F.A.O.

| Date | Mintage | F | VF | XF | Unc | BU |
|---|---|---|---|---|---|---|
| 1974 | 5,000,000 | — | — | 0.15 | 0.35 | — |
| 1975 | 4,000,000 | — | — | 0.15 | 0.35 | — |
| 1976 | 4,000,000 | — | — | 0.15 | 0.35 | — |
| 1977 | 4,000,000 | — | — | 0.15 | 0.35 | — |
| 1978 | 141,744,000 | — | — | 0.15 | 0.30 | — |
| 1979 | — | — | — | 0.15 | 0.40 | — |

**10 POISHA** **KM# 11.1** **Composition:** Aluminum **Series:** F.A.O.

| Date | Mintage | F | VF | XF | Unc | BU |
|---|---|---|---|---|---|---|
| 1977 | 48,000,000 | — | — | 0.15 | 0.30 | — |
| 1978 | 77,518,000 | — | — | 0.15 | 0.30 | — |
| 1979 | 170,112,000 | — | — | 0.15 | 0.30 | — |
| 1980 | 200,000,000 | — | — | 0.15 | 0.30 | — |

**10 POISHA** **KM# 11.2** **Composition:** Aluminum

| Date | Mintage | F | VF | XF | Unc | BU |
|---|---|---|---|---|---|---|
| 1981 | — | — | — | 0.25 | 0.50 | — |
| 1983 | 142,848,000 | — | — | 0.15 | 0.30 | — |
| 1984 | 57,152,000 | — | — | 0.15 | 0.30 | — |

**25 POISHA** **KM# 3** **Composition:** Steel **Obverse:** Rohy

| Date | Mintage | F | VF | XF | Unc | BU |
|---|---|---|---|---|---|---|
| 1973 | Est. 25,072,000 | — | — | 0.25 | 0.75 | — |

**25 POISHA** **KM# 8** **Composition:** Steel **Series:** F.A.O.

| Date | Mintage | F | VF | XF | Unc | BU |
|---|---|---|---|---|---|---|
| 1974 | 5,000,000 | — | — | 0.20 | 0.50 | — |
| 1975 | 6,000,000 | — | — | 0.20 | 0.50 | — |
| 1976 | 6,000,000 | — | — | 0.20 | 0.50 | — |
| 1977 | 51,300,000 | — | — | 0.15 | 0.35 | — |
| 1978 | 66,750,000 | — | — | 0.15 | 0.35 | — |
| 1979 | — | — | — | 0.15 | 0.35 | — |

**25 POISHA** **KM# 12** **Composition:** Steel **Series:** F.A.O.

| Date | Mintage | F | VF | XF | Unc | BU |
|---|---|---|---|---|---|---|
| 1977 | 45,300,000 | — | — | 0.15 | 0.40 | — |
| 1978 | 66,750,000 | — | — | 0.15 | 0.40 | — |
| 1979 | 56,704,000 | — | — | 0.15 | 0.40 | — |
| 1980 | 228,992,000 | — | — | 0.15 | 0.40 | — |
| 1981 | 45,072,000 | — | — | 0.15 | 0.40 | — |
| 1983 | 96,128,000 | — | — | 0.15 | 0.35 | — |
| 1984 | 203,872,000 | — | — | 0.15 | 0.35 | — |
| 1991 | 50,002,000 | — | — | 0.15 | 0.35 | — |

**50 POISHA** **KM# 4** **Composition:** Steel

| Date | Mintage | F | VF | XF | Unc | BU |
|---|---|---|---|---|---|---|
| 1973 | 18,000,000 | — | 0.25 | 0.75 | 2.50 | — |

**50 POISHA** **KM# 13** **Composition:** Steel **Series:** F.A.O.

| Date | Mintage | F | VF | XF | Unc | BU |
|---|---|---|---|---|---|---|
| 1977 | 12,700,000 | — | — | 0.20 | 0.75 | — |
| 1978 | 37,300,000 | — | — | 0.20 | 0.75 | — |
| 1979 | 2,208,000 | — | — | 0.20 | 0.75 | — |
| 1980 | 124,512,000 | — | — | 0.20 | 0.50 | — |
| 1981 | 36,680,000 | — | — | 0.20 | 0.75 | — |
| 1983 | 31,392,000 | — | — | 0.20 | 0.75 | — |
| 1984 | 168,608,000 | — | — | 0.20 | 0.50 | — |
| 1994 | — | — | — | 0.20 | 0.50 | — |

**TAKA** **KM# 9.1** **Composition:** Copper-Nickel **Series:** F.A.O. **Obverse:** Stylized family **Reverse:** Shapla flower

| Date | Mintage | F | VF | XF | Unc | BU |
|---|---|---|---|---|---|---|
| 1975 | 4,000,000 | — | 0.15 | 0.45 | 1.00 | — |
| 1976 | — | — | 0.15 | 0.45 | 1.00 | — |
| 1977 | — | — | 0.15 | 0.45 | 1.00 | — |

**TAKA** **KM# 17** **Weight:** 31.3500 g. **Composition:** 0.9250 Silver .9323 oz. ASW **Subject:** 20th Victory Day **Obverse:** Seven portraits **Reverse:** National memorial

| Date | Mintage | F | VF | XF | Unc | BU |
|---|---|---|---|---|---|---|
| 1991 Proof | — | Value: 32.50 | | | | |

**TAKA** **KM# 14** **Weight:** 31.3500 g. **Composition:** 0.9250 Silver .9323 oz. ASW **Reverse:** Olympics - Runners with Torch

| Date | Mintage | F | VF | XF | Unc | BU |
|---|---|---|---|---|---|---|
| 1992 Proof | Est. 40,000 | Value: 32.50 | | | | |

**TAKA** **KM# 9.2** **Composition:** Steel **Note:** Non-magnetic. Varieties exist.

| Date | Mintage | F | VF | XF | Unc | BU |
|---|---|---|---|---|---|---|
| 1992 | — | — | 15.00 | 0.45 | 1.00 | — |
| 1993 | — | — | 0.15 | 0.45 | 1.00 | — |
| 1995 | — | — | 0.15 | 0.45 | 1.00 | — |

**TAKA** **KM# 15** **Weight:** 31.3500 g. **Composition:** 0.9250 Silver .9323 oz. ASW **Subject:** Engangered Wildlife **Reverse:** Deer

| Date | Mintage | F | VF | XF | Unc | BU |
|---|---|---|---|---|---|---|
| 1993 Proof | Est. 15,000 | Value: 37.50 | | | | |

**TAKA** **KM# 16** **Weight:** 31.3500 g. **Composition:** 0.9250 Silver .9323 oz. ASW **Subject:** World Cup Soccer, 1994

| Date | Mintage | F | VF | XF | Unc | BU |
|---|---|---|---|---|---|---|
| 1993 Proof | 40,000 | Value: 35.00 | | | | |

**TAKA** **KM# 9.3** **Composition:** Brass

| Date | Mintage | F | VF | XF | Unc | BU |
|---|---|---|---|---|---|---|
| 1996 | — | — | 0.20 | 0.65 | 1.85 | — |

**5 TAKA** **KM# 18.1** **Weight:** 7.8700 g. **Composition:** Steel **Obverse:** Shapla flower **Reverse:** Bridge

| Date | Mintage | F | VF | XF | Unc | BU |
|---|---|---|---|---|---|---|
| 1994 | — | — | — | — | 1.75 | — |

**5 TAKA** **KM# 18.2** **Weight:** 8.1700 g. **Composition:** Steel **Obverse:** Shapla flower, thicker design

| Date | Mintage | F | VF | XF | Unc | BU |
|---|---|---|---|---|---|---|
| 1996 | — | — | — | — | 2.25 | — |

# BARBADOS

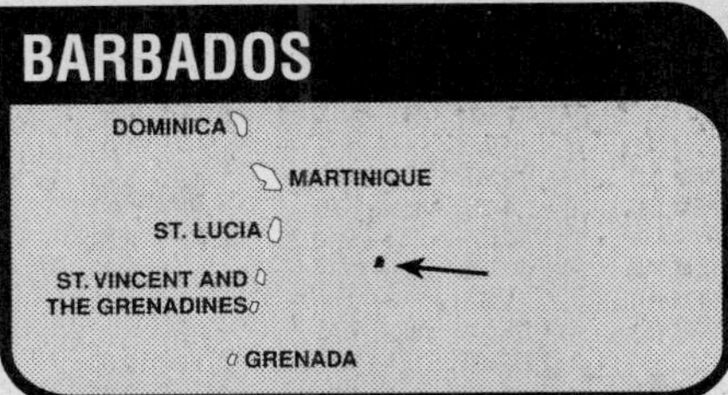


Barbados, an independent state within the British Commonwealth, is located in the Windward Islands of the West Indies east of St. Vincent. The coral island has an area of 166 sq. mi. (430 sq. km.) and a population of 269,000. Capital: Bridgetown. The economy is based on sugar and tourism. Sugar, petroleum products, molasses, and rum are exported.

Barbados was named by the Portuguese who achieved the first landing on the island in 1563. British sailors landed at the site of present-day Holetown in 1624. Barbados was under uninterrupted British control from the time of the first British settlement in 1627 until it obtained independence on Nov. 30, 1966. It is a member of the Commonwealth of Nations. Elizabeth II is Head of State as Queen of Barbados.

Unmarked side cut pieces of Spanish and Spanish Colonial 1, 2 and 8 reales were the principal coinage medium of 18th-century Barbados. The "Neptune" tokens issued by Sir Phillip Gibbs, a local plantation owner, circulated freely but were never established as legal coinage. The coinage and banknotes of the British Caribbean Territories (Eastern Group) were employed prior to 1973 when Barbados issued a decimal coinage.

**RULERS**

British, until 1966

**MINT MARKS**

FM - Franklin Mint, U.S.A.*

None - Royal Mint

***NOTE**: From 1975-1985 the Franklin Mint produced coinage in up to 3 different qualities. Qualities of issue are designated in ( ) after each date and are defined as follows:

**(M) MATTE** - Normal circulation strike or a dull finish produced by sandblasting special uncirculated (polish finish) or proof quality dies.

**(U) SPECIAL UNCIRCULATED** - Polished or proof-like in appearance without any frosted features.

**(P) PROOF** - The highest quality obtainable having mirror-like fields and frosted features.

**MONETARY SYSTEM**

100 Cents = 1 Dollar

## INDEPENDENT SOVEREIGN STATE

### within the British Commonwealth.

## DECIMAL COINAGE

**CENT** **KM# 10** **Composition:** Bronze

| Date | Mintage | F | VF | XF | Unc | BU |
|---|---|---|---|---|---|---|
| 1973 | 5,000,000 | — | — | 0.10 | 0.25 | — |
| 1973FM (M) | 7,500 | — | — | — | 1.00 | — |
| 1973FM (P) | 97,000 | Value: 0.50 | | | | |
| 1974FM (M) | 8,708 | — | — | — | 1.00 | — |
| 1974FM (P) | 36,000 | Value: 0.50 | | | | |
| 1975FM (M) | 5,000 | — | — | — | 0.75 | — |
| 1975FM (U) | 1,360 | — | — | — | 1.00 | — |
| 1975FM (P) | 20,000 | Value: 0.50 | | | | |
| 1977FM (M) | 2,102 | — | — | — | 0.75 | — |
| 1977FM (U) | 468 | — | — | — | 3.00 | — |
| 1977FM (P) | 5,014 | Value: 0.50 | | | | |
| 1978 | 4,807,000 | — | — | 0.10 | 0.25 | — |
| 1978FM (M) | 2,000 | — | — | — | 1.00 | — |
| 1978FM (U) | 2,517 | — | — | — | 1.50 | — |
| 1978FM (P) | 4,436 | Value: 1.00 | | | | |
| 1979 | 5,606,000 | — | — | 0.10 | 0.25 | — |
| 1979FM (M) | 1,500 | — | — | — | 1.00 | — |
| 1979FM (U) | 523 | — | — | — | 2.50 | — |
| 1979FM (P) | 4,126 | Value: 1.00 | | | | |
| 1980 | 14,400,000 | — | — | 0.10 | 0.25 | — |
| 1980FM (M) | 1,500 | — | — | — | 1.00 | — |
| 1980FM (U) | 649 | — | — | — | 2.00 | — |
| 1980FM (P) | 2,111 | Value: 1.50 | | | | |
| 1981 | 10,160,000 | — | — | 0.10 | 0.25 | — |
| 1981FM (M) | 1,500 | — | — | — | 1.00 | — |
| 1981FM (U) | 327 | — | — | — | 2.00 | — |
| 1981FM (P) | 943 | Value: 1.50 | | | | |
| 1982 | 5,040,000 | — | — | 0.10 | 0.25 | — |
| 1982FM (U) | 1,500 | — | — | — | 1.25 | — |
| 1982FM (P) | 843 | Value: 1.50 | | | | |
| 1983FM (M) | 1,500 | — | — | — | 1.00 | — |
| 1983FM (U) | — | — | — | — | 1.25 | — |
| 1983FM (P) | 459 | Value: 1.50 | | | | |
| 1984 | 5,008,000 | — | — | 0.10 | 0.25 | — |
| 1984FM (M) | 868 | — | — | — | 1.25 | — |
| 1984FM (P) | — | Value: 1.50 | | | | |
| 1985 | — | — | — | 0.10 | 0.25 | — |
| 1986 | — | — | — | 0.10 | 0.25 | — |
| 1987 | 10,000,000 | — | — | 0.10 | 0.25 | — |
| 1988 | 12,136,000 | — | — | 0.10 | 0.25 | — |
| 1989 | — | — | — | 0.10 | 0.25 | — |
| 1990 | — | — | — | 0.10 | 0.25 | — |
| 1991 | — | — | — | 0.10 | 0.25 | — |

**CENT** **KM# 11** **Composition:** Brass **Reverse:** South Point Lighthouse

| Date | Mintage | F | VF | XF | Unc | BU |
|---|---|---|---|---|---|---|
| 1973 | 3,000,000 | — | 0.10 | 0.15 | 0.35 | — |
| 1973FM (M) | 7,500 | — | — | — | 1.25 | — |
| 1973FM (P) | 97,000 | Value: 0.75 | | | | |
| 1974FM (M) | 8,708 | — | — | — | 1.25 | — |
| 1974FM (P) | 36,000 | Value: 0.75 | | | | |
| 1975FM (M) | 5,000 | — | — | — | 1.00 | — |
| 1975FM (U) | 1,360 | — | — | — | 1.25 | — |
| 1975FM (P) | 20,000 | Value: 0.75 | | | | |
| 1977FM (M) | 2,100 | — | — | — | 2.00 | — |
| 1977FM (U) | 468 | — | — | — | 3.00 | — |
| 1977FM (P) | 5,014 | Value: 0.75 | | | | |
| 1978FM (M) | 2,000 | — | — | — | 0.75 | — |
| 1978FM (U) | 2,517 | — | — | — | 2.75 | — |
| 1978FM (P) | 4,436 | Value: 1.25 | | | | |
| 1979 | 4,800,000 | — | 0.10 | 0.15 | 0.35 | — |
| 1979FM (M) | 1,500 | — | — | — | 0.75 | — |
| 1979FM (U) | 523 | — | — | — | 2.75 | — |
| 1979FM (P) | 4,126 | Value: 1.25 | | | | |
| 1980FM (M) | 1,500 | — | — | — | 1.00 | — |
| 1980FM (U) | 649 | — | — | — | 2.25 | — |
| 1980FM (P) | 2,111 | Value: 1.75 | | | | |
| 1981FM (M) | 1,500 | — | — | — | 1.00 | — |
| 1981FM (U) | 327 | — | — | — | 2.25 | — |
| 1981FM (P) | 943 | Value: 1.75 | | | | |
| 1982 | 2,100,000 | — | 0.10 | 0.15 | 0.35 | — |
| 1982FM (U) | 1,500 | — | — | — | 1.50 | — |
| 1982FM (P) | 843 | Value: 1.75 | | | | |
| 1983FM (M) | 1,500 | — | — | — | 1.50 | — |
| 1983FM (U) | — | — | — | — | 1.50 | — |
| 1983FM (P) | 459 | Value: 1.75 | | | | |
| 1984FM | 1,737 | — | — | — | 1.50 | — |
| 1984FM (P) | — | Value: 2.00 | | | | |
| 1985 | — | — | — | — | 0.25 | — |
| 1986 | — | — | — | — | 0.25 | — |
| 1988 | 4,200,000 | — | — | — | 0.25 | — |
| 1989 | — | — | — | — | 0.25 | — |
| 1991 | — | — | — | — | 0.25 | — |
| 1994 | — | — | — | — | 0.25 | — |
| 1996 | — | — | — | — | 0.25 | — |
| 1997 | — | — | — | — | 0.25 | — |
| 1998 | — | — | — | — | 0.25 | — |
| 1999 | — | — | — | — | 0.25 | — |

**CENT** **KM# 19** **Composition:** Copper Plated Zinc **Subject:** 10th Anniversary of Independence

| Date | Mintage | F | VF | XF | Unc | BU |
|---|---|---|---|---|---|---|
| ND(1976) | 6,406,000 | — | — | 0.10 | 0.20 | — |
| ND(1976)FM (M) | 5,000 | — | — | — | 0.50 | — |
| ND(1976)FM (U) | 996 | — | — | — | 1.00 | — |
| ND(1976)FM (P) | 12,000 | Value: 0.50 | | | | |

**CENT** **KM# 10a** **Composition:** Copper Plated Zinc

| Date | Mintage | F | VF | XF | Unc | BU |
|---|---|---|---|---|---|---|
| 1992 | — | — | — | 0.10 | 0.25 | — |
| 1993 | — | — | — | 0.10 | 0.25 | — |
| 1995 | — | — | — | 0.10 | 0.25 | — |
| 1996 | — | — | — | 0.10 | 0.25 | — |
| 1997 | — | — | — | 0.10 | 0.25 | — |
| 1998 | — | — | — | 0.10 | 0.25 | — |
| 1999 | — | — | — | 0.10 | 0.25 | — |

**5 CENTS** **KM# 20** **Composition:** Brass **Subject:** 10th Anniversary of Independence

| Date | Mintage | F | VF | XF | Unc | BU |
|---|---|---|---|---|---|---|
| ND(1976)FM (M) | 5,000 | — | — | — | 1.00 | — |
| ND(1976)FM (U) | 12,000 | — | — | — | 1.00 | — |
| ND(1976)FM (P) | — | Value: 0.75 | | | | |

**10 CENTS** **KM# 12** **Composition:** Copper-Nickel **Reverse:** Bonaparte Tern

| Date | Mintage | F | VF | XF | Unc | BU |
|---|---|---|---|---|---|---|
| 1973 | 4,000,000 | — | 0.10 | 0.15 | 0.50 | — |
| 1973FM (M) | 5,000 | — | — | — | 1.50 | — |
| 1973FM (P) | 97,000 | Value: 1.00 | | | | |
| 1974FM (M) | 6,208 | — | — | — | 1.50 | — |
| 1974FM (P) | 36,000 | Value: 1.00 | | | | |
| 1975FM (M) | 2,500 | — | — | — | 1.00 | — |
| 1975FM (U) | 1,360 | — | — | — | 1.50 | — |
| 1975FM (P) | 20,000 | Value: 1.00 | | | | |
| 1977FM (M) | 2,100 | — | — | — | 1.00 | — |
| 1977FM (U) | 468 | — | — | — | 4.00 | — |
| 1977FM (P) | 5,014 | Value: 1.00 | | | | |
| 1978FM (M) | 2,000 | — | — | — | 1.00 | — |
| 1978FM (U) | 2,517 | — | — | — | 3.00 | — |
| 1978FM (P) | 4,436 | Value: 1.50 | | | | |
| 1979 | 2,500,000 | — | 0.10 | 0.20 | 0.60 | — |
| 1979FM (M) | 1,500 | — | — | — | 2.50 | — |
| 1979FM (U) | 523 | — | — | — | 3.00 | — |
| 1979FM (P) | 4,126 | Value: 1.50 | | | | |
| 1980 | 3,500,000 | — | 0.10 | 0.15 | 0.50 | — |
| 1980FM (M) | 1,500 | — | — | — | 1.00 | — |
| 1980FM (U) | 649 | — | — | — | 2.50 | — |
| 1980FM (P) | 2,111 | Value: 2.00 | | | | |
| 1981FM (M) | 1,500 | — | — | — | 1.00 | — |
| 1981FM (U) | 327 | — | — | — | 2.50 | — |
| 1981FM (P) | 943 | Value: 2.00 | | | | |
| 1982FM (U) | 1,500 | — | — | — | 1.75 | — |
| 1982FM (P) | 843 | Value: 2.00 | | | | |
| 1983FM (M) | 1,500 | — | — | — | 1.75 | — |
| 1983FM (U) | — | — | — | — | 1.75 | — |
| 1983FM (P) | 459 | Value: 2.00 | | | | |
| 1984 | 3,400,000 | — | 0.10 | 0.15 | 0.50 | — |
| 1984FM (P) | — | Value: 2.25 | | | | |
| 1985 | — | — | 0.10 | 0.15 | 0.50 | — |
| 1986 | — | — | 0.10 | 0.15 | 0.50 | — |
| 1987 | 3,500,000 | — | 0.10 | 0.15 | 0.50 | — |
| 1988 | — | — | 0.10 | 0.15 | 0.50 | — |
| 1989 | — | — | 0.10 | 0.15 | 0.50 | — |
| 1990 | — | — | 0.10 | 0.15 | 0.50 | — |
| 1992 | — | — | 0.10 | 0.15 | 0.50 | — |
| 1995 | — | — | 0.10 | 0.15 | 0.50 | — |
| 1996 | — | — | 0.10 | 0.15 | 0.50 | — |
| 1998 | — | — | 0.10 | 0.15 | 0.50 | — |
| 2000 | — | — | 0.10 | 0.15 | 0.50 | — |
| 2001 | — | — | 0.10 | 0.15 | 0.50 | — |

**10 CENTS** **KM# 21** **Composition:** Copper-Nickel **Subject:** 10th Anniversary of Independence

| Date | Mintage | F | VF | XF | Unc | BU |
|---|---|---|---|---|---|---|
| ND(1976)FM (M) | 2,500 | — | — | — | 0.75 | — |
| ND(1976)FM (U) | 996 | — | — | — | 1.75 | — |
| ND(1976)FM (P) | 12,000 | Value: 1.50 | | | | |

**25 CENTS** **KM# 13** **Composition:** Copper-Nickel **Reverse:** Morgan Lewis Sugar Mill

| Date | Mintage | F | VF | XF | Unc | BU |
|---|---|---|---|---|---|---|
| 1973 | 6,000,000 | — | 0.15 | 0.30 | 0.60 | — |
| 1973FM (M) | 4,300 | — | — | — | 1.75 | — |
| 1973FM (P) | 97,000 | Value: 1.25 | | | | |
| 1974FM (M) | 5,508 | — | — | — | 1.75 | — |
| 1974FM (P) | 36,000 | Value: 1.25 | | | | |
| 1975FM (M) | 1,800 | — | — | — | 1.25 | — |
| 1975FM (U) | 1,360 | — | — | — | 1.75 | — |
| 1975FM (P) | 20,000 | Value: 1.25 | | | | |
| 1977FM (M) | 2,100 | — | — | — | 1.00 | — |
| 1977FM (U) | 468 | — | — | — | 4.25 | — |
| 1977FM (P) | 5,014 | Value: 1.25 | | | | |
| 1978 | 2,407,000 | — | 0.20 | 0.40 | 0.80 | — |
| 1978FM (M) | 2,000 | — | — | — | 1.00 | — |
| 1978FM (U) | 2,517 | — | — | — | 3.25 | — |
| 1978FM (P) | 4,436 | Value: 1.75 | | | | |
| 1979 | 1,200,000 | — | 0.20 | 0.40 | 0.80 | — |
| 1979FM (M) | 1,500 | — | — | — | 1.00 | — |
| 1979FM (U) | 523 | — | — | — | 3.00 | — |
| 1979FM (P) | 4,126,000 | Value: 1.75 | | | | |
| 1980 | 2,700,000 | — | 0.15 | 0.30 | 0.60 | — |
| 1980FM (M) | 1,500 | — | — | — | 3.00 | — |
| 1980FM (U) | 649 | — | — | — | 2.75 | — |
| 1980FM (P) | 2,111 | Value: 2.25 | | | | |
| 1981 | 4,365,000 | — | 0.15 | 0.30 | 0.60 | — |
| 1981FM (M) | 1,500 | — | — | — | 3.00 | — |
| 1981FM (U) | 327 | — | — | — | 2.75 | — |
| 1981FM (P) | 943 | Value: 2.25 | | | | |
| 1982FM (U) | 1,500 | — | — | — | 2.00 | — |
| 1982FM (P) | 843 | Value: 2.25 | | | | |
| 1983FM (M) | 1,500 | — | — | — | 2.00 | — |
| 1983FM (U) | — | — | — | — | 2.00 | — |
| 1983FM (P) | 459 | Value: 2.25 | | | | |
| 1984FM | 868 | — | — | — | 2.00 | — |
| 1984FM (P) | — | Value: 2.50 | | | | |
| 1985 | | — | 0.15 | 0.30 | 0.60 | — |
| 1986 | | — | 0.15 | 0.30 | 0.60 | — |
| 1987 | 3,150,000 | — | — | — | 2.00 | — |
| 1988 | | — | 0.15 | 0.30 | 0.60 | — |
| 1989 | | — | 0.15 | 0.30 | 0.60 | — |
| 1990 | | — | 0.15 | 0.30 | 0.60 | — |
| 1994 | — | — | 0.15 | 0.30 | 0.60 | — |
| 1996 | — | — | 0.15 | 0.30 | 0.60 | — |
| 1998 | — | — | 0.15 | 0.30 | 0.60 | — |
| 2000 | — | — | 0.15 | 0.30 | 0.60 | — |

**25 CENTS** **KM# 22** **Composition:** Copper-Nickel **Subject:** 10th Anniversary of Independence

| Date | Mintage | F | VF | XF | Unc | BU |
|---|---|---|---|---|---|---|
| ND(1976)FM (M) | 1,800 | — | — | — | 1.25 | — |
| ND(1976)FM (U) | 996 | — | — | — | 2.00 | — |
| ND(1976)FM (P) | 12,000 | Value: 1.50 | | | | |

**DOLLAR** **KM# 14.1** **Composition:** Copper-Nickel **Reverse:** Flying Fish

| Date | Mintage | F | VF | XF | Unc | BU |
|---|---|---|---|---|---|---|
| 1973 | 3,955,000 | — | 0.60 | 0.75 | 1.00 | — |
| 1973FM (M) | 3,000 | — | — | — | 2.00 | — |
| 1973FM (P) | 97,000 | Value: 1.50 | | | | |
| 1974FM (M) | 4,208 | — | — | — | 2.00 | — |
| 1974FM (P) | 36,000 | Value: 1.50 | | | | |
| 1975FM (M) | 500 | — | — | — | 3.50 | — |
| 1975FM (U) | 1,360 | — | — | — | 2.00 | — |
| 1975FM (P) | 20,000 | Value: 1.50 | | | | |
| 1977FM (M) | 600 | — | — | — | 5.00 | — |
| 1977FM (U) | 468 | — | — | — | 4.50 | — |
| 1977FM (P) | 5,014 | Value: 2.50 | | | | |
| 1978FM (U) | 1,017 | — | — | — | 3.50 | — |
| 1978FM (P) | 4,436 | Value: 2.50 | | | | |
| 1979 | 2,000,000 | — | 0.75 | 1.25 | 1.75 | — |
| 1979FM (M) | 600 | — | — | — | 3.00 | — |
| 1979FM (U) | 523 | — | — | — | 3.50 | — |
| 1979FM (P) | 4,126 | Value: 2.50 | | | | |
| 1980FM (M) | 600 | — | — | — | 3.50 | — |
| 1980FM (U) | 649 | — | — | — | 3.50 | — |
| 1980FM (P) | 2,111 | Value: 3.00 | | | | |
| 1981FM (M) | 600 | — | — | — | 3.00 | — |
| 1981FM (U) | 327 | — | — | — | 3.50 | — |
| 1981FM (P) | 943 | Value: 3.50 | | | | |
| 1982FM (U) | 600 | — | — | — | 3.00 | — |
| 1982FM (P) | 843 | Value: 3.50 | | | | |
| 1983FM (M) | 600 | — | — | — | 3.00 | — |
| 1983FM (U) | — | — | — | — | 3.00 | — |
| 1983FM (P) | 459 | Value: 4.00 | | | | |
| 1984FM | 469 | — | — | — | 3.50 | — |
| 1984FM (P) | — | Value: 4.50 | | | | |
| 1985 | — | — | — | — | 1.00 | — |
| 1986 | — | — | — | — | 1.00 | — |

**DOLLAR** **KM# 23** **Composition:** Copper-Nickel **Subject:** 10th Anniversary of Independence

| Date | Mintage | F | VF | XF | Unc | BU |
|---|---|---|---|---|---|---|
| ND(1976)FM (M) | 500 | — | — | — | 4.00 | — |
| ND(1976)FM (U) | 996 | — | — | — | 2.50 | — |
| ND(1976)FM (P) | 12,000 | Value: 2.00 | | | | |

**DOLLAR** **KM# 14.2** **Composition:** Copper-Nickel

| Date | Mintage | F | VF | XF | Unc | BU |
|---|---|---|---|---|---|---|
| 1988 | 3,145,000 | — | — | — | 2.25 | — |
| 1989 | — | — | — | — | 2.25 | — |
| 1994 | — | — | — | — | 2.25 | — |

**DOLLAR** **KM# 57** **Weight:** 10.0000 g. **Composition:** 0.5000 Silver .1607 oz. ASW **Reverse:** Bust of Queen Mother

| Date | Mintage | F | VF | XF | Unc | BU |
|---|---|---|---|---|---|---|
| 1994 Proof | Est. 50,000 | Value: 28.00 | | | | |

**DOLLAR** **KM# 65** **Weight:** 9.9400 g. **Composition:** 0.9250 Silver .2956 oz. ASW **Subject:** Queen Mother's 95th Birthday **Obverse:** National arms **Reverse:** Queen Mother's portrait

| Date | Mintage | F | VF | XF | Unc | BU |
|---|---|---|---|---|---|---|
| 1995 Proof | Est. 50,000 | Value: 35.00 | | | | |

**2 DOLLARS** **KM# 15** **Composition:** Copper-Nickel **Reverse:** Staghorn Coral

| Date | Mintage | F | VF | XF | Unc | BU |
|---|---|---|---|---|---|---|
| 1973FM (M) | 3,000 | — | — | — | 4.00 | — |
| 1973FM (P) | 97,000 | Value: 4.50 | | | | |
| 1974FM (M) | 4,208 | — | — | — | 4.00 | — |
| 1974FM (P) | 36,000 | Value: 4.50 | | | | |
| 1975FM (M) | 500 | — | — | — | 5.00 | — |
| 1975FM (U) | 1,360 | — | — | — | 4.00 | — |
| 1975FM (P) | 20,000 | Value: 4.50 | | | | |
| 1977FM (M) | 600 | — | — | — | 4.50 | — |
| 1977FM (U) | 468 | — | — | — | 5.50 | — |
| 1977FM (P) | 5,014 | Value: 4.50 | | | | |
| 1978FM (U) | 1,017 | — | — | — | 5.00 | — |
| 1978FM (P) | 4,436 | Value: 4.00 | | | | |
| 1979FM (M) | 600 | — | — | — | 4.50 | — |

| Date | Mintage | F | VF | XF | Unc | BU |
|---|---|---|---|---|---|---|
| 1979FM (U) | 523 | — | — | — | 5.00 | — |
| 1979FM (P) | 4,126 | Value: 4.00 | | | | |
| 1980FM (M) | 600 | — | — | — | 4.50 | — |
| 1980FM (U) | 649 | — | — | — | 4.00 | — |
| 1980FM (P) | 2,111 | Value: 4.00 | | | | |
| 1981FM (M) | 600 | — | — | — | 4.50 | — |
| 1981FM (U) | 327 | — | — | — | 4.50 | — |
| 1981FM (P) | 943 | Value: 4.00 | | | | |
| 1982FM (U) | 600 | — | — | — | 4.50 | — |
| 1982FM (P) | 843 | Value: 4.00 | | | | |
| 1983FM (U) | — | — | — | — | 4.50 | — |
| 1983FM (P) | 459 | Value: 4.00 | | | | |
| 1984FM (U) | 473 | — | — | — | 4.50 | — |
| 1984FM (P) | — | Value: 4.50 | | | | |

**2 DOLLARS** **KM# 24** **Composition:** Copper-Nickel **Subject:** 10th Anniversary of Independence

| Date | Mintage | F | VF | XF | Unc | BU |
|---|---|---|---|---|---|---|
| ND(1976)FM (M) | 500 | — | — | — | 5.00 | — |
| ND(1976)FM (U) | 996 | — | — | — | 5.00 | — |
| ND(1976)FM (P) | 12,000 | Value: 4.00 | | | | |

**4 DOLLARS** **KM# A9** **Composition:** Copper-Nickel **Series:** F.A.O

| Date | Mintage | F | VF | XF | Unc | BU |
|---|---|---|---|---|---|---|
| 1970 | 30,000 | — | 3.50 | 7.00 | 12.50 | — |
| 1970 Proof | 2,000 | Value: 22.50 | | | | |

**5 DOLLARS** **KM# 16a** **Weight:** 31.1000 g. **Composition:** 0.8000 Silver .7999 oz. ASW

| Date | Mintage | F | VF | XF | Unc | BU |
|---|---|---|---|---|---|---|
| 1973FM (M) | 2,750 | — | — | — | 11.50 | — |
| 1973FM (P) | 97,000 | Value: 7.00 | | | | |
| 1974FM (P) | 36,000 | Value: 8.00 | | | | |
| 1975FM (P) | 20,000 | Value: 9.00 | | | | |
| 1977FM (P) | 5,014 | Value: 11.50 | | | | |
| 1978FM (P) | 4,436 | Value: 11.50 | | | | |
| 1979FM (P) | 4,126 | Value: 11.50 | | | | |
| 1980FM (P) | 2,111 | Value: 14.50 | | | | |
| 1981FM (P) | 835 | Value: 22.00 | | | | |
| 1982FM (P) | 658 | Value: 22.00 | | | | |
| 1983FM (P) | 130 | Value: 32.00 | | | | |
| 1984FM (P) | — | Value: 32.00 | | | | |

**5 DOLLARS** **KM# 16** **Composition:** Copper-Nickel **Subject:** Shell Fountain in Bridgetown's Trafalgar Square **Obverse:** Similar to 2 Dollars, KM#15

| Date | Mintage | F | VF | XF | Unc | BU |
|---|---|---|---|---|---|---|
| 1974FM (M) | 3,958 | — | — | — | 5.00 | — |
| 1975FM (M) | 250 | — | — | — | 8.00 | — |
| 1975FM (U) | 1,360 | — | — | — | 5.00 | — |
| 1977FM (M) | 600 | — | — | — | 5.00 | — |
| 1977FM (U) | 468 | — | — | — | 5.00 | — |
| 1978FM (U) | 1,017 | — | — | — | 5.00 | — |
| 1979FM (M) | 600 | — | — | — | 5.00 | — |
| 1979FM (U) | 523 | — | — | — | 5.00 | — |
| 1980FM (M) | 600 | — | — | — | 5.00 | — |
| 1980FM (U) | 649 | — | — | — | 5.00 | — |
| 1981FM (M) | 600 | — | — | — | 5.00 | — |
| 1981FM (U) | 1,156 | — | — | — | 5.00 | — |
| 1982FM (U) | 600 | — | — | — | 5.00 | — |
| 1982FM (P) | 843 | — | — | — | 5.00 | — |
| 1983FM (M) | 600 | — | — | — | 5.00 | — |
| 1983FM (U) | 261 | — | — | — | 5.00 | — |
| 1984FM | 470 | — | — | — | 5.00 | — |

**5 DOLLARS** **KM# 25** **Composition:** Copper-Nickel **Subject:** 10th Anniversary of Independence **Reverse:** Similar to KM#16

| Date | Mintage | F | VF | XF | Unc | BU |
|---|---|---|---|---|---|---|
| ND(1976)FM (M) | 250 | — | — | — | 25.00 | — |
| ND(1976)FM (U) | 996 | — | — | — | 12.50 | — |

**5 DOLLARS** **KM# 25a** **Weight:** 31.1000 g. **Composition:** 0.8000 Silver .7999 oz. ASW

| Date | Mintage | F | VF | XF | Unc | BU |
|---|---|---|---|---|---|---|
| ND(1976)FM (P) | 12,000 | Value: 15.00 | | | | |

**5 DOLLARS** **KM# 54** **Weight:** 28.5500 g. **Composition:** 0.9250 Silver .8492 oz. ASW **Reverse:** World Cup Soccer

| Date | Mintage | F | VF | XF | Unc | BU |
|---|---|---|---|---|---|---|
| 1994 Proof | Est. 10,000 | Value: 37.50 | | | | |

**5 DOLLARS** **KM# 55** **Weight:** 28.2800 g. **Composition:** 0.9250 Silver .8411 oz. ASW **Subject:** UN Global SIDS Conference **Obverse:** Coat of arms **Reverse:** Stylized tropical island view

| Date | Mintage | F | VF | XF | Unc | BU |
|---|---|---|---|---|---|---|
| 1994 Proof | 2,000 | Value: 40.00 | | | | |

**5 DOLLARS** **KM# 58** **Weight:** 31.4700 g. **Composition:** 0.9250 Silver .9359 oz. ASW **Reverse:** Queen Mother's Engagement Portrait

| Date | Mintage | F | VF | XF | Unc | BU |
|---|---|---|---|---|---|---|
| 1994 Proof | Est. 20,000 | Value: 50.00 | | | | |

**5 DOLLARS** **KM# 59** **Weight:** 28.2800 g. **Composition:** 0.9250 Silver .8411 oz. ASW **Reverse:** Pedro A. Campo

| Date | Mintage | F | VF | XF | Unc | BU |
|---|---|---|---|---|---|---|
| 1994 Proof | Est. 10,000 | Value: 50.00 | | | | |

**5 DOLLARS** **KM# 62** **Composition:** Copper-Nickel **Subject:** 50th Anniversary - United Nations

| Date | Mintage | F | VF | XF | Unc | BU |
|---|---|---|---|---|---|---|
| 1995 | — | — | — | — | 8.00 | — |

**5 DOLLARS** **KM# 62a** **Weight:** 28.2800 g. **Composition:** 0.9250 Silver .8411 oz. ASW

| Date | Mintage | F | VF | XF | Unc | BU |
|---|---|---|---|---|---|---|
| 1995 Proof | Est. 105,000 | Value: 32.50 | | | | |

**5 DOLLARS** KM# 63 **Weight:** 28.2800 g. **Composition:** 0.9250 Silver .8411 oz. ASW **Reverse:** First European Settlers, 1625

| Date | Mintage | F | VF | XF | Unc | BU |
|---|---|---|---|---|---|---|
| 1995 Proof | Est. 15,000 | Value: 40.00 | | | | |

**5 DOLLARS** KM# 67 **Weight:** 28.1000 g. **Composition:** 0.9250 Silver .8357 oz. ASW **Subject:** Eternal Flame **Obverse:** National arms. **Reverse:** Denomination and eternal flame. **Edge:** Reeded. **Shape:** Octagonal. **Size:** 38.6 mm.

| Date | Mintage | F | VF | XF | Unc | BU |
|---|---|---|---|---|---|---|
| 1999-2000 Proof | — | Value: 60.00 | | | | |

**10 DOLLARS** KM# 17a **Weight:** 37.9000 g. **Composition:** 0.9250 Silver 1.1271 oz. ASW

| Date | Mintage | F | VF | XF | Unc | BU |
|---|---|---|---|---|---|---|
| 1973FM (M) | 2,750 | — | — | — | 15.00 | — |
| 1973FM (P) | 97,000 | Value: 11.50 | | | | |
| 1974FM (P) | 57,000 | Value: 11.50 | | | | |
| 1975FM (P) | 29,000 | Value: 11.50 | | | | |
| 1977FM (P) | 7,212 | Value: 15.00 | | | | |
| 1978FM (P) | 7,079 | Value: 15.00 | | | | |
| 1979FM (P) | 6,534 | Value: 15.00 | | | | |
| 1980FM (P) | 3,618 | Value: 17.50 | | | | |
| 1981FM (P) | 835 | Value: 45.00 | | | | |

**10 DOLLARS** KM# 17 **Composition:** Copper-Nickel **Subject:** Neptune, God of the Sea **Obverse:** Similar to 2 Dollars, KM#15

| Date | Mintage | F | VF | XF | Unc | BU |
|---|---|---|---|---|---|---|
| 1974FM (M) | 3,958 | — | — | — | 10.00 | — |
| 1975FM (M) | 250 | — | — | — | 20.00 | — |
| 1975FM (U) | 1,360 | — | — | — | 12.50 | — |
| 1977FM (M) | 600 | — | — | — | 12.50 | — |

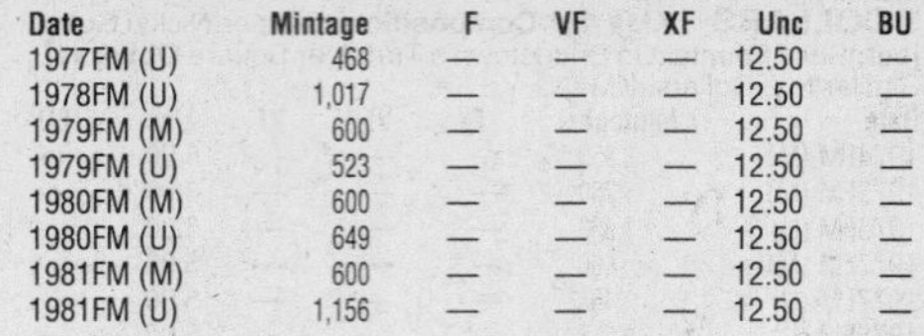

| Date | Mintage | F | VF | XF | Unc | BU |
|---|---|---|---|---|---|---|
| 1977FM (U) | 468 | — | — | — | 12.50 | — |
| 1978FM (U) | 1,017 | — | — | — | 12.50 | — |
| 1979FM (M) | 600 | — | — | — | 12.50 | — |
| 1979FM (U) | 523 | — | — | — | 12.50 | — |
| 1980FM (M) | 600 | — | — | — | 12.50 | — |
| 1980FM (U) | 649 | — | — | — | 12.50 | — |
| 1981FM (M) | 600 | — | — | — | 12.50 | — |
| 1981FM (U) | 1,156 | — | — | — | 12.50 | — |

**10 DOLLARS** KM# 26 **Composition:** Copper-Nickel **Subject:** 10th Anniversary of Independence **Reverse:** Similar to KM#17

| Date | Mintage | F | VF | XF | Unc | BU |
|---|---|---|---|---|---|---|
| ND(1976)FM (M) | 250 | — | — | — | 30.00 | — |
| ND(1976)FM (U) | 996 | — | — | — | 15.00 | — |

**10 DOLLARS** KM# 26a **Weight:** 37.9000 g. **Composition:** 0.9250 Silver 1.1271 oz. ASW

| Date | Mintage | F | VF | XF | Unc | BU |
|---|---|---|---|---|---|---|
| ND(1976)FM (P) | 16,000 | Value: 15.00 | | | | |

**10 DOLLARS** KM# 34 **Composition:** Copper-Nickel **Subject:** 10th Anniversary of the Central Bank of Barbados **Obverse:** Similar to KM#26

| Date | Mintage | F | VF | XF | Unc | BU |
|---|---|---|---|---|---|---|
| 1982FM (U) | 600 | — | — | — | 55.00 | — |

**10 DOLLARS** KM# 34a **Weight:** 35.5200 g. **Composition:** 0.9250 Silver 1.0564 oz. ASW

| Date | Mintage | F | VF | XF | Unc | BU |
|---|---|---|---|---|---|---|
| 1982FM (P) | 851 | Value: 45.00 | | | | |

**10 DOLLARS** KM# 36 **Composition:** Copper-Nickel **Subject:** Pelican

| Date | Mintage | F | VF | XF | Unc | BU |
|---|---|---|---|---|---|---|
| 1983FM (M) | 600 | — | — | — | 50.00 | — |
| 1983FM (U) | 141 | — | — | — | 100 | — |

**10 DOLLARS** KM# 36a **Weight:** 35.5200 g. **Composition:** 0.9250 Silver 1.0564 oz. ASW

| Date | Mintage | F | VF | XF | Unc | BU |
|---|---|---|---|---|---|---|
| 1983FM (P) | 679 | Value: 115 | | | | |

**10 DOLLARS** KM# 40 **Weight:** 35.5200 g. **Composition:** 0.9250 Silver 1.0564 oz. ASW **Subject:** Dolphins

| Date | Mintage | F | VF | XF | Unc | BU |
|---|---|---|---|---|---|---|
| 1984FM (M) | — | — | — | — | — | — |
| 1984FM (P) | 469 | Value: 165 | | | | |

**10 DOLLARS** KM# 50 **Weight:** 28.2800 g. **Composition:** 0.9250 Silver .8411 oz. ASW **Subject:** International Cricket Belt Buckle

| Date | Mintage | F | VF | XF | Unc | BU |
|---|---|---|---|---|---|---|
| 1991 Proof | 5,000 | Value: 55.00 | | | | |

**10 DOLLARS** KM# 52 **Weight:** 23.3300 g. **Composition:** 0.9250 Silver .6938 oz. ASW **Subject:** Discovery of America - Columbus and Native American - Ship and Scroll

| Date | Mintage | F | VF | XF | Unc | BU |
|---|---|---|---|---|---|---|
| 1991 Matte | 750 | Value: 65.00 | | | | |
| 1991 Proof | Est. 25,000 | Value: 35.00 | | | | |

**10 DOLLARS** KM# 53 **Weight:** 23.3300 g. **Composition:** 0.9250 Silver .6938 oz. ASW **Subject:** Discovery of America - Columbus and Tribal Chief - Scroll

| Date | Mintage | F | VF | XF | Unc | BU |
|---|---|---|---|---|---|---|
| 1992 Matte | 500 | Value: 65.00 | | | | |
| 1992 Proof | Est. 25,000 | Value: 35.00 | | | | |

**10 DOLLARS** KM# 61 **Weight:** 23.3300 g. **Composition:** 0.9250 Silver .6938 oz. ASW **Subject:** 1992 Summer Olympics - Sailboards

| Date | Mintage | F | VF | XF | Unc | BU |
|---|---|---|---|---|---|---|
| 1992 Proof | 10,000 | Value: 50.00 | | | | |

**10 DOLLARS** KM# 60 **Weight:** 7.7800 g. **Composition:** 0.5830 Gold .1458 oz. AGW **Subject:** Queen Mother's Engagement Portrait

| Date | Mintage | F | VF | XF | Unc | BU |
|---|---|---|---|---|---|---|
| 1995 Proof | Est. 5,000 | Value: 150 | | | | |

**10 DOLLARS** KM# 66 **Weight:** 28.2800 g. **Composition:** 0.9250 Silver .8410 oz. ASW **Subject:** 50th Anniversary of the University of the West Indies **Obverse:** National arms **Reverse:** University arms, dates

| Date | Mintage | F | VF | XF | Unc | BU |
|---|---|---|---|---|---|---|
| 1998 Proof | 1,000 | Value: 55.00 | | | | |

**20 DOLLARS** KM# 46 **Weight:** 23.3300 g. **Composition:** 0.9250 Silver .6938 oz. ASW **Subject:** Decade For Women

| Date | Mintage | F | VF | XF | Unc | BU |
|---|---|---|---|---|---|---|
| 1985 Proof | 1,633 | Value: 45.00 | | | | |

**20 DOLLARS** KM# 49 **Weight:** 23.3300 g. **Composition:** 0.9250 Silver .6938 oz. ASW **Reverse:** Summer Olympics - Hurdler

| Date | Mintage | F | VF | XF | Unc | BU |
|---|---|---|---|---|---|---|
| 1988 | 15,000 | — | — | — | 28.00 | — |

**25 DOLLARS** KM# 27 **Weight:** 28.2800 g. **Composition:** 0.9250 Silver .8410 oz. ASW **Subject:** Coronation Jubilee **Obverse:** Portrait of Queen Elizabeth II

| Date | Mintage | F | VF | XF | Unc | BU |
|---|---|---|---|---|---|---|
| 1978FM (M) | 300 | — | — | — | 90.00 | — |
| 1978FM (U) | 69 | — | — | — | 250 | — |
| 1978FM (P) | 8,728 | Value: 16.00 | | | | |

**25 DOLLARS** KM# 30 **Weight:** 30.2800 g. **Composition:** 0.5000 Silver .4868 oz. ASW **Subject:** 10th Anniversary of Caribbean Development Bank

| Date | Mintage | F | VF | XF | Unc | BU |
|---|---|---|---|---|---|---|
| 1980FM (P) Proof | 2,345 | Value: 25.00 | | | | |

**25 DOLLARS** KM# 31 **Weight:** 30.2800 g. **Composition:** 0.5000 Silver .4868 oz. ASW **Subject:** Caribbean Festival of Arts **Obverse:** Similar to KM#30

| Date | Mintage | F | VF | XF | Unc | BU |
|---|---|---|---|---|---|---|
| 1981FM (P) | 1,008 | Value: 30.00 | | | | |

**25 DOLLARS** **KM# 37 Weight:** 30.2800 g. **Composition:** 0.5000 Silver .4868 oz. ASW **Subject:** 30th Anniversary Coronation of Queen Elizabeth II

| Date | Mintage | F | VF | XF | Unc | BU |
|---|---|---|---|---|---|---|
| 1983FM (P) | 2,951 | Value: 22.50 | | | | |

**25 DOLLARS** **KM# 43 Weight:** 28.2800 g. **Composition:** 0.9250 Silver .8410 oz. ASW **Subject:** Royal Visit

| Date | Mintage | F | VF | XF | Unc | BU |
|---|---|---|---|---|---|---|
| 1985 | Est. 5,000 | — | — | — | 32.50 | — |

**25 DOLLARS** **KM# 43a Weight:** 47.5400 g. **Composition:** 0.9170 Gold 1.4013 oz. AGW **Subject:** Royal Visit

| Date | Mintage | F | VF | XF | Unc | BU |
|---|---|---|---|---|---|---|
| 1985 | Est. 250 | Value: 950 | | | | |

**25 DOLLARS** **KM# 44 Weight:** 28.2800 g. **Composition:** 0.5000 Silver .4546 oz. ASW **Subject:** Commonwealth Games

| Date | Mintage | F | VF | XF | Unc | BU |
|---|---|---|---|---|---|---|
| 1986 | Est. 50,000 | — | — | — | 25.00 | — |

**25 DOLLARS** **KM# 44a Weight:** 28.2800 g. **Composition:** 0.9250 Silver .8410 oz. ASW

| Date | Mintage | F | VF | XF | Unc | BU |
|---|---|---|---|---|---|---|
| 1986 | Est. 20,000 | Value: 30.00 | | | | |

**50 DOLLARS** **KM# 32 Weight:** 27.3500 g. **Composition:** 0.5000 Silver .4397 oz. ASW **Subject:** World Food Day - Black Belly Sheep

| Date | Mintage | F | VF | XF | Unc | BU |
|---|---|---|---|---|---|---|
| 1981FM (U) | 6,012 | — | — | — | 35.00 | — |

**50 DOLLARS** **KM# 42 Weight:** 16.8500 g. **Composition:** 0.5000 Silver .2709 oz. ASW **Series:** F.A.O. **Reverse:** Four-wing Flying Fish

| Date | Mintage | F | VF | XF | Unc | BU |
|---|---|---|---|---|---|---|
| 1984 | 3,600 | — | — | — | 32.50 | — |

**50 DOLLARS** **KM# 47 Weight:** 33.6250 g. **Composition:** 0.9250 Silver 1.0000 oz. ASW **Subject:** 350th Anniversary of Parliament

| Date | Mintage | F | VF | XF | Unc | BU |
|---|---|---|---|---|---|---|
| ND(1989) Proof | Est. 5,000 | Value: 35.00 | | | | |

**50 DOLLARS** **KM# 51 Weight:** 15.9800 g. **Composition:** 0.9170 Gold .4709 oz. AGW **Subject:** International Cricket Belt Buckle **Reverse:** Cricket player on belt buckle **Note:** Similar to 10 Dollars, KM#50.

| Date | Mintage | F | VF | XF | Unc | BU |
|---|---|---|---|---|---|---|
| 1991 Proof | 500 | Value: 530 | | | | |

**50 DOLLARS** **KM# 56 Weight:** 15.9800 g. **Composition:** 0.9170 Gold .4709 oz. AGW **Subject:** UN Global SIDS Conference

| Date | Mintage | F | VF | XF | Unc | BU |
|---|---|---|---|---|---|---|
| 1994 Proof | 100 | Value: 550 | | | | |

**100 DOLLARS** **KM# 18 Weight:** 6.2100 g. **Composition:** 0.5000 Gold .0998 oz. AGW **Subject:** 350th Anniversary - The English Ship - Olive Blossom

| Date | Mintage | F | VF | XF | Unc | BU |
|---|---|---|---|---|---|---|
| ND(1975)FM (M) | 50 | — | — | — | 250 | — |
| ND(1975)FM (U) | 16,000 | — | — | — | 50.00 | — |
| ND(1975)FM (P) | 23,000 | Value: 65.00 | | | | |

**100 DOLLARS** **KM# 28 Weight:** 4.0600 g. **Composition:** 0.9000 Gold .1174 oz. AGW **Subject:** Human Rights

| Date | Mintage | F | VF | XF | Unc | BU |
|---|---|---|---|---|---|---|
| 1978 | 1,114 | — | — | — | 125 | — |

**100 DOLLARS** **KM# 28a Weight:** 5.0500 g. **Composition:** 0.9000 Gold .1461 oz. AGW

| Date | Mintage | F | VF | XF | Unc | BU |
|---|---|---|---|---|---|---|
| 1978 Proof | Inc. above | Value: 150 | | | | |

**100 DOLLARS** **KM# 38 Weight:** 6.2100 g. **Composition:** 0.5000 Gold .0998 oz. AGW **Subject:** Neptune, God of the Sea

| Date | Mintage | F | VF | XF | Unc | BU |
|---|---|---|---|---|---|---|
| 1983FM (U) | 3 | — | — | — | — | — |
| 1983FM (P) | 484 | Value: 220 | | | | |

**100 DOLLARS** **KM# 39 Weight:** 6.2100 g. **Composition:** 0.5000 Gold .0998 oz. AGW **Subject:** Triton, Son of Neptune

| Date | Mintage | F | VF | XF | Unc | BU |
|---|---|---|---|---|---|---|
| 1984FM (P) | 1,103 | Value: 165 | | | | |

**100 DOLLARS** **KM# 41 Weight:** 6.2100 g. **Composition:** 0.5000 Gold .0998 oz. AGW **Subject:** Smphitrite, Wife of Neptune

| Date | Mintage | F | VF | XF | Unc | BU |
|---|---|---|---|---|---|---|
| 1985FM (P) | 1,276 | Value: 160 | | | | |

**100 DOLLARS** **KM# 48 Weight:** 15.9760 g. **Composition:** 0.9170 Gold .4709 oz. AGW **Subject:** 350th Anniversary of Parliament

| Date | Mintage | F | VF | XF | Unc | BU |
|---|---|---|---|---|---|---|
| ND(1989)FM | Est. 500 | Value: 350 | | | | |

**150 DOLLARS** **KM# 33** **Weight:** 7.1300 g. **Composition:** 0.5000 Gold .1146 oz. AGW **Subject:** National Flower - Poinciana

| Date | Mintage | F | VF | XF | Unc | BU |
|---|---|---|---|---|---|---|
| 1981FM (U) | 7 | — | — | — | — | — |
| 1981FM (P) | 1,140 | Value: 115 | | | | |

**200 DOLLARS** **KM# 29** **Weight:** 8.1200 g. **Composition:** 0.9000 Gold .2349 oz. AGW **Subject:** Year of the Child

| Date | Mintage | F | VF | XF | Unc | BU |
|---|---|---|---|---|---|---|
| 1979 | 1,121 | — | — | — | 225 | — |

**200 DOLLARS** **KM# 29a** **Weight:** 10.1000 g. **Composition:** 0.9000 Gold .2922 oz. AGW

| Date | Mintage | F | VF | XF | Unc | BU |
|---|---|---|---|---|---|---|
| 1979 Proof | Inc. above | Value: 275 | | | | |

**250 DOLLARS** **KM# 35** **Weight:** 6.6000 g. **Composition:** 0.9000 Gold .1910 oz. AGW **Subject:** 250th Anniversary of Birth of George Washington

| Date | Mintage | F | VF | XF | Unc | BU |
|---|---|---|---|---|---|---|
| 1982FM (P) | 802 | Value: 150 | | | | |

**250 DOLLARS** **KM# 45** **Weight:** 47.5400 g. **Composition:** 0.9170 Gold 1.4017 oz. AGW **Subject:** Commonwealth Games **Note:** Similar to 25 Dollars, KM#44.

| Date | Mintage | F | VF | XF | Unc | BU |
|---|---|---|---|---|---|---|
| 1986 Proof | 150 | Value: 1,000 | | | | |

## MINT SETS

| KM# | Date | Mintage | Identification | Issue Price | Mkt Val |
|---|---|---|---|---|---|
| MS1 | 1973 | 2,500 | KM#10-15, 16a, 17a | 25.00 | 25.00 |
| MS2 | 1974 | 3,708 | KM#10-17 | 25.00 | 20.00 |
| MS3 | 1975 | 1,360 | KM#10-17 | 27.50 | 22.50 |
| MS4 | 1976 | 996 | KM#19-26 | 27.50 | 30.00 |
| MS5 | 1977 | 468 | KM#10-17 | 27.50 | 30.00 |
| MS6 | 1978 | 517 | KM#10-17 | 29.00 | 30.00 |
| MS7 | 1979 | 523 | KM#10-17 | 29.00 | 30.00 |
| MS8 | 1980 | 649 | KM#10-17 | 30.00 | 30.00 |
| MS9 | 1981 | 327 | KM#10-17 | 30.00 | 35.00 |
| MS10 | 1982 | — | KM#10-16, 34 | 35.00 | 45.00 |
| MS11 | 1983 | 141 | KM#10-16, 36 | 35.50 | 100 |
| MS12 | 1989 | — | KM#10-14.1 | 17.00 | 17.00 |

## PROOF SETS

| KM# | Date | Mintage | Identification | Issue Price | Mkt Val |
|---|---|---|---|---|---|
| PS1 | 1973 | 97,454 | KM#109-15, 16a, 17a | 37.50 | 30.00 |
| PS2 | 1974 | 35,600 | KM#10-15, 16a, 17a | 50.00 | 30.00 |
| PS3 | 1975 | 20,458 | KM#10-15, 16a, 17a | 55.00 | 30.00 |
| PS4 | 1976 | 11,929 | KM#19-24, 25a, 26a | 55.00 | 40.00 |
| PS5 | 1977 | 5,014 | KM#10-15, 16a, 17a | 55.00 | 35.00 |
| PS6 | 1978 | 4,436 | KM#10-15, 16a, 17a | 58.00 | 37.50 |
| PS7 | 1979 | 4,126 | KM#10-15, 16a, 17a | 60.00 | 37.50 |
| PS8 | 1980 | 2,011 | KM#10-15, 16a, 17a | 117 | 45.00 |
| PS9 | 1980 | — | KM#16a, 17a | 115 | 32.50 |
| PS10 | 1981 | — | KM#10-15, 16a, 17a | 117 | 80.00 |
| PS11 | 1982 | — | KM#10-15, 16a, 34a | 117 | 80.00 |
| PS12 | 1983 | — | KM#10-15, 16a, 36a | — | 170 |
| PS13 | 1984 | — | KM#10-15, 16a, 40 | 132 | 200 |

# BELARUS

Belarus (Byelorussia, Belorussia, or White Russia- formerly the Belorussian S.S.R.) is situated along the western Dvina and Dnieper Rivers, bounded in the west by Poland, to the north by Latvia and Lithuania, to the east by Russia and the south by the Ukraine. It has an area of 80,154 sq. mi. (207,600 sq. km.) and a population of 4.8 million. Capital: Minsk. Chief products: peat, salt, and agricultural products including flax, fodder and grasses for cattle breeding and dairy products.

There never existed an independent state of Byelorussia. Until the partitions of Poland at the end of the 18th century, the history of Byelorussia is identical with that of Lithuania.

When Russia incorporated the whole of Byelorussia into its territories in 1795, it claimed to be recovering old Russian lands and denied that the Byelorussians were a separate nation. Significant efforts for independence did not occur until 1918 and were met by external antagonism from German, Polish, and Russian influences.

Soviet and anti-Communist sympathies continued to reflect the political and social unrest of the U.S.S.R. for Byelorussia. Finally, on August 25, 1991, following an unsuccessful coup, the Supreme Soviet adopted a declaration of independence, and the "Republic of Belarus" was proclaimed in September. In December, it became a founder member of the CIS.

**MONETARY SYSTEM**
100 Kapeek = 1 Rouble

## REPUBLIC

### STANDARD COINAGE

**ROUBLE** **KM# 6a** **Weight:** 28.5100 g. **Composition:** 0.9250 Silver .8479 oz. ASW

| Date | Mintage | F | VF | XF | Unc | BU |
|---|---|---|---|---|---|---|
| 1996 Proof | 20,000 | Value: 35.00 | | | | |

**ROUBLE** **KM# 7** **Composition:** Copper-Nickel **Subject:** Olympics **Obverse:** National arms **Reverse:** Gymnast on the rings

| Date | Mintage | F | VF | XF | Unc | BU |
|---|---|---|---|---|---|---|
| 1996 Prooflike | — | — | — | — | 12.50 | — |

**ROUBLE** **KM# 8** **Composition:** Copper-Nickel **Subject:** Olympics **Obverse:** National arms **Reverse:** Rhythmic gymnast

| Date | Mintage | F | VF | XF | Unc | BU |
|---|---|---|---|---|---|---|
| 1996 Prooflike | — | — | — | — | 12.50 | — |

**ROUBLE** **KM# 31** **Weight:** 7.9800 g. **Composition:** 0.9167 Gold .2532 oz. AGW **Subject:** United Nations 50th Anniversary **Obverse:** National arms **Reverse:** Crane flying over map and U.N. logo

| Date | Mintage | F | VF | XF | Unc | BU |
|---|---|---|---|---|---|---|
| 1996 Proof | 5,000 | Value: 185 | | | | |

**ROUBLE** **KM# 9** **Weight:** 7.9800 g. **Composition:** 0.9167 Gold .2532 oz. AGW **Subject:** Third Anniversary of Independence **Obverse:** National arms **Reverse:** Monument

| Date | Mintage | F | VF | XF | Unc | BU |
|---|---|---|---|---|---|---|
| 1997 Prooflike | — | — | — | — | 12.50 | — |

**ROUBLE** **KM# 34** **Weight:** 7.9800 g. **Composition:** 0.9167 Gold .2532 oz. AGW **Subject:** Olympics **Obverse:** National arms **Reverse:** Biathlon skier with rifle

| Date | Mintage | F | VF | XF | Unc | BU |
|---|---|---|---|---|---|---|
| 1997 Prooflike | 5,000 | — | — | — | 12.50 | — |

**ROUBLE** **KM# 36** **Weight:** 7.9800 g. **Composition:** 0.9167 Gold .2532 oz. AGW **Subject:** Olympics **Reverse:** 2 hockey players

| Date | Mintage | F | VF | XF | Unc | BU |
|---|---|---|---|---|---|---|
| 1997 Prooflike | 5,000 | — | — | — | 12.50 | — |

**ROUBLE** KM# 18 **Weight:** 7.9800 g. **Composition:** 0.9167 Gold .2532 oz. AGW **Subject:** Architecture of Belarus **Obverse:** National arms **Reverse:** Castle at Mir

| Date | Mintage | F | VF | XF | Unc | BU |
|---|---|---|---|---|---|---|
| 1998 Proof | — | Value: 11.50 | | | | |

**ROUBLE** KM# 19 **Weight:** 7.9800 g. **Composition:** 0.9167 Gold .2532 oz. AGW **Subject:** Cities of Belarus **Obverse:** National arms **Reverse:** Walled City of Polatsk with city arms

| Date | Mintage | F | VF | XF | Unc | BU |
|---|---|---|---|---|---|---|
| 1998 Proof | — | Value: 11.50 | | | | |

**ROUBLE** KM# 20 **Weight:** 7.9800 g. **Composition:** 0.9167 Gold .2532 oz. AGW **Subject:** 200th Anniversary - Birth of A. Mitskevich - Poet **Obverse:** National arms **Reverse:** Mitskevich portrait, dates

| Date | Mintage | F | VF | XF | Unc | BU |
|---|---|---|---|---|---|---|
| 1998 Proof | — | Value: 11.50 | | | | |

**ROUBLE** KM# 21 **Weight:** 7.9800 g. **Composition:** 0.9167 Gold .2532 oz. AGW **Subject:** Olympics **Obverse:** National arms and denomination **Reverse:** Hurdlers, Olympic crest

| Date | Mintage | F | VF | XF | Unc | BU |
|---|---|---|---|---|---|---|
| 1998 Proof | — | Value: 11.50 | | | | |

**ROUBLE** KM# 22 **Weight:** 7.9800 g. **Composition:** 0.9167 Gold .2532 oz. AGW **Subject:** Cities of Belarus **Obverse:** National arms **Reverse:** Minsk view with city arms

| Date | Mintage | F | VF | XF | Unc | BU |
|---|---|---|---|---|---|---|
| 1999 Proof | — | Value: 11.50 | | | | |

**ROUBLE** KM# 23 **Weight:** 7.9800 g. **Composition:** 0.9167 Gold .2532 oz. AGW **Subject:** 100th Anniversary - Birth of Mikhas Lynkou **Obverse:** National arms **Reverse:** Head of Lynkou facing right

| Date | Mintage | F | VF | XF | Unc | BU |
|---|---|---|---|---|---|---|
| 1999 Proof | — | Value: 11.50 | | | | |

**ROUBLE** KM# 40 **Weight:** 14.5000 g. **Composition:** Copper-Nickel **Subject:** G.N. Glebats **Obverse:** National arms **Reverse:** Glebats portrait with 2 smaller portraits, dates **Edge:** Reeded

| Date | Mintage | F | VF | XF | Unc | BU |
|---|---|---|---|---|---|---|
| 1999 Proof | — | Value: 11.50 | | | | |

**ROUBLE** KM# 41 **Composition:** Copper-Nickel **Subject:** 2000 Years **Obverse:** National arms **Reverse:** Bethlehem view

| Date | Mintage | F | VF | XF | Unc | BU |
|---|---|---|---|---|---|---|
| 1999 Proof | — | Value: 11.50 | | | | |

**10 ROUBLES** KM# 24 **Weight:** 16.9600 g. **Composition:** 0.9250 Silver .5044 oz. ASW **Subject:** 200th Anniversary - Birth of A. Mitskevich **Obverse:** National arms **Reverse:** Portrait Mitskevich facing left, dates

| Date | Mintage | F | VF | XF | Unc | BU |
|---|---|---|---|---|---|---|
| 1998 Proof | — | Value: 28.50 | | | | |

**10 ROUBLES** KM# 25 **Weight:** 16.9600 g. **Composition:** 0.9250 Silver .5044 oz. ASW **Subject:** G.N. Glebats - Theatre Artist **Obverse:** National arms **Reverse:** Glebats portrait with 2 smaller portraits, dates

| Date | Mintage | F | VF | XF | Unc | BU |
|---|---|---|---|---|---|---|
| 1999 Proof | — | Value: 28.50 | | | | |

**10 ROUBLES** KM# 26 **Weight:** 16.9600 g. **Composition:** 0.9250 Silver .5044 oz. ASW **Subject:** 100th Anniversary - Birth of Mikhas Lynkou **Obverse:** National arms **Reverse:** Head of Lynkou facing right, dates

| Date | Mintage | F | VF | XF | Unc | BU |
|---|---|---|---|---|---|---|
| 1999 Proof | — | Value: 28.50 | | | | |

**20 ROUBLES** KM# 13 **Weight:** 33.8400 g. **Composition:** 0.9250 Silver 1.0064 oz. ASW **Subject:** Olympics **Obverse:** National arms and denomination **Reverse:** Olympic crest, gymnast on rings

| Date | Mintage | F | VF | XF | Unc | BU |
|---|---|---|---|---|---|---|
| 1996 Proof | 1,000 | Value: 50.00 | | | | |

**20 ROUBLES** KM# 14 **Weight:** 33.8400 g. **Composition:** 0.9250 Silver 1.0064 oz. ASW **Subject:** Olympics **Obverse:** National arms **Reverse:** Ribbon dancer

| Date | Mintage | F | VF | XF | Unc | BU |
|---|---|---|---|---|---|---|
| 1996 Proof | 1,000 | Value: 50.00 | | | | |

**20 ROUBLES** **KM# 10** **Weight:** 34.7400 g. **Composition:** 0.9000 Silver 1.0052 oz. ASW **Subject:** Monument of Independence **Obverse:** National emblem

| Date | Mintage | F | VF | XF | Unc | BU |
|---|---|---|---|---|---|---|
| 1997 Proof | 2,000 | Value: 45.00 | | | | |

**20 ROUBLES** **KM# 11** **Weight:** 34.7400 g. **Composition:** 0.9000 Silver 1.0052 oz. ASW **Subject:** Russia-Belarus State Treaty **Obverse:** National emblem **Reverse:** 2 city views with respective national emblems

| Date | Mintage | F | VF | XF | Unc | BU |
|---|---|---|---|---|---|---|
| 1997 Proof | — | Value: 45.00 | | | | |

**20 ROUBLES** **KM# 12** **Weight:** 31.4800 g. **Composition:** 0.9990 Silver 1.0110 oz. ASW **Subject:** 75th Anniversary - Banking System **Obverse:** National emblem **Reverse:** Bank building

| Date | Mintage | F | VF | XF | Unc | BU |
|---|---|---|---|---|---|---|
| 1997 Proof | — | Value: 50.00 | | | | |

**20 ROUBLES** **KM# 15** **Weight:** 31.0300 g. **Composition:** 0.9250 Silver .9228 oz. ASW **Subject:** Olympics **Obverse:** National arms **Reverse:** Biathalon skier

| Date | Mintage | F | VF | XF | Unc | BU |
|---|---|---|---|---|---|---|
| 1997 Proof | Est. 1,000 | Value: 35.00 | | | | |

**20 ROUBLES** **KM# 16** **Weight:** 31.1500 g. **Composition:** 0.9250 Silver .9264 oz. ASW **Subject:** Olympics **Obverse:** National arms **Reverse:** 2 hockey players

| Date | Mintage | F | VF | XF | Unc | BU |
|---|---|---|---|---|---|---|
| 1997 Proof | Est. 1,000 | Value: 35.00 | | | | |

**20 ROUBLES** **KM# 27** **Weight:** 33.5200 g. **Composition:** 0.9250 Silver .9969 oz. ASW **Subject:** Architecture of Belarus **Obverse:** National arms **Reverse:** Castle and Mir and seal

| Date | Mintage | F | VF | XF | Unc | BU |
|---|---|---|---|---|---|---|
| 1998 Proof | — | Value: 35.00 | | | | |

**20 ROUBLES** **KM# 28** **Weight:** 33.5200 g. **Composition:** 0.9250 Silver .9969 oz. ASW **Subject:** Cities of Belarus **Obverse:** National arms **Reverse:** Polatsk with city arms above

| Date | Mintage | F | VF | XF | Unc | BU |
|---|---|---|---|---|---|---|
| 1998 Proof | — | Value: 35.00 | | | | |

**20 ROUBLES** **KM# 29** **Weight:** 33.5200 g. **Composition:** 0.9250 Silver .9969 oz. ASW **Subject:** Olympics **Obverse:** National arms and denomination **Reverse:** Hurdlers, Olympic crest

| Date | Mintage | F | VF | XF | Unc | BU |
|---|---|---|---|---|---|---|
| 1998 Proof | — | Value: 35.00 | | | | |

**20 ROUBLES** **KM# 17** **Weight:** 33.9000 g. **Composition:** 0.9250 Silver 1.0082 oz. ASW **Subject:** 80th Anniversary - Financial System **Obverse:** National arms **Reverse:** Anniversary logo

| Date | Mintage | F | VF | XF | Unc | BU |
|---|---|---|---|---|---|---|
| 1999 Proof | — | Value: 32.50 | | | | |

**20 ROUBLES** **KM# 30** **Weight:** 33.5200 g. **Composition:** 0.9250 Silver .9969 oz. ASW **Subject:** Cities of Belarus **Obverse:** National arms **Reverse:** Minsk view with city arms

| Date | Mintage | F | VF | XF | Unc | BU |
|---|---|---|---|---|---|---|
| 1999 Proof | — | Value: 35.00 | | | | |

**20 ROUBLES** **KM# 42** **Weight:** 33.8600 g. **Composition:** 0.9250 Silver 1.0070 oz. ASW **Subject:** 2000 Years of Christianity **Obverse:** National arms **Reverse:** Bethlehem view **Edge:** Reeded

| Date | Mintage | F | VF | XF | Unc | BU |
|---|---|---|---|---|---|---|
| 1999 Proof | — | Value: 35.00 | | | | |

**20 ROUBLES** **KM# 43** **Weight:** 33.8600 g. **Composition:** 0.9250 Silver 1.0070 oz. ASW **Subject:** Jubilee 2000 **Obverse:** National arms **Reverse:** 3 churches

| Date | Mintage | F | VF | XF | Unc | BU |
|---|---|---|---|---|---|---|
| 1999 Proof | — | Value: 35.00 | | | | |

**50 ROUBLES** **KM# 32** **Weight:** 7.7800 g. **Composition:** 0.9990 Gold .2499 oz. AGW **Subject:** Olympics **Obverse:** National arms **Reverse:** Ribbon dancer

| Date | Mintage | F | VF | XF | Unc | BU |
|---|---|---|---|---|---|---|
| 1996 Proof | 500 | Value: 220 | | | | |

**50 ROUBLES** **KM# 33** **Weight:** 7.7800 g. **Composition:** 0.9990 Gold .2499 oz. AGW **Reverse:** Gymnast on rings

| Date | Mintage | F | VF | XF | Unc | BU |
|---|---|---|---|---|---|---|
| 1996 Proof | 500 | Value: 220 | | | | |

**50 ROUBLES** **KM# 35** **Weight:** 7.7800 g. **Composition:** 0.9990 Gold .2499 oz. AGW **Reverse:** Skier with rifle

| Date | Mintage | F | VF | XF | Unc | BU |
|---|---|---|---|---|---|---|
| 1997 Proof | 500 | Value: 220 | | | | |

**50 ROUBLES** **KM# 37** **Weight:** 7.7800 g. **Composition:** 0.9990 Gold .2499 oz. AGW **Reverse:** 2 hockey players

| Date | Mintage | F | VF | XF | Unc | BU |
|---|---|---|---|---|---|---|
| 1997 Proof | 500 | Value: 220 | | | | |

**50 ROUBLES** **KM# 38** **Weight:** 7.7800 g. **Composition:** 0.9990 Gold .2499 oz. AGW **Reverse:** 2 hurdlers

| Date | Mintage | F | VF | XF | Unc | BU |
|---|---|---|---|---|---|---|
| 1997 Proof | 500 | Value: 220 | | | | |

# BELGIAN CONGO

The Belgian Congo and Ruanda-Urundi were united administratively from 1925 to 1960. Ruanda-Urundi was made a U.N. Trust territory in 1946. Coins for these 2 areas were made jointly between 1952 and 1960. Ruanda-Urundi became the Republic of Rwanda on June 1, 1962.

**MONETARY SYSTEM**

100 Centimes = 1 Franc

## PROVINCE

### DECIMAL COINAGE

**CENTIME** **KM# 15** **Composition:** Copper

| Date | Mintage | F | VF | XF | Unc | BU |
|---|---|---|---|---|---|---|
| 1910 | 2,000,000 | 1.00 | 2.00 | 3.00 | 9.00 | — |
| 1919 | 500,000 | 1.00 | 2.00 | 3.00 | 10.00 | — |

**2 CENTIMES** **KM# 16** **Composition:** Copper

| Date | Mintage | F | VF | XF | Unc | BU |
|---|---|---|---|---|---|---|
| 1910 | 1,500,000 | 1.00 | 3.00 | 7.00 | 25.00 | — |
| 1919 | 500,000 | 1.50 | 3.50 | 10.00 | 30.00 | — |

**5 CENTIMES** **KM# 12** **Composition:** Copper-Nickel

| Date | Mintage | F | VF | XF | Unc | BU |
|---|---|---|---|---|---|---|
| 1909 | 1,800,000 | 5.00 | 12.50 | 40.00 | 100 | — |

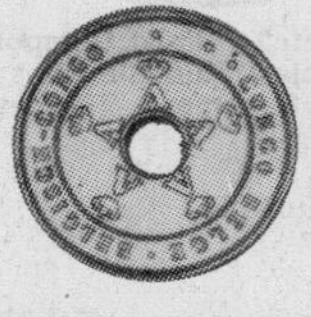

**5 CENTIMES** **KM# 17** **Composition:** Copper-Nickel

| Date | Mintage | F | VF | XF | Unc | BU |
|---|---|---|---|---|---|---|
| 1910(H) | 6,000,000 | 0.75 | 1.50 | 3.50 | 16.00 | — |
| 1911(H) | 5,000,000 | 0.75 | 1.50 | 3.50 | 16.00 | — |
| 1917(H) | 1,000,000 | 3.00 | 7.00 | 18.00 | 55.00 | — |
| 1917(H) Proof | — | Value: 175 | | | | |
| 1919(H) | 3,000,000 | 1.50 | 3.00 | 7.00 | 25.00 | — |
| 1919 | 6,850,000 | 0.50 | 1.00 | 2.50 | 16.00 | — |
| 1920 | 2,740,000 | 0.50 | 1.00 | 3.50 | 18.00 | — |
| 1921 | 17,260,000 | 0.25 | 0.75 | 1.50 | 10.00 | — |
| 1921(H) | 3,000,000 | 1.00 | 2.00 | 6.00 | 20.00 | — |
| 1925 | 11,000,000 | 0.25 | 0.75 | 2.00 | 10.00 | — |
| 1926/5 | 5,770,000 | 2.25 | 4.50 | — | — | — |
| 1926 | Inc. above | 0.25 | 1.00 | 2.00 | 9.00 | — |
| 1927 | 2,000,000 | 0.50 | 1.00 | 2.50 | 10.00 | — |
| 1928/6 | 1,500,000 | 2.00 | 4.00 | 8.00 | 20.00 | — |
| 1928 | Inc. above | 0.75 | 1.25 | 3.00 | 10.00 | — |

**10 CENTIMES** **KM# 13** **Composition:** Copper-Nickel

| Date | Mintage | F | VF | XF | Unc | BU |
|---|---|---|---|---|---|---|
| 1909 | 1,500,000 | 8.00 | 20.00 | 70.00 | 160 | — |

**10 CENTIMES** **KM# 18** **Composition:** Copper-Nickel

| Date | Mintage | F | VF | XF | Unc | BU |
|---|---|---|---|---|---|---|
| 1910 | 5,000,000 | 0.50 | 1.00 | 3.00 | 15.00 | — |
| 1911 | 5,000,000 | 0.50 | 1.00 | 3.00 | 15.00 | — |
| 1917(H) | 500,000 | 5.00 | 10.00 | 25.00 | 75.00 | — |
| 1919 | 3,430,000 | 0.50 | 1.00 | 3.50 | 16.50 | — |
| 1919(H) | 1,500,000 | 0.75 | 1.25 | 4.00 | 18.00 | — |
| 1920 | 1,510,000 | 0.75 | 1.25 | 4.00 | 18.00 | — |
| 1921 | 13,540,000 | 0.25 | 0.75 | 2.00 | 10.00 | — |
| 1921(H) | 3,000,000 | 0.75 | 1.50 | 3.50 | 16.50 | — |
| 1922 | 14,950,000 | 0.25 | 1.00 | 2.50 | 10.00 | — |
| 1924 | 3,600,000 | 0.50 | 1.50 | 3.00 | 15.00 | — |
| 1925/4 | 4,800,000 | 2.00 | 4.00 | 8.00 | 50.00 | — |
| 1925 | Inc. above | 0.25 | 1.00 | 3.00 | 15.00 | — |
| 1927 | 2,020,000 | 0.25 | 1.00 | 3.00 | 12.00 | — |
| 1928/7 | 5,600,000 | 1.00 | 3.00 | 8.00 | 40.00 | — |
| 1928 | Inc. above | 0.25 | 1.00 | 3.00 | 12.00 | — |

**20 CENTIMES** **KM# 14** **Composition:** Copper-Nickel

| Date | Mintage | F | VF | XF | Unc | BU |
|---|---|---|---|---|---|---|
| 1909 | 300,000 | 10.00 | 25.00 | 65.00 | 180 | — |

**20 CENTIMES** **KM# 19** **Composition:** Copper-Nickel

| Date | Mintage | F | VF | XF | Unc | BU |
|---|---|---|---|---|---|---|
| 1910 | 1,000,000 | 2.00 | 5.00 | 12.00 | 40.00 | — |
| 1911 | 1,250,000 | 1.50 | 4.00 | 10.00 | 35.00 | — |

**20 CENTIMES** **KM# 22** **Composition:** Copper-Nickel **Reverse:** French legend **Rev. Legend:** CONGO BELGE

| Date | Mintage | F | VF | XF | Unc | BU |
|---|---|---|---|---|---|---|
| 1921 | 4,000,000 | 0.60 | 2.00 | 8.00 | 27.50 | — |
| 1922 | 6,000,000 | 0.60 | 2.00 | 8.00 | 27.50 | — |
| 1923 | 7,200,000 | 0.60 | 2.00 | 8.00 | 27.50 | — |
| 1924 | 1,096,000 | 0.75 | 3.00 | 10.00 | 32.50 | — |
| 1925 | 16,104,000 | 0.60 | 2.00 | 7.00 | 25.00 | — |
| 1926/5 | 16,000,000 | 1.00 | 4.00 | 12.00 | 45.00 | — |
| 1926 | Inc. above | 0.60 | 2.00 | 8.00 | 25.00 | — |
| 1927 | 10,000,000 | 0.60 | 2.00 | 8.00 | 27.50 | — |
| 1929/7 | 7,504,000 | 0.60 | 2.00 | 9.00 | 32.00 | — |
| 1929/8 | Inc. above | 1.00 | 4.00 | 15.00 | 90.00 | — |
| 1929 | Inc. above | 0.60 | 2.00 | 7.00 | 25.00 | — |

**20 CENTIMES** **KM# 23** **Composition:** Copper-Nickel **Reverse:** Flemish legend **Rev. Legend:** BELGISCH CONGO

| Date | Mintage | F | VF | XF | Unc | BU |
|---|---|---|---|---|---|---|
| 1921 | 4,000,000 | 0.60 | 2.00 | 8.00 | 32.00 | — |
| 1922 | 5,592,000 | 0.60 | 2.00 | 7.00 | 27.50 | — |
| 1923 | 7,208,000 | 1.00 | 5.00 | 16.50 | 70.00 | — |

| Date | Mintage | F | VF | XF | Unc | BU |
|---|---|---|---|---|---|---|
| 1923 | Inc. above | 0.60 | 2.00 | 7.00 | 25.00 | — |
| 1924 | 7,000,000 | 0.60 | 2.00 | 8.00 | 27.50 | — |
| 1925/4 | 10,600,000 | 1.50 | 7.00 | 20.00 | 90.00 | — |
| 1925 | Inc. above | 0.60 | 2.00 | 7.00 | 27.50 | — |
| 1926 | 25,200,000 | 0.60 | 2.00 | 7.00 | 25.00 | — |
| 1927 | 4,800,000 | 0.60 | 2.00 | 8.00 | 27.50 | — |
| 1928 | 7,484,000 | 0.60 | 2.00 | 7.00 | 25.00 | — |
| 1929/8 | 116,000 | 25.00 | 50.00 | 75.00 | 120 | — |
| 1929 | Inc. above | 20.00 | 40.00 | 70.00 | 100 | — |

**FRANC** **KM# 20** **Composition:** Copper-Nickel **Reverse:** French legend **Rev. Legend:** CONGO BELGE

| Date | Mintage | F | VF | XF | Unc | BU |
|---|---|---|---|---|---|---|
| 1920 | 4,000,000 | 0.85 | 2.75 | 10.00 | 37.50 | — |
| 1922 | 5,000,000 | 0.85 | 2.75 | 9.00 | 32.00 | — |
| 1923/2 | 5,000,000 | 2.00 | 7.00 | 16.00 | 45.00 | — |
| 1923 | Inc. above | 0.85 | 2.75 | 9.00 | 32.00 | — |
| 1924 | 6,030,000 | 0.85 | 2.75 | 9.00 | 35.00 | — |
| 1925 | 10,470,000 | 0.85 | 2.75 | 9.00 | 32.00 | — |
| 1926/5 | 12,500,000 | 2.00 | 7.00 | 16.50 | 50.00 | — |
| 1926 | Inc. above | 0.85 | 2.75 | 8.00 | 30.00 | — |
| 1927 | 15,250,000 | 0.85 | 2.75 | 8.00 | 30.00 | — |
| 1929 | 5,763,000 | 0.85 | 2.75 | 9.00 | 32.00 | — |
| 1930 | 5,000,000 | 0.85 | 2.75 | 10.00 | 40.00 | — |

**FRANC** **KM# 21** **Composition:** Copper-Nickel **Reverse:** Flemish legend **Rev. Legend:** BELGISCH CONGO

| Date | Mintage | F | VF | XF | Unc | BU |
|---|---|---|---|---|---|---|
| 1920 | 475,000 | 2.00 | 5.00 | 16.50 | 50.00 | — |
| 1921 | 3,525,000 | 0.85 | 3.00 | 9.00 | 37.50 | — |
| 1922 | 5,000,000 | 0.85 | 3.00 | 9.00 | 37.50 | — |
| 1923/2 | 7,362,000 | 2.00 | 5.00 | 17.00 | 55.00 | — |
| 1923 | Inc. above | 0.85 | 2.75 | 9.00 | 32.00 | — |
| 1924 | 4,608,000 | 0.85 | 3.00 | 10.00 | 37.50 | — |
| 1925 | 9,530,000 | 0.85 | 2.75 | 9.00 | 32.00 | — |
| 1926/5 | 17,000,000 | 2.00 | 5.00 | 17.00 | 55.00 | — |
| 1926 | Inc. above | 0.85 | 2.75 | 9.00 | 32.00 | — |
| 1928 | 9,250,000 | 0.85 | 2.75 | 9.00 | 32.00 | — |
| 1929 | 4,250,000 | 0.85 | 3.00 | 10.00 | 37.50 | — |

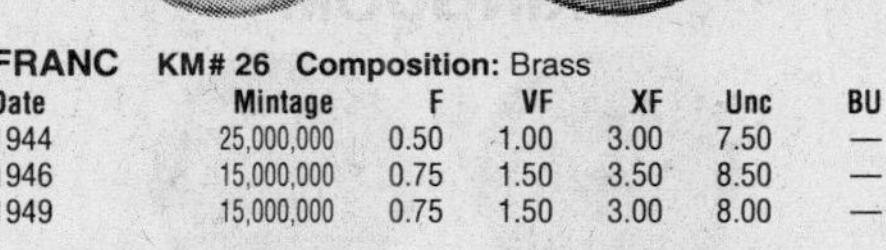


**FRANC** **KM# 26** **Composition:** Brass

| Date | Mintage | F | VF | XF | Unc | BU |
|---|---|---|---|---|---|---|
| 1944 | 25,000,000 | 0.50 | 1.00 | 3.00 | 7.50 | — |
| 1946 | 15,000,000 | 0.75 | 1.50 | 3.50 | 8.50 | — |
| 1949 | 15,000,000 | 0.75 | 1.50 | 3.00 | 8.00 | — |

**2 FRANCS** **KM# 25** **Composition:** Brass

| Date | Mintage | F | VF | XF | Unc | BU |
|---|---|---|---|---|---|---|
| 1943 | 25,000,000 | 2.50 | 4.50 | 9.00 | 40.00 | — |

**2 FRANCS** **KM# 28** **Composition:** Brass

| Date | Mintage | F | VF | XF | Unc | BU |
|---|---|---|---|---|---|---|
| 1946 | 13,000,000 | 1.00 | 2.00 | 3.50 | 12.00 | — |
| 1947 | 12,000,000 | 1.00 | 2.00 | 4.00 | 15.00 | — |

**5 FRANCS** **KM# 24** **Composition:** Nickel-Bronze

| Date | Mintage | F | VF | XF | Unc | BU |
|---|---|---|---|---|---|---|
| 1936 | 2,600,000 | 5.00 | 10.00 | 20.00 | 95.00 | — |
| 1937 | 11,400,000 | 4.00 | 12.00 | 25.00 | 100 | — |

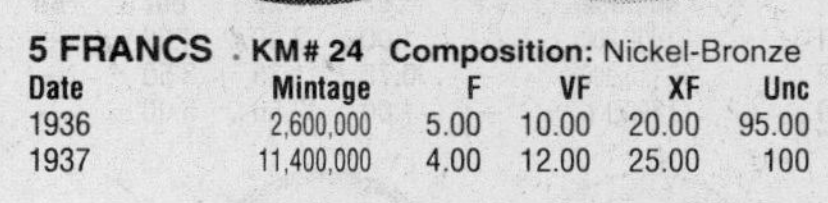


**5 FRANCS** **KM# 29** **Composition:** Brass

| Date | Mintage | F | VF | XF | Unc | BU |
|---|---|---|---|---|---|---|
| 1947 | 10,000,000 | 3.00 | 7.00 | 15.00 | 50.00 | — |

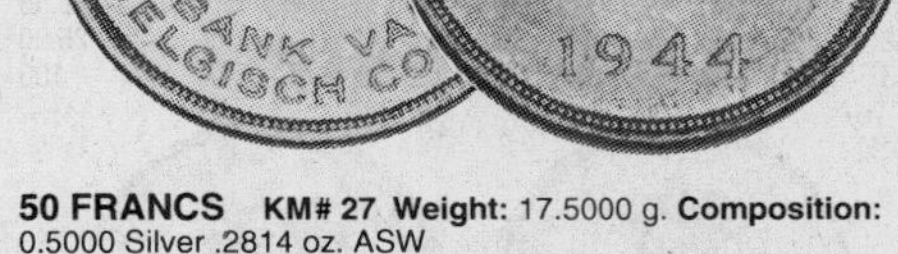


**50 FRANCS** **KM# 27** **Weight:** 17.5000 g. **Composition:** 0.5000 Silver .2814 oz. ASW

| Date | Mintage | F | VF | XF | Unc | BU |
|---|---|---|---|---|---|---|
| 1944 | 1,000,000 | 20.00 | 50.00 | 90.00 | 175 | — |

# RUANDA-URUNDI

## PROVINCE

### DECIMAL COINAGE

**FRANC** **KM# 4** **Composition:** Aluminum

| Date | Mintage | F | VF | XF | Unc | BU |
|---|---|---|---|---|---|---|
| 1957 | 10,000,000 | — | 0.50 | 1.00 | 2.00 | — |
| 1958 | 20,000,000 | — | 0.50 | 1.00 | 2.00 | — |
| 1959 | 20,000,000 | — | 0.50 | 1.00 | 2.00 | — |
| 1960 | 20,000,000 | — | 0.50 | 1.00 | 2.00 | — |

**5 FRANCS** KM# 1 **Composition:** Brass

| Date | Mintage | F | VF | XF | Unc | BU |
|---|---|---|---|---|---|---|
| 1952 | 10,000,000 | — | 2.50 | 5.00 | 10.00 | — |

**5 FRANCS** KM# 3 **Composition:** Aluminum

| Date | Mintage | F | VF | XF | Unc | BU |
|---|---|---|---|---|---|---|
| 1956 DB | 10,000,000 | — | 1.00 | 2.00 | 4.00 | — |
| 1958 DB | 26,110,000 | — | 0.75 | 1.75 | 3.50 | — |
| 1959 DB | 3,890,000 | — | 1.00 | 2.50 | 5.00 | — |

**50 CENTIMES** KM# 2 **Composition:** Aluminum

| Date | Mintage | F | VF | XF | Unc | BU |
|---|---|---|---|---|---|---|
| 1954 DB | 4,700,000 | — | 0.35 | 0.75 | 2.00 | — |
| 1955 DB | 20,300,000 | — | 0.15 | 0.60 | 1.50 | — |

## ESSAIS

| KM# | Date | Mintage | Identification | Mkt Val |
|---|---|---|---|---|
| E1 | 1952 | — | 5 Francs. | 35.00 |
| E2 | 1954 | — | 50 Centimes. | 25.00 |
| E3 | 1954 | — | 50 Centimes. Silver. | 100 |

| KM# | Date | Mintage | Identification | Mkt Val |
|---|---|---|---|---|
| E4 | 1956 | — | 5 Francs. | 30.00 |

| KM# | Date | Mintage | Identification | Mkt Val |
|---|---|---|---|---|
| E5 | 1957 | — | Franc. | 20.00 |
| E6 | 1960 | — | Franc. Bronze. | 90.00 |

# BELGIUM

The Kingdom of Belgium, a constitutional monarchy in northwest Europe, has an area of 11,780 sq. mi. (30,519 sq. km.) and a population of 10.1 million, chiefly Dutch-speaking Flemish and French-speaking Walloons. Capital: Brussels. Agriculture, dairy farming, and the processing of raw materials for re-export are the principal industries. Beurs voor Diamant in Antwerp is the world's largest diamond trading center. Iron and steel, machinery motor vehicles, chemicals, textile yarns and fabrics comprise the principal exports.

At the Congress of Vienna in 1815 the area was reunited with the Netherlands, but in 1830 independence was gained and the constitutional monarchy of Belgium was established. A large part of the Duchy of Luxembourg was incorporated into Belgium and the first king was Leopold I of Saxe-Coburg-Gotha. It was invaded by the German Army in August, 1914 and the German forces carried on a devastating occupation of most of the territory until the Armistice. Belgium joined the League of Nations. On May 10, 1940 it was invaded again by the German army. The Belgian and Allied forces were quickly overwhelmed and were evacuated through Dunkirk. Allied troops reached Belgium again in Sept. 1944. Prince Charles, Count of Flanders, assumed King Leopold's responsibilities until liberation by the U.S. Army in Austria on May 8, 1945. As of January 1, 1989, Belgium became a federal kingdom.

**RULERS**

Leopold II, 1865-1909
Albert I, 1909-1934
Leopold III, 1934-1950
Baudouin I, 1951-1993
Albert II, 1993-

**MINT MARKS**

Angel head - Brussels

**MINTMASTERS INITIALS & PRIVY MARKS**

(b) - bird - Vogelier
Lamb head – Lambret

**NOTE**: Beginning in 1987, the letters "qp" appear on the coins - (quality proof)

**MONETARY SYSTEM**

100 Centimes = 1 Franc
1 Ecu - 1 Euro

**LEGENDS**

Belgian coins are usually inscribed either in Dutch, French or both. However some modern coins are being inscribed in Latin or German. The language used is best told by noting the spelling of the name of the country.

(Fr) French: BELGIQUE or BELGES
(Du) Dutch: BELGIE or BELGEN
(La) Latin: BELGICA
(Ge) German: BELGIEN

Many Belgian coins are collected by what is known as Position A and Position B edges. Some dates command a premium depending on the position which are as follows:

Position A: Coins with portrait side down having upright edge lettering.
Position B: Coins with portrait side up having upright edge lettering.

# KINGDOM

**CENTIME** KM# 33.1 **Composition:** Copper **Obverse:** Legend in French **Obv. Legend:** DES BELGES

| Date | Mintage | F | VF | XF | Unc | BU |
|---|---|---|---|---|---|---|
| 1901/801 Near 1 | 3,743,000 | 0.50 | 1.50 | 3.50 | 15.00 | — |
| 1901/801 Far 1 | Inc. above | 0.50 | 1.50 | 3.50 | 15.00 | — |
| 1901 | Inc. above | 0.25 | 0.50 | 1.50 | 5.00 | — |
| 1902/802 Near 2 | 2,847,000 | 1.00 | 2.00 | 7.50 | 20.00 | — |
| 1902/802 Far 2 | Inc. above | 1.00 | 2.00 | 7.50 | 20.00 | — |
| 1902/801 | Inc. above | 1.00 | 2.00 | 7.50 | 25.00 | — |
| 1902/1 | Inc. above | 1.00 | 2.00 | 7.50 | 20.00 | — |
| 1902 | Inc. above | 0.20 | 0.50 | 1.50 | 5.00 | — |
| 1907 | 3,967,000 | 0.20 | 0.50 | 1.50 | 5.00 | — |

**CENTIME** KM# 34.1 **Composition:** Copper **Obverse:** Legend in Dutch **Obv. Legend:** DER BELGEN

| Date | Mintage | F | VF | XF | Unc | BU |
|---|---|---|---|---|---|---|
| 1901/899 | Inc. above | 0.75 | 2.25 | 4.50 | 10.00 | — |
| 1901 | Inc. above | 0.25 | 0.50 | 1.50 | 5.00 | — |
| 1902/1 | 2,482,000 | 1.25 | 3.50 | 9.00 | 15.00 | — |
| 1902 | Inc. above | 0.25 | 0.75 | 2.00 | 7.00 | — |
| 1907 | 3,966,000 | 0.25 | 0.75 | 1.50 | 5.00 | — |

**CENTIME** KM# 33.2 **Composition:** Copper **Note:** Thin flan.

| Date | Mintage | F | VF | XF | Unc | BU |
|---|---|---|---|---|---|---|
| 1901 | Inc. above | 1.00 | 1.50 | 4.00 | 12.50 | — |
| 1902 | Inc. above | 1.00 | 1.50 | 6.00 | 15.00 | — |

**CENTIME** KM# 34.2 **Composition:** Copper **Note:** Thin flan.

| Date | Mintage | F | VF | XF | Unc | BU |
|---|---|---|---|---|---|---|
| 1901 | Inc. above | 1.00 | 1.50 | 8.00 | 25.00 | — |
| 1902 | Inc. above | 1.00 | 1.50 | 8.00 | 25.00 | — |

**CENTIME** KM# 33.3 **Composition:** Copper **Reverse:** Additional stop in signature... BRAEMT.F.

| Date | Mintage | F | VF | XF | Unc | BU |
|---|---|---|---|---|---|---|
| 1902 | Inc. above | 1.00 | 2.00 | 10.00 | 30.00 | — |

**CENTIME** KM# 76 **Composition:** Copper **Obverse:** Legend in French **Obv. Legend:** DES BELGES

| Date | Mintage | F | VF | XF | Unc | BU |
|---|---|---|---|---|---|---|
| 1912 | 2,540,000 | 0.20 | 0.50 | 2.50 | 7.00 | — |
| 1914 | 870,000 | 0.25 | 0.75 | 3.50 | 10.00 | — |

**CENTIME** KM# 77 **Composition:** Copper **Obverse:** Legend in Dutch **Obv. Legend:** DER BELGEN

| Date | Mintage | F | VF | XF | Unc | BU |
|---|---|---|---|---|---|---|
| 1912 | 2,542,000 | 0.20 | 0.50 | 1.50 | 5.00 | — |

**2 CENTIMES** KM# 35.1 **Composition:** Copper **Obverse:** Legend in French **Obv. Legend:** DES BELGES

| Date | Mintage | F | VF | XF | Unc | BU |
|---|---|---|---|---|---|---|
| 1902 | 2,490,000 | 0.15 | 0.50 | 4.00 | 12.00 | — |
| 1905 | 4,981,000 | 0.15 | 0.35 | 2.00 | 7.00 | — |
| 1909/5 | 4,983,000 | 0.75 | 1.50 | 8.00 | 25.00 | — |
| 1909 | Inc. above | 0.15 | 0.35 | 2.00 | 7.00 | — |

**2 CENTIMES** KM# 36 **Composition:** Copper **Obverse:** Legend in Dutch **Obv. Legend:** DER BELGEN

| Date | Mintage | F | VF | XF | Unc | BU |
|---|---|---|---|---|---|---|
| 1902 | 2,488,000 | 0.15 | 1.50 | 3.00 | 10.00 | — |
| 1905/2 | 4,986,000 | 1.50 | 3.00 | 15.00 | 40.00 | — |
| 1905 | Inc. above | 0.15 | 1.00 | 2.00 | 7.00 | — |
| 1909 | 565,000 | 0.50 | 2.00 | 12.00 | 25.00 | — |

**2 CENTIMES** KM# 35.2 **Composition:** Copper **Note:** Thin flan.

| Date | Mintage | F | VF | XF | Unc | BU |
|---|---|---|---|---|---|---|
| 1902 | Inc. above | 3.00 | 5.00 | 35.00 | 100 | — |

**2 CENTIMES** KM# 65 **Composition:** Copper **Obverse:** Legend in Dutch **Obv. Legend:** DER BELGEN

| Date | Mintage | F | VF | XF | Unc | BU |
|---|---|---|---|---|---|---|
| 1910 | 1,248,000 | 0.25 | 0.50 | 3.00 | 7.00 | — |
| 1911 Large date | 6,441,000 | 0.15 | 0.35 | 1.50 | 5.00 | — |
| 1911 Small date | Inc. above | 0.15 | 0.35 | 1.50 | 5.00 | — |
| 1912 | 1,602,000 | 0.35 | 0.50 | 2.00 | 6.00 | — |
| 1919 | 4,998,000 | 0.15 | 0.35 | 0.75 | 3.00 | — |

**2 CENTIMES** **KM# 64** **Composition:** Copper **Obverse:** Legend in French **Obv. Legend:** DES BELGES

| Date | Mintage | F | VF | XF | Unc | BU |
|---|---|---|---|---|---|---|
| 1911 | 645,000 | 1.50 | 3.00 | 14.00 | 40.00 | — |
| 1912/1 | 4,928,000 | 1.00 | 2.00 | 8.00 | 20.00 | — |
| 1912 | Inc. above | 0.15 | 0.50 | 2.00 | 5.00 | — |
| 1914 | 491,000 | 1.00 | 2.50 | 12.00 | 30.00 | — |
| 1919/4 | 5,000,000 | 0.75 | 1.00 | 5.00 | 10.00 | — |
| 1919 | Inc. above | 0.15 | 0.25 | 1.00 | 3.00 | — |

**5 CENTIMES** **KM# 40.1** **Composition:** Copper-Nickel **Obverse:** Legend in French **Obv. Legend:** DES BELGES

| Date | Mintage | F | VF | XF | Unc | BU |
|---|---|---|---|---|---|---|
| 1901 | — | 10.00 | 16.00 | 65.00 | 140 | — |

**5 CENTIMES** **KM# 44** **Composition:** Copper-Nickel **Reverse:** Lion of different design

| Date | Mintage | F | VF | XF | Unc | BU |
|---|---|---|---|---|---|---|
| 1901 | 2,494,000 | 3.00 | 8.00 | 35.00 | 70.00 | — |

**5 CENTIMES** **KM# 45** **Composition:** Copper-Nickel **Obverse:** Legend in Dutch **Obv. Legend:** DER BELGEN **Reverse:** Lion of different lower design

| Date | Mintage | F | VF | XF | Unc | BU |
|---|---|---|---|---|---|---|
| 1901 | 2,491,000 | 3.00 | 8.00 | 35.00 | 70.00 | — |

**5 CENTIMES** **KM# 46** **Composition:** Copper-Nickel **Obverse:** Legend in French, small date **Obv. Legend:** BELGIQUE

| Date | Mintage | F | VF | XF | Unc | BU |
|---|---|---|---|---|---|---|
| 1901 | 202,000 | 15.00 | 30.00 | 75.00 | 150 | — |
| 1902/1 | 1,416,000 | 0.50 | 2.00 | 9.00 | 20.00 | — |
| 1902 | Inc. above | 0.25 | 1.50 | 6.00 | 14.00 | — |
| 1903 | 864,000 | 1.00 | 4.00 | 15.00 | 30.00 | — |

**5 CENTIMES** **KM# 47** **Composition:** Copper-Nickel **Obverse:** Legend in Dutch, small date **Obv. Legend:** BELGIE

| Date | Mintage | F | VF | XF | Unc | BU |
|---|---|---|---|---|---|---|
| 1902/1 | 1,485,000 | 1.75 | 5.50 | 22.50 | 45.00 | — |
| 1902 | Inc. above | 0.15 | 1.50 | 7.00 | 20.00 | — |
| 1903 | 1,002,000 | 1.00 | 5.00 | 20.00 | 40.00 | — |

**5 CENTIMES** **KM# 54** **Composition:** Copper-Nickel **Obverse:** Legend in French, large date **Obv. Legend:** BELGIQUE

| Date | Mintage | F | VF | XF | Unc | BU |
|---|---|---|---|---|---|---|
| 1904 | 5,814,000 | 0.15 | 0.35 | 2.00 | 7.00 | — |
| 1905/4 | 9,575,000 | 0.30 | 1.00 | 3.00 | 10.00 | — |
| 1905 | Inc. above | 0.15 | 0.35 | 2.00 | 7.00 | — |
| 1905 WICHAUX (error) | Inc. above | 2.00 | 5.00 | 25.00 | 60.00 | — |
| 1905 A. MICHAUX | Inc. above | 1.00 | 3.50 | 15.00 | 40.00 | — |
| 1906/5 | 8,463,000 | 0.30 | 1.50 | 3.00 | 10.00 | — |
| 1906 | Inc. above | 0.15 | 0.35 | 2.00 | 6.00 | — |
| 1907 | 993,000 | 1.00 | 3.00 | 12.00 | 22.00 | — |

**5 CENTIMES** **KM# 55** **Composition:** Copper-Nickel **Obverse:** Legend in Dutch, large date **Obv. Legend:** BELGIE

| Date | Mintage | F | VF | XF | Unc | BU |
|---|---|---|---|---|---|---|
| 1904 | 5,812,000 | 0.15 | 0.35 | 2.00 | 7.00 | — |
| 1905/3 | 7,002,000 | 0.35 | 2.50 | 15.00 | 30.00 | — |
| 1905/4 | Inc. above | 0.30 | 1.50 | 10.00 | 25.00 | — |
| 1905 | Inc. above | 0.15 | 0.35 | 2.00 | 7.00 | — |
| 1905 Without cross | Inc. above | — | 1.50 | 12.50 | 20.00 | — |
| 1906 | 11,016,000 | 0.15 | 0.35 | 2.00 | 7.00 | — |
| 1906 Without cross | Inc. above | 2.00 | 5.00 | 15.00 | 35.00 | — |
| 1907 | 998,000 | 1.00 | 2.00 | 10.00 | 22.00 | — |

**5 CENTIMES** **KM# 66** **Composition:** Copper-Nickel **Obverse:** Legend in French **Obv. Legend:** BELGIQUE **Reverse:** Plain field above 5

| Date | Mintage | F | VF | XF | Unc | BU |
|---|---|---|---|---|---|---|
| 1910 | 8,011,000 | 0.10 | 0.35 | 1.25 | 6.00 | — |
| 1913/0 | 5,005,000 | 0.20 | 0.75 | 2.25 | 10.00 | — |
| 1913 | Inc. above | 0.10 | 0.40 | 1.50 | 7.00 | — |
| 1914 | 1,004,000 | 1.00 | 3.00 | 8.00 | 20.00 | — |
| 1920/10 | 10,040,000 | 0.10 | 1.00 | 3.00 | 7.00 | — |
| 1920 | Inc. above | 0.10 | 0.35 | 1.25 | 4.00 | — |
| 1922/0 | 12,640,000 | 0.10 | 1.50 | 4.00 | 9.00 | — |
| 1922/1 | Inc. above | 0.10 | 1.50 | 3.50 | 9.00 | — |
| 1922 | Inc. above | 0.10 | 0.35 | 1.25 | 4.00 | — |
| 1923/13 | 9,000,000 | 0.10 | 0.75 | 2.50 | 8.00 | — |
| 1923 | Inc. above | 0.10 | 0.35 | 1.25 | 4.00 | — |
| 1925/13 | 15,860,000 | 0.10 | 0.50 | 2.00 | 8.00 | — |
| 1925 | Inc. above | 0.10 | 0.35 | 1.25 | 4.00 | — |
| 1926/5 | 7,000,000 | 0.10 | 1.00 | 2.50 | 8.00 | — |
| 1926 | Inc. above | 0.10 | 0.35 | 1.25 | 4.00 | — |
| 1927 | 2,000,000 | 0.10 | 1.00 | 2.50 | 9.00 | — |
| 1928 | 12,507,000 | 0.10 | 0.35 | 1.25 | 5.00 | — |
| 1932 Inc. KM93 | — | 5.00 | 15.00 | 50.00 | 150 | — |

**5 CENTIMES** **KM# 67** **Composition:** Copper-Nickel **Obverse:** Legend in Dutch **Obv. Legend:** BELGIE **Reverse:** Plain field above 5

| Date | Mintage | F | VF | XF | Unc | BU |
|---|---|---|---|---|---|---|
| 1910 | 8,033,000 | 0.10 | 0.35 | 1.25 | 8.00 | — |
| 1914 | 6,040,000 | 0.10 | 0.35 | 1.25 | 4.00 | — |
| 1920/10 | 10,030,000 | 0.10 | 0.50 | 3.00 | 12.00 | — |
| 1920 | Inc. above | 0.10 | 0.35 | 1.25 | 4.00 | — |
| 1921/11 | 4,200,000 | 0.10 | 1.00 | 2.50 | 12.00 | — |
| 1921 | Inc. above | 0.10 | 1.00 | 2.00 | 9.00 | — |
| 1922/12 | 13,180,000 | 0.10 | 1.00 | 2.50 | 8.00 | — |
| 1922/0 | Inc. above | 0.10 | 1.00 | 3.00 | 9.00 | — |
| 1922 | Inc. above | 0.10 | 0.35 | 1.25 | 4.00 | — |
| 1923/13 | 3,530,000 | 0.10 | 1.00 | 3.00 | 14.00 | — |
| 1923 | Inc. above | 0.10 | 0.75 | 2.00 | 7.00 | — |
| 1924/11 | 5,260,000 | 0.10 | 1.00 | 2.50 | 9.00 | — |
| 1924/14 | Inc. above | 0.10 | 0.50 | 1.75 | 8.00 | — |
| 1924 | Inc. above | 0.10 | 0.35 | 1.25 | 4.00 | — |
| 1925/13 | 13,000,000 | 0.10 | 1.00 | 2.50 | 8.00 | — |
| 1925/15 High 2 | Inc. above | 0.10 | 1.00 | 2.00 | 9.00 | — |
| 1925/15 Level 2 | Inc. above | 0.10 | 1.00 | 2.00 | 9.00 | — |
| 1925/3 | Inc. above | 0.10 | 0.60 | 2.00 | 9.00 | — |
| 1925 | Inc. above | 0.10 | 0.35 | 1.25 | 4.00 | — |
| 1927 | 6,938,000 | 0.10 | 0.35 | 1.25 | 6.00 | — |
| 1928/3 | 6,252,000 | 0.10 | 0.75 | 2.50 | 9.00 | — |
| 1928 | Inc. above | 0.10 | 0.35 | 1.25 | 6.00 | — |
| 1930 Inc. KM94 | — | 5.00 | 15.00 | 50.00 | 150 | — |
| 1931 Inc. KM94 | — | 7.50 | 18.00 | 60.00 | 170 | — |

**5 CENTIMES** **KM# 80** **Composition:** Zinc **Obverse:** Legend in French **Obv. Legend:** BELGIQUE-BELGIE **Note:** German Occupation WW I

| Date | Mintage | F | VF | XF | Unc | BU |
|---|---|---|---|---|---|---|
| 1915 | 10,199,000 | 0.15 | 2.00 | 4.00 | 15.00 | — |
| 1916 | 45,464,000 | 0.10 | 0.60 | 2.00 | 5.00 | — |

**5 CENTIMES** **KM# 94** **Composition:** Nickel-Brass **Obverse:** Legend in Dutch **Obv. Legend:** BELGIE **Reverse:** Star added above 5

| Date | Mintage | F | VF | XF | Unc | BU |
|---|---|---|---|---|---|---|
| 1930 | 3,000,000 | 0.10 | 0.20 | 0.35 | 3.00 | — |
| 1931 | 7,430,000 | 0.10 | 0.20 | 0.35 | 3.00 | — |

**5 CENTIMES** **KM# 93** **Composition:** Nickel-Brass **Obverse:** Legend in French **Obv. Legend:** BELGIQUE **Reverse:** Star added above 5

| Date | Mintage | F | VF | XF | Unc | BU |
|---|---|---|---|---|---|---|
| 1932 | 5,520,000 | 0.10 | 0.20 | 0.35 | 3.00 | — |

**5 CENTIMES** **KM# 110.1** **Composition:** Nickel-Brass **Obverse:** Legend in French **Obv. Legend:** BELGIQUE-BELGIE

| Date | Mintage | F | VF | XF | Unc | BU |
|---|---|---|---|---|---|---|
| 1938 | 4,970,000 | 0.10 | 0.20 | 0.75 | 2.00 | — |
| 1939 | — | — | — | — | — | — |

**Note:** Struck at a later date

**5 CENTIMES** **KM# 110.2** **Composition:** Nickel-Brass **Note:** Medal alignment.

| Date | Mintage | F | VF | XF | Unc | BU |
|---|---|---|---|---|---|---|
| 1938 | Inc. above | 1.25 | 3.00 | 8.00 | 30.00 | — |

**5 CENTIMES** **KM# 111** **Composition:** Nickel-Brass **Obverse:** Legend in Dutch **Obv. Legend:** BELGIE-BELGIQUE

| Date | Mintage | F | VF | XF | Unc | BU |
|---|---|---|---|---|---|---|
| 1939 | 3,000,000 | 0.10 | 0.20 | 0.75 | 2.00 | — |
| 1940 | 1,970,000 | 0.20 | 0.50 | 1.50 | 5.00 | — |

**5 CENTIMES** **KM# 124** **Composition:** Nickel-Brass **Obverse:** Legend in Dutch **Obv. Legend:** BELGIE-BELGIQUE

| Date | Mintage | F | VF | XF | Unc | BU |
|---|---|---|---|---|---|---|
| 1941 | 4,000,000 | 0.15 | 0.75 | 2.50 | 8.00 | — |
| 1942 | 18,430,000 | 0.10 | 0.20 | 0.50 | 3.00 | — |

**5 CENTIMES** **KM# 123** **Composition:** Nickel-Brass **Obverse:** Legend in French **Obv. Legend:** BELGIQUE-BELGIE **Note:** German Occupation WW II

| Date | Mintage | F | VF | XF | Unc | BU |
|---|---|---|---|---|---|---|
| 1941 | 10,000,000 | 0.10 | 0.20 | 1.00 | 4.00 | — |
| 1943 | 7,606,000 | 0.10 | 0.20 | 1.00 | 4.00 | — |

**10 CENTIMES** **KM# 42** **Composition:** Copper-Nickel **Obverse:** Legend in French **Obv. Legend:** DES BELGES

| Date | Mintage | F | VF | XF | Unc | BU |
|---|---|---|---|---|---|---|
| 1901 | 551,000 | 30.00 | 50.00 | 150 | 275 | — |

**10 CENTIMES** **KM# 43** **Composition:** Copper-Nickel **Obverse:** Legend in Dutch **Obv. Legend:** DER BELGEN

| Date | Mintage | F | VF | XF | Unc | BU |
|---|---|---|---|---|---|---|
| 1901 | 556,000 | 30.00 | 50.00 | 140 | 250 | — |

**10 CENTIMES** **KM# 48** **Composition:** Copper-Nickel **Obverse:** Legend in French, small date **Obv. Legend:** BELGIQUE

| Date | Mintage | F | VF | XF | Unc | BU |
|---|---|---|---|---|---|---|
| 1901 | 582,000 | 6.00 | 15.00 | 40.00 | 130 | — |
| 1902/1 | 5,866,000 | 0.50 | 3.00 | 7.00 | 20.00 | — |
| 1902 | Inc. above | 0.15 | 1.00 | 3.00 | 12.00 | — |
| 1903 | 763,000 | 1.00 | 4.00 | 10.00 | 30.00 | — |

**10 CENTIMES** **KM# 49** **Composition:** Copper-Nickel **Obverse:** Legend in Dutch, small date **Obv. Legend:** BELGIE

| Date | Mintage | F | VF | XF | Unc | BU |
|---|---|---|---|---|---|---|
| 1902 | 1,560,000 | 0.20 | 1.00 | 5.00 | 15.00 | — |
| 1903/2 | — | 0.50 | 1.25 | 7.00 | 18.00 | — |
| 1903 | 5,658,000 | 0.20 | 1.00 | 12.00 | 30.00 | — |

**10 CENTIMES** **KM# 52** **Composition:** Copper-Nickel **Obverse:** Legend in French, large date **Obv. Legend:** BELGIQUE

| Date | Mintage | F | VF | XF | Unc | BU |
|---|---|---|---|---|---|---|
| 1903 | Inc. above | 2.00 | 7.00 | 17.00 | 40.00 | — |
| 1904 | 16,354,000 | 0.15 | 1.00 | 3.00 | 10.00 | — |
| 1905/4 | 14,392,000 | 0.25 | 1.00 | 5.00 | 18.00 | — |
| 1905 | Inc. above | 0.15 | 0.60 | 2.00 | 10.00 | — |
| 1906/5 | 1,483,000 | 0.50 | 1.50 | 5.00 | 18.00 | — |
| 1906 | Inc. above | 0.25 | 0.75 | 3.50 | 12.00 | — |

**10 CENTIMES** **KM# 53** **Composition:** Copper-Nickel **Obverse:** Legend in Dutch, large date **Obv. Legend:** BELGIE

| Date | Mintage | F | VF | XF | Unc | BU |
|---|---|---|---|---|---|---|
| 1903 | Inc. above | 1.00 | 4.00 | 10.00 | 20.00 | — |
| 1904 | 16,834,000 | 0.20 | 0.50 | 2.00 | 7.00 | — |
| 1905/3 | 13,758,000 | 0.35 | 1.00 | 3.00 | 15.00 | — |
| 1905/4 | Inc. above | 0.30 | 1.00 | 3.00 | 15.00 | — |
| 1905 | Inc. above | 0.20 | 0.50 | 2.00 | 8.00 | — |
| 1906/5 Point above center of 6 | 2,017,000 | 0.50 | 1.25 | 4.00 | 15.00 | — |
| 1906/5 Point above right side of 6 | Inc. above | 0.50 | 1.25 | 4.00 | 15.00 | — |
| 1906 | Inc. above | 0.10 | 0.75 | 2.50 | 9.00 | — |

**10 CENTIMES** **KM# 85.1** **Composition:** Copper-Nickel **Obverse:** Legend in French **Obv. Legend:** BELGIQUE

| Date | Mintage | F | VF | XF | Unc | BU |
|---|---|---|---|---|---|---|
| 1911 Struck at a later date | — | — | — | — | — | — |
| 1920 | 6,520,000 | 0.15 | 0.40 | 1.50 | 8.00 | — |
| 1921 | 7,215,000 | 0.15 | 0.20 | 1.00 | 7.00 | — |
| 1923 | 20,625,000 | 0.10 | 0.20 | 1.00 | 6.00 | — |
| 1926/3 | 6,916,000 | 0.20 | 0.75 | 3.00 | 12.00 | — |
| 1926/5 | Inc. above | 0.20 | 0.75 | 3.00 | 12.00 | — |
| 1926 | Inc. above | 0.15 | 0.20 | 1.00 | 7.00 | — |
| 1927 | 8,125,000 | 0.15 | 0.20 | 1.00 | 6.00 | — |
| 1928/3 | 6,895,000 | 0.20 | 1.00 | 4.50 | 16.00 | — |
| 1928 | Inc. above | 0.15 | 0.20 | 1.00 | 7.00 | — |
| 1929 | 12,260,000 | 0.15 | 0.20 | 1.00 | 6.00 | — |

**10 CENTIMES** **KM# 81** **Composition:** Zinc **Obverse:** Legend in French **Obv. Legend:** BELGIQUE-BELGIE **Note:** German Occupation. All of KM#81 have dots after the date. The 1916 is distinguished by a period after the date.

| Date | Mintage | F | VF | XF | Unc | BU |
|---|---|---|---|---|---|---|
| 1915 | 9,681,000 | 0.25 | 1.50 | 4.00 | 15.00 | — |
| 1916 | 37,382,000 | 0.15 | 0.75 | 3.00 | 12.00 | — |
| 1916. | Inc. above | 10.00 | 17.50 | 70.00 | 150 | — |
| 1917 | 1,447,000 | 17.50 | 25.00 | 85.00 | 200 | — |

**10 CENTIMES** **KM# 85.2** **Composition:** Copper-Nickel **Reverse:** Single line below ES of CES

| Date | Mintage | F | VF | XF | Unc | BU |
|---|---|---|---|---|---|---|
| 1920 | Inc. above | 0.50 | 1.00 | 3.00 | 10.00 | — |
| 1921 | Inc. above | 1.00 | 2.50 | 9.00 | 30.00 | — |

**10 CENTIMES** **KM# 86** **Composition:** Copper-Nickel **Obverse:** Legend in Dutch **Obv. Legend:** BELGIE **Reverse:** Plain field above 10

| Date | Mintage | F | VF | XF | Unc | BU |
|---|---|---|---|---|---|---|
| 1920 | 5,050,000 | 0.15 | 0.20 | 1.00 | 7.00 | — |
| 1921 | 7,580,000 | 0.15 | 0.20 | 1.00 | 6.00 | — |
| 1922 | 6,250,000 | 0.15 | 0.20 | 1.00 | 6.00 | — |
| 1924 | 5,825,000 | 0.15 | 0.20 | 1.00 | 7.00 | — |
| 1925/4 | 8,160,000 | 0.20 | 0.40 | 2.00 | 9.00 | — |
| 1925 | Inc. above | 0.10 | 0.20 | 1.00 | 6.00 | — |
| 1926/5 | 6,250,000 | 0.20 | 0.40 | 2.00 | 9.00 | — |
| 1926 | Inc. above | 0.15 | 0.20 | 1.00 | 6.00 | — |
| 1927 | 10,625,000 | 0.15 | 0.20 | 1.00 | 6.00 | — |
| 1928/5 | 6,750,000 | 0.20 | 0.40 | 2.00 | 9.00 | — |
| 1928 | Inc. above | 0.15 | 0.20 | 1.00 | 6.00 | — |
| 1929 | 4,668,000 | 0.15 | 0.20 | 1.00 | 8.00 | — |
| 1930 | — | 15.00 | 30.00 | 100 | 250 | — |

**10 CENTIMES** **KM# 95.1** **Composition:** Nickel-Brass **Obverse:** Legend in French **Obv. Legend:** BELGIQUE **Reverse:** Star added above 10

| Date | Mintage | F | VF | XF | Unc | BU |
|---|---|---|---|---|---|---|
| 1930/20 | 2,000,000 | 50.00 | 75.00 | 200 | 375 | — |
| 1930 | Inc. above | 20.00 | 30.00 | 100 | 250 | — |
| 1931 | 6,270,000 | 1.00 | 2.00 | 8.00 | 20.00 | — |
| 1932 | 1,270,000 | 35.00 | 50.00 | 175 | 350 | — |
| 1932 A instead of signature | Inc. above | 50.00 | 100 | 240 | 500 | — |

**10 CENTIMES** **KM# 96** **Composition:** Nickel-Brass **Obverse:** Legend in Dutch **Obv. Legend:** BELGIE **Reverse:** Star added above 10

| Date | Mintage | F | VF | XF | Unc | BU |
|---|---|---|---|---|---|---|
| 1930 | 1,581,000 | 0.30 | 0.75 | 3.00 | 10.00 | — |
| 1931 | 5,000,000 | 25.00 | 40.00 | 125 | 250 | — |

**10 CENTIMES** **KM# 95.2** **Composition:** Nickel-Brass **Reverse:** Single line below ES of CES

| Date | Mintage | F | VF | XF | Unc | BU |
|---|---|---|---|---|---|---|
| 1931 | Inc. above | 2.00 | 5.00 | 15.00 | 40.00 | — |
| 1932 | Inc. above | 45.00 | 90.00 | 200 | 500 | — |

**10 CENTIMES** **KM# 112** **Composition:** Nickel-Brass **Obverse:** Legend in French **Obv. Legend:** BELGIQUE-BELGIE

| Date | Mintage | F | VF | XF | Unc | BU |
|---|---|---|---|---|---|---|
| 1938 | 6,000,000 | 0.10 | 0.25 | 0.50 | 1.50 | — |
| 1939 | 7,000,000 | 0.50 | 1.00 | 3.00 | 8.00 | — |

**10 CENTIMES** **KM# 113.1** **Composition:** Nickel-Brass **Obverse:** Legend in Dutch **Obv. Legend:** BELGIE-BELGIQUE

| Date | Mintage | F | VF | XF | Unc | BU |
|---|---|---|---|---|---|---|
| 1939 | 8,425,000 | 0.10 | 0.25 | 0.50 | 1.50 | — |

**10 CENTIMES** **KM# 113.2** **Composition:** Nickel-Brass **Note:** Thin flan.

| Date | Mintage | F | VF | XF | Unc | BU |
|---|---|---|---|---|---|---|
| 1939 | Inc. above | 1.25 | 3.00 | 10.00 | 35.00 | — |

**10 CENTIMES** **KM# 126** **Composition:** Zinc **Obverse:** Legend in Dutch **Obv. Legend:** BELGIE-BELGIQUE **Note:**

| Date | Mintage | F | VF | XF | Unc | BU |
|---|---|---|---|---|---|---|
| 1941 | 7,000,000 | 0.15 | 0.25 | 1.50 | 6.00 | — |
| 1942 | 21,000,000 | 0.15 | 0.25 | 1.50 | 4.00 | — |
| 1943 | 22,000,000 | 0.15 | 0.25 | 1.50 | 4.00 | — |
| 1944 | 28,140,000 | 0.15 | 0.25 | 1.50 | 4.00 | — |
| 1945 | 8,000,000 | 0.15 | 0.50 | 2.00 | 6.00 | — |
| 1946 | 5,370,000 | 0.15 | 0.50 | 2.00 | 6.00 | — |

**10 CENTIMES** **KM# 125** **Composition:** Zinc **Obverse:** Legend in French **Obv. Legend:** BELGIQUE-BELGIE **Note:** German Occupation WW II.

| Date | Mintage | F | VF | XF | Unc | BU |
|---|---|---|---|---|---|---|
| 1941 | 10,000,000 | 0.15 | 0.25 | 1.50 | 4.00 | — |
| 1942 | 17,000,000 | 0.15 | 0.25 | 1.50 | 4.00 | — |
| 1943 | 22,500,000 | 0.15 | 0.25 | 1.50 | 4.00 | — |
| 1945 | — | — | — | — | — | — |
| **Note:** Struck at a later date | | | | | | |
| 1946 | Est. 10,370,000 | — | — | — | — | — |
| **Note:** Not released for circulation | | | | | | |

**20 CENTIMES** **KM# 146** **Composition:** Bronze **Obverse:** Legend in French **Obv. Legend:** BELGIQUE

| Date | Mintage | F | VF | XF | Unc | BU |
|---|---|---|---|---|---|---|
| 1953 | 14,150,000 | — | 0.10 | 0.20 | 0.50 | — |
| 1953 CENTIMES not touching rim | — | — | 0.10 | 0.75 | 2.50 | — |
| 1954 | — | — | 400 | 600 | 800 | — |
| 1957 | 13,300,000 | — | — | 0.10 | 0.25 | — |
| 1958 | 8,700,000 | — | — | 0.10 | 0.25 | — |
| 1959 | 19,670,000 | — | — | 0.10 | 0.25 | — |
| 1962 | 410,000 | — | 6.00 | 10.00 | 12.50 | — |
| 1963 | 2,550,000 | 0.10 | 0.20 | 0.50 | 1.00 | — |

**20 CENTIMES** **KM# 147.1** **Composition:** Bronze **Obverse:** Legend in Dutch **Obv. Legend:** BELGIE

| Date | Mintage | F | VF | XF | Unc | BU |
|---|---|---|---|---|---|---|
| 1954 | 50,130,000 | — | — | 0.10 | 0.20 | — |
| 1960 | 7,530,000 | — | — | 0.10 | 0.25 | — |

**20 CENTIMES** **KM# 147.2** **Composition:** Bronze **Obverse:** CENTIMES touching rim

| Date | Mintage | F | VF | XF | Unc | BU |
|---|---|---|---|---|---|---|
| 1954 | Inc. above | — | 0.15 | 0.75 | 2.50 | — |
| 1960 | Inc. above | — | 0.15 | 0.75 | 2.50 | — |

**25 CENTIMES** **KM# 62** **Composition:** Copper-Nickel **Obverse:** Legend in French **Obv. Legend:** BELGIQUE

| Date | Mintage | F | VF | XF | Unc | BU |
|---|---|---|---|---|---|---|
| 1908 | 4,007,000 | 0.50 | 4.00 | 30.00 | 75.00 | — |
| 1909/8 | 1,998,000 | 4.00 | 30.00 | 110 | 200 | — |
| 1909 | Inc. above | 1.00 | 8.00 | 40.00 | 90.00 | — |

**25 CENTIMES** **KM# 63** **Composition:** Copper-Nickel **Obverse:** Legend in Dutch **Obv. Legend:** BELGIE

| Date | Mintage | F | VF | XF | Unc | BU |
|---|---|---|---|---|---|---|
| 1908 | 4,011,000 | 0.50 | 4.00 | 30.00 | 75.00 | — |

**25 CENTIMES** **KM# 69** **Composition:** Copper-Nickel **Obverse:** Legend in Dutch **Obv. Legend:** BELGIE

| Date | Mintage | F | VF | XF | Unc | BU |
|---|---|---|---|---|---|---|
| 1910 | 2,006,000 | 0.15 | 1.00 | 8.00 | 25.00 | — |
| 1911 | — | — | — | — | — | — |
| **Note:** Struck at a later date | | | | | | |
| 1913 | 2,010,000 | 0.15 | 1.00 | 8.00 | 20.00 | — |
| 1921 | 11,173,000 | 0.15 | 0.25 | 2.00 | 6.00 | — |
| 1922/1 | 14,200,000 | 0.20 | 1.00 | 5.00 | 25.00 | — |
| 1922 | Inc. above | 0.15 | 0.25 | 2.00 | 6.00 | — |
| 1926/3 | 6,400,000 | 0.35 | 1.25 | 9.00 | 25.00 | — |
| 1926 | Inc. above | 0.10 | 0.40 | 2.00 | 6.00 | — |
| 1927/3 | 3,799,000 | 0.35 | 1.25 | 8.00 | 25.00 | — |
| 1927 | Inc. above | 0.10 | 0.25 | 2.00 | 8.00 | — |
| 1928 | 9,200,000 | 0.10 | 0.25 | 2.00 | 6.00 | — |
| 1929 | 8,980,000 | 0.10 | 0.25 | 2.00 | 6.00 | — |

**25 CENTIMES** **KM# 68.1** **Composition:** Copper-Nickel **Obverse:** Legend in French **Obv. Legend:** BELGIQUE

| Date | Mintage | F | VF | XF | Unc | BU |
|---|---|---|---|---|---|---|
| 1913 | 2,011,000 | 0.15 | 0.75 | 6.00 | 20.00 | — |
| 1920 | 2,844,000 | 0.15 | 0.50 | 5.00 | 18.00 | — |
| 1921 | 7,464,000 | 0.10 | 0.25 | 2.00 | 8.00 | — |
| 1922 | 7,600,000 | 0.10 | 0.25 | 2.00 | 6.00 | — |
| 1923 | 11,356,000 | 0.15 | 0.25 | 2.00 | 6.00 | — |
| 1926/3 | 1,300,000 | 1.00 | 2.00 | 12.00 | 30.00 | — |
| 1926 | Inc. above | 0.50 | 1.00 | 7.00 | 25.00 | — |
| 1927/3 | 8,800,000 | 1.00 | 2.00 | 20.00 | 35.00 | — |
| 1927 | Inc. above | 0.10 | 0.25 | 2.00 | 6.00 | — |
| 1928 | 4,351,000 | 0.10 | 0.25 | 2.00 | 8.00 | — |
| 1929 | 9,600,000 | 0.10 | 0.25 | 2.00 | 6.00 | — |

**25 CENTIMES** **KM# 82** **Composition:** Zinc **Obverse:** Legend in French **Obv. Legend:** BELGIQUE-BELGIE **Note:** German Occupation WW I

| Date | Mintage | F | VF | XF | Unc | BU |
|---|---|---|---|---|---|---|
| 1915 | 8,080,000 | 0.50 | 2.00 | 9.00 | 25.00 | — |
| 1916 | 10,671,000 | 0.50 | 2.00 | 7.00 | 20.00 | — |
| 1917 | 3,555,000 | 2.00 | 4.00 | 18.00 | 50.00 | — |
| 1918 | 5,489,000 | 1.00 | 3.00 | 12.00 | 30.00 | — |

**25 CENTIMES** **KM# 68.2** **Composition:** Copper-Nickel **Reverse:** Single line below ES of CES

| Date | Mintage | F | VF | XF | Unc | BU |
|---|---|---|---|---|---|---|
| 1920 | Inc. above | 0.50 | 1.00 | 8.00 | 25.00 | — |
| 1921 | Inc. above | 0.35 | 0.75 | 5.00 | 15.00 | — |

**25 CENTIMES** **KM# 114.1** **Composition:** Nickel-Brass **Obverse:** Legend in French **Obv. Legend:** BELGIQUE-BELGIE

| Date | Mintage | F | VF | XF | Unc | BU |
|---|---|---|---|---|---|---|
| 1938 | 7,200,000 | — | 0.25 | 1.00 | 4.00 | — |
| 1939 | 7,732,000 | — | 0.25 | 1.00 | 4.00 | — |

**25 CENTIMES** **KM# 115.1** **Composition:** Nickel-Brass **Obverse:** Legend in Dutch **Obv. Legend:** BELGIE-BELGIQUE

| Date | Mintage | F | VF | XF | Unc | BU |
|---|---|---|---|---|---|---|
| 1938 | 14,932,000 | — | 0.25 | 1.00 | 3.00 | — |

**25 CENTIMES** **KM# 115.2** **Composition:** Nickel-Brass **Note:** Medal alignment.

| Date | Mintage | F | VF | XF | Unc | BU |
|---|---|---|---|---|---|---|
| 1938 | Inc. above | 1.75 | 3.00 | 10.00 | 30.00 | — |

**25 CENTIMES** **KM# 114.2** **Composition:** Nickel-Brass **Note:** Medal alignment.

| Date | Mintage | F | VF | XF | Unc | BU |
|---|---|---|---|---|---|---|
| 1939 | Inc. above | 1.75 | 3.00 | 10.00 | 30.00 | — |

**25 CENTIMES** **KM# 131** **Composition:** Zinc **Obverse:** Legend in French **Obv. Legend:** BELGIQUE-BELGIE **Note:** German Occupation WW II

| Date | Mintage | F | VF | XF | Unc | BU |
|---|---|---|---|---|---|---|
| 1941 Rare | — | — | — | — | — | — |
| 1942 | 14,400,000 | — | 0.20 | 0.75 | 3.00 | — |
| 1943 | 21,600,000 | — | 0.20 | 0.75 | 3.00 | — |
| 1945 | — | — | — | — | — | — |
| **Note:** Struck at a later date | | | | | | |
| 1946 | 21,428,000 | — | 0.20 | 0.75 | 3.00 | — |
| 1947 | Est. 300,000 | — | — | — | — | — |
| **Note:** Not released for circulation | | | | | | |

**25 CENTIMES** **KM# 132** **Composition:** Zinc **Obverse:** Legend in Dutch **Obv. Legend:** BELGIE-BELGIQUE

| Date | Mintage | F | VF | XF | Unc | BU |
|---|---|---|---|---|---|---|
| 1942 | 14,400,000 | — | 0.20 | 0.75 | 3.00 | — |
| 1943 | 21,600,000 | — | 0.20 | 0.75 | 3.00 | — |
| 1944 | 25,960,000 | — | 0.20 | 0.75 | 3.00 | — |
| 1945 | 8,200,000 | — | 0.25 | 1.25 | 4.00 | — |
| 1946 | 11,652,000 | — | 0.20 | 0.75 | 3.00 | — |
| 1947 | Est. 316,000 | — | — | — | — | — |
| **Note:** Not released for circulation | | | | | | |

**25 CENTIMES** **KM# 154.2** **Composition:** Copper-Nickel **Note:** Medal alignment. Struck at Brussels Mint. Mint mark - Angel Head. Mintmaster Vogelier's privy mark - Bird.

| Date | Mintage | F | VF | XF | Unc | BU |
|---|---|---|---|---|---|---|
| 1964 | Inc. above | — | — | 5.00 | 12.00 | — |
| 1965 | Inc. above | — | — | 5.00 | 15.00 | — |
| 1966 | Inc. above | — | — | 5.00 | 12.00 | — |
| 1967 | Inc. above | — | — | 6.00 | 15.00 | — |
| 1969 | Inc. above | — | — | 5.00 | 12.00 | — |
| 1971 | Inc. above | — | — | 6.00 | 15.00 | — |
| 1972 | Inc. above | — | — | 5.00 | 12.00 | — |

**25 CENTIMES** **KM# 153.2** **Composition:** Copper-Nickel **Note:** Medal alignment. Struck at the Brussels Mint. Mint mark - Angel Head. Mintmaster Vogelier's privy mark - Bird.

| Date | Mintage | F | VF | XF | Unc | BU |
|---|---|---|---|---|---|---|
| 1964 | Inc. above | — | — | 5.00 | 12.00 | — |
| 1965 | Inc. above | — | — | 10.00 | 25.00 | — |
| 1967 | Inc. above | — | — | 10.00 | 25.00 | — |
| 1970 | Inc. above | — | — | 5.00 | 12.00 | — |
| 1971 | Inc. above | — | — | 5.00 | 12.00 | — |
| 1974 | Inc. above | — | — | 10.00 | 25.00 | — |

**25 CENTIMES** **KM# 153.1** **Composition:** Copper-Nickel **Obverse:** Legend in French **Obv. Legend:** BELGIQUE **Note:** Struck at Brussels Mint. Mint mark - Angel Head. Mintmaster Vogelier's privy mark - Bird.

| Date | Mintage | F | VF | XF | Unc | BU |
|---|---|---|---|---|---|---|
| 1964 | 21,770,000 | — | — | 0.10 | 0.15 | — |
| 1965 | 11,440,000 | — | — | 0.10 | 0.15 | — |
| 1966 | 19,990,000 | — | — | 0.10 | 0.15 | — |
| 1967 | 6,820,000 | — | — | 0.10 | 0.15 | — |
| 1968 | 25,250,000 | — | — | 0.10 | 0.15 | — |
| 1969 | 7,670,000 | — | — | 0.10 | 0.15 | — |
| 1970 | 27,000,000 | — | — | 0.10 | 0.15 | — |
| 1971 | 16,000,000 | — | — | 0.10 | 0.15 | — |
| 1972 | 20,000,000 | — | — | 0.10 | 0.15 | — |
| 1973 | 12,500,000 | — | — | 0.10 | 0.15 | — |
| 1974 | 20,000,000 | — | — | 0.10 | 0.15 | — |
| 1975 | 12,000,000 | — | — | 0.10 | 0.15 | — |

**25 CENTIMES** **KM# 154.1** **Composition:** Copper-Nickel **Obverse:** Legend in Dutch **Obv. Legend:** BELGIE **Note:** Struck at Brussels Mint. Mint mark - Angel Head. Mintmaster Vogelier's privy mark - Bird.

| Date | Mintage | F | VF | XF | Unc | BU |
|---|---|---|---|---|---|---|
| 1964 | 21,300,000 | — | — | 0.10 | 0.15 | — |
| 1965 | 7,900,000 | — | — | 0.10 | 0.15 | — |
| 1966 | 23,420,000 | — | — | 0.10 | 0.15 | — |
| 1967 | 7,720,000 | — | — | 0.10 | 0.15 | — |
| 1968 | 22,750,000 | — | — | 0.10 | 0.15 | — |
| 1969 | 25,190,000 | — | — | 0.10 | 0.15 | — |
| 1970 | 12,000,000 | — | — | 0.10 | 0.15 | — |
| 1971 | 16,000,000 | — | — | 0.10 | 0.15 | — |
| 1972 | 20,000,000 | — | — | 0.10 | 0.15 | — |
| 1973 | 12,500,000 | — | — | 0.10 | 0.15 | — |
| 1974 | 20,000,000 | — | — | 0.10 | 0.15 | — |
| 1975 | 12,000,000 | — | — | 0.10 | 0.15 | — |

**50 CENTIMES** **KM# 50** **Weight:** 2.5000 g. **Composition:** 0.8350 Silver .0671 oz. ASW **Obverse:** Legend in French **Obv. Legend:** DES BELGES

| Date | Mintage | F | VF | XF | Unc | BU |
|---|---|---|---|---|---|---|
| 1901 | 3,000,000 | 2.00 | 12.00 | 50.00 | 100 | — |

**50 CENTIMES** **KM# 51** **Weight:** 2.5000 g. **Composition:** 0.8350 Silver .0671 oz. ASW **Obverse:** Legend in Dutch **Obv. Legend:** DER BELGEN

| Date | Mintage | F | VF | XF | Unc | BU |
|---|---|---|---|---|---|---|
| 1901 | 3,000,000 | 2.00 | 12.00 | 50.00 | 100 | — |

**50 CENTIMES** **KM#60.1** **Weight:** 2.5000 g. **Composition:** 0.8350 Silver .0671 oz. ASW **Obverse:** Legend in French **Obv. Legend:** DES BELGES

| Date | Mintage | F | VF | XF | Unc | BU |
|---|---|---|---|---|---|---|
| 1907 | 545,000 | 3.00 | 5.00 | 18.00 | 50.00 | — |
| 1909 | 2,503,000 | 1.00 | 2.50 | 10.00 | 27.00 | — |

**50 CENTIMES** **KM#60.2** **Weight:** 2.5000 g. **Composition:** 0.8350 Silver .0671 oz. ASW **Obverse:** Without period in signature

| Date | Mintage | F | VF | XF | Unc | BU |
|---|---|---|---|---|---|---|
| 1907 | Inc. above | 4.00 | 10.00 | 25.00 | 75.00 | — |
| 1909 | Inc. above | 2.00 | 5.00 | 12.00 | 35.00 | — |

**50 CENTIMES** **KM#61.1** **Weight:** 2.5000 g. **Composition:** 0.8350 Silver .0671 oz. ASW **Obverse:** Legend in Dutch **Obv. Legend:** DER BELGEN

| Date | Mintage | F | VF | XF | Unc | BU |
|---|---|---|---|---|---|---|
| 1907 | 545,000 | 3.00 | 10.00 | 25.00 | 45.00 | — |
| 1909 | 2,510,000 | 1.00 | 2.50 | 9.00 | 25.00 | — |

**50 CENTIMES** **KM#61.3** **Weight:** 2.5000 g. **Composition:** 0.8350 Silver .0671 oz. ASW **Obverse:** Without periods in signature

| Date | Mintage | F | VF | XF | Unc | BU |
|---|---|---|---|---|---|---|
| 1909 | Inc. above | 2.00 | 6.00 | 17.50 | 50.00 | — |

**50 CENTIMES** **KM#61.2** **Weight:** 2.5000 g. **Composition:** 0.8350 Silver .0671 oz. ASW **Note:** Medal alignment

| Date | Mintage | F | VF | XF | Unc | BU |
|---|---|---|---|---|---|---|
| 1909 | Inc. above | 12.50 | 15.00 | 40.00 | 125 | — |

**50 CENTIMES** **KM# 70** **Weight:** 2.5000 g. **Composition:** 0.8350 Silver .0671 oz. ASW **Obverse:** Legend in French **Obv. Legend:** DES BELGES

| Date | Mintage | F | VF | XF | Unc | BU |
|---|---|---|---|---|---|---|
| 1910 | 1,900,000 | 1.00 | 2.00 | 9.00 | 25.00 | — |
| 1911 | 2,063,000 | 1.00 | 3.00 | 10.00 | 30.00 | — |
| 1912 | 1,000,000 | 0.50 | 1.00 | 1.50 | 6.00 | — |
| 1914 | 240,000 | 2.50 | 5.00 | 20.00 | 65.00 | — |

**50 CENTIMES** **KM# 71** **Weight:** 2.5000 g. **Composition:** 0.8350 Silver .0671 oz. ASW **Obverse:** Legend in Dutch **Obv. Legend:** DER BELGEN

| Date | Mintage | F | VF | XF | Unc | BU |
|---|---|---|---|---|---|---|
| 1910 | 1,900,000 | 1.00 | 3.00 | 10.00 | 35.00 | — |
| 1911 | 2,063,000 | 0.50 | 1.00 | 1.50 | 6.00 | — |
| 1912 | 1,000,000 | 0.50 | 1.00 | 1.50 | 6.00 | — |

**50 CENTIMES** **KM# 83** **Composition:** Zinc **Obverse:** Legend in Dutch **Obv. Legend:** BELGIE-BELGIQUE **Note:** German Occupation WW I

| Date | Mintage | F | VF | XF | Unc | BU |
|---|---|---|---|---|---|---|
| 1918 | 7,394,000 | 0.50 | 3.00 | 10.00 | 25.00 | — |

**50 CENTIMES** **KM# 87** **Composition:** Nickel **Obverse:** Legend in French **Obv. Legend:** BELGIQUE

| Date | Mintage | F | VF | XF | Unc | BU |
|---|---|---|---|---|---|---|
| 1922 | 6,180,000 | 0.15 | 0.25 | 0.50 | 3.00 | — |
| 1923 | 8,820,000 | 0.15 | 0.25 | 0.50 | 3.00 | — |
| 1927 | 1,750,000 | 0.15 | 0.30 | 0.50 | 3.00 | — |
| 1928 | 3,000,000 | 0.15 | 0.35 | 1.00 | 4.00 | — |
| 1929 | 1,000,000 | 0.25 | 0.50 | 3.00 | 10.00 | — |
| 1930 | 1,000,000 | 0.25 | 0.50 | 3.00 | 10.00 | — |
| 1932/23 | 2,530,000 | 1.00 | 3.00 | 10.00 | 25.00 | — |
| 1932 | Inc. above | 0.15 | 0.50 | 1.00 | 4.00 | — |
| 1933 | 2,861,000 | 0.15 | 0.25 | 0.75 | 4.00 | — |

**50 CENTIMES** **KM# 88** **Composition:** Nickel **Obverse:** Legend in Dutch **Obv. Legend:** BELGIE

| Date | Mintage | F | VF | XF | Unc | BU |
|---|---|---|---|---|---|---|
| 1922 | — | — | — | — | — | — |
| **Note:** Struck at a later date | | | | | | |
| 1923 | 15,000,000 | 0.20 | 0.25 | 0.50 | 3.00 | — |
| 1928/3 | 10,000,000 | 0.25 | 0.50 | 3.00 | 10.00 | — |
| 1928 | Inc. above | 0.20 | 0.25 | 0.50 | 3.00 | — |
| 1930/20 | 2,252,000 | 0.50 | 2.00 | 3.50 | 12.00 | — |
| 1930 | Inc. above | 0.20 | 0.75 | 2.50 | 6.00 | — |
| 1932 | 2,000,000 | 0.20 | 0.50 | 1.00 | 4.00 | — |
| 1933 | 1,189,000 | 1.00 | 2.00 | 4.00 | 12.00 | — |
| 1934 | 935,000 | 50.00 | 80.00 | 140 | 250 | — |

**50 CENTIMES** **KM# 118** **Composition:** Nickel **Obverse:** Legend in French **Obv. Legend:** BELGIQUE-BELGIE **Note:** Striking interrupted by the war. Seems to have never been officially released into circulation.

| Date | Mintage | F | VF | XF | Unc | BU |
|---|---|---|---|---|---|---|
| 1939 | 15,500,000 | 200 | 400 | 800 | 1,200 | — |

**50 CENTIMES** **KM# 144** **Composition:** Bronze **Obverse:** Legend in French **Obv. Legend:** BELGIQUE **Reverse:** Large head

| Date | Mintage | F | VF | XF | Unc | BU |
|---|---|---|---|---|---|---|
| 1952 | 3,520,000 | — | 0.10 | 0.25 | 1.00 | — |
| 1953 | 22,620,000 | — | — | 0.10 | 0.35 | — |

**50 CENTIMES** **KM# 145** **Composition:** Bronze **Obverse:** Legend in Dutch **Obv. Legend:** BELGIE **Reverse:** Large head

| Date | Mintage | F | VF | XF | Unc | BU |
|---|---|---|---|---|---|---|
| 1952 | 5,830,000 | — | 0.10 | 0.25 | 1.00 | — |
| 1953 | 22,930,000 | — | — | 0.10 | 0.35 | — |
| 1954 | 15,730,000 | — | — | 0.10 | 0.35 | — |

**50 CENTIMES** **KM# 148.2** **Composition:** Bronze **Note:** Medal alignment.

| Date | Mintage | F | VF | XF | Unc | BU |
|---|---|---|---|---|---|---|
| 1953 | Inc. above | — | — | 2.00 | 6.50 | — |
| 1959 | Inc. above | — | — | 2.00 | 5.00 | — |
| 1965 | Inc. above | — | — | 2.00 | 4.00 | — |
| 1966 | Inc. above | — | — | 2.00 | 4.00 | — |
| 1967 | Inc. above | — | — | 2.00 | 4.00 | — |
| 1969 | Inc. above | — | — | 2.00 | 4.00 | — |
| 1974 | Inc. above | — | — | 2.00 | 4.00 | — |
| 1976 | Inc. above | — | — | 2.00 | 4.00 | — |
| 1980 | — | — | — | 2.00 | 4.00 | — |

**50 CENTIMES** **KM# 149.2** **Composition:** Bronze **Note:** Medal alignment.

| Date | Mintage | F | VF | XF | Unc | BU |
|---|---|---|---|---|---|---|
| 1953 | Inc. above | — | — | 2.00 | 6.50 | — |
| 1958 | Inc. above | — | — | 2.00 | 6.50 | — |
| 1967 | Inc. above | — | — | 2.00 | 6.50 | — |
| 1969 | Inc. above | — | — | 2.00 | 6.50 | — |
| 1977 | Inc. above | — | — | 2.00 | 6.50 | — |
| 1979 | Inc. above | — | — | 2.00 | 6.50 | — |
| 1981 | Inc. above | — | — | 2.00 | 6.50 | — |

**50 CENTIMES** **KM# 148.1** **Composition:** Bronze **Obverse:** Legend in French **Obv. Legend:** BELGIQUE **Reverse:** Smaller head

| Date | Mintage | F | VF | XF | Unc | BU |
|---|---|---|---|---|---|---|
| 1955 | 29,160,000 | — | — | 0.10 | 0.25 | — |
| 1958 | 9,750,000 | — | — | 0.10 | 0.25 | — |
| 1959 | 17,350,000 | — | — | 0.10 | 0.20 | — |
| 1962 | 6,160,000 | — | — | 0.10 | 0.15 | — |
| 1964 | 5,860,000 | — | — | 0.10 | 0.15 | — |
| 1965 | 10,320,000 | — | — | 0.10 | 0.15 | — |
| 1966 | 11,040,000 | — | — | 0.10 | 0.15 | — |
| 1967 | 7,200,000 | — | — | 0.10 | 0.15 | — |
| 1968 | 2,000,000 | — | — | 0.10 | 0.20 | — |
| 1969 | 10,000,000 | — | — | 0.10 | 0.15 | — |
| 1970 | 16,000,000 | — | — | 0.10 | 0.15 | — |
| 1971 | 1,250,000 | — | — | 0.10 | 0.20 | — |
| 1972 | 3,000,000 | — | — | 0.10 | 0.15 | — |
| 1973 | 3,000,000 | — | — | 0.10 | 0.15 | — |
| 1974 | 5,000,000 | — | — | 0.10 | 0.15 | — |
| 1974 Wide rim | Inc. above | — | — | 0.10 | 0.15 | — |
| 1975 | 7,000,000 | — | — | 0.10 | 0.15 | — |
| 1976 | 8,000,000 | — | — | 0.10 | 0.15 | — |
| 1977 | 13,000,000 | — | — | 0.10 | 0.15 | — |
| 1978 | 2,500,000 | — | — | 0.10 | 0.15 | — |
| 1979 | 20,000,000 | — | — | 0.10 | 0.15 | — |
| 1980 | 20,000,000 | — | — | 0.10 | 0.15 | — |
| 1981 | 2,000,000 | — | — | 0.10 | 0.15 | — |
| 1982 | 7,000,000 | — | — | 0.10 | 0.15 | — |
| 1983 | 14,100,000 | — | — | 0.10 | 0.15 | — |
| 1985 | 6,000,000 | — | — | 0.10 | 0.15 | — |
| 1987 | 9,000,000 | — | — | 0.10 | 0.15 | — |
| 1988 | 4,500,000 | — | — | 0.10 | 0.15 | — |
| 1989 | 60,000 | — | — | — | 0.50 | — |
| 1990 | 60,000 | — | — | — | 0.50 | — |
| 1991 | 60,000 | — | — | — | 0.50 | — |
| 1992 | 7,060,000 | — | — | 0.10 | 0.15 | — |
| 1993 | — | — | — | 0.10 | 0.15 | — |
| 1994 | 10,000,000 | — | — | 0.10 | 0.15 | — |
| 1995 | 60,000 | — | — | — | 0.50 | — |
| 1996 | 4,320,000 | — | — | 0.10 | 0.15 | — |
| 1997 | 95,060,000 | — | — | — | 0.10 | — |
| 1998 | 75,060,000 | — | — | — | 0.10 | — |
| 1999 | 60,000 | — | — | — | 0.50 | — |
| 2000 | 60,000 | — | — | — | 0.50 | — |

**50 CENTIMES** **KM# 149.1** **Composition:** Bronze **Reverse:** Smaller head; legend in Dutch **Rev. Legend:** BELGIE

| Date | Mintage | F | VF | XF | Unc | BU |
|---|---|---|---|---|---|---|
| 1956 | 5,640,000 | — | — | 0.10 | 0.25 | — |
| 1957 | 13,800,000 | — | — | 0.10 | 0.25 | — |
| 1958 | 19,480,000 | — | — | 0.10 | 0.20 | — |
| 1962 | 4,150,000 | — | — | 0.10 | 0.15 | — |
| 1963 | 1,110,000 | — | — | 0.10 | 0.15 | — |
| 1964 | 10,340,000 | — | — | 0.10 | 0.15 | — |
| 1965 | 9,590,000 | — | — | 0.10 | 0.15 | — |
| 1966 | 6,930,000 | — | — | 0.10 | 0.15 | — |
| 1967 | 6,970,000 | — | — | 0.10 | 0.15 | — |
| 1968 | 2,000,000 | — | — | 0.10 | 0.20 | — |
| 1969 | 10,000,000 | — | — | 0.10 | 0.15 | — |
| 1970 | 12,000,000 | — | — | 0.10 | 0.15 | — |
| 1971 | 1,250,000 | — | — | 0.10 | 0.20 | — |
| 1972 | 7,000,000 | — | — | 0.10 | 0.15 | — |
| 1973 | 3,000,000 | — | — | 0.10 | 0.15 | — |
| 1974 | 5,000,000 | — | — | 0.10 | 0.15 | — |
| 1975 | 7,000,000 | — | — | 0.10 | 0.15 | — |
| 1976 | 8,000,000 | — | — | 0.10 | 0.15 | — |
| 1977 | 13,000,000 | — | — | 0.10 | 0.15 | — |
| 1978 | 2,500,000 | — | — | 0.10 | 0.15 | — |
| 1979 | 40,000,000 | — | — | 0.10 | 0.15 | — |
| 1980 | 20,000,000 | — | — | 0.10 | 0.15 | — |
| 1981 | 2,000,000 | — | — | 0.10 | 0.15 | — |
| 1982 | 7,000,000 | — | — | 0.10 | 0.15 | — |
| 1983 | 14,100,000 | — | — | 0.10 | 0.15 | — |
| 1985 | 6,000,000 | — | — | 0.10 | 0.15 | — |
| 1987 | 9,000,000 | — | — | 0.10 | 0.15 | — |
| 1988 | 9,000,000 | — | — | 0.10 | 0.15 | — |
| 1989 | 60,000 | — | — | — | 0.50 | — |
| 1990 | 60,000 | — | — | — | 0.50 | — |
| 1991 | 60,000 | — | — | — | 0.50 | — |
| 1992 | 7,060,000 | — | — | 0.10 | 0.15 | — |
| 1993 | 1,040,000 | — | — | 0.10 | 0.15 | — |
| 1994 | 10,000,000 | — | — | 0.10 | 0.15 | — |
| 1995 | 60,000 | — | — | — | 0.50 | — |
| 1996 | 60,000 | — | — | — | 0.50 | — |
| 1997 | 95,060,000 | — | — | — | 0.10 | — |
| 1998 | 75,060,000 | — | — | — | 0.10 | — |
| 1999 | — | — | — | — | 0.50 | — |
| 2000 | — | — | — | — | 0.50 | — |

**FRANC** **KM# 56.1** **Weight:** 5.0000 g. **Composition:** 0.8350 Silver .1342 oz. ASW **Obverse:** Legend in French **Obv. Legend:** DES BELGES

| Date | Mintage | F | VF | XF | Unc | BU |
|---|---|---|---|---|---|---|
| 1904 | 803,000 | 4.00 | 14.00 | 40.00 | 75.00 | — |
| 1909 | 2,250,000 | 2.00 | 10.00 | 30.00 | 45.00 | — |

**FRANC** **KM# 56.2** **Weight:** 5.0000 g. **Composition:** 0.8350 Silver .1342 oz. ASW **Obverse:** Without period in signature

| Date | Mintage | F | VF | XF | Unc | BU |
|---|---|---|---|---|---|---|
| 1904 | Inc. above | 7.00 | 25.00 | 60.00 | 90.00 | — |
| 1909 | Inc. above | 2.50 | 10.00 | 30.00 | 45.00 | — |

**FRANC** KM# 57.1 **Weight:** 5.0000 g. **Composition:** 0.8350 Silver .1342 oz. ASW **Obverse:** Legend in Dutch **Obv. Legend:** DER BELGEN

| Date | Mintage | F | VF | XF | Unc | BU |
|---|---|---|---|---|---|---|
| 1904 | 803,000 | 5.00 | 20.00 | 40.00 | 75.00 | — |
| 1909 | 2,250,000 | 2.00 | 10.00 | 30.00 | 45.00 | — |

**FRANC** KM# 57.2 **Weight:** 5.0000 g. **Composition:** 0.8350 Silver .1342 oz. ASW **Obverse:** Without period in signature

| Date | Mintage | F | VF | XF | Unc | BU |
|---|---|---|---|---|---|---|
| 1904 | Inc. above | 10.00 | 60.00 | 110 | 200 | — |
| 1909 | Inc. above | 3.00 | 10.00 | 30.00 | 45.00 | — |

**FRANC** KM# 72.1 **Weight:** 5.0000 g. **Composition:** 0.8350 Silver .1342 oz. ASW **Obverse:** Legend in French **Obv. Legend:** DES BELGES

| Date | Mintage | F | VF | XF | Unc | BU |
|---|---|---|---|---|---|---|
| 1910 | 2,190,000 | 1.00 | 3.00 | 8.00 | 25.00 | — |
| 1911 | 2,810,000 | 0.75 | 1.50 | 5.00 | 12.00 | — |
| 1912 | 3,250,000 | 0.75 | 1.50 | 2.50 | 7.00 | — |
| 1913 | 3,000,000 | 0.75 | 1.50 | 2.50 | 7.00 | — |
| 1914 | 10,563,000 | 0.75 | 1.50 | 2.50 | 7.00 | — |
| 1917 | 8,540,000 | 350 | 700 | 1,500 | 2,000 | — |
| 1918 | 1,469,000 | 300 | 600 | 1,400 | 2,000 | — |

**FRANC** KM# 73.1 **Weight:** 5.0000 g. **Composition:** 0.8350 Silver .1342 oz. ASW **Obverse:** Legend in Dutch **Obv. Legend:** DER BELGEN

| Date | Mintage | F | VF | XF | Unc | BU |
|---|---|---|---|---|---|---|
| 1910 | 2,750,000 | 1.00 | 4.00 | 15.00 | 35.00 | — |
| 1911 | 2,250,000 | 0.75 | 1.50 | 5.00 | 10.00 | — |
| 1912 | 3,250,000 | 0.75 | 1.50 | 2.50 | 7.00 | — |
| 1913 | 3,000,000 | 0.75 | 1.50 | 2.50 | 7.00 | — |
| 1914 | 10,222,000 | 0.75 | 1.50 | 2.50 | 7.00 | — |
| 1918 | — | 300 | 600 | 1,400 | 2,000 | — |

**FRANC** KM# 72.2 **Weight:** 5.0000 g. **Composition:** 0.8350 Silver .1342 oz. ASW **Note:** Medal alignment.

| Date | Mintage | F | VF | XF | Unc | BU |
|---|---|---|---|---|---|---|
| 1914 | Inc. above | 4.50 | 12.50 | 50.00 | 125 | — |

**FRANC** KM# 73.2 **Weight:** 5.0000 g. **Composition:** 0.8350 Silver .1342 oz. ASW **Note:** Medal alignment.

| Date | Mintage | F | VF | XF | Unc | BU |
|---|---|---|---|---|---|---|
| 1914 | Inc. above | 4.50 | 12.50 | 50.00 | 125 | — |

**FRANC** KM# 89 **Composition:** Nickel **Obverse:** Legend in French **Obv. Legend:** BELGIQUE

| Date | Mintage | F | VF | XF | Unc | BU |
|---|---|---|---|---|---|---|
| 1922 | 14,000,000 | 0.15 | 0.25 | 1.00 | 3.00 | — |
| 1923 | 22,500,000 | 0.15 | 0.25 | 1.00 | 3.00 | — |
| 1928/3 | 5,000,000 | 0.25 | 1.50 | 5.00 | 12.00 | — |
| 1928/7 | Inc. above | 0.25 | 1.50 | 5.00 | 12.00 | — |
| 1928 | Inc. above | 0.15 | 0.25 | 1.00 | 4.00 | — |
| 1929 | 7,415,000 | 0.15 | 0.25 | 1.00 | 3.50 | — |
| 1930 | 5,365,000 | 0.15 | 0.25 | 1.00 | 3.50 | — |
| 1931 | — | 250 | 500 | 1,000 | 1,800 | — |
| 1933 | 1,998,000 | 0.25 | 1.50 | 5.00 | 12.00 | — |
| 1934/24 | 10,263,000 | 0.25 | 1.50 | 4.00 | 20.00 | — |
| 1934 | Inc. above | 0.15 | 0.25 | 1.00 | 3.00 | — |

**FRANC** KM# 90 **Composition:** Nickel **Obverse:** Legend in Dutch **Obv. Legend:** BELGIE

| Date | Mintage | F | VF | XF | Unc | BU |
|---|---|---|---|---|---|---|
| 1922 | 19,000,000 | 0.15 | 0.25 | 1.00 | 3.00 | — |
| 1923/2 | 17,500,000 | 0.20 | 1.50 | 4.00 | 12.00 | — |
| 1923 | Inc. above | 0.15 | 0.25 | 1.00 | 3.00 | — |
| 1928/3 | 4,975,000 | 0.20 | 2.00 | 5.00 | 12.00 | — |
| 1928/7 | Inc. above | 0.20 | 2.00 | 5.00 | 12.00 | — |
| 1928 | Inc. above | 0.15 | 0.50 | 2.00 | 7.00 | — |
| 1929 | 10,365,000 | 0.15 | 0.25 | 1.00 | 3.00 | — |
| 1933 | 786,000 | 200 | 400 | 600 | 1,200 | — |
| 1934/24 | 8,025,000 | 0.35 | 2.50 | 7.00 | 20.00 | — |
| 1934 | Inc. above | 0.15 | 0.50 | 1.00 | 3.00 | — |
| 1935/23 | 2,238,000 | 1.50 | 4.00 | 12.00 | 20.00 | — |
| 1935 | Inc. above | 0.25 | 0.75 | 2.00 | 6.00 | — |

**FRANC** KM# 119 **Composition:** Nickel **Obverse:** Legend in French **Obv. Legend:** BELGIQUE-BELGIE

| Date | Mintage | F | VF | XF | Unc | BU |
|---|---|---|---|---|---|---|
| 1939 | 46,865,000 | 0.15 | 0.25 | 0.50 | 1.50 | — |
| 1940 | — | — | — | — | — | — |

**Note:** Struck at a later date

**FRANC** KM# 120 **Composition:** Nickel **Obverse:** Legend in Dutch **Obv. Legend:** BELGIE-BELGIQUE

| Date | Mintage | F | VF | XF | Unc | BU |
|---|---|---|---|---|---|---|
| 1939 | 36,000,000 | 0.15 | 0.25 | 0.50 | 1.50 | — |
| 1940 | 10,865,000 | 0.20 | 0.40 | 0.75 | 2.50 | — |

**FRANC** KM# 127 **Composition:** Zinc **Obverse:** Legend in French **Obv. Legend:** BELGIQUE-BELGIE **Note:** German Occupation WW II

| Date | Mintage | F | VF | XF | Unc | BU |
|---|---|---|---|---|---|---|
| 1941 | 16,000,000 | 0.20 | 0.75 | 1.50 | 6.00 | — |
| 1942 | 25,000,000 | 0.20 | 0.75 | 1.50 | 4.00 | — |
| 1943 | 28,000,000 | 0.20 | 0.75 | 1.50 | 4.00 | — |
| 1947 | 3,175,000 | 60.00 | 125 | 400 | 700 | — |

**FRANC** KM# 128 **Composition:** Zinc **Obverse:** Legend in Dutch **Obv. Legend:** BELGIE-BELGIQUE

| Date | Mintage | F | VF | XF | Unc | BU |
|---|---|---|---|---|---|---|
| 1942 | 42,000,000 | 0.20 | 0.75 | 1.50 | 4.00 | — |
| 1943 | 28,000,000 | 0.20 | 0.75 | 1.50 | 4.00 | — |
| 1944 | 24,190,000 | 0.20 | 0.75 | 1.50 | 4.00 | — |
| 1945 | 15,930,000 | 0.20 | 1.00 | 2.00 | 7.00 | — |
| 1946 | 36,000,000 | 0.20 | 0.75 | 1.50 | 4.00 | — |
| 1947 | 3,000,000 | 25.00 | 40.00 | 100 | 200 | — |

**FRANC** KM# 142.1 **Composition:** Copper-Nickel **Obverse:** Legend in French **Obv. Legend:** BELGIQUE

| Date | Mintage | F | VF | XF | Unc | BU |
|---|---|---|---|---|---|---|
| 1950 | 13,630,000 | — | — | 0.10 | 3.00 | — |
| 1951 | 51,025,000 | — | — | 0.10 | 2.00 | — |
| 1952 | 53,205,000 | — | — | 0.10 | 2.00 | — |
| 1954 | 4,980,000 | — | 0.10 | 0.25 | 3.00 | — |
| 1955 | 3,960,000 | — | 0.10 | 0.25 | 3.00 | — |
| 1956 | 10,000,000 | — | — | 0.10 | 1.00 | — |
| 1958 | 31,750,000 | — | — | 0.10 | 1.00 | — |
| 1959 | 9,000,000 | — | — | 0.10 | 1.00 | — |
| 1960 | 10,000,000 | — | — | 0.10 | 0.50 | — |
| 1961 | 5,030,000 | — | — | 0.10 | 0.50 | — |
| 1962 | 12,250,000 | — | — | 0.10 | 0.50 | — |
| 1963 | 18,700,000 | — | — | 0.10 | 0.50 | — |
| 1964 | 10,110,000 | — | — | 0.10 | 0.50 | — |
| 1965 | 10,185,000 | — | — | 0.10 | 0.50 | — |
| 1966 | 16,430,000 | — | — | 0.10 | 0.50 | — |
| 1967 | 32,945,000 | — | — | 0.10 | 0.30 | — |
| 1968 | 8,000,000 | — | — | 0.10 | 0.30 | — |
| 1969 | 21,950,000 | — | — | 0.10 | 0.30 | — |
| 1970 | 35,500,000 | — | — | 0.10 | 0.30 | — |
| 1971 | 10,000,000 | — | — | 0.10 | 0.30 | — |
| 1972 | 35,000,000 | — | — | 0.10 | 0.30 | — |
| 1973 | 42,500,000 | — | — | 0.10 | 0.30 | — |
| 1974 | 30,000,000 | — | — | 0.10 | 0.30 | — |
| 1975 | 80,000,000 | — | — | 0.10 | 0.30 | — |
| 1976 | 18,000,000 | — | — | 0.10 | 0.30 | — |
| 1977 | 68,500,000 | — | — | 0.10 | 0.30 | — |
| 1978 | 47,500,000 | — | — | 0.10 | 0.30 | — |
| 1979 | 25,000,000 | — | — | 0.10 | 0.30 | — |
| 1980 | 66,500,000 | — | — | 0.10 | 0.30 | — |
| 1981 | 2,000,000 | 0.10 | 0.20 | 0.50 | 0.75 | — |
| 1988 | 17,500,000 | — | — | 0.10 | 0.30 | — |

**FRANC** KM# 143.1 **Composition:** Copper-Nickel **Reverse:** Legend in Dutch **Rev. Legend:** BELGIE

| Date | Mintage | F | VF | XF | Unc | BU |
|---|---|---|---|---|---|---|
| 1950 | 10,000,000 | — | — | 0.10 | 3.00 | — |
| 1951 | 53,750,000 | — | — | 0.10 | 2.00 | — |
| 1952 | 49,145,000 | — | — | 0.10 | 2.00 | — |
| 1953 | 9,915,000 | — | — | 0.10 | 2.00 | — |
| 1954 | 4,940,000 | — | 0.10 | 0.25 | 3.00 | — |
| 1955 | 3,960,000 | — | 0.10 | 0.25 | 3.00 | — |
| 1956 | 10,040,000 | — | — | 0.10 | 1.00 | — |
| 1957 | 18,315,000 | — | — | 0.10 | 1.00 | — |
| 1958 | 17,365,000 | — | — | 0.10 | 1.00 | — |
| 1959 | 5,830,000 | — | — | 0.10 | 1.00 | — |
| 1960 | 5,555,000 | — | — | 0.10 | 0.50 | — |
| 1961 | 9,350,000 | — | — | 0.10 | 0.50 | — |
| 1962 | 10,720,000 | — | — | 0.10 | 0.50 | — |
| 1963 | 23,460,000 | — | — | 0.10 | 0.50 | — |
| 1964 | 7,430,000 | — | — | 0.10 | 0.50 | — |
| 1965 | 11,190,000 | — | — | 0.10 | 0.50 | — |
| 1966 | 20,990,000 | — | — | 0.10 | 0.50 | — |
| 1967 | 27,470,000 | — | — | 0.10 | 0.50 | — |
| 1968 | 8,170,000 | — | — | 0.10 | 0.30 | — |
| 1969 | 21,730,000 | — | — | 0.10 | 0.30 | — |
| 1970 | 35,730,000 | — | — | 0.10 | 0.30 | — |
| 1971 | 10,000,000 | — | — | 0.10 | 0.30 | — |
| 1972 | 35,000,000 | — | — | 0.10 | 0.30 | — |
| 1973 | 42,500,000 | — | — | 0.10 | 0.30 | — |
| 1974 | 30,000,000 | — | — | 0.10 | 0.30 | — |
| 1975 | 80,000,000 | — | — | 0.10 | 0.30 | — |
| 1976 | 18,000,000 | — | — | 0.10 | 0.30 | — |
| 1977 | 68,500,000 | — | — | 0.10 | 0.30 | — |
| 1978 | 47,500,000 | — | — | 0.10 | 0.30 | — |
| 1979 | 50,000,000 | — | — | 0.10 | 0.30 | — |
| 1980 | 66,500,000 | — | — | 0.10 | 0.30 | — |
| 1981 | 2,000,000 | — | — | 0.10 | 0.50 | — |
| 1988 | 17,500,000 | — | — | 0.10 | 0.30 | — |

**FRANC** KM# 143.2 **Composition:** Copper-Nickel **Note:** Medal alignment

| Date | Mintage | F | VF | XF | Unc | BU |
|---|---|---|---|---|---|---|
| 1951 | Inc. above | — | 3.00 | 9.00 | 20.00 | — |
| 1952 | Inc. above | — | 3.00 | 9.00 | 20.00 | — |
| 1956 | Inc. above | — | 3.00 | 9.00 | 20.00 | — |
| 1957 | Inc. above | — | 3.00 | 9.00 | 20.00 | — |
| 1958 | Inc. above | — | 3.00 | 9.00 | 20.00 | — |
| 1964 | Inc. above | — | 3.00 | 9.00 | 20.00 | — |
| 1970 | Inc. above | — | 3.00 | 9.00 | 20.00 | — |
| 1971 | Inc. above | — | 3.00 | 9.00 | 20.00 | — |
| 1973 | Inc. above | — | 3.00 | 9.00 | 20.00 | — |
| 1976 | Inc. above | — | 3.00 | 9.00 | 20.00 | — |
| 1977 | Inc. above | — | 3.00 | 9.00 | 20.00 | — |
| 1979 | Inc. above | — | 3.00 | 9.00 | 20.00 | — |
| 1981 | Inc. above | — | 3.00 | 9.00 | 20.00 | — |

**FRANC** KM# 142.2 **Composition:** Copper-Nickel **Note:** Medal alignment

| Date | Mintage | F | VF | XF | Unc | BU |
|---|---|---|---|---|---|---|
| 1952 | Inc. above | — | 3.00 | 9.00 | 20.00 | — |
| 1956 | Inc. above | — | 3.00 | 9.00 | 20.00 | — |
| 1958 | Inc. above | — | 3.00 | 9.00 | 20.00 | — |
| 1959 | Inc. above | — | 3.00 | 9.00 | 20.00 | — |
| 1963 | Inc. above | — | 3.00 | 9.00 | 20.00 | — |
| 1965 | Inc. above | — | 3.00 | 9.00 | 20.00 | — |
| 1966 | Inc. above | — | 3.00 | 9.00 | 25.00 | — |
| 1969 | Inc. above | — | 3.00 | 9.00 | 25.00 | — |
| 1970 | Inc. above | — | 3.00 | 9.00 | 25.00 | — |
| 1974 | Inc. above | — | 3.00 | 9.00 | 25.00 | — |
| 1975 | Inc. above | — | 3.00 | 9.00 | 25.00 | — |
| 1977 | Inc. above | — | 3.00 | 9.00 | 25.00 | — |
| 1978 | Inc. above | — | 3.00 | 9.00 | 25.00 | — |
| 1979 | Inc. above | — | 3.00 | 9.00 | 25.00 | — |
| 1988 | Inc. above | — | 3.00 | 9.00 | 25.00 | — |

**FRANC** **KM# 171** **Composition:** Nickel Plated Iron **Obverse:** Dutch legend. **Obv. Legend:** BOUDEWIJN I **Reverse:** Legend in Dutch **Rev. Legend:** BELGIE

| Date | Mintage | F | VF | XF | Unc | BU |
|---|---|---|---|---|---|---|
| 1989 | 200,060,000 | — | — | — | 0.35 | — |
| 1990 | 200,060,000 | — | — | — | 0.35 | — |
| 1991 | 200,060,000 | — | — | — | 0.35 | — |
| 1992 | 60,000 | — | — | — | 1.25 | — |
| 1993 | 15,060,000 | — | — | — | 0.35 | — |

**FRANC** **KM# 170** **Composition:** Nickel Plated Iron **Obverse:** French legend. **Obv. Legend:** BAUDOUIN I **Reverse:** Legend in Dutch **Rev. Legend:** BELGIE

| Date | Mintage | F | VF | XF | Unc | BU |
|---|---|---|---|---|---|---|
| 1989 | 200,060,000 | — | — | — | 0.35 | — |
| 1990 | 200,060,000 | — | — | — | 0.35 | — |
| 1991 | 200,060,000 | — | — | — | 0.35 | — |
| 1992 | 60,000 | — | — | — | 1.25 | — |
| 1993 | 15,060,000 | — | — | — | 0.35 | — |

**FRANC** **KM# 188** **Composition:** Nickel Plated Iron **Reverse:** Legend in Dutch **Rev. Legend:** BELGIE

| Date | Mintage | F | VF | XF | Unc | BU |
|---|---|---|---|---|---|---|
| 1994 | 75,060,000 | — | — | — | 0.30 | — |
| 1995 | 75,060,000 | — | — | — | 0.30 | — |
| 1996 | 75,060,000 | — | — | — | 0.30 | — |
| 1997 | 95,060,000 | — | — | — | 0.30 | — |
| 1998 | 75,060,000 | — | — | — | 0.30 | — |
| 1999 | 60,000 | — | — | — | 1.00 | — |
| 2000 | 60,000 | — | — | — | 1.00 | — |

**FRANC** **KM# 187** **Composition:** Nickel Plated Iron **Obverse:** Albert II **Reverse:** Legend in French **Rev. Legend:** BELGIQUE **Note:** Struck at Brussels Mint. Mint mark - Angel Head. Unknown mintmaster's privy mark - scales.

| Date | Mintage | F | VF | XF | Unc | BU |
|---|---|---|---|---|---|---|
| 1994 | 75,060,000 | — | — | — | 0.30 | — |
| 1995 | 75,060,000 | — | — | — | 0.30 | — |
| 1996 | 75,060,000 | — | — | — | 0.30 | — |
| 1997 | 95,060,000 | — | — | — | 0.30 | — |
| 1998 | 75,060,000 | — | — | — | 0.30 | — |
| 1999 | 60,000 | — | — | — | 1.00 | — |
| 2000 | 60,000 | — | — | — | 1.00 | — |

**2 FRANCS (2 Frank)** **KM# 58.1** **Weight:** 10.0000 g. **Composition:** 0.8350 Silver .2685 oz. ASW **Obverse:** Legend in French **Obv. Legend:** DES BELGES

| Date | Mintage | F | VF | XF | Unc | BU |
|---|---|---|---|---|---|---|
| 1904 | 400,000 | 6.00 | 10.00 | 45.00 | 90.00 | — |
| 1909 | 1,088,000 | 2.50 | 5.00 | 25.00 | 50.00 | — |

**2 FRANCS (2 Frank)** **KM# 58.2** **Weight:** 10.0000 g. **Composition:** 0.8350 Silver .2685 oz. ASW **Obverse:** Without period in signature

| Date | Mintage | F | VF | XF | Unc | BU |
|---|---|---|---|---|---|---|
| 1904 | Inc. above | 9.00 | 15.00 | 60.00 | 100 | — |
| 1909 | Inc. above | 10.00 | 20.00 | 75.00 | 200 | — |

**2 FRANCS (2 Frank)** **KM# 59.1** **Weight:** 10.0000 g. **Composition:** 0.8350 Silver .2685 oz.. ASW **Obverse:** Legend in Dutch **Obv. Legend:** DER BELGEN

| Date | Mintage | F | VF | XF | Unc | BU |
|---|---|---|---|---|---|---|
| 1904 | 400,000 | 5.00 | 10.00 | 45.00 | 90.00 | — |
| 1909 | 1,088,000 | 2.50 | 4.00 | 25.00 | 50.00 | — |

**2 FRANCS (2 Frank)** **KM# 59.2** **Weight:** 10.0000 g. **Composition:** 0.8350 Silver .2685 oz. ASW **Obverse:** Without period in signature

| Date | Mintage | F | VF | XF | Unc | BU |
|---|---|---|---|---|---|---|
| 1904 | Inc. above | 12.50 | 30.00 | 75.00 | 200 | — |
| 1909 | Inc. above | 7.00 | 15.00 | 45.00 | 90.00 | — |

**2 FRANCS (2 Frank)** **KM# 74** **Weight:** 10.0000 g. **Composition:** 0.8350 Silver .2685 oz. ASW **Obverse:** Legend in French **Obv. Legend:** DES BELGES

| Date | Mintage | F | VF | XF | Unc | BU |
|---|---|---|---|---|---|---|
| 1910 | 800,000 | 2.50 | 4.00 | 15.00 | 50.00 | — |
| 1911 | 1,000,000 | 2.00 | 3.00 | 10.00 | 30.00 | — |
| 1912 | 375,000 | 3.00 | 5.00 | 20.00 | 55.00 | — |

**2 FRANCS (2 Frank)** **KM# 75** **Weight:** 10.0000 g. **Composition:** 0.8350 Silver .2685 oz. ASW **Obverse:** Legend in Dutch **Obv. Legend:** DER BELGEN

| Date | Mintage | F | VF | XF | Unc | BU |
|---|---|---|---|---|---|---|
| 1911 | 1,775,000 | 2.00 | 3.00 | 10.00 | 30.00 | — |
| 1912 | 375,000 | 2.50 | 4.00 | 20.00 | 50.00 | — |

**2 FRANCS (2 Frank)** **KM# 91.1** **Composition:** Nickel **Obverse:** Legend in French **Obv. Legend:** BELGIQUE

| Date | Mintage | F | VF | XF | Unc | BU |
|---|---|---|---|---|---|---|
| 1923 | 7,500,000 | 0.50 | 1.50 | 8.00 | 15.00 | — |
| 1930/20 | 1,250,000 | 12.00 | 20.00 | 140 | 250 | — |
| 1930 | Inc. above | 10.00 | 17.00 | 100 | 200 | — |

**2 FRANCS (2 Frank)** **KM# 92** **Composition:** Nickel **Obverse:** Legend in Dutch **Obv. Legend:** BELGIE

| Date | Mintage | F | VF | XF | Unc | BU |
|---|---|---|---|---|---|---|
| 1923 | 6,500,000 | 0.25 | 1.50 | 7.00 | 15.00 | — |
| 1924 | 1,000,000 | 5.00 | 15.00 | 65.00 | 125 | — |
| 1930/20 | 1,252,000 | 15.00 | 40.00 | 125 | 250 | — |
| 1930 | Inc. above | 8.00 | 15.00 | 100 | 200 | — |

**2 FRANCS (2 Frank)** **KM# 91.2** **Composition:** Nickel **Note:** Medal alignment

| Date | Mintage | F | VF | XF | Unc | BU |
|---|---|---|---|---|---|---|
| 1923 | Inc. above | 5.00 | 8.00 | 45.00 | 110 | — |

**2 FRANCS (2 Frank)** **KM# 133** **Composition:** Zinc Coated Steel **Obverse:** Legend in French **Obv. Legend:** BELGIQUE-BELGIE **Note:** Allied Occupation issue. Made in U.S.A. on blanks for 1943 cents.

| Date | Mintage | F | VF | XF | Unc | BU |
|---|---|---|---|---|---|---|
| 1944 | 25,000,000 | 0.25 | 0.50 | 1.50 | 5.00 | — |

**2 FRANCS (2 Frank)** **KM# 133a** **Composition:** Silver **Note:** Made in error in U.S.A. on blanks for Netherlands 25 cents.

| Date | Mintage | F | VF | XF | Unc | BU |
|---|---|---|---|---|---|---|
| 1944 | — | 100 | 200 | 300 | 400 | — |

**5 FRANCS - 5 FRANK (Un / Een Belga)** **KM# 97.1** **Composition:** Nickel **Obverse:** Legend in French **Obv. Legend:** DES BELGES **Reverse:** Value: UN BELGA **Note:** All dates exist in position A and B, values are the same.

| Date | Mintage | F | VF | XF | Unc | BU |
|---|---|---|---|---|---|---|
| 1930 | 1,600,000 | 1.50 | 6.00 | 12.00 | 20.00 | — |
| 1931 | 9,032,000 | 1.00 | 4.00 | 10.00 | 15.00 | — |
| 1932 | 3,600,000 | 1.50 | 7.00 | 14.00 | 25.00 | — |
| 1933 | 1,387,000 | 6.00 | 15.00 | 35.00 | 50.00 | — |
| 1934 | 1,000,000 | 30.00 | 75.00 | 160 | 250 | — |

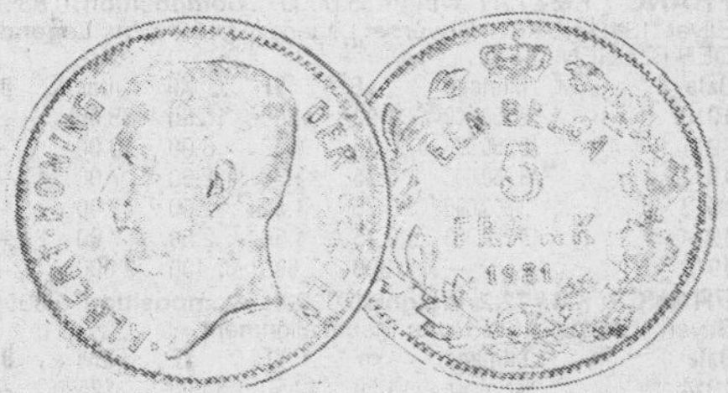

**5 FRANCS - 5 FRANK (Un / Een Belga)** **KM# 98** **Composition:** Nickel **Obverse:** Legend in Dutch **Obv. Legend:** DER BELGEN **Reverse:** Value: EEN BELGA **Note:** All dates exist in position A and B, values are the same.

| Date | Mintage | F | VF | XF | Unc | BU |
|---|---|---|---|---|---|---|
| 1930 | 5,086,000 | 2.00 | 8.00 | 16.00 | 25.00 | — |
| 1931 | 5,336,000 | 1.50 | 6.00 | 12.00 | 20.00 | — |
| 1932 | 3,683,000 | 1.50 | 7.00 | 14.00 | 25.00 | — |
| 1933 | 2,514,000 | 8.00 | 20.00 | 40.00 | 60.00 | — |

**5 FRANCS - 5 FRANK (Un / Een Belga)** **KM# 97.2** **Composition:** Nickel **Note:** Medal alignment. Edge varieties exist.

| Date | Mintage | F | VF | XF | Unc | BU |
|---|---|---|---|---|---|---|
| 1930 | Inc. above | 17.50 | 50.00 | 150 | 300 | — |

**5 FRANCS - 5 FRANK (Un / Een Belga)** **KM# 109.2** **Composition:** Nickel **Note:** Medal alignment. Edge varieties exist.

| Date | Mintage | F | VF | XF | Unc | BU |
|---|---|---|---|---|---|---|
| 1936 | Inc. above | 15.00 | 45.00 | 130 | 300 | — |

**5 FRANCS - 5 FRANK (Un / Een Belga)** **KM# 108.2** **Composition:** Nickel **Note:** Medal alignment.

| Date | Mintage | F | VF | XF | Unc | BU |
|---|---|---|---|---|---|---|
| 1936 | Inc. above | 17.50 | 55.00 | 150 | 350 | — |

**5 FRANCS - 5 FRANK (Un / Een Belga)** **KM# 108.1** **Composition:** Nickel **Reverse:** Legend in French **Rev. Legend:** BELGIQUE **Note:** Both dates exist in position A and B, values are the same.

| Date | Mintage | F | VF | XF | Unc | BU |
|---|---|---|---|---|---|---|
| 1936 | 650,000 | 6.00 | 20.00 | 50.00 | 85.00 | — |
| 1937 | 1,848,000 | 6.00 | 17.50 | 40.00 | 70.00 | — |

**5 FRANCS - 5 FRANK (Un / Een Belga) KM# 109.1**
**Composition:** Nickel **Reverse:** Legend in Dutch **Rev. Legend:** BELGIE **Note:** Both dates exist in position A and B, values are the same.

| Date | Mintage | F | VF | XF | Unc | BU |
|---|---|---|---|---|---|---|
| 1936 | 2,498,000 | 4.00 | 15.00 | 35.00 | 60.00 | — |
| 1937 | — | — | — | — | — | — |

**5 FRANCS - 5 FRANK (Un / Een Belga) KM# 116.1**
**Composition:** Nickel **Obverse:** Legend in French **Obv. Legend:** BELGIQUE-BELGIE **Note:** Milled edge, lettering with crown.

| Date | Mintage | F | VF | XF | Unc | BU |
|---|---|---|---|---|---|---|
| 1938 Position A | 11,419,000 | 0.20 | 0.75 | 3.00 | 6.00 | — |
| 1938 Position B | Inc. above | 0.30 | 1.00 | 4.00 | 7.00 | — |

**5 FRANCS - 5 FRANK (Un / Een Belga) KM# 117.1**
**Composition:** Nickel **Obverse:** Legend in Dutch **Obv. Legend:** BELGIE-BELGIQUE **Note:** Milled edge, lettering with crown.

| Date | Mintage | F | VF | XF | Unc | BU |
|---|---|---|---|---|---|---|
| 1938 Position A | 3,200,000 | 7.00 | 15.00 | 50.00 | 125 | — |
| 1938 Position B | Inc. above | 7.00 | 15.00 | 50.00 | 125 | — |
| 1939 Position A | 8,219,000 | 7.50 | 20.00 | 80.00 | 175 | — |
| 1939 Position B | Inc. above | 7.50 | 20.00 | 80.00 | 175 | — |

**5 FRANCS - 5 FRANK (Un / Een Belga) KM# 117.2**
**Composition:** Nickel **Note:** Milled edge, lettering with star.

| Date | Mintage | F | VF | XF | Unc | BU |
|---|---|---|---|---|---|---|
| 1938 Position A | Inc. above | 6.00 | 20.00 | 70.00 | 160 | — |
| 1938 Position B | Inc. above | 6.00 | 20.00 | 70.00 | 160 | — |
| 1939 Position A | Inc. above | 0.15 | 0.50 | 1.25 | 4.00 | — |
| 1939 Position B | Inc. above | 0.15 | 0.50 | 1.25 | 4.00 | — |

**5 FRANCS - 5 FRANK (Un / Een Belga) KM# 116.3**
**Composition:** Nickel **Note:** Milled edge, without lettering (error).

| Date | Mintage | F | VF | XF | Unc | BU |
|---|---|---|---|---|---|---|
| 1938 | Inc. above | 40.00 | 70.00 | 135 | 300 | — |

**5 FRANCS - 5 FRANK (Un / Een Belga) KM# 117.3**
**Composition:** Nickel **Note:** Milled edge, without lettering (error).

| Date | Mintage | F | VF | XF | Unc | BU |
|---|---|---|---|---|---|---|
| 1939 | Inc. above | 30.00 | 60.00 | 175 | 350 | — |

**5 FRANCS - 5 FRANK (Un / Een Belga) KM# 116.2**
**Composition:** Nickel **Note:** Milled edge, lettering with star.

| Date | Mintage | F | VF | XF | Unc | BU |
|---|---|---|---|---|---|---|
| 1939 Position A | Inc. above | 200 | 500 | 900 | 1,750 | — |
| 1939 Position B | Inc. above | 200 | 500 | 900 | 1,750 | — |

**5 FRANCS - 5 FRANK (Un / Een Belga) KM# 129.1**
**Composition:** Zinc **Obverse:** Legend in French **Obv. Legend:** DES BELGES **Note:** German Occupation WW II

| Date | Mintage | F | VF | XF | Unc | BU |
|---|---|---|---|---|---|---|
| 1941 | 15,200,000 | 0.35 | 0.75 | 2.50 | 10.00 | — |
| 1943 | 16,236,000 | 0.35 | 0.75 | 2.00 | 10.00 | — |
| 1944 | 1,868,000 | 0.75 | 3.00 | 12.00 | 35.00 | — |
| 1945 | 3,200,000 | 0.50 | 1.00 | 6.00 | 15.00 | — |
| 1946 | 4,452,000 | 1.00 | 4.50 | 15.00 | 40.00 | — |
| 1947 | 3,100,000 | 20.00 | 40.00 | 110 | 300 | — |

**5 FRANCS - 5 FRANK (Un / Een Belga) KM# 130**
**Composition:** Zinc **Obverse:** Legend in Dutch **Obv. Legend:** DER BELGEN

| Date | Mintage | F | VF | XF | Unc | BU |
|---|---|---|---|---|---|---|
| 1941 | 27,544,000 | 0.30 | 0.50 | 2.50 | 10.00 | — |
| 1945 | 3,200,000 | 15.00 | 30.00 | 75.00 | 200 | — |
| 1946 Rare | 4,000,000 | — | — | — | — | — |
| 1947 | 36,000 | 75.00 | 150 | 375 | 750 | — |

**5 FRANCS - 5 FRANK (Un / Een Belga) KM# 129.2**
**Composition:** Zinc **Note:** Medal alignment.

| Date | Mintage | F | VF | XF | Unc | BU |
|---|---|---|---|---|---|---|
| 1943 | Inc. above | 5.00 | 15.00 | 50.00 | 130 | — |

**5 FRANCS - 5 FRANK (Un / Een Belga) KM# 134.1**
**Composition:** Copper-Nickel **Obverse:** Legend in French **Obv. Legend:** BELGIQUE

| Date | Mintage | F | VF | XF | Unc | BU |
|---|---|---|---|---|---|---|
| 1948 | 5,304,000 | — | — | 0.20 | 4.00 | — |
| 1949 | 38,752,000 | — | — | 0.20 | 2.00 | — |
| 1950 | 23,948,000 | — | — | 0.20 | 2.00 | — |
| 1958 | 9,088,000 | — | — | 0.20 | 1.00 | — |
| 1961 | 6,000,000 | — | — | 0.20 | 0.50 | — |
| 1962 | 6,576,000 | — | — | 0.20 | 0.50 | — |
| 1963 | 11,144,000 | — | — | 0.20 | 0.35 | — |
| 1964 | 3,520,000 | — | — | 0.20 | 0.40 | — |
| 1965 | 11,988,000 | — | — | 0.20 | 0.35 | — |
| 1966 | 6,772,000 | — | — | 0.20 | 0.40 | — |
| 1967 | 13,268,000 | — | — | 0.20 | 0.35 | — |
| 1968 | 5,192,000 | — | — | 0.20 | 0.40 | — |
| 1969 | 22,235,000 | — | — | 0.20 | 0.35 | — |
| 1969 Without engraver's name | Inc. above | — | 2.50 | 9.00 | 20.00 | — |
| 1970 | 2,000,000 | — | — | 0.20 | 0.45 | — |
| 1971 | 15,000,000 | — | — | 0.20 | 0.35 | — |
| 1972 | 17,500,000 | — | — | 0.20 | 0.35 | — |
| 1973 | 10,000,000 | — | — | 0.20 | 0.35 | — |
| 1974 | 25,000,000 | — | — | 0.20 | 0.35 | — |
| 1975 | 34,000,000 | — | — | 0.20 | 0.35 | — |
| 1976 | 7,500,000 | — | — | 0.20 | 0.40 | — |
| 1977 | 22,500,000 | — | — | 0.20 | 0.35 | — |
| 1978 | 27,500,000 | — | — | 0.20 | 0.35 | — |
| 1979 | 5,000,000 | — | — | 0.20 | 0.40 | — |
| 1980 | 11,000,000 | — | — | 0.20 | 0.35 | — |
| 1981 | 2,000,000 | — | — | 0.20 | 0.40 | — |

**5 FRANCS - 5 FRANK (Un / Een Belga) KM# 135.1**
**Composition:** Copper-Nickel **Obverse:** Legend in Dutch **Obv. Legend:** BELGIE

| Date | Mintage | F | VF | XF | Unc | BU |
|---|---|---|---|---|---|---|
| 1948 | 4,800,000 | — | — | 0.20 | 4.00 | — |
| 1949 | 31,500,000 | — | — | 0.20 | 2.00 | — |
| 1950 | 34,728,000 | — | — | 0.20 | 2.00 | — |
| 1958 | 2,672,000 | — | — | 0.20 | 4.00 | — |
| 1960 | 5,896,000 | — | — | 0.20 | 0.75 | — |
| 1961 | 4,120,000 | — | — | 0.20 | 0.50 | — |
| 1962 | 7,624,000 | — | — | 0.20 | 0.50 | — |
| 1963 | 6,136,000 | — | — | 0.20 | 0.40 | — |
| 1964 | 8,128,000 | — | — | 0.20 | 0.40 | — |
| 1965 | 9,956,000 | — | — | 0.20 | 0.40 | — |
| 1966 | 7,136,000 | — | — | 0.20 | 0.40 | — |
| 1967 | 16,132,000 | — | — | 0.20 | 0.35 | — |
| 1968 | 3,200,000 | — | — | 0.20 | 0.40 | — |
| 1969 | 21,500,000 | — | — | 0.20 | 0.35 | — |
| 1970 | 2,000,000 | — | — | 0.20 | 0.45 | — |
| 1971 | 15,000,000 | — | — | 0.20 | 0.35 | — |
| 1972 | 17,500,000 | — | — | 0.20 | 0.35 | — |
| 1972 Without engraver's name | Inc. above | — | 2.50 | 9.00 | 20.00 | — |
| 1973 | 10,000,000 | — | — | 0.20 | 0.35 | — |
| 1974 | 25,000,000 | — | — | 0.20 | 0.35 | — |
| 1975 | 34,000,000 | — | — | 0.20 | 0.35 | — |
| 1976 | 7,500,000 | — | — | 0.20 | 0.40 | — |
| 1977 | 22,500,000 | — | — | 0.20 | 0.35 | — |
| 1978 | 27,500,000 | — | — | 0.20 | 0.35 | — |
| 1979 | 10,000,000 | — | — | 0.20 | 0.35 | — |
| 1980 | 11,000,000 | — | — | 0.20 | 0.35 | — |
| 1981 | 2,000,000 | — | — | 0.20 | 0.40 | — |

**5 FRANCS - 5 FRANK (Un / Een Belga) KM# 134.2**
**Composition:** Copper-Nickel **Note:** Medal alignment.

| Date | Mintage | F | VF | XF | Unc | BU |
|---|---|---|---|---|---|---|
| 1949 | Inc. above | — | 4.00 | 10.00 | 30.00 | — |
| 1950 | Inc. above | — | 4.00 | 10.00 | 30.00 | — |
| 1958 | Inc. above | — | 4.00 | 10.00 | 30.00 | — |
| 1962 | Inc. above | — | 4.00 | 10.00 | 30.00 | — |
| 1963 | Inc. above | — | 4.00 | 10.00 | 30.00 | — |
| 1965 | Inc. above | — | 4.00 | 10.00 | 30.00 | — |
| 1966 | Inc. above | — | 4.00 | 10.00 | 30.00 | — |
| 1969 | Inc. above | — | 4.00 | 10.00 | 30.00 | — |
| 1975 | Inc. above | — | 4.00 | 10.00 | 30.00 | — |
| 1977 | Inc. above | — | 4.00 | 10.00 | 30.00 | — |

**5 FRANCS - 5 FRANK (Un / Een Belga) KM# 135.2**
**Composition:** Copper-Nickel **Note:** Medal alignment.

| Date | Mintage | F | VF | XF | Unc | BU |
|---|---|---|---|---|---|---|
| 1950 | Inc. above | — | 4.00 | 10.00 | 30.00 | — |
| 1962 | Inc. above | — | 4.00 | 10.00 | 30.00 | — |
| 1963 | Inc. above | — | 4.00 | 10.00 | 30.00 | — |
| 1965 | Inc. above | — | 4.00 | 10.00 | 30.00 | — |
| 1966 | Inc. above | — | 4.00 | 10.00 | 30.00 | — |
| 1969 | Inc. above | — | 4.00 | 10.00 | 30.00 | — |
| 1974 | Inc. above | — | 4.00 | 10.00 | 30.00 | — |

**5 FRANCS - 5 FRANK (Un / Een Belga) KM# 163**
**Composition:** Brass Or Aluminum-Bronze **Reverse:** Legend in French **Rev. Legend:** BELGIQUE

| Date | Mintage | F | VF | XF | Unc | BU |
|---|---|---|---|---|---|---|
| 1986 | 208,400,000 | — | — | 0.35 | 0.65 | — |
| 1987 | 22,500,000 | — | — | 0.35 | 0.65 | — |
| 1988 | 26,500,000 | — | — | 0.35 | 0.65 | — |
| 1989 | 60,000 | — | — | — | 2.00 | — |
| 1990 | 60,000 | — | — | — | 2.00 | — |
| 1991 | 60,000 | — | — | — | 2.00 | — |
| 1992 | 5,060,000 | — | — | 0.35 | 0.65 | — |
| 1993 | 15,060,000 | — | — | 0.35 | 0.65 | — |

**5 FRANCS - 5 FRANK (Un / Een Belga) KM# 164**
**Composition:** Brass Or Aluminum-Bronze **Reverse:** Legend in Dutch **Rev. Legend:** BELGIE

| Date | Mintage | F | VF | XF | Unc | BU |
|---|---|---|---|---|---|---|
| 1986 | 208,400,000 | — | — | 0.35 | 0.65 | — |
| 1987 | 22,500,000 | — | — | 0.35 | 0.65 | — |
| 1988 | 26,500,000 | — | — | 0.35 | 0.65 | — |
| 1989 | 60,000 | — | — | — | 2.00 | — |
| 1990 | 60,000 | — | — | — | 2.00 | — |
| 1991 | 60,000 | — | — | — | 2.00 | — |
| 1992 | 5,060,000 | — | — | 0.35 | 0.65 | — |
| 1993 | 15,060,000 | — | — | 0.35 | 0.65 | — |

**5 FRANCS - 5 FRANK (Un / Een Belga) KM# 189**
**Composition:** Aluminum-Bronze **Obverse:** Albert II **Reverse:** Legend in French **Rev. Legend:** BELGIQUE **Note:** Struck at Brussels Mint. Mint mark - Angel Head. Unknown Mintmaster's privy mark - Scales.

| Date | Mintage | F | VF | XF | Unc | BU |
|---|---|---|---|---|---|---|
| 1994 | 30,060,000 | — | — | — | 0.50 | — |
| 1995 | 60,000 | — | — | — | 5.00 | — |
| 1996 | 14,485,000 | — | — | — | 0.50 | — |
| 1997 | 60,000 | — | — | — | 5.00 | — |
| 1998 | 6,500,000 | — | — | — | 2.00 | — |

**5 FRANCS - 5 FRANK (Un / Een Belga) KM# 190**
**Composition:** Aluminum-Bronze **Reverse:** Legend in Dutch **Rev. Legend:** BELGIE **Note:** Struck at Brussels Mint. Mint mark - Angel Head. Unknown mintmaster's privy mark - Scales.

| Date | Mintage | F | VF | XF | Unc | BU |
|---|---|---|---|---|---|---|
| 1994 | 30,060,000 | — | — | — | 0.50 | — |
| 1995 | 60,000 | — | — | — | 5.00 | — |
| 1996 | 3,133,000 | — | — | — | 2.00 | — |
| 1997 | 6,000 | — | — | — | 5.00 | — |
| 1998 | 6,500,000 | — | — | — | 1.00 | — |
| 1999 | 60,000 | — | — | — | 5.00 | — |
| 2000 | 60,000 | — | — | — | 5.00 | — |

**10 FRANCS - 10 FRANK (Deux / Twee Belgas) KM# 99**
**Composition:** Nickel **Subject:** Independence Cenntennial **Reverse:** Legend in French **Rev. Legend:** BELGIQUE **Note:** Exists in position A or B, values are the same.

| Date | Mintage | F | VF | XF | Unc | BU |
|---|---|---|---|---|---|---|
| 1930 | 2,699,000 | 25.00 | 70.00 | 130 | 200 | — |

**10 FRANCS - 10 FRANK (Deux / Twee Belgas) KM# 100**
**Composition:** Nickel **Reverse:** Legend in Dutch **Rev. Legend:** BELGIE **Note:** Exists in position A or B, values are the same.

| Date | Mintage | F | VF | XF | Unc | BU |
|---|---|---|---|---|---|---|
| 1930 | 3,000,000 | 30.00 | 75.00 | 140 | 250 | — |

**10 FRANCS - 10 FRANK (Deux / Twee Belgas) KM# 155.2**
**Composition:** Nickel **Note:** Medal alignment. Struck at Brussels Mint. Mint mark - Angel Head. Mintmaster Vogelier's privy mark - Bird.

| Date | Mintage | F | VF | XF | Unc | BU |
|---|---|---|---|---|---|---|
| 1969 | Inc. above | — | 6.00 | 12.00 | 35.00 | — |
| 1974 | Inc. above | — | 6.00 | 12.00 | 35.00 | — |
| 1977 | Inc. above | — | 6.00 | 12.00 | 35.00 | — |
| 1978 | Inc. above | — | 6.00 | 12.00 | 30.00 | — |

**10 FRANCS - 10 FRANK (Deux / Twee Belgas) KM# 155.1**
**Composition:** Nickel **Reverse:** Legend in French **Rev. Legend:** BELGIQUE **Note:** Struck at Brussels Mint. Mint mark - Angel Head. Mintmaster Vogelier's privy mark - Bird.

| Date | Mintage | F | VF | XF | Unc | BU |
|---|---|---|---|---|---|---|
| 1969 | 22,235,000 | — | — | 0.40 | 0.70 | — |
| 1970 | 9,500,000 | — | — | 0.40 | 0.70 | — |
| 1971 | 15,000,000 | — | — | 0.40 | 0.70 | — |
| 1972 | 10,000,000 | — | — | 0.40 | 0.70 | — |
| 1973 | 10,000,000 | — | — | 0.40 | 0.70 | — |
| 1974 | 5,000,000 | — | — | 0.40 | 0.70 | — |
| 1975 | 5,000,000 | — | — | 0.40 | 0.70 | — |
| 1976 | 7,500,000 | — | — | 0.40 | 0.70 | — |
| 1977 | 7,000,000 | — | — | 0.40 | 0.70 | — |
| 1978 | 2,500,000 | — | — | 0.60 | 1.50 | — |
| 1979 | 5,000,000 | — | — | 0.60 | 1.50 | — |

**10 FRANCS - 10 FRANK (Deux / Twee Belgas) KM# 156.1**
**Composition:** Nickel **Reverse:** Legend in Dutch **Rev. Legend:** BELGIE **Note:** Struck at Brussels Mint. Mint mark - Angel Head. Mintmaster Vogelier's privy mark - Bird.

| Date | Mintage | F | VF | XF | Unc | BU |
|---|---|---|---|---|---|---|
| 1969 | 21,500,000 | — | — | 0.40 | 0.70 | — |
| 1970 | 10,000,000 | — | — | 0.40 | 0.70 | — |
| 1971 | 15,000,000 | — | — | 0.40 | 0.70 | — |
| 1972 | 10,000,000 | — | — | 0.40 | 0.70 | — |
| 1973 | 10,000,000 | — | — | 0.40 | 0.70 | — |
| 1974 | 5,000,000 | — | — | 0.40 | 0.70 | — |
| 1975 | 5,000,000 | — | — | 0.40 | 0.70 | — |
| 1976 | 7,500,000 | — | — | 0.40 | 0.70 | — |
| 1977 | 7,000,000 | — | — | 0.40 | 0.70 | — |
| 1978 | 2,500,000 | — | — | 0.60 | 1.50 | — |
| 1979 | 10,000,000 | — | — | 0.60 | 1.50 | — |

**10 FRANCS - 10 FRANK (Deux / Twee Belgas) KM# 156.2**
**Composition:** Nickel **Note:** Medal alignment. Struck at Brussels Mint. Mint mark - Angel Head. Mintmaster Vogelier's privy mark - Bird.

| Date | Mintage | F | VF | XF | Unc | BU |
|---|---|---|---|---|---|---|
| 1971 | Inc. above | — | 6.00 | 12.00 | 35.00 | — |
| 1976 | Inc. above | — | 6.00 | 12.00 | 35.00 | — |

**20 FRANCS (20 Frank) KM# 78 Weight:** 6.4516 g. **Composition:** 0.9000 Gold .1867 oz. AGW **Obverse:** Legend in French **Obv. Legend:** DES BELGES

| Date | Mintage | F | VF | XF | Unc | BU |
|---|---|---|---|---|---|---|
| 1914 Position A | 125,000 | — | BV | 75.00 | 110 | — |
| 1914 Position B | Inc. above | 125 | 250 | 700 | 1,000 | — |

**20 FRANCS (20 Frank) KM# 79 Weight:** 6.4516 g. **Composition:** 0.9000 Gold .1867 oz. AGW **Obverse:** Legend in Dutch **Obv. Legend:** DER BELGEN

| Date | Mintage | F | VF | XF | Unc | BU |
|---|---|---|---|---|---|---|
| 1914 Position A | 125,000 | — | BV | 75.00 | 110 | — |
| 1914 Position B | Inc. above | BV | 80.00 | 90.00 | 130 | — |

**20 FRANCS - 20 FRANK (Vier / Quatre Belgas) KM# 101.1**
**Composition:** Nickel **Obverse:** Legend in French **Obv. Legend:** DES BELGES **Note:** All dates exist in position A and B, values are the same.

| Date | Mintage | F | VF | XF | Unc | BU |
|---|---|---|---|---|---|---|
| 1931 | 3,957,000 | 20.00 | 45.00 | 100 | 140 | — |
| 1932 | 5,472,000 | 15.00 | 40.00 | 90.00 | 130 | — |
| 1934 | — | — | — | — | — | — |

Note: Struck at a later date

**20 FRANCS - 20 FRANK (Vier / Quatre Belgas) KM# 102**
**Composition:** Nickel **Obverse:** Legend in Dutch **Obv. Legend:** DER BELGEN **Note:** All dates exist in position A and B, values are the same.

| Date | Mintage | F | VF | XF | Unc | BU |
|---|---|---|---|---|---|---|
| 1931 | 2,600,000 | 25.00 | 50.00 | 110 | 160 | — |
| 1932 | 6,950,000 | 15.00 | 40.00 | 90.00 | 130 | — |
| 1934 | — | — | — | — | — | — |

Note: Struck at a later date

**20 FRANCS - 20 FRANK (Vier / Quatre Belgas) KM# 101.2**
**Composition:** Nickel **Note:** Medal alignment. Edge varieties exist.

| Date | Mintage | F | VF | XF | Unc | BU |
|---|---|---|---|---|---|---|
| 1932 | Inc. above | 65.00 | 175 | 400 | 600 | — |

**20 FRANCS - 20 FRANK (Vier / Quatre Belgas) KM# 103.1 Weight:** 11.0000 g. **Composition:** 0.6800 Silver .2405 oz. ASW **Obverse:** Legend in French **Obv. Legend:** DES BELGES

| Date | Mintage | F | VF | XF | Unc | BU |
|---|---|---|---|---|---|---|
| 1933 Position A | 200,000 | 22.50 | 40.00 | 90.00 | 175 | — |
| 1933 Position B | Inc. above | 25.00 | 45.00 | 100 | 200 | — |
| 1934 Position A | 12,300,000 | BV | 2.00 | 4.00 | 8.00 | — |
| 1934 Position B | Inc. above | 1.50 | 2.50 | 4.50 | 9.00 | — |

**20 FRANCS - 20 FRANK (Vier / Quatre Belgas) KM# 104.1 Weight:** 11.0000 g. **Composition:** 0.6800 Silver .2405 oz. ASW **Obverse:** Legend in Dutch **Obv. Legend:** DER BELGEN

| Date | Mintage | F | VF | XF | Unc | BU |
|---|---|---|---|---|---|---|
| 1933 Position A | 200,000 | 14.00 | 30.00 | 60.00 | 110 | — |
| 1933 Position B | Inc. above | 16.00 | 32.50 | 65.00 | 125 | — |
| 1934 Position A | 12,300,000 | BV | 2.00 | 4.00 | 8.00 | — |
| 1934 Position B | Inc. above | 1.50 | 2.50 | 4.50 | 9.00 | — |

**20 FRANCS - 20 FRANK (Vier / Quatre Belgas) KM# 105 Weight:** 11.0000 g. **Composition:** 0.6800 Silver .2405 oz. ASW **Note:** Both dates exist in position A and B, values are the same. Coins dated 1934 exist with and without umlauts above E in BELGIE.

| Date | Mintage | F | VF | XF | Unc | BU |
|---|---|---|---|---|---|---|
| 1934 | 1,250,000 | 2.00 | 4.00 | 8.00 | 15.00 | — |
| 1935 | 10,760,000 | BV | 2.50 | 5.00 | 7.00 | — |

**20 FRANCS - 20 FRANK (Vier / Quatre Belgas) KM# 103.2 Weight:** 11.0000 g. **Composition:** 0.6800 Silver .2405 oz. ASW **Note:** Medal alignment.

| Date | Mintage | F | VF | XF | Unc | BU |
|---|---|---|---|---|---|---|
| 1934 | Inc. above | 35.00 | 80.00 | 190 | 400 | — |

**20 FRANCS - 20 FRANK (Vier / Quatre Belgas) KM# 104.2 Weight:** 11.0000 g. **Composition:** 0.6800 Silver .2405 oz. ASW **Note:** Medal alignment.

| Date | Mintage | F | VF | XF | Unc | BU |
|---|---|---|---|---|---|---|
| 1934 | Inc. above | 30.00 | 70.00 | 170 | 350 | — |

**20 FRANCS - 20 FRANK (Vier / Quatre Belgas) KM# 140.2 Weight:** 8.0000 g. **Composition:** 0.8350 Silver .2148 oz. ASW **Note:** Medal alignment.

| Date | Mintage | F | VF | XF | Unc | BU |
|---|---|---|---|---|---|---|
| 1949 | Inc. above | 15.00 | 35.00 | 75.00 | 125 | — |
| 1950 | Inc. above | 15.00 | 35.00 | 75.00 | 125 | — |

**20 FRANCS - 20 FRANK (Vier / Quatre Belgas) KM# 141.2 Weight:** 8.0000 g. **Composition:** 0.8350 Silver .2148 oz. ASW **Note:** Medal alignment.

| Date | Mintage | F | VF | XF | Unc | BU |
|---|---|---|---|---|---|---|
| 1949 | Inc. above | 20.00 | 35.00 | 85.00 | 135 | — |
| 1951 | Inc. above | 15.00 | 40.00 | 95.00 | 150 | — |

**20 FRANCS - 20 FRANK (Vier / Quatre Belgas)** **KM# 140.1 Weight:** 8.0000 g. **Composition:** 0.8350 Silver .2148 oz. ASW **Obverse:** Legend in French **Obv. Legend:** BELGIQUE

| Date | Mintage | F | VF | XF | Unc | BU |
|---|---|---|---|---|---|---|
| 1949 | 4,600,000 | BV | 1.50 | 3.50 | 5.00 | — |
| 1950 | 12,957,000 | BV | 1.50 | 3.00 | 5.00 | — |
| 1951 | — | — | — | — | — | — |
| 1953 | 3,953,000 | BV | 2.00 | 4.00 | 7.00 | — |
| 1954 | 4,835,000 | 12.00 | 20.00 | 60.00 | 100 | — |
| 1955 | 1,730,000 | 150 | 250 | 650 | 900 | — |

**20 FRANCS - 20 FRANK (Vier / Quatre Belgas)** **KM# 141.1 Weight:** 8.0000 g. **Composition:** 0.8350 Silver .2148 oz. ASW **Obverse:** Legend in Dutch **Obv. Legend:** BELGIE

| Date | Mintage | F | VF | XF | Unc | BU |
|---|---|---|---|---|---|---|
| 1949 | 5,545,000 | BV | 1.50 | 3.50 | 5.00 | — |
| 1950 | — | 150 | 400 | 600 | 1,000 | — |
| 1951 | 7,885,000 | BV | 1.50 | 3.00 | 5.00 | — |
| 1953 | 6,625,000 | BV | 1.50 | 3.00 | 7.00 | — |
| 1954 | 5,323,000 | 8.00 | 15.00 | 50.00 | 80.00 | — |
| 1955 | 3,760,000 | 15.00 | 50.00 | 125 | 200 | — |

**20 FRANCS - 20 FRANK (Vier / Quatre Belgas)** **KM# 159 Composition:** Nickel-Bronze **Reverse:** Legend in French **Rev. Legend:** BELGIQUE

| Date | Mintage | F | VF | XF | Unc | BU |
|---|---|---|---|---|---|---|
| 1980 | 60,000,000 | — | — | 0.70 | 1.00 | — |
| 1981 | 60,000,000 | — | — | 0.70 | 1.00 | — |
| 1982 | 54,000,000 | — | — | 0.70 | 1.00 | — |
| 1989 | 60,000 | — | — | — | 3.50 | — |
| 1990 | 60,000 | — | — | — | 3.50 | — |
| 1991 | 60,000 | — | — | — | 3.50 | — |
| 1992 | 2,610,000 | — | — | 0.70 | 1.00 | — |
| 1993 | 7,540,000 | — | — | 0.70 | 1.00 | — |

**20 FRANCS - 20 FRANK (Vier / Quatre Belgas)** **KM# 160 Composition:** Nickel-Bronze **Reverse:** Legend in Dutch **Rev. Legend:** BELGIE

| Date | Mintage | F | VF | XF | Unc | BU |
|---|---|---|---|---|---|---|
| 1980 | 60,000,000 | — | — | 0.70 | 1.00 | — |
| 1981 | 60,000,000 | — | — | 0.70 | 1.00 | — |
| 1982 | 54,000,000 | — | — | 0.70 | 1.00 | — |
| 1989 | 60,000 | — | — | — | 3.50 | — |
| 1990 | 60,000 | — | — | — | 3.50 | — |
| 1991 | 60,000 | — | — | — | 3.50 | — |
| 1992 | 2,610,000 | — | — | 0.70 | 1.00 | — |
| 1993 | 7,540,000 | — | — | 0.70 | 1.00 | — |

**20 FRANCS - 20 FRANK (Vier / Quatre Belgas)** **KM# 191 Composition:** Nickel-Bronze **Obverse:** Albert II **Reverse:** Legend in French **Rev. Legend:** BELGIQUE **Note:** Struck at Brussels Mint. Mint mark - Angel Head. Unknown mintmaster's privy mark - Scales.

| Date | Mintage | F | VF | XF | Unc | BU |
|---|---|---|---|---|---|---|
| 1994 | 12,560,000 | — | — | 0.70 | 1.00 | — |
| 1995 | 60,000 | — | — | — | 7.50 | — |
| 1996 | 60,000 | — | — | — | 7.50 | — |
| 1997 | 60,000 | — | — | — | 7.50 | — |
| 1998 | 3,000,000 | — | — | — | 3.75 | — |
| 1999 | 60,000 | — | — | — | 7.50 | — |
| 2000 | 60,000 | — | — | — | 7.50 | — |

**20 FRANCS - 20 FRANK (Vier / Quatre Belgas)** **KM# 192 Composition:** Nickel-Bronze **Reverse:** Legend in Dutch **Rev. Legend:** BELGIE **Note:** Struck at Brussels Mint. Mint mark - Angel Head. Unknown mintmaster's privy mark - Scales.

| Date | Mintage | F | VF | XF | Unc | BU |
|---|---|---|---|---|---|---|
| 1994 | 12,560,000 | — | — | 0.70 | 1.00 | — |
| 1995 | 60,000 | — | — | — | 7.50 | — |
| 1996 | 11,352,000 | — | — | — | 7.50 | — |
| 1997 | 60,000 | — | — | — | 7.50 | — |
| 1998 | 300,000 | — | — | — | 3.75 | — |
| 1999 | 60,000 | — | — | — | 7.50 | — |
| 2000 | 60,000 | — | — | — | 7.50 | — |

**50 FRANCS (50 Frank)** **KM# 106.1 Weight:** 22.0000 g. **Composition:** 0.6800 Silver .4810 oz. ASW **Subject:** Brussels Exposition and Railway Centennial **Obv. Legend:** DE BELGIQUE **Reverse:** Legend in French **Rev. Legend:** DE FER BELGES **Note:** Exists in positions A and B, values are the same.

| Date | Mintage | F | VF | XF | Unc | BU |
|---|---|---|---|---|---|---|
| 1935 | 140,000 | 40.00 | 70.00 | 110 | 180 | — |

**50 FRANCS (50 Frank)** **KM# 107.1 Weight:** 22.0000 g. **Composition:** 0.6800 Silver .4810 oz. ASW **Obv. Legend:** BELGIE **Reverse:** Legend in Dutch **Rev. Legend:** DER BELGISCHE **Note:** Exists in positions A and B, values are the same.

| Date | Mintage | F | VF | XF | Unc | BU |
|---|---|---|---|---|---|---|
| 1935 | 140,000 | 50.00 | 100 | 150 | 225 | — |

**50 FRANCS (50 Frank)** **KM# 106.2 Weight:** 22.0000 g. **Composition:** 0.6800 Silver .4810 oz. ASW **Note:** Medal alignment. Exists in positions A and B, values are the same.

| Date | Mintage | F | VF | XF | Unc | BU |
|---|---|---|---|---|---|---|
| 1935 | Inc. above | 200 | 300 | 500 | 800 | — |

**50 FRANCS (50 Frank)** **KM# 107.2 Weight:** 22.0000 g. **Composition:** 0.6800 Silver .4810 oz. ASW **Note:** Medal alignment. Exists in positions A and B, values are the same.

| Date | Mintage | F | VF | XF | Unc | BU |
|---|---|---|---|---|---|---|
| 1935 | Inc. above | 300 | 600 | 900 | 1,500 | — |

**50 FRANCS (50 Frank)** **KM# 121.1 Weight:** 20.0000 g. **Composition:** 0.8350 Silver .5369 oz. ASW **Reverse:** Legend in French **Rev. Legend:** BELGIQUE: BELGIE **Note:** Both dates exists in positions A and B, values are the same.

| Date | Mintage | F | VF | XF | Unc | BU |
|---|---|---|---|---|---|---|
| 1939 | 1,000,000 | BV | 8.00 | 12.00 | 18.00 | — |
| 1940 | 631,000 | BV | 10.00 | 18.00 | 27.50 | — |

**50 FRANCS (50 Frank)** **KM# 121.2 Weight:** 20.0000 g. **Composition:** 0.8350 Silver .5369 oz. ASW **Reverse:** Without cross on crown **Note:** Both dates exists in positions A and B, values are the same.

| Date | Mintage | F | VF | XF | Unc | BU |
|---|---|---|---|---|---|---|
| 1939 | Inc. above | 5.00 | 10.00 | 15.00 | 25.00 | — |
| 1940 | Inc. above | 7.00 | 15.00 | 20.00 | 35.00 | — |

**50 FRANCS (50 Frank)** **KM# 122.1 Weight:** 20.0000 g. **Composition:** 0.8350 Silver .5369 oz. ASW **Reverse:** Legend in Dutch **Rev. Legend:** BELGIE: BELGIQUE **Note:** Both dates exists in positions A and B, values are the same.

| Date | Mintage | F | VF | XF | Unc | BU |
|---|---|---|---|---|---|---|
| 1939 | 1,000,000 | BV | 8.00 | 12.00 | 18.00 | — |
| 1940 | 631,000 | BV | 10.00 | 20.00 | 30.00 | — |

**50 FRANCS (50 Frank)** **KM# 122.2 Weight:** 20.0000 g. **Composition:** 0.8350 Silver .5369 oz. ASW **Reverse:** Without cross on crown **Note:** Both dates exists in positions A and B, values are the same.

| Date | Mintage | F | VF | XF | Unc | BU |
|---|---|---|---|---|---|---|
| 1939 | Inc. above | 6.00 | 15.00 | 20.00 | 30.00 | — |
| 1940 | Inc. above | 15.00 | 20.00 | 40.00 | 60.00 | — |

**50 FRANCS (50 Frank)** **KM# 122.3 Weight:** 20.0000 g. **Composition:** 0.8350 Silver .5369 oz. ASW **Reverse:** Triangle in 3rd arms from left, cross on crown **Note:** Both dates exists in positions A and B, values are the same.

| Date | Mintage | F | VF | XF | Unc | BU |
|---|---|---|---|---|---|---|
| 1940 | Inc. above | 15.00 | 25.00 | 35.00 | 50.00 | — |

**50 FRANCS (50 Frank)** **KM# 122.4 Weight:** 20.0000 g. **Composition:** 0.8350 Silver .5369 oz. ASW **Reverse:** Without cross on crown **Note:** Both dates exists in positions A and B, values are the same.

| Date | Mintage | F | VF | XF | Unc | BU |
|---|---|---|---|---|---|---|
| 1940 | Inc. above | 30.00 | 60.00 | 100 | 150 | — |

**50 FRANCS (50 Frank)** **KM# 138.1 Weight:** 18.0000 g. **Composition:** 0.8350 Silver .4832 oz. ASW **Obverse:** Legend in French **Obv. Legend:** BELGIQUE

| Date | Mintage | F | VF | XF | Unc | BU |
|---|---|---|---|---|---|---|
| 1948 | 1,000,000 | BV | 2.75 | 4.00 | 7.00 | — |
| 1949 | 106,000 | 12.50 | 25.00 | 40.00 | 60.00 | — |
| 1950 | 2,807,000 | BV | 2.75 | 4.00 | 7.00 | — |
| 1954 | 2,517,000 | BV | 2.75 | 4.00 | 7.00 | — |

**50 FRANCS (50 Frank)** **KM# 137 Weight:** 12.5000 g. **Composition:** 0.8350 Silver .3356 oz. ASW **Obverse:** Legend in Dutch **Obv. Legend:** BELGIE

| Date | Mintage | F | VF | XF | Unc | BU |
|---|---|---|---|---|---|---|
| 1948 | 3,000,000 | BV | 2.00 | 3.00 | 6.00 | — |
| 1950 | 4,110,000 | BV | 2.00 | 3.00 | 6.00 | — |
| 1951 | 1,698,000 | BV | 2.00 | 3.00 | 6.00 | — |
| 1954 | 2,978,000 | BV | 2.00 | 3.00 | 6.00 | — |

**50 FRANCS (50 Frank)** **KM# 136.2 Weight:** 12.5000 g. **Composition:** 0.8350 Silver .3356 oz. ASW **Note:** Medal alignment.

| Date | Mintage | F | VF | XF | Unc | BU |
|---|---|---|---|---|---|---|
| 1949 | Inc. above | 10.00 | 30.00 | 90.00 | 175 | — |

**50 FRANCS (50 Frank)** **KM# 150.2 Weight:** 12.5000 g. **Composition:** 0.8350 Silver .3356 oz. ASW **Note:** Medal alignment.

| Date | Mintage | F | VF | XF | Unc | BU |
|---|---|---|---|---|---|---|
| 1958 | Inc. above | 18.00 | 45.00 | 100 | 180 | — |

**50 FRANCS (50 Frank)** **KM# 151.2 Weight:** 12.5000 g. **Composition:** 0.8350 Silver .3356 oz. ASW **Note:** Medal alignment.

| Date | Mintage | F | VF | XF | Unc | BU |
|---|---|---|---|---|---|---|
| 1958 | Inc. above | 15.00 | 35.00 | 75.00 | 125 | — |

**50 FRANCS (50 Frank)** **KM# 150.1** **Weight:** 12.5000 g. **Composition:** 0.8350 Silver .3356 oz. ASW **Subject:** Brussels World Fair **Obverse:** Legend in French **Obv. Legend:** DES BELGES

| Date | Mintage | F | VF | XF | Unc | BU |
|---|---|---|---|---|---|---|
| 1958 | 476,000 | BV | 4.00 | 7.50 | 10.00 | — |

**50 FRANCS (50 Frank)** **KM# 151.1** **Weight:** 12.5000 g. **Composition:** 0.8350 Silver .3356 oz. ASW **Obverse:** Legend in Dutch **Obv. Legend:** DER BELGEN

| Date | Mintage | F | VF | XF | Unc | BU |
|---|---|---|---|---|---|---|
| 1958 | 382,000 | BV | 4.00 | 7.50 | 10.00 | — |

**50 FRANCS (50 Frank)** **KM# 152.1** **Weight:** 12.5000 g. **Composition:** 0.8350 Silver .3356 oz. ASW **Subject:** King Baudouin Marriage

| Date | Mintage | F | VF | XF | Unc | BU |
|---|---|---|---|---|---|---|
| 1960 | 500,000 | BV | 4.00 | 6.00 | 9.00 | — |

**50 FRANCS (50 Frank)** **KM# 152.2** **Weight:** 12.5000 g. **Composition:** 0.8350 Silver .3356 oz. ASW **Note:** Medal alignment.

| Date | Mintage | F | VF | XF | Unc | BU |
|---|---|---|---|---|---|---|
| 1960 | Inc. above | 12.50 | 30.00 | 60.00 | 120 | — |

**50 FRANCS (50 Frank)** **KM# 168** **Composition:** Nickel **Reverse:** Legend in French **Rev. Legend:** BELGIQUE

| Date | Mintage | F | VF | XF | Unc | BU |
|---|---|---|---|---|---|---|
| 1987 | 30,000,000 | — | — | 2.00 | 4.00 | — |
| 1988 | 3,500,000 | — | — | 2.00 | 4.00 | — |
| 1989 | 15,060,000 | — | — | 2.00 | 4.00 | — |
| 1990 | 15,060,000 | — | — | 2.00 | 4.00 | — |
| 1991 | 3,500,000 | — | — | 2.00 | 4.00 | — |
| 1992 | 15,060,000 | — | — | 2.00 | 4.00 | — |
| 1993 | 15,060,000 | — | — | 2.00 | 4.00 | — |

**50 FRANCS (50 Frank)** **KM# 169** **Composition:** Nickel **Reverse:** Legend in Dutch **Rev. Legend:** BELGIE

| Date | Mintage | F | VF | XF | Unc | BU |
|---|---|---|---|---|---|---|
| 1987 | 30,000,000 | — | — | 2.00 | 4.00 | — |
| 1988 | 3,500,000 | — | — | 2.00 | 4.00 | — |
| 1989 | 15,060,000 | — | — | 2.00 | 4.00 | — |
| 1990 | 15,060,000 | — | — | 2.00 | 4.00 | — |
| 1991 | 3,500,000 | — | — | 2.00 | 4.00 | — |

| Date | Mintage | F | VF | XF | Unc | BU |
|---|---|---|---|---|---|---|
| 1992 | 15,060,000 | — | — | 2.00 | 4.00 | — |
| 1993 | 15,060,000 | — | — | 2.00 | 4.00 | — |

**50 FRANCS (50 Frank)** **KM# 193** **Composition:** Nickel **Obverse:** Albert II **Reverse:** Legend in French **Rev. Legend:** BELGIQUE **Note:** Struck at Brussels Mint. Mint mark - Angel Head. Unknown mintmaster's privy mark - Scales.

| Date | Mintage | F | VF | XF | Unc | BU |
|---|---|---|---|---|---|---|
| 1994 | 5,000,000 | — | — | — | 3.00 | — |
| 1995 | 60,000 | — | — | — | 10.00 | — |
| 1996 | 60,000 | — | — | — | 10.00 | — |
| 1997 | 60,000 | — | — | — | 10.00 | — |
| 1998 | 3,000,000 | — | — | — | 4.50 | — |
| 1999 | 60,000 | — | — | — | 10.00 | — |
| 2000 | 60,000 | — | — | — | 10.00 | — |

**50 FRANCS (50 Frank)** **KM# 194** **Composition:** Nickel **Obverse:** Albert II **Reverse:** Legend in Dutch **Rev. Legend:** BELGIE **Note:** Struck at Brussels Mint. Mint mark - Angel Head. Unknown mintmaster's privy mark - Scales.

| Date | Mintage | F | VF | XF | Unc | BU |
|---|---|---|---|---|---|---|
| 1994 | 5,000,000 | — | — | — | 4.50 | — |
| 1995 | 60,000 | — | — | — | 10.00 | — |
| 1996 | 60,000 | — | — | — | 10.00 | — |
| 1997 | 60,000 | — | — | — | 10.00 | — |
| 1998 | 3,000,000 | — | — | — | 4.50 | — |
| 1999 | 60,000 | — | — | — | 10.00 | — |
| 2000 | 60,000 | — | — | — | 10.00 | — |

**50 FRANCS (50 Frank)** **KM# 213.1** **Composition:** Nickel **Subject:** European Soccer Championship **Obverse:** Head of Albert II left **Reverse:** Soccer ball, legend in French **Rev. Legend:** BELGIQUE

**Edge:** Reeded

| Date | Mintage | F | VF | XF | Unc | BU |
|---|---|---|---|---|---|---|
| 2000 | 500,000 | — | — | — | 3.75 | — |

**50 FRANCS (50 Frank)** **KM# 214.1** **Composition:** Nickel **Subject:** European Soccer Championship **Obverse:** Head of Albert II left **Reverse:** Soccer ball, legend in Dutch **Rev. Legend:** BELGIE **Edge:** Reeded

| Date | Mintage | F | VF | XF | Unc | BU |
|---|---|---|---|---|---|---|
| 2000 | 500,000 | — | — | — | 3.75 | — |

**50 FRANCS (50 Frank)** **KM# 213.2** **Composition:** Nickel **Note:** Medal alignment.

| Date | Mintage | F | VF | XF | Unc | BU |
|---|---|---|---|---|---|---|
| 2000 | — | Value: 15.00 | | | | |

**50 FRANCS (50 Frank)** **KM# 214.2** **Composition:** Nickel **Note:** Medal alignment.

| Date | Mintage | F | VF | XF | Unc | BU |
|---|---|---|---|---|---|---|
| 2000 | — | Value: 15.00 | | | | |

**100 FRANCS (100 Frank)** **KM# 136.1** **Weight:** 12.5000 g. **Composition:** 0.8350 Silver .3356 oz. ASW **Obverse:** Legend in French **Obv. Legend:** BELGIQUE

| Date | Mintage | F | VF | XF | Unc | BU |
|---|---|---|---|---|---|---|
| 1948 | 2,000,000 | BV | 2.00 | 3.00 | 6.00 | — |
| **Note:** Exists in position A and B, values are the same | | | | | | |
| 1949 | 4,354,000 | BV | 2.00 | 3.00 | 6.00 | — |
| 1950 | — | 200 | 400 | 800 | 1,750 | — |
| 1951 | 2,904,000 | BV | 2.00 | 3.00 | 6.00 | — |
| 1954 | 3,232,000 | BV | 7.50 | 15.00 | 25.00 | — |

**100 FRANCS (100 Frank)** **KM# 139.1** **Weight:** 18.0000 g. **Composition:** 0.8350 Silver .4832 oz. ASW **Obverse:** Legend in Dutch **Obv. Legend:** BELGIE

| Date | Mintage | F | VF | XF | Unc | BU |
|---|---|---|---|---|---|---|
| 1948 | 1,000,000 | BV | 2.75 | 4.00 | 7.00 | — |
| 1949 | 2,271,000 | BV | 2.75 | 4.00 | 7.00 | — |
| 1950 | — | 300 | 500 | 850 | 1,200 | — |
| 1951 | 4,691,000 | BV | 2.75 | 4.00 | 7.00 | — |

**100 FRANCS (100 Frank)** **KM# 138.2** **Weight:** 18.0000 g. **Composition:** 0.8350 Silver .4832 oz. ASW **Note:** Medal alignment.

| Date | Mintage | F | VF | XF | Unc | BU |
|---|---|---|---|---|---|---|
| 1948 | Inc. above | 10.00 | 40.00 | 90.00 | 220 | — |
| 1950 | Inc. above | 10.00 | 40.00 | 90.00 | 200 | — |

**100 FRANCS (100 Frank)** **KM# 139.2** **Weight:** 18.0000 g. **Composition:** 0.8350 Silver .4832 oz. ASW **Note:** Medal alignment.

| Date | Mintage | F | VF | XF | Unc | BU |
|---|---|---|---|---|---|---|
| 1948 | Inc. above | 10.00 | 40.00 | 90.00 | 200 | — |
| 1949 | Inc. above | 7.50 | 30.00 | 75.00 | 160 | — |
| 1951 | Inc. above | 10.00 | 40.00 | 90.00 | 200 | — |

**200 FRANCS (200 Frank)** **KM# 215** **Composition:** Silver **Subject:** The Universe **Obverse:** Legend in French **Obv. Legend:** BELGIQUE

| Date | Mintage | F | VF | XF | Unc | BU |
|---|---|---|---|---|---|---|
| 2000 | 50,000 | — | — | — | 10.00 | — |
| 2000 (qp) Proof | 10,000 | Value: 30.00 | | | | |

**200 FRANCS (200 Frank)** **KM# 216** **Composition:** Silver **Subject:** Nature **Obverse:** Legend in Dutch **Obv. Legend:** BELGIE

| Date | Mintage | F | VF | XF | Unc | BU |
|---|---|---|---|---|---|---|
| 2000 | 50,000 | — | — | — | 10.00 | — |
| 2000 (qp) Proof | 10,000 | Value: 30.00 | | | | |

**200 FRANCS (200 Frank)** **KM# 217** **Composition:** Silver **Subject:** The City **Obverse:** Legend in German **Obv. Legend:** BELGIEN

| Date | Mintage | F | VF | XF | Unc | BU |
|---|---|---|---|---|---|---|
| 2000 | 50,000 | — | — | — | 10.00 | — |
| 2000 (qp) Proof | 10,000 | — | — | — | 30.00 | — |

**250 FRANCS (250 Frank)** **KM# 157.1** **Weight:** 25.0000 g. **Composition:** 0.8350 Silver .6711 oz. ASW **Subject:** Silver Jubilee of King Baudouin **Obverse:** Legend in French **Obv. Legend:** ROI DES BELGES **Edge:** Reeded **Note:** Struck at Brussels Mint. Mint mark - Angel Head. Mintmaster Vogelier's privy mark - Bird.

| Date | Mintage | F | VF | XF | Unc | BU |
|---|---|---|---|---|---|---|
| 1976 Large B, slant 5 | 1,000,000 | — | BV | 5.00 | 8.00 | — |
| 1976 Small B, upright 5 | Inc. above | BV | 8.00 | 10.00 | 15.00 | |

**250 FRANCS (250 Frank)** **KM# 157.2** **Weight:** 25.0000 g. **Composition:** 0.8350 Silver .6711 oz. ASW **Edge:** Stars **Note:** Struck at Brussels Mint. Mint mark - Angel Head. Mintmaster Vogelier's privy mark - Bird.

| Date | Mintage | F | VF | XF | Unc | BU |
|---|---|---|---|---|---|---|
| 1976 Prooflike | 100,000 | — | — | — | 15.00 | — |

**250 FRANCS (250 Frank)** **KM# 158.1** **Weight:** 25.0000 g. **Composition:** 0.8350 Silver .6711 oz. ASW **Obverse:** Legend in Dutch **Obv. Legend:** KONING DER BELGEN **Edge:** Reeded **Note:** Struck at Brussels Mint. Mint mark - Angel Head. Mintmaster Vogelier's privy mark - Bird.

| Date | Mintage | F | VF | XF | Unc | BU |
|---|---|---|---|---|---|---|
| 1976 Large B, slant 5 | 1,000,000 | — | BV | 5.00 | 8.00 | — |
| 1976 Small B, upright 5 | Inc. above | BV | 10.00 | 18.50 | 30.00 | — |

**250 FRANCS (250 Frank)** **KM# 158.2** **Weight:** 25.0000 g. **Composition:** 0.8350 Silver .6711 oz. ASW **Edge:** Stars **Note:** Struck at Brussels Mint. Mint mark - Angel Head. Mintmaster Vogelier's privy mark - Bird.

| Date | Mintage | F | VF | XF | Unc | BU |
|---|---|---|---|---|---|---|
| 1976 Prooflike | 100,000 | — | — | — | 15.00 | — |

**250 FRANCS (250 Frank)** **KM# 195** **Weight:** 18.7500 g. **Composition:** 0.9250 Silver .5571 oz. ASW **Subject:** BE-NE-LUX Treaty **Note:** Struck at Brussels Mint. Mint mark - Angel Head. Unknown mintmaster's privy mark - Scales.

| Date | Mintage | F | VF | XF | Unc | BU |
|---|---|---|---|---|---|---|
| 1994 | 90,000 | — | — | — | 14.00 | — |
| 1994 Proof | 1,800 | Value: 45.00 | | | | |

**250 FRANCS (250 Frank)** **KM# 199** **Weight:** 18.7500 g. **Composition:** 0.9250 Silver .5571 oz. ASW **Subject:** Death of Queen Astrid **Note:** Struck at Brussels Mint. Mint mark - Angel Head. Unknown mintmaster's privy mark - Scales.

| Date | Mintage | F | VF | XF | Unc | BU |
|---|---|---|---|---|---|---|
| 1995 | 177,000 | — | — | — | 14.00 | — |
| 1995 Proof | 25,000 | Value: 35.00 | | | | |

**250 FRANCS (250 Frank)** **KM# 202** **Weight:** 18.7500 g. **Composition:** 0.9250 Silver .5571 oz. ASW **Subject:** 20th Anniversary - King Baudouin Foundation **Obverse:** Royal couple and monogram **Reverse:** Denomination, stylized design and royal monogram

| Date | Mintage | F | VF | XF | Unc | BU |
|---|---|---|---|---|---|---|
| ND(1996) | 100,000 | — | — | — | 14.00 | — |
| ND(1996) Proof | 25,000 | Value: 25.00 | | | | |

**250 FRANCS (250 Frank)** **KM# 207** **Weight:** 18.7500 g. **Composition:** 0.9250 Silver .5571 oz. ASW **Subject:** 60th Birthday - Queen Paola **Obverse:** Denomination **Reverse:** Portrait **Note:** Struck at Brussels Mint. Mint mark - Angel Head. Unknown mintmaster's privy mark - Scales.

| Date | Mintage | F | VF | XF | Unc | BU |
|---|---|---|---|---|---|---|
| 1997 | — | — | — | — | 12.00 | — |
| 1997 Proof | 25,000 | Value: 25.00 | | | | |

**250 FRANCS (250 Frank)** **KM# 208** **Weight:** 18.7500 g. **Composition:** 0.9250 Silver .5571 oz. ASW **Subject:** King Boudewijn - Queen Fabiola **Obverse:** King and Queen's portraits **Reverse:** Pelican with nestlings

| Date | Mintage | F | VF | XF | Unc | BU |
|---|---|---|---|---|---|---|
| ND(1998) | — | — | — | — | 12.00 | — |
| ND(1998) Proof | 25,000 | Value: 25.00 | | | | |

**250 FRANCS (250 Frank)** **KM# 209** **Weight:** 18.7500 g. **Composition:** 0.9250 Silver .5571 oz. ASW **Subject:** 40th Wedding Anniversary - King Alber and Queen Paola **Obverse:** King and Queen's conjoining busts left **Reverse:** St. Gudule Cathedral and city hall **Edge:** Reeded

| Date | Mintage | F | VF | XF | Unc | BU |
|---|---|---|---|---|---|---|
| ND(1999) | 100,000 | — | — | — | 12.00 | — |
| ND(1999) Proof | 25,000 | Value: 25.00 | | | | |

**250 FRANCS (250 Frank)** **KM# 218** **Weight:** 18.7500 g. **Composition:** 0.9250 Silver .5571 oz. ASW **Subject:** Marriage of Prince Philip and Princess Mathilde **Reverse:** 2 hands joined on a rose

| Date | Mintage | F | VF | XF | Unc | BU |
|---|---|---|---|---|---|---|
| 1999 | 200,000 | — | — | — | 12.00 | — |
| 1999 Proof | 25,000 | Value: 25.00 | | | | |

**500 FRANCS** **KM# 232** **Weight:** 23.1100 g. **Composition:** 0.7200 Silver .5350 oz. ASW **Subject:** European Union **Obverse:** 'E' emblem and map. **Reverse:** Europa riding a bull. Roman numeral date. **Edge:** Plain. **Size:** 37 mm.

| Date | Mintage | F | VF | XF | Unc | BU |
|---|---|---|---|---|---|---|
| 2001 Proof | — | Value: 35.00 | | | | |

**500 FRANCS (500 Frank)** **KM# 165** **Weight:** 25.0000 g. **Composition:** 0.5100 Silver .4099 oz. ASW **Obverse:** KM#161 **Reverse:** KM#162 **Note:** Mule. Struck at Brussels Mint. Mint mark - Angel Head. Mintmaster Vogelier's privy mark - Bird.

| Date | Mintage | F | VF | XF | Unc | BU |
|---|---|---|---|---|---|---|
| 1980 | — | — | — | — | 1,000 | — |

**500 FRANCS (500 Frank)** **KM# 161** **Composition:** Silver Clad Copper-Nickel **Subject:** 150th Anniversary of Independence **Obverse:** French legend. **Reverse:** French legend **Note:** Struck at Brussels Mint. Mint mark - Angel Head. Mintmaster Vogelier's privy mark - Bird.

| Date | Mintage | F | VF | XF | Unc | BU |
|---|---|---|---|---|---|---|
| 1980 | 1,000,000 | — | — | — | 12.00 | — |

**500 FRANCS (500 Frank)** **KM# 161a** **Weight:** 25.0000 g. **Composition:** 0.5100 Silver .4099 oz. ASW **Obverse:** French legend. **Reverse:** French legend **Note:** Struck at Brussels Mint. Mint mark - Angel Head. Mintmaster Vogelier's privy mark - Bird.

| Date | Mintage | F | VF | XF | Unc | BU |
|---|---|---|---|---|---|---|
| 1980 Proof | 53,000 | Value: 27.00 | | | | |

**500 FRANCS (500 Frank)** **KM# 162** **Composition:** Silver Clad Copper-Nickel **Obverse:** Dutch legend. **Reverse:** Dutch legend **Note:** Struck at Brussels Mint. Mint mark - Angel Head. Mintmaster Vogelier's privy mark - Bird.

| Date | Mintage | F | VF | XF | Unc | BU |
|---|---|---|---|---|---|---|
| 1980 | 1,000,000 | — | — | — | 12.00 | — |

**500 FRANCS (500 Frank)** **KM# 162a** **Weight:** 25.0000 g. **Composition:** 0.5100 Silver .4099 oz. ASW **Reverse:** Dutch legend **Note:** Struck at Brussels Mint. Mint mark - Angel Head. Mintmaster Vogelier's privy mark - Bird.

| Date | Mintage | F | VF | XF | Unc | BU |
|---|---|---|---|---|---|---|
| 1980 Proof | 52,000 | Value: 27.00 | | | | |

**500 FRANCS (500 Frank)** **KM# 178** **Weight:** 22.8500 g. **Composition:** 0.8330 Silver .6120 oz. ASW **Subject:** 60th Birthday of King Baudouin **Reverse:** Dutch legends

| Date | Mintage | F | VF | XF | Unc | BU |
|---|---|---|---|---|---|---|
| 1990 | 475,000 | — | — | — | 17.00 | — |
| 1990 Proof | 10,000 | Value: 35.00 | | | | |

**500 FRANCS (500 Frank)** **KM# 179** **Weight:** 22.8500 g. **Composition:** 0.8330 Silver .6120 oz. ASW **Subject:** 60th Birthday of King Baudouin **Reverse:** French legends

| Date | Mintage | F | VF | XF | Unc | BU |
|---|---|---|---|---|---|---|
| 1990 | 475,000 | — | — | — | 17.00 | — |
| 1990 Proof | 10,000 | Value: 35.00 | | | | |

**500 FRANCS (500 Frank)** **KM# 180** **Weight:** 22.8500 g. **Composition:** 0.8330 Silver .6120 oz. ASW **Subject:** 60th Birthday of King Baudouin **Reverse:** German legends

| Date | Mintage | F | VF | XF | Unc | BU |
|---|---|---|---|---|---|---|
| 1990 | 50,000 | — | — | — | 17.00 | — |
| 1990 Proof | 10,000 | Value: 35.00 | | | | |

**500 FRANCS (500 Frank)** **KM# 196** **Weight:** 22.8500 g. **Composition:** 0.8330 Silver .6120 oz. ASW **Subject:** 40th Year of Reign **Obverse:** Stylized design around **Reverse:** Crown above, denomination, year below, dutch legend

| Date | Mintage | F | VF | XF | Unc | BU |
|---|---|---|---|---|---|---|
| 1991 | — | — | — | — | 15.00 | — |
| 1991 Proof | 10,000 | Value: 25.00 | | | | |

**500 FRANCS (500 Frank)** **KM# 197** **Weight:** 22.8500 g. **Composition:** 0.8330 Silver .6120 oz. ASW **Subject:** 40th Year of Reign **Obverse:** Stylized design around **Reverse:** Crown above, denomination, year below, French legend

| Date | Mintage | F | VF | XF | Unc | BU |
|---|---|---|---|---|---|---|
| 1991 | — | — | — | — | 15.00 | — |
| 1991 Proof | 10,000 | Value: 25.00 | | | | |

**500 FRANCS (500 Frank)** **KM# 198** **Weight:** 22.8500 g. **Composition:** 0.8330 Silver .6120 oz. ASW **Subject:** 40th Year of Reign **Obverse:** Stylized design around **Reverse:** Crown above, denomination, year below, German legend

| Date | Mintage | F | VF | XF | Unc | BU |
|---|---|---|---|---|---|---|
| 1991 | — | — | — | — | 15.00 | — |
| 1991 Proof | 10,000 | Value: 25.00 | | | | |

**500 FRANCS (500 Frank)** **KM# 186** **Weight:** 22.8500 g. **Composition:** 0.8330 Silver .6120 oz. ASW **Subject:** Europalaia - Mexico Exposition **Note:** Struck at Brussels Mint. Mint mark - Angel Head. Unknown mintmaster's privy mark - Scales.

| Date | Mintage | F | VF | XF | Unc | BU |
|---|---|---|---|---|---|---|
| 1993 | 52,000 | — | — | — | 15.00 | — |
| 1993 Proof | — | Value: 25.00 | | | | |

**500 FRANCS (500 Frank)** **KM# 212** **Weight:** 22.8500 g. **Composition:** 0.9250 Silver .6975 oz. ASW **Subject:** Brussels - European Culture Capital **Obverse:** Denomination and European map **Reverse:** Portraits of Albert and Elizabeth in ruffled collars **Edge:** Plain

| Date | Mintage | F | VF | XF | Unc | BU |
|---|---|---|---|---|---|---|
| ND(1999) | 200,000 | — | — | — | 20.00 | — |
| ND(1999) (qp) Proof | 30,000 | Value: 35.00 | | | | |

**500 FRANCS (500 Frank)** **KM# 219** **Weight:** 22.8500 g. **Composition:** 0.9250 Silver .6975 oz. ASW **Subject:** Europe: Charles V **Obverse:** Map and denomination. **Reverse:** Charles V of Spain and building. **Edge:** Plain. **Size:** 37 mm.

| Date | Mintage | F | VF | XF | Unc | BU |
|---|---|---|---|---|---|---|
| ND(2000) | — | — | — | — | 20.00 | — |
| 2000 Proof | 40,000 | Value: 35.00 | | | | |

**500 FRANCS (500 Frank)** **KM# 222** **Weight:** 22.8500 g. **Composition:** 0.9250 Silver .6795 oz. ASW **Subject:** Europe: Europa and the Bull **Obverse:** Map and denomination. **Reverse:** Europa sitting on a bull. **Edge:** Plain. **Size:** 37 mm.

| Date | Mintage | F | VF | XF | Unc | BU |
|---|---|---|---|---|---|---|
| 2001 Proof | 40,000 | Value: 47.50 | | | | |

**5000 FRANCS** **KM# 210** **Weight:** 15.5500 g. **Composition:** 0.9990 Gold .4994 oz. AGW **Subject:** Brussels - European Culture Capital **Obverse:** Denomination and European map **Reverse:** Portraits of Albert and Elizabeth in ruffled collars **Edge:** Plain

| Date | Mintage | F | VF | XF | Unc | BU |
|---|---|---|---|---|---|---|
| ND(1999) (qp) Proof | 2,000 | Value: 325 | | | | |

**5000 FRANCS** **KM# 220** **Weight:** 15.5500 g. **Composition:** 0.9990 Gold .4994 oz. AGW **Subject:** Europe: Charles V **Obverse:** Map and denomination. **Reverse:** Charles V of Spain with building. **Edge:** Plain. **Size:** 29 mm.

| Date | Mintage | F | VF | XF | Unc | BU |
|---|---|---|---|---|---|---|
| ND(2000) (qp) Proof | 2,000 | Value: 325 | | | | |

**5000 FRANCS** **KM# 223** **Weight:** 15.5500 g. **Composition:** 0.9990 Gold .4994 oz. AGW **Subject:** Europe: Europa and the Bull **Obverse:** Map and denomination. **Reverse:** Europa sitting on a bull. **Edge:** Plain. **Size:** 29 mm.

| Date | Mintage | F | VF | XF | Unc | BU |
|---|---|---|---|---|---|---|
| 2001 Proof | 2,000 | Value: 325 | | | | |

## TRADE COINAGE

### European Currency Units

**5 ECU** **KM# 166** **Weight:** 22.8500 g. **Composition:** 0.8330 Silver .6120 oz. ASW **Subject:** 30th Anniversary - Treaties of Rome **Reverse:** Bust of Charles V right

| Date | Mintage | F | VF | XF | Unc | BU |
|---|---|---|---|---|---|---|
| 1987 | 985,000 | — | — | — | 10.00 | — |
| 1987 (qp) Proof | 15,000 | Value: 50.00 | | | | |
| 1988 (qp) Proof | 15,000 | Value: 50.00 | | | | |

**5 ECU** **KM# 183** **Weight:** 22.8500 g. **Composition:** 0.8330 Silver .6120 oz. ASW **Reverse:** Charlemagne

| Date | Mintage | F | VF | XF | Unc | BU |
|---|---|---|---|---|---|---|
| 1991 (qp) Proof | 10,000 | Value: 45.00 | | | | |

**5 ECU** **KM# 185** **Weight:** 22.8500 g. **Composition:** 0.9250 Silver .6796 oz. ASW **Subject:** Belgian Presidency of the E.C. **Obverse:** King Baudouin

| Date | Mintage | F | VF | XF | Unc | BU |
|---|---|---|---|---|---|---|
| 1993 (qp) Proof | 25,000 | Value: 35.00 | | | | |

**5 ECU** **KM# 200** **Weight:** 22.8500 g. **Composition:** 0.9250 Silver .6796 oz. ASW **Subject:** 50th Anniversary - United Nations

| Date | Mintage | F | VF | XF | Unc | BU |
|---|---|---|---|---|---|---|
| 1995 (qp) Proof | 125,000 | Value: 27.00 | | | | |

**5 ECU** **KM# 203** **Weight:** 22.8500 g. **Composition:** 0.9250 Silver .6796 oz. ASW **Subject:** 50th Anniversary - UNICEF **Obverse:** Royal couple **Reverse:** UNICEF logo

| Date | Mintage | F | VF | XF | Unc | BU |
|---|---|---|---|---|---|---|
| 1996 (qp) Proof | Est. 40,000 | Value: 28.00 | | | | |

**5 ECU** **KM# 205** **Weight:** 22.8500 g. **Composition:** 0.9250 Silver .6796 oz. ASW **Subject:** 40th Anniversary - Treaty of Rome **Obverse:** Portraits of Albert II and Baudouin **Reverse:** European Union map

| Date | Mintage | F | VF | XF | Unc | BU |
|---|---|---|---|---|---|---|
| 1997 (qp) Proof | Est. 30,000 | Value: 30.00 | | | | |

**5 ECU** **KM# 221** **Weight:** 22.8500 g. **Composition:** 0.9250 Silver .6796 oz. ASW **Subject:** 50th Anniversary - Human Rights Declaration

| Date | Mintage | F | VF | XF | Unc | BU |
|---|---|---|---|---|---|---|
| 1998 (qp) Proof | 30,000 | Value: 27.00 | | | | |

**10 ECU** **KM# 172** **Weight:** 3.1100 g. **Composition:** 0.9990 Gold .1000 oz. AGW **Reverse:** Charles V bust right

| Date | Mintage | F | VF | XF | Unc | BU |
|---|---|---|---|---|---|---|
| 1989 (qp) Proof | 2,000 | Value: 150 | | | | |
| 1990 (qp) Proof | 5,000 | Value: 100 | | | | |

**10 ECU** **KM# 176** **Ring Composition:** 0.8330 Silver **Center Weight:** 5.3000 g. **Center Composition:** 0.9000 Gold .1000 oz. ASW AGW **Subject:** 60th Birthday of King Baudouin

| Date | Mintage | F | VF | XF | Unc | BU |
|---|---|---|---|---|---|---|
| 1990 (qp) Proof | 42,000 | Value: 50.00 | | | | |

**10 ECU** **KM# 181** **Ring Composition:** 0.8330 Silver **Center Weight:** 5.3000 g. **Center Composition:** 0.9000 Gold .1000 oz. ASW AGW **Subject:** 40th Year of Reign of King Baudouin

| Date | Mintage | F | VF | XF | Unc | BU |
|---|---|---|---|---|---|---|
| 1991 (qp) Proof | 16,000 | Value: 80.00 | | | | |

**20 ECU** **KM# 177** **Ring Composition:** 0.8330 Silver **Center Weight:** 10.5000 g. **Center Composition:** 0.9000 Gold .2000 oz. ASW AGW **Subject:** 60th Birthday of King Baudouin

| Date | Mintage | F | VF | XF | Unc | BU |
|---|---|---|---|---|---|---|
| 1990 (qp) | 35,000 | Value: 100 | | | | |

**20 ECU** **KM# 182** **Ring Composition:** 0.8330 Silver **Center Weight:** 10.5000 g. **Center Composition:** 0.9000 Gold .2000 oz. ASW AGW **Subject:** 40th Year of Reign of King Baudouin

| Date | Mintage | F | VF | XF | Unc | BU |
|---|---|---|---|---|---|---|
| 1991 (qp) | 13,000 | Value: 160 | | | | |

**25 ECU** **KM# 173** **Weight:** 7.7750 g. **Composition:** 0.9990 Gold .2500 oz. AGW **Reverse:** Diocletian bust right

| Date | Mintage | F | VF | XF | Unc | BU |
|---|---|---|---|---|---|---|
| 1989 | 30,000 | — | — | BV | 90.00 | — |
| 1989 (qp) Proof | 2,000 | Value: 200 | | | | |
| 1990 (qp) Proof | 5,000 | Value: 95.00 | | | | |

**50 ECU** **KM# 167** **Weight:** 17.2800 g. **Composition:** 0.9000 Gold .5000 oz. AGW **Subject:** 30th Anniversary - Treaties of Rome **Obverse:** Charles V bust right

| Date | Mintage | F | VF | XF | Unc | BU |
|---|---|---|---|---|---|---|
| 1987 | 1,502,000 | — | — | BV | 140 | — |
| 1987 (qp) Proof | 15,000 | Value: 250 | | | | |
| 1988 (qp) Proof | 15,000 | Value: 250 | | | | |

**50 ECU** **KM# 174** **Weight:** 15.5550 g. **Composition:** 0.9990 Gold .5000 oz. AGW **Reverse:** Charlemagne

| Date | Mintage | F | VF | XF | Unc | BU |
|---|---|---|---|---|---|---|
| 1989 | 60,000 | — | — | BV | 170 | — |
| 1989 (qp) Proof | 2,000 | Value: 400 | | | | |
| 1990 (qp) Proof | 5,000 | Value: 200 | | | | |

**50 ECU** **KM# 184** **Weight:** 15.5550 g. **Composition:** 0.9990 Gold .5000 oz. AGW **Reverse:** Charlemagne bust right

| Date | Mintage | F | VF | XF | Unc | BU |
|---|---|---|---|---|---|---|
| 1991 | — | — | — | — | — | — |
| 1991 (qp) Proof | 4,000 | Value: 300 | | | | |

**50 ECU** **KM# 213** **Weight:** 15.5550 g. **Composition:** 0.9990 Gold .5000 oz. AGW **Subject:** Belgian Presidency of the E.C.

| Date | Mintage | F | VF | XF | Unc | BU |
|---|---|---|---|---|---|---|
| 1993 (qp) Proof | 10,000 | Value: 250 | | | | |

**50 ECU** **KM# 201** **Weight:** 15.5550 g. **Composition:** 0.9990 Gold .5000 oz. AGW **Subject:** 50th Anniversary - United Nations

| Date | Mintage | F | VF | XF | Unc | BU |
|---|---|---|---|---|---|---|
| 1995 (qp) Proof | 2,500 | Value: 250 | | | | |

**50 ECU** **KM# 204** **Weight:** 15.5550 g. **Composition:** 0.9990 Gold .5000 oz. AGW **Subject:** 50th Anniversary - UNICEF **Obverse:** Royal couple **Reverse:** UNICEF logo

| Date | Mintage | F | VF | XF | Unc | BU |
|---|---|---|---|---|---|---|
| 1996 (qp) Proof | 2,500 | Value: 270 | | | | |

**50 ECU** **KM# 206 Weight:** 15.5550 g. **Composition:** 0.9990 Gold .5000 oz. AGW **Subject:** 40th Anniversary - Treaty of Rome **Obverse:** Portraits of Albert II and Baudouin **Reverse:** European Union map

| Date | Mintage | F | VF | XF | Unc | BU |
|---|---|---|---|---|---|---|
| 1997 (qp) Proof | 2,500 | Value: 270 | | | | |

**50 ECU** **KM# 211 Weight:** 15.5550 g. **Composition:** 0.9990 Gold .5000 oz. AGW **Subject:** 50th Anniversary - Human Rights Declaration

| Date | Mintage | F | VF | XF | Unc | BU |
|---|---|---|---|---|---|---|
| 1998 (qp) Proof | 2,500 | Value: 270 | | | | |

**100 ECU** **KM# 175 Weight:** 31.1030 g. **Composition:** 0.9990 Gold 1.0000 oz. AGW **Reverse:** Maria Theresa

| Date | Mintage | F | VF | XF | Unc | BU |
|---|---|---|---|---|---|---|
| 1989 | 50,000 | — | — | BV | 325 | — |
| 1989 (qp) Proof | 2,000 | Value: 750 | | | | |
| 1990 (qp) Proof | 5,000 | Value: 400 | | | | |

## PATTERNS

Including off metal strikes

| KM# | Date | Mintage | Identification | Mkt Val |
|---|---|---|---|---|
| Pn93 | 1901 | — | 5 Centimes. Brass Plated Nickel. | — |
| Pn94 | 1901 | — | 5 Centimes. Copper-Iron Alloy. KM#45 | — |
| Pn95 | 1901 | — | 5 Centimes. Copper. Designer's initials as A.M.; KM#46 | — |
| Pn96 | 1901 | — | 5 Centimes. Copper. Thin flan, KM#46 | — |
| Pn97 | 1901 | — | 10 Centimes. Nickel. KM#48 | — |
| Pn98 | 1901 | — | 10 Centimes. Copper-Nickel. | — |
| Pn100 | 1901 | — | 50 Centimes. Silver. | — |
| Pn101 | 1901 | — | Franc. Silver. | — |
| Pn102 | 1901 | — | Franc. Silver. Head left. Lion with constitution | — |
| Pn103 | 1901 | — | 2 Francs. Silver. | — |
| Pn104 | 1901 | — | 2 Francs. Silver. Head left. Lion with constitution. Reeded edge | — |
| Pn99 | 1901 | — | 50 Centimes. Copper. KM#50 | 250 |
| Pn105 | 1902 | — | 5 Centimes. Nickel. | 100 |
| Pn107 | 19xx | — | Franc. Nickel-Brass. | 400 |
| Pn108 | 1902 | — | Franc. Silver. Reeded edgeSmall portrait, KM#56.1 | 350 |
| Pn109 | 1902 | — | Franc. Silver. Plain edgeSmall portrait, KM#56.1 | 350 |
| Pn106 | 1902 | — | 5 Centimes. Copper-Nickel. Without center hole; KM#47. | — |
| Pn112 | 1903 | — | Franc. Silver. | — |
| Pn113 | 1903 | — | Franc. Silver. | — |
| Pn114 | 1903 | — | Franc. Silver. | — |
| Pn115 | 1903 | — | Franc. Silver. | — |
| Pn116 | 1903 | — | Franc. Silver. | — |
| Pn117 | 1903 | — | Franc. Silver. | — |
| Pn118 | 1903 | — | Franc. Silver. | — |
| Pn119 | 1903 | — | Franc. Silver. | — |
| Pn110 | 1903 | — | Franc. Silver. Reeded edgeSmall portrait, KM#56.1 | 350 |
| Pn111 | 1903 | — | Franc. Silver. Plain edgeSmall portrait, KM#56.1 | 350 |
| Pn136 | 1904 | — | 50 Centimes. Silver. Plain edgeKM#60.1 | — |
| Pn137 | 1904 | — | 50 Centimes. Silver. Reeded edgeKM#60.1 | — |
| Pn138 | 1904 | — | 50 Centimes. Silver. Smaller designs, KM#60.1 | — |
| Pn139 | 1904 | — | Franc. Silver. Reeded edgeThin flan, KM#56.1. | — |
| Pn140 | 1904 | — | Franc. Silver. Plain edgeThick flan, KM#56.1. | — |
| Pn141 | 1904 | — | 2 Francs. Silver. Plain edgeKM#58.1. | — |
| Pn142 | 1904 | — | 2 Francs. Silver. Reeded edgeThin flan, KM#58.1. | — |

| KM# | Date | Mintage | Identification | Mkt Val |
|---|---|---|---|---|
| Pn143 | 1904 | — | 2 Francs. Silver. Plain edgeThick flan, KM#58.1. | — |
| Pn144 | 1904 | — | 2 Francs. Silver. Plain edgeKM#59.1. | — |
| Pn145 | 1904 | — | 2 Francs. Silver. Reeded edgeThin flan, KM#59.1. | — |
| Pn146 | 1904 | — | 2 Francs. Silver. Plain edgeThick flan, KM#59.1. | — |
| Pn147 | 1906 | — | 5 Centimes. Nickel-Brass. Restrike, KM#93. | — |
| Pn148 | 1907 | — | Centime. Copper. Reeded edgeThick flan, KM#34.1. | — |
| Pn149 | 1907 | — | 25 Centimes. Copper-Nickel. | — |
| Pn150 | 1909 | — | Franc. Silver. Reeded edgeKM#73.1 | — |
| Pn151 | 1910 | — | 5 Centimes. Gold. Not holed, KM#67 | — |
| Pn152 | 1910 | — | 5 Centimes. Silver. Not holed, KM#67 | — |
| Pn153 | 1910 | — | 5 Centimes. Bronze. Not holed, KM#67 | — |
| Pn154 | 1910 | — | 5 Centimes. Aluminum. Not holed, KM#67 | — |
| Pn155 | 1910 | — | Franc. Silver. Reeded edgeKM#72. | — |
| Pn156 | 1910 | — | Franc. Silver. Reeded edgeThick planchet, KM#72. | — |
| Pn157 | 1910 | — | Franc. Silver. Reeded edgeThin planchet, KM#72. | — |
| Pn158 | 1910 | — | Franc. Silver. Designer's name as Devreese, KM#72. | — |
| Pn159 | 1910 | — | Franc. Silver. Plain edgeKM#73.1 | — |
| Pn160 | 1910 | — | 2 Francs. Silver. Plain edgeKM#74. | — |
| Pn161 | 1911 | — | Centime. Copper. Restrike. | — |
| Pn162 | 1911 | — | 10 Centimes. Copper. Not holed. | — |
| Pn163 | 1911 | — | 10 Centimes. Brass. Holed. | — |
| Pn164 | 1911 | — | 10 Centimes. Copper-Nickel. Not holed. | — |
| Pn165 | 1911 | — | 10 Centimes. Gold. KM#85.1. | — |
| Pn166 | 1911 | — | 10 Centimes. Silver. KM#85.1. | — |
| Pn167 | 1911 | — | 10 Centimes. Bronze. KM#85.1. | — |
| Pn168 | 1911 | — | 10 Centimes. Copper. KM#85.1. | — |
| Pn169 | 1911 | — | 10 Centimes. Aluminum. KM#85.1. | — |
| Pn170 | 1911 | — | 10 Centimes. Gold. KM#86 | — |
| Pn171 | 1911 | — | 10 Centimes. Silver. KM#86. | — |
| Pn172 | 1911 | — | 10 Centimes. Bronze. KM#86. | — |
| Pn173 | 1911 | — | 10 Centimes. Copper. KM#86. | — |
| Pn174 | 1911 | — | 10 Centimes. Aluminum. KM#86. | — |
| Pn175 | 1911 | — | Franc. Reeded edgeDesigner's name as Devreese, KM#73. | — |
| Pn176 | 1911 | — | Franc. Plain edge. Designer's name as Devreese, KM#73. | — |
| Pn181 | 1911 | — | 20 Francs. Brass Plated Copper. | — |
| Pn182 | 1911 | — | 20 Francs. Nickel. | — |
| Pn183 | 1911 | — | 20 Francs. Gold. Dutch legend. | — |
| Pn184 | 1911 | — | 20 Francs. Gold. French legend. | — |
| Pn185 | 1911 | — | 20 Francs. Pewter. | — |
| Pn186 | 1911 | — | 100 Francs. Aluminum-Nickel. Dutch legend. | — |
| Pn187 | 1911 | — | 100 Francs. Aluminum-Nickel. French legend. | — |
| Pn188 | 1911 | — | 100 Francs. Silver. Reeded edge | — |
| Pn177 | 1911 | — | 2 Francs. Copper. KM#74. | 350 |
| Pn178 | 1911 | — | 2 Francs. Gold. | 1,500 |
| Pn179 | 1911 | — | 10 Francs. Gold. Dutch legend. | 2,000 |
| Pn180 | 1911 | — | 10 Francs. Gold. French legend. | 2,000 |
| Pn190 | 1912 | — | 10 Francs. Gold. Dutch legend. | 2,000 |
| Pn191 | 1912 | — | 10 Francs. Gold. French legend. | 2,000 |
| Pn193 | 1912 | 3 | 100 Francs. Gold. Dutch legend. | 16,000 |
| Pn194 | 1912 | 6 | 100 Francs. Gold. French legend. | 12,500 |
| Pn189 | 1912/1 | — | Centime. Copper. Restrike, ESSAI. | — |
| Pn192 | 1912 | — | 10 Francs. Gold. Reeded edge | — |
| Pn195 | 1914 | — | 2 Francs. Silver. Unadopted portrait. ESSAI/MONETAIRE/1914 | — |
| Pn196 | (1915) | — | Centime. Zinc. | — |
| Pn197 | 1915 | — | 5 Centimes. Copper-Iron Bi-Metal. Reeded edge KM#66. | — |
| Pn198 | 1915 | — | 10 Centimes. Copper-Iron Bi-Metal. KM#681. | — |
| Pn199 | 1915 | — | 25 Centimes. Pot Metal. | — |
| Pn200 | 1916 | — | 10 Centimes. Copper-Iron Bi-Metal. KM#81. | — |
| Pn201 | 1917 | — | 10 Centimes. Silver. Plain edge KM#81. | — |

| KM# | Date | Mintage | Identification | Mkt Val |
|---|---|---|---|---|
| Pn202 | 1918 | — | 25 Centimes. Silver. Plain edge KM#82. | — |
| Pn203 | (1918) | — | 25 Centimes. Copper-Iron Bi-Metal. 2 branches around legend. ESSAI MONETAIRE. Legend around 25 CES | — |
| Pn204 | (1918) | — | 25 Centimes. Zinc. Legend around 25 CENT.. Lion, ESSAI | — |
| Pn205 | (1918) | — | 25 Centimes. Silver. 16 sided. | — |
| Pn206 | 1918 | — | 50 Centimes. Gold. KM#83. | — |
| Pn207 | 1918 | — | 50 Centimes. Silver. KM#83. | — |
| Pn208 | 1918 | — | 50 Centimes. Tan Bronze. KM#83. | — |
| Pn209 | 1918 | — | 50 Centimes. Red Bronze. KM#83. | — |
| Pn210 | 1918 | — | 50 Centimes. Aluminum. KM#83. | — |
| Pn211 | 1918 | — | 50 Centimes. Silver. Not holed. | — |
| Pn212 | 1918 | — | 50 Centimes. Nickel. Not holed. | — |
| Pn213 | 1918 | — | 50 Centimes. Copper-Nickel. Not holed. | — |
| Pn214 | 1920 | — | 5 Centimes. Nickel. Reeded edge Not holed, KM#66. | — |
| PnA215 | 1920 | — | 20 Francs. Silver. Victory and Peace | 400 |
| Pn216 | 1921 | — | 5 Centimes. Nickel. KM#69 | — |
| Pn217 | 1922 | — | 5 Centimes. Nickel-Brass. Restrike, KM#94 | — |
| Pn218 | 1922 | — | 50 Centimes. Bronze. | — |
| Pn219 | 1922 | — | 50 Centimes. Silver. Plain edge KM#87 | — |
| Pn220 | 1922 | — | 50 Centimes. Bronze. Plain edge KM#87 | — |
| Pn221 | 1922 | — | 50 Centimes. Aluminum. Plain edge KM#87 | — |
| Pn222 | 1922 | — | 50 Centimes. Nickel. Plain edge KM#87 | — |
| Pn223 | 1922 | — | 50 Centimes. Copper. Plain edge KM#87 | — |
| Pn224 | 1922 | — | 50 Centimes. Copper-Tin Alloy. Plain edge KM#87 | — |
| Pn225 | 1922 | — | 50 Centimes. Silver. Reeded edge KM#87 | — |
| Pn226 | 1922 | — | 50 Centimes. Bronze. Reeded edge KM#87 | — |
| Pn227 | 1922 | — | 50 Centimes. Aluminum. Reeded edge KM#87 | — |
| Pn228 | 1922 | — | 50 Centimes. Nickel. Reeded edge KM#87 | — |
| Pn229 | 1922 | — | 50 Centimes. Copper. Reeded edge KM#87 | — |
| Pn230 | 1922 | — | 50 Centimes. Copper-Tin Alloy. Reeded edge KM#87 | — |
| Pn231 | 1922 | — | 50 Centimes. Silver. Plain edge KM#88 | — |
| Pn232 | 1922 | — | 50 Centimes. Bronze. Plain edge KM#88 | — |
| Pn233 | 1922 | — | 50 Centimes. Aluminum. Plain edge KM#88 | — |
| Pn234 | 1922 | — | 50 Centimes. Copper. Plain edge KM#88 | — |
| Pn235 | 1922 | — | 50 Centimes. Copper-Tin Alloy. Plain edge KM#88 | — |
| Pn236 | 1922 | — | 50 Centimes. Silver. Reeded edge KM#88 | — |
| Pn237 | 1922 | — | 50 Centimes. Bronze. Reeded edge KM#88 | — |
| Pn238 | 1922 | — | 50 Centimes. Aluminum. Reeded edge KM#88 | — |
| Pn239 | 1922 | — | 50 Centimes. Copper. Reeded edge KM#88 | — |
| Pn240 | 1922 | — | 50 Centimes. Copper-Tin Alloy. Reeded edge KM#88 | — |
| Pn241 | 1922 | — | Franc. Silver. Plain edge KM#89 | — |
| Pn242 | 1922 | — | Franc. Bronze. Plain edge KM#89 | — |
| Pn243 | 1922 | — | Franc. Aluminum. Plain edge KM#89 | — |
| Pn244 | 1922 | — | Franc. Copper. Plain edge KM#89 | — |
| Pn245 | 1922 | — | Franc. Copper-Tin Alloy. Plain edge KM#89 | — |
| Pn246 | 1922 | — | Franc. Silver. Reeded edge KM#89 | — |
| Pn247 | 1922 | — | Franc. Bronze. Reeded edge KM#89 | — |
| Pn248 | 1922 | — | Franc. Aluminum. Reeded edge KM#89 | — |
| Pn249 | 1922 | — | Franc. Copper. Reeded edge KM#89 | — |
| Pn250 | 1922 | — | Franc. Copper-Tin Alloy. Reeded edge KM#89 | — |
| Pn251 | 1922 | — | Franc. Silver. Plain edge KM#90 | — |
| Pn252 | 1922 | — | Franc. Bronze. Plain edge KM#90 | — |
| Pn253 | 1922 | — | Franc. Aluminum. Plain edge KM#90 | — |
| Pn254 | 1922 | — | Franc. Nickel. Plain edge Irregular flan, KM#90. | — |
| Pn255 | 1922 | — | Franc. Copper. Plain edge KM#90. | — |
| Pn256 | 1922 | — | Franc. Copper-Tin Alloy. Plain edge KM#90. | — |
| Pn257 | 1922 | — | Franc. Silver. Reeded edge KM#90. | — |
| Pn258 | 1922 | — | Franc. Bronze. Reeded edge KM#90. | — |
| Pn259 | 1922 | — | Franc. Aluminum. Reeded edge KM#90. | — |
| Pn260 | 1922 | — | Franc. Copper. Reeded edge KM#90. | — |
| Pn261 | 1922 | — | Franc. Copper-Tin Alloy. Reeded edge KM#90. | — |
| Pn262 | 1922 | — | Franc. Nickel. KM#89. KM#90 | — |

| KM# | Date | Mintage | Identification | Mkt Val |
|---|---|---|---|---|
| Pn263 | 1923 | — | 2 Francs. Silver. ESSAI, KM#91.1. | — |
| Pn264 | 1923 | — | 2 Francs. Bronze. ESSAI, KM#91.1. | — |
| Pn265 | 1923 | — | 2 Francs. Aluminum. ESSAI, KM#91.1. | — |
| Pn266 | 1923 | — | 2 Francs. Copper-Tin Alloy. ESSAI, KM#91.1. | — |
| Pn267 | 1926 | — | 5 Francs. Red Bronze. ESSAI | — |
| Pn268 | 1926 | — | 5 Francs. Silver. Head left. Wreath with 5 FR within | — |
| Pn269 | 1926 | — | 5 Francs. Bronze. Head left. Wreath with 5 FR within | — |
| Pn270 | 1926 | — | 5 Francs. Nickel. Head left. Wreath with 5 FR within | — |
| Pn271 | 1926 | — | 5 Francs. Copper-Tin Alloy. Head left. Wreath with 5 FR within | — |
| Pn272 | 1926 | — | 5 Francs. Silver. Crown above 5 Francs | — |
| Pn273 | 1926 | — | 5 Francs. Bronze. Crown above 5 Francs | — |
| Pn274 | 1926 | — | 5 Francs. Nickel. Crown above 5 Francs | — |
| Pn275 | 1926 | — | 5 Francs. Copper-Tin Alloy. Crown above 5 Francs | — |
| Pn276 | 1926 | — | 5 Francs. Silver. Crown above oak wreath, 5 Francs within | — |
| Pn277 | 1926 | — | 5 Francs. Bronze. Crown above oak wreath, 5 Francs within | — |
| Pn278 | 1926 | — | 5 Francs. Copper-Tin Alloy. Crown above oak wreath, 5 Francs within | — |
| Pn279 | 1926 | — | 5 Francs. Gold. Wreath, UN BELGA CINQ FRANCS | — |
| Pn280 | 1926 | — | 5 Francs. Silver. Wreath, UN BELGA CINQ FRANCS | — |
| Pn281 | 1926 | — | 5 Francs. Bronze. Wreath, UN BELGA CINQ FRANCS | — |
| Pn282 | 1926 | — | 5 Francs. Nickel. Wreath, UN BELGA CINQ FRANCS | — |
| Pn283 | 1926 | — | 5 Francs. Copper-Tin Alloy. Wreath, UN BELGA CINQ FRANCS | — |
| Pn284 | 1926 | — | 5 Francs. Gold. Lion in shield, SF flanking | — |
| Pn285 | 1926 | — | 5 Francs. Silver. Lion in shield, SF flanking | — |
| Pn286 | 1926 | — | 5 Francs. Bronze. Lion in shield, SF flanking | — |
| Pn287 | 1926 | — | 5 Francs. Nickel. Lion in shield, SF flanking | — |
| Pn288 | 1926 | — | 5 Francs. Copper-Tin Alloy. Lion in shield, SF flanking | — |
| Pn289 | 1927 | — | 5 Francs. Silver. Head by Bonnetain. 2 laurel branches, UN BELGA/OU/5 FRANCS/ESSAI | — |
| Pn290 | 1927 | — | 5 Francs. Copper. Head by Bonnetain. 2 laurel branches, UN BELGA/OU/5 FRANCS/ESSAI | — |
| Pn291 | 1927 | — | 5 Francs. Copper-Tin Alloy. Head by Bonnetain. 2 laurel branches, UN BELGA/OU/5 FRANCS/ESSAI | — |
| Pn292 | 1927 | — | 5 Francs. Nickel. | — |
| Pn293 | 1929 | — | 5 Centimes. Not holed, KM#67. | — |
| Pn294 | 1929 | — | 10 Centimes. Nickel. Not holed, ESSAI, KM#85.1. | — |
| Pn295 | 1929 | — | 10 Centimes. Gold. KM#85.1. | — |
| Pn296 | 1929 | — | 10 Centimes. Silver. KM#85.1. | — |
| Pn297 | 1929 | — | 10 Centimes. Bronze. KM#85.1. | — |
| Pn298 | 1929 | — | 10 Centimes. Copper. KM#85.1. | — |
| Pn299 | 1929 | — | 10 Centimes. Aluminum. KM#85.1. | — |
| Pn300 | 1929 | — | 25 Centimes. Gold. ESSAI, KM#68.1. | — |
| Pn301 | 1929 | — | 25 Centimes. Silver. ESSAI, KM#68.1. | — |
| Pn302 | 1929 | — | 25 Centimes. Bronze. ESSAI, KM#68.1. | — |
| Pn303 | 1929 | — | 25 Centimes. Copper. ESSAI, KM#68.1. | — |
| Pn304 | 1929 | — | 25 Centimes. Aluminum. ESSAI, KM#68.1. | — |
| Pn305 | 1929 | — | 25 Centimes. Gold. ESSAI, KM#69. | — |
| Pn306 | 1929 | — | 25 Centimes. Silver. ESSAI, KM#69. | — |
| Pn307 | 1929 | — | 25 Centimes. Bronze. ESSAI, KM#69. | — |
| Pn308 | 1929 | — | 25 Centimes. Copper. ESSAI, KM#69. | — |
| Pn309 | 1929 | — | 25 Centimes. Aluminum. ESSAI, KM#69. | — |
| Pn310 | 1929 | — | 5 Francs. Nickel. | — |
| Pn311 | 1929 | — | 5 Francs. Bronze. | — |
| Pn312 | 1930 | — | 2 Francs. Copper. KM#92. | — |
| Pn313 | 1930 | — | 2 Francs. Matte Bronze. KM#92. | — |
| Pn315 | 1930 | — | 20 Francs. Silver. | — |

| KM# | Date | Mintage | Identification | Mkt Val |
|---|---|---|---|---|
| Pn314 | 1930 | — | 10 Francs. Brass. | 250 |
| Pn317 | 1931 | — | 20 Francs. Bronze. French legend. | 250 |
| Pn318 | 1931 | — | 20 Francs. Bronze. Dutch legend. | 250 |
| Pn316 | 1931 | — | Franc. Nickel. | — |
| Pn319 | 1932 | — | 5 Centimes. Copper-Nickel. | — |
| Pn320 | 1932 | — | 5 Centimes. Dupriez's design. | — |
| Pn321 | 1932 | — | 5 Centimes. Copper. Not holed, KM#93. | — |
| Pn322 | 1932 | — | 50 Centimes. Nickel. KM#87. KM#88. Reeded edge | — |
| Pn323 | 1932 | — | 50 Centimes. Nickel. KM#87. KM#88. Plain edge | — |
| Pn324 | 1933 | — | 5 Francs. Silver. | — |
| Pn325 | 1933 | — | 10 Francs. Nickel. | — |
| Pn326 | 1933 | — | 10 Francs. Nickel. DEUX BELGAS/OU/10 FRANCS | — |
| Pn327 | 1933 | — | 50 Francs. Silver. 10/BELGAS/50/FRANCS within 2 oak branches. Plain edge | — |
| Pn328 | 1933 | — | 50 Francs. Silver. Cross ornaments on edge . | — |
| Pn329 | 1933 | — | 50 Francs. Silver. Reeded edge | — |
| Pn330 | 1933 | — | 50 Francs. Silver. Small head of Albert within pellet circle. Value within 2 laurel branches | — |
| Pn331 | 1933 | — | 50 Francs. Silver. Bust by Bonnetain. Value within laurel branches | — |
| Pn333 | 1933 | — | 100 Francs. By Devreese | — |
| Pn332 | 1933 | — | 100 Francs. Silver. Bust by Bonnetain. 20/BELGAS/100/ FRANCS wtihin 2 laurel branches | — |
| Pn334 | 1933 | — | 100 Francs. L'UNION FAIT LA FORCE/100 FRSBy Devreese | — |
| Pn335 | 1933 | — | 100 Francs. Bronze. 20/BELGAS/100 FRANCS between 2 branches | — |
| Pn336 | 1933 | — | 500 Francs. Bronze. 20/BELGAS/500/FRANCS between laurel and oak branches | — |
| Pn337 | 1933 | — | 500 Francs. Nickel. | — |

| KM# | Date | Mintage | Identification | Mkt Val |
|---|---|---|---|---|
| Pn338 | 1934 | — | 5 Francs. Bronze. | 100 |
| Pn339 | 1934 | — | 20 Francs. Bronze. | 125 |
| Pn346 | 1935 | — | 40 Francs. 0.6800 Silver. Lettered edge | 14,000 |
| Pn363 | 1935 | — | 50 Francs. 0.6800 Silver. Plain edge | 600 |
| Pn340 | 1935 | — | Franc. Copper-Tin Alloy. Reeded edge | — |
| Pn341 | 1935 | — | Franc. Nickel. Reeded edge | — |
| Pn342 | 1935 | — | Franc. Silver. Allegory of Belgium kneeling left; BELGIQUE \ BELGIE at sides. Caducesus between IF and date. Plain edge | — |
| Pn343 | 1935 | — | Franc. Silver. Allegory of Belgium kneeling left. Plain edge | — |
| Pn344 | 1935 | — | Franc. Copper. Allegory of Belgium kneeling left. Plain edge | — |
| Pn345 | 1935 | — | Franc. Nickel. Allegory of Belgium kneeling left. Plain edge | — |
| Pn347 | 1935 | — | 40 Francs. Silver. Plain edge Restrike. | — |
| Pn348 | 1935 | — | 40 Francs. Copper-Tin Alloy. Lettered edge Expo commemorative. | — |
| Pn349 | 1935 | — | 40 Francs. Gold. Reeded edge Expo commemorative. | — |
| Pn350 | 1935 | — | 40 Francs. Silver. Reeded edge Expo commemorative. | — |
| Pn351 | 1935 | — | 40 Francs. Bronze. Reeded edge Expo commemorative. | — |
| Pn352 | 1935 | — | 40 Francs. Copper. Reeded edge Expo commemorative. | — |
| Pn353 | 1935 | — | 40 Francs. Copper-Tin Alloy. Reeded edge Expo commemorative. | — |
| Pn354 | 1935 | — | 40 Francs. Nickel. Reeded edge Expo commemorative. | — |
| Pn355 | 1935 | — | 40 Francs. Aluminum. Reeded edge Expo commemorative. | — |
| Pn356 | 1935 | — | 40 Francs. Gold. Expo commemorative, thin planchet | — |
| Pn357 | 1935 | — | 40 Francs. Silver. Expo commemorative, thin planchet | — |
| Pn358 | 1935 | — | 40 Francs. Bronze. Expo commemorative, thin planchet | — |
| Pn359 | 1935 | — | 40 Francs. Copper. Expo commemorative, thin planchet | — |
| Pn360 | 1935 | — | 40 Francs. Copper-Tin Alloy. Expo commemorative. | — |
| Pn361 | 1935 | — | 40 Francs. Nickel. Expo commemorative, thin planchet | — |
| Pn362 | 1935 | — | 40 Francs. Aluminum. Expo commemorative, thin planchet | — |
| Pn364 | 1935 | — | 50 Francs. Silver. Plain edge KM#106.1. | — |
| Pn365 | 1935 | — | 50 Francs. Copper. Plain edge KM#106.1. | — |
| Pn366 | 1935 | — | 50 Francs. Copper-Tin Alloy. Plain edge KM#106.1. | — |
| Pn367 | 1935 | — | 50 Francs. Copper-Tin Alloy. edge inscription. KM#106.1. | — |
| Pn368 | 1935 | — | 50 Francs. Gold. Reeded edge KM#106.1. | — |
| Pn369 | 1935 | — | 50 Francs. Silver. Reeded edge KM#106.1. | — |
| Pn370 | 1935 | — | 50 Francs. Bronze. Reeded edge KM#106.1. | — |

| KM# | Date | Mintage | Identification | Mkt Val |
|---|---|---|---|---|
| Pn371 | 1935 | — | 50 Francs. Copper. Reeded edge KM#106.1. | — |
| Pn372 | 1935 | — | 50 Francs. Copper-Tin Alloy. Reeded edge KM#106.1. | — |
| Pn373 | 1935 | — | 50 Francs. Aluminum. Reeded edge KM#106.1. | — |
| Pn374 | 1935 | — | 50 Francs. Silver. Plain edge KM#107.1. | — |
| Pn375 | 1935 | — | 50 Francs. Copper-Tin Alloy. Plain edge KM#107.1. | — |
| Pn376 | 1935 | — | 50 Francs. Bronze. edge inscription, KM#107.1. | — |
| Pn377 | 1935 | — | 50 Francs. Copper-Tin Alloy. Reeded edge KM#107.1. | — |
| Pn378 | 1936 | — | 5 Francs. Nickel. | — |
| Pn379 | 1938 | — | 5 Centimes. Copper-Tin Alloy. KM#110.1 | — |
| Pn380 | 1938 | — | 5 Centimes. Bronze. KM#110.1 | — |
| Pn381 | 1938 | — | 5 Centimes. Tin. Not holed, KM#110.1 | — |
| Pn382 | 1938 | — | 10 Centimes. Copper-Tin Alloy. Thin planchet, KM#112. | — |
| Pn383 | 1938 | — | 10 Centimes. Copper-Tin Alloy. Thick planchet, KM#112. | — |
| Pn384 | 1938 | — | 10 Centimes. Bronze. KM#112. | — |
| Pn385 | 1938 | — | 10 Centimes. Copper-Tin Alloy. Large letters, not holed. | — |
| Pn386 | 1938 | — | 25 Centimes. Nickel. Large shields. | — |
| Pn387 | 1938 | — | 25 Centimes. Copper-Tin Alloy. Not holed. | — |
| Pn388 | 1938 | — | 20 Francs. Silver. | — |
| Pn389 | 1938 | — | 20 Francs. Silver. Similar to KM#121. | — |
| Pn390 | 1938 | — | 20 Francs. Bronze. Similar to KM#121. | — |
| Pn391 | 1938 | — | 20 Francs. Copper. Similar to KM#121. | — |
| Pn392 | 1938 | — | 20 Francs. Copper-Tin Alloy. Similar to KM#121. | — |
| Pn393 | 1938 | — | 20 Francs. Nickel. Similar to KM#121. | — |
| Pn394 | 1938 | — | 20 Francs. Silver. | — |
| Pn395 | 1938 | — | 20 Francs. Copper-Tin Alloy. | — |
| Pn396 | 1938 | — | 20 Francs. Tin. | — |
| Pn397 | 1938 | — | 20 Francs. Silver. Thick planchet. | — |
| Pn398 | 1938 | — | 20 Francs. Copper-Tin Alloy. Thick planchet. | — |
| Pn399 | 1938 | — | 20 Francs. Tin. Thick planchet. | — |
| Pn400 | 1938 | — | 20 Francs. Silver. Small portrait. | — |
| Pn401 | 1938 | — | 20 Francs. Bronze. Small portrait. | — |
| Pn402 | 1938 | — | 20 Francs. Copper-Tin Alloy. Small portrait. | — |
| Pn403 | 1938 | — | 20 Francs. Tin. Small portrait. | — |
| Pn404 | 1938 | — | 50 Francs. Silver. Plain edge KM#121.1. | — |
| Pn405 | 1938 | — | 50 Francs. Copper-Tin Alloy. Plain edge KM#121.1. | — |
| Pn406 | 1938 | — | 50 Francs. Copper. Plain edge | — |
| Pn407 | 1938 | — | 50 Francs. Copper. Plain edge ESSAI | — |
| Pn408 | 1939 | — | 25 Centimes. Copper-Tin Alloy. Not holed, KM#114.1. | — |
| Pn409 | 1939 | — | 25 Centimes. Bronze. KM#114.1. | — |
| Pn410 | 1939 | — | Franc. Nickel. KM#120. | — |
| Pn411 | 1939 | — | Franc. Bronze. Reeded edge KM#120. | — |
| Pn412 | 1939 | — | Franc. Copper-Tin Alloy. Reeded edge KM#120. | — |
| Pn413 | 1939 | — | 50 Francs. Copper-Tin Alloy. Lettered edge KM#121.1. | — |
| Pn414 | 1939 | — | 50 Francs. Bronze. Lettered edge KM#121.1. | — |
| Pn415 | 1940 | — | Franc. Nickel. Restrike, KM#119. | — |
| Pn416 | 1940 | — | 5 Francs. Copper-Tin Alloy. Portrait by Rau, Leopold III ROI DE BELGES. 5/FRANCS/1940 between oak and laurel brnaches | — |
| Pn417 | 1940 | — | 5 Francs. Copper-Tin Alloy. Portrait by RauThick planchet. | — |
| Pn418 | 1940 | — | 5 Francs. Copper-Tin Alloy. Portrait by Rau. KM#108.1 | — |
| Pn419 | 1940 | — | 5 Francs. Copper-Tin Alloy. Portrait by Rau. KM#108.1Thick planchet. | — |
| Pn420 | 1940 | — | 5 Francs. Copper-Tin Alloy. Leopold III | — |
| Pn421 | 1940 | — | 5 Francs. Copper-Tin Alloy. Leopold IIIThick planchet. | — |
| Pn422 | 1940 | — | 5 Francs. Nickel. Leopold III. Reeded edge | — |
| Pn423 | 1940 | — | 5 Francs. Nickel. Leopold III. Reeded edge Thick planchet. | — |
| Pn424 | 1940 | — | 5 Francs. Silver. Leopold III. KM#108.1 | — |
| Pn425 | 1940 | — | 5 Francs. Silver. Leopold III. KM#108.1Thick planchet. | — |
| Pn426 | 1940 | — | 5 Francs. Copper-Tin Alloy. Leopold III, ROI DES BELGES. KM#108.1Thick planchet. | — |
| Pn427 | 1941 | — | 10 Centimes. Silver. Reeded edge KM#130. | — |
| Pn428 | 1941 | — | 5 Francs. Silver. Reeded edge KM#130. | — |
| Pn429 | 1944 | — | 2 Francs. Silver. KM#133. | — |
| Pn430 | 1948 | — | 100 Francs. Copper. ESSAI, KM#138. | — |
| Pn431 | 1948 | — | 100 Francs. Copper. ESSAI, KM#139.1. | — |
| Pn432 | 1949 | — | 5 Francs. Copper. KM#134.1. | — |
| Pn433 | 1949 | — | 5 Francs. Copper. KM#135.1. | — |
| Pn434 | 1949 | — | 50 Francs. Bronze. | — |
| Pn435 | 1949 | — | 100 Francs. Silver. | — |
| Pn436 | 1949 | — | 100 Francs. Silver. | — |
| Pn437 | 1949 | — | 1000 Francs. Bronze. Plain edge | — |
| Pn438 | 1949 | — | 1000 Francs. Silver. | — |
| Pn440 | | — | 1000 Francs. Bronze. | — |
| Pn441 | 1949 | — | 1000 Francs. Bronze. Milled edge | — |
| Pn439 | 1949 | — | 1000 Francs. Gold. ESSAI | 10,920 |
| Pn442 | 1951 | — | 20 Francs. Copper. ESSAI, KM#140.1 | — |
| Pn443 | 1951 | — | 20 Francs. Copper. ESSAI, KM#141.1 | — |
| Pn444 | 1951 | — | 20 Francs. Copper. ESSAI, KM#136.1. | — |
| Pn445 | 1951 | — | 50 Francs. Copper. ESSAI, KM#137 | — |
| Pn446 | 1952 | — | Franc. Copper. KM#142.1 | — |
| Pn447 | 1952 | — | Franc. Copper. KM#143.1 | — |

## PIEFORTS

| KM# | Date | Mintage | Identification | Mkt Val |
|---|---|---|---|---|
| P6 | 1918 | — | 50 Centimes. Zinc. Plain edge Not holed, KM#83. | — |
| P7 | 1920 | — | 25 Centimes. Nickel. Plain edge KM#68.1. | — |
| P8 | 1926 | — | 5 Centimes. Copper. Plain edge Not holed, KM#66. | — |
| P9 | 1935 | — | Franc. Silver. | — |
| P10 | 1935 | — | Franc. Copper. | — |
| P11 | 1935 | — | Franc. Nickel. | — |
| P12 | 1989 | — | 100 Ecu. Gold. KM#175 | 1,000 |

## TRIAL STRIKES

| KM# | Date | Mintage | Identification | Mkt Val |
|---|---|---|---|---|
| TS5 | 1903 | — | Franc. Pewter. UnifaceRectangle planchet. | — |
| TS6 | 1904 | — | Franc. Pewter. UnifaceRectangle planchet. | — |
| TS7 | (1904) | — | 2 Francs. Lead. Uniface | 50.00 |
| TS8 | 1910 | — | 2 Francs. Portrait, uniface. | — |
| TS9 | 1910 | — | 2 Francs. KM#74Uniface. | — |
| TS10 | 1911 | — | 20 Francs. Gold. Error obverse. | — |
| TS11 | 1911 | — | 20 Francs. Aluminum. Error obverse. | — |
| TS12 | 1918 | — | 50 Centimes. Klippe. | — |
| TS13 | 1926 | — | 5 Francs. Nickel. Klippe. | — |
| TS14 | 1933 | — | 10 Francs. Silver. Legend within 2 branches | — |
| TS15 | 1933 | — | 50 Francs. Silver. Irregular flan. | — |
| TS16 | 1949 | — | 1000 Francs. Red Copper. Klippe | — |
| TS17 | 1949 | — | 1000 Francs. Yellow Copper. Klippe | — |
| TS18 | 1949 | — | 1000 Francs. Red Copper. Klippe | — |
| TS19 | 1949 | — | 1000 Francs. Yellow Copper. Klippe | — |
| TS20 | 1949 | — | 1000 Francs. Silver. Klippe | — |

## "FDC" SETS

| KM# | Date | Mintage | Identification | Issue Price | Mkt Val |
|---|---|---|---|---|---|
| SS1 | 1970 | 5,000 | KM#135, 143, 149, 154, 156 DU | 0.60 | 130 |
| SS2 | 1970 | 5,000 | KM#134, 142, 148, 153, 155 FR | 0.60 | 130 |
| SS3 | 1971 | 10,000 | KM#135, 143, 149, 154, 156 DU | 0.63 | 55.00 |
| SS4 | 1971 | 10,000 | KM#134, 142, 148, 153, 155 FR | 0.63 | 55.00 |
| SS5 | 1972 | 10,000 | KM#135, 143, 149, 154, 156 DU | 0.70 | 80.00 |
| SS6 | 1972 | 10,000 | KM#134, 142, 148, 153, 155 FR | 0.70 | 80.00 |
| SS7 | 1973 | 16,778 | KM#135, 143, 149, 154, 156 DU | 0.80 | 30.00 |
| SS8 | 1973 | 15,000 | KM#134, 142, 148, 153, 155 FR | 0.80 | 30.00 |
| SS9 | 1974 | 20,608 | KM#135, 143, 149, 154, 156 DU | 1.10 | 22.00 |
| SS10 | 1974 | 19,000 | KM#134, 142, 148, 153, 155 FR | 1.10 | 22.00 |
| SS11 | 1975 | 45,752 | KM#135, 143, 149, 154, 156 DU, 134, 142, 148, 153, 155 FR | 2.50 | 8.00 |
| SS12 | 1976 | 15,000 | KM#135, 143, 149, 156, 158.1 DU, 134, 142, 148, 155, 157.1 FR | 20.75 | 60.00 |
| SS13 | 1977 | 45,938 | KM#135, 143, 149, 156 DU, 134, 142, 148, 155 FR | 2.65 | 5.00 |
| SS14 | 1978 | 46,237 | KM#135, 143, 149, 156 DU, 134, 142, 148, 155 FR | 4.00 | 6.00 |
| SS15 | 1979 | 49,997 | KM#135, 143, 149, 156 DU, 134, 142, 148, 155 FR | 4.00 | 5.00 |
| SS16 | 1980 | 60,000 | KM#135, 143, 149, 160 DU, 134, 142, 148, 159 FR | 4.00 | 5.00 |
| SS17 | 1981 | 54,331 | KM#135, 143, 149, 160 DU, 134, 142, 148, 159 FR | 3.25 | 5.00 |

## MINT SETS

| KM# | Date | Mintage | Identification | Issue Price | Mkt Val |
|---|---|---|---|---|---|
| MS1 | 1989 | 60,000 | KM#149, 160, 164, 169, 171 DU; 148, 159, 163, 168, 170 FR | 11.00 | 25.00 |
| MS2 | 1990 | 60,000 | KM#149, 160, 164, 169, 171 DU; 148, 159, 163, 168, 170 FR | 13.00 | 18.00 |
| MS3 | 1991 | 60,000 | KM#149, 160, 164, 169, 171 DU; 148, 159, 163, 168, 170 FR | 13.00 | 10.00 |
| MS4 | 1991 | — | KM#196-198 | — | 30.00 |
| MS5 | 1992 | 60,000 | KM#149, 160, 164, 169, 171 DU; 148, 159, | 15.00 | 10.00 |
| MS6 | 1993 | 40,000 | KM#149, 160, 164, 169, 171 DU; 148, 159, 163, 168, 170 FR | 15.00 | 10.00 |
| MS7 | 1994 | 60,000 | KM#148.1, 149.1, 187-194, medal | 15.00 | 12.00 |
| MS8 | 1995 | 60,000 | KM#148.1, 149.1, 187-194, medal | 15.00 | 16.00 |
| MS9 | 1996 | 60,000 | KM#148.1, 149.1, 187-194, medal | 15.00 | 12.00 |
| MS10 | 1997 | 60,000 | KM#148.1, 149.1, 187-194, medal | — | 14.00 |
| MS11 | 1998 | 60,000 | KM#148.1, 149.1, 187-194 | 15.00 | 12.00 |
| MS12 | 1999 | 60,000 | KM#148.1, 149.1, 187-194 | 15.00 | 12.00 |
| MS13 | 2000 | 60,000 | KM#148.1, 149.1, 187-194 | 15.00 | 12.00 |

## PROOF SETS

| KM# | Date | Mintage | Identification | Issue Price | Mkt Val |
|---|---|---|---|---|---|
| PS1 | 1987 | 15,000 | KM#166-167 | 395 | 300 |
| PS2 | 1988 | 15,000 | KM#166-167 | 395 | 300 |
| PS3 | 1989 | 2,000 | KM#172-175 | 1,300 | 1,500 |
| PS4 | 1990 | 5,000 | KM#172-175 | 1,300 | 900 |
| PS5 | 1990 | 10,000 | KM#178-180 | 100 | 110 |
| PS6 | 1991 | 10,000 | KM#196-198 | 100 | 80.00 |
| PS7 | 2000 | 10,000 | KM#215-217 | 75.00 | 80.00 |

# GHENT

# GERMAN OCCUPATION WWI

## TOKEN COINAGE

**50 CENTIMES** **KM# Tn1a** **Composition:** Iron **Reverse:** Thick "50"

| Date | Mintage | F | VF | XF | Unc | BU |
|---|---|---|---|---|---|---|
| 1915 | Inc. above | 3.00 | 6.00 | 12.00 | 35.00 | — |

**50 CENTIMES** **KM# Tn1** **Composition:** Iron **Obverse:** Brass and iron **Reverse:** Copper plated **Note:** Similar to KM#Tn1a, thin "50".

| Date | Mintage | F | VF | XF | Unc | BU |
|---|---|---|---|---|---|---|
| 1915 | 512,000 | 3.00 | 6.00 | 12.00 | 35.00 | — |

**FRANKEN** **KM# Tn2** **Composition:** Iron **Obverse:** Brass **Reverse:** Copper plated

| Date | Mintage | F | VF | XF | Unc | BU |
|---|---|---|---|---|---|---|
| 1915 | 370,000 | 5.00 | 8.00 | 15.00 | 40.00 | — |

**FRANKEN** **KM# Tn2a** **Composition:** Iron **Reverse:** 11. 1919 instead of 1.1. 1919

| Date | Mintage | F | VF | XF | Unc | BU |
|---|---|---|---|---|---|---|
| 1915 | Inc. above | 3.75 | 7.50 | 15.00 | 40.00 | — |

**FRANKEN** **KM# Tn3** **Composition:** Gilt Copper **Obverse:** Lion in circle, STAD GENT VILLE DE GAND around **Reverse:** 1915 1 FR in circle, UIT BETAALBAAR 1 JANUARI 1918 REMBOURSABLE 1 JANVIER 1920 along sides of square **Note:** Square. This token was struck in 1920 for the benefit of charity.

| Date | Mintage | F | VF | XF | Unc | BU |
|---|---|---|---|---|---|---|
| 1915 | — | 30.00 | 60.00 | 120 | 250 | — |

**2 FRANKEN** **KM# Tn4** **Composition:** Iron **Obverse:** Brass and iron **Reverse:** Copper plated

| Date | Mintage | F | VF | XF | Unc | BU |
|---|---|---|---|---|---|---|
| 1915 | 314,000 | 5.00 | 10.00 | 20.00 | 50.00 | — |

**2 FRANKEN** KM# Tn5 **Composition:** Gilt Copper **Obverse:** Arms in circle, STAD GENT FIDES ET AMOR around **Reverse:** 1928 2 FRANK in circle, UIT BETAAL BAAR JANUARI 1922 PAX ET LABOR around **Note:** This token was struck in 1920 for the benefit of charity.

| Date | Mintage | F | VF | XF | Unc | BU |
|---|---|---|---|---|---|---|
| 1918 | — | 25.00 | 50.00 | 100 | 200 | — |

**5 FRANKEN** KM# Tn6 **Composition:** Iron **Obverse:** Brass plated **Reverse:** Brass plated

| Date | Mintage | F | VF | XF | Unc | BU |
|---|---|---|---|---|---|---|
| 1917 | 108,000 | 17.50 | 30.00 | 45.00 | 100 | — |

**5 FRANKEN** KM# Tn7 **Composition:** Iron

| Date | Mintage | F | VF | XF | Unc | BU |
|---|---|---|---|---|---|---|
| 1918 | 339,000 | 12.50 | 22.50 | 35.00 | 80.00 | — |

# BELIZE (British Honduras)

Belize, formerly British Honduras, but now an independent member of the British Commonwealth, is situated in Central America south of Mexico and east and north of Guatemala, with an area of 8,867 sq. mi. (22,960 sq. km.) and a population of *242,000. Capital: Belmopan. Tourism now augments Belize's economy, in addition to sugar, citrus fruits, chicle and hardwoods which are exported.

In Dec. 1975, the U.N. General Assembly adopted a resolution supporting the right of the people of Belize to self-determination, and asking Britain and Guatemala to renew their negotiations on the future of Belize. Independence was obtained on Sept. 21, 1981. Elizabeth II is Head of State as Queen of Belize.

**RULERS**

British, until 1981

**MINT MARKS**

H - Birmingham Mint

No mm - Royal Mint

**MONETARY SYSTEM**

**commencing 1864**

100 Cents = 1 Dollar

## BRITISH COLONIAL & CONSTITUTIONAL

### DECIMAL COINAGE

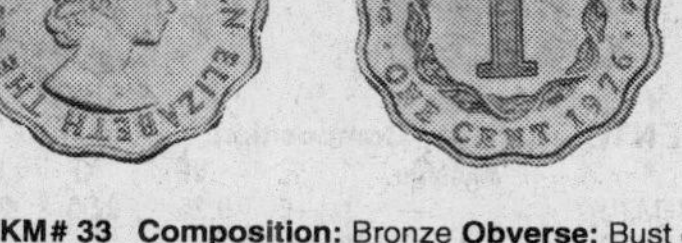

**CENT** KM# 33 **Composition:** Bronze **Obverse:** Bust of Queen Elizabeth right **Reverse:** Denomination within circle **Edge:** Scalloped

| Date | Mintage | F | VF | XF | Unc | BU |
|---|---|---|---|---|---|---|
| 1973 | 400,000 | — | — | 0.10 | 0.25 | — |
| 1974 | 2,000,000 | — | — | 0.10 | 0.20 | — |
| 1975 | Inc. above | — | — | 0.10 | 0.15 | — |
| 1976 | 3,000,000 | — | — | 0.10 | 0.15 | — |

**CENT** KM# 38 **Composition:** Bronze **Reverse:** Swallow-tailed kite

| Date | Mintage | F | VF | XF | Unc | BU |
|---|---|---|---|---|---|---|
| 1974FM (M) | 225,000 | — | — | 0.40 | 0.75 | — |
| 1974FM (P) | 21,000 | Value: 1.25 | | | | |

**CENT** KM# 38a **Weight:** 3.0200 g. **Composition:** 0.9250 Silver .0898 oz. ASW **Reverse:** Swallow-tailed kite

| Date | Mintage | F | VF | XF | Unc | BU |
|---|---|---|---|---|---|---|
| 1974FM (P) | 31,000 | Value: 2.50 | | | | |

**CENT** KM# 46 **Composition:** Bronze **Reverse:** Swallow-tailed kite **Edge:** Scalloped

| Date | Mintage | F | VF | XF | Unc | BU |
|---|---|---|---|---|---|---|
| 1975FM (M) | 118,000 | — | — | 0.10 | 0.75 | — |
| 1975FM (U) | 1,095 | — | — | 0.20 | 1.00 | — |
| 1975FM (P) | 8,794 | Value: 1.00 | | | | |
| 1976FM (M) | 126,000 | — | — | 0.10 | 0.75 | — |
| 1976FM (U) | 759 | — | — | 0.20 | 1.00 | — |
| 1976FM (P) | 4,893 | Value: 1.00 | | | | |

**CENT** KM# 46a **Weight:** 3.0200 g. **Composition:** 0.9250 Silver .0898 oz. ASW **Reverse:** Swallow-tailed kite **Edge:** Scalloped

| Date | Mintage | F | VF | XF | Unc | BU |
|---|---|---|---|---|---|---|
| 1975FM (P) | 13,000 | Value: 2.00 | | | | |
| 1976FM (P) | 5,897 | Value: 2.00 | | | | |
| 1977FM (P) | 3,197 | Value: 2.00 | | | | |
| 1978FM (P) | 3,342 | Value: 2.00 | | | | |
| 1979FM (P) | 2,445 | Value: 2.00 | | | | |
| 1980FM (P) | 1,826 | Value: 2.00 | | | | |
| 1981FM (P) | 615 | Value: 2.50 | | | | |

**CENT** KM# 33a **Composition:** Aluminum **Obverse:** Bust of Queen Elizabeth right **Reverse:** Denomination within circle **Edge:** Scalloped

| Date | Mintage | F | VF | XF | Unc | BU |
|---|---|---|---|---|---|---|
| 1976 | 2,049,999 | — | — | 0.10 | 0.15 | — |
| 1979 | 2,505,000 | — | — | 0.10 | 0.15 | — |
| 1980 | 1,505,000 | — | — | 0.10 | 0.15 | — |
| 1982 | — | — | — | 0.10 | 0.15 | — |
| 1983 | — | — | — | 0.10 | 0.15 | — |
| 1986 | — | — | — | 0.10 | 0.15 | — |
| 1987 | — | — | — | 0.10 | 0.15 | — |
| 1989 | — | — | — | 0.10 | 0.15 | — |
| 1991 | — | — | — | 0.10 | 0.15 | — |
| 1996 | — | — | — | 0.10 | 0.15 | — |

**CENT** KM# 46b **Composition:** Aluminum **Reverse:** Swallow-tailed kite **Edge:** Scalloped

| Date | Mintage | F | VF | XF | Unc | BU |
|---|---|---|---|---|---|---|
| 1977FM (U) | 126,000 | — | — | 0.10 | 0.20 | — |
| 1977FM (P) | 2,107 | Value: 1.00 | | | | |
| 1978FM (U) | 125,000 | — | — | 0.10 | 0.20 | — |
| 1978FM (P) | 1,671 | Value: 1.00 | | | | |
| 1979FM (U) | 808 | — | — | 0.15 | 0.75 | — |
| 1979FM (P) | 1,287 | Value: 1.00 | | | | |
| 1980FM (U) | 761 | — | — | 0.15 | 0.75 | — |
| 1980FM (P) | 920 | Value: 1.00 | | | | |
| 1981FM (U) | 297 | — | — | 0.15 | 0.75 | — |
| 1981FM (P) | 643 | Value: 1.00 | | | | |

**CENT** KM# 83 **Composition:** Aluminum **Reverse:** Swallow-tailed kite **Edge:** Scalloped

| Date | Mintage | F | VF | XF | Unc | BU |
|---|---|---|---|---|---|---|
| 1982FM (U) | — | — | 0.15 | 0.25 | 1.50 | — |
| 1982FM (P) | — | Value: 2.00 | | | | |
| 1983FM (U) | — | — | 0.15 | 0.25 | 1.50 | — |
| 1983FM (P) | — | Value: 2.00 | | | | |

**CENT** KM# 83a **Weight:** 3.0200 g. **Composition:** 0.9250 Silver .0898 oz. ASW **Reverse:** Swallow-tailed kite **Edge:** Scalloped

| Date | Mintage | F | VF | XF | Unc | BU |
|---|---|---|---|---|---|---|
| 1982FM (P) | 381 | Value: 6.50 | | | | |
| 1983FM (P) | 336 | Value: 6.50 | | | | |

**CENT** KM# 90 **Composition:** Aluminum **Reverse:** Swallow-tailed kite **Edge:** Scalloped

| Date | Mintage | F | VF | XF | Unc | BU |
|---|---|---|---|---|---|---|
| 1984FM (U) | — | — | 0.15 | 0.25 | 1.50 | — |
| 1984FM (P) | — | Value: 2.00 | | | | |

**CENT** KM# 90a **Weight:** 3.0200 g. **Composition:** 0.9250 Silver .0898 oz. ASW **Reverse:** Swallow-tailed kite **Edge:** Scalloped

| Date | Mintage | F | VF | XF | Unc | BU |
|---|---|---|---|---|---|---|
| 1984FM (P) | — | Value: 6.50 | | | | |
| 1985 Proof | 212 | Value: 7.50 | | | | |

**CENT** KM# 114 **Composition:** Aluminum **Obverse:** New portrait of Queen Elizabeth II.

| Date | Mintage | F | VF | XF | Unc | BU |
|---|---|---|---|---|---|---|
| 1992 | — | — | — | 0.10 | 0.15 | — |
| 1994 | — | — | — | 0.10 | 0.15 | — |
| 1996 | — | — | — | 0.10 | 0.15 | — |

**5 CENTS** **KM# 34** **Composition:** Nickel-Brass **Obverse:** Bust of Queen Elizabeth II right **Reverse:** Denomination within circle

| Date | Mintage | F | VF | XF | Unc | BU |
|---|---|---|---|---|---|---|
| 1973 | 210,000 | — | — | 0.50 | 1.00 | — |
| 1974 | 210,000 | — | — | 0.50 | 1.00 | — |
| 1975 | 420,000 | — | — | 0.15 | 0.40 | — |
| 1976 | 570,000 | — | — | 0.15 | 0.40 | — |
| 1979 | — | — | — | 0.15 | 0.40 | — |

**5 CENTS** **KM# 39** **Composition:** Nickel-Brass **Reverse:** Fork-tailed flycatcher

| Date | Mintage | F | VF | XF | Unc | BU |
|---|---|---|---|---|---|---|
| 1974FM (M) | 50,000 | — | — | 0.25 | 1.25 | — |
| 1974FM (P) | 21,000 | Value: 1.50 | | | | |

**5 CENTS** **KM# 39a** **Weight:** 4.3500 g. **Composition:** 0.9250 Silver .1293 oz. ASW **Reverse:** Fork-tailed flycatcher

| Date | Mintage | F | VF | XF | Unc | BU |
|---|---|---|---|---|---|---|
| 1974FM (P) | 31,000 | Value: 3.00 | | | | |

**5 CENTS** **KM# 47** **Composition:** Nickel-Brass **Reverse:** Fork-tailed flycatcher

| Date | Mintage | F | VF | XF | Unc | BU |
|---|---|---|---|---|---|---|
| 1975FM (M) | 24,000 | — | — | 0.25 | 1.50 | — |
| 1975FM (U) | 1,095 | — | — | 0.25 | 1.50 | — |
| 1975FM (P) | 8,794 | Value: 1.25 | | | | |
| 1976FM (M) | 25,000 | — | — | 0.25 | 1.50 | — |
| 1976FM (U) | 759 | — | — | 0.25 | 1.50 | — |
| 1976FM (P) | 4,893 | Value: 1.25 | | | | |

**5 CENTS** **KM# 47a** **Weight:** 4.3500 g. **Composition:** 0.9250 Silver .1293 oz. ASW **Reverse:** Fork-tailed flycatcher

| Date | Mintage | F | VF | XF | Unc | BU |
|---|---|---|---|---|---|---|
| 1975FM (P) | 13,000 | Value: 2.50 | | | | |
| 1976FM (P) | 5,897 | Value: 2.50 | | | | |
| 1977FM (P) | 3,197 | Value: 2.50 | | | | |
| 1978FM (P) | 3,342 | Value: 2.50 | | | | |
| 1979FM (P) | 2,445 | Value: 2.50 | | | | |
| 1980FM (P) | 1,826 | Value: 2.50 | | | | |
| 1981FM (P) | 615 | Value: 3.00 | | | | |

**5 CENTS** **KM# 34a** **Composition:** Aluminum **Obverse:** Bust of Queen Elizabeth II right **Reverse:** Denomination within circle

| Date | Mintage | F | VF | XF | Unc | BU |
|---|---|---|---|---|---|---|
| 1976 | 1,000,000 | — | — | 0.10 | 0.25 | — |
| 1979 | 960,000 | — | — | 0.10 | 0.25 | — |
| 1980 | 1,040,000 | — | — | 0.10 | 0.25 | — |
| 1986 | — | — | — | 0.10 | 0.25 | — |
| 1987 | — | — | — | 0.10 | 0.25 | — |
| 1989 | — | — | — | 0.10 | 0.25 | — |
| 1991 | — | — | — | 0.10 | 0.25 | — |
| 1992 | — | — | — | 0.10 | 0.25 | — |
| 1993 | — | — | — | 0.10 | 0.25 | — |
| 1994 | — | — | — | 0.10 | 0.25 | — |

**5 CENTS** **KM# 47b** **Composition:** Aluminum **Reverse:** Fork-tailed flycatcher

| Date | Mintage | F | VF | XF | Unc | BU |
|---|---|---|---|---|---|---|
| 1977FM (U) | 26,000 | — | — | 0.10 | 0.50 | — |
| 1977FM (P) | 2,107 | Value: 1.50 | | | | |
| 1978FM (U) | 25,000 | — | — | 0.10 | 0.50 | — |
| 1978FM (P) | 1,671 | Value: 1.50 | | | | |
| 1979FM (U) | 808 | — | — | 0.15 | 0.75 | — |
| 1979FM (P) | 1,287 | — | — | 0.25 | 1.75 | — |
| 1980FM (U) | 761 | — | — | 0.15 | 0.75 | — |
| 1980FM (P) | 920 | Value: 1.75 | | | | |
| 1981FM (U) | 297 | — | — | 0.15 | 0.75 | — |
| 1981FM (P) | 643 | Value: 1.75 | | | | |

**5 CENTS** **KM# 64** **Composition:** Aluminum **Series:** World Food Day **Obverse:** Bust of Queen Elizabeth right **Reverse:** Denomination

| Date | Mintage | F | VF | XF | Unc | BU |
|---|---|---|---|---|---|---|
| 1981 | — | — | — | 0.10 | 0.35 | — |

**5 CENTS** **KM# 84** **Composition:** Aluminum **Reverse:** Fork-tailed flycatcher

| Date | Mintage | F | VF | XF | Unc | BU |
|---|---|---|---|---|---|---|
| 1982FM (U) | — | — | 0.15 | 0.35 | 1.50 | — |
| 1982FM (P) | — | Value: 2.50 | | | | |
| 1983FM (U) | — | — | 0.15 | 0.35 | 1.50 | — |
| 1983FM (P) | — | Value: 2.50 | | | | |

**5 CENTS** **KM# 84a** **Weight:** 4.3500 g. **Composition:** 0.9250 Silver .1293 oz. ASW **Reverse:** Fork-tailed flycatcher

| Date | Mintage | F | VF | XF | Unc | BU |
|---|---|---|---|---|---|---|
| 1982FM (P) | 381 | Value: 12.00 | | | | |
| 1983FM (P) | 479 | Value: 12.00 | | | | |

**5 CENTS** **KM# 91** **Composition:** Aluminum

| Date | Mintage | F | VF | XF | Unc | BU |
|---|---|---|---|---|---|---|
| 1984FM (U) | — | — | 0.25 | 0.50 | 2.00 | — |
| 1984FM (P) | — | Value: 2.50 | | | | |

**5 CENTS** **KM# 91a** **Weight:** 4.3500 g. **Composition:** 0.9250 Silver .1293 oz. ASW

| Date | Mintage | F | VF | XF | Unc | BU |
|---|---|---|---|---|---|---|
| 1984FM (P) | — | Value: 12.00 | | | | |
| 1985 | 212 | Value: 13.50 | | | | |

**5 CENTS** **KM# 115** **Composition:** Aluminum

| Date | Mintage | F | VF | XF | Unc | BU |
|---|---|---|---|---|---|---|
| 1992 | — | — | — | 0.10 | 0.20 | — |
| 1993 | — | — | — | 0.10 | 0.20 | — |

**10 CENTS** **KM# 35** **Composition:** Copper-Nickel **Obverse:** Bust of Queen Elizabeth right **Reverse:** Denomination within circle

| Date | Mintage | F | VF | XF | Unc | BU |
|---|---|---|---|---|---|---|
| 1974 | 100,000 | — | 0.15 | 0.35 | 0.60 | — |
| 1975 | 200,000 | — | 0.10 | 0.25 | 0.50 | — |
| 1976 | 700,000 | — | 0.10 | 0.20 | 0.45 | — |
| 1979 | 800,000 | — | 0.10 | 0.20 | 0.40 | — |
| 1980 | — | — | 0.10 | 0.20 | 0.40 | — |
| 1981 | — | — | 0.10 | 0.20 | 0.40 | — |
| 1992 | — | — | 0.10 | 0.20 | 0.40 | — |

**10 CENTS** **KM# 40** **Composition:** Copper-Nickel **Reverse:** Long-tailed hermit

| Date | Mintage | F | VF | XF | Unc | BU |
|---|---|---|---|---|---|---|
| 1974FM (M) | 27,000 | — | — | 0.50 | 2.00 | — |
| 1974FM (P) | 21,000 | Value: 1.75 | | | | |

**10 CENTS** **KM# 40a** **Weight:** 2.7900 g. **Composition:** 0.9250 Silver .0829 oz. ASW **Reverse:** Long-tailed hermit

| Date | Mintage | F | VF | XF | Unc | BU |
|---|---|---|---|---|---|---|
| 1974FM (P) | 31,000 | Value: 3.50 | | | | |

**10 CENTS** **KM# 48** **Composition:** Copper-Nickel **Reverse:** Long-tailed hermit

| Date | Mintage | F | VF | XF | Unc | BU |
|---|---|---|---|---|---|---|
| 1975FM (M) | 12,000 | — | — | 0.25 | 1.50 | — |
| 1975FM (U) | 1,095 | — | — | 0.30 | 2.00 | — |
| 1975FM (P) | 8,794 | Value: 1.50 | | | | |
| 1976FM (M) | 13,000 | — | — | 0.25 | 1.50 | — |
| 1976FM (U) | 759 | — | — | 0.35 | 2.50 | — |
| 1976FM (P) | 4,893 | Value: 1.50 | | | | |
| 1977FM (U) | 14,000 | — | — | 0.25 | 1.50 | — |
| 1977FM (P) | 2,107 | Value: 2.00 | | | | |
| 1978FM (U) | 13,000 | — | — | 0.25 | 1.50 | — |
| 1978FM (P) | 1,671 | Value: 2.00 | | | | |
| 1979FM (U) | 808 | — | — | 0.25 | 1.50 | — |
| 1979FM (P) | 1,287 | Value: 2.50 | | | | |
| 1980FM (U) | 761 | — | — | 0.25 | 1.50 | — |
| 1980FM (P) | 920 | Value: 2.50 | | | | |
| 1981FM (U) | 297 | — | — | 0.25 | 1.50 | — |
| 1981FM (P) | 643 | Value: 2.50 | | | | |

**10 CENTS** **KM# 48a** **Weight:** 2.7900 g. **Composition:** 0.9250 Silver .0829 oz. ASW **Reverse:** Long-tailed hermit

| Date | Mintage | F | VF | XF | Unc | BU |
|---|---|---|---|---|---|---|
| 1975FM (P) | 13,000 | Value: 3.00 | | | | |
| 1976FM (P) | 5,897 | Value: 3.00 | | | | |
| 1977FM (P) | 3,197 | Value: 3.00 | | | | |
| 1978FM (P) | 3,342 | Value: 3.00 | | | | |
| 1979FM (P) | 2,445 | Value: 3.00 | | | | |
| 1980FM (P) | 1,826 | Value: 3.00 | | | | |
| 1981FM (P) | 615 | Value: 4.00 | | | | |

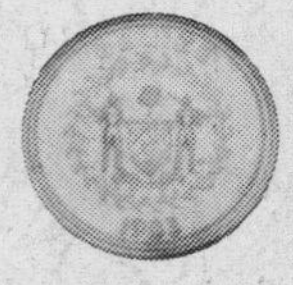
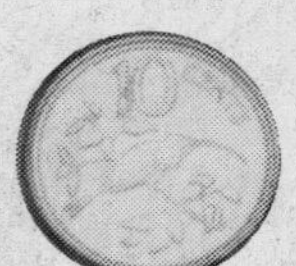

**10 CENTS** **KM# 85** **Composition:** Copper-Nickel **Reverse:** Long-tailed hermit

| Date | Mintage | F | VF | XF | Unc | BU |
|---|---|---|---|---|---|---|
| 1982FM (U) | — | — | 0.25 | 0.50 | 2.50 | — |
| 1982FM (P) | — | Value: 3.50 | | | | |
| 1983FM (U) | — | — | 0.25 | 0.50 | 2.50 | — |
| 1983FM (P) | — | Value: 3.50 | | | | |

**10 CENTS** **KM# 85a** **Weight:** 2.7900 g. **Composition:** 0.9250 Silver .0829 oz. ASW **Reverse:** Long-tailed hermit

| Date | Mintage | F | VF | XF | Unc | BU |
|---|---|---|---|---|---|---|
| 1982FM (P) | 381 | Value: 13.50 | | | | |
| 1983FM (P) | 312 | Value: 13.50 | | | | |

**10 CENTS** **KM# 92** **Composition:** Copper-Nickel **Reverse:** Long-tailed hermit

| Date | Mintage | F | VF | XF | Unc | BU |
|---|---|---|---|---|---|---|
| 1984FM (U) | — | — | 0.25 | 0.50 | 2.50 | — |
| 1984FM (P) | — | Value: 3.50 | | | | |

**10 CENTS** **KM# 92a** **Weight:** 2.7900 g. **Composition:** 0.9250 Silver .0829 oz. ASW **Reverse:** Long-tailed hermit

| Date | Mintage | F | VF | XF | Unc | BU |
|---|---|---|---|---|---|---|
| 1984FM (P) Proof | — | Value: 13.50 | | | | |
| 1985 Proof | 212 | Value: 15.50 | | | | |

**10 CENTS** **KM# 116** **Composition:** Copper-Nickel **Obverse:** New portrait of Queen Elizabeth II.

| Date | Mintage | F | VF | XF | Unc | BU |
|---|---|---|---|---|---|---|
| 1992 | — | — | — | 0.15 | 0.40 | — |

**25 CENTS** **KM# 36** **Composition:** Copper-Nickel **Obverse:** Bust of Queen Elizabeth right **Reverse:** Denomination within circle

| Date | Mintage | F | VF | XF | Unc | BU |
|---|---|---|---|---|---|---|
| 1974 | 100,000 | — | 0.35 | 0.65 | 1.25 | — |
| 1975 | 200,000 | — | 0.20 | 0.35 | 0.75 | — |
| 1976 | 790,000 | — | 0.20 | 0.35 | 0.75 | — |
| 1979 | 500,000 | — | 0.20 | 0.35 | 0.75 | — |
| 1980 | — | — | 0.20 | 0.35 | 0.75 | — |
| 1981 | — | — | 0.20 | 0.35 | 0.75 | — |
| 1986 | — | — | 0.20 | 0.35 | 0.75 | — |
| 1987 | — | — | 0.20 | 0.35 | 0.75 | — |
| 1988 | — | — | 0.20 | 0.35 | 0.75 | — |
| 1989 | — | — | 0.20 | 0.35 | 0.75 | — |
| 1991 | — | — | 0.20 | 0.35 | 0.75 | — |
| 1992 | — | — | 0.20 | 0.35 | 0.75 | — |
| 1993 | — | — | 0.20 | 0.35 | 0.75 | — |
| 1994 | — | — | 0.20 | 0.35 | 0.75 | — |

**25 CENTS** **KM# 41** **Composition:** Copper-Nickel **Reverse:** Blue-crowned motmot

| Date | Mintage | F | VF | XF | Unc | BU |
|---|---|---|---|---|---|---|
| 1974FM (M) | 13,000 | — | — | 1.00 | 3.50 | — |
| 1974FM (P) | 21,000 | Value: 2.50 | | | | |

**25 CENTS** **KM# 41a** **Weight:** 6.6000 g. **Composition:** 0.9250 Silver .1962 oz. ASW **Reverse:** Blue-crowned motmot

| Date | Mintage | F | VF | XF | Unc | BU |
|---|---|---|---|---|---|---|
| 1974FM (P) | 31,000 | Value: 5.00 | | | | |

**25 CENTS** **KM# 49** **Composition:** Copper-Nickel **Reverse:** Blue-crowned motmot

| Date | Mintage | F | VF | XF | Unc | BU |
|---|---|---|---|---|---|---|
| 1975FM (M) | 4,716 | — | — | 0.40 | 3.00 | — |
| 1975FM (U) | 1,095 | — | — | 0.40 | 3.00 | — |
| 1975FM (P) | 8,794 | Value: 2.50 | | | | |
| 1976FM (M) | 5,000 | — | — | 0.50 | 4.00 | — |
| 1976FM (U) | 759 | — | — | 0.45 | 3.50 | — |
| 1976FM (P) | 4,893 | Value: 2.50 | | | | |
| 1977FM (U) | 5,520 | — | — | 0.30 | 2.00 | — |
| 1977FM (P) | 2,107 | Value: 2.75 | | | | |
| 1978FM (U) | 5,458 | — | — | 0.30 | 2.00 | — |
| 1978FM (P) | 1,671 | Value: 2.75 | | | | |
| 1979FM (U) | 808 | — | — | 0.40 | 3.00 | — |
| 1979FM (P) | 1,287 | Value: 3.00 | | | | |
| 1980FM (U) | 761 | — | — | 0.40 | 3.00 | — |
| 1980FM (P) | 920 | Value: 3.00 | | | | |
| 1981FM (U) | 297 | — | — | 0.40 | 3.00 | — |
| 1981FM (P) | 643 | Value: 3.00 | | | | |

**25 CENTS** **KM# 49a** **Weight:** 6.6000 g. **Composition:** 0.9250 Silver .1962 oz. ASW **Reverse:** Blue-crowned motmot

| Date | Mintage | F | VF | XF | Unc | BU |
|---|---|---|---|---|---|---|
| 1975FM (P) | 13,000 | Value: 3.50 | | | | |
| 1976FM (P) | 5,897 | Value: 3.50 | | | | |
| 1977FM (P) | 3,197 | Value: 3.50 | | | | |
| 1978FM (P) | 3,342 | Value: 3.50 | | | | |
| 1979FM (P) | 2,445 | Value: 3.50 | | | | |
| 1980FM (P) | 1,826 | Value: 3.50 | | | | |
| 1981FM (P) | 615 | Value: 5.00 | | | | |

**25 CENTS** **KM# 86** **Composition:** Copper-Nickel **Reverse:** Blue-crowned motmot

| Date | Mintage | F | VF | XF | Unc | BU |
|---|---|---|---|---|---|---|
| 1982FM (U) | — | — | 0.50 | 1.00 | 4.00 | — |
| 1982FM (P) | — | Value: 5.00 | | | | |
| 1983FM (U) | — | — | 0.50 | 1.00 | 4.00 | — |
| 1983FM (P) | — | Value: 5.00 | | | | |

**25 CENTS** **KM# 86a** **Weight:** 6.6000 g. **Composition:** 0.9250 Silver .1962 oz. ASW **Reverse:** Blue-crowned motmot

| Date | Mintage | F | VF | XF | Unc | BU |
|---|---|---|---|---|---|---|
| 1982FM (P) | 381 | Value: 18.50 | | | | |
| 1983FM (P) | 314 | Value: 18.50 | | | | |

**25 CENTS** **KM# 93** **Composition:** Copper-Nickel **Reverse:** Blue-crowned motmot

| Date | Mintage | F | VF | XF | Unc | BU |
|---|---|---|---|---|---|---|
| 1984FM (U) | — | — | 0.50 | 1.00 | 4.00 | — |
| 1984FM (P) | — | Value: 5.00 | | | | |

**25 CENTS** **KM# 93a** **Weight:** 6.6000 g. **Composition:** 0.9250 Silver .1962 oz. ASW **Reverse:** Blue-crowned motmot

| Date | Mintage | F | VF | XF | Unc | BU |
|---|---|---|---|---|---|---|
| 1984FM (P) | — | Value: 18.50 | | | | |
| 1985 Proof | 212 | Value: 22.50 | | | | |

**25 CENTS** **KM# 77** **Composition:** Copper-Nickel **Subject:** World Forestry Congress **Obverse:** Bust of Queen Elizabeth right **Reverse:** Denomination

| Date | Mintage | F | VF | XF | Unc | BU |
|---|---|---|---|---|---|---|
| 1985 | — | — | 0.25 | 0.40 | 0.85 | — |

**25 CENTS** **KM# 117** **Composition:** Copper-Nickel **Obverse:** New portrait of Queen Elizabeth II.

| Date | Mintage | F | VF | XF | Unc | BU |
|---|---|---|---|---|---|---|
| 1991 | — | — | 0.20 | 0.35 | 0.75 | — |
| 1992 | — | — | 0.20 | 0.35 | 0.75 | — |
| 1993 | — | — | 0.20 | 0.35 | 0.75 | — |

**50 CENTS** **KM# 37** **Composition:** Copper-Nickel **Obverse:** Bust of Queen Elizabeth right **Reverse:** Denomination within circle

| Date | Mintage | F | VF | XF | Unc | BU |
|---|---|---|---|---|---|---|
| 1974 | 123,000 | — | 0.50 | 1.50 | 3.00 | — |
| 1975 | Inc. above | — | 0.40 | 0.75 | 2.00 | — |
| 1976 | 312,000 | — | 0.40 | 0.75 | 2.00 | — |
| 1979 | 125,000 | — | 0.50 | 1.50 | 3.00 | — |
| 1980 | — | — | 0.40 | 0.75 | 1.75 | — |
| 1989 | — | — | 0.40 | 0.75 | 1.75 | — |
| 1991 | — | — | 0.40 | 0.75 | 1.75 | — |
| 1992 | — | — | 0.40 | 0.75 | 1.75 | — |
| 1993 | — | — | 0.40 | 0.75 | 1.75 | — |

**50 CENTS** **KM# 42** **Composition:** Copper-Nickel **Reverse:** Frigate bird

| Date | Mintage | F | VF | XF | Unc | BU |
|---|---|---|---|---|---|---|
| 1974FM (M) | 8,806 | — | — | 0.40 | 4.00 | — |
| 1974FM (P) | 21,000 | Value: 3.50 | | | | |

**50 CENTS** **KM# 42a** **Weight:** 9.9400 g. **Composition:** 0.9250 Silver .3197 oz. ASW **Reverse:** Frigate bird

| Date | Mintage | F | VF | XF | Unc | BU |
|---|---|---|---|---|---|---|
| 1974FM (P) | 31,000 | Value: 7.50 | | | | |

**50 CENTS** **KM# 50** **Composition:** Copper-Nickel **Reverse:** Frigate bird

| Date | Mintage | F | VF | XF | Unc | BU |
|---|---|---|---|---|---|---|
| 1975FM (M) | 2,358 | — | — | 0.65 | 6.00 | — |
| 1975FM (U) | 1,095 | — | — | 0.45 | 4.50 | — |
| 1975FM (P) | 8,794 | Value: 4.00 | | | | |
| 1976FM (M) | 3,259 | — | — | 0.55 | 5.00 | — |
| 1976FM (U) | 759 | — | — | 0.55 | 5.00 | — |
| 1976FM (P) | 4,893 | Value: 4.00 | | | | |
| 1977FM (U) | 3,540 | — | — | 0.45 | 4.00 | — |
| 1977FM (P) | 2,107 | Value: 4.00 | | | | |
| 1978FM (U) | 2,958 | — | — | 0.45 | 4.00 | — |
| 1978FM (P) | 1,671 | Value: 4.00 | | | | |
| 1979FM (U) | 808 | — | — | 0.55 | 5.00 | — |
| 1979FM (P) | 1,287 | Value: 4.00 | | | | |
| 1980FM (U) | 761 | — | — | 0.55 | 5.00 | — |
| 1980FM (P) | 920 | Value: 5.00 | | | | |
| 1981FM (U) | 297 | — | — | 0.55 | 5.00 | — |
| 1981FM (P) | 643 | Value: 5.00 | | | | |

**50 CENTS** **KM# 50a** **Weight:** 9.9400 g. **Composition:** 0.9250 Silver .3197 oz. ASW **Reverse:** Frigate bird

| Date | Mintage | F | VF | XF | Unc | BU |
|---|---|---|---|---|---|---|
| 1975FM (P) | 13,000 | Value: 6.50 | | | | |
| 1976FM (P) | 5,897 | Value: 6.50 | | | | |
| 1977FM (P) | 3,197 | Value: 6.50 | | | | |
| 1978FM (P) | 3,342 | Value: 6.50 | | | | |
| 1979FM (P) | 2,445 | Value: 6.50 | | | | |
| 1980FM (P) | 1,826 | Value: 6.50 | | | | |
| 1981FM (P) | 615 | Value: 8.50 | | | | |

**50 CENTS** **KM# 87** **Composition:** Copper-Nickel **Reverse:** Frigate bird

| Date | Mintage | F | VF | XF | Unc | BU |
|---|---|---|---|---|---|---|
| 1982FM (U) | — | — | 0.75 | 1.50 | 6.50 | — |
| 1982FM (P) | — | Value: 7.50 | | | | |
| 1983FM (U) | — | — | 0.75 | 1.50 | 6.50 | — |
| 1983FM (P) | — | Value: 7.50 | | | | |

**50 CENTS** **KM# 87a** **Weight:** 9.9400 g. **Composition:** 0.9250 Silver .3197 oz. ASW **Reverse:** Frigate bird

| Date | Mintage | F | VF | XF | Unc | BU |
|---|---|---|---|---|---|---|
| 1982FM (P) | 381 | Value: 27.50 | | | | |
| 1983FM (P) | 312 | Value: 27.50 | | | | |

**50 CENTS** **KM# 94** **Composition:** Copper-Nickel **Reverse:** Frigate bird

| Date | Mintage | F | VF | XF | Unc | BU |
|---|---|---|---|---|---|---|
| 1984FM (U) | — | — | 0.75 | 1.50 | 6.50 | — |
| 1984FM (P) | — | Value: 7.50 | | | | |

**50 CENTS** **KM# 94a** **Weight:** 9.9400 g. **Composition:** 0.9250 Silver .3197 oz. ASW **Reverse:** Frigate bird

| Date | Mintage | F | VF | XF | Unc | BU |
|---|---|---|---|---|---|---|
| 1984FM (P) | — | Value: 27.50 | | | | |
| 1985 Proof | 212 | Value: 32.50 | | | | |

**50 CENTS** **KM# 118** **Composition:** Copper-Nickel **Obverse:** New portrait of Queen Elizabeth II.

| Date | Mintage | F | VF | XF | Unc | BU |
|---|---|---|---|---|---|---|
| 1992 | — | — | 0.40 | 0.75 | 1.75 | — |
| 1993 | — | — | 0.40 | 0.75 | 1.75 | — |

**DOLLAR** **KM# 43** **Composition:** Copper-Nickel **Reverse:** Scarlet macaw

| Date | Mintage | F | VF | XF | Unc | BU |
|---|---|---|---|---|---|---|
| 1974FM (M) | 6,656 | — | — | 1.00 | 5.00 | — |
| 1974FM (P) | 21,000 | Value: 5.00 | | | | |
| 1975FM (M) | 1,182 | — | — | 1.50 | 8.00 | — |
| 1975FM (U) | 1,095 | — | — | 0.75 | 5.00 | — |
| 1975FM (P) | 8,794 | Value: 5.00 | | | | |
| 1976FM (M) | 1,250 | — | — | 1.50 | 8.00 | — |
| 1976FM (U) | 759 | — | — | 1.25 | 6.00 | — |
| 1976FM (P) | 4,893 | Value: 5.00 | | | | |
| 1977FM (U) | 1,770 | — | — | 1.00 | 5.00 | — |
| 1977FM (P) | 2,107 | Value: 6.00 | | | | |
| 1978FM (U) | 1,708 | — | — | 1.00 | 5.00 | — |
| 1978FM (P) | 1,671 | Value: 6.00 | | | | |
| 1979FM (U) | 808 | — | — | 1.25 | 5.50 | — |
| 1979FM (P) | 1,287 | Value: 6.00 | | | | |
| 1980FM (U) | 761 | — | — | 1.25 | 5.50 | — |
| 1980FM (P) | 920 | Value: 6.00 | | | | |
| 1981FM (U) | 297 | — | — | 1.50 | 7.50 | — |
| 1981FM (P) | 643 | Value: 8.50 | | | | |

**DOLLAR** **KM# 43a** **Weight:** 19.8900 g. **Composition:** 0.9250 Silver .5915 oz. ASW **Reverse:** Scarlet macaw

| Date | Mintage | F | VF | XF | Unc | BU |
|---|---|---|---|---|---|---|
| 1974FM (P) | 31,000 | Value: 9.00 | | | | |
| 1975FM (P) | 13,000 | Value: 9.00 | | | | |
| 1976FM (P) | 5,897 | Value: 10.00 | | | | |
| 1977FM (P) | 3,197 | Value: 10.00 | | | | |
| 1978FM (P) | 3,342 | Value: 10.00 | | | | |
| 1979FM (P) | 2,445 | Value: 10.00 | | | | |
| 1980FM (P) | 1,826 | Value: 10.00 | | | | |
| 1981FM (P) | 615 | Value: 12.50 | | | | |

**DOLLAR** **KM# 88** **Composition:** Copper-Nickel **Reverse:** Scarlet macaw

| Date | Mintage | F | VF | XF | Unc | BU |
|---|---|---|---|---|---|---|
| 1982FM (U) | — | — | 1.50 | 3.00 | 7.50 | — |
| 1982FM (P) | — | Value: 8.50 | | | | |
| 1983FM (U) | — | — | 1.50 | 3.00 | 7.50 | — |
| 1983FM (P) | — | Value: 8.50 | | | | |

**DOLLAR** **KM# 88a** **Weight:** 19.8900 g. **Composition:** 0.9250 Silver .5915 oz. ASW **Reverse:** Scarlet macaw

| Date | Mintage | F | VF | XF | Unc | BU |
|---|---|---|---|---|---|---|
| 1982FM (P) | 381 | Value: 37.50 | | | | |
| 1983FM (P) | 1,589 | Value: 37.50 | | | | |

**DOLLAR** **KM# 95** **Composition:** Copper-Nickel **Reverse:** Scarlet macaw

| Date | Mintage | F | VF | XF | Unc | BU |
|---|---|---|---|---|---|---|
| 1984FM (U) | — | — | 1.50 | 3.00 | 7.50 | — |
| 1984FM (P) | — | Value: 8.50 | | | | |

**DOLLAR** **KM# 95a** **Weight:** 19.8900 g. **Composition:** 0.9250 Silver .5915 oz. ASW **Reverse:** Scarlet macaw

| Date | Mintage | F | VF | XF | Unc | BU |
|---|---|---|---|---|---|---|
| 1984FM (P) | — | Value: 37.50 | | | | |
| 1985 Proof | 212 | Value: 45.00 | | | | |

**DOLLAR** **KM# 99** **Composition:** Nickel-Brass **Reverse:** Columbus' three ships

| Date | Mintage | F | VF | XF | Unc | BU |
|---|---|---|---|---|---|---|
| 1990 | — | — | — | — | 2.25 | — |
| 1991 | — | — | — | — | 2.25 | — |
| 1992 | — | — | — | — | 2.25 | — |

**DOLLAR** **KM# 99a** **Weight:** 9.0000 g. **Composition:** 0.9250 Silver .2676 oz. ASW **Reverse:** Columbus' three ships

| Date | Mintage | F | VF | XF | Unc | BU |
|---|---|---|---|---|---|---|
| 1990 Proof | Est. 5,000 | Value: 32.50 | | | | |

**2 DOLLARS** **KM# 100** **Composition:** Copper-Nickel **Subject:** Queen Mother's 90th birthday

| Date | Mintage | F | VF | XF | Unc | BU |
|---|---|---|---|---|---|---|
| ND(1990) | — | — | — | — | 6.00 | — |

**2 DOLLARS** **KM# 100a** **Weight:** 28.2800 g. **Composition:** 0.9250 Silver .8411 oz. ASW **Subject:** Queen Mother's 90th birthday

| Date | Mintage | F | VF | XF | Unc | BU |
|---|---|---|---|---|---|---|
| ND(1990) Proof | Est. 10,000 | Value: 45.00 | | | | |

**2 DOLLARS** **KM# 119** **Weight:** 28.2800 g. **Composition:** 0.9250 Silver .8411 oz. ASW **Subject:** 40th anniversary - coronation of Queen Elizabeth II

| Date | Mintage | F | VF | XF | Unc | BU |
|---|---|---|---|---|---|---|
| ND(1993) Proof | Est. 10,000 | Value: 45.00 | | | | |

**2 DOLLARS** **KM# 131** **Composition:** Copper-Nickel **Subject:** Battle of St. George's Caye **Obverse:** National arms **Reverse:** Oar-powered landing craft shorebound

| Date | Mintage | F | VF | XF | Unc | BU |
|---|---|---|---|---|---|---|
| ND(1998) | — | — | — | — | 5.00 | — |

**2 DOLLARS** **KM# 132** **Weight:** 28.2800 g. **Composition:** 0.9250 Silver .8410 oz. ASW **Subject:** Heritage Protection **Obverse:** National arms. **Reverse:** Large building, people, leopard and arms. **Edge:** Reeded. **Size:** 38.6 mm.

| Date | Mintage | F | VF | XF | Unc | BU |
|---|---|---|---|---|---|---|
| 1998 Proof | 5,000 | Value: 55.00 | | | | |

**5 DOLLARS** **KM# 44** **Composition:** Copper-Nickel **Reverse:** Keel-billed toucan

| Date | Mintage | F | VF | XF | Unc | BU |
|---|---|---|---|---|---|---|
| 1974FM (M) | 4,936 | — | — | 2.75 | 5.00 | — |
| 1974FM (P) | 21,000 | Value: 6.50 | | | | |
| 1975FM (M) | 237 | — | — | 5.00 | 22.50 | — |
| 1975FM (U) | 1,095 | — | — | 2.75 | 5.00 | — |
| 1975FM (P) | 8,794 | Value: 6.50 | | | | |
| 1976FM (M) | 250 | — | — | 5.00 | 20.00 | — |
| 1976FM (U) | 759 | — | — | 2.75 | 5.00 | — |
| 1976FM (P) | 4,893 | Value: 6.50 | | | | |
| 1977FM (U) | 720 | — | — | 2.75 | 6.50 | — |
| 1977FM (P) | 2,107 | Value: 7.50 | | | | |
| 1978FM (U) | 708 | — | — | 2.75 | 6.50 | — |
| 1978FM (P) | 1,671 | Value: 7.50 | | | | |
| 1979FM (U) | 808 | — | — | 2.75 | 5.00 | — |
| 1979FM (P) | 1,287 | Value: 7.50 | | | | |
| 1980FM (U) | 761 | — | — | 2.75 | 5.00 | — |
| 1980FM (P) | 920 | Value: 7.50 | | | | |
| 1981FM (U) | 297 | — | — | 2.75 | 6.50 | — |
| 1981FM (P) | 643 | Value: 8.50 | | | | |

**5 DOLLARS** **KM# 44a** **Weight:** 26.4000 g. **Composition:** 0.9250 Silver .7851 oz. ASW **Reverse:** Keel-billed toucan

| Date | Mintage | F | VF | XF | Unc | BU |
|---|---|---|---|---|---|---|
| 1974FM (P) | 31,000 | Value: 8.50 | | | | |
| 1975FM (P) | 13,000 | Value: 9.00 | | | | |
| 1976FM (P) | 5,897 | Value: 11.50 | | | | |
| 1977FM (P) | 3,197 | Value: 11.50 | | | | |
| 1978FM (P) | 3,342 | Value: 11.50 | | | | |
| 1979FM (P) | 2,445 | Value: 11.50 | | | | |
| 1980FM (P) | 1,826 | Value: 11.50 | | | | |
| 1981FM (P) | 615 | Value: 16.00 | | | | |

**5 DOLLARS** **KM# 89** **Composition:** Copper-Nickel **Reverse:** Keel-billed toucan

| Date | Mintage | F | VF | XF | Unc | BU |
|---|---|---|---|---|---|---|
| 1982FM (U) | — | — | 2.00 | 4.00 | 12.00 | — |
| 1982FM (P) | — | Value: 15.00 | | | | |
| 1983FM (U) | — | — | 2.00 | 4.00 | 12.00 | — |
| 1983FM (P) | — | Value: 15.00 | | | | |

**5 DOLLARS** **KM# 89a** **Weight:** 26.4000 g. **Composition:** 0.9250 Silver .7851 oz. ASW **Reverse:** Keel-billed toucan

| Date | Mintage | F | VF | XF | Unc | BU |
|---|---|---|---|---|---|---|
| 1982FM (P) | 381 | Value: 50.00 | | | | |
| 1983FM (P) | 311 | Value: 50.00 | | | | |

**5 DOLLARS** **KM# 96** **Composition:** Copper-Nickel **Reverse:** Keel-billed toucan

| Date | Mintage | F | VF | XF | Unc | BU |
|---|---|---|---|---|---|---|
| 1984FM (U) | — | — | 2.00 | 4.00 | 12.00 | — |
| 1984FM (P) | — | Value: 15.00 | | | | |

**5 DOLLARS** **KM# 96a** **Weight:** 26.4000 g. **Composition:** 0.9250 Silver .7851 oz. ASW **Reverse:** Keel-billed toucan

| Date | Mintage | F | VF | XF | Unc | BU |
|---|---|---|---|---|---|---|
| 1984FM (P) | — | Value: 50.00 | | | | |
| 1985 | 212 | Value: 60.00 | | | | |

**5 DOLLARS** **KM# 107** **Weight:** 28.2800 g. **Composition:** 0.9250 Silver .8411 oz. ASW **Subject:** 50th anniversary - Battle of El Alamein - Field Marshall Rommel **Obverse:** Portrait of Queen Elizabeth II **Reverse:** Similar to 50 Dollars, KM#111

| Date | Mintage | F | VF | XF | Unc | BU |
|---|---|---|---|---|---|---|
| 1992 Proof | Est. 5,000 | Value: 45.00 | | | | |

**5 DOLLARS** **KM# 108** **Weight:** 28.2800 g. **Composition:** 0.9250 Silver .8411 oz. ASW **Subject:** 50th anniversary - Battle of El Alamein - Lt. Gen. Montgomery **Obverse:** Portrait of Queen Elizabeth II **Reverse:** Similar to 250 Dollars, KM#113

| Date | Mintage | F | VF | XF | Unc | BU |
|---|---|---|---|---|---|---|
| 1992 Proof | Est. 5,000 | Value: 45.00 | | | | |

**5 DOLLARS** **KM# 126** **Weight:** 28.2800 g. **Composition:** 0.9250 Silver .8411 oz. ASW **Subject:** Queen Mother - Balmoral Castle

| Date | Mintage | F | VF | XF | Unc | BU |
|---|---|---|---|---|---|---|
| 1995 Proof | Est. 40,000 | Value: 50.00 | | | | |

**10 DOLLARS** **KM# 45** **Composition:** Copper-Nickel **Reverse:** Great curassow

| Date | Mintage | F | VF | XF | Unc | BU |
|---|---|---|---|---|---|---|
| 1974FM (M) | 4,726 | — | — | 3.50 | 6.50 | — |
| 1974FM (P) | 21,000 | Value: 8.00 | | | | |
| 1975FM (M) | 117 | — | — | 12.50 | 45.00 | — |
| 1975FM (U) | 1,095 | — | — | 3.50 | 10.00 | — |
| 1975FM (P) | 8,794 | Value: 9.00 | | | | |
| 1976FM (M) | 125 | — | — | 10.00 | 35.00 | — |
| 1976FM (U) | 759 | — | — | 3.50 | 10.00 | — |
| 1976FM (P) | 4,893 | Value: 10.00 | | | | |
| 1977FM (U) | 645 | — | — | 4.00 | 12.00 | — |
| 1977FM (P) | 2,107 | Value: 12.50 | | | | |
| 1978FM (U) | 583 | — | — | 5.00 | 12.00 | — |
| 1978FM (P) | 1,671 | Value: 12.50 | | | | |

**10 DOLLARS** **KM# 45a** **Weight:** 29.8000 g. **Composition:** 0.9250 Silver .8863 oz. ASW **Reverse:** Great curassow

| Date | Mintage | F | VF | XF | Unc | BU |
|---|---|---|---|---|---|---|
| 1974FM (P) | 31,000 | Value: 10.00 | | | | |
| 1975FM (P) | 13,000 | Value: 11.50 | | | | |
| 1976FM (P) | 5,897 | Value: 12.50 | | | | |
| 1977FM (P) | 3,197 | Value: 14.00 | | | | |
| 1978FM (P) | 3,342 | Value: 14.00 | | | | |

**10 DOLLARS** **KM# 57** **Composition:** Copper-Nickel **Obverse:** Similar to Dollar, KM#43 **Reverse:** Flying jabirus

| Date | Mintage | F | VF | XF | Unc | BU |
|---|---|---|---|---|---|---|
| 1979FM (U) | 808 | — | — | 5.00 | 18.00 | — |
| 1979FM (P) | 1,287 | Value: 25.00 | | | | |

**10 DOLLARS** **KM# 57a** **Weight:** 29.8000 g. **Composition:** 0.9250 Silver .8863 oz. ASW **Obverse:** Similar to Dollar, KM#43 **Reverse:** Flying jabirus

| Date | Mintage | F | VF | XF | Unc | BU |
|---|---|---|---|---|---|---|
| 1979FM (P) | 2,445 | Value: 40.00 | | | | |

**10 DOLLARS** **KM# 60** **Composition:** Copper-Nickel **Reverse:** Scarlet ibis

| Date | Mintage | F | VF | XF | Unc | BU |
|---|---|---|---|---|---|---|
| 1980FM (U) | 761 | — | — | 5.00 | 25.00 | — |
| 1980FM (P) | 920 | Value: 28.00 | | | | |

**10 DOLLARS** **KM# 60a** **Weight:** 25.5000 g. **Composition:** 0.9250 Silver .7583 oz. ASW **Reverse:** Scarlet ibis

| Date | Mintage | F | VF | XF | Unc | BU |
|---|---|---|---|---|---|---|
| 1980FM (P) | 1,826 | Value: 50.00 | | | | |

**10 DOLLARS** **KM# 65** **Composition:** Copper-Nickel **Obverse:** Similar to Dollar, KM#43 **Reverse:** Roseate spoonbill

| Date | Mintage | F | VF | XF | Unc | BU |
|---|---|---|---|---|---|---|
| 1981FM (U) | 297 | — | 7.50 | 15.00 | 40.00 | — |
| 1981FM (P) | 643 | Value: 50.00 | | | | |

**10 DOLLARS** **KM# 65a** **Weight:** 25.5000 g. **Composition:** 0.9250 Silver .7583 oz. ASW **Obverse:** Similar to Dollar, KM#43 **Reverse:** Roseate spoonbill

| Date | Mintage | F | VF | XF | Unc | BU |
|---|---|---|---|---|---|---|
| 1981FM (P) | 615 | Value: 75.00 | | | | |

**10 DOLLARS** KM# 69 **Composition:** Copper-Nickel **Obverse:** Similar to Dollar, KM#80 **Reverse:** Yellow-crowned Amazon parrot

| Date | Mintage | F | VF | XF | Unc | BU |
|---|---|---|---|---|---|---|
| 1982FM (U) | — | — | 10.00 | 20.00 | 50.00 | — |
| 1982FM (P) | — | Value: 65.00 | | | | |

**10 DOLLARS** KM#69a **Weight:** 25.5000 g. **Composition:** 0.9250 Silver .7583 oz. ASW **Obverse:** Similar to Dollar, KM#80 **Reverse:** Yellow-crowned Amazon parrot

| Date | Mintage | F | VF | XF | Unc | BU |
|---|---|---|---|---|---|---|
| 1982FM (P) | 381 | Value: 120 | | | | |

**10 DOLLARS** KM# 80 **Composition:** Copper-Nickel **Obverse:** KM#69 **Reverse:** KM#45 **Note:** Mule.

| Date | Mintage | F | VF | XF | Unc | BU |
|---|---|---|---|---|---|---|
| 1982FM (U) | — | — | — | — | 25.00 | — |

**10 DOLLARS** KM# 71 **Composition:** Copper-Nickel **Reverse:** Ringed kingfisher

| Date | Mintage | F | VF | XF | Unc | BU |
|---|---|---|---|---|---|---|
| 1983FM (U) | — | — | 10.00 | 20.00 | 50.00 | — |
| 1983FM (P) | — | Value: 65.00 | | | | |

**10 DOLLARS** KM#71a **Weight:** 25.5000 g. **Composition:** 0.9250 Silver .7583 oz. ASW **Reverse:** Ringed kingfisher

| Date | Mintage | F | VF | XF | Unc | BU |
|---|---|---|---|---|---|---|
| 1983FM (P) | 334 | Value: 135 | | | | |

**10 DOLLARS** KM# 75 **Composition:** Copper-Nickel **Reverse:** Laughing falcon

| Date | Mintage | F | VF | XF | Unc | BU |
|---|---|---|---|---|---|---|
| 1984FM (U) | — | — | — | — | 50.00 | — |
| 1984FM (P) | — | Value: 60.00 | | | | |

**10 DOLLARS** KM#75a **Weight:** 25.5000 g. **Composition:** 0.9250 Silver .7583 oz. ASW **Reverse:** Laughing falcon

| Date | Mintage | F | VF | XF | Unc | BU |
|---|---|---|---|---|---|---|
| 1984FM (P) | — | Value: 115 | | | | |
| 1985 Proof | 212 | Value: 135 | | | | |

**10 DOLLARS** KM# 102 **Composition:** Copper-Nickel **Subject:** 10th anniversary of independence

| Date | Mintage | F | VF | XF | Unc | BU |
|---|---|---|---|---|---|---|
| ND(1991) | 1,000,000 | — | — | — | 8.50 | — |

**10 DOLLARS** KM# 102a **Weight:** 28.2800 g. **Composition:** 0.9250 Silver .8411 oz. ASW **Subject:** 10th anniversary of independence

| Date | Mintage | F | VF | XF | Unc | BU |
|---|---|---|---|---|---|---|
| ND(1991) Proof | Est. 1,000 | Value: 37.50 | | | | |

**10 DOLLARS** KM#104 **Weight:** 28.2800 g. **Composition:** 0.9250 Silver .8411 oz. ASW **Subject:** 10th anniversary of Central Bank **Reverse:** Jabiru stork

| Date | Mintage | F | VF | XF | Unc | BU |
|---|---|---|---|---|---|---|
| 1992 Proof | Est. 1,000 | Value: 45.00 | | | | |

**10 DOLLARS** KM# 109 **Weight:** 155.6000 g. **Composition:** 0.9990 Silver 5.0032 oz. ASW **Subject:** 50th anniversary - Battle of El Alamein - Lt. Gen. Montgomery **Obverse:** Portrait of Queen Elizabeth II **Reverse:** Similar to 250 Dollars, KM#113

| Date | Mintage | F | VF | XF | Unc | BU |
|---|---|---|---|---|---|---|
| 1992 Proof | Est. 2,500 | Value: 150 | | | | |

**10 DOLLARS** KM#121 **Weight:** 28.2800 g. **Composition:** 0.9250 Silver .8411 oz. ASW **Subject:** Royal visit **Obverse:** Queen's portrait **Reverse:** Cameo portraits above flowers

| Date | Mintage | F | VF | XF | Unc | BU |
|---|---|---|---|---|---|---|
| 1994 Proof | — | Value: 42.50 | | | | |

**10 DOLLARS** KM#123 **Weight:** 28.2800 g. **Composition:** 0.9250 Silver .8411 oz. ASW **Subject:** World Cup soccer

| Date | Mintage | F | VF | XF | Unc | BU |
|---|---|---|---|---|---|---|
| 1994 Proof | Est. 10,000 | Value: 45.00 | | | | |

**10 DOLLARS** KM#124 **Weight:** 28.2800 g. **Composition:** 0.9250 Silver .8411 oz. ASW **Reverse:** Carrack sailing ship

| Date | Mintage | F | VF | XF | Unc | BU |
|---|---|---|---|---|---|---|
| 1995 Proof | Est. 15,000 | Value: 40.00 | | | | |

**10 DOLLARS** KM#125 **Weight:** 28.2800 g. **Composition:** 0.9250 Silver .8411 oz. ASW **Series:** Endangered wildlife **Reverse:** Howler monkey on branch

| Date | Mintage | F | VF | XF | Unc | BU |
|---|---|---|---|---|---|---|
| 1995 Proof | Est. 10,000 | Value: 45.00 | | | | |

**10 DOLLARS** **KM# 127** **Weight:** 28.2800 g. **Composition:** 0.9250 Silver .8411 oz. ASW **Series:** Olympic Games 1996 **Obverse:** Wreathed arms **Reverse:** Female softball player

| Date | Mintage | F | VF | XF | Unc | BU |
|---|---|---|---|---|---|---|
| 1996 Proof | Est. 10,000 | Value: 45.00 | | | | |

**10 DOLLARS** **KM# 128** **Weight:** 28.2800 g. **Composition:** 0.9250 Silver .8411 oz. ASW **Subject:** Battle of St. George's Caye **Obverse:** National arms **Reverse:** Oar-powered gunboats

| Date | Mintage | F | VF | XF | Unc | BU |
|---|---|---|---|---|---|---|
| ND(1998) Proof | — | Value: 55.00 | | | | |

**10 DOLLARS** **KM# 130** **Weight:** 28.2800 g. **Composition:** 0.9250 Silver .8411 oz. ASW **Subject:** 50th anniversary - University of the West Indies **Obverse:** National arms **Reverse:** University arms

| Date | Mintage | F | VF | XF | Unc | BU |
|---|---|---|---|---|---|---|
| ND(1999) Proof | 1,000 | Value: 55.00 | | | | |

**20 DOLLARS** **KM# 79** **Weight:** 23.3300 g. **Composition:** 0.9250 Silver .6938 oz. ASW **Series:** Los Angeles Olympics **Obverse:** National arms **Reverse:** Bicyclist

| Date | Mintage | F | VF | XF | Unc | BU |
|---|---|---|---|---|---|---|
| 1984 Proof | 1,050 | Value: 45.00 | | | | |

**20 DOLLARS** **KM# 82** **Weight:** 23.3300 g. **Composition:** 0.9250 Silver .6938 oz. ASW **Series:** Decade for Women **Obverse:** National arms

| Date | Mintage | F | VF | XF | Unc | BU |
|---|---|---|---|---|---|---|
| 1985 Proof | Est. 20,000 | Value: 27.50 | | | | |

**25 DOLLARS** **KM# 54** **Weight:** 27.8100 g. **Composition:** 0.9250 Silver .8270 oz. ASW **Subject:** 25th Anniversary of Coronation **Obverse:** Queen Elizabeth II

| Date | Mintage | F | VF | XF | Unc | BU |
|---|---|---|---|---|---|---|
| 1978FM (U) | 352 | — | — | 22.00 | 50.00 | — |
| 1978FM (P) | 8,438 | Value: 16.50 | | | | |

**25 DOLLARS** **KM# 61** **Weight:** 30.2800 g. **Composition:** 0.5000 Silver .4686 oz. ASW **Subject:** 10th anniversary - Caribbean development bank

| Date | Mintage | F | VF | XF | Unc | BU |
|---|---|---|---|---|---|---|
| 1980FM (P) | 2,647 | Value: 25.00 | | | | |

**25 DOLLARS** **KM# 72** **Weight:** 30.2800 g. **Composition:** 0.5000 Silver .4686 oz. ASW **Subject:** 30th anniversary of Coronation

| Date | Mintage | F | VF | XF | Unc | BU |
|---|---|---|---|---|---|---|
| 1983FM (P) | 2,944 | Value: 22.50 | | | | |

**25 DOLLARS** **KM# 78** **Weight:** 28.2800 g. **Composition:** 0.9250 Silver .8411 oz. ASW **Subject:** Royal visit

| Date | Mintage | F | VF | XF | Unc | BU |
|---|---|---|---|---|---|---|
| 1985 Proof | Est. 5,000 | Value: 22.50 | | | | |

**25 DOLLARS** **KM# 97 Weight:** 28.2800 g. **Composition:** 0.9250 Silver .8411 oz. ASW **Subject:** 500th anniversary - Columbus discovery of America

| Date | Mintage | F | VF | XF | Unc | BU |
|---|---|---|---|---|---|---|
| 1989 Proof | Est. 5,000 | Value: 35.00 | | | | |

**25 DOLLARS** **KM# 106 Weight:** 28.2800 g. **Composition:** 0.9250 Silver .8411 oz. ASW **Series:** 25th Olympic Games **Reverse:** Hurdlers

| Date | Mintage | F | VF | XF | Unc | BU |
|---|---|---|---|---|---|---|
| 1992 Proof | 30,000 | Value: 27.50 | | | | |

**25 DOLLARS** **KM# 110 Weight:** 3.1300 g. **Composition:** 0.9990 Gold .1 oz. AGW **Subject:** 50th anniversary - Battle of El Alamein **Obverse:** Portrait of Queen Elizabeth II **Reverse:** 4 tanks

| Date | Mintage | F | VF | XF | Unc | BU |
|---|---|---|---|---|---|---|
| 1992 Proof | Est. 500 | Value: 100 | | | | |

**50 DOLLARS** **KM# 66 Weight:** 1.5000 g. **Composition:** 0.5000 Gold .0241 oz. AGW **Reverse:** White-necked Jacobin hummingbird

| Date | Mintage | F | VF | XF | Unc | BU |
|---|---|---|---|---|---|---|
| 1981FM (U) | 200 | — | — | — | 65.00 | — |
| 1981FM (P) | 2,873 | Value: 50.00 | | | | |

**50 DOLLARS** **KM# 81 Weight:** 129.6000 g. **Composition:** 0.9250 Silver 3.8547 oz. ASW **Subject:** Bird conservation **Obverse:** Similar to 25 Dollars, KM#72 **Reverse:** Red-footed booby

| Date | Mintage | F | VF | XF | Unc | BU |
|---|---|---|---|---|---|---|
| 1985 Proof | Est. 10,000 | Value: 80.00 | | | | |

**50 DOLLARS** **KM# 111 Weight:** 7.8100 g. **Composition:** 0.9990 Gold .2511 oz. AGW **Subject:** 50th anniversary - Battle of El Alamein **Obverse:** Portrait of Queen Elizabeth II **Reverse:** Field Marshall Rommel

| Date | Mintage | F | VF | XF | Unc | BU |
|---|---|---|---|---|---|---|
| 1992 Proof | Est. 500 | Value: 250 | | | | |

**100 DOLLARS** **KM# 51 Weight:** 6.2100 g. **Composition:** 0.5000 Gold .0998 oz. AGW **Subject:** 30th anniversary of United Nations

| Date | Mintage | F | VF | XF | Unc | BU |
|---|---|---|---|---|---|---|
| 1975FM (M) | 100 | — | — | — | 200 | — |
| 1975FM (U) | 2,028 | — | — | — | 60.00 | — |
| 1975FM (P) | 8,126 | Value: 55.00 | | | | |

**100 DOLLARS** **KM# 52 Weight:** 6.2100 g. **Composition:** 0.5000 Gold .0998 oz. AGW **Reverse:** Ancient Mayan symbols

| Date | Mintage | F | VF | XF | Unc | BU |
|---|---|---|---|---|---|---|
| 1976FM (M) | 216 | — | — | — | 175 | — |
| 1976FM (P) | 11,000 | Value: 55.00 | | | | |

**100 DOLLARS** **KM# 53 Weight:** 6.2100 g. **Composition:** 0.5000 Gold .0998 oz. AGW **Reverse:** Kinich Ahau, Mayan sun god

| Date | Mintage | F | VF | XF | Unc | BU |
|---|---|---|---|---|---|---|
| 1977FM (M) | 200 | — | — | — | 135 | — |
| 1977FM (U) | 51 | — | — | — | 350 | — |
| 1977FM (P) | 7,859 | Value: 55.00 | | | | |

**100 DOLLARS** **KM# 55 Weight:** 6.2100 g. **Composition:** 0.5000 Gold .0998 oz. AGW **Reverse:** Itzamna Mayan god

| Date | Mintage | F | VF | XF | Unc | BU |
|---|---|---|---|---|---|---|
| 1978FM (U) | 351 | — | — | — | 150 | — |
| 1978FM (P) | 7,178 | Value: 55.00 | | | | |

**100 DOLLARS** **KM# 58 Weight:** 6.2100 g. **Composition:** 0.5000 Gold .0998 oz. AGW **Reverse:** Queen angelfish

| Date | Mintage | F | VF | XF | Unc | BU |
|---|---|---|---|---|---|---|
| 1979FM (U) | 400 | — | — | — | 125 | — |
| 1979FM (P) | 4,465 | Value: 80.00 | | | | |

**100 DOLLARS** **KM# 59 Weight:** 6.4700 g. **Composition:** 0.5000 Gold .1040 oz. AGW **Reverse:** Star of Bethlehem

| Date | Mintage | F | VF | XF | Unc | BU |
|---|---|---|---|---|---|---|
| 1979FM (U) | — | — | — | — | 120 | — |
| 1979FM (P) | — | Value: 70.00 | | | | |

**100 DOLLARS** **KM# 62 Weight:** 6.2100 g. **Composition:** 0.5000 Gold .0998 oz. AGW **Reverse:** Moorish idol reef fish

| Date | Mintage | F | VF | XF | Unc | BU |
|---|---|---|---|---|---|---|
| 1980FM (U) | 400 | — | — | — | 150 | — |
| 1980FM (P) | 3,993 | Value: 90.00 | | | | |

**100 DOLLARS** **KM# 63 Weight:** 6.2100 g. **Composition:** 0.5000 Gold .0998 oz. AGW **Reverse:** Orchids

| Date | Mintage | F | VF | XF | Unc | BU |
|---|---|---|---|---|---|---|
| 1980FM (U) | 250 | — | — | — | 140 | — |
| 1980FM (P) | 2,454 | Value: 85.00 | | | | |

**100 DOLLARS** **KM# 67** **Weight:** 6.2100 g. **Composition:** 0.5000 Gold .0998 oz. AGW **Reverse:** Yellow swallowtail butterfly

| Date | Mintage | F | VF | XF | Unc | BU |
|---|---|---|---|---|---|---|
| 1981FM (U) | 200 | — | — | — | 180 | — |
| 1981FM (P) | 1,658 | Value: 200 | | | | |

**100 DOLLARS** **KM# 68** **Weight:** 6.2100 g. **Composition:** 0.5000 Gold .0998 oz. AGW **Subject:** National independence

| Date | Mintage | F | VF | XF | Unc | BU |
|---|---|---|---|---|---|---|
| 1981FM (U) | 50 | — | — | — | 325 | — |
| 1981FM (P) | 1,401 | Value: 125 | | | | |

**100 DOLLARS** **KM# 70** **Weight:** 6.2100 g. **Composition:** 0.5000 Gold .0998 oz. AGW **Reverse:** Kinkajou

| Date | Mintage | F | VF | XF | Unc | BU |
|---|---|---|---|---|---|---|
| 1982FM (U) | 10 | — | — | — | 450 | — |
| 1982FM (P) | 586 | Value: 175 | | | | |

**100 DOLLARS** **KM# 73** **Weight:** 6.2100 g. **Composition:** 0.5000 Gold .0998 oz. AGW **Reverse:** Margay jungle cat

| Date | Mintage | F | VF | XF | Unc | BU |
|---|---|---|---|---|---|---|
| 1983FM (U) | 20 | — | — | — | 400 | — |
| 1983FM (P) | 494 | Value: 200 | | | | |

**100 DOLLARS** **KM# 74** **Weight:** 6.2100 g. **Composition:** 0.5000 Gold .0998 oz. AGW **Reverse:** White-tailed deer

| Date | Mintage | F | VF | XF | Unc | BU |
|---|---|---|---|---|---|---|
| 1984FM (P) | 965 | Value: 150 | | | | |

**100 DOLLARS** **KM# 76** **Weight:** 6.2100 g. **Composition:** 0.5000 Gold .0998 oz. AGW **Reverse:** Ocelot

| Date | Mintage | F | VF | XF | Unc | BU |
|---|---|---|---|---|---|---|
| 1985FM (P) Proof | 899 | Value: 220 | | | | |

**100 DOLLARS** **KM# 103** **Weight:** 15.9760 g. **Composition:** 0.9170 Gold .4708 oz. AGW **Subject:** 10th anniversary of independence **Note:** Similar to 10 Dollars, KM#102.

| Date | Mintage | F | VF | XF | Unc | BU |
|---|---|---|---|---|---|---|
| 1991 Proof | Est. 500 | Value: 550 | | | | |

**100 DOLLARS** **KM# 112** **Weight:** 15.6000 g. **Composition:** 0.9990 Gold .5016 oz. AGW **Subject:** 50th anniversary - Battle of El Alamein **Obverse:** Portrait of Queen Elizabeth II **Reverse:** Infantry advancing

| Date | Mintage | F | VF | XF | Unc | BU |
|---|---|---|---|---|---|---|
| 1992 Proof | Est. 500 | Value: 500 | | | | |

**100 DOLLARS** **KM# 129** **Weight:** 15.9700 g. **Composition:** 0.9170 Gold .4707 oz. AGW **Subject:** Battle of St. George's Caye **Note:** Similar to KM#128.

| Date | Mintage | F | VF | XF | Unc | BU |
|---|---|---|---|---|---|---|
| ND(1998) Proof | — | Value: 675 | | | | |

**250 DOLLARS** **KM# 56** **Weight:** 8.8100 g. **Composition:** 0.9000 Gold .2549 oz. AGW **Reverse:** Jaguar

| Date | Mintage | F | VF | XF | Unc | BU |
|---|---|---|---|---|---|---|
| 1978FM (U) | 200 | — | — | — | 225 | — |
| 1978FM (P) | Est. 3,399 | Value: 235 | | | | |

**Note:** 1,712 pieces were used in first-day covers

**250 DOLLARS** **KM# 98** **Weight:** 15.9800 g. **Composition:** 0.9170 Gold .4708 oz. AGW **Subject:** 500th anniversary of Columbus discovery of America

| Date | Mintage | F | VF | XF | Unc | BU |
|---|---|---|---|---|---|---|
| 1989 Proof | Est. 500 | Value: 375 | | | | |

**250 DOLLARS** **KM# 105** **Weight:** 15.9800 g. **Composition:** 0.9170 Gold .4708 oz. AGW **Subject:** 10th anniversary of Central Bank **Reverse:** Jabiru stork **Note:** Similar to KM#104.

| Date | Mintage | F | VF | XF | Unc | BU |
|---|---|---|---|---|---|---|
| 1992 | Est. 500 | Value: 375 | | | | |

**250 DOLLARS** **KM# 113** **Weight:** 31.2100 g. **Composition:** 0.9990 Gold 1.0035 oz. AGW **Subject:** 50th anniversary - Battle of El Alamein **Obverse:** Portrait of Queen Elizabeth II **Reverse:** Lt. Gen. Montgomery

| Date | Mintage | F | VF | XF | Unc | BU |
|---|---|---|---|---|---|---|
| 1992 Proof | Est. 500 | Value: 750 | | | | |

**500 DOLLARS** **KM# 101** **Weight:** 47.5400 g. **Composition:** 0.9170 Gold 1.4018 oz. AGW **Subject:** Royal visit **Note:** Similar to KM#78.

| Date | Mintage | F | VF | XF | Unc | BU |
|---|---|---|---|---|---|---|
| 1985 Proof | Est. 250 | Value: 1,000 | | | | |

**500 DOLLARS** **KM# 120** **Weight:** 47.5400 g. **Composition:** 0.9170 Gold 1.4018 oz. AGW **Subject:** 40th anniversary - coronation of Queen Elizabeth II

| Date | Mintage | F | VF | XF | Unc | BU |
|---|---|---|---|---|---|---|
| 1993 Proof | Est. 100 | Value: 1,150 | | | | |

**500 DOLLARS** **KM# 122** **Weight:** 47.5400 g. **Composition:** 0.9170 Gold 1.4018 oz. AGW **Subject:** Royal visit **Reverse:** Cameo portraits

| Date | Mintage | F | VF | XF | Unc | BU |
|---|---|---|---|---|---|---|
| 1994 Proof | — | Value: 1,150 | | | | |

## PIEFORTS

| KM# | Date | Mintage | Identification | Mkt Val |
|---|---|---|---|---|
| P1 | 1990 | 1,000 | Dollar. 0.9250 Silver. KM99a. | 60.00 |

## MINT SETS

| KM# | Date | Mintage | Identification | Issue Price | Mkt Val |
|---|---|---|---|---|---|
| MS1 | 1974 | 4,506 | KM38-45 | 20.00 | 20.00 |
| MS2 | 1975 | 1,095 | KM43-50 | 27.50 | 30.00 |
| MS3 | 1976 | 759 | KM43-50 | 27.50 | 32.00 |
| MS4 | 1977 | — | KM43-45, 46b -47b, 48-50 | 27.50 | 30.00 |
| MS5 | 1978 | 458 | KM43-45, 46b-47b, 48-50 | 28.50 | 32.00 |
| MS6 | 1979 | 808 | KM43-44, 46b-47b, 48-50, 57 | 28.50 | 32.00 |
| MS7 | 1980 | 761 | KM43-44, 46b-47b, 48-50, 60 | 29.50 | 40.00 |
| MS8 | 1981 | 297 | KM43-44, 46b-47b, 48-50, 65 | 29.50 | 60.00 |
| MS9 | 1982 | — | KM69, 83-89 | 29.50 | 60.00 |
| MS10 | 1983 | — | KM71, 83-89 | 29.50 | 65.00 |
| MS11 | 1984 | — | KM75, 90-96 | — | 75.00 |
| MS12 | 1992 | — | KM33a, 34a, 35-37, 99 | 24.00 | 24.00 |

## PROOF SETS

| KM# | Date | Mintage | Identification | Issue Price | Mkt Val |
|---|---|---|---|---|---|
| PS1 | 1974 | 21,470 | KM38-45 | 35.00 | 18.00 |
| PS2 | 1974 | 31,368 | KM38a-45a | 100 | 40.00 |
| PS3 | 1975 | 8,794 | KM43-50 | 37.50 | 22.00 |
| PS4 | 1975 | 13,275 | KM43a-50a | 110 | 40.00 |
| PS5 | 1976 | 4,893 | KM43-50 | 37.50 | 25.00 |
| PS6 | 1976 | 5,897 | KM43a-50a | 110 | 45.00 |
| PS7 | 1977 | 2,107 | KM43-45, 46b-47b, 48-50 | 37.50 | 30.00 |
| PS8 | 1977 | 3,197 | KM43a-50a | 110 | 47.50 |
| PS9 | 1978 | 1,671 | KM43-45, 46b, 47b, 48-50 | 39.50 | 30.00 |
| PS10 | 1978 | 3,342 | KM43a-50a | 110 | 47.50 |
| PS11 | 1979 | 1,287 | KM43-44, 46b-47b, 48-50, 57 | 41.50 | 35.00 |
| PS12 | 1979 | 2,445 | KM43a-44a, 46a-50a, 57a | 112 | 70.00 |
| PS13 | 1980 | 920 | KM43-44, 46b-47b, 48-50, 60 | 41.50 | 40.00 |
| PS14 | 1980 | 1,826 | KM43a-44a, 46a-50a, 60a | 222 | 80.00 |
| PS15 | 1981 | 643 | KM43-44, 46b-47b, 48-50, 65 | 41.50 | 60.00 |
| PS16 | 1981 | 615 | KM43a-44a, 46a-50a, 65a | — | 115 |
| PS17 | 1982 | — | KM69, 83-89 | 49.50 | 75.00 |
| PS18 | 1982 | 381 | KM69a, 83a-89a | 222 | 285 |
| PS19 | 1983 | 306 | KM71, 83-89 | 37.00 | 70.00 |
| PS20 | 1983 | 241 | KM71a, 83a-89a | 197 | 300 |
| PS21 | 1984 | — | KM75, 90-96 | 37.00 | 65.00 |
| PS22 | 1984 | 397 | KM75a, 90a-96a | 197 | 280 |
| PS23 | 1985 | 212 | KM75a, 90a-96a | — | 325 |
| PS24 | 1992 | 500 | KM110-113 | 1,600 | 1,600 |
| PS25 | 1992 | — | KM107-108 | 100 | 100 |

# BENIN (Dahomey)

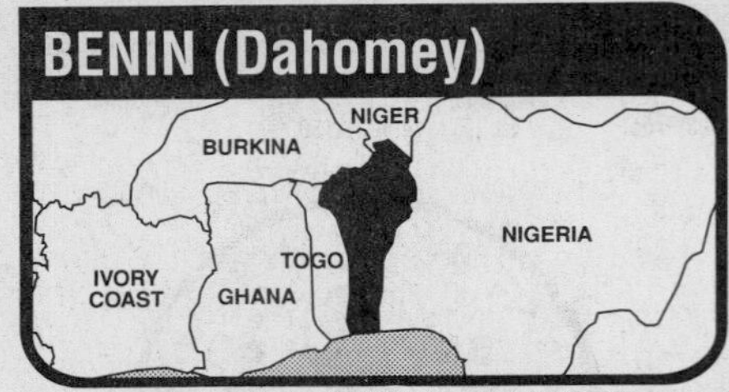


The Republic of Benin (formerly the Republic of Dahomey), located on the south side of the African bulge between Togo and Nigeria, has an area of 43,500 sq. mi. (112,620 sq. km.) and a population of 5.5 million. Capital: Porto-Novo. The principal industry of Benin, one of the poorest countries of West Africa, is the processing of palm oil products. Palm kernel oil, peanuts, cotton, and coffee are exported.

## PEOPLES REPUBLIC

### STANDARD COINAGE

**200 FRANCS** **KM# 10** **Composition:** Copper **Reverse:** Sailing ship - Preussen

| Date | Mintage | F | VF | XF | Unc | BU |
|---|---|---|---|---|---|---|
| 1993 | — | — | — | — | 7.50 | — |
| 1993 Proof | 100 | Value: 55.00 | | | | |

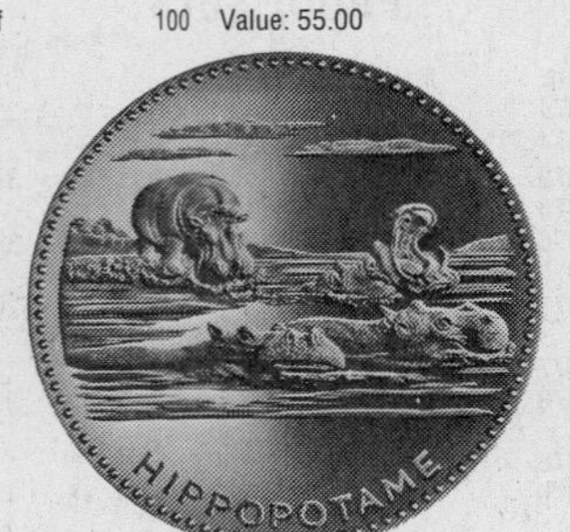

**200 FRANCS** **KM# 8** **Composition:** Copper-Nickel **Series:** Prehistoric Animals **Reverse:** Dinosaurs - Acanthopholis

| Date | Mintage | F | VF | XF | Unc | BU |
|---|---|---|---|---|---|---|
| 1994 | — | — | — | — | 20.00 | — |

**200 FRANCS** **KM# 15** **Composition:** Copper **Series:** Prehistoric Animals **Reverse:** Dinosaurs - Tyrannosaurus Rex

| Date | Mintage | F | VF | XF | Unc | BU |
|---|---|---|---|---|---|---|
| 1994 | — | — | — | — | 14.00 | — |
| 1994 Proof | 100 | Value: 55.00 | | | | |

**200 FRANCS** **KM# 16** **Composition:** Copper-Nickel **Subject:** United Nations - 50 Years **Reverse:** Family in boat

| Date | Mintage | F | VF | XF | Unc | BU |
|---|---|---|---|---|---|---|
| ND(1995) | — | — | — | — | 8.50 | — |

**200 FRANCS** **KM# 17** **Composition:** Nickel-Bonded Steel And Enamel **Reverse:** WWI Austrian Hansa - Brandenburg D. I

| Date | Mintage | F | VF | XF | Unc | BU |
|---|---|---|---|---|---|---|
| 1995 | 25,000 | — | — | — | 30.00 | — |

**200 FRANCS** **KM# 23** **Composition:** Copper **Series:** Prehistoric Animals **Obverse:** National arms **Reverse:** Iguanodon

| Date | Mintage | F | VF | XF | Unc | BU |
|---|---|---|---|---|---|---|
| 1995 Proof | 100 | Value: 65.00 | | | | |

**200 FRANCS** **KM# 25** **Composition:** Copper-Nickel **Series:** Sydney 2000 **Obverse:** National arms **Reverse:** Classic sculpture and racing scullcraft

| Date | Mintage | F | VF | XF | Unc | BU |
|---|---|---|---|---|---|---|
| 1999 | 10,000 | — | — | — | 7.50 | — |

**500 FRANCS** **KM# 3** **Weight:** 12.0000 g. **Composition:** 0.9990 Silver .3858 oz. ASW **Subject:** 1992 World Cup Soccer **Reverse:** Soccer - Goalie

| Date | Mintage | F | VF | XF | Unc | BU |
|---|---|---|---|---|---|---|
| 1992 | Est. 10,000 | — | — | — | 45.00 | — |

**500 FRANCS** **KM# 14** **Weight:** 14.0000 g. **Composition:** 0.9990 Silver .4497 oz. ASW **Reverse:** Soccer - Eifel Tower, flag and ball **Edge Lettering:** 1995 World Cup Soccer

| Date | Mintage | F | VF | XF | Unc | BU |
|---|---|---|---|---|---|---|
| 1995 Proof | 30,000 | Value: 22.50 | | | | |

**1000 FRANCS** **KM# 2** **Weight:** 19.9100 g. **Composition:** 0.9990 Silver .6402 oz. ASW **Reverse:** National map in radient sun.

| Date | Mintage | F | VF | XF | Unc | BU |
|---|---|---|---|---|---|---|
| ND(1992) Proof | 1,000 | Value: 38.50 | | | | |

**1000 FRANCS** **KM# 4** **Weight:** 20.0000 g. **Composition:** 0.9990 Silver .6430 oz. ASW **Series:** Olympics **Reverse:** Gymnast

| Date | Mintage | F | VF | XF | Unc | BU |
|---|---|---|---|---|---|---|
| 1992 Proof | Est. 5,000 | Value: 28.00 | | | | |

**1000 FRANCS** **KM# 5** **Weight:** 20.0000 g. **Composition:** 0.9990 Silver .6430 oz. ASW **Subject:** 1992 World Cup Soccer **Reverse:** Player kicking ball

| Date | Mintage | F | VF | XF | Unc | BU |
|---|---|---|---|---|---|---|
| 1992 Proof | Est. 10,000 | Value: 35.00 | | | | |

**1000 FRANCS** **KM# 1** **Weight:** 19.9100 g. **Composition:** 0.9990 Silver .6402 oz. ASW **Note:** Five hands holding jar

| Date | Mintage | F | VF | XF | Unc | BU |
|---|---|---|---|---|---|---|
| ND(1992) Proof | 1,000 | Value: 38.00 | | | | |

**1000 FRANCS** **KM# 6** **Weight:** 20.0000 g. **Composition:** 0.9990 Silver .6430 oz. ASW **Subject:** Protection of Nature **Reverse:** Elephant

| Date | Mintage | F | VF | XF | Unc | BU |
|---|---|---|---|---|---|---|
| 1993 Proof | — | Value: 60.00 | | | | |

**1000 FRANCS** **KM# 7** **Weight:** 20.0000 g. **Composition:** 0.9990 Silver .6430 oz. ASW **Reverse:** Sailing ship - Preussen

| Date | Mintage | F | VF | XF | Unc | BU |
|---|---|---|---|---|---|---|
| 1993 | 100 | — | — | — | 110 | — |
| 1993 Proof | — | Value: 32.50 | | | | |

**1000 FRANCS** **KM# 27** **Weight:** 20.0000 g. **Composition:** 0.9990 Silver .6430 oz. ASW **Series:** Protection of Nature **Reverse:** Elephant

| Date | Mintage | F | VF | XF | Unc | BU |
|---|---|---|---|---|---|---|
| 1993 Proof | — | Value: 35.00 | | | | |

**1000 FRANCS** **KM# 9** **Weight:** 15.8600 g. **Composition:** 0.9940 Silver .5095 oz. ASW **Series:** Dinosaurs **Reverse:** Tyrannosaurus Rex

| Date | Mintage | F | VF | XF | Unc | BU |
|---|---|---|---|---|---|---|
| 1994 Proof | — | Value: 50.00 | | | | |

**1000 FRANCS** **KM# 12** **Weight:** 20.0000 g. **Composition:** 0.9990 Silver .6424 oz. ASW **Series:** 1996 Olympics **Reverse:** Three runners

| Date | Mintage | F | VF | XF | Unc | BU |
|---|---|---|---|---|---|---|
| 1995 Proof | 15,000 | Value: 28.00 | | | | |

**1000 FRANCS** **KM# 13** **Weight:** 20.0000 g. **Composition:** 0.9990 Silver .6424 oz. ASW **Subject:** 32 Years of Independence

| Date | Mintage | F | VF | XF | Unc | BU |
|---|---|---|---|---|---|---|
| 1995 Proof | 2,000 | Value: 35.00 | | | | |

**1000 FRANCS** **KM# 18** **Weight:** 20.0000 g. **Composition:** 0.9990 Silver .6424 oz. ASW **Reverse:** WWI Austrian Hansa - Brandenburg D. I

| Date | Mintage | F | VF | XF | Unc | BU |
|---|---|---|---|---|---|---|
| 1995 Proof | 15,000 | Value: 45.00 | | | | |

**1000 FRANCS** KM# 28 **Weight:** 20.0000 g. **Composition:** 0.9990 Silver .6424 oz. ASW **Series:** Prehistoric Animals **Reverse:** Iguanodon **Edge:** Plain

| Date | Mintage | F | VF | XF | Unc | BU |
|---|---|---|---|---|---|---|
| 1995 Proof | — | Value: 35.00 | | | | |

**1000 FRANCS** KM# 20 **Weight:** 15.0000 g. **Composition:** 0.9990 Silver .4817 oz. ASW **Subject:** 1996 World Cup Soccer **Obverse:** National arms **Reverse:** Two multi-colored soccer players

| Date | Mintage | F | VF | XF | Unc | BU |
|---|---|---|---|---|---|---|
| 1996 Proof | — | Value: 45.00 | | | | |

**1000 FRANCS** KM# 19 **Weight:** 20.0000 g. **Composition:** 0.9990 Silver .6424 oz. ASW **Note:** Multi-colored panther.

| Date | Mintage | F | VF | XF | Unc | BU |
|---|---|---|---|---|---|---|
| 1996 Proof | — | Value: 60.00 | | | | |

**1000 FRANCS** KM# 21 **Weight:** 15.0000 g. **Composition:** 0.9990 Silver .4817 oz. ASW **Series:** 2000 Summer Olympics **Obverse:** National arms **Reverse:** Multi-colored shot-putter and Olympic torch

| Date | Mintage | F | VF | XF | Unc | BU |
|---|---|---|---|---|---|---|
| 1997 | 100 | — | — | — | 110 | — |
| 1997 Proof | — | Value: 40.00 | | | | |

**1000 FRANCS** KM# 24 **Weight:** 20.0000 g. **Composition:** 0.9990 Silver .6430 oz. ASW **Series:** 2000 Summer Olympics **Obverse:** National arms **Reverse:** Two runners and statue

| Date | Mintage | F | VF | XF | Unc | BU |
|---|---|---|---|---|---|---|
| 1997 | 100 | — | — | — | 75.00 | — |
| 1997 Proof | 7,500 | Value: 32.50 | | | | |

**1000 FRANCS** KM# 26 **Weight:** 20.1300 g. **Composition:** 0.9990 Silver .6465 oz. ASW **Series:** 2000 Summer Olympics **Obverse:** National arms **Reverse:** Classic statue and racing scullcraft

| Date | Mintage | F | VF | XF | Unc | BU |
|---|---|---|---|---|---|---|
| 1999 Proof | 5,000 | Value: 35.00 | | | | |

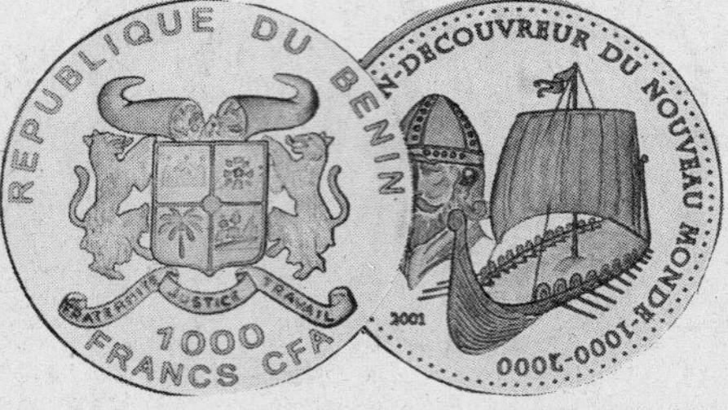


**1000 FRANCS** KM# 37 **Weight:** 14.9500 g. **Composition:** 0.9990 Silver .4802 oz. ASW **Subject:** Leif Ericksson **Obverse:** National arms. **Reverse:** Head of Eriksson at left, Viking ship at right. **Edge:** Plain. **Size:** 35 mm.

| Date | Mintage | F | VF | XF | Unc | BU |
|---|---|---|---|---|---|---|
| 2001 Proof | — | Value: 30.00 | | | | |

**6000 FRANCS** KM# 11 **Weight:** 20.1300 g. **Composition:** 0.9990 Silver .6465 oz. ASW **Series:** Protection of Nature **Reverse:** Elephant

| Date | Mintage | F | VF | XF | Unc | BU |
|---|---|---|---|---|---|---|
| 1993 Proof | — | Value: 60.00 | | | | |

**6000 FRANCS** KM# 22 **Weight:** 28.3400 g. **Composition:** 0.9250 Silver .8248 oz. ASW **Subject:** 50th Anniversary U.N. **Obverse:** National arms **Reverse:** Family in boat

| Date | Mintage | F | VF | XF | Unc | BU |
|---|---|---|---|---|---|---|
| ND(1995) Proof | — | Value: 42.50 | | | | |

**15000 FRANCS** KM# 34 **Weight:** 500.0000 g. **Composition:** 0.9990 Silver 16.0593 oz. ASW **Subject:** Wildlife Protection **Obverse:** National arms. **Reverse:** Multicolor crocodile. **Edge:** Reeded. **Size:** 84.8 mm. **Note:** Illustration reduced. Actual size: 84.8mm.

| Date | Mintage | F | VF | XF | Unc | BU |
|---|---|---|---|---|---|---|
| 1996 Proof | — | Value: 450 | | | | |

**20000 FRANCS** KM# 36 **Weight:** 846.0152 g. **Composition:** 0.9990 Silver 27.2 oz. ASW **Subject:** African Fauna **Obverse:** National arms. **Reverse:** Multicolor zebra. **Edge:** Plain. **Size:** 90.4 mm. **Note:** Illustration reduced. Actual size: 90.4mm.

| Date | Mintage | F | VF | XF | Unc | BU |
|---|---|---|---|---|---|---|
| 1997 Proof | — | Value: 700 | | | | |

**30000 FRANCS** KM# 29 **Weight:** 15.5500 g. **Composition:** 0.9990 Gold .4494 oz. AGW **Obverse:** National arms **Reverse:** Map in radiant sun **Edge:** Reeded

| Date | Mintage | F | VF | XF | Unc | BU |
|---|---|---|---|---|---|---|
| ND(1992) Proof | Est. 100 | Value: 450 | | | | |

**100000 FRANCS** KM# 30 **Weight:** 31.1035 g. **Composition:** 0.9990 Gold 1.0000 oz. AGW **Obverse:** National arms **Reverse:** President **Edge:** Reeded

| Date | Mintage | F | VF | XF | Unc | BU |
|---|---|---|---|---|---|---|
| 1992 Rare | Est. 10 | — | — | — | — | — |

## PIEFORTS

| KM# | Date | Mintage | Identification | Mkt Val |
|---|---|---|---|---|
| P1 | 1997 | — | 1000 Francs. KM#21 | 135 |
| P2 | 1997 | — | 1000 Francs. KM#24. | 125 |
| P3 | 1999 | — | 1000 Francs. KM#26. | 85.00 |

# BERMUDA

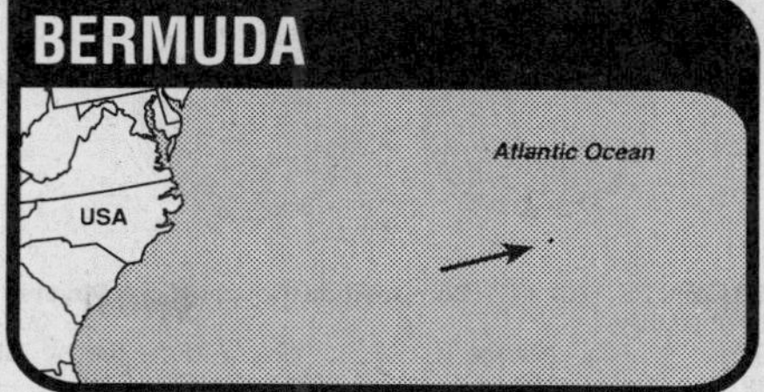


The Parliamentary British Colony of Bermuda, situated in the western Atlantic Ocean 660 miles (1,062 km.) east of North Carolina, has an area of 20.6 sq. mi. (53 sq. km.) and a population of 61,600. Capital: Hamilton. Concentrated essences, beauty preparations, and cut flowers are exported. Most Bermudians derive their livelihood from tourism.

Bermuda was discovered by Juan de Bermudez, a Spanish navigator, in about 1503. British influence dates from 1609 when a group of Virginia-bound British colonists under the command of Sir George Somers was shipwrecked on the islands for 10 months. The islands were settled in 1612 by 60 British colonists from the Virginia Colony and became a crown colony in 1684. The earliest coins issued for the island were the "Hogge Money" series of 2, 3, 6 and 12 pence, the name derived from the pig in the obverse design, a recognition of the quantity of such animals then found there. The next issue for Bermuda was the Birmingham coppers of 1793; all locally circulating coinage was demonetized in 1842, when the currency of the United Kingdom became standard. Internal autonomy was obtained by the constitution of June 8, 1968.

In February, 1970, Bermuda converted from its former currency, which was sterling, to a decimal currency, the dollar unit which is equal to one U.S. dollar. On July 31, 1972, Bermuda severed its monetary link with the British pound sterling and pegged its dollar to be the same gold value as the U.S. dollar.

**RULERS**
British

**MINT MARKS**
CHI - Valcambi, Switzerland
FM - Franklin Mint, U.S.A.*

***NOTE**: From 1975-1985 the Franklin Mint produced coinage in up to 3 different qualities. Qualities of issue are designated in ( ) after each date and are defined as follows:

**(M) MATTE** - Normal circulation strike or a dull finish produced by sandblasting special uncirculated (polish finish) or proof quality dies.

**(U) SPECIAL UNCIRCUALTED** - Polished or proof-like in appearance without any frosted features.

**(P) PROOF** - The highest quality obtainable having mirror-like fields and frosted features.

**MONETARY SYSTEM**
12 Pence = 1 Shilling
20 Shillings = 1 Pound

# BRITISH ADMINISTRATION

## POUND STERLING COINAGE

**CROWN** KM#13 **Weight:** 28.2800 g. **Composition:** 0.9250 Silver .8411 oz. ASW **Subject:** 350th anniversary - colony founding

| Date | Mintage | F | VF | XF | Unc | BU |
|---|---|---|---|---|---|---|
| 1959 | 100,000 | BV | 5.00 | 7.00 | 12.50 | — |
| 1959 Matte proof | — | Value: 1,000 | | | | |

**Note:** Mintage: 6-10

**CROWN** KM#14 **Weight:** 22.6200 g. **Composition:** 0.5000 Silver .3636 oz. ASW

| Date | Mintage | F | VF | XF | Unc | BU |
|---|---|---|---|---|---|---|
| 1964 | 470,000 | — | — | BV | 4.00 | — |
| 1964 Proof | 30,000 | Value: 6.00 | | | | |

## DECIMAL COINAGE

100 Cents = 1 Dollar

**CENT** KM# 15 **Composition:** Bronze **Reverse:** Wild boar

| Date | Mintage | F | VF | XF | Unc | BU |
|---|---|---|---|---|---|---|
| 1970 | 5,500,000 | — | — | 0.10 | 0.20 | — |
| 1970 Proof | 11,000 | Value: 0.50 | | | | |
| 1971 | 4,256,000 | — | — | 0.10 | 0.20 | — |
| 1973 | 2,144,000 | — | — | 0.10 | 0.20 | — |
| 1974 | 856,000 | — | — | 0.10 | 0.25 | — |
| 1975 | 1,000,000 | — | — | 0.10 | 0.20 | — |
| 1976 | 1,000,000 | — | — | 0.10 | 0.20 | — |
| 1977 | 2,000,000 | — | — | 0.10 | 0.20 | — |
| 1978 | 3,160,000 | — | — | 0.10 | 0.20 | — |
| 1980 | 3,520,000 | — | — | 0.10 | 0.20 | — |
| 1981 | 3,200,000 | — | — | 0.10 | 0.20 | — |
| 1982 | 320,000 | — | — | 0.10 | 0.20 | — |
| 1983 | 800,000 | — | — | 0.10 | 0.20 | — |
| 1983 Proof | 10,000 | Value: 1.00 | | | | |
| 1984 | 800,000 | — | — | 0.10 | 0.20 | — |
| 1985 | — | — | — | 0.10 | 0.20 | — |

**CENT** KM# 44 **Composition:** Bronze **Reverse:** Wild boar

| Date | Mintage | F | VF | XF | Unc | BU |
|---|---|---|---|---|---|---|
| 1986 | 960,000 | — | — | 0.10 | 0.20 | — |
| 1986 Proof | Inc. above | Value: 2.00 | | | | |
| 1987 | — | — | — | 0.10 | 0.20 | — |
| 1988 | — | — | — | 0.10 | 0.20 | — |
| 1990 | — | — | — | 0.10 | 0.20 | — |
| 1991 | — | — | — | 0.10 | 0.20 | — |

**CENT** KM# 44a **Composition:** Steel **Reverse:** Wild boar **Note:** Copper coated.

| Date | Mintage | F | VF | XF | Unc | BU |
|---|---|---|---|---|---|---|
| 1988 | — | — | — | — | 2.50 | — |

**CENT** KM# 44b **Composition:** Copper Plated Zinc **Reverse:** Wild boar

| Date | Mintage | F | VF | XF | Unc | BU |
|---|---|---|---|---|---|---|
| 1991 | — | — | — | 0.10 | 0.20 | — |
| 1993 | — | — | — | 0.10 | 0.20 | — |
| 1994 | — | — | — | 0.10 | 0.20 | — |
| 1995 | — | — | — | 0.10 | 0.20 | — |
| 1996 | — | — | — | 0.10 | 0.20 | — |
| 1997 | — | — | — | 0.10 | 0.20 | — |

**CENT** KM# 44c **Weight:** 3.7000 g. **Composition:** 0.9250 Silver .11 oz. ASW **Reverse:** Wild boar **Note:** In sets only.

| Date | Mintage | F | VF | XF | Unc | BU |
|---|---|---|---|---|---|---|
| 1995 | 2,000 | — | — | — | 4.00 | — |

**CENT** KM# 44d **Weight:** 6.2000 g. **Composition:** 0.9170 Gold .1827 oz. AGW **Reverse:** Wild boar **Note:** In sets only.

| Date | Mintage | F | VF | XF | Unc | BU |
|---|---|---|---|---|---|---|
| 1995 | 500 | — | — | — | 135 | — |

**CENT** **KM# 107** **Composition:** Copper Plated Zinc **Obverse:** Queen's portrait Obv. Designer: Rank-Broadley **Reverse:** Wild boar

| Date | Mintage | F | VF | XF | Unc | BU |
|---|---|---|---|---|---|---|
| 1999 | — | — | — | — | 0.40 | — |
| 1999 Proof | 2,500 | Value: 2.50 | | | | |
| 2000 | — | — | — | — | 0.50 | — |
| 2000 Proof | — | Value: 2.50 | | | | |

**5 CENTS** **KM# 16** **Composition:** Copper-Nickel **Reverse:** Queen angel fish

| Date | Mintage | F | VF | XF | Unc | BU |
|---|---|---|---|---|---|---|
| 1970 | 2,190,000 | — | 0.10 | 0.15 | 0.35 | — |
| 1970 Proof | 11,000 | Value: 0.50 | | | | |
| 1974 | 310,000 | — | 0.10 | 0.15 | 0.35 | — |
| 1975 | 500,000 | — | 0.10 | 0.15 | 0.35 | — |
| 1977 | 500,000 | — | 0.10 | 0.15 | 0.35 | — |
| 1979 | 500,000 | — | 0.10 | 0.15 | 0.35 | — |
| 1980 | 1,100,000 | — | 0.10 | 0.15 | 0.35 | — |
| 1981 | 900,000 | — | 0.10 | 0.15 | 0.35 | — |
| 1982 | 200,000 | — | 0.10 | 0.15 | 0.35 | — |
| 1983 | 800,000 | — | 0.10 | 0.15 | 0.35 | — |
| 1983 Proof | 10,000 | Value: 1.50 | | | | |
| 1984 | 500,000 | — | 0.10 | 0.15 | 0.35 | — |
| 1985 | — | — | 0.10 | 0.15 | 0.35 | — |

**5 CENTS** **KM# 45** **Composition:** Copper-Nickel **Reverse:** Queen angel fish

| Date | Mintage | F | VF | XF | Unc | BU |
|---|---|---|---|---|---|---|
| 1986 | 700,000 | — | 0.10 | 0.15 | 0.35 | — |
| 1986 Proof | Inc. above | Value: 2.50 | | | | |
| 1987 | — | — | 0.10 | 0.15 | 0.35 | — |
| 1988 | — | — | 0.10 | 0.15 | 0.35 | — |
| 1990 | — | — | 0.10 | 0.15 | 0.35 | — |
| 1993 | — | — | 0.10 | 0.15 | 0.35 | — |
| 1994 | — | — | 0.10 | 0.15 | 0.35 | — |
| 1995 | — | — | 0.10 | 0.15 | 0.35 | — |
| 1997 | — | — | 0.10 | 0.15 | 0.35 | — |

**5 CENTS** **KM# 45a** **Weight:** 5.7000 g. **Composition:** 0.9250 Silver .1695 oz. ASW **Reverse:** Queen angel fish **Note:** In sets only.

| Date | Mintage | F | VF | XF | Unc | BU |
|---|---|---|---|---|---|---|
| 1995 | 2,000 | — | — | — | 8.00 | — |

**5 CENTS** **KM# 45b** **Weight:** 5.7000 g. **Composition:** 0.9170 Gold .2859 oz. AGW **Reverse:** Queen angel fish **Note:** In sets only.

| Date | Mintage | F | VF | XF | Unc | BU |
|---|---|---|---|---|---|---|
| 1995 | 500 | — | — | — | 200 | — |

**5 CENTS** **KM# 108** **Composition:** Copper-Nickel **Obverse:** Queen's portrait Obv. Designer: Rank-Broadley **Reverse:** Queen angel fish

| Date | Mintage | F | VF | XF | Unc | BU |
|---|---|---|---|---|---|---|
| 1999 | — | — | — | — | 0.75 | — |
| 1999 Proof | 2,500 | Value: 3.50 | | | | |
| 2000 | — | — | — | — | 0.75 | — |
| 2000 Proof | — | Value: 3.50 | | | | |

**10 CENTS** **KM# 17** **Composition:** Copper-Nickel **Reverse:** Bermuda lily

| Date | Mintage | F | VF | XF | Unc | BU |
|---|---|---|---|---|---|---|
| 1970 | 2,500,000 | — | 0.10 | 0.15 | 0.35 | — |
| 1970 Proof | 11,000 | Value: 0.50 | | | | |
| 1971 | 2,000,000 | — | 0.10 | 0.15 | 0.35 | — |
| 1978 | 500,000 | — | 0.10 | 0.15 | 0.40 | — |
| 1979 | 800,000 | — | 0.10 | 0.15 | 0.40 | — |
| 1980 | 1,100,000 | — | 0.10 | 0.15 | 0.35 | — |
| 1981 | 1,300,000 | — | 0.10 | 0.15 | 0.35 | — |
| 1982 | 400,000 | — | 0.10 | 0.15 | 0.40 | — |
| 1983 | 1,000,000 | — | 0.10 | 0.15 | 0.35 | — |
| 1983 Proof | 10,000 | Value: 2.00 | | | | |
| 1984 | 500,000 | — | 0.10 | 0.15 | 0.40 | — |
| 1985 | — | — | 0.10 | 0.15 | 0.40 | — |

**10 CENTS** **KM# 46** **Composition:** Copper-Nickel **Reverse:** Bermuda lily

| Date | Mintage | F | VF | XF | Unc | BU |
|---|---|---|---|---|---|---|
| 1986 | 350,000 | — | 0.10 | 0.15 | 0.40 | — |
| 1986 Proof | Inc. above | Value: 3.50 | | | | |
| 1987 | — | — | 0.10 | 0.15 | 0.40 | — |
| 1988 | — | — | 0.10 | 0.15 | 0.40 | — |
| 1990 | — | — | 0.10 | 0.15 | 0.40 | — |
| 1993 | — | — | 0.10 | 0.15 | 0.40 | — |
| 1994 | — | — | 0.10 | 0.15 | 0.40 | — |
| 1995 | — | — | 0.10 | 0.15 | 0.40 | — |
| 1996 | — | — | 0.10 | 0.15 | 0.40 | — |
| 1997 | — | — | 0.10 | 0.15 | 0.40 | — |

**10 CENTS** **KM# 46a** **Weight:** 2.8000 g. **Composition:** 0.9250 Silver .0833 oz. ASW **Reverse:** Bermuda lily **Note:** In sets only.

| Date | Mintage | F | VF | XF | Unc | BU |
|---|---|---|---|---|---|---|
| 1995 | 2,000 | — | — | — | 10.00 | — |

**10 CENTS** **KM# 46b** **Weight:** 4.7500 g. **Composition:** 0.9170 Gold .14 oz. AGW **Reverse:** Bermuda lily **Note:** In sets only.

| Date | Mintage | F | VF | XF | Unc | BU |
|---|---|---|---|---|---|---|
| 1995 | 500 | — | — | — | 135 | — |

**10 CENTS** **KM# 109** **Composition:** Copper-Nickel **Obverse:** Queen's portrait Obv. Designer: Rank-Broadley **Reverse:** Bermuda lily

| Date | Mintage | F | VF | XF | Unc | BU |
|---|---|---|---|---|---|---|
| 1999 | — | — | — | — | 0.85 | — |
| 1999 Proof | 2,500 | Value: 6.00 | | | | |
| 2000 | — | — | — | — | 0.85 | — |
| 2000 Proof | — | Value: 6.00 | | | | |

**25 CENTS** **KM# 18** **Composition:** Copper-Nickel **Reverse:** Yellow-billed tropical bird

| Date | Mintage | F | VF | XF | Unc | BU |
|---|---|---|---|---|---|---|
| 1970 | 1,500,000 | — | 0.30 | 0.50 | 1.25 | — |
| 1970 Proof | 11,000 | Value: 2.00 | | | | |
| 1973 | 1,000,000 | — | 0.30 | 0.50 | 1.25 | — |
| 1979 | 570,000 | — | 0.30 | 0.50 | 1.25 | — |
| 1980 | 1,120,000 | — | 0.30 | 0.50 | 1.25 | — |
| 1981 | 2,200,000 | — | 0.30 | 0.50 | 1.25 | — |
| 1982 | 160,000 | — | 0.30 | 0.50 | 1.50 | — |
| 1983 | 600,000 | — | 0.30 | 0.50 | 1.25 | — |
| 1983 Proof | 10,000 | Value: 2.50 | | | | |
| 1984 | 400,000 | — | 0.30 | 0.50 | 1.25 | — |
| 1985 | — | — | 0.30 | 0.50 | 1.25 | — |

**25 CENTS** **KM# 32** **Composition:** Copper-Nickel **Subject:** 375th anniversary of Bermuda **Obverse:** Similar to KM#18 **Reverse:** Arms of the Bermudas

| Date | Mintage | F | VF | XF | Unc | BU |
|---|---|---|---|---|---|---|
| 1984 | — | — | — | 1.50 | 4.50 | — |

**25 CENTS** **KM# 32a** **Weight:** 5.9600 g. **Composition:** 0.9250 Silver .1772 oz. ASW **Subject:** 375th anniversary of Bermuda **Obverse:** Similar to KM#18 **Reverse:** Arms of the Bermudas

| Date | Mintage | F | VF | XF | Unc | BU |
|---|---|---|---|---|---|---|
| 1984 Proof | 1,750 | Value: 18.50 | | | | |

**25 CENTS** **KM# 33** **Composition:** Copper-Nickel **Subject:** 375th anniversary of Bermuda **Obverse:** Similar to KM#18 **Reverse:** City of Hamilton

| Date | Mintage | F | VF | XF | Unc | BU |
|---|---|---|---|---|---|---|
| 1984 | — | — | — | 1.00 | 4.50 | — |

**25 CENTS** **KM# 33a** **Weight:** 5.9600 g. **Composition:** 0.9250 Silver .1772 oz. ASW **Subject:** 375th anniversary of Bermuda **Obverse:** Similar to KM#18 **Reverse:** City of Hamilton

| Date | Mintage | F | VF | XF | Unc | BU |
|---|---|---|---|---|---|---|
| 1984 Proof | 1,750 | Value: 18.50 | | | | |

**25 CENTS** **KM# 34** **Composition:** Copper-Nickel **Subject:** 375th anniversary of Bermuda **Obverse:** Similar to KM#18 **Reverse:** Town of St. George

| Date | Mintage | F | VF | XF | Unc | BU |
|---|---|---|---|---|---|---|
| 1984 | — | — | — | 1.50 | 4.50 | — |

**25 CENTS** **KM# 34a** **Weight:** 5.9600 g. **Composition:** 0.9250 Silver .1772 oz. ASW **Subject:** 375th anniversary of Bermuda **Obverse:** Similar to KM#18 **Reverse:** Town of St. George

| Date | Mintage | F | VF | XF | Unc | BU |
|---|---|---|---|---|---|---|
| 1984 Proof | 1,750 | Value: 18.50 | | | | |

**25 CENTS** **KM# 35** **Composition:** Copper-Nickel **Subject:** 375th anniversary of Bermuda **Obverse:** Similar to KM#18 **Reverse:** Warwick Parish

| Date | Mintage | F | VF | XF | Unc | BU |
|---|---|---|---|---|---|---|
| 1984 | — | — | — | 1.50 | 4.50 | — |

**25 CENTS** **KM# 35a** **Weight:** 5.9600 g. **Composition:** 0.9250 Silver .1772 oz. ASW **Subject:** 375th anniversary of Bermuda **Obverse:** Similar to KM#18 **Reverse:** Warwick Parish

| Date | Mintage | F | VF | XF | Unc | BU |
|---|---|---|---|---|---|---|
| 1984 Proof | 1,750 | Value: 18.50 | | | | |

**25 CENTS** **KM# 36** **Composition:** Copper-Nickel **Subject:** 375th anniversary of Bermuda **Obverse:** Similar to KM#18 **Reverse:** Smith's Parish

| Date | Mintage | F | VF | XF | Unc | BU |
|---|---|---|---|---|---|---|
| 1984 | — | — | — | 1.50 | 4.50 | — |

**25 CENTS** **KM# 36a** **Weight:** 5.9600 g. **Composition:** 0.9250 Silver .1772 oz. ASW **Subject:** 375th anniversary of Bermuda **Obverse:** Similar to KM#18 **Reverse:** Smith's Parish

| Date | Mintage | F | VF | XF | Unc | BU |
|---|---|---|---|---|---|---|
| 1984 Proof | 1,750 | Value: 18.50 | | | | |

**25 CENTS** **KM# 37** **Composition:** Copper-Nickel **Subject:** 375th anniversary of Bermuda **Obverse:** Similar to KM#18 **Reverse:** Devonshire Parish

| Date | Mintage | F | VF | XF | Unc | BU |
|---|---|---|---|---|---|---|
| 1984 | — | — | — | 1.50 | 4.50 | — |

**25 CENTS** **KM# 37a** **Weight:** 5.9600 g. **Composition:** 0.9250 Silver .1772 oz. ASW **Subject:** 375th anniversary of Bermuda **Obverse:** Similar to KM#18 **Reverse:** Devonshire Parish

| Date | Mintage | F | VF | XF | Unc | BU |
|---|---|---|---|---|---|---|
| 1984 Proof | 1,750 | Value: 18.50 | | | | |

**25 CENTS** **KM# 38** **Composition:** Copper-Nickel **Subject:** 375th anniversary of Bermuda **Obverse:** Similar to KM#18 **Reverse:** Sandy's Parish

| Date | Mintage | F | VF | XF | Unc | BU |
|---|---|---|---|---|---|---|
| 1984 | — | — | — | 1.50 | 4.50 | — |

**25 CENTS** **KM# 38a** **Weight:** 5.9600 g. **Composition:** 0.9250 Silver .1772 oz. ASW **Subject:** 375th anniversary of Bermuda **Obverse:** Similar to KM#18 **Reverse:** Sandy's Parish

| Date | Mintage | F | VF | XF | Unc | BU |
|---|---|---|---|---|---|---|
| 1984 Proof | 1,750 | Value: 18.50 | | | | |

**25 CENTS** **KM# 39** **Composition:** Copper-Nickel **Subject:** 375th anniversary of Bermuda **Obverse:** Similar to KM#18 **Reverse:** Hamilton Parish

| Date | Mintage | F | VF | XF | Unc | BU |
|---|---|---|---|---|---|---|
| 1984 | — | — | — | 1.50 | 4.50 | — |

**25 CENTS** **KM# 39a** **Weight:** 5.9600 g. **Composition:** 0.9250 Silver .1772 oz. ASW **Subject:** 375th anniversary of Bermuda **Obverse:** Similar to KM#18 **Reverse:** Hamilton Parish

| Date | Mintage | F | VF | XF | Unc | BU |
|---|---|---|---|---|---|---|
| 1984 Proof | 1,750 | Value: 18.50 | | | | |

**25 CENTS** **KM# 40** **Composition:** Copper-Nickel **Subject:** 375th anniversary of Bermuda **Obverse:** Similar to KM#18 **Reverse:** Southampton Parish

| Date | Mintage | F | VF | XF | Unc | BU |
|---|---|---|---|---|---|---|
| 1984 | — | — | — | 1.50 | 4.50 | — |

**25 CENTS** **KM# 40a** **Weight:** 5.9600 g. **Composition:** 0.9250 Silver .1772 oz. ASW **Subject:** 375th anniversary of Bermuda **Obverse:** Similar to KM#18 **Reverse:** Southampton Parish

| Date | Mintage | F | VF | XF | Unc | BU |
|---|---|---|---|---|---|---|
| 1984 Proof | 1,750 | Value: 18.50 | | | | |

**25 CENTS** **KM# 41** **Composition:** Copper-Nickel **Subject:** 375th anniversary of Bermuda **Obverse:** Similar to KM#18 **Reverse:** Pembroke Parish

| Date | Mintage | F | VF | XF | Unc | BU |
|---|---|---|---|---|---|---|
| 1984 | — | — | — | 1.50 | 4.50 | — |

**25 CENTS** **KM# 41a** **Weight:** 5.9600 g. **Composition:** 0.9250 Silver .1772 oz. ASW **Subject:** 375th anniversary of Bermuda **Obverse:** Similar to KM#18 **Reverse:** Pembroke Parish

| Date | Mintage | F | VF | XF | Unc | BU |
|---|---|---|---|---|---|---|
| 1984 Proof | 1,750 | Value: 18.50 | | | | |

**25 CENTS** **KM# 42** **Composition:** Copper-Nickel **Subject:** 375th anniversary of Bermuda **Obverse:** Similar to KM#18 **Reverse:** Paget Parish

| Date | Mintage | F | VF | XF | Unc | BU |
|---|---|---|---|---|---|---|
| 1984 | — | — | — | 1.50 | 4.50 | — |

**25 CENTS** **KM# 42a** **Weight:** 5.9600 g. **Composition:** 0.9250 Silver .1772 oz. ASW **Subject:** 375th anniversary of Bermuda **Obverse:** Similar to KM#18 **Reverse:** Paget Parish

| Date | Mintage | F | VF | XF | Unc | BU |
|---|---|---|---|---|---|---|
| 1984 Proof | 1,750 | Value: 18.50 | | | | |

**25 CENTS** **KM# 47** **Composition:** Copper-Nickel **Subject:** 375th anniversary of Bermuda **Obverse:** Similar to KM#18 **Reverse:** Paget Parish

| Date | Mintage | F | VF | XF | Unc | BU |
|---|---|---|---|---|---|---|
| 1986 | 560,000 | — | 0.30 | 0.40 | 0.75 | |
| 1986 Proof | Inc. above | Value: 6.00 | | | | |
| 1987 | — | — | 0.30 | 0.40 | 0.75 | — |
| 1988 | — | — | 0.30 | 0.40 | 0.75 | — |
| 1993 | — | — | 0.30 | 0.40 | 0.75 | — |
| 1994 | — | — | 0.30 | 0.40 | 0.75 | — |
| 1995 | — | — | 0.30 | 0.40 | 0.75 | — |
| 1996 | — | — | 0.30 | 0.40 | 0.75 | — |
| 1997 | — | — | 0.30 | 0.40 | 0.75 | — |

**25 CENTS** **KM# 47a** **Weight:** 7.0000 g. **Composition:** 0.9250 Silver .2082 oz. ASW **Subject:** 375th anniversary of Bermuda **Obverse:** Similar to KM#18 **Reverse:** Paget Parish **Note:** In sets only.

| Date | Mintage | F | VF | XF | Unc | BU |
|---|---|---|---|---|---|---|
| 1995 | 2,000 | — | — | — | 18.00 | — |

**25 CENTS** **KM# 47b** **Weight:** 11.7000 g. **Composition:** 0.9170 Gold .3448 oz. AGW **Subject:** 375th anniversary of Bermuda **Obverse:** Similar to KM#18 **Reverse:** Paget Parish **Note:** In sets only.

| Date | Mintage | F | VF | XF | Unc | BU |
|---|---|---|---|---|---|---|
| 1995 | 500 | — | — | — | 225 | — |

**25 CENTS** **KM# 110** **Composition:** Copper-Nickel **Obverse:** Queen's portrait Obv. Designer: Rank-Broadley **Reverse:** Bermuda longtail bird

| Date | Mintage | F | VF | XF | Unc | BU |
|---|---|---|---|---|---|---|
| 1999 | — | — | — | — | 1.50 | — |
| 1999 Proof | 2,500 | Value: 12.00 | | | | |
| 2000 | — | — | — | — | 1.50 | — |
| 2000 Proof | — | Value: 9.00 | | | | |

**50 CENTS** **KM# 19** **Composition:** Copper-Nickel

| Date | Mintage | F | VF | XF | Unc | BU |
|---|---|---|---|---|---|---|
| 1970 | 1,000,000 | — | 0.60 | 0.75 | 1.00 | — |
| 1970 Proof | 11,000 | Value: 2.00 | | | | |
| 1978 | 200,000 | — | 0.60 | 0.85 | 1.25 | — |
| 1980 | 60,000 | — | 0.60 | 0.85 | 1.50 | — |
| 1981 | 100,000 | — | 0.60 | 0.85 | 1.25 | — |
| 1982 | 80,000 | — | 0.60 | 0.85 | 1.50 | — |
| 1983 | 60,000 | — | 0.60 | 0.85 | 1.50 | — |
| 1983 Proof | 10,000 | Value: 4.50 | | | | |
| 1984 | 40,000 | — | 0.60 | 0.85 | 1.50 | — |
| 1985 | — | — | 0.60 | 0.85 | 1.50 | — |

**50 CENTS** **KM# 48** **Composition:** Copper-Nickel

| Date | Mintage | F | VF | XF | Unc | BU |
|---|---|---|---|---|---|---|
| 1986 | 60,000 | — | 0.60 | 0.85 | 1.50 | — |
| 1986 Proof | Inc. above | Value: 7.50 | | | | |
| 1988 | — | — | 0.60 | 0.85 | 1.50 | — |

**DOLLAR** **KM# 20** **Weight:** 28.2800 g. **Composition:** 0.8000 Silver .7273 oz. ASW

| Date | Mintage | F | VF | XF | Unc | BU |
|---|---|---|---|---|---|---|
| 1970 Proof | 11,000 | Value: 15.00 | | | | |

**DOLLAR** KM# 22 **Weight:** 28.2800 g. **Composition:** 0.5000 Silver .4546 oz. ASW **Subject:** Silver wedding anniversary

| Date | Mintage | F | VF | XF | Unc | BU |
|---|---|---|---|---|---|---|
| 1972 | 75,000 | — | — | — | 7.50 | — |

**DOLLAR** KM# 22a **Weight:** 28.2800 g. **Composition:** 0.9250 Silver .8411 oz. ASW **Subject:** Silver wedding anniversary

| Date | Mintage | F | VF | XF | Unc | BU |
|---|---|---|---|---|---|---|
| 1972 Proof | 15,000 | Value: 12.00 | | | | |

**DOLLAR** KM# 28 **Composition:** Copper-Nickel **Subject:** Wedding of Prince Charles and Lady Diana **Obverse:** Similar to KM#20

| Date | Mintage | F | VF | XF | Unc | BU |
|---|---|---|---|---|---|---|
| 1981 | 65,000 | — | — | — | 7.00 | — |

**DOLLAR** KM# 28a **Weight:** 28.2800 g. **Composition:** 0.9250 Silver .8411 oz. ASW **Subject:** Wedding of Prince Charles and Lady Diana **Obverse:** Similar to KM#20

| Date | Mintage | F | VF | XF | Unc | BU |
|---|---|---|---|---|---|---|
| 1981 Proof | 17,000 | Value: 17.50 | | | | |

**DOLLAR** KM# 30 **Composition:** Nickel-Brass **Subject:** Cahow over Bermuda **Obverse:** Similar to KM#20

| Date | Mintage | F | VF | XF | Unc | BU |
|---|---|---|---|---|---|---|
| 1983 | 250,000 | — | — | — | 4.00 | — |
| 1983 Proof | 10,000 | Value: 7.00 | | | | |

**DOLLAR** KM# 43 **Composition:** Copper-Nickel **Subject:** Cruise ship tourism

| Date | Mintage | F | VF | XF | Unc | BU |
|---|---|---|---|---|---|---|
| 1985 | 11,000 | — | — | — | 5.00 | — |

**DOLLAR** KM# 43a **Weight:** 28.2800 g. **Composition:** 0.9250 Silver .8411 oz. ASW **Subject:** Cruise ship tourism

| Date | Mintage | F | VF | XF | Unc | BU |
|---|---|---|---|---|---|---|
| 1985 | 2,500 | — | — | — | 25.00 | — |
| 1985 Proof | 4,000 | Value: 25.00 | | | | |

**DOLLAR** KM# 49 **Composition:** Copper-Nickel **Series:** World Wildlife Fund **Reverse:** Sea turtle

| Date | Mintage | F | VF | XF | Unc | BU |
|---|---|---|---|---|---|---|
| 1986 | — | — | — | — | 12.00 | — |

**DOLLAR** KM# 49a **Weight:** 28.2800 g. **Composition:** 0.9250 Silver .8411 oz. ASW **Series:** World Wildlife Fund **Reverse:** Sea turtle

| Date | Mintage | F | VF | XF | Unc | BU |
|---|---|---|---|---|---|---|
| 1986 | Est. 10,000 | — | — | — | 17.50 | — |
| 1986 Proof | Est. 25,000 | Value: 22.50 | | | | |

**DOLLAR** KM# 50 **Composition:** Nickel-Brass **Obverse:** Similar to KM#43 **Reverse:** Cahow over Bermuda

| Date | Mintage | F | VF | XF | Unc | BU |
|---|---|---|---|---|---|---|
| 1986 Proof | — | Value: 12.50 | | | | |

**DOLLAR** KM# 52 **Composition:** Copper-Nickel **Subject:** 50th anniversary of commercial aviation **Reverse:** Amphibious plane

| Date | Mintage | F | VF | XF | Unc | BU |
|---|---|---|---|---|---|---|
| 1987 | — | — | — | — | 7.00 | — |

**DOLLAR** KM# 52a **Weight:** 28.2800 g. **Composition:** 0.6250 Silver .8411 oz. ASW **Subject:** 50th anniversary of commercial aviation **Reverse:** Amphibious plane

| Date | Mintage | F | VF | XF | Unc | BU |
|---|---|---|---|---|---|---|
| 1987 | 4,000 | — | — | — | 20.00 | — |
| 1987 Proof | 5,000 | Value: 27.50 | | | | |

**DOLLAR** KM# 55 **Composition:** Copper-Nickel **Subject:** Railroad

| Date | Mintage | F | VF | XF | Unc | BU |
|---|---|---|---|---|---|---|
| 1988 | — | — | — | — | 7.00 | — |

**DOLLAR** KM# 56a **Weight:** 9.2000 g. **Composition:** 0.9250 Silver .2736 oz. ASW

| Date | Mintage | F | VF | XF | Unc | BU |
|---|---|---|---|---|---|---|
| 1988 Proof | Est. 3,000 | Value: 25.00 | | | | |
| 1995 | 2,000 | — | — | — | 40.00 | — |

**Note:** In sets only.

**DOLLAR** KM# 56 **Composition:** Nickel-Brass **Note:** Circulation type.

| Date | Mintage | F | VF | XF | Unc | BU |
|---|---|---|---|---|---|---|
| 1988 | — | — | — | — | 3.00 | — |
| 1993 | 15,000 | — | — | — | 5.00 | — |

**Note:** In sets only.

| Date | Mintage | F | VF | XF | Unc | BU |
|---|---|---|---|---|---|---|
| 1996 | — | — | — | — | 3.00 | — |
| 1997 | — | — | — | — | 3.00 | — |

**DOLLAR** KM# 55a **Weight:** 28.2800 g. **Composition:** 0.9250 Silver .8411 oz. ASW **Subject:** Railroad

| Date | Mintage | F | VF | XF | Unc | BU |
|---|---|---|---|---|---|---|
| 1988 | — | — | — | — | 20.00 | — |
| 1988 Proof | — | Value: 30.00 | | | | |

**DOLLAR** KM# 61 **Composition:** Copper-Nickel **Subject:** Monarch Conservation Project

| Date | Mintage | F | VF | XF | Unc | BU |
|---|---|---|---|---|---|---|
| 1989 | — | — | — | — | 8.00 | — |

**DOLLAR** KM# 61a **Weight:** 28.2800 g. **Composition:** 0.9250 Silver .8411 oz. ASW **Subject:** Monarch Conservation Project

| Date | Mintage | F | VF | XF | Unc | BU |
|---|---|---|---|---|---|---|
| 1989 | Est. 5,000 | — | — | — | 22.50 | — |
| 1989 Proof | Est. 5,000 | Value: 37.50 | | | | |

**DOLLAR** KM# 67 **Composition:** Copper-Nickel **Subject:** Queen Mother's 90th birthday

| Date | Mintage | F | VF | XF | Unc | BU |
|---|---|---|---|---|---|---|
| 1990 | — | — | — | — | 5.00 | — |

**DOLLAR** KM# 67a **Weight:** 28.2800 g. **Composition:** 0.9250 Silver .8411 oz. ASW **Subject:** Queen Mother's 90th birthday

| Date | Mintage | F | VF | XF | Unc | BU |
|---|---|---|---|---|---|---|
| 1990 Proof | 1,473 | Value: 50.00 | | | | |

**DOLLAR** KM# 78 **Composition:** Bronze **Series:** Olympics **Obverse:** Portrait of Queen Elizabeth **Reverse:** Rings, similar to 5 Dollars, KM#79

| Date | Mintage | F | VF | XF | Unc | BU |
|---|---|---|---|---|---|---|
| 1992 Proof | Est. 250 | Value: 35.00 | | | | |

**DOLLAR** KM# 85 **Weight:** 31.4700 g. **Composition:** 0.9250 Silver .9359 oz. ASW **Series:** 1992 Olympics **Reverse:** Sailboats

| Date | Mintage | F | VF | XF | Unc | BU |
|---|---|---|---|---|---|---|
| ND(1993) Proof | Est. 25,000 | Value: 50.00 | | | | |

**DOLLAR** KM# 56b **Weight:** 15.5000 g. **Composition:** 0.9170 Gold .4568 oz. AGW

| Date | Mintage | F | VF | XF | Unc | BU |
|---|---|---|---|---|---|---|
| 1995 | 500 | — | — | — | 450 | — |

**Note:** In sets only.

**DOLLAR** **KM# 91** **Composition:** Copper-Nickel **Subject:** International Senior Games

| Date | Mintage | F | VF | XF | Unc | BU |
|---|---|---|---|---|---|---|
| 1996 | 1,000 | — | — | — | 25.00 | — |

**DOLLAR** **KM# 94** **Composition:** Copper-Nickel **Subject:** Queen Elizabeth II's 70th birthday **Obverse:** Queen's portrait **Reverse:** Horse-drawn carriage

| Date | Mintage | F | VF | XF | Unc | BU |
|---|---|---|---|---|---|---|
| ND(1996) | — | — | — | — | 12.00 | — |

**DOLLAR** **KM# 105** **Weight:** 28.2800 g. **Composition:** 0.9250 Silver .8416 oz. ASW **Series:** Olympic Games **Obverse:** Queen's portrait **Reverse:** Horse jumping

| Date | Mintage | F | VF | XF | Unc | BU |
|---|---|---|---|---|---|---|
| 1996 Proof | — | Value: 50.00 | | | | |

**DOLLAR** **KM# 95** **Composition:** Copper-Nickel **Subject:** Wreck of the Sea Venture **Obverse:** Queen's portrait **Reverse:** Shipwreck from Bermudan arms

| Date | Mintage | F | VF | XF | Unc | BU |
|---|---|---|---|---|---|---|
| 1997 | — | — | — | — | 12.00 | — |

**DOLLAR** **KM# 119** **Weight:** 28.2800 g. **Composition:** 0.9250 Silver .8410 oz. ASW **Subject:** World Wildlife Fund - Conserving Nature **Obverse:** Queen's head right. **Reverse:** Bermuda Rock Skink (Eumeces longirostris) on rock. **Edge:** Reeded. **Size:** 39 mm.

| Date | Mintage | F | VF | XF | Unc | BU |
|---|---|---|---|---|---|---|
| 1997 Proof | — | Value: 37.50 | | | | |

**DOLLAR** **KM# 104** **Composition:** Copper-Nickel **Obverse:** Queen's portrait **Reverse:** Ship and map

| Date | Mintage | F | VF | XF | Unc | BU |
|---|---|---|---|---|---|---|
| 1998 | — | — | — | — | 12.00 | — |

**DOLLAR** **KM# 111** **Composition:** Nickel-Brass **Obverse:** Queen's portrait Obv. Designer: Rank-Broadley **Reverse:** Sailboat

| Date | Mintage | F | VF | XF | Unc | BU |
|---|---|---|---|---|---|---|
| 1999 | — | — | — | — | 3.00 | — |
| 1999 Proof | 2,500 | Value: 25.00 | | | | |
| 2000 | — | — | — | — | 3.00 | — |
| 2000 Proof | — | Value: 25.00 | | | | |

**DOLLAR** **KM# 117** **Weight:** 28.2800 g. **Composition:** Copper-Nickel **Subject:** Tall Ships **Obverse:** Queen's head right. **Reverse:** Three-masted sailing ship. **Edge:** Reeded. **Size:** 38.6 mm.

| Date | Mintage | F | VF | XF | Unc | BU |
|---|---|---|---|---|---|---|
| 2000 | 10,000 | — | — | — | 15.00 | — |

**DOLLAR** **KM# 117a** **Weight:** 28.2800 g. **Composition:** 0.9250 Silver .8410 oz. ASW **Subject:** Tall Ships **Obverse:** Queen's head right. **Reverse:** Three-masted sailing ship. **Edge:** Reeded. **Size:** 38.6 mm.

| Date | Mintage | F | VF | XF | Unc | BU |
|---|---|---|---|---|---|---|
| 2000 Proof | 1,500 | Value: 400 | | | | |

**2 DOLLARS** **KM# 64** **Weight:** 28.2800 g. **Composition:** 0.9250 Silver .8411 oz. ASW **Reverse:** Cicada insects

| Date | Mintage | F | VF | XF | Unc | BU |
|---|---|---|---|---|---|---|
| 1990 Proof | 2,500 | Value: 30.00 | | | | |

**2 DOLLARS** **KM# 65** **Weight:** 28.2800 g. **Composition:** 0.9250 Silver .8411 oz. ASW **Subject:** Wildlife **Reverse:** Tree frog

| Date | Mintage | F | VF | XF | Unc | BU |
|---|---|---|---|---|---|---|
| 1990 Proof | 2,500 | Value: 35.00 | | | | |

**2 DOLLARS** **KM# 68** **Weight:** 28.2800 g. **Composition:** 0.9250 Silver .8411 oz. ASW **Reverse:** Yellow-crowned night heron

| Date | Mintage | F | VF | XF | Unc | BU |
|---|---|---|---|---|---|---|
| 1991 Proof | Est. 2,500 | Value: 30.00 | | | | |

**2 DOLLARS** **KM# 69** **Weight:** 28.2800 g. **Composition:** 0.9250 Silver .8411 oz. ASW **Reverse:** Spiny lobster

| Date | Mintage | F | VF | XF | Unc | BU |
|---|---|---|---|---|---|---|
| 1991 Proof | Est. 2,500 | Value: 30.00 | | | | |

**2 DOLLARS** **KM# 71** **Weight:** 28.2800 g. **Composition:** 0.9250 Silver .8411 oz. ASW **Reverse:** Bluebird feeding nestling

| Date | Mintage | F | VF | XF | Unc | BU |
|---|---|---|---|---|---|---|
| 1992 Proof | Est. 2,500 | Value: 37.50 | | | | |

**2 DOLLARS** **KM# 72** **Weight:** 28.2800 g. **Composition:** 0.9250 Silver .8411 oz. ASW **Reverse:** Cedar tree

| Date | Mintage | F | VF | XF | Unc | BU |
|---|---|---|---|---|---|---|
| 1992 Proof | Est. 2,500 | Value: 30.00 | | | | |

**2 DOLLARS** **KM# 81** **Weight:** 23.0000 g. **Composition:** 0.9250 Silver .684 oz. ASW **Subject:** 200 years of Bermudan coinage

| Date | Mintage | F | VF | XF | Unc | BU |
|---|---|---|---|---|---|---|
| 1993 Proof | 5,000 | Value: 40.00 | | | | |

**2 DOLLARS** **KM# 83** **Weight:** 28.2800 g. **Composition:** 0.9250 Silver .8411 oz. ASW **Reverse:** Humpback whale

| Date | Mintage | F | VF | XF | Unc | BU |
|---|---|---|---|---|---|---|
| 1993 Proof | Est. 2,500 | Value: 45.00 | | | | |

**2 DOLLARS** **KM# 84** **Weight:** 28.2800 g. **Composition:** 0.9250 Silver .8411 oz. ASW **Reverse:** Bermuda longtail bird

| Date | Mintage | F | VF | XF | Unc | BU |
|---|---|---|---|---|---|---|
| 1993 Proof | Est. 2,500 | Value: 40.00 | | | | |

**2 DOLLARS** **KM# 89** **Weight:** 28.2800 g. **Composition:** 0.9250 Silver .8411 oz. ASW **Subject:** City of Hamilton's 200th anniversary **Reverse:** Ship at dock

| Date | Mintage | F | VF | XF | Unc | BU |
|---|---|---|---|---|---|---|
| 1993 Proof | 250 | Value: 70.00 | | | | |

**2 DOLLARS** **KM# 86** **Weight:** 27.2800 g. **Composition:** 0.9250 Silver .8411 oz. ASW **Subject:** Royal visit **Reverse:** Map

| Date | Mintage | F | VF | XF | Unc | BU |
|---|---|---|---|---|---|---|
| 1994 Proof | — | Value: 40.00 | | | | |

**2 DOLLARS** **KM# 87** **Weight:** 28.2800 g. **Composition:** 0.9250 Silver .8411 oz. ASW **Reverse:** Longsnout seahorse

| Date | Mintage | F | VF | XF | Unc | BU |
|---|---|---|---|---|---|---|
| 1994 Proof | Est. 2,500 | Value: 50.00 | | | | |

**2 DOLLARS** **KM# 88** **Weight:** 28.2800 g. **Composition:** 0.9250 Silver .8411 oz. ASW **Reverse:** Lightbourn's fusinus (seashell)

| Date | Mintage | F | VF | XF | Unc | BU |
|---|---|---|---|---|---|---|
| 1994 Proof | Est. 2,500 | Value: 50.00 | | | | |

**2 DOLLARS** **KM# 116** **Weight:** 28.2800 g. **Composition:** Copper-Nickel **Subject:** Millennium **Obverse:** Queen's head right. **Reverse:** Radiant sun with sailing ship dividing dates 1999-2000 above map. **Edge:** Scalloped. **Size:** 38.6 mm.

| Date | Mintage | F | VF | XF | Unc | BU |
|---|---|---|---|---|---|---|
| 1999-2000 | — | — | — | — | 25.00 | — |

**2 DOLLARS** **KM# 116a** **Weight:** 28.2800 g. **Composition:** 0.9250 Silver .8410 oz. ASW **Subject:** Millennium **Obverse:** Queen's head right. **Reverse:** Radiant sun behind sailing ship dividing dates 1999-2000 above map. **Edge:** Scalloped. **Size:** 38.6 mm.

| Date | Mintage | F | VF | XF | Unc | BU |
|---|---|---|---|---|---|---|
| 1999-2000 Proof | — | Value: 65.00 | | | | |

**3 DOLLARS** **KM# 92** **Weight:** 20.0000 g. **Composition:** 0.9250 Silver .5948 oz. ASW **Subject:** Bermuda Triangle **Obverse:** Queen's portrait **Reverse:** Map, compass, capsizing ship **Note:** Similar to 60 Dollars, KM#93.

| Date | Mintage | F | VF | XF | Unc | BU |
|---|---|---|---|---|---|---|
| 1996 Proof | 5,000 | Value: 75.00 | | | | |

**3 DOLLARS** **KM# 99** **Weight:** 20.2500 g. **Composition:** 0.9250 Silver .6022 oz. ASW **Subject:** Wreck of the Sea Venture **Obverse:** Queen's portrait **Reverse:** Ship wreck scene

| Date | Mintage | F | VF | XF | Unc | BU |
|---|---|---|---|---|---|---|
| 1997 Proof | Est. 6,500 | Value: 50.00 | | | | |

**3 DOLLARS** **KM# 106** **Weight:** 20.0000 g. **Composition:** 0.9250 Silver .5948 oz. ASW **Obverse:** Queen's portrait **Reverse:** Sailing ship, map

| Date | Mintage | F | VF | XF | Unc | BU |
|---|---|---|---|---|---|---|
| 1998 Proof | Est. 6,500 | Value: 50.00 | | | | |

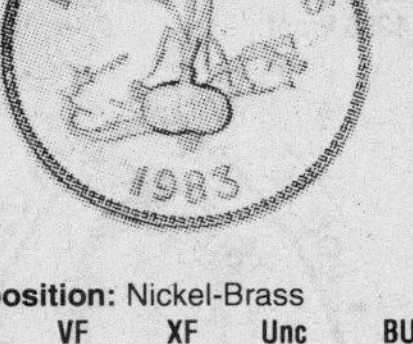


**5 DOLLARS** **KM# 31** **Composition:** Nickel-Brass

| Date | Mintage | F | VF | XF | Unc | BU |
|---|---|---|---|---|---|---|
| 1983 | 100,000 | — | — | — | 6.00 | — |
| 1983 Proof | 10,000 | Value: 10.00 | | | | |

**5 DOLLARS** **KM# 51** **Composition:** Brass **Obverse:** Similar to Dollar, KM#43 **Reverse:** Onion superimposed over Bermuda map

| Date | Mintage | F | VF | XF | Unc | BU |
|---|---|---|---|---|---|---|
| 1986 Proof | — | Value: 12.50 | | | | |

**5 DOLLARS** KM# 54 **Weight:** 155.5150 g. **Composition:** 0.9990 Silver 5 oz. ASW **Subject:** Sea Venture wreck **Obverse:** Similar to Dollar, KM#43 **Reverse:** Sailing ship **Size:** 65 mm. **Note:** Illustration reduced.

| Date | Mintage | F | VF | XF | Unc | BU |
|---|---|---|---|---|---|---|
| 1987 Proof | Est. 20,000 | Value: 75.00 | | | | |

**5 DOLLARS** KM# 62 **Weight:** 155.5150 g. **Composition:** 0.9990 Silver 5 oz. ASW **Subject:** San Antonio **Obverse:** Portrait of Queen Elizabeth **Reverse:** Sailing ship **Size:** 65 mm. **Note:** Illustration reduced.

| Date | Mintage | F | VF | XF | Unc | BU |
|---|---|---|---|---|---|---|
| 1988 Proof | 1,500 | Value: 135 | | | | |

**5 DOLLARS** KM# 79 **Weight:** 155.5150 g. **Composition:** 0.9990 Silver 5 oz. ASW **Series:** Olympics **Obverse:** Portrait of Queen Elizabeth **Reverse:** Rings **Size:** 65 mm. **Note:** Illustration reduced.

| Date | Mintage | F | VF | XF | Unc | BU |
|---|---|---|---|---|---|---|
| 1992 Proof | Est. 1,250 | Value: 135 | | | | |

**5 DOLLARS** KM# 90 **Weight:** 56.5600 g. **Composition:** 0.9250 Silver 1.6822 oz. ASW **Subject:** 375th anniversary of Bermudan Parliament

| Date | Mintage | F | VF | XF | Unc | BU |
|---|---|---|---|---|---|---|
| 1995 Proof | 375 | Value: 130 | | | | |

**5 DOLLARS** KM# 120 **Weight:** 28.2800 g. **Composition:** 0.9250 Silver .8410 oz. ASW **Subject:** Gombey Dancers **Obverse:** Queen's head right. **Reverse:** Multicolor costumed dancers. **Edge:** Reeded. **Size:** 38.6 mm.

| Date | Mintage | F | VF | XF | Unc | BU |
|---|---|---|---|---|---|---|
| 2001 Proof | 3,500 | Value: 65.00 | | | | |

**9 DOLLARS** KM# 96 **Weight:** 155.5175 g. **Composition:** 0.9990 Silver 5 oz. ASW **Subject:** Bermuda Triangle **Obverse:** Queen's portrait **Reverse:** Map, compass, capsizing ship **Note:** Similar to 60 Dollars, KM#93.

| Date | Mintage | F | VF | XF | Unc | BU |
|---|---|---|---|---|---|---|
| 1996 Proof | Est. 1,000 | Value: 200 | | | | |

**9 DOLLARS** KM# 100 **Weight:** 155.5175 g. **Composition:** 0.9990 Silver 5 oz. ASW **Subject:** Wreck of the Sea Venture **Obverse:** Queen's portrait **Reverse:** Ship wreck scene **Note:** Similar to 60 Dollars, KM#102.

| Date | Mintage | F | VF | XF | Unc | BU |
|---|---|---|---|---|---|---|
| 1997 Proof | Est. 1,000 | Value: 200 | | | | |

**9 DOLLARS** KM# 112 **Weight:** 155.5200 g. **Composition:** 0.9990 Silver 4.9951 oz. ASW **Subject:** Bermuda Triangle **Obverse:** Queen's portrait **Reverse:** Map and ship, The Deliverance

| Date | Mintage | F | VF | XF | Unc | BU |
|---|---|---|---|---|---|---|
| 1998 Proof | Est. 1,000 | Value: 200 | | | | |

**10 DOLLARS** KM# 57 **Weight:** 3.1340 g. **Composition:** 0.9990 Gold .1007 oz. AGW **Subject:** Hogge money **Reverse:** Wild pig

| Date | Mintage | F | VF | XF | Unc | BU |
|---|---|---|---|---|---|---|
| 1989 Proof | 500 | Value: 100 | | | | |

**10 DOLLARS** KM# 74 **Weight:** 3.1340 g. **Composition:** 0.9990 Gold .1007 oz. AGW **Subject:** Hogge money **Reverse:** Ship

| Date | Mintage | F | VF | XF | Unc | BU |
|---|---|---|---|---|---|---|
| 1990 Proof | 500 | Value: 100 | | | | |

**10 DOLLARS** KM# 66 **Weight:** 3.1340 g. **Composition:** 0.9990 Gold .1007 oz. AGW **Subject:** Wildlife **Reverse:** Tree frog **Note:** Similar to 2 Dollars, KM#65.

| Date | Mintage | F | VF | XF | Unc | BU |
|---|---|---|---|---|---|---|
| 1990 | 1,000 | — | — | — | 75.00 | — |

**10 DOLLARS** KM# 70 **Weight:** 3.1340 g. **Composition:** 0.9990 Gold .1007 oz. AGW **Obverse:** Queen Elizabeth II **Reverse:** Yellow-crowned night heron

| Date | Mintage | F | VF | XF | Unc | BU |
|---|---|---|---|---|---|---|
| 1991 Proof | Est. 2,500 | Value: 70.00 | | | | |

**10 DOLLARS** KM# 73 **Weight:** 3.1340 g. **Composition:** 0.9990 Gold .1007 oz. AGW **Reverse:** Bluebird feeding nestling **Note:** Similar to KM#71.

| Date | Mintage | F | VF | XF | Unc | BU |
|---|---|---|---|---|---|---|
| 1992 Proof | Est. 2,500 | Value: 70.00 | | | | |

**15 DOLLARS** KM# 118 **Weight:** 15.9700 g. **Composition:** 0.9990 Gold .5129 oz. AGW **Subject:** Tall Ships **Obverse:** Queen's head right. **Reverse:** Three-masted sailing ship. **Edge:** Reeded. **Size:** 28.4 mm.

| Date | Mintage | F | VF | XF | Unc | BU |
|---|---|---|---|---|---|---|
| 2000 Proof | 1,500 | Value: 400 | | | | |

**20 DOLLARS** KM# 21 **Weight:** 7.9881 g. **Composition:** 0.9170 Gold .2355 oz. AGW **Reverse:** Cahow in flight.

| Date | Mintage | F | VF | XF | Unc | BU |
|---|---|---|---|---|---|---|
| 1970 Proof | 1,000 | Value: 230 | | | | |

**25 DOLLARS** KM# 23 **Composition:** Copper-Nickel **Subject:** Royal visit

| Date | Mintage | F | VF | XF | Unc | BU |
|---|---|---|---|---|---|---|
| 1975FM (M) | 1,193 | — | — | — | 45.00 | — |
| 1975FM (U) | 100 | — | — | — | 60.00 | — |

**25 DOLLARS** KM# 23a **Weight:** 48.7000 g. **Composition:** 0.9250 Silver 1.4483 oz. ASW **Subject:** Royal visit

| Date | Mintage | F | VF | XF | Unc | BU |
|---|---|---|---|---|---|---|
| 1975FM (P) Proof | 15,000 | Value: 25.00 | | | | |

**25 DOLLARS** **KM# 25** **Weight:** 54.7500 g. **Composition:** 0.9250 Silver 1.6283 oz. ASW **Subject:** Queen's silver jubilee

| Date | Mintage | F | VF | XF | Unc | BU |
|---|---|---|---|---|---|---|
| 1977Chi | 10,000 | — | — | — | 35.00 | — |
| 1977Chi Proof | 11,000 | Value: 40.00 | | | | |
| 1977 | Est. 520 | — | — | — | 250 | — |

**Note:** Struck at the Royal Canadian Mint.

| Date | Mintage | F | VF | XF | Unc | BU |
|---|---|---|---|---|---|---|
| 1977 Proof | Est. 550 | Value: 270 | | | | |

**Note:** Struck at the Royal Canadian Mint.

**25 DOLLARS** **KM# 53** **Weight:** 31.1000 g. **Composition:** 0.9990 Palladium 1 oz. **Subject:** Sea Venture **Reverse:** Ship

| Date | Mintage | F | VF | XF | Unc | BU |
|---|---|---|---|---|---|---|
| 1987 Proof | Est. 20,000 | Value: 1,150 | | | | |

**25 DOLLARS** **KM# 63** **Weight:** 31.1000 g. **Composition:** 0.9990 Palladium 1 oz. **Subject:** Ship wreck of San Antonio **Obverse:** Portrait of Queen Elizabeth

| Date | Mintage | F | VF | XF | Unc | BU |
|---|---|---|---|---|---|---|
| 1988 Proof | 2,000 | Value: 1,250 | | | | |

**25 DOLLARS** **KM# 58** **Weight:** 7.8140 g. **Composition:** 0.9990 Gold .2512 oz. AGW **Subject:** Hogge money **Reverse:** Ship

| Date | Mintage | F | VF | XF | Unc | BU |
|---|---|---|---|---|---|---|
| 1989 Proof | 500 | Value: 220 | | | | |

**25 DOLLARS** **KM# 75** **Weight:** 7.8140 g. **Composition:** 0.9990 Gold .2512 oz. AGW **Subject:** Hogge money **Reverse:** Wild pig

| Date | Mintage | F | VF | XF | Unc | BU |
|---|---|---|---|---|---|---|
| 1990 Proof | 500 | Value: 220 | | | | |

**30 DOLLARS** **KM# 97** **Weight:** 15.5518 g. **Composition:** 0.9990 Gold .5 oz. AGW **Subject:** Bermuda Triangle **Obverse:** Queen's portrait **Reverse:** Map, compass, capsizing ship **Note:** Similar to 60 Dollars, KM#93.

| Date | Mintage | F | VF | XF | Unc | BU |
|---|---|---|---|---|---|---|
| 1996 Proof | Est. 1,500 | Value: 500 | | | | |

**30 DOLLARS** **KM# 101** **Weight:** 15.5518 g. **Composition:** 0.9990 Gold .5 oz. AGW **Subject:** Wreck of the Sea Venture **Obverse:** Queen's portrait **Reverse:** Ship wreck scene **Note:** Similar to 60 Dollars, KM#102.

| Date | Mintage | F | VF | XF | Unc | BU |
|---|---|---|---|---|---|---|
| 1997 Proof | Est. 1,500 | Value: 500 | | | | |

**30 DOLLARS** **KM# 113** **Weight:** 15.5500 g. **Composition:** 0.9990 Gold .4994 oz. AGW **Obverse:** Queen's portrait **Reverse:** Map, ship, The Deliverance **Note:** Similar to 60 Dollars, KM#112.

| Date | Mintage | F | VF | XF | Unc | BU |
|---|---|---|---|---|---|---|
| 1998 Proof | Est. 1,500 | Value: 500 | | | | |

**50 DOLLARS** **KM# 26** **Weight:** 4.0500 g. **Composition:** 0.9000 Gold .1172 oz. AGW **Subject:** Queen's silver jubilee

| Date | Mintage | F | VF | XF | Unc | BU |
|---|---|---|---|---|---|---|
| 1977Chi | 3,950 | — | — | — | 75.00 | — |
| 1977Chi Proof | 4,070 | Value: 85.00 | | | | |
| 1977 | Est. 520 | — | — | — | 250 | — |

**Note:** Struck at the Royal Canadian Mint

| Date | Mintage | F | VF | XF | Unc | BU |
|---|---|---|---|---|---|---|
| 1977 Proof | Est. 580 | Value: 250 | | | | |

**Note:** Struck at the Royal Canadian Mint

**50 DOLLARS** **KM# 59** **Weight:** 15.6080 g. **Composition:** 0.9990 Gold .5018 oz. AGW **Subject:** Hogge money **Reverse:** Wild pig

| Date | Mintage | F | VF | XF | Unc | BU |
|---|---|---|---|---|---|---|
| 1989 Proof | 500 | Value: 250 | | | | |

**50 DOLLARS** **KM# 76** **Weight:** 15.6080 g. **Composition:** 0.9990 Gold .5018 oz. AGW **Subject:** Hogge money **Reverse:** Ship

| Date | Mintage | F | VF | XF | Unc | BU |
|---|---|---|---|---|---|---|
| 1990 Proof | 500 | Value: 250 | | | | |

**60 DOLLARS** **KM# 93** **Weight:** 31.4890 g. **Composition:** 0.9990 Gold 1.0124 oz. AGW **Subject:** Bermuda Triangle **Obverse:** Queen's portrait **Reverse:** Map, compass, capsizing ship

| Date | Mintage | F | VF | XF | Unc | BU |
|---|---|---|---|---|---|---|
| 1996 Proof | 1,500 | Value: 900 | | | | |

**60 DOLLARS** **KM# 102** **Weight:** 31.4890 g. **Composition:** 0.9990 Gold 1.0124 oz. AGW **Subject:** Wreck of the Sea Venture **Obverse:** Queen's portrait **Reverse:** Ship wreck scene

| Date | Mintage | F | VF | XF | Unc | BU |
|---|---|---|---|---|---|---|
| 1997 Proof | Est. 1,500 | Value: 900 | | | | |

**60 DOLLARS** **KM# 114** **Weight:** 31.4800 g. **Composition:** 0.9990 Gold 1.0111 oz. AGW **Obverse:** Queen's portrait **Reverse:** Map, ship, The Deliverance

| Date | Mintage | F | VF | XF | Unc | BU |
|---|---|---|---|---|---|---|
| 1998 Proof | Est. 1,500 | Value: 900 | | | | |

**100 DOLLARS** **KM# 24** **Weight:** 7.0300 g. **Composition:** 0.9000 Gold .2034 oz. AGW **Subject:** Royal visit

| Date | Mintage | F | VF | XF | Unc | BU |
|---|---|---|---|---|---|---|
| 1975FM (M) | 25 | — | — | — | 350 | — |
| 1975FM (M) | 19,000 | — | — | — | 95.00 | — |
| 1975FM (M) Proof | 27,000 | Value: 100 | | | | |

**100 DOLLARS** **KM# 27** **Weight:** 8.1000 g. **Composition:** 0.9000 Gold .2344 oz. AGW **Subject:** Queen's silver jubilee

| Date | Mintage | F | VF | XF | Unc | BU |
|---|---|---|---|---|---|---|
| 1977Chi | 6,225 | — | — | — | 110 | — |
| 1977Chi Proof | 5,613 | Value: 135 | | | | |
| 1977 | Est. 2,312 | — | — | — | 200 | — |

**Note:** Struck at the Royal Canadian Mint

| Date | Mintage | F | VF | XF | Unc | BU |
|---|---|---|---|---|---|---|
| 1977 Proof | Est. 1,887 | Value: 240 | | | | |

**Note:** Struck at the Royal Canadian Mint

**100 DOLLARS** **KM#60** **Weight:** 31.2100 g. **Composition:** 0.9990 Gold 1.0035 oz. AGW **Subject:** Hogge money **Reverse:** Ship

| Date | Mintage | F | VF | XF | Unc | BU |
|---|---|---|---|---|---|---|
| 1989 Proof | 500 | Value: 600 | | | | |

**100 DOLLARS** **KM#77** **Weight:** 31.2100 g. **Composition:** 0.9990 Gold 1.0035 oz. AGW **Subject:** Hogge money **Reverse:** Wild pig

| Date | Mintage | F | VF | XF | Unc | BU |
|---|---|---|---|---|---|---|
| 1990 Proof | 500 | Value: 600 | | | | |

**100 DOLLARS** **KM#80** **Weight:** 47.5400 g. **Composition:** 0.9170 Gold 1.4017 oz. AGW **Series:** Olympics **Subject:** Portrait of Queen Elizabeth II **Reverse:** Rings, similar to 5 Dollars, KM#79

| Date | Mintage | F | VF | XF | Unc | BU |
|---|---|---|---|---|---|---|
| 1992 Proof | Est. 250 | Value: 950 | | | | |

**180 DOLLARS** **KM# 98** **Weight:** 155.5175 g. **Composition:** 0.9990 Gold 5 oz. AGW **Subject:** Bermuda Triangle **Obverse:** Queen's portrait **Reverse:** Map, compass, capsizing ship **Note:** Similar to 60 Dollars, KM#93.

| Date | Mintage | F | VF | XF | Unc | BU |
|---|---|---|---|---|---|---|
| 1996 Proof | Est. 1,500 | Value: 3,000 | | | | |

**180 DOLLARS** **KM# 103** **Weight:** 155.5175 g. **Composition:** 0.9990 Gold 5 oz. AGW **Subject:** Wreck of the Sea Venture **Obverse:** Queen's portrait **Reverse:** Ship wreck scene **Note:** Similar to 60 Dollars, KM#102.

| Date | Mintage | F | VF | XF | Unc | BU |
|---|---|---|---|---|---|---|
| 1997 Proof | Est. 99 | Value: 4,000 | | | | |

**180 DOLLARS** **KM# 115** **Weight:** 155.5200 g. **Composition:** 0.9990 Gold 4.9951 oz. AGW **Obverse:** Queen's portrait **Reverse:** Map, ship, The Deliverance **Note:** Similar to 60 Dollars, KM#114.

| Date | Mintage | F | VF | XF | Unc | BU |
|---|---|---|---|---|---|---|
| 1998 Proof | Est. 99 | Value: 4,000 | | | | |

**200 DOLLARS** **KM#82** **Weight:** 28.5000 g. **Composition:** 0.9990 Gold .9154 oz. AGW **Subject:** 200 years - Bermudan coinage

| Date | Mintage | F | VF | XF | Unc | BU |
|---|---|---|---|---|---|---|
| 1993 Proof | 200 | Value: 550 | | | | |

**250 DOLLARS** **KM#29** **Weight:** 15.9760 g. **Composition:** 0.9170 Gold .471 oz. AGW **Subject:** Wedding of Prince Charles and Lady Diana **Obverse:** Similar to 20 Dollars, KM#21

| Date | Mintage | F | VF | XF | Unc | BU |
|---|---|---|---|---|---|---|
| 1981 | 217 | — | — | — | 550 | — |
| 1981 Proof | 790 | Value: 400 | | | | |

## PIEFORTS

| KM# | Date | Mintage | Identification | Issue Price | Mkt Val |
|---|---|---|---|---|---|
| P1 | 1981 | 690 | 250 Dollars. 31.9520 g. KM29. | 920 | 750 |
| P2 | 1988 | 500 | Dollar. 0.9250 Silver. 16.8000 g. KM56a. | 35.00 | 175 |

## MINT SETS

| KM# | Date | Mintage | Identification | Issue Price | Mkt Val |
|---|---|---|---|---|---|
| MS1 | 1970 | 90,000 | KM15-19 | 3.25 | 4.00 |
| MS2 | 1977Chi | — | KM25-27 | 175 | 235 |
| MSA2 | 1977 | — | KM25-27 | — | 685 |
| MS3 | 1977Chi | — | KM26-27 | 150 | 200 |
| MS4 | 1984 | 3,350 | KM32-42 | 24.95 | 27.50 |
| MS5 | 1993 | 15,000 | KM44b, 45-47, 56 | — | 10.00 |
| MS6 | 1995 | 2,000 | KM44c, 45a-47a, 56a | 100 | 80.00 |
| MS7 | 1999 | 5,000 | KM107-111 | 15.00 | 15.00 |

## PROOF SETS

| KM# | Date | Mintage | Identification | Issue Price | Mkt Val |
|---|---|---|---|---|---|
| PS1 | 1970 | 10,000 | KM15-20 | 24.00 | 20.00 |
| PS2 | 1970 | 1,000 | KM15-21 | 216 | 280 |
| PSA2 | 1977 | — | KM25-27 | — | 760 |
| PS3 | 1977Chi | — | KM25-27 | 245 | 325 |
| PS4 | 1977Chi | — | KM26-27 | 210 | 275 |
| PS5 | 1981 | 500 | KM28a, 29, (P1), numbered set | 1,500 | 1,050 |
| PS6 | 1983 | 6,474 | KM15-19, 30, 31 | 30.00 | 30.00 |
| PS7 | 1984 | 1,750 | KM32a-42a | 250 | 200 |
| PS8 | 1986 | — | KM44-48, 50-51 | 50.00 | 42.50 |
| PS10 | 1989 | 500 | KM57-60 | 1,495 | 1,250 |
| PS11 | 1990 | 500 | KM74-77 | — | 1,250 |
| PS12 | 1992 | 250 | KM78-80 | 1,075 | 1,250 |
| PS13 | 1992 | 500 | KM71-72 | 75.00 | 100 |
| PS14 | 1995 | 500 | KM44d, 45b-47b, 56b | 1,100 | 1,200 |
| PS15 | 1996 | 1,000 | KM96-97 | — | 700 |
| PS16 | 1999 | 2,500 | KM107-111 | 50.00 | 50.00 |

# BHUTAN

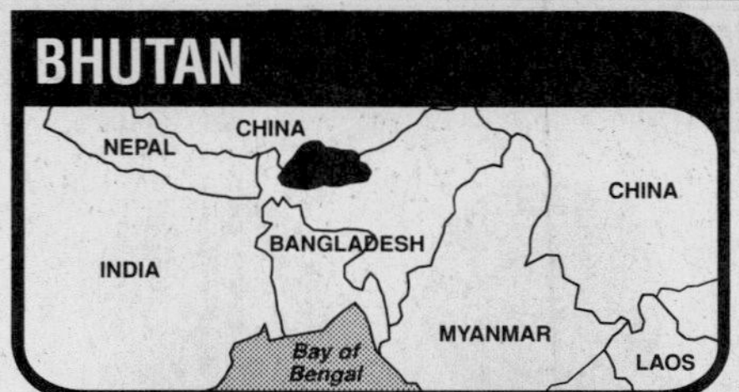


The Kingdom of Bhutan, a landlocked Himalayan country bordered by Tibet and India, has an area of 18,150 sq. mi. (47,000 sq. km.) and a population of *2.03 million. Capital: Thimphu. Virtually the entire population is engaged in agricultural and pastoral activities. Rice, wheat, barley, and yak butter are produced in sufficient quantity to make the country self-sufficient in food. The economy of Bhutan is primitive and many transactions are conducted on a barter basis.

Bhutan's early history is obscure, but is thought to have resembled that of rural medieval Europe. The country was conquered by Tibet in the 9th century, and a dual temporal and spiritual rule developed which operated until the mid-19th century, when the southern part of the country was occupied by the British and annexed to British India. Bhutan was established as a hereditary monarchy in 1907, and in 1910 agreed to British control of its external affairs. In 1949, India and Bhutan concluded a treaty whereby India assumed Britain's role in subsidizing Bhutan and guiding its foreign affairs. In 1971 Bhutan became a full member of the United Nations.

**RULERS**

Ugyen Wangchuck, 1907-1926
Jigme Wangchuck, 1926-1952
Jigme Dorji Wangchuck, 1952-1972
Jigme Singye Wangchuck, 1972-

## KINGDOM

### under British Adminstration.

### HAMMERED 'DUMP' COINAGE

Period III
1835-1910AD

'Sa'

**1/2 RUPEE (Deb)** **KM# A7** **Composition:** Copper Or Brass **Obverse:** Small "Sa" at upper right

| Date | Mintage | Good | VG | F | VF | XF |
|---|---|---|---|---|---|---|
| ND | — | 1.00 | 2.25 | 4.50 | 7.50 | — |

'Sa'

**1/2 RUPEE (Deb)** **KM# 7.1** **Composition:** Copper Or Brass **Obverse:** "Sa" at lower left

| Date | Mintage | Good | VG | F | VF | XF |
|---|---|---|---|---|---|---|
| ND | — | 1.00 | 1.50 | 3.00 | 6.00 | — |

**1/2 RUPEE (Deb)** **KM# 7.1a** **Weight:** 1.8500 g. **Composition:** Copper Or Brass **Obverse:** "Sa" at lower left **Note:** Small flan.

| Date | Mintage | Good | VG | F | VF | XF |
|---|---|---|---|---|---|---|
| ND | — | 1.00 | 1.50 | 3.00 | 6.00 | — |

**1/2 RUPEE (Deb)** **KM# 7.2** **Composition:** Copper Or Brass **Obverse:** Dots added

| Date | Mintage | Good | VG | F | VF | XF |
|---|---|---|---|---|---|---|
| ND | — | 1.00 | 1.50 | 3.00 | 6.00 | — |

**1/2 RUPEE (Deb)** **KM# 7.3** **Composition:** Copper Or Brass **Obverse:** "Sa" at upper right

| Date | Mintage | Good | VG | F | VF | XF |
|---|---|---|---|---|---|---|
| ND | — | 1.00 | 1.50 | 3.00 | 6.00 | — |

**1/2 RUPEE (Deb)** **KM# 7.4** **Composition:** Copper Or Brass **Obverse:** Large "Sa" below 5 pellets

| Date | Mintage | Good | VG | F | VF | XF |
|---|---|---|---|---|---|---|
| ND | — | 1.00 | 1.50 | 3.00 | 6.00 | — |

**1/2 RUPEE (Deb)** **KM# 7.5** **Composition:** Copper Or Brass **Obverse:** Large "Sa" below swastika

| Date | Mintage | Good | VG | F | VF | XF |
|---|---|---|---|---|---|---|
| ND | — | 1.00 | 1.50 | 3.00 | 6.00 | — |

**1/2 RUPEE (Deb)** **KM# 7.6** **Composition:** Copper Or Brass **Reverse:** Branch

| Date | Mintage | Good | VG | F | VF | XF |
|---|---|---|---|---|---|---|
| ND | — | 1.00 | 1.50 | 3.00 | 6.00 | — |

**1/2 RUPEE (Deb)** **KM# A8.1** **Composition:** Copper Or Brass **Obv. Legend:** Retrograde **Rev. Legend:** Retrograde

| Date | Mintage | Good | VG | F | VF | XF |
|---|---|---|---|---|---|---|
| ND | — | 1.00 | 2.00 | 3.50 | 7.00 | — |

**1/2 RUPEE (Deb)** **KM# A8.2** **Composition:** Copper Or Brass **Reverse:** Dots added

| Date | Mintage | Good | VG | F | VF | XF |
|---|---|---|---|---|---|---|
| ND | — | 1.00 | 1.50 | 3.00 | 6.00 | — |

**1/2 RUPEE (Deb)** **KM# A8.3** **Composition:** Copper Or Brass **Reverse:** 4 pellets

| Date | Mintage | Good | VG | F | VF | XF |
|---|---|---|---|---|---|---|
| ND | — | 1.00 | 1.50 | 3.00 | 6.00 | — |

**1/2 RUPEE (Deb)** **KM# A8.4** **Composition:** Copper Or Brass **Obverse:** 2 dots above crescent

| Date | Mintage | Good | VG | F | VF | XF |
|---|---|---|---|---|---|---|
| ND | — | 1.00 | 1.50 | 3.00 | 6.00 | — |

**1/2 RUPEE (Deb)** **KM# 8.1** **Composition:** Copper Or Brass **Obverse:** X above crescent

| Date | Mintage | Good | VG | F | VF | XF |
|---|---|---|---|---|---|---|
| ND | — | 1.00 | 1.50 | 3.00 | 6.00 | — |

**1/2 RUPEE (Deb)** **KM# 8.2** **Composition:** Copper Or Brass **Obverse:** 1 or 2 dots in center inscription

| Date | Mintage | Good | VG | F | VF | XF |
|---|---|---|---|---|---|---|
| ND | — | 0.50 | 1.00 | 2.00 | 4.00 | — |

**1/2 RUPEE (Deb)** **KM# 8.3** **Composition:** Copper Or Brass **Obverse:** Crescent above "+" at left

| Date | Mintage | Good | VG | F | VF | XF |
|---|---|---|---|---|---|---|
| ND | — | 1.00 | 2.00 | 3.50 | 7.00 | — |

**1/2 RUPEE (Deb)** **KM# 8.4** **Composition:** Copper Or Brass **Obverse:** "+" above crescent

| Date | Mintage | Good | VG | F | VF | XF |
|---|---|---|---|---|---|---|
| ND | — | 1.00 | 2.00 | 3.50 | 7.00 | — |

**1/2 RUPEE (Deb)** **KM# 8.6** **Composition:** Copper Or Brass **Obverse:** Low "+" at left

| Date | Mintage | Good | VG | F | VF | XF |
|---|---|---|---|---|---|---|
| ND | — | 1.00 | 2.00 | 3.50 | 7.00 | — |

**1/2 RUPEE (Deb)** **KM# 8.7** **Composition:** Copper Or Brass **Obverse:** 3 pellets at left, low "+" at right

| Date | Mintage | Good | VG | F | VF | XF |
|---|---|---|---|---|---|---|
| ND | — | 1.00 | 2.00 | 3.50 | 7.00 | — |

**1/2 RUPEE (Deb)** **KM# 8.8** **Composition:** Copper Or Brass **Obverse:** Hooks added **Reverse:** 4 pellets

| Date | Mintage | Good | VG | F | VF | XF |
|---|---|---|---|---|---|---|
| ND | — | 1.00 | 2.00 | 3.50 | 7.00 | — |

**1/2 RUPEE (Deb)** **KM# 8.9** **Composition:** Copper Or Brass **Obverse:** 2 rows of pellets, high "+" at right

| Date | Mintage | Good | VG | F | VF | XF |
|---|---|---|---|---|---|---|
| ND | — | 1.00 | 2.00 | 3.50 | 7.00 | — |

**1/2 RUPEE (Deb)** **KM# 9.1** **Composition:** Copper Or Brass **Obverse:** Swastika

| Date | Mintage | Good | VG | F | VF | XF |
|---|---|---|---|---|---|---|
| ND | — | 2.00 | 3.00 | 5.00 | 9.00 | — |

**1/2 RUPEE (Deb)** **KM# 9.2** **Composition:** Copper Or Brass **Obverse:** Swastika reversed

| Date | Mintage | Good | VG | F | VF | XF |
|---|---|---|---|---|---|---|
| ND | — | 2.00 | 3.00 | 5.00 | 9.00 | — |

'Wang'

**1/2 RUPEE (Deb)** **KM# 10** **Composition:** Copper Or Brass

| Date | Mintage | Good | VG | F | VF | XF |
|---|---|---|---|---|---|---|
| ND | — | 3.00 | 5.00 | 8.00 | 12.00 | — |

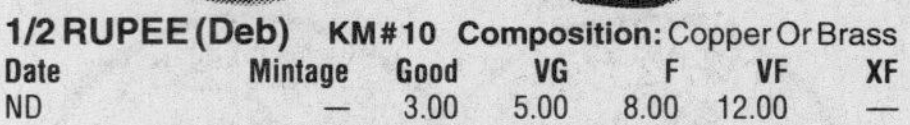

**1/2 RUPEE (Deb)** **KM# 11** **Composition:** Copper Or Brass

| Date | Mintage | Good | VG | F | VF | XF |
|---|---|---|---|---|---|---|
| ND | — | 3.00 | 5.00 | 8.00 | 12.00 | — |

**1/2 RUPEE (Deb)** **KM# 11a** **Composition:** Copper Or Brass

| Date | Mintage | Good | VG | F | VF | XF |
|---|---|---|---|---|---|---|
| ND | — | 3.00 | 5.00 | 8.00 | 12.00 | — |

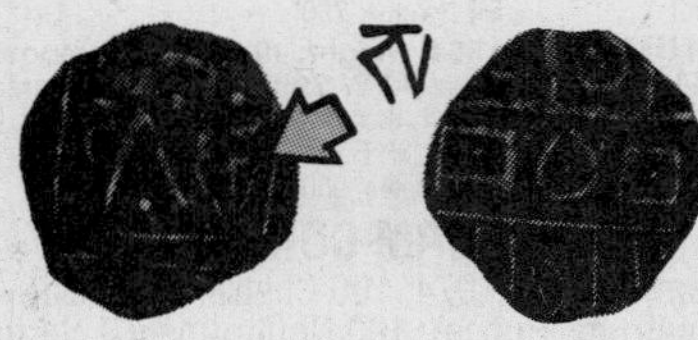

**1/2 RUPEE (Deb)** **KM# 11b** **Composition:** Copper Or Brass

| Date | Mintage | Good | VG | F | VF | XF |
|---|---|---|---|---|---|---|
| ND | — | 3.00 | 5.00 | 8.00 | 12.00 | — |

**1/2 RUPEE (Deb)** **KM# 12** **Composition:** Copper Or Brass **Obverse:** Rosette **Reverse:** Swastika

| Date | Mintage | Good | VG | F | VF | XF |
|---|---|---|---|---|---|---|
| ND | — | 3.00 | 5.00 | 8.00 | 12.00 | — |

**1/2 RUPEE (Deb)** **KM# 13** **Composition:** Copper Or Brass **Obverse:** Rosette **Reverse:** 2 fish

| Date | Mintage | Good | VG | F | VF | XF |
|---|---|---|---|---|---|---|
| ND | — | 3.00 | 5.00 | 8.00 | 12.00 | — |

**1/2 RUPEE (Deb)** **KM# 14** **Composition:** Copper Or Brass **Reverse:** 2 fish **Note:** Varieties exist.

| Date | Mintage | Good | VG | F | VF | XF |
|---|---|---|---|---|---|---|
| ND | — | 2.00 | 3.00 | 5.00 | 9.00 | — |

**1/2 RUPEE (Deb)** **KM# 15** **Composition:** Copper Or Brass **Obverse:** Knot **Reverse:** Conch shell

| Date | Mintage | Good | VG | F | VF | XF |
|---|---|---|---|---|---|---|
| ND | — | 1.50 | 2.50 | 4.00 | 8.00 | — |

## HAMMERED 'DUMP' COINAGE

Period IV
1910-1927

**1/2 RUPEE (Deb)** **KM# 16** **Composition:** Copper

| Date | Mintage | Good | VG | F | VF | XF |
|---|---|---|---|---|---|---|
| ND | — | 2.00 | 3.50 | 7.50 | 12.00 | — |

**1/2 RUPEE (Deb)** **KM# 17** **Composition:** Silver

| Date | Mintage | Good | VG | F | VF | XF |
|---|---|---|---|---|---|---|
| ND | — | 10.00 | 15.00 | 25.00 | 35.00 | — |

**1/2 RUPEE (Deb)** **KM# 17a** **Composition:** Copper **Note:** Obverse is similar to KM#17, but symbols on reverse are arranged differently.

| Date | Mintage | Good | VG | F | VF | XF |
|---|---|---|---|---|---|---|

**1/2 RUPEE (Deb)** **KM# 18** **Composition:** Silver

| Date | Mintage | Good | VG | F | VF | XF |
|---|---|---|---|---|---|---|
| ND | — | 10.00 | 15.00 | 25.00 | 35.00 | — |

**1/2 RUPEE (Deb)** **KM# 18a** **Composition:** Copper **Note:** Obverse is similar to KM#18, but symbols on reverse are arranged differently.

| Date | Mintage | Good | VG | F | VF | XF |
|---|---|---|---|---|---|---|
| ND | — | 2.00 | 3.50 | 5.00 | 9.00 | — |

**1/2 RUPEE (Deb)** **KM# 18b** **Composition:** Brass **Reverse:** Different reverse than KM18, this was heretofore an unpublished variety.

| Date | Mintage | Good | VG | F | VF | XF |
|---|---|---|---|---|---|---|
| ND | — | 2.00 | 3.50 | 5.00 | 9.00 | — |

**1/2 RUPEE (Deb)** **KM# 19** **Composition:** Silver

| Date | Mintage | Good | VG | F | VF | XF |
|---|---|---|---|---|---|---|
| ND | — | 10.00 | 15.00 | 25.00 | 35.00 | — |

**1/2 RUPEE (Deb)** **KM# 19a** **Composition:** Copper **Note:** Obverse is similar to KM#19, but symbols on reverse are arranged differently.

| Date | Mintage | Good | VG | F | VF | XF |
|---|---|---|---|---|---|---|
| ND | — | 2.00 | 3.50 | 5.00 | 9.00 | — |

**1/2 RUPEE (Deb)** **KM# 20** **Composition:** Silver

| Date | Mintage | Good | VG | F | VF | XF |
|---|---|---|---|---|---|---|
| ND | — | 10.00 | 15.00 | 25.00 | 35.00 | — |

**1/2 RUPEE (Deb)** **KM# 20a** **Composition:** Copper **Note:** Obverse is similar to KM#20, but symbols on reverse are arranged differently.

| Date | Mintage | Good | VG | F | VF | XF |
|---|---|---|---|---|---|---|
| ND | — | 3.00 | 4.50 | 6.00 | 10.00 | — |

**1/2 RUPEE (Deb)** **KM# 21** **Composition:** Copper

| Date | Mintage | Good | VG | F | VF | XF |
|---|---|---|---|---|---|---|
| ND | — | 1.50 | 2.50 | 3.50 | 6.00 | — |

**1/2 RUPEE (Deb)** **KM# 22** **Composition:** Copper **Obverse:** Interlacing opposite of KM#21 **Reverse:** Interlacing opposite of KM#21 **Note:** Varieties exist.

| Date | Mintage | Good | VG | F | VF | XF |
|---|---|---|---|---|---|---|
| ND | — | 1.50 | 2.50 | 3.50 | 6.00 | — |

## GENERAL COINAGE

**PICE** **KM# 23.1** **Weight:** 7.0000 g. **Composition:** Bronze **Size:** 26.5 mm. **Note:** Similar to KM#23.2.

| Date | Mintage | F | VF | XF | Unc | BU |
|---|---|---|---|---|---|---|
| 1928 | — | 22.50 | 40.00 | 65.00 | 100 | — |

**PICE** **KM# 23.2** **Weight:** 4.9000 g. **Composition:** Bronze **Size:** 25.1 mm. **Note:** Actually struck in 1931.

| Date | Mintage | F | VF | XF | Unc | BU |
|---|---|---|---|---|---|---|
| 1928 | 10,000 | 20.00 | 35.00 | 60.00 | 90.00 | — |
| 1928 Proof | — | Value: 100 | | | | |

**PICE** **KM# A27** **Weight:** 3.3000 g. **Composition:** Bronze

| Date | Mintage | F | VF | XF | Unc | BU |
|---|---|---|---|---|---|---|
| ND | — | — | — | — | — | — |

**PICE** **KM# 27** **Weight:** 2.9000 g. **Composition:** Bronze **Note:** Actually struck in 1951 and 1955. Later strikes of 1955 dates differ in detail because of recut dies.

| Date | Mintage | F | VF | XF | Unc | BU |
|---|---|---|---|---|---|---|
| ND | Est. 1,260,000 | 0.75 | 1.00 | 1.50 | 2.25 | — |

**1/2 RUPEE** **KM# 26** **Composition:** Nickel **Obverse:** Legend normal **Note:** 5.78-5.90 grams.

| Date | Mintage | F | VF | XF | Unc | BU |
|---|---|---|---|---|---|---|
| ND(1928) | 20,000 | 2.00 | 3.00 | 4.50 | 7.00 | — |
| **Note:** Actually struck in 1951. | | | | | | |
| ND(1950) | 202,000 | 1.50 | 2.50 | 3.00 | 4.50 | — |
| **Note:** Actually struck in 1955. | | | | | | |

**1/2 RUPEE** **KM# 24** **Composition:** Silver **Note:** 5.83-.5.85 grams.

| Date | Mintage | F | VF | XF | Unc | BU |
|---|---|---|---|---|---|---|
| ND(1928) | 50,000 | 10.00 | 15.00 | 22.50 | 35.00 | — |
| **Note:** Actually struck in 1929. | | | | | | |
| ND(1928) Proof | — | Value: 100 | | | | |

**1/2 RUPEE** **KM# 25** **Composition:** Silver **Obverse:** Legend modified **Note:** Actually struck in 1930.

| Date | Mintage | F | VF | XF | Unc | BU |
|---|---|---|---|---|---|---|
| ND(1928) | Inc. above | 10.00 | 15.00 | 22.50 | 35.00 | — |

**1/2 RUPEE** **KM# 28** **Weight:** 5.0800 g. **Composition:** Nickel **Obverse:** Legend normal **Note:** Actually struck in 1967-1968.

| Date | Mintage | F | VF | XF | Unc | BU |
|---|---|---|---|---|---|---|
| ND(1950) | 10,000,000 | 0.75 | 1.00 | 1.50 | 2.25 | — |

## DECIMAL COINAGE

**RUPEE** **KM# 31** **Composition:** Copper-Nickel **Subject:** 40th anniversary - accession of Jigme Wangchuk

| Date | Mintage | F | VF | XF | Unc | BU |
|---|---|---|---|---|---|---|
| 1966 | 10,000 | — | 0.50 | 0.75 | 1.50 | — |
| 1966 Proof | 6,000 | Value: 1.50 | | | | |

**25 NAYA PAISA** **KM# 29** **Composition:** Copper-Nickel **Subject:** 40th anniversary - accession of Jigme Wangchuk

| Date | Mintage | F | VF | XF | Unc | BU |
|---|---|---|---|---|---|---|
| 1966 | 10,000 | — | 0.20 | 0.40 | 0.75 | — |
| 1966 Proof | 6,000 | Value: 1.00 | | | | |

**50 NAYA PAISA** **KM# 30** **Composition:** Copper-Nickel **Subject:** 40th anniversary - accession of Jigme Wangchuk

| Date | Mintage | F | VF | XF | Unc | BU |
|---|---|---|---|---|---|---|
| 1966 | 10,000 | — | 0.25 | 0.50 | 1.00 | — |
| 1966 Proof | 6,000 | Value: 1.50 | | | | |

**3 RUPEE** **KM# 32** **Composition:** Copper-Nickel **Subject:** 40th anniversary - accession of Jigme Wangchuk

| Date | Mintage | F | VF | XF | Unc | BU |
|---|---|---|---|---|---|---|
| 1966 | 5,826 | — | — | — | 5.00 | — |
| 1966 Proof | 6,000 | Value: 6.50 | | | | |

**3 RUPEE** **KM# 32a** **Weight:** 28.2800 g. **Composition:** 0.9250 Silver .8411 oz. ASW **Subject:** 40th anniversary - accession of Jigme Wangchuk

| Date | Mintage | F | VF | XF | Unc | BU |
|---|---|---|---|---|---|---|
| 1966 | — | — | — | — | 375 | — |
| 1966 Proof | 2,000 | Value: 25.00 | | | | |
| 1966 Matte proof | — | Value: 375 | | | | |

**SERTUM** **KM# 33** **Weight:** 7.9800 g. **Composition:** 0.9170 Gold .2352 oz. AGW **Subject:** 40th anniversary - accession of Jigme Wangchuk

| Date | Mintage | F | VF | XF | Unc | BU |
|---|---|---|---|---|---|---|
| 1966 | 2,300 | — | — | — | 125 | — |
| 1966 Proof | 598 | Value: 165 | | | | |

**SERTUM** **KM# 33a** **Weight:** 9.8400 g. **Composition:** 0.9500 Platinum .3005 oz. APW **Subject:** 40th anniversary - accession of Jigme Wangchuk

| Date | Mintage | F | VF | XF | Unc | BU |
|---|---|---|---|---|---|---|
| 1966 Proof | 72 | Value: 300 | | | | |

**SERTUM** **KM# 36** **Weight:** 7.9800 g. **Composition:** 0.9170 Gold .2352 oz. AGW

| Date | Mintage | F | VF | XF | Unc | BU |
|---|---|---|---|---|---|---|
| 1970 | 3,111 | — | — | — | 125 | — |

**2 SERTUMS** **KM# 34** **Weight:** 15.9800 g. **Composition:** 0.9170 Gold .4711 oz. AGW **Subject:** 40th anniversary - accession of Jigme Wangchuk

| Date | Mintage | F | VF | XF | Unc | BU |
|---|---|---|---|---|---|---|
| 1966 | 800 | — | — | — | 225 | — |
| 1966 Proof | 598 | Value: 300 | | | | |

**2 SERTUMS** **KM# 34a** **Weight:** 19.6700 g. **Composition:** 0.9500 Platinum .6008 oz. APW **Subject:** 40th anniversary - accession of Jigme Wangchuk

| Date | Mintage | F | VF | XF | Unc | BU |
|---|---|---|---|---|---|---|
| 1966 Proof | 72 | Value: 420 | | | | |

**5 SERTUMS** **KM# 35** **Weight:** 39.9400 g. **Composition:** 0.9170 Gold 1.1776 oz. AGW **Subject:** 40th anniversary - accession of Jigme Wangchuk

| Date | Mintage | F | VF | XF | Unc | BU |
|---|---|---|---|---|---|---|
| 1966 | 800 | — | — | — | 500 | — |
| 1966 Proof | 598 | Value: 700 | | | | |

**5 SERTUMS** **KM# 35a** **Weight:** 49.1800 g. **Composition:** 0.9500 Platinum 1.5022 oz. APW **Subject:** 40th anniversary - accession of Jigme Wangchuk

| Date | Mintage | F | VF | XF | Unc | BU |
|---|---|---|---|---|---|---|
| 1966 Proof | 72 | Value: 950 | | | | |

## REFORM COINAGE

Commencing 1974; 100 Chetrums (Paisa) = 1 Ngultrum (Rupee); 100 Ngultrums = 1 Sertum

**5 CHETRUMS** **KM# 37** **Composition:** Aluminum

| Date | Mintage | F | VF | XF | Unc | BU |
|---|---|---|---|---|---|---|
| 1974 | — | — | 0.10 | 0.20 | 0.50 | — |
| 1974 Proof | 1,000 | Value: 1.25 | | | | |
| 1975 | — | — | 0.10 | 0.15 | 0.20 | — |
| 1975 Proof | — | Value: 1.25 | | | | |

**5 CHHERTUM** **KM# 45** **Composition:** Bronze

| Date | Mintage | F | VF | XF | Unc | BU |
|---|---|---|---|---|---|---|
| 1979 | — | — | 0.10 | 0.20 | 0.50 | — |
| 1979 Proof | — | Value: 1.00 | | | | |

**10 CHETRUMS** **KM# 38** **Composition:** Aluminum

| Date | Mintage | F | VF | XF | Unc | BU |
|---|---|---|---|---|---|---|
| 1974 | — | — | 0.15 | 0.25 | 0.50 | — |
| 1974 Proof | 1,000 | Value: 1.50 | | | | |

**10 CHETRUMS** **KM# 43** **Composition:** Aluminum **Series:** F.A.O. and International Women's Year

| Date | Mintage | F | VF | XF | Unc | BU |
|---|---|---|---|---|---|---|
| 1975 | 4,000,000 | — | 0.15 | 0.25 | 0.65 | — |
| 1975 Proof | — | Value: 2.50 | | | | |

**10 CHHERTUM** **KM# 46** **Composition:** Bronze

| Date | Mintage | F | VF | XF | Unc | BU |
|---|---|---|---|---|---|---|
| 1979 | — | — | 0.15 | 0.30 | 1.00 | — |
| 1979 Proof | — | Value: 2.00 | | | | |

**20 CHETRUMS** **KM# 39** **Composition:** Aluminum-Bronze **Series:** F.A.O.

| Date | Mintage | F | VF | XF | Unc | BU |
|---|---|---|---|---|---|---|
| 1974 | 1,194,000 | — | 0.15 | 0.25 | 0.50 | — |
| 1974 Prooflike | — | — | — | — | 1.50 | — |

**Note:** In mint sets only.

| Date | Mintage | |
|---|---|---|
| 1974 Proof | 1,000 | Value: 2.00 |

**25 CHETRUMS** **KM# 40.1** **Composition:** Copper-Nickel **Reverse:** Type I

| Date | Mintage | F | VF | XF | Unc | BU |
|---|---|---|---|---|---|---|
| 1974 | — | — | 0.10 | 0.20 | 0.75 | — |
| 1974 Proof | 1,000 | Value: 3.00 | | | | |

**25 CHETRUMS** **KM# 40.2** **Composition:** Copper-Nickel **Reverse:** Type II

| Date | Mintage | F | VF | XF | Unc | BU |
|---|---|---|---|---|---|---|
| 1974 | — | — | 0.10 | 0.20 | 0.75 | — |
| 1975 | — | — | 0.10 | 0.20 | 0.75 | — |
| 1975 Proof | — | Value: 3.00 | | | | |

**25 CHHERTUM** **KM# 47** **Composition:** Copper-Nickel

| Date | Mintage | F | VF | XF | Unc | BU |
|---|---|---|---|---|---|---|
| 1979 | — | — | 0.25 | 0.50 | 1.25 | — |
| 1979 Proof | — | Value: 4.00 | | | | |

**25 CHHERTUM** **KM# 47a** **Composition:** Steel **Note:** Aluminum-bronze clad.

| Date | Mintage | F | VF | XF | Unc | BU |
|---|---|---|---|---|---|---|
| 1979 | — | — | — | — | 2.50 | — |

**50 CHHERTUM** **KM# 48** **Composition:** Copper-Nickel

| Date | Mintage | F | VF | XF | Unc | BU |
|---|---|---|---|---|---|---|
| 1979 | — | — | 0.25 | 0.65 | 1.50 | — |
| 1979 Proof | — | Value: 5.00 | | | | |

**NGULTRUM** **KM# 41** **Composition:** Copper-Nickel

| Date | Mintage | F | VF | XF | Unc | BU |
|---|---|---|---|---|---|---|
| 1974 | — | — | 0.20 | 0.50 | 1.25 | — |
| 1974 Proof | 1,000 | Value: 5.00 | | | | |

| Date | Mintage | F | VF | XF | Unc | BU |
|---|---|---|---|---|---|---|
| 1975 | — | — | 0.20 | 0.50 | 1.25 | — |
| 1975 Proof | — | Value: 5.00 | | | | |

**NGULTRUM** **KM# 49** **Composition:** Copper-Nickel

| Date | Mintage | F | VF | XF | Unc | BU |
|---|---|---|---|---|---|---|
| 1979 | — | — | 0.30 | 0.75 | 2.00 | — |
| 1979 Proof | — | Value: 5.50 | | | | |

**NGULTRUM** **KM# 49a** **Composition:** Copper-Nickel Clad Steel

| Date | Mintage | F | VF | XF | Unc | BU |
|---|---|---|---|---|---|---|
| 1979 | — | — | — | — | 3.00 | — |

**3 NGULTRUMS** **KM# 50** **Composition:** Copper-Nickel

| Date | Mintage | F | VF | XF | Unc | BU |
|---|---|---|---|---|---|---|
| 1979 | — | — | 1.25 | 2.50 | 5.50 | — |
| 1979 Proof | — | Value: 8.50 | | | | |

**3 NGULTRUMS** **KM# 50a** **Weight:** 28.2800 g. **Composition:** 0.9250 Silver .8411 oz. ASW

| Date | Mintage | F | VF | XF | Unc | BU |
|---|---|---|---|---|---|---|
| 1979 Proof | Est. 10,000 | Value: 32.50 | | | | |

**15 NGULTRUMS** **KM# 42** **Weight:** 22.3000 g. **Composition:** 0.5000 Silver .3584 oz. ASW **Series:** F.A.O.

| Date | Mintage | F | VF | XF | Unc | BU |
|---|---|---|---|---|---|---|
| 1974 | 30,000 | — | — | — | 8.00 | — |
| 1974 Prooflike | — | — | — | — | 10.00 | — |

**Note:** In mint sets only.

| Date | Mintage | |
|---|---|---|
| 1974 Proof | 1,000 | Value: 42.50 |

**30 NGULTRUMS** **KM# 44** **Weight:** 25.0000 g. **Composition:** 0.5000 Silver .4018 oz. ASW **Series:** F.A.O. and International Women's Year

| Date | Mintage | F | VF | XF | Unc | BU |
|---|---|---|---|---|---|---|
| 1975 | 14,000 | — | — | — | 10.00 | — |
| 1975 Proof | — | Value: 20.00 | | | | |

**50 NGULTRUMS** **KM# 54** **Weight:** 28.2800 g. **Composition:** 0.9250 Silver .8411 oz. ASW **Series:** World Food Day

| Date | Mintage | F | VF | XF | Unc | BU |
|---|---|---|---|---|---|---|
| 1981 | 15,000 | — | — | — | 32.50 | — |
| 1981 Proof | 5,000 | Value: 45.00 | | | | |

**50 NGULTRUMS** **KM# 83** **Composition:** Copper-Nickel **Subject:** 50 years - United Nations

| Date | Mintage | F | VF | XF | Unc | BU |
|---|---|---|---|---|---|---|
| 1995 | — | — | — | — | 8.00 | — |

**100 NGULTRUMS** **KM# 58** **Weight:** 23.3300 g. **Composition:** 0.9250 Silver .6938 oz. ASW **Series:** Decade for Women

| Date | Mintage | F | VF | XF | Unc | BU |
|---|---|---|---|---|---|---|
| 1984 Proof | 1,050 | Value: 28.00 | | | | |

**100 NGULTRUMS** **KM# 84** **Composition:** Copper-Nickel **Subject:** St. Paul's Walden Bury Palace

| Date | Mintage | F | VF | XF | Unc | BU |
|---|---|---|---|---|---|---|
| 1995 | Est. 35,000 | — | — | — | 12.50 | — |

**100 NGULTRUMS** **KM# 103** **Weight:** 20.0000 g. **Composition:** 0.9250 Silver .5948 oz. ASW **Subject:** Olympic Games 2000 **Obverse:** National arms. **Reverse:** Archer at left sighting in on target at right. **Edge:** Reeded. **Size:** 34 mm.

| Date | Mintage | F | VF | XF | Unc | BU |
|---|---|---|---|---|---|---|
| 1998 Proof | — | Value: 17.50 | | | | |

**200 NGULTRUMS** **KM# 57** **Weight:** 28.2800 g. **Composition:** 0.9250 Silver .8411 oz. ASW **Series:** International Year of Disabled Persons

| Date | Mintage | F | VF | XF | Unc | BU |
|---|---|---|---|---|---|---|
| 1981 | 10,000 | — | — | — | 40.00 | — |
| 1981 Proof | 10,000 | Value: 45.00 | | | | |

**200 NGULTRUMS** **KM# 55** **Weight:** 28.2800 g. **Composition:** 0.9250 Silver .8411 oz. ASW **Subject:** 75th anniversary of monarchy

| Date | Mintage | F | VF | XF | Unc | BU |
|---|---|---|---|---|---|---|
| 1982(1983) | 10,000 | — | — | — | 30.00 | — |
| 1982(1983) Proof | 5,000 | Value: 40.00 | | | | |

**200 NGULTRUMS** **KM# 86** **Weight:** 10.0000 g. **Composition:** 0.5000 Silver .1607 oz. ASW **Series:** Olympics **Reverse:** 2 basketball players

| Date | Mintage | F | VF | XF | Unc | BU |
|---|---|---|---|---|---|---|
| 1996 | Est. 10,000 | — | — | — | 20.00 | — |

**200 NGULTRUMS** **KM# 87** **Weight:** 10.0000 g. **Composition:** 0.5000 Silver .1607 oz. ASW **Series:** Olympics **Reverse:** Skiing scene

| Date | Mintage | F | VF | XF | Unc | BU |
|---|---|---|---|---|---|---|
| 1996 | Est. 50,000 | — | — | — | 15.00 | — |

**300 NGULTRUMS** **KM# 61** **Weight:** 28.2800 g. **Composition:** 0.9250 Silver .8411 oz. ASW **Subject:** World Championship Soccer

| Date | Mintage | F | VF | XF | Unc | BU |
|---|---|---|---|---|---|---|
| 1990 Proof | 20,000 | Value: 35.00 | | | | |

**300 NGULTRUMS** **KM# 65** **Weight:** 31.4700 g. **Composition:** 0.9250 Silver .9359 oz. ASW **Series:** Endangered wildlife **Reverse:** Snow leopard

| Date | Mintage | F | VF | XF | Unc | BU |
|---|---|---|---|---|---|---|
| 1991 Proof | Est. 25,000 | Value: 35.00 | | | | |

**300 NGULTRUMS** **KM# 63** **Weight:** 28.2800 g. **Composition:** 0.9250 Silver .8411 oz. ASW **Subject:** Solar system

| Date | Mintage | F | VF | XF | Unc | BU |
|---|---|---|---|---|---|---|
| 1992 Proof | — | Value: 32.50 | | | | |

**300 NGULTRUMS KM# 72 Weight:** 31.4700 g. **Composition:** 0.9250 Silver .9359 oz. ASW **Subject:** World Cup soccer

| Date | Mintage | F | VF | XF | Unc | BU |
|---|---|---|---|---|---|---|
| 1992 Proof | 20,000 | Value: 27.50 | | | | |

**300 NGULTRUMS KM# 77 Weight:** 31.4700 g. **Composition:** 0.9250 Silver .9359 oz. ASW **Series:** 1992 Olympic Games **Reverse:** Boxer

| Date | Mintage | F | VF | XF | Unc | BU |
|---|---|---|---|---|---|---|
| 1992 Proof | 20,000 | Value: 20.00 | | | | |

**300 NGULTRUMS KM# 78 Weight:** 31.3200 g. **Composition:** 0.9250 Silver .9314 oz. ASW **Subject:** World Championship Soccer **Reverse:** Ball in flight

| Date | Mintage | F | VF | XF | Unc | BU |
|---|---|---|---|---|---|---|
| 1993 Proof | 30,000 | Value: 40.00 | | | | |

**300 NGULTRUMS KM# 74 Weight:** 31.4700 g. **Composition:** 0.9250 Silver .9359 oz. ASW **Series:** 1994 Olympic Games **Reverse:** Speed skating

| Date | Mintage | F | VF | XF | Unc | BU |
|---|---|---|---|---|---|---|
| 1992 Proof | 40,000 | Value: 22.50 | | | | |

**300 NGULTRUMS KM# 66 Weight:** 31.4700 g. **Composition:** 0.9250 Silver .9359 oz. ASW **Subject:** 40th anniversary - coronation of Queen Elizabeth II

| Date | Mintage | F | VF | XF | Unc | BU |
|---|---|---|---|---|---|---|
| 1993 Proof | Est. 10,000 | Value: 32.50 | | | | |

**300 NGULTRUMS KM# 79 Weight:** 31.3200 g. **Composition:** 0.9250 Silver .9314 oz. ASW **Series:** Olympic Games **Reverse:** Soccer

| Date | Mintage | F | VF | XF | Unc | BU |
|---|---|---|---|---|---|---|
| 1993 Proof | 30,000 | Value: 25.00 | | | | |

**300 NGULTRUMS KM# 75 Weight:** 31.4700 g. **Composition:** 0.9250 Silver .9359 oz. ASW **Series:** Endangered wildlife **Reverse:** Golden langur monkey

| Date | Mintage | F | VF | XF | Unc | BU |
|---|---|---|---|---|---|---|
| 1992 Proof | — | Value: 32.50 | | | | |

**300 NGULTRUMS KM# 67 Weight:** 31.4700 g. **Composition:** 0.9250 Silver .9359 oz. ASW **Series:** Endangered wildlife **Reverse:** Takin

| Date | Mintage | F | VF | XF | Unc | BU |
|---|---|---|---|---|---|---|
| 1993 Proof | Est. 10,000 | Value: 37.50 | | | | |

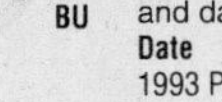

**300 NGULTRUMS KM# 89 Weight:** 31.3200 g. **Composition:** 0.9250 Silver .9314 oz. ASW **Subject:** Maurice Ravel **Obverse:** National emblem **Reverse:** Portrait, musician, dancer, and dates

| Date | Mintage | F | VF | XF | Unc | BU |
|---|---|---|---|---|---|---|
| 1993 Proof | — | Value: 42.50 | | | | |

**300 NGULTRUMS KM# 76 Weight:** 31.4700 g. **Composition:** 0.9250 Silver .9359 oz. ASW **Series:** 1992 Olympic Games **Reverse:** Archery

| Date | Mintage | F | VF | XF | Unc | BU |
|---|---|---|---|---|---|---|
| 1992 Proof | 20,000 | Value: 18.50 | | | | |

**300 NGULTRUMS KM# 68 Weight:** 31.4700 g. **Composition:** 0.9250 Silver .9359 oz. ASW **Subject:** Protect our world **Reverse:** Elephant, rhino, tree, and tiger

| Date | Mintage | F | VF | XF | Unc | BU |
|---|---|---|---|---|---|---|
| 1993 Proof | Est. 10,000 | Value: 50.00 | | | | |

**300 NGULTRUMS KM# 69 Weight:** 31.3200 g. **Composition:** 0.9250 Silver .9314 oz. ASW **Subject:** Protect our world **Reverse:** Rain forest

| Date | Mintage | F | VF | XF | Unc | BU |
|---|---|---|---|---|---|---|
| 1994 Proof | Est. 10,000 | Value: 45.00 | | | | |

**300 NGULTRUMS** **KM# 73** **Weight:** 31.3200 g. **Composition:** 0.9250 Silver .9314 oz. ASW **Series:** 1996 Olympic Games **Reverse:** Basketball

| Date | Mintage | F | VF | XF | Unc | BU |
|---|---|---|---|---|---|---|
| 1994 Proof | 30,000 | Value: 25.00 | | | | |

**300 NGULTRUMS** **KM# 88** **Weight:** 31.4500 g. **Composition:** 0.9250 Silver .9353 oz. ASW **Series:** Endangered wildlife **Reverse:** Kalij pheasant

| Date | Mintage | F | VF | XF | Unc | BU |
|---|---|---|---|---|---|---|
| 1994 Proof | — | Value: 37.50 | | | | |

**300 NGULTRUMS** **KM# 81** **Weight:** 31.4500 g. **Composition:** 0.9250 Silver .9353 oz. ASW **Subject:** Joao Cabral **Obverse:** National emblem **Reverse:** 2 explorers

| Date | Mintage | F | VF | XF | Unc | BU |
|---|---|---|---|---|---|---|
| 1994 Proof | Est. 10,000 | Value: 32.50 | | | | |

**300 NGULTRUMS** **KM# 80** **Weight:** 28.2800 g. **Composition:** 0.9250 Silver .8411 oz. ASW **Subject:** 50th anniversary - United Nations

| Date | Mintage | F | VF | XF | Unc | BU |
|---|---|---|---|---|---|---|
| 1995 Proof | Est. 100,000 | Value: 32.50 | | | | |

**300 NGULTRUMS** **KM# 90** **Weight:** 31.5000 g. **Composition:** 0.9250 Silver .9368 oz. ASW **Subject:** Chinese lunar year **Obverse:** National emblem **Reverse:** Seated monkey

| Date | Mintage | F | VF | XF | Unc | BU |
|---|---|---|---|---|---|---|
| 1996 Proof | — | Value: 28.50 | | | | |

**300 NGULTRUMS** **KM# 98** **Weight:** 31.5000 g. **Composition:** 0.9250 Silver .9368 oz. ASW **Subject:** Chinese lunar year **Obverse:** National emblem **Reverse:** Stylized dragon

| Date | Mintage | F | VF | XF | Unc | BU |
|---|---|---|---|---|---|---|
| 1996 Proof | — | Value: 30.00 | | | | |

**300 NGULTRUMS** **KM# 91** **Weight:** 31.5000 g. **Composition:** 0.9250 Silver .9368 oz. ASW **Subject:** Chinese lunar year **Obverse:** National emblem **Reverse:** Stylized rooster

| Date | Mintage | F | VF | XF | Unc | BU |
|---|---|---|---|---|---|---|
| 1996 Proof | — | Value: 28.50 | | | | |

**300 NGULTRUMS** **KM# 93** **Weight:** 31.5000 g. **Composition:** 0.9250 Silver .9368 oz. ASW **Subject:** Chinese lunar year **Obverse:** National emblem **Reverse:** Stylized pig

| Date | Mintage | F | VF | XF | Unc | BU |
|---|---|---|---|---|---|---|
| 1996 Proof | — | Value: 28.50 | | | | |

**300 NGULTRUMS** **KM# 94** **Weight:** 31.5000 g. **Composition:** 0.9250 Silver .9368 oz. ASW **Subject:** Chinese lunar year **Obverse:** National emblem **Reverse:** Stylized rat

| Date | Mintage | F | VF | XF | Unc | BU |
|---|---|---|---|---|---|---|
| 1996 Proof | — | Value: 30.00 | | | | |

**300 NGULTRUMS** **KM# 95** **Weight:** 31.5000 g. **Composition:** 0.9250 Silver .9368 oz. ASW **Subject:** Chinese lunar year **Obverse:** National emblem **Reverse:** Stylized ox

| Date | Mintage | F | VF | XF | Unc | BU |
|---|---|---|---|---|---|---|
| 1996 Proof | — | Value: 28.50 | | | | |

**300 NGULTRUMS** **KM# 96** **Weight:** 31.5000 g. **Composition:** 0.9250 Silver .9368 oz. ASW **Subject:** Chinese lunar year **Obverse:** National emblem **Reverse:** Stylized tiger

| Date | Mintage | F | VF | XF | Unc | BU |
|---|---|---|---|---|---|---|
| 1996 Proof | — | Value: 30.00 | | | | |

**300 NGULTRUMS** **KM# 92** **Weight:** 31.5000 g. **Composition:** 0.9250 Silver .9368 oz. ASW **Subject:** Chinese lunar year **Obverse:** National emblem **Reverse:** Stylized dog

| Date | Mintage | F | VF | XF | Unc | BU |
|---|---|---|---|---|---|---|
| 1996 Proof | — | Value: 28.50 | | | | |

**300 NGULTRUMS** KM# 97 **Weight:** 31.5000 g. **Composition:** 0.9250 Silver .9368 oz. ASW **Subject:** Chinese lunar year **Obverse:** National emblem **Reverse:** Stylized rabbit

| Date | Mintage | F | VF | XF | Unc | BU |
|---|---|---|---|---|---|---|
| 1996 Proof | — | Value: 28.50 | | | | |

**300 NGULTRUMS** KM# 99 **Weight:** 31.5000 g. **Composition:** 0.9250 Silver .9368 oz. ASW **Subject:** Chinese lunar year **Obverse:** National emblem **Reverse:** Stylized snake

| Date | Mintage | F | VF | XF | Unc | BU |
|---|---|---|---|---|---|---|
| 1996 Proof | — | Value: 30.00 | | | | |

**300 NGULTRUMS** KM# 100 **Weight:** 31.5000 g. **Composition:** 0.9250 Silver .9368 oz. ASW **Subject:** Chinese lunar year **Obverse:** National emblem **Reverse:** Stylized horse

| Date | Mintage | F | VF | XF | Unc | BU |
|---|---|---|---|---|---|---|
| 1996 Proof | — | Value: 28.50 | | | | |

**300 NGULTRUMS** KM# 101 **Weight:** 31.5000 g. **Composition:** 0.9250 Silver .9368 oz. ASW **Subject:** Chinese lunar year **Obverse:** National emblem **Reverse:** Stylized ram

| Date | Mintage | F | VF | XF | Unc | BU |
|---|---|---|---|---|---|---|
| 1996 Proof | — | Value: 28.50 | | | | |

**300 NGULTRUMS** KM# 102 **Weight:** 1.2441 g. **Composition:** 0.9990 Gold .04 oz. AGW **Obverse:** National emblem **Reverse:** Mask

| Date | Mintage | F | VF | XF | Unc | BU |
|---|---|---|---|---|---|---|
| 1997 Proof | — | Value: 45.00 | | | | |

**SERTUM** KM# 51 **Weight:** 7.9800 g. **Composition:** 0.9170 Gold .2352 oz. AGW **Obverse:** Similar to 5 Sertums, KM#35 **Reverse:** 2 dragons around inner circle

| Date | Mintage | F | VF | XF | Unc | BU |
|---|---|---|---|---|---|---|
| 1979 | 1,000 | — | — | — | 125 | — |
| 1979 Proof | 1,000 | Value: 160 | | | | |

**SERTUM** KM# 51a **Weight:** 9.8500 g. **Composition:** 0.9500 Platinum .3008 oz. APW **Obverse:** Similar to 5 Sertums, KM#35 **Reverse:** 2 dragons around inner circle

| Date | Mintage | F | VF | XF | Unc | BU |
|---|---|---|---|---|---|---|
| 1979 Proof | — | Value: 300 | | | | |

**SERTUM** KM# 56 **Weight:** 7.9900 g. **Composition:** 0.9170 Gold .2356 oz. AGW **Subject:** 75th anniversary of monarchy

| Date | Mintage | F | VF | XF | Unc | BU |
|---|---|---|---|---|---|---|
| 1982(1983) | 1,000 | — | — | — | 135 | — |
| 1982(1983) Proof | 1,000 | Value: 165 | | | | |

**SERTUM** KM# 85 **Weight:** 1.2442 g. **Composition:** 0.9999 Gold .04 oz. AGW **Subject:** 40th anniversary - Queen Elizabeth II's coronation

| Date | Mintage | F | VF | XF | Unc | BU |
|---|---|---|---|---|---|---|
| 1995 | Est. 250,000 | — | — | — | 50.00 | — |

**2 SERTUMS** KM# 52 **Weight:** 15.9800 g. **Composition:** 0.9170 Gold .4711 oz. AGW **Obverse:** Similar to 5 Sertums, KM#35 **Reverse:** 2 dragons around inner circle

| Date | Mintage | F | VF | XF | Unc | BU |
|---|---|---|---|---|---|---|
| 1979 | 1,000 | — | — | — | 225 | — |
| 1979 Proof | 1,000 | Value: 285 | | | | |

**2 SERTUMS** KM# 52a **Weight:** 19.7000 g. **Composition:** 0.9500 Platinum .6017 oz. APW **Obverse:** Similar to 5 Sertums, KM#35 **Reverse:** 2 dragons around inner circle

| Date | Mintage | F | VF | XF | Unc | BU |
|---|---|---|---|---|---|---|
| 1979 Proof | — | Value: 420 | | | | |

**2 SERTUMS** KM# 60 **Weight:** 15.9800 g. **Composition:** 0.9170 Gold .4711 oz. AGW **Series:** International Year of Disabled Persons

| Date | Mintage | F | VF | XF | Unc | BU |
|---|---|---|---|---|---|---|
| 1981 | — | — | — | — | 700 | — |
| 1981 Proof | — | Value: 900 | | | | |

**5 SERTUMS** KM# 53 **Weight:** 39.9400 g. **Composition:** 0.9170 Gold 1.1776 oz. AGW **Obverse:** Similar to 5 Sertums, KM#35 **Reverse:** 2 dragons around inner circle

| Date | Mintage | F | VF | XF | Unc | BU |
|---|---|---|---|---|---|---|
| 1979 | 1,000 | — | — | — | 500 | — |
| 1979 Proof | 1,000 | Value: 675 | | | | |

**5 SERTUMS** KM# 53a **Weight:** 49.2000 g. **Composition:** 0.9500 Platinum 1.5022 oz. APW **Obverse:** Similar to 5 Sertums, KM#35 **Reverse:** 2 dragons around inner circle

| Date | Mintage | F | VF | XF | Unc | BU |
|---|---|---|---|---|---|---|
| 1979 Proof | — | Value: 950 | | | | |

**5 SERTRUMS** KM# 64 **Weight:** 7.7760 g. **Composition:** 0.5833 Gold .1458 oz. AGW **Series:** Endangered wildlife **Reverse:** Black-necked crane

| Date | Mintage | F | VF | XF | Unc | BU |
|---|---|---|---|---|---|---|
| 1992 Proof | 2,000 | Value: 85.00 | | | | |

**5 SERTRUMS** KM# 70 **Weight:** 7.7760 g. **Composition:** 0.5833 Gold .1458 oz. AGW **Series:** 1992 Olympics **Reverse:** Archer

| Date | Mintage | F | VF | XF | Unc | BU |
|---|---|---|---|---|---|---|
| 1993 Proof | Est. 3,000 | Value: 125 | | | | |

**5 SERTRUMS** KM# 71 **Weight:** 7.7760 g. **Composition:** 0.5833 Gold .1458 oz. AGW **Subject:** World Cup '94 soccer

| Date | Mintage | F | VF | XF | Unc | BU |
|---|---|---|---|---|---|---|
| 1993 Proof | Est. 2,000 | Value: 125 | | | | |

**5 SERTRUMS** KM# 82 **Weight:** 7.7760 g. **Composition:** 0.5833 Gold .1458 oz. AGW **Series:** Olympics **Subject:** Tae kwon do **Obverse:** National emblem **Reverse:** Karate practitioner

| Date | Mintage | F | VF | XF | Unc | BU |
|---|---|---|---|---|---|---|
| 1994 Proof | Est. 3,000 | Value: 125 | | | | |

## MEDALLIC COINAGE

**25 NGULTRUMS** KM# 59 **Composition:** Copper-Nickel **Series:** International Games **Reverse:** Boxing

| Date | Mintage | F | VF | XF | Unc | BU |
|---|---|---|---|---|---|---|
| 1984 Proof | — | Value: 10.00 | | | | |

**25 NGULTRUMS** KM# 62 **Composition:** Copper-Nickel **Series:** International Games **Obverse:** National emblem and legends **Reverse:** Shot put

| Date | Mintage | F | VF | XF | Unc | BU |
|---|---|---|---|---|---|---|
| 1984 Proof | — | Value: 10.00 | | | | |

## PIEFORTS

| KM# | Date | Mintage | Identification | Mkt Val |
|---|---|---|---|---|
| P1 | 1981 | — | 2 Sertums. KM60. | 1,450 |
| P2 | 1981 | Est. 1,100 | 200 Ngultrums. KM57. | 300 |

## MINT SETS

| KM# | Date | Mintage | Identification | Issue Price | Mkt Val |
|---|---|---|---|---|---|
| MS1 | 1966 (3) | 300 | KM33-35 | 175 | 850 |
| MS3 | 1974 (4) | | KM37-38, 40-41 | 6.00 | 3.00 |
| MS2 | 1974 (2) | | KM39, 42 | 4.00 | 11.50 |
| MS4 | 1979 (3) | 1,000 | KM51-53 | 1,575 | 850 |

## PROOF SETS

| KM# | Date | Mintage | Identification | Issue Price | Mkt Val |
|---|---|---|---|---|---|
| PS1 | 1966 (4) | 6,000 | KM29-32 | 11.50 | 8.50 |
| PS2 | 1966 (3) | 598 | KM33-35 | 300 | 1,175 |
| PS3 | 1966 (3) | 72 | KM33a-35a | 685 | 1,675 |
| PS4 | 1974 (6) | 1,000 | KM37-42 | 18.00 | 65.00 |
| PS5 | 1975 (5) | | KM37, 40-41, 43-44; rare | — | — |
| PS6 | 1979 (5) | 20,000 | KM45-49 | 30.00 | 15.00 |
| PS7 | 1979 (3) | 1,000 | KM51-53 | 2,100 | 1,125 |
| PS8 | 1979 (3) | | KM51a-53a | 2,400 | 1,675 |

# BIAFRA

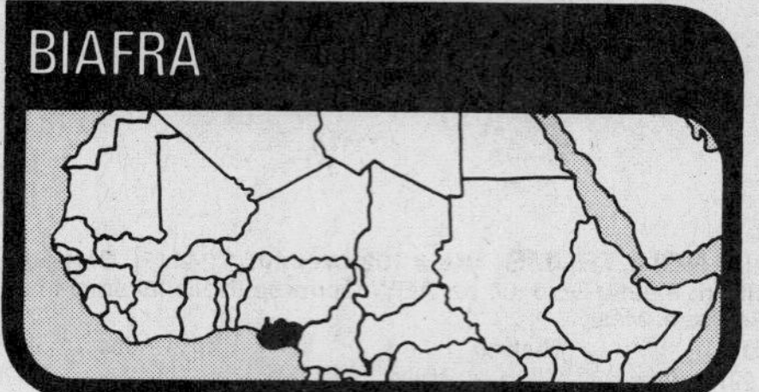

On May 30, 1967, the Eastern Region of the Republic of Nigeria, an area occupied principally by the proud and resourceful Ibo tribe, seceded from Nigeria and proclaimed itself the independent Republic of Biafra with Odumegwu Ojukwu as Chief of State. Civil war erupted and raged for 31 months. Casualties, including civilian, were about two million, the majority succumbing to malnutrition and disease. Biafra surrendered to the federal government on January 15, 1970.

**MONETARY SYSTEM**
12 Pence = 1 Shilling
20 Shillings = 1 Pound

## INDEPENDANT REPUBLIC OF BIAFRA

### STANDARD COINAGE

**3 PENCE** KM# 1 **Composition:** Aluminum

| Date | Mintage | F | VF | XF | Unc | BU |
|---|---|---|---|---|---|---|
| 1969 | — | — | 15.00 | 20.00 | 30.00 | — |

**6 PENCE** KM# 12 **Composition:** Aluminum **Obverse:** Value: 6 PENCE

| Date | Mintage | F | VF | XF | Unc | BU |
|---|---|---|---|---|---|---|
| 1969 2 pieces known | — | — | — | — | — | — |

**SHILLING** KM# 2 **Composition:** Aluminum

| Date | Mintage | F | VF | XF | Unc | BU |
|---|---|---|---|---|---|---|
| 1969 | — | — | 10.00 | 15.00 | 22.50 | — |

**SHILLING** KM# 3 **Composition:** Aluminum **Obverse:** Value: ONE SHILLING

| Date | Mintage | F | VF | XF | Unc | BU |
|---|---|---|---|---|---|---|
| 1969 | — | — | — | 250 | 350 | — |

**2-1/2 SHILLING** KM# 4 **Composition:** Aluminum

| Date | Mintage | F | VF | XF | Unc | BU |
|---|---|---|---|---|---|---|
| 1969 | — | — | 11.50 | 17.50 | 30.00 | — |

**CROWN** KM# 5 **Composition:** Silver **Subject:** Independence and Liberty

| Date | Mintage | F | VF | XF | Unc | BU |
|---|---|---|---|---|---|---|
| 1969 Rare | — | — | — | — | — | — |

**POUND** KM# 6 **Weight:** 19.7600 g. **Composition:** 0.7500 Silver .4765 oz. ASW

| Date | Mintage | F | VF | XF | Unc | BU |
|---|---|---|---|---|---|---|
| 1969 | — | — | — | 75.00 | 95.00 | — |

**POUND** KM# 7 **Weight:** 3.9940 g. **Composition:** 0.9170 Gold .1177 oz. AGW **Subject:** 2nd Anniversary of Independence **Obverse:** Similar to 25 Pounds, KM#11

| Date | Mintage | F | VF | XF | Unc | BU |
|---|---|---|---|---|---|---|
| 1969 Proof | 3,000 | Value: 65.00 | | | | |

**2 POUNDS** KM# 8 **Weight:** 7.9881 g. **Composition:** 0.9170 Gold .2354 oz. AGW **Subject:** 2nd Anniversary of Independence **Obverse:** Similar to 25 Pounds, KM#11

| Date | Mintage | F | VF | XF | Unc | BU |
|---|---|---|---|---|---|---|
| 1969 Proof | 3,000 | Value: 130 | | | | |

**5 POUNDS** **KM# 9** **Weight:** 15.9761 g. **Composition:** 0.9170 Gold .4710 oz. AGW **Subject:** 2nd Anniversary of Independence **Obverse:** Similar to 25 Pounds, KM#11

| Date | Mintage | F | VF | XF | Unc | BU |
|---|---|---|---|---|---|---|
| 1969 Proof | 3,000 | Value: 260 | | | | |

**10 POUNDS** **KM# 10** **Weight:** 39.9403 g. **Composition:** 0.9170 Gold 1.1776 oz. AGW **Subject:** 2nd Anniversary of Independence **Obverse:** Similar to 25 Pounds, KM#11

| Date | Mintage | F | VF | XF | Unc | BU |
|---|---|---|---|---|---|---|
| 1969 Proof | 3,000 | Value: 625 | | | | |

**25 POUNDS** **KM# 11** **Weight:** 79.8805 g. **Composition:** 0.9170 Gold 2.3553 oz. AGW **Subject:** 2nd Anniversary of Independence

| Date | Mintage | F | VF | XF | Unc | BU |
|---|---|---|---|---|---|---|
| 1969 Proof | 3,000 | Value: 1,275 | | | | |

## PROOF SETS

| KM# | Date | Mintage | Identification | Issue Price | Mkt Val |
|---|---|---|---|---|---|
| PS1 | 1969 | 3,000 | KM7-11 | 464 | 2,350 |

# BOHEMIA & MORAVIA

Bohemia, a western province in the Czech Republic, was combined with the majority of Moravia in central Czechoslovakia (excluding parts of north and south Moravia which were joined with Silesia in 1938) to form the German protectorate in March, 1939, after the German invasion. Toward the end of war in 1945 the protectorate was dissolved and Bohemia and Moravia once again became part of Czechoslovakia.

**MONETARY SYSTEM**
100 Haleru = 1 Koruna

## GERMAN PROTECTORATE

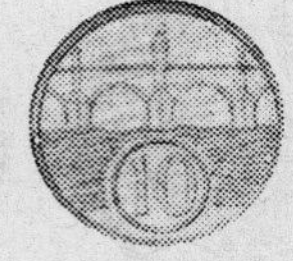

**10 HALERU** **KM# 1** **Composition:** Zinc

| Date | Mintage | F | VF | XF | Unc | BU |
|---|---|---|---|---|---|---|
| 1940 | 82,114,000 | 0.25 | 0.50 | 1.00 | 6.00 | — |
| 1941 | Inc. above | 0.25 | 0.50 | 1.00 | 7.50 | — |
| 1942 | Inc. above | 0.25 | 0.50 | 1.00 | 7.50 | — |
| 1943 | Inc. above | 0.50 | 0.75 | 1.50 | 10.00 | — |
| 1944 | Inc. above | 0.75 | 1.50 | 2.50 | 12.00 | — |

**20 HALERU** **KM# 2** **Composition:** Zinc

| Date | Mintage | F | VF | XF | Unc | BU |
|---|---|---|---|---|---|---|
| 1940 | 106,526,000 | 0.25 | 0.50 | 1.00 | 7.50 | — |
| 1941 | Inc. above | 0.25 | 0.50 | 1.00 | 7.50 | — |
| 1942 | Inc. above | 0.25 | 0.50 | 1.00 | 7.50 | — |
| 1943 | Inc. above | 0.50 | 0.75 | 1.50 | 10.00 | — |
| 1944 | Inc. above | 0.50 | 1.00 | 1.75 | 12.00 | — |

**50 HALERU** **KM# 3** **Composition:** Zinc

| Date | Mintage | F | VF | XF | Unc | BU |
|---|---|---|---|---|---|---|
| 1940 | 53,270,000 | 0.35 | 0.75 | 1.25 | 10.00 | — |
| 1941 | Inc. above | 0.35 | 0.75 | 1.25 | 10.00 | — |
| 1942 | Inc. above | 0.35 | 0.75 | 1.25 | 10.00 | — |
| 1943 | Inc. above | 0.75 | 1.50 | 3.00 | 15.00 | — |
| 1944 | Inc. above | 0.35 | 0.75 | 1.25 | 10.00 | — |

**KORUNA** **KM# 4** **Composition:** Zinc

| Date | Mintage | F | VF | XF | Unc | BU |
|---|---|---|---|---|---|---|
| 1941 | 102,817,000 | 0.50 | 0.75 | 1.50 | 12.50 | — |
| 1942 | Inc. above | 0.50 | 0.75 | 1.50 | 12.50 | — |
| 1943 | Inc. above | 0.50 | 0.75 | 1.50 | 12.50 | — |
| 1944 | Inc. above | 0.50 | 0.75 | 1.50 | 12.50 | — |

# BOLIVIA

The Republic of Bolivia, a landlocked country in west central South America, has an area of 424,165 sq. mi. (1,098,580 sq. km.) and a population of *8.33 million. Its capitals are: La Paz (administrative) and Sucre (constitutional). Principal exports are tin, zinc, antimony, tungsten, petroleum, natural gas, cotton and coffee.

Much of present-day Bolivia was first dominated by the Tiahuanaco Culture ca.400 BC. It had in turn been incorporated into the Inca Empire by 1440AD prior to the arrival of the Spanish, in 1535, who reduced the Indian population to virtual slavery. When Joseph Napoleon was placed upon the throne of occupied Spain in 1809, a fervor of revolutionary activity quickened throughout Alto Peru - culminating in the 1809 Proclamation of Liberty. Sixteen bloody years of struggle ensued before the republic, named for the famed liberator Simon Bolivar, was established on August 6, 1825. Since then Bolivia has survived more than 16 constitutions, 78 Presidents, 3 military juntas and over 160 revolutions.

**MINT MARKS**
A - Paris
(a) - Paris, privy marks only
CHI - Valcambia
H - Heaton
KN - Kings' Norton

**MONETARY SYSTEM**
100 Centavos = 1 Boliviano

## REPUBLIC

### REFORM COINAGE

1870 - 1951

The low quality of steel used for production of dies from the beginning of Republican coinage thru the late 1890’s resulted in most series having multiple dies with differences in spacing, dots and even style of letters and numbers. Only major differences or errors will be listed.

**5 CENTAVOS** **KM# 173.3** **Composition:** Copper-Nickel **Reverse:** Cornucopia and torch flank date

| Date | Mintage | F | VF | XF | Unc | BU |
|---|---|---|---|---|---|---|
| 1902 | 2,000,000 | 0.50 | 1.25 | 5.00 | 15.00 | — |
| 1907 | 2,000,000 | 1.75 | 3.75 | 7.50 | 20.00 | — |
| 1908 | 3,000,000 | 0.50 | 1.00 | 4.00 | 15.00 | — |
| 1909 | — | 2.00 | 4.00 | 9.00 | 25.00 | — |

**5 CENTAVOS** **KM# 173.1** **Composition:** Copper-Nickel **Note:** Coins dated 1893, 1918 and 1919 medal rotation were struck at the Heaton Mint.

| Date | Mintage | F | VF | XF | Unc | BU |
|---|---|---|---|---|---|---|
| 1909 | 4,000,000 | 0.50 | 1.00 | 4.00 | 15.00 | — |
| 1918 | 530,000 | 1.25 | 2.00 | 6.00 | 15.00 | — |
| 1919 | 4,370,000 | 3.00 | 5.00 | 10.00 | 25.00 | — |

**5 CENTAVOS** **KM# 178** **Composition:** Copper-Nickel

| Date | Mintage | F | VF | XF | Unc | BU |
|---|---|---|---|---|---|---|
| 1935 | 5,000,000 | 0.50 | 1.00 | 3.00 | 9.00 | — |

**10 CENTAVOS** KM# 174.3 **Composition:** Copper-Nickel **Reverse:** Cornucopia and torch flank date

| Date | Mintage | F | VF | XF | Unc | BU |
|---|---|---|---|---|---|---|
| 1901 | — | 17.50 | 27.50 | 45.00 | 75.00 | — |
| 1902 | 8,500,000 | 0.50 | 1.00 | 4.00 | 15.00 | — |
| 1907/2 | 4,000,000 | 1.25 | 2.50 | 7.00 | 20.00 | — |
| 1907 | Inc. above | 0.50 | 1.00 | 4.00 | 15.00 | — |
| 1908 | 6,000,000 | 0.50 | 1.00 | 4.00 | 15.00 | — |
| 1909 | 8,000,000 | 0.50 | 1.00 | 4.00 | 15.00 | — |

**10 CENTAVOS** KM# 174.1 **Composition:** Copper-Nickel **Reverse:** Without privy marks **Note:** Coins dated 1893, 1918 and 1919 medal rotation were struck at the Heaton Mint.

| Date | Mintage | F | VF | XF | Unc | BU |
|---|---|---|---|---|---|---|
| 1918 | 1,335,000 | 2.50 | 5.00 | 7.50 | 15.00 | — |
| 1919 | 6,165,000 | 0.50 | 1.00 | 3.00 | 10.00 | — |

**10 CENTAVOS** KM# 179.1 **Composition:** Copper-Nickel **Reverse:** Wide O in value

| Date | Mintage | F | VF | XF | Unc | BU |
|---|---|---|---|---|---|---|
| 1935 | 10,000,000 | 0.50 | 1.00 | 2.50 | 10.00 | — |
| 1936 | 10,000,000 | 0.50 | 1.00 | 2.50 | 10.00 | — |

**10 CENTAVOS** KM# 180 **Composition:** Copper-Nickel

| Date | Mintage | F | VF | XF | Unc | BU |
|---|---|---|---|---|---|---|
| 1937 | 20,000,000 | 0.50 | 1.00 | 2.50 | 10.00 | — |

**10 CENTAVOS** KM# 179.2 **Composition:** Copper-Nickel **Reverse:** Narrow O in value

| Date | Mintage | F | VF | XF | Unc | BU |
|---|---|---|---|---|---|---|
| 1939 | — | 0.50 | 1.00 | 2.50 | 10.00 | — |

**10 CENTAVOS** KM# 179a **Composition:** Zinc

| Date | Mintage | F | VF | XF | Unc | BU |
|---|---|---|---|---|---|---|
| 1942 (p) | 10,000,000 | 0.50 | 1.00 | 2.50 | 10.00 | — |

**20 CENTAVOS** KM# 159.2 **Weight:** 4.6000 g. **Composition:** 0.9000 Silver .1331 oz. ASW **Note:** Reduced size dates and lettering, bar below CENTS. The small bar usually found below "S" in "9DS" is missing in the 1886-1888 and 1902 dates, Mint mark in monogram.

| Date | Mintage | VG | F | VF | XF | Unc |
|---|---|---|---|---|---|---|
| 1901PTS MM | 40,000 | 2.50 | 5.00 | 13.50 | 20.00 | — |
| 1901PTS MM/.WM | — | 2.50 | 5.00 | 16.50 | 35.00 | — |
| 1902PTS MM | — | 6.50 | 10.00 | 20.00 | 50.00 | — |
| 1903PTS MM | 10,000 | 10.00 | 15.00 | 30.00 | 75.00 | — |
| 1904PTS MM | — | 7.00 | 12.00 | 20.00 | 50.00 | — |
| 1907PTS MM | — | 45.00 | 90.00 | 150 | 300 | — |

**20 CENTAVOS** KM# 176 **Weight:** 4.0000 g. **Composition:** 0.8330 Silver .1071 oz. ASW

| Date | Mintage | F | VF | XF | Unc | BU |
|---|---|---|---|---|---|---|
| 1909H | 1,500,000 | 2.50 | 5.00 | 15.00 | 35.00 | — |
| 1909H Proof | — | Value: 500 | | | | |

**20 CENTAVOS** KM# 183 **Composition:** Zinc **Note:** Medal rotation strike.

| Date | Mintage | F | VF | XF | Unc | BU |
|---|---|---|---|---|---|---|
| 1942 (p) | 10,000,000 | 1.00 | 2.00 | 6.00 | 20.00 | — |

**50 CENTAVOS (1/2 Boliviano)** KM# 175.1 **Weight:** 11.5000 g. **Composition:** 0.9000 Silver .3328 oz. ASW **Note:** Mint mark in monogram.

| Date | Mintage | VG | F | VF | XF | Unc |
|---|---|---|---|---|---|---|
| 1901/0PTS MM | — | BV | 7.00 | 18.50 | 37.50 | — |
| 1901PTS MM | Inc. above | BV | 3.50 | 8.00 | 16.50 | — |
| 1902PTS MM | 1,530,000 | BV | 3.50 | 8.00 | 16.50 | — |
| 1903/2PTS MM | 690,000 | BV | 5.00 | 16.00 | 37.50 | — |
| 1903PTS MM | Inc. above | BV | 3.50 | 8.00 | 16.50 | — |
| 1904PTS MM | 1,290,000 | BV | 3.50 | 8.00 | 16.50 | — |
| 1905PTS MM | 1,690,000 | BV | 3.50 | 8.00 | 16.50 | — |
| 1905PTS AB | Inc. above | BV | 3.50 | 8.00 | 16.50 | — |
| 1906PTS MM | 630,000 | BV | 4.50 | 10.00 | 21.50 | — |
| 1906PTS AB | 5,500,000 | BV | 3.50 | 8.00 | 16.50 | — |
| 1907PTS MM | 50,000 | BV | 4.50 | 10.00 | 21.50 | — |
| 1908PTS MM | — | BV | 3.50 | 8.00 | 16.50 | — |
| 1908PTS MM Inverted 8 | — | BV | 10.00 | 25.00 | 50.00 | — |

**50 CENTAVOS (1/2 Boliviano)** KM# 177 **Weight:** 10.0000 g. **Composition:** 0.8330 Silver .2678 oz. ASW

| Date | Mintage | VG | F | VF | XF | Unc |
|---|---|---|---|---|---|---|
| 1909H | 1,400,000 | BV | 5.00 | 10.00 | 25.00 | — |
| 1909H | — | Value: 500 | | | | |

**50 CENTAVOS (1/2 Boliviano)** KM# 181 **Composition:** Copper Nickel **Note:** Most melted upon receipt in Bolivia. Medal rotation strike.

| Date | Mintage | F | VF | XF | Unc | BU |
|---|---|---|---|---|---|---|
| 1937 | 8,000,000 | 10.00 | 25.00 | 45.00 | 75.00 | — |

**50 CENTAVOS (1/2 Boliviano)** KM# 182 **Composition:** Copper Nickel **Note:** Medal rotation strike.

| Date | Mintage | F | VF | XF | Unc | BU |
|---|---|---|---|---|---|---|
| 1939 | — | 0.25 | 0.50 | 1.00 | 5.00 | — |

**50 CENTAVOS (1/2 Boliviano)** KM# 182a.1 **Composition:** Bronze **Note:** Medal rotation strike.

| Date | Mintage | F | VF | XF | Unc | BU |
|---|---|---|---|---|---|---|
| 1942 (p) | 10,000,000 | 0.35 | 0.60 | 1.25 | 5.00 | — |

**50 CENTAVOS (1/2 Boliviano)** KM# 182a.2 **Composition:** Bronze **Note:** Restrike - poor detail. Medal rotation strike.

| Date | Mintage | F | VF | XF | Unc | BU |
|---|---|---|---|---|---|---|
| 1942 | 5,310,000 | 0.25 | 0.50 | 1.00 | 4.00 | — |

**BOLIVIANO** KM# 184 **Composition:** Bronze **Note:** Medal rotation strike. Mint mark in monogram.

| Date | Mintage | F | VF | XF | Unc | BU |
|---|---|---|---|---|---|---|
| 1951PTS | 10,000,000 | 0.10 | 0.20 | 0.50 | 2.00 | — |
| 1951PTS Proof | 10 | Value: 200 | | | | |
| 1951PTS H | 15,000,000 | 0.10 | 0.20 | 0.40 | 1.75 | — |
| 1951PTS KN | 15,000,000 | 0.25 | 0.50 | 1.00 | 3.00 | — |

**5 BOLIVIANOS** KM# 185 **Composition:** Bronze **Note:** Medal rotation strike.

| Date | Mintage | F | VF | XF | Unc | BU |
|---|---|---|---|---|---|---|
| 1951 | 7,000,000 | 0.25 | 0.50 | 1.00 | 3.50 | — |
| 1951 Proof | — | Value: 150 | | | | |
| 1951 H | 15,000,000 | 0.25 | 0.50 | 1.00 | 3.50 | — |
| 1951 KN | 15,000,000 | 0.60 | 0.90 | 1.50 | 4.00 | — |

**10 BOLIVIANOS (1 Bolivar)** **KM# 186** **Composition:** Bronze **Note:** Medal rotation strike.

| Date | Mintage | F | VF | XF | Unc | BU |
|---|---|---|---|---|---|---|
| 1951 | 40,000,000 | 0.60 | 1.00 | 1.75 | 3.50 | — |
| 1951 Proof | — | — | — | — | — | — |

## MONETARY REFORM COINAGE

1,000,000 Peso Bolivianos = 1 Boliviano;
100 Centavos = 1 Boliviano

**2 CENTAVOS** **KM# 200** **Composition:** Stainless Steel

| Date | Mintage | F | VF | XF | Unc | BU |
|---|---|---|---|---|---|---|
| 1987 | 20,000,000 | — | — | — | 0.35 | — |

**5 CENTAVOS** **KM# 201** **Composition:** Stainless Steel

| Date | Mintage | F | VF | XF | Unc | BU |
|---|---|---|---|---|---|---|
| 1987 | 20,000,000 | — | — | — | 0.50 | — |

**10 CENTAVOS** **KM# 202** **Composition:** Stainless Steel

| Date | Mintage | F | VF | XF | Unc | BU |
|---|---|---|---|---|---|---|
| 1987 | 20,000,000 | — | — | — | 0.65 | — |
| 1991 | 23,000,000 | — | — | — | 0.50 | — |
| 1995 | 14,000,000 | — | — | — | 0.50 | — |
| 1997 | 33,000,000 | — | — | — | 0.50 | — |

**10 CENTAVOS** **KM# 202a** **Composition:** Copper Clad Steel

| Date | Mintage | F | VF | XF | Unc | BU |
|---|---|---|---|---|---|---|
| 1997 | — | — | — | — | 0.50 | — |

**20 CENTAVOS** **KM# 203** **Composition:** Stainless Steel

| Date | Mintage | F | VF | XF | Unc | BU |
|---|---|---|---|---|---|---|
| 1987 | 20,000,000 | — | — | — | 0.75 | — |
| 1991 | 20,000,000 | — | — | — | 0.65 | — |
| 1995 | 14,000,000 | — | — | — | 0.65 | — |
| 1997 | 19,000,000 | — | — | — | 0.65 | — |

**50 CENTAVOS** **KM# 204** **Composition:** Stainless Steel

| Date | Mintage | F | VF | XF | Unc | BU |
|---|---|---|---|---|---|---|
| 1987 | 15,000,000 | — | — | — | 1.00 | — |
| 1991 | 20,000,000 | — | — | — | 0.75 | — |
| 1995 | 14,000,000 | — | — | — | 0.75 | — |
| 1997 | 15,000,000 | — | — | — | 0.75 | — |

**BOLIVIANO** **KM# 205** **Composition:** Stainless Steel

| Date | Mintage | F | VF | XF | Unc | BU |
|---|---|---|---|---|---|---|
| 1987 | 10,000,000 | — | — | — | 1.75 | — |
| 1991 | 20,000,000 | — | — | — | 1.00 | — |
| 1995 | 9,000,000 | — | — | — | 1.00 | — |
| 1997 | 17,000,000 | — | — | — | 1.00 | — |

**BOLIVIANO** **KM# 210** **Weight:** 27.0000 g. **Composition:** 0.9250 Silver .8030 oz. ASW **Subject:** 70th Anniversary - Bolivian Central Bank **Obverse:** National arms **Reverse:** Denomination above bank emblem

| Date | Mintage | F | VF | XF | Unc | BU |
|---|---|---|---|---|---|---|
| 1998 Proof | 1,000 | Value: 65.00 | | | | |

**2 BOLIVIANOS** **KM# 206.1** **Composition:** Stainless Steel

| Date | Mintage | F | VF | XF | Unc | BU |
|---|---|---|---|---|---|---|
| 1991 | 18,000,000 | — | — | — | 2.00 | — |

**2 BOLIVIANOS** **KM# 206.2** **Composition:** Stainless Steel **Size:** 29mm mm. **Note:** Increased size.

| Date | Mintage | F | VF | XF | Unc | BU |
|---|---|---|---|---|---|---|
| 1995 | 11,000,000 | — | — | — | 2.00 | — |
| 1997 | — | — | — | — | 2.00 | — |

**10 BOLIVIANOS** **KM# 207** **Weight:** 27.0000 g. **Composition:** 0.9250 Silver .8029 oz. ASW **Series:** Ibero - American

| Date | Mintage | F | VF | XF | Unc | BU |
|---|---|---|---|---|---|---|
| 1991 Proof | Est. 50,000 | Value: 55.00 | | | | |

**10 BOLIVIANOS** **KM# 209** **Weight:** 27.1300 g. **Composition:** 0.9250 Silver .8068 oz. ASW **Series:** Ibero - American **Obverse:** Bolivian arms **Reverse:** Folk dancer

| Date | Mintage | F | VF | XF | Unc | BU |
|---|---|---|---|---|---|---|
| 1997 Proof | 33,000 | Value: 55.00 | | | | |

**50 BOLIVIANOS** **KM# 211** **Weight:** 27.0000 g. **Composition:** 0.9250 Silver .8030 oz. ASW **Subject:** 450th Anniversary of La Paz **Obverse:** National arms **Reverse:** City arms above church building

| Date | Mintage | F | VF | XF | Unc | BU |
|---|---|---|---|---|---|---|
| 1998 Proof | 2,000 | Value: 65.00 | | | | |

## REFORM COINAGE

1965-1979; 100 Centavos = 1 Peso Boliviano

**5 CENTAVOS** **KM# 187** **Composition:** Copper Clad Steel

| Date | Mintage | F | VF | XF | Unc | BU |
|---|---|---|---|---|---|---|
| 1965 | 10,000,000 | 0.20 | 0.30 | 0.65 | 1.50 | — |
| 1970 | 100,000 | 0.20 | 0.30 | 0.65 | 2.00 | — |

**10 CENTAVOS** **KM# 188** **Composition:** Copper Clad Steel

| Date | Mintage | F | VF | XF | Unc | BU |
|---|---|---|---|---|---|---|
| 1965 | 10,000,000 | 0.10 | 0.25 | 0.50 | 1.50 | — |
| 1967 | — | 0.10 | 0.20 | 0.40 | 1.00 | — |
| 1969 | 5,700,000 | 0.10 | 0.20 | 0.40 | 1.00 | — |
| 1971 | 200,000 | 0.15 | 0.25 | 0.50 | 1.00 | — |
| 1972 | 100,000 | 0.20 | 0.40 | 0.80 | 1.50 | — |
| 1973 | 6,000,000 | 0.10 | 0.20 | 0.40 | 1.00 | — |

**20 CENTAVOS** **KM# 189** **Composition:** Nickel Clad Steel

| Date | Mintage | F | VF | XF | Unc | BU |
|---|---|---|---|---|---|---|
| 1965 | 5,000,000 | 0.20 | 0.40 | 0.70 | 2.00 | — |
| 1967 | — | 0.20 | 0.40 | 0.65 | 1.75 | — |
| 1970 | 400,000 | 0.20 | 0.40 | 0.80 | 2.50 | — |
| 1971 | 400,000 | 0.20 | 0.40 | 0.80 | 2.50 | — |
| 1973 | 5,000,000 | 0.20 | 0.40 | 0.60 | 1.50 | — |

**25 CENTAVOS** **KM# 193** **Composition:** Nickel Clad Steel

| Date | Mintage | F | VF | XF | Unc | BU |
|---|---|---|---|---|---|---|
| 1971 | — | 0.15 | 0.30 | 0.60 | 1.00 | — |
| 1972 | 9,998,000 | 0.15 | 0.30 | 0.60 | 1.00 | — |

**50 CENTAVOS** **KM# 190** **Composition:** Nickel Clad Steel

| Date | Mintage | F | VF | XF | Unc | BU |
|---|---|---|---|---|---|---|
| 1965 | 10,000,000 | — | 0.25 | 0.65 | 1.75 | — |
| 1967 | — | — | 0.25 | 0.65 | 1.25 | — |
| 1972 | — | — | 0.25 | 0.65 | 1.25 | — |
| 1973 | 5,000,000 | — | 0.25 | 0.65 | 1.25 | — |
| 1974 | 15,000,000 | — | 0.25 | 0.65 | 1.25 | — |
| 1978 | 5,000,000 | — | 0.25 | 0.65 | 1.25 | — |
| 1980 | 3,600,000 | — | 0.25 | 0.65 | 1.25 | — |

**PESO BOLIVIANOS** **KM# 192** **Composition:** Nickel Clad Steel **Series:** F.A.O.

| Date | Mintage | F | VF | XF | Unc | BU |
|---|---|---|---|---|---|---|
| 1968 | 10,000,000 | 0.20 | 0.35 | 0.80 | 1.75 | — |
| 1969 | — | 0.20 | 0.35 | 0.80 | 1.75 | — |
| 1970 | 10,000,000 | 0.15 | 0.25 | 0.80 | 1.75 | — |
| 1972 | — | 0.20 | 0.35 | 0.80 | 1.75 | — |
| 1973 | 5,000,000 | 0.15 | 0.25 | 0.80 | 1.75 | — |
| 1974 small date | 15,000,000 | 0.15 | 0.25 | 0.80 | 1.75 | — |
| 1978 | 10,000,000 | 0.15 | 0.25 | 0.80 | 1.75 | — |
| 1980 large date | 2,993,000 | 0.15 | 0.25 | 0.80 | 1.75 | — |

**PESO BOLIVIANOS** **KM# 191** **Composition:** Nickel Clad Steel **Series:** F.A.O.

| Date | Mintage | F | VF | XF | Unc | BU |
|---|---|---|---|---|---|---|
| ND(1968) | 40,000 | — | 2.50 | 3.50 | 6.50 | — |

**5 PESOS BOLIVIANOS** **KM# 197** **Composition:** Nickel Clad Steel

| Date | Mintage | F | VF | XF | Unc | BU |
|---|---|---|---|---|---|---|
| 1976 | 20,000,000 | 0.65 | 1.25 | 2.50 | 5.00 | — |
| 1978 | 10,000,000 | 0.65 | 1.25 | 2.50 | 5.00 | — |
| 1980 | 5,231,000 | 0.65 | 1.25 | 2.50 | 5.00 | — |

**100 PESOS BOLIVIANOS** **KM# 194** **Weight:** 10.0000 g. **Composition:** 0.9330 Silver .3000 oz. ASW **Subject:** 150th Anniversary of Independence

| Date | Mintage | F | VF | XF | Unc | BU |
|---|---|---|---|---|---|---|
| ND(1975) | 160,000 | BV | 3.50 | 5.00 | 8.50 | — |

**200 PESOS BOLIVIANOS** **KM# 198** **Weight:** 23.3300 g. **Composition:** 0.9250 Silver .6938 oz. ASW **Subject:** International Year of the Child

| Date | Mintage | F | VF | XF | Unc | BU |
|---|---|---|---|---|---|---|
| 1979 | 15,000 | Value: 16.50 | | | | |

**250 PESOS BOLIVIANOS** **KM# 195** **Weight:** 15.0000 g. **Composition:** 0.9330 Silver .4500 oz. ASW **Subject:** 150th Anniversary of Independence

| Date | Mintage | F | VF | XF | Unc | BU |
|---|---|---|---|---|---|---|
| ND(1975) | 140,000 | BV | 4.00 | 6.00 | 12.50 | — |

**500 PESOS BOLIVIANOS** **KM# 196** **Weight:** 22.0000 g. **Composition:** 0.9330 Silver .6600 oz. ASW **Subject:** 150th Anniversary of Independence

| Date | Mintage | F | VF | XF | Unc | BU |
|---|---|---|---|---|---|---|
| ND(1975) | 100,000 | BV | 6.00 | 12.00 | 20.00 | — |

**4000 PESOS BOLIVIANOS** **KM# 199** **Weight:** 17.1700 g. **Composition:** 0.9000 Gold .4968 oz. AGW **Subject:** International Year of the Child

| Date | Mintage | F | VF | XF | Unc | BU |
|---|---|---|---|---|---|---|
| 1979 Proof | 6,315 | Value: 200 | | | | |

## MEDALLIC COINAGE

1952 - Gold Bullion

**3-1/2 GRAMOS (5 Bolivianos)** **KM# MB1** **Weight:** 3.8900 g. **Composition:** 0.9000 Gold .1125 oz. AGW **Subject:** 1952 Revolution Commemorative

| Date | Mintage | F | VF | XF | Unc | BU |
|---|---|---|---|---|---|---|
| 1952(a) | 29,000 | — | — | —BV+20% | | — |

**7 GRAMOS (10 Bolivianos)** **KM# MB2** **Weight:** 7.7800 g. **Composition:** 0.9000 Gold .2251 oz. AGW **Subject:** 1952 Revolution Commemorative

| Date | Mintage | F | VF | XF | Unc | BU |
|---|---|---|---|---|---|---|
| 1952(a) | 79,000 | — | — | —BV+15% | | — |

**14 GRAMOS (20 Bolivianos)** **KM# MB3** **Weight:** 15.5600 g. **Composition:** 0.9000 Gold .4502 oz. AGW **Subject:** 1952 Revolution Commemorative

| Date | Mintage | F | VF | XF | Unc | BU |
|---|---|---|---|---|---|---|
| 1952(a) | 7,142 | — | — | — | BV+10% | — |

**35 GRAMOS (50 Bolivianos)** **KM# MB4** **Weight:** 38.9000 g. **Composition:** 0.9000 Gold 1.1257 oz. AGW **Subject:** 1952 Revolution Commemorative

| Date | Mintage | F | VF | XF | Unc | BU |
|---|---|---|---|---|---|---|
| 1952(a) | 2,857 | — | — | — | BV+10% | — |

## PATTERNS

Including off metal strikes

| KM# | Date | Mintage | Identification | Mkt Val |
|---|---|---|---|---|
| Pn54 | 1902 | — | 20 Centavos. Brass. Struck at La Paz. | 75.00 |
| Pn55 | 1902 | — | (No Denomination). Brass. Struck at La Paz. 1/2 Medio Boliviano/20 Centavos error. | 75.00 |

| KM# | Date | Mintage | Identification | Mkt Val |
|---|---|---|---|---|
| Pn56 | 1902 | — | 50 Centavos. Brass. | 100 |
| Pn57 | 1942 | — | 50 Centavos. Silver. Struck at La Paz. KM#182a.1. | 200 |
| Pn58 | 1952 | — | 35 Gramos. Brass. Struck at La Paz. KM MB4. | — |

## PIEFORTS

| KM# | Date | Mintage | Identification | Issue Price | Mkt Val |
|---|---|---|---|---|---|
| P9 | 1979 | 90 | 200 Pesos. KM#198. | — | 200 |
| P10 | 1979 | 47 | 4000 Pesos. KM#199. | — | 1,000 |

## TRIAL STRIKES

| KM# | Date | Mintage | Identification | Issue Price | Mkt Val |
|---|---|---|---|---|---|
| Ts1 | (1909) | — | 20 Centavos. Silver. 23.2mm mm. Uniface. | — | — |

## MINT SETS

| KM# | Date | Mintage | Identification | Issue Price | Mkt Val |
|---|---|---|---|---|---|
| MS1 | 1952 | — | KM#MB1-MB4; Market Value is BV+10% | — | — |

# BOPHUTHATSWANA

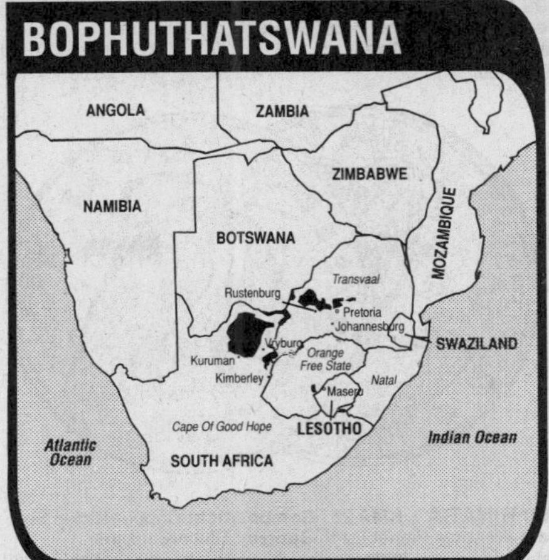


Bophuthatswana is a group of non-contiguous black enclaves located partially in Bechuanaland, Botswana and in the northwestern area of South Africa. Established in 1977, it ceased to exist with the end of apartheid in 1994. Population: 1,382,637. Capital: Mmabatho. The exportation of platinum is their main source of income.

The Botswana people have occupied their general area from the beginnings of their history. In 1871 the British recognized their sovereignty. In 1895 their land, known as British Bechuanaland, was claimed by the British and the Boers. The people were scattered across the sub-continent.

## SOVEREIGN ENCLAVE

### GOLD BULLION MEDALLIC COINAGE

**NKWE** **KM# M1** **Weight:** 16.9660 g. **Composition:** 0.9170 Gold .5 oz. AGW **Subject:** 10th Anniversary of Independence **Note:** Similar to Lowe, KM#2.

| Date | Mintage | F | VF | XF | Unc | BU |
|---|---|---|---|---|---|---|
| 1987 Proof | — | Value: 275 | | | | |

### PLATINUM BULLION MEDALLIC COINAGE

**LOWE** **KM# M2** **Weight:** 31.2100 g. **Composition:** 0.9995 Platinum 1 oz. APW **Subject:** 10th Anniversary of Independence

| Date | Mintage | F | VF | XF | Unc | BU |
|---|---|---|---|---|---|---|
| 1987 Proof | — | Value: 700 | | | | |

# BOSNIA – HERZEGOVINA

The Republic of Bosnia-Herzegovina borders Croatia to the north and west, Serbia to the east and Montenegro in the south-east with only 12.4 mi. of coastline. The total land area is 19,735 sq. mi. (51,129 sq. km.). They have a population of *4.34 million. Capital: Sarajevo. Electricity, mining and agriculture are leading industries.

After the defeat of Germany in WWII, during which Bosnia was under the control of Pavelic of Croatia, a new Socialist Republic was formed under Marshall Tito having six constituent republics, all subservient, quite similar to the constitution of the U.S.S.R. Military and civil loyalty was with Tito, not with Moscow. In Jan. 1990, the Yugoslav Government announced a rewriting of the Constitution, abolishing the Communist Party's monopoly of power. Opposition parties were legalized in July 1990. On Oct. 15, 1991 the National Assembly adopted a "Memorandum on Sovereignty", the envisaged Bosnian autonomy within a Yugoslav federation. In March 1992, an agreement was reached under EC auspices by Moslems, Serbs and Croats to set up 3 autonomous ethnic communities under a central Bosnian authority. Independence was declared on April 5, 1992. The 2 Serbian members of government resigned and fighting broke out between all 3 ethnic communities. The Dayton (Ohio) Peace Accord was signed in 1995, which recognized the Federation of Bosnia-Herzegovina and the Srpska (Serbian) Republic. Both governments maintain separate military forces, school systems, etc. The United Nations is currently providing humanitarian aid while a recent peace treaty allowed NATO "Peace Keeping" forces to be deployed in Dec. 1995 replacing the United Nations troops previously acting in a similar role.

**MINT MARKS**

PM - Pobjoy Mint

**MONETARY SYSTEM**

1 Dinara = 100 Para, 1992-1998

1 Convertible Marka = 100 Convertible Feniga = 1 Deutschemark 1998-

**NOTE**: German Marks and Yugoslavian Dinara circulate freely.

## REPUBLIC

### STANDARD COINAGE

**10 FENINGA** **KM# 115** **Composition:** Copper-Plated-Steel **Obverse:** Denomination on map **Reverse:** Triangle and stars

| Date | Mintage | F | VF | XF | Unc | BU |
|---|---|---|---|---|---|---|
| 1998 | — | — | — | — | 0.50 | — |
| 2000 | — | — | — | — | 0.50 | — |

**20 FENINGA** **KM# 116** **Composition:** Copper-Plated-Steel **Obverse:** Denomination on map **Reverse:** Triangle and stars

| Date | Mintage | F | VF | XF | Unc | BU |
|---|---|---|---|---|---|---|
| 1998 | — | — | — | — | 1.00 | — |
| 2000 | — | — | — | — | 1.00 | — |

**50 FENINGA** KM# 117 **Composition:** Copper-Plated-Steel **Obverse:** Denomination on map **Reverse:** Triangle and stars

| Date | Mintage | F | VF | XF | Unc | BU |
|---|---|---|---|---|---|---|
| 1998 | — | — | — | — | 2.25 | — |
| 2000 | — | — | — | — | 2.25 | — |

## DINARA COINAGE

**500 DINARA** KM# 1 **Composition:** Copper-Nickel **Series:** Preserve Planet Earth **Subject:** Brontosaurus

| Date | Mintage | F | VF | XF | Unc | BU |
|---|---|---|---|---|---|---|
| 1993 Proof | — | Value: 8.50 | | | | |

**500 DINARA** KM# 4 **Composition:** Copper-Nickel **Series:** Preserve Planet Earth **Subject:** Tyrannosaurus Rex

| Date | Mintage | F | VF | XF | Unc | BU |
|---|---|---|---|---|---|---|
| 1993 Proof | — | Value: 10.00 | | | | |

**500 DINARA** KM# 23 **Composition:** Copper-Nickel **Series:** Preserve Planet Earth **Subject:** Gray Wolf

| Date | Mintage | F | VF | XF | Unc | BU |
|---|---|---|---|---|---|---|
| 1994 Proof | — | — | — | — | 9.00 | — |

**500 DINARA** KM# 24 **Composition:** Copper-Nickel **Series:** Preserve Planet Earth **Subject:** Black Bears

| Date | Mintage | F | VF | XF | Unc | BU |
|---|---|---|---|---|---|---|
| 1994 Proof | — | — | — | — | 9.00 | — |

**500 DINARA** KM# 25 **Composition:** Copper-Nickel **Series:** Preserve Planet Earth **Subject:** River Kingfisher

| Date | Mintage | F | VF | XF | Unc | BU |
|---|---|---|---|---|---|---|
| 1994 | — | — | — | — | 9.00 | — |

**500 DINARA** KM# 20 **Composition:** Copper-Nickel **Series:** Preserve Planet Earth **Subject:** Eohippus **Note:** Similar to 10,000 Dinara, KM#22.

| Date | Mintage | F | VF | XF | Unc | BU |
|---|---|---|---|---|---|---|
| 1994 Proof | — | — | — | — | 9.00 | — |

**500 DINARA** KM# 39 **Composition:** Copper-Nickel **Series:** Preserve Planet Earth **Subject:** Przewalskii Horses **Note:** Similar to 750 Dinara, KM#40.

| Date | Mintage | F | VF | XF | Unc | BU |
|---|---|---|---|---|---|---|
| 1995 | — | — | — | — | 9.00 | — |

**500 DINARA** KM# 42 **Composition:** Copper-Nickel **Series:** Preserve Planet Earth **Subject:** Hedgehogs **Note:** Similar to 750 Dinara, KM#40.

| Date | Mintage | F | VF | XF | Unc | BU |
|---|---|---|---|---|---|---|
| 1995 | — | — | — | — | 9.00 | — |

**500 DINARA** KM# 64 **Composition:** Copper-Nickel **Series:** European Youth Olympics **Subject:** Flame **Note:** Similar to 750 Dinara, KM#66.

| Date | Mintage | F | VF | XF | Unc | BU |
|---|---|---|---|---|---|---|
| 1995 | — | — | — | — | 8.50 | — |

**500 DINARA** KM# 65 **Composition:** Copper-Nickel **Series:** European Youth Olympics **Subject:** Rings **Note:** Similar to 750 Dinara, KM#67.

| Date | Mintage | F | VF | XF | Unc | BU |
|---|---|---|---|---|---|---|
| 1995 | — | — | — | — | 8.50 | — |

**500 DINARA** KM# 76 **Composition:** Copper-Nickel **Series:** Preserve Planet Earth **Subject:** Hoopoe Birds **Note:** Similar to 750 Dinara, KM#77.

| Date | Mintage | F | VF | XF | Unc | BU |
|---|---|---|---|---|---|---|
| 1996 | — | — | — | — | 8.50 | — |

**500 DINARA** KM# 79 **Composition:** Copper-Nickel **Series:** Preserve Planet Earth **Subject:** Goosander Birds **Note:** Similar to 750 Dinars, KM#80.

| Date | Mintage | F | VF | XF | Unc | BU |
|---|---|---|---|---|---|---|
| 1996 | — | — | — | — | 8.50 | — |

**500 DINARA** KM# 52 **Composition:** Copper-Nickel **Series:** Olympics **Subject:** Long Jump **Note:** Similar to 750 Dinara, KM#56.

| Date | Mintage | F | VF | XF | Unc | BU |
|---|---|---|---|---|---|---|
| 1996 | — | — | — | — | 8.50 | — |

**500 DINARA** KM# 53 **Composition:** Copper-Nickel **Series:** Olympics **Subject:** Sprinter **Note:** Similar to 750 Dinara, KM#57.

| Date | Mintage | F | VF | XF | Unc | BU |
|---|---|---|---|---|---|---|
| 1996 | — | — | — | — | 8.50 | — |

**500 DINARA** KM# 54 **Composition:** Copper-Nickel **Series:** Olympics **Subject:** Wrestlers **Note:** Similar to 750 Dinara, KM#58.

| Date | Mintage | F | VF | XF | Unc | BU |
|---|---|---|---|---|---|---|
| 1996 | — | — | — | — | 8.50 | — |

**500 DINARA** KM# 55 **Composition:** Copper-Nickel **Series:** Olympics **Subject:** Fencers **Note:** Similar to 750 Dinara, KM#59.

| Date | Mintage | F | VF | XF | Unc | BU |
|---|---|---|---|---|---|---|
| 1996 | — | — | — | — | 8.50 | — |

**500 DINARA** KM# 95 **Composition:** Copper-Nickel **Subject:** Jurassic Park **Obverse:** Arms above bridge **Reverse:** Tyrannosaurus Rex, Jurassic Park logo **Note:** Similar to 750 Dinara, KM#96.

| Date | Mintage | F | VF | XF | Unc | BU |
|---|---|---|---|---|---|---|
| 1997 | — | — | — | — | 10.00 | — |

**750 DINARA** KM# 2 **Weight:** 28.2800 g. **Composition:** 0.9250 Silver .8411 oz. ASW **Series:** Preserve Planet Earth **Subject:** Brontosaurus

| Date | Mintage | F | VF | XF | Unc | BU |
|---|---|---|---|---|---|---|
| 1993 Proof | Est. 30,000 | Value: 37.50 | | | | |

**750 DINARA** KM# 5 **Weight:** 28.2800 g. **Composition:** 0.9250 Silver .8411 oz. ASW **Series:** Preserve Planet Earth **Subject:** Tyrannosaurus Rex

| Date | Mintage | F | VF | XF | Unc | BU |
|---|---|---|---|---|---|---|
| 1993 Proof | Est. 30,000 | Value: 37.50 | | | | |

**750 DINARA** KM# 7 **Weight:** 28.2800 g. **Composition:** 0.9250 Silver .8411 oz. ASW **Series:** Olympics **Subject:** Bobsledding

| Date | Mintage | F | VF | XF | Unc | BU |
|---|---|---|---|---|---|---|
| 1993 Proof | Est. 30,000 | Value: 45.00 | | | | |

**750 DINARA** KM# 9 **Weight:** 28.2800 g. **Composition:** 0.9250 Silver .8411 oz. ASW **Series:** Olympics **Subject:** Downhill Skiing

| Date | Mintage | F | VF | XF | Unc | BU |
|---|---|---|---|---|---|---|
| 1993 Proof | Est. 30,000 | Value: 45.00 | | | | |

**750 DINARA** **KM# 11** **Weight:** 28.2800 g. **Composition:** 0.9250 Silver .8411 oz. ASW **Series:** Olympics **Subject:** Cross Country Skiing

| Date | Mintage | F | VF | XF | Unc | BU |
|---|---|---|---|---|---|---|
| 1993 Proof | Est. 30,000 | Value: 45.00 | | | | |

**750 DINARA** **KM# 13** **Weight:** 28.2800 g. **Composition:** 0.9250 Silver .8411 oz. ASW **Series:** Olympics **Subject:** Pairs Figure Skating

| Date | Mintage | F | VF | XF | Unc | BU |
|---|---|---|---|---|---|---|
| 1993 Proof | Est. 30,000 | Value: 45.00 | | | | |

**750 DINARA** **KM# 26** **Weight:** 28.2800 g. **Composition:** 0.9250 Silver .8411 oz. ASW **Series:** Preserve Planet Earth **Subject:** Wolf

| Date | Mintage | F | VF | XF | Unc | BU |
|---|---|---|---|---|---|---|
| 1994 Proof | Est. 30,000 | Value: 37.50 | | | | |

**750 DINARA** **KM# 27** **Weight:** 28.2800 g. **Composition:** 0.9250 Silver .8411 oz. ASW **Series:** Preserve Planet Earth **Subject:** Black Bears

| Date | Mintage | F | VF | XF | Unc | BU |
|---|---|---|---|---|---|---|
| 1994 Proof | Est. 30,000 | Value: 32.50 | | | | |

**750 DINARA** **KM# 28** **Weight:** 28.2800 g. **Composition:** 0.9250 Silver .8411 oz. ASW **Series:** Preserve Planet Earth **Subject:** River Kingfisher

| Date | Mintage | F | VF | XF | Unc | BU |
|---|---|---|---|---|---|---|
| 1994 Proof | Est. 30,000 | Value: 32.50 | | | | |

**750 DINARA** **KM# 21** **Weight:** 28.2800 g. **Composition:** 0.9250 Silver .8411 oz. ASW **Series:** Preserve Planet Earth **Subject:** Eohippu **Note:** Similar to 10,000 Dinara, KM#22.

| Date | Mintage | F | VF | XF | Unc | BU |
|---|---|---|---|---|---|---|
| 1994 Proof | Est. 30,000 | Value: 32.50 | | | | |

**750 DINARA** **KM# 40** **Weight:** 28.2800 g. **Composition:** 0.9250 Silver .8411 oz. ASW **Series:** Preserve Planet Earth **Subject:** Przewalskii Horses

| Date | Mintage | F | VF | XF | Unc | BU |
|---|---|---|---|---|---|---|
| 1995 Proof | Est. 30,000 | Value: 32.50 | | | | |

**750 DINARA** **KM# 43** **Weight:** 28.2800 g. **Composition:** 0.9250 Silver .8411 oz. ASW **Series:** Preserve Planet Earth **Subject:** Hedgehogs

| Date | Mintage | F | VF | XF | Unc | BU |
|---|---|---|---|---|---|---|
| 1995 Proof | Est. 30,000 | Value: 35.00 | | | | |

**750 DINARA** **KM# 66** **Weight:** 28.2800 g. **Composition:** 0.9250 Silver .8411 oz. ASW **Series:** European Youth Olympics **Subject:** Flame

| Date | Mintage | F | VF | XF | Unc | BU |
|---|---|---|---|---|---|---|
| 1995 Proof | Est. 30,000 | Value: 37.50 | | | | |

**750 DINARA** **KM# 67** **Weight:** 28.2800 g. **Composition:** 0.9250 Silver .8411 oz. ASW **Series:** European Youth Olympics **Subject:** Rings

| Date | Mintage | F | VF | XF | Unc | BU |
|---|---|---|---|---|---|---|
| 1995 Proof | Est. 30,000 | Value: 37.50 | | | | |

**750 DINARA** **KM# 56** **Weight:** 28.2800 g. **Composition:** 0.9250 Silver .8411 oz. ASW **Series:** Olympics **Subject:** Long Jump

| Date | Mintage | F | VF | XF | Unc | BU |
|---|---|---|---|---|---|---|
| 1996 Proof | Est. 30,000 | Value: 35.00 | | | | |

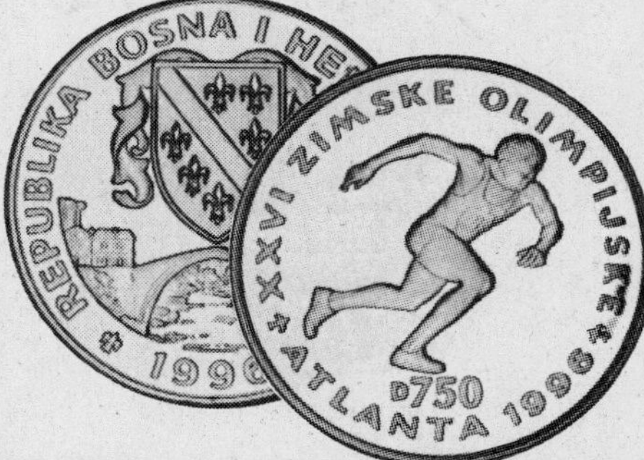


**750 DINARA** **KM# 57** **Weight:** 28.2800 g. **Composition:** 0.9250 Silver .8411 oz. ASW **Series:** Olympics **Subject:** Sprinter

| Date | Mintage | F | VF | XF | Unc | BU |
|---|---|---|---|---|---|---|
| 1996 Proof | Est. 30,000 | Value: 35.00 | | | | |

**750 DINARA** **KM# 58** **Weight:** 28.2800 g. **Composition:** 0.9250 Silver .8411 oz. ASW **Series:** Olympics **Subject:** Wrestlers

| Date | Mintage | F | VF | XF | Unc | BU |
|---|---|---|---|---|---|---|
| 1996 Proof | Est. 30,000 | Value: 35.00 | | | | |

**750 DINARA** KM# 59 **Weight:** 28.2800 g. **Composition:** 0.9250 Silver .8411 oz. ASW **Series:** Olympics **Subject:** Fencers

| Date | Mintage | F | VF | XF | Unc | BU |
|---|---|---|---|---|---|---|
| 1996 Proof | Est. 30,000 | Value: 35.00 | | | | |

**750 DINARA** KM# 77 **Weight:** 28.2800 g. **Composition:** 0.9250 Silver .8411 oz. ASW **Series:** Preserve Planet Earth **Subject:** Hoopoe Birds

| Date | Mintage | F | VF | XF | Unc | BU |
|---|---|---|---|---|---|---|
| 1996 Proof | Est. 30,000 | Value: 32.50 | | | | |

**750 DINARA** KM# 80 **Weight:** 28.2800 g. **Composition:** 0.9250 Silver .8411 oz. ASW **Series:** Preserve Planet Earth **Subject:** Goosander Birds

| Date | Mintage | F | VF | XF | Unc | BU |
|---|---|---|---|---|---|---|
| 1996 Proof | Est. 30,000 | Value: 32.50 | | | | |

**750 DINARA** KM# 96 **Weight:** 28.2800 g. **Composition:** 0.9250 Silver .8411 oz. ASW **Subject:** Jurassic Park **Obverse:** Arms above bridge **Reverse:** Tyrannosaurus Rex, Jurassic Park logo

| Date | Mintage | F | VF | XF | Unc | BU |
|---|---|---|---|---|---|---|
| 1997 Proof | Est. 10,000 | Value: 48.00 | | | | |

**10000 DINARA** KM# 12 **Weight:** 6.2200 g. **Composition:** 0.9990 Gold .1998 oz. AGW **Series:** Olympics **Subject:** Cross Country Skiing **Obverse:** Similar to KM#6 **Reverse:** Cross country skier **Note:** Similar to 750 Dinara, KM#11.

| Date | Mintage | F | VF | XF | Unc | BU |
|---|---|---|---|---|---|---|
| 1993 Proof | Est. 5,000 | Value: 175 | | | | |

**10000 DINARA** KM# 14 **Weight:** 6.2200 g. **Composition:** 0.9990 Gold .1998 oz. AGW **Series:** Olympics **Subject:** Pairs Figure Skating **Obverse:** Similar to KM#6 **Reverse:** Pair skating **Note:** Similar to 750 Dinara, KM#13.

| Date | Mintage | F | VF | XF | Unc | BU |
|---|---|---|---|---|---|---|
| 1993 Proof | Est. 5,000 | Value: 175 | | | | |

**10000 DINARA** KM# 3 **Weight:** 6.2200 g. **Composition:** 0.9990 Gold .1998 oz. AGW **Series:** Preserve Planet Earth **Subject:** Brontosaurus

| Date | Mintage | F | VF | XF | Unc | BU |
|---|---|---|---|---|---|---|
| 1993 Proof | Est. 5,000 | Value: 170 | | | | |

**10000 DINARA** KM# 6 **Weight:** 6.2200 g. **Composition:** 0.9990 Gold .1998 oz. AGW **Series:** Preserve Planet Earth **Subject:** Tyrannosaurus Rex

| Date | Mintage | F | VF | XF | Unc | BU |
|---|---|---|---|---|---|---|
| 1993 Proof | Est. 5,000 | Value: 170 | | | | |

**10000 DINARA** KM# 8 **Weight:** 6.2200 g. **Composition:** 0.9990 Gold .1998 oz. AGW **Series:** Olympics **Subject:** Bobsledding **Obverse:** Similar to KM#6 **Reverse:** 2 bobsledders starting race **Note:** Similar to 750 Dinara, KM#7.

| Date | Mintage | F | VF | XF | Unc | BU |
|---|---|---|---|---|---|---|
| 1993 Proof | Est. 5,000 | Value: 175 | | | | |

**10000 DINARA** KM# 10 **Weight:** 6.2200 g. **Composition:** 0.9990 Gold .1998 oz. AGW **Series:** Olympics **Subject:** Downhill Skiing **Obverse:** Similar to KM#6 **Reverse:** Downhill skier **Note:** Similar to 750 Dinara, KM#9.

| Date | Mintage | F | VF | XF | Unc | BU |
|---|---|---|---|---|---|---|
| 1993 | Est. 5,000 | Value: 175 | | | | |

**10000 DINARA** KM# 22 **Weight:** 6.2200 g. **Composition:** 0.9990 Gold .1998 oz. AGW **Series:** Preserve Planet Earth **Subject:** Eohippu

| Date | Mintage | F | VF | XF | Unc | BU |
|---|---|---|---|---|---|---|
| 1994 Proof | Est. 5,000 | Value: 170 | | | | |

**10000 DINARA** KM# 29 **Weight:** 6.2200 g. **Composition:** 0.9990 Gold .1998 oz. AGW **Series:** Preserve Planet Earth **Subject:** Wolf **Reverse:** Wolf walking right **Note:** Similar to 750 Dinara, KM#26.

| Date | Mintage | F | VF | XF | Unc | BU |
|---|---|---|---|---|---|---|
| 1994 Proof | 5,000 | Value: 170 | | | | |

**10000 DINARA** KM# 30 **Weight:** 6.2200 g. **Composition:** 0.9990 Gold .1998 oz. AGW **Series:** Preserve Planet Earth **Subject:** Black Bears **Reverse:** Black bear and cub walking right **Note:** Similar to 750 Dinara, KM#27.

| Date | Mintage | F | VF | XF | Unc | BU |
|---|---|---|---|---|---|---|
| 1994 Proof | 5,000 | Value: 170 | | | | |

**10000 DINARA** KM# 31 **Weight:** 6.2200 g. **Composition:** 0.9990 Gold .1998 oz. AGW **Series:** Preserve Planet Earth **Subject:** Kingfisher **Reverse:** Kingfisher left with fish in bill **Note:** Similar to 750 Dinara, KM#28.

| Date | Mintage | F | VF | XF | Unc | BU |
|---|---|---|---|---|---|---|
| 1994 Proof | 5,000 | Value: 170 | | | | |

**10000 DINARA** KM# 41 **Weight:** 6.2200 g. **Composition:** 0.9990 Gold .1998 oz. AGW **Series:** Preserve Planet Earth **Subject:** Przewalskii Horses **Note:** Similar to 750 Dinara, KM#40.

| Date | Mintage | F | VF | XF | Unc | BU |
|---|---|---|---|---|---|---|
| 1995 Proof | Est. 5,000 | Value: 170 | | | | |

**10000 DINARA** KM# 44 **Weight:** 6.2200 g. **Composition:** 0.9990 Gold .1998 oz. AGW **Series:** Preserve Planet Earth **Subject:** Hedgehogs **Note:** Similar to 750 Dinara, KM#43.

| Date | Mintage | F | VF | XF | Unc | BU |
|---|---|---|---|---|---|---|
| 1995 Proof | Est. 5,000 | Value: 170 | | | | |

**10000 DINARA** KM# 60 **Weight:** 6.2200 g. **Composition:** 0.9990 Gold .1998 oz. AGW **Series:** Olympics **Subject:** Long Jump **Obverse:** Coat of arms above bridge **Reverse:** Jumper **Note:** Similar to 750 Dinara, KM#56.

| Date | Mintage | F | VF | XF | Unc | BU |
|---|---|---|---|---|---|---|
| 1996 Proof | Est. 5,000 | Value: 190 | | | | |

**10000 DINARA** KM# 61 **Weight:** 6.2200 g. **Composition:** 0.9990 Gold .1998 oz. AGW **Series:** Olympics **Subject:** Sprinter **Obverse:** Coat of arms **Reverse:** Sprinter **Note:** Similar to 750 Dinara, KM#57.

| Date | Mintage | F | VF | XF | Unc | BU |
|---|---|---|---|---|---|---|
| 1996 Proof | Est. 5,000 | Value: 190 | | | | |

**10000 DINARA** KM# 62 **Weight:** 6.2200 g. **Composition:** 0.9990 Gold .1998 oz. AGW **Series:** Olympics **Subject:** Wrestlers **Obverse:** Coat of arms **Reverse:** Wrestlers **Note:** Similar to 750 Dinara, KM#58.

| Date | Mintage | F | VF | XF | Unc | BU |
|---|---|---|---|---|---|---|
| 1996 Proof | Est. 5,000 | Value: 190 | | | | |

**10000 DINARA** KM# 63 **Weight:** 6.2200 g. **Composition:** 0.9990 Gold .1998 oz. AGW **Series:** Olympics **Subject:** Fencers **Obverse:** Coat of arms **Reverse:** Fencers **Note:** Similar to 750 Dinara, KM#59.

| Date | Mintage | F | VF | XF | Unc | BU |
|---|---|---|---|---|---|---|
| 1996 Proof | Est. 5,000 | Value: 190 | | | | |

**10000 DINARA** KM# 78 **Weight:** 6.2200 g. **Composition:** 0.9990 Gold .1998 oz. AGW **Series:** Preserve Planet Earth **Subject:** Hoopoe Birds **Note:** Similar to 750 Dinara, KM#77.

| Date | Mintage | F | VF | XF | Unc | BU |
|---|---|---|---|---|---|---|
| 1996 Proof | Est. 5,000 | Value: 175 | | | | |

**10000 DINARA** KM# 81 **Weight:** 6.2200 g. **Composition:** 0.9990 Gold .1998 oz. AGW **Series:** Preserve Planet Earth **Subject:** Goosander Birds **Note:** Similar to 750 Dinara, KM#80.

| Date | Mintage | F | VF | XF | Unc | BU |
|---|---|---|---|---|---|---|
| 1996 Proof | Est. 5,000 | Value: 175 | | | | |

**10000 DINARA** KM# 97 **Weight:** 6.2200 g. **Composition:** 0.9990 Gold .1998 oz. AGW **Subject:** Jurassic Park **Note:** Similar to 750 Dinara, KM#96.

| Date | Mintage | F | VF | XF | Unc | BU |
|---|---|---|---|---|---|---|
| 1997 Proof | Est. 2,500 | Value: 175 | | | | |

## MARKA / MARAKA COINAGE

**KONVERTIBLE MARKA** KM# 118 **Weight:** 4.9000 g. **Composition:** Nickel Plated Steel **Obverse:** Denomination. **Reverse:** Coat of arms above date. **Edge:** Reeded and plain sections. **Size:** 23.23 mm.

| Date | Mintage | F | VF | XF | Unc | BU |
|---|---|---|---|---|---|---|
| 2000 | — | — | — | — | 5.50 | — |

**2 KONVERTIBLE MARKA** KM# 119 **Ring Composition:** Nickel-Brass **Center Weight:** 6.9000 g. **Center Composition:** Copper-Nickel **Obverse:** Denomination. **Reverse:** Dove of peace. **Edge:** Reeded and plain sections. **Size:** 25.75 mm.

| Date | Mintage | F | VF | XF | Unc | BU |
|---|---|---|---|---|---|---|
| 2000 | — | — | — | — | 11.50 | — |

**5 MARKA** KM# 111 **Composition:** Copper-Nickel **Subject:** Summer Olympics 2000 **Obverse:** Arms above bridge **Reverse:** Javelin thrower

| Date | Mintage | F | VF | XF | Unc | BU |
|---|---|---|---|---|---|---|
| 1998 | — | — | — | — | 8.50 | — |

**5 MARKA** KM# 98 **Composition:** Copper-Nickel **Subject:** Princess Diana **Obverse:** Arms above bridge **Reverse:** Portrait and map **Note:** Similar to 10 Marka, KM#99.

| Date | Mintage | F | VF | XF | Unc | BU |
|---|---|---|---|---|---|---|
| 1998 | — | — | — | — | 8.50 | — |

**10 MARKA** **KM# 99** **Weight:** 28.2800 g. **Composition:** 0.9250 Silver .8410 oz. ASW **Subject:** Princess Diana **Obverse:** Arms above bridge **Reverse:** Portrait and map

| Date | Mintage | F | VF | XF | Unc | BU |
|---|---|---|---|---|---|---|
| 1998 Proof | Est. 10,000 | Value: 50.00 | | | | |

**10 MARKA** **KM# 112** **Weight:** 28.2800 g. **Composition:** 0.9250 Silver .8410 oz. ASW **Subject:** Summer Olympics 2000 **Obverse:** Arms above bridge **Reverse:** Javelin thrower

| Date | Mintage | F | VF | XF | Unc | BU |
|---|---|---|---|---|---|---|
| 1998 Proof | Est. 10,000 | Value: 50.00 | | | | |

**20 MARKA** **KM# 100** **Weight:** 1.2441 g. **Composition:** 0.9999 Gold .0400 oz. AGW **Subject:** Princess Diana **Obverse:** Arms above bridge **Reverse:** Portrait and map **Note:** Similar to 10 Marka, KM#99.

| Date | Mintage | F | VF | XF | Unc | BU |
|---|---|---|---|---|---|---|
| 1998 Proof | Est. 10,000 | Value: 50.00 | | | | |

**50 MARKA** **KM# 101** **Weight:** 3.1103 g. **Composition:** 0.9999 Gold .1000 oz. AGW **Subject:** Princess Diana **Obverse:** Arms above bridge **Reverse:** Portrait and map **Note:** Similar to 10 Marka, KM#99.

| Date | Mintage | F | VF | XF | Unc | BU |
|---|---|---|---|---|---|---|
| 1998 Proof | Est. 7,500 | Value: 100 | | | | |

**100 MARKA** **KM# 113** **Weight:** 6.2206 g. **Composition:** 0.9999 Gold .2000 oz. AGW **Subject:** Summer Olympics 2000 **Obverse:** Arms above bridge **Reverse:** Javelin thrower **Note:** Similar to 10 Marka, KM#112.

| Date | Mintage | F | VF | XF | Unc | BU |
|---|---|---|---|---|---|---|
| 1998 Proof | Est. 5,000 | Value: 185 | | | | |

**100 MARKA** **KM# 102** **Weight:** 6.2206 g. **Composition:** 0.9999 Gold .2000 oz. AGW **Subject:** Princess Diana **Obverse:** Arms above bridge **Reverse:** Portrait and map **Note:** Similar to 10 Marka, KM#99.

| Date | Mintage | F | VF | XF | Unc | BU |
|---|---|---|---|---|---|---|
| 1998 Proof | Est. 5,000 | Value: 185 | | | | |

**250 MARKA** **KM# 103** **Weight:** 15.5517 g. **Composition:** 0.9999 Gold .5000 oz. AGW **Subject:** Princess Diana **Obverse:** Arms above bridge **Reverse:** Portrait and map **Note:** Similar to 10 Marka, KM#99.

| Date | Mintage | F | VF | XF | Unc | BU |
|---|---|---|---|---|---|---|
| 1998 Proof | Est. 3,000 | Value: 365 | | | | |

## TRADE COINAGE

**1/25 DUKAT** **KM# 15** **Weight:** 1.2440 g. **Composition:** 0.9999 Gold .0400 oz. AGW **Subject:** Hajj- Kaaba in Mecca **Note:** Similar to 1 Dukat, KM#19.

| Date | Mintage | F | VF | XF | Unc | BU |
|---|---|---|---|---|---|---|
| 1993 Proof | Est. 25,000 | Value: 40.00 | | | | |

**1/10 DUKAT** **KM# 16** **Weight:** 3.1103 g. **Composition:** 0.9999 Gold .1000 oz. AGW **Subject:** Hajj - Kaaba in Mecca **Note:** Similar to 1 Dukat, KM#19.

| Date | Mintage | F | VF | XF | Unc | BU |
|---|---|---|---|---|---|---|
| 1993 Proof | Est. 20,000 | Value: 80.00 | | | | |

**1/5 DUKAT** **KM# 17** **Weight:** 6.2200 g. **Composition:** 0.9999 Gold .2000 oz. AGW **Subject:** Hajj - Kaaba in Mecca **Note:** Similar to 1 Dukat, KM#19.

| Date | Mintage | F | VF | XF | Unc | BU |
|---|---|---|---|---|---|---|
| 1993 Proof | Est. 5,000 | Value: 160 | | | | |

**1/10 DUKAT** **KM# 18** **Weight:** 15.5510 g. **Composition:** 0.9999 Gold .5000 oz. AGW **Subject:** Hajj - Kaaba in Mecca **Note:** Similar to 1 Dukat, KM#19.

| Date | Mintage | F | VF | XF | Unc | BU |
|---|---|---|---|---|---|---|
| 1993 Proof | Est. 5,000 | Value: 320 | | | | |

**DUKAT** **KM# 19** **Weight:** 31.1030 g. **Composition:** 0.9999 Gold 1.0000 oz. AGW **Subject:** Hajj - Kaaba in Mecca

| Date | Mintage | F | VF | XF | Unc | BU |
|---|---|---|---|---|---|---|
| 1993 Proof | Est. 5,000 | Value: 600 | | | | |
| 1994 Proof | — | Value: 600 | | | | |

**1/25 SUVERENA** **KM# 32** **Weight:** 1.2441 g. **Composition:** 0.9999 Gold .0400 oz. AGW **Subject:** Lipizzaner Stallion **Note:** Similar to 1 Suverena, KM#37a.

| Date | Mintage | F | VF | XF | Unc | BU |
|---|---|---|---|---|---|---|
| 1994 Proof | — | Value: 50.00 | | | | |

**1/25 SUVERENA** **KM# 45** **Weight:** 1.2441 g. **Composition:** 0.9999 Gold .0400 oz. AGW **Subject:** English Hack **Note:** Similar to 1 Suverena, KM#51.

| Date | Mintage | F | VF | XF | Unc | BU |
|---|---|---|---|---|---|---|
| 1995 Proof | Est. 15,000 | Value: 50.00 | | | | |

**1/25 SUVERENA** **KM# 70** **Weight:** 1.2441 g. **Composition:** 0.9999 Gold .0400 oz. AGW **Subject:** Hanoverian Stallion **Note:** Similar to 1 Suverena, KM#76.

| Date | Mintage | F | VF | XF | Unc | BU |
|---|---|---|---|---|---|---|
| 1996 Proof | Est. 15,000 | Value: 50.00 | | | | |

**1/25 SUVERENA** **KM# 89** **Weight:** 1.2441 g. **Composition:** 0.9999 Gold .0400 oz. AGW **Subject:** The Arab **Note:** Similar to 1 Suverena, KM#95.

| Date | Mintage | F | VF | XF | Unc | BU |
|---|---|---|---|---|---|---|
| 1997 Proof | Est. 15,000 | Value: 50.00 | | | | |

**1/25 SUVERENA** **KM# 104** **Weight:** 1.2441 g. **Composition:** 0.9999 Gold .0400 oz. AGW **Subject:** Chinese Horse **Obverse:** Arms above bridge **Reverse:** Horse **Note:** Similar to 1 Suverena, KM#108.

| Date | Mintage | F | VF | XF | Unc | BU |
|---|---|---|---|---|---|---|
| 1998 Proof | Est. 15,000 | Value: 50.00 | | | | |

**1/10 SUVERENA** **KM# 33** **Weight:** 3.1103 g. **Composition:** 0.9999 Gold .1000 oz. AGW **Subject:** Lipizzaner Stallion **Note:** Similar to 1 Suverena, KM#37a.

| Date | Mintage | F | VF | XF | Unc | BU |
|---|---|---|---|---|---|---|
| 1994 Proof | — | Value: 100 | | | | |

**1/10 SUVERENA** **KM# 46** **Weight:** 3.1103 g. **Composition:** 0.9999 Gold .1000 oz. AGW **Subject:** English Hack **Note:** Similar to 1 Suverena, KM#51.

| Date | Mintage | F | VF | XF | Unc | BU |
|---|---|---|---|---|---|---|
| 1995 Proof | Est. 10,000 | Value: 100 | | | | |

**1/10 SUVERENA** **KM# 71** **Weight:** 3.1103 g. **Composition:** 0.9999 Gold .1000 oz. AGW **Subject:** Hanoverian Stallion **Note:** Similar to 1 Suverena, KM#76.

| Date | Mintage | F | VF | XF | Unc | BU |
|---|---|---|---|---|---|---|
| 1996 Proof | Est. 10,000 | Value: 100 | | | | |

**1/10 SUVERENA** **KM# 90** **Weight:** 3.1103 g. **Composition:** 0.9999 Gold .1000 oz. AGW **Subject:** The Arab **Note:** Similar to 1 Suverena, KM#95.

| Date | Mintage | F | VF | XF | Unc | BU |
|---|---|---|---|---|---|---|
| 1997 Proof | Est. 10,000 | Value: 100 | | | | |

**1/10 SUVERENA** **KM# 105** **Weight:** 3.1103 g. **Composition:** 0.9999 Gold .1000 oz. AGW **Subject:** Chinese Horse **Obverse:** Arms above bridge **Reverse:** Horse **Note:** Similar to 1 Suverena, KM#108.

| Date | Mintage | F | VF | XF | Unc | BU |
|---|---|---|---|---|---|---|
| 1998 Proof | Est. 10,000 | Value: 100 | | | | |

**1/5 SUVERENA** **KM# 34** **Weight:** 6.2207 g. **Composition:** 0.9999 Gold .2000 oz. AGW **Subject:** Lipizzaner Stallion **Note:** Similar to 1 Suverena, KM#37a.

| Date | Mintage | F | VF | XF | Unc | BU |
|---|---|---|---|---|---|---|
| 1994 Proof | — | Value: 180 | | | | |

**1/5 SUVERENA** **KM# 47** **Weight:** 6.2207 g. **Composition:** 0.9999 Gold .2000 oz. AGW **Subject:** English Hack **Note:** Similar to 1 Suverena, KM#51.

| Date | Mintage | F | VF | XF | Unc | BU |
|---|---|---|---|---|---|---|
| 1995 Proof | Est. 5,000 | Value: 180 | | | | |

**1/5 SUVERENA** **KM# 72** **Weight:** 6.2207 g. **Composition:** 0.9999 Gold .2000 oz. AGW **Subject:** Hanoverian Stallion **Note:** Similar to 1 Suverena, KM#76.

| Date | Mintage | F | VF | XF | Unc | BU |
|---|---|---|---|---|---|---|
| 1996 Proof | Est. 5,000 | Value: 180 | | | | |

**1/5 SUVERENA** **KM# 91** **Weight:** 6.2207 g. **Composition:** 0.9999 Gold .2000 oz. AGW **Subject:** The Arab **Note:** Similar to 1 Suverena, KM#95.

| Date | Mintage | F | VF | XF | Unc | BU |
|---|---|---|---|---|---|---|
| 1997 Proof | Est. 5,000 | Value: 180 | | | | |

**1/5 SUVERENA** **KM# 106** **Weight:** 6.2207 g. **Composition:** 0.9999 Gold .2000 oz. AGW **Subject:** Chinese Horse **Obverse:** Arms above bridge **Reverse:** Horse **Note:** Similar to 1 Suverena, KM#108.

| Date | Mintage | F | VF | XF | Unc | BU |
|---|---|---|---|---|---|---|
| 1998 Proof | Est. 5,000 | Value: 175 | | | | |

**1/2 SUVERENA** **KM# 35** **Weight:** 15.5517 g. **Composition:** 0.9999 Gold .5000 oz. AGW **Subject:** Lipizzaner Stallion **Note:** Similar to 1 Suverena, KM#37a.

| Date | Mintage | F | VF | XF | Unc | BU |
|---|---|---|---|---|---|---|
| 1994 Proof | — | Value: 365 | | | | |

**1/2 SUVERENA** **KM# 48** **Weight:** 15.5517 g. **Composition:** 0.9999 Gold .5000 oz. AGW **Subject:** English Hack **Note:** Similar to 1 Suverena, KM#51.

| Date | Mintage | F | VF | XF | Unc | BU |
|---|---|---|---|---|---|---|
| 1995 Proof | Est. 2,500 | Value: 365 | | | | |

**1/2 SUVERENA** **KM# 73** **Weight:** 15.5517 g. **Composition:** 0.9999 Gold .5000 oz. AGW **Subject:** Hanoverian Stallion **Note:** Similar to 1 Suverena, KM#76.

| Date | Mintage | F | VF | XF | Unc | BU |
|---|---|---|---|---|---|---|
| 1996 Proof | Est. 2,500 | Value: 365 | | | | |

**1/2 SUVERENA** **KM# 92** **Weight:** 15.5517 g. **Composition:** 0.9999 Gold .5000 oz. AGW **Subject:** The Arab **Note:** Similar to 1 Suverena, KM#95.

| Date | Mintage | F | VF | XF | Unc | BU |
|---|---|---|---|---|---|---|
| 1997 Proof | Est. 2,500 | Value: 365 | | | | |

**1/2 SUVERENA** **KM# 107** **Weight:** 15.5517 g. **Composition:** 0.9999 Gold .5000 oz. AGW **Subject:** Chinese Horse **Obverse:** Arms above bridge **Reverse:** Horse **Note:** Similar to 1 Suverena, KM#108.

| Date | Mintage | F | VF | XF | Unc | BU |
|---|---|---|---|---|---|---|
| 1998 Proof | Est. 2,500 | Value: 365 | | | | |

**SUVERENA** **KM# 37a** **Weight:** 31.1035 g. **Composition:** 0.9999 Gold 1.0000 oz. AGW

| Date | Mintage | F | VF | XF | Unc | BU |
|---|---|---|---|---|---|---|
| 1994 Proof | — | Value: 700 | | | | |

**SUVERENA** **KM# 36** **Composition:** Copper-Nickel **Subject:** Lipizzaner Stallion **Obverse:** Arms **Reverse:** Lipizzaner Stallion rearing **Note:** Similar to KM#37a.

| Date | Mintage | F | VF | XF | Unc | BU |
|---|---|---|---|---|---|---|
| 1994 | — | — | — | — | 8.50 | — |

**SUVERENA** **KM# 37** **Weight:** 31.1035 g. **Composition:** 0.9999 Silver 1.0000 oz. ASW **Note:** Similar to KM#37a.

| Date | Mintage | F | VF | XF | Unc | BU |
|---|---|---|---|---|---|---|
| 1994 Proof | — | Value: 50.00 | | | | |

**SUVERENA** **KM# 49** **Composition:** Copper-Nickel **Subject:** English Hack **Note:** Similar to 1 Suverena, KM#51.

| Date | Mintage | F | VF | XF | Unc | BU |
|---|---|---|---|---|---|---|
| 1995 | — | — | — | — | 9.00 | — |

**SUVERENA** **KM# 50** **Weight:** 31.1035 g. **Composition:** 0.9999 Silver 1.0000 oz. ASW

| Date | Mintage | F | VF | XF | Unc | BU |
|---|---|---|---|---|---|---|
| 1995 Proof | Est. 30,000 | Value: 50.00 | | | | |

**SUVERENA** **KM# 51** **Weight:** 31.1035 g. **Composition:** 0.9999 Gold 1.0000 oz. AGW

| Date | Mintage | F | VF | XF | Unc | BU |
|---|---|---|---|---|---|---|
| 1995 Proof | Est. 850 | Value: 700 | | | | |

**SUVERENA** **KM# 75** **Weight:** 31.1035 g. **Composition:** 0.9999 Silver 1.0000 oz. ASW **Note:** Similar to 1 Suverena, KM#76.

| Date | Mintage | F | VF | XF | Unc | BU |
|---|---|---|---|---|---|---|
| 1996 Proof | Est. 30,000 | Value: 50.00 | | | | |

**SUVERENA** **KM# 74** **Composition:** Copper-Nickel **Subject:** Hanoverian Stallion **Note:** Similar to KM#76.

| Date | Mintage | F | VF | XF | Unc | BU |
|---|---|---|---|---|---|---|
| 1996 | — | — | — | — | 8.50 | — |

**SUVERENA** **KM# A76** **Weight:** 31.1035 g. **Composition:** 0.9999 Gold 1.0000 oz. AGW **Subject:** Hanoverian Stallion

| Date | Mintage | F | VF | XF | Unc | BU |
|---|---|---|---|---|---|---|
| 1996 Proof | 850 | Value: 700 | | | | |

**SUVERENA** **KM# 93** **Composition:** Copper-Nickel **Subject:** The Arab **Obverse:** National arms over bridge **Reverse:** Arabian horse

| Date | Mintage | F | VF | XF | Unc | BU |
|---|---|---|---|---|---|---|
| 1997 | — | — | — | — | 10.00 | — |

**SUVERENA** **KM# 93a** **Weight:** 31.1035 g. **Composition:** 0.9999 Silver 1.0000 oz. ASW

| Date | Mintage | F | VF | XF | Unc | BU |
|---|---|---|---|---|---|---|
| 1997 Proof | Est. 30,000 | Value: 50.00 | | | | |

**SUVERENA** **KM# 93b** **Weight:** 31.1035 g. **Composition:** 0.9999 Gold 1.0000 oz. AGW

| Date | Mintage | F | VF | XF | Unc | BU |
|---|---|---|---|---|---|---|
| 1997 Proof | 850 | Value: 700 | | | | |

**SUVERENA** **KM# 108** **Composition:** Copper-Nickel **Subject:** Chinese Horse **Obverse:** Arms over bridge **Reverse:** Horse

| Date | Mintage | F | VF | XF | Unc | BU |
|---|---|---|---|---|---|---|
| 1998 | — | — | — | — | 10.00 | — |

**SUVERENA** **KM# 108a** **Weight:** 31.1035 g. **Composition:** 0.9999 Silver 1.0000 oz. ASW

| Date | Mintage | F | VF | XF | Unc | BU |
|---|---|---|---|---|---|---|
| 1998 Proof | Est. 30,000 | Value: 50.00 | | | | |

**SUVERENA** **KM# 109** **Weight:** 31.1035 g. **Composition:** 0.9999 Gold 1.0000 oz. AGW **Note:** Similar to KM#108.

| Date | Mintage | F | VF | XF | Unc | BU |
|---|---|---|---|---|---|---|
| 1998 Proof | — | Value: 700 | | | | |

**14 ECUS** **KM# 82** **Weight:** 10.0000 g. **Composition:** 0.9250 Silver .8921 oz. ASW **Subject:** International Day of Peace

| Date | Mintage | F | VF | XF | Unc | BU |
|---|---|---|---|---|---|---|
| 1993 Proof | Est. 20,000 | Value: 45.00 | | | | |

**14 ECUS** **KM# 83** **Weight:** 10.0000 g. **Composition:** 0.9250 Silver .8921 oz. ASW **Subject:** Peace - Teddy Bear

| Date | Mintage | F | VF | XF | Unc | BU |
|---|---|---|---|---|---|---|
| 1994 Proof | 20,000 | Value: 50.00 | | | | |

**14 ECUS** **KM# 84** **Weight:** 10.1000 g. **Composition:** 0.9250 Silver .3004 oz. ASW **Subject:** Peace - Allegorical Europa

| Date | Mintage | F | VF | XF | Unc | BU |
|---|---|---|---|---|---|---|
| 1995 Proof | Est. 20,000 | Value: 27.50 | | | | |

**14 ECUS + 2** **KM# 85** **Weight:** 9.9700 g. **Composition:** 0.9990 Silver .3205 oz. ASW **Subject:** War Relief Funding - Sarajevo Mosque

| Date | Mintage | F | VF | XF | Unc | BU |
|---|---|---|---|---|---|---|
| 1993 Proof | 20,000 | Value: 30.00 | | | | |

**21 ECUS ++3** **KM# 86** **Weight:** 15.5600 g. **Composition:** 0.9990 Silver .5002 oz. ASW **Subject:** War Relief Funding - Sarajevo Mosque **Note:** Similar to 14 Ecus + 2, KM#M1.

| Date | Mintage | F | VF | XF | Unc | BU |
|---|---|---|---|---|---|---|
| 1993 Proof | Est. 15,000 | Value: 60.00 | | | | |

**70 ECUS + 10** **KM# 87** **Weight:** 6.2200 g. **Composition:** 0.9990 Gold .2000 oz. AGW **Subject:** War Relief Funding - Sarajevo Mosque **Obverse:** Coat of arms above bridge **Reverse:** Dove of peace above Sarajevo Mosque **Note:** Similar to 14 Ecus + 2, KM#M1.

| Date | Mintage | F | VF | XF | Unc | BU |
|---|---|---|---|---|---|---|
| 1993 Proof | Est. 5,000 | Value: 165 | | | | |

**14 EURO** **KM# 88** **Weight:** 10.0000 g. **Composition:** 0.9250 Silver .2974 oz. ASW **Subject:** Peace **Obverse:** Arms over bridge **Reverse:** Rose and the word PEACE in many languages

| Date | Mintage | F | VF | XF | Unc | BU |
|---|---|---|---|---|---|---|
| 1996 Proof | Est. 20,000 | Value: 35.00 | | | | |

**14 EURO** **KM# 110** **Weight:** 10.0000 g. **Composition:** 0.9250 Silver .2974 oz. ASW **Subject:** Peace II **Obverse:** Arms over bridge **Reverse:** Dove in flight

| Date | Mintage | F | VF | XF | Unc | BU |
|---|---|---|---|---|---|---|
| 1998 Proof | Est. 20,000 | Value: 40.00 | | | | |

**14 EURO** **KM# 114** **Weight:** 10.0000 g. **Composition:** 0.9250 Silver .2974 oz. ASW **Subject:** The Tree of Stability **Obverse:** National arms above bridge **Reverse:** Woman planting oak tree

| Date | Mintage | F | VF | XF | Unc | BU |
|---|---|---|---|---|---|---|
| 1999 Proof | Est. 20,000 | Value: 40.00 | | | | |

## MINT SETS

| KM# | Date | Mintage | Identification | Issue Price | Mkt Val |
|---|---|---|---|---|---|
| MS1 | 2000 (5) | — | KM#115, 116, 117, 118, 119 | 20.00 | 22.00 |

## PROOF SETS

| KM# | Date | Mintage | Identification | Issue Price | Mkt Val |
|---|---|---|---|---|---|
| PS1 | 1996 (5) | 500 | KM#70-73, 76 | — | 1,400 |

# BOTSWANA

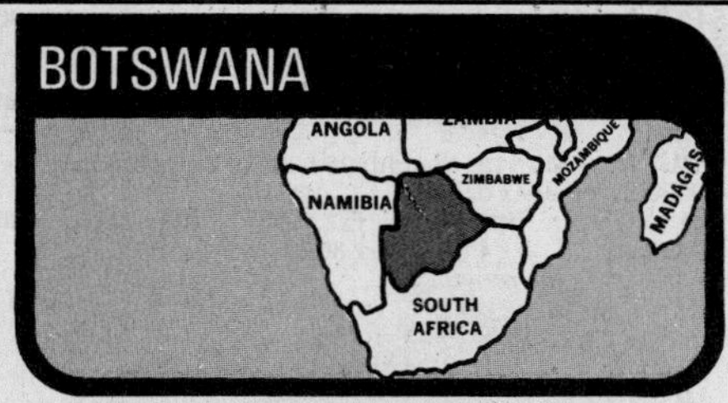


The Republic of Botswana (formerly Bechuanaland), located in south central Africa between Namibia and Zimbabwe, has an area of 224,607 sq. mi. (600,370 sq. km.) and a population of *1.62 million. Capital: Gaborone. Botswana is a member of a Customs Union with South Africa, Lesotho, and Swaziland. The economy is primarily pastoral with a rapidly developing mining industry, of which diamonds, copper and nickel are the chief elements. Meat products and diamonds comprise 85 percent of the exports.

Little is known of the origin of the peoples of Botswana. The early inhabitants, the Bushmen, did not develop a recorded history and are now dying out. The ancestors of the present Botswana residents probably arrived about 1600AD in Bantu migrations from the north and east. Bechuanaland was first united early in the 19th century under Chief Khama III to more effectively resist incursions by the Boer trekkers from Transvaal and by the neighboring Matabeles. As the Boer threat intensified, appeals for protection were made to the British Government, which proclaimed the whole of Bechuanaland a British protectorate in 1885. In 1895, the southern part of the protectorate was annexed to Cape Province. The northern part, known as the Bechuanaland Protectorate, remained under British administration until it became the independent Republic of Botswana on Sept. 30, 1966. Botswana is a member of the Commonwealth of Nations. The president is Chief of State and Head of government.

**MINT MARKS**

B - Berne

**MONETARY SYSTEM**

100 Cents = 1 Thebe

## REPUBLIC

### STANDARD COINAGE

**50 CENTS** **KM# 1** **Weight:** 10.0000 g. **Composition:** 0.8000 Silver .2572 oz. ASW **Subject:** Independence Commemorative

| Date | Mintage | F | VF | XF | Unc | BU |
|---|---|---|---|---|---|---|
| ND(1966)B | 40,000 | — | 2.50 | 3.50 | 5.00 | — |
| ND(1966)B Proof | 10,000 | Value: 7.50 | | | | |

**10 THEBE** **KM# 2** **Weight:** 11.2900 g. **Composition:** 0.9000 Gold .3270 oz. AGW **Subject:** Independence Commemorative

| Date | Mintage | F | VF | XF | Unc | BU |
|---|---|---|---|---|---|---|
| ND(1966)B | 5,100 | — | — | — | 160 | — |

### REFORM COINAGE

100 Thebe = 1 Pula

**THEBE** **KM# 3** **Composition:** Aluminum **Reverse:** Turako

| Date | Mintage | F | VF | XF | Unc | BU |
|---|---|---|---|---|---|---|
| 1976 | 15,000,000 | — | 0.10 | 0.15 | 0.25 | — |
| 1976 Proof | 26,000 | Value: 0.75 | | | | |
| 1981 Proof | 10,000 | Value: 1.00 | | | | |
| 1983 | 5,000,000 | — | 0.10 | 0.20 | 0.35 | — |
| 1984 | 5,000,000 | — | 0.10 | 0.20 | 0.35 | — |
| 1985 | — | — | 0.10 | 0.20 | 0.35 | — |
| 1987 | — | — | 0.10 | 0.20 | 0.30 | — |
| 1988 | — | — | 0.10 | 0.20 | 0.30 | — |
| 1989 | — | — | 0.10 | 0.20 | 0.30 | — |
| 1991 | — | — | 0.10 | 0.20 | 0.30 | — |

**2 THEBE** **KM# 14** **Composition:** Bronze **Subject:** World Food Day **Reverse:** Millet

| Date | Mintage | F | VF | XF | Unc | BU |
|---|---|---|---|---|---|---|
| 1981 | 9,990,000 | — | 0.15 | 0.25 | 0.50 | — |
| 1981 Proof | 10,000 | Value: 1.00 | | | | |
| 1985 | — | — | 0.15 | 0.25 | 0.50 | — |

**5 THEBE** **KM# 4** **Composition:** Bronze **Reverse:** Toko **Edge:** Reeded

| Date | Mintage | F | VF | XF | Unc | BU |
|---|---|---|---|---|---|---|
| 1976 | 3,000,000 | — | 0.15 | 0.25 | 0.50 | — |
| 1976 Proof | 26,000 | Value: 1.00 | | | | |
| 1977 | 250,000 | — | 0.15 | 0.25 | 0.50 | — |
| 1979 | 200,000 | — | 0.15 | 0.25 | 0.50 | — |
| 1980 | 1,000,000 | — | 0.15 | 0.25 | 0.50 | — |
| 1981 | 4,990,000 | — | 0.15 | 0.25 | 0.50 | — |
| 1981 Proof | 10,000 | Value: 1.25 | | | | |
| 1984 | 2,000,000 | — | 0.15 | 0.25 | 0.50 | — |
| 1985 | — | — | 0.15 | 0.25 | 0.50 | — |
| 1988 | — | — | 0.15 | 0.25 | 0.50 | — |
| 1989 | — | — | 0.15 | 0.25 | 0.50 | — |

**5 THEBE** **KM# 4a.1** **Composition:** Bronze Clad Steel **Edge:** Plain

| Date | Mintage | F | VF | XF | Unc | BU |
|---|---|---|---|---|---|---|
| 1991 | — | — | 0.15 | 0.25 | 0.50 | — |

**5 THEBE** **KM# 4a.2** **Composition:** Bronze Clad Steel **Edge:** Reeded **Note:** Modified design.

| Date | Mintage | F | VF | XF | Unc | BU |
|---|---|---|---|---|---|---|
| 1996 | — | — | 0.15 | 0.25 | 0.50 | — |

**5 THEBE** **KM# 26** **Composition:** Bronze Clad Steel **Obverse:** National arms **Reverse:** Toko bird

| Date | Mintage | F | VF | XF | Unc | BU |
|---|---|---|---|---|---|---|
| 1998 | — | — | 0.15 | 0.25 | 0.50 | — |

**10 THEBE** **KM# 5** **Composition:** Copper-Nickel **Reverse:** South African Oryx

| Date | Mintage | F | VF | XF | Unc | BU |
|---|---|---|---|---|---|---|
| 1976 | 1,500,000 | — | 0.25 | 0.40 | 0.75 | — |
| 1976 Proof | 26,000 | Value: 1.50 | | | | |
| 1977 | 500,000 | — | 0.25 | 0.40 | 0.75 | — |
| 1979 | 750,000 | — | 0.25 | 0.40 | 0.75 | — |
| 1980 | — | — | 0.25 | 0.40 | 0.75 | — |
| 1981 | 2,590,000 | — | 0.25 | 0.40 | 0.75 | — |
| 1981 Proof | 10,000 | Value: 1.75 | | | | |
| 1984 | 4,000,000 | — | 0.20 | 0.30 | 0.60 | — |
| 1985 | — | — | 0.20 | 0.30 | 0.60 | — |
| 1989 | — | — | 0.20 | 0.30 | 0.60 | — |

**10 THEBE** **KM# 5a** **Composition:** Nickel Clad Steel

| Date | Mintage | F | VF | XF | Unc | BU |
|---|---|---|---|---|---|---|
| 1991 | — | — | 0.20 | 0.30 | 0.65 | — |

**10 THEBE** **KM# 27** **Composition:** Nickel Clad Steel **Obverse:** National arms **Reverse:** South African Oryx

| Date | Mintage | F | VF | XF | Unc | BU |
|---|---|---|---|---|---|---|
| 1998 | — | — | 0.20 | 0.30 | 0.65 | — |

**25 THEBE** **KM# 6** **Composition:** Copper-Nickel **Reverse:** Zebu

| Date | Mintage | F | VF | XF | Unc | BU |
|---|---|---|---|---|---|---|
| 1976 | 1,500,000 | — | 0.25 | 0.55 | 1.50 | — |
| 1976 Proof | 26,000 | Value: 2.00 | | | | |
| 1977 | 265,000 | — | 0.25 | 0.60 | 1.75 | — |
| 1980 | — | — | 0.25 | 0.60 | 1.35 | — |
| 1981 | 740,000 | — | 0.25 | 0.60 | 1.35 | — |
| 1981 Proof | 10,000 | Value: 2.50 | | | | |
| 1982 | 400,000 | — | 0.25 | 0.60 | 1.75 | — |
| 1984 | 2,000,000 | — | 0.25 | 0.55 | 1.35 | — |
| 1985 | — | — | 0.30 | 0.60 | 1.35 | — |
| 1989 | — | — | 0.30 | 0.60 | 1.35 | — |

**25 THEBE** **KM# 6a** **Composition:** Nickel Clad Steel

| Date | Mintage | F | VF | XF | Unc | BU |
|---|---|---|---|---|---|---|
| 1991 | — | — | 0.30 | 0.60 | 1.35 | — |

**25 THEBE** **KM# 28** **Composition:** Nickel Clad Steel **Obverse:** National arms **Reverse:** Zebu bull

| Date | Mintage | F | VF | XF | Unc | BU |
|---|---|---|---|---|---|---|
| 1998 | — | — | 0.30 | 0.60 | 1.35 | — |

**50 THEBE** **KM# 7** **Composition:** Copper-Nickel **Reverse:** African Fish Eagle

| Date | Mintage | F | VF | XF | Unc | BU |
|---|---|---|---|---|---|---|
| 1976 | 266,000 | — | 0.65 | 1.35 | 2.25 | — |
| 1976 Proof | 26,000 | Value: 3.00 | | | | |
| 1977 | 250,000 | — | 0.65 | 1.35 | 2.25 | — |
| 1980 | — | — | 0.65 | 1.35 | 2.25 | — |
| 1981 Proof | 10,000 | Value: 3.50 | | | | |
| 1984 | 2,000,000 | — | 0.65 | 1.35 | 2.25 | — |
| 1985 | — | — | 0.65 | 1.35 | 2.25 | — |

**50 THEBE** **KM# 7a** **Composition:** Nickel Clad Steel

| Date | Mintage | F | VF | XF | Unc | BU |
|---|---|---|---|---|---|---|
| 1991 | — | — | 0.65 | 1.35 | 2.25 | — |

**50 THEBE** **KM# 29** **Composition:** Nickel Clad Steel **Obverse:** National arms **Reverse:** African Fish Eagle

| Date | Mintage | F | VF | XF | Unc | BU |
|---|---|---|---|---|---|---|
| 1998 | — | — | 0.50 | 1.00 | 2.00 | — |

**PULA** **KM# 8** **Composition:** Copper-Nickel **Reverse:** Zebra

| Date | Mintage | F | VF | XF | Unc | BU |
|---|---|---|---|---|---|---|
| 1976 | 166,000 | — | 1.50 | 2.50 | 5.00 | — |
| 1976 Proof | 26,000 | Value: 6.00 | | | | |
| 1977 | 500,000 | — | 1.50 | 2.50 | 4.50 | — |
| 1981 | — | — | 1.50 | 2.50 | 4.50 | — |
| 1981 Proof | 10,000 | Value: 6.50 | | | | |
| 1985 | — | — | 1.50 | 2.50 | 4.50 | — |
| 1987 | — | — | 1.50 | 2.50 | 4.50 | — |

**PULA** **KM# 24** **Composition:** Nickel-Brass **Reverse:** Zebra

| Date | Mintage | F | VF | XF | Unc | BU |
|---|---|---|---|---|---|---|
| 1991 | — | — | 1.00 | 1.75 | 3.50 | — |

**2 PULA** **KM# 17** **Weight:** 28.2800 g. **Composition:** 0.5000 Silver .4546 oz. ASW **Subject:** Commonwealth Games

| Date | Mintage | F | VF | XF | Unc | BU |
|---|---|---|---|---|---|---|
| 1986 | Est. 50,000 | — | — | — | 12.50 | — |

**2 PULA** **KM# 17a** **Weight:** 28.2800 g. **Composition:** 0.9250 Silver .8411 oz. ASW

| Date | Mintage | F | VF | XF | Unc | BU |
|---|---|---|---|---|---|---|
| 1986 Proof | Est. 20,000 | Value: 25.00 | | | | |

**2 PULA** **KM# 18** **Weight:** 28.2800 g. **Composition:** 0.9250 Silver .8411 oz. ASW **Subject:** Wildlife **Reverse:** Slaty Egret

| Date | Mintage | F | VF | XF | Unc | BU |
|---|---|---|---|---|---|---|
| 1986 Proof | Est. 25,000 | Value: 24.00 | | | | |

**2 PULA** **KM# 22** **Weight:** 28.2800 g. **Composition:** 0.9250 Silver .8411 oz. ASW **Subject:** Save The Children Fund **Obverse:** Coat of arms **Reverse:** Child milking goat

| Date | Mintage | F | VF | XF | Unc | BU |
|---|---|---|---|---|---|---|
| 1989 Proof | Est. 20,000 | Value: 30.00 | | | | |

**2 PULA** **KM# 25** **Composition:** Nickel-Brass **Subject:** Wildlife **Reverse:** Rhinoceros

| Date | Mintage | F | VF | XF | Unc | BU |
|---|---|---|---|---|---|---|
| 1994 | — | — | 1.75 | 2.75 | 5.50 | — |

**5 PULA** **KM# 9** **Weight:** 28.2800 g. **Composition:** 0.5000 Silver .4546 oz. ASW **Subject:** 10th Anniversary of Independence

| Date | Mintage | F | VF | XF | Unc | BU |
|---|---|---|---|---|---|---|
| ND(1976) | 31,000 | — | — | — | 15.00 | — |

**5 PULA** **KM# 9a** **Weight:** 28.2800 g. **Composition:** 0.9250 Silver .8411 oz. ASW

| Date | Mintage | F | VF | XF | Unc | BU |
|---|---|---|---|---|---|---|
| ND(1976) Proof | 22,000 | Value: 22.50 | | | | |

**5 PULA** **KM# 11** **Weight:** 28.5000 g. **Composition:** 0.5000 Silver .4582 oz. ASW **Subject:** Wildlife **Obverse:** Similar to KM#15 **Reverse:** Gemsbok

| Date | Mintage | F | VF | XF | Unc | BU |
|---|---|---|---|---|---|---|
| 1978 | 4,026 | — | — | — | 22.50 | — |

**5 PULA** **KM# 11a** **Weight:** 28.5000 g. **Composition:** 0.9250 Silver .8477 oz. ASW

| Date | Mintage | F | VF | XF | Unc | BU |
|---|---|---|---|---|---|---|
| 1978 Proof | 4,172 | Value: 30.00 | | | | |

**5 PULA** **KM# 15** **Weight:** 28.5000 g. **Composition:** 0.9250 Silver .8477 oz. ASW **Subject:** International Year of Disabled Persons

| Date | Mintage | F | VF | XF | Unc | BU |
|---|---|---|---|---|---|---|
| 1981 | 13,000 | — | — | — | 22.50 | — |
| 1981 Proof | 11,000 | Value: 32.50 | | | | |

**5 PULA** **KM# 19** **Weight:** 15.9800 g. **Composition:** 0.9170 Gold .4711 oz. AGW **Subject:** Wildlife **Reverse:** Red Lechwes

| Date | Mintage | F | VF | XF | Unc | BU |
|---|---|---|---|---|---|---|
| 1986 Proof | Est. 5,000 | Value: 300 | | | | |

**5 PULA** **KM# 20** **Composition:** Copper-Nickel **Subject:** Pope's Visit

| Date | Mintage | F | VF | XF | Unc | BU |
|---|---|---|---|---|---|---|
| 1988 | Est. 50,000 | — | — | — | 8.50 | — |

**5 PULA** **KM# 20a** **Weight:** 28.2800 g. **Composition:** 0.9250 Silver .8411 oz. ASW

| Date | Mintage | F | VF | XF | Unc | BU |
|---|---|---|---|---|---|---|
| 1988 Proof | Est. 5,000 | Value: 45.00 | | | | |

**5 PULA** **KM# 21** **Weight:** 28.2800 g. **Composition:** 0.9250 Silver .8411 oz. ASW **Subject:** 1988 Summer Olympics **Reverse:** Runners

| Date | Mintage | F | VF | XF | Unc | BU |
|---|---|---|---|---|---|---|
| 1988 Proof | 25,000 | Value: 25.00 | | | | |

**Note:** A copper-nickel strike variety of this coin does not exist

**5 PULA** **KM# 23** **Weight:** 10.0000 g. **Composition:** 0.9170 Gold .2948 oz. AGW **Subject:** Save the Children Fund

| Date | Mintage | F | VF | XF | Unc | BU |
|---|---|---|---|---|---|---|
| 1989 Proof | Est. 3,000 | Value: 350 | | | | |

**5 PULA** **KM# 30** **Ring Composition:** Brass **Center Weight:** 6.2000 g. **Center Composition:** Copper-Nickel **Obverse:** National arms. **Reverse:** Caterpillar on plant. **Edge:** Reeded. **Size:** 23.4 mm.

| Date | Mintage | F | VF | XF | Unc | BU |
|---|---|---|---|---|---|---|
| 2000 | — | — | — | — | 4.50 | — |

**10 PULA** **KM# 12** **Weight:** 35.0000 g. **Composition:** 0.5000 Silver .5627 oz. ASW **Subject:** Wildlife **Obverse:** Similar to 5 Pula, KM#21 **Reverse:** Klipspringer

| Date | Mintage | F | VF | XF | Unc | BU |
|---|---|---|---|---|---|---|
| 1978 | 4,088 | — | — | — | 25.00 | — |

**10 PULA** **KM# 12a** **Weight:** 35.0000 g. **Composition:** 0.9250 Silver 1.0408 oz. ASW

| Date | Mintage | F | VF | XF | Unc | BU |
|---|---|---|---|---|---|---|
| 1978 Proof | 3,989 | Value: 35.00 | | | | |

**150 PULA** **KM# 10** **Weight:** 15.9800 g. **Composition:** 0.9170 Gold .4711 oz. AGW **Subject:** 10th Anniversary of Independence

| Date | Mintage | F | VF | XF | Unc | BU |
|---|---|---|---|---|---|---|
| ND(1976) | 2,520 | — | — | — | 225 | — |
| ND(1976) Proof | 2,000 | Value: 265 | | | | |

**150 PULA** **KM# 13** **Weight:** 33.4370 g. **Composition:** 0.9000 Gold .9676 oz. AGW **Subject:** Wildlife **Reverse:** Brown Hyaena

| Date | Mintage | F | VF | XF | Unc | BU |
|---|---|---|---|---|---|---|
| 1978 | 664 | — | — | — | 525 | — |
| 1978 Proof | 219 | Value: 950 | | | | |

**150 PULA** **KM# 16** **Weight:** 15.9800 g. **Composition:** 0.9170 Gold .4711 oz. AGW **Subject:** International Year of Disabled Persons

| Date | Mintage | F | VF | XF | Unc | BU |
|---|---|---|---|---|---|---|
| 1981 | 4,158 | — | — | — | 225 | — |
| 1981 Proof | 4,155 | Value: 265 | | | | |

## PIEFORTS

| KM# | Date | Mintage | Identification | Issue Price | Mkt Val |
|---|---|---|---|---|---|
| P1 | 1981 | 1,000 | 5 Pula. KM#15. | — | 65.00 |
| P2 | 1981 | 510 | 150 Pula. KM#16. | — | 1,150 |

## MINT SETS

| KM# | Date | Mintage | Identification | Issue Price | Mkt Val |
|---|---|---|---|---|---|
| MS1 | 1978 (2) | — | KM#11, 12 | — | 50.00 |

## PROOF SETS

| KM# | Date | Mintage | Identification | Issue Price | Mkt Val |
|---|---|---|---|---|---|
| PS1 | 1976 (6) | 20,000 | KM#3-8 | 18.00 | 14.50 |
| PS2 | 1978 (2) | — | KM#11a, 12a | — | 65.00 |
| PS3 | 1981 (7) | 10,000 | KM#3-8, 14 | 33.00 | 17.50 |

# BRAZIL

The Federative Republic of Brazil, which comprises half the continent of South America and is the only Latin American country deriving its culture and language from Portugal, has an area of 3,286,488 sq. mi. (8,511,965 sq. km.) and a population of *169.2 million. Capital: Brasilia. The economy of Brazil is as varied and complex as any in the developing world. Agriculture is a mainstay of the economy, while only 4 percent of the area is under cultivation. Known mineral resources are almost unlimited in variety and size of reserves. A large, relatively sophisticated industry ranges from basic steel and chemical production to finished consumer goods. Coffee, cotton, iron ore and cocoa are the chief exports.

Brazil was discovered and claimed for Portugal by Admiral Pedro Alvares Cabral in 1500. Portugal established a settlement in 1532 and proclaimed the area a royal colony in 1549. During the Napoleonic Wars, Dom Joao VI established the seat of Portuguese government in Rio de Janeiro. When he returned to Portugal, his son Dom Pedro I declared Brazil's independence on Sept. 7, 1822, and became emperor of Brazil. The Empire of Brazil was maintained until 1889 when the federal republic was established. The Federative Republic was established in 1946 by terms of a constitution drawn up by a constituent assembly. Following a coup in 1964 the armed forces retained overall control under a dictatorship until civilian government was restored on March 15, 1985. The current constitution was adopted in 1988.

**MINT MARKS**

(a) - Paris, privy marks only
A - Berlin 1913
B - Bahia

**MONETARY SYSTEM**

**(1833-1942)**

1000 Reis = 1 Milreis

**(1942-1967)**

100 Centavos = 1 Cruzeiro

# REPUBLIC

## DECIMAL COINAGE

1889-1942

**20 REIS** **KM# 490** **Composition:** Bronze

| Date | Mintage | F | VF | XF | Unc | BU |
|---|---|---|---|---|---|---|
| 1901 | 713,000 | 1.00 | 4.50 | 9.50 | 20.00 | — |
| 1904 | 850,000 | 1.00 | 4.50 | 9.50 | 20.00 | — |
| 1905 | 1,075,000 | 3.50 | 7.00 | 14.50 | 48.00 | — |
| 1906 | 215,000 | 2.00 | 5.00 | 12.00 | 30.00 | — |
| 1908 | 4,558,000 | 1.00 | 4.50 | 9.50 | 20.00 | — |
| 1909 | 1,215,000 | 5.00 | 10.00 | 22.00 | 95.00 | — |
| 1910 | 828,000 | 1.00 | 4.50 | 9.50 | 20.00 | — |
| 1911 | 1,545,000 | 1.00 | 4.50 | 9.50 | 20.00 | — |
| 1912 | 480,000 | 1.00 | 4.50 | 9.50 | 25.00 | — |

**20 REIS** **KM# 516** **Composition:** Copper-Nickel

| Date | Mintage | F | VF | XF | Unc | BU |
|---|---|---|---|---|---|---|
| 1918 | 373,000 | 0.25 | 0.50 | 2.00 | 4.50 | — |
| 1919 | 2,870,000 | 0.25 | 0.50 | 1.00 | 3.50 | — |
| 1920 | 825,000 | 0.25 | 0.50 | 1.25 | 4.50 | — |
| 1921 | 1,020,000 | 0.25 | 0.50 | 1.25 | 4.50 | — |

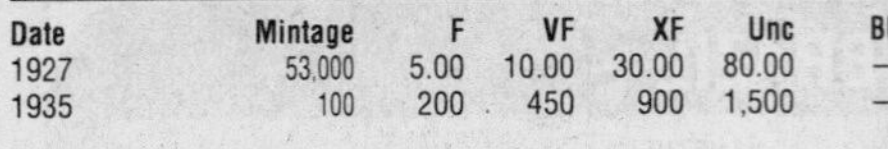

| Date | Mintage | F | VF | XF | Unc | BU |
|---|---|---|---|---|---|---|
| 1927 | 53,000 | 5.00 | 10.00 | 30.00 | 80.00 | — |
| 1935 | 100 | 200 | 450 | 900 | 1,500 | — |

**40 REIS** **KM# 491** **Composition:** Bronze **Reverse:** FC above star

| Date | Mintage | F | VF | XF | Unc | BU |
|---|---|---|---|---|---|---|
| 1901 | 525,000 | 0.75 | 2.00 | 3.00 | 14.50 | — |
| 1907 | 218,000 | 0.75 | 2.00 | 3.00 | 14.50 | — |
| 1908 | 4,639,000 | 0.75 | 2.00 | 3.00 | 14.50 | — |
| 1909 | 4,226,000 | 0.75 | 2.00 | 3.50 | 16.50 | — |
| 1910 | 848,000 | 0.75 | 2.00 | 4.00 | 18.50 | — |
| 1911 | 1,660,000 | 0.75 | 2.00 | 4.00 | 18.50 | — |
| 1912 | 819,000 | 1.00 | 2.50 | 4.50 | 21.50 | — |

**50 REIS** **KM# 517** **Composition:** Copper-Nickel

| Date | Mintage | F | VF | XF | Unc | BU |
|---|---|---|---|---|---|---|
| 1918 | 558,000 | 0.15 | 0.35 | 0.75 | 5.50 | — |
| 1919 | 558,000 | 0.15 | 0.35 | 0.75 | 5.50 | — |
| 1920 | 72,000 | 0.40 | 1.00 | 3.50 | 15.00 | — |
| 1921 | 682,000 | 0.15 | 0.35 | 0.75 | 5.50 | — |
| 1922 | 176,000 | 0.40 | 1.00 | 3.50 | 15.00 | — |
| 1925 | 128,000 | 0.40 | 1.50 | 4.00 | 18.50 | — |
| 1926 | 194,000 | 0.40 | 1.50 | 4.00 | 18.50 | — |
| 1931 | 20,000 | 2.00 | 10.00 | 40.00 | 80.00 | — |
| 1935 | 100 | 125 | 300 | 800 | 1,500 | — |

**100 REIS** **KM# 503** **Composition:** Copper-Nickel **Note:** Date in romal numerals.

| Date | Mintage | F | VF | XF | Unc | BU |
|---|---|---|---|---|---|---|
| 1901 | 15,775,000 | 0.40 | 1.50 | 3.25 | 18.50 | — |

**100 REIS** **KM# 518** **Composition:** Copper-Nickel

| Date | Mintage | F | VF | XF | Unc | BU |
|---|---|---|---|---|---|---|
| 1918 | 600,000 | 0.40 | 1.50 | 3.25 | 16.50 | — |
| 1919 | 1,219,000 | 0.40 | 1.50 | 3.25 | 16.50 | — |
| 1920 | 1,251,000 | 0.40 | 1.50 | 3.25 | 16.50 | — |
| 1921 | 853,000 | 0.40 | 1.50 | 3.25 | 16.50 | — |
| 1922 | 347,000 | 0.40 | 1.50 | 4.75 | 18.50 | — |
| 1923 | 956,000 | 0.40 | 1.50 | 4.75 | 18.50 | — |
| 1924 | 1,478,000 | 1.00 | 2.50 | 8.50 | 23.50 | — |
| 1925 | 2,502,000 | 0.30 | 1.25 | 2.75 | 16.50 | — |
| 1926 | 1,807,000 | 0.50 | 1.50 | 4.75 | 18.50 | — |
| 1927 | 1,451,000 | 0.30 | 1.25 | 2.75 | 16.50 | — |
| 1928 | 1,514,000 | 0.30 | 1.25 | 2.75 | 16.50 | — |
| 1929 | 2,503,000 | 0.30 | 1.25 | 2.75 | 16.50 | — |
| 1930 | 2,398,000 | 0.30 | 1.25 | 2.75 | 16.50 | — |
| 1931 | 2,500,000 | 0.25 | 1.00 | 2.25 | 16.50 | — |
| 1932 | 948,000 | 0.25 | 1.00 | 2.25 | 16.50 | — |
| 1933 | 1,314,000 | 0.25 | 1.00 | 2.25 | 16.50 | — |
| 1934 | 3,614,000 | 0.25 | 1.00 | 2.25 | 16.50 | — |
| 1935 | 3,442,000 | 0.25 | 1.00 | 2.25 | 16.50 | — |

**100 REIS** **KM# 527** **Composition:** Copper-Nickel **Subject:** 400th Anniversary of Colonization **Obverse:** Cazique Tibirica

| Date | Mintage | F | VF | XF | Unc | BU |
|---|---|---|---|---|---|---|
| 1932 | 1,012,000 | 0.50 | 1.00 | 2.25 | 6.50 | — |

**100 REIS** **KM# 536** **Composition:** Copper-Nickel **Reverse:** Admiral Marques Tamandare

| Date | Mintage | F | VF | XF | Unc | BU |
|---|---|---|---|---|---|---|
| 1936 | 3,928,000 | 0.20 | 0.50 | 1.50 | 3.00 | — |
| 1937 | 7,905,000 | 0.10 | 0.35 | 1.00 | 2.50 | — |
| 1938 | 8,618,000 | 0.10 | 0.35 | 1.00 | 2.50 | — |

**100 REIS** **KM# 544** **Composition:** Copper-Nickel **Reverse:** Dr. Getulio Vargas **Edge:** Fluted

| Date | Mintage | F | VF | XF | Unc | BU |
|---|---|---|---|---|---|---|
| 1938 | 8,106,000 | 0.10 | 0.20 | 0.50 | 1.50 | — |
| 1940 | 8,797,000 | 0.10 | 0.20 | 0.50 | 1.50 | — |
| 1942 | 1,285,000 | 0.10 | 0.20 | 0.50 | 1.50 | — |

**Note:** The 1942 issue has a deeper yellow cast due to higher copper content

**200 REIS** **KM# 504** **Composition:** Copper-Nickel **Note:** Date in roman numerals.

| Date | Mintage | F | VF | XF | Unc | BU |
|---|---|---|---|---|---|---|
| 1901 | 12,625,000 | 0.35 | 1.00 | 2.00 | 12.50 | — |

**200 REIS** **KM# 519** **Composition:** Copper-Nickel

| Date | Mintage | F | VF | XF | Unc | BU |
|---|---|---|---|---|---|---|
| 1918 | 625,000 | 0.35 | 1.00 | 2.00 | 14.00 | — |
| 1919 | 882,000 | 0.35 | 1.00 | 2.00 | 14.00 | — |
| 1920 | 1,657,000 | 0.35 | 1.00 | 2.00 | 14.00 | — |
| 1921 | 1,135,000 | 0.35 | 1.00 | 2.00 | 14.00 | — |
| 1922 | 678,000 | 0.35 | 1.00 | 2.00 | 14.00 | — |
| 1923 | 1,655,000 | 0.35 | 1.00 | 2.00 | 14.00 | — |
| 1924 | 1,750,000 | 0.35 | 1.00 | 2.00 | 14.00 | — |
| 1925 | 2,081,999 | 0.35 | 1.00 | 2.00 | 14.00 | — |
| 1926 | 324,000 | 1.00 | 3.00 | 8.00 | 21.50 | — |
| 1927 | 1,806,000 | 0.35 | 1.00 | 2.00 | 14.00 | — |
| 1928 | 782,000 | 0.35 | 1.00 | 2.00 | 14.00 | — |
| 1929 | 2,440,000 | 0.25 | 1.00 | 2.00 | 14.00 | — |
| 1930 | 1,697,000 | 0.25 | 1.00 | 2.00 | 14.00 | — |
| 1931 | 1,830,000 | 0.25 | 1.00 | 2.00 | 14.00 | — |
| 1932 | 761,000 | 0.25 | 1.00 | 2.00 | 14.00 | — |
| 1933 | 173,000 | 0.35 | 1.00 | 2.00 | 14.00 | — |
| 1934 | 612,000 | 0.25 | 1.00 | 2.00 | 14.00 | — |
| 1935 | 1,329,000 | 0.25 | 1.00 | 2.00 | 14.00 | — |

**200 REIS** **KM# 528** **Composition:** Copper-Nickel **Subject:** 400th Anniversary of Colonization **Reverse:** Ship

| Date | Mintage | F | VF | XF | Unc | BU |
|---|---|---|---|---|---|---|
| ND(1932) | 596,000 | 0.75 | 1.75 | 3.50 | 15.00 | — |

**200 REIS** **KM# 537** **Composition:** Copper-Nickel **Obverse:** Train **Reverse:** Viscount de Maua

| Date | Mintage | F | VF | XF | Unc | BU |
|---|---|---|---|---|---|---|
| 1936 | 2,256,000 | 0.30 | 0.75 | 2.00 | 8.50 | — |
| 1937 | 6,506,000 | 0.30 | 0.75 | 2.00 | 8.50 | — |
| 1938 | 5,787,000 | 0.30 | 0.75 | 2.00 | 8.50 | — |

**200 REIS** **KM# 545** **Composition:** Copper-Nickel **Reverse:** Dr. Getulio Vargas **Edge:** Fluted

| Date | Mintage | F | VF | XF | Unc | BU |
|---|---|---|---|---|---|---|
| 1938 | 7,666,000 | 0.20 | 0.50 | 0.85 | 2.75 | — |
| 1940 | 10,161,000 | 0.15 | 0.40 | 0.60 | 2.25 | — |
| 1942 | 1,966,000 | 0.15 | 0.40 | 0.60 | 2.25 | — |

**Note:** The 1942 issue has a yellow cast due to higher copper content

**300 REIS** **KM# 538** **Composition:** Copper-Nickel **Obverse:** Harp **Reverse:** Antonio Carlos Gomes

| Date | Mintage | F | VF | XF | Unc | BU |
|---|---|---|---|---|---|---|
| 1936 | 3,029,000 | 0.30 | 1.25 | 4.00 | 11.50 | — |
| 1937 | 4,507,000 | 0.30 | 1.25 | 4.00 | 11.50 | — |
| 1938 | 3,753,000 | 0.30 | 1.25 | 4.00 | 11.50 | — |

**300 REIS** **KM# 546** **Composition:** Copper-Nickel **Reverse:** Dr. Getulio Vargas **Edge:** Fluted

| Date | Mintage | F | VF | XF | Unc | BU |
|---|---|---|---|---|---|---|
| 1938 | 12,080,000 | 0.20 | 0.35 | 0.50 | 2.25 | — |
| 1940 | 8,124,000 | 0.20 | 0.35 | 0.50 | 2.25 | — |
| 1942 | 2,020,000 | 0.25 | 0.40 | 0.75 | 3.25 | — |

**Note:** The 1942 issue has a yellow cast due to higher copper content

**400 REIS** **KM# 505** **Composition:** Copper-Nickel **Note:** Date in roman numerals.

| Date | Mintage | F | VF | XF | Unc | BU |
|---|---|---|---|---|---|---|
| 1901 | 5,531,000 | 1.50 | 3.00 | 6.00 | 26.00 | — |

**400 REIS** **KM# 515** **Composition:** Copper-Nickel

| Date | Mintage | F | VF | XF | Unc | BU |
|---|---|---|---|---|---|---|
| 1914 | 646,000 | 15.00 | 35.00 | 75.00 | 150 | — |

**Note:** This is considered a pattern by many authorities

**400 REIS** **KM# 520** **Composition:** Copper-Nickel

| Date | Mintage | F | VF | XF | Unc | BU |
|---|---|---|---|---|---|---|
| 1918 | 491,000 | 0.75 | 2.00 | 5.50 | 17.00 | — |
| 1919 | 891,000 | 0.75 | 2.00 | 5.50 | 17.00 | — |
| 1920 | 1,521,000 | 0.75 | 2.00 | 5.50 | 17.00 | — |
| 1921 | 871,000 | 0.50 | 1.75 | 5.50 | 17.00 | — |
| 1922 | 1,275,000 | 0.50 | 1.75 | 5.50 | 17.00 | — |
| 1923 | 764,000 | 0.50 | 1.75 | 5.50 | 17.00 | — |
| 1925 | 2,048,000 | 0.50 | 1.75 | 5.50 | 17.00 | — |
| 1926 | 1,034,000 | 0.50 | 1.75 | 5.50 | 17.00 | — |
| 1927 | 738,000 | 0.50 | 1.75 | 5.50 | 17.00 | — |
| 1929 | 869,000 | 0.50 | 1.75 | 5.50 | 17.00 | — |
| 1930 | 1,030,999 | 0.50 | 1.75 | 5.50 | 17.00 | — |
| 1931 | 1,431,000 | 0.50 | 1.75 | 5.50 | 17.00 | — |
| 1932 | 588,000 | 0.50 | 1.75 | 5.50 | 17.00 | — |
| 1935 | 225,000 | 0.50 | 1.75 | 5.50 | 17.00 | — |

**400 REIS** **KM# 529** **Composition:** Copper-Nickel **Subject:** 400th Anniversary of Colonization

| Date | Mintage | F | VF | XF | Unc | BU |
|---|---|---|---|---|---|---|
| ND(1932) | 416,000 | 1.00 | 2.75 | 4.75 | 11.50 | — |

**400 REIS** **KM# 539** **Composition:** Copper-Nickel **Obverse:** Oil lamp **Reverse:** Oswaldo Cruz

| Date | Mintage | F | VF | XF | Unc | BU |
|---|---|---|---|---|---|---|
| 1936 | 2,079,000 | 0.50 | 1.00 | 2.75 | 8.50 | — |
| 1937 | 3,111,000 | 0.50 | 1.00 | 2.75 | 8.50 | — |
| 1938 | 2,681,000 | 0.50 | 1.00 | 2.75 | 8.50 | — |

**400 REIS** **KM# 547** **Composition:** Copper-Nickel **Reverse:** Dr. Getulio Vargas **Edge:** Fluted

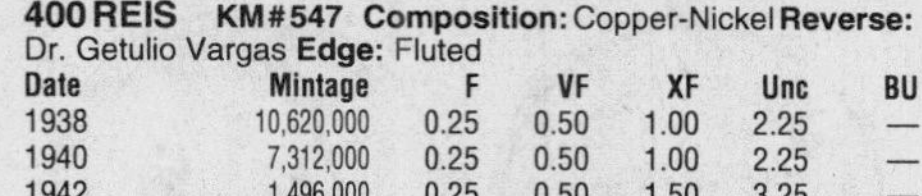

| Date | Mintage | F | VF | XF | Unc | BU |
|---|---|---|---|---|---|---|
| 1938 | 10,620,000 | 0.25 | 0.50 | 1.00 | 2.25 | — |
| 1940 | 7,312,000 | 0.25 | 0.50 | 1.00 | 2.25 | — |
| 1942 | 1,496,000 | 0.25 | 0.50 | 1.50 | 3.25 | — |

**Note:** The 1942 issue has a yellow cast due to higher copper content

**500 REIS** **KM# 506** **Weight:** 5.0000 g. **Composition:** 0.9000 Silver .1446 oz. ASW

| Date | Mintage | F | VF | XF | Unc | BU |
|---|---|---|---|---|---|---|
| 1906 | 352,000 | BV | 2.75 | 4.75 | 14.00 | — |
| 1907 | 1,282,000 | BV | 2.75 | 4.75 | 14.00 | — |
| 1908 | 498,000 | BV | 2.75 | 4.75 | 14.00 | — |
| 1911 | 8,000 | 20.00 | 35.00 | 70.00 | 150 | — |
| 1912 | Est. 222,000 | 20.00 | 40.00 | 80.00 | 200 | — |

**500 REIS** **KM# 509** **Weight:** 5.0000 g. **Composition:** 0.9000 Silver .1446 oz. ASW

| Date | Mintage | F | VF | XF | Unc | BU |
|---|---|---|---|---|---|---|

**500 REIS** **KM# 512** **Weight:** 5.0000 g. **Composition:** 0.9000 Silver .1446 oz. ASW

| Date | Mintage | F | VF | XF | Unc | BU |
|---|---|---|---|---|---|---|
| 1913 A | — | 1.25 | 2.50 | 4.50 | 15.00 | — |

**500 REIS** **KM# 521.1** **Composition:** Aluminum-Bronze **Subject:** Independence Centennial

| Date | Mintage | F | VF | XF | Unc | BU |
|---|---|---|---|---|---|---|
| ND(1922) | 13,744,000 | 0.25 | 0.60 | 1.25 | 4.75 | — |

**500 REIS** **KM# 521.2** **Composition:** Aluminum-Bronze **Note:** Error: BBASIL instead of BRASIL

| Date | Mintage | F | VF | XF | Unc | BU |
|---|---|---|---|---|---|---|
| ND(1922) | Inc. above | 17.50 | 35.00 | 55.00 | 120 | — |

**500 REIS** **KM# 524** **Composition:** Aluminum-Bronze

| Date | Mintage | F | VF | XF | Unc | BU |
|---|---|---|---|---|---|---|
| 1924 | 7,400,000 | 0.30 | 0.75 | 1.50 | 7.00 | — |
| 1927 | 2,725,000 | 0.30 | 0.75 | 1.50 | 7.00 | — |
| 1928 | 9,432,000 | 0.30 | 0.75 | 1.50 | 7.00 | — |
| 1930 | 146,000 | 1.00 | 2.00 | 3.75 | 9.00 | — |

**500 REIS** **KM# 530** **Composition:** Aluminum-Bronze **Subject:** 400th Anniversary of Colonization

| Date | Mintage | F | VF | XF | Unc | BU |
|---|---|---|---|---|---|---|
| ND(1932) | 34,000 | 1.50 | 4.00 | 11.50 | 18.50 | — |

**500 REIS** **KM# 533** **Weight:** 4.0000 g. **Composition:** Aluminum-Bronze **Reverse:** Diogo Feijo; CB on truncation

| Date | Mintage | F | VF | XF | Unc | BU |
|---|---|---|---|---|---|---|
| 1935 | 14,000 | 2.00 | 9.00 | 25.00 | 45.00 | — |

**500 REIS** **KM# 540** **Weight:** 5.0000 g. **Composition:** Aluminum-Bronze **Reverse:** Diogo Feijo

| Date | Mintage | F | VF | XF | Unc | BU |
|---|---|---|---|---|---|---|
| 1936 | 1,326,000 | 0.60 | 1.25 | 4.75 | 9.00 | — |
| 1937 | Inc. above | 0.60 | 1.25 | 4.75 | 9.00 | — |
| 1938 | — | 0.60 | 1.25 | 4.75 | 9.00 | — |

**500 REIS** **KM# 549** **Weight:** 5.0000 g. **Composition:** Aluminum-Bronze **Reverse:** Joaquim Machado de Assis

| Date | Mintage | F | VF | XF | Unc | BU |
|---|---|---|---|---|---|---|
| 1939 | 5,928,000 | 0.50 | 1.00 | 3.00 | 8.00 | — |

**1000 REIS** **KM# 507** **Weight:** 10.0000 g. **Composition:** 0.9000 Silver .2894 oz. ASW **Edge:** Reeded

| Date | Mintage | F | VF | XF | Unc | BU |
|---|---|---|---|---|---|---|
| 1906 | 420,000 | BV | 4.75 | 8.50 | 23.50 | — |
| 1907 | 1,282,000 | BV | 4.75 | 8.50 | 23.50 | — |
| 1908 | 1,624,000 | BV | 4.75 | 8.50 | 23.50 | — |
| 1909 | 816,000 | BV | 4.75 | 8.50 | 23.50 | — |
| 1910 | 2,354,000 | BV | 4.75 | 8.50 | 23.50 | — |
| 1911 | 2,810,000 | BV | 4.75 | 8.50 | 23.50 | — |
| 1912 | Est. 1,570,000 | BV | 4.75 | 8.50 | 23.50 | — |

**1000 REIS** **KM# 510** **Weight:** 10.0000 g. **Composition:** 0.9000 Silver .2894 oz. ASW

| Date | Mintage | F | VF | XF | Unc | BU |
|---|---|---|---|---|---|---|
| 1912 | Inc. above | 3.75 | 5.50 | 10.00 | 32.50 | — |
| 1913 | 2,525,000 | 3.75 | 5.50 | 10.00 | 32.50 | — |

**1000 REIS** **KM# 513** **Weight:** 10.0000 g. **Composition:** 0.9000 Silver .2894 oz. ASW

| Date | Mintage | F | VF | XF | Unc | BU |
|---|---|---|---|---|---|---|
| 1913 A | — | BV | 3.25 | 6.00 | 17.50 | — |

**1000 REIS** **KM# 522.1** **Composition:** Aluminum-Bronze **Subject:** Independence Centennial

| Date | Mintage | F | VF | XF | Unc | BU |
|---|---|---|---|---|---|---|
| ND(1922) | 16,698,000 | 0.40 | 0.60 | 2.00 | 5.50 | — |

**1000 REIS** **KM# 522.2** **Composition:** Aluminum-Bronze **Note:** Error: BBASIL instead of BRASIL

| Date | Mintage | F | VF | XF | Unc | BU |
|---|---|---|---|---|---|---|
| ND(1922) | Inc. above | 2.50 | 5.00 | 10.00 | 18.00 | — |

**1000 REIS** **KM# 525** **Composition:** Aluminum-Bronze **Obverse:** Monogram left of knot

| Date | Mintage | F | VF | XF | Unc | BU |
|---|---|---|---|---|---|---|
| 1924 | 9,354,000 | 0.50 | 1.00 | 2.25 | 7.50 | — |
| 1925 | 6,205,000 | 0.50 | 1.00 | 2.25 | 7.50 | — |
| 1927 | 35,817,000 | 0.50 | 1.00 | 2.25 | 7.50 | — |
| 1928 | 1,899,000 | 0.50 | 1.00 | 2.25 | 7.50 | — |
| 1929 | 83,000 | 3.50 | 14.00 | 45.00 | 100 | — |
| 1930 | 45,000 | 3.50 | 14.00 | 45.00 | 100 | — |
| 1931 | 200,000 | 1.00 | 4.50 | 8.00 | 14.00 | — |

**1000 REIS** **KM# 531** **Composition:** Aluminum-Bronze **Subject:** 400th Anniversary of Colonization **Obverse:** Martim Affonso da Sousa

| Date | Mintage | F | VF | XF | Unc | BU |
|---|---|---|---|---|---|---|
| (1932) | 56,000 | 2.00 | 4.00 | 7.50 | 15.00 | — |

**1000 REIS** **KM# 534** **Composition:** Aluminum-Bronze **Reverse:** Jose de Anchieta; CB under chin

| Date | Mintage | F | VF | XF | Unc | BU |
|---|---|---|---|---|---|---|
| 1935 | 138,000 | 1.00 | 2.00 | 4.00 | 9.00 | — |

**1000 REIS** **KM# 541** **Composition:** Aluminum-Bronze **Reverse:** Jose de Anchieta, LGCB under chin **Note:** Size reduced.

| Date | Mintage | F | VF | XF | Unc | BU |
|---|---|---|---|---|---|---|
| 1936 | 926,000 | 0.50 | 1.00 | 2.50 | 7.00 | — |
| 1937 | Inc. above | 0.50 | 1.00 | 2.50 | 7.00 | — |
| 1938 LGCB under chin | — | 0.50 | 1.00 | 2.50 | 7.00 | — |
| 1938 CB under chin | — | 0.50 | 1.00 | 2.50 | 7.00 | — |

**1000 REIS** **KM# 550** **Composition:** Aluminum-Bronze **Reverse:** Tobias Barreto de Menezes; BR monogram right of bust

| Date | Mintage | F | VF | XF | Unc | BU |
|---|---|---|---|---|---|---|
| 1939 | 9,586,000 | 0.25 | 0.75 | 2.00 | 6.50 | — |

**2000 REIS** **KM# 508** **Weight:** 20.0000 g. **Composition:** 0.9000 Silver .5787 oz. ASW

| Date | Mintage | F | VF | XF | Unc | BU |
|---|---|---|---|---|---|---|
| 1906 | 256,000 | 4.75 | 9.00 | 16.50 | 55.00 | — |
| 1907 | 2,863,000 | BV | 6.00 | 11.50 | 45.00 | — |
| 1908 | 1,707,000 | BV | 6.00 | 11.50 | 45.00 | — |
| 1910 | 585,000 | 4.75 | 9.00 | 16.50 | 55.00 | — |
| 1911 | 1,929,000 | BV | 6.00 | 11.50 | 45.00 | — |
| 1912 | 741,000 | 4.75 | 9.00 | 16.50 | 55.00 | — |

**2000 REIS** **KM# 511** **Weight:** 20.0000 g. **Composition:** 0.9000 Silver .5787 oz. ASW **Reverse:** Arms break behind

| Date | Mintage | F | VF | XF | Unc | BU |
|---|---|---|---|---|---|---|
| 1912 | Inc. above | 6.00 | 11.50 | 23.50 | 58.00 | — |
| 1913 | 395,000 | 6.00 | 11.50 | 23.50 | 62.00 | — |

**2000 REIS** **KM# 514** **Weight:** 20.0000 g. **Composition:** 0.9000 Silver .5787 oz. ASW **Reverse:** Continuous legend

| Date | Mintage | F | VF | XF | Unc | BU |
|---|---|---|---|---|---|---|
| 1913 A | — | 4.75 | 9.00 | 14.50 | 42.50 | — |

**2000 REIS** **KM# 523** **Weight:** 7.9000 g. **Composition:** 0.9000 Silver .2285 oz. ASW **Subject:** Independence Centennial

| Date | Mintage | F | VF | XF | Unc | BU |
|---|---|---|---|---|---|---|
| ND(1922) | 1,560,000 | BV | 2.75 | 3.75 | 8.50 | — |

**2000 REIS** **KM# 523a** **Weight:** 7.9000 g. **Composition:** 0.5000 Silver .1269 oz. ASW

| Date | Mintage | F | VF | XF | Unc | BU |
|---|---|---|---|---|---|---|
| ND(1922) | Inc. above | BV | 2.75 | 3.75 | 8.50 | — |

**Note:** Struck in both .900 and .500 fine silver, but can only be distinguished by analysis (and color), on worn specimens

**2000 REIS** **KM# 526** **Weight:** 7.9000 g. **Composition:** 0.5000 Silver .1269 oz. ASW

| Date | Mintage | F | VF | XF | Unc | BU |
|---|---|---|---|---|---|---|
| 1924 | 9,147,000 | BV | 1.50 | 3.75 | 12.00 | — |
| 1925 | 723,000 | BV | 1.50 | 3.75 | 12.00 | — |
| 1926 | 1,787,000 | BV | 1.50 | 3.75 | 12.00 | — |
| 1927 | 1,008,999 | BV | 2.50 | 4.75 | 14.00 | — |
| 1928 | 1,250,000 | BV | 1.50 | 3.75 | 12.00 | — |
| 1929 | 1,744,000 | BV | 1.50 | 3.75 | 12.00 | — |
| 1930 | 1,240,000 | BV | 1.50 | 3.75 | 12.00 | — |
| 1931 | 546,000 | BV | 1.50 | 3.75 | 12.00 | — |
| 1934 | 938,000 | BV | 1.50 | 3.75 | 12.00 | — |

**2000 REIS** **KM# 532** **Weight:** 7.9000 g. **Composition:** 0.5000 Silver .1269 oz. ASW **Subject:** 400th Anniversary of Colonization **Obverse:** John III

| Date | Mintage | F | VF | XF | Unc | BU |
|---|---|---|---|---|---|---|
| ND(1922) | 695,000 | 2.00 | 2.50 | 4.75 | 14.00 | — |

**2000 REIS** **KM# 535** **Weight:** 7.9000 g. **Composition:** 0.5000 Silver .1269 oz. ASW **Reverse:** Duke of Caxias; CB below chin

| Date | Mintage | F | VF | XF | Unc | BU |
|---|---|---|---|---|---|---|
| 1935 | 2,131,000 | BV | 1.50 | 3.75 | 12.50 | — |

**2000 REIS** KM# 542 **Composition:** Aluminum-Bronze **Reverse:** Duke of Caxias **Edge:** Reeded

| Date | Mintage | F | VF | XF | Unc | BU |
|---|---|---|---|---|---|---|
| 1936 | 665,000 | 0.50 | 1.00 | 2.00 | 5.50 | — |
| 1937 | Inc. above | 0.50 | 1.00 | 2.00 | 5.50 | — |
| 1938 | — | 2.50 | 4.75 | 11.50 | 28.00 | — |

**2000 REIS** KM# 548 **Composition:** Aluminum-Bronze **Edge:** Plain **Note:** Polygonal planchet.

| Date | Mintage | F | VF | XF | Unc | BU |
|---|---|---|---|---|---|---|
| 1937 | — | 25.00 | 50.00 | 125 | 300 | — |
| 1938 | — | 0.75 | 1.50 | 3.25 | 7.50 | — |

**2000 REIS** KM# 551 **Composition:** Aluminum-Bronze **Reverse:** Floriano Peixoto

| Date | Mintage | F | VF | XF | Unc | BU |
|---|---|---|---|---|---|---|
| 1939 | 5,048,000 | 0.50 | 1.00 | 2.00 | 5.50 | — |

**5000 REIS** KM# 543 **Weight:** 10.0000 g. **Composition:** 0.6000 Silver .1929 oz. ASW **Reverse:** Alberto Santos Dumont

| Date | Mintage | F | VF | XF | Unc | BU |
|---|---|---|---|---|---|---|
| 1936 | 1,986,000 | BV | 2.00 | 3.50 | 8.50 | — |
| 1937 | 414,000 | BV | 2.00 | 3.50 | 8.50 | — |
| 1938 | 994,000 | BV | 2.00 | 3.50 | 8.50 | — |

**10000 REIS** KM# 496 **Weight:** 8.9645 g. **Composition:** 0.9170 Gold .2643 oz. AGW

| Date | Mintage | F | VF | XF | Unc | BU |
|---|---|---|---|---|---|---|
| 1898 | 216 | 250 | 500 | 1,500 | 2,000 | — |
| 1901 | 111 | 150 | 250 | 700 | 1,150 | — |
| 1902 Unique | — | — | — | — | — | — |
| 1903 | 391 | 150 | 250 | 700 | 1,150 | — |
| 1904 | 541 | 150 | 250 | 700 | 1,150 | — |
| 1906 | 572 | 150 | 250 | 700 | 1,150 | — |
| 1907 | 878 | 150 | 250 | 600 | 1,100 | — |
| 1908 | 689 | 150 | 250 | 600 | 1,100 | — |
| 1909 | 1,069 | 150 | 250 | 600 | 1,100 | — |
| 1911 | 137 | 175 | 350 | 800 | 1,350 | — |
| 1914 | 969 | 250 | 500 | 1,500 | 2,400 | — |
| 1915 | 4,314 | 250 | 500 | 1,400 | 2,000 | — |
| 1916 | 4,720 | 150 | 250 | 700 | 1,150 | — |
| 1919 | 526 | 150 | 250 | 700 | 1,150 | — |
| 1921 | 2,435 | 150 | 250 | 600 | 1,000 | — |
| 1922 Rare | 6 | — | — | — | — | — |

**20000 REIS** KM# 497 **Weight:** 17.9290 g. **Composition:** 0.9170 Gold .5286 oz. AGW

| Date | Mintage | F | VF | XF | Unc | BU |
|---|---|---|---|---|---|---|
| 1894 | 4,267 | BV | 300 | 550 | 1,100 | — |
| 1901 | 784 | BV | 350 | 700 | 1,350 | — |
| 1902 | 884 | BV | 350 | 700 | 1,350 | — |
| 1903 | 675 | BV | 350 | 700 | 1,350 | — |
| 1904 | 444 | BV | 350 | 700 | 1,350 | — |
| 1906 | 396 | BV | 500 | 900 | 1,600 | — |
| 1907 | 3,310 | BV | 300 | 550 | 1,100 | — |
| 1908 | 6,001,000 | BV | 300 | 550 | 1,100 | — |
| 1909 | 4,427 | BV | 300 | 550 | 1,100 | — |
| 1910 | 5,119 | BV | 300 | 550 | 1,100 | — |
| 1911 | 8,467 | BV | 300 | 550 | 1,100 | — |
| 1912 | 4,878 | BV | 300 | 550 | 1,100 | — |
| 1913 | 5,182 | BV | 300 | 600 | 1,200 | — |
| 1914 | 1,980 | BV | 350 | 700 | 1,400 | — |
| 1917 | 2,269 | BV | 400 | 800 | 1,550 | — |
| 1918 | 1,216 | BV | 400 | 800 | 1,550 | — |
| 1921 | 5,924 | BV | 300 | 600 | 1,200 | — |
| 1922 | 2,681 | BV | 400 | 800 | 1,550 | — |

## REFORM COINAGE

100 Centavos = 1 Cruzeiro; 1942-1967

**10 CENTAVOS** KM# 555 **Composition:** Copper-Nickel **Obverse:** Getulio Vargas **Note:** KM#555 has a very light yellowish appearance while KM#555a is a deeper yellow.

| Date | Mintage | F | VF | XF | Unc | BU |
|---|---|---|---|---|---|---|
| 1942 | 3,826,000 | — | 0.35 | 0.50 | 1.00 | — |
| 1943 | 13,565,000 | — | 0.25 | 0.35 | 0.75 | — |

**10 CENTAVOS** KM# 555a **Composition:** Aluminum-Bronze **Note:** KM#555 has a very light yellowish appearance while KM#555a is a deeper yellow.

| Date | Mintage | F | VF | XF | Unc | BU |
|---|---|---|---|---|---|---|
| 1943 | Inc. above | — | 0.25 | 0.35 | 0.75 | — |
| 1944 | 12,617,000 | — | 0.25 | 0.60 | 1.00 | — |
| 1945 | 24,674,000 | — | 0.25 | 0.60 | 1.00 | — |
| 1946 | 35,159,000 | — | 0.25 | 0.60 | 1.00 | — |
| 1947 | 20,664,000 | — | 0.25 | 0.35 | 0.75 | — |

**10 CENTAVOS** KM# 561 **Composition:** Aluminum-Bronze **Obverse:** Jose Bonifacio de Andrada e Silva

| Date | Mintage | F | VF | XF | Unc | BU |
|---|---|---|---|---|---|---|
| 1947 | Inc. above | — | 0.15 | 0.20 | 0.35 | — |
| 1948 | 45,041,000 | — | 0.15 | 0.20 | 0.35 | — |
| 1949 | 21,763,000 | — | 0.15 | 0.20 | 0.35 | — |
| 1950 | 16,329,999 | — | 0.15 | 0.20 | 0.35 | — |
| 1951 | 15,561,000 | — | 0.10 | 0.15 | 0.35 | — |
| 1952 | 10,966,000 | — | 0.10 | 0.20 | 0.50 | — |
| 1953 | 25,883,000 | — | 0.10 | 0.15 | 0.35 | — |
| 1954 | 17,031,000 | — | 0.10 | 0.15 | 0.35 | — |
| 1955 | 25,172,000 | — | 0.10 | 0.15 | 0.35 | — |

**10 CENTAVOS** KM# 564 **Composition:** Aluminum **Obverse:** National Arms

| Date | Mintage | F | VF | XF | Unc | BU |
|---|---|---|---|---|---|---|
| 1956 | 741,000 | — | 0.10 | 0.15 | 0.50 | — |
| 1957 | 25,311,000 | — | 0.10 | 0.15 | 0.25 | — |
| 1958 | 5,813,000 | — | 0.10 | 0.15 | 0.25 | — |
| 1959 | 2,611,000 | — | 0.10 | 0.15 | 0.25 | — |
| 1960 | 624,000 | — | 0.10 | 0.15 | 0.50 | — |
| 1961 | 951,000 | — | 0.10 | 0.15 | 0.50 | — |

**20 CENTAVOS** KM# 556 **Composition:** Copper-Nickel **Obverse:** Getulio Vargas **Note:** KM#556 has a very light yellowish appearance while KM#556a is a deeper yellow.

| Date | Mintage | F | VF | XF | Unc | BU |
|---|---|---|---|---|---|---|
| 1942 | 3,007,000 | — | 0.25 | 0.50 | 1.00 | — |
| 1943 | 13,392,000 | — | 0.15 | 0.40 | 0.75 | — |

**20 CENTAVOS** KM# 556a **Composition:** Aluminum-Bronze **Note:** KM#556 has a very light yellowish appearance while KM#556a is a deeper yellow.

| Date | Mintage | F | VF | XF | Unc | BU |
|---|---|---|---|---|---|---|
| 1943 | Inc. above | — | 0.15 | 0.35 | 0.75 | — |
| 1944 | 12,673,000 | — | 0.15 | 0.35 | 0.75 | — |

**Note:** Coins dated 1944 exist with and without designer's initials and straight or curved backed 9 in date

| Date | Mintage | F | VF | XF | Unc | BU |
|---|---|---|---|---|---|---|
| 1945 | 61,632,000 | — | 0.15 | 0.35 | 0.60 | — |
| 1946 | 31,526,000 | — | 0.15 | 0.35 | 0.60 | — |
| 1947 | 36,422,000 | — | 0.15 | 0.35 | 0.75 | — |
| 1948 | 39,671,000 | — | 0.15 | 0.35 | 0.75 | — |

**20 CENTAVOS** KM# 562 **Composition:** Aluminum-Bronze **Obverse:** Ruy Barbosa

| Date | Mintage | F | VF | XF | Unc | BU |
|---|---|---|---|---|---|---|
| 1948 | Inc. above | — | 0.15 | 0.25 | 0.50 | — |
| 1949 | 24,805,000 | — | 0.15 | 0.25 | 0.50 | — |
| 1950 | 15,145,000 | — | 0.15 | 0.25 | 0.50 | — |
| 1951 | 14,964,000 | — | 0.15 | 0.25 | 0.50 | — |
| 1952 | 10,942,000 | — | 0.15 | 0.25 | 0.50 | — |
| 1953 | 25,585,000 | — | 0.15 | 0.25 | 0.50 | — |
| 1954 | 16,477,000 | — | 0.15 | 0.25 | 0.50 | — |
| 1955 | 25,122,000 | — | 0.15 | 0.25 | 0.50 | — |
| 1956 | 6,716,000 | — | 0.15 | 0.25 | 0.50 | — |

**20 CENTAVOS** KM# 565 **Composition:** Aluminum **Obverse:** National Arms **Note:** Varieties exist in the thickness of the planchet for year 1956.

| Date | Mintage | F | VF | XF | Unc | BU |
|---|---|---|---|---|---|---|
| 1956 | Inc. above | — | 0.10 | 0.25 | 0.50 | — |
| 1957 | 27,110,000 | — | 0.10 | 0.20 | 0.40 | — |
| 1958 | 8,552,000 | — | 0.10 | 0.20 | 0.40 | — |
| 1959 | 4,810,000 | — | 0.10 | 0.20 | 0.40 | — |
| 1960 | 510,000 | — | 0.10 | 0.25 | 0.50 | — |
| 1961 | 2,332,000 | — | 0.10 | 0.20 | 0.40 | — |

**50 CENTAVOS** KM# 557 **Composition:** Copper-Nickel **Obverse:** Getulio Vargas **Note:** KM#557 has a very light yellowish appearance while KM#557a is a deeper yellow.

| Date | Mintage | F | VF | XF | Unc | BU |
|---|---|---|---|---|---|---|
| 1942 | 2,358,000 | — | 0.40 | 0.75 | 1.50 | — |
| 1943 | 13,392,000 | — | 0.35 | 0.50 | 1.00 | — |

**50 CENTAVOS** KM# 557a **Composition:** Aluminum-Bronze **Note:** KM#557 has a very light yellowish appearance while KM#557a is a deeper yellow.

| Date | Mintage | F | VF | XF | Unc | BU |
|---|---|---|---|---|---|---|
| 1943 | Inc. above | — | 0.30 | 0.50 | 1.00 | — |
| 1944 | 12,102,000 | — | 0.30 | 0.50 | 1.00 | — |
| 1945 | 73,222,000 | — | 0.30 | 0.50 | 1.00 | — |
| 1946 | 13,941,000 | — | 0.30 | 0.50 | 1.00 | — |
| 1947 | 23,588,000 | — | 0.20 | 0.50 | 1.00 | — |

**50 CENTAVOS** **KM# 563** **Composition:** Aluminum-Bronze **Obverse:** General Eurico Gaspar Dutra

| Date | Mintage | F | VF | XF | Unc | BU |
|---|---|---|---|---|---|---|
| 1948 | 32,023,000 | — | 0.15 | 0.25 | 0.50 | — |
| 1949 | 11,392,000 | — | 0.15 | 0.25 | 0.50 | — |
| 1950 | 7,804,000 | — | 0.15 | 0.35 | 0.75 | — |
| 1951 | 7,523,000 | — | 0.15 | 0.35 | 0.75 | — |
| 1952 | 6,863,000 | — | 0.15 | 0.35 | 0.75 | — |
| 1953 | 17,372,000 | — | 0.15 | 0.25 | 0.50 | — |
| 1954 | 11,353,000 | — | 0.15 | 0.25 | 0.50 | — |
| 1955 | 27,150,000 | — | 0.15 | 0.25 | 0.50 | — |
| 1956 | 32,130,000 | — | 0.15 | 0.25 | 0.50 | — |

**50 CENTAVOS** **KM# 566** **Composition:** Aluminum-Bronze **Obverse:** National arms

| Date | Mintage | F | VF | XF | Unc | BU |
|---|---|---|---|---|---|---|
| 1956 | Inc. above | — | 0.15 | 0.25 | 0.50 | — |

**50 CENTAVOS** **KM# 569** **Composition:** Aluminum **Obverse:** National Arms

| Date | Mintage | F | VF | XF | Unc | BU |
|---|---|---|---|---|---|---|
| 1957 | 49,350,000 | — | 0.10 | 0.20 | 0.35 | — |
| 1958 | 59,815,000 | — | 0.10 | 0.20 | 0.35 | — |
| 1959 | 32,891,000 | — | 0.10 | 0.20 | 0.35 | — |
| 1960 | 15,997,000 | — | 0.10 | 0.20 | 0.35 | — |
| 1961 | 18,456,000 | — | 0.10 | 0.20 | 0.35 | — |

**CRUZEIRO** **KM# 558** **Composition:** Aluminum-Bronze **Obverse:** Topographical map

| Date | Mintage | F | VF | XF | Unc | BU |
|---|---|---|---|---|---|---|
| 1942 | 381,000 | — | 0.50 | 1.00 | 3.50 | — |
| 1943 | 2,728,000 | — | 0.25 | 0.50 | 1.00 | — |
| 1944 | 3,820,000 | — | 0.25 | 0.50 | 1.00 | — |
| 1945 | 32,543,999 | — | 0.25 | 0.50 | 0.75 | — |
| 1946 | 49,794,000 | — | 0.25 | 0.50 | 1.00 | — |
| 1947 | 15,391,000 | — | 0.25 | 0.50 | 1.00 | — |
| 1949 | 7,889,000 | — | 0.25 | 0.50 | 1.00 | — |
| 1950 | 5,163,000 | — | 0.25 | 0.50 | 1.00 | — |
| 1951 | 3,757,000 | — | 0.25 | 0.50 | 1.00 | — |
| 1952 | 1,769,000 | — | 0.50 | 1.00 | 3.50 | — |
| 1953 | 5,195,000 | — | 0.25 | 0.50 | 1.00 | — |
| 1954 | 1,145,000 | — | 0.25 | 0.50 | 1.50 | — |
| 1955 | 1,758,000 | — | 0.25 | 0.50 | 1.00 | — |
| 1956 | 668,000 | — | 6.00 | 12.00 | 20.00 | — |

**CRUZEIRO** **KM# 567** **Composition:** Aluminum-Bronze **Obverse:** National Arms

| Date | Mintage | F | VF | XF | Unc | BU |
|---|---|---|---|---|---|---|
| 1956 | Inc. above | — | 0.20 | 0.35 | 0.65 | — |

**CRUZEIRO** **KM# 570** **Composition:** Aluminum **Obverse:** National Arms

| Date | Mintage | F | VF | XF | Unc | BU |
|---|---|---|---|---|---|---|
| 1957 | 11,849,000 | — | 0.20 | 0.75 | 2.50 | — |
| 1958 | 15,443,000 | — | 0.20 | 1.00 | 3.00 | — |
| 1959 | 25,010,000 | — | 0.20 | 0.75 | 2.50 | — |
| 1960 | 35,267,000 | — | 0.20 | 0.75 | 2.50 | — |
| 1961 | 22,181,000 | — | 0.20 | 1.00 | 3.00 | — |

**2 CRUZEIROS** **KM# 559** **Composition:** Aluminum-Bronze **Obverse:** Topographical map

| Date | Mintage | F | VF | XF | Unc | BU |
|---|---|---|---|---|---|---|
| 1942 | 276,000 | — | 0.75 | 1.50 | 4.00 | — |
| 1943 | 1,929,000 | — | 0.25 | 0.50 | 1.00 | — |
| 1944 | 3,820,000 | — | 0.25 | 0.50 | 1.00 | — |
| 1945 | 32,543,999 | — | 0.20 | 0.40 | 1.00 | — |
| 1946 | 33,650,000 | — | 0.20 | 0.40 | 1.00 | — |
| 1947 | 9,908,000 | — | 0.20 | 0.40 | 1.00 | — |
| 1949 | 11,252,000 | — | 0.20 | 0.40 | 1.00 | — |
| 1950 | 7,754,000 | — | 0.25 | 0.50 | 1.00 | — |
| 1951 | 390,000 | — | 0.40 | 1.00 | 3.00 | — |
| 1952 | 1,456,000 | — | 1.00 | 2.00 | 5.00 | — |
| 1953 | 3,582,000 | — | 0.20 | 0.40 | 1.00 | — |
| 1954 | 1,197,000 | — | 0.25 | 1.00 | 2.00 | — |
| 1955 | 1,838,000 | — | 0.20 | 0.50 | 1.00 | — |
| 1956 | — | — | 2.00 | 4.00 | 10.00 | — |

**2 CRUZEIROS** **KM# 568** **Composition:** Aluminum-Bronze **Obverse:** National Arms

| Date | Mintage | F | VF | XF | Unc | BU |
|---|---|---|---|---|---|---|
| 1956 | Inc. above | — | 0.20 | 0.40 | 1.50 | — |

**2 CRUZEIROS** **KM# 571** **Composition:** Aluminum **Obverse:** National Arms

| Date | Mintage | F | VF | XF | Unc | BU |
|---|---|---|---|---|---|---|
| 1957 | 194,000 | — | 0.20 | 0.30 | 1.25 | — |
| 1958 | 13,687,000 | — | 0.15 | 0.25 | 1.00 | — |
| 1959 | 20,894,000 | — | 0.15 | 0.25 | 1.00 | — |
| 1960 | 19,624,000 | — | 0.15 | 0.25 | 1.00 | — |
| 1961 | 24,924,000 | — | 0.15 | 0.25 | 1.00 | — |

**5 CRUZEIROS** **KM# 560** **Composition:** Aluminum-Bronze **Obverse:** Topographical map

| Date | Mintage | F | VF | XF | Unc | BU |
|---|---|---|---|---|---|---|
| 1942 | 115,000 | — | 1.00 | 3.00 | 8.00 | — |
| 1943 | 222,000 | — | 0.75 | 2.00 | 6.50 | — |

**10 CRUZEIROS** **KM# 572** **Composition:** Aluminum

| Date | Mintage | F | VF | XF | Unc | BU |
|---|---|---|---|---|---|---|
| 1965 | 19,656,000 | — | 0.10 | 0.20 | 0.50 | — |

**20 CRUZEIROS** **KM# 573** **Composition:** Aluminum

| Date | Mintage | F | VF | XF | Unc | BU |
|---|---|---|---|---|---|---|
| 1965 | 25,930,000 | — | 0.15 | 0.25 | 0.75 | — |

**50 CRUZEIROS** **KM# 574** **Composition:** Copper-Nickel

| Date | Mintage | F | VF | XF | Unc | BU |
|---|---|---|---|---|---|---|
| 1965 | 18,001,000 | — | 0.15 | 0.35 | 1.00 | — |

## REFORM COINAGE

1000 Old Cruzeiros = 1 Cruzeiro Novo (New); 100 Centavos = 1 (New) Cruzeiro; 1967-1985

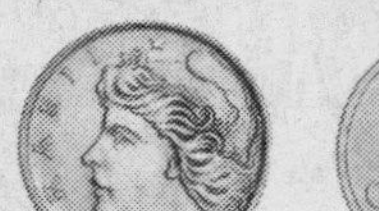

**CENTAVO** **KM# 575.1** **Composition:** Stainless Steel

| Date | Mintage | F | VF | XF | Unc | BU |
|---|---|---|---|---|---|---|
| 1967 | 57,499,000 | — | — | — | 0.15 | — |

**CENTAVO** **KM# 575.2** **Composition:** Stainless Steel **Note:** Thinner planchet.

| Date | Mintage | F | VF | XF | Unc | BU |
|---|---|---|---|---|---|---|
| 1969 | 243,855,000 | — | — | — | 0.15 | — |
| 1975 | — | — | — | 0.15 | 0.30 | — |
| 1976 | — | — | — | 0.15 | 0.30 | — |

**CENTAVO** **KM# 585** **Composition:** Stainless Steel **Series:** F.A.O **Subject:** Sugar Cane

| Date | Mintage | F | VF | XF | Unc | BU |
|---|---|---|---|---|---|---|
| 1975 | 31,700,000 | — | — | 0.15 | 0.30 | — |
| 1976 | 18,355,000 | — | — | — | 0.20 | — |
| 1977 | 100,000 | — | — | — | 0.20 | — |
| 1978 | 50,000 | — | — | 0.15 | 0.30 | — |

**CENTAVO** **KM# 589** **Composition:** Stainless Steel **Series:** F.A.O **Subject:** Soja

| Date | Mintage | F | VF | XF | Unc | BU |
|---|---|---|---|---|---|---|
| 1979 | 100,000 | — | 0.15 | 0.35 | 1.00 | — |
| 1980 | 60,000 | — | 0.15 | 0.35 | 1.00 | — |
| 1981 | 100,000 | — | 0.15 | 0.35 | 1.00 | — |
| 1982 | 100,000 | — | 0.15 | 0.35 | 1.00 | — |
| 1983 | — | — | 0.15 | 0.35 | 1.00 | — |
| 1984 | — | — | 0.15 | 0.35 | 1.00 | — |

**2 CENTAVOS** **KM# 576.1** **Composition:** Stainless Steel

| Date | Mintage | F | VF | XF | Unc | BU |
|---|---|---|---|---|---|---|
| 1967 | 65,226,000 | — | — | — | 0.25 | — |

**2 CENTAVOS** **KM# 576.2** **Composition:** Stainless Steel
**Note:** Thinner planchet.

| Date | Mintage | F | VF | XF | Unc | BU |
|---|---|---|---|---|---|---|
| 1969 | Est. 134,298,000 | — | — | — | 0.50 | — |

**Note:** Mintage figure includes coins struck through 1974 dated 1969

| Date | Mintage | F | VF | XF | Unc | BU |
|---|---|---|---|---|---|---|
| 1975 | — | — | — | 0.25 | 0.75 | — |
| 1976 | — | — | — | 0.25 | 0.75 | — |

**2 CENTAVOS** **KM# 586** **Composition:** Stainless Steel **Series:** F.A.O **Subject:** Soja

| Date | Mintage | F | VF | XF | Unc | BU |
|---|---|---|---|---|---|---|
| 1975 | 31,400,000 | — | — | — | 0.25 | — |
| 1976 | 18,754,000 | — | — | — | 0.25 | — |
| 1977 | 100,000 | — | — | — | 0.25 | — |
| 1978 | 50,000 | — | — | 0.20 | 0.50 | — |

**5 CENTAVOS** **KM# 577.1** **Composition:** Stainless Steel

| Date | Mintage | F | VF | XF | Unc | BU |
|---|---|---|---|---|---|---|
| 1967 | 69,304,000 | — | — | 0.20 | 0.50 | — |

**5 CENTAVOS** **KM# 577.2** **Composition:** Stainless Steel
**Note:** Thinner planchet.

| Date | Mintage | F | VF | XF | Unc | BU |
|---|---|---|---|---|---|---|
| 1969 | Est. 345,071,000 | — | — | 0.20 | 0.50 | — |

**Note:** Mintage figure includes coins struck through 1974 dated 1969

| Date | Mintage | F | VF | XF | Unc | BU |
|---|---|---|---|---|---|---|
| 1975 | — | — | — | 0.20 | 0.50 | — |
| 1976 | — | — | — | 0.20 | 0.50 | — |

**5 CENTAVOS** **KM# 587.1** **Composition:** Stainless Steel **Series:** F.A.O **Subject:** Zebu **Reverse:** Plain 5

| Date | Mintage | F | VF | XF | Unc | BU |
|---|---|---|---|---|---|---|
| 1975 | 44,500,000 | — | — | 0.20 | 0.50 | — |
| 1976 | 134,267,000 | — | — | 0.20 | 0.50 | — |
| 1977 | 85,360 | — | — | 0.20 | 0.50 | — |
| 1978 | 34,090,000 | — | — | 0.20 | 0.65 | — |

**5 CENTAVOS** **KM# 587.2** **Composition:** Stainless Steel **Reverse:** 5 over wavy lines

| Date | Mintage | F | VF | XF | Unc | BU |
|---|---|---|---|---|---|---|
| 1975 | Inc. above | — | — | 0.20 | 0.50 | — |
| 1976 | Inc. above | — | — | 0.20 | 0.50 | — |
| 1977 | Inc. above | — | — | 0.20 | 0.50 | — |
| 1978 | Inc. above | — | — | 0.20 | 0.65 | — |

**10 CENTAVOS** **KM# 578.1** **Composition:** Copper-Nickel

| Date | Mintage | F | VF | XF | Unc | BU |
|---|---|---|---|---|---|---|
| 1967 | 22,420,000 | — | — | 0.20 | 0.50 | — |

**10 CENTAVOS** **KM# 578.2** **Composition:** Copper-Nickel
**Note:** Thinner planchet.

| Date | Mintage | F | VF | XF | Unc | BU |
|---|---|---|---|---|---|---|
| 1970 | Est. 134,070,000 | — | — | 0.20 | 0.40 | — |

**Note:** Mintage figure includes coins struck through 1974 dated 1970

**10 CENTAVOS** **KM# 578.1a** **Composition:** Stainless Steel

| Date | Mintage | F | VF | XF | Unc | BU |
|---|---|---|---|---|---|---|
| 1974 | 114,598,000 | — | — | 0.20 | 0.40 | — |
| 1975 | — | — | — | 0.20 | 0.40 | — |
| 1976 | — | — | — | 0.20 | 0.40 | — |
| 1977 | 225,213,000 | — | — | 0.20 | 0.40 | — |
| 1978 | 225,000,000 | — | — | 0.20 | 0.40 | — |
| 1979 | 100,000 | — | — | 0.20 | 0.40 | — |

**20 CENTAVOS** **KM# 579.1** **Composition:** Copper-Nickel

| Date | Mintage | F | VF | XF | Unc | BU |
|---|---|---|---|---|---|---|
| 1967 | 123,610,000 | — | — | 0.20 | 0.50 | — |
| 1970 | — | — | — | 0.20 | 0.50 | — |

**20 CENTAVOS** **KM# 579.2** **Composition:** Copper-Nickel
**Note:** Thinner planchet.

| Date | Mintage | F | VF | XF | Unc | BU |
|---|---|---|---|---|---|---|
| 1970 | Est. 384,894,000 | — | — | 0.20 | 0.60 | — |

**Note:** Mintage figure includes coins struck through 1974 dated 1970

**20 CENTAVOS** **KM# 579.1a** **Composition:** Stainless Steel

| Date | Mintage | F | VF | XF | Unc | BU |
|---|---|---|---|---|---|---|
| 1975 | 102,367,000 | — | — | 0.20 | 0.50 | — |
| 1976 | — | — | — | 0.20 | 0.50 | — |
| 1977 | 240,001,000 | — | — | 0.20 | 0.50 | — |
| 1978 | 255,000,000 | — | — | 0.20 | 0.50 | — |
| 1979 | 116,000 | — | — | 0.20 | 0.50 | — |

**50 CENTAVOS** **KM# 580** **Composition:** Nickel

| Date | Mintage | F | VF | XF | Unc | BU |
|---|---|---|---|---|---|---|
| 1967 | 12,987,000 | — | 0.25 | 0.50 | 1.25 | — |

**50 CENTAVOS** **KM# 580a** **Composition:** Copper-Nickel **Edge:** Reeded.

| Date | Mintage | F | VF | XF | Unc | BU |
|---|---|---|---|---|---|---|
| 1970 | 503,895,000 | — | 0.20 | 0.35 | 1.00 | — |
| 1975 | — | — | 0.20 | 0.35 | 1.00 | — |

**50 CENTAVOS** **KM# 580b** **Composition:** Stainless Steel **Edge:** Plain.

| Date | Mintage | F | VF | XF | Unc | BU |
|---|---|---|---|---|---|---|
| 1975 | 79,062,000 | — | 0.20 | 0.35 | 1.00 | — |
| 1976 | — | — | 0.20 | 0.35 | 1.00 | — |
| 1977 | 160,019,000 | — | 0.20 | 0.35 | 1.00 | — |
| 1978 | 200,000,000 | — | 0.20 | 0.35 | 1.00 | — |
| 1979 | 104,000 | — | 0.20 | 0.35 | 1.00 | — |

**CRUZEIRO** **KM# 581** **Composition:** Nickel

| Date | Mintage | F | VF | XF | Unc | BU |
|---|---|---|---|---|---|---|
| 1970 | Est. 48,930,000 | — | 0.25 | 0.50 | 1.00 | — |

**Note:** Mintage figure includes coins struck through 1972 dated 1970

| Date | Mintage | F | VF | XF | Unc | BU |
|---|---|---|---|---|---|---|
| 1970 Proof | 18,000 | Value: 3.00 | | | | |

**CRUZEIRO** **KM# 582** **Composition:** Nickel **Subject:** 150th Anniversary of Independence

| Date | Mintage | F | VF | XF | Unc | BU |
|---|---|---|---|---|---|---|
| 1972 Lettered edge | 5,600,000 | — | 0.35 | 0.85 | 1.65 | — |
| 1972 Plain edge | Inc. above | — | 0.35 | 0.85 | 1.65 | — |

**Note:** Coins with plain edge are believed by some to be errors

| Date | Mintage | F | VF | XF | Unc | BU |
|---|---|---|---|---|---|---|
| 1972 Lettered edge; Proof | — | Value: 3.00 | | | | |
| 1972 Plain edge; Proof | — | Value: 3.00 | | | | |

**Note:** Coins with plain edge are believed by some to be errors

**CRUZEIRO** **KM# 581a** **Composition:** Copper-Nickel

| Date | Mintage | F | VF | XF | Unc | BU |
|---|---|---|---|---|---|---|
| 1975 | 21,613,000 | — | 0.20 | 0.45 | 1.00 | — |
| 1976 | — | — | 0.20 | 0.45 | 1.00 | — |
| 1977 | 98,000 | — | 0.20 | 0.45 | 1.00 | — |
| 1978 | 77,000 | — | 0.20 | 0.45 | 1.00 | — |

**CRUZEIRO** **KM# 590** **Composition:** Stainless Steel **Subject:** Sugar Cane

| Date | Mintage | F | VF | XF | Unc | BU |
|---|---|---|---|---|---|---|
| 1979 | 596,000 | — | 0.15 | 0.25 | 0.65 | — |
| 1980 | 690,497,000 | — | 0.15 | 0.25 | 0.65 | — |
| 1981 | 560,000,000 | — | 0.15 | 0.25 | 0.65 | — |
| 1982 | 300,000,000 | — | 0.15 | 0.25 | 0.65 | — |
| 1983 | 100,000 | — | 0.15 | 0.25 | 0.65 | — |
| 1984 | 62,100,000 | — | 0.15 | 0.25 | 0.65 | — |

**CRUZEIRO** **KM# 598** **Composition:** Stainless Steel **Series:** F.A.O **Subject:** Sugar Cane

| Date | Mintage | F | VF | XF | Unc | BU |
|---|---|---|---|---|---|---|
| 1985 | 10,000,000 | — | — | 0.20 | 0.50 | — |

**5 CRUZEIROS** **KM# 591** **Composition:** Stainless Steel **Subject:** Coffee Plant

| Date | Mintage | F | VF | XF | Unc | BU |
|---|---|---|---|---|---|---|
| 1980 | 288,200,000 | — | 0.20 | 0.35 | 0.75 | — |
| 1981 | 82,000,000 | — | 0.20 | 0.35 | 0.75 | — |
| 1982 | 108,000,000 | — | 0.20 | 0.35 | 0.75 | — |
| 1983 | 113,400,000 | — | 0.20 | 0.35 | 0.75 | — |
| 1984 | 243,000,000 | — | 0.20 | 0.35 | 0.75 | — |

**5 CRUZEIROS** **KM# 599** **Composition:** Stainless Steel **Series:** F.A.O **Subject:** Coffee

| Date | Mintage | F | VF | XF | Unc | BU |
|---|---|---|---|---|---|---|
| 1985 | 10,000,000 | — | 0.20 | 0.40 | 0.85 | — |

**10 CRUZEIROS** KM# 588 **Weight:** 11.3000 g. **Composition:** 0.8000 Silver .2906 oz. ASW **Subject:** 10th Anniversary of Central Bank **Obverse:** Humberto de Alencar Castelo Branco

| Date | Mintage | F | VF | XF | Unc | BU |
|---|---|---|---|---|---|---|
| 1975 | 20,000 | — | — | — | 55.00 | — |

**10 CRUZEIROS** KM# 592.1 **Composition:** Stainless Steel

| Date | Mintage | F | VF | XF | Unc | BU |
|---|---|---|---|---|---|---|
| 1980 | 100,010,000 | — | — | 0.50 | 0.75 | — |
| 1981 | 200,000,000 | — | — | 0.50 | 0.75 | — |
| 1982 | 331,000,000 | — | — | 0.50 | 0.75 | — |
| 1983 | 390,000,000 | — | — | 0.50 | 0.75 | — |
| 1984 | 390,000,000 | — | — | 0.50 | 0.75 | — |

**10 CRUZEIROS** KM# 592.2 **Composition:** Stainless Steel **Note:** Reduced weight.

| Date | Mintage | F | VF | XF | Unc | BU |
|---|---|---|---|---|---|---|
| 1985 | 201,000,000 | — | — | 0.50 | 0.75 | — |
| 1986 | — | — | — | 0.50 | 0.75 | — |

**20 CRUZEIROS** KM# 583 **Weight:** 18.0000 g. **Composition:** 0.9000 Silver .5208 oz. ASW **Subject:** 150th Anniversary of Independence

| Date | Mintage | F | VF | XF | Unc | BU |
|---|---|---|---|---|---|---|
| 1972 A | 250,000 | — | BV | 6.00 | 10.00 | — |

**20 CRUZEIROS** KM# 593.1 **Composition:** Stainless Steel **Subject:** Francis of Assisi Church

| Date | Mintage | F | VF | XF | Unc | BU |
|---|---|---|---|---|---|---|
| 1981 | 88,297,000 | — | — | 0.25 | 0.85 | — |
| 1982 | 158,200,000 | — | — | 0.20 | 0.65 | — |
| 1983 | 312,000,000 | — | — | 0.20 | 0.65 | — |
| 1984 | 226,000,000 | — | — | 0.20 | 0.65 | — |

**20 CRUZEIROS** KM# 593.2 **Composition:** Stainless Steel **Note:** Reduced weight.

| Date | Mintage | F | VF | XF | Unc | BU |
|---|---|---|---|---|---|---|
| 1985 | 205,000,000 | — | — | 0.20 | 0.65 | — |
| 1986 | — | — | — | 0.20 | 0.65 | — |

**50 CRUZEIROS** KM# 594.1 **Composition:** Stainless Steel

| Date | Mintage | F | VF | XF | Unc | BU |
|---|---|---|---|---|---|---|
| 1981 | 57,000,000 | — | — | 0.35 | 1.00 | — |
| 1982 | 134,000,000 | — | — | 0.20 | 0.65 | — |
| 1983 | 181,800,000 | — | — | 0.20 | 0.65 | — |
| 1984 | 292,418,000 | — | — | 0.20 | 0.65 | — |

**50 CRUZEIROS** KM# 594.2 **Composition:** Stainless Steel **Note:** Reduced weight.

| Date | Mintage | F | VF | XF | Unc | BU |
|---|---|---|---|---|---|---|
| 1985 | 180,000,000 | — | — | 0.20 | 0.65 | — |
| 1986 | — | — | — | 0.20 | 0.65 | — |

**100 CRUZEIROS** KM# 595 **Composition:** Stainless Steel

| Date | Mintage | F | VF | XF | Unc | BU |
|---|---|---|---|---|---|---|
| 1985 | 162,000,000 | — | — | 0.20 | 0.40 | — |
| 1986 | — | — | — | — | 0.35 | — |

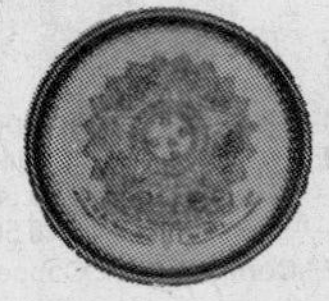

**200 CRUZEIROS** KM# 596 **Composition:** Stainless Steel

| Date | Mintage | F | VF | XF | Unc | BU |
|---|---|---|---|---|---|---|
| 1985 | 55,000,000 | — | — | 0.25 | 0.50 | — |
| 1986 | — | — | — | — | 0.40 | — |

**300 CRUZEIROS** KM# 584 **Weight:** 16.6500 g. **Composition:** 0.9200 Gold .4925 oz. AGW **Subject:** 150th Anniversary of Independence

| Date | Mintage | F | VF | XF | Unc | BU |
|---|---|---|---|---|---|---|
| 1972 A | 30,000 | — | — | — | 300 | — |

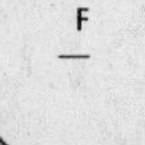

**500 CRUZEIROS** KM# 597 **Composition:** Stainless Steel

| Date | Mintage | F | VF | XF | Unc | BU |
|---|---|---|---|---|---|---|
| 1985 | 74,000,000 | — | — | 0.35 | 1.00 | — |
| 1986 | — | — | — | — | 0.65 | — |

## REFORM COINAGE

1000 Cruzeiros Novos = 1 Cruzado; 100 Centavos = 1 Cruzado; 1986-1989

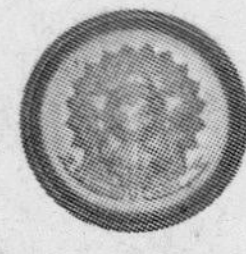

**CENTAVO** KM# 600 **Composition:** Stainless Steel

| Date | Mintage | F | VF | XF | Unc | BU |
|---|---|---|---|---|---|---|
| 1986 | 100,000,000 | — | — | — | 0.15 | — |
| 1987 | 1,000,000 | — | — | — | 0.20 | — |
| 1988 | 1,000,000 | — | — | — | 0.20 | — |

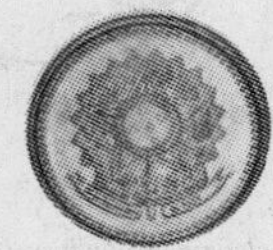

**5 CENTAVOS** KM# 601 **Composition:** Stainless Steel

| Date | Mintage | F | VF | XF | Unc | BU |
|---|---|---|---|---|---|---|
| 1986 | 99,282,000 | — | — | — | 0.15 | — |
| 1987 | 1,000,000 | — | — | — | 0.20 | — |
| 1988 | 1,000,000 | — | — | — | 0.20 | — |

**10 CENTAVOS** KM# 602 **Composition:** Stainless Steel

| Date | Mintage | F | VF | XF | Unc | BU |
|---|---|---|---|---|---|---|
| 1986 | 200,000,000 | — | — | — | 0.15 | — |
| 1987 | 245,628,000 | — | — | — | 0.15 | — |
| 1988 | 21,293,000 | — | — | — | 0.20 | — |

**20 CENTAVOS** KM# 603 **Composition:** Stainless Steel

| Date | Mintage | F | VF | XF | Unc | BU |
|---|---|---|---|---|---|---|
| 1986 | 140,000,000 | — | — | — | 0.20 | — |
| 1987 | 157,500,000 | — | — | — | 0.20 | — |
| 1988 | 16,000,000 | — | — | — | 0.25 | — |

**50 CENTAVOS** KM# 604 **Composition:** Stainless Steel

| Date | Mintage | F | VF | XF | Unc | BU |
|---|---|---|---|---|---|---|
| 1986 | 200,000,000 | — | — | — | 0.35 | — |
| 1987 | 201,884,000 | — | — | — | 0.35 | — |
| 1988 | 131,255,000 | — | — | — | 0.35 | — |

**CRUZADO** KM# 605 **Composition:** Stainless Steel

| Date | Mintage | F | VF | XF | Unc | BU |
|---|---|---|---|---|---|---|
| 1986 | — | — | — | — | 1.00 | — |
| 1987 | 383,087,000 | — | — | — | 0.45 | — |
| 1988 | 321,216,000 | — | — | — | 0.45 | — |

**5 CRUZADOS** KM# 606 **Composition:** Stainless Steel

| Date | Mintage | F | VF | XF | Unc | BU |
|---|---|---|---|---|---|---|
| 1986 | — | — | — | — | 1.50 | — |
| 1987 | 141,000,000 | — | — | — | 0.65 | — |
| 1988 | 291,906,000 | — | — | — | 0.65 | — |

**10 CRUZADOS** KM# 607 **Composition:** Stainless Steel

| Date | Mintage | F | VF | XF | Unc | BU |
|---|---|---|---|---|---|---|
| 1987 | 131,500,000 | — | — | — | 1.75 | — |
| 1988 | 457,977,000 | — | — | — | 0.85 | — |

**100 CRUZADOS** **KM# 608** **Composition:** Stainless Steel **Subject:** Abolition of Slavery Centennial - Male

| Date | Mintage | F | VF | XF | Unc | BU |
|---|---|---|---|---|---|---|
| ND | 200,000 | — | — | 1.00 | 3.00 | — |

**100 CRUZADOS** **KM# 609** **Composition:** Stainless Steel **Subject:** Abolition of Slavery Centennial - Female

| Date | Mintage | F | VF | XF | Unc | BU |
|---|---|---|---|---|---|---|
| ND | 200,000 | — | — | 1.00 | 3.00 | — |

**100 CRUZADOS** **KM# 610** **Composition:** Stainless Steel **Subject:** Abolition of Slavery Centennial - Child

| Date | Mintage | F | VF | XF | Unc | BU |
|---|---|---|---|---|---|---|
| ND | 200,000 | — | — | 1.00 | 3.00 | — |

## REFORM COINAGE

1000 Old Cruzados = 1 Novo Cruzado; 1989-1990

**CENTAVO** **KM# 611** **Composition:** Stainless Steel

| Date | Mintage | F | VF | XF | Unc | BU |
|---|---|---|---|---|---|---|
| 1989 | — | — | — | — | 0.35 | — |
| 1990 | — | — | — | — | 0.35 | — |

**5 CENTAVOS** **KM# 612** **Composition:** Stainless Steel

| Date | Mintage | F | VF | XF | Unc | BU |
|---|---|---|---|---|---|---|
| 1989 | — | — | — | — | 0.45 | — |
| 1990 | — | — | — | — | 0.45 | — |
| 1991 | — | — | — | — | 0.45 | — |
| 1992 | — | — | — | — | 0.45 | — |

**10 CENTAVOS** **KM# 613** **Composition:** Stainless Steel

| Date | Mintage | F | VF | XF | Unc | BU |
|---|---|---|---|---|---|---|
| 1989 | — | — | — | — | 0.60 | — |
| 1990 | — | — | — | — | 0.60 | — |
| 1991 | — | — | — | — | 0.60 | — |

| Date | Mintage | F | VF | XF | Unc | BU |
|---|---|---|---|---|---|---|
| 1992 | — | — | — | — | 0.60 | — |
| 1993 | — | — | — | — | 0.60 | — |

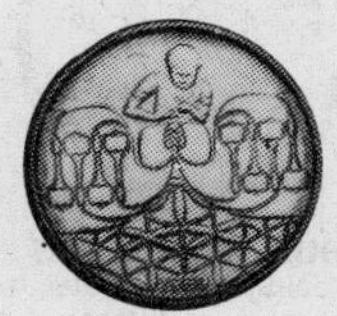

**50 CENTAVOS** **KM# 614** **Composition:** Stainless Steel

| Date | Mintage | F | VF | XF | Unc | BU |
|---|---|---|---|---|---|---|
| 1989 | — | — | — | — | 1.25 | — |
| 1990 | — | — | — | — | 1.25 | — |
| 1991 | — | — | — | — | 1.25 | — |
| 1992 | — | — | — | — | 1.25 | — |

**NOVO CRUZADO** **KM# 615** **Composition:** Stainless Steel **Subject:** Centennial of the Republic

| Date | Mintage | F | VF | XF | Unc | BU |
|---|---|---|---|---|---|---|
| ND | — | — | — | — | 2.00 | — |

**200 NOVOS CRUZADOS** **KM# 616** **Weight:** 13.4700 g. **Composition:** 0.9990 Silver .4331 oz. ASW **Subject:** Centennial of the Republic

| Date | Mintage | F | VF | XF | Unc | BU |
|---|---|---|---|---|---|---|
| ND Proof | 30,000 | Value: 35.00 | | | | |

## REFORM COINAGE

100 Centavos = 1 Cruzeiro; 1 Novo Cruzado = 1 Cruzeiro; 1990-1993

**CRUZEIRO** **KM# 617** **Composition:** Stainless Steel

| Date | Mintage | F | VF | XF | Unc | BU |
|---|---|---|---|---|---|---|
| 1990 | — | — | — | — | 0.35 | — |

**5 CRUZEIROS** **KM# 618.1** **Composition:** Stainless Steel

| Date | Mintage | F | VF | XF | Unc | BU |
|---|---|---|---|---|---|---|
| 1990 | — | — | — | — | 0.45 | — |

**5 CRUZEIROS** **KM# 618.2** **Composition:** Stainless Steel **Note:** Thinner planchet.

| Date | Mintage | F | VF | XF | Unc | BU |
|---|---|---|---|---|---|---|
| 1991 | — | — | — | — | 0.45 | — |
| 1992 | — | — | — | — | 0.45 | — |

**10 CRUZEIROS** **KM# 619.1** **Composition:** Stainless Steel

| Date | Mintage | F | VF | XF | Unc | BU |
|---|---|---|---|---|---|---|
| 1990 | — | — | — | — | 0.50 | — |

**10 CRUZEIROS** **KM# 619.2** **Composition:** Stainless Steel **Note:** Thinner planchet.

| Date | Mintage | F | VF | XF | Unc | BU |
|---|---|---|---|---|---|---|
| 1991 | — | — | — | — | 0.50 | — |
| 1992 | — | — | — | — | 0.50 | — |

**50 CRUZEIROS** **KM# 620.1** **Composition:** Stainless Steel

| Date | Mintage | F | VF | XF | Unc | BU |
|---|---|---|---|---|---|---|
| 1990 | — | — | — | — | 0.65 | — |

**50 CRUZEIROS** **KM# 620.2** **Composition:** Stainless Steel **Note:** Thinner planchet.

| Date | Mintage | F | VF | XF | Unc | BU |
|---|---|---|---|---|---|---|
| 1991 | — | — | — | — | 0.60 | — |
| 1992 | — | — | — | — | 0.60 | — |

**100 CRUZEIROS** **KM# 623** **Composition:** Stainless Steel **Subject:** Manatee

| Date | Mintage | F | VF | XF | Unc | BU |
|---|---|---|---|---|---|---|
| 1992 | — | — | — | — | 0.65 | — |
| 1993 | — | — | — | — | 0.65 | — |

**500 CRUZEIROS** **KM# 621** **Weight:** 27.0000 g. **Composition:** 0.9250 Silver .8029 oz. ASW **Subject:** Ibero - American Series

| Date | Mintage | F | VF | XF | Unc | BU |
|---|---|---|---|---|---|---|
| 1991 Proof | 70,000 | Value: 55.00 | | | | |

**500 CRUZEIROS** **KM# 624** **Composition:** Stainless Steel **Subject:** Loggerhead Sea Turtle

| Date | Mintage | F | VF | XF | Unc | BU |
|---|---|---|---|---|---|---|
| 1992 | — | — | — | — | 0.75 | — |
| 1993 | — | — | — | — | 0.75 | — |

**1000 CRUZEIROS** **KM# 626** **Composition:** Stainless Steel **Subject:** Fish - Acara

| Date | Mintage | F | VF | XF | Unc | BU |
|---|---|---|---|---|---|---|
| 1992 | — | — | — | — | 0.85 | — |
| 1993 | — | — | — | — | 0.85 | — |

**2000 CRUZEIROS** **KM# 622** **Weight:** 28.2000 g. **Composition:** 0.9250 Silver .7977 oz. ASW **Subject:** U.N. Conference on Environment and Development - Hummingbird and Flower

| Date | Mintage | F | VF | XF | Unc | BU |
|---|---|---|---|---|---|---|
| 1992 Proof | 50,000 | Value: 50.00 | | | | |

**5000 CRUZEIROS** **KM# 625** **Composition:** Stainless Steel **Subject:** 200th Anniversary of Tiradentes' Death

| Date | Mintage | F | VF | XF | Unc | BU |
|---|---|---|---|---|---|---|
| ND | — | — | — | — | 2.50 | — |

## REFORM COINAGE

1000 Cruzeiros = 1 Cruzeiro Real; 1993 - June 30, 1994

**5 CRUZEIROS REAIS** **KM# 627** **Composition:** Stainless Steel **Subject:** Macaw Parrots - Arara

| Date | Mintage | F | VF | XF | Unc | BU |
|---|---|---|---|---|---|---|
| 1993 | — | — | — | — | 0.60 | — |
| 1994 | — | — | — | — | 0.60 | — |

**10 CRUZEIROS REAL** **KM# 628** **Composition:** Stainless Steel **Subject:** Anteater - Tamandua

| Date | Mintage | F | VF | XF | Unc | BU |
|---|---|---|---|---|---|---|
| 1993 | — | — | — | — | 0.75 | — |
| 1994 | — | — | — | — | 0.75 | — |

**50 CRUZEIROS REAIS** **KM# 629** **Composition:** Stainless Steel **Subject:** Mother Jaguar and Cub

| Date | Mintage | F | VF | XF | Unc | BU |
|---|---|---|---|---|---|---|
| 1993 | — | — | — | — | 0.85 | — |
| 1994 | — | — | — | — | 0.85 | — |

**100 CRUZEIROS REAIS** **KM# 630** **Composition:** Stainless Steel **Subject:** Maned Wolf

| Date | Mintage | F | VF | XF | Unc | BU |
|---|---|---|---|---|---|---|
| 1993 | — | — | — | — | 1.50 | — |
| 1994 | — | — | — | — | 1.50 | — |

## REFORM COINAGE

2750 Cruzeiros Reals = 1 Real; 100 Centavos = 1 Real; July 1, 1994 --

**CENTAVO** **KM# 631** **Composition:** Stainless Steel

| Date | Mintage | F | VF | XF | Unc | BU |
|---|---|---|---|---|---|---|
| 1994 | — | — | — | — | 0.35 | — |
| 1995 | — | — | — | — | 0.35 | — |
| 1996 | — | — | — | — | 0.35 | — |
| 1997 | — | — | — | — | 0.35 | — |

**CENTAVO** **KM# 647** **Composition:** Copper Plated Steel **Subject:** Cabra; **Obverse:** Cabral's portrait **Reverse:** Denomination

| Date | Mintage | F | VF | XF | Unc | BU |
|---|---|---|---|---|---|---|
| 1998 | — | — | — | — | 0.35 | — |
| 1999 | — | — | — | — | 0.10 | — |
| 2000 | — | — | — | — | 0.10 | — |

**5 CENTAVOS** **KM# 632** **Composition:** Stainless Steel

| Date | Mintage | F | VF | XF | Unc | BU |
|---|---|---|---|---|---|---|
| 1994 | — | — | — | — | 0.45 | — |
| 1995 | — | — | — | — | 0.45 | — |
| 1996 | — | — | — | — | 0.45 | — |
| 1997 | — | — | — | — | 0.45 | — |

**5 CENTAVOS** **KM# 648** **Composition:** Copper Plated Steel **Subject:** Tiradentes **Obverse:** Tiradente's portrait **Reverse:** Denomination

| Date | Mintage | F | VF | XF | Unc | BU |
|---|---|---|---|---|---|---|
| 1998 | — | — | — | — | 0.45 | — |
| 1999 | — | — | — | — | 0.45 | — |
| 2000 | — | — | — | — | 0.45 | — |

**10 CENTAVOS** **KM# 633** **Composition:** Stainless Steel

| Date | Mintage | F | VF | XF | Unc | BU |
|---|---|---|---|---|---|---|
| 1994 | — | — | — | — | 0.60 | — |
| 1995 | — | — | — | — | 0.60 | — |
| 1996 | — | — | — | — | 0.60 | — |
| 1997 | — | — | — | — | 0.60 | — |

**10 CENTAVOS** **KM# 641** **Composition:** Stainless Steel **Series:** F.A.O. **Subject:** Seedling in Hand

| Date | Mintage | F | VF | XF | Unc | BU |
|---|---|---|---|---|---|---|
| 1995 | 10,000,000 | — | — | — | 0.65 | — |

**10 CENTAVOS** **KM# 649.1** **Composition:** Brass Plated Steel **Subject:** Pedro I **Obverse:** Bust of Pedro, Horseman with sword in left hand **Reverse:** Denomination **Note:** Majority of mintage recalled and melted.

| Date | Mintage | F | VF | XF | Unc | BU |
|---|---|---|---|---|---|---|
| 1997 | — | — | — | — | — | — |
| 1998 | — | — | — | — | — | — |

**10 CENTAVOS** **KM# 649.2** **Composition:** Brass Plated Steel **Obverse:** Bust of Pedro, Horseman with sword in right hand

| Date | Mintage | F | VF | XF | Unc | BU |
|---|---|---|---|---|---|---|
| 1998 | — | — | — | — | 0.60 | — |
| 1999 | — | — | — | — | 0.60 | — |
| 2000 | — | — | — | — | 0.60 | — |

**25 CENTAVOS** **KM# 634** **Composition:** Stainless Steel

| Date | Mintage | F | VF | XF | Unc | BU |
|---|---|---|---|---|---|---|
| 1994 | — | — | — | — | 0.75 | — |
| 1995 | — | — | — | — | 0.75 | — |

**25 CENTAVOS** **KM# 642** **Composition:** Stainless Steel **Series:** F.A.O **Subject:** Farmer Working

| Date | Mintage | F | VF | XF | Unc | BU |
|---|---|---|---|---|---|---|
| 1995 | 10,000,000 | — | — | — | 0.80 | — |

**25 CENTAVOS** **KM# 650** **Composition:** Brass Plated Steel **Series:** F **Subject:** Deodoro **Obverse:** Deodoro's portrait and national emblem **Reverse:** Denomination

| Date | Mintage | F | VF | XF | Unc | BU |
|---|---|---|---|---|---|---|
| 1998 | — | — | — | — | 0.75 | — |
| 1999 | — | — | — | — | 0.75 | — |
| 2000 | — | — | — | — | 0.75 | — |

**50 CENTAVOS** **KM# 635** **Composition:** Stainless Steel **Series:** F

| Date | Mintage | F | VF | XF | Unc | BU |
|---|---|---|---|---|---|---|
| 1994 | — | — | — | — | 1.25 | — |
| 1995 | — | — | — | — | 1.25 | — |

**50 CENTAVOS** **KM# 651** **Composition:** Copper-Nickel **Series:** F **Subject:** Rio Branco **Obverse:** Rio Branco's portrait **Reverse:** Denomination

| Date | Mintage | F | VF | XF | Unc | BU |
|---|---|---|---|---|---|---|
| 1998 | — | — | — | — | 1.25 | — |
| 1999 | — | — | — | — | 1.25 | — |
| 2000 | — | — | — | — | 1.25 | — |

**REAL** **KM# 636** **Composition:** Stainless Steel **Series:** F

| Date | Mintage | F | VF | XF | Unc | BU |
|---|---|---|---|---|---|---|
| 1994 | — | — | — | — | 2.50 | — |
| 1997 | — | — | — | — | 2.50 | — |

**REAL** **KM# 652** **Ring Composition:** Brass **Center Composition:** Copper-Nickel **Series:** F **Obverse:** Allegorical portrait **Reverse:** Denomination

| Date | Mintage | F | VF | XF | Unc | BU |
|---|---|---|---|---|---|---|
| 1998 | — | — | — | — | 2.65 | — |
| 1999 | — | — | — | — | 2.65 | — |
| 2000 | — | — | — | — | 2.65 | — |

**REAL** **KM# 653** **Center Composition:** Copper-Nickel **Series:** F **Subject:** Universal Declaration of Human Rights **Obverse:** Globe **Reverse:** Denomination

| Date | Mintage | F | VF | XF | Unc | BU |
|---|---|---|---|---|---|---|
| 1998 | — | — | — | — | 2.75 | — |

**2 REAIS** **KM# 637** **Weight:** 27.0000 g. **Composition:** 0.9250 Silver .8029 oz. ASW **Series:** F **Subject:** 300th Anniversary - First Brazilian Mint

| Date | Mintage | F | VF | XF | Unc | BU |
|---|---|---|---|---|---|---|
| 1994 Proof | 10,000 | Value: 65.00 | | | | |

**2 REAIS** **KM# 643** **Weight:** 27.0000 g. **Composition:** 0.9250 Silver .8029 oz. ASW **Series:** F **Subject:** Ayrton Senna - Race Driver

| Date | Mintage | F | VF | XF | Unc | BU |
|---|---|---|---|---|---|---|
| 1995 Proof | 10,000 | Value: 75.00 | | | | |

**3 REAIS** **KM# 640** **Weight:** 11.5000 g. **Composition:** 0.9250 Silver .3420 oz. ASW **Series:** F **Subject:** 30th Anniversary - Central Bank

| Date | Mintage | F | VF | XF | Unc | BU |
|---|---|---|---|---|---|---|
| ND Proof | Est. 10,000 | Value: 40.00 | | | | |

**3 REAIS** **KM# 645** **Weight:** 11.5000 g. **Composition:** 0.9250 Silver .3420 oz. ASW **Series:** F **Subject:** Centennial of Belo Horizonte **Obverse:** Denomination **Reverse:** Collage, name, dates

| Date | Mintage | F | VF | XF | Unc | BU |
|---|---|---|---|---|---|---|
| 1997 Proof | Est. 20,000 | Value: 40.00 | | | | |

**4 REAIS** **KM# 638** **Weight:** 27.0000 g. **Composition:** 0.9250 Silver .8030 oz. ASW **Series:** F **Subject:** World Cup Soccer

| Date | Mintage | F | VF | XF | Unc | BU |
|---|---|---|---|---|---|---|
| 1994 Proof | Est. 10,000 | Value: 75.00 | | | | |

**5 REAIS** **KM# 654** **Weight:** 28.0000 g. **Composition:** 0.9990 Silver .8993 oz. ASW **Subject:** 500 Years - Discovery of Brazil **Obverse:** Partial compass face and feathers. **Reverse:** Indian at left, ship at right, partial compass face and feathers at lower right. **Edge:** Reeded. **Size:** 40 mm.

| Date | Mintage | F | VF | XF | Unc | BU |
|---|---|---|---|---|---|---|
| ND(2000) Proof | — | Value: 65.00 | | | | |

**20 REAIS** **KM# 639** **Weight:** 8.0000 g. **Composition:** 0.9000 Gold .2315 oz. AGW **Series:** F **Subject:** World CUp Soccer **Obverse:** Hand held trophy **Reverse:** Denomination in net. Similar to 4 Reais, KM#638

| Date | Mintage | F | VF | XF | Unc | BU |
|---|---|---|---|---|---|---|
| 1994 Proof | Est. 2,000 | Value: 245 | | | | |

**20 REAIS** **KM# 644** **Weight:** 8.0000 g. **Composition:** 0.9000 Gold .2315 oz. AGW **Series:** F **Subject:** Ayrton Senna - Race Driver

| Date | Mintage | F | VF | XF | Unc | BU |
|---|---|---|---|---|---|---|
| 1995 Proof | 5,000 | Value: 245 | | | | |

**20 REAIS** **KM# 655** **Weight:** 8.0000 g. **Composition:** 0.9000 Gold .2315 oz. AGW **Subject:** 500 Years - Discovery of Brazil **Obverse:** Partial compass face and feathers at right, anniversary dates at left. **Reverse:** Ornamented map. **Edge:** Reeded. **Size:** 22 mm.

| Date | Mintage | F | VF | XF | Unc | BU |
|---|---|---|---|---|---|---|
| ND(2000) Proof | — | Value: 245 | | | | |

## LEPROSARIUM COINAGE

**100 REIS** **KM# L1** **Composition:** Brass **Issuer:** Colonia Santa Teresa

| Date | Mintage | F | VF | XF | Unc | BU |
|---|---|---|---|---|---|---|
| ND(ca.1940) Rare | — | 175 | 250 | 400 | — | — |

**200 REIS** **KM# L2** **Composition:** Brass **Issuer:** Colonia Santa Teresa

| Date | Mintage | F | VF | XF | Unc | BU |
|---|---|---|---|---|---|---|
| ND(ca.1940) | — | 200 | 300 | 500 | — | — |

**300 REIS** **KM# L3** **Composition:** Brass **Issuer:** Colonia Santa Teresa

| Date | Mintage | F | VF | XF | Unc | BU |
|---|---|---|---|---|---|---|
| ND(ca.1940) Rare | — | 250 | 350 | 550 | — | — |

**500 REIS** **KM# L4** **Composition:** Brass **Issuer:** Colonia Santa Teresa

| Date | Mintage | F | VF | XF | Unc | BU |
|---|---|---|---|---|---|---|
| ND(ca.1940) Rare | — | 300 | 400 | 600 | — | — |

**1000 REIS** **KM# L5** **Composition:** Brass **Issuer:** Colonia Santa Teresa

| Date | Mintage | F | VF | XF | Unc | BU |
|---|---|---|---|---|---|---|
| ND(ca.1940) Rare | — | 350 | 500 | 700 | — | — |

**1.00 REIS** **KM# L6** **Composition:** Brass **Issuer:** Santa Casa de Misericordia

| Date | Mintage | F | VF | XF | Unc | BU |
|---|---|---|---|---|---|---|
| ND(ca.1920) Rare | — | — | — | — | — | — |

**2.00 REIS** **KM# L7** **Composition:** Brass **Issuer:** Santa Casa de Misericordia

| Date | Mintage | F | VF | XF | Unc | BU |
|---|---|---|---|---|---|---|
| ND(ca.1920) | — | — | 250 | 450 | — | — |

**5.00 REIS** **KM# L8** **Composition:** Brass **Issuer:** Santa Casa de Misericordia

| Date | Mintage | F | VF | XF | Unc | BU |
|---|---|---|---|---|---|---|
| ND(ca.1920) Rare | — | — | — | — | — | — |

**1.000 REIS** **KM# L9** **Composition:** Brass **Issuer:** Santa Casa de Misericordia

| Date | Mintage | F | VF | XF | Unc | BU |
|---|---|---|---|---|---|---|
| ND(ca.1920) Rare | — | — | — | — | — | — |

**5.000 REIS** **KM# L10** **Composition:** Brass **Issuer:** Santa Casa de Misericordia

| Date | Mintage | F | VF | XF | Unc | BU |
|---|---|---|---|---|---|---|
| ND(ca.1920) Rare | — | — | — | — | — | — |

## COUNTERMARKED COINAGE

1932 Revolution - Private Issues

## PATTERNS

Including off metal strikes

| KM# | Date | Mintage | Identification | Mkt Val |
|---|---|---|---|---|
| Pn179 | 1901 | — | 100 Reis. Nickel-Silver. | 185 |
| Pn180 | 1901 | — | 100 Reis. Nickel. Birmingham Mint | 185 |
| Pn181 | 1901 | — | 100 Reis. Nickel. Hamburg Mint | 185 |
| Pn182 | 1901 | — | 100 Reis. Silver. | 285 |
| Pn183 | 1901 | — | 100 Reis. Gold. | 1,150 |
| Pn184 | 1901 | — | 200 Reis. Nickel-Silver. | 235 |
| Pn185 | 1901 | — | 200 Reis. Nickel. Birmingham Mint | 235 |
| Pn186 | 1901 | — | 200 Reis. Nickel. Hamburg Mint | 235 |
| Pn187 | 1901 | — | 200 Reis. Silver. | 285 |
| Pn188 | 1901 | — | 200 Reis. Gold. | 1,900 |
| Pn189 | 1901 | — | 400 Reis. Nickel-Silver. | 235 |
| Pn190 | 1901 | — | 400 Reis. Nickel. Birmingham Mint | 235 |
| Pn192 | 1901 | — | 400 Reis. Silver. | 575 |
| Pn193 | 1901 | — | 400 Reis. Gold. | 2,850 |
| Pn191 | 1901 | — | 400 Reis. Nickel. Hamburg Mint | 235 |
| Pn194 | 1902 | — | 100 Reis. Nickel. MCMI. 1902. | 375 |
| Pn195 | 1907 | — | 100 Reis. Silver. | 375 |
| Pn196 | 1907 | — | 200 Reis. Silver. | 575 |
| Pn197 | 1907 | — | 500 Reis. Silver. | 375 |
| Pn198 | 1907 | — | 1000 Reis. Silver. | 375 |
| Pn199 | 1907 | — | 2000 Reis. Silver. | 375 |
| Pn200 | 1908 | — | 50 Reis. Silver. | 375 |
| Pn201 | 1908 | — | 500 Reis. Silver. | 375 |
| Pn202 | 1908 | — | 1000 Reis. Silver. | 375 |
| Pn203 | 1908 | — | 2000 Reis. Silver. | 375 |
| Pn204 | 1910 | — | 40 Reis. Silver. | 375 |
| Pn205 | 1910 | — | 1000 Reis. Silver. | 375 |
| Pn206 | 1910 | — | 2000 Reis. Silver. | 425 |
| Pn207 | 1912 | — | 2000 Reis. Copper. | 325 |
| Pn208 | 1913 | — | 1000 Reis. Copper. | 325 |
| Pn209 | 1914 | — | 50 Reis. Silver. | 325 |

| KM# | Date | Mintage | Identification | Mkt Val |
|---|---|---|---|---|
| Pn210 | 1914 | — | 400 Reis. Nickel. | 325 |

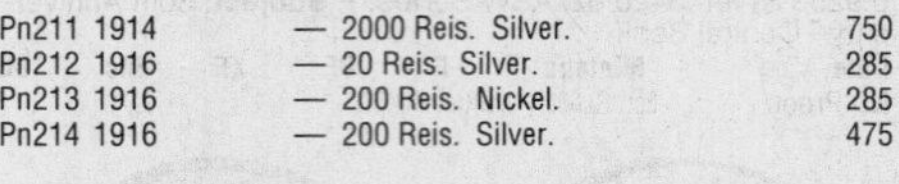

| KM# | Date | Mintage | Identification | Mkt Val |
|---|---|---|---|---|
| Pn211 | 1914 | — | 2000 Reis. Silver. | 750 |
| Pn212 | 1916 | — | 20 Reis. Silver. | 285 |
| Pn213 | 1916 | — | 200 Reis. Nickel. | 285 |
| Pn214 | 1916 | — | 200 Reis. Silver. | 475 |

| KM# | Date | Mintage | Identification | Mkt Val |
|---|---|---|---|---|
| Pn215 | 1916 | — | 2000 Reis. Silver. | 750 |
| Pn216 | 1917 | — | 50 Reis. Nickel. | 325 |
| Pn217 | 1917 | — | 100 Reis. Nickel. | 325 |

| KM# | Date | Mintage | Identification | Mkt Val |
|---|---|---|---|---|
| Pn218 | 1917 | — | 200 Reis. Nickel. | 325 |
| Pn219 | 1917 | — | 400 Reis. Nickel. | 325 |
| Pn220 | 1917 | — | 500 Reis. Nickel. | 375 |
| Pn221 | 1917 | — | 1000 Reis. Nickel. | 325 |
| Pn222 | 1917 | — | 2000 Reis. Nickel. | 325 |
| Pn223 | 1918 | — | 20 Reis. Nickel. | 235 |
| Pn224 | 1918 | — | 20 Reis. Nickel. Large planchet. | 185 |
| Pn225 | 1918 | — | 20 Reis. Silver. | 325 |
| Pn226 | 1918 | — | 2000 Reis. Nickel. Center hole. | 285 |
| Pn227 | 1921 | — | 1000 Reis. | 185 |
| Pn228 | 1921 | — | 2000 Reis. | 375 |
| Pn229 | 1921 | — | 10000 Reis. Gold. | 950 |
| Pn230 | 1921 | — | 20000 Reis. Gold. | 950 |
| Pn231 | 1922 | — | 50 Reis. Copper-Nickel. | 285 |
| Pn232 | 1922 | — | 50 Reis. Nickel-Silver. | 185 |
| Pn233 | 1922 | — | 500 Reis. Aluminum-Bronze. | 185 |
| Pn234 | 1922 | — | 500 Reis. Silver. Large planchet. | 185 |

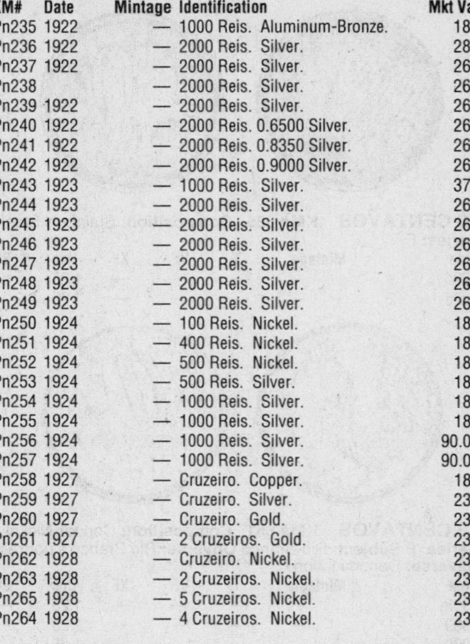

| KM# | Date | Mintage | Identification | Mkt Val |
|---|---|---|---|---|
| Pn235 | 1922 | — | 1000 Reis. Aluminum-Bronze. | 185 |
| Pn236 | 1922 | — | 2000 Reis. Silver. | 285 |
| Pn237 | 1922 | — | 2000 Reis. Silver. | 265 |
| Pn238 | | — | 2000 Reis. Silver. | 265 |
| Pn239 | 1922 | — | 2000 Reis. Silver. | 265 |
| Pn240 | 1922 | — | 2000 Reis. 0.6500 Silver. | 265 |
| Pn241 | 1922 | — | 2000 Reis. 0.8350 Silver. | 265 |
| Pn242 | 1922 | — | 2000 Reis. 0.9000 Silver. | 265 |
| Pn243 | 1923 | — | 1000 Reis. Silver. | 375 |
| Pn244 | 1923 | — | 2000 Reis. Silver. | 265 |
| Pn245 | 1923 | — | 2000 Reis. Silver. | 265 |
| Pn246 | 1923 | — | 2000 Reis. Silver. | 265 |
| Pn247 | 1923 | — | 2000 Reis. Silver. | 265 |
| Pn248 | 1923 | — | 2000 Reis. Silver. | 265 |
| Pn249 | 1923 | — | 2000 Reis. Silver. | 265 |
| Pn250 | 1924 | — | 100 Reis. Nickel. | 185 |
| Pn251 | 1924 | — | 400 Reis. Nickel. | 185 |
| Pn252 | 1924 | — | 500 Reis. Nickel. | 185 |
| Pn253 | 1924 | — | 500 Reis. Silver. | 185 |
| Pn254 | 1924 | — | 1000 Reis. Silver. | 185 |
| Pn255 | 1924 | — | 1000 Reis. Silver. | 185 |
| Pn256 | 1924 | — | 1000 Reis. Silver. | 90.00 |
| Pn257 | 1924 | — | 1000 Reis. Silver. | 90.00 |
| Pn258 | 1927 | — | Cruzeiro. Copper. | 185 |
| Pn259 | 1927 | — | Cruzeiro. Silver. | 235 |
| Pn260 | 1927 | — | Cruzeiro. Gold. | 235 |
| Pn261 | 1927 | — | 2 Cruzeiros. Gold. | 235 |
| Pn262 | 1928 | — | Cruzeiro. Nickel. | 235 |
| Pn263 | 1928 | — | 2 Cruzeiros. Nickel. | 235 |
| Pn265 | 1928 | — | 5 Cruzeiros. Nickel. | 235 |
| Pn264 | 1928 | — | 4 Cruzeiros. Nickel. | 235 |

| KM# | Date | Mintage | Identification | Mkt Val |
|---|---|---|---|---|
| Pn266 | 1928 | — | 10 Cruzeiros. Nickel. | 375 |
| Pn267 | 1931 | — | 10 Reis. Silver. | 185 |
| Pn268 | 1932 | — | 100 Reis. Nickel-Silver. St. Vincent. | 185 |
| Pn269 | 1932 | — | 100 Reis. Silver. St. Vincent. | 375 |
| Pn270 | 1932 | — | 200 Reis. Nickel-Silver. | 235 |
| Pn271 | 1932 | — | 200 Reis. Copper-Nickel. St. Vincent. | 235 |
| Pn272 | 1932 | — | 200 Reis. Silver. St. Vincent. | 235 |
| Pn273 | 1932 | — | 400 Reis. Nickel-Silver. | 265 |
| Pn274 | 1932 | — | 400 Reis. Silver. St. Vincent. | 265 |
| Pn275 | 1932 | — | 500 Reis. Copper. Large planchet. | 265 |
| Pn276 | 1932 | — | 1000 Reis. Copper. St. Vincent. | 285 |
| Pn277 | 1932 | — | 1000 Reis. Aluminum-Bronze. Arms. | 285 |
| Pn278 | 1932 | — | 1000 Reis. Silver. | 285 |
| Pn279 | 1932 | — | 1000 Reis. Silver. Large planchet. | 375 |
| Pn280 | 1932 | — | 2000 Reis. Silver. St. Vincent. | 265 |
| Pn281 | 1935 | — | 200 Reis. Nickel. Large planchet. | 185 |
| Pn282 | 1935 | — | 400 Reis. Silver. | 185 |
| Pn283 | 1935 | — | 500 Reis. Nickel. 3.8500 g. | 375 |
| Pn284 | 1935 | — | 500 Reis. Nickel-Silver. 6.0000 g. | 375 |
| Pn285 | 1935 | — | 1000 Reis. Copper. | 185 |
| Pn286 | 1935 | — | 1000 Reis. Nickel. | 185 |
| Pn287 | 1935 | — | 1000 Reis. Nickel-Silver. | 375 |
| Pn288 | 1935 | — | 1000 Reis. Silver. | 375 |
| Pn289 | 1935 | — | 2000 Reis. Zinc. | 285 |

| KM# | Date | Mintage | Identification | Mkt Val |
|---|---|---|---|---|
| Pn290 | 1935 | — | 2000 Reis. Bronze. | 265 |
| Pn291 | 1935 | — | 2000 Reis. Copper. | 265 |
| Pn292 | 1935 | — | 2000 Reis. Nickel-Silver. | 375 |
| Pn293 | 1935 | — | 2000 Reis. Silver. | 325 |
| Pn294 | 1936 | — | 100 Reis. Nickel-Silver. | 185 |
| Pn295 | 1936 | — | 100 Reis. Silver. | 325 |
| Pn296 | 1936 | — | 200 Reis. Nickel-Silver. | 90.00 |
| Pn297 | 1936 | — | 200 Reis. Silver. | 90.00 |
| Pn298 | 1936 | — | 300 Reis. Nickel-Silver. | 90.00 |
| Pn299 | 1936 | — | 400 Reis. Nickel-Silver. | 90.00 |
| Pn300 | 1936 | — | 400 Reis. Silver. | 90.00 |
| Pn301 | 1936 | — | 500 Reis. Nickel-Silver. | 90.00 |
| Pn302 | 1936 | — | 500 Reis. Silver. | 90.00 |
| Pn303 | 1936 | — | 1000 Reis. Nickel-Silver. | 90.00 |
| Pn304 | 1936 | — | 1000 Reis. Silver. | 90.00 |
| Pn305 | 1936 | — | 2000 Reis. Nickel-Silver. | 90.00 |
| Pn306 | 1936 | — | 5000 Reis. Zinc. | 90.00 |
| Pn307 | 1936 | — | 5000 Reis. Nickel-Silver. | 90.00 |
| Pn308 | 1936 | — | 5000 Reis. Silver. | 90.00 |

| KM# | Date | Mintage | Identification | Mkt Val |
|---|---|---|---|---|
| Pn309 | 1937 | — | 100 Reis. Nickel. | 90.00 |
| Pn310 | 1937 | — | 300 Reis. Nickel-Silver. | 90.00 |
| Pn311 | 1937 | — | 300 Reis. Nickel. | 90.00 |
| Pn312 | 1938 | — | 200 Reis. Nickel. | 90.00 |
| Pn313 | 1938 | — | 2000 Reis. Copper. | 90.00 |
| Pn314 | 1939 | — | 500 Reis. Nickel. | 90.00 |
| Pn315 | 1939 | — | 1000 Reis. | 90.00 |
| Pn316 | 1939 | — | 2000 Reis. Aluminum-Bronze. | 90.00 |
| Pn317 | 1939 | — | 2000 Reis. Aluminum-Bronze. Peixoto. | 90.00 |
| Pn318 | 1940 | — | 10 Centavos. Silver. | 90.00 |
| Pn319 | 1940 | — | 100 Reis. Copper-Nickel. | 90.00 |
| Pn320 | 1940 | — | 100 Reis. Nickel. | 90.00 |
| Pn321 | 1940 | — | 200 Reis. Copper-Nickel. | 90.00 |
| Pn322 | 1940 | — | 200 Reis. Nickel. | 90.00 |
| Pn323 | 1940 | — | 300 Reis. Copper-Nickel. | 90.00 |
| Pn324 | 1940 | — | 300 Reis. Nickel. | 90.00 |
| Pn325 | 1940 | — | 400 Reis. Copper-Nickel. | 90.00 |
| Pn326 | 1940 | — | 400 Reis. Nickel. | 90.00 |
| Pn327 | 1941 | — | 10 Centavos. Nickel. | 90.00 |
| Pn328 | 1941 | — | 10 Centavos. Nickel-Silver. | 90.00 |
| Pn329 | 1941 | — | 50 Centavos. Brass. | 90.00 |
| Pn330 | 1941 | — | 50 Centavos. Nickel. | 90.00 |
| Pn331 | 1941 | — | 50 Centavos. Nickel-Silver. | 90.00 |
| Pn332 | 1941 | — | 50 Centavos. Nickel-Silver. | 90.00 |
| Pn333 | 1941 | — | 50 Centavos. Silver. | 90.00 |
| Pn334 | 1941 | — | 50 Centavos. Silver. | 90.00 |
| Pn335 | 1941 | — | Cruzeiro. Nickel-Silver. | 90.00 |
| Pn336 | 1941 | — | 2 Cruzeiros. Nickel. | 90.00 |
| Pn337 | 1941 | — | 2 Cruzeiros. Nickel-Silver. | 45.00 |
| Pn338 | 1941 | — | 2 Cruzeiros. Silver. | 65.00 |
| Pn339 | 1942 | — | 100 Reis. Nickel. | 45.00 |
| Pn340 | 1942 | — | 200 Reis. Nickel. | 45.00 |
| Pn341 | 1942 | — | 300 Reis. Nickel. | 45.00 |
| Pn342 | 1942 | — | 400 Reis. Nickel. | 45.00 |
| Pn343 | 1942 | — | 2 Cruzeiros. Nickel. | 45.00 |
| Pn344 | 1942 | — | 2 Cruzeiros. Nickel-Silver. | 45.00 |
| Pn345 | 1943 | — | 10 Centavos. Nickel-Silver. | 45.00 |
| Pn346 | 1943 | — | 20 Centavos. Nickel-Silver. | 45.00 |
| Pn347 | 1943 | — | 20 Centavos. Silver. | 45.00 |
| Pn348 | 1943 | — | 50 Centavos. Nickel-Silver. | 45.00 |
| Pn349 | 1943 | — | Cruzeiro. Silver. | 45.00 |
| Pn350 | 1945 | — | 10 Centavos. Nickel-Silver. | 45.00 |
| Pn351 | 1945 | — | 10 Centavos. Silver. | 45.00 |
| Pn352 | 1945 | — | 50 Centavos. Nickel-Silver. | 45.00 |
| Pn353 | 1945 | — | 50 Centavos. Silver. | 45.00 |
| Pn354 | 1945 | — | Cruzeiro. Nickel. | 45.00 |
| Pn355 | 1945 | — | Cruzeiro. Nickel-Silver. | 45.00 |
| Pn356 | 1947 | — | 20 Centavos. Aluminum-Bronze. | 150 |
| Pn357 | 1947 | — | 50 Centavos. Aluminum-Bronze. | 150 |
| Pn358 | 1947 | — | 2 Cruzeiros. Aluminum-Bronze. | 90.00 |
| Pn360 | 1950 | — | Cruzeiro. Silver. | 55.00 |
| Pn361 | 1950 | — | Cruzeiro. Gold. | — |
| Pn362 | 1955 | — | 50 Centavos. Aluminum. | 45.00 |
| Pn363 | 1956 | — | 10 Centavos. Aluminum. Arms. | 45.00 |
| Pn364 | 1956 | — | 10 Centavos. Aluminum-Bronze. Arms. | 45.00 |
| Pn365 | 1956 | — | 10 Centavos. Aluminum-Bronze. Bonifacio. | 45.00 |
| Pn366 | 1956 | — | 20 Centavos. Aluminum-Bronze. | 45.00 |
| Pn367 | 1956 | — | 50 Centavos. Aluminum. | 45.00 |
| Pn368 | 1956 | — | Cruzeiro. Aluminum. | 45.00 |
| Pn369 | 1961 | — | 2 Cruzeiros. Aluminum-Bronze. | 90.00 |
| Pn370 | 1962 | — | 5 Cruzeiros. | 90.00 |
| Pn371 | 1963 | — | 5 Cruzeiros. Aluminum. Map. | 90.00 |
| Pn372 | 1963 | — | 5 Cruzeiros. Aluminum. Arms. | 90.00 |
| Pn373 | 1963 | — | 5 Cruzeiros. Aluminum-Bronze. Arms. | 90.00 |
| Pn374 | 1964 | — | 5 Cruzeiros. Aluminum. | 90.00 |
| Pn375 | 1964 | — | 10 Cruzeiros. Aluminum. | 90.00 |
| Pn376 | 1964 | — | 20 Cruzeiros. Aluminum. | 90.00 |
| Pn377 | 1964 | — | 50 Cruzeiros. Nickel. | 90.00 |
| Pn378 | 1964 | — | 100 Cruzeiros. Nickel. | 90.00 |
| Pn379 | 1964 | — | 200 Cruzeiros. Nickel. | 90.00 |
| Pn380 | 1965 | — | 5 Cruzeiros. Aluminum. Map. | 90.00 |
| Pn381 | 1965 | — | 5 Cruzeiros. Aluminum. Arms. | 90.00 |
| Pn382 | 1966 | — | Centavo. Stainless Steel. | 90.00 |
| Pn383 | 1966 | — | 2 Centavos. Stainless Steel. | 90.00 |
| Pn384 | 1966 | — | 5 Centavos. Stainless Steel. | 90.00 |
| Pn385 | 1966 | — | 5 Centavos. Nickel. | 90.00 |
| Pn386 | 1966 | — | 10 Centavos. Copper-Nickel. | 90.00 |
| Pn387 | 1966 | — | 20 Centavos. Copper-Nickel. | 90.00 |
| Pn388 | 1967 | — | 10 Centavos. Stainless Steel. | 90.00 |
| Pn389 | 1972 | — | 20 Cruzeiros. 0.9000 Silver. KM#583. | 90.00 |

## PROVAS

| KM# | Date | Mintage | Identification | Mkt Val |
|---|---|---|---|---|
| Pr1 | 1967 | — | Cruzeiro. Nickel. PROVA. | 45.00 |
| Pr2 | 1967 | — | Cruzeiro. Nickel. PROVA. | 45.00 |
| Pr3 | 1970 | — | 20 Centavos. Stainless Steel. KM#579.1. | 45.00 |
| Pr4 | 1970 | — | 50 Centavos. Stainless Steel. | 45.00 |
| Pr5 | 1972 | — | Cruzeiro. Nickel. Y#94. | 150 |
| Pr6 | 1972 | — | 20 Cruzeiros. Silver. KM#583. | 45.00 |
| Pr7 | 1972 | — | 300 Cruzeiros. Brass. KM#584. | 115 |
| Pr8 | 1972 | — | 300 Cruzeiros. Gold. KM#584. | 325 |
| Pr9 | 1974 | — | 10 Centavos. Stainless Steel. KM#578.1a. | 45.00 |
| Pr10 | 1974 | — | Cruzeiro. Nickel. KM#581. | 45.00 |
| Pr11 | 1975 | — | Centavo. Stainless Steel. KM#585. | 45.00 |
| Pr12 | 1975 | — | 2 Centavos. Stainless Steel. KM#586. | 45.00 |
| Pr13 | 1975 | — | 5 Centavos. Stainless Steel. KM#587.1. | 45.00 |
| Pr14 | 1975 | — | 10 Centavos. Stainless Steel. KM#578.1a. | 45.00 |
| Pr15 | 1975 | — | 50 Centavos. Stainless Steel. KM#580b. | 45.00 |
| Pr16 | 1975 | — | 10 Cruzeiros. Silver. KM#588. | 70.00 |
| Pr17 | 1976 | — | Centavo. Silver. KM#585. | 70.00 |
| Pr18 | 1976 | — | 2 Centavos. Stainless Steel. KM#586. | 28.00 |
| Pr19 | 1976 | — | 5 Centavos. Stainless Steel. KM#587.1. | 45.00 |
| Pr20 | 1980 | 5,000 | Centavo. Steel. KM#589. | 28.00 |
| Pr21 | 1980 | 5,000 | 10 Centavos. Steel. | 28.00 |
| Pr23 | 1980 | 5,000 | Cruzeiro. Steel. KM#590. | 28.00 |
| Pr22 | 1980 | 5,000 | 50 Centavos. Steel. | 28.00 |
| Pr24 | 1980 | 5,000 | 5 Cruzeiros. Steel. KM#591. | 28.00 |
| Pr25 | 1980 | 5,000 | 10 Cruzeiros. Steel. KM#592. | 28.00 |
| PrA26 | 1988 | — | 100 Cruzados. Stainless Steel. KM#608. | 45.00 |
| PrB26 | 1988 | — | 100 Cruzados. Stainless Steel. KM#609. | 45.00 |
| PrC26 | 1988 | — | 100 Cruzados. Stainless Steel. KM#610. | 45.00 |
| Pr26 | 1989 | — | Centavo. Steel. KM#611. | 38.00 |
| Pr27 | 1989 | — | 5 Centavos. Steel. KM#612. | 38.00 |
| Pr28 | 1989 | — | 10 Centavos. Steel. KM#613. | 42.00 |
| Pr29 | 1989 | — | 50 Centavos. Steel. KM#614. | 45.00 |
| Pr30 | | — | 200 Novos Cruzados. 0.9990 Silver. KM#616. | 90.00 |
| Pr31 | 1990 | — | Cruzeiro. Steel. KM#617. | 38.00 |
| Pr32 | 1990 | — | 5 Cruzeiros. Steel. KM#618. | 38.00 |
| Pr33 | 1990 | — | 10 Cruzeiros. Steel. KM#619. | 42.00 |
| Pr34 | 1990 | — | 50 Cruzeiros. Steel. KM#620. | 45.00 |
| Pr35 | 1991 | — | 500 Cruzeiros. 0.9250 Silver. KM#621. | 90.00 |

| KM# | Date | Mintage | Identification | Mkt Val |
|---|---|---|---|---|
| Pr36 | 1992 | — | 2000 Cruzeiros. Silver. KM#622. | 140 |

| KM# | Date | Mintage | Identification | Mkt Val |
|---|---|---|---|---|
| Pr37 | | — | 5000 Cruzeiros. Steel. KM#625. | 80.00 |

| KM# | Date | Mintage | Identification | Mkt Val |
|---|---|---|---|---|
| Pr38 | 1994 | — | 4 Reais. 0.9250 Silver. KM#638. | 155 |

## TRIAL STRIKES

| KM# | Date | Mintage | Identification | Mkt Val |
|---|---|---|---|---|
| TS4 | 1948 | — | 1000 Cruzeiros. Uniface. | 750 |

## MINT SETS

| KM# | Date | Mintage | Identification | Issue Price | Mkt Val |
|---|---|---|---|---|---|
| MS1 | 1972 (2) | — | KM#582-583 | — | 12.50 |

This area, site of the ancient Mayan civilization, was sighted by Columbus in 1502, and settled by shipwrecked English seamen in 1638. British buccaneers settled the former capital of Belize in the 17th century. Britain claimed administrative right over the area after the emancipation of Central America from Spain. In 1825, Imperial coins were introduced into the colony and were rated against the Spanish dollar and Honduran currency. It was declared a colony subordinate to Jamaica in 1862 and was established as the separate Crown Colony of British Honduras in 1884. In May, 1885 an order in Council authorized coins for the colony, with the first shipment arriving in July. While the Guatemalan peso was originally the standard of value, in 1894 the colony changed to the gold standard, based on the U.S. gold dollar. The anti-British Peoples United Party, which attained power in 1954, won a constitution, effective in 1964 which established self-government under a British appointed governor. British Honduras became Belize on June 1, 1973, following the passage of a surprise bill by the Peoples United Party, but the constitutional relationship with Britain remained unchanged.

**MONETARY SYSTEM**

commencing 1864
100 Cents = 1 Dollar

# BRITISH COLONY

## DECIMAL COINAGE

**CENT** KM# 11 **Composition:** Bronze

| Date | Mintage | F | VF | XF | Unc | BU |
|---|---|---|---|---|---|---|
| 1904 | 50,000 | 6.00 | 15.00 | 50.00 | 90.00 | — |
| 1904 Proof | — | Value: 200 | | | | |
| 1904 Matte Proof | — | Value: 1,550 | | | | |
| 1906 | 50,000 | 12.00 | 27.50 | 65.00 | 225 | — |
| 1906 Matte Proof | — | Value: 1,050 | | | | |
| 1909 | 25,000 | 35.00 | 80.00 | 150 | 300 | — |

**CENT** KM# 15 **Composition:** Bronze

| Date | Mintage | F | VF | XF | Unc | BU |
|---|---|---|---|---|---|---|
| 1911 | 50,000 | 60.00 | 100 | 200 | 500 | — |
| 1912H | 50,000 | 85.00 | 160 | 250 | 600 | — |
| 1913 | 25,000 | 100 | 200 | 300 | 700 | — |

**CENT** KM# 19 **Composition:** Bronze

| Date | Mintage | F | VF | XF | Unc | BU |
|---|---|---|---|---|---|---|
| 1914 | 175,000 | 3.00 | 7.50 | 25.00 | 120 | — |
| 1916H | 125,000 | 3.50 | 8.50 | 27.50 | 125 | — |
| 1918 | 40,000 | 7.00 | 15.00 | 40.00 | 150 | — |
| 1919 | 50,000 | 7.00 | 15.00 | 40.00 | 150 | — |
| 1924 | 50,000 | 7.00 | 15.00 | 40.00 | 125 | — |
| 1924 Proof | — | Value: 250 | | | | |
| 1926 | 50,000 | 5.00 | 12.00 | 35.00 | 125 | — |
| 1926 Proof | — | Value: 225 | | | | |
| 1936 | 40,000 | 2.00 | 5.00 | 20.00 | 65.00 | — |
| 1936 Proof | 50 | Value: 170 | | | | |

**CENT** KM# 21 **Composition:** Bronze

| Date | Mintage | F | VF | XF | Unc | BU |
|---|---|---|---|---|---|---|
| 1937 | 80,000 | 0.75 | 4.00 | 12.00 | 75.00 | — |
| 1937 Proof | — | Value: 170 | | | | |
| 1939 | 50,000 | 2.00 | 7.00 | 20.00 | 150 | — |
| 1939 Proof | — | Value: 100 | | | | |
| 1942 | 50,000 | 2.00 | 7.00 | 20.00 | 150 | — |
| 1942 Proof | — | Value: 125 | | | | |
| 1943 | 100,000 | 1.00 | 5.00 | 15.00 | 125 | — |
| 1943 Proof | — | Value: 150 | | | | |
| 1944 | 100,000 | 2.00 | 7.00 | 20.00 | 150 | — |
| 1944 Proof | — | Value: 200 | | | | |
| 1945 | 130,000 | 0.75 | 2.00 | 7.50 | 50.00 | — |
| 1945 Proof | — | Value: 120 | | | | |
| 1947 | 100,000 | 0.75 | 2.50 | 10.00 | 70.00 | — |
| 1947 Proof | — | Value: 150 | | | | |

**CENT** KM# 24 **Composition:** Bronze **Obv. Legend:** Without EMPEROR OF INDIA

| Date | Mintage | F | VF | XF | Unc | BU |
|---|---|---|---|---|---|---|
| 1949 | 100,000 | 0.60 | 1.50 | 4.00 | 16.50 | — |
| 1949 Proof | — | Value: 135 | | | | |
| 1950 | 100,000 | 0.40 | 1.00 | 2.50 | 6.50 | — |
| 1950 Proof | — | Value: 135 | | | | |
| 1951 | 100,000 | 0.60 | 1.50 | 4.00 | 16.50 | — |
| 1951 Proof | — | Value: 135 | | | | |

**CENT** KM# 27 **Composition:** Bronze

| Date | Mintage | F | VF | XF | Unc | BU |
|---|---|---|---|---|---|---|
| 1954 | 200,000 | 0.50 | 0.75 | 1.00 | 5.00 | — |
| 1954 Proof | — | Value: 150 | | | | |

**CENT** KM# 30 **Composition:** Bronze

| Date | Mintage | F | VF | XF | Unc | BU |
|---|---|---|---|---|---|---|
| 1956 | 200,000 | 0.10 | 0.25 | 0.50 | 3.50 | — |
| 1956 Proof | — | Value: 80.00 | | | | |
| 1958 | 400,000 | 1.00 | 2.00 | 9.00 | 80.00 | — |
| 1958 Proof | — | Value: 80.00 | | | | |
| 1959 | 200,000 | 1.00 | 2.50 | 10.00 | 100 | — |
| 1959 Proof | — | Value: 100 | | | | |
| 1961 | 800,000 | — | 0.15 | 0.25 | 0.50 | — |
| 1961 Proof | — | Value: 80.00 | | | | |
| 1964 | 300,000 | — | 0.10 | 0.30 | 0.90 | — |
| 1965 | 400,000 | — | — | 0.10 | 0.50 | — |
| 1966 | 100,000 | — | — | 0.10 | 0.50 | — |
| 1967 | 400,000 | — | — | 0.10 | 0.50 | — |
| 1968 | 200,000 | — | — | 0.10 | 0.50 | — |
| 1969 | 520,000 | — | — | 0.10 | 0.40 | — |
| 1970 | 120,000 | — | — | 0.10 | 0.40 | — |
| 1971 | 800,000 | — | — | 0.10 | 0.40 | — |
| 1972 | 800,000 | — | — | 0.10 | 0.40 | — |
| 1973 | 400,000 | — | — | 0.10 | 0.40 | — |

**5 CENTS** **KM# 14** **Composition:** Copper-Nickel

| Date | Mintage | F | VF | XF | Unc | BU |
|---|---|---|---|---|---|---|
| 1907 | 10,000 | 25.00 | 50.00 | 100 | 250 | — |
| 1909 | 10,000 | 25.00 | 50.00 | 100 | 250 | — |

**5 CENTS** **KM# 16** **Composition:** Copper-Nickel

| Date | Mintage | F | VF | XF | Unc | BU |
|---|---|---|---|---|---|---|
| 1911 | 10,000 | 25.00 | 50.00 | 100 | 250 | — |
| 1912H | 20,000 | 10.00 | 25.00 | 55.00 | 175 | — |
| 1912H Proof | — | Value: 550 | | | | |
| 1916H | 20,000 | 10.00 | 25.00 | 55.00 | 175 | — |
| 1918 | 20,000 | 10.00 | 25.00 | 55.00 | 175 | — |
| 1919 | 20,000 | 8.00 | 20.00 | 50.00 | 160 | — |
| 1936 | 60,000 | 2.50 | 5.00 | 20.00 | 75.00 | — |
| 1936 Proof | 50 | Value: 450 | | | | |

**5 CENTS** **KM# 22** **Composition:** Copper-Nickel

| Date | Mintage | F | VF | XF | Unc | BU |
|---|---|---|---|---|---|---|
| 1939 | 20,000 | 3.00 | 6.00 | 25.00 | 75.00 | — |
| 1939 Proof | — | Value: 275 | | | | |

**5 CENTS** **KM# 22a** **Composition:** Nickel-Brass

| Date | Mintage | F | VF | XF | Unc | BU |
|---|---|---|---|---|---|---|
| 1942 | 30,000 | 5.00 | 15.00 | 65.00 | 200 | — |
| 1942 Proof | — | Value: 300 | | | | |
| 1943 | 40,000 | 2.00 | 12.00 | 60.00 | 190 | — |
| 1944 | 50,000 | 1.50 | 10.00 | 50.00 | 175 | — |
| 1944 Proof | — | Value: 275 | | | | |
| 1945 | 65,000 | 1.00 | 5.00 | 15.00 | 75.00 | — |
| 1945 Proof | — | Value: 150 | | | | |
| 1947 | 40,000 | 1.50 | 5.00 | 15.00 | 85.00 | — |
| 1947 Proof | — | Value: 185 | | | | |

**5 CENTS** **KM# 25** **Composition:** Nickel-Brass
**Obv. Legend:** Without EMPEROR OF INDIA

| Date | Mintage | F | VF | XF | Unc | BU |
|---|---|---|---|---|---|---|
| 1949 | 40,000 | 1.50 | 3.00 | 10.00 | 50.00 | — |
| 1949 Proof | — | Value: 150 | | | | |
| 1950 | 225,000 | 0.40 | 1.00 | 4.00 | 30.00 | — |
| 1950 Proof | — | Value: 200 | | | | |
| 1952 | 100,000 | 0.50 | 2.00 | 6.00 | 35.00 | — |
| 1952 Proof | — | Value: 250 | | | | |

**5 CENTS** **KM# 31** **Composition:** Nickel-Brass

| Date | Mintage | F | VF | XF | Unc | BU |
|---|---|---|---|---|---|---|
| 1956 | 100,000 | 0.20 | 0.50 | 3.00 | 75.00 | — |
| 1956 Proof | — | Value: 125 | | | | |
| 1957 | 100,000 | 0.30 | 0.75 | 1.50 | 10.00 | — |
| 1957 Proof | — | Value: 175 | | | | |
| 1958 | 200,000 | 0.30 | 1.00 | 7.50 | 90.00 | — |
| 1958 Proof | — | Value: 125 | | | | |
| 1959 | 100,000 | 0.40 | 2.00 | 10.00 | 100 | — |
| 1959 Proof | — | Value: 185 | | | | |
| 1961 | 100,000 | 0.30 | 0.75 | 2.50 | 35.00 | — |
| 1961 Proof | — | Value: 120 | | | | |
| 1962 | 200,000 | 0.15 | 0.35 | 0.65 | 2.00 | — |
| 1962 Proof | — | Value: 115 | | | | |
| 1963 | 100,000 | 0.10 | 0.20 | 0.50 | 1.50 | — |
| 1963 Proof | — | Value: 175 | | | | |
| 1964 | 100,000 | 0.10 | 0.15 | 0.35 | 1.00 | — |
| 1965 | 150,000 | — | 0.10 | 0.25 | 0.75 | — |
| 1966 | 150,000 | — | 0.10 | 0.20 | 0.60 | — |
| 1968 | 200,000 | — | 0.10 | 0.15 | 0.50 | — |
| 1969 | 540,000 | — | 0.10 | 0.15 | 0.50 | — |
| 1970 | 240,000 | — | 0.10 | 0.15 | 0.50 | — |
| 1971 | 450,000 | — | 0.10 | 0.15 | 0.50 | — |
| 1972 | 200,000 | — | 0.10 | 0.15 | 0.50 | — |
| 1973 | 210,000 | — | 0.10 | 0.15 | 0.75 | — |

**10 CENTS** **KM# 20** **Weight:** 2.3240 g. **Composition:** 0.9250 Silver .0691 oz. ASW

| Date | Mintage | F | VF | XF | Unc | BU |
|---|---|---|---|---|---|---|
| 1918 | 10,000 | 15.00 | 25.00 | 100 | 350 | — |
| 1919 | 10,000 | 15.00 | 25.00 | 100 | 350 | — |
| 1936 | 30,000 | 6.00 | 12.00 | 25.00 | 100 | — |
| 1936 Proof | 50 | Value: 325 | | | | |

**10 CENTS** **KM# 23** **Weight:** 2.3240 g. **Composition:** 0.9250 Silver .0691 oz. ASW

| Date | Mintage | F | VF | XF | Unc | BU |
|---|---|---|---|---|---|---|
| 1939 | 20,000 | 3.00 | 7.00 | 20.00 | 60.00 | — |
| 1939 Proof | — | Value: 300 | | | | |
| 1942 | 10,000 | 10.00 | 20.00 | 60.00 | 250 | — |
| 1943 | 20,000 | 3.00 | 6.00 | 45.00 | 250 | — |
| 1944 | 30,000 | 2.50 | 5.00 | 35.00 | 150 | — |
| 1944 Proof | — | Value: 250 | | | | |
| 1946 | 10,000 | 5.00 | 12.00 | 45.00 | 200 | — |
| 1946 Proof | — | Value: 450 | | | | |

**10 CENTS** **KM# 32** **Composition:** Copper-Nickel

| Date | Mintage | F | VF | XF | Unc | BU |
|---|---|---|---|---|---|---|
| 1956 | 100,000 | 0.40 | 1.00 | 2.00 | 7.50 | — |
| 1956 Proof | — | Value: 200 | | | | |
| 1959 | 100,000 | 0.60 | 1.50 | 2.00 | 37.50 | — |
| 1959 Proof | — | Value: 135 | | | | |
| 1961 | 50,000 | 0.30 | 0.75 | 1.25 | 3.00 | — |
| 1961 Proof | — | Value: 135 | | | | |
| 1963 | 50,000 | 0.20 | 0.50 | 0.75 | 2.00 | — |
| 1963 Proof | — | Value: 135 | | | | |
| 1964 | 60,000 | 0.15 | 0.25 | 0.50 | 1.00 | — |
| 1965/6 | 200,000 | 5.00 | 10.00 | 20.00 | 40.00 | — |
| 1965 | Inc. above | — | 0.10 | 0.15 | 0.50 | — |
| 1970 | — | — | 0.10 | 0.15 | 0.75 | — |

**25 CENTS** **KM# 9** **Weight:** 5.8100 g. **Composition:** 0.9250 Silver .1728 oz. ASW

| Date | Mintage | F | VF | XF | Unc | BU |
|---|---|---|---|---|---|---|
| 1901 | 20,000 | 20.00 | 35.00 | 125 | 400 | — |
| 1901 Proof | 30 | Value: 650 | | | | |

**25 CENTS** **KM# 12** **Weight:** 5.8100 g. **Composition:** 0.9250 Silver .1728 oz. ASW

| Date | Mintage | F | VF | XF | Unc | BU |
|---|---|---|---|---|---|---|
| 1906 | 30,000 | 15.00 | 30.00 | 110 | 375 | — |
| 1907 | 60,000 | 10.00 | 25.00 | 95.00 | 325 | — |

**25 CENTS** **KM# 17** **Weight:** 5.8100 g. **Composition:** 0.9250 Silver .1728 oz. ASW

| Date | Mintage | F | VF | XF | Unc | BU |
|---|---|---|---|---|---|---|
| 1911 | 14,000 | 25.00 | 60.00 | 150 | 400 | — |
| 1919 | 40,000 | 8.00 | 17.50 | 75.00 | 250 | — |

**25 CENTS** **KM# 26** **Composition:** Copper-Nickel

| Date | Mintage | F | VF | XF | Unc | BU |
|---|---|---|---|---|---|---|
| 1952 | 75,000 | 2.00 | 5.00 | 50.00 | 200 | — |
| 1952 Proof | — | Value: 250 | | | | |

**25 CENTS** **KM# 29** **Composition:** Copper-Nickel

| Date | Mintage | F | VF | XF | Unc | BU |
|---|---|---|---|---|---|---|
| 1955 | 75,000 | 0.40 | 1.00 | 3.50 | 15.00 | — |
| 1955 Proof | — | Value: 150 | | | | |
| 1960 | 75,000 | 0.40 | 1.00 | 5.00 | 100 | — |
| 1960 Proof | — | Value: 250 | | | | |
| 1962 | 50,000 | 0.30 | 0.50 | 1.00 | 2.50 | — |
| 1962 Proof | — | Value: 150 | | | | |
| 1963 | 50,000 | 0.30 | 0.50 | 2.00 | 7.50 | — |
| 1963 Proof | — | Value: 150 | | | | |
| 1964 | 100,000 | 0.30 | 0.50 | 0.75 | 1.50 | — |
| 1965 | 75,000 | — | 0.50 | 1.00 | 2.00 | — |
| 1966 | 75,000 | 0.40 | 1.00 | 2.00 | 8.00 | — |
| 1968 | 125,000 | 0.25 | 0.50 | 1.00 | 2.00 | — |
| 1970 | — | 0.20 | 0.35 | 0.75 | 1.50 | — |
| 1971 | 150,000 | 0.20 | 0.30 | 0.50 | 1.50 | — |
| 1972 | 200,000 | 0.20 | 0.30 | 0.50 | 1.50 | — |
| 1973 | 100,000 | 0.20 | 0.30 | 0.60 | 1.75 | — |

**50 CENTS** **KM# 10** **Weight:** 11.6200 g. **Composition:** 0.9250 Silver .3456 oz. ASW

| Date | Mintage | F | VF | XF | Unc | BU |
|---|---|---|---|---|---|---|
| 1895 | 36,000 | 15.00 | 40.00 | 120 | 400 | — |
| 1901 | 10,000 | 35.00 | 80.00 | 350 | 1,000 | — |
| 1901 Prof | 30 | Value: 1,000 | | | | |

**50 CENTS** KM# 13 **Weight:** 11.6200 g. **Composition:** 0.9250 Silver .3456 oz. ASW

| Date | Mintage | F | VF | XF | Unc | BU |
|---|---|---|---|---|---|---|
| 1906 | 15,000 | 20.00 | 60.00 | 225 | 600 | — |
| 1907 | 19,000 | 18.00 | 55.00 | 170 | 500 | — |

**50 CENTS** KM# 18 **Weight:** 11.6200 g. **Composition:** 0.9250 Silver .3456 oz. ASW

| Date | Mintage | F | VF | XF | Unc | BU |
|---|---|---|---|---|---|---|
| 1911 | 12,000 | 30.00 | 75.00 | 250 | 850 | — |
| 1919 | 40,000 | 20.00 | 40.00 | 150 | 400 | — |
| 1919 Proof | — | Value: 1,250 | | | | |

**50 CENTS** KM# 28 **Composition:** Copper-Nickel

| Date | Mintage | F | VF | XF | Unc | BU |
|---|---|---|---|---|---|---|
| 1954 | 75,000 | 0.30 | 0.50 | 1.00 | 4.00 | — |
| 1954 Proof | — | Value: 175 | | | | |
| 1962 | 50,000 | 0.30 | 0.50 | 1.50 | 5.00 | — |
| 1962 Proof | — | Value: 200 | | | | |
| 1964 | 50,000 | 0.30 | 0.50 | 1.50 | 3.50 | — |
| 1965 | 25,000 | 1.00 | 3.00 | 5.00 | 22.50 | — |
| 1966 | 25,000 | 0.75 | 2.00 | 4.00 | 15.00 | — |
| 1971 | 30,000 | 0.30 | 0.50 | 1.50 | 3.50 | — |

## PROOF SETS

| KM# | Date | Mintage | Identification | Issue Price | Mkt Val |
|---|---|---|---|---|---|
| PS1 | 1894 (5) | 25 | KM#6-10 | — | 3,000 |
| PS2 | 1901 (2) | 30 | KM#9, 10 | — | 2,500 |
| PS3 | 1936 (3) | 50 | KM#16, 19, 20 | — | 1,000 |
| PS4 | 1939 (3) | — | KM#21-23 | — | 675 |
| PS5 | 1949 (2) | — | KM#24, 25 | — | 300 |
| PS6 | 1950 (2) | — | KM#24, 25 | — | 350 |
| PS7 | 1954 (2) | — | KM#27, 28 | — | 300 |
| PS8 | 1956 (3) | — | KM#30-32 | — | 400 |
| PS9 | 1958 (2) | — | KM#30, 31 | — | 200 |

British North Borneo (now known as *Sabah*), a former British protectorate and crown colony, occupies the northern tip of the island of Borneo. The island of Labuan, which lies 6 miles off the northwest coast of the island of Borneo, was attached to Singapore settlement in 1907. It became an independent settlement of the Straits Colony in 1912 and was incorporated with British North Borneo in 1946. In 1963 it became part of Malaysia.

**RULERS**
British

**MINT MARKS**
H - Heaton, Birmingham

**MONETARY SYSTEM**
100 Cents = 1 Straits Dollar

## BRITISH PROTECTORATE

### STANDARD COINAGE

**1/2 CENT** KM# 1 **Composition:** Bronze

| Date | Mintage | F | VF | XF | Unc | BU |
|---|---|---|---|---|---|---|
| 1907H | 1,000,000 | 15.00 | 30.00 | 45.00 | 130 | — |

**CENT** KM# 3 **Composition:** Copper-Nickel

| Date | Mintage | F | VF | XF | Unc | BU |
|---|---|---|---|---|---|---|
| 1904H | 2,000,000 | 2.00 | 3.50 | 8.50 | 22.50 | — |
| 1921H | 1,000,000 | 2.00 | 3.50 | 12.50 | 27.50 | — |
| 1935H | 1,000,000 | 1.25 | 2.50 | 6.50 | 22.50 | — |
| 1938H | 1,000,000 | 1.25 | 2.50 | 6.50 | 22.50 | — |
| 1941H | 1,000,000 | 1.25 | 2.50 | 6.50 | 22.50 | — |

**CENT** KM# 2 **Composition:** Bronze

| Date | Mintage | F | VF | XF | Unc | BU |
|---|---|---|---|---|---|---|
| 1907H | 1,000,000 | 20.00 | 50.00 | 75.00 | 140 | — |
| 1907H Proof | — | Value: 400 | | | | |

**2-1/2 CENT** KM# 4 **Composition:** Copper-Nickel

| Date | Mintage | F | VF | XF | Unc | BU |
|---|---|---|---|---|---|---|
| 1903H | 2,000,000 | 2.50 | 5.00 | 20.00 | 50.00 | — |
| 1903H Proof | — | Value: 300 | | | | |
| 1920H | 280,000 | 5.00 | 15.00 | 35.00 | 80.00 | — |

**5 CENTS** KM# 5 **Composition:** Copper-Nickel

| Date | Mintage | F | VF | XF | Unc | BU |
|---|---|---|---|---|---|---|
| 1903H | 1,000,000 | 2.50 | 5.00 | 15.00 | 42.50 | — |
| 1920H | 100,000 | 5.00 | 10.00 | 32.00 | 65.00 | — |
| 1921H | 500,000 | 2.50 | 5.00 | 15.00 | 45.00 | — |
| 1927H | 150,000 | 3.00 | 5.00 | 15.00 | 45.00 | — |
| 1928H | 150,000 | 2.00 | 4.00 | 12.00 | 40.00 | — |
| 1938H | 500,000 | 1.50 | 3.00 | 7.50 | 22.50 | — |
| 1940H | 500,000 | 1.50 | 3.00 | 7.50 | 22.50 | — |
| 1941H | 1,000,000 | 1.50 | 3.00 | 7.50 | 22.50 | — |

**25 CENTS** KM# 6 **Weight:** 2.8300 g. **Composition:** 0.5000 Silver .0454 oz. ASW

| Date | Mintage | F | VF | XF | Unc | BU |
|---|---|---|---|---|---|---|
| 1929H | 400,000 | 7.00 | 15.00 | 35.00 | 80.00 | — |
| 1929H Proof | — | Value: 175 | | | | |

The Colony of the Virgin Islands, a British colony situated in the Caribbean Sea northeast of Puerto Rico and west of the Leeward Islands, has an area of 59 sq. mi. (155 sq. km.) and a population of 13,000. Capital: Road Town. The principal islands of the 36-island group are Tortola, Virgin Gorda, Anegada, and Jost Van Dyke. The chief industries are fishing and stock raising. Fish, livestock and bananas are exported.

The Virgin Islands were discovered by Columbus in 1493, and named by him, Las Virgienes, in honor of St. Ursula and her companions. The British Virgin Islands were formerly part of the administration of the Leeward Islands but received a separate administration as a Crown Colony in 1950. A new constitution promulgated in 1967 provided for a ministerial form of government headed by the Governor.

The Government of the British Virgin Islands issued the first official coinage in its history on June 30, 1973, in honor of 300 years of constitutional government in the islands. U.S. coins and currency continue to be the primary medium of exchange, though the coinage of the British Virgin Islands is legal tender.

# BRITISH COLONY

## STANDARD COINAGE

**CENT KM# 1 Composition:** Bronze **Reverse:** Green-throated Carib and Antillean Crested Hummingbird

| Date | Mintage | F | VF | XF | Unc | BU |
|---|---|---|---|---|---|---|
| 1973FM | 53,000 | — | — | 0.10 | 0.50 | — |
| 1973FM (P) | 181,000 | Value: 1.00 | | | | |
| 1974FM | 22,000 | — | — | 0.10 | 0.50 | — |
| 1974FM (P) | 94,000 | Value: 1.00 | | | | |
| 1975FM (M) | 6,000 | — | — | 0.10 | 0.75 | — |
| 1975FM (U) | 2,351 | — | — | 0.10 | 0.50 | — |
| 1975FM (P) | 32,000 | Value: 1.00 | | | | |
| 1976FM (M) | 12,000 | — | — | 0.10 | 0.50 | — |
| 1976FM (U) | 996 | — | — | 0.10 | 0.50 | — |
| 1976FM (P) | 15,000 | Value: 1.00 | | | | |
| 1977FM (M) | 500 | — | — | 0.25 | 2.00 | — |
| 1977FM (U) | 782 | — | — | 0.10 | 0.50 | — |
| 1977FM (P) | 7,218 | Value: 1.00 | | | | |
| 1978FM (U) | 1,443 | — | — | 0.10 | 0.50 | — |
| 1978FM (P) | 7,059 | Value: 1.00 | | | | |
| 1979FM (U) | 680 | — | — | 0.10 | 0.50 | — |
| 1979FM (P) | 5,304 | Value: 1.00 | | | | |
| 1980FM (U) | 1,007 | — | — | 0.10 | 0.50 | — |
| 1980FM (P) | 3,421 | Value: 1.00 | | | | |
| 1981FM (U) | 472 | — | — | 0.10 | 0.50 | — |
| 1981FM (P) | 1,124 | Value: 1.50 | | | | |
| 1982FM (U) | — | — | — | 0.10 | 0.50 | — |
| 1982FM (P) | — | Value: 1.50 | | | | |
| 1983FM (U) | — | — | — | 0.10 | 0.50 | — |
| 1983FM (P) | — | Value: 1.50 | | | | |
| 1984FM (P) | — | Value: 1.50 | | | | |

**CENT KM# 9 Weight:** 1.7500 g. **Composition:** 0.9250 Silver .0520 oz. ASW **Subject:** Queen's Silver Jubilee

| Date | Mintage | F | VF | XF | Unc | BU |
|---|---|---|---|---|---|---|
| 1977FM (P) | 17,000 | Value: 2.50 | | | | |

**CENT KM# 16 Weight:** 1.7500 g. **Composition:** 0.9250 Silver .0520 oz. ASW **Subject:** Coronation Jubilee **Note:** Similar to KM#1.

| Date | Mintage | F | VF | XF | Unc | BU |
|---|---|---|---|---|---|---|
| 1978FM (P) | 6,196 | Value: 3.50 | | | | |

**CENT KM# 42 Composition:** Bronze **Reverse:** Hawksbill Turtle

| Date | Mintage | F | VF | XF | Unc | BU |
|---|---|---|---|---|---|---|
| 1985FM (P) | — | Value: 2.00 | | | | |

**CENT KM# 42a Weight:** 1.7500 g. **Composition:** 0.9250 Silver .0520 oz. ASW

| Date | Mintage | F | VF | XF | Unc | BU |
|---|---|---|---|---|---|---|
| 1985FM (P) | 1,474 | Value: 5.00 | | | | |

**5 CENTS KM# 2 Composition:** Copper-Nickel **Reverse:** Zenaida Dove

| Date | Mintage | F | VF | XF | Unc | BU |
|---|---|---|---|---|---|---|
| 1973FM | 26,000 | — | — | 0.15 | 0.75 | — |
| 1973FM (P) | 181,000 | Value: 1.25 | | | | |
| 1974FM | 18,000 | — | — | 0.15 | 0.75 | — |
| 1974FM (P) | 94,000 | Value: 1.25 | | | | |
| 1975FM (M) | 3,800 | — | — | 0.20 | 1.00 | — |
| 1975FM (U) | 2,351 | — | — | 0.15 | 0.75 | — |
| 1975FM (P) | 32,000 | Value: 1.25 | | | | |
| 1976FM (M) | 4,800 | — | — | 0.20 | 1.00 | — |
| 1976FM (U) | 996 | — | — | 0.15 | 0.75 | — |
| 1976FM (P) | 15,000 | Value: 1.25 | | | | |
| 1977FM (M) | 500 | — | — | 0.35 | 3.50 | — |
| 1977FM (U) | 782 | — | — | 0.15 | 0.75 | — |
| 1977FM (P) | 7,218 | Value: 1.25 | | | | |
| 1978FM (U) | 1,443 | — | — | 0.15 | 0.75 | — |
| 1978FM (P) | 7,059 | Value: 1.25 | | | | |
| 1979FM (U) | 680 | — | — | 0.15 | 0.75 | — |
| 1979FM (P) | 5,304 | Value: 1.25 | | | | |
| 1980FM (U) | 1,007 | — | — | 0.15 | 0.75 | — |
| 1980FM (P) | 3,421 | Value: 1.25 | | | | |
| 1981FM (U) | 472 | — | — | 0.15 | 0.75 | — |
| 1981FM (P) | 1,124 | Value: 1.25 | | | | |
| 1982FM (U) | — | — | — | 0.15 | 0.75 | — |
| 1982FM (P) | — | Value: 1.25 | | | | |
| 1983FM (U) | — | — | — | 0.15 | 0.75 | — |
| 1983FM (P) | — | Value: 1.25 | | | | |
| 1984FM (P) | — | Value: 1.25 | | | | |

**5 CENTS KM# 10 Weight:** 3.5500 g. **Composition:** 0.9250 Silver .1055 oz. ASW **Subject:** Queen's Silver Jubilee

| Date | Mintage | F | VF | XF | Unc | BU |
|---|---|---|---|---|---|---|
| 1977FM (P) | 17,000 | Value: 3.00 | | | | |

**5 CENTS KM# 17 Weight:** 3.5500 g. **Composition:** 0.9250 Silver .1055 oz. ASW **Subject:** Coronation Jubilee

| Date | Mintage | F | VF | XF | Unc | BU |
|---|---|---|---|---|---|---|
| ND(1978)FM (P) | 6,196 | Value: 4.50 | | | | |

**5 CENTS KM# 43 Composition:** Copper-Nickel **Reverse:** Bonito Fish

| Date | Mintage | F | VF | XF | Unc | BU |
|---|---|---|---|---|---|---|
| 1985FM (P) | — | Value: 2.00 | | | | |

**5 CENTS KM# 43a Weight:** 3.5550 g. **Composition:** 0.9250 Silver .1055 oz. ASW

| Date | Mintage | F | VF | XF | Unc | BU |
|---|---|---|---|---|---|---|
| 1985FM (P) | 1,471 | Value: 5.50 | | | | |

**10 CENTS KM# 3 Composition:** Copper-Nickel **Reverse:** Ringed Kingfisher

| Date | Mintage | F | VF | XF | Unc | BU |
|---|---|---|---|---|---|---|
| 1973FM (U) | 23,000 | — | — | 0.20 | 1.00 | — |
| 1973FM (P) | 181,000 | Value: 1.50 | | | | |
| 1974FM (U) | 13,000 | — | — | 0.20 | 1.00 | — |
| 1974FM (P) | 94,000 | Value: 1.50 | | | | |
| 1975FM (M) | 2,000 | — | — | 0.20 | 1.25 | — |
| 1975FM (U) | 2,351 | — | — | 0.20 | 1.00 | — |
| 1975FM (P) | 32,000 | Value: 1.50 | | | | |
| 1976FM (M) | 3,000 | — | — | 0.20 | 1.00 | — |
| 1976FM (U) | 996 | — | — | 0.20 | 1.00 | — |
| 1976FM (P) | 15,000 | Value: 1.50 | | | | |
| 1977FM (M) | 500 | — | — | 0.45 | 4.00 | |
| 1977FM (U) | 782 | — | — | 0.20 | 1.00 | — |
| 1977FM (P) | 7,218 | Value: 1.50 | | | | |
| 1978FM (U) | 1,443 | — | — | 0.20 | 1.00 | — |
| 1978FM (P) | 7,059 | Value: 1.50 | | | | |
| 1979FM (U) | 680 | — | — | 0.20 | 1.00 | — |
| 1979FM (P) | 5,304 | Value: 1.50 | | | | |
| 1980FM (U) | 1,007 | — | — | 0.20 | 1.00 | — |
| 1980FM (P) | 3,421 | Value: 1.50 | | | | |
| 1981FM (U) | 472 | — | — | 0.20 | 1.00 | — |
| 1981FM (P) | 1,124 | Value: 1.50 | | | | |
| 1982FM (U) | — | — | — | 0.20 | 1.00 | — |
| 1982FM (P) | — | Value: 1.50 | | | | |
| 1983FM (U) | — | — | — | 0.20 | 1.00 | — |
| 1983FM (P) | — | Value: 1.50 | | | | |
| 1984FM (P) | — | Value: 1.50 | | | | |

**10 CENTS KM# 11 Weight:** 6.4000 g. **Composition:** 0.9250 Silver .1903 oz. ASW **Subject:** Queen's Silver Jubilee

| Date | Mintage | F | VF | XF | Unc | BU |
|---|---|---|---|---|---|---|
| 1977FM (P) | 17,000 | Value: 5.00 | | | | |

**10 CENTS KM# 18 Weight:** 6.4000 g. **Composition:** 0.9250 Silver .1903 oz. ASW **Subject:** Coronation Jubilee

| Date | Mintage | F | VF | XF | Unc | BU |
|---|---|---|---|---|---|---|
| ND(1978)FM (P) | 6,196 | Value: 6.50 | | | | |

**10 CENTS KM# 44 Composition:** Copper-Nickel **Reverse:** Great Barracuda

| Date | Mintage | F | VF | XF | Unc | BU |
|---|---|---|---|---|---|---|
| 1985FM (P) | — | Value: 3.00 | | | | |

**10 CENTS KM# 44a Weight:** 6.4000 g. **Composition:** 0.9250 Silver .1903 oz. ASW

| Date | Mintage | F | VF | XF | Unc | BU |
|---|---|---|---|---|---|---|
| 1985FM (P) | 1,474 | Value: 7.50 | | | | |

**25 CENTS** **KM# 4** **Composition:** Silver **Reverse:** Mangrove Cuckoo

| Date | Mintage | F | VF | XF | Unc | BU |
|---|---|---|---|---|---|---|
| 1973FM | 21,000 | — | — | 0.30 | 1.50 | — |
| 1973FM (P) | 181,000 | Value: 1.75 | | | | |
| 1974FM | 12,000 | — | — | 0.30 | 1.50 | — |
| 1974FM (P) | 94,000 | Value: 1.75 | | | | |
| 1975FM (M) | 1,000 | — | — | 0.35 | 3.00 | — |
| 1975FM (U) | 2,351 | — | — | 0.30 | 1.50 | — |
| 1975FM (P) | 32,000 | Value: 1.75 | | | | |
| 1976FM (M) | 2,000 | — | — | 0.30 | 2.00 | — |
| 1976FM (U) | 996 | — | — | 0.30 | 1.50 | — |
| 1976FM (P) | 15,000 | Value: 1.75 | | | | |
| 1977FM (M) | 500 | — | — | 0.50 | 5.00 | — |
| 1977FM (U) | 782 | — | — | 0.30 | 1.50 | — |
| 1977FM (P) | 7,218 | Value: 1.75 | | | | |
| 1978FM (U) | 1,443 | — | — | 0.30 | 1.50 | — |
| 1978FM (P) | 7,059 | Value: 1.75 | | | | |
| 1979FM (U) | 680 | — | — | 0.30 | 1.50 | — |
| 1979FM (P) | 5,304 | Value: 1.75 | | | | |
| 1980FM (U) | 1,007 | — | — | 0.30 | 1.50 | — |
| 1980FM (P) | 3,421 | Value: 1.75 | | | | |
| 1981FM (U) | 472 | — | — | 0.30 | 1.50 | — |
| 1981FM (P) | 1,124 | Value: 1.75 | | | | |
| 1982FM (U) | — | — | — | 0.30 | 1.50 | — |
| 1982FM (P) | — | Value: 1.75 | | | | |
| 1983FM (U) | — | — | — | 0.30 | 1.50 | — |
| 1983FM (P) | — | Value: 1.75 | | | | |
| 1984FM (P) | — | Value: 1.75 | | | | |

**25 CENTS** **KM# 12** **Weight:** 8.8100 g. **Composition:** 0.9250 Silver .2620 oz. ASW **Subject:** Queen's Silver Jubilee

| Date | Mintage | F | VF | XF | Unc | BU |
|---|---|---|---|---|---|---|
| 1977FM (P) | 17,000 | Value: 7.00 | | | | |

**25 CENTS** **KM# 19** **Weight:** 8.8100 g. **Composition:** 0.9250 Silver .2620 oz. ASW **Subject:** Coronation Jubilee

| Date | Mintage | F | VF | XF | Unc | BU |
|---|---|---|---|---|---|---|
| ND(1978)FM (P) | 6,196 | Value: 8.50 | | | | |

**25 CENTS** **KM# 45** **Composition:** Copper-Nickel **Reverse:** Blue Marlin

| Date | Mintage | F | VF | XF | Unc | BU |
|---|---|---|---|---|---|---|
| 1985FM (P) | — | Value: 5.00 | | | | |

**25 CENTS** **KM# 45a** **Weight:** 8.8100 g. **Composition:** 0.9250 Silver .2620 oz. ASW

| Date | Mintage | F | VF | XF | Unc | BU |
|---|---|---|---|---|---|---|
| 1985FM (P) | 1,480 | Value: 12.50 | | | | |

**50 CENTS** **KM# 5** **Composition:** Copper-Nickel **Reverse:** Brown Pelican

| Date | Mintage | F | VF | XF | Unc | BU |
|---|---|---|---|---|---|---|
| 1973FM | 20,000 | — | — | 0.75 | 2.50 | — |
| 1973FM (P) | 181,000 | Value: 2.50 | | | | |
| 1974FM | 12,000 | — | — | 0.75 | 2.00 | — |
| 1974FM (P) | 94,000 | Value: 2.50 | | | | |
| 1975FM (M) | 1,000 | — | — | 1.00 | 5.00 | — |
| 1975FM (U) | 2,351 | — | — | 0.75 | 2.50 | — |
| 1975FM (P) | 32,000 | Value: 2.50 | | | | |
| 1976FM (M) | 2,000 | — | — | 0.75 | 3.00 | — |
| 1976FM (U) | 996 | — | — | 0.75 | 2.50 | — |
| 1976FM (P) | 15,000 | Value: 2.50 | | | | |
| 1977FM (M) | 600 | — | — | 1.00 | 6.00 | — |
| 1977FM (U) | 782 | — | — | 0.75 | 2.50 | — |
| 1977FM (P) | 7,218 | Value: 2.50 | | | | |
| 1978FM (U) | 1,543 | — | — | 0.75 | 2.50 | — |
| 1978FM (P) | 7,059 | Value: 2.50 | | | | |
| 1979FM (U) | 680 | — | — | 0.75 | 2.50 | — |
| 1979FM (P) | 5,304 | Value: 2.50 | | | | |
| 1980FM (U) | 1,007 | — | — | 0.75 | 2.50 | — |
| 1980FM (P) | 3,421 | Value: 2.50 | | | | |
| 1981FM (U) | 472 | — | — | 0.75 | 2.50 | — |
| 1981FM (P) | 1,124 | Value: 2.50 | | | | |
| 1982FM (U) | — | — | — | 0.75 | 2.50 | — |
| 1982FM (P) | — | Value: 2.50 | | | | |
| 1983FM (U) | — | — | — | 0.75 | 2.50 | — |
| 1983FM (P) | — | Value: 2.50 | | | | |
| 1984FM (P) | — | Value: 2.50 | | | | |

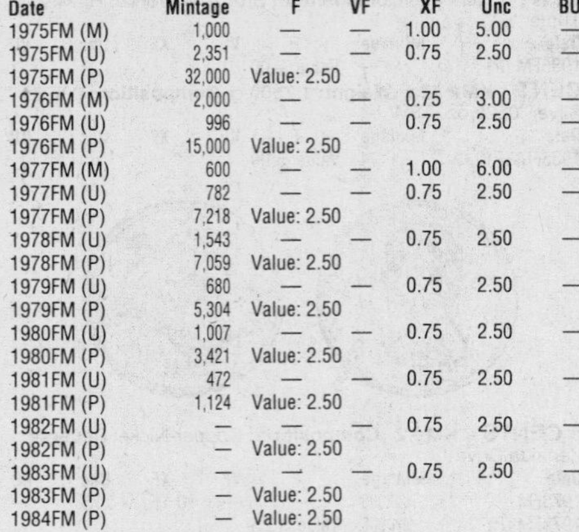

**50 CENTS** **KM# 13** **Weight:** 16.7200 g. **Composition:** 0.9250 Silver .4972 oz. ASW **Subject:** Queen's Silver Jubilee

| Date | Mintage | F | VF | XF | Unc | BU |
|---|---|---|---|---|---|---|
| 1977FM (P) | 17,000 | Value: 10.00 | | | | |

**50 CENTS** **KM# 20** **Weight:** 16.7200 g. **Composition:** 0.9250 Silver .4972 oz. ASW **Subject:** Coronation Jubilee

| Date | Mintage | F | VF | XF | Unc | BU |
|---|---|---|---|---|---|---|
| ND(1978)FM (P) | 6,196 | Value: 11.50 | | | | |

**50 CENTS** **KM# 46** **Composition:** Copper-Nickel **Reverse:** Dolphin

| Date | Mintage | F | VF | XF | Unc | BU |
|---|---|---|---|---|---|---|
| 1985FM (P) | — | Value: 7.00 | | | | |

**50 CENTS** **KM# 46a** **Weight:** 16.7200 g. **Composition:** 0.9250 Silver .4972 oz. ASW

| Date | Mintage | F | VF | XF | Unc | BU |
|---|---|---|---|---|---|---|
| 1985FM (P) | 1,406 | Value: 22.50 | | | | |

**DOLLAR** **KM# 6a** **Weight:** 25.7000 g. **Composition:** 0.9250 Silver .7643 oz. ASW

| Date | Mintage | F | VF | XF | Unc | BU |
|---|---|---|---|---|---|---|
| 1973FM (M) | 20,000 | — | — | 8.00 | 11.00 | — |
| 1973FM (P) | 181,000 | Value: 8.50 | | | | |
| 1974FM (P) | 94,000 | Value: 9.00 | | | | |
| 1975FM (P) | 32,000 | Value: 11.00 | | | | |
| 1976FM (P) | 15,000 | Value: 11.00 | | | | |
| 1977FM (P) | 7,218 | Value: 12.00 | | | | |
| 1978FM (P) | 7,059 | Value: 12.00 | | | | |
| 1979FM (P) | 5,304 | Value: 12.50 | | | | |
| 1980FM (P) | 3,421 | Value: 13.50 | | | | |
| 1981FM (P) | 1,124 | Value: 14.50 | | | | |
| 1982FM (P) | 1,865 | Value: 15.00 | | | | |
| 1983FM (P) | 478 | Value: 22.00 | | | | |
| 1984FM (P) | — | Value: 15.00 | | | | |

**DOLLAR** **KM# 6** **Composition:** Copper-Nickel **Reverse:** Magnificent Frigate

| Date | Mintage | F | VF | XF | Unc | BU |
|---|---|---|---|---|---|---|
| 1974FM (M) | 12,000 | — | — | 2.50 | 6.50 | — |
| 1974FM (U) | — | — | — | — | — | — |
| 1975FM (M) | 800 | — | — | 2.50 | 8.00 | — |
| 1975FM (U) | 2,351 | — | — | 2.50 | 6.50 | — |
| 1976FM (M) | 1,800 | — | — | 2.50 | 6.50 | — |
| 1976FM (U) | 996 | — | — | 2.50 | 8.00 | — |
| 1977FM (M) | 800 | — | — | 2.50 | 8.00 | — |
| 1977FM (U) | 782 | — | — | 2.50 | 8.00 | — |
| 1978FM (U) | 1,743 | — | — | 2.50 | 6.50 | — |
| 1979FM (U) | 680 | — | — | 2.50 | 8.00 | — |
| 1980FM (U) | 1,007 | — | — | 2.50 | 6.50 | — |
| 1981FM (U) | 472 | — | — | 2.50 | 8.00 | — |
| 1982FM (U) | — | — | — | 2.50 | 8.00 | — |
| 1983FM (U) | — | — | — | 2.50 | 8.00 | — |

**DOLLAR** **KM# 14** **Weight:** 25.7000 g. **Composition:** 0.9250 Silver .7643 oz. ASW **Subject:** Queen's Silver Jubilee

| Date | Mintage | F | VF | XF | Unc | BU |
|---|---|---|---|---|---|---|
| 1977FM (P) | 17,000 | Value: 15.00 | | | | |

**DOLLAR** **KM# 21** **Weight:** 25.7000 g. **Composition:** 0.9250 Silver .7643 oz. ASW **Subject:** Coronation Jubilee

| Date | Mintage | F | VF | XF | Unc | BU |
|---|---|---|---|---|---|---|
| ND(1978)FM (P) | 6,196 | Value: 17.50 | | | | |

**DOLLAR** **KM# 47** **Composition:** Copper-Nickel **Reverse:** Butterfly Fish

| Date | Mintage | F | VF | XF | Unc | BU |
|---|---|---|---|---|---|---|
| 1985FM (P) | — | Value: 30.00 | | | | |

**DOLLAR** **KM# 47a** **Weight:** 24.7400 g. **Composition:** 0.9250 Silver .7358 oz. ASW

| Date | Mintage | F | VF | XF | Unc | BU |
|---|---|---|---|---|---|---|
| 1985FM (P) | 1,372 | Value: 42.50 | | | | |

**DOLLAR** **KM# 169** **Composition:** Copper-Nickel **Subject:** 500th Anniversary - Columbus' First Voyage to America **Obverse:** Queen's portrait **Reverse:** VIGILATE on banner below shield with woman and twelve lamps

| Date | Mintage | F | VF | XF | Unc | BU |
|---|---|---|---|---|---|---|
| ND(1992) | — | Value: 25.00 | | | | |

**DOLLAR** **KM# 172** **Composition:** Copper-Nickel **Subject:** Queen Mother's 100th Birthday **Obverse:** Queen's head right **Reverse:** Queen Mother facing **Edge:** Reeded

| Date | Mintage | F | VF | XF | Unc | BU |
|---|---|---|---|---|---|---|
| 2000 | 100,000 | — | — | — | 7.50 | — |

**DOLLAR** **KM# 175** **Composition:** Copper-Nickel **Subject:** 1st Anniversary - Earl and Countess of Wessex **Obverse:** Queen's head right **Reverse:** 1/2 figures of Earl and Countess of Wessex facing, date below **Edge:** Reeded

| Date | Mintage | F | VF | XF | Unc | BU |
|---|---|---|---|---|---|---|
| 2000 | — | — | — | — | 7.50 | — |

**5 DOLLARS** **KM# 24** **Composition:** Copper-Nickel **Reverse:** Snowy Egret

| Date | Mintage | F | VF | XF | Unc | BU |
|---|---|---|---|---|---|---|
| 1979FM (U) | 680 | — | — | — | 45.00 | — |

**5 DOLLARS** **KM# 24a** **Weight:** 40.5000 g. **Composition:** 0.9250 Silver 1.2044 oz. ASW

| Date | Mintage | F | VF | XF | Unc | BU |
|---|---|---|---|---|---|---|
| 1979FM (P) | 5,304 | Value: 30.00 | | | | |

**5 DOLLARS** **KM# 26** **Composition:** Copper-Nickel **Reverse:** Great Blue Heron

| Date | Mintage | F | VF | XF | Unc | BU |
|---|---|---|---|---|---|---|
| 1980FM (U) | 1,007 | — | — | — | 42.50 | — |

**5 DOLLARS** **KM# 26a** **Weight:** 40.5000 g. **Composition:** 0.9250 Silver 1.2044 oz. ASW

| Date | Mintage | F | VF | XF | Unc | BU |
|---|---|---|---|---|---|---|
| 1980FM (P) | 3,421 | Value: 32.50 | | | | |

**5 DOLLARS** **KM# 30** **Composition:** Copper-Nickel **Subject:** Royal Tern **Obverse:** Similar to 50 Cents, KM#13

| Date | Mintage | F | VF | XF | Unc | BU |
|---|---|---|---|---|---|---|
| 1981FM (U) | 472 | — | — | — | 50.00 | — |

**5 DOLLARS** **KM# 30a** **Weight:** 40.5000 g. **Composition:** 0.9250 Silver 1.2044 oz. ASW

| Date | Mintage | F | VF | XF | Unc | BU |
|---|---|---|---|---|---|---|
| 1981FM (P) | 1,124 | Value: 35.00 | | | | |

**5 DOLLARS** **KM# 33** **Composition:** Copper-Nickel **Reverse:** White-tailed Tropic Birds

| Date | Mintage | F | VF | XF | Unc | BU |
|---|---|---|---|---|---|---|
| 1982FM (U) | — | — | — | — | 32.50 | — |

**5 DOLLARS** **KM# 33a** **Weight:** 40.5000 g. **Composition:** 0.9250 Silver 1.2044 oz. ASW

| Date | Mintage | F | VF | XF | Unc | BU |
|---|---|---|---|---|---|---|
| 1982FM (P) | 1,865 | Value: 35.00 | | | | |

**5 DOLLARS** **KM# 35** **Composition:** Copper-Nickel **Subject:** Yellow Warblers **Obverse:** Similar to 50 Cents, KM#13

| Date | Mintage | F | VF | XF | Unc | BU |
|---|---|---|---|---|---|---|
| 1983FM (U) | — | — | — | — | 45.00 | — |

**5 DOLLARS** **KM# 35a** **Weight:** 40.5000 g. **Composition:** 0.9250 Silver 1.2044 oz. ASW

| Date | Mintage | F | VF | XF | Unc | BU |
|---|---|---|---|---|---|---|
| 1983FM (P) | 478 | Value: 55.00 | | | | |
| 1984FM (P) | — | Value: 55.00 | | | | |

**10 DOLLARS** **KM# 36** **Weight:** 30.2800 g. **Composition:** 0.5000 Silver .4868 oz. ASW **Subject:** 30th Anniversary - Coronation of Queen Elizabeth II

| Date | Mintage | F | VF | XF | Unc | BU |
|---|---|---|---|---|---|---|
| 1983FM (P) | 2,957 | Value: 17.50 | | | | |

**10 DOLLARS** **KM# 157** **Composition:** Copper-Nickel **Subject:** Discovery of America - Columbus Landing

| Date | Mintage | F | VF | XF | Unc | BU |
|---|---|---|---|---|---|---|
| ND(1992)FM (P) | — | Value: 12.50 | | | | |

**10 DOLLARS** KM#173 **Weight:** 28.2800 g. **Composition:** 0.9250 Silver .8410 oz. ASW **Obverse:** Queen's head right **Reverse:** 1/2 bust Queen Mother facing **Edge:** Reeded

| Date | Mintage | F | VF | XF | Unc | BU |
|---|---|---|---|---|---|---|
| 2000 | 10,000 | Value: 47.50 | | | | |

**10 DOLLARS** KM#176 **Weight:** 28.2800 g. **Composition:** 0.9250 Silver .8410 oz. ASW **Subject:** 1st Anniversary - Earl and Countess of Wessex **Obverse:** Queen's head right **Reverse:** 1/2 figures of Earl and Countess of Wessex facing, date below **Edge:** Reeded

| Date | Mintage | F | VF | XF | Unc | BU |
|---|---|---|---|---|---|---|
| 2000 | 10,000 | Value: 47.50 | | | | |

**20 DOLLARS** KM# 48 **Weight:** 19.0900 g. **Composition:** 0.9250 Silver .5678 oz. ASW **Subject:** Crossed Cannons

| Date | Mintage | F | VF | XF | Unc | BU |
|---|---|---|---|---|---|---|
| 1985FM (P) | — | Value: 16.50 | | | | |

**20 DOLLARS** KM# 49 **Weight:** 19.0900 g. **Composition:** 0.9250 Silver .5678 oz. ASW **Subject:** Porcelain Cup **Obverse:** Similar to KM#48

| Date | Mintage | F | VF | XF | Unc | BU |
|---|---|---|---|---|---|---|
| 1985FM (P) | — | Value: 16.50 | | | | |

**20 DOLLARS** KM# 50 **Weight:** 19.0900 g. **Composition:** 0.9250 Silver .5678 oz. ASW **Subject:** Sextant **Obverse:** Similar to KM#48

| Date | Mintage | F | VF | XF | Unc | BU |
|---|---|---|---|---|---|---|
| 1985FM (P) | — | Value: 16.50 | | | | |

**20 DOLLARS** KM# 51 **Weight:** 19.0900 g. **Composition:** 0.9250 Silver .5678 oz. ASW **Subject:** Emerald and Gold Ring **Obverse:** Similar to KM#48

| Date | Mintage | F | VF | XF | Unc | BU |
|---|---|---|---|---|---|---|
| 1985FM (P) | — | Value: 16.50 | | | | |

**20 DOLLARS** KM# 52 **Weight:** 19.0900 g. **Composition:** 0.9250 Silver .5678 oz. ASW **Subject:** Gold Doubloon on 1702 **Obverse:** Similar to KM#48

| Date | Mintage | F | VF | XF | Unc | BU |
|---|---|---|---|---|---|---|
| 1985FM (P) | — | Value: 16.50 | | | | |

**20 DOLLARS** KM# 53 **Weight:** 19.0900 g. **Composition:** 0.9250 Silver .5678 oz. ASW **Subject:** Anchor **Obverse:** Similar to KM#48

| Date | Mintage | F | VF | XF | Unc | BU |
|---|---|---|---|---|---|---|
| 1985FM (P) | — | Value: 16.50 | | | | |

**20 DOLLARS** KM# 54 **Weight:** 19.0900 g. **Composition:** 0.9250 Silver .5678 oz. ASW **Subject:** Brass Nocturnal **Obverse:** Similar to KM#48

| Date | Mintage | F | VF | XF | Unc | BU |
|---|---|---|---|---|---|---|
| 1985FM (P) | — | Value: 16.50 | | | | |

**20 DOLLARS** KM# 55 **Weight:** 19.0900 g. **Composition:** 0.9250 Silver .5678 oz. ASW **Subject:** Sword Guillon **Obverse:** Similar to KM#48

| Date | Mintage | F | VF | XF | Unc | BU |
|---|---|---|---|---|---|---|
| 1985FM (P) Proof | — | Value: 16.50 | | | | |

**20 DOLLARS** KM# 56 **Weight:** 19.0900 g. **Composition:** 0.9250 Silver .5678 oz. ASW **Subject:** Gold Bar **Obverse:** Similar to KM#48

| Date | Mintage | F | VF | XF | Unc | BU |
|---|---|---|---|---|---|---|
| 1985FM (P) | — | Value: 16.50 | | | | |

**20 DOLLARS** KM# 57 **Weight:** 19.0900 g. **Composition:** 0.9250 Silver .5678 oz. ASW **Subject:** Gold Escudo **Obverse:** Similar to KM#48 **Reverse:** Obverse and reverse of gold escudo of 1733

| Date | Mintage | F | VF | XF | Unc | BU |
|---|---|---|---|---|---|---|
| 1985FM (P) | — | Value: 16.50 | | | | |

**20 DOLLARS** **KM# 58** **Weight:** 19.0900 g. **Composition:** 0.9250 Silver .5678 oz. ASW **Subject:** Ivory Sundial **Obverse:** Similar to KM#48

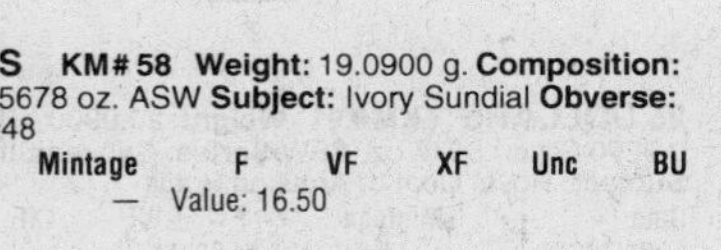

| Date | Mintage | F | VF | XF | Unc | BU |
|---|---|---|---|---|---|---|
| 1985FM (P) | — | Value: 16.50 | | | | |

**20 DOLLARS** **KM# 59** **Weight:** 19.0900 g. **Composition:** 0.9250 Silver .5678 oz. ASW **Subject:** Gold Monstrance **Obverse:** Similar to KM#48

| Date | Mintage | F | VF | XF | Unc | BU |
|---|---|---|---|---|---|---|
| 1985FM (P) | — | Value: 16.50 | | | | |

**20 DOLLARS** **KM# 60** **Weight:** 19.0900 g. **Composition:** 0.9250 Silver .5678 oz. ASW **Subject:** Teapot **Obverse:** Similar to KM#48

| Date | Mintage | F | VF | XF | Unc | BU |
|---|---|---|---|---|---|---|
| 1985FM (P) | — | Value: 16.50 | | | | |

**20 DOLLARS** **KM# 61** **Weight:** 19.0900 g. **Composition:** 0.9250 Silver .5678 oz. ASW **Subject:** Brass Religious Medallion **Obverse:** Similar to KM#48

| Date | Mintage | F | VF | XF | Unc | BU |
|---|---|---|---|---|---|---|
| 1985FM (P) | — | Value: 16.50 | | | | |

**20 DOLLARS** **KM# 62** **Weight:** 19.0900 g. **Composition:** 0.9250 Silver .5678 oz. ASW **Subject:** Astrolable **Obverse:** Similar to KM#48

| Date | Mintage | F | VF | XF | Unc | BU |
|---|---|---|---|---|---|---|
| 1985FM (P) | — | Value: 16.50 | | | | |

**20 DOLLARS** **KM# 64** **Weight:** 19.0900 g. **Composition:** 0.9250 Silver .5678 oz. ASW **Subject:** Porcelain Bottle **Obverse:** Similar to KM#48

| Date | Mintage | F | VF | XF | Unc | BU |
|---|---|---|---|---|---|---|
| 1985FM (P) | — | Value: 16.50 | | | | |

**20 DOLLARS** **KM# 65** **Weight:** 19.0900 g. **Composition:** 0.9250 Silver .5678 oz. ASW **Subject:** Ship and Dutch Cannons **Obverse:** Similar to KM#48

| Date | Mintage | F | VF | XF | Unc | BU |
|---|---|---|---|---|---|---|
| 1985FM (P) | — | Value: 16.50 | | | | |

**20 DOLLARS** **KM# 67** **Weight:** 19.0900 g. **Composition:** 0.9250 Silver .5678 oz. ASW **Subject:** Ship's Stern Lantern **Obverse:** Similar to KM#48

| Date | Mintage | F | VF | XF | Unc | BU |
|---|---|---|---|---|---|---|
| 1985FM (P) | — | Value: 16.50 | | | | |

**20 DOLLARS** **KM# 68** **Weight:** 19.0900 g. **Composition:** 0.9250 Silver .5678 oz. ASW **Subject:** Brass Dividers **Obverse:** Similar to KM#48

| Date | Mintage | F | VF | XF | Unc | BU |
|---|---|---|---|---|---|---|
| 1985FM (P) | — | Value: 16.50 | | | | |

**20 DOLLARS** **KM# 69** **Weight:** 19.0900 g. **Composition:** 0.9250 Silver .5678 oz. ASW **Subject:** Gold Cross **Obverse:** Similar to KM#48

| Date | Mintage | F | VF | XF | Unc | BU |
|---|---|---|---|---|---|---|
| 1985FM (P) | — | Value: 16.50 | | | | |

**20 DOLLARS** **KM# 70** **Weight:** 19.0900 g. **Composition:** 0.9250 Silver .5678 oz. ASW **Subject:** Perfume Bottle **Obverse:** Similar to KM#48

| Date | Mintage | F | VF | XF | Unc | BU |
|---|---|---|---|---|---|---|
| 1985FM (P) | — | Value: 16.50 | | | | |

**20 DOLLARS** **KM# 71** **Weight:** 19.0900 g. **Composition:** 0.9250 Silver .5678 oz. ASW **Subject:** Pocket Watch **Obverse:** Similar to KM#48

| Date | Mintage | F | VF | XF | Unc | BU |
|---|---|---|---|---|---|---|
| 1985FM (P) | — | Value: 16.50 | | | | |

**20 DOLLARS** KM# 72 **Weight:** 19.0900 g. **Composition:** 0.9250 Silver .5678 oz. ASW **Subject:** Gold Bracelet and Button **Obverse:** Similar to KM#48

| Date | Mintage | F | VF | XF | Unc | BU |
|---|---|---|---|---|---|---|
| 1985FM (P) | — | Value: 16.50 | | | | |

**20 DOLLARS** KM# 63.1 **Weight:** 19.0900 g. **Composition:** 0.9250 Silver .5678 oz. ASW **Subject:** Bells **Obverse:** Similar to KM#48 **Note:** FM mint mark at right.

| Date | Mintage | F | VF | XF | Unc | BU |
|---|---|---|---|---|---|---|
| 1985FM (P) | — | Value: 16.50 | | | | |

**20 DOLLARS** KM# 63.2 **Weight:** 19.0900 g. **Composition:** 0.9250 Silver .5678 oz. ASW **Note:** FM mint mark in center.

| Date | Mintage | F | VF | XF | Unc | BU |
|---|---|---|---|---|---|---|
| 1985FM (P) | — | Value: 16.50 | | | | |

**20 DOLLARS** KM# 66 **Weight:** 19.0900 g. **Composition:** 0.9250 Silver .5678 oz. ASW **Obverse:** Similar to KM#48 **Note:** Spanish Colonial 8 Reales, Cob coin.

| Date | Mintage | F | VF | XF | Unc | BU |
|---|---|---|---|---|---|---|
| 1985FM (P) | — | Value: 16.50 | | | | |

**25 DOLLARS** KM# 22 **Weight:** 28.1000 g. **Composition:** 0.9250 Silver .8356 oz. ASW **Subject:** Coronation Jubilee **Obverse:** Portrait of Queen

| Date | Mintage | F | VF | XF | Unc | BU |
|---|---|---|---|---|---|---|
| 1978FM (P) | 8,438 | Value: 25.00 | | | | |

**25 DOLLARS** KM# 27 **Weight:** 1.5000 g. **Composition:** 0.5000 Gold .0241 oz. AGW **Reverse:** Diving Osprey

| Date | Mintage | F | VF | XF | Unc | BU |
|---|---|---|---|---|---|---|
| 1980FM (P) Proof | 11,000 | Value: 50.00 | | | | |

**25 DOLLARS** KM# 31.1 **Weight:** 1.5000 g. **Composition:** 0.5000 Gold .0241 oz. AGW **Reverse:** Caribbean Sparrow Hawk

| Date | Mintage | F | VF | XF | Unc | BU |
|---|---|---|---|---|---|---|
| 1981FM (P) Proof | 2,513 | Value: 60.00 | | | | |

**25 DOLLARS** KM# 31.2 **Weight:** 1.5000 g. **Composition:** 0.5000 Gold .0241 oz. AGW **Obverse:** Error. Without FM mint mark

| Date | Mintage | F | VF | XF | Unc | BU |
|---|---|---|---|---|---|---|
| 1981 (P) Proof | — | Value: 70.00 | | | | |

**25 DOLLARS** KM# 41 **Weight:** 1.5000 g. **Composition:** 0.5000 Gold .0241 oz. AGW **Reverse:** Hawk

| Date | Mintage | F | VF | XF | Unc | BU |
|---|---|---|---|---|---|---|
| 1982FM (P) Proof | 3,819 | Value: 52.20 | | | | |

**25 DOLLARS** KM# 37 **Weight:** 1.5000 g. **Composition:** 0.5000 Gold .0241 oz. AGW **Reverse:** Merlin Hawk

| Date | Mintage | F | VF | XF | Unc | BU |
|---|---|---|---|---|---|---|
| 1983FM (P) Proof | 5,949 | Value: 50.00 | | | | |

**25 DOLLARS** KM# 40 **Weight:** 1.5000 g. **Composition:** 0.5000 Gold .0241 oz. AGW **Reverse:** Peregrine Falcon

| Date | Mintage | F | VF | XF | Unc | BU |
|---|---|---|---|---|---|---|
| 1984FM (P) Proof | 97 | Value: 115 | | | | |

**25 DOLLARS** KM# 73 **Weight:** 1.5000 g. **Composition:** 0.5000 Gold .0241 oz. AGW **Reverse:** Marsh Hawk

| Date | Mintage | F | VF | XF | Unc | BU |
|---|---|---|---|---|---|---|
| 1985FM (P) Proof | 1,294 | Value: 80.00 | | | | |

**25 DOLLARS** KM# 90 **Weight:** 20.0900 g. **Composition:** 0.9250 Silver .5977 oz. ASW **Series:** Sunken Ship Treasures **Subject:** Ornamental Lock Plate

| Date | Mintage | F | VF | XF | Unc | BU |
|---|---|---|---|---|---|---|
| 1988FM (P) Proof | — | Value: 26.00 | | | | |

**25 DOLLARS** KM# 91 **Weight:** 20.0900 g. **Composition:** 0.9250 Silver .5977 oz. ASW **Series:** Sunken Ship Treasures **Subject:** Royal Coat of Arms on Bottle

| Date | Mintage | F | VF | XF | Unc | BU |
|---|---|---|---|---|---|---|
| 1988FM (P) Proof | — | Value: 26.00 | | | | |

**25 DOLLARS** KM# 92 **Weight:** 20.0900 g. **Composition:** 0.9250 Silver .5977 oz. ASW **Series:** Sunken Ship Treasures **Subject:** Finger Ring

| Date | Mintage | F | VF | XF | Unc | BU |
|---|---|---|---|---|---|---|
| 1988FM (P) Proof | — | Value: 26.00 | | | | |

**25 DOLLARS** KM# 93 **Weight:** 20.0900 g. **Composition:** 0.9250 Silver .5977 oz. ASW **Series:** Sunken Ship Treasures **Subject:** Hour Glass

| Date | Mintage | F | VF | XF | Unc | BU |
|---|---|---|---|---|---|---|
| 1988FM (P) Proof | — | Value: 26.00 | | | | |

**25 DOLLARS** KM# 94 **Weight:** 20.0900 g. **Composition:** 0.9250 Silver .5977 oz. ASW **Series:** Sunken Ship Treasures **Subject:** Dagger and Scabbard

| Date | Mintage | F | VF | XF | Unc | BU |
|---|---|---|---|---|---|---|
| 1988FM (P) Proof | — | Value: 26.00 | | | | |

**25 DOLLARS** **KM# 95** **Weight:** 20.0900 g. **Composition:** 0.9250 Silver .5977 oz. ASW **Series:** Sunken Ship Treasures **Subject:** Jewel Encrusted Cross

| Date | Mintage | F | VF | XF | Unc | BU |
|---|---|---|---|---|---|---|
| 1988FM (P) Proof | — | Value: 26.00 | | | | |

**25 DOLLARS** **KM# 96** **Weight:** 20.0900 g. **Composition:** 0.9250 Silver .5977 oz. ASW **Series:** Sunken Ship Treasures **Subject:** Crossed Keys

| Date | Mintage | F | VF | XF | Unc | BU |
|---|---|---|---|---|---|---|
| 1988FM (P) Proof | — | Value: 26.00 | | | | |

**25 DOLLARS** **KM# 97** **Weight:** 20.0900 g. **Composition:** 0.9250 Silver .5977 oz. ASW **Series:** Sunken Ship Treasures **Subject:** Belt Buckle

| Date | Mintage | F | VF | XF | Unc | BU |
|---|---|---|---|---|---|---|
| 1988FM (P) | — | Value: 26.00 | | | | |

**25 DOLLARS** **KM# 98** **Weight:** 20.0900 g. **Composition:** 0.9250 Silver .5977 oz. ASW **Series:** Sunken Ship Treasures **Subject:** American Bottle

| Date | Mintage | F | VF | XF | Unc | BU |
|---|---|---|---|---|---|---|
| 1988FM (P) | — | Value: 26.00 | | | | |

**25 DOLLARS** **KM# 99** **Weight:** 20.0900 g. **Composition:** 0.9250 Silver .5977 oz. ASW **Series:** Sunken Ship Treasures **Subject:** Religious Medallion

| Date | Mintage | F | VF | XF | Unc | BU |
|---|---|---|---|---|---|---|
| 1988FM (P) | — | Value: 26.00 | | | | |

**25 DOLLARS** **KM# 100** **Weight:** 20.0900 g. **Composition:** 0.9250 Silver .5977 oz. ASW **Series:** Sunken Ship Treasures **Subject:** Baby Figurines

| Date | Mintage | F | VF | XF | Unc | BU |
|---|---|---|---|---|---|---|
| 1988FM (P) | — | Value: 26.00 | | | | |

**25 DOLLARS** **KM# 101** **Weight:** 20.0900 g. **Composition:** 0.9250 Silver .5977 oz. ASW **Series:** Sunken Ship Treasures **Subject:** Insignia of the Royal

| Date | Mintage | F | VF | XF | Unc | BU |
|---|---|---|---|---|---|---|
| 1988FM (P) | — | Value: 26.00 | | | | |

**25 DOLLARS** **KM# 102** **Weight:** 20.0900 g. **Composition:** 0.9250 Silver .5977 oz. ASW **Series:** Sunken Ship Treasures **Subject:** Engraved Printing Block

| Date | Mintage | F | VF | XF | Unc | BU |
|---|---|---|---|---|---|---|
| 1988FM (P) | — | Value: 26.00 | | | | |

**25 DOLLARS** **KM# 103** **Weight:** 20.0900 g. **Composition:** 0.9250 Silver .5977 oz. ASW **Series:** Sunken Ship Treasures **Subject:** Antique Clock

| Date | Mintage | F | VF | XF | Unc | BU |
|---|---|---|---|---|---|---|
| 1988FM (P) | — | Value: 26.00 | | | | |

**25 DOLLARS** **KM# 132** **Weight:** 20.0900 g. **Composition:** 0.9250 Silver .5977 oz. ASW **Subject:** Flintlock Pistol

| Date | Mintage | F | VF | XF | Unc | BU |
|---|---|---|---|---|---|---|
| 1988FM (P) | — | Value: 26.00 | | | | |

**25 DOLLARS** **KM# 133** **Weight:** 20.0900 g. **Composition:** 0.9250 Silver .5977 oz. ASW **Subject:** Stylized Fish Statue

| Date | Mintage | F | VF | XF | Unc | BU |
|---|---|---|---|---|---|---|
| 1988FM (P) | — | Value: 26.00 | | | | |

**25 DOLLARS** **KM# 134** **Weight:** 20.0900 g. **Composition:** 0.9250 Silver .5977 oz. ASW **Subject:** Mortar and Pestle

| Date | Mintage | F | VF | XF | Unc | BU |
|---|---|---|---|---|---|---|
| 1988FM (P) | — | Value: 26.00 | | | | |

**25 DOLLARS** **KM# 135** **Weight:** 20.0900 g. **Composition:** 0.9250 Silver .5977 oz. ASW **Subject:** Open Mouthed Dragon Head Sculpture

| Date | Mintage | F | VF | XF | Unc | BU |
|---|---|---|---|---|---|---|
| 1988FM (P) | — | Value: 26.00 | | | | |

**25 DOLLARS** **KM# 136** **Weight:** 20.0900 g. **Composition:** 0.9250 Silver .5977 oz. ASW **Subject:** Military Mortar

| Date | Mintage | F | VF | XF | Unc | BU |
|---|---|---|---|---|---|---|
| 1988FM (P) | — | Value: 26.00 | | | | |

**25 DOLLARS** **KM# 137** **Weight:** 20.0900 g. **Composition:** 0.9250 Silver .5977 oz. ASW **Subject:** Seated Figure Sculpture

| Date | Mintage | F | VF | XF | Unc | BU |
|---|---|---|---|---|---|---|
| 1988FM (P) | — | Value: 26.00 | | | | |

**25 DOLLARS** **KM# 138** **Weight:** 20.0900 g. **Composition:** 0.9250 Silver .5977 oz. ASW **Subject:** Lion Sculpture

| Date | Mintage | F | VF | XF | Unc | BU |
|---|---|---|---|---|---|---|
| 1988FM (P) | — | Value: 26.00 | | | | |

**25 DOLLARS** **KM# 139** **Weight:** 20.0900 g. **Composition:** 0.9250 Silver .5977 oz. ASW **Subject:** Violin

| Date | Mintage | F | VF | XF | Unc | BU |
|---|---|---|---|---|---|---|
| 1988FM (P) | — | Value: 26.00 | | | | |

**25 DOLLARS** **KM# 140** **Weight:** 20.0900 g. **Composition:** 0.9250 Silver .5977 oz. ASW **Subject:** Chalice

| Date | Mintage | F | VF | XF | Unc | BU |
|---|---|---|---|---|---|---|
| 1988FM (P) | — | Value: 26.00 | | | | |

**25 DOLLARS** **KM# 141** **Weight:** 20.0900 g. **Composition:** 0.9250 Silver .5977 oz. ASW **Subject:** Pitcher

| Date | Mintage | F | VF | XF | Unc | BU |
|---|---|---|---|---|---|---|
| 1988FM (P) | — | Value: 26.00 | | | | |

**25 DOLLARS** **KM# 142** **Weight:** 20.0900 g. **Composition:** 0.9250 Silver .5977 oz. ASW **Subject:** Cannon

| Date | Mintage | F | VF | XF | Unc | BU |
|---|---|---|---|---|---|---|
| 1988FM (P) | — | Value: 26.00 | | | | |

**25 DOLLARS** **KM# 104** **Weight:** 21.5400 g. **Composition:** 0.9250 Silver .6406 oz. ASW **Series:** Discovery of America **Subject:** Columbus Planning Voyage

| Date | Mintage | F | VF | XF | Unc | BU |
|---|---|---|---|---|---|---|
| ND(1992)FM (P) | — | Value: 32.00 | | | | |

**25 DOLLARS** **KM# 105** **Weight:** 21.5400 g. **Composition:** 0.9250 Silver .6406 oz. ASW **Series:** Discovery of America **Subject:** Columbus Lecturing

| Date | Mintage | F | VF | XF | Unc | BU |
|---|---|---|---|---|---|---|
| ND(1992)FM (P) | — | Value: 32.00 | | | | |

**25 DOLLARS** **KM# 106** **Weight:** 21.5400 g. **Composition:** 0.9250 Silver .6406 oz. ASW **Series:** Discovery of America **Subject:** Queen Isabella Offering Jewels

| Date | Mintage | F | VF | XF | Unc | BU |
|---|---|---|---|---|---|---|
| ND(1992)FM (P) | — | Value: 32.00 | | | | |

**25 DOLLARS** **KM# 107** **Weight:** 21.5400 g. **Composition:** 0.9250 Silver .6406 oz. ASW **Series:** Discovery of America **Subject:** Columbus Aboard Ship

| Date | Mintage | F | VF | XF | Unc | BU |
|---|---|---|---|---|---|---|
| ND(1992)FM (P) | — | Value: 32.00 | | | | |

**25 DOLLARS** **KM# 108** **Weight:** 21.5400 g. **Composition:** 0.9250 Silver .6406 oz. ASW **Series:** Discovery of America **Subject:** Columbus on Horseback

| Date | Mintage | F | VF | XF | Unc | BU |
|---|---|---|---|---|---|---|
| ND(1992)FM (P) | — | Value: 32.00 | | | | |

**25 DOLLARS** **KM# 109** **Weight:** 21.5400 g. **Composition:** 0.9250 Silver .6406 oz. ASW **Series:** Discovery of America **Subject:** Ship Under Full Sail

| Date | Mintage | F | VF | XF | Unc | BU |
|---|---|---|---|---|---|---|
| ND(1992)FM | — | Value: 32.00 | | | | |

**25 DOLLARS** **KM# 110** **Weight:** 21.5400 g. **Composition:** 0.9250 Silver .6406 oz. ASW **Series:** Discovery of America **Subject:** Ship At Anchor

| Date | Mintage | F | VF | XF | Unc | BU |
|---|---|---|---|---|---|---|
| ND(1992)FM (P) | — | Value: 32.00 | | | | |

**25 DOLLARS** **KM# 111** **Weight:** 21.5400 g. **Composition:** 0.9250 Silver .6406 oz. ASW **Series:** Discovery of America **Subject:** Natives Offering Gifts

| Date | Mintage | F | VF | XF | Unc | BU |
|---|---|---|---|---|---|---|
| ND(1992)FM (P) | — | Value: 32.00 | | | | |

**25 DOLLARS** **KM# 112** **Weight:** 21.5400 g. **Composition:** 0.9250 Silver .6406 oz. ASW **Series:** Discovery of America **Subject:** Shipwreck

| Date | Mintage | F | VF | XF | Unc | BU |
|---|---|---|---|---|---|---|
| ND(1992)FM (P) | — | Value: 32.00 | | | | |

**25 DOLLARS** **KM# 113** **Weight:** 21.5400 g. **Composition:** 0.9250 Silver .6406 oz. ASW **Series:** Discovery of America **Subject:** Royal Banquet

| Date | Mintage | F | VF | XF | Unc | BU |
|---|---|---|---|---|---|---|
| ND(1992)FM (P) | — | Value: 32.00 | | | | |

**25 DOLLARS** **KM# 114** **Weight:** 21.5400 g. **Composition:** 0.9250 Silver .6406 oz. ASW **Series:** Discovery of America **Subject:** Columbus Predicting Lunar Eclipse to Natives

| Date | Mintage | F | VF | XF | Unc | BU |
|---|---|---|---|---|---|---|
| ND(1992)FM (P) | — | Value: 32.00 | | | | |

**25 DOLLARS** **KM# 115** **Weight:** 21.5400 g. **Composition:** 0.9250 Silver .6406 oz. ASW **Series:** Discovery of America **Subject:** Columbus on Shore

| Date | Mintage | F | VF | XF | Unc | BU |
|---|---|---|---|---|---|---|
| ND(1992)FM (P) | — | Value: 32.00 | | | | |

**25 DOLLARS** **KM# 116** **Weight:** 21.5400 g. **Composition:** 0.9250 Silver .6406 oz. ASW **Series:** Discovery of America **Subject:** Spanish Figures

| Date | Mintage | F | VF | XF | Unc | BU |
|---|---|---|---|---|---|---|
| ND(1992)FM (P) | — | Value: 32.00 | | | | |

**25 DOLLARS** **KM# 117** **Weight:** 21.5400 g. **Composition:** 0.9250 Silver .6406 oz. ASW **Series:** Discovery of America **Subject:** Columbus With Shore Party

| Date | Mintage | F | VF | XF | Unc | BU |
|---|---|---|---|---|---|---|
| ND(1992)FM (P) | — | Value: 32.00 | | | | |

**25 DOLLARS** **KM# 118** **Weight:** 21.5400 g. **Composition:** 0.9250 Silver .6406 oz. ASW **Series:** Discovery of America **Subject:** Death of Columbus

| Date | Mintage | F | VF | XF | Unc | BU |
|---|---|---|---|---|---|---|
| ND(1992)FM (P) | — | Value: 32.00 | | | | |

**25 DOLLARS** **KM# 122** **Weight:** 21.5400 g. **Composition:** 0.9250 Silver .6406 oz. ASW **Series:** Discovery of America **Subject:** Columbus Bowing Before King Ferdinand

| Date | Mintage | F | VF | XF | Unc | BU |
|---|---|---|---|---|---|---|
| ND(1992)FM (P) | — | Value: 32.00 | | | | |

**25 DOLLARS** **KM# 123** **Weight:** 21.5400 g. **Composition:** 0.9250 Silver .6406 oz. ASW **Series:** Discovery of America **Subject:** Columbus Before Queen Isabella

| Date | Mintage | F | VF | XF | Unc | BU |
|---|---|---|---|---|---|---|
| ND(1992)FM (P) | — | Value: 32.00 | | | | |

**25 DOLLARS** **KM# 124** **Weight:** 21.5400 g. **Composition:** 0.9250 Silver .6406 oz. ASW **Series:** Discovery of America **Subject:** Columbus Before King Ferdinand and Queen Isabella

| Date | Mintage | F | VF | XF | Unc | BU |
|---|---|---|---|---|---|---|
| ND(1992)FM (P) | — | Value: 32.00 | | | | |

**25 DOLLARS** **KM# 125** **Weight:** 21.5400 g. **Composition:** 0.9250 Silver .6406 oz. ASW **Series:** Discovery of America **Subject:** Columbus Getting Provisions For His Ships

| Date | Mintage | F | VF | XF | Unc | BU |
|---|---|---|---|---|---|---|
| ND(1992)FM (P) | — | Value: 32.00 | | | | |

**25 DOLLARS** **KM# 126** **Weight:** 21.5400 g. **Composition:** 0.9250 Silver .6406 oz. ASW **Series:** Discovery of America **Subject:** 4 Sailing Ships

| Date | Mintage | F | VF | XF | Unc | BU |
|---|---|---|---|---|---|---|
| ND(1992)FM (P) | — | Value: 32.00 | | | | |

**25 DOLLARS** **KM# 127** **Weight:** 21.5400 g. **Composition:** 0.9250 Silver .6406 oz. ASW **Series:** Discovery of America **Subject:** Columbus Navigating By Stars

| Date | Mintage | F | VF | XF | Unc | BU |
|---|---|---|---|---|---|---|
| ND(1992)FM (P) | — | Value: 32.00 | | | | |

**25 DOLLARS** **KM# 128** **Weight:** 21.5400 g. **Composition:** 0.9250 Silver .6406 oz. ASW **Series:** Discovery of America **Subject:** Sighting Land

| Date | Mintage | F | VF | XF | Unc | BU |
|---|---|---|---|---|---|---|
| ND(1992)FM (P) | — | Value: 32.00 | | | | |

**25 DOLLARS** **KM# 129** **Weight:** 21.5400 g. **Composition:** 0.9250 Silver .6406 oz. ASW **Series:** Discovery of America **Subject:** Columbus Claiming the Newly Discovered Land

| Date | Mintage | F | VF | XF | Unc | BU |
|---|---|---|---|---|---|---|
| ND(1992)FM (P) | — | Value: 32.00 | | | | |

**25 DOLLARS** **KM# 130** **Weight:** 21.5400 g. **Composition:** 0.9250 Silver .6406 oz. ASW **Series:** Discovery of America **Subject:** Columbus Seated on Shore with Shipwreck Offshore

| Date | Mintage | F | VF | XF | Unc | BU |
|---|---|---|---|---|---|---|
| ND(1992)FM (P) | — | Value: 32.00 | | | | |

**25 DOLLARS** **KM# 131** **Weight:** 21.5400 g. **Composition:** 0.9250 Silver .6406 oz. ASW **Series:** Discovery of America **Subject:** Columbus As Prisoner

| Date | Mintage | F | VF | XF | Unc | BU |
|---|---|---|---|---|---|---|
| ND(1992)FM (P) | — | Value: 32.00 | | | | |

**25 DOLLARS** **KM# 143** **Weight:** 20.0900 g. **Composition:** 0.9250 Silver .5977 oz. ASW **Series:** Endangered Wildlife **Subject:** African Elephants

| Date | Mintage | F | VF | XF | Unc | BU |
|---|---|---|---|---|---|---|
| 1993FM (P) | — | Value: 40.00 | | | | |

**25 DOLLARS** **KM# 144** **Weight:** 20.0900 g. **Composition:** 0.9250 Silver .5977 oz. ASW **Series:** Endangered Wildlife **Subject:** Mountain Gorilla

| Date | Mintage | F | VF | XF | Unc | BU |
|---|---|---|---|---|---|---|
| 1993FM (P) | — | Value: 40.00 | | | | |

**25 DOLLARS** **KM# 145** **Weight:** 20.0900 g. **Composition:** 0.9250 Silver .5977 oz. ASW **Series:** Endangered Wildlife **Subject:** Cape Mountain Zebra

| Date | Mintage | F | VF | XF | Unc | BU |
|---|---|---|---|---|---|---|
| 1993FM (P) | — | Value; 35.00 | | | | |

**25 DOLLARS** **KM# 146** **Weight:** 20.0900 g. **Composition:** 0.9250 Silver .5977 oz. ASW **Series:** Endangered Wildlife **Subject:** Polar Bear

| Date | Mintage | F | VF | XF | Unc | BU |
|---|---|---|---|---|---|---|
| 1993FM (P) | — | Value: 35.00 | | | | |

**25 DOLLARS** **KM# 147** **Weight:** 20.0900 g. **Composition:** 0.9250 Silver .5977 oz. ASW **Series:** Endangered Wildlife **Subject:** Bald Eagle

| Date | Mintage | F | VF | XF | Unc | BU |
|---|---|---|---|---|---|---|
| 1993FM (P) | — | Value: 32.50 | | | | |

**25 DOLLARS** **KM# 148** **Weight:** 20.0900 g. **Composition:** 0.9250 Silver .5977 oz. ASW **Series:** Endangered Wildlife **Subject:** Snow Leopard

| Date | Mintage | F | VF | XF | Unc | BU |
|---|---|---|---|---|---|---|
| 1993FM (P) | — | Value: 35.00 | | | | |

**25 DOLLARS** **KM# 149** **Weight:** 20.0900 g. **Composition:** 0.9250 Silver .5977 oz. ASW **Series:** Endangered Wildlife **Subject:** Javan Rhinoceros

| Date | Mintage | F | VF | XF | Unc | BU |
|---|---|---|---|---|---|---|
| 1993FM (P) | — | Value: 37.50 | | | | |

**25 DOLLARS** **KM# 150** **Weight:** 20.0900 g. **Composition:** 0.9250 Silver .5977 oz. ASW **Series:** Endangered Wildlife **Subject:** Asian Lion

| Date | Mintage | F | VF | XF | Unc | BU |
|---|---|---|---|---|---|---|
| 1993FM (P) | — | Value: 45.00 | | | | |

**25 DOLLARS** **KM# 151** **Weight:** 20.0900 g. **Composition:** 0.9250 Silver .5977 oz. ASW **Series:** Endangered Wildlife **Subject:** Giant Panda

| Date | Mintage | F | VF | XF | Unc | BU |
|---|---|---|---|---|---|---|
| 1993FM (P) | — | Value: 37.50 | | | | |

**25 DOLLARS** **KM# 152** **Weight:** 20.0900 g. **Composition:** 0.9250 Silver .5977 oz. ASW **Series:** Endangered Wildlife **Subject:** Golden Lion Tamarin

| Date | Mintage | F | VF | XF | Unc | BU |
|---|---|---|---|---|---|---|
| 1993FM (P) | — | Value: 35.00 | | | | |

**25 DOLLARS** **KM# 153** **Weight:** 20.0900 g. **Composition:** 0.9250 Silver .5977 oz. ASW **Series:** Endangered Wildlife **Subject:** Pere David's Deer

| Date | Mintage | F | VF | XF | Unc | BU |
|---|---|---|---|---|---|---|
| 1993FM (P) | — | Value: 32.50 | | | | |

**25 DOLLARS** **KM# 154** **Weight:** 20.0900 g. **Composition:** 0.9250 Silver .5977 oz. ASW **Series:** Endangered Wildlife **Subject:** Spectacled Bear

| Date | Mintage | F | VF | XF | Unc | BU |
|---|---|---|---|---|---|---|
| 1993FM (P) | — | Value: 40.00 | | | | |

**25 DOLLARS** **KM# 155** **Weight:** 20.0900 g. **Composition:** 0.9250 Silver .5977 oz. ASW **Series:** Endangered Wildlife **Obverse:** Queen's head right. **Reverse:** Parrot on tree branch. **Edge:** Reeded. **Size:** 40 mm.

| Date | Mintage | F | VF | XF | Unc | BU |
|---|---|---|---|---|---|---|
| 1993FM (P) | — | Value: 40.00 | | | | |

**25 DOLLARS** **KM# 158** **Weight:** 21.5900 g. **Composition:** 0.9250 Silver .6420 oz. ASW **Series:** Endangered Wildlife **Subject:** Black-footed Ferrets **Obverse:** Queen's portrait **Reverse:** Pair of black-footed ferrets, one standing

| Date | Mintage | F | VF | XF | Unc | BU |
|---|---|---|---|---|---|---|
| 1993FM Proof | — | Value: 35.00 | | | | |

**25 DOLLARS** **KM# 159** **Weight:** 21.5900 g. **Composition:** 0.9250 Silver .6420 oz. ASW **Series:** Endangered Wildlife **Subject:** Rock Lizard **Obverse:** Queen's portrait **Reverse:** Large lizard

| Date | Mintage | F | VF | XF | Unc | BU |
|---|---|---|---|---|---|---|
| 1993FM Proof | — | Value: 37.50 | | | | |

**25 DOLLARS** **KM#160** **Weight:** 21.5900 g. **Composition:** 0.9250 Silver .6420 oz. ASW **Series:** Endangered Wildlife **Subject:** Parma Wallaby **Obverse:** Queen's portrait **Reverse:** Two kangaroo-like creatures, one with offspring

| Date | Mintage | F | VF | XF | Unc | BU |
|---|---|---|---|---|---|---|
| 1993FM Proof | — | Value: 35.00 | | | | |

**25 DOLLARS** **KM#161** **Weight:** 21.5900 g. **Composition:** 0.9250 Silver .6420 oz. ASW **Series:** Endangered Wildlife **Subject:** Sea Turtle **Obverse:** Queen's portrait **Reverse:** Pair of leatherback turtles and Portuguese Man-o-War jelly fish

| Date | Mintage | F | VF | XF | Unc | BU |
|---|---|---|---|---|---|---|
| 1993FM Proof | — | Value: 40.00 | | | | |

**25 DOLLARS** **KM#170** **Weight:** 21.3500 g. **Composition:** 0.9250 Silver .6349 oz. ASW **Series:** Endangered Wildlife **Subject:** Cheetah **Obverse:** Queen's portrait **Reverse:** Cheetah running left

| Date | Mintage | F | VF | XF | Unc | BU |
|---|---|---|---|---|---|---|
| 1993FM Proof | — | Value: 35.00 | | | | |

**25 DOLLARS** **KM#171** **Weight:** 21.3500 g. **Composition:** 0.9250 Silver .6349 oz. ASW **Series:** Endangered Wildlife **Subject:** Bison **Obverse:** Queen's portrait **Reverse:** Bison in forest

| Date | Mintage | F | VF | XF | Unc | BU |
|---|---|---|---|---|---|---|
| 1993FM Proof | — | Value: 32.50 | | | | |

**25 DOLLARS** **KM#178** **Weight:** 21.6000 g. **Composition:** 0.9250 Silver .6424 oz. ASW **Series:** Endangered Wildlife **Obverse:** Queen's head right. **Reverse:** Three flamingos and four nests. **Edge:** Reeded. **Size:** 40 mm.

| Date | Mintage | F | VF | XF | Unc | BU |
|---|---|---|---|---|---|---|
| 1993 Proof | — | Value: 40.00 | | | | |

**25 DOLLARS** **KM#179** **Weight:** 20.9000 g. **Composition:** 0.9250 Silver .5977 oz. ASW **Obverse:** Queen's head right. **Reverse:** Front half of tiger stalking left. **Rev. Legend:** Endangered Wildlife **Edge:** Reeded. **Size:** 40 mm.

| Date | Mintage | F | VF | XF | Unc | BU |
|---|---|---|---|---|---|---|
| 1993FM Proof | — | Value: 35.00 | | | | |

**25 DOLLARS** **KM#165** **Weight:** 21.5900 g. **Composition:** 0.9250 Silver .6420 oz. ASW **Series:** Endangered Wildlife **Subject:** Seals **Obverse:** Queen's portrait **Reverse:** Two seals playing

| Date | Mintage | F | VF | XF | Unc | BU |
|---|---|---|---|---|---|---|
| 1997 | — | — | — | — | 40.00 | — |

**25 DOLLARS** **KM#166** **Weight:** 21.5900 g. **Composition:** 0.9250 Silver .6420 oz. ASW **Series:** Endangered Wildlife **Subject:** Sea Otter **Obverse:** Queen's portrait **Reverse:** Sea otter holding a sea urchin

| Date | Mintage | F | VF | XF | Unc | BU |
|---|---|---|---|---|---|---|
| 1997 | — | — | — | — | 35.00 | — |

**25 DOLLARS** **KM#167** **Weight:** 21.5900 g. **Composition:** 0.9250 Silver .6420 oz. ASW **Series:** Endangered Wildlife **Subject:** Antelope **Obverse:** Queen's portrait **Reverse:** Pair of sparring antelope

| Date | Mintage | F | VF | XF | Unc | BU |
|---|---|---|---|---|---|---|
| 1997 | — | — | — | — | 32.50 | — |

**25 DOLLARS** **KM#168** **Weight:** 21.5900 g. **Composition:** 0.9250 Silver .6420 oz. ASW **Series:** Endangered Wildlife **Subject:** Humpback Whale **Obverse:** Queen's portrait **Reverse:** Diving whale

| Date | Mintage | F | VF | XF | Unc | BU |
|---|---|---|---|---|---|---|
| 1997 | — | — | — | — | 37.50 | — |

**50 DOLLARS** **KM# 28** **Weight:** 2.6800 g. **Composition:** 0.5000 Gold .0430 oz. AGW **Subject:** Golden Dove of Christmas

| Date | Mintage | F | VF | XF | Unc | BU |
|---|---|---|---|---|---|---|
| 1980 Proof | 6,379 | Value: 65.00 | | | | |

**50 DOLLARS** **KM# 75** **Weight:** 2.0687 g. **Composition:** 0.5000 Gold .0332 oz. AGW **Subject:** Flute Player

| Date | Mintage | F | VF | XF | Unc | BU |
|---|---|---|---|---|---|---|
| 1988 Proof | — | Value: 55.00 | | | | |

**50 DOLLARS** **KM# 76** **Weight:** 2.0687 g. **Composition:** 0.5000 Gold .0332 oz. AGW **Subject:** Bird's Head Staff

| Date | Mintage | F | VF | XF | Unc | BU |
|---|---|---|---|---|---|---|
| 1988 Proof | — | Value: 55.00 | | | | |

**50 DOLLARS** **KM# 77** **Weight:** 2.0687 g. **Composition:** 0.5000 Gold .0332 oz. AGW **Subject:** Double Spouted Vessel

| Date | Mintage | F | VF | XF | Unc | BU |
|---|---|---|---|---|---|---|
| 1988 Proof | — | Value: 55.00 | | | | |

**50 DOLLARS** **KM# 78** **Weight:** 2.0687 g. **Composition:** 0.5000 Gold .0332 oz. AGW **Subject:** Deer-top Bell

| Date | Mintage | F | VF | XF | Unc | BU |
|---|---|---|---|---|---|---|
| 1988 Proof | — | Value: 55.00 | | | | |

**50 DOLLARS** **KM# 79** **Weight:** 2.0687 g. **Composition:** 0.5000 Gold .0332 oz. AGW **Subject:** Two Headed Animal

| Date | Mintage | F | VF | XF | Unc | BU |
|---|---|---|---|---|---|---|
| 1988 Proof | — | Value: 55.00 | | | | |

**50 DOLLARS** **KM# 80** **Weight:** 2.0687 g. **Composition:** 0.5000 Gold .0332 oz. AGW **Subject:** Turtle

| Date | Mintage | F | VF | XF | Unc | BU |
|---|---|---|---|---|---|---|
| 1988 Proof | — | Value: 55.00 | | | | |

**50 DOLLARS** **KM# 81** **Weight:** 2.0687 g. **Composition:** 0.5000 Gold .0332 oz. AGW **Subject:** Frog

| Date | Mintage | F | VF | XF | Unc | BU |
|---|---|---|---|---|---|---|
| 1988 Proof | — | Value: 55.00 | | | | |

**50 DOLLARS** **KM# 82** **Weight:** 2.0687 g. **Composition:** 0.5000 Gold .0332 oz. AGW **Subject:** Mixtec Mask

| Date | Mintage | F | VF | XF | Unc | BU |
|---|---|---|---|---|---|---|
| 1988 Proof | — | Value: 55.00 | | | | |

**50 DOLLARS** KM# 83 **Weight:** 2.0687 g. **Composition:** 0.5000 Gold .0332 oz. AGW **Subject:** Chimu Gold Beaker

| Date | Mintage | F | VF | XF | Unc | BU |
|---|---|---|---|---|---|---|
| 1988 Proof | — | Value: 55.00 | | | | |

**50 DOLLARS** KM# 84 **Weight:** 2.0687 g. **Composition:** 0.5000 Gold .0332 oz. AGW **Subject:** Bird Vessel

| Date | Mintage | F | VF | XF | Unc | BU |
|---|---|---|---|---|---|---|
| 1988 Proof | — | Value: 55.00 | | | | |

**50 DOLLARS** KM# 85 **Weight:** 2.0687 g. **Composition:** 0.5000 Gold .0332 oz. AGW **Subject:** Ceremonial Headdress

| Date | Mintage | F | VF | XF | Unc | BU |
|---|---|---|---|---|---|---|
| 1988 Proof | — | Value: 55.00 | | | | |

**50 DOLLARS** KM# 86 **Weight:** 2.0687 g. **Composition:** 0.5000 Gold .0332 oz. AGW **Subject:** Sacrifical Knife

| Date | Mintage | F | VF | XF | Unc | BU |
|---|---|---|---|---|---|---|
| 1988 Proof | — | Value: 55.00 | | | | |

**50 DOLLARS** KM# 87 **Weight:** 2.0687 g. **Composition:** 0.5000 Gold .0332 oz. AGW **Subject:** Ceremonial Dancer

| Date | Mintage | F | VF | XF | Unc | BU |
|---|---|---|---|---|---|---|
| 1988 Proof | — | Value: 55.00 | | | | |

**50 DOLLARS** KM# 88 **Weight:** 2.0687 g. **Composition:** 0.5000 Gold .0332 oz. AGW **Subject:** Spanish Colonial Gold Coin

| Date | Mintage | F | VF | XF | Unc | BU |
|---|---|---|---|---|---|---|
| 1988 Proof | — | Value: 55.00 | | | | |

**50 DOLLARS** KM# 89 **Weight:** 2.0687 g. **Composition:** 0.5000 Gold .0332 oz. AGW **Subject:** Crossed Hands

| Date | Mintage | F | VF | XF | Unc | BU |
|---|---|---|---|---|---|---|
| 1988 Proof | — | Value: 55.00 | | | | |

**100 DOLLARS** KM# 7 **Weight:** 7.1000 g. **Composition:** 0.9000 Gold .2054 oz. AGW **Subject:** Royal Tern

| Date | Mintage | F | VF | XF | Unc | BU |
|---|---|---|---|---|---|---|
| 1975FM (M) Rare | 10 | — | — | — | — | — |
| 1975FM (U) | 13,000 | — | — | — | 110 | — |
| 1975FM (P) | Est. 23,000 | Value: 135 | | | | |

**Note:** Includes 8,754 in First Day Covers

**100 DOLLARS** KM# 8 **Weight:** 7.1000 g. **Composition:** 0.9000 Gold .2054 oz. AGW **Subject:** 50th Birthday of Queen Elizabeth II

| Date | Mintage | F | VF | XF | Unc | BU |
|---|---|---|---|---|---|---|
| 1976FM (M) Rare | 10 | — | — | — | — | — |
| 1976FM (U) | 1,752 | — | — | — | 125 | — |
| 1976FM (P) | 12,000 | Value: 150 | | | | |

**100 DOLLARS** KM# 15 **Weight:** 7.1000 g. **Composition:** 0.9000 Gold .2054 oz. AGW **Subject:** Queen's Silver Jubilee

| Date | Mintage | F | VF | XF | Unc | BU |
|---|---|---|---|---|---|---|
| 1977FM (U) Rare | 10 | — | — | — | — | — |
| 1977FM (P) | 6,715 | Value: 150 | | | | |

**100 DOLLARS** KM# 23 **Weight:** 7.1000 g. **Composition:** 0.9000 Gold .2054 oz. AGW **Subject:** Coronation Jubilee

| Date | Mintage | F | VF | XF | Unc | BU |
|---|---|---|---|---|---|---|
| 1978FM (P) | 5,772 | Value: 160 | | | | |

**100 DOLLARS** KM# 25 **Weight:** 7.1000 g. **Composition:** 0.9000 Gold .2054 oz. AGW **Subject:** Sir Francis Drake

| Date | Mintage | F | VF | XF | Unc | BU |
|---|---|---|---|---|---|---|
| 1979FM (P) | 3,216 | Value: 175 | | | | |

**100 DOLLARS** KM# 29 **Weight:** 7.1000 g. **Composition:** 0.9000 Gold .2054 oz. AGW **Subject:** 400th Anniversary of Drake's Voyage

| Date | Mintage | F | VF | XF | Unc | BU |
|---|---|---|---|---|---|---|
| 1980 Proof | 5,412 | Value: 125 | | | | |

**100 DOLLARS** KM# 32 **Weight:** 7.1000 g. **Composition:** 0.9000 Gold .2054 oz. AGW **Subject:** Knighting of Sir Francis Drake

| Date | Mintage | F | VF | XF | Unc | BU |
|---|---|---|---|---|---|---|
| 1981FM (P) | 1,321 | Value: 180 | | | | |

**100 DOLLARS** KM# 34 **Weight:** 7.1000 g. **Composition:** 0.9000 Gold .2054 oz. AGW **Subject:** 30th Anniversary - Reign of Queen Elizabeth II

| Date | Mintage | F | VF | XF | Unc | BU |
|---|---|---|---|---|---|---|
| 1982FM (P) | 620 | Value: 250 | | | | |

**100 DOLLARS** KM# 38 **Weight:** 7.1000 g. **Composition:** 0.9000 Gold .2054 oz. AGW **Subject:** 30th Anniversary - Coronation of Queen Elizabeth II

| Date | Mintage | F | VF | XF | Unc | BU |
|---|---|---|---|---|---|---|
| 1983FM (P) | 624 | Value: 250 | | | | |

**100 DOLLARS** KM# 39 **Weight:** 7.1000 g. **Composition:** 0.9000 Gold .2054 oz. AGW **Subject:** Flora - Ginger Thomas

| Date | Mintage | F | VF | XF | Unc | BU |
|---|---|---|---|---|---|---|
| 1984FM (P) | 25 | Value: 475 | | | | |

**100 DOLLARS** KM# 74 **Weight:** 7.1000 g. **Composition:** 0.9000 Gold .2054 oz. AGW **Subject:** Sir Francis Drake's West Indian Voyage

| Date | Mintage | F | VF | XF | Unc | BU |
|---|---|---|---|---|---|---|
| 1985FM (P) | 772 | Value: 200 | | | | |

**100 DOLLARS** KM# 119 **Weight:** 4.1180 g. **Composition:** 0.5000 Gold .0662 oz. AGW **Subject:** Discovery of America - King Ferdinand of Spain

| Date | Mintage | F | VF | XF | Unc | BU |
|---|---|---|---|---|---|---|
| ND(1991)FM (P) | — | Value: 110 | | | | |

**100 DOLLARS** KM# 162 **Weight:** 4.1180 g. **Composition:** 0.5000 Gold .0662 oz. AGW **Subject:** The Pinta **Obverse:** Queen's portrait **Reverse:** Ship sailing right

| Date | Mintage | F | VF | XF | Unc | BU |
|---|---|---|---|---|---|---|
| ND(1994) Proof | — | Value: 125 | | | | |

**100 DOLLARS** KM# 174 **Weight:** 6.2200 g. **Composition:** 0.9990 Gold .2000 oz. AGW **Subject:** Queen Mother's 100th Birthday **Obverse:** Queen's head right **Reverse:** 1/2 bust of Queen Mother facing **Edge:** Reeded

| Date | Mintage | F | VF | XF | Unc | BU |
|---|---|---|---|---|---|---|
| 2000 Proof | 5,000 | Value: 175 | | | | |

**250 DOLLARS** KM# 120 **Weight:** 8.0494 g. **Composition:** 0.5000 Gold .1294 oz. AGW **Subject:** Discovery of America - Queen Isabella of Spain

| Date | Mintage | F | VF | XF | Unc | BU |
|---|---|---|---|---|---|---|
| ND(1991)FM (P) | — | Value: 265 | | | | |

**250 DOLLARS** KM# 163 **Weight:** 8.0494 g. **Composition:** 0.5000 Gold .1294 oz. AGW **Subject:** The Nina **Obverse:** Queen's portrait **Reverse:** Ship sailing left

| Date | Mintage | F | VF | XF | Unc | BU |
|---|---|---|---|---|---|---|
| ND(1994) Proof | — | Value: 285 | | | | |

**500 DOLLARS** KM# 121 **Weight:** 19.8126 g. **Composition:** 0.5000 Gold .3185 oz. AGW **Subject:** Discovery of America - Christopher Columbus

| Date | Mintage | F | VF | XF | Unc | BU |
|---|---|---|---|---|---|---|
| ND(1991)FM (P) | — | Value: 550 | | | | |

**500 DOLLARS** KM# 164 **Weight:** 19.8126 g. **Composition:** 0.5000 Gold .3185 oz. AGW **Subject:** The Santa Maria **Obverse:** Queen's portrait **Reverse:** Ship sailing left, no gulls

| Date | Mintage | F | VF | XF | Unc | BU |
|---|---|---|---|---|---|---|
| ND(1994) Proof | — | Value: 575 | | | | |

**1000 DOLLARS** KM# 156 **Weight:** 14.8000 g. **Composition:** 0.9990 Platinum .4758 oz. APW **Subject:** Discovery of America - 3 Ships Sailing

| Date | Mintage | F | VF | XF | Unc | BU |
|---|---|---|---|---|---|---|
| ND(1992) Proof | — | Value: 1,150 | | | | |

## MINT SETS

| KM# | Date | Mintage | Identification | Issue Price | Mkt Val |
|---|---|---|---|---|---|
| MS1 | 1973 (6) | 18,402 | KM#1-5, 6a | 11.50 | 8.00 |
| MS2 | 1974 (6) | 9,474 | KM#1-6 | 10.00 | 8.00 |
| MS3 | 1975 (6) | 2,351 | KM#1-6 | 12.50 | 10.00 |
| MS4 | 1976 (6) | 996 | KM#1-6 | 13.50 | 12.00 |
| MS5 | 1977 (6) | 782 | KM#1-6 | 12.50 | 12.00 |
| MS6 | 1978 (6) | 943 | KM#1-6 | 13.00 | 12.00 |
| MS7 | 1979 (7) | 680 | KM#1-6, 24 | 20.00 | 25.00 |
| MS8 | 1980 (7) | 1,007 | KM#1-6, 26 | 21.00 | 25.00 |
| MS9 | 1981 (9) | 472 | KM#1-6, 30 | 20.00 | 30.00 |
| MS10 | 1982 (7) | — | KM#1-6, 33 | 28.50 | 35.00 |
| MS11 | 1983 (7) | 203 | KM#1-6, 35 | 22.00 | 50.00 |

## PROOF SETS

| KM# | Date | Mintage | Identification | Issue Price | Mkt Val |
|---|---|---|---|---|---|
| PS1 | 1973 (6) | 146,581 | KM#1-5, 6a. Includes 34,418 proofs in First Day Covers | 15.00 | 15.00 |
| PS2 | 1974 (6) | 93,555 | KM#1-5, 6a | 20.00 | 16.50 |
| PS3 | 1975 (6) | 32,244 | KM#1-5, 6a | 25.00 | 18.50 |
| PS4 | 1976 (6) | 15,003 | KM#1-5, 6a | 25.00 | 18.50 |
| PS5 | 1977 (6) | 7,218 | KM#1-5, 6a | 26.00 | 20.00 |
| PS6 | 1977 (6) | 17,366 | KM#9-14 | 60.00 | 40.00 |
| PS7 | 1978 (6) | 7,059 | KM#1-5, 6a | 25.00 | 20.00 |
| PS8 | 1978 (6) | 6,196 | KM#16-21 | — | 40.00 |
| PS9 | 1979 (7) | 5,304 | KM#1-5, 6a, 24a | 39.50 | 37.50 |
| PS10 | 1980 (7) | 3,421 | KM#105, 6a, 26a | 97.00 | 47.50 |
| PS11 | 1981 (7) | 1,124 | KM#1-5, 6a, 30a | 97.00 | 60.00 |
| PS12 | 1982 (7) | — | KM#1-5, 6a, 33a | 97.00 | 60.00 |
| PS13 | 1983 (7) | 478 | KM#1-5, 6a, 35a | 77.00 | 65.00 |
| PS14 | 1984 (7) | 5,000 | KM#1-5, 6a, 35a | 77.00 | 60.00 |
| PS15 | 1985 (6) | — | KM#42-47 | 20.50 | 45.00 |
| PS16 | 1985 (6) | — | KM#42a-47a | 76.00 | 95.00 |
| PS17 | ND (1991) (3) | — | KM#119-121 | 975 | 950 |
| PS18 | ND (1994) (3) | — | KM#162-164 | 975 | 985 |

# BRITISH WEST AFRICA

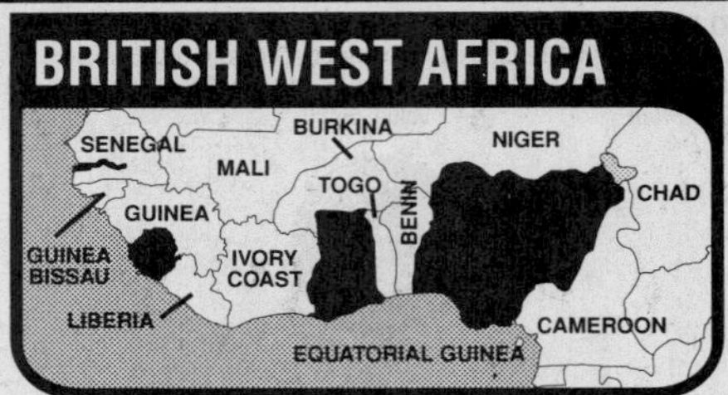


British West Africa was an administrative grouping of the four former British West African colonies of Gambia, Sierra Leone, Nigeria and Gold Coast (now Ghana). All are now independent republics and members of the British Commonwealth of Nations. See separate entries for individual statistics and history.

The Bank of British West Africa became the banker to the Colonial Government in 1894 and held this status until 1912. As such they were responsible for maintaining a proper supply of silver coinage for the colonies.

Through the subsidiary efforts of the Governor of Lagos, Nigeria a specific British West African coinage was put into use between 1907 and 1911. These coins bear the inscription, NIGERIA-BRITISH WEST AFRICA.

The four colonies were supplied with a common coinage and banknotes by the West African Currency Board from 1912 through 1958. This coinage bore the inscription BRITISH WEST AFRICA. The coinage, which includes three denominations of 1936 bearing the name of Edward VIII, is obsolete.

For later coinage see Gambia, Ghana, Sierra Leone and Nigeria.

**RULERS**

British, until 1958

**MINT MARKS**

G-J.R. Gaunt & Sons, Birmingham
H - Heaton Mint, Birmingham
K, KN - King's Norton, Birmingham
SA - Pretoria, South Africa
No mm - Royal Mint, London

**MONETARY SYSTEM**

12 Pence = 1 Shilling
20 Shillings = 1 Pound

# BRITISH COLONIES

## POUND COINAGE

**1/10 PENNY** KM# 1 **Composition:** Aluminum

| Date | Mintage | F | VF | XF | Unc | BU |
|---|---|---|---|---|---|---|
| 1907 | 1,254,000 | 2.00 | 4.00 | 10.00 | 20.00 | — |
| 1908 | 8,363,000 | 1.00 | 3.00 | 6.00 | 15.00 | — |
| 1908 Proof | — | Value: 300 | | | | |

**1/10 PENNY** KM# 3 **Composition:** Copper-Nickel

| Date | Mintage | F | VF | XF | Unc | BU |
|---|---|---|---|---|---|---|
| 1908 | 9,600,000 | 0.30 | 0.50 | 1.00 | 2.00 | — |
| 1909 | 4,800,000 | 0.40 | 0.75 | 1.50 | 5.00 | — |
| 1910 | 7,200,000 | 0.50 | 1.00 | 2.00 | 7.50 | — |

**1/10 PENNY** KM# 4 **Composition:** Copper-Nickel

| Date | Mintage | F | VF | XF | Unc | BU |
|---|---|---|---|---|---|---|
| 1911H | 7,200,000 | 1.50 | 3.50 | 7.50 | 15.00 | — |

**1/10 PENNY** **KM# 7** **Composition:** Copper-Nickel
**Rev. Legend:** Without NIGERIA

| Date | Mintage | F | VF | XF | Unc | BU |
|---|---|---|---|---|---|---|
| 1912H | 10,800,000 | 0.30 | 0.75 | 1.50 | 4.00 | — |
| 1913 | 4,632,000 | 1.00 | 2.00 | 3.50 | 6.50 | — |
| 1913H | 1,080,000 | 0.30 | 0.75 | 1.50 | 3.50 | — |
| 1914 | 1,200,000 | 3.00 | 5.00 | 10.00 | 22.50 | — |
| 1914H | 20,088,000 | 0.50 | 1.25 | 2.00 | 5.00 | — |
| 1915H | 10,032,000 | 0.30 | 0.75 | 1.50 | 5.00 | — |
| 1916H | 480,000 | 25.00 | 50.00 | 75.00 | 150 | — |
| 1917H | 9,384,000 | 2.00 | 3.00 | 5.00 | 15.00 | — |
| 1919H | 912,000 | 1.25 | 2.00 | 4.00 | 7.50 | — |
| 1919KN | 480,000 | 10.00 | 25.00 | 50.00 | 75.00 | — |
| 1920H | 1,560,000 | 2.00 | 3.00 | 5.00 | 10.00 | — |
| 1920KN | 12,996,000 | 0.40 | 1.00 | 3.00 | 5.00 | — |
| 1920KN Proof | — | Value: 125 | | | | |
| 1922KN | 7,265,000 | 1.00 | 1.75 | 4.50 | 12.00 | — |
| 1923KN | 12,000,000 | 0.30 | 0.75 | 1.50 | 5.00 | — |
| 1925 | 2,400,000 | 5.00 | 10.00 | 20.00 | 40.00 | — |
| 1925H | 12,000,000 | 2.00 | 3.00 | 5.00 | 12.00 | — |
| 1925KN | 12,000,000 | 0.75 | 1.50 | 3.00 | 8.00 | — |
| 1926 | 12,000,000 | 0.75 | 1.50 | 2.50 | 6.00 | — |
| 1927 | 3,984,000 | 0.20 | 0.50 | 1.50 | 3.00 | — |
| 1927 Proof | — | Value: 150 | | | | |
| 1928 | 11,760,000 | 0.20 | 0.50 | 1.50 | 3.00 | — |
| 1928 Proof | — | Value: 150 | | | | |
| 1928H | 2,964,000 | 0.20 | 0.50 | 1.50 | 3.00 | — |
| 1928KN | 3,151,000 | 2.00 | 3.00 | 6.00 | 15.00 | — |
| 1930 | 9,600,000 | 2.00 | 3.00 | 6.00 | 15.00 | — |
| 1930 Proof | — | Value: 150 | | | | |
| 1931 | 9,840,000 | 0.20 | 0.50 | 1.00 | 3.00 | — |
| 1931 Proof | — | Value: 150 | | | | |
| 1932 | 3,600,000 | 0.20 | 0.50 | 1.50 | 5.00 | — |
| 1932 Proof | — | Value: 150 | | | | |
| 1933 | 7,200,000 | 0.20 | 0.50 | 1.50 | 3.50 | — |
| 1933 Proof | — | Value: 150 | | | | |
| 1934 | 4,800,000 | 0.75 | 1.50 | 3.00 | 6.00 | — |
| 1934 Proof | — | Value: 150 | | | | |
| 1935 | 13,200,000 | 0.75 | 1.50 | 3.00 | 7.50 | — |
| 1935 Proof | — | Value: 150 | | | | |
| 1936 | 9,720,000 | 0.20 | 0.50 | 1.00 | 3.00 | — |
| 1936 Proof | — | Value: 150 | | | | |

**1/10 PENNY** **KM# 14** **Composition:** Copper-Nickel

| Date | Mintage | F | VF | XF | Unc | BU |
|---|---|---|---|---|---|---|
| 1936 | 5,880,000 | 0.25 | 0.50 | 1.00 | 2.50 | — |
| 1936 Proof | — | Value: 200 | | | | |
| 1936H | 1,404,000 | 50.00 | 75.00 | 125 | 250 | — |
| 1936H Proof | — | Value: 300 | | | | |
| 1936KN | 3,000,000 | 1.00 | 2.00 | 3.50 | 9.00 | — |
| 1936KN Proof | — | Value: 200 | | | | |

**1/10 PENNY** **KM# 20** **Composition:** Copper-Nickel

| Date | Mintage | F | VF | XF | Unc | BU |
|---|---|---|---|---|---|---|
| 1938 | 12,000,000 | 0.10 | 0.25 | 0.50 | 1.50 | — |
| 1938 Proof | — | Value: 125 | | | | |
| 1938H | 1,596,000 | 5.00 | 8.00 | 12.00 | 22.50 | — |
| 1938H Proof | — | Value: 100 | | | | |
| 1939 | 9,840,000 | 0.25 | 0.50 | 1.00 | 3.50 | — |
| 1939 Proof | — | Value: 200 | | | | |
| 1940 | 13,920,000 | 0.25 | 0.50 | 1.00 | 2.00 | — |
| 1940 Proof | — | Value: 125 | | | | |
| 1941 | 16,560,000 | 1.00 | 2.00 | 4.00 | 8.00 | — |
| 1941 Proof | — | Value: 125 | | | | |
| 1942 | 12,360,000 | 1.00 | 2.50 | 4.50 | 10.00 | — |
| 1942 Proof | — | Value: 125 | | | | |
| 1943 | 22,560,000 | 1.00 | 2.50 | 5.00 | 10.00 | — |
| 1944 | 10,440,000 | 1.00 | 2.50 | 5.00 | 10.00 | — |
| 1944 Proof | — | Value: 150 | | | | |
| 1945 | 25,706,000 | 0.50 | 1.00 | 1.75 | 6.00 | — |
| 1945 Proof | — | Value: 125 | | | | |
| 1946 | 2,803,000 | 1.00 | 2.00 | 4.00 | 9.00 | — |
| 1946 Proof | — | Value: 125 | | | | |
| 1946H | 5,004,000 | 1.00 | 2.00 | 4.00 | 9.00 | — |
| 1946KN | 1,152,000 | 0.25 | 0.50 | 1.00 | 3.00 | — |
| 1946KN Proof | — | Value: 125 | | | | |
| 1947 | 4,202,000 | 0.50 | 1.00 | 2.00 | 5.00 | — |
| 1947 Proof | — | Value: 125 | | | | |
| 1947KN | 3,900,000 | 200 | 300 | 500 | 600 | — |

**1/10 PENNY** **KM# 26** **Composition:** Copper-Nickel
**Obv. Legend:** Without IND: IMP:

| Date | Mintage | F | VF | XF | Unc | BU |
|---|---|---|---|---|---|---|
| 1949H | 3,700,000 | 1.00 | 2.00 | 3.00 | 6.00 | — |
| 1949KN | 3,036,000 | 1.00 | 2.00 | 3.00 | 5.00 | — |
| 1950KN | 13,200,000 | 0.25 | 0.50 | 1.00 | 2.50 | — |
| 1950KN Proof | — | Value: 150 | | | | |

**1/10 PENNY** **KM# 26a** **Composition:** Bronze

| Date | Mintage | F | VF | XF | Unc | BU |
|---|---|---|---|---|---|---|
| 1952 | 15,060,000 | 0.50 | 1.00 | 2.00 | 6.00 | — |
| 1952 Proof | — | Value: 150 | | | | |

**1/10 PENNY** **KM# 32** **Composition:** Bronze

| Date | Mintage | F | VF | XF | Unc | BU |
|---|---|---|---|---|---|---|
| 1954 | 4,800,000 | 0.50 | 1.00 | 2.00 | 4.00 | — |
| 1954 Proof | — | Value: 150 | | | | |
| 1956 | 2,400,000 | 100 | 200 | 400 | 700 | — |
| 1956 Proof | — | Value: 750 | | | | |
| 1957 | 7,200,000 | 60.00 | 120 | 220 | 325 | — |
| 1957 Proof | — | Value: 600 | | | | |

**1/2 PENNY** **KM# 5** **Composition:** Copper-Nickel

| Date | Mintage | F | VF | XF | Unc | BU |
|---|---|---|---|---|---|---|
| 1911H | 3,360,000 | 4.00 | 12.00 | 25.00 | 40.00 | — |

**1/2 PENNY** **KM# 8** **Composition:** Copper-Nickel
**Rev. Legend:** Without NIGERIA

| Date | Mintage | F | VF | XF | Unc | BU |
|---|---|---|---|---|---|---|
| 1912H | 3,120,000 | 2.00 | 5.00 | 7.00 | 20.00 | — |
| 1913 | 1,382,000 | 150 | 250 | 300 | 500 | — |
| 1913H | 216,000 | 5.00 | 10.00 | 17.50 | 30.00 | — |
| 1914 | 240,000 | 10.00 | 20.00 | 35.00 | 60.00 | — |
| 1914H | 586,000 | 20.00 | 30.00 | 50.00 | 75.00 | — |
| 1914K | 3,360,000 | 3.00 | 6.00 | 17.50 | 30.00 | — |
| 1914K Proof | — | Value: 225 | | | | |

**Note:** Issued with East Africa KM#11 in a double (4 pc.) specimen set

| Date | Mintage | F | VF | XF | Unc | BU |
|---|---|---|---|---|---|---|
| 1915K | 3,577,000 | 1.00 | 2.00 | 4.00 | 15.00 | — |
| 1916H | 4,046,000 | 1.00 | 3.00 | 5.00 | 15.00 | — |
| 1917H | 214,000 | 6.00 | 12.00 | 28.00 | 50.00 | — |
| 1918H | 490,000 | 2.50 | 5.00 | 10.00 | 30.00 | — |
| 1919H | 4,950,000 | 1.25 | 2.50 | 6.00 | 20.00 | — |
| 1919KN | 3,861,000 | 1.25 | 2.50 | 7.50 | 25.00 | — |
| 1920H | 26,285,000 | 1.50 | 3.00 | 7.50 | 15.00 | — |
| 1920KN | 13,844,000 | 0.50 | 3.00 | 8.50 | 16.50 | — |
| 1922KN | 5,817,000 | 300 | 500 | 750 | 1,200 | — |
| 1927 | 528,000 | 20.00 | 30.00 | 65.00 | 135 | — |
| 1927 Proof | — | Value: 225 | | | | |
| 1929 | 336,000 | 6.00 | 22.00 | 47.50 | 95.00 | — |
| 1929 Proof | — | Value: 225 | | | | |
| 1931 | 96,000 | 500 | 800 | 1,200 | 1,500 | — |
| 1931 Proof | — | Value: 225 | | | | |
| 1932 | 960,000 | 2.50 | 15.00 | 35.00 | 55.00 | — |
| 1932 Proof | — | Value: 225 | | | | |
| 1933 | 2,122,000 | 12.00 | 23.50 | 55.00 | 110 | — |
| 1933 Proof | — | Value: 225 | | | | |
| 1934 | 1,694,000 | 2.50 | 15.00 | 35.00 | 75.00 | — |
| 1934 Proof | — | Value: 225 | | | | |
| 1935 | 3,271,000 | 1.00 | 3.00 | 18.00 | 35.00 | — |
| 1935 Proof | — | Value: 225 | | | | |
| 1936 | 5,400,000 | 2.50 | 5.00 | 18.00 | 32.00 | — |
| 1936 | — | Value: 225 | | | | |

**1/2 PENNY** **KM# 15** **Composition:** Copper-Nickel

| Date | Mintage | F | VF | XF | Unc | BU |
|---|---|---|---|---|---|---|
| 1936 | 14,760,000 | 0.25 | 0.50 | 1.00 | 2.50 | — |
| 1936 Proof | — | Value: 200 | | | | |
| 1936H | 2,400,000 | 1.00 | 2.00 | 5.00 | 12.50 | — |
| 1936H Proof | — | Value: 200 | | | | |
| 1936KN | 2,298,000 | 0.65 | 1.25 | 2.25 | 4.00 | — |
| 1936KN Proof | — | Value: 200 | | | | |

**1/2 PENNY** **KM# 18** **Composition:** Copper-Nickel

| Date | Mintage | F | VF | XF | Unc | BU |
|---|---|---|---|---|---|---|
| 1937H | 4,800,000 | 0.40 | 0.85 | 1.50 | 4.00 | — |
| 1937H Proof | — | Value: 125 | | | | |
| 1937KN | 5,577,000 | 0.40 | 0.85 | 3.00 | 5.00 | — |
| 1940KN | 2,410,000 | 2.00 | 4.00 | 6.00 | 15.00 | — |
| 1940KN Proof | — | Value: 125 | | | | |
| 1941H | 2,400,000 | 0.40 | 2.00 | 4.00 | 12.00 | — |
| 1942 | 4,800,000 | 0.40 | 0.85 | 2.00 | 8.50 | — |
| 1943 | 3,360,000 | 0.50 | 1.00 | 5.00 | 10.00 | — |
| 1944 | 3,600,000 | 1.00 | 3.00 | 7.00 | 20.00 | — |
| 1944 Proof | — | Value: 125 | | | | |
| 1946 | 3,600,000 | 0.25 | 1.00 | 3.00 | 7.00 | — |
| 1946 Proof | — | Value: 125 | | | | |
| 1947H | 15,218,000 | 0.35 | 0.75 | 1.25 | 5.00 | — |
| 1947KN | 12,000,000 | 0.40 | 0.85 | 2.00 | 6.00 | — |

**1/2 PENNY** **KM# 27** **Composition:** Copper-Nickel
**Obv. Legend:** Without IND: IMP:

| Date | Mintage | F | VF | XF | Unc | BU |
|---|---|---|---|---|---|---|
| 1949H | 5,909,000 | 1.50 | 3.50 | 8.00 | 22.00 | — |
| 1949KN | 3,413,000 | 1.50 | 3.50 | 8.00 | 25.00 | — |
| 1951 | 3,468,000 | 1.50 | 3.50 | 9.00 | 25.00 | — |
| 1951 Proof | — | Value: 250 | | | | |

**1/2 PENNY** **KM# 27a** **Composition:** Bronze

| Date | Mintage | F | VF | XF | Unc | BU |
|---|---|---|---|---|---|---|
| 1952 | 11,332,000 | 0.25 | 0.50 | 1.50 | 5.50 | — |
| 1952 Proof | — | Value: 150 | | | | |
| 1952H | 27,603,000 | 0.20 | 0.35 | 0.75 | 2.00 | — |
| 1952KN | 4,800,000 | 0.50 | 2.00 | 5.00 | 10.00 | — |

**PENNY** **KM# 2** **Composition:** Copper-Nickel

| Date | Mintage | F | VF | XF | Unc | BU |
|---|---|---|---|---|---|---|
| 1907 | 863,000 | 2.00 | 5.00 | 9.00 | 20.00 | — |
| 1908 | 3,217,000 | 2.00 | 4.00 | 8.00 | 17.50 | — |

| Date | Mintage | F | VF | XF | Unc | BU |
|---|---|---|---|---|---|---|
| 1909 | 960,000 | 3.50 | 9.00 | 18.00 | 45.00 | — |
| 1910 | 2,520,000 | 2.75 | 7.00 | 12.00 | 25.00 | — |

**PENNY** KM# 6 **Composition:** Copper-Nickel

| Date | Mintage | F | VF | XF | Unc | BU |
|---|---|---|---|---|---|---|
| 1911H | 1,920,000 | 15.00 | 40.00 | 80.00 | 150 | — |

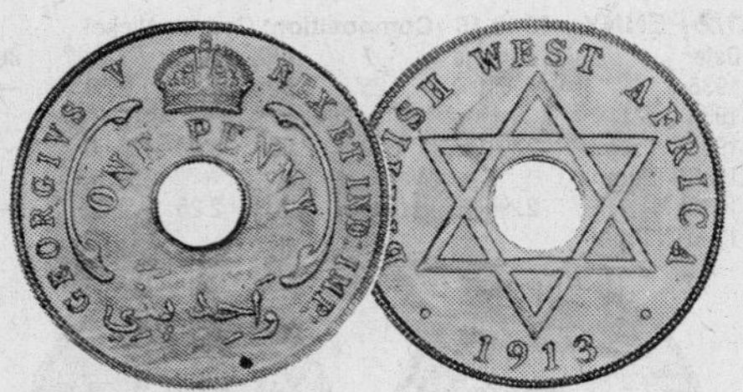

**PENNY** KM# 9 **Composition:** Copper-Nickel
**Rev. Legend:** Without NIGERIA

| Date | Mintage | F | VF | XF | Unc | BU |
|---|---|---|---|---|---|---|
| 1912H | 1,560,000 | 1.50 | 3.00 | 7.50 | 22.50 | — |
| 1913 | 1,680,000 | 7.50 | 15.00 | 30.00 | 75.00 | — |
| 1913H | 144,000 | 5.00 | 10.00 | 17.50 | 35.00 | — |
| 1914 | 3,000,000 | 2.50 | 5.00 | 10.00 | 22.50 | — |
| 1914H | 72,000 | 35.00 | 50.00 | 100 | 200 | — |
| 1915H | 3,295,000 | 1.25 | 2.00 | 5.00 | 15.00 | — |
| 1916H | 3,461,000 | 1.25 | 2.00 | 7.00 | 20.00 | — |
| 1917H | 444,000 | 5.00 | 7.00 | 18.00 | 45.00 | — |
| 1918H | 994,000 | 7.50 | 15.00 | 35.00 | 75.00 | — |
| 1919H | 21,864,000 | 1.25 | 2.50 | 5.00 | 15.00 | — |
| 1919KN | 264,000 | 7.50 | 15.00 | 25.00 | 50.00 | — |
| 1920H | 37,870,000 | 1.00 | 1.75 | 3.50 | 12.50 | — |
| 1920KN | 20,685,000 | 1.00 | 2.00 | 5.00 | 17.50 | — |
| 1922KN | 3,971,000 | 400 | 750 | 1,000 | 1,500 | — |
| 1926 | 8,039,999 | 2.00 | 4.00 | 10.00 | 30.00 | — |
| 1927 | 792,000 | 25.00 | 45.00 | 85.00 | 200 | — |
| 1927 Proof | — | Value: 225 | | | | |
| 1928 | 6,672,000 | 2.00 | 4.00 | 10.00 | 25.00 | — |
| 1928 Proof | — | Value: 225 | | | | |
| 1929 | 636,000 | 20.00 | 35.00 | 50.00 | 100 | — |
| 1929 Proof | — | Value: 225 | | | | |
| 1933 | 2,806,000 | 2.00 | 14.00 | 32.50 | 65.00 | — |
| 1933 Proof | — | Value: 225 | | | | |
| 1934 | 2,640,000 | 3.50 | 15.00 | 35.00 | 75.00 | — |
| 1934 Proof | — | Value: 225 | | | | |
| 1935 | 8,551,000 | 1.25 | 12.50 | 27.50 | 45.00 | — |
| 1935 Proof | — | Value: 225 | | | | |
| 1936 | 7,368,000 | 1.25 | 3.50 | 10.00 | 25.00 | — |
| 1936 Proof | — | Value: 225 | | | | |

**PENNY** KM# 16 **Composition:** Copper-Nickel

| Date | Mintage | F | VF | XF | Unc | BU |
|---|---|---|---|---|---|---|
| 1936 | 7,992,000 | 0.50 | 1.00 | 3.50 | 7.00 | — |
| 1936 Proof | — | Value: 250 | | | | |
| 1936H | 12,600,000 | 0.35 | 0.75 | 1.00 | 2.25 | — |
| 1936H Proof | — | Value: 250 | | | | |
| 1936KN | 12,512,000 | 0.35 | 0.75 | 1.00 | 2.25 | — |
| 1936KN Proof | — | Value: 250 | | | | |

**PENNY** KM# 17 **Composition:** Copper-Nickel **Obverse:** East Africa, KM#24 **Reverse:** KM#16 **Note:** Mule.

| Date | Mintage | F | VF | XF | Unc | BU |
|---|---|---|---|---|---|---|
| 1936H | — | 125 | 150 | 225 | 350 | — |

**PENNY** KM# 19 **Composition:** Copper-Nickel

| Date | Mintage | F | VF | XF | Unc | BU |
|---|---|---|---|---|---|---|
| 1937H | 11,999,000 | 0.50 | 0.75 | 1.25 | 2.00 | — |
| 1937H Proof | — | Value: 200 | | | | |
| 1937KN | 11,999,000 | 0.50 | 0.75 | 1.25 | 2.00 | — |
| 1937KN Proof | — | Value: 200 | | | | |
| 1940 | 3,840,000 | 0.50 | 0.75 | 1.25 | 2.00 | — |
| 1940 Proof | — | — | — | — | — | — |
| 1940H | 2,400,000 | 0.50 | 0.75 | 3.00 | 8.00 | — |
| 1940KN | 2,400,000 | 0.75 | 1.50 | 4.50 | 10.00 | — |
| 1941 | 6,960,000 | 0.35 | 0.75 | 1.25 | 3.50 | — |
| 1941 Proof | — | — | — | — | — | — |
| 1942 | 18,840,000 | 0.30 | 0.60 | 1.00 | 3.00 | — |
| 1943 | 28,920,000 | 0.30 | 0.60 | 1.00 | 3.00 | — |
| 1943H | 7,140,000 | 2.00 | 5.00 | 10.00 | 20.00 | — |
| 1944 | 19,440,000 | 0.30 | 0.60 | 1.00 | 4.00 | — |
| 1945 | 6,072,000 | 0.45 | 0.90 | 1.75 | 5.00 | — |
| 1945 Proof | — | Value: 150 | | | | |
| 1945H | 9,000,000 | 1.00 | 2.00 | 4.50 | 10.00 | — |
| 1945KN | 9,557,000 | 0.75 | 1.50 | 3.00 | 7.00 | — |
| 1946H | 10,446,000 | 0.85 | 1.75 | 3.75 | 8.00 | — |
| 1946KN | 11,976,000 | 0.30 | 0.60 | 1.00 | 5.00 | — |
| 1946SA | 1,020,000 | 250 | 500 | 750 | 1,150 | — |
| 1947H | 12,443,000 | 0.30 | 0.60 | 1.00 | 5.00 | — |
| 1947KN | 9,829,000 | 0.30 | 0.60 | 1.00 | 5.00 | — |
| 1947SA | 58,980,000 | 0.30 | 0.60 | 1.00 | 4.50 | — |

**PENNY** KM# 25 **Composition:** Copper-Nickel **Obverse:** KM#16 **Reverse:** KM#19 **Note:** Mule.

| Date | Mintage | F | VF | XF | Unc | BU |
|---|---|---|---|---|---|---|
| 1945H | — | 2,000 | 3,000 | 4,000 | 6,000 | — |

**PENNY** KM# 30 **Composition:** Copper-Nickel
**Obv. Legend:** Without IND: IMPL

| Date | Mintage | F | VF | XF | Unc | BU |
|---|---|---|---|---|---|---|
| 1951 | 1,258,000 | 7.50 | 12.50 | 27.50 | 45.00 | — |
| 1951 Proof | — | Value: 250 | | | | |
| 1951KN | 2,692,000 | 6.00 | 10.00 | 20.00 | 35.00 | — |

**PENNY** KM# 30a **Composition:** Bronze

| Date | Mintage | F | VF | XF | Unc | BU |
|---|---|---|---|---|---|---|
| 1952 | 10,542,000 | 0.75 | 1.50 | 3.00 | 8.50 | — |
| 1952 Proof | — | Value: 175 | | | | |
| 1952H | 30,794,000 | 0.20 | 0.40 | 0.60 | 3.00 | — |
| 1952KN | 45,398,000 | 0.20 | 0.40 | 0.60 | 3.00 | — |
| 1952KN Proof | — | Value: 175 | | | | |

**PENNY** KM# 33 **Composition:** Bronze

| Date | Mintage | F | VF | XF | Unc | BU |
|---|---|---|---|---|---|---|
| 1956H | 13,503,000 | 0.75 | 1.50 | 3.50 | 9.00 | — |
| 1956KN | 13,500,000 | 0.30 | 0.60 | 2.50 | 8.00 | — |
| 1957 | 9,000,000 | 0.75 | 1.50 | 6.00 | 13.50 | — |
| 1957 Proof | — | Value: 150 | | | | |
| 1957H | 5,340,000 | 1.00 | 2.50 | 8.00 | 20.00 | — |
| 1957KN | 5,600,000 | 1.00 | 2.50 | 6.00 | 16.00 | — |
| 1958 | 12,200,000 | 0.75 | 1.50 | 4.00 | 13.50 | — |
| 1958 Proof | — | Value: 125 | | | | |
| 1958KN | Inc. above | 0.75 | 1.50 | 3.00 | 10.00 | — |

**PENNY** KM# 34 **Composition:** Bronze **Obverse:** KM#30 **Reverse:** KM#33 **Note:** Mule.

| Date | Mintage | F | VF | XF | Unc | BU |
|---|---|---|---|---|---|---|
| 1956H | — | 60.00 | 90.00 | 150 | 250 | — |

**3 PENCE** KM# 10 **Weight:** 1.1438 g. **Composition:** 0.9250 Silver .0420 oz. ASW

| Date | Mintage | F | VF | XF | Unc | BU |
|---|---|---|---|---|---|---|
| 1913 | 240,000 | 3.50 | 7.50 | 12.50 | 30.00 | — |
| 1913 Proof | — | Value: 250 | | | | |
| 1913H | 496,000 | 2.00 | 4.00 | 7.50 | 25.00 | — |
| 1914H | 1,560,000 | 1.00 | 2.00 | 7.50 | 25.00 | — |
| 1915H | 270,000 | 18.00 | 25.00 | 50.00 | 100 | — |
| 1916H | 820,000 | 10.00 | 15.00 | 30.00 | 65.00 | — |
| 1917H | 3,600,000 | 1.50 | 2.50 | 7.50 | 25.00 | — |
| 1918H | 1,722,000 | 1.75 | 3.50 | 8.00 | 20.00 | — |
| 1919H | 19,826,000 | 1.00 | 2.00 | 6.00 | 15.00 | — |
| 1919H Proof | — | Value: 200 | | | | |

**3 PENCE** KM# 10a **Weight:** 1.1438 g. **Composition:** 0.5000 Silver .0227 oz. ASW

| Date | Mintage | F | VF | XF | Unc | BU |
|---|---|---|---|---|---|---|
| 1920H | 3,616,000 | 25.00 | 50.00 | 80.00 | 175 | — |

**3 PENCE** KM# 10b **Composition:** Tin-Brass

| Date | Mintage | F | VF | XF | Unc | BU |
|---|---|---|---|---|---|---|
| 1920KN Unique | — | — | — | — | — | — |
| **Note:** Mint mark on obverse below bust | | | | | | |
| 1920KN | 19,000,000 | 1.00 | 5.00 | 12.50 | 25.00 | — |
| 1920KN Proof | — | Value: 75.00 | | | | |
| 1925 | 8,800,000 | 1.50 | 5.00 | 20.00 | 40.00 | — |
| 1926 | 1,600,000 | 10.00 | 25.00 | 50.00 | 85.00 | — |
| 1927 | 800,000 | 20.00 | 40.00 | 100 | 200 | — |
| 1928 | 1,760,000 | 10.00 | 35.00 | 70.00 | 125 | — |
| 1928 Proof | — | Value: 175 | | | | |
| 1933 | 2,800,000 | 2.00 | 4.50 | 18.00 | 40.00 | — |
| 1933 Proof | — | Value: 200 | | | | |
| 1934 | 6,400,000 | 1.00 | 12.50 | 20.00 | 35.00 | — |
| 1934 Proof | — | Value: 200 | | | | |
| 1935 | 11,560,000 | 1.00 | 12.50 | 20.00 | 35.00 | — |
| 1935 Proof | — | Value: 200 | | | | |
| 1936 | 17,160,000 | 1.00 | 3.50 | 15.00 | 28.00 | — |
| 1936 Proof | — | Value: 200 | | | | |
| 1936H | 1,000,000 | 15.00 | 25.00 | 45.00 | 85.00 | — |
| 1936H Proof | — | Value: 200 | | | | |
| 1936KN | 2,037,999 | 10.00 | 15.00 | 30.00 | 65.00 | — |

**3 PENCE** **KM# 21** **Composition:** Copper-Nickel

| Date | Mintage | F | VF | XF | Unc | BU |
|---|---|---|---|---|---|---|
| 1938H | 7,000,000 | 0.30 | 0.60 | 2.50 | 7.50 | — |
| 1938H Proof | — | Value: 200 | | | | |
| 1938KN | 9,056,000 | 0.35 | 0.75 | 2.50 | 8.00 | — |
| 1938KN Proof | — | Value: 250 | | | | |
| 1939H | 16,500,000 | 0.30 | 0.60 | 2.00 | 5.00 | — |
| 1939H Proof | — | Value: 300 | | | | |
| 1939KN | 15,500,000 | 0.30 | 0.60 | 2.00 | 8.00 | — |
| 1939KN Proof | — | Value: 200 | | | | |
| 1940H | 3,862,000 | 0.50 | 1.00 | 2.50 | 7.50 | — |
| 1940KN | 10,000,000 | 0.30 | 0.60 | 2.00 | 5.00 | — |
| 1941H | 5,032,000 | 0.40 | 0.85 | 3.50 | 9.00 | — |
| 1943H | 5,106,000 | 0.40 | 0.85 | 6.00 | 15.00 | — |
| 1943KN | 9,502,000 | 0.40 | 0.85 | 3.50 | 9.00 | — |
| 1944KN | 2,536,000 | 0.40 | 0.85 | 6.50 | 15.00 | — |
| 1945H | 998,000 | 3.00 | 5.00 | 10.00 | 20.00 | — |
| 1945KN | 3,000,000 | 0.40 | 0.85 | 5.00 | 12.50 | — |
| 1946KN | 7,488,000 | 0.40 | 0.85 | 3.50 | 9.00 | — |
| 1947H | 10,000,000 | 0.35 | 0.75 | 3.50 | 8.00 | — |
| 1947KN | 11,248,000 | 0.40 | 0.85 | 3.50 | 8.00 | — |

**3 PENCE** **KM# 35** **Composition:** Copper-Nickel

| Date | Mintage | F | VF | XF | Unc | BU |
|---|---|---|---|---|---|---|
| 1957H | 800,000 | 30.00 | 50.00 | 125 | 300 | — |

**6 PENCE** **KM# 11** **Weight:** 2.8276 g. **Composition:** 0.9250 Silver .0841 oz. ASW

| Date | Mintage | F | VF | XF | Unc | BU |
|---|---|---|---|---|---|---|
| 1913 | 560,000 | 3.00 | 5.00 | 12.00 | 35.00 | — |
| 1913 Proof | — | Value: 350 | | | | |
| 1913H | 400,000 | 3.00 | 5.00 | 15.00 | 37.50 | — |
| 1914H | 952,000 | 2.75 | 5.00 | 17.50 | 40.00 | — |
| 1916H | 400,000 | 5.00 | 10.00 | 30.00 | 60.00 | — |
| 1917H | 2,400,000 | 3.00 | 5.00 | 16.50 | 37.50 | — |
| 1918H | 1,160,000 | 2.00 | 5.00 | 16.50 | 37.50 | — |
| 1919H | 8,676,000 | 2.00 | 3.50 | 11.50 | 22.00 | — |
| 1919H Proof | — | Value: 200 | | | | |

**6 PENCE** **KM# 11a** **Weight:** 2.8276 g. **Composition:** 0.5000 Silver .0454 oz. ASW

| Date | Mintage | F | VF | XF | Unc | BU |
|---|---|---|---|---|---|---|
| 1920H | 2,948,000 | 12.50 | 30.00 | 50.00 | 175 | — |
| 1920H Proof | — | Value: 275 | | | | |

**6 PENCE** **KM# 11b** **Composition:** Tin-Brass

| Date | Mintage | F | VF | XF | Unc | BU |
|---|---|---|---|---|---|---|
| 1920KN | 12,000,000 | 1.00 | 5.00 | 20.00 | 37.50 | — |
| 1920KN Proof | — | Value: 125 | | | | |
| 1923H | 2,000,000 | 5.00 | 12.50 | 50.00 | 95.00 | — |
| 1924 | 1,000,000 | 15.00 | 30.00 | 80.00 | 150 | — |
| 1924H | 1,000,000 | 15.00 | 30.00 | 80.00 | 150 | — |
| 1924KN | 1,000,000 | 15.00 | 30.00 | 80.00 | 150 | — |
| 1925 | 2,800,000 | 3.50 | 7.00 | 30.00 | 60.00 | — |
| 1928 | 400,000 | 25.00 | 50.00 | 150 | 250 | — |
| 1928 Proof | — | Value: 200 | | | | |
| 1933 | 1,000,000 | 20.00 | 40.00 | 100 | 175 | — |
| 1933 Proof | — | Value: 225 | | | | |
| 1935 | 4,000,000 | 5.00 | 12.50 | 25.00 | 50.00 | — |
| 1935 Proof | — | Value: 225 | | | | |
| 1936 | 10,400,000 | 7.50 | 15.00 | 25.00 | 50.00 | — |
| 1936 Proof | — | Value: 225 | | | | |
| 1936H | 480,000 | 25.00 | 50.00 | 125 | 200 | — |
| 1936H Proof | — | Value: 225 | | | | |
| 1936KN | 2,696,000 | 15.00 | 25.00 | 35.00 | 70.00 | — |
| 1936KN Proof | — | Value: 225 | | | | |

**6 PENCE** **KM# 22** **Composition:** Nickel-Brass

| Date | Mintage | F | VF | XF | Unc | BU |
|---|---|---|---|---|---|---|
| 1938 | 12,114,000 | 0.50 | 1.00 | 2.00 | 8.00 | — |
| 1938 Proof | — | Value: 200 | | | | |
| 1940 | 17,829,000 | 0.75 | 1.50 | 3.00 | 10.00 | — |
| 1940 Proof | — | Value: 200 | | | | |
| 1942 | 1,600,000 | 2.50 | 4.00 | 10.00 | 20.00 | — |
| 1943 | 10,586,000 | 0.75 | 1.75 | 5.00 | 11.00 | — |
| 1944 | 1,814,000 | 2.00 | 3.00 | 15.00 | 30.00 | — |
| 1945 | 4,000,000 | 1.00 | 2.00 | 12.50 | 25.00 | — |
| 1945 Proof | — | Value: 200 | | | | |
| 1946 | 4,000,000 | 2.50 | 5.00 | 25.00 | 50.00 | — |
| 1946 Proof | — | Value: 225 | | | | |
| 1947 | 6,120,000 | 0.50 | 1.50 | 5.00 | 15.00 | — |
| 1947 Proof | — | Value: 175 | | | | |

**6 PENCE** **KM# 31** **Composition:** Nickel-Brass
**Obv. Legend:** Without IND: IMP:

| Date | Mintage | F | VF | XF | Unc | BU |
|---|---|---|---|---|---|---|
| 1952 | 2,544,000 | — | — | — | 250 | — |
| 1952 Proof | — | Value: 300 | | | | |

**Note:** This type was never released into circulation and the majority of the mintage was melted down at Riverside Metal Company in New Jersey. Approximately 167 pieces avoided the furnace and found their way into the numismtic market

**SHILLING** **KM# 12** **Weight:** 5.6552 g. **Composition:** 0.9250 Silver .1682 oz. ASW

| Date | Mintage | F | VF | XF | Unc | BU |
|---|---|---|---|---|---|---|
| 1913 | 8,800,000 | 2.75 | 4.00 | 12.50 | 22.50 | — |
| 1913 Proof | — | Value: 400 | | | | |
| 1913H | 3,540,000 | 10.00 | 20.00 | 40.00 | 100 | — |
| 1914 | 3,000,000 | 2.75 | 4.00 | 15.00 | 35.00 | — |
| 1914H | 11,292,000 | 2.75 | 4.00 | 12.50 | 30.00 | — |
| 1915H | 254,000 | 20.00 | 40.00 | 80.00 | 150 | — |
| 1916H | 11,838,000 | 2.75 | 4.00 | 15.00 | 35.00 | — |
| 1917H | 15,018,000 | 2.75 | 4.00 | 15.00 | 35.00 | — |
| 1918H | 9,486,000 | 2.75 | 5.50 | 17.50 | 40.00 | — |
| 1918H Proof | — | Value: 200 | | | | |
| 1919 | 2,000,000 | 10.00 | 15.00 | 30.00 | 55.00 | — |
| 1919H | 992,000 | 15.00 | 30.00 | 65.00 | 100 | — |
| 1919H Proof | — | Value: 200 | | | | |
| 1920 | 828,000 | 22.50 | 40.00 | 85.00 | 150 | — |

**SHILLING** **KM# 12a** **Composition:** Tin-Brass

| Date | Mintage | F | VF | XF | Unc | BU |
|---|---|---|---|---|---|---|
| 1920KN Unique | — | — | — | — | — | — |

**Note:** Mint mark on obverse below bust

| Date | Mintage | F | VF | XF | Unc | BU |
|---|---|---|---|---|---|---|
| 1920G | 16,000 | 1,000 | 2,000 | 2,500 | 3,000 | — |
| 1920KN | 38,800,000 | 1.50 | 5.00 | 12.50 | 32.50 | — |
| 1920KN Proof | — | Value: 200 | | | | |
| 1922KN | 32,324,000 | 2.00 | 6.50 | 35.00 | 70.00 | — |
| 1923H | 24,384,000 | 4.00 | 7.50 | 25.00 | 45.00 | — |
| 1923KN | 5,000,000 | 8.00 | 15.00 | 50.00 | 90.00 | — |
| 1924 | 17,000,000 | 2.00 | 6.50 | 30.00 | 60.00 | — |
| 1924H | 9,567,000 | 10.00 | 20.00 | 65.00 | 125 | — |
| 1924KN | 7,000,000 | 7.50 | 15.00 | 40.00 | 80.00 | — |
| 1925 | 19,800,000 | 4.00 | 8.00 | 18.00 | 45.00 | — |
| 1926 | 19,952,000 | 2.00 | 5.00 | 10.00 | 40.00 | — |
| 1927 | 22,248,000 | 1.50 | 4.00 | 8.50 | 35.00 | — |
| 1927 Proof | — | Value: 250 | | | | |
| 1928 | 10,000,000 | 20.00 | 35.00 | 75.00 | 225 | — |
| 1928 Proof | — | Value: 300 | | | | |
| 1936 | 70,200,000 | 3.00 | 6.50 | 11.00 | 32.50 | — |
| 1936 Proof | — | Value: 225 | | | | |
| 1936H | 10,920,000 | 12.50 | 22.50 | 35.00 | 75.00 | — |
| 1936KN | 14,962,000 | 2.00 | 5.00 | 15.00 | 42.50 | — |
| 1936KN Proof | — | Value: 200 | | | | |

**SHILLING** **KM# 23** **Composition:** Nickel-Brass

| Date | Mintage | F | VF | XF | Unc | BU |
|---|---|---|---|---|---|---|
| 1938 | 57,806,000 | 0.50 | 1.25 | 4.50 | 12.00 | — |
| 1938 Proof | — | Value: 200 | | | | |
| 1939 | 55,472,000 | 0.50 | 1.25 | 6.50 | 18.00 | — |
| 1939 Proof | — | Value: 200 | | | | |
| 1940 | 40,311,000 | 0.50 | 1.25 | 5.50 | 15.00 | — |
| 1940 Proof | — | Value: 200 | | | | |
| 1942 | 42,000,000 | 0.50 | 1.25 | 6.50 | 18.00 | — |
| 1943 | 133,600,000 | 0.50 | 1.25 | 5.50 | 15.00 | — |
| 1945 | 8,010,000 | 1.00 | 1.50 | 12.00 | 25.00 | — |
| 1945 Proof | — | Value: 200 | | | | |
| 1945H | 12,864,000 | 2.00 | 3.50 | 15.00 | 35.00 | — |
| 1945KN | 11,120,000 | 1.00 | 2.00 | 12.00 | 25.00 | — |
| 1946 | 37,350,000 | 1.00 | 2.00 | 15.00 | 35.00 | — |
| 1946 Proof | — | Value: 200 | | | | |
| 1946H | — | 750 | 1,000 | 2,000 | 4,000 | — |
| 1947 | 99,200,000 | 0.50 | 1.00 | 4.50 | 12.00 | — |
| 1947 Proof | — | Value: 200 | | | | |
| 1947H | 10,000,000 | 1.50 | 3.00 | 15.00 | 30.00 | — |
| 1947KN | 10,384,000 | 0.50 | 1.00 | 6.50 | 16.50 | — |

**SHILLING** **KM# 28** **Composition:** Tin-Brass
**Obv. Legend:** Without IND: IMP:

| Date | Mintage | F | VF | XF | Unc | BU |
|---|---|---|---|---|---|---|
| 1949 | 70,000,000 | 0.50 | 2.50 | 12.00 | 25.00 | — |
| 1949 Proof | — | Value: 175 | | | | |
| 1949H | 10,000,000 | 1.25 | 4.00 | 12.50 | 27.50 | — |
| 1949KN | 10,016,000 | 1.25 | 4.00 | 12.50 | 27.50 | — |
| 1949KN Proof | — | Value: 200 | | | | |
| 1951 | 35,346,000 | 1.25 | 5.00 | 15.00 | 30.00 | — |
| 1951 Proof | — | Value: 175 | | | | |
| 1951H | 10,000,000 | 1.25 | 5.00 | 15.00 | 30.00 | — |
| 1951KN | 16,832,000 | 1.25 | 5.00 | 15.00 | 30.00 | — |
| 1952 | 98,654,000 | 0.50 | 1.00 | 3.00 | 9.00 | — |
| 1952 Proof | — | Value: 200 | | | | |
| 1952H | 44,096,000 | 0.50 | 1.00 | 2.00 | 7.50 | — |
| 1952KN | 41,653,000 | 0.50 | 1.00 | 2.00 | 6.00 | — |
| 1952KN Proof | — | Value: 175 | | | | |

**2 SHILLING** **KM# 13** **Weight:** 11.3104 g. **Composition:** 0.9250 Silver .3364 oz. ASW

| Date | Mintage | F | VF | XF | Unc | BU |
|---|---|---|---|---|---|---|
| 1913 | 2,100,000 | 5.00 | 8.00 | 16.50 | 45.00 | — |
| 1913 Proof | — | Value: 500 | | | | |
| 1913H | 1,176,000 | 6.00 | 15.00 | 27.50 | 55.00 | — |
| 1914 | 330,000 | 15.00 | 50.00 | 125 | 200 | — |
| 1914H | 637,000 | 10.00 | 25.00 | 35.00 | 75.00 | — |
| 1915H | 66,000 | 25.00 | 60.00 | 100 | 175 | — |
| 1916H | 9,824,000 | 5.00 | 15.00 | 30.00 | 60.00 | — |
| 1917H | 1,059,000 | 15.00 | 40.00 | 85.00 | 150 | — |
| 1917H Proof | — | Value: 300 | | | | |
| 1918H | 7,294,000 | 5.00 | 12.00 | 27.50 | 55.00 | — |
| 1919 | 2,000,000 | 6.00 | 20.00 | 40.00 | 85.00 | — |
| 1919H | 10,866,000 | 4.50 | 10.00 | 32.00 | 65.00 | — |
| 1919H Proof | — | Value: 200 | | | | |
| 1920 | 683,000 | 30.00 | 60.00 | 175 | 250 | — |

**2 SHILLING** **KM# 13a** **Weight:** 11.3104 g. **Composition:** 0.5000 Silver .1818 oz. ASW

| Date | Mintage | F | VF | XF | Unc | BU |
|---|---|---|---|---|---|---|
| 1920H | 1,926,000 | 30.00 | 55.00 | 100 | 275 | — |

**2 SHILLING** **KM# 13b** **Composition:** Tin-Brass

| Date | Mintage | F | VF | XF | Unc | BU |
|---|---|---|---|---|---|---|
| 1920KN | 15,856,000 | 2.50 | 5.00 | 15.00 | 40.00 | — |
| 1920KN Proof | — | Value: 250 | | | | |
| 1922 | 10,000,000 | 3.00 | 9.00 | 17.50 | 55.00 | — |
| 1922KN | 5,500,000 | 6.00 | 15.00 | 30.00 | 75.00 | — |
| 1922KN Proof | — | Value: 250 | | | | |
| 1923H | 12,696,000 | 4.00 | 12.00 | 22.50 | 65.00 | — |
| 1924 | 1,500,000 | 8.00 | 20.00 | 40.00 | 90.00 | — |
| 1925 | 3,700,000 | 4.00 | 12.00 | 25.00 | 70.00 | — |
| 1926 | 11,500,000 | 4.50 | 15.00 | 45.00 | 80.00 | — |
| 1927 | 11,100,000 | 6.00 | 20.00 | 60.00 | 100 | — |
| 1927 Proof | — | Value: 250 | | | | |
| 1928 | 7,900,000 | 1,500 | 2,000 | 3,000 | 5,000 | — |
| 1928 Proof | — | Value: 3,000 | | | | |
| 1936 | 32,939,999 | 5.00 | 12.00 | 35.00 | 60.00 | — |
| 1936 Proof | — | Value: 250 | | | | |
| 1936H | 8,703,000 | 6.00 | 18.00 | 45.00 | 75.00 | — |
| 1936KN | 8,794,000 | 6.00 | 18.00 | 45.00 | 75.00 | — |

**2 SHILLING** KM# 24 **Composition:** Nickel-Brass

| Date | Mintage | F | VF | XF | Unc | BU |
|---|---|---|---|---|---|---|
| 1938H | 32,000,000 | 1.00 | 2.00 | 3.50 | 15.00 | — |
| 1938KN | 27,852,000 | 1.00 | 2.00 | 3.50 | 15.00 | — |
| **Note:** Grained edge variety exists | | | | | | |
| 1939H | 5,750,000 | 2.00 | 5.00 | 15.00 | 35.00 | — |
| 1939KN | 6,250,000 | 1.00 | 4.00 | 12.00 | 30.00 | — |
| 1939KN Proof | — | Value: 200 | | | | |
| 1942KN | 10,000,000 | 1.25 | 4.50 | 14.00 | 30.00 | — |
| 1946H | 10,500,000 | 1.25 | 4.00 | 12.00 | 27.50 | — |
| 1946KN | 4,800,000 | 1.25 | 7.00 | 22.00 | 42.50 | — |
| 1947H | 5,055,000 | 1.00 | 6.00 | 20.00 | 40.00 | — |
| 1947KN | 4,200,000 | 1.25 | 7.00 | 22.00 | 42.50 | — |

**2 SHILLING** KM# 29 **Composition:** Nickel-Brass
**Obv. Legend:** Winthout IND: IMP:

| Date | Mintage | F | VF | XF | Unc | BU |
|---|---|---|---|---|---|---|
| 1949H | 7,500,000 | 1.25 | 7.00 | 22.00 | 40.00 | — |
| 1949KN | 7,576,000 | 1.25 | 6.00 | 20.00 | 35.00 | — |
| 1951H | 6,566,000 | 1.25 | 7.00 | 22.00 | 40.00 | — |
| 1951H Proof | — | Value: 250 | | | | |
| 1952H | 4,410,000 | 2.00 | 8.00 | 22.50 | 42.00 | — |
| 1952KN | 1,236,000 | 8.00 | 20.00 | 50.00 | 75.00 | — |

## PATTERNS

Including off metal strikes

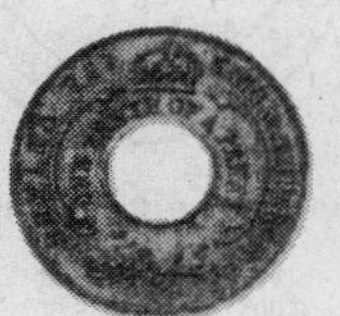

| KM# | Date | Mintage | Identification | Mkt Val |
|---|---|---|---|---|
| Pn1 | 1906 | 4 | 1/10 Penny. Aluminum. | 3,000 |
| Pn2 | 1906 | — | Penny. Copper-Nickel. Two varieties known, tick and thin flan. | 3,000 |
| Pn3 | 1920 | — | Shilling. Silver. 6.2700 g. | 1,500 |
| PnA4 | 1920 | — | Penny. Brass. #KM9. | 1,800 |
| Pn4 | 1920 | — | 2 Shilling. Silver. Uniface. | 250 |
| Pn5 | 1925 | — | Shilling. Nickel-Brass. Bare headed. ROYAL MINT 1925 edge. | 2,000 |
| Pn6 | 1936 | — | Shilling. Nickel-Brass. Security edge. Raised word SPECIMEN in field above date. | 500 |
| Pn7 | 1936 | — | Shilling. Nickel-Brass. Fine reeded edge. Word SPECIMEN in field above date. | 400 |
| Pn8 | 1936 | — | Shilling. Nickel-Brass. Security edge. Raised word SPECIMEN in field above date. | 500 |
| Pn9 | 1936 | — | Shilling. Nickel-Brass. Coarser reeded edge. Without word SPECIMEN. | 1,500 |
| PnA10 | 1937 | — | Penny. Bronze. KM#19. | 1,000 |
| Pn10 | 1938 | — | 2 Shilling. Nickel-Brass. Security edge. Raised word SPECIMEN in field. | 800 |
| Pn11 | 1952 | — | 2 Shilling. Nickel-Brass. Raised word SPECIMEN in field below date. | 400 |
| Pn12 | | — | Shilling. Nickel-Brass. KM#13b. Raided word MODEL. | 1,000 |

## TRIAL STRIKES

| KM# | Date | Mintage | Identification | Mkt Val |
|---|---|---|---|---|
| TS1 | 1952 | — | Shilling. Steel. Raised word TRIAL vertical in field on both sides. | 100 |
| TS2 | 1952 | — | Shilling. Nickel. Raised word TRIAL vertical in field on both sides. | 100 |
| TS3 | 1952 | — | Shilling. Steel. Raised word TRIAL vertical. Raised word TRIAL horizontal. | 125 |
| TS4 | 1952 | — | Shilling. Nickel. Raised word TRIAL vertical. Raised word TRIAL horizontal. | 85.00 |

## SPECIMEN SETS (SS)

| KM# | Date | Mintage | Identification | Issue Price | Mkt Val |
|---|---|---|---|---|---|
| SS1 | 1913 (8) | 14 | KM10-13 | — | 1,250 |
| SS2 | 1913 (4) | 200 | KM10-13 | — | 550 |
| SS3 | 1919H (8) | 2 | KM10-13 | — | 1,500 |
| SS4 | 1920KN (8) | 36 | KM10b-11b, 12a, 13b | — | 1,150 |
| SSA5 | 1920KN (4) | 4 | KM10b-11b, 12a, 13b | — | — |
| SS5 | 1928 (4) | — | KM10b-11b, 12a, 13b | — | 1,000 |
| SS6 | 1936H (3) | — | KM14-16 | — | 450 |
| SS7 | 1952 (4) | — | KM26a-27a, 30a, 31 | — | 750 |

Negara Brunei Darussalam (State of Brunei), an independent sultanate on the northwest coast of the island of Borneo, has an area of 2,226 sq. mi. (5,765 sq. km.) and a population of *326,000. Capital: Bandar Seri Begawan. Crude oil and rubber are exported.

Magellan was the first European to visit Brunei in 1521. It was a powerful state, ruling over northern Borneo and adjacent islands from the 16th to the 19th century. Brunei became a British protectorate in 1888 and a British dependency in 1905. The Constitution of 1959 restored control over internal affairs to the sultan, while delegating responsibility for defense and foreign affairs to Britain. On January 1, 1984 it became independent.

**TITLES**

Negri Brunei نكري بروني

**RULERS**

Sultan Hashim Jalal, 1885-1906
British 1906-1950
Sultan Sir Omar Ali Saifuddin III, 1950-1967
Sultan Hassanal Bolkiah I, 1967-

**MONETARY SYSTEM**

100 Sen = 1 Dollar

# SULTANATE

## DECIMAL COINAGE

100 Sen = 1 Dollar (Ringgit)

**SEN** KM# 4 **Composition:** Bronze

| Date | Mintage | F | VF | XF | Unc | BU |
|---|---|---|---|---|---|---|
| 1967 | 1,000,000 | — | 0.15 | 0.35 | 0.75 | — |

**SEN** KM# 9 **Composition:** Bronze

| Date | Mintage | F | VF | XF | Unc | BU |
|---|---|---|---|---|---|---|
| 1968 | 60,000 | — | 0.25 | 0.50 | 1.75 | — |
| 1970 | 140,000 | — | 0.10 | 0.20 | 0.50 | — |
| 1970 Proof | 4,000 | Value: 4.00 | | | | |
| 1971 | 400,000 | — | 0.10 | 0.15 | 0.40 | — |
| 1973 | 120,000 | — | 0.20 | 0.40 | 1.50 | — |
| 1974 | 640,000 | — | — | 0.10 | 0.30 | — |
| 1976 | 140,000 | — | — | 0.10 | 0.30 | — |
| 1977 | 140,000 | — | — | 0.10 | 0.30 | — |

**SEN** KM# 15 **Composition:** Bronze **Obv. Legend:** Without numeral 'I' in title

| Date | Mintage | F | VF | XF | Unc | BU |
|---|---|---|---|---|---|---|
| 1977 | 280,000 | — | — | 0.10 | 0.20 | — |
| 1978 | 269,000 | — | — | 0.10 | 0.15 | — |
| 1979 | 250,000 | — | 0.10 | 0.20 | 0.50 | — |
| 1979 Proof | 10,000 | Value: 2.00 | | | | |
| 1980 | 260,000 | — | — | 0.10 | 0.15 | — |
| 1981 | 540,000 | — | — | 0.10 | 0.15 | — |
| 1982 | 100,000 | — | — | 0.30 | 1.50 | — |
| 1983 | 500,000 | — | — | 0.10 | 0.15 | — |
| 1984 | 400,000 | — | — | 0.10 | 0.15 | — |
| 1984 Proof | 3,000 | Value: 2.00 | | | | |
| 1985 | 200,000 | — | — | 0.10 | 0.15 | — |
| 1985 Proof | — | Value: 2.00 | | | | |
| 1986 | 101,000 | — | — | — | 0.15 | — |
| 1986 Proof | 7,000 | Value: 2.00 | | | | |

**SEN KM# 15a Composition:** Copper Clad Steel

| Date | Mintage | F | VF | XF | Unc | BU |
|---|---|---|---|---|---|---|
| 1986 | 102,000 | — | — | — | 0.30 | — |
| 1987 | 390,000 | — | — | — | 0.30 | — |
| 1988 | 500,000 | — | — | — | 0.30 | — |
| 1989 | 601,000 | — | — | — | 0.30 | — |
| 1990 | 680,000 | — | — | — | 0.30 | — |
| 1991 | 680,000 | — | — | — | 0.30 | — |
| 1992 | 887,000 | — | — | — | 0.30 | — |
| 1993 | 948,000 | — | — | — | 0.30 | — |

**SEN KM# 15b Weight:** 2.9200 g. **Composition:** 0.9250 Silver .0869 oz. ASW

| Date | Mintage | F | VF | XF | Unc | BU |
|---|---|---|---|---|---|---|
| 1987 Proof | 2,000 | Value: 3.00 | | | | |
| 1988 Proof | 2,000 | Value: 3.00 | | | | |
| 1989 Proof | 2,000 | Value: 3.00 | | | | |
| 1990 Proof | 2,000 | Value: 3.00 | | | | |
| 1991 Proof | 2,000 | Value: 3.00 | | | | |
| 1992 Proof | 2,000 | Value: 3.00 | | | | |
| 1993 Proof | 2,000 | Value: 3.00 | | | | |

**SEN KM# 42 Weight:** 3.1000 g. **Composition:** 0.9250 Silver .0922 oz. ASW **Subject:** 25 Years - Currency Board **Obverse:** Sultan's portrait **Reverse:** Mosque **Edge:** Reeded

| Date | Mintage | F | VF | XF | Unc | BU |
|---|---|---|---|---|---|---|
| 1992 Proof | — | — | — | — | — | — |
| 1992 | 2,000 | — | — | — | 5.00 | — |

**SEN KM# 34 Composition:** Copper Clad Steel

| Date | Mintage | F | VF | XF | Unc | BU |
|---|---|---|---|---|---|---|
| 1993 | 948,000 | — | — | — | 0.50 | — |
| 1994 | — | — | — | — | 0.50 | — |
| 1995 | — | — | — | — | 0.50 | — |
| 1996 | — | — | — | — | 0.50 | — |

**SEN KM# 54 Composition:** Copper Clad Steel **Subject:** 10 Years of Independence **Obverse:** Sultan's portrait **Reverse:** National arms

| Date | Mintage | F | VF | XF | Unc | BU |
|---|---|---|---|---|---|---|
| ND (1994) | — | — | — | — | 1.00 | — |

**SEN KM# 54a Weight:** 3.1000 g. **Composition:** 0.9250 Silver .0922 oz. ASW **Subject:** 10 Years of Independence **Obverse:** Sultan's portrait **Reverse:** National arms

| Date | Mintage | F | VF | XF | Unc | BU |
|---|---|---|---|---|---|---|
| ND (1994) Proof | 1,980 | Value: 7.00 | | | | |

**5 SEN KM# 5 Composition:** Copper-Nickel

| Date | Mintage | F | VF | XF | Unc | BU |
|---|---|---|---|---|---|---|
| 1967 | 1,160,000 | — | 0.20 | 0.40 | 1.00 | — |

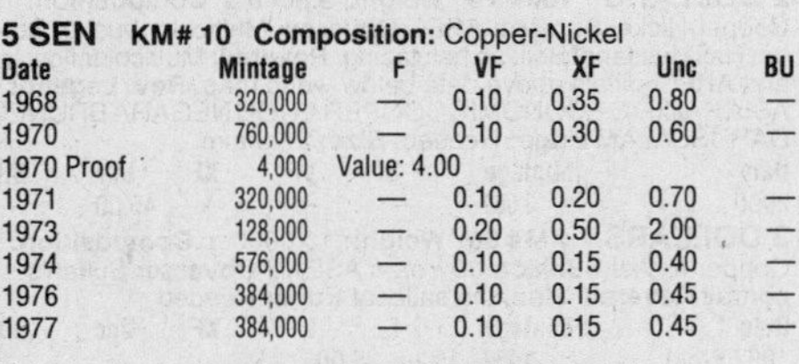

**5 SEN KM# 10 Composition:** Copper-Nickel

| Date | Mintage | F | VF | XF | Unc | BU |
|---|---|---|---|---|---|---|
| 1968 | 320,000 | — | 0.10 | 0.35 | 0.80 | — |
| 1970 | 760,000 | — | 0.10 | 0.30 | 0.60 | — |
| 1970 Proof | 4,000 | Value: 4.00 | | | | |
| 1971 | 320,000 | — | 0.10 | 0.20 | 0.70 | — |
| 1973 | 128,000 | — | 0.20 | 0.50 | 2.00 | — |
| 1974 | 576,000 | — | 0.10 | 0.15 | 0.40 | — |
| 1976 | 384,000 | — | 0.10 | 0.15 | 0.45 | — |
| 1977 | 384,000 | — | 0.10 | 0.15 | 0.45 | — |

**5SEN KM#16 Composition:** Copper-Nickel **Obv. Legend:** Without numerial 'I' in title

| Date | Mintage | F | VF | XF | Unc | BU |
|---|---|---|---|---|---|---|
| 1977 | 920,000 | — | — | 0.10 | 0.30 | — |
| 1978 | 640,000 | — | — | 0.10 | 0.30 | — |
| 1979 | 650,000 | — | 0.10 | 0.20 | 0.50 | — |
| 1979 Proof | 10,000 | Value: 3.00 | | | | |
| 1980 | 640,000 | — | — | 0.10 | 0.30 | — |
| 1981 | 960,000 | — | — | 0.10 | 0.30 | — |
| 1982 | 240,000 | — | — | 0.50 | 2.00 | — |
| 1983 | 1,280,000 | — | — | 0.10 | 0.30 | — |
| 1984 | 800,000 | — | — | 0.10 | 0.30 | — |
| 1984 Proof | 3,000 | Value: 3.00 | | | | |
| 1985 | 800,000 | — | — | 0.10 | 0.30 | — |
| 1985 Proof | — | Value: 3.00 | | | | |
| 1986 | 189,000 | — | — | — | 0.30 | — |
| 1986 Proof | 7,000 | Value: 3.00 | | | | |
| 1987 | 960,000 | — | — | — | 0.30 | — |
| 1988 | 820,000 | — | — | — | 0.30 | — |
| 1989 | 1,504,000 | — | — | — | 0.30 | — |
| 1990 | 1,340,000 | — | — | — | 0.30 | — |
| 1991 | 1,340,000 | — | — | — | 0.30 | — |
| 1992 | 1,900,000 | — | — | — | 0.30 | — |
| 1993 | 1,951,000 | — | — | — | 0.30 | — |

**5 SEN KM# 16a Weight:** 1.6500 g. **Composition:** 0.9250 Silver .0490 oz. ASW

| Date | Mintage | F | VF | XF | Unc | BU |
|---|---|---|---|---|---|---|
| 1987 Proof | 2,000 | Value: 3.00 | | | | |
| 1988 Proof | 2,000 | Value: 3.00 | | | | |
| 1989 Proof | 2,000 | Value: 3.00 | | | | |
| 1990 Proof | 2,000 | Value: 3.00 | | | | |
| 1991 Proof | 2,000 | Value: 3.00 | | | | |
| 1992 Proof | 2,000 | Value: 3.00 | | | | |
| 1993 Proof | 2,000 | Value: 3.00 | | | | |

**5 SEN KM# 43 Weight:** 1.9000 g. **Composition:** 0.9250 Silver .0565 oz. ASW **Subject:** 25 Years - Currency Board **Obverse:** Sultan's portrait **Reverse:** Mosque **Edge:** Reeded

| Date | Mintage | F | VF | XF | Unc | BU |
|---|---|---|---|---|---|---|
| 1992 Proof | 2,000 | Value: 7.00 | | | | |

**5 SEN KM# 35 Composition:** Copper-Nickel

| Date | Mintage | F | VF | XF | Unc | BU |
|---|---|---|---|---|---|---|
| 1993 | 1,951,000 | — | — | — | 0.50 | — |
| 1994 | — | — | — | — | 0.50 | — |
| 1996 | — | — | — | — | 0.50 | — |

**5 SEN KM# 55 Composition:** Copper-Nickel .0565 oz. **Subject:** 10 Years of Independence **Obverse:** Sultan's portrait **Reverse:** National arms

| Date | Mintage | F | VF | XF | Unc | BU |
|---|---|---|---|---|---|---|
| ND (1994) | 3,000 | — | — | — | 1.50 | — |

**5 SEN KM# 55a Weight:** 1.9000 g. **Composition:** 0.9250 Silver .0565 oz. ASW **Subject:** 10 Years of Independence **Obverse:** Sultan's portrait **Reverse:** National arms

| Date | Mintage | F | VF | XF | Unc | BU |
|---|---|---|---|---|---|---|
| ND (1994) Proof | 1,980 | Value: 9.00 | | | | |

**10 SEN KM# 6 Composition:** Copper-Nickel

| Date | Mintage | F | VF | XF | Unc | BU |
|---|---|---|---|---|---|---|
| 1967 | 3,510,000 | — | 0.15 | 0.35 | 0.75 | — |

**10 SEN KM# 11 Composition:** Copper-Nickel

| Date | Mintage | F | VF | XF | Unc | BU |
|---|---|---|---|---|---|---|
| 1968 | 580,000 | — | 0.10 | 0.25 | 0.60 | — |
| 1970 | 1,360,000 | — | 0.10 | 0.20 | 0.50 | — |
| 1970 Proof | 4,000 | Value: 4.00 | | | | |
| 1971 | 420,000 | — | 0.10 | 0.20 | 0.50 | — |
| 1973 | 300,000 | — | 0.10 | 0.25 | 0.60 | — |
| 1974 | 1,410,000 | — | 0.10 | 0.20 | 0.50 | — |
| 1976 | 920,000 | — | 0.10 | 0.20 | 0.50 | — |
| 1977 | 920,000 | — | — | 0.15 | 0.40 | — |

**10 SEN KM# 17 Composition:** Copper-Nickel **Obv. Legend:** Without numeral 'I' in title

| Date | Mintage | F | VF | XF | Unc | BU |
|---|---|---|---|---|---|---|
| 1977 | 1,800,000 | — | 0.10 | 0.15 | 0.40 | — |
| 1978 | 1,080,000 | — | — | 0.10 | 0.30 | — |
| 1979 | 2,050,000 | — | — | 0.10 | 0.30 | — |
| 1979 Proof | 10,000 | Value: 4.00 | | | | |
| 1980 | 2,840,000 | — | — | 0.10 | 0.25 | — |
| 1981 | 976,000 | — | — | 0.10 | 0.25 | — |
| 1983 | 1,080,000 | — | — | 0.10 | 0.25 | — |
| 1984 | 1,400,000 | — | — | 0.10 | 0.25 | — |
| 1984 Proof | 3,000 | Value: 4.25 | | | | |
| 1985 | 1,540,000 | — | — | 0.10 | 0.25 | — |
| 1985 Proof | — | Value: 4.25 | | | | |
| 1986 | 2,181,000 | — | — | — | 0.25 | — |
| 1986 Proof | 7,000 | Value: 4.25 | | | | |
| 1987 | 2,560,000 | — | — | — | 0.25 | — |
| 1988 | 960,000 | — | — | — | 0.25 | — |
| 1989 | 1,000,000 | — | — | — | 0.25 | — |
| 1990 | 1,800,000 | — | — | — | 0.25 | — |
| 1991 | 1,800,000 | — | — | — | 0.25 | — |
| 1992 | 3,839,000 | — | — | — | 0.25 | — |
| 1993 | 3,973,000 | — | — | — | 0.25 | — |

**10 SEN KM# 17a Weight:** 3.3500 g. **Composition:** 0.9250 Silver .0996 oz. ASW **Obv. Legend:** Without numeral 'I' in title

| Date | Mintage | F | VF | XF | Unc | BU |
|---|---|---|---|---|---|---|
| 1987 Proof | 2,000 | Value: 6.00 | | | | |
| 1988 Proof | 2,000 | Value: 6.00 | | | | |
| 1989 Proof | 2,000 | Value: 6.00 | | | | |
| 1990 Proof | 2,000 | Value: 6.00 | | | | |
| 1991 Proof | 2,000 | Value: 6.00 | | | | |
| 1992 Proof | 2,000 | Value: 6.00 | | | | |
| 1993 Proof | 2,000 | Value: 6.00 | | | | |

**10 SEN KM# 44 Weight:** 3.5000 g. **Composition:** 0.9250 Silver .1041 oz. ASW **Obverse:** Sultan's portrait **Reverse:** Mosque **Edge:** Reeded

| Date | Mintage | F | VF | XF | Unc | BU |
|---|---|---|---|---|---|---|
| 1992 Proof | 2,000 | Value: 10.00 | | | | |

**10 SEN KM# 36 Composition:** Copper-Nickel

| Date | Mintage | F | VF | XF | Unc | BU |
|---|---|---|---|---|---|---|
| 1993 | 3,973,000 | — | — | — | 0.75 | — |
| 1994 | — | — | — | — | 0.75 | — |
| 1996 | — | — | — | — | 0.75 | — |

**10 SEN KM# 56a Weight:** 3.5000 g. **Composition:** 0.9250 Silver .1041 oz. ASW **Subject:** 10 Years of Independence **Obverse:** Sultan's portrait **Reverse:** National arms

| Date | Mintage | F | VF | XF | Unc | BU |
|---|---|---|---|---|---|---|
| ND (1994) Proof | 1,980 | Value: 12.00 | | | | |

**10 SEN KM# 56 Composition:** Copper-Nickel **Subject:** 10 Years of Independence **Obverse:** Sultan's portrait **Reverse:** National arms

| Date | Mintage | F | VF | XF | Unc | BU |
|---|---|---|---|---|---|---|
| ND (1994) | 3,000 | — | — | — | 2.00 | — |

**20 SEN KM# 7 Composition:** Copper-Lead Alloy

| Date | Mintage | F | VF | XF | Unc | BU |
|---|---|---|---|---|---|---|
| 1967 | 2,130,000 | — | 0.35 | 1.00 | 2.00 | — |

**20 SEN KM# 12 Composition:** Copper-Nickel

| Date | Mintage | F | VF | XF | Unc | BU |
|---|---|---|---|---|---|---|
| 1968 | 510,000 | — | 0.20 | 0.50 | 1.00 | — |
| 1970 | 850,000 | — | 0.15 | 0.35 | 0.85 | — |
| 1970 Proof | 4,000 | Value: 4.00 | | | | |
| 1971 | 450,000 | — | 0.20 | 0.50 | 1.00 | — |
| 1973 | 450,000 | — | 0.20 | 0.50 | 1.00 | — |
| 1974 | 700,000 | — | 0.15 | 0.35 | 0.85 | — |
| 1976 | 640,000 | — | 0.15 | 0.35 | 0.85 | — |
| 1977 | 640,000 | — | 0.15 | 0.35 | 0.85 | — |

**20 SEN** **KM# 18** **Composition:** Copper-Nickel **Obv. Legend:** Without numeral 'I' in title

| Date | Mintage | F | VF | XF | Unc | BU |
|---|---|---|---|---|---|---|
| 1977 | 1,200,000 | — | 0.10 | 0.25 | 0.75 | — |
| 1978 | 720,000 | — | 0.15 | 0.40 | 1.00 | — |
| 1979 | 1,060,000 | — | 0.20 | 0.50 | 1.25 | — |
| 1979 Proof | 10,000 | Value: 4.50 | | | | |
| 1980 | 1,540,000 | — | 0.10 | 0.20 | 0.50 | — |
| 1981 | 2,140,000 | — | 0.10 | 0.20 | 0.50 | — |
| 1982 | 120,000 | — | 1.50 | 4.50 | 9.00 | — |
| 1983 | 1,350,000 | — | 0.10 | 0.15 | 0.40 | — |
| 1984 | 750,000 | — | 0.10 | 0.15 | 0.40 | — |
| 1984 Proof | 3,000 | Value: 4.75 | | | | |
| 1985 | 1,000,000 | — | 0.10 | 0.15 | 0.40 | — |
| 1985 Proof | — | Value: 4.75 | | | | |
| 1986 | 2,639,000 | — | — | — | 0.40 | — |
| 1986 Proof | 7,000 | Value: 4.75 | | | | |
| 1987 | 2,400,000 | — | — | — | 0.40 | — |
| 1988 | 560,000 | — | — | — | 0.40 | — |
| 1989 | 500,000 | — | — | — | 0.40 | — |
| 1990 | 720,000 | — | — | — | 0.40 | — |
| 1991 | 725,000 | — | — | — | 0.40 | — |
| 1992 | 2,432,000 | — | — | — | 0.40 | — |
| 1993 | 2,521,000 | — | — | — | 0.40 | — |

**20 SEN** **KM# 18a** **Weight:** 6.5100 g. **Composition:** 0.9250 Silver .1936 oz. ASW **Obv. Legend:** Without numeral 'I' in title

| Date | Mintage | F | VF | XF | Unc | BU |
|---|---|---|---|---|---|---|
| 1987 Proof | 2,000 | Value: 10.00 | | | | |
| 1988 Proof | 2,000 | Value: 10.00 | | | | |
| 1989 Proof | 2,000 | Value: 10.00 | | | | |
| 1990 Proof | 2,000 | Value: 10.00 | | | | |
| 1991 Proof | 2,000 | Value: 10.00 | | | | |
| 1992 Proof | 2,000 | Value: 10.00 | | | | |
| 1993 Proof | 2,000 | Value: 10.00 | | | | |

**20 SEN** **KM# 45** **Weight:** 6.7000 g. **Composition:** 0.9250 Silver .1993 oz. ASW **Subject:** 25 Years - Currency Board **Obverse:** Sultan's portrait **Reverse:** Mosque **Edge:** Reeded

| Date | Mintage | F | VF | XF | Unc | BU |
|---|---|---|---|---|---|---|
| 1992 Proof | 2,000 | Value: 12.00 | | | | |

**20 SEN** **KM# 37** **Composition:** Copper-Nickel

| Date | Mintage | F | VF | XF | Unc | BU |
|---|---|---|---|---|---|---|
| 1993 | — | — | — | — | 1.25 | — |
| 1994 | — | — | — | — | 1.25 | — |

**20 SEN** **KM# 57** **Composition:** Copper-Nickel **Subject:** 10 Years of Independence **Obverse:** Sultan's portrait **Reverse:** National arms

| Date | Mintage | F | VF | XF | Unc | BU |
|---|---|---|---|---|---|---|
| ND (1994) | 3,000 | — | — | — | 2.50 | — |

**20 SEN** **KM# 57a** **Weight:** 6.7000 g. **Composition:** 0.9250 Silver .1993 oz. ASW **Subject:** 10 Years of Independence **Obverse:** Sultan's portrait **Reverse:** National arms

| Date | Mintage | F | VF | XF | Unc | BU |
|---|---|---|---|---|---|---|
| ND (1994) Proof | 1,980 | Value: 15.00 | | | | |

**50 SEN** **KM# 8** **Composition:** Copper-Nickel

| Date | Mintage | F | VF | XF | Unc | BU |
|---|---|---|---|---|---|---|
| 1967 | 788,000 | — | 0.75 | 1.75 | 3.50 | — |

**50 SEN** **KM# 13** **Composition:** Copper-Nickel

| Date | Mintage | F | VF | XF | Unc | BU |
|---|---|---|---|---|---|---|
| 1968 | 212,000 | — | 0.30 | 1.00 | 1.75 | — |
| 1970 | 300,000 | — | 0.30 | 1.00 | 1.75 | — |
| 1970 Proof | 4,000 | Value: 6.50 | | | | |
| 1971 | 320,000 | — | 0.30 | 1.00 | 1.75 | — |
| 1973 | 140,000 | — | 0.50 | 2.50 | 4.00 | — |
| 1974 | 244,000 | — | 0.30 | 1.00 | 1.75 | — |
| 1976 | 240,000 | — | 0.30 | 1.00 | 1.75 | — |
| 1977 | 240,000 | — | 0.30 | 1.00 | 1.75 | — |

**50 SEN** **KM# 19** **Composition:** Copper-Nickel **Obv. Legend:** Without numeral 'I' in titles

| Date | Mintage | F | VF | XF | Unc | BU |
|---|---|---|---|---|---|---|
| 1977 | 499,000 | — | 0.30 | 0.85 | 1.65 | — |
| 1978 | 264,000 | — | 0.30 | 0.85 | 1.65 | — |
| 1979 | 730,000 | — | 0.30 | 0.85 | 1.65 | — |
| 1979 Proof | 10,000 | Value: 6.50 | | | | |
| 1980 | 536,000 | — | 0.30 | 0.45 | 0.85 | — |
| 1981 | 960,000 | — | 0.30 | 0.40 | 0.75 | — |
| 1982 | 136,000 | — | 1.00 | 3.00 | 7.00 | — |
| 1983 | 408,000 | — | 0.30 | 0.40 | 0.75 | — |
| 1984 | 320,000 | — | 0.30 | 0.40 | 0.75 | — |
| 1984 Proof | 3,000 | Value: 6.75 | | | | |
| 1985 | 450,000 | — | 0.30 | 0.40 | 0.75 | — |
| 1985 Proof | — | — | — | — | — | — |
| 1986 | 1,067,000 | — | — | — | 0.75 | — |
| 1986 Proof | 7,000 | Value: 6.75 | | | | |
| 1987 | 1,120,000 | — | — | — | 0.75 | — |
| 1988 | 250,000 | — | — | — | 0.75 | — |
| 1989 | 500,000 | — | — | — | 0.75 | — |
| 1990 | 472,000 | — | — | — | 0.75 | — |
| 1991 | 508,000 | — | — | — | 0.75 | — |
| 1992 | 1,072,000 | — | — | — | 0.75 | — |
| 1993 | 1,102,000 | — | — | — | 0.75 | — |

**50 SEN** **KM# 19a** **Weight:** 10.8200 g. **Composition:** 0.9250 Silver .3218 oz. ASW **Obv. Legend:** Without numeral 'I' in titles

| Date | Mintage | F | VF | XF | Unc | BU |
|---|---|---|---|---|---|---|
| 1987 Proof | 2,000 | Value: 15.00 | | | | |
| 1988 Proof | 2,000 | Value: 15.00 | | | | |
| 1989 Proof | 2,000 | Value: 15.00 | | | | |
| 1990 Proof | 2,000 | Value: 15.00 | | | | |
| 1991 Proof | 2,000 | Value: 15.00 | | | | |
| 1992 Proof | 2,000 | Value: 15.00 | | | | |
| 1993 Proof | 2,000 | Value: 15.00 | | | | |

**50 SEN** **KM# 46** **Weight:** 11.1000 g. **Composition:** 0.9250 Silver .3301 oz. ASW **Subject:** 25 Years - Currency Board **Obverse:** Sultan's portrait **Reverse:** Mosque

| Date | Mintage | F | VF | XF | Unc | BU |
|---|---|---|---|---|---|---|
| 1992 Proof | 2,000 | Value: 20.00 | | | | |

**50 SEN** **KM# 38** **Composition:** Copper-Nickel

| Date | Mintage | F | VF | XF | Unc | BU |
|---|---|---|---|---|---|---|
| 1993 | — | — | — | — | 2.25 | — |
| 1994 | — | — | — | — | 2.25 | — |

**50 SEN** **KM# 58** **Composition:** Copper-Nickel **Subject:** 10 Years of Independence` **Obverse:** Sultan's portrait **Reverse:** National arms

| Date | Mintage | F | VF | XF | Unc | BU |
|---|---|---|---|---|---|---|
| ND (1994) | 3,000 | — | — | — | 4.50 | — |

**50 SEN** **KM# 58a** **Weight:** 11.1000 g. **Composition:** 0.9250 Silver .3301 oz. ASW **Subject:** 10 Years of Independence` **Obverse:** Sultan's portrait **Reverse:** National arms

| Date | Mintage | F | VF | XF | Unc | BU |
|---|---|---|---|---|---|---|
| ND (1994) Proof | 1,980 | Value: 20.00 | | | | |

**50 SEN** **KM# 64** **Composition:** Copper-Nickel **Subject:** Sultan's 50th Birthday **Obverse:** Sultan's portrait **Reverse:** Waterfront building

| Date | Mintage | F | VF | XF | Unc | BU |
|---|---|---|---|---|---|---|
| ND (1996) Proof | 500 | Value: 25.00 | | | | |

**DOLLAR** **KM# 14** **Composition:** Copper-Nickel

| Date | Mintage | F | VF | XF | Unc | BU |
|---|---|---|---|---|---|---|
| 1970 Proof | 5,000 | Value: 37.50 | | | | |

**DOLLAR** **KM# 20** **Composition:** Copper-Nickel **Obv. Legend:** Without numeral 'I' in title

| Date | Mintage | F | VF | XF | Unc | BU |
|---|---|---|---|---|---|---|
| 1979 Proof | 10,000 | Value: 20.00 | | | | |
| 1984 | 5,000 | — | — | — | 10.00 | — |
| 1984 Proof | 3,000 | Value: 22.00 | | | | |
| 1985 | 15,000 | — | — | — | 8.00 | — |
| 1985 Proof | 10,000 | Value: 20.00 | | | | |
| 1986 | 10,000 | — | — | — | 8.00 | — |
| 1986 Proof | 7,000 | Value: 22.00 | | | | |
| 1987 | 2,000 | — | — | — | 10.00 | — |
| 1988 | 2,000 | — | — | — | 10.00 | — |
| 1989 | 2,000 | — | — | — | 10.00 | — |
| 1990 | 3,000 | — | — | — | 10.00 | — |
| 1991 | 3,000 | — | — | — | 10.00 | — |
| 1992 | — | — | — | — | 10.00 | — |
| 1993 | — | — | — | — | 10.00 | — |

**DOLLAR** **KM# 20a** **Weight:** 18.0500 g. **Composition:** 0.9250 Silver .5368 oz. ASW **Obv. Legend:** Without numeral 'I' in title

| Date | Mintage | F | VF | XF | Unc | BU |
|---|---|---|---|---|---|---|
| 1987 Proof | 2,000 | Value: 40.00 | | | | |
| 1988 Proof | 2,000 | Value: 40.00 | | | | |
| 1989 Proof | 2,000 | Value: 40.00 | | | | |
| 1990 Proof | 2,000 | Value: 40.00 | | | | |
| 1991 Proof | 2,000 | Value: 40.00 | | | | |
| 1992 Proof | 2,000 | Value: 40.00 | | | | |
| 1993 Proof | 2,000 | Value: 40.00 | | | | |

**DOLLAR** **KM# 47** **Weight:** 18.2000 g. **Composition:** 0.9250 Silver .5413 oz. ASW **Subject:** 25th Anniversary of Brunei Currency Board **Obverse:** Sultan Hassanal Bolkiah **Obv. Legend:** Mosque

| Date | Mintage | F | VF | XF | Unc | BU |
|---|---|---|---|---|---|---|
| 1992 Proof | 2,000 | Value: 40.00 | | | | |

**DOLLAR** **KM# 47a** **Composition:** 0.9170 Gold **Subject:** 25th Anniversary of Brunei Currency Board **Obverse:** Sultan Hassanal Bolkian **Obv. Legend:** Mosque

| Date | Mintage | F | VF | XF | Unc | BU |
|---|---|---|---|---|---|---|
| 1992 Proof | 1,000 | Value: 300 | | | | |

**DOLLAR** **KM# 59** **Composition:** Copper-Nickel **Subject:** 10 Years of Independence **Obverse:** Sultan's portrait **Obv. Legend:** National arms

| Date | Mintage | F | VF | XF | Unc | BU |
|---|---|---|---|---|---|---|
| ND (1994) | 3,000 | — | — | — | 8.00 | — |

**DOLLAR** **KM# 59a** **Weight:** 18.2000 g. **Composition:** 0.9250 Silver .5413 oz. ASW **Subject:** 10 Years of Independence **Obverse:** Sultan's portrait **Obv. Legend:** National arms

| Date | Mintage | F | VF | XF | Unc | BU |
|---|---|---|---|---|---|---|
| ND (1994) Proof | 1,980 | — | — | — | — | — |

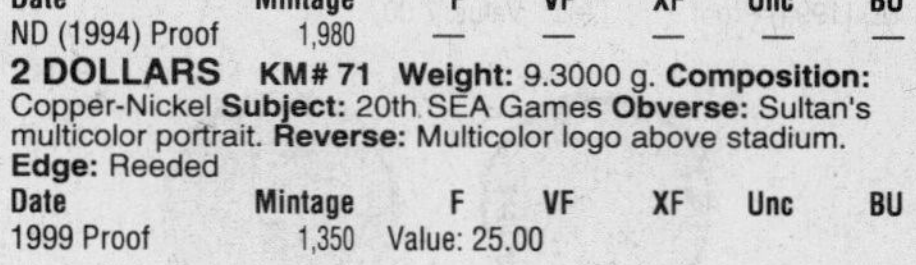

**2 DOLLARS** **KM# 71** **Weight:** 9.3000 g. **Composition:** Copper-Nickel **Subject:** 20th SEA Games **Obverse:** Sultan's multicolor portrait. **Reverse:** Multicolor logo above stadium. **Edge:** Reeded

| Date | Mintage | F | VF | XF | Unc | BU |
|---|---|---|---|---|---|---|
| 1999 Proof | 1,350 | Value: 25.00 | | | | |

**2 DOLLARS** **KM# 74** **Weight:** 9.8000 g. **Composition:** Copper-Nickel **Subject:** APEC **Obverse:** Multicolor bust of Sultan Haji Hassanal Bolkiah half facing. **Reverse:** Multicolor flower and APEC initials above date below world map. **Rev. Legend:** ASIA PACIFIC ECONOMIC COOPERATION NEGARA BRUNEI DARUSSALAM **Edge:** Reeded. **Size:** 27.3 mm.

| Date | Mintage | F | VF | XF | Unc | BU |
|---|---|---|---|---|---|---|
| 2000 | 3,000 | — | — | — | 45.00 | — |

**3 DOLLARS** **KM# 68** **Weight:** 10.0000 g. **Composition:** Copper-Nickel **Subject:** 30 Years ASEAN **Obverse:** Sultan's portrait **Reverse:** Map and sailboat **Edge:** Reeded

| Date | Mintage | F | VF | XF | Unc | BU |
|---|---|---|---|---|---|---|
| 1997 Proof | 1,250 | Value: 35.00 | | | | |

**5 DOLLARS** **KM# 23** **Composition:** Copper-Nickel **Subject:** Year of Hejira 1400 **Obv. Legend:** Without numeral 'I' in title

| Date | Mintage | F | VF | XF | Unc | BU |
|---|---|---|---|---|---|---|
| AH1400(1979) | 10,000 | — | 3.50 | 12.50 | 22.50 | — |

**5 DOLLARS** **KM# 48** **Composition:** 0.9170 Gold **Subject:** 25th Anniversary of Brunei Currency Board **Obverse:** Sultan Hassanal Bolkiah

**Reverse:** Mosque

| Date | Mintage | F | VF | XF | Unc | BU |
|---|---|---|---|---|---|---|
| 1992 Proof | 1,000 | Value: 350 | | | | |

**5 DOLLARS** **KM# 60** **Composition:** Copper-Nickel **Subject:** 10 Years of Independence **Obverse:** Sultan's portrait **Reverse:** National arms

| Date | Mintage | F | VF | XF | Unc | BU |
|---|---|---|---|---|---|---|
| ND (1994) | 3,000 | — | — | — | 16.00 | — |

**5 DOLLARS** **KM# 60a** **Weight:** 28.2800 g. **Composition:** 0.9250 Silver .8410 oz. ASW **Subject:** 10 Years of Independence **Obverse:** Sultan's portrait **Reverse:** National arms

| Date | Mintage | F | VF | XF | Unc | BU |
|---|---|---|---|---|---|---|
| ND (1994) Proof | 1,980 | Value: 35.00 | | | | |

**10 DOLLARS** **KM# 21** **Weight:** 28.2800 g. **Composition:** 0.9250 Silver .8411 oz. ASW **Subject:** 10th Anniversary of Brunei Currency Board **Obv. Legend:** Without numeral 'I' in title

| Date | Mintage | F | VF | XF | Unc | BU |
|---|---|---|---|---|---|---|
| 1977 Proof | 10,000 | Value: 60.00 | | | | |

**10 DOLLARS** **KM# 26** **Composition:** Copper-Nickel **Subject:** Independence Day

| Date | Mintage | F | VF | XF | Unc | BU |
|---|---|---|---|---|---|---|
| 1984 | 15,000 | — | — | — | 20.00 | — |
| 1984 Proof | 5,000 | Value: 45.00 | | | | |

**10 DOLLARS** **KM# 49** **Composition:** 0.9170 Gold **Subject:** 25th Anniversary of Brunei Currency Board **Obverse:** Sultan Hassanal Bolkiah **Reverse:** Mosque

| Date | Mintage | F | VF | XF | Unc | BU |
|---|---|---|---|---|---|---|
| 1992 Proof | 1,000 | Value: 400 | | | | |

**10 DOLLARS** **KM# 61a** **Weight:** 30.7000 g. **Composition:** 0.9250 Silver .9130 oz. ASW **Subject:** 10 Years of Independence **Obverse:** Sultan's portrait **Reverse:** National arms

| Date | Mintage | F | VF | XF | Unc | BU |
|---|---|---|---|---|---|---|
| ND (1994) | 3,000 | — | — | — | 30.00 | — |
| ND (1994) Proof | 2,500 | Value: 55.00 | | | | |

**10 DOLLARS** **KM# 61** **Composition:** Copper-Nickel **Subject:** 10 Years of Independence **Obverse:** Sultan's portrait **Reverse:** National arms

| Date | Mintage | F | VF | XF | Unc | BU |
|---|---|---|---|---|---|---|
| ND | 3,000 | — | — | — | 18.00 | — |

**20 DOLLARS** **KM# 32** **Weight:** 28.2800 g. **Composition:** 0.9250 Silver .8411 oz. ASW **Subject:** 20th Anniversary of Brunei Currency Board

| Date | Mintage | F | VF | XF | Unc | BU |
|---|---|---|---|---|---|---|
| 1987 Proof | 3,000 | Value: 70.00 | | | | |

**20 DOLLARS** **KM# 29** **Weight:** 28.2800 g. **Composition:** 0.9250 Silver .8411 oz. ASW **Subject:** 20th Anniversary of Coronation

| Date | Mintage | F | VF | XF | Unc | BU |
|---|---|---|---|---|---|---|
| ND (1988) | 5,000 | — | — | — | 30.00 | — |
| ND (1988) Proof | 1,000 | Value: 85.00 | | | | |

**20 DOLLARS** **KM# 72** **Weight:** 62.2000 g. **Composition:** 0.9990 Silver 2.0000 oz. ASW **Subject:** 20th SEA Games **Obverse:** Sultan's multicolor portrait. **Reverse:** Multicolor logo above stadium **Edge:** Reeded

| Date | Mintage | F | VF | XF | Unc | BU |
|---|---|---|---|---|---|---|
| 1999 Proof | 850 | Value: 100 | | | | |

**25 DOLLARS** **KM# 50** **Weight:** 31.1000 g. **Composition:** 0.9250 Silver .9249 oz. ASW **Subject:** 25th Anniversary of Brunei Currency Board **Obverse:** Sultan Hassanal Bolkiah **Reverse:** Mosque **Size:** 38.7 mm.

| Date | Mintage | F | VF | XF | Unc | BU |
|---|---|---|---|---|---|---|
| 1992 Proof | 2,000 | Value: 75.00 | | | | |

**25 DOLLARS** **KM# 39** **Composition:** Copper-Nickel **Subject:** 25th Anniversary of Accession

| Date | Mintage | F | VF | XF | Unc | BU |
|---|---|---|---|---|---|---|
| ND (1992) Proof | 7,500 | Value: 35.00 | | | | |

**25 DOLLARS** **KM# 39a** **Composition:** 0.9170 Gold **Subject:** 25th Anniversary of Accession

| Date | Mintage | F | VF | XF | Unc | BU |
|---|---|---|---|---|---|---|
| ND (1992) Proof | — | Value: 550 | | | | |

**30 DOLLARS** **KM# 70** **Weight:** 31.1000 g. **Composition:** 0.9170 Gold .9169 oz. AGW **Subject:** 30 Years - ASEAN **Obverse:** Sultan Hassanal Bolkiah **Reverse:** ASEAN logo

| Date | Mintage | F | VF | XF | Unc | BU |
|---|---|---|---|---|---|---|
| 1997 Proof | 800 | Value: 575 | | | | |

**30 DOLLARS** **KM# 69** **Weight:** 62.2070 g. **Composition:** 0.9990 Silver 2.0000 oz. ASW **Subject:** 30 Years - ASEAN **Obverse:** Sultan Hassanal Bolkiah **Reverse:** 7 multicolored flags.

| Date | Mintage | F | VF | XF | Unc | BU |
|---|---|---|---|---|---|---|
| 1997 Proof | 1,000 | Value: 135 | | | | |

**50 DOLLARS** **KM# 67** **Weight:** 31.1035 g. **Composition:** 0.9170 Gold 1.0000 oz. AGW **Subject:** 50th Birthday - Sultan Hassanal Bolkian **Obverse:** Sultan Hassanal Bolkiah **Reverse:** Mosque

| Date | Mintage | F | VF | XF | Unc | BU |
|---|---|---|---|---|---|---|
| ND (1996) Proof | 500 | Value: 650 | | | | |

**50 DOLLARS** **KM# 24** **Weight:** 28.2800 g. **Composition:** 0.9250 Silver .8411 oz. ASW **Subject:** Year of Hejira 1400 **Obv. Legend:** Without numeral 'I' in title

| Date | Mintage | F | VF | XF | Unc | BU |
|---|---|---|---|---|---|---|
| AH1400 (1980)(1979) Proof | 3,000 | Value: 145 | | | | |

**50 DOLLARS** **KM# 40** **Weight:** 30.7000 g. **Composition:** 0.9250 Silver .9130 oz. ASW **Subject:** 25th Anniversary of Accession **Reverse:** Royal procession. **Edge:** Reeded. **Size:** 42 mm.

| Date | Mintage | F | VF | XF | Unc | BU |
|---|---|---|---|---|---|---|
| ND (1992) Proof | 3,500 | Value: 50.00 | | | | |

**50 DOLLARS** **KM# 40a** **Composition:** 0.9170 Gold **Subject:** 25th Anniversary of Accession **Obverse:** Sultan Hassanal Bolkiah **Reverse:** Royal procession

| Date | Mintage | F | VF | XF | Unc | BU |
|---|---|---|---|---|---|---|
| ND (1992) | — | — | — | — | — | — |

**50 DOLLARS** **KM# 51** **Composition:** 0.9170 Gold **Subject:** 25th Anniversary of Brunei Currency Board **Obverse:** Sultan Hassanal Bolkiah

**Reverse:** Mosque

| Date | Mintage | F | VF | XF | Unc | BU |
|---|---|---|---|---|---|---|
| 1992 Proof | 1,000 | Value: 450 | | | | |

**50 DOLLARS** **KM# 65** **Weight:** 62.2070 g. **Composition:** 0.9990 Silver 2.0000 oz. ASW **Subject:** 50th Birthday - Sultan Hassanal Bolkiah **Obverse:** Sultan Hassanal Bolkiah's multicolor portrait. **Reverse:** Buildings on waterfront

| Date | Mintage | F | VF | XF | Unc | BU |
|---|---|---|---|---|---|---|
| ND Proof | 500 | Value: 175 | | | | |

**50 DOLLARS** **KM# 66** **Weight:** 62.2070 g. **Composition:** 0.9990 Silver 2.0000 oz. ASW **Subject:** 50th Birthday - Sultan Hassanal Bolkiah **Obverse:** Sultan Bolkian arms **Reverse:** Building

| Date | Mintage | F | VF | XF | Unc | BU |
|---|---|---|---|---|---|---|
| ND (1996) Proof | 500 | Value: 225 | | | | |

**100 DOLLARS** **KM# 27** **Weight:** 28.2800 g. **Composition:** 0.9250 Silver .8411 oz. ASW **Subject:** Independence Day

| Date | Mintage | F | VF | XF | Unc | BU |
|---|---|---|---|---|---|---|
| 1984 | 5,000 | — | — | — | 140 | — |
| 1984 Proof | 2,000 | Value: 185 | | | | |

**100 DOLLARS** **KM# 33** **Weight:** 13.5000 g. **Composition:** 0.9170 Gold .3976 oz. AGW **Subject:** 20th Anniversary of Brunei Currency Board

| Date | Mintage | F | VF | XF | Unc | BU |
|---|---|---|---|---|---|---|
| 1987 Proof | 1,000 | Value: 450 | | | | |

**100 DOLLARS** **KM# 30** **Weight:** 31.1000 g. **Composition:** 0.9250 Silver .9250 oz. ASW **Subject:** 20th Anniversary of Coronation

| Date | Mintage | F | VF | XF | Unc | BU |
|---|---|---|---|---|---|---|
| ND (1988) Proof | 2,000 | Value: 175 | | | | |

**100 DOLLARS** **KM# 52** **Composition:** 917.0000 Gold **Subject:** 25th Anniversary of Brunei Currency Board **Obverse:** Sultan Hassanal Bolkiah **Reverse:** Mosque

| Date | Mintage | F | VF | XF | Unc | BU |
|---|---|---|---|---|---|---|
| 1992 Proof | 1,000 | Value: 550 | | | | |

**100 DOLLARS** **KM# 62** **Composition:** 917.0000 White Gold **Subject:** 10th Years of Independence **Obverse:** Sultan Hassanal Bolkiah **Reverse:** National arms

| Date | Mintage | F | VF | XF | Unc | BU |
|---|---|---|---|---|---|---|
| ND (1994) | 1,980 | — | — | — | 475 | — |
| ND (1994) Proof | 1,500 | Value: 525 | | | | |

**200 DOLLARS** **KM# 73** **Weight:** 31.1000 g. **Composition:** 0.9170 Gold .9169 oz. AGW **Subject:** 20th SEA Games **Obverse:** Sultan Hassanal Bolkiah **Reverse:** Multicolor logo above stadium

| Date | Mintage | F | VF | XF | Unc | BU |
|---|---|---|---|---|---|---|
| 1999 Proof | 450 | Value: 650 | | | | |

**250 DOLLARS** **KM# 53** **Composition:** 0.9170 Gold **Subject:** 25th Anniversary of Brunei Currency Board **Obverse:** Sultan Hassanal Bolkiah **Reverse:** Mosque

| Date | Mintage | F | VF | XF | Unc | BU |
|---|---|---|---|---|---|---|
| 1992 Proof | 1,000 | Value: 700 | | | | |

**500 DOLLARS** **KM# 41** **Weight:** 50.0000 g. **Composition:** 0.9170 Gold 1.4727 oz. AGW **Subject:** 25th Anniversary of Accession **Obverse:** Sultan's portrait. **Reverse:** Other portrait.

| Date | Mintage | F | VF | XF | Unc | BU |
|---|---|---|---|---|---|---|
| ND (1992) Proof | 1,500 | Value: 1,350 | | | | |

**750 DOLLARS** **KM# 25** **Weight:** 15.9800 g. **Composition:** 0.9170 Gold .4711 oz. AGW **Subject:** Year of Hejira 1400

| Date | Mintage | F | VF | XF | Unc | BU |
|---|---|---|---|---|---|---|
| AH1400 (1980)(1979) Proof | 1,000 | Value: 650 | | | | |

**1000 DOLLARS** **KM# 22** **Weight:** 50.0000 g. **Composition:** 0.9170 Gold 1.4742 oz. AGW **Subject:** 10th Anniversary of Sultan's Coronation

| Date | Mintage | F | VF | XF | Unc | BU |
|---|---|---|---|---|---|---|
| ND (1978) Proof | 1,000 | Value: 1,450 | | | | |

**1000 DOLLARS** **KM# 28** **Weight:** 50.0000 g. **Composition:** 0.9170 Gold 1.4742 oz. AGW **Subject:** Independence Day **Obverse:** Bust of Sultan Bolkiah half right **Reverse:** Off shore oil rig

| Date | Mintage | F | VF | XF | Unc | BU |
|---|---|---|---|---|---|---|
| 1984 | 4,000 | — | — | — | 1,000 | — |
| 1984 Proof | 1,000 | Value: 1,150 | | | | |

**1000 DOLLARS** **KM# 31** **Weight:** 50.0000 g. **Composition:** 0.9170 Gold 1.4742 oz. AGW **Subject:** 20th Anniversary of Coronation

| Date | Mintage | F | VF | XF | Unc | BU |
|---|---|---|---|---|---|---|
| (1988) Proof | 1,000 | Value: 1,100 | | | | |

**1000 DOLLARS** **KM# 63** **Composition:** 0.9990 Gold **Subject:** 10 Years of Independence **Obverse:** Sultan Hassanal Bolkiah **Reverse:** National arms

| Date | Mintage | F | VF | XF | Unc | BU |
|---|---|---|---|---|---|---|
| ND (1994) | 980 | — | — | — | 1,275 | — |
| ND (1994) Proof | 1,000 | Value: 1,325 | | | | |

## PROOF SETS

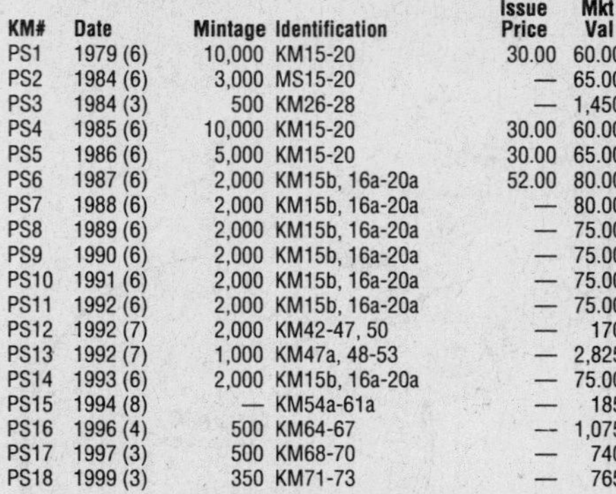

| KM# | Date | Mintage | Identification | Issue Price | Mkt Val |
|---|---|---|---|---|---|
| PSA1 | 1970 (5) | — | KM9-13 | — | 22.50 |
| PS1 | 1979 (6) | 10,000 | KM15-20 | 30.00 | 60.00 |
| PS2 | 1984 (6) | 3,000 | MS15-20 | — | 65.00 |
| PS3 | 1984 (3) | 500 | KM26-28 | — | 1,450 |
| PS4 | 1985 (6) | 10,000 | KM15-20 | 30.00 | 60.00 |
| PS5 | 1986 (6) | 5,000 | KM15-20 | 30.00 | 65.00 |
| PS6 | 1987 (6) | 2,000 | KM15b, 16a-20a | 52.00 | 80.00 |
| PS7 | 1988 (6) | 2,000 | KM15b, 16a-20a | — | 80.00 |
| PS8 | 1989 (6) | 2,000 | KM15b, 16a-20a | — | 75.00 |
| PS9 | 1990 (6) | 2,000 | KM15b, 16a-20a | — | 75.00 |
| PS10 | 1991 (6) | 2,000 | KM15b, 16a-20a | — | 75.00 |
| PS11 | 1992 (6) | 2,000 | KM15b, 16a-20a | — | 75.00 |
| PS12 | 1992 (7) | 2,000 | KM42-47, 50 | — | 170 |
| PS13 | 1992 (7) | 1,000 | KM47a, 48-53 | — | 2,825 |
| PS14 | 1993 (6) | 2,000 | KM15b, 16a-20a | — | 75.00 |
| PS15 | 1994 (8) | — | KM54a-61a | — | 185 |
| PS16 | 1996 (4) | 500 | KM64-67 | — | 1,075 |
| PS17 | 1997 (3) | 500 | KM68-70 | — | 740 |
| PS18 | 1999 (3) | 350 | KM71-73 | — | 765 |

## SPECIMEN SETS (SS)

| KM# | Date | Mintage | Identification | Issue Price | Mkt Val |
|---|---|---|---|---|---|
| MS2 | 1984 (6) | 5,000 | KM15-20 | — | 15.00 |
| MS3 | 1984 (3) | 500 | KM26-28 | — | 1,250 |
| MS4 | 1985 (6) | 15,000 | KM15-20 | 10.00 | 22.50 |
| MS5 | 1986 (6) | 10,000 | KM15-20 | 10.00 | 22.50 |
| MS6 | 1987 (6) | 3,000 | KM15a, 16-20 | 15.60 | 22.50 |
| MS7 | 1988 (6) | 2,000 | KM15a, 16-20 | 15.60 | 22.50 |
| MS8 | 1989 (6) | 2,000 | KM15a, 16-20 | — | 22.50 |
| MS9 | 1990 (6) | 3,000 | KM15a, 16-20 | — | 22.50 |
| MS10 | 1991 (6) | 3,000 | KM15a, 16-20 | — | 22.50 |
| MS11 | 1994 (8) | — | KM54-61 | — | 50.00 |

# BULGARIA

The Republic of Bulgaria, formerly the Peoples Republic of Bulgaria, a Balkan country on the Black Sea in southeastern Europe, has an area of 42,855 sq. mi. (110,910 sq. km.) and a population of *8.31 million. Capital: Sofia. Agriculture remains a key component of the economy but industrialization, particularly heavy industry, has been emphasized since the late 1940s. Machinery, tobacco and cigarettes, wines and spirits, clothing and metals are the chief exports.

The area now occupied by Bulgaria was conquered by the Bulgars, an Asiatic tribe, in the 7th century. Bulgarian kingdoms continued to exist on the Bulgarian peninsula until it came under Turkish rule in 1395. In 1878, after nearly 500 years of Turkish rule, Bulgaria was made a principality under Turkish suzerainty. Union seven years later with Eastern Rumelia created a Balkan state with borders approximating those of present-day Bulgaria. A Bulgarian kingdom, fully independent of Turkey, was proclaimed Sept. 22, 1908. During WWI Bulgaria had been aligned with Germany. After the Armistice certain land concessions were given to Greece and Romania. In 1934 King Boris III suspended all political parties and established a dictatorial monarchy. In 1938 the military began rearming through the aide of the Anglo-French loan. As WW II developed, Bulgaria again supported the Germans but protected their Jewish community. Boris died mysteriously in 1943 and Simeon II became King at the age of six. The country was then ruled by a pro-Nazi regency until it was liberated by Soviet forces in 1944.

The monarchy was abolished and Simeon was ousted by plebiscite in 1946 and Bulgaria became a Peoples Republic on the Soviet pattern. After democratic reforms in 1989 the name was changed to the Republic of Bulgaria.

Coinage of the Peoples Republic features a number of politically oriented commemoratives.

**RULERS**

Ferdinand I, as Prince, 1887-1908
As King, 1908-1918
Boris III, 1918-1943

**MINT MARKS**

A - Berlin
(a) Cornucopia & torch - Paris
BP - Budapest
H - Heaton Mint, Birmingham
KB - Kormoczbanya
(p) Poissy - Thunderbolt

**MONETARY SYSTEM**

100 Stotinki = 1 Lev

# TURKISH PRINCIPALITY

## STANDARD COINAGE

**STOTINKA** **KM# 22.1** **Composition:** Bronze **Ruler:** Ferdinand I as Prince **Reverse:** Privy marks and design name below denomination

| Date | Mintage | F | VF | XF | Unc | BU |
|---|---|---|---|---|---|---|
| 1901 | 20,000,000 | 1.00 | 2.00 | 6.00 | 12.50 | — |

**STOTINKA** **KM# 22.2** **Composition:** Bronze **Ruler:** Ferdinand I as Prince **Reverse:** Without privy marks and designer name

| Date | Mintage | F | VF | XF | Unc | BU |
|---|---|---|---|---|---|---|
| 1912 | 20,000,000 | 0.50 | 1.00 | 2.50 | 5.00 | — |

**2 STOTINKI** **KM# 23.1** **Composition:** Bronze **Ruler:** Ferdinand I **Reverse:** Privy marks and designer name below denomination

| Date | Mintage | F | VF | XF | Unc | BU |
|---|---|---|---|---|---|---|
| 1901(a) | 40,000,000 | 1.00 | 2.00 | 5.00 | 10.00 | — |

**2 STOTINKI** **KM# 23.2** **Composition:** Bronze **Reverse:** Without privy marks and designer name

| Date | Mintage | F | VF | XF | Unc | BU |
|---|---|---|---|---|---|---|
| 1912 | 40,000,000 | 0.50 | 1.00 | 2.00 | 4.00 | — |

**5 STOTINKI** **KM# 24** **Composition:** Copper-Nickel

| Date | Mintage | F | VF | XF | Unc | BU |
|---|---|---|---|---|---|---|
| 1906 | 14,000,000 | 0.20 | 0.60 | 2.00 | 5.00 | — |
| 1912 | 14,000,000 | 0.20 | 0.40 | 1.00 | 2.50 | — |
| 1913 | 20,000,000 | 0.20 | 0.40 | 1.00 | 2.50 | — |
| 1913 Proof | — | — | — | — | — | — |

**5 STOTINKI** **KM# 24a** **Composition:** Zinc

| Date | Mintage | F | VF | XF | Unc | BU |
|---|---|---|---|---|---|---|
| 1917 | 53,200,000 | 0.60 | 1.00 | 2.50 | 6.00 | — |

**10 STOTINKI** **KM# 25** **Composition:** Copper-Nickel

| Date | Mintage | F | VF | XF | Unc | BU |
|---|---|---|---|---|---|---|
| 1906 | 13,000,000 | 0.50 | 1.00 | 2.50 | 6.00 | — |
| 1912 | 13,000,000 | 0.20 | 0.40 | 1.00 | 2.50 | — |
| 1912 Proof | — | — | — | — | — | — |
| 1913 | 20,000,000 | 0.20 | 0.40 | 1.00 | 2.50 | — |

**10 STOTINKI** **KM# 25a** **Composition:** Zinc

| Date | Mintage | F | VF | XF | Unc | BU |
|---|---|---|---|---|---|---|
| 1917 | 59,100,000 | 0.40 | 1.00 | 2.00 | 5.00 | — |
| 1917 Proof | — | Value: 125 | | | | |

**20 STOTINKI** **KM# 26** **Composition:** Copper-Nickel

| Date | Mintage | F | VF | XF | Unc | BU |
|---|---|---|---|---|---|---|
| 1906 | 10,000,000 | 0.50 | 1.50 | 3.50 | 10.00 | — |
| 1912 | 10,000,000 | 0.20 | 0.50 | 1.25 | 5.00 | — |
| 1913 | 5,000,000 | 0.20 | 0.50 | 1.50 | 5.50 | — |
| 1913 | — | — | — | — | — | — |

**20 STOTINKI** **KM# 26a** **Composition:** Zinc

| Date | Mintage | F | VF | XF | Unc | BU |
|---|---|---|---|---|---|---|
| 1917 | 40,000,000 | 0.50 | 1.75 | 4.00 | 8.50 | — |
| 1917 Proof | — | Value: 125 | | | | |

# KINGDOM

## STANDARD COINAGE

**50 STOTINKI** **KM# 27** **Weight:** 2.5000 g. **Composition:** 0.8350 Silver .0671 oz. ASW

| Date | Mintage | F | VF | XF | Unc | BU |
|---|---|---|---|---|---|---|
| 1910 | 400,000 | 1.75 | 3.50 | 6.00 | 14.00 | — |

**50 STOTINKI** **KM# 30** **Weight:** 2.5000 g. **Composition:** 0.8350 Silver .0671 oz. ASW

| Date | Mintage | F | VF | XF | Unc | BU |
|---|---|---|---|---|---|---|
| 1912 | 2,000,000 | 1.00 | 2.00 | 4.50 | 10.00 | — |
| 1913 | 3,000,000 | 1.00 | 2.00 | 3.50 | 8.00 | — |
| 1916 | 4,562,000 | 50.00 | 100 | 175 | 275 | — |

**50 STOTINKI** **KM# 46** **Weight:** 2.5000 g. **Composition:** 0.8350 Aluminum-Bronze .0671 oz.

| Date | Mintage | F | VF | XF | Unc | BU |
|---|---|---|---|---|---|---|
| 1937 | 60,200,000 | 0.25 | 0.50 | 1.00 | 2.50 | — |

**LEV** **KM# 28** **Weight:** 5.0000 g. **Composition:** 0.8350 Silver .1342 oz. ASW

| Date | Mintage | F | VF | XF | Unc | BU |
|---|---|---|---|---|---|---|
| 1910 | 3,000,000 | 2.00 | 4.00 | 7.00 | 16.00 | — |

**LEV** **KM# 31** **Weight:** 5.0000 g. **Composition:** 0.8350 Silver .1342 oz. ASW

| Date | Mintage | F | VF | XF | Unc | BU |
|---|---|---|---|---|---|---|
| 1912 | 2,000,000 | 2.00 | 3.00 | 5.50 | 12.50 | — |
| 1913 | 3,500,000 | 2.00 | 3.00 | 5.00 | 10.00 | — |
| 1916 | 4,569,000 | 100 | 200 | 350 | 600 | — |

**LEV** **KM# 35** **Composition:** Aluminum

| Date | Mintage | F | VF | XF | Unc | BU |
|---|---|---|---|---|---|---|
| 1923 | 40,000,000 | 2.50 | 5.00 | 12.00 | 35.00 | — |

**LEV** **KM# 37** **Composition:** Copper-Nickel

| Date | Mintage | F | VF | XF | Unc | BU |
|---|---|---|---|---|---|---|
| 1925 | 35,000,000 | 0.20 | 0.50 | 1.00 | 2.50 | — |
| 1925(p) | 34,982,000 | 0.25 | 0.60 | 1.25 | 3.00 | — |

**Note:** The Poissy issue bears the thunderbolt mint mark

**LEV** **KM# 37a** **Composition:** Iron

| Date | Mintage | F | VF | XF | Unc | BU |
|---|---|---|---|---|---|---|
| 1941 | 10,000,000 | 3.00 | 6.00 | 15.00 | 40.00 | — |

**2 LEVA** **KM# 29** **Weight:** 10.0000 g. **Composition:** 0.8350 Silver .2685 oz. ASW

| Date | Mintage | F | VF | XF | Unc | BU |
|---|---|---|---|---|---|---|
| 1910 | 400,000 | 4.50 | 7.50 | 16.00 | 45.00 | — |

**2 LEVA** **KM# 32** **Weight:** 10.0000 g. **Composition:** 0.8350 Silver .2685 oz. ASW

| Date | Mintage | F | VF | XF | Unc | BU |
|---|---|---|---|---|---|---|
| 1912 | 1,000,000 | 4.00 | 6.00 | 12.00 | 20.00 | — |
| 1913 | 500,000 | 4.00 | 6.00 | 12.00 | 20.00 | — |
| 1916 | 2,286,000 | 200 | 400 | 700 | 1,150 | — |

**2 LEVA** **KM# 36** **Composition:** Aluminum

| Date | Mintage | F | VF | XF | Unc | BU |
|---|---|---|---|---|---|---|
| 1923 | 20,000,000 | 3.00 | 6.00 | 15.00 | 50.00 | — |

**2 LEVA** **KM# 38** **Composition:** Copper-Nickel

| Date | Mintage | F | VF | XF | Unc | BU |
|---|---|---|---|---|---|---|
| 1925 | 20,000,000 | 0.40 | 0.80 | 1.75 | 4.00 | — |
| 1925(p) | 20,000,000 | 0.50 | 1.00 | 2.00 | 4.50 | — |

**Note:** The Poissy issue bears the thunderbolt privy mark

**2 LEVA** **KM# 38a** **Composition:** Iron

| Date | Mintage | F | VF | XF | Unc | BU |
|---|---|---|---|---|---|---|
| 1941 | 15,000,000 | 0.75 | 1.50 | 3.50 | 10.00 | — |

**2 LEVA** **KM# 49** **Composition:** Iron

| Date | Mintage | F | VF | XF | Unc | BU |
|---|---|---|---|---|---|---|
| 1943 | 35,000,000 | 0.75 | 1.50 | 4.50 | 15.00 | — |

**5 LEVA** **KM# 39** **Composition:** Copper-Nickel

| Date | Mintage | F | VF | XF | Unc | BU |
|---|---|---|---|---|---|---|
| 1930 | 20,001,000 | 0.60 | 1.25 | 2.75 | 7.00 | — |

**5 LEVA** **KM# 39a** **Composition:** Iron

| Date | Mintage | F | VF | XF | Unc | BU |
|---|---|---|---|---|---|---|
| 1941 | 15,000,000 | 1.00 | 3.00 | 6.00 | 20.00 | — |

**5 LEVA** **KM# 39b** **Composition:** Nickel Clad Steel

| Date | Mintage | F | VF | XF | Unc | BU |
|---|---|---|---|---|---|---|
| 1943 | 36,000,000 | 0.50 | 1.00 | 2.00 | 5.50 | — |

**10 LEVA** **KM# 40** **Composition:** Copper-Nickel

| Date | Mintage | F | VF | XF | Unc | BU |
|---|---|---|---|---|---|---|
| 1930 | 15,001,000 | 0.75 | 1.50 | 3.50 | 9.00 | — |

**10 LEVA** **KM# 40a** **Composition:** Iron

| Date | Mintage | F | VF | XF | Unc | BU |
|---|---|---|---|---|---|---|
| 1941 | 2,200,000 | 6.00 | 12.00 | 25.00 | 65.00 | — |

**10 LEVA** **KM# 40b** **Composition:** Nickel Clad Steel

| Date | Mintage | F | VF | XF | Unc | BU |
|---|---|---|---|---|---|---|
| 1943 | 25,000,000 | 0.60 | 1.25 | 3.00 | 7.50 | — |

**20 LEVA** **KM# 33** **Weight:** 6.4516 g. **Composition:** 0.9000 Gold .1867 oz. AGW **Subject:** Declaration of Independence

| Date | Mintage | F | VF | XF | Unc | BU |
|---|---|---|---|---|---|---|
| 1912 | 75,000 | 100 | 175 | 275 | 450 | — |
| 1912 Proof | — | Value: 2,000 | | | | |

**20 LEVA** **KM# 41** **Weight:** 4.0000 g. **Composition:** 0.5000 Silver .0643 oz. ASW

| Date | Mintage | F | VF | XF | Unc | BU |
|---|---|---|---|---|---|---|
| 1930BP | 10,016,000 | 1.00 | 2.00 | 3.50 | 8.50 | — |

**20 LEVA** **KM# 47** **Composition:** Copper-Nickel

| Date | Mintage | F | VF | XF | Unc | BU |
|---|---|---|---|---|---|---|
| 1940A | 6,650,000 | 0.50 | 1.00 | 2.00 | 5.00 | — |

**50 LEVA** **KM# 42** **Weight:** 10.0000 g. **Composition:** 0.5000 Silver .1607 oz. ASW

| Date | Mintage | F | VF | XF | Unc | BU |
|---|---|---|---|---|---|---|
| 1930BP | 9,028,000 | 2.50 | 4.50 | 8.50 | 20.00 | — |

**50 LEVA** **KM# 44** **Weight:** 10.0000 g. **Composition:** 0.5000 Silver .1607 oz. ASW

| Date | Mintage | F | VF | XF | Unc | BU |
|---|---|---|---|---|---|---|
| 1934 | 3,001,000 | 2.00 | 4.00 | 7.00 | 16.00 | — |
| 1934 Proof | — | — | — | — | — | — |

**50 LEVA** **KM# 48** **Composition:** Copper-Nickel

| Date | Mintage | F | VF | XF | Unc | BU |
|---|---|---|---|---|---|---|
| 1940A | 12,340,000 | 0.75 | 1.50 | 3.00 | 7.50 | — |

**50 LEVA** **KM# 48a** **Composition:** Nickel Clad Steel

| Date | Mintage | F | VF | XF | Unc | BU |
|---|---|---|---|---|---|---|
| 1943A | 15,000,000 | 1.00 | 2.00 | 4.00 | 9.00 | — |

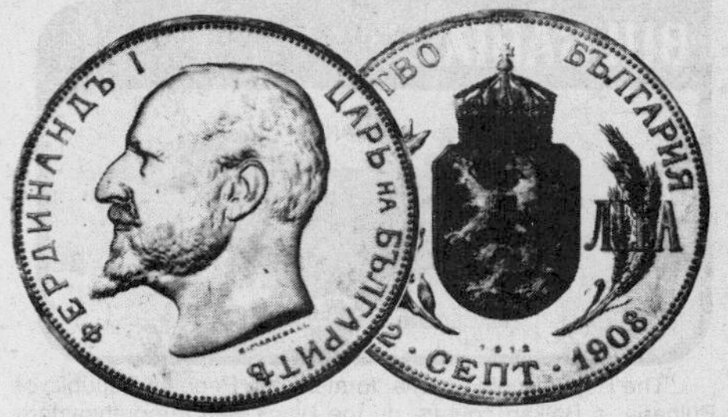

**100 LEVA** **KM# 34** **Weight:** 32.2580 g. **Composition:** 0.9000 Gold .9334 oz. AGW **Subject:** Declaration of Independence

| Date | Mintage | F | VF | XF | Unc | BU |
|---|---|---|---|---|---|---|
| 1912 | 5,000 | 600 | 900 | 1,850 | 3,000 | — |
| 1912 Proof | — | Value: 3,500 | | | | |

**100 LEVA** **KM# 43** **Weight:** 20.0000 g. **Composition:** 0.5000 Silver .3215 oz. ASW

| Date | Mintage | F | VF | XF | Unc | BU |
|---|---|---|---|---|---|---|
| 1930BP | 1,556,000 | BV | 6.00 | 12.00 | 30.00 | — |

**100 LEVA** **KM# 45** **Weight:** 20.0000 g. **Composition:** 0.5000 Silver .3215 oz. ASW

| Date | Mintage | F | VF | XF | Unc | BU |
|---|---|---|---|---|---|---|
| 1934 | 2,506,000 | BV | 4.50 | 7.50 | 13.50 | — |
| 1934 Proof | — | — | — | — | — | — |
| 1937 | 2,207,000 | BV | 4.50 | 7.50 | 13.50 | — |

## MEDALLIC COINAGE

Originally produced as a jewelry item. A similar piece with Russian legends also exists and is found listed in "Unusual World Coins", 3rd edition, Krause Publications.

**4 DUKAT** **KM# M1** **Weight:** 13.9600 g. **Composition:** 0.9860 Gold .4425 oz. AGW **Countermark:** Crown and government mark

| Date | Mintage | F | VF | XF | Unc | BU |
|---|---|---|---|---|---|---|
| 1910 | — | 225 | 250 | 275 | 500 | — |
| 1911 | — | 250 | 275 | 300 | 525 | — |
| 1912 | — | 225 | 250 | 275 | 500 | — |
| 1914 | — | 275 | 400 | 500 | 900 | — |

| Date | Mintage | F | VF | XF | Unc | BU |
|---|---|---|---|---|---|---|
| 1917 | — | 275 | 400 | 500 | 900 | — |
| 1918 | — | 250 | 275 | 300 | 525 | — |
| 1919 | — | 300 | 400 | 500 | 900 | — |

**Note:** Values above are for holed or holed and plugged specimens; unholed specimens command 5 times the values indicated

**4 DUKAT** **KM# M2** **Weight:** 13.9600 g. **Composition:** 0.9860 Gold .4425 oz. AGW **Countermark:** Crown and government mark

| Date | Mintage | F | VF | XF | Unc | BU |
|---|---|---|---|---|---|---|
| 1926 | — | 350 | 450 | 600 | 900 | — |

**Note:** Values above are for holed or holed and plugged specimens; unholed specimens command 5 times the values indicated

# PEOPLES REPUBLIC

## STANDARD COINAGE

**STOTINKA** **KM# 50** **Composition:** Brass

| Date | Mintage | F | VF | XF | Unc | BU |
|---|---|---|---|---|---|---|
| 1951 | — | — | — | 0.10 | 0.25 | — |

**STOTINKA** **KM# 59** **Composition:** Brass **Obverse:** Date 9 / IX / 1944 on ribbon

| Date | Mintage | F | VF | XF | Unc | BU |
|---|---|---|---|---|---|---|
| 1962 | — | — | — | 0.10 | 0.25 | — |
| 1970 | — | — | 0.20 | 0.50 | 2.00 | — |

**STOTINKA** **KM# 84** **Composition:** Brass **Obverse:** 2 dates on ribbon, '681-1944' **Note:** Edge varieties exist.

| Date | Mintage | F | VF | XF | Unc | BU |
|---|---|---|---|---|---|---|
| 1974 | — | — | — | 0.10 | 0.15 | — |
| 1979 Proof | 2,000 | Value: 1.50 | | | | |
| 1980 Proof | 2,000 | Value: 1.50 | | | | |
| 1981 | 137 | — | — | — | 2.00 | — |
| 1988 | — | — | — | 0.10 | 0.15 | — |
| 1989 | — | — | — | 0.10 | 0.15 | — |
| 1990 | — | — | — | 0.10 | 0.15 | — |

**STOTINKA** **KM# 111** **Composition:** Brass **Subject:** 1300th Anniversary of Bulgaria

| Date | Mintage | F | VF | XF | Unc | BU |
|---|---|---|---|---|---|---|
| 1981 | — | — | 0.10 | 0.20 | 0.50 | — |
| 1981 Proof | — | Value: 2.00 | | | | |

**2 STOTINKI** **KM# 60** **Composition:** Brass **Obverse:** Date 9 • IX • 1944 on ribbon

| Date | Mintage | F | VF | XF | Unc | BU |
|---|---|---|---|---|---|---|
| 1962 | — | — | — | 0.10 | 0.25 | — |

**2 STOTINKI** **KM# 85** **Composition:** Brass **Obverse:** 2 dates on ribbon, '681-1944'

| Date | Mintage | F | VF | XF | Unc | BU |
|---|---|---|---|---|---|---|
| 1974 | — | — | — | 0.10 | 0.25 | — |
| 1979 Proof | 2,000 | Value: 2.00 | | | | |
| 1980 Proof | 2,000 | Value: 2.00 | | | | |
| 1981 Rare | 20 | — | — | — | — | — |
| 1988 | — | — | — | 0.10 | 0.25 | — |
| 1989 | — | — | — | 0.10 | 0.25 | — |
| 1990 | — | — | — | 0.10 | 0.25 | — |

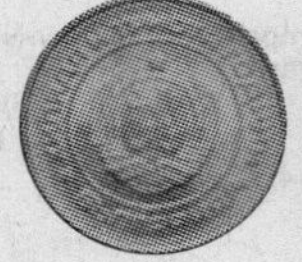

**2 STOTINKI** **KM# 112** **Composition:** Brass **Subject:** 1300th Anniversary of Bulgaria

| Date | Mintage | F | VF | XF | Unc | BU |
|---|---|---|---|---|---|---|
| 1981 | — | — | 0.10 | 0.20 | 0.60 | — |
| 1981 Proof | — | Value: 2.50 | | | | |

**3 STOTINKI** **KM# 51** **Composition:** Brass

| Date | Mintage | F | VF | XF | Unc | BU |
|---|---|---|---|---|---|---|
| 1951 | — | — | 0.10 | 0.25 | 0.75 | — |

**5 STOTINKI** **KM# 52** **Composition:** Brass

| Date | Mintage | F | VF | XF | Unc | BU |
|---|---|---|---|---|---|---|
| 1951 | — | 0.10 | 0.15 | 0.25 | 0.75 | — |

**5 STOTINKI** **KM# 61** **Composition:** Brass **Obverse:** Date 9 • IX • 1944 on ribbon

| Date | Mintage | F | VF | XF | Unc | BU |
|---|---|---|---|---|---|---|
| 1962 | — | — | 0.10 | 0.20 | 0.50 | — |

**5 STOTINKI** **KM# 86** **Composition:** Brass **Obverse:** 2 dates on ribbon '681-1944'

| Date | Mintage | F | VF | XF | Unc | BU |
|---|---|---|---|---|---|---|
| 1974 | — | — | 0.10 | 0.15 | 0.25 | — |
| 1979 Proof | 2,000 | Value: 2.00 | | | | |
| 1980 Proof | 2,000 | Value: 2.00 | | | | |
| 1988 | — | — | — | 0.15 | 0.25 | — |
| 1989 | — | — | — | 0.15 | 0.25 | — |
| 1990 | — | — | — | 0.15 | 0.25 | — |

**5 STOTINKI** **KM# 113** **Composition:** Brass **Subject:** 1300th Anniversary of Bulgaria

| Date | Mintage | F | VF | XF | Unc | BU |
|---|---|---|---|---|---|---|
| 1981 | — | — | 0.10 | 0.25 | 0.75 | — |
| 1981 Proof | — | Value: 2.50 | | | | |

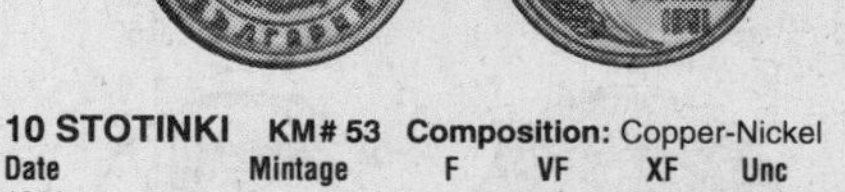

**10 STOTINKI** **KM# 53** **Composition:** Copper-Nickel

| Date | Mintage | F | VF | XF | Unc | BU |
|---|---|---|---|---|---|---|
| 1951 | — | — | 0.10 | 0.20 | 0.40 | — |

**10 STOTINKI** **KM# 62** **Composition:** Nickel-Brass **Obverse:** Date 9 • IX • 1944 on ribbon

| Date | Mintage | F | VF | XF | Unc | BU |
|---|---|---|---|---|---|---|
| 1962 | — | — | 0.10 | 0.20 | 0.40 | — |

**10 STOTINKI** **KM# 87** **Composition:** Nickel-Brass **Obverse:** 2 dates on arms, '681-1944'

| Date | Mintage | F | VF | XF | Unc | BU |
|---|---|---|---|---|---|---|
| 1974 | — | — | 0.10 | 0.15 | 0.25 | — |
| 1979 Proof | 2,000 | Value: 3.50 | | | | |
| 1980 Proof | 2,000 | Value: 3.50 | | | | |
| 1988 | — | — | — | 0.15 | 0.25 | — |
| 1989 | — | — | — | 0.15 | 0.25 | — |
| 1990 | — | — | — | 0.15 | 0.25 | — |

**10 STOTINKI** **KM# 114** **Composition:** Copper-Nickel **Subject:** 1300th Anniversary of Bulgaria

| Date | Mintage | F | VF | XF | Unc | BU |
|---|---|---|---|---|---|---|
| 1981 | — | — | 0.20 | 0.50 | 1.50 | — |
| 1981 Proof | — | Value: 3.50 | | | | |

**20 STOTINKI** **KM# 55** **Composition:** Copper-Nickel

| Date | Mintage | F | VF | XF | Unc | BU |
|---|---|---|---|---|---|---|
| 1952 | — | 1.00 | 2.50 | 7.50 | 20.00 | — |
| 1954 | — | 0.10 | 0.25 | 0.75 | 1.50 | — |

**20 STOTINKI** **KM# 63** **Composition:** Nickel-Brass **Obverse:** Date 9 • IX • 1944 on ribbon

| Date | Mintage | F | VF | XF | Unc | BU |
|---|---|---|---|---|---|---|
| 1962 | — | 0.10 | 0.20 | 0.30 | 0.75 | — |

**20 STOTINKI** **KM# 88** **Composition:** Nickel-Brass **Obverse:** 2 dates on ribbon, '681-1944'

| Date | Mintage | F | VF | XF | Unc | BU |
|---|---|---|---|---|---|---|
| 1974 | — | 0.10 | 0.20 | 0.30 | 0.60 | — |
| 1979 Proof | 2,000 | Value: 3.50 | | | | |
| 1980 Proof | 2,000 | Value: 3.50 | | | | |
| 1988 | — | — | — | 0.30 | 0.60 | — |
| 1989 | — | — | — | 0.30 | 0.60 | — |
| 1990 | — | — | — | 0.30 | 0.60 | — |

**20 STOTINKI** **KM# 115** **Composition:** Copper-Nickel **Subject:** 1300th Anniversary of Bulgaria

| Date | Mintage | F | VF | XF | Unc | BU |
|---|---|---|---|---|---|---|
| 1981 | — | — | 0.25 | 0.65 | 2.00 | — |
| 1981 Proof | — | Value: 4.00 | | | | |

**25 STOTINKI** **KM# 54** **Composition:** Copper-Nickel

| Date | Mintage | F | VF | XF | Unc | BU |
|---|---|---|---|---|---|---|
| 1951 | — | 0.10 | 0.20 | 0.50 | 1.00 | — |

**50 STOTINKI** **KM# 56** **Composition:** Copper-Nickel

| Date | Mintage | F | VF | XF | Unc | BU |
|---|---|---|---|---|---|---|
| 1959 | — | 0.10 | 0.20 | 0.40 | 0.80 | — |

**50 STOTINKI** **KM# 64** **Composition:** Nickel-Brass **Obverse:** Date 9 • IX • 1944 on ribbon

| Date | Mintage | F | VF | XF | Unc | BU |
|---|---|---|---|---|---|---|
| 1962 | — | 0.10 | 0.40 | 0.65 | 1.00 | — |

**50 STOTINKI** **KM# 89** **Composition:** Nickel-Brass **Obverse:** 2 dates on ribbon, '681-1944'

| Date | Mintage | F | VF | XF | Unc | BU |
|---|---|---|---|---|---|---|
| 1974 | — | 0.10 | 0.40 | 0.65 | 1.50 | — |
| 1979 Proof | 2,000 | Value: 4.00 | | | | |
| 1980 Proof | 2,000 | Value: 4.00 | | | | |
| 1988 | — | — | — | 0.50 | 1.00 | — |
| 1989 | — | — | — | 0.50 | 1.00 | — |
| 1990 | — | — | — | 0.50 | 1.00 | — |

**50 STOTINKI** **KM# 98** **Composition:** Copper-Nickel **Subject:** University Games at Sofia

| Date | Mintage | F | VF | XF | Unc | BU |
|---|---|---|---|---|---|---|
| 1977 | 2,000,000 | 0.20 | 0.40 | 0.75 | 1.50 | — |

**50 STOTINKI** **KM# 116** **Composition:** Copper-Nickel **Subject:** 1300th Anniversary of Bulgaria

| Date | Mintage | F | VF | XF | Unc | BU |
|---|---|---|---|---|---|---|
| 1981 | — | — | 0.30 | 0.60 | 1.80 | — |
| 1981 Proof | — | Value: 4.00 | | | | |

**LEV** **KM# 57** **Composition:** Copper-Nickel **Obverse:** Date 9 • IX • 1944 on ribbon

| Date | Mintage | F | VF | XF | Unc | BU |
|---|---|---|---|---|---|---|
| 1960 | — | 0.10 | 0.25 | 0.60 | 1.00 | — |

**LEV** **KM# 58** **Composition:** Nickel-Brass

| Date | Mintage | F | VF | XF | Unc | BU |
|---|---|---|---|---|---|---|
| 1962 | — | — | 0.50 | 1.00 | 1.50 | — |

**LEV** **KM# 74** **Composition:** Nickel-Brass **Subject:** 25th Anniversary of Socialist Revolution

| Date | Mintage | F | VF | XF | Unc | BU |
|---|---|---|---|---|---|---|
| 1969 | 3,700,000 | 0.35 | 0.60 | 1.25 | 2.50 | — |

**LEV** **KM# 76** **Composition:** Nickel-Brass **Subject:** 90th Anniversary Liberation From Turks

| Date | Mintage | F | VF | XF | Unc | BU |
|---|---|---|---|---|---|---|
| 1969 | 2,150,000 | 0.35 | 0.65 | 1.50 | 2.75 | — |

**LEV** **KM# 90** **Composition:** Nickel-Brass **Obverse:** 2 dates '681-1944' on ribbon

| Date | Mintage | F | VF | XF | Unc | BU |
|---|---|---|---|---|---|---|
| 1974 | — | — | 0.50 | 1.00 | 2.00 | — |
| 1979 Proof | 2,000 | Value: 6.00 | | | | |
| 1980 Proof | 2,000 | Value: 6.00 | | | | |
| 1988 | — | — | — | 0.75 | 2.00 | — |
| 1989 | — | — | — | 0.75 | 2.00 | — |
| 1990 | — | — | — | 0.75 | 2.00 | — |

**LEV** **KM# 94** **Composition:** Bronze **Subject:** 100th Anniversary of the "April Uprising" against the Turks

| Date | Mintage | F | VF | XF | Unc | BU |
|---|---|---|---|---|---|---|
| 1976 | 300,000 | 0.35 | 0.60 | 1.25 | 2.50 | — |
| 1976 Proof | — | Value: 4.00 | | | | |

**LEV** **KM# 107** **Composition:** Copper-Nickel **Subject:** World Cup Soccer Games in Spain

| Date | Mintage | F | VF | XF | Unc | BU |
|---|---|---|---|---|---|---|
| 1980 | 220,000 | — | 0.60 | 1.25 | 2.50 | — |
| 1980 Proof | 30,000 | Value: 3.50 | | | | |

**LEV** **KM# 117** **Composition:** Copper-Nickel **Subject:** 1300th Anniversary of Bulgaria

| Date | Mintage | F | VF | XF | Unc | BU |
|---|---|---|---|---|---|---|
| 1981 | — | — | 0.50 | 1.00 | 2.00 | — |
| 1981 Proof | — | — | — | — | — | — |

**LEV** **KM# 118** **Composition:** Copper-Nickel **Subject:** International Hunting Exposition

| Date | Mintage | F | VF | XF | Unc | BU |
|---|---|---|---|---|---|---|
| 1981 | 250,000 | — | 0.60 | 1.25 | 2.50 | — |
| 1981 Proof | 50,000 | Value: 3.50 | | | | |

**LEV** **KM# 119** **Composition:** Copper-Nickel **Subject:** Russo-Bulgarian Friendship **Note:** The same reverse die was used for both Bulgaria 1 Lev, KM#19 and Russia 1 Rouble, KM#189.

| Date | Mintage | F | VF | XF | Unc | BU |
|---|---|---|---|---|---|---|
| 1981 | 250,000 | — | 0.60 | 1.25 | 2.50 | — |
| 1981 Proof | 50,000 | Value: 3.50 | | | | |

**LEV KM# 175 Composition:** Copper-Nickel **Series:** 1980 Winter Olympics **Reverse:** Hockey player

| Date | Mintage | F | VF | XF | Unc | BU |
|---|---|---|---|---|---|---|
| 1987 | — | — | — | — | 2.50 | — |
| 1987 Proof | 300,000 | Value: 3.50 | | | | |

**LEV KM# 176 Composition:** Copper-Nickel **Series:** Summer Olympics **Reverse:** Sprinters

| Date | Mintage | F | VF | XF | Unc | BU |
|---|---|---|---|---|---|---|
| 1988 | — | — | — | — | 2.50 | — |
| 1988 Proof | 300,000 | Value: 3.50 | | | | |

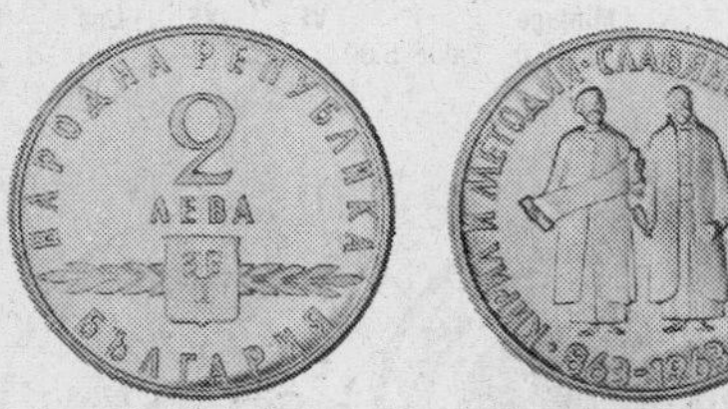

**2 LEVA KM# 65 Weight:** 8.8889 g. **Composition:** 0.9000 Silver .2572 oz. ASW **Subject:** 1100th Anniversary - Slovanic Alphabet

| Date | Mintage | F | VF | XF | Unc | BU |
|---|---|---|---|---|---|---|
| ND(1963) Proof | 10,000 | Value: 7.50 | | | | |

**2 LEVA KM# 69 Weight:** 8.8889 g. **Composition:** 0.9000 Silver .2572 oz. ASW **Subject:** 20th Anniversary Peoples Republic

| Date | Mintage | F | VF | XF | Unc | BU |
|---|---|---|---|---|---|---|
| ND(1964) Proof | 20,000 | Value: 7.50 | | | | |

**2 LEVA KM# 73 Composition:** Copper-Nickel **Subject:** 1050th Anniversary - Death of Ochridsky

| Date | Mintage | F | VF | XF | Unc | BU |
|---|---|---|---|---|---|---|
| ND(1966) | 506,000 | — | 1.00 | 2.00 | 4.00 | — |

**2 LEVA KM# 75 Composition:** Copper-Nickel **Subject:** 25th Anniversary of Socialist Revolution

| Date | Mintage | F | VF | XF | Unc | BU |
|---|---|---|---|---|---|---|
| 1969 | 1,500,000 | — | 0.75 | 1.75 | 3.50 | — |

**2 LEVA KM# 77 Composition:** Copper-Nickel **Subject:** 90th Anniversary - Liberation from Turks

| Date | Mintage | F | VF | XF | Unc | BU |
|---|---|---|---|---|---|---|
| 1969 | 1,900,000 | — | 0.75 | 1.75 | 3.50 | — |

**2 LEVA KM# 80 Composition:** Nickel-Brass **Subject:** 150th Anniversary - Birth of Dobri Chintulov

| Date | Mintage | F | VF | XF | Unc | BU |
|---|---|---|---|---|---|---|
| 1972 | 100,000 | — | 1.25 | 2.50 | 4.50 | — |

**2 LEVA KM# 95.1 Composition:** Copper-Nickel **Subject:** 100th Anniversary of the "April Uprising" against the Turks

| Date | Mintage | F | VF | XF | Unc | BU |
|---|---|---|---|---|---|---|
| 1976 | Est. 300,000 | — | 0.75 | 1.50 | 3.00 | — |
| 1976 Proof | — | Value: 5.00 | | | | |

**2 LEVA KM# 95.2 Composition:** Copper-Nickel **Edge:** Lettered

| Date | Mintage | F | VF | XF | Unc | BU |
|---|---|---|---|---|---|---|
| 1976 | 138 | — | — | — | — | — |

**2 LEVA KM# 108 Composition:** Copper-Nickel **Subject:** World Cup Soccer Games in Spain

| Date | Mintage | F | VF | XF | Unc | BU |
|---|---|---|---|---|---|---|
| 1980 | 220,000 | — | 0.60 | 1.20 | 2.50 | — |
| 1980 Proof | 30,000 | Value: 4.50 | | | | |

**2 LEVA KM# 110 Composition:** Copper-Nickel **Subject:** 100th Anniversary - Birth of Yordan Yovkov

| Date | Mintage | F | VF | XF | Unc | BU |
|---|---|---|---|---|---|---|
| 1980 | 200,000 | — | 1.00 | 2.50 | 4.50 | — |

**2 LEVA KM# 120 Composition:** Copper-Nickel **Subject:** International Hunting Exposition

| Date | Mintage | F | VF | XF | Unc | BU |
|---|---|---|---|---|---|---|
| 1981 | 250,000 | — | 0.75 | 1.50 | 3.00 | — |
| 1981 Proof | 50,000 | Value: 5.00 | | | | |

**2 LEVA KM# 121 Composition:** Copper-Nickel **Subject:** 1300th Anniversary of Nationhood **Reverse:** Equestrian figure

| Date | Mintage | F | VF | XF | Unc | BU |
|---|---|---|---|---|---|---|
| 1981 | — | — | — | — | 2.50 | — |
| 1981 Proof | — | Value: 4.00 | | | | |

**2 LEVA KM# 122 Composition:** Copper-Nickel **Subject:** 1300th Anniversary of Nationhood **Reverse:** Mother and child

| Date | Mintage | F | VF | XF | Unc | BU |
|---|---|---|---|---|---|---|
| 1981 Proof | — | Value: 4.00 | | | | |

**2 LEVA KM# 123 Composition:** Copper-Nickel **Subject:** 1300th Anniversary of Nationhood **Reverse:** Dimitrov

| Date | Mintage | F | VF | XF | Unc | BU |
|---|---|---|---|---|---|---|
| 1981 | — | — | — | — | 3.50 | — |
| 1981 Proof | — | Value: 5.00 | | | | |

**2 LEVA KM# 124 Composition:** Copper-Nickel **Subject:** 1300th Anniversary of Nationhood **Reverse:** King and saint

| Date | Mintage | F | VF | XF | Unc | BU |
|---|---|---|---|---|---|---|
| 1981 | — | — | — | — | 2.50 | — |
| 1981 Proof | — | Value: 4.00 | | | | |

**2 LEVA** **KM# 125** **Composition:** Copper-Nickel **Subject:** 1300th Anniversary of Nationhood **Reverse:** Soldier

| Date | Mintage | F | VF | XF | Unc | BU |
|---|---|---|---|---|---|---|
| 1981 | — | — | — | — | 2.50 | — |
| 1981 Proof | — | Value: 4.00 | | | | |

**2 LEVA** **KM# 126** **Composition:** Copper-Nickel **Subject:** 1300th Anniversary of Nationhood **Reverse:** Clandestine meeting

| Date | Mintage | F | VF | XF | Unc | BU |
|---|---|---|---|---|---|---|
| 1981 Proof | — | Value: 4.00 | | | | |

**2 LEVA** **KM# 127** **Composition:** Copper-Nickel **Subject:** 1300th Anniversary of Nationhood **Reverse:** Cyrillic alphabet

| Date | Mintage | F | VF | XF | Unc | BU |
|---|---|---|---|---|---|---|
| 1981 | — | — | — | — | 2.50 | — |
| 1981 Proof | — | Value: 4.00 | | | | |

**2 LEVA** **KM# 128** **Composition:** Copper-Nickel **Subject:** 1300th Anniversary of Nationhood **Reverse:** Rila Monastary

| Date | Mintage | F | VF | XF | Unc | BU |
|---|---|---|---|---|---|---|
| 1981 | — | — | — | — | 2.50 | — |
| 1981 Proof | — | Value: 4.00 | | | | |

**2 LEVA** **KM# 129** **Composition:** Copper-Nickel **Subject:** 1300th Anniversary of Nationhood **Reverse:** Russky monument

| Date | Mintage | F | VF | XF | Unc | BU |
|---|---|---|---|---|---|---|
| 1981 Proof | — | Value: 4.50 | | | | |

**2 LEVA** **KM# 130** **Composition:** Copper-Nickel **Subject:** 1300th Anniversary of Nationhood **Reverse:** Bojana church

| Date | Mintage | F | VF | XF | Unc | BU |
|---|---|---|---|---|---|---|
| 1981 Proof | 300,000 | Value: 4.50 | | | | |

**2 LEVA** **KM# 161** **Composition:** Copper-Nickel **Subject:** 1300th Anniversary of Nationhood - Oboriste Assembly

| Date | Mintage | F | VF | XF | Unc | BU |
|---|---|---|---|---|---|---|
| 1981 Proof | 300,000 | Value: 4.50 | | | | |

**2 LEVA** **KM# 162** **Composition:** Copper-Nickel **Subject:** 1300th Anniversary of Nationhood - Uprising of Assen and Peter

| Date | Mintage | F | VF | XF | Unc | BU |
|---|---|---|---|---|---|---|
| 1981 Proof | 300,000 | Value: 4.50 | | | | |

**2 LEVA** **KM# 163** **Composition:** Copper-Nickel **Subject:** 1300th Anniversary of Nationhood - 100th Anniversary of Serbo-Bulgarian War

| Date | Mintage | F | VF | XF | Unc | BU |
|---|---|---|---|---|---|---|
| 1981 Proof | — | Value: 4.50 | | | | |

**2 LEVA** **KM# 155** **Composition:** Copper-Nickel **Subject:** Soccer

| Date | Mintage | F | VF | XF | Unc | BU |
|---|---|---|---|---|---|---|
| 1986 Proof | 100,000 | Value: 4.00 | | | | |

**2 LEVA** **KM# 158** **Composition:** Copper-Nickel **Subject:** World Championship of Rhythmic Gymnastics

| Date | Mintage | F | VF | XF | Unc | BU |
|---|---|---|---|---|---|---|
| 1987 Proof | 300,000 | Value: 3.50 | | | | |

**2 LEVA** **KM# 159** **Composition:** Copper-Nickel **Series:** Winter Olympics **Reverse:** Skier

| Date | Mintage | F | VF | XF | Unc | BU |
|---|---|---|---|---|---|---|
| 1987 World Championship of Rhythmic Gymnastics | 300,000 | Value: 5.00 | | | | |

**2 LEVA** **KM# 165** **Composition:** Copper-Nickel **Subject:** 100th Anniversary of Sophia University

| Date | Mintage | F | VF | XF | Unc | BU |
|---|---|---|---|---|---|---|
| 1988 Proof | — | Value: 4.00 | | | | |

**2 LEVA** **KM# 166** **Composition:** Copper-Nickel **Subject:** Soviet-Bulgarian Space Flight

| Date | Mintage | F | VF | XF | Unc | BU |
|---|---|---|---|---|---|---|
| 1988 Proof | 300,000 | Value: 3.00 | | | | |

**2 LEVA** **KM# 177** **Composition:** Copper-Nickel **Series:** Summer Olympics **Reverse:** High jumper

| Date | Mintage | F | VF | XF | Unc | BU |
|---|---|---|---|---|---|---|
| 1988 Proof | 300,000 | Value: 3.50 | | | | |

**2 LEVA** **KM# 188** **Composition:** Copper-Nickel **Subject:** Sophia Universtiy **Note:** Similar to 20 Leva, KM#173.

| Date | Mintage | F | VF | XF | Unc | BU |
|---|---|---|---|---|---|---|
| 1988 Proof | 300,000 | Value: 3.00 | | | | |

**2 LEVA** **KM# 178** **Composition:** Copper-Nickel **Subject:** Sports **Reverse:** Rowers

| Date | Mintage | F | VF | XF | Unc | BU |
|---|---|---|---|---|---|---|
| 1989 Proof | 300,000 | Value: 3.00 | | | | |

**5 LEVA** **KM# 66** **Weight:** 16.6667 g. **Composition:** 0.9000 Silver .4823 oz. ASW **Subject:** 1100th Anniversary Slavic Alphabet

| Date | Mintage | F | VF | XF | Unc | BU |
|---|---|---|---|---|---|---|
| ND(1963) Proof | 5,000 | Value: 13.50 | | | | |

**5 LEVA** **KM# 70** **Weight:** 16.6667 g. **Composition:** 0.9000 Silver .4823 oz. ASW **Subject:** 20th Anniversary Peoples Republic

| Date | Mintage | F | VF | XF | Unc | BU |
|---|---|---|---|---|---|---|
| ND(1964) Proof | 10,000 | Value: 13.50 | | | | |

**5 LEVA** **KM# 78** **Weight:** 20.5000 g. **Composition:** 0.9000 Silver .5932 oz. ASW **Subject:** 120th Anniversary - Birth of Ivan Vazov

| Date | Mintage | F | VF | XF | Unc | BU |
|---|---|---|---|---|---|---|
| 1970 | 370,000 | — | — | 4.50 | 7.00 | — |
| 1970 Proof | 110,000 | Value: 8.00 | | | | |

**5 LEVA** **KM# 79** **Weight:** 20.5000 g. **Composition:** 0.9000 Silver .5932 oz. ASW **Subject:** 150th Anniversary - Birth of Georgi S. Rakovski

| Date | Mintage | F | VF | XF | Unc | BU |
|---|---|---|---|---|---|---|
| 1971 Prooflike | 300,000 | — | — | — | — | — |

**5 LEVA** **KM# 81** **Weight:** 20.5000 g. **Composition:** 0.9000 Silver .5932 oz. ASW **Subject:** 250th Anniversary - Birth of Paisii Hilendarski

| Date | Mintage | F | VF | XF | Unc | BU |
|---|---|---|---|---|---|---|
| 1972 Proof | 200,000 | Value: 8.00 | | | | |

**5 LEVA** **KM# 82** **Weight:** 20.5000 g. **Composition:** 0.9000 Silver .5932 oz. ASW **Subject:** Centennial - Death of Vasil Levski

| Date | Mintage | F | VF | XF | Unc | BU |
|---|---|---|---|---|---|---|
| 1973 Proof | 200,000 | Value: 8.00 | | | | |

**5 LEVA** **KM# 83** **Weight:** 20.5000 g. **Composition:** 0.9000 Silver .5932 oz. ASW **Subject:** 50th Anniversary - Anti-fascist Uprising

| Date | Mintage | F | VF | XF | Unc | BU |
|---|---|---|---|---|---|---|
| 1973 Proof | 200,000 | Value: 8.00 | | | | |

**5 LEVA** **KM# 91** **Weight:** 20.5000 g. **Composition:** 0.9000 Silver .5932 oz. ASW **Subject:** 50th Anniversary - Death of Alexander Stamboliiski

| Date | Mintage | F | VF | XF | Unc | BU |
|---|---|---|---|---|---|---|
| 1974 Proof | 200,000 | Value: 8.50 | | | | |

**5 LEVA** **KM# 92** **Weight:** 20.5000 g. **Composition:** 0.9000 Silver .5932 oz. ASW **Subject:** 30th Anniversary - Liberation from Fascism

| Date | Mintage | F | VF | XF | Unc | BU |
|---|---|---|---|---|---|---|
| 1974 Proof | 200,000 | Value: 8.50 | | | | |

**5 LEVA** **KM# 96** **Weight:** 20.5000 g. **Composition:** 0.9000 Silver .5932 oz. ASW **Subject:** Centennial - Death of Khristo Botev

| Date | Mintage | F | VF | XF | Unc | BU |
|---|---|---|---|---|---|---|
| 1976 Proof | 200,000 | Value: 8.50 | | | | |

**5 LEVA** **KM# 97** **Weight:** 20.5000 g. **Composition:** 0.5000 Silver .3295 oz. ASW **Subject:** 100th Anniversary of the "April Uprising" against the Turks

| Date | Mintage | F | VF | XF | Unc | BU |
|---|---|---|---|---|---|---|
| 1976 Proof | 200,000 | Value: 8.50 | | | | |

**5 LEVA** **KM# 99** **Weight:** 20.5000 g. **Composition:** 0.5000 Silver .3295 oz. ASW **Subject:** 150th Anniversary - Birth of Petko Slaveykov

| Date | Mintage | F | VF | XF | Unc | BU |
|---|---|---|---|---|---|---|
| 1977 Proof | 200,000 | Value: 8.50 | | | | |

**5 LEVA** **KM# 100** **Weight:** 20.5000 g. **Composition:** 0.5000 Silver .3295 oz. ASW **Subject:** 100th Anniversary - Birth of Peio Javoroff

| Date | Mintage | F | VF | XF | Unc | BU |
|---|---|---|---|---|---|---|
| 1978 Proof | 200,000 | Value: 8.50 | | | | |

**5 LEVA** **KM# 101** **Weight:** 20.5000 g. **Composition:** 0.5000 Silver .3295 oz. ASW **Subject:** 100th Anniversary - National Library

| Date | Mintage | F | VF | XF | Unc | BU |
|---|---|---|---|---|---|---|
| ND(1978) Proof | 200,000 | Value: 8.50 | | | | |

**5 LEVA** **KM# 103** **Weight:** 20.5000 g. **Composition:** 0.5000 Silver .3295 oz. ASW **Subject:** 100th Anniversary - Communication Systems

| Date | Mintage | F | VF | XF | Unc | BU |
|---|---|---|---|---|---|---|
| 1979 | 35,000 | — | — | — | 8.50 | — |
| 1979 Proof | 15,000 | Value: 12.50 | | | | |

**5 LEVA** **KM# 109** **Composition:** Copper-Nickel **Subject:** World Cup Soccer Games in Spain

| Date | Mintage | F | VF | XF | Unc | BU |
|---|---|---|---|---|---|---|
| 1980 | 220,000 | — | — | — | 3.50 | — |
| 1980 Proof | 30,000 | Value: 6.00 | | | | |

**5 LEVA** **KM# 131** **Composition:** Copper-Nickel **Subject:** International Hunting Exposition

| Date | Mintage | F | VF | XF | Unc | BU |
|---|---|---|---|---|---|---|
| 1981 | 250,000 | — | — | — | 4.50 | — |
| 1981 Proof | 50,000 | Value: 7.00 | | | | |

**5 LEVA** **KM# 132** **Composition:** Copper-Nickel **Subject:** 1300th Anniversary of Nationhood - Friendship with Hungary

| Date | Mintage | F | VF | XF | Unc | BU |
|---|---|---|---|---|---|---|
| 1981 | — | — | — | — | 3.50 | — |
| 1981 Proof | — | Value: 7.00 | | | | |

**5 LEVA** **KM# 140** **Composition:** Copper-Nickel **Subject:** 100th Anniversary - Birth of Vladimir Dimitrov

| Date | Mintage | F | VF | XF | Unc | BU |
|---|---|---|---|---|---|---|
| 1982 Proof | 3,000 | Value: 5.00 | | | | |

**5 LEVA** **KM# 141** **Composition:** Copper-Nickel **Subject:** 40th Anniversary - Birth of Lyudmila Zhivkova

| Date | Mintage | F | VF | XF | Unc | BU |
|---|---|---|---|---|---|---|
| 1982 Proof | 20,000 | Value: 5.00 | | | | |

**5 LEVA** **KM# 142** **Composition:** Copper-Nickel **Subject:** 2nd International Children's Assembly

| Date | Mintage | F | VF | XF | Unc | BU |
|---|---|---|---|---|---|---|
| 1982 Proof | 200,000 | Value: 4.00 | | | | |

**5 LEVA** **KM# 151** **Composition:** Copper-Nickel **Subject:** 3rd International Children's Assembly

| Date | Mintage | F | VF | XF | Unc | BU |
|---|---|---|---|---|---|---|
| 1985 Proof | 100,000 | Value: 4.00 | | | | |

**5 LEVA** **KM# 152** **Composition:** Copper-Nickel **Subject:** 90th Anniversary of Tourism Movement - Konstantinov

| Date | Mintage | F | VF | XF | Unc | BU |
|---|---|---|---|---|---|---|
| 1985 Proof | 100,000 | Value: 4.50 | | | | |

**5 LEVA** **KM# 153** **Composition:** Copper-Nickel **Subject:** 4th Anniversary of UNESCO

| Date | Mintage | F | VF | XF | Unc | BU |
|---|---|---|---|---|---|---|
| 1985 Proof | 100,000 | Value: 4.50 | | | | |

**5 LEVA** **KM# 154** **Composition:** Copper-Nickel **Subject:** Young Inventors' Exposition

| Date | Mintage | F | VF | XF | Unc | BU |
|---|---|---|---|---|---|---|
| 1985 Proof | 100,000 | Value: 4.50 | | | | |

**5 LEVA** **KM# 167.1** **Composition:** Copper-Nickel **Subject:** Chiprovo Uprising **Edge:** Plain

| Date | Mintage | F | VF | XF | Unc | BU |
|---|---|---|---|---|---|---|
| 1988 Proof | 100,000 | Value: 4.50 | | | | |

**5 LEVA** **KM# 167.2** **Composition:** Copper-Nickel **Edge:** Reeded

| Date | Mintage | F | VF | XF | Unc | BU |
|---|---|---|---|---|---|---|
| 1988 Proof | — | Value: 5.00 | | | | |

**5 LEVA** **KM# 168** **Composition:** Copper-Nickel **Subject:** 20th Anniversary - Dimitar and Karadzha

| Date | Mintage | F | VF | XF | Unc | BU |
|---|---|---|---|---|---|---|
| 1988 Proof | 100,000 | Value: 4.00 | | | | |

**5 LEVA** **KM# 170** **Composition:** Copper-Nickel **Subject:** Childrens' Assembly

| Date | Mintage | F | VF | XF | Unc | BU |
|---|---|---|---|---|---|---|
| 1988 Proof | 100,000 | Value: 4.00 | | | | |

**5 LEVA** **KM# 169** **Composition:** Copper-Nickel **Note:** Kremikovski

| Date | Mintage | F | VF | XF | Unc | BU |
|---|---|---|---|---|---|---|
| 1988 Proof | 200,000 | Value: 4.00 | | | | |

**5 LEVA** **KM# 179** **Composition:** Copper-Nickel **Subject:** 200th Birthday of Aprilov

| Date | Mintage | F | VF | XF | Unc | BU |
|---|---|---|---|---|---|---|
| 1989 Proof | 100,000 | Value: 4.00 | | | | |

**5 LEVA** **KM# 180** **Composition:** Copper-Nickel **Subject:** 250th Anniversary - Birth of Vrachanski

| Date | Mintage | F | VF | XF | Unc | BU |
|---|---|---|---|---|---|---|
| 1989 Proof | 100,000 | Value: 4.00 | | | | |

**10 LEVA** **KM# 67** **Weight:** 8.4444 g. **Composition:** 0.9000 Gold .2443 oz. AGW **Subject:** 1100th Anniversary - Slavic Alphabet

| Date | Mintage | F | VF | XF | Unc | BU |
|---|---|---|---|---|---|---|
| ND(1963) Proof | 7,000 | Value: 165 | | | | |

**10 LEVA** **KM# 71** **Weight:** 8.4444 g. **Composition:** 0.9000 Gold .2443 oz. AGW **Subject:** 20th Anniversary - Peoples Republic **Reverse:** Head of Georgi Dmitrov left.

| Date | Mintage | F | VF | XF | Unc | BU |
|---|---|---|---|---|---|---|
| ND(1964) Proof | 10,000 | Value: 125 | | | | |

**10 LEVA** **KM# 93.1** **Weight:** 29.9500 g. **Composition:** 0.9000 Silver .8666 oz. ASW **Subject:** 10th Olympic Congress **Edge:** Inscription in Latin

| Date | Mintage | F | VF | XF | Unc | BU |
|---|---|---|---|---|---|---|
| 1975 Proof | 50,000 | Value: 16.50 | | | | |

**10 LEVA** **KM# 93.2** **Weight:** 29.9500 g. **Composition:** 0.9000 Silver .8666 oz. ASW **Edge:** Inscription in Cyrillic

| Date | Mintage | F | VF | XF | Unc | BU |
|---|---|---|---|---|---|---|
| 1975 Proof | 50,000 | Value: 16.50 | | | | |

**10 LEVA** **KM# 102** **Weight:** 29.8500 g. **Composition:** 0.5000 Silver .4798 oz. ASW **Subject:** 100th Anniversary - Liberation from Turks

| Date | Mintage | F | VF | XF | Unc | BU |
|---|---|---|---|---|---|---|
| ND(1978) Proof | 200,000 | Value: 12.50 | | | | |

**10 LEVA** **KM# 104** **Weight:** 23.3280 g. **Composition:** 0.9250 Silver .6938 oz. ASW **Series:** International Year of the Child

| Date | Mintage | F | VF | XF | Unc | BU |
|---|---|---|---|---|---|---|
| 1979 Proof | 20,000 | Value: 22.50 | | | | |

**10 LEVA** **KM# 105** **Weight:** 14.0000 g. **Composition:** 0.5000 Silver .2251 oz. ASW **Subject:** Bulgarian-Soviet Cosmonaut Flight

| Date | Mintage | F | VF | XF | Unc | BU |
|---|---|---|---|---|---|---|
| 1979 Proof | 35,000 | Value: 20.00 | | | | |

**10 LEVA** **KM# 105a** **Weight:** 23.8500 g. **Composition:** 0.9000 Silver .6901 oz. ASW

| Date | Mintage | F | VF | XF | Unc | BU |
|---|---|---|---|---|---|---|
| 1979 Proof | 15,000 | Value: 28.50 | | | | |

**10 LEVA** **KM# 143** **Weight:** 18.8800 g. **Composition:** 0.5000 Silver .3035 oz. ASW **Subject:** Soccer Games **Reverse:** Ball and net

| Date | Mintage | F | VF | XF | Unc | BU |
|---|---|---|---|---|---|---|
| 1982 Proof | 1,000 | Value: 22.50 | | | | |

**10 LEVA** **KM# 144** **Weight:** 18.8800 g. **Composition:** 0.5000 Silver .3035 oz. ASW **Subject:** Soccer Games **Reverse:** Players

| Date | Mintage | F | VF | XF | Unc | BU |
|---|---|---|---|---|---|---|
| 1982 Proof | 1,000 | Value: 21.50 | | | | |

**10 LEVA** **KM# 146** **Weight:** 23.3300 g. **Composition:** 0.9250 Silver .6939 oz. ASW **Series:** Winter Olypics **Reverse:** Skier

| Date | Mintage | F | VF | XF | Unc | BU |
|---|---|---|---|---|---|---|
| 1984 Proof | 12,000 | Value: 14.50 | | | | |

**10 LEVA** **KM# 149** **Weight:** 23.3300 g. **Composition:** 0.9250 Silver .6939 oz. ASW **Subject:** International Decade for Women

| Date | Mintage | F | VF | XF | Unc | BU |
|---|---|---|---|---|---|---|
| 1984 Proof | 2,152 | Value: 32.50 | | | | |

**10 LEVA** **KM# 157** **Weight:** 18.7500 g. **Composition:** 0.6400 Silver .3858 oz. ASW **Reverse:** Cosmonauts

| Date | Mintage | F | VF | XF | Unc | BU |
|---|---|---|---|---|---|---|
| 1985 Proof | 2,500 | Value: 32.50 | | | | |

**10 LEVA** **KM# 184** **Weight:** 18.7500 g. **Composition:** 0.6400 Silver .3858 oz. ASW **Series:** 1988 Winter Olympics **Reverse:** Hockey player

| Date | Mintage | F | VF | XF | Unc | BU |
|---|---|---|---|---|---|---|
| 1987 Proof | 15,000 | Value: 20.00 | | | | |

**10 LEVA** **KM# 185** **Weight:** 18.7500 g. **Composition:** 0.6400 Silver .3858 oz. ASW **Series:** Summer Olympics **Reverse:** Sprinters

| Date | Mintage | F | VF | XF | Unc | BU |
|---|---|---|---|---|---|---|
| 1988 Proof | 30,000 | Value: 15.00 | | | | |

**10 LEVA** **KM# 244** **Weight:** 10.3500 g. **Composition:** 0.8000 Silver .2662 oz. ASW **Subject:** The Year 2000 **Obverse:** National arms above date with pierced zeros. **Reverse:** Bell above date with pierced zeros. **Edge:** Plain. **Size:** 33.9 mm.

| Date | Mintage | F | VF | XF | Unc | BU |
|---|---|---|---|---|---|---|
| 2000 Proof | — | Value: 50.00 | | | | |

**20 LEVA** **KM# 68** **Weight:** 16.8889 g. **Composition:** 0.9000 Gold .4887 oz. AGW **Subject:** 100th Anniversary - Slavic Alphabet

| Date | Mintage | F | VF | XF | Unc | BU |
|---|---|---|---|---|---|---|
| ND(1963) Proof | 3,000 | Value: 325 | | | | |

**20 LEVA** **KM# 72** **Weight:** 16.8889 g. **Composition:** 0.9000 Gold .4887 oz. AGW **Subject:** 20th Anniversary - Peoples Republic **Reverse:** Head of Georgi Dmitrov left

| Date | Mintage | F | VF | XF | Unc | BU |
|---|---|---|---|---|---|---|
| ND(1964) Proof | 5,000 | Value: 250 | | | | |

**20 LEVA** **KM# 106** **Weight:** 21.8000 g. **Composition:** 0.5000 Silver .3505 oz. ASW **Subject:** Centennial of Sophia as Capital

| Date | Mintage | F | VF | XF | Unc | BU |
|---|---|---|---|---|---|---|
| 1979 | 35,000 | — | — | — | 20.00 | — |

**20 LEVA** **KM# 106a** **Weight:** 32.0000 g. **Composition:** 0.9000 Silver .9260 oz. ASW

| Date | Mintage | F | VF | XF | Unc | BU |
|---|---|---|---|---|---|---|
| 1979 Proof | 15,000 | Value: 35.00 | | | | |

**20 LEVA** **KM# 133** (KM133.1) **Weight:** 14.0000 g. **Composition:** 0.5000 Silver .2250 oz. ASW **Subject:** 40th Anniversary - Birth of Lyudmila Zhivkova **Obverse:** Denomination between emblems of Children's Assembly and Year of the Child. **Reverse:** Head of Lyudmila Zhivkova left.

| Date | Mintage | F | VF | XF | Unc | BU |
|---|---|---|---|---|---|---|
| 1982 Proof | 10,000 | Value: 20.00 | | | | |

**20 LEVA** **Weight:** 14.0000 g. **Composition:** 0.5000 Silver .2250 oz. ASW **Obverse:** Denomination between emblems of Children's Assembly and Year of the Child

| Date | Mintage | F | VF | XF | Unc | BU |
|---|---|---|---|---|---|---|
| 1982 Proof | — | Value: 150 | | | | |

**20 LEVA** **KM# 164** **Weight:** 11.2200 g. **Composition:** 0.5000 Silver .1804 oz. ASW **Note:** Vasil Levsky

| Date | Mintage | F | VF | XF | Unc | BU |
|---|---|---|---|---|---|---|
| 1987 Proof | 100,000 | Value: 12.50 | | | | |

**20 LEVA** **KM# 171** **Weight:** 11.3900 g. **Composition:** 0.5000 Silver .1830 oz. ASW **Subject:** Bulgarian Railways

| Date | Mintage | F | VF | XF | Unc | BU |
|---|---|---|---|---|---|---|
| 1988 Proof | 100,000 | Value: 11.50 | | | | |

**20 LEVA** **KM# 172** **Weight:** 11.2200 g. **Composition:** 0.5000 Silver .1804 oz. ASW **Subject:** 110th Anniversary of Liberation

| Date | Mintage | F | VF | XF | Unc | BU |
|---|---|---|---|---|---|---|
| 1988 Proof | 100,000 | Value: 11.50 | | | | |

**20 LEVA** **KM# 173** **Weight:** 11.5500 g. **Composition:** 0.5000 Silver .1855 oz. ASW **Subject:** 100th Anniversary of Sophia University

| Date | Mintage | F | VF | XF | Unc | BU |
|---|---|---|---|---|---|---|
| 1988 Proof | 100,000 | Value: 12.50 | | | | |

**20 LEVA** **KM# 174** **Weight:** 11.1900 g. **Composition:** 0.5000 Silver .1803 oz. ASW **Subject:** Soviet-Bulgarian Space Flight

| Date | Mintage | F | VF | XF | Unc | BU |
|---|---|---|---|---|---|---|
| 1988 Proof | 100,000 | Value: 12.50 | | | | |

**20 LEVA** **KM# 181** **Composition:** Copper-Nickel-Zinc

| Date | Mintage | F | VF | XF | Unc | BU |
|---|---|---|---|---|---|---|
| 1989 Proof | — | Value: 8.00 | | | | |

**20 LEVA** **KM# 183** **Weight:** 12.1300 g. **Composition:** 0.5000 Silver .2138 oz. ASW **Subject:** Academy of Science

| Date | Mintage | F | VF | XF | Unc | BU |
|---|---|---|---|---|---|---|
| 1989 Proof | 100,000 | Value: 12.50 | | | | |

**25 LEVA** **KM# 134** **Weight:** 14.0000 g. **Composition:** 0.5000 Silver .2250 oz. ASW **Subject:** 1300th Anniversary of Nationhood

| Date | Mintage | F | VF | XF | Unc | BU |
|---|---|---|---|---|---|---|
| 1981 Proof | Est. 100,000 | Value: 22.50 | | | | |

**25 LEVA** **KM# 145** **Weight:** 14.0000 g. **Composition:** 0.5000 Silver .2250 oz. ASW **Subject:** 100th Anniversary - Birth of George Dimitrov

| Date | Mintage | F | VF | XF | Unc | BU |
|---|---|---|---|---|---|---|
| 1982 Proof | 15,000 | Value: 12.50 | | | | |

**25 LEVA** **KM# 148** **Weight:** 14.0000 g. **Composition:** 0.5000 Silver .2250 oz. ASW **Subject:** 40th Anniversary of Peoples Republic

| Date | Mintage | F | VF | XF | Unc | BU |
|---|---|---|---|---|---|---|
| ND(1984) Proof | 100,000 | Value: 11.50 | | | | |

**25 LEVA** **KM# 156.1** **Weight:** 23.3300 g. **Composition:** 0.9250 Silver .6939 oz. ASW **Subject:** Soccer

| Date | Mintage | F | VF | XF | Unc | BU |
|---|---|---|---|---|---|---|
| 1986 Proof | 10,000 | Value: 25.00 | | | | |

**25 LEVA** **KM# 160** **Weight:** 23.3300 g. **Composition:** 0.9250 Silver .6939 oz. ASW **Series:** Winter Olympics **Reverse:** Skier

| Date | Mintage | F | VF | XF | Unc | BU |
|---|---|---|---|---|---|---|
| 1987 Proof | 15,000 | Value: 20.00 | | | | |

**25 LEVA** **KM# 189** **Weight:** 23.3800 g. **Composition:** 0.9250 Silver .6954 oz. ASW **Series:** 1992 Summer Olympics **Reverse:** Two rowers

| Date | Mintage | F | VF | XF | Unc | BU |
|---|---|---|---|---|---|---|
| 1989 Proof | 80,000 | Value: 15.00 | | | | |

**25 LEVA** **KM# 156.2** **Weight:** 23.3300 g. **Composition:** 0.9250 Silver .6939 oz. ASW **Reverse:** Without date in field above eagle's head

| Date | Mintage | F | VF | XF | Unc | BU |
|---|---|---|---|---|---|---|
| 1986 Proof | Inc. above | Value: 30.00 | | | | |

**25 LEVA** **KM# 186** **Weight:** 23.3300 g. **Composition:** 0.9250 Silver .6939 oz. ASW **Series:** Summer Olympics **Subject:** High Jump

| Date | Mintage | F | VF | XF | Unc | BU |
|---|---|---|---|---|---|---|
| 1988 Proof | 30,000 | Value: 21.50 | | | | |

**25 LEVA** **KM# 190** **Weight:** 23.3800 g. **Composition:** 0.9250 Silver .6954 oz. ASW **Series:** 1992 Winter Olympics **Obverse:** Similar to KM#189 **Reverse:** Figure skaters

| Date | Mintage | F | VF | XF | Unc | BU |
|---|---|---|---|---|---|---|
| 1989 Proof | 80,000 | Value: 16.50 | | | | |

**25 LEVA** **KM# 194** **Weight:** 23.3300 g. **Composition:** 0.9250 Silver .6939 oz. ASW **Subject:** Soccer **Reverse:** Player

| Date | Mintage | F | VF | XF | Unc | BU |
|---|---|---|---|---|---|---|
| 1986 Proof | 10,000 | Value: 20.00 | | | | |

**25 LEVA** **KM# 187** **Weight:** 23.3300 g. **Composition:** 0.9250 Silver .6939 oz. ASW **Subject:** Soccer **Reverse:** Two players

| Date | Mintage | F | VF | XF | Unc | BU |
|---|---|---|---|---|---|---|
| 1989 Proof | Est. 10,000 | Value: 25.00 | | | | |

**25 LEVA** **KM# 193** **Weight:** 23.3800 g. **Composition:** 0.9250 Silver .6954 oz. ASW **Subject:** Wildlife **Reverse:** Mother bear and cubs

| Date | Mintage | F | VF | XF | Unc | BU |
|---|---|---|---|---|---|---|
| 1989 Proof | — | Value: 32.50 | | | | |

**25 LEVA** **KM# 191** **Weight:** 23.3800 g. **Composition:** 0.9250 Silver .6954 oz. ASW **Subject:** Soccer **Reverse:** Globe, net, and shoe

| Date | Mintage | F | VF | XF | Unc | BU |
|---|---|---|---|---|---|---|
| 1990 Proof | 20,000 | Value: 22.50 | | | | |

**25 LEVA** **KM# 192** **Weight:** 23.3800 g. **Composition:** 0.9250 Silver .6954 oz. ASW **Subject:** Soccer **Obverse:** Similar to KM#193 **Reverse:** Ball design

| Date | Mintage | F | VF | XF | Unc | BU |
|---|---|---|---|---|---|---|
| 1990 Proof | 20,000 | Value: 24.00 | | | | |

**25 LEVA** **KM# 195** **Weight:** 23.3800 g. **Composition:** 0.9250 Silver .6954 oz. ASW **Series:** Winter Olympics **Reverse:** Cross-country skiers

| Date | Mintage | F | VF | XF | Unc | BU |
|---|---|---|---|---|---|---|
| 1990 Proof | 80,000 | Value: 15.00 | | | | |

**25 LEVA** **KM# 196** **Weight:** 23.3800 g. **Composition:** 0.9250 Silver .6954 oz. ASW **Series:** Summer Olympics **Reverse:** Runners

| Date | Mintage | F | VF | XF | Unc | BU |
|---|---|---|---|---|---|---|
| 1990 Proof | 80,000 | Value: 15.00 | | | | |

**25 LEVA** **KM# 197** **Weight:** 23.3800 g. **Composition:** 0.9250 Silver .6954 oz. ASW **Subject:** Wildlife **Reverse:** Lynx

| Date | Mintage | F | VF | XF | Unc | BU |
|---|---|---|---|---|---|---|
| 1990 Proof | — | Value: 32.50 | | | | |

**50 LEVA** **KM# 135** **Weight:** 20.5000 g. **Composition:** 0.9000 Silver .5932 oz. ASW **Subject:** 1300th Anniversary of Nationhood **Obverse:** Dates above denomination **Reverse:** Equestrian figure

| Date | Mintage | F | VF | XF | Unc | BU |
|---|---|---|---|---|---|---|
| 1981 Proof | Est. 10,000 | Value: 22.50 | | | | |

**50 LEVA** **KM# 136** **Weight:** 20.5000 g. **Composition:** 0.9000 Silver .5932 oz. ASW **Subject:** 1300th Anniversary of Nationhood **Obverse:** Head of Georgi Dmitrov left.

| Date | Mintage | F | VF | XF | Unc | BU |
|---|---|---|---|---|---|---|
| 1981 Proof | 1,000 | Value: 25.00 | | | | |

**50 LEVA** **KM# 137** **Weight:** 20.5000 g. **Composition:** 0.9000 Silver .5932 oz. ASW **Subject:** 1300th Anniversary of Nationhood **Reverse:** Mother and child

| Date | Mintage | F | VF | XF | Unc | BU |
|---|---|---|---|---|---|---|
| 1981 Proof | 1,000 | Value: 30.00 | | | | |

**50 LEVA** **KM# 138** **Weight:** 20.5000 g. **Composition:** 0.9000 Silver .5932 oz. ASW **Subject:** 1300th Anniversary of Nationhood

| Date | Mintage | F | VF | XF | Unc | BU |
|---|---|---|---|---|---|---|
| 1981 Proof | Est. 10,000 | Value: 22.50 | | | | |

**50 LEVA** KM# 182 **Composition:** Copper-Nickel-Zinc

| Date | Mintage | F | VF | XF | Unc | BU |
|---|---|---|---|---|---|---|
| 1989 Proof | — | Value: 12.00 | | | | |

**100 LEVA** KM# 150 **Weight:** 8.4444 g. **Composition:** 0.9000 Gold .2443 oz. AGW **Subject:** International Womens Decade **Note:** .076 Silver, .024 Copper

| Date | Mintage | F | VF | XF | Unc | BU |
|---|---|---|---|---|---|---|
| 1984 Proof | 500 | Value: 200 | | | | |

**100 LEVA** KM# 150a **Weight:** 8.4444 g. **Composition:** 0.9000 Gold .2443 oz. AGW **Note:** .100 Copper

| Date | Mintage | F | VF | XF | Unc | BU |
|---|---|---|---|---|---|---|
| 1984 | 15,000 | — | — | — | 185 | — |

**1000 LEVA** KM# 139 **Weight:** 16.8800 g. **Composition:** 0.9000 Gold .4885 oz. AGW **Subject:** 1300th Anniversary of Nationhood

| Date | Mintage | F | VF | XF | Unc | BU |
|---|---|---|---|---|---|---|
| 1981 Proof | 2,000 | Value: 385 | | | | |

## REPUBLIC

### STANDARD COINAGE

**10 STOTINKI** KM# 199 **Composition:** Nickel-Brass **Note:** Ancient lion sculpture.

| Date | Mintage | F | VF | XF | Unc | BU |
|---|---|---|---|---|---|---|
| 1992 | — | — | — | — | 0.25 | — |

**20 STOTINKI** KM# 200 **Composition:** Nickel-Brass **Note:** Ancient lion sculpture.

| Date | Mintage | F | VF | XF | Unc | BU |
|---|---|---|---|---|---|---|
| 1992 | — | — | — | — | 0.35 | — |

**50 STOTINKI** KM# 201 **Composition:** Nickel-Brass **Note:** Ancient lion sculpture.

| Date | Mintage | F | VF | XF | Unc | BU |
|---|---|---|---|---|---|---|
| 1992 | — | — | — | — | 0.50 | — |

**LEV** KM# 202 **Composition:** Nickel-Brass **Note:** Madara horseman

| Date | Mintage | F | VF | XF | Unc | BU |
|---|---|---|---|---|---|---|
| 1992 | — | — | — | — | 0.75 | — |

**2 LEVA** KM# 203 **Composition:** Nickel-Brass **Note:** Madara horseman

| Date | Mintage | F | VF | XF | Unc | BU |
|---|---|---|---|---|---|---|
| 1992 | — | — | — | — | 1.25 | — |

**5 LEVA** KM# 204 **Composition:** Nickel-Brass **Note:** Madara horseman

| Date | Mintage | F | VF | XF | Unc | BU |
|---|---|---|---|---|---|---|
| 1992 | — | — | — | — | 1.75 | — |

**10 LEVA** KM# 205 **Composition:** Copper-Nickel **Note:** Madara horseman

| Date | Mintage | F | VF | XF | Unc | BU |
|---|---|---|---|---|---|---|
| 1992 | — | — | — | — | 2.50 | — |

**10 LEVA** KM# 224 **Composition:** Brass **Note:** Reduced size and metal change.

| Date | Mintage | F | VF | XF | Unc | BU |
|---|---|---|---|---|---|---|
| 1997 | — | — | — | — | 1.25 | — |

**20 LEVA** KM# 228 **Composition:** Brass **Obverse:** Madara horseman **Reverse:** Denomination

| Date | Mintage | F | VF | XF | Unc | BU |
|---|---|---|---|---|---|---|
| 1997 | — | — | — | — | 1.50 | — |

**50 LEVA** KM# 198 **Weight:** 10.0700 g. **Composition:** 0.9250 Silver .2995 oz. ASW **Series:** Olympics **Subject:** Downhill skiing

| Date | Mintage | F | VF | XF | Unc | BU |
|---|---|---|---|---|---|---|
| 1992 Proof | 100,000 | Value: 11.50 | | | | |

**50 LEVA** KM# 213 **Composition:** Copper-Nickel **Subject:** Centennial of Olympics in Bulgaria

| Date | Mintage | F | VF | XF | Unc | BU |
|---|---|---|---|---|---|---|
| 1994 Proof | Est. 50,000 | Value: 5.00 | | | | |

**50 LEVA** KM# 225 **Composition:** Brass **Obverse:** Madera horseman **Reverse:** Denomination

| Date | Mintage | F | VF | XF | Unc | BU |
|---|---|---|---|---|---|---|
| 1997 | — | — | — | — | 1.75 | — |

**100 LEVA** KM# 226 **Weight:** 23.2300 g. **Composition:** 0.9250 Silver .6908 oz. ASW **Obverse:** Denomination **Reverse:** Eagle descending on prey

| Date | Mintage | F | VF | XF | Unc | BU |
|---|---|---|---|---|---|---|
| 1992 Proof | — | Value: 30.00 | | | | |

**100 LEVA** **KM# 212** **Weight:** 23.2300 g. **Composition:** 0.9250 Silver .6908 oz. ASW **Note:** Old Ship Radetsky

| Date | Mintage | F | VF | XF | Unc | BU |
|---|---|---|---|---|---|---|
| 1992 Proof | Est. 30,000 | Value: 28.00 | | | | |

**100 LEVA** **KM# 209** **Weight:** 23.3300 g. **Composition:** 0.9250 Silver .6939 oz. ASW **Series:** 1994 Olympics **Reverse:** Bobsled

| Date | Mintage | F | VF | XF | Unc | BU |
|---|---|---|---|---|---|---|
| 1993 Proof | 60,000 | Value: 22.50 | | | | |

**100 LEVA** **KM# 210** **Weight:** 23.3300 g. **Composition:** 0.9250 Silver .6939 oz. ASW **Subject:** 1994 World Cup Soccer

| Date | Mintage | F | VF | XF | Unc | BU |
|---|---|---|---|---|---|---|
| 1993 Proof | 30,000 | Value: 28.50 | | | | |

**100 LEVA** **KM# 227** **Weight:** 23.3300 g. **Composition:** 0.9250 Silver .6939 oz. ASW **Obverse:** Denomination **Reverse:** Ibex

| Date | Mintage | F | VF | XF | Unc | BU |
|---|---|---|---|---|---|---|
| 1993 Proof | — | Value: 30.00 | | | | |

**100 LEVA** **KM# 231** **Weight:** 23.3300 g. **Composition:** 0.9250 Silver .6939 oz. ASW **Obverse:** Denomination **Reverse:** Parliament building

| Date | Mintage | F | VF | XF | Unc | BU |
|---|---|---|---|---|---|---|
| 1993 Proof | Est. 30,000 | Value: 30.00 | | | | |

**500 LEVA** **KM# 206** **Weight:** 33.6250 g. **Composition:** 0.9250 Silver 1.0000 oz. ASW **Subject:** European Community - St. Theodor Stratilat **Obverse:** ECU monogram and date in circle of stars

| Date | Mintage | F | VF | XF | Unc | BU |
|---|---|---|---|---|---|---|
| 1993 Proof | 5,000 | Value: 32.50 | | | | |

**500 LEVA** **KM# 211** **Weight:** 23.0000 g. **Composition:** 0.9250 Silver .6840 oz. ASW **Subject:** World Cup Soccer

| Date | Mintage | F | VF | XF | Unc | BU |
|---|---|---|---|---|---|---|
| 1994 Proof | Est. 30,000 | Value: 32.50 | | | | |

**500 LEVA** **KM# 219** **Weight:** 10.0000 g. **Composition:** 0.9250 Silver .2974 oz. ASW **Subject:** Soccer **Obverse:** Denomination **Reverse:** Two soccer players

| Date | Mintage | F | VF | XF | Unc | BU |
|---|---|---|---|---|---|---|
| 1996 Proof | 60,000 | Value: 25.00 | | | | |

**500 LEVA** **KM# 229** **Composition:** Copper-Nickel-Zinc **Subject:** NATO **Obverse:** Denomination **Reverse:** City arms and NATO flag

| Date | Mintage | F | VF | XF | Unc | BU |
|---|---|---|---|---|---|---|
| 1997 | 30,000 | — | — | — | 5.00 | — |

**1000 LEVA** **KM# 214** **Weight:** 23.3300 g. **Composition:** 0.9250 Silver .6939 oz. ASW **Series:** 50 Years - F.A.O. **Reverse:** Wheat and globe

| Date | Mintage | F | VF | XF | Unc | BU |
|---|---|---|---|---|---|---|
| 1995 Proof | 30,000 | Value: 32.50 | | | | |

**1000 LEVA** **KM# 215** **Weight:** 23.3300 g. **Composition:** 0.9250 Silver .6939 oz. ASW **Subject:** 100 Years of Olympic Games **Reverse:** Equestrian

| Date | Mintage | F | VF | XF | Unc | BU |
|---|---|---|---|---|---|---|
| 1995 Proof | 60,000 | Value: 30.00 | | | | |

**1000 LEVA** **KM# 220** **Weight:** 23.3300 g. **Composition:** 0.9250 Silver .6939 oz. ASW **Subject:** Sailing Ship Kaliakra **Obverse:** Denomination **Reverse:** Sailing ship

| Date | Mintage | F | VF | XF | Unc | BU |
|---|---|---|---|---|---|---|
| 1996 Proof | 30,000 | Value: 35.00 | | | | |

**1000 LEVA** **KM# 232** **Weight:** 23.3300 g. **Composition:** 0.9250 Silver .6938 oz. ASW **Subject:** UNICEF **Obverse:** Denomination **Reverse:** Singing child, UNICEF logo

| Date | Mintage | F | VF | XF | Unc | BU |
|---|---|---|---|---|---|---|
| 1997 Proof | 25,000 | Value: 30.00 | | | | |

**1000 LEVA** **KM# 216** **Weight:** 23.3300 g. **Composition:** 0.9250 Silver .6939 oz. ASW **Subject:** 110 Years - Union of Eastern Rumelia with the Bulgarian principality

| Date | Mintage | F | VF | XF | Unc | BU |
|---|---|---|---|---|---|---|
| 1995 Proof | 30,000 | Value: 32.50 | | | | |

**1000 LEVA** **KM# 221** **Weight:** 23.3300 g. **Composition:** 0.9250 Silver .6939 oz. ASW **Series:** Olympics **Obverse:** Denomination **Reverse:** Speed skater

| Date | Mintage | F | VF | XF | Unc | BU |
|---|---|---|---|---|---|---|
| 1996 Proof | 60,000 | Value: 30.00 | | | | |

**1000 LEVA** **KM# 233** **Weight:** 23.3300 g. **Composition:** 0.9250 Silver .6938 oz. ASW **Subject:** World Cup Soccer - France 1998 **Obverse:** Denomination **Reverse:** Three soccer players

| Date | Mintage | F | VF | XF | Unc | BU |
|---|---|---|---|---|---|---|
| 1997 Proof | — | Value: 35.00 | | | | |

**1000 LEVA** **KM# 217** **Weight:** 33.6250 g. **Composition:** 0.9250 Silver 1.0000 oz. ASW **Subject:** Rozhen Peak Astronomical Observatory

| Date | Mintage | F | VF | XF | Unc | BU |
|---|---|---|---|---|---|---|
| 1995 Proof | 50,000 | Value: 32.50 | | | | |

**1000 LEVA** **KM# 222** **Weight:** 33.6250 g. **Composition:** 0.9250 Silver 1.0000 oz. ASW **Subject:** St. Ivan of Rila **Obverse:** ECU monogram **Reverse:** Standing saint, church, and denomination

| Date | Mintage | F | VF | XF | Unc | BU |
|---|---|---|---|---|---|---|
| 1996 Proof | 50,000 | Value: 32.50 | | | | |

**1000 LEVA** **KM# 239** **Composition:** Copper-Nickel-Zinc **Subject:** Bulgarian Telegraphic Agency Centennial **Obverse:** Crowned arms **Reverse:** World map and logo

| Date | Mintage | F | VF | XF | Unc | BU |
|---|---|---|---|---|---|---|
| 1998 Proof | — | Value: 5.50 | | | | |

**5000 LEVA** **KM# 207** **Weight:** 8.6400 g. **Composition:** 0.9000 Gold .2500 oz. AGW **Subject:** European Community - Slavonic Alphabet

| Date | Mintage | F | VF | XF | Unc | BU |
|---|---|---|---|---|---|---|
| 1993 Proof | Est. 2,500 | Value: 200 | | | | |

**5000 LEVA** KM# 243 **Weight:** 10.0000 g. **Composition:** 0.9250 Silver .2974 oz. ASW **Obverse:** National arms **Reverse:** Building above "EURO"

| Date | Mintage | F | VF | XF | Unc | BU |
|---|---|---|---|---|---|---|
| 1998 Proof | — | Value: 18.50 | | | | |

**10000 LEVA** KM# 208 **Weight:** 15.5670 g. **Composition:** 0.9990 Platinum .4999 oz. APW **Subject:** European Community - Desislava **Obverse:** Similar to 5000 Leva, KM#207

| Date | Mintage | F | VF | XF | Unc | BU |
|---|---|---|---|---|---|---|
| 1993 Proof | Est. 2,500 | Value: 450 | | | | |

**10000 LEVA** KM# 218 **Weight:** 8.6400 g. **Composition:** 0.9000 Gold .2500 oz. AGW **Reverse:** St. Alexander Nevski Cathedral

| Date | Mintage | F | VF | XF | Unc | BU |
|---|---|---|---|---|---|---|
| 1994 Proof | 30,000 | Value: 285 | | | | |

**10000 LEVA** KM# 234 **Weight:** 23.3300 g. **Composition:** 0.9250 Silver .6938 oz. ASW **Subject:** 120th Anniversary of Liberation **Obverse:** National arms **Reverse:** Decorated soldier wtih flag

| Date | Mintage | F | VF | XF | Unc | BU |
|---|---|---|---|---|---|---|
| 1998 Proof | 20,000 | Value: 40.00 | | | | |

**10000 LEVA** KM# 235 **Weight:** 23.3300 g. **Composition:** 0.9250 Silver .6938 oz. ASW **Subject:** United Europe **Obverse:** Rider of Madara over dead lion **Reverse:** Ancient cup and map

| Date | Mintage | F | VF | XF | Unc | BU |
|---|---|---|---|---|---|---|
| 1998 Proof | — | Value: 40.00 | | | | |

**20000 LEVA** KM# 236 **Weight:** 1.5552 g. **Composition:** 0.9990 Gold .0500 oz. AGW **Subject:** Czar Ivan Alexander **Obverse:** Stylized lion **Reverse:** Four human figure sculptures

| Date | Mintage | F | VF | XF | Unc | BU |
|---|---|---|---|---|---|---|
| 1998 Proof | — | Value: 75.00 | | | | |

## REFORM COINAGE

**STOTINKA** KM# 237 **Composition:** Brass **Obverse:** Madara horseman **Reverse:** Denomination

| Date | Mintage | F | VF | XF | Unc | BU |
|---|---|---|---|---|---|---|
| 1999 | — | — | — | — | 0.25 | — |

**2 STOTINKI** KM# 238 **Composition:** Brass **Obverse:** Madara horseman **Reverse:** Denomination

| Date | Mintage | F | VF | XF | Unc | BU |
|---|---|---|---|---|---|---|
| 1999 | — | — | — | — | 0.35 | — |

**5 STOTINKI** KM# A239 **Composition:** Brass **Obverse:** Madara horseman **Reverse:** Denomination

| Date | Mintage | F | VF | XF | Unc | BU |
|---|---|---|---|---|---|---|
| 1999 | — | — | — | — | 0.50 | — |

**10 STOTINKI** KM# 240 **Composition:** Copper-Nickel **Obverse:** Madara horseman **Reverse:** Denomination

| Date | Mintage | F | VF | XF | Unc | BU |
|---|---|---|---|---|---|---|
| 1999 | — | — | — | — | 0.65 | — |

**20 STOTINKI** KM# 241 **Composition:** Copper-Nickel **Obverse:** Madara horseman **Reverse:** Denomination

| Date | Mintage | F | VF | XF | Unc | BU |
|---|---|---|---|---|---|---|
| 1999 | — | — | — | — | 0.85 | — |

**50 STOTINKI** KM# 242 **Composition:** Copper-Nickel **Obverse:** Madara horseman **Reverse:** Denomination

| Date | Mintage | F | VF | XF | Unc | BU |
|---|---|---|---|---|---|---|
| 1999 | — | — | — | — | 1.25 | — |

## ESSAIS

| KM# | Date | Mintage | Identification | Mkt Val |
|---|---|---|---|---|
| E5 | 1925 | — | 2 Leva. Copper-Nickel. | 150 |

## PIEFORTS

| KM# | Date | Mintage | Identification | Mkt Val |
|---|---|---|---|---|
| P3 | 1979 | 2,000 | 10 Leva. KM#104 | 65.00 |

## TRIAL STRIKES

| KM# | Date | Mintage | Identification | Mkt Val |
|---|---|---|---|---|
| TS1 | 1901 | — | 2 Stotinki. Bronze. Uniface. | — |
| TS2 | 1901 | — | 2 Stotinki. Bronze. Uniface. | — |

## PATTERNS

Including off metal strikes

| KM# | Date | Mintage | Identification | Mkt Val |
|---|---|---|---|---|
| PnA6 | 1923 | — | Lev. Aluminum. Similar to KM#35 | — |

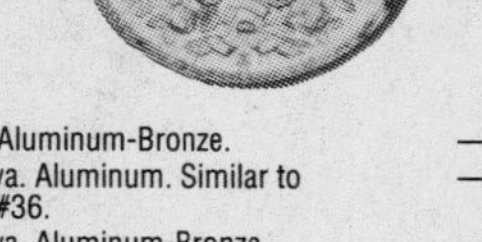

| KM# | Date | Mintage | Identification | Mkt Val |
|---|---|---|---|---|
| Pn6 | 1923 | — | Lev. Aluminum-Bronze. | — |
| PnA8 | 1923 | — | 2 Leva. Aluminum. Similar to KM#36. | — |
| Pn8 | 1923 | — | 2 Leva. Aluminum-Bronze. | — |
| Pn7 | 1923 | — | 2 Leva. Aluminum. | 275 |
| Pn9 | 1928 | 2 | 5 Leva. | — |
| Pn10 | 1930 | 2 | 5 Leva. | — |

| KM# | Date | Mintage | Identification | Mkt Val |
|---|---|---|---|---|
| Pn11 | 1930 | 2 | 10 Leva. | — |
| Pn12 | 1950 | — | 5 Leva. | — |

| KM# | Date | Mintage | Identification | Mkt Val |
|---|---|---|---|---|
| Pn13 | 1984 | 1,500 | 10 Leva. Copper-Nickel. Reeded edge. PROBA I; KM#146. | 35.00 |

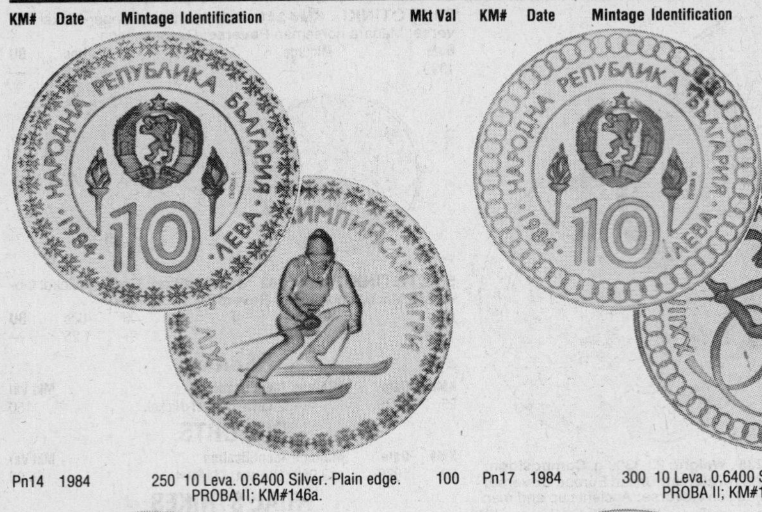

| KM# | Date | Mintage | Identification | Mkt Val |
|---|---|---|---|---|
| Pn14 | 1984 | 250 | 10 Leva. 0.6400 Silver. Plain edge. PROBA II; KM#146a. | 100 |
| Pn17 | 1984 | 300 | 10 Leva. 0.6400 Silver. Plain edge. PROBA II; KM#147a | 150 |

| KM# | Date | Mintage | Identification | Mkt Val |
|---|---|---|---|---|
| Pn15 | 1984 | 50 | 10 Leva. 0.9250 Silver. Lettered edge. SPECIMEN; KM#146a. | 200 |
| Pn18 | 1984 | 50 | 10 Leva. 0.9250 Silver. Lettered edge. SPECIMEN; KM#147a | 265 |
| Pn16 | 1984 | 2,000 | 10 Leva. Copper-Nickel. Reeded edge. PROBA I; KM#147 | 55.00 |

## MINT SETS

| KM# | Date | Mintage | Identification | Issue Price | Mkt Val |
|---|---|---|---|---|---|
| MS2 | 1999 (6) | — | KM#237-242, plus medal | — | 12.00 |
| MS1 | 1981 (3) | — | KM#118, 120, 131 | — | 20.00 |

## PROOF SETS

| KM# | Date | Mintage | Identification | Issue Price | Mkt Val |
|---|---|---|---|---|---|
| PS5 | 1963/73 (8) | — | KM#65-66, 69-70, 78-79, 80-81 mixed date set, REPUBLIQUE DE BULGARIE | — | 155 |
| PS7 | 1980 (7) | 2,000 | KM#84-90 | — | 22.50 |
| PS1 | 1912 (2) | — | KM#33-34 | — | 5,500 |
| PS2 | 1962/66 (9) | — | KM#58-64 (1962), 73 (1966) | — | — |
| PS3 | 1963 (2) | 5,000 | KM#65-66 | — | 27.50 |
| PS4 | 1964 (2) | 10,000 | KM#69-70 | — | 27.50 |
| PS6 | 1979 (7) | 2,000 | KM#84-90 | — | 22.50 |

# BURUNDI

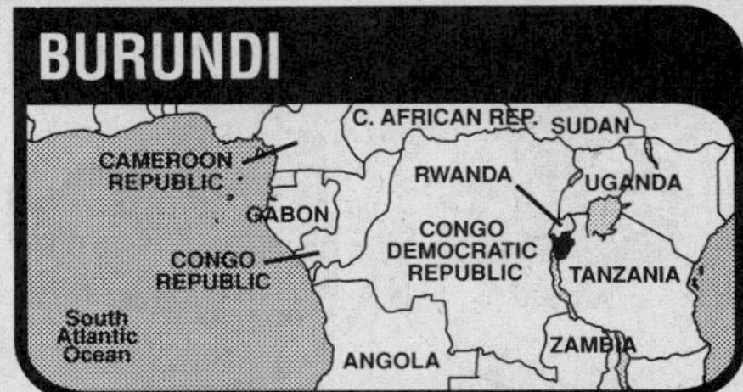


The Republic of Burundi, a landlocked country in central Africa, was a kingdom with a feudalistic society, caste system and Mwami (king) for more than 400 years before independence. It has an area of 10,740 sq. mi. (27,830 sq. km.) and a population of 6.3 million. Capital: Bujumbura. Plagued by poor soil, irregular rainfall and a single-crop economy, coffee, Burundi is barely able to feed itself. Coffee and tea are exported.

Although the area was visited by European explorers and missionaries in the latter half of the 19th century, it wasn't until the 1890s that it, together with Rwanda, fell under European domination as part of German East Africa. Following World War I, the territory was mandated to Belgium by the League of Nations and administered with the Belgian Congo. After World War II it became a U.N. Trust Territory. Limited self-government was established by U.N.-supervised elections in 1961. Burundi gained independence as a kingdom under Mwami Mwambutsa IV on July 1, 1962. The republic was established by military coup in 1966.

**NOTE**: For earlier coinage see Belgian Congo, and Rwanda and Burundi. For previously listed coinage dated 1966, coins of Mwambutsa IV and Ntare V, refer to *UNUSUAL WORLD COINS*, 3rd edition, Krause Publications, 1992.

**RULERS**

Mwambutsa IV, 1962-1966
Ntare V, 1966

**MINT MARKS**

PM - Pobjoy Mint
(b) - Privy Marks, Brussels

**MONETARY SYSTEM**

100 Centimes = 1 Franc

## KINGDOM

### STANDARD COINAGE

**FRANC** KM# 6 **Composition:** Brass

| Date | Mintage | F | VF | XF | Unc | BU |
|---|---|---|---|---|---|---|
| 1965 | 10,000,000 | — | 0.75 | 1.50 | 3.00 | — |

**5 FRANCS** KM# 1 **Composition:** Copper Nickel **Subject:** Burundi Independence

| Date | Mintage | F | VF | XF | Unc | BU |
|---|---|---|---|---|---|---|
| 1962 | — | — | — | — | — | — |
| 1962 Proof | — | — | — | — | — | — |

**5 FRANCS** KM# 1a **Weight:** 24.1100 g. **Composition:** 0.9000 Silver .6976 oz. ASW **Subject:** Burundi Independence

| Date | Mintage | F | VF | XF | Unc | BU |
|---|---|---|---|---|---|---|
| 1962 Proof | — | — | — | — | — | — |

**10 FRANCS** **KM# 2** **Weight:** 3.2000 g. **Composition:** 0.9000 Gold .0926 oz. AGW **Subject:** Burundi Independence

| Date | Mintage | F | VF | XF | Unc | BU |
|---|---|---|---|---|---|---|
| 1962 Proof | 7,500 | Value: 65.00 | | | | |

**10 FRANCS** **KM# 7** **Weight:** 3.0000 g. **Composition:** 0.9000 Gold .0868 oz. AGW **Subject:** 50th Anniversary - Reign of Mwambutsa IV

| Date | Mintage | F | VF | XF | Unc | BU |
|---|---|---|---|---|---|---|
| ND(1965) | — | — | — | — | 50.00 | — |
| ND(1965) Proof | 5,000 | Value: 65.00 | | | | |

**25 FRANCS** **KM# 3** **Weight:** 8.0000 g. **Composition:** 0.9000 Gold .2315 oz. AGW **Subject:** Burundi Independence

| Date | Mintage | F | VF | XF | Unc | BU |
|---|---|---|---|---|---|---|
| 1962 Proof | 15,000 | Value: 125 | | | | |

**25 FRANCS** **KM# 8** **Weight:** 7.5000 g. **Composition:** 0.9000 Gold .217 oz. AGW **Subject:** 50th Anniversary - Reign of Mwambutsa IV

| Date | Mintage | F | VF | XF | Unc | BU |
|---|---|---|---|---|---|---|
| ND(1965) | — | — | — | — | 120 | — |
| ND(1965) Proof | 5,000 | Value: 135 | | | | |

**50 FRANCS** **KM# 4** **Weight:** 16.0000 g. **Composition:** 0.9000 Gold .4630 oz. AGW **Subject:** Burundi Independence

| Date | Mintage | F | VF | XF | Unc | BU |
|---|---|---|---|---|---|---|
| 1962 Proof | 3,500 | Value: 320 | | | | |

**50 FRANCS** **KM# 9** **Weight:** 15.0000 g. **Composition:** 0.9000 Gold .4340 oz. AGW **Subject:** 50th Anniversary - Reign of Mwambutsa IV

| Date | Mintage | F | VF | XF | Unc | BU |
|---|---|---|---|---|---|---|
| ND(1965) | — | — | — | — | 215 | — |
| ND(1965) Proof | 5,000 | Value: 285 | | | | |

**100 FRANCS** **KM# 5** **Weight:** 32.0000 g. **Composition:** 0.9000 Gold .9260 oz. AGW **Subject:** Burundi Independence

| Date | Mintage | F | VF | XF | Unc | BU |
|---|---|---|---|---|---|---|
| 1962 Proof | 2,500 | Value: 580 | | | | |

**100 FRANCS** **KM# 10** **Weight:** 30.0000 g. **Composition:** 0.9000 Gold .8681 oz. AGW **Subject:** 50th Anniversary - Reign of Mwambutsa IV

| Date | Mintage | F | VF | XF | Unc | BU |
|---|---|---|---|---|---|---|
| ND(1965) | — | — | — | — | 450 | — |
| ND(1965) Proof | 5,000 | Value: 520 | | | | |

## REPUBLIC
### 1966-.
### MEDALLIC COINAGE

**10 FRANCS** **KM# M1** **Weight:** 1.5000 g. **Composition:** Billon **Subject:** 50th Anniversary - Reign of Mwambutsa IV **Obverse:** Portrait of late King Mwambutsa IV

| Date | Mintage | F | VF | XF | Unc | BU |
|---|---|---|---|---|---|---|
| ND(1966) Prooflike | 6,000 | — | — | — | — | — |

**10 FRANCS** **KM# M6** **Weight:** 1.5000 g. **Composition:** Billon **Subject:** Coronation of Ntare V **Obverse:** Portrait of Ntare V

| Date | Mintage | F | VF | XF | Unc | BU |
|---|---|---|---|---|---|---|
| ND(1966) Prooflike | 6,000 | — | — | — | — | — |

**25 FRANCS** **KM# M2** **Weight:** 3.2000 g. **Composition:** Billon **Subject:** 50th Anniversary - Reign of Mwambutsa IV **Obverse:** Portrait of late King Mwambutsa IV

| Date | Mintage | F | VF | XF | Unc | BU |
|---|---|---|---|---|---|---|
| ND(1966) Prooflike | 6,000 | — | — | — | 37.50 | — |

**25 FRANCS** **KM# M7** **Weight:** 3.2000 g. **Composition:** Billon **Subject:** Coronation of Ntare V **Obverse:** Portrait of Ntare V

| Date | Mintage | F | VF | XF | Unc | BU |
|---|---|---|---|---|---|---|
| ND(1966) Prooflike | 6,000 | — | — | — | — | — |

**50 FRANCS** **KM# M3** **Weight:** 5.2000 g. **Composition:** Billon **Subject:** 50th Anniversary - Reign of Mwambutsa IV **Obverse:** Portrait of late King Mwambutsa IV

| Date | Mintage | F | VF | XF | Unc | BU |
|---|---|---|---|---|---|---|
| ND(1966) Prooflike | 6,000 | — | — | — | — | — |

**50 FRANCS** **KM# M8** **Weight:** 5.2000 g. **Composition:** Billon **Subject:** Coronation of Ntare V **Obverse:** Portrait of Ntare V

| Date | Mintage | F | VF | XF | Unc | BU |
|---|---|---|---|---|---|---|
| ND(1966) Prooflike | 6,000 | — | — | — | — | — |

**100 FRANCS** **KM# M4** **Weight:** 10.3000 g. **Composition:** Billon **Subject:** 50th Anniversary - Reign of Mwambutsa IV **Obverse:** Portrait of late King Mwambutsa IV

| Date | Mintage | F | VF | XF | Unc | BU |
|---|---|---|---|---|---|---|
| ND(1966) Prooflike | 16,000 | — | — | — | — | — |

**100 FRANCS** **KM# M9** **Weight:** 10.3000 g. **Composition:** Billon **Subject:** Coronation of Ntare V **Obverse:** Portrait of Ntare V

| Date | Mintage | F | VF | XF | Unc | BU |
|---|---|---|---|---|---|---|
| ND(1966) Prooflike | 16,000 | — | — | — | — | — |

**500 FRANCS** **KM# M5** **Composition:** Billon **Subject:** 50th Anniversary - Reign of Mwambutsa IV **Obverse:** Portrait of late King Mwambutsa IV

| Date | Mintage | F | VF | XF | Unc | BU |
|---|---|---|---|---|---|---|
| ND(1966) Prooflike | — | — | — | — | — | — |

**500 FRANCS** KM# M10 **Composition:** Billon **Subject:** Coronation of Ntare V **Obverse:** Portrait of Ntare V

| Date | Mintage | F | VF | XF | Unc | BU |
|---|---|---|---|---|---|---|
| ND(1966) Prooflike | — | — | — | — | — | — |

## STANDARD COINAGE

**FRANC** KM# 18 **Composition:** Aluminum

| Date | Mintage | F | VF | XF | Unc | BU |
|---|---|---|---|---|---|---|
| 1970 | 10,000,000 | 2.00 | 4.50 | 7.50 | 17.50 | — |

**FRANC** KM# 19 **Composition:** Aluminum

| Date | Mintage | F | VF | XF | Unc | BU |
|---|---|---|---|---|---|---|
| 1976 | 5,000,000 | — | 0.30 | 0.75 | 1.75 | — |
| 1980 | — | — | 0.20 | 0.65 | 1.75 | — |
| 1990PM | — | — | 0.15 | 0.50 | 1.50 | — |
| 1993PM | — | — | 0.15 | 0.50 | 1.50 | — |

**5 FRANCS** KM# 16 **Composition:** Aluminum

| Date | Mintage | F | VF | XF | Unc | BU |
|---|---|---|---|---|---|---|
| 1968(b) | 2,000,000 | — | 0.25 | 0.85 | 2.00 | — |
| 1969(b) | 2,000,000 | — | 0.25 | 0.85 | 2.00 | — |
| 1971(b) | 2,000,000 | — | 0.25 | 0.85 | 2.00 | — |

**5 FRANCS** KM# 20 **Composition:** Aluminum

| Date | Mintage | F | VF | XF | Unc | BU |
|---|---|---|---|---|---|---|
| 1976 | 2,000,000 | — | 0.25 | 0.65 | 1.75 | — |
| 1980 | — | — | 0.25 | 0.65 | 1.75 | — |

**10 FRANCS** KM# 11 **Weight:** 3.2000 g. **Composition:** 0.9000 Gold .0926 oz. AGW **Subject:** 1st Anniversary of Republic

| Date | Mintage | F | VF | XF | Unc | BU |
|---|---|---|---|---|---|---|
| 1967 Proof | — | Value: 85.00 | | | | |

**10 FRANCS** KM# 17 **Composition:** Copper Nickel **Series:** F.A.O. **Subject:** 1st Anniversary of Republic

| Date | Mintage | F | VF | XF | Unc | BU |
|---|---|---|---|---|---|---|
| 1968 | 2,000,000 | — | 0.75 | 1.50 | 3.50 | — |
| 1971 | 2,000,000 | — | 0.75 | 1.50 | 3.50 | — |

**20 FRANCS** KM# 12 **Weight:** 6.4000 g. **Composition:** 0.9000 Gold .1852 oz. AGW **Subject:** 1st Anniversary of Republic

| Date | Mintage | F | VF | XF | Unc | BU |
|---|---|---|---|---|---|---|
| ND(1967) Proof | — | Value: 115 | | | | |

**25 FRANCS** KM# 13 **Weight:** 8.0000 g. **Composition:** 0.9000 Gold .2315 oz. AGW **Subject:** 1st Anniversary of Republic

| Date | Mintage | F | VF | XF | Unc | BU |
|---|---|---|---|---|---|---|
| ND(1967) Proof | — | Value: 135 | | | | |

**50 FRANCS** KM# 14 **Weight:** 16.0000 g. **Composition:** 0.9000 Gold .4630 oz. AGW **Subject:** 1st Anniversary of Republic

| Date | Mintage | F | VF | XF | Unc | BU |
|---|---|---|---|---|---|---|
| ND(1967) Proof | — | Value: 285 | | | | |

**100 FRANCS** KM# 15 **Weight:** 32.0000 g. **Composition:** 0.9000 Gold .9261 oz. AGW **Subject:** 1st Anniversary of Republic

| Date | Mintage | F | VF | XF | Unc | BU |
|---|---|---|---|---|---|---|
| ND(1967) Proof | — | Value: 585 | | | | |

## PROOF SETS

| KM# | Date | Mintage | Identification | Issue Price | Mkt Val |
|---|---|---|---|---|---|
| PS1 | 1962 (4) | 2,500 | KM2-5 | — | 1,100 |
| PS2 | 1965 (4) | 5,000 | KM7-10 | — | 1,100 |
| PS3 | 1967 (5) | — | KM11-15 | — | 1,200 |

# CAMBODIA

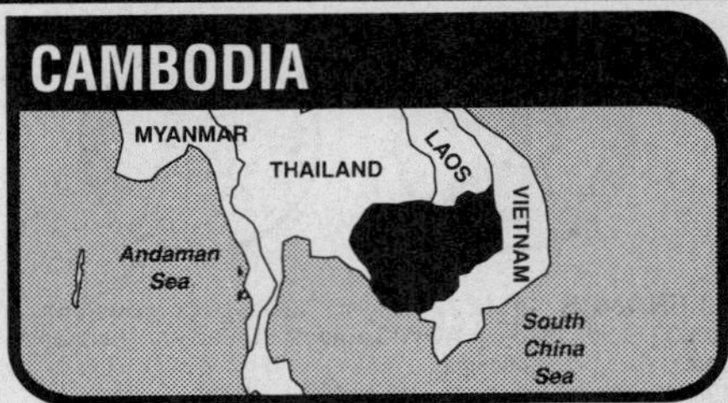


The State of Cambodia, formerly Democratic Kampuchea and the Khmer Republic, a land of paddy fields and forest-clad hills located on the Indo-Chinese peninsula, fronting on the Gulf of Thailand, has an area of 70,238 sq. mi. (181,040 sq. km.) and a population of *11.21 million. Capital: Phnom Penh. Agriculture is the basis of the economy, with rice the chief crop. Native industries include cattle breeding, weaving and rice milling. Rubber, cattle, corn, and timber are exported.

The region was the nucleus of the Khmer empire which flourished from the 5th to the 12th century and attained an excellence in art and architecture still evident in the magnificent ruins at Angkor. The Khmer empire once ruled over much of Southeast Asia, but began to decline in the 13th century as the Thai and Vietnamese invaded the region and attached its territories. At the request of the Cambodian king, a French protectorate attached to Cochin-China was established over the country in 1863, saving it from dissolution, and in 1885, Cambodia was included in the French Union of Indo-China.

France established a constitutional monarchy for Cambodia within the French Union in 1949. The 1954 Geneva Convention resulted in full independence for the Kingdom of Cambodia. King Sihanouk abdicated to his father and won the office of Prime Minister.

Prince Sihanouk was toppled by a bloodless coup led by Lon Nol in March of 1970. Sihanouk moved to Peking to head a government-in-exile. On Oct. 9, 1970, Cambodia became the Khmer Republic, and Lon Nol its President. The government of Lon Nol was in turn toppled, April 17, 1975, by the Khmer Rouge insurgents who took control of the government and renamed the country Democratic Kampuchea.

The Khmer Rouge completely eliminated the economy and created a state without money, exchange or barter while exterminating about 2 million Cambodians. These atrocities were finally halted at the beginning of 1979 when the Vietnamese regulars and Cambodian rebels launched an offensive that drove the Khmer Rouge out of Phnom Penh and the country acquired another new title - The Peoples Republic of Kampuchea.

In 1993 Prince Norodom Sihanouk returned to Kampuchea to lead the Supreme National Council.

**RULERS**

**Kings of Cambodia**
Norodom I, 1835-1904
Sisowath, 1904-1927
Sisowath Monivong, 1927-1941
Norodom Sihanouk, 1941-1955
Norodom Suramarit, 1955-1960
Heng Samrin, 1979-1985
Hun Sen, 1985-1991
Norodom Sihanouk, 1991-1993
Chairman, Supreme National Council
King, 1993-

**MINT MARKS**
(a) - Paris, privy marks only
(k) - Key, Havana, Cuba

**MONETARY SYSTEM**

**(Until 1860)**

2 Att = 1 Pe (Pey)
4 Pe = 1 Fuang (Fuong)
8 Fuang = 1 Tical
4 Salong = 1 Tical

**(Commencing 1860)**

100 Centimes = 1 Franc

# KINGDOM

## TOKEN COINAGE

**10 CENTIMES** KM# Tn1 **Composition:** Brass **Issuer:** Panom Penh Royal Palace. **Obv. Legend:** SOMDACH PREA NÒRÒDOM... **Size:** 26 mm.

| Date | Mintage | F | VF | XF | Unc | BU |
|---|---|---|---|---|---|---|
| ND (1875-1904) | — | — | 125 | — | 175 | — |

**15 CENTIMES** **KM# Tn3** **Composition:** Brass **Issuer:** Panom Penh Royal Palace. **Obv. Legend:** SOMDACH PREA NÒRÒDOM... **Size:** 26 mm.

| Date | Mintage | F | VF | XF | Unc | BU |
|---|---|---|---|---|---|---|
| ND (1875-1904) | — | — | 175 | — | 225 | — |

**25 CENTIMES** **KM# Tn4** **Composition:** Brass **Issuer:** Panom Penh Royal Palace. **Obv. Legend:** SOMDACH PREA NÒRÒDOM... **Size:** 26 mm.

| Date | Mintage | F | VF | XF | Unc | BU |
|---|---|---|---|---|---|---|
| ND (1875-1904) | — | — | 200 | — | 250 | — |

## INDEPENDANT KINGDOM

**10 CENTIMES** **KM# 51** **Composition:** Aluminum

| Date | Mintage | F | VF | XF | Unc | BU |
|---|---|---|---|---|---|---|
| 1953(a) | 4,000 | 0.25 | 0.45 | 0.85 | 2.00 | — |

**20 CENTIMES** **KM# 52** **Composition:** Aluminum

| Date | Mintage | F | VF | XF | Unc | BU |
|---|---|---|---|---|---|---|
| 1953(a) | 3,000 | 0.25 | 0.65 | 1.50 | 3.00 | — |

**20 CENTIMES** **KM# 55** **Composition:** Aluminum

| Date | Mintage | F | VF | XF | Unc | BU |
|---|---|---|---|---|---|---|
| 1959(a) | 1,004 | 0.15 | 0.25 | 0.60 | 1.00 | — |

**50 CENTIMES** **KM# 53** **Composition:** Aluminum

| Date | Mintage | F | VF | XF | Unc | BU |
|---|---|---|---|---|---|---|
| 1953(a) | 3,170 | 0.45 | 0.85 | 2.00 | 4.00 | — |

**10 SEN** **KM# 54** **Composition:** Aluminum

| Date | Mintage | F | VF | XF | Unc | BU |
|---|---|---|---|---|---|---|
| 1959(a) | 1,000 | 0.10 | 0.20 | 0.35 | 0.65 | — |

**50 SEN** **KM# 56** **Composition:** Aluminum

| Date | Mintage | F | VF | XF | Unc | BU |
|---|---|---|---|---|---|---|
| 1959(a) | 3,399 | 0.20 | 0.35 | 0.75 | 1.50 | — |

## KHMER REPUBLIC
### 1970 - 1975.

**RIEL** **KM# 59** **Composition:** Copper-Nickel **Series:** F.A.O

| Date | Mintage | F | VF | XF | Unc | BU |
|---|---|---|---|---|---|---|
| 1970 | 5,000 | — | — | 7.50 | 16.50 | — |

**Note:** According to the Royal Mint of Great Britain, this coin was minted at the Llantrissant Branch Mint in 1972 but dated 1969. According to the FAO, the coin was to have been dated 1971, but was "not minted" due to the fall of the Cambodian government in 1970. However, this coin was released in limited numbers in 1983. The photograph of the coin, supplied by the FAO, is dated 1970. This type is currently available from many sources in the numismatic market

**5000 RIELS** **KM# 60** **Weight:** 19.0100 g. **Composition:** 0.9250 Silver .5654 oz. ASW **Obverse:** Temple of Angkor Wat

| Date | Mintage | F | VF | XF | Unc | BU |
|---|---|---|---|---|---|---|
| 1974 | 500 | — | — | — | 65.00 | — |
| 1974 Proof | 800 | Value: 65.00 | | | | |

**5000 RIELS** **KM# 61** **Weight:** 19.0100 g. **Composition:** 0.9250 Silver .5654 oz. ASW **Obverse:** Cambodian dancers **Reverse:** Similar to KM#60.

| Date | Mintage | F | VF | XF | Unc | BU |
|---|---|---|---|---|---|---|
| 1974 | 500 | — | — | — | 85.00 | — |
| 1974 Proof | 800 | Value: 85.00 | | | | |

**10000 RIELS** **KM# 62** **Weight:** 38.0300 g. **Composition:** 0.9250 Silver 1.1310 oz. ASW **Obverse:** Bust of President Lon Nol left **Reverse:** Similar to 5,000 Riels, KM#60

| Date | Mintage | F | VF | XF | Unc | BU |
|---|---|---|---|---|---|---|
| 1974 | 500 | — | — | — | 110 | — |
| 1974 Proof | 800 | Value: 110 | | | | |

**10000 RIELS** **KM# 63** **Weight:** 38.0300 g. **Composition:** 0.9250 Silver 1.1310 oz. ASW **Obverse:** Celestial dancer **Reverse:** Similar to 5,000 Riels, KM#60

| Date | Mintage | F | VF | XF | Unc | BU |
|---|---|---|---|---|---|---|
| 1974 | 500 | — | — | — | 140 | — |
| 1974 Proof | 800 | Value: 140 | | | | |

**50000 RIELS** **KM# 64** **Weight:** 6.7100 g. **Composition:** 0.9000 Gold .1941 oz. AGW **Obverse:** Cambodian dancers

| Date | Mintage | F | VF | XF | Unc | BU |
|---|---|---|---|---|---|---|
| 1974 | 3,250 | — | — | — | 135 | — |
| 1974 Proof | 2,300 | Value: 190 | | | | |

**50000 RIELS** **KM# 65** **Weight:** 6.7100 g. **Composition:** 0.9000 Gold .1941 oz. AGW **Obverse:** Celestial dancer

| Date | Mintage | F | VF | XF | Unc | BU |
|---|---|---|---|---|---|---|
| 1974 | 450 | — | — | — | 245 | — |
| 1974 Proof | 300 | Value: 350 | | | | |

**100000 RIELS** **KM# 66** **Weight:** 19.1700 g. **Composition:** 0.9000 Gold .5547 oz. AGW **Obverse:** Bust of Presdient Lon Nol left **Reverse:** Similar to 50,000 Riels, KM#65

| Date | Mintage | F | VF | XF | Unc | BU |
|---|---|---|---|---|---|---|
| 1974 | 250 | — | — | — | 425 | — |
| 1974 Proof | 100 | Value: 685 | | | | |

# PEOPLE'S REPUBLIC OF KAMPUCHEA
## 1979 - 1990.

**5 SEN** **KM# 69** **Composition:** Aluminum

| Date | Mintage | F | VF | XF | Unc | BU |
|---|---|---|---|---|---|---|
| 1979 | — | — | 0.60 | 1.25 | 3.00 | — |

**4 RIELS** **KM# 71** **Composition:** Copper-Nickel **Subject:** Cambodian Transportation **Reverse:** Old sailing ship

| Date | Mintage | F | VF | XF | Unc | BU |
|---|---|---|---|---|---|---|
| 1988(k) | 1,500 | — | — | — | 12.50 | — |

**4 RIELS** **KM# 75** **Composition:** Copper-Nickel **Subject:** 700th Anniversary of Swiss Unity

| Date | Mintage | F | VF | XF | Unc | BU |
|---|---|---|---|---|---|---|
| ND (1988) | 15,000 | — | — | — | 10.00 | — |

**4 RIELS** **KM# 91** **Composition:** Copper **Reverse:** Angkot Wat Temples

| Date | Mintage | F | VF | XF | Unc | BU |
|---|---|---|---|---|---|---|
| ND (1988) | — | — | — | — | 7.50 | — |

**4 RIELS** **KM# 74** **Composition:** Copper-Nickel **Subject:** World Championship Soccer - Italy

| Date | Mintage | F | VF | XF | Unc | BU |
|---|---|---|---|---|---|---|
| 1989 | 2,000 | — | — | — | 7.50 | — |

**4 RIELS** **KM# 90** **Composition:** Copper **Reverse:** Angkor Wat Temples

| Date | Mintage | F | VF | XF | Unc | BU |
|---|---|---|---|---|---|---|
| 1989 | — | — | — | — | 8.50 | — |

**20 RIELS** **KM# 70** **Weight:** 12.0600 g. **Composition:** 0.9990 Silver .3855 oz. ASW **Subject:** Cambodian Transportation **Reverse:** Old sailing ship

| Date | Mintage | F | VF | XF | Unc | BU |
|---|---|---|---|---|---|---|
| 1988(k) | 3,000 | — | — | — | 30.00 | — |

**20 RIELS** **KM# 72** **Weight:** 12.0600 g. **Composition:** 0.9990 Silver .3855 oz. ASW **Subject:** World Championship Soccer - Mexico

| Date | Mintage | F | VF | XF | Unc | BU |
|---|---|---|---|---|---|---|
| 1988 | 5,000 | — | — | — | 30.00 | — |

**20 RIELS** **KM# 73** **Weight:** 16.0000 g. **Composition:** 0.9990 Silver .5145 oz. ASW **Subject:** 700th Anniversary of Swiss Unity - 1991

| Date | Mintage | F | VF | XF | Unc | BU |
|---|---|---|---|---|---|---|
| ND Proof | 2,000 | Value: 50.00 | | | | |

**20 RIELS** **KM# 78** **Weight:** 12.0000 g. **Composition:** 0.9990 Silver .3855 oz. ASW **Subject:** European Soccer Championship - Germany

| Date | Mintage | F | VF | XF | Unc | BU |
|---|---|---|---|---|---|---|
| 1988(k) | 5,000 | — | — | — | 40.00 | — |

**20 RIELS** **KM# 76** **Weight:** 16.0000 g. **Composition:** 0.9990 Silver .5145 oz. ASW **Reverse:** Angkor Wat Temples

| Date | Mintage | F | VF | XF | Unc | BU |
|---|---|---|---|---|---|---|
| 1989 Proof | 2,000 | Value: 40.00 | | | | |

**20 RIELS** **KM# 79** **Weight:** 16.0000 g. **Composition:** 0.9990 Silver .5145 oz. ASW **Subject:** World Championship Soccer - Italy

| Date | Mintage | F | VF | XF | Unc | BU |
|---|---|---|---|---|---|---|
| 1989 Proof | 10,000 | Value: 28.00 | | | | |

**20 RIELS** **KM# 80** **Weight:** 16.0000 g. **Composition:** 0.9990 Silver .5145 oz. ASW **Subject:** Summer Olympics **Reverse:** Fencers

| Date | Mintage | F | VF | XF | Unc | BU |
|---|---|---|---|---|---|---|
| 1989 Proof | 10,000 | Value: 32.50 | | | | |

**20 RIELS** **KM# 81** **Weight:** 16.0000 g. **Composition:** 0.9990 Silver .5145 oz. ASW **Subject:** Winter Olympics **Reverse:** Skier

| Date | Mintage | F | VF | XF | Unc | BU |
|---|---|---|---|---|---|---|
| 1989 Proof | 5,000 | Value: 35.00 | | | | |

**40 RIELS** **KM#77** **Weight:** 3.1500 g. **Composition:** 0.9990 Gold .1012 oz. AGW **Obverse:** Similar to KM#82. **Reverse:** Angkor Wat Temples

| Date | Mintage | F | VF | XF | Unc | BU |
|---|---|---|---|---|---|---|
| 1989 | 500 | — | — | — | 120 | — |

**40 RIELS** **KM#82** **Weight:** 3.1500 g. **Composition:** 0.9990 Gold .1012 oz. AGW **Reverse:** Folklore and dance

| Date | Mintage | F | VF | XF | Unc | BU |
|---|---|---|---|---|---|---|
| 1990 | 500 | Value: 150 | | | | |

## STATE OF CAMBODIA
### 1990 - 1993.

**4 RIELS** **KM# 83** **Composition:** Nickel Plated Steel **Subject:** Olympics **Reverse:** Tennis

| Date | Mintage | F | VF | XF | Unc | BU |
|---|---|---|---|---|---|---|
| 1991 | 5,000 | — | — | — | 13.50 | — |

**4 RIELS** **KM#86** **Composition:** Copper-Nickel **Series:** Prehistoric Animals **Reverse:** Cryptocleidus

| Date | Mintage | F | VF | XF | Unc | BU |
|---|---|---|---|---|---|---|
| 1993 | — | — | — | — | 24.00 | — |

**4 RIELS** **KM#89** **Composition:** Copper-Nickel **Series:** Prehistoric Animals **Reverse:** Anatosaurus

| Date | Mintage | F | VF | XF | Unc | BU |
|---|---|---|---|---|---|---|
| 1994 | — | — | — | — | 24.00 | — |

**20 RIELS** **KM# 84** **Weight:** 11.9600 g. **Composition:** 0.9990 Silver .3845 oz. ASW **Subject:** World Cup Soccer - 1994 **Reverse:** Player kicking ball

| Date | Mintage | F | VF | XF | Unc | BU |
|---|---|---|---|---|---|---|
| 1991 | 30,000 | — | — | — | 30.00 | — |

**20 RIELS** **KM# 88** **Weight:** 11.9600 g. **Composition:** 0.9990 Silver .3845 oz. ASW **Subject:** World Cup Soccer - 1994 **Reverse:** 2 players kicking ball

| Date | Mintage | F | VF | XF | Unc | BU |
|---|---|---|---|---|---|---|
| 1992 Proof | — | Value: 42.50 | | | | |

**20 RIELS** **KM# 85** **Weight:** 19.9500 g. **Composition:** 0.9990 Silver .6408 oz. ASW **Subject:** Protection of Nature **Obverse:** Similar to KM#84 **Reverse:** Asian elephants

| Date | Mintage | F | VF | XF | Unc | BU |
|---|---|---|---|---|---|---|
| 1993 Proof | — | Value: 45.00 | | | | |

**20 RIELS** **KM# 87** **Weight:** 16.0600 g. **Composition:** 0.9990 Silver .5145 oz. ASW **Series:** Prehistoric Animals **Obverse:** Similar to KM#84. **Reverse:** Indricotherium

| Date | Mintage | F | VF | XF | Unc | BU |
|---|---|---|---|---|---|---|
| 1993 | — | Value: 40.00 | | | | |

**20 RIELS** **KM# 96** **Weight:** 16.1000 g. **Composition:** 0.9990 Silver .5171 oz. ASW **Series:** Prehistoric Animals **Obverse:** National flag **Reverse:** Nothosaurus at water's edge **Edge:** Plain

| Date | Mintage | F | VF | XF | Unc | BU |
|---|---|---|---|---|---|---|
| 1994 Proof | — | Value: 50.00 | | | | |

## KINGDOM OF CAMBODIA
### 1993 -

**50 RIELS** **KM# 92** **Composition:** Steel

| Date | Mintage | F | VF | XF | Unc | BU |
|---|---|---|---|---|---|---|
| BE2538-1994 | — | — | — | — | 0.25 | — |

**100 RIELS** **KM# 93** **Composition:** Steel **Obverse:** 3 towered building

| Date | Mintage | F | VF | XF | Unc | BU |
|---|---|---|---|---|---|---|
| BE2538-1994 | — | — | — | — | 0.50 | — |

**200 RIELS** **KM# 94** **Composition:** Steel **Obverse:** 2 Ceremonial bowls

| Date | Mintage | F | VF | XF | Unc | BU |
|---|---|---|---|---|---|---|
| BE2538-1994 | — | — | — | — | 1.00 | — |

**500 RIELS** **KM# 95** **Ring Composition:** Brass **Center Composition:** Steel **Obverse:** Royal emblem

| Date | Mintage | F | VF | XF | Unc | BU |
|---|---|---|---|---|---|---|
| BE2538-1994 | — | — | — | — | 3.50 | — |

## ESSAIS

| KM# | Date | Mintage | Identification | Issue Price | Mkt Val |
|---|---|---|---|---|---|
| E9 | 1953 | 1,200 | 10 Centimes. | — | 20.00 |
| E10 | 1953 | 1,200 | 20 Centimes. | — | 22.00 |
| E11 | 1953 | 1,200 | 50 Centimes. | — | 25.00 |

## PATTERNS

Including off metal strikes

| KM# | Date | Mintage | Identification | Mkt Val |
|---|---|---|---|---|
| Pn15 | 1902 | — | 4 Francs. Silver. Palace at Pnom-Penh | 250 |

## PIEFORTS

| KM# | Date | Mintage | Identification | Mkt Val |
|---|---|---|---|---|
| P12 | 1989 | 110 | 20 Riels. 0.9990 Silver. KM80. | 125 |
| P13 | 1989 | 110 | 20 Riels. 0.9990 Silver. KM76. | 125 |

## PIEFORTS WITH ESSAI

Double thickness

Standard metals unless otherwise noted.

| KM# | Date | Mintage | Identification | Issue Price | Mkt Val |
|---|---|---|---|---|---|
| PE9 | 1953 | 104 | 10 Centimes. | — | 50.00 |
| PE10 | 1953 | 104 | 20 Centimes. | — | 65.00 |
| PE11 | 1953 | 104 | 50 Centimes. | — | 80.00 |

## MINT SETS

| KM# | Date | Mintage | Identification | Issue Price | Mkt Val |
|---|---|---|---|---|---|
| MS1 | 1953 (3) | — | KM51,-53 | — | 10.00 |
| MS2 | 1974 (7) | 250 | KM60-66 | — | 1,175 |
| MS3 | 1974 (4) | 500 | KM60-63 | — | 365 |
| MS4 | BE2538 (1994) (4) | — | KM92-95 with 7 laminated banknotes | 0.38 | 7.50 |

## PROOF SETS

| KM# | Date | Mintage | Identification | Issue Price | Mkt Val |
|---|---|---|---|---|---|
| PS1 | 1974 (7) | 100 | KM60-66 | — | 1,600 |
| PS2 | 1974 (4) | 800 | KM60-63 | — | 365 |

# CAMEROON

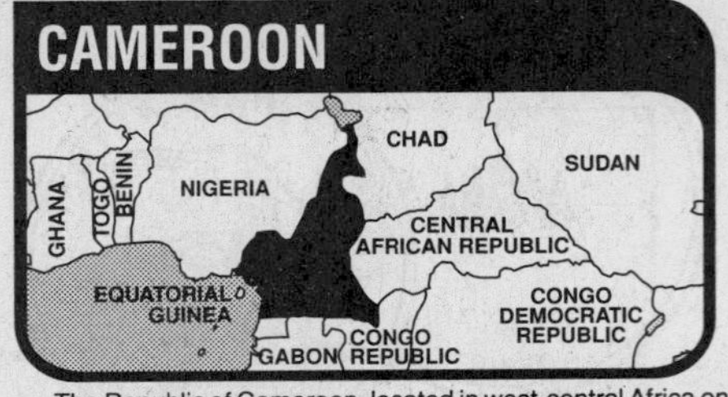


The Republic of Cameroon, located in west-central Africa on the Gulf of Guinea, has an area of 183,569 sq. mi. (475,445 sq. km.) and a population of *15.13 million. Capital: Yaounde. About 90 percent of the labor force is employed on the land; cash crops account for 80 percent of the country's export revenue. Cocoa, coffee, aluminum, cotton, rubber, and timber are exported.

European contact with what is now the United Republic of Cameroon began in the 16th century with the voyage of Portuguese navigator Fernando Po. The following three centuries saw continuous activity by Spanish, Dutch, and British traders and missionaries. The land was spared colonial rule until 1884, when treaties with tribal chiefs brought German domination. In 1919, the League of Nations divided the Cameroons between Great Britain and France, with the larger eastern area going to France. The French and British mandates were converted into United Nations trusteeships in 1946. French Cameroon became the independent Cameroon Republic on Jan. 1, 1960. The federation of East (French) and West (British) Cameroon was established in 1961 when the southern part of British Cameroon voted for reunification with the Cameroon Republic, and the northern part for union with Nigeria Cameroon joined the Commonwealth of Nations in November 1995.

Coins of French Equatorial Africa and of the monetary unions identified as the Equatorial African States and Central African States are also current in Cameroon.

**MINT MARKS**

(a) - Paris, privy marks only

SA - Pretoria, 1943

**MONETARY SYSTEM**

100 Centimes = 1 Franc

# FRENCH MANDATE

## STANDARD COINAGE

**50 CENTIMES** **KM# 1** **Composition:** Aluminum-Bronze

| Date | Mintage | F | VF | XF | Unc | BU |
|---|---|---|---|---|---|---|
| 1924(a) | 4,000,000 | 1.50 | 3.50 | 22.00 | 90.00 | — |
| 1925(a) | 2,500,000 | 2.00 | 5.00 | 25.00 | 100 | — |
| 1926(a) | 7,800,000 | 1.00 | 2.00 | 15.00 | 70.00 | — |

**50 CENTIMES** **KM# 4** **Composition:** Bronze

| Date | Mintage | F | VF | XF | Unc | BU |
|---|---|---|---|---|---|---|
| 1943SA | 4,000,000 | 2.00 | 3.50 | 7.00 | 18.00 | — |

**50 CENTIMES** **KM# 6** **Composition:** Bronze **Obverse:** LIBRE added to legend

| Date | Mintage | F | VF | XF | Unc | BU |
|---|---|---|---|---|---|---|
| 1943SA | 4,000,000 | 2.50 | 5.50 | 12.00 | 25.00 | — |

**FRANC** **KM# 2** **Composition:** Aluminum-Bronze

| Date | Mintage | F | VF | XF | Unc | BU |
|---|---|---|---|---|---|---|
| 1924(a) | 3,000,000 | 2.00 | 4.00 | 20.00 | 90.00 | — |
| 1925(a) | 1,722,000 | 3.00 | 6.00 | 30.00 | 125 | — |
| 1926(a) | 11,928,000 | 1.00 | 2.00 | 12.00 | 60.00 | — |

**FRANC** **KM# 5** **Composition:** Bronze

| Date | Mintage | F | VF | XF | Unc | BU |
|---|---|---|---|---|---|---|
| 1943SA | 3,000,000 | 2.50 | 4.50 | 17.50 | 40.00 | — |

**FRANC** **KM# 7** **Composition:** Bronze **Obverse:** LIBRE added to legend

| Date | Mintage | F | VF | XF | Unc | BU |
|---|---|---|---|---|---|---|
| 1943SA | 3,000,000 | 3.50 | 6.50 | 20.00 | 45.00 | — |

**FRANC** **KM# 8** **Composition:** Aluminum

| Date | Mintage | F | VF | XF | Unc | BU |
|---|---|---|---|---|---|---|
| 1948(a) | 8,000,000 | 0.15 | 0.35 | 0.85 | 1.75 | — |

**2 FRANCS** **KM# 3** **Composition:** Aluminum-Bronze

| Date | Mintage | F | VF | XF | Unc | BU |
|---|---|---|---|---|---|---|
| 1924(a) | 500,000 | 5.00 | 15.00 | 65.00 | 185 | — |
| 1925(a) | 100,000 | 8.00 | 25.00 | 100 | 275 | — |

**2 FRANCS** **KM# 9** **Composition:** Aluminum

| Date | Mintage | F | VF | XF | Unc | BU |
|---|---|---|---|---|---|---|
| 1948(a) | 5,000,000 | 0.65 | 1.25 | 2.00 | 5.00 | — |

# REPUBLIC

## STANDARD COINAGE

**50 FRANCS** **KM# 13** **Composition:** Copper-Nickel **Subject:** Independence Commemorative **Obverse:** Three Giant Eland **Reverse:** Denomination

| Date | Mintage | F | VF | XF | Unc | BU |
|---|---|---|---|---|---|---|
| 1960(a) | 1,154,000 | 2.00 | 3.50 | 5.50 | 10.00 | — |

**100 FRANCS** **KM# 14** **Composition:** Nickel **Obverse:** Three Giant Eland **Reverse:** Denomination **Note:** KM#14 was issued double thick and should not be considered a piefort.

| Date | Mintage | F | VF | XF | Unc | BU |
|---|---|---|---|---|---|---|
| 1966(a) | 9,950,000 | 1.00 | 2.00 | 4.50 | 10.00 | — |
| 1967(a) | 10,000,000 | 1.00 | 2.00 | 4.50 | 10.00 | — |
| 1968(a) | 11,000,000 | 1.00 | 2.00 | 4.50 | 10.00 | — |

**100 FRANCS** **KM# 15** **Composition:** Nickel **Obverse:** Three Giant Eland **Reverse:** Denomination **Note:** Refer also to Equatorial African States and Central African States.

| Date | Mintage | F | VF | XF | Unc | BU |
|---|---|---|---|---|---|---|
| 1971(a) | 15,000,000 | 2.00 | 3.00 | 6.00 | 12.50 | — |
| 1972(a) | 20,000,000 | 2.00 | 3.00 | 6.00 | 12.50 | — |

**100 FRANCS** **KM# 16** **Composition:** Nickel **Obverse:** KM#17 **Reverse:** KM#15

| Date | Mintage | F | VF | XF | Unc | BU |
|---|---|---|---|---|---|---|
| 1972(a) | — | 6.50 | 12.50 | 22.50 | 45.00 | — |

**100 FRANCS** **KM# 17** **Composition:** Nickel **Obverse:** Three Giant Eland **Reverse:** Denomination

| Date | Mintage | F | VF | XF | Unc | BU |
|---|---|---|---|---|---|---|
| 1975(a) | — | 1.00 | 2.00 | 3.00 | 5.50 | — |
| 1980(a) | — | 1.00 | 2.00 | 3.00 | 5.50 | — |
| 1982(a) | — | 0.75 | 1.50 | 2.50 | 4.50 | — |
| 1983(a) | — | 0.75 | 1.50 | 2.50 | 4.50 | — |
| 1984(a) | — | 0.75 | 1.50 | 2.50 | 4.50 | — |
| 1986(a) | — | 0.75 | 1.50 | 2.50 | 4.50 | — |

**500 FRANCS** **KM# 23** **Composition:** Copper-Nickel

| Date | Mintage | F | VF | XF | Unc | BU |
|---|---|---|---|---|---|---|
| 1985(a) | — | 2.00 | 3.50 | 5.50 | 10.00 | — |
| 1986(a) | — | 2.00 | 3.50 | 5.50 | 10.00 | — |
| 1988(a) | — | 2.00 | 3.50 | 5.50 | 10.00 | — |

**1000 FRANCS** **KM# 18** **Weight:** 3.5000 g. **Composition:** 0.9000 Gold .1012 oz. AGW **Subject:** 10th Anniversary of Independence

| Date | Mintage | F | VF | XF | Unc | BU |
|---|---|---|---|---|---|---|
| 1970 Proof | 4,000 | Value: 75.00 | | | | |

**3000 FRANCS** **KM# 19** **Weight:** 10.5000 g. **Composition:** 0.9000 Gold .3038 oz. AGW **Subject:** 10th Anniversary of Independence

| Date | Mintage | F | VF | XF | Unc | BU |
|---|---|---|---|---|---|---|
| 1970 Proof | 4,000 | Value: 185 | | | | |

**Note:** With or without cornucopia mint mark on reverse

**5000 FRANCS** **KM# 20** **Weight:** 17.5000 g. **Composition:** 0.9000 Gold .5064 oz. AGW **Subject:** 10th Anniversary of Independence

| Date | Mintage | F | VF | XF | Unc | BU |
|---|---|---|---|---|---|---|
| 1970 Proof | 4,000 | Value: 300 | | | | |

**10000 FRANCS** **KM# 21** **Weight:** 35.0000 g. **Composition:** 0.9000 Gold 1.0128 oz. AGW **Subject:** 10th Anniversary of Independence

| Date | Mintage | F | VF | XF | Unc | BU |
|---|---|---|---|---|---|---|
| 1970 Proof | 4,000 | Value: 650 | | | | |

**20000 FRANCS** **KM# 22** **Weight:** 70.0000 g. **Composition:** 0.9000 Gold 2.0257 oz. AGW **Subject:** 10th Anniversary of Independence **Obverse:** Similar to 10,000 Francs, KM#21

| Date | Mintage | F | VF | XF | Unc | BU |
|---|---|---|---|---|---|---|
| 1970 Proof | 4,000 | Value: 1,150 | | | | |

## TOKEN COINAGE

**50 CENTIMES** **KM# TN3** **Composition:** Brass **Issuer:** Societe Nationale **Obverse:** SOCIETE NATIONALE DU CAMEROUN in legend **Reverse:** 50c

| Date | Mintage | VG | F | VF | XF | Unc |
|---|---|---|---|---|---|---|
| ND | — | 40.00 | 100 | 175 | 320 | — |

**FRANC** **KM# Tn4** **Composition:** Brass **Reverse:** 50c **Note:** Similar to KM#TN3.

| Date | Mintage | VG | F | VF | XF | Unc |
|---|---|---|---|---|---|---|
| ND | — | 50.00 | 120 | 220 | 375 | — |

## ESSAIS

Standard metals unless otherwise noted

| KM# | Date | Mintage | Identification | Issue Price | Mkt Val |
|---|---|---|---|---|---|
| E1 | 1924 | — | 50 Centimes. KM1 | — | 85.00 |
| E2 | 1924 | — | Franc. KM2 | — | 100 |

| KM# | Date | Mintage | Identification | Issue Price | Mkt Val |
|---|---|---|---|---|---|
| E3 | 1924 | — | 2 Francs. KM3 | — | 125 |
| E4 | 1943 | — | 1/2 Franc. | — | 600 |
| E5 | 1948 | 2,000 | Franc. Copper-Nickel. KM8 | — | 30.00 |
| E6 | 1948 | 2,000 | 2 Francs. Copper-Nickel. KM9 | — | 35.00 |
| E7 | 1958 | 2,030 | 5 Francs. KM24 | — | 15.00 |
| E8 | 1958 | 2,030 | 10 Francs. KM25 | — | 17.50 |
| E9 | 1958 | 2,030 | 25 Francs. KM26 | — | 20.00 |
| E10 | 1960 | 1,500 | 50 Francs. KM13 | — | 27.50 |
| E11 | 1966 | 1,200 | 100 Francs. KM14 | — | 22.50 |
| E12 | 1970 | — | 1000 Francs. Bronze. KM18 | — | 95.00 |
| E13 | 1971 | 1,550 | 100 Francs. KM15 | — | 22.50 |
| E14 | 1971 | 6 | 100 Francs. Gold. KM15 | — | 1,250 |
| E15 | 1972 | 1,550 | 100 Francs. KM16 | — | 30.00 |
| E16 | 1975 | 1,700 | 100 Francs. KM17 | — | 22.50 |
| E17 | 1985 | — | 500 Francs. KM23 | — | 35.00 |

## PIEFORTS WITH ESSAI

Double thickness - Standard metals unless otherwise noted

| KM# | Date | Mintage | Identification | Issue Price | Mkt Val |
|---|---|---|---|---|---|
| PE1 | 1948 | 104 | Franc. KM8 | — | 60.00 |
| PE2 | 1948 | 104 | 2 Francs. KM9 | — | 75.00 |
| PE3 | 1948 | — | 2 Francs. KM9, double piefort | — | 250 |
| PE4 | 1948 | — | 2 Francs. Copper-Nickel. KM9 | — | 250 |

## PROOF SETS

| KM# | Date | Mintage | Identification | Issue Price | Mkt Val |
|---|---|---|---|---|---|
| PS1 | 1970 (5) | 4,000 | KM18-22 | — | 2,350 |

# CANADA

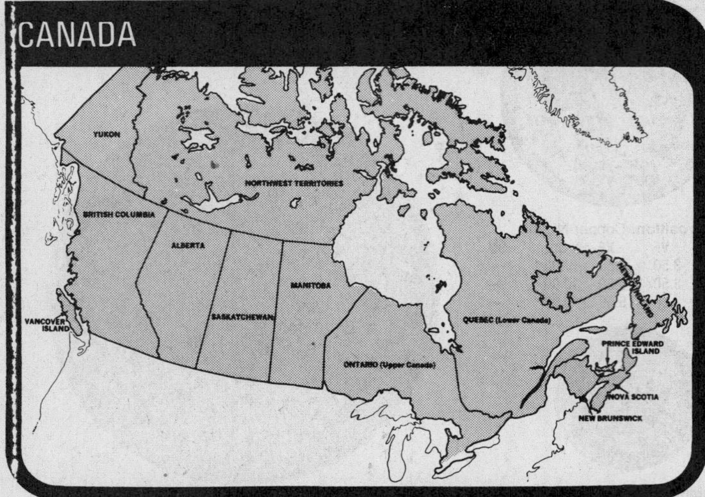


Canada is located to the north of the United States, and spans the full breadth of the northern portion of North America from Atlantic to Pacific oceans, except for the State of Alaska. It has a total area of 3,850,000 sq. mi. (9,971,550 sq. km.) and a population of 30.29 million. Capital: Ottawa.

Jacques Cartier, a French explorer, took possession of Canada for France in 1534, and for more than a century the history of Canada was that of a French colony. Samuel de Champlain helped to establish the first permanent colony in North America, in 1604 at Port Royal, Acadia – now Annapolis Royal, Nova Scotia. Four years later he founded the settlement in Quebec.

The British settled along the coast to the south while the French, motivated by a grand design, pushed into the interior. France's plan for a great American empire was to occupy the Mississippi heartland of the country, and from there to press in upon the narrow strip of English coastal settlements from the west. Inevitably, armed conflict erupted between the French and the British; consequently, Britain acquired Hudson Bay, Newfoundland and Nova Scotia from the French in 1713. British control of the rest of New France was secured in 1763, largely because of James Wolfe's great victory over Montcalm near Quebec in 1759.

During the American Revolution, Canada became a refuge for great numbers of American Royalists, most of whom settled in Ontario, thereby creating an English majority west of the Ottawa River. The ethnic imbalance contravened the effectiveness of the prevailing French type of government, and in 1791 the Constitutional act was passed by the British parliament, dividing Canada at the Ottawa River into two parts, each with its own government: Upper Canada, chiefly English and consisting of the southern section of what is now Ontario; and Lower Canada, chiefly French and consisting principally of the southern section of Quebec. Subsequent revolt by dissidents in both sections caused the British government to pass the Union Act, July 23, 1840, which united Lower and Upper Canada (as Canada East and Canada West) to form the Province of Canada, with one council and one assembly in which the two sections had equal numbers.

The union of the two provinces did not encourage political stability; the equal strength of the French and British made the task of government all but impossible. A further change was made with the passage of the British North American Act, which took effect on July 1, 1867, and established Canada as the first federal union in the British Empire. Four provinces entered the union at first: Upper Canada as Ontario, Lower Canada as Quebec, Nova Scotia and New Brunswick. The Hudson Bay Company's territories were acquired in 1869 out of which were formed the provinces of Manitoba, Saskatchewan and Alberta. British Columbia joined in 1871 and Prince Edward Island in 1873. Canada took over the Arctic Archipelago in 1895. In 1949 Newfoundland came into the confederation.

In the early years, Canada's coins were struck in England at the Royal Mint in London or at the Heaton Mint in Birmingham. Issues struck at the Royal Mint do not bear a mint mark, but those produced by Heaton carry an "H". All Canadian coins have been struck since January 2, 1908, at the Royal Canadian Mints at Ottawa and recently at Winnipeg except for some 1968 pure nickel dimes struck at the U.S. Mint in Philadelphia, and do not bear mint marks. Ottawa's mint mark (C) does not appear on some 20th Century Newfoundland issues, however, as it does on English type sovereigns struck there from 1908 through 1918.

Canada is a member of the Commonwealth of Nations. Elizabeth II is Head of State as Queen of Canada.

**RULERS:**
British 1763-

**MONETARY SYSTEM**
1 Dollar = 100 Cents

## CONFEDERATION

### CIRCULATION COINAGE

**CENT** **Weight:** 3.2400 g. **Composition:** Bronze

| KM | Date | Mintage | VG-8 | F-12 | VF-20 | XF-40 | MS-60 | MS-63 | Proof |
|---|---|---|---|---|---|---|---|---|---|
| 7 | 1901 | 4,100,000 | 1.50 | 2.50 | 3.00 | 5.00 | 22.00 | 70.00 | — |

**CENT** **Weight:** 3.2400 g. **Composition:** Bronze

| KM | Date | Mintage | VG-8 | F-12 | VF-20 | XF-40 | MS-60 | MS-63 | Proof |
|---|---|---|---|---|---|---|---|---|---|
| 8 | 1902 | 3,000,000 | 1.25 | 1.50 | 2.00 | 5.00 | 13.00 | 45.00 | — |
| | 1903 | 4,000,000 | 1.25 | 1.50 | 2.00 | 4.00 | 18.00 | 50.00 | — |
| | 1904 | 2,500,000 | 1.50 | 2.00 | 3.25 | 5.00 | 25.00 | 75.00 | — |
| | 1905 | 2,000,000 | 2.50 | 4.00 | 5.00 | 7.00 | 30.00 | 85.00 | — |
| | 1906 | 4,100,000 | 1.25 | 1.50 | 2.00 | 4.00 | 22.00 | 125 | — |
| | 1907 | 2,400,000 | 1.25 | 2.00 | 3.00 | 5.00 | 25.00 | 90.00 | — |
| | 1907H | 800,000 | 8.00 | 11.00 | 16.00 | 30.00 | 80.00 | 350 | — |
| | 1908 | 2,401,506 | 1.25 | 2.00 | 3.00 | 5.00 | 22.00 | 80.00 | 150 |
| | 1909 | 3,973,339 | 1.25 | 1.50 | 2.00 | 4.00 | 18.00 | 65.00 | — |
| | 1910 | 5,146,487 | 1.25 | 1.50 | 2.00 | 3.00 | 13.00 | 65.00 | — |

**CENT** **Weight:** 3.2400 g. **Composition:** Bronze

| KM | Date | Mintage | VG-8 | F-12 | VF-20 | XF-40 | MS-60 | MS-63 | Proof |
|---|---|---|---|---|---|---|---|---|---|
| 15 | 1911 | 4,663,486 | 0.75 | 1.25 | 1.75 | 3.50 | 15.00 | 50.00 | 250 |

**CENT** **Weight:** 3.2400 g. **Composition:** Bronze

| KM | Date | Mintage | VG-8 | F-12 | VF-20 | XF-40 | MS-60 | MS-63 | Proof |
|---|---|---|---|---|---|---|---|---|---|
| 21 | 1912 | 5,107,642 | 0.75 | 1.00 | 1.50 | 2.50 | 15.00 | 50.00 | — |
| | 1913 | 5,735,405 | 0.75 | 1.00 | 1.50 | 2.50 | 15.00 | 75.00 | — |
| | 1914 | 3,405,958 | 0.75 | 1.00 | 1.50 | 2.50 | 25.00 | 90.00 | — |
| | 1915 | 4,932,134 | 0.75 | 1.00 | 1.50 | 2.50 | 18.00 | 65.00 | — |
| | 1916 | 11,022,367 | 0.50 | 0.65 | 0.90 | 2.00 | 12.00 | 45.00 | — |
| | 1917 | 11,899,254 | 0.50 | 0.65 | 0.90 | 1.50 | 8.00 | 40.00 | — |
| | 1918 | 12,970,798 | 0.50 | 0.65 | 0.90 | 1.50 | 8.00 | 40.00 | — |
| | 1919 | 11,279,634 | 0.50 | 0.65 | 0.90 | 1.50 | 8.00 | 40.00 | — |
| | 1920 | 6,762,247 | 0.50 | 0.65 | 0.90 | 1.50 | 10.00 | 50.00 | — |

**CENT** **Weight:** 3.2400 g. **Composition:** Bronze

| KM | Date | Mintage | VG-8 | F-12 | VF-20 | XF-40 | MS-60 | MS-63 | Proof |
|---|---|---|---|---|---|---|---|---|---|
| 28 | 1920 | 15,483,923 | 0.25 | 0.50 | 1.00 | 2.00 | 7.00 | 30.00 | — |
| | 1921 | 7,601,627 | 0.50 | 0.75 | 1.75 | 3.00 | 18.00 | 90.00 | — |
| | 1922 | 1,243,635 | 8.75 | 10.00 | 14.50 | 22.00 | 130 | 500 | — |
| | 1923 | 1,019,002 | 14.25 | 16.25 | 23.00 | 34.00 | 200 | 1,000 | — |
| | 1924 | 1,593,195 | 3.00 | 4.00 | 5.00 | 10.00 | 70.00 | 300 | — |
| | 1925 | 1,000,622 | 10.00 | 12.00 | 18.75 | 28.00 | 130 | 500 | — |
| | 1926 | 2,143,372 | 2.25 | 3.00 | 4.50 | 8.75 | 65.00 | 250 | — |
| | 1927 | 3,553,928 | 0.90 | 1.25 | 2.25 | 4.00 | 30.00 | 110 | — |
| | 1928 | 9,144,860 | 0.15 | 0.30 | 0.65 | 1.50 | 10.00 | 50.00 | — |
| | 1929 | 12,159,840 | 0.15 | 0.30 | 0.65 | 1.50 | 10.00 | 50.00 | — |
| | 1930 | 2,538,613 | 1.35 | 1.80 | 3.00 | 5.00 | 30.00 | 110 | — |
| | 1931 | 3,842,776 | 0.65 | 1.00 | 1.75 | 3.50 | 25.00 | 100 | — |
| | 1932 | 21,316,190 | 0.15 | 0.20 | 0.50 | 1.50 | 9.00 | 40.00 | — |
| | 1933 | 12,079,310 | 0.15 | 0.20 | 0.50 | 1.50 | 9.00 | 40.00 | — |
| | 1934 | 7,042,358 | 0.20 | 0.30 | 0.75 | 1.50 | 9.00 | 40.00 | — |
| | 1935 | 7,526,400 | 0.20 | 0.30 | 0.75 | 1.50 | 9.00 | 35.00 | — |
| | 1936 | 8,768,769 | 0.15 | 0.20 | 0.75 | 1.50 | 9.00 | 30.00 | — |
| | 1936 dot below date; Rare | 678,823 | — | — | — | — | — | — | — |

**Note:** Only one possible business strike is known to exist. No other examples (or possible business strikes) have ever surfaced.

| KM | Date | Mintage | VG-8 | F-12 | VF-20 | XF-40 | MS-60 | MS-63 | Proof |
|---|---|---|---|---|---|---|---|---|---|
| | 1936 dot below date, specimen, 3 known | — | — | — | — | — | — | — | — |

**Note:** At the David Akers auction of the John Jay Pittman collection (Part 1, 10-97), a gem specimen realized $121,000. At the David Akers auction of the John Jay Pittman collection (Part 3, 10-99), a near choice specimen realized $115,000.

**CENT** Weight: 3.2400 g. **Composition:** Bronze

| KM | Date | Mintage | VG-8 | F-12 | VF-20 | XF-40 | MS-60 | MS-63 | Proof |
|---|---|---|---|---|---|---|---|---|---|
| 32 | 1937 | 10,040,231 | 0.40 | 0.75 | 1.00 | 1.50 | 2.25 | 7.00 | — |
| | 1938 | 18,365,608 | 0.30 | 0.65 | 0.90 | 1.00 | 2.00 | 6.50 | — |
| | 1939 | 21,600,319 | 0.25 | 0.50 | 0.75 | 0.90 | 1.75 | 5.00 | — |
| | 1940 | 85,740,532 | 0.10 | 0.15 | 0.25 | 0.50 | 1.50 | 5.50 | — |
| | 1941 | 56,336,011 | 0.10 | 0.15 | 0.25 | 0.50 | 4.00 | 50.00 | — |
| | 1942 | 76,113,708 | 0.10 | 0.15 | 0.25 | 0.50 | 4.00 | 40.00 | — |
| | 1943 | 89,111,969 | 0.10 | 0.15 | 0.25 | 0.50 | 1.50 | 25.00 | — |
| | 1944 | 44,131,216 | 0.20 | 0.25 | 0.30 | 0.60 | 5.50 | 70.00 | — |
| | 1945 | 77,268,591 | 0.10 | 0.15 | 0.20 | 0.30 | 1.00 | 14.00 | — |
| | 1946 | 56,662,071 | 0.10 | 0.15 | 0.20 | 0.30 | 1.00 | 5.00 | — |
| | 1947 | 31,093,901 | 0.10 | 0.15 | 0.20 | 0.30 | 1.00 | 6.00 | — |
| | 1947 maple leaf | 47,855,448 | 0.10 | 0.15 | 0.20 | 0.30 | 1.00 | 5.00 | — |

**CENT** Weight: 3.2400 g. **Composition:** Bronze **Obverse:** Modified legend

| KM | Date | Mintage | VG-8 | F-12 | VF-20 | XF-40 | MS-60 | MS-63 | Proof |
|---|---|---|---|---|---|---|---|---|---|
| 41 | 1948 | 25,767,779 | — | 0.10 | 0.25 | 0.60 | 2.25 | 20.00 | — |
| | 1949 | 33,128,933 | — | 0.10 | 0.15 | 0.25 | 1.25 | 6.00 | — |
| | 1950 | 60,444,992 | — | 0.10 | 0.15 | 0.25 | 0.85 | 6.00 | — |
| | 1951 | 80,430,379 | — | 0.10 | 0.15 | 0.20 | 0.85 | 8.00 | — |
| | 1952 | 67,631,736 | — | 0.10 | 0.15 | 0.20 | 0.85 | 4.00 | — |

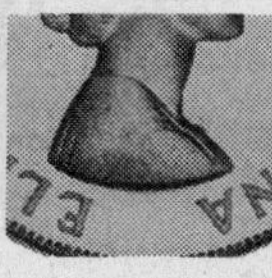

**CENT** Weight: 3.2400 g. **Composition:** Bronze **Obverse:** Elizabeth II effigy **Obv. Designer:** Gillick

| KM | Date | Mintage | VG-8 | F-12 | VF-20 | XF-40 | MS-60 | MS-63 | Proof |
|---|---|---|---|---|---|---|---|---|---|
| 49 | 1953 without strap | 67,806,016 | 0.15 | 0.20 | 0.25 | 0.30 | 0.65 | 1.50 | — |
| | 1953 with strap | Inc. above | 0.50 | 1.00 | 1.50 | 2.50 | 10.00 | 35.00 | — |
| | 1954 with strap | 22,181,760 | 0.10 | 0.15 | 0.30 | 0.40 | 1.00 | 4.00 | — |
| | 1954 without strap, proof-like only | Inc. above | — | — | — | — | 150 | 250 | — |
| | 1955 with strap | 56,403,193 | — | 0.10 | 0.15 | 0.20 | 0.35 | 1.00 | — |
| | 1955 without strap | Inc. above | 80.00 | 110 | 150 | 225 | 400 | 1,000 | — |
| | 1956 | 78,658,535 | — | — | — | 0.10 | 0.50 | 0.90 | — |
| | 1957 | 100,601,792 | — | — | — | 0.10 | 0.25 | 0.50 | — |
| | 1958 | 59,385,679 | — | — | — | 0.10 | 0.25 | 0.50 | — |
| | 1959 | 83,615,343 | — | — | — | 0.10 | 0.25 | 0.30 | — |
| | 1960 | 75,772,775 | — | — | — | 0.10 | 0.25 | 0.30 | — |
| | 1961 | 139,598,404 | — | — | — | — | 0.15 | 0.20 | — |
| | 1962 | 227,244,069 | — | — | — | — | 0.10 | 0.20 | — |
| | 1963 | 279,076,334 | — | — | — | — | 0.10 | 0.20 | — |
| | 1964 | 484,655,322 | — | — | — | — | 0.10 | 0.20 | — |

**CENT** Weight: 3.2400 g. **Composition:** Bronze **Obverse:** Elizabeth II effigy **Obv. Designer:** Machin

| KM | Date | Mintage | VG-8 | F-12 | VF-20 | XF-40 | MS-60 | MS-63 | Proof |
|---|---|---|---|---|---|---|---|---|---|
| 59.1 | 1965 sm. beads, pointed 5 | 304,441,082 | — | — | — | 0.45 | 1.00 | 4.00 | — |
| | 1965 sm. beads, blunt 5 | Inc. above | — | — | — | — | 0.20 | 0.30 | — |
| | 1965 lg. beads, pointed 5 | Inc. above | — | — | 3.00 | 5.00 | 12.00 | 30.00 | — |
| | 1965 lg. beads, blunt 5 | Inc. above | — | — | — | 0.10 | 0.20 | 0.40 | — |
| | 1966 | 184,151,087 | — | — | — | — | 0.10 | 0.20 | — |
| | 1968 | 329,695,772 | — | — | — | — | 0.10 | 0.20 | — |
| | 1969 | 335,240,929 | — | — | — | — | 0.10 | 0.20 | — |
| | 1970 | 311,145,010 | — | — | — | — | 0.10 | 0.20 | — |
| | 1971 | 298,228,936 | — | — | — | — | 0.10 | 0.20 | — |
| | 1972 | 451,304,591 | — | — | — | — | 0.10 | 0.20 | — |
| | 1973 | 457,059,852 | — | — | — | — | 0.10 | 0.20 | — |
| | 1974 | 692,058,489 | — | — | — | — | 0.10 | 0.20 | — |
| | 1975 | 642,318,000 | — | — | — | — | 0.10 | 0.20 | — |
| | 1976 | 701,122,890 | — | — | — | — | 0.10 | 0.20 | — |
| | 1977 | 453,762,670 | — | — | — | — | 0.10 | 0.20 | — |
| | 1978 | 911,170,647 | — | — | — | — | 0.10 | 0.20 | — |

**CENT** Weight: 3.2400 g. **Composition:** Bronze **Obverse:** Elizabeth II effigy. Smaller bust **Obv. Designer:** Machin

| KM | Date | Mintage | VG-8 | F-12 | VF-20 | XF-40 | MS-60 | MS-63 | Proof |
|---|---|---|---|---|---|---|---|---|---|
| 59.2 | 1979 | 754,394,064 | — | — | — | — | 0.10 | 0.20 | — |

**CENT** Weight: 2.8000 g. **Composition:** Bronze **Obverse:** Elizabeth II effigy **Obv. Designer:** Machin **Note:** Reduced weight.

| KM | Date | Mintage | VG-8 | F-12 | VF-20 | XF-40 | MS-60 | MS-63 | Proof |
|---|---|---|---|---|---|---|---|---|---|
| 127 | 1980 | 912,052,318 | — | — | — | — | 0.10 | 0.15 | — |
| | 1981 | 1,209,468,500 | — | — | — | — | 0.10 | 0.15 | — |
| | 1981 Proof | 199,000 | — | — | — | — | — | — | 1.50 |

**CENT** Weight: 2.5000 g. **Composition:** Bronze **Obverse:** Elizabeth II effigy **Obv. Designer:** Machin **Edge:** Multisided. **Note:** Reduced weight.

| KM | Date | Mintage | VG-8 | F-12 | VF-20 | XF-40 | MS-60 | MS-63 | Proof |
|---|---|---|---|---|---|---|---|---|---|
| 132 | 1982 | 911,001,000 | — | — | — | — | 0.10 | 0.15 | — |
| | 1982 Proof | 180,908 | — | — | — | — | — | — | 1.50 |
| | 1983 | 975,510,000 | — | — | — | — | 0.10 | 0.15 | — |
| | 1983 Proof | 168,000 | — | — | — | — | — | — | 1.50 |
| | 1984 | 838,225,000 | — | — | — | — | 0.10 | 0.15 | — |
| | 1984 Proof | 161,602 | — | — | — | — | — | — | 1.50 |
| | 1985 pointed 5 | 771,772,500 | — | — | — | 5.00 | 10.00 | 18.50 | — |
| | 1985 blunt 5 | Inc. above | — | — | — | — | 0.10 | 0.15 | — |
| | 1985 blunt 5, proof | 157,037 | — | — | — | — | — | — | 1.50 |
| | 1986 | 740,335,000 | — | — | — | — | 0.10 | 0.15 | — |
| | 1986 Proof | 175,745 | — | — | — | — | — | — | 1.50 |
| | 1987 | 774,549,000 | — | — | — | — | 0.10 | 0.15 | — |
| | 1987 Proof | 179,004 | — | — | — | — | — | — | 1.50 |
| | 1988 | 482,676,752 | — | — | — | — | 0.10 | 0.15 | — |
| | 1988 Proof | 175,259 | — | — | — | — | — | — | 1.50 |
| | 1989 | 1,077,347,200 | — | — | — | — | 0.10 | 0.15 | — |
| | 1989 Proof | 170,928 | — | — | — | — | — | — | 1.50 |

**CENT** Weight: 2.5000 g. **Composition:** Bronze **Obverse:** Elizabeth II effigy **Obv. Designer:** dePedery-Hunt

| KM | Date | Mintage | VG-8 | F-12 | VF-20 | XF-40 | MS-60 | MS-63 | Proof |
|---|---|---|---|---|---|---|---|---|---|
| 181 | 1990 | 218,035,000 | — | — | — | — | 0.10 | 0.15 | — |
| | 1990 Proof | 140,649 | — | — | — | — | — | — | 2.50 |
| | 1991 | 831,001,000 | — | — | — | — | 0.10 | 0.15 | — |
| | 1991 Proof | 131,888 | — | — | — | — | — | — | 3.50 |
| | 1993 | 752,034,000 | — | — | — | — | 0.10 | 0.15 | — |
| | 1993 Proof | 145,065 | — | — | — | — | — | — | 2.00 |
| | 1994 | 639,516,000 | — | — | — | — | 0.10 | 0.15 | — |
| | 1994 Proof | 146,424 | — | — | — | — | — | — | 2.50 |
| | 1995 | 624,983,000 | — | — | — | — | 0.10 | 0.15 | — |
| | 1996 | 445,746,000 | — | — | — | — | 0.10 | 0.15 | — |
| | 1996 Proof | — | — | — | — | — | — | — | 2.50 |

**CENT** **Composition:** Copper Plated Zinc

| KM | Date | Mintage | VG-8 | F-12 | VF-20 | XF-40 | MS-60 | MS-63 | Proof |
|---|---|---|---|---|---|---|---|---|---|
| 181a | 1996 | 445,746,000 | — | — | — | — | 0.10 | 0.15 | 2.50 |

**CENT** **Composition:** Bronze-Plated Zinc **Edge:** Round and plain.

| KM | Date | Mintage | VG-8 | F-12 | VF-20 | XF-40 | MS-60 | MS-63 | Proof |
|---|---|---|---|---|---|---|---|---|---|
| 289 | 1997 | 506,928,000 | — | — | — | — | 0.10 | 0.15 | — |
| | 1997 Proof | — | — | — | — | — | — | — | 2.75 |
| | 1998 | — | — | — | — | — | 0.10 | 0.15 | — |
| | 1998 Proof | — | — | — | — | — | — | — | 3.00 |
| | 1998W | — | — | — | — | — | — | 1.75 | — |
| | 1999 | — | — | — | — | — | 0.10 | 0.15 | — |
| | 1999 Proof | — | — | — | — | — | — | — | 4.00 |
| | 1999W | — | — | — | — | — | — | — | — |
| | 2000 | — | — | — | — | — | 0.10 | 0.15 | — |
| | 2000W | — | — | — | — | — | — | 1.75 | — |
| | 2000 Proof | — | — | — | — | — | — | — | 4.00 |

**CENT** **Composition:** Bronze

| KM | Date | Mintage | VG-8 | F-12 | VF-20 | XF-40 | MS-60 | MS-63 | Proof |
|---|---|---|---|---|---|---|---|---|---|
| 289a | 1998 In Specimen sets only | — | — | — | — | — | — | 0.75 | — |

**5 CENTS** Weight: 1.1620 g. **Composition:** 0.9250 Silver 0.0346 oz. ASW

| KM | Date | Mintage | VG-8 | F-12 | VF-20 | XF-40 | MS-60 | MS-63 | Proof |
|---|---|---|---|---|---|---|---|---|---|
| 2 | 1901 | 2,000,000 | 2.75 | 4.00 | 8.00 | 18.00 | 100 | 325 | — |

**5 CENTS** Weight: 1.1620 g. **Composition:** 0.9250 Silver 0.0346 oz. ASW

| KM | Date | Mintage | VG-8 | F-12 | VF-20 | XF-40 | MS-60 | MS-63 | Proof |
|---|---|---|---|---|---|---|---|---|---|
| 9 | 1902 | 2,120,000 | 1.50 | 2.00 | 3.25 | 7.00 | 30.00 | 50.00 | — |
| | 1902 lg. broad H | 2,200,000 | 1.50 | 2.00 | 3.25 | 7.00 | 30.00 | 50.00 | — |
| | 1902 sm. narrow H | Inc. above | 5.00 | 9.00 | 20.00 | 35.00 | 80.00 | 150 | — |

**5 CENTS** Weight: 1.1620 g. **Composition:** 0.9250 Silver 0.0346 oz. ASW

| KM | Date | Mintage | VG-8 | F-12 | VF-20 | XF-40 | MS-60 | MS-63 | Proof |
|---|---|---|---|---|---|---|---|---|---|
| 13 | 1903 22 leaves | 1,000,000 | 4.00 | 7.00 | 14.00 | 30.00 | 120 | 280 | — |
| | 1903H 21 leaves | 2,640,000 | 1.75 | 3.00 | 7.00 | 13.00 | 90.00 | 200 | — |
| | 1904 | 2,400,000 | 1.75 | 3.00 | 7.00 | 18.00 | 140 | 400 | — |
| | 1905 | 2,600,000 | 1.75 | 3.00 | 6.00 | 12.00 | 85.00 | 200 | — |
| | 1906 | 3,100,000 | 1.50 | 2.00 | 4.00 | 8.00 | 65.00 | 175 | — |
| | 1907 | 5,200,000 | 1.50 | 2.00 | 4.00 | 7.00 | 45.00 | 125 | — |
| | 1908 | 1,220,524 | 4.00 | 6.50 | 12.00 | 25.00 | 85.00 | 150 | — |
| | 1909 round leaves | 1,983,725 | 2.00 | 2.50 | 7.00 | 15.00 | 125 | 350 | — |
| | 1909 pointed leaves | Inc. above | 6.00 | 11.00 | 25.00 | 50.00 | 300 | 1,000 | — |
| | 1910 pointed leaves | 3,850,325 | 1.50 | 1.75 | 3.25 | 7.00 | 45.00 | 75.00 | — |
| | 1910 round leaves | Inc. above | 8.50 | 13.50 | 28.00 | 70.00 | 320 | 1,100 | — |

**5 CENTS** Weight: 1.1620 g. **Composition:** 0.9250 Silver 0.0346 oz. ASW

| KM | Date | Mintage | VG-8 | F-12 | VF-20 | XF-40 | MS-60 | MS-63 | Proof |
|---|---|---|---|---|---|---|---|---|---|
| 16 | 1911 | 3,692,350 | 1.25 | 2.00 | 4.00 | 8.00 | 50.00 | 85.00 | — |

**5 CENTS** Weight: 1.1620 g. **Composition:** 0.9250 Silver 0.0346 oz. ASW

| KM | Date | Mintage | VG-8 | F-12 | VF-20 | XF-40 | MS-60 | MS-63 | Proof |
|---|---|---|---|---|---|---|---|---|---|
| 22 | 1912 | 5,863,170 | 1.25 | 2.00 | 3.00 | 6.00 | 45.00 | 125 | — |
| | 1913 | 5,488,048 | 1.25 | 1.75 | 2.50 | 5.00 | 20.00 | 40.00 | — |
| | 1914 | 4,202,179 | 1.25 | 2.00 | 3.00 | 6.00 | 45.00 | 110 | — |

| KM | Date | Mintage | VG-8 | F-12 | VF-20 | XF-40 | MS-60 | MS-63 | Proof |
|---|---|---|---|---|---|---|---|---|---|
| | 1915 | 1,172,258 | 5.50 | 10.50 | 20.00 | 40.00 | 175 | 400 | — |
| | 1916 | 2,481,675 | 1.75 | 3.00 | 5.00 | 11.00 | 75.00 | 175 | — |
| | 1917 | 5,521,373 | 1.25 | 1.75 | 2.00 | 4.00 | 25.00 | 60.00 | — |
| | 1918 | 6,052,298 | 1.25 | 1.75 | 2.00 | 4.00 | 25.00 | 50.00 | — |
| | 1919 | 7,835,400 | 1.25 | 1.75 | 2.00 | 4.00 | 25.00 | 50.00 | — |

**5 CENTS** **Weight:** 1.1664 g. **Composition:** 0.8000 Silver .0300 oz. ASW

| KM | Date | Mintage | VG-8 | F-12 | VF-20 | XF-40 | MS-60 | MS-63 | Proof |
|---|---|---|---|---|---|---|---|---|---|
| 22a | 1920 | 10,649,851 | 1.25 | 1.75 | 2.00 | 4.00 | 20.00 | 35.00 | — |
| | 1921 | 2,582,495 | 1,450 | 1,850 | 2,400 | 3,150 | 5,500 | 12,500 | — |

**Note:** Approximately 460 known; balance remelted. Stack's A.G. Carter Jr. Sale (12-89) choice BU, finest known, realized $57,200.

**5 CENTS** **Composition:** Nickel

| KM | Date | Mintage | VG-8 | F-12 | VF-20 | XF-40 | MS-60 | MS-63 | Proof |
|---|---|---|---|---|---|---|---|---|---|
| 29 | 1922 | 4,794,119 | 0.25 | 0.75 | 1.75 | 7.00 | 35.00 | 75.00 | — |
| | 1923 | 2,502,279 | 0.40 | 1.25 | 3.50 | 12.00 | 75.00 | 200 | — |
| | 1924 | 3,105,839 | 0.30 | 0.70 | 2.50 | 7.00 | 60.00 | 150 | — |
| | 1925 | 201,921 | 25.00 | 35.00 | 65.00 | 155 | 800 | 2,500 | — |
| | 1926 near 6 | 938,162 | 1.50 | 4.00 | 12.00 | 40.00 | 300 | 1,200 | — |
| | 1926 far 6 | Inc. above | 60.00 | 85.00 | 150 | 275 | 1,000 | 3,000 | — |
| | 1927 | 5,285,627 | 0.25 | 0.65 | 1.75 | 6.50 | 45.00 | 110 | — |
| | 1928 | 4,577,712 | 0.25 | 0.65 | 1.75 | 6.50 | 40.00 | 90.00 | — |
| | 1929 | 5,611,911 | 0.25 | 0.65 | 1.75 | 6.50 | 45.00 | 130 | — |
| | 1930 | 3,704,673 | 0.25 | 0.65 | 1.75 | 6.50 | 70.00 | 150 | — |
| | 1931 | 5,100,830 | 0.25 | 0.65 | 2.00 | 10.25 | 75.00 | 325 | — |
| | 1932 | 3,198,566 | 0.25 | 0.65 | 2.25 | 10.50 | 75.00 | 200 | — |
| | 1933 | 2,597,867 | 0.40 | 1.00 | 4.00 | 13.00 | 150 | 500 | — |
| | 1934 | 3,827,304 | 0.25 | 0.65 | 3.00 | 10.75 | 80.00 | 275 | — |
| | 1935 | 3,900,000 | 0.25 | 0.65 | 1.75 | 6.50 | 70.00 | 180 | — |
| | 1936 | 4,400,450 | 0.25 | 0.65 | 1.75 | 6.50 | 40.00 | 85.00 | — |

**5 CENTS** **Composition:** Nickel

| KM | Date | Mintage | VG-8 | F-12 | VF-20 | XF-40 | MS-60 | MS-63 | Proof |
|---|---|---|---|---|---|---|---|---|---|
| 33 | 1937 dot | 4,593,263 | 0.20 | 0.30 | 1.25 | 2.50 | 9.00 | 22.00 | — |
| | 1938 | 3,898,974 | 0.20 | 1.00 | 2.00 | 7.00 | 50.00 | 100 | — |
| | 1939 | 5,661,123 | 0.20 | 0.30 | 1.25 | 3.00 | 30.00 | 55.00 | — |
| | 1940 | 13,920,197 | 0.15 | 0.20 | 0.75 | 2.25 | 12.00 | 35.00 | — |
| | 1941 | 8,681,785 | 0.10 | 0.20 | 0.75 | 2.25 | 15.00 | 42.00 | — |
| | 1942 round | 6,847,544 | 0.20 | 0.25 | 0.75 | 1.75 | 12.00 | 35.00 | — |

**5 CENTS** **Composition:** Tombac

| KM | Date | Mintage | VG-8 | F-12 | VF-20 | XF-40 | MS-60 | MS-63 | Proof |
|---|---|---|---|---|---|---|---|---|---|
| 39 | 1942 - 12 sided | 3,396,234 | 0.40 | 0.65 | 1.25 | 1.75 | 3.00 | 9.00 | — |

**5 CENTS** **Composition:** Nickel

| KM | Date | Mintage | VG-8 | F-12 | VF-20 | XF-40 | MS-60 | MS-63 | Proof |
|---|---|---|---|---|---|---|---|---|---|
| 39a | 1946 | 6,952,684 | 0.15 | 0.25 | 0.50 | 2.00 | 8.00 | 18.00 | — |
| | 1947 | 7,603,724 | 0.15 | 0.25 | 0.50 | 1.25 | 6.50 | 12.50 | — |
| | 1947 dot | Inc. above | 12.00 | 15.00 | 22.00 | 50.00 | 150 | 250 | — |
| | 1947 maple leaf | 9,595,124 | 0.15 | 0.25 | 0.50 | 1.25 | 6.00 | 12.00 | — |

**5 CENTS** **Composition:** Nickel **Obverse:** Modified legend

| KM | Date | Mintage | VG-8 | F-12 | VF-20 | XF-40 | MS-60 | MS-63 | Proof |
|---|---|---|---|---|---|---|---|---|---|
| 42 | 1948 | 1,810,789 | 0.40 | 0.50 | 1.00 | 3.00 | 12.00 | 20.00 | — |
| | 1949 | 13,037,090 | 0.15 | 0.20 | 0.35 | 0.75 | 4.00 | 7.00 | — |
| | 1950 | 11,970,521 | 0.15 | 0.20 | 0.35 | 0.75 | 4.00 | 7.00 | — |

**5 CENTS** **Composition:** Chromium And Nickel-Plated Steel

| KM | Date | Mintage | VG-8 | F-12 | VF-20 | XF-40 | MS-60 | MS-63 | Proof |
|---|---|---|---|---|---|---|---|---|---|
| 42a | 1951 Low relief | 4,313,410 | 0.15 | 0.25 | 0.50 | 0.85 | 2.50 | 4.50 | — |

**Note:** "A" in GRATIA points between denticles

| KM | Date | Mintage | VG-8 | F-12 | VF-20 | XF-40 | MS-60 | MS-63 | Proof |
|---|---|---|---|---|---|---|---|---|---|
| | 1951 High relief | Inc. above | 325 | 425 | 550 | 950 | 1,400 | 1,850 | — |

**Note:** "A" in GRATIA points to a denticle

| KM | Date | Mintage | VG-8 | F-12 | VF-20 | XF-40 | MS-60 | MS-63 | Proof |
|---|---|---|---|---|---|---|---|---|---|
| | 1952 | 10,891,148 | 0.15 | 0.25 | 0.50 | 0.85 | 3.00 | 5.00 | — |

**5 CENTS** **Composition:** Chromium And Nickel-Plated Steel **Obverse:** Elizabeth II effigy **Obv. Designer:** Gillick **Shape:** 12-sided

| KM | Date | Mintage | VG-8 | F-12 | VF-20 | XF-40 | MS-60 | MS-63 | Proof |
|---|---|---|---|---|---|---|---|---|---|
| 50 | 1953 without strap | 16,635,552 | 0.15 | 0.25 | 0.40 | 1.00 | 3.00 | 4.50 | — |
| | 1953 without strap, near leaf | Inc. above | 75.00 | 125 | 175 | 300 | 600 | 1,500 | — |
| | 1953 with strap, far leaf | Inc. above | 75.00 | 100 | 150 | 250 | 450 | 1,500 | — |
| | 1953 with strap | Inc. above | 0.15 | 0.25 | 0.45 | 1.00 | 3.50 | 7.00 | — |
| | 1954 | 6,998,662 | 0.15 | 0.25 | 0.50 | 1.00 | 4.00 | 8.00 | — |

**5 CENTS** **Composition:** Nickel

| KM | Date | Mintage | VG-8 | F-12 | VF-20 | XF-40 | MS-60 | MS-63 | Proof |
|---|---|---|---|---|---|---|---|---|---|
| 50a | 1955 | 5,355,028 | 0.15 | 0.25 | 0.40 | 0.75 | 2.50 | 4.50 | — |
| | 1956 | 9,399,854 | — | 0.20 | 0.30 | 0.45 | 1.50 | 3.00 | — |
| | 1957 | 7,387,703 | — | — | 0.25 | 0.30 | 1.25 | 3.00 | — |
| | 1958 | 7,607,521 | — | — | 0.25 | 0.30 | 1.25 | 3.00 | — |
| | 1959 | 11,552,523 | — | — | — | 0.20 | 0.40 | 1.00 | — |
| | 1960 | 37,157,433 | — | — | — | 0.15 | 0.35 | 0.70 | — |
| | 1961 | 47,889,051 | — | — | — | — | 0.20 | 0.40 | — |
| | 1962 | 46,307,305 | — | — | — | — | 0.20 | 0.40 | — |

**5 CENTS** **Composition:** Nickel **Shape:** Round

| KM | Date | Mintage | VG-8 | F-12 | VF-20 | XF-40 | MS-60 | MS-63 | Proof |
|---|---|---|---|---|---|---|---|---|---|
| 57 | 1963 | 43,970,320 | — | — | — | — | 0.20 | 0.35 | — |
| | 1964 | 78,075,068 | — | — | — | — | 0.20 | 0.35 | — |
| | 1964 extra water line | — | 8.00 | 10.00 | 12.00 | 15.00 | 25.00 | 40.00 | — |

**5 CENTS** **Composition:** Nickel **Obverse:** Elizabeth II effigy **Obv. Designer:** Machin

| KM | Date | Mintage | VG-8 | F-12 | VF-20 | XF-40 | MS-60 | MS-63 | Proof |
|---|---|---|---|---|---|---|---|---|---|
| 60.1 | 1965 | 84,876,018 | — | — | — | — | 0.20 | 0.30 | — |
| | 1966 | 27,976,648 | — | — | — | — | 0.20 | 0.30 | — |
| | 1968 | 101,930,379 | — | — | — | — | 0.20 | 0.30 | — |
| | 1969 | 27,830,229 | — | — | — | — | 0.20 | 0.30 | — |
| | 1970 | 5,726,010 | — | — | — | 0.20 | 0.35 | 0.75 | — |
| | 1971 | 27,312,609 | — | — | — | — | 0.20 | 0.30 | — |
| | 1972 | 62,417,387 | — | — | — | — | 0.20 | 0.30 | — |
| | 1973 | 53,507,435 | — | — | — | — | 0.20 | 0.30 | — |
| | 1974 | 94,704,645 | — | — | — | — | 0.20 | 0.30 | — |
| | 1975 | 138,882,000 | — | — | — | — | 0.20 | 0.30 | — |
| | 1976 | 55,140,213 | — | — | — | — | 0.20 | 0.30 | — |
| | 1977 | 89,120,791 | — | — | — | — | 0.20 | 0.30 | — |
| | 1978 | 137,079,273 | — | — | — | — | 0.20 | 0.30 | — |

**5 CENTS** **Composition:** Nickel **Obverse:** Smaller bust

| KM | Date | Mintage | VG-8 | F-12 | VF-20 | XF-40 | MS-60 | MS-63 | Proof |
|---|---|---|---|---|---|---|---|---|---|
| 60.2 | 1979 | 186,295,825 | — | — | — | — | 0.20 | 0.30 | — |
| | 1980 | 134,878,000 | — | — | — | — | 0.20 | 0.30 | — |
| | 1981 | 99,107,900 | — | — | — | — | 0.20 | 0.30 | — |
| | 1981 Proof | 199,000 | — | — | — | — | — | — | 1.50 |

**5 CENTS** **Composition:** Copper-Nickel

| KM | Date | Mintage | VG-8 | F-12 | VF-20 | XF-40 | MS-60 | MS-63 | Proof |
|---|---|---|---|---|---|---|---|---|---|
| 60.2a | 1982 | 64,924,400 | — | — | — | — | 0.20 | 0.30 | — |
| | 1982 Proof | 180,908 | — | — | — | — | — | — | 1.50 |
| | 1983 | 72,596,000 | — | — | — | — | 0.20 | 0.30 | — |
| | 1983 Proof | 168,000 | — | — | — | — | — | — | 1.50 |
| | 1984 | 84,088,000 | — | — | — | — | 0.20 | 0.30 | — |
| | 1984 Proof | 161,602 | — | — | — | — | — | — | 1.50 |
| | 1985 | 126,618,000 | — | — | — | — | 0.20 | 0.30 | — |
| | 1985 Proof | 157,037 | — | — | — | — | — | — | 1.50 |
| | 1986 | 156,104,000 | — | — | — | — | 0.20 | 0.30 | — |
| | 1986 Proof | 175,745 | — | — | — | — | — | — | 1.50 |
| | 1987 | 106,299,000 | — | — | — | — | 0.10 | 0.20 | — |
| | 1987 Proof | 179,004 | — | — | — | — | — | — | 1.50 |
| | 1988 | 75,025,000 | — | — | — | — | 0.10 | 0.20 | — |
| | 1988 Proof | 175,259 | — | — | — | — | — | — | 1.50 |
| | 1989 | 141,570,538 | — | — | — | — | 0.10 | 0.20 | — |
| | 1989 Proof | 170,928 | — | — | — | — | — | — | 1.50 |

**5 CENTS** **Composition:** Copper-Nickel **Obverse:** Elizabeth II effigy **Obv. Designer:** dePedery-Hunt

| KM | Date | Mintage | VG-8 | F-12 | VF-20 | XF-40 | MS-60 | MS-63 | Proof |
|---|---|---|---|---|---|---|---|---|---|
| 182 | 1990 | 42,537,000 | — | — | — | — | 0.10 | 0.20 | — |
| | 1990 Proof | 140,649 | — | — | — | — | — | — | 2.50 |
| | 1991 | 10,931,000 | — | — | — | — | 0.20 | 0.70 | — |
| | 1991 Proof | 131,888 | — | — | — | — | — | — | 7.00 |

| KM | Date | Mintage | VG-8 | F-12 | VF-20 | XF-40 | MS-60 | MS-63 | Proof |
|---|---|---|---|---|---|---|---|---|---|
| | 1993 | 86,877,000 | — | — | — | — | 0.10 | 0.20 | — |
| | 1993 Proof | 143,065 | — | — | — | — | — | — | 2.50 |
| | 1994 | 99,352,000 | — | — | — | — | 0.10 | 0.20 | — |
| | 1994 Proof | 146,424 | — | — | — | — | — | — | 3.00 |
| | 1995 | 78,528,000 | — | — | — | — | 0.10 | 0.20 | — |
| | 1995 Proof | 50,000 | — | — | — | — | — | — | 2.50 |
| | 1996 far 6 | 36,686,000 | — | — | — | — | 0.75 | 1.50 | — |
| | 1996 near 6 | Inc. above | — | — | — | — | 0.10 | 0.20 | — |
| | 1996 Proof | — | — | — | — | — | — | — | 2.50 |
| | 1997 Proof | — | — | — | — | — | — | — | 2.50 |
| | 1997 | 27,354,000 | — | — | — | — | 0.10 | 0.20 | — |
| | 1998 | 156,873,000 | — | — | — | — | 0.10 | 0.20 | — |
| | 1998 Proof | — | — | — | — | — | — | — | 2.50 |
| | 1998W | — | — | — | — | — | — | 1.50 | — |
| | 1999 | 124,861,000 | — | — | — | — | 0.10 | 0.20 | — |
| | 1999 Proof | — | — | — | — | — | — | — | 2.50 |
| | 1999W | — | — | — | — | — | — | — | — |
| | 2000 Proof | — | — | — | — | — | — | — | 2.50 |
| | 2000 | 108,514,000 | — | — | — | — | 0.10 | 0.20 | — |
| | 2000W | — | — | — | — | — | — | 1.50 | — |
| | 2001 Proof | — | — | — | — | — | — | — | 2.50 |
| | 2001 | — | — | — | — | — | 0.10 | 0.20 | — |

**5 CENTS** **Weight:** 3.9000 g. **Composition:** Nickel Plated Steel **Obverse:** Queen's head right. **Reverse:** Beaver. **Edge:** Reeded. **Size:** 21.2 mm.

| KM | Date | Mintage | VG-8 | F-12 | VF-20 | XF-40 | MS-60 | MS-63 | Proof |
|---|---|---|---|---|---|---|---|---|---|
| 182b | 1999 P | Est. 20,000 | — | — | — | — | — | 15.00 | — |
| | 2000 P | Est. 2,300,000 | — | — | — | — | 1.50 | 2.25 | — |
| | 2001 P | — | — | — | — | — | 0.20 | 0.35 | — |
| | 2002 P | — | — | — | — | — | 0.20 | 0.35 | — |

**5 CENTS** **Weight:** 5.3500 g. **Composition:** 0.9250 Silver 0.1591 oz. ASW

| KM | Date | Mintage | VG-8 | F-12 | VF-20 | XF-40 | MS-60 | MS-63 | Proof |
|---|---|---|---|---|---|---|---|---|---|
| 182a | 1999 | — | — | — | — | — | — | — | 5.00 |
| | 2000 | — | — | — | — | — | — | — | 5.00 |
| | 2001 | — | — | — | — | — | — | — | 5.00 |

**10 CENTS** **Weight:** 2.3240 g. **Composition:** 0.9250 Silver 0.0691 oz. ASW **Obverse:** Victoria bust left

| KM | Date | Mintage | VG-8 | F-12 | VF-20 | XF-40 | MS-60 | MS-63 | Proof |
|---|---|---|---|---|---|---|---|---|---|
| 3 | 1901 | 1,200,000 | 6.75 | 10.50 | 25.00 | 60.00 | 150 | 390 | — |

**10 CENTS** **Weight:** 2.3240 g. **Composition:** 0.9250 Silver 0.0691 oz. ASW **Obverse:** Edward VII bust right

| KM | Date | Mintage | VG-8 | F-12 | VF-20 | XF-40 | MS-60 | MS-63 | Proof |
|---|---|---|---|---|---|---|---|---|---|
| 10 | 1902 | 720,000 | 3.50 | 9.00 | 20.00 | 50.00 | 250 | 650 | — |
| | 1902H | 1,100,000 | 2.75 | 5.00 | 12.50 | 28.00 | 75.00 | 200 | — |
| | 1903 | 500,000 | 8.00 | 20.00 | 50.00 | 150 | 800 | 1,900 | — |
| | 1903H | 1,320,000 | 4.50 | 7.00 | 20.00 | 42.00 | 200 | 450 | — |
| | 1904 | 1,000,000 | 4.50 | 9.00 | 30.00 | 65.00 | 250 | 450 | — |
| | 1905 | 1,000,000 | 4.00 | 10.00 | 30.00 | 80.00 | 350 | 800 | — |
| | 1906 | 1,700,000 | 2.75 | 7.50 | 15.00 | 40.00 | 200 | 400 | — |
| | 1907 | 2,620,000 | 2.75 | 7.50 | 15.00 | 30.00 | 180 | 350 | — |
| | 1908 | 776,666 | 5.00 | 10.00 | 27.00 | 65.00 | 180 | 250 | — |
| | 1909 Victorian leaves, similar to 1902-1908 coinage | 1,697,200 | 3.50 | 9.00 | 25.00 | 60.00 | 285 | 800 | — |
| | 1909 broad leaves, similar to 1910-1912 coinage | Inc. above | 5.50 | 12.00 | 30.00 | 70.00 | 375 | 1,000 | — |
| | 1910 | 4,468,331 | 2.75 | 5.00 | 12.50 | 28.00 | 100 | 250 | — |

**10 CENTS** **Weight:** 2.3240 g. **Composition:** 0.9250 Silver 0.0691 oz. ASW

| KM | Date | Mintage | VG-8 | F-12 | VF-20 | XF-40 | MS-60 | MS-63 | Proof |
|---|---|---|---|---|---|---|---|---|---|
| 17 | 1911 | 2,737,584 | 3.00 | 7.00 | 12.00 | 30.00 | 80.00 | 180 | — |

**10 CENTS** **Weight:** 2.3240 g. **Composition:** 0.9250 Silver 0.0691 oz. ASW

| KM | Date | Mintage | VG-8 | F-12 | VF-20 | XF-40 | MS-60 | MS-63 | Proof |
|---|---|---|---|---|---|---|---|---|---|
| 23 | 1912 | 3,235,557 | 1.75 | 2.50 | 6.00 | 22.00 | 150 | 400 | — |
| | 1913 sm. leaves | 3,613,937 | 1.50 | 2.25 | 5.00 | 17.50 | 80.00 | 250 | — |
| | 1913 lg. leaves | Inc. above | 70.00 | 125 | 250 | 650 | 4,000 | 10,000 | — |
| | 1914 | 2,549,811 | 1.50 | 2.50 | 5.50 | 18.50 | 80.00 | 350 | — |
| | 1915 | 688,057 | 4.00 | 10.00 | 22.00 | 70.00 | 225 | 550 | — |
| | 1916 | 4,218,114 | 1.25 | 1.50 | 4.00 | 11.00 | 60.00 | 200 | — |
| | 1917 | 5,011,988 | 1.00 | 1.50 | 3.00 | 8.75 | 40.00 | 70.00 | — |
| | 1918 | 5,133,602 | 1.00 | 1.50 | 3.00 | 6.00 | 35.00 | 65.00 | — |
| | 1919 | 7,877,722 | 1.00 | 1.50 | 3.00 | 6.00 | 35.00 | 65.00 | — |

**10 CENTS** **Weight:** 2.3328 g. **Composition:** 0.8000 Silver 0.0600 oz. ASW

| KM | Date | Mintage | VG-8 | F-12 | VF-20 | XF-40 | MS-60 | MS-63 | Proof |
|---|---|---|---|---|---|---|---|---|---|
| 23a | 1920 | 6,305,345 | 1.00 | 1.50 | 3.00 | 8.00 | 40.00 | 75.00 | — |
| | 1921 | 2,469,562 | 1.25 | 2.00 | 4.00 | 12.50 | 50.00 | 150 | — |
| | 1928 | 2,458,602 | 1.00 | 1.75 | 4.00 | 8.00 | 40.00 | 100 | — |
| | 1929 | 3,253,888 | 1.00 | 2.25 | 3.50 | 8.00 | 40.00 | 90.00 | — |
| | 1930 | 1,831,043 | 1.00 | 2.50 | 4.50 | 9.00 | 40.00 | 90.00 | — |
| | 1931 | 2,067,421 | 1.00 | 1.75 | 4.00 | 8.00 | 40.00 | 90.00 | — |
| | 1932 | 1,154,317 | 1.50 | 2.50 | 6.00 | 15.00 | 60.00 | 120 | — |
| | 1933 | 672,368 | 2.00 | 3.00 | 8.00 | 25.00 | 100 | 275 | — |
| | 1934 | 409,067 | 3.00 | 6.00 | 16.00 | 40.00 | 200 | 400 | — |
| | 1935 | 384,056 | 3.50 | 6.00 | 15.00 | 40.00 | 200 | 400 | — |
| | 1936 | 2,460,871 | 0.60 | 1.25 | 3.00 | 6.00 | 30.00 | 65.00 | — |
| | 1936 dot on rev. Specimen, 4 known | — | — | — | — | — | — | — | — |

**Note:** At the David Akers sale of the John Jay Pittman collection, Part 1, 10-97, a gem specimen realized $120,000.

**10 CENTS** **Weight:** 2.3328 g. **Composition:** 0.8000 Silver 0.0600 oz. ASW

| KM | Date | Mintage | VG-8 | F-12 | VF-20 | XF-40 | MS-60 | MS-63 | Proof |
|---|---|---|---|---|---|---|---|---|---|
| 34 | 1937 | 2,500,095 | 0.50 | 1.00 | 2.25 | 3.75 | 8.00 | 12.00 | — |
| | 1938 | 4,197,323 | 1.00 | 2.00 | 3.25 | 6.50 | 40.00 | 55.00 | — |
| | 1939 | 5,501,748 | 0.70 | 1.50 | 2.50 | 5.00 | 30.00 | 40.00 | — |
| | 1940 | 16,526,470 | BV | 0.50 | 1.50 | 3.00 | 10.00 | 20.00 | — |
| | 1941 | 8,716,386 | BV | 1.50 | 2.50 | 6.00 | 25.00 | 60.00 | — |
| | 1942 | 10,214,011 | BV | 0.50 | 1.25 | 4.00 | 20.00 | 30.00 | — |
| | 1943 | 21,143,229 | BV | 0.50 | 1.25 | 4.00 | 11.00 | 20.00 | — |
| | 1944 | 9,383,582 | BV | 0.50 | 1.50 | 4.50 | 15.00 | 25.00 | — |
| | 1945 | 10,979,570 | BV | 0.50 | 1.25 | 4.00 | 11.00 | 15.00 | — |
| | 1946 | 6,300,066 | BV | 1.00 | 2.00 | 4.50 | 20.00 | 30.00 | — |
| | 1947 | 4,431,926 | BV | 1.25 | 2.50 | 6.00 | 20.00 | 30.00 | — |
| | 1947 maple leaf | 9,638,793 | BV | 0.50 | 1.50 | 3.00 | 7.00 | 10.00 | — |

**10 CENTS** **Weight:** 2.3328 g. **Composition:** 0.8000 Silver 0.0600 oz. ASW **Obverse:** Modified legend

| KM | Date | Mintage | VG-8 | F-12 | VF-20 | XF-40 | MS-60 | MS-63 | Proof |
|---|---|---|---|---|---|---|---|---|---|
| 43 | 1948 | 422,741 | 2.00 | 3.50 | 7.50 | 13.00 | 30.00 | 45.00 | — |
| | 1949 | 11,336,172 | — | BV | 0.85 | 2.00 | 6.00 | 10.00 | — |
| | 1950 | 17,823,075 | — | BV | 0.65 | 1.50 | 5.00 | 7.00 | — |
| | 1951 | 15,079,265 | — | BV | 0.50 | 1.50 | 4.00 | 7.00 | — |
| | 1952 | 10,474,455 | — | BV | 0.50 | 1.50 | 3.00 | 5.00 | — |

**10 CENTS** **Weight:** 2.3328 g. **Composition:** 0.8000 Silver 0.0600 oz. ASW **Obverse:** Elizabeth II effigy **Obv. Designer:** Gillick

| KM | Date | Mintage | VG-8 | F-12 | VF-20 | XF-40 | MS-60 | MS-63 | Proof |
|---|---|---|---|---|---|---|---|---|---|
| 51 | 1953 without straps | 17,706,395 | — | — | BV | 1.25 | 2.00 | 4.00 | — |
| | 1953 with straps | Inc. above | — | — | BV | 1.25 | 3.00 | 5.00 | — |
| | 1954 | 4,493,150 | — | BV | 1.00 | 2.25 | 5.00 | 8.00 | — |
| | 1955 | 12,237,294 | — | — | BV | 0.75 | 2.00 | 4.00 | — |
| | 1956 | 16,732,844 | — | — | BV | 0.75 | 2.00 | 3.50 | — |
| | 1956 dot below date | Inc. above | — | 1.00 | 2.00 | 3.00 | 8.00 | 15.00 | — |
| | 1957 | 16,110,229 | — | — | — | 0.70 | 1.00 | 1.50 | — |
| | 1958 | 10,621,236 | — | — | — | 0.70 | 1.00 | 1.50 | — |
| | 1959 | 19,691,433 | — | — | — | 0.70 | 0.75 | 1.25 | — |
| | 1960 | 45,446,835 | — | — | — | BV | 0.50 | 1.00 | — |
| | 1961 | 26,850,859 | — | — | — | BV | 0.50 | 1.00 | — |
| | 1962 | 41,864,335 | — | — | — | BV | 0.50 | 1.00 | — |
| | 1963 | 41,916,208 | — | — | — | BV | 0.50 | 1.00 | — |
| | 1964 | 49,518,549 | — | — | — | BV | 0.50 | 1.00 | — |

**10 CENTS** **Weight:** 2.3328 g. **Composition:** 0.8000 Silver 0.0600 oz. ASW **Obverse:** Elizabeth II effigy **Obv. Designer:** Machin

| KM | Date | Mintage | VG-8 | F-12 | VF-20 | XF-40 | MS-60 | MS-63 | Proof |
|---|---|---|---|---|---|---|---|---|---|
| 61 | 1965 | 56,965,392 | — | — | — | BV | 0.50 | 0.75 | — |
| | 1966 | 34,567,898 | — | — | — | BV | 0.50 | 0.75 | — |

OTTAWA

**10 CENTS** **Weight:** 2.3328 g. **Composition:** 0.8000 Silver 0.0600 oz. ASW

| KM | Date | Mintage | VG-8 | F-12 | VF-20 | XF-40 | MS-60 | MS-63 | Proof |
|---|---|---|---|---|---|---|---|---|---|
| 72 | 1968 Ottawa reeding | 70,460,000 | — | — | — | BV | 0.50 | 0.75 | — |

**10 CENTS** **Composition:** Nickel

| KM | Date | Mintage | VG-8 | F-12 | VF-20 | XF-40 | MS-60 | MS-63 | Proof |
|---|---|---|---|---|---|---|---|---|---|
| 72a | 1968 Ottawa reeding | 87,412,930 | — | — | — | 0.15 | 0.25 | 0.35 | — |

**10 CENTS** **Composition:** Nickel

| KM | Date | Mintage | VG-8 | F-12 | VF-20 | XF-40 | MS-60 | MS-63 | Proof |
|---|---|---|---|---|---|---|---|---|---|
| 73 | 1968 Philadelphia reeding | 85,170,000 | — | — | — | 0.15 | 0.25 | 0.35 | — |
| | 1969 lg. date, lg. ship, 10-20 known | — | — | 4,750 | 6,600 | 10,000 | 14,150 | — | — |

**10 CENTS** **Composition:** Nickel **Reverse:** Redesigned smaller ship

| KM | Date | Mintage | VG-8 | F-12 | VF-20 | XF-40 | MS-60 | MS-63 | Proof |
|---|---|---|---|---|---|---|---|---|---|
| 77.1 | 1969 | 55,833,929 | — | — | — | 0.15 | 0.25 | 0.35 | — |
| | 1970 | 5,249,296 | — | — | — | 0.25 | 0.45 | 0.95 | — |
| | 1971 | 41,016,968 | — | — | — | 0.15 | 0.25 | 0.35 | — |
| | 1972 | 60,169,387 | — | — | — | 0.15 | 0.25 | 0.35 | — |
| | 1973 | 167,715,435 | — | — | — | 0.15 | 0.25 | 0.35 | — |
| | 1974 | 201,566,565 | — | — | — | 0.15 | 0.25 | 0.35 | — |
| | 1975 | 207,680,000 | — | — | — | 0.15 | 0.25 | 0.35 | — |
| | 1976 | 95,018,533 | — | — | — | 0.15 | 0.25 | 0.35 | — |
| | 1977 | 128,452,206 | — | — | — | 0.15 | 0.25 | 0.35 | — |
| | 1978 | 170,366,431 | — | — | — | 0.15 | 0.25 | 0.35 | — |

**10 CENTS** **Composition:** Nickel **Obverse:** Smaller bust

| KM | Date | Mintage | VG-8 | F-12 | VF-20 | XF-40 | MS-60 | MS-63 | Proof |
|---|---|---|---|---|---|---|---|---|---|
| 77.2 | 1979 | 237,321,321 | — | — | — | 0.15 | 0.25 | 0.35 | — |
| | 1980 | 170,111,533 | — | — | — | 0.15 | 0.25 | 0.35 | — |
| | 1981 | 123,912,900 | — | — | — | 0.15 | 0.25 | 0.35 | — |
| | 1981 Proof | 199,000 | — | — | — | — | — | — | 1.50 |
| | 1982 | 93,475,000 | — | — | — | 0.15 | 0.25 | 0.35 | — |
| | 1982 Proof | 180,908 | — | — | — | — | — | — | 1.50 |
| | 1983 | 111,065,000 | — | — | — | 0.15 | 0.25 | 0.35 | — |
| | 1983 Proof | 168,000 | — | — | — | — | — | — | 1.50 |
| | 1984 | 121,690,000 | — | — | — | 0.15 | 0.25 | 0.35 | — |
| | 1984 Proof | 161,602 | — | — | — | — | — | — | 1.50 |
| | 1985 | 143,025,000 | — | — | — | 0.15 | 0.25 | 0.35 | — |
| | 1985 Proof | 157,037 | — | — | — | — | — | — | 1.50 |
| | 1986 | 168,620,000 | — | — | — | 0.15 | 0.25 | 0.35 | — |
| | 1986 Proof | 175,745 | — | — | — | — | — | — | 1.50 |
| | 1987 | 147,309,000 | — | — | — | 0.15 | 0.25 | 0.35 | — |
| | 1987 Proof | 179,004 | — | — | — | — | — | — | 1.50 |
| | 1988 | 162,998,558 | — | — | — | 0.15 | 0.25 | 0.35 | — |
| | 1988 Proof | 175,259 | — | — | — | — | — | — | 1.50 |
| | 1989 | 199,104,414 | — | — | — | 0.15 | 0.25 | 0.35 | — |
| | 1989 Proof | 170,528 | — | — | — | — | — | — | 1.50 |

**10 CENTS** **Composition:** Nickel **Obverse:** Elizabeth II effigy **Obv. Designer:** dePedery-Hunt

| KM | Date | Mintage | VG-8 | F-12 | VF-20 | XF-40 | MS-60 | MS-63 | Proof |
|---|---|---|---|---|---|---|---|---|---|
| 183 | 1990 | 65,023,000 | — | — | — | 0.15 | 0.25 | 0.35 | — |
| | 1990 Proof | 140,649 | — | — | — | — | — | — | 2.50 |
| | 1991 | 50,397,000 | — | — | — | 0.15 | 0.25 | 0.35 | — |
| | 1991 Proof | 131,888 | — | — | — | — | — | — | 4.00 |
| | 1993 | 135,569,000 | — | — | — | 0.15 | 0.25 | 0.35 | — |
| | 1993 Proof | 143,065 | — | — | — | — | — | — | 2.00 |
| | 1994 | 145,800,000 | — | — | — | 0.15 | 0.25 | 0.35 | — |
| | 1994 Proof | 146,424 | — | — | — | — | — | — | 2.50 |
| | 1995 | 123,875,000 | — | — | — | 0.15 | 0.25 | 0.35 | — |
| | 1995 Proof | 50,000 | — | — | — | — | — | — | 2.50 |
| | 1996 Proof | — | — | — | — | — | — | — | — |
| | 1996 | 51,814,000 | — | — | — | — | — | — | — |
| | 1997 | 203,514,000 | — | — | — | — | — | — | — |
| | 1997 Proof | — | — | — | — | — | — | — | — |
| | 1998 Proof | — | — | — | — | — | — | — | — |
| | 1998 | 203,514,000 | — | — | — | 0.15 | 0.25 | 0.35 | — |
| | 1998W | — | — | — | — | — | — | 1.50 | — |
| | 1999 | 258,462,000 | — | — | — | 0.15 | 0.25 | 0.35 | — |
| | 1999 Proof | — | — | — | — | — | — | — | — |
| | 2000 Proof | — | — | — | — | — | — | — | — |
| | 2000 | 159,125,000 | — | — | — | 0.15 | 0.25 | 0.35 | — |
| | 2000W | — | — | — | — | — | — | 1.50 | — |

**10 CENTS** **Weight:** 2.4000 g. **Composition:** 0.9250 Silver 0.0713 oz. ASW

| KM | Date | Mintage | VG-8 | F-12 | VF-20 | XF-40 | MS-60 | MS-63 | Proof |
|---|---|---|---|---|---|---|---|---|---|
| 183a | 1998 Proof | — | — | — | — | — | — | — | 4.00 |
| | 19980 Proof | — | — | — | — | — | — | — | 4.00 |
| | 1999 Proof | — | — | — | — | — | — | — | 5.00 |
| | 2000 Proof | — | — | — | — | — | — | — | 5.00 |
| | 2001 Proof | — | — | — | — | — | — | — | 5.00 |

**10 CENTS** **Composition:** Nickel Plated Steel **Obverse:** Queen's head right. **Reverse:** Sailboat. **Edge:** Reeded. **Size:** 18 mm.

| KM | Date | Mintage | VG-8 | F-12 | VF-20 | XF-40 | MS-60 | MS-63 | Proof |
|---|---|---|---|---|---|---|---|---|---|
| 183b | 1999 P | Est. 20,000 | — | — | — | — | — | 15.00 | — |
| | 2000 P | — | — | — | — | — | 0.30 | 0.65 | — |
| | 2001 P | — | — | — | — | — | 0.30 | 0.65 | — |
| | 2002 P | — | — | — | — | — | — | 0.50 | — |

**25 CENTS** **Weight:** 5.8100 g. **Composition:** 0.9250 Silver 0.1728 oz. ASW

| KM | Date | Mintage | VG-8 | F-12 | VF-20 | XF-40 | MS-60 | MS-63 | Proof |
|---|---|---|---|---|---|---|---|---|---|
| 5 | 1901 | 640,000 | 6.00 | 9.75 | 27.00 | 80.00 | 350 | 975 | — |

**25 CENTS** **Weight:** 5.8100 g. **Composition:** 0.9250 Silver 0.1728 oz. ASW

| KM | Date | Mintage | VG-8 | F-12 | VF-20 | XF-40 | MS-60 | MS-63 | Proof |
|---|---|---|---|---|---|---|---|---|---|
| 11 | 1902 | 464,000 | 7.00 | 12.00 | 35.00 | 110 | 500 | 1,450 | — |
| | 1902H | 800,000 | 4.00 | 7.25 | 32.00 | 60.00 | 200 | 400 | — |
| | 1903 | 846,150 | 5.00 | 12.00 | 35.00 | 110 | 400 | 1,450 | — |
| | 1904 | 400,000 | 10.00 | 28.00 | 80.00 | 250 | 1,250 | 4,000 | — |
| | 1905 | 800,000 | 5.50 | 15.00 | 65.00 | 160 | 1,350 | 5,000 | — |
| | 1906 large crown | 1,237,843 | 5.00 | 7.25 | 27.00 | 70.00 | 350 | 1,200 | — |
| | 1906 small crown; Rare | Inc. above | — | — | — | — | — | — | — |
| | 1907 | 2,088,000 | 4.00 | 7.25 | 27.00 | 70.00 | 325 | 1,000 | — |
| | 1908 | 495,016 | 6.00 | 12.00 | 45.00 | 125 | 300 | 700 | — |
| | 1909 | 1,335,929 | 5.00 | 9.00 | 40.00 | 150 | 485 | 1,450 | — |

**25 CENTS** **Weight:** 5.8319 g. **Composition:** 0.9250 Silver 0.1734 oz. ASW

| KM | Date | Mintage | VG-8 | F-12 | VF-20 | XF-40 | MS-60 | MS-63 | Proof |
|---|---|---|---|---|---|---|---|---|---|
| 11a | 1910 | 3,577,569 | 3.00 | 7.25 | 26.00 | 60.00 | 200 | 500 | — |

**25 CENTS** **Weight:** 5.8319 g. **Composition:** 0.9250 Silver 0.1734 oz. ASW

| KM | Date | Mintage | VG-8 | F-12 | VF-20 | XF-40 | MS-60 | MS-63 | Proof |
|---|---|---|---|---|---|---|---|---|---|
| 18 | 1911 | 1,721,341 | 4.00 | 12.00 | 25.00 | 60.00 | 200 | 350 | — |

**25 CENTS** **Weight:** 5.8319 g. **Composition:** 0.9250 Silver 0.1734 oz. ASW

| KM | Date | Mintage | VG-8 | F-12 | VF-20 | XF-40 | MS-60 | MS-63 | Proof |
|---|---|---|---|---|---|---|---|---|---|
| 24 | 1912 | 2,544,199 | 2.25 | 3.50 | 10.00 | 30.00 | 250 | 1,000 | — |
| | 1913 | 2,213,595 | 2.25 | 3.50 | 10.00 | 30.00 | 200 | 850 | — |
| | 1914 | 1,215,397 | 2.50 | 4.00 | 15.00 | 40.00 | 400 | 1,500 | — |
| | 1915 | 242,382 | 6.00 | 22.00 | 95.00 | 300 | 1,750 | 5,000 | — |
| | 1916 | 1,462,566 | 1.75 | 3.25 | 10.00 | 25.00 | 150 | 500 | — |
| | 1917 | 3,365,644 | 1.75 | 3.00 | 7.00 | 15.00 | 100 | 175 | — |
| | 1918 | 4,175,649 | 1.75 | 3.00 | 6.00 | 15.00 | 75.00 | 150 | — |
| | 1919 | 5,852,262 | 1.75 | 3.00 | 6.00 | 15.00 | 75.00 | 150 | — |

**25 CENTS** **Weight:** 5.8319 g. **Composition:** 0.8000 Silver 0.1500 oz. ASW

| KM | Date | Mintage | VG-8 | F-12 | VF-20 | XF-40 | MS-60 | MS-63 | Proof |
|---|---|---|---|---|---|---|---|---|---|
| 24a | 1920 | 1,975,278 | 1.75 | 3.00 | 8.00 | 22.00 | 125 | 375 | — |
| | 1921 | 597,337 | 7.00 | 16.00 | 55.00 | 175 | 825 | 2,250 | — |
| | 1927 | 468,096 | 15.00 | 28.00 | 65.00 | 175 | 550 | 1,200 | — |
| | 1928 | 2,114,178 | 1.75 | 3.00 | 8.00 | 22.00 | 110 | 275 | — |
| | 1929 | 2,690,562 | 1.75 | 2.75 | 8.00 | 22.00 | 110 | 275 | — |
| | 1930 | 968,748 | 1.75 | 3.50 | 10.00 | 25.00 | 175 | 450 | — |
| | 1931 | 537,815 | 1.75 | 3.50 | 12.00 | 27.50 | 175 | 450 | — |
| | 1932 | 537,994 | 2.50 | 4.00 | 13.00 | 30.00 | 175 | 450 | — |
| | 1933 | 421,282 | 3.00 | 4.50 | 15.00 | 30.00 | 150 | 250 | — |
| | 1934 | 384,350 | 3.50 | 6.00 | 22.00 | 45.00 | 175 | 450 | — |
| | 1935 | 537,772 | 3.50 | 5.00 | 17.50 | 42.00 | 125 | 275 | — |
| | 1936 | 972,094 | 1.75 | 3.50 | 8.00 | 15.00 | 70.00 | 150 | — |
| | 1936 dot | 153,322 | 20.00 | 40.00 | 110 | 225 | 600 | 1,400 | — |

**Note:** David Akers John Jay Pittman sale Part Three, 10-99, nearly Choice Unc. realized $6,900.

**25 CENTS** **Weight:** 5.8319 g. **Composition:** 0.8000 Silver 0.1500 oz. ASW

| KM | Date | Mintage | VG-8 | F-12 | VF-20 | XF-40 | MS-60 | MS-63 | Proof |
|---|---|---|---|---|---|---|---|---|---|
| 35 | 1937 | 2,690,176 | 1.00 | 1.50 | 2.25 | 3.50 | 10.00 | 25.00 | — |
| | 1938 | 3,149,245 | 1.00 | 1.50 | 3.25 | 5.00 | 40.00 | 85.00 | — |
| | 1939 | 3,532,495 | 1.00 | 1.50 | 2.25 | 4.50 | 35.00 | 75.00 | — |
| | 1940 | 9,583,650 | BV | 1.00 | 1.50 | 2.50 | 10.00 | 20.00 | — |
| | 1941 | 6,654,672 | BV | 1.00 | 1.50 | 2.50 | 10.00 | 20.00 | — |
| | 1942 | 6,935,871 | BV | 1.00 | 1.50 | 2.50 | 10.00 | 20.00 | — |
| | 1943 | 13,559,575 | BV | 1.00 | 1.50 | 2.50 | 10.00 | 20.00 | — |
| | 1944 | 7,216,237 | BV | 1.00 | 1.50 | 2.50 | 15.00 | 25.00 | — |
| | 1945 | 5,296,495 | BV | 1.00 | 1.50 | 2.00 | 10.00 | 20.00 | — |
| | 1946 | 2,210,810 | BV | 1.50 | 3.00 | 5.00 | 30.00 | 45.00 | — |
| | 1947 | 1,524,554 | BV | 1.50 | 4.00 | 8.00 | 30.00 | 55.00 | — |

| KM | Date | Mintage | VG-8 | F-12 | VF-20 | XF-40 | MS-60 | MS-63 | Proof |
|---|---|---|---|---|---|---|---|---|---|
| | 1947 dot after 7 | Inc. above | 25.00 | 30.00 | 50.00 | 85.00 | 175 | 375 | — |
| | 1947 maple leaf | 4,393,938 | BV | 1.00 | 2.00 | 3.00 | 10.00 | 20.00 | — |

**25 CENTS** **Weight:** 5.8319 g. **Composition:** 0.8000 Silver 0.1500 oz. ASW **Obverse:** Modified legend

| KM | Date | Mintage | VG-8 | F-12 | VF-20 | XF-40 | MS-60 | MS-63 | Proof |
|---|---|---|---|---|---|---|---|---|---|
| 44 | 1948 | 2,564,424 | BV | 1.50 | 3.00 | 5.00 | 35.00 | 70.00 | — |
| | 1949 | 7,988,830 | — | BV | 1.25 | 2.00 | 5.00 | 11.00 | — |
| | 1950 | 9,673,335 | — | BV | 1.25 | 1.50 | 4.00 | 9.00 | — |
| | 1951 | 8,290,719 | — | BV | 1.25 | 1.50 | 3.00 | 8.00 | — |
| | 1952 | 8,859,642 | — | BV | 1.25 | 1.50 | 3.00 | 7.00 | — |

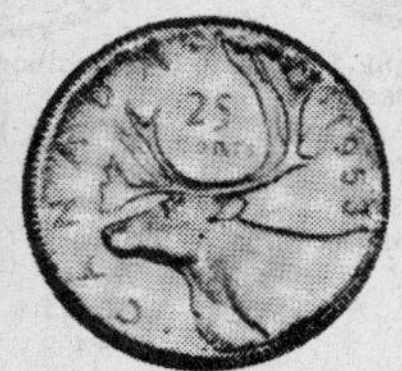

**25 CENTS** **Weight:** 5.8319 g. **Composition:** 0.8000 Silver 0.1500 oz. ASW **Obverse:** Elizabeth II effigy **Obv. Designer:** Gillick

| KM | Date | Mintage | VG-8 | F-12 | VF-20 | XF-40 | MS-60 | MS-63 | Proof |
|---|---|---|---|---|---|---|---|---|---|
| 52 | 1953 without strap | 10,546,769 | — | BV | 1.25 | 1.50 | 3.00 | 7.00 | — |
| | 1953 with strap | Inc. above | — | BV | 1.25 | 1.50 | 4.00 | 12.00 | — |
| | 1954 | 2,318,891 | BV | 1.25 | 2.00 | 4.00 | 15.00 | 25.00 | — |
| | 1955 | 9,552,505 | — | — | BV | 1.25 | 2.50 | 5.00 | — |
| | 1956 | 11,269,353 | — | — | BV | 1.25 | 2.00 | 4.00 | — |
| | 1957 | 12,770,190 | — | — | BV | 1.00 | 1.50 | 3.00 | — |
| | 1958 | 9,336,910 | — | — | BV | 1.00 | 1.50 | 3.00 | — |
| | 1959 | 13,503,461 | — | — | — | BV | 1.25 | 1.50 | — |
| | 1960 | 22,835,327 | — | — | — | BV | 1.00 | 1.50 | — |
| | 1961 | 18,164,368 | — | — | — | BV | 1.00 | 1.50 | — |
| | 1962 | 29,559,266 | — | — | — | BV | 1.00 | 1.25 | — |
| | 1963 | 21,180,652 | — | — | — | BV | 1.00 | 1.25 | — |
| | 1964 | 36,479,343 | — | — | — | BV | 1.00 | 1.25 | — |

**25 CENTS** **Weight:** 5.8319 g. **Composition:** 0.8000 Silver 0.1500 oz. ASW **Obverse:** Elizabeth II effigy **Obv. Designer:** Machin

| KM | Date | Mintage | VG-8 | F-12 | VF-20 | XF-40 | MS-60 | MS-63 | Proof |
|---|---|---|---|---|---|---|---|---|---|
| 62 | 1965 | 44,708,869 | — | — | — | BV | 1.00 | 1.25 | — |
| | 1966 | 25,626,315 | — | — | — | BV | 1.00 | 1.25 | — |

**25 CENTS** **Weight:** 5.8319 g. **Composition:** 0.5000 Silver 0.0937 oz. ASW **Obverse:** Elizabeth II effigy **Obv. Designer:** Machin

| KM | Date | Mintage | VG-8 | F-12 | VF-20 | XF-40 | MS-60 | MS-63 | Proof |
|---|---|---|---|---|---|---|---|---|---|
| 62a | 1968 | 71,464,000 | — | — | — | BV | 0.75 | 1.25 | — |

**25 CENTS** **Composition:** Nickel **Obverse:** Elizabeth II effigy **Obv. Designer:** Machin

| KM | Date | Mintage | VG-8 | F-12 | VF-20 | XF-40 | MS-60 | MS-63 | Proof |
|---|---|---|---|---|---|---|---|---|---|
| 62b | 1968 | 88,686,931 | — | — | — | 0.30 | 0.50 | 0.75 | — |
| | 1969 | 133,037,929 | — | — | — | 0.30 | 0.50 | 0.75 | — |
| | 1970 | 10,302,010 | — | — | — | 0.30 | 1.25 | 2.25 | — |
| | 1971 | 48,170,428 | — | — | — | 0.30 | 0.50 | 0.75 | — |
| | 1972 | 43,743,387 | — | — | — | 0.30 | 0.50 | 0.75 | — |
| | 1974 | 192,360,598 | — | — | — | 0.30 | 0.50 | 0.75 | — |
| | 1975 | 141,148,000 | — | — | — | 0.30 | 0.50 | 0.75 | — |
| | 1976 | 86,898,261 | — | — | — | 0.30 | 0.50 | 0.75 | — |
| | 1977 | 99,634,555 | — | — | — | 0.30 | 0.50 | 0.75 | — |
| | 1978 | 176,475,408 | — | — | — | 0.30 | 0.50 | 0.75 | — |

**25 CENTS** **Composition:** Nickel **Obverse:** Elizabeth II effigy, smaller bust **Obv. Designer:** Machin

| KM | Date | Mintage | VG-8 | F-12 | VF-20 | XF-40 | MS-60 | MS-63 | Proof |
|---|---|---|---|---|---|---|---|---|---|
| 74 | 1979 | 131,042,905 | — | — | — | 0.30 | 0.50 | 0.75 | — |
| | 1980 | 76,178,000 | — | — | — | 0.30 | 0.50 | 0.75 | — |
| | 1981 | 131,580,272 | — | — | — | 0.30 | 0.50 | 0.75 | — |
| | 1981 Proof | 199,000 | — | — | — | — | — | — | 2.00 |
| | 1982 | 171,926,000 | — | — | — | 0.30 | 0.50 | 0.75 | — |
| | 1982 Proof | 180,908 | — | — | — | — | — | — | 2.00 |
| | 1983 | 13,162,000 | — | — | — | 0.30 | 0.75 | 1.50 | — |
| | 1983 Proof | 168,000 | — | — | — | — | — | — | 3.00 |
| | 1984 | 121,668,000 | — | — | — | 0.30 | 0.50 | 0.75 | — |
| | 1984 Proof | 161,602 | — | — | — | — | — | — | 2.00 |
| | 1985 | 158,734,000 | — | — | — | 0.30 | 0.50 | 0.75 | — |
| | 1985 Proof | 157,037 | — | — | — | — | — | — | 2.00 |
| | 1986 | 132,220,000 | — | — | — | 0.30 | 0.50 | 0.75 | — |
| | 1986 Proof | 175,745 | — | — | — | — | — | — | 2.00 |
| | 1987 | 53,408,000 | — | — | — | 0.30 | 0.65 | 1.25 | — |
| | 1987 Proof | 179,004 | — | — | — | — | — | — | 2.00 |
| | 1988 | 80,368,473 | — | — | — | 0.30 | 0.50 | 1.00 | — |
| | 1988 Proof | 175,259 | — | — | — | — | — | — | 2.00 |
| | 1989 | 119,796,307 | — | — | — | 0.30 | 0.50 | 0.75 | — |
| | 1989 Proof | 170,928 | — | — | — | — | — | — | 2.00 |

**25 CENTS** **Composition:** Nickel **Obverse:** Elizabeth II effigy **Obv. Designer:** dePedery-Hunt

| KM | Date | Mintage | VG-8 | F-12 | VF-20 | XF-40 | MS-60 | MS-63 | Proof |
|---|---|---|---|---|---|---|---|---|---|
| 184 | 1990 | 31,258,000 | — | — | — | 0.30 | 0.50 | 1.00 | — |
| | 1990 Proof | 140,649 | — | — | — | — | — | — | 2.50 |
| | 1991 | 459,000 | — | — | 2.00 | 4.00 | 8.00 | 12.00 | — |
| | 1991 Proof | 131,888 | — | — | — | — | — | — | 20.00 |
| | 1993 | 73,758,000 | — | — | — | 0.30 | 0.65 | 1.00 | — |
| | 1993 Proof | 143,065 | — | — | — | — | — | — | 2.00 |
| | 1994 | 77,670,000 | — | — | — | 0.30 | 0.65 | 1.00 | — |
| | 1994 Proof | 146,424 | — | — | — | — | — | — | 3.00 |
| | 1995 | 89,210,000 | — | — | — | 0.30 | 0.65 | 1.00 | — |
| | 1995 Proof | 50,000 | — | — | — | — | — | — | 3.00 |
| | 1996 Proof | — | — | — | — | — | — | — | 3.00 |
| | 1996 | 28,106,000 | — | — | — | — | — | 2.50 | — |
| | 1997 | — | — | — | — | — | — | 2.50 | — |
| | 1997 Proof | — | — | — | — | — | — | — | 3.00 |
| | 1998W | — | — | — | — | — | — | 5.00 | — |
| | 1999 | — | — | — | — | — | — | 2.50 | — |
| | 1999 Proof | — | — | — | — | — | — | — | 3.00 |
| | 2000 Proof | — | — | — | — | — | — | — | 3.00 |
| | 2000 | — | — | — | — | — | — | 2.50 | — |
| | 2000W | — | — | — | — | — | — | 5.00 | — |
| | 2001 Proof | — | — | — | — | — | — | — | 3.00 |
| | 2001 | 8,250,000 | — | — | — | — | — | 3.00 | — |

**25 CENTS** **Weight:** 5.9000 g. **Composition:** 0.9250 Silver 0.1754 oz. ASW

| KM | Date | Mintage | VG-8 | F-12 | VF-20 | XF-40 | MS-60 | MS-63 | Proof |
|---|---|---|---|---|---|---|---|---|---|

**25 CENTS** **Composition:** Nickel Plated Steel

| KM | Date | Mintage | VG-8 | F-12 | VF-20 | XF-40 | MS-60 | MS-63 | Proof |
|---|---|---|---|---|---|---|---|---|---|
| 184b | 1999 P | Est. 20,000 | — | — | — | — | — | 20.00 | — |
| | 2001 P | — | — | — | — | — | 0.60 | 1.00 | — |
| | 2002 P | — | — | — | — | — | 0.60 | 1.00 | — |

**50 CENTS** **Weight:** 11.6200 g. **Composition:** 0.9250 Silver .3456 oz. ASW

| KM | Date | Mintage | VG-8 | F-12 | VF-20 | XF-40 | MS-60 | MS-63 | Proof |
|---|---|---|---|---|---|---|---|---|---|
| 6 | 1901 | 80,000 | 42.00 | 70.00 | 165 | 400 | 4,200 | 10,500 | — |

**50 CENTS** **Weight:** 11.6200 g. **Composition:** 0.9250 Silver .3456 oz. ASW

| KM | Date | Mintage | VG-8 | F-12 | VF-20 | XF-40 | MS-60 | MS-63 | Proof |
|---|---|---|---|---|---|---|---|---|---|
| 12 | 1902 | 120,000 | 11.00 | 22.50 | 85.00 | 200 | 1,100 | 3,000 | — |
| | 1903H | 140,000 | 16.00 | 35.00 | 100 | 225 | 1,100 | 3,000 | — |
| | 1904 | 60,000 | 85.00 | 150 | 285 | 625 | 2,650 | 7,000 | — |
| | 1905 | 40,000 | 100 | 200 | 425 | 1,000 | 4,000 | 10,000 | — |
| | 1906 | 350,000 | 10.00 | 25.00 | 70.00 | 190 | 1,000 | 3,000 | — |
| | 1907 | 300,000 | 8.00 | 25.00 | 70.00 | 200 | 1,000 | 3,500 | — |
| | 1908 | 128,119 | 14.75 | 45.00 | 125 | 275 | 800 | 1,650 | — |
| | 1909 | 302,118 | 13.00 | 40.00 | 150 | 350 | 2,000 | 6,000 | — |
| | 1910 Victorian leaves | 649,521 | 8.00 | 25.00 | 75.00 | 225 | 1,100 | 3,500 | — |

**50 CENTS** **Weight:** 11.6638 g. **Composition:** 0.9250 Silver .3461 oz. ASW

| KM | Date | Mintage | VG-8 | F-12 | VF-20 | XF-40 | MS-60 | MS-63 | Proof |
|---|---|---|---|---|---|---|---|---|---|
| 12a | 1910 Edwardian leaves | Inc. above | 8.00 | 22.00 | 65.00 | 200 | 1,000 | 3,150 | — |

**50 CENTS** **Weight:** 11.6638 g. **Composition:** 0.9250 Silver .3461 oz. ASW

| KM | Date | Mintage | VG-8 | F-12 | VF-20 | XF-40 | MS-60 | MS-63 | Proof |
|---|---|---|---|---|---|---|---|---|---|
| 19 | 1911 | 209,972 | 6.00 | 55.00 | 200 | 425 | 1,100 | 2,900 | — |

**50 CENTS** **Weight:** 11.6638 g. **Composition:** 0.9250 Silver .3461 oz. ASW **Obverse:** Modified legend

| KM | Date | Mintage | VG-8 | F-12 | VF-20 | XF-40 | MS-60 | MS-63 | Proof |
|---|---|---|---|---|---|---|---|---|---|
| 25 | 1912 | 285,867 | 4.00 | 16.00 | 65.00 | 175 | 850 | 2,200 | — |
| | 1913 | 265,889 | 4.00 | 16.00 | 85.00 | 200 | 1,100 | 4,000 | — |
| | 1914 | 160,128 | 8.00 | 40.00 | 120 | 375 | 2,000 | 6,000 | — |
| | 1916 | 459,070 | 3.00 | 9.00 | 35.00 | 95.00 | 550 | 1,800 | — |
| | 1917 | 752,213 | 3.00 | 7.00 | 25.00 | 70.00 | 350 | 950 | — |
| | 1918 | 754,989 | 3.00 | 6.00 | 20.00 | 60.00 | 300 | 800 | — |
| | 1919 | 1,113,429 | 3.00 | 6.00 | 20.00 | 60.00 | 300 | 1,100 | — |

**50 CENTS** **Weight:** 11.6638 g. **Composition:** 0.8000 Silver .3000 oz. ASW

| KM | Date | Mintage | VG-8 | F-12 | VF-20 | XF-40 | MS-60 | MS-63 | Proof |
|---|---|---|---|---|---|---|---|---|---|
| 25a | 1920 | 584,691 | 3.00 | 7.00 | 25.00 | 90.00 | 400 | 950 | — |
| | 1921 75 to 100 known | — | 12,000 | 17,000 | 20,750 | 21,000 | 35,000 | 45,000 | — |
| | **Note:** David Akers John Jay Pittman sale, Part Three, 10-99, Gem Unc. realized $63,250 | | | | | | | | |
| | 1929 | 228,328 | 3.00 | 7.00 | 25.00 | 75.00 | 375 | 900 | — |
| | 1931 | 57,581 | 6.00 | 18.00 | 60.00 | 175 | 725 | 1,700 | — |
| | 1932 | 19,213 | 90.00 | 125 | 300 | 600 | 2,800 | 7,000 | — |
| | 1934 | 39,539 | 10.00 | 20.00 | 60.00 | 175 | 500 | 1,150 | — |
| | 1936 | 38,550 | 10.00 | 18.00 | 50.00 | 135 | 400 | 900 | — |

**50 CENTS** **Weight:** 11.6638 g. **Composition:** 0.8000 Silver .3000 oz. ASW

| KM | Date | Mintage | VG-8 | F-12 | VF-20 | XF-40 | MS-60 | MS-63 | Proof |
|---|---|---|---|---|---|---|---|---|---|
| 36 | 1937 | 192,016 | 2.00 | 3.00 | 4.50 | 7.00 | 20.00 | 50.00 | — |
| | 1938 | 192,018 | 3.00 | 4.00 | 8.00 | 22.00 | 90.00 | 275 | — |
| | 1939 | 287,976 | 2.50 | 3.50 | 5.50 | 13.00 | 60.00 | 170 | — |
| | 1940 | 1,996,566 | BV | 1.75 | 2.50 | 4.00 | 18.00 | 60.00 | — |
| | 1941 | 1,714,874 | BV | 1.75 | 2.50 | 4.00 | 18.00 | 60.00 | — |
| | 1942 | 1,974,164 | BV | 1.75 | 2.50 | 4.00 | 18.00 | 60.00 | — |
| | 1943 | 3,109,583 | BV | 1.75 | 2.50 | 4.00 | 18.00 | 60.00 | — |
| | 1944 | 2,460,205 | BV | 1.75 | 2.50 | 4.00 | 18.00 | 60.00 | — |
| | 1945 | 1,959,528 | BV | 1.75 | 2.50 | 4.00 | 18.00 | 60.00 | — |
| | 1946 | 950,235 | BV | 2.00 | 3.50 | 7.00 | 40.00 | 110 | — |
| | 1946 hoof in 6 | Inc. above | 10.00 | 20.00 | 35.00 | 100 | 900 | 2,000 | — |
| | 1947 straight 7 | 424,885 | BV | 2.50 | 3.50 | 9.00 | 50.00 | 160 | — |
| | 1947 curved 7 | Inc. above | BV | 2.50 | 3.50 | 9.00 | 50.00 | 160 | — |
| | 1947 maple leaf, straight 7 | 38,433 | 14.00 | 18.00 | 25.00 | 50.00 | 125 | 230 | — |
| | 1947 maple leaf, curved 7 | Inc. above | 800 | 1,000 | 1,250 | 1,750 | 2,750 | 5,500 | — |

**50 CENTS** **Weight:** 11.6638 g. **Composition:** 0.8000 Silver .3000 oz. ASW **Obverse:** Modified legend

| KM | Date | Mintage | VG-8 | F-12 | VF-20 | XF-40 | MS-60 | MS-63 | Proof |
|---|---|---|---|---|---|---|---|---|---|
| 45 | 1948 | 37,784 | 35.00 | 42.00 | 50.00 | 75.00 | 110 | 175 | — |
| | 1949 | 858,991 | BV | 2.00 | 3.50 | 7.00 | 25.00 | 100 | — |
| | 1949 hoof over 9 | Inc. above | 5.00 | 10.00 | 18.00 | 45.00 | 225 | 550 | — |
| | 1950 no lines | 2,384,179 | 2.50 | 4.00 | 7.00 | 15.00 | 110 | 175 | — |
| | 1950 lines in 0 | Inc. above | BV | 1.75 | 2.75 | 3.50 | 8.00 | 20.00 | — |
| | 1951 | 2,421,730 | BV | 1.50 | 2.50 | 3.00 | 6.00 | 17.00 | — |
| | 1952 | 2,596,465 | BV | 1.50 | 2.50 | 3.00 | 6.00 | 11.00 | — |

**50 CENTS** **Weight:** 11.6638 g. **Composition:** 0.8000 Silver .3000 oz. ASW **Obverse:** Elizabeth II Effigy **Obv. Designer:** Gillick

| KM | Date | Mintage | VG-8 | F-12 | VF-20 | XF-40 | MS-60 | MS-63 | Proof |
|---|---|---|---|---|---|---|---|---|---|
| 53 | 1953 small date | 1,630,429 | — | BV | 2.00 | 2.50 | 4.50 | 10.00 | — |
| | 1953 lg. date, straps | Inc. above | — | BV | 2.50 | 3.00 | 10.00 | 22.00 | — |
| | 1953 lg. date without straps | Inc. above | BV | 2.00 | 3.50 | 9.00 | 50.00 | 90.00 | — |
| | 1954 | 506,305 | BV | 2.00 | 3.50 | 7.00 | 18.00 | 30.00 | — |
| | 1955 | 753,511 | — | BV | 2.50 | 3.50 | 10.00 | 20.00 | — |
| | 1956 | 1,379,499 | — | BV | 2.00 | 2.50 | 4.50 | 9.00 | — |
| | 1957 | 2,171,689 | — | BV | — | 1.75 | 3.50 | 6.00 | — |
| | 1958 | 2,957,266 | — | BV | — | 1.75 | 3.00 | 5.50 | — |

**50 CENTS** **Weight:** 11.6638 g. **Composition:** 0.8000 Silver .3000 oz. ASW **Reverse:** New shield

| KM | Date | Mintage | VG-8 | F-12 | VF-20 | XF-40 | MS-60 | MS-63 | Proof |
|---|---|---|---|---|---|---|---|---|---|
| 56 | 1959 horizontal shading | 3,095,535 | — | — | BV | 1.75 | 2.50 | 4.50 | — |
| | 1960 | 3,488,897 | — | — | — | BV | 2.25 | 3.25 | — |
| | 1961 | 3,584,417 | — | — | — | BV | 2.00 | 3.00 | — |
| | 1962 | 5,208,030 | — | — | — | BV | 1.75 | 3.00 | — |
| | 1963 | 8,348,871 | — | — | — | BV | 1.75 | 3.00 | — |
| | 1964 | 9,377,676 | — | — | — | BV | 1.75 | 3.00 | — |

**50 CENTS** **Weight:** 11.6638 g. **Composition:** 0.8000 Silver .3000 oz. ASW **Obverse:** Elizabeth II effigy **Obv. Designer:** Machin

| KM | Date | Mintage | VG-8 | F-12 | VF-20 | XF-40 | MS-60 | MS-63 | Proof |
|---|---|---|---|---|---|---|---|---|---|
| 63 | 1965 | 12,629,974 | — | — | — | BV | 1.75 | 3.00 | — |
| | 1966 | 7,920,496 | — | — | — | BV | 1.75 | 3.00 | — |

1968-76

1977

1978-

**50 CENTS** **Composition:** Nickel

| KM | Date | Mintage | VG-8 | F-12 | VF-20 | XF-40 | MS-60 | MS-63 | Proof |
|---|---|---|---|---|---|---|---|---|---|
| 75.1 | 1968 | 3,966,932 | — | — | — | 0.50 | 0.65 | 1.00 | — |
| | 1969 | 7,113,929 | — | — | — | 0.50 | 0.65 | 1.00 | — |
| | 1970 | 2,429,526 | — | — | — | 0.50 | 0.65 | 1.00 | — |
| | 1971 | 2,166,444 | — | — | — | 0.50 | 0.65 | 1.00 | — |
| | 1972 | 2,515,632 | — | — | — | 0.50 | 0.65 | 1.00 | — |
| | 1973 | 2,546,096 | — | — | — | 0.50 | 0.65 | 1.00 | — |
| | 1974 | 3,436,650 | — | — | — | 0.50 | 0.65 | 1.00 | — |
| | 1975 | 3,710,000 | — | — | — | 0.50 | 0.65 | 1.00 | — |
| | 1976 | 2,940,719 | — | — | — | 0.50 | 0.65 | 1.00 | — |

**50 CENTS** **Composition:** Nickel **Obverse:** Smaller bust

| KM | Date | Mintage | VG-8 | F-12 | VF-20 | XF-40 | MS-60 | MS-63 | Proof |
|---|---|---|---|---|---|---|---|---|---|
| 75.2 | 1977 | 709,839 | — | — | 0.50 | 0.75 | 1.35 | 2.00 | — |

**50 CENTS** **Composition:** Nickel **Reverse:** Redesigned arms

| KM | Date | Mintage | VG-8 | F-12 | VF-20 | XF-40 | MS-60 | MS-63 | Proof |
|---|---|---|---|---|---|---|---|---|---|
| 75.3 | 1978 square jewels | 3,341,892 | — | — | — | 0.50 | 0.65 | 1.00 | — |
| | 1978 round jewels | Inc. above | — | — | 0.50 | 2.50 | 3.00 | 4.00 | — |

| KM | Date | Mintage | VG-8 | F-12 | VF-20 | XF-40 | MS-60 | MS-63 | Proof |
|---|---|---|---|---|---|---|---|---|---|
| | 1979 | 3,425,000 | — | — | — | 0.50 | 0.65 | 1.00 | — |
| | 1980 | 1,574,000 | — | — | — | 0.50 | 0.65 | 1.00 | — |
| | 1981 | 2,690,272 | — | — | — | 0.50 | 0.65 | 1.00 | — |
| | 1981 Proof | 199,000 | — | — | — | — | — | — | 3.00 |
| | 1982 small beads | 2,236,674 | — | — | — | 20.00 | 40.00 | 60.00 | — |
| | 1982 small beads; Proof | 180,908 | — | — | — | — | — | — | 3.00 |
| | 1982 large beads | Inc. above | — | — | — | 0.50 | 0.65 | 1.00 | — |
| | 1983 | 1,177,000 | — | — | — | 0.50 | 0.65 | 1.00 | — |
| | 1983 Proof | 168,000 | — | — | — | — | — | — | 3.00 |
| | 1984 | 1,502,989 | — | — | — | 0.50 | 0.65 | 1.00 | — |
| | 1984 Proof | 161,602 | — | — | — | — | — | — | 3.00 |
| | 1985 | 2,188,374 | — | — | — | 0.50 | 0.65 | 1.00 | — |
| | 1985 Proof | 157,037 | — | — | — | — | — | — | 3.00 |
| | 1986 | 781,400 | — | — | — | 0.50 | 1.00 | 1.25 | — |
| | 1986 Proof | 175,745 | — | — | — | — | — | — | 3.00 |
| | 1987 | 373,000 | — | — | — | 0.50 | 1.00 | 1.50 | — |
| | 1987 Proof | 179,004 | — | — | — | — | — | — | 3.50 |
| | 1988 | 220,000 | — | — | — | 0.50 | 1.00 | 1.50 | — |
| | 1988 Proof | 175,259 | — | — | — | — | — | — | 3.00 |
| | 1989 | 266,419 | — | — | — | 0.50 | 1.00 | 1.75 | — |
| | 1989 Proof | 170,928 | — | — | — | — | — | — | 3.00 |

**50 CENTS** **Composition:** Nickel **Obverse:** Elizabeth II effigy **Obv. Designer:** dePedery-Hunt

| KM | Date | Mintage | VG-8 | F-12 | VF-20 | XF-40 | MS-60 | MS-63 | Proof |
|---|---|---|---|---|---|---|---|---|---|
| 185 | 1990 | 207,000 | — | — | — | 0.50 | 1.25 | 1.75 | — |
| | 1990 Proof | 140,649 | — | — | — | — | — | — | 5.00 |
| | 1991 | 490,000 | — | — | — | 0.50 | 0.85 | 1.00 | — |
| | 1991 Proof | 131,888 | — | — | — | — | — | — | 7.00 |
| | 1993 | 393,000 | — | — | — | 0.50 | 0.85 | 1.00 | — |
| | 1993 Proof | 143,065 | — | — | — | — | — | — | 3.00 |
| | 1994 | 987,000 | — | — | — | 0.50 | 0.75 | 1.00 | — |
| | 1994 Proof | 146,424 | — | — | — | — | — | — | 4.00 |
| | 1995 | 626,000 | — | — | — | 0.50 | 0.75 | 1.00 | — |
| | 1995 Proof | 50,000 | — | — | — | — | — | — | 4.00 |
| | 1996 | 458,000 | — | — | — | 0.50 | 0.65 | 1.00 | — |
| | 1996 | — | — | — | — | — | — | — | — |

**50 CENTS** **Weight:** 11.6380 g. **Composition:** 0.9250 Silver .3461 oz. ASW

| KM | Date | Mintage | VG-8 | F-12 | VF-20 | XF-40 | MS-60 | MS-63 | Proof |
|---|---|---|---|---|---|---|---|---|---|

**50 CENTS** **Composition:** Nickel **Reverse:** Redesigned arms

| KM | Date | Mintage | VG-8 | F-12 | VF-20 | XF-40 | MS-60 | MS-63 | Proof |
|---|---|---|---|---|---|---|---|---|---|
| 290 | 1997 Proof | — | — | — | — | — | — | — | — |
| | 1997 | 387,000 | — | — | — | 0.50 | 0.65 | 1.00 | — |
| | 1998 | 308,000 | — | — | — | 0.50 | 0.65 | 1.00 | — |
| | 1998 Proof | — | — | — | — | — | — | — | — |
| | 1998W | — | — | — | — | — | — | 2.00 | — |
| | 1999 | 496,000 | — | — | — | 0.50 | 0.65 | 1.00 | — |
| | 1999 Proof | — | — | — | — | — | — | — | — |
| | 2000 Proof | — | — | — | — | — | — | — | — |
| | 2000 | 559,000 | — | — | — | 0.50 | 0.65 | 1.00 | — |
| | 2000W | — | — | — | — | — | — | 2.00 | — |

**50 CENTS** **Weight:** 11.6380 g. **Composition:** 0.9250 Silver .3461 oz. ASW

| KM | Date | Mintage | VG-8 | F-12 | VF-20 | XF-40 | MS-60 | MS-63 | Proof |
|---|---|---|---|---|---|---|---|---|---|

**50 CENTS** **Composition:** Nickel Plated Steel **Reverse:** Redesigned arms

| KM | Date | Mintage | VG-8 | F-12 | VF-20 | XF-40 | MS-60 | MS-63 | Proof |
|---|---|---|---|---|---|---|---|---|---|
| 290b | 1999 | Est. 20,000 | — | — | — | — | — | 15.00 | — |
| | 2001 | — | — | — | — | — | 1.50 | 4.00 | — |
| | 2002 | — | — | — | — | — | 1.50 | 4.00 | — |

**DOLLAR** **Weight:** 23.3276 g. **Composition:** 0.8000 Silver 0.6000 oz. ASW **Reverse:** Voyageur

| KM | Date | Mintage | F-12 | VF-20 | XF-40 | AU-50 | MS-60 | MS-63 | Proof |
|---|---|---|---|---|---|---|---|---|---|
| 31 | 1936 | 339,600 | 8.50 | 12.50 | 16.50 | 21.50 | 35.00 | 72.00 | 5,000 |

**DOLLAR** **Weight:** 23.3276 g. **Composition:** 0.8000 Silver 0.6000 oz. ASW **Reverse:** Voyageur

| KM | Date | Mintage | F-12 | VF-20 | XF-40 | AU-50 | MS-60 | MS-63 | Proof |
|---|---|---|---|---|---|---|---|---|---|
| 37 | 1937 | 207,406 | 9.00 | 9.50 | 11.00 | 13.00 | 25.00 | 65.00 | — |
| | 1937 Mirror Proof | 1,295 | — | — | — | — | — | — | 650 |
| | 1937 Matte Proof | Inc. above | — | — | — | — | — | — | 250 |
| | 1938 | 90,304 | 23.50 | 32.00 | 40.00 | 50.00 | 65.00 | 175 | 6,000 |
| | 1945 | 38,391 | 65.00 | 90.00 | 110 | 125 | 175 | 450 | 2,000 |
| | 1946 | 93,055 | 12.50 | 22.50 | 31.00 | 37.50 | 65.00 | 225 | 1,800 |
| | 1947 pointed 7 | | 55.00 | 70.00 | 85.00 | 110 | 275 | 900 | 3,500 |
| | 1947 blunt 7 | 65,595 | 35.00 | 50.00 | 70.00 | 90.00 | 110 | 225 | 4,500 |
| | 1947 maple leaf | 21,135 | 100 | 130 | 150 | 160 | 225 | 450 | 1,800 |

**DOLLAR** **Weight:** 23.3276 g. **Composition:** 0.8000 Silver 0.6000 oz. ASW **Obverse:** Modified left legend **Reverse:** Voyageur

| KM | Date | Mintage | F-12 | VF-20 | XF-40 | AU-50 | MS-60 | MS-63 | Proof |
|---|---|---|---|---|---|---|---|---|---|
| 46 | 1948 | 18,780 | 300 | 350 | 400 | 500 | 600 | 900 | 3,000 |
| | 1950 with 4 water lines | 261,002 | 5.00 | 7.00 | 9.00 | 12.00 | 15.00 | 28.00 | 800 |
| | 1950 arnprior with 2-1/2 water lines | Inc. above | 6.50 | 8.50 | 12.50 | 16.00 | 25.00 | 75.00 | 1,500 |
| | 1951 with 4 water lines | 416,395 | 4.00 | 5.00 | 6.50 | 7.50 | 9.00 | 22.50 | 650 |
| | 1951 arnprior with 2-1/2 water lines | Inc. above | 15.00 | 30.00 | 45.00 | 60.00 | 100 | 250 | 1,500 |
| | 1952 with 4 water lines | 406,148 | 4.00 | 5.00 | 6.50 | 7.50 | 10.00 | 22.50 | 1,250 |
| | 1952 short water lines, arnprior type | Inc. above | 8.00 | 12.00 | 15.00 | 18.00 | 25.00 | 60.00 | 1,750 |
| | 1952 without water lines | Inc. above | 5.00 | 6.00 | 8.00 | 10.00 | 16.50 | 30.00 | — |

**DOLLAR** **Weight:** 23.3276 g. **Composition:** 0.8000 Silver 0.6000 oz. ASW **Obverse:** Elizabeth II effigy **Obv. Designer:** Gillick **Reverse:** Voyageur **Note:** All genuine circulation strike 1955 Arnprior dollars have a die break running along the top of TI in the word GRATIA on the obverse.

| KM | Date | Mintage | F-12 | VF-20 | XF-40 | AU-50 | MS-60 | MS-63 | Proof |
|---|---|---|---|---|---|---|---|---|---|
| 54 | 1953 without strap, wire rim | 1,074,578 | BV | 3.90 | 4.50 | 5.00 | 7.00 | 13.00 | 400 |
| | 1953 with strap, flat rim | Inc. above | BV | 3.90 | 4.50 | 5.00 | 7.00 | 13.00 | — |
| | 1954 | 246,606 | 4.00 | 6.00 | 8.00 | 10.00 | 16.50 | 31.50 | — |
| | 1955 with 4 water lines | 268,105 | 4.50 | 6.00 | 8.00 | 10.00 | 15.00 | 25.00 | — |
| | 1955 arnprior with 1-1/2 water lines* and die break | Inc. above | 40.00 | 45.00 | 55.00 | 65.00 | 75.00 | 140 | — |
| | 1956 | 209,092 | 7.00 | 9.00 | 12.50 | 15.50 | 19.00 | 30.00 | — |
| | 1957 with 4 water lines | 496,389 | — | BV | 4.75 | 5.50 | 7.50 | 11.00 | — |
| | 1957 with 1 water line | Inc. above | 4.50 | 5.50 | 7.50 | 8.50 | 10.00 | 20.00 | — |
| | 1959 | 1,443,502 | — | — | — | BV | 5.00 | 6.50 | — |
| | 1960 | 1,420,486 | — | — | — | BV | 5.00 | 6.50 | — |
| | 1961 | 1,262,231 | — | — | — | BV | 5.00 | 6.50 | — |
| | 1962 | 1,884,789 | — | — | — | BV | 5.00 | 6.50 | — |
| | 1963 | 4,179,981 | — | — | — | BV | 5.00 | 6.50 | — |

**DOLLAR** **Weight:** 23.3276 g. **Composition:** 0.8000 Silver 0.6000 oz. ASW **Obverse:** Elizabeth II effigy **Obv. Designer:** Machin **Reverse:** Voyageur

| KM | Date | Mintage | F-12 | VF-20 | XF-40 | AU-50 | MS-60 | MS-63 | Proof |
|---|---|---|---|---|---|---|---|---|---|
| 64.1 | 1965 small beads, pointed 5 | 10,768,569 | — | — | — | BV | 4.00 | 6.00 | — |
| | 1965 small beads, blunt 5 | Inc. above | — | — | — | BV | 4.00 | 6.00 | — |
| | 1965 large beads, blunt 5 | Inc. above | — | — | — | BV | 4.00 | 6.00 | — |
| | 1965 large beads, pointed 5 | Inc. above | — | — | — | BV | 4.75 | 8.00 | — |
| | 1965 medium beads, pointed 5 | Inc. above | BV | 5.00 | 7.00 | 9.00 | 12.00 | 25.00 | — |
| | 1966 large beads | 9,912,178 | — | — | — | BV | 4.00 | 6.00 | — |
| | 1966 small beads | 485 | — | — | 750 | 1,000 | 1,350 | 1,550 | — |

**DOLLAR** **Composition:** Nickel **Obverse:** Large bust **Reverse:** Voyageur **Size:** 32 mm.

| KM | Date | Mintage | MS-63 | P/L | Proof |
|---|---|---|---|---|---|
| 76.1 | 1968 | 5,579,714 | 1.25 | — | — |
| | 1968 | 1,408,143 | — | 1.75 | — |
| | 1969 | 4,809,313 | 1.25 | — | — |
| | 1969 | 594,258 | — | 2.00 | — |
| | 1972 | 2,676,041 | 1.50 | — | — |
| | 1972 | 405,865 | — | 2.50 | — |

**DOLLAR** **Weight:** 23.3276 g. **Composition:** 0.5000 Silver 0.3750 oz. ASW **Obverse:** Smaller bust **Reverse:** Voyageur **Size:** 36 mm.

| KM | Date | Mintage | MS-63 | P/L | Proof |
|---|---|---|---|---|---|
| 64.2a | 1972 Proof | 341,598 | — | — | 5.00 |

**Note:** Specimen $5.50.

**DOLLAR** **Composition:** Nickel **Reverse:** Voyageur **Size:** 32 mm. **Note:** Only known in prooflike sets with 1976 obverse slightly modified.

| KM | Date | Mintage | MS-63 | P/L | Proof |
|---|---|---|---|---|---|
| 76.3 | 1975 mule w/1976 obv. | Inc. above | — | — | — |

**DOLLAR** **Composition:** Nickel **Obverse:** Smaller bust **Reverse:** Voyageur **Size:** 32 mm.

| KM | Date | Mintage | MS-63 | P/L | Proof |
|---|---|---|---|---|---|
| 76.2 | 1975 | 3,256,000 | 1.50 | — | — |
| | 1975 | 322,325 | — | 2.50 | — |
| | 1976 | 2,498,204 | 1.50 | — | — |
| | 1976 | 274,106 | — | 2.50 | — |

**DOLLAR** **Composition:** Nickel **Reverse:** Voyageur modified **Size:** 32 mm mm.

| KM | Date | Mintage | MS-63 | P/L | Proof |
|---|---|---|---|---|---|
| 117 | 1977 | 1,393,745 | 1.50 | — | — |

**DOLLAR** **Composition:** Nickel **Reverse:** Voyageur **Size:** 32 mm. **Note:** Modified design.

| KM | Date | Mintage | MS-63 | P/L | Proof |
|---|---|---|---|---|---|
| 120.1 | 1978 | 2,948,488 | 1.50 | — | — |
| | 1979 | 2,954,842 | 1.50 | — | — |
| | 1980 | 3,291,221 | 1.50 | — | — |
| | 1981 | 2,778,900 | 1.50 | — | — |
| | 1982 | 1,098,500 | 1.50 | 2.50 | — |
| | 1982 Proof | 180,908 | — | — | 5.25 |
| | 1983 | 2,267,525 | 1.50 | 4.00 | — |
| | 1983 Proof | 166,779 | — | — | 5.25 |
| | 1984 | 1,223,486 | 1.50 | — | — |
| | 1984 Proof | 161,602 | — | — | 6.00 |
| | 1985 | 3,104,092 | 1.50 | 3.50 | — |
| | 1985 Proof | 153,950 | — | — | 7.00 |
| | 1986 | 3,089,225 | 2.00 | 4.00 | — |
| | 1986 Proof | 176,224 | — | — | 7.50 |
| | 1987 | 287,330 | 3.50 | 5.00 | — |
| | 1987 Proof | 175,686 | — | — | 7.50 |

**DOLLAR** **Composition:** Nickel **Reverse:** Voyageur **Size:** 32 mm. **Note:** Modified design.

| KM | Date | Mintage | MS-63 | P/L | Spec. |
|---|---|---|---|---|---|
| 120.2 | 1985 mule w/New Zealand 50 cent, KM-37 obverse | — | 1,200 | — | — |

**DOLLAR** **Composition:** Aureate-Bronze Plated Nickel **Obverse:** Elizabeth II effigy **Obv. Designer:** Machin **Reverse:** Loon

| KM | Date | Mintage | MS-63 | P/L | Proof |
|---|---|---|---|---|---|
| 157 | 1987 | 205,405,000 | 2.25 | — | — |
| | 1987 Proof | 178,120 | — | — | 8.00 |
| | 1988 | 138,893,539 | 2.25 | 4.00 | — |
| | 1988 Proof | 175,259 | — | — | 6.75 |
| | 1989 | 184,773,902 | 3.00 | 4.00 | — |
| | 1989 Proof | 170,928 | — | — | 6.75 |

**DOLLAR** **Composition:** Nickel **Obverse:** Elizabeth II effigy **Obv. Designer:** dePedery-Hunt **Reverse:** Loon

| KM | Date | Mintage | MS-63 | P/L | Proof |
|---|---|---|---|---|---|
| 186 | 1990 | 68,402,000 | 1.75 | 4.00 | — |
| | 1990 Proof | 140,649 | — | — | 7.00 |
| | 1991 | 23,156,000 | 1.75 | 6.50 | — |
| | 1991 Proof | — | — | — | 13.00 |
| | 1993 | 33,662,000 | 2.00 | 3.00 | — |
| | 1993 Proof | — | — | — | 6.00 |
| | 1994 | 36,237,000 | 2.00 | 3.50 | — |
| | 1994 Proof | — | — | — | 7.00 |
| | 1995 | 41,813,000 | 3.00 | 4.50 | — |
| | 1995 Proof | — | — | — | 7.00 |
| | 1996 | 17,101,000 | 2.00 | 6.00 | — |
| | 1996 Proof | — | — | — | 7.50 |
| | 1997 | — | 5.00 | 6.00 | — |
| | 1997 Proof | — | — | — | 8.00 |
| | 1998 | — | 5.00 | 6.00 | — |
| | 1998 Proof | — | — | — | 10.00 |
| | 1998W | — | — | 4.50 | — |
| | 1999 | — | 5.00 | 6.00 | — |
| | 1999 Proof | — | — | — | 8.00 |
| | 2000 | — | 5.00 | 6.00 | — |
| | 2000 | — | — | — | 8.00 |

**5 DOLLARS** **Weight:** 8.3592 g. **Composition:** 0.9000 Gold 0.2419 oz. AGW

| KM | Date | Mintage | F-12 | VF-20 | XF-40 | AU-50 | MS-60 | MS-63 |
|---|---|---|---|---|---|---|---|---|
| 26 | 1912 | 165,680 | 110 | 125 | 150 | 175 | 225 | 550 |
| | 1913 | 98,832 | 110 | 125 | 150 | 175 | 225 | 550 |
| | 1914 | 31,122 | 150 | 250 | 300 | 400 | 625 | 1,750 |

**10 DOLLARS** **Weight:** 16.7185 g. **Composition:** 0.9000 Gold 0.4838 oz. AGW

| KM | Date | Mintage | F-12 | VF-20 | XF-40 | AU-50 | MS-60 | MS-63 |
|---|---|---|---|---|---|---|---|---|
| 27 | 1912 | 74,759 | 225 | 275 | 325 | 375 | 500 | 2,000 |
| | 1913 | 149,232 | 225 | 275 | 325 | 375 | 525 | 2,650 |
| | 1914 | 140,068 | 225 | 275 | 350 | 400 | 575 | 2,750 |

**SOVEREIGN** **Weight:** 7.9881 g. **Composition:** 0.9170 Gold .2354 oz. AGW **Reverse:** Mint mark below horse's rear hooves

| KM | Date | Mintage | VG-8 | F-12 | VF-20 | XF-40 | MS-60 | MS-63 | Proof |
|---|---|---|---|---|---|---|---|---|---|
| 14 | 1908C | 636 | — | 1,000 | 1,750 | 2,000 | 2,700 | 3,000 | — |
| | 1909C | 16,273 | — | 110 | 170 | 200 | 475 | 1,600 | — |
| | 1910C | 28,012 | — | 100 | 150 | 180 | 475 | 2,000 | — |

**SOVEREIGN** **Weight:** 7.9881 g. **Composition:** 0.9170 Gold 0.2354 oz. AGW

| KM | Date | Mintage | VG-8 | F-12 | VF-20 | XF-40 | MS-60 | MS-63 | Proof |
|---|---|---|---|---|---|---|---|---|---|
| 20 | 1911C | 256,946 | — | BV | BV | 80.00 | 100 | 165 | — |
| | 1913C | 3,715 | — | 350 | 450 | 550 | 1,000 | 2,300 | — |
| | 1914C | 14,871 | — | 175 | 250 | 325 | 400 | 800 | — |
| | 1916C about 20 known | — | — | 7,920 | 12,500 | 11,000 | 16,000 | 25,000 | — |

**Note:** Stacks' A.G. Carter Jr. Sale 12-89 Gem BU realized $82,500.

| KM | Date | Mintage | VG-8 | F-12 | VF-20 | XF-40 | MS-60 | MS-63 | Proof |
|---|---|---|---|---|---|---|---|---|---|
| 20 | 1917C | 58,845 | — | BV | BV | 85.00 | 125 | 400 | — |
| | 1918C | 106,514 | — | BV | BV | 85.00 | 135 | 600 | — |

| KM | Date | Mintage | VG-8 | F-12 | VF-20 | XF-40 | MS-60 | MS-63 | Proof |
|---|---|---|---|---|---|---|---|---|---|
| | 1919C | 135,889 | — | BV | BV | 85.00 | 125 | 500 | — |

## COMMEMORATIVE COINAGE

**CENT** **Composition:** Bronze **Subject:** Confederation Centennial

| KM | Date | Mintage | VG-8 | F-12 | VF-20 | XF-40 | MS-60 | MS-63 | Proof |
|---|---|---|---|---|---|---|---|---|---|
| 65 | ND(1967) | 345,140,645 | — | — | — | — | 0.10 | 0.20 | 1.00 |

**CENT** **Composition:** Bronze **Subject:** Confederation 125

| KM | Date | Mintage | VG-8 | F-12 | VF-20 | XF-40 | MS-60 | MS-63 | Proof |
|---|---|---|---|---|---|---|---|---|---|
| 204 | ND(1992) | 673,512,000 | — | — | — | — | 0.10 | 0.15 | — |
| | ND(1992) Proof | 147,061 | — | — | — | — | — | — | 2.50 |

**CENT** **Weight:** 5.6700 g. **Composition:** 0.9250 Copper-Plated Silver 0.1677 oz. **Subject:** 90th Anniversary Royal Canadian Mint - 1908-1998

| KM | Date | Mintage | VG-8 | F-12 | VF-20 | XF-40 | MS-60 | MS-63 | Proof |
|---|---|---|---|---|---|---|---|---|---|
| 309 | ND(1998) | 25,000 | — | — | — | — | — | 16.00 | — |

**CENT** **Weight:** 5.6700 g. **Composition:** 0.9250 Silver .1677 oz. ASW **Subject:** 90th Anniversary Royal Canadian Mint - 1908-1998 **Obverse:** With "Canada" added to bust

| KM | Date | Mintage | VG-8 | F-12 | VF-20 | XF-40 | MS-60 | MS-63 | Proof |
|---|---|---|---|---|---|---|---|---|---|
| 332 | ND(2000) Proof | 25,000 | — | — | — | — | — | — | 16.00 |

**3 CENTS** **Weight:** 31.1035 g. **Composition:** 0.9250 Silver .1600 oz. ASW **Subject:** 1st Canadian Postage Stamp **Obverse:** Queen's head right. **Reverse:** Partial stamp design. **Edge:** Plain. **Size:** 21.1 mm.

| KM | Date | Mintage | MS-63 | Proof |
|---|---|---|---|---|
| 410 | 2001 Proof | 90,000 | — | 25.00 |

**5 CENTS** **Composition:** Tombac **Subject:** Victory

| KM | Date | Mintage | VG-8 | F-12 | VF-20 | XF-40 | MS-60 | MS-63 | Proof |
|---|---|---|---|---|---|---|---|---|---|
| 40 | 1943 | 24,760,256 | 0.20 | 0.30 | 0.40 | 0.85 | 2.00 | 6.00 | — |
| | 1944 1 known | 8,000 | — | — | — | — | — | — | — |

**5 CENTS** **Composition:** Chrome Plated Steel

| KM | Date | Mintage | VG-8 | F-12 | VF-20 | XF-40 | MS-60 | MS-63 | Proof |
|---|---|---|---|---|---|---|---|---|---|
| 40a | 1944 | 11,532,784 | 0.15 | 0.25 | 0.45 | 1.00 | 2.00 | 4.00 | — |
| | 1945 | 18,893,216 | 0.15 | 0.25 | 0.45 | 1.00 | 2.00 | 4.00 | — |

**5 CENTS** **Composition:** Nickel **Subject:** Nickel Bicentennial

| KM | Date | Mintage | VG-8 | F-12 | VF-20 | XF-40 | MS-60 | MS-63 | Proof |
|---|---|---|---|---|---|---|---|---|---|
| 48 | ND(1951) | 9,028,507 | 0.15 | 0.20 | 0.25 | 0.50 | 1.75 | 3.50 | — |

**5 CENTS** **Composition:** Copper Nickel **Subject:** Confederation Centennial

| KM | Date | Mintage | VG-8 | F-12 | VF-20 | XF-40 | MS-60 | MS-63 | Proof |
|---|---|---|---|---|---|---|---|---|---|
| 66 | ND(1967) | 36,876,574 | — | — | — | — | 0.20 | 0.30 | 1.00 |

**5 CENTS** **Composition:** Copper-Nickel **Subject:** Confederation 125

| KM | Date | Mintage | VG-8 | F-12 | VF-20 | XF-40 | MS-60 | MS-63 | Proof |
|---|---|---|---|---|---|---|---|---|---|
| 205 | ND(1992) | 53,732,000 | — | — | — | — | 0.10 | 0.20 | — |
| | ND(1992) Proof | 147,061 | — | — | — | — | — | — | 4.00 |

**5 CENTS** **Weight:** 1.1670 g. **Composition:** 0.9250 Silver .0347 oz. ASW **Subject:** 90th Anniversary Royal Canadian Mint

| KM | Date | Mintage | VG-8 | F-12 | VF-20 | XF-40 | MS-60 | MS-63 | Proof |
|---|---|---|---|---|---|---|---|---|---|
| 310 | ND(1998) | 25,000 | — | — | — | — | — | 12.00 | — |

| KM | Date | Mintage | VG-8 | F-12 | VF-20 | XF-40 | MS-60 | MS-63 | Proof |
|---|---|---|---|---|---|---|---|---|---|
| | ND(1998) Proof | 25,000 | — | — | — | — | — | — | 12.00 |

**5 CENTS** **Composition:** 0.9250 Silver **Subject:** First French-Canadian Regiment

| KM | Date | Mintage | VG-8 | F-12 | VF-20 | XF-40 | MS-60 | MS-63 | Proof |
|---|---|---|---|---|---|---|---|---|---|
| 400 | 2000 Proof | — | — | — | — | — | — | — | 11.50 |

**5 CENTS** **Weight:** 5.3500 g. **Composition:** 0.9250 Silver .1591 oz. ASW **Subject:** Royal Military College **Obverse:** Queen's head right. **Reverse:** Marching cadets and arch. **Edge:** Plain. **Size:** 21.2 mm.

| KM | Date | Mintage | VG-8 | F-12 | VF-20 | XF-40 | MS-60 | MS-63 | Proof |
|---|---|---|---|---|---|---|---|---|---|
| 413 | 2001 Proof | — | — | — | — | — | — | — | 11.50 |

**10 CENTS** **Weight:** 2.3328 g. **Composition:** 0.8000 Silver 0.0600 oz. ASW **Subject:** Confederation Centennial

| KM | Date | Mintage | VG-8 | F-12 | VF-20 | XF-40 | MS-60 | MS-63 | Proof |
|---|---|---|---|---|---|---|---|---|---|
| 67 | ND(1967) | 62,998,215 | — | — | — | BV | 0.50 | 1.00 | 2.00 |

**10 CENTS** **Weight:** 2.3328 g. **Composition:** 0.5000 Silver 0.0372 oz. ASW **Subject:** Confederation Centennial

| KM | Date | Mintage | VG-8 | F-12 | VF-20 | XF-40 | MS-60 | MS-63 | Proof |
|---|---|---|---|---|---|---|---|---|---|
| 67a | ND(1967) | Inc. above | — | — | — | BV | 0.50 | 1.00 | — |

**10 CENTS** **Composition:** Nickel **Subject:** Confederation 125

| KM | Date | Mintage | VG-8 | F-12 | VF-20 | XF-40 | MS-60 | MS-63 | Proof |
|---|---|---|---|---|---|---|---|---|---|
| 206 | ND(1992) | 174,476,000 | — | — | — | — | 0.25 | 0.35 | — |
| | ND(1992) Proof | 147,061 | — | — | — | — | — | — | 3.00 |

**10 CENTS** **Weight:** 2.4000 g. **Composition:** 0.9250 Silver .0714 oz. ASW **Subject:** John Cabot

| KM | Date | Mintage | VG-8 | F-12 | VF-20 | XF-40 | MS-60 | MS-63 | Proof |
|---|---|---|---|---|---|---|---|---|---|
| 299 | ND(1997) Proof | 49,848 | — | — | — | — | — | — | 17.50 |

**10 CENTS** **Weight:** 2.3200 g. **Composition:** 0.9250 Silver .0690 oz. ASW **Subject:** 90th Anniversary Royal Canadian Mint

| KM | Date | Mintage | VG-8 | F-12 | VF-20 | XF-40 | MS-60 | MS-63 | Proof |
|---|---|---|---|---|---|---|---|---|---|
| 311 | ND(1998) Matte | 25,000 | — | — | — | — | — | — | 10.00 |
| | ND(1998) Proof | 25,000 | — | — | — | — | — | — | 10.00 |

**10 CENTS** **Weight:** 2.4000 g. **Composition:** 0.9250 Silver .0714 oz. ASW **Subject:** First Canadian Credit Union **Obverse:** Queen's head right. **Reverse:** Alphonse Desjardins' house, (founder of the first credit union in Canada). **Edge:** Reeded. **Size:** 18 mm.

| KM | Date | Mintage | VG-8 | F-12 | VF-20 | XF-40 | MS-60 | MS-63 | Proof |
|---|---|---|---|---|---|---|---|---|---|
| 409 | ND(2000) Proof | 66,336 | — | — | — | — | — | — | 11.00 |

**10 CENTS** **Weight:** 1.7700 g. **Composition:** Nickel Plated Steel **Subject:** Year of the Volunteer **Obverse:** Queen's head right. **Reverse:** Three portraits and radiant sun. **Edge:** Reeded. **Size:** 18 mm.

| KM | Date | Mintage | VG-8 | F-12 | VF-20 | XF-40 | MS-60 | MS-63 | Proof |
|---|---|---|---|---|---|---|---|---|---|
| 412 | 2001P Proof | — | — | — | — | — | — | — | — |

**10 CENTS** **Weight:** 2.4000 g. **Composition:** 0.9250 Silver .0714 oz. ASW **Subject:** Year of the Volunteer **Obverse:** Queen's head right. **Reverse:** 3 conjoined busts above banner, radiant sun below. **Edge:** Reeded. **Size:** 18 mm.

| KM | Date | Mintage | MS-63 | Proof |
|---|---|---|---|---|
| 412a | 2001P Proof | 50,000 | — | 12.50 |

**25 CENTS** **Weight:** 5.8319 g. **Composition:** 0.8000 Silver 0.1500 oz. ASW **Subject:** Confederation Centennial

| KM | Date | Mintage | VG-8 | F-12 | VF-20 | XF-40 | MS-60 | MS-63 | Proof |
|---|---|---|---|---|---|---|---|---|---|
| 68 | ND(1967) | 48,855,500 | — | — | — | BV | 1.00 | 1.75 | — |

**25 CENTS** **Weight:** 5.8319 g. **Composition:** 0.5000 Silver 0.0937 oz. ASW **Subject:** Confederation Centennial

| KM | Date | Mintage | VG-8 | F-12 | VF-20 | XF-40 | MS-60 | MS-63 | Proof |
|---|---|---|---|---|---|---|---|---|---|
| 68a | ND(1967) | Inc. above | — | — | — | BV | 1.00 | 1.75 | — |

**25 CENTS** **Composition:** Nickel **Subject:** RCMP Centennial **Note:** 120 beads.

| KM | Date | Mintage | VG-8 | F-12 | VF-20 | XF-40 | MS-60 | MS-63 | Proof |
|---|---|---|---|---|---|---|---|---|---|
| 81.1 | ND(1973) | 134,958,587 | — | — | — | 0.30 | 0.50 | 0.80 | — |

**25 CENTS** **Composition:** Nickel **Subject:** RCMP Centennial **Note:** 132 beads.

| KM | Date | Mintage | VG-8 | F-12 | VF-20 | XF-40 | MS-60 | MS-63 | Proof |
|---|---|---|---|---|---|---|---|---|---|
| 81.2 | ND(1973) | Inc. above | 30.00 | 50.00 | 60.00 | 70.00 | 85.00 | 110 | — |

**25 CENTS** **Composition:** Nickel **Subject:** Confederation 125

| KM | Date | Mintage | VG-8 | F-12 | VF-20 | XF-40 | MS-60 | MS-63 | Proof |
|---|---|---|---|---|---|---|---|---|---|
| 207 | ND(1992) | 442,986 | — | — | — | — | — | 12.50 | — |
| | ND(1992) Proof | 147,061 | — | — | — | — | — | — | 20.00 |

**25 CENTS** **Composition:** Nickel **Series:** 125th Anniversary of Confederation **Subject:** New Brunswick

| KM | Date | Mintage | VG-8 | F-12 | VF-20 | XF-40 | MS-60 | MS-63 | Proof |
|---|---|---|---|---|---|---|---|---|---|
| 203 | ND(1992) | 12,174,000 | — | — | — | — | 0.35 | 0.75 | — |

**25 CENTS** **Weight:** 5.8319 g. **Composition:** 0.9250 Silver 0.1734 oz. ASW **Series:** 125th Anniversary of Confederation **Subject:** New Brunswick

| KM | Date | Mintage | VG-8 | F-12 | VF-20 | XF-40 | MS-60 | MS-63 | Proof |
|---|---|---|---|---|---|---|---|---|---|
| 203a | ND(1992) Proof | 149,579 | — | — | — | — | — | — | 7.50 |

**25 CENTS** **Composition:** Nickel **Series:** 125th Anniversary of Confederation **Subject:** North West Territories

| KM | Date | Mintage | VG-8 | F-12 | VF-20 | XF-40 | MS-60 | MS-63 | Proof |
|---|---|---|---|---|---|---|---|---|---|
| 212 | ND(1992) | 12,582,000 | — | — | — | — | 0.35 | 0.75 | — |

**25 CENTS** **Weight:** 5.8319 g. **Composition:** 0.9250 Silver 0.1734 oz. ASW **Series:** 125th Anniversary of Confederation **Subject:** North West Territories

| KM | Date | Mintage | VG-8 | F-12 | VF-20 | XF-40 | MS-60 | MS-63 | Proof |
|---|---|---|---|---|---|---|---|---|---|
| 212a | ND(1992) Proof | 149,579 | — | — | — | — | — | — | 7.50 |

**25 CENTS** **Composition:** Nickel **Series:** 125th Anniversary of Confederation **Subject:** Newfoundland

| KM | Date | Mintage | VG-8 | F-12 | VF-20 | XF-40 | MS-60 | MS-63 | Proof |
|---|---|---|---|---|---|---|---|---|---|
| 213 | ND(1992) | 11,405,000 | — | — | — | — | 0.35 | 0.75 | — |

**25 CENTS** **Weight:** 5.8319 g. **Composition:** 0.9250 Silver 0.1734 oz. ASW **Series:** 125th Anniversary of Confederation **Subject:** Newfoundland

| KM | Date | Mintage | VG-8 | F-12 | VF-20 | XF-40 | MS-60 | MS-63 | Proof |
|---|---|---|---|---|---|---|---|---|---|
| 213a | ND(1992) Proof | 149,579 | — | — | — | — | — | — | 7.50 |

**25 CENTS** **Composition:** Nickel **Series:** 125th Anniversary of Confederation **Subject:** Manitoba

| KM | Date | Mintage | VG-8 | F-12 | VF-20 | XF-40 | MS-60 | MS-63 | Proof |
|---|---|---|---|---|---|---|---|---|---|
| 214 | ND(1992) | 11,349,000 | — | — | — | — | 0.35 | 0.75 | — |

**25 CENTS** **Weight:** 5.8319 g. **Composition:** 0.9250 Silver 0.1734 oz. ASW **Series:** 125th Anniversary of Confederation **Subject:** Manitoba

| KM | Date | Mintage | VG-8 | F-12 | VF-20 | XF-40 | MS-60 | MS-63 | Proof |
|---|---|---|---|---|---|---|---|---|---|
| 214a | ND(1992) Proof | 149,579 | — | — | — | — | — | — | 7.50 |

**25 CENTS** **Composition:** Nickel **Series:** 125th Anniversary of Confederation **Subject:** Yukon

| KM | Date | Mintage | VG-8 | F-12 | VF-20 | XF-40 | MS-60 | MS-63 | Proof |
|---|---|---|---|---|---|---|---|---|---|
| 220 | ND(1992) | 10,388,000 | — | — | — | — | 0.35 | 0.75 | — |

**25 CENTS** **Weight:** 5.8319 g. **Composition:** 0.9250 Silver 0.1734 oz. ASW **Series:** 125th Anniversary of Confederation **Subject:** Yukon

| KM | Date | Mintage | VG-8 | F-12 | VF-20 | XF-40 | MS-60 | MS-63 | Proof |
|---|---|---|---|---|---|---|---|---|---|
| 220a | ND(1992) Proof | 149,579 | — | — | — | — | — | — | 7.50 |

**25 CENTS** **Composition:** Nickel **Series:** 125th Anniversary of Confederation **Subject:** Alberta

| KM | Date | Mintage | VG-8 | F-12 | VF-20 | XF-40 | MS-60 | MS-63 | Proof |
|---|---|---|---|---|---|---|---|---|---|
| 221 | ND(1992) | 12,133,000 | — | — | — | — | 0.35 | 0.75 | — |

**25 CENTS** **Weight:** 5.8319 g. **Composition:** 0.9250 Silver 0.1734 oz. ASW **Series:** 125th Anniversary of Confederation **Subject:** Alberta

| KM | Date | Mintage | VG-8 | F-12 | VF-20 | XF-40 | MS-60 | MS-63 | Proof |
|---|---|---|---|---|---|---|---|---|---|
| 221a | ND(1992) Proof | — | — | — | — | — | — | — | 7.50 |

**25 CENTS** **Composition:** Nickel **Series:** 125th Anniversary of Confederation **Subject:** Prince Edward Island

| KM | Date | Mintage | VG-8 | F-12 | VF-20 | XF-40 | MS-60 | MS-63 | Proof |
|---|---|---|---|---|---|---|---|---|---|
| 222 | ND(1992) | 13,001,000 | — | — | — | — | 0.35 | 0.75 | — |

**25 CENTS** **Weight:** 5.8319 g. **Composition:** 0.9250 Silver 0.1734 oz. ASW **Series:** 125th Anniversary of Confederation **Subject:** Prince Edward Island

| KM | Date | Mintage | VG-8 | F-12 | VF-20 | XF-40 | MS-60 | MS-63 | Proof |
|---|---|---|---|---|---|---|---|---|---|
| 222a | ND(1992) Proof | 149,579 | — | — | — | — | — | — | 7.50 |

**25 CENTS** **Composition:** Nickel **Series:** 125th Anniversary of Confederation **Subject:** Ontario

| KM | Date | Mintage | VG-8 | F-12 | VF-20 | XF-40 | MS-60 | MS-63 | Proof |
|---|---|---|---|---|---|---|---|---|---|
| 223 | ND(1992) | 14,263,000 | — | — | — | — | 0.35 | 0.75 | — |

**25 CENTS** **Weight:** 5.8319 g. **Composition:** 0.9250 Silver 0.1734 oz. ASW **Series:** 125th Anniversary of Confederation **Subject:** Ontario

| KM | Date | Mintage | VG-8 | F-12 | VF-20 | XF-40 | MS-60 | MS-63 | Proof |
|---|---|---|---|---|---|---|---|---|---|
| 223a | ND(1992) Proof | 149,579 | — | — | — | — | — | — | 7.50 |

**25 CENTS** **Composition:** Nickel **Series:** 125th Anniversary of Confederation **Subject:** Nova Scotia

| KM | Date | Mintage | VG-8 | F-12 | VF-20 | XF-40 | MS-60 | MS-63 | Proof |
|---|---|---|---|---|---|---|---|---|---|
| 231 | ND(1992) | 13,600,000 | — | — | — | — | 0.35 | 0.75 | — |

**25 CENTS** **Weight:** 5.8319 g. **Composition:** 0.9250 Silver 0.1734 oz. ASW **Series:** 125th Anniversary of Confederation **Subject:** Nova Scotia

| KM | Date | Mintage | VG-8 | F-12 | VF-20 | XF-40 | MS-60 | MS-63 | Proof |
|---|---|---|---|---|---|---|---|---|---|
| 231a | ND(1992) Proof | 149,579 | — | — | — | — | — | — | 7.50 |

**25 CENTS** **Composition:** Nickel **Series:** 125th Anniversary of Confederation **Subject:** British Columbia

| KM | Date | Mintage | VG-8 | F-12 | VF-20 | XF-40 | MS-60 | MS-63 | Proof |
|---|---|---|---|---|---|---|---|---|---|
| 232 | ND(1992) | 14,001,000 | — | — | — | — | 0.35 | 0.75 | — |

**25 CENTS** **Weight:** 5.8319 g. **Composition:** 0.9250 Silver 0.1734 oz. ASW **Series:** 125th Anniversary of Confederation **Subject:** British Columbia

| KM | Date | Mintage | VG-8 | F-12 | VF-20 | XF-40 | MS-60 | MS-63 | Proof |
|---|---|---|---|---|---|---|---|---|---|
| 232a | ND(1992) Proof | 149,579 | — | — | — | — | — | — | 7.50 |

**25 CENTS** **Composition:** Nickel **Series:** 125th Anniversary of Confederation **Subject:** Saskatchewan

| KM | Date | Mintage | VG-8 | F-12 | VF-20 | XF-40 | MS-60 | MS-63 | Proof |
|---|---|---|---|---|---|---|---|---|---|
| 233 | ND(1992) | 14,165,000 | — | — | — | — | 0.35 | 0.75 | — |

**25 CENTS** **Weight:** 5.8319 g. **Composition:** 0.9250 Silver 0.1734 oz. ASW **Series:** 125th Anniversary of Confederation **Subject:** Saskatchewan

| KM | Date | Mintage | VG-8 | F-12 | VF-20 | XF-40 | MS-60 | MS-63 | Proof |
|---|---|---|---|---|---|---|---|---|---|
| 233a | ND(1992) Proof | 149,579 | — | — | — | — | — | — | 7.50 |

**25 CENTS** **Composition:** Nickel **Series:** 125th Anniversary of Confederation **Subject:** Quebec

| KM | Date | Mintage | VG-8 | F-12 | VF-20 | XF-40 | MS-60 | MS-63 | Proof |
|---|---|---|---|---|---|---|---|---|---|
| 234 | ND(1992) | 13,607,000 | — | — | — | — | 0.35 | 0.75 | — |

**25 CENTS** **Weight:** 5.8319 g. **Composition:** 0.9250 Silver 0.1734 oz. ASW **Series:** 125th Anniversary of Confederation **Subject:** Quebec

| KM | Date | Mintage | VG-8 | F-12 | VF-20 | XF-40 | MS-60 | MS-63 | Proof |
|---|---|---|---|---|---|---|---|---|---|
| 234a | ND(1992) Proof | 149,579 | — | — | — | — | — | — | 7.50 |

**25 CENTS** **Subject:** 90th Anniversary Royal Canadian Mint

| KM | Date | Mintage | VG-8 | F-12 | VF-20 | XF-40 | MS-60 | MS-63 | Proof |
|---|---|---|---|---|---|---|---|---|---|
| 312 | ND(1998) Matte | 25,000 | — | — | — | — | — | — | 15.00 |

**25 CENTS** **Composition:** Nickel **Series:** Millennium **Subject:** January **Reverse:** Totem pole, portraits

| KM | Date | Mintage | VG-8 | F-12 | VF-20 | XF-40 | MS-60 | MS-63 | Proof |
|---|---|---|---|---|---|---|---|---|---|
| 342 | 1999 | | — | — | — | — | 0.50 | 0.70 | — |

**25 CENTS** **Weight:** 5.8319 g. **Composition:** 0.9250 Silver 0.1734 oz. ASW **Series:** Millennium **Subject:** January **Reverse:** Totem pole, portraits

| KM | Date | Mintage | VG-8 | F-12 | VF-20 | XF-40 | MS-60 | MS-63 | Proof |
|---|---|---|---|---|---|---|---|---|---|
| 342a | 1999 Proof | | — | — | — | — | — | — | 8.00 |

**25 CENTS** **Composition:** Nickel **Series:** Millennium **Subject:** February **Reverse:** Native petroglyphs

| KM | Date | Mintage | VG-8 | F-12 | VF-20 | XF-40 | MS-60 | MS-63 | Proof |
|---|---|---|---|---|---|---|---|---|---|
| 343 | 1999 | | — | — | — | — | 0.50 | 0.70 | — |

**25 CENTS** **Weight:** 5.8319 g. **Composition:** 0.9250 Silver 0.1734 oz. ASW **Series:** Millennium **Subject:** February **Reverse:** Native petroglyphs

| KM | Date | Mintage | VG-8 | F-12 | VF-20 | XF-40 | MS-60 | MS-63 | Proof |
|---|---|---|---|---|---|---|---|---|---|
| 343a | 1999 Proof | | | | | | | | 8.00 |

**25 CENTS** **Composition:** Nickel **Series:** Millennium **Subject:** March **Reverse:** Lumberjack

| KM | Date | Mintage | VG-8 | F-12 | VF-20 | XF-40 | MS-60 | MS-63 | Proof |
|---|---|---|---|---|---|---|---|---|---|
| 344 | 1999 | | — | — | — | — | 0.50 | 0.70 | — |

**25 CENTS** **Weight:** 5.8319 g. **Composition:** 0.9250 Silver 0.1734 oz. ASW **Series:** Millennium **Subject:** March **Reverse:** Lumberjack

| KM | Date | Mintage | VG-8 | F-12 | VF-20 | XF-40 | MS-60 | MS-63 | Proof |
|---|---|---|---|---|---|---|---|---|---|
| 344a | 1999 Proof | | — | — | — | — | — | — | 8.00 |

**25 CENTS** **Composition:** Nickel **Series:** Millennium **Subject:** April **Reverse:** Owl, polar bear

| KM | Date | Mintage | VG-8 | F-12 | VF-20 | XF-40 | MS-60 | MS-63 | Proof |
|---|---|---|---|---|---|---|---|---|---|
| 345 | 1999 | — | — | — | — | — | 0.50 | 0.70 | — |

**25 CENTS** **Weight:** 5.8319 g. **Composition:** 0.9250 Silver 0.1734 oz. ASW **Series:** Millennium **Subject:** April **Reverse:** Owl, polar bear

| KM | Date | Mintage | VG-8 | F-12 | VF-20 | XF-40 | MS-60 | MS-63 | Proof |
|---|---|---|---|---|---|---|---|---|---|
| 345a | 1999 Proof | — | — | — | — | — | — | — | 8.00 |

**25 CENTS** **Composition:** Nickel **Series:** Millennium **Subject:** May **Reverse:** Voyageurs in canoe

| KM | Date | Mintage | VG-8 | F-12 | VF-20 | XF-40 | MS-60 | MS-63 | Proof |
|---|---|---|---|---|---|---|---|---|---|
| 346 | 1999 | — | — | — | — | — | 0.50 | 0.70 | — |

**25 CENTS** **Weight:** 5.8319 g. **Composition:** 0.9250 Silver 0.1734 oz. ASW **Series:** Millennium **Subject:** May **Reverse:** Voyageurs in canoe

| KM | Date | Mintage | VG-8 | F-12 | VF-20 | XF-40 | MS-60 | MS-63 | Proof |
|---|---|---|---|---|---|---|---|---|---|
| 346a | 1999 Proof | — | — | — | — | — | — | — | 8.00 |

**25 CENTS** **Composition:** Nickel **Series:** Millennium **Subject:** June **Reverse:** 19th-century locomotive

| KM | Date | Mintage | VG-8 | F-12 | VF-20 | XF-40 | MS-60 | MS-63 | Proof |
|---|---|---|---|---|---|---|---|---|---|
| 347 | 1999 | — | — | — | — | — | 0.50 | 0.70 | — |

**25 CENTS** **Weight:** 5.8319 g. **Composition:** 0.9250 Silver 0.1734 oz. ASW **Series:** Millennium **Subject:** June **Reverse:** 19th-century locomotive

| KM | Date | Mintage | VG-8 | F-12 | VF-20 | XF-40 | MS-60 | MS-63 | Proof |
|---|---|---|---|---|---|---|---|---|---|
| 347a | 1999 Proof | — | — | — | — | — | — | — | 8.00 |

**25 CENTS** **Composition:** Nickel **Series:** Millennium **Subject:** July **Reverse:** 6 stylized portraits

| KM | Date | Mintage | VG-8 | F-12 | VF-20 | XF-40 | MS-60 | MS-63 | Proof |
|---|---|---|---|---|---|---|---|---|---|
| 348 | 1999 | — | — | — | — | — | 0.50 | 0.70 | — |

**25 CENTS** **Weight:** 5.8319 g. **Composition:** 0.9250 Silver 0.1734 oz. ASW **Series:** Millennium **Subject:** July **Reverse:** 6 stylized portraits

| KM | Date | Mintage | VG-8 | F-12 | VF-20 | XF-40 | MS-60 | MS-63 | Proof |
|---|---|---|---|---|---|---|---|---|---|
| 348a | 1999 Proof | — | — | — | — | — | — | — | 8.00 |

**25 CENTS** **Composition:** Nickel **Series:** Millennium **Subject:** August **Reverse:** Hay harvesting

| KM | Date | Mintage | VG-8 | F-12 | VF-20 | XF-40 | MS-60 | MS-63 | Proof |
|---|---|---|---|---|---|---|---|---|---|
| 349 | 1999 | — | — | — | — | — | 0.50 | 0.70 | — |

**25 CENTS** **Weight:** 5.8319 g. **Composition:** 0.9250 Silver 0.1734 oz. ASW **Series:** Millennium **Subject:** August **Reverse:** Hay harvesting

| KM | Date | Mintage | VG-8 | F-12 | VF-20 | XF-40 | MS-60 | MS-63 | Proof |
|---|---|---|---|---|---|---|---|---|---|
| 349a | 1999 Proof | — | — | — | — | — | — | — | 8.00 |

**25 CENTS** **Composition:** Nickel **Series:** Millennium **Subject:** September **Reverse:** Childlike artwork

| KM | Date | Mintage | VG-8 | F-12 | VF-20 | XF-40 | MS-60 | MS-63 | Proof |
|---|---|---|---|---|---|---|---|---|---|
| 350 | 1999 | — | — | — | — | — | 0.50 | 0.70 | — |

**25 CENTS** **Weight:** 5.8319 g. **Composition:** 0.9250 Silver 0.1734 oz. ASW **Series:** Millennium **Subject:** September **Reverse:** Childlike artwork

| KM | Date | Mintage | VG-8 | F-12 | VF-20 | XF-40 | MS-60 | MS-63 | Proof |
|---|---|---|---|---|---|---|---|---|---|
| 350a | 1999 Proof | — | — | — | — | — | — | — | 8.00 |

**25 CENTS** **Composition:** Nickel **Series:** Millennium **Subject:** October **Reverse:** Aboriginal artwork

| KM | Date | Mintage | VG-8 | F-12 | VF-20 | XF-40 | MS-60 | MS-63 | Proof |
|---|---|---|---|---|---|---|---|---|---|
| 351 | 1999 | — | — | — | — | — | 0.50 | 0.70 | — |

**25 CENTS** **Weight:** 5.8319 g. **Composition:** 0.9250 Silver 0.1734 oz. ASW **Series:** Millennium **Subject:** October **Reverse:** Aboriginal artwork

| KM | Date | Mintage | VG-8 | F-12 | VF-20 | XF-40 | MS-60 | MS-63 | Proof |
|---|---|---|---|---|---|---|---|---|---|
| 351a | 1999 Proof | — | — | — | — | — | — | — | 8.00 |

**25 CENTS** **Composition:** Nickel **Series:** Millennium **Subject:** November **Reverse:** Bush plane with landing skis

| KM | Date | Mintage | VG-8 | F-12 | VF-20 | XF-40 | MS-60 | MS-63 | Proof |
|---|---|---|---|---|---|---|---|---|---|
| 352 | 1999 | — | — | — | — | — | 0.50 | 0.70 | — |

**25 CENTS** **Weight:** 5.8319 g. **Composition:** 0.9250 Silver 0.1734 oz. ASW **Series:** Millennium **Subject:** November **Reverse:** Bush plane with landing skis

| KM | Date | Mintage | VG-8 | F-12 | VF-20 | XF-40 | MS-60 | MS-63 | Proof |
|---|---|---|---|---|---|---|---|---|---|
| 352a | 1999 Proof | — | — | — | — | — | — | — | 8.00 |

**25 CENTS** **Composition:** Nickel **Series:** Millennium **Subject:** December **Reverse:** Eclectic geometric design

| KM | Date | Mintage | VG-8 | F-12 | VF-20 | XF-40 | MS-60 | MS-63 | Proof |
|---|---|---|---|---|---|---|---|---|---|

**25 CENTS** **Weight:** 5.8319 g. **Composition:** 0.9250 Silver 0.1734 oz. ASW **Series:** Millennium **Subject:** December **Reverse:** Eclectic geometric design

| KM | Date | Mintage | VG-8 | F-12 | VF-20 | XF-40 | MS-60 | MS-63 | Proof |
|---|---|---|---|---|---|---|---|---|---|
| 353a | 1999 Proof | — | — | — | — | — | — | — | 8.00 |

**25 CENTS** **Composition:** Nickel **Subject:** Health **Reverse:** Ribbon and caduceus

| KM | Date | Mintage | VG-8 | F-12 | VF-20 | XF-40 | MS-60 | MS-63 | Proof |
|---|---|---|---|---|---|---|---|---|---|
| 373 | 2000 | — | — | — | — | — | 0.50 | 0.70 | — |

**25 CENTS** **Composition:** 0.9250 Silver **Subject:** Health **Reverse:** Ribbon and caduceus

| KM | Date | Mintage | VG-8 | F-12 | VF-20 | XF-40 | MS-60 | MS-63 | Proof |
|---|---|---|---|---|---|---|---|---|---|

**25 CENTS** **Composition:** Nickel **Subject:** Freedom **Reverse:** 2 children and rising sun

| KM | Date | Mintage | VG-8 | F-12 | VF-20 | XF-40 | MS-60 | MS-63 | Proof |
|---|---|---|---|---|---|---|---|---|---|
| 374 | 2000 | — | — | — | — | — | 0.50 | 0.70 | — |

**25 CENTS** **Composition:** 0.9250 Silver **Subject:** Freedom **Reverse:** 2 children and rising sun

| KM | Date | Mintage | VG-8 | F-12 | VF-20 | XF-40 | MS-60 | MS-63 | Proof |
|---|---|---|---|---|---|---|---|---|---|
| 374a | 2000 Proof | — | — | — | — | — | — | — | 8.00 |

**25 CENTS** **Composition:** 0.9250 Silver **Subject:** Family **Reverse:** Circular native carvings

| KM | Date | Mintage | VG-8 | F-12 | VF-20 | XF-40 | MS-60 | MS-63 | Proof |
|---|---|---|---|---|---|---|---|---|---|
| 375a | 2000 Proof | — | — | — | — | — | — | — | 8.00 |

**25 CENTS** **Composition:** Nickel **Subject:** Family **Reverse:** Circular native carvings

| KM | Date | Mintage | VG-8 | F-12 | VF-20 | XF-40 | MS-60 | MS-63 | Proof |
|---|---|---|---|---|---|---|---|---|---|
| 375 | 2000 | — | — | — | — | — | 0.50 | 0.70 | — |

**25 CENTS** **Composition:** Nickel **Subject:** Community **Reverse:** Map on globe

| KM | Date | Mintage | VG-8 | F-12 | VF-20 | XF-40 | MS-60 | MS-63 | Proof |
|---|---|---|---|---|---|---|---|---|---|
| 376 | 2000 | — | — | — | — | — | 0.50 | 0.70 | — |

**25 CENTS** **Composition:** 0.9250 Silver **Subject:** Community **Reverse:** Map on globe

| KM | Date | Mintage | VG-8 | F-12 | VF-20 | XF-40 | MS-60 | MS-63 | Proof |
|---|---|---|---|---|---|---|---|---|---|
| 376a | 2000 Proof | — | — | — | — | — | — | — | 8.00 |

**25 CENTS** **Composition:** Nickel **Subject:** Harmony **Reverse:** Maple leaf

| KM | Date | Mintage | VG-8 | F-12 | VF-20 | XF-40 | MS-60 | MS-63 | Proof |
|---|---|---|---|---|---|---|---|---|---|
| 377 | 2000 | — | — | — | — | — | 0.50 | 0.70 | — |

**25 CENTS** **Composition:** 0.9250 Silver **Subject:** Harmony **Reverse:** Maple leaf

| KM | Date | Mintage | VG-8 | F-12 | VF-20 | XF-40 | MS-60 | MS-63 | Proof |
|---|---|---|---|---|---|---|---|---|---|
| 377a | 2000 Proof | — | — | — | — | — | — | — | 8.00 |

**25 CENTS** **Composition:** Nickel **Subject:** Wisdom **Reverse:** Man with young child

| KM | Date | Mintage | VG-8 | F-12 | VF-20 | XF-40 | MS-60 | MS-63 | Proof |
|---|---|---|---|---|---|---|---|---|---|
| 378 | 2000 | — | — | — | — | — | 0.50 | 0.70 | — |

**25 CENTS** **Composition:** 0.9250 Silver **Subject:** Wisdom **Reverse:** Man with young child

| KM | Date | Mintage | VG-8 | F-12 | VF-20 | XF-40 | MS-60 | MS-63 | Proof |
|---|---|---|---|---|---|---|---|---|---|
| 378a | 2000 Proof | — | — | — | — | — | — | — | 8.00 |

**25 CENTS** **Composition:** Nickel **Subject:** Creativity **Reverse:** Canoe full of children

| KM | Date | Mintage | VG-8 | F-12 | VF-20 | XF-40 | MS-60 | MS-63 | Proof |
|---|---|---|---|---|---|---|---|---|---|
| 379 | 2000 | — | — | — | — | — | 0.50 | 0.70 | — |

**25 CENTS** **Composition:** 0.9250 Silver **Subject:** Creativity **Reverse:** Canoe full of children

| KM | Date | Mintage | VG-8 | F-12 | VF-20 | XF-40 | MS-60 | MS-63 | Proof |
|---|---|---|---|---|---|---|---|---|---|
| 379a | 2000 Proof | — | — | — | — | — | — | — | 8.00 |

**25 CENTS** **Composition:** Nickel **Subject:** Ingenuity **Reverse:** Crescent-shaped city views

| KM | Date | Mintage | VG-8 | F-12 | VF-20 | XF-40 | MS-60 | MS-63 | Proof |
|---|---|---|---|---|---|---|---|---|---|
| 380 | 2000 | — | — | — | — | — | 0.50 | 0.70 | — |

**25 CENTS** **Composition:** 0.9250 Silver **Subject:** Ingenuity **Reverse:** Crescent-shaped city view

| KM | Date | Mintage | VG-8 | F-12 | VF-20 | XF-40 | MS-60 | MS-63 | Proof |
|---|---|---|---|---|---|---|---|---|---|
| 380a | 2000 Proof | — | — | — | — | — | — | — | 8.00 |

**25 CENTS** **Composition:** Nickel **Subject:** Achievement **Reverse:** Rocket above jagged design

| KM | Date | Mintage | VG-8 | F-12 | VF-20 | XF-40 | MS-60 | MS-63 | Proof |
|---|---|---|---|---|---|---|---|---|---|
| 381 | 2000 | — | — | — | — | — | 0.50 | 0.70 | — |

**25 CENTS** **Composition:** 0.9250 Silver **Subject:** Achievement **Reverse:** Rocket above jagged design

| KM | Date | Mintage | VG-8 | F-12 | VF-20 | XF-40 | MS-60 | MS-63 | Proof |
|---|---|---|---|---|---|---|---|---|---|
| 381a | 2000 Proof | — | — | — | — | — | — | — | 8.00 |

**25 CENTS** **Composition:** Nickel **Subject:** Natural legacy **Reverse:** Environmental elements

| KM | Date | Mintage | VG-8 | F-12 | VF-20 | XF-40 | MS-60 | MS-63 | Proof |
|---|---|---|---|---|---|---|---|---|---|
| 382 | 2000 | — | — | — | — | — | 0.50 | 0.70 | — |

**25 CENTS** **Composition:** 0.9250 Silver **Subject:** Natural legacy **Reverse:** Environmental elements

| KM | Date | Mintage | VG-8 | F-12 | VF-20 | XF-40 | MS-60 | MS-63 | Proof |
|---|---|---|---|---|---|---|---|---|---|
| 382a | 2000 Proof | — | — | — | — | — | — | — | 8.00 |

**25 CENTS** **Composition:** Nickel **Subject:** Celebration **Reverse:** Fireworks, children behind flag

| KM | Date | Mintage | VG-8 | F-12 | VF-20 | XF-40 | MS-60 | MS-63 | Proof |
|---|---|---|---|---|---|---|---|---|---|
| 383 | 2000 | — | — | — | — | — | 0.50 | 0.70 | — |

**25 CENTS** **Composition:** 0.9250 Silver **Subject:** Celebration **Reverse:** Fireworks, children behind flag

| KM | Date | Mintage | VG-8 | F-12 | VF-20 | XF-40 | MS-60 | MS-63 | Proof |
|---|---|---|---|---|---|---|---|---|---|
| 383a | 2000 Proof | — | — | — | — | — | — | — | 8.00 |

**25 CENTS** **Composition:** Nickel **Subject:** Pride **Reverse:** 2 with three small maple leaves on large maple leaf

| KM | Date | Mintage | VG-8 | F-12 | VF-20 | XF-40 | MS-60 | MS-63 | Proof |
|---|---|---|---|---|---|---|---|---|---|
| 384.2 | 2000 | — | — | — | — | — | 0.50 | 0.70 | — |

**25 CENTS** **Composition:** 0.9250 Silver **Subject:** Pride **Reverse:** 2 with 3 small maple leaves on large maple leaf

| KM | Date | Mintage | VG-8 | F-12 | VF-20 | XF-40 | MS-60 | MS-63 | Proof |
|---|---|---|---|---|---|---|---|---|---|
| 384.2a | 2000 Proof | — | — | — | — | — | — | — | 8.00 |

**25 CENTS** **Composition:** Nickel **Subject:** Pride **Reverse:** Red with 3 small maple leaves on large maple leaf **Note:** Colorized version.

| KM | Date | Mintage | VG-8 | F-12 | VF-20 | XF-40 | MS-60 | MS-63 | Proof |
|---|---|---|---|---|---|---|---|---|---|
| 384.1 | 2000 | — | — | — | — | — | — | 6.50 | — |

**25 CENTS** **Weight:** 5.0600 g. **Composition:** Nickel Plated Steel **Subject:** Spirit of Canada **Obverse:** Queen's head right. **Reverse:** Maple leaf at center, children holding hands below. **Edge:** Reeded. **Size:** 23.9 mm.

| KM | Date | Mintage | VG-8 | F-12 | VF-20 | XF-40 | MS-60 | MS-63 | Proof |
|---|---|---|---|---|---|---|---|---|---|
| 419 | 2001 | — | — | — | — | — | — | — | — |

**50 CENTS** **Weight:** 11.6638 g. **Composition:** 0.8000 Silver .3000 oz. ASW **Subject:** Confederation centennial

| KM | Date | Mintage | VG-8 | F-12 | VF-20 | XF-40 | MS-60 | MS-63 | Proof |
|---|---|---|---|---|---|---|---|---|---|
| 69 | ND(1967) | 4,211,392 | — | — | — | 2.00 | 2.75 | 5.00 | — |

**50 CENTS** **Composition:** Nickel **Subject:** Confederation 125

| KM | Date | Mintage | VG-8 | F-12 | VF-20 | XF-40 | MS-60 | MS-63 | Proof |
|---|---|---|---|---|---|---|---|---|---|
| 208 | ND(1992) | 445,000 | — | — | — | 0.50 | 0.75 | 1.00 | — |
|  | ND(1992) Proof | 147,061 | — | — | — | — | — | — | 5.00 |

**50 CENTS** **Weight:** 11.6638 g. **Composition:** 0.9250 Silver .3461 oz. ASW **Subject:** Atlantic puffin

| KM | Date | Mintage | VG-8 | F-12 | VF-20 | XF-40 | MS-60 | MS-63 | Proof |
|---|---|---|---|---|---|---|---|---|---|
| 261 | 1995 Proof | — | — | — | — | — | — | — | 13.50 |

**50 CENTS** **Weight:** 11.6638 g. **Composition:** 0.9250 Silver .3461 oz. ASW **Subject:** Whooping crane

| KM | Date | Mintage | VG-8 | F-12 | VF-20 | XF-40 | MS-60 | MS-63 | Proof |
|---|---|---|---|---|---|---|---|---|---|
| 262 | 1995 Proof | — | — | — | — | — | — | — | 13.50 |

**50 CENTS** **Weight:** 11.6638 g. **Composition:** 0.9250 Silver .3461 oz. ASW **Subject:** Gray jays

| KM | Date | Mintage | VG-8 | F-12 | VF-20 | XF-40 | MS-60 | MS-63 | Proof |
|---|---|---|---|---|---|---|---|---|---|
| 263 | 1995 Proof | — | — | — | — | — | — | — | 13.50 |

**50 CENTS** **Weight:** 11.6638 g. **Composition:** 0.9250 Silver .3461 oz. ASW **Subject:** White-tailed ptarmigans

| KM | Date | Mintage | VG-8 | F-12 | VF-20 | XF-40 | MS-60 | MS-63 | Proof |
|---|---|---|---|---|---|---|---|---|---|
| 264 | 1995 Proof | — | — | — | — | — | — | — | 13.50 |

**50 CENTS** **Weight:** 11.6638 g. **Composition:** 0.9250 Silver .3461 oz. ASW **Subject:** Moose calf

| KM | Date | Mintage | VG-8 | F-12 | VF-20 | XF-40 | MS-60 | MS-63 | Proof |
|---|---|---|---|---|---|---|---|---|---|
| 283 | 1996 Proof | — | — | — | — | — | — | — | 12.00 |

**50 CENTS** **Weight:** 11.6638 g. **Composition:** 0.9250 Silver .3461 oz. ASW **Subject:** Wood ducklings

| KM | Date | Mintage | VG-8 | F-12 | VF-20 | XF-40 | MS-60 | MS-63 | Proof |
|---|---|---|---|---|---|---|---|---|---|
| 284 | 1996 Proof | — | — | — | — | — | — | — | 12.00 |

**50 CENTS** **Weight:** 11.6638 g. **Composition:** 0.9250 Silver .3461 oz. ASW **Subject:** Cougar kittens

| KM | Date | Mintage | VG-8 | F-12 | VF-20 | XF-40 | MS-60 | MS-63 | Proof |
|---|---|---|---|---|---|---|---|---|---|
| 285 | 1996 Proof | — | — | — | — | — | — | — | 12.00 |

**50 CENTS** **Weight:** 11.6638 g. **Composition:** 0.9250 Silver .3461 oz. ASW **Subject:** Black bear cubs

| KM | Date | Mintage | VG-8 | F-12 | VF-20 | XF-40 | MS-60 | MS-63 | Proof |
|---|---|---|---|---|---|---|---|---|---|
| 286 | 1996 Proof | — | — | — | — | — | — | — | 12.00 |

**50 CENTS** **Weight:** 11.6638 g. **Composition:** 0.9250 Silver .3461 oz. ASW **Subject:** Duck tolling retriever

| KM | Date | Mintage | VG-8 | F-12 | VF-20 | XF-40 | MS-60 | MS-63 | Proof |
|---|---|---|---|---|---|---|---|---|---|
| 292 | 1997 Proof | — | — | — | — | — | — | — | 12.00 |

**50 CENTS** **Weight:** 11.6638 g. **Composition:** 0.9250 Silver .3461 oz. ASW **Subject:** Labrador retriever

| KM | Date | Mintage | VG-8 | F-12 | VF-20 | XF-40 | MS-60 | MS-63 | Proof |
|---|---|---|---|---|---|---|---|---|---|
| 293 | 1997 Proof | — | — | — | — | — | — | — | 12.00 |

**50 CENTS** **Weight:** 11.6638 g. **Composition:** 0.9250 Silver .3461 oz. ASW **Subject:** Newfoundland

| KM | Date | Mintage | VG-8 | F-12 | VF-20 | XF-40 | MS-60 | MS-63 | Proof |
|---|---|---|---|---|---|---|---|---|---|
| 294 | 1997 Proof | — | — | — | — | — | — | — | 12.00 |

**50 CENTS** **Weight:** 11.6638 g. **Composition:** 0.9250 Silver .3461 oz. ASW **Subject:** Eskimo dog

| KM | Date | Mintage | VG-8 | F-12 | VF-20 | XF-40 | MS-60 | MS-63 | Proof |
|---|---|---|---|---|---|---|---|---|---|
| 295 | 1997 Proof | — | — | — | — | — | — | — | 12.00 |

**50 CENTS** **Weight:** 11.6638 g. **Composition:** 0.9250 Silver .3461 oz. ASW **Subject:** 90th Anniversary Royal Canadian Mint

| KM | Date | Mintage | VG-8 | F-12 | VF-20 | XF-40 | MS-60 | MS-63 | Proof |
|---|---|---|---|---|---|---|---|---|---|
| 313 | ND(1998) Matte | 25,000 | — | — | — | — | — | — | 20.00 |
| | ND(1998) Proof | 25,000 | — | — | — | — | — | — | 20.00 |

**50 CENTS** **Weight:** 11.6638 g. **Composition:** 0.9250 Silver .3461 oz. ASW **Subject:** 110 years Canadian speed and figure skating

| KM | Date | Mintage | VG-8 | F-12 | VF-20 | XF-40 | MS-60 | MS-63 | Proof |
|---|---|---|---|---|---|---|---|---|---|
| 314 | ND(1998) Proof | — | — | — | — | — | — | — | 12.00 |

**50 CENTS** **Weight:** 11.6638 g. **Composition:** 0.9250 Silver .3461 oz. ASW **Subject:** 100 years Canadian ski racing

| KM | Date | Mintage | VG-8 | F-12 | VF-20 | XF-40 | MS-60 | MS-63 | Proof |
|---|---|---|---|---|---|---|---|---|---|
| 315 | ND(1998) Proof | — | — | — | — | — | — | — | 12.00 |

**50 CENTS** **Weight:** 11.6638 g. **Composition:** 0.9250 Silver .3461 oz. ASW **Subject:** Killer whales

| KM | Date | Mintage | VG-8 | F-12 | VF-20 | XF-40 | MS-60 | MS-63 | Proof |
|---|---|---|---|---|---|---|---|---|---|
| 318 | 1998 Proof | — | — | — | — | — | — | — | 10.00 |

**50 CENTS** **Weight:** 11.6638 g. **Composition:** 0.9250 Silver .3461 oz. ASW **Subject:** Humpback whale

| KM | Date | Mintage | VG-8 | F-12 | VF-20 | XF-40 | MS-60 | MS-63 | Proof |
|---|---|---|---|---|---|---|---|---|---|
| 319 | 1998 Proof | — | — | — | — | — | — | — | 10.00 |

**50 CENTS** **Weight:** 11.6638 g. **Composition:** 0.9250 Silver .3461 oz. ASW **Subject:** Beluga whale

| KM | Date | Mintage | VG-8 | F-12 | VF-20 | XF-40 | MS-60 | MS-63 | Proof |
|---|---|---|---|---|---|---|---|---|---|
| 320 | 1998 Proof | — | — | — | — | — | — | — | 10.00 |

**50 CENTS** **Weight:** 11.6638 g. **Composition:** 0.9250 Silver .3461 oz. ASW **Subject:** Blue whale

| KM | Date | Mintage | VG-8 | F-12 | VF-20 | XF-40 | MS-60 | MS-63 | Proof |
|---|---|---|---|---|---|---|---|---|---|
| 321 | 1998 Proof | — | — | — | — | — | — | — | 10.00 |

**50 CENTS** **Weight:** 11.6638 g. **Composition:** 0.9250 Silver .3461 oz. ASW **Subject:** 110 years Canadian soccer

| KM | Date | Mintage | VG-8 | F-12 | VF-20 | XF-40 | MS-60 | MS-63 | Proof |
|---|---|---|---|---|---|---|---|---|---|
| 327 | ND(1998) Proof | — | — | — | — | — | — | — | 12.00 |

**50 CENTS** **Weight:** 11.6638 g. **Composition:** 0.9250 Silver .3461 oz. ASW **Subject:** 20 years Canadian auto racing

| KM | Date | Mintage | VG-8 | F-12 | VF-20 | XF-40 | MS-60 | MS-63 | Proof |
|---|---|---|---|---|---|---|---|---|---|
| 328 | ND(1998) Proof | — | — | — | — | — | — | — | 12.00 |

**50 CENTS** **Weight:** 11.6638 g. **Composition:** 0.9250 Silver .3461 oz. ASW **Subject:** 1904 Canadian open

| KM | Date | Mintage | VG-8 | F-12 | VF-20 | XF-40 | MS-60 | MS-63 | Proof |
|---|---|---|---|---|---|---|---|---|---|
| 333 | 1999 Proof | — | — | — | — | — | — | — | 13.50 |

**50 CENTS** **Weight:** 11.6638 g. **Composition:** 0.9250 Silver .3461 oz. ASW **Subject:** First U.S.-Canadian yacht race

| KM | Date | Mintage | VG-8 | F-12 | VF-20 | XF-40 | MS-60 | MS-63 | Proof |
|---|---|---|---|---|---|---|---|---|---|
| 334 | 1999 Proof | — | — | — | — | — | — | — | 12.00 |

**50 CENTS** **Weight:** 11.6638 g. **Composition:** 0.9250 Silver .3461 oz. ASW **Series:** Canadian cats **Subject:** Cymric

| KM | Date | Mintage | VG-8 | F-12 | VF-20 | XF-40 | MS-60 | MS-63 | Proof |
|---|---|---|---|---|---|---|---|---|---|
| 335 | 1999 Proof | — | — | — | — | — | — | — | 12.00 |

**50 CENTS** **Weight:** 11.6638 g. **Composition:** 0.9250 Silver .3461 oz. ASW **Series:** Canadian cats **Subject:** Tonkinese

| KM | Date | Mintage | VG-8 | F-12 | VF-20 | XF-40 | MS-60 | MS-63 | Proof |
|---|---|---|---|---|---|---|---|---|---|
| 336 | 1999 Proof | — | — | — | — | — | — | — | 12.00 |

**50 CENTS** **Weight:** 11.6638 g. **Composition:** 0.9250 Silver .3461 oz. ASW **Series:** Canadian cats **Subject:** Cougar

| KM | Date | Mintage | VG-8 | F-12 | VF-20 | XF-40 | MS-60 | MS-63 | Proof |
|---|---|---|---|---|---|---|---|---|---|
| 337 | 1999 Proof | — | — | — | — | — | — | — | 12.00 |

**50 CENTS** **Weight:** 11.6638 g. **Composition:** 0.9250 Silver .3461 oz. ASW **Series:** Canadian cats **Subject:** Lynx

| KM | Date | Mintage | VG-8 | F-12 | VF-20 | XF-40 | MS-60 | MS-63 | Proof |
|---|---|---|---|---|---|---|---|---|---|
| 338 | 1999 Proof | — | — | — | — | — | — | — | 12.00 |

**50 CENTS** **Composition:** 0.9250 Silver **Subject:** Ice hockey **Reverse:** 4 hockey players

| KM | Date | Mintage | VG-8 | F-12 | VF-20 | XF-40 | MS-60 | MS-63 | Proof |
|---|---|---|---|---|---|---|---|---|---|
| 385 | ND(2000) Proof | — | — | — | — | — | — | — | 12.00 |

**50 CENTS** **Composition:** 0.9250 Silver **Subject:** Curling **Reverse:** Motion study of a curler

| KM | Date | Mintage | VG-8 | F-12 | VF-20 | XF-40 | MS-60 | MS-63 | Proof |
|---|---|---|---|---|---|---|---|---|---|
| 386 | ND(2000) Proof | — | — | — | — | — | — | — | 12.00 |

**50 CENTS** **Composition:** 0.9250 Silver **Subject:** Great horned owl

| KM | Date | Mintage | VG-8 | F-12 | VF-20 | XF-40 | MS-60 | MS-63 | Proof |
|---|---|---|---|---|---|---|---|---|---|
| 389 | 2000 Proof | — | — | — | — | — | — | — | 12.00 |

**50 CENTS** **Composition:** 0.9250 Silver **Subject:** Red-tail hawk

| KM | Date | Mintage | VG-8 | F-12 | VF-20 | XF-40 | MS-60 | MS-63 | Proof |
|---|---|---|---|---|---|---|---|---|---|
| 390 | 2000 Proof | — | — | — | — | — | — | — | 12.00 |

**50 CENTS** **Composition:** 0.9250 Silver **Subject:** Osprey

| KM | Date | Mintage | VG-8 | F-12 | VF-20 | XF-40 | MS-60 | MS-63 | Proof |
|---|---|---|---|---|---|---|---|---|---|
| 391 | 2000 Proof | — | — | — | — | — | — | — | 12.00 |

**50 CENTS** **Composition:** 0.9250 Silver **Subject:** Bald eagle

| KM | Date | Mintage | VG-8 | F-12 | VF-20 | XF-40 | MS-60 | MS-63 | Proof |
|---|---|---|---|---|---|---|---|---|---|
| 392 | 2000 Proof | — | — | — | — | — | — | — | 12.00 |

**50 CENTS** **Composition:** 0.9250 Silver **Subject:** Steeplechase

| KM | Date | Mintage | VG-8 | F-12 | VF-20 | XF-40 | MS-60 | MS-63 | Proof |
|---|---|---|---|---|---|---|---|---|---|
| 393 | 2000 Proof | — | — | — | — | — | — | — | 12.00 |

**50 CENTS** **Composition:** 0.9250 Silver **Subject:** Bowling

| KM | Date | Mintage | VG-8 | F-12 | VF-20 | XF-40 | MS-60 | MS-63 | Proof |
|---|---|---|---|---|---|---|---|---|---|
| 394 | 2000 Proof | — | — | — | — | — | — | — | 12.00 |

**50 CENTS** **Weight:** 9.3000 g. **Composition:** 0.9250 Silver .2766 oz. ASW **Series:** Festivals - Quebec **Obverse:** Queen's head right. **Reverse:** Snowman and Chateau Frontenac. **Edge:** Reeded. **Size:** 27.13 mm.

| KM | Date | Mintage | VG-8 | F-12 | VF-20 | XF-40 | MS-60 | MS-63 | Proof |
|---|---|---|---|---|---|---|---|---|---|
| 420 | 2001 Proof | — | — | — | — | — | — | — | 15.00 |

**50 CENTS** **Weight:** 9.3000 g. **Composition:** 0.9250 Silver .2766 oz. ASW **Series:** Festivals - Nunavut **Obverse:** Queen's head right. **Reverse:** Dancer, dog sled and snowmobiles. **Edge:** Reeded. **Size:** 27.13 mm.

| KM | Date | Mintage | VG-8 | F-12 | VF-20 | XF-40 | MS-60 | MS-63 | Proof |
|---|---|---|---|---|---|---|---|---|---|
| 421 | 2001 Proof | — | — | — | — | — | — | — | 15.00 |

**50 CENTS** **Weight:** 9.3000 g. **Composition:** 0.9250 Silver .2766 oz. ASW **Series:** Festivals - Newfoundland **Obverse:** Queen's head right. **Reverse:** Sailor and musical people. **Edge:** Reeded. **Size:** 27.13 mm.

| KM | Date | Mintage | VG-8 | F-12 | VF-20 | XF-40 | MS-60 | MS-63 | Proof |
|---|---|---|---|---|---|---|---|---|---|
| 422 | 2001 Proof | — | — | — | — | — | — | — | 15.00 |

**50 CENTS** **Weight:** 9.3000 g. **Composition:** 0.9250 Silver .2766 oz. ASW **Series:** Festivals - Prince Edward Island **Obverse:** Queen's head right. **Reverse:** Family, juggler and building. **Edge:** Reeded. **Size:** 27.13 mm.

| KM | Date | Mintage | VG-8 | F-12 | VF-20 | XF-40 | MS-60 | MS-63 | Proof |
|---|---|---|---|---|---|---|---|---|---|
| 423 | 2001 Proof | — | — | — | — | — | — | — | 15.00 |

**50 CENTS** **Weight:** 9.3000 g. **Composition:** 0.9250 Silver .2766 oz. ASW **Series:** Folklore - The Sled **Obverse:** Queen's head right. **Reverse:** Family scene. **Edge:** Reeded. **Size:** 27.13 mm.

| KM | Date | Mintage | VG-8 | F-12 | VF-20 | XF-40 | MS-60 | MS-63 | Proof |
|---|---|---|---|---|---|---|---|---|---|
| 424 | 2001 Proof | — | — | — | — | — | — | — | 17.00 |

**50 CENTS** **Weight:** 9.3000 g. **Composition:** 0.9250 Silver .2766 oz. ASW **Series:** Folklore - The Maiden's Cave **Obverse:** Queen's head right. **Reverse:** Woman shouting. **Edge:** Reeded. **Size:** 27.13 mm.

| KM | Date | Mintage | VG-8 | F-12 | VF-20 | XF-40 | MS-60 | MS-63 | Proof |
|---|---|---|---|---|---|---|---|---|---|
| 425 | 2001 Proof | — | — | — | — | — | — | — | 17.00 |

**50 CENTS** **Weight:** 9.3000 g. **Composition:** 0.9250 Silver .2766 oz. ASW **Series:** Folklore - The Small Jumpers **Obverse:** Queen's head right. **Reverse:** Jumping children on seashore. **Edge:** Reeded. **Size:** 27.13 mm.

| KM | Date | Mintage | VG-8 | F-12 | VF-20 | XF-40 | MS-60 | MS-63 | Proof |
|---|---|---|---|---|---|---|---|---|---|
| 426 | 2001 Proof | — | — | — | — | — | — | — | 17.00 |

**DOLLAR** **Weight:** 23.3276 g. **Composition:** 0.8000 Silver 0.6000 oz. ASW **Subject:** Silver Jubilee

| KM | Date | Mintage | F-12 | VF-20 | XF-40 | AU-50 | MS-60 | MS-63 | Proof |
|---|---|---|---|---|---|---|---|---|---|
| 30 | 1935 | 428,707 | 11.50 | 17.50 | 28.00 | 32.00 | 36.50 | 60.00 | 4,500 |

**DOLLAR** **Weight:** 23.3276 g. **Composition:** 0.8000 Silver 0.6000 oz. ASW **Subject:** Royal Visit

| KM | Date | Mintage | F-12 | VF-20 | XF-40 | AU-50 | MS-60 | MS-63 | Proof |
|---|---|---|---|---|---|---|---|---|---|
| 38 | 1939 | 1,363,816 | 5.00 | 6.00 | 7.00 | 8.50 | 11.50 | 20.00 | — |
| | 1939 Matte specimen | — | — | — | — | — | — | — | 475 |

**DOLLAR** **Weight:** 23.3276 g. **Composition:** 0.8000 Silver 0.6000 oz. ASW **Subject:** Newfoundland

| KM | Date | Mintage | F-12 | VF-20 | XF-40 | AU-50 | MS-60 | MS-63 | Proof |
|---|---|---|---|---|---|---|---|---|---|
| 47 | 1949 | 672,218 | 9.00 | 11.00 | 16.50 | 21.50 | 25.00 | 30.00 | — |
| | 1949 Specimen proof | — | — | — | — | — | — | — | 1,200 |

**DOLLAR** **Weight:** 23.3276 g. **Composition:** 0.8000 Silver 0.6000 oz. ASW **Subject:** British Columbia

| KM | Date | Mintage | F-12 | VF-20 | XF-40 | AU-50 | MS-60 | MS-63 | Proof |
|---|---|---|---|---|---|---|---|---|---|
| 55 | ND(1958) | 3,039,630 | BV | 3.50 | 4.50 | 5.00 | 6.50 | 10.00 | — |

**DOLLAR** **Weight:** 23.3276 g. **Composition:** 0.8000 Silver 0.6000 oz. ASW **Subject:** Charlottetown

| KM | Date | Mintage | F-12 | VF-20 | XF-40 | AU-50 | MS-60 | MS-63 | Proof |
|---|---|---|---|---|---|---|---|---|---|
| 58 | ND(1964) | 7,296,832 | — | — | — | BV | 4.00 | 5.00 | — |
| | ND(1964) Specimen proof | Inc. above | — | — | — | — | — | — | 250 |

**DOLLAR** **Weight:** 23.3276 g. **Composition:** 0.8000 Silver 0.6000 oz. ASW **Subject:** Confederation Centennial **Reverse:** Goose

| KM | Date | Mintage | MS-63 | P/L | Proof |
|---|---|---|---|---|---|
| 70 | ND(1967) | 6,767,496 | 6.00 | 7.00 | 10.00 |

**DOLLAR** **Composition:** Nickel **Subject:** Manitoba **Size:** 32 mm.

| KM | Date | Mintage | MS-63 | P/L | Proof |
|---|---|---|---|---|---|
| 78 | 1970 | 4,140,058 | 2.00 | — | — |
| | 1970 | 645,869 | — | 2.50 | — |

**DOLLAR** **Composition:** Nickel **Subject:** British Columbia **Size:** 32 mm.

| KM | Date | Mintage | MS-63 | P/L | Proof |
|---|---|---|---|---|---|
| 79 | 1971 | 4,260,781 | 2.00 | — | — |
| | 1971 | 468,729 | — | 2.25 | — |

**DOLLAR** **Weight:** 23.3276 g. **Composition:** 0.5000 Silver 0.3750 oz. ASW **Subject:** British Columbia **Size:** 36 mm.

| KM | Date | Mintage | MS-63 | P/L | Spec. |
|---|---|---|---|---|---|
| 80 | 1971 | 585,674 | — | — | 5.50 |

**DOLLAR** **Weight:** 23.3276 g. **Composition:** 0.5000 Silver 0.3750 oz. ASW **Subject:** Mountie **Size:** 36 mm.

| KM | Date | Mintage | MS-63 | P/L | Spec. |
|---|---|---|---|---|---|
| 83 | 1973 | 1,031,271 | — | — | 5.50 |

**DOLLAR** **Note:** Mountie Dollar in blue case with R.C.M.P. crest.

| KM | Date | Mintage | MS-63 | P/L | Spec. |
|---|---|---|---|---|---|
| 83v | 1973 | Inc. above | — | — | 15.00 |

**DOLLAR** **Composition:** Nickel **Subject:** Prince Edward Island **Size:** 32 mm.

| KM | Date | Mintage | MS-63 | P/L | Proof |
|---|---|---|---|---|---|
| 82 | 1973 | 3,196,452 | 2.00 | — | — |
| | 1973 (c) | 466,881 | — | 2.50 | — |

**DOLLAR** **Composition:** Nickel **Subject:** Winnipeg Centennial **Size:** 32 mm.

| KM | Date | Mintage | MS-63 | P/L | Proof |
|---|---|---|---|---|---|
| 88 | 1974 | 2,799,363 | 2.00 | — | — |
| | 1974 (c) | 363,786 | — | 2.50 | — |

**DOLLAR** **Composition:** 0.5000 Silver **Subject:** Winnipeg Centennial **Size:** 36 mm.

| KM | Date | Mintage | MS-63 | P/L | Spec. |
|---|---|---|---|---|---|
| 88a | 1974 | 728,947 | — | — | 5.50 |

**DOLLAR** **Weight:** 23.3276 g. **Composition:** 0.5000 Silver 0.3750 oz. ASW **Subject:** Calgary **Size:** 36 mm.

| KM | Date | Mintage | MS-63 | P/L | Spec. |
|---|---|---|---|---|---|
| 97 | 1975 | 930,956 | — | — | 5.50 |

**DOLLAR** **Weight:** 23.3276 g. **Composition:** 0.5000 Silver 0.3750 oz. ASW **Subject:** Parliament Library **Size:** 36 mm.

| KM | Date | Mintage | MS-63 | P/L | Spec. |
|---|---|---|---|---|---|
| 106 | 1976 | 578,708 | — | — | 6.00 |
| | 1976 blue case VIP | Inc. above | — | — | 15.00 |

**DOLLAR** **Weight:** 23.3276 g. **Composition:** 0.5000 Silver 0.3750 oz. ASW **Subject:** Silver Jubilee **Size:** 36 mm.

| KM | Date | Mintage | MS-63 | P/L | Spec. |
|---|---|---|---|---|---|
| 118 | 1977 red case VIP | Inc. above | — | — | — |
| | 1977 | 744,848 | — | — | 5.00 |

**DOLLAR** **Weight:** 23.3276 g. **Composition:** 0.5000 Silver 0.3750 oz. ASW **Subject:** XI Commonwealth Games **Size:** 36 mm.

| KM | Date | Mintage | MS-63 | P/L | Spec. |
|---|---|---|---|---|---|
| 121 | 1978 | 709,602 | — | — | 5.00 |

**DOLLAR** **Weight:** 23.3276 g. **Composition:** 0.5000 Silver 0.3750 oz. ASW **Subject:** Griffon **Size:** 36 mm.

| KM | Date | Mintage | MS-63 | P/L | Spec. |
|---|---|---|---|---|---|
| 124 | 1979 | 826,695 | — | — | 8.00 |

**DOLLAR** **Weight:** 23.3276 g. **Composition:** 0.5000 Silver 0.3750 oz. ASW **Subject:** Arctic Territories **Size:** 36 mm.

| KM | Date | Mintage | MS-63 | P/L | Spec. |
|---|---|---|---|---|---|
| 128 | 1980 | 539,617 | — | — | 17.50 |

**DOLLAR** **Weight:** 23.3276 g. **Composition:** 0.5000 Silver 0.3750 oz. ASW **Subject:** Transcontinental Railroad **Size:** 36 mm.

| KM | Date | Mintage | MS-63 | P/L | Proof |
|---|---|---|---|---|---|
| 130 | 1981 | 699,494 | 7.50 | — | 13.50 |

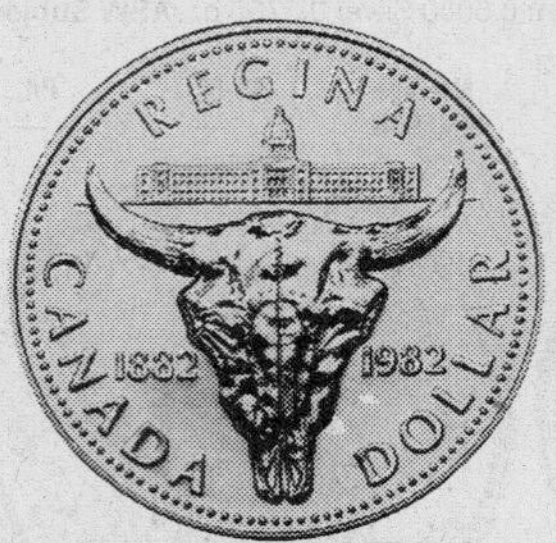

**DOLLAR** **Weight:** 23.3276 g. **Composition:** 0.5000 Silver 0.3750 oz. ASW **Subject:** Regina **Size:** 36 mm.

| KM | Date | Mintage | MS-63 | P/L | Proof |
|---|---|---|---|---|---|
| 133 | 1982 | 144,930 | 7.50 | — | — |
| | 1982 Proof | 758,958 | — | — | 5.00 |

**DOLLAR** **Composition:** Nickel **Subject:** Constitution **Size:** 32 mm.

| KM | Date | Mintage | MS-63 | P/L | Proof |
|---|---|---|---|---|---|
| 134 | 1982 | 9,709,422 | 3.00 | 6.00 | — |

**DOLLAR** **Weight:** 23.3276 g. **Composition:** 0.5000 Silver 0.3750 oz. ASW **Subject:** Edmonton University Games **Size:** 36 mm.

| KM | Date | Mintage | MS-63 | P/L | Proof |
|---|---|---|---|---|---|
| 138 | 1983 | 159,450 | 5.00 | — | — |
| | 1983 Proof | 506,847 | — | — | 6.00 |

**DOLLAR** **Weight:** 23.3276 g. **Composition:** 0.5000 Silver 0.3750 oz. ASW **Subject:** Toronto Sesquicentennial **Size:** 36 mm.

| KM | Date | Mintage | MS-63 | P/L | Proof |
|---|---|---|---|---|---|
| 140 | 1984 | 133,610 | 7.50 | — | — |
| | 1984 Proof | 732,542 | — | — | 5.00 |

**DOLLAR** **Composition:** Nickel **Subject:** Jacques Cartier **Size:** 32 mm.

| KM | Date | Mintage | MS-63 | P/L | Proof |
|---|---|---|---|---|---|
| 141 | 1984 | 7,009,323 | 2.25 | — | — |
| | 1984 Proof | 87,760 | — | — | 6.50 |

**DOLLAR** **Weight:** 23.3276 g. **Composition:** 0.5000 Silver 0.3750 oz. ASW **Subject:** National Parks/Moose **Size:** 36 mm.

| KM | Date | Mintage | MS-63 | P/L | Proof |
|---|---|---|---|---|---|
| 143 | 1985 | 163,314 | 7.50 | — | — |
| | 1985 Proof | 733,354 | — | — | 6.00 |

**DOLLAR** **Weight:** 23.3276 g. **Composition:** 0.5000 Silver 0.3750 oz. ASW **Subject:** Vancouver **Size:** 36 mm.

| KM | Date | Mintage | MS-63 | P/L | Proof |
|---|---|---|---|---|---|
| 149 | 1986 | 125,949 | 7.50 | — | — |
| | 1986 Proof | 680,004 | — | — | 6.25 |

**DOLLAR** **Weight:** 23.3276 g. **Composition:** 0.5000 Silver 0.3750 oz. ASW **Subject:** John Davis **Size:** 36 mm.

| KM | Date | Mintage | MS-63 | P/L | Proof |
|---|---|---|---|---|---|
| 154 | 1987 | 118,722 | 7.50 | — | — |
| | 1987 Proof | 602,374 | — | — | 9.00 |

**DOLLAR** **Weight:** 23.3276 g. **Composition:** 0.5000 Silver 0.3750 oz. ASW **Subject:** Ironworks **Size:** 36 mm.

| KM | Date | Mintage | MS-63 | P/L | Proof |
|---|---|---|---|---|---|
| 161 | 1988 | 106,872 | 15.00 | — | — |
| | 1988 Proof | 255,013 | — | — | 17.50 |

**DOLLAR** **Weight:** 23.3276 g. **Composition:** 0.5000 Silver 0.3750 oz. ASW **Subject:** MacKenzie River **Size:** 36 mm.

| KM | Date | Mintage | MS-63 | P/L | Proof |
|---|---|---|---|---|---|
| 168 | 1989 | 99,774 | 12.00 | — | — |
| | 1989 Proof | 244,062 | — | — | 17.50 |

**DOLLAR** **Weight:** 23.3276 g. **Composition:** 0.5000 Silver 0.3750 oz. ASW **Subject:** Henry Kelsey **Size:** 36 mm.

| KM | Date | Mintage | MS-63 | P/L | Proof |
|---|---|---|---|---|---|
| 170 | 1990 | 99,455 | 8.50 | — | — |
| | 1990 Proof | 254,959 | — | — | 12.50 |

**DOLLAR** **Weight:** 23.3276 g. **Composition:** 0.5000 Silver 0.3750 oz. ASW **Subject:** S.S. Frontenac **Size:** 36 mm.

| KM | Date | Mintage | MS-63 | P/L | Proof |
|---|---|---|---|---|---|
| 179 | 1991 | 73,843 | 9.50 | — | — |
| | 1991 Proof | 195,424 | — | — | 22.50 |

**DOLLAR** **Weight:** 25.1750 g. **Composition:** 0.9250 Silver 0.7487 oz. ASW **Subject:** Stagecoach service **Size:** 36 mm.

| KM | Date | Mintage | MS-63 | P/L | Proof |
|---|---|---|---|---|---|
| 210 | 1992 | 78,160 | 9.50 | — | — |
| | 1992 Proof | 187,612 | — | — | 12.50 |

**DOLLAR** **Composition:** Aureate **Subject:** Loon **Size:** 32 mm.

| KM | Date | Mintage | MS-63 | P/L | Proof |
|---|---|---|---|---|---|
| 209 | ND(1992) | 4,242,085 | 2.00 | 4.00 | 8.00 |

**DOLLAR** **Composition:** Aureate **Subject:** Parliament **Size:** 26 mm.

| KM | Date | Mintage | MS-63 | P/L | Proof |
|---|---|---|---|---|---|
| 218 | ND(1992) | 23,915,000 | 2.25 | 5.00 | — |
| | ND(1992) Proof | 24,227 | — | — | 9.00 |

**DOLLAR** **Weight:** 25.1750 g. **Composition:** 0.9250 Silver 0.7487 oz. ASW **Subject:** Stanley Cup hockey **Size:** 36 mm.

| KM | Date | Mintage | MS-63 | P/L | Proof |
|---|---|---|---|---|---|
| 235 | 1993 | 88,150 | 9.50 | — | — |
| | 1993 Proof | 294,314 | — | — | 12.50 |

**DOLLAR** **Weight:** 25.1750 g. **Composition:** 0.9250 Silver 0.7487 oz. ASW **Subject:** Last RCMP sled-dog patrol **Size:** 36 mm.

| KM | Date | Mintage | MS-63 | P/L | Proof |
|---|---|---|---|---|---|
| 251 | 1994 | 61,561 | 12.00 | — | — |
| | 1994 Proof | 170,374 | — | — | 24.50 |

**DOLLAR** **Composition:** Aureate **Subject:** War Memorial **Size:** 26 mm.

| KM | Date | Mintage | MS-63 | P/L | Proof |
|---|---|---|---|---|---|
| 248 | 1994 | 15,000,000 | 2.25 | — | — |
| | 1994 Proof | 54,524 | — | — | 10.00 |

**DOLLAR** **Composition:** Aureate **Subject:** Peacekeeping Monument in Ottawa **Size:** 26 mm.

| KM | Date | Mintage | MS-63 | P/L | Proof |
|---|---|---|---|---|---|
| 258 | 1995 | — | 2.25 | — | — |
| | 1995 Proof | 43,293 | — | — | 10.00 |

**DOLLAR** **Weight:** 25.1750 g. **Composition:** 0.9250 Silver 0.7487 oz. ASW **Subject:** Hudson Bay Co. **Size:** 36 mm.

| KM | Date | Mintage | MS-63 | P/L | Proof |
|---|---|---|---|---|---|
| 259 | 1995 | 61,819 | 10.00 | — | — |
| | 1995 Proof | 166,259 | — | — | 17.00 |

**DOLLAR** **Weight:** 25.1750 g. **Composition:** 0.9250 Silver 0.7487 oz. ASW **Subject:** McIntosh Apple **Size:** 36 mm.

| KM | Date | Mintage | MS-63 | P/L | Proof |
|---|---|---|---|---|---|
| 274 | 1996 | 58,834 | 12.00 | — | — |
| | 1996 Proof | 133,779 | — | — | 20.00 |

**DOLLAR** **Weight:** 25.1750 g. **Composition:** 0.9250 Silver 0.7487 oz. ASW **Subject:** 25th Anniversary Hockey Victory **Size:** 36 mm.

| KM | Date | Mintage | MS-63 | P/L | Proof |
|---|---|---|---|---|---|
| 282 | ND(1997) | 155,252 | 10.75 | — | — |
| | ND(1997) Proof | 184,965 | — | — | 23.50 |

**DOLLAR** **Composition:** Aureate **Subject:** Loon Dollar 10th Anniversary **Size:** 26 mm.

| KM | Date | Mintage | MS-63 | P/L | Proof |
|---|---|---|---|---|---|
| 291 | 1997 | — | — | 10.00 | — |

**DOLLAR** **Weight:** 25.1750 g. **Composition:** 0.9250 Silver 0.7487 oz. ASW **Subject:** Loon Dollar 10th Anniversary **Size:** 36 mm.

| KM | Date | Mintage | MS-63 | P/L | Proof |
|---|---|---|---|---|---|
| 296 | 1997 Proof | 24,995 | — | — | 65.00 |

**DOLLAR** **Weight:** 25.1750 g. **Composition:** 0.9250 Silver 0.7487 oz. ASW **Subject:** 120th Anniversary Royal Canadian Mounted Police **Size:** 36 mm. **Note:** Individually cased prooflikes, proofs or specimens are from broken-up prooflike or specimen sets.

| KM | Date | Mintage | MS-63 | P/L | Proof |
|---|---|---|---|---|---|
| 306 | 1998 | 79,777 | — | 12.00 | — |
| | 1998 Proof | 120,172 | — | — | 21.50 |

**DOLLAR** **Weight:** 25.1750 g. **Composition:** 0.9250 Silver 0.7487 oz. ASW **Subject:** International Year of Old Persons **Size:** 36 mm.

| KM | Date | Mintage | MS-63 | P/L | Proof |
|---|---|---|---|---|---|
| 355 | 1999 Proof | 24,976 | — | — | 32.50 |

**DOLLAR** **Weight:** 25.1750 g. **Composition:** 0.9250 Silver 0.7487 oz. ASW **Subject:** Discovery of Queen Charlotte Isle **Size:** 36 mm.

| KM | Date | Mintage | MS-63 | P/L | Proof |
|---|---|---|---|---|---|
| 356 | ND(1999) | 67,655 | — | 12.00 | — |
| | ND(1999) Proof | 126,435 | — | — | 22.50 |

**DOLLAR** **Weight:** 25.1750 g. **Composition:** 0.9250 Silver 0.7487 oz. ASW **Subject:** Voyage of Discovery **Reverse:** Human and space shuttle **Size:** 36 mm.

| KM | Date | Mintage | MS-63 | P/L | Proof |
|---|---|---|---|---|---|
| 401 | 2000 | 60,100 | — | 12.00 | — |
| | 2000 Proof | 114,130 | — | — | 22.50 |

**DOLLAR** **Weight:** 25.1750 g. **Composition:** 0.9250 Silver 0.7487 oz. ASW **Subject:** National Ballet **Obverse:** Queen's head right. **Reverse:** Ballet dancers. **Edge:** Reeded. **Size:** 36 mm.

| KM | Date | Mintage | MS-63 | P/L | Proof |
|---|---|---|---|---|---|
| 414 | 2001 | 65,000 | — | — | — |
| | 2001 Proof | 225,000 | — | — | 21.50 |

**2 DOLLARS** **Ring Weight:** 5.0958 g. **Ring Composition:** Silver 0.1638 oz. ASW **Center Weight:** 5.7456 g. **Center Composition:** Gold 0.1847 oz. AGW **Reverse:** Polar bear **Size:** 32 mm.

| KM | Date | Mintage | MS-63 | P/L | Proof |
|---|---|---|---|---|---|
| 270a | 1996 Proof | 5,000 | — | — | 175 |

**2 DOLLARS** **Ring Composition:** Silver 0.7434 oz. ASW **Center Weight:** 25.0000 g. **Center Composition:** 0.9250 Gold Plated Silver **Reverse:** Polar bear

| KM | Date | Mintage | MS-63 | P/L | Proof |
|---|---|---|---|---|---|
| 270b | 1996 Proof | 10,000 | — | — | 50.00 |

**2 DOLLARS** **Ring Composition:** Nickel **Center Composition:** Aluminum-Bronze **Reverse:** Polar bear **Size:** 28 mm. **Note:** The Type III design has two lines outlining the star.

| KM | Date | Mintage | MS-63 | P/L | Proof |
|---|---|---|---|---|---|
| 270 | 1996 | 375,483,000 | 3.25 | 5.00 | 10.00 |
| | 1997 | 16,942,000 | 3.25 | — | — |
| | 1998 | 4,926,000 | 3.25 | — | — |
| | 1998W | — | — | 4.00 | — |
| | 1999 | — | 3.25 | — | — |
| | 2000 | — | 3.25 | — | — |
| | 2000W | — | — | — | — |
| | 2001 | — | 3.25 | — | — |

**2 DOLLARS** **Ring Composition:** 0.9250 Silver 0.2626 oz. ASW **Center Weight:** 8.8300 g. **Center Composition:** 0.9250 Gold Plated Silver **Reverse:** Polar bear

| KM | Date | Mintage | MS-63 | P/L | Proof |
|---|---|---|---|---|---|
| 270c | 1997 Proof | — | — | — | 10.00 |
| | 19980 Proof | — | — | — | 12.00 |
| | 1999 Proof | — | — | — | 12.00 |
| | 2000 Proof | — | — | — | 12.00 |
| | 2001 Proof | — | — | — | 12.00 |

**2 DOLLARS** **Ring Composition:** Nickel **Center Composition:** Aluminum-Bronze **Subject:** Nunavut

| KM | Date | Mintage | MS-63 | P/L | Proof |
|---|---|---|---|---|---|
| 357 | 1999 | — | 3.50 | — | — |

**2 DOLLARS** **Ring Weight:** 5.8600 g. **Ring Composition:** 0.9250 Silver .1743 oz. ASW **Center Weight:** 2.9600 g. **Center Composition:** 0.9250 Gold Plated Silver .0880 oz. ASW AGW **Subject:** Nunavut **Obverse:** Queen's head right. **Reverse:** Drum dancer. **Edge:** Interrupted reeding. **Size:** 28 mm.

| KM | Date | Mintage | MS-63 | P/L | Proof |
|---|---|---|---|---|---|
| 357a | 1999 Proof | — | — | — | 14.00 |

**2 DOLLARS** **Ring Weight:** 6.3140 g. **Ring Composition:** 0.1708 White Gold .0347 oz. AGW **Center Weight:** 5.0900 g. **Center Composition:** 0.9167 Gold .15 oz. AGW **Subject:** Nunavut **Obverse:** Queen's head right. **Reverse:** Drum dancer.

| KM | Date | Mintage | MS-63 | P/L | Proof |
|---|---|---|---|---|---|
| 357b | 1999 Proof | 10,000 | — | — | 175 |

**2 DOLLARS** **Ring Composition:** Nickel**Center Weight:** 5.9000 g. **Center Composition:** Aluminum-Bronze **Subject:** Knowledge **Reverse:** Polar bear and 2 cubs **Edge:** Reeded and plain sections. **Size:** 23.88 mm.

| KM | Date | Mintage | MS-63 | P/L | Proof |
|---|---|---|---|---|---|
| 399 | 2000 | — | 3.50 | — | — |

**2 DOLLARS** **Ring Composition:** 0.1708 Gold **Center Composition:** 0.9167 Gold **Subject:** Knowledge **Reverse:** Polar bear and two cubs right.

| KM | Date | Mintage | MS-63 | P/L | Proof |
|---|---|---|---|---|---|
| 399b | 2000 Proof | — | — | — | 175 |

**2 DOLLARS** **Ring Composition:** 0.9250 Silver **Center Composition:** 0.9250 Gold Plated Silver **Subject:** Knowledge **Reverse:** Polar bear and 2 cubs **Note:** Gold plated.

| KM | Date | Mintage | MS-63 | P/L | Proof |
|---|---|---|---|---|---|
| 399a | 2000 Proof | 40,000 | — | — | 12.00 |

**5 DOLLARS** **Weight:** 24.3000 g. **Composition:** 0.9250 Silver 0.7227 oz. ASW **Subject:** 1976 Montreal Olympics **Reverse:** Sailboat "Kingston" **Size:** 38 mm. **Note:** Series I.

| KM | Date | Mintage | MS-63 | Proof |
|---|---|---|---|---|
| 84 | 1973 | — | 5.00 | — |
| | 1973 Proof | 165,203 | — | 6.25 |

**5 DOLLARS** **Composition:** 0.9250 Silver 0.7227 oz. ASW **Subject:** 1976 Montreal Olympics **Reverse:** North American map **Note:** Series I.

| KM | Date | Mintage | MS-63 | Proof |
|---|---|---|---|---|
| 85 | 1973 | — | 5.00 | — |
| | 1973 Proof | 165,203 | — | 6.25 |

**5 DOLLARS** **Weight:** 24.3000 g. **Composition:** 0.9250 Silver 0.7227 oz. ASW **Subject:** 1976 Montreal Olympics **Reverse:** Olympic rings **Size:** 38 mm. **Note:** Series II.

| KM | Date | Mintage | MS-63 | Proof |
|---|---|---|---|---|
| 89 | 1974 | — | 5.00 | — |
| | 1974 Proof | 97,431 | — | 6.25 |

**5 DOLLARS** **Weight:** 24.3000 g. **Composition:** 0.9250 Silver 0.7227 oz. ASW **Subject:** 1976 Montreal Olympics **Reverse:** Athlete with torch **Size:** 38 mm. **Note:** Series II.

| KM | Date | Mintage | MS-63 | Proof |
|---|---|---|---|---|
| 90 | 1974 | — | 5.00 | — |
| | 1974 Proof | 97,431 | — | 6.25 |

**5 DOLLARS** **Weight:** 24.3000 g. **Composition:** 0.9250 Silver 0.7227 oz. ASW **Subject:** 1976 Montreal Olympics **Reverse:** Rowing **Size:** 38 mm. **Note:** Series III.

| KM | Date | Mintage | MS-63 | Proof |
|---|---|---|---|---|
| 91 | 1974 | — | 5.00 | — |
| | 1974 Proof | 104,684 | — | 6.25 |

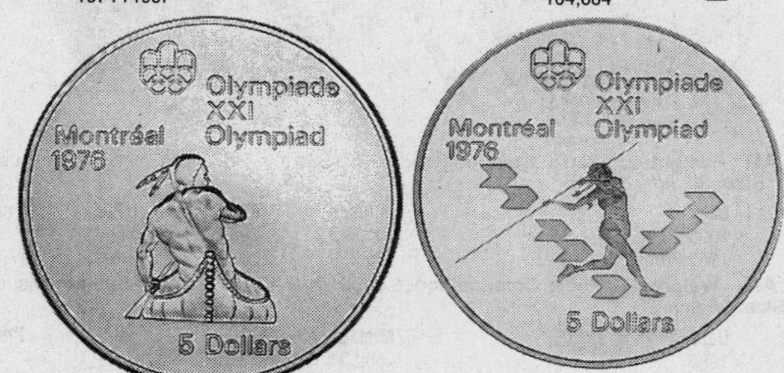


**5 DOLLARS** **Weight:** 24.3000 g. **Composition:** 0.9250 Silver 0.7227 oz. ASW **Subject:** 1976 Montreal Olympics **Reverse:** Canoeing **Size:** 38 mm. **Note:** Series III.

| KM | Date | Mintage | MS-63 | Proof |
|---|---|---|---|---|
| 92 | 1974 | — | 5.00 | — |
| | 1974 Proof | 104,684 | — | 6.25 |

**5 DOLLARS** **Weight:** 24.3000 g. **Composition:** 0.9250 Silver 0.7227 oz. ASW **Subject:** 1976 Montreal Olympics **Reverse:** Marathon **Size:** 38 mm. **Note:** Series IV.

| KM | Date | Mintage | MS-63 | Proof |
|---|---|---|---|---|
| 98 | 1975 | — | 5.00 | — |
| | 1975 Proof | 89,155 | — | 6.25 |

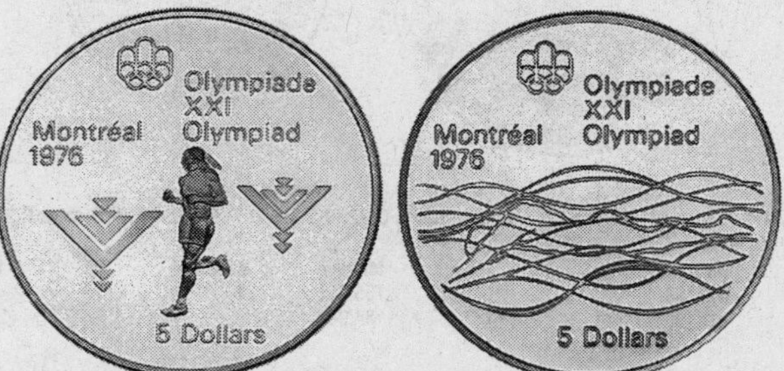


**5 DOLLARS** **Weight:** 24.3000 g. **Composition:** 0.9250 Silver 0.7227 oz. ASW **Subject:** 1976 Montreal Olympics **Reverse:** Women's javelin **Size:** 38 mm. **Note:** Series IV.

| KM | Date | Mintage | MS-63 | Proof |
|---|---|---|---|---|
| 99 | 1975 | — | 5.00 | — |
| | 1975 Proof | 89,155 | — | 6.25 |

**5 DOLLARS** **Weight:** 24.3000 g. **Composition:** 0.9250 Silver 0.7227 oz. ASW **Subject:** 1976 Montreal Olympics **Reverse:** Swimmer **Size:** 38 mm. **Note:** Series V.

| KM | Date | Mintage | MS-63 | Proof |
|---|---|---|---|---|
| 100 | 1975 | — | 5.00 | — |
| | 1975 Proof | 89,155 | — | 6.25 |

**5 DOLLARS** **Weight:** 24.3000 g. **Composition:** 0.9250 Silver 0.7227 oz. ASW **Subject:** 1976 Montreal Olympics **Reverse:** Diver **Size:** 38 mm. **Note:** Series V.

| KM | Date | Mintage | MS-63 | Proof |
|---|---|---|---|---|
| 101 | 1975 | — | 5.00 | — |
| | 1975 Proof | 89,155 | — | 6.25 |

**5 DOLLARS** **Weight:** 24.3000 g. **Composition:** 0.9250 Silver 0.7227 oz. ASW **Subject:** 1976 Montreal Olympics **Reverse:** Fencing **Size:** 38 mm. **Note:** Series VI.

| KM | Date | Mintage | MS-63 | Proof |
|---|---|---|---|---|
| 107 | 1976 | — | 5.00 | — |
| | 1976 Proof | 82,302 | — | 6.50 |

**5 DOLLARS** **Weight:** 24.3000 g. **Composition:** 0.9250 Silver 0.7227 oz. ASW **Subject:** 1976 Montreal Olympics **Obv. Legend:** Boxing **Size:** 38 mm. **Note:** Series VI.

| KM | Date | Mintage | MS-63 | Proof |
|---|---|---|---|---|
| 108 | 1976 | — | 5.00 | — |
| | 1976 Proof | 82,302 | — | 6.50 |

**5 DOLLARS** **Weight:** 24.3000 g. **Composition:** 0.9250 Silver 0.7227 oz. ASW **Subject:** 1976 Montreal Olympics **Reverse:** Olympic village **Size:** 38 mm. **Note:** Series VII.

| KM | Date | Mintage | MS-63 | Proof |
|---|---|---|---|---|
| 109 | 1976 | — | 5.00 | — |
| | 1976 Proof | 76,908 | — | 6.50 |

**5 DOLLARS** **Weight:** 24.3000 g. **Composition:** 0.9250 Silver 0.7227 oz. ASW **Subject:** 1976 Montreal Olympics **Reverse:** Olympic flame **Size:** 38 mm. **Note:** Series VII.

| KM | Date | Mintage | MS-63 | Proof |
|---|---|---|---|---|
| 110 | 1976 | — | 5.00 | — |
| | 1976 Proof | 79,102 | — | 6.50 |

**5 DOLLARS** **Weight:** 31.3900 g. **Composition:** 0.9999 Silver 1.0091 oz. ASW **Subject:** Dr. Norman Bethune

| KM | Date | Mintage | MS-63 | Proof |
|---|---|---|---|---|
| 316 | 1998 in proof sets only | 61,000 | — | 35.00 |

**5 DOLLARS** **Composition:** Copper-Zinc-Nickel **Reverse:** Viking ship under sail **Note:** Sold in sets with Norway 20 kroner, KM#465.

| KM | Date | Mintage | MS-63 | Proof |
|---|---|---|---|---|
| 398 | 1999 Proof | — | — | 16.50 |

**10 DOLLARS** **Weight:** 48.6000 g. **Composition:** 0.9250 Silver 1.4454 oz. ASW **Subject:** 1976 Montreal Olympics **Reverse:** Montreal skyline **Size:** 87 mm. **Note:** Series I.

| KM | Date | Mintage | MS-63 | Proof |
|---|---|---|---|---|
| 87 | 1973 | — | 10.00 | — |
| | 1973 Proof | 165,203 | — | 11.50 |

**10 DOLLARS** **Weight:** 48.6000 g. **Composition:** 0.9250 Silver 1.4454 oz. ASW **Subject:** 1976 Montreal Olympics **Reverse:** World map **Size:** 45 mm. **Note:** Series I.

| KM | Date | Mintage | MS-63 | Proof |
|---|---|---|---|---|
| 86.1 | 1973 | 103,426 | 10.00 | — |
| | 1973 Proof | 165,203 | — | 11.50 |

**10 DOLLARS** **Weight:** 48.6000 g. **Composition:** 0.9250 Silver 1.4454 oz. ASW **Subject:** 1976 Montreal Olympics **Reverse:** World map **Size:** 45 mm. **Note:** Series I.

| KM | Date | Mintage | MS-63 | Proof |
|---|---|---|---|---|
| 86.2 | 1974 Error: mule | 320 | 300 | — |

**10 DOLLARS** **Weight:** 48.6000 g. **Composition:** 0.9250 Silver 1.4454 oz. ASW **Subject:** 1976 Montreal Olympics **Reverse:** Head of Zeus **Size:** 45 mm. **Note:** Series II.

| KM | Date | Mintage | MS-63 | Proof |
|---|---|---|---|---|
| 93 | 1974 | — | 10.00 | — |
| | 1974 Proof | 104,684 | — | 11.50 |

**10 DOLLARS** **Weight:** 48.6000 g. **Composition:** 0.9250 Silver 1.4454 oz. ASW **Subject:** 1976 Montreal Olympics **Reverse:** Temple of Zeus **Size:** 45 mm. **Note:** Series II.

| KM | Date | Mintage | MS-63 | Proof |
|---|---|---|---|---|
| 94 | 1974 | — | 10.00 | — |
| | 1974 Proof | 104,684 | — | 11.50 |

**10 DOLLARS** **Weight:** 48.6000 g. **Composition:** 0.9250 Silver 1.4454 oz. ASW **Subject:** 1976 Montreal Olympics **Reverse:** Cycling **Size:** 45 mm. **Note:** Series III.

| KM | Date | Mintage | MS-63 | Proof |
|---|---|---|---|---|
| 95 | 1974 | — | 10.00 | — |
| | 1974 Proof | 97,431 | — | 11.50 |

**10 DOLLARS** **Weight:** 48.6000 g. **Composition:** 0.9250 Silver 1.4454 oz. ASW **Subject:** 1976 Montreal Olympics **Reverse:** Lacrosse **Size:** 45 mm. **Note:** Series III.

| KM | Date | Mintage | MS-63 | Proof |
|---|---|---|---|---|
| 96 | 1974 | — | 10.00 | — |
| | 1974 Proof | 97,431 | — | 11.50 |

**10 DOLLARS** **Weight:** 48.6000 g. **Composition:** 0.9250 Silver 1.4454 oz. ASW **Subject:** 1976 Montreal Olympics **Reverse:** Men's hurdles **Size:** 45 mm. **Note:** Series IV.

| KM | Date | Mintage | MS-63 | Proof |
|---|---|---|---|---|
| 102 | 1975 | — | 10.00 | — |
| | 1975 Proof | 82,302 | — | 11.50 |

**10 DOLLARS** **Weight:** 48.6000 g. **Composition:** 0.9250 Silver 1.4454 oz. ASW **Subject:** 1976 Montreal Olympics **Reverse:** Women's shot put **Size:** 45 mm. **Note:** Series IV.

| KM | Date | Mintage | MS-63 | Proof |
|---|---|---|---|---|
| 103 | 1975 | — | 10.00 | — |
| | 1975 Proof | 82,302 | — | 11.50 |

**10 DOLLARS** **Weight:** 48.6000 g. **Composition:** 0.9250 Silver 1.4454 oz. ASW **Subject:** 1976 Montreal Olympics **Reverse:** Sailing **Size:** 45 mm. **Note:** Series V.

| KM | Date | Mintage | MS-63 | Proof |
|---|---|---|---|---|
| 104 | 1975 | — | 10.00 | — |
| | 1975 Proof | 89,155 | — | 11.50 |

**10 DOLLARS** **Weight:** 48.6000 g. **Composition:** 0.9250 Silver 1.4454 oz. ASW **Subject:** 1976 Montreal Olympics **Reverse:** Canoeing **Size:** 45 mm. **Note:** Series V.

| KM | Date | Mintage | MS-63 | Proof |
|---|---|---|---|---|
| 105 | 1975 | — | 10.00 | — |
| | 1975 Proof | 89,155 | — | 11.50 |

**10 DOLLARS** **Weight:** 48.6000 g. **Composition:** 0.9250 Silver 1.4454 oz. ASW **Subject:** 1976 Montreal Olympics **Reverse:** Football **Size:** 45 mm. **Note:** Series VI.

| KM | Date | Mintage | MS-63 | Proof |
|---|---|---|---|---|
| 111 | 1976 | — | 10.00 | — |
| | 1976 Proof | 76,908 | — | 12.00 |

**10 DOLLARS** **Weight:** 48.6000 g. **Composition:** 0.9250 Silver 1.4454 oz. ASW **Subject:** 1976 Montreal Olympics **Reverse:** Field hockey **Size:** 45 mm. **Note:** Series VI.

| KM | Date | Mintage | MS-63 | Proof |
|---|---|---|---|---|
| 112 | 1976 | — | 10.00 | — |
| | 1976 Proof | 76,908 | — | 12.00 |

**10 DOLLARS** **Weight:** 48.6000 g. **Composition:** 0.9250 Silver 1.4454 oz. ASW **Subject:** 1976 Montreal Olympics **Reverse:** Olympic Stadium **Size:** 45 mm mm. **Note:** Series VII.

| KM | Date | Mintage | MS-63 | Proof |
|---|---|---|---|---|
| 113 | 1976 | — | 10.00 | — |
| | 1976 Proof | 79,102 | — | 12.00 |

**10 DOLLARS** **Weight:** 48.6000 g. **Composition:** 0.9250 Silver 1.4454 oz. ASW **Subject:** 1976 Montreal Olympics **Reverse:** Olympic Velodrome **Size:** 45 mm. **Note:** Series VII.

| KM | Date | Mintage | MS-63 | Proof |
|---|---|---|---|---|
| 114 | 1976 | — | 10.00 | — |
| | 1976 Proof | 79,102 | — | 12.00 |

**15 DOLLARS** **Weight:** 33.6300 g. **Composition:** 0.9250 Silver 1.0000 oz. ASW **Subject:** 1992 Olympics **Reverse:** Coaching track **Size:** 39 mm.

| KM | Date | Mintage | MS-63 | Proof |
|---|---|---|---|---|
| 215 | 1992 Proof | 275,000 | — | 28.00 |

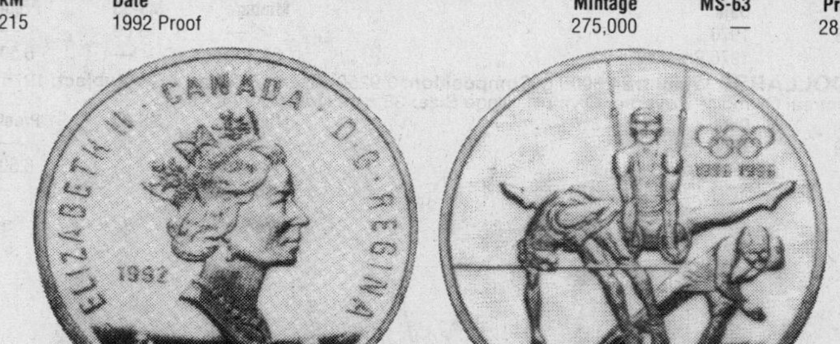


**15 DOLLARS** **Weight:** 33.6300 g. **Composition:** 0.9250 Silver 1.0000 oz. ASW **Subject:** 1992 Olympics **Reverse:** High jump, rings, speed skating

| KM | Date | Mintage | MS-63 | Proof |
|---|---|---|---|---|
| 216 | 1992 Proof | 275,000 | — | 28.00 |

**15 DOLLARS** **Ring Weight:** 33.6300 g. **Ring Composition:** 0.9250 Silver 1.0000 oz. ASW **Center Weight:** 0.3700 g. **Center Composition:** 0.9999 Gold 0.0118 oz. AGW **Subject:** Year of the Tiger **Size:** 32 mm.

| KM | Date | Mintage | MS-63 | Proof |
|---|---|---|---|---|
| 304 | 1998 Proof | 68,888 | — | 180 |

**15 DOLLARS** **Ring Weight:** 33.6300 g. **Ring Composition:** 0.9250 Silver 1.0000 oz. ASW **Center Weight:** 0.3700 g. **Center Composition:** 0.9999 Gold 0.0118 oz. AGW **Subject:** Year of the Rabbitt

| KM | Date | Mintage | MS-63 | Proof |
|---|---|---|---|---|
| 331 | 1999 Proof | — | — | 40.00 |

**15 DOLLARS** **Ring Weight:** 33.6300 g. **Ring Composition:** 0.9250 Silver 1 oz. ASW **Center Weight:** 0.3700 g. **Center Composition:** 0.9999 Gold 0.0118 oz. AGW **Subject:** Year of the Dragon

| KM | Date | Mintage | MS-63 | Proof |
|---|---|---|---|---|
| 387 | 2000 Proof | — | — | 55.00 |

**15 DOLLARS** **Weight:** 33.6300 g. **Composition:** 0.9250 Silver 1 oz. ASW **Subject:** Year of the Snake **Obverse:** Queen's head right. **Reverse:** Snake within circle of lunar calendar signs. **Edge:** Reeded. **Size:** 40 mm.

| KM | Date | Mintage | MS-63 | Proof |
|---|---|---|---|---|
| 415 | 2001 Proof | — | — | 50.00 |

**20 DOLLARS** **Weight:** 18.2733 g. **Composition:** 0.9000 Gold 0.5288 oz. AGW **Subject:** Centennial

| KM | Date | Mintage | MS-63 | Proof |
|---|---|---|---|---|
| 71 | 1967 Proof | 337,688 | — | 185 |

**20 DOLLARS** **Weight:** 33.6300 g. **Composition:** 0.9250 Silver 1.0000 oz. ASW **Subject:** 1988 Calgary Olympics **Reverse:** Downhill skier **Edge:** Lettered **Size:** 40 mm.

| KM | Date | Mintage | MS-63 | Proof |
|---|---|---|---|---|
| 145 | 1985 Proof | 406,360 | — | 21.50 |
| | 1985 Plain edge; Proof | Inc. above | — | 175 |

**20 DOLLARS** **Weight:** 33.6300 g. **Composition:** 0.9250 Silver 1.0000 oz. ASW **Subject:** 1988 Calgary Olympics **Reverse:** Speed skater **Edge:** Lettered **Size:** 40 mm.

| KM | Date | Mintage | MS-63 | Proof |
|---|---|---|---|---|
| 146 | 1985 Proof | 354,222 | — | 21.50 |
| | 1985 Plain edge; Proof | Inc. above | — | 175 |

**20 DOLLARS** **Weight:** 33.6300 g. **Composition:** 0.9250 Silver 1.0000 oz. ASW **Subject:** 1988 Calgary Olympics **Reverse:** Biathlon **Edge:** Lettered **Size:** 40 mm.

| KM | Date | Mintage | MS-63 | Proof |
|---|---|---|---|---|
| 147 | 1986 Proof | 308,086 | — | 21.50 |
| | 1986 Plain edge; Proof | Inc. above | — | 175 |

**20 DOLLARS** **Weight:** 33.6300 g. **Composition:** 0.9250 Silver 1.0000 oz. ASW **Subject:** 1988 Calgary Olympics **Reverse:** Hockey **Edge:** Lettered **Size:** 40 mm.

| KM | Date | Mintage | MS-63 | Proof |
|---|---|---|---|---|
| 148 | 1986 Proof | 396,602 | — | 21.50 |
| | 1986 Plain edge; Proof | Inc. above | — | 175 |

**20 DOLLARS** **Weight:** 33.6300 g. **Composition:** 0.9250 Silver 1.0000 oz. ASW **Subject:** 1988 Calgary Olympics **Reverse:** Cross-country skier **Size:** 40 mm.

| KM | Date | Mintage | MS-63 | Proof |
|---|---|---|---|---|
| 150 | 1986 Proof | 303,199 | — | 21.50 |

**20 DOLLARS** **Weight:** 33.6300 g. **Composition:** 0.9250 Silver 1.0000 oz. ASW **Subject:** 1988 Calgary Olympics **Reverse:** Free-style skier **Edge:** Lettered **Size:** 40 mm.

| KM | Date | Mintage | MS-63 | Proof |
|---|---|---|---|---|
| 151 | 1986 Proof | 294,322 | — | 21.50 |
| | 1986 Plain edge; Proof | Inc. above | — | 175 |

**20 DOLLARS** **Weight:** 34.1070 g. **Composition:** 0.9250 Silver 1.0000 oz. ASW **Subject:** 1988 Calgary Olympics **Reverse:** Figure skater **Size:** 40 mm.

| KM | Date | Mintage | MS-63 | Proof |
|---|---|---|---|---|
| 155 | 1987 Proof | 334,875 | — | 21.50 |

**20 DOLLARS** **Weight:** 34.1070 g. **Composition:** 0.9250 Silver 1.0000 oz. ASW **Subject:** 1988 Calgary Olympics **Reverse:** Curling **Size:** 40 mm.

| KM | Date | Mintage | MS-63 | Proof |
|---|---|---|---|---|
| 156 | 1987 Proof | 286,457 | — | 21.50 |

**20 DOLLARS** **Weight:** 34.1070 g. **Composition:** 0.9250 Silver 1.0000 oz. ASW **Subject:** 1988 Calgary Olympics **Reverse:** Ski jumper **Size:** 40 mm.

| KM | Date | Mintage | MS-63 | Proof |
|---|---|---|---|---|
| 159 | 1987 Proof | 290,954 | — | 21.50 |

**20 DOLLARS** **Weight:** 34.1070 g. **Composition:** 0.9250 Silver 1.0000 oz. ASW **Subject:** 1988 Calgary Olympics **Reverse:** Bobsled **Size:** 40 mm.

| KM | Date | Mintage | MS-63 | Proof |
|---|---|---|---|---|
| 160 | 1987 Proof | 274,326 | — | 21.50 |

**20 DOLLARS** **Weight:** 31.1030 g. **Composition:** 0.9250 Silver 0.9743 oz. ASW **Subject:** Aviation **Reverse:** Lancaster/Fauquier **Size:** 38 mm.

| KM | Date | Mintage | MS-63 | Proof |
|---|---|---|---|---|
| 172 | 1990 Proof | 43,596 | — | 125 |

**20 DOLLARS** **Weight:** 31.1030 g. **Composition:** 0.9250 Silver 0.9743 oz. ASW **Subject:** Aviation **Reverse:** Anson and Harvard **Size:** 38 mm.

| KM | Date | Mintage | MS-63 | Proof |
|---|---|---|---|---|
| 173 | 1990 Proof | 41,844 | — | 45.00 |

**20 DOLLARS** **Weight:** 31.1030 g. **Composition:** 0.9250 Silver 0.9743 oz. ASW **Subject:** Aviation **Reverse:** Silver Dart **Size:** 38 mm.

| KM | Date | Mintage | MS-63 | Proof |
|---|---|---|---|---|
| 196 | 1991 Proof | 28,791 | — | 37.50 |

**20 DOLLARS** **Weight:** 31.1030 g. **Composition:** 0.9250 Silver 0.9742 oz. ASW **Subject:** Aviation **Reverse:** de Haviland Beaver **Size:** 38 mm.

| KM | Date | Mintage | MS-63 | Proof |
|---|---|---|---|---|
| 197 | 1991 Proof | 29,399 | — | 37.50 |

**20 DOLLARS** **Weight:** 31.1030 g. **Composition:** 0.9250 Silver 0.9743 oz. ASW **Subject:** Aviation **Reverse:** Curtiss JN-4 Canick ("Jenny") **Size:** 38 mm.

| KM | Date | Mintage | MS-63 | Proof |
|---|---|---|---|---|
| 224 | 1992 Proof | 33,105 | — | 37.50 |

**20 DOLLARS** **Weight:** 31.1030 g. **Composition:** 0.9250 Silver 0.9743 oz. ASW **Subject:** Aviation **Reverse:** de Haviland Gypsy Moth **Size:** 38 mm.

| KM | Date | Mintage | MS-63 | Proof |
|---|---|---|---|---|
| 225 | 1992 Proof | 32,537 | — | 37.50 |

**20 DOLLARS** **Weight:** 31.1030 g. **Composition:** 0.9250 Silver 0.0257 oz. ASW **Subject:** Aviation **Reverse:** Fairchild 71C float plane **Size:** 38 mm.

| KM | Date | Mintage | MS-63 | Proof |
|---|---|---|---|---|
| 236 | 1993 Proof | 32,199 | — | 37.50 |

**20 DOLLARS** **Weight:** 31.1030 g. **Composition:** 0.9250 Silver 0.9743 oz. ASW **Subject:** Aviation **Reverse:** Lockheed 14 **Size:** 38 mm.

| KM | Date | Mintage | MS-63 | Proof |
|---|---|---|---|---|
| 237 | 1993 Proof | 32,550 | — | 37.50 |

**20 DOLLARS** **Weight:** 31.1030 g. **Composition:** 0.9250 Silver 0.9743 oz. ASW **Subject:** Aviation **Reverse:** Curtiss HS-2L seaplane **Size:** 38 mm.

| KM | Date | Mintage | MS-63 | Proof |
|---|---|---|---|---|
| 246 | 1994 Proof | 31,242 | — | 37.50 |

**20 DOLLARS** **Weight:** 31.1030 g. **Composition:** 0.9250 Silver 0.9743 oz. ASW **Subject:** Aviation **Reverse:** Vickers Vedette **Size:** 38 mm.

| KM | Date | Mintage | MS-63 | Proof |
|---|---|---|---|---|
| 247 | 1994 Proof | 30,880 | — | 37.50 |

**20 DOLLARS** **Weight:** 31.1030 g. **Composition:** 0.9250 Silver 0.9743 oz. ASW **Subject:** Aviation **Reverse:** C-FEA1 Fleet Cannuck **Size:** 38 mm.

| KM | Date | Mintage | MS-63 | Proof |
|---|---|---|---|---|
| 271 | 1995 Proof | 17,438 | — | 37.50 |

**20 DOLLARS** **Weight:** 31.1030 g. **Composition:** 0.9250 Silver 0.9743 oz. ASW **Subject:** Aviation **Reverse:** DHC-1 Chipmunk **Size:** 38 mm.

| KM | Date | Mintage | MS-63 | Proof |
|---|---|---|---|---|
| 272 | 1995 Proof | 17,722 | — | 37.50 |

**20 DOLLARS** **Weight:** 31.1030 g. **Composition:** 0.9250 Silver 0.9743 oz. ASW **Subject:** Aviation **Reverse:** CF-100 Cannuck **Size:** 38 mm.

| KM | Date | Mintage | MS-63 | Proof |
|---|---|---|---|---|
| 276 | 1996 Proof | 18,508 | — | 37.50 |

**20 DOLLARS** **Weight:** 31.1030 g. **Composition:** 0.9250 Silver 0.9743 oz. ASW **Subject:** Aviation **Obv. Legend:** CF-105 Arrow **Size:** 38 mm.

| KM | Date | Mintage | MS-63 | Proof |
|---|---|---|---|---|
| 277 | 1996 Proof | 27,163 | — | 50.00 |

**20 DOLLARS** **Weight:** 31.1030 g. **Composition:** 0.9250 Silver 0.9743 oz. ASW **Subject:** Aviation **Reverse:** Canadair F-86 Sabre **Size:** 38 mm.

| KM | Date | Mintage | MS-63 | Proof |
|---|---|---|---|---|
| 297 | 1997 Proof | 14,389 | — | 37.50 |

**20 DOLLARS** **Weight:** 31.1030 g. **Composition:** 0.9250 Silver 0.9743 oz. ASW **Subject:** Aviation **Reverse:** Canadair CT-114 Tutor **Size:** 38 mm.

| KM | Date | Mintage | MS-63 | Proof |
|---|---|---|---|---|
| 298 | 1997 Proof | 15,669 | — | 37.50 |

**20 DOLLARS** **Weight:** 31.1030 g. **Composition:** 0.9250 Silver 0.9743 oz. ASW **Subject:** Aviation **Reverse:** CP-107 Argus **Size:** 38 mm.

| KM | Date | Mintage | MS-63 | Proof |
|---|---|---|---|---|
| 329 | 1998 Proof | 50,000,000 | — | 37.50 |

**20 DOLLARS** **Weight:** 31.1030 g. **Composition:** 0.9250 Silver 0.9743 oz. ASW **Subject:** Aviation **Reverse:** CP-215 Waterbomber **Size:** 38 mm.

| KM | Date | Mintage | MS-63 | Proof |
|---|---|---|---|---|
| 330 | 1998 Proof | 50,000,000 | — | 37.50 |

**20 DOLLARS** **Weight:** 31.1030 g. **Composition:** 0.9250 Silver 0.9743 oz. ASW **Subject:** Aviation **Reverse:** DHC-6 Twin Otter **Size:** 38 mm.

| KM | Date | Mintage | MS-63 | Proof |
|---|---|---|---|---|
| 339 | 1999 Proof | 50,000,000 | — | 37.50 |

**20 DOLLARS** **Weight:** 31.1030 g. **Composition:** 0.9250 Silver 0.9743 oz. ASW **Subject:** Aviation **Reverse:** DHC-8 Dash 8 **Size:** 38 mm.

| KM | Date | Mintage | MS-63 | Proof |
|---|---|---|---|---|
| 340 | 1999 Proof | 50,000,000 | — | 37.50 |

**20 DOLLARS** **Composition:** 0.9250 Silver **Subject:** First Canadian locomotive **Reverse:** Locomotive below multicolored cameo **Size:** 38 mm.

| KM | Date | Mintage | MS-63 | Proof |
|---|---|---|---|---|
| 395 | 2000 Proof | — | — | 40.00 |

**20 DOLLARS** **Composition:** 0.9250 Silver **Subject:** First Canadian self-propelled car **Reverse:** Car below multicolored cameo **Size:** 38 mm.

| KM | Date | Mintage | MS-63 | Proof |
|---|---|---|---|---|
| 396 | 2000 Proof | — | — | 40.00 |

**20 DOLLARS** **Composition:** 0.9250 Silver **Subject:** Bluenose sailboat **Reverse:** Boat below multicolored cameo **Size:** 38 mm.

| KM | Date | Mintage | MS-63 | Proof |
|---|---|---|---|---|
| 397 | 2000 Proof | — | — | 100 |

**20 DOLLARS** **Weight:** 31.1035 g. **Composition:** 0.9250 Silver .9250 oz. ASW **Subject:** First Canadian Steel Boiler Steam Locomotive **Obverse:** Queen's head right. **Reverse:** Locomotive and cameo hologram. **Edge:** Reeded and plain sections. **Size:** 38 mm.

| KM | Date | Mintage | MS-63 | Proof |
|---|---|---|---|---|
| 411 | 2001 Proof | 15,000 | — | 40.00 |

**20 DOLLARS** **Weight:** 31.1030 g. **Composition:** 0.9250 Silver .9250 oz. ASW **Series:** Transportation - The Marco Polo **Obverse:** Queen's head right. **Reverse:** Sailship with hologram cameo. **Edge:** Reeded and plain sections. **Size:** 38 mm.

| KM | Date | Mintage | MS-63 | Proof |
|---|---|---|---|---|
| 427 | 2001 Proof | 15,000 | — | 40.00 |

**20 DOLLARS** **Weight:** 31.1030 g. **Composition:** 0.9250 Silver .9250 oz. ASW **Series:** Transportation - Russell Touring Car **Obverse:** Queen's head right. **Reverse:** Russell touring car with hologram cameo. **Edge:** Reeded and plain sections. **Size:** 38 mm.

| KM | Date | Mintage | MS-63 | Proof |
|---|---|---|---|---|
| 428 | 2001 Proof | 15,000 | — | 40.00 |

**100 DOLLARS** **Weight:** 13.3375 g. **Composition:** 0.5830 Gold 0.2500 oz. AGW **Subject:** 1976 Montreal Olympics **Obverse:** Beaded borders **Size:** 27 mm.

| KM | Date | Mintage | MS-63 | Proof |
|---|---|---|---|---|
| 115 | 1976 | 650,000 | 85.00 | — |

**100 DOLLARS** **Weight:** 16.9655 g. **Composition:** 0.9170 Gold 0.5000 oz. AGW **Subject:** 1976 Montreal Olympics **Obverse:** Plain borders **Size:** 25 mm.

| KM | Date | Mintage | MS-63 | Proof |
|---|---|---|---|---|
| 116 | 1976 Proof | 337,342 | — | 160 |

**100 DOLLARS** **Weight:** 16.9655 g. **Composition:** 0.9170 Gold 0.5000 oz. AGW **Subject:** Queen's silver jubilee

| KM | Date | Mintage | MS-63 | Proof |
|---|---|---|---|---|
| 119 | ND(1977) Proof | 180,396 | — | 165 |

**100 DOLLARS** **Weight:** 16.9655 g. **Composition:** 0.9170 Gold 0.5000 oz. AGW **Subject:** Canadian unification

| KM | Date | Mintage | MS-63 | Proof |
|---|---|---|---|---|
| 122 | 1978 Proof | 200,000 | — | 165 |

**100 DOLLARS** **Weight:** 16.9655 g. **Composition:** 0.9170 Gold 0.5000 oz. AGW **Subject:** International Year of the Child

| KM | Date | Mintage | MS-63 | Proof |
|---|---|---|---|---|
| 126 | 1979 Proof | 250,000 | — | 160 |

**100 DOLLARS** **Weight:** 16.9655 g. **Composition:** 0.9170 Gold 0.5000 oz. AGW **Subject:** Arctic Territories

| KM | Date | Mintage | MS-63 | Proof |
|---|---|---|---|---|
| 129 | 1980 Proof | 300,000 | — | 165 |

**100 DOLLARS** **Weight:** 16.9655 g. **Composition:** 0.9170 Gold 0.5000 oz. AGW **Subject:** National anthem

| KM | Date | Mintage | MS-63 | Proof |
|---|---|---|---|---|
| 131 | 1981 Proof | 102,000 | — | 170 |

**100 DOLLARS** **Weight:** 16.9655 g. **Composition:** 0.9170 Gold 0.5000 oz. AGW **Subject:** New Constitution

| KM | Date | Mintage | MS-63 | Proof |
|---|---|---|---|---|
| 137 | 1982 Proof | 121,708 | — | 165 |

**100 DOLLARS** **Weight:** 16.9655 g. **Composition:** 0.9170 Gold 0.5000 oz. AGW **Subject:** 400th Anniversary of St. John's, Newfoundland

| KM | Date | Mintage | MS-63 | Proof |
|---|---|---|---|---|
| 139 | ND(1983) Proof | 83,128 | — | 165 |

**100 DOLLARS** **Weight:** 16.9655 g. **Composition:** 0.9170 Gold 0.5000 oz. AGW **Subject:** Jacques Cartier

| KM | Date | Mintage | MS-63 | Proof |
|---|---|---|---|---|
| 142 | ND(1984) Proof | 67,662 | — | 170 |

**100 DOLLARS** **Weight:** 16.9655 g. **Composition:** 0.9170 Gold 0.5000 oz. AGW **Subject:** National Parks **Reverse:** Big-horn sheep

| KM | Date | Mintage | MS-63 | Proof |
|---|---|---|---|---|
| 144 | ND(1985) Proof | 61,332 | — | 170 |

**100 DOLLARS** **Weight:** 16.9655 g. **Composition:** 0.9170 Gold 0.5000 oz. AGW **Subject:** Peace

| KM | Date | Mintage | MS-63 | Proof |
|---|---|---|---|---|
| 152 | 1986 Proof | 76,409 | — | 165 |

**100 DOLLARS** **Weight:** 13.3375 g. **Composition:** 0.5830 Gold 0.2500 oz. AGW **Subject:** 1988 Calgary Olympics **Reverse:** Torch and logo

| KM | Date | Mintage | MS-63 | Proof |
|---|---|---|---|---|
| 158 | 1987 lettered edge; Proof | 142,750 | — | 90.00 |
| | 1987 plain edge; Proof | Inc. above | — | 350 |

**100 DOLLARS** **Weight:** 13.3375 g. **Composition:** 0.5830 Gold 0.2500 oz. AGW **Subject:** Whales

| KM | Date | Mintage | MS-63 | Proof |
|---|---|---|---|---|
| 162 | 1988 Proof | 52,594 | — | 90.00 |

**100 DOLLARS** **Weight:** 13.3375 g. **Composition:** 0.5830 Gold 0.2500 oz. AGW **Subject:** Sainte-Marie

| KM | Date | Mintage | MS-63 | Proof |
|---|---|---|---|---|
| 169 | ND(1989) Proof | 59,657 | — | 90.00 |

**100 DOLLARS** **Weight:** 13.3375 g. **Composition:** 0.5830 Gold 0.2500 oz. AGW **Subject:** International Literacy Year

| KM | Date | Mintage | MS-63 | Proof |
|---|---|---|---|---|
| 171 | 1990 Proof | 49,940 | — | 90.00 |

**100 DOLLARS** **Weight:** 13.3375 g. **Composition:** 0.5830 Gold 0.2500 oz. AGW **Subject:** S.S. Empress of India

| KM | Date | Mintage | MS-63 | Proof |
|---|---|---|---|---|
| 180 | 1991 Proof | 33,966 | — | 90.00 |

**100 DOLLARS** **Weight:** 13.3375 g. **Composition:** 0.5830 Gold 0.2500 oz. AGW **Subject:** Montreal

| KM | Date | Mintage | MS-63 | Proof |
|---|---|---|---|---|
| 211 | 1992 Proof | 28,162 | — | 95.00 |

**100 DOLLARS** **Weight:** 13.3375 g. **Composition:** 0.5830 Gold 0.2500 oz. AGW **Subject:** Antique Automobiles

| KM | Date | Mintage | MS-63 | Proof |
|---|---|---|---|---|
| 245 | 1993 Proof | 25,971 | — | 100 |

**100 DOLLARS** **Weight:** 13.3375 g. **Composition:** 0.5830 Gold 0.2500 oz. AGW **Subject:** World War II Home Front

| KM | Date | Mintage | MS-63 | Proof |
|---|---|---|---|---|
| 249 | 1994 Proof | 16,201 | — | 125 |

**100 DOLLARS** **Weight:** 13.3375 g. **Composition:** 0.5830 Gold 0.2500 oz. AGW **Subject:** Louisbourg

| KM | Date | Mintage | MS-63 | Proof |
|---|---|---|---|---|
| 260 | 1995 Proof | 16,916 | — | 125 |

**100 DOLLARS** **Weight:** 13.3375 g. **Composition:** 0.5830 Gold 0.2500 oz. AGW **Subject:** Klondike Gold Rush Centennial

| KM | Date | Mintage | MS-63 | Proof |
|---|---|---|---|---|
| 273 | ND(1996) Proof | 17,973 | — | 135 |

**100 DOLLARS** **Weight:** 13.3375 g. **Composition:** 0.5830 Gold 0.2500 oz. AGW **Subject:** Alexander Graham Bell

| KM | Date | Mintage | MS-63 | Proof |
|---|---|---|---|---|
| 287 | 1997 Proof | 14,775 | — | 155 |

**100 DOLLARS** **Weight:** 13.3375 g. **Composition:** 0.5830 Gold 0.2500 oz. AGW **Subject:** Discovery of Insulin

| KM | Date | Mintage | MS-63 | Proof |
|---|---|---|---|---|
| 307 | 1998 Proof | 11,220 | — | 155 |

**100 DOLLARS** **Weight:** 13.3375 g. **Composition:** 0.5830 Gold 0.2500 oz. AGW **Subject:** 50th Anniversary Newfoundland Unity With Canada

| KM | Date | Mintage | MS-63 | Proof |
|---|---|---|---|---|
| 341 | 1999 Proof | 10,242 | — | 170 |

**100 DOLLARS** **Weight:** 13.3375 g. **Composition:** 0.5830 Gold 0.2500 oz. AGW **Subject:** McClure's Arctic expedition

| KM | Date | Mintage | MS-63 | Proof |
|---|---|---|---|---|
| 402 | 2000 Proof | 9,767 | — | 185 |

**100 DOLLARS** **Weight:** 13.3375 g. **Composition:** 0.5830 Gold 0.2500 oz. AGW **Subject:** Library of Parliament **Obverse:** Queen's head right. **Reverse:** Statue in domed building. **Edge:** Reeded. **Size:** 27 mm.

| KM | Date | Mintage | MS-63 | Proof |
|---|---|---|---|---|
| 416 | 2001 Proof | 10,000 | — | 185 |

**150 DOLLARS** **Weight:** 13.6100 g. **Composition:** 0.7500 Gold .3282 oz. AGW **Subject:** Year of the Dragon

| KM | Date | Mintage | MS-63 | Proof |
|---|---|---|---|---|
| 388 | 2000 Proof | 8,851 | — | 475 |

**150 DOLLARS** **Weight:** 13.6100 g. **Composition:** 0.7500 Gold .3282 oz. AGW **Subject:** Year of the Snake **Obverse:** Queen's head right. **Reverse:** Multicolor snake hologram. **Edge:** Reeded. **Size:** 28 mm.

| KM | Date | Mintage | MS-63 | Proof |
|---|---|---|---|---|
| 417 | 2001 Proof | 6,888 | — | 265 |

**175 DOLLARS** **Weight:** 16.9700 g. **Composition:** 0.9170 Gold 0.5000 oz. AGW **Subject:** 1992 Olympics **Reverse:** Passing the torch

| KM | Date | Mintage | MS-63 | Proof |
|---|---|---|---|---|
| 217 | 1992 Proof | 22,092 | — | 210 |

**200 DOLLARS** **Weight:** 17.1060 g. **Composition:** 0.9170 Gold 0.5042 oz. AGW **Subject:** Canadian flag silver jubilee **Size:** 29 mm.

| KM | Date | Mintage | MS-63 | Proof |
|---|---|---|---|---|
| 178 | 1990 Proof | 20,980 | — | 175 |

**200 DOLLARS** **Weight:** 17.1060 g. **Composition:** 0.9170 Gold 0.5042 oz. AGW **Subject:** Hockey **Size:** 29 mm.

| KM | Date | Mintage | MS-63 | Proof |
|---|---|---|---|---|
| 202 | 1991 Proof | 10,215 | — | 200 |

**200 DOLLARS** **Weight:** 17.1060 g. **Composition:** 0.9170 Gold 0.5042 oz. AGW **Subject:** Niagara Falls **Size:** 29 mm.

| KM | Date | Mintage | MS-63 | Proof |
|---|---|---|---|---|
| 230 | 1992 Proof | 9,465 | — | 250 |

**200 DOLLARS** **Weight:** 17.1350 g. **Composition:** 0.9170 Gold 0.5500 oz. AGW **Subject:** Mounted police **Size:** 29 mm.

| KM | Date | Mintage | MS-63 | Proof |
|---|---|---|---|---|
| 244 | 1993 Proof | 10,807 | — | 190 |

**200 DOLLARS** **Weight:** 17.1350 g. **Composition:** 0.9170 Gold 0.5500 oz. AGW **Subject:** Novel: Anne of Green Gables **Size:** 29 mm.

| KM | Date | Mintage | MS-63 | Proof |
|---|---|---|---|---|
| 250 | 1994 Proof | 10,655 | — | 210 |

**200 DOLLARS** **Weight:** 17.1350 g. **Composition:** 0.9170 Gold 0.5500 oz. AGW **Subject:** Maple-syrup production **Size:** 29 mm.

| KM | Date | Mintage | MS-63 | Proof |
|---|---|---|---|---|
| 265 | 1995 Proof | 6,579 | — | 225 |

**200 DOLLARS** **Weight:** 17.1350 g. **Composition:** 0.9170 Gold 0.5500 oz. AGW **Subject:** Transcontinental Canadian Railway **Size:** 29 mm.

| KM | Date | Mintage | MS-63 | Proof |
|---|---|---|---|---|
| 275 | 1996 Proof | 8,047 | — | 265 |

**200 DOLLARS** **Weight:** 17.1350 g. **Composition:** 0.9170 Gold 0.5500 oz. AGW **Subject:** Haida mask **Size:** 29 mm.

| KM | Date | Mintage | MS-63 | Proof |
|---|---|---|---|---|
| 288 | 1997 Proof | 11,610 | — | 350 |

**200 DOLLARS** **Weight:** 17.1350 g. **Composition:** 0.9170 Gold 0.5500 oz. AGW **Subject:** Legendary white buffalo **Size:** 29 mm.

| KM | Date | Mintage | MS-63 | Proof |
|---|---|---|---|---|
| 317 | 1998 Proof | 7,149 | — | 275 |

**200 DOLLARS** **Weight:** 17.1350 g. **Composition:** 0.9170 Gold 0.5500 oz. AGW **Subject:** Mikmaq butterfly **Size:** 29 mm.

| KM | Date | Mintage | MS-63 | Proof |
|---|---|---|---|---|
| 358 | 1999 Proof | 6,510 | — | 280 |

**200 DOLLARS** **Weight:** 17.1350 g. **Composition:** 0.9170 Gold 0.5500 oz. AGW **Subject:** Motherhood **Reverse:** Inuit mother with infant **Size:** 29 mm.

| KM | Date | Mintage | MS-63 | Proof |
|---|---|---|---|---|
| 403 | 2000 Proof | 6,284 | — | 280 |

**200 DOLLARS** **Weight:** 17.1350 g. **Composition:** 0.9170 Gold 0.5500 oz. AGW **Subject:** Cornelius David Krieghoff **Obverse:** Queen's head right. **Reverse:** Farm homestead circa 1856. **Edge:** Reeded. **Size:** 29 mm.

| KM | Date | Mintage | MS-63 | Proof |
|---|---|---|---|---|
| 418 | 2001 Proof | 10,000 | — | 275 |

**350 DOLLARS** **Weight:** 38.0500 g. **Composition:** 0.9999 Gold 1.2233 oz. AGW **Subject:** Flowers of Canada's Coat of Arms

| KM | Date | Mintage | MS-63 | Proof |
|---|---|---|---|---|
| 308 | 1998 Proof | 664 | — | 725 |

**350 DOLLARS** **Weight:** 38.0500 g. **Composition:** 0.9999 Gold 1.2233 oz. AGW **Subject:** Lady's slipper

| KM | Date | Mintage | MS-63 | Proof |
|---|---|---|---|---|
| 370 | 1999 Proof | 1,990 | — | 665 |

**350 DOLLARS** **Weight:** 38.0500 g. **Composition:** 0.9999 Gold 1.2233 oz. AGW **Subject:** Pacific Dogwood

| KM | Date | Mintage | MS-63 | Proof |
|---|---|---|---|---|
| 404 | 2000 Proof | 1,506 | — | 665 |

**350 DOLLARS** **Weight:** 38.0500 g. **Composition:** 0.9999 Gold 1.2233 oz. AGW **Subject:** The Mayflower Flower **Obverse:** Queen's head right. **Reverse:** Two flowers. **Edge:** Reeded. **Size:** 34 mm.

| KM | Date | Mintage | MS-63 | Proof |
|---|---|---|---|---|
| 433 | 2001 Proof | — | — | 676 |

## SILVER BULLION COINAGE

**5 DOLLARS** **Weight:** 31.1000 g. **Composition:** 0.9999 Silver 1.0000 oz. ASW **Obverse:** Elizabeth II effigy **Obv. Designer:** Machin **Reverse:** Maple leaf

| KM | Date | Mintage | MS-63 | Proof |
|---|---|---|---|---|
| 163 | 1988 | 1,155,931 | 8.00 | — |
| | 1989 | 3,288,235 | 7.25 | — |
| | 1989 Proof | 43,965 | — | 28.50 |

**5 DOLLARS** **Weight:** 31.1000 g. **Composition:** 0.9999 Silver 1.0000 oz. ASW **Obverse:** New Elizabeth II effigy **Obv. Designer:** de Pedery-Hunt **Reverse:** Maple leaf

| KM | Date | Mintage | MS-63 | Proof |
|---|---|---|---|---|
| 187 | 1990 | 1,708,800 | 8.00 | — |
| | 1991 | 644,300 | 10.00 | — |
| | 1992 | 343,800 | 9.50 | — |
| | 1993 | 889,946 | 7.50 | — |
| | 1994 | 1,133,900 | 7.75 | — |
| | 1995 | 326,244 | 8.50 | — |
| | 1996 | 250,445 | 11.00 | — |
| | 1997 | 100,970 | 12.00 | — |
| | 1998 Tiger privy mark | 25,000 | 13.50 | — |
| | 1998 Proof; 20 Years ANS privy mark | — | — | 35.00 |
| | 1998 Titanic privy mark | 26,000 | 15.00 | — |
| | 1998 R.C.M.P. privy mark | 25,000 | 15.00 | — |
| | 1998 90th Anniversary R.C.M. privy mark | 13,025 | 16.50 | — |
| | 1999 Rabbit privy mark | 25,000 | 13.50 | — |
| | 2000 Expo Hanover privy mark | — | 18.50 | — |
| | 2001 Snake privy mark | 25,000 | 13.50 | — |

**5 DOLLARS** **Weight:** 31.1000 g. **Composition:** 0.9999 Silver 1 oz. ASW **Reverse:** Maple leaf with fireworks privy mark

| KM | Date | Mintage | MS-63 | Proof |
|---|---|---|---|---|
| 363 | 1999/2000 | 298,775 | 9.50 | — |

**50 DOLLARS** **Weight:** 311.0350 g. **Composition:** 0.9999 Silver 10.0000 oz. ASW **Subject:** 10th Anniversary Silver Maple Leaf

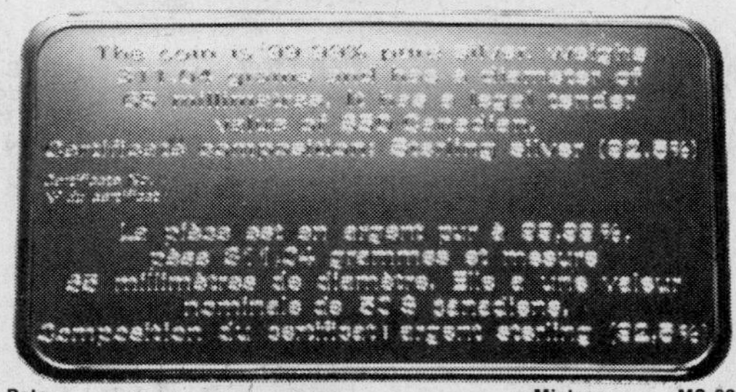

| KM | Date | Mintage | MS-63 | Proof |
|---|---|---|---|---|
| 326 | 1998 Proof | 25,000,000 | — | 125 |

## GOLD BULLION COINAGE

**DOLLAR** **Weight:** 1.5551 g. **Composition:** 0.9999 Gold 0.05 oz. AGW

| KM | Date | Mintage | MS-63 | Proof |
|---|---|---|---|---|
| 238 | 1993 | 37,080 | BV+37% | — |
| | 1994 | 78,860 | BV+37% | — |
| | 1995 | 85,920 | BV+37% | — |
| | 1996 | 56,520 | BV+37% | — |
| | 1997 | 59,720 | BV+37% | — |
| | 1998 | 44,260 | BV+37% | — |
| | 1999 Maple leaf with oval "20 Years ANS" privy mark | — | BV+46% | — |

**DOLLAR** **Weight:** 1.5551 g. **Composition:** 0.9999 Gold 0.05 oz. AGW **Reverse:** Maple leaf hologram

| KM | Date | Mintage | MS-63 | Proof |
|---|---|---|---|---|
| 365 | 1999 | — | — | — |

**2 DOLLARS** **Weight:** 2.0735 g. **Composition:** 0.9999 Gold 0.0666 oz. AGW **Reverse:** Maple leaf

| KM | Date | Mintage | MS-63 | Proof |
|---|---|---|---|---|
| 256 | 1994 | 5,493 | 55.00 | — |

**5 DOLLARS** **Weight:** 3.1200 g. **Composition:** 0.9999 Gold .1000 oz. AGW **Obverse:** Elizabeth II effigy **Obv. Designer:** Machin **Reverse:** Maple leaf

| KM | Date | Mintage | MS-63 | Proof |
|---|---|---|---|---|
| 135 | 1982 | 246,000 | BV+14% | — |
| | 1983 | 304,000 | BV+14% | — |
| | 1984 | 262,000 | BV+14% | — |
| | 1985 | 398,000 | BV+14% | — |
| | 1986 | 529,516 | BV+14% | — |
| | 1987 | 459,000 | BV+14% | — |
| | 1988 | 506,500 | BV+14% | — |
| | 1989 | 539,000 | BV+14% | — |
| | 1989 Proof | 16,992 | — | 50.00 |

**5 DOLLARS** **Weight:** 3.1200 g. **Composition:** 0.9999 Gold 0.1000 oz. AGW **Obverse:** Elizabeth II effigy **Obv. Designer:** dePedery-Hunt **Reverse:** Maple leaf

| KM | Date | Mintage | MS-63 | Proof |
|---|---|---|---|---|
| 188 | 1990 | 476,000 | BV+14% | — |
| | 1991 | 322,000 | BV+14% | — |
| | 1992 | 384,000 | BV+14% | — |
| | 1993 | 248,630 | BV+14% | — |
| | 1994 | 313,150 | BV+14% | — |
| | 1995 | 294,890 | BV+14% | — |
| | 1996 | 179,220 | BV+14% | — |
| | 1997 | 188,540 | BV+14% | — |
| | 1998 | 301,940 | BV+14% | — |
| | 1999 Maple leaf with oval "20 Years ANS" privy mark | — | BV+19% | — |

**5 DOLLARS** **Weight:** 3.1200 g. **Composition:** 0.9999 Gold 0.1000 oz. AGW **Reverse:** Maple leaf hologram

| KM | Date | Mintage | MS-63 | Proof |
|---|---|---|---|---|
| 366 | 1999 | — | — | — |

**10 DOLLARS** **Weight:** 7.7850 g. **Composition:** 0.9999 Gold 0.2500 oz. AGW **Obverse:** Elizabeth II effigy **Obv. Designer:** Machin **Reverse:** Maple leaf

| KM | Date | Mintage | MS-63 | Proof |
|---|---|---|---|---|
| 136 | 1982 | 184,000 | BV+10% | — |
| | 1983 | 308,800 | BV+10% | — |
| | 1984 | 242,400 | BV+10% | — |
| | 1985 | 620,000 | BV+10% | — |
| | 1986 | 915,200 | BV+10% | — |
| | 1987 | 376,000 | BV+10% | — |
| | 1988 | 436,000 | BV+10% | — |
| | 1989 | 328,800 | BV+10% | — |
| | 1989 Proof | 6,998 | — | 125 |

**10 DOLLARS** **Weight:** 7.7850 g. **Composition:** 0.9999 Gold 0.2500 oz. AGW **Obverse:** Elizabeth II effigy **Obv. Designer:** dePedery-Hunt **Reverse:** Maple leaf

| KM | Date | Mintage | MS-63 | Proof |
|---|---|---|---|---|
| 189 | 1990 | 253,600 | BV+10% | — |
| | 1991 | 166,400 | BV+10% | — |
| | 1992 | 179,600 | BV+10% | — |
| | 1993 | 158,452 | BV+10% | — |
| | 1994 | 148,792 | BV+10% | — |
| | 1995 | 127,596 | BV+10% | — |
| | 1996 | 89,148 | BV+10% | — |
| | 1997 | 98,104 | BV+10% | — |
| | 1998 | 85,472 | BV+10% | — |
| | 1999 Maple leaf with oval "20 Years ANS" privy mark | — | BV+15% | — |

**10 DOLLARS** **Weight:** 7.7850 g. **Composition:** 0.9999 Gold 0.2500 oz. AGW **Reverse:** Maple leaf hologram

| KM | Date | Mintage | MS-63 | Proof |
|---|---|---|---|---|
| 367 | 1999 | — | — | — |

**20 DOLLARS** **Weight:** 15.5515 g. **Composition:** 0.9999 Gold 0.5000 oz. AGW **Obverse:** Elizabeth II effigy **Obv. Designer:** Machin **Size:** 32 mm. mm.

| KM | Date | Mintage | MS-63 | Proof |
|---|---|---|---|---|
| 153 | 1986 | 529,200 | BV+7% | — |
| | 1987 | 332,800 | BV+7% | — |
| | 1988 | 538,400 | BV+7% | — |
| | 1989 | 259,200 | BV+7% | — |
| | 1989 Proof | 6,998 | — | 225 |

**20 DOLLARS** **Weight:** 15.5515 g. **Composition:** 0.9999 Gold 0.5000 oz. AGW **Obverse:** Elizabeth II effigy **Obv. Designer:** dePedery-Hunt **Reverse:** Maple leaf

| KM | Date | Mintage | MS-63 | Proof |
|---|---|---|---|---|
| 190 | 1990 | 174,400 | BV+7% | — |
| | 1991 | 96,200 | BV+7% | — |
| | 1992 | 108,000 | BV+7% | — |
| | 1993 | 99,492 | BV+7% | — |
| | 1994 | 104,766 | BV+7% | — |
| | 1995 | 103,162 | BV+7% | — |
| | 1996 | 66,246 | BV+7% | — |
| | 1997 | 63,354 | BV+7% | — |
| | 1998 | 65,366 | BV+7% | — |
| | 1999 Maple leaf with oval "20 Years ANS" privy mark | — | BV+12% | — |

**20 DOLLARS** **Weight:** 15.5515 g. **Composition:** 0.9999 Gold 0.5000 oz. AGW **Reverse:** Maple leaf hologram

| KM | Date | Mintage | MS-63 | Proof |
|---|---|---|---|---|
| 368 | 1999 | — | — | — |

**50 DOLLARS** **Weight:** 31.1030 g. **Composition:** 0.9990 Gold 1.0000 oz. AGW **Reverse:** Maple leaf flanked by .9999

| KM | Date | Mintage | MS-63 | Proof |
|---|---|---|---|---|
| 125.1 | 1979 | 1,000,000 | BV+4% | — |
| | 1980 | 1,251,500 | BV+4% | — |
| | 1981 | 863,000 | BV+4% | — |
| | 1982 | 883,000 | BV+4% | — |

**50 DOLLARS** **Weight:** 31.1030 g. **Composition:** 0.9999 Gold 1.0000 oz. AGW **Reverse:** Maple leaf flanked by .9999

| KM | Date | Mintage | MS-63 | Proof |
|---|---|---|---|---|
| 125.2 | 1983 | 843,000 | BV+4% | — |
| | 1984 | 1,067,500 | BV+4% | — |
| | 1985 | 1,908,000 | BV+4% | — |
| | 1986 | 779,115 | BV+4% | — |
| | 1987 | 978,000 | BV+4% | — |
| | 1988 | 826,500 | BV+4% | — |
| | 1989 | 856,000 | BV+4% | — |
| | 1989 Proof | 17,781 | — | 350 |

**50 DOLLARS** **Weight:** 31.1030 g. **Composition:** 0.9999 Gold 1.000 oz. AGW **Obverse:** Elizabeth II effigy **Obv. Designer:** dePedery-Hunt **Reverse:** Maple leaf flanked by .9999

| KM | Date | Mintage | MS-63 | Proof |
|---|---|---|---|---|
| 191 | 1990 | 815,000 | BV+4% | — |
| | 1991 | 290,000 | BV+4% | — |
| | 1992 | 368,900 | BV+4% | — |
| | 1993 | 321,413 | BV+4% | — |
| | 1994 | 180,357 | BV+4% | — |
| | 1995 | 208,729 | BV+4% | — |
| | 1996 | 143,682 | BV+4% | — |
| | 1997 | 478,211 | BV+4% | — |
| | 1998 | 593,704 | BV+4% | — |
| | 1999 Maple leaf with oval "20 Years ANS" privy mark | — | BV+7% | — |

**50 DOLLARS** **Weight:** 31.1030 g. **Composition:** 0.9999 Gold 1 oz. AGW **Reverse:** Mountie

| KM | Date | Mintage | MS-63 | Proof |
|---|---|---|---|---|
| 305 | 1997 | 12,913 | 335 | — |

**50 DOLLARS** **Weight:** 31.1030 g. **Composition:** 0.9999 Gold 1.0000 oz. AGW **Reverse:** Maple leaf hologram

| KM | Date | Mintage | MS-63 | Proof |
|---|---|---|---|---|
| 369 | 1999 | — | — | — |

**50 DOLLARS** **Weight:** 31.1030 g. **Composition:** 0.9999 Gold 1.0000 oz. AGW **Reverse:** Maple leaf with fireworks privy mark

| KM | Date | Mintage | MS-63 | Proof |
|---|---|---|---|---|
| 364 | 1999/2000 | — | — | — |

## PLATINUM BULLION COINAGE

**DOLLAR** **Weight:** 1.5552 g. **Composition:** 0.9995 Platinum 0.0500 oz. APW **Reverse:** Maple leaf

| KM | Date | Mintage | MS-63 | Proof |
|---|---|---|---|---|
| 239 | 1993 | 2,120 | BV+35% | — |
| | 1994 | 4,260 | BV+35% | — |
| | 1995 | 460 | BV+35% | — |
| | 1996 | 1,640 | BV+35% | — |
| | 1997 | 1,340 | BV+35% | — |
| | 1998 | 2,000 | BV+35% | — |
| | 1999 | 2,000 | BV+35% | — |

**2 DOLLARS** **Weight:** 2.0735 g. **Composition:** 0.9995 Platinum 0.0666 oz. APW **Reverse:** Maple leaf

| KM | Date | Mintage | MS-63 | Proof |
|---|---|---|---|---|
| 257 | 1994 | 1,470 | 250 | — |

**5 DOLLARS** **Weight:** 3.1203 g. **Composition:** 0.9995 Platinum 0.1000 oz. APW **Obverse:** Elizabeth II effigy **Obv. Designer:** Machin

| KM | Date | Mintage | MS-63 | Proof |
|---|---|---|---|---|
| 164 | 1988 | 74,000 | BV+18% | — |
| | 1989 | 18,000 | BV+18% | — |
| | 1989 Proof | 11,999 | — | 75.00 |

**5 DOLLARS** **Weight:** 3.1203 g. **Composition:** 0.9995 Platinum 0.1000 oz. APW **Obverse:** Elizabeth II effigy **Obv. Designer:** dePedery-Hunt

| KM | Date | Mintage | MS-63 | Proof |
|---|---|---|---|---|
| 192 | 1990 | 9,000 | BV+18% | — |
| | 1991 | 13,000 | BV+18% | — |
| | 1992 | 16,000 | BV+18% | — |
| | 1993 | 14,020 | BV+18% | — |
| | 1994 | 19,190 | BV+18% | — |
| | 1995 | 8,940 | BV+18% | — |
| | 1996 | 8,820 | BV+18% | — |
| | 1997 | 7,050 | BV+18% | — |
| | 1998 | 5,710 | BV+18% | — |
| | 1999 | 2,000 | BV+18% | — |

**10 DOLLARS** **Weight:** 7.7857 g. **Composition:** 0.9995 Platinum 0.2500 oz. APW **Obverse:** Elizabeth II effigy **Obv. Designer:** Machin **Reverse:** Maple leaf

| KM | Date | Mintage | MS-63 | Proof |
|---|---|---|---|---|
| 165 | 1988 | 93,600 | BV+13% | — |
| | 1989 | 3,200 | BV+13% | — |
| | 1989 Proof | 1,999 | — | 175 |

**10 DOLLARS** **Weight:** 7.7857 g. **Composition:** 0.9995 Platinum 0.2500 oz. APW **Obverse:** Elizabeth II effigy **Obv. Designer:** dePedery-Hunt **Reverse:** Maple leaf

| KM | Date | Mintage | MS-63 | Proof |
|---|---|---|---|---|
| 193 | 1990 | 1,600 | BV+13% | — |
| | 1991 | 7,200 | BV+13% | — |
| | 1992 | 11,600 | BV+13% | — |
| | 1993 | 8,048 | BV+13% | — |
| | 1994 | 9,456 | BV+13% | — |
| | 1995 | 6,524 | BV+13% | — |
| | 1996 | 6,160 | BV+13% | — |
| | 1997 | 4,552 | BV+13% | — |
| | 1998 | 3,816 | BV+13% | — |
| | 1999 | 2,000 | BV+13% | — |

**20 DOLLARS** **Weight:** 15.5519 g. **Composition:** 0.9995 Platinum 0.5000 oz. APW **Obverse:** Elizabeth II effigy **Obv. Designer:** Machin **Reverse:** Maple leaf

| KM | Date | Mintage | MS-63 | Proof |
|---|---|---|---|---|
| 166 | 1988 | 23,600 | BV+9% | — |
| | 1989 | 4,800 | BV+9% | — |
| | 1989 Proof | 1,999 | — | 350 |

**20 DOLLARS** **Weight:** 15.5519 g. **Composition:** 0.9995 Platinum 0.5000 oz. APW **Obverse:** Elizabeth II effigy **Obv. Designer:** dePedery-Hunt **Reverse:** Maple leaf

| KM | Date | Mintage | MS-63 | Proof |
|---|---|---|---|---|
| 194 | 1990 | 2,600 | BV+9% | — |
| | 1991 | 5,600 | BV+9% | — |
| | 1992 | 12,800 | BV+9% | — |
| | 1993 | 6,022 | BV+9% | — |
| | 1994 | 6,710 | BV+9% | — |
| | 1995 | 6,308 | BV+9% | — |
| | 1996 | 5,490 | BV+9% | — |
| | 1997 | 3,990 | BV+9% | — |
| | 1998 | 5,486 | BV+9% | — |
| | 1999 | 500 | 325 | — |

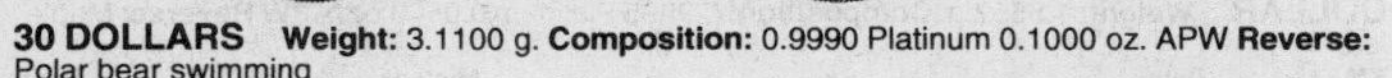

**30 DOLLARS** **Weight:** 3.1100 g. **Composition:** 0.9990 Platinum 0.1000 oz. APW **Reverse:** Polar bear swimming

| KM | Date | Mintage | MS-63 | Proof |
|---|---|---|---|---|
| 174 | 1990 Proof | 2,629 | — | 70.00 |

**30 DOLLARS** **Weight:** 3.1100 g. **Composition:** 0.9990 Platinum 0.1000 oz. APW **Reverse:** Snowy owl

| KM | Date | Mintage | MS-63 | Proof |
|---|---|---|---|---|
| 198 | 1991 Proof | 3,500 | — | 85.00 |

**30 DOLLARS** **Weight:** 3.1100 g. **Composition:** 0.9990 Platinum 0.1000 oz. APW **Reverse:** Cougar head and shoulders

| KM | Date | Mintage | MS-63 | Proof |
|---|---|---|---|---|
| 226 | 1992 Proof | 3,500 | — | 85.00 |

**30 DOLLARS** **Weight:** 3.1100 g. **Composition:** 0.9990 Platinum 0.1000 oz. APW **Reverse:** Arctic fox

| KM | Date | Mintage | MS-63 | Proof |
|---|---|---|---|---|
| 240 | 1993 Proof | 3,500 | — | 100 |

**30 DOLLARS** **Weight:** 3.1100 g. **Composition:** 0.9990 Platinum 0.1000 oz. APW **Reverse:** Sea otter **Note:** 1,500 sets only.

| KM | Date | Mintage | MS-63 | Proof |
|---|---|---|---|---|
| 252 | 1994 Proof | 1,500 | — | 110 |

**30 DOLLARS** **Weight:** 3.1100 g. **Composition:** 0.9990 Platinum 0.1000 oz. APW **Reverse:** Canadian lynx

| KM | Date | Mintage | MS-63 | Proof |
|---|---|---|---|---|
| 266 | 1995 Proof | 620 | — | 100 |

**30 DOLLARS** **Weight:** 3.1100 g. **Composition:** 0.9990 Platinum 0.1000 oz. APW **Reverse:** Falcon portrait

| KM | Date | Mintage | MS-63 | Proof |
|---|---|---|---|---|
| 278 | 1996 Proof | 489 | — | 100 |

**30 DOLLARS** **Weight:** 3.1320 g. **Composition:** 0.9995 Platinum 0.1006 oz. APW **Reverse:** Bison head

| KM | Date | Mintage | MS-63 | Proof |
|---|---|---|---|---|
| 300 | 1997 Proof | 5,000 | — | 100 |

**30 DOLLARS** **Weight:** 3.1100 g. **Composition:** 0.9990 Platinum 0.1 oz. APW **Reverse:** Grey wolf

| KM | Date | Mintage | MS-63 | Proof |
|---|---|---|---|---|
| 322 | ND(1998) Proof | 2,000 | — | 100 |

**30 DOLLARS** **Weight:** 3.1320 g. **Composition:** 0.9995 Platinum 0.1006 oz. APW **Reverse:** Musk ox

| KM | Date | Mintage | MS-63 | Proof |
|---|---|---|---|---|
| 359 | 1999 Proof | 1,500 | — | 100 |

**30 DOLLARS** **Weight:** 3.1320 g. **Composition:** 0.9995 Platinum .1006 oz. APW **Reverse:** Pronghorn antelope head

| KM | Date | Mintage | MS-63 | Proof |
|---|---|---|---|---|
| 405 | 2000 Proof | 600 | — | 100 |

**30 DOLLARS** **Weight:** 3.1320 g. **Composition:** 0.9995 Platinum .1006 oz. APW **Subject:** Platinum Collector Bullion **Obverse:** Queen's head right. **Reverse:** Duck's head. **Edge:** Reeded. **Size:** 16 mm.

| KM | Date | Mintage | MS-63 | Proof |
|---|---|---|---|---|
| 429 | 2001 Proof | — | — | 100 |

**50 DOLLARS** **Weight:** 31.1030 g. **Composition:** 0.9995 Platinum 1.0000 oz. APW **Obverse:** Elizabeth II effigy **Obv. Designer:** Machin **Reverse:** Maple leaf

| KM | Date | Mintage | MS-63 | Proof |
|---|---|---|---|---|
| 167 | 1988 | 37,500 | BV+4% | — |
| | 1989 | 10,000 | BV+4% | — |
| | 1989 Proof | 5,965 | — | 700 |

**50 DOLLARS** **Weight:** 31.1030 g. **Composition:** 0.9995 Platinum 1.0000 oz. APW **Obverse:** Elizabeth II effigy **Obv. Designer:** dePedery-Hunt **Reverse:** Maple leaf

| KM | Date | Mintage | MS-63 | Proof |
|---|---|---|---|---|
| 195 | 1990 | 15,100 | BV+4% | — |
| | 1991 | 31,900 | BV+4% | — |
| | 1992 | 40,500 | BV+4% | — |
| | 1993 | 17,666 | BV+4% | — |
| | 1994 | 36,245 | BV+4% | — |
| | 1995 | 25,829 | BV+4% | — |
| | 1996 | 62,273 | BV+4% | — |
| | 1997 | 25,480 | BV+4% | — |
| | 1998 | 10,403 | BV+4% | — |
| | 1999 | 1,300 | 480 | — |

**75 DOLLARS** **Weight:** 7.7760 g. **Composition:** 0.9990 Platinum 0.2500 oz. APW **Reverse:** Polar bear resting

| KM | Date | Mintage | MS-63 | Proof |
|---|---|---|---|---|
| 175 | 1990 Proof | 2,629 | — | 155 |

**75 DOLLARS** **Weight:** 7.7760 g. **Composition:** 0.9990 Platinum 0.2500 oz. APW **Reverse:** Snowy owls perched on branch

| KM | Date | Mintage | MS-63 | Proof |
|---|---|---|---|---|
| 199 | 1991 Proof | 3,500 | — | 175 |

**75 DOLLARS** **Weight:** 7.7760 g. **Composition:** 0.9990 Platinum 0.2500 oz. APW **Reverse:** Cougar prowling

| KM | Date | Mintage | MS-63 | Proof |
|---|---|---|---|---|
| 227 | 1992 Proof | 3,500 | — | 175 |

**75 DOLLARS** **Weight:** 7.7760 g. **Composition:** 0.9990 Platinum 0.2500 oz. APW **Reverse:** Two Arctic foxes

| KM | Date | Mintage | MS-63 | Proof |
|---|---|---|---|---|
| 241 | 1993 Proof | 3,500 | — | 195 |

**75 DOLLARS** **Weight:** 7.7760 g. **Composition:** 0.9990 Platinum 0.2500 oz. APW **Reverse:** Sea otter eating urchin

| KM | Date | Mintage | MS-63 | Proof |
|---|---|---|---|---|
| 253 | 1994 Proof | 1,500 | — | 215 |

**75 DOLLARS** **Weight:** 7.7760 g. **Composition:** 0.9990 Platinum 0.2500 oz. APW **Reverse:** Two lynx kittens

| KM | Date | Mintage | MS-63 | Proof |
|---|---|---|---|---|
| 267 | 1995 Proof | 1,500 | — | 195 |

**75 DOLLARS** **Weight:** 7.7760 g. **Composition:** 0.9990 Platinum 0.2500 oz. APW **Reverse:** Peregrine falcon, diving falcon

| KM | Date | Mintage | MS-63 | Proof |
|---|---|---|---|---|
| 279 | 1996 Proof | 1,500 | — | 195 |

**75 DOLLARS** **Weight:** 7.7760 g. **Composition:** 0.9990 Platinum 0.2500 oz. APW **Reverse:** Two bison calves

| KM | Date | Mintage | MS-63 | Proof |
|---|---|---|---|---|
| 301 | 1997 Proof | 1,500 | — | 195 |

**75 DOLLARS** **Weight:** 7.7760 g. **Composition:** 0.9990 Platinum 0.2500 oz. APW **Reverse:** Gray wolf

| KM | Date | Mintage | MS-63 | Proof |
|---|---|---|---|---|
| 323 | 1998 Proof | 1,000 | — | 195 |

**75 DOLLARS** **Weight:** 7.7760 g. **Composition:** 0.9990 Platinum 0.2500 oz. APW **Reverse:** Musk ox

| KM | Date | Mintage | MS-63 | Proof |
|---|---|---|---|---|
| 360 | 1999 Proof | 500 | — | 195 |

**75 DOLLARS** **Weight:** 7.7760 g. **Composition:** 0.9990 Platinum .25 oz. APW **Reverse:** Standing pronghorn antelope

| KM | Date | Mintage | MS-63 | Proof |
|---|---|---|---|---|
| 406 | 2000 Proof | 600 | — | 195 |

**75 DOLLARS** **Weight:** 7.8000 g. **Composition:** 0.9995 Platinum .2506 oz. APW **Subject:** Platinum Collector Bullion **Obverse:** Queen's head right. **Reverse:** Duck in flight. **Edge:** Reeded. **Size:** 20 mm.

| KM | Date | Mintage | MS-63 | Proof |
|---|---|---|---|---|
| 430 | 2001 Proof | — | — | 195 |

**150 DOLLARS** **Weight:** 15.5520 g. **Composition:** 0.9990 Platinum 0.5000 oz. APW **Reverse:** Polar bear walking

| KM | Date | Mintage | MS-63 | Proof |
|---|---|---|---|---|
| 176 | 1990 Proof | 2,629 | — | 310 |

**150 DOLLARS** **Weight:** 15.5520 g. **Composition:** 0.9990 Platinum 0.5000 oz. APW **Reverse:** Snowy owl flying

| KM | Date | Mintage | MS-63 | Proof |
|---|---|---|---|---|
| 200 | 1991 Proof | 3,500 | — | 335 |

**150 DOLLARS** **Weight:** 15.5520 g. **Composition:** 0.9990 Platinum 0.5000 oz. APW **Reverse:** Cougar mother and cub

| KM | Date | Mintage | MS-63 | Proof |
|---|---|---|---|---|
| 228 | 1992 Proof | 3,500 | — | 335 |

**150 DOLLARS** **Weight:** 15.5520 g. **Composition:** 0.9990 Platinum 0.5000 oz. APW **Reverse:** Arctic fox by lake

| KM | Date | Mintage | MS-63 | Proof |
|---|---|---|---|---|
| 242 | 1993 Proof | 3,500 | — | 370 |

**150 DOLLARS** **Weight:** 15.5520 g. **Composition:** 0.9990 Platinum 0.5000 oz. APW **Reverse:** Sea otter mother carrying pup

| KM | Date | Mintage | MS-63 | Proof |
|---|---|---|---|---|
| 254 | 1994 | 1,500 | — | 400 |

**150 DOLLARS** **Weight:** 15.5520 g. **Composition:** 0.9990 Platinum 0.5000 oz. APW **Reverse:** Prowling lynx

| KM | Date | Mintage | MS-63 | Proof |
|---|---|---|---|---|
| 268 | 1995 Proof | 226 | — | 365 |

**150 DOLLARS** **Weight:** 15.5520 g. **Composition:** 0.9990 Platinum 0.5000 oz. APW **Reverse:** Peregrine falcon - falcon on branch

| KM | Date | Mintage | MS-63 | Proof |
|---|---|---|---|---|
| 280 | 1996 Proof | 100 | — | 365 |

**150 DOLLARS** **Weight:** 15.5520 g. **Composition:** 0.9990 Platinum 0.5000 oz. APW **Reverse:** Bison bull

| KM | Date | Mintage | MS-63 | Proof |
|---|---|---|---|---|
| 302 | 1997 Proof | 4,000 | — | 365 |

**150 DOLLARS** **Weight:** 15.5520 g. **Composition:** 0.9990 Platinum 0.5000 oz. APW **Reverse:** Two gray wolf cubs

| KM | Date | Mintage | MS-63 | Proof |
|---|---|---|---|---|
| 324 | 1998 Proof | 2,000 | — | 365 |

**150 DOLLARS** **Weight:** 15.5520 g. **Composition:** 0.9990 Platinum 0.5000 oz. APW **Reverse:** Musk ox

| KM | Date | Mintage | MS-63 | Proof |
|---|---|---|---|---|
| 361 | 1999 Proof | 500 | — | 370 |

**150 DOLLARS** **Weight:** 15.5520 g. **Composition:** 0.9990 Platinum .5 oz. APW **Reverse:** Two pronghorn antelope

| KM | Date | Mintage | MS-63 | Proof |
|---|---|---|---|---|
| 407 | 2000 Proof | 600 | — | 375 |

**150 DOLLARS** **Weight:** 15.5900 g. **Composition:** 0.9995 Platinum .5010 oz. APW **Subject:** Platinum Collector Bullion **Obverse:** Queen's head right. **Reverse:** Two ducks. **Edge:** Reeded. **Size:** 25 mm.

| KM | Date | Mintage | MS-63 | Proof |
|---|---|---|---|---|
| 431 | 2001 Proof | — | — | 375 |

**300 DOLLARS** **Weight:** 31.1035 g. **Composition:** 0.9990 Platinum 1.0000 oz. APW **Reverse:** Polar bear mother and cub

| KM | Date | Mintage | MS-63 | Proof |
|---|---|---|---|---|
| 177 | 1990 Proof | 2,629 | — | 675 |

**300 DOLLARS** **Weight:** 31.1035 g. **Composition:** 0.9990 Platinum 1.0000 oz. APW **Reverse:** Snowy owl with chicks

| KM | Date | Mintage | MS-63 | Proof |
|---|---|---|---|---|
| 201 | 1991 Proof | 3,500 | — | 710 |

**300 DOLLARS** **Weight:** 31.1035 g. **Composition:** 0.9990 Platinum 1.0000 oz. APW **Reverse:** Cougar resting in tree

| KM | Date | Mintage | MS-63 | Proof |
|---|---|---|---|---|
| 229 | 1992 Proof | 3,500 | — | 710 |

**300 DOLLARS** **Weight:** 31.1035 g. **Composition:** 0.9990 Platinum 1.0000 oz. APW **Reverse:** Mother fox and three kits

| KM | Date | Mintage | MS-63 | Proof |
|---|---|---|---|---|
| 243 | 1993 Proof | 3,500 | — | 740 |

**300 DOLLARS** **Weight:** 31.1035 g. **Composition:** 0.9990 Platinum 1.0000 oz. APW **Reverse:** Two otters swimming

| KM | Date | Mintage | MS-63 | Proof |
|---|---|---|---|---|
| 255 | 1994 | — | — | 800 |

**300 DOLLARS** **Weight:** 31.1035 g. **Composition:** 0.9990 Platinum 1.0000 oz. APW **Reverse:** Female lynx and three kittens

| KM | Date | Mintage | MS-63 | Proof |
|---|---|---|---|---|
| 269 | 1995 Proof | 1,500 | — | 725 |

**300 DOLLARS** **Weight:** 31.1035 g. **Composition:** 0.9990 Platinum 1.0000 oz. APW **Reverse:** Peregrine falcon feeding nestlings

| KM | Date | Mintage | MS-63 | Proof |
|---|---|---|---|---|
| 281 | 1996 Proof | 1,500 | — | 725 |

**300 DOLLARS** **Weight:** 31.1035 g. **Composition:** 0.9990 Platinum 1.0000 oz. APW **Reverse:** Bison family

| KM | Date | Mintage | MS-63 | Proof |
|---|---|---|---|---|
| 303 | 1997 Proof | 1,500 | — | 725 |

**300 DOLLARS** **Weight:** 31.1035 g. **Composition:** 0.9990 Platinum 1.0000 oz. APW **Reverse:** Gray wolf and two cubs

| KM | Date | Mintage | MS-63 | Proof |
|---|---|---|---|---|
| 325 | 1998 | 1,000 | — | 725 |

**300 DOLLARS** **Weight:** 31.1035 g. **Composition:** 0.9990 Platinum 1.0000 oz. APW **Reverse:** Musk ox

| KM | Date | Mintage | MS-63 | Proof |
|---|---|---|---|---|
| 362 | 1999 Proof | 500 | — | 735 |

**300 DOLLARS** **Weight:** 31.1035 g. **Composition:** 0.9990 Platinum 1.0000 oz. APW **Reverse:** Four pronghorn antelope

| KM | Date | Mintage | MS-63 | Proof |
|---|---|---|---|---|
| 408 | 2000 Proof | 600 | — | 750 |

**300 DOLLARS** **Weight:** 31.1600 g. **Composition:** 0.9995 Platinum 1.0013 oz. APW **Subject:** Platinum Collector Bullion **Obverse:** Queen's head right. **Reverse:** Two standing ducks. **Edge:** Reeded. **Size:** 30 mm.

| KM | Date | Mintage | MS-63 | Proof |
|---|---|---|---|---|
| 432 | 2001 Proof | — | — | 750 |

## CUSTOM PROOF-LIKE SETS (CPL)

| KM | Date | Mintage | Identification | Issue Price | Mkt Val |
|---|---|---|---|---|---|
| CPL1 | 1971 | 33,517 | KM59.1 (2pcs.), 60.1, 62b-75.1, 77.1 | 6.50 | 5.00 |
| CPL2 | 1971 | 38,198 | KM59.1 (2pcs.), 60.1, 62b, 75.1-77.1 | 6.50 | 5.00 |
| CPL3 | 1973 | 35,676 | KM59.1 (2pcs.), 60.1, 75.1, 77.1, 81.1 | 6.50 | 4.75 |
| CPL4 | 1973 | — | KM59.1 (2pcs.), 60.1, 75.1, 77.1, 81.1 | 6.50 | 140 |
| CPL5 | 1974 | 44,296 | KM59.1 (2pcs.), 60.1, 62b-75.1, 88 | 8.00 | 5.00 |
| CPL6 | 1975 | 36,851 | KM59.1 (2pcs.), 60.1, 62b-75.1, 76.2, | 8.00 | 5.00 |
| CPL7 | 1976 | 28,162 | KM59.1 (2pcs.), 60.1, 62b-75.1, 76.2, | 8.00 | 5.50 |
| CPL8 | 1977 | 44,198 | KM59.1 (2pcs.), 60.1, 62b-75.2, 77.1, | 8.15 | 5.50 |
| CPL9 | 1978 | 41,000 | KM59.1 (2pcs.), 60.1, 62b-75.3, 77.1, | — | 5.50 |
| CPL10 | 1979 | 31,174 | KM59.1 (2pcs.), 60.2, 74, 75.3, 77.2, 120 | 10.75 | 5.50 |
| CPL11 | 1980 | 41,447 | KM60.2, 74, 75.3, 77.2, 120, 127 (2pcs.) | 10.75 | 6.00 |

## MINT SETS

| KM | Date | Mintage | Identification | Issue Price | Mkt Val |
|---|---|---|---|---|---|
| MS1 | 1973 | — | KM84-87, Olympic Commemoratives, Series I | 45.00 | 30.00 |
| MS2 | 1974 | — | KM89-90, 93-94; Olympic Commemoratives, Series II | 48.00 | 30.00 |
| MS3 | 1974 | — | KM91-92, 95-96; Olympic Commemorative, Series III | 48.00 | 30.00 |
| MS4 | 1975 | — | KM98-99, 102-103; Olympic Commemoratives, Series IV | 48.00 | 30.00 |
| MS5 | 1975 | — | KM100-101, 104-105; Olympic Commemoratives, Series V | 60.00 | 30.00 |
| MS6 | 1976 | — | KM107-108, 111-112; Olympic Commemoratives, Series VI | 60.00 | 30.00 |
| MS7 | 1976 | — | KM109-110, 113-114; Olympic Commemoratives, Series VII | 60.00 | 30.00 |

## OLYMPIC COMMEMORATIVES (OCP)

| KM | Date | Mintage | Identification | Issue Price | Mkt Val |
|---|---|---|---|---|---|
| OCP1 | 1973 | — | KM84-87, Series I | 78.50 | 37.50 |
| OCP2 | 1974 | — | KM89, 90, 93, 94, Series II | 88.50 | 37.50 |
| OCP3 | 1974 | — | KM91, 92, 95, 96, SeriesIII | 88.50 | 37.50 |
| OCP4 | 1975 | — | KM98, 99, 102, 103, SeriesIV | 88.50 | 37.50 |
| OCP5 | 1975 | — | KM100, 101, 104, 105, Series V | 88.50 | 37.50 |
| OCP6 | 1976 | — | KM107, 108, 111, 112, Series VI | 88.50 | 38.50 |
| OCP7 | 1976 | — | KM109, 110, 113, 114, Series VII | 88.50 | 38.50 |

## PROOF SETS

| KM | Date | Mintage | Identification | Issue Price | Mkt Val |
|---|---|---|---|---|---|
| PS10 | 1989 | 6,823 | KM125.2, 135-136, 153 | 1,190 | 800 |
| PS11 | 1989 | 1,995 | KM164-167 | 1,700 | 1,150 |
| PS12 | 1989 | 2,550 | KM125.2, 163, 167 | 1,530 | 1,100 |
| PS13 | 1989 | 9,979 | KM135, 163-164 | 165 | 155 |
| PS14 | 1990 | 158,068 | KM170, 181-186 | 41.00 | 22.50 |
| PS16 | 1991 | 14,629 | KM179, 181-186 | — | 45.00 |
| PS19 | 1992 | 147,061 | KM204-210 | 42.75 | 25.00 |
| PS2 | 1982 | 180,908 | KM60.2a, 74, 75.3, 77.2, 120, 132, 133 | 36.00 | 11.00 |
| PS21 | 1993 | 143,065 | KM181-186, 235 | 42.75 | 18.00 |
| PS24 | 1994 | 99,121 | KM181-186, 251 | 43.00 | 28.00 |
| PS26 | 1995 | — | KM181-186, 259 | 37.45 | 25.00 |
| PS3 | 1983 | 166,779 | KM60.2a, 74, 75.3, 77.2, 120, 132, 138 | 36.00 | 12.50 |
| PS39 | 1998 | 25,000 | KM309-313 | 73.50 | 55.00 |
| PS4 | 1984 | 161,602 | KM60.2a, 74, 75.3, 77.2, 120, 132, 140 | 30.00 | 13.50 |
| PS40 | 1998 | 61,000 | KM316 w/China Y-727 | 72.50 | 40.00 |
| PS43 | 1998 | 25,000 | KM310-313, 332 | 73.50 | 55.00 |
| PS48 | 2000 | — | KM373a-348a | 101 | 90.00 |
| PS49 | 2000 | — | KM389-392 | 44.00 | 40.00 |
| PS5 | 1985 | 157,037 | KM60.2a, 74, 75.3, 77.2, 120, 132, 143 | 30.00 | 14.00 |
| PS50 | 2000 | 600 | KM405-408 | 1,416 | 1,420 |
| PS6 | 1986 | 175,745 | KM60.2a, 74, 75.3, 77.2, 120, 132, 149 | 30.00 | 14.00 |
| PS7 | 1987 | 179,004 | KM60.2a, 74, 75.3, 77.2, 120, 132, 154 | 34.00 | 14.00 |
| PS8 | 1988 | 175,259 | KM60.2a, 74, 75.3, 77.2, 132, 157, 161 | 37.50 | 22.50 |
| PS9 | 1989 | 170,928 | KM60.2a, 74, 75.3, 77.2, 132, 157, 168 | 40.00 | 22.50 |
| PS1 | 1981 | 199,000 | KM60.2, 74, 75.3, 77.2, 120, 127, 130 | 36.00 | 17.50 |
| PS15 | 1990 | 2,629 | KM174-177 | 1,720 | 1,100 |
| PS17 | 1991 | 873 | KM198-201 | 1,760 | 1,150 |
| PS18 | 1992 | 84,397 | KM203a, 212a-214a, 218, 220a-223a, | — | 75.00 |
| PS20 | 1992 | 3,500 | KM226-229 | 1,680 | 1,200 |
| PS22 | 1993 | 3,500 | KM240-243 | 1,329 | 1,300 |
| PS23 | 1994 | 47,303 | KM181-186, 248 | 47.50 | 35.00 |
| PS25 | 1994 | 1,500 | KM252-255 | 915 | 1,450 |
| PS27 | 1995 | 50,000 | KM181-185, 258, 259 | 49.45 | 35.00 |
| PS28 | 1995 | — | KM261-264 | 42.00 | 50.00 |
| PS29 | 1995 | 682 | KM266-269 | 1,555 | 1,400 |
| PS30 | 1995 | — | KM261-262 | 22.00 | 21.00 |
| PS31 | 1995 | — | KM263-264 | 22.00 | 21.00 |
| PS32 | 1996 | 423 | KM278-281 | 1,555 | 1,400 |
| PS33 | 1996 | — | KM181a-185a, 186, 274 | 49.00 | 40.00 |
| PS34 | 1996 | — | KM283-286 | 44.45 | 45.00 |
| PS35 | 1997 | — | KM182a-184a, 209, 270c, 282, 289, | 60.00 | 40.00 |
| PS36 | 1997 | — | KM292-295 | 44.45 | 35.00 |
| PS37 | 1997 | — | KM300-303 | 1,530 | 1,400 |
| PS38 | 1998 | — | KM182a-184a, 186, 270b, 289, 290a, | 59.45 | 55.00 |
| PS41 | 1998 | — | KM318-321 | 44.45 | 38.00 |
| PS42 | 1998 | 1,000 | KM322-325 | 1,552 | 1,400 |
| PS44 | 1998 | — | KM182a-184a, 186, 270c, 289, 290a, | 59.45 | 60.00 |
| PS45 | 1999 | — | KM335-338 | 39.95 | 40.00 |
| PS46 | 1999 | — | KM342a-353a | 99.45 | 90.00 |
| PS47 | 1999 | — | KM359-362 | 1,425 | 1,450 |
| PS51 | 2001 | — | KM#429, 430, 431, 432 | — | 1,420 |

## PROOF-LIKE DOLLARS

| KM | Date | Mintage | Identification | Issue Price | Mkt Val |
|---|---|---|---|---|---|
| D1.1 | 1951 | — | KM46, Canoe | | 175 |
| D1.2 | 1951 | — | KM46, Arnprior | | 700 |
| D15 | 1965 | 2,904,352 | KM64, Canoe | — | 4.50 |
| D16 | 1966 | 672,514 | KM64, Canoe | — | 4.50 |
| D2.1 | 1952 | — | KM46, water lines | | 1,200 |
| D2.2 | 1952 | — | KM46, without water lines | | 175 |
| D3 | 1953 | 1,200 | KM54, Canoe w/shoulder fold | — | 300 |
| D5 | 1955 | 7,950 | KM54, Canoe | 1.25 | 100 |
| D7 | 1957 | 16,241 | KM54, Canoe | 1.25 | 22.00 |
| D4 | 1954 | 5,300 | KM54, Canoe | 1.25 | 125 |
| D5a | 1955 | — | KM54, Arnprior | 1.25 | 150 |
| D6 | 1956 | 10,212 | KM54, Canoe | 1.25 | 50.00 |
| D8 | 1958 | 33,237 | KM55, British Columbia | 1.25 | 18.00 |
| D9 | 1959 | 45,160 | KM54, Canoe | 1.25 | 10.00 |
| D10 | 1960 | 82,728 | KM54, Canoe | 1.25 | 7.00 |
| D11 | 1961 | 120,928 | KM54, Canoe | 1.25 | 7.00 |
| D12 | 1962 | 248,901 | KM54, Canoe | 1.25 | 6.00 |
| D13 | 1963 | 963,525 | KM54, Canoe | 1.25 | 4.50 |
| D14 | 1964 | 2,862,441 | KM58, Charlottetown | 1.25 | 4.50 |
| D17 | 1967 | 1,036,176 | KM70, Confederation | — | 6.50 |

## PROOF-LIKE SETS (PL)

| KM | Date | Mintage | Identification | Issue Price | Mkt Val |
|---|---|---|---|---|---|
| PL1 | 1953 | 1,200 | KM49 w/o straps, 50-54 | 2.20 | 1,250 |
| PL2 | 1953 | — | KM49-54 | 2.20 | 760 |
| PL33 | 1981 | 186,250 | KM60.2, 74, 75.3, 77.2, 120, 123 | 5.00 | 3.25 |
| PL34 | 1982 | 203,287 | KM60.2, 74, 75.3, 77.2, 120, 123 | 6.00 | 2.50 |
| PL36 | 1983 | 190,838 | KM60.2a, 74, 75.3, 77.2, 120, 132 | 5.00 | 6.00 |
| PL37 | 1984 | 181,249 | KM60.2a, 74, 75.3, 77.2, 120, 132 | 5.25 | 5.00 |
| PL38 | 1985 | 173,924 | KM60.2a, 74, 75.3, 77.2, 120, 132 | 5.25 | 6.00 |
| PL39 | 1986 | 167,338 | KM60.2a, 74, 75.3, 77.2, 120, 132 | 5.25 | 6.50 |
| PL40 | 1987 | 212,136 | KM60.2a, 74, 75.3, 77.2, 120, 132 | 5.25 | 5.00 |
| PL41 | 1988 | 182,048 | KM60.2a, 74, 75.3, 77.2, 132, 157 | 6.05 | 5.50 |
| PL42 | 1989 | 173,622 | KM60.2a, 74, 75.3, 77.2, 132, 157 | 6.60 | 8.50 |
| PL43 | 1990 | 170,791 | KM181-186 | 7.40 | 8.50 |
| PL44 | 1991 | 147,814 | KM181-186 | 7.40 | 25.00 |
| PL45 | 1992 | 217,597 | KM204-209 | 8.25 | 11.00 |
| PL46 | 1993 | 171,680 | KM181-186 | 8.25 | 4.50 |
| PL47 | 1994 | 141,676 | KM181-185, 258 | 8.50 | 6.00 |
| PL48 | 1994 | 18,794 | KM181-185, 258 (Oh Canada holder) | — | 10.00 |
| PL49 | 1995 | 143,892 | KM181-186 | 6.95 | 6.50 |
| PL50 | 1995 | 50,927 | KM181-186 (Oh Canada holder) | 14.65 | 10.00 |
| PL51 | 1995 | 36,443 | KM181-186 (Baby Gift holder) | — | 11.00 |
| PL52 | 1996 | 116,736 | KM181-186 | — | 13.50 |
| PL53 | 1996 | 29,747 | KM181-186 (Baby Gift holder) | — | 15.00 |
| PL63 | 1999 | — | KM342-353 | 16.95 | 12.00 |
| PL64 | 2000 | — | KM373-384 | 16.95 | 12.00 |
| PL3 | 1954 | 3,000 | KM49-54 | 2.50 | 200 |
| PL4 | 1954 | — | KM49 w/o straps, 50-54 | 2.50 | 470 |
| PL5 | 1955 | 6,300 | KM49, 50a, 51-54 | 2.50 | 140 |
| PL6 | 1955 | — | KM49, 50a, 51-54, Arnprior | 2.50 | 220 |
| PL7 | 1956 | 6,500 | KM49, 50a, 51-54 | 2.50 | 80.00 |
| PL8 | 1957 | 11,862 | KM49, 50a, 51-54 | 2.50 | 50.00 |
| PL9 | 1958 | 18,259 | KM49, 50a, 51-53, 55 | 2.50 | 45.00 |
| PL10 | 1959 | 31,577 | KM49, 50a, 51, 52, 54, 56 | 2.50 | 20.00 |
| PL11 | 1960 | 64,097 | KM49, 50a, 51, 52, 54, 56 | 3.00 | 12.75 |
| PL12 | 1961 | 98,373 | KM49, 50a, 51, 52, 54, 56 | 3.00 | 12.50 |
| PL13 | 1962 | 200,950 | KM49, 50a, 51, 52, 54, 56 | 3.00 | 10.00 |
| PL14 | 1963 | 673,006 | KM49, 51, 52, 54, 56, 57 | 3.00 | 7.00 |
| PL15 | 1964 | 1,653,162 | KM49, 51, 52, 56-58 | 3.00 | 7.00 |
| PL16 | 1965 | 2,904,352 | KM59.1-60.1, 61-63, 64.1 | 4.00 | 7.00 |
| PL17 | 1966 | 672,514 | KM59.1-60.1, 61-63, 64.1 | 4.00 | 7.00 |
| PL18 | 1967 | 961,887 | KM65-70 (pliofilm flat pack) | 4.00 | 11.00 |
| PL18A | 1967 | 70,583 | KM65-70 and Silver Medal (red box) | 12.00 | 15.25 |
| PL18B | 1967 | 337,688 | KM65-71 (black box) | 40.00 | 200 |
| PL19 | 1968 | 521,641 | KM59.1-60.1, 62b, 72a, 75.1-76.1 | 4.00 | 2.25 |
| PL20 | 1969 | 326,203 | KM59.1-60.1, 62b, 75.1-77.1 | 4.00 | 2.75 |
| PL21 | 1970 | 349,120 | KM59.1-60.1, 62b, 75.1, 77.1, 78 | 4.00 | 3.25 |
| PL22 | 1971 | 253,311 | KM59.1-60.1, 62b, 75.1, 77.1, 79 | 4.00 | 2.25 |
| PL23 | 1972 | 224,275 | KM59.1-60.1, 62b-77.1 | 4.00 | 2.75 |
| PL24 | 1973 | 243,695 | KM59.1-60.1, 62b-75.1 obv. 120 | 4.00 | 3.50 |
| PL25 | 1973 | — | KM59.1-60.1, 62b-75.1 obv. 132 bead | 4.00 | 110 |
| PL26 | 1974 | 213,589 | KM59.1-60.1, 62b-75.1, 77.1, 88 | 5.00 | 2.75 |

| KM | Date | Mintage | Identification | Issue Price | Mkt Val |
|---|---|---|---|---|---|
| PL27.1 | 1975 | 197,372 | KM59.1, 60.1, 62b-75.1, 76.2, 77.1 | 5.00 | 2.25 |
| PL27.2 | 1975 | — | KM59.1, 60.1, 62b-75.1, 76.3, 77.1 | 5.00 | — |
| PL28 | 1976 | 171,737 | KM59.1, 60.1, 62b-75.1, 76.2, 77.1 | 5.15 | 2.75 |
| PL29 | 1977 | 225,307 | KM59.1, 60.1, 62b, 75.2, 77.1, 117.1 | 5.15 | 2.75 |
| PL30 | 1978 | 260,000 | KM59.1-60.1, 62b, 75.3, 77.1, 120 | 5.25 | 2.75 |
| PL31 | 1979 | 187,624 | KM59.2-60.2, 74, 75.3, 77.2, 120 | 6.25 | 2.75 |
| PL32 | 1980 | 410,842 | KM60.2, 74, 75.3, 77.2, 120, 127 | 6.50 | 4.50 |
| PL54 | 1996 | — | KM181a-185a, 186 | 8.95 | 9.50 |
| PL55 | 1996 | — | KM181a-185a, 186 (Oh Canada holder) | 14.65 | 12.00 |
| PL56 | 1996 | — | KM181a-185a, 186 (Baby Gift holder) | — | 12.00 |
| PL57 | 1997 | — | KM182a-184a, 209, 270, 289-290 | 10.45 | 9.50 |
| PL58 | 1997 | — | KM182a-184a, 270, 289-291 (Oh Canada holder) | 16.45 | 16.25 |
| PL59 | 1997 | — | KM182a-184a, 209, 270, 289-290 (Baby Gift holder) | 18.50 | 16.75 |
| PL60 | 1998 | — | KM182-184, 186, 270, 289-290 | 10.45 | 12.00 |
| PL61 | 1998 | — | KM182-184, 186, 270, 289-290 (Oh Canada holder) | 16.45 | 16.25 |
| PL62 | 1998 | — | KM182-184, 186, 270, 289-290 (Tiny | 16.45 | 14.75 |

## SPECIMEN SETS (SS)

| KM | Date | Mintage | Identification | Issue Price | Mkt Val |
|---|---|---|---|---|---|
| SS1 | 1858 | — | KM1-4, Reeded edge | — | 6,000 |
| SS15 | 1908 | 1,000 | KM8, 10-13 | — | 2,200 |
| SS2 | 1858 | — | KM1-4, Plain edge | — | 6,000 |
| SS3 | 1858 | — | KM1-4; Double Set | — | 12,500 |
| SS40 | 1947 | — | KM32, 34-36(7 curved), 37(7 pointed), | — | 8,500 |
| SS41 | 1947 | — | KM32, 34-36(7 curved), 37(blunt 7), 39a | — | 6,200 |
| SS42 | 1947 | — | KM32, 34-36(7 curved right), 37, 39a | — | 4,250 |
| SS49 | 1953 | 28 | KM49 w/o straps, 50-54 | — | 1,850 |
| SS50 | 1953 | — | KM49 w/ straps, 50-54 | — | 875 |
| SS67 | 1981 | 71,300 | KM60.2, 74, 75.3, 77.2, 120, 127; Regular Specimen Sets Resumed | 10.00 | 6.00 |
| SS68 | 1982 | 62,298 | KM60.2a, 74, 75.3, 77.2, 120, 132; Regular Specimen Sets Resumed | 11.50 | 6.00 |
| SS69 | 1983 | 60,329 | KM60.2a, 74, 75.3, 77.2, 120, 132; Regular Specimen Sets Resumed | 12.75 | 6.00 |
| SS70 | 1984 | 60,400 | KM60.2a, 74, 75.3, 77.2, 120, 132; Regular Specimen Sets Resumed | 10.00 | 6.00 |
| SS71 | 1985 | 61,553 | KM60.2a, 74, 75.3, 77.2, 120, 132; Regular Specimen Sets Resumed | 10.00 | 6.50 |
| SS72 | 1986 | 67,152 | KM60.2a, 74, 75.3, 77.2, 120, 132; Regular Specimen Sets Resumed | 10.00 | 6.50 |
| SS72A | 1987 | 75,194 | KM60.2a, 74, 75.3, 77.2, 120, 132; Regular Specimen Sets Resumed | 11.00 | 7.00 |
| SS73 | 1988 | 70,205 | KM60.2a, 74, 75.3, 77.2, 132, 157; Regular Specimen Sets Resumed | 12.30 | 8.00 |
| SS74 | 1989 | 75,306 | KM60.2a, 74, 75.3, 77.2, 132, 157; Regular Specimen Sets Resumed | 14.50 | 13.25 |
| SS75 | 1990 | 76,611 | KM181-186; Regular Specimen Sets Resumed | 15.50 | 14.50 |
| SS76 | 1991 | 68,552 | KM181-186; Regular Specimen Sets Resumed | 15.50 | 32.50 |
| SS77 | 1992 | 78,328 | KM204-209; Regular Specimen Sets Resumed | 16.25 | 21.00 |
| SS78 | 1993 | 77,351 | KM181-186; Regular Specimen Sets Resumed | 16.25 | 14.75 |
| SS79 | 1994 | 77,349 | KM181-186; Regular Specimen Sets Resumed | 16.50 | 16.25 |
| SS80 | 1995 | — | KM181-186; Regular Specimen Sets Resumed | 13.95 | 16.25 |
| SS84 | 1998 | — | KM182-184, 186, 270, 289, 290; Regular Specimen Sets Resumed | 19.95 | 19.00 |
| SS4 | 1858 | — | KM1 (overdate), 2-4; Double Set | — | 14,000 |
| SS5 | 1870 | 100 | KM2, 3, 5, 6 (reeded edges) | — | 12,500 |
| SS6 | 1870 | — | KM2, 3, 5, 6; Double Set (plain edges) | — | 25,000 |
| SS7 | 1872 | — | KM2, 3, 5, 6 | — | 12,500 |
| SS8 | 1875 | — | KM2 (Large date), 3, 5 | — | 20,000 |
| SS9 | 1880 | — | KM2, 3, 5 (Narrow 0) | — | 7,000 |
| SS10 | 1881 | — | KM7, 2, 3, 5, 6 | — | 12,000 |
| SS11 | 1892 | — | KM3, 5 | — | 10,000 |
| SS12 | 1902 | 100 | KM8-12 | — | 10,000 |
| SS13 | 1902 | — | KM9 (Large H), 10, 11 | — | 6,500 |
| SS14 | 1903 | — | KM10, 12, 13 | — | 7,000 |
| SS16 | 1911 | 1,000 | KM15-19 | — | 5,500 |
| SS17 | 1911/12 | 5 | KM15-20, 26-27 | — | 52,250 |
| SS18 | 1921 | — | KM22-25, 28 | — | 80,000 |
| SS19 | 1922 | — | KM28, 29 | — | 800 |
| SS20 | 1923 | — | KM28, 29 | — | 1,600 |
| SS21 | 1924 | — | KM28, 29 | — | 1,400 |
| SS22 | 1925 | — | KM28, 29 | — | 2,725 |
| SS23 | 1926 | — | KM28, 29 (Near 6) | — | 1,800 |
| SS24 | 1927 | — | KM24a, 28, 29 | — | 3,200 |
| SS25 | 1928 | — | KM23a, 24a, 28, 29 | — | 2,800 |
| SS26 | 1929 | — | KM23a,-25a, 28, 29 | — | 10,000 |
| SS27 | 1930 | — | KM23a, 24a. 28, 29 | — | 6,500 |
| SS28 | 1931 | — | KM23a-25a, 28, 29 | — | 8,500 |
| SS29 | 1932 | — | KM23a-25a, 28, 29 | — | 10,000 |
| SS30 | 1934 | — | KM23-25, 28, 29 | — | 8,500 |
| SS31 | 1936 | — | KM23-25, 28, 29 | — | 8,500 |
| SS32 | 1936 | — | KM23a(dot), 24a(dot), 25a, 28(dot), 29, | — | — |
| SS33 | 1937 | 1,025 | KM32-37, Matte Finish | — | 750 |
| SS34 | 1937 | — | KM32-35, Mirror Fields | — | 500 |
| SS35 | 1937 | 75 | KM32-37, Mirror Fields | — | 1,550 |
| SS36 | 1938 | — | KM32-37 | — | 18,250 |
| SS-A36 | 1939 | — | KM32-35, 38, Matte Finish | — | — |
| SS-B36 | 1939 | — | KM32-35, 38, Mirror Fields | — | — |
| SS-C36 | 1942 | — | KM32, 33 | — | 300 |
| SS-D36 | 1943 | — | KM32, 40 | — | 300 |
| SS-A37 | 1944 | — | KM32, 40a | — | 300 |
| SS37 | 1944 | 3 | KM32, 34-37, 40a | — | 11,300 |
| SS-A38 | 1945 | — | KM32, 40a | — | 300 |
| SS38 | 1945 | 6 | KM32, 34-37, 40a | — | 4,650 |
| SS39 | 1946 | 15 | KM32, 34-37, 39a | — | 4,000 |
| SS43 | 1948 | 30 | KM41-46 | — | 4,250 |
| SS44 | 1949 | 20 | KM41-45, 47 | — | 3,200 |
| SS44A | 1949 | — | KM47 | — | 1,550 |
| SS45 | 1950 | 12 | KM41-46 | — | 1,650 |
| SS46 | 1950 | — | KM41-45, 46 (Arnprior) | — | 3,175 |
| SS47 | 1951 | 12 | KM41, 48, 42a, 43-46 (w/water lines) | — | 2,725 |
| SS48 | 1952 | 2,317 | KM41, 42a, 43-46 (water lines) | — | 3,175 |
| SS48A | 1952 | — | KM41, 42a, 43-46 (w/o water lines) | — | 3,175 |
| SS51 | 1964 | — | KM49, 51, 52, 56-58 | — | 450 |
| SS52 | 1965 | — | KM59.1-60.1, 61-63, 64.1 | — | 450 |
| SS56 | 1971 | 66,860 | KM59.1-60.1, 62b-75.1, 77.1, 79 (2pcs.); Double Dollar Prestige Sets | 12.00 | 9.50 |
| SS57 | 1972 | 36,349 | KM59.1,-60.1, 62b-75.1, 76.1 (2pcs.), 77; Double Dollar Prestige Sets | 12.00 | 14.50 |
| SS58 | 1973 | 119,819 | KM59.1-60.1, 75.1, 77.1, 81.1, 82, 83; Double Dollar Prestige Sets | 12.00 | 10.00 |
| SS59 | 1973 | — | KM59.1-60.1, 75.1, 77.1, 81.2, 82, 83; Double Dollar Prestige Sets | — | 125 |
| SS60 | 1974 | 85,230 | KM59.1-60.1, 62b-75.1, 77.1, 88, 88a; Double Dollar Prestige Sets | 15.00 | 10.00 |
| SS61 | 1975 | 97,263 | KM59.1-60.1, 62b-75.1, 76.2, 77.1, 97; Double Dollar Prestige Sets | 15.00 | 10.00 |
| SS62 | 1976 | 87,744 | KM59.1-60, 62b-75.1, 76.2, 77.1, 106; Double Dollar Prestige Sets | 16.00 | 10.00 |
| SS63 | 1977 | 142,577 | KM59.1-60.1, 62b, 75.2, 77.1, 117.1, 118; Double Dollar Prestige Sets | 16.50 | 10.00 |
| SS64 | 1978 | 147,000 | KM59.1-60.1, 62b, 75.3, 77.1, 120, 121; Double Dollar Prestige Sets | 16.50 | 10.00 |
| SS65 | 1979 | 155,698 | KM59.2-60.2, 74, 75.3, 77.2, 120, 124; Double Dollar Prestige Sets | 18.50 | 11.50 |
| SS66 | 1980 | 162,875 | KM60.2, 74-75.3, 77.2, 120, 127, 128; Double Dollar Prestige Sets | 30.50 | 22.50 |
| SS82 | 1996 | — | KM181a-185a, 186; Regular Specimen Sets Resumed | 18.95 | 20.00 |
| SS83 | 1997 | — | KM182a-184a, 270, 289-291; Regular Specimen Sets Resumed | 19.95 | 22.00 |
| SS85 | 1998 | — | KM182-184, 186, 270, 289a, 290; Regular Specimen Sets Resumed | 19.95 | 20.00 |

## V.I.P. SPECIMEN SETS (VS)

| KM | Date | Mintage | Identification | Issue Price | Mkt Val |
|---|---|---|---|---|---|
| VS1 | 1969 | 4 | | — | 5,850 |
| VS2 | 1970 | 100 | KM59.1-60.1, 74.1-75.1, 77.1, 78 | — | 525 |
| VS3 | 1971 | 69 | KM59.1-60.1, 74.1-75.1, 77.1, 79(2pcs) | — | 375 |
| VS4 | 1972 | 25 | KM59.1-60.1, 74.1-75.1, 76.1, (2pcs), | — | 435 |
| VS5 | 1973 | 26 | KM59.1-60.1, 75.1, 77.1, 81.1, 82, 83 | — | 435 |
| VS6 | 1974 | 72 | KM59.1-60.1, 74.1-75.1, 77.1, 88, 88a | — | 375 |
| VS7 | 1975 | 94 | KM59.1-60.1, 74.1-75.1, 76.2, 77.1, 97 | — | 375 |
| VS8 | 1976 | — | KM59.1-60.1, 74.1-75.1, 76.2, 77.1, 106 | — | 375 |

The Republic of Cape Verde, Africa's smallest republic, is located in the Atlantic Ocean, about 370 miles (595 km.) west of Dakar, Senegal, off the coast of Africa. The 14-island republic has an area of 1,557 sq. mi. (4,033 sq. km.) and a population of 435,983. Capital: Praia. The refueling of ships and aircraft is the chief economic function of the country. Fishing is important and agriculture is widely practiced, but the Cape Verdes are not self-sufficient in food. Fish products, salt, bananas, and shellfish are exported.

The date of discovery of the islands is uncertain. Possibly they were visited by Venetian captain Alvise Cadamosto in 1456. Portuguese navigator Diogo Gomes claimed them for Portugal in May of 1460. Settlement began two years later. The early importance and wealth of the islands, which caused them to be attacked by Sir Francis Drake and the Dutch, resulted from the monopoly of the Guinea slave trade granted the inhabitants in 1466. Poverty and famine occasioned by frequent periods of severe drought have marked the history of the country since abolition of the slave trade in 1876.

After 500 years of Portuguese rule, the Cape Verdes became independent on July 5, 1975. At the first general election, all seats of the new national assembly were won by the Party for the Independence of Guinea-Bissau and Cape Verde (PAIGC). The PAIGC linked the two former colonies into one state. Antonio Mascarenhas Monteiro won the first free presidential election in 1991.

**RULERS**

Portuguese, until 1975

**MONETARY SYSTEM**

100 Centavos = 1 Escudo

# PORTUGUESE COLONY

## COLONIAL COINAGE

**5 CENTAVOS** KM# 1 **Composition:** Bronze

| Date | Mintage | F | VF | XF | Unc | BU |
|---|---|---|---|---|---|---|
| 1930 | 1,000,000 | 0.75 | 1.50 | 3.00 | 7.00 | — |

**10 CENTAVOS** KM# 2 **Composition:** Bronze

| Date | Mintage | F | VF | XF | Unc | BU |
|---|---|---|---|---|---|---|
| 1930 | 1,500,000 | 0.75 | 1.50 | 3.50 | 10.00 | — |

**20 CENTAVOS** KM# 3 **Composition:** Bronze

| Date | Mintage | F | VF | XF | Unc | BU |
|---|---|---|---|---|---|---|
| 1930 | 1,500,000 | 1.00 | 2.00 | 4.00 | 11.50 | — |

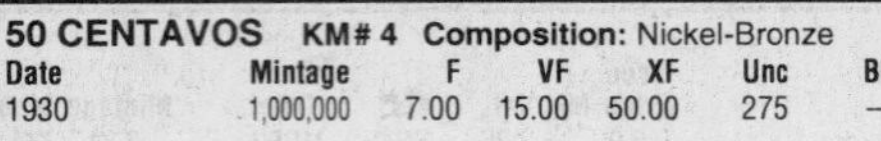

**50 CENTAVOS** KM# 4 **Composition:** Nickel-Bronze

| Date | Mintage | F | VF | XF | Unc | BU |
|---|---|---|---|---|---|---|
| 1930 | 1,000,000 | 7.00 | 15.00 | 50.00 | 275 | — |

**50 CENTAVOS** KM# 6 **Composition:** Nickel-Bronze

| Date | Mintage | F | VF | XF | Unc | BU |
|---|---|---|---|---|---|---|
| 1949 | 1,000,000 | 0.50 | 1.00 | 2.50 | 6.00 | — |

**50 CENTAVOS** KM# 11 **Composition:** Bronze

| Date | Mintage | F | VF | XF | Unc | BU |
|---|---|---|---|---|---|---|
| 1968 | 1,000,000 | 0.25 | 0.50 | 1.00 | 2.50 | — |

**ESCUDO** KM# 5 **Composition:** Nickel-Bronze

| Date | Mintage | F | VF | XF | Unc | BU |
|---|---|---|---|---|---|---|
| 1930 | 50,000 | 15.00 | 35.00 | 85.00 | 350 | — |

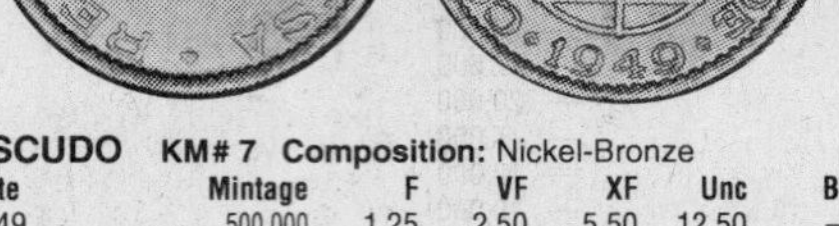

**ESCUDO** KM# 7 **Composition:** Nickel-Bronze

| Date | Mintage | F | VF | XF | Unc | BU |
|---|---|---|---|---|---|---|
| 1949 | 500,000 | 1.25 | 2.50 | 5.50 | 12.50 | — |

**ESCUDO** KM# 8 **Composition:** Bronze

| Date | Mintage | F | VF | XF | Unc | BU |
|---|---|---|---|---|---|---|
| 1953 | 250,000 | 1.00 | 2.00 | 4.50 | 10.00 | — |
| 1968 | 500,000 | 0.50 | 1.00 | 2.00 | 5.00 | — |

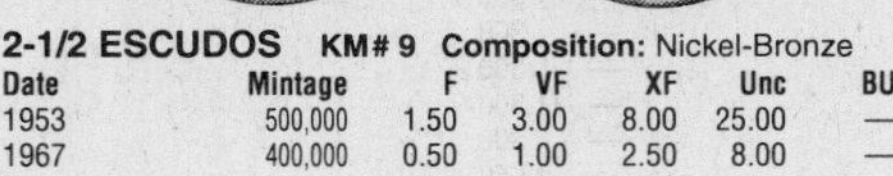

**2-1/2 ESCUDOS** KM# 9 **Composition:** Nickel-Bronze

| Date | Mintage | F | VF | XF | Unc | BU |
|---|---|---|---|---|---|---|
| 1953 | 500,000 | 1.50 | 3.00 | 8.00 | 25.00 | — |
| 1967 | 400,000 | 0.50 | 1.00 | 2.50 | 8.00 | — |

**5 ESCUDOS** KM# 12 **Composition:** Nickel-Bronze

| Date | Mintage | F | VF | XF | Unc | BU |
|---|---|---|---|---|---|---|
| 1968 | 200,000 | 0.75 | 1.50 | 3.50 | 10.00 | — |

**10 ESCUDOS** KM# 10 **Weight:** 5.0000 g. **Composition:** 0.7200 Silver .1158 oz. ASW

| Date | Mintage | F | VF | XF | Unc | BU |
|---|---|---|---|---|---|---|
| 1953 | 400,000 | 1.50 | 3.00 | 6.00 | 18.00 | — |

# REPUBLIC

## DECIMAL COINAGE

**20 CENTAVOS** KM# 15 **Composition:** Aluminum

| Date | Mintage | F | VF | XF | Unc | BU |
|---|---|---|---|---|---|---|
| 1977 | — | 0.10 | 0.20 | 0.30 | 0.50 | — |
| 1980 | — | 0.10 | 0.20 | 0.30 | 0.50 | — |

**50 CENTAVOS** KM# 16 **Composition:** Aluminum

| Date | Mintage | F | VF | XF | Unc | BU |
|---|---|---|---|---|---|---|
| 1977 | — | 0.15 | 0.25 | 0.40 | 0.75 | — |
| 1930 | — | 0.15 | 0.25 | 0.40 | 0.75 | — |

**ESCUDO** KM# 17 **Composition:** Nickel-Bronze **Series:** F.A.O.

| Date | Mintage | F | VF | XF | Unc | BU |
|---|---|---|---|---|---|---|
| 1977 | 1,000,000 | 0.25 | 0.50 | 0.85 | 1.75 | — |
| 1980 | — | 0.25 | 0.50 | 0.85 | 1.75 | — |

**ESCUDO** KM# 23 **Composition:** Brass Plated Steel **Subject:** 10th Anniversary of Independence

| Date | Mintage | F | VF | XF | Unc | BU |
|---|---|---|---|---|---|---|
| 1985 | — | — | — | 0.85 | 1.75 | — |
| 1985 Proof | — | — | — | — | — | — |

**ESCUDO** **KM# 23a** **Weight:** 4.0000 g. **Composition:** 0.9250 Silver .1190 oz. ASW **Subject:** 10th Anniversary of Independence

| Date | Mintage | F | VF | XF | Unc | BU |
|---|---|---|---|---|---|---|
| 1985 Proof | — | Value: 20.00 | | | | |

**ESCUDO** **KM# 23b** **Weight:** 6.0000 g. **Composition:** 0.7500 Gold .1447 oz. AGW **Subject:** 10th Anniversary of Independence

| Date | Mintage | F | VF | XF | Unc | BU |
|---|---|---|---|---|---|---|
| 1985 Proof | 50 | Value: 250 | | | | |

**ESCUDO** **KM# 27** **Composition:** Brass Plated Steel **Reverse:** Tartaruga Sea Turtle

| Date | Mintage | F | VF | XF | Unc | BU |
|---|---|---|---|---|---|---|
| 1994 | — | — | — | — | 1.00 | — |

**2-1/2 ESCUDOS** **KM# 18** **Composition:** Nickel-Bronze **Series:** F.A.O.

| Date | Mintage | F | VF | XF | Unc | BU |
|---|---|---|---|---|---|---|
| 1977 | 1,200,000 | 0.25 | 0.50 | 0.85 | 1.75 | — |
| 1980 | — | 0.25 | 0.50 | 0.85 | 1.75 | — |
| 1982 | — | 0.25 | 0.50 | 0.85 | 1.75 | — |

**5 ESCUDOS** **KM# 28** **Composition:** Copper Plated Steel **Reverse:** Osprey.

| Date | Mintage | F | VF | XF | Unc | BU |
|---|---|---|---|---|---|---|
| 1994 | — | — | — | — | 1.50 | — |

**5 ESCUDOS** **KM# 31** **Composition:** Copper Plated Steel **Reverse:** Flowers - Contra Bruxas

| Date | Mintage | F | VF | XF | Unc | BU |
|---|---|---|---|---|---|---|
| 1994 | — | — | — | — | 1.00 | — |

**5 ESCUDOS** **KM# 36** **Composition:** Copper Plated Steel **Reverse:** Sailboat - Belmira

| Date | Mintage | F | VF | XF | Unc | BU |
|---|---|---|---|---|---|---|
| 1994 | — | — | — | — | 1.00 | — |

**10 ESCUDOS** **KM# 19** **Composition:** Copper-Nickel **Reverse:** Eduardo Mondlane

| Date | Mintage | F | VF | XF | Unc | BU |
|---|---|---|---|---|---|---|
| 1977 | — | 0.25 | 0.50 | 1.00 | 2.00 | — |
| 1980 | — | 0.25 | 0.50 | 1.00 | 2.00 | — |
| 1982 | — | 0.20 | 0.40 | 0.75 | 1.50 | — |

**10 ESCUDOS** **KM# 24** **Composition:** Copper-Nickel **Subject:** 10th Anniversary of Independence

| Date | Mintage | F | VF | XF | Unc | BU |
|---|---|---|---|---|---|---|
| 1985 Proof | — | — | — | — | — | — |
| 1985 | — | — | — | — | 2.00 | — |

**10 ESCUDOS** **KM# 24a** **Weight:** 9.0000 g. **Composition:** 0.9250 Silver .2677 oz. ASW **Subject:** 10th Anniversary of Independence

| Date | Mintage | F | VF | XF | Unc | BU |
|---|---|---|---|---|---|---|
| 1985 Proof | — | Value: 25.00 | | | | |

**10 ESCUDOS** **KM# 24b** **Weight:** 9.0000 g. **Composition:** 0.7500 Gold .2170 oz. AGW **Subject:** 10th Anniversary of Independence

| Date | Mintage | F | VF | XF | Unc | BU |
|---|---|---|---|---|---|---|
| 1985 Proof | 50 | Value: 400 | | | | |

**10 ESCUDOS** **KM# 29** **Composition:** Nickel Plated Steel **Reverse:** Brown-headed Kingfisher.

| Date | Mintage | F | VF | XF | Unc | BU |
|---|---|---|---|---|---|---|
| 1994 | — | — | — | — | 2.00 | — |

**10 ESCUDOS** **KM# 32** **Composition:** Nickel Plated Steel **Reverse:** Flowers - Lingua De Vaca

| Date | Mintage | F | VF | XF | Unc | BU |
|---|---|---|---|---|---|---|
| 1994 | — | — | — | — | 1.25 | — |

**10 ESCUDOS** **KM# 41** **Composition:** Nickel Plated Steel **Obverse:** National emblem **Reverse:** Sail ship **Note:** Carvalho

| Date | Mintage | F | VF | XF | Unc | BU |
|---|---|---|---|---|---|---|
| 1994 | — | — | — | — | 1.25 | — |

**20 ESCUDOS** **KM# 20** **Composition:** Copper-Nickel **Reverse:** Domingos Ramos

| Date | Mintage | F | VF | XF | Unc | BU |
|---|---|---|---|---|---|---|
| 1977 | — | 0.35 | 0.65 | 1.25 | 2.75 | — |
| 1980 | — | 0.35 | 0.65 | 1.25 | 2.75 | — |
| 1982 | — | 0.25 | 0.50 | 0.85 | 1.75 | — |

**20 ESCUDOS** **KM# 30** **Composition:** Nickel Plated Steel **Reverse:** Brown Booby.

| Date | Mintage | F | VF | XF | Unc | BU |
|---|---|---|---|---|---|---|
| 1994 | — | — | — | — | 3.00 | — |

**20 ESCUDOS** **KM# 33** **Composition:** Nickel Plated Steel **Reverse:** Flowers - Carqueja

| Date | Mintage | F | VF | XF | Unc | BU |
|---|---|---|---|---|---|---|
| 1994 | — | — | — | — | 2.00 | — |

**20 ESCUDOS** **KM# 42** **Composition:** Nickel Plated Steel **Obverse:** National emblem **Reverse:** Sail ship **Note:** Novas de Alegria

| Date | Mintage | F | VF | XF | Unc | BU |
|---|---|---|---|---|---|---|
| 1994 | — | — | — | — | 2.00 | — |

**50 ESCUDOS** **KM# 21** **Composition:** Copper-Nickel **Reverse:** Amilcar Lopes Cabral

| Date | Mintage | F | VF | XF | Unc | BU |
|---|---|---|---|---|---|---|
| 1977 | — | 1.00 | 1.50 | 2.50 | 4.50 | — |
| 1980 | — | 1.00 | 1.50 | 2.50 | 4.50 | — |

**50 ESCUDOS** **KM# 22** **Composition:** Copper-Nickel **Series:** F.A.O. **Subject:** World Fisheries Conference

| Date | Mintage | F | VF | XF | Unc | BU |
|---|---|---|---|---|---|---|
| 1984 | Est. 115,000 | — | — | — | 7.50 | — |

**50 ESCUDOS** **KM# 22a** **Weight:** 16.0000 g. **Composition:** 0.9250 Silver .4759 oz. ASW **Series:** F.A.O. **Subject:** World Fisheries Conference

| Date | Mintage | F | VF | XF | Unc | BU |
|---|---|---|---|---|---|---|
| 1984 Proof | Est. 20,000 | Value: 47.50 | | | | |

**50 ESCUDOS** **KM# 22b** **Weight:** 27.0000 g. **Composition:** 0.9170 Gold .7958 oz. AGW **Series:** .F.A.O. **Subject:** World Fisheries Conference

| Date | Mintage | F | VF | XF | Unc | BU |
|---|---|---|---|---|---|---|
| 1984 Proof | Est. 100,000 | Value: 1,500 | | | | |

**50 ESCUDOS** KM# 37 **Weight:** 27.0000 g. **Composition:** 0.9170 Gold .7958 oz. AGW **Reverse:** Cape Verde Sparrow.

| Date | Mintage | F | VF | XF | Unc | BU |
|---|---|---|---|---|---|---|
| 1994 | — | — | — | — | 7.50 | — |

**50 ESCUDOS** KM# 44 **Composition:** Nickel Plated Steel 8 oz. **Obverse:** National emblem **Reverse:** Macelina flowers

| Date | Mintage | F | VF | XF | Unc | BU |
|---|---|---|---|---|---|---|
| 1994 | — | — | — | — | 5.00 | — |

**50 ESCUDOS** KM# 43 **Composition:** Nickel Plated Steel 8 oz. **Obverse:** National emblem **Reverse:** Sail ship **Note:** Senhor das Areias

| Date | Mintage | F | VF | XF | Unc | BU |
|---|---|---|---|---|---|---|
| 1994 | — | — | — | — | 5.00 | — |

**100 ESCUDOS** KM# 25 **Composition:** Copper-Nickel 8 oz. **Subject:** Papal Visit

| Date | Mintage | F | VF | XF | Unc | BU |
|---|---|---|---|---|---|---|
| 1990 | — | — | — | — | 8.00 | — |

**100 ESCUDOS** KM# 25a **Weight:** 33.4000 g. **Composition:** 0.9000 Gold .9666 oz. AGW **Subject:** Papal Visit

| Date | Mintage | F | VF | XF | Unc | BU |
|---|---|---|---|---|---|---|
| 1990 Proof | — | — | — | — | — | — |

**100 ESCUDOS** KM# 38 **Ring Composition:** Bronze **Center Composition:** Copper-Nickel **Reverse:** Saiao Flowers

| Date | Mintage | F | VF | XF | Unc | BU |
|---|---|---|---|---|---|---|
| 1994 | — | — | — | — | 8.00 | — |

**100 ESCUDOS** KM# 38a **Ring Composition:** Brass **Center Composition:** Copper-Nickel

| Date | Mintage | F | VF | XF | Unc | BU |
|---|---|---|---|---|---|---|
| 1994 | — | — | — | — | 8.00 | — |

**100 ESCUDOS** KM# 39 **Ring Composition:** Bronze **Center Composition:** Copper-Nickel **Reverse:** Raza Lark.

| Date | Mintage | F | VF | XF | Unc | BU |
|---|---|---|---|---|---|---|
| 1994 | — | — | — | — | 12.50 | — |

**100 ESCUDOS** KM# 39a **Ring Composition:** Brass **Center Composition:** Copper-Nickel **Reverse:** Calhandra do Ilheu Raso bird

| Date | Mintage | F | VF | XF | Unc | BU |
|---|---|---|---|---|---|---|
| 1994 | — | — | — | — | 12.50 | — |

**100 ESCUDOS** KM# 40 **Ring Composition:** Bronze **Center Composition:** Copper-Nickel **Reverse:** Sailship Medalan

| Date | Mintage | F | VF | XF | Unc | BU |
|---|---|---|---|---|---|---|
| 1994 | — | — | — | — | 9.00 | — |

**100 ESCUDOS** KM# 40a **Ring Composition:** Brass **Center Composition:** Copper-Nickel

| Date | Mintage | F | VF | XF | Unc | BU |
|---|---|---|---|---|---|---|
| 1994 | — | — | — | — | 9.00 | — |

**200 ESCUDOS** KM# 34 **Composition:** Copper-Nickel **Series:** F.A.O. **Reverse:** Water

| Date | Mintage | F | VF | XF | Unc | BU |
|---|---|---|---|---|---|---|
| 1995 | — | — | — | — | 8.00 | — |

**200 ESCUDOS** KM# 35 **Composition:** Copper-Nickel **Subject:** 20th Year of Independence

| Date | Mintage | F | VF | XF | Unc | BU |
|---|---|---|---|---|---|---|
| ND (1995) | — | — | — | — | 8.00 | — |

**250 ESCUDOS** KM# 13 **Weight:** 16.4000 g. **Composition:** 0.9000 Silver .4745 oz. ASW **Subject:** 1st Anniversary of Independence

| Date | Mintage | F | VF | XF | Unc | BU |
|---|---|---|---|---|---|---|
| 1976 | 13,000 | — | — | — | 16.50 | — |
| 1976 Proof | 3,525 | Value: 32.50 | | | | |

**1000 ESCUDOS** KM# 26 **Weight:** 28.1100 g. **Composition:** 0.9250 Silver .8361 oz. ASW **Subject:** Tordesilhas Treaty

| Date | Mintage | F | VF | XF | Unc | BU |
|---|---|---|---|---|---|---|
| ND (1994) | — | — | — | — | 25.00 | — |
| ND (1994) Proof | Est. 10,000 | Value: 45.00 | | | | |

**2500 ESCUDOS** KM# 14 **Weight:** 8.0000 g. **Composition:** 0.9000 Gold .2315 oz. AGW **Subject:** 1st Anniversary of Independence

| Date | Mintage | F | VF | XF | Unc | BU |
|---|---|---|---|---|---|---|
| 1976 Proof | 3,409 | Value: 220 | | | | |

## PIEFORTS

| KM# | Date | Mintage | Identification | Mkt Val |
|---|---|---|---|---|
| P1 | 1984 | 520 | 50 Escudos. 0.9250 Silver. KM22a | 75.00 |

## PROVAS

| KM# | Date | Mintage | Identification | Mkt Val |
|---|---|---|---|---|
| Pr1 | 1930 | — | 5 Centavos. Stamped "PROVA" in field. KM1 | 35.00 |
| Pr2 | 1930 | — | 10 Centavos. Stamped "PROVA" in field. KM2 | 35.00 |
| Pr3 | 1930 | — | 20 Centavos. Stamped "PROVA" in field. KM3 | 35.00 |
| Pr4 | 1930 | — | 50 Centavos. Stamped "PROVA" in field. KM4 | 75.00 |
| Pr5 | 1930 | — | Escudo. Stamped "PROVA" in field. KM5 | 100 |
| Pr6 | 1949 | — | 50 Centavos. Stamped "PROVA" in field. KM6 | 30.00 |
| Pr7 | 1949 | — | Escudo. Stamped "PROVA" in field. KM7 | 35.00 |
| Pr8 | 1953 | — | Escudo. Stamped "PROVA" in field. KM8 | 35.00 |
| Pr9 | 1953 | — | 2-1/2 Escudos. Stamped "PROVA" in field. KM9 | 30.00 |
| Pr10 | 1953 | — | 10 Escudos. Stamped "PROVA" in field. KM10 | 35.00 |
| Pr11 | 1954 | — | Escudo. Stamped "PROVA" in field. | 20.00 |
| Pr12 | 1954 | — | 2-1/2 Escudos. Stamped "PROVA" in field. | 30.00 |
| Pr13 | 1955 | — | Escudo. Stamped "PROVA" in field. | 20.00 |
| Pr14 | 1955 | — | 2-1/2 Escudos. Stamped "PROVA" in field. | 30.00 |
| Pr15 | 1956 | — | Escudo. Stamped "PROVA" in field. | 20.00 |
| Pr16 | 1956 | — | 2-1/2 Escudos. Stamped "PROVA" in field. | 30.00 |
| Pr17 | 1957 | — | Escudo. Stamped "PROVA" in field. | 20.00 |
| Pr18 | 1957 | — | 2-1/2 Escudos. Stamped "PROVA" in field. | 30.00 |
| Pr19 | 1958 | — | Escudo. Stamped "PROVA" in field. | 20.00 |
| Pr20 | 1958 | — | 2-1/2 Escudos. Stamped "PROVA" in field. | 30.00 |
| Pr21 | 1959 | — | Escudo. Stamped "PROVA" in field. | 20.00 |
| Pr22 | 1959 | — | 2-1/2 Escudos. Stamped "PROVA" in field. | 30.00 |
| Pr23 | 1960 | — | Escudo. Stamped "PROVA" in field. | 20.00 |
| Pr24 | 1960 | — | 2-1/2 Escudos. Stamped "PROVA" in field. | 30.00 |
| Pr25 | 1961 | — | Escudo. Stamped "PROVA" in field. | 20.00 |
| Pr26 | 1961 | — | 2-1/2 Escudos. Stamped "PROVA" in field. | 30.00 |
| Pr27 | 1962 | — | Escudo. Stamped "PROVA" in field. | 20.00 |
| Pr28 | 1962 | — | 2-1/2 Escudos. Stamped "PROVA" in field. | 30.00 |
| Pr29 | 1963 | — | Escudo. Stamped "PROVA" in field. | 20.00 |
| Pr30 | 1963 | — | 2-1/2 Escudos. Stamped "PROVA" in field. | 30.00 |
| Pr31 | 1964 | — | Escudo. Stamped "PROVA" in field. | 20.00 |
| Pr32 | 1964 | — | 2-1/2 Escudos. Stamped "PROVA" in field. | 30.00 |
| Pr33 | 1965 | — | Escudo. Stamped "PROVA" in field. | 20.00 |
| Pr34 | 1965 | — | 2-1/2 Escudos. Stamped "PROVA" in field. | 30.00 |
| Pr35 | 1966 | — | Escudo. Stamped "PROVA" in field. | 20.00 |
| Pr36 | 1966 | — | 2-1/2 Escudos. Stamped "PROVA" in field. | 30.00 |
| Pr37 | 1967 | — | Escudo. Stamped "PROVA" in field. | 15.00 |
| Pr38 | 1967 | — | 2-1/2 Escudos. Stamped "PROVA" in field. KM9 | 20.00 |
| Pr39 | 1968 | — | 50 Centavos. Stamped "PROVA" in field. KM11 | 15.00 |
| Pr40 | 1968 | — | Escudo. Stamped "PROVA" in field. KM8 | 20.00 |
| Pr41 | 1968 | — | 5 Escudos. Stamped "PROVA" in field. KM12 | 25.00 |

## PROOF SETS

| KM# | Date | Mintage | Identification | Issue Price | Mkt Val |
|---|---|---|---|---|---|
| PS1 | (4) | — | KM13-14 1976, KM17-18 | — | 300 |
| PS2 | 1985 (2) | — | KM23a, 24a | — | 50.00 |

# CAYMAN ISLANDS

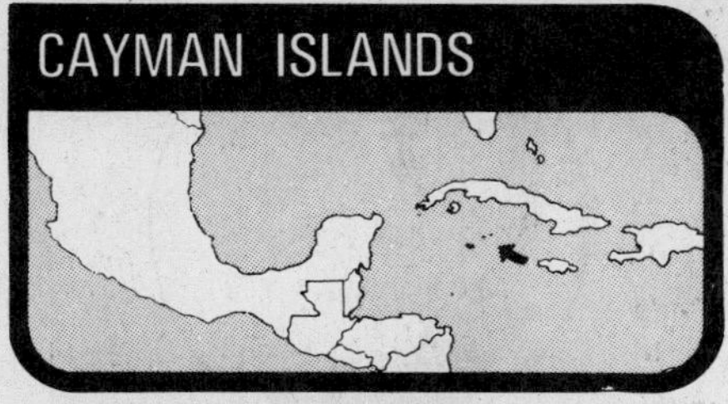

The Cayman Islands is a dependent territory of the United Kingdom with the British monarch as head of state. It is situated about 180 miles (290 km.) northwest of Jamaica, consists of three islands: Grand Cayman, Little Cayman, and Cayman Brac. The islands have an area of 102 sq. mi. (259 sq. km.) and a population of 33,200. Capital: George Town. Seafaring, commerce, banking, and tourism are the principal industries. Rope, turtle shells, and sharkskins are exported.

The islands were discovered by Columbus in 1503, and named by him Tortugas (Spanish for turtles') because of the great number of turtles in the nearby waters. Ceded to Britain in 1670, they were colonized from Jamaica by the British and remained dependencies of Jamaica until 1959, when they became a unit territory within the Federation of the West Indies. They became a separate colony when the Federation was dissolved in 1962. Since 1972 a form of self-government has existed, with the Governor responsible for defense and certain other affairs.

While the islands used Jamaican currency for much of their history, the Caymans issued its first national coinage in 1972. The $25 gold and silver commemorative coins issued in 1972 to celebrate the silver wedding anniversary of Queen Elizabeth II and Prince Philip are the first coins in 300 years of Commonwealth coinage to portray a member of the British royal family other than the reigning monarch.

**RULERS**
British

**MINT MARKS**
CHI - Valcambi
FM - Franklin Mint, U.S.A.*

**MONETARY SYSTEM**
100 Cents = 1 Dollar

## BRITISH COLONY

### DECIMAL COINAGE

**CENT** **KM# 1** **Composition:** Bronze **Reverse:** Great Caiman Thrush

| Date | Mintage | F | VF | XF | Unc | BU |
|---|---|---|---|---|---|---|
| 1972 | 2,155,000 | — | — | 0.10 | 0.25 | — |
| 1972 Proof | 11,000 | Value: 0.50 | | | | |
| 1973 Proof | 9,988 | Value: 0.50 | | | | |
| 1974 Proof | 30,000 | Value: 0.50 | | | | |
| 1975 Proof | 7,175 | Value: 0.50 | | | | |
| 1976 Proof | 3,044 | Value: 0.50 | | | | |
| 1977 | 1,800,000 | — | — | 0.10 | 0.25 | — |
| 1977 Proof | 1,970 | Value: 1.00 | | | | |
| 1979FM Proof | 4,247 | Value: 0.50 | | | | |
| 1980FM | — | — | — | 0.10 | 0.25 | — |
| 1980FM Proof | 1,215 | Value: 1.25 | | | | |
| 1981FM Proof | 865 | Value: 1.50 | | | | |
| 1982FM Proof | 589 | Value: 1.50 | | | | |
| 1982 | — | — | — | 0.10 | 0.25 | — |
| 1983FM Proof | — | Value: 1.50 | | | | |
| 1984FM Proof | — | Value: 1.50 | | | | |
| 1986 | 1,000 | Value: 1.50 | | | | |

**CENT** **KM# 26** **Composition:** Bronze **Subject:** 25th Anniversary of Coronation

| Date | Mintage | F | VF | XF | Unc | BU |
|---|---|---|---|---|---|---|
| 1978 Proof | 1,303 | Value: 2.00 | | | | |

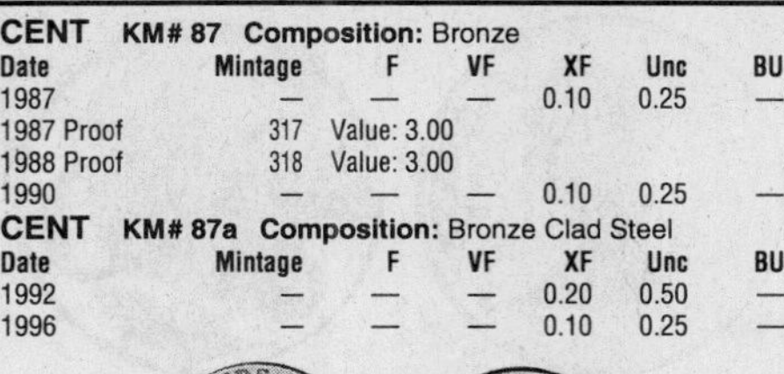

**CENT** **KM# 87** **Composition:** Bronze

| Date | Mintage | F | VF | XF | Unc | BU |
|---|---|---|---|---|---|---|
| 1987 | — | — | — | 0.10 | 0.25 | — |
| 1987 Proof | 317 | Value: 3.00 | | | | |
| 1988 Proof | 318 | Value: 3.00 | | | | |
| 1990 | — | — | — | 0.10 | 0.25 | — |

**CENT** **KM# 87a** **Composition:** Bronze Clad Steel

| Date | Mintage | F | VF | XF | Unc | BU |
|---|---|---|---|---|---|---|
| 1992 | — | — | — | 0.20 | 0.50 | — |
| 1996 | — | — | — | 0.10 | 0.25 | — |

**CENT** **KM# 131** **Weight:** 2.5300 g. **Composition:** Bronze Plated Steel **Obverse:** Queen's head right. **Reverse:** Great Caiman thrush. **Edge:** Reeded. **Size:** 17 mm.

| Date | Mintage | F | VF | XF | Unc | BU |
|---|---|---|---|---|---|---|
| 1999 | — | — | — | — | 0.50 | — |

**5 CENTS** **KM# 2** **Composition:** Copper-Nickel **Reverse:** Prawn **Note:** 1973 Uncirculates were not released to circulation.

| Date | Mintage | F | VF | XF | Unc | BU |
|---|---|---|---|---|---|---|
| 1972 | 300,000 | — | — | 0.10 | 0.25 | — |
| 1972 Proof | 12,000 | Value: 0.50 | | | | |
| 1973 | 200,000 | — | — | — | 0.50 | — |
| **Note:** 1973 Business strikes were not released to circulation | | | | | | |
| 1973 Proof | 9,988 | Value: 0.50 | | | | |
| 1974 Proof | 30,000 | Value: 0.50 | | | | |
| 1975 Proof | 7,175 | Value: 0.50 | | | | |
| 1976 Proof | 3,044 | Value: 0.50 | | | | |
| 1977 | 600,000 | — | — | 0.10 | 0.20 | — |
| 1977 Proof | 1,980 | Value: 0.50 | | | | |
| 1979 Proof | 4,247 | Value: 0.50 | | | | |
| 1980 Proof | — | Value: 2.00 | | | | |
| 1981 Proof | — | Value: 2.50 | | | | |
| 1982 | — | — | — | 0.10 | 0.20 | — |
| 1982 Proof | — | Value: 2.50 | | | | |
| 1983 Proof | — | Value: 2.50 | | | | |
| 1984 Proof | — | Value: 2.50 | | | | |
| 1986 | 1,000 | Value: 2.50 | | | | |

**5 CENTS** **KM# 27** **Composition:** Copper-Nickel **Subject:** 25th Anniversary of Coronation **Reverse:** Prawn

| Date | Mintage | F | VF | XF | Unc | BU |
|---|---|---|---|---|---|---|
| 1978 Proof | 1,303 | Value: 3.00 | | | | |

**5 CENTS** **KM# 88** **Composition:** Copper-Nickel

| Date | Mintage | F | VF | XF | Unc | BU |
|---|---|---|---|---|---|---|
| 1987 | — | — | — | 0.10 | 0.25 | — |
| 1987 Proof | 317 | Value: 5.00 | | | | |
| 1988 Proof | 318 | Value: 5.00 | | | | |
| 1990 | — | — | — | 0.10 | 0.25 | — |

**5 CENTS** **KM# 88a** **Composition:** Nickel Clad Steel

| Date | Mintage | F | VF | XF | Unc | BU |
|---|---|---|---|---|---|---|
| 1992 | — | — | — | 0.20 | 0.50 | — |
| 1996 | — | — | — | 0.10 | 0.25 | — |

**5 CENTS** **KM# 132** **Weight:** 2.0000 g. **Composition:** Nickel Clad Steel **Obverse:** Queen's head right. **Reverse:** Prawn. **Edge:** Plain. **Size:** 18 mm.

| Date | Mintage | F | VF | XF | Unc | BU |
|---|---|---|---|---|---|---|
| 1999 | — | — | — | — | 0.50 | — |

**10 CENTS** **KM# 3** **Composition:** Copper-Nickel **Reverse:** Green Turtle

| Date | Mintage | F | VF | XF | Unc | BU |
|---|---|---|---|---|---|---|
| 1972 | 550,000 | — | 0.15 | 0.20 | 0.50 | — |
| 1972 Proof | 11,000 | Value: 0.75 | | | | |
| 1973 | 200,000 | — | — | — | 1.00 | — |
| **Note:** 1973 Business strikes were not released to circulation | | | | | | |
| 1973 Proof | 9,988 | Value: 0.75 | | | | |
| 1974 Proof | 30,000 | Value: 0.75 | | | | |
| 1975 Proof | 7,175 | Value: 0.75 | | | | |
| 1976 Proof | 3,044 | Value: 0.75 | | | | |
| 1977 | 960,000 | — | 0.15 | 0.20 | 0.50 | — |
| 1977 Proof | 1,980 | Value: 0.75 | | | | |
| 1979FM Proof | 4,247 | Value: 0.75 | | | | |
| 1980FM Proof | 1,215 | Value: 3.00 | | | | |
| 1981FM Proof | 865 | Value: 3.00 | | | | |
| 1982 | — | — | 0.15 | 0.20 | 0.50 | — |
| 1982FM Proof | 589 | Value: 3.00 | | | | |
| 1983FM Proof | — | Value: 3.00 | | | | |
| 1984FM Proof | — | Value: 3.00 | | | | |
| 1986 | 1,000 | Value: 3.00 | | | | |

**10 CENTS** **KM# 28** **Composition:** Copper-Nickel **Subject:** 25th Anniversary of Coronation

| Date | Mintage | F | VF | XF | Unc | BU |
|---|---|---|---|---|---|---|
| 1978 Proof | 1,304 | Value: 3.50 | | | | |

**10 CENTS** **KM# 89** **Composition:** Copper-Nickel

| Date | Mintage | F | VF | XF | Unc | BU |
|---|---|---|---|---|---|---|
| 1987 | — | — | 0.15 | 0.20 | 0.50 | — |
| 1987 Proof | 317 | Value: 6.00 | | | | |
| 1988 Proof | 318 | Value: 6.00 | | | | |
| 1990 | — | — | 0.15 | 0.20 | 0.50 | — |

**10 CENTS** **KM# 89a** **Composition:** Nickel Clad Steel

| Date | Mintage | F | VF | XF | Unc | BU |
|---|---|---|---|---|---|---|
| 1992 | — | — | 0.25 | 0.40 | 1.00 | — |
| 1996 | — | — | 0.20 | 0.30 | 0.75 | — |

**10 CENTS** **KM# 133** **Weight:** 3.4300 g. **Composition:** Nickel Clad Steel **Obverse:** Queen's head right. **Reverse:** Green turtle. **Edge:** Reeded. **Size:** 21 mm.

| Date | Mintage | F | VF | XF | Unc | BU |
|---|---|---|---|---|---|---|
| 1999 | — | — | — | — | 1.00 | — |

**25 CENTS** **KM# 4** **Composition:** Copper-Nickel

| Date | Mintage | F | VF | XF | Unc | BU |
|---|---|---|---|---|---|---|
| 1972 | 350,000 | — | 0.30 | 0.50 | 1.00 | — |
| 1972 Proof | 11,000 | Value: 1.00 | | | | |
| 1973 | 100,000 | — | — | — | 2.00 | — |
| **Note:** 1973 Business strikes were not released to circulation | | | | | | |
| 1973 Proof | 9,988 | Value: 1.00 | | | | |

| Date | Mintage | F | VF | XF | Unc | BU |
|---|---|---|---|---|---|---|
| 1974 Proof | 30,000 | Value: 1.00 | | | | |
| 1975 Proof | 7,175 | Value: 1.00 | | | | |
| 1976 Proof | 3,044 | Value: 1.00 | | | | |
| 1977 | 520,000 | — | 0.30 | 0.50 | 1.00 | — |
| 1977 Proof | 1,980 | Value: 1.00 | | | | |
| 1979FM Proof | 4,247 | Value: 1.00 | | | | |
| 1980FM Proof | 1,215 | Value: 3.50 | | | | |
| 1981FM Proof | 865 | Value: 4.00 | | | | |
| 1982 | — | — | 0.30 | 0.50 | 1.00 | — |
| 1982FM Proof | 589 | Value: 4.00 | | | | |
| 1983FM Proof | — | Value: 4.00 | | | | |
| 1984FM Proof | — | Value: 4.00 | | | | |
| 1986 Proof | 1,000 | Value: 4.00 | | | | |

**25 CENTS KM# 29 Composition:** Copper-Nickel **Subject:** 25th Anniversary of Coronation **Reverse:** Similar to KM#4

| Date | Mintage | F | VF | XF | Unc | BU |
|---|---|---|---|---|---|---|
| 1978 Proof | 1,303 | Value: 4.00 | | | | |

**25 CENTS KM# 90 Composition:** Copper-Nickel

| Date | Mintage | F | VF | XF | Unc | BU |
|---|---|---|---|---|---|---|
| 1987 | — | — | 0.30 | 0.50 | 1.00 | — |
| 1987 Proof | 317 | Value: 8.00 | | | | |
| 1988 Proof | 318 | Value: 8.00 | | | | |
| 1990 | — | — | 0.30 | 0.50 | 1.00 | — |

**25 CENTS KM# 90a Composition:** Nickel Clad Steel

| Date | Mintage | F | VF | XF | Unc | BU |
|---|---|---|---|---|---|---|
| 1992 | — | — | 0.45 | 0.75 | 1.50 | — |
| 1996 | — | — | 0.35 | 0.60 | 1.25 | — |

**25 CENTS KM# 134 Weight:** 5.0400 g. **Composition:** Nickel-Clad Steel **Obverse:** Queen's head right. **Reverse:** Sailboat. **Edge:** Reeded. **Size:** 24.2 mm.

| Date | Mintage | F | VF | XF | Unc | BU |
|---|---|---|---|---|---|---|
| 1999 | — | — | — | — | 1.50 | — |

**50 CENTS KM# 5 Weight:** 10.3000 g. **Composition:** 0.9250 Silver .3063 oz. ASW **Reverse:** Caribbean Emperor Fish

| Date | Mintage | F | VF | XF | Unc | BU |
|---|---|---|---|---|---|---|
| 1972 | 500 | Value: 12.50 | | | | |
| 1972 Proof | 11,000 | Value: 4.00 | | | | |
| 1973 Proof | 9,988 | Value: 4.00 | | | | |
| 1974 Proof | 30,000 | Value: 4.00 | | | | |
| 1975 Proof | 7,175 | Value: 4.00 | | | | |
| 1976 Proof | 3,044 | Value: 4.50 | | | | |
| 1977 Proof | 1,980 | Value: 4.50 | | | | |
| 1979FM Proof | 4,247 | Value: 4.50 | | | | |
| 1980FM Proof | 1,215 | Value: 5.00 | | | | |
| 1981FM Proof | 865 | Value: 6.50 | | | | |
| 1982FM Proof | 589 | Value: 6.50 | | | | |

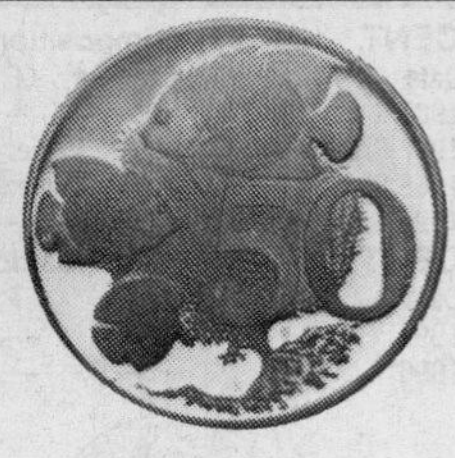

**50 CENTS KM# 30 Weight:** 10.3000 g. **Composition:** 0.9250 Silver **Subject:** 25th Anniversary of Coronation

| Date | Mintage | F | VF | XF | Unc | BU |
|---|---|---|---|---|---|---|
| 1978 Proof | 2,169 | Value: 8.00 | | | | |

**50 CENTS KM# 73 Weight:** 10.3000 g. **Composition:** 9.2500 Silver **Obverse:** Similar to KM#5 **Reverse:** Morning Glory

| Date | Mintage | F | VF | XF | Unc | BU |
|---|---|---|---|---|---|---|
| 1983FM Proof | — | Value: 15.00 | | | | |
| 1984FM Proof | 411 | Value: 15.00 | | | | |
| 1986 Proof | 1,000 | Value: 15.00 | | | | |

**50 CENTS KM# 91 Weight:** 10.3000 g. **Composition:** 0.9250 Silver .3063 oz. ASW **Obverse:** Similar to 5 Dollars, KM#81

| Date | Mintage | F | VF | XF | Unc | BU |
|---|---|---|---|---|---|---|
| 1987 Proof | 317 | Value: 20.00 | | | | |
| 1988 Proof | 318 | Value: 20.00 | | | | |

**DOLLAR KM# 6 Weight:** 18.0000 g. **Composition:** 0.9250 Silver .5353 oz. ASW **Reverse:** Flamboyant

| Date | Mintage | F | VF | XF | Unc | BU |
|---|---|---|---|---|---|---|
| 1972 | 500 | — | — | — | 15.00 | — |
| 1972 Proof | 11,000 | Value: 4.50 | | | | |
| 1973 Proof | 9,988 | Value: 4.50 | | | | |
| 1974 Proof | 30,000 | Value: 4.50 | | | | |
| 1975 Proof | 7,175 | Value: 5.00 | | | | |
| 1976 Proof | 3,044 | Value: 7.00 | | | | |
| 1977 Proof | 1,980 | Value: 7.00 | | | | |
| 1979FM Proof | 4,247 | Value: 7.00 | | | | |
| 1980FM Proof | 1,215 | Value: 9.00 | | | | |
| 1981FM Proof | 865 | Value: 10.00 | | | | |
| 1982FM Proof | 589 | Value: 10.00 | | | | |

**DOLLAR KM# 31 Weight:** 18.0000 g. **Composition:** 0.9250 Silver .5353 oz. ASW **Subject:** 25th Anniversary of Coronation

| Date | Mintage | F | VF | XF | Unc | BU |
|---|---|---|---|---|---|---|
| 1978 Proof | 2,168 | Value: 12.00 | | | | |

**DOLLAR KM# 74 Weight:** 18.0000 g. **Composition:** 0.9250 Silver .5353 oz. ASW **Obverse:** Similar to 50 Cents, KM#5 **Reverse:** Pineapple

| Date | Mintage | F | VF | XF | Unc | BU |
|---|---|---|---|---|---|---|
| 1983FM Proof | 1,686 | Value: 16.00 | | | | |
| 1984FM Proof | 456 | Value: 16.00 | | | | |
| 1986 Proof | 1,000 | Value: 16.00 | | | | |

**DOLLAR KM# 92 Weight:** 18.0000 g. **Composition:** 0.9250 Silver .5353 oz. ASW **Obverse:** Similar to 5 Dollars, KM#81

| Date | Mintage | F | VF | XF | Unc | BU |
|---|---|---|---|---|---|---|
| 1987 Proof | 317 | Value: 22.00 | | | | |
| 1988 Proof | 318 | Value: 22.00 | | | | |

**DOLLAR KM# 103 Weight:** 18.1400 g. **Composition:** 0.9250 Silver .5395 oz. ASW **Reverse:** Green Turtle

| Date | Mintage | F | VF | XF | Unc | BU |
|---|---|---|---|---|---|---|
| 1990 Proof | Est. 5,000 | Value: 60.00 | | | | |

**DOLLAR KM# 111 Weight:** 18.1400 g. **Composition:** 0.9250 Silver .5395 oz. ASW **Reverse:** Rock Iquana

| Date | Mintage | F | VF | XF | Unc | BU |
|---|---|---|---|---|---|---|
| 1992 Proof | Est. 5,000 | Value: 55.00 | | | | |

**DOLLAR KM# 116 Weight:** 18.1400 g. **Composition:** 0.9250 Silver .5395 oz. ASW **Reverse:** Cayman Ironwood Tree

| Date | Mintage | F | VF | XF | Unc | BU |
|---|---|---|---|---|---|---|
| 1994 Proof | Est. 10,000 | Value: 37.50 | | | | |

**DOLLAR** **KM# 118** **Weight:** 28.2800 g. **Composition:** 0.9250 Silver .8411 oz. ASW **Subject:** Royal Visit **Reverse:** Royal Couple above yacht "Britannia"

| Date | Mintage | F | VF | XF | Unc | BU |
|---|---|---|---|---|---|---|
| 1994 Proof | Est. 10,000 | Value: 50.00 | | | | |

**DOLLAR** **KM# 120** **Weight:** 28.2800 g. **Composition:** 0.9250 Silver .8411 oz. ASW **Reverse:** Queen Mother's arms

| Date | Mintage | F | VF | XF | Unc | BU |
|---|---|---|---|---|---|---|
| 1994 Proof | Est. 20,000 | Value: 45.00 | | | | |

**DOLLAR** **KM# 121** **Weight:** 28.2800 g. **Composition:** 0.9250 Silver .8411 oz. ASW **Reverse:** Sir Francis Drake

| Date | Mintage | F | VF | XF | Unc | BU |
|---|---|---|---|---|---|---|
| 1994 Proof | Est. 10,000 | Value: 32.50 | | | | |

**DOLLAR** **KM# 125** **Weight:** 28.2800 g. **Composition:** 0.9250 Silver .8411 oz. ASW **Reverse:** Rock Iquana

| Date | Mintage | F | VF | XF | Unc | BU |
|---|---|---|---|---|---|---|
| 1995 Proof | Est. 10,000 | Value: 55.00 | | | | |

**DOLLAR** **KM# 124** **Weight:** 28.2800 g. **Composition:** 0.9250 Silver .8411 oz. ASW **Subject:** Olympics **Reverse:** 2 Sail Boats

| Date | Mintage | F | VF | XF | Unc | BU |
|---|---|---|---|---|---|---|
| 1996 Proof | Est. 30,000 | Value: 30.00 | | | | |

**DOLLAR** **KM# 122** **Weight:** 18.1400 g. **Composition:** 0.9250 Silver .5394 oz. ASW **Reverse:** Amazona Leucocephala Caymanesis - Parrot

| Date | Mintage | F | VF | XF | Unc | BU |
|---|---|---|---|---|---|---|
| 1996 Proof | Est. 10,000 | Value: 50.00 | | | | |

**2 DOLLARS** **KM# 7** **Weight:** 29.4500 g. **Composition:** 0.9250 Silver .8758 oz. ASW **Obverse:** Similar to 50 cents, KM#5 **Reverse:** Great Blue Heron

| Date | Mintage | F | VF | XF | Unc | BU |
|---|---|---|---|---|---|---|
| 1972 | 500 | — | — | — | 20.00 | — |
| 1972 Proof | 11,000 | Value: 7.50 | | | | |
| 1973 Proof | 9,988 | Value: 7.50 | | | | |
| 1974 Proof | 30,000 | Value: 7.50 | | | | |
| 1975 Proof | 5,390 | Value: 8.50 | | | | |
| 1976 Proof | 3,044 | Value: 12.50 | | | | |
| 1977 Proof | 1,980 | Value: 12.50 | | | | |
| 1979FM Proof | 4,247 | Value: 12.50 | | | | |
| 1980FM Proof | 1,215 | Value: 18.00 | | | | |
| 1981FM Proof | 865 | Value: 20.00 | | | | |
| 1982FM Proof | 589 | Value: 20.00 | | | | |
| 1986 Proof | 1,000 | Value: 18.00 | | | | |

**2 DOLLARS** **KM# 32** **Weight:** 29.4500 g. **Composition:** 0.9250 Silver .8758 oz. ASW **Subject:** 25th Anniversary of Coronation

| Date | Mintage | F | VF | XF | Unc | BU |
|---|---|---|---|---|---|---|
| 1978 Proof | 2,169 | Value: 22.50 | | | | |

**2 DOLLARS** **KM# 75** **Weight:** 29.4500 g. **Composition:** 0.9250 Silver .8758 oz. ASW **Obv. Legend:** Parrot

| Date | Mintage | F | VF | XF | Unc | BU |
|---|---|---|---|---|---|---|
| 1983FM Proof | 409 | Value: 45.00 | | | | |
| 1984FM Proof | 200 | Value: 55.00 | | | | |

**2 DOLLARS** **KM# 93** **Weight:** 29.4500 g. **Composition:** 0.9250 Silver .8758 oz. ASW **Obverse:** Similar to 5 Dollars, KM#81 **Reverse:** Great Blue Heron

| Date | Mintage | F | VF | XF | Unc | BU |
|---|---|---|---|---|---|---|
| 1987 Proof | 317 | Value: 45.00 | | | | |
| 1988 Proof | 318 | Value: 45.00 | | | | |

**2 DOLLARS** **KM# 114** **Weight:** 28.2800 g. **Composition:** 0.9250 Silver .8411 oz. ASW **Reverse:** Wreck of the "Ten Sails"

| Date | Mintage | F | VF | XF | Unc | BU |
|---|---|---|---|---|---|---|
| 1994 Proof | 15,000 | Value: 30.00 | | | | |

**2 DOLLARS** **KM# 127** **Weight:** 28.2800 g. **Composition:** 0.9250 Silver .8411 oz. ASW **Subject:** 25th Anniversary - Currency Board **Obverse:** Queen's portrait **Reverse:** Coins and arms in inner circle

| Date | Mintage | F | VF | XF | Unc | BU |
|---|---|---|---|---|---|---|
| ND Proof | Est. 2,000 | Value: 55.00 | | | | |

**2 DOLLARS** **KM# 128** **Weight:** 28.2800 g. **Composition:** 0.9250 Silver .8411 oz. ASW **Subject:** Queen's Golden Wedding Anniversary **Obverse:** Queen's portrait **Reverse:** Royal couple in carriage above gold plated sheild

| Date | Mintage | F | VF | XF | Unc | BU |
|---|---|---|---|---|---|---|
| 1997 Proof | Est. 30,000 | Value: 57.00 | | | | |

**2 DOLLARS** **KM# 129** **Weight:** 28.2800 g. **Composition:** 0.9250 Silver .8411 oz. ASW **Obverse:** Queen's portrait **Reverse:** Schooners "Arbutus I" and "Goldfield" under sail

| Date | Mintage | F | VF | XF | Unc | BU |
|---|---|---|---|---|---|---|
| 1997 Proof | Est. 5,000 | Value: 60.00 | | | | |

**2 DOLLARS** **KM# 130** **Weight:** 15.5520 g. **Composition:** 0.9990 Silver .4995 oz. ASW **Subject:** Millennium **Obverse:** Queen's portrait **Reverse:** Ornate clock above denomination **Edge:** Scalloped

| Date | Mintage | F | VF | XF | Unc | BU |
|---|---|---|---|---|---|---|
| 2000 Proof | 30 | Value: 47.50 | | | | |

**5 DOLLARS** **KM# 8** **Weight:** 35.5000 g. **Composition:** 0.9250 Silver 1.0557 oz. ASW

| Date | Mintage | F | VF | XF | Unc | BU |
|---|---|---|---|---|---|---|
| 1972 | 500 | — | — | — | 35.00 | — |
| 1972 Proof | 11,000 | Value: 7.50 | | | | |

| Date | Mintage | F | VF | XF | Unc | BU |
|---|---|---|---|---|---|---|
| 1973 Proof | 17,000 | Value: 7.50 | | | | |
| 1974 Proof | 26,000 | Value: 7.50 | | | | |
| 1975 Proof | 7,753 | Value: 9.00 | | | | |
| 1976 Proof | 5,177 | Value: 9.00 | | | | |
| 1977 Proof | 3,525 | Value: 10.00 | | | | |
| 1979FM Proof | — | Value: 17.50 | | | | |
| 1980FM Proof | — | Value: 20.00 | | | | |
| 1981FM Proof | — | Value: 22.00 | | | | |
| 1984FM Proof | — | Value: 22.00 | | | | |
| 1986 Proof | 1,000 | Value: 22.00 | | | | |

**5 DOLLARS** **KM# 33** **Weight:** 35.5000 g. **Composition:** 0.9250 Silver 1.0557 oz. ASW **Subject:** 25th Anniversary of Coronation

| Date | Mintage | F | VF | XF | Unc | BU |
|---|---|---|---|---|---|---|
| 1978 Proof | 2,168 | Value: 27.50 | | | | |

**5 DOLLARS** **KM# 70** **Weight:** 35.5000 g. **Composition:** 0.9250 Silver 1.0557 oz. ASW **Subject:** 150th Anniversary of Parliamentary Government **Obverse:** Similar to 50 Cents, KM#5

| Date | Mintage | F | VF | XF | Unc | BU |
|---|---|---|---|---|---|---|
| 1982FM Proof | 1,105 | Value: 40.00 | | | | |

**5 DOLLARS** **KM# 76** **Weight:** 35.5000 g. **Composition:** 0.9250 Silver 1.0557 oz. ASW **Subject:** Royal Visit

| Date | Mintage | F | VF | XF | Unc | BU |
|---|---|---|---|---|---|---|
| 1983FM Proof | 419 | Value: 37.50 | | | | |

**5 DOLLARS** **KM# 81** **Weight:** 28.2800 g. **Composition:** 0.9250 Silver .8411 oz. ASW **Subject:** 250th Anniversary of Royal Land Grant

| Date | Mintage | F | VF | XF | Unc | BU |
|---|---|---|---|---|---|---|
| 1985 Proof | Est. 1,000 | Value: 31.50 | | | | |

**5 DOLLARS** **KM# 80** **Weight:** 28.2800 g. **Composition:** 0.5000 Silver .4547 oz. ASW **Subject:** Commonwealth Games

| Date | Mintage | F | VF | XF | Unc | BU |
|---|---|---|---|---|---|---|
| 1986 | 50,000 | — | — | — | 12.50 | — |

**5 DOLLARS** **KM# 80a** **Weight:** 28.2800 g. **Composition:** 0.9250 Silver .8411 oz. ASW **Reverse:** Commonwealth games

| Date | Mintage | F | VF | XF | Unc | BU |
|---|---|---|---|---|---|---|
| 1986 Proof | Est. 20,000 | Value: 25.00 | | | | |

**5 DOLLARS** **KM# 85** **Weight:** 28.2800 g. **Composition:** 0.9250 Silver .8411 oz. ASW **Subject:** Queen Elizabeth II and Philip's 40th Wedding Anniversary

| Date | Mintage | F | VF | XF | Unc | BU |
|---|---|---|---|---|---|---|
| ND (1987) Proof | Est. 2,000 | Value: 32.50 | | | | |

**5 DOLLARS** **KM# 85a** **Weight:** 35.6400 g. **Composition:** 0.9250 Silver 1.0560 oz. ASW **Subject:** Queen Elizabeth II and Philip's 40th Wedding Anniversary

| Date | Mintage | F | VF | XF | Unc | BU |
|---|---|---|---|---|---|---|
| ND (1987) Proof | 317 | Value: 90.00 | | | | |

**5 DOLLARS** **KM# 95** **Weight:** 28.2800 g. **Composition:** 0.9250 Silver .8411 oz. ASW **Subject:** World Wildlife Fund **Reverse:** Cuban Amazon

| Date | Mintage | F | VF | XF | Unc | BU |
|---|---|---|---|---|---|---|
| 1987 Proof | — | Value: 32.50 | | | | |

**5 DOLLARS** **KM# 96** **Weight:** 28.2800 g. **Composition:** 0.9250 Silver .8411 oz. ASW **Subject:** 50th Anniversary of Columbus' Discovery of America

| Date | Mintage | F | VF | XF | Unc | BU |
|---|---|---|---|---|---|---|
| 1988 Proof | 10,000 | Value: 30.00 | | | | |

**5 DOLLARS** **KM# 94.1** **Weight:** 28.2800 g. **Composition:** 0.9250 Silver .8411 oz. ASW **Subject:** Seoul Olympics **Obverse:** Denomination below portrait

| Date | Mintage | F | VF | XF | Unc | BU |
|---|---|---|---|---|---|---|
| 1988 Proof | 20,000 | Value: 27.50 | | | | |

**5 DOLLARS** **KM# 94.2** **Weight:** 35.6400 g. **Composition:** 0.9250 Silver 1.0560 oz. ASW **Subject:** Seoul Olympics **Obverse:** Date below portrait

| Date | Mintage | F | VF | XF | Unc | BU |
|---|---|---|---|---|---|---|
| 1988 Proof | 318 | Value: 200 | | | | |

**5 DOLLARS** **KM# 98** **Weight:** 28.2800 g. **Composition:** 0.9250 Silver .8411 oz. ASW **Subject:** Visit of Princess Alexandra **Note:** Similar to 250 Dollars, KM#99.

| Date | Mintage | F | VF | XF | Unc | BU |
|---|---|---|---|---|---|---|
| 1988 Proof | Est. 5,000 | Value: 35.00 | | | | |



**5 DOLLARS** **KM# 100** **Weight:** 28.2800 g. **Composition:** 0.9250 Silver .8411 oz. ASW **Subject:** 100 Years of Postal Service

| Date | Mintage | F | VF | XF | Unc | BU |
|---|---|---|---|---|---|---|
| ND (1989) Proof | 10,000 | Value: 40.00 | | | | |

**5 DOLLARS** **KM# 102** **Weight:** 28.2800 g. **Composition:** 0.9250 Silver .8411 oz. ASW **Subject:** Save the Children Fund

| Date | Mintage | F | VF | XF | Unc | BU |
|---|---|---|---|---|---|---|
| 1989 Proof | Est. 20,000 | Value: 22.50 | | | | |

**5 DOLLARS** **KM# 108** **Weight:** 28.2800 g. **Composition:** 0.9250 Silver .8411 oz. ASW **Subject:** Queen Mother's Birth Centennial

| Date | Mintage | F | VF | XF | Unc | BU |
|---|---|---|---|---|---|---|
| ND (1990) Proof | Est. 10,000 | Value: 25.00 | | | | |

**5 DOLLARS** **KM# 109** **Weight:** 28.2800 g. **Composition:** 0.9250 Silver .8411 oz. ASW **Subject:** 20th Anniversary of the Currency Board

| Date | Mintage | F | VF | XF | Unc | BU |
|---|---|---|---|---|---|---|
| ND (1991) Proof | Est. 2,500 | Value: 45.00 | | | | |

**5 DOLLARS** **KM# 110** **Weight:** 28.2800 g. **Composition:** 0.9250 Silver .8411 oz. ASW **Subject:** 1992 Olympics - Barcelona

| Date | Mintage | F | VF | XF | Unc | BU |
|---|---|---|---|---|---|---|
| 1992 Proof | Est. 50,000 | Value: 27.50 | | | | |

**5 DOLLARS** **KM# 112** **Weight:** 28.2800 g. **Composition:** 0.9250 Silver .8411 oz. ASW **Subject:** 40th Anniversary - Coronation of Queen Elizabeth

| Date | Mintage | F | VF | XF | Unc | BU |
|---|---|---|---|---|---|---|
| ND (1993) Proof | Est. 10,000 | Value: 37.50 | | | | |

**5 DOLLARS** **KM# 126** **Weight:** 28.2800 g. **Composition:** 0.9250 Silver .8411 oz. ASW **Subject:** 70th Birthday of Queen Elizabeth II **Obverse:** Queen's portrait **Reverse:** The Queen on horseback

| Date | Mintage | F | VF | XF | Unc | BU |
|---|---|---|---|---|---|---|
| ND (1996) Proof | Est. 13,000 | Value: 45.00 | | | | |

**10 DOLLARS** **KM# 68** **Composition:** Copper-Nickel **Subject:** Wedding of Prince Charles and Lady Diana

| Date | Mintage | F | VF | XF | Unc | BU |
|---|---|---|---|---|---|---|
| 1981 | — | — | — | — | 7.50 | — |

**10 DOLLARS** **KM# 68a** **Weight:** 28.2800 g. **Composition:** 0.9250 Silver .8411 oz. ASW **Subject:** Wedding of Prince Charles and lady Diana

| Date | Mintage | F | VF | XF | Unc | BU |
|---|---|---|---|---|---|---|
| 1981 Proof | 40,000 | Value: 20.00 | | | | |

**10 DOLLARS** **KM# 72** **Weight:** 27.8900 g. **Composition:** 0.9250 Silver .8295 oz. ASW **Subject:** International Year of the Child

| Date | Mintage | F | VF | XF | Unc | BU |
|---|---|---|---|---|---|---|
| 1982 Proof | 6,616 | Value: 21.50 | | | | |

**10 DOLLARS** **KM# 77** **Weight:** 23.4500 g. **Composition:** 0.9250 Silver .6975 oz. ASW **Subject:** Royal Visit

| Date | Mintage | F | VF | XF | Unc | BU |
|---|---|---|---|---|---|---|
| 1983FM Proof | 10,000 | Value: 30.00 | | | | |

**25 DOLLARS** **KM# 9** **Weight:** 51.3500 g. **Composition:** 0.9250 Silver 1.5271 oz. ASW **Subject:** Queen Elizabeth II and Philip's 25th Wedding Anniversary

| Date | Mintage | F | VF | XF | Unc | BU |
|---|---|---|---|---|---|---|
| 1972 | 186,000 | — | — | — | 25.00 | — |
| 1972 Proof | 26,000 | Value: 30.00 | | | | |

**25 DOLLARS** **KM# 9a** **Weight:** 15.7500 g. **Composition:** 0.5000 Gold .2222 oz. AGW **Subject:** Queen Elizabeth II and Philip's 25th Wedding Anniversary

| Date | Mintage | F | VF | XF | Unc | BU |
|---|---|---|---|---|---|---|
| 1972 | 7,706 | — | — | — | 120 | — |
| 1972 Proof | 21,000 | Value: 135 | | | | |

**25 DOLLARS** **KM# 10** **Weight:** 51.3500 g. **Composition:** 0.9250 Silver 1.5271 oz. ASW **Subject:** Churchill Centenary

| Date | Mintage | F | VF | XF | Unc | BU |
|---|---|---|---|---|---|---|
| 1974 | 1,200 | — | — | — | 32.50 | — |
| 1974 Proof | 12,000 | Value: 30.00 | | | | |

**Note:** 4300 sets were issued in proof containing KM#10 and Turks & Caicos Islands 20 Crowns KM#2 with an issue price of $80.00

**25 DOLLARS** **KM# 14** **Weight:** 51.3500 g. **Composition:** 0.9250 Silver 1.5271 oz. ASW **Subject:** Queen's Silver Jubliee

| Date | Mintage | F | VF | XF | Unc | BU |
|---|---|---|---|---|---|---|
| 1977 | 3,600 | — | — | — | 45.00 | — |
| 1977 Proof | 7,854 | Value: 45.00 | | | | |

**25 DOLLARS** **KM# 16** **Weight:** 51.3500 g. **Composition:** 0.9250 Silver 1.5271 oz. ASW **Obverse:** Portrait Queen Elizabeth right **Reverse:** Queen Mary I

| Date | Mintage | F | VF | XF | Unc | BU |
|---|---|---|---|---|---|---|
| 1977 Proof | 2,720 | Value: 50.00 | | | | |

**25 DOLLARS** **KM# 17** **Weight:** 51.3500 g. **Composition:** 0.9250 Silver 1.5271 oz. ASW **Obverse:** Portrait Queen Elizabeth right **Reverse:** Queen Elizabeth I

| Date | Mintage | F | VF | XF | Unc | BU |
|---|---|---|---|---|---|---|
| 1977 Proof | 2,677 | Value: 50.00 | | | | |

**25 DOLLARS** **KM# 18** **Weight:** 51.3500 g. **Composition:** 0.9250 Silver 1.5271 oz. ASW **Obverse:** Portrait Queen Elizabeth right **Reverse:** Queen Mary II

| Date | Mintage | F | VF | XF | Unc | BU |
|---|---|---|---|---|---|---|
| 1977 Proof | 2,653 | Value: 50.00 | | | | |

**25 DOLLARS** **KM# 19** **Weight:** 51.3500 g. **Composition:** 0.9250 Silver 1.5271 oz. ASW **Obverse:** Portrait Queen Elizabeth right **Reverse:** Queen Anne

| Date | Mintage | F | VF | XF | Unc | BU |
|---|---|---|---|---|---|---|
| 1977 Proof | 2,630 | Value: 50.00 | | | | |

**25 DOLLARS** **KM# 20** **Weight:** 51.3500 g. **Composition:** 0.9250 Silver 1.5271 oz. ASW **Obverse:** Portrait Queen Elizabeth right **Reverse:** Queen Victoria

| Date | Mintage | F | VF | XF | Unc | BU |
|---|---|---|---|---|---|---|
| 1977 Proof | 2,623 | Value: 50.00 | | | | |

**25 DOLLARS** **KM# 36** **Weight:** 51.3500 g. **Composition:** 0.9250 Silver 1.5271 oz. ASW **Subject:** 25th Anniversary of Coronation **Obverse:** Portrait Queen Elizabeth right **Reverse:** Ampulla

| Date | Mintage | F | VF | XF | Unc | BU |
|---|---|---|---|---|---|---|
| 1978 Proof | 5,000 | Value: 45.00 | | | | |

**25 DOLLARS** **KM# 37** **Weight:** 51.3500 g. **Composition:** 0.9250 Silver 1.5271 oz. ASW **Subject:** 25th Anniversary of Coronation **Obverse:** Portrait Queen Elizabeth right **Reverse:** Orb

| Date | Mintage | F | VF | XF | Unc | BU |
|---|---|---|---|---|---|---|
| 1978 Proof | 5,000 | Value: 45.00 | | | | |

**25 DOLLARS** **KM# 38** **Weight:** 51.3500 g. **Composition:** 0.9250 Silver 1.5271 oz. ASW **Subject:** 25th Anniversary of Coronation **Obverse:** Portrait Queen Elizabeth right **Reverse:** St. Edward's crown

| Date | Mintage | F | VF | XF | Unc | BU |
|---|---|---|---|---|---|---|
| 1978 Proof | 5,000 | Value: 45.00 | | | | |

**25 DOLLARS** **KM# 39** **Weight:** 51.3500 g. **Composition:** 0.9250 Silver 1.5271 oz. ASW **Subject:** 25th Anniversary of Coronation **Obverse:** Portrait Queen Elizabeth right **Reverse:** Coronation chair

| Date | Mintage | F | VF | XF | Unc | BU |
|---|---|---|---|---|---|---|
| 1978 Proof | 5,000 | Value: 45.00 | | | | |

**25 DOLLARS** **KM# 40** **Weight:** 51.3500 g. **Composition:** 0.9250 Silver 1.5271 oz. ASW **Subject:** 25th Anniversary of Coronation **Obverse:** Portrait Queen Elizabeth right **Reverse:** Royal scepter

| Date | Mintage | F | VF | XF | Unc | BU |
|---|---|---|---|---|---|---|
| 1978 Proof | 5,000 | Value: 45.00 | | | | |

**25 DOLLARS** **KM# 41** **Weight:** 51.3500 g. **Composition:** 0.9250 Silver 1.5271 oz. ASW **Subject:** 25th Anniversary of Coronation **Obverse:** Queen's portrait, date between dots **Reverse:** Spoon

| Date | Mintage | F | VF | XF | Unc | BU |
|---|---|---|---|---|---|---|
| 1978 Proof | 5,000 | Value: 45.00 | | | | |

**25 DOLLARS** **KM# 48** **Weight:** 35.6400 g. **Composition:** 0.5000 Silver .5729 oz. ASW **Obverse:** Portrait Queen Elizabeth right **Reverse:** Saxon Kings

| Date | Mintage | F | VF | XF | Unc | BU |
|---|---|---|---|---|---|---|
| 1980CHI Proof | 12,000 | Value: 35.00 | | | | |

**25 DOLLARS** **KM# 49** **Weight:** 35.6400 g. **Composition:** 0.5000 Silver .5729 oz. ASW **Obverse:** Portrait Queen Elizabeth right **Reverse:** Norman Kings

| Date | Mintage | F | VF | XF | Unc | BU |
|---|---|---|---|---|---|---|
| 1980CHI Proof | 12,000 | Value: 35.00 | | | | |

**25 DOLLARS** **KM# 50** **Weight:** 35.6400 g. **Composition:** 0.5000 Silver .5729 oz. ASW **Reverse:** House of Plantagenet - I

| Date | Mintage | F | VF | XF | Unc | BU |
|---|---|---|---|---|---|---|
| 1980CHI Proof | 12,000 | Value: 35.00 | | | | |

**25 DOLLARS** **KM# 51** **Weight:** 35.6400 g. **Composition:** 0.5000 Silver .5729 oz. ASW **Obverse:** Similar to KM#50 **Reverse:** House of Plantagenet - II

| Date | Mintage | F | VF | XF | Unc | BU |
|---|---|---|---|---|---|---|
| 1980CHI Proof | 12,000 | Value: 35.00 | | | | |

**25 DOLLARS** **KM# 52** **Weight:** 35.6400 g. **Composition:** 0.5000 Silver .5729 oz. ASW **Reverse:** House of Lancaster

| Date | Mintage | F | VF | XF | Unc | BU |
|---|---|---|---|---|---|---|
| 1980CHI Proof | 12,000 | Value: 35.00 | | | | |

**25 DOLLARS** KM# 53 **Weight:** 35.6400 g. **Composition:** 0.5000 Silver .5729 oz. ASW **Obverse:** Similar to KM#52 **Reverse:** House of York

| Date | Mintage | F | VF | XF | Unc | BU |
|---|---|---|---|---|---|---|
| 1980CHI Proof | 12,000 | Value: 35.00 | | | | |

**25 DOLLARS** KM# 54 **Weight:** 35.6400 g. **Composition:** 0.5000 Silver .5729 oz. ASW **Obverse:** Similar to KM#52 **Reverse:** House of Tudor

| Date | Mintage | F | VF | XF | Unc | BU |
|---|---|---|---|---|---|---|
| 1980CHI Proof | 12,000 | Value: 35.00 | | | | |

**25 DOLLARS** KM# 55 **Weight:** 35.6400 g. **Composition:** 0.5000 Silver .5729 oz. ASW **Obverse:** Similar to KM#52 **Reverse:** House of Stuart & Orange

| Date | Mintage | F | VF | XF | Unc | BU |
|---|---|---|---|---|---|---|
| 1980CHI Proof | 12,000 | Value: 35.00 | | | | |

**25 DOLLARS** KM# 56 **Weight:** 35.6400 g. **Composition:** 0.5000 Silver .5729 oz. ASW **Obverse:** Similar to KM#52 **Reverse:** House of Hanover

| Date | Mintage | F | VF | XF | Unc | BU |
|---|---|---|---|---|---|---|
| 1980CHI Proof | 12,000 | Value: 35.00 | | | | |

**25 DOLLARS** KM# 57 **Weight:** 35.6400 g. **Composition:** 0.5000 Silver .5729 oz. ASW **Obverse:** Similar to KM#52 **Reverse:** House of Saxe-Coburg and Windsor

| Date | Mintage | F | VF | XF | Unc | BU |
|---|---|---|---|---|---|---|
| 1980CHI Proof | 12,000 | Value: 35.00 | | | | |

**25 DOLLARS** KM# 78 **Weight:** 64.8000 g. **Composition:** 0.9250 Silver 1.9273 oz. ASW **Subject:** Royal Visit **Obverse:** Portrait Queen Elizabeth II right

| Date | Mintage | F | VF | XF | Unc | BU |
|---|---|---|---|---|---|---|
| 1983FM Proof | 5,000 | Value: 45.00 | | | | |

**25 DOLLARS** KM# 104 **Weight:** 3.1340 g. **Composition:** 0.9990 Gold .1006 oz. AGW **Subject:** Winston Churchill - Evacuation of Dunkirk **Obverse:** Portrait Queen Elizabeth II right

| Date | Mintage | F | VF | XF | Unc | BU |
|---|---|---|---|---|---|---|
| 1990 Proof | Est. 500 | Value: 100 | | | | |

**50 DOLLARS** KM# 12 **Weight:** 64.9400 g. **Composition:** 0.9250 Silver 1.9314 oz. ASW **Subject:** Sovereign Queens of England **Obverse:** Portrait Queen Elizabeth II right

| Date | Mintage | F | VF | XF | Unc | BU |
|---|---|---|---|---|---|---|
| 1975 | 33,000 | — | — | — | 45.00 | — |
| 1975 Proof | 7,800 | Value: 50.00 | | | | |
| 1976 | 1,292 | — | — | — | 55.00 | — |
| 1976 Proof | 2,843 | Value: 55.00 | | | | |
| 1977 | 2,400 | — | — | — | 55.00 | — |
| 1977 Proof | Inc. above | Value: 55.00 | | | | |

**50 DOLLARS** KM# 21 **Weight:** 11.3400 g. **Composition:** 0.5000 Gold .1823 oz. AGW **Reverse:** Queen Mary I

| Date | Mintage | F | VF | XF | Unc | BU |
|---|---|---|---|---|---|---|
| 1977 Proof | 1,999 | Value: 115 | | | | |

**50 DOLLARS** KM# 22 **Weight:** 11.3400 g. **Composition:** 0.5000 Gold .1823 oz. AGW **Reverse:** Queen Elizabeth I

| Date | Mintage | F | VF | XF | Unc | BU |
|---|---|---|---|---|---|---|
| 1977 Proof | 1,969 | Value: 115 | | | | |

**50 DOLLARS** KM# 23 **Weight:** 11.3400 g. **Composition:** 0.5000 Gold .1823 oz. AGW **Reverse:** Queen Mary II

| Date | Mintage | F | VF | XF | Unc | BU |
|---|---|---|---|---|---|---|
| 1977 Proof | 1,961 | Value: 115 | | | | |

**50 DOLLARS** KM# 24 **Weight:** 11.3400 g. **Composition:** 0.5000 Gold .1823 oz. AGW **Reverse:** Queen Anne

| Date | Mintage | F | VF | XF | Unc | BU |
|---|---|---|---|---|---|---|
| 1977 Proof | 1,938 | Value: 115 | | | | |

**50 DOLLARS** KM# 25 **Weight:** 11.3400 g. **Composition:** 0.5000 Gold .1823 oz. AGW **Reverse:** Queen Victoria

| Date | Mintage | F | VF | XF | Unc | BU |
|---|---|---|---|---|---|---|
| 1977 Proof | 1,932 | Value: 115 | | | | |

**50 DOLLARS** KM# 42 **Weight:** 11.3400 g. **Composition:** 0.5000 Gold .1823 oz. AGW **Subject:** 25th Anniversary of Coronation **Obv. Legend:** Ampulla

| Date | Mintage | F | VF | XF | Unc | BU |
|---|---|---|---|---|---|---|
| 1978 Proof | 771 | Value: 120 | | | | |

**50 DOLLARS** KM# 43 **Weight:** 11.3400 g. **Composition:** 0.5000 Gold .1823 oz. AGW **Subject:** 25th Anniversary of Coronation **Obv. Legend:** Orb

| Date | Mintage | F | VF | XF | Unc | BU |
|---|---|---|---|---|---|---|
| 1978 Proof | 771 | Value: 120 | | | | |

**50 DOLLARS** KM# 44 **Weight:** 11.3400 g. **Composition:** 0.5000 Gold .1823 oz. AGW **Subject:** 25th Anniversary of Coronation **Reverse:** St. Edward's Crown

| Date | Mintage | F | VF | XF | Unc | BU |
|---|---|---|---|---|---|---|
| 1978 Proof | 771 | Value: 120 | | | | |

**50 DOLLARS** KM# 45 **Weight:** 11.3400 g. **Composition:** 0.5000 Gold .1823 oz. AGW **Subject:** 25th Anniversary of Coronation **Reverse:** Chair

| Date | Mintage | F | VF | XF | Unc | BU |
|---|---|---|---|---|---|---|
| 1978 Proof | 771 | Value: 120 | | | | |

**50 DOLLARS** KM# 46 **Weight:** 11.3400 g. **Composition:** 0.5000 Gold .1823 oz. AGW **Subject:** 25th Anniversary of Coronation **Reverse:** Scepter

| Date | Mintage | F | VF | XF | Unc | BU |
|---|---|---|---|---|---|---|
| 1978 Proof | 771 | Value: 120 | | | | |

**50 DOLLARS** KM# 47 **Weight:** 11.3400 g. **Composition:** 0.5000 Gold .1823 oz. AGW **Subject:** 25th Anniversary of Coronation **Reverse:** Spoon

| Date | Mintage | F | VF | XF | Unc | BU |
|---|---|---|---|---|---|---|
| 1978 Proof | 771 | Value: 120 | | | | |

**50 DOLLARS** KM# 34 **Weight:** 64.9400 g. **Composition:** 0.9250 Silver 1.9314 oz. ASW **Reverse:** Coronation Anniversary legend added to KM#12

| Date | Mintage | F | VF | XF | Unc | BU |
|---|---|---|---|---|---|---|
| 1978 Proof | 5,775 | Value: 60.00 | | | | |

**50 DOLLARS** KM# 58 **Weight:** 11.3400 g. **Composition:** 0.5000 Gold .1823 oz. AGW **Obverse:** Portrait Queen Elizabeth II right **Reverse:** Saxon Kings

| Date | Mintage | F | VF | XF | Unc | BU |
|---|---|---|---|---|---|---|
| 1980 Proof | 10,000 | Value: 110 | | | | |

**50 DOLLARS** KM# 59 **Weight:** 11.3400 g. **Composition:** 0.5000 Gold .1823 oz. AGW **Obverse:** Portrait Queen Elizabeth II right **Reverse:** Norman Kings

| Date | Mintage | F | VF | XF | Unc | BU |
|---|---|---|---|---|---|---|
| 1980 Proof | 10,000 | Value: 110 | | | | |

**50 DOLLARS** KM# 60 **Weight:** 11.3400 g. **Composition:** 0.5000 Gold .1823 oz. AGW **Obverse:** Portrait Queen Elizabeth II right **Reverse:** House of Plantagenet - I

| Date | Mintage | F | VF | XF | Unc | BU |
|---|---|---|---|---|---|---|
| 1980 Proof | 11,000 | Value: 110 | | | | |

**50 DOLLARS** KM# 61 **Weight:** 11.3400 g. **Composition:** 0.5000 Gold .1823 oz. AGW **Obverse:** Portrait Queen Elizabeth II right **Reverse:** House of Plantagenet - II

| Date | Mintage | F | VF | XF | Unc | BU |
|---|---|---|---|---|---|---|
| 1980 Proof | 11,000 | Value: 110 | | | | |

**50 DOLLARS** KM# 62 **Weight:** 11.3400 g. **Composition:** 0.5000 Gold .1823 oz. AGW **Obverse:** Portrait Queen Elizabeth II right **Reverse:** House of Lancaster

| Date | Mintage | F | VF | XF | Unc | BU |
|---|---|---|---|---|---|---|
| 1980 Proof | 11,000 | Value: 110 | | | | |

**50 DOLLARS** KM# 63 **Weight:** 11.3400 g. **Composition:** 0.5000 Gold .1823 oz. AGW **Obverse:** Portrait Queen Elizabeth II right **Reverse:** House of York

| Date | Mintage | F | VF | XF | Unc | BU |
|---|---|---|---|---|---|---|
| 1980 Proof | 11,000 | Value: 110 | | | | |

**50 DOLLARS** KM# 64 **Weight:** 11.3400 g. **Composition:** 0.5000 Gold .1823 oz. AGW **Obverse:** Portrait Queen Elizabeth II right **Reverse:** House of Tudor

| Date | Mintage | F | VF | XF | Unc | BU |
|---|---|---|---|---|---|---|
| 1980 Proof | 11,000 | Value: 110 | | | | |

**50 DOLLARS** KM# 65 **Weight:** 11.3400 g. **Composition:** 0.5000 Gold .1823 oz. AGW **Obverse:** Portrait Queen Elizabeth II right **Reverse:** House of Stuart and Oranage

| Date | Mintage | F | VF | XF | Unc | BU |
|---|---|---|---|---|---|---|
| 1980 Proof | 11,000 | Value: 110 | | | | |

**50 DOLLARS** KM# 66 **Weight:** 11.3400 g. **Composition:** 0.5000 Gold .1823 oz. AGW **Obverse:** Portrait Queen Elizabeth II right **Reverse:** House of Hanover

| Date | Mintage | F | VF | XF | Unc | BU |
|---|---|---|---|---|---|---|
| 1980 Proof | 11,000 | Value: 110 | | | | |

**50 DOLLARS** KM# 67 **Weight:** 11.3400 g. **Composition:** 0.5000 Gold .1823 oz. AGW **Obverse:** Portrait Queen Elizabeth II right **Reverse:** House of Saxe-Coburg and Windsor

| Date | Mintage | F | VF | XF | Unc | BU |
|---|---|---|---|---|---|---|
| 1980 Proof | 11,000 | Value: 110 | | | | |

**50 DOLLARS** **KM# 71** **Weight:** 5.0000 g. **Composition:** 0.9000 Gold .1447 oz. AGW **Subject:** 150th Anniversary of Parliamentary Government

| Date | Mintage | F | VF | XF | Unc | BU |
|---|---|---|---|---|---|---|
| 1982 Proof | 585 | Value: 115 | | | | |

**50 DOLLARS** **KM# 79** **Weight:** 5.1900 g. **Composition:** 0.9170 Gold .1530 oz. AGW **Subject:** Royal Visit

| Date | Mintage | F | VF | XF | Unc | BU |
|---|---|---|---|---|---|---|
| 1983 | 5,000 | — | — | — | 110 | — |

**50 DOLLARS** **KM# 83** **Weight:** 129.6000 g. **Composition:** 0.9250 Silver 3.8547 oz. ASW **Subject:** Bird Conservation **Reverse:** Snowy Egret

| Date | Mintage | F | VF | XF | Unc | BU |
|---|---|---|---|---|---|---|
| 1985 Proof | 10,000 | Value: 90.00 | | | | |

**50 DOLLARS** **KM# 105** **Weight:** 7.8140 g. **Composition:** 0.9990 Gold .2509 oz. AGW **Reverse:** Winston Churchill - spitfires Over Dover

| Date | Mintage | F | VF | XF | Unc | BU |
|---|---|---|---|---|---|---|
| 1990 Proof | Est. 500 | Value: 200 | | | | |

**50 DOLLARS** **KM# 115** **Weight:** 15.9800 g. **Composition:** 0.9170 Gold .4708 oz. AGW **Reverse:** Wreck of the Ten Sails

| Date | Mintage | F | VF | XF | Unc | BU |
|---|---|---|---|---|---|---|
| 1994 Proof | Est. 200 | Value: 500 | | | | |

**100 DOLLARS** **KM# 11** **Weight:** 22.6801 g. **Composition:** 0.5000 Gold .3646 oz. AGW **Subject:** Churchill Centenary

| Date | Mintage | F | VF | XF | Unc | BU |
|---|---|---|---|---|---|---|
| 1974 | 1,400 | — | — | — | 180 | — |
| 1974 Proof | 6,300 | Value: 200 | | | | |

**100 DOLLARS** **KM# 13** **Weight:** 22.6801 g. **Composition:** 0.5000 Gold .3646 oz. AGW **Obverse:** Portrait Queen Elizabeth II right **Reverse:** Sovereign Queens of England

| Date | Mintage | F | VF | XF | Unc | BU |
|---|---|---|---|---|---|---|
| 1975 | 8,053 | — | — | — | 175 | — |
| 1975 Proof | 4,950 | Value: 190 | | | | |
| 1976 | 2,028 | — | — | — | 200 | — |
| 1976 Proof | 3,560 | Value: 225 | | | | |
| 1977 | — | — | — | — | 200 | — |
| 1977 Proof | 2,845 | Value: 225 | | | | |

**100 DOLLARS** **KM# 15** **Weight:** 22.6801 g. **Composition:** 0.5000 Gold .3646 oz. AGW **Subject:** Queen's Silver Jubilee

| Date | Mintage | F | VF | XF | Unc | BU |
|---|---|---|---|---|---|---|
| 1977 | 562 | — | — | — | 185 | — |
| 1977 Proof | 4,386 | Value: 200 | | | | |

**100 DOLLARS** **KM# 35** **Weight:** 22.6801 g. **Composition:** 0.5000 Gold .3646 oz. AGW **Reverse:** Similar to KM#13, but with Coronation Anniversary legend

| Date | Mintage | F | VF | XF | Unc | BU |
|---|---|---|---|---|---|---|
| 1978 Proof | 1,973 | Value: 240 | | | | |

**100 DOLLARS** **KM# 69** **Weight:** 8.0352 g. **Composition:** 0.9170 Gold .2369 oz. AGW **Subject:** Wedding of Prince Charles and Lady Diana

| Date | Mintage | F | VF | XF | Unc | BU |
|---|---|---|---|---|---|---|
| 1981 Proof | 11,000 | Value: 150 | | | | |

**100 DOLLARS** **KM# 97** **Weight:** 15.9800 g. **Composition:** 0.9170 Gold .4708 oz. AGW **Subject:** 500th Anniversary of Columbus' Discovery of America

| Date | Mintage | F | VF | XF | Unc | BU |
|---|---|---|---|---|---|---|
| 1988 Proof | 380 | Value: 350 | | | | |

**100 DOLLARS** **KM# 101** **Weight:** 15.9800 g. **Composition:** 0.9170 Gold .4708 oz. AGW **Subject:** 100 Years of Postal Service **Reverse:** Similar to 5 Dollars, KM#100

| Date | Mintage | F | VF | XF | Unc | BU |
|---|---|---|---|---|---|---|
| 1989 Proof | 93 | Value: 475 | | | | |

**100 DOLLARS** **KM# 106** **Weight:** 15.6080 g. **Composition:** 0.9990 Gold .5013 oz. AGW **Obverse:** Portrait Queen Elizabeth II right **Reverse:** Winston Churchill - Evacuation of Dunkirk

| Date | Mintage | F | VF | XF | Unc | BU |
|---|---|---|---|---|---|---|
| 1990 Proof | 500 | Value: 375 | | | | |

**100 DOLLARS** **KM# 117** **Weight:** 30.5000 g. **Composition:** 0.9170 Gold .8974 oz. AGW **Obverse:** Portrait Queen Elizabeth right **Reverse:** Cayman Ironwood Tree

| Date | Mintage | F | VF | XF | Unc | BU |
|---|---|---|---|---|---|---|
| 1994 Proof | Est. 15,000 | Value: 620 | | | | |

**100 DOLLARS** **KM# 123** **Weight:** 15.9800 g. **Composition:** 0.9170 Gold .4708 oz. AGW **Obverse:** Portrait Queen Elizabeth right **Reverse:** Amazona Leucocephala Caymanesis - Parrot

| Date | Mintage | F | VF | XF | Unc | BU |
|---|---|---|---|---|---|---|
| 1996 Proof | Est. 150 | Value: 450 | | | | |

**250 DOLLARS** **KM# 82** **Weight:** 47.5400 g. **Composition:** 0.9170 Gold 1.4001 oz. AGW **Subject:** 250th Anniversary of Royal Land Grant **Note:** Similar to 5 Dollars, KM#81.

| Date | Mintage | F | VF | XF | Unc | BU |
|---|---|---|---|---|---|---|
| 1985 Proof | Est. 250 | Value: 850 | | | | |

**250 DOLLARS** **KM# 84** **Weight:** 47.5400 g. **Composition:** 0.9170 Gold 1.4001 oz. AGW **Subject:** Commonwealth Games **Obverse:** Portrait Queen Elizabeth right **Reverse:** Long jumper

| Date | Mintage | F | VF | XF | Unc | BU |
|---|---|---|---|---|---|---|
| 1986 Proof | 64 | Value: 975 | | | | |

**250 DOLLARS** **KM# 86** **Weight:** 47.5400 g. **Composition:** 0.9170 Gold 1.4001 oz. AGW **Subject:** Queen Elizabeth II and Philip's 40th Wedding Anniversary **Obverse:** Portrait Queen Elizabeth right **Reverse:** E & P monogram

| Date | Mintage | F | VF | XF | Unc | BU |
|---|---|---|---|---|---|---|
| ND Proof | 75 | Value: 950 | | | | |

**250 DOLLARS** KM# 99 **Weight:** 47.5400 g. **Composition:** 0.9170 Gold 1.4001 oz. AGW **Subject:** Visit of Princess Alexander

| Date | Mintage | F | VF | XF | Unc | BU |
|---|---|---|---|---|---|---|
| 1988 Proof | 86 | Value: 950 | | | | |

**250 DOLLARS** KM# 107 **Weight:** 31.2100 g. **Composition:** 0.9990 Gold 1.0014 oz. AGW **Obverse:** Portrait Queen Elizabeth right **Reverse:** Winston Churchill - Spitfires Over Dover

| Date | Mintage | F | VF | XF | Unc | BU |
|---|---|---|---|---|---|---|
| 1990 Proof | Est. 500 | Value: 975 | | | | |

**250 DOLLARS** KM# 113 **Weight:** 47.5400 g. **Composition:** 0.9170 Gold 1.4013 oz. AGW **Subject:** 40th Anniversary - Coronation of Queen Elizabeth II

| Date | Mintage | F | VF | XF | Unc | BU |
|---|---|---|---|---|---|---|
| 1993 Proof | Est. 100 | Value: 1,000 | | | | |

**250 DOLLARS** KM# 119 **Weight:** 47.5400 g. **Composition:** 0.9170 Gold 1.4013 oz. AGW **Subject:** Royal Visit **Obverse:** Portrait Queen Elizabeth **Reverse:** Royal couple above yacht "Britannia"

| Date | Mintage | F | VF | XF | Unc | BU |
|---|---|---|---|---|---|---|
| 1994 Proof | 200 | Value: 1,000 | | | | |

## PIEFORTS

| KM# | Date | Mintage | Identification | Issue Price | Mkt Val |
|---|---|---|---|---|---|
| P1 | 1982 | 74 | 10 Dollars. KIM72 | 250 | 120 |

## MINT SETS

| KM# | Date | Mintage | Identification | Issue Price | Mkt Val |
|---|---|---|---|---|---|
| MS1 | 1987 (4) | — | KM87-90 | — | 5.00 |
| MS2 | 1992 (4) | — | KM87a-90a | 8.00 | 8.00 |
| MS3 | 1996 (4) | — | KM87a-90a | — | 12.00 |

## PROOF SETS

| KM# | Date | Mintage | Identification | Issue Price | Mkt Val |
|---|---|---|---|---|---|
| PS1 | 1972 (8) | 10,757 | KM1-8 | 40.00 | 25.00 |
| PS2 | 1973 (8) | 9,988 | KM1-8 | 40.00 | 25.00 |
| PS3 | 1974 (8) | 15,387 | KM1-8 | 40.00 | 25.00 |
| PS4 | 1974 (2) | 2,400 | KM10-11 | 245 | 200 |
| PS5 | 1975 (8) | 5,390 | KM1-8 | 54.50 | 28.00 |
| PS6 | 1975 (6) | 1,785 | KM1-6 | 31.50 | 10.00 |
| PS7 | 1975 (2) | 3,650 | KM12-13 | 293 | 235 |
| PS8 | 1976 (8) | 3,044 | KM1-8 | 54.50 | 30.00 |
| PS9 | 1976 (2) | 1,531 | KM12-13 | 293 | 265 |
| PS11 | 1977 (8) | 1,970 | KM1-8 | 52.50 | 35.00 |
| PS12 | 1977 (6) | 2,445 | KM12, 16-20 | 315 | 310 |
| PS13 | 1977 (6) | 1,932 | KM13, 21-25 | 651 | 700 |
| PS14 | 1977 (2) | 223 | KM14-15 | 290 | 250 |
| PS15 | 1978 (8) | 1,303 | KM26-33 | 79.50 | 60.00 |
| PS16 | 1978 (6) | 5,000 | KM36-41 | 306 | 270 |
| PS17 | 1978 (6) | 771 | KM42-47 | 600 | 750 |
| PS18 | 1979 (8) | 4,427 | KM1-8 | 117 | 50.00 |
| PS19 | 1980 (8) | 1,215 | KM1-8 | 147 | 45.00 |
| PS20 | 1980 (10) | — | KM48-57 | — | 350 |
| PS21 | 1981 (8) | 865 | KM1-8 | 147 | 50.00 |
| PS22 | 1982 (8) | 589 | KM1-7, 70 | 147 | 65.00 |
| PS23 | 1983 (8) | 348 | KM1-4, 73-76 | 157 | 125 |
| PS24 | 1984 (8) | — | KM1-4, 8, 73-75 | 159 | 120 |
| PS25 | 1986 (8) | 330 | KM1-4, 7-8, 73-74 | 150 | 85.00 |
| PS26 | 1987 (8) | 317 | KM85a, 87-93 | 160 | 200 |
| PS27 | 1988 (8) | 318 | KM87-93, 94.2 | 170 | 300 |
| PS28 | 1990 (4) | 500 | KM104-107 | 1,650 | 1,650 |

# CENTRAL AFRICAN REPUBLIC

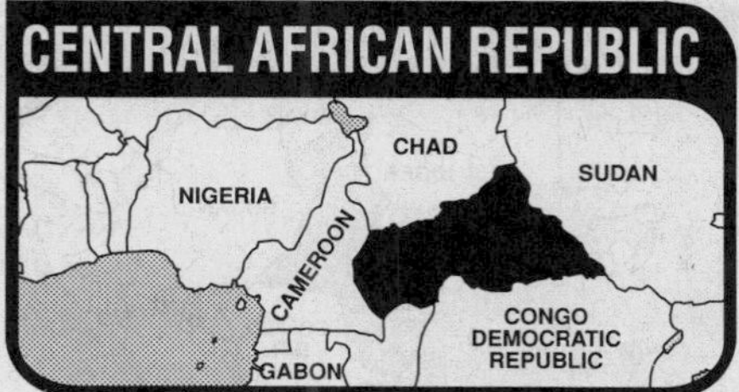


The Central African Republic, a landlocked country in Central Africa, bounded by Chad on the north, Cameroon on the west, Congo (Brazzaville) and Congo Democratic Republic, (formerly Zaire) on the south and the Sudan on the east, has an area of 240,324 sq. mi. (622,984 sq. km.) and a population of 3.2 million. Capital: Bangui. Deposits of uranium, iron ore, manganese and copper remain to be developed. Diamonds, cotton, timber and coffee are exported.

The area that is now the Central African Republic was constituted as the French territory of Ubangi-Shari in 1894. It was united with Chad in 1905 and joined with Middle Congo and Gabon in 1910, becoming one of the four territories of French Equatorial Africa. Upon dissolution of the federation on Dec. 1, 1958, the constituent territories became fully autonomous members of the French Community. Ubangi-Shari proclaimed its complete independence as the Central African Republic on Aug. 13, 1960.

On Jan. 1, 1966, Col. Jean-Bedel Bokassa, Chief of Staff of the Armed Forces, overthrew the government of President David Dacko and assumed power as president of the republic. President Bokassa abolished the constitution of 1959 and dissolved the National Assembly. In 1975 the Congress of the sole political party appointed Bokassa president for life. The republic became a constitutional monarchy on Dec. 4, 1976; President Bokassa was named Emperor Bokassa I. Bokassa was ousted as Central African emperor in a bloodless takeover of the government led by former president David Dacko on Sept. 20, 1979, and the African nation proclaimed once again a republic.

**NOTE**: For earlier coinage see French Equatorial Africa and Equatorial African States including later coinage as listed in Central African States.

**RULERS**

French, until 1960

Marshal Jean-Bedel Bokassa, 1976-1979

**MINT MARKS**

(a) - Paris, privy marks only

**MONETARY SYSTEM**

100 Centimes = 1 Franc

# FIRST REPUBLIC

## DECIMAL COINAGE

**100 FRANCS** KM# 6 **Composition:** Nickel **Obverse:** Three Giant Eland **Reverse:** Denomination

| Date | Mintage | F | VF | XF | Unc | BU |
|---|---|---|---|---|---|---|
| 1971 | 3,500,000 | 5.00 | 8.00 | 13.50 | 28.00 | — |
| 1972 | — | 5.00 | 8.00 | 13.50 | 28.00 | — |
| 1974 | — | 6.00 | 12.00 | 20.00 | 40.00 | — |

**100 FRANCS** KM# 7 **Composition:** Nickel **Obverse:** Three Giant Eland **Reverse:** Denomination

| Date | Mintage | F | VF | XF | Unc | BU |
|---|---|---|---|---|---|---|
| 1975 | — | 4.50 | 7.50 | 12.50 | 22.50 | — |
| 1976 | — | 2.00 | 3.50 | 6.00 | 10.00 | — |
| 1979 | — | 6.00 | 13.50 | 20.00 | 35.00 | — |
| 1982 | — | 2.75 | 4.50 | 8.00 | 15.00 | — |
| 1983 | — | 2.75 | 4.50 | 9.00 | 20.00 | — |
| 1984 | — | 2.50 | 4.00 | 7.00 | 11.50 | — |
| 1985 | — | 2.50 | 4.00 | 7.00 | 11.50 | — |
| 1988 | — | 2.50 | 4.00 | 7.00 | 11.50 | — |
| 1990 | — | 2.00 | 3.50 | 6.00 | 10.00 | — |

**1000 FRANCS** KM# 1 **Weight:** 3.5000 g. **Composition:** 0.9000 Gold .1012 oz. AGW **Subject:** 10th Anniversary of Independence **Obverse:** Bust of President Jean Bedel Bokasso

| Date | Mintage | F | VF | XF | Unc | BU |
|---|---|---|---|---|---|---|
| 1970 Proof | 4,000 | Value: 90.00 | | | | |

**3000 FRANCS** KM# 2 **Weight:** 10.5000 g. **Composition:** 0.9000 Gold .3038 oz. AGW **Subject:** 10th Anniversary of Independence

| Date | Mintage | F | VF | XF | Unc | BU |
|---|---|---|---|---|---|---|
| 1970 Proof | 4,000 | Value: 210 | | | | |

**5000 FRANCS** KM# 3 **Weight:** 17.5000 g. **Composition:** 0.9000 Gold .5064 oz. AGW **Subject:** 10th Anniversary of Independence; 1972 Munich Olympics **Obverse:** Similar to 3000 Francs, KM#2 **Reverse:** Wrestlers

| Date | Mintage | F | VF | XF | Unc | BU |
|---|---|---|---|---|---|---|
| 1970 Proof | 4,000 | Value: 350 | | | | |

**10000 FRANCS** KM# 4 **Weight:** 35.0000 g. **Composition:** 0.9000 Gold 1.0128 oz. AGW **Subject:** 10th Anniversary of Independence; ONU 24th Anniversary **Obverse:** Similar to 3000 Francs, KM#2

| Date | Mintage | F | VF | XF | Unc | BU |
|---|---|---|---|---|---|---|
| 1970 Proof | 4,000 | Value: 700 | | | | |

**20000 FRANCS** KM# 5 **Weight:** 70.0000 g. **Composition:** 0.9000 Gold 2.025728 oz. AGW **Subject:** 10th Anniversary of Independence; Operation Bohassa

| Date | Mintage | F | VF | XF | Unc | BU |
|---|---|---|---|---|---|---|
| 1970 Proof | 4,000 | Value: 1,420 | | | | |

# EMPIRE

## DECIMAL COINAGE

**100 FRANCS** KM# 8 **Composition:** Nickel **Obverse:** Three Giant Eland **Rev. Legend:** EMPIRE CENTRAFRICAIN

| Date | Mintage | F | VF | XF | Unc | BU |
|---|---|---|---|---|---|---|
| 1978 (a) | — | 30.00 | 60.00 | 160 | 450 | — |

# SECOND REPUBLIC

## DECIMAL COINAGE

**100 FRANCS** KM# 11 **Composition:** Copper-Nickel

| Date | Mintage | F | VF | XF | Unc | BU |
|---|---|---|---|---|---|---|
| 1985 | — | 7.50 | 15.00 | 30.00 | 55.00 | — |
| 1986 | — | 7.50 | 15.00 | 30.00 | 55.00 | — |

## ESSAIS

| KM# | Date | Mintage | Identification | Issue Price | Mkt Val |
|---|---|---|---|---|---|
| E1 | 1970 | — | 1000 Francs. Bronze. KM1. | — | 100 |
| E2 | 1971 | 1,450 | 100 Francs. KM6. | — | 25.00 |
| E3 | 1971 | 4 | 100 Francs. Gold. KM6. | — | 1,250 |
| E4 | 1975 | 1,700 | 100 Francs. KM7 | — | 22.00 |
| E5 | 1978 | 1,900 | 100 Francs. KM8 | — | 150 |
| E6 | 1985 | 1,700 | 500 Francs. KM11 | — | 45.00 |

## PROOF SETS

| KM# | Date | Mintage | Identification | Issue Price | Mkt Val |
|---|---|---|---|---|---|
| PS1 | 1970 (5) | 40,000 | KM1-5 | 375 | 2,765 |

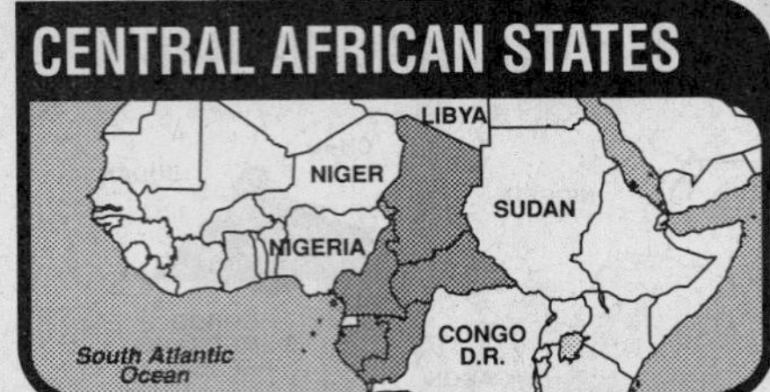


The Central African States, a monetary union comprised of Equatorial Guinea (a former Spanish possession), the former French possessions and now independent states of the Republic of Congo (Brazzaville), Gabon, Central African Republic, Chad and Cameroon, issues a common currency for the member states from a common central bank. The monetary unit, the African Financial Community franc, is tied to and supported by the French franc.

In 1960, an attempt was made to form a union of the newly independent republics of Chad, Congo, Central Africa and Gabon. The proposal was discarded when Chad refused to become a constituent member. The four countries then linked into an Equatorial Customs Unit, to which Cameroon became an associate member in 1961. A more extensive cooperation of the five republics, identified as the Central African Customs and Economic Union, was entered into force at the beginning of 1966.

In 1974 the Central Bank of the Equatorial African States, which had issued coins and paper currency in its own name and with the names of the constituent member nations, changed its name to the Bank of the Central African States. Equatorial Guinea converted to the CFA currency system issuing its first 100 Franc in 1985.

For earlier coinage see French Equatorial Africa.

**Country Code Letters**

To observe the movement of coinage throughout the states, the country of origin in which the coin is intended to circulate is designated by the following additional code letters:

A = Chad
B = Central African Republic
C = Congo
D = Gabon
E = Cameroon

By 1996 this practice was discontinued as the strategy had proved to be inconclusive.

# REPUBLIC OF CONGO

## STANDARD COINAGE

**FRANC** KM# 8 **Composition:** Aluminum **Obverse:** Three giant eland.
**Reverse:** Denomination

| Date | Mintage | F | VF | XF | Unc | BU |
|---|---|---|---|---|---|---|
| 1974(a) | — | 0.30 | 0.60 | 1.00 | 2.50 | — |
| 1976(a) | — | 0.30 | 0.60 | 1.00 | 2.50 | — |
| 1978(a) | — | 0.20 | 0.40 | 0.80 | 2.00 | — |
| 1979(a) | — | 0.20 | 0.40 | 0.80 | 2.00 | — |
| 1982(a) | — | 0.20 | 0.40 | 0.80 | 2.00 | — |
| 1985(a) | — | 0.20 | 0.40 | 0.80 | 2.00 | — |
| 1986(a) | — | 0.20 | 0.40 | 0.80 | 2.00 | — |
| 1988(a) | — | 0.20 | 0.40 | 0.80 | 2.00 | — |
| 1990(a) | — | 0.20 | 0.40 | 0.80 | 2.00 | — |
| 1992(a) | — | 0.20 | 0.40 | 0.80 | 2.00 | — |

**5 FRANCS** KM# 7 **Composition:** Aluminum-Bronze **Obverse:** Three giant eland **Reverse:** Denomination

| Date | Mintage | F | VF | XF | Unc | BU |
|---|---|---|---|---|---|---|
| 1973(a) | — | 0.15 | 0.30 | 0.60 | 1.65 | — |
| 1975(a) | — | 0.15 | 0.30 | 0.60 | 1.65 | — |
| 1976(a) | — | 0.15 | 0.30 | 0.60 | 1.65 | — |
| 1977(a) | — | 0.15 | 0.30 | 0.60 | 1.65 | — |
| 1978(a) | — | 0.15 | 0.30 | 0.60 | 1.65 | — |
| 1979(a) | — | 0.15 | 0.30 | 0.60 | 1.65 | — |
| 1980(a) | — | 0.15 | 0.30 | 0.60 | 1.35 | — |
| 1981(a) | — | 0.15 | 0.30 | 0.60 | 1.35 | — |
| 1982(a) | — | 0.15 | 0.30 | 0.60 | 1.35 | — |
| 1983(a) | — | 0.15 | 0.30 | 0.60 | 1.35 | — |
| 1984(a) | — | 0.15 | 0.30 | 0.60 | 1.35 | — |
| 1985(a) | — | 0.15 | 0.30 | 0.60 | 1.35 | — |
| 1992(a) | — | 0.15 | 0.30 | 0.60 | 1.35 | — |

**10 FRANCS** KM# 9 **Composition:** Aluminum-Bronze **Obverse:** Three giant eland **Reverse:** Denomination

| Date | Mintage | F | VF | XF | Unc | BU |
|---|---|---|---|---|---|---|
| 1974(a) | — | 0.20 | 0.35 | 0.75 | 2.00 | — |
| 1975(a) | — | 0.20 | 0.35 | 0.75 | 2.00 | — |
| 1976(a) | — | 0.20 | 0.35 | 0.75 | 2.00 | — |
| 1977(a) | — | 0.20 | 0.35 | 0.75 | 2.00 | — |
| 1978(a) | — | 0.20 | 0.35 | 0.75 | 2.00 | — |
| 1979(a) | — | 0.20 | 0.35 | 0.75 | 2.00 | — |
| 1980(a) | — | 0.20 | 0.35 | 0.65 | 1.35 | — |
| 1981(a) | — | 0.20 | 0.35 | 0.65 | 1.35 | — |
| 1982(a) | — | 0.20 | 0.35 | 0.65 | 1.35 | — |
| 1983(a) | — | 0.20 | 0.35 | 0.65 | 1.35 | — |
| 1984(a) | — | 0.20 | 0.35 | 0.65 | 1.35 | — |
| 1985(a) | — | 0.20 | 0.35 | 0.65 | 1.35 | — |
| 1992(a) | — | 0.20 | 0.35 | 0.65 | 1.35 | — |
| 1996(a) | — | 0.20 | 0.35 | 0.75 | 1.65 | — |

**25 FRANCS** KM# 10 **Composition:** Aluminum-Bronze **Obverse:** Three giant eland **Reverse:** Denomination

| Date | Mintage | F | VF | XF | Unc | BU |
|---|---|---|---|---|---|---|
| 1975(a) | — | 0.50 | 1.00 | 1.75 | 3.00 | — |
| 1976(a) | — | 0.50 | 1.00 | 1.50 | 2.75 | — |
| 1978(a) | — | 0.50 | 1.00 | 1.50 | 2.75 | — |
| 1982(a) | — | 0.35 | 0.75 | 1.25 | 2.50 | — |
| 1983(a) | — | 0.35 | 0.75 | 1.25 | 2.50 | — |
| 1984(a) | — | 0.35 | 0.75 | 1.25 | 2.50 | — |
| 1985(a) | — | 0.35 | 0.75 | 1.25 | 2.50 | — |
| 1986(a) | — | 0.35 | 0.75 | 1.25 | 2.50 | — |
| 1996(a) | — | 0.35 | 0.75 | 1.25 | 2.50 | — |

**50 FRANCS** KM# 11 **Composition:** Nickel **Obverse:** Three giant eland **Reverse:** Denomination

| Date | Mintage | F | VF | XF | Unc | BU |
|---|---|---|---|---|---|---|
| 1976(a) A | 10,000,000 | 2.00 | 3.50 | 7.50 | 12.00 | — |
| 1976(a) B | Inc. above | 2.00 | 3.50 | 7.50 | 12.00 | — |
| 1976(a) C | Inc. above | 1.00 | 2.00 | 4.00 | 7.00 | — |
| 1976(a) D | Inc. above | 1.00 | 2.00 | 4.00 | 7.00 | — |
| 1976(a) E | Inc. above | 1.00 | 2.00 | 4.00 | 7.50 | — |
| 1977(a) A | — | 2.00 | 3.50 | 7.50 | 12.00 | — |
| 1977(a) B | — | 2.00 | 3.50 | 7.50 | 12.00 | — |
| 1977(a) C | — | 1.00 | 2.00 | 4.00 | 7.00 | — |
| 1977(a) D | — | 1.00 | 2.00 | 4.00 | 7.00 | — |
| 1977(a) E | — | 1.00 | 2.00 | 4.00 | 7.50 | — |
| 1978(a) A | — | 2.00 | 3.50 | 7.50 | 12.00 | — |
| 1978(a) B | — | 2.00 | 3.50 | 7.50 | 12.00 | — |
| 1978(a) C | — | 1.00 | 2.00 | 4.00 | 7.00 | — |
| 1978(a) D | — | 1.00 | 2.00 | 4.00 | 7.00 | — |
| 1979(a) E | — | 1.00 | 2.00 | 4.00 | 7.50 | — |
| 1980(a) A | — | 1.50 | 2.75 | 5.50 | 11.50 | — |
| 1980(a) C | — | 0.75 | 1.50 | 3.50 | 6.00 | — |
| 1981(a) C | — | 0.75 | 1.50 | 3.50 | 6.00 | — |
| 1981(a) D | — | 0.85 | 1.75 | 3.75 | 6.50 | — |
| 1982(a) A | — | 1.50 | 2.75 | 5.50 | 11.50 | — |
| 1983(a) B | — | 0.75 | 1.50 | 3.50 | 6.00 | — |
| 1983(a) D | — | 0.75 | 1.50 | 3.50 | 6.00 | — |
| 1983(a) E | — | 0.75 | 1.50 | 3.50 | 6.00 | — |
| 1984(a) A | — | 1.50 | 2.75 | 5.50 | 11.50 | — |
| 1984(a) B | — | 1.50 | 2.75 | 5.50 | 11.50 | — |
| 1984(a) C | — | 0.75 | 1.50 | 3.50 | 6.00 | — |
| 1984(a) D | — | 0.75 | 1.50 | 3.50 | 6.00 | — |
| 1985(a) A | — | 1.50 | 2.75 | 5.50 | 11.50 | — |
| 1985(a) B | — | 1.50 | 2.75 | 5.50 | 11.50 | — |
| 1985(a) D | — | 0.75 | 1.50 | 3.50 | 6.00 | — |
| 1986(a) B | — | 1.50 | 2.75 | 5.50 | 11.50 | — |
| 1986(a) E | — | 0.85 | 1.75 | 3.75 | 6.50 | — |
| 1988(a) B | — | 1.50 | 2.75 | 5.50 | 11.50 | — |
| 1989(a) A | — | 1.50 | 2.75 | 5.50 | 11.50 | — |
| 1990(a) B | — | 1.50 | 2.75 | 5.50 | 11.50 | — |

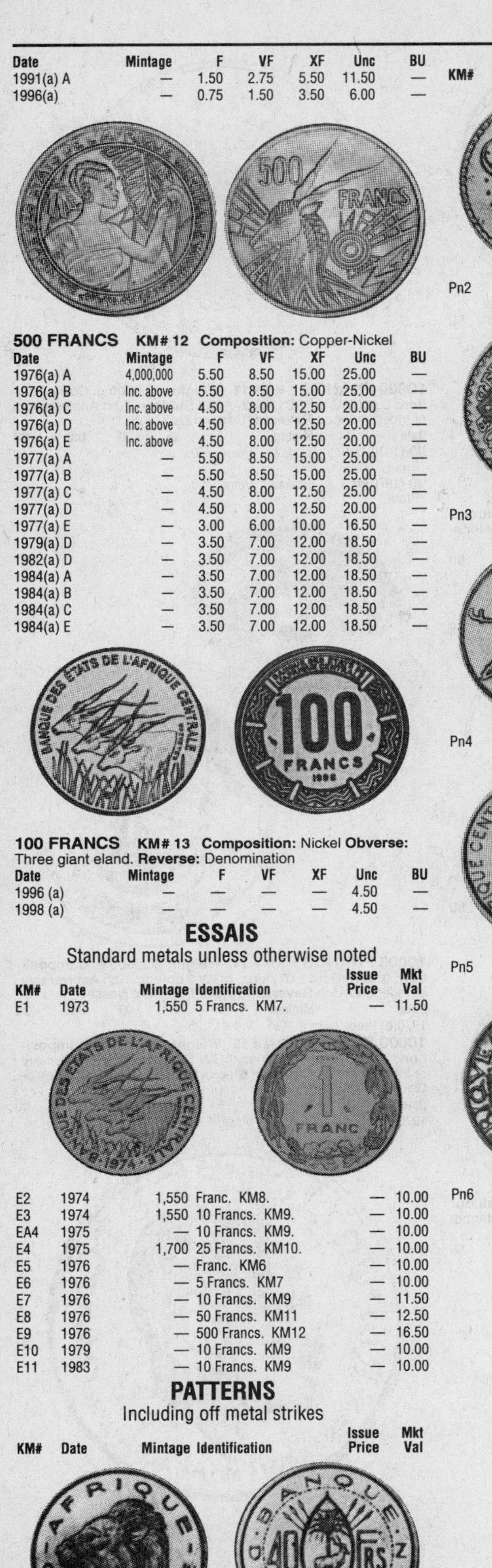

| Date | Mintage | F | VF | XF | Unc | BU |
|---|---|---|---|---|---|---|
| 1991(a) A | — | 1.50 | 2.75 | 5.50 | 11.50 | — |
| 1996(a) | — | 0.75 | 1.50 | 3.50 | 6.00 | — |

**500 FRANCS** KM# 12 **Composition:** Copper-Nickel

| Date | Mintage | F | VF | XF | Unc | BU |
|---|---|---|---|---|---|---|
| 1976(a) A | 4,000,000 | 5.50 | 8.50 | 15.00 | 25.00 | — |
| 1976(a) B | Inc. above | 5.50 | 8.50 | 15.00 | 25.00 | — |
| 1976(a) C | Inc. above | 4.50 | 8.00 | 12.50 | 20.00 | — |
| 1976(a) D | Inc. above | 4.50 | 8.00 | 12.50 | 20.00 | — |
| 1976(a) E | Inc. above | 4.50 | 8.00 | 12.50 | 20.00 | — |
| 1977(a) A | — | 5.50 | 8.50 | 15.00 | 25.00 | — |
| 1977(a) B | — | 5.50 | 8.50 | 15.00 | 25.00 | — |
| 1977(a) C | — | 4.50 | 8.00 | 12.50 | 25.00 | — |
| 1977(a) D | — | 4.50 | 8.00 | 12.50 | 20.00 | — |
| 1977(a) E | — | 3.00 | 6.00 | 10.00 | 16.50 | — |
| 1979(a) D | — | 3.50 | 7.00 | 12.00 | 18.50 | — |
| 1982(a) D | — | 3.50 | 7.00 | 12.00 | 18.50 | — |
| 1984(a) A | — | 3.50 | 7.00 | 12.00 | 18.50 | — |
| 1984(a) B | — | 3.50 | 7.00 | 12.00 | 18.50 | — |
| 1984(a) C | — | 3.50 | 7.00 | 12.00 | 18.50 | — |
| 1984(a) E | — | 3.50 | 7.00 | 12.00 | 18.50 | — |

**100 FRANCS** KM# 13 **Composition:** Nickel **Obverse:** Three giant eland. **Reverse:** Denomination

| Date | Mintage | F | VF | XF | Unc | BU |
|---|---|---|---|---|---|---|
| 1996 (a) | — | — | — | — | 4.50 | — |
| 1998 (a) | — | — | — | — | 4.50 | — |

## ESSAIS

Standard metals unless otherwise noted

| KM# | Date | Mintage | Identification | Issue Price | Mkt Val |
|---|---|---|---|---|---|
| E1 | 1973 | 1,550 | 5 Francs. KM7. | — | 11.50 |
| E2 | 1974 | 1,550 | Franc. KM8. | — | 10.00 |
| E3 | 1974 | 1,550 | 10 Francs. KM9. | — | 10.00 |
| EA4 | 1975 | — | 10 Francs. KM9. | — | 10.00 |
| E4 | 1975 | 1,700 | 25 Francs. KM10. | — | 10.00 |
| E5 | 1976 | — | Franc. KM6 | — | 10.00 |
| E6 | 1976 | — | 5 Francs. KM7 | — | 10.00 |
| E7 | 1976 | — | 10 Francs. KM9 | — | 11.50 |
| E8 | 1976 | — | 50 Francs. KM11 | — | 12.50 |
| E9 | 1976 | — | 500 Francs. KM12 | — | 16.50 |
| E10 | 1979 | — | 10 Francs. KM9 | — | 10.00 |
| E11 | 1983 | — | 10 Francs. KM9 | — | 10.00 |

## PATTERNS

Including off metal strikes

| KM# | Date | Mintage | Identification | Issue Price | Mkt Val |
|---|---|---|---|---|---|
| Pn1 | 1956 | 33 | 40 Francs. Aluminum-Bronze. | — | 375 |

| KM# | Date | Mintage | Identification | Issue Price | Mkt Val |
|---|---|---|---|---|---|
| Pn2 | 1956 | 33 | 40 Francs. Aluminum-Bronze. | — | 375 |
| Pn3 | 1956 | 33 | 40 Francs. Aluminum-Bronze. | — | 375 |
| Pn4 | 1956 | 33 | 40 Francs. Aluminum-Bronze. | — | 375 |
| Pn5 | 1956 | 33 | 40 Francs. Aluminum-Bronze. | — | 375 |
| Pn6 | 1956 | 33 | 40 Francs. Aluminum-Bronze. | — | 375 |

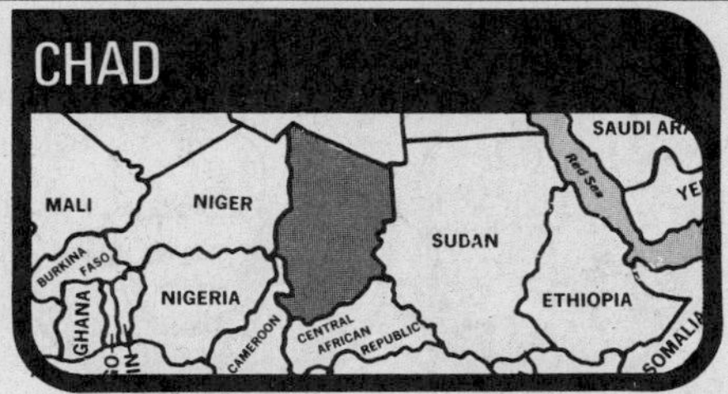


The Republic of Chad, a landlocked country of central Africa, is the largest country of former French Equatorial Africa. It has an area of 495,755 sq. mi. (1,284,000 sq. km.) and a population of *7.27 million. Capital: N'Djamena. An expanding livestock industry produces camels, cattle and sheep. Cotton (the chief product), ivory and palm oil are important exports.

Although supposedly known to Ptolemy, the Chad area was first visited by white men in 1823. Exaggerated estimates of its economic importance led to a race for its possession (1890-93), which resulted in the territory being divided by treaty between Great Britain, France and Germany. As a consequence of World War I, the German area was mandated to France in 1919. Chad was absorbed into the colony of French Equatorial Africa, as part of Ubangi-Shari, in 1910 and became a separate colony in 1920. Upon dissolution of French Equatorial Africa in 1959, the component states became autonomous members of the French Union. Chad became an independent republic on Aug. 11, 1960.

**NOTE**: For earlier and related coinage see French Equatorial Africa and the Equatorial African States. For later coinage see Central African States.

**MINT MARKS**

(a) - Paris, privy marks only
(b) = Brussels
NI - Numismatic Italiana, Arezzo, Italy

**COMMEMORATIVE EDGE INSCRIPTIONS**

1960 LIBERTE PROGRESS SOLIDARITE
1970/REPUBLIQUE DU TCHAD

# REPUBLIC

## DECIMAL COINAGE

**100 FRANCS** KM# 1 **Weight:** 5.0000 g. **Composition:** 0.9250 Silver .0957 oz. ASW **Subject:** 10th Anniversary of Independence **Reverse:** Robert Francis Kennedy

| Date | Mintage | F | VF | XF | Unc | BU |
|---|---|---|---|---|---|---|
| 1970(b) Proof | 975 | Value: 85.00 | | | | |

**100 FRANCS** KM# 2 **Composition:** Nickel **Obverse:** Three Giant Eland **Reverse:** Denomination

| Date | Mintage | F | VF | XF | Unc | BU |
|---|---|---|---|---|---|---|
| 1971(a) | 5,000,000 | 10.00 | 17.50 | 27.50 | 45.00 | — |
| 1972(a) | 5,000,000 | 10.00 | 17.50 | 27.50 | 45.00 | — |

**100 FRANCS** KM# 3 **Composition:** Nickel

| Date | Mintage | F | VF | XF | Unc | BU |
|---|---|---|---|---|---|---|
| 1975(a) | — | 9.00 | 15.00 | 22.00 | 35.00 | — |
| 1978(a) | — | 12.00 | 20.00 | 28.00 | 45.00 | — |
| 1980(a) | — | 10.00 | 17.50 | 25.00 | 40.00 | — |
| 1982(a) | — | 9.00 | 15.00 | 22.00 | 35.00 | — |
| 1984(a) | — | 9.00 | 15.00 | 22.00 | 35.00 | — |
| 1985(a) | — | 7.00 | 12.00 | 20.00 | 30.00 | — |
| 1988(a) | — | 7.00 | 12.00 | 20.00 | 30.00 | — |
| 1990(a) | — | 7.00 | 12.00 | 20.00 | 30.00 | — |

**200 FRANCS** **KM# 4** **Weight:** 15.0000 g. **Composition:** 0.9250 Silver .4461 oz. ASW **Subject:** 10th Anniversary of Independence **Reverse:** Martin Luther King, Jr

| Date | Mintage | F | VF | XF | Unc | BU |
|---|---|---|---|---|---|---|
| 1970(b) Proof | 952 | Value: 150 | | | | |

**200 FRANCS** **KM# 5** **Weight:** 15.0000 g. **Composition:** 0.8000 Silver .3858 oz. ASW **Subject:** 10th Anniversary of Independence **Reverse:** Charles de Gaulle

| Date | Mintage | F | VF | XF | Unc | BU |
|---|---|---|---|---|---|---|
| 1970(b) Proof | 442 | Value: 185 | | | | |

**200 FRANCS** **KM# 6** **Weight:** 15.0000 g. **Composition:** 0.8000 Silver .3858 oz. ASW **Subject:** 10th Anniversary of Independence **Reverse:** Egypt's President Nasser

| Date | Mintage | F | VF | XF | Unc | BU |
|---|---|---|---|---|---|---|
| 1970(b) Proof | 435 | Value: 150 | | | | |

**300 FRANCS** **KM# 7** **Weight:** 25.0000 g. **Composition:** 0.9250 Silver .8922 oz. ASW **Subject:** 10th Anniversary of Independence **Reverse:** John Fitzgerald Kennedy

| Date | Mintage | F | VF | XF | Unc | BU |
|---|---|---|---|---|---|---|
| 1970(b) Proof | 504 | Value: 500 | | | | |

**500 FRANCS** **KM# 13** **Composition:** Copper-Nickel

| Date | Mintage | F | VF | XF | Unc | BU |
|---|---|---|---|---|---|---|
| 1985(a) | — | 15.00 | 22.00 | 35.00 | 50.00 | — |

**1000 FRANCS** **KM# 8** **Weight:** 3.5000 g. **Composition:** 0.9000 Gold .1012 oz. AGW **Subject:** 10th Anniversary of Independence **Reverse:** Commandant Lamy

| Date | Mintage | F | VF | XF | Unc | BU |
|---|---|---|---|---|---|---|
| ND (1970)(a)NI Proof | 4,000 | Value: 180 | | | | |
| ND (1970)(a)NI Proof | Inc. above | Value: 180 | | | | |

**3000 FRANCS** **KM# 9** **Weight:** 10.5000 g. **Composition:** 0.9000 Gold .3038 oz. AGW **Subject:** 10th Anniversary of Independence **Reverse:** Governor Eboue

| Date | Mintage | F | VF | XF | Unc | BU |
|---|---|---|---|---|---|---|
| ND (1970)(a)NI | 4,000 | Value: 225 | | | | |
| ND (1970)NI | Inc. above | Value: 225 | | | | |

**5000 FRANCS** **KM# 10** **Weight:** 17.5000 g. **Composition:** 0.9000 Gold .5064 oz. AGW **Subject:** 10th Anniversary of Independence **Reverse:** General Leclerc

| Date | Mintage | F | VF | XF | Unc | BU |
|---|---|---|---|---|---|---|
| ND (1970)(a)NI Proof | 4,000 | Value: 345 | | | | |
| ND (1970)NI Proof | Inc. above | Value: 345 | | | | |

**10000 FRANCS** **KM# 11** **Weight:** 36.0000 g. **Composition:** 0.9000 Gold 1.0128 oz. AGW **Subject:** 10th Anniversary of Independence **Reverse:** General De Gaulle

| Date | Mintage | F | VF | XF | Unc | BU |
|---|---|---|---|---|---|---|
| ND (1970)(a)NI Proof | 4,000 | Value: 750 | | | | |
| ND (1970)NI Proof | Inc. above | Value: 750 | | | | |

**10000 FRANCS** **KM# 14** **Weight:** 36.0000 g. **Composition:** 0.9000 Gold 1.0128 oz. AGW **Subject:** 10th Anniversary of Independence **Reverse:** Egypt's President Nasser

| Date | Mintage | F | VF | XF | Unc | BU |
|---|---|---|---|---|---|---|
| 1970(b) Proof | 205 | Value: 1,250 | | | | |

**10000 FRANCS** **KM# 15** **Weight:** 36.0000 g. **Composition:** 0.9000 Gold 1.0128 oz. AGW **Subject:** 10th Anniversary of Independence **Obverse:** Map of Africa **Reverse:** Charles de Gaulle facing

| Date | Mintage | F | VF | XF | Unc | BU |
|---|---|---|---|---|---|---|
| 1970 Proof | 90 | Value: 1,450 | | | | |

**20000 FRANCS** KM# 12 **Weight:** 70.0000 g. **Composition:** 0.9000 Gold 2.0257 oz. AGW **Subject:** 10th Anniversary of Independence **Reverse:** Francois Tombalbaye

| Date | Mintage | F | VF | XF | Unc | BU |
|---|---|---|---|---|---|---|
| ND (1970)(a)NI Proof | Est. 4,000 | Value: 1,750 | | | | |
| ND (1970)NI Proof | Inc. above | Value: 1,750 | | | | |

## ESSAIS

Standard metals unless otherwise noted

| KM# | Date | Mintage | Identification | Issue Price | Mkt Val |
|---|---|---|---|---|---|
| E1 | 1970 | — | 10000 Francs. Copper-Nickel-Aluminum. KM11. | — | 125 |

| KM# | Date | Mintage | Identification | Issue Price | Mkt Val |
|---|---|---|---|---|---|
| E3 | 1971 | 1,700 | 100 Francs. KM2. | — | 23.50 |
| E4 | 1971 | 4 | 100 Francs. Gold. KM2. | — | 1,250 |
| E5 | 1975 | 1,700 | 100 Francs. KM3. | — | 22.50 |

| KM# | Date | Mintage | Identification | Issue Price | Mkt Val |
|---|---|---|---|---|---|
| E6 | 1985 | 1,700 | 500 Francs. KM13. | — | 70.00 |

## PROOF SETS

| KM# | Date | Mintage | Identification | Issue Price | Mkt Val |
|---|---|---|---|---|---|
| PS2 | 1970 (3) | — | KM1, 4, 7 | 33.00 | 735 |
| PS1 | 1970 (5) | 4,000 | KM8-12 | 412 | 3,250 |

# CHILE

The Republic of Chile, a ribbon-like country on the Pacific coast of southern South America, has an area of 292,135 sq. mi. (756,950 sq. km.) and a population of *15.21 million. Capital: Santiago. Historically, the economic base of Chile has been the rich mineral deposits of its northern provinces. Copper has accounted for more than 75 percent of Chile's export earnings in recent years. Other important mineral exports are iron ore, iodine and nitrate of soda. Fresh fruits and vegetables, as well as wine are increasingly significant in inter-hemispheric trade.

Diego de Almargo was the first Spaniard to attempt to wrest Chile from the Incas and Araucanian tribes in 1536. He failed, and was followed by Pedro de Valdivia, a favorite of Pizarro, who founded Santiago in 1541. When the Napoleonic Wars involved Spain, leaving the constituent parts of the Spanish Empire to their own devices, Chilean patriots formed a national government and proclaimed the country's independence, Sept. 18, 1810. Independence however, was not secured until Feb. 12, 1818, after a bitter struggle led by Bernardo O'Higgins and San Martin. Despite a long steady history of monetary devaluation, reflected in declining weight and fineness in its currency, Chile developed a strong democracy. This was displaced when rampant inflation characterized chaotic and subsequently repressive governments in the mid to late 20th century.

**RULERS**
Spanish until 1818

**MINT MARKS**
So - Santiago

**MONETARY SYSTEM**
16 Reales = 1 Escudo

## REPUBLIC

### DECIMAL COINAGE

**CENTAVO** KM# 161 **Composition:** Copper

| Date | Mintage | VG | F | VF | XF | Unc |
|---|---|---|---|---|---|---|
| 1904 | 970,000 | 0.50 | 1.00 | 2.00 | 6.00 | — |
| 1908 | 174,000 | 0.65 | 1.25 | 3.00 | 9.00 | — |
| 1919 | 173,000 | 0.50 | 1.00 | 2.50 | 8.50 | — |

**2 CENTAVOS** KM# 164 **Composition:** Copper

| Date | Mintage | F | VF | XF | Unc | BU |
|---|---|---|---|---|---|---|
| 1919 | 147,000 | 1.50 | 3.00 | 6.00 | 17.50 | — |

**2-1/2 CENTAVOS (Dos I Medio)** KM# 162 **Composition:** Copper

| Date | Mintage | F | VF | XF | Unc | BU |
|---|---|---|---|---|---|---|
| 1904 | 277,000 | 2.75 | 7.50 | 20.00 | 50.00 | — |
| 1906/4 | 161,000 | 3.50 | 10.00 | 22.00 | 55.00 | — |
| 1906 | Inc. above | 3.50 | 10.00 | 22.00 | 55.00 | — |
| 1907/4 | 262,000 | 2.75 | 7.50 | 20.00 | 45.00 | — |
| 1907 | Inc. above | 2.75 | 7.50 | 20.00 | 45.00 | — |
| **Note:** Varieties exist for 1907 dated coins | | | | | | |
| 1908/4 | 201,000 | 2.50 | 7.00 | 19.00 | 45.00 | — |
| 1908 | Inc. above | 2.50 | 7.00 | 19.00 | 45.00 | — |

**5 CENTAVOS** KM# 155.2 **Weight:** 1.0000 g. **Composition:** 0.5000 Silver .0160 oz. ASW **Obverse:** 0.5 below condor **Note:** Varieties exist with 0.5, 0.5., 0/5.5., 0,5 or 05. below condor.

| Date | Mintage | F | VF | XF | Unc | BU |
|---|---|---|---|---|---|---|
| 1901/801 | 2,109,000 | 3.00 | 5.00 | 8.50 | 22.00 | — |
| 1901/891 | Inc. above | 3.00 | 5.00 | 8.50 | 22.00 | — |
| 1901 | Inc. above | 2.00 | 3.00 | 5.00 | 16.00 | — |
| 1904/894 | 2,527,000 | — | — | — | — | — |
| 1904/1 | Inc. above | 3.50 | 7.00 | 12.50 | 30.00 | — |
| 1904 | Inc. above | 2.00 | 3.00 | 5.00 | 16.00 | — |
| 1906/4 | 713,000 | — | — | — | — | — |
| 1906 | Inc. above | 2.00 | 3.00 | 6.00 | 18.50 | — |
| 1907 | 2,791,000 | 2.00 | 3.00 | 5.00 | 16.00 | — |
| 1909/899 | — | 2.50 | 4.00 | 7.00 | 20.00 | — |

**5 CENTAVOS** KM# 155.2a **Weight:** 1.0000 g. **Composition:** 0.4000 Silver .0128 oz. ASW

| Date | Mintage | F | VF | XF | Unc | BU |
|---|---|---|---|---|---|---|
| 1908 | 3,642,000 | 2.00 | 3.00 | 5.00 | 10.00 | — |
| 1909/1 | 1,177,000 | 2.00 | 4.00 | 6.00 | 12.50 | — |
| 1909 | Inc. above | 2.00 | 4.00 | 6.00 | 12.50 | — |
| 1909/8 | Inc. above | 2.00 | 4.00 | 6.00 | 12.50 | — |
| 1910/01 | 1,587,000 | 2.00 | 3.00 | 5.00 | 10.00 | — |
| 1910 | Inc. above | 2.00 | 3.00 | 5.00 | 10.00 | — |
| 1911 | 847,000 | 2.00 | 4.00 | 6.00 | 12.50 | — |
| 1913/2 | 2,573,000 | 2.00 | 5.00 | 10.00 | 20.00 | — |
| **Note:** Varieties exist with a dot below 1 in date for 1913 | | | | | | |
| 1913 | Inc. above | 2.00 | 3.00 | 5.00 | 10.00 | — |
| **Note:** Varieties exist with a dot below 1 in date for 1913 | | | | | | |
| 1919 | | 1.50 | 3.00 | 5.00 | 10.00 | — |

**5 CENTAVOS** KM# 155.3 **Weight:** 1.0000 g. **Composition:** 0.4500 Silver .0144 oz. ASW **Obverse:** 0.45 below condor

| Date | Mintage | F | VF | XF | Unc | BU |
|---|---|---|---|---|---|---|
| 1915 | 2,250,000 | 1.50 | 3.00 | 5.00 | 10.00 | — |
| **Note:** 1915 exists with flat and curved top on 5 | | | | | | |
| 1916/1 | 4,337,000 | 1.50 | 3.50 | 6.00 | 12.00 | — |
| 1916/5 | Inc. above | 1.50 | 0.50 | 6.00 | 12.00 | — |
| 1916 | Inc. above | 1.50 | 3.00 | 5.00 | 10.00 | — |
| 1919/1 | 1,494,000 | 3.00 | 5.00 | 10.00 | 20.00 | — |
| 1919/5 | Inc. above | 2.00 | 4.00 | 6.00 | 12.00 | — |
| 1919 | Inc. above | 3.00 | 5.00 | 10.00 | 20.00 | — |

**5 CENTAVOS** KM# 165 **Composition:** Copper-Nickel **Obverse:** Without designer's name O. ROTY at bottom **Note:** Varieties exist.

| Date | Mintage | F | VF | XF | Unc | BU |
|---|---|---|---|---|---|---|
| 1920 | 718,000 | 1.00 | 1.50 | 3.00 | 10.00 | — |
| 1921 | 2,406,000 | 0.50 | 1.25 | 2.00 | 5.00 | — |
| 1922 | 3,872,000 | 0.50 | 1.25 | 2.00 | 5.00 | — |
| 1923 | 2,150,000 | 0.50 | 1.25 | 2.00 | 5.00 | — |
| 1925 | 994,000 | 0.50 | 1.25 | 2.00 | 5.00 | — |
| 1926 | 594,000 | 1.50 | 2.50 | 3.00 | 6.50 | — |
| 1927 | 1,276,000 | 0.50 | 1.00 | 2.00 | 5.00 | — |
| 1928 | 5,197,000 | 0.50 | 1.00 | 2.00 | 5.00 | — |
| 1933 | 3,000,000 | 5.00 | 10.00 | 17.50 | 45.00 | — |
| 1934 | Inc. above | 0.25 | 0.50 | 1.00 | 2.00 | — |
| 1936 | 2,000,000 | 0.25 | 0.50 | 1.00 | 2.00 | — |
| 1937 | 2,000,000 | 0.25 | 0.50 | 1.00 | 2.00 | — |
| 1938 | 2,000,000 | 0.25 | 0.50 | 1.00 | 2.00 | — |

**10 CENTAVOS** **KM# 156.2** **Weight:** 2.0000 g. **Composition:** 0.5000 Silver .0321 oz. ASW **Obverse:** 0.5 below condor **Note:** Varieties exist for dated coins with 0.5, 0,5, 0.5. or 0.5/9 below condor.

| Date | Mintage | F | VF | XF | Unc | BU |
|---|---|---|---|---|---|---|
| 1900 | 104,000 | 20.00 | 35.00 | 50.00 | 85.00 | — |
| 1901/801 | Inc. above | 10.00 | 20.00 | 30.00 | 50.00 | — |
| 1901/891 | Inc. above | 15.00 | 25.00 | 35.00 | 60.00 | — |
| 1901 | Inc. above | 15.00 | 25.00 | 40.00 | 100 | — |
| 1904/899 | 779,000 | 2.00 | 3.50 | 7.00 | 16.50 | — |
| 1904 | Inc. above | 2.50 | 4.50 | 9.00 | 20.00 | — |
| 1906 | 139,000 | 2.50 | 4.50 | 8.50 | 18.00 | — |
| 1907 | 3,151,000 | 2.00 | 3.50 | 7.00 | 16.50 | — |

**10 CENTAVOS** **KM# 156.2a** **Weight:** 1.5000 g. **Composition:** 0.4000 Silver .0192 oz. ASW **Note:** Varities exist.

| Date | Mintage | F | VF | XF | Unc | BU |
|---|---|---|---|---|---|---|
| 1908 | 4,149,000 | 1.00 | 2.00 | 4.50 | 12.00 | — |
| 1908/inverted 6 | — | 1.50 | 3.00 | 6.00 | 15.00 | — |
| 1909/8 | 2,964,000 | 1.50 | 3.00 | 6.00 | 15.00 | — |
| 1909 | Inc. above | 1.00 | 2.00 | 4.50 | 12.00 | — |
| 1913 | 1,269,000 | 1.50 | 3.00 | 6.00 | 15.00 | — |
| 1919 | 883,000 | 2.50 | 5.00 | 9.00 | 18.50 | — |
| 1920 | 2,109,000 | 1.00 | 2.00 | 4.50 | 12.00 | — |

**10 CENTAVOS** **KM# 156.3** **Weight:** 1.5000 g. **Composition:** 0.4500 Silver .0217 oz. ASW **Obverse:** 0.45 below condor

| Date | Mintage | F | VF | XF | Unc | BU |
|---|---|---|---|---|---|---|
| 1915 | 1,620,000 | 1.00 | 1.50 | 3.00 | 6.50 | — |
| 1916 | 2,855,000 | 1.00 | 1.50 | 3.00 | 6.50 | — |
| 1917 | 736,000 | 1.50 | 2.50 | 5.00 | 12.50 | — |
| 1918 | Inc. above | 1.50 | 2.50 | 5.00 | 12.50 | — |

**10 CENTAVOS** **KM# 166** **Composition:** Copper-Nickel **Obverse:** Without designer's name O. ROTY at bottom **Edge:** Plain

| Date | Mintage | F | VF | XF | Unc | BU |
|---|---|---|---|---|---|---|
| 1920 | 451,000 | 1.50 | 3.50 | 5.00 | 10.00 | — |
| 1921 | 2,654,000 | 0.50 | 0.75 | 1.50 | 3.00 | — |
| 1922 | 4,017,000 | 0.50 | 0.75 | 1.50 | 3.00 | — |
| 1923 | 3,356,000 | 0.50 | 0.75 | 7.00 | 16.50 | — |
| 1924 | 1,445,000 | 0.50 | 0.75 | 1.50 | 3.00 | — |
| 1925 | 2,665,000 | 0.50 | 0.75 | 1.50 | 3.00 | — |
| 1927 | 523,000 | 1.00 | 2.00 | 3.00 | 6.00 | — |
| 1928 | 3,052,000 | 0.50 | 0.75 | 1.50 | 3.00 | — |
| 1932 | 1,500,000 | 0.75 | 1.00 | 2.00 | 4.00 | — |
| 1933/2 | 5,800,000 | — | — | — | — | — |
| 1933 | Inc. above | 0.25 | 0.50 | 1.00 | 2.00 | — |
| 1934 | 900,000 | 0.50 | 0.75 | 1.50 | 3.00 | — |
| 1935 | 1,500,000 | 0.50 | 0.75 | 1.50 | 3.00 | — |
| 1936 | 3,300,000 | 0.25 | 0.50 | 1.00 | 2.00 | — |
| 1937 | 2,000,000 | 0.25 | 0.50 | 1.00 | 2.00 | — |
| 1938 | 5,000,000 | 0.25 | 0.50 | 1.00 | 2.00 | — |
| 1939 | 1,200,000 | 0.25 | 0.50 | 1.00 | 2.00 | — |
| 1940 | 6,100,000 | 0.25 | 0.50 | 1.00 | 2.00 | — |
| 1941 | 900,000 | 1.00 | 2.00 | 3.00 | 6.00 | — |

**20 CENTAVOS** **KM# 151.2** **Weight:** 4.0000 g. **Composition:** 0.5000 Silver .0643 oz. ASW **Obverse:** 0.5 below condor **Note:** Varieties with 0.5 or 0.5. exist.

| Date | Mintage | F | VF | XF | Unc | BU |
|---|---|---|---|---|---|---|
| 1900/899 | 334,000 | 60.00 | 80.00 | — | — | — |
| 1900 | Inc. above | 30.00 | 40.00 | 80.00 | 150 | — |
| 1906/896 | 866,000 | 2.50 | 4.00 | 6.00 | 15.00 | — |
| 1906 | Inc. above | 2.00 | 3.50 | 4.50 | 9.00 | — |
| 1907/895 | 7,625,000 | 2.00 | 3.00 | 4.00 | 8.50 | — |
| 1907 | Inc. above | 1.00 | 2.00 | 3.00 | 7.50 | — |

**20 CENTAVOS** **KM# 151.3** **Weight:** 3.0000 g. **Composition:** 0.4000 Silver .0385 oz. ASW **Obverse:** Without 0.5 below condor

| Date | Mintage | F | VF | XF | Unc | BU |
|---|---|---|---|---|---|---|
| 1907 | 1,201,000 | 1.00 | 1.50 | 3.00 | 7.50 | — |
| 1908 | 5,869,000 | 0.75 | 1.25 | 2.50 | 6.50 | — |
| 1909 | 1,080,000 | 0.75 | 1.25 | 2.50 | 6.50 | — |
| 1913/1 | 3,507,000 | — | — | — | — | — |
| 1913/50 | Inc. above | 0.75 | 1.25 | 2.50 | 6.50 | — |
| 1913 | Inc. above | 1.50 | 2.50 | 4.00 | 9.00 | — |
| 1919 | 3,749,000 | 0.75 | 1.25 | 2.50 | 6.50 | — |
| 1920 | 4,189,000 | 0.75 | 1.25 | 2.50 | 6.50 | — |

**20 CENTAVOS** **KM# 151.4** **Weight:** 3.0000 g. **Composition:** 0.4500 Silver .0434 oz. ASW **Obverse:** 0.45 below condor

| Date | Mintage | F | VF | XF | Unc | BU |
|---|---|---|---|---|---|---|
| 1916 | 3,377,000 | 2.00 | 3.00 | 5.00 | 10.00 | — |

**20 CENTAVOS** **KM# 167.1** **Composition:** Copper-Nickel **Obverse:** Without designer's name O. ROTY at bottom **Reverse:** Large 20 **Edge:** Plain

| Date | Mintage | F | VF | XF | Unc | BU |
|---|---|---|---|---|---|---|
| 1920 | 499,000 | 1.00 | 2.50 | 5.50 | 13.50 | — |
| 1921 | 6,547,000 | 0.35 | 0.75 | 1.25 | 3.50 | — |
| 1922 | 8,261,000 | 0.35 | 0.75 | 1.25 | 3.50 | — |
| 1923 | 5,439,000 | 0.35 | 0.75 | 1.25 | 3.50 | — |
| 1924 | 16,096,000 | 0.35 | 0.75 | 1.25 | 3.50 | — |
| 1925 Varieties exist with dot under 5 in date for 1925 | 9,830,000 | 0.35 | 0.75 | 1.25 | 3.50 | — |
| 1929 | 9,685,000 | 0.35 | 0.75 | 1.25 | 3.50 | — |

**20 CENTAVOS** **KM# 167.2** **Composition:** Copper-Nickel **Obverse:** Without designer's name **Reverse:** Small 20

| Date | Mintage | F | VF | XF | Unc | BU |
|---|---|---|---|---|---|---|
| 1925 | — | — | — | — | — | — |
| 1932 | — | 0.50 | 1.00 | 2.00 | 4.50 | — |
| 1933/ Reversed 33 | 59,000,000 | — | — | — | — | — |
| 1933 | Inc. above | 0.35 | 0.75 | 1.25 | 3.50 | — |
| 1937 | — | 0.50 | 1.00 | 2.00 | 4.50 | — |

**20 CENTAVOS** **KM# 167.4** **Composition:** Copper-Nickel **Obverse:** With designer's name O. ROTY at bottom

| Date | Mintage | F | VF | XF | Unc | BU |
|---|---|---|---|---|---|---|
| 1929 | Inc. above | 1.00 | 2.50 | 5.00 | 10.00 | — |

**20 CENTAVOS** **KM# 167.3** **Composition:** Copper-Nickel **Obverse:** With designer's name O. ROTY at bottom

| Date | Mintage | F | VF | XF | Unc | BU |
|---|---|---|---|---|---|---|
| 1932 | — | 0.35 | 0.75 | 1.25 | 3.50 | — |
| 1933/ Reversed 33 | 1,000,000 | 1.00 | 1.50 | 2.50 | 6.00 | — |
| 1933 | Inc. above | 0.35 | 0.75 | 1.25 | 3.50 | — |
| 1937 | — | 0.35 | 0.75 | 1.25 | 3.50 | — |
| 1938 | 3,043,000 | 0.35 | 0.75 | 1.25 | 3.50 | — |
| 1939 3/reversed 3 | 5,283,000 | 1.00 | 1.50 | 2.50 | 6.00 | — |
| 1939 | Inc. above | 0.35 | 0.75 | 1.25 | 3.50 | — |
| 1940 | 9,300,000 | 0.35 | 0.75 | 1.25 | 3.00 | — |
| 1941 | 3,000,000 | 0.35 | 0.75 | 1.25 | 3.50 | — |

**20 CENTAVOS** **KM# 177** **Composition:** Copper **Obverse:** Bust of General Bernardo O'Higgins, Thenot on truncation

| Date | Mintage | F | VF | XF | Unc | BU |
|---|---|---|---|---|---|---|
| 1942 | 30,000,000 | 0.15 | 0.25 | 0.50 | 1.65 | — |
| 1943 | 396,000,000 | 0.15 | 0.25 | 0.50 | 1.65 | — |
| 1944 | 29,100,000 | 0.15 | 0.25 | 0.50 | 1.65 | — |
| 1945 | 11,400,000 | 0.15 | 0.25 | 0.50 | 1.65 | — |
| 1946 | 13,800,000 | 0.15 | 0.25 | 0.50 | 1.65 | — |
| 1947 | 15,700,000 | 0.15 | 0.25 | 0.50 | 1.65 | — |
| 1948 | 15,200,000 | 0.15 | 0.25 | 0.50 | 1.65 | — |
| 1949 | 14,700,000 | 0.15 | 0.25 | 0.50 | 1.65 | — |
| 1950 | 15,200,000 | 0.15 | 0.25 | 0.50 | 1.65 | — |
| 1951 | 14,700,000 | 0.15 | 0.25 | 0.50 | 1.65 | — |
| 1952 | 15,500,000 | 0.15 | 0.25 | 0.50 | 1.65 | — |
| 1953 | 7,800,000 | 0.15 | 0.25 | 0.50 | 1.65 | — |

**40 CENTAVOS** **KM# 163** **Weight:** 6.0000 g. **Composition:** 0.4000 Silver .0771 oz. ASW

| Date | Mintage | F | VF | XF | Unc | BU |
|---|---|---|---|---|---|---|
| 1907 | 56,000 | 15.00 | 25.00 | 50.00 | 125 | — |
| 1908 | 1,452,000 | 3.50 | 7.00 | 15.00 | 35.00 | — |

**50 CENTAVOS** **KM# 160** **Weight:** 10.0000 g. **Composition:** 0.7000 Silver .2250 oz. ASW **Note:** Varieties with 0.7 or 0.7. exist.

| Date | Mintage | F | VF | XF | Unc | BU |
|---|---|---|---|---|---|---|
| 1902 | 2,022,000 | 3.50 | 6.00 | 12.00 | 28.00 | — |
| 1903 | 1,111,000 | 3.50 | 6.00 | 12.00 | 28.00 | — |
| 1905 | 1,075,000 | 3.50 | 6.00 | 12.00 | 28.00 | — |

**50 CENTAVOS** **KM# 178** **Composition:** Copper **Obverse:** Bust of General Bernardo O'Higgins, Thenot on truncation **Edge:** Plain

| Date | Mintage | F | VF | XF | Unc | BU |
|---|---|---|---|---|---|---|
| 1942 | 4,715,000 | 1.00 | 2.00 | 5.00 | — | — |

**PESO** **KM# 152.2** **Weight:** 20.0000 g. **Composition:** 0.7000 Silver .4501 oz. ASW **Obverse:** 0.7 below condor

| Date | Mintage | F | VF | XF | Unc | BU |
|---|---|---|---|---|---|---|
| 1902 | 178,000 | 8.00 | 17.50 | 35.00 | 65.00 | — |
| 1903 | 372,000 | 6.00 | 12.50 | 18.50 | 42.50 | — |
| 1905 | 429,000 | 6.00 | 12.50 | 18.50 | 42.50 | — |

PESO KM# 152.3 Weight: 12.0000 g. Composition: 0.9000 Silver .3472 oz. ASW Obverse: 0.9 below condor

| Date | Mintage | F | VF | XF | Unc | BU |
|---|---|---|---|---|---|---|
| 1910 | 2,166,000 | 4.00 | 6.00 | 12.00 | 22.50 | — |

PESO KM# 152.4 Weight: 9.0000 g. Composition: 0.7200 Silver .2083 oz. ASW Obverse: 0.72 below condor

| Date | Mintage | F | VF | XF | Unc | BU |
|---|---|---|---|---|---|---|
| 1915 | 6,032,000 | 3.75 | 5.00 | 6.50 | 15.00 | — |
| 1917 | 3,033,000 | 4.00 | 5.50 | 8.00 | 17.50 | — |

PESO KM# 152.5 Weight: 9.0000 g. Composition: 0.5000 Silver .1446 oz. ASW Obverse: 0.5 below condor

| Date | Mintage | F | VF | XF | Unc | BU |
|---|---|---|---|---|---|---|
| 1921 | 2,287,000 | 2.25 | 3.50 | 5.00 | 10.00 | — |
| 1922 | 2,718,000 | 2.25 | 3.50 | 5.00 | 10.00 | — |

PESO KM# 152.6 Weight: 9.0000 g. Composition: 0.5000 Silver .1446 oz. ASW Note: Struck with medal rotation.

| Date | Mintage | F | VF | XF | Unc | BU |
|---|---|---|---|---|---|---|
| 1924 | 1,748,000 | 2.25 | 3.50 | 5.00 | 10.00 | — |
| 1925 Varieties of 1925 dated coins exist with flat and curved tops | 2,037,000 | 2.25 | 3.50 | 5.00 | 10.00 | — |

PESO KM# 171.2 Weight: 9.0000 g. Composition: 0.5000 Silver .1446 oz. ASW Reverse: Thick 1 in denomination Note: Varieties 0.5 and 0,5 exist. Total of 2,431,608 pieces dated 1921-1927 were melted down in 1932.

| Date | Mintage | F | VF | XF | Unc | BU |
|---|---|---|---|---|---|---|
| 1927So | — | 4.00 | 6.00 | 10.00 | 18.00 | — |

PESO KM# A171.1 Weight: 9.0000 g. Composition: 0.5000 Silver .1446 oz. ASW Obverse: KM#152.5 Reverse: KM#171 Note: Without mint mark. Mule.

| Date | Mintage | F | VF | XF | Unc | BU |
|---|---|---|---|---|---|---|
| 1927 | — | 15.00 | 30.00 | 45.00 | 90.00 | — |

PESO KM# 171.1 Weight: 9.0000 g. Composition: 0.5000 Silver .1446 oz. ASW Reverse: Thin 1 in denomination

| Date | Mintage | F | VF | XF | Unc | BU |
|---|---|---|---|---|---|---|
| 1927So | 3,890,000 | 4.00 | 6.00 | 10.00 | 18.00 | — |

PESO KM# 174 Weight: 6.0000 g. Composition: 0.4000 Silver .0771 oz. ASW

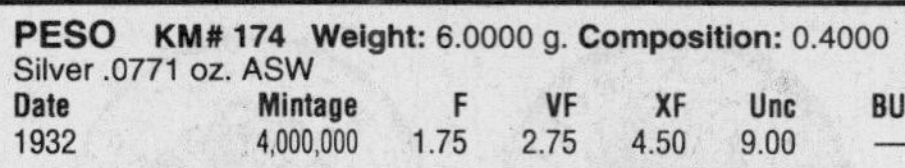

| Date | Mintage | F | VF | XF | Unc | BU |
|---|---|---|---|---|---|---|
| 1932 | 4,000,000 | 1.75 | 2.75 | 4.50 | 9.00 | — |

PESO KM# 176.1 Composition: Copper-Nickel

| Date | Mintage | F | VF | XF | Unc | BU |
|---|---|---|---|---|---|---|
| 1933 | 29,976,000 | 0.35 | 0.75 | 1.75 | 3.50 | — |

PESO KM# 176.2 Composition: Copper-Nickel Obverse: O ROTY incuse on rock base

| Date | Mintage | F | VF | XF | Unc | BU |
|---|---|---|---|---|---|---|
| 1940 | 150,000 | 1.50 | 2.50 | 3.50 | 7.50 | — |

PESO KM# 179 Composition: Copper Obverse: General Bernardo O'Higgins

| Date | Mintage | F | VF | XF | Unc | BU |
|---|---|---|---|---|---|---|
| 1942 | 15,150,000 | 0.10 | 0.35 | 1.00 | 4.00 | — |
| 1943 | 16,900,000 | 0.10 | 0.35 | 1.00 | 4.00 | — |
| 1944 | 12,050,000 | 0.10 | 0.35 | 1.00 | 5.00 | — |
| 1945 | 7,600,000 | 0.10 | 0.35 | 1.00 | 5.00 | — |
| 1946 | 2,050,000 | 0.10 | 0.35 | 1.50 | 7.50 | — |
| 1947 | 2,200,000 | 0.10 | 0.35 | 1.50 | 7.50 | — |
| 1948 | 5,900,000 | 0.10 | 0.25 | 0.75 | 3.75 | — |
| 1949 | 7,100,000 | 0.10 | 0.20 | 0.45 | 2.25 | — |
| 1950 | 7,250,000 | 0.10 | 0.20 | 0.45 | 2.25 | — |
| 1951 | 8,150,000 | 0.10 | 0.20 | 0.45 | 2.25 | — |
| 1952 | 10,400,000 | 0.10 | 0.20 | 0.45 | 2.25 | — |
| 1953 Short top 5 | 17,200,000 | 0.10 | 0.20 | 0.40 | 1.50 | — |
| 1953 Long top 5 | Inc. above | 0.10 | 0.20 | 0.40 | 1.50 | — |
| 1954 | 7,566,000 | 0.10 | 0.20 | 0.40 | 1.50 | — |

PESO KM# 179a Composition: Aluminum

| Date | Mintage | F | VF | XF | Unc | BU |
|---|---|---|---|---|---|---|
| 1954 | 43,550,000 | 0.10 | 0.15 | 0.25 | 0.40 | — |
| 1955 | 69,050,000 | 0.10 | 0.15 | 0.25 | 0.40 | — |
| 1956 | 58,250,000 | 0.10 | 0.15 | 0.25 | 0.40 | — |
| 1956 Proof | — | — | — | — | — | — |
| 1957 | 49,250,000 | 0.10 | 0.15 | 0.25 | 0.40 | — |
| 1958 | 29,900 | 0.10 | 0.15 | 0.25 | 0.40 | — |

2 PESOS KM# 172 Weight: 18.0000 g. Composition: 0.5000 Silver .2893 oz. ASW Note: Varieties 0.5 and 0,5 with curved top and flat top 5 exist. 459,510 pieces were melted down in 1932.

| Date | Mintage | F | VF | XF | Unc | BU |
|---|---|---|---|---|---|---|
| 1927 | 1,060,000 | BV | 4.00 | 9.00 | 18.50 | — |

5 PESOS KM# 159 Weight: 2.9955 g. Composition: 0.9170 Gold .0883 oz. AGW

| Date | Mintage | F | VF | XF | Unc | BU |
|---|---|---|---|---|---|---|
| 1900 | 1,265,000 | 50.00 | 90.00 | 120 | 150 | — |
| 1911 | 1,399 | — | — | 200 | 350 | — |

5 PESOS KM# 173.1 Weight: 25.0000 g. Composition: 0.9000 Silver .7234 oz. ASW Reverse: Wide 5

| Date | Mintage | F | VF | XF | Unc | BU |
|---|---|---|---|---|---|---|
| 1927 | 965,000 | 10.00 | 13.50 | 20.00 | 45.00 | — |

5 PESOS KM# 173.2 Weight: 25.0000 g. Composition: 0.9000 Silver .7234 oz. ASW Reverse: Narrow 5 Note: Varieties 0.9 and 0,9 exist. 436,510 pieces of KM#173.1 and #173.2 were melted down in 1932.

| Date | Mintage | F | VF | XF | Unc | BU |
|---|---|---|---|---|---|---|
| 1927 | Inc. above | 10.00 | 13.50 | 20.00 | 45.00 | — |

5 PESOS KM# 180 Composition: Aluminum

| Date | Mintage | F | VF | XF | Unc | BU |
|---|---|---|---|---|---|---|
| 1956 | 1,600,000 | 0.15 | 0.35 | 0.50 | 0.85 | — |

5 PESOS KM# 182 Weight: 22.5000 g. Composition: 0.9990 Silver .7228 oz. ASW Subject: 150th Anniversary of Naval Academy Reverse: Bust of Arturo Prat

| Date | Mintage | F | VF | XF | Unc | BU |
|---|---|---|---|---|---|---|
| 1968 Proof | 1,200 | Value: 25.00 | | | | |

10 PESOS KM# 157 Weight: 5.9910 g. Composition: 0.9170 Gold .1766 oz. AGW

| Date | Mintage | F | VF | XF | Unc | BU |
|---|---|---|---|---|---|---|
| 1901 | 1,651,000 | BV | 100 | 125 | 200 | — |

**10 PESOS** KM# 181 **Composition:** Aluminum

| Date | Mintage | F | VF | XF | Unc | BU |
|---|---|---|---|---|---|---|
| 1956 | 13,100,000 | 0.15 | 0.35 | 0.50 | 0.75 | — |
| 1957 | 28,800,000 | 0.15 | 0.35 | 0.50 | 0.75 | — |
| 1958 | 44,500,000 | 0.15 | 0.35 | 0.50 | 0.75 | — |
| 1959 | 10,220,000 | 0.25 | 0.50 | 1.00 | 1.50 | — |

**10 PESOS** KM# 183 **Weight:** 45.0000 g. **Composition:** 0.9990 Silver 1.4455 oz. ASW **Subject:** Arrival of Liberation Fleet in 1820

| Date | Mintage | F | VF | XF | Unc | BU |
|---|---|---|---|---|---|---|
| 1968 Proof | 1,215 | Value: 85.00 | | | | |

**20 PESOS** KM# 158 **Weight:** 11.9821 g. **Composition:** 0.9170 Gold .3532 oz. AGW

| Date | Mintage | F | VF | XF | Unc | BU |
|---|---|---|---|---|---|---|
| 1906 | 41,000 | — | BV | 165 | 275 | — |
| 1907 | 12,000 | — | BV | 165 | 275 | — |
| 1908 | 26,000 | — | BV | 165 | 275 | — |
| 1910 | 28,000 | — | BV | 165 | 275 | — |
| 1911 | 17,000 | — | BV | 165 | 275 | — |
| 1913/11 | 18,000 | — | BV | 165 | 275 | — |
| 1913 | Inc. above | — | BV | 165 | 275 | — |
| 1914 | 22,000 | — | BV | 165 | 275 | — |
| 1915 | 65,000 | — | BV | 165 | 275 | — |
| 1916 | 36,000 | — | BV | 165 | 275 | — |
| 1917 | 717,000 | — | BV | 165 | 275 | — |

**20 PESOS** KM# 168 **Weight:** 4.0679 g. **Composition:** 0.9000 Gold .1177 oz. AGW

| Date | Mintage | F | VF | XF | Unc | BU |
|---|---|---|---|---|---|---|
| 1926 | 85,000 | — | BV | 65.00 | 90.00 | — |
| 1958 | 500 | BV | 65.00 | 125 | 200 | — |
| 1959 | 25,000 | — | — | BV | 70.00 | — |
| 1961 | 20,000 | — | — | BV | 70.00 | — |
| 1964 | — | — | — | BV | 70.00 | — |
| 1976 | 99,000 | — | — | BV | 70.00 | — |
| 1977 | 38,000 | — | — | BV | 70.00 | — |
| 1979 | 30,000 | — | — | BV | 70.00 | — |
| 1980 | 30,000 | — | — | BV | 70.00 | — |

**20 PESOS** KM# 188 **Weight:** 4.0679 g. **Composition:** 0.9000 Gold .1177 oz. AGW **Reverse:** Coat of arms on ornamental vines

| Date | Mintage | F | VF | XF | Unc | BU |
|---|---|---|---|---|---|---|
| 1976 | Inc. above | — | BV | 65.00 | 90.00 | — |

**50 PESOS** KM# 169 **Weight:** 10.1698 g. **Composition:** 0.9000 Gold .2943 oz. AGW

| Date | Mintage | F | VF | XF | Unc | BU |
|---|---|---|---|---|---|---|
| 1926 | 126,000 | — | BV | 120 | 150 | — |
| 1958 | 10,000 | — | — | BV | 150 | — |
| 1961 | 20,000 | — | — | BV | 150 | — |
| 1962 | 30,000 | — | — | BV | 150 | — |
| 1965 | — | — | — | BV | 150 | — |
| 1966 | — | — | — | BV | 150 | — |
| 1967 | — | — | — | BV | 150 | — |
| 1968 | — | — | — | BV | 150 | — |
| 1969 | — | — | — | BV | 150 | — |
| 1970 | — | — | — | — | 650 | — |
| 1974 | — | — | — | BV | 150 | — |

**50 PESOS** KM# 184 **Weight:** 10.1698 g. **Composition:** 0.9000 Gold .2943 oz. AGW **Subject:** 150th Anniversary of Military Academy

| Date | Mintage | F | VF | XF | Unc | BU |
|---|---|---|---|---|---|---|
| 1968 Proof | 2,515 | Value: 185 | | | | |

**100 PESOS** KM# 170 **Weight:** 20.3397 g. **Composition:** 0.9000 Gold .5886 oz. AGW

| Date | Mintage | F | VF | XF | Unc | BU |
|---|---|---|---|---|---|---|
| 1926 | 678,000 | — | BV | 200 | 285 | — |

**100 PESOS** KM# 175 **Weight:** 20.3397 g. **Composition:** 0.9000 Gold .5886 oz. AGW **Obverse:** Revised bust and legend style **Reverse:** Revised legend style

| Date | Mintage | F | VF | XF | Unc | BU |
|---|---|---|---|---|---|---|
| 1932 | 9,315 | — | BV | 325 | 425 | — |
| 1946 | 260,000 | — | — | BV | 265 | — |
| 1947 | 540,000 | — | — | BV | 265 | — |
| 1948 | 420,000 | — | — | BV | 265 | — |
| 1949 | 310,000 | — | — | BV | 265 | — |
| 1950 | 20,000 | — | — | BV | 265 | — |
| 1951 | 145,000 | — | — | BV | 265 | — |
| 1952 | 245,000 | — | — | BV | 265 | — |
| 1953 | 175,000 | — | — | BV | 265 | — |
| 1954 | 190,000 | — | — | BV | 265 | — |
| 1955 | 150,000 | — | — | BV | 265 | — |
| 1956 | 60,000 | — | — | BV | 265 | — |
| 1957 | 40,000 | — | — | BV | 265 | — |
| 1958 | 157,000 | — | — | BV | 265 | — |
| 1959 | 90,000 | — | — | BV | 265 | — |
| 1960 | 200,000 | — | — | BV | 265 | — |
| 1961 | 295,000 | — | — | BV | 265 | — |
| 1962 | 260,000 | — | — | BV | 265 | — |
| 1963 | 210,000 | — | — | BV | 265 | — |
| 1964 | — | — | — | BV | 265 | — |
| 1968 | — | — | — | BV | 265 | — |
| 1969 | — | — | — | BV | 265 | — |
| 1970 | — | — | — | BV | 265 | — |
| 1971 | — | — | — | BV | 265 | — |
| 1972 | — | — | — | BV | 265 | — |
| 1973 | — | — | — | BV | 265 | — |
| 1974 | — | — | — | BV | 265 | — |
| 1976 | 172,000 | — | — | BV | 265 | — |
| 1977 | 25,000 | — | — | BV | 265 | — |
| 1979 | 100,000 | — | — | BV | 265 | — |
| 1980 | 50,000 | — | — | BV | 265 | — |

**100 PESOS** KM# 185 **Weight:** 20.3397 g. **Composition:** 0.9000 Gold .5886 oz. AGW **Subject:** 150th Anniversary of National Coinage

| Date | Mintage | F | VF | XF | Unc | BU |
|---|---|---|---|---|---|---|
| 1968 Proof | 1,815 | Value: 375 | | | | |

**200 PESOS** KM# 186 **Weight:** 40.6794 g. **Composition:** 0.9000 Gold 1.1771 oz. AGW **Subject:** 150th Anniversary of San Martin's passage through Andes Mountains

| Date | Mintage | F | VF | XF | Unc | BU |
|---|---|---|---|---|---|---|
| 1968 Proof | 965 | Value: 750 | | | | |

**500 PESOS** KM# 187 **Weight:** 101.6985 g. **Composition:** 0.9000 Gold 2.9427 oz. AGW **Subject:** 150th Anniversary of National Flag

| Date | Mintage | F | VF | XF | Unc | BU |
|---|---|---|---|---|---|---|
| 1968 Proof | — | Value: 1,950 | | | | |

## REFORM COINAGE

10 Pesos = 1 Centesimo; 100 Centesimos = 1 Escudo

**1/2 CENTESIMO** KM# 192 **Composition:** Aluminum

| Date | Mintage | F | VF | XF | Unc | BU |
|---|---|---|---|---|---|---|
| 1962 | 3,750,000 | — | 0.10 | 0.30 | 0.50 | — |
| 1962 Proof | — | — | — | — | — | — |
| 1963 | 8,100,000 | — | 0.10 | 0.30 | 0.50 | — |

**CENTESIMO** KM# 189 **Composition:** Aluminum

| Date | Mintage | F | VF | XF | Unc | BU |
|---|---|---|---|---|---|---|
| 1960 | 20,160,000 | — | 0.35 | 0.75 | 1.25 | — |
| 1961 | Inc. above | — | 0.15 | 0.30 | 0.50 | — |
| 1962 | 26,320,000 | — | 0.15 | 0.30 | 0.50 | — |
| 1963 | 27,100,000 | — | 0.15 | 0.30 | 0.50 | — |

**2 CENTESIMOS** KM# 193 **Composition:** Aluminum-Bronze

| Date | Mintage | F | VF | XF | Unc | BU |
|---|---|---|---|---|---|---|
| 1960 | 2,050,000 | — | — | — | 50.00 | — |
| **Note:** Not released for circulation | | | | | | |
| 1964 | 2,050,000 | — | — | 0.10 | 1.00 | — |
| 1965 | 32,550,000 | — | — | 0.10 | 1.00 | — |
| 1966 | 31,800,000 | — | — | 0.10 | 1.00 | — |
| 1967 | 34,750,000 | — | — | 0.10 | 1.00 | — |
| 1968 | 29,400,000 | — | — | 0.10 | 1.00 | — |
| 1969 | — | — | — | — | 2.50 | — |
| 1969 Proof | — | Value: 50.00 | | | | |
| 1970 | 20,250,000 | — | — | 0.10 | 1.00 | — |

**5 CENTESIMOS** KM# 190 **Composition:** Aluminum-Bronze

| Date | Mintage | F | VF | XF | Unc | BU |
|---|---|---|---|---|---|---|
| 1960 Proof | — | Value: 100 | | | | |
| 1961 | 12,000 | — | 2.50 | 5.00 | 10.00 | — |
| 1962 | — | — | — | — | — | — |
| 1964 | 16,628,000 | — | 0.10 | 0.15 | 1.00 | — |
| 1965 | 27,680,000 | — | 0.10 | 0.15 | 1.00 | — |
| 1966 | 32,360,000 | — | 0.10 | 0.15 | 1.00 | — |
| 1967 | 19,680,000 | — | 0.10 | 0.15 | 1.00 | — |
| 1968 | 4,400,000 | — | 0.10 | 0.15 | 1.00 | — |
| 1968 Proof | — | Value: 50.00 | | | | |
| 1969 | 13,200,000 | — | — | — | 3.50 | — |
| 1969 Proof | — | Value: 50.00 | | | | |
| 1970 | 30,680,000 | — | 0.10 | 0.15 | 1.00 | — |
| 1971 | 16,080,000 | — | 0.10 | 0.15 | 1.00 | — |

**10 CENTESIMOS** KM# 191 **Composition:** Aluminum-Bronze

| Date | Mintage | F | VF | XF | Unc | BU |
|---|---|---|---|---|---|---|
| 1960 | — | — | 2.00 | 3.50 | 6.50 | — |
| 1961 | 1,915,000 | — | 0.10 | 0.20 | 1.00 | — |
| 1962 | 1,480,000 | — | 0.10 | 0.20 | 1.00 | — |
| 1963 Small date | 10,980,000 | — | 0.10 | 0.20 | 1.00 | — |
| 1964 | 27,070,000 | — | 0.10 | 0.20 | 1.00 | — |
| 1965 | 49,480,000 | — | 0.10 | 0.20 | 1.00 | — |
| 1966 | 60,680,000 | — | 0.10 | 0.20 | 1.00 | — |
| 1967 | 27,520,000 | — | 0.10 | 0.25 | 1.00 | — |
| 1968 | 8,040,000 | — | 0.10 | 0.20 | 1.00 | — |
| 1969 | 15,660,000 | — | — | — | 3.50 | — |
| 1970 Large date | 42,080,000 | — | 0.10 | 0.20 | 1.00 | — |

**10 CENTESIMOS** KM# 194 **Composition:** Aluminum-Bronze **Obverse:** Bust of Bernardo O'Higgins

| Date | Mintage | F | VF | XF | Unc | BU |
|---|---|---|---|---|---|---|
| 1971 | 99,700,000 | — | — | 0.10 | 0.15 | — |

**20 CENTESIMOS** KM# 195 **Composition:** Aluminum-Bronze **Obverse:** Bust of Jose Manuel Balmaceda

| Date | Mintage | F | VF | XF | Unc | BU |
|---|---|---|---|---|---|---|
| 1971 | 89,200,000 | — | — | 0.10 | 0.20 | — |
| 1972 | — | — | 0.10 | 0.20 | 1.00 | — |

**50 CENTESIMOS** KM# 196 **Composition:** Aluminum-Bronze **Obverse:** Bust of Manuel Rodriguez

| Date | Mintage | F | VF | XF | Unc | BU |
|---|---|---|---|---|---|---|
| 1971 | 58,300,000 | — | 0.10 | 0.15 | 0.25 | — |

**50CENTESIMOS** KM# 197 **Composition:** Copper-Nickel **Obverse:** Bust of Jose Miguel Carrera

| Date | Mintage | F | VF | XF | Unc | BU |
|---|---|---|---|---|---|---|
| 1971 | 160,900,000 | — | 0.10 | 0.20 | 0.40 | — |
| 1972 | Inc. above | — | 0.10 | 0.20 | 0.40 | — |
| 1972 Proof | — | Value: 50.00 | | | | |

**2 ESCUDOS** KM# 198 **Composition:** Copper-Nickel **Obverse:** Caupolican, Chief of Araucanian Indians

| Date | Mintage | F | VF | XF | Unc | BU |
|---|---|---|---|---|---|---|
| 1971 | 106 | — | — | — | 125 | — |
| **Note:** Not released for circulation | | | | | | |
| 1971 Proof | — | Value: 50.00 | | | | |

**5 ESCUDOS** KM# 199 **Composition:** Copper-Nickel

| Date | Mintage | F | VF | XF | Unc | BU |
|---|---|---|---|---|---|---|
| 1971 | — | — | 0.10 | 0.25 | 0.75 | — |
| 1972 | — | — | 0.10 | 0.25 | 0.75 | — |
| 1972 Proof | — | Value: 50.00 | | | | |

**5 ESCUDOS** KM# 199a **Composition:** Aluminum

| Date | Mintage | F | VF | XF | Unc | BU |
|---|---|---|---|---|---|---|
| 1972 | — | — | 0.10 | 0.15 | 0.20 | — |

**10 ESCUDOS** KM# 200 **Composition:** Aluminum

| Date | Mintage | F | VF | XF | Unc | BU |
|---|---|---|---|---|---|---|
| 1974 | 33,750,000 | — | 0.10 | 0.15 | 0.35 | — |
| 1974 Proof | — | Value: 50.00 | | | | |
| 1975 | 31,600,000 | — | 0.10 | 0.15 | 0.35 | — |

**50 ESCUDOS** KM# 201 **Composition:** Nickel-Brass

| Date | Mintage | F | VF | XF | Unc | BU |
|---|---|---|---|---|---|---|
| 1974 | 5,700,000 | — | 0.15 | 0.25 | 0.60 | — |
| 1975 | 20,300,000 | — | 0.15 | 0.20 | 0.50 | — |

**100 ESCUDOS** KM# 202

| Date | Mintage | F | VF | XF | Unc | BU |
|---|---|---|---|---|---|---|
| 1974 | 32,100,000 | — | 0.20 | 0.35 | 0.75 | — |
| 1975 | 65,600,000 | — | 0.20 | 0.35 | 0.75 | — |

## REFORM COINAGE

100 Centavos = 1 Peso; 1000 Old Escudos = 1 Peso

**CENTAVO** KM# 203 **Composition:** Aluminum

| Date | Mintage | F | VF | XF | Unc | BU |
|---|---|---|---|---|---|---|
| 1975 | 2,000,000 | — | 0.10 | 0.15 | 0.50 | — |

**5 CENTAVOS** KM# 204 **Composition:** Aluminum-Bronze

| Date | Mintage | F | VF | XF | Unc | BU |
|---|---|---|---|---|---|---|
| 1975 | 5,400,000 | — | — | 0.10 | 0.25 | — |
| 1976 | 6,600,000 | — | — | 0.10 | 0.25 | — |

**5 CENTAVOS** KM# 204a **Composition:** Aluminum

| Date | Mintage | F | VF | XF | Unc | BU |
|---|---|---|---|---|---|---|
| 1976 | 5,000,000 | — | — | 0.10 | 0.25 | — |

**10 CENTAVOS** KM# 205 **Composition:** Aluminum-Bronze

| Date | Mintage | F | VF | XF | Unc | BU |
|---|---|---|---|---|---|---|
| 1975 | 8,600,000 | — | — | 0.10 | 0.25 | — |
| 1976 | 9,000,000 | — | — | 0.10 | 0.25 | — |

**10 CENTAVOS** **KM# 205a** **Composition:** Aluminum

| Date | Mintage | F | VF | XF | Unc | BU |
|---|---|---|---|---|---|---|
| 1976 | 6,600,000 | — | — | 0.10 | 0.25 | — |
| 1977 | 57,800,000 | — | — | 0.10 | 0.25 | — |
| 1978 | 58,050,000 | — | — | 0.10 | 0.25 | — |
| 1979 | 101,950,000 | — | — | 0.10 | 0.25 | — |

**50 CENTAVOS** **KM# 206** **Composition:** Copper-Nickel

| Date | Mintage | F | VF | XF | Unc | BU |
|---|---|---|---|---|---|---|
| 1975 | 38,000,000 | — | — | 0.10 | 0.25 | — |
| 1976 | 1,000,000 | — | 0.50 | 1.00 | 2.00 | — |
| 1977 | 10,000,000 | — | — | 0.10 | 0.25 | — |

**50 CENTAVOS** **KM# 206a** **Composition:** Aluminum-Bronze

| Date | Mintage | F | VF | XF | Unc | BU |
|---|---|---|---|---|---|---|
| 1978 | 19,250,000 | — | — | 0.10 | 0.25 | — |
| 1979 | 28,000,000 | — | — | 0.10 | 0.25 | — |

**PESO** **KM# 207** **Composition:** Copper-Nickel **Obverse:** Bust of Bernardo O'Higgins **Obv. Legend:** BERNARDO O'HIGGINS

| Date | Mintage | F | VF | XF | Unc | BU |
|---|---|---|---|---|---|---|
| 1975 | 51,000,000 | — | 0.10 | 0.15 | 0.25 | — |

**PESO** **KM# 208** **Composition:** Copper-Nickel **Obverse:** Bust of Bernardo O'Higgins **Obv. Legend:** LIBERTADOR. B. O'HIGGINS

| Date | Mintage | F | VF | XF | Unc | BU |
|---|---|---|---|---|---|---|
| 1976 | 30,000,000 | — | — | 0.10 | 0.25 | — |
| 1977 | 20,000,000 | — | — | 0.10 | 0.25 | — |

**PESO** **KM# 208a** **Composition:** Aluminum-Bronze

| Date | Mintage | F | VF | XF | Unc | BU |
|---|---|---|---|---|---|---|
| 1978 | 39,706,000 | — | — | 0.10 | 0.25 | — |
| 1979 | 63,000,000 | — | — | 0.10 | 0.25 | — |

**PESO** **KM# 216.1** **Composition:** Aluminum-Bronze **Note:** Reduced size, 17 millimeter. Wide date.

| Date | Mintage | F | VF | XF | Unc | BU |
|---|---|---|---|---|---|---|
| 1981 | 40,000,000 | — | — | 0.10 | 0.20 | — |
| 1984 | 60,000,000 | — | — | 0.10 | 0.20 | — |
| 1985 | 20,000,000 | — | — | 0.10 | 0.20 | — |
| 1986 | 45,000,000 | — | — | 0.10 | 0.20 | — |
| 1987 | 80,000,000 | — | — | 0.10 | 0.20 | — |

**PESO** **KM# 216.2** **Composition:** Aluminum-Bronze **Note:** Narrow date.

| Date | Mintage | F | VF | XF | Unc | BU |
|---|---|---|---|---|---|---|
| 1988 | 105,000,000 | — | — | 0.10 | 0.20 | — |
| 1989 | 205,000,000 | — | — | 0.10 | 0.20 | — |
| 1990 | 140,000,000 | — | — | 0.10 | 0.20 | — |
| 1991 | 140,000,000 | — | — | 0.10 | 0.20 | — |
| 1992 | — | — | — | 0.10 | 0.20 | — |

**PESO** **KM# 231** **Composition:** Aluminum **Note:** Varieties exist.

| Date | Mintage | F | VF | XF | Unc | BU |
|---|---|---|---|---|---|---|
| 1992 | — | — | — | — | 0.10 | — |
| 1993 | — | — | — | — | 0.10 | — |
| 1994 | — | — | — | — | 0.10 | — |
| 1995 | — | — | — | — | 0.10 | — |
| 1996 | — | — | — | — | 0.10 | — |
| 1998 | — | — | — | — | 0.10 | — |

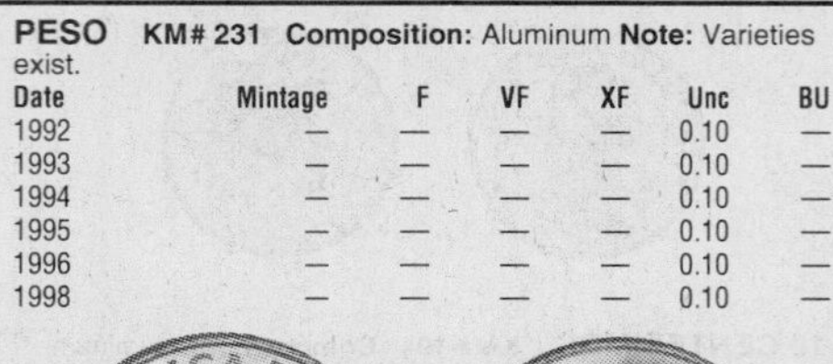

**5 PESOS** **KM# 209** **Composition:** Copper-Nickel **Subject:** 3rd Anniversary of New Government

| Date | Mintage | F | VF | XF | Unc | BU |
|---|---|---|---|---|---|---|
| 1976 | 2,100,000 | — | 0.15 | 0.25 | 2.00 | — |
| 1977 | 28,300,000 | — | 0.15 | 0.25 | 2.00 | — |
| 1978 | 11,704,000 | — | 0.15 | 0.25 | 2.00 | — |
| 1980 | 8,200,000 | — | 0.15 | 0.25 | 2.00 | — |

**5 PESOS** **KM# 217.1** **Composition:** Nickel-Brass 19 oz. **Note:** Wide date, 19 millimeters.

| Date | Mintage | F | VF | XF | Unc | BU |
|---|---|---|---|---|---|---|
| 1981 | 17,000,000 | — | — | 0.10 | 0.50 | — |
| 1982 | 20,000,000 | — | — | 0.10 | 0.50 | — |
| 1984 | 12,000,000 | — | — | 0.10 | 0.50 | — |
| 1985 | 16,000,000 | — | — | 0.10 | 0.50 | — |
| 1986 | 16,000,000 | — | — | 0.10 | 0.50 | — |
| 1987 | 8,000,000 | — | — | 0.10 | 0.50 | — |

**5 PESOS** **KM# 217.2** **Composition:** Nickel-Brass **Note:** Narrow date.

| Date | Mintage | F | VF | XF | Unc | BU |
|---|---|---|---|---|---|---|
| 1988 | 27,000,000 | — | — | 0.10 | 0.50 | — |
| 1989 | 32,000,000 | — | — | 0.10 | 0.50 | — |
| 1990 | 23,000,000 | — | — | 0.10 | 0.50 | — |

**5 PESOS** **KM# 229** **Composition:** Nickel-Brass **Obverse:** Bust of Bernardo O'Higgins right **Reverse:** Denomination, date

| Date | Mintage | F | VF | XF | Unc | BU |
|---|---|---|---|---|---|---|
| 1990 | 8,000,000 | — | — | 0.10 | 0.50 | — |
| 1991 | 2,000,000 | — | — | 0.10 | 0.50 | — |
| 1992 | — | — | — | 0.10 | 0.50 | — |

**5 PESOS** **KM# 232** **Composition:** Aluminum-Bronze **Note:** Varieties exist.

| Date | Mintage | F | VF | XF | Unc | BU |
|---|---|---|---|---|---|---|
| 1992 | — | — | — | 0.10 | 0.35 | — |
| 1993 | — | — | — | 0.10 | 0.35 | — |
| 1994 | — | — | — | 0.10 | 0.35 | — |
| 1995 | — | — | — | 0.10 | 0.35 | — |
| 1996 | — | — | — | 0.10 | 0.35 | — |
| 1997 | — | — | — | 0.10 | 0.35 | — |
| 1998 | — | — | — | 0.10 | 0.35 | — |

**10 PESOS** **KM# 210** **Composition:** Copper-Nickel **Subject:** 3rd Anniversary of New Government

| Date | Mintage | F | VF | XF | Unc | BU |
|---|---|---|---|---|---|---|
| 1976 | 2,100,000 | — | 0.10 | 0.20 | 1.25 | — |
| 1977 | 30,000,000 | — | 0.10 | 0.20 | 1.00 | — |
| 1978 | 20,004,000 | — | 0.10 | 0.20 | 1.00 | — |
| 1979 | 7,000,000 | — | 0.10 | 0.20 | 1.00 | — |
| 1980 | 20,000,000 | — | 0.10 | 0.20 | 1.00 | — |

**10 PESOS** **KM# 211** **Weight:** 44.8000 g. **Composition:** 0.9990 Silver 1.4390 oz. ASW **Subject:** 3rd Anniversary of New Government

| Date | Mintage | F | VF | XF | Unc | BU |
|---|---|---|---|---|---|---|
| ND(1976) Proof | 1,000 | Value: 115 | | | | |

**10 PESOS** **KM# 218.1** **Composition:** Nickel-Brass **Note:** Wide date, narrow rim.

| Date | Mintage | F | VF | XF | Unc | BU |
|---|---|---|---|---|---|---|
| 1981 | 55,000,000 | — | 0.10 | 0.20 | 0.50 | — |
| 1982 | 45,000,000 | — | 0.10 | 0.20 | 0.50 | — |
| 1984 | 30,000,000 | — | 0.10 | 0.20 | 0.50 | — |
| 1985 | 400,000 | — | 0.50 | 1.50 | 3.50 | — |
| 1986 | 25,000,000 | — | 0.10 | 0.20 | 0.50 | — |
| 1987 | 8,000,000 | — | 0.10 | 0.20 | 0.50 | — |

**10 PESOS** **KM# 218.2** **Composition:** Nickel-Brass **Note:** Narrow date.

| Date | Mintage | F | VF | XF | Unc | BU |
|---|---|---|---|---|---|---|
| 1988 | 45,000,000 | — | 0.10 | 0.20 | 0.50 | — |
| 1989 | 73,000,000 | — | 0.10 | 0.20 | 0.50 | — |

**10 PESOS** **KM# 218.3** **Composition:** Nickel-Brass **Note:** Wide rim.

| Date | Mintage | F | VF | XF | Unc | BU |
|---|---|---|---|---|---|---|
| 1990 | 10,000,000 | — | 0.10 | 0.20 | 0.50 | — |

**10 PESOS** **KM# 228.1** **Composition:** Nickel-Brass **Obverse:** Small bust of Bernardo O'Higgins right, wide rim

| Date | Mintage | F | VF | XF | Unc | BU |
|---|---|---|---|---|---|---|
| 1990 | 5,000,000 | — | 0.10 | 0.20 | 0.50 | — |
| 1993 | — | — | 0.10 | 0.20 | 0.50 | — |

**10 PESOS** **KM# 228.2** **Composition:** Nickel-Brass **Obverse:** Large bust of Bernardo O'Higgins right, normal rim

| Date | Mintage | F | VF | XF | Unc | BU |
|---|---|---|---|---|---|---|
| 1990 | 25,000,000 | — | 0.10 | 0.20 | 0.50 | — |
| 1991 | — | — | 0.10 | 0.20 | 0.50 | — |
| 1992 | — | — | 0.10 | 0.20 | 0.50 | — |
| 1993 | — | — | 0.10 | 0.20 | 0.50 | — |
| 1994 | — | — | 0.10 | 0.20 | 0.50 | — |
| 1995 | — | — | 0.10 | 0.20 | 0.50 | — |
| 1996 | — | — | 0.10 | 0.20 | 0.50 | — |
| 1997 | — | — | 0.10 | 0.20 | 0.50 | — |
| 1998 | — | — | 0.10 | 0.20 | 0.50 | — |

**50 PESOS** KM# 212 **Weight:** 10.1500 g. **Composition:** 0.9000 Gold .2937 oz. AGW **Subject:** 3rd Anniversary of New Government

| Date | Mintage | F | VF | XF | Unc | BU |
|---|---|---|---|---|---|---|
| ND(1976) | 1,900 | — | — | — | 200 | — |
| ND(1976) Proof | Inc. above | Value: 225 | | | | |

**50 PESOS** KM# 219.1 **Composition:** Aluminum-Bronze **Note:** Wide date.

| Date | Mintage | F | VF | XF | Unc | BU |
|---|---|---|---|---|---|---|
| 1981 | 12,000,000 | — | 0.25 | 0.50 | 1.25 | — |
| 1982 | 14,000,000 | — | 0.25 | 0.50 | 1.25 | — |
| 1985 | 400,000 | — | 0.60 | 1.50 | 3.50 | — |
| 1986 | 1,000,000 | — | 0.25 | 0.50 | 1.25 | — |
| 1987 | 4,000,000 | — | 0.25 | 0.50 | 1.25 | — |

**50 PESOS** KM# 219.2 **Composition:** Aluminum-Bronze **Note:** Narrow date.

| Date | Mintage | F | VF | XF | Unc | BU |
|---|---|---|---|---|---|---|
| 1988 | 4,800,000 | — | 0.25 | 0.50 | 1.25 | — |
| 1989 | 4,000,000 | — | 0.25 | 0.50 | 1.25 | — |
| 1991 | 10,845,000 | — | 0.25 | 0.50 | 1.25 | — |
| 1992 | — | — | 0.25 | 0.50 | 1.25 | — |
| 1993 | — | — | 0.25 | 0.50 | 1.25 | — |
| 1994 | — | — | 0.25 | 0.50 | 1.25 | — |
| 1995 | — | — | 0.25 | 0.50 | 1.25 | — |

**100 PESOS** KM# 213 **Weight:** 20.3000 g. **Composition:** 0.9000 Gold .5874 oz. AGW **Subject:** 3rd Anniversary of New Government

| Date | Mintage | F | VF | XF | Unc | BU |
|---|---|---|---|---|---|---|
| 1976 | 2,900 | — | — | — | 350 | — |
| 1976 Proof | 100 | Value: 750 | | | | |

**100 PESOS** KM# 226.1 **Composition:** Aluminum-Bronze **Note:** Wide date with pointed 9.

| Date | Mintage | F | VF | XF | Unc | BU |
|---|---|---|---|---|---|---|
| 1981 | 10,000,000 | — | 0.50 | 0.75 | 2.50 | — |
| 1983 | — | — | 0.50 | 0.75 | 2.50 | — |
| 1984 | 8,000,000 | — | 0.50 | 0.75 | 2.50 | — |
| 1985 | 15,000,000 | — | 0.50 | 0.75 | 2.50 | — |
| 1986 | 11,000,000 | — | 0.50 | 0.75 | 2.50 | — |
| 1987 | 15,000,000 | — | 0.50 | 0.75 | 2.50 | — |

**100 PESOS** KM# 226.2 **Composition:** Aluminum-Bronze **Note:** Narrow date with curved 9.

| Date | Mintage | F | VF | XF | Unc | BU |
|---|---|---|---|---|---|---|
| 1989 | 20,000,000 | — | 0.50 | 0.75 | 2.50 | — |
| 1991 | 4,320,000 | — | 0.50 | 0.75 | 2.50 | — |
| 1992 | — | — | 0.50 | 0.75 | 2.50 | — |
| 1993 | — | — | 0.50 | 0.75 | 2.50 | — |
| 1994 | — | — | 0.50 | 0.75 | 2.50 | — |
| 1995 | — | — | 0.50 | 0.75 | 2.50 | — |
| 1996 | — | — | 0.50 | 0.75 | 2.50 | — |
| 1997 | — | — | 0.50 | 0.75 | 2.50 | — |

**500 PESOS** KM# 214 **Weight:** 102.2700 g. **Composition:** 0.9000 Gold 2.9595 oz. AGW **Subject:** 3rd Anniversary of New Government **Note:** Similar to 100 Pesos, KM#213.

| Date | Mintage | F | VF | XF | Unc | BU |
|---|---|---|---|---|---|---|
| 1976 | 500 | — | — | — | 1,850 | — |
| 1976 Proof | 700 | Value: 1,850 | | | | |

**500 PESOS** KM# 235 **Ring Composition:** Copper-Nickel **Center Weight:** 6.5000 g. **Center Composition:** Aluminum-Bronze **Subject:** Cardenal Raul Silva Henrique **Obverse:** Bust of Henrique in inner ring facing left. **Reverse:** Denomination with date below. **Edge:** Reeded. **Size:** 25.9 mm.

| Date | Mintage | F | VF | XF | Unc | BU |
|---|---|---|---|---|---|---|
| 2000 | — | — | — | — | 6.00 | — |

**2000 PESOS** KM# 233 **Weight:** 8.2000 g. **Composition:** 0.5000 Silver .1318 oz. ASW **Subject:** 250th Anniversary of the Mint

| Date | Mintage | F | VF | XF | Unc | BU |
|---|---|---|---|---|---|---|
| 1993 | 50,000 | — | — | — | 16.50 | — |

**10000 PESOS** KM# 230 **Weight:** 27.0000 g. **Composition:** 0.9250 Silver .8029 oz. ASW **Series:** Ibero - American

| Date | Mintage | F | VF | XF | Unc | BU |
|---|---|---|---|---|---|---|
| 1991 Proof | 75,000 | Value: 45.00 | | | | |

## SILVER BULLION COINAGE

**1/4 ONZA** KM# 223 **Weight:** 7.7770 g. **Composition:** 0.9990 Silver .2500 oz. ASW **Subject:** 10th Anniversary of National Liberation

| Date | Mintage | F | VF | XF | Unc | BU |
|---|---|---|---|---|---|---|
| ND(1983) Proof | 1,000 | Value: 12.50 | | | | |

**1/2 ONZA** KM# 224 **Weight:** 15.5530 g. **Composition:** 0.9990 Silver .5000 oz. ASW **Subject:** 10th Anniversary of National Liberation

| Date | Mintage | F | VF | XF | Unc | BU |
|---|---|---|---|---|---|---|
| ND(1983) Proof | 1,000 | Value: 25.00 | | | | |

**ONZA** KM# 225 **Weight:** 31.1070 g. **Composition:** 0.9990 Silver 1.0000 oz. ASW **Subject:** 10th Anniversary of National Liberation

| Date | Mintage | F | VF | XF | Unc | BU |
|---|---|---|---|---|---|---|
| ND(1983) Proof | 1,000 | Value: 45.00 | | | | |

**ONZA** KM# 234 **Weight:** 31.1035 g. **Composition:** 0.9990 Silver 1.0000 oz. ASW **Subject:** Numismatic Association of Chile **Obverse:** Similar to 4 Escudos, KM#2 **Reverse:** Similar to 1/2 Real, KM#90 obverse

| Date | Mintage | F | VF | XF | Unc | BU |
|---|---|---|---|---|---|---|
| ND(1999) Proof | 75 | Value: 55.00 | | | | |

## GOLD BULLION COINAGE

**1/4 ONZA** **KM# 220** **Weight:** 8.6400 g. **Composition:** 0.9000 Gold .2500 oz. AGW **Subject:** 10th Anniversary of National Liberation **Note:** Similar to KM#223.

| Date | Mintage | F | VF | XF | Unc | BU |
|---|---|---|---|---|---|---|
| ND(1983) | 1,000 | — | — | — | 175 | — |

**1/2 ONZA** **KM# 221** **Weight:** 17.2800 g. **Composition:** 0.9000 Gold .5000 oz. AGW **Subject:** 10th Anniversary of National Liberation **Note:** Similar to KM#224.

| Date | Mintage | F | VF | XF | Unc | BU |
|---|---|---|---|---|---|---|
| ND(1983) | 1,000 | — | — | — | 350 | — |

**ONZA** **KM# 227** **Weight:** 31.1000 g. **Composition:** 0.9990 Gold 1.0000 oz. AGW

| Date | Mintage | F | VF | XF | Unc | BU |
|---|---|---|---|---|---|---|
| 1948 | 1,950 | — | — | — | 800 | — |

**ONZA** **KM# 215** **Weight:** 31.1000 g. **Composition:** 0.9990 Gold 1.0000 oz. AGW **Obverse:** Crowned arms **Reverse:** Crowned pillars and worlds

| Date | Mintage | F | VF | XF | Unc | BU |
|---|---|---|---|---|---|---|
| 1978 | — | — | — | — | 750 | — |
| 1979 | 1,580 | — | — | — | 600 | — |
| 1980 | 1,730 | — | — | — | 600 | — |
| 1981 | 200 | — | — | — | 700 | — |
| 1983 | 999 | — | — | — | 650 | — |
| 1983 Proof | 1 | — | — | — | — | — |

**ONZA** **KM# 222** **Weight:** 34.5590 g. **Composition:** 0.9000 Gold 1.0000 oz. AGW **Subject:** 10th Anniversary of National Liberation **Note:** Similar to KM#225.

| Date | Mintage | F | VF | XF | Unc | BU |
|---|---|---|---|---|---|---|
| 1983 | 1,000 | — | — | — | 675 | — |

## PATTERNS

Including off metal strikes

| KM# | Date | Mintage | Identification | Mkt Val |
|---|---|---|---|---|
| PnA26 | 1908 | — | 5 Centavos. Copper-Nickel. | — |
| PnB26 | 1908 | — | 10 Centavos. Brass. | — |
| Pn26 | 1914 | — | Peso. Silver. | 300 |
| PnA27 | 1914 | — | 2 Pesos. Silver. Piefort, large flan. | 500 |
| Pn27 | 1914 | — | 2 Pesos. Silver. Piefort, small flan. | 500 |
| Pn28 | 1916 | — | 20 Centavos. Silver. 4.0000 g. | — |
| Pn29 | 1916 | — | 20 Centavos. Silver. 4.0400 g. | — |
| Pn30 | 1917 | — | 10 Centavos. Silver. 1.9000 g. | — |
| Pn31 | 1917 | — | 10 Centavos. Silver. 2.5200 g. | — |
| Pn32 | 1919 | — | 5 Centavos. Copper-Nickel. | — |
| Pn33 | 1919 | — | 5 Centavos. Silver. 1.4900 g. | — |
| Pn34 | 1919 | — | 5 Centavos. Silver. 1.5300 g. | — |
| Pn35 | 1919 | — | 10 Centavos. Copper-Nickel. | — |
| Pn36 | 1919 | — | 20 Centavos. Copper-Nickel. | — |
| Pn37 | 19xx | — | 10 Centavos. Copper-Nickel. Center hole. | — |
| Pn38 | 1926 | — | Peso. Silver. | 550 |
| Pn39 | 1926 | — | Peso. Silver. Fineness added. | 550 |
| Pn40 | 1926 | — | Peso. Silver. Coat of arms. Without fineness. | 600 |
| Pn41 | 1926 | — | 2 Pesos. Silver. Condor. Coat of arms. Without fineness. | 1,000 |
| Pn42 | 1926 | — | 2 Pesos. Silver. Indian. Star in wreath. "5" fineness, Pn#43. | 600 |
| Pn43 | 1926 | — | 2 Pesos. Silver. Indian. Star in wreath. "72" fineness, Pn44. | 600 |
| Pn44 | 1926 | — | 5 Pesos. | 1,500 |
| Pn45 | 1926 | — | 5 Pesos. Silver. Weak or no fineness (effaced from die). | 1,500 |
| Pn46 | 1926 | — | 5 Pesos. Silver. | 1,250 |
| Pn47 | 1927 | — | Peso. Copper-Nickel. | 250 |
| Pn48 | 1927 | — | Peso. Silver. | 500 |
| Pn49 | 1927 | — | 5 Pesos. Silver. | 1,000 |
| Pn50 | 1929 | — | 20 Centavos. Copper-Nickel. Center hole. | 125 |
| Pn51 | 1929 | — | 20 Centavos. Copper-Nickel. Pn49 but "CHILE" on reverse instead of "20" | 125 |
| Pn52 | 1929 | — | Peso. Silver. | 250 |
| Pn53 | ND (1929) | — | Peso. Silver. Without country, date or fineness. | 250 |
| Pn54 | ND (1929) | — | Peso. Silver. Similar to Pn52, without mountains on obverse. | 250 |
| Pn55 | 1930 | — | 20 Centavos. Copper-Nickel. Center hole. | 125 |
| Pn56 | 1930 | — | 20 Centavos. Copper-Nickel. Pn54 but "20" instead of "CHILE" on obverse. | 125 |
| Pn57 | 1930 | — | Peso. Silver. Worker and factory. Value. | 300 |
| Pn58 | 1930 | — | 2 Pesos. Copper-Nickel. Condor. Value and date in wreath. | 325 |
| PnA59 | 1933 | — | Peso. Nickel. KM#176.1. | — |
| Pn59 | 1933 | — | Peso. Copper-Nickel. Condor. Value and date in wreath. | 250 |
| PnA60 | 1933 | — | Peso. Copper-Nickel. Condor. Value and date in wreath. Mint punched cancelled. | 250 |
| Pn62 | ND (1938) | — | 5 Pesos. Silver. Without date. | 300 |
| Pn60 | 1938 | — | 5 Pesos. Brass. | — |
| Pn61 | 1938 | — | 5 Pesos. Copper-Nickel. | — |
| PnA62 | ND (1938) | — | 5 Pesos. (No Composition). Plain edge. Aluminum-Bronze or Silver. | — |
| PnA63 | 1941 | — | 20 Centavos. Bronze. | — |
| Pn63 | 1942 | — | Peso. Copper. Like KM#179, but smaller diameter. | 100 |
| Pn64 | 1947 | — | 100 Pesos. Copper. | — |
| Pn65 | 1948 | — | Onza. Silver. | 75.00 |
| Pn65a | 1948 | — | Onza. Copper. | 25.00 |
| PnA66 | 1951 | — | 10 Pesos. Aluminum-Bronze. Thick flan. | — |
| Pn66 | 1953 | — | 20 Centavos. Aluminum. | — |
| Pn67 | 1956 | — | 5 Pesos. Brass. KM#180. | — |
| Pn68 | 1959 | — | 10 Pesos. Brass. KM#181. | — |
| Pn69 | 1960 | — | 2 Centesimos. Brass. Uniface. | — |
| Pn70 | 1960 | — | 2 Centesimos. Copper-Nickel. | 60.00 |
| PnA70 | 1960 | — | 2 Centesimos. Aluminum-Bronze. | — |
| Pn71 | 1960 | — | 5 Centesimos. Copper. KM#190. | 70.00 |
| Pn72 | 1960 | — | 5 Centesimos. Copper-Nickel. Plain edge. KM#190. | 90.00 |
| Pn73 | 1960 | — | 5 Centesimos. Copper-Nickel. Milled edge. KM#190. | 75.00 |
| Pn74 | 1960 | — | 10 Centesimos. Copper. KM#191. | 60.00 |
| Pn75 | 1960 | — | 10 Centesimos. Copper-Nickel. KM#191. | 40.00 |
| Pn76 | 1960 | — | 10 Centesimos. Brass. KM#191. | — |
| Pn77 | 1960 | — | 10 Centesimos. Brass. | — |
| Pn78 | 1960 | — | 10 Centesimos. Aluminum-Bronze. Legend. Arms flanked by C-M. | 65.00 |
| Pn79 | 1960 | — | 10 Centesimos. Copper-Nickel. Legend. Arms flanked by C-M. | 65.00 |
| Pn80 | 1964 | — | 2 Centesimos. Copper-Nickel. KM#193. | 75.00 |
| Pn81 | 1968 | — | 100 Pesos. Copper. Center hole. | 125 |
| Pn82 | 1969 | — | Peso. Copper-Nickel. Ten sided. Ten sided, arms with "C.M." below. | 100 |
| Pn83 | 1971 | — | Peso. Nickel. | — |
| PnB84 | 1971 | — | 2 Escudos. Silver. KM#198. | — |
| PnC84 | 1972 | — | 5 Escudos. Silver. KM#199. | — |
| PnA84 | 1972 | — | Escudo. Silver. KM197. | — |
| | 1972 | — | Escudo. Silver. KM#197. | — |
| Pn84 | 1974 | — | 10 Escudos. Aluminum. | — |
| Pn85 | 1979 | 5 | 100 Pesos. 0.5000 Silver. Equestrian statue of O'Higgins. | — |

## PIEFORTS

| KM# | Date | Mintage | Identification | Mkt Val |
|---|---|---|---|---|
| P4 | 1951 | — | 10 Pesos. Aluminum-Bronze. KM#181. | 125 |

## TRIAL STRIKES

| KM# | Date | Mintage | Identification | Mkt Val |
|---|---|---|---|---|
| TS7 | (1960) | — | 10 Centesimos. Copper-Nickel. Coat of arms flanked by C-M. Coat of arms flanked by C-M. | 60.00 |
| TS8 | (1960) | — | 10 Centesimos. Aluminum-Bronze. Coat of arms flanked by C-M. Coat of arms flanked by C-M. | 50.00 |

## PROOF SETS

| KM# | Date | Mintage | Identification | Issue Price | Mkt Val |
|---|---|---|---|---|---|
| PS1 | 1968 (6) | — | KM#182-187. Total of 12,000 coins struck for each denomination including those available singly | 560 | 3,350 |
| PS2 | 1968 (4) | — | KM#184-187. Total of 12,000 coins struck for each denomination including those available singly | 528 | 3,250 |
| PS3 | 1968 (2) | — | KM#182, 183. Total of 12,000 coins struck for each denomination including those available singly | 31.50 | 100 |
| PS4 | 1971/2 (3) | — | KM#197 (1972), KM#198 (1971), KM#199 (1972). Total of 12,000 coins struck for each denomination including those available singly | — | 150 |

# a map of the CHINESE PROVINCES

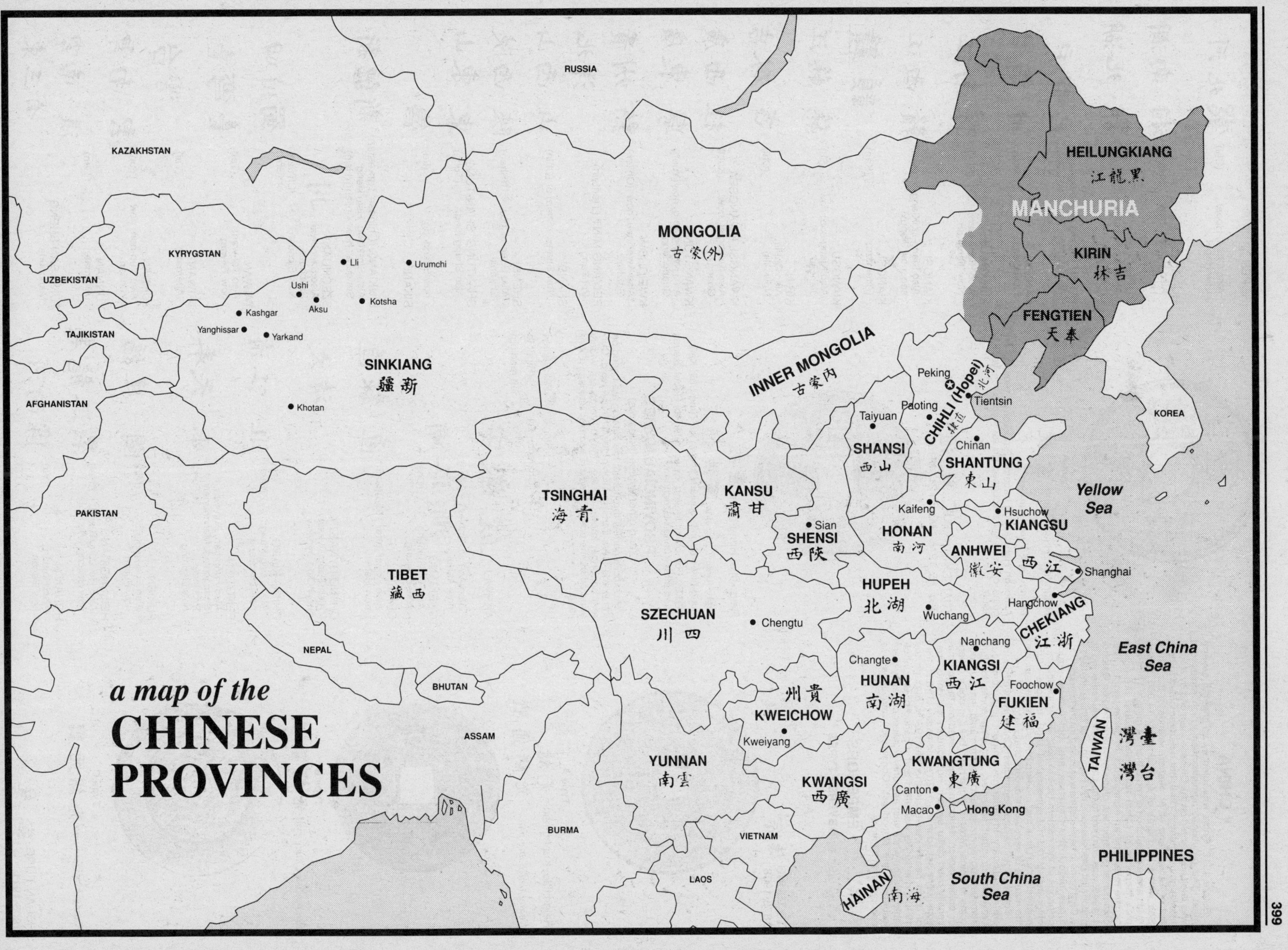

# CHINA

Before 1912, China was ruled by an imperial government. The republican administration which replaced it was itself supplanted on the Chinese mainland by a communist government in 1949, but it has remained in control of Taiwan and other offshore islands in the China Sea with a land area of approximately 14,000 square miles and a population of more than 14 million. The People's Republic of China administers some 3.7 million square miles and an estimated 1.19 billion people. This communist government, officially established on October 1, 1949, was admitted to the United Nations, replacing its nationalist predecessor, the Republic of China, in 1971.

Cast coins in base metals were used in China many centuries before the Christian era, but locally struck coinages of the western type in gold, silver, copper and other metals did not appear until 1888. In spite of the relatively short time that modern coins have been in use, the number of varieties is exceptionally large.

Both Nationalist and Communist China, as well as the pre-revolutionary Imperial government and numerous provincial or other agencies, including some foreign-administered agencies and governments, have issued coins in China. Most of these have been in dollar (yuan) or dollar-fraction denominations, based on the internationally used dollar system, but coins in tael denominations were issued in the 1920's and earlier. The striking of coins nearly ceased in the late 1930's through the 1940's due to the war effort and a period of uncontrollable inflation while vast amounts of paper currency were issued by the Nationalist, Communist and Japanese occupation institutions.

## EMPERORS

### OBVERSE TYPES

TE TSUNG 德宗
1875-1908

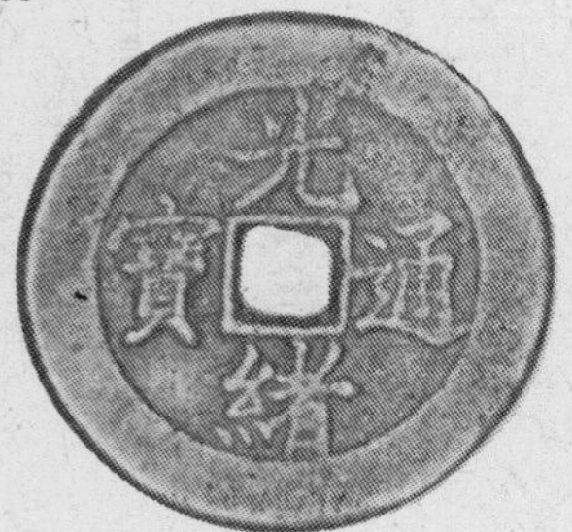

**Type A**

Reign title: Kuang-hsu 光緒

*Kuang-hsu T'ung-pao* 光緒通寶

**Type B**

*Kuang-hsu Chung-pao* 光緒重寶

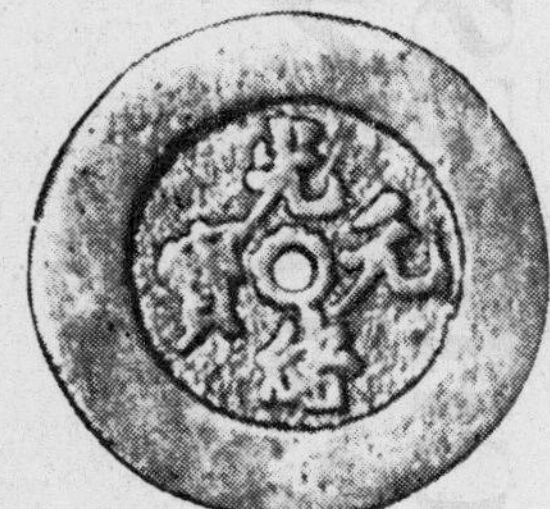

**Type C**

*Kuang-hsu Yuan-pao* 光緒元寶

HSUAN T'UNG 宣統
1908-1911

**Type A**

Reign title: Hsuan-t'ung 宣統

*Hsuan-t'ung T'ung-pao*

Although Hsuan-t'ung became Emperor in 1908, all the coins of his reign are based on an Accession year of 1909.

YUAN SHIH KAI 宣統通
Dec. 15, 1915 - March 21, 1916

Reign title: Hung-hsien 憲洪

*Hung-hsien T'ung-pao* 憲洪 通寶

Hung-hsien (more popularly known as Yuan Shih Kai).

**NOTE:** For other legend types refer to Rebel Issues listed after Yunnan-Szechuan.

## PROVINCIAL NAMES

(and other source indicators)

Provincial names throughout the catalog are based on the Wade-Giles transliteration of the Chinese word. Current spellings, known as the "Pinyin" form, are widely adopted by the printed media. Example: Sinkiang = Xinjiang.

| | Single Character (1) | Full Names (Right to left reading) |
|---|---|---|
| ANHWEI<br>Also An-hwi, Anhui, now Anhui (Wan) | 皖 | 徽安 |
| CHEKIANG<br>Also Cheh-kiang, now Zhejiang (Che) | 浙 | 江浙 |
| CHIHLI<br>Also Hopei (after 1928) now Hebei (Chih) | 直 | 隸直 |
| CH'ING DYNASTY<br>Also Tsing Dynasty, now Qing Dynasty | | 清大 |
| CHING-KIANG<br>Also Tsing-kiang now Qingjiang (Huai) | 淮 | 江清 |
| FENGTIEN<br>Also Fung-tien, Fun-tien, Shengching, Manchurian Provinces, now Liaoning (Feng) | 奉 | 天奉 |
| FUKIEN<br>Also Foo-kien, F.K., now Fujian (Min) | 閩 | 建福 |
| HEILUNGKIANG<br>Also Hei Lung Kiang, now Heilongjiang (Hei) | 黑 | 江龍黑 |
| HONAN<br>Also Ho-nan, now Henan (Yu) | 豫 | 南河 |
| HOPEH<br>Also Chihli, Hopei, now Hebei (Chi) | 冀 | 北河 |
| HUNAN<br>Also Hu-nan, now Hunan (Hsiang) | 湘 | 南湖 |
| HUPEH<br>Also Hupei, Hu-peh, now Hubei (O) | 鄂 | 北湖 |
| HU PU (Board of Revenue)<br>Also Hu Poo, Hoo Poo (Hu) | 户 | 部户 |
| KANSU<br>Now Gansu (Kan) | 甘 | 肅甘 |
| KIANGNAN<br>Also Kiang Nan Now Jiangnan (Ning) | 甯 | 南江 |
| KIANGSI<br>Also Kiang-si, Kiang-see, now Jiangxi (Kan) | 贛 | 西江 |
| KIANGSI<br>(Alternate) (Kan) | 贑 | 贛 |
| KIANGSU<br>Also Kiang-soo, now Jiangsu (Su) | 蘇 | 蘇江 |
| KIRIN<br>Also Chi-lin Now Jilin (Chi) | 吉 | 林吉 |
| KWANGSI, KWANGSEA<br>Also Kwang-si, now Guangxi (Kuei) | 桂 | 西廣 |
| KWANGTUNG<br>Also Kwang-tung, now Guangdong (Yueh) | 粵 | 東廣 |
| KWEICHOW<br>Also Kweichou, now Guizhou (Ch'ien) | 黔 | 州貴 |
| PEIYANG MINT (Tientsin)<br>Pei Yang | | 洋北 |
| SHANSI<br>Now Shanxi (Shan) or (Chin) | 山 | 西山 |
| SHENSI<br>Also Shen-si, now Shaanxi (Shan) | 陝 | 西陝 |
| SHANTUNG, SHAN-TUNG<br>Also Shang-tung, (Tung) | 東 | 東山 |
| now Shandong (Lu) | 魯 | |
| SIKANG | | |
| SINKIANG (Chinese Turkestan)<br>Also Sin-kiang, Hsin kiang Sungarei, now Xinjiang (Hsin) | 新 | 疆新 |
| SZECHUAN<br>Also Szechwan, Szechuen, Now Sichuan (Ch'uan) or (Shu) | 川<br>蜀 | 川四 |
| TAIWAN<br>Also Tai-wan, now Taiwan (Tai) | 臺 | 湾臺 |
| TAIWAN<br>(Alternate) (Tai) | | 灣台 |
| YUNNAN<br>Also Yun-nan, now Yunnan (Yun) | 雲 | 南雲 |
| YUNNAN<br>(Alternate) (Tien) | 滇 | 南雲 |
| TUNG SAN SHENG<br>Manchuria | | 省三東 |

YUNNAN-SZECHUAN 滇川

## GOVERNMENTAL NAMES
(and other source indicators)

| | Full Names (Right to left reading) |
|---|---|
| CHITUNG (Japanese puppet) | 府政東冀 |
| CHINESE SOVIET REPUBLIC | 國和共埃維蘇華中 |
| MANCHOUKUO (Japanese puppet) | 國洲滿大 |
| MENGCHIANG (Japanese puppet) | (2)行銀疆蒙 |
| PEOPLES REPUBLIC OF CHINA (Communist) | (3) 中華人民共和國 |
| REPUBLIC OF CHINA (Nationalist) | 國民華中 |
| NORTH CHINA (Japanese puppet) | 行銀備準合聯國中 |

(1) Single-character designators for provincial or regional mints are used primarily on copper coins of the Tai Ching Ti Kuo series.
(2) Vertical readings predominate.
(3) Reads left to right.
(4) For lists of mints in Sinkiang, see that section.

## ADDITIONAL CHARACTERS

The additional characters illustrated and defined below are found on the reverse of cast bronze cash coins, usually above the square center hole. In the period covered by this catalog the following mints produced cash coins with these additional marks: Board of Revenue and Board of Works in Peking, Kweichow, Aksu and Ili in Sinkiang, Shantung, Szechuan, and all three mints listed in Yunnan.

| | | | | | |
|---|---|---|---|---|---|
| 一 | I,Yi | 十一 | Shih i | 心 | Hsin |
| 二 | Erh | 合 | Ho | 宇 | Yu |
| 三 | San | 工 | Kung | 宙 | Chou |
| 四 | Szu | 主 | Chu | 來 | Lai |
| 五 | Wu | 川 | Ch'uan | 往 | Wang |
| 六 | Liu | 之 | Chih | 晋 | Chin |
| 七 | Ch'i | 正 | Cheng | 村 | Ts'un |
| 八 | Pa | 又 | Yu | 日 | Jih |
| 九 | Chiu | 山 | Shan | 列 | Lieh |
| 十 | Shih | 大 | Ta | 仁 | Jen |
| 主 | Chu | 中 | Chung | 丰 | Feng |
| 上 | Shang | 順 | Shun | 云 | Yun |
| 手 | Shou | 天 | T'ien | 利 | Li |

Kung 穴 Fen 分 —

## MINT MARK IDENTIFIER

There are more than 30 different mints covered in the following text. For ease in identification the more common varieties are illustrated with the Manchu legend.

Boo-Ciowan (Peking) BOARD OF REVENUE

Boo Yuwan (Peking) BOARD OF PUBLIC WORKS

Boo Hu
Hu Mint
ANHWEI

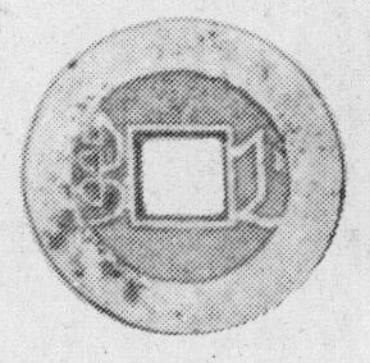

Boo Je
Che Mint
Hangchow
CHEKIANG

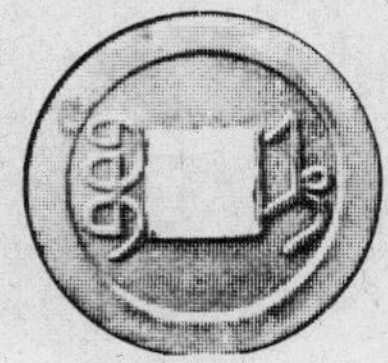

Boo Ji
Chihli Mint
Paoting
CHIHLI

Boo Gi
Chi Mint
Chichow
CHIHLI

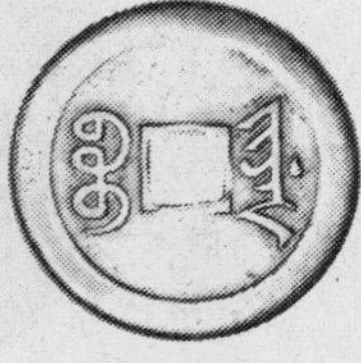

Boo Jiyen
Ching Mint
Tientsin
CHIHLI
(Through Hsien-Feng era)

Boo Fung
FENGTIEN

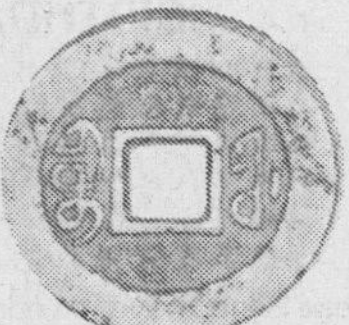

Boo Fu
Fu Mint
Fuchou
FUKIEN

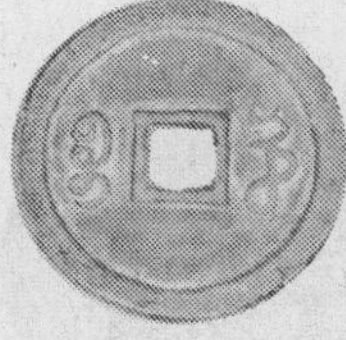

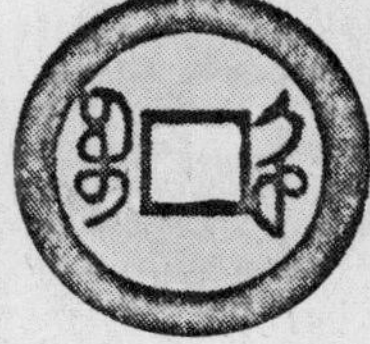

Boo Ho
Ho Mint
K'aifeng
HONAN

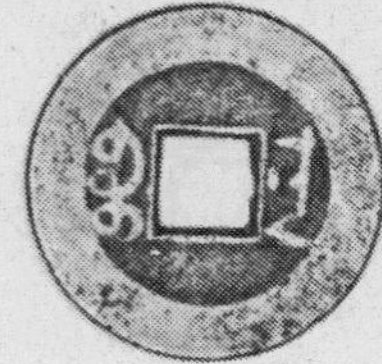

Boo Nan
Nan Mint
Ch'ang-sha
HUNAN

Boo De
Teh Mint
Chengte
CHIHLI

Boo U
Wu Mint
Wuch'ang
HUPEH

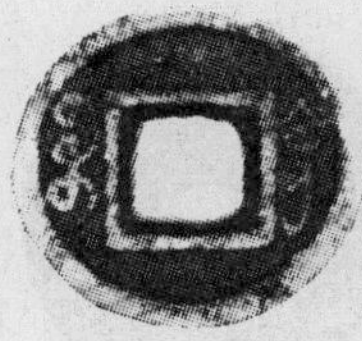

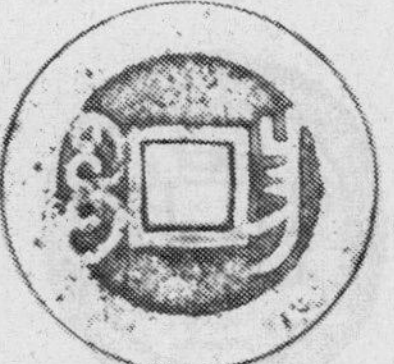

Boo Gung
Kungchang KANSU
Nanchang KIANGSI

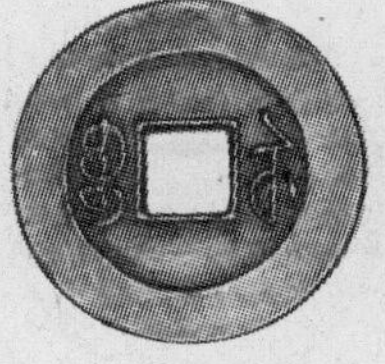

Boo Su
Su Mint
Soohow
KIANGSU

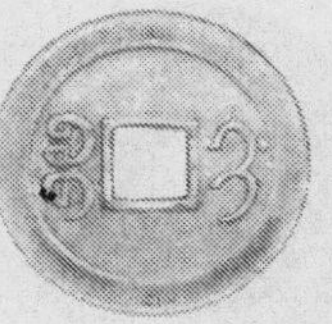

Boo Gi
Chi Mint
KIRIN
(Kuang-hsu era)

Boo Gui
Kuelin
KWANGSI

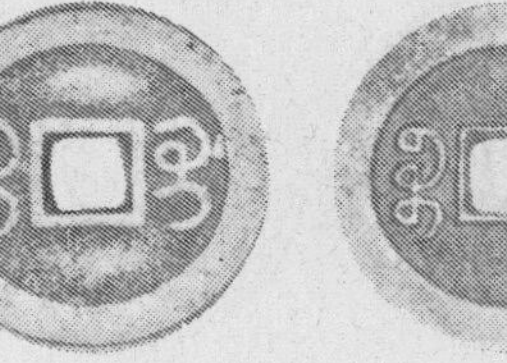

Boo Guwang
Canton
KWANGTUNG

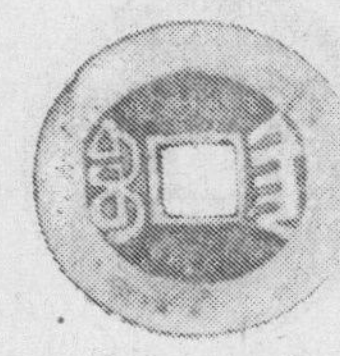

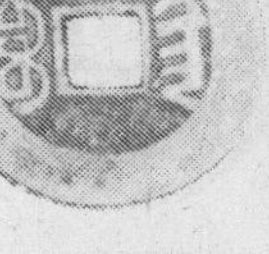

Boo Giyan
Kweiyang
KWEICHOW

Boo Jin
Taiyuan
SHANSI

Boo Ji
Chinan
SHANTUNG

Boo Cuwan
Chengtu
SZECHUAN

Boo San
Shan Mint
Sian
SHENSI

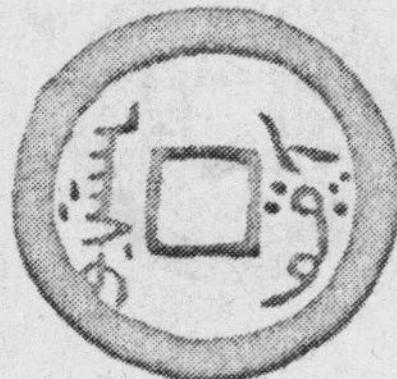

Aksu (Hocheng)
SINKIANG

Ili (Hweiyuan)
SINKIANG

Kotsha (Kuche)
SINKIANG

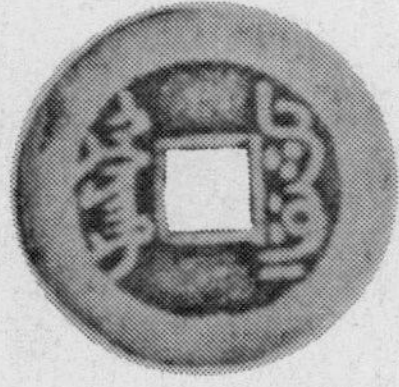

Kashgar (Shufu)
SINKIANG

Khotan (Hotien)
SINKIANG

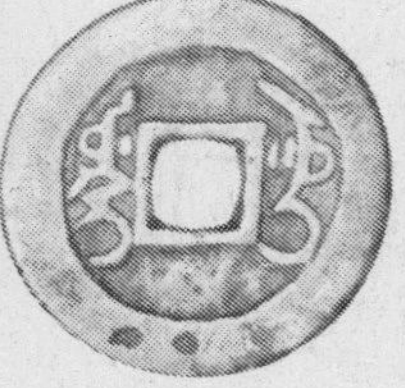

Urumchi (Tihwa)
SINKIANG

Ushi (Wushih)
SINKIANG

Yarkand (Soche)
SINKIANG

Tai Mint
TAIWAN

Boo Yon
Yun Mint
Yunnanfu
YUNNAN

Boo Dong
Tung Mint
Tungch'uan
YUNNAN

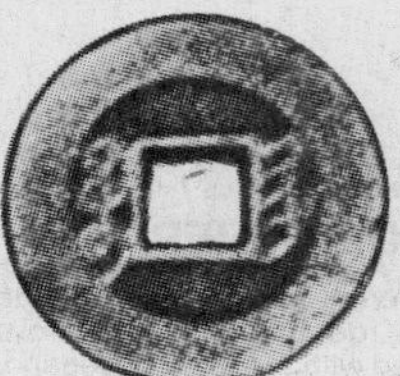

Taku (Dagu) Mint
TIENTSIN

Chou Mint
Location uncertain
(Refer to Yunnan)

## NON-CIRCULATING ISSUES

Along with regular circulation coinage produced by the various mints certain cash types were cast in various sizes with the emperor's reign title on the obverse but with various characters and/or symbols not found in our mint identifiers. This listing is not complete but it will benefit the collector as an aid to proper identification.

## PALACE ISSUES

(Palace Cash)

Usually 1-6 mace in weight, made of 60% copper and 40% zinc. Made for distribution in the palace during new year. Usually given to eunuchs and guards. Recipients hung them under lamps - "lamp 'hanging' money."

**Rev. leg: *T'ien-hsia T'ai-p'ing***
**"Peace under Heaven."**

The market value is about $60.00-100.00 in VF condition.

**Obv: Kuang-hsu**
**Hsuan-t'ung**

**Rev: *I-t'ung T'ien-hsia***

**"Unify the whole country".**

The market value is about $50.00-70.00 in VF condition.

## BIRTHDAY CASH

壽 福

These issues have the normal reign title on the obverse but the reverse has two Chinese characters 'Fu' in normal or seal script (happiness), at right and 'Shou' (birthday) at left. The market value is about $60.00-$100.00 in F/VF condition. Some are palace issues, but most are made by private sources as good luck amulets.

Kuang-hsu

## NUMERALS

| NUMBER | CONVENTIONAL | FORMAL | COMMERCIAL |
|---|---|---|---|
| 1 | 一 元 | 壹 弌 | 〡 |
| 2 | 二 | 弍 貳 | 〢 |
| 3 | 三 | 叁 弎 | 〣 |
| 4 | 四 | 肆 | 〤 |
| 5 | 五 | 伍 | 〥 |
| 6 | 六 | 陸 | 〦 |
| 7 | 七 | 柒 | 〧 |
| 8 | 八 | 捌 | 〨 |
| 9 | 九 | 玖 | 〩 |
| 10 | 十 | 拾 什 | 十 |
| 20 | 十 二 or 廿 | 拾貳 | 〢十 |
| 25 | 五 十 二 or 五廿 | 伍拾貳 | 〢十〥 |
| 30 | 十 三 or 卅 | 拾叁 | 〣十 |
| 100 | 百 一 | 佰壹 | 〡百 |
| 1,000 | 千 一 | 仟壹 | 〡千 |
| 10,000 | 萬 一 | 萬壹 | 〡万 |
| 100,000 | 萬十 億一 | 萬拾 億壹 | 十万 |
| 1,000,000 | 萬百一 | 萬佰壹 | 〡百万 |

**NOTE:** This table has been adapted from *Chinese Bank Notes* by Ward Smith and Brian Matravers.

## MONETARY UNITS

| Dollar Amounts | | |
|---|---|---|
| DOLLAR (*Yuan*) | 元 or 員 | 圓 or 圜 |
| HALF DOLLAR (*Pan Yuan*) | 圓 半 | 元中 |
| 50¢ (*Chiao/Hao*) | 角伍 | 毫伍 |
| 10¢ (*Chiao/Hao*) | 角壹 | 毫壹 |
| 1¢ (*Fen/Hsien*) | 分壹 | 仙壹 |

| Copper and Cash Coin Amounts | | | |
|---|---|---|---|
| COPPER (*Mei*) | 枚 | CASH (*Wen*) | 文 |

| Tael Amounts | |
|---|---|
| 1 TAEL (*Liang*) | 兩 |
| HALF TAEL (*Pan Liang*) | 兩半 |
| 5 MACE (*Wu Ch'ien*) | 錢伍 |
| 1 MACE (*I Ch'ien*) | 錢壹 |
| 1 CANDEREEN (*I Fen*) | 分壹 |

| Common Prefixes | | | |
|---|---|---|---|
| COPPER (*T'ung*) | 銅 | GOLD (*Chin*) | 金 |
| SILVER (*Yin*) | 銀 | Ku Ping (*Tael*)* | 平庫 |

**NOTE:** This table has been adapted from *Chinese Bank Notes* by Ward Smith and Brian Matravers.

## MONETARY SYSTEM

### Cash Coin System

800-1600 Cash = 1 Tael
400 Sinkiang 'red' cash = 1 Tael

In theory, 1000 cash were equal to a tael of silver, but in actuality the rate varied from time to time and place to place.

### Dollar System

10 Cash (Wen, Ch'ien) = 1 Cent (Fen, Hsien)
10 Cents = 1 Chiao (Hao)
100 Cents = 1 Dollar (Yuan)
1 Dollar = 0.72 Tael

Imperial silver coins normally bore no denomination, but were inscribed with their weights as follows:

1 Dollar = 7 Mace and 2 Candareens
50 Cents = 3 Mace and 6 Candareens
20 Cents = 1 Mace and 4.4 Candareens
10 Cents = 7.2 Candareens
5 Cents = 3.6 Candareens

**NOTE:** *Candareen* is spelled *Candarin* and misspelled as *Caindarin* on Kirin Province Imperial coinage.

### Tael System

10 Li = 1 Fen (Candareen)
10 Fen (Candareen) = 1 Ch'ien (Mace)
10 Ch'ien (Mace) = 1 Liang (Tael)

## DATING

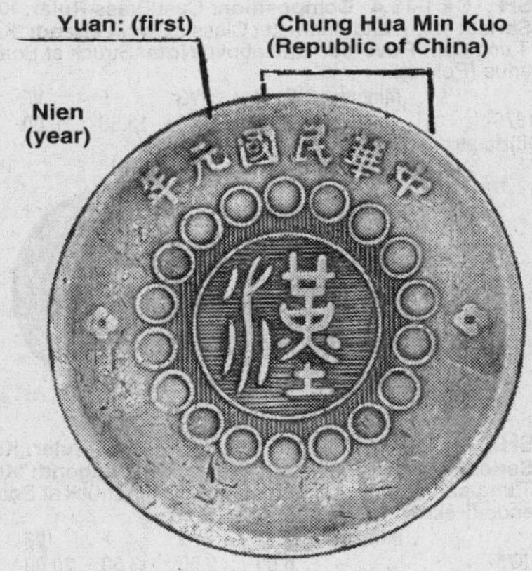


Most struck Chinese coins are dated by year within a given period, such as the regnal eras or the republican periods. A 1907 issue, for example, would be dated in the 33rd year of the Kuang Hsu era (1875 + 33 - 1 = 1907) or a 1926 issue is dated in the 15th year of the Republic (1912 + 15 - 1 = 1926). The mathematical discrepancy in both instances is accounted for by the fact that the first year is included in the elapsed time. Modern Chinese Communist coins are dated in western numerals using the western calendar, but earlier issues use conventional Chinese numerals. The coins of the Republic of China (Taiwan) are also dated in the year of the Republic, which is added to equal the calendar year. Still another method is a 60-year, repeating cycle, outlined in the table below. The date is shown by the combination of two characters, the first from the top row and the second from the column at left. In this catalog, when a cyclical date is used, the abbreviation CD appears before the AD date.

Dates not in parentheses are those which appear on the coins. For undated coins, dates appearing in parentheses are the years in which the coin was actually minted. Undated coins for which the year of minting is unknown are listed with ND (No Date) in the date or year column.

### CYCLICAL DATES

| | 庚 | 辛 | 壬 | 癸 | 甲 | 乙 | 丙 | 丁 | 戊 | 己 |
|---|---|---|---|---|---|---|---|---|---|---|
| 戌 | 1850<br>1910 | | 1862<br>1922 | | 1874<br>1934 | | 1886<br>1946 | | 1838<br>1898 | |
| 亥 | | 1851<br>1911 | | 1863<br>1923 | | 1875<br>1935 | | 1887<br>1947 | | 1839<br>1899 |
| 子 | 1840<br>1900 | | 1852<br>1912 | | 1864<br>1924 | | 1876<br>1936 | | 1888<br>1948 | |
| 丑 | | 1841<br>1901 | | 1853<br>1913 | | 1865<br>1925 | | 1877<br>1937 | | 1889<br>1949 |
| 寅 | 1830<br>1890 | | 1842<br>1902 | | 1854<br>1914 | | 1866<br>1926 | | 1878<br>1938 | |
| 卯 | | 1831<br>1891 | | 1843<br>1903 | | 1855<br>1915 | | 1867<br>1927 | | 1879<br>1939 |
| 辰 | 1880<br>1940 | | 1832<br>1892 | | 1844<br>1904 | | 1856<br>1916 | | 1868<br>1928 | |
| 巳 | | 1881<br>1941 | | 1833<br>1893 | | 1845<br>1905 | | 1857<br>1917 | | 1869<br>1929 |
| 午 | 1870<br>1930 | | 1882<br>1942 | | 1834<br>1894 | | 1846<br>1906 | | 1858<br>1918 | |
| 未 | | 1871<br>1931 | | 1883<br>1943 | | 1835<br>1895 | | 1847<br>1907 | | 1859<br>1919 |
| 申 | 1860<br>1920 | | 1872<br>1932 | | 1884<br>1944 | | 1836<br>1896 | | 1848<br>1908 | |
| 酉 | | 1861<br>1921 | | 1873<br>1933 | | 1885<br>1945 | | 1837<br>1897 | | 1849<br>1909 |

**NOTE:** This table has been adapted from *Chinese Bank Notes* by Ward Smith and Brian Matravers.

### GRADING

Chinese coins should not be graded entirely by western standards. In addition to Fine, Very Fine, Extremely Fine (XF), and Uncirculated, the type of strike should be considered weak, medium or sharp strike. China had no rigid minting rules as we know them. For instance, Kirin (Jilin). and Sinkiang (Xinjiang) Provinces used some dies made of iron - hence, they wore out rapidly. Some communist army issues were apparently struck by crude hand methods on soft dies (it is hard to find two coins of the same die!). In general, especially for some minor coins, dies were used until they were worn well beyond western standards. Subsequently, one could have an uncirculated coin struck from worn dies with little of the design or letters still visible, but still uncirculated! All prices quoted are for well-struck (sharp struck), well-centered specimens. Most silver coins can be found from very fine to uncirculated. Some copper coins are difficult to find except in poorer grades.

## REFERENCES

The following references have been used for this section:

**K - Edward Kann - Illustrated Catalog of Chinese Coins.**

**Hsu - T.K. Hsu - Illustrated Catalog of Chinese Coins, 1981 edition.**

**W - A.M. Tracey Woodward - The Minted Ten-Cash Coins of China.**

**NOTE:** The die struck 10 and 20 Cash coins are often found silver plated. This was not done at the mint. They were apparently plated to be passed to the unwary as silver coins.

## IDENTIFICATION

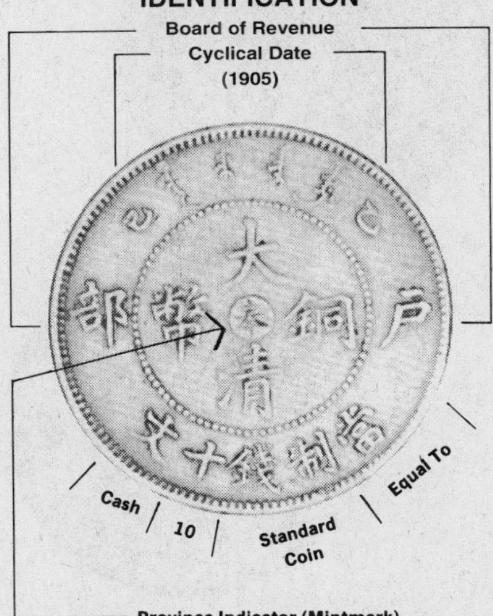


/Cash/ 10 / Standard / Equal To /

## DRAGON TYPES

(Chinese Imperial Coins)

Side View Dragon-left (Silver Coins)

First used by the Kwangtung Mint in 1889. This was the standard (though not the only) dragon used on silver coins. Normally there is no circle around the dragon. Note the fireball beneath the dragon's chin. Normally there are seven flames on the fireball.

Side View Dragon-left (Copper Coins)

First used on copper coins in 1901 or 1902. The dragon may be circled or uncircled. Many varieties exist, with three to seven flames on the fireball.

Side View Dragon-right (Silver Coins)

First appears on the second series of Fukien. The dragon is redesigned with the dragon's body reversed.

Flying Dragon

Introduced in 1901. Copied from the dragon on Japanese coins. China used this dragon only on copper coins (with one rare exception). Note that the clouds around the dragon's body are curly and snake-like instead of puffy like those around the side view dragon. The fireball now appears as a pearl which the dragon is about to grasp, and normally has no flames. This dragon is normally circled.

Front View Dragon

Introduced about 1904, this type of dragon was not used by many mints. The dragon is usually uncircled and has few clouds around its body. Note the tiny mountain under the cloud beneath the fireball.

Tai Ch'ing Ti Kuo Dragon

In 1905 China carried out a coinage reform which standardized the designs of copper coins. All mints were ordered to use the same obverse and reverse designs, but to place a mint mark in the center of the obverse.

## SYCEE (INGOTS)

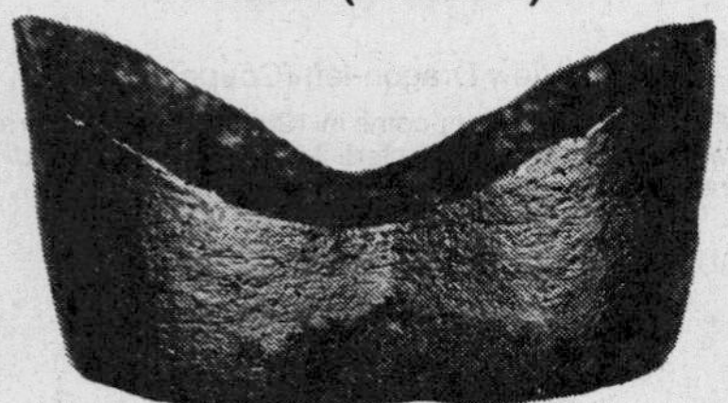

Prior to 1889 the general coinage issued by the Chinese government was the copper-alloy cash coin. Despite occasional shortlived experiments with silver and gold coinage, and disregarding paper money which tended to be unreliable, the government expected the people to get by solely with cash coins. This system worked well for individuals making purchases for themselves, but was unsatisfactory for trade and large business transactions, since a dollar's worth of cash coins weighed about four pounds. As a result, a private currency consisting of silver ingots, usually stamped by the firm which made them, came into use. These were the sycee ingots.

It is not known when these ingots first came into use. Some sources date them to the Yuan (Mongol) dynasty but they are certainly much older. Examples are known from as far back as the Han dynasty (206 BC - 220 AD) but prior to the Sung era (960 - 1280AD) they were used mainly for hoarding wealth. The development of commerce by the Sung dynasty, however, required the use of silver or gold to pay for large purchases. By the Mongol period (1280-1368) silver ingots and paper money had become the dominant currencies, especially for trade. The western explorers who traveled to China during this period (such as Marco Polo) mention both paper money and sycee but not a single one refers to cash coins.

During the Ming dynasty (1368-1644) trade fell off and the use of silver decreased. But toward the end of that dynasty, Dutch and British ships began a new China trade and sycee once again became common. During the 19th and early 20th centuries, the trade in sycee became enormous. Most of the sycee around today are from this period. In 1935 the Chinese government and in 1939 Sinkiang banned the use of sycee and it soon disappeared.

The word sycee (pronounced "sigh - see") is a western corruption of the Chinese word hsi-szu ("fine silk") or hsi yin ("fine silver") and is first known to have appeared in the English language in the late 1600's. By the early 1700's the word appeared regularly in the records of the British East India Company. Westerners also called these ingots "boat money" or "shoe money" owing to the fact that the most common type of ingot resembles a Chinese shoe. The Chinese, however, called the ingots by a variety of names, the most common of which were yuan pao, wen - yin (fine silver) and yin-ting (silver ingot).

The ingots were cast in molds (giving them their characteristic shapes) and while the metal was still semi liquid, the inscription was impressed. It was due to this procedure that the sides of some sycee are higher than the center. The manufacturers were usually silver firms, often referred to as lu fang's, and after the sycee was finished it was occasionally tested and marked by the kung ku (public assayer).

Sycee were not circulated as we understand it. One didn't usually carry a sycee to market and spend it. Usually the ingots were used as a means of carrying a large amount of money on trips (as we would carry $100 bills instead of $5 bills) or for storing wealth. Large transactions between merchants or banks were paid by means of crates of sycee - each containing 60 fifty tael ingots.

Sycee are known in a variety of shapes the most common of which are the shoe or boat shaped, drum shaped, and loaf shaped (rectangular or hourglass-shaped, with a generally flat surface). Other shapes include one that resembles a double headed axe (this is the oldest type known), one that is square and flat, and others that are "fancy" (in the form of fish, butterflies, leaves, etc.).

Sycee have no denominations as they were simply ingots that passed by weight. Most are in more or less standard weights, however, the most common being 1, 5, 10 and 50 taels. Other weights known include 1/10, 1/5, 1/4, 1/3, 1/2, 2/3, 72/100 (this is the weight of a dollar), 3/4, 2, 3, 4, 6, 7, 8 and 25 taels. Most of the pieces weighing less than 5 taels were used as gifts or souvenirs.

The actual weight of any given value of sycee varied considerably due to the fact that the tael was not a single weight but a general term for a wide range of local weight standards. The weight of the tael varied depending upon location and type of tael in question. For example in one town, the weight of a tael of rice, of silver and of stones may each be different. In addition, the fineness of silver also varied depending upon location and type of tael in question. It was not true, as westerners often wrote, that sycee were made of pure silver. For most purposes, a weight of 37 grams may be used for the tael.

**Weights and Current Market Value of Sycee (Weights are approximate)**

| | | |
|---|---|---|
| 1/2 tael | 17-19 grams | 26.00 |
| 72/100 tael | 25-27 grams | 36.00 |
| 1 tael | 35-38 grams | 46.00 |
| 2 taels | 70-75 grams | 70.00 |
| 3 taels | 100-140 grams | 85.00 |
| 5 taels | 175-190 grams | 110.00 |
| 7 taels | 240-260 grams | 125.00 |
| 10 taels | 350-380 grams | 250.00 |
| 25 taels | 895-925 grams | 3500. |
| 50 taels | 1790-1850 grams | 2000. |
| 50 taels, square | 1790-1850 grams | 1600. |

## SZECHUAN WARLORD ISSUE

### 200 CASH

**Obv: Mirror image of normal coin, Y#459.**

**NOTE:** Certain coins found with degenerate or reversed English legends are usually considered to be local warlord issues while some authorities insist on referring to them as contemporary counterfeits.

# CHINA

## EMPIRE

### GENERAL CAST COINAGE

**CASH C# 1-16.2 Composition:** Cast Brass **Ruler:** Kuang-hsü **Series:** Thousand Character Classic **Obv. Legend:** "Kuang-hsü T'ung-pao" **Reverse:** "Chou" above **Note:** Struck at Board of Revenue (Peking).

| Date | Mintage | Good | VG | F | VF | XF |
|---|---|---|---|---|---|---|
| ND(1875-1908)Hu-pu | — | 6.00 | 9.00 | 13.50 | 20.00 | — |

**CASH C# 1-16.3 Composition:** Cast Brass **Ruler:** Kuang-hsü **Series:** Thousand Character Classic **Obv. Legend:** "Kuang-hsü T'ung-pao" **Reverse:** "Jih" above **Note:** Struck at Board of Revenue (Peking).

| Date | Mintage | Good | VG | F | VF | XF |
|---|---|---|---|---|---|---|
| ND(1875-1908)Hu-pu | — | 6.00 | 9.00 | 13.50 | 20.00 | — |

**CASH C# 1-16.4 Composition:** Cast Brass **Ruler:** Kuang-hsü **Series:** Thousand Character Classic **Obv. Legend:** "Kuang-hsü T'ung-pao" **Reverse:** "Lai" above **Note:** Struck at Board of Revenue (Peking).

| Date | Mintage | Good | VG | F | VF | XF |
|---|---|---|---|---|---|---|
| ND(1875-1908)Hu-pu | — | 6.00 | 9.00 | 13.50 | 20.00 | — |

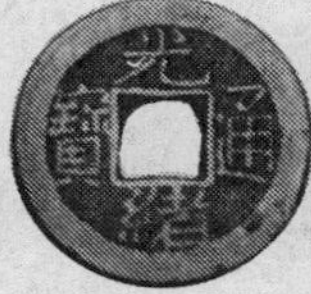 

**CASH C# 1-16.5 Composition:** Cast Brass **Ruler:** Kuang-hsü **Series:** Thousand Character Classic **Obv. Legend:** "Kuang-hsü T'ung-pao" **Reverse:** "Lieh" above **Note:** Struck at Board of Revenue (Peking).

| Date | Mintage | Good | VG | F | VF | XF |
|---|---|---|---|---|---|---|
| ND(1875-1908)Hu-pu | — | 6.00 | 9.00 | 13.50 | 20.00 | — |

**CASH C# 1-16.6 Composition:** Cast Brass **Ruler:** Kuang-hsü **Series:** Thousand Character Classic **Obv. Legend:** "Kuang-hsü T'ung-pao" **Reverse:** "Wang" above **Note:** Struck at Board of Revenue (Peking).

| Date | Mintage | Good | VG | F | VF | XF |
|---|---|---|---|---|---|---|
| ND(1875-1908)Hu-pu | — | 6.00 | 9.00 | 13.50 | 20.00 | — |

**CASH C# 1-16.7 Composition:** Cast Brass **Ruler:** Kuang-hsü **Series:** Thousand Character Classic **Obv. Legend:** "Kuang-hsü T'ung-pao" **Reverse:** "Yu" above **Note:** Struck at Board of Revenue (Peking).

| Date | Mintage | Good | VG | F | VF | XF |
|---|---|---|---|---|---|---|
| ND(1875-1908)Hu-pu | — | 6.00 | 9.00 | 13.50 | 20.00 | — |

**CASH C# 1-16.10 Composition:** Cast Brass **Ruler:** Kuang-hsü **Series:** Thousand Character Classic **Obv. Legend:** "Kuang-hsü T'ung-pao" **Reverse:** "Shou" above **Note:** Struck at Board of Revenue (Peking).

| Date | Mintage | Good | VG | F | VF | XF |
|---|---|---|---|---|---|---|
| ND(1875-1908)Hu-pu | — | 6.00 | 9.00 | 13.50 | 20.00 | — |

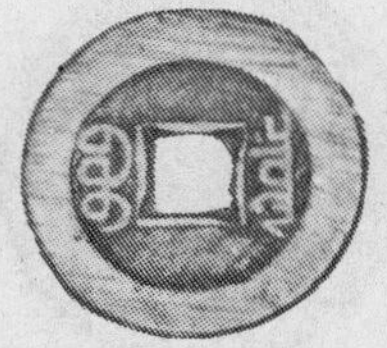

**CASH C# 1-16 Composition:** Cast Brass **Ruler:** Kuang-hsü **Obv. Legend:** "Kuang-hsü T'ung-pao" **Note:** Struck at Board of Revenue (Peking).

| Date | Mintage | Good | VG | F | VF | XF |
|---|---|---|---|---|---|---|
| ND(1875-1908)Hu-pu | — | 1.50 | 2.00 | 2.75 | 4.00 | — |

**Note:** For crude cast, red copper issues, see Sinkiang General coinage

**CASH C# 1-16.1 Composition:** Cast Brass **Ruler:** Kuang-hsü **Series:** Thousand Character Classic **Obv. Legend:** "Kuang-hsü T'ung-pao" **Reverse:** "Chih" above **Note:** Struck at Board of Revenue (Peking). Sch.#1578.

| Date | Mintage | Good | VG | F | VF | XF |
|---|---|---|---|---|---|---|
| ND(1875-1908)Hu-pu | — | 6.00 | 9.00 | 13.50 | 20.00 | — |

**CASH C# 1-16.8 Composition:** Cast Brass **Ruler:** Kuang-hsü **Obv. Legend:** "Kuang-hsü T'ung-pao" **Reverse:** Dot below **Note:** Struck at Board of Revenue (Peking).

| Date | Mintage | Good | VG | F | VF | XF |
|---|---|---|---|---|---|---|
| ND(1899-1901)Hu-pu | — | 1.75 | 3.00 | 4.00 | 6.00 | — |

**CASH C# 1-16.9 Composition:** Cast Brass **Ruler:** Kuang-hsü **Obv. Legend:** "Kuang-hsü T'ung-pao" **Reverse:** Dot above **Note:** Struck at Board of Revenue (Peking).

| Date | Mintage | Good | VG | F | VF | XF |
|---|---|---|---|---|---|---|
| ND(1899-1901)Hu-pu | — | 1.75 | 3.00 | 4.00 | 6.00 | — |

**CASH C# 2-15 Composition:** Cast Brass **Ruler:** Kuang-hsü **Obverse:** Inscription: "Kuang-hsü T'ung-pao" **Note:** Struck at Board of Public Works (Peking).

| Date | Mintage | Good | VG | F | VF | XF |
|---|---|---|---|---|---|---|
| ND(1875-1908)Kung-pu | — | 1.50 | 3.00 | 6.00 | 7.00 | — |

**Note:** For crude cast copper strikes, see Sinkiang General Coinage

**CASH C# 2-15.1 Composition:** Cast Brass **Ruler:** Kuang-hsü **Series:** Thousand Character Classic **Obv. Legend:** "Kuang-hsü T'ung-pao" **Reverse:** "Chou" above **Note:** Struck at Board of Public Works (Peking).

| Date | Mintage | Good | VG | F | VF | XF |
|---|---|---|---|---|---|---|
| ND(1899-1901Kung-pu | — | 6.00 | 10.00 | 15.00 | 20.00 | — |

**CASH C# 2-15.2 Composition:** Cast Brass **Ruler:** Kuang-hsü **Series:** Thousand Character Classic **Obv. Legend:** "Kuang-hsü T'ung-pao" **Reverse:** "Lai" above **Note:** Struck at Board of Public Works (Peking).

| Date | Mintage | Good | VG | F | VF | XF |
|---|---|---|---|---|---|---|
| ND(1899-1901)Kung-pu | — | 6.00 | 10.00 | 15.00 | 20.00 | — |

**CASH C# 2-15.3 Composition:** Cast Brass **Ruler:** Kuang-hsü **Series:** Thousand Character Classic **Obv. Legend:** "Kuang-hsü T'ung-pao" **Reverse:** "Lieh" above **Note:** Struck at Board of Public Works (Peking).

| Date | Mintage | Good | VG | F | VF | XF |
|---|---|---|---|---|---|---|
| ND(1899-1901Kung-pu | — | 6.00 | 10.00 | 15.00 | 20.00 | — |

**CASH C# 2-15.4 Composition:** Cast Brass **Ruler:** Kuang-hsü **Series:** Thousand Character Classic **Obv. Legend:** "Kuang-hsü T'ung-pao" **Reverse:** "Yu" above **Note:** Struck at Board of Public Works (Peking).

| Date | Mintage | Good | VG | F | VF | XF |
|---|---|---|---|---|---|---|
| ND(1899-1901)Kung-pu | — | 6.00 | 10.00 | 15.00 | 20.00 | — |

**CASH C# 2-15.5 Composition:** Cast Brass **Ruler:** Kuang-hsü **Series:** Thousand Character Classic **Obv. Legend:** "Kuang-hsü T'ung-pao" **Reverse:** "Jih" above **Note:** Struck at Board of Public Works (Peking).

| Date | Mintage | Good | VG | F | VF | XF |
|---|---|---|---|---|---|---|
| ND(1899-1901)Kung-pu | — | 6.00 | 10.00 | 15.00 | 20.00 | — |

**CASH C# 2-15.6 Composition:** Cast Brass **Ruler:** Kuang-hsü **Series:** Thousand Character Classic **Obv. Legend:** "Kuang-hsü T'ung-pao" **Reverse:** "Wang" above **Note:** Struck at Board of Public Works (Peking).

| Date | Mintage | Good | VG | F | VF | XF |
|---|---|---|---|---|---|---|
| ND(1899-1901)Kung-pu | — | 6.00 | 10.00 | 15.00 | 20.00 | — |

**CASH C# 2-15.7 Composition:** Cast Brass **Ruler:** Kuang-hsü **Series:** Thousand Character Classic **Obv. Legend:** "Kuang-hsü T'ung-pao" **Reverse:** "Jih" above, dot below **Note:** Struck at Board of Public Works (Peking).

| Date | Mintage | Good | VG | F | VF | XF |
|---|---|---|---|---|---|---|
| ND(1899-1901)Kung-pu | — | 6.00 | 10.00 | 15.00 | 20.00 | — |

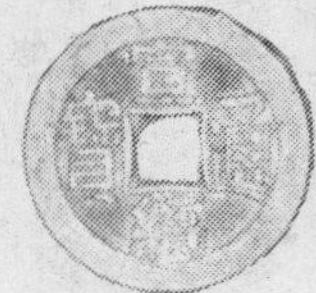
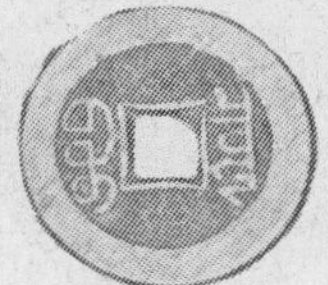

**CASH C# 1-19.1 Composition:** Cast Brass **Ruler:** Hsüan-t'ung **Obv. Legend:** "Hsüan-t'ung T'ung-pao" **Note:** Struck at Board of Revenue (Peking).

| Date | Mintage | Good | VG | F | VF | XF |
|---|---|---|---|---|---|---|
| ND(1909-11)Hu-pu | — | 5.50 | 7.00 | 10.00 | 15.00 | — |

**CASH C# 1-19.2 Composition:** Cast Brass **Ruler:** Hsüan-t'ung **Obv. Legend:** "Hsüan-t'ung T'ung-pao" **Note:** Struck at Board of Revenue (Peking).

| Date | Mintage | Good | VG | F | VF | XF |
|---|---|---|---|---|---|---|
| ND(1909-11)Hu-pu | — | 10.00 | 15.00 | 25.00 | 30.00 | — |

**CASH C# 1-19a Composition:** Iron **Ruler:** Hsüan-t'ung **Obv. Legend:** "Hsüan-t'ung T'ung-pao" **Note:** Struck at Board of Revenue (Peking).

| Date | Mintage | Good | VG | F | VF | XF |
|---|---|---|---|---|---|---|
| ND(1909-11)Hu-pu | — | 12.00 | 20.00 | 30.00 | 50.00 | — |

**5 CASH C# 2-5 Composition:** Cast Brass **Ruler:** Hsien-feng **Obv. Legend:** "Hsien-feng Chung-pao" **Note:** Struck at Board of Public Works (Peking). (Size varies: 28-32 milimeters.)

| Date | Mintage | Good | VG | F | VF | XF |
|---|---|---|---|---|---|---|
| ND(1851-61)Kung-pu | — | 10.00 | 12.50 | 17.50 | 35.00 | — |

**5 CASH C# 2-16 Composition:** Cast Brass **Ruler:** Kuang-hsü **Obv. Legend:** "Kuang-hsü Chung-pao" **Note:** Struck at Board of Public Works (Peking).

| Date | Mintage | Good | VG | F | VF | XF |
|---|---|---|---|---|---|---|
| ND(1875-1908)Kung-pu | — | 200 | 350 | 500 | 700 | — |

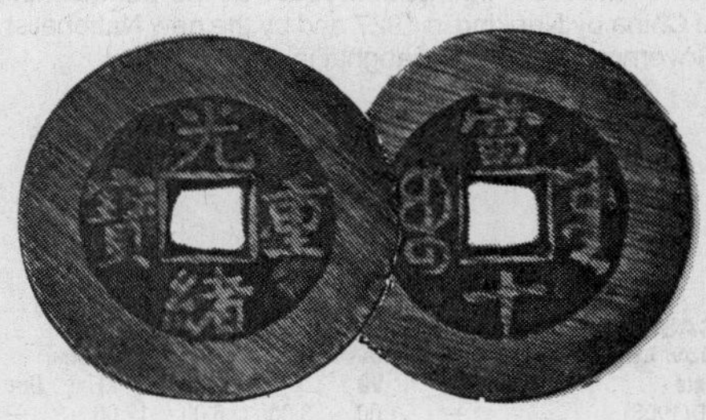

**10 CASH C# 2-17 Composition:** Cast Brass **Ruler:** Kuang-hsü **Obv. Legend:** "Kuang-hsü T'ung-pao" **Reverse:** Normal Shih(10) below **Note:** Struck at Board of Public Works (Peking). (Size varies: 31-32 milimeters.)

| Date | Mintage | Good | VG | F | VF | XF |
|---|---|---|---|---|---|---|
| ND(1875-1908) | — | 4.50 | 7.50 | 10.00 | 25.00 | — |

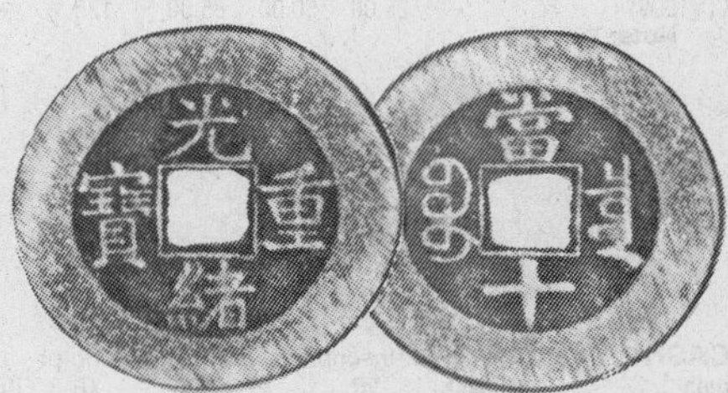

**10 CASH C# 1-17 Composition:** Cast Brass **Ruler:** Kuang-hsü **Obv. Legend:** "Kuang-hsü Chung-pao" **Reverse:** Normal "Shih" for 10 below **Size:** 30 mm. **Note:** Struck at Board of Revenue (Peking).

| Date | Mintage | Good | VG | F | VF | XF |
|---|---|---|---|---|---|---|
| ND(1875-1908)Hu-pu | — | 3.00 | 5.00 | 8.00 | 10.00 | — |

**10 CASH C# 1-18 Composition:** Cast Brass **Ruler:** Kuang-hsü **Obv. Legend:** "Kuang-hsü Chung-pao" **Reverse:** Official "Shih" for 10 below **Size:** 28 mm. **Note:** Struck at Board of Revenue (Peking).

| Date | Mintage | Good | VG | F | VF | XF |
|---|---|---|---|---|---|---|
| ND(1875-1908)Hu-pu | — | 4.50 | 7.50 | 10.00 | 15.00 | — |

**10 CASH C# 1-18.1 Composition:** Cast Brass **Ruler:** Kuang-hsü **Obv. Legend:** "Kuang-hsü Chung-pao" **Reverse:** Official "Shih" for 10 below **Size:** 22 mm. **Note:** Struck at Board of Revenue (Peking).

| Date | Mintage | Good | VG | F | VF | XF |
|---|---|---|---|---|---|---|
| ND(1875-1908)Hu-pu | — | 6.00 | 9.00 | 15.00 | 20.00 | — |

**10 CASH C# 2-18 Composition:** Cast Brass **Ruler:** Kuang-hsü **Obv. Legend:** "Kuang-hsü T'ung-pao" **Reverse:** Official Shih(10) below **Note:** Struck at Board of Public Works (Peking).

| Date | Mintage | Good | VG | F | VF | XF |
|---|---|---|---|---|---|---|
| ND(1880-1908) | — | 6.00 | 10.00 | 15.00 | 35.00 | — |

## STANDARD UNIFIED GENERAL COINAGE

A Central mint opened at Tientsin in 1905, was made responsible for producing most of the dies for the Tai Ch'ing "Hupoo" coinage and for the 1910 and 1911 unified coinage. The mint was burned down in 1912 but resumed operations in 1914 with Yuan Shih-kai dollar issues. It continued producing dies for selected branch mints until 1921. It was superseded as the Central mint of China by Nanking in 1927 and by the new Nationalist Government mint at Shanghai in 1933.

**CASH** **Y# 7** **Composition:** Brass **Ruler:** Kuang-hsü **Obv. Legend:** "Kuang-hsü" **Reverse:** Dragon **Note:** Struck.

| Date | Mintage | VG | F | VF | XF | Unc |
|---|---|---|---|---|---|---|
| CD(1908) | — | 1.00 | 3.00 | 6.00 | 12.00 | — |

**CASH** **Y# 18** **Composition:** Brass **Ruler:** Hsüan-t'ung **Obv. Legend:** "Hsüan-t'ung " **Reverse:** Dragon **Note:** Struck.

| Date | Mintage | VG | F | VF | XF | Unc |
|---|---|---|---|---|---|---|
| CD(1909) | — | 25.00 | 50.00 | 85.00 | 135 | — |

Note: Inc. Y25

**CASH** **Y# 25** **Obverse:** Inscription: Tai-ch'ing T'ung-pi

| Date | Mintage | VG | F | VF | XF | Unc |
|---|---|---|---|---|---|---|
| ND(1909) | 92,126,000 | 1.00 | 1.50 | 2.00 | 3.00 | — |

**2 CASH** **Y# 8** **Composition:** Copper **Ruler:** Kuang-hsü **Obverse:** Inscription: Tai-ch'ing T'ung-pi **Reverse:** Dragon

| Date | Mintage | VG | F | VF | XF | Unc |
|---|---|---|---|---|---|---|
| CD(1905) Hu-pu | — | 2.50 | 4.50 | 10.00 | 17.50 | — |
| CD(1906) Hu-pu | — | 3.00 | 6.00 | 10.00 | 25.00 | — |

**2 CASH** **Y# 8.1** **Composition:** Copper **Ruler:** Kuang-hsü **Obverse:** Inscription: Tai-ch'ing T'ung-pi; four dots divide legend **Reverse:** Dragon

| Date | Mintage | VG | F | VF | XF | Unc |
|---|---|---|---|---|---|---|
| CD(1907) | — | 7.00 | 18.00 | 25.00 | 40.00 | — |

**2 CASH** **Y# A18** **Composition:** Copper **Ruler:** Hsüan-t'ung **Obverse:** Inscription: Hsüan-t'ung

| Date | Mintage | VG | F | VF | XF | Unc |
|---|---|---|---|---|---|---|
| CD(1909) Rare | 13,353,000 | — | — | — | — | — |

**5 CASH** **Y# 3** **Composition:** Copper **Ruler:** Kuang-hsü **Obverse:** Inscription: Kuang-hsü Yüan-pao **Reverse:** Dragon **Rev. Legend:** HU POO

| Date | Mintage | VG | F | VF | XF | Unc |
|---|---|---|---|---|---|---|
| ND(1903-05) Hu-pu | 3,671,000 | 7.00 | 14.00 | 21.00 | 35.00 | — |

**5 CASH** **Composition:** Copper **Ruler:** Kuang-hsü **Obverse:** Inscription: Kuang-hsü Yüan-pao **Obv. Legend:** Kuang-hsü Nien-tsao **Reverse:** Dragon; smaller legend **Rev. Legend:** HU POO

| Date | Mintage | VG | F | VF | XF | Unc |
|---|---|---|---|---|---|---|
| ND(1903-05) Reported, not confirmed | — | — | — | — | — | — |

**5 CASH** **Y# 9** **Composition:** Copper **Ruler:** Kuang-hsü **Obverse:** Inscription: Tai-ch'ing T'ung-pi **Reverse:** Dragon; smaller legend **Rev. Legend:** Kuang-hsu

| Date | Mintage | VG | F | VF | XF | Unc |
|---|---|---|---|---|---|---|
| CD(1905) | — | 5.00 | 10.00 | 20.00 | 35.00 | — |
| CD(1906) Rare | — | — | — | — | — | — |

**5 CASH** **Y# 9.1** **Composition:** Copper **Ruler:** Kuang-hsu **Obverse:** Inscription: Tai-ch'ing T'ung-pi; four dots divide legend **Obv. Legend:** Kuang-hsü **Reverse:** Dragon

| Date | Mintage | VG | F | VF | XF | Unc |
|---|---|---|---|---|---|---|
| CD(1907) | — | 16.50 | 40.00 | 75.00 | 125 | — |

**5 CASH** **Y# 19** **Composition:** Copper **Ruler:** Hsüan-t'ung **Obv. Legend:** Hsüan-t'ung

| Date | Mintage | VG | F | VF | XF | Unc |
|---|---|---|---|---|---|---|
| CD(1909) | 2,170,000 | — | — | 850 | 1,200 | — |

**10 CASH** **Y# 4** **Composition:** Copper **Ruler:** Kuang-hsu **Obverse:** Inscription: Kuang-hsü Yüan-pao **Obv. Legend:** Hsüan-t'ung **Reverse:** Side view dragon **Rev. Legend:** HU POO

| Date | Mintage | F | VF | XF | Unc | BU |
|---|---|---|---|---|---|---|
| ND(1903-05) | 281,171,000 | 2.00 | 3.50 | 6.00 | 25.00 | — |

**10 CASH** **Y# 4.1** **Composition:** Copper **Ruler:** Kuang-hsü **Reverse:** Side view dragon; different rosettes; smaller legend **Rev. Legend:** HU POO

| Date | Mintage | F | VF | XF | Unc | BU |
|---|---|---|---|---|---|---|
| ND(1903-05) | Inc. above | 1.00 | 2.00 | 5.00 | 20.00 | — |

**10 CASH** **Y# 10** **Composition:** Copper **Ruler:** Kuang-hsü **Obverse:** Inscription: Tai-ch'ing T'ung-pi **Reverse:** Side view dragon **Rev. Legend:** Kuang-hsü Nien-tsao TAI-CHING-TI-KUO...

| Date | Mintage | F | VF | XF | Unc | BU |
|---|---|---|---|---|---|---|
| CD(1905) | Inc. above | 1.50 | 3.00 | 5.00 | 25.00 | — |

**10 CASH** **Y# 10.1** **Composition:** Copper **Ruler:** Kuang-hsü **Obverse:** Inscription: Tai-ch'ing T'ung-pi **Reverse:** Different dragon; larger legend **Rev. Legend:** TAI-CHING-TI-KUO...

| Date | Mintage | F | VF | XF | Unc | BU |
|---|---|---|---|---|---|---|
| CD(1905) | — | 25.00 | 65.00 | 110 | 200 | — |

**10 CASH** **Y# 10.2** **Composition:** Copper **Ruler:** Kuang-hsü **Obverse:** Inscription: Tai-ch'ing T'ung-pi **Reverse:** Dragon **Rev. Legend:** Kuang-hsü Nien-tsao TAI-CHING-TI-KUO

| Date | Mintage | F | VF | XF | Unc | BU |
|---|---|---|---|---|---|---|
| CD(1906) | — | 0.75 | 1.50 | 3.00 | 20.00 | — |

**10 CASH** **Y# 10.3** **Composition:** Copper **Ruler:** Kuang-hsü **Obverse:** Inscription: Tai-ch'ing T'ung-pi; without dots **Reverse:** Dragon; legend without dot after KUO **Rev. Legend:** Kuang-hsü Nien-tsao TAI-CHING-TI-KUO

| Date | Mintage | F | VF | XF | Unc | BU |
|---|---|---|---|---|---|---|
| CD(1907) | — | 1.00 | 2.00 | 4.50 | 18.00 | — |

**10 CASH** **Y# 10.4** **Composition:** Copper **Ruler:** Kuang-hsü **Obverse:** Inscription: Tai-ch'ing T'ung-pi **Reverse:** Dragon; legend with dot after KUO **Rev. Legend:** Kuang-hsü Nien-tsao TAI-CHING-TI-KUO.

| Date | Mintage | F | VF | XF | Unc | BU |
|---|---|---|---|---|---|---|
| CD(1907) | — | 1.00 | 2.00 | 4.50 | 18.00 | — |

**10 CASH** **Y# 10.4a** **Composition:** Brass **Ruler:** Kuang-hsü **Obverse:** Inscription: Tai-ch'ing T'ung-pi; without dots **Reverse:** Dragon **Rev. Legend:** Kuang-hsü Nien-tsao TAI-CHING-TI-KUO.

| Date | Mintage | F | VF | XF | Unc | BU |
|---|---|---|---|---|---|---|
| CD(1907) | — | 5.50 | 20.00 | 35.00 | 80.00 | — |

**10 CASH** **Y# 10.5** **Composition:** Copper **Ruler:** Kuang-hsü **Obverse:** Inscription: Tai-ch'ing T'ung-pi; four dots divide legend **Reverse:** Dragon **Rev. Legend:** Kuang-hsü Nien-tsao TAI-CHING-TI-KUO.

| Date | Mintage | F | VF | XF | Unc | BU |
|---|---|---|---|---|---|---|
| CD(1907) | — | 1.00 | 2.00 | 4.50 | 18.00 | — |

**10 CASH Y# 10.5a Composition:** Brass **Ruler:** Kuang-hsü **Obverse:** Inscription: Tai-ch'ing T'ung-pi **Reverse:** Dragon **Rev. Legend:** Kuang-hsü Nien-tsao TAI-CHING-TI-KUO.

| Date | Mintage | F | VF | XF | Unc | BU |
|---|---|---|---|---|---|---|
| CD(1907) | — | 5.50 | 15.00 | 30.00 | 85.00 | — |

**10 CASH Y# 20 Composition:** Copper **Ruler:** Hsüan-t'ung **Obverse:** Inscription: Tai-ch'ing T'ung-pi **Reverse:** Waves below dragon **Rev. Legend:** Hsüan-t'ung Nien-tsao TAI-CHING-TI-KUO.

| Date | Mintage | F | VF | XF | Unc | BU |
|---|---|---|---|---|---|---|
| CD(1909) | — | 1.00 | 2.00 | 4.00 | 22.50 | — |

**10 CASH Y# 20.1 Composition:** Copper **Ruler:** Hsüan-t'ung **Obverse:** Inscription: Tai-ch'ing T'ung-pi **Reverse:** Rosette below dragon, U of KUO inverted A **Rev. Legend:** Hsüan-t'ung Nien-tsao TAI-CHING-TI-KUO.

| Date | Mintage | F | VF | XF | Unc | BU |
|---|---|---|---|---|---|---|
| CD(1909) | — | 5.50 | 12.00 | 25.00 | 60.00 | — |

**Note:** Although this coin bears no indication of its origin, it was minted in the Manchurian Provinces ca.1922

**10 CASH Y# 20x Composition:** Copper **Ruler:** Hsüan-t'ung **Obverse:** Inscription: Tai-ch'ing T'ung-pi; rosette in center **Reverse:** Dragon **Rev. Legend:** Hsüan-t'ung Nien-tsao TAI-CHING-TI-KUO.

| Date | Mintage | F | VF | XF | Unc | BU |
|---|---|---|---|---|---|---|
| CD(1909) | — | 10.00 | 20.00 | 30.00 | 80.00 | — |

**Note:** Although this coin bears no indication of its origin, it was minted in Kirin Province

**10 CASH Y# 27 Composition:** Bronze **Ruler:** Hsüan-t'ung **Obverse:** Inscription: Tai-ch'ing T'ung-pi; dragon **Rev. Legend:** Hsüan-t'ung...

| Date | Mintage | F | VF | XF | Unc | BU |
|---|---|---|---|---|---|---|
| 3(1911) | 95,585,000 | 2.50 | 4.00 | 8.00 | 40.00 | — |
| 3(1911) Rare | — | — | — | — | — | — |

**10 CASH Y# 27a Composition:** Brass **Ruler:** Hsüan-t'ung **Obverse:** Inscription: Tai-ch'ing T'ung-pi; dragon **Rev. Legend:** Hsüan-t'ung...

| Date | Mintage | F | VF | XF | Unc | BU |
|---|---|---|---|---|---|---|
| 3(1911) | — | 30.00 | 45.00 | 95.00 | 150 | — |

**20 CASH Y# 5 Composition:** Copper **Ruler:** Kuang-hsü **Obverse:** Inscription: Kuang-hsü Yüan-pao **Reverse:** Dragon **Rev. Legend:** HU POO

| Date | Mintage | VG | F | VF | XF | Unc |
|---|---|---|---|---|---|---|
| ND(1903) Restrike | — | 0.50 | 1.00 | 2.00 | 3.00 | — |

**20 CASH Y# 5.1 Composition:** Copper **Ruler:** Kuang-hsü **Obverse:** Inscription: Kuang-hsü Yüan-pao; four-point rosette in center **Reverse:** Dragon **Rev. Legend:** HU POO

| Date | Mintage | VG | F | VF | XF | Unc |
|---|---|---|---|---|---|---|
| ND(1903) Restrike | — | 2.50 | 6.00 | 12.00 | 25.00 | — |

**20 CASH Y# 5.2 Composition:** Copper **Ruler:** Kuang-hsü **Obverse:** Inscription: Kuang-hsü Yüan-pao **Reverse:** Head of dragon and clouds redesigned **Rev. Legend:** HU POO

| Date | Mintage | VG | F | VF | XF | Unc |
|---|---|---|---|---|---|---|
| ND(1903) Restrike | — | 2.50 | 6.00 | 12.00 | 25.00 | — |

**Note:** Y#5-5.2 were struck at the Wuchang Mint in 1917 from unused dies prepared in 1903

from unused dies prepared in 1903.

**20 CASH Y# 5a Composition:** Copper **Ruler:** Kuang-hsü **Obverse:** Inscription: Kuang-hsü Yüan-pao **Reverse:** Dragon in circle of dots **Rev. Legend:** HU POO

| Date | Mintage | VG | F | VF | XF | Unc |
|---|---|---|---|---|---|---|
| ND(1903-05) | — | 30.00 | 50.00 | 85.00 | 125 | — |

**20 CASH Y# 11 Composition:** Copper **Ruler:** Kuang-hsü **Obverse:** Inscription: Tai-ch'ing T'ung-pi **Reverse:** Dragon **Rev. Legend:** Kuang-hsü Nien-tsao, TAI-CHING-TI-KUO

| Date | Mintage | VG | F | VF | XF | Unc |
|---|---|---|---|---|---|---|
| CD(1905) | — | 12.50 | 30.00 | 50.00 | 75.00 | — |

**20 CASH Y# 11.1 Composition:** Copper **Ruler:** Kuang-hsü **Obverse:** Inscription: Tai-ch'ing T'ung-pi **Reverse:** Dragon **Rev. Legend:** Kuang-hsü Nien-tsao, TAI-CHING-TI-KUO

| Date | Mintage | VG | F | VF | XF | Unc |
|---|---|---|---|---|---|---|
| CD(1906) | — | 12.50 | 30.00 | 50.00 | 75.00 | — |

**20 CASH Y# 11.3a Composition:** Brass **Ruler:** Kuang-hsü **Obverse:** Inscription: Tai-ch'ing T'ung-pi **Reverse:** Dragon **Rev. Legend:** Kuang-hsü Nien-tsao, TAI-CHING-TI-KUO

| Date | Mintage | VG | F | VF | XF | Unc |
|---|---|---|---|---|---|---|
| CD(1907) | — | 3.50 | 8.00 | 15.00 | 30.00 | — |

**20 CASH Y# 11.2 Composition:** Copper **Ruler:** Kuang-hsü **Obverse:** Inscription: Tai-ch'ing T'ung-pi; dots around date **Reverse:** Dragon **Rev. Legend:** Kuang-hsü Nien-tsao, TAI-CHING-TI-KUO **Note:** 1.2-1.7 milimeters thick.

| Date | Mintage | VG | F | VF | XF | Unc |
|---|---|---|---|---|---|---|
| CD(1907) | — | 0.60 | 1.50 | 2.00 | 4.00 | — |

**20 CASH Y# 11.3 Composition:** Copper **Ruler:** Kuang-hsü **Obverse:** Inscription: Tai-ch'ing T'ung-pi **Reverse:** Dragon **Rev. Legend:** Kuang-hsü Nien-tsao, TAI-CHING-TI-KUO **Note:** 2.0-2.3 milimeters thick.

| Date | Mintage | VG | F | VF | XF | Unc |
|---|---|---|---|---|---|---|
| CD(1907) | — | 2.50 | 6.00 | 12.00 | 25.00 | — |

**20 CASH Y# 21.2 Composition:** Copper **Ruler:** Hsüan-t'ung **Obverse:** Inscription: Tai-ch'ing T'ung-pi **Reverse:** Without dot between KUO and COPPER; six waves beneath dragon **Rev. Legend:** Hsüan-t'ung Nien-tsao, TAI-CHING-TI-KUO... **Note:** 2.0-2.3 milimeters thick.

| Date | Mintage | VG | F | VF | XF | Unc |
|---|---|---|---|---|---|---|
| CD(1909) | — | 1.25 | 3.00 | 6.00 | 10.00 | — |

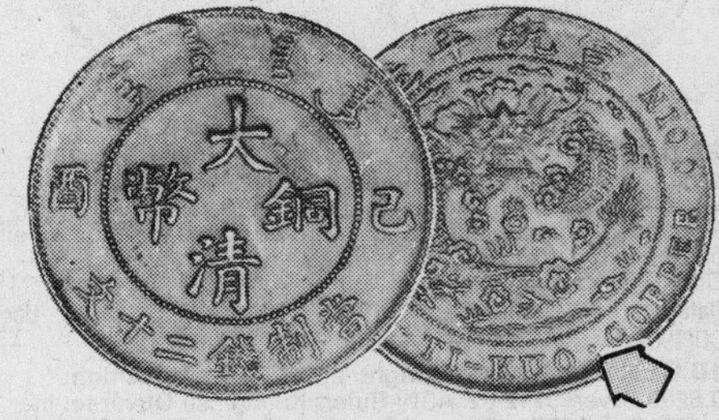

**20 CASH Y# 21.1 Composition:** Copper **Ruler:** Hsüan-t'ung **Obverse:** Inscription: Tai-ch'ing T'ung-pi **Reverse:** Without dot between KUO and COPPER; six waves beneath dragon **Rev. Legend:** Hsüan-t'ung Nien-tsao, TAI-CHING-TI-KUO... **Note:** 1.2-1.7 milimeters thick.

| Date | Mintage | VG | F | VF | XF | Unc |
|---|---|---|---|---|---|---|
| CD(1909) | — | 1.25 | 3.00 | 6.00 | 10.00 | — |

**20 CASH Y# 21 Composition:** Brass **Ruler:** Hsüan-t'ung **Obverse:** Inscription: Tai-ch'ing T'ung-pi **Reverse:** With dot between KUO and COPPER; six waves beneath dragon **Rev. Legend:** Hsüan-t'ung Nien-tsao, TAI-CHING-TI-KUA...

| Date | Mintage | VG | F | VF | XF | Unc |
|---|---|---|---|---|---|---|
| CD(1909) | — | 1.00 | 2.50 | 5.00 | 10.00 | — |

**20 CASH** **Y# 21.3** **Composition:** Copper **Ruler:** Hsüan-t'ung **Obverse:** Inscription: Tai-ch'ing T'ung-pi **Reverse:** Without dot between KUO and COPPER; rosette beneath dragon **Rev. Legend:** Hsüan-t'ung Nien-tsao, TAI-CHING-TI-KUO...

| Date | Mintage | VG | F | VF | XF | Unc |
|---|---|---|---|---|---|---|
| CD(1909) (restrike) | — | 6.00 | 15.00 | 40.00 | 70.00 | — |

**Note:** Although this coin bears no indication of its origin, it was minted in the Manchurian Provinces ca.1922

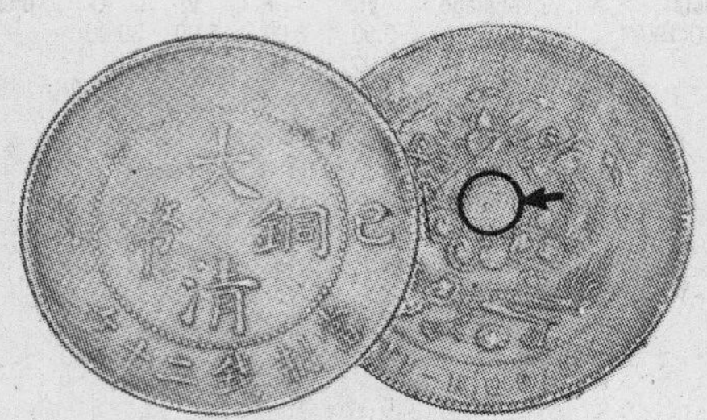

**20 CASH** **Y# 21.4** **Composition:** Copper **Ruler:** Hsüan-t'ung **Obverse:** Inscription: Tai-ch'ing T'ung-pi **Reverse:** Without dot between KUO and COPPER; dot below dragon's chin **Rev. Legend:** Hsüan-t'ung Nien-tsao, TAI-CHING-TI-KUO...

| Date | Mintage | VG | F | VF | XF | Unc |
|---|---|---|---|---|---|---|
| CD(1909) (restrike) | — | 3.50 | 8.50 | 16.00 | 30.00 | — |

**Note:** Although this coin bears no indication of its origin, it was minted in the Manchurian Provinces ca.1922

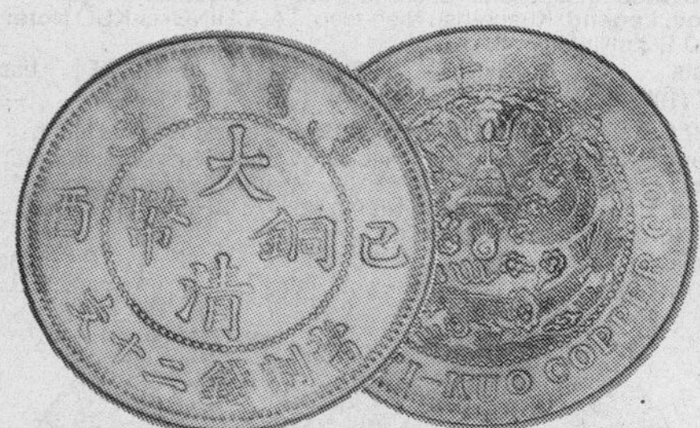

**20 CASH** **Y# 21.5** **Composition:** Copper **Ruler:** Hsüan-t'ung **Obverse:** Inscription: Tai-ch'ing T'ung-pi; inner circle of large dots **Reverse:** Without dot between KUO and COPPER; five crude waves beneath dragon with redesigned forehead; inner circle of large dots **Rev. Legend:** Hsüan-t'ung Nien-tsao, TAI-CHING-TI-KUO...

| Date | Mintage | VG | F | VF | XF | Unc |
|---|---|---|---|---|---|---|
| CD(1909) | — | 1.25 | 3.00 | 6.00 | 16.00 | — |

**10 CENTS** **K# 215** **Weight:** 2.7000 g. **Composition:** 0.8200 Silver .0712 oz. ASW **Ruler:** Kuang-hsü **Obverse:** Inscription: Tai-ch'ing T'ung-pi **Reverse:** Dragon **Rev. Legend:** Kuang-hsü Nien-tsao, TAI-CHING-TI-KUO...

| Date | Mintage | F | VF | XF | Unc | BU |
|---|---|---|---|---|---|---|
| CD(1907) | — | 85.00 | 150 | 250 | 400 | — |

**10 CENTS** **Y# 12** **Weight:** 2.7000 g. **Composition:** 0.8200 Silver .0712 oz. ASW **Ruler:** Kuang-hsü **Obverse:** Inscription: Kuang-hsü Yüan-pao **Reverse:** Dragon **Rev. Legend:** Kuang-hsü Nien-tsao, TAI-CHING-TI-KUO...

| Date | Mintage | F | VF | XF | Unc | BU |
|---|---|---|---|---|---|---|
| ND(1908) | — | 30.00 | 40.00 | 90.00 | 200 | — |

**10 CENTS** **K# 222** **Weight:** 3.2000 g. **Composition:** 0.6500 Silver .0669 oz. ASW **Ruler:** Hsüan-t'ung **Obverse:** Inscription: Tai-ch'ing Yin-pi **Reverse:** Dragon **Rev. Legend:** Hsüan-t'ung Nien-tsao

| Date | Mintage | F | VF | XF | Unc | BU |
|---|---|---|---|---|---|---|
| ND(1910) | — | 85.00 | 150 | 250 | 500 | — |
| ND(1910) Proof | — | Value: 750 | | | | |

**10 CENTS** **Y# 28** **Weight:** 2.7000 g. **Composition:** Silver **Ruler:** Hsüan-t'ung **Obverse:** Inscription: Tai-ch'ing Yin-pi **Obv. Legend:** Hsüan-t'ung **Reverse:** Dragon **Rev. Legend:** Hsüan-t'ung Nien-tsao

| Date | Mintage | F | VF | XF | Unc | BU |
|---|---|---|---|---|---|---|
| 3(1911) | — | 15.00 | 30.00 | 75.00 | 180 | — |

**Note:** Refer to Hunan Republic 10 Cents, K#762

**20 CENTS** **K# 214** **Weight:** 5.5000 g. **Composition:** 0.8200 Silver .1450 oz. ASW **Ruler:** Kuang-hsü **Obverse:** Inscription: Tai-ch'ing Yin-pi **Reverse:** Dragon **Rev. Legend:** Kuang-hsü Nien-tsao, TAI-CHING-TI-KUO...

| Date | Mintage | F | VF | XF | Unc | BU |
|---|---|---|---|---|---|---|
| CD(1907) | — | 100 | 150 | 250 | 450 | — |

**20 CENTS** **K# 217w** **Weight:** 5.3000 g. **Composition:** 0.8200 Silver .1450 oz. ASW **Ruler:** Kuang-hsü **Obverse:** Inscription: Kuang-hsü Yüan-pao **Reverse:** Dragon **Rev. Legend:** Kuang-hsü Nien-tsao, TAI-CHING-TI-KUO... with "COPPER COIN" (error)

| Date | Mintage | F | VF | XF | Unc | BU |
|---|---|---|---|---|---|---|
| ND(1908) Rare | — | — | — | — | — | — |

**20 CENTS** **Y# 13** **Weight:** 5.3000 g. **Composition:** 0.8200 Silver .1450 oz. ASW **Ruler:** Kuang-hsü **Obverse:** Inscription: Kuang-hsü Yüan-pao **Reverse:** Dragon **Rev. Legend:** Kuang-hsü Nien-tsao, TAI-CHING-TI-KUO...

| Date | Mintage | F | VF | XF | Unc | BU |
|---|---|---|---|---|---|---|
| ND(1908) | — | 60.00 | 100 | 150 | 260 | — |

**20 CENTS** **Y# 29** **Weight:** 5.4000 g. **Composition:** 0.8200 Silver .1450 oz. ASW **Ruler:** Hsüan-t'ung **Obverse:** Inscription: Tai-ch'ing Yin-pi **Obv. Legend:** Hsüan-t'ung **Reverse:** Dragon

| Date | Mintage | F | VF | XF | Unc | BU |
|---|---|---|---|---|---|---|
| 3(1911) | — | 50.00 | 100 | 175 | 350 | — |

**25 CENTS** **K# 221** **Weight:** 6.7000 g. **Composition:** 0.8000 Silver .1724 oz. ASW **Ruler:** Hsüan-t'ung **Obverse:** Inscription: Tai-ch'ing Yin-pi **Obv. Legend:** Hsüan-t'ung Nien-tsao **Reverse:** Dragon

| Date | Mintage | F | VF | XF | Unc | BU |
|---|---|---|---|---|---|---|
| ND(1910) | 1,410,000 | 200 | 400 | 750 | 1,200 | — |
| ND(1910) Proof | — | Value: 2,000 | | | | |

**50 CENTS** **K# 213** **Weight:** 13.6000 g. **Composition:** 0.8600 Silver .3761 oz. ASW **Ruler:** Kuang-hsü **Obverse:** Inscription: Tai-ch'ing Yin-pi **Reverse:** Dragon **Rev. Legend:** Kuang-hsü Nien-tsao, TAI-CHING-TI-KUO...

| Date | Mintage | F | VF | XF | Unc | BU |
|---|---|---|---|---|---|---|
| CD(1907) | — | 125 | 300 | 550 | 1,000 | — |

**50 CENTS** **Y# 23** **Weight:** 13.4000 g. **Composition:** 0.8000 Silver .3447 oz. ASW **Ruler:** Hsüan-t'ung **Obverse:** Inscription: Tai-ch'ing Yin-pi **Reverse:** Dragon **Rev. Legend:** Hsüan-t'ung Nien-tsao

| Date | Mintage | F | VF | XF | Unc | BU |
|---|---|---|---|---|---|---|
| ND(1910) | 1,571,000 | 40.00 | 70.00 | 150 | 450 | — |
| ND(1910) Proof | — | Value: 750 | | | | |

**50 CENTS** **Y# 30** **Weight:** 13.4000 g. **Composition:** 0.8000 Silver .3447 oz. ASW **Ruler:** Hsüan-t'ung **Obverse:** Inscription: Tai-ch'ing Yin-pi **Obv. Legend:** Hsüan-t'ung **Reverse:** Dragon

| Date | Mintage | F | VF | XF | Unc | BU |
|---|---|---|---|---|---|---|
| 3(1911) | Inc. above | 250 | 500 | 800 | 1,500 | — |
| 3(1911) Proof | — | Value: 2,000 | | | | |

**DOLLAR** K# 212 **Weight:** 26.9000 g. **Composition:** 0.9000 Silver .7785 oz. ASW **Ruler:** Kuang-hsü **Obverse:** Inscription: Tai-ch'ing Yin-pi **Reverse:** Dragon **Rev. Legend:** Kuang-hsü Nien-tsao, TAI-CHING-TI-KOU...

| Date | Mintage | F | VF | XF | Unc | BU |
|---|---|---|---|---|---|---|
| CD(1907) | — | 200 | 350 | 700 | 1,400 | — |

**DOLLAR** Y# 14 **Weight:** 26.9000 g. **Composition:** 0.9000 Silver .7785 oz. ASW **Ruler:** Kuang-hsü **Obverse:** Inscription: Kuang-hsü Yüan-pao **Reverse:** Dragon **Rev. Legend:** Kuang-hsü Nien-tsao, TAI-CHING-TI-KOU...

| Date | Mintage | F | VF | XF | Unc | BU |
|---|---|---|---|---|---|---|
| ND(1908) | — | 20.00 | 35.00 | 75.00 | 300 | — |

**DOLLAR** K# 219 **Weight:** 26.9000 g. **Composition:** 0.9000 Silver .7785 oz. ASW **Ruler:** Hsüan-t'ung **Obverse:** Inscription: Tai-ch'ing Yin-pi **Reverse:** Dragon **Rev. Legend:** Hsüan-t'ung Nien-tsao

| Date | Mintage | F | VF | XF | Unc | BU |
|---|---|---|---|---|---|---|
| ND(1910) | — | 125 | 300 | 600 | 1,000 | — |
| ND(1910) Proof | — | Value: 2,100 | | | | |

**DOLLAR** Y# 31 **Weight:** 26.9000 g. **Composition:** 0.9000 Silver .7785 oz. ASW **Ruler:** Hsüan-t'ung **Obverse:** Inscription: Tai-ch'ing Yin-pi **Obv. Legend:** Hsüan-t'ung **Reverse:** Dragon

| Date | Mintage | F | VF | XF | Unc | BU |
|---|---|---|---|---|---|---|
| 3(1911) | 77,153,000 | 18.00 | 25.00 | 50.00 | 300 | — |

**Note:** Struck at the Tientsin, Nanking, and Wuchang Mints without distinctive marks

**DOLLAR** Y# 31.1 **Weight:** 26.9000 g. **Composition:** 0.9000 Silver .7785 oz. ASW **Ruler:** Hsüan-t'ung **Obverse:** Inscription: Tai-ch'ing Yin-pi **Obv. Legend:** Hsüan-t'ung **Reverse:** Dragon; "dot" after DOLLAR

| Date | Mintage | F | VF | XF | Unc | BU |
|---|---|---|---|---|---|---|
| 3(1911) | Inc. above | 25.00 | 40.00 | 75.00 | 350 | — |

## PATTERNS

### Standard Unified General

| KM# | Date | Mintage | Identification | Mkt Val |
|---|---|---|---|---|
| Pn3 | | — | Cash. Brass. Hsu4 | 400 |
| Pn4 | | — | Cash. Brass. Hsu4a, square hole. | 400 |
| Pn5 | | — | Cash. Brass. Hsu4b, without hole. | 400 |
| Pn6 | | — | Cash. Copper. Y#7. | 400 |
| Pn7 | | — | Cash. Brass. Y#25; without hole. | 400 |
| Pn8 | (1907) | — | Dollar. Copper. K212. | — |
| Pn9 | (1908) | — | 20 Cents. Nickel. Milled edge. K217w. | — |
| Pn10 | (1910) | — | 10 Cents. Nickel. K222. | — |
| PnA11 | (1910) | — | 25 Cents. Plain edge. K221. | — |
| Pn11 | (1910) | — | Li. Copper. Hsu33. | 400 |
| Pn12 | (1910) | — | 5 Li. Copper. Hsu34. | 550 |
| Pn13 | (1910) | — | 5 Li. Bronze. | 550 |
| Pn14 | (1910) | — | 2 Cash. Copper. Hsu13. | 400 |
| Pn15 | (1910) | — | 2 Cash. Brass. With hole, Hsu13. | 400 |
| Pn16 | (1910) | — | Fen. Copper. Hsu35. | 600 |
| Pn17 | (1910) | — | Fen. Bronze. | 600 |
| Pn18 | (1910) | — | 2 Fen. Copper. Hsu36. | 1,000 |
| Pn19 | (1910) | — | 2 Fen. Bronze. | 1,000 |

| KM# | Date | Mintage | Identification | Mkt Val |
|---|---|---|---|---|
| Pn20 | 3(1911) | — | 5 Cash. Copper. Y26; Hsu30. | 600 |
| Pn21 | 3(1911) | — | 5 Cash. Bronze. Y26a. | 600 |
| Pn22 | 3(1911) | — | 20 Cash. Copper. Hsu32. | 700 |
| Pn23 | 3(1911) | — | 20 Cash. Bronze. | 700 |

| KM# | Date | Mintage | Identification | Mkt Val |
|---|---|---|---|---|
| Pn40 | 3(1911) | — | Dollar. Silver. K223. | 4,700 |
| Pn41 | 3(1911) | — | Dollar. Silver. K223a. | 1,800 |
| Pn44 | 3(1911) | — | Dollar. Silver. K225. | 8,000 |
| Pn45 | 3(1911) | — | Dollar. Silver. K226. | 4,500 |
| Pn42 | 3(1911) | — | Dollar. Silver. K223b. | — |
| Pn43 | 3(1911) | — | Dollar. Silver. K224. | — |

## PATTERNS

### Peking Tael Series

| KM# | Date | Mintage | Identification | Mkt Val |
|---|---|---|---|---|
| Pn29 | 29(1903) | — | 5 Fen. Silver. K931. | 600 |

| KM# | Date | Mintage | Identification | Mkt Val |
|---|---|---|---|---|
| Pn30 | 29(1903) | — | Ch'len. Silver. K930. | 750 |
| Pn31 | 29(1903) | — | 2 Ch'len. Silver. K929. | 1,250 |
| Pn31a | 29(1903) | — | 2 Ch'len. Gold. K929v. | 8,500 |
| Pn32 | 29(1903) | — | 5 Ch'len. Silver. K928. | 3,000 |
| Pn33 | 29(1903) | — | Liang. Silver. K927. | 9,350 |
| Pn33a | 29(1903) | — | Liang. Gold. K927v. | 35,000 |
| Pn34 | (1906) | — | Ch'len. Silver. K937. | 550 |
| Pn35 | (1906) | — | 2 Ch'len. Silver. K936. | 675 |
| Pn36 | (1906) | — | 5 Ch'len. Silver. K935. | 750 |
| Pn37 | (1906) | — | Liang. Silver. K934. | 1,750 |
| Pn38 | (1906) | — | Liang. Gold. K1540. | 24,750 |
| Pn39 | (1907) | — | Liang. Gold. K1541. | 24,750 |
| Pn39a | (1907) | — | Liang. Silver. K1541y. | 3,500 |
| Pn46 | (1908) | — | 20 Cents. Nickel. K217y. | — |
| Pn47 | (1910) | — | 10 Cents. Nickel. K222y. | 125 |

## TRIAL STRIKES

| KM# | Date | Mintage | Identification | Mkt Val |
|---|---|---|---|---|
| TS3 | 1(1910) | — | Fen. White Metal. Hsu35, KM#Pn13. Uniface. | 125 |

## PROOF SETS

| KM# | Date | Mintage | Identification | Issue Price | Mkt Val |
|---|---|---|---|---|---|
| PS1 | ND(1910) (4) | — | Y#23, K#219, 221, 222 | — | — |

# ANHWEI PROVINCE

**Anhui**

A province located in eastern China. Made a separate province during the Manchu dynasty in the 17th century. Principally agricultural with some mining of coal and iron ore. Spanish-American 8 Reales saw wide circulation in this province until the end of World War I. The provincial mint at Anking began operations in 1897, closed in 1899, and later reopened in 1902. The primary production of the mint was cash coins but included a series of silver coinage.

## EMPIRE

### MILLED COINAGE

**5 CASH** Y# 35 **Composition:** Copper **Ruler:** Kuang-hsü **Obv. Legend:** Kuang-hsü Yüan-pao **Reverse:** Circled dragon **Rev. Legend:** AN-HWEI

| Date | Mintage | VG | F | VF | XF | Unc |
|---|---|---|---|---|---|---|
| ND(1902) | — | 125 | 175 | 250 | 350 | — |

**5 CASH** Y# 35.1 **Composition:** Copper **Ruler:** Kuang-hsü **Obv. Legend:** Kuang-hsü Yüan-pao **Reverse:** Uncircled dragon **Rev. Legend:** AN-HUI

| Date | Mintage | VG | F | VF | XF | Unc |
|---|---|---|---|---|---|---|
| ND(c. 1902) Rare | — | — | — | — | — | — |

**10 CASH** Y# 36 **Composition:** Copper **Ruler:** Kuang-hsü **Obverse:** Inscription: Kuang-hsü Yü-pao **Reverse:** Letter "N" backwards in "AN-HWEI" and in "TEN"

| Date | Mintage | VG | F | VF | XF | Unc |
|---|---|---|---|---|---|---|
| ND(1902-1906) | — | 6.00 | 12.00 | 20.00 | 40.00 | — |

**10 CASH** Y# 34a **Composition:** Copper **Ruler:** Kuang-hsü **Obv. Legend:** Kuang-hsü Yüan-pao **Reverse:** Letter "A" inverted, denomination ONE SEN

| Date | Mintage | VG | F | VF | XF | Unc |
|---|---|---|---|---|---|---|
| ND(1902) | — | 50.00 | 80.00 | 125 | 350 | — |

**10 CASH** Y# 34a.1 **Composition:** Copper **Ruler:** Kuang-hsü **Obv. Legend:** Kuang-hsü Yüan-pao **Reverse:** Letter "A" corrected, denomination ONE SEN

| Date | Mintage | VG | F | VF | XF | Unc |
|---|---|---|---|---|---|---|
| ND(1902) | — | 40.00 | 65.00 | 100 | 250 | — |

**10 CASH** Y# 36.1 **Composition:** Copper **Ruler:** Kuang-hsü **Obverse:** Small Manchu in center, inscription: Kuang-hsü Yü-pao **Reverse:** Rosettes close together, letter "N" corrected **Edge:** Plain

| Date | Mintage | VG | F | VF | XF | Unc |
|---|---|---|---|---|---|---|
| ND(1902-1906) | — | 1.00 | 2.50 | 5.00 | 10.00 | — |

**10 CASH** Y# 36.1a **Composition:** Copper **Ruler:** Kuang-hsü **Obverse:** Small Manchu in center, inscription: Kuang-hsü Yü-pao **Reverse:** Rosettes close together, letter "N" corrected **Edge:** Milled

| Date | Mintage | VG | F | VF | XF | Unc |
|---|---|---|---|---|---|---|
| ND(1902-1906) Rare | — | — | — | — | — | — |

**10 CASH** Y# 34 **Composition:** Copper **Ruler:** Kuang-hsü **Obv. Legend:** Kuang-hsü Yüan-pao **Reverse:** Denomination: ONE CEN **Note:** May show various stages of recutting of "C" in "CEN."

| Date | Mintage | VG | F | VF | XF | Unc |
|---|---|---|---|---|---|---|
| ND1902 | — | 35.00 | 50.00 | 85.00 | 150 | — |

**10 CASH** Y# 36.2 **Composition:** Copper **Ruler:** Kuang-hsü **Obverse:** Smaller, redesigned rosettes, larger Manchu words in center, inscription: Kuang-hsü Yüan-pao **Reverse:** Rosettes close together, larger clouds around redesigned dragon

| Date | Mintage | VG | F | VF | XF | Unc |
|---|---|---|---|---|---|---|
| ND(1902-1906) | — | 1.50 | 4.00 | 6.00 | 10.00 | — |

**10 CASH** Y# 36.3 **Composition:** Copper **Ruler:** Kuang-hsü **Obverse:** Rosettes crude and heavy, inscription: Kuang-hsü Yü-pao **Reverse:** Rosettes close together, dragon's head redesigned

| Date | Mintage | VG | F | VF | XF | Unc |
|---|---|---|---|---|---|---|
| ND(1902-1908) | — | 5.00 | 12.00 | 17.50 | 35.00 | — |

**10 CASH** Y# 36.4 **Composition:** Copper **Ruler:** Kuang-hsü **Obverse:** Inscription: Kuang-hsü Yü-pao **Reverse:** Rosettes far apart

| Date | Mintage | VG | F | VF | XF | Unc |
|---|---|---|---|---|---|---|
| ND(1902-1906) | — | 1.00 | 2.50 | 5.00 | 10.00 | — |

**10 CASH** Y# 36a **Composition:** Copper **Ruler:** Kuang-hsü **Obverse:** Small rosette at center, legend with 5 characters at bottom, inscription: Kuang-hsü Yü-pao **Reverse:** Large English legend above dragon, without TEN CASH

| Date | Mintage | VG | F | VF | XF | Unc |
|---|---|---|---|---|---|---|
| ND(1902-1906) | — | 1.00 | 2.50 | 5.00 | 12.00 | — |

**10 CASH** Y# 36a.1 **Composition:** Copper **Ruler:** Kuang-hsü **Obverse:** Small rosette, inscription: Kuang-hsu Yuan-pao **Reverse:** Small English legend above dragon

| Date | Mintage | VG | F | VF | XF | Unc |
|---|---|---|---|---|---|---|
| ND(1902-1906) | — | 1.50 | 3.00 | 6.00 | 15.00 | — |

**10 CASH** Y# 36a.2 **Composition:** Copper **Ruler:** Kuang-hsü **Obverse:** Inscription: Kuang-hsü Yüan-pao **Reverse:** Small English legend with larger clouds around dragon and only one cloud below dragon's tail

| Date | Mintage | VG | F | VF | XF | Unc |
|---|---|---|---|---|---|---|
| ND(1902-1906) | — | 2.00 | 5.00 | 8.00 | 18.00 | — |

**10 CASH** Y# 36a.3 **Composition:** Copper **Ruler:** Kuang-hsü **Obverse:** Large rosette at center, legend with 2 characters at bottom, inscription: Kuang-hsü Yüan-pao

| Date | Mintage | VG | F | VF | XF | Unc |
|---|---|---|---|---|---|---|
| ND(1902-1906) | — | 1.00 | 2.50 | 5.00 | 10.00 | — |

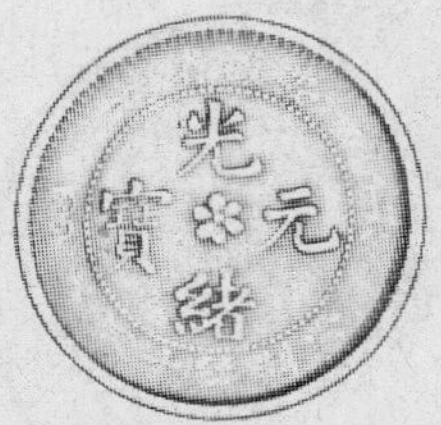

**10 CASH** Y# 36a.4 **Composition:** Copper **Ruler:** Kuang-hsü **Obverse:** Large rosette at center, legend with 5 characters at bottom, inscription: Kuang-hsü Yüan-pao

| Date | Mintage | VG | F | VF | XF | Unc |
|---|---|---|---|---|---|---|
| ND(1902-1906) | — | 1.25 | 2.50 | 5.00 | 10.00 | — |

**10 CASH** Y# 36a.5 **Composition:** Copper **Ruler:** Kuang-hsü **Obverse:** Legend with 2 characters at bottom, inscription: Kuang-hsü Yüan-pao **Reverse:** Small English legend above dragon

| Date | Mintage | VG | F | VF | XF | Unc |
|---|---|---|---|---|---|---|
| ND(1902-1906) | — | 3.50 | 7.50 | 15.00 | 30.00 | — |

**10 CASH** Y# 36a.6 **Composition:** Copper **Ruler:** Kuang-hsü **Obverse:** Slightly smaller rosette at center with right Manchu word slightly higher than on Y#36a.5, inscription: Kuang-hsü Yüan-pao **Reverse:** Small English legend above dragon

| Date | Mintage | VG | F | VF | XF | Unc |
|---|---|---|---|---|---|---|
| ND(1902-1906) | — | 1.00 | 2.50 | 5.00 | 10.00 | — |

**10 CASH** **Y# 38a** **Composition:** Copper **Ruler:** Kuang-hsü **Obverse:** Legend with 2 characters at bottom, inscription: Kuang-hsü Yüan-pao **Reverse:** Ten spelled TOEN

| Date | Mintage | VG | F | VF | XF | Unc |
|---|---|---|---|---|---|---|
| ND(1902-1906) | — | 8.00 | 15.00 | 30.00 | 50.00 | — |

**10 CASH** **Y# 38a.1** **Composition:** Copper **Ruler:** Kuang-hsü **Obverse:** Legend with 5 characters at bottom, inscription: Kuang-hsü Yüan-pao **Reverse:** Ten spelled TOEN

| Date | Mintage | VG | F | VF | XF | Unc |
|---|---|---|---|---|---|---|
| ND(1902-1906) | — | 35.00 | 70.00 | 150 | 250 | — |

**10 CASH** **Y# 38b** **Composition:** Copper **Ruler:** Kuang-hsü **Obverse:** Legend with 2 characters at bottom, inscription: Kuang-hsü Yüan-pao **Reverse:** Without TEN CASH

| Date | Mintage | VG | F | VF | XF | Unc |
|---|---|---|---|---|---|---|
| ND(1902-1906) | — | 5.00 | 12.00 | 25.00 | 65.00 | — |

**10 CASH** **Y# 38b.1** **Composition:** Copper **Ruler:** Kuang-hsü **Obverse:** Legend with 5 characters at bottom, inscription: Kuang-hsü Yüan-pao

| Date | Mintage | VG | F | VF | XF | Unc |
|---|---|---|---|---|---|---|
| ND(1902-1906) | — | 15.00 | 35.00 | 50.00 | 140 | — |

**10 CASH** **Y# 39** **Composition:** Copper **Ruler:** Kuang-hsü **Obverse:** Legend with 7 characters at bottom, inscription: Kuang-hsü Yüan-pao **Reverse:** Rosettes at side and AN-HUI above dragon

| Date | Mintage | VG | F | VF | XF | Unc |
|---|---|---|---|---|---|---|
| ND(1902-1906) Rare | — | — | — | — | — | — |

**10 CASH** **Y# 39.1** **Composition:** Copper **Ruler:** Kuang-hsü **Obverse:** Inscription: Kuang-hsü Yüan-pao **Reverse:** Stars at sides and AN-HUI above dragon

| Date | Mintage | VG | F | VF | XF | Unc |
|---|---|---|---|---|---|---|
| ND(1902-1906) Rare | — | — | — | — | — | — |

**10 CASH** **Y# 39.2** **Composition:** Copper **Ruler:** Kuang-hsü **Obverse:** Inscription: Kuang-hsü Yüan-pao **Reverse:** AN-HUI, upright dragon **Note:** Square-holed center.

| Date | Mintage | VG | F | VF | XF | Unc |
|---|---|---|---|---|---|---|
| ND(1902-1906) Rare | — | — | — | — | — | — |

**10 CASH** **Y# 10a** **Composition:** Copper **Ruler:** Kuang-hsü **Obverse:** Large mint mark at center, inscription: Tai-ch'ing T'ung-pi **Rev. Legend:** Kuang-hsü Nien-tsao, TAI-CHING-TI-KUO ...

| Date | Mintage | VG | F | VF | XF | Unc |
|---|---|---|---|---|---|---|
| CD(1906) | — | 1.00 | 2.50 | 5.00 | 10.00 | — |

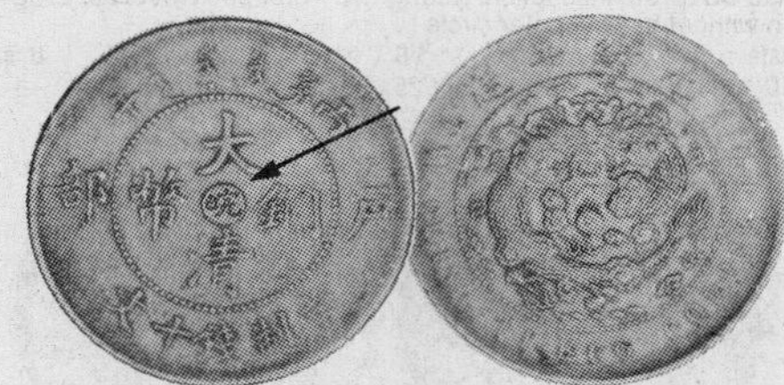

**10 CASH** **Y# 10a.1** **Composition:** Copper **Ruler:** Kuang-hsü **Obverse:** Small mint mark at center, inscription: Tai-ch'ing T'ung-pi **Rev. Legend:** Kuang-hsü Nien-tsao, TAI-CHING-TI-KUO ...

| Date | Mintage | VG | F | VF | XF | Unc |
|---|---|---|---|---|---|---|
| CD(1906) | — | 1.50 | 3.00 | 6.00 | 12.00 | — |

**10 CASH** **Y# 10a.2** **Composition:** Copper **Ruler:** Kuang-hsü **Obverse:** More finely engraved, cloud near dragon's lower foot shaped like a 3, inscription: Tai-ch'ing T'ung-pi **Reverse:** More finely engraved **Rev. Legend:** Kuang-hsü Nien-tsao, TAI-CHING-TI-KUO ...

| Date | Mintage | VG | F | VF | XF | Unc |
|---|---|---|---|---|---|---|
| CD(1906) | — | 1.00 | 2.50 | 5.00 | 10.00 | — |

**10 CASH** **Y# 20a** **Composition:** Copper **Ruler:** Hsüan-t'ung **Obverse:** Inscription: Tai-ch'ing T'ung-pi **Rev. Legend:** Hsüan-t'ung Nien-tsao, TAI-CHING-TI-KUO ...

| Date | Mintage | VG | F | VF | XF | Unc |
|---|---|---|---|---|---|---|
| CD(1909) | — | 12.50 | 25.00 | 50.00 | 125 | — |

**10 CASH** **Y# 20a.1** **Composition:** Copper **Ruler:** Hsüan-t'ung **Obverse:** Inscription: Tai-ch'ing T'ung-pi **Reverse:** Dot after COIN **Rev. Legend:** Hsüan-t'ung Nien-tsao, TAI-CHING-TI-KUO ...

| Date | Mintage | VG | F | VF | XF | Unc |
|---|---|---|---|---|---|---|
| CD(1909) | — | 35.00 | 65.00 | 130 | 225 | — |

**20 CASH** **Y# 37** **Composition:** Copper **Ruler:** Kuang-hsü **Obverse:** Inscription: Kuang-hsü Yüan-pao

| Date | Mintage | VG | F | VF | XF | Unc |
|---|---|---|---|---|---|---|
| ND(1902) | — | 375 | 750 | 1,100 | 1,500 | — |

**20 CASH** **Y# 11a** **Composition:** Copper **Ruler:** Kuang-hsü **Obverse:** Inscription: Tai-ch'ing T'ung-pi **Reverse:** Inscription: Kuang-hsü Nien-tsao, TAI-CHING-TI-KUO ...

| Date | Mintage | VG | F | VF | XF | Unc |
|---|---|---|---|---|---|---|
| CD(1906) | — | 37.50 | 75.00 | 150 | 300 | — |

**20 CENTS** **Y# 43.5** **Weight:** 5.3000 g. **Composition:** 0.9200 Silver .1397 oz. ASW **Ruler:** Kuang-hsü **Obverse:** Inscription: Kuang-hsü Yüan-pao **Reverse:** Dragon

| Date | Mintage | F | VF | XF | Unc | BU |
|---|---|---|---|---|---|---|
| ND(1901) 1 known | — | — | — | — | — | — |

**Note:** D.K.E. Ching Sale 6-91 VF++ realized $2,420.

## MILITARY TOKEN COINAGE

Given to An-hui Imperial troops by the Military Bureau for faithful and/or meritorious service.

**10 CASH** **KM# W45** **Composition:** Copper **Ruler:** Kuang-hsü **Issuer:** Anhwei Military Bureau **Obverse:** Large central Chinese character "Cheang" (reward) **Obv. Legend:** An-hui Wu Dih Buh Yuen **Reverse:** Legend around dragon **Rev. Legend:** AN-HWEI***TEN CASH***

| Date | Mintage | VG | F | VF | XF | Unc |
|---|---|---|---|---|---|---|
| ND | — | 125 | 225 | 375 | 550 | — |

**10 CASH** **KM# W46** **Composition:** Copper **Ruler:** Kuang-hsü **Issuer:** Anhwei Military Bureau **Reverse:** Legend around Dragon **Rev. Legend:** AN-HWEI***TEN CASH***

| Date | Mintage | VG | F | VF | XF | Unc |
|---|---|---|---|---|---|---|
| ND | — | 125 | 225 | 375 | 550 | — |

**10 CASH** **KM# W47** **Composition:** Copper **Ruler:** Kuang-hsü **Issuer:** Anhwei Military Bureau **Reverse:** Legend without TEN CASH

| Date | Mintage | VG | F | VF | XF | Unc |
|---|---|---|---|---|---|---|
| ND | — | 125 | 225 | 375 | 550 | — |

# CHEKIANG PROVINCE

**Zhejiang**

A province located along the east coast of China. Although the smallest of the Chinese mainland provinces, it is one of the most densely populated. Economic interests are mostly agricultural with iron and coal mining and some fishing. A small mint opened in 1897. This was replaced by a larger mint which operated briefly 1898-99. Other mints opened in 1903 and 1905. These were merged with the Fukien Mint in 1906-07.

## EMPIRE

### PROVINCIAL CAST COINAGE

**CASH** C# 4-19.1 **Composition:** Cast Brass **Ruler:** Kuang - Hsü **Reverse:** More angular mint mark

| Date | Mintage | Good | VG | F | VF | XF |
|---|---|---|---|---|---|---|
| ND(1875-1908) | — | 2.00 | 3.00 | 4.00 | 6.00 | — |

**CASH** **Composition:** Cast Zinc **Ruler:** Kuang - Hsü

| Date | Mintage | Good | VG | F | VF | XF |
|---|---|---|---|---|---|---|
| ND(1875-1908) Rare | — | — | — | — | — | — |

**CASH** C# 4-19 **Composition:** Cast Brass **Ruler:** Kuang - Hsü **Obverse:** Type A **Reverse:** Mint mark as C#4-1

| Date | Mintage | Good | VG | F | VF | XF |
|---|---|---|---|---|---|---|
| ND(1875-1908) | — | 3.00 | 4.50 | 6.50 | 12.00 | — |

### MILLED COINAGE

**2 CASH** Y# 8b **Composition:** Copper **Ruler:** Kuang - Hsü **Obverse:** Inscription: Tai-ch'ing T'ung-pi **Reverse:** Dragon

| Date | Mintage | VG | F | VF | XF | Unc |
|---|---|---|---|---|---|---|
| CD(1906) | — | 5.00 | 10.00 | 16.00 | 30.00 | — |

**5 CASH** Y# 9b **Composition:** Copper **Ruler:** Kuang - Hsü **Obverse:** Inscription: Tai-ch'ing T'ung-pi **Rev. Legend:** Kuang-hsü Nien-tsao, TAI-CHING-TI-KUO ...

| Date | Mintage | VG | F | VF | XF | Unc |
|---|---|---|---|---|---|---|
| CD(1906) | — | 5.00 | 10.00 | 16.00 | 30.00 | — |

**10 CASH** Y# 49 **Composition:** Copper **Ruler:** Kuang - Hsü **Obverse:** Ball in circle in center, inscription: Kuang-hsü Yüan-pao **Reverse:** Dragon

| Date | Mintage | VG | F | VF | XF | Unc |
|---|---|---|---|---|---|---|
| ND(1903-1906) | — | 0.50 | 1.50 | 2.50 | 4.50 | — |

**10 CASH** Y# 49.1 **Composition:** Copper **Ruler:** Kuang - Hsü **Obverse:** Rosette at center and large Manchu "Boo" at left, inscription: Kuang-hsü Yüan-pao **Reverse:** Dragon

| Date | Mintage | VG | F | VF | XF | Unc |
|---|---|---|---|---|---|---|
| ND(1903-1906) | — | 0.50 | 1.50 | 2.50 | 4.50 | — |

**10 CASH** Y# 49.1a **Composition:** Brass **Ruler:** Kuang - Hsü **Obverse:** Rosette at center and large Manchu "Boo" at left, inscription: Kuang-hsü Yüan-pao **Reverse:** Dragon

| Date | Mintage | VG | F | VF | XF | Unc |
|---|---|---|---|---|---|---|
| ND(1903-1906) | — | 2.00 | 4.00 | 8.00 | 15.00 | — |

**10 CASH** Y# 49.2 **Composition:** Copper **Ruler:** Kuang - Hsü **Obverse:** Inscription: Kuang-hsü Yüan-pao **Reverse:** Dragon **Note:** Similar to Y#49.1a.

| Date | Mintage | VG | F | VF | XF | Unc |
|---|---|---|---|---|---|---|
| ND(1903-1906) | — | 0.75 | 1.50 | 3.00 | 6.00 | — |

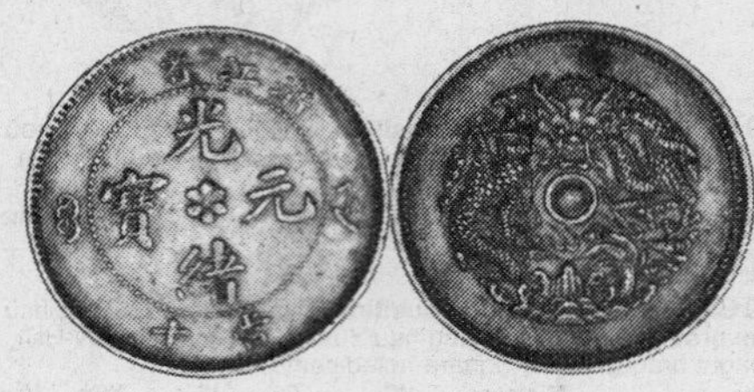

**10 CASH** Y# 49.3 **Composition:** Copper **Ruler:** Kuang - Hsü **Obverse:** Rosette at center and small Manchu word at left, inscription: Kuang-hsü Yüan-pao **Reverse:** Small, cramped dragon with few clouds around body

| Date | Mintage | VG | F | VF | XF | Unc |
|---|---|---|---|---|---|---|
| ND(1903-1906) | — | 0.75 | 1.50 | 3.00 | 6.00 | — |

**10 CASH** Y# 49.4 **Composition:** Copper **Ruler:** Kuang - Hsü **Obverse:** Inscription: Kuang-hsü Yüan-pao **Reverse:** Dragon without ball in center circle

| Date | Mintage | VG | F | VF | XF | Unc |
|---|---|---|---|---|---|---|
| ND(1903-1906) | — | 1.25 | 2.50 | 5.00 | 10.00 | — |

**10 CASH** Y# 49a **Composition:** Brass **Ruler:** Kuang - Hsü **Obverse:** Legend has 4 characters at bottom, inscription: Kuang-hsü Yüan-pao **Reverse:** Dragon

| Date | Mintage | VG | F | VF | XF | Unc |
|---|---|---|---|---|---|---|
| ND(1903-1906) | — | 3.00 | 6.00 | 11.00 | 20.00 | — |

**10 CASH** Y# 49b **Composition:** Copper **Ruler:** Kuang - Hsü **Obverse:** Inscription: Kuang-hsü Yüan-pao **Reverse:** Dragon

| Date | Mintage | VG | F | VF | XF | Unc |
|---|---|---|---|---|---|---|
| ND(1903-1906) | — | 6.00 | 12.00 | 25.00 | 45.00 | — |

**10 CASH** Y# 10b **Composition:** Copper **Ruler:** Kuang - Hsü **Obverse:** Inscription: Tai-ch'ing T'ung-pi **Reverse:** Dragon **Rev. Legend:** Kuang hsü Nien-tsao, TAI-CHING-TI-KUO with KUO spelled KIIO

| Date | Mintage | VG | F | VF | XF | Unc |
|---|---|---|---|---|---|---|
| CD(1906) | — | 1.00 | 2.00 | 4.00 | 8.00 | — |

**10 CASH** Y# 10b.1 **Composition:** Copper **Ruler:** Kuang - Hsü **Obverse:** Inscription: Tai-ch'ing T'ung-pi **Reverse:** Dragon **Rev. Legend:** Kuang hsü Nien-tsao, TAI-CHING-TI-KUO with KUO spelled KUO

| Date | Mintage | VG | F | VF | XF | Unc |
|---|---|---|---|---|---|---|
| CD(1906) | — | 2.50 | 5.00 | 10.00 | 20.00 | — |

**Note:** Chekiang and other 10 Cash coin types found struck over Korean 5 Fun coins are known. Why they were restruck in China is unknown.

**20 CASH** Y# 50 **Composition:** Copper **Ruler:** Kuang - Hsü **Obverse:** Inscription: Kuang-hsü Yüan-pao **Reverse:** Dragon **Note:** Two planchet sizes exist.

| Date | Mintage | VG | F | VF | XF | Unc |
|---|---|---|---|---|---|---|
| ND(1903-1904) | — | 100 | 200 | 350 | 600 | — |

**20 CASH** Y# 11b **Composition:** Copper **Ruler:** Kuang - Hsü **Obverse:** Inscription: Tai-ch'ing T'ung-Pi **Rev. Legend:** Kuang-hsü Nien-tsao, TAI-CHING-TI-KUO ...

| Date | Mintage | VG | F | VF | XF | Unc |
|---|---|---|---|---|---|---|
| CD(1906) | — | 60.00 | 100 | 200 | 350 | — |

## REPUBLIC

### MILLED COINAGE

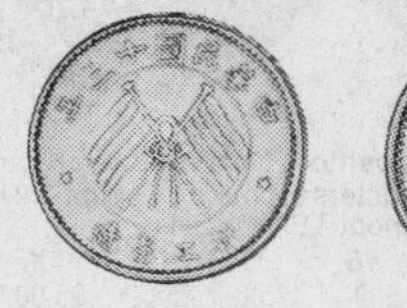

**10 CENTS** Y# 371 **Weight:** 2.6500 g. **Composition:** 0.6500 Silver .0554 oz. ASW **Obverse:** Crossed flags

| Date | Mintage | F | VF | XF | Unc | BU |
|---|---|---|---|---|---|---|
| 13(1924) | 4,464,000 | 4.00 | 7.00 | 10.00 | 25.00 | — |

**20 CENTS** Y# 373 **Weight:** 5.3000 g. **Composition:** Silver **Reverse:** Large value "20"

| Date | Mintage | F | VF | XF | Unc | BU |
|---|---|---|---|---|---|---|
| 13(1924)(1924) | — | 300 | 500 | 700 | 1,500 | — |

### PATTERNS

Including off metal strikes

| KM# | Date | Mintage | Identification | Mkt Val |
|---|---|---|---|---|
| Pn6 | (1902) | — | 20 Cents. Silver. CHE-KIANG. K121-I. | 1,500 |
| Pn7 | (1902) | — | Dollar. Silver. CHE-KIANG. K 119-I. | 20,000 |
| Pn4 | (1902) | — | 5 Cents. Silver. CHE-KIANG. K123-I. | 2,100 |

| KM# | Date | Mintage | Identification | Mkt Val |
|---|---|---|---|---|
| Pn5 | (1902) | — | 10 Cents. Silver. CHE-KIANG. K122-I. | 1,500 |
| Pn8 | (1902) | — | Dollar. Copper. CHE-KIANG. K 119-I. | 1,150 |

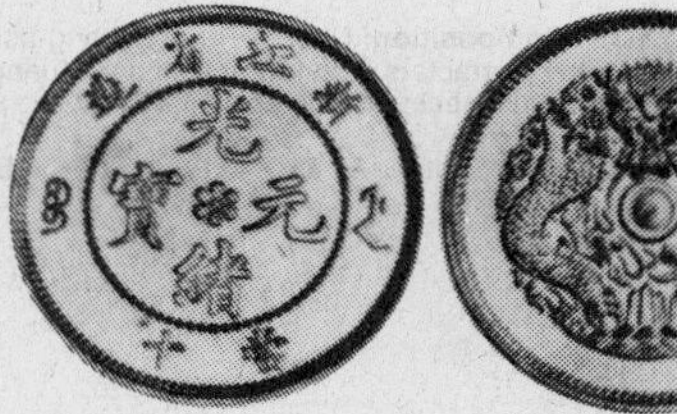

| KM# | Date | Mintage | Identification | Mkt Val |
|---|---|---|---|---|
| Pn9 | (1903) | — | 10 Cash. Copper. Y49.3a. | 200 |
| Pn10 | (1903) | — | 10 Cash. White copper. Y49.3a. W132. | — |
| Pn11 | 13(1924) | — | 20 Cents. Silver. Crossed flags. Y372. | 1,100 |

# CHIHLI PROVINCE

**Hebei, Hopei**

A province located in northeastern China which contains the eastern end of the Great Wall. An important producer of coal and some iron ore. In 1928 the provincial name was changed from Chihli to Hopei. The Paoting mint was established in 1745 and only produced cast cash coins.

A mint for struck cash was established in 1888 and the mint for the Peiyang silver coinage was added in 1896. This was destroyed during the Boxer Rebellion. A replacement mint was built in 1902 for the provincial coinage and merged with the Tientsin (Tianjin) Central mint in 1910.

## EMPIRE

### PROVINCIAL CAST COINAGE

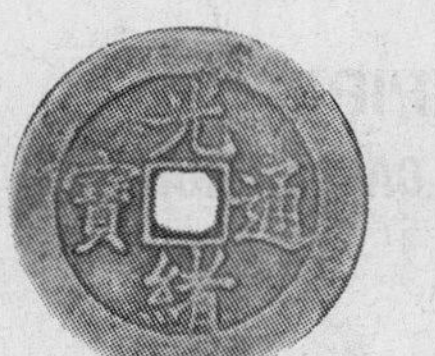

**CASH C# 8-1 Composition:** Cast Brass **Ruler:** Kuang-hsü **Obverse:** Inscription: Kuang-hsü T'ung-pao **Reverse:** Inscription: Manchu Boo-jiyen **Note:** Struck at Ching (Peiyang Arsenal-Tientsin).

| Date | Mintage | Good | VG | F | VF | XF |
|---|---|---|---|---|---|---|
| ND(1875-1908) | — | 2.50 | 4.50 | 7.50 | 12.00 | — |

**CASH C# 3-1.1 Composition:** Cast Brass **Ruler:** Kuang-hsü **Obverse:** Inscription: Kuang-hsü Tung-pao **Reverse:** Type 1 mint mark, inscription: Manchu, Boo-gu **Note:** Struck at Taku Naval Arsenal.

| Date | Mintage | Good | VG | F | VF | XF |
|---|---|---|---|---|---|---|
| ND(1875-1908) | — | 120 | 180 | 275 | 400 | — |

**CASH C# 3-1.2 Composition:** Cast Brass **Ruler:** Kuang-hsü **Obverse:** Inscription: Kuang-hsü Tung-pao **Reverse:** Type 2 mint mark, inscription: Manchu, Boo-gu **Note:** Struck at Taku Naval Arsenal.

| Date | Mintage | Good | VG | F | VF | XF |
|---|---|---|---|---|---|---|
| ND(1875-1908) | — | 20.00 | 30.00 | 50.00 | 75.00 | — |

**CASH C# 8-1.2 Composition:** Cast Brass **Ruler:** Kuang-hsü **Obverse:** Inscription: Kuang-hsü T'ung-pao **Reverse:** Dot below, inscription: Manchu Boo-jiyen **Note:** Struck at Ching (Peiyang Arsenal-Tientsin).

| Date | Mintage | Good | VG | F | VF | XF |
|---|---|---|---|---|---|---|
| ND(1875-1908) | — | 2.00 | 3.50 | 6.00 | 10.00 | — |

**CASH C# 8-1.1 Composition:** Cast Brass **Ruler:** Kuang-hsü **Obverse:** Inscription: Kuang-hsü T'ung-pao **Reverse:** Dot above, inscription: Manchu Boo-jiyen **Note:** Struck at Ching (Peiyang Arsenal-Tientsin).

| Date | Mintage | Good | VG | F | VF | XF |
|---|---|---|---|---|---|---|
| ND(1875-1908) | — | 2.75 | 4.50 | 7.50 | 15.00 | — |

**CASH C# 8-1.3 Composition:** Cast Brass **Ruler:** Kuang-hsü **Obverse:** Inscription: Kuang-hsü T'ung-pao **Reverse:** 2 dots below, inscription: Manchu Boo-jiyen **Note:** Struck at Ching (Peiyang Arsenal-Tientsin).

| Date | Mintage | Good | VG | F | VF | XF |
|---|---|---|---|---|---|---|
| ND(1875-1908) | — | 3.50 | 5.50 | 9.00 | 15.00 | — |

**CASH C# 8-1.4 Composition:** Cast Brass **Ruler:** Kuang-hsü **Obverse:** Inscription: Kuang-hsü T'ung-pao **Reverse:** Circle above, inscription: Manchu Boo-jiyen **Note:** Struck at Ching (Peiyang Arsenal-Tientsin).

| Date | Mintage | Good | VG | F | VF | XF |
|---|---|---|---|---|---|---|
| ND(1875-1908) | — | 3.50 | 5.50 | 9.00 | 18.00 | — |

**CASH C# 8-1.5 Composition:** Cast Brass **Ruler:** Kuang-hsü **Obverse:** Inscription: Kuang-hsü T'ung-pao **Reverse:** Circle below, inscription: Manchu Boo-jiyen **Note:** Struck at Ching (Peiyang Arsenal-Tientsin).

| Date | Mintage | Good | VG | F | VF | XF |
|---|---|---|---|---|---|---|
| ND(1875-1908) | — | 3.50 | 5.50 | 9.00 | 18.00 | — |

**CASH C# 8-1.6 Composition:** Cast Brass **Ruler:** Kuang-hsü **Obverse:** Inscription: Kuang-hsü T'ung-pao **Reverse:** Crescent above, inscription: Manchu Boo-jiyen **Note:** Struck at Ching (Peiyang Arsenal-Tientsin).

| Date | Mintage | Good | VG | F | VF | XF |
|---|---|---|---|---|---|---|
| ND(1875-1908) | — | 3.50 | 5.50 | 9.00 | 18.00 | — |

**CASH C# 8-1.7 Composition:** Cast Brass **Ruler:** Kuang-hsü **Obverse:** Inscription: Kuang-hsü T'ung-pao **Reverse:** Crescent below, inscription: Manchu Boo-jiyen **Note:** Struck at Ching (Peiyang Arsenal-Tientsin).

| Date | Mintage | Good | VG | F | VF | XF |
|---|---|---|---|---|---|---|
| ND(1875-1908) | — | 2.00 | 3.75 | 7.50 | 17.00 | — |

**CASH C# 8-1.8 Composition:** Cast Brass **Ruler:** Kuang-hsü **Obverse:** Inscription: Kuang-hsü T'ung-pao **Reverse:** Dash below, inscription: Manchu Boo-jiyen **Note:** Struck at Ching (Peiyang Arsenal-Tientsin). Varieties exist with dots and crescents in different corners on reverse and also with incuse dots.

| Date | Mintage | Good | VG | F | VF | XF |
|---|---|---|---|---|---|---|
| ND(1875-1908) | — | 2.00 | 3.75 | 7.50 | 15.00 | — |

### MILLED COINAGE

**CASH Y# 66 Composition:** Brass **Ruler:** Kuang-hsü **Obverse:** Inscription: Kuang-hsü T'ung-pao **Note:** Struck at Ching (Peiyang Arsenal-Tientsin).

| Date | Mintage | VG | F | VF | XF | Unc |
|---|---|---|---|---|---|---|
| ND(1904-1907) | — | 4.00 | 6.00 | 12.00 | 25.00 | — |

**CASH Y# 7c Composition:** Brass **Ruler:** Kuang-hsü **Obv. Legend:** Kuang-hsü **Reverse:** Dragon **Note:** Struck at Ching (Peiyang Arsenal-Tientsin).

| Date | Mintage | VG | F | VF | XF | Unc |
|---|---|---|---|---|---|---|
| CD(1908) | — | 2.50 | 4.50 | 7.50 | 13.50 | — |

**2 CASH Y# 8c (Y82) Composition:** Copper **Ruler:** Kuang-hsü **Note:** Struck at Ching (Peiyang Arsenal-Tientsin).

| Date | Mintage | VG | F | VF | XF | Unc |
|---|---|---|---|---|---|---|
| (1906) Rare | — | — | — | — | — | — |

**5 CASH Y# 9c Composition:** Copper **Ruler:** Kuang-hsü **Obverse:** Inscription: Tai-ch'ing T'ung-pi **Rev. Legend:** Kuang-hsü Nien-tsao, TAI-CHING-TI-KUO ... **Note:** Struck at Ching (Peiyang Arsenal-Tientsin).

| Date | Mintage | VG | F | VF | XF | Unc |
|---|---|---|---|---|---|---|
| CD(1906) | — | 10.00 | 20.00 | 35.00 | 48.00 | — |

**10 CASH Y# 67 Composition:** Copper **Ruler:** Kuang-hsü **Obverse:** Inscription: Kuang-hsü Yüan-pao **Reverse:** Side-view square-mouth dragon, hole in center of rosette **Rev. Legend:** PEI YANG **Note:** Struck at Ching (Peiyang Arsenal-Tientsin).

| Date | Mintage | VG | F | VF | XF | Unc |
|---|---|---|---|---|---|---|
| ND(c. 1906) | — | 1.00 | 2.00 | 2.50 | 4.00 | — |

**Note:** Mulings exist with obverse of Kwangtung (Guangdong) Y#192 and reverse of Chihli Y#67. Refer to Kwangtung listings.

**10 CASH Y# 67.1 Composition:** Copper **Ruler:** Kuang-hsü **Obverse:** Inscription: Kuang-hsü Yüan-pao **Reverse:** Dragon with round mouth **Note:** Struck at Ching (Peiyang Arsenal-Tientsin).

| Date | Mintage | VG | F | VF | XF | Unc |
|---|---|---|---|---|---|---|
| ND(c. 1906) | — | 1.00 | 2.00 | 2.50 | 4.00 | — |

**10 CASH Y# 67.2 Composition:** Copper **Ruler:** Kuang-hsü **Obverse:** Inscription: Kuang-hsü Yüan-pao **Reverse:** Dot in center of rosettes, dragon with square mouth **Note:** Struck at Ching (Peiyang Arsenal-Tientsin).

| Date | Mintage | VG | F | VF | XF | Unc |
|---|---|---|---|---|---|---|
| ND(c. 1906) | — | 1.00 | 2.00 | 2.50 | 4.00 | — |

**10 CASH Y# 67.3 Composition:** Copper **Ruler:** Kuang-hsü **Obverse:** Inscription: Kuang-hsü Yüan-pao **Reverse:** Dot in center of rosettes, dragon with round mouth **Note:** Struck at Ching (Peiyang Arsenal-Tientsin).

| Date | Mintage | VG | F | VF | XF | Unc |
|---|---|---|---|---|---|---|
| ND(c. 1906) | — | 1.00 | 2.00 | 2.50 | 4.00 | — |

**10 CASH Y# 67.4 Composition:** Copper **Ruler:** Kuang-hsü **Obverse:** Inscription: Kuang-hsü Yüan-pao **Reverse:** Redesigned dragon with smaller body and smaller English legends **Note:** Struck at Ching (Peiyang Arsenal-Tientsin).

| Date | Mintage | VG | F | VF | XF | Unc |
|---|---|---|---|---|---|---|
| ND(c. 1906) | — | 1.50 | 3.50 | 7.00 | 15.00 | — |

**10 CASH Y# 10c Composition:** Copper **Ruler:** Kuang-hsü **Obverse:** Inscription: Tai-ch'ing T'ung-pi **Rev. Legend:** Kuang-hsü Nien-tsao, TAI-CHING-TI-KUO ... **Note:** Struck at Ching (Peiyang Arsenal-Tientsin).

| Date | Mintage | VG | F | VF | XF | Unc |
|---|---|---|---|---|---|---|
| CD(1906) | — | 1.00 | 2.00 | 3.00 | 5.00 | — |

**20 CASH** Y# 68 **Composition:** Copper **Ruler:** Kuang-hsü **Note:** Struck at Ching (Peiyang Arsenal-Tientsin).

| Date | Mintage | VG | F | VF | XF | Unc |
|---|---|---|---|---|---|---|
| ND(c. 1906) | — | 20.00 | 30.00 | 40.00 | 100 | — |

**20 CASH** Y# 68a **Composition:** Brass **Ruler:** Kuang-hsü **Obverse:** Inscription: Kuang-hsü Yüan-pao **Reverse:** Side view dragon **Rev. Legend:** PEI YANG **Note:** Struck at Ching (Peiyang Arsenal-Tientsin).

| Date | Mintage | VG | F | VF | XF | Unc |
|---|---|---|---|---|---|---|
| ND(c. 1906) Rare | — | — | — | — | — | — |

**20 CASH** Y# 68.1 **Composition:** Copper **Ruler:** Kuang-hsü **Obverse:** Inscription: Kuang-hsü Yüan-pao **Reverse:** Smaller lettering **Note:** Struck at Ching (Peiyang Arsenal-Tientsin).

| Date | Mintage | VG | F | VF | XF | Unc |
|---|---|---|---|---|---|---|
| ND(c. 1906) | — | 25.00 | 35.00 | 50.00 | 120 | — |

**20 CASH** Y# 11c **Composition:** Copper **Ruler:** Kuang-hsü **Obverse:** Inscription: Tai-ch'ing T'ung-pi **Rev. Legend:** Kuang-hsü Nien-tsao, TAI-CHING-TI-KUO ... **Note:** Struck at Ching (Peiyang Arsenal-Tientsin).

| Date | Mintage | VG | F | VF | XF | Unc |
|---|---|---|---|---|---|---|
| CD(1906) | — | 15.00 | 30.00 | 60.00 | 120 | — |

**20 CENTS** Y# 71a **Weight:** 5.3000 g. **Composition:** 0.8200 Silver .1397 oz. ASW **Ruler:** Kuang-hsü **Obverse:** Inscription: Kuang-hsü Yüan-pao **Reverse:** Side view dragon, legend at bottom **Rev. Legend:** PEI YANG **Note:** Struck at Ching (Peiyang Arsenal-Tientsin).

| Date | Mintage | F | VF | XF | Unc | BU |
|---|---|---|---|---|---|---|
| 31(1905) | 161,000 | 35.00 | 75.00 | 150 | 350 | — |

**DOLLAR** Y# 73 **Weight:** 26.7000 g. **Composition:** 0.9000 Silver .7727 oz. ASW **Ruler:** Kuang-hsü **Obverse:** Similar to Y#73.2, inscription: Kuang-hsü Yüan-pao **Reverse:** Side view dragon, legend at bottom **Rev. Legend:** PEI YANG **Note:** Struck at Ching (Peiyang Arsenal-Tientsin).

| Date | Mintage | F | VF | XF | Unc | BU |
|---|---|---|---|---|---|---|
| 25(1899) | 1,566,000 | 25.00 | 40.00 | 75.00 | 450 | — |
| 26(1900) | — | 40.00 | 75.00 | 125 | 750 | — |
| 29(1903) | 22,018,000 | 12.00 | 17.00 | 35.00 | 150 | — |

**DOLLAR** Y# 73.1 **Weight:** 26.7000 g. **Composition:** 0.9000 Silver .7727 oz. ASW **Ruler:** Kuang-hsü **Obverse:** Inscription: Kuang-hsü Yüan-pao **Reverse:** Side view dragon, legend at bottom, period after legend **Rev. Legend:** PEI YANG **Note:** Struck at Ching (Peiyang Arsenal-Tientsin).

| Date | Mintage | F | VF | XF | Unc | BU |
|---|---|---|---|---|---|---|
| 29(1903) | Inc. above | 12.50 | 17.00 | 40.00 | 200 | — |

**DOLLAR** Y# 73.2 **Weight:** 26.7000 g. **Composition:** 0.9000 Silver .7727 oz. ASW **Ruler:** Kuang-hsü **Obverse:** Inscription: Kuang-hsü Yüan-pao **Reverse:** Thinner side-view dragon, legend at bottom, year as "33rd" **Rev. Legend:** PEI YANG **Note:** Struck at Ching (Peiyang Arsenal-Tientsin).

| Date | Mintage | F | VF | XF | Unc | BU |
|---|---|---|---|---|---|---|
| 33(1907) | 2,341,000 | 15.00 | 25.00 | 50.00 | 250 | — |
| 34(1908) | — | 12.50 | 20.00 | 38.00 | 175 | — |

**DOLLAR** Y# 73.3 **Weight:** 26.7000 g. **Composition:** 0.9000 Silver .7727 oz. ASW **Ruler:** Kuang-hsü **Obverse:** Inscription: Kuang-hsü Yüan-pao **Reverse:** Side view dragon, legend at bottom, short center spine to tail **Rev. Legend:** PEI YANG **Note:** Struck at Ching (Peiyang Arsenal-Tientsin). Restruck during Republican times.

| Date | Mintage | F | VF | XF | Unc | BU |
|---|---|---|---|---|---|---|
| 34(1908) | — | 12.00 | 15.00 | 30.00 | 150 | — |

**DOLLAR** Y# 73.4 **Weight:** 26.7000 g. **Composition:** 0.9000 Silver .7727 oz. ASW **Ruler:** Kuang-hsü **Obverse:** Inscription: Kuang-hsü Yüan-pao **Reverse:** Side view dragon, legend at bottom, crosslet 4 in date **Rev. Legend:** PEI YANG **Note:** Struck at Ching (Peiyang Arsenal-Tientsin). Restruck during Republican times.

| Date | Mintage | F | VF | XF | Unc | BU |
|---|---|---|---|---|---|---|
| 34(1908) | — | 50.00 | 125 | 250 | 600 | — |

**TAEL** Y# 74 **Weight:** 51.2000 g. **Composition:** Silver **Ruler:** Kuang-hsü **Obverse:** Inscription: Kuang-hsü Yüan-pao **Reverse:** Side view dragon, legend at bottom **Rev. Legend:** PEI YANG **Note:** Struck at Ching (Peiyang Arsenal-Tientsin).

| Date | Mintage | F | VF | XF | Unc | BU |
|---|---|---|---|---|---|---|
| 33(1907) | — | 2,000 | 3,500 | 5,000 | 10,000 | — |

**TAEL** Y# 74.1 **Weight:** 51.2000 g. **Composition:** Silver **Ruler:** Kuang-hsü **Obverse:** Inscription: Kuang-hsü Yüan-pao **Reverse:** Side view dragon, legend at bottom, 3 dots on pearl arranged horizontally **Rev. Legend:** PEI YANG **Note:** Struck at Ching (Peiyang Arsenal-Tientsin).

| Date | Mintage | F | VF | XF | Unc | BU |
|---|---|---|---|---|---|---|
| 33(1907) | — | 2,000 | 3,500 | 5,000 | 10,000 | — |

**TAEL** Y# 74.2 **Weight:** 51.2000 g. **Composition:** Silver **Ruler:** Kuang-hsü **Obverse:** Inscription: Kuang-hsü Yüan-pao **Reverse:** Side view dragon, legend at bottom, 3 dots on pearl arranged in arc **Rev. Legend:** PEI YANG **Note:** Struck at Ching (Peiyang Arsenal-Tientsin).

| Date | Mintage | F | VF | XF | Unc | BU |
|---|---|---|---|---|---|---|
| 33(1907) | — | 2,000 | 3,500 | 5,000 | 10,000 | — |

## PATTERNS

### Including off metal strikes

| KM# | Date | Mintage | Identification | Mkt Val |
|---|---|---|---|---|
| Pn6 | 29(1903) | — | Dollar. Brass. Y73. | — |
| Pn7 | 33(1907) | — | Tael. Gold. Y74. | — |

# FENGTIEN PROVINCE

**(Fungtien)**

**Liaoning**

The southernmost province of the Three Eastern Provinces was known by a variety of names including Fengtien, Shengching, and Liaoning. The modern Mukden (Fengtien Province) Mint operated from 1897 to 1931.

## EMPIRE

### PROVINCIAL CAST COINAGE

**CASH** C# 9-1 **Composition:** Cast Brass **Ruler:** Kuang-hsü **Obverse:** Type A, inscription: Kuang-hsü T'ung-pao **Reverse:** Inscription: Manchu Boo-fung **Note:** Struck at Fung (Fengtien).

| Date | Mintage | Good | VG | F | VF | XF |
|---|---|---|---|---|---|---|
| ND(1875-1908) | — | 20.00 | 30.00 | 50.00 | — | — |

### MILLED COINAGE

**5 CASH** Y# 19e **Composition:** Copper **Ruler:** Hsüan-t'ung **Obverse:** Inscription: Tai-ching T'ung-pi **Rev. Legend:** Hsüan-t'ung Nien-tsao, TAI-CHING-TI-KUO ...

| Date | Mintage | VG | F | VF | XF | Unc |
|---|---|---|---|---|---|---|
| CD(1909) | — | 37.50 | 75.00 | 125 | 200 | — |

**10 CASH** Y# 88 **Composition:** Brass **Ruler:** Kuang-hsü **Obverse:** Inscription: Kuang-hsü Yüan-pao **Rev. Legend:** Province named spelled FEN-TIEN

| Date | Mintage | VG | F | VF | XF | Unc |
|---|---|---|---|---|---|---|
| CD(1903) | — | 50.00 | 90.00 | 135 | 225 | — |

**10 CASH** Y# 89 **Composition:** Brass **Ruler:** Kuang-hsü **Obverse:** Inscription: Kuang-hsü Yüan-pao **Rev. Legend:** FUNG-TIEN PROVINCE

| Date | Mintage | VG | F | VF | XF | Unc |
|---|---|---|---|---|---|---|
| CD(1903) | — | 3.75 | 7.50 | 25.00 | 40.00 | — |
| CD(1904) | — | 1.25 | 3.00 | 5.00 | 8.00 | — |
| CD(1905) | — | 1.50 | 4.50 | 10.00 | 12.00 | — |
| CD(1906) | 35,036,000 | 3.00 | 6.00 | 25.00 | 35.00 | — |

**10 CASH** Y# 89.1 **Composition:** Brass **Ruler:** Kuang-hsü **Obverse:** Manchu words in center reversed, inscription: Kuang-hsü Yüan-pao **Rev. Legend:** FUNG-TIEN PROVINCE

| Date | Mintage | F | VF | XF | Unc | BU |
|---|---|---|---|---|---|---|
| CD(1903) | — | 85.00 | 150 | 250 | — | — |

**10 CASH** Y# 89.2 **Composition:** Brass **Ruler:** Kuang-hsü **Obverse:** Inscription: Kuang-hsü Yüan-pao **Reverse:** Large pearl **Rev. Legend:** FUNG-TIEN PROVINCE

| Date | Mintage | F | VF | XF | Unc | BU |
|---|---|---|---|---|---|---|
| CD(1905) | — | 2.00 | 4.00 | 8.00 | 24.00 | — |

**10 CASH** Y# 10e **Composition:** Copper **Ruler:** Kuang-hsü **Obverse:** Inscription: Tai-ch'ing T'ung-pi **Reverse:** Small pearl **Rev. Legend:** Kuang-hsü Nien-tsao, TAI-CHING-TI KUO ...

| Date | Mintage | F | VF | XF | Unc | BU |
|---|---|---|---|---|---|---|
| CD(1905) | — | 4.00 | 8.00 | 15.00 | 30.00 | — |

**10 CASH** Y# 10e.1 **Composition:** Copper **Ruler:** Kuang-hsü **Obverse:** Inscription: Tai-ch'ing T'ung-pi **Reverse:** Large pearl **Rev. Legend:** Kuang-hsü Nien-tsao, TAI-CHING-TI KUO ...

| Date | Mintage | F | VF | XF | Unc | BU |
|---|---|---|---|---|---|---|
| CD(1905) | — | 4.00 | 8.00 | 15.00 | 30.00 | — |

**10 CASH** Y# 10e.2 **Composition:** Copper **Ruler:** Kuang-hsü **Obverse:** Mint mark on spherical disc in center, inscription: Tai-ch'ing T'ung-pi **Reverse:** Large pearl **Rev. Legend:** Kuang-hsü Nien-tsao, TAI-CHING-TI KUO ...

| Date | Mintage | F | VF | XF | Unc | BU |
|---|---|---|---|---|---|---|
| (1907) | 130,000 | 3.00 | 6.00 | 20.00 | — | — |

**10 CASH** Y# 10e.3 **Composition:** Copper **Ruler:** Kuang-hsü **Obverse:** Mint mark on flat disc in center, inscription: Tai-ch'ing T'ung-pi **Rev. Legend:** Kuang-hsü Nien-tsao, TAI-CHING-TI KUO ...

| Date | Mintage | F | VF | XF | Unc | BU |
|---|---|---|---|---|---|---|
| CD(1907) | Inc. above | 1.50 | 3.00 | 6.00 | 20.00 | — |

**10 CASH** Y# 81 **Composition:** Copper **Ruler:** Kuang-hsü **Obverse:** Type A

| Date | Mintage | VG | F | VF | XF | Unc |
|---|---|---|---|---|---|---|
| ND | — | 40.00 | 60.00 | 90.00 | 200 | — |

**Note:** Seven varieties exist

**10 CASH** Y# 20e **Composition:** Copper **Ruler:** Hsüan-t'ung **Obverse:** Mint mark on flat disc in center, inscription: Tai-ch'ing T'ung-pi **Rev. Legend:** Hsüan-T'ung Nien-tsao, TAI-CH-ING-TI-KUO ...

| Date | Mintage | F | VF | XF | Unc | BU |
|---|---|---|---|---|---|---|
| CD(1909) | — | 8.00 | 17.50 | 30.00 | — | — |

**10 CASH** Y# W286 **Composition:** Copper **Ruler:** Kuang-hsü **Obverse:** Inscription: Tai-ch'ing T'ung-pi **Rev. Legend:** Kuang-hsü Nien-tsao, TAI-CHING-TI-KUO ... **Note:** Mule, obverse Y#20e, reverse Y#10e.

| Date | Mintage | F | VF | XF | Unc | BU |
|---|---|---|---|---|---|---|
| CD(1909) 6 known | — | — | — | — | — | — |

**20 CASH** Y# 90 **Composition:** Brass **Ruler:** Kuang-hsü **Obverse:** Inscription: Kuang-hsü Yüan-pao **Rev. Legend:** FUNG TIEN PROVINCE

| Date | Mintage | VG | F | VF | XF | Unc |
|---|---|---|---|---|---|---|
| CD(1903) | — | 75.00 | 100 | 125 | 175 | — |
| CD(1904) | — | 5.50 | 11.00 | 22.50 | 55.00 | — |
| CD(1905) | — | 9.00 | 18.00 | 25.00 | 60.00 | — |

**20 CASH** Y# 11e **Composition:** Brass **Ruler:** Kuang-hsü **Obverse:** Inscription: Tai-ching T'ung-pi **Rev. Legend:** Kuang-hsü Nien-tsao, TAI-CHING-TI-KUO ...

| Date | Mintage | VG | F | VF | XF | Unc |
|---|---|---|---|---|---|---|
| CD(1905) | — | 4.00 | 7.00 | 20.00 | 40.00 | — |
| CD(1907) | — | 6.00 | 12.00 | 25.00 | 50.00 | — |

**20 CASH** Y# 21e **Composition:** Brass **Ruler:** Hsüan-t'ung **Obverse:** Inscription: Tai-ching T'ung-pi **Rev. Legend:** Hsüan-t'ung Nien-tsao, TAI-CHING-TI-KUO ...

| Date | Mintage | VG | F | VF | XF | Unc |
|---|---|---|---|---|---|---|
| CD(1909) | — | 25.00 | 60.00 | 110 | 175 | — |

**20 CENTS** Y# 91 **Composition:** Silver **Ruler:** Kuang-hsü **Obverse:** Inscription: Kuang-hsü Yüan-pao **Reverse:** Side view dragon, 8 rows of scales on dragon **Rev. Legend:** FUNG-TIEN PROVINCE **Size:** 24 mm.

| Date | Mintage | F | VF | XF | Unc | BU |
|---|---|---|---|---|---|---|
| CD(1904) | — | 8.00 | 14.00 | 25.00 | 70.00 | — |

**20 CENTS** Y# 91.1 **Composition:** Silver **Ruler:** Kuang-hsü **Obverse:** Inscription: Kuang-hsü Yüan-pao **Reverse:** Side view dragon, 5 rows of scales on dragon **Rev. Legend:** FUNG-TIEN PROVINCE

| Date | Mintage | F | VF | XF | Unc | BU |
|---|---|---|---|---|---|---|
| CD(1904) | — | 9.00 | 16.00 | 30.00 | 80.00 | — |

**DOLLAR** Y# 92 **Weight:** 26.4000 g. **Composition:** 0.8500 Silver .7215 oz. ASW **Ruler:** Kuang-hsü **Obverse:** Inscription: Kuang-hsü Yüan-pao **Reverse:** Side view dragon **Rev. Legend:** FUNG-TIEN PROVINCE

| Date | Mintage | F | VF | XF | Unc | BU |
|---|---|---|---|---|---|---|
| CD(1903) | 262,000 | 120 | 200 | 500 | 1,500 | — |

**DOLLAR** Y# 92.1 **Weight:** 26.4000 g. **Composition:** 0.8500 Silver .7215 oz. ASW **Ruler:** Kuang-hsü **Obverse:** Manchu "Boo-funs" in center are reversed, inscription: Kuang-hsü Yüan-pao **Reverse:** Side view dragon **Rev. Legend:** FUNG-TIEN PROVINCE

| Date | Mintage | F | VF | XF | Unc | BU |
|---|---|---|---|---|---|---|
| CD(1903) | Inc. above | 150 | 300 | 600 | 1,800 | — |

## TOKEN COINAGE

**10 CENTS** KM# TnA1 **Composition:** Copper **Ruler:** Kuang-hsü **Obverse:** Dragon **Reverse:** Tang-shih (10)

| Date | Mintage | F | VF | XF | Unc | BU |
|---|---|---|---|---|---|---|
| ND(c. 1904) | — | — | 900 | 1,500 | 2,500 | — |

**DOLLAR** KM# Tn1Y# W242 **Composition:** Copper **Ruler:** Kuang-hsü **Obverse:** Reverse of 10 Cash, Y#10e, small spiral on pearl **Reverse:** Inscription: Tang-yuan (1 Dollar)

| Date | Mintage | F | VF | XF | Unc | BU |
|---|---|---|---|---|---|---|
| ND(c. 1904) | — | — | 550 | 900 | 1,500 | — |

**DOLLAR** KM# Tn1a **Composition:** Brass **Ruler:** Kuang-hsü **Obverse:** Reverse of 10 Cash, Y#10e, small spiral on pearl **Reverse:** Inscription: Tang-yuan (1 Dollar)

| Date | Mintage | F | VF | XF | Unc | BU |
|---|---|---|---|---|---|---|
| ND(c. 1904) | — | — | 550 | 900 | 1,500 | — |

**100 CENTS** **KM# Tn2Y# W243** **Composition:** Copper **Ruler:** Kuang-hsü **Obverse:** Dragon, large spiral on pearl **Obv. Legend:** FUNG TIEN PROVINCE **Reverse:** Inscription: Tang Pai **Note:** Silver forgeries exist.

| Date | Mintage | F | VF | XF | Unc | BU |
|---|---|---|---|---|---|---|
| ND(c. 1904) | — | — | 550 | 900 | 1,500 | — |

**100 CENTS** **KM# Tn3** **Composition:** Brass **Ruler:** Kuang-hsü **Obv. Legend:** FUNG-TIEN PROVINCE **Reverse:** Inscription: Tang Pai **Note:** Silver forgeries exist.

| Date | Mintage | F | VF | XF | Unc | BU |
|---|---|---|---|---|---|---|
| ND(c. 1904) | — | — | — | — | — | — |

## PATTERNS

Including off metal strikes

| KM# | Date | Mintage | Identification | Mkt Val |
|---|---|---|---|---|
| Pn2A | (c. 1902) | — | 10 Cents. Brass. Regular provincial design. | — |
| Pn3 | (c. 1902) | — | 20 Cents. Brass. Regular provincial design. | — |
| Pn6 | (c. 1902) | — | 50 Cents. Brass. Error, TENG-TIEN. | — |
| Pn7 | (c. 1902) | — | Dollar. Aluminum. Error, TENG-TIEN. | — |
| Pn10 | (c. 1902) | — | 10 Cash. Copper. | — |
| Pn8 | (c. 1902) | — | Dollar. Silver. Error, TENG-TIEN. | — |
| Pn4 | (c. 1902) | — | 20 Cents. Brass. Error, TENG-TIEN. | — |
| Pn5 | (c. 1902) | — | 20 Cents. Silver. FENG-TIEN. | — |
| Pn9 | (c. 1902) | — | Dollar. Brass. Error, TENG-TIEN. | — |
| Pn11 | 1903 | — | 10 Cash. Copper. Y88. | — |
| Pn18 | 1903 | — | Tael. Silver. K931-I. | — |
| Pn14 | 1903 | — | 20 Cash. Copper. Y90. | 200 |
| Pn12 | 1903 | — | 10 Cash. Copper. Y89. | — |
| Pn13 | 1903 | — | 10 Cash. Copper. Y89.1. | — |
| Pn15 | 1904 | — | 10 Cash. Copper. Y89. | — |
| Pn16 | 1905 | — | 10 Cash. Copper. Y89. | — |
| Pn17 | 1905 | — | 20 Cash. Copper. Y90. | — |

**Note:** Superior Goodman sale 6-91 about XF realized $187,000. (Pn18)

# FUKIEN PROVINCE

**Fujian**

A province located on the southeastern coast of China, including the island of Taiwan until it became its own separate province in 1885. Although known mainly as an agricultural area, forestry and some mining, particularly iron ore and coal, are also important to the economy. The Foochow Mint operated throughout the Manchu dynasty. The Viceroy's or City mint was opened in 1896 for struck coinage. Two other mints were established in 1905, the Mamoi Arsenal Mint which struck the Custom-House issues until it closed in 1906, and the West Mint which later became the main Fukien (Fujian) Mint. It closed between 1914 and 1920. Various subsidiary mints were in operation from 1924 to 1925.

## EMPIRE

### PROVINCIAL CAST COINAGE

**CASH** **C# 10-25** **Composition:** Cast Brass **Ruler:** Kuang-Hsü **Obverse:** Inscription: Kuang hsü T'ung-pao **Reverse:** Inscription: Manchu Boo-fun **Note:** Struck at Fun (Foochow). Sch. #1581.

| Date | Mintage | Good | VG | F | VF | XF |
|---|---|---|---|---|---|---|
| ND(1875-1908) | — | 0.85 | 1.50 | 2.50 | 3.50 | — |

**CASH** **C# 10-25.1** **Composition:** Cast Brass **Ruler:** Kuang - Hsü **Obverse:** Inscription: Kuang hsü T'ung-pao **Reverse:** Dot at top of hole, inscription: Manchu "Boo-fu" **Note:** Struck at Fun (Foochow).

| Date | Mintage | Good | VG | F | VF | XF |
|---|---|---|---|---|---|---|
| ND(1875-1908) | — | 2.50 | 4.00 | 6.50 | 10.00 | — |

**CASH** **C# 10-25.2** **Composition:** Cast Brass **Ruler:** Kuang - Hsü **Obverse:** Inscription: Kuang hsü T'ung-pao **Reverse:** Inverted, inscription: Manchu "Boo-fu" **Note:** Struck at Fun (Foochow).

| Date | Mintage | Good | VG | F | VF | XF |
|---|---|---|---|---|---|---|
| ND(1875-1908) | — | — | — | — | — | — |

### MILLED COINAGE

**CASH** **Y# 106** **Composition:** Brass **Ruler:** Hsüan - T'ung **Obverse:** Inscription: Hsüan-t'ung T'ung-pao **Reverse:** Inscription: Manchu Boo-fu **Note:** Struck at Fu (Fuchow).

| Date | Mintage | VG | F | VF | XF | Unc |
|---|---|---|---|---|---|---|
| ND(1909/11) | — | 15.00 | 25.00 | 50.00 | 80.00 | — |

**CASH** **Y# 95** **Composition:** Brass **Ruler:** Kuang - Hsü **Obverse:** Inscription: Kuang hsü T'ung-pao **Reverse:** Inscription: Manchu Boo-fung **Note:** Struck at Fu (Fuchow).

| Date | Mintage | VG | F | VF | XF | Unc |
|---|---|---|---|---|---|---|
| ND(1908) | — | 6.00 | 10.00 | 15.00 | 30.00 | — |

**CASH** **Y# 7f** **Composition:** Brass **Ruler:** Kuang - Hsü **Obverse:** Inscription: Kuang hsü **Reverse:** Dragon **Note:** Struck at Fu (Fuchow).

| Date | Mintage | VG | F | VF | XF | Unc |
|---|---|---|---|---|---|---|
| CD(1908) | — | 35.00 | 75.00 | 110 | 175 | — |

**2 CASH** **Y# 8f** **Composition:** Brass **Obverse:** Inscription: Tai-ching T'ung-pi **Reverse:** Dragon **Note:** Struck at Fu (Fuchow).

| Date | Mintage | VG | F | VF | XF | Unc |
|---|---|---|---|---|---|---|
| CD(1906) | — | 3.00 | 8.00 | 14.00 | 25.00 | — |

**5 CASH** **Y# 99** **Composition:** Copper **Ruler:** Kuang - Hsü **Obverse:** Inscription: Kuang-hsü Yüan-pao **Reverse:** Dragon **Rev. Legend:** FOO-KIEN **Note:** Struck at Fu (Fuchow).

| Date | Mintage | VG | F | VF | XF | Unc |
|---|---|---|---|---|---|---|
| ND(1901-1903) | 590,000 | 18.00 | 25.00 | 37.50 | 60.00 | — |

**5 CASH** **Y# 99a** **Composition:** Brass **Ruler:** Kuang - Hsü **Obverse:** Inscription: Kuang-hsü Yüan-pao **Reverse:** Dragon **Rev. Legend:** FOO-KIEN **Note:** Struck at Fu (Fuchow).

| Date | Mintage | VG | F | VF | XF | Unc |
|---|---|---|---|---|---|---|
| ND(1901-1903) | — | 12.00 | 25.00 | 50.00 | 75.00 | — |

**10 CASH** **Y# 97** **Composition:** Copper **Ruler:** Kuang - Hsü **Obverse:** Large characters at left and right, inscription: Kuang-hsü Yüan-pao **Reverse:** Dragon **Rev. Legend:** F.K. CUSTOM-HOUSE **Note:** Struck at Fu (Fuchow).

| Date | Mintage | F | VF | XF | Unc | BU |
|---|---|---|---|---|---|---|
| ND(1901-1905) | 417,031,000 | 1.50 | 2.50 | 8.00 | 25.00 | — |

**10 CASH** **Y# 97.1** **Composition:** Copper **Ruler:** Kuang - Hsü **Obverse:** Small characters at left and right sides, inscription: Kuang-hsü Yüan-pao **Reverse:** Dragon **Rev. Legend:** F.K. CUSTOM-HOUSE **Note:** Struck at Fu (Fuchow).

| Date | Mintage | F | VF | XF | Unc | BU |
|---|---|---|---|---|---|---|
| ND(1901-1905) | Inc. above | 2.00 | 4.00 | 10.00 | 30.00 | — |

**10 CASH** **Y# 98** **Composition:** Copper **Ruler:** Kuang - Hsü **Obverse:** Inscription: Kuang-hsü Yüan-pao **Reverse:** Dragon **Rev. Legend:** FOO-KIEN CUSTOM **Note:** Struck at Fu (Fuchow).

| Date | Mintage | F | VF | XF | Unc | BU |
|---|---|---|---|---|---|---|
| ND(1901-1905) | Inc. above | 100 | 150 | 250 | — | — |

**10 CASH** **Y# 100** **Composition:** Copper **Ruler:** Kuang - Hsü **Obverse:** Inscription: Kuang-hsü Yüan-pao **Reverse:** 1 cloud left of pearl, dragon **Rev. Legend:** FOO-KIEN **Note:** Struck at Fu (Fuchow).

| Date | Mintage | F | VF | XF | Unc | BU |
|---|---|---|---|---|---|---|
| ND(1901-1905) | Inc. above | 3.00 | 6.00 | 9.00 | 30.00 | — |

**10 CASH** **Y# 100.1** **Composition:** Copper **Ruler:** Kuang - Hsü **Obverse:** Inscription: Kuang-hsü Yüan-pao **Reverse:** 3 clouds left of pearl and without cloud above tip of dragon's tail, dragon **Rev. Legend:** FOO-KIEN **Note:** Struck at Fu (Fuchow).

| Date | Mintage | F | VF | XF | Unc | BU |
|---|---|---|---|---|---|---|
| ND(1901-1905) | Inc. above | 2.00 | 4.00 | 7.00 | 25.00 | — |

**10 CASH** **Y# 100.2** **Composition:** Copper **Ruler:** Kuang - Hsü **Obverse:** Inscription: Kuang-hsü Yüan-pao **Reverse:** 3 clouds left of pearl and a cloud above tip of dragon's tail, dragon **Rev. Legend:** FOO-KIEN **Note:** Struck at Fu (Fuchow).

| Date | Mintage | F | VF | XF | Unc | BU |
|---|---|---|---|---|---|---|
| ND(1901-1905) | Inc. above | 1.00 | 2.00 | 4.00 | 25.00 | — |

**10 CASH** **Y# 100.3** **Composition:** Copper **Ruler:** Kuang - Hsü **Obverse:** Inscription: Kuang-hsü Yüan-pao **Reverse:** Dragon, denomination: 10 CASHES **Rev. Legend:** FOO-KIEN **Note:** Struck at Fu (Fuchow).

| Date | Mintage | F | VF | XF | Unc | BU |
|---|---|---|---|---|---|---|
| ND(1901-1905) | Inc. above | 12.00 | 20.00 | 45.00 | — | — |

**10 CASH** **Y# 100.2a** **Composition:** Brass **Ruler:** Kuang - Hsü **Obverse:** Inscription: Kuang-hsü Yüan-pao **Reverse:** Dragon **Rev. Legend:** FOO-KIEN **Note:** Struck at Fu (Fuchow).

| Date | Mintage | F | VF | XF | Unc | BU |
|---|---|---|---|---|---|---|
| ND(1901-1905) | Inc. above | — | — | — | — | — |

**10 CASH** **Y# 10f** **Composition:** Copper **Ruler:** Kuang - Hsü **Obverse:** Inscription: Tai-ch'ing T'ung-pi **Reverse:** Dragon, inscription: denomination 10 CASHES **Rev. Legend:** Kuang-hsü Nien-tsao, TAI-CHING-TI-KUO ... **Note:** Struck at Fu (Fuchow).

| Date | Mintage | F | VF | XF | Unc | BU |
|---|---|---|---|---|---|---|
| CD(1906) | — | 0.75 | 1.50 | 3.00 | 20.00 | — |

**10 CASH** **Y# 20f** **Composition:** Copper **Ruler:** Hsüan - T'ung **Obverse:** Inscription: Tai-ch'ing T'ung-pi **Reverse:** Dragon **Rev. Legend:** Hsüan-tung Nien-tsao, TAI-CHING-TI-KUO ... **Note:** Struck at Fu (Fuchow).

| Date | Mintage | F | VF | XF | Unc | BU |
|---|---|---|---|---|---|---|
| CD(1909) | — | 50.00 | 85.00 | 125 | — | — |

**20 CASH** **Y# 101** **Composition:** Copper **Ruler:** Kuang - Hsü **Obverse:** Inscription: Kuang-hsü Yüan-pao **Reverse:** Dragon **Rev. Legend:** FOO-KIEN **Note:** Struck at Fu (Fuchow).

| Date | Mintage | VG | F | VF | XF | Unc |
|---|---|---|---|---|---|---|
| ND(1901-1902) | 18,000 | 12.00 | 30.00 | 45.00 | 75.00 | — |

**5 CENTS** **Y# 102** **Weight:** 1.3500 g. **Composition:** 0.8200 Silver .0356 oz. ASW **Ruler:** Kuang - Hsü **Obverse:** Legend with 5 characters at top, inscription: Kuang-hsü Yüan-pao **Reverse:** Side view dragon left **Note:** Struck at Fu (Fuchow).

| Date | Mintage | F | VF | XF | Unc | BU |
|---|---|---|---|---|---|---|
| ND(1896-1903) | — | 7.00 | 13.00 | 22.50 | 60.00 | — |

**5 CENTS** **Y# 102.1** **Weight:** 1.3500 g. **Composition:** 0.8200 Silver .0356 oz. ASW **Ruler:** Kuang - Hsü **Obverse:** Legend with four characters at top, inscription: Kuang-hsü Yüan-pao **Reverse:** Rosette at either side of side view dragon right **Note:** Struck at Fu (Fuchow).

| Date | Mintage | F | VF | XF | Unc | BU |
|---|---|---|---|---|---|---|
| ND(1903-1908) | — | 3.00 | 8.00 | 20.00 | 40.00 | — |

**5 CENTS** **Y# 102.2** **Weight:** 1.3500 g. **Composition:** 0.8200 Silver .0356 oz. ASW **Ruler:** Kuang - Hsü **Obverse:** Inscription: Kuang-hsü Yüan-pao **Reverse:** Rosette above dragon's head **Note:** Struck at Fu (Fuchow).

| Date | Mintage | F | VF | XF | Unc | BU |
|---|---|---|---|---|---|---|
| ND(1903-1908) | — | 6.00 | 12.00 | 25.00 | 50.00 | — |

**5 CENTS** **Y# 102.3** **Weight:** 1.3500 g. **Composition:** 0.8200 Silver .0356 oz. ASW **Ruler:** Kuang - Hsü **Obverse:** Inscription: Kuang-hsü Yüan-pao **Rev. Legend:** PROVINCE FOO-KIRN **Note:** Struck at Fu (Fuchow).

| Date | Mintage | F | VF | XF | Unc | BU |
|---|---|---|---|---|---|---|
| ND(1903-1908) | — | — | — | — | — | — |

**10 CENTS** **Y# 103** **Weight:** 2.7000 g. **Composition:** 0.8200 Silver .0712 oz. ASW **Ruler:** Kuang - Hsü **Obverse:** Legend with 5 characters at top, inscription: Kuang-hsü Yüan-pao **Reverse:** Rosette at either side of side view dragon left **Note:** Struck at Fu (Fuchow).

| Date | Mintage | F | VF | XF | Unc | BU |
|---|---|---|---|---|---|---|
| ND(1896-1903) | 13,425,000 | 5.00 | 9.00 | 17.50 | 35.00 | — |

**10 CENTS** **Y# 103.1** **Weight:** 2.7000 g. **Composition:** 0.8200 Silver .0712 oz. ASW **Ruler:** Kuang - Hsü **Obverse:** Inscription: Kuang-hsü Yüan-pao **Reverse:** Dot at either side of side view dragon left **Note:** Struck at Fu (Fuchow).

| Date | Mintage | F | VF | XF | Unc | BU |
|---|---|---|---|---|---|---|
| ND(1896-1903) | Inc. above | 8.00 | 15.00 | 30.00 | 60.00 | — |

**10 CENTS** **Y# 103.2** **Weight:** 2.7000 g. **Composition:** 0.8200 Silver .0712 oz. ASW **Ruler:** Kuang - Hsü **Obverse:** Legend has 4 characters at top, inscription: Kuang-hsü Yüan-pao **Reverse:** Small side view dragon right **Note:** Struck at Fu (Fuchow).

| Date | Mintage | F | VF | XF | Unc | BU |
|---|---|---|---|---|---|---|
| ND(1903-1908) | Inc. above | 3.00 | 6.00 | 12.00 | 30.00 | — |

**10 CENTS** **Y# 103.3** **Weight:** 2.7000 g. **Composition:** 0.8200 Silver .0712 oz. ASW **Ruler:** Kuang - Hsü **Obverse:** Legend has 4 characters at top, inscription: Kuang-hsü Yüan-pao **Reverse:** Large side view dragon right **Note:** Struck at Fu (Fuchow).

| Date | Mintage | F | VF | XF | Unc | BU |
|---|---|---|---|---|---|---|
| ND(1903-1908) | Inc. above | 6.00 | 12.00 | 24.00 | 50.00 | — |

**20 CENTS** **Y# 104** **Weight:** 5.4000 g. **Composition:** 0.8200 Silver .1424 oz. ASW **Ruler:** Kuang - Hsü **Obverse:** Legend has 5 characters at top, inscription: Kuang-hsü Yüan-pao **Reverse:** Dot at either side of side view dragon left **Note:** Struck at Fu (Fuchow).

| Date | Mintage | F | VF | XF | Unc | BU |
|---|---|---|---|---|---|---|
| ND(1896-1903) | 31,772,000 | 3.00 | 6.00 | 12.50 | 30.00 | — |

**20 CENTS** **Y# 104.1** **Weight:** 5.4000 g. **Composition:** 0.8200 Silver .1424 oz. ASW **Ruler:** Kuang - Hsü **Obverse:** Inscription: Kuang-hsü Yüan-pao **Reverse:** Rosette at either side of side view dragon left **Note:** Struck at Fu (Fuchow).

| Date | Mintage | F | VF | XF | Unc | BU |
|---|---|---|---|---|---|---|
| ND(1898-1903) | Inc. above | 3.00 | 6.00 | 12.50 | 30.00 | — |

**20 CENTS** **Y# 104.2** **Weight:** 5.4000 g. **Composition:** 0.8200 Silver .1424 oz. ASW **Ruler:** Kuang - Hsü **Obverse:** Legend has 4 characters at top, inscription: Kuang-hsü Yüan-pao **Reverse:** Side view dragon right **Note:** Struck at Fu (Fuchow). Variety with large side view dragon right on reverse exists.

| Date | Mintage | F | VF | XF | Unc | BU |
|---|---|---|---|---|---|---|
| ND(1903-1908) | Inc. above | 3.00 | 6.00 | 12.50 | 30.00 | — |

# REPUBLIC

## PROVINCIAL CAST COINAGE

**CASH** **Y# 374** **Composition:** Cast Brass **Obverse:** Inscription: Fu-chien T'ung-pao **Reverse:** 6 stripes on right flag

| Date | Mintage | VG | F | VF | XF | Unc |
|---|---|---|---|---|---|---|
| ND(c. 1912) | — | 50.00 | 80.00 | 125 | 165 | — |

**2 CASH** **Y# 375** **Composition:** Cast Brass **Obverse:** Inscription: Fu-chien T'ung-pao **Reverse:** 5 stripes on right flag

| Date | Mintage | VG | F | VF | XF | Unc |
|---|---|---|---|---|---|---|
| ND(c. 1912) | — | 12.50 | 17.50 | 22.50 | 30.00 | — |

**2 CASH** **Y# 375.1** **Composition:** Cast Brass **Obverse:** Inscription: Fu-chien T'ung-pao **Reverse:** 6 stripes on right flag

| Date | Mintage | VG | F | VF | XF | Unc |
|---|---|---|---|---|---|---|
| ND(c. 1912) | — | 30.00 | 50.00 | 80.00 | 125 | — |

## MILLED COINAGE

**10 CASH** **Y# 379** **Composition:** Copper **Obverse:** Inscription: Chung-hua Yüan-pao **Rev. Legend:** FOO-KIEN COPPER COIN

| Date | Mintage | F | VF | XF | Unc | BU |
|---|---|---|---|---|---|---|
| ND(c. 1912) | — | 4.00 | 8.00 | 15.00 | 35.00 | — |

**10 CASH** Y# 379a **Composition:** Brass **Obverse:** Inscription: Chung-hua Yüan-pao **Rev. Legend:** FOO-KIEN COPPER COIN

| Date | Mintage | F | VF | XF | Unc | BU |
|---|---|---|---|---|---|---|
| ND(c. 1912) | — | 37.50 | 50.00 | 87.50 | 125 | — |

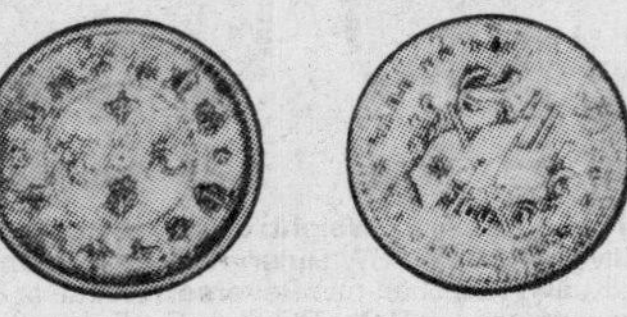

**10 CENTS** Y# 380 **Weight:** 2.6000 g. **Composition:** Silver **Obverse:** Inscription: Chung-hua Yüan-pao

| Date | Mintage | F | VF | XF | Unc | BU |
|---|---|---|---|---|---|---|
| ND(c. 1912) | — | 30.00 | 80.00 | 180 | 300 | — |

**10 CENTS** Y# 382 **Weight:** 2.6000 g. **Composition:** Silver **Obverse:** Inscription: Chung-hua Yüan-pao

| Date | Mintage | F | VF | XF | Unc | BU |
|---|---|---|---|---|---|---|
| ND(c. 1913) | — | 2.50 | 5.00 | 9.00 | 20.00 | — |

**10 CENTS** Y# 380a **Weight:** 2.6000 g. **Composition:** Silver **Obverse:** Different legend in center, inscription: Chung-hua Yüan-pao **Note:** Similar to Y#380.

| Date | Mintage | F | VF | XF | Unc | BU |
|---|---|---|---|---|---|---|
| CD1924 | — | 50.00 | 85.00 | 150 | 250 | — |

**10 CENTS** Y# 388 **Weight:** 2.6000 g. **Composition:** Silver **Subject:** Canton martyrs

| Date | Mintage | F | VF | XF | Unc | BU |
|---|---|---|---|---|---|---|
| 17(1928) | — | 7.50 | 15.00 | 30.00 | 50.00 | — |
| 20(1931) | — | 10.00 | 25.00 | 50.00 | 75.00 | — |

**10 CENTS** Y# 390 **Weight:** 2.6000 g. **Composition:** Silver **Subject:** Canton martyrs

| Date | Mintage | F | VF | XF | Unc | BU |
|---|---|---|---|---|---|---|
| 21(1932) | — | 100 | 150 | 200 | 375 | — |

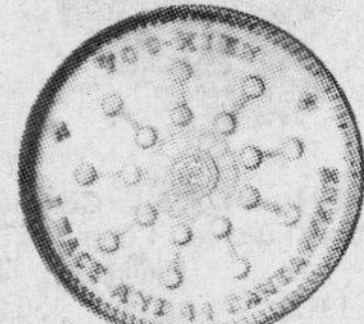

**20 CENTS** Y# 377 **Weight:** 5.0000 g. **Composition:** Silver **Obverse:** Inscription: Chung-hua Yüan-pao

| Date | Mintage | F | VF | XF | Unc | BU |
|---|---|---|---|---|---|---|
| CD1911 | — | 10.00 | 20.00 | 35.00 | 100 | — |

**20 CENTS** Y# A381 **Weight:** 5.4000 g. **Composition:** Silver **Obverse:** Inscription: Chung-hua Yüan-pao

| Date | Mintage | F | VF | XF | Unc | BU |
|---|---|---|---|---|---|---|
| ND(1912) | — | 3.50 | 7.00 | 15.00 | 25.00 | — |

**20 CENTS** Y# 381 **Weight:** 5.3000 g. **Composition:** Silver **Obverse:** Rosettes at sides, dot in middle of rosette center **Reverse:** Rosettes at sides

| Date | Mintage | F | VF | XF | Unc | BU |
|---|---|---|---|---|---|---|
| CD1923 | — | 3.50 | 7.00 | 10.00 | 25.00 | — |

**20 CENTS** Y# 383 **Weight:** 5.2000 g. **Composition:** Silver **Note:** Kann dates this coin 1913, but evidence suggests that it was struck in 1923.

| Date | Mintage | F | VF | XF | Unc | BU |
|---|---|---|---|---|---|---|
| ND(1923) | — | 3.00 | 5.00 | 10.00 | 20.00 | — |

**20 CENTS** Y# 381.1 **Weight:** 5.3000 g. **Composition:** Silver **Reverse:** MADE spelled MAIE in legend

| Date | Mintage | F | VF | XF | Unc | BU |
|---|---|---|---|---|---|---|
| CD1923 | — | 3.50 | 7.50 | 12.50 | 30.00 | — |

**20 CENTS** Y# 381.2 **Weight:** 5.3000 g. **Composition:** Silver **Rev. Legend:** MADEIN FOO-KIENMINT

| Date | Mintage | F | VF | XF | Unc | BU |
|---|---|---|---|---|---|---|
| CD1923 | — | 3.50 | 7.50 | 12.50 | 30.00 | — |

**20 CENTS** Y# 381.3 **Weight:** 5.3000 g. **Composition:** Silver **Obverse:** Without dot in middle of center rosette, 5-pointed star at sides in place of rosette

| Date | Mintage | F | VF | XF | Unc | BU |
|---|---|---|---|---|---|---|
| CD1923 | — | 10.00 | 12.50 | 17.50 | 35.00 | — |

**20 CENTS** Y# 381.4 **Weight:** 5.0000 g. **Composition:** Silver **Obverse:** Different legend in center

| Date | Mintage | F | VF | XF | Unc | BU |
|---|---|---|---|---|---|---|
| CD1924 | — | 5.00 | 8.00 | 15.00 | 35.00 | — |

**20 CENTS** Y# 383a **Weight:** 5.7000 g. **Composition:** Silver

| Date | Mintage | F | VF | XF | Unc | BU |
|---|---|---|---|---|---|---|
| 13(1924) | — | 35.00 | 50.00 | 70.00 | 90.00 | — |

**20 CENTS** Y# 384 **Weight:** 5.0000 g. **Composition:** Silver **Subject:** Northern Expedition

| Date | Mintage | F | VF | XF | Unc | BU |
|---|---|---|---|---|---|---|
| 16(1927) | — | 200 | 300 | 400 | 600 | — |

**20 CENTS** Y# 385 **Weight:** 5.3000 g. **Composition:** Silver **Subject:** Northern Expedition

| Date | Mintage | F | VF | XF | Unc | BU |
|---|---|---|---|---|---|---|
| 16(1927) | — | 600 | 950 | 1,250 | 1,750 | — |

**20 CENTS** Y# 389.1 **Weight:** 5.3000 g. **Composition:** Silver **Subject:** Canton martyrs **Obverse:** 2 rows of bricks at right of gate

| Date | Mintage | F | VF | XF | Unc | BU |
|---|---|---|---|---|---|---|
| 17(1928) | — | 5.00 | 7.50 | 12.50 | 30.00 | — |
| 20(1931) | — | 7.50 | 12.00 | 20.00 | 60.00 | — |

**20 CENTS** Y# 389.2 **Weight:** 5.5000 g. **Composition:** Silver **Subject:** Canton martyrs **Obverse:** Half brick in 3rd row of bricks at right of gate

| Date | Mintage | F | VF | XF | Unc | BU |
|---|---|---|---|---|---|---|
| 17(1928) | — | 4.00 | 6.50 | 10.00 | 30.00 | — |
| 20(1931) | — | 6.00 | 10.00 | 16.50 | 50.00 | — |

**20 CENTS** Y# 389.3 **Weight:** 5.5000 g. **Composition:** Silver **Subject:** Canton martyrs **Reverse:** 6-pointed star in legend

| Date | Mintage | F | VF | XF | Unc | BU |
|---|---|---|---|---|---|---|
| 20(1931) | — | — | — | — | — | — |

**20 CENTS** Y# 391 **Weight:** 5.3000 g. **Composition:** Silver **Subject:** Canton martyrs

| Date | Mintage | F | VF | XF | Unc | BU |
|---|---|---|---|---|---|---|
| 21(1932) | — | 40.00 | 65.00 | 100 | 250 | — |

## PATTERNS

Including off metal strikes

| KM# | Date | Mintage | Identification | Mkt Val |
|---|---|---|---|---|
| Pn3 | (c. 1912) | — | 2 Cash. Cast Brass. "Fu-chien Sheng-tsao." | 300 |
| Pn5 | (c. 1912) | — | 2 Cash. Cast Brass. "Min-sheng T'ung-pao." | 300 |
| Pn4 | (c. 1912) | — | 2 Cash. Cast Brass. "Fu-chien T'ung-pao." | 300 |
| Pn6 | 16(1927) | — | 20 Cents. Silver. 5.0000 g. Sun Yat-sen Memorial. K712. | 600 |
| Pn7 | 17(1928) | — | 20 Cents. Brass. Y389.1. | — |
| Pn8 | 21(1932) | — | 20 Cents. Brass. Y391. | — |

# HEILUNGKIANG PROVINCE

**Heilongjiang**

The northwesternmost of the former Three Eastern Provinces, bordering on Siberia. Though very large in extent, it is only sparsely populated, for wide areas are desert land. Economically the district was always backward. Heilungkiang (Heilongjiang) Province had no mint of its own, and seemingly no silver money bearing its name was ever placed in circulation although Imperial patterns in the standard dragon design exist for at least the dollar and 50 cent denominations. During the beginning of the 20th century it was suggested to contract for silver coins from the Berlin Mint.

## PATTERNS

Including off metal strikes

| KM# | Date | Mintage | Identification | Mkt Val |
|---|---|---|---|---|
| Pn1 | ND(1903) | — | 50 Cents. Brass. KM584x. | 2,500 |
| Pn2 | ND(1903) | — | Dollar. Silver. | — |
| Pn3 | ND(1903) | — | Dollar. Brass. | 6,000 |
| Pn4 | ND(1903) | — | Dollar. Silver Plated Brass. | 6,000 |

# HONAN PROVINCE

**Henan**

A province in east-central China. As well as being one of the most densely populated provinces it is also one of the most important agriculturally. It is the area of earliest settlement in China and has housed the capital during various dynasties. The Kaifeng Mint issued coins from its opening in 1647 through most of the rulers of the Manchu dynasty. In 1905 a modern mint opened at Kaifeng but closed in 1914. A mint in Loyang opened in 1924.

# EMPIRE

## PROVINCIAL CAST COINAGE

**CASH** **C# 11-9** **Composition:** Cast Brass **Ruler:** Kuang-hsü **Obverse:** Inscription: Kuang-hsü T'ung-pao **Reverse:** Inscription: Manchu Boo-ho **Note:** Struck at Ho (K'aifeng).

| Date | Mintage | Good | VG | F | VF | XF |
|---|---|---|---|---|---|---|
| ND(1875-1908) | — | 4.00 | 8.00 | 10.00 | 12.00 | — |

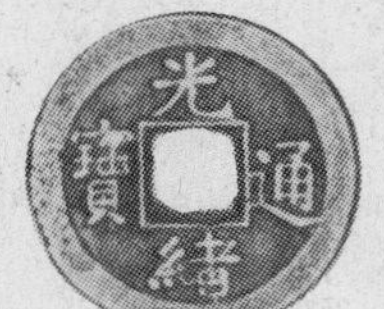

**CASH** **C# 11-9.1** **Composition:** Cast Brass **Ruler:** Kuang-hsü **Obverse:** Inscription: Kuang-hsü T'ung-pao **Reverse:** Circle above, inscription: Manchu Boo-ho **Note:** Struck at Ho (K'aifeng).

| Date | Mintage | Good | VG | F | VF | XF |
|---|---|---|---|---|---|---|
| ND(1875-1908) | — | 5.00 | 9.00 | 13.50 | 35.00 | — |

**CASH** **C# 11-9.2** **Composition:** Cast Brass **Ruler:** Kuang-hsü **Obverse:** Inscription: Kuang-hsü T'ung-pao **Reverse:** Circle below, inscription: Manchu Boo-ho **Note:** Struck at Ho (K'aifeng).

| Date | Mintage | Good | VG | F | VF | XF |
|---|---|---|---|---|---|---|
| ND(1875-1908) | — | 5.00 | 9.00 | 13.50 | 25.00 | — |

**CASH** **C# 11-9.3** **Composition:** Cast Brass **Ruler:** Kuang-hsü **Obverse:** Inscription: Kuang-hsü T'ung-pao **Reverse:** Crescent above, inscription: Manchu Boo-ho **Note:** Struck at Ho (K'aifeng).

| Date | Mintage | Good | VG | F | VF | XF |
|---|---|---|---|---|---|---|
| ND(1875-1908) | — | 5.00 | 9.00 | 13.50 | 25.00 | — |

**CASH** **C# 11-9.4** **Composition:** Cast Brass **Ruler:** Kuang-hsü **Obverse:** Inscription: Kuang-hsü T'ung-pao **Reverse:** Crescent below, inscription: Manchu Boo-ho **Note:** Struck at Ho (K'aifeng).

| Date | Mintage | Good | VG | F | VF | XF |
|---|---|---|---|---|---|---|
| ND(1875-1908) | — | 5.00 | 9.00 | 13.50 | 25.00 | — |

**CASH** **C# 11-9.5** **Composition:** Cast Brass **Ruler:** Kuang-hsü **Obverse:** Inscription: Kuang-hsü T'ung-pao **Reverse:** Crescent above, dot below, inscription: Manchu Boo-ho **Note:** Struck at Ho (K'aifeng). Sch. #1571.

| Date | Mintage | Good | VG | F | VF | XF |
|---|---|---|---|---|---|---|
| ND(1875-1908) | — | 5.00 | 9.00 | 13.50 | 25.00 | — |

**CASH** **C# 11-9.6** **Composition:** Cast Brass **Ruler:** Kuang-hsü **Obverse:** Inscription: Kuang-hsü T'ung-pao **Reverse:** Dot above, inscription: Manchu Boo-ho **Note:** Struck at Ho (K'aifeng).

| Date | Mintage | Good | VG | F | VF | XF |
|---|---|---|---|---|---|---|
| ND(1875-1908) | — | 5.00 | 9.00 | 13.50 | 20.00 | — |

**CASH** **C# 11-9.7** **Composition:** Cast Brass **Ruler:** Kuang-hsü **Obverse:** Inscription: Kuang-hsü T'ung-pao **Reverse:** Dot below, inscription: Manchu Boo-ho **Note:** Struck at Ho (K'aifeng).

| Date | Mintage | Good | VG | F | VF | XF |
|---|---|---|---|---|---|---|
| ND(1875-1908) | — | 5.00 | 9.00 | 13.50 | 20.00 | — |

**CASH** **C# 11-9.8** **Composition:** Cast Brass **Ruler:** Kuang-hsü **Obverse:** Inscription: Kuang-hsü T'ung-pao **Reverse:** Dot at upper left, inscription: Manchu Boo-ho **Note:** Struck at Ho (K'aifeng). Crescent and dot varieties exist.

| Date | Mintage | Good | VG | F | VF | XF |
|---|---|---|---|---|---|---|
| ND(1875-1908) | — | 5.00 | 9.00 | 13.50 | 20.00 | — |

**CASH** **C# 3-1.1a** **Composition:** Cast Zinc **Ruler:** Kuang-hsü **Obverse:** Inscription: Kuang-hsü T'ung-pao **Reverse:** Dot at upper left, inscription: Manchu Boo-ho **Note:** Struck at Ho (K'aifeng).

| Date | Mintage | Good | VG | F | VF | XF |
|---|---|---|---|---|---|---|
| ND(1875-1908) Rare | — | — | — | — | — | — |

## MILLED COINAGE

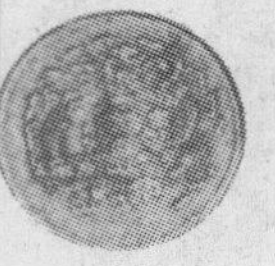

**CASH** **Y# 7g** **Composition:** Brass **Ruler:** Kuang-hsü **Obv. Legend:** Kuang-hsü **Reverse:** Side view dragon

| Date | Mintage | VG | F | VF | XF | Unc |
|---|---|---|---|---|---|---|
| CD1908 | — | 10.00 | 25.00 | 42.50 | 75.00 | — |

**CASH** **Y# 7ga** **Composition:** Copper **Ruler:** Kuang-hsü **Obv. Legend:** Kuang-hsü **Reverse:** Side view dragon

| Date | Mintage | VG | F | VF | XF | Unc |
|---|---|---|---|---|---|---|
| CD1908 | — | 20.00 | 50.00 | 85.00 | 150 | — |

**10 CASH** **Y# 108** **Composition:** Copper **Ruler:** Kuang-hsü **Obverse:** Inscription: Kuang-hsü Yüan-pao **Reverse:** Circled dragon without mountain below pearl with 3 flames

| Date | Mintage | VG | F | VF | XF | Unc |
|---|---|---|---|---|---|---|
| ND(1905) | — | 4.00 | 10.00 | 20.00 | 45.00 | — |

**10 CASH** **Y# 108.1** **Composition:** Copper **Ruler:** Kuang-hsü **Obverse:** Inscription: Kuang-hsü Yüan-pao **Reverse:** Circled dragon without mountain below pearl with 5 flames

| Date | Mintage | VG | F | VF | XF | Unc |
|---|---|---|---|---|---|---|
| ND(1905) | — | 1.00 | 2.00 | 4.50 | 9.00 | — |

**10 CASH** **Y# 108.2** **Composition:** Copper **Ruler:** Kuang-hsü **Obverse:** Inscription: Kuang-hsü Yüan-pao **Reverse:** Circled dragon, mountain below pearl, very small English lettering

| Date | Mintage | VG | F | VF | XF | Unc |
|---|---|---|---|---|---|---|
| ND(1905) | — | 6.00 | 15.00 | 30.00 | 50.00 | — |

**10 CASH** **Y# 108.3** **Composition:** Copper **Ruler:** Kuang-hsü **Obverse:** Inscription: Kuang-hsü Yüan-pao **Reverse:** Circled dragon, large English legend

| Date | Mintage | VG | F | VF | XF | Unc |
|---|---|---|---|---|---|---|
| ND(1905) | — | 5.00 | 10.00 | 15.00 | 30.00 | — |

**10 CASH** **Y# 108a** **Composition:** Brass **Ruler:** Kuang-hsü **Obverse:** Raised sphere yin-yang in center, inscription: Kuang-hsü Yüan-pao **Reverse:** Uncircled dragon, Honan spelled HOU-NAN **Note:** Dies made in Japan.

| Date | Mintage | VG | F | VF | XF | Unc |
|---|---|---|---|---|---|---|
| ND(1905) Rare | — | — | — | — | — | — |

**10 CASH** **Y# 108a.1** **Composition:** Copper **Ruler:** Kuang-hsü **Obverse:** Inscription: Kuang-hsü Yüan-pao **Reverse:** Uncircled dragon

| Date | Mintage | VG | F | VF | XF | Unc |
|---|---|---|---|---|---|---|
| ND(1905) | — | 1.00 | 3.00 | 5.00 | 10.00 | — |

**10 CASH** **Y# 108a.2** **Composition:** Copper **Ruler:** Kuang-hsü **Obverse:** Curved line on raised yin-yang slanted more, inscription: Kuang-hsü Yüan-pao **Reverse:** Uncircled dragon

| Date | Mintage | VG | F | VF | XF | Unc |
|---|---|---|---|---|---|---|
| ND(1905) | — | 1.00 | 3.00 | 5.00 | 10.00 | — |

**10 CASH** **Y# 108a.3** **Composition:** Copper **Ruler:** Kuang-hsü **Obverse:** Flat yin-yang slanted more, inscription: Kuang-hsü Yüan-pao **Reverse:** Circled dragon, plain pearl **Note:** Dies made in United States.

| Date | Mintage | VG | F | VF | XF | Unc |
|---|---|---|---|---|---|---|
| ND(1905) | — | 0.75 | 2.50 | 4.00 | 8.00 | — |

**10 CASH** **Y# 108a.3a** **Composition:** Brass **Ruler:** Kuang-hsü **Obverse:** Inscription: Kuang-hsü Yüan-pao **Reverse:** Dragon

| Date | Mintage | VG | F | VF | XF | Unc |
|---|---|---|---|---|---|---|
| ND(1905) | — | 2.50 | 5.00 | 10.00 | 20.00 | — |

**10 CASH** **Y# 108a.4** **Composition:** Copper **Ruler:** Kuang-hsü **Obverse:** Inscription: Kuang-hsü Yüan-pao **Reverse:** Dragon, incuse swirl in pearl **Note:** Dies made in United States.

| Date | Mintage | VG | F | VF | XF | Unc |
|---|---|---|---|---|---|---|
| ND(1905) | — | 1.00 | 3.00 | 5.00 | 12.00 | — |

**10 CASH** **Y# 10g** **Composition:** Copper **Ruler:** Kuang-hsü **Obverse:** Inscription: Tai-ch'ing T'ung-pi **Reverse:** Dragon, period after COIN in legend **Rev. Legend:** Kuang-hsü Nien-tsao, TAI-CHING-TI-KUO ...

| Date | Mintage | VG | F | VF | XF | Unc |
|---|---|---|---|---|---|---|
| CD(1906) | 132,000,000 | 0.85 | 2.00 | 5.00 | 10.00 | — |

**10 CASH** **Y# 10g.1** **Composition:** Copper **Ruler:** Kuang-hsü **Obverse:** Inscription: Tai-ch'ing T'ung-pi **Reverse:** Dragon, period after COPPER in legend **Rev. Legend:** Kuang-hsü Nien-tsao, TAI-CHING-TI-KUO ...

| Date | Mintage | VG | F | VF | XF | Unc |
|---|---|---|---|---|---|---|
| CD(1906) | — | 1.25 | 3.00 | 6.00 | 10.00 | — |

**10 CASH** **Y# 10g.2** **Composition:** Copper **Ruler:** Kuang-hsü **Obverse:** Inscription: Tai-ch'ing T'ung-pi **Reverse:** Dragon **Rev. Legend:** Kuang-hsü Nien-tsao, TAI-CHING-TI-KUO ... **Note:** Cyclical dates at sides.

| Date | Mintage | VG | F | VF | XF | Unc |
|---|---|---|---|---|---|---|
| CD(1907) Rare | — | — | — | — | — | — |

**10 CASH** **Y# 20g** **Composition:** Copper **Ruler:** Hsüan-t'ung **Obverse:** Inscription: Tai-ch'ing T'ung-pi **Reverse:** Dragon **Rev. Legend:** Hsüan-t'ung Nien-tsao, TAI-CHING-TI-KUO ... **Note:** Normally encountered with weak legends.

| Date | Mintage | VG | F | VF | XF | Unc |
|---|---|---|---|---|---|---|
| CD(1909) | — | 20.00 | 40.00 | 60.00 | 125 | — |
| CD(1911) | — | 5.00 | 15.00 | 25.00 | 50.00 | — |

## REPUBLIC

### MILLED COINAGE

**10 CASH** **Y# A392** **Composition:** Copper

| Date | Mintage | F | VF | XF | Unc | BU |
|---|---|---|---|---|---|---|
| ND(1913-1914) | — | 1.00 | 2.00 | 6.00 | 20.00 | — |

**10 CASH** **Y# A392.1** **Composition:** Copper **Obverse:** Without lines above and below rosettes

| Date | Mintage | F | VF | XF | Unc | BU |
|---|---|---|---|---|---|---|
| ND(1913-1914) | — | 1.00 | 2.00 | 6.00 | 20.00 | — |

**10 CASH** **Y# A392.2** **Composition:** Copper **Reverse:** Letter "S" in CASH backwards

| Date | Mintage | F | VF | XF | Unc | BU |
|---|---|---|---|---|---|---|
| ND(c. 1920) | — | 17.50 | 30.00 | 60.00 | — | — |

**10 CASH** **Y# 392** **Composition:** Copper **Reverse:** TEN CASH in legend in larger letters

| Date | Mintage | F | VF | XF | Unc | BU |
|---|---|---|---|---|---|---|
| ND(c. 1920) | — | 0.75 | 1.50 | 4.00 | 18.00 | — |

**10 CASH** **Y# 392.1** **Composition:** Copper **Obverse:** Rosette in center higher in relation to heart-shaped leaves below

| Date | Mintage | F | VF | XF | Unc | BU |
|---|---|---|---|---|---|---|
| ND(c. 1920) | — | 2.00 | 3.50 | 6.00 | 20.00 | — |

**20 CASH** **Y# 393** **Composition:** Copper **Reverse:** Legend has 6 characters at bottom

| Date | Mintage | Good | VG | F | VF | XF |
|---|---|---|---|---|---|---|
| ND(c. 1920) | — | 1.25 | 2.50 | 5.00 | 10.00 | 30.00 |

**20 CASH** **Y# 393.1** **Composition:** Copper **Reverse:** Legend has 5 characters at bottom

| Date | Mintage | Good | VG | F | VF | XF |
|---|---|---|---|---|---|---|
| ND(c. 1920) | — | 1.00 | 2.00 | 4.00 | 6.00 | 20.00 |

**20 CASH** **Y# 393.2** **Composition:** Copper **Reverse:** CHINA replaces HO-NAN in legend

| Date | Mintage | Good | VG | F | VF | XF |
|---|---|---|---|---|---|---|
| ND(c. 1921) | — | 12.50 | 25.00 | 45.00 | 175 | — |

**20 CASH** **Y# A397** **Composition:** Copper **Reverse:** Star above flags

| Date | Mintage | Good | VG | F | VF | XF |
|---|---|---|---|---|---|---|
| 20(1931) | — | — | 500 | 1,500 | 3,000 | — |

**50 CASH** **Y# 394** **Composition:** Copper **Reverse:** Short flag poles

| Date | Mintage | Good | VG | F | VF | XF |
|---|---|---|---|---|---|---|
| ND(c. 1920) | — | 2.00 | 5.00 | 10.00 | 20.00 | 60.00 |

**50 CASH** **Y# 394.1** **Composition:** Copper **Reverse:** Long flag poles

| Date | Mintage | Good | VG | F | VF | XF |
|---|---|---|---|---|---|---|
| ND(c. 1920) | — | 2.00 | 5.00 | 10.00 | 20.00 | 60.00 |

**50 CASH** **Y# 394b** **Composition:** Brass

| Date | Mintage | Good | VG | F | VF | XF |
|---|---|---|---|---|---|---|
| ND(c. 1920) | — | 10.00 | 20.00 | 40.00 | 80.00 | 225 |

**50 CASH** **Y# 394a** **Composition:** Brass **Reverse:** CHINA replaces HONAN in legend

| Date | Mintage | Good | VG | F | VF | XF |
|---|---|---|---|---|---|---|
| ND(c. 1921) | — | 6.50 | 12.50 | 25.00 | 60.00 | 175 |

**50 CASH** **Y# 397** **Composition:** Brass

| Date | Mintage | Good | VG | F | VF | XF |
|---|---|---|---|---|---|---|
| 20(1931) | — | 50.00 | 120 | 200 | 330 | — |

**100 CASH** **Y# 395** **Composition:** Copper **Reverse:** Small star in right flag, tassels 4 millimeters long

| Date | Mintage | Good | VG | F | VF | XF |
|---|---|---|---|---|---|---|
| ND(c. 1928) | — | 3.00 | 5.00 | 10.00 | 25.00 | 75.00 |

**100 CASH** **Y# 395.1** **Composition:** Copper **Reverse:** Tassels 5 millimeters long

| Date | Mintage | Good | VG | F | VF | XF |
|---|---|---|---|---|---|---|
| ND(c. 1928) | — | 3.75 | 6.50 | 12.50 | 30.00 | 90.00 |

**100 CASH** **Y# 395.2** **Composition:** Copper **Reverse:** Large star in right flag

| Date | Mintage | Good | VG | F | VF | XF |
|---|---|---|---|---|---|---|
| ND(c. 1928) | — | — | — | — | — | — |

**100 CASH** **Y# 398** **Composition:** Copper

| Date | Mintage | Good | VG | F | VF | XF |
|---|---|---|---|---|---|---|
| 20(1931) | — | 30.00 | 60.00 | 95.00 | 150 | — |

**200 CASH** **Y# 396** **Composition:** Copper **Reverse:** Large square inside right flag

| Date | Mintage | Good | VG | F | VF | XF |
|---|---|---|---|---|---|---|
| ND(c. 1928) | — | 3.00 | 5.00 | 10.00 | 25.00 | 75.00 |

**200 CASH** **Y# 396.1** **Composition:** Copper **Reverse:** Small square and small star inside right flag

| Date | Mintage | Good | VG | F | VF | XF |
|---|---|---|---|---|---|---|
| ND(c. 1928) | — | 2.50 | 4.50 | 9.00 | 25.00 | 75.00 |

**200 CASH** **Y# 396.2** **Composition:** Copper **Reverse:** Small square and large star inside right flag

| Date | Mintage | Good | VG | F | VF | XF |
|---|---|---|---|---|---|---|
| ND(c. 1928) | — | 2.50 | 4.50 | 9.00 | 25.00 | 75.00 |

**200 CASH** **Y# 396a** **Composition:** Brass **Reverse:** Small square and large star inside right flag

| Date | Mintage | Good | VG | F | VF | XF |
|---|---|---|---|---|---|---|
| ND(c. 1928) | — | 6.00 | 15.00 | 22.50 | 45.00 | 135 |

## PATTERNS

Including off metal strikes

| KM# | Date | Mintage | Identification | Mkt Val |
|---|---|---|---|---|
| Pn1 | (1909) | — | 2 Cash. Brass. | — |
| Pn2 | (1909) | — | 5 Cash. Copper. Y19g. | — |
| Pn3 | (1909) | — | 20 Cash. Copper. Y21g. | — |

# HUNAN PROVINCE

A province in south-central China. Mining of coal, antimony, tungsten and tin is important as well as raising varied agricultural products. The Changsha Mint produced Cash coins from early in the Manchu dynasty. Its facility for struck coinage opened in 1897, and two further copper mints were added in 1905. All three mints were closed down in 1907, but one mint was reopened at a later date and produced vast quantities of republican copper coinage until 1926.

## EMPIRE

### PROVINCIAL CAST COINAGE

**CASH** **C# 12-7** **Composition:** Cast Brass **Ruler:** Kuang-hsü **Obverse:** Inscription: Kuang-hsü T'ung-pao **Reverse:** Inscription: Manchu Boo-nan **Note:** Struck at Nan (Ch'angsha)

| Date | Mintage | Good | VG | F | VF | XF |
|---|---|---|---|---|---|---|
| ND(1875-1908) | — | 7.50 | 15.00 | 21.50 | 30.00 | — |

### MILLED COINAGE

**10 CASH** **Y# 112** **Composition:** Copper **Ruler:** Kuang-hsü **Obverse:** Inscription: Kuang-hsü Yüan-pao; rosette in ceetner with center of petals depressed; Manchu words at sides, "Tan Shih" at bottom **Reverse:** Narrow spacing in HU-NAN above dragon

| Date | Mintage | F | VF | XF | Unc | BU |
|---|---|---|---|---|---|---|
| ND(1902-06) | — | 1.00 | 2.00 | 5.00 | 20.00 | — |

**10 CASH** **Y# 112.1** **Composition:** Copper **Ruler:** Kuang-hsü **Obverse:** Inscription: Kuang-hsü Yüan-pao **Reverse:** Dragon; wide spacing in HU-NAN

| Date | Mintage | F | VF | XF | Unc | BU |
|---|---|---|---|---|---|---|
| ND(1902-06) | — | 2.25 | 4.00 | 9.00 | 30.00 | — |

**10 CASH** Y# 112.2 **Composition:** Copper **Ruler:** Kuang-hsü **Obverse:** Inscription: Kuang-hsü Yüan-pao; petals of rosettes not depressed **Reverse:** Dragon

| Date | Mintage | F | VF | XF | Unc | BU |
|---|---|---|---|---|---|---|
| ND(1902-06) | — | 1.50 | 2.50 | 6.00 | 20.00 | — |

**10 CASH** Y# 112.3 **Composition:** Copper **Ruler:** Kuang-hsü **Obverse:** Inscription: Kuang-hsü Yüan-pao; two Manchu words in center, "T'ung Yuan" at bottom **Reverse:** Dragon

| Date | Mintage | F | VF | XF | Unc | BU |
|---|---|---|---|---|---|---|
| ND(1902-06) | — | 3.00 | 6.00 | 10.00 | 30.00 | — |

**10 CASH** Y# 112.4 **Composition:** Copper **Ruler:** Kuang-hsü **Obverse:** Inscription: Kuang-hsü Yüan-pao **Reverse:** Dragon; narrow spacing in HU-NAN

| Date | Mintage | F | VF | XF | Unc | BU |
|---|---|---|---|---|---|---|
| ND(1902-06) | — | 1.50 | 2.50 | 6.00 | 20.00 | — |

**10 CASH** Y# 112.5 **Composition:** Copper **Ruler:** Kuang-hsü **Obverse:** Inscription: Kuang-hsü Yüan-pao; rosette in center, "Tan Shih" at bottom **Reverse:** Dragon; ring around pearl

| Date | Mintage | F | VF | XF | Unc | BU |
|---|---|---|---|---|---|---|
| ND(1902-06) | — | 1.25 | 2.00 | 4.00 | 18.00 | — |

**10 CASH** Y# 112.6 **Composition:** Copper **Ruler:** Kuang-hsü **Obverse:** Inscription: Kuang-hsü Yüan-pao; centers of petals on rosette depressed **Reverse:** Dragon

| Date | Mintage | F | VF | XF | Unc | BU |
|---|---|---|---|---|---|---|
| ND(1902-06) | — | 1.50 | 2.50 | 6.00 | 20.00 | — |

**10 CASH** Y# 112.7 **Composition:** Copper **Ruler:** Kuang-hsü **Obverse:** Inscription: Kuang-hsü Yüan-pao; two Manchu words in center, "T'ung Yuan" at bottom **Reverse:** Dragon; ring around pearl

| Date | Mintage | F | VF | XF | Unc | BU |
|---|---|---|---|---|---|---|
| ND(1902-06) | — | 1.50 | 2.50 | 6.00 | 20.00 | — |

**10 CASH** Y# 112.8 **Composition:** Copper **Ruler:** Kuang-hsü **Obverse:** Inscription: Kuang-hsü Yüan-pao; larger characters at left and right, and different characters below **Reverse:** Dragon redesigned and small star at either side

| Date | Mintage | F | VF | XF | Unc | BU |
|---|---|---|---|---|---|---|
| ND(1902-06) | — | 5.00 | 10.00 | 17.50 | 40.00 | — |

**10 CASH** Y# 112.9 **Composition:** Copper **Ruler:** Kuang-hsü **Obverse:** Inscription: Kuang-hsü Yüan-pao; rosette in center; legend: four characters at bottom **Reverse:** Redesigned dragon without pearl; rosette at either side

| Date | Mintage | F | VF | XF | Unc | BU |
|---|---|---|---|---|---|---|
| ND(1902-06) | — | 7.50 | 15.00 | 30.00 | 75.00 | — |

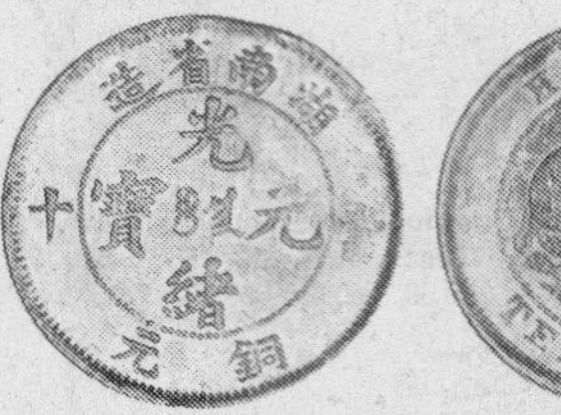

**10 CASH** Y# 112.10 **Composition:** Copper **Ruler:** Kuang-hsü **Obverse:** Inscription: Kuang-hsü Yüan-pao; two Manchu words in center with dot between; "T'ung Yuan" at bottom **Reverse:** Dragon

| Date | Mintage | F | VF | XF | Unc | BU |
|---|---|---|---|---|---|---|
| ND(1902-06) | — | 1.00 | 2.00 | 4.00 | 18.00 | — |

**10 CASH** Y# 112.11 **Composition:** Copper **Ruler:** Kuang-hsü **Obverse:** Inscription: Kuang-hsü Yüan-pao; without dot between Manchu words, "T'ung Yuan" at bottom **Reverse:** Dragon

| Date | Mintage | F | VF | XF | Unc | BU |
|---|---|---|---|---|---|---|
| ND(1902-06) | — | 1.00 | 2.00 | 4.00 | 18.00 | — |

**10 CASH** Y# 112.12 **Composition:** Copper **Ruler:** Kuang-hsü **Obverse:** Inscription: Kuang-hsü Yüan-pao; smaller 15.5 milimeter inner circle, with larger beads, "T'ung Yuan" at bottom **Reverse:** Dragon

| Date | Mintage | F | VF | XF | Unc | BU |
|---|---|---|---|---|---|---|
| ND(1902-06) | — | 1.00 | 2.00 | 4.00 | 18.00 | — |

**10 CASH** Y# 112.13 **Composition:** Copper **Ruler:** Kuang-hsü **Obverse:** Inscription: Kuang-hsü Yüan-pao; two Manchu words in center, 18.4 milimeter inner circle; "Huang T'ung" at bottom **Reverse:** Dragon

| Date | Mintage | F | VF | XF | Unc | BU |
|---|---|---|---|---|---|---|
| ND(1902-06) | — | 25.00 | 45.00 | 80.00 | — | — |

**10 CASH** Y# 112.14 **Composition:** Copper **Ruler:** Kuang-hsü **Obverse:** Inscription: Kuang-hsü Yüan-pao; smaller 17.5 milimeter inner circle; "Huang T'ung Yuan" at bottom **Reverse:** Dragon

| Date | Mintage | F | VF | XF | Unc | BU |
|---|---|---|---|---|---|---|
| ND(1902-06) | — | 25.00 | 45.00 | 80.00 | — | — |

**10 CASH** Y# 113 **Composition:** Copper **Ruler:** Kuang-hsü **Obverse:** Inscription: Kuang-hsü Yüan-pao **Obv. Legend:** Six characters at bottom **Reverse:** Flying dragon **Edge:** Reeded

| Date | Mintage | F | VF | XF | Unc | BU |
|---|---|---|---|---|---|---|
| ND(1902-06) | — | 4.00 | 8.00 | 15.00 | 40.00 | — |

**10 CASH** Y# 113.1 **Composition:** Copper **Ruler:** Kuang-hsü **Obverse:** Inscription: Kuang-hsü Yüan-pao **Obv. Legend:** Inverted U in HU-NAN **Reverse:** Dragon **Edge:** Reeded

| Date | Mintage | F | VF | XF | Unc | BU |
|---|---|---|---|---|---|---|
| ND(1902-06) | — | 12.50 | 25.00 | 45.00 | — | — |

**10 CASH** Y# 113a **Composition:** Brass **Ruler:** Kuang-hsü **Obverse:** Inscription: Kuang-hsü Yüan-pao **Obv. Legend:** Three characters at bottom **Reverse:** Dragon

| Date | Mintage | F | VF | XF | Unc | BU |
|---|---|---|---|---|---|---|
| ND(1902-06) | — | 3.50 | 6.00 | 12.50 | 35.00 | — |

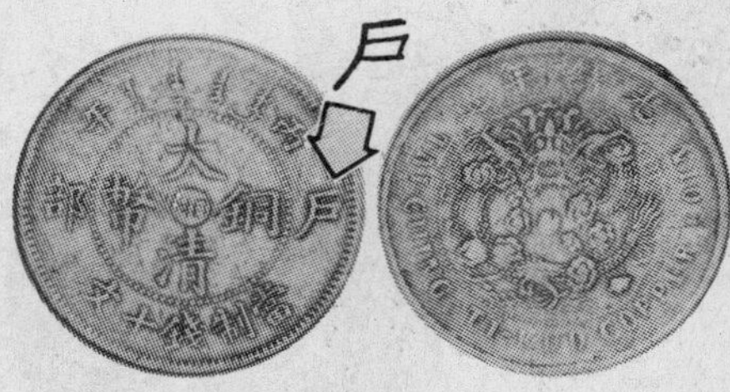


**10 CASH** Y# 10h **Composition:** Copper **Ruler:** Kuang-hsü **Obverse:** Inscription: Tai-ch'ing T'ung-pi; upper and lower parts of character "Hu" connected **Reverse:** Dragon; dot between Chinese characters above dragon **Rev. Legend:** Kuang-hsü Nien-tsao, TAI-CHING-TI-KUO...

| Date | Mintage | F | VF | XF | Unc | BU |
|---|---|---|---|---|---|---|
| CD(1906) | — | 17.50 | 35.00 | 70.00 | — | — |

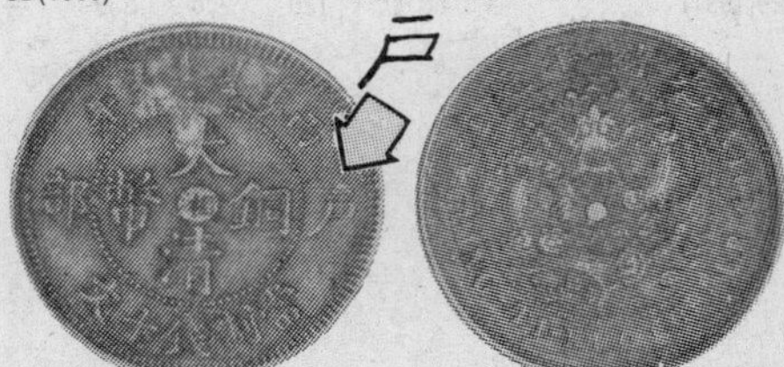


**10 CASH** Y# 10h.1 **Composition:** Copper **Ruler:** Kuang-hsü **Obverse:** Inscription: Tai-ch'ing T'ung-pi; upper and lower parts of character "Hu" not connected **Reverse:** Dragon; dot between Chinese characters at top **Rev. Legend:** Kuang-hsü Nien-tsao, TAI-CHING-TI-KUO...

| Date | Mintage | F | VF | XF | Unc | BU |
|---|---|---|---|---|---|---|
| CD(1906) | — | 17.50 | 35.00 | 70.00 | — | — |

**10 CASH** Y# 10h.2 **Composition:** Copper **Ruler:** Kuang-hsü **Obverse:** Inscription: Tai-ch'ing T'ung-pi; similar to Y#10h.1 **Reverse:** Dragon; seven flames on pearl **Rev. Legend:** Kuang-hsü Nien-tsao, TAI-CHING-TI-KUO...

| Date | Mintage | F | VF | XF | Unc | BU |
|---|---|---|---|---|---|---|
| CD(1906) | — | 2.00 | 4.00 | 8.00 | 22.00 | — |

**10 CASH** **Y# 10h.3** **Composition:** Copper **Ruler:** Kuang-hsü **Obverse:** Inscription: Tai-ch'ing T'ung-pi **Reverse:** Dragon; seven-flame pearl ornamented with toothlike projections **Rev. Legend:** Kuang-hsü Nien-tsao, TAI-CHING-TI-KUO...

| Date | Mintage | F | VF | XF | Unc | BU |
|---|---|---|---|---|---|---|
| CD(1906) | — | 2.00 | 3.50 | 6.00 | 18.00 | — |

**10 CASH** **Y# 10h.4** **Composition:** Copper **Ruler:** Kuang-hsü **Obverse:** Inscription: Tai-ch'ing T'ung-pi **Reverse:** Dragon; four flames on pearl **Rev. Legend:** Kuang-hsü Nien-tsao, TAI-CHING-TI-KUO...

| Date | Mintage | F | VF | XF | Unc | BU |
|---|---|---|---|---|---|---|
| CD(1906) | — | 3.00 | 6.00 | 10.00 | 22.00 | — |

**10 CASH** **Y# 10h.5** **Composition:** Copper **Ruler:** Kuang-hsü **Obverse:** Inscription: Tai-ch'ing T'ung-pi **Reverse:** Redesigned dragon with high waves beneath **Rev. Legend:** Kuang-hsü Nien-tsao, TAI-CHING-TI-KUO...

| Date | Mintage | F | VF | XF | Unc | BU |
|---|---|---|---|---|---|---|
| CD(1906) | — | 40.00 | 80.00 | 150 | — | — |

**10 CASH** **Y# 10h.6** **Composition:** Copper **Ruler:** Kuang-hsü **Obverse:** Inscription: Tai-ch'ing T'ung-pi; character "Hu" connected **Reverse:** Redesigned dragon, dot between COPPER COIN **Rev. Legend:** Kuang-hsü Nien-tsao, TAI-CHING-TI-KUO...

| Date | Mintage | F | VF | XF | Unc | BU |
|---|---|---|---|---|---|---|
| CD(1906) | — | 12.50 | 20.00 | 40.00 | — | — |

**10 CASH** **Y# 10h.7** **Composition:** Copper **Ruler:** Kuang-hsü **Obverse:** Inscription: Tai-ch'ing T'ung-pi; character "Hu" connected **Reverse:** Redesigned dragon with five flames on pearl **Rev. Legend:** Kuang-hsü Nien-tsao, TAI-CHING-TI-KUO... **Note:** Cross-reference numbers: Woodward #342 and #343

| Date | Mintage | F | VF | XF | Unc | BU |
|---|---|---|---|---|---|---|
| CD(1906) | — | 30.00 | 45.00 | 75.00 | — | — |

## BULLION COINAGE

### Mace/Tael Series

**CH'IEN (MACE)** **K# 951** **Weight:** 3.7000 g. **Composition:** Silver **Obverse:** Two lines of two characters each **Reverse:** Two lines of one character each **Note:** Provincial type.

| Date | Mintage | VG | F | VF | XF | Unc |
|---|---|---|---|---|---|---|
| ND(ca.1906) | — | 30.00 | 50.00 | 70.00 | 100 | — |

**CH'IEN (MACE)** **K# 971** **Weight:** 3.7000 g. **Composition:** Silver **Obverse:** Three lines of two characters each **Reverse:** Two lines of three characters each **Note:** Merchant type.

| Date | Mintage | VG | F | VF | XF | Unc |
|---|---|---|---|---|---|---|
| ND(ca.1908) | — | 30.00 | 50.00 | 70.00 | 120 | — |

**CH'IEN (MACE)** **K# 973** **Weight:** 3.7000 g. **Composition:** Silver **Obverse:** Two lines of two characters each **Reverse:** Two lines of one character each **Note:** Merchant type.

| Date | Mintage | VG | F | VF | XF | Unc |
|---|---|---|---|---|---|---|
| ND(ca.1908) | — | 30.00 | 50.00 | 70.00 | 120 | — |

**CH'IEN (MACE)** **K# 984/5** **Weight:** 3.7000 g. **Composition:** Silver **Obverse:** Two lines of three characters each **Reverse:** Two lines of one character each **Note:** Merchant type.

| Date | Mintage | VG | F | VF | XF | Unc |
|---|---|---|---|---|---|---|
| ND(ca.1908) | — | 30.00 | 50.00 | 70.00 | 120 | — |

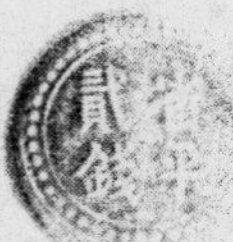

**2 CH'IEN (MACE)** **K# 950** **Weight:** 7.3000 g. **Composition:** Silver **Obverse:** Two lines of two characters each **Reverse:** Two lines of two characters each **Note:** Provincial type.

| Date | Mintage | VG | F | VF | XF | Unc |
|---|---|---|---|---|---|---|
| ND(ca.1906) | — | 35.00 | 55.00 | 75.00 | 110 | — |

**2 CH'IEN (MACE)** **K# 960** **Weight:** 7.3000 g. **Composition:** Silver **Obverse:** Three lines of two characters each **Reverse:** Two lines of three characters each **Note:** Provincial type.

| Date | Mintage | VG | F | VF | XF | Unc |
|---|---|---|---|---|---|---|
| ND(ca.1906) | — | 35.00 | 55.00 | 75.00 | 110 | — |

**2 CH'IEN (MACE)** **K# 970** **Weight:** 7.3000 g. **Composition:** Silver **Obverse:** Three lines of two characters each **Reverse:** Two lines of three characters each **Note:** Ta Ch'ing Bank type.

| Date | Mintage | VG | F | VF | XF | Unc |
|---|---|---|---|---|---|---|
| ND(ca.1908) | — | 35.00 | 55.00 | 75.00 | 130 | — |

**2 CH'IEN (MACE)** **K# 972** **Weight:** 7.3000 g. **Composition:** Silver **Obverse:** Two lines of two characters each **Reverse:** Two lines of two characters each **Note:** Merchant type.

| Date | Mintage | VG | F | VF | XF | Unc |
|---|---|---|---|---|---|---|
| ND(ca.1908) | — | 35.00 | 55.00 | 75.00 | 130 | — |

**2 CH'IEN (MACE)** **K# 982/3** **Weight:** 7.3000 g. **Composition:** Silver **Obverse:** Two lines of three characters each **Reverse:** Two lines of two characters each **Note:** Merchant type.

| Date | Mintage | VG | F | VF | XF | Unc |
|---|---|---|---|---|---|---|
| ND(ca.1908) | — | 35.00 | 55.00 | 75.00 | 110 | — |

**3 CH'IEN (MACE)** **K# 949** **Weight:** 10.7000 g. **Composition:** Silver **Obverse:** Two lines of three characters each **Reverse:** Two lines of three characters each **Note:** Provincial type.

| Date | Mintage | VG | F | VF | XF | Unc |
|---|---|---|---|---|---|---|
| ND(ca.1906) | — | 37.50 | 60.00 | 85.00 | 120 | — |

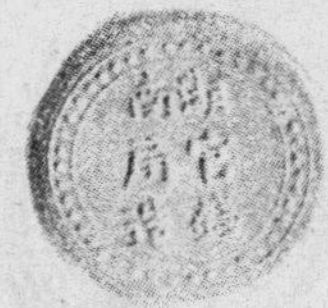

**3 CH'IEN (MACE)** **K# 959** **Weight:** 10.7000 g. **Composition:** Silver **Obverse:** Three lines of two characters each **Reverse:** Two lines of three characters each **Note:** Provincial type.

| Date | Mintage | VG | F | VF | XF | Unc |
|---|---|---|---|---|---|---|
| ND(ca.1906) | — | 37.50 | 60.00 | 85.00 | 120 | — |

**3 CH'IEN (MACE)** **K# 969** **Weight:** 10.7000 g. **Composition:** Silver **Obverse:** Three lines of two characters each **Reverse:** Two lines of three characters each **Note:** Ta Ch'ing Bank type.

| Date | Mintage | VG | F | VF | XF | Unc |
|---|---|---|---|---|---|---|
| ND(ca.1908) | — | 37.50 | 60.00 | 85.00 | 140 | — |

**3 CH'IEN (MACE)** **K# 981** **Weight:** 10.7000 g. **Composition:** Silver **Obverse:** Two lines of three characters each **Reverse:** Two lines of three characters each **Note:** Merchant type.

| Date | Mintage | VG | F | VF | XF | Unc |
|---|---|---|---|---|---|---|
| ND(ca.1908) | — | 37.50 | 60.00 | 85.00 | 140 | — |

**3 CH'IEN (MACE)** **K# 981a** **Weight:** 10.7000 g. **Composition:** Silver **Note:** Merchant type; "official" character for three.

| Date | Mintage | VG | F | VF | XF | Unc |
|---|---|---|---|---|---|---|
| ND(ca.1908) | — | 37.50 | 60.00 | 85.00 | 120 | — |

**4 CH'IEN (MACE)** **K# 948** **Weight:** 14.3000 g. **Composition:** Silver **Obverse:** Two lines of three characters each **Reverse:** Two lines of three characters each **Note:** Provincial type.

| Date | Mintage | VG | F | VF | XF | Unc |
|---|---|---|---|---|---|---|
| ND(ca.1906) | — | 40.00 | 65.00 | 90.00 | 125 | — |

**4 CH'IEN (MACE)** **K# 958** **Weight:** 14.3000 g. **Composition:** Silver **Obverse:** Three lines of two characters each **Reverse:** Two lines of three characters each **Note:** Provincial type.

| Date | Mintage | VG | F | VF | XF | Unc |
|---|---|---|---|---|---|---|
| ND(ca.1906) | — | 40.00 | 65.00 | 90.00 | 125 | — |

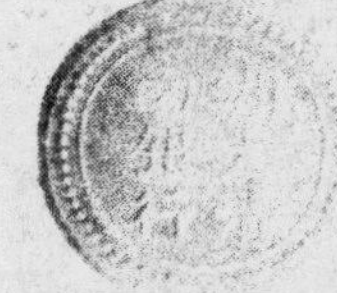

**4 CH'IEN (MACE)** **K# 968** **Weight:** 14.3000 g. **Composition:** Silver **Obverse:** Three lines of two characters each **Reverse:** Two lines of three characters each **Note:** Ta Ch'ing Bank type.

| Date | Mintage | VG | F | VF | XF | Unc |
|---|---|---|---|---|---|---|
| ND(ca.1908) | — | 40.00 | 65.00 | 90.00 | 135 | — |

**4 CH'IEN (MACE)** **K# 980** **Weight:** 14.3000 g. **Composition:** Silver **Obverse:** Two lines of three characters each **Reverse:** Two lines of three characters each **Note:** Merchant type.

| Date | Mintage | VG | F | VF | XF | Unc |
|---|---|---|---|---|---|---|
| ND(ca.1908) | — | 40.00 | 65.00 | 90.00 | 135 | — |

**5 CH'IEN (MACE)** **K# 947** **Weight:** 18.3000 g. **Composition:** Silver **Obverse:** Two lines of three characters each **Reverse:** Two lines of three characters each **Note:** Provincial type.

| Date | Mintage | VG | F | VF | XF | Unc |
|---|---|---|---|---|---|---|
| ND(ca.1906) | — | 42.50 | 70.00 | 100 | 140 | — |

**5 CH'IEN (MACE)** **K# 957** **Weight:** 18.3000 g. **Composition:** Silver **Obverse:** Three lines of two characters each **Reverse:** Two lines of three characters each **Note:** Provincial type.

| Date | Mintage | VG | F | VF | XF | Unc |
|---|---|---|---|---|---|---|
| ND(ca.1906_) | — | 42.50 | 70.00 | 100 | 140 | — |

**5 CH'IEN (MACE)** **K# 967** **Weight:** 18.3000 g. **Composition:** Silver **Obverse:** Three lines of two characters each **Reverse:** Two lines of three characters each **Note:** Ta Ch'ing Bank type.

| Date | Mintage | VG | F | VF | XF | Unc |
|---|---|---|---|---|---|---|
| ND(ca.1908) | — | 42.50 | 70.00 | 100 | 150 | — |

**5 CH'IEN (MACE)** **K# 979** **Weight:** 18.3000 g. **Composition:** Silver **Obverse:** Two lines of three characters each **Reverse:** Two lines of three characters each **Note:** Merchant type.

| Date | Mintage | VG | F | VF | XF | Unc |
|---|---|---|---|---|---|---|
| ND(ca.1908) | — | 42.50 | 70.00 | 100 | 150 | — |

**6 CH'IEN (MACE)** **K# 946** **Weight:** 21.4000 g. **Composition:** Silver **Obverse:** Two lines of three characters each **Reverse:** Two lines of three characters each **Note:** Provincial type.

| Date | Mintage | VG | F | VF | XF | Unc |
|---|---|---|---|---|---|---|
| ND(ca.1906) | — | 45.00 | 75.00 | 110 | 150 | — |

**6 CH'IEN (MACE)** **K# 956** **Weight:** 21.4000 g. **Composition:** Silver **Obverse:** Three lines of two characters each **Reverse:** Two lines of three characters each **Note:** Provincial type.

| Date | Mintage | VG | F | VF | XF | Unc |
|---|---|---|---|---|---|---|
| ND(ca.1906) | — | 45.00 | 75.00 | 110 | 150 | — |

**6 CH'IEN (MACE)** **K# 966** **Weight:** 21.4000 g. **Composition:** Silver **Obverse:** Three lines of two characters each **Reverse:** Two lines of three characters each **Note:** Ta Ch'ing Bank type.

| Date | Mintage | VG | F | VF | XF | Unc |
|---|---|---|---|---|---|---|
| ND(ca.1908) | — | 45.00 | 75.00 | 110 | 185 | — |

**6 CH'IEN (MACE)** **K# 978** **Weight:** 21.4000 g. **Composition:** Silver **Obverse:** Two lines of three characters each **Reverse:** Two lines of three characters each **Note:** Merchant type.

| Date | Mintage | VG | F | VF | XF | Unc |
|---|---|---|---|---|---|---|
| ND(ca.1908) | — | 45.00 | 75.00 | 110 | 185 | — |

**7 CH'IEN (MACE)** **K# 945** **Weight:** 25.9000 g. **Composition:** Silver **Obverse:** Two lines of three characters each **Reverse:** Two lines of three characters each **Note:** Provincial type.

| Date | Mintage | VG | F | VF | XF | Unc |
|---|---|---|---|---|---|---|
| ND(ca.1906) | — | 45.00 | 75.00 | 110 | 150 | — |

**7 CH'IEN (MACE)** **K# 955** **Weight:** 25.9000 g. **Composition:** Silver **Obverse:** Three lines of two characters each **Reverse:** Two lines of three characters each **Note:** Provincial type.

| Date | Mintage | VG | F | VF | XF | Unc |
|---|---|---|---|---|---|---|
| ND(ca.1906) | — | 45.00 | 75.00 | 110 | 150 | — |

**7 CH'IEN (MACE)** **K# 965** **Weight:** 25.9000 g. **Composition:** Silver **Obverse:** Three lines of two characters each **Reverse:** Two lines of three characters each **Note:** Ta Ch'ing Bank type.

| Date | Mintage | VG | F | VF | XF | Unc |
|---|---|---|---|---|---|---|
| ND(ca.1908) | — | 45.00 | 75.00 | 110 | 185 | — |

**7 CH'IEN (MACE)** **K# 977** **Weight:** 25.9000 g. **Composition:** Silver **Obverse:** Two lines of three characters each **Reverse:** Two lines of three characters each **Note:** Merchant type.

| Date | Mintage | VG | F | VF | XF | Unc |
|---|---|---|---|---|---|---|
| ND(ca.1908) | — | 45.00 | 75.00 | 110 | 185 | — |

**8 CH'IEN (MACE)** **K# 944** **Weight:** 29.2000 g. **Composition:** Silver **Obverse:** Two lines of three characters each **Reverse:** Two lines of three characters each **Note:** Provincial type.

| Date | Mintage | VG | F | VF | XF | Unc |
|---|---|---|---|---|---|---|
| ND(ca.1906) | — | 50.00 | 75.00 | 125 | 175 | — |

**8 CH'IEN (MACE)** **K# 954** **Weight:** 29.2000 g. **Composition:** Silver **Obverse:** Three lines of two characters each **Reverse:** Two lines of three characters each **Note:** Provincial type.

| Date | Mintage | VG | F | VF | XF | Unc |
|---|---|---|---|---|---|---|
| ND(ca.1906) | — | 50.00 | 75.00 | 125 | 175 | — |

**8 CH'IEN (MACE)** **K# 964** **Weight:** 29.2000 g. **Composition:** Silver **Obverse:** Three lines of two characters each **Reverse:** Two lines of three characters each **Note:** Ta Ch'ing Bank type.

| Date | Mintage | VG | F | VF | XF | Unc |
|---|---|---|---|---|---|---|
| ND(ca.1908) | — | 50.00 | 75.00 | 125 | 175 | — |

**8 CH'IEN (MACE)** **K# 976** **Weight:** 29.2000 g. **Composition:** Silver **Obverse:** Two lines of three characters each **Reverse:** Two lines of three characters each **Note:** Merchant type.

| Date | Mintage | VG | F | VF | XF | Unc |
|---|---|---|---|---|---|---|
| ND(ca.1908) | — | 50.00 | 75.00 | 125 | 175 | — |

**9 CH'IEN (MACE)** **K# 943** **Weight:** 29.2000 g. **Composition:** Silver **Obverse:** Two lines of three characters each **Reverse:** Two lines of three characters each **Note:** Provincial type.

| Date | Mintage | VG | F | VF | XF | Unc |
|---|---|---|---|---|---|---|
| ND(ca.1906) | — | 50.00 | 75.00 | 125 | 175 | — |

**9 CH'IEN (MACE)** **K# 953** **Weight:** 29.2000 g. **Composition:** Silver **Obverse:** Three lines of two characters each **Reverse:** Two lines of three characters each **Note:** Provincial type.

| Date | Mintage | VG | F | VF | XF | Unc |
|---|---|---|---|---|---|---|
| ND(ca.1906) | — | 50.00 | 75.00 | 125 | 175 | — |

**9 CH'IEN (MACE)** **K# 963** **Weight:** 29.2000 g. **Composition:** Silver **Obverse:** Three lines of two characters each **Reverse:** Two lines of three characters each **Note:** Ta Ch'ing Bank type.

| Date | Mintage | VG | F | VF | XF | Unc |
|---|---|---|---|---|---|---|
| ND(ca.1908) | — | 50.00 | 75.00 | 125 | 200 | — |

**9 CH'IEN (MACE)** **K# 975** **Weight:** 29.2000 g. **Composition:** Silver **Obverse:** Two lines of three characters each **Reverse:** Two lines of three characters each **Note:** Merchant type.

| Date | Mintage | VG | F | VF | XF | Unc |
|---|---|---|---|---|---|---|
| ND(ca.1908) | — | 50.00 | 75.00 | 125 | 200 | — |

**LIANG (Tael)** **K# 942** **Weight:** 35.9000 g. **Composition:** Silver **Obverse:** Two lines of three characters each **Reverse:** Two lines of three characters each **Note:** Provincial type.

| Date | Mintage | VG | F | VF | XF | Unc |
|---|---|---|---|---|---|---|
| ND(ca.1906) | — | 60.00 | 100 | 150 | 225 | — |

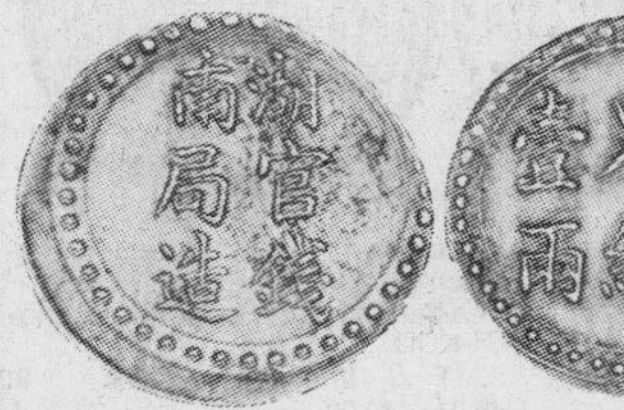

**LIANG (Tael)** **K# 952** **Weight:** 35.9000 g. **Composition:** Silver **Obverse:** Three lines of two characters each **Reverse:** Two lines of three characters each **Note:** Provincial type.

| Date | Mintage | VG | F | VF | XF | Unc |
|---|---|---|---|---|---|---|
| ND(ca.1906) | — | 60.00 | 100 | 140 | 200 | — |

**LIANG (Tael)** **K# 962** **Weight:** 35.9000 g. **Composition:** Silver **Obverse:** Three lines of two characters each **Reverse:** Two lines of three characters each **Note:** Ta Ch'ing Bank type.

| Date | Mintage | VG | F | VF | XF | Unc |
|---|---|---|---|---|---|---|
| ND(ca.1908) | — | 45.00 | 75.00 | 110 | 165 | — |

**LIANG (Tael)** **K# 942r** **Weight:** 35.9000 g. **Composition:** Silver **Obverse:** Three lines of four characters each

| Date | Mintage | VG | F | VF | XF | Unc |
|---|---|---|---|---|---|---|
| ND(ca.1908) Rare | — | — | — | — | — | — |

**LIANG (Tael)** K# 974 **Weight:** 35.9000 g. **Composition:** Silver **Obverse:** Two lines of three characters each **Reverse:** Two lines of three characters each **Note:** Merchant type.

| Date | Mintage | VG | F | VF | XF | Unc |
|---|---|---|---|---|---|---|
| ND(ca.1908) | — | 90.00 | 150 | 225 | 325 | — |

## TRANSITIONAL COINAGE

**10 CASH** Y# 401.1 **Composition:** Copper **Ruler:** Hung-hsien **Obv. Legend:** THE FIRST YEAR OF HUNG SHUAN **Rev. Legend:** Hung-hsien Yüan-nien

| Date | Mintage | VG | F | VF | XF | Unc |
|---|---|---|---|---|---|---|
| 1(1915)(1915) | — | 35.00 | 60.00 | 100 | 150 | — |

**10 CASH** Y# 401.2 **Composition:** Copper **Ruler:** Hung-hsien **Obverse:** Wider space in legend

| Date | Mintage | VG | F | VF | XF | Unc |
|---|---|---|---|---|---|---|
| 1(1915)(1915) | — | 10.00 | 20.00 | 30.00 | 45.00 | — |

# REPUBLIC

## MILLED COINAGE

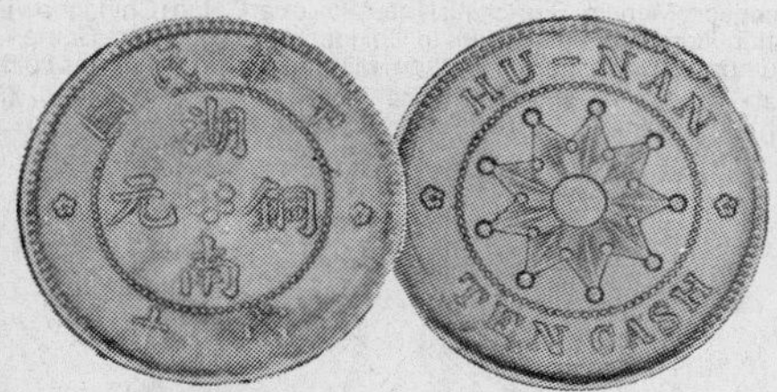

**10 CASH** Y# 399 **Composition:** Copper **Obverse:** Large rosette **Reverse:** Center of star convex

| Date | Mintage | F | VF | XF | Unc | BU |
|---|---|---|---|---|---|---|
| ND(1912) | — | 2.00 | 4.00 | 7.50 | 24.00 | — |

**10 CASH** Y# 399a **Composition:** Brass

| Date | Mintage | F | VF | XF | Unc | BU |
|---|---|---|---|---|---|---|
| ND(1912) | — | 5.00 | 10.00 | 17.50 | 45.00 | — |

**10 CASH** Y# 399.1 **Composition:** Copper **Obverse:** Small rosette **Reverse:** Center of star convex

| Date | Mintage | F | VF | XF | Unc | BU |
|---|---|---|---|---|---|---|
| ND(1912) | — | 2.00 | 4.00 | 7.00 | 24.00 | — |

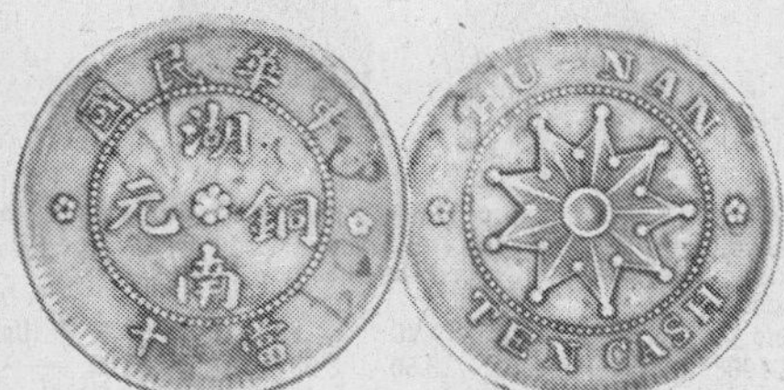

**10 CASH** Y# 399.2 **Composition:** Copper **Reverse:** Center of star concave; star outlined

| Date | Mintage | F | VF | XF | Unc | BU |
|---|---|---|---|---|---|---|
| ND(1912) | — | 2.25 | 4.50 | 8.50 | 26.00 | — |

**10 CASH** Y# 399.3 **Composition:** Copper **Reverse:** Star not outlined

| Date | Mintage | F | VF | XF | Unc | BU |
|---|---|---|---|---|---|---|
| ND(1912) | — | 2.25 | 4.50 | 8.50 | 26.00 | — |

**10 CASH** Y# 399.4 **Composition:** Copper **Obverse:** Large rosette **Reverse:** Center of star concave

| Date | Mintage | F | VF | XF | Unc | BU |
|---|---|---|---|---|---|---|
| ND(1912) | — | 2.25 | 4.50 | 8.50 | 26.00 | — |

**10 CASH** Y# 399.5 **Composition:** Copper **Note:** Mule. General Issue, Y#306.

| Date | Mintage | F | VF | XF | Unc | BU |
|---|---|---|---|---|---|---|
| ND(1912) | — | — | — | — | — | — |

**10 CASH** Y# 402 **Composition:** Copper **Subject:** Provincial Constitution **Obverse:** Rosette above flags

| Date | Mintage | VG | F | VF | XF | Unc |
|---|---|---|---|---|---|---|
| 11(1922) | — | 15.00 | 25.00 | 38.00 | 60.00 | — |

**10 CASH** Y# 402.1 **Composition:** Copper **Obverse:** Star above flags

| Date | Mintage | VG | F | VF | XF | Unc |
|---|---|---|---|---|---|---|
| 11(1922) | — | 18.50 | 26.00 | 40.00 | 65.00 | — |

**20 CASH** Y# 400b **Composition:** Brass

| Date | Mintage | VG | F | VF | XF | Unc |
|---|---|---|---|---|---|---|
| ND(1912) | — | 1.65 | 4.00 | 10.00 | 20.00 | — |

**20 CASH** Y# 400.2 **Composition:** Copper

| Date | Mintage | VG | F | VF | XF | Unc |
|---|---|---|---|---|---|---|
| ND(1919) | — | 0.60 | 1.00 | 3.00 | 6.00 | — |

**20 CASH** Y# 400.3 **Composition:** Copper **Obverse:** 25 small curls in ribbon at base of plant

| Date | Mintage | VG | F | VF | XF | Unc |
|---|---|---|---|---|---|---|
| ND(1919) | — | 0.60 | 1.00 | 3.00 | 6.00 | — |

**20 CASH** Y# 400.4 **Composition:** Copper **Obverse:** Smaller rice grains **Reverse:** Floral ornament at left smaller

| Date | Mintage | VG | F | VF | XF | Unc |
|---|---|---|---|---|---|---|
| ND(1919) | — | 0.60 | 1.00 | 3.00 | 6.00 | — |

**20 CASH** Y# 400.5 **Composition:** Copper **Obverse:** Thin ribbon at base of plant

| Date | Mintage | VG | F | VF | XF | Unc |
|---|---|---|---|---|---|---|
| ND(1919) | — | 0.60 | 1.00 | 3.00 | 6.00 | — |

**20 CASH** Y# 400.6 **Composition:** Copper **Reverse:** Small pentagonal rosette above crossed flags

| Date | Mintage | VG | F | VF | XF | Unc |
|---|---|---|---|---|---|---|
| ND(1919) | — | 0.60 | 1.00 | 3.00 | 6.00 | — |

**20 CASH** Y# 400.7 **Composition:** Copper **Reverse:** Larger star-shaped rosette above crossed flags

| Date | Mintage | VG | F | VF | XF | Unc |
|---|---|---|---|---|---|---|
| ND(1919) | — | 1.00 | 2.50 | 4.00 | 7.00 | — |

**20 CASH** Y# 400.7b **Composition:** Brass

| Date | Mintage | VG | F | VF | XF | Unc |
|---|---|---|---|---|---|---|
| ND(1919) | — | 1.65 | 4.00 | 8.00 | 15.00 | — |

**20 CASH** Y# 400.8 **Composition:** Copper **Obverse:** Larger star-shaped rosette above flags

| Date | Mintage | VG | F | VF | XF | Unc |
|---|---|---|---|---|---|---|
| ND(1919) | — | 1.00 | 2.50 | 4.00 | 7.00 | — |

**20 CASH** Y# 400.9 **Composition:** Copper **Reverse:** Sharp pointed star above crossed flags

| Date | Mintage | VG | F | VF | XF | Unc |
|---|---|---|---|---|---|---|
| ND(1919) | — | 1.00 | 2.50 | 4.00 | 7.00 | — |

**20 CASH** Y# 400.10 **Composition:** Copper **Reverse:** Sharp 5-pointed star above rosette, above crossed flags

| Date | Mintage | VG | F | VF | XF | Unc |
|---|---|---|---|---|---|---|
| ND(1919) | — | 20.00 | 25.00 | 30.00 | 35.00 | — |

**20 CASH** Y# 400.11 **Composition:** Copper **Reverse:** Similar to Y#400.2; no dot in rosette above flags

| Date | Mintage | VG | F | VF | XF | Unc |
|---|---|---|---|---|---|---|
| ND(1919) | — | — | — | — | — | — |

**20 CASH** Y# 400a **Composition:** Copper **Obverse:** Denomination: 20 CASH

| Date | Mintage | VG | F | VF | XF | Unc |
|---|---|---|---|---|---|---|
| ND(1919) | — | 50.00 | 75.00 | 100 | 150 | — |

**20 CASH** Y# 400 **Composition:** Copper **Reverse:** Rosette above flags, five characters at bottom in legend

| Date | Mintage | VG | F | VF | XF | Unc |
|---|---|---|---|---|---|---|
| ND(1919) | — | 1.25 | 3.00 | 7.50 | 15.00 | — |

**20 CASH** Y# 403.1 **Composition:** Copper **Subject:** Provincial Constitution

| Date | Mintage | VG | F | VF | XF | Unc |
|---|---|---|---|---|---|---|
| 11(1922) | — | 22.50 | 35.00 | 65.00 | 90.00 | — |

**20 CASH** Y# 403.2 **Composition:** Copper

| Date | Mintage | VG | F | VF | XF | Unc |
|---|---|---|---|---|---|---|
| 11(1922) | — | 35.00 | 75.00 | 100 | 150 | — |

**10 CENTS** K# 762 **Composition:** Silver **Ruler:** Hung-hsien **Obverse:** Inscription: Chung-hua Yin-pi **Obv. Legend:** Hung-hsien Yüan-nien **Reverse:** "Flying" dragon

| Date | Mintage | F | VF | XF | Unc | BU |
|---|---|---|---|---|---|---|
| ND(1915) | — | 250 | 550 | 900 | 1,400 | — |

**Note:** Though Kann calls this coin as Essay, contemporary reports indicate that the coin actually circulated briefly in 1915. Not to be confused with Y#28, the obverse of which has a different legend in Chinese. (See General Issues - Empire.)

**DOLLAR** Y# 404 **Weight:** 27.4000 g. **Composition:** Silver **Subject:** Provincial Constitution

| Date | Mintage | F | VF | XF | Unc | BU |
|---|---|---|---|---|---|---|
| 11(1922) | — | 125 | 250 | 400 | 800 | — |

## PATTERNS

Including off metal strikes

| KM# | Date | Mintage | Identification | Mkt Val |
|---|---|---|---|---|
| Pn4 | (1902) | — | 10 Cash. Copper. Three characters at bottom, Y#112.10. | 850 |
| Pn5 | (1902) | — | 10 Cash. Copper. Three characters at bottom, Y#112.12. | 350 |

**Note:** Two Heaton (Birmingham) proof patterns for a proposed brass coinage which wasn't adopted. Dies were recut with only 2 characters for issue.

| KM# | Date | Mintage | Identification | Mkt Val |
|---|---|---|---|---|
| Pn7 | (1915) | — | 10 Cents. Copper. Plain edge. K#762y | 450 |
| Pn6 | (1915) | — | 10 Cents. Nickel. Plain edge. K#762x | — |
| Pn9 | 11(1922) | — | Dollar. Silver. General Chao Heng-ti | — |
| Pn10 | 11(1922) | — | Dollar. Copper. General Chao Heng-ti | — |

# HUPEH PROVINCE

Hubei

A province located in east-central China. Hilly, with some lakes and swamps, it has rich coal and iron deposits plus a varied agricultural program. The Wuchang Mint had been active from early in the Manchu dynasty and its modern equipment began operations in 1895. It probably closed in 1929.

## EMPIRE

### PROVINCIAL CAST COINAGE

**CASH** C# 13-11 **Composition:** Cast Brass **Ruler:** Kuang-hsü **Obverse:** Inscription: Kuang-hsü T'ung-pao **Reverse:** Inscription: Manchu Boo-ching **Note:** Struck at Ching (Chingchow).

| Date | Mintage | Good | VG | F | VF | XF |
|---|---|---|---|---|---|---|
| ND(1875-1908) | — | 12.50 | 20.00 | 30.00 | 45.00 | — |

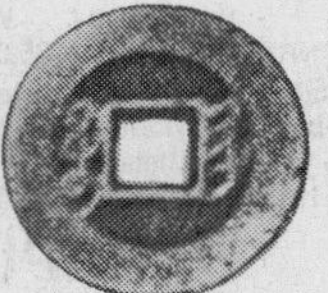

**CASH** C# 13-11.1 **Composition:** Cast Brass **Ruler:** Kuang-hsü **Obverse:** Inscription: Kuang-hsü T'ung-pao **Reverse:** Inscription: Manchu Boo-ching **Note:** Struck at Ching (Chingchow). Attribution of this mint mark to Chingchow is uncertain. Some authorities claim the Taku (Dagu) Mint in Tientsin struck this coin.

| Date | Mintage | Good | VG | F | VF | XF |
|---|---|---|---|---|---|---|
| ND(1875-1908) | — | 12.00 | 15.00 | 22.50 | 30.00 | — |

### MILLED COINAGE

**CASH** Y# 121 **Composition:** Brass **Ruler:** Kuang-hsü **Obverse:** Inscription: Kuang-hsü Yüan-pao **Reverse:** Dragon **Note:** Struck at Ching (Chingchow).

| Date | Mintage | VG | F | VF | XF | Unc |
|---|---|---|---|---|---|---|
| ND(1906) | 66,474,000 | 8.00 | 12.00 | 18.00 | 25.00 | — |

**CASH** Y# 7j **Composition:** Brass **Ruler:** Kuang-hsü **Obverse:** Small mint mark on small disc in center **Obv. Legend:** Kuang-hsü **Reverse:** Dragon **Note:** Struck at Ching (Chingchow).

| Date | Mintage | VG | F | VF | XF | Unc |
|---|---|---|---|---|---|---|
| CD1908 | Inc. above | 3.50 | 8.00 | 15.00 | 25.00 | — |

**CASH** Y# 7j.1 **Composition:** Brass **Ruler:** Kuang-hsü **Obverse:** Large mint mark on small disc in center **Obv. Legend:** Kuang-hsü **Reverse:** Dragon **Note:** Struck at Ching (Chingchow).

| Date | Mintage | VG | F | VF | XF | Unc |
|---|---|---|---|---|---|---|
| CD1908 | Inc. above | 3.50 | 8.00 | 15.00 | 25.00 | — |

**2 CASH** Y# 8j **Composition:** Copper **Ruler:** Kuang-hsü **Obverse:** Inscription: Tai-ch'ing T'ung-pi **Reverse:** Dragon **Note:** Struck at Ching (Chingchow).

| Date | Mintage | VG | F | VF | XF | Unc |
|---|---|---|---|---|---|---|
| CD(1906) | 844,000 | 50.00 | 80.00 | 125 | 200 | — |

**5 CASH** **Y# 9j** **Composition:** Copper **Ruler:** Kuang-hsü **Obverse:** Inscription: Tai-ch'ing T'ung-pi **Rev. Legend:** Kuang-hsü Nien-tsao, TAI-CHING-TI-KUO ... **Size:** 24 mm. **Note:** Struck at Ching (Chingchow).

| Date | Mintage | VG | F | VF | XF | Unc |
|---|---|---|---|---|---|---|
| CD(1906) | 9,846,000 | 5.00 | 9.00 | 15.00 | 30.00 | — |

**5 CASH** **Y# 9j.1** **Composition:** Copper **Ruler:** Kuang-hsü **Obverse:** Inscription: Tai-ch'ing T'ung-pi **Reverse:** Dragon redesigned **Rev. Legend:** Kuang-hsü Nien-tsao, TAI-CHING-TI-KUO ... **Size:** 23 mm. **Note:** Struck at Ching (Chingchow).

| Date | Mintage | VG | F | VF | XF | Unc |
|---|---|---|---|---|---|---|
| CD(1906) | Inc. above | 6.00 | 11.00 | 17.50 | 35.00 | — |

**10 CASH** **Y# 120** **Composition:** Copper **Ruler:** Kuang-hsü **Obverse:** 8-petalled rosette, inscription: Kuang-hsü Yüan-pao **Reverse:** Circled dragon **Note:** Struck at Ching (Chingchow).

| Date | Mintage | F | VF | XF | Unc | BU |
|---|---|---|---|---|---|---|
| ND(1902-1905) | 4,475,000 | 5.00 | 8.00 | 15.00 | 35.00 | — |

**10 CASH** **Y# 120a.9** **Composition:** Copper **Ruler:** Kuang-hsü **Obverse:** Square in circle, inscription: Kuang-hsü Yüan-pao **Reverse:** Dragon, hyphen in HU-PEH **Note:** Struck at Ching (Chingchow).

| Date | Mintage | F | VF | XF | Unc | BU |
|---|---|---|---|---|---|---|
| ND(1902-1905) | Inc. above | 4.00 | 7.50 | 15.00 | 30.00 | — |

**10 CASH** **Y# 120a** **Composition:** Copper **Ruler:** Kuang-hsü **Obverse:** Inscription: Kuang-hsü Yüan-pao **Reverse:** Uncircled large dragon **Note:** Struck at Ching (Chingchow).

| Date | Mintage | F | VF | XF | Unc | BU |
|---|---|---|---|---|---|---|
| ND(1902-1905) | Inc. above | 3.50 | 7.00 | 13.50 | 30.00 | — |

**10 CASH** **Y# 120a.1** **Composition:** Copper **Ruler:** Kuang-hsü **Obverse:** Inscription: Kuang-hsü Yüan-pao **Reverse:** Slightly larger English letters, wide face on dragon **Note:** Struck at Ching (Chingchow).

| Date | Mintage | F | VF | XF | Unc | BU |
|---|---|---|---|---|---|---|
| ND(1902-1905) | Inc. above | 1.00 | 2.00 | 3.00 | 20.00 | — |

**10 CASH** **Y# 120a.2** **Composition:** Copper **Ruler:** Kuang-hsü **Obverse:** Inscription: Kuang-hsü Yüan-pao **Reverse:** Large pearl with many spines, narrower face on dragon **Note:** Struck at Ching (Chingchow).

| Date | Mintage | F | VF | XF | Unc | BU |
|---|---|---|---|---|---|---|
| ND(1902-1905) | Inc. above | 0.75 | 1.50 | 2.75 | 20.00 | — |

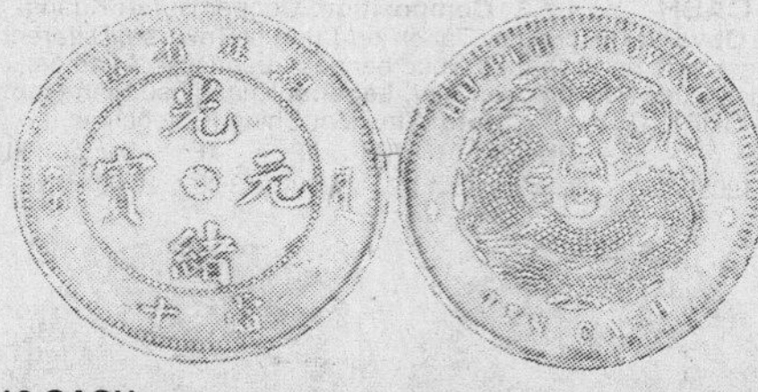

**10 CASH** **Y# 120a.3** **Composition:** Copper **Ruler:** Kuang-hsü **Obverse:** Inscription: Kuang-hsü Yüan-pao **Reverse:** Smaller pearl with fewer spines on dragon **Note:** Struck at Ching (Chingchow). Commonly found with medal alignment but also exists with coin alignment.

| Date | Mintage | F | VF | XF | Unc | BU |
|---|---|---|---|---|---|---|
| ND(1902-1905) | Inc. above | 0.75 | 1.50 | 2.75 | 20.00 | — |

**10 CASH** **Y# 120a.3a** **Composition:** Brass **Ruler:** Kuang-hsü **Obverse:** Inscription: Kuang-hsü Yüan-pao **Reverse:** Dragon **Note:** Struck at Ching (Chingchow).

| Date | Mintage | F | VF | XF | Unc | BU |
|---|---|---|---|---|---|---|
| ND(1902-1905) | Inc. above | — | — | — | — | — |

**10 CASH** **Y# 120a.4** **Composition:** Copper **Ruler:** Kuang-hsü **Obverse:** 5-petalled rosette, small Manchu word at right, inscription: Kuang-hsü Yüan-pao **Reverse:** 4 dots in shape of cross at either side of dragon, PROVINCE spelled PHOVINCE, with "V" an inverted "A" **Note:** Struck at Ching (Chingchow).

| Date | Mintage | F | VF | XF | Unc | BU |
|---|---|---|---|---|---|---|
| ND(1902-1905) | Inc. above | 1.00 | 2.00 | 3.00 | 20.00 | — |

**10 CASH** **Y# 120a.5** **Composition:** Copper **Ruler:** Kuang-hsü **Obverse:** Large Manchu at right, inscription: Kuang-hsü Yüan-pao **Reverse:** "R" in PROVINCE inverted, "V" an inverted "A", dragon **Note:** Struck at Ching (Chingchow).

| Date | Mintage | F | VF | XF | Unc | BU |
|---|---|---|---|---|---|---|
| ND(1902-1905) | Inc. above | 1.00 | 2.00 | 3.00 | 20.00 | — |

**10 CASH** **Y# 120a.6** **Composition:** Copper **Ruler:** Kuang-hsü **Obverse:** Inscription: Kuang-hsü Yüan-pao **Reverse:** 6-pointed star at either side of dragon, hyphen in HU-PEH **Note:** Struck at Ching (Chingchow).

| Date | Mintage | F | VF | XF | Unc | BU |
|---|---|---|---|---|---|---|
| ND(1902-1905) | Inc. above | 1.00 | 2.00 | 3.00 | 20.00 | — |

**10 CASH** **Y# 120a.7** **Composition:** Copper **Ruler:** Kuang-hsü **Obverse:** Inscription: Kuang-hsü Yüan-pao **Reverse:** 6-pointed star at either side of dragon, without hyphen in HU-PEH **Note:** Struck at Ching (Chingchow).

| Date | Mintage | F | VF | XF | Unc | BU |
|---|---|---|---|---|---|---|
| ND(1902-1905) | Inc. above | 1.50 | 3.00 | 6.00 | 22.00 | — |

**10 CASH** **Y# 120a.8** **Composition:** Copper **Ruler:** Kuang-hsü **Obverse:** 5-petalled rosette and small Manchu, inscription: Kuang-hsü Yüan-pao **Reverse:** Dragon, very small pearl **Note:** Struck at Ching (Chingchow).

| Date | Mintage | F | VF | XF | Unc | BU |
|---|---|---|---|---|---|---|
| ND(1902-1905) | Inc. above | 3.50 | 6.00 | 12.00 | 25.00 | — |

**10 CASH** **Y# 120a.10** **Composition:** Copper **Ruler:** Kuang-hsü **Obverse:** Square in circle, inscription: Kuang-hsü Yüan-pao **Reverse:** Dragon, without hyphen in HU-PEH **Note:** Struck at Ching (Chingchow).

| Date | Mintage | F | VF | XF | Unc | BU |
|---|---|---|---|---|---|---|
| ND(1902-1905) | Inc. above | 1.50 | 2.50 | 5.00 | 25.00 | — |

**10 CASH** **Y# 122** **Composition:** Copper **Ruler:** Kuang-hsü **Obverse:** Second character from right at top is larger, 6-petalled rosette, inscription: Kuang-hsü Yüan-pao **Reverse:** Front view dragon **Note:** Struck at Ching (Chingchow).

| Date | Mintage | F | VF | XF | Unc | BU |
|---|---|---|---|---|---|---|
| ND(1902-1905) | Inc. above | 0.60 | 1.50 | 3.00 | 20.00 | — |

**10 CASH** **Y# 122.1** **Composition:** Copper **Ruler:** Kuang-hsü **Obverse:** Second character from right "Pei" smaller, inscription: Kuang-hsü Yüan-pao **Reverse:** Dragon **Note:** Struck at Ching (Chingchow).

| Date | Mintage | F | VF | XF | Unc | BU |
|---|---|---|---|---|---|---|
| ND(1902-1905) | Inc. above | 0.50 | 1.50 | 3.00 | 20.00 | — |

**10 CASH** **Y# 122.3** **Composition:** Copper **Ruler:** Kuang-hsü **Obverse:** Inscription: Kuang-hsü Yüan-pao **Reverse:** Clouds above dragon's head, 2 clouds below pearl instead of 1 **Note:** Struck at Ching (Chingchow).

| Date | Mintage | F | VF | XF | Unc | BU |
|---|---|---|---|---|---|---|
| ND(1902-1905) | Inc. above | 2.00 | 5.00 | 10.00 | 35.00 | — |

**10 CASH** **Y# 122.4** **Composition:** Copper **Ruler:** Kuang-hsü **Obverse:** Inscription: Kuang-hsü Yüan-pao **Reverse:** Dragon, small circle around lower part of pearl, without dots on either side of mountain **Note:** Struck at Ching (Chingchow).

| Date | Mintage | F | VF | XF | Unc | BU |
|---|---|---|---|---|---|---|
| ND(1902-1905) | Inc. above | 2.00 | 5.00 | 10.00 | 35.00 | — |

**10 CASH** **Y# 122.5** **Composition:** Copper **Ruler:** Kuang-hsü **Obverse:** Inscription: Kuang-hsü Yüan-pao **Reverse:** Dragon, larger circle around larger pearl, larger English letters **Note:** Struck at Ching (Chingchow).

| Date | Mintage | F | VF | XF | Unc | BU |
|---|---|---|---|---|---|---|
| ND(1902-1905) | Inc. above | 2.00 | 5.00 | 10.00 | 25.00 | — |

**10 CASH** **Y# 122a** **Composition:** Copper **Ruler:** Kuang-hsü **Obverse:** Inscription: Kuang-hsü Yüan-pao **Reverse:** Circled front view of dragon **Note:** Struck at Ching (Chingchow).

| Date | Mintage | F | VF | XF | Unc | BU |
|---|---|---|---|---|---|---|
| ND(1902-1905) | — | 125 | 175 | 225 | — | — |

**10 CASH** **Y# 10j** **Composition:** Copper **Ruler:** Kuang-hsü **Obverse:** Inscription: Tai-ch'ing T'ung-pi **Reverse:** Dragon, 7 flames on pearl **Rev. Legend:** Kuang hsü Nien-tsao, TAI-CHING-TI-KUO ... **Note:** Struck at Ching (Chingchow).

| Date | Mintage | F | VF | XF | Unc | BU |
|---|---|---|---|---|---|---|
| CD(1906) | 1,865,558,000 | 0.75 | 1.00 | 2.00 | 20.00 | — |

**10 CASH** **Y# 10j.1** **Composition:** Copper **Ruler:** Kuang-hsü **Obverse:** Inscription: Tai-ch'ing T'ung-pi **Reverse:** Redesigned dragon with wide lips, cloud-shaped bar below pearl with 5 flames **Rev. Legend:** Kuang hsü Nien-tsao, TAI-CHING-TI-KUO ... **Note:** Struck at Ching (Chingchow). 28-29 millimeters.

| Date | Mintage | F | VF | XF | Unc | BU |
|---|---|---|---|---|---|---|
| CD(1906) | Inc. above | 2.00 | 5.00 | 10.00 | 25.00 | — |

**10 CASH** **Y# 10j.2** **Composition:** Copper **Ruler:** Kuang-hsü **Obverse:** Inscription: Tai-ch'ing T'ung-pi **Reverse:** Dragon **Rev. Legend:** Kuang hsü Nien-tsao, TAI-CHING-TI-KUO ... **Size:** 30 mm. **Note:** Struck at Ching (Chingchow).

| Date | Mintage | F | VF | XF | Unc | BU |
|---|---|---|---|---|---|---|
| CD(1906) | Inc. above | 2.00 | 5.00 | 10.00 | 25.00 | — |

**10 CASH** **Y# 10j.3** **Composition:** Copper **Ruler:** Kuang-hsü **Obverse:** Inscription: Tai-ch'ing T'ung-pi **Reverse:** Different dragon with hook-shaped cloud beneath, pearl with 4 flames, large incuse swirl on pearl **Rev. Legend:** Kuang hsü Nien-tsao, TAI-CHING-TI-KUO ... **Note:** Struck at Ching (Chingchow).

| Date | Mintage | F | VF | XF | Unc | BU |
|---|---|---|---|---|---|---|
| CD(1906) | Inc. above | 1.00 | 2.00 | 3.00 | 20.00 | — |

**10 CASH** **Y# 10j.4** **Composition:** Copper **Ruler:** Kuang-hsü **Obverse:** Inscription: Tai-ch'ing T'ung-pi **Reverse:** Dragon, small incuse swirl on pearl with 4 flames **Rev. Legend:** Kuang hsü Nien-tsao, TAI-CHING-TI-KUO ... **Note:** Struck at Ching (Chingchow).

| Date | Mintage | F | VF | XF | Unc | BU |
|---|---|---|---|---|---|---|
| CD(1906) | Inc. above | 0.50 | 1.00 | 2.00 | 20.00 | — |

**10 CASH** **Y# 10j.5** **Composition:** Copper **Ruler:** Kuang-hsü **Obverse:** Inscription: Tai-ch'ing T'ung-pi **Reverse:** Dragon, swirl on pearl in relief with 4 flames **Rev. Legend:** Kuang hsü Nien-tsao, TAI-CHING-TI-KUO ... **Note:** Struck at Ching (Chingchow).

| Date | Mintage | F | VF | XF | Unc | BU |
|---|---|---|---|---|---|---|
| CD(1906) | Inc. above | 0.75 | 1.00 | 2.00 | 20.00 | — |

**10 CASH** **Y# 20j** **Composition:** Copper **Ruler:** Hsüan-t'ung **Obverse:** Inscription: Tai-ch'ing T'ung-pi **Reverse:** Dragon, large incuse swirl on pearl **Rev. Legend:** Hsüan-t'ung Nien-tsao, TAI-CHING-TI-KUO ... **Note:** Struck at Ching (Chingchow).

| Date | Mintage | F | VF | XF | Unc | BU |
|---|---|---|---|---|---|---|
| CD(1909) | 371,577,000 | 1.50 | 3.00 | 6.00 | 25.00 | — |

**10 CASH** **Y# 20j.2** **Composition:** Copper **Ruler:** Hsüan-t'ung **Obverse:** CD1909 over CD1906, inscription: Tai-ch'ing T'ung-pi **Reverse:** Dragon **Rev. Legend:** Hsüan-t'ung Nien-tsao, TAI-CHING-TI-KUO ... **Note:** Struck at Ching (Chingchow).

| Date | Mintage | F | VF | XF | Unc | BU |
|---|---|---|---|---|---|---|
| CD(1909/1906) | — | — | — | — | — | — |

**10 CASH** **Y# 20j.1** **Composition:** Copper **Ruler:** Hsüan-t'ung **Obverse:** Inscription: Tai-ch'ing T'ung-pi **Reverse:** Dragon, small swirl in relief on pearl **Rev. Legend:** Hsüan-t'ung Nien-tsao, TAI-CHING-TI-KUO ... **Note:** Struck at Ching (Chingchow).

| Date | Mintage | F | VF | XF | Unc | BU |
|---|---|---|---|---|---|---|
| CD(1909) | Inc. above | 1.50 | 3.00 | 6.00 | 25.00 | — |

**10 CASH** **Y# 20j.3** **Composition:** Copper **Ruler:** Hsüan-t'ung **Obverse:** Characters "Hsuan T'ung" re-engraved over characeters "Kuang Hsu," inscription: Tai-ch'ing T'ung-pi **Reverse:** Dragon **Rev. Legend:** Hsüan-t'ung Nien-tsao, TAI-CHING-TI-KUO ... **Note:** Struck at Ching (Chingchow).

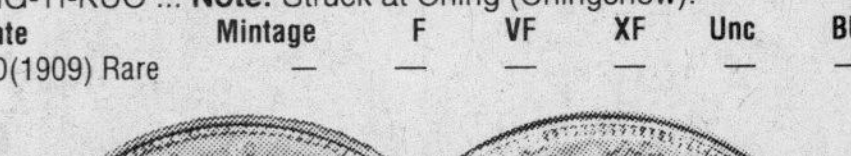

| Date | Mintage | F | VF | XF | Unc | BU |
|---|---|---|---|---|---|---|
| CD(1909) Rare | — | — | — | — | — | — |

**20 CASH** **Y# 11j** **Composition:** Copper **Ruler:** Kuang-hsü **Obverse:** Inscription: Tai-ch'ing T'ung-pi **Reverse:** Dragon **Rev. Legend:** Kuang-hsü Nien-tsao, TAI-CHING-TI-KUO ... **Note:** Struck at Ching (Chingchow).

| Date | Mintage | VG | F | VF | XF | Unc |
|---|---|---|---|---|---|---|
| CD(1906) | 3,710,000 | 100 | 250 | 375 | 625 | — |

**DOLLAR** Y# 127.1 **Weight:** 26.7000 g. **Composition:** 0.9000 Silver .7727 oz. ASW **Ruler:** Kuang-hsü **Obverse:** Inscription: Kuang-hsü Yüan-pao **Reverse:** Without "Pen Sheng" at either side of dragon **Note:** Struck at Ching (Chingchow).

| Date | Mintage | F | VF | XF | Unc | BU |
|---|---|---|---|---|---|---|
| ND(1895-1907) | 19,935,000 | 20.00 | 30.00 | 50.00 | 250 | — |

**DOLLAR** Y# 131 **Weight:** 27.0000 g. **Composition:** 0.9000 Silver .7814 oz. ASW **Ruler:** Hsüan-t'ung **Obverse:** Inscription: Hsüan-t'ung Yüan-pao **Reverse:** Dragon **Note:** Struck at Ching (Chingchow).

| Date | Mintage | F | VF | XF | Unc | BU |
|---|---|---|---|---|---|---|
| ND(1909-1911) | 2,703,000 | 20.00 | 30.00 | 50.00 | 200 | — |

**5 CENTS** Y# 123 **Weight:** 1.3500 g. **Composition:** 0.8200 Silver .0356 oz. ASW **Ruler:** Kuang-hsü **Obverse:** Inscription: Kuang-hsü Yüan-pao **Reverse:** Dragon **Rev. Legend:** Kuang-hsü Nien-tsao, TAI-CHING-TI-KUO ... **Note:** Struck at Ching (Chingchow).

| Date | Mintage | F | VF | XF | Unc | BU |
|---|---|---|---|---|---|---|
| ND(1895-1905) | 4,278,000 | 50.00 | 100 | 150 | 250 | — |

**10 CENTS** Y# 124.1 **Weight:** 2.7000 g. **Composition:** 0.8200 Silver .0712 oz. ASW **Ruler:** Kuang-hsü **Obverse:** Inscription: Kuang-hsü Yüan-pao **Reverse:** Without characters beside dragon, 2 varieties of edge milling **Rev. Legend:** Kuang-hsü Nien-tsao, TAI-CHING-TI-KUO ... **Note:** Struck at Ching (Chingchow).

| Date | Mintage | F | VF | XF | Unc | BU |
|---|---|---|---|---|---|---|
| ND(1895-1907) | — | 2.00 | 4.00 | 7.50 | 20.00 | — |

**10 CENTS** Y# 129 **Composition:** Silver **Ruler:** Hsüan-t'ung **Obverse:** Inscription: Hsüan-t'ung Yüan-pao **Reverse:** Dragon **Rev. Legend:** Kuang-hsü Nien-tsao, TAI-CHING-TI-KUO ... **Note:** Struck at Ching (Chingchow).

| Date | Mintage | F | VF | XF | Unc | BU |
|---|---|---|---|---|---|---|
| ND(1909) | — | 150 | 300 | 450 | 750 | — |

**20 CENTS** Y# 125.1 **Weight:** 5.3000 g. **Composition:** 0.8200 Silver .1397 oz. ASW **Ruler:** Kuang-hsü **Obverse:** Inscription: Kuang-hsü Yüan-pao **Reverse:** Without characters beside dragon **Note:** Struck at Ching (Chingchow).

| Date | Mintage | F | VF | XF | Unc | BU |
|---|---|---|---|---|---|---|
| ND(1895-1907) | — | 5.00 | 10.00 | 15.00 | 30.00 | — |

**20 CENTS** Y# 130 **Composition:** Silver **Ruler:** Hsüan-t'ung **Obverse:** Inscription: Hsüan-t'ung Yüan-pao **Reverse:** Dragon **Note:** Struck at Ching (Chingchow).

| Date | Mintage | F | VF | XF | Unc | BU |
|---|---|---|---|---|---|---|
| ND(1909) | — | 250 | 500 | 850 | 1,250 | — |

**50 CENTS** Y# 126 **Weight:** 13.5000 g. **Composition:** 0.8600 Silver .3733 oz. ASW **Ruler:** Hsüan-t'ung **Obverse:** Inscription: Kuang-hsü Yüan-pao **Reverse:** Dragon **Note:** Struck at Ching (Chingchow).

| Date | Mintage | F | VF | XF | Unc | BU |
|---|---|---|---|---|---|---|
| ND(1895-1905) | — | 35.00 | 65.00 | 120 | 250 | — |

## BULLION COINAGE/TAEL SYSTEM

**TAEL** Y# 128.1 **Weight:** 37.7000 g. **Composition:** 0.8770 Silver 1.0631 oz. ASW **Ruler:** Kuang-hsü **Obverse:** Large inscription: Kuang-hsü Yin-pi **Reverse:** Two dragons forming circle **Note:** Struck at Ching (Chingchow).

| Date | Mintage | F | VF | XF | Unc | BU |
|---|---|---|---|---|---|---|
| 30(1904) | 648,000 | 325 | 600 | 1,800 | 3,000 | — |

**TAEL** Y# 128.2 **Weight:** 37.7000 g. **Composition:** 0.8770 Silver 1.0631 oz. ASW **Ruler:** Kuang-hsü **Obverse:** Smaller inscription: Kuang-hsü Yin-pi **Reverse:** Two dragons forming circle **Note:** Struck at Ching (Chingchow).

| Date | Mintage | F | VF | XF | Unc | BU |
|---|---|---|---|---|---|---|
| 30(1904) | Inc. above | 200 | 300 | 600 | 1,400 | — |

# REPUBLIC

## MILLED COINAGE

**20 CASH** Y# A405 **Composition:** Brass **Note:** Attribution is uncertain. Probably minted in Szechuan (Sichuan).

| Date | Mintage | VG | F | VF | XF | Unc |
|---|---|---|---|---|---|---|
| ND(c. 1914) | — | 40.00 | 85.00 | 115 | 165 | — |

**50 CASH** Y# 405 **Composition:** Copper Or Brass **Note:** Crude strike. Similar coins dated Yr. 1 and Yr. 8 are known, but their status is uncertain.

| Date | Mintage | Good | VG | F | VF | XF |
|---|---|---|---|---|---|---|
| 3(1914) | — | 375 | 575 | 850 | 1,100 | — |
| 7(1918) | — | 250 | 400 | 600 | 850 | — |

**50 CASH** Y# 405.1 **Composition:** Copper Or Brass **Note:** Machine strike. Not to be confused with Szechuan (Sichuan) Y#449.

| Date | Mintage | Good | VG | F | VF | XF |
|---|---|---|---|---|---|---|
| 7(1918) | — | 375 | 575 | 850 | 1,100 | — |

**20 CENTS** Y# 406 **Weight:** 5.2000 g. **Composition:** Silver **Obverse:** Characters "Tsao" at left and "Hu" at right of military bust of Yüan Shih-kai left **Note:** Do not confuse with Y#327 (see Republic-general issues).

| Date | Mintage | F | VF | XF | Unc | BU |
|---|---|---|---|---|---|---|
| 9(1920) | — | 75.00 | 125 | 200 | 500 | — |

## PATTERNS

Including off metal strikes

| KM# | Date | Mintage | Identification | Mkt Val |
|---|---|---|---|---|
| PnA6 | (1902) | — | 10 Cash. White copper. Y122.5. W518. | — |
| Pn6 | (1902) | — | 10 Cash. Brass. W480. | — |
| PnA7 | 3(1911) | — | 10 Cents. Pewter. K48y. | — |
| Pn7 | 1(1916) | — | 10 Cents. White Metal. K764x. | — |

# KANSU PROVINCE

**Gansu**

A province located in north-central China with a contrast of mountains and sandy plains. The west end of the Great Wall with its branches lies in Kansu (Gansu). Kansu (Gansu) was the eastern end of the "Silk Road" that led to central and western Asia. Two mints issued Cash coins. It has been reported, but not confirmed, that the Lanchow Mint operated as late as 1949.

## REPUBLIC

### MILLED COINAGE

**20 CASH** **Y# C407** **Composition:** Copper **Note:** Struck at Kansu.

| Date | Mintage | VG | F | VF | XF | Unc |
|---|---|---|---|---|---|---|
| ND(1920) | — | — | — | — | — | — |

**50 CASH** **Y# D407** **Composition:** Copper **Note:** Struck at Kansu.

| Date | Mintage | VG | F | VF | XF | Unc |
|---|---|---|---|---|---|---|
| ND(1920) | — | 70.00 | 150 | 250 | — | — |

**50 CASH** **Y# 408** **Composition:** Copper

| Date | Mintage | VG | F | VF | XF | Unc |
|---|---|---|---|---|---|---|
| 15(1926) | 2,564,000 | 85.00 | 175 | 275 | 450 | — |

**50 CASH** **Y# A408** **Composition:** Copper

| Date | Mintage | VG | F | VF | XF | Unc |
|---|---|---|---|---|---|---|
| ND(1927) | — | 500 | 900 | 1,500 | — | — |

**100 CASH** **Y# 409** **Composition:** Copper

| Date | Mintage | VG | F | VF | XF | Unc |
|---|---|---|---|---|---|---|
| 15(1926) | — | 35.00 | 50.00 | 100 | 150 | — |

**DOLLAR** **Y# 407** **Weight:** 26.6000 g. **Composition:** Silver **Obverse:** Military bust of Yüan Shih-kai left, "Su" at left, "Kan" at right

| Date | Mintage | F | VF | XF | Unc | BU |
|---|---|---|---|---|---|---|
| 3(1914) | — | 125 | 200 | 350 | 800 | — |

**DOLLAR** **Y# 410** **Weight:** 26.6000 g. **Composition:** Silver **Obverse:** Facing bust of Sun Yat-sen

| Date | Mintage | F | VF | XF | Unc | BU |
|---|---|---|---|---|---|---|
| 17(1928) | — | 175 | 300 | 500 | 1,000 | — |

## PATTERNS

Including off metal strikes

| KM# | Date | Mintage | Identification | Mkt Val |
|---|---|---|---|---|
| Pn2 | ND(ca.1928) | — | 10 Cash. Copper. | — |
| Pn4 | 17(1928) | — | 50 Cash. Copper. | — |
| Pn1 | ND(ca.1928) | — | 5 Cash. Copper. Hsu#385. | 650 |
| Pn3 | ND(1928) | — | 5 Fen. Copper. Hsu#383. | 300 |
| Pn5 | ND(ca.1928) | — | 10 Fen. Copper. Hsu#384. | 400 |

# KIANGNAN

A district in eastern China made up of Anhwei (Anhui) and Kiangsu (Jiangsu) provinces. In 1667 the province of Kiangnan was divided into the present provinces of Anhwei (Anhui) and Kiangsu (Jiangsu). In 1723 Nanking, formerly the capital of Kiangnan, was made the capital of Liang-Chiang Chiang (an administrative area consisting of Anhwei (Anhui), Kiangsu (Jiangsu), and Kiangsi (Jiangxi) provinces).

Always highly regarded because of location, agriculture and manufacturing, Kiangnan has frequently been sought after by contending forces.

The Nanking Mint had been active during imperial times. Modern minting facilities began operations in 1897. A second mint was planned for the Kiangnan Arsenal in Shanghai in 1905. Mints for copper coins also operated in Chingkiang (Qingjiang) in central Kiangsu and at Soochow which is further south. A silver mint was planned for Shanghai in 1921. The Nanking Mint, the most important of the group, burned down in 1929. The Nationalist Government Central Mint was completed in Shanghai in 1930 and opened in 1933.

## EMPIRE

### MILLED COINAGE

The initials HAH, SY, CH and TH are those of mint officials and were placed on the coins as a guarantee of the coin's fineness. The 5-, 10-, and 20-cent coins are often found without a decimal point between the numbers on the reverse. The 1904 dated dollar was restruck during Republican times.

**CASH** **Y# 7k** **Composition:** Brass **Ruler:** Kuang-Hsü **Obverse:** Bottom horizontal stroke in mint mark extends beyond outside vertical strokes **Obv. Legend:** Kuang-hsü **Reverse:** Dragon

| Date | Mintage | VG | F | VF | XF | Unc |
|---|---|---|---|---|---|---|
| CD(1908) | 25,450,000 | 2.50 | 4.50 | 8.50 | 16.00 | — |

**CASH** **Y# 7k.1** **Composition:** Brass **Ruler:** Kuang-Hsü **Obverse:** Bottom horizontal stroke in mint mark does not extend beyond outside vertical strokes **Obv. Legend:** Kuang-hsü **Reverse:** Dragon

| Date | Mintage | VG | F | VF | XF | Unc |
|---|---|---|---|---|---|---|
| CD(1908) | Inc. above | 3.50 | 6.50 | 12.50 | 21.50 | — |

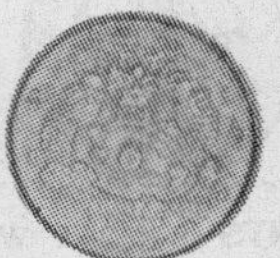

**2 CASH** **8k** **Composition:** Brass **Ruler:** Kuang-Hsü

| Date | Mintage | VG | F | VF | XF | Unc |
|---|---|---|---|---|---|---|
| CD(1906) | — | — | — | — | — | — |

**5 CASH** Y# 9k.1 **Composition:** Copper **Ruler:** Kuang-Hsü **Obverse:** Inscription: Tai-ch'ing T'ung-pi; mint mark incused on raised disk **Reverse:** Dragon **Rev. Legend:** Kuang-hsü Nien-tsao, TAI-CHING-TI-KUO...

| Date | Mintage | VG | F | VF | XF | Unc |
|---|---|---|---|---|---|---|
| CD(1906) | — | 35.00 | 65.00 | 100 | 150 | — |

**5 CASH** Y# 9k.1a **Composition:** Brass **Ruler:** Kuang-Hsü **Obverse:** Inscription: Tai-ch'ing T'ung-pi **Reverse:** Dragon **Rev. Legend:** Kuang-hsü Nien-tsao, TAI-CHING-TI-KUO...

| Date | Mintage | VG | F | VF | XF | Unc |
|---|---|---|---|---|---|---|
| CD(1906) | — | 45.00 | 90.00 | 125 | 200 | — |

**5 CASH** Y# 9k.2 **Composition:** Copper **Ruler:** Kuang-Hsü **Obverse:** Inscription: Tai-ch'ing T'ung-pi; mint mark in relief at center without disk **Reverse:** Dragon **Rev. Legend:** Kuang-hsü Nien-tsao, TAI-CHING-TI-KUO...

| Date | Mintage | VG | F | VF | XF | Unc |
|---|---|---|---|---|---|---|
| CD(1906) | — | 45.00 | 90.00 | 125 | 200 | — |

**10 CASH** Y# 135 **Composition:** Copper **Ruler:** Kuang-Hsü **Obverse:** Inscription: Kuang-hsü Yüan-pao **Reverse:** Dragon **Edge:** Reeded

| Date | Mintage | F | VF | XF | Unc | BU |
|---|---|---|---|---|---|---|
| ND(ca.1902) | — | 30.00 | 60.00 | 100 | — | — |

**10 CASH** Y# 135.1 **Composition:** Copper **Ruler:** Kuang-Hsü **Obverse:** Inscription: Kuang-hsü Yüan-pao **Reverse:** Dragon **Edge:** Plain

| Date | Mintage | F | VF | XF | Unc | BU |
|---|---|---|---|---|---|---|
| ND(ca.1902) | — | 30.00 | 60.00 | 100 | — | — |

**10 CASH** Y# 135.2 **Composition:** Copper **Ruler:** Kuang-Hsü **Obverse:** Inscription: Kuang-hsü Yüan-pao; small Manchu words in center **Reverse:** Dragon

| Date | Mintage | F | VF | XF | Unc | BU |
|---|---|---|---|---|---|---|
| CD(ca.1902) | — | 1.50 | 3.00 | 5.00 | 20.00 | — |

**10 CASH** Y# 135.3 **Composition:** Copper **Ruler:** Kuang-Hsü **Obverse:** Inscription: Kuang-hsü Yüan-pao; large Manchu words in center **Reverse:** Dragon

| Date | Mintage | F | VF | XF | Unc | BU |
|---|---|---|---|---|---|---|
| CD(ca.1902) | — | 6.50 | 12.50 | 25.00 | 45.00 | — |

**10 CASH** Y# C140 **Composition:** Copper **Ruler:** Kuang-Hsü **Obverse:** Inscription: Kuang-hsü Yüan-pao; Kiang-nan **Reverse:** Dragon **Rev. Legend:** KIANG-SOO **Note:** Mule; often confused with Y#162.

| Date | Mintage | F | VF | XF | Unc | BU |
|---|---|---|---|---|---|---|
| ND(ca.1902) | — | 150 | 200 | 250 | — | — |
| CD(1902) | — | — | — | — | — | — |

**10 CASH** Y# 135.4 **Composition:** Copper **Ruler:** Kuang-Hsü **Obverse:** Inscription: Kuang-hsü Yüan-pao **Reverse:** Dragon

| Date | Mintage | F | VF | XF | Unc | BU |
|---|---|---|---|---|---|---|
| CD(1903) | — | 4.00 | 5.00 | 7.00 | 24.00 | — |

**10 CASH** Y# 135.5 **Composition:** Copper **Ruler:** Kuang-Hsü **Obverse:** Inscription: Kuang-hsü Yüan-pao **Reverse:** Dragon; cloud above letter T looks like number 3

| Date | Mintage | F | VF | XF | Unc | BU |
|---|---|---|---|---|---|---|
| CD(1904) | 351,974,000 | 1.00 | 2.00 | 5.00 | 20.00 | — |

**10 CASH** Y# 135.6 **Composition:** Copper **Ruler:** Kuang-Hsü **Obverse:** Inscription: Kuang-hsü Yüan-pao **Reverse:** Dragon; cloud above T redesigned; CASH spelled GASH

| Date | Mintage | F | VF | XF | Unc | BU |
|---|---|---|---|---|---|---|
| CD(1904) | Inc. above | 4.50 | 9.00 | 17.50 | 45.00 | — |

**10 CASH** Y# 135.7 **Composition:** Copper **Ruler:** Kuang-Hsü **Obverse:** Inscription: Kuang-hsü Yüan-pao **Reverse:** Thin-tailed dragon; third design of cloud above letter T

| Date | Mintage | F | VF | XF | Unc | BU |
|---|---|---|---|---|---|---|
| CD(1904) | Inc. above | 1.50 | 3.00 | 5.00 | 20.00 | — |

**10 CASH** Y# 135.8 **Composition:** Copper **Ruler:** Kuang-Hsü **Obverse:** Inscription: Kuang-hsü Yüan-pao **Reverse:** Fewer clouds around dragon; scales on dragon's body different, pearl smaller

| Date | Mintage | F | VF | XF | Unc | BU |
|---|---|---|---|---|---|---|
| CD(1904) | Inc. above | 4.50 | 9.00 | 17.50 | 45.00 | — |

**Note:** This coin is believed to be counterfeit

**10 CASH** Y# 135.9 **Composition:** Copper **Ruler:** Kuang-Hsü **Obverse:** Inscription: Kuang-hsü Yüan-pao **Reverse:** Small rosette at either side of dragon

| Date | Mintage | F | VF | XF | Unc | BU |
|---|---|---|---|---|---|---|
| CD(1905) | 496,020,000 | 1.00 | 2.00 | 5.00 | 20.00 | — |

**10 CASH** Y# 135.10 **Composition:** Copper **Ruler:** Kuang-Hsü **Obverse:** Inscription: Kuang-hsü Yüan-pao **Reverse:** Large oblong rosettes at either side of dragon

| Date | Mintage | F | VF | XF | Unc | BU |
|---|---|---|---|---|---|---|
| CD(1905) | Inc. above | 1.50 | 3.00 | 5.00 | 20.00 | — |

**10 CASH** Y# 138 **Composition:** Copper **Ruler:** Kuang-Hsü **Obverse:** Inscription: Kuang-hsü Yüan-pao **Reverse:** Dragon; denomination: TEN-CASH

| Date | Mintage | F | VF | XF | Unc | BU |
|---|---|---|---|---|---|---|
| CD(1905) | Inc. above | 3.50 | 6.00 | 12.00 | 30.00 | — |

**10 CASH** Y# 138.1 **Composition:** Copper **Ruler:** Kuang-Hsü **Obverse:** Inscription: Kuang-hsü Yüan-pao; rosette in center **Reverse:** Dragon; without hyphen in TEN CASH

| Date | Mintage | F | VF | XF | Unc | BU |
|---|---|---|---|---|---|---|
| CD(1905) | Inc. above | 0.75 | 1.50 | 5.00 | 20.00 | — |

**10 CASH** Y# B140 **Composition:** Copper **Ruler:** Kuang-Hsü **Obverse:** Inscription: Kuang-hsü Yüan-pao; Y#138 **Reverse:** Dragon; Y#10k **Note:** Mule

| Date | Mintage | F | VF | XF | Unc | BU |
|---|---|---|---|---|---|---|
| CD(1905) | Inc. above | 30.00 | 50.00 | 70.00 | — | — |

**10 CASH** **Y# D140** **Composition:** Copper **Ruler:** Kuang-Hsü **Obverse:** Inscription: Kuang-hsü Yüan-pao; Y#138.1 **Reverse:** Dragon; Y#135 **Note:** Mule

| Date | Mintage | F | VF | XF | Unc | BU |
|---|---|---|---|---|---|---|
| CD(1905) | Inc. above | 100 | 150 | 200 | — | — |

**Note:** Other Kiangnan mules exist, dated 1902 and 1903

**10 CASH** **Y# A140** **Composition:** Copper **Ruler:** Kuang-Hsü **Obverse:** Inscription: Tai-ch'ing T'ung-Pi; Y#10k.2 **Reverse:** Dragon; Y#138 **Note:** Mule

| Date | Mintage | F | VF | XF | Unc | BU |
|---|---|---|---|---|---|---|
| CD(1906) | Inc. above | 25.00 | 40.00 | 60.00 | — | — |

**10 CASH** **Y# 140.2** **Composition:** Copper **Ruler:** Kuang-Hsü **Obverse:** Inscription: Tai-ch'ing T'ung-pi, Y#10k **Reverse:** Dragon, Y#138 **Note:** Mule; mint mark incuse on raised disk.

| Date | Mintage | F | VF | XF | Unc | BU |
|---|---|---|---|---|---|---|
| CD(1906) | Inc. above | 3.00 | 5.00 | 12.00 | 30.00 | — |

**10 CASH** **Y# 140.1 (Y140)** **Composition:** Copper **Ruler:** Kuang-Hsü **Obverse:** Inscription: Tai-ch'ing T'ung-Pi; Y#10k **Reverse:** Dragon; Y#138 **Note:** Mule; raised or incused mint mark.

| Date | Mintage | F | VF | XF | Unc | BU |
|---|---|---|---|---|---|---|
| CD(1906) | Inc. above | 3.00 | 5.00 | 12.00 | 30.00 | — |

**10 CASH** **Y# 10k** **Composition:** Copper **Ruler:** Kuang-Hsü **Obverse:** Inscription: Tai-ch'ing T'ung-pi; mint mark in relief on raised disc **Reverse:** Dragon with wide face and incuse eyes **Rev. Legend:** Kuang-hsü Nien-tsao, TAI-CHING-TI-KUO...

| Date | Mintage | F | VF | XF | Unc | BU |
|---|---|---|---|---|---|---|
| CD(1906) | 504,800,000 | 1.25 | 2.50 | 5.00 | 20.00 | — |

**10 CASH** **Y# 10k.1** **Composition:** Copper **Ruler:** Kuang-Hsü **Obverse:** Inscription: Tai-ch'ing T'ung-pi **Reverse:** Dragon with narrower face and raised dots for eyes **Rev. Legend:** Kuang-hsü Nien-tsao, TAI-CHING-TI-KUO...

| Date | Mintage | F | VF | XF | Unc | BU |
|---|---|---|---|---|---|---|
| CD(1906) | Inc. above | 1.25 | 2.50 | 5.00 | 20.00 | — |

**10 CASH** **Y# 10k.2** **Composition:** Copper **Ruler:** Kuang-Hsü **Obverse:** Inscription: Tai-ch'ing T'ung-pi; mint mark in relief without raised disc **Reverse:** Dragon with wide face and incuse eyes **Rev. Legend:** Kuang-hsü Nien-tsao, TAI-CHING-TI-KUO...

| Date | Mintage | F | VF | XF | Unc | BU |
|---|---|---|---|---|---|---|
| CD(1906) | Inc. above | 1.00 | 2.50 | 5.00 | 20.00 | — |

**10 CASH** **Y# 10k.3** **Composition:** Copper **Ruler:** Kuang-Hsü **Obverse:** Inscription: Tai-ch'ing T'ung-pi **Reverse:** Dragon with narrow face and raised dots for eyes **Rev. Legend:** Kuang-hsü Nien-tsao, TAI-CHING-TI-KUO...

| Date | Mintage | F | VF | XF | Unc | BU |
|---|---|---|---|---|---|---|
| CD(1906) | Inc. above | 1.00 | 2.50 | 5.00 | 20.00 | — |

**10 CASH** **Y# 10k.4** **Composition:** Copper **Ruler:** Kuang-Hsü **Obverse:** Inscription: Tai-ch'ing T'ung-pi; mint mark incuse on raised disc **Reverse:** Dragon **Rev. Legend:** Kuang-hsü Nien-tsao, TAI-CHING-TI-KUO...

| Date | Mintage | F | VF | XF | Unc | BU |
|---|---|---|---|---|---|---|
| CD(1906) | Inc. above | 12.50 | 25.00 | 45.00 | — | — |

**10 CASH** **Y# 10k.4a** **Composition:** Brass **Ruler:** Kuang-Hsü **Obverse:** Inscription: Tai-ch'ing T'ung-pi **Reverse:** Dragon **Rev. Legend:** Kuang-hsü Nien-tsao, TAI-CHING-TI-KUO...

| Date | Mintage | F | VF | XF | Unc | BU |
|---|---|---|---|---|---|---|
| CD(1906) | — | — | — | — | — | — |

**10 CASH** **Y# 10k.5** **Composition:** Copper **Ruler:** Kuang-Hsü **Obverse:** Inscription: Tai-ch'ing T'ung-pi; mint mark incuse on raised disc **Reverse:** Dragon with wide face; seven flames on pearl **Rev. Legend:** Kuang-hsü Nien-tsao, TAI-CHING-TI-KUO...

| Date | Mintage | F | VF | XF | Unc | BU |
|---|---|---|---|---|---|---|
| CD(1907) | 552,000,000 | 1.50 | 3.00 | 5.00 | 20.00 | — |

**10 CASH** **Y# 10k.6** **Composition:** Copper **Ruler:** Kuang-Hsü **Obverse:** Inscription: Tai-ch'ing T'ung-pi **Reverse:** Different dragon with narrow face an small mouth; five flames on pearl; dot after COIN **Rev. Legend:** Kuang-hsü Nien-tsao, TAI-CHING-TI-KUO...

| Date | Mintage | F | VF | XF | Unc | BU |
|---|---|---|---|---|---|---|
| CD(1907) | Inc. above | 1.00 | 2.00 | 4.50 | 20.00 | — |

**10 CASH** **Y# 10k.6a** **Composition:** Brass **Ruler:** Kuang-Hsü **Obverse:** Inscription: Tai-ch'ing T'ung-pi **Reverse:** Dragon **Rev. Legend:** Kuang-hsü Nien-tsao, TAI-CHING-TI-KUO...

| Date | Mintage | F | VF | XF | Unc | BU |
|---|---|---|---|---|---|---|
| CD(1907) | Inc. above | 9.00 | 17.50 | 30.00 | — | — |

**10 CASH** **Y# 10k.7** **Composition:** Copper **Ruler:** Kuang-Hsü **Obverse:** Inscription: Tai-ch'ing T'ung-pi **Reverse:** Dragon with large mouth and redesigned head; flame below pearl has long tail which touches dragon's body; KUO spelled KIIO **Rev. Legend:** Kuang-hsü Nien-tsao, TAI-CHING-TI-KUO...

| Date | Mintage | F | VF | XF | Unc | BU |
|---|---|---|---|---|---|---|
| CD(1907) | Inc. above | 1.00 | 2.50 | 5.00 | 20.00 | — |

**10 CASH** **Y# 10k.8** **Composition:** Copper **Ruler:** Kuang-Hsü **Obverse:** Inscription: Tai-ch'ing T'ung-pi **Reverse:** Tail of flame below pearl does not touch dragon's body; dash after word COIN; KUO spelled KUO **Rev. Legend:** Kuang-hsü Nien-tsao, TAI-CHING-TI-KUO...

| Date | Mintage | F | VF | XF | Unc | BU |
|---|---|---|---|---|---|---|
| CD(1907) | Inc. above | 1.00 | 2.50 | 5.00 | 20.00 | — |

**10 CASH** **Y# 10k.9** **Composition:** Copper **Ruler:** Kuang-Hsü **Obverse:** Inscription: Tai-ch'ing T'ung-pi **Reverse:** Dragon with square mouth; letter K in KUO larger than other letters; without dot or dash after COIN **Rev. Legend:** Kuang-hsü Nien-tsao, TAI-CHING-TI-KUO...

| Date | Mintage | F | VF | XF | Unc | BU |
|---|---|---|---|---|---|---|
| CD(1907) | Inc. above | 1.00 | 2.25 | 4.50 | 20.00 | — |

**10 CASH** **Y# 10k.9a** **Composition:** Copper **Ruler:** Kuang-Hsü **Obverse:** Inscription: Tai-ch'ing T'ung-pi **Reverse:** Large flat-faced dragon **Rev. Legend:** Kuang-hsü Nien-tsao, TAI-CHING-TI-KUO...

| Date | Mintage | F | VF | XF | Unc | BU |
|---|---|---|---|---|---|---|
| CD(1907) | — | — | — | — | — | — |

**10 CASH** **Y# E140** **Composition:** Copper **Ruler:** Kuang-Hsü **Obverse:** Inscription: Tai-ch'ing T'ung-pi; Y#10.5 **Reverse:** Dragon; Kiangnan Y#138.1 **Note:** Mule

| Date | Mintage | F | VF | XF | Unc | BU |
|---|---|---|---|---|---|---|
| CD(1907) | — | 100 | 225 | 300 | — | — |

**10 CASH** **Y# 10k.10** **Composition:** Copper **Ruler:** Kuang-Hsü **Obverse:** Inscription: Tai-ch'ing T'ung-pi: mint mark incuse on raised disc **Reverse:** Dragon with small moutn; five flame pearl; dot after COIN; KUO spelled KUO **Rev. Legend:** Kuang-hsü Nien-tsao, TAI-CHING-TI-KUO...

| Date | Mintage | F | VF | XF | Unc | BU |
|---|---|---|---|---|---|---|
| CD(1908) | 442,750,000 | 1.00 | 2.50 | 5.00 | 20.00 | — |

**10 CASH** **Y# 10k.11** **Composition:** Copper **Ruler:** Kuang-Hsü **Obverse:** Inscription: Tai-ch'ing T'ung-pi **Reverse:** Dragon has large mouth and redesigned head; tail on cloud beneath pearl touches dragon's body; KUO spelled KIIO **Rev. Legend:** Kuang-hsü Nien-tsao, TAI-CHING-TI-KUO...

| Date | Mintage | F | VF | XF | Unc | BU |
|---|---|---|---|---|---|---|
| CD(1908) | Inc. above | 1.00 | 2.00 | 4.00 | 20.00 | — |

**10 CASH** Y# 10k.12 **Composition:** Copper **Ruler:** Kuang-Hsü **Obverse:** Inscription: Tai-ch'ing T'ung-pi **Reverse:** Dragon; dash after COIN; KUO spelled KUO **Rev. Legend:** Kuang-hsü Nien-tsao, TAI-CHING-TI-KUO...

| Date | Mintage | F | VF | XF | Unc | BU |
|---|---|---|---|---|---|---|
| CD(1908) | Inc. above | 1.50 | 3.00 | 5.00 | 20.00 | — |

**10 CASH** Y# 10k.13 **Composition:** Copper **Ruler:** Kuang-Hsü **Obverse:** Inscription: Tai-ch'ing T'ung-pi **Reverse:** Dragon's head redesigned; without dot or dash after COIN; KUO spelled KIIO **Rev. Legend:** Kuang-hsü Nien-tsao, TAI-CHING-TI-KUO...

| Date | Mintage | F | VF | XF | Unc | BU |
|---|---|---|---|---|---|---|
| CD(1908) | Inc. above | 1.00 | 2.00 | 4.00 | 20.00 | — |

**Note:** Most of the 1907 and 1908 ten cash above have copper spelled GOPPER

**5 CENTS** Y# 141a **Weight:** 13.0000 g. **Composition:** 0.8200 Silver .0343 oz. ASW **Ruler:** Kuang-Hsü **Obverse:** Inscription: Kuang-hsü Yüan-pao **Reverse:** Without circle around dragon

| Date | Mintage | F | VF | XF | Unc | BU |
|---|---|---|---|---|---|---|
| ND(1898) | Inc. above | 10.00 | 15.00 | 30.00 | 50.00 | — |
| CD(1899) | 3,812 | 50.00 | 100 | 150 | 300 | — |
| CD(1900) | 618,000 | 10.00 | 15.00 | 30.00 | 50.00 | — |
| CD(1901) | — | 50.00 | 75.00 | 150 | 275 | — |

**10 CENTS** Y# 142a.5 **Weight:** 2.6000 g. **Composition:** 0.8200 Silver .0343 oz. ASW **Ruler:** Kuang-Hsü **Obverse:** Inscription: Kuang-hsü Yüan-pao; without initials **Reverse:** Large English letters

| Date | Mintage | F | VF | XF | Unc | BU |
|---|---|---|---|---|---|---|
| CD(1901) | 7,794,000 | 2.50 | 4.50 | 9.00 | 30.00 | — |

**10 CENTS** Y# 142a.6 **Weight:** 2.6000 g. **Composition:** 0.8200 Silver .0343 oz. ASW **Ruler:** Kuang-Hsü **Obverse:** Inscription: Kuang-hsü Yüan-pao; without initials **Reverse:** Small English letters

| Date | Mintage | F | VF | XF | Unc | BU |
|---|---|---|---|---|---|---|
| CD(1901) | Inc. above | 2.50 | 4.50 | 9.00 | 30.00 | — |

**10 CENTS** Y# 142a.7 **Weight:** 2.6000 g. **Composition:** 0.8200 Silver .0343 oz. ASW **Ruler:** Kuang-Hsü **Obverse:** Inscription: Kuang-hsü Yüan-pao; initials "HAH" **Reverse:** Large rosettes beside dragon

| Date | Mintage | F | VF | XF | Unc | BU |
|---|---|---|---|---|---|---|
| CD(1901) | Inc. above | 3.50 | 6.50 | 12.50 | 35.00 | — |

**10 CENTS** Y# 142a.8 **Weight:** 2.6000 g. **Composition:** 0.8200 Silver .0343 oz. ASW **Ruler:** Kuang-Hsü **Obverse:** Inscription: Kuang-hsü Yüan-pao **Reverse:** Small rosettes beside dragon

| Date | Mintage | F | VF | XF | Unc | BU |
|---|---|---|---|---|---|---|
| CD(1901) | Inc. above | 3.50 | 6.50 | 12.50 | 35.00 | — |

**10 CENTS** Y# 142a.9 **Weight:** 2.6000 g. **Composition:** 0.8200 Silver .0343 oz. ASW **Ruler:** Kuang-Hsü **Obverse:** Inscription: Kuang-hsü Yüan-pao **Reverse:** Large stars beside dragon

| Date | Mintage | F | VF | XF | Unc | BU |
|---|---|---|---|---|---|---|
| CD(1902) | 3,778,000 | 3.00 | 5.50 | 10.00 | 30.00 | — |

**10 CENTS** Y# 142a.10 **Weight:** 2.6000 g. **Composition:** 0.8200 Silver .0343 oz. ASW **Ruler:** Kuang-Hsü **Obverse:** Inscription: Kuang-hsü Yüan-pao **Reverse:** Small stars beside dragon

| Date | Mintage | F | VF | XF | Unc | BU |
|---|---|---|---|---|---|---|
| CD(1902) | Inc. above | 4.00 | 7.00 | 12.00 | 50.00 | — |

**10 CENTS** Y# 142a.11 **Weight:** 2.6000 g. **Composition:** 0.8200 Silver .0343 oz. ASW **Ruler:** Kuang-Hsü **Obverse:** Inscription: Kuang-hsü Yüan-pao; large rosette

| Date | Mintage | F | VF | XF | Unc | BU |
|---|---|---|---|---|---|---|
| CD(1903) | 1,161,000 | 10.00 | 25.00 | 50.00 | 90.00 | — |

**10 CENTS** Y# 142a.12 **Weight:** 2.6000 g. **Composition:** 0.8200 Silver .0343 oz. ASW **Ruler:** Kuang-Hsü **Obverse:** Inscription: Kuang-hsü Yüan-pao; small rosette

| Date | Mintage | F | VF | XF | Unc | BU |
|---|---|---|---|---|---|---|
| CD(1903) | Inc. above | 10.00 | 25.00 | 50.00 | 90.00 | — |

**10 CENTS** Y# 142a.13 **Weight:** 2.6000 g. **Composition:** 0.8200 Silver .0343 oz. ASW **Ruler:** Kuang-Hsü **Obverse:** Inscription: Kuang-hsü Yüan-pao; initials "HAH TH"

| Date | Mintage | F | VF | XF | Unc | BU |
|---|---|---|---|---|---|---|
| CD(1904) | 897,000 | 5.00 | 10.00 | 25.00 | 75.00 | — |

**10 CENTS** Y# 142a.14 **Weight:** 2.6000 g. **Composition:** 0.8200 Silver .0343 oz. ASW **Ruler:** Kuang-Hsü **Obverse:** Inscription: Kuang-hsü Yüan-pao; initials "SY" upside down

| Date | Mintage | F | VF | XF | Unc | BU |
|---|---|---|---|---|---|---|
| CD(1905) | 681,000 | 5.00 | 10.00 | 25.00 | 75.00 | — |

**10 CENTS** Y# 146 **Weight:** 2.6000 g. **Composition:** 0.8200 Silver .0343 oz. ASW **Ruler:** Hsüan-T'ung **Obverse:** Inscription: Hsüan-t'ung Yüan-pao **Reverse:** Dragon

| Date | Mintage | F | VF | XF | Unc | BU |
|---|---|---|---|---|---|---|
| ND(1911) | Est. 820,000 | 10.00 | 25.00 | 50.00 | 90.00 | — |

**Note:** Includes 590,000 pieces struck in debased silver in 1916

**20 CENTS** Y# 143 **Weight:** 5.3000 g. **Composition:** 0.8200 Silver .1397 oz. ASW **Ruler:** Kuang-Hsü **Obverse:** Inscription: Kuang-hsü Yüan-pao; rosettes at 2 abd 10 o'clock **Reverse:** Circle around dragon

| Date | Mintage | F | VF | XF | Unc | BU |
|---|---|---|---|---|---|---|
| ND(1898) | 7,000,000 | 17.50 | 40.00 | 70.00 | 180 | — |

**20 CENTS** Y# 143a.6 **Weight:** 5.3000 g. **Composition:** 0.8200 Silver .1397 oz. ASW **Ruler:** Kuang-Hsü **Obverse:** Inscription: Kuang-hsü Yüan-pao; without initials

| Date | Mintage | F | VF | XF | Unc | BU |
|---|---|---|---|---|---|---|
| CD(1901) | 47,114,000 | 4.50 | 8.00 | 15.00 | 50.00 | — |

**20 CENTS** Y# 143a.14 **Weight:** 5.3000 g. **Composition:** 0.8200 Silver .1397 oz. ASW **Ruler:** Kuang-Hsü **Obverse:** Inscription: Kuang-hsü Yüan-pao **Rev. Legend:** ...MACI...

| Date | Mintage | F | VF | XF | Unc | BU |
|---|---|---|---|---|---|---|
| CD(1901) | Inc. above | 5.00 | 10.00 | 25.00 | 60.00 | — |

**20 CENTS** Y# 143a.7 **Weight:** 5.3000 g. **Composition:** 0.8200 Silver .1397 oz. ASW **Ruler:** Kuang-Hsü **Obverse:** Inscription: Kuang-hsü Yüan-pao; initials "HAH"

| Date | Mintage | F | VF | XF | Unc | BU |
|---|---|---|---|---|---|---|
| CD(1901) | Inc. above | 3.50 | 5.00 | 10.00 | 50.00 | — |

**20 CENTS** Y# 143a.8 **Weight:** 5.3000 g. **Composition:** 0.8200 Silver .1397 oz. ASW **Ruler:** Kuang-Hsü **Obverse:** Inscription: Kuang-hsü Yüan-pao

| Date | Mintage | F | VF | XF | Unc | BU |
|---|---|---|---|---|---|---|
| CD(1902) | 15,754,000 | 4.00 | 6.50 | 12.50 | 50.00 | — |

**20 CENTS** Y# 143a.9 **Weight:** 5.3000 g. **Composition:** 0.8200 Silver .1397 oz. ASW **Ruler:** Kuang-Hsü **Obverse:** Inscription: Kuang-hsü Yüan-pao; rosette in outer legend

| Date | Mintage | F | VF | XF | Unc | BU |
|---|---|---|---|---|---|---|
| CD(1903) | 2,432,000 | 10.00 | 20.00 | 50.00 | 100 | — |

**20 CENTS** Y# 143a.10 **Weight:** 5.3000 g. **Composition:** 0.8200 Silver .1397 oz. ASW **Ruler:** Kuang-Hsü **Obverse:** Inscription: Kuang-hsü Yüan-pao; without rosette

| Date | Mintage | F | VF | XF | Unc | BU |
|---|---|---|---|---|---|---|
| CD(1903) | Inc. above | 12.50 | 25.00 | 50.00 | 150 | — |

**20 CENTS** Y# 143a.11 **Weight:** 5.3000 g. **Composition:** 0.8200 Silver .1397 oz. ASW **Ruler:** Kuang-Hsü **Obverse:** Inscription: Kuang-hsü Yüan-pao; initials "HAH TH"

| Date | Mintage | F | VF | XF | Unc | BU |
|---|---|---|---|---|---|---|
| CD(1904) | 1,172,000 | 15.00 | 35.00 | 55.00 | 120 | — |

**20 CENTS** Y# 143a.12 **Weight:** 5.3000 g. **Composition:** 0.8200 Silver .1397 oz. ASW **Ruler:** Kuang-Hsü **Obverse:** Inscription: Kuang-hsü Yüan-pao; without initials

| Date | Mintage | F | VF | XF | Unc | BU |
|---|---|---|---|---|---|---|
| CD(1905) | 828,000 | 10.00 | 25.00 | 45.00 | 120 | — |

**20 CENTS** Y# 143a.13 **Weight:** 5.3000 g. **Composition:** 0.8200 Silver .1397 oz. ASW **Ruler:** Kuang-Hsü **Obverse:** Inscription: Kuang-hsü Yüan-pao; initials "SY"

| Date | Mintage | F | VF | XF | Unc | BU |
|---|---|---|---|---|---|---|
| CD(1905) | Inc. above | 9.00 | 22.00 | 35.00 | 100 | — |

**20 CENTS** Y# 147 **Weight:** 5.3000 g. **Composition:** 0.8200 Silver .1397 oz. ASW **Ruler:** Hsüan-T'ung **Obverse:** Inscription: Hsüan-T'ung Yüan-pao **Reverse:** Dragon

| Date | Mintage | F | VF | XF | Unc | BU |
|---|---|---|---|---|---|---|
| ND(1911) | 2,320,000 | 20.00 | 50.00 | 80.00 | 150 | — |

**Note:** Includes 2,005,000 pieces struck in debased silver in 1916

**DOLLAR** Y# 145a.6 **Weight:** 26.7000 g. **Composition:** 0.9000 Silver **Ruler:** Kuang-Hsü **Obverse:** Inscription: Kuang-hsü Yüan-pao; bold initials "HAH" without rosette **Reverse:** Petals of rosettes separated from each other

| Date | Mintage | F | VF | XF | Unc | BU |
|---|---|---|---|---|---|---|
| CD(1901) | Inc. above | 65.00 | 125 | 200 | 500 | — |

**DOLLAR** Y# 145a.7 **Weight:** 26.7000 g. **Composition:** 0.9000 Silver **Ruler:** Kuang-Hsü **Obverse:** Inscription: Kuang-hsü Yüan-pao; initials "HAH" and rosette **Reverse:** Petals of rosettes run together

| Date | Mintage | F | VF | XF | Unc | BU |
|---|---|---|---|---|---|---|
| CD(1901) | Inc. above | 20.00 | 35.00 | 75.00 | 275 | — |

**DOLLAR** Y# 145a.5 **Weight:** 26.7000 g. **Composition:** 0.9000 Silver **Ruler:** Kuang-Hsü **Obverse:** Inscription: Kuang-hsü Yüan-pao; without initials **Note:** Cross-reference number K#86.

| Date | Mintage | F | VF | XF | Unc | BU |
|---|---|---|---|---|---|---|
| CD(1901) | 2,377,000 | 150 | 200 | 300 | 1,250 | — |

**DOLLAR** Y# 145a.21 **Weight:** 26.7000 g. **Composition:** 0.9000 Silver **Ruler:** Kuang-Hsü **Obverse:** Inscription: Kuang-hsü Yüan-pao; fine initials "HAH" without rosette **Reverse:** Similar to Y#145a.6 **Note:** Cross-reference number K#90.

| Date | Mintage | F | VF | XF | Unc | BU |
|---|---|---|---|---|---|---|
| CD(1901) | Inc. above | 65.00 | 125 | 200 | 500 | — |

**DOLLAR** Y# 145a.22 **Weight:** 26.7000 g. **Composition:** 0.9000 Silver **Ruler:** Kuang-Hsü **Obverse:** Inscription: Kuang-hsü Yüan-pao; cross of six dots at upper right **Reverse:** Similar to Y#145a.6 **Note:** Cross-reference number K#90b.

| Date | Mintage | F | VF | XF | Unc | BU |
|---|---|---|---|---|---|---|
| CD(1901) | Inc. above | 100 | 200 | 350 | 1,000 | — |

**DOLLAR** Y# 145a.8 **Weight:** 25.7000 g. **Composition:** 0.9000 Silver **Ruler:** Kuang-Hsü **Obverse:** Inscription: Kuang-hsü Yüan-pao; small date, small "HAH" **Reverse:** Similar to Y#145a.4 **Note:** Cross-reference number K#94.

| Date | Mintage | F | VF | XF | Unc | BU |
|---|---|---|---|---|---|---|
| CD(1902) | 3,562,000 | 25.00 | 50.00 | 100 | 300 | — |

**DOLLAR** Y# 145a.9 **Weight:** 27.0000 g. **Composition:** 0.9000 Silver **Ruler:** Kuang-Hsü **Obverse:** Inscription: Kuang-hsü Yüan-pao; larger date, larger "HAH"

| Date | Mintage | F | VF | XF | Unc | BU |
|---|---|---|---|---|---|---|
| CD(1902) | Inc. above | 25.00 | 50.00 | 100 | 300 | — |

**DOLLAR** Y# 145a.10 **Weight:** 26.9000 g. **Composition:** 0.9000 Silver **Ruler:** Kuang-Hsü **Obverse:** Inscription: Kuang-hsü Yüan-pao; "HAH" and rosettes in outer ring **Note:** Cross-reference number K#96.

| Date | Mintage | F | VF | XF | Unc | BU |
|---|---|---|---|---|---|---|
| CD(1903) | 1,489,000 | 40.00 | 85.00 | 175 | 400 | — |

**DOLLAR** Y# 145a.11 **Weight:** 27.0000 g. **Composition:** 0.9000 Silver **Ruler:** Kuang-Hsü **Obverse:** Inscription: Kuang-hsü Yüan-pao; without rosette in outer ring **Note:** Cross-reference number K#96c.

| Date | Mintage | F | VF | XF | Unc | BU |
|---|---|---|---|---|---|---|
| CD(1903) | Inc. above | 400 | 600 | 900 | 2,000 | — |

**DOLLAR** Y# 145a.12 **Weight:** 26.7000 g. **Composition:** 0.9000 Silver **Ruler:** Kuang-Hsü **Obverse:** Inscription: Kuang-hsü Yüan-pao; initials "HAH" and "CH" without dots or rosettes **Reverse:** Similar to Y#145a.4 **Note:** Cross-reference number K#99.

| Date | Mintage | F | VF | XF | Unc | BU |
|---|---|---|---|---|---|---|
| CD(1904) | 44,725,000 | 15.00 | 25.00 | 40.00 | 200 | — |

**DOLLAR** Y# 145a.13 **Weight:** 27.0000 g. **Composition:** 0.9000 Silver **Ruler:** Kuang-Hsü **Obverse:** Inscription: Kuang-hsü Yüan-pao; dot at either side

| Date | Mintage | F | VF | XF | Unc | BU |
|---|---|---|---|---|---|---|
| CD(1904) | Inc. above | 15.00 | 25.00 | 40.00 | 200 | — |

**DOLLAR** Y# 145a.19 **Weight:** 27.0000 g. **Composition:** 0.9000 Silver **Ruler:** Kuang-Hsü **Obverse:** Inscription: Kuang-hsü Yüan-pao; dot at either side, without four central characters

| Date | Mintage | F | VF | XF | Unc | BU |
|---|---|---|---|---|---|---|
| CD(1904) | — | — | — | — | — | — |

**DOLLAR** Y# 145a.14 **Weight:** 27.0000 g. **Composition:** 0.9000 Silver **Ruler:** Kuang-Hsü **Obverse:** Inscription: Kuang-hsü Yüan-pao **Reverse:** Dot to left of numeral 7

| Date | Mintage | F | VF | XF | Unc | BU |
|---|---|---|---|---|---|---|
| CD(1904) | Inc. above | 15.00 | 25.00 | 40.00 | 150 | — |

**DOLLAR** Y# 145a.15 **Weight:** 27.0000 g. **Composition:** 0.9000 Silver **Ruler:** Kuang-Hsü **Obverse:** Inscription: Kuang-hsü Yüan-pao; four-petalled rosette at either side "HAH" and "CH"

| Date | Mintage | F | VF | XF | Unc | BU |
|---|---|---|---|---|---|---|
| CD(1904) | Inc. above | 50.00 | 125 | 200 | 500 | — |

**DOLLAR** Y# 145a.16 **Weight:** 27.0000 g. **Composition:** 0.9000 Silver **Ruler:** Kuang-Hsü **Obverse:** Inscription: Kuang-hsü Yüan-pao; initials "HAH" and "TH"

| Date | Mintage | F | VF | XF | Unc | BU |
|---|---|---|---|---|---|---|
| CD(1904) | Inc. above | 50.00 | 100 | 200 | 500 | — |

**DOLLAR** Y# 145a.17 **Weight:** 27.1000 g. **Composition:** 0.9000 Silver **Ruler:** Kuang-Hsü **Obverse:** Inscription: Kuang-hsü Yüan-pao; initials "SY" **Reverse:** Similar to Y#145a.10

| Date | Mintage | F | VF | XF | Unc | BU |
|---|---|---|---|---|---|---|
| CD(1905) | 634,000 | 35.00 | 65.00 | 200 | 600 | — |

## PATTERNS

Including off metal strikes

| KM# | Date | Mintage | Identification | Mkt Val |
|---|---|---|---|---|
| Pn4 | (1906) | — | 20 Cash. Copper. Y#11k | — |
| Pn3 | (1906) | — | 2 Cash. Copper. Y#8k | 2,000 |

# KIANGSI PROVINCE

**Jiangxi, Kiangsee**

A province located in southeastern China. Mostly hilly with some mountains on the borders that produce coal and tungsten. Some of China's finest porcelain comes from this province. Kiangsi was visited by Marco Polo. A mint was opened in Nanchang in 1729, closed in 1733, reopened in 1736 and operated with reasonable continuity from that time. Modern machinery was introduced in 1901 although it only produced copper coins. The mint closed amidst internal problems in the 1920's.

## EMPIRE

### PROVINCIAL CAST COINAGE

**CASH** C#15-9 **Composition:** Cast Brass **Ruler:** Kuang-hsü **Obverse:** Type A **Reverse:** Type 1 mint mark

| Date | Mintage | Good | VG | F | VF | XF |
|---|---|---|---|---|---|---|
| ND(1875-1908) | — | 4.50 | 6.50 | 12.00 | 15.00 | — |

**10 CASH** C# 15-10 **Composition:** Cast Brass **Ruler:** Kuang-hsü **Obverse:** Type B

| Date | Mintage | Good | VG | F | VF | XF |
|---|---|---|---|---|---|---|
| ND(1875-1908) Rare | — | — | — | — | — | — |

### MILLED COINAGE

Many Kiangsi (Jiangxi) coins have a six-petalled rosette in the center of the obverse, arranged so that two sides of the rosette are formed by two petals in line with each other. The remainng two sides have a single petal, standing out from the rest. The direction that these single petals point, determines whether the rosette is horizontal or vertical. A horizontal rosette has the single petals pointing left and right, while the single petals of the vertical rosette point up and down.

**10 CASH** **Y# 149** **Composition:** Copper **Ruler:** Kuang-hsü **Obverse:** Vertical rosette at center, inscription: Kuang-hsü Yüan-pao **Reverse:** Province name spelled KIANG-SEE

| Date | Mintage | VG | F | VF | XF | Unc |
|---|---|---|---|---|---|---|
| ND(c. 1902) | — | 3.50 | 8.00 | 12.50 | 22.50 | — |

**10 CASH** **Y# 149.1** **Composition:** Copper **Ruler:** Kuang-hsü **Obverse:** Horizontal rosette at center, inscription: Kuang-hsü Yüan-pao

| Date | Mintage | VG | F | VF | XF | Unc |
|---|---|---|---|---|---|---|
| ND(c. 1902) | — | 3.50 | 8.00 | 12.50 | 22.50 | — |

**10 CASH** **Y# 149.2** **Composition:** Copper **Ruler:** Kuang-hsü **Obverse:** Different Manchu word at right, inscription: Kuang-hsü Yüan-pao **Reverse:** Circled dragon **Note:** May be a pattern.

| Date | Mintage | VG | F | VF | XF | Unc |
|---|---|---|---|---|---|---|
| ND(c. 1902) Rare | — | — | — | — | — | — |

**10 CASH** **Y# 150** **Composition:** Copper **Ruler:** Kuang-hsü **Obverse:** Manchu "Pao Yuan" at 3 and 9 o'clock, inscription: Kuang-hsü Yüan-pao **Reverse:** Province name spelled KIANG-SI, 2 stars at either side of dragon

| Date | Mintage | F | VF | XF | Unc | BU |
|---|---|---|---|---|---|---|
| ND(c. 1902) | — | 6.00 | 11.00 | 17.50 | 35.00 | — |

**10 CASH** **Y# 150.1** **Composition:** Copper **Ruler:** Kuang-hsü **Obverse:** Manchu "Pao Ch'ang" at center and Chinese reading "Ku P'ing" at 3 and 9 o'clock, inscription: Kuang-hsü Yüan-pao

| Date | Mintage | F | VF | XF | Unc | BU |
|---|---|---|---|---|---|---|
| ND(c. 1902) | — | 3.00 | 6.00 | 12.00 | 25.00 | — |

**10 CASH** **Y# 150.2** **Composition:** Copper **Ruler:** Kuang-hsü **Obverse:** Manchu "Pao Ch'ang" at 3 and 9 o'clock, horizontal rosette in center, inscription: Kuang-hsü Yüan-pao

| Date | Mintage | F | VF | XF | Unc | BU |
|---|---|---|---|---|---|---|
| ND(c. 1902) | — | 1.00 | 2.00 | 5.00 | 20.00 | — |

**10 CASH** **Y# 150.2a** **Composition:** Brass **Ruler:** Kuang-hsü **Obverse:** Inscription: Kuang-hsü Yüan-pao

| Date | Mintage | F | VF | XF | Unc | BU |
|---|---|---|---|---|---|---|
| ND(c. 1902) | — | 5.00 | 10.00 | 20.00 | 40.00 | — |

**10 CASH** **Y# 150.3** **Composition:** Copper **Ruler:** Kuang-hsü **Obverse:** Vertical rosette in center, inscription: Kuang-hsü Yüan-pao

| Date | Mintage | F | VF | XF | Unc | BU |
|---|---|---|---|---|---|---|
| ND(c. 1902) | — | 1.00 | 2.00 | 5.00 | 20.00 | — |

**10 CASH** **Y# 150.4** **Composition:** Copper **Ruler:** Kuang-hsü **Obverse:** Horizontal rosette, inscription: Kuang-hsü Yüan-pao **Reverse:** 1 star at either side of dragon, large English lettering

| Date | Mintage | F | VF | XF | Unc | BU |
|---|---|---|---|---|---|---|
| ND(c. 1902) | — | 1.00 | 2.00 | 5.00 | 20.00 | — |

**10 CASH** **Y# 150.4a** **Composition:** Brass **Ruler:** Kuang-hsü **Obverse:** Horizontal rosette, inscription: Kuang-hsü Yüan-pao **Reverse:** 1 star at either side of dragon, large English lettering

| Date | Mintage | F | VF | XF | Unc | BU |
|---|---|---|---|---|---|---|
| ND(c. 1902) | — | 5.00 | 9.00 | 17.50 | 35.00 | — |

**10 CASH** **Y# 150.5** **Composition:** Copper **Ruler:** Kuang-hsü **Obverse:** Vertical rosette, inscription: Kuang-hsü Yüan-pao

| Date | Mintage | F | VF | XF | Unc | BU |
|---|---|---|---|---|---|---|
| ND(c. 1902) | — | 1.00 | 2.00 | 5.00 | 20.00 | — |

**10 CASH** **Y# 150.6** **Composition:** Copper **Ruler:** Kuang-hsü **Obverse:** Inscription: Kuang-hsü Yüan-pao **Reverse:** Smaller English lettering, 1 star at either side of dragon

| Date | Mintage | F | VF | XF | Unc | BU |
|---|---|---|---|---|---|---|
| ND(c. 1902) | — | 1.00 | 2.00 | 5.00 | 20.00 | — |

**10 CASH** **Y# 150.7** **Composition:** Copper **Ruler:** Kuang-hsü **Obverse:** Small rosette center, inscription: Kuang-hsü Yüan-pao **Reverse:** 1 star at either side of dragon

| Date | Mintage | F | VF | XF | Unc | BU |
|---|---|---|---|---|---|---|
| ND(c. 1902) | — | 6.00 | 11.00 | 17.50 | 35.00 | — |

**10 CASH** **Y# 150.8** **Composition:** Copper **Ruler:** Kuang-hsü **Obverse:** Inscription: Kuang-hsü Yüan-pao **Reverse:** 3 stars at either side of dragon

| Date | Mintage | F | VF | XF | Unc | BU |
|---|---|---|---|---|---|---|
| ND(c. 1902) | — | 12.50 | 20.00 | 30.00 | 60.00 | — |

**10 CASH** **Y# 152** **Composition:** Copper **Ruler:** Kuang-hsü **Obverse:** Manchu "Pao Ch'ang" at 3 and 9 o'clock, inscription: Kuang-hsü Yüan-pao **Reverse:** Province name spelled KIANG-SI, front view dragon, mountain below pearl

| Date | Mintage | VG | F | VF | XF | Unc |
|---|---|---|---|---|---|---|
| ND(c. 1902) | — | 2.50 | 4.00 | 6.00 | 12.00 | — |

**10 CASH** **Y# 152.1** **Composition:** Copper **Ruler:** Kuang-hsü **Obverse:** Horizontal rosette in center, Manchu "Pao Ch'ang" at 3 and 9 o'clock, inscription: Kuang-hsü Yüan-pao

| Date | Mintage | VG | F | VF | XF | Unc |
|---|---|---|---|---|---|---|
| ND(c. 1902) | — | 2.50 | 4.00 | 6.00 | 12.00 | — |

**10 CASH** **Y# 152.2** **Composition:** Copper **Ruler:** Kuang-hsü **Obverse:** Horizontal rosette in center, Manchu "Pao Ch'ang" at 3 and 9 o'clock, small character "10," inscription: Kuang-hsü Yüan-pao

| Date | Mintage | VG | F | VF | XF | Unc |
|---|---|---|---|---|---|---|
| ND(c. 1902) | — | 5.00 | 12.00 | 17.50 | 27.50 | — |

**10 CASH** **Y# 152.3** **Composition:** Copper **Ruler:** Kuang-hsü **Obverse:** Horizontal rosette in center, Manchu "Pao Ch'ang" at 3 and 9 o'clock, large character "10," inscription: Kuang-hsü Yüan-pao **Reverse:** Without mountain below dragon

| Date | Mintage | VG | F | VF | XF | Unc |
|---|---|---|---|---|---|---|
| ND(c. 1902) | — | 3.50 | 8.00 | 12.00 | 17.50 | — |

**10 CASH** **Y# 152.7** **Composition:** Copper **Ruler:** Kuang-hsü **Obverse:** Vertical rosette in center, inscription: Kuang-hsü Yüan-pao

| Date | Mintage | VG | F | VF | XF | Unc |
|---|---|---|---|---|---|---|
| ND(c. 1902) | — | — | — | — | — | — |

**10 CASH** **Y# 152.4** **Composition:** Copper **Ruler:** Kuang-hsü **Obverse:** Horizontal rosette in center, small character "10," inscription: Kuang-hsü Yüan-pao

| Date | Mintage | VG | F | VF | XF | Unc |
|---|---|---|---|---|---|---|
| ND(c. 1902) | — | 3.50 | 8.00 | 12.00 | 17.50 | — |

**10 CASH** **Y# 152.5** **Composition:** Copper **Ruler:** Kuang-hsü **Obverse:** Manchu "Pao Ch'ang" in center, Chinese "K'u P'ing" at 3 and 9 o'clock, inscription: Kuang-hsü Yüan-pao **Reverse:** Without mountain below pearl, dragon's body repositioned

| Date | Mintage | VG | F | VF | XF | Unc |
|---|---|---|---|---|---|---|
| ND(c. 1902) | — | 3.50 | 8.50 | 12.50 | 17.50 | — |

**10 CASH** **Y# 152.6** **Composition:** Copper **Ruler:** Kuang-hsü **Obverse:** Inscription: Kuang-hsü Yüan-pao **Reverse:** Mountain below dragon

| Date | Mintage | VG | F | VF | XF | Unc |
|---|---|---|---|---|---|---|
| ND(c. 1902) | — | 3.25 | 7.50 | 11.00 | 16.00 | — |

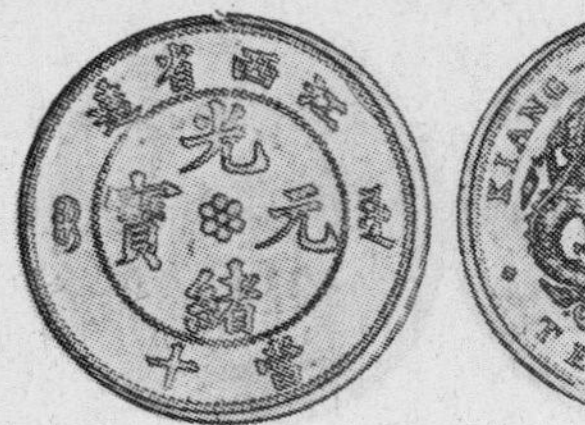


**10 CASH** **Y# 153** **Composition:** Copper **Ruler:** Kuang-hsü **Obverse:** Inscription: Kuang-hsü Yüan-pao **Reverse:** Legend above front view dragon **Rev. Legend:** KIANG-SEE PROVINCE **Note:** Found with and without a swirl on the pearl below dragon's mouth.

| Date | Mintage | VG | F | VF | XF | Unc |
|---|---|---|---|---|---|---|
| ND(c. 1902) | — | 2.00 | 4.50 | 7.00 | 11.00 | — |

**10 CASH** **Y# 153.1** **Composition:** Copper **Ruler:** Kuang-hsü **Obverse:** Manchu "Pao Ch'ang" at center and Chinese "K'u P'ing" at 3 and 9 o'clock, inscription: Kuang-hsü Yüan-pao **Note:** Found with and without a swirl on the pearl below dragon's mouth.

| Date | Mintage | VG | F | VF | XF | Unc |
|---|---|---|---|---|---|---|
| ND(c. 1902) | — | 0.80 | 2.00 | 3.50 | 7.00 | — |

**10 CASH** **Y# 153.2** **Composition:** Copper **Ruler:** Kuang-hsü **Obverse:** Small Manchu "Pao Ch'ang" at 3 and 9 o'clock, small horizontal rosette in center, inscription: Kuang-hsü Yüan-pao **Note:** Found with and without a swirl on the pearl below dragon's mouth.

| Date | Mintage | VG | F | VF | XF | Unc |
|---|---|---|---|---|---|---|
| ND(c. 1902) | — | 0.80 | 2.00 | 3.50 | 7.00 | — |

**10 CASH** **Y# 153.3** **Composition:** Copper **Ruler:** Kuang-hsü **Obverse:** Small vertical rosette in center, inscription: Kuang-hsü Yüan-pao **Note:** Found with and without a swirl on the pearl below dragon's mouth.

| Date | Mintage | VG | F | VF | XF | Unc |
|---|---|---|---|---|---|---|
| ND(c. 1902) | — | 2.00 | 5.00 | 10.00 | 17.50 | — |

**10 CASH** **Y# 154** **Composition:** Copper **Ruler:** Kuang-hsü **Obverse:** Inscription: Kuang-hsü Yüan-pao **Reverse:** Legend above flying dragon **Rev. Legend:** KIANG SI

| Date | Mintage | VG | F | VF | XF | Unc |
|---|---|---|---|---|---|---|
| ND(c. 1902) | — | 40.00 | 60.00 | 80.00 | 100 | — |

**10 CASH** **Y# 10m** **Composition:** Copper **Ruler:** Kuang-hsü **Obverse:** Inscription: Tai-ch'ing T'ung-pi **Reverse:** Dragon's eyes in relief **Rev. Legend:** Kuang-hsü Nien-tsao, TAI-CHING-TI-KUO ...

| Date | Mintage | VG | F | VF | XF | Unc |
|---|---|---|---|---|---|---|
| CD(1906) | — | 1.25 | 3.00 | 6.00 | 12.00 | — |

**10 CASH** **Y# 10m.1** **Composition:** Copper **Ruler:** Kuang-hsü **Obverse:** Inscription: Tai-ch'ing T'ung-pi **Reverse:** Dragon's eyes incuse **Rev. Legend:** Kuang-hsü Nien-tsao, TAI-CHING-TI-KUO ...

| Date | Mintage | VG | F | VF | XF | Unc |
|---|---|---|---|---|---|---|
| CD(1906) | — | 1.25 | 3.00 | 6.00 | 12.00 | — |

**10 CASH** **Y# 10m.2** **Composition:** Copper **Ruler:** Kuang-hsü **Obverse:** Inscription: Tai-ch'ing T'ung-pi **Reverse:** Dragon redesigned, small faint cloud beneath pearl **Rev. Legend:** Kuang-hsü Nien-tsao, TAI-CHING-TI-KUO ...

| Date | Mintage | VG | F | VF | XF | Unc |
|---|---|---|---|---|---|---|
| CD(1906) | — | 5.00 | 12.00 | 17.50 | 30.00 | — |

# REPUBLIC

## MILLED COINAGE

**10 CASH** **Y# 412** **Composition:** Copper **Obverse:** Date appears at 3 and 9 o'clock **Obv. Legend:** Chiang-hsi Sheng-tsao **Reverse:** 9-pointed star inside circle and 5-petalled rosette at 3 and 9 o'clock

| Date | Mintage | VG | F | VF | XF | Unc |
|---|---|---|---|---|---|---|
| CD(1911) | — | 200 | 300 | 450 | 650 | — |

**10 CASH** **Y# 412a** **Composition:** Copper **Obverse:** Horizontal rosette in center with Chinese characters "Chiang Hsi" above and below **Reverse:** 6-petalled rosette at either side

| Date | Mintage | VG | F | VF | XF | Unc |
|---|---|---|---|---|---|---|
| CD1912 | — | 1.25 | 3.00 | 5.00 | 9.00 | — |

**10 CASH** **Y# 412a.1** **Composition:** Copper **Obverse:** Small, vertical rosette in center

| Date | Mintage | VG | F | VF | XF | Unc |
|---|---|---|---|---|---|---|
| CD1912 | — | 1.25 | 3.00 | 5.00 | 9.00 | — |

**10 CASH** **Y# 412a.2** **Composition:** Copper **Obverse:** Large, vertical rosette in center; thick, large-center characters **Reverse:** Small, 5-petalled rosettes at either side

| Date | Mintage | VG | F | VF | XF | Unc |
|---|---|---|---|---|---|---|
| CD(1912) | — | 6.00 | 12.00 | 17.50 | 27.50 | — |

**10 CASH** **Y# 412a.3** **Composition:** Copper **Obverse:** Large, vertical rosette in center; thin-center characters

| Date | Mintage | VG | F | VF | XF | Unc |
|---|---|---|---|---|---|---|
| CD(1912) | — | 1.25 | 3.00 | 5.00 | 10.00 | — |

## REBEL COINAGE

"Ta Han" was a rebel issue made before the revolution. Not only a symbol of defiance, this coin indicated secret membership. Ching law subjected those carrying these coins to execution.

**10 CASH** **Y# 411** **Composition:** Copper **Obverse:** Mint mark incused on raised-disc center with Chinese characters on 4 sides, "Ta-Han T'ung-pi" character value in outer ring at bottom **Reverse:** Ring of 9 balls without inscription

| Date | Mintage | VG | F | VF | XF | Unc |
|---|---|---|---|---|---|---|
| CD(1911) Rare | — | — | — | — | — | — |

# KIANGSU-KIANGSOO PROVINCE

**Jiangsu**

A province located on the east coast of China. One of the smallest and most densely populated of all Chinese provinces. A mint opened in Soochow in 1667, but closed shortly after in 1670. A new mint opened in 1734 for producing cast coins and had continuous operation until about 1870. Modern equipment was introduced in 1898 and a second mint was opened in 1904. Both mints closed down production in 1906. Taels were produced in Shanghai by local silversmiths as early as 1856. These saw limited circulation in the immediate area.

# EMPIRE

## PROVINCIAL CAST COINAGE

**CASH C# 16-12 Composition:** Cast Brass **Ruler:** Kuang-hsü **Obverse:** Inscription: Kuang-hsü T'ung-pao **Reverse:** Inscription: Manchu Boo-su **Note:** Struck at Su (Soochow).

| Date | Mintage | Good | VG | F | VF | XF |
|---|---|---|---|---|---|---|
| ND(1875-1908) | — | 2.25 | 4.50 | 8.00 | 13.00 | — |

**CASH C# 16-12.1 Composition:** Cast Brass **Ruler:** Kuang-hsü **Obverse:** Inscription: Kuang-hsü T'ung-pao **Reverse:** Circle above, inscription: Manchu Boo-su **Note:** Struck at Su (Soochow).

| Date | Mintage | Good | VG | F | VF | XF |
|---|---|---|---|---|---|---|
| ND(1875-1908) | — | 3.00 | 6.00 | 10.00 | 16.00 | — |

**CASH C# 16-12.2 Composition:** Cast Brass **Ruler:** Kuang-hsü **Obverse:** Inscription: Kuang-hsü T'ung-pao **Reverse:** Crescent above, inscription: Manchu Boo-su **Note:** Struck at Su (Soochow).

| Date | Mintage | Good | VG | F | VF | XF |
|---|---|---|---|---|---|---|
| ND(1875-1908) | — | 3.00 | 6.00 | 10.00 | 16.00 | — |

## MILLED COINAGE

**5 CASH Y# 158 Composition:** Copper **Ruler:** Kuang-hsü **Obverse:** Inscription: Kuang-hsü Yüan-pao **Reverse:** Side view dragon, EIVE for FIVE

| Date | Mintage | F | VF | XF | Unc | BU |
|---|---|---|---|---|---|---|
| ND(1901) | — | 32.50 | 55.00 | 100 | — | — |

**5 CASH Y# 9n Composition:** Brass **Ruler:** Kuang-hsü **Obverse:** Inscription: Tai-ching T'ung-pi **Rev. Legend:** Kuang-hsü Nien-tasao, TAI-CHING-TI-KUO ...

| Date | Mintage | F | VF | XF | Unc | BU |
|---|---|---|---|---|---|---|
| CD(1906) | — | 75.00 | 125 | 200 | — | — |

**10 CASH Y# 162 Composition:** Brass **Ruler:** Kuang-hsü **Obverse:** Manchu words at center, without rosettes, inscription: Kuang-hsü Yüan-pao **Edge:** Reeded

| Date | Mintage | F | VF | XF | Unc | BU |
|---|---|---|---|---|---|---|
| ND(c. 1902) | — | 3.75 | 6.00 | 12.00 | 32.00 | — |

**10 CASH Y# 162.1 Composition:** Brass **Ruler:** Kuang-hsü **Obverse:** Manchu in center, rosettes at 2 and 10 o'clock, inscription: Kuang-hsü Yüan-pao

| Date | Mintage | F | VF | XF | Unc | BU |
|---|---|---|---|---|---|---|
| ND(c. 1902) | — | 1.00 | 2.00 | 5.00 | 20.00 | — |

**10 CASH Y# 162.2 Composition:** Brass **Ruler:** Kuang-hsü **Obverse:** Inscription: Kuang-hsü Yüan-pao **Edge:** Plain

| Date | Mintage | F | VF | XF | Unc | BU |
|---|---|---|---|---|---|---|
| ND(c. 1902) | — | 1.00 | 2.00 | 5.00 | 20.00 | — |

**10 CASH Y# 162.3 Composition:** Brass **Ruler:** Kuang-hsü **Obverse:** Tiny rosettes, inscription: Kuang-hsü Yüan-pao **Reverse:** Tiny rosettes **Edge:** Reeded

| Date | Mintage | F | VF | XF | Unc | BU |
|---|---|---|---|---|---|---|
| ND(c. 1902) | — | 1.25 | 2.50 | 5.00 | 20.00 | — |

**10 CASH Y# 162.4 Composition:** Brass **Ruler:** Kuang-hsü **Obverse:** Rosette center, Manchu at 3 and 9 o'clock, inscription: Kuang-hsü Yüan-pao

| Date | Mintage | F | VF | XF | Unc | BU |
|---|---|---|---|---|---|---|
| ND(c. 1902) | — | 1.00 | 2.00 | 5.00 | 20.00 | — |

**10 CASH Y# 162.5 Composition:** Brass **Ruler:** Kuang-hsü **Obverse:** Inscription: Kuang-hsü Yüan-pao **Edge:** Plain

| Date | Mintage | F | VF | XF | Unc | BU |
|---|---|---|---|---|---|---|
| ND(c. 1902) | — | 1.00 | 2.00 | 5.00 | 20.00 | — |

**10 CASH Y# 162.6 Composition:** Brass **Ruler:** Kuang-hsü **Obverse:** Rosette center, large Manchu at 3 and 9 o'clock, higher than on Y#162.4, inscription: Kuang-hsü Yüan-pao **Edge:** Reeded

| Date | Mintage | F | VF | XF | Unc | BU |
|---|---|---|---|---|---|---|
| ND(c. 1902) | — | 1.50 | 2.50 | 5.00 | 20.00 | — |

**10 CASH Y# 162.7 Composition:** Copper **Ruler:** Kuang-hsü **Obverse:** Inscription: Kuang-hsü Yüan-pao **Edge:** Plain

| Date | Mintage | F | VF | XF | Unc | BU |
|---|---|---|---|---|---|---|
| ND(c. 1902) | — | 1.50 | 2.50 | 5.00 | 25.00 | — |

**10 CASH Y# 162.7a Composition:** Brass **Ruler:** Kuang-hsü **Obverse:** Inscription: Kuang-hsü Yüan-pao

| Date | Mintage | F | VF | XF | Unc | BU |
|---|---|---|---|---|---|---|
| ND(c. 1902) Rare | — | — | — | — | — | — |

**10 CASH Y# 162.8 Composition:** Copper **Ruler:** Kuang-hsü **Obverse:** Manchu "Boo-su" at center, inscription: Kuang-hsü Yüan-pao **Edge:** Reeded

| Date | Mintage | F | VF | XF | Unc | BU |
|---|---|---|---|---|---|---|
| CD(1902) | — | 2.00 | 4.00 | 7.50 | 25.00 | — |

**10 CASH Y# 162.13 Composition:** Copper **Ruler:** Kuang-hsü **Obverse:** Inscription: Kuang-hsü Yüan-pao **Edge:** Plain

| Date | Mintage | F | VF | XF | Unc | BU |
|---|---|---|---|---|---|---|
| CD(1902) | — | — | — | — | — | — |

**10 CASH Y# B162 Composition:** Copper **Ruler:** Kuang-hsü **Obverse:** Kiangsu Y#162.8, inscription: Kuang-hsü Yüan-pao **Reverse:** Kiangnan Y#135 **Note:** Mule.

| Date | Mintage | F | VF | XF | Unc | BU |
|---|---|---|---|---|---|---|
| CD(1902) | — | 90.00 | 150 | 250 | — | — |

**10 CASH Y# 162.9 Composition:** Copper **Ruler:** Kuang-hsü **Obverse:** Manchu "Boo-su" at center, inscription: Kuang-hsü Yüan-pao **Edge:** Reeded

| Date | Mintage | F | VF | XF | Unc | BU |
|---|---|---|---|---|---|---|
| CD(1903) | — | 5.00 | 7.50 | 12.00 | 32.00 | — |

**10 CASH Y# C162 Composition:** Copper **Ruler:** Kuang-hsü **Obverse:** Kiangsu Y#162.9, inscription: Kuang-hsü Yüan-pao **Reverse:** Kiangnan Y#135 **Note:** Mule.

| Date | Mintage | F | VF | XF | Unc | BU |
|---|---|---|---|---|---|---|
| CD(1903) | — | 90.00 | 150 | 250 | — | — |

**10 CASH Y# 160 Composition:** Brass **Ruler:** Kuang-hsü **Obverse:** Inscription: Kuang-hsü Yüan-pao **Reverse:** Cloud below all 3 letters of SOO

| Date | Mintage | F | VF | XF | Unc | BU |
|---|---|---|---|---|---|---|
| ND(1904-1905) | — | 2.50 | 4.00 | 8.00 | 24.00 | — |

**10 CASH Y# 160.1 Composition:** Brass **Ruler:** Kuang-hsü **Obverse:** Inscription: Kuang-hsü Yüan-pao **Reverse:** Cloud below first 2 letters of SOO, Manchu "Boo" at 9 o'clock higher, dragon's body thinner

| Date | Mintage | F | VF | XF | Unc | BU |
|---|---|---|---|---|---|---|
| (1904-1905) | — | 2.50 | 4.00 | 8.00 | 24.00 | — |

**10 CASH Y# 162.10 Composition:** Copper **Ruler:** Kuang-hsü **Obverse:** Rosette center, small Manchu "Boo-su" at 3 and 9 o'clock, inscription: Kuang-hsü Yüan-pao **Edge:** Plain

| Date | Mintage | F | VF | XF | Unc | BU |
|---|---|---|---|---|---|---|
| CD(1905) | — | 1.00 | 2.00 | 5.00 | 20.00 | — |

**10 CASH Y# 162.11 Composition:** Copper **Ruler:** Kuang-hsü **Obverse:** Larger Manchu "Boo-su", inscription: Kuang-hsü Yüan-pao

| Date | Mintage | F | VF | XF | Unc | BU |
|---|---|---|---|---|---|---|
| CD(1905) | — | 2.50 | 5.00 | 8.00 | 25.00 | — |

**10 CASH** **Y# 162.12** **Composition:** Copper **Ruler:** Kuang-hsü **Obverse:** Inscription: Kuang-hsü Yüan-pao **Reverse:** Kiang-su spelled KIANG-COO **Note:** Considered a contemporary counterfiet by some authorities.

| Date | Mintage | F | VF | XF | Unc | BU |
|---|---|---|---|---|---|---|
| CD(1905) | — | 250 | 500 | 750 | — | — |

**10 CASH** **Y# A162** **Composition:** Copper **Ruler:** Kuang-hsü **Obverse:** Kiangsu Y#162, inscription: Kuang-hsü Yüan-pao **Reverse:** Kiangnan Y#135 **Note:** Mule.

| Date | Mintage | F | VF | XF | Unc | BU |
|---|---|---|---|---|---|---|
| ND(c.1905) | — | 90.00 | 150 | 250 | — | — |

**10 CASH** **Y# 10n** **Composition:** Copper **Ruler:** Kuang-hsü **Obverse:** Mint mark incused on raised disc, inscription: Tai-ch'ing T'ung-pi **Rev. Legend:** Kuang-hsü Nien-tsao, TAI-CHING-TI-KUO ... **Edge:** Plain

| Date | Mintage | F | VF | XF | Unc | BU |
|---|---|---|---|---|---|---|
| CD(1906) | — | 2.50 | 5.00 | 10.00 | 30.00 | — |

**10 CASH** **Y# 10n.1** **Composition:** Copper **Ruler:** Kuang-hsü **Obverse:** Mint mark incused on raised disc, inscription: Tai-ch'ing T'ung-pi **Rev. Legend:** Kuang-hsü Nien-tsao, TAI-CHING-TI-KUO ... **Edge:** Reeded

| Date | Mintage | F | VF | XF | Unc | BU |
|---|---|---|---|---|---|---|
| CD(1906) | — | 6.00 | 11.00 | 17.50 | 40.00 | — |

**10 CASH** **Y# 10n.2** **Composition:** Copper **Ruler:** Kuang-hsü **Obverse:** Mint mark in relief in field at center without raised disc, inscription: Tai-ch'ing T'ung-pi **Rev. Legend:** Kuang-hsü Nien-tsao, TAI-CHING-TI-KUO ... **Edge:** Plain

| Date | Mintage | F | VF | XF | Unc | BU |
|---|---|---|---|---|---|---|
| CD(1906) | — | 6.00 | 11.00 | 17.50 | 40.00 | — |

**20 CASH** **Y# 163** **Composition:** Copper **Ruler:** Kuang-hsü **Obverse:** Inscription: Kuang-hsü Yüan-pao **Reverse:** Dragon

| Date | Mintage | VG | F | VF | XF | Unc |
|---|---|---|---|---|---|---|
| ND(c. 1902) | — | 17.50 | 32.50 | 45.00 | 65.00 | — |

**20 CASH** **Y# 163a** **Composition:** Brass **Ruler:** Kuang-hsü **Obverse:** Inscription: Kuang-hsü Yüan-pao **Reverse:** Dragon

| Date | Mintage | VG | F | VF | XF | Unc |
|---|---|---|---|---|---|---|
| ND(c. 1902) | — | 30.00 | 45.00 | 70.00 | 110 | — |

**20 CASH** **Y# 11n.1** **Composition:** Copper **Ruler:** Kuang-hsü **Obverse:** Inscription: Tai-ch'ing T'ung-pi **Rev. Legend:** Kuang-hsü Nien-tsao, TAI-CHING-TI-KUO ...

| Date | Mintage | VG | F | VF | XF | Unc |
|---|---|---|---|---|---|---|
| CD(1906) | — | 25.00 | 40.00 | 60.00 | 90.00 | — |

**20 CASH** **Y# 11n.1a** **Composition:** Brass **Ruler:** Kuang-hsü **Obverse:** Inscription: Tai-ch'ing T'ung-pi **Rev. Legend:** Kuang-hsü Nien-tsao, TAI-CHING-TI-KUO ...

| Date | Mintage | VG | F | VF | XF | Unc |
|---|---|---|---|---|---|---|
| CD(1906) | — | 35.00 | 60.00 | 90.00 | 150 | — |

## MILLED COINAGE

### Chingkiang Series

**10 CASH** **Y# 77** **Composition:** Copper **Ruler:** Kuang-hsü **Obverse:** Large character at 3 o'clock, inscription: Kuang-hsü Yüan-pao **Edge:** Reeded **Note:** Struck at Chingkiang.

| Date | Mintage | F | VF | XF | Unc | BU |
|---|---|---|---|---|---|---|
| ND(1905) | — | 2.50 | 4.00 | 7.50 | 25.00 | — |

**10 CASH** **Y# 77.1** **Composition:** Copper **Ruler:** Kuang-hsü **Obverse:** Large character at 3 o'clock, inscription: Kuang-hsü Yüan-pao **Edge:** Plain **Note:** Struck at Chingkiang.

| Date | Mintage | F | VF | XF | Unc | BU |
|---|---|---|---|---|---|---|
| ND(1905) | — | 2.50 | 4.00 | 7.50 | 25.00 | — |

**10 CASH** **Y# 77.2** **Composition:** Copper **Ruler:** Kuang-hsü **Obverse:** Ring around center dot in rosette, inscription: Kuang-hsü Yüan-pao **Edge:** Reeded **Note:** Struck at Chingkiang.

| Date | Mintage | F | VF | XF | Unc | BU |
|---|---|---|---|---|---|---|
| ND(1905) | — | 3.00 | 5.00 | 10.00 | 30.00 | — |

**10 CASH** **Y# 77.3** **Composition:** Copper **Ruler:** Kuang-hsü **Obverse:** Ring around center dot in rosette, inscription: Kuang-hsü Yüan-pao **Edge:** Plain **Note:** Struck at Chingkiang.

| Date | Mintage | F | VF | XF | Unc | BU |
|---|---|---|---|---|---|---|
| ND(1905) | — | 9.00 | 12.00 | 15.00 | 35.00 | — |

**10 CASH** **Y# 77.4** **Composition:** Copper **Ruler:** Kuang-hsü **Obverse:** Smaller character at 3 o'clock, inscription: Kuang-hsü Yüan-pao **Edge:** Reeded **Note:** Struck at Chingkiang.

| Date | Mintage | F | VF | XF | Unc | BU |
|---|---|---|---|---|---|---|
| ND(1905) | — | 3.50 | 6.00 | 12.00 | 32.00 | — |

**10 CASH** **Y# 77.5** **Composition:** Copper **Ruler:** Kuang-hsü **Obverse:** Smaller character at 3 o'clock, inscription: Kuang-hsü Yüan-pao **Edge:** Plain **Note:** Struck at Chingkiang.

| Date | Mintage | F | VF | XF | Unc | BU |
|---|---|---|---|---|---|---|
| ND(1905) | — | 3.50 | 6.00 | 12.00 | 32.00 | — |

**10 CASH** **Y# 77.6** **Composition:** Copper **Ruler:** Kuang-hsü **Obverse:** Without rosette, inscription: Kuang-hsü Yüan-pao **Edge:** Reeded **Note:** Struck at Chingkiang.

| Date | Mintage | F | VF | XF | Unc | BU |
|---|---|---|---|---|---|---|
| ND(1905) | — | 3.00 | 5.00 | 10.00 | 30.00 | — |

**10 CASH** **Y# 77.7** **Composition:** Copper **Ruler:** Kuang-hsü **Obverse:** Without rosette, inscription: Kuang-hsü Yüan-pao **Edge:** Plain **Note:** Struck at Chingkiang.

| Date | Mintage | F | VF | XF | Unc | BU |
|---|---|---|---|---|---|---|
| ND(1905) | — | 8.00 | 10.00 | 15.00 | 35.00 | — |

**10 CASH** **Y# 78** **Composition:** Copper **Ruler:** Kuang-hsü **Obverse:** Large character at 3 o'clock, inscription: Kuang-hsü Yüan-pao **Edge:** Reeded **Note:** Struck at Chingkiang.

| Date | Mintage | F | VF | XF | Unc | BU |
|---|---|---|---|---|---|---|
| ND(1905) | — | 1.50 | 3.00 | 5.00 | 20.00 | — |

**10 CASH** **Y# 78.1** **Composition:** Copper **Ruler:** Kuang-hsü **Obverse:** Large character at 3 o'clock, inscription: Kuang-hsü Yüan-pao **Edge:** Plain **Note:** Struck at Chingkiang.

| Date | Mintage | F | VF | XF | Unc | BU |
|---|---|---|---|---|---|---|
| ND(1905) | — | 3.00 | 5.00 | 10.00 | 30.00 | — |

**10 CASH** **Y# 78.2** **Composition:** Copper **Ruler:** Kuang-hsü **Obverse:** Small character at 3 o'clock, inscription: Kuang-hsü Yüan-pao **Edge:** Reeded **Note:** Struck at Chingkiang.

| Date | Mintage | F | VF | XF | Unc | BU |
|---|---|---|---|---|---|---|
| ND(1905) | — | 1.00 | 2.00 | 5.00 | 20.00 | — |

**10 CASH** **Y# 78.3** **Composition:** Copper **Ruler:** Kuang-hsü **Obverse:** Small character at 3 o'clock, inscription: Kuang-hsü Yüan-pao **Edge:** Plain **Note:** Struck at Chingkiang.

| Date | Mintage | F | VF | XF | Unc | BU |
|---|---|---|---|---|---|---|
| ND(1905) | — | 1.00 | 2.00 | 5.00 | 20.00 | — |

**10 CASH** **Y# 78.4** **Composition:** Copper **Ruler:** Kuang-hsü **Obverse:** Without rosette, inscription: Kuang-hsü Yüan-pao **Edge:** Reeded **Note:** Struck at Chingkiang.

| Date | Mintage | F | VF | XF | Unc | BU |
|---|---|---|---|---|---|---|
| ND(1905) | — | 3.50 | 6.00 | 15.00 | 35.00 | — |

**10 CASH** **Y# 10d** **Composition:** Copper **Ruler:** Kuang-hsü **Obverse:** Small mint mark in center, without center raised disc Inscription: Tai-ch'ing T-ung-pi **Reverse:** 5 flames on pearl **Rev. Legend:** Kuang-hsü Nien-tsao, TAI-CHING-TI-KUO ... **Note:** Struck at Chingkiang.

| Date | Mintage | F | VF | XF | Unc | BU |
|---|---|---|---|---|---|---|
| CD(1906) | — | 25.00 | 50.00 | 100 | — | — |

**10 CASH** **Y# 10d.1** **Composition:** Copper **Ruler:** Kuang-hsü **Obverse:** Small mint mark, inscription: Tai-ch'ing T-ung-pi **Reverse:** 7 flames on pearl **Rev. Legend:** Kuang-hsü Nien-tsao, TAI-CHING-TI-KUO ... **Note:** Struck at Chingkiang.

| Date | Mintage | F | VF | XF | Unc | BU |
|---|---|---|---|---|---|---|
| CD(1906) | — | 1.50 | 2.50 | 5.00 | 20.00 | — |

**10 CASH** **Y# 10d.2** **Composition:** Copper **Ruler:** Kuang-hsü **Obverse:** Inscription: Tai-ch'ing T-ung-pi **Reverse:** 9 flames on pearl **Rev. Legend:** Kuang-hsü Nien-tsao, TAI-CHING-TI-KUO ... **Note:** Struck at Chingkiang.

| Date | Mintage | F | VF | XF | Unc | BU |
|---|---|---|---|---|---|---|
| CD(1906) | — | 1.00 | 2.00 | 5.00 | 20.00 | — |

**10 CASH Y# 10d.3 Composition:** Copper **Ruler:** Kuang-hsü **Obverse:** Large mint mark, inscription: Tai-ch'ing T-ung-pi **Reverse:** 5 flames on pearl **Rev. Legend:** Kuang-hsü Nien-tsao, TAI-CHING-TI-KUO ... **Note:** Struck at Chingkiang.

| Date | Mintage | F | VF | XF | Unc | BU |
|---|---|---|---|---|---|---|
| CD(1906) | — | 1.50 | 2.50 | 5.00 | 20.00 | — |

**10 CASH Y# 10d.4 Composition:** Copper **Ruler:** Kuang-hsü **Obverse:** Inscription: Tai-ch'ing T-ung-pi **Reverse:** 7 flames on pearl **Rev. Legend:** Kuang-hsü Nien-tsao, TAI-CHING-TI-KUO ... **Note:** Struck at Chingkiang.

| Date | Mintage | F | VF | XF | Unc | BU |
|---|---|---|---|---|---|---|
| CD(1906) | — | 1.50 | 2.50 | 5.00 | 20.00 | — |

**10 CASH Y# 10d.5 Composition:** Copper **Ruler:** Kuang-hsü **Obverse:** Inscription: Tai-ch'ing T-ung-pi **Reverse:** 9 flames on pearl **Rev. Legend:** Kuang-hsü Nien-tsao, TAI-CHING-TI-KUO ... **Note:** Struck at Chingkiang.

| Date | Mintage | F | VF | XF | Unc | BU |
|---|---|---|---|---|---|---|
| CD(1906) | — | 1.50 | 2.50 | 5.00 | 20.00 | — |

**10 CASH Y# 10d.6 Composition:** Copper **Ruler:** Kuang-hsü **Obverse:** Mint mark incused on raised disc, inscription: Tai-ch'ing T-ung-pi **Rev. Legend:** Kuang-hsü Nien-tsao, TAI-CH-ING-TI-KUO ... **Note:** Struck at Chingkiang. Trial piece.

| Date | Mintage | F | VF | XF | Unc | BU |
|---|---|---|---|---|---|---|
| CD(1906) | — | — | — | — | — | — |

**Note:** 10 Cash coins of Kiangsu (Jiangsu) and Chingkiang are often found plated with a silvery material. This was not done at the mint. Apparently they were plated so they could be passed to the unwary as silver coins.

## PATTERNS

Including off metal strikes

| KM# | Date | Mintage | Identification | Mkt Val |
|---|---|---|---|---|
| Pn2 | (c. 1901) | — | 2 Cash. Brass. Y159. | 200 |
| Pn3 | (1906) | — | 2 Cash. Brass. Y8n. | 200 |
| Pn4 | (c. 1906) | — | 5 Cash. Brass. EIVE for FIVE. Y161.1. | 300 |

| KM# | Date | Mintage | Identification | Mkt Val |
|---|---|---|---|---|
| Pn6 | (c. 1906) | — | 10 Cash. White copper. Y162.5, W826. | — |
| Pn7 | (1906) | — | 20 Cash. Copper. Character "Huai" in center. Y11d. | — |
| Pn5 | (c. 1906) | — | 5 Cash. Copper. EIVE for FIVE. Y161.1a. | 300 |

## KIRIN PROVINCE

**Jilin**

A province of northeast China that was formed in 1945. Before that it was one of the three original provinces of Manchuria. Besides growing corn, wheat and tobacco, there is also coal mining. An arsenal in Kirin (Jilin) opened in 1881 and was chosen as a source for coinage attempts. In 1884 Tael trials were struck and regular coinage began in 1895. Modern equipment was installed in a new mint in Kirin (Jilin) in 1901. The issues of this mint were very prolific and many varieties exist due to the use of hand cut dies for the earlier issues. The mint burned down in 1911.

## EMPIRE

### PROVINCIAL CAST COINAGE

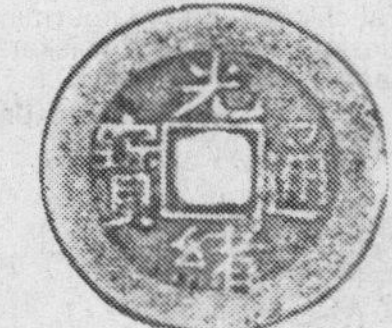

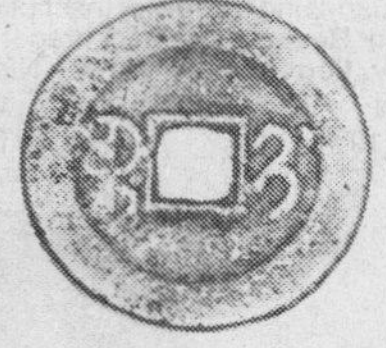

**CASH C# 17-1 Composition:** Cast Brass **Ruler:** Kuang-hsü

| Date | Mintage | Good | VG | F | VF | XF |
|---|---|---|---|---|---|---|
| ND(1875-1908) | — | 15.00 | 25.00 | 35.00 | 50.00 | — |

**Note:** This coin is sometimes erroneously attributed to Chi-chou (Chichow) in Chihli (Hebei) province, which used this mint mark in the Hsien-feng and earlier reigns

**10 CASH Composition:** Cast Brass **Ruler:** Kuang-hsü

| Date | Mintage | Good | VG | F | VF | XF |
|---|---|---|---|---|---|---|
| ND(1875-1908) Rare | — | — | — | — | — | — |

**Note:** Previously listed 10 Cash, Chilin Mint, C#17-2 has been determined to be a fantasy

### MILLED COINAGE

Errors in the English legends are very common in the Kirin coinage. It has been estimated there are over 2500 die varieties of Kirin (Jilin) silver coins and more than 1000 varieties of copper 10 Cash. Listed here are basic types and major varieties only.

**2 CASH Y# 175 Composition:** Bronze **Ruler:** Kuang-hsü **Obverse:** Inscription: Kuang-hsü T'ung-pao **Note:** Struck at Chi (Chilin). Mint mark: Manchu Boo-gi.

| Date | Mintage | VG | F | VF | XF | Unc |
|---|---|---|---|---|---|---|
| ND(ca.1905) | — | 80.00 | 120 | 160 | 250 | — |

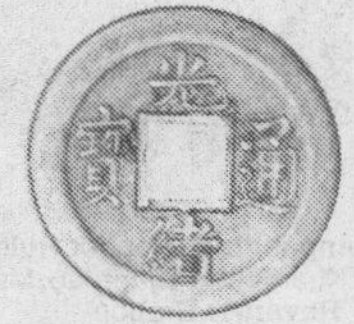

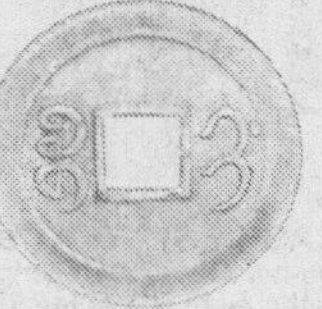

**10 CASH HSU# 481 Composition:** Brass **Ruler:** Kuang-hsü **Obverse:** Inscription: Kuang-hsü T'ung-pao **Note:** Four minor varieties exist.

| Date | Mintage | F | VF | XF | Unc | BU |
|---|---|---|---|---|---|---|
| ND(ca.1900) | — | 30.00 | 50.00 | 75.00 | 100 | — |

**Note:** This coin is sometimes erroneously attributed to Chi-chou (Chichow) in Chihli (Hebei) province, which used this mint mark in the Hsien-feng and earlier reigns

**10 CASH(ES) Y# 176 Composition:** Copper **Ruler:** Kuang-hsü **Obverse:** Inscription: Kuang-hsü Yüan-pao **Reverse:** Dragon

| Date | Mintage | VG | F | VF | XF | Unc |
|---|---|---|---|---|---|---|
| ND(ca.1901) | — | 35.00 | 60.00 | 90.00 | 125 | — |

**10 CASH(ES) Y# 176.1 Composition:** Copper **Ruler:** Kuang-hsü **Obverse:** Inscription: Kuang-hsü Yüan-pao **Reverse:** Thinner dragon

| Date | Mintage | VG | F | VF | XF | Unc |
|---|---|---|---|---|---|---|
| ND(ca.1901) | — | 35.00 | 60.00 | 90.00 | 125 | — |

**10 CASH(ES) Y# 174 Composition:** Bronze **Ruler:** Kuang-hsü **Obverse:** Inscription: Kuang-hsü Yüan-pao **Note:** Struck at Chi (Chilin). Mint mark: Manchu Chi.

| Date | Mintage | VG | F | VF | XF | Unc |
|---|---|---|---|---|---|---|
| ND(1901) Rare | — | — | — | — | — | — |

**10 CASH(ES) Y# 177 Composition:** Copper **Ruler:** Kuang-hsü **Obverse:** Inscription: Kuang-hsü Yüan-pao; small rosettes **Reverse:** Dragon; large rosettes

| Date | Mintage | VG | F | VF | XF | Unc |
|---|---|---|---|---|---|---|
| ND(ca.1903) | — | 5.00 | 10.00 | 15.00 | 25.00 | — |

**10 CASH(ES) Y# 177.1 Composition:** Copper **Ruler:** Kuang-hsü **Obverse:** Inscription: Kuang-hsü Yüan-pao **Reverse:** Dragon; small stars

| Date | Mintage | VG | F | VF | XF | Unc |
|---|---|---|---|---|---|---|
| ND(ca.1903) | — | 5.00 | 10.00 | 15.00 | 25.00 | — |

**10 CASH(ES)** **Y# 177.2** **Composition:** Copper **Ruler:** Kuang-hsü **Obverse:** Inscription: Kuang-hsü Yüan-pao; small stars **Reverse:** Dragon; large rosettes

| Date | Mintage | VG | F | VF | XF | Unc |
|---|---|---|---|---|---|---|
| ND(ca.1903) | — | 5.00 | 10.00 | 17.50 | 30.00 | — |

**10 CASH(ES)** **Y# 177.3** **Composition:** Copper **Ruler:** Kuang-hsü **Obverse:** Inscription: Kuang-hsü Yüan-pao; small stars **Reverse:** Dragon; small stars

| Date | Mintage | VG | F | VF | XF | Unc |
|---|---|---|---|---|---|---|
| ND(ca.1903) | — | 5.00 | 10.00 | 15.00 | 25.00 | — |

**10 CASH(ES)** **Y# 177.3a** **Composition:** Brass **Ruler:** Kuang-hsü **Obverse:** Inscription: Kuang-hsü Yüan-pao **Reverse:** Dragon

| Date | Mintage | VG | F | VF | XF | Unc |
|---|---|---|---|---|---|---|
| ND(ca.1903) | — | 5.00 | 10.00 | 17.50 | 30.00 | — |

**10 CASH(ES)** **Y# 177.4** **Composition:** Brass **Ruler:** Kuang-hsü **Obverse:** Inscription: Kuang-hsü Yüan-pao; large stars **Reverse:** Dragon; large stars

| Date | Mintage | VG | F | VF | XF | Unc |
|---|---|---|---|---|---|---|
| ND(ca.1903) | — | 4.00 | 7.00 | 12.00 | 17.50 | — |

**10 CASH(ES)** **Y# 177.5** **Composition:** Brass **Ruler:** Kuang-hsü **Obverse:** Inscription: Kuang-hsü Yüan-pao; large stars **Reverse:** Dragon; large rosettes

| Date | Mintage | VG | F | VF | XF | Unc |
|---|---|---|---|---|---|---|
| ND(ca.1903) | — | 4.00 | 7.00 | 12.00 | 17.50 | — |

**10 CASH(ES)** **Y# 177.6** **Composition:** Brass **Ruler:** Kuang-hsü **Obverse:** Inscription: Kuang-hsü Yüan-pao; medium rosettes **Reverse:** Dragon

| Date | Mintage | VG | F | VF | XF | Unc |
|---|---|---|---|---|---|---|
| ND(ca.1903) | — | 4.00 | 7.00 | 12.00 | 17.50 | — |

**10 CASH(ES)** **Y# 177.7** **Composition:** Brass **Ruler:** Kuang-hsü **Obverse:** Inscription: Kuang-hsü Yüan-pao **Reverse:** Dragon; CASHES spelled Cashis

| Date | Mintage | VG | F | VF | XF | Unc |
|---|---|---|---|---|---|---|
| ND(ca.1903) | — | 60.00 | 100 | 160 | 250 | — |

**Note:** It is difficult to differentiate the stars and rosettes on worn coins; the rosettes have a raised dot in the center while the stars have a hole in the center; it has been estimated that 1000 varieties of Y#177 exist

**10 CASH(ES)** **Y# 20p** **Composition:** Copper **Ruler:** Hsüan-t'ung **Obverse:** Inscription: Tai-ch'ing T'ung-pi; very small mint mark **Rev. Legend:** Hsüan-t'ung Nien-tsao, TAI-CHING-TI-KUO...

| Date | Mintage | VG | F | VF | XF | Unc |
|---|---|---|---|---|---|---|
| CD(1909) | — | 8.00 | 15.00 | 25.00 | 40.00 | — |

**10 CASH(ES)** **Y# 20p.1** **Composition:** Copper **Ruler:** Hsüan-t'ung **Obverse:** Inscription: Tai-ch'ing T'ung-pi; larger mint mark **Reverse:** Head of dragon, redesigned with more whiskers **Rev. Legend:** Hsüan-t'ung Nien-tsao, TAI-CHING-TI-KUO...

| Date | Mintage | VG | F | VF | XF | Unc |
|---|---|---|---|---|---|---|
| CD(1909) | — | 10.00 | 17.50 | 30.00 | 45.00 | — |

**10 CASH(ES)** **Y# 20p.2** **Composition:** Copper **Ruler:** Hsüan-t'ung **Obverse:** Inscription: Tai-ch'ing T'ung-pi; larger mint mark **Reverse:** Dragon similar to Y#20p **Rev. Legend:** Hsüan-t'ung Nien-tsao, TAI-CHING-TI-KUO...

| Date | Mintage | VG | F | VF | XF | Unc |
|---|---|---|---|---|---|---|
| CD(1909) | — | 10.00 | 17.50 | 30.00 | 45.00 | — |

**Note:** For Y#20x refer to General Issues-Empire

**10 CASH(ES)** **Y# 20p.3** **Composition:** Copper **Ruler:** Hsüan-t'ung **Obverse:** Inscription: Tai-ch'ing T'ung-pi; Y#20p **Reverse:** General Issue - Empire Y#20.1 **Rev. Legend:** Hsüan-t'ung Nien-tsao, TAI-CHING-TI-KUO... **Note:** Mule.

| Date | Mintage | VG | F | VF | XF | Unc |
|---|---|---|---|---|---|---|
| CD(1909) 2 known | — | — | — | — | 3,500 | — |

**Note:** Though dated 1909, minted at Mukden ca.1922

**20 CASH(ES)** **Y# 178** **Composition:** Copper **Ruler:** Kuang-hsü **Obverse:** Inscription: Kuang-hsü Yüan-pao **Reverse:** Dragon

| Date | Mintage | VG | F | VF | XF | Unc |
|---|---|---|---|---|---|---|
| ND(1903) | — | 35.00 | 65.00 | 100 | 175 | — |

**20 CASH(ES)** **Y# A176** **Composition:** Copper **Ruler:** Kuang-hsü **Obverse:** Inscription: Kuang-hsü Yüan-pao; Manchu in center, eight characters below **Reverse:** Dragon

| Date | Mintage | VG | F | VF | XF | Unc |
|---|---|---|---|---|---|---|
| ND(1903) | — | 80.00 | 200 | 400 | 700 | — |

**20 CASH(ES)** **Y# A176.1** **Composition:** Copper **Ruler:** Kuang-hsü **Obverse:** Inscription: Kuang-hsü Yüan-pao; rosette in center, three characters below **Reverse:** Dragon

| Date | Mintage | VG | F | VF | XF | Unc |
|---|---|---|---|---|---|---|
| ND(1903) | — | 80.00 | 225 | 425 | 725 | — |

**20 CASH(ES)** **Y# 21p** **Composition:** Copper **Ruler:** Kuang-hsü **Obverse:** Inscription: Tai-ch'ing T'ung-pi **Reverse:** Dragon **Rev. Legend:** Hsüan-t'ung Nien-tsao, TAI-CHING-TI-KUO...

| Date | Mintage | VG | F | VF | XF | Unc |
|---|---|---|---|---|---|---|
| CD(1909) | — | 120 | 250 | 450 | 750 | — |

**30 CASHES** **Y# E176** **Composition:** Brass **Ruler:** Kuang-hsü **Obverse:** Inscription: Kuang-hsü T'ung-pao **Reverse:** Side view dragon

| Date | Mintage | VG | F | VF | XF | Unc |
|---|---|---|---|---|---|---|
| CD(1901) Rare | — | — | — | — | — | — |

**50 CASHES** **Y# B176** **Composition:** Brass **Ruler:** Kuang-hsü **Obverse:** Inscription: Kuang-hsü T'ung-pao **Reverse:** Side view dragon

| Date | Mintage | Good | VG | F | VF | XF |
|---|---|---|---|---|---|---|
| CD(1901) 3 known | — | — | — | — | — | — |

**Note:** D.K.E. Ching Sale 6-91 VG-F realized $3,410; a similar 20 Cashes and silver 50 Cent have been reported and are believed to be fantasies by some authorities

**100 CASHES** **Y# F176** **Composition:** Brass **Ruler:** Kuang-hsü **Obverse:** Inscription: Kuang-hsü T'ung-pao **Reverse:** Side view dragon

| Date | Mintage | VG | F | VF | XF | Unc |
|---|---|---|---|---|---|---|
| CD(1901) | — | — | — | — | — | — |

**10 COPPERS** **Y# C176** **Composition:** Brass **Ruler:** Kuang-hsü **Obverse:** Inscription: Kuang-hsü Yüan-pao **Reverse:** Dragon **Note:** Similar to 50 Cashes, Y#B176

| Date | Mintage | VG | F | VF | XF | Unc |
|---|---|---|---|---|---|---|
| CD(1901) | — | — | — | — | — | — |

**5 CENTS** **Y# 179.1** **Weight:** 1.2700 g. **Composition:** Silver **Ruler:** Kuang-hsü **Obverse:** Inscription: Kuang-hsü Yüan-pao **Reverse:** Side view dragon; without crosses flanking weight

| Date | Mintage | F | VF | XF | Unc | BU |
|---|---|---|---|---|---|---|
| ND(ca.1898) | — | 5.00 | 10.00 | 20.00 | 50.00 | — |
| CD(1899) | — | 6.50 | 12.50 | 25.00 | 60.00 | — |
| **Note:** Cross-reference number K#394 | | | | | | |
| CD(1900) | — | 10.00 | 20.00 | 30.00 | 75.00 | — |
| **Note:** Cross-reference number K#416 | | | | | | |
| CD(1906) | — | 6.50 | 12.50 | 25.00 | 60.00 | — |
| **Note:** Cross-reference number K#549 | | | | | | |
| CD(1907) | — | 8.00 | 15.00 | 25.00 | 60.00 | — |
| CD(1908) Rare | — | — | — | — | — | — |

**5 CENTS** **Y# 179a** **Weight:** 1.2700 g. **Composition:** Silver **Ruler:** Kuang-hsü **Obverse:** Inscription: Kuang-hsü Yüan-pao; Yin-yang in center **Reverse:** Side view dragon

| Date | Mintage | F | VF | XF | Unc | BU |
|---|---|---|---|---|---|---|
| CD(1900) | — | 7.50 | 15.00 | 30.00 | 60.00 | — |
| CD(1901) | — | 5.50 | 11.50 | 25.00 | 50.00 | — |
| **Note:** Cross-reference number K#444 | | | | | | |
| CD(1902) | — | 6.50 | 12.50 | 25.00 | 60.00 | — |
| **Note:** Cross-reference number K#465 | | | | | | |

| Date | Mintage | F | VF | XF | Unc | BU |
|---|---|---|---|---|---|---|
| CD(1903) | — | 12.50 | 25.00 | 50.00 | 100 | — |

**Note:** Cross-reference number K#481

| Date | Mintage | F | VF | XF | Unc | BU |
|---|---|---|---|---|---|---|
| CD(1904) | — | 10.00 | 15.00 | 30.00 | 70.00 | — |

**Note:** Cross-reference number K#510

| Date | Mintage | F | VF | XF | Unc | BU |
|---|---|---|---|---|---|---|
| CD(1905) | — | 7.50 | 15.00 | 30.00 | 65.00 | — |

**Note:** Cross-reference number K#533

**10 CENTS** **Y# 180.1** **Weight:** 2.5500 g. **Composition:** Silver **Ruler:** Kuang-hsü **Obverse:** Inscription: Kuang-hsü Yüan-pao; large flower vase center **Reverse:** Side view dragon; without crosses flanking weight

| Date | Mintage | F | VF | XF | Unc | BU |
|---|---|---|---|---|---|---|
| ND(ca.1898) | — | 5.50 | 11.50 | 22.50 | 50.00 | — |
| CD(1899) | — | 6.50 | 12.50 | 25.00 | 60.00 | — |

**Note:** Cross-reference number K#393

| Date | Mintage | F | VF | XF | Unc | BU |
|---|---|---|---|---|---|---|
| CD(1900) | — | 6.50 | 12.50 | 25.00 | 60.00 | — |

**Note:** Cross-reference number K#416

| Date | Mintage | F | VF | XF | Unc | BU |
|---|---|---|---|---|---|---|
| CD(1906) | — | 6.50 | 12.50 | 25.00 | 60.00 | — |

**Note:** Cross-reference number K#546

| Date | Mintage | F | VF | XF | Unc | BU |
|---|---|---|---|---|---|---|
| CD(1907) | — | 45.00 | 90.00 | 150 | 250 | — |

**10 CENTS** **Y# 180a** **Weight:** 2.5500 g. **Composition:** Silver **Ruler:** Kuang-hsü **Obverse:** Inscription: Kuang-hsü Yüan-pao; Yin-yang in center **Reverse:** Side view dragon

| Date | Mintage | F | VF | XF | Unc | BU |
|---|---|---|---|---|---|---|
| CD(1900) | — | 7.50 | 15.00 | 30.00 | 75.00 | — |
| CD(1901) | — | 5.50 | 11.50 | 22.50 | 50.00 | — |

**Note:** Cross-reference number K#440

| Date | Mintage | F | VF | XF | Unc | BU |
|---|---|---|---|---|---|---|
| CD(1902) | — | 7.50 | 15.00 | 30.00 | 65.00 | — |

**Note:** Cross-reference number K#464

| Date | Mintage | F | VF | XF | Unc | BU |
|---|---|---|---|---|---|---|
| CD(1903) | — | 9.00 | 18.50 | 37.50 | 85.00 | — |

**Note:** Cross-reference number K#481

| Date | Mintage | F | VF | XF | Unc | BU |
|---|---|---|---|---|---|---|
| CD(1904) | — | 35.00 | 60.00 | 100 | 250 | — |
| CD(1905) | — | 6.50 | 11.50 | 22.50 | 50.00 | — |

**10 CENTS** **Y# 180c** **Weight:** 2.5500 g. **Composition:** Silver **Ruler:** Kuang-hsü **Obverse:** Inscription: Kuang-hsü Yüan-pao; numeral 1 in center **Reverse:** Side view dragon

| Date | Mintage | F | VF | XF | Unc | BU |
|---|---|---|---|---|---|---|
| CD(1908) | — | 70.00 | 125 | 175 | 350 | — |

**20 CENTS** **Y# 181** **Weight:** 5.1000 g. **Composition:** Silver **Ruler:** Kuang-hsü **Obverse:** Inscription: Kuang-hsü Yüan-pao; flower vase center **Reverse:** Side view dragon

| Date | Mintage | F | VF | XF | Unc | BU |
|---|---|---|---|---|---|---|
| ND(ca.1898) | — | 7.50 | 15.00 | 30.00 | 60.00 | — |
| CD(1899) | — | 6.50 | 12.50 | 25.00 | 50.00 | — |
| CD(1900) | — | 7.50 | 15.00 | 30.00 | 60.00 | — |
| CD(1906) | | 6.50 | 12.50 | 25.00 | 50.00 | — |
| CD(1907) | | 6.50 | 12.50 | 25.00 | 50.00 | — |
| CD(1908) | | 90.00 | 175 | 300 | 500 | — |

**20 CENTS** **Y# 181a** **Weight:** 5.1000 g. **Composition:** Silver **Ruler:** Kuang-hsü **Obverse:** Inscription: Kuang-hsü Yüan-pao; Yin-yang in center **Reverse:** Side view dragon

| Date | Mintage | F | VF | XF | Unc | BU |
|---|---|---|---|---|---|---|
| CD(1900) | — | 7.50 | 15.00 | 30.00 | 60.00 | — |
| CD(1901) | 22,508,000 | 6.50 | 12.50 | 25.00 | 50.00 | — |
| CD(1902) | Inc. above | 6.50 | 12.50 | 25.00 | 50.00 | — |
| CD(1903) | Inc. above | 6.50 | 12.50 | 25.00 | 50.00 | — |
| CD(1904) | Inc. above | 6.50 | 12.50 | 25.00 | 50.00 | — |
| CD(1905) | Inc. above | 6.50 | 12.50 | 25.00 | 50.00 | — |

**20 CENTS** **Y# 181c** **Weight:** 5.1000 g. **Composition:** Silver **Ruler:** Kuang-hsü **Obverse:** Inscription: Kuang-hsü Yüan-pao; numeral 2 center **Reverse:** Side view dragon

| Date | Mintage | F | VF | XF | Unc | BU |
|---|---|---|---|---|---|---|
| CD(1908) | Inc. above | 25.00 | 50.00 | 85.00 | 150 | — |

**20 CENTS** **Y# 181b** **Weight:** 5.1000 g. **Composition:** Silver **Ruler:** Kuang-hsü **Obverse:** Inscription: Kuang-hsü Yüan-pao; Manchu words in center **Reverse:** Side view dragon

| Date | Mintage | F | VF | XF | Unc | BU |
|---|---|---|---|---|---|---|
| CD(1908) | Inc. above | 50.00 | 100 | 150 | 275 | — |

**20 CENTS** **Y# 22.2** **Weight:** 5.1000 g. **Composition:** Silver **Ruler:** Hsüan-t'ung **Obverse:** Inscription: Hsüan-t'ung Yüan-pao; mint mark in circle at center **Reverse:** Side view dragon

| Date | Mintage | F | VF | XF | Unc | BU |
|---|---|---|---|---|---|---|
| ND(1909) | — | 35.00 | 70.00 | 125 | 225 | — |

**20 CENTS** **Y# 22** **Weight:** 5.1000 g. **Composition:** Silver **Ruler:** Hsüan-t'ung **Obverse:** Inscription: Hsüan-t'ung Yüan-pao; mint mark in relief on raised disc at center **Reverse:** Side view dragon

| Date | Mintage | F | VF | XF | Unc | BU |
|---|---|---|---|---|---|---|
| ND(1909) | — | 35.00 | 70.00 | 125 | 225 | — |

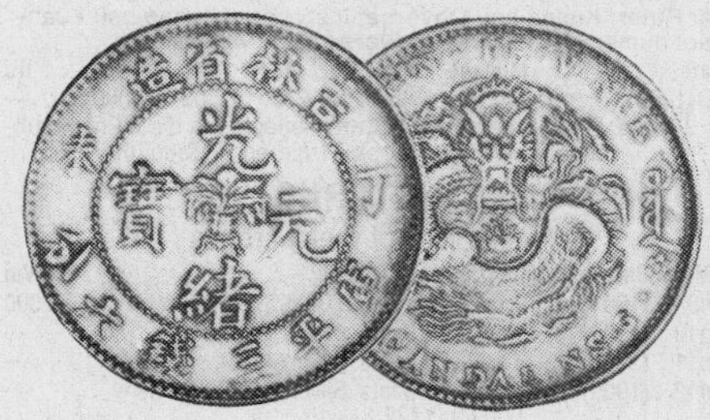

**50 CENTS** **Y# 182.3** **Weight:** 13.1000 g. **Composition:** Silver **Ruler:** Kuang-hsü **Obverse:** Inscription: Kuang-hsü Yüan-pao **Reverse:** Side view dragon

| Date | Mintage | F | VF | XF | Unc | BU |
|---|---|---|---|---|---|---|
| CD(1899) | — | 25.00 | 45.00 | 80.00 | 200 | — |
| CD(1900) | — | 20.00 | 35.00 | 60.00 | 150 | — |
| CD(1906) | — | 20.00 | 35.00 | 60.00 | 150 | — |
| CD(1907) | — | 20.00 | 35.00 | 60.00 | 150 | — |
| CD(1908) | — | 50.00 | 80.00 | 125 | 300 | — |

**50 CENTS** **Y# 182a.1** **Weight:** 13.1000 g. **Composition:** Silver **Ruler:** Kuang-hsü **Obverse:** Inscription: Kuang-hsü Yüan-pao; redesigned yin-yang in center **Reverse:** Side view dragon

| Date | Mintage | F | VF | XF | Unc | BU |
|---|---|---|---|---|---|---|
| CD(1901) | — | 20.00 | 35.00 | 60.00 | 150 | — |
| CD(1902) | — | 20.00 | 35.00 | 60.00 | 150 | — |
| CD(1903) | — | 25.00 | 40.00 | 65.00 | 165 | — |

| Date | Mintage | F | VF | XF | Unc | BU |
|---|---|---|---|---|---|---|
| CD(1904) | — | 20.00 | 35.00 | 60.00 | 150 | — |
| CD(1905) | — | 15.00 | 30.00 | 50.00 | 140 | — |

**50 CENTS** **Y# 182b** **Weight:** 13.1000 g. **Composition:** Silver **Ruler:** Kuang-hsü **Obverse:** Inscription: Kuang-hsü Yüan-pao; Manchu words in center **Reverse:** Side view dragon

| Date | Mintage | F | VF | XF | Unc | BU |
|---|---|---|---|---|---|---|
| CD(1908) | — | 75.00 | 150 | 275 | 450 | — |

**DOLLAR** **Y# 183** **Weight:** 26.1000 g. **Composition:** Silver **Ruler:** Kuang-hsü **Obverse:** Inscription: Kuang-hsü Yüan-pao; flower vase center **Reverse:** Side view dragon; small rosettes before and after weight: 7 CANDARINS 2 or 7 CAINDARINS 2

| Date | Mintage | F | VF | XF | Unc | BU |
|---|---|---|---|---|---|---|
| ND(ca.1898) | — | 60.00 | 100 | 250 | 500 | — |
| CD(1899) | — | 60.00 | 100 | 250 | 500 | — |
| CD(1900) | — | 60.00 | 100 | 300 | 600 | — |
| CD(1906) | — | 60.00 | 100 | 250 | 500 | — |
| CD(1907) | — | 125 | 175 | 300 | 650 | — |
| CD(1908) | — | 600 | 1,000 | 2,500 | 5,000 | — |

**DOLLAR** **Y# 183a.1** **Weight:** 26.1000 g. **Composition:** Silver **Ruler:** Kuang-hsü **Obverse:** Inscription: Kuang-hsü Yüan-pao; redesigned Yin-yang in center **Reverse:** Coarse-scaled, beady-eyed dragon

| Date | Mintage | F | VF | XF | Unc | BU |
|---|---|---|---|---|---|---|
| CD(1901) | — | 75.00 | 125 | 200 | 550 | — |
| CD(1902) | — | 75.00 | 125 | 200 | 500 | — |

**DOLLAR** Y# 183a.2 **Weight:** 26.1000 g. **Composition:** Silver **Ruler:** Kuang-hsü **Obverse:** Inscription: Kuang-hsü Yüan-pao **Reverse:** Fine dot-scaled, beady-eyed dragon

| Date | Mintage | F | VF | XF | Unc | BU |
|---|---|---|---|---|---|---|
| CD(1902) | — | 60.00 | 125 | 200 | 500 | — |
| CD(1903) | — | 75.00 | 125 | 200 | 400 | — |
| CD(1904) | — | 75.00 | 125 | 175 | 300 | — |
| CD(1905) | — | 75.00 | 125 | 175 | 300 | — |

**DOLLAR** Y# 183a.3 **Weight:** 26.1000 g. **Composition:** Silver **Ruler:** Kuang-hsü **Obverse:** Inscription: Kuang-hsü Yüan-pao **Reverse:** Fine oval-scaled, round-eyed dragon

| Date | Mintage | F | VF | XF | Unc | BU |
|---|---|---|---|---|---|---|
| CD(1905) | — | 50.00 | 100 | 175 | 400 | — |

**DOLLAR** Y# 183.1 **Weight:** 26.1000 g. **Composition:** Silver **Ruler:** Kuang-hsü **Obverse:** Inscription: Kuang-hsü Yüan-pao; large rosettes **Reverse:** Side view dragon; without rosettes flanking weight

| Date | Mintage | F | VF | XF | Unc | BU |
|---|---|---|---|---|---|---|
| ND(ca.1905) | — | 750 | 1,350 | 2,500 | 4,500 | — |

**DOLLAR** Y# 183.2 **Weight:** 26.1000 g. **Composition:** Silver **Ruler:** Kuang-hsü **Obverse:** Inscription: Kuang-hsü Yüan-pao **Reverse:** Side view dragon **Rev. Legend:** 3.2 CAINDARINS 2 (error)

| Date | Mintage | F | VF | XF | Unc | BU |
|---|---|---|---|---|---|---|
| CD(1906) | — | 175 | 250 | 350 | 750 | — |

**DOLLAR** Y# 183.3 **Weight:** 26.1000 g. **Composition:** Silver **Ruler:** Kuang-hsü **Obverse:** Inscription: Kuang-hsü Yüan-pao; small rosettes **Reverse:** Side view dragon; small rosettes before and after weight 7 CANDARINS 2

| Date | Mintage | F | VF | XF | Unc | BU |
|---|---|---|---|---|---|---|
| ND(ca.1906) | — | 100 | 135 | 175 | 500 | — |

**DOLLAR** Y# 183.4 **Weight:** 26.1000 g. **Composition:** Silver **Ruler:** Kuang-hsü **Obverse:** Inscription: Kuang-hsü Yüan-pao; small leaves out of left basket **Reverse:** Side view dragon; similar to Y#183.2

| Date | Mintage | F | VF | XF | Unc | BU |
|---|---|---|---|---|---|---|
| ND(ca.1906) | — | 60.00 | 100 | 150 | 400 | — |

**DOLLAR** Y# 183b **Weight:** 26.1000 g. **Composition:** Silver **Ruler:** Kuang-hsü **Obverse:** Inscription: Kuang-hsü Yüan-pao: Manchu words in center **Reverse:** Side view dragon

| Date | Mintage | F | VF | XF | Unc | BU |
|---|---|---|---|---|---|---|
| CD(1908) | — | 500 | 1,000 | 2,000 | 3,500 | — |

**DOLLAR** Y# 183c **Weight:** 26.1000 g. **Composition:** Silver **Ruler:** Kuang-hsü **Obverse:** Inscription: Kuang-hsü Yüan-pao: numeral 11 in center **Reverse:** Side view dragon

| Date | Mintage | F | VF | XF | Unc | BU |
|---|---|---|---|---|---|---|
| CD(1908) | — | 550 | 1,250 | 2,500 | 4,000 | — |

**Note:** The numeral 11 in center reflects the discount in subsidiary coinage; it took 11 dimes to equal the dollar

## PATTERNS

Including off metal strikes

| KM# | Date | Mintage | Identification | Mkt Val |
|---|---|---|---|---|
| Pn9 | (1901) | — | 20 Dollars. Gold. | 21,500 |
| Pn10 | (1902) | — | 50 Cents. Brass. Y#182a.1 | — |
| Pn11 | (1908) | — | 20 Cents. Zinc. Y#181c | — |
| Pn12 | (1909) | — | 20 Cents. Silver. K#583, formerly Y#22.1 | — |

# KWANGSI-KWANGSEA

**Guangxi**

A hilly region in southeast China with many forests. Large amounts of rice are grown adjacent to the many rivers. A mint opened in Kweilin in 1667, closed in 1670, reopened in 1679, closed again in 1681. It reopened in the mid-1700's and was a rather prolific issuer of Cash coins. In 1905 the government allowed modern mints to be established in Kwangsi (Guangxi) at Nanning (1905) and Kweilin (1905). The Nanning Mint began operation in 1919 and closed in 1923. In 1920 a new mint was opened at Wuchow and operated sporadically until 1929. In 1938 part of the Shanghai Central Mint was moved to Kweilin where it operated until at least 1945 and perhaps as late as 1949.

## EMPIRE

### PROVINCIAL CAST COINAGE

**CASH** C#18-9 **Composition:** Cast Brass **Ruler:** Kuang-hsü **Obverse:** Inscription: Kuang-hsü T'ung-pao **Reverse:** Inscription: Manchu Boo-gui **Note:** Struck at Kue (Kuelin).

| Date | Mintage | Good | VG | F | VF | XF |
|---|---|---|---|---|---|---|
| ND(1875-1908) | — | 5.50 | 8.50 | 13.50 | 25.00 | — |

## REPUBLIC

### MILLED COINAGE

**CENT** Y# 413 **Composition:** Brass **Obv. Legend:** KWANG-SEA

| Date | Mintage | F | VF | XF | Unc | BU |
|---|---|---|---|---|---|---|
| (1919) | — | 150 | 250 | 400 | — | — |

**CENT** Y# 413a **Composition:** Brass **Obv. Legend:** KWANG-SI

| Date | Mintage | F | VF | XF | Unc | BU |
|---|---|---|---|---|---|---|
| 8(1919) | — | 40.00 | 75.00 | 150 | — | — |

**CENT** Y# 347 **Composition:** Brass **Reverse:** Large "Kuei" mint mark below Pu

| Date | Mintage | F | VF | XF | Unc | BU |
|---|---|---|---|---|---|---|
| 28(1939) Rare | — | — | — | — | — | — |

**CENT** Y# 347.1 **Composition:** Brass **Reverse:** Small "Kuei" mint mark below Pu

| Date | Mintage | F | VF | XF | Unc | BU |
|---|---|---|---|---|---|---|
| 28(1939) Rare | — | — | — | — | — | — |

**5 CENTS** Y# A415 **Composition:** Copper-Nickel **Reverse:** Large "5" in sprays

| Date | Mintage | F | VF | XF | Unc | BU |
|---|---|---|---|---|---|---|
| 12(1923) | — | 150 | 250 | 400 | 600 | — |

**10 CENTS** Y# 414 **Weight:** 2.7000 g. **Composition:** Silver

| Date | Mintage | F | VF | XF | Unc | BU |
|---|---|---|---|---|---|---|
| 9(1920) | — | 60.00 | 100 | 150 | 250 | — |

**20 CENTS** Y# 415 **Weight:** 5.3000 g. **Composition:** Silver **Rev. Legend:** KWANG-SEA

| Date | Mintage | F | VF | XF | Unc | BU |
|---|---|---|---|---|---|---|
| 8(1919) | — | 50.00 | 75.00 | 100 | 175 | — |
| 9(1920) | — | 70.00 | 100 | 150 | 250 | — |

**20 CENTS** Y# 415a **Weight:** 5.3000 g. **Composition:** Silver **Rev. Legend:** KWANG-SI

| Date | Mintage | F | VF | XF | Unc | BU |
|---|---|---|---|---|---|---|
| 8(1919) | — | 10.00 | 25.00 | 40.00 | 125 | — |
| 9(1920) | — | 10.00 | 20.00 | 45.00 | 100 | — |
| 11(1922) | — | 10.00 | 15.00 | 40.00 | 100 | — |
| 12(1923) | — | 4.00 | 9.00 | 20.00 | 40.00 | — |
| 13(1924) | — | 4.00 | 7.50 | 12.50 | 25.00 | — |
| 14(1925) | — | 4.00 | 7.50 | 12.50 | 25.00 | — |

**20 CENTS** **Y# 415a.1** **Weight:** 5.3000 g. **Composition:** Silver **Obverse:** Character "Kuei" in center instead of dot

| Date | Mintage | F | VF | XF | Unc | BU |
|---|---|---|---|---|---|---|
| 13(1924) | — | 80.00 | 100 | 150 | 250 | — |

**20 CENTS** **Y# 415b** **Weight:** 5.3000 g. **Composition:** Silver **Obverse:** Tiny character "Hsi" on dot center **Reverse:** Wreath added around "20"

| Date | Mintage | F | VF | XF | Unc | BU |
|---|---|---|---|---|---|---|
| 15(1926) | — | 3.50 | 6.50 | 10.00 | 20.00 | — |
| 16(1927) | — | 3.50 | 6.50 | 10.00 | 20.00 | — |

**20 CENTS** **Y# 416** **Weight:** 5.3000 g. **Composition:** Silver **Reverse:** Elephant nose rock at Kueilin

| Date | Mintage | F | VF | XF | Unc | BU |
|---|---|---|---|---|---|---|
| 38(1949) | — | 90.00 | 150 | 200 | 350 | — |

## PIEFORTS

| KM# | Date | Mintage | Identification | Mkt Val |
|---|---|---|---|---|
| P1 | 19(1921) | — | 10 Cents. Bronze. Y414c. KM#Pn5. | 250 |
| P2 | 10(1921) | — | 10 Cents. Brass. 3.2900 g. Y414b. KM#Pn4. | 150 |

## PATTERNS

Including off metal strikes

| KM# | Date | Mintage | Identification | Mkt Val |
|---|---|---|---|---|
| Pn1 | (1905) | — | 10 Cash. Copper. | — |
| Pn2 | (1906) | — | 10 Cash. Copper. | — |
| Pn3 | 10(1921) | — | 10 Cents. Copper. 2.11-2.22 grams. Y414a, K746-IIx. | 110 |
| Pn7 | 10(1921) | — | 20 Cents. Copper. 4.68-4.97 grams. Y415c, K746-Ix. | 100 |
| Pn5 | 10(1921) | — | 10 Cents. Bronze. Y414c. | 140 |
| Pn8 | 10(1921) | — | 20 Cents. Bronze. Y415d. | — |
| Pn4 | 10(1921) | — | 10 Cents. Brass. Y414b. | — |
| Pn9 | 10(1921) | — | 20 Cents. Brass. Y415e. | — |
| Pn6 | 10(1921) | — | 10 Cents. Silver. Y414f. | — |
| Pn10 | 10(1921) | — | 20 Cents. Silver. 4.8700 g. Y415f. | 750 |

# KWANGTUNG PROVINCE

**Guangdong**

A province located on the southeast coast of China. Kwangtung (Guangdong) lies mostly in the tropics and has both mountains and plains. Its coastline is nearly 800 miles long and provides many good harbors. Because of the location of Guangzhou (Canton) in the province, Kwangtung (Guangdong) was the first to be visited by seaborne foreign traders. Hong Kong was ceded to Great Britain after the First Opium War in 1841. Kowloon was later ceded to Britain in 1860 and the New Territories (100 year lease) in 1898 and Macao to Portugal in 1887, Kwangchowwan was leased to France in 1898 (a property was restored in 1946). A modern mint opened in Guangzhou (Canton) in 1889 with Edward Wyon as superintendent. The mint was a large issuer of coins until it closed in 1931. The Nationalists reopened the mint briefly in 1949, striking a few silver dollars, before abandoning the mainland for their retreat to Taiwan.

The large island of Hainan was split off from Kwangtung (Guangdong) Province in 1988 and established as a separate province.

Hong Kong was returned to China by Britain on July 1, 1997 and established as a special administrative region, retaining its own coinage. Macao returns to China a few weeks before the end of 1999.

# EMPIRE

## PROVINCIAL CAST COINAGE

**CASH** **C# 19-7** **Composition:** Cast Brass **Ruler:** Kuang-hsü **Obverse:** Inscription: Kuang-hsü T'ung-pao **Reverse:** Inscription: Manchu Boo-guwang **Note:** Struck at Kwang (Canton).

| Date | Mintage | Good | VG | F | VF | XF |
|---|---|---|---|---|---|---|
| ND(1875-1908) | — | 12.00 | 22.00 | 32.00 | 45.00 | — |

## MILLED COINAGE

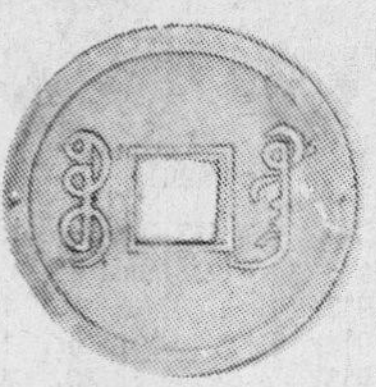

**CASH** **Y# 190** **Composition:** Brass **Ruler:** Kuang-hsü **Obverse:** "Kuang" in a different style, inscription: Kuang-hsü T'ung-pao **Reverse:** Inscription: Manchu Boo-guwang **Note:** Struck at Kwang (Canton)

| Date | Mintage | F | VF | XF | Unc | BU |
|---|---|---|---|---|---|---|
| ND(1890-1908) | 1,059,253,000 | 0.10 | 0.25 | 1.00 | 2.00 | — |

**CASH** **Y# 191** **Composition:** Brass **Ruler:** Kuang-hsü **Obverse:** Inscription: Kuang-hsü T'ung-pao **Reverse:** Inscription: Manchu Boo-guwang **Note:** Struck at Kwang (Canton).

| Date | Mintage | F | VF | XF | Unc | BU |
|---|---|---|---|---|---|---|
| ND(1906-1908) | — | 0.10 | 0.25 | 1.00 | 3.00 | — |

**CASH** **Y# 204** **Composition:** Brass **Obverse:** Inscription: Hsüan-t'ung T'uang pao **Reverse:** Inscription: Manchu Boo-guwang **Note:** Struck at Kwang (Canton).

| Date | Mintage | F | VF | XF | Unc | BU |
|---|---|---|---|---|---|---|
| ND(1909-1911) | — | 0.50 | 1.00 | 2.00 | 5.00 | — |

**10 CASH** **Y# 20r** **Composition:** Copper **Ruler:** Hsuan-T'ung **Obverse:** Inscription: Tai-ch'ing T'ung-pi **Reverse:** Dragon **Rev. Legend:** Hsüan-t'ung Nien-tsao, TAI-CHING-TI KUO ...

| Date | Mintage | F | VF | XF | Unc | BU |
|---|---|---|---|---|---|---|
| CD(1909) | — | 1.50 | 3.00 | 5.00 | 25.00 | — |

**CENT (10 Cash)** **Y# 192** **Composition:** Copper **Ruler:** Kuang-hsü **Obverse:** Inscription: Kuang-hsü Yuan-pao **Obv. Legend:** 6 characters at bottom **Reverse:** Dragon, ONE CENT

| Date | Mintage | F | VF | XF | Unc | BU |
|---|---|---|---|---|---|---|
| ND(1900-1906) | — | 0.75 | 1.50 | 3.00 | 20.00 | — |

**CENT (10 Cash)** **Y# A192** **Composition:** Copper **Ruler:** Kuang-hsü **Obverse:** Y#192, inscription: Kuang-hsü Yuan-pao **Reverse:** Chihli 10 Cash, Y#67, dragon **Note:** Mule.

| Date | Mintage | F | VF | XF | Unc | BU |
|---|---|---|---|---|---|---|
| ND | — | 25.00 | 35.00 | 50.00 | 125 | — |

**CENT (10 Cash)** **Y# 193** **Composition:** Copper **Ruler:** Kuang-hsü **Obverse:** Inscription: Kuang-hsü Yuan-pao **Obv. Legend:** 7 characters at bottom **Reverse:** Dragon, TEN CASH **Note:** Varieties in lettering exist.

| Date | Mintage | F | VF | XF | Unc | BU |
|---|---|---|---|---|---|---|
| ND(1900-1906) | — | 1.00 | 2.00 | 4.00 | 20.00 | — |

**CENT (10 Cash)** **Y# A193** **Composition:** Copper **Ruler:** Kuang-hsü **Obverse:** Y#192, inscription: Kuang-hsü Yuan-pao **Reverse:** Y#193, dragon, TEN CASH **Note:** Mule.

| Date | Mintage | F | VF | XF | Unc | BU |
|---|---|---|---|---|---|---|
| ND(c. 1906) | — | 20.00 | 28.50 | 40.00 | 100 | — |

**CENT (10 Cash)** **Y# 10r** **Composition:** Copper **Ruler:** Kuang-hsü **Obverse:** Inscription: Tai-ch'ing T'ung-pi **Reverse:** Dragon **Rev. Legend:** Kuang-hsü Nien-tsao, TAI-CHING-TI KUO ...

| Date | Mintage | F | VF | XF | Unc | BU |
|---|---|---|---|---|---|---|
| CD(1906) | 79,000,000 | 1.00 | 2.00 | 4.00 | 20.00 | — |
| CD(1907) | 46,000,000 | 1.00 | 2.00 | 4.00 | 20.00 | — |
| CD(1908) | 62,736,000 | 1.00 | 2.00 | 4.00 | 20.00 | — |

**CENT (10 Cash)** **Y# B193** **Composition:** Copper **Ruler:** Kuang-hsü **Obverse:** Y#193, inscription: Kuang-hsü Yuan-pao **Reverse:** Y#192, dragon **Note:** Mule.

| Date | Mintage | F | VF | XF | Unc | BU |
|---|---|---|---|---|---|---|
| ND(c. 1906) | — | 20.00 | 28.50 | 40.00 | 100 | — |

**CENT** **KM# B192** (KM1) **Composition:** Copper **Ruler:** Kuang-hsü **Obverse:** Inscription: Kuang-hsü Yüan-pao **Note:** Previous W#896.

| Date | Mintage | VG | F | VF | XF | Unc |
|---|---|---|---|---|---|---|
| ND(ca.1906) | — | — | 65.00 | 100 | 150 | 225 |

**5 CENTS** **Y# 199** **Weight:** 1.3000 g. **Composition:** 0.8200 Silver .0343 oz. ASW **Ruler:** Kuang-hsü **Obverse:** Inscription: Kuang-hsü Yüan-pao **Reverse:** English legend around dragon

| Date | Mintage | F | VF | XF | Unc | BU |
|---|---|---|---|---|---|---|
| ND(1890-1905) | — | 3.50 | 6.00 | 10.00 | 30.00 | — |

**10 CENTS** **Y# 200** **Weight:** 2.7000 g. **Composition:** 0.8200 Silver .0712 oz. ASW **Ruler:** Kuang-hsü **Obverse:** Inscription: Kuang-hsü Yüan-pao **Reverse:** English legends around dragon

| Date | Mintage | F | VF | XF | Unc | BU |
|---|---|---|---|---|---|---|
| ND(1890-1908) | — | 2.00 | 4.00 | 6.00 | 15.00 | — |

**20 CENTS** **Y# 201** **Weight:** 5.5000 g. **Composition:** 0.8000 Silver .1415 oz. ASW **Ruler:** Kuang-hsü **Obverse:** Inscription: Kuang-hsü Yüan-pao **Reverse:** Dragon

| Date | Mintage | F | VF | XF | Unc | BU |
|---|---|---|---|---|---|---|
| ND(1890-1908) | — | 1.50 | 2.50 | 3.50 | 10.00 | — |
| ND(1890-1908) Proof, 10 known | — | Value: 400 | | | | |

**20 CENTS** Y# 205 **Weight:** 5.5000 g. **Composition:** 0.8000 Silver .1415 oz. ASW **Ruler:** Hsuan-T'ung **Obverse:** Inscription: Hsüan-t'ung Yüan-pao **Reverse:** Dragon **Note:** Two varieties of edge reeding known.

| Date | Mintage | F | VF | XF | Unc | BU |
|---|---|---|---|---|---|---|
| ND(1909-1911) | 94,774,000 | 4.50 | 6.00 | 9.00 | 20.00 | — |

**50 CENTS** Y# 202 **Weight:** 13.5000 g. **Composition:** 0.8600 Silver .3733 oz. ASW **Ruler:** Kuang-hsü **Obverse:** Inscription: Kuang-hsü Yuan-pao **Reverse:** English legends around dragon

| Date | Mintage | F | VF | XF | Unc | BU |
|---|---|---|---|---|---|---|
| ND(1890-1905) | — | 20.00 | 40.00 | 75.00 | 250 | — |
| ND(1890-1905) Proof | — | Value: 650 | | | | |

**DOLLAR** Y# 203 **Weight:** 27.0000 g. **Composition:** 0.9000 Silver .7814 oz. ASW **Ruler:** Kuang-hsü **Obverse:** Inscription: Kuang-hsü Yuan-pao **Reverse:** English legends around dragon

| Date | Mintage | F | VF | XF | Unc | BU |
|---|---|---|---|---|---|---|
| ND(1890-1908) | — | 15.00 | 25.00 | 50.00 | 350 | — |
| ND(1890-1908) Proof | — | Value: 1,000 | | | | |

**DOLLAR** Y# 206 **Weight:** 27.0000 g. **Composition:** 0.9000 Silver .7814 oz. ASW **Obverse:** Inscription: Hsüan-t'ung Yüan-pao **Reverse:** Dragon

| Date | Mintage | F | VF | XF | Unc | BU |
|---|---|---|---|---|---|---|
| ND(1909-1911) | — | 15.00 | 25.00 | 50.00 | 300 | — |

# REPUBLIC

## MILLED COINAGE

**CENT** Y# 417 **Composition:** Bronze

| Date | Mintage | F | VF | XF | Unc | BU |
|---|---|---|---|---|---|---|
| 1(1912) | 18,836,000 | 1.50 | 2.25 | 5.00 | 22.00 | — |
| 3(1914) | 14,750,000 | 1.50 | 2.25 | 5.00 | 22.00 | — |
| 4(1915) | 6,350,000 | 4.00 | 6.00 | 15.00 | 35.00 | — |
| 5(1916) | 18,388,000 | 2.00 | 3.00 | 7.50 | 30.00 | — |
| 7(1918) | — | 7.50 | 12.50 | 20.00 | 45.00 | — |

**CENT** Y# 417a **Composition:** Brass

| Date | Mintage | F | VF | XF | Unc | BU |
|---|---|---|---|---|---|---|
| 1(1912) | Inc. above | — | — | — | — | — |
| 3(1914) | Inc. above | 2.00 | 5.00 | 10.00 | 25.00 | — |
| 4(1915) | Inc. above | 3.00 | 7.50 | 15.00 | 30.00 | — |
| 5(1916) | Inc. above | 1.25 | 3.00 | 6.00 | 20.00 | — |

**2 CENTS** Y# 418 **Composition:** Brass

| Date | Mintage | F | VF | XF | Unc | BU |
|---|---|---|---|---|---|---|
| 7(1918) | — | 30.00 | 50.00 | 90.00 | 175 | — |

**2 CENTS** Y# 418a **Composition:** Copper

| Date | Mintage | F | VF | XF | Unc | BU |
|---|---|---|---|---|---|---|
| 7(1918) Rare | — | — | — | — | — | — |

**5 CENTS** Y# 420 **Composition:** Copper-Nickel **Reverse:** Large "5" in sprays

| Date | Mintage | F | VF | XF | Unc | BU |
|---|---|---|---|---|---|---|
| 8(1919) | 916,000 | 1.00 | 2.00 | 3.00 | 5.00 | — |

**5 CENTS** Y# 421 **Composition:** Copper-Nickel **Reverse:** Flag

| Date | Mintage | F | VF | XF | Unc | BU |
|---|---|---|---|---|---|---|
| 10(1921) | 666,000 | 1.25 | 3.00 | 6.50 | 12.50 | — |

**5 CENTS** Y# 420a **Composition:** Copper-Nickel **Reverse:** Large "5" in sprays

| Date | Mintage | F | VF | XF | Unc | BU |
|---|---|---|---|---|---|---|
| 12(1923) | 480,000 | 1.00 | 2.00 | 3.00 | 5.00 | — |

**10 CENTS** Y# 422 **Weight:** 2.7000 g. **Composition:** Silver **Reverse:** Large "10"

| Date | Mintage | F | VF | XF | Unc | BU |
|---|---|---|---|---|---|---|
| 2(1913) | 8,798,000 | 2.00 | 4.00 | 5.00 | 10.00 | — |
| 3(1914) | Inc. above | 2.50 | 4.00 | 5.00 | 10.00 | — |
| 11(1922) | — | 4.00 | 7.00 | 10.00 | 25.00 | — |

**10 CENTS** Y# 425 **Weight:** 2.5000 g. **Composition:** Silver **Reverse:** Bust of Sun Yat-sen

| Date | Mintage | F | VF | XF | Unc | BU |
|---|---|---|---|---|---|---|
| 18(1929) | 48,960,000 | 1.50 | 3.00 | 5.00 | 8.00 | — |

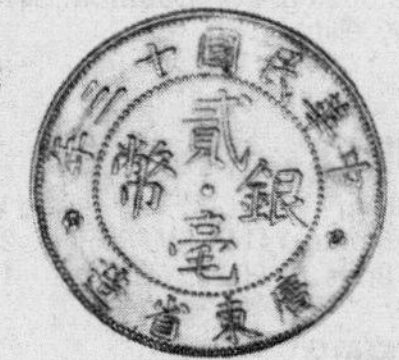

**20 CENTS** Y# 423 **Weight:** 5.4000 g. **Composition:** Silver **Note:** The fineness of many of these 20-cent pieces, especially those dated Yr. 13 (1924), is as low as .500. In 1924 the Anhwei (Anhui) Mint secretly produced quantities of Kwangtung (Guangdong) 20-cent pieces that were only .400 fine.

| Date | Mintage | F | VF | XF | Unc | BU |
|---|---|---|---|---|---|---|
| 1(1912) | 88,000,000 | 1.25 | 2.50 | 6.00 | 12.00 | — |
| 2(1913) | 109,974,000 | 1.25 | 2.50 | 6.00 | 12.00 | — |
| 3(1914) | 41,691,000 | 1.25 | 2.50 | 6.00 | 12.00 | — |
| 4(1915) | 22,332,000 | 4.00 | 10.00 | 30.00 | 65.00 | — |
| 7(1918) | — | 1.25 | 2.50 | 5.00 | 10.00 | — |
| 8(1919) | 195,000,000 | 0.75 | 1.50 | 3.00 | 5.00 | — |
| 9(1920) | 197,000,000 | 0.75 | 1.50 | 3.00 | 5.00 | — |
| 10(1921) | 402,250,000 | 0.75 | 1.50 | 3.00 | 5.00 | — |
| 11(1922) | 350,000,000 | 0.75 | 1.50 | 3.00 | 5.00 | — |
| 12(1923) | 4,400,000 | 2.25 | 3.50 | 7.00 | 20.00 | — |
| 13(1924) | 55,109,000 | 2.25 | 3.50 | 8.25 | 20.00 | — |

**20 CENTS** Y# 424 **Weight:** 5.3000 g. **Composition:** Silver **Reverse:** Bust of Sun Yat-sen

| Date | Mintage | F | VF | XF | Unc | BU |
|---|---|---|---|---|---|---|
| 13(1924) | — | 25.00 | 45.00 | 70.00 | 175 | — |

**20 CENTS** Y# 426 **Weight:** 5.3000 g. **Composition:** Silver **Obverse:** Value in sprays **Reverse:** Bust of Sun Yat-sen

| Date | Mintage | F | VF | XF | Unc | BU |
|---|---|---|---|---|---|---|
| 17(1928) | 28,530,000 | 25.00 | 40.00 | 60.00 | 150 | — |
| 18(1929) | 779,738,000 | 0.75 | 1.50 | 2.50 | 5.00 | — |
| 19(1930) 1 known | — | — | — | — | 3,500 | — |

## PATTERNS

Including off metal strikes

| KM# | Date | Mintage | Identification | Mkt Val |
|---|---|---|---|---|
| Pn16 | (c. 1902) | — | 1/2 Cent. Copper. Circled "flying" dragon. | — |
| Pn17 | (1904) | — | Tael. Silver. K932. | — |
| | | | **Note:** Superior Goodman sale 6-91 proof realized $41,800. | |
| PnA18 | (1904) | — | Tael. Pewter. 6 millimeters thick. K932x. | — |
| Pn18 | (1904) | — | Tael. White Metal. K932y. | — |
| PnA19 | (1906) | — | 20 Cash. Copper. TCTK. | — |
| Pn19 | 3(1914) | — | 10 Cents. Copper. Y422. | — |
| PnA20 | 4(1915) | — | Cent. Red Copper. Y417. | — |
| PnB20 | 5(1916) | — | Cent. Red Copper. Y417. | — |
| PnC20 | 7(1918) | — | Cent. Red Copper. Y417. | — |
| Pn20 | 8(1919) | — | 20 Cents. Copper. Y423. | 150 |
| Pn21 | 9(1920) | — | 20 Cents. Copper. Y423. | 150 |
| Pn22 | 10(1921) | — | 20 Cents. Copper. Y423. | 150 |
| Pn-A23 | 11(1922) | — | 20 Cents. Copper. Y423. | 150 |
| Pn23 | 13(1924) | — | 20 Cents. Gold. Y424. | — |
| Pn24 | 17(1928) | — | 20 Cents. Copper. Y426. | — |
| Pn25 | 18(1929) | — | 20 Cents. Copper. Y426. | — |

| KM# | Date | Mintage | Identification | Mkt Val |
|---|---|---|---|---|
| Pn26 | (c. 1929) | — | 20 Cents. Gold. Y426. | 800 |
| Pn27 | 25(1936) | — | Cent. Bronze. Sun Yat Sen. | 3,000 |
| Pn28 | 25(1936) | — | Cent. Copper. | 700 |

# KWEICHOW PROVINCE

**Guizhou**

A province located in southern China. It is basically a plateau region that is somewhat remote from the general traffic of China. The Kweichow Mint opened in 1730 and produced Cash coins until the end of the reign of Kuang Hsu. The Republic issues for this province are enigmatic as to their origin, as a mint supposedly did not exist in Kweichow (Guizhou) at this time.

## EMPIRE

### PROVINCIAL CAST COINAGE

The Kweichow (Guizhou) Provincial Cash Coinage obviously copied from contemporary Japanese coins, are still a mystery. Even as late as the 1920s, Kweichow (Guizhou) was a very primitive area. It is highly unlikely that the coins were made there in the 1880s and 1890s. It is possible that they were minted elsewhere, possibly in one of the central coastal provinces.

**CASH** **C#20-9** **Composition:** Cast Brass **Ruler:** Kuang-hsü **Obverse:** Inscription: Kuang-hsü T'ung-pao **Reverse:** Inscription: Manchu Boo-jiyan **Note:** Struck at Kweiyang.

| Date | Mintage | Good | VG | F | VF | XF |
|---|---|---|---|---|---|---|
| ND(1875-1908 | — | 4.00 | 7.50 | 10.00 | 15.00 | — |

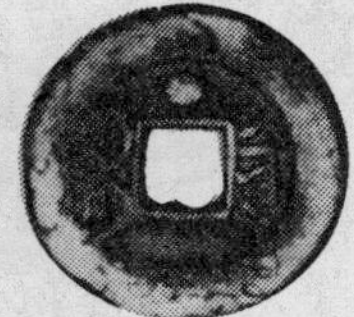

**CASH** **C# 20-9.1** **Composition:** Cast Brass **Ruler:** Kuang-hsü **Obverse:** Inscription: Kuang-hsü T'ung-pao **Reverse:** Inscription: Manchu Boo-jiyan, dot above **Note:** Struck at Kweiyang.

| Date | Mintage | Good | VG | F | VF | XF |
|---|---|---|---|---|---|---|
| ND(1875-1908) | — | 5.00 | 9.00 | 12.50 | 18.50 | — |

**CASH** **C# 20-9.2** **Composition:** Cast Brass **Ruler:** Kuang-hsü **Obverse:** Inscription: Kuang-hsü T'ung-pao **Reverse:** Inscription: Manchu Boo-jiyan, Chinese "Kung" above **Note:** Struck at Kweiyang.

| Date | Mintage | Good | VG | F | VF | XF |
|---|---|---|---|---|---|---|
| ND(1875-1908) | — | 8.50 | 11.50 | 16.50 | 25.00 | — |

## REPUBLIC

### MILLED COINAGE

**DOLLAR** **Y# 428** **Weight:** 25.8000 g. **Composition:** Silver **Subject:** First road in Kweichow

| Date | Mintage | F | VF | XF | Unc | BU |
|---|---|---|---|---|---|---|
| 17(1928) | 648,000 | 350 | 550 | 1,200 | 3,000 | — |

**Note:** This coin is known as the "Auto Dollar" as it purports to portray the governor's automobile; minor varieties exist in Chinese legends and automobile design

**DOLLAR** **Y# 433** **Weight:** 26.4000 g. **Composition:** Silver

| Date | Mintage | F | VF | XF | Unc | BU |
|---|---|---|---|---|---|---|
| 38(1949) | — | 400 | 700 | 1,250 | 3,000 | — |

**Note:** This coin is known as the "Bamboo Dollar"

**1/2 CENT** **Y# A429** **Composition:** Copper

| Date | Mintage | VG | F | VF | XF | Unc |
|---|---|---|---|---|---|---|
| 38(1949) | — | 450 | 750 | — | — | — |

**1/2 CENT** **Y# A429a** **Composition:** Brass

| Date | Mintage | VG | F | VF | XF | Unc |
|---|---|---|---|---|---|---|
| 38(1949) | — | 300 | 450 | — | — | — |

**1/2 CENT** **Y# A429a.2** **Composition:** Brass **Obverse:** Narrow, thick characters

| Date | Mintage | VG | F | VF | XF | Unc |
|---|---|---|---|---|---|---|
| 38(1949) | — | 450 | 650 | — | — | — |

**10 CENTS** **Y# 429** **Composition:** Antimony

| Date | Mintage | VG | F | VF | XF | Unc |
|---|---|---|---|---|---|---|
| 20(1931) | — | 250 | 450 | 650 | 900 | — |

**20 CENTS** **Y# 430** **Composition:** Silver

| Date | Mintage | F | VF | XF | Unc | BU |
|---|---|---|---|---|---|---|
| 38(1949) | — | 125 | 200 | 300 | 425 | — |

**20 CENTS** **Y# 431** **Composition:** Silver

| Date | Mintage | F | VF | XF | Unc | BU |
|---|---|---|---|---|---|---|
| 38(1949) | — | — | — | — | 3,750 | — |

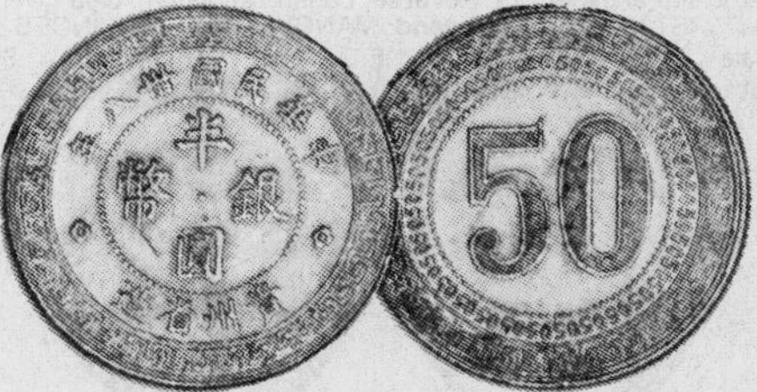

**50 CENTS** **Y# 432** **Composition:** Silver

| Date | Mintage | F | VF | XF | Unc | BU |
|---|---|---|---|---|---|---|
| 38(1949) | — | — | 1,750 | 3,000 | 5,300 | — |

# MANCHURIAN PROVINCES

## EMPIRE

### MILLED COINAGE

**10 CENTS** **Y# 209** **Weight:** 2.6000 g. **Composition:** 0.8900 Silver .0744 oz. ASW **Ruler:** Kuang-Hsü **Obverse:** Incscription: Kuang-hsü Yüan-pao **Reverse:** Legend at bottom **Rev. Legend:** MANCHURIAN PROVINCES

| Date | Mintage | F | VF | XF | Unc | BU |
|---|---|---|---|---|---|---|
| 33(1907) | 1,079,000 | 10.00 | 25.00 | 40.00 | 100 | — |

**20 CENTS** **Y# 210** **Weight:** 5.2000 g. **Composition:** 0.8900 Silver .1488 oz. ASW **Ruler:** Kuang-Hsü **Obverse:** Incscription: Kuang-hsü Yüan-pao; one dot at either side **Reverse:** Legend at bottom **Rev. Legend:** MANCHURIAN PROVINCES

| Date | Mintage | F | VF | XF | Unc | BU |
|---|---|---|---|---|---|---|
| 33(1907) | — | 20.00 | 30.00 | 60.00 | 120 | — |

**20 CENTS** **Y# 210a.1** **Weight:** 5.2000 g. **Composition:** 0.8900 Silver .1388 oz. ASW **Ruler:** Kuang-Hsü **Obverse:** Incscription: Kuang-hsü Yüan-pao; three rosettes at either side **Reverse:** Legend at bottom **Rev. Legend:** MANCHURIAN PROVINCES

| Date | Mintage | F | VF | XF | Unc | BU |
|---|---|---|---|---|---|---|
| 33(ca.1908) | 249,219,000 | 9.00 | 17.50 | 35.00 | 70.00 | — |

**20 CENTS** **Y# 210a.2** **Weight:** 5.2000 g. **Composition:** 0.8900 Silver .1388 oz. ASW **Ruler:** Kuang-Hsü **Obverse:** Incscription: Kuang-hsü Yüan-pao; one rosette at either side **Reverse:** Legend at bottom **Rev. Legend:** MANCHURIAN PROVINCES

| Date | Mintage | F | VF | XF | Unc | BU |
|---|---|---|---|---|---|---|
| 33(ca.1908) | Inc. above | 6.00 | 12.00 | 20.00 | 60.00 | — |

**20 CENTS** **Y# 213.2** **Weight:** 5.2000 g. **Composition:** 0.8900 Silver .1388 oz. ASW **Ruler:** Hsüan-t'ung **Obverse:** Incscription:Hsüan-t'ung Yüan-pao; one large-petalled rosette at

either side **Reverse:** Legend at bottom; date as 1ST YEAR **Rev. Legend:** MANCHURIAN PROVINCES

| Date | Mintage | F | VF | XF | Unc | BU |
|---|---|---|---|---|---|---|
| 1(1909) | Inc. above | 4.00 | 8.50 | 15.00 | 40.00 | — |

**20 CENTS** **Y# 213** **Weight:** 5.2000 g. **Composition:** 0.8900 Silver .1388 oz. ASW **Ruler:** Hsüan-t'ung **Obverse:** Incscription:Hsüan-t'ung Yüan-pao; two small stars flanking ond large star at either side **Reverse:** Legend at bottom; date given as FIRST YEAR **Rev. Legend:** MANCHURIAN PROVINCES

| Date | Mintage | F | VF | XF | Unc | BU |
|---|---|---|---|---|---|---|
| 1(ca.1910) | Inc. above | 4.00 | 7.50 | 12.50 | 30.00 | — |

**20 CENTS** **Y# 213.1** **Weight:** 5.2000 g. **Composition:** 0.8900 Silver .1388 oz. ASW **Ruler:** Hsüan-t'ung **Obverse:** Incscription:Hsüan-t'ung Yüan-pao; one small star at either side **Reverse:** Legend at bottom **Rev. Legend:** MANCHURIAN PROVINCES

| Date | Mintage | F | VF | XF | Unc | BU |
|---|---|---|---|---|---|---|
| 1(ca.1910) | Inc. above | 4.00 | 8.50 | 15.00 | 35.00 | — |

**20 CENTS** **Y# 213.3** **Weight:** 5.2000 g. **Composition:** 0.8900 Silver .1388 oz. ASW **Ruler:** Hsüan-t'ung **Obverse:** Incscription:Hsüan-t'ung Yüan-pao; one large star between two dots **Reverse:** Legend at bottom **Rev. Legend:** MANCHURIAN PROVINCES

| Date | Mintage | F | VF | XF | Unc | BU |
|---|---|---|---|---|---|---|
| 1(ca.1910) | Inc. above | 4.00 | 8.50 | 15.00 | 35.00 | — |

**20 CENTS** **Y# 213a** **Weight:** 5.2000 g. **Composition:** 0.8900 Silver .1388 oz. ASW **Ruler:** Hsüan-t'ung **Obverse:** Incscription:Hsüan-t'ung Yüan-pao; Manchu "Boo-fu" at center **Reverse:** Error in legend **Rev. Legend:** MANCHURIAN PROVIENCES

| Date | Mintage | F | VF | XF | Unc | BU |
|---|---|---|---|---|---|---|
| ND(ca.1911) | Inc. above | 4.00 | 8.50 | 15.00 | 35.00 | — |

**20 CENTS** **Y# 213a.6** **Weight:** 5.2000 g. **Composition:** 0.8900 Silver .1388 oz. ASW **Ruler:** Hsüan-t'ung **Obverse:** Incscription:Hsüan-t'ung Yüan-pao; without Manchu "Boo-fu" at center **Reverse:** Error in legend **Rev. Legend:** MANCHURIAN PROVIENCES

| Date | Mintage | F | VF | XF | Unc | BU |
|---|---|---|---|---|---|---|
| ND(ca.1912) | Inc. above | 5.00 | 10.00 | 20.00 | 40.00 | — |

**20 CENTS** **Y# 213a.4** **Weight:** 5.2000 g. **Composition:** 0.7000 Silver .1170 oz. ASW **Ruler:** Hsüan-t'ung **Obverse:** Incscription:Hsüan-t'ung Yüan-pao; without Manchu "Boo-fu" at center **Reverse:** Legend at bottom **Rev. Legend:** MANCHURIAN PROVINCES

| Date | Mintage | F | VF | XF | Unc | BU |
|---|---|---|---|---|---|---|
| ND(ca.1913) | Inc. above | 5.00 | 10.00 | 20.00 | 40.00 | — |

**20 CENTS** **Y# 213a.1** **Weight:** 5.2000 g. **Composition:** 0.7000 Silver .1170 oz. ASW **Ruler:** Hsüan-t'ung **Obverse:** Incscription:Hsüan-t'ung Yüan-pao; five-pettaled rosette in center with dot in center of rosette; dot below side rosettes **Reverse:** Legend at bottom **Rev. Legend:** MANCHURIAN PROVINCES

| Date | Mintage | F | VF | XF | Unc | BU |
|---|---|---|---|---|---|---|
| ND(ca.1914-15) | Inc. above | 4.00 | 8.50 | 15.00 | 30.00 | — |

**20 CENTS** **Y# 213a.2** **Weight:** 5.2000 g. **Composition:** 0.7000 Silver .1170 oz. ASW **Ruler:** Hsüan-t'ung **Obverse:** Incscription:Hsüan-t'ung Yüan-pao; with dot below side rosettes **Reverse:** Legend at bottom **Rev. Legend:** MANCHURIAN PROVINCES

| Date | Mintage | F | VF | XF | Unc | BU |
|---|---|---|---|---|---|---|
| ND(ca.1914-15) | Inc. above | 4.00 | 8.50 | 15.00 | 30.00 | — |

**20 CENTS** **Y# 213a.3** **Weight:** 5.2000 g. **Composition:** 0.7000 Silver .1170 oz. ASW **Ruler:** Hsüan-t'ung **Obverse:** Incscription:Hsüan-t'ung Yüan-pao; with dot in center of five-pettalled rosette **Reverse:** Legend at bottom **Rev. Legend:** MANCHURIAN PROVINCES

| Date | Mintage | F | VF | XF | Unc | BU |
|---|---|---|---|---|---|---|
| ND(ca.1914-15) | Inc. above | 4.00 | 8.50 | 15.00 | 30.00 | — |

**50 CENTS** **Y# 211** **Weight:** 13.1000 g. **Composition:** 0.8900 Silver .3749 oz. ASW **Ruler:** Kuang-Hsü **Obverse:** Incscription: Kuang-Hsü Yüan-pao **Reverse:** Legend at bottom **Rev. Legend:** MANCHURIAN PROVINCES

| Date | Mintage | F | VF | XF | Unc | BU |
|---|---|---|---|---|---|---|
| 33(1907) | — | 150 | 300 | 500 | 1,000 | — |

**DOLLAR** **Y# 212** **Weight:** 26.4000 g. **Composition:** 0.8900 Silver .7555 oz. ASW **Ruler:** Kuang-Hsü **Obverse:** Incscription: Kuang-Hsü Yüan-pao **Reverse:** Legend at bottom **Rev. Legend:** MANCHURIAN PROVINCES

| Date | Mintage | F | VF | XF | Unc | BU |
|---|---|---|---|---|---|---|
| 33(1907) | — | 200 | 400 | 700 | 1,500 | — |

# REPUBLIC

## MILLED COINAGE

**CENT** **Y# 434** **Composition:** Copper **Obv. Legend:** Chung-hua Min-kuo... **Reverse:** Sunburst in floral sprays

| Date | Mintage | F | VF | XF | Unc | BU |
|---|---|---|---|---|---|---|
| 18(1929) | — | 2.00 | 3.00 | 5.00 | 25.00 | — |

**CENT** **Y# 434a** **Composition:** Brass **Obv. Legend:** Chung-hua Min-kuo... **Reverse:** Sunburst in floral sprays

| Date | Mintage | F | VF | XF | Unc | BU |
|---|---|---|---|---|---|---|
| 18(1929) | — | — | — | — | — | — |

## PATTERNS

Including off metal strikes

| KM# | Date | Mintage | Identification | Mkt Val |
|---|---|---|---|---|
| Pn1 | 18(1929) | — | Dollar. Silver. | — |
| | | | **Note:** Superior Goodman sale 6-91 choice AU realized, $22,000 | |
| Pn2 | 18(1929) | — | Fen. Copper. Y#434 with formal Chinese "One Fen" | — |

# SHANSI PROVINCE

**Shanxi**

A province located in northeastern China that has some of the richest coal deposits in the world. Parts of the Great Wall cross the province. Extensive agriculture of early China started here. Cited as a "model province" in the new Chinese Republic. Intermittently active mints from 1645. The modern mint was established in 1919. It operated until the mid-1920's and closed because of the public's resistance against the coins that were being produced.

# EMPIRE

## PROVINCIAL CAST COINAGE

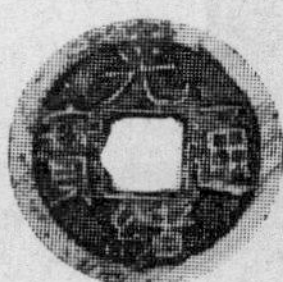

**CASH** **C# 21-8** **Composition:** Cast Brass **Ruler:** Kuang-hsu **Obverse:** Inscription: Kuang-hsu T'ung-pao **Reverse:** Manchu "Boo-Jin" **Note:** Struck at Chin (Taiyuan).

| Date | Mintage | Good | VG | F | VF | XF |
|---|---|---|---|---|---|---|
| ND(1875-1908) | — | 6.50 | 11.50 | 17.50 | 35.00 | — |

# REPUBLIC

## MILLED COINAGE

**20 CENTS Y# 217 Weight:** 4.8000 g. **Composition:** Silver **Ruler:** Hsuan-Tung **Obverse:** Inscription: Hsuan-t'ung Yuan-pao **Reverse:** Side view dragon

| Date | Mintage | VG | F | VF | XF | Unc |
|---|---|---|---|---|---|---|
| ND(ca.1911) | — | 100 | 175 | 300 | 450 | — |

**Note:** Several varieties exist similar to Y#217, but struck more crudely in base metal and with different Chinese legends at the top of the obverse. English legends are usually blundered. These were struck about 1913 and thought to be warlord issues. Do not confuse these with coins of Fengtien (Liaoning), from which this was copied.

**10 CASH (1 Cent) Y# A435 Composition:** Copper **Obverse:** Crossed flags **Reverse:** Value in wheat sprays

| Date | Mintage | F | VF | XF | Unc | BU |
|---|---|---|---|---|---|---|
| ND(ca.1912) | — | 100 | 150 | 220 | — | — |

## PATTERNS

Including off metal strikes

| KM# | Date | Mintage | Identification | Mkt Val |
|---|---|---|---|---|
| Pn2 | (1925)(14) | — | 5 Cents. Nickel. K823. | — |

# SHANTUNG PROVINCE

**Shandong**

A province located on the northeastern coast of China. Confucius was born in this province. Parts of the province were leased to Great Britain and to Germany. Farming, fishing and mining are the chief occupations. A mint was opened at Tsinan in 1647 and was an intermittent producer for the empire. A modern mint was opened at Tsinan in 1905, but closed in 1906. Patterns were prepared between 1926-1933 in anticipation of a new coinage, but none were struck for circulation.

# EMPIRE

## PROVINCIAL CAST COINAGE

**CASH C# 22-6 Composition:** Cast Brass **Ruler:** Kuang-hsü **Reverse:** Type 1 mint mark, inscription: Manchu Boo-ji **Note:** Struck at Chi (Chinan).

| Date | Mintage | Good | VG | F | VF | XF |
|---|---|---|---|---|---|---|
| ND(1875-1908) | — | 10.00 | 18.50 | 27.50 | 40.00 | — |

**Note:** Refer to Tungchuan, Yünnan Province, for one-cash C#27 series coins previously listed here.

## MILLED COINAGE

**2 CASH Y# 8s Composition:** Copper **Ruler:** Kuang-hsü **Obverse:** Inscription: Tai-ch'ing T'ung-pi **Reverse:** Dragon

| Date | Mintage | VG | F | VF | XF | Unc |
|---|---|---|---|---|---|---|
| CD1906 | — | 12.00 | 25.00 | 35.00 | 70.00 | — |

**10 CASH Y# 220 Composition:** Copper **Ruler:** Kuang-hsü **Obverse:** Inscription: Kuang-hsü Yüan-pao **Reverse:** Side view dragon

| Date | Mintage | VG | F | VF | XF | Unc |
|---|---|---|---|---|---|---|
| ND(1904-1905) | — | 3.25 | 8.00 | 15.00 | 30.00 | 55.00 |

**10 CASH Y# 221 Composition:** Copper **Ruler:** Kuang-hsü **Obverse:** Thin Manchu words in center, flying dragon, inscription: Kuang-hsü Yüan-pao **Reverse:** SHANTUNG

| Date | Mintage | VG | F | VF | XF | Unc |
|---|---|---|---|---|---|---|
| ND(1904-1905) | — | 2.75 | 7.00 | 11.00 | 17.50 | 40.00 |

**10 CASH Y# 221.1 Composition:** Copper **Ruler:** Kuang-hsü **Obverse:** Thick Manchu in center, flying dragon, inscription: Kuang-hsü Yüan-pao

| Date | Mintage | VG | F | VF | XF | Unc |
|---|---|---|---|---|---|---|
| ND(1904-1905) | — | 1.50 | 3.50 | 7.00 | 14.00 | 30.00 |

**10 CASH Y# 221.2 Composition:** Copper **Ruler:** Kuang-hsü **Obverse:** Smaller stars, flying dragon, inscription: Kuang-hsü Yüan-pao

| Date | Mintage | VG | F | VF | XF | Unc |
|---|---|---|---|---|---|---|
| ND(1904-1905) | — | 1.50 | 3.50 | 7.00 | 14.00 | 30.00 |

**10 CASH Y# 221.3 Composition:** Copper **Ruler:** Kuang-hsü **Obverse:** Similar to Y#220, flying dragon, inscription: Kuang-hsü Yüan-pao **Reverse:** Similar to Y#221

| Date | Mintage | VG | F | VF | XF | Unc |
|---|---|---|---|---|---|---|
| ND(1904-1905) | — | 62.50 | 125 | 200 | 300 | — |

**10 CASH Y# 221a Composition:** Copper **Ruler:** Kuang-hsü **Obverse:** Thick Manchu in center, flying dragon, inscription: Kuang-hsü Yüan-pao **Reverse:** SHANG-TUNG

| Date | Mintage | VG | F | VF | XF | Unc |
|---|---|---|---|---|---|---|
| ND(1904-1905) | — | 1.00 | 2.50 | 4.00 | 7.50 | 20.00 |

**10 CASH Y# 221a.1 Composition:** Copper **Ruler:** Kuang-hsü **Obverse:** Thin Manchu in center, flying dragon, inscription: Kuang-hsü Yüan-pao

| Date | Mintage | VG | F | VF | XF | Unc |
|---|---|---|---|---|---|---|
| ND(1904-1905) | — | 2.00 | 5.00 | 10.00 | 17.50 | 40.00 |

**10 CASH Y# 10s Composition:** Brass **Ruler:** Kuang-hsü **Obverse:** Inscription: Tai-ch'ing T'ung-pi **Reverse:** 6 large waves below dragon **Rev. Legend:** Kuang-hsü Nien-tsao, TAI-CHING-TI-KUO ...

| Date | Mintage | F | VF | XF | Unc | BU |
|---|---|---|---|---|---|---|
| CD(1906) | — | 6.00 | 10.00 | 17.50 | 40.00 | — |

**10 CASH Y# 10s.1 Composition:** Copper **Ruler:** Kuang-hsü **Obverse:** Inscription: Tai-ch'ing T'ung-pi **Rev. Legend:** Kuang-hsü Nien-tsao, TAI-CHING-TI-KUO ...

| Date | Mintage | F | VF | XF | Unc | BU |
|---|---|---|---|---|---|---|
| CD(1906) | — | 7.50 | 12.50 | 25.00 | 50.00 | — |

**10 CASH Y# 10s.1a Composition:** Copper **Ruler:** Kuang-hsü **Obverse:** Inscription: Tai-ch'ing T'ung-pi **Reverse:** 5 small waves below dragon **Rev. Legend:** Kuang-hsü Nien-tsao, TAI-CHING-TI-KUO ...

| Date | Mintage | F | VF | XF | Unc | BU |
|---|---|---|---|---|---|---|
| CD(1906) | — | 5.00 | 10.00 | 17.50 | 40.00 | — |

**10 CASH Y# 10s.2a Composition:** Copper **Ruler:** Kuang-hsü **Obverse:** Inscription: Tai-ch'ing T'ung-pi **Reverse:** Dragon with larger forehead and narrower face, pearl redesigned **Rev. Legend:** Kuang-hsü Nien-tsao, TAI-CHING-TI-KUO ...

| Date | Mintage | F | VF | XF | Unc | BU |
|---|---|---|---|---|---|---|
| CD(1906) | — | 8.00 | 15.00 | 30.00 | 60.00 | — |

## PATTERNS

Including off metal strikes

| KM# | Date | Mintage | Identification | Mkt Val |
|---|---|---|---|---|
| Pn1 | (1851) | — | 10 Cash. Cast Brass. C22-7. | — |
| Pn2 | (1851) | — | 50 Cash. Cast Brass. C22-3. | — |
| Pn3 | (1851) | — | 100 Cash. Cast Brass. C22-4. | — |
| Pn7 | 15(1926) | — | 10 Dollars. Gold. K1536. | 2,500 |
| Pn9 | 15(1926) | — | 20 Dollars. Gold. K1535. | 3,000 |
| Pn8 | 15(1926) | — | 10 Dollars. Pewter. K1536y. | — |
| Pn10 | 15(1926) | — | 20 Dollars. Pewter. K1535y. | — |
| Pn11 | 21(1932) | — | 20 Cash. Copper. Wide flan. | — |

| KM# | Date | Mintage | Identification | Mkt Val |
|---|---|---|---|---|
| Pn12 | 22(1933) | — | 2 Cents. Nickel. K827. | — |

| KM# | Date | Mintage | Identification | Mkt Val |
|---|---|---|---|---|
| Pn13 | 22(1933) | — | 20 Cash. Copper. | — |

## SHENSI PROVINCE

**Shaanxi**

A province located in central China that is a rich agricultural area. A very important province in the early development of China. An active imperial mint was located at Sian (Xi'an).

# EMPIRE

## PROVINCIAL CASH COINAGE

**CASH** **C# 23-13** **Composition:** Cast Brass **Ruler:** Kuang-hsü **Obverse:** Type A

| Date | Mintage | Good | VG | F | VF | XF |
|---|---|---|---|---|---|---|
| ND(1875-1908) | — | 20.00 | 35.00 | 50.00 | 75.00 | — |

**10 CASH** **C# 23-14** **Composition:** Cast Brass **Ruler:** Kuang-hsü **Obverse:** Type B

| Date | Mintage | Good | VG | F | VF | XF |
|---|---|---|---|---|---|---|
| ND(1875-1908) Rare | — | — | — | — | — | — |

# REPUBLIC

## MILLED COINAGE

One is 2/100 of Large Dollar Coin = 2 Cent

**CENT** **Y# 435** **Composition:** Copper **Obverse:** Crossed flags **Obv. Legend:** IMTYPIF: "I Mei Ta Yuan Pi I (1) Fen" (One is 1/100 of Large Dollar Coin = 1 Cent) **Reverse:** Value above wheat sprays

| Date | Mintage | VG | F | VF | XF | Unc |
|---|---|---|---|---|---|---|
| ND(c. 1928) | — | 25.00 | 40.00 | 70.00 | 150 | — |

**2 CENTS** **Y# 436** **Composition:** Copper **Obverse:** Crossed flags, star between flags **Obv. Legend:** IMTYPEF: "I Mei Ta Yuan Pi Erh (2) Fen" **Reverse:** Value above wheat sprays **Note:** Dentilated borders.

| Date | Mintage | VG | F | VF | XF | Unc |
|---|---|---|---|---|---|---|
| ND(c. 1928) | — | 35.00 | 60.00 | 90.00 | 150 | — |

**2 CENTS** **Y# 436.1** **Composition:** Copper **Obverse:** Crossed flags, without star between flags **Obv. Legend:** IMTYPEF: "I Mei Ta Yuan Pi Erh (2) Fen" **Reverse:** Value above wheat sprays **Note:** Large Chinese legends.

| Date | Mintage | VG | F | VF | XF | Unc |
|---|---|---|---|---|---|---|
| ND(c. 1928) | — | 15.00 | 25.00 | 40.00 | 75.00 | — |

**2 CENTS** **Y# 436.2** **Composition:** Copper **Obverse:** Crossed flags, star in center **Obv. Legend:** IMTYPEF: "I Mei Ta Yuan Pi Erh (2) Fen" **Reverse:** Value above wheat sprays, star in center

| Date | Mintage | VG | F | VF | XF | Unc |
|---|---|---|---|---|---|---|
| ND(c. 1928) | — | 40.00 | 75.00 | 120 | 225 | — |

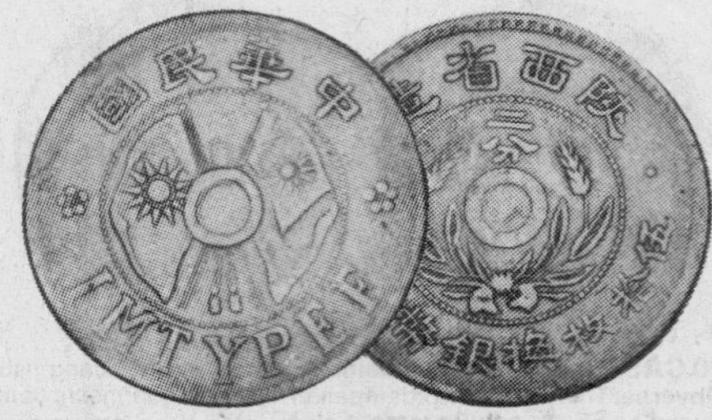

**2 CENTS** **Y# 436.3** **Composition:** Copper **Obverse:** Crossed flags, without star between flags **Obv. Legend:** IMTYPEF: "I Mei Ta Yuan Pi Erh (2) Fen" **Reverse:** Value above wheat sprays **Note:** Small Chinese legends.

| Date | Mintage | VG | F | VF | XF | Unc |
|---|---|---|---|---|---|---|
| ND(c. 1928) | — | 25.00 | 50.00 | 80.00 | 125 | — |

**2 CENTS** **Y# 436.4** **Composition:** Copper **Obverse:** Crossed flags **Obv. Legend:** IMTYPEF: "I Mei Ta Yuan Pi Erh (2) Fen" **Reverse:** Value above wheat sprays **Note:** Pearled borders.

| Date | Mintage | VG | F | VF | XF | Unc |
|---|---|---|---|---|---|---|
| ND(c. 1928) | — | 50.00 | 80.00 | 120 | 200 | — |

**2 CENTS** **Y# 436.5** **Composition:** Copper **Obverse:** Crossed flags, similar to Y#436.2 but with star between flags **Obv. Legend:** IMTYPEF: "I Mei Ta Yuan Pi Erh (2) Fen" **Reverse:** Value above wheat sprays **Note:** Large Chinese legends.

| Date | Mintage | VG | F | VF | XF | Unc |
|---|---|---|---|---|---|---|
| ND(c. 1928) | — | 40.00 | 75.00 | 120 | 225 | — |

## SIKANG PROVINCE

Created in 1928 from the western frontier region of Szechuan Province. It was dissolved in 1955, being divided between Szechuan (Sichuan) Province and Tibet.

# REPUBLIC

## MILLED COINAGE

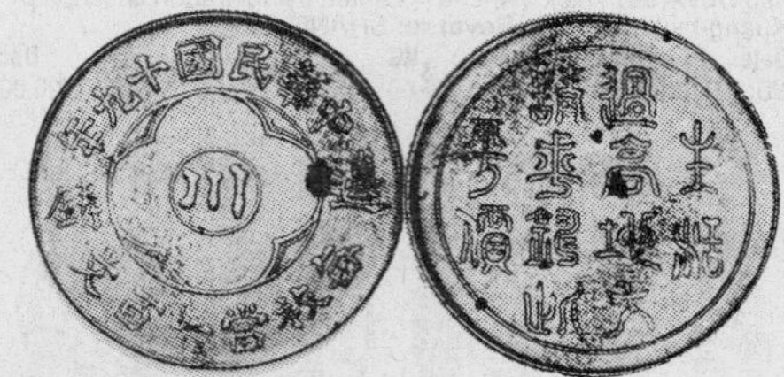

**100 CASH** **KM# 1** **Composition:** Copper

| Date | Mintage | VG | F | VF | XF | Unc |
|---|---|---|---|---|---|---|
| (1926)(15) | — | 150 | 225 | 300 | 400 | — |
| (1930)(19) | — | 125 | 150 | 200 | 300 | — |

**100 CASH** **KM# 2** **Composition:** Brass

| Date | Mintage | VG | F | VF | XF | Unc |
|---|---|---|---|---|---|---|
| (1930)(19) | — | 125 | 150 | 225 | 375 | — |

**Note:** Previously listed in Szechuan (Sichuan) Province as Y466, 466a.

## SINKIANG PROVINCE

**Hsinkiang, Xinjiang**
**"New Dominion"**

An autonomous region in western China, often referred to as Chinese Turkestan. High mountains surround 2000 ft. tableland on three sides with a large desert in center of this province. Many salt lakes, mining and some farming and oil. Inhabited by early man and was referred to as the "Silk Route" to the West. Sinkiang (Xinjiang) has been historically under the control of many factions, including Genghis Khan. It became a province in 1884. China has made claim to Sinkiang (Xinjiang) for many, many years. This rule has been more nominal than actual. Sinkiang (Xinjiang) had eight imperial mints, only three of which were in operation toward the end of the reign of Kuang Hsu. Only two mints operated during the early years of the republic. In 1949, due to a drastic coin shortage and lack of confidence in the inflated paper money, it was planned to mint some dollars in Sinkiang (Xinjiang). These did not see much circulation, however, due to the defeat of the nationalists, though they have recently appeared in considerable numbers in today's market.

**PATTERNS**

NOTE: A number of previously listed cast coins of Sinkiang Province are now known to be patterns - "mother" cash or "seed" cash for which no circulating issues are known. The following coins are, therefore, no longer listed. Most were probably manufactured in Beijing. They are generally made of brass rather than the purer copper usual to Sinkiang. The following coins are, therefore, no longer listed here: Craig #30-9, 30-11a, 30-12a, 30-14, 30-15a, 30-16, 30-17, 28-4.1, 28-8a, 28-9a,28-9c, 28-10, 31-1a, 31-1v, 31-2, 32-4, 32-5, 33-12, 33-21, 34-2, 34-3, 35-5a and 35-6.

**MONETARY SYSTEM**

2 Pul = 1 Cash
2 Cash = 5 Li
4 Cash = 10 Li = 1 Fen
25 Cash = 10 Fen = 1 Miscal = 1 Ch'ien, Mace, Tanga
10 Miscals (Mace) = 1 Liang (Tael or Sar)
20 Miscals (Tangas) = 1 Tilla

**MINT NAME**

**LOCAL MINT NAMES AND MARKS**
**MINT + CHINESE + TURKI + MANCHU**

Aksu 城阿 اقصو

Ili, now Yining (Gulja) 犂伊 الي

Kashgar, now Kashi 什喀 کشقر

Khotan, now Hotan 闐和 خوتن

Kotsha, (Kuche) کوتشر

Kuche, now Kuqa 車庫 کوچا

Ti-hua, now Dihua, refer to Urumchi 化廸

Urumchi, now Urumqi 化廸 ارومجي

Ushi, now Wushi (Uqturpan) 什烏 اوش

沙吉英

Yangihissar, now Yengisar

羌爾葉 يارقند

Yarkand, now Shache (Yarkant)

# EMPIRE

## PROVINCIAL CAST COINAGE

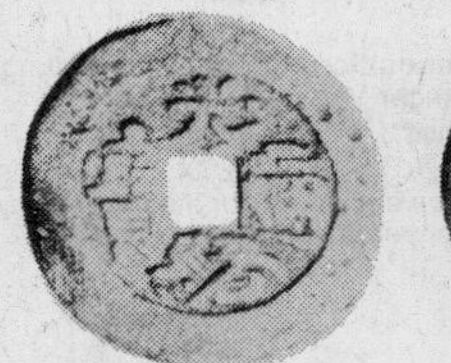
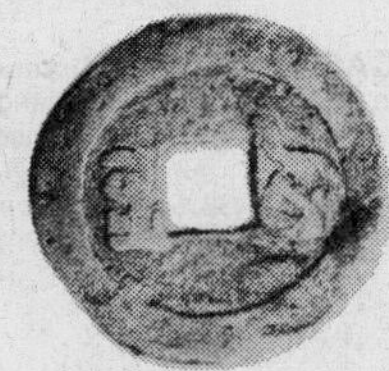

**CASH** **C# 33-23** **Composition:** Cast Copper **Ruler:** Kuang-hsü **Obverse:** Inscription: "Kuang-hsü T'ung-pao" **Note:** Struck at Kuche (Kucha)

| Date | Mintage | Good | VG | F | VF | XF |
|---|---|---|---|---|---|---|
| ND(1875-1908) | — | 6.00 | 8.00 | 12.00 | 20.00 | — |

**10 CASH** **C# 30-18** **Composition:** Cast Copper **Ruler:** Kuang-hsü **Obverse:** Inscription: Kuang-hsü T'ung-pao **Reverse:** Character "A" (for Asku) above center hole, "Asku" in Turki at right, in Manchu at left **Note:** Cast at Aksu Mint.

| Date | Mintage | Good | VG | F | VF | XF |
|---|---|---|---|---|---|---|
| ND(1875-1908) | — | 1.50 | 2.50 | 4.00 | 8.00 | — |

**10 CASH** **C# 30-18.1** **Composition:** Cast Copper **Ruler:** Kuang-hsü **Reverse:** "Asku" in Manchu at right, in Turki at left **Note:** Cast at Aksu Mint.

| Date | Mintage | Good | VG | F | VF | XF |
|---|---|---|---|---|---|---|
| ND(1875-1908) | — | 7.50 | 12.50 | 19.00 | 35.00 | — |

**10 CASH** **C# 32-6** **Composition:** Cast Copper **Ruler:** Kuang-hsü **Obverse:** Inscription: Kuang-hsü T'ung-pao **Reverse:** "Kashgar" in Turki at left, in Manchu at right, "K'a" (Kashgar) above **Note:** Struck at the Kashgar Mint.

| Date | Mintage | Good | VG | F | VF | XF |
|---|---|---|---|---|---|---|
| ND(1875-1908) | — | 5.00 | 9.50 | 15.00 | 25.00 | — |

**10 CASH** **C# 32-6.1** **Composition:** Cast Copper **Ruler:** Kuang-hsü **Obverse:** Inscription: Kuang-hsü T'ung-pao **Reverse:** "Manchu Boo-Kashgar" (right-left) **Note:** Struck at the Kashgar Mint.

| Date | Mintage | Good | VG | F | VF | XF |
|---|---|---|---|---|---|---|
| ND(1875-1908) | — | 5.00 | 9.50 | 15.00 | 25.00 | — |

**10 CASH** **C# 30-19** **Composition:** Cast Copper **Ruler:** Kuang-hsü **Reverse:** Character "K'a" (for Kashgar) above **Note:** Cast at Aksu Mint.

| Date | Mintage | Good | VG | F | VF | XF |
|---|---|---|---|---|---|---|
| ND(1886-1908) | — | 2.00 | 4.50 | 6.50 | 13.50 | — |

**Note:** Cast in the Aksu Mint for the Kashgar Mint, beginning in 1886 during the reign of Kuang-Hsu

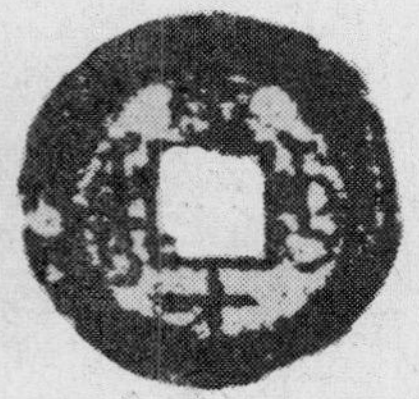

**10 CASH** **C# 34-4** **Composition:** Cast Copper **Ruler:** Hsüan-t'ung **Reverse:** "K'u" (Kuche) above, "Ushi" in Manchu and Turki right and left

| Date | Mintage | Good | VG | F | VF | XF |
|---|---|---|---|---|---|---|
| ND(1909-1911) | — | 50.00 | 80.00 | 150 | — | — |

**Note:** Cast in Ushi to the order of the Kuche Mint; it is the last of the "red" copper cash

## GENERAL CAST COINAGE

**CASH** **KM# 11** **Composition:** Cast Copper **Ruler:** Kuang-hsü **Reverse:** Similar to KM#10 but entire reverse is in inverted mirror image **Note:** Struck at Kuche (Kucha)

| Date | Mintage | Good | VG | F | VF | XF |
|---|---|---|---|---|---|---|
| ND(1875-1908) | — | 3.50 | 6.00 | 9.00 | 13.50 | — |

**CASH** **KM# 10** **Composition:** Cast Copper **Ruler:** Kuang-hsü **Obverse:** Inscription: Kuang-hsü T'ung-pao **Reverse:** Inscription: Manchu "Boo Ciowan" for Hu-pu Board of Revenue **Note:** Struck at Kuche.

| Date | Mintage | Good | VG | F | VF | XF |
|---|---|---|---|---|---|---|
| ND(1875-1908) | — | 1.50 | 3.50 | 6.00 | 9.50 | — |

**CASH** **KM# 12** **Composition:** Cast Copper **Ruler:** Kuang-hsü **Obverse:** Inscription: Kuang-hsü T'ung-pao **Reverse:** Similar to KM#11 **Note:** Struck at Kuche.

| Date | Mintage | Good | VG | F | VF | XF |
|---|---|---|---|---|---|---|
| ND(1875-1908) | — | 1.50 | 3.50 | 6.00 | 9.50 | — |

**CASH** **KM# 13** **Composition:** Cast Copper **Ruler:** Kuang-hsü **Obverse:** Inscription: Kuang-hsü T'ung-pao **Reverse:** "Boo Chaun" or "Yuan" (illiterate Manchu) **Note:** Struck at Kuche.

| Date | Mintage | Good | VG | F | VF | XF |
|---|---|---|---|---|---|---|
| ND(1875-1908) | — | 1.50 | 3.50 | 6.00 | 9.50 | — |

**CASH** **KM# 14** **Composition:** Cast Copper **Ruler:** Kuang-hsü **Obverse:** Inscription: Kuang-hsü T'ung-pao **Reverse:** "Boo Choan" (illiterate Manchu) **Note:** Struck at Kuche.

| Date | Mintage | Good | VG | F | VF | XF |
|---|---|---|---|---|---|---|
| ND(1875-1908) | — | 1.50 | 3.00 | 5.00 | 8.50 | — |

**Note:** The five one-cash varieties listed above could be confused with Beijing issues C1-16 or C2-15, but they are much more crudely cast, and are made of red copper rather than brass; see Landon Ross, 1986, Numismatics International Bulletin 20(3) for a more detailed review

**10 CASH** **KM# 8** **Composition:** Cast Copper **Ruler:** Kuang-hsü **Obverse:** Inscription: "Kuang-hsü T'ung-pao" **Reverse:** "Manchu Boo Hsin" with "Hsin" (new, but here standing for the Tihwa (now Urumqi) Mint) above **Note:** Cast at Tihwa Mint.

| Date | Mintage | Good | VG | F | VF | XF |
|---|---|---|---|---|---|---|
| ND(1875-1908) | — | 3.50 | 5.00 | 7.50 | 15.00 | — |

**10 CASH** **KM# 9** **Composition:** Cast Copper **Ruler:** Kuang-hsü **Obverse:** Inscription: "Kuang-hsü T'ung-pao" **Reverse:** "Manchu Boo Hsin" (for Tihwa Mint) with "Hsin" (new) above **Note:** Cast at Tihwa Mint.

| Date | Mintage | Good | VG | F | VF | XF |
|---|---|---|---|---|---|---|
| ND(1875-1908) | — | 3.00 | 4.50 | 7.00 | 15.00 | — |

**10 CASH** **KM# 7.1** **Composition:** Cast Copper **Ruler:** Kuang-hsü **Obverse:** Inscription: "Kuang-hsü T'ung-pao" **Reverse:** "Pao Ku" with "K'u" (for Kuche) above **Note:** Struck at Kuche.

| Date | Mintage | Good | VG | F | VF | XF |
|---|---|---|---|---|---|---|
| ND(1875-1908) | — | 1.50 | 3.00 | 5.00 | 10.00 | — |

**10 CASH** **KM# 7.2** **Composition:** Cast Copper **Ruler:** Kuang-hsü **Reverse:** "Pao" (for Kuche) at left reversed **Note:** Struck at Kuche.

| Date | Mintage | Good | VG | F | VF | XF |
|---|---|---|---|---|---|---|
| ND(1875-1908) | — | 7.50 | 13.50 | 22.50 | 35.00 | — |

**10 CASH** **C# 33-16** **Composition:** Cast Copper **Ruler:** Kuang-hsü **Obverse:** Inscription: "Kuang-hsü T'ung-pao" **Note:** Cast at Kuche (Kucha)

| Date | Mintage | Good | VG | F | VF | XF |
|---|---|---|---|---|---|---|
| ND(1875-1908) | — | 10.00 | 20.00 | 30.00 | 50.00 | — |

**10 CASH** **C# 33-19** **Composition:** Cast Copper **Ruler:** Kuang-hsü **Obverse:** Inscription: "Kuang-hsü T'ung-paoi" **Reverse:** Inscription: "Manchu Boo-kuce", kuce in simple style **Note:** Cast at Kuche (Kucha) Mint.

| Date | Mintage | Good | VG | F | VF | XF |
|---|---|---|---|---|---|---|
| ND(1875-1908) | — | 2.00 | 3.00 | 10.00 | 18.00 | — |

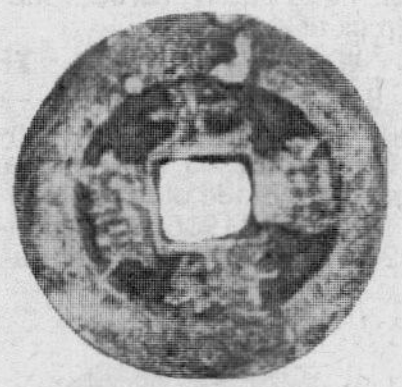

**10 CASH** **C# 33-18** **Composition:** Cast Copper **Ruler:** Kuang-hsü **Reverse:** Character "K'u" above **Note:** Struck at Kuche (Kucha)

| Date | Mintage | Good | VG | F | VF | XF |
|---|---|---|---|---|---|---|
| ND1875-1908) | — | 7.50 | 12.00 | 17.50 | 35.00 | — |

**10 CASH** **C# 33-18.1** **Composition:** Cast Copper **Ruler:** Kuang-hsü **Reverse:** Semi-circle at lower right **Note:** Struck at Kuche (Kucha)

| Date | Mintage | Good | VG | F | VF | XF |
|---|---|---|---|---|---|---|
| ND(1875-1908) | — | 7.50 | 13.50 | 22.50 | 35.00 | — |

**10 CASH** **Composition:** Cast Copper **Ruler:** Kuang-hsü **Obverse:** Type A-1 **Reverse:** "Pao Yuan?" (left-right) with "K'a" (for Kashgar) above

| Date | Mintage | Good | VG | F | VF | XF |
|---|---|---|---|---|---|---|
| ND | — | — | — | — | — | — |

**Note:** Reported, not confirmed.

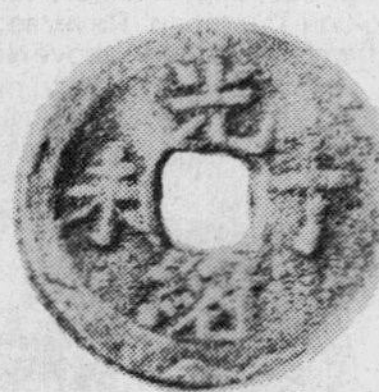

**10 CASH** **KM# 16** **Composition:** Cast Copper **Ruler:** Kuang-hsü Ting Wei **Reverse:** "Boo-yuan?" with "Hsin" (new) above

| Date | Mintage | Good | VG | F | VF | XF |
|---|---|---|---|---|---|---|
| CD(1907) | — | 7.50 | 17.50 | 30.00 | — | — |

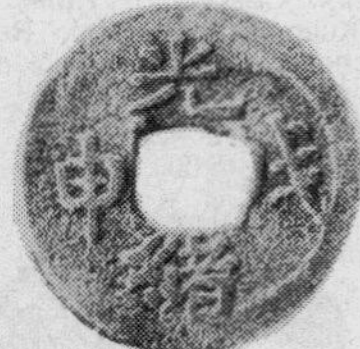

**10 CASH** **KM# 17** **Composition:** Cast Copper **Ruler:** Kuang-hsü **Obverse:** Inscription: "Kuang-hsü Wu-shen"

| Date | Mintage | Good | VG | F | VF | XF |
|---|---|---|---|---|---|---|
| CD(1908) | — | 11.50 | 25.00 | 45.00 | — | — |

## MILLED COINAGE

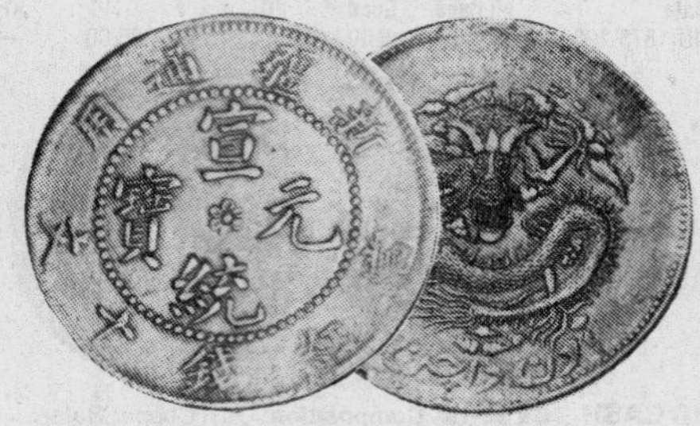

**10 CASH** **Y# 2.1** **Composition:** Copper **Ruler:** Hsüan-t'ung **Obverse:** Inscription: Hsüan-t'ung Yüan-pao **Reverse:** Without Chinese legend above side-view dragon

| Date | Mintage | Good | VG | F | VF | XF |
|---|---|---|---|---|---|---|
| ND(ca.1909) | — | 25.00 | 42.50 | 75.00 | 175 | — |

**10 CASH** **Y# 2.2** **Composition:** Copper **Ruler:** Hsüan-t'ung **Obverse:** Inscription: Hsüan-t'ung Yüan-pao **Reverse:** Chinese legend with "Nien" (year) added above dragon

| Date | Mintage | Good | VG | F | VF | XF |
|---|---|---|---|---|---|---|
| CD(1910) | — | 25.00 | 42.50 | 75.00 | 175 | — |
| CD(1911) | — | 30.00 | 50.00 | 100 | 200 | — |

**10 CASH** **Y# 2a** **Composition:** Copper **Ruler:** Hsüan-t'ung **Obverse:** Inscription: Hsüan-t'ung Yüan-pao; large characters within center circle

| Date | Mintage | F | VF | XF | Unc | BU |
|---|---|---|---|---|---|---|
| CD(1910) | — | — | — | 25.00 | 35.00 | — |

**Note:** Modern copy

**10 CASH** **Y# 2.3** **Composition:** Copper **Ruler:** Hsüan-t'ung **Obverse:** Inscription: Hsüan-t'ung Yüan-pao; double ring around star in center

| Date | Mintage | Good | VG | F | VF | XF |
|---|---|---|---|---|---|---|
| CD(1911) | — | 30.00 | 50.00 | 100 | 200 | — |

**10 CASH** **Y# A38.1** **Composition:** Copper **Ruler:** Hung-hsien **Obverse:** Chinese legend "Hung-hsien T'ung-pi" in inner dotted circle **Note:** Struck at the Kashgar Mint.

| Date | Mintage | Good | VG | F | VF | XF |
|---|---|---|---|---|---|---|
| AH1334 | — | 120 | 180 | 250 | — | — |

**10 CASH** **Y# A38.2** **Composition:** Copper **Ruler:** Hung-hsien **Note:** Struck at the Kashgar Mint.

| Date | Mintage | Good | VG | F | VF | XF |
|---|---|---|---|---|---|---|
| AH1334 | — | 120 | 180 | 250 | — | — |

**Note:** Y#A38.1 and A38.2 were issued for the brief reign of Yuan Shih-kai as Emperor Hung-hsien (1916)

**FEN, 5 LI** **Y# 1** **Composition:** Copper **Ruler:** Kuang-hsü **Obverse:** Inscription: Kuang-hsü Yüan-pao; large dots in circle, dentilated rims **Reverse:** Front view dragon **Note:** Two varieties are reported.

| Date | Mintage | Good | VG | F | VF | XF |
|---|---|---|---|---|---|---|
| ND(ca.1906) | — | 150 | 200 | 350 | 550 | — |

**FEN, 5 LI** **Y# 1a** **Composition:** Copper **Ruler:** Kuang-hsü **Obverse:** Inscription: Kuang-hsü Yüan-pao; small dots in circle, dotted rims **Reverse:** Front view dragon

| Date | Mintage | F | VF | XF | Unc | BU |
|---|---|---|---|---|---|---|
| ND(ca.1906) Modern copy | — | — | — | 25.00 | 35.00 | — |

**Note:** The legend on this coin states that it is valued at 1 Fen 5 Li of silver (about 15 Cash); the coin is the size of a normal 10 Cash piece of Sinkiang (Xinjiang), but these pieces are usually larger than those of the other provinces; for this reason, it is assumed the coin was overvalued to benefit the government

**2 FEN 5 LI** **Y# A1** **Composition:** Copper **Ruler:** Kuang-hsü **Obverse:** Inscription: Kuang-hsü Yüan-pao **Reverse:** Front view dragon

| Date | Mintage | Good | VG | F | VF | XF |
|---|---|---|---|---|---|---|
| ND(ca.1906) Rare | — | — | — | — | — | — |

**Note:** This denomination was recalled shortly after issue and the dies re-engraved 1 Fen and 5 Li to produce Y#1; do not confuse poorly re-engraved Chinese numeral "172" examples of Y#1 for Y#A1; note the difference in spacing of the Chinese characters below the rosettes between Y#1 and Y#A1

**2 FEN 5 LI** **Y# B1** **Composition:** Copper **Ruler:** Kuang-hsü **Obverse:** Inscription: Kuang-hsü Yüan-pao **Reverse:** Side view dragon

| Date | Mintage | Good | VG | F | VF | XF |
|---|---|---|---|---|---|---|
| ND(ca.1906) Rare | — | — | — | — | — | — |

**Note:** Status unknown

**MISCAL (Mace)** **Y# B16** **Weight:** 3.5000 g. **Composition:** Silver **Ruler:** Kuang-hsü **Obverse:** Inscription: Kuang-hsü Yin-yüan; "Kashgar" at right, value at left **Note:** Struck at Kashgar Mint.

| Date | Mintage | VG | F | VF | XF | Unc |
|---|---|---|---|---|---|---|
| AH1331 Error for 1321 | — | 50.00 | 85.00 | 175 | 250 | — |
| AH1322 | — | 50.00 | 85.00 | 175 | 250 | — |

**MISCAL (Mace)** **Y# C16** **Weight:** 3.5000 g. **Composition:** Silver **Ruler:** Kuang-hsü **Obverse:** "Kash-gar" in Chinese at right and left of value **Reverse:** Turki inscription in sprays **Note:** Struck at Kashgar Mint.

| Date | Mintage | VG | F | VF | XF | Unc |
|---|---|---|---|---|---|---|
| AH1322 | — | 45.00 | 70.00 | 125 | 200 | — |

**MISCAL (Mace)** **Y# A20.2** **Weight:** 3.5000 g. **Composition:** Silver **Ruler:** Kuang-hsü **Obverse:** Turki at right and left of value, date at lower right **Reverse:** Side view dragon **Note:** Struck at Kashgar Mint.

| Date | Mintage | VG | F | VF | XF | Unc |
|---|---|---|---|---|---|---|
| AH1323 | — | 200 | 350 | 600 | 1,000 | — |

**MISCAL (Mace)** **Y# A20.3** **Weight:** 3.5000 g. **Composition:** Silver **Ruler:** Kuang-hsü **Obverse:** Inverted Turki legends at right and left of value **Note:** Struck at Kashgar Mint.

| Date | Mintage | VG | F | VF | XF | Unc |
|---|---|---|---|---|---|---|
| AH1323 | — | 200 | 350 | 600 | 1,000 | — |

**MISCAL (Mace)** **Y# 3** **Weight:** 3.5000 g. **Composition:** Silver **Ruler:** Kuang-hsü **Obverse:** Outer legend: Turki without dot in center **Reverse:** Without Turki legend

| Date | Mintage | VG | F | VF | XF | Unc |
|---|---|---|---|---|---|---|
| ND(1905) | — | 75.00 | 125 | 200 | 325 | — |

**MISCAL (Mace)** **Y# 3.1** **Weight:** 3.5000 g. **Composition:** Silver **Ruler:** Kuang-hsü **Obverse:** Legend: Turki with dot in center **Reverse:** Without Turki legend

| Date | Mintage | VG | F | VF | XF | Unc |
|---|---|---|---|---|---|---|
| ND(1905) | — | 75.00 | 125 | 200 | 325 | — |

**MISCAL (Mace)** **Y# 3.2** **Weight:** 3.5000 g. **Composition:** Silver **Ruler:** Kuang-hsü **Obverse:** Without outer Turki legend **Reverse:** Turki legend

| Date | Mintage | VG | F | VF | XF | Unc |
|---|---|---|---|---|---|---|
| ND(1905) | — | 325 | 550 | 900 | 1,500 | — |

**MISCAL (Mace)** **Y# 3.3** **Weight:** 3.5000 g. **Composition:** Silver **Ruler:** Kuang-hsü **Obverse:** Without outer Turki legend **Reverse:** Without outer Turki legend

| Date | Mintage | VG | F | VF | XF | Unc |
|---|---|---|---|---|---|---|
| ND(1905) | — | 90.00 | 150 | 250 | 400 | — |

**MISCAL (Mace)** **Y# A20.1** **Weight:** 3.5000 g. **Composition:** Silver **Ruler:** Kuang-hsü **Obverse:** Turki at right and left of value, date at lower left **Reverse:** Side view dragon

| Date | Mintage | VG | F | VF | XF | Unc |
|---|---|---|---|---|---|---|
| AH1323 | — | 200 | 350 | 600 | 1,000 | — |

**MISCAL (Mace)** **Y# 10** **Weight:** 3.5000 g. **Composition:** Silver **Ruler:** Kuang-hsü **Obverse:** Without outer Turki legend **Reverse:** Legend above dragon, 1 MACE below **Rev. Legend:** SUNGAREI

| Date | Mintage | VG | F | VF | XF | Unc |
|---|---|---|---|---|---|---|
| ND(1906) | — | 110 | 225 | 400 | 650 | — |

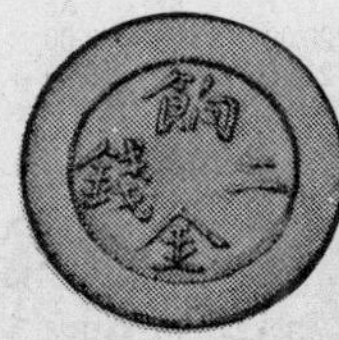

**GOLD MISCAL (Mace)** **Y# 9** **Weight:** 7.8000 g. **Composition:** Gold **Ruler:** Kuang-hsü **Obverse:** Narrow-spaced Chinese "2" **Reverse:** Turki legend around uncircled dragon

| Date | Mintage | F | VF | XF | Unc | BU |
|---|---|---|---|---|---|---|
| ND(ca.1906) | — | 750 | 1,350 | 2,000 | 2,800 | — |

**GOLD MISCAL (Mace)** **Y# 9.1** **Weight:** 7.8000 g. **Composition:** Gold **Ruler:** Kuang-hsü **Obverse:** Wide-spaced Chinese "2" **Reverse:** Redesigned dragon

| Date | Mintage | F | VF | XF | Unc | BU |
|---|---|---|---|---|---|---|
| ND(ca.1906) | — | 750 | 1,350 | 2,000 | 2,800 | — |

**GOLD MISCAL (Mace)** **Y# 8** **Weight:** 3.9000 g. **Composition:** Gold **Ruler:** Kuang-hsü **Reverse:** Turki legend around uncircled dragon

| Date | Mintage | F | VF | XF | Unc | BU |
|---|---|---|---|---|---|---|
| ND(ca.1907) | — | 400 | 650 | 950 | 1,350 | — |

**GOLD MISCAL (Mace)** **Y# 8.2** **Weight:** 3.9000 g. **Composition:** Gold **Ruler:** Kuang-hsü **Reverse:** Turki legend at left differs

| Date | Mintage | F | VF | XF | Unc | BU |
|---|---|---|---|---|---|---|
| ND(ca.1907) | — | 450 | 750 | 1,150 | 1,650 | — |

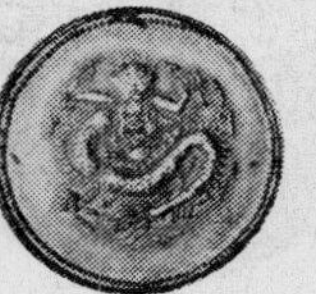

**GOLD MISCAL (Mace)** **Y# 8.1** **Weight:** 3.9000 g. **Composition:** Gold **Ruler:** Kuang-hsü **Reverse:** Without Turki legend around uncircled dragon

| Date | Mintage | F | VF | XF | Unc | BU |
|---|---|---|---|---|---|---|
| ND(ca.1907) | — | 750 | 1,250 | 1,850 | 2,650 | — |

**GOLD MISCAL (Mace)** **Y# 8.3** **Weight:** 3.9000 g. **Composition:** Gold **Ruler:** Kuang-hsü **Reverse:** Turki legend in outer circle

| Date | Mintage | F | VF | XF | Unc | BU |
|---|---|---|---|---|---|---|
| ND(ca.1907) | — | 550 | 950 | 1,350 | 2,000 | — |

**2 MISCALS (2 Mace)** **Y# 17a** **Weight:** 7.2000 g. **Composition:** Silver **Ruler:** Kuang-hsü **Obverse:** Inscription: Kuang-hsü Yin-yüan between Kashgar and value **Note:** Struck at Kashgar Mint.

| Date | Mintage | VG | F | VF | XF | Unc |
|---|---|---|---|---|---|---|
| AH1311 | — | — | — | — | — | — |
| Note: Error | | | | | | |
| AH1312 | — | 12.50 | 22.50 | 32.50 | 50.00 | — |
| AH1313 | — | 12.50 | 22.50 | 32.50 | 50.00 | — |
| AH1314 | — | 12.50 | 22.50 | 32.50 | 50.00 | — |
| AH1315 | — | 12.50 | 22.50 | 32.50 | 50.00 | — |
| AH1317 | — | 12.50 | 22.50 | 32.50 | 50.00 | — |
| AH1319 | — | 12.50 | 22.50 | 32.50 | 50.00 | — |
| AH1320 | — | 17.50 | 30.00 | 45.00 | 75.00 | — |

**2 MISCALS (2 Mace)** **Y# 17a.1** **Weight:** 7.2000 g. **Composition:** Silver **Ruler:** Kuang-hsü **Obverse:** Inscription: Kuang-hsü Yin-yüan between "K'a Tsao" at right, value at left **Note:** Struck at Kashgar Mint.

| Date | Mintage | VG | F | VF | XF | Unc |
|---|---|---|---|---|---|---|
| AH1320 Rare | — | — | — | — | — | — |
| AH1321 | — | 17.50 | 30.00 | 45.00 | 75.00 | — |
| AH1322 | — | 20.00 | 35.00 | 55.00 | 100 | — |

**2 MISCALS (2 Mace)** **Y# 33** **Composition:** Cast Copper **Ruler:** Kuang-hsü **Obverse:** Inscription: "Kuang-hsü Yin-yüan" between "Tihwa" and value with normal Ërh (2) at left **Reverse:** Inscription: Turki in floral wreath **Note:** Struck at Tihwa Mint.

| Date | Mintage | VG | F | VF | XF | Unc |
|---|---|---|---|---|---|---|
| AH1321 | — | 15.00 | 22.00 | 55.00 | 90.00 | — |
| AH1322 | — | 15.00 | 22.00 | 55.00 | 90.00 | — |
| AH1323 | — | 17.50 | 30.00 | 55.00 | 90.00 | — |

**2 MISCALS (2 Mace)** **Y# 33.1** **Composition:** Cast Copper **Ruler:** Kuang-hsü **Obverse:** Inscription: "Kuang-hsü Yin-yüan" between "Tihwa" and value with official Ërh (2) at left **Reverse:** Inscription: Turki in floral wreath **Note:** Struck at Tihwa Mint.

| Date | Mintage | VG | F | VF | XF | Unc |
|---|---|---|---|---|---|---|
| AH1323 | — | 15.00 | 22.00 | 55.00 | 90.00 | — |
| AH1324 | — | 15.00 | 22.00 | 55.00 | 90.00 | — |
| AH1325 | — | 15.00 | 22.00 | 55.00 | 90.00 | — |

**2 MISCALS (2 Mace)** **Y# B20.1** **Weight:** 7.2000 g. **Composition:** Silver **Obv. Legend:** Chinese and Turki around inscription Kuang-hsü Yüan-pao **Reverse:** Dragon **Note:** Struck at Kashgar Mint.

| Date | Mintage | VG | F | VF | XF | Unc |
|---|---|---|---|---|---|---|
| AH1323 | — | 175 | 300 | 500 | 850 | — |

**2 MISCALS (2 Mace)** **Y# B20.2** **Weight:** 7.2000 g. **Composition:** Silver **Obv. Legend:** Chinese and Turki around inscription Kuang-hsü Yüan-pao **Reverse:** Dragon **Note:** Struck at Kashgar Mint.

| Date | Mintage | VG | F | VF | XF | Unc |
|---|---|---|---|---|---|---|
| AH1323 | — | 175 | 300 | 500 | 850 | — |

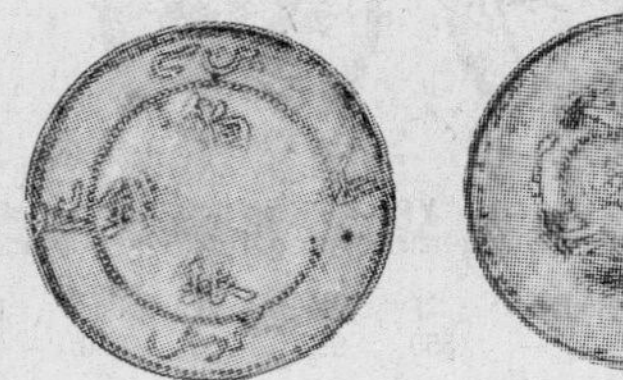

**2 MISCALS (2 Mace)** Y# 4 **Weight:** 7.2000 g. **Composition:** Silver **Ruler:** Kuang-hsü **Obverse:** Turki outer legend **Reverse:** Without Turki legend

| Date | Mintage | VG | F | VF | XF | Unc |
|---|---|---|---|---|---|---|
| ND(1905) | — | 50.00 | 75.00 | 150 | 400 | — |

**2 MISCALS (2 Mace)** Y# 4.1 **Weight:** 7.2000 g. **Composition:** Silver **Ruler:** Kuang-hsü **Obverse:** Continuous Turki outer legend **Reverse:** Without Turki legend

| Date | Mintage | VG | F | VF | XF | Unc |
|---|---|---|---|---|---|---|
| ND(1905) | — | 100 | 150 | 250 | 325 | — |

**2 MISCALS (2 Mace)** Y# 4.2 **Weight:** 7.2000 g. **Composition:** Silver **Ruler:** Kuang-hsü **Obverse:** Without outer Turki legend **Reverse:** Turki legend

| Date | Mintage | VG | F | VF | XF | Unc |
|---|---|---|---|---|---|---|
| ND(1905) | — | 150 | 250 | 400 | 650 | — |

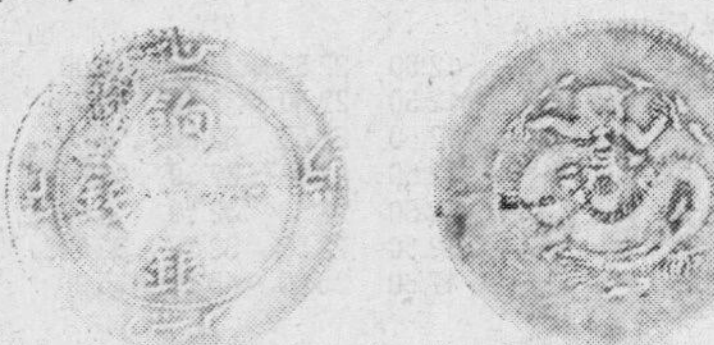

**2 MISCALS (2 Mace)** Y# 4.3 **Weight:** 7.2000 g. **Composition:** Silver **Ruler:** Kuang-hsü **Reverse:** Redesigned dragon without Turki legends

| Date | Mintage | VG | F | VF | XF | Unc |
|---|---|---|---|---|---|---|
| ND(1905) | — | 150 | 250 | 400 | 650 | — |

**2 MISCALS (2 Mace)** Y# 4.4 **Weight:** 7.2000 g. **Composition:** Silver **Ruler:** Kuang-hsü **Obverse:** Turki outer legend **Reverse:** Circled dragon without Turki legend

| Date | Mintage | VG | F | VF | XF | Unc |
|---|---|---|---|---|---|---|
| ND(1905) Rare | — | — | — | — | — | — |

**2 MISCALS (2 Mace)** Y# 11 **Weight:** 7.2000 g. **Composition:** Silver **Ruler:** Kuang-hsü **Reverse:** Legend above dragon, 2 MACE below **Rev. Legend:** SUNGAREI

| Date | Mintage | VG | F | VF | XF | Unc |
|---|---|---|---|---|---|---|
| ND(1906) | — | 200 | 425 | 850 | 1,350 | — |

**2 MISCALS (2 Mace)** Y# 23 **Weight:** 7.2000 g. **Composition:** Silver **Obv. Legend:** Chinese and Turki around inscription Ta-Ch'ing Yin-pi **Reverse:** Dragon in circle surrounded by sprays

| Date | Mintage | VG | F | VF | XF | Unc |
|---|---|---|---|---|---|---|
| AH1324 Rare | — | — | — | — | — | — |
| AH1325 | — | 20.00 | 40.00 | 65.00 | 110 | — |
| AH1326 | — | 20.00 | 40.00 | 65.00 | 110 | — |
| AH1327 | — | 25.00 | 50.00 | 80.00 | 150 | — |
| AH1329 | — | 35.00 | 65.00 | 110 | 175 | — |

**2 MISCALS (2 Mace)** Y# 29 **Weight:** 7.2000 g. **Composition:** Silver **Obverse:** Turki legend around Yin-Yüan Êrh-ch'ien within a beaded circle **Reverse:** Double ring around small dragon, floral pattern outside without legend **Note:** Struck at Kashgar Mint.

| Date | Mintage | VG | F | VF | XF | Unc |
|---|---|---|---|---|---|---|
| AH1329 | — | 55.00 | 90.00 | 150 | 250 | — |

**2 MISCALS (2 Mace)** Y# 29.1 **Weight:** 7.2000 g. **Composition:** Silver **Obverse:** Yin-yüan Êrh-ch'ien **Reverse:** Turki legend below larger dragon within single circle **Note:** Struck at Kashgar Mint.

| Date | Mintage | VG | F | VF | XF | Unc |
|---|---|---|---|---|---|---|
| AH1329 | — | 75.00 | 125 | 200 | 325 | — |

**3 MISCALS** Y# 18a **Weight:** 10.5000 g. **Composition:** Silver **Ruler:** Kuang-hsü **Obverse:** Inscription: Kuang-hsü Yin-yüan between Kashgar and value **Reverse:** Turki in floral wreath **Note:** Struck at Kashgar Mint.

| Date | Mintage | VG | F | VF | XF | Unc |
|---|---|---|---|---|---|---|
| AH1319 | — | 10.00 | 20.00 | 32.50 | 65.00 | — |
| AH1320 | — | 10.00 | 20.00 | 32.50 | 65.00 | — |

**3 MISCALS** Y# 18a.1 **Weight:** 10.5000 g. **Composition:** Silver **Ruler:** Kuang-hsü **Obverse:** Inscription: "Kuang-hsü Yin-yüan" between "K'a Tsao" and value **Reverse:** Turki in floral wreath **Note:** Struck at Kashgar Mint.

| Date | Mintage | VG | F | VF | XF | Unc |
|---|---|---|---|---|---|---|
| AH1320 | — | 10.00 | 20.00 | 32.50 | 65.00 | — |
| AH1321 | — | 10.00 | 20.00 | 32.50 | 65.00 | — |
| AH1322 | — | 10.00 | 20.00 | 32.50 | 65.00 | — |

**3 MISCALS** Y# 34 **Weight:** 10.3000 g. **Composition:** Silver **Ruler:** Kuang-hsü **Obverse:** Inscription: "Kuang-hsü Yin-yüan" between "Tihwa" and value with normal "San" (3) at left **Reverse:** Inscription: Turki in floral wreath **Note:** Struck at the Tihwa Mint.

| Date | Mintage | VG | F | VF | XF | Unc |
|---|---|---|---|---|---|---|
| AH1321 | — | 17.50 | 30.00 | 75.00 | 110 | — |
| AH1322 | — | 17.50 | 30.00 | 75.00 | 110 | — |
| AH1323 | — | 17.50 | 30.00 | 75.00 | 110 | — |

**3 MISCALS** Y# 35 **Weight:** 17.9000 g. **Composition:** Silver **Ruler:** Kuang-hsü **Obverse:** Inscription: "Kuang-hsü Yin-yüan" between "Tihwa" and value with normal "Wu" (5) at left **Reverse:** Inscription: Turki in floral wreath **Note:** Struck at the Tihwa Mint.

| Date | Mintage | VG | F | VF | XF | Unc |
|---|---|---|---|---|---|---|
| AH1321 | — | 20.00 | 35.00 | 70.00 | 125 | — |
| AH1322 | — | 20.00 | 35.00 | 70.00 | 125 | — |
| AH1323 | — | 20.00 | 35.00 | 70.00 | 125 | — |

**3 MISCALS** Y# 35a **Weight:** 17.9000 g. **Composition:** Silver **Ruler:** Kuang-hsü **Obverse:** Inscription: "Kuang-hsü Yin-yüan" between "Tihwa" and value with official "Wu" (5) at left **Reverse:** Inscription: Turki in floral wreath **Note:** Struck at the Tihwa Mint.

| Date | Mintage | VG | F | VF | XF | Unc |
|---|---|---|---|---|---|---|
| AH1323 | — | 20.00 | 40.00 | 70.00 | 125 | — |
| AH1324 | — | 15.00 | 30.00 | 60.00 | 100 | — |
| AH1325 | — | 15.00 | 30.00 | 60.00 | 100 | — |

**3 MISCALS** Y# 34a **Weight:** 10.3000 g. **Composition:** Silver **Ruler:** Kuang-hsü **Obverse:** Inscription: "Kuang-hsü Yin-yüan" between "Tihwa" and value with official "San" (3) at left **Reverse:** Inscription: Turki in floral wreath **Note:** Struck at the Tihwa Mint.

| Date | Mintage | VG | F | VF | XF | Unc |
|---|---|---|---|---|---|---|
| AH1323 | — | 10.00 | 20.00 | 32.50 | 65.00 | — |
| AH1324 | — | 10.00 | 20.00 | 32.50 | 65.00 | — |
| AH1325 | — | 10.00 | 20.00 | 32.50 | 65.00 | — |

**3 MISCALS** Y# 20 **Weight:** 10.5000 g. **Composition:** Silver **Ruler:** Kuang-hsü **Obv. Legend:** Turki and Chinese around inscription: "Ta-ch'ing Yüan-pao" with normal "San" (3) in Chinese at bottom **Note:** Struck at Kashgar Mint.

| Date | Mintage | VG | F | VF | XF | Unc |
|---|---|---|---|---|---|---|
| AH1323 | — | 85.00 | 175 | 275 | 450 | — |

**3 MISCALS** Y# 20.1 **Weight:** 10.5000 g. **Composition:** Silver **Ruler:** Kuang-hsü **Obv. Legend:** Turki and Chinese around inscription: "Ta-ch'ing Yüan-pao" with official "San" (3) in Chinese at bottom **Note:** Struck at Kashgar Mint.

| Date | Mintage | VG | F | VF | XF | Unc |
|---|---|---|---|---|---|---|
| AH1323 | — | 100 | 200 | 325 | 550 | — |

**3 MISCALS** Y# 20.2 **Weight:** 10.5000 g. **Composition:** Silver **Ruler:** Kuang-hsü **Obv. Legend:** Turki and Chinese around inscription: "Ta-ch'ing Yüan-pao" with official "San" (3) in Chinese at bottom, date at lower right **Note:** Struck at the Kashgar Mint.

| Date | Mintage | VG | F | VF | XF | Unc |
|---|---|---|---|---|---|---|
| AH1323 | — | 100 | 200 | 365 | 600 | — |

**3 MISCALS** Y# 30 **Weight:** 10.5000 g. **Composition:** Silver **Obverse:** Inscription: "Yin-yüan San-ch'ien" **Reverse:** Turki

legend below snall, side view dragon in circle **Note:** Struck at the Kashgar Mint.

| Date | Mintage | VG | F | VF | XF | Unc |
|---|---|---|---|---|---|---|
| AH1329 | — | 200 | 350 | 600 | 1,000 | — |

**4 MISCALS (4 Mace)** **Y# 5** **Weight:** 14.2000 g. **Composition:** Silver **Ruler:** Kuang-hsü

| Date | Mintage | VG | F | VF | XF | Unc |
|---|---|---|---|---|---|---|
| ND(1905) | — | 85.00 | 125 | 200 | 400 | — |

**5 MISCALS** **Y# 19a** **Weight:** 17.2000 g. **Composition:** Silver **Ruler:** Kuang-hsü **Obverse:** Inscription: "Kuang-hsü Yin-yüan" between "Kashgar" and value; Chinese characters "K'a Shih" at right **Reverse:** Inscription: Turki within sprays **Note:** Struck at the Kashgar Mint.

| Date | Mintage | VG | F | VF | XF | Unc |
|---|---|---|---|---|---|---|
| AH1311 Error | — | — | — | — | — | — |
| AH1313 | — | 17.50 | 25.00 | 40.00 | 70.00 | — |
| AH1314 | — | 17.50 | 25.00 | 40.00 | 70.00 | — |
| AH1315 | — | 17.50 | 25.00 | 40.00 | 70.00 | — |
| AH1316 | — | 17.50 | 25.00 | 40.00 | 70.00 | — |
| AH1317 | — | 17.50 | 25.00 | 40.00 | 70.00 | — |
| AH1319 | — | 17.50 | 25.00 | 40.00 | 70.00 | — |
| AH1320 | — | 17.50 | 25.00 | 40.00 | 70.00 | — |

**5 MISCALS** **Y# 19a.1** **Weight:** 17.2000 g. **Composition:** Silver **Ruler:** Kuang-hsü **Obverse:** Inscription: "Kuang-hsü Yin-yüan" between "K'a Tsao" at right, value at left **Note:** Struck at the Kashgar Mint.

| Date | Mintage | VG | F | VF | XF | Unc |
|---|---|---|---|---|---|---|
| AH1311 Error | — | — | — | — | — | — |
| AH1321 | — | 10.00 | 17.50 | 30.00 | 60.00 | — |
| AH1322 | — | 10.00 | 17.50 | 30.00 | 60.00 | — |

**5 MISCALS** **Y# 21.1** **Weight:** 17.2000 g. **Composition:** Silver **Obverse:** Date at lower right **Note:** Struck at the Kashgar Mint.

| Date | Mintage | VG | F | VF | XF | Unc |
|---|---|---|---|---|---|---|
| AH1323 | — | 20.00 | 30.00 | 45.00 | 75.00 | — |

**5 MISCALS** **Y# 21.7** **Weight:** 17.2000 g. **Composition:** Silver **Ruler:** Kuang-hsü **Obverse:** Date at upper right **Note:** Struck at the Kashgar Mint.

| Date | Mintage | VG | F | VF | XF | Unc |
|---|---|---|---|---|---|---|
| AH1323 | — | 20.00 | 30.00 | 45.00 | 75.00 | — |

**5 MISCALS** **Y# 21.2** **Weight:** 17.2000 g. **Composition:** Silver **Ruler:** Kuang-hsü **Obverse:** Inverted Turki legend, date at lower right **Note:** Struck at the Kashgar Mint.

| Date | Mintage | VG | F | VF | XF | Unc |
|---|---|---|---|---|---|---|
| AH1323 | — | 22.50 | 35.00 | 60.00 | 100 | — |

**5 MISCALS** **Y# 21.3** **Weight:** 17.2000 g. **Composition:** Silver **Ruler:** Kuang-hsü **Obverse:** Normal "Wu" (5) at bottom, date at lower right **Note:** Struck at the Kashgar Mint.

| Date | Mintage | VG | F | VF | XF | Unc |
|---|---|---|---|---|---|---|
| AH1323 Rare | — | — | — | — | — | — |

**5 MISCALS** **Y# 21.4** **Weight:** 17.2000 g. **Composition:** Silver **Ruler:** Kuang-hsü **Obverse:** Date at upper left **Reverse:** Side view dragon's tail points to left **Note:** Struck at the Kashgar Mint.

| Date | Mintage | VG | F | VF | XF | Unc |
|---|---|---|---|---|---|---|
| AH1323 | — | 15.00 | 25.00 | 50.00 | 90.00 | — |

**5 MISCALS** **Y# 21.5** **Weight:** 17.2000 g. **Composition:** Silver **Ruler:** Kuang-hsü **Obverse:** Date at lower right **Note:** Struck at the Kashgar Mint.

| Date | Mintage | VG | F | VF | XF | Unc |
|---|---|---|---|---|---|---|
| AH1323 | — | 15.00 | 25.00 | 50.00 | 90.00 | — |

**5 MISCALS** **Y# 21.6** **Weight:** 17.2000 g. **Composition:** Silver **Ruler:** Kuang-hsü **Obverse:** Inverted Turki legend, date at lower right **Note:** Struck at the Kashgar Mint.

| Date | Mintage | VG | F | VF | XF | Unc |
|---|---|---|---|---|---|---|
| AH1323 | — | 20.00 | 35.00 | 80.00 | 135 | — |

**5 MISCALS** **Y# 21** **Weight:** 17.2000 g. **Composition:** Silver **Ruler:** Kuang-hsü **Obv. Legend:** Chinese and Turki around inscription: "Ta-ch'ing Yüan-pao", date at upper left **Reverse:** Side view dragon's tail points to right **Note:** Cross-reference number: K#1110. Struck at the Kashgar Mint.

| Date | Mintage | VG | F | VF | XF | Unc |
|---|---|---|---|---|---|---|
| AH1323 | — | 20.00 | 30.00 | 45.00 | 75.00 | — |

**5 MISCALS** **Y# 25** **Weight:** 17.2000 g. **Composition:** Silver **Ruler:** Kuang-hsü **Obverse:** "Kashgar Tsao" at top between standard Turki legend; inscription: "Ta-ch'ing Yin-pi" **Note:** Struck at the Kashgar Mint.

| Date | Mintage | VG | F | VF | XF | Unc |
|---|---|---|---|---|---|---|
| ND(ca.1906) | — | 22.50 | 40.00 | 85.00 | 150 | — |

**5 MISCALS** **Y# 25.1** **Weight:** 17.2000 g. **Composition:** Silver **Obverse:** Date at left or upper left **Note:** Struck at the Kashgar Mint.

| Date | Mintage | VG | F | VF | XF | Unc |
|---|---|---|---|---|---|---|
| AH1325 | — | 22.50 | 40.00 | 85.00 | 150 | — |
| AH1326 | — | 22.50 | 40.00 | 85.00 | 150 | — |
| AH1327 | — | 22.50 | 40.00 | 85.00 | 150 | — |

**5 MISCALS** **Y# 25.3** **Weight:** 17.2000 g. **Composition:** Silver **Obverse:** Inverted Turki legend, date at upper right, right, or lower right **Note:** Struck at the Kashgar Mint.

| Date | Mintage | VG | F | VF | XF | Unc |
|---|---|---|---|---|---|---|
| AH1325 | — | 17.50 | 25.00 | 75.00 | 110 | — |
| AH1326 | — | 17.50 | 25.00 | 75.00 | 110 | — |
| AH1328 | — | 17.50 | 25.00 | 75.00 | 110 | — |

Note: Error for 1326

**5 MISCALS** **Y# 25.4** **Weight:** 17.2000 g. **Composition:** Silver **Obverse:** "Kashgar" at top between standard Turki legend with date at upper right **Note:** Struck at the Kashgar Mint.

| Date | Mintage | VG | F | VF | XF | Unc |
|---|---|---|---|---|---|---|
| AH1325 | — | 20.00 | 35.00 | 100 | 150 | — |

**5 MISCALS** **Y# 25.9** **Weight:** 17.2000 g. **Composition:** Silver **Obverse:** Similar to Y#25.4 **Reverse:** Floral sprays reversed **Note:** Struck at the Kashgar Mint.

| Date | Mintage | VG | F | VF | XF | Unc |
|---|---|---|---|---|---|---|
| AH1325 | — | 50.00 | 100 | 165 | 275 | — |

**5 MISCALS** **Y# 25.10** **Weight:** 17.2000 g. **Composition:** Silver **Obverse:** Date at upper left **Reverse:** Standard florals **Note:** Struck at the Kashgar Mint.

| Date | Mintage | VG | F | VF | XF | Unc |
|---|---|---|---|---|---|---|
| AH1325 | — | 50.00 | 100 | 165 | 275 | — |

**5 MISCALS** **Y# 25.11** **Weight:** 17.2000 g. **Composition:** Silver **Obverse:** Date at upper left **Reverse:** Three rosettes at top **Note:** Struck at the Kashgar Mint.

| Date | Mintage | VG | F | VF | XF | Unc |
|---|---|---|---|---|---|---|
| AH1325 | — | 600 | 800 | 1,000 | 1,200 | — |

**5 MISCALS** **Y# 25.2** **Weight:** 17.2000 g. **Composition:** Silver **Note:** Similar to Y#25.1. Varieties exist in date placement. Struck at the Kashgar Mint.

| Date | Mintage | VG | F | VF | XF | Unc |
|---|---|---|---|---|---|---|
| AH1325 | — | 22.50 | 40.00 | 85.00 | 150 | — |
| AH1326 | — | 22.50 | 40.00 | 85.00 | 150 | — |
| AH1327 | — | 22.50 | 40.00 | 85.00 | 150 | — |

**5 MISCALS** **Y# 25.8** **Weight:** 17.2000 g. **Composition:** Silver **Obverse:** Date at upper left or left **Note:** Varieties exist. Struck at the Kashgar Mint.

| Date | Mintage | VG | F | VF | XF | Unc |
|---|---|---|---|---|---|---|
| AH1325 | — | 17.50 | 25.00 | 75.00 | 110 | — |

**5 MISCALS** **Y# 27** **Weight:** 17.2000 g. **Composition:** Silver **Ruler:** Hsüan-t'ung **Obverse:** "Kashgar" at top, Turki below; inscription: "Hsüan-t'ung Yin-pi", star in center **Note:** Struck at the Kashgar Mint.

| Date | Mintage | VG | F | VF | XF | Unc |
|---|---|---|---|---|---|---|
| AH1327 | — | 20.00 | 30.00 | 65.00 | 110 | — |
| AH1328 | — | 25.00 | 50.00 | 90.00 | 150 | — |

**5 MISCALS** **Y# 27.1** **Weight:** 17.2000 g. **Composition:** Silver **Ruler:** Hsüan-t'ung **Obverse:** Official "Wu" (5) at right, dot in center **Note:** Struck at the Kashgar Mint.

| Date | Mintage | VG | F | VF | XF | Unc |
|---|---|---|---|---|---|---|
| AH1328 | — | 35.00 | 65.00 | 150 | 225 | — |

**5 MISCALS** **Y# 27.2** **Weight:** 17.2000 g. **Composition:** Silver **Ruler:** Hsüan-t'ung **Obverse:** Rosette in center **Note:** Struck at the Kashgar Mint.

| Date | Mintage | VG | F | VF | XF | Unc |
|---|---|---|---|---|---|---|
| AH1329 | — | 50.00 | 100 | 200 | 275 | — |

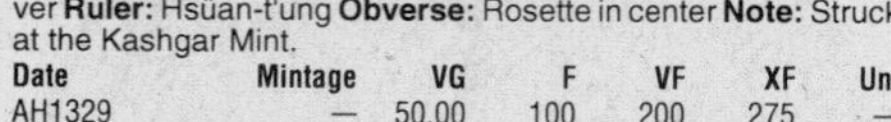

**5 MISCALS** **Y# A28** (**Y27.3**) **Weight:** 17.2000 g. **Composition:** Silver **Ruler:** Hsüan-t'ung **Obverse:** "Kashgar" at top, normal "Wu" (5) at right, star in center; inscription: "Hsüan-t'ung Yüan-pao" **Reverse:** Side view dragon **Note:** Struck at the Kashgar Mint.

| Date | Mintage | VG | F | VF | XF | Unc |
|---|---|---|---|---|---|---|
| AH1329 | — | 17.50 | 25.00 | 75.00 | 110 | — |

**5 MISCALS** **Y# A28.1** (**Y27.4**) **Weight:** 17.2000 g. **Composition:** Silver **Ruler:** Hsüan-t'ung **Obverse:** Dot in center **Reverse:** Side view dragon **Note:** Struck at the Kashgar Mint.

| Date | Mintage | VG | F | VF | XF | Unc |
|---|---|---|---|---|---|---|
| AH1329 | — | 17.50 | 25.00 | 75.00 | 110 | — |

**5 MISCALS** **Y# A28.2** (**Y27.5**) **Weight:** 17.2000 g. **Composition:** Silver **Ruler:** Hsüan-t'ung **Obverse:** Rosette in center **Reverse:** Side view dragon **Note:** Struck at the Kashgar Mint.

| Date | Mintage | VG | F | VF | XF | Unc |
|---|---|---|---|---|---|---|
| AH1329 | — | 17.50 | 25.00 | 75.00 | 110 | — |

**5 MISCALS** **Y# A28.3** (**Y27.6**) **Weight:** 17.2000 g. **Composition:** Silver **Ruler:** Hsüan-t'ung **Obverse:** Official "Wu" (5) at right, star in center **Reverse:** Side view dragon **Note:** Struck at the Kashgar Mint.

| Date | Mintage | VG | F | VF | XF | Unc |
|---|---|---|---|---|---|---|
| AH1329 | — | 17.50 | 25.00 | 75.00 | 110 | — |

**5 MISCALS** **Y# 31.2** **Weight:** 17.2000 g. **Composition:** Silver **Ruler:** Kuang-hsü **Obverse:** Rosettes in outer field **Note:** Struck at the Kashgar Mint.

| Date | Mintage | VG | F | VF | XF | Unc |
|---|---|---|---|---|---|---|
| AH1329 | — | 50.00 | 100 | 165 | 275 | — |

**5 MISCALS** **Y# 31.3** **Weight:** 17.2000 g. **Composition:** Silver **Ruler:** Kuang-hsü **Reverse:** Rosettes in center **Note:** Struck at the Kashgar Mint.

| Date | Mintage | VG | F | VF | XF | Unc |
|---|---|---|---|---|---|---|
| AH1329 | — | 22.50 | 75.00 | 100 | 150 | — |

**5 MISCALS** **Y# 31** **Weight:** 17.2000 g. **Composition:** Silver **Ruler:** Kuang-hsü **Obv. Legend:** Legend "Kashgar" at top, Turki below around side view dragon, star at center and at right **Reverse:** Inscription: "Hsiang-yin" (ration silver) between value **Note:** Varieties with two and three tail spines on dragon exist. Struck at the Kashgar Mint.

| Date | Mintage | VG | F | VF | XF | Unc |
|---|---|---|---|---|---|---|
| AH1329 | — | 20.00 | 40.00 | 100 | 150 | — |
| AH1330 | — | 20.00 | 40.00 | 100 | 150 | — |
| AH1321 Error for 1331 | — | 20.00 | 40.00 | 100 | 150 | — |
| AH1331 | — | 20.00 | 40.00 | 100 | 150 | — |

**5 MISCALS (5 Mace)** **Y# 6** **Weight:** 17.9000 g. **Composition:** Silver **Ruler:** Kuang-hsü **Obverse:** Without dot or rosette in center **Reverse:** Uncircled dragon

| Date | Mintage | VG | F | VF | XF | Unc |
|---|---|---|---|---|---|---|
| ND(1905) | — | 15.00 | 25.00 | 60.00 | 175 | — |

**5 MISCALS (5 Mace)** **Y# 6.1** **Weight:** 17.9000 g. **Composition:** Silver **Ruler:** Kuang-hsü **Reverse:** Circled dragon, without rosettes

| Date | Mintage | VG | F | VF | XF | Unc |
|---|---|---|---|---|---|---|
| ND(1905) | — | 15.00 | 25.00 | 50.00 | 90.00 | — |

**5 MISCALS (5 Mace)** **Y# 6.2** **Weight:** 17.9000 g. **Composition:** Silver **Ruler:** Kuang-hsü **Reverse:** Large rosettes at sides of dragon

| Date | Mintage | VG | F | VF | XF | Unc |
|---|---|---|---|---|---|---|
| ND(1905) | — | 15.00 | 25.00 | 50.00 | 90.00 | — |

**5 MISCALS (5 Mace)** **Y# 6.3** **Weight:** 17.9000 g. **Composition:** Silver **Ruler:** Kuang-hsü **Obverse:** Dot in center **Reverse:** Without rosettes, circled dragon

| Date | Mintage | VG | F | VF | XF | Unc |
|---|---|---|---|---|---|---|
| ND(1905) | — | 15.00 | 25.00 | 50.00 | 90.00 | — |

**5 MISCALS (5 Mace)** **Y# 6.4** **Weight:** 17.9000 g. **Composition:** Silver **Ruler:** Kuang-hsü **Obverse:** Cross in center

| Date | Mintage | VG | F | VF | XF | Unc |
|---|---|---|---|---|---|---|
| ND(1905) | — | 15.00 | 25.00 | 50.00 | 90.00 | — |

**5 MISCALS (5 Mace)** **Y# 6.5** **Weight:** 17.9000 g. **Composition:** Silver **Ruler:** Kuang-hsü **Obverse:** Large rosette in center, middle of which is depressed

| Date | Mintage | VG | F | VF | XF | Unc |
|---|---|---|---|---|---|---|
| ND(1905) | — | 15.00 | 25.00 | 50.00 | 90.00 | — |

**5 MISCALS (5 Mace)** **Y# 6.6** **Weight:** 17.9000 g. **Composition:** Silver **Ruler:** Kuang-hsü **Obverse:** Eight-petalled rosette in center, middle of which is raised **Reverse:** Small rosettes at sides of dragon

| Date | Mintage | VG | F | VF | XF | Unc |
|---|---|---|---|---|---|---|
| ND(1905) | — | 15.00 | 25.00 | 50.00 | 90.00 | — |

**5 MISCALS (5 Mace)** Y# 6.7 **Weight:** 17.9000 g. **Composition:** Silver **Ruler:** Kuang-hsü **Reverse:** Bat above uncircled dragon's head

| Date | Mintage | VG | F | VF | XF | Unc |
|---|---|---|---|---|---|---|
| ND(1905) | — | 175 | 300 | 450 | 700 | — |

**5 MISCALS (5 Mace)** Y# 6.8 **Weight:** 17.9000 g. **Composition:** Silver **Ruler:** Kuang-hsü **Reverse:** Turki legend around uncircled dragon

| Date | Mintage | VG | F | VF | XF | Unc |
|---|---|---|---|---|---|---|
| ND(1905) | — | 400 | 600 | — | — | — |

**5 MISCALS (5 Mace)** Y# 6.9 **Weight:** 17.9000 g. **Composition:** Silver **Ruler:** Kuang-hsü **Reverse:** Legend above uncircled dragon, 5 MACE below **Rev. Legend:** SUNGAREI

| Date | Mintage | VG | F | VF | XF | Unc |
|---|---|---|---|---|---|---|
| ND(1906) Rare | — | — | — | — | — | — |

**Note:** Some authorities consider this coin a fantasy

**5 MISCALS (5 Mace)** Y# 6.10 **Weight:** 17.9000 g. **Composition:** Silver **Ruler:** Kuang-hsü **Reverse:** Without SUNGREI, with four bats and many clouds around dragon

| Date | Mintage | VG | F | VF | XF | Unc |
|---|---|---|---|---|---|---|
| ND(1906) Rare | — | — | — | — | — | — |

**5 MISCALS (5 Mace)** Y# 6.11 **Weight:** 17.9000 g. **Composition:** Silver **Ruler:** Kuang-hsü **Obverse:** Turki legend rotated **Reverse:** Bat above dragon's head

| Date | Mintage | VG | F | VF | XF | Unc |
|---|---|---|---|---|---|---|
| ND(1906) Rare | — | — | — | — | — | — |

**SAR (Tael)** Y# 7 **Weight:** 35.5000 g. **Composition:** Silver **Ruler:** Kuang-hsü **Obverse:** Without Turki legend **Reverse:** Without Turki legend, rosettes at sides of uncircled dtagon

| Date | Mintage | VG | F | VF | XF | Unc |
|---|---|---|---|---|---|---|
| ND(1905) | — | 25.00 | 40.00 | 60.00 | 140 | — |

**SAR (Tael)** Y# 7.1 **Weight:** 35.5000 g. **Composition:** Silver **Ruler:** Kuang-hsü **Reverse:** Turki legend around circled dragon, without rosettes

| Date | Mintage | VG | F | VF | XF | Unc |
|---|---|---|---|---|---|---|
| ND(1905) | — | 40.00 | 65.00 | 100 | 300 | — |

**SAR (Tael)** Y# 7.2 **Weight:** 35.5000 g. **Composition:** Silver **Ruler:** Kuang-hsü **Reverse:** Turki legend around uncircled dragon

| Date | Mintage | VG | F | VF | XF | Unc |
|---|---|---|---|---|---|---|
| ND(1905) | — | 500 | 850 | 1,250 | 1,600 | — |

**SAR (Tael)** Y# 7.3 **Weight:** 35.5000 g. **Composition:** Silver **Ruler:** Kuang-hsü **Obverse:** Outer Turki legend, rosette in center **Reverse:** Without Turki legend, with rosettes at sides of uncircled dragon

| Date | Mintage | VG | F | VF | XF | Unc |
|---|---|---|---|---|---|---|
| ND(1905) | — | 35.00 | 50.00 | 70.00 | 150 | — |

**SAR (Tael)** Y# 26 **Weight:** 35.2000 g. **Composition:** Silver **Obverse:** Chinese "Kashgar" at top wtih Turki "Kashgar" to left; inscription: "Ta-ch'ing Yin-pi" **Reverse:** Side view dragon in sprays **Note:** Struck at the Kashgar Mint.

| Date | Mintage | VG | F | VF | XF | Unc |
|---|---|---|---|---|---|---|
| AH1325 | — | 200 | 300 | 500 | 850 | — |

**SAR (Tael)** Y# 26.2 **Weight:** 35.2000 g. **Composition:** Silver **Obverse:** Chinese "Kashgar" at top wtih Turki "Kashgar" to right **Note:** Struck at the Kashgar Mint.

| Date | Mintage | VG | F | VF | XF | Unc |
|---|---|---|---|---|---|---|
| AH1325 | — | 300 | 500 | 700 | 1,200 | — |

**SAR (Tael)** Y# 26.1 **Weight:** 35.2000 g. **Composition:** Silver **Obverse:** "Kashgar Tsao" at top **Note:** Struck at the Kashgar Mint.

| Date | Mintage | VG | F | VF | XF | Unc |
|---|---|---|---|---|---|---|
| AH1325 | — | 1,200 | 2,750 | 5,000 | 7,000 | — |

# REPUBLIC

## PROVINCIAL CAST COINAGE

**10 CASH** Y# 37.2 **Composition:** Cast Copper **Ruler:** Kuang-hsü **Note:** Reduced size; Struck at the Aksu Mint.

| Date | Mintage | Good | VG | F | VF | XF |
|---|---|---|---|---|---|---|
| ND(ca.1912) | — | 35.00 | 55.00 | 80.00 | — | — |

**10 CASH** Y# 37.1 **Composition:** Cast Copper **Ruler:** Kuang-hsü **Note:** Struck at the Aksu Mint.

| Date | Mintage | Good | VG | F | VF | XF |
|---|---|---|---|---|---|---|
| ND(ca.1912) | — | 35.00 | 55.00 | 80.00 | — | — |

## MILLED COINAGE

**5 CASH** **Y# A36.1** **Composition:** Copper **Obverse:** Large Chinese inscription: "Chung-hua Min-kuo" between "T'ung-pi" **Rev. Legend:** Chinese outer, Turki inner, around flag **Note:** Struck at the Kashgar Mint.

| Date | Mintage | Good | VG | F | VF | XF |
|---|---|---|---|---|---|---|
| ND(ca.1912) | — | 275 | 375 | 500 | 700 | — |

**5 CASH** **Y# A36.2** **Composition:** Copper **Obverse:** Small Chinese inscription: "Chung-hua Min-kuo" between "T'ung-pi" **Rev. Legend:** Chinese outer, Turki inner, around flag **Note:** Struck at the Kashgar Mint.

| Date | Mintage | Good | VG | F | VF | XF |
|---|---|---|---|---|---|---|
| ND(ca.1912) | — | 275 | 375 | 500 | 700 | — |

**5 CASH** **Y# 36** **Composition:** Copper **Obv. Legend:** Chinese around inscription "Chung-hua Min-kuo" **Reverse:** Inscription: Turki above and below crossed flags **Note:** Struck at the Kashgar Mint.

| Date | Mintage | Good | VG | F | VF | XF |
|---|---|---|---|---|---|---|
| AH1331 | — | 100 | 135 | 225 | 350 | — |

寶

**10 CASH** **Y# B39.1** **Composition:** Copper **Obverse:** Large character "Shih" (ten), normal "Pao"

| Date | Mintage | Good | VG | F | VF | XF |
|---|---|---|---|---|---|---|
| ND | — | 8.50 | 15.00 | 25.00 | 37.50 | 65.00 |

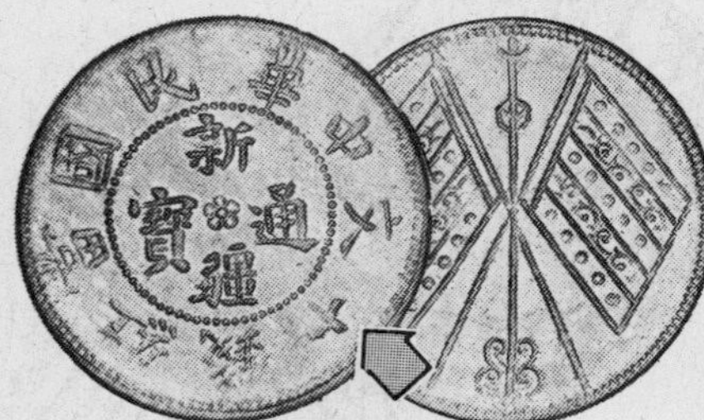

**10 CASH** **Y# B39.2** **Composition:** Copper **Obverse:** Small character "Shih" (ten) **Reverse:** Small crossed flags

| Date | Mintage | Good | VG | F | VF | XF |
|---|---|---|---|---|---|---|
| ND | — | 12.50 | 25.00 | 35.00 | 50.00 | 85.00 |

寶

**10 CASH** **Y# B39.3** **Composition:** Copper **Obverse:** Elaborate character "Pao"

| Date | Mintage | Good | VG | F | VF | XF |
|---|---|---|---|---|---|---|
| ND | — | — | — | — | — | — |

**10 CASH** **Y# 38.2** **Composition:** Copper **Reverse:** Modified Turki legend with date at bottom **Note:** Struck at the Kashgar Mint.

| Date | Mintage | Good | VG | F | VF | XF |
|---|---|---|---|---|---|---|
| AH1331 | — | 8.50 | 12.50 | 17.50 | 30.00 | — |
| AH1332 | — | 8.50 | 12.50 | 17.50 | 30.00 | — |
| AH1334 | — | 8.50 | 12.50 | 17.50 | 30.00 | — |
| AH1335 | — | 8.50 | 12.50 | 17.50 | 30.00 | — |

**10 CASH** **Y# B36.1** **Composition:** Copper **Obverse:** Large Chinese inscription: "Chung-hua Min-kuo" between "T'ung-pi" **Rev. Legend:** Chinese outer, Turki inner, around flag **Note:** Struck at the Kashgar Mint.

| Date | Mintage | Good | VG | F | VF | XF |
|---|---|---|---|---|---|---|
| ND(ca.1912) | — | 25.00 | 37.50 | 50.00 | 85.00 | — |

**10 CASH** **Y# B36.2** **Composition:** Copper **Obverse:** Small Chinese inscription: "Chung-hua Min-kuo" between "T'ung-pi" **Rev. Legend:** Chinese outer, Turki inner, around flag **Note:** Struck at the Kashgar Mint.

| Date | Mintage | Good | VG | F | VF | XF |
|---|---|---|---|---|---|---|
| ND(ca.1912) | — | 25.00 | 37.50 | 50.00 | 85.00 | — |

**10 CASH** **Y# A39.1** **Composition:** Copper **Reverse:** Large crossed flags with vertical stirpes

| Date | Mintage | Good | VG | F | VF | XF |
|---|---|---|---|---|---|---|
| CD1(1912) | — | 7.50 | 13.50 | 18.50 | 28.50 | 49.50 |

**10 CASH** **Y# A39.2** **Composition:** Copper **Reverse:** Small crossed flags with vertical stirpes

| Date | Mintage | Good | VG | F | VF | XF |
|---|---|---|---|---|---|---|
| CD1(1912) | — | 7.00 | 12.00 | 16.50 | 25.50 | 47.50 |

**Note:** This type exists with a great variety of the "Shih" (ten), and "Pao" characters

**10 CASH** **Y# 38.1** **Composition:** Copper **Obverse:** Chinese legend: "Shih Wen" (10 Cash) at upper left **Reverse:** Date at upper center **Note:** Struck at the Kashgar Mint.

| Date | Mintage | Good | VG | F | VF | XF |
|---|---|---|---|---|---|---|
| ND(ca.1913) | — | 7.50 | 15.00 | 20.00 | 35.00 | — |
| AH1332 | — | 7.50 | 15.00 | 20.00 | 35.00 | — |
| AH1333 | — | 7.50 | 15.00 | 20.00 | 35.00 | — |
| AH1334 | — | 7.50 | 15.00 | 20.00 | 35.00 | — |

**10 CASH** **Y# F38** **Composition:** Copper **Ruler:** Kuang-hsü **Obverse:** Chinese characters "Shih Wen" (10 Wen) at lower left **Reverse:** Upper Turki legend inverted

| Date | Mintage | Good | VG | F | VF | XF |
|---|---|---|---|---|---|---|
| AH1332 | — | 35.00 | 65.00 | 85.00 | 125 | — |

**10 CASH** **Y# 38.6** **Composition:** Copper **Reverse:** Single flower in lower Turki legend **Note:** Struck at the Kashgar Mint.

| Date | Mintage | Good | VG | F | VF | XF |
|---|---|---|---|---|---|---|
| AH1334 | — | — | — | — | — | — |

**10 CASH** **Y# 38.7** **Composition:** Copper **Reverse:** Without flowers or florals in Turki legends **Note:** Struck at the Kashgar Mint.

| Date | Mintage | Good | VG | F | VF | XF |
|---|---|---|---|---|---|---|
| AH1334 | — | — | — | — | — | — |

**10 CASH** **Y# 38.5** **Composition:** Copper **Obverse:** Outer Chinese legend wtihout "Shih" of "Kashgar" at lower left **Reverse:** Turki legend in florals with "Zarb Kashgar" at top, similar to Y#A38.2 **Note:** Struck at the Kashgar Mint.

| Date | Mintage | Good | VG | F | VF | XF |
|---|---|---|---|---|---|---|
| AH1334(1915) | — | 37.50 | 60.00 | 100 | 150 | — |

**10 CASH** **Y# 38.3** **Composition:** Copper **Obverse:** Two lower right Chinese characters different **Reverse:** AH date at top **Note:** Struck at the Kashgar Mint.

| Date | Mintage | Good | VG | F | VF | XF |
|---|---|---|---|---|---|---|
| AH133-4(1916) | — | 50.00 | 75.00 | 125 | 200 | — |

**10 CASH** **Y# 38a.1** **Composition:** Copper **Obverse:** Chinese date at upper right with rosette; Chinese legend in inner circle **Obv. Legend:** "Chung-hua Min-kuo: **Note:** Struck at the Kashgar Mint.

| Date | Mintage | Good | VG | F | VF | XF |
|---|---|---|---|---|---|---|
| AH1339(1921) | — | 5.00 | 10.00 | 15.00 | 25.00 | — |
| AH1340(1921) | — | 5.00 | 10.00 | 15.00 | 25.00 | — |

**10 CASH** **Y# 38b.1** **Composition:** Copper **Obverse:** Chinese legend "Min-kuo T'ung-yüan" in inner circle with "Kashgar" at right **Note:** Struck at the Kashgar Mint.

| Date | Mintage | Good | VG | F | VF | XF |
|---|---|---|---|---|---|---|
| AH1340 | — | 15.00 | 30.00 | 40.00 | 65.00 | — |

**10 CASH** **Y# 38b.2** **Composition:** Copper **Obverse:** Outer Chinese legend rotated **Note:** Struck at the Kashgar Mint.

| Date | Mintage | Good | VG | F | VF | XF |
|---|---|---|---|---|---|---|
| AH134x | — | 15.00 | 30.00 | 40.00 | 65.00 | — |

**10 CASH** **Y# C39** **Composition:** Copper

| Date | Mintage | Good | VG | F | VF | XF |
|---|---|---|---|---|---|---|
| CD1921 Status unknown; rare | — | — | — | — | — | — |

**10 CASH** **Y# 38a.3** **Composition:** Copper **Reverse:** Turki legend rearranged **Note:** Struck at the Kashgar Mint.

| Date | Mintage | Good | VG | F | VF | XF |
|---|---|---|---|---|---|---|
| AH1339(1921) | — | 5.00 | 10.00 | 15.00 | 25.00 | — |
| AH134x(1921) | — | 5.00 | 10.00 | 15.00 | 25.00 | — |

**10 CASH** **Y# A44.1** **Composition:** Copper **Note:** Struck at the Kashgar Mint.

| Date | Mintage | Good | VG | F | VF | XF |
|---|---|---|---|---|---|---|
| 11(1922) | — | 50.00 | 75.00 | 100 | 125 | — |

**10 CASH** **Y# 38a.5** **Composition:** Copper **Obverse:** Crowded Chinese year "11"

| Date | Mintage | Good | VG | F | VF | XF |
|---|---|---|---|---|---|---|
| AH1340(1922) | — | 25.00 | 40.00 | 65.00 | 100 | — |

**10 CASH** **Y# A44.2** **Composition:** Copper **Note:** Flags reversed; Struck at the Kashgar Mint.

| Date | Mintage | Good | VG | F | VF | XF |
|---|---|---|---|---|---|---|
| 11(1922) | — | 50.00 | 75.00 | 100 | 125 | — |

**10 CASH** **Y# 38a.2** **Composition:** Copper **Obverse:** Outer Chinese legend without "Shih" of "Kashgar" at upper left **Note:** Struck at the Kashgar Mint.

| Date | Mintage | Good | VG | F | VF | XF |
|---|---|---|---|---|---|---|
| AH134x(1922) | — | 5.00 | 10.00 | 15.00 | 25.00 | — |

**10 CASH** **Y# B38b.1** **Composition:** Copper **Obverse:** Legend in inner circle **Obv. Legend:** "MinKuo T'ung Yuan" **Reverse:** Turki legend in solid sunburst **Note:** Struck at the Kashgar Mint.

| Date | Mintage | Good | VG | F | VF | XF |
|---|---|---|---|---|---|---|
| AH1346 | — | 125 | 175 | 300 | 400 | — |

**10 CASH** **Y# B38b.2** **Composition:** Copper **Obverse:** Similar to Y#B838d **Reverse:** Similar to Y#B38b.1 **Note:** Struck at the Kashgar Mint.

| Date | Mintage | Good | VG | F | VF | XF |
|---|---|---|---|---|---|---|
| AH1346 | — | 150 | 200 | 350 | 500 | — |

**10 CASH** **Y# B38c.1** **Composition:** Copper **Obverse:** Chinese character "Jih" in solid sunburst

| Date | Mintage | Good | VG | F | VF | XF |
|---|---|---|---|---|---|---|
| CD(1928) | — | 175 | 275 | 425 | 600 | — |

**10 CASH** **Y# B38c.4** **Composition:** Copper **Obv. Legend:** Cyclic date at left and right like Y#B38.4

| Date | Mintage | Good | VG | F | VF | XF |
|---|---|---|---|---|---|---|
| CD(1928) | — | 175 | 275 | 425 | 600 | — |

**10 CASH** **Y# B38.1** **Composition:** Copper **Obverse:** Chinese legend in inner circle; Chinese date at left and right of upper legend **Obv. Legend:** "Chung Hua Min Kuo" **Reverse:** Chinese characters "T'ung Yuan" in solid sunburst

| Date | Mintage | Good | VG | F | VF | XF |
|---|---|---|---|---|---|---|
| CD(1928) | — | 40.00 | 80.00 | 120 | 200 | — |

**10 CASH** **Y# B38c.2** **Composition:** Copper **Obverse:** Like B38c.1 **Reverse:** Chinese character "Jih" in rayed sunburst **Note:** Struck at the Kashgar Mint.

| Date | Mintage | Good | VG | F | VF | XF |
|---|---|---|---|---|---|---|
| CD(1928) | — | 175 | 275 | 425 | 600 | — |

**10 CASH** **Y# B38c.3** **Composition:** Copper **Obverse:** Like Y#B38b.1 **Reverse:** Like Y#B38c.1 **Note:** Struck at the Kashgar Mint.

| Date | Mintage | Good | VG | F | VF | XF |
|---|---|---|---|---|---|---|
| CD(1928) | — | 175 | 275 | 425 | 600 | — |

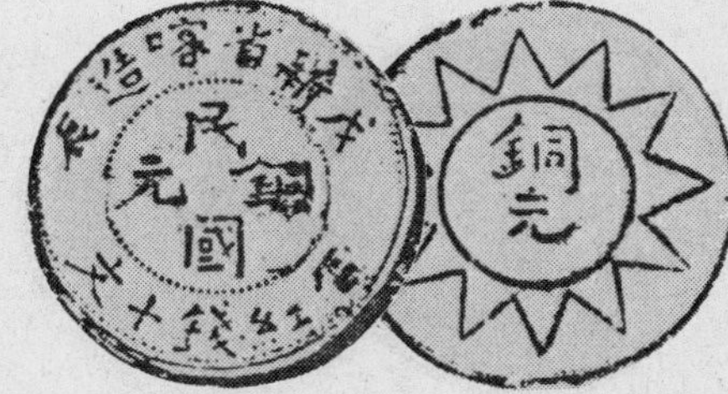

**10 CASH** **Y# B38d** **Composition:** Copper **Obverse:** Chinese legend in inner circle **Obv. Legend:** "Min Kuo T'ung Yuan" **Reverse:** Chinese characters "T'ung Yuan" in solid sunburst **Note:** Struck at the Kashgar Mint.

| Date | Mintage | Good | VG | F | VF | XF |
|---|---|---|---|---|---|---|
| CD(1928) | — | 125 | 175 | 300 | 400 | — |

**10 CASH** **Y# B38.2** **Composition:** Copper **Obverse:** Upper legend **Obv. Legend:** "Hsinchiang Kashgar Tsao" **Reverse:** Small Chinese characters "T'ung Yuan" in outlined sunburst **Note:** Struck at the Kashgar Mint.

| Date | Mintage | Good | VG | F | VF | XF |
|---|---|---|---|---|---|---|
| CD(1928) | — | 30.00 | 70.00 | 100 | 180 | — |

**Note:** A similar coin with same upper legend and cyclical date 1929 at sides is reported

**10 CASH** **Y# B38.3** **Composition:** Copper **Obverse:** Upper legend **Obv. Legend:** "Hsinchiang Kash Tsao" **Reverse:** Large Chinese characters "T'ung Yuan" in outlined sunburst **Note:** Struck at the Kashgar Mint.

| Date | Mintage | Good | VG | F | VF | XF |
|---|---|---|---|---|---|---|
| CD(1928) | — | 15.00 | 23.00 | 30.00 | 50.00 | — |

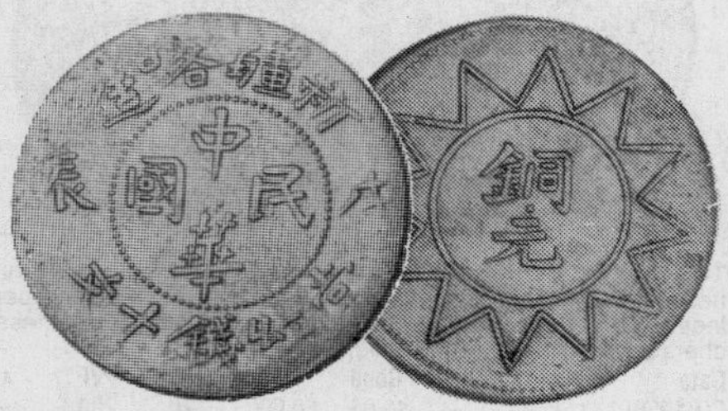

**10 CASH** **Y# B38.4** **Composition:** Copper **Obverse:** Chinese date at left and right **Reverse:** Chinese characters "T'ung Yuan" in outlined sunburst **Note:** Struck at the Kashgar Mint.

| Date | Mintage | Good | VG | F | VF | XF |
|---|---|---|---|---|---|---|
| CD(1928) | — | 3.00 | 5.50 | 8.00 | 16.00 | — |
| CD(1929) | — | 5.00 | 7.50 | 15.00 | 25.00 | — |

**10 CASH** **Y# B38.5** **Composition:** Copper **Reverse:** Chinese characters "T'ung Yuan" in outlined finely rayed sunburst **Note:** Struck at the Kashgar Mint.

| Date | Mintage | Good | VG | F | VF | XF |
|---|---|---|---|---|---|---|
| CD(1928) | — | 60.00 | 90.00 | 140 | 200 | — |

**10 CASH** **Y# B38.6** **Composition:** Copper **Obverse:** Upper legend **Reverse:** "Hsinchiang Kashgar Tsao" **Note:** Struck at the Kashgar Mint.

| Date | Mintage | Good | VG | F | VF | XF |
|---|---|---|---|---|---|---|
| CD(1929) | — | 40.00 | 60.00 | 100 | 170 | — |

**10 CASH** **Y# 40.1** **Composition:** Copper **Obverse:** Chinese legend in inner circle with "Hsin Chiang" at upper right **Obv. Legend:** Chung Hua Min Kuo **Reverse:** Flags with solid sunbursts with inner circles

| Date | Mintage | Good | VG | F | VF | XF |
|---|---|---|---|---|---|---|
| CD(1929) | — | 7.00 | 12.00 | 16.50 | 25.00 | 40.00 |
| CD(1930) Rare | — | — | — | — | — | — |

**Note:** The cyclical date character at left exists closed, which is rare, and open for CD1929

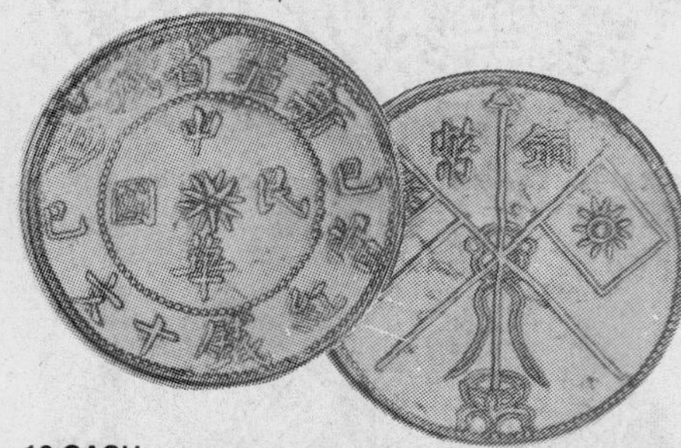

**10 CASH** **Y# 40.2** **Composition:** Copper **Obverse:** Large starburst in center **Reverse:** Long streamers

| Date | Mintage | Good | VG | F | VF | XF |
|---|---|---|---|---|---|---|
| CD(1929) Rare | — | 7.00 | 12.00 | 16.50 | 25.00 | 40.00 |

**Note:** Y#40 inscribed "Sheng Ch'eng" (provincial capital) in upper legend refers to Tihwa (Urumchi now Urumqi)

**10 CASH** **Y# B38a.1** **Composition:** Copper **Obverse:** Chinese characters for date to left and right of "Chung Hua Min Kuo" in inner circle **Reverse:** Turki legend in oulined subnurst **Note:** Struck at the Kashgar Mint.

| Date | Mintage | Good | VG | F | VF | XF |
|---|---|---|---|---|---|---|
| CD(1929) | — | 100 | 165 | 250 | 350 | — |

**10 CASH** **Y# B38a.2** **Composition:** Copper **Obverse:** Upper legend **Obv. Legend:** "Hsinchiang Kashgar Tsao" **Note:** Struck at the Kashgar Mint.

| Date | Mintage | Good | VG | F | VF | XF |
|---|---|---|---|---|---|---|
| CD(1929) | — | 75.00 | 100 | 125 | 150 | — |

**10 CASH** **Y# 44.1** **Composition:** Copper **Obverse:** Upper legend **Obv. Legend:** "Hsinchiang Kashgar Tsao" **Reverse:** Flags with wide outlined sungursts; flags at right with inner circle **Note:** Struck at the Kashgar Mint.

| Date | Mintage | Good | VG | F | VF | XF |
|---|---|---|---|---|---|---|
| CD(1929) | — | 5.00 | 8.50 | 17.50 | 32.50 | — |

**10 CASH** **Y# 44.2** **Composition:** Copper **Obverse:** Small eight-petalled rosette in center **Reverse:** Flag at right without inner circle **Note:** Struck at the Kashgar Mint.

| Date | Mintage | Good | VG | F | VF | XF |
|---|---|---|---|---|---|---|
| CD(1929) | — | 4.50 | 7.50 | 12.00 | 16.00 | — |
| CD(1930) | — | 4.50 | 7.50 | 12.00 | 16.00 | — |

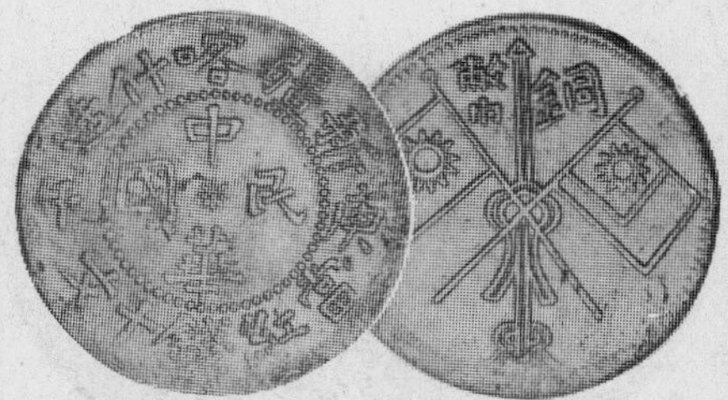

**10 CASH** **Y# 44.6** **Composition:** Copper **Reverse:** Reversed flags with large solid sunbursts **Note:** Struck at the Kashgar Mint.

| Date | Mintage | Good | VG | F | VF | XF |
|---|---|---|---|---|---|---|
| CD(1929) | — | 3.00 | 7.00 | 13.00 | 18.00 | — |
| CD(1930) | — | 4.00 | 8.00 | 15.00 | 20.00 | — |

**10 CASH** **Y# 44.8** **Composition:** Copper **Obverse:** Uper legend **Obv. Legend:** "Hsinchiang Kash Tsao" **Note:** Struck at the Kashgar Mint.

| Date | Mintage | Good | VG | F | VF | XF |
|---|---|---|---|---|---|---|
| CD(1929) | — | 75.00 | 100 | 125 | 150 | — |

**10 CASH** **Y# 44.9** **Composition:** Copper **Reverse:** Reversed flags with large "flower petal" outlined sunbursts **Note:** Struck at the Kashgar Mint.

| Date | Mintage | Good | VG | F | VF | XF |
|---|---|---|---|---|---|---|
| CD(1930) | — | 4.00 | 8.00 | 15.00 | 20.00 | — |

**10 CASH** **Y# 44.7** **Composition:** Copper **Reverse:** Reversed flags with small solid sunbursts **Note:** Struck at the Kashgar Mint.

| Date | Mintage | Good | VG | F | VF | XF |
|---|---|---|---|---|---|---|
| CD(1930) | — | 25.00 | 50.00 | 100 | 165 | — |

**10 CASH** **Y# 44.10** **Composition:** Copper **Reverse:** Flags reversed **Note:** Struck at the Kashgar Mint.

| Date | Mintage | Good | VG | F | VF | XF |
|---|---|---|---|---|---|---|
| CD(1930) | — | — | — | — | — | — |

**10 CASH** Y# 44.3 **Composition:** Copper **Obverse:** Star with rays in center **Note:** Struck at the Kashgar Mint.

| Date | Mintage | Good | VG | F | VF | XF |
|---|---|---|---|---|---|---|
| CD(1930) | — | 8.50 | 17.50 | 22.50 | 37.50 | — |

**10 CASH** Y# 44.4 **Composition:** Copper **Obverse:** Eight-petalled rosette in center **Reverse:** Flags with narrow outlined sunbursts **Note:** Struck at the Kashgar Mint.

| Date | Mintage | Good | VG | F | VF | XF |
|---|---|---|---|---|---|---|
| CD(1930) | — | 10.00 | 20.00 | 35.00 | 55.00 | — |

**10 CASH** Y# 40.3 **Composition:** Copper **Obverse:** Cyclical date at upper right in legend **Note:** Struck at the Kashgar Mint.

| Date | Mintage | Good | VG | F | VF | XF |
|---|---|---|---|---|---|---|
| CD(1930) Rare | — | — | — | — | — | — |

**10 CASH** Y# 44.5 **Composition:** Copper **Reverse:** Flags with solid sunbursts **Note:** Struck at the Kashgar Mint.

| Date | Mintage | Good | VG | F | VF | XF |
|---|---|---|---|---|---|---|
| CD(1933) | — | 4.00 | 8.00 | 15.00 | 20.00 | — |

**20 CASH** Y# 48 **Composition:** Copper **Note:** Struck at the Kashgar Mint.

| Date | Mintage | Good | VG | F | VF | XF |
|---|---|---|---|---|---|---|
| AH133x(1921) Rare | — | — | — | — | — | — |

**20 CASH** Y# A41.1 **Composition:** Copper **Obverse:** Chinese legend in inner circle with "Hsin Kiang" at upper right **Obv. Legend:** Chung Hua Min Kuo

| Date | Mintage | Good | VG | F | VF | XF |
|---|---|---|---|---|---|---|
| CD(1929) | — | 75.00 | 125 | 200 | 300 | — |
| CD(1930) | — | 85.00 | 140 | 225 | 335 | — |

**Note:** Y#A41.1 inscribed "Sheng Ch'eng" (provincial capital) in upper legend refers to Tihwa (Urumchi now Urumqi)

**20 CASH** Y# A41.2 **Composition:** Copper **Obv. Legend:** Cyclical date at upper right

| Date | Mintage | Good | VG | F | VF | XF |
|---|---|---|---|---|---|---|
| CD(1930) Rare | — | — | — | — | — | — |

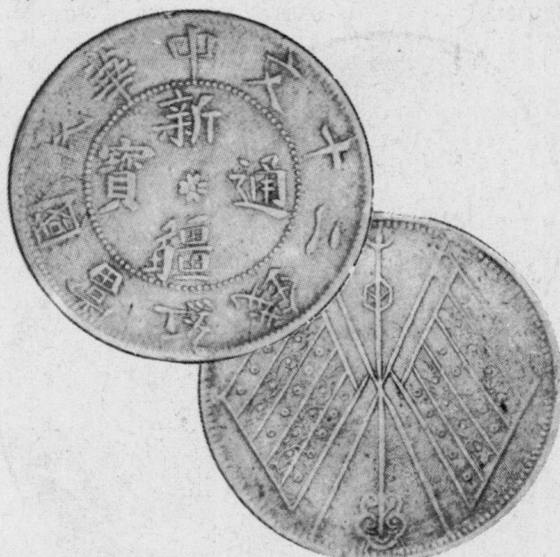

**20 CASH** Y# 39.1 **Composition:** Copper **Obverse:** Eight-petalled rosette in center **Reverse:** Two stripes in flags have arabesques

| Date | Mintage | VG | F | VF | XF | Unc |
|---|---|---|---|---|---|---|
| ND | — | 10.00 | 16.50 | 20.00 | 27.50 | — |

**20 CASH** Y# 39.2 **Composition:** Copper **Obverse:** Five-petalled rosette in center

| Date | Mintage | VG | F | VF | XF | Unc |
|---|---|---|---|---|---|---|
| ND | — | 50.00 | 100 | 150 | 225 | — |

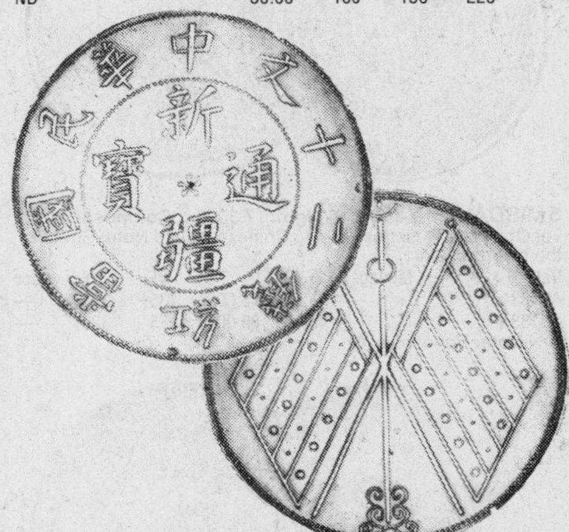

**20 CASH** Y# 39.3 **Composition:** Copper **Reverse:** Without arabesques in flag

| Date | Mintage | F | VF | XF | Unc | BU |
|---|---|---|---|---|---|---|
| ND Restrike | — | — | — | 50.00 | 75.00 | — |

**5 MISCALS** Y# 43 **Weight:** 17.3000 g. **Composition:** Silver **Obverse:** Stars dividing Chinese legends **Reverse:** Crossed flags dividing Turki legend **Note:** Struck at the Kashgar Mint.

| Date | Mintage | VG | F | VF | XF | Unc |
|---|---|---|---|---|---|---|
| AH1331 | — | 40.00 | 75.00 | 160 | 275 | — |
| AH1332 | — | 40.00 | 75.00 | 160 | 275 | — |

**5 MISCALS** Y# 43.1 **Weight:** 17.3000 g. **Composition:** Silver **Obverse:** Rosettes dividing Chinese legend **Note:** Varieties exist; Struck at the Kashgar Mint.

| Date | Mintage | VG | F | VF | XF | Unc |
|---|---|---|---|---|---|---|
| AH1330 | — | 35.00 | 65.00 | 135 | 225 | — |
| AH1331 | — | 35.00 | 65.00 | 135 | 225 | — |

| Date | Mintage | VG | F | VF | XF | Unc |
|---|---|---|---|---|---|---|
| AH1332 | — | 35.00 | 65.00 | 135 | 225 | — |
| AH13-32 | — | 35.00 | 65.00 | 135 | 225 | — |

**5 MISCALS** Y# 43.3 **Weight:** 17.3000 g. **Composition:** Silver **Obverse:** Rosette in center, floral arrangements dividing Chinese legend **Note:** Varieties exist; Struck at the Kashgar Mint.

| Date | Mintage | VG | F | VF | XF | Unc |
|---|---|---|---|---|---|---|
| AH13-32 | — | 40.00 | 75.00 | 160 | 275 | — |
| AH133-4 | — | 45.00 | 85.00 | 185 | 325 | — |

**5 MISCALS** Y# 43.2 **Weight:** 17.3000 g. **Composition:** Silver **Obverse:** Rosettes dividing Chinese legend **Note:** Struck at the Kashgar Mint.

| Date | Mintage | VG | F | VF | XF | Unc |
|---|---|---|---|---|---|---|
| AH1334 | — | 45.00 | 85.00 | 185 | 325 | — |
| AH133-4 | — | 45.00 | 85.00 | 185 | 325 | — |

**Note:** Varieties exist.

**5 MISCALS** Y# 43.4 **Weight:** 17.3000 g. **Composition:** Silver **Obverse:** Stars divide rotated outer Chinese legend **Note:** Struck at the Kashgar Mint.

| Date | Mintage | VG | F | VF | XF | Unc |
|---|---|---|---|---|---|---|
| AHx13x(ca.1916) | — | — | — | — | — | — |

**Note:** Considered contemporary forgeries by some experts

**5 MISCALS (5 Mace)** Y# 41 **Weight:** 17.9000 g. **Composition:** Silver **Reverse:** Two stripes in flags have arabesques

| Date | Mintage | VG | F | VF | XF | Unc |
|---|---|---|---|---|---|---|
| 1(1912) | — | 40.00 | 65.00 | 150 | 200 | — |

**5 MISCALS (5 Mace)** Y# 41a **Weight:** 17.9000 g. **Composition:** Silver **Reverse:** Four stripes in flags have arabesques

| Date | Mintage | VG | F | VF | XF | Unc |
|---|---|---|---|---|---|---|
| 1(1912) | — | 40.00 | 65.00 | 150 | 200 | — |

**SAR (Tael)** Y# 42 **Weight:** 35.9000 g. **Composition:** Silver **Reverse:** Two stripes in flags have arabesques

| Date | Mintage | VG | F | VF | XF | Unc |
|---|---|---|---|---|---|---|
| CD1(1912) | — | 60.00 | 100 | 200 | 350 | — |

**SAR (Tael)** Y# 42a **Weight:** 35.9000 g. **Composition:** Silver **Obverse:** Similar to Y#42 **Reverse:** Four stripes in flags have arabesques

| Date | Mintage | VG | F | VF | XF | Unc |
|---|---|---|---|---|---|---|
| CD1(1912) | — | 60.00 | 100 | 200 | 350 | — |

**SAR (Tael)** Y# 45 **Weight:** 35.0000 g. **Composition:** Silver **Obverse:** Large characters **Reverse:** Rosette at top between wheat ears

| Date | Mintage | VG | F | VF | XF | Unc |
|---|---|---|---|---|---|---|
| ND(1917) | — | 15.00 | 20.00 | 32.50 | 50.00 | — |

**SAR (Tael)** Y# 45.1 **Weight:** 35.0000 g. **Composition:** Silver **Obverse:** Similar to Y#45 but with small characters **Reverse:** Without rosette at top

| Date | Mintage | VG | F | VF | XF | Unc |
|---|---|---|---|---|---|---|
| ND(1917) | — | 15.00 | 20.00 | 32.50 | 50.00 | — |

**SAR (Tael)** Y# 45.2 **Weight:** 35.0000 g. **Composition:** Silver **Reverse:** Rosette at top between branches

| Date | Mintage | VG | F | VF | XF | Unc |
|---|---|---|---|---|---|---|
| ND(1918) | — | 20.00 | 25.00 | 42.50 | 75.00 | — |

**DOLLAR** Y# 46 **Composition:** Silver **Obverse:** Similar to Y#46.2 but with larger Chinese characters **Reverse:** Think pointed base "1"

| Date | Mintage | VG | F | VF | XF | Unc |
|---|---|---|---|---|---|---|
| 38(1949) | — | 12.50 | 20.00 | 32.50 | 50.00 | — |

**DOLLAR** Y# 46.1 **Composition:** Silver **Obverse:** Similar to Y#46.2 but with larger Chinese characters **Reverse:** Think pointed base "1" with large serif

| Date | Mintage | VG | F | VF | XF | Unc |
|---|---|---|---|---|---|---|
| 38(1949) | — | 12.50 | 20.00 | 30.50 | 50.00 | — |

**DOLLAR** Y# 46.2 **Composition:** Silver **Obverse:** Smaller Chinese characters **Reverse:** Thin pointed base "1"

| Date | Mintage | VG | F | VF | XF | Unc |
|---|---|---|---|---|---|---|
| 38(1949) | — | 12.50 | 20.00 | 32.50 | 50.00 | — |

**DOLLAR** Y# 46.3 **Composition:** Silver **Reverse:** Square-based "1"

| Date | Mintage | VG | F | VF | XF | Unc |
|---|---|---|---|---|---|---|
| 38(1949) | — | 15.00 | 25.00 | 45.00 | 80.00 | — |

**DOLLAR** Y# 46.4 **Composition:** Silver **Obverse:** Outlined Chinese characters "Yüan" in center

| Date | Mintage | VG | F | VF | XF | Unc |
|---|---|---|---|---|---|---|
| 38(1949) | — | 15.00 | 25.00 | 60.00 | 100 | — |

**DOLLAR** Y# 46.5 **Composition:** Silver **Note:** 9-4-9-1 (1949) at bottom

| Date | Mintage | VG | F | VF | XF | Unc |
|---|---|---|---|---|---|---|
| 1949(1949) | — | 75.00 | 125 | 175 | 250 | — |

# ISLAMIC REPUBLIC OF EASTERN TURKESTAN

## MILLED COINAGE

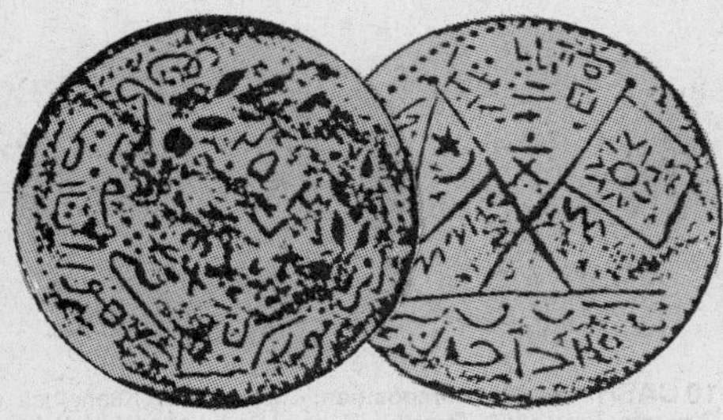

**20 CASH** Y# E38.2 **Composition:** Copper **Reverse:** Flags reversed

| Date | Mintage | Good | VG | F | VF | XF |
|---|---|---|---|---|---|---|
| AH1352 | — | 50.00 | 100 | 150 | 200 | — |

**Note:** Considered contemporary forgeries by some experts

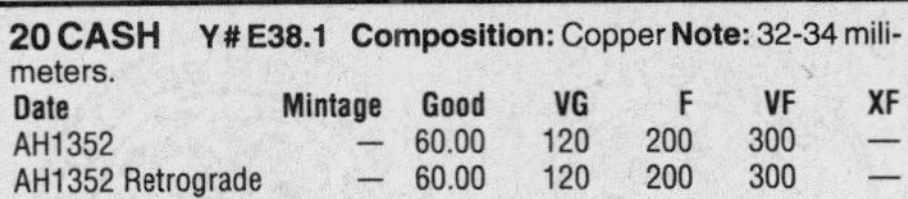

**20 CASH** Y# E38.1 **Composition:** Copper **Note:** 32-34 milimeters.

| Date | Mintage | Good | VG | F | VF | XF |
|---|---|---|---|---|---|---|
| AH1352 | — | 60.00 | 120 | 200 | 300 | — |
| AH1352 Retrograde | — | 60.00 | 120 | 200 | 300 | — |

**MISCAL** Y# E39 **Composition:** Silver **Obverse:** Turki legend around central Turki legend **Obv. Legend:** "Sharket Turkhestan Cumhuriyet Islamiyesi" around "Muskuk, sanah 1252" **Reverse:** Turki legend: "Zarb Kashgar"

| Date | Mintage | Good | VG | F | VF | XF |
|---|---|---|---|---|---|---|
| AH1352 Rare | — | — | — | — | — | — |

**Note:** Varieties of sun with eight and nine rays exist

# ULGHURISTAN REPUBLIC

A rebel Islamic republic that sought independence from China. The rebellion was quickly crushed. Coins of the Republic were all made by overstriking on Kashgar Republic 10 Cach coins.

## MILLED COINAGE

**10 CASH** Y# D38.1 **Composition:** Copper **Reverse:** Flag at right without fringe

| Date | Mintage | Good | VG | F | VF | XF |
|---|---|---|---|---|---|---|
| AH1352 | — | 50.00 | 100 | 160 | 250 | — |

**10 CASH** Y# D38.2 **Composition:** Copper **Reverse:** Flag at right with partial fringe

| Date | Mintage | Good | VG | F | VF | XF |
|---|---|---|---|---|---|---|
| AH1352 | — | 50.00 | 100 | 160 | 250 | — |

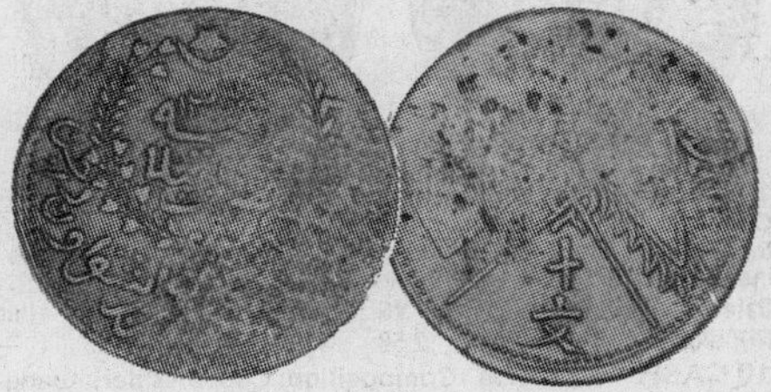

**10 CASH** Y# D38.3 **Composition:** Copper **Reverse:** Flag at right with full fringe

| Date | Mintage | Good | VG | F | VF | XF |
|---|---|---|---|---|---|---|
| AH1352 | — | 50.00 | 100 | 160 | 250 | — |

**Note:** Encountered overstruck on various earlier Republican Series 10 Cash

**20 CASH** Y# G38 **Composition:** Copper **Obverse:** Similar to 20 Cash, Y#E38.3 **Reverse:** Small flag at left

| Date | Mintage | Good | VG | F | VF | XF |
|---|---|---|---|---|---|---|
| AH1352 | — | — | — | — | — | — |

**20 CASH** Y# E38.3 **Composition:** Copper **Reverse:** Sun in partial frame in left flag, denomination given as two wen (sic) **Note:** Size varies 32-34 milimeters.

| Date | Mintage | Good | VG | F | VF | XF |
|---|---|---|---|---|---|---|
| AH1352 Rare | — | — | — | — | — | — |

**20 CASH** Y# E38.4 **Composition:** Copper **Reverse:** Large sun in national flag at left **Note:** Varieties exist.

| Date | Mintage | Good | VG | F | VF | XF |
|---|---|---|---|---|---|---|
| AH1352 | — | 50.00 | 100 | 150 | 200 | — |

**Note:** Crudely cut Chinese denomination appears as 2 instead of 20; also encountered overstruck on 10 Cash, Y#44 varieties

## PATTERNS

Including off metal strikes

| KM# | Date | Mintage | Identification | Mkt Val |
|---|---|---|---|---|
| Pn6 | (ca.1906) | — | 5 Mace. Silver. Without bats around large dragon. | — |
| Pn7 | (ca.1906) | — | 7 Mace. Silver. SUNGAREI. 2 Candareens, Y#12. | — |
| Pn30 | 1324 | — | Tael. Silver. | — |
| Pn1 | (ca.1906) | — | Mace. Copper. SUNGAREI. Y#10 | 1,600 |
| Pn3 | (ca.1906) | — | 2 Mace. Copper. SUNGAREI. | 1,200 |
| Pn2 | (ca.1906) | — | 2 Mace. Silver. SUNGAREI. Y#11 | 3,000 |
| Pn4 | (ca.1906) | — | 4 Mace. Silver. SUNGAREI. | 8,000 |
| Pn5 | (ca.1906) | — | 4 Mace. Brass. SUNGAREI. | 1,250 |

# SUIYUAN PROVINCE

In November 1913, the central government grouped together 19 Mongolian and 12 Shansi districts to form the Suiyuan Special Administrative Zone. In 1928, the name was changed to Suiyuan Province. The province was joined with other Mongolian provinces to form Inner Mongolia after the communist takeover in 1949.

## REPUBLIC

## MILLED COINAGE

**FEN** KM# 3 **Composition:** Shell Casing Brass **Obverse:** White Tower **Reverse:** Ancient spade coin between Yi and Fen

| Date | Mintage | VG | F | VF | XF | Unc |
|---|---|---|---|---|---|---|
| 1949(38)(1949) | — | 175 | 250 | 350 | 550 | — |

**5 FEN** KM# 5 **Composition:** Shell Casing Brass **Obverse:** White Tower **Reverse:** Ancient spade coin between Wu(5) and Fen

| Date | Mintage | VG | F | VF | XF | Unc |
|---|---|---|---|---|---|---|
| 1949(38)(1949) | — | 600 | 750 | 1,000 | 1,350 | — |

# SZECHUAN PROVINCE

### Sichuan

A province located in south-central China. The largest of the traditional Chinese provinces, Szechuan (Sichuan) is a plateau region watered by many rivers. These rivers carry much trading traffic. Agriculture or mining are the occupational choices of most of the populace. In World War II the national capital was moved to Chungking in Szechuan (Sichuan). Chengtu was an active imperial mint that opened in 1732 and was in practically continuous operation until the advent of modern equipment. Modern minting was introduced in the province when Chengtu began milled coinage in 1898. A mint was authorized for Chungking in 1905 but it did not begin operations until 1913. The Chengtu Mint was looted by soldiers in 1925. The last republic issues from Szechuan (Sichuan) were dated 1932.

The machinery for the first Szechuan (Sichuan) Mint was produced in New Jersey and the dies were engraved in Philadelphia. The mint was opened in 1898, but closed within a few months and did not reopen until 1901. There is no doubt now that Y#234-238 (K#145-149) were the first issues of this mint, contrary to the Kann listings.

# EMPIRE

## PROVINCIAL CAST COINAGE

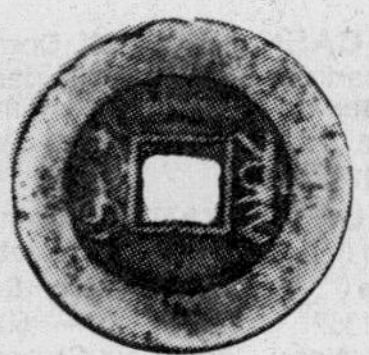

**CASH** C#24-9 **Composition:** Cast Brass **Ruler:** Kuang-hsü **Obverse:** Inscription: Kuang-hsü T'ung-pao **Reverse:** Inscription: Manchu Boo-Cuwan **Note:** Struck at Chuan (Cheng tu)

| Date | Mintage | Good | VG | F | VF | XF |
|---|---|---|---|---|---|---|
| ND(1875-1908) | — | 4.50 | 7.50 | 11.50 | 22.50 | — |

## MILLED COINAGE

**5 CASH** Y# 225 **Composition:** Copper **Ruler:** Kuang-hsü **Obverse:** Inscription: Kuang-hsü Yüan-pao; Manchu at center **Reverse:** Side view dragon

| Date | Mintage | VG | F | VF | XF | Unc |
|---|---|---|---|---|---|---|
| ND(1903-04) | 85,000 | 50.00 | 70.00 | 100 | 150 | — |

**5 CASH** Y# 225a **Composition:** Brass **Ruler:** Kuang-hsü **Obverse:** Inscription: Kuang-hsü Yüan-pao

| Date | Mintage | VG | F | VF | XF | Unc |
|---|---|---|---|---|---|---|
| ND(1903-04) Rare | Inc. above | — | — | — | — | — |

**5 CASH** Y# A229 (YA228) **Composition:** Brass **Ruler:** Kuang-hsü **Obverse:** Inscription: Kuang-hsü Yüan-pao; Y#228 **Reverse:** Y#225

| Date | Mintage | VG | F | VF | XF | Unc |
|---|---|---|---|---|---|---|
| ND(1903-04) | Inc. above | 100 | 140 | 200 | 300 | — |

**5 CASH** Y# 228 **Composition:** Brass **Ruler:** Kuang-hsü **Obverse:** Inscription: Kuang-hsü Yüan-pao; flower at center **Reverse:** Flying dragon

| Date | Mintage | VG | F | VF | XF | Unc |
|---|---|---|---|---|---|---|
| ND(1903-04) | Inc. above | 350 | 500 | 750 | — | — |

**10 CASH** Y# 226 **Composition:** Copper **Ruler:** Kuang-hsü **Obverse:** Inscription: Kuang-hsü Yüan-pao; with thick Manchu in center, large rosettes

| Date | Mintage | VG | F | VF | XF | Unc |
|---|---|---|---|---|---|---|
| ND(1903-05) | 95,960,000 | 12.50 | 25.00 | 35.00 | 60.00 | — |

**10 CASH** Y# 226.1 **Composition:** Copper **Ruler:** Kuang-hsü **Obverse:** Inscription: Kuang-hsü Yüan-pao; with thin Manchu in center, small rosettes

| Date | Mintage | VG | F | VF | XF | Unc |
|---|---|---|---|---|---|---|
| ND(1903-05) | Inc. above | 22.50 | 45.00 | 70.00 | 125 | — |

**10 CASH** Y# 226.2 **Composition:** Copper **Ruler:** Kuang-hsü **Obverse:** Inscription: Kuang-hsü Yüan-pao; with large rosettes

| Date | Mintage | VG | F | VF | XF | Unc |
|---|---|---|---|---|---|---|
| ND(1903-05) | Inc. above | 20.00 | 40.00 | 60.00 | 100 | — |

**10 CASH** Y# 229 **Composition:** Copper **Ruler:** Kuang-hsü **Obverse:** Inscription: Kuang-hsü Yüan-pao; legend with two characters at bottom, 6-9 milimeters apart **Reverse:** Trident-shaped flame on dragon's body below letters CHU

| Date | Mintage | VG | F | VF | XF | Unc |
|---|---|---|---|---|---|---|
| ND(1903-05) | Inc. above | 4.00 | 6.50 | 10.00 | 17.50 | — |

**10 CASH** Y# 229.1 **Composition:** Copper **Ruler:** Kuang-hsü **Obverse:** Inscription: Kuang-hsü Yüan-pao; legend with characters at bottom, 4-5 milimeters apart

| Date | Mintage | VG | F | VF | XF | Unc |
|---|---|---|---|---|---|---|
| ND(1903-05) | Inc. above | 4.00 | 6.50 | 10.00 | 17.50 | — |

**10 CASH** Y# 229.2 **Composition:** Copper **Ruler:** Kuang-hsü **Obverse:** Inscription: Kuang-hsü Yüan-pao; with Manchu at 3 o'clock is lower in relation to center characters

| Date | Mintage | VG | F | VF | XF | Unc |
|---|---|---|---|---|---|---|
| ND(1903-05) | Inc. above | 4.00 | 6.50 | 10.00 | 17.50 | — |

**10 CASH** Y# 229.3 **Composition:** Copper **Ruler:** Kuang-hsü **Obverse:** Inscription: Kuang-hsü Yüan-pao; with characters 6-9 milimeters apart **Reverse:** Trident-shaped flame below letters HUE

| Date | Mintage | VG | F | VF | XF | Unc |
|---|---|---|---|---|---|---|
| ND(1903-05) | Inc. above | 4.00 | 6.50 | 10.00 | 17.50 | — |

**10 CASH** Y# 229.3a **Composition:** Brass **Ruler:** Kuang-hsü **Obverse:** Inscription: Kuang-hsü Yüan-pao

| Date | Mintage | VG | F | VF | XF | Unc |
|---|---|---|---|---|---|---|
| ND(1903-05) | Inc. above | 4.00 | 6.50 | 10.00 | 17.50 | — |

**10 CASH** Y# 229.4 **Composition:** Brass **Ruler:** Kuang-hsü **Obverse:** Inscription: Kuang-hsü Yüan-pao; with characters 4-5 milimeters apart

| Date | Mintage | VG | F | VF | XF | Unc |
|---|---|---|---|---|---|---|
| ND(1903-05) | Inc. above | 4.00 | 6.50 | 10.00 | 17.50 | — |

**10 CASH** Y# 229.5 **Composition:** Brass **Ruler:** Kuang-hsü **Obverse:** Inscription: Kuang-hsü Yüan-pao; with bottom characters 6-9 milimeters apart **Reverse:** Without trident-shaped flame, instead a cloud pointing to the letter U

| Date | Mintage | VG | F | VF | XF | Unc |
|---|---|---|---|---|---|---|
| ND(1903-05) | Inc. above | 2.50 | 4.00 | 7.50 | 12.00 | — |

**10 CASH** Y# 229.5a **Composition:** Copper **Ruler:** Kuang-hsü **Obverse:** Inscription: Kuang-hsü Yüan-pao

| Date | Mintage | VG | F | VF | XF | Unc |
|---|---|---|---|---|---|---|
| ND(1903-05) | Inc. above | 3.00 | 5.00 | 10.00 | 15.00 | — |

**10 CASH** Y# 229.6 **Composition:** Brass **Ruler:** Kuang-hsü **Obverse:** Inscription: Kuang-hsü Yüan-pao; with characters 4-5 milimeters apart

| Date | Mintage | VG | F | VF | XF | Unc |
|---|---|---|---|---|---|---|
| ND(1903-05) | Inc. above | 4.00 | 6.00 | 10.00 | 17.50 | — |

**10 CASH** Y# 229.6a **Composition:** Copper **Ruler:** Kuang-hsü **Obverse:** Inscription: Kuang-hsü Yüan-pao

| Date | Mintage | VG | F | VF | XF | Unc |
|---|---|---|---|---|---|---|
| ND(1903-05) | Inc. above | 2.00 | 3.00 | 5.50 | 10.00 | — |

**10 CASH** Y# 229.7 **Composition:** Brass **Ruler:** Kuang-hsü **Obverse:** Inscription: Kuang-hsü Yüan-pao; with Manchu at 3 o'clock is lower

| Date | Mintage | VG | F | VF | XF | Unc |
|---|---|---|---|---|---|---|
| ND(1903-05) | Inc. above | 3.75 | 6.00 | 10.00 | 17.50 | — |

**10 CASH** Y# 229.7a **Composition:** Copper **Ruler:** Kuang-hsü **Obverse:** Inscription: Kuang-hsü Yüan-pao

| Date | Mintage | VG | F | VF | XF | Unc |
|---|---|---|---|---|---|---|
| ND(1903-05) | Inc. above | 2.00 | 3.50 | 6.00 | 9.00 | — |

**10 CASH** Y# 229.8 **Composition:** Brass **Ruler:** Kuang-hsü **Obverse:** Inscription: Kuang-hsü Yüan-pao; with characters 4-5 milimeters apart **Reverse:** Without cloud below CHU, high point of dragon's body below letter C, tail joins body above S in CASH

| Date | Mintage | VG | F | VF | XF | Unc |
|---|---|---|---|---|---|---|
| ND(1903-05) | Inc. above | 4.00 | 6.00 | 9.00 | 17.50 | — |

**10 CASH** Y# 229.8a **Composition:** Copper **Ruler:** Kuang-hsü **Obverse:** Inscription: Kuang-hsü Yüan-pao

| Date | Mintage | VG | F | VF | XF | Unc |
|---|---|---|---|---|---|---|
| ND(1903-05) | Inc. above | 2.00 | 3.50 | 6.00 | 9.00 | — |

**10 CASH** Y# 229.9 **Composition:** Copper **Ruler:** Kuang-hsü **Obverse:** Inscription: Kuang-hsü Yüan-pao **Reverse:** High point of dragon's body below letter H, tail joins body above letter C in CASH

| Date | Mintage | VG | F | VF | XF | Unc |
|---|---|---|---|---|---|---|
| ND(1903-05) | Inc. above | 2.00 | 3.50 | 6.00 | 9.00 | — |

**10 CASH** Y# 231 **Composition:** Copper **Ruler:** Kuang-hsü **Obverse:** Inscription: Kuang-hsü Yüan-pao

| Date | Mintage | VG | F | VF | XF | Unc |
|---|---|---|---|---|---|---|
| ND(1903-05) | Inc. above | 150 | 200 | 225 | 275 | — |

**10 CASH** Y# 10t **Composition:** Copper **Ruler:** Kuang-hsü **Obverse:** Inscription: Ta-ch'ing T'ung-pi **Rev. Legend:** Kuang-hsü Nien-tsao, TAI-CHING-TI-KUO...

| Date | Mintage | VG | F | VF | XF | Unc |
|---|---|---|---|---|---|---|
| CD(1906) | 337,748,000 | 1.00 | 1.50 | 3.00 | 6.00 | — |

**10 CASH** Y# 20t.1 **Composition:** Copper **Ruler:** Hsüan-t'ung **Obverse:** Inscription: Ta-ch'ing T'ung-pi; with bottom of

Manchu word at 11 o'clock curls to left **Rev. Legend:** Hsüan-t'ung Nien-tsao, TAI-CHING-TI-KUO...

| Date | Mintage | VG | F | VF | XF | Unc |
|---|---|---|---|---|---|---|
| CD(1909) | 231,930,000 | 1.00 | 1.50 | 3.00 | 6.00 | — |

**10 CASH** **Y# 20t.1a** **Composition:** Brass **Ruler:** Hsüan-t'ung **Obverse:** Inscription: Ta-ch'ing T'ung-pi **Rev. Legend:** Hsüan-t'ung Nien-tsao, TAI-CHING-TI-KUO...

| Date | Mintage | VG | F | VF | XF | Unc |
|---|---|---|---|---|---|---|
| CD(1909) | Inc. above | 3.00 | 5.00 | 10.00 | 15.00 | — |

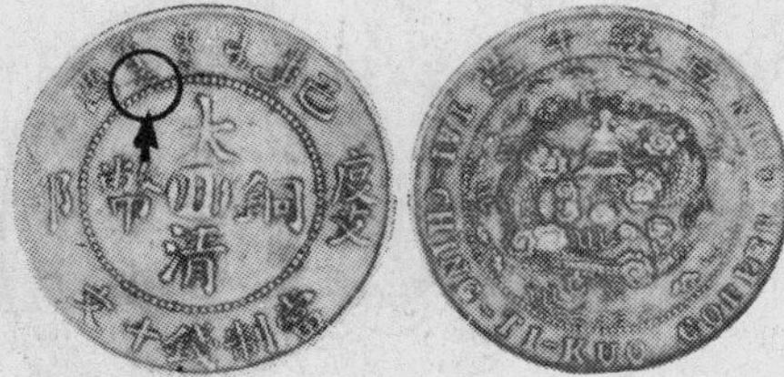

**10 CASH** **Y# 20t.2** **Composition:** Copper **Ruler:** Hsüan-t'ung **Obverse:** Inscription: Ta-ch'ing T'ung-pi; with bottom of Manchu word at 11 o'clock curls to right **Rev. Legend:** Hsüan-t'ung Nien-tsao, TAI-CHING-TI-KUO...

| Date | Mintage | VG | F | VF | XF | Unc |
|---|---|---|---|---|---|---|
| CD(1909) | Inc. above | 5.00 | 9.00 | 12.00 | 17.50 | — |

**20 CASH** **Y# 227** **Composition:** Copper **Ruler:** Kuang-hsü **Obverse:** Inscription: Kuang-hsü Yüan-pao

| Date | Mintage | VG | F | VF | XF | Unc |
|---|---|---|---|---|---|---|
| ND(1903-05) | 25,319,000 | 100 | 125 | 175 | 250 | — |

**20 CASH** **Y# 230** **Composition:** Copper **Ruler:** Kuang-hsü **Obverse:** Inscription: Kuang-hsü Yüan-pao; with small Manchu at 3 and 9 o'clock **Reverse:** Trident flame points to E of SZE

| Date | Mintage | VG | F | VF | XF | Unc |
|---|---|---|---|---|---|---|
| ND(1903-05) | Inc. above | 10.00 | 15.00 | 30.00 | 50.00 | — |

**20 CASH** **Y# 230.3** **Composition:** Copper **Ruler:** Kuang-hsü **Obverse:** Inscription: Kuang-hsü Yüan-pao; with large Manchu **Reverse:** Trident flame below ZE

| Date | Mintage | VG | F | VF | XF | Unc |
|---|---|---|---|---|---|---|
| ND(1903-05) | Inc. above | 15.00 | 30.00 | 50.00 | 80.00 | — |

**20 CASH** **Y# 230.4** **Composition:** Copper **Ruler:** Kuang-hsü **Obverse:** Inscription: Kuang-hsü Yüan-pao **Reverse:** Trident flame below CHU of CHUEN, large letters

| Date | Mintage | VG | F | VF | XF | Unc |
|---|---|---|---|---|---|---|
| ND(1903-05) | — | 30.00 | 60.00 | 100 | 160 | — |

**20 CASH** **Y# 230.5** **Composition:** Copper **Ruler:** Kuang-hsü **Obverse:** Inscription: Kuang-hsü Yüan-pao **Reverse:** Trident flame points to E of CHUEN, small letters

| Date | Mintage | VG | F | VF | XF | Unc |
|---|---|---|---|---|---|---|
| ND(1903-05) | Inc. above | — | — | — | — | — |

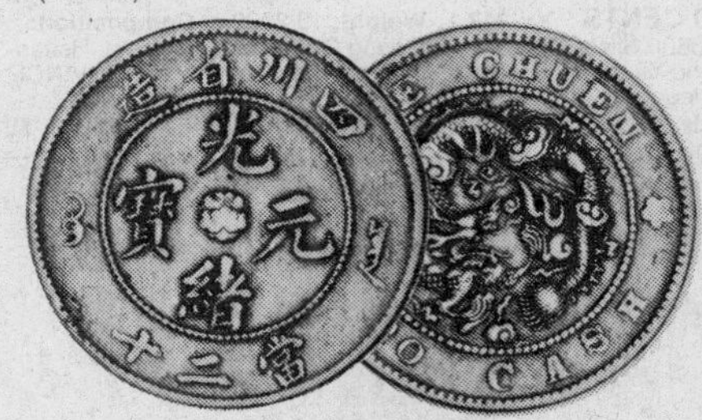

**20 CASH** **Y# 230.6** **Composition:** Copper **Ruler:** Kuang-hsü **Obverse:** Inscription: Kuang-hsü Yüan-pao; with different small Manchu **Reverse:** Large 5-petalled rosettes, dragon differs

| Date | Mintage | VG | F | VF | XF | Unc |
|---|---|---|---|---|---|---|
| ND(1903-05) | Inc. above | 12.50 | 20.00 | 35.00 | 60.00 | — |

**20 CASH** **Y# 230.7a** **Composition:** Brass **Ruler:** Kuang-hsü **Obverse:** Inscription: Kuang-hsü Yüan-pao; with small Manchu **Reverse:** Larger cloud below CHUEN

| Date | Mintage | VG | F | VF | XF | Unc |
|---|---|---|---|---|---|---|
| ND(1903-05) | Inc. above | 15.00 | 25.00 | 40.00 | 70.00 | — |

**20 CASH** **Y# 230.1** **Composition:** Copper **Ruler:** Kuang-hsü **Obverse:** Inscription: Kuang-hsü Yüan-pao; with large Manchu at 3 and 9 o'clock **Reverse:** Large trident flame points to C of CHUEN **Note:** Varieties exist.

| Date | Mintage | VG | F | VF | XF | Unc |
|---|---|---|---|---|---|---|
| ND(1903-05) | Inc. above | 30.00 | 50.00 | 80.00 | 150 | — |

**20 CASH** **Y# 11t** **Composition:** Copper **Obverse:** Inscription: Ta-ch'ing T'ung-pi

| Date | Mintage | VG | F | VF | XF | Unc |
|---|---|---|---|---|---|---|
| CD(1906) | 51,028,000 | 10.00 | 22.50 | 35.00 | 60.00 | — |

**20 CASH** **Y# 21t.1** **Composition:** Copper **Obverse:** Inscription: Ta-ch'ing T'ung-pi; with bottom of Manchu word at 11 o'clock curls right

| Date | Mintage | VG | F | VF | XF | Unc |
|---|---|---|---|---|---|---|
| CD(1909) | 33,414,000 | 15.00 | 27.50 | 40.00 | 70.00 | — |

**20 CASH** **Y# 21t.2** **Composition:** Copper **Obverse:** Inscription: Ta-ch'ing T'ung-pi; with bottom of Manchu word at 11 o'clock curls left

| Date | Mintage | VG | F | VF | XF | Unc |
|---|---|---|---|---|---|---|
| CD(1909) | — | 15.00 | 27.50 | 40.00 | 70.00 | — |

**20 CASH** **Y# 21t.1a** **Composition:** Brass **Obverse:** Inscription: Ta-ch'ing T'ung-pi

| Date | Mintage | VG | F | VF | XF | Unc |
|---|---|---|---|---|---|---|
| CD(1909) | Inc. above | 25.00 | 35.00 | 65.00 | 100 | — |

**5 CENTS** **Y# 234** **Weight:** 1.3000 g. **Composition:** 0.8200 Silver .0343 oz. ASW **Ruler:** Kuang-hsü **Obverse:** Inscription: Kuang-hsü Yüan-pao

| Date | Mintage | F | VF | XF | Unc | BU |
|---|---|---|---|---|---|---|
| ND(1898; 1901-08) | 671,000 | 12.50 | 17.50 | 30.00 | 80.00 | — |

**5 CENTS** **Y# 234.1** **Weight:** 1.3000 g. **Composition:** 0.8200 Silver .0343 oz. ASW **Ruler:** Kuang-hsü **Obverse:** Inscription: Kuang-hsü Yüan-pao **Reverse:** With errors in the English legend

| Date | Mintage | F | VF | XF | Unc | BU |
|---|---|---|---|---|---|---|
| ND(1901-08) | Inc. above | 15 00 | 25.00 | 40.00 | 90.00 | — |

**5 CENTS** **Y# 239** **Weight:** 1.3000 g. **Composition:** 0.8200 Silver .0343 oz. ASW **Ruler:** Hsüan-t'ung **Obverse:** Inscription: Hsüan-t'ung Yüan-pao

| Date | Mintage | F | VF | XF | Unc | BU |
|---|---|---|---|---|---|---|
| ND(1910) | 566,000 | 20.00 | 30.00 | 55.00 | 120 | — |

**10 CENTS** **Y# 235** **Weight:** 2.6000 g. **Composition:** 0.8200 Silver .0686 oz. ASW **Ruler:** Kuang-hsü **Obverse:** Inscription: Kuang-hsü Yüan-pao

| Date | Mintage | F | VF | XF | Unc | BU |
|---|---|---|---|---|---|---|
| ND(1898; 1901-08) | 1,274,000 | 10.00 | 20.00 | 30.00 | 90.00 | — |

**10 CENTS** **Y# 240** **Weight:** 2.6000 g. **Composition:** 0.8200 Silver .0686 oz. ASW **Ruler:** Hsüan-t'ung **Obverse:** Inscription: Hsüan-t'ung Yüan-pao

| Date | Mintage | F | VF | XF | Unc | BU |
|---|---|---|---|---|---|---|
| ND(1909-11) | 278,000 | 25.00 | 30.00 | 55.00 | 120 | — |

**20 CENTS** **Y# 236** **Weight:** 5.3000 g. **Composition:** 0.8200 Silver .1397 oz. ASW **Ruler:** Kuang-hsü **Obverse:** Inscription: Kuang-hsü Yüan-pao **Reverse:** Five flames on pearl

| Date | Mintage | F | VF | XF | Unc | BU |
|---|---|---|---|---|---|---|
| ND(1898; 1901-08) | 897,000 | 10.00 | 20.00 | 40.00 | 100 | — |

**20 CENTS** **Y# 236.1** **Weight:** 5.3000 g. **Composition:** 0.8200 Silver .1397 oz. ASW **Ruler:** Kuang-hsü **Obverse:** Inscription: Kuang-hsü Yüan-pao **Reverse:** Six flames on pearl

| Date | Mintage | F | VF | XF | Unc | BU |
|---|---|---|---|---|---|---|
| ND(1898; 1901-08) | Inc. above | 10.00 | 20.00 | 40.00 | 100 | — |

**20 CENTS** **Y# 236.2** **Weight:** 5.3000 g. **Composition:** 0.8200 Silver .1397 oz. ASW **Ruler:** Kuang-hsü **Obverse:** Inscription: Kuang-hsü Yüan-pao **Reverse:** Seven flames on pearl

| Date | Mintage | F | VF | XF | Unc | BU |
|---|---|---|---|---|---|---|
| ND(1898; 1901-08) | Inc. above | 10.00 | 20.00 | 40.00 | 100 | — |

**20 CENTS** **Y# 236.3** **Weight:** 5.3000 g. **Composition:** 0.8200 Silver .1397 oz. ASW **Ruler:** Kuang-hsü **Obverse:** Inscription: Kuang-hsü Yüan-pao **Reverse:** Various errors in English legend

| Date | Mintage | F | VF | XF | Unc | BU |
|---|---|---|---|---|---|---|
| ND(1901-08) | Inc. above | 15.00 | 25.00 | 50.00 | 125 | — |

**20 CENTS** **Y# 241** **Weight:** 5.3000 g. **Composition:** 0.8200 Silver .1397 oz. ASW **Ruler:** Hsüan-t'ung **Obverse:** Inscription: Hsüan-t'ung Yüan-pao

| Date | Mintage | F | VF | XF | Unc | BU |
|---|---|---|---|---|---|---|
| ND(1909-11) Rare | 41,000 | — | — | — | — | — |

**50 CENTS** **Y# 237** **Weight:** 13.2000 g. **Composition:** 0.8600 Silver .3650 oz. ASW **Ruler:** Kuang-hsü **Obverse:** Inscription: Kuang-hsü Yüan-pao **Reverse:** Dragon with narrow face, small cross at either side, large fireball

| Date | Mintage | F | VF | XF | Unc | BU |
|---|---|---|---|---|---|---|
| ND(1898; 1901-08) | 474,000 | 22.50 | 40.00 | 100 | 300 | — |

**50 CENTS** **Y# 237.1** **Weight:** 13.2000 g. **Composition:** 0.8600 Silver .3650 oz. ASW **Ruler:** Kuang-hsü **Obverse:** Inscription: Kuang-hsü Yüan-pao **Reverse:** Various errors in English legend

| Date | Mintage | F | VF | XF | Unc | BU |
|---|---|---|---|---|---|---|
| ND(1901-08) | Inc. above | 25.00 | 50.00 | 100 | 225 | — |

**50 CENTS** **Y# 237.2** **Weight:** 13.2000 g. **Composition:** 0.8600 Silver .3650 oz. ASW **Ruler:** Kuang-hsü **Obverse:** Inscription: Kuang-hsü Yüan-pao **Reverse:** Dragon with tapering face and small chin, small fireball, small cross at either side of dragon

| Date | Mintage | F | VF | XF | Unc | BU |
|---|---|---|---|---|---|---|
| ND(1901-08) | Inc. above | — | 40.00 | 100 | 200 | — |

**50 CENTS** **Y# 237.3** **Weight:** 13.2000 g. **Composition:** 0.8600 Silver .3650 oz. ASW **Ruler:** Kuang-hsü **Obverse:** Inscription: Kuang-hsü Yüan-pao **Reverse:** Dragon with wide face and smaller fireball, thicker spines on top of dragon's head, small cross at either side of dragon

| Date | Mintage | F | VF | XF | Unc | BU |
|---|---|---|---|---|---|---|
| ND(1901-08) | Inc. above | 22.50 | 40.00 | 100 | 200 | — |

**50 CENTS** **Y# 242** **Weight:** 13.2000 g. **Composition:** 0.8600 Silver **Ruler:** Hsüan-t'ung **Obverse:** Inscription: Hsüan-t'ung Yüan-pao

| Date | Mintage | F | VF | XF | Unc | BU |
|---|---|---|---|---|---|---|
| ND(1909-11) | 38,000 | 75.00 | 130 | 180 | 325 | — |

**50 CENTS** **Y# 242.1** **Weight:** 13.2000 g. **Composition:** 0.8600 Silver **Ruler:** Hsüan-t'ung **Obverse:** Inscription: Hsüan-t'ung Yüan-pao **Reverse:** Inverted A in place of V in PROVINCE in legend

| Date | Mintage | F | VF | XF | Unc | BU |
|---|---|---|---|---|---|---|
| ND(1901-11) | Inc. above | 75.00 | 130 | 180 | 325 | — |

**DOLLAR** **Y# 238** **Weight:** 26.8000 g. **Composition:** 0.9000 Silver .7756 oz. ASW **Ruler:** Kuang-hsü **Obverse:** Inscription: Kuang-hsü Yüan-pao **Reverse:** Dragon with narrow face and large fireball, small cross at either side of dragon

| Date | Mintage | F | VF | XF | Unc | BU |
|---|---|---|---|---|---|---|
| ND(1901-08) | 6,487,000 | 20.00 | 30.00 | 75.00 | 500 | — |

**DOLLAR** **Y# 238.1** **Weight:** 26.8000 g. **Composition:** 0.9000 Silver .7756 oz. ASW **Ruler:** Kuang-hsü **Obverse:** Inscription: Kuang-hsü Yüan-pao **Reverse:** Inverted A instead of V in PROVINCE in legend

| Date | Mintage | F | VF | XF | Unc | BU |
|---|---|---|---|---|---|---|
| ND(1901-08) | Inc. above | 17.50 | 25.00 | 70.00 | 500 | — |

**DOLLAR** **Y# 238.2** **Weight:** 26.8000 g. **Composition:** 0.9000 Silver .7756 oz. ASW **Ruler:** Kuang-hsü **Obverse:** Inscription: Kuang-hsü Yüan-pao **Reverse:** Dragon with wider face and flatter pearl, small cross at either side of dragon

| Date | Mintage | F | VF | XF | Unc | BU |
|---|---|---|---|---|---|---|
| ND(1901-08) | Inc. above | 15.00 | 20.00 | 70.00 | 500 | — |

**DOLLAR** **Y# 238.3** **Weight:** 26.8000 g. **Composition:** 0.9000 Silver .7756 oz. ASW **Ruler:** Kuang-hsü **Obverse:** Inscription: Kuang-hsü Yüan-pao **Reverse:** 7 MACE and 3 CANDAREENS instead of 2 CANDAREENS

| Date | Mintage | F | VF | XF | Unc | BU |
|---|---|---|---|---|---|---|
| ND(1901-08) | Inc. above | 35.00 | 60.00 | 125 | 750 | — |

**DOLLAR** **Y# 243** **Weight:** 26.8000 g. **Composition:** 0.9000 Silver .7756 oz. ASW **Ruler:** Hsüan-t'ung **Obverse:** Inscription: Hsüan-t'ung Yüan-pao **Reverse:** Large spines on dragon's body

| Date | Mintage | F | VF | XF | Unc | BU |
|---|---|---|---|---|---|---|
| ND(1909-11) | 2,846,000 | 15.00 | 25.00 | 75.00 | 500 | — |

**DOLLAR** **Y# 243.1** **Weight:** 26.8000 g. **Composition:** 0.9000 Silver .7756 oz. ASW **Ruler:** Hsüan-t'ung **Obverse:** Inscription: Hsüan-t'ung Yüan-pao **Reverse:** Inverted A instead of V in PROVINCE

| Date | Mintage | F | VF | XF | Unc | BU |
|---|---|---|---|---|---|---|
| ND(1909-11) | Inc. above | 15.00 | 30.00 | 75.00 | 500 | — |

**DOLLAR** **Y# 243.2** **Weight:** 26.8000 g. **Composition:** 0.9000 Silver .7756 oz. ASW **Ruler:** Hsüan-t'ung **Obverse:** Inscription: Hsüan-t'ung Yüan-pao **Reverse:** Small spines on dragon's body

| Date | Mintage | F | VF | XF | Unc | BU |
|---|---|---|---|---|---|---|
| ND(1909-11) | Inc. above | 65.00 | 100 | 200 | 600 | — |

# REPUBLIC

## CUT MILLED COINAGE

**50 CASH** **Y# 459y** **Composition:** Brass **Note:** 200 Cash, Y#459 cut into quarters.

| Date | Mintage | VG | F | VF | XF | Unc |
|---|---|---|---|---|---|---|
| 2(1913) | — | 30.00 | 35.00 | 40.00 | 50.00 | — |

**100 CASH** **Y# 459x** **Composition:** Copper Or Brass **Note:** 200 Cash, Y#459 cut in half.

| Date | Mintage | VG | F | VF | XF | Unc |
|---|---|---|---|---|---|---|
| 2(1913) | — | 3.50 | 9.50 | 17.00 | 45.00 | — |

## MILLED CASH COINAGE

**5 CASH** **Y# 441a** **Composition:** Brass

| Date | Mintage | VG | F | VF | XF | Unc |
|---|---|---|---|---|---|---|
| 1(1912) | Inc. above | — | — | — | — | — |

**5 CASH** **Y# 441b** **Composition:** Silver

| Date | Mintage | VG | F | VF | XF | Unc |
|---|---|---|---|---|---|---|
| 1(1912) | — | — | — | 1,000 | 1,500 | — |

**Note:** Modern forgeries of Y#441 in copper and of Y#441b in silver exist

**5 CASH** Y# 443 **Composition:** Copper

| Date | Mintage | VG | F | VF | XF | Unc |
|---|---|---|---|---|---|---|
| 1(1912) | Inc. above | 35.00 | 70.00 | 110 | 150 | — |

**5 CASH** Y# 443a **Composition:** Brass

| Date | Mintage | VG | F | VF | XF | Unc |
|---|---|---|---|---|---|---|
| 1(1912) Rare | — | — | — | — | — | — |

**5 CASH** Y# 446 **Composition:** Copper

| Date | Mintage | VG | F | VF | XF | Unc |
|---|---|---|---|---|---|---|
| 1(1912) Rare | Inc. above | — | — | — | — | — |

**5 CASH** Y# 446a **Composition:** Brass

| Date | Mintage | VG | F | VF | XF | Unc |
|---|---|---|---|---|---|---|
| 1(1912) Rare | Inc. above | — | — | — | — | — |

**5 CASH** Y# 441 **Composition:** Copper **Note:** Varieties exist.

| Date | Mintage | VG | F | VF | XF | Unc |
|---|---|---|---|---|---|---|
| 1(1912) | 471,000 | 40.00 | 80.00 | 130 | 250 | — |

**10 CASH** Y# 447 **Composition:** Copper **Obverse:** Two rosettes

| Date | Mintage | VG | F | VF | XF | Unc |
|---|---|---|---|---|---|---|
| 1(1912) | 108,618,000 | 1.75 | 3.00 | 10.00 | 20.00 | — |
| 2(1913) | Inc. above | 6.00 | 15.00 | 25.00 | 50.00 | — |

**10 CASH** Y# 447a **Composition:** Brass

| Date | Mintage | VG | F | VF | XF | Unc |
|---|---|---|---|---|---|---|
| 1(1912) | Inc. above | 0.80 | 1.50 | 2.50 | 5.00 | — |
| 2(1913) | Inc. above | 1.65 | 4.00 | 8.00 | 20.00 | — |

**10 CASH** Y# 447.1a **Composition:** Brass **Obverse:** Three rosettes

| Date | Mintage | VG | F | VF | XF | Unc |
|---|---|---|---|---|---|---|
| 2(1913) Rare | Inc. above | — | — | — | — | — |

## DECIMAL COINAGE

**10 CASH** Y# 475 **Composition:** Red Copper **Obverse:** Characters in five-petalled flower **Reverse:** Denomination above sun

| Date | Mintage | VG | F | VF | XF | Unc |
|---|---|---|---|---|---|---|
| 19(1930) Rare | — | — | — | — | — | — |

**20 CASH** Y# 448 **Composition:** Copper **Obverse:** Two rosettes

| Date | Mintage | VG | F | VF | XF | Unc |
|---|---|---|---|---|---|---|
| 1(1912) | 115,061,000 | 1.00 | 2.50 | 5.00 | 15.00 | — |

**Note:** Character for "first" instead of number one in date

**20 CASH** Y# 448a **Composition:** Brass

| Date | Mintage | VG | F | VF | XF | Unc |
|---|---|---|---|---|---|---|
| 1(1912) | Inc. above | 0.75 | 1.50 | 2.50 | 6.00 | — |
| 2(1913) | Inc. above | 1.00 | 2.00 | 3.50 | 7.00 | — |

**Note:** Character for "first" instead of number one in date

**20 CASH** Y# 448.1 **Composition:** Copper **Obverse:** Three rosettes

| Date | Mintage | VG | F | VF | XF | Unc |
|---|---|---|---|---|---|---|
| 2(1913) | Inc. above | 250 | 350 | 450 | 800 | — |
| 3(1914) | Inc. above | 250 | 350 | 450 | 800 | — |

**20 CASH** Y# 448.1a **Composition:** Brass

| Date | Mintage | VG | F | VF | XF | Unc |
|---|---|---|---|---|---|---|
| 2(1913) | Inc. above | 2.50 | 6.00 | 12.00 | 25.00 | — |
| 3(1914) | Inc. above | 2.50 | 6.00 | 12.00 | 25.00 | — |

**Note:** There are many varieties of this 20 Cash; small and large rosettes; open and closed size characters and exaggerated size character with horns

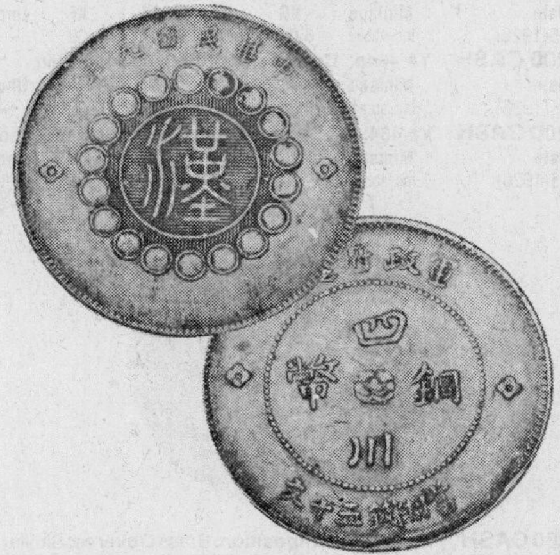

**50 CASH** Y# 449 **Composition:** Copper **Reverse:** Small flower in center

| Date | Mintage | VG | F | VF | XF | Unc |
|---|---|---|---|---|---|---|
| 1(1912) | 489,382,000 | 2.00 | 4.00 | 7.00 | 15.00 | — |

**50 CASH** Y# 449a **Composition:** Brass

| Date | Mintage | VG | F | VF | XF | Unc |
|---|---|---|---|---|---|---|
| 1(1912) | Inc. above | 1.50 | 3.50 | 6.00 | 10.00 | — |

**50 CASH** Y# 449.1 **Composition:** Copper **Reverse:** Larger flower in center

| Date | Mintage | VG | F | VF | XF | Unc |
|---|---|---|---|---|---|---|
| 1(1912) | Inc. above | 2.00 | 5.00 | 10.00 | 20.00 | — |

**50 CASH** Y# 449.1a **Composition:** Brass

| Date | Mintage | VG | F | VF | XF | Unc |
|---|---|---|---|---|---|---|
| 1(1912) | Inc. above | 2.50 | 6.00 | 12.50 | 25.00 | — |

**Note:** A Yr. 7 is reported, but its authenticity is not verified

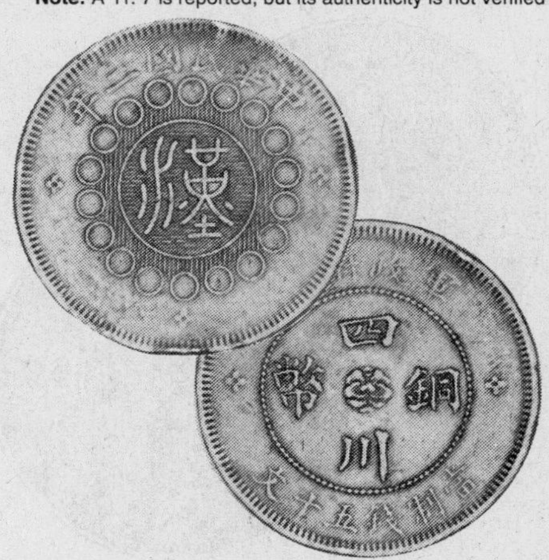

**50 CASH** Y# 449.2 **Composition:** Copper **Obverse:** Three rosettes **Reverse:** Small flower in center

| Date | Mintage | VG | F | VF | XF | Unc |
|---|---|---|---|---|---|---|
| 2(1913) | Inc. above | 2.25 | 5.50 | 11.00 | 22.00 | — |

**50 CASH** Y# 449.2a **Composition:** Brass

| Date | Mintage | VG | F | VF | XF | Unc |
|---|---|---|---|---|---|---|
| 2(1913) | Inc. above | 2.25 | 5.50 | 11.00 | 22.00 | — |
| 3(1914) | Inc. above | 2.25 | 5.50 | 11.00 | 22.00 | — |

**50 CASH** Y# 462 **Composition:** Copper

| Date | Mintage | VG | F | VF | XF | Unc |
|---|---|---|---|---|---|---|
| 15(1926) | 90,000 | 18.50 | 35.00 | 65.00 | 100 | — |

**50 CASH** Y# 462a **Composition:** Brass

| Date | Mintage | VG | F | VF | XF | Unc |
|---|---|---|---|---|---|---|
| 15(1926) | Inc. above | 16.50 | 32.50 | 55.00 | 80.00 | — |

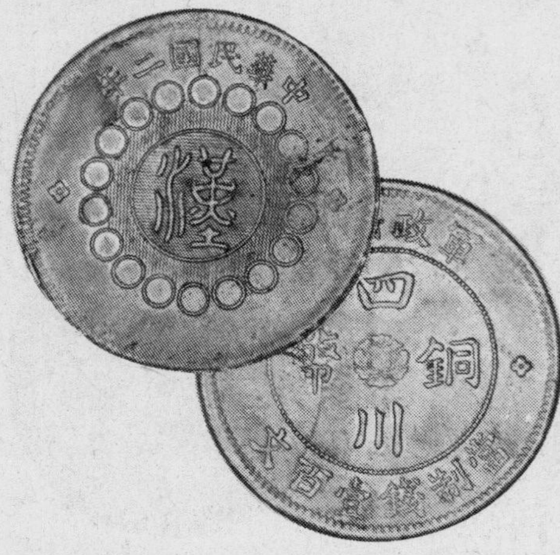

**100 CASH** **Y# 450** **Composition:** Copper **Obverse:** Two rosettes **Reverse:** Large flower in center

| Date | Mintage | VG | F | VF | XF | Unc |
|---|---|---|---|---|---|---|
| 2(1913) | 399,212,000 | 2.50 | 6.00 | 8.50 | 17.50 | — |
| 3(1914) | — | 30.00 | 40.00 | 50.00 | 60.00 | — |

**100 CASH** **Y# 450a** **Composition:** Brass

| Date | Mintage | VG | F | VF | XF | Unc |
|---|---|---|---|---|---|---|
| 2(1913) | Inc. above | 1.50 | 3.00 | 6.00 | 10.00 | — |

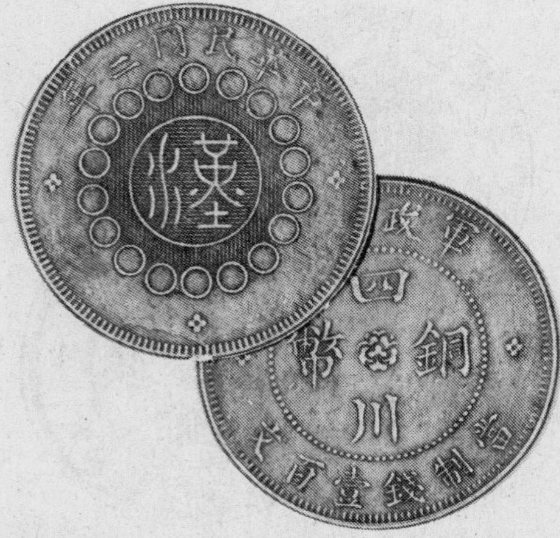

**100 CASH** **Y# 450.1** **Composition:** Copper **Obverse:** Three rosettes **Reverse:** Small flower in center

| Date | Mintage | VG | F | VF | XF | Unc |
|---|---|---|---|---|---|---|
| 2(1913) | Inc. above | 3.50 | 9.00 | 15.00 | 25.00 | — |
| 3(1914) | — | — | — | — | — | — |

**100 CASH** **Y# 463** **Composition:** Copper

| Date | Mintage | VG | F | VF | XF | Unc |
|---|---|---|---|---|---|---|
| 15(1926) | 7,055,000 | 3.50 | 9.00 | 15.00 | 25.00 | — |

**100 CASH** **Y# 463a** **Composition:** Brass

| Date | Mintage | VG | F | VF | XF | Unc |
|---|---|---|---|---|---|---|
| 15(1926) | Inc. above | 3.25 | 8.00 | 12.50 | 20.00 | — |

**Note:** Two reverse varieties known; often struck over older 10 Cash coins

**200 CASH** **Y# 459a** **Composition:** Brass

| Date | Mintage | VG | F | VF | XF | Unc |
|---|---|---|---|---|---|---|
| 2(1913) | Inc. above | 20.00 | 40.00 | 80.00 | 125 | — |

**200 CASH** **Y# 459.1** **Composition:** Copper **Obverse:** Tassels draped over flag poles

| Date | Mintage | VG | F | VF | XF | Unc |
|---|---|---|---|---|---|---|
| 2(1913) | Inc. above | 6.00 | 10.00 | 25.00 | 40.00 | — |

**200 CASH** **Y# 459.1a** **Composition:** Brass

| Date | Mintage | VG | F | VF | XF | Unc |
|---|---|---|---|---|---|---|
| 2(1913) | — | 4.50 | 8.00 | 20.00 | 35.00 | — |

**200 CASH** **Y# 459.2** **Composition:** Copper **Reverse:** Smaller stars at sides

| Date | Mintage | VG | F | VF | XF | Unc |
|---|---|---|---|---|---|---|
| 2(1913) | Inc. above | 5.00 | 9.00 | 22.50 | 37.50 | — |

**Note:** For cut segments refer to 50 Cash, Y#459y and 100 Cash, Y#459x

**200 CASH** **Y# 464** **Composition:** Copper **Edge:** Plain

| Date | Mintage | VG | F | VF | XF | Unc |
|---|---|---|---|---|---|---|
| 15(1926) | 404,644,000 | 4.00 | 12.00 | 17.00 | 35.00 | — |

**200 CASH** **Y# 464.1** **Composition:** Copper **Edge:** Reeded

| Date | Mintage | VG | F | VF | XF | Unc |
|---|---|---|---|---|---|---|
| 15(1926) | Inc. above | 6.00 | 15.00 | 25.00 | 45.00 | — |

**200 CASH** **Y# 464a** **Composition:** Brass **Edge:** Plain

| Date | Mintage | VG | F | VF | XF | Unc |
|---|---|---|---|---|---|---|
| 15(1926) | Inc. above | 4.50 | 12.00 | 17.00 | 35.00 | — |

**200 CASH** **Y# 464.1a** **Composition:** Brass **Edge:** Reeded

| Date | Mintage | VG | F | VF | XF | Unc |
|---|---|---|---|---|---|---|
| 15(1926) | Inc. above | — | — | — | — | — |

**200 CASH** **Y# 464.2** **Composition:** Brass **Obverse:** Similar to Y#464 **Reverse:** Dot within first 0 of 200

| Date | Mintage | VG | F | VF | XF | Unc |
|---|---|---|---|---|---|---|
| 15(1926) | Inc. above | — | — | — | — | — |

**Note:** Many varieties: open and closed buds; overstruck on earlier pieces and on virgin flans; different sizes and thicknesses

**2 CENTS** **Y# 476** **Composition:** Copper

| Date | Mintage | VG | F | VF | XF | Unc |
|---|---|---|---|---|---|---|
| 19(1930)(1930) Rare | — | — | — | — | — | — |

**2 CENTS** **Y# 476a** **Composition:** Brass

| Date | Mintage | VG | F | VF | XF | Unc |
|---|---|---|---|---|---|---|
| 19(1930)(1930) | — | — | — | — | — | — |

**10 CENTS** **Y# 453** **Weight:** 2.6000 g. **Composition:** Silver

| Date | Mintage | F | VF | XF | Unc | BU |
|---|---|---|---|---|---|---|
| 1(1912) | 370,000 | 25.00 | 40.00 | 75.00 | 150 | — |

**10 CENTS** **Y# 468** **Composition:** Copper-Nickel

| Date | Mintage | F | VF | XF | Unc | BU |
|---|---|---|---|---|---|---|
| ND(ca.1926) | — | 12.50 | 20.00 | 45.00 | 70.00 | — |

**10 CENTS** **Y# 468a** **Composition:** Silver

| Date | Mintage | F | VF | XF | Unc | BU |
|---|---|---|---|---|---|---|
| ND(ca.1926) | — | 35.00 | 75.00 | 125 | 200 | — |

**10 CENTS** **Y# 468b** **Composition:** Iron

| Date | Mintage | F | VF | XF | Unc | BU |
|---|---|---|---|---|---|---|
| ND(ca.1926) | — | 20.00 | 50.00 | 70.00 | 125 | — |

**20 CENTS** **Y# 454** **Weight:** 5.2000 g. **Composition:** Silver

| Date | Mintage | F | VF | XF | Unc | BU |
|---|---|---|---|---|---|---|
| 1(1912) | 95,000 | 50.00 | 85.00 | 150 | 300 | — |

**20 CENTS** **K# 795** **Weight:** 5.2000 g. **Composition:** Silver **Subject:** Tibetan War

| Date | Mintage | F | VF | XF | Unc | BU |
|---|---|---|---|---|---|---|
| 1923 | — | 60.00 | 175 | 250 | 500 | — |

**Note:** Authenticity not established

**50 CENTS** **Y# 455** **Weight:** 12.9000 g. **Composition:** Silver

| Date | Mintage | F | VF | XF | Unc | BU |
|---|---|---|---|---|---|---|
| 1(1912) | 37,942,000 | 15.00 | 25.00 | 50.00 | 125 | — |
| 2(1913) Rare | Inc. above | — | — | — | — | — |

**50 CENTS** Y# 473 **Weight:** 10.5000 g. **Composition:** Silver **Subject:** Sun Yat-sen

| Date | Mintage | F | VF | XF | Unc | BU |
|---|---|---|---|---|---|---|
| 17(1928) | Inc. above | 100 | 450 | 600 | 1,000 | — |

**DOLLAR** Y# 456 **Weight:** 25.6000 g. **Composition:** Silver

| Date | Mintage | F | VF | XF | Unc | BU |
|---|---|---|---|---|---|---|
| 1(1912) | 55,670,000 | 12.50 | 20.00 | 55.00 | 125 | — |
| 2(1913) Rare | Inc. above | — | — | — | — | — |

**DOLLAR** Y# 456.1 **Weight:** 25.6000 g. **Composition:** Silver **Reverse:** Right hand character with two dots instead of horizontal stroke

| Date | Mintage | F | VF | XF | Unc | BU |
|---|---|---|---|---|---|---|
| 1(1912) | Inc. above | 25.00 | 50.00 | 100 | 250 | — |

**Note:** Silver content ranged from 0.880 to 0.500 fine

**DOLLAR** Y# 474 **Weight:** 25.5000 g. **Composition:** Silver **Subject:** Sun Yat-sen

| Date | Mintage | F | VF | XF | Unc | BU |
|---|---|---|---|---|---|---|
| 17(1928) | Inc. above | 400 | 600 | 850 | 1,400 | — |

## PATTERNS

Including off metal strikes

| KM# | Date | Mintage | Identification | Mkt Val |
|---|---|---|---|---|
| Pn16 | (ca.1901) | — | 20 Cents. Aluminum. Dragon type. | — |
| Pn17 | (1902) | — | 5 Cents. Brass. K#149y | 200 |
| Pn18 | (1902) | — | 10 Cents. Brass. K#148y | 250 |
| Pn19 | (1902) | — | 20 Cents. Brass. K#147y | 300 |
| Pn20 | (1902) | — | 50 Cents. Brass. K#146y | 400 |
| Pn21 | (1902) | — | Dollar. Brass. K#145y | 800 |
| Pn24 | (1906) | — | 2 Cash. Copper. Y#8t | — |
| Pn25 | (1906) | — | 5 Cash. Copper. Y#9t | — |
| Pn23 | (1908) | — | 5 Cash. Brass. | — |
| Pn22 | (1908) | — | Cash. Brass. Y#7t | 300 |
| Pn26 | (ca.1912) | — | 10 Cents. Copper. | — |
| Pn27 | 1(1912) | — | 50 Cents. Copper. Y#455 | — |
| Pn28 | (ca.1926) | — | 10 Cents. Brass. Y#468 | — |
| Pn29 | 17(1928) | — | Dollar. Copper. Y#474 | — |
| Pn30 | (1941) | — | 50 Cents. Temple. Spade. World War II | — |

# YUNNAN PROVINCE

A province located in south China bordering Burma, Laos and Vietnam. It is very mountainous with many lakes. Yunnan was the home of various active imperial mints. A modern mint was established at Kunming in 1905 and the first struck copper coins were issued in 1906 and the first struck silver coins in 1908. General Tang Chi-yao issued coins in gold, silver and copper with his portrait in 1919. The last Republican coins were struck here in 1949.

## EMPIRE

### PROVINCIAL CAST COINAGE

**CASH** C# 26-9 **Composition:** Cast Brass **Ruler:** Kuang-hsü **Obverse:** Inscription: Kuang-hsü T'ung-pao **Reverse:** Inscription: Manchu Boo-yôn **Note:** Struck at Yün Yünnanfu.

| Date | Mintage | Good | VG | F | VF | XF |
|---|---|---|---|---|---|---|
| ND(1875-1908) | — | 2.00 | 4.00 | 6.50 | 9.00 | — |

**CASH** C# 27-6 **Composition:** Cast Brass **Ruler:** Kuang-hsü **Obverse:** Inscription: Kuang-hsü T'ung-pao **Reverse:** Inscription: Manchu Boo-dong **Note:** Struck at Tung Tungch'uan.

| Date | Mintage | Good | VG | F | VF | XF |
|---|---|---|---|---|---|---|
| ND(1875-1908) | — | 4.00 | 6.50 | 9.00 | 15.00 | — |

**CASH** C# 27-6.1 **Composition:** Cast Brass **Ruler:** Kuang-hsü **Obverse:** Inscription: Kuang-hsü T'ung-pao **Reverse:** Inscription: Manchu Boo-dong; "Chin" above **Note:** Struck at Tung Tungch'uan.

| Date | Mintage | Good | VG | F | VF | XF |
|---|---|---|---|---|---|---|
| ND(1875-1908) | — | 5.00 | 7.50 | 10.00 | 15.00 | — |

**CASH** C# 27-6.2 **Composition:** Cast Brass **Ruler:** Kuang-hsü **Obverse:** Inscription: Kuang-hsü T'ung-pao **Reverse:** Inscription: Manchu Boo-dong; "Ts'un" below **Note:** Struck at Tung Tungch'uan.

| Date | Mintage | Good | VG | F | VF | XF |
|---|---|---|---|---|---|---|
| ND(1875-1908) | — | 5.00 | 7.50 | 10.00 | 15.00 | — |

**CASH** C# 26-9.1 **Composition:** Cast Brass **Ruler:** Kuang-hsü **Obverse:** Inscription: Kuang-hsü T'ung-pao **Reverse:** Inscription: Manchu Boo-yôn; "Kung" above **Note:** Struck at Yün Yünnanfu.

| Date | Mintage | Good | VG | F | VF | XF |
|---|---|---|---|---|---|---|
| ND(1875-1908) | — | 2.00 | 5.00 | 7.50 | 10.00 | — |

**CASH** C# 26-9.2 **Composition:** Cast Brass **Ruler:** Kuang-hsü **Obverse:** Inscription: Kuang-hsü T'ung-pao **Reverse:** Inscription: Manchu Boo-yôn; "Ssu" (four) above **Note:** Struck at Yün Yünnanfu.

| Date | Mintage | Good | VG | F | VF | XF |
|---|---|---|---|---|---|---|
| ND(1875-1908) | — | 2.50 | 5.00 | 7.50 | 10.00 | — |

**CASH** C# 26-9.3 **Composition:** Cast Brass **Ruler:** Kuang-hsü **Obverse:** Inscription: Kuang-hsü T'ung-pao **Reverse:** Inscription: Manchu Boo-yôn; "Chin" above **Note:** Struck at Yün Yünnanfu.

| Date | Mintage | Good | VG | F | VF | XF |
|---|---|---|---|---|---|---|
| ND(1875-1908) | — | 2.50 | 5.00 | 7.50 | 10.00 | — |

**CASH** C# 26-9.4 **Composition:** Cast Brass **Ruler:** Kuang-hsü **Obverse:** Inscription: Kuang-hsü T'ung-pao **Reverse:** Inscription: Manchu Boo-yôn; crescent above, dot below **Note:** Struck at Yün Yünnanfu.

| Date | Mintage | Good | VG | F | VF | XF |
|---|---|---|---|---|---|---|
| ND(1875-1908) | — | 2.50 | 5.00 | 7.50 | 12.00 | — |

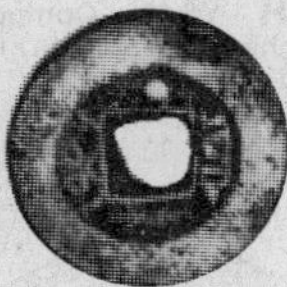

**CASH** C# 26-9.5 **Composition:** Cast Brass **Ruler:** Kuang-hsü **Obverse:** Inscription: Kuang-hsü T'ung-pao **Reverse:** Inscription: Manchu Boo-yôn; dot above hole **Note:** Struck at Yün Yünnanfu.

| Date | Mintage | Good | VG | F | VF | XF |
|---|---|---|---|---|---|---|
| ND(1875-1908) | — | 2.50 | 5.00 | 7.50 | 12.00 | — |

**CASH** C# 26-11 **Composition:** Cast Brass **Ruler:** Hsüan-t'ung **Obverse:** Inscription: Hsuan-t'ung T'ung-pao **Reverse:** Inscription: Manchu Boo-yôn; "Kung" above hole **Note:** Struck at Yün Yünnanfu.

| Date | Mintage | Good | VG | F | VF | XF |
|---|---|---|---|---|---|---|
| ND(1909-11) | — | 75.00 | 100 | 150 | 220 | — |

**CASH** C# 27-7 **Composition:** Cast Brass **Ruler:** Hsüan-t'ung **Obverse:** Inscription: Hsuan-t'ung T'ung-pao **Reverse:** Inscription: Manchu Boo-dong; "Ts'un" below **Note:** Struck at Tung Tungch'uan.

| Date | Mintage | Good | VG | F | VF | XF |
|---|---|---|---|---|---|---|
| ND(1909-11) Rare | — | — | — | — | — | — |

**CASH** C# 26-12 **Composition:** Cast Brass **Ruler:** Hsüan-t'ung **Obverse:** Inscription: Hsuan-t'ung T'ung-pao **Reverse:** Inscription: Manchu Boo-yôn; "Shan" above hole **Note:** Struck at Yün Yünnanfu.

| Date | Mintage | Good | VG | F | VF | XF |
|---|---|---|---|---|---|---|
| ND(1909-11) | — | 30.00 | 40.00 | 50.00 | 100 | — |

**CASH** C# 26-13 **Composition:** Cast Brass **Ruler:** Hsüan-t'ung **Obverse:** Inscription: Hsuan-t'ung T'ung-pao **Reverse:** Inscription: Manchu Boo-yôn; without character above hole **Note:** Struck at Yün Yünnanfu.

| Date | Mintage | Good | VG | F | VF | XF |
|---|---|---|---|---|---|---|
| ND(1909-11) | — | 35.00 | 45.00 | 55.00 | 100 | — |

### MILLED COINAGE

**10 CASH** Y# 10u **Composition:** Copper **Obverse:** Inscription: Tai-ching T'ung-pi with large mint mark "Yun" in center **Reverse:** Side view dragon

| Date | Mintage | VG | F | VF | XF | Unc |
|---|---|---|---|---|---|---|
| CD(1906) | 36,701,000 | 10.00 | 22.00 | 35.00 | 60.00 | — |

**10 CASH** Y# 10u.1 **Composition:** Copper **Obverse:** Inscription: Tai-ching T'ung-pi with small mint mark "Yun" in center **Reverse:** Side view dragon

| Date | Mintage | VG | F | VF | XF | Unc |
|---|---|---|---|---|---|---|
| CD(1906) | Inc. above | 25.00 | 55.00 | 85.00 | 125 | — |

**10 CASH** Y# 10v **Composition:** Copper **Obverse:** Inscription: Tai-ching T'ung-pi with mint mark "Tien" in center **Reverse:** Side view dragon

| Date | Mintage | VG | F | VF | XF | Unc |
|---|---|---|---|---|---|---|
| CD(1906) | Inc. above | 12.50 | 30.00 | 40.00 | 65.00 | — |

**20 CASH** Y# 11u **Composition:** Copper **Obverse:** Inscription: Tai-ching T'ung-pi with large mint mark "Yun" in center **Reverse:** Side view dragon

| Date | Mintage | VG | F | VF | XF | Unc |
|---|---|---|---|---|---|---|
| CD(1906) | 645,000 | 125 | 175 | 225 | 275 | — |

**20 CASH** Y# 11u.1 **Composition:** Copper **Obverse:** Inscription: Tai-ching T'ung-pi with small mint mark "Yun" in center **Reverse:** Side view dragon

| Date | Mintage | VG | F | VF | XF | Unc |
|---|---|---|---|---|---|---|
| CD(1906) | — | 150 | 275 | 400 | 550 | — |

**20 CASH** Y# 11v.1 **Composition:** Copper **Obverse:** Inscription: Tai-ching T'ung-pi with mint mark "Tien" in center **Reverse:** Side view dragon

| Date | Mintage | VG | F | VF | XF | Unc |
|---|---|---|---|---|---|---|
| CD(1906) | Inc. above | 150 | 275 | 400 | 550 | — |

**20 CASH** Y# 11v.1a **Composition:** Brass **Obverse:** Inscription: Tai-ching T'ung-pi **Reverse:** Side view dragon

| Date | Mintage | VG | F | VF | XF | Unc |
|---|---|---|---|---|---|---|
| CD(1906) | Inc. above | 175 | 350 | 450 | 600 | — |

**20 CENTS** Y# 252 **Composition:** Brass **Ruler:** Kuang-hsü **Obverse:** Inscription: Kuang-hsü Yuan-pao **Reverse:** Side view dragon **Note:** Many minor varieties.

| Date | Mintage | F | VF | XF | Unc | BU |
|---|---|---|---|---|---|---|
| ND(1908) | 532,000 | 18.50 | 35.00 | 60.00 | 125 | — |

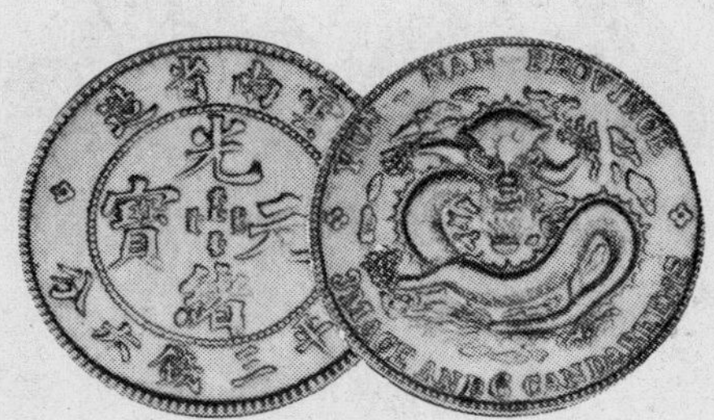

**50 CENTS** Y# 253 **Weight:** 13.2000 g. **Composition:** 0.8000 Silver .3395 oz. ASW **Ruler:** Kuang-hsü **Obverse:** Inscription: Kuang-hsü Yuan-pao **Reverse:** Side view dragon

| Date | Mintage | F | VF | XF | Unc | BU |
|---|---|---|---|---|---|---|
| ND(1908) | — | 7.50 | 15.00 | 20.00 | 85.00 | — |

**50 CENTS** Y# 259 **Weight:** 13.2000 g. **Composition:** 0.8000 Silver .3395 oz. ASW **Ruler:** Hsüan-t'ung **Obverse:** Inscription: Hsüan-t'ung-pao **Reverse:** Side view dragon; seven flames on pearl

| Date | Mintage | F | VF | XF | Unc | BU |
|---|---|---|---|---|---|---|
| ND(1909-11) | — | 7.00 | 13.50 | 22.50 | 90.00 | — |

**50 CENTS** Y# 259.1 **Weight:** 13.2000 g. **Composition:** 0.8000 Silver .3395 oz. ASW **Ruler:** Hsüan-t'ung **Obverse:** Inscription: Hsüan-t'ung-pao **Reverse:** Side view dragon; nine flames on pearl

| Date | Mintage | F | VF | XF | Unc | BU |
|---|---|---|---|---|---|---|
| ND(1909-11) | — | 7.00 | 13.50 | 22.50 | 90.00 | — |

**DOLLAR** Y# 254 **Weight:** 26.8000 g. **Composition:** 0.9000 Silver .7755 oz. ASW **Ruler:** Kuang-hsü **Obverse:** Inscription: Kuang-hsü Yüan-pao **Reverse:** Side view dragon

| Date | Mintage | F | VF | XF | Unc | BU |
|---|---|---|---|---|---|---|
| ND(1908) | — | 15.00 | 30.00 | 65.00 | 300 | — |

**DOLLAR** Y# 260 **Weight:** 26.8000 g. **Composition:** 0.9000 Silver .7755 oz. ASW **Ruler:** Hsüan-t'ung **Obverse:** Inscription: Hsüan-t'ung T'ung-pao **Obv. Legend:** Four characters at top **Reverse:** Side view dragon

| Date | Mintage | F | VF | XF | Unc | BU |
|---|---|---|---|---|---|---|
| ND(1909-11) | — | 15.00 | 25.00 | 60.00 | 300 | — |

**DOLLAR** Y# 260.1 **Weight:** 26.8000 g. **Composition:** 0.9000 Silver .7755 oz. ASW **Ruler:** Hsüan-t'ung **Obverse:** Inscription: Hsüan-t'ung T'ung-pao **Obv. Legend:** Seven characters at top **Reverse:** Side view dragon

| Date | Mintage | F | VF | XF | Unc | BU |
|---|---|---|---|---|---|---|
| CD1910 | — | — | — | — | 32,500 | — |

# REPUBLIC

## TRANSITIONAL COINAGE

In the name of the Republic

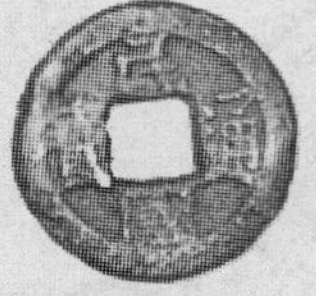

**CASH** KM# 5 **Composition:** Cast Copper Or Brass **Obverse:** Inscription: Min-kuo T'ung-pao **Reverse:** Inscription: "Tung-ch'uan" **Note:** Struck at Tung (Tungch'uan) Mint.

| Date | Mintage | Good | VG | F | VF | XF |
|---|---|---|---|---|---|---|
| ND(1912) | — | 20.00 | 30.00 | 40.00 | 65.00 | — |

**CASH** KM# 5a **Composition:** Cast Copper Or Brass **Obverse:** Inscription: Min-kuo T'ung-pao **Reverse:** Inscription: "Boo-yön" **Note:** Struck at Yün Yünnan-fu.

| Date | Mintage | Good | VG | F | VF | XF |
|---|---|---|---|---|---|---|
| ND(1912) | — | 100 | 125 | 180 | — | — |

**10 CASH** KM# 4 **Composition:** Brass **Obverse:** Inscription: Min-kuo T'ung-pao

| Date | Mintage | Good | VG | F | VF | XF |
|---|---|---|---|---|---|---|
| ND(1912) | — | 15.00 | 25.00 | 35.00 | 50.00 | — |

## RESTRUCK IMPERIAL COINAGE

The following imperial coins are reign-dated 1875-1908. These coins were apparently restruck from previously unused dies at intervals from 1911 through to 1949, and with a progressively reduced silver content. The dates and silver content shown are approximate.

**10 CENTS** Y# 255 **Weight:** 2.6500 g. **Composition:** 0.6500 Silver .0554 oz. ASW **Obverse:** Inscription: Kuang-hsü Yuan-pao **Reverse:** Side view dragon with two circles beneath pearl

| Date | Mintage | F | VF | XF | Unc | BU |
|---|---|---|---|---|---|---|
| ND(1911-15) | 902,000 | 15.00 | 30.00 | 45.00 | 90.00 | — |

**20 CENTS** Y# 256 **Weight:** 5.3000 g. **Composition:** 0.8000 Silver .1363 oz. ASW **Obverse:** Inscription: Kuang-hsü Yuan-pao **Reverse:** Side view dragon with two circles beneath pearl

| Date | Mintage | F | VF | XF | Unc | BU |
|---|---|---|---|---|---|---|
| ND(1911-15) | — | 12.50 | 17.50 | 32.50 | 75.00 | — |

**20 CENTS** Y# 256a **Weight:** 5.3000 g. **Composition:** 0.6500 Silver .1108 oz. ASW **Obverse:** Inscription: Kuang-hsü Yuan-pao **Reverse:** Side view dragon with three circles beneath pearl

| Date | Mintage | F | VF | XF | Unc | BU |
|---|---|---|---|---|---|---|
| ND(1911-15) | — | 12.50 | 22.50 | 37.50 | 75.00 | — |

**20 CENTS** Y# 256b **Weight:** 5.3000 g. **Composition:** 0.4000 Silver .0682 oz. ASW **Obverse:** Inscription: Kuang-hsü Yuan-pao **Reverse:** Side view dragon with two or three circles beneath pearl

| Date | Mintage | F | VF | XF | Unc | BU |
|---|---|---|---|---|---|---|
| ND(1920-31) | — | — | — | — | — | — |

**50 CENTS** **Y# 257** **Weight:** 13.2000 g. **Composition:** 0.8000 Silver .3395 oz. ASW **Obverse:** Inscription: Kuang-hsü Yuan-pao **Reverse:** Side view dragon with two circles below pearl

| Date | Mintage | F | VF | XF | Unc | BU |
|---|---|---|---|---|---|---|
| ND(1911-15) | — | 5.50 | 8.00 | 12.00 | 30.00 | — |

**50 CENTS** **Y# 257.1** **Weight:** 13.2000 g. **Composition:** 0.8000 Silver .3395 oz. ASW **Obverse:** Inscription: Kuang-hsü Yuan-pao **Reverse:** Side view dragon with three circles below pearl

| Date | Mintage | F | VF | XF | Unc | BU |
|---|---|---|---|---|---|---|
| ND(1911-15) | — | 5.00 | 7.00 | 10.00 | 20.00 | — |

**50 CENTS** **Y# 257.2** **Weight:** 13.2000 g. **Composition:** 0.5000 Silver .2122 oz. ASW **Obverse:** Inscription: Kuang-hsü Yuan-pao **Reverse:** Side view dragon with four circles below pearl

| Date | Mintage | F | VF | XF | Unc | BU |
|---|---|---|---|---|---|---|
| ND(1920-31) | — | 5.00 | 6.00 | 9.00 | 20.00 | — |

**Note:** There are more than 30 minor varieties of Y#257

**50 CENTS** **Y# 257.3** **Weight:** 13.2000 g. **Composition:** 0.5000 Silver - Billon **Obverse:** Inscription: Kuang-hsü Yuan-pao **Reverse:** Side view dragon with two circles beneath pearl, large circle around center circle of rosettes

| Date | Mintage | F | VF | XF | Unc | BU |
|---|---|---|---|---|---|---|
| ND(1949) | — | — | — | — | — | — |

**DOLLAR** **Y# 258** **Weight:** 26.8000 g. **Composition:** 0.9000 Silver .7755 oz. ASW **Obverse:** Inscription: Kuang-hsü Yuan-pao **Reverse:** Side view dragon with one circle below pearl

| Date | Mintage | F | VF | XF | Unc | BU |
|---|---|---|---|---|---|---|
| ND(1911-15) | — | 15.00 | 20.00 | 35.00 | 250 | — |

**DOLLAR** **Y# 258.1** **Weight:** 26.8000 g. **Composition:** 0.9000 Silver .7755 oz. ASW **Obverse:** Inscription: Kuang-hsü Yuan-pao **Reverse:** Side view dragon with four circles below pearl

| Date | Mintage | F | VF | XF | Unc | BU |
|---|---|---|---|---|---|---|
| ND(1920-22) | — | 15.00 | 20.00 | 35.00 | 250 | — |

## STANDARD COINAGE

**CENT** **Y# 488** **Composition:** Brass **Obv. Legend:** Chung-hua Min-kuo above crossed flags

| Date | Mintage | VG | F | VF | XF | Unc |
|---|---|---|---|---|---|---|
| 21(1932) Rare | — | — | — | — | — | — |

**2 CENTS** **Y# 489** **Composition:** Brass **Obv. Legend:** Chung-hua Min-kuo above crossed flags

| Date | Mintage | VG | F | VF | XF | Unc |
|---|---|---|---|---|---|---|
| 21(1932) | — | 175 | 325 | 500 | 750 | — |

**50 CASH** **Y# 478** **Composition:** Brass **Obverse:** Bust of General T'ang Chi-yao facing **Note:** (ca.1919)

| Date | Mintage | VG | F | VF | XF | Unc |
|---|---|---|---|---|---|---|
| ND | — | 10.00 | 20.00 | 40.00 | 70.00 | — |

**50 CASH** **Y# 478a** **Composition:** Copper **Obverse:** Bust of General T'ang Chi-yao facing **Note:** (ca.1919)

| Date | Mintage | VG | F | VF | XF | Unc |
|---|---|---|---|---|---|---|
| ND | — | 20.00 | 40.00 | 80.00 | 125 | — |

**5 CENTS** **Y# 485** **Composition:** Copper-Nickel **Reverse:** Flag

| Date | Mintage | VG | F | VF | XF | Unc |
|---|---|---|---|---|---|---|
| 12(1923) | — | 22.50 | 32.50 | 47.50 | 75.00 | — |

**5 CENTS** **Y# 490** **Composition:** Copper **Obv. Legend:** Chung-hua Min-kuo above crossed flags

| Date | Mintage | VG | F | VF | XF | Unc |
|---|---|---|---|---|---|---|
| 21(1932) | — | 125 | 175 | 250 | 350 | — |

**10 CENTS** **Y# 486** **Composition:** Copper-Nickel **Reverse:** Flag **Edge:** Reeded

| Date | Mintage | VG | F | VF | XF | Unc |
|---|---|---|---|---|---|---|
| 12(1923) | — | 1.75 | 2.50 | 3.75 | 7.50 | — |

**10 CENTS** **Y# 486.1** **Composition:** Copper-Nickel **Reverse:** Flag **Edge:** Unreeded

| Date | Mintage | VG | F | VF | XF | Unc |
|---|---|---|---|---|---|---|
| 12(1923) | — | 2.50 | 4.00 | 6.50 | 12.50 | — |

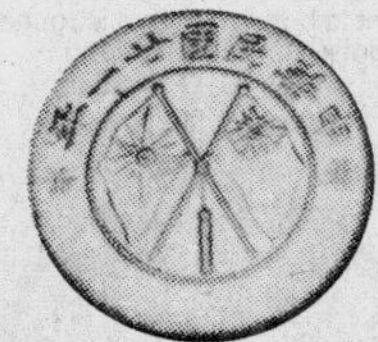

**20 CENTS** **Y# 491** **Weight:** 5.6000 g. **Composition:** Silver **Obverse:** Crossed flags

| Date | Mintage | F | VF | XF | Unc | BU |
|---|---|---|---|---|---|---|
| 21(1932) | — | 3.00 | 5.00 | 8.00 | 20.00 | — |

**20 CENTS** **Y# 493** **Weight:** 5.6000 g. **Composition:** Silver **Reverse:** Provincial capitol

| Date | Mintage | F | VF | XF | Unc | BU |
|---|---|---|---|---|---|---|
| 38(1949) | — | 5.00 | 7.50 | 12.50 | 40.00 | — |

**50 CENTS** **Y# 480** **Weight:** 13.1000 g. **Composition:** 0.8500 Silver **Obverse:** Bust of General T'ang Chi-yao right **Reverse:** Crossed flags **Note:** (ca.1916)

| Date | Mintage | F | VF | XF | Unc | BU |
|---|---|---|---|---|---|---|
| ND | — | 10.00 | 20.00 | 45.00 | 120 | — |

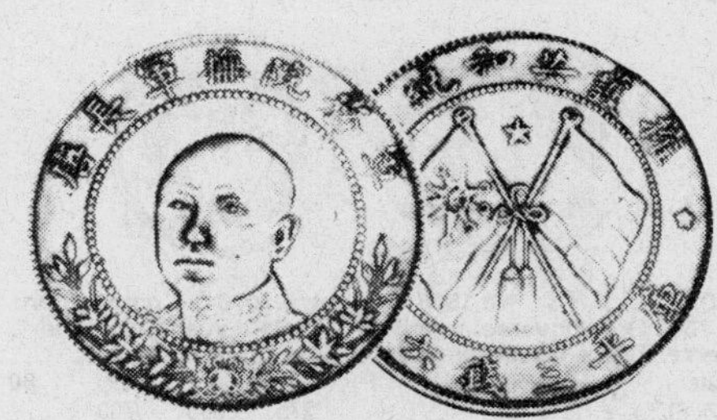

**50 CENTS** **Y# 479** **Weight:** 13.1000 g. **Composition:** 0.8500 Silver **Obverse:** Bust of General T'ang Chi-yao facing **Reverse:** Crossed flags **Note:** (ca.1917)

| Date | Mintage | F | VF | XF | Unc | BU |
|---|---|---|---|---|---|---|
| ND | — | 7.50 | 12.00 | 17.50 | 35.00 | — |

**50 CENTS** **Y# 479.1** **Weight:** 13.1000 g. **Composition:** 0.8500 Silver **Obverse:** Bust of General T'ang Chi-yao facing **Reverse:** Crossed flags with circle in center of flag at left **Note:** (ca.1917)

| Date | Mintage | F | VF | XF | Unc | BU |
|---|---|---|---|---|---|---|
| ND | — | 7.50 | 12.00 | 17.50 | 35.00 | — |

**50 CENTS** **Y# 492** **Weight:** 13.1000 g. **Composition:** 0.5000 Silver

| Date | Mintage | F | VF | XF | Unc | BU |
|---|---|---|---|---|---|---|
| 21(1932) | — | 5.00 | 8.00 | 10.00 | 15.00 | — |

**5 DOLLARS** **K# 1521** **Composition:** Gold **Obverse:** Inscription: "Equal to 5 (silver) Dollars" **Note:** Uniface; Similar to 10 Dollars, K#1520.

| Date | Mintage | F | VF | XF | Unc | BU |
|---|---|---|---|---|---|---|
| ND(1917) Rare | — | — | — | — | — | — |

**5 DOLLARS** **Y# 481** **Weight:** 4.5000 g. **Composition:** 0.7500 Gold **Obverse:** Bust of General T'ang Chi-yao facing **Reverse:** With numeral 2 below flag tassels

| Date | Mintage | F | VF | XF | Unc | BU |
|---|---|---|---|---|---|---|
| ND(1919) | Est. 60,000 | 200 | 300 | 400 | 600 | — |

**5 DOLLARS** **K# 1529** **Weight:** 4.5000 g. **Composition:** 0.7500 Gold **Obverse:** Inscription: Wu(5)-Yüan Chin-pi **Reverse:** Tien in wheat sprays

| Date | Mintage | F | VF | XF | Unc | BU |
|---|---|---|---|---|---|---|
| ND(1925) | — | — | 275 | 500 | 700 | — |

**10 DOLLARS** K# 1520 **Composition:** Gold **Obverse:** Inscription: "Equal to 10 Silver Dollars" **Note:** Uniface.

| Date | Mintage | F | VF | XF | Unc | BU |
|---|---|---|---|---|---|---|
| ND Rare | — | — | — | — | — | — |

**10 DOLLARS** Y# 482 **Weight:** 8.5000 g. **Composition:** 0.7500 Gold **Obverse:** Bust of General T'ang Chi-yao facing **Reverse:** With numeral 1 below flag tassels

| Date | Mintage | F | VF | XF | Unc | BU |
|---|---|---|---|---|---|---|
| ND(1919) | 900,000 | 250 | 350 | 450 | 600 | — |

**10 DOLLARS** Y# 482.1 **Weight:** 8.5000 g. **Composition:** 0.7500 Gold **Obverse:** Bust of General T'ang Chi-yao facing **Reverse:** Without numeral 1 below flag tassels

| Date | Mintage | F | VF | XF | Unc | BU |
|---|---|---|---|---|---|---|
| ND(1919) | Inc. above | 200 | 350 | 450 | 600 | — |

**10 DOLLARS** K# 1528 **Weight:** 8.5000 g. **Composition:** 0.7500 Gold **Obverse:** Inscription: Shih(10)-yüan Chin-pi **Reverse:** Tien in wheat sprays

| Date | Mintage | F | VF | XF | Unc | BU |
|---|---|---|---|---|---|---|
| ND(1925) | — | — | 275 | 500 | 700 | — |

### PATTERNS

Including off metal strikes

| KM# | Date | Mintage | Identification | Mkt Val |
|---|---|---|---|---|
| Pn1 | (ca.1902) | — | Cash. Brass. Tungch'uwan | — |
| Pn2 | (1908) | — | 10 Cash. Copper. | 250 |
| Pn3 | (1908) | — | 50 Cents. Copper. Y#253. | 200 |
| Pn4 | (1908) | — | 50 Cents. Brass. Y#253. | 250 |
| Pn5 | (1908) | — | 50 Cents. Copper. Y#257. | 200 |
| Pn6 | (1908) | — | Dollar. Copper. Y#254. | 350 |
| Pn7 | (1925) | — | 5 Dollars. Silver. | 200 |
| Pn8 | (1925) | — | 10 Dollars. Silver. | 300 |
| Pn9 | (1925) | — | 10 Dollars. Pewter. K#1528y. | — |

## YUNNAN-SZECHUAN

Yunnan-Sichuan

These two coins have a 2-character mint mark in the center of the obverse, indicating the provinces of Yunnan and Szechuan (Sichuan).

## EMPIRE

### PROVINCIAL CAST COINAGE

**10 CASH** Y# 10w **Composition:** Copper **Ruler:** Kuang-hsu **Obverse:** Inscription: Ta-ching T'ung-pi **Rev. Legend:** Kuang-hsu Nien-tsao, TAI-CHING-TI-KUO...

| Date | Mintage | VG | F | VF | XF | Unc |
|---|---|---|---|---|---|---|
| CD(1906) | — | 20.00 | 40.00 | 60.00 | 110 | — |

**20 CASH** Y# 11w **Composition:** Copper **Ruler:** Kuang-hsu **Obverse:** Inscription: Ta-ch'ing T'ung-pi **Rev. Legend:** Kuang-hsu Nien-tsao, TAI-CHING-TI-KUO...

| Date | Mintage | VG | F | VF | XF | Unc |
|---|---|---|---|---|---|---|
| CD(1906) | — | 100 | 150 | 200 | 250 | — |

# REPUBLIC OF CHINA

## REPUBLIC

### TRANSITIONAL COINAGE

**5 CASH (5 Wen)** KM# 1 **Composition:** Copper **Ruler:** Hung-hsien **Obverse:** Inscription: Hung-hsien T'ung-pao

| Date | Mintage | Good | VG | F | VF | XF |
|---|---|---|---|---|---|---|
| ND(1916) Rare | — | — | — | — | — | — |

**Note:** Questionable, believed to be a fantasy by some authorities

**10 CASH (10 Wen)** KM# 2 **Composition:** Bronze **Ruler:** Hung-hsien **Obverse:** Inscription: Hung-hsien T'ung-pao **Note:** Uniface.

| Date | Mintage | Good | VG | F | VF | XF |
|---|---|---|---|---|---|---|
| ND(1916) Rare | — | — | — | — | — | — |

**Note:** Questionable, believed to be a fantasy by some authorities

### STANDARD COINAGE

**10 CASH (10 Wen)** Y# 301a **Composition:** Brass

| Date | Mintage | F | VF | XF | Unc | BU |
|---|---|---|---|---|---|---|
| ND(ca.1912) | — | — | — | — | — | — |

**10 CASH (10 Wen)** Y# 301.2 **Composition:** Copper **Obverse:** Second character from right in bottom legend is rounded **Reverse:** Double circle with two dots separating legend

| Date | Mintage | F | VF | XF | Unc | BU |
|---|---|---|---|---|---|---|
| ND(ca.1912) | — | 0.50 | 1.00 | 2.50 | 16.00 | — |

**10 CASH (10 Wen)** Y# 301.4 **Composition:** Copper **Obverse:** Large star on flag extending to edges of flag **Reverse:** Double circle with six-pointed stars separating legend

| Date | Mintage | F | VF | XF | Unc | BU |
|---|---|---|---|---|---|---|
| ND(ca.1912) | — | 10.00 | 15.00 | 25.00 | 65.00 | — |

**10 CASH (10 Wen)** Y# 301.4a **Composition:** Brass

| Date | Mintage | F | VF | XF | Unc | BU |
|---|---|---|---|---|---|---|
| ND(ca.1912) | — | — | — | — | — | — |

**10 CASH (10 Wen)** Y# 301.5 **Composition:** Copper **Obverse:** Flower wtih many stems **Reverse:** Single circle

| Date | Mintage | F | VF | XF | Unc | BU |
|---|---|---|---|---|---|---|
| ND(ca.1912) | — | 0.75 | 1.50 | 3.00 | 20.00 | — |

**10 CASH (10 Wen)** Y# 301.6 **Composition:** Copper **Obverse:** Flower wtih fewer stems **Reverse:** Single circle

| Date | Mintage | F | VF | XF | Unc | BU |
|---|---|---|---|---|---|---|
| ND(ca.1912) | — | 0.75 | 1.50 | 3.00 | 20.00 | — |

**10 CASH (10 Wen)** Y# 301 **Composition:** Copper **Reverse:** Double circle with small rosettes separating legend **Note:** Struck at Nanking.

| Date | Mintage | F | VF | XF | Unc | BU |
|---|---|---|---|---|---|---|
| ND(ca.1912) | — | 0.50 | 0.75 | 1.50 | 15.00 | — |

**10 CASH (10 Wen)** Y# 301.3 **Composition:** Copper **Obverse:** Small star on flag **Reverse:** Double circle with six-pointed stars separating legend **Note:** Struck at Nanking.

| Date | Mintage | F | VF | XF | Unc | BU |
|---|---|---|---|---|---|---|
| ND(ca.1912) | — | 0.75 | 1.50 | 3.00 | 18.00 | — |

**10 CASH (10 Wen)** Y# 301.1 **Composition:** Copper **Obverse:** Second character from right in bottom legend is rounded **Reverse:** Double circle with three dots separating legend **Note:** Unknown mint.

| Date | Mintage | F | VF | XF | Unc | BU |
|---|---|---|---|---|---|---|
| ND(ca.1912) | — | 1.00 | 2.00 | 5.00 | 22.00 | — |

**10 CASH (10 Wen)** **Y# 309** **Composition:** Copper **Note:** Struck at Tientsin.

| Date | Mintage | F | VF | XF | Unc | BU |
|---|---|---|---|---|---|---|
| ND(1914-17) | — | 10.00 | 20.00 | 40.00 | 120 | — |

**Note:** Pieces with L. GIORGI near rim are patterns

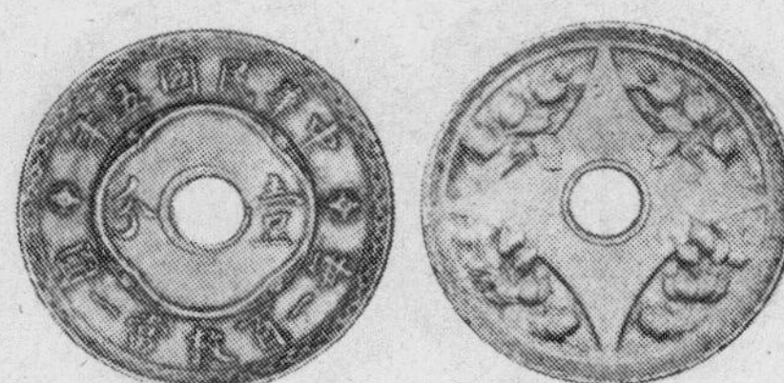

**10 CASH (10 Wen)** **Y# 324** **Composition:** Bronze **Note:** Struck at Tientsin.

| Date | Mintage | F | VF | XF | Unc | BU |
|---|---|---|---|---|---|---|
| 5(1916)(1916) | — | 5.00 | 10.00 | 20.00 | 50.00 | — |

**Note:** Pieces with L. GIORGI near rim are patterns

**10 CASH (10 Wen)** **Y# 307** **Composition:** Copper **Obverse:** One large rosette on either side **Reverse:** Slender leaves and short ribbon **Note:** Struck at Taiyüan, Shensi.

| Date | Mintage | F | VF | XF | Unc | BU |
|---|---|---|---|---|---|---|
| ND(1919) | 421,138,000 | 0.50 | 1.00 | 3.00 | 14.00 | — |

**10 CASH (10 Wen)** **Y# 307.1** **Composition:** Copper **Reverse:** Larger leaves and longer ribbon

| Date | Mintage | F | VF | XF | Unc | BU |
|---|---|---|---|---|---|---|
| ND(1919) | Inc. above | 10.00 | 20.00 | 40.00 | 100 | — |

**10 CASH (10 Wen)** **Y# 307a** **Composition:** Copper **Obverse:** Three rosettes on either side, ornate right flag **Reverse:** Long ribbon

| Date | Mintage | F | VF | XF | Unc | BU |
|---|---|---|---|---|---|---|
| ND(1919) | Inc. above | 1.00 | 2.00 | 4.00 | 12.50 | — |

**10 CASH (10 Wen)** **Y# 307b** **Composition:** Brass

| Date | Mintage | F | VF | XF | Unc | BU |
|---|---|---|---|---|---|---|
| ND(1919) | — | — | — | — | — | — |

**10 CASH (10 Wen)** **Y# 307a.1** **Composition:** Copper **Reverse:** Short ribbon and smaller wheat ears

| Date | Mintage | F | VF | XF | Unc | BU |
|---|---|---|---|---|---|---|
| ND(1919) | Inc. above | 10.00 | 20.00 | 40.00 | 100 | — |

**10 CASH (10 Wen)** **Y# 303.5** **Composition:** Brass **Obverse:** Large rosettes **Note:** Similar to Y#307a.1.

| Date | Mintage | F | VF | XF | Unc | BU |
|---|---|---|---|---|---|---|
| ND(ca.1920) | — | — | — | — | — | — |

**10 CASH (10 Wen)** **Y# 302** **Composition:** Copper **Reverse:** Vine above leaf at 12-o'clock; wreath tied at bottom; M-shaped leaves at base of wheat ears **Note:** Struck at Anhwei

| Date | Mintage | F | VF | XF | Unc | BU |
|---|---|---|---|---|---|---|
| ND(ca.1920) | — | 0.60 | 1.50 | 3.00 | 18.00 | — |

**10 CASH (10 Wen)** **Y# 304** **Composition:** Copper **Obverse:** Circled flag flanked by pentagonal rosettes **Note:** Struck at Anhwei.

| Date | Mintage | F | VF | XF | Unc | BU |
|---|---|---|---|---|---|---|
| ND(ca.1920) | — | 11.50 | 21.50 | 42.50 | 85.00 | — |

**10 CASH (10 Wen)** **Y# 305** **Composition:** Copper **Reverse:** Chrysanthemum **Note:** Struck at Changsha, Hunan.

| Date | Mintage | F | VF | XF | Unc | BU |
|---|---|---|---|---|---|---|
| ND(ca.1920) | — | 15.00 | 25.00 | 50.00 | 115 | — |

**10 CASH (10 Wen)** **Y# 306.1** **Composition:** Copper **Note:** Struck at Changsha, Hunan.

| Date | Mintage | F | VF | XF | Unc | BU |
|---|---|---|---|---|---|---|
| ND(ca.1920) | — | 0.50 | 1.25 | 3.00 | 14.00 | — |

**10 CASH (10 Wen)** **Y# 302a** **Composition:** Brass

| Date | Mintage | F | VF | XF | Unc | BU |
|---|---|---|---|---|---|---|
| ND(ca.1920) | — | — | — | — | — | — |

**10 CASH (10 Wen)** **Y# 302.1** **Composition:** Copper **Reverse:** Larger wheat ears

| Date | Mintage | F | VF | XF | Unc | BU |
|---|---|---|---|---|---|---|
| ND(ca.1920) | — | 1.00 | 3.50 | 6.50 | 20.00 | — |

**10 CASH (10 Wen)** **Y# 302.2** **Composition:** Copper **Reverse:** Vine beneath leaf at 12-o'clock; wreath not tied at bottom; without M-shaped leaves at base of wheat ears

| Date | Mintage | F | VF | XF | Unc | BU |
|---|---|---|---|---|---|---|
| ND(ca.1920) | — | 1.50 | 4.00 | 8.00 | 20.00 | — |

**10 CASH (10 Wen)** **Y# 302.3** **Composition:** Copper **Reverse:** Leaves pointing clockwise

| Date | Mintage | F | VF | XF | Unc | BU |
|---|---|---|---|---|---|---|
| ND(ca.1920) | — | 30.00 | 40.00 | 60.00 | 100 | — |

**10 CASH (10 Wen)** **Y# 303** **Composition:** Copper **Obverse:** Small star-shaped rosettes **Reverse:** Small four-petalled rosettes separating legend

| Date | Mintage | F | VF | XF | Unc | BU |
|---|---|---|---|---|---|---|
| ND(ca.1920) | — | 0.50 | 1.00 | 2.00 | 15.00 | — |

**10 CASH (10 Wen)** **Y# 303.1** **Composition:** Copper **Obverse:** Left flag's star in relief

| Date | Mintage | F | VF | XF | Unc | BU |
|---|---|---|---|---|---|---|
| ND(ca.1920) | — | 0.50 | 1.00 | 2.00 | 15.00 | — |

**10 CASH (10 Wen)** **Y# 303a** **Composition:** Brass **Obverse:** Stars replace rosettes

| Date | Mintage | F | VF | XF | Unc | BU |
|---|---|---|---|---|---|---|
| ND(ca.1920) | — | 1.50 | 4.00 | 10.00 | 22.50 | — |

**10 CASH (10 Wen)** **Y# 303.3** **Composition:** Copper **Obverse:** Large rosettes replace stars **Reverse:** Stars separating legend

| Date | Mintage | F | VF | XF | Unc | BU |
|---|---|---|---|---|---|---|
| ND(ca.1920) | — | 3.00 | 6.25 | 12.50 | 25.00 | — |

**10 CASH (10 Wen)** **Y# 303.4** **Composition:** Copper **Obverse:** Very smallpentagonal rosettes

| Date | Mintage | F | VF | XF | Unc | BU |
|---|---|---|---|---|---|---|
| ND(ca.1920) | — | 0.75 | 1.50 | 3.00 | 15.00 | — |

**10 CASH (10 Wen)** **Y# 303.4a** **Composition:** Brass

| Date | Mintage | F | VF | XF | Unc | BU |
|---|---|---|---|---|---|---|
| ND(ca.1920) | — | 3.00 | 6.25 | 12.50 | 25.00 | — |

**10 CASH (10 Wen)** **Y# 306b** **Composition:** Brass

| Date | Mintage | F | VF | XF | Unc | BU |
|---|---|---|---|---|---|---|
| ND(ca.1920) | — | 1.00 | 2.50 | 5.00 | 18.00 | — |

**10 CASH (10 Wen)** **Y# 306.1b** **Composition:** Copper **Obverse:** Y#306.1 **Reverse:** Y#306.4

| Date | Mintage | F | VF | XF | Unc | BU |
|---|---|---|---|---|---|---|
| ND(ca.1920) | — | 5.00 | 7.50 | 14.00 | 30.00 | — |

**10 CASH (10 Wen)** **Y# 306.2** **Composition:** Copper **Obverse:** Dot on either side of upper legend

| Date | Mintage | F | VF | XF | Unc | BU |
|---|---|---|---|---|---|---|
| ND(ca.1920) | — | 1.00 | 2.00 | 3.50 | 15.00 | — |

**10 CASH (10 Wen)** **Y# 306.2b** **Composition:** Brass

| Date | Mintage | F | VF | XF | Unc | BU |
|---|---|---|---|---|---|---|
| ND(ca.1920) | — | 1.25 | 3.00 | 5.00 | 15.00 | — |

**10 CASH (10 Wen)** **Y# 306.3** **Composition:** Copper **Obverse:** Star between flags

| Date | Mintage | F | VF | XF | Unc | BU |
|---|---|---|---|---|---|---|
| ND(ca.1920) | — | 20.00 | 40.00 | 75.00 | — | — |

**10 CASH (10 Wen)** **Y# 306.4** **Composition:** Copper **Obverse:** Elongated rosettes, different characters in bottom legend **Reverse:** Thin leaf blade between lower wheat ears

| Date | Mintage | F | VF | XF | Unc | BU |
|---|---|---|---|---|---|---|
| ND(ca.1920) | — | 27.50 | 55.00 | 85.00 | 210 | — |

**10 CASH (10 Wen)** **Y# 306a** **Composition:** Copper **Obverse:** Five characters in lower legend

| Date | Mintage | F | VF | XF | Unc | BU |
|---|---|---|---|---|---|---|
| ND(ca.1920) | — | 5.00 | 12.00 | 25.00 | 65.00 | — |

**10 CASH (10 Wen)** **Y# 311** **Composition:** Copper **Note:** Struck at Kalgan.

| Date | Mintage | F | VF | XF | Unc | BU |
|---|---|---|---|---|---|---|
| 13(1924)(1924) | — | 175 | 350 | 500 | 850 | — |

**10 CASH (10 Wen)** **Y# 324a** **Composition:** Bronze

| Date | Mintage | F | VF | XF | Unc | BU |
|---|---|---|---|---|---|---|
| 22(1933)(1933) | — | 8.00 | 15.00 | 30.00 | 100 | — |

**10 CASH (10 Wen)** **Y# 347** **Composition:** Copper

| Date | Mintage | F | VF | XF | Unc | BU |
|---|---|---|---|---|---|---|
| 25(1936) | 311,780,000 | 0.40 | 0.75 | 1.75 | 2.50 | — |
| 26(1937) | 307,198,000 | 0.45 | 1.00 | 1.50 | 3.00 | — |
| 27(1938) | 12,000,000 | 3.00 | 5.00 | 8.00 | 16.00 | — |
| 28(1939) | 75,000,000 | 2.00 | 4.00 | 7.00 | 15.00 | — |

**20 CASH (20 Wen)** **Y# 308b** **Composition:** Cast Brass

| Date | Mintage | Good | VG | F | VF | XF |
|---|---|---|---|---|---|---|
| 8(1919) | — | 10.00 | 15.00 | 18.50 | 25.00 | — |

**Note:** A "warlord" issue; refer to note under Szechuan - Republic

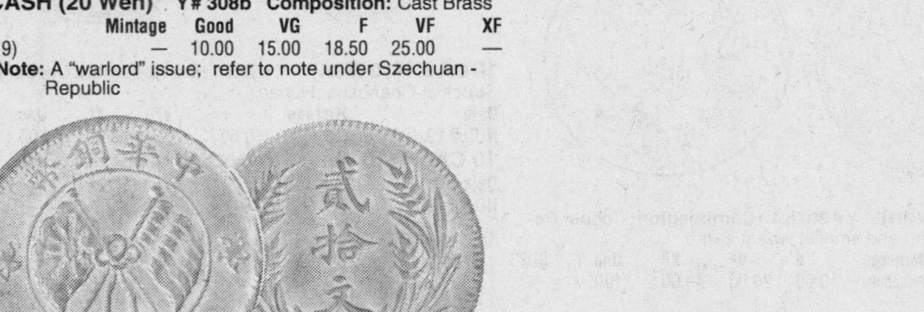

**20 CASH (20 Wen)** **Y# 308** **Composition:** Copper **Note:** Struck at Taiyüan, Shansi.

| Date | Mintage | F | VF | XF | Unc | BU |
|---|---|---|---|---|---|---|
| 8(1919) | 200,861,000 | 1.50 | 3.00 | 7.50 | 30.00 | — |

**20 CASH (20 Wen)** **Y# 310** **Composition:** Copper **Note:** Struck at Tientsin.

| Date | Mintage | F | VF | XF | Unc | BU |
|---|---|---|---|---|---|---|
| ND(ca.19210 | — | 15.00 | 30.00 | 70.00 | 135 | — |

**Note:** Some sources date these 20 Cash pieces bearing crossed flags ca.1912, but many were not struck until the 1920s; this coin is usually found weakly struck and lightweight

**20 CASH (20 Wen)** **Y# 308a** **Composition:** Copper **Obverse:** Four rosettes added between legends

| Date | Mintage | F | VF | XF | Unc | BU |
|---|---|---|---|---|---|---|
| 10(1921) | Inc. above | 1.00 | 2.50 | 6.00 | 30.00 | — |

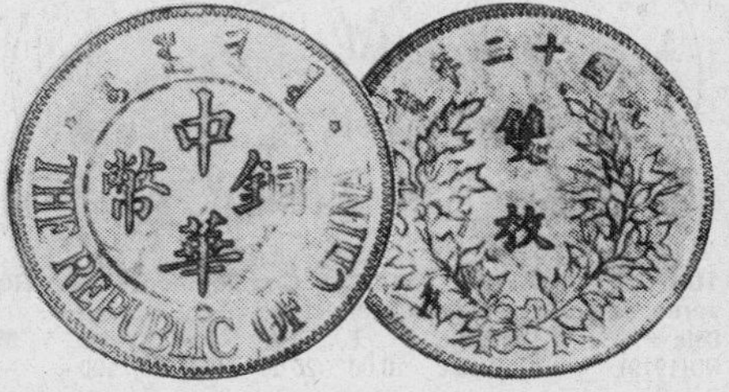

**20 CASH (20 Wen)** **Y# 312** **Composition:** Copper **Note:** Struck at Kalgan.

| Date | Mintage | F | VF | XF | Unc | BU |
|---|---|---|---|---|---|---|
| 13(1924)(1924) | — | 10.00 | 30.00 | 70.00 | 135 | — |

**Note:** This coin is usually found weakly struck

**20 CASH (20 Wen)** **HSU# 9** **Composition:** Copper **Note:** Nationailst commemorative.

| Date | Mintage | F | VF | XF | Unc | BU |
|---|---|---|---|---|---|---|
| ND(1927-28) | — | 225 | 400 | 650 | 900 | — |

**500 CASH (500 Wen)** **HSU# 445a** **Composition:** Copper **Subject:** Nationalist Commemorative

| Date | Mintage | F | VF | XF | Unc | BU |
|---|---|---|---|---|---|---|
| ND(1927/8) Rare | 12 | — | — | — | — | — |

**1/2 CENT (5 Li)** **Y# 323** **Composition:** Bronze **Note:** Struck at Tientsin.

| Date | Mintage | F | VF | XF | Unc | BU |
|---|---|---|---|---|---|---|
| 25(1916) | 1,789,000 | 5.00 | 10.00 | 20.00 | 45.00 | — |

**1/2 CENT (1/2 Fen)** **Y# 346** **Composition:** Bronze

| Date | Mintage | F | VF | XF | Unc | BU |
|---|---|---|---|---|---|---|
| 25(1936) | 64,720,000 | 0.75 | 1.50 | 3.00 | 7.50 | — |
| 28(1939) Rare | — | — | — | — | — | — |

**CENT (1 Fen)** **Y# 355** **Composition:** Aluminum

| Date | Mintage | F | VF | XF | Unc | BU |
|---|---|---|---|---|---|---|
| 29(1940) | 150,000,000 | 0.10 | 0.25 | 0.50 | 1.50 | — |

**CENT (1 Fen)** **Y# 357** **Composition:** Brass

| Date | Mintage | F | VF | XF | Unc | BU |
|---|---|---|---|---|---|---|
| 29(1940) | 50,000,000 | 0.75 | 1.00 | 2.00 | 4.00 | — |

**CENT (1 Fen)** **Y# 363** **Composition:** Bronze

| Date | Mintage | F | VF | XF | Unc | BU |
|---|---|---|---|---|---|---|
| 37(1948)(1948) | — | 4.00 | 10.00 | 15.00 | 20.00 | — |

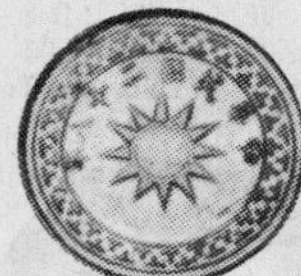

**CENT (1 Hsien)** **Y# 353** **Composition:** Brass **Note:** Shi Kwan Cent.

| Date | Mintage | F | VF | XF | Unc | BU |
|---|---|---|---|---|---|---|
| 28(1939)(1939) | — | 40.00 | 60.00 | 120 | 200 | — |

**2 CENTS (2 Fen)** **Y# 325a** **Composition:** Bronze

| Date | Mintage | F | VF | XF | Unc | BU |
|---|---|---|---|---|---|---|
| 22(1933) | — | 40.00 | 60.00 | 95.00 | 150 | — |

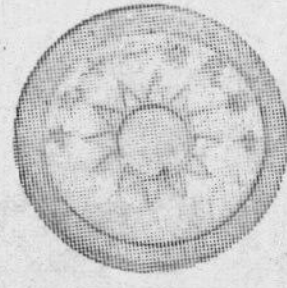

**2 CENTS (2 Fen)** **Y# 358** **Composition:** Brass

| Date | Mintage | F | VF | XF | Unc | BU |
|---|---|---|---|---|---|---|
| 29(1940) | — | 0.50 | 1.00 | 1.50 | 2.00 | — |
| 30(1941) Rare | — | — | — | — | — | — |

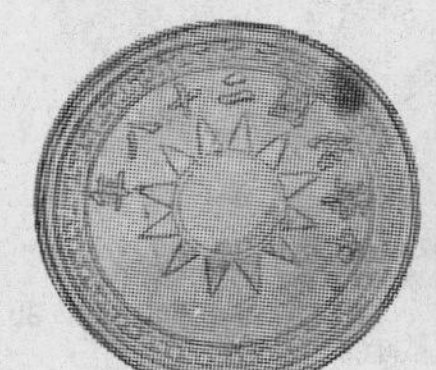

**2 CENTS (2 Hsien)** **Y# 354** **Composition:** Brass

| Date | Mintage | F | VF | XF | Unc | BU |
|---|---|---|---|---|---|---|
| 28(1939) | 300,000,000 | 10.00 | 15.00 | 25.00 | 50.00 | — |

**5 CENTS (5 Fen)** **Y# 348** **Composition:** Nickel

| Date | Mintage | F | VF | XF | Unc | BU |
|---|---|---|---|---|---|---|
| 25(1936) | 72,844,000 | 1.00 | 1.50 | 3.00 | 6.00 | — |
| 27(1938) | 34,325,000 | 2.50 | 4.50 | 8.00 | 15.00 | — |
| 28(1939) | 6,000,000 | 10.00 | 15.00 | 25.00 | 50.00 | — |

**5 CENTS (5 Fen)** **Y# 348.1** **Composition:** Nickel **Reverse:** A mint mark below spade (Vienna)

| Date | Mintage | F | VF | XF | Unc | BU |
|---|---|---|---|---|---|---|
| 25(1936) | 20,000,000 | 1.00 | 2.00 | 3.50 | 15.00 | — |

**5 CENTS (5 Fen)** **Y# 348.2** **Composition:** Nickel **Obverse:** Character "P'ing" on both sides of portrait

| Date | Mintage | F | VF | XF | Unc | BU |
|---|---|---|---|---|---|---|
| 25(1936) | — | 50.00 | 80.00 | 125 | 175 | — |

**5 CENTS (5 Fen)** **Y# 348.3** **Composition:** Nickel **Obverse:** Character "Ch'ing" on both sides of portrait

| Date | Mintage | F | VF | XF | Unc | BU |
|---|---|---|---|---|---|---|
| 25(1936) | — | 50.00 | 80.00 | 125 | 175 | — |

**5 CENTS (5 Fen)** **Y# 356** **Composition:** Aluminum

| Date | Mintage | F | VF | XF | Unc | BU |
|---|---|---|---|---|---|---|
| 29(1940) | 350,000,000 | 0.50 | 1.00 | 2.50 | 4.00 | — |

**5 CENTS (5 Fen)** **Y# 359** **Composition:** Copper-Nickel

| Date | Mintage | F | VF | XF | Unc | BU |
|---|---|---|---|---|---|---|
| 29(1940) | 57,000,000 | 0.25 | 1.50 | 2.50 | 5.00 | — |
| 30(1941) | 96,000,000 | 0.25 | 1.50 | 2.50 | 6.00 | — |

**10 CENTS (1 Chiao)** **K# 602b** **Weight:** 2.3000 g. **Composition:** Silver **Note:** Edge engraied with circles.

| Date | Mintage | F | VF | XF | Unc | BU |
|---|---|---|---|---|---|---|
| ND(1912) | — | — | 700 | 850 | 1,500 | — |

**10 CENTS (1 Chiao)** **K# 602** **Weight:** 2.3000 g. **Composition:** Silver **Note:** Similar to 1 Dollar, Y#318, vertical reeding.

| Date | Mintage | F | VF | XF | Unc | BU |
|---|---|---|---|---|---|---|
| ND(1912) | — | 200 | 500 | 700 | 1,250 | — |

**10 CENTS (1 Chiao)** **Y# 326** **Weight:** 2.7000 g. **Composition:** 0.7000 Silver .607 oz. ASW

| Date | Mintage | F | VF | XF | Unc | BU |
|---|---|---|---|---|---|---|
| 3(1914) | — | 5.00 | 10.00 | 17.50 | 40.00 | — |
| 5(1916) | — | 20.00 | 35.00 | 50.00 | 100 | — |

**10 CENTS (1 Chiao)** **Y# 334** **Composition:** Silver **Note:** Pu Yi wedding.

| Date | Mintage | F | VF | XF | Unc | BU |
|---|---|---|---|---|---|---|
| 15(1926) | — | 5.00 | 12.00 | 25.00 | 60.00 | — |

**10 CENTS (1 Chiao)** **Y# 339** **Weight:** 2.5000 g. **Composition:** Silver **Note:** Death of Sun Yat-sen.

| Date | Mintage | F | VF | XF | Unc | BU |
|---|---|---|---|---|---|---|
| 16(1927) | — | 25.00 | 40.00 | 70.00 | 135 | — |

**10 CENTS (1 Chiao)** **Y# 349** **Composition:** Nickel

| Date | Mintage | F | VF | XF | Unc | BU |
|---|---|---|---|---|---|---|
| 25(1936) | 73,866,000 | 0.60 | 1.00 | 3.00 | 7.50 | — |
| 27(1938) | 110,203,000 | 2.00 | 4.25 | 8.00 | 20.00 | — |
| 28(1939) | 68,000,000 | 1.50 | 3.50 | 10.00 | 27.50 | — |

**10 CENTS (1 Chiao)** **Y# 349a** **Composition:** Non-Magnetic Nickel Alloy

| Date | Mintage | F | VF | XF | Unc | BU |
|---|---|---|---|---|---|---|
| 25(1936) | 1,000,000 | 18.00 | 30.00 | 35.00 | 65.00 | — |

**Note:** All of the Y#349 coins were supposed to have been minted in pure nickel at the Shanghai Mint. However, in 1936 a warloard had the Tientsin Mint produce about one million 10 Cent pieces of heavily alloyed nickel. The result is that the Shanghai pieces are attracted to a magnet while the Tientsin pieces are not.

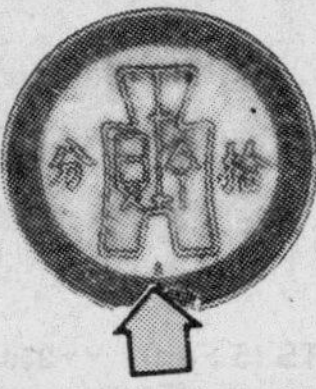

**10 CENTS (1 Chiao)** Y# 349.1 **Composition:** Nickel **Reverse:** A mint mark below spade (Vienna Mint)

| Date | Mintage | F | VF | XF | Unc | BU |
|---|---|---|---|---|---|---|
| 25(1936)A | 60,000,000 | 1.00 | 2.00 | 8.00 | 25.00 | — |

**10 CENTS (1 Chiao)** Y# 360 **Composition:** Copper-Nickel **Edge:** Reeded

| Date | Mintage | F | VF | XF | Unc | BU |
|---|---|---|---|---|---|---|
| 29(1940) | 68,000,000 | 0.50 | 2.50 | 8.00 | 15.00 | — |
| 30(1941) | 254,000,000 | 0.50 | 1.50 | 2.50 | 5.00 | — |
| 31(1942) | 10,000,000 | 25.00 | 60.00 | 80.00 | 120 | — |

**10 CENTS (1 Chiao)** Y# 360.1 **Composition:** Copper-Nickel **Edge:** Plain

| Date | Mintage | F | VF | XF | Unc | BU |
|---|---|---|---|---|---|---|
| 29(1940) Rare | Inc. above | — | — | — | — | — |
| 30(1941) | Inc. above | 2.00 | 7.50 | 10.00 | 15.00 | — |

**20 CENTS (2 Chiao)** Y# 317 **Weight:** 5.2000 g. **Composition:** Silver **Note:** Founding of the Republic.

| Date | Mintage | F | VF | XF | Unc | BU |
|---|---|---|---|---|---|---|
| ND(19121) | 155,000 | 15.00 | 20.00 | 35.00 | 80.00 | — |

**20 CENTS (2 Chiao)** Y# 327 **Weight:** 5.4000 g. **Composition:** 0.7000 Silver .1215 oz. ASW

| Date | Mintage | F | VF | XF | Unc | BU |
|---|---|---|---|---|---|---|
| 3(1914) | — | 3.00 | 5.00 | 9.00 | 35.00 | — |
| 5(1916) | — | 3.00 | 5.00 | 10.00 | 45.00 | — |
| 9(1920) | — | 100 | 250 | 300 | 500 | — |

**20 CENTS (2 Chiao)** Y# 335 **Weight:** 5.2000 g. **Composition:** Silver **Note:** Pu Yi wedding.

| Date | Mintage | F | VF | XF | Unc | BU |
|---|---|---|---|---|---|---|
| 15(1926) | — | 10.00 | 15.00 | 30.00 | 80.00 | — |

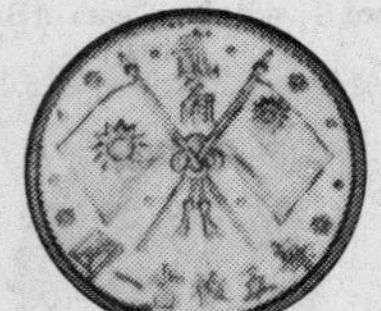

**20 CENTS (2 Chiao)** Y# 340 **Weight:** 5.3000 g. **Composition:** Silver **Note:** Death of Sun Yat-sen

| Date | Mintage | F | VF | XF | Unc | BU |
|---|---|---|---|---|---|---|
| 16(1927)(1927) | — | 15.00 | 25.00 | 40.00 | 100 | — |

**20 CENTS (20 Fen)** Y# 350 **Composition:** Nickel

| Date | Mintage | F | VF | XF | Unc | BU |
|---|---|---|---|---|---|---|
| 25(1936) | 49,620,000 | 0.50 | 2.50 | 6.00 | 10.00 | — |
| 27(1938) | 61,248,000 | 1.00 | 2.00 | 7.00 | 12.00 | — |
| 28(1939) | 38,000,000 | 2.00 | 5.00 | 10.00 | 15.00 | — |

**20 CENTS (20 Fen)** Y# 350.1 **Composition:** Nickel **Reverse:** A mint mark below spade (Vienna Mint)

| Date | Mintage | F | VF | XF | Unc | BU |
|---|---|---|---|---|---|---|
| 25(1936) | 40,000,000 | 1.00 | 2.00 | 3.50 | 6.00 | — |

**20 CENTS (20 Fen)** Y# 361 **Composition:** Copper-Nickel

| Date | Mintage | F | VF | XF | Unc | BU |
|---|---|---|---|---|---|---|
| 31(1942) | 32,300,000 | 0.40 | 1.00 | 2.25 | 4.00 | — |

**50 CENTS (1/2 Yuan)** Y# 328 **Weight:** 13.6000 g. **Composition:** 0.7000 Silver .3060 oz. ASW

| Date | Mintage | F | VF | XF | Unc | BU |
|---|---|---|---|---|---|---|
| 3(1914) | — | 20.00 | 30.00 | 50.00 | 100 | — |

**50 CENTS (1/2 Yuan)** Y# 362 **Composition:** Copper-Nickel

| Date | Mintage | F | VF | XF | Unc | BU |
|---|---|---|---|---|---|---|
| 31(1942) | 57,000,000 | 1.50 | 3.00 | 7.50 | 15.00 | — |
| 32(1943) | 4,000,000 | 3.50 | 9.50 | 17.50 | 30.00 | — |

**DOLLAR (Yuan)** Y# 318 **Weight:** 26.9000 g. **Composition:** 0.9000 Silver .7785 oz. ASW **Subject:** Sun Yat-sen Founding of the Republic **Reverse:** Two five-pointed stars dividing legend at top

| Date | Mintage | F | VF | XF | Unc | BU |
|---|---|---|---|---|---|---|
| ND(1912) | — | 100 | 150 | 300 | 650 | — |

**DOLLAR (Yuan)** Y# 318.1 **Weight:** 26.9000 g. **Composition:** 0.9000 Silver .7785 oz. ASW **Obverse:** Dot below ear

| Date | Mintage | F | VF | XF | Unc | BU |
|---|---|---|---|---|---|---|
| ND(1912) | — | — | — | — | — | — |

**Note:** For similar issue with rosettes see Y#318a.1 (1927)

**DOLLAR (Yuan)** Y# 319 **Weight:** 27.3000 g. **Composition:** 0.9000 Silver .7900 oz. ASW **Obverse:** Similar to Y#318

| Date | Mintage | F | VF | XF | Unc | BU |
|---|---|---|---|---|---|---|
| ND(1912) | — | 80.00 | 125 | 200 | 450 | — |

**DOLLAR (Yuan)** Y# 320 **Weight:** 26.5000 g. **Composition:** Silver **Subject:** Li Yüan-hung Founding of Republic **Reverse:** Similar to Y#319

| Date | Mintage | F | VF | XF | Unc | BU |
|---|---|---|---|---|---|---|
| ND(1912) | — | 125 | 250 | 400 | 700 | — |

**DOLLAR (Yuan)** Y# 320.1 **Weight:** 26.5000 g. **Composition:** Silver **Rev. Legend:** OE for OF

| Date | Mintage | F | VF | XF | Unc | BU |
|---|---|---|---|---|---|---|
| ND(1912) | — | 150 | 275 | 450 | 750 | — |

**DOLLAR (Yuan)** Y# 320.2 **Weight:** 26.5000 g. **Composition:** Silver **Rev. Legend:** CIIINA for CHINA

| Date | Mintage | F | VF | XF | Unc | BU |
|---|---|---|---|---|---|---|
| ND(1912) | — | 150 | 275 | 450 | 750 | — |

**DOLLAR (Yuan)** Y# 321 **Weight:** 26.5000 g. **Composition:** Silver **Subject:** Li Yüan-hung Founding of Republic

| Date | Mintage | F | VF | XF | Unc | BU |
|---|---|---|---|---|---|---|
| ND(1912) | — | 50.00 | 100 | 150 | 250 | — |

**DOLLAR (Yuan)** **Y# 321.1** **Weight:** 26.5000 g. **Composition:** Silver **Reverse:** H of "THE" in legend engraved as I I

| Date | Mintage | F | VF | XF | Unc | BU |
|---|---|---|---|---|---|---|
| ND(1912) | — | 60.00 | 125 | 175 | 275 | — |

**DOLLAR (Yuan)** **Y# 329.2** **Weight:** 26.4000 g. **Composition:** 0.8900 Silver .7555 oz. ASW **Edge:** Ornamented with alternating T's

| Date | Mintage | F | VF | XF | Unc | BU |
|---|---|---|---|---|---|---|
| 3`914)(1914) | — | 30.00 | 80.00 | 500 | 1,000 | — |

**DOLLAR (Yuan)** **Y# 329.3** **Weight:** 26.4000 g. **Composition:** 0.8900 Silver .7555 oz. ASW **Edge:** Plain

| Date | Mintage | F | VF | XF | Unc | BU |
|---|---|---|---|---|---|---|
| 3(1914) | — | 20.00 | 40.00 | 300 | 500 | — |

**DOLLAR (Yuan)** **Y# 329.1** **Weight:** 26.4000 g. **Composition:** 0.8900 Silver .7555 oz. ASW **Note:** Edge engrailed with circles

| Date | Mintage | F | VF | XF | Unc | BU |
|---|---|---|---|---|---|---|
| 3(1914) | — | 30.00 | 80.00 | 500 | 1,000 | — |

**DOLLAR (Yuan)** **Y# 329.4** **Weight:** 26.4000 g. **Composition:** 0.8900 Silver .7555 oz. ASW **Note:** Tiny circle in ribbon bow. This is a mint mark, but it is not clear what mint is indicated.

| Date | Mintage | F | VF | XF | Unc | BU |
|---|---|---|---|---|---|---|
| 3(1914) | — | 15.00 | 30.00 | 70.00 | 125 | — |

**DOLLAR (Yuan)** **Y# 329** **Weight:** 26.4000 g. **Composition:** 0.8900 Silver .7555 oz. ASW **Subject:** Yüan Shih-kai **Obverse:** Six characters above head **Note:** Vertical reeding.

| Date | Mintage | F | VF | XF | Unc | BU |
|---|---|---|---|---|---|---|
| 3(1914) | — | 7.00 | 12.00 | 15.00 | 25.00 | — |

**DOLLAR (Yuan)** **Y# 322** **Weight:** 26.7000 g. **Composition:** 0.9000 Silver .7474 oz. ASW **Subject:** Yüan Shih-kai Founding of Republic **Note:** 2.8 milimeters thickness.

| Date | Mintage | F | VF | XF | Unc | BU |
|---|---|---|---|---|---|---|
| ND | 20,000 | 60.00 | 125 | 250 | 375 | — |

**DOLLAR (Yuan)** **Y# 322.1** **Weight:** 26.7000 g. **Composition:** 0.9000 Silver .7474 oz. ASW **Note:** 3.25 milimeters thickness.

| Date | Mintage | F | VF | XF | Unc | BU |
|---|---|---|---|---|---|---|
| ND(ca.1918) | — | 60.00 | 125 | 250 | 375 | — |

**Note:** A restrike made about 1918 for collectors

**DOLLAR (Yuan)** **Y# 330** **Weight:** 8.1500 g. **Composition:** 0.8500 Gold .2227 oz. AGW **Ruler:** Hung-hsien

| Date | Mintage | F | VF | XF | Unc | BU |
|---|---|---|---|---|---|---|
| 8(1919) | — | — | 2,000 | 2,850 | 4,000 | — |

**DOLLAR (Yuan)** **Y# 329.6** **Weight:** 26.4000 g. **Composition:** 0.8900 Silver .7555 oz. ASW **Obverse:** Seven characters above head

| Date | Mintage | F | VF | XF | Unc | BU |
|---|---|---|---|---|---|---|
| 8(1919) | — | 10.00 | 15.00 | 35.00 | 100 | — |
| 9(1920) | — | 7.00 | 10.00 | 15.00 | 25.00 | — |
| 10(1921) | — | 7.00 | 10.00 | 15.00 | 25.00 | — |

**DOLLAR (Yuan)** **Y# 329.5** **Weight:** 26.4000 g. **Composition:** 0.8900 Silver .7555 oz. ASW **Edge:** Oblique reeding

| Date | Mintage | F | VF | XF | Unc | BU |
|---|---|---|---|---|---|---|
| 10(1921) | — | 17.50 | 30.00 | 35.00 | 50.00 | — |

**DOLLAR (Yuan)** **Y# 332** **Weight:** 26.8000 g. **Composition:** Silver **Ruler:** Hung-hsien **Subject:** Inauguration of Hung-hsien Regime **Obverse:** Bust of Hung-hsien in military uniform with plumed hat facing **Reverse:** Winged dragon left

| Date | Mintage | F | VF | XF | Unc | BU |
|---|---|---|---|---|---|---|
| ND(1917) | — | 125 | 250 | 400 | 650 | — |

**DOLLAR (Yuan)** **K# 676** **Weight:** 26.5000 g. **Composition:** Silver **Subject:** President Hsu Shih-chang **Edge:** Reeded

| Date | Mintage | F | VF | XF | Unc | BU |
|---|---|---|---|---|---|---|
| 10(1921) | — | 150 | 300 | 500 | 750 | — |

**DOLLAR (Yuan)** **K# 676.1** **Weight:** 26.5000 g. **Composition:** Silver **Edge:** Plain

| Date | Mintage | F | VF | XF | Unc | BU |
|---|---|---|---|---|---|---|
| 10(1921) | — | 300 | 600 | 800 | 1,200 | — |

**DOLLAR (Yuan)** **Y# 336** **Weight:** 26.8000 g. **Composition:** Silver **Subject:** Pu Yi Wedding **Reverse:** Value in small characters

| Date | Mintage | F | VF | XF | Unc | BU |
|---|---|---|---|---|---|---|
| 12(1923) | — | 175 | 350 | 600 | 1,200 | — |

**DOLLAR (Yuan)** **Y# 336.1** **Weight:** 26.8000 g. **Composition:** Silver **Subject:** Pu Yi Wedding **Reverse:** Value in large characters

| Date | Mintage | F | VF | XF | Unc | BU |
|---|---|---|---|---|---|---|
| 12(1923) | — | 300 | 600 | 1,000 | 2,400 | — |

**DOLLAR (Yuan)** **K# 677** **Weight:** 26.7000 g. **Composition:** Silver **Obverse:** Bust of President Tsao Kun facing

| Date | Mintage | F | VF | XF | Unc | BU |
|---|---|---|---|---|---|---|
| ND(1923) | 50,000 | 100 | 200 | 300 | 450 | — |

**DOLLAR (Yuan)** **K# 678** **Weight:** 26.7000 g. **Composition:** Silver **Obverse:** Bust of President Tsao Kun in military uniform

| Date | Mintage | F | VF | XF | Unc | BU |
|---|---|---|---|---|---|---|
| ND(1923) | — | — | 200 | 300 | 450 | — |

**DOLLAR (Yuan)** **K# 683** **Composition:** Silver **Obverse:** Bust of President Tuan Chi-jui facing

| Date | Mintage | F | VF | XF | Unc | BU |
|---|---|---|---|---|---|---|
| ND(1924) | — | 100 | 200 | 300 | 600 | — |

**DOLLAR (Yuan)** **K# 609** **Weight:** 27.0000 g. **Composition:** Silver **Obverse:** Bust of Sun Yat-sen **Note:** Sun Yat-sen Memorial

| Date | Mintage | F | VF | XF | Unc | BU |
|---|---|---|---|---|---|---|
| 16(1927) | 480 | 700 | 1,500 | 2,750 | 5,000 | — |

**DOLLAR (Yuan)** **Y# 318a.1** **Weight:** 27.0000 g. **Composition:** 0.8900 Silver .7727 oz. ASW **Obverse:** Bust of Sun Yat-sen left **Reverse:** Two rosettes dividing legend at top; mausoleum in Nanking **Edge:** Incuse reeding

| Date | Mintage | F | VF | XF | Unc | BU |
|---|---|---|---|---|---|---|
| ND(1927) | — | 7.00 | 9.00 | 12.50 | 22.50 | — |

**DOLLAR (Yuan)** **Y# 318a.2** **Weight:** 27.0000 g. **Composition:** 0.8900 Silver .7727 oz. ASW **Edge:** Reeding in relief

| Date | Mintage | F | VF | XF | Unc | BU |
|---|---|---|---|---|---|---|
| ND(1927) | — | 7.00 | 9.00 | 12.50 | 22.50 | — |

**Note:** Varieties exist with errors in the English legend. For similar coins with 5-pointed stars dividing legends, see Y#318 (1912). In 1949 the Canton Mint restruck Memento dollars. There are modern restrikes in red copper and brass.

**DOLLAR (Yuan)** **K# 690** **Weight:** 26.5000 g. **Composition:** Silver **Obverse:** Bust of General Chu Yu-pu facing

| Date | Mintage | F | VF | XF | Unc | BU |
|---|---|---|---|---|---|---|
| (1927) | — | — | — | 6,500 | 9,500 | — |

**DOLLAR (Yuan)** **Y# 344** **Weight:** 26.7000 g. **Composition:** 0.8800 Silver .7555 oz. ASW **Reverse:** Birds above junk, rising sun

| Date | Mintage | F | VF | XF | Unc | BU |
|---|---|---|---|---|---|---|
| 21(1932) | 2,260,000 | 125 | 200 | 300 | 600 | — |

**DOLLAR (Yuan)** **Y# 345** **Weight:** 26.7000 g. **Composition:** 0.8800 Silver .7555 oz. ASW **Reverse:** Without birds above junkor rising sun

| Date | Mintage | F | VF | XF | Unc | BU |
|---|---|---|---|---|---|---|
| 23(1933) | 46,400,000 | 12.50 | 15.00 | 20.00 | 45.00 | — |
| 24(1934) | 128,740,000 | 9.00 | 12.50 | 15.00 | 25.00 | — |

**Note:** In 1949, three U.S. mints restruck a total of 30 million "Junk Dollars" dated Year 23

**DOLLAR (Yuan)** **Y# 333** **Weight:** 7.0500 g. **Composition:** Red Gold **Ruler:** Hung-hsien **Obverse:** Bust of Hung-hsien left **Reverse:** Winged dragon left

| Date | Mintage | F | VF | XF | Unc | BU |
|---|---|---|---|---|---|---|
| 1(1916) | — | — | 2,000 | 3,500 | 5,000 | — |

**DOLLAR (Yuan)** **Y# 333a** **Weight:** 7.0500 g. **Composition:** Yellow Gold **Ruler:** Hung-hsien

| Date | Mintage | F | VF | XF | Unc | BU |
|---|---|---|---|---|---|---|
| 1(1916) | — | — | 2,000 | 3,500 | 5,000 | — |

**20 DOLLARS** **Y# 331** **Weight:** 16.3000 g. **Composition:** 0.8500 Gold .4456 oz. AGW **Ruler:** Hung-hsien

| Date | Mintage | F | VF | XF | Unc | BU |
|---|---|---|---|---|---|---|
| 8(1919) | — | — | — | 4,500 | 7,500 | — |

## TOKEN COINAGE

**FEN** **KM# Tn1** **Composition:** Brass **Note:** Struck at Shansi Arsenal

| Date | Mintage | F | VF | XF | Unc | BU |
|---|---|---|---|---|---|---|
| 17(1928) | — | 75.00 | 125 | 175 | 300 | — |

**Note:** This token is usually found with small punch marks near center on obverse and reverse

**2 FEN** **KM# Tn2** **Composition:** Brass **Note:** Struck at Shansi Arsenal

| Date | Mintage | F | VF | XF | Unc | BU |
|---|---|---|---|---|---|---|
| 17(1928)(1928) | — | 150 | 250 | 400 | 650 | — |

**Note:** This token has always been found with small punch marks near center on obverse and reverse

**5 FEN** **KM# Tn3** **Composition:** Brass **Note:** Struck at Shansi Arsenal; similar to 2 Fen, KM#Tn2.

| Date | Mintage | F | VF | XF | Unc | BU |
|---|---|---|---|---|---|---|
| 17(1928) | — | 450 | 750 | 1,250 | — | — |

**Note:** This token has always been found with small punch marks near center on obverse and reverse

**10 FEN** **KM# Tn4** **Composition:** Brass **Note:** Struck at Shansi Arsenal; similar to 2 Fen, KM#Tn2.

| Date | Mintage | F | VF | XF | Unc | BU |
|---|---|---|---|---|---|---|
| 17(1928) | — | 450 | 750 | 1,250 | — | — |

**Note:** This token has always been found with small punch marks near center on obverse and reverse

## PATTERNS

Including off metal strikes

| KM# | Date | Mintage | Identification | Mkt Val |
|---|---|---|---|---|
| Pn2 | (1912) | — | Cash. Copper Or Brass. | — |
| Pn3 | (1912) | — | Cash. Zinc. | — |
| Pn4 | (1912) | — | Cash. Iron. | — |
| PnA6 | (1912) | — | 10 Cash. Copper. Similar to Pn5 but larger bust; W972. | — |
| Pn6 | (1912) | — | 10 Cash. Gold. | — |
| Pn8 | (1912) | — | Dollar. Gold. Y#318 | — |
| PnA10 | (1912) | — | Dollar. Silver. Li Yuan-hung | — |
| Pn11 | (1912) | — | Dollar. Eyes in relief. Chin Teh-chuen, K#672a. | — |

**Note:** Authenticity in doubt

| KM# | Date | Mintage | Identification | Mkt Val |
|---|---|---|---|---|
| Pn5 | (1912) | — | 10 Cash. Copper. Hsu13 | 1,000 |
| Pn7 | (1912) | — | 20 Cents. Gold. Y#317 | 1,500 |
| Pn9 | (1912) | — | Dollar. Gold. Y#318 - K#1550 | 6,500 |
| Pn10 | (1912) | — | Dollar. Silver. Chin Teh-chuen, K#672 | 25,000 |
| Pn12 | (1912) | — | Dollar. Bronze. K#672x | 4,000 |

**Note:** Authenticity in doubt

| KM# | Date | Mintage | Identification | Mkt Val |
|---|---|---|---|---|
| Pn16 | 3(1914) | — | 5 Cents. Silver. Milled edge. Essay, K#815c; with G. L. | 350 |
| Pn17 | 3(1914) | — | 5 Cents. Copper. Essay, K#815x | 225 |
| Pn20 | 3(1914) | — | 10 Cents. Silver. With G. L., K#659a | 700 |
| Pn21 | 3(1914) | — | 10 Cents. Copper. Y#326 | 45.00 |
| Pn22 | 3(1914) | — | 10 Cents. Nickel. Y#326 | 350 |
| Pn23 | 3(1914) | — | 20 Cents. Silver. With G. L.; K#657a | 900 |
| Pn24 | 3(1914) | — | 20 Cents. Copper. Y#327 | 65.00 |
| Pn25 | 3(1914) | — | 20 Cents. Nickel. Y#327 | 375 |
| Pn26 | 3(1914) | — | 20 Cents. Pewter. Y#327 | 300 |

| KM# | Date | Mintage | Identification | Mkt Val |
|---|---|---|---|---|
| Pn27 | 3(1914) | — | 50 Cents. Silver. With L. GIORGI; Yuan Shih-kai, K#655a. | 1,150 |

| KM# | Date | Mintage | Identification | Mkt Val |
|---|---|---|---|---|
| Pn28 | (1914) | — | Dollar. Silver. With L. GIORGI; Yuan Shih-kai, K#642a. | 1,250 |
| Pn29 | (1914) | — | Dollar. Gold. With L. GIORGI, Yuan Shih-kai; K#1558 | 8,500 |
| Pn30 | (1914) | — | Dollar. Silver. Yuan Shih-kai, plumes of hat touch rim; K#644. | 2,500 |
| Pn31 | (1914) | — | Dollar. Silver. With L. GIORGI; Yuan Shih-kai, K#645 | 2,500 |

| KM# | Date | Mintage | Identification | Mkt Val |
|---|---|---|---|---|
| Pn32 | 3(1914) | — | Dollar. Silver. K#643 | 2,250 |
| Pn33 | 3(1914) | — | Dollar. Silver. With L. GIORGI; K#643a | 2,250 |
| Pn34 | (1914) | — | Dollar. Copper. Y#322 | 500 |
| Pn35 | (1914) | — | Dollar. Brass. Y#322 | 600 |
| Pn37 | (1914) | — | Dollar. Copper. Y#329 | 450 |
| Pn38 | (1914) | — | Dollar. Brass. Y#329 | 400 |
| PnA39 | (1914) | — | 5 Dollars. K#1517 | 3,500 |
| Pn13 | 3(1914) | — | 5 Cents. Nickel. K#815 | — |
| Pn14 | 3(1914) | — | 5 Cents. Nickel. Plain edge. Essay, K#815a | — |
| Pn15 | 3(1914) | — | 5 Cents. Nickel. Milled edge. Essay, K#815b; with G. L. | — |
| Pn18 | 3(1914) | — | 5 Cents. Pewter. Plain edge. Essay, K#815y | — |
| Pn19 | 3(1914) | — | 5 Cents. Copper. With G. L., essay, K#815z | — |
| Pn36 | (1914) | — | Dollar. Gold. Y#329 | — |

| KM# | Date | Mintage | Identification | Mkt Val |
|---|---|---|---|---|
| PnA13 | (1914) | — | 10 Cash. Copper. With L. GEORGI; Y#309. | 800 |
| Pn41 | 5(1916) | — | 10 Cash. Copper. With L. GIORGI; Y#324.3 | — |
| Pn43 | 5(1916) | — | 20 Cents. Copper. Y#327 | — |
| Pn45 | (1916) | — | Dollar. White Metal. Y#332 | — |
| Pn50 | 1(1916) | — | 10 Dollars. Gold. With L. G.; K#1515a | — |
| Pn51 | 1(1916) | — | 10 Dollars. Copper. With L. G.; K#1515y | — |
| Pn54 | 1(1916) | — | 10 Dollars. Silver. Y#333 | — |
| Pn39 | 5(1916) | — | 1/2 Cent. Copper. Without center hole; Y#323 | 350 |

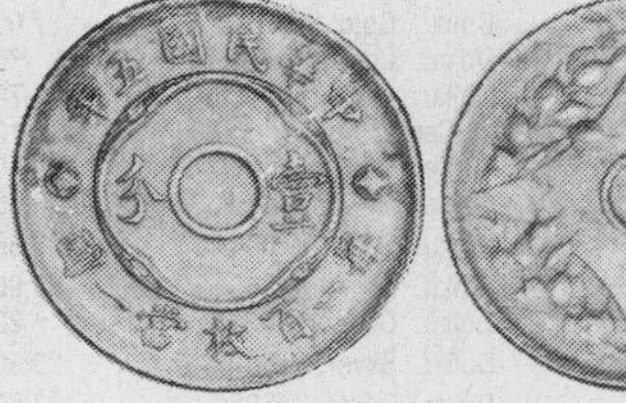

| KM# | Date | Mintage | Identification | Mkt Val |
|---|---|---|---|---|
| Pn40 | 5(1916) | — | 10 Cash. Copper. Without center hole; Y#324 | 400 |

| KM# | Date | Mintage | Identification | Mkt Val |
|---|---|---|---|---|
| Pn42 | 5(1916) | — | 20 Cash. Copper. Hsu44 | 650 |
| Pn44 | (1916) | — | Dollar. Gold. Y#332 | 6,000 |
| Pn47 | (1916) | — | Dollar. Silver. With L. GIORGI; plumes don't touch rim; K#663a. | 17,500 |
| Pn48 | (1916) | — | Dollar. Silver. With L. GIORGI; K#663d | 10,000 |
| Pn52 | (1916) | — | Dollar. Silver. Plumes of hat touch rim; K#664 | 3,750 |
| Pn53 | (1916) | — | Dollar. Gold. With L. GIORGI; K#1560 | 20,000 |
| Pn55 | 1(1916) | — | 10 Dollars. Copper. Y#333 | 375 |
| Pn56 | 8(1919) | — | 10 Cash. Copper. Hsu29 | 1,000 |
| Pn57 | 8(1919) | — | 10 Cash. Copper. Hsu30 | 1,000 |
| Pn59 | 8(1919) | — | 10 Dollars. Copper. Y#330 | 325 |
| Pn60 | 8(1919) | — | 10 Dollars. Brass. Y#330 | 325 |
| Pn61 | 8(1919) | — | 20 Dollars. Copper. Y#331 | 485 |
| PnA62 | 9(1920) | — | 50 Cents. Gold. Ni Szh Ching | 6,000 |
| PnB62 | 9(1920) | — | Dollar. Brass. K#666v | 300 |
| PnC62 | 9(1920) | — | Dollar. Pewter. K#666y | 200 |
| Pn62 | 10(1921) | — | Dollar. Gold. K#676 | 6,500 |

| KM# | Date | Mintage | Identification | Mkt Val |
|---|---|---|---|---|
| Pn63 | 10(1921) | — | Dollar. Silver. Reeded edge. K#676a.1 | 900 |
| Pn64 | 10(1921) | — | Dollar. Silver. Plain edge. K#676a.2 | 750 |
| Pn65 | 10(1921) | — | Dollar. Gold. Reeded edge. K#1570 | 9,350 |
| Pn66 | 10(1921) | — | Dollar. Gold. Plain edge. K#1570a | 9,350 |
| Pn67 | (1923) | — | Dollar. Gold. K#1572 | 9,900 |
| Pn68 | (1923) | — | Dollar. Copper. K#677x | 450 |
| Pn69 | (1923) | — | Dollar. Brass. K#677y | 450 |
| Pn70 | 12(1923) | — | Dollar. Gold. Y#336 | 8,500 |
| Pn71 | 12(1923) | — | Dollar. Copper. Y#336 | — |
| Pn72 | 12(1923) | — | Dollar. Gold. Y#336.1 | — |
| Pn73 | (1924) | — | Dollar. Gold. K#1577 | 7,000 |
| Pn74 | (1924) | — | Dollar. Copper. K#683x | 700 |
| Pn75 | (1924) | — | Dollar. Pewter. K#683y | 700 |
| Pn76 | 15(1926) | — | 10 Cents. Copper. Y#334 | 125 |
| Pn77 | 15(1926) | — | 10 Cents. Lead. Y#334 | 90.00 |
| Pn78 | 15(1926) | — | 20 Cents. Copper. Y#335 | 65.00 |
| PnA79 | 15(1926) | — | Dollar. Silver. K#604 | 82,500 |
| Pn79 | 15(1926) | — | Dollar. Silver. K#685 | 20,900 |
| Pn83 | (1927) | — | Dollar. Copper. Y#318 | 225 |
| Pn84 | (1927) | — | Dollar. Silver. K#687 | 25,000 |
| Pn85 | 16(1927) | — | Dollar. Silver. K#686 | 27,500 |
| Pn80 | 16(1927) | — | 10 Cents. Copper. Y#339 | — |
| Pn81 | 16(1927) | — | 10 Cents. Gold. Y#339 | — |
| Pn82 | (1927) | — | Dollar. Gold. Y#318 | — |
| Pn86 | (1928) | — | 20 Cash. Copper. Y#337 | — |
| Pn87 | (1928) | — | 20 Cash. Copper. Similar to 1 Chiao. | — |

| KM# | Date | Mintage | Identification | Mkt Val |
|---|---|---|---|---|
| Pn90 | 17(1928) | — | Dollar. Silver. K#688 | 4,500 |
| Pn91 | 17(1928) | — | Dollar. Copper. K#688x | 3,500 |
| PnA92 | 17(1928) | — | Dollar. Gold. K#688z | 19,800 |
| Pn92 | 17(1928) | — | Dollar. Pewter. K#688y | 6,500 |
| Pn94 | 18(1929) | — | 10 Cents. Copper-Nickel. Vienna; K#617yVI | 850 |

| KM# | Date | Mintage | Identification | Mkt Val |
|---|---|---|---|---|
| Pn97 | 18(1929) | — | Dollar. Silver. Italian; K#614 | 1,250 |
| Pn98 | 18(1929) | — | Dollar. Silver. With designer's name. K#614a | 2,500 |

| KM# | Date | Mintage | Identification | Mkt Val |
|---|---|---|---|---|
| Pn99 | 18(1929) | — | Dollar. Silver. English; K#615 | 650 |

| KM# | Date | Mintage | Identification | Mkt Val |
|---|---|---|---|---|
| Pn100 | 18(1929) | — | Dollar. Silver. American; K#616 | 600 |
| Pn101 | 18(1929) | — | Dollar. Silver. Austrian; K#61 | 600 |
| Pn102 | 18(1929) | — | Dollar. Silver. Japanese; K#618 | 900 |

**Note:** In 1929 China invited several mints to submit designs for a new Sun Yat-sen Dollar, with his bust on one side and a junk on the other. All designs were very much alike, differing mainly in details of the portrait, the waves, and the junk.

| KM# | Date | Mintage | Identification | Mkt Val |
|---|---|---|---|---|
| Pn103 | 18(1929) | — | 10 Cents. Silver. K#617yIII | 850 |
| Pn104 | 18(1929) | — | 20 Cents. Silver. K#617yII | 850 |
| Pn105 | 18(1929) | — | 50 Cents. Silver. K#617yI | 850 |
| Pn106 | 18(1929) | — | Dollar. Silver. K#610 | 11,000 |
| Pn107 | 18(1929) | — | 20 Cents. Silver. K#611 | 5,000 |
| Pn93 | 18(1929) | — | 20 Cents. Silver. K#611 | — |
| Pn95 | 18(1929) | — | 20 Cents. Copper-Nickel. Vienna; K#617yV | — |
| Pn96 | 18(1929) | — | 50 Cents. Copper-Nickel. Vienna; K#617yIV | — |
| Pn108 | 18(1929) | — | Dollar. Silver. Wreath. K#612 | — |
| Pn109 | (1929) | — | Dollar. Silver. Memento. K#620 | — |
| Pn110 | (1929) | — | Dollar. Copper. K#620x | — |
| Pn111 | (1929) | — | Dollar. White Metal. K#620y | — |
| Pn112 | (1929) | — | Dollar. Silver. Wreath. K#620k | — |
| Pn113 | (1929) | — | Dollar. White Metal. K#620m | — |
| Pn114 | 21(1932) | — | Cent. Bronze. | — |
| Pn115 | 21(1932) | — | Cent. Bronze. Without center hole | — |
| Pn136 | 21(1932) | — | Dollar. Copper. K#628x | — |
| Pn118 | 21(1932) | — | 2 Cents. Nickel. Milled edge. K#830 | 1,200 |
| Pn119 | 21(1932) | — | 2 Cents. Nickel. Plain edge. K#830a | 1,200 |
| Pn120 | 21(1932) | — | 2 Cents. Nickel. Without center hole; K#830b | 2,000 |
| Pn121 | 21(1932) | — | 5 Cents. Nickel. Milled edge. K#829 | 550 |
| Pn122 | 21(1932) | — | 5 Cents. Nickel. Plain edge. K#829a | 550 |
| Pn123 | 21(1932) | — | 5 Cents. Nickel. Without center; K#829b | 550 |
| Pn137 | 21(1932) | — | Dollar. Copper. Y#344 | 275 |
| Pn138 | 22(1933) | — | Dollar. Copper. Y#345 | — |
| Pn139 | 23(1934) | — | Dollar. Copper. Y#345 | — |

| KM# | Date | Mintage | Identification | Mkt Val |
|---|---|---|---|---|
| Pn141 | 24(1935) | — | 5 Cents. Copper. K#833x | — |
| Pn143 | 24(1935) | — | 10 Cents. Copper. K#832x | — |
| Pn145 | 24(1935) | — | 20 Cents. Copper. K#831x | — |
| PnA146 | 24(1935) | — | 1/2 Dollar. Silver. K#625k | — |
| PnB146 | 24(1935) | — | 1/2 Dollar. Copper. K#625x | — |
| Pn146 | 24(1935) | — | Dollar. Silver. K#625 | — |
| Pn147 | 24(1935) | — | Dollar. Copper. Y#345 | — |
| Pn140 | 24(1935) | — | 5 Cents. Nickel. K#833 | 400 |

| KM# | Date | Mintage | Identification | Mkt Val |
|---|---|---|---|---|
| Pn142 | 24(1935) | — | 10 Cents. Nickel. K#832 | 400 |
| Pn144 | 24(1935) | — | 20 Cents. Nickel. K#831 | 400 |
| Pn146a | 24(1935) | — | Dollar. Copper Or Brass. Reduced size Pn146 | 1,550 |
| Pn157 | 25(1936) | — | 10 Cents. Nickel. Character "Ch'ing" in field or on portrait. | 450 |
| Pn158 | 25(1936) | — | 10 Cents. Nickel. Character "P'ing" in field or on portrait. | 450 |
| Pn159 | 25(1936) | — | 10 Cents. Nickel. Character "Ch'ing" on side of portrait. | 450 |
| Pn160 | 25(1936) | — | 10 Cents. Nickel. Character "P'ing" on side of portrait. | 450 |
| Pn168 | 25(1936) | — | 20 Cents. Pewter. Y#350 | 75.00 |

| KM# | Date | Mintage | Identification | Mkt Val |
|---|---|---|---|---|
| Pn174 | 25(1936) | — | Dollar. Silver. K#632 | 4,000 |

| KM# | Date | Mintage | Identification | Mkt Val |
|---|---|---|---|---|
| Pn178 | 25(1936) | — | Dollar. Silver. Chiang Kai-shek | 25,000 |
| Pn179 | 25(1936) | — | Dollar. Copper. Chiang Kai-shek | 7,500 |
| Pn148 | 25//1936 | — | Mei. Copper. Character "Chin". | — |
| Pn149 | 25//1936 | — | Mei. Copper. | — |
| Pn150 | 25//1936 | — | 2 Mei. Copper. | — |
| Pn151 | 25//1936 | — | 5 Mei. Copper. | — |
| Pn152 | 25//1936 | — | 10 Mei. Copper. | — |
| Pn153 | 25//1936 | — | 50 Mei. Copper. | — |
| Pn154 | 25//1936 | — | 20 Wen. Copper. | — |
| Pn155 | 25//1936 | — | Fen. Copper. | — |
| Pn156 | 25(1936) | — | 5 Cents. Copper. Y#348 | — |

| KM# | Date | Mintage | Identification | Mkt Val |
|---|---|---|---|---|
| Pn161 | 25(1936) | — | 10 Cents. Copper. Y#349 | — |
| Pn162 | 25(1936) | — | 10 Cents. Aluminum. Y#349 | — |
| Pn163 | 25(1936) | — | 10 Cents. Aluminum-Bronze. Y#349 | — |
| Pn164 | 25(1936) | — | 10 Cents. Lead. Y#349 | — |
| Pn165 | 25(1936) | — | 20 Cents. Copper. Y#350 | — |
| Pn166 | 25(1936) | — | 20 Cents. Aluminum. Y#350 | — |
| Pn167 | 25(1936) | — | 20 Cents. Aluminum-Bronze. Y#350 | — |
| Pn169 | 25(1936) | — | 50 Cents. Silver. K#635 | — |
| Pn170 | 25(1936) | — | 50 Cents. Silver. K#633 | — |
| Pn171 | 25(1936) | — | 50 Cents. Silver. Similar to K#633 without Greek border. | — |
| Pn172 | 25(1936) | — | Dollar. Silver. K#634 | — |
| Pn173 | 25(1936) | — | Dollar. Silver. Similar to K#632 without Greek border. | — |
| Pn175 | 25(1936) | — | Dollar. Copper. K#632x | — |
| Pn176 | 25(1936) | — | Dollar. Nickel. K#632y | — |
| Pn177 | 25(1936) | — | Dollar. Brass. K#632z | — |
| PnA155 | 25//1936 | — | 1/2 Fen. Copper. Character "P'ing" lower. | — |

**Note:** This may also exist with character under spade on reverse

| KM# | Date | Mintage | Identification | Mkt Val |
|---|---|---|---|---|
| PnA156 | 25//1936 | — | Fen. Copper. Character "P'ing" lower. | — |
| PnB156 | 25//1936 | — | Fen. Copper. Character "P'ing" under spade. | — |
| PnC156 | 25//1936 | — | Fen. Copper. Character "Ch'ing" lower. | — |
| PnD156 | 25//1936 | — | Fen. Copper. Character "Ch'ing" under spade. | — |
| Pn183 | 26(1937) | — | 20 Cents. Nickel. Y#350.1 | — |
| Pn184 | 26(1937)S | — | 50 Cents. Silver. K#637 | — |
| Pn185 | 26(1937)S | — | Dollar. Silver. K#636 | — |
| Pn180 | 26(1937) | — | 5 Cents. Nickel. Y#348.2 | — |
| Pn181 | 26(1937) | — | 10 Cents. Nickel. "P'ing" on side of portrait; Y#349.7 | — |
| Pn189 | 27(1938) | — | 20 Cents. Pewter. Y#350 | 150 |
| Pn186 | 27(1938) | — | 5 Cents. Copper. Y#348 | — |
| Pn187 | 27(1938) | — | 10 Cents. Copper. Y#349 | — |
| Pn188 | 27(1938) | — | 20 Cents. Copper. Y#350 | — |
| Pn190 | 28(1939) | — | 5 Cents. Copper. Y#348 | — |
| Pn191 | 28(1939) | — | 5 Cents. Brass. Y#348 | — |
| PnA192 | 28(1939) | — | 20 Cents. Copper. K#857x | 175 |
| PnB192 | 29(1940) | — | 1/2 Dollar. Copper. | 250 |

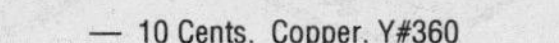

| KM# | Date | Mintage | Identification | Mkt Val |
|---|---|---|---|---|
| Pn192 | 30(1941) | — | 10 Cents. Copper. Y#360 | 250 |

| KM# | Date | Mintage | Identification | Mkt Val |
|---|---|---|---|---|
| PnA194 | 30(1941) | — | 20 Cents. Nickel. K#863 IV | 250 |
| PnC194 | 30(1941) | — | 1/2 Dollar. Nickel. K#863 III | 500 |
| Pn193 | 30(1941) | — | 10 Cents. Brass. Y#360 | — |
| PnB194 | 30(1941) | — | 1/2 Dollar. Silver. K#696x | — |
| Pn194 | 31(1942) | — | 10 Cents. Copper-Nickel. Character "Kuei" below the spade. | — |
| Pn195 | 31(1942) | — | 10 Cents. Copper. Y#360 | — |
| Pn196 | 31(1942) | — | 10 Cents. Brass. Y#360 | — |
| Pn197 | 31(1942) | — | 20 Cents. Copper-Nickel. Character "Kuei" below spade. | — |
| Pn198 | 31(1942) | — | 20 Cents. Copper. Y#361 | — |
| Pn199 | 31(1942) | — | 50 Cents. Copper-Nickel. Character "Kuei" between legs of space. K#866m | — |
| Pn200 | 31(1942) | — | 50 Cents. Copper. Y#362 | 200 |
| Pn201 | 31(1942) | — | 50 Cents. Bronze. Y#362 | 200 |
| Pn202 | 31(1942) | — | 50 Cents. Silver. Y#362 | 500 |
| Pn203 | 32(1943) | — | 50 Cents. Copper. Y#362 | 200 |
| Pn204 | 32(1943) | — | 50 Cents. Bronze. Y#362 | 200 |
| PnA203 | 32(1943) | — | 50 Cents. Copper-Nickel. Character "Kuei" between legs of spade. | — |
| PnA205 | 37(1948) | — | 50 Cents. Silver. Ch'ing right; K#698 | — |
| Pn205 | 37(1948) | — | Dollar. Silver. K#637yII | — |
| Pn206 | 37(1948) | — | 2 Dollars. Silver. K#637yI; denomination | 200 |

## PATTERNS

### Gold Standard

KM#Pn124-135 were intended to be a gold standard coinage, but was not adopted. Though inscribed "One Yuan Dollar", the proposed unit was called a "Sun".

| KM# | Date | Mintage | Identification | Mkt Val |
|---|---|---|---|---|
| Pn124 | 21(1932) | — | 10 Cents. Silver. K#631 | — |
| Pn125 | 21(1932) | — | 10 Cents. Silver. Plain edge. K#631a | — |
| Pn126 | 21(1932) | — | 10 Cents. Copper. K#631 | — |
| Pn127 | 21(1932) | — | 20 Cents. Silver. Milled edge. K#630 | — |
| Pn128 | 21(1932) | — | 20 Cents. Silver. Plain edge. K#630a | — |
| Pn129 | 21(1932) | — | 20 Cents. Copper. K#630x | — |
| Pn132 | 21(1932) | — | 1/2 Dollar. Copper. K#629x | — |
| Pn133 | 21(1932) | — | Dollar. Silver. Milled edge. K#628 | — |
| Pn130 | 21(1932) | — | 1/2 Dollar. Silver. Milled edge. K#629 | 4,000 |
| Pn131 | 21(1932) | — | 1/2 Dollar. Silver. Plain edge. K#629a | 4,000 |
| Pn134 | 21(1932) | — | Dollar. Silver. Plain edge. K#628a | 10,000 |
| Pn135 | 21(1932) | — | Dollar. Silver. Cherry blossom edge | 10,000 |

## TRIAL STRIKES

| KM# | Date | Mintage | Identification | Mkt Val |
|---|---|---|---|---|
| TS1 | (1912) | — | Dollar. Silver. Uniface. Chin Techuan; K#672b | 8,000 |
| TS2 | 37(1948) | — | 50 Cents. Silver. 4.9800 g. K#698w | 750 |

# TAIWAN

## REPUBLIC

### STANDARD COINAGE

**CHIAO** Y# 531 **Composition:** Bronze **Obverse:** Sun Yat-sen

| Date | Mintage | F | VF | XF | Unc | BU |
|---|---|---|---|---|---|---|
| 38(1949) | 157,600,000 | 0.10 | 0.30 | 1.00 | 4.00 | — |

**CHIAO** Y# 533 **Composition:** Aluminum

| Date | Mintage | F | VF | XF | Unc | BU |
|---|---|---|---|---|---|---|
| 44(1955) | 583,980,000 | — | 0.10 | 0.15 | 1.00 | — |

**CHIAO** Y# 545 **Composition:** Aluminum

| Date | Mintage | F | VF | XF | Unc | BU |
|---|---|---|---|---|---|---|
| 56(1967) | 89,999,000 | — | 0.10 | 0.15 | 0.75 | — |
| 59(1970) | 30,000,000 | — | 0.10 | 0.25 | 1.00 | — |
| 60(1971) | 19,925,000 | — | 0.20 | 0.40 | 1.50 | — |
| 61(1972) | 11,141,000 | 0.10 | 0.40 | 0.60 | 2.00 | — |
| 62(1973) | 111,400,000 | — | — | 0.10 | 0.75 | — |
| 63(1974) | 71,930,000 | — | 0.10 | 0.25 | 1.00 | — |

**2 CHIAO** Y# 534 **Composition:** Aluminum **Obverse:** Sun Yat-sen

| Date | Mintage | F | VF | XF | Unc | BU |
|---|---|---|---|---|---|---|
| 39(1950) | 327,495,000 | — | 0.10 | 0.50 | 3.00 | — |

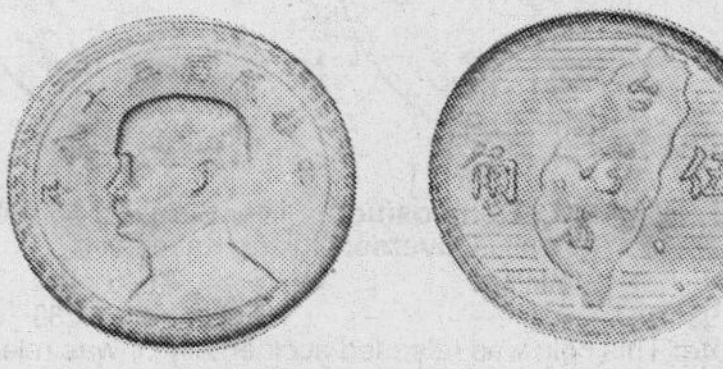

**5 CHIAO** Y# 532 **Weight:** 5.0000 g. **Composition:** 0.7200 Silver .1157 oz. ASW **Obverse:** Sun Yat-sen

| Date | Mintage | F | VF | XF | Unc | BU |
|---|---|---|---|---|---|---|
| ND38(1949) | — | 1.50 | 2.00 | 3.50 | 5.00 | — |

**5 CHIAO** Y# 535 **Composition:** Brass

| Date | Mintage | F | VF | XF | Unc | BU |
|---|---|---|---|---|---|---|
| 43(1954) | 279,624,000 | — | 0.10 | 0.25 | 1.00 | — |

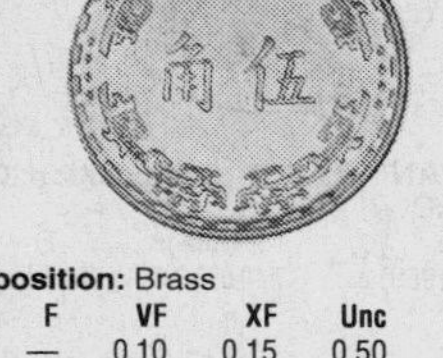

**5 CHIAO** Y# 546 **Composition:** Brass

| Date | Mintage | F | VF | XF | Unc | BU |
|---|---|---|---|---|---|---|
| 56(1967) | 109,999,000 | — | 0.10 | 0.15 | 0.50 | — |
| 59(1970) | 6,010,000 | 0.15 | 0.30 | 0.60 | 1.25 | — |
| 60(1971) | 4,434,000 | 0.20 | 0.40 | 0.80 | 1.50 | — |
| 61(1972) | 21,171,000 | — | 0.10 | 0.20 | 1.00 | — |
| 62(1973) | 88,840,000 | — | 0.10 | 0.20 | 1.00 | — |
| 69(1980) | 3,972,000 | — | 0.10 | 0.20 | 1.00 | — |
| 70(1981) | 100,000,000 | — | 0.10 | 0.20 | 1.00 | — |

**5 CHIAO** **Y# 550** **Composition:** Bronze

| Date | Mintage | F | VF | XF | Unc | BU |
|---|---|---|---|---|---|---|
| 70(1981) | 103,800,000 | — | 0.10 | 0.20 | 1.00 | — |
| 70(1981) Proof | — | Value: 10.00 | | | | |
| 75(1986) | 22,000,000 | — | 0.10 | 0.20 | 1.00 | — |
| 77(1988) | 10,000,000 | — | 0.15 | 0.30 | 1.25 | — |

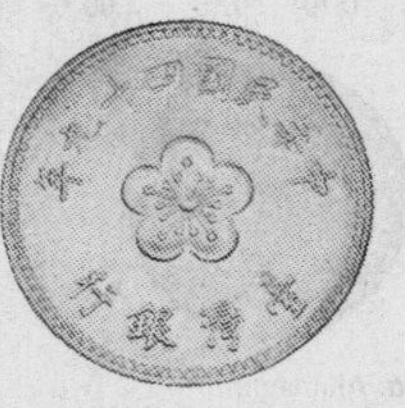

**YUAN** **Y# 536** **Composition:** Copper-Nickel-Zinc

| Date | Mintage | F | VF | XF | Unc | BU |
|---|---|---|---|---|---|---|
| 49(1960) | 321,717,000 | — | 0.10 | 0.20 | 0.50 | — |
| 59(1970) | 48,800,000 | 0.10 | 0.20 | 0.50 | 1.00 | — |
| 60(1971) | 41,532,000 | 0.10 | 0.20 | 0.50 | 1.00 | — |
| 61(1972) | 105,309,000 | — | 0.10 | 0.20 | 0.50 | — |
| 62(1973) | 353,924,000 | — | 0.10 | 0.20 | 0.50 | — |
| 63(1974) | 535,605,000 | — | 0.10 | 0.20 | 0.50 | — |
| 64(1975) | 456,874,000 | — | 0.10 | 0.20 | 0.50 | — |
| 65(1976) | 634,497,000 | — | 0.10 | 0.20 | 0.50 | — |
| 66(1977) | 116,900,000 | — | 0.10 | 0.20 | 0.50 | — |
| 67(1978) | 104,245,000 | — | 0.10 | 0.20 | 0.50 | — |
| 68(1979) | — | 0.10 | 0.20 | 0.50 | 0.80 | — |
| 69(1980) | 113,900,000 | — | 0.10 | 0.20 | 0.50 | — |

**YUAN** **Y# A537** **Composition:** Silver **Subject:** 50th Anniversary of the Republic **Obverse:** Chiang Kai-shek

| Date | Mintage | F | VF | XF | Unc | BU |
|---|---|---|---|---|---|---|
| ND50(1961) | — | — | — | — | 280 | — |

**Note:** This coin was released accidentally or was released and quickly withdrawn and is very scarce today

**YUAN** **Y# 543** **Composition:** Copper-Nickel **Subject:** 80th Birthday of Chiang Kai-shek

| Date | Mintage | F | VF | XF | Unc | BU |
|---|---|---|---|---|---|---|
| ND55(1966) | — | 0.15 | 0.25 | 0.40 | 1.00 | — |

**YUAN** **Y# 547** **Composition:** Copper-Nickel-Zinc **Series:** F.A.O

| Date | Mintage | F | VF | XF | Unc | BU |
|---|---|---|---|---|---|---|
| 58(1969) | 10,000,000 | 0.15 | 0.25 | 0.40 | 1.00 | — |

**YUAN** **Y# 551** **Composition:** Bronze **Obverse:** Chiang Kai-shek

| Date | Mintage | F | VF | XF | Unc | BU |
|---|---|---|---|---|---|---|
| 70(1981) | 1,080,000,000 | — | — | 0.10 | 0.15 | — |
| 70(1981) Proof | — | Value: 12.50 | | | | |
| 71(1982) | 780,000,000 | — | — | 0.10 | 0.15 | — |
| 72(1983) | 420,000,000 | — | — | 0.10 | 0.15 | — |
| 73(1984) | 110,000,000 | — | — | 0.10 | 0.15 | — |
| 74(1985) | 200,000,000 | — | — | 0.10 | 0.15 | — |
| 75(1986) | 200,000,000 | — | — | 0.10 | 0.15 | — |
| 76(1987) | 110,000,000 | — | — | 0.10 | 0.15 | — |
| 77(1988) | 40,000,000 | — | — | 0.20 | 0.50 | — |
| 81(1992) | — | — | — | 0.15 | 0.25 | — |
| 82(1993) | — | — | — | 0.15 | 0.25 | — |
| 83(1994) | — | — | — | 0.15 | 0.25 | — |
| 84(1995) | — | — | — | 0.15 | 0.25 | — |
| 85(1996) | — | — | — | 0.15 | 0.25 | — |

**5 YUAN** **Y# 537** **Composition:** Copper-Nickel **Obverse:** Sun Yat-sen

| Date | Mintage | F | VF | XF | Unc | BU |
|---|---|---|---|---|---|---|
| ND54(1965) | — | 0.25 | 0.75 | 1.50 | 5.00 | — |

**5 YUAN** **Y# 548** **Composition:** Copper-Nickel **Obverse:** Chiang Kai-shek

| Date | Mintage | F | VF | XF | Unc | BU |
|---|---|---|---|---|---|---|
| 59(1970) | 12,360,000 | 0.15 | 0.40 | 0.80 | 1.50 | — |
| 60(1971) | 20,575,000 | 0.15 | 0.35 | 0.50 | 1.00 | — |
| 61(1972) | 27,998,000 | 0.15 | 0.35 | 0.50 | 1.00 | — |
| 62(1973) | 50,122,000 | 0.15 | 0.35 | 0.50 | 0.80 | — |
| 63(1974) | 418,068,000 | 0.15 | 0.35 | 0.50 | 0.80 | — |
| 64(1975) | 39,520,000 | 0.15 | 0.35 | 0.50 | 0.80 | — |
| 65(1976) | 140,000,000 | 0.15 | 0.35 | 0.50 | 0.80 | — |
| 66(1977) | 50,260,000 | 0.15 | 0.35 | 0.50 | 0.80 | — |
| 67(1978) | 78,082,000 | 0.15 | 0.35 | 0.50 | 0.80 | — |
| 68(1979) | — | 0.15 | 0.35 | 0.50 | 0.80 | — |
| 69(1980) | 273,000,000 | 0.15 | 0.35 | 0.50 | 0.80 | — |
| 70(1981) | 162,000,000 | 0.15 | 0.35 | 0.50 | 0.80 | — |

**5 YUAN** **Y# 552** **Composition:** Copper-Nickel

| Date | Mintage | F | VF | XF | Unc | BU |
|---|---|---|---|---|---|---|
| 70(1981) | 522,432,000 | — | 0.15 | 0.20 | 0.50 | — |
| 70(1981) Proof | — | Value: 12.50 | | | | |
| 71(1982) | 6,600,000 | — | 0.15 | 0.20 | 0.50 | — |
| 72(1983) | 34,000,000 | — | 0.15 | 0.20 | 0.50 | — |
| 73(1984) | 280,000,000 | — | 0.15 | 0.20 | 0.50 | — |
| 77(1988) | 200,000,000 | — | 0.15 | 0.20 | 0.50 | — |
| 78(1989) | — | — | 0.15 | 0.20 | 0.50 | — |

**10 YUAN** **Y# 538** **Composition:** Copper-Nickel **Obverse:** Sun Yat-sen

| Date | Mintage | F | VF | XF | Unc | BU |
|---|---|---|---|---|---|---|
| ND54(1965) | — | 0.50 | 1.00 | 2.00 | 6.00 | — |

**10 YUAN** **Y# 553** **Composition:** Copper-Nickel **Obverse:** Chiang Kai-shek

| Date | Mintage | F | VF | XF | Unc | BU |
|---|---|---|---|---|---|---|
| 70(1981) | 123,000,000 | — | 0.30 | 0.40 | 0.65 | — |
| 70(1981) Proof | — | Value: 15.00 | | | | |
| 71(1982) | 361,000,000 | — | 0.30 | 0.40 | 0.65 | — |
| 72(1983) | 196,000,000 | — | 0.30 | 0.40 | 0.65 | — |
| 73(1984) | 220,000,000 | — | 0.30 | 0.40 | 0.65 | — |
| Note: | | | | | | |
| 74(1985) | 200,000,000 | — | 0.30 | 0.40 | 0.65 | — |
| 75(1986) | 100,000,000 | — | 0.30 | 0.40 | 0.65 | — |
| 76(1987) | 90,000,000 | — | 0.30 | 0.40 | 0.65 | — |
| 77(1988) | 100,000,000 | — | 0.30 | 0.40 | 0.65 | — |
| 78(1989) | — | — | 0.30 | 0.40 | 0.65 | — |
| 79(1990) | — | — | 0.30 | 0.40 | 0.65 | — |
| 80(1991) | — | — | 0.30 | 0.40 | 0.65 | — |
| 81(1992) | — | — | 0.30 | 0.40 | 0.65 | — |
| 82(1993) | — | — | 0.30 | 0.40 | 0.65 | — |
| 83(1994) | — | — | 0.30 | 0.40 | 0.65 | — |

**10 YUAN** **Y# 555** **Composition:** Copper-Nickel **Subject:** 50th Anniversary - Taiwan's Liberation from Japan

| Date | Mintage | F | VF | XF | Unc | BU |
|---|---|---|---|---|---|---|
| ND84(1995) | — | — | — | — | 2.25 | — |

**10 YUAN** **Y# 558** **Composition:** Copper-Nickel **Subject:** 50th Anniversary - Taiwan Yuan (Dollar) **Obverse:** Coins **Reverse:** Anniversary dates above denomination

| Date | Mintage | F | VF | XF | Unc | BU |
|---|---|---|---|---|---|---|
| ND88(1999) | 30,000,000 | — | — | — | 2.75 | — |

**10 YUAN** **Y# 560** **Weight:** 7.5000 g. **Composition:** Copper-Nickel **Subject:** Year of the Dragon **Obverse:** Dragon **Reverse:** Stylized dragon above denomination

| Date | Mintage | F | VF | XF | Unc | BU |
|---|---|---|---|---|---|---|
| 89(2000) | — | — | — | — | 2.75 | — |

**10 YUAN** **Y# 567** **Weight:** 7.4300 g. **Composition:** Copper-Nickel **Subject:** 90th Anniversary of the Republic **Obverse:** Bust of Sun Yat-sen facing. **Reverse:** Holographic design and denomination. **Edge:** Reeded. **Size:** 26 mm.

| Date | Mintage | F | VF | XF | Unc | BU |
|---|---|---|---|---|---|---|
| 90 (2001) | — | — | — | — | 2.50 | — |

**20 YUAN** **Y# 565** **Ring Composition:** Brass **Center Weight:** 8.4000 g. **Center Composition:** Copper-Nickel **Obverse:** Male portrait. **Reverse:** Three boats. **Edge:** Reeded. **Size:** 26.8 mm.

| Date | Mintage | F | VF | XF | Unc | BU |
|---|---|---|---|---|---|---|
| 90 (2001) | — | — | — | — | 3.50 | — |

**50 YUAN** **Y# 539** **Weight:** 17.1000 g. **Composition:** 0.7500 Silver .4123 oz. ASW **Obverse:** Sun Yat-sen

| Date | Mintage | F | VF | XF | Unc | BU |
|---|---|---|---|---|---|---|
| ND54(1965) | — | — | — | 10.00 | 20.00 | — |

**50 YUAN** **Y# 554** **Composition:** Brass

| Date | Mintage | F | VF | XF | Unc | BU |
|---|---|---|---|---|---|---|
| 81(1992) | — | — | 0.50 | 1.00 | 3.50 | — |
| 82(1993) | — | — | 0.50 | 1.00 | 3.50 | — |

**50 YUAN** **Y# 556** **Ring Composition:** Copper-Nickel **Center Composition:** Brass **Obverse:** Parliament building

| Date | Mintage | F | VF | XF | Unc | BU |
|---|---|---|---|---|---|---|
| 85(1996) | — | — | — | — | 5.75 | — |
| 86(1997) | — | — | — | — | 5.75 | — |

**50 YUAN** **Y# 562** **Weight:** 15.5680 g. **Composition:** 0.9990 Silver .5004 oz. ASW **Subject:** Late President - Chiang Ching-Kuo **Obverse:** Bust of Ching-kuo facing. **Reverse:** Mausoleum above denomination. **Edge:** Reeded. **Size:** 33 mm.

| Date | Mintage | F | VF | XF | Unc | BU |
|---|---|---|---|---|---|---|
| 87 (1998) | 70,000 | — | — | — | 25.00 | — |

**50 YUAN** **Y# 559** **Weight:** 15.5500 g. **Composition:** 0.9250 Silver .4624 oz. ASW **Subject:** 50 Years - Taiwan Yuan (Dollar) **Obverse:** Coins **Reverse:** Denomination including coin design and dates

| Date | Mintage | F | VF | XF | Unc | BU |
|---|---|---|---|---|---|---|
| 88(1999) | 390,000 | — | — | — | 20.00 | — |

**50 YUAN** **Y# 564** **Weight:** 15.5680 g. **Composition:** 0.9990 Silver .5004 oz. ASW **Subject:** Year 2000 **Obverse:** Celestial globe. **Reverse:** Dragon. **Edge:** Reeded. **Size:** 33 mm.

| Date | Mintage | F | VF | XF | Unc | BU |
|---|---|---|---|---|---|---|
| 89 (2000) | 120,000 | — | — | — | 25.00 | — |

**100 YUAN** **Y# 540** **Weight:** 22.2100 g. **Composition:** 0.7500 Silver .5335 oz. ASW **Obverse:** Sun Yat-sen

| Date | Mintage | F | VF | XF | Unc | BU |
|---|---|---|---|---|---|---|
| 54(1965) | — | — | — | 12.50 | 25.00 | — |

**100 YUAN** **Y# 561** **Weight:** 15.5680 g. **Composition:** 0.9990 Silver .5000 oz. ASW **Subject:** 50th Anniversary - 2-28 Incident **Obverse:** Monument. **Reverse:** Geometrical design. **Edge:** Reeded. **Size:** 33 mm.

| Date | Mintage | F | VF | XF | Unc | BU |
|---|---|---|---|---|---|---|
| ND (1997) | 55,000 | — | — | — | 25.00 | — |

**200 YUAN** **Y# 557** **Weight:** 31.1350 g. **Composition:** 0.9990 Silver 1.0000 oz. ASW **Subject:** First Popular Election Vote **Obverse:** Portrait of President Lee Teng-hui and Vice President Lien Chan **Reverse:** National emblem above text

| Date | Mintage | F | VF | XF | Unc | BU |
|---|---|---|---|---|---|---|
| 85(1996) Proof | — | Value: 65.00 | | | | |

**200 YUAN** **Y# 566** **Weight:** 31.3500 g. **Composition:** 0.9990 Silver 1.0069 oz. ASW **Subject:** Second Popular Vote Presidential Election **Obverse:** Bust of the President and Vice-president. **Reverse:** National emblem above inscription. **Edge:** Reeded. **Size:** 38 mm.

| Date | Mintage | F | VF | XF | Unc | BU |
|---|---|---|---|---|---|---|
| 89 (2000) | — | — | — | — | 75.00 | — |

**1000 YUAN** **Y# 541** **Weight:** 15.0000 g. **Composition:** 0.9000 Gold .4340 oz. AGW **Obverse:** Sun Yat-sen

| Date | Mintage | F | VF | XF | Unc | BU |
|---|---|---|---|---|---|---|
| 54(1965) | — | — | — | — | 275 | — |

**1000 YUAN** Y# 563 **Weight:** 15.5540 g. **Composition:** 0.9990 Gold .5000 oz. AGW **Subject:** Late President - Chiang Ching-kuo **Obverse:** Bust of Ching-kuo facing. **Reverse:** Mausoleum. **Edge:** Reeded. **Size:** 25 mm.

| Date | Mintage | F | VF | XF | Unc | BU |
|---|---|---|---|---|---|---|
| 87 (1998) | 30,000 | — | — | — | 275 | — |

**2000 YUAN** Y# 542 **Weight:** 30.0000 g. **Composition:** 0.9000 Gold .8681 oz. AGW **Obverse:** Sun Yat-sen

| Date | Mintage | F | VF | XF | Unc | BU |
|---|---|---|---|---|---|---|
| 54(1965) | — | — | — | — | 525 | — |

**2000 YUAN** Y# 544 **Weight:** 31.0600 g. **Composition:** 0.9000 Gold .8988 oz. AGW **Subject:** 80th Birthday of Chiang Kai-shek

| Date | Mintage | F | VF | XF | Unc | BU |
|---|---|---|---|---|---|---|
| 55(1966) | — | — | — | — | 550 | — |

## PATTERNS

Yuan System; Including off metal strikes

KG numbers in reference to "Coinage of the Chinese Emigre Government 1949-1957" by E. Kann and D. Graham.

| KM# | Date | Mintage | Identification | Mkt Val |
|---|---|---|---|---|
| Pn1 | 38(1949) | — | Chiao. Bronze. KG#12a | 150 |
| PnA17 | 38(1949) | — | 20 Yuan. Bronze. | 1,200 |
| Pn2 | 38(1949) | — | Chiao. Aluminum. KG#12b | 150 |
| Pn3 | 38(1949) | — | Chiao. Copper. KG#12c | 150 |
| Pn4 | 38(1949) | — | Chiao. Copper. KG#12d | 150 |
| Pn5 | 38(1949) | — | Chiao. Aluminum. K#12e; without reeded edge | 150 |

| KM# | Date | Mintage | Identification | Mkt Val |
|---|---|---|---|---|
| Pn6 | 38(1949) | — | Chiao. Copper. k#13 | 150 |

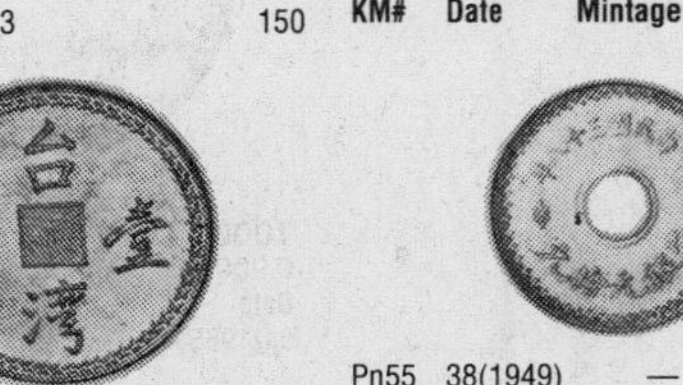

| KM# | Date | Mintage | Identification | Mkt Val |
|---|---|---|---|---|
| Pn7 | 38(1949) | — | Chiao. Copper. KG#14 | 150 |
| Pn8 | 38(1949) | — | 5 Chiao. Aluminum-Bronze. KG#15a | 350 |
| Pn9 | 38(1949) | — | 5 Chiao. Aluminum. KG#15b | 250 |
| Pn10 | 38(1949) | — | 5 Chiao. Silver. KG#16 | 400 |
| Pn11 | 38(1949) | — | 5 Chiao. Copper. KG#16a | 300 |
| Pn12 | 38(1949) | — | 5 Chiao. Silver. KG#17 | 375 |
| Pn13 | 38(1949) | — | 5 Chiao. Silver. KG#18 | 600 |
| Pn14 | 38(1949) | — | 5 Chiao. Silver. KG#19 | 725 |
| Pn15 | 38(1949) | — | 5 Chiao. Silver. KG#20 | 400 |
| Pn16 | 38(1949) | — | Yuan. Silver. KG#21i | 400 |
| Pn17 | 39(1950) | — | 2 Chiao. Aluminum. Reeded edge. KG#21a | 150 |
| Pn18 | 39(1950) | — | 2 Chiao. Aluminum-Bronze. KG#21b | 150 |
| Pn19 | 39(1950) | — | 2 Chiao. Aluminum-Bronze. KG#21c; without reeded edge | 150 |
| Pn20 | 39(1950) | — | 2 Chiao. Copper. KG#21d | 150 |
| Pn21 | 39(1950) | — | Yuan. Silver. | 700 |
| Pn22 | 39(1950) | — | Yuan. Copper-Nickel. | 300 |
| Pn23 | 39(1950) | — | Yuan. Copper-Nickel. | 300 |
| Pn24 | 39(1950) | — | Yuan. Aluminum-Bronze. KG#22a | 200 |
| Pn25 | 39(1950) | — | Yuan. Aluminum. KG#22b | 350 |
| Pn26 | 43(1954) | — | 5 Chiao. Aluminum-Bronze. KG#23 | 300 |
| Pn27 | 43(1954) | — | 5 Chiao. Aluminum-Bronze. Reeded edge. KG#23a | 300 |
| Pn28 | 43(1954) | — | 5 Chiao. Copper. KG#23b | 300 |
| Pn29 | 43(1954) | — | 5 Chiao. Aluminum-Bronze. KG#23c | 300 |
| Pn30 | 43(1954) | — | 5 Chiao. Aluminum-Bronze. KG#24 | 300 |
| Pn31 | 43(1954) | — | 5 Chiao. Aluminum-Bronze. KG#25 | 300 |
| Pn32 | 43(1954) | — | 5 Chiao. Aluminum-Bronze. KG#25a | 300 |
| Pn33 | 43(1954) | — | 5 Chiao. Bronze. KG#26a | 300 |
| Pn34 | 44(1955) | — | Chiao. Aluminum. Simplified "TAI", KG#27a | 175 |
| Pn35 | 44(1955) | — | Chiao. Bronze. KG#27b | 175 |
| Pn36 | 45(1956) | — | 2 Chiao. Copper-Nickel. Y#534 | 175 |
| PnA37 | 45(1956) | — | Yuan. Copper-Nickel. Ocean unlined. | — |
| PnB37 | 45(1956) | — | Yuan. Aluminum-Bronze. Pn37 with simplified "TAI" character. | — |
| Pn37 | 45(1956) | — | Yuan. Copper-Nickel. | 300 |

| KM# | Date | Mintage | Identification | Mkt Val |
|---|---|---|---|---|
| Pn38 | 48(1959) | — | Yuan. Nickel. | 350 |
| Pn39 | 48(1959) | — | Yuan. Nickel-Silver. | 250 |
| Pn40 | 49(1960) | — | Yuan. Nickel-Silver. Y#536 | 250 |
| Pn41 | 49(1960) | — | Yuan. Nickel-Silver. Large flan | 275 |
| Pn42 | 49(1960) | — | Yuan. Nickel-Silver. With Taiwan-sheng | 275 |
| Pn43 | 49(1960) | — | Yuan. Nickel-Silver. With 1 Yuan | 275 |
| Pn44 | 49(1960) | — | Yuan. Nickel-Silver. With 1 Kinmen | 275 |
| Pn45 | 49(1960) | — | 5 Yuan. Nickel. | — |
| Pn46 | 49(1960) | — | 5 Yuan. Nickel. Ancient Chinese symbols | — |
| PnA47 | 50(1961) | — | Yuan. Copper-Nickel. Y#536 | — |
| Pn47 | 50(1961) | — | Yuan. Nickel-Silver. Sun Yat-sen. | 225 |
| Pn48 | 50(1961) | — | Yuan. Nickel-Aluminum. Chiang Kai-shek. | 225 |
| Pn49 | 50(1961) | — | Yuan. Nickel-Silver. Similar to Pn48 but eleven characters above bust. | 225 |
| PnA49 | 50(1961) | — | Yuan. Nickel. Chiang Kai-shek | 225 |
| PnB49 | 50(1961) | — | Yuan. Nickel-Aluminum. Chiang Kai-shek | 225 |
| Pn50 | 51(1962) | — | 5 Yuan. Nickel. | 300 |
| Pn51 | 53(1964) | — | 5 Yuan. Copper-Nickel. | 300 |
| Pn52 | 54(1965) | — | 10 Yuan. Copper-Nickel. Clouds replace mountains. Y#538 | 400 |
| Pn53 | 54(1965) | — | 10 Yuan. Copper-Nickel. Without clouds. Y#538 | 400 |
| Pn54 | 55(1966) | — | 2000 Yuan. Gilt Silver. Madam and President Chiang. Y#544 | 650 |
| Pn65 | 62(1973) | — | 5 Yuan. Gold. Y#548 | 1,250 |
| Pn66 | 64(1975) | — | Yuan. Gold. Y#536 | 850 |
| Pn67 | 64(1975) | — | Yuan. Aluminum. Y#536 | 200 |

## PATTERNS

Tael System; Including off metal strikes

KG numbers in reference to "Coinage of the Chinese Emigre Government 1949-1957" by E. Kann and D. Graham.

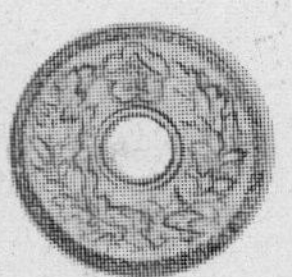

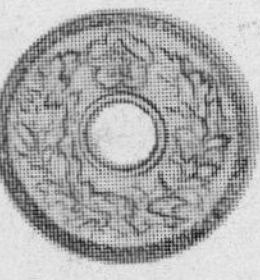

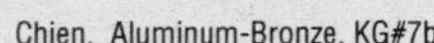

| KM# | Date | Mintage | Identification | Mkt Val |
|---|---|---|---|---|
| Pn55 | 38(1949) | — | Chien. Aluminum-Bronze. KG#7b | 350 |
| Pn56 | 38(1949) | — | Chien. Silver. KG#6a | 500 |
| Pn57 | 38(1949) | — | Chien. Aluminum-Bronze. KG#6b | 350 |
| Pn58 | 38(1949) | — | 2 Chien. Aluminum-Bronze. KG#4b | 350 |

| KM# | Date | Mintage | Identification | Mkt Val |
|---|---|---|---|---|
| Pn59 | 38(1949) | — | 2-1/2 Chien. Aluminum-Bronze. KG#3b | 350 |

| KM# | Date | Mintage | Identification | Mkt Val |
|---|---|---|---|---|
| Pn60 | 38(1949) | — | 5 Chien. Aluminum-Bronze. KG#2b | 350 |
| Pn62 | 45(1956) | — | 2-1/2 Chien. Copper-Nickel. | 250 |
| Pn63 | 45(1956) | — | 2-1/2 Chien. Aluminum-Bronze. | 250 |
| Pn64 | 45(1956) | — | 2-1/2 Chien. Aluminum. | 250 |

## MINT SETS

| KM# | Date | Mintage | Identification | Issue Price | Mkt Val |
|---|---|---|---|---|---|
| MS1 | 1965 (4) | — | Y#537-540 | — | 75.00 |
| MS2 | 88(1999) (2) | 260,000 | Y#558-559 | — | 25.00 |

## PROOF SETS

| KM# | Date | Mintage | Identification | Issue Price | Mkt Val |
|---|---|---|---|---|---|
| PS10 | 90(2001) (5) | 150,000 | Y#550-554 | 29.40 | 35.00 |
| PS2 | 82(1993) (5) | 50,000 | Y#550-554 | 14.75 | 300 |
| PS3 | 83(1994) (5) | 70,000 | Y#550-554 | 14.75 | 80.00 |
| PS4 | 84(1995) (5) | 70,000 | Y#550-554 | 17.65 | 57.50 |
| PS5 | 85(1996) (5) | 70,000 | Y#550-554 | 17.65 | 62.50 |
| PS6 | 86(1997) (5) | 70,000 | Y#550-554 | 17.65 | 62.50 |
| PS7 | 87(1998) (5) | 100,000 | Y#550-554 | 20.60 | 35.00 |
| PS8 | 88(1999) (5) | 100,000 | Y#550-554 | 20.60 | 35.00 |
| PS9 | 89(2000) (5) | 100,000 | Y#550-554 | 22.05 | 62.50 |
| PS1 | 70(1981) (4) | — | Y#550-553 | — | 50.00 |

## CHINA-JAPANESE PUPPET STATES

Shortly after World War I the greatest external threat to the territorial integrity of China was posed by Japan, which urgently needed room for an expanding population and raw materials for its industrial and military machines, and which recognized the necessity of controlling all of China if it was to realize its plan of dominating the rest of the Asiatic and South Sea countries. The Japanese had large investments in Manchuria (a name given by non-Chinese to the three northeastern provinces of China), which allowed them privileges that compromised Chinese sovereignty. The educated of China were not reconciled to Japan's growing power in Manchuria, and the resultant friction occasioned a series of vexing incidents, which Japan decided to circumvent by direct action. On the night of Sept. 18-19, 1931, with a contrived incident for an excuse, Japanese forces seized the city of Mukden (Shenyang), and within a few weeks completely demolished Chinese power north of the Great Wall.

In Feb. 1932, after the Japanese occupation of Manchuria, they set up Manchoukuo as an independent republic. Jehol (Rehe) was occupied by the Japanese in 1933 and added to Manchoukuo. Manchoukuo was established as an empire in 1934 with the deposed Manchu emperor Hsuan T'ung (the late Henry Pu Yi) as the puppet emperor K'ang Te. Lacking the means to face the Japanese armies in the field, the Chinese could only trade space for time.

Not content with confining its control of China to the areas north of the Great Wall, the Japanese launched a major campaign in 1937, and by the fall of 1938 had occupied in addition to Manchuria the provinces of Hopei (Hebei) and Chahar, most of the port cities, and the major cities as far west as Hankow (Hankou), now part of Wuhan. In addition, they dominated or threatened the provinces of Suiyuan, Shansi (Shanxi) and Shantung (Shandong). Still the Chinese did not yield. The struggle was prolonged until the advent of World War II, which brought about the defeat of Japan and the return of the puppet states to Chinese control.

As the victorious Japanese armies swept deeper into China, Japan established central banks under control of the Bank of Japan in the conquered provinces for the purpose of establishing control over banking and finance in the puppet states, and eventually in all of China. These included the Chi Tung Bank, which had its main office in Tientsin (Tianjin) with branches in Peking (Beijing), Chinan (Jinan) and Tangshan, the Federal Reserve Bank of China with its main office in Peking (Beijing) and branches in 37 other cities; and the Hua Hsing Bank with its main office in Shanghai and two branches. The puppet states of Manchukuo, previously detailed in this introduction, and Mengchiang, which comprised a greater part of Inner Mongolia, were also major coin-issuing entities.

## EAST HOPEI

AUTONOMOUS

The Chi Tung Bank was the banking institution of the "East Hopei Anti-Comintern Autonomous Government" established by the Japanese in 1936 to undermine the political position of China in the northwest provinces. It issued both coins and notes between 1937 and 1939 with a restraint uncharacteristic of the puppet banks of the China-Japanese puppet states.

## ANTI-COMINTERN AUTONOMOUS GOVERNMENT

### STANDARD COINAGE

**5 LI Y# 516 Composition:** Copper **Issuer:** Chi Tung Bank **Obverse:** Japanese character 'first" **Reverse:** Value in grain stalks

| Date | Mintage | F | VF | XF | Unc | BU |
|---|---|---|---|---|---|---|
| 26(1937) | — | 10.00 | 20.00 | 35.00 | 100 | — |

**FEN Y# 517 Composition:** Copper **Issuer:** Chi Tung Bank **Obverse:** Japanese character 'first" **Reverse:** Value in grain stalks

| Date | Mintage | F | VF | XF | Unc | BU |
|---|---|---|---|---|---|---|
| 26(1937)(1937) | — | 3.00 | 6.00 | 9.00 | 30.00 | — |

**5 FEN Y# 518 Composition:** Copper-Nickel **Issuer:** Chi Tung Bank **Obverse:** Japanese character 'first" **Reverse:** Value in grain stalks

| Date | Mintage | F | VF | XF | Unc | BU |
|---|---|---|---|---|---|---|
| 26(1937)(1937) | — | 2.50 | 4.50 | 6.50 | 25.00 | — |

**CHIAO Y# 519 Composition:** Copper-Nickel **Issuer:** Chi Tung Bank **Obverse:** T'ien-ning Pagoda in Peking **Reverse:** Value in grain stalks

| Date | Mintage | F | VF | XF | Unc | BU |
|---|---|---|---|---|---|---|
| 26(1937)(1937) | — | 2.50 | 4.50 | 6.50 | 22.50 | — |

**2 CHIAO Y# 520 Composition:** Copper-Nickel **Issuer:** Chi Tung Bank **Obverse:** T'ien-ning Pagoda in Peking **Reverse:** Value in grain stalks

| Date | Mintage | F | VF | XF | Unc | BU |
|---|---|---|---|---|---|---|
| 26(1937)(1937) | — | 3.00 | 6.00 | 10.00 | 35.00 | — |

## MANCHOUKUO

The former Japanese puppet state of Manchoukuo (largely Manchuria), comprising the northeastern Chinese provinces of Fengtien (Liaoning), Kirin (Jilin), Heilungkiang (Heilongjiang) and Jehol (Rehe), had an area of 503,143 sq. mi. (1,303,134 sq. km.) and a population of 43.3 million. Capital: Changchun, renamed Hsinking. The area is rich in fertile soil, timber and mineral resources, including coal, iron and gold.

Until the closing years of the 19th century when Chinese influence became predominant, Manchuria was chiefly a domain of the tribal Manchus and their Mongol allies. Coincident with the rise of Chinese influence, foreign imperialistic powers began to appreciate the value of the area to their expansionist philosophy. Japan, overpopulated and poor in resources, desired it as a source of raw materials and for increased living area. Russia wanted it as the eastern terminus of the Trans-Siberian railway that was to unite its Asian empire. The inevitable conflict of Japanese, Chinese and Russian interests required that one or more of the powers be eliminated. After eliminating Russia in their war of 1904-05, Japan eliminated China on the night of Sept. 18, 1931, when, on the pretext of a contrived incident, it moved militarily to seize control of the Three Eastern Provinces. Early in 1932 Japan declared Manchuria independent by virtue of a voluntary separatist movement and established the state of Manchoukuo. To give the puppet state an aura of legitimacy, the deposed emperor of the former Manchu dynasty was recalled from retirement and designated "chief executive ". The area was restored to China at the end of World War II.

**RULERS**
Ta T'ung, 1932-1934
K'ang Te, 1934-1945

The puppet emperor under the assumed name of K'ang Te was previously the last emperor of China (P'u-yi, or Hsuan T'ung, 1909-11).

**MONETARY SYSTEM**
10 Li = 1 Fen
10 Fen = 1 Chiao

**IDENTIFICATION OF REIGN CHARACTERS**

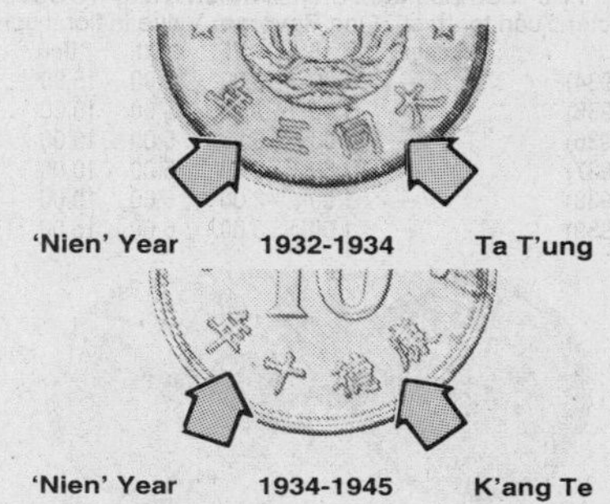


**DATE ABBREVIATIONS**
TT - Ta T'ung
KT - K'ang Te

**NOTE**: Uncirculated aluminum coins without any planchet defects are worth up to twice the market valuations given.

## JAPANESE OCCUPATION

### STANDARD COINAGE

**5 LI Y# 1 Composition:** Bronze **Ruler:** Ta -T'ung **Obverse:** Flag **Reverse:** Value in floral sprays

| Date | Mintage | F | VF | XF | Unc | BU |
|---|---|---|---|---|---|---|
| TT 2(1933) | — | 20.00 | 35.00 | 50.00 | 100 | — |
| TT 3(1934) | — | 4.00 | 9.00 | 15.00 | 30.00 | — |

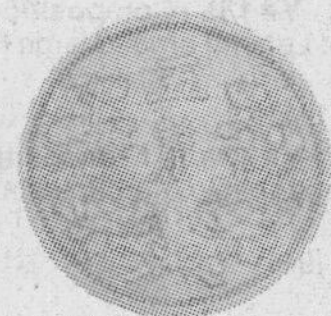

**5 LI Y# 5 Composition:** Bronze **Ruler:** K'ang -Te **Obverse:** Character Yuan for "first", Flag **Reverse:** Value in floral sprays

| Date | Mintage | F | VF | XF | Unc | BU |
|---|---|---|---|---|---|---|
| KT 1(1934) | — | 3.00 | 7.50 | 10.00 | 25.00 | — |
| KT 2(1935) | — | 3.00 | 7.50 | 10.00 | 25.00 | — |
| KT 3(1936) | — | 17.50 | 27.50 | 40.00 | 70.00 | — |
| KT 4(1937) | — | 4.00 | 10.00 | 12.50 | 27.50 | — |
| KT 6(1939) | — | 150 | 200 | 275 | 375 | — |

**FEN** Y# 2 **Composition:** Bronze **Ruler:** Ta -T'ung **Obverse:** Flag **Reverse:** Value in floral sprays

| Date | Mintage | F | VF | XF | Unc | BU |
|---|---|---|---|---|---|---|
| TT 3(1933) | — | 2.00 | 4.00 | 8.00 | 25.00 | — |
| TT 4(1934) | — | 1.50 | 3.00 | 5.00 | 20.00 | — |

**FEN** Y# 6 **Composition:** Bronze **Ruler:** K'ang -Te **Obverse:** Character Yuan for "first", Flag **Reverse:** Value in floral sprays

| Date | Mintage | F | VF | XF | Unc | BU |
|---|---|---|---|---|---|---|
| KT 1(1934) | — | 1.00 | 3.00 | 6.00 | 15.00 | — |
| KT 2(1935) | — | 1.00 | 3.00 | 5.00 | 10.00 | — |
| KT 3(1936) | — | 1.00 | 3.00 | 5.00 | 10.00 | — |
| KT 4(1937) | — | 1.00 | 3.00 | 5.00 | 10.00 | — |
| KT 5(1938) | — | 1.00 | 3.00 | 5.00 | 10.00 | — |
| KT 6(1939) | — | 1.00 | 3.00 | 6.00 | 15.00 | — |

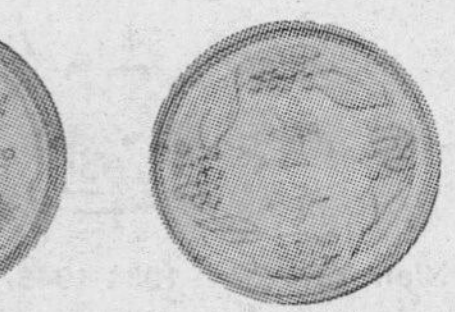

**FEN** Y# 9 **Composition:** Aluminum **Ruler:** K'ang -Te **Obverse:** National symbol **Reverse:** Value in floral wreath

| Date | Mintage | F | VF | XF | Unc | BU |
|---|---|---|---|---|---|---|
| KT 6(1939) | — | 0.40 | 0.75 | 2.00 | 5.00 | — |
| KT 7(1940) | — | 0.40 | 0.75 | 2.00 | 5.00 | — |
| KT 8(1941) | — | 0.40 | 0.75 | 2.00 | 5.00 | — |
| KT 9(1942) | — | 0.40 | 0.75 | 2.00 | 5.00 | — |
| KT 10(1943) | — | 0.40 | 0.75 | 2.00 | 5.00 | — |

**FEN** Y# 13 **Composition:** Aluminum **Ruler:** K'ang -Te **Obverse:** Legend around large "1" **Reverse:** Floral wreath

| Date | Mintage | F | VF | XF | Unc | BU |
|---|---|---|---|---|---|---|
| KT 10(1943) | — | 0.75 | 2.00 | 5.00 | 10.00 | — |
| KT 11(1944) | — | 0.75 | 2.00 | 5.00 | 10.00 | — |

**FEN** Y# 13a **Composition:** Red Fiber **Ruler:** K'ang -Te **Obverse:** Legend around large "1" **Reverse:** Floral wreath

| Date | Mintage | VG | F | VF | XF | Unc |
|---|---|---|---|---|---|---|
| KT 12(1945) | — | 0.50 | 1.25 | 3.00 | 6.00 | — |

**FEN** Y# 13a.1 **Composition:** Brown Fiber **Ruler:** K'ang -Te **Obverse:** Legend around large "1" **Reverse:** Floral wreath

| Date | Mintage | VG | F | VF | XF | Unc |
|---|---|---|---|---|---|---|
| KT 12(1945) | — | 1.50 | 4.00 | 10.00 | 15.00 | — |

**5 FEN** Y# 3 **Composition:** Copper-Nickel **Ruler:** Ta -T'ung **Obverse:** Lotus flower **Reverse:** Pearl above value between facing dragons

| Date | Mintage | F | VF | XF | Unc | BU |
|---|---|---|---|---|---|---|
| TT 2(1933) | — | 0.75 | 2.00 | 5.00 | 15.00 | — |
| TT 3(1934) | — | 0.40 | 1.00 | 2.00 | 10.00 | — |

Narrow Design

Wide Design

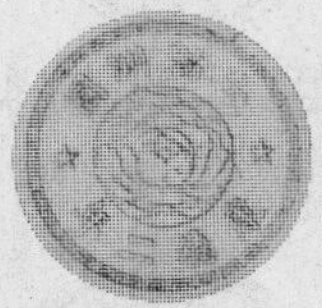

**5 FEN** Y# 7 **Composition:** Copper-Nickel **Ruler:** K'ang -Te **Obverse:** Character Yuan for "first" **Reverse:** Pearl above value between facing dragons

| Date | Mintage | F | VF | XF | Unc | BU |
|---|---|---|---|---|---|---|
| KT 1(1934) | — | 0.60 | 1.50 | 3.00 | 6.00 | — |
| KT 2(1935) | — | 0.60 | 1.50 | 3.00 | 6.00 | — |
| KT 3(1936) | — | 0.60 | 1.50 | 3.00 | 6.00 | — |
| **Note:** Narrow border design | | | | | | |
| KT 3(1936) | — | 1.25 | 3.00 | 6.00 | 12.00 | — |
| **Note:** Wide border design | | | | | | |
| KT 4(1937) | — | 1.00 | 2.00 | 4.00 | 7.50 | — |
| KT 6(1939) | — | 1.00 | 2.00 | 4.00 | 7.50 | — |

**5 FEN** Y# 11 **Composition:** Aluminum **Ruler:** K'ang -Te **Obverse:** Legend around large "5" **Reverse:** National symbol above value in floral sprays

| Date | Mintage | F | VF | XF | Unc | BU |
|---|---|---|---|---|---|---|
| KT 7(1940) | — | 0.60 | 1.50 | 3.00 | 6.00 | — |
| KT 8(1941) | — | 0.40 | 0.75 | 2.00 | 4.00 | — |
| KT 9(1942) | — | 0.40 | 0.75 | 2.00 | 4.00 | — |
| KT 10(1943) | — | 0.40 | 0.75 | 2.00 | 4.00 | — |

**5 FEN** Y# A13 **Composition:** Aluminum **Ruler:** K'ang -Te **Obverse:** Legend around small "5" **Reverse:** Wreath

| Date | Mintage | F | VF | XF | Unc | BU |
|---|---|---|---|---|---|---|
| KT 10(1943) | — | 1.00 | 2.50 | 5.00 | 12.50 | — |
| KT 11(1944) | — | 1.00 | 2.50 | 5.00 | 12.50 | — |

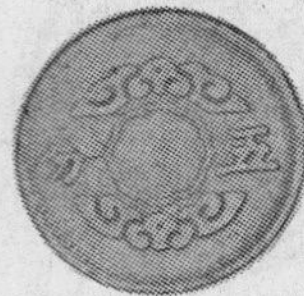

**5 FEN** Y# A13a **Composition:** Red Fiber **Ruler:** K'ang -Te **Obverse:** Legend around small "5" **Reverse:** Wreath

| Date | Mintage | VG | F | VF | XF | Unc |
|---|---|---|---|---|---|---|
| KT 11(1944) | — | 1.00 | 2.00 | 3.50 | 7.00 | — |
| KT 12(1945) | — | 60.00 | 75.00 | 100 | — | — |

**5 FEN** Y# A13a.1 **Composition:** Brown Fiber **Ruler:** K'ang -Te **Obverse:** Legend around small "5" **Reverse:** Floral wreath

| Date | Mintage | VG | F | VF | XF | Unc |
|---|---|---|---|---|---|---|
| KT 11(1944) | — | 4.00 | 10.00 | 15.00 | 25.00 | — |

**CHIAO (10 Fen)** Y# 4 **Composition:** Copper-Nickel **Ruler:** Ta -T'ung **Obverse:** Lotus flower **Reverse:** Pearl above value between facing dragons

| Date | Mintage | F | VF | XF | Unc | BU |
|---|---|---|---|---|---|---|
| TT 2(1933) | — | 1.50 | 3.00 | 7.00 | 15.00 | — |
| TT 3(1934) | — | 0.80 | 2.00 | 3.75 | 12.50 | — |

**CHIAO (10 Fen)** Y# 8 **Composition:** Copper-Nickel **Ruler:** K'ang -Te **Obverse:** Character Yuan for "first" **Reverse:** Pearl above value between facing dragons

| Date | Mintage | F | VF | XF | Unc | BU |
|---|---|---|---|---|---|---|
| KT 1(1934) | — | 0.80 | 2.00 | 3.00 | 8.00 | — |
| KT 2(1935) | — | 0.80 | 2.00 | 3.00 | 8.00 | — |
| KT 5(1938) | — | 0.80 | 2.00 | 3.00 | 8.00 | — |
| KT 6(1939) | — | 0.80 | 2.00 | 3.00 | 8.00 | — |
| KT 6(1939) Proof | — | — | — | — | — | — |

**CHIAO (10 Fen)** Y# 10 **Composition:** Copper-Nickel **Ruler:** K'ang -Te **Obverse:** Dragon head facing **Reverse:** National symbol above value in floral sprays

| Date | Mintage | F | VF | XF | Unc | BU |
|---|---|---|---|---|---|---|
| KT 7(1940) | — | 1.00 | 3.00 | 5.00 | 12.50 | — |

**CHIAO (10 Fen)** Y# 12 **Composition:** Aluminum **Ruler:** K'ang -Te **Obverse:** Legend around "10" on "Fundo" weight outline **Reverse:** National symbol above value in floral sprays

| Date | Mintage | F | VF | XF | Unc | BU |
|---|---|---|---|---|---|---|
| KT 7(1940) | — | 0.80 | 2.00 | 3.00 | 8.00 | — |
| KT 8(1941) | — | 0.80 | 2.00 | 3.00 | 8.00 | — |
| KT 9(1942) | — | 0.80 | 2.00 | 3.00 | 8.00 | — |
| KT 10(1943) | — | 275 | 400 | 500 | 600 | — |

**CHIAO (10 Fen)** Y# 14 **Composition:** Aluminum **Ruler:** K'ang -Te **Reverse:** Legend around large "10"

| Date | Mintage | F | VF | XF | Unc | BU |
|---|---|---|---|---|---|---|
| KT 10(1943) | — | 1.50 | 3.00 | 5.00 | 12.50 | — |

## BULLION COINAGE

These gold ingots, issued under the authority of the Japanese military, were issued and held by the Bank of Manchoukuo in the early 1930s. Although they carry Chinese legends, they were not made by or for the Chinese market.

**TAEL** KM# 1.1 **Weight:** 31.2500 g. **Composition:** 1.0000 Gold 1.0048 oz. AGW **Obverse:** Character "Fu" "Happiness" **Reverse:** 24K/1000 all in outline **Size:** 30 mm.

| Date | Mintage | F | VF | XF | Unc | BU |
|---|---|---|---|---|---|---|
| ND(1932) | — | — | 450 | 650 | 900 | — |

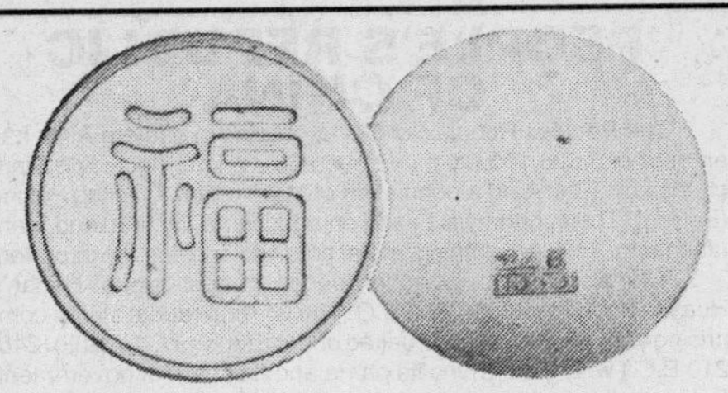

**TAEL** KM# 1.2 **Weight:** 31.2500 g. **Composition:** 1.0000 Gold 1.0048 oz. AGW **Obverse:** Character "Fu" (happiness) **Reverse:** 1000 in outline, 24K above

| Date | Mintage | F | VF | XF | Unc | BU |
|---|---|---|---|---|---|---|
| ND(1932) | — | — | 450 | 650 | 900 | — |

**TAEL** KM# 2 **Composition:** Gold 1.5000 oz. AGW **Obverse:** Character "Fu" (happiness) **Size:** 37 mm.

| Date | Mintage | F | VF | XF | Unc | BU |
|---|---|---|---|---|---|---|
| ND(1932) | — | — | 950 | 1,250 | 1,500 | — |

**TAEL** KM# 3 **Weight:** 31.2500 g. **Composition:** 1.0000 Gold 1.0048 oz. AGW **Obverse:** Character "Shuang-hsi" (Double happiness) **Size:** 30 mm.

| Date | Mintage | F | VF | XF | Unc | BU |
|---|---|---|---|---|---|---|
| ND(1932) | — | — | 1,200 | 1,550 | 1,950 | — |

**TAEL** KM# 4 **Weight:** 31.2500 g. **Composition:** 1.0000 Gold 1.0048 oz. AGW **Obverse:** Character "Fu" (happiness) in center, characters "Fu-kuei Wan-nien" top-bottom-right-left (Richness, honor (for) 10,000 years) **Reverse:** "24K/1000" over 4 characters in frame

| Date | Mintage | F | VF | XF | Unc | BU |
|---|---|---|---|---|---|---|
| ND(1932) | — | — | 950 | 1,250 | 1,500 | — |

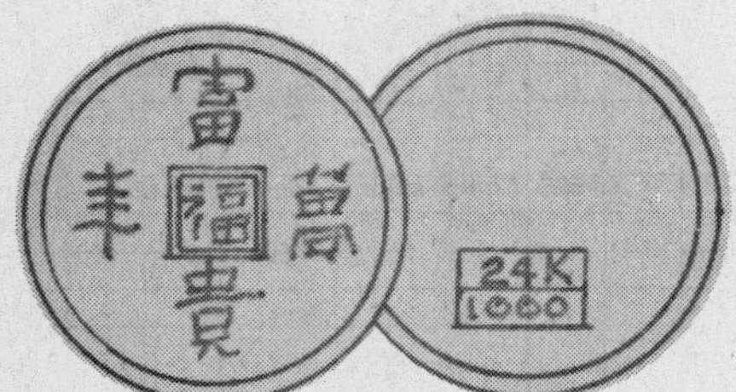

**TAEL** KM# 5 **Weight:** 31.2500 g. **Composition:** 1.0000 Gold 1.0048 oz. AGW **Obverse:** Character "Fu" (happiness) in center, characters "Fu-kuei Wan-nien" top-bottom-right-left (richness, honor (for) 10,000 years) **Reverse:** "24K/1000" over 4 characters in frame

| Date | Mintage | F | VF | XF | Unc | BU |
|---|---|---|---|---|---|---|
| ND(1932) | — | — | 950 | 1,250 | 1,500 | — |

**TAEL** KM# 6 **Weight:** 31.2500 g. **Composition:** 1.0000 Gold 1.0048 oz. AGW **Obverse:** Character "Shou" (Longevity) **Reverse:** "24K" over ""1000" in frame

| Date | Mintage | F | VF | XF | Unc | BU |
|---|---|---|---|---|---|---|
| ND(1932) | — | — | 950 | 1,250 | 1,500 | — |

**TAEL** KM# 7 **Composition:** Gold 1.5000 oz. AGW **Obverse:** Character "Shou" (longevity) **Size:** 37 mm.

| Date | Mintage | F | VF | XF | Unc | BU |
|---|---|---|---|---|---|---|
| ND(1932) | — | — | 1,450 | 1,850 | 2,250 | — |

**TAEL** KM# 8 **Weight:** 31.2500 g. **Composition:** 1.0000 Gold 1.0048 oz. AGW **Obverse:** Character "Lu" (Prosperity) **Size:** 30 mm.

| Date | Mintage | F | VF | XF | Unc | BU |
|---|---|---|---|---|---|---|
| ND(1932) | — | — | 950 | 1,250 | 1,500 | — |

## PATTERNS

Including off metal strikes

| KM# | Date | Mintage | Identification | Mkt Val |
|---|---|---|---|---|
| Pn1 | KT5(1938) | — | 5 Chiao. Copper-Nickel. Medieval emperor's bust. Portrait. | — |
| Pn2 | KT5(1938) | — | 5 Chiao. Copper-Nickel. Two facing phoenix. Chinese characters. | — |

| KM# | Date | Mintage | Identification | Mkt Val |
|---|---|---|---|---|
| Pn3 | KT9(1942) | — | Chiao. Silver. Specimen | 400 |
| Pn4 | KT9(1942) | — | Chiao. Copper-Nickel. Specimen | 250 |
| Pn5 | KT9(1942) | — | Chiao. Brass. Specimen | 200 |
| Pn6 | KT9(1942) | — | Chiao. Nickel-Bronze. Specimen | 200 |
| Pn7 | KT12(1945) | — | Fen. Copper Plated Steel. Y#13a | — |

# MENG CHIANG

As Japanese troops moved into North China in 1937, the political situation became fluid in several provinces bordering on Manchoukuo, which were sometimes referred to as Inner Mongolia. On September 27, 1937, the Chanan Bank was established. As the situation became more settled the Japanese effected the merger of two local banks with the Bank of Chanan under a new title, Meng Chiang (Mongolian Borderlands or Mongol Territory) Bank. The Meng Chiang Bank was organized on November 27 and opened on December 1, 1937, with headquarters in Kalgan (Zhangjiakou) and branch offices in about a dozen locations throughout the region. Its notes were declared the exclusive currency for the area. The bank closed at the end of the war.

## JAPANESE OCCUPATION

### STANDARD COINAGE

**5 CHIAO** Y# 521 **Composition:** Copper-Nickel **Obverse:** Legend in floral design **Reverse:** Value in facing dragons

| Date | Mintage | F | VF | XF | Unc | BU |
|---|---|---|---|---|---|---|
| 27(1938) | — | 3.50 | 6.50 | 10.00 | 25.00 | — |

### PATTERNS

Including off metal strikes

Note: "KK" indicates Kublai Khan dating system

| KM# | Date | Mintage | Identification | Mkt Val |
|---|---|---|---|---|
| Pn3 | 738(1943) | — | Chiao. Aluminum. Ram's head. | 2,250 |

| KM# | Date | Mintage | Identification | Mkt Val |
|---|---|---|---|---|
| Pn2 | 738(1943) | — | 5 Fen. Aluminum. Ram's head. | 1,650 |
| Pn1 | 738(1943) | — | Fen. Aluminum. Ram's head. | — |

# PROVISIONAL GOVT. OF CHINA

In late 1937 the Japanese North China Expeditionary Army established the "Provisional Government of China" at Peking (Beijing).

### FEDERAL RESERVE BANK

The Federal Reserve Bank of China was opened in 1938 by Japanese military authorities in Peking (Beijing). It was the puppet financial agency of the Japanese in northeast China. The puppet bank issued both coins and currency, but in modest amounts.

## JAPANESE OCCUPATION

### STANDARD COINAGE

**FEN** Y# 523 **Composition:** Aluminum **Issuer:** Federal Reserve Bank **Obverse:** Legend around FR Bank symbol **Reverse:** Temple of Heaven

| Date | Mintage | F | VF | XF | Unc | BU |
|---|---|---|---|---|---|---|
| 30(1941) | — | 0.50 | 1.00 | 2.50 | 7.00 | — |
| 31(1942) | — | 0.50 | 1.00 | 2.00 | 6.00 | — |
| 32(1943) | — | 3.00 | 6.00 | 10.00 | 30.00 | — |

**5 FEN** Y# 524 **Composition:** Aluminum **Issuer:** Federal Reserve Bank **Obverse:** Legend around FR Bank symbol **Reverse:** Temple of Heaven **Note:** The 5 Fen pieces were struck on thick (1 gram) and then (.8 gram) planchets.

| Date | Mintage | F | VF | XF | Unc | BU |
|---|---|---|---|---|---|---|
| 30(1941) | — | 0.75 | 2.00 | 4.00 | 10.00 | — |
| 31(1942) | — | 1.00 | 2.50 | 5.00 | 15.00 | — |
| 32(1943) | — | 3.50 | 7.50 | 15.00 | 45.00 | — |

**CHIAO** Y# 525 **Composition:** Aluminum **Issuer:** Federal Reserve Bank **Obverse:** Legend around FR Bank symbol **Reverse:** Temple of Heaven **Note:** The 1 Chiao pieces were struck on thick (1.5 gram), thin (1.2 gram), and very thin (1.0 gram) planchets.

| Date | Mintage | F | VF | XF | Unc | BU |
|---|---|---|---|---|---|---|
| 30(1941) | — | 0.40 | 1.00 | 2.00 | 6.00 | — |
| 31(1942) | — | 0.40 | 1.00 | 2.00 | 6.00 | — |
| 32(1943) | — | 1.50 | 3.00 | 6.50 | 20.00 | — |

### PATTERNS

Including off metal strikes

| KM# | Date | Mintage | Identification | Mkt Val |
|---|---|---|---|---|
| Pn1 | 30(1941) | — | Fen. Silver. KM#523, R.Y.30. | 700 |
| Pn2 | 30(1941) | — | 5 Fen. Silver. KM#524, R.Y.30. | 700 |

# REFORMED GOVT. OF CHINA

On March 28, 1938 the Japanese Central China Expeditionary Army established the Reformed Government of the Republic of China at Nanking (Nanjing).

### HUA HSING COMMERCIAL BANK

The Hua Hsing Commerce Bank was a financial agency created and established by the government of Japan and its puppet authorities in Shanghai in May 1939. Notes and coins were issued until sometime in 1941, with the quantities restricted by Chinese aversion to accepting them.

## JAPANESE OCCUPATION

### STANDARD COINAGE

**FEN** Y# A522 **Composition:** Bronze **Obverse:** Legend around character "Hua" above pair of wings **Reverse:** Stylized character divides value

| Date | Mintage | F | VF | XF | Unc | BU |
|---|---|---|---|---|---|---|
| 29(1940)(1940) | — | 100 | 200 | 300 | 400 | — |

**10 FEN** Y# 522 **Composition:** Copper-Nickel **Obverse:** Legend around character "Hua" above pair of wings **Reverse:** Floral bouquet divides value

| Date | Mintage | F | VF | XF | Unc | BU |
|---|---|---|---|---|---|---|
| 29(1940)(1940) | — | 1.00 | 2.00 | 3.50 | 7.00 | — |

**Note:** Metal Alloys vary

### PATTERNS

Including off metal strikes

| KM# | Date | Mintage | Identification | Mkt Val |
|---|---|---|---|---|
| Pn1 | 29(1940) | — | Fen. Copper-Nickel. | 650 |
| Pn2 | 29(1940) | — | Fen. Silver. | 750 |

| KM# | Date | Mintage | Identification | Mkt Val |
|---|---|---|---|---|
| Pn3 | 29(1940) | — | 5 Fen. Copper-Nickel. Liu-ho Pagoda. | 650 |

| KM# | Date | Mintage | Identification | Mkt Val |
|---|---|---|---|---|
| Pn4 | 29(1940) | — | 20 Fen. Copper-Nickel. Junk. | 2,250 |

# PEOPLE'S REPUBLIC OF CHINA

The Peoples Republic of China, located in eastern Asia, has an area of 3,696,100 sq. mi. (9,596,960 sq. km.) (including Manchuria and Tibet) and a population of *1.20 billion. Capital: Peking (Beijing). The economy is based on agriculture, mining, and manufacturing. Textiles, clothing, metal ores, tea and rice are exported.

China's ancient civilization began in east-central Henan's Huayang county, 2800-2300 B.C. The warring feudal states comprising early China were first united under Emperor Ch'in Shih (246-210 B.C.) who gave China its name and first central government. Subsequent dynasties alternated brilliant cultural achievements with internal disorder until the Empire was brought down by the revolution of 1911, and the Republic of China installed in its place. Chinese culture attained a pre-eminence in art, literature and philosophy, but a traditional backwardness in industry and administration ill prepared China for the demands of 19th century Western expansionism which exposed it to military and political humiliations, and mandated a drastic revision of political practice in order to secure an accommodation with the modern world.

The Republic of 1911 barely survived the stress of World War I, and was subsequently all but shattered by the rise of nationalism and the emergence of the Chinese Communist movement. Moscow, which practiced a policy of cooperation between Communists and other parties in movements for national liberation, sought to establish an entente between the Chinese Communist Party and the Kuomintang ('National Peoples Party') of Sun Yat-sen. The ensuing cooperation was based on little more than the hope each had of using the other.

An increasingly uneasy association between the Kuomintang and the Chinese Communist Party developed and continued until April 12, 1927, when Chiang Kai-shek, Sun Yat-sen's political heir, instituted a bloody purge to stamp out the Communists within the Kuomintang and the government and virtually paralyzed their ranks throughout China. Some time after the mid-1927 purges, the Chinese Communist Party turned to armed force to resist Chiang Kai-shek and during the period of 1930-34 acquired control over large parts of Kiangsi (Jiangxi), Fukien (Fujian), Hunan and Hupeh (Hubei). The Nationalist Nanking government responded with a series of campaigns against the soviet power bases and, by October of 1934, succeeded in driving the remnants of the Communist army to a refuge in Shensi (Shaanxi) Province. There the Communists reorganized under the leadership of Mao Tse-tung, defeated the Nationalist forces, and on Sept. 21, 1949, established the Peoples Republic of China. Thereafter relations between Russia and Communist China steadily deteriorated until 1958, when China emerged as an independent center of Communist power.

### SOVIET PERIOD

Prior to 1949, the People's Republic of China did not exist as such, but the Communists did control areas known as Soviets. Most of the Soviets were established on the borders of two or more provinces and were named according to the provinces involved. Thus there were such soviets as the Kiangsi-Hunan Soviet, the Hunan-Hupeh-Kiangsi Soviet, the Hupeh-Honan-Anhwei Soviet and others. In 1931 some of the soviets in the southern Kiangsi area were consolidated into the Chinese Soviet Republic, which lasted until the Long March of 1934.

### MONETARY SYSTEM

**Before 1949**

10 Cash (Wen) = 1 Cent (Fen)
100 Cents (Fen) = 1 Dollar (Yuan)

**After 1949**

10 Fen (Cents) = 1 Jiao
10 Jiao = 1 Renminbi Yuan

### MINT MARKS

(b) - Beijing (Peking)
(s) - Shanghai
(y) - Shenyang (Mukden)

# CHINESE SOVIET REPUBLIC

In November, 1931, the first congress of the Chinese Soviet proclaimed and established the "Chinese Soviet Republic" under the Chairmanship of Mao Tse-Tung.

## CONSOLIDATED SOVIET REPUBLIC

### STANDARD COINAGE

**CENT** Y# 506 **Composition:** Copper **Ruler:** Mao Tse-Tung

| Date | Mintage | VG | F | VF | XF | Unc |
|---|---|---|---|---|---|---|
| ND(ca.1932) | — | 10.00 | 20.00 | 30.00 | 50.00 | — |

**CENT** Y# 506a **Composition:** Copper **Ruler:** Mao Tse-Tung **Reverse:** Sharp star

| Date | Mintage | F | VF | XF | Unc | BU |
|---|---|---|---|---|---|---|
| ND(ca.1960) Restrike | — | — | — | 8.00 | 20.00 | — |

**5 CENTS** Y# 507 **Composition:** Copper **Ruler:** Mao Tse-Tung **Edge:** Plain **Note:** Varieties exist.

| Date | Mintage | VG | F | VF | XF | Unc |
|---|---|---|---|---|---|---|
| ND(ca.1932) | — | 20.00 | 30.00 | 50.00 | 85.00 | — |

**5 CENTS** Y# 507.1 **Composition:** Copper **Ruler:** Mao Tse-Tung **Edge:** Reeded **Note:** Varieties exist.

| Date | Mintage | VG | F | VF | XF | Unc |
|---|---|---|---|---|---|---|
| ND(ca.1932) | — | 20.00 | 30.00 | 50.00 | 85.00 | — |

**5 CENTS** Y# 507a **Composition:** Copper **Ruler:** Mao Tse-Tung

| Date | Mintage | F | VF | XF | Unc | BU |
|---|---|---|---|---|---|---|
| ND(ca.1960) Restrike | — | — | — | 10.00 | 25.00 | — |

**20 CENTS** Y# 508 **Weight:** 5.5000 g. **Composition:** Silver **Ruler:** Mao Tse-Tung **Note:** Many minor varieties exist.

| Date | Mintage | VG | F | VF | XF | Unc |
|---|---|---|---|---|---|---|
| 1932 | — | 15.00 | 25.00 | 40.00 | 75.00 | — |
| 1933 | — | 10.00 | 20.00 | 30.00 | 65.00 | — |

**DOLLAR** KM# 5 **Composition:** Silver **Ruler:** Mao Tse-Tung **Obverse:** Crude facing portrait of Lenin **Reverse:** Hammer, sickle, and value within ornamental wreath

| Date | Mintage | VG | F | VF | XF | Unc |
|---|---|---|---|---|---|---|
| 1931 Rare | — | — | — | — | — | — |

## PATTERNS

Including off metal strikes

| KM# | Date | Mintage | Identification | Issue Price | Mkt Val |
|---|---|---|---|---|---|
| Pn1 | 1932 | — | 20 Cents, Copper, Y#508 | | — |

# HSIANG-O-HSI SOVIET

## SOVIET CONTROLLED PROVINCE

### STANDARD COINAGE

**FEN** KM# 1 **Composition:** Copper **Obverse:** Legend around large star **Reverse:** Denomination within wreath, legend around

| Date | Mintage | VG | F | VF | XF | Unc |
|---|---|---|---|---|---|---|
| ND(1931) Rare | — | — | — | — | — | — |

# HUNAN SOVIET

## SOVIET CONTROLLED PROVINCE

### STANDARD COINAGE

**DOLLAR** KM# 1.1 (KM1) **Composition:** Silver **Obverse:** Large star. **Obv. Legend:** "Hu-nan Sheng Su-wei-ai Cheng-fu"

| Date | Mintage | VG | F | VF | XF | Unc |
|---|---|---|---|---|---|---|
| 1931 | — | 180 | 300 | — | — | — |

**DOLLAR** KM# 1.2 **Composition:** Silver **Obverse:** Small star.

| Date | Mintage | VG | F | VF | XF | Unc |
|---|---|---|---|---|---|---|
| 1931 | — | 80.00 | 180 | 300 | — | — |

# HUPEH-HONAN-ANHWEI SOVIET

The Hupeh-Honan-Anhwei Soviet District was a large revolutionary base. It was formerly made up of three separate special districts: East Hupeh, South Honan and West Anhwei which united until after 1930. Between 1931 and 1932 this Bank has issued a quantity of copper and silver coins as well as banknotes.

## SOVIET CONTROLLED PROVINCE

### STANDARD COINAGE

**DOLLAR** Y# 503 **Weight:** 26.8000 g. **Composition:** Silver **Reverse:** Lower legend appears in crude Russian **Rev. Legend:** "SOVETS...."

| Date | Mintage | VG | F | VF | XF | Unc |
|---|---|---|---|---|---|---|
| 1932 | — | 250 | 575 | 750 | 1,000 | — |

**Note:** Attribution of Y#503 to the Hupeh-Honan-Anhwei Soviet is not definite.

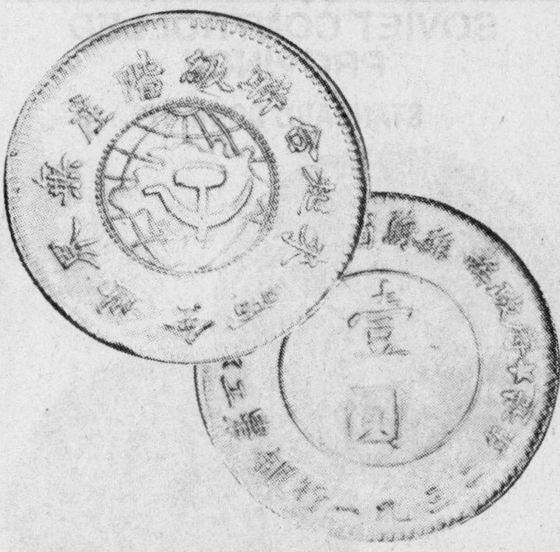

**DOLLAR** Y# 504 **Weight:** 27.2000 g. **Composition:** Silver

| Date | Mintage | VG | F | VF | XF | Unc |
|---|---|---|---|---|---|---|
| 1932 | — | 175 | 275 | 400 | 700 | — |

# MIN-CHE-KAN SOVIET

(Fukien-Chekiang-Kiangsi)

## SOVIET CONTROLLED PROVINCE

### STANDARD COINAGE

**DOLLAR** KM# 1 **Composition:** Silver **Obverse:** Profile bust of Lenin

| Date | Mintage | VG | F | VF | XF | Unc |
|---|---|---|---|---|---|---|
| 1934 | — | — | — | — | — | — |

**Note:** Authenticity in doubt

**DOLLAR** KM# 2 **Composition:** Silver **Obverse:** 15 character legend around globe with hammer and sickle

| Date | Mintage | VG | F | VF | XF | Unc |
|---|---|---|---|---|---|---|
| 1934 | — | — | — | — | — | — |

**Note:** Authenticity in doubt

## P'ING CHIANG COUNTY SOVIET

## SOVIET CONTROLLED PROVINCE

### STANDARD COINAGE

**DOLLAR** KM# 1 **Composition:** Silver **Obverse:** Legend in 8 Chinese characters **Obv. Legend:** "P'ing Chiang..."

| Date | Mintage | VG | F | VF | XF | Unc |
|---|---|---|---|---|---|---|
| 1931 Rare | — | — | — | — | — | — |

## SHENSI-NORTH SOVIET

## SOVIET CONTROLLED PROVINCE

### STANDARD COINAGE

Date is given in the 5th year of the Chinese Soviet Republic. They were issued after the "Long March".

**DOLLAR** KM# 1.1 **Composition:** Silver **Reverse:** Value in plain field, yr.5 at bottom

| Date | Mintage | VG | F | VF | XF | Unc |
|---|---|---|---|---|---|---|
| 5(1935)(1935) | — | 1,750 | 2,250 | 2,850 | — | — |

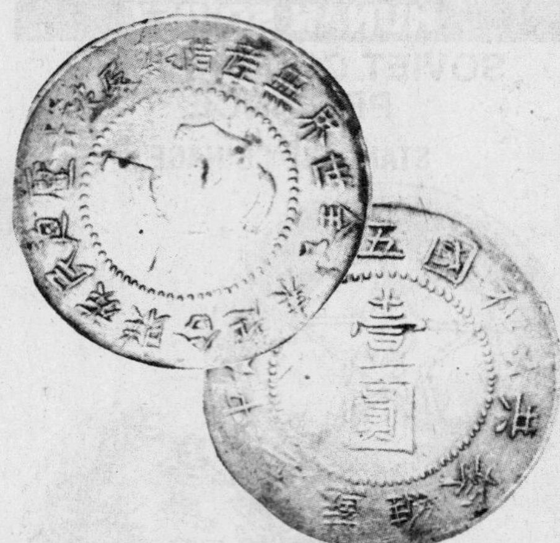

**DOLLAR** KM# 1.2 **Composition:** Silver **Obverse:** Star at left, slightly lower **Reverse:** Legend rotated with yr.5 at top

| Date | Mintage | VG | F | VF | XF | Unc |
|---|---|---|---|---|---|---|
| 5(1935)(1935) | — | 1,750 | 2,250 | 2,850 | — | — |

**DOLLAR** KM# 2 **Composition:** Silver **Reverse:** Value within wheat stalks

| Date | Mintage | VG | F | VF | XF | Unc |
|---|---|---|---|---|---|---|
| 5(1935)(1935) | — | 2,500 | 3,000 | 3,500 | — | — |

## SZECHUAN-SHENSI SOVIET

## SOVIET CONTROLLED PROVINCE

### STANDARD COINAGE

**200 CASH** Y# 510 **Composition:** Copper

| Date | Mintage | Good | VG | F | VF | XF |
|---|---|---|---|---|---|---|
| 1933 | — | 25.00 | 50.00 | 80.00 | 140 | — |

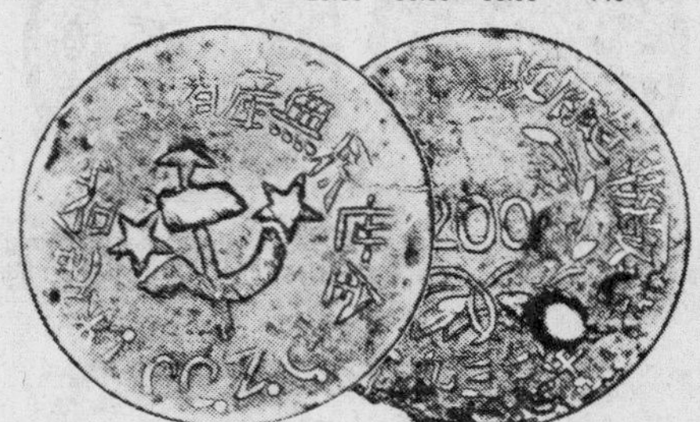

**200 CASH** Y# 510.1 **Composition:** Copper **Reverse:** Small 200 at center

| Date | Mintage | Good | VG | F | VF | XF |
|---|---|---|---|---|---|---|
| 1933 | — | 25.00 | 50.00 | 80.00 | 140 | — |

**200 CASH** Y# 510.2 **Composition:** Copper **Reverse:** Large 200 at center

| Date | Mintage | Good | VG | F | VF | XF |
|---|---|---|---|---|---|---|
| 1933 | — | 25.00 | 50.00 | 80.00 | 140 | — |

**200 CASH** Y# 510.3 **Composition:** Copper **Reverse:** Square 0's in 200 at center

| Date | Mintage | Good | VG | F | VF | XF |
|---|---|---|---|---|---|---|
| 1933 | — | 30.00 | 60.00 | 100 | 175 | — |

**200 CASH** **Y# 510.4** **Composition:** Copper **Obverse:** Solid hammer and sickle reversed **Reverse:** 200 retrograde at center

| Date | Mintage | Good | VG | F | VF | XF |
|---|---|---|---|---|---|---|
| 1933 | — | 35.00 | 70.00 | 115 | 200 | — |

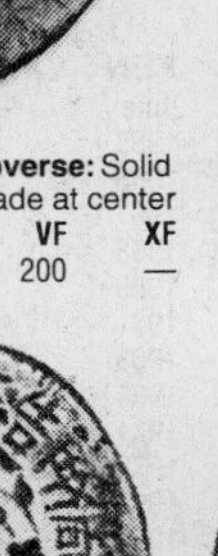

**200 CASH** **Y# 510.5** **Composition:** Copper **Obverse:** Shaded hammer and sickle reversed **Note:** Varieties exist.

| Date | Mintage | Good | VG | F | VF | XF |
|---|---|---|---|---|---|---|
| 1933 | — | 30.00 | 60.00 | 100 | 175 | — |

**200 CASH** **Y# 511.1** **Composition:** Copper **Obverse:** Date with open 3 and backwards 4

| Date | Mintage | VG | F | VF | XF | Unc |
|---|---|---|---|---|---|---|
| 1934 | — | 22.50 | 45.00 | 75.00 | 135 | — |

**200 CASH** **Y# 511.2** **Composition:** Copper **Obverse:** Date with 4 corrected

| Date | Mintage | VG | F | VF | XF | Unc |
|---|---|---|---|---|---|---|
| 1934 | — | 22.50 | 45.00 | 75.00 | 135 | — |

**200 CASH** **Y# 511** **Composition:** Copper **Obverse:** Date with closed 3 and backwards 4 **Note:** Modern forgeries of this variety exist.

| Date | Mintage | VG | F | VF | XF | Unc |
|---|---|---|---|---|---|---|
| 1934 | — | 22.50 | 45.00 | 75.00 | 135 | — |

**200 CASH** **Y# 511a** **Composition:** Copper **Obverse:** Date with 4 corrected

| Date | Mintage | F | VF | XF | Unc | BU |
|---|---|---|---|---|---|---|
| 1934 Restrike | — | — | — | 12.50 | 25.00 | — |

**Note:** Many varieties of 200 Cash pieces exist; well struck, usually found in choice condition; unlisted varieties do not carry a premium

**500 CASH** **Y# 512** **Composition:** Copper **Obverse:** Small stars flanking date

| Date | Mintage | VG | F | VF | XF | Unc |
|---|---|---|---|---|---|---|
| 1934 | — | 75.00 | 100 | 175 | 275 | — |

**500 CASH** **Y# 512.1** **Composition:** Copper **Obverse:** Large stars flanking date; hammer handle across lower leg of star

| Date | Mintage | VG | F | VF | XF | Unc |
|---|---|---|---|---|---|---|
| 1934 | — | 50.00 | 100 | 160 | 250 | — |

**500 CASH** **Y# 512.2** **Composition:** Copper **Obverse:** Hammer handle extends between right leg of star **Note:** 33-34 milimeters.

| Date | Mintage | VG | F | VF | XF | Unc |
|---|---|---|---|---|---|---|
| 1934 | — | 50.00 | 100 | 150 | 225 | — |

**Note:** Many varieties of 500 Cash pieces exist; unlisted varieties do not carry a premium

**DOLLAR** **Y# 513.2** **Weight:** 26.3000 g. **Composition:** Silver **Reverse:** Small solid stars

| Date | Mintage | VG | F | VF | XF | Unc |
|---|---|---|---|---|---|---|
| 1933 Rare | — | — | — | — | — | — |
| 1934 | — | 100 | 175 | 250 | 375 | — |

**DOLLAR** **Y# 513.3** **Weight:** 26.3000 g. **Composition:** Silver **Reverse:** Outlined stars

| Date | Mintage | VG | F | VF | XF | Unc |
|---|---|---|---|---|---|---|
| 1934 | — | 100 | 200 | 275 | 400 | — |

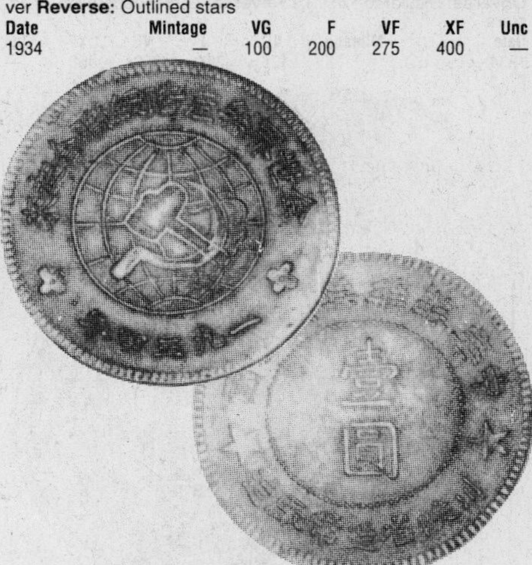

**DOLLAR** **Y# 513.5** **Weight:** 26.3000 g. **Composition:** Silver **Reverse:** Large solid stars

| Date | Mintage | VG | F | VF | XF | Unc |
|---|---|---|---|---|---|---|
| 1934 | — | 100 | 200 | 275 | 400 | — |

**DOLLAR** **Y# 513.4** **Weight:** 26.3000 g. **Composition:** Silver **Obverse:** Similar to Y#513.1 **Reverse:** Pentagram stars **Note:** Many minor varieties exist.

| Date | Mintage | VG | F | VF | XF | Unc |
|---|---|---|---|---|---|---|
| 1934 | — | 75.00 | 150 | 225 | 350 | — |

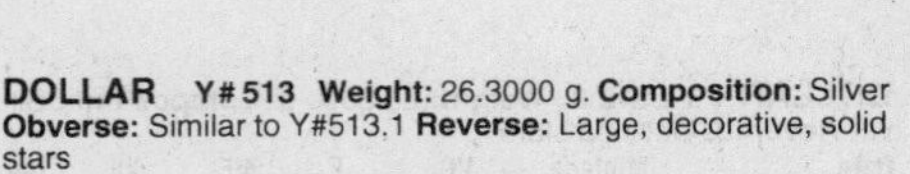

**DOLLAR** **Y# 513** **Weight:** 26.3000 g. **Composition:** Silver **Obverse:** Similar to Y#513.1 **Reverse:** Large, decorative, solid stars

| Date | Mintage | VG | F | VF | XF | Unc |
|---|---|---|---|---|---|---|
| 1934 | — | 125 | 225 | 300 | 450 | — |

**DOLLAR** **Y# 513.1** **Weight:** 26.3000 g. **Composition:** Silver **Reverse:** Medium solid stars

| Date | Mintage | VG | F | VF | XF | Unc |
|---|---|---|---|---|---|---|
| 1934 | — | 100 | 175 | 250 | 375 | — |

## UNCERTAIN ORIGIN COINAGE

**DOLLAR** **K# 650k** **Weight:** 26.4000 g. **Composition:** Silver **Countermark:** Three Chinese characters in rectangular box **Obverse:** Countermark meaning <i>SOVIET</i> **Note:** Countermark on Y#329.

| Date | Mintage | VG | F | VF | XF | Unc |
|---|---|---|---|---|---|---|
| ND | — | 125 | 200 | 325 | 600 | — |

## WAN-HSI-PEI-SOVIET

(Northwest Anhwei)

## SOVIET CONTROLLED PROVINCE

### STANDARD COINAGE

**50 CASH** **KM# 1** **Composition:** Copper **Obverse:** Legend around globe with hammer and sickle **Reverse:** Value in star within wreath, all within legend

| Date | Mintage | VG | F | VF | XF | Unc |
|---|---|---|---|---|---|---|
| ND(1931-32) Rare | — | — | — | — | — | — |

**50 CASH** **KM# 2** **Composition:** Copper **Reverse:** Value in circle, Chinese legend above, Western legend below

| Date | Mintage | VG | F | VF | XF | Unc |
|---|---|---|---|---|---|---|
| ND(1931-32) Rare | — | — | — | — | — | — |

# PEOPLES REPUBLIC

### STANDARD COINAGE

**FEN** **Y# 1** **Composition:** Aluminum

| Date | Mintage | F | VF | XF | Unc | BU |
|---|---|---|---|---|---|---|
| 1955 | — | 0.20 | 0.50 | 1.50 | 5.00 | — |
| 1956 | — | 0.40 | 1.00 | 2.50 | 7.50 | — |
| 1957 | — | 0.60 | 1.50 | 3.50 | 10.00 | — |
| 1958 | — | 0.10 | 0.25 | 0.75 | 2.50 | — |
| 1959 | — | 0.10 | 0.25 | 0.75 | 2.50 | — |
| 1961 | — | 0.10 | 0.25 | 0.75 | 2.50 | — |
| 1963 | — | 0.10 | 0.25 | 0.50 | 1.50 | — |
| 1964 | — | 0.10 | 0.25 | 0.50 | 1.00 | — |
| 1971 | — | 0.10 | 0.25 | 0.50 | 1.00 | — |
| 1972 | — | 0.10 | 0.25 | 0.50 | 1.00 | — |
| 1973 | — | 0.10 | 0.25 | 0.50 | 1.50 | — |
| 1974 | — | 0.10 | 0.25 | 0.50 | 1.00 | — |
| 1975 | 500,000 | 0.10 | 0.25 | 0.50 | 1.00 | — |
| 1976 | — | — | 0.10 | 0.25 | 0.50 | — |
| 1977 | — | — | 0.10 | 0.25 | 0.50 | — |
| 1978 | — | — | 0.10 | 0.25 | 0.50 | — |
| 1979 | — | — | 0.10 | 0.25 | 0.50 | — |
| 1980 | — | — | 0.10 | 0.25 | 0.50 | — |
| 1980 Proof | — | Value: 1.00 | | | | |
| 1981 | — | — | 0.10 | 0.25 | 0.50 | — |
| 1981 Proof | — | Value: 1.00 | | | | |
| 1982 | — | — | — | 0.25 | 0.50 | — |
| 1982 Proof | — | Value: 1.00 | | | | |
| 1983 | 2,412,000 | — | — | 0.10 | 0.25 | — |
| 1984 | 3,283,000 | — | — | 0.10 | 0.25 | — |
| 1985 | — | — | — | 0.10 | 0.25 | — |
| 1985 Proof | — | Value: 1.00 | | | | |
| 1986 | — | — | — | 0.10 | 0.25 | — |
| 1986 Proof | — | Value: 1.00 | | | | |
| 1987 | — | — | — | 0.10 | 0.25 | — |
| 1991 | — | — | — | 0.10 | 0.25 | — |
| 1991 Proof | — | Value: 1.00 | | | | |
| 1992 | — | — | — | 0.10 | 0.25 | — |
| 1992 Proof | — | Value: 1.00 | | | | |
| 1993 In sets only | — | — | — | — | 0.75 | — |
| 1993 Proof | — | Value: 1.00 | | | | |
| 1994 In sets only | — | — | — | — | 0.75 | — |
| 1994 Proof | — | Value: 1.00 | | | | |
| 1995 In sets only | — | — | — | — | 0.75 | — |
| 1995 Proof | — | Value: 1.00 | | | | |
| 1996 In sets only | — | — | — | — | 0.75 | — |
| 1996 Proof | — | Value: 1.00 | | | | |
| 1997 | — | — | — | 0.10 | 0.25 | — |

**2 FEN** **Y# 2** **Composition:** Aluminum

| Date | Mintage | F | VF | XF | Unc | BU |
|---|---|---|---|---|---|---|
| 1956 | — | 0.10 | 0.25 | 0.75 | 1.50 | — |
| 1959 | — | 0.20 | 0.50 | 1.00 | 4.00 | — |
| 1960 | — | 0.20 | 0.50 | 1.00 | 4.00 | — |
| 1961 | — | 0.10 | 0.25 | 0.75 | 1.50 | — |
| 1962 | — | 0.10 | 0.25 | 0.75 | 1.50 | — |
| 1963 | — | 0.10 | 0.25 | 0.75 | 1.50 | — |
| 1964 | — | 0.10 | 0.25 | 0.50 | 1.25 | — |
| 1974 | — | 0.10 | 0.25 | 0.50 | 1.50 | — |
| 1975 | — | 0.10 | 0.25 | 0.50 | 1.00 | — |
| 1976 | — | 0.10 | 0.25 | 0.50 | 1.00 | — |
| 1977 | 360,000 | 0.10 | 0.25 | 0.50 | 0.75 | — |
| 1978 | — | 0.10 | 0.20 | 0.40 | 0.60 | — |
| 1979 | — | 0.10 | 0.20 | 0.40 | 0.60 | — |
| 1980 | — | 0.10 | 0.20 | 0.40 | 0.60 | — |
| 1980 Proof | — | Value: 1.00 | | | | |
| 1981 | — | 0.10 | 0.20 | 0.40 | 0.60 | — |
| 1981 Proof | — | Value: 1.00 | | | | |
| 1982 | — | 0.10 | 0.20 | 0.40 | 0.60 | — |
| 1982 Proof | — | Value: 1.00 | | | | |
| 1983 | 1,790,000 | — | 0.10 | 0.20 | 0.35 | — |
| 1984 | 1,963,000 | — | 0.10 | 0.20 | 0.35 | — |
| 1985 | — | — | 0.10 | 0.20 | 0.35 | — |
| 1985 Proof | — | Value: 1.00 | | | | |
| 1986 | — | — | 0.15 | 0.35 | 0.75 | — |
| 1986 Proof | — | Value: 1.00 | | | | |
| 1987 | — | — | 0.10 | 0.20 | 0.35 | — |
| 1988 | — | — | 0.10 | 0.20 | 0.35 | — |
| 1989 | — | — | 0.10 | 0.20 | 0.35 | — |

| Date | Mintage | F | VF | XF | Unc | BU |
|---|---|---|---|---|---|---|
| 1990 | — | — | 0.10 | 0.20 | 0.35 | — |
| 1991 | — | — | 0.10 | 0.20 | 0.35 | — |
| 1991 Proof | — | Value: 1.00 | | | | |
| 1992 | — | — | 0.10 | 0.20 | 0.35 | — |
| 1992 Proof | — | Value: 1.00 | | | | |
| 1993 In sets only | — | — | — | — | 0.75 | — |
| 1993 Proof | — | Value: 1.00 | | | | |
| 1994 In sets only | — | — | — | — | 0.75 | — |
| 1994 Proof | — | Value: 1.00 | | | | |
| 1995 In sets only | — | — | — | — | 0.75 | — |
| 1995 Proof | — | Value: 1.00 | | | | |
| 1996 In sets only | — | — | — | — | 0.75 | — |
| 1996 Proof | — | Value: 1.00 | | | | |

**5 FEN** **Y# 3** **Composition:** Aluminum

| Date | Mintage | F | VF | XF | Unc | BU |
|---|---|---|---|---|---|---|
| 1955 | — | 0.30 | 0.75 | 2.00 | 10.00 | — |
| 1956 | — | 0.15 | 0.35 | 0.75 | 2.00 | — |
| 1957 | — | 0.15 | 0.35 | 0.75 | 2.50 | — |
| 1974 | — | 0.15 | 0.25 | 0.50 | 1.50 | — |
| 1975 | — | 0.15 | 0.25 | 0.50 | 1.50 | — |
| 1976 | 350,000 | 0.15 | 0.25 | 0.50 | 0.75 | — |
| 1979 | — | 0.15 | 0.35 | 0.75 | 2.00 | — |
| 1980 | — | 0.15 | 0.25 | 0.50 | 0.75 | — |
| 1980 Proof | — | Value: 1.00 | | | | |
| 1981 | — | 0.15 | 0.25 | 0.50 | 0.75 | — |
| 1981 Proof | — | Value: 1.00 | | | | |
| 1982 | — | 0.15 | 0.25 | 0.50 | 0.75 | — |
| 1982 Proof | — | Value: 1.00 | | | | |
| 1983 | 484,000 | — | 0.15 | 0.25 | 0.45 | — |
| 1984 | 600,000 | — | 0.15 | 0.25 | 0.45 | — |
| 1985 | — | — | 0.15 | 0.25 | 0.45 | — |
| 1985 Proof | — | Value: 1.00 | | | | |
| 1986 | — | — | 0.15 | 0.25 | 0.45 | — |
| 1986 Proof | — | Value: 1.00 | | | | |
| 1987 | — | — | 0.15 | 0.25 | 0.45 | — |
| 1988 | — | — | 0.15 | 0.25 | 0.45 | — |
| 1989 | — | — | 0.15 | 0.25 | 0.45 | — |
| 1990 | — | — | 0.15 | 0.25 | 0.45 | — |
| 1991 | — | — | 0.15 | 0.25 | 0.45 | — |
| 1991 Proof | — | Value: 1.00 | | | | |
| 1992 | — | — | 0.15 | 0.25 | 0.45 | — |
| 1992 Proof | — | Value: 1.00 | | | | |
| 1993 In sets only | — | — | — | — | 0.75 | — |
| 1993 Proof | — | Value: 1.00 | | | | |
| 1994 In sets only | — | — | — | — | 0.75 | — |
| 1994 Proof | — | Value: 1.00 | | | | |
| 1995 In sets only | — | — | — | — | 0.75 | — |
| 1995 Proof | — | Value: 1.00 | | | | |
| 1996 In sets only | — | — | — | — | 0.75 | — |
| 1996 Proof | — | Value: 1.00 | | | | |

**JIAO** **Y# 24** **Composition:** Copper-Zinc

| Date | Mintage | F | VF | XF | Unc | BU |
|---|---|---|---|---|---|---|
| 1980 | — | — | — | — | 0.50 | — |
| 1980 Proof | — | Value: 1.00 | | | | |
| 1981 | — | — | — | — | 0.50 | — |
| 1981 Proof | — | Value: 1.00 | | | | |
| 1982 Proof | — | Value: 1.00 | | | | |
| 1983 | 3,100,000 | — | — | — | 0.50 | — |
| 1984 | 3,500,000 | — | — | — | 0.50 | — |
| 1985 Proof | — | Value: 1.00 | | | | |
| 1986 Proof | — | Value: 1.00 | | | | |

**JIAO** **Y# 148** **Composition:** Brass **Series:** 6th National Games **Subject:** Gymnast

| Date | Mintage | F | VF | XF | Unc | BU |
|---|---|---|---|---|---|---|
| 1987 | 10,570,000 | — | — | 1.00 | 2.00 | — |

**JIAO** **Y# 149** **Composition:** Brass **Series:** 6th National Games **Subject:** Soccer

| Date | Mintage | F | VF | XF | Unc | BU |
|---|---|---|---|---|---|---|
| 1987 | Inc. above | — | — | 1.00 | 2.00 | — |

**JIAO** **Y# 150** **Composition:** Brass **Series:** 6th National Games **Subject:** Volleyball

| Date | Mintage | F | VF | XF | Unc | BU |
|---|---|---|---|---|---|---|
| 1987 | Inc. above | — | — | 1.00 | 2.00 | — |

**JIAO** **Y# 328** **Composition:** Aluminum **Reverse:** Peony blossom

| Date | Mintage | F | VF | XF | Unc | BU |
|---|---|---|---|---|---|---|
| 1991 | — | — | — | — | 0.50 | — |
| 1991 Proof | — | Value: 1.00 | | | | |
| 1992 | — | — | — | — | 0.50 | — |
| 1992 Proof | — | Value: 1.00 | | | | |
| 1993 | — | — | — | — | 0.50 | — |
| 1993 Proof | — | Value: 1.00 | | | | |
| 1994 | — | — | — | — | 0.50 | — |
| 1994 Proof | — | Value: 1.00 | | | | |
| 1995 | — | — | — | — | 0.50 | — |
| 1995 Proof | — | Value: 1.00 | | | | |
| 1996 | — | — | — | — | 0.50 | — |
| 1996 Proof | — | Value: 1.00 | | | | |
| 1997 | — | — | — | — | 0.50 | — |

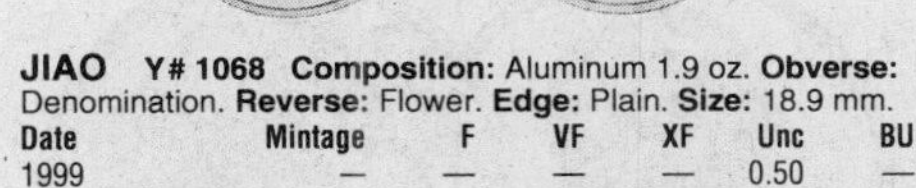

**JIAO** **Y# 1068** **Composition:** Aluminum 1.9 oz. **Obverse:** Denomination. **Reverse:** Flower. **Edge:** Plain. **Size:** 18.9 mm.

| Date | Mintage | F | VF | XF | Unc | BU |
|---|---|---|---|---|---|---|
| 1999 | — | — | — | — | 0.50 | — |

**2 JIAO** **Y# 25** **Composition:** Copper-Zinc

| Date | Mintage | F | VF | XF | Unc | BU |
|---|---|---|---|---|---|---|
| 1980 | — | — | — | — | 0.60 | — |
| 1980 Proof | — | Value: 1.25 | | | | |
| 1981 | — | — | — | — | 0.60 | — |
| 1981 Proof | — | Value: 1.25 | | | | |
| 1982 Proof | — | Value: 1.25 | | | | |
| 1983 | 4,200,000 | — | — | — | 0.60 | — |
| 1984 | 2,500,000 | — | — | — | 0.60 | — |
| 1985 Proof | — | Value: 1.25 | | | | |
| 1986 Proof | — | Value: 1.25 | | | | |

**5 JIAO** **Y# 26** **Composition:** Copper-Zinc

| Date | Mintage | F | VF | XF | Unc | BU |
|---|---|---|---|---|---|---|
| 1980 | — | — | — | — | 0.75 | — |
| 1980 Proof | — | Value: 1.50 | | | | |
| 1981 | — | — | — | — | 0.75 | — |
| 1981 Proof | — | Value: 1.50 | | | | |
| 1982 Proof | — | Value: 1.50 | | | | |
| 1983 | 3,000,000 | — | — | — | 0.75 | — |
| 1984 | 3,500,000 | — | — | — | 0.75 | — |
| 1985 | — | — | — | — | 0.75 | — |
| 1985 Proof | — | Value: 1.50 | | | | |
| 1986 Proof | — | Value: 1.50 | | | | |

**5 JIAO** **Y# 53** **Weight:** 2.2000 g. **Composition:** 0.9000 Silver .0637 oz. ASW **Reverse:** Marco Polo

| Date | Mintage | F | VF | XF | Unc | BU |
|---|---|---|---|---|---|---|
| 1983 Proof | 7,050 | Value: 90.00 | | | | |

**5 JIAO** **Y# 205** **Weight:** 2.0000 g. **Composition:** 0.9990 Silver .0643 oz. ASW **Reverse:** Phoenix and dragon representing good luck.

| Date | Mintage | F | VF | XF | Unc | BU |
|---|---|---|---|---|---|---|
| 1989 Proof | 55,000 | Value: 10.00 | | | | |

**5 JIAO** **Y# 329** **Composition:** Brass

| Date | Mintage | F | VF | XF | Unc | BU |
|---|---|---|---|---|---|---|
| 1991 | — | — | — | — | 1.00 | — |
| 1991 Proof | — | Value: 1.50 | | | | |
| 1992 | — | — | — | — | 1.00 | — |
| 1992 Proof | — | Value: 1.50 | | | | |
| 1993 | — | — | — | — | 1.00 | — |
| 1993 Proof | — | Value: 1.50 | | | | |
| 1994 | — | — | — | — | 1.00 | — |
| 1994 Proof | — | Value: 1.50 | | | | |
| 1995 | — | — | — | — | 1.00 | — |
| 1995 Proof | — | Value: 1.50 | | | | |
| 1996 | — | — | — | — | 1.00 | — |
| 1996 Proof | — | Value: 1.50 | | | | |
| 1997 | — | — | — | — | 1.00 | — |
| 1998 | — | — | — | — | 1.00 | — |

**YUAN** **Y# 10** **Composition:** Brass **Series:** 1980 Olympics **Subject:** Archery

| Date | Mintage | F | VF | XF | Unc | BU |
|---|---|---|---|---|---|---|
| 1980 Proof | 40,000 | Value: 11.50 | | | | |

**YUAN** **Y# 11** **Composition:** Brass **Series:** 1980 Olympics **Subject:** Wrestling

| Date | Mintage | F | VF | XF | Unc | BU |
|---|---|---|---|---|---|---|
| 1980 Proof | 40,000 | Value: 11.50 | | | | |

**YUAN** **Y# 12** **Composition:** Brass **Series:** 1980 Olympics **Subject:** Equestrian **Obverse:** Similar to Y#14

| Date | Mintage | F | VF | XF | Unc | BU |
|---|---|---|---|---|---|---|
| 1980 Proof | 40,000 | Value: 11.50 | | | | |

**YUAN** **Y# 13** **Composition:** Brass **Series:** 1980 Olympics **Subject:** Soccer **Obverse:** State seal

| Date | Mintage | F | VF | XF | Unc | BU |
|---|---|---|---|---|---|---|
| 1980 Proof | 40,000 | Value: 11.50 | | | | |

**YUAN** **Y# 14** **Composition:** Brass **Series:** 1980 Olympics **Subject:** Alpine Skiing

| Date | Mintage | F | VF | XF | Unc | BU |
|---|---|---|---|---|---|---|
| 1980 Proof | 29,000 | Value: 13.50 | | | | |

**YUAN** **Y# 15** **Composition:** Brass **Series:** 1980 Olympics **Subject:** Speed Skating

| Date | Mintage | F | VF | XF | Unc | BU |
|---|---|---|---|---|---|---|
| 1980 Proof | 29,000 | Value: 13.50 | | | | |

**YUAN** **Y# 16** **Composition:** Brass **Series:** 1980 Olympics **Subject:** Figure Skating

| Date | Mintage | F | VF | XF | Unc | BU |
|---|---|---|---|---|---|---|
| 1980 Proof | 29,000 | Value: 13.50 | | | | |

**YUAN** **Y# 17** **Composition:** Brass **Series:** 1980 Olympics **Subject:** Biathlon

| Date | Mintage | F | VF | XF | Unc | BU |
|---|---|---|---|---|---|---|
| 1980 Proof | 29,000 | Value: 13.50 | | | | |

**YUAN** **Y# 27** **Composition:** Copper-Nickel

| Date | Mintage | F | VF | XF | Unc | BU |
|---|---|---|---|---|---|---|
| 1980 | — | — | — | — | 2.00 | — |
| 1980 Proof | — | Value: 3.00 | | | | |
| 1981 | — | — | — | — | 2.00 | — |
| 1981 Proof | — | Value: 3.00 | | | | |
| 1982 Proof | — | Value: 3.00 | | | | |
| 1983 | 3,100,000 | — | — | — | 2.00 | — |
| 1984 | 4,100,000 | — | — | — | 2.00 | — |
| 1985 | — | — | — | — | 2.00 | — |
| 1985 Proof | — | Value: 3.00 | | | | |
| 1986 Proof | — | Value: 3.00 | | | | |

**YUAN** **Y# 34** **Composition:** Brass **Subject:** World Cup Soccer

| Date | Mintage | F | VF | XF | Unc | BU |
|---|---|---|---|---|---|---|
| 1982 Proof | 20,000 | Value: 12.50 | | | | |

**YUAN** **Y# 58** **Composition:** Brass **Reverse:** Panda

| Date | Mintage | F | VF | XF | Unc | BU |
|---|---|---|---|---|---|---|
| 1983 Proof | 30,000 | Value: 12.00 | | | | |
| 1984 Proof | 30,000 | Value: 12.00 | | | | |

**YUAN** **Y# 85** **Composition:** Copper-Nickel **Subject:** 35th Anniversary - Peoples Republic

| Date | Mintage | F | VF | XF | Unc | BU |
|---|---|---|---|---|---|---|
| ND(1984) | 20,410,000 | — | — | — | 6.00 | — |
| ND(1984) Proof | — | Value: 7.50 | | | | |

**YUAN** **Y# 86** **Composition:** Copper-Nickel **Subject:** 35th Anniversary - Peoples Republic

| Date | Mintage | F | VF | XF | Unc | BU |
|---|---|---|---|---|---|---|
| ND(1984) | Inc. above | — | — | — | 6.00 | — |
| ND(1984) Proof | — | Value: 7.50 | | | | |

**YUAN** **Y# 87** **Composition:** Copper-Nickel **Subject:** 35th Anniversary - Peoples Republic

| Date | Mintage | F | VF | XF | Unc | BU |
|---|---|---|---|---|---|---|
| ND(1984) | Inc. above | — | — | — | 6.00 | — |
| ND(1984) Proof | — | Value: 7.50 | | | | |

**YUAN** **Y# 96** **Composition:** Copper-Nickel **Subject:** 20th Anniversary - Tibet Autonomous Region

| Date | Mintage | F | VF | XF | Unc | BU |
|---|---|---|---|---|---|---|
| 1985 | 2,612,000 | — | — | 3.00 | 8.50 | — |
| 1985 Proof | 10,000 | Value: 12.00 | | | | |

**YUAN** **Y# 109** **Composition:** Copper-Nickel **Subject:** 30th Anniversary - Xinjiang Autonomous Region

| Date | Mintage | F | VF | XF | Unc | BU |
|---|---|---|---|---|---|---|
| 1985 | 4,500,000 | — | — | 2.00 | 6.00 | — |
| 1985 Proof | 10,000 | Value: 7.50 | | | | |

**YUAN** **Y# 151** **Composition:** Copper-Nickel **Subject:** Year of Peace

| Date | Mintage | F | VF | XF | Unc | BU |
|---|---|---|---|---|---|---|
| 1986 | 27,048,000 | — | — | — | 6.50 | — |

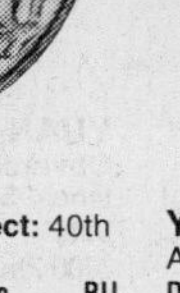

**YUAN** **Y# 140** **Composition:** Copper-Nickel **Subject:** 40th Anniversary - Mongolian Autonomous Region

| Date | Mintage | F | VF | XF | Unc | BU |
|---|---|---|---|---|---|---|
| 1987 | 9,054,000 | — | — | 2.00 | 6.00 | — |

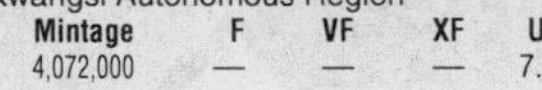

**YUAN** **Y# 198** **Composition:** Copper-Nickel **Subject:** 30th Anniversary - Kwangsi Autonomous Region

| Date | Mintage | F | VF | XF | Unc | BU |
|---|---|---|---|---|---|---|
| 1988 | 4,072,000 | — | — | — | 7.00 | — |

**YUAN** **Y# 211** **Composition:** Copper-Nickel **Subject:** 30th Anniversary - Ningxia Autonomous Region

| Date | Mintage | F | VF | XF | Unc | BU |
|---|---|---|---|---|---|---|
| 1988 | 1,560,000 | — | — | — | 7.50 | — |

**YUAN** **Y# 212** **Composition:** Copper-Nickel **Subject:** 40th Anniversary - Peoples Bank

| Date | Mintage | F | VF | XF | Unc | BU |
|---|---|---|---|---|---|---|
| 1988 | 2,068,000 | — | — | 5.00 | 14.00 | — |

**YUAN** **Y# 204** **Composition:** Copper-Nickel **Subject:** 40th Anniversary - Peoples Republic

| Date | Mintage | F | VF | XF | Unc | BU |
|---|---|---|---|---|---|---|
| 1989 | 2,000,000 | — | — | — | 5.00 | — |

**YUAN** **Y# 264** **Composition:** Nickel Clad Steel **Series:** XI Asian Games **Reverse:** Sword Dancer

| Date | Mintage | F | VF | XF | Unc | BU |
|---|---|---|---|---|---|---|
| 1990 | 25,608,000 | — | — | — | 4.00 | — |

**YUAN** **Y# 265** **Composition:** Nickel Clad Steel **Series:** XI Asian Games **Reverse:** Female Archer

| Date | Mintage | F | VF | XF | Unc | BU |
|---|---|---|---|---|---|---|
| 1990 | Inc. above | — | — | — | 4.00 | — |

**YUAN** **Y# 279** **Composition:** Nickel Clad Steel **Subject:** Planting Trees Festival **Reverse:** Head of young woman

| Date | Mintage | F | VF | XF | Unc | BU |
|---|---|---|---|---|---|---|
| 1991 | 10,000,000 | — | — | — | 2.75 | — |

**YUAN** **Y# 280** **Composition:** Nickel Clad Steel **Subject:** Planting Trees Festival **Reverse:** Globe

| Date | Mintage | F | VF | XF | Unc | BU |
|---|---|---|---|---|---|---|
| 1991 | 10,000,000 | — | — | — | 2.75 | — |

**YUAN** **Y# 281** **Composition:** Nickel Clad Steel **Subject:** Planting Trees Festival **Reverse:** Seedling

| Date | Mintage | F | VF | XF | Unc | BU |
|---|---|---|---|---|---|---|
| 1991 | 10,000,000 | — | — | — | 2.75 | — |

**YUAN** **Y# 284** **Composition:** Nickel Plated Steel **Subject:** 1st Meeting of Chinese Communist Party **Reverse:** House of Shanghai

| Date | Mintage | F | VF | XF | Unc | BU |
|---|---|---|---|---|---|---|
| 1991 | 30,000,000 | — | — | — | 2.50 | — |

**YUAN** **Y# 285** **Composition:** Nickel Plated Steel **Subject:** Party Meeting During Long March in 1935 **Reverse:** House in Zunyi, Kweichow Province

| Date | Mintage | F | VF | XF | Unc | BU |
|---|---|---|---|---|---|---|
| 1991 | 30,000,000 | — | — | — | 2.50 | — |

**YUAN** **Y# 286** **Composition:** Nickel Plated Steel **Subject:** 1978 Party Conference - Tianamen Square

| Date | Mintage | F | VF | XF | Unc | BU |
|---|---|---|---|---|---|---|
| 1991 | 30,000,000 | — | — | — | 2.50 | — |

**YUAN** **Y# 316** **Composition:** Nickel Plated Steel **Subject:** Women's World Soccer Championship **Reverse:** Goalie

| Date | Mintage | F | VF | XF | Unc | BU |
|---|---|---|---|---|---|---|
| 1991 | 10,000,000 | — | — | — | 2.50 | — |

**YUAN** **Y# 317** **Composition:** Nickel Plated Steel **Subject:** Women's World Soccer Championship **Reverse:** Player

| Date | Mintage | F | VF | XF | Unc | BU |
|---|---|---|---|---|---|---|
| 1991 | 10,000,000 | — | — | — | 2.50 | — |

**YUAN** **Y# 330** **Composition:** Nickel Clad Steel

| Date | Mintage | F | VF | XF | Unc | BU |
|---|---|---|---|---|---|---|
| 1991 | — | — | — | — | 1.50 | — |
| 1991 Proof | — | Value: 2.50 | | | | |
| 1992 | — | — | — | — | 1.50 | — |
| 1992 Proof | — | Value: 2.50 | | | | |
| 1993 | — | — | — | — | 1.50 | — |
| 1993 Proof | — | Value: 2.50 | | | | |
| 1994 | — | — | — | — | 1.50 | — |
| 1994 Proof | — | Value: 2.50 | | | | |
| 1995 | — | — | — | — | 1.50 | — |
| 1995 Proof | — | Value: 2.50 | | | | |
| 1996 | — | — | — | — | 1.50 | — |
| 1996 Proof | — | Value: 2.50 | | | | |
| 1997 | — | — | — | — | 1.50 | — |
| 1997 Proof | — | Value: 2.50 | | | | |

**YUAN** **Y# 364** **Composition:** Nickel Clad Steel **Subject:** 10th Anniversary - Constitution

| Date | Mintage | F | VF | XF | Unc | BU |
|---|---|---|---|---|---|---|
| 1992 | 10,000,000 | — | — | — | 2.50 | — |

**YUAN** **Y# 365** **Composition:** Nickel Clad Steel **Subject:** 100th Birthday of Ching Ling - 2nd Wife of Sun Yat-sen

| Date | Mintage | F | VF | XF | Unc | BU |
|---|---|---|---|---|---|---|
| 1993 | 10,448,000 | — | — | — | 3.50 | — |

**YUAN** **Y# 399** **Composition:** Nickel Clad Steel **Subject:** 100th Anniversary - Birth of Chairman Mao

| Date | Mintage | F | VF | XF | Unc | BU |
|---|---|---|---|---|---|---|
| 1993 | 20,000,000 | — | — | — | 3.50 | — |
| 1993 Prooflike | — | — | — | — | 5.00 | — |

**YUAN** **Y# 455** **Composition:** Nickel Clad Steel **Series:** Children's Year **Reverse:** 2 children

| Date | Mintage | F | VF | XF | Unc | BU |
|---|---|---|---|---|---|---|
| 1994 | — | — | — | — | 2.50 | — |

**YUAN** **Y# 487** **Composition:** Nickel Plated Steel **Subject:** Table Tennis

| Date | Mintage | F | VF | XF | Unc | BU |
|---|---|---|---|---|---|---|
| 1995 | 10,000,000 | — | — | — | 3.50 | — |
| 1995 Proof | 20,000 | Value: 6.50 | | | | |

**YUAN** **Y# 528** **Composition:** Nickel Plated Steel **Subject:** 50th Anniversary - Defeat of Fascism and Japan

| Date | Mintage | F | VF | XF | Unc | BU |
|---|---|---|---|---|---|---|
| 1995 | 10,000,000 | — | — | — | 3.50 | — |

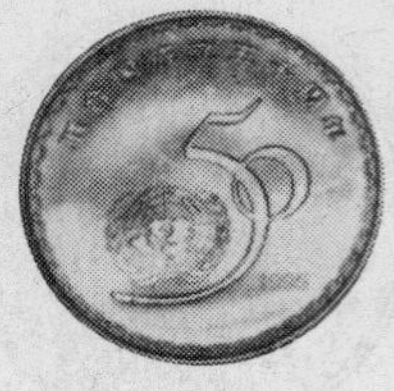

**YUAN** **Y# 529** **Composition:** Nickel Plated Steel **Subject:** 50th Anniversary - United Nations

| Date | Mintage | F | VF | XF | Unc | BU |
|---|---|---|---|---|---|---|
| 1995 | 10,000,000 | — | — | — | 3.00 | — |

**YUAN** **Y# 530** **Composition:** Nickel Plated Steel **Subject:** 4th UN Women's Conference

| Date | Mintage | F | VF | XF | Unc | BU |
|---|---|---|---|---|---|---|
| 1995 | 10,000,000 | — | — | — | 3.00 | — |

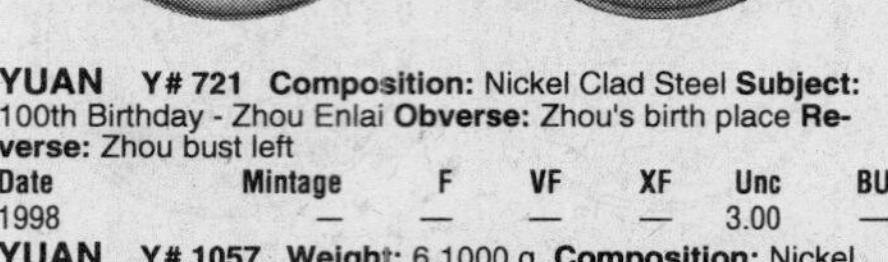

**YUAN** **Y# 721** **Composition:** Nickel Clad Steel **Subject:** 100th Birthday - Zhou Enlai **Obverse:** Zhou's birth place **Reverse:** Zhou bust left

| Date | Mintage | F | VF | XF | Unc | BU |
|---|---|---|---|---|---|---|
| 1998 | — | — | — | — | 3.00 | — |

**YUAN** **Y# 1057** **Weight:** 6.1000 g. **Composition:** Nickel Clad Steel **Subject:** Liu Shao-chi **Obverse:** Building, denomination and date. **Reverse:** Bust of Shao-chi left. **Edge Lettering:** ZHONGGUO twice. **Size:** 24.9 mm.

| Date | Mintage | F | VF | XF | Unc | BU |
|---|---|---|---|---|---|---|
| 1998 | — | — | — | — | 3.00 | — |

**YUAN** **Y# 1058** **Weight:** 6.1000 g. **Composition:** Nickel Clad Steel **Subject:** 50th Anniversary - People's Political Consultative Conference **Obverse:** Building. **Reverse:** Coat of arms. **Size:** 24.9 mm.

| Date | Mintage | F | VF | XF | Unc | BU |
|---|---|---|---|---|---|---|
| 1999 | — | — | — | — | 3.00 | — |

**YUAN** **Y# 1037** **Weight:** 6.1000 g. **Composition:** Nickel Clad Steel **Subject:** Dunhuang Cave **Obverse:** Pagoda **Reverse:** Standing and floating figures **Edge:** "RMB" 3 times

| Date | Mintage | F | VF | XF | Unc | BU |
|---|---|---|---|---|---|---|
| 2000 | — | — | — | — | 4.00 | — |

**YUAN** **Y# 1069** **Composition:** Nickel Clad Steel 6.03 oz. **Obverse:** Denomination. **Reverse:** Flower. **Edge:** "RMB" three times. **Size:** 24.9 mm.

| Date | Mintage | F | VF | XF | Unc | BU |
|---|---|---|---|---|---|---|
| 2000 Proof | — | — | — | — | 3.50 | — |

**3 YUAN** **Y# 307** **Weight:** 1.0000 g. **Composition:** 0.9990 Gold .0321 oz. AGW **Obverse:** Temple of Heaven

| Date | Mintage | F | VF | XF | Unc | BU |
|---|---|---|---|---|---|---|
| 1991 Proof | — | Value: 30.00 | | | | |

**3 YUAN** **Y# 362** **Weight:** 15.0000 g. **Composition:** 0.9000 Silver .4340 oz. ASW **Subject:** Ancient Chinese Coins

| Date | Mintage | F | VF | XF | Unc | BU |
|---|---|---|---|---|---|---|
| 1992 Proof | 23,000 | Value: 16.50 | | | | |

**3 YUAN** **Y# 363** **Weight:** 15.0000 g. **Composition:** 0.9000 Silver .4340 oz. ASW **Subject:** Ancient Chinese Paper

| Date | Mintage | F | VF | XF | Unc | BU |
|---|---|---|---|---|---|---|
| 1992 Proof | Est. 20,000 | Value: 16.50 | | | | |

**3 YUAN** **Y# 403** **Weight:** 15.0000 g. **Composition:** 0.9000 Silver .4340 oz. ASW **Subject:** Chinese gods Fu, Lu and Shu **Note:** Similar to 500 Yuan, Y#407.

| Date | Mintage | F | VF | XF | Unc | BU |
|---|---|---|---|---|---|---|
| 1993 Proof | 20,000 | Value: 18.50 | | | | |

**3 YUAN** **Y# 733** **Weight:** 15.0000 g. **Composition:** 0.9000 Silver .4340 oz. ASW **Subject:** Yin and Yang Concept **Obverse:** Great Wall tower **Reverse:** Chinese gods Fu, Lu and Shu with Yin Yang symbol

| Date | Mintage | F | VF | XF | Unc | BU |
|---|---|---|---|---|---|---|
| 1995 Proof | — | Value: 16.50 | | | | |

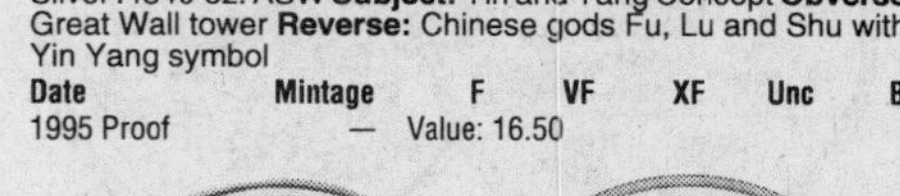

**3 YUAN** **Y# 734** **Weight:** 15.0000 g. **Composition:** 0.9000 Silver .4340 oz. ASW **Subject:** Great Wall of China **Obverse:** Great Wall view **Reverse:** Great Wall construction scene

| Date | Mintage | F | VF | XF | Unc | BU |
|---|---|---|---|---|---|---|
| 1995 Proof | — | Value: 16.50 | | | | |

**5 YUAN** **Y# 48** **Weight:** 1.5552 g. **Composition:** 0.9990 Gold .0500 oz. AGW

| Date | Mintage | F | VF | XF | Unc | BU |
|---|---|---|---|---|---|---|
| 1983 Proof | 58,000 | Value: 65.00 | | | | |

**5 YUAN** **Y# 54** **Weight:** 22.2200 g. **Composition:** 0.9000 Silver .6430 oz. ASW **Reverse:** Marco Polo

| Date | Mintage | F | VF | XF | Unc | BU |
|---|---|---|---|---|---|---|
| 1983 Proof | 15,000 | Value: 50.00 | | | | |

**5 YUAN** **Y# 61** **Weight:** 8.4500 g. **Composition:** 0.8000 Silver .2173 oz. ASW **Series:** 1984 Summer and Winter Olympics **Reverse:** High Jumper

| Date | Mintage | F | VF | XF | Unc | BU |
|---|---|---|---|---|---|---|
| 1984 Proof | 10,000 | Value: 25.00 | | | | |

**5 YUAN** **Y# 68** **Weight:** 22.2200 g. **Composition:** 0.9000 Silver .6430 oz. ASW **Subject:** Soldier Statues from Archaeological Discovery

| Date | Mintage | F | VF | XF | Unc | BU |
|---|---|---|---|---|---|---|
| 1984 Proof | 14,000 | Value: 20.00 | | | | |

**5 YUAN** **Y# 69** **Weight:** 22.2200 g. **Composition:** 0.9000 Silver .6430 oz. ASW **Subject:** Soldier Statues from Archaeological Discovery

| Date | Mintage | F | VF | XF | Unc | BU |
|---|---|---|---|---|---|---|
| 1984 Proof | 14,000 | Value: 20.00 | | | | |

**5 YUAN** **Y# 70** **Weight:** 22.2200 g. **Composition:** 0.9000 Silver .6430 oz. ASW **Subject:** Soldier Statues from Archaeological Discovery

| Date | Mintage | F | VF | XF | Unc | BU |
|---|---|---|---|---|---|---|
| 1984 Proof | 14,000 | Value: 20.00 | | | | |

**5 YUAN** **Y# 71** **Weight:** 22.2200 g. **Composition:** 0.9000 Silver .6430 oz. ASW **Subject:** Soldier Statues from Archaeological Discovery

| Date | Mintage | F | VF | XF | Unc | BU |
|---|---|---|---|---|---|---|
| 1984 Proof | 14,000 | Value: 20.00 | | | | |

**5 YUAN** **Y# 73** **Weight:** 1.5552 g. **Composition:** 0.9990 Gold .0500 oz. AGW

| Date | Mintage | F | VF | XF | Unc | BU |
|---|---|---|---|---|---|---|
| 1984 Proof | 86,000 | Value: 40.00 | | | | |

**5 YUAN** **Y# 80** **Weight:** 1.5552 g. **Composition:** 0.9990 Gold .0500 oz. AGW

| Date | Mintage | F | VF | XF | Unc | BU |
|---|---|---|---|---|---|---|
| 1985 Proof | 217,000 | Value: 55.00 | | | | |

**5 YUAN** **Y# 90** **Weight:** 22.2200 g. **Composition:** 0.9000 Silver .6430 oz. ASW **Subject:** Founders of Chinese Culture **Obverse:** State seal **Reverse:** Lao-Tse riding water buffalo

| Date | Mintage | F | VF | XF | Unc | BU |
|---|---|---|---|---|---|---|
| 1985 Proof | 8,175 | Value: 28.50 | | | | |

**5 YUAN** **Y# 91** **Weight:** 22.2200 g. **Composition:** 0.9000 Silver .6430 oz. ASW **Subject:** Founders of Chinese Culture **Reverse:** Qu Yuan

| Date | Mintage | F | VF | XF | Unc | BU |
|---|---|---|---|---|---|---|
| 1985 Proof | 8,175 | Value: 28.50 | | | | |

**5 YUAN** **Y# 92** **Weight:** 22.2200 g. **Composition:** 0.9000 Silver .6430 oz. ASW **Subject:** Founders of Chinese Culture **Reverse:** Sun Wu

| Date | Mintage | F | VF | XF | Unc | BU |
|---|---|---|---|---|---|---|
| 1985 Proof | 8,175 | Value: 28.50 | | | | |

**5 YUAN** **Y# 93** **Weight:** 22.2200 g. **Composition:** 0.9000 Silver .6430 oz. ASW **Subject:** Founders of Chinese Culture **Reverse:** Chen Sheng and Wu Guang

| Date | Mintage | F | VF | XF | Unc | BU |
|---|---|---|---|---|---|---|
| 1985 Proof | 8,175 | Value: 28.50 | | | | |

**5 YUAN** **Y# 101** **Weight:** 1.5552 g. **Composition:** 0.9990 Gold .0500 oz. AGW

| Date | Mintage | F | VF | XF | Unc | BU |
|---|---|---|---|---|---|---|
| 1986 | 53,000 | — | — | — | 35.00 | — |
| 1986 P Proof | 98,000 | Value: 40.00 | | | | |

**5 YUAN** **Y# 106** **Weight:** 22.2200 g. **Composition:** 0.9000 Silver .6430 oz. ASW **Subject:** Wildlife **Reverse:** Giant Panda

| Date | Mintage | F | VF | XF | Unc | BU |
|---|---|---|---|---|---|---|
| 1986 | 20,000 | — | — | — | 30.00 | — |
| 1986 Proof | 20,000 | Value: 45.00 | | | | |

**5 YUAN** **Y# 112** **Weight:** 18.6100 g. **Composition:** 0.9250 Silver .5535 oz. ASW **Subject:** Soccer

| Date | Mintage | F | VF | XF | Unc | BU |
|---|---|---|---|---|---|---|
| 1986 Proof | 8,500 | Value: 25.00 | | | | |

**5 YUAN** **Y# 112a** **Weight:** 17.0600 g. **Composition:** 0.8000 Silver .4388 oz. ASW

| Date | Mintage | F | VF | XF | Unc | BU |
|---|---|---|---|---|---|---|
| 1986 Satin finish | — | — | — | — | 40.00 | — |

**5 YUAN** **Y# 113** **Weight:** 22.2200 g. **Composition:** 0.9000 Silver .6367 oz. ASW **Subject:** Chinese Culture - Cai Lun - Paper Making

| Date | Mintage | F | VF | XF | Unc | BU |
|---|---|---|---|---|---|---|
| 1986 Proof | 9,675 | Value: 22.50 | | | | |

**5 YUAN** **Y# 114** **Weight:** 22.2200 g. **Composition:** 0.9000 Silver .6367 oz. ASW **Subject:** Chinese Culture - Zhang Heng - Astronomer

| Date | Mintage | F | VF | XF | Unc | BU |
|---|---|---|---|---|---|---|
| 1986 Proof | 9,675 | Value: 22.50 | | | | |

**5 YUAN** **Y# 115** **Weight:** 22.2200 g. **Composition:** 0.9000 Silver .6367 oz. ASW **Subject:** Chinese Culture - Zu Chong Zhi - Mathematician

| Date | Mintage | F | VF | XF | Unc | BU |
|---|---|---|---|---|---|---|
| 1986 Proof | 9,675 | Value: 22.50 | | | | |

**5 YUAN** **Y# 116** **Weight:** 22.2200 g. **Composition:** 0.9000 Silver .6367 oz. ASW **Subject:** Chinese Culture - Sima Qian - Historian

| Date | Mintage | F | VF | XF | Unc | BU |
|---|---|---|---|---|---|---|
| 1986 Proof | 9,675 | Value: 22.50 | | | | |

**5 YUAN** **Y# 119** **Weight:** 18.6100 g. **Composition:** 0.9250 Silver .5535 oz. ASW **Subject:** Year of Peace

| Date | Mintage | F | VF | XF | Unc | BU |
|---|---|---|---|---|---|---|
| 1986 Proof | 1,350 | Value: 200 | | | | |

**5 YUAN** **Y# 132** **Weight:** 22.2200 g. **Composition:** 0.9000 Silver .6367 oz. ASW **Obverse:** Great Wall **Reverse:** The Ship Empress of China

| Date | Mintage | F | VF | XF | Unc | BU |
|---|---|---|---|---|---|---|
| 1986 | 75,000 | — | — | — | 17.50 | — |

**5 YUAN** **Y# 197** **Weight:** 18.6100 g. **Composition:** 0.9250 Silver .5535 oz. ASW **Subject:** Soccer **Reverse:** 2 Players

| Date | Mintage | F | VF | XF | Unc | BU |
|---|---|---|---|---|---|---|
| 1986 | 1,000 | — | — | — | 55.00 | — |

**5 YUAN** **Y# 197a** **Weight:** 16.8300 g. **Composition:** 0.8000 Silver .4328 oz. ASW

| Date | Mintage | F | VF | XF | Unc | BU |
|---|---|---|---|---|---|---|
| 1986 Proof | 4,000 | Value: 30.00 | | | | |

**5 YUAN** **Y# 124** **Weight:** 1.5552 g. **Composition:** 0.9990 Gold .0500 oz. AGW

| Date | Mintage | F | VF | XF | Unc | BU |
|---|---|---|---|---|---|---|
| 1987(s) | 99,000 | — | — | — | 35.00 | — |
| 1987(y) | 39,000 | — | — | — | 35.00 | — |
| 1987 P Proof | 10,000 | Value: 40.00 | | | | |

**5 YUAN** **Y# 135** **Weight:** 31.4700 g. **Composition:** 0.9000 Silver .9107 oz. ASW **Reverse:** Poet Li Bai

| Date | Mintage | F | VF | XF | Unc | BU |
|---|---|---|---|---|---|---|
| 1987 Proof | 4,000 | Value: 23.50 | | | | |

**5 YUAN** **Y# 136** **Weight:** 31.4700 g. **Composition:** 0.9000 Silver .9107 oz. ASW **Reverse:** Poet Du Fu

| Date | Mintage | F | VF | XF | Unc | BU |
|---|---|---|---|---|---|---|
| 1987 Proof | 4,000 | Value: 23.50 | | | | |

**5 YUAN** **Y# 137** **Weight:** 31.4700 g. **Composition:** 0.9000 Silver .9107 oz. ASW **Subject:** Bridge Builder - Li Chun

| Date | Mintage | F | VF | XF | Unc | BU |
|---|---|---|---|---|---|---|
| 1987 Proof | 4,000 | Value: 24.00 | | | | |

**5 YUAN** **Y# 138** **Weight:** 31.4700 g. **Composition:** 0.9000 Silver .9107 oz. ASW **Subject:** Princess Chen Wen and Song Zan Gan Bu

| Date | Mintage | F | VF | XF | Unc | BU |
|---|---|---|---|---|---|---|
| 1987 Proof | 4,000 | Value: 24.00 | | | | |

**5 YUAN** **Y# 129** **Weight:** 31.4700 g. **Composition:** 0.9000 Silver .9107 oz. ASW **Series:** Winter Olympics **Reverse:** Downhill Skier

| Date | Mintage | F | VF | XF | Unc | BU |
|---|---|---|---|---|---|---|
| 1988 Proof | 17,000 | Value: 60.00 | | | | |

**5 YUAN** **Y# 130** **Weight:** 31.4700 g. **Composition:** 0.9000 Silver .9107 oz. ASW **Series:** Summer Olympics **Reverse:** Woman Hurdler

| Date | Mintage | F | VF | XF | Unc | BU |
|---|---|---|---|---|---|---|
| 1988 Proof | 20,000 | Value: 32.50 | | | | |

**5 YUAN** **Y# 152** **Weight:** 1.5552 g. **Composition:** 0.9990 Gold .0500 oz. AGW **Reverse:** Panda pawing bamboo

| Date | Mintage | F | VF | XF | Unc | BU |
|---|---|---|---|---|---|---|
| 1988 | 482,000 | — | — | — | 35.00 | — |
| 1988 Proof | 11,000 | Value: 40.00 | | | | |

**5 YUAN** **Y# 160** **Weight:** 22.2200 g. **Composition:** 0.9000 Silver .6430 oz. ASW **Subject:** Military Hero of Song Dynasty - Yue Fei

| Date | Mintage | F | VF | XF | Unc | BU |
|---|---|---|---|---|---|---|
| 1988 Proof | 13,000 | Value: 22.50 | | | | |

**5 YUAN** **Y# 161** **Weight:** 22.2200 g. **Composition:** 0.9000 Silver .6430 oz. ASW **Subject:** Bi Sheng - Inventor of Movable-type Printing

| Date | Mintage | F | VF | XF | Unc | BU |
|---|---|---|---|---|---|---|
| 1988 Proof | 14,000 | Value: 22.50 | | | | |

**5 YUAN** **Y# 162** **Weight:** 22.2200 g. **Composition:** 0.9000 Silver .6430 oz. ASW **Subject:** Su Shi - Song Dynasty Poet

| Date | Mintage | F | VF | XF | Unc | BU |
|---|---|---|---|---|---|---|
| 1988 Proof | 9,500 | Value: 22.50 | | | | |

**5 YUAN** **Y# 163** **Weight:** 22.2200 g. **Composition:** 0.9000 Silver .6430 oz. ASW **Subject:** Li Qingzhao - Poetess of Song Dynasty

| Date | Mintage | F | VF | XF | Unc | BU |
|---|---|---|---|---|---|---|
| 1988 Proof | 13,000 | Value: 22.50 | | | | |

**5 YUAN** **Y# 171** **Weight:** 27.0000 g. **Composition:** 0.9000 Silver .7812 oz. ASW **Series:** Olympics **Reverse:** Sailboat Racing

| Date | Mintage | F | VF | XF | Unc | BU |
|---|---|---|---|---|---|---|
| 1988 Proof | 20,000 | Value: 32.50 | | | | |

**5 YUAN** **Y# 172** **Weight:** 27.0000 g. **Composition:** 0.9000 Silver .7812 oz. ASW **Series:** Olympics **Subject:** Fencing

| Date | Mintage | F | VF | XF | Unc | BU |
|---|---|---|---|---|---|---|
| 1988 Proof | 20,000 | Value: 30.00 | | | | |

**5 YUAN** **Y# 213** **Weight:** 22.2200 g. **Composition:** 0.9000 Silver .6431 oz. ASW **Subject:** Kublai Khan - Emperor

| Date | Mintage | F | VF | XF | Unc | BU |
|---|---|---|---|---|---|---|
| 1989 Proof | 10,000 | Value: 25.00 | | | | |

**5 YUAN** **Y# 214** **Weight:** 22.2200 g. **Composition:** 0.9000 Silver .6431 oz. ASW **Subject:** Guan Hanqing - Playwright

| Date | Mintage | F | VF | XF | Unc | BU |
|---|---|---|---|---|---|---|
| 1989 Proof | 8,000 | Value: 27.50 | | | | |

**5 YUAN** **Y# 215** **Weight:** 22.2200 g. **Composition:** 0.9000 Silver .6431 oz. ASW **Subject:** Guo Shoujing - Scientist

| Date | Mintage | F | VF | XF | Unc | BU |
|---|---|---|---|---|---|---|
| 1989 Proof | 8,500 | Value: 27.50 | | | | |

**5 YUAN** **Y# 216** **Weight:** 22.2200 g. **Composition:** 0.9000 Silver .6431 oz. ASW **Subject:** Huang Daopo - Inventor of Water Wheel

| Date | Mintage | F | VF | XF | Unc | BU |
|---|---|---|---|---|---|---|
| 1989 Proof | 8,000 | Value: 27.50 | | | | |

**5 YUAN** **Y# 230** **Weight:** 22.2200 g. **Composition:** 0.9000 Silver .6431 oz. ASW **Series:** Save The Children Fund

| Date | Mintage | F | VF | XF | Unc | BU |
|---|---|---|---|---|---|---|
| 1989 | 20,000 | — | — | — | 30.00 | — |

**5 YUAN** Y# 243 **Weight:** 27.0000 g. **Composition:** 0.9250 Silver .8030 oz. ASW **Subject:** Soccer **Reverse:** 2 Players

| Date | Mintage | F | VF | XF | Unc | BU |
|---|---|---|---|---|---|---|
| 1989 Proof | 30,000 | Value: 25.00 | | | | |

**5 YUAN** Y# 187 **Weight:** 1.5552 g. **Composition:** 0.9990 Gold .0500 oz. AGW **Series:** Olympics **Note:** Similar to 100 Yuan, Y#191.

| Date | Mintage | F | VF | XF | Unc | BU |
|---|---|---|---|---|---|---|
| 1989 | 334,000 | — | — | — | 35.00 | — |
| 1989 Proof | — | Value: 45.00 | | | | |

**5 YUAN** Y# 238 **Weight:** 1.5552 g. **Composition:** 0.9990 Gold .0500 oz. AGW **Note:** Similar to 100 Yuan, Y#242.

| Date | Mintage | F | VF | XF | Unc | BU |
|---|---|---|---|---|---|---|
| 1990 | — | — | — | — | 35.00 | — |
| 1990 Proof | 5,000 | Value: 45.00 | | | | |

**5 YUAN** Y# 257 **Weight:** 15.0000 g. **Composition:** 0.9000 Silver .4341 oz. ASW **Subject:** Bronze Archaeological Finds **Reverse:** Elephant Pitcher

| Date | Mintage | F | VF | XF | Unc | BU |
|---|---|---|---|---|---|---|
| 1990 Proof | 5,000 | Value: 28.50 | | | | |

**5 YUAN** Y# 258 **Weight:** 15.0000 g. **Composition:** 0.9000 Silver .4341 oz. ASW **Subject:** Bronze Archaeological Finds **Reverse:** Mythical Creature

| Date | Mintage | F | VF | XF | Unc | BU |
|---|---|---|---|---|---|---|
| 1990 Proof | 5,000 | Value: 28.50 | | | | |

**5 YUAN** Y# 259 **Weight:** 15.0000 g. **Composition:** 0.9000 Silver .4341 oz. ASW **Subject:** Bronze Archaeological Finds **Reverse:** Rhinoceros

| Date | Mintage | F | VF | XF | Unc | BU |
|---|---|---|---|---|---|---|
| 1990 Proof | 5,000 | Value: 28.50 | | | | |

**5 YUAN** Y# 260 **Weight:** 15.0000 g. **Composition:** 0.9000 Silver .4341 oz. ASW **Subject:** Bronze Archaeological Finds **Reverse:** Leopard

| Date | Mintage | F | VF | XF | Unc | BU |
|---|---|---|---|---|---|---|
| 1990 Proof | 5,000 | Value: 28.50 | | | | |

**5 YUAN** Y# 297 **Weight:** 27.0000 g. **Composition:** 0.9250 Silver .8030 oz. ASW **Subject:** Soccer **Reverse:** 2 Players

| Date | Mintage | F | VF | XF | Unc | BU |
|---|---|---|---|---|---|---|
| 1990 Proof | 30,000 | Value: 27.50 | | | | |

**5 YUAN** Y# 298 **Weight:** 27.0000 g. **Composition:** 0.9250 Silver .8030 oz. ASW **Subject:** Soccer **Reverse:** Goalie

| Date | Mintage | F | VF | XF | Unc | BU |
|---|---|---|---|---|---|---|
| 1990 Proof | 30,000 | Value: 27.50 | | | | |

**5 YUAN** Y# 302 **Weight:** 22.2200 g. **Composition:** 0.9000 Silver .6431 oz. ASW **Subject:** Luo Guanzhong - Historian

| Date | Mintage | F | VF | XF | Unc | BU |
|---|---|---|---|---|---|---|
| 1990 | — | — | — | — | 20.00 | — |

**5 YUAN** Y# 303 **Weight:** 22.2200 g. **Composition:** 0.9000 Silver .6431 oz. ASW **Subject:** Li Zicheng - Revolutionary

| Date | Mintage | F | VF | XF | Unc | BU |
|---|---|---|---|---|---|---|
| 1990 | — | — | — | — | 20.00 | — |

**5 YUAN** Y# 304 **Weight:** 22.2200 g. **Composition:** 0.9000 Silver .6431 oz. ASW **Subject:** Li Shi Zhen - Herbalist

| Date | Mintage | F | VF | XF | Unc | BU |
|---|---|---|---|---|---|---|
| 1990 | — | — | — | — | 20.00 | — |

**5 YUAN** Y# 305 **Weight:** 22.2200 g. **Composition:** 0.9000 Silver .6431 oz. ASW **Subject:** Zheng He - Seafarer

| Date | Mintage | F | VF | XF | Unc | BU |
|---|---|---|---|---|---|---|
| 1990 | — | — | — | — | 20.00 | — |

**5 YUAN** Y# 322 **Weight:** 22.2200 g. **Composition:** 0.9000 Silver .6431 oz. ASW **Subject:** Song Yingxing - Scientist

| Date | Mintage | F | VF | XF | Unc | BU |
|---|---|---|---|---|---|---|
| 1991 Proof | 25,000 | Value: 22.50 | | | | |

**5 YUAN** Y# 323 **Weight:** 22.2200 g. **Composition:** 0.9000 Silver .6431 oz. ASW **Subject:** Cao Xueqin - Writer

| Date | Mintage | F | VF | XF | Unc | BU |
|---|---|---|---|---|---|---|
| 1991 Proof | Est. 25,000 | Value: 22.50 | | | | |

**5 YUAN** Y# 324 **Weight:** 22.2200 g. **Composition:** 0.9000 Silver .6431 oz. ASW **Subject:** Lin Zexu - High Ranking Official

| Date | Mintage | F | VF | XF | Unc | BU |
|---|---|---|---|---|---|---|
| 1991 Proof | 25,000 | Value: 22.50 | | | | |

**5 YUAN** Y# 325 **Weight:** 22.2200 g. **Composition:** 0.9000 Silver .6431 oz. ASW **Subject:** Hong Xuquan - Revolutionary

| Date | Mintage | F | VF | XF | Unc | BU |
|---|---|---|---|---|---|---|
| 1991 Proof | 25,000 | Value: 22.50 | | | | |

**5 YUAN** Y# 309 **Weight:** 1.5552 g. **Composition:** 0.9990 Gold .0500 oz. AGW **Note:** Similar to 100 Yuan, Y#313.

| Date | Mintage | F | VF | XF | Unc | BU |
|---|---|---|---|---|---|---|
| 1991 | — | — | — | — | 45.00 | — |
| 1991 Proof | — | Value: 50.00 | | | | |

**5 YUAN** Y# 341 **Weight:** 1.5552 g. **Composition:** 0.9990 Gold .0500 oz. AGW **Note:** Similar to 100 Yuan, Y#345.

| Date | Mintage | F | VF | XF | Unc | BU |
|---|---|---|---|---|---|---|
| 1992 | — | — | — | — | 45.00 | — |
| 1992 Proof | — | Value: 50.00 | | | | |

**5 YUAN** Y# 331 **Weight:** 22.2200 g. **Composition:** 0.9000 Silver .6431 oz. ASW **Subject:** Archeological Finds **Obverse:** Great Wall **Reverse:** Ancient Ships and Shipbuilding

| Date | Mintage | F | VF | XF | Unc | BU |
|---|---|---|---|---|---|---|
| 1992 Proof | 15,000 | Value: 27.50 | | | | |

**5 YUAN** Y# 332 **Weight:** 22.2200 g. **Composition:** 0.9000 Silver .6431 oz. ASW **Subject:** First Compass

| Date | Mintage | F | VF | XF | Unc | BU |
|---|---|---|---|---|---|---|
| 1992 Proof | 15,000 | Value: 25.00 | | | | |

**5 YUAN** Y# 333 **Weight:** 22.2200 g. **Composition:** 0.9000 Silver .6431 oz. ASW **Subject:** First Seismograph

| Date | Mintage | F | VF | XF | Unc | BU |
|---|---|---|---|---|---|---|
| 1992 Proof | 15,000 | Value: 25.00 | | | | |

**5 YUAN** Y# 334 **Weight:** 22.2200 g. **Composition:** 0.9000 Silver .6431 oz. ASW **Subject:** Ancient Kite Flying

| Date | Mintage | F | VF | XF | Unc | BU |
|---|---|---|---|---|---|---|
| 1992 Proof | 15,000 | Value: 25.00 | | | | |

**5 YUAN** Y# 335 **Weight:** 22.2200 g. **Composition:** 0.9000 Silver .6431 oz. ASW **Reverse:** Bronze Age Metal Working Scene

| Date | Mintage | F | VF | XF | Unc | BU |
|---|---|---|---|---|---|---|
| 1992 Proof | 15,000 | Value: 25.00 | | | | |

**5 YUAN** Y# 548 **Weight:** 22.2200 g. **Composition:** 0.9000 Silver .6430 oz. ASW **Subject:** United Nationsl Environmental Protection **Obverse:** State seal **Reverse:** Woman drawing water from stream

| Date | Mintage | F | VF | XF | Unc | BU |
|---|---|---|---|---|---|---|
| 1992 Proof | 20,000 | Value: 40.00 | | | | |

**5 YUAN** Y# 549 **Weight:** 22.2200 g. **Composition:** 0.9000 Silver .6430 oz. ASW **Obverse:** State seal **Reverse:** Zheng Chenggong portrait.

| Date | Mintage | F | VF | XF | Unc | BU |
|---|---|---|---|---|---|---|
| 1992 Proof | — | Value: 17.50 | | | | |

**5 YUAN** Y# 550 **Weight:** 22.2200 g. **Composition:** 0.9000 Silver .6430 oz. ASW **Obverse:** State seal **Reverse:** Cai Wenji, writer

| Date | Mintage | F | VF | XF | Unc | BU |
|---|---|---|---|---|---|---|
| 1992 Proof | Est. 7,000 | Value: 20.00 | | | | |

**5 YUAN** Y# 551 **Weight:** 22.2200 g. **Composition:** 0.9000 Silver .6430 oz. ASW **Obverse:** State seal **Reverse:** Hua Mulan, soldier

| Date | Mintage | F | VF | XF | Unc | BU |
|---|---|---|---|---|---|---|
| 1992 Proof | Est. 7,000 | Value: 28.00 | | | | |

**5 YUAN** Y# 552 **Weight:** 22.2200 g. **Composition:** 0.9000 Silver .6430 oz. ASW **Obverse:** State seal **Reverse:** Wang Zhaojun, princess, peacemaker.

| Date | Mintage | F | VF | XF | Unc | BU |
|---|---|---|---|---|---|---|
| 1992 Proof | Est. 7,000 | Value: 20.00 | | | | |

**5 YUAN** Y# 676 **Weight:** 15.0000 g. **Composition:** 0.9000 Silver .4350 oz. ASW **Subject:** Taiwan Scenery Series **Obverse:** Great Wall **Reverse:** Tall, narrow building

| Date | Mintage | F | VF | XF | Unc | BU |
|---|---|---|---|---|---|---|
| 1992 Proof | 2,000 | Value: 32.00 | | | | |

**5 YUAN** Y# 677 **Weight:** 15.0000 g. **Composition:** 0.9000 Silver .4350 oz. ASW **Reverse:** Pondside building

| Date | Mintage | F | VF | XF | Unc | BU |
|---|---|---|---|---|---|---|
| 1992 Proof | 2,000 | Value: 32.00 | | | | |

**5 YUAN** **Y# 678** **Weight:** 15.0000 g. **Composition:** 0.9000 Silver .4350 oz. ASW **Reverse:** Hillside building

| Date | Mintage | F | VF | XF | Unc | BU |
|---|---|---|---|---|---|---|
| 1992 Proof | 2,000 | Value: 32.00 | | | | |

**5 YUAN** **Y# 679** **Weight:** 15.0000 g. **Composition:** 0.9000 Silver .4350 oz. ASW **Reverse:** 3 buildings joined by bridges

| Date | Mintage | F | VF | XF | Unc | BU |
|---|---|---|---|---|---|---|
| 1992 Proof | 2,000 | Value: 32.00 | | | | |

**5 YUAN** **Y# 750** **Weight:** 15.0000 g. **Composition:** 0.9000 Silver .4340 oz. ASW **Subject:** Archeological Finds **Obverse:** National emblem **Reverse:** Resting deer with long antlers

| Date | Mintage | F | VF | XF | Unc | BU |
|---|---|---|---|---|---|---|
| 1992 Proof | 3,000 | Value: 35.00 | | | | |

**5 YUAN** **Y# 751** **Weight:** 15.0000 g. **Composition:** 0.9000 Silver .4340 oz. ASW **Subject:** Archeological Finds **Obverse:** National emblem **Reverse:** Tiger

| Date | Mintage | F | VF | XF | Unc | BU |
|---|---|---|---|---|---|---|
| 1992 Proof | 3,000 | Value: 35.00 | | | | |

**5 YUAN** **Y# 752** **Weight:** 15.0000 g. **Composition:** 0.9000 Silver .4340 oz. ASW **Subject:** Archeological Finds **Obverse:** National emblem **Reverse:** Big horn sheep

| Date | Mintage | F | VF | XF | Unc | BU |
|---|---|---|---|---|---|---|
| 1992 Proof | 3,000 | Value: 35.00 | | | | |

**5 YUAN** **Y# 753** **Weight:** 15.0000 g. **Composition:** 0.9000 Silver .4340 oz. ASW **Subject:** Archeological Finds **Obverse:** National emblem **Reverse:** Changzin court lantern

| Date | Mintage | F | VF | XF | Unc | BU |
|---|---|---|---|---|---|---|
| 1992 Proof | 3,000 | Value: 35.00 | | | | |

**5 YUAN** **Y# 393** **Weight:** 15.0000 g. **Composition:** 0.9000 Silver .4341 oz. ASW **Reverse:** Marco Polo

| Date | Mintage | F | VF | XF | Unc | BU |
|---|---|---|---|---|---|---|
| 1992 Proof | 12,000 | Value: 22.50 | | | | |

**5 YUAN** **Y# 553** **Weight:** 22.2200 g. **Composition:** 0.9000 Silver .6430 oz. ASW **Obverse:** State seal **Reverse:** Xiao Zhuo, strategist

| Date | Mintage | F | VF | XF | Unc | BU |
|---|---|---|---|---|---|---|
| 1993 Proof | Est. 7,000 | Value: 28.00 | | | | |

**5 YUAN** **Y# 558** **Weight:** 22.2200 g. **Composition:** 0.9000 Silver .6430 oz. ASW **Subject:** Mathematical Definiation of Zero **Obverse:** State seal **Reverse:** Mathematicians, abacus

| Date | Mintage | F | VF | XF | Unc | BU |
|---|---|---|---|---|---|---|
| 1993 Proof | 15,000 | Value: 22.00 | | | | |

**5 YUAN** **Y# 559** **Weight:** 22.2200 g. **Composition:** 0.9000 Silver .6430 oz. ASW **Subject:** Invention of the Stirrup **Obverse:** Great Wall **Reverse:** Early polo game

| Date | Mintage | F | VF | XF | Unc | BU |
|---|---|---|---|---|---|---|
| 1993 Proof | 15,000 | Value: 22.00 | | | | |

**5 YUAN** **Y# 560** **Weight:** 22.2200 g. **Composition:** 0.9000 Silver .6430 oz. ASW **Subject:** The Terracotta Army **Obverse:** Great Wall **Reverse:** The unearthing of the terracotta figurines

| Date | Mintage | F | VF | XF | Unc | BU |
|---|---|---|---|---|---|---|
| 1993 Proof | 15,000 | Value: 22.00 | | | | |

**5 YUAN** **Y# 359** **Composition:** Copper **Reverse:** 2 Pandas eating bamboo

| Date | Mintage | F | VF | XF | Unc | BU |
|---|---|---|---|---|---|---|
| 1993 | 2,000,000 | — | — | — | 12.00 | — |

**5 YUAN** **Y# 377** **Weight:** 22.2200 g. **Composition:** 0.9000 Silver .6431 oz. ASW **Subject:** Chin-Yin Yang

| Date | Mintage | F | VF | XF | Unc | BU |
|---|---|---|---|---|---|---|
| 1993 Proof | 15,000 | Value: 35.00 | | | | |

**5 YUAN** **Y# 392** **Weight:** 15.5517 g. **Composition:** 0.9990 Silver .5000 oz. ASW **Reverse:** Panda facing forward

| Date | Mintage | F | VF | XF | Unc | BU |
|---|---|---|---|---|---|---|
| 1993 | — | — | — | — | 17.50 | — |

**5 YUAN** **Y# 400** **Weight:** 22.2200 g. **Composition:** 0.9000 Silver .6431 oz. ASW **Subject:** Invention of the Umbrella

| Date | Mintage | F | VF | XF | Unc | BU |
|---|---|---|---|---|---|---|
| 1993 Proof | 15,000 | Value: 20.00 | | | | |

**5 YUAN** **Y# 483** **Weight:** 1.5552 g. **Composition:** 0.9995 Platinum .0500 oz. APW **Reverse:** Panda seated on rock

| Date | Mintage | F | VF | XF | Unc | BU |
|---|---|---|---|---|---|---|
| 1993 Proof | — | Value: 50.00 | | | | |

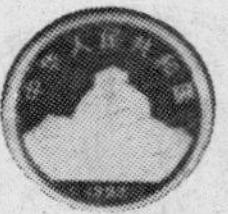

**5 YUAN** **Y# 498** **Weight:** 1.5552 g. **Composition:** 0.9990 Gold .0500 oz. AGW **Subject:** Goddess of Mercy

| Date | Mintage | F | VF | XF | Unc | BU |
|---|---|---|---|---|---|---|
| 1993 Prooflike | 15,000 | — | — | — | 35.00 | — |

**5 YUAN** **Y# 500** **Weight:** 1.5552 g. **Composition:** 0.9990 Gold .0500 oz. AGW **Reverse:** Goddess Kuan Yin - Seated in Flowers

| Date | Mintage | F | VF | XF | Unc | BU |
|---|---|---|---|---|---|---|
| 1993 Proof | 1,000 | Value: 55.00 | | | | |

**5 YUAN** **Y# 534** **Weight:** 22.2200 g. **Composition:** 0.9000 Silver .6431 oz. ASW **Subject:** Chou En-Lai **Obverse:** State emblem

| Date | Mintage | F | VF | XF | Unc | BU |
|---|---|---|---|---|---|---|
| 1993 Proof | 25,000 | Value: 22.50 | | | | |

**5 YUAN** **Y# 535** **Weight:** 22.2200 g. **Composition:** 0.9000 Silver .6431 oz. ASW **Subject:** Liu Shaoqi

| Date | Mintage | F | VF | XF | Unc | BU |
|---|---|---|---|---|---|---|
| 1993 Proof | 25,000 | Value: 22.50 | | | | |

**5 YUAN** **Y# 536** **Weight:** 22.2200 g. **Composition:** 0.9000 Silver .6431 oz. ASW **Subject:** Chu Teh

| Date | Mintage | F | VF | XF | Unc | BU |
|---|---|---|---|---|---|---|
| 1993 Proof | 25,000 | Value: 22.50 | | | | |

**5 YUAN** **Y# 537** **Weight:** 22.2200 g. **Composition:** 0.9000 Silver .6431 oz. ASW **Subject:** Li Da-Chao

| Date | Mintage | F | VF | XF | Unc | BU |
|---|---|---|---|---|---|---|
| 1993 Proof | 25,000 | Value: 22.50 | | | | |

**5 YUAN** **Y# 610** **Weight:** 1.5552 g. **Composition:** 0.9990 Gold .0500 oz. AGW **Obverse:** Panda pawing bamboo

| Date | Mintage | F | VF | XF | Unc | BU |
|---|---|---|---|---|---|---|
| 1993 | — | — | — | — | 37.50 | — |
| 1993 Proof | — | Value: 50.00 | | | | |

**5 YUAN** **Y# 768** **Weight:** 15.0000 g. **Composition:** 0.9000 Silver .4340 oz. ASW **Subject:** Archeological Finds **Obverse:** State seal **Reverse:** Ox lantern

| Date | Mintage | F | VF | XF | Unc | BU |
|---|---|---|---|---|---|---|
| 1993 Proof | 3,000 | Value: 35.00 | | | | |

**5 YUAN** **Y# 769** **Weight:** 15.0000 g. **Composition:** 0.9000 Silver .4340 oz. ASW **Subject:** Archeological Finds **Obverse:** National emblem **Reverse:** Human figure lantern

| Date | Mintage | F | VF | XF | Unc | BU |
|---|---|---|---|---|---|---|
| 1993 Proof | 3,000 | Value: 35.00 | | | | |

**5 YUAN** **Y# 770** **Weight:** 15.0000 g. **Composition:** 0.9000 Silver .4340 oz. ASW **Subject:** Archeological Finds **Obverse:** National emblem **Reverse:** Horse statue

| Date | Mintage | F | VF | XF | Unc | BU |
|---|---|---|---|---|---|---|
| 1993 Proof | 3,000 | Value: 35.00 | | | | |

**5 YUAN** **Y# 771** **Weight:** 15.0000 g. **Composition:** 0.9000 Silver .4340 oz. ASW **Subject:** Archeological Finds **Obverse:** National emblem **Reverse:** Pig statue

| Date | Mintage | F | VF | XF | Unc | BU |
|---|---|---|---|---|---|---|
| 1993 Proof | 2,000 | Value: 35.00 | | | | |

**5 YUAN** **Y# 441** **Weight:** 15.0000 g. **Composition:** 0.9000 Silver .4341 oz. ASW **Obverse:** Great Wall **Reverse:** Taiwan Temple Buddha Statue **Note:** Similar to 50 Yuan, Y#445.

| Date | Mintage | F | VF | XF | Unc | BU |
|---|---|---|---|---|---|---|
| 1993 Proof | 1,000 | Value: 35.00 | | | | |

**5 YUAN** **Y# 442** **Weight:** 15.0000 g. **Composition:** 0.9000 Silver .4341 oz. ASW **Subject:** Taiwan Temple **Obverse:** Great Wall **Reverse:** Large temple **Note:** Similar to 50 Yuan, Y#446.

| Date | Mintage | F | VF | XF | Unc | BU |
|---|---|---|---|---|---|---|
| 1993 Proof | 1,000 | Value: 35.00 | | | | |

**5 YUAN** **Y# 443** **Weight:** 15.0000 g. **Composition:** 0.9000 Silver .4341 oz. ASW **Subject:** Taiwan Temple **Obverse:** Great Wall **Reverse:** Small temple **Note:** Similar to 50 Yuan, Y#447.

| Date | Mintage | F | VF | XF | Unc | BU |
|---|---|---|---|---|---|---|
| 1993 Proof | 1,000 | Value: 35.00 | | | | |

**5 YUAN** **Y# 444** **Weight:** 15.0000 g. **Composition:** 0.9000 Silver .4341 oz. ASW **Subject:** Taiwan Temple **Obverse:** Great Wall **Reverse:** Tower temple **Note:** Similar to 50 Yuan, Y#448.

| Date | Mintage | F | VF | XF | Unc | BU |
|---|---|---|---|---|---|---|
| 1993 Proof | 1,000 | Value: 35.00 | | | | |

**5 YUAN** **Y# 773** **Weight:** 1.5552 g. **Composition:** 0.9990 Gold .0500 oz. AGW **Subject:** Mount Song **Obverse:** Great Wall **Reverse:** Temple **Note:** Similar to 10 Yuan, Y#420.

| Date | Mintage | F | VF | XF | Unc | BU |
|---|---|---|---|---|---|---|
| 1993 Proof | 8,888 | Value: 35.00 | | | | |

**5 YUAN** **Y# 419** **Weight:** 1.5552 g. **Composition:** 0.9990 Gold .0500 oz. AGW **Reverse:** Unicorn

| Date | Mintage | F | VF | XF | Unc | BU |
|---|---|---|---|---|---|---|
| 1994 Proof | 31,000 | Value: 65.00 | | | | |

**5 YUAN** **Y# 431** **Weight:** 1.5552 g. **Composition:** 0.9990 Gold .0500 oz. AGW

| Date | Mintage | F | VF | XF | Unc | BU |
|---|---|---|---|---|---|---|
| 1994 | 35,000 | — | — | — | 45.00 | — |
| 1994 Proof | — | Value: 50.00 | | | | |

**5 YUAN** **Y# 436** **Weight:** 15.5517 g. **Composition:** 0.9990 Silver .5000 oz. ASW **Reverse:** Panda approaching water

| Date | Mintage | F | VF | XF | Unc | BU |
|---|---|---|---|---|---|---|
| 1994 | — | — | — | — | 20.00 | — |

**5 YUAN** **Y# 506** **Weight:** 15.5517 g. **Composition:** 0.9990 Silver .5000 oz. ASW **Reverse:** Goddess Kuan Yin - with child

| Date | Mintage | F | VF | XF | Unc | BU |
|---|---|---|---|---|---|---|
| 1994 Proof | 3,000 | Value: 27.50 | | | | |

**5 YUAN** **Y# 507** **Weight:** 15.5517 g. **Composition:** 0.9990 Silver .5000 oz. ASW **Reverse:** Goddess Kuan Yin - with bottle

| Date | Mintage | F | VF | XF | Unc | BU |
|---|---|---|---|---|---|---|
| 1994 Proof | 3,000 | Value: 27.50 | | | | |

**5 YUAN** **Y# 508** **Weight:** 15.5517 g. **Composition:** 0.9990 Silver .5000 oz. ASW **Reverse:** Goddess Kuan Yin - standing

| Date | Mintage | F | VF | XF | Unc | BU |
|---|---|---|---|---|---|---|
| 1994 Proof | 3,000 | Value: 27.50 | | | | |

**5 YUAN** **Y# 509** **Weight:** 15.5517 g. **Composition:** 0.9990 Silver .5000 oz. ASW **Reverse:** Goddess Kuan Yin - seated

| Date | Mintage | F | VF | XF | Unc | BU |
|---|---|---|---|---|---|---|
| 1994 Proof | 3,000 | Value: 27.50 | | | | |

**5 YUAN** **Y# 616** **Weight:** 22.2200 g. **Composition:** 0.9000 Silver .6430 oz. ASW **Subject:** Oriental Inventions **Obverse:** Great Wall **Reverse:** First tuned bells

| Date | Mintage | F | VF | XF | Unc | BU |
|---|---|---|---|---|---|---|
| 1994 Proof | 15,000 | Value: 20.00 | | | | |

**5 YUAN** **Y# 617** **Weight:** 22.2200 g. **Composition:** 0.9000 Silver .6430 oz. ASW **Subject:** Oriental Inventions **Obverse:** Great Wall **Reverse:** First silken fabric

| Date | Mintage | F | VF | XF | Unc | BU |
|---|---|---|---|---|---|---|
| 1994 Proof | 15,000 | Value: 20.00 | | | | |

**5 YUAN** **Y# 618** **Weight:** 22.2200 g. **Composition:** 0.9000 Silver .6430 oz. ASW **Subject:** Oriental Invention **Obverse:** Great Wall **Reverse:** First records of comets

| Date | Mintage | F | VF | XF | Unc | BU |
|---|---|---|---|---|---|---|
| 1994 Proof | 15,000 | Value: 20.00 | | | | |

**5 YUAN** **Y# 619** **Weight:** 22.2200 g. **Composition:** 0.9000 Silver .6430 oz. ASW **Subject:** Oriental Inventions **Obverse:** Great Wall **Reverse:** First masts for sailing

| Date | Mintage | F | VF | XF | Unc | BU |
|---|---|---|---|---|---|---|
| 1994 Proof | 15,000 | Value: 20.00 | | | | |

**5 YUAN** **Y# 620** **Weight:** 22.2200 g. **Composition:** 0.9000 Silver .6430 oz. ASW **Subject:** Oriental Inventions **Obverse:** Great Wall **Reverse:** First chain pumps used to draw water

| Date | Mintage | F | VF | XF | Unc | BU |
|---|---|---|---|---|---|---|
| 1994 Proof | 15,000 | Value: 20.00 | | | | |

**5 YUAN** **Y# 481** **Weight:** 22.2200 g. **Composition:** 0.9000 Silver .6430 oz. ASW **Reverse:** Sea Goddess

| Date | Mintage | F | VF | XF | Unc | BU |
|---|---|---|---|---|---|---|
| 1995 Proof | 8,000,000 | Value: 23.50 | | | | |

**5 YUAN** **Y# 516** **Weight:** 22.2200 g. **Composition:** 0.9000 Silver .6430 oz. ASW **Reverse:** Goddess Kuan Yin - with Lotus flower

| Date | Mintage | F | VF | XF | Unc | BU |
|---|---|---|---|---|---|---|
| 1995 Proof | 3,000 | Value: 27.50 | | | | |

**5 YUAN** **Y# 517** **Weight:** 22.2200 g. **Composition:** 0.9000 Silver .6430 oz. ASW **Reverse:** Goddess Kuan Yin - with wheel

| Date | Mintage | F | VF | XF | Unc | BU |
|---|---|---|---|---|---|---|
| 1995 Proof | 3,000 | Value: 27.50 | | | | |

**5 YUAN** **Y# 518** **Weight:** 22.2200 g. **Composition:** 0.9000 Silver .6430 oz. ASW **Reverse:** Goddess Kuan Yin - with sceptre

| Date | Mintage | F | VF | XF | Unc | BU |
|---|---|---|---|---|---|---|
| 1995 Proof | 3,000 | Value: 27.50 | | | | |

**5 YUAN** **Y# 519** **Weight:** 22.2200 g. **Composition:** 0.9000 Silver .6430 oz. ASW **Reverse:** Goddess Kuan Yin - with bowl

| Date | Mintage | F | VF | XF | Unc | BU |
|---|---|---|---|---|---|---|
| 1995 Proof | 3,000 | Value: 27.50 | | | | |

**5 YUAN** **Y# 547** **Composition:** Bronze **Reverse:** Golden Monkey

| Date | Mintage | F | VF | XF | Unc | BU |
|---|---|---|---|---|---|---|
| 1995 | — | — | — | — | 10.00 | — |

**5 YUAN** **Y# 600** **Weight:** 22.2200 g. **Composition:** 0.9000 Silver .6430 oz. ASW **Reverse:** 2 men leading camel

| Date | Mintage | F | VF | XF | Unc | BU |
|---|---|---|---|---|---|---|
| 1995 Proof | 15,000 | Value: 30.00 | | | | |

**5 YUAN** **Y# 601** **Weight:** 22.2200 g. **Composition:** 0.9000 Silver .6430 oz. ASW **Reverse:** Dancer

| Date | Mintage | F | VF | XF | Unc | BU |
|---|---|---|---|---|---|---|
| 1995 Proof | 15,000 | Value: 27.50 | | | | |

**5 YUAN** **Y# 602** **Weight:** 22.2200 g. **Composition:** 0.9000 Silver .6430 oz. ASW **Reverse:** Silk merchant and customer

| Date | Mintage | F | VF | XF | Unc | BU |
|---|---|---|---|---|---|---|
| 1995 Proof | 15,000 | Value: 27.50 | | | | |

**5 YUAN** **Y# 603** **Weight:** 22.2200 g. **Composition:** 0.9000 Silver .6430 oz. ASW **Reverse:** Silk spinner

| Date | Mintage | F | VF | XF | Unc | BU |
|---|---|---|---|---|---|---|
| 1995 Proof | Est. 15,000 | Value: 27.50 | | | | |

**5 YUAN** **Y# 628 (Y629)** **Weight:** 22.2200 g. **Composition:** 0.9000 Silver .6430 oz. ASW **Subject:** Oriental Inventions **Obverse:** Great Wall **Reverse:** Individual block printing

| Date | Mintage | F | VF | XF | Unc | BU |
|---|---|---|---|---|---|---|
| 1995 Proof | 15,000 | Value: 20.00 | | | | |

**5 YUAN** **Y# 630** **Weight:** 22.2200 g. **Composition:** 0.9000 Silver .6430 oz. ASW **Subject:** Oriental Inventions **Obverse:** Great Wall **Reverse:** Potter

| Date | Mintage | F | VF | XF | Unc | BU |
|---|---|---|---|---|---|---|
| 1995 Proof | 15,000 | Value: 20.00 | | | | |

**5 YUAN** **Y# 640** **Weight:** 1.5552 g. **Composition:** 0.9990 Gold .0500 oz. AGW **Reverse:** Panda holding bamboo stick

| Date | Mintage | F | VF | XF | Unc | BU |
|---|---|---|---|---|---|---|
| 1995 | — | — | — | — | 45.00 | — |

**5 YUAN** **Y# 736** **Weight:** 1.5552 g. **Composition:** 0.9990 Gold .0500 oz. AGW **Obverse:** Eastern unicorn **Reverse:** Western unicorn with offspring

| Date | Mintage | F | VF | XF | Unc | BU |
|---|---|---|---|---|---|---|
| 1995 Proof | 20,000 | Value: 70.00 | | | | |

**5 YUAN** **Y# 791** **Weight:** 15.7717 g. **Composition:** 0.9990 Silver .5000 oz. ASW **Obverse:** Temple of Heaven **Reverse:** Panda climbing tree branch

| Date | Mintage | F | VF | XF | Unc | BU |
|---|---|---|---|---|---|---|
| 1995 Proof | — | Value: 32.50 | | | | |

**5 YUAN** **Y# 794** **Weight:** 22.2223 g. **Composition:** 0.9000 Silver .6430 oz. ASW **Subject:** Chinese Culture Series **Obverse:** Great Wall seen through arch **Reverse:** Pagoda of Six Harmonies

| Date | Mintage | F | VF | XF | Unc | BU |
|---|---|---|---|---|---|---|
| 1995 Proof | 20,000 | Value: 37.50 | | | | |

**5 YUAN** **Y# 795** **Weight:** 22.2223 g. **Composition:** 0.9000 Silver .6430 oz. ASW **Subject:** Chinese Culture Series **Obverse:** Great Wall seen through arch **Reverse:** Mencius seated at table

| Date | Mintage | F | VF | XF | Unc | BU |
|---|---|---|---|---|---|---|
| 1995 Proof | 20,000 | Value: 37.50 | | | | |

**5 YUAN** **Y# 796** **Weight:** 22.2223 g. **Composition:** 0.9000 Silver .6430 oz. ASW **Subject:** Chinese Culture Series **Obverse:** Great Wall seen through arch **Reverse:** Tang Taizong seated

| Date | Mintage | F | VF | XF | Unc | BU |
|---|---|---|---|---|---|---|
| 1995 Proof | 20,000 | Value: 37.50 | | | | |

**5 YUAN** **Y# 797** **Weight:** 22.2223 g. **Composition:** 0.9000 Silver .6430 oz. ASW **Subject:** Chinese Culture Series **Obverse:** Great Wall seen through arch **Reverse:** Lion dance

| Date | Mintage | F | VF | XF | Unc | BU |
|---|---|---|---|---|---|---|
| 1995 Proof | 20,000 | Value: 37.50 | | | | |

**5 YUAN** **Y# 798** **Weight:** 22.2223 g. **Composition:** 0.9000 Silver .6430 oz. ASW **Subject:** Chinese Culture Series **Obverse:** Great Wall seen through arch **Reverse:** Female opera role

| Date | Mintage | F | VF | XF | Unc | BU |
|---|---|---|---|---|---|---|
| 1995 Proof | 20,000 | Value: 37.50 | | | | |

**5 YUAN** **Y# 629** **Weight:** 20.0000 g. **Composition:** 0.9000 Silver **Subject:** Oriental Inventions - Chinese game of Go **Obverse:** The Great Wall. **Reverse:** Two people playing Go. **Size:** 36 mm.

| Date | Mintage | F | VF | XF | Unc | BU |
|---|---|---|---|---|---|---|
| 1995 Proof | — | Value: 22.50 | | | | |

**5 YUAN** **Y# 627** **Weight:** 22.2200 g. **Composition:** 0.9000 Silver .6430 oz. ASW **Subject:** Oriental Inventions **Obverse:** Great Wall **Reverse:** Soldiers with cannon and gunpowder **Note:** Similar to 50 Yuan, Y#632.

| Date | Mintage | F | VF | XF | Unc | BU |
|---|---|---|---|---|---|---|
| 1995 Proof | 15,000 | Value: 20.00 | | | | |

**5 YUAN** **Y# 631** **Weight:** 22.2200 g. **Composition:** 0.9000 Silver .6430 oz. ASW **Subject:** Oriental Inventions **Obverse:** Great Wall **Reverse:** Teacher with chart of human body **Note:** Similar to 50 Yuan, Y#636.

| Date | Mintage | F | VF | XF | Unc | BU |
|---|---|---|---|---|---|---|
| 1995 Proof | 15,000 | Value: 20.00 | | | | |

**5 YUAN** **Y# 581** **Weight:** 1.5552 g. **Composition:** 0.9990 Gold .0500 oz. AGW **Reverse:** Panda in tree looking down

| Date | Mintage | F | VF | XF | Unc | BU |
|---|---|---|---|---|---|---|
| 1996 | — | — | — | — | 50.00 | — |

**5 YUAN** **Y# 581a** **Weight:** 1.5552 g. **Composition:** 0.9990 Platinum .0500 oz. APW

| Date | Mintage | F | VF | XF | Unc | BU |
|---|---|---|---|---|---|---|
| 1996 | 5,000 | — | — | — | 75.00 | — |

**5 YUAN** **Y# 604** **Weight:** 22.2200 g. **Composition:** 0.9000 Silver .6430 oz. ASW **Reverse:** Caravan route market scene

| Date | Mintage | F | VF | XF | Unc | BU |
|---|---|---|---|---|---|---|
| 1996 Proof | 15,000 | Value: 45.00 | | | | |

**5 YUAN** **Y# 605** **Weight:** 22.2200 g. **Composition:** 0.9000 Silver .6430 oz. ASW **Reverse:** Fairy above Magao Sanctuary

| Date | Mintage | F | VF | XF | Unc | BU |
|---|---|---|---|---|---|---|
| 1996 Proof | 15,000 | Value: 45.00 | | | | |

**5 YUAN** **Y# 606** **Weight:** 22.2200 g. **Composition:** 0.9000 Silver .6430 oz. ASW **Reverse:** Various historic sculptures

| Date | Mintage | F | VF | XF | Unc | BU |
|---|---|---|---|---|---|---|
| 1996 Proof | 15,000 | Value: 45.00 | | | | |

**5 YUAN** **Y# 607** **Weight:** 22.2200 g. **Composition:** 0.9000 Silver .6430 oz. ASW **Reverse:** Musicians on camel

| Date | Mintage | F | VF | XF | Unc | BU |
|---|---|---|---|---|---|---|
| 1996 Proof | 15,000 | Value: 45.00 | | | | |

**5 YUAN** **Y# 729** **Composition:** Bronze **Obverse:** State emblem **Reverse:** Tiger

| Date | Mintage | F | VF | XF | Unc | BU |
|---|---|---|---|---|---|---|
| 1996 | — | — | — | — | 12.00 | — |

**5 YUAN** **Y# 730** **Composition:** Bronze **Obverse:** State emblem **Reverse:** Pair of dolphins

| Date | Mintage | F | VF | XF | Unc | BU |
|---|---|---|---|---|---|---|
| 1996 | — | — | — | — | 12.00 | — |

**5 YUAN** **Y# 740** **Weight:** 1.5552 g. **Composition:** 0.9990 Gold .0500 oz. AGW **Obverse:** Eastern unicorn **Reverse:** Head of western unicorn

| Date | Mintage | F | VF | XF | Unc | BU |
|---|---|---|---|---|---|---|
| 1996 | — | — | — | — | 40.00 | — |
| 1996 Proof | 5,000 | Value: 80.00 | | | | |

**5 YUAN** **Y# 740a** **Weight:** 1.5552 g. **Composition:** 0.9990 Platinum .0500 oz. APW

| Date | Mintage | F | VF | XF | Unc | BU |
|---|---|---|---|---|---|---|
| 1996 | — | — | — | — | 75.00 | — |

**5 YUAN** **Y# 847** **Weight:** 15.5517 g. **Composition:** 0.9990 Silver .5000 oz. ASW **Obverse:** Temple of Heaven **Reverse:** Panda seated on shore

| Date | Mintage | F | VF | XF | Unc | BU |
|---|---|---|---|---|---|---|
| 1996 | — | — | — | — | 18.50 | — |

**5 YUAN** **Y# 871** **Weight:** 22.2223 g. **Composition:** 0.9000 Silver .6430 oz. ASW **Subject:** Chinese Inventions and Discoveries Series **Obverse:** Great Wall **Reverse:** Three musicians

| Date | Mintage | F | VF | XF | Unc | BU |
|---|---|---|---|---|---|---|
| 1996 Proof | 15,000 | Value: 30.00 | | | | |

**5 YUAN** **Y# 872** **Weight:** 22.2223 g. **Composition:** 0.9000 Silver .6430 oz. ASW **Subject:** Chinese Inventions and Discoveries Series **Obverse:** Great Wall **Reverse:** Suspension bridge

| Date | Mintage | F | VF | XF | Unc | BU |
|---|---|---|---|---|---|---|
| 1996 Proof | 15,000 | Value: 30.00 | | | | |

**5 YUAN** **Y# 873** **Weight:** 22.2223 g. **Composition:** 0.9000 Silver .6430 oz. ASW **Subject:** Chinese Inventions and Discoveries Series **Obverse:** Great Wall **Reverse:** Astronomical clock

| Date | Mintage | F | VF | XF | Unc | BU |
|---|---|---|---|---|---|---|
| 1996 Proof | 15,000 | Value: 30.00 | | | | |

**5 YUAN** **Y# 874** **Weight:** 22.2223 g. **Composition:** 0.9000 Silver .6430 oz. ASW **Subject:** Chinese Inventions and Discoveries Series **Obverse:** Great Wall **Reverse:** Sailing ship

| Date | Mintage | F | VF | XF | Unc | BU |
|---|---|---|---|---|---|---|
| 1996 Proof | 15,000 | Value: 30.00 | | | | |

**5 YUAN** **Y# 875** **Weight:** 22.2223 g. **Composition:** 0.9000 Silver .6430 oz. ASW **Subject:** Chinese Inventions and Discoveries Series **Obverse:** Great Wall **Reverse:** Horse cart

| Date | Mintage | F | VF | XF | Unc | BU |
|---|---|---|---|---|---|---|
| 1996 Proof | 15,000 | Value: 30.00 | | | | |

**5 YUAN** **Y# 883** **Weight:** 15.5517 g. **Composition:** 0.9990 Silver .5000 oz. ASW **Obverse:** Eastern unicorn **Reverse:** Western unicorn

| Date | Mintage | F | VF | XF | Unc | BU |
|---|---|---|---|---|---|---|
| 1996 Proof | — | Value: 25.00 | | | | |

**5 YUAN** **Y# 885** **Weight:** 1.5552 g. **Composition:** 0.9990 Gold .0500 oz. AGW **Subject:** Goddess Guanyin **Obverse:** Temple **Reverse:** Goddess holding flower

| Date | Mintage | F | VF | XF | Unc | BU |
|---|---|---|---|---|---|---|
| 1996 Proof | — | Value: 35.00 | | | | |

**5 YUAN** **Y# 953** **Weight:** 1.5551 g. **Composition:** 0.9990 Platinum .0500 oz. APW **Obverse:** Eastern unicorn **Reverse:** Western unicorn

| Date | Mintage | F | VF | XF | Unc | BU |
|---|---|---|---|---|---|---|
| 1996 Prooflike | 8,000 | — | — | — | 75.00 | — |
| 1996 Proof | 5,000 | Value: 65.00 | | | | |

**5 YUAN** **Y# 982** **Weight:** 1.5552 g. **Composition:** 0.9990 Gold .0500 oz. AGW **Subject:** Pu Tuo Mountain

| Date | Mintage | F | VF | XF | Unc | BU |
|---|---|---|---|---|---|---|
| 1997 | 35,000 | — | — | — | 30.00 | — |

**5 YUAN** **Y# 728** **Weight:** 15.6300 g. **Composition:** 0.9990 Silver .5020 oz. ASW **Obverse:** Temple of Heaven **Reverse:** Panda crossing stream

| Date | Mintage | F | VF | XF | Unc | BU |
|---|---|---|---|---|---|---|
| 1997 Proof | — | Value: 20.00 | | | | |

**5 YUAN** **Y# 731** **Composition:** Bronze **Obverse:** State emblem **Reverse:** Created Ibis

| Date | Mintage | F | VF | XF | Unc | BU |
|---|---|---|---|---|---|---|
| 1997 | — | — | — | — | 12.00 | — |

**5 YUAN** **Y# 732** **Composition:** Bronze **Obverse:** State emblem **Reverse:** Red Crested Crane

| Date | Mintage | F | VF | XF | Unc | BU |
|---|---|---|---|---|---|---|
| 1997 | — | — | — | — | 12.00 | — |

**5 YUAN** **Y# 892** **Weight:** 15.5517 g. **Composition:** 0.9990 Silver .5000 oz. ASW **Obverse:** Temple of Heaven **Reverse:** Panda on branch

| Date | Mintage | F | VF | XF | Unc | BU |
|---|---|---|---|---|---|---|
| 1997 Proof | — | Value: 15.00 | | | | |

**5 YUAN** **Y# 893** **Weight:** 15.5517 g. **Composition:** 0.9990 Silver .5000 oz. ASW **Obverse:** Similar to Y#892 with additional legend on Hong Kong's return **Reverse:** Panda crossing stream

| Date | Mintage | F | VF | XF | Unc | BU |
|---|---|---|---|---|---|---|
| 1997 | 30,000 | — | — | — | 20.00 | — |

**5 YUAN** **Y# 911** **Weight:** 15.5517 g. **Composition:** 0.9990 Silver .5000 oz. ASW **Obverse:** 2 Eastern unicorns **Reverse:** 1 Western unicorn

| Date | Mintage | F | VF | XF | Unc | BU |
|---|---|---|---|---|---|---|
| 1997 Proof | — | Value: 20.00 | | | | |

**5 YUAN** **Y# 916** **Weight:** 15.5517 g. **Composition:** 0.9990 Silver .5000 oz. ASW **Subject:** Traditional Chinese Mascot **Obverse:** Ornamental column **Reverse:** Child holding carp

| Date | Mintage | F | VF | XF | Unc | BU |
|---|---|---|---|---|---|---|
| 1997 | 80,000 | — | — | — | 20.00 | — |

**5 YUAN** **Y# 958** **Weight:** 1.5551 g. **Composition:** 0.9990 Platinum .0500 oz. APW **Obverse:** 2 Eastern unicorns **Reverse:** 1 Western unicorn

| Date | Mintage | F | VF | XF | Unc | BU |
|---|---|---|---|---|---|---|
| 1997 Proof | 5,000 | Value: 50.00 | | | | |

**5 YUAN** **Y# 962** **Weight:** 15.6000 g. **Composition:** 0.9990 Silver .5000 oz. ASW **Subject:** Panda **Reverse:** Multicolor panda and flora. **Edge:** Reeded. **Size:** 36 mm.

| Date | Mintage | F | VF | XF | Unc | BU |
|---|---|---|---|---|---|---|
| 1997 | 100,000 | — | — | — | 20.00 | — |

**5 YUAN** **Y# 716** **Weight:** 1.5552 g. **Composition:** 0.9990 Gold .0500 oz. AGW **Obverse:** Temple of Heaven **Reverse:** Panda on branch **Note:** Similar to 100 Yuan, Y#720.

| Date | Mintage | F | VF | XF | Unc | BU |
|---|---|---|---|---|---|---|
| 1997 | — | — | — | — | 40.00 | — |

**Note:** Exists in large and small date varieties

**5 YUAN** **Y# 940** **Composition:** Bronze **Subject:** Brown-eared Pheasant **Obverse:** State seal **Reverse:** Denomination above pheasant

| Date | Mintage | F | VF | XF | Unc | BU |
|---|---|---|---|---|---|---|
| 1998 | — | — | — | — | 10.00 | — |

**5 YUAN** **Y# 941** **Composition:** Bronze **Subject:** Chinese Alligator **Obverse:** State seal **Reverse:** Denomination above alligator

| Date | Mintage | F | VF | XF | Unc | BU |
|---|---|---|---|---|---|---|
| 1998 | — | — | — | — | 10.00 | — |

**5 YUAN** **Y# 964** **Weight:** 15.5517 g. **Composition:** 0.9990 Silver .5000 oz. ASW **Reverse:** Multicolor panda

| Date | Mintage | F | VF | XF | Unc | BU |
|---|---|---|---|---|---|---|
| 1998 | 100,000 | — | — | — | 20.00 | — |

**5 YUAN** **Y# 990** **Weight:** 1.5600 g. **Composition:** 0.9990 Gold .0500 oz. AGW **Obverse:** Temple of Heaven **Reverse:** Panda seated on rock

| Date | Mintage | F | VF | XF | Unc | BU |
|---|---|---|---|---|---|---|
| 1998 | — | — | — | — | 35.00 | — |

**Note:** Exists in large and small date varieties

**5 YUAN** **Y# 981** **Weight:** 1.5600 g. **Composition:** 0.9990 Gold .0500 oz. AGW **Obverse:** Temple of Heaven **Reverse:** Panda on ledge

| Date | Mintage | F | VF | XF | Unc | BU |
|---|---|---|---|---|---|---|
| 1999 | — | — | — | — | 35.00 | — |

**Note:** Exists in large and small date varieties

**5 YUAN** **Y# 945** **Weight:** 1.5600 g. **Composition:** 0.9990 Gold .0500 oz. AGW **Obverse:** Temple of Heaven **Reverse:** Panda seated on leaves **Note:** Similar to 100 Yuan, KM#949.

| Date | Mintage | F | VF | XF | Unc | BU |
|---|---|---|---|---|---|---|
| 2000 | — | — | — | — | 35.00 | — |

**Note:** Domestic Chinese examples struck with mirror fields, overseas examples struck with frosted fields

**10 YUAN** **Y# 44** **Weight:** 15.0000 g. **Composition:** 0.8500 Silver .4099 oz. ASW **Subject:** Year of the Pig

| Date | Mintage | F | VF | XF | Unc | BU |
|---|---|---|---|---|---|---|
| 1983 Proof | 6,790 | Value: 285 | | | | |

**10 YUAN** **Y# 49** **Weight:** 3.1103 g. **Composition:** 0.9990 Gold .1000 oz. AGW

| Date | Mintage | F | VF | XF | Unc | BU |
|---|---|---|---|---|---|---|
| 1983 | 74,000 | — | — | — | 55.00 | — |

**10 YUAN** **Y# 55** **Weight:** 1.2000 g. **Composition:** 0.9000 Gold .0347 oz. AGW **Subject:** Marco Polo

| Date | Mintage | F | VF | XF | Unc | BU |
|---|---|---|---|---|---|---|
| 1983 Proof | 50,000 | Value: 50.00 | | | | |

**10 YUAN** **Y# 57** **Weight:** 27.0000 g. **Composition:** 0.9000 Silver .7813 oz. ASW **Subject:** Pandas

| Date | Mintage | F | VF | XF | Unc | BU |
|---|---|---|---|---|---|---|
| 1983 Proof | 10,000 | Value: 175 | | | | |
| 1983 Frosted Proof | Inc. above | Value: 200 | | | | |

**10 YUAN** **Y# 59** **Weight:** 15.0000 g. **Composition:** 0.8500 Silver .4099 oz. ASW **Subject:** Year of thé Rat

| Date | Mintage | F | VF | XF | Unc | BU |
|---|---|---|---|---|---|---|
| 1984 Proof | 11,000 | Value: 100 | | | | |

**10 YUAN** **Y# 62** **Weight:** 16.8100 g. **Composition:** 0.9250 Silver .5000 oz. ASW **Subject:** Women's Decade

| Date | Mintage | F | VF | XF | Unc | BU |
|---|---|---|---|---|---|---|
| ND(1984) Proof | 4,000 | Value: 50.00 | | | | |

**10 YUAN** **Y# 63** **Weight:** 16.8100 g. **Composition:** 0.9250 Silver .5000 oz. ASW **Series:** Olympics **Subject:** Volleyball

| Date | Mintage | F | VF | XF | Unc | BU |
|---|---|---|---|---|---|---|
| 1984 | 1,000 | — | — | — | 65.00 | — |

**10 YUAN** **Y# 63a** **Weight:** 17.0600 g. **Composition:** 0.8000 Silver .4388 oz. ASW

| Date | Mintage | F | VF | XF | Unc | BU |
|---|---|---|---|---|---|---|
| 1984 Proof | 4,500 | Value: 30.00 | | | | |

**10 YUAN** **Y# 64** **Weight:** 17.0600 g. **Composition:** 0.8000 Silver .4388 oz. ASW **Series:** Olympics **Subject:** Speed Skating

| Date | Mintage | F | VF | XF | Unc | BU |
|---|---|---|---|---|---|---|
| 1984 Proof | 6,000 | Value: 40.00 | | | | |

**10 YUAN** **Y# 67** **Weight:** 27.0000 g. **Composition:** 0.9250 Silver .8031 oz. ASW **Subject:** Pandas

| Date | Mintage | F | VF | XF | Unc | BU |
|---|---|---|---|---|---|---|
| 1984 Proof | 10,000 | Value: 80.00 | | | | |

**10 YUAN** **Y# 74** **Weight:** 3.1103 g. **Composition:** 0.9990 Gold .1000 oz. AGW

| Date | Mintage | F | VF | XF | Unc | BU |
|---|---|---|---|---|---|---|
| 1984 | 85,000 | — | — | — | 55.00 | — |

**10 YUAN** **Y# 88** **Weight:** 27.0000 g. **Composition:** 0.9000 Silver .7813 oz. ASW **Subject:** 110th Anniversary - Birth of Dr. Cheng Jiageng

| Date | Mintage | F | VF | XF | Unc | BU |
|---|---|---|---|---|---|---|
| 1984 Proof | 6,000 | Value: 55.00 | | | | |

**10 YUAN** **Y# 78** **Weight:** 15.0000 g. **Composition:** 0.9000 Silver .4341 oz. ASW **Subject:** Year of the Ox

| Date | Mintage | F | VF | XF | Unc | BU |
|---|---|---|---|---|---|---|
| 1985 Proof | 22,000 | Value: 35.00 | | | | |

**10 YUAN** **Y# 81** **Weight:** 3.1103 g. **Composition:** 0.9990 Gold .1000 oz. AGW

| Date | Mintage | F | VF | XF | Unc | BU |
|---|---|---|---|---|---|---|
| 1985 | 150,000 | — | — | — | 60.00 | — |

**10 YUAN** **Y# 95** **Weight:** 27.0000 g. **Composition:** 0.9000 Silver .7813 oz. ASW **Subject:** Pandas

| Date | Mintage | F | VF | XF | Unc | BU |
|---|---|---|---|---|---|---|
| 1985 Proof | 10,000 | Value: 80.00 | | | | |

**10 YUAN** **Y# 97** **Weight:** 34.5600 g. **Composition:** 0.9000 Silver 1.0000 oz. ASW **Subject:** 20th Anniversary - Tibet Autonomous Region

| Date | Mintage | F | VF | XF | Unc | BU |
|---|---|---|---|---|---|---|
| 1985 Proof | 3,000 | Value: 50.00 | | | | |

**10 YUAN** **Y# 110** **Weight:** 34.5600 g. **Composition:** 0.9000 Silver 1.0000 oz. ASW **Subject:** 30th Anniversary - Xinjiang Autonomous Region

| Date | Mintage | F | VF | XF | Unc | BU |
|---|---|---|---|---|---|---|
| 1985 Proof | 1,400 | Value: 60.00 | | | | |

**10 YUAN** **Y# 98** **Weight:** 15.0000 g. **Composition:** 0.9000 Silver .4341 oz. ASW **Subject:** Year of the Tiger

| Date | Mintage | F | VF | XF | Unc | BU |
|---|---|---|---|---|---|---|
| 1986 Proof | 15,000 | Value: 55.00 | | | | |

**10 YUAN** **Y# 102** **Weight:** 3.1103 g. **Composition:** 0.9990 Gold .1000 oz. AGW

| Date | Mintage | F | VF | XF | Unc | BU |
|---|---|---|---|---|---|---|
| 1986 | 45,000 | — | — | — | 55.00 | — |
| 1986 P Proof | 10,000 | Value: 60.00 | | | | |

**10 YUAN** **Y# 111** **Weight:** 29.1900 g. **Composition:** 0.9250 Silver .8682 oz. ASW **Subject:** 120th Anniversary - Birth of Sun Yat-sen **Reverse:** Sun Yat-sen's residence

| Date | Mintage | F | VF | XF | Unc | BU |
|---|---|---|---|---|---|---|
| 1986 Proof | 8,450 | Value: 50.00 | | | | |

**10 YUAN** **Y# 121** **Weight:** 15.0000 g. **Composition:** 0.9000 Silver .4341 oz. ASW **Subject:** Year of the Rabbit **Obverse:** Yellow Crane Pavilion above legend **Reverse:** 2 rabbits above denomination

| Date | Mintage | F | VF | XF | Unc | BU |
|---|---|---|---|---|---|---|
| 1987 Proof | 14,000 | Value: 90.00 | | | | |

**10 YUAN** **Y# 125** **Weight:** 3.1103 g. **Composition:** 0.9990 Gold .1000 oz. AGW

| Date | Mintage | F | VF | XF | Unc | BU |
|---|---|---|---|---|---|---|
| 1987(s) | 99,000 | — | — | — | 55.00 | — |
| 1987(y) | 37,000 | — | — | — | 55.00 | — |
| 1987 P Proof | 10,000 | Value: 60.00 | | | | |

**10 YUAN Y#133 Weight:** 31.1000 g. **Composition:** 0.9990 Silver 1.0000 oz. ASW

| Date | Mintage | F | VF | XF | Unc | BU |
|---|---|---|---|---|---|---|
| 1987 Proof | 31,000 | Value: 35.00 | | | | |

**10 YUAN Y#141 Weight:** 15.0000 g. **Composition:** 0.9000 Silver .4341 oz. ASW **Subject:** Year of the Dragon

| Date | Mintage | F | VF | XF | Unc | BU |
|---|---|---|---|---|---|---|
| 1988 Proof | 15,000 | Value: 65.00 | | | | |

**10 YUAN Y# 153 Ring Weight:** 31.1035 g. **Ring Composition:** 0.9990 Silver 1.0000 oz. ASW **Center Weight:** 3.1103 g. **Center Composition:** 0.9990 Gold .1000 oz. AGW **Reverse:** Panda pawing bamboo

| Date | Mintage | F | VF | XF | Unc | BU |
|---|---|---|---|---|---|---|
| 1988 | 290,000 | — | — | — | 55.00 | — |
| 1988 Proof | 11,000 | Value: 60.00 | | | | |

**10 YUAN Y#165 Weight:** 27.0000 g. **Composition:** 0.9250 Silver .5056 oz. ASW **Subject:** Rare Animal Protection **Reverse:** Crested Ibis

| Date | Mintage | F | VF | XF | Unc | BU |
|---|---|---|---|---|---|---|
| 1988 Proof | 35,000 | Value: 30.00 | | | | |

**10 YUAN Y#166 Weight:** 27.0000 g. **Composition:** 0.9250 Silver .5056 oz. ASW **Subject:** Rare Animal Protection **Reverse:** Baiji Dolphins

| Date | Mintage | F | VF | XF | Unc | BU |
|---|---|---|---|---|---|---|
| 1988 Proof | 35,000 | Value: 32.50 | | | | |

**10 YUAN Y#174 Weight:** 31.1000 g. **Composition:** 0.9990 Silver 1.0000 oz. ASW **Subject:** Year of the Dragon

| Date | Mintage | F | VF | XF | Unc | BU |
|---|---|---|---|---|---|---|
| 1988 Proof | 20,000 | Value: 65.00 | | | | |

**10 YUAN Y#177 Weight:** 15.0000 g. **Composition:** 0.8500 Silver .4100 oz. ASW **Subject:** Year of the Snake **Obverse:** Shanhaiguan City Gate

| Date | Mintage | F | VF | XF | Unc | BU |
|---|---|---|---|---|---|---|
| 1989 Proof | 15,000 | Value: 40.00 | | | | |

**10 YUAN Y#183 Weight:** 31.1000 g. **Composition:** 0.9990 Silver 1.0000 oz. ASW **Subject:** Year of the Snake **Obverse:** State seal

| Date | Mintage | F | VF | XF | Unc | BU |
|---|---|---|---|---|---|---|
| 1989 Proof | 6,000 | Value: 135 | | | | |

**10 YUAN Y#186 Weight:** 31.1000 g. **Composition:** 0.9990 Silver 1.0000 oz. ASW **Reverse:** Baby Panda

| Date | Mintage | F | VF | XF | Unc | BU |
|---|---|---|---|---|---|---|
| 1989 | 250,000 | — | — | — | 18.50 | — |
| 1989 Proof | 25,000 | Value: 32.50 | | | | |

**10 YUAN Y#199 Weight:** 27.0000 g. **Composition:** 0.9250 Silver .8031 oz. ASW **Subject:** 1990 Asian Games **Obverse:** Monument, stadium, Great Wall segment and sun **Reverse:** Weight lifter

| Date | Mintage | F | VF | XF | Unc | BU |
|---|---|---|---|---|---|---|
| 1989 Proof | 20,000 | Value: 30.00 | | | | |

**10 YUAN Y#200 Weight:** 27.0000 g. **Composition:** 0.9250 Silver .8031 oz. ASW **Subject:** 1990 Asian Games **Obverse:** Monument, stadium, Great Wall segment and sun **Reverse:** Diver

| Date | Mintage | F | VF | XF | Unc | BU |
|---|---|---|---|---|---|---|
| 1989 Proof | 20,000 | Value: 30.00 | | | | |

**10 YUAN Y#201 Weight:** 27.0000 g. **Composition:** 0.9250 Silver .8031 oz. ASW **Subject:** 1990 Asian Games **Obverse:** Monument, stadium, Great Wall segment and sun **Reverse:** Tennis player

| Date | Mintage | F | VF | XF | Unc | BU |
|---|---|---|---|---|---|---|
| 1989 Proof | 20,000 | Value: 30.00 | | | | |

**10 YUAN Y#202 Weight:** 27.0000 g. **Composition:** 0.9250 Silver .8031 oz. ASW **Subject:** 1990 Asian Games **Obverse:** Monument, stadium, Great Wall segment and sun **Reverse:** Bicyclist

| Date | Mintage | F | VF | XF | Unc | BU |
|---|---|---|---|---|---|---|
| 1989 Proof | 20,000 | Value: 30.00 | | | | |

**10 YUAN** **Y#235** **Weight:** 27.0000 g. **Composition:** 0.9250 Silver .8031 oz. ASW **Subject:** 40th Anniversary of Peoples Republic **Reverse:** Tiananmen Square

| Date | Mintage | F | VF | XF | Unc | BU |
|---|---|---|---|---|---|---|
| ND(1989) Proof | 5,000 | Value: 35.00 | | | | |

**10 YUAN** **Y#236** **Weight:** 27.0000 g. **Composition:** 0.9250 Silver .8031 oz. ASW **Subject:** 40th Anniversary of Peoples Republic **Reverse:** Great Wall

| Date | Mintage | F | VF | XF | Unc | BU |
|---|---|---|---|---|---|---|
| ND(1989) Proof | 5,000 | Value: 35.00 | | | | |

**10 YUAN** **Y#248** **Weight:** 27.0000 g. **Composition:** 0.9250 Silver .8031 oz. ASW **Subject:** Endangered Animals **Obverse:** State seal **Reverse:** Japanese deer

| Date | Mintage | F | VF | XF | Unc | BU |
|---|---|---|---|---|---|---|
| 1989 Proof | 10,000 | Value: 32.50 | | | | |

**10 YUAN** **Y#249** **Weight:** 27.0000 g. **Composition:** 0.9250 Silver .8031 oz. ASW **Subject:** Endangered Animals **Obverse:** State seal **Reverse:** Red-crowned crane

| Date | Mintage | F | VF | XF | Unc | BU |
|---|---|---|---|---|---|---|
| 1989 Proof | 10,000 | Value: 32.50 | | | | |

**10 YUAN** **Y#188** **Weight:** 3.1103 g. **Composition:** 0.9990 Gold .1000 oz. AGW **Note:** Similar to 100 Yuan, Y#191.

| Date | Mintage | F | VF | XF | Unc | BU |
|---|---|---|---|---|---|---|
| 1989 | 128,000 | — | — | — | 55.00 | — |
| 1989 Proof | 8,000 | Value: 60.00 | | | | |

**10 YUAN** **Y#206** **Weight:** 1.0000 g. **Composition:** 0.9990 Gold .0322 oz. AGW **Reverse:** Phoenix and dragon

| Date | Mintage | F | VF | XF | Unc | BU |
|---|---|---|---|---|---|---|
| 1990 Proof | 34,000 | Value: 35.00 | | | | |

**10 YUAN** **Y#221** **Weight:** 15.0000 g. **Composition:** 0.8500 Silver .4100 oz. ASW **Subject:** Year of the Horse **Obverse:** Temple of Confucius

| Date | Mintage | F | VF | XF | Unc | BU |
|---|---|---|---|---|---|---|
| 1990 Proof | 15,000 | Value: 45.00 | | | | |

**10 YUAN** **Y#222** **Weight:** 31.1000 g. **Composition:** 0.9990 Silver 1.0000 oz. ASW **Subject:** Year of the Horse

| Date | Mintage | F | VF | XF | Unc | BU |
|---|---|---|---|---|---|---|
| 1990 Proof | 12,000 | Value: 40.00 | | | | |

**10 YUAN** **Y#237** **Weight:** 31.1000 g. **Composition:** 0.9990 Silver 1.0000 oz. ASW **Reverse:** Panda

| Date | Mintage | F | VF | XF | Unc | BU |
|---|---|---|---|---|---|---|
| 1990 | 200,000 | — | — | — | 20.00 | — |
| 1990 Proof | 20,000 | Value: 35.00 | | | | |

**10 YUAN** **Y#239** **Weight:** 3.1100 g. **Composition:** 0.9990 Gold .0322 oz. AGW **Reverse:** Panda

| Date | Mintage | F | VF | XF | Unc | BU |
|---|---|---|---|---|---|---|
| 1990 | — | — | — | — | 55.00 | — |
| 1990 Proof | 5,000 | Value: 65.00 | | | | |

**10 YUAN** **Y#244** **Weight:** 27.0000 g. **Composition:** 0.9250 Silver .8031 oz. ASW **Subject:** Homer - Poet

| Date | Mintage | F | VF | XF | Unc | BU |
|---|---|---|---|---|---|---|
| 1990 Proof | 30,000 | Value: 22.50 | | | | |

**10 YUAN** **Y#245** **Weight:** 27.0000 g. **Composition:** 0.9250 Silver .8031 oz. ASW **Subject:** William Shakespeare

| Date | Mintage | F | VF | XF | Unc | BU |
|---|---|---|---|---|---|---|
| 1990 Proof | 30,000 | Value: 25.00 | | | | |

**10 YUAN** **Y#246** **Weight:** 27.0000 g. **Composition:** 0.9250 Silver .8031 oz. ASW **Subject:** Ludwig Van Beethoven

| Date | Mintage | F | VF | XF | Unc | BU |
|---|---|---|---|---|---|---|
| 1990 Proof | 30,000 | Value: 25.00 | | | | |

**10 YUAN** **Y#247** **Weight:** 27.0000 g. **Composition:** 0.9250 Silver .8031 oz. ASW **Subject:** Thomas Alva Edison

| Date | Mintage | F | VF | XF | Unc | BU |
|---|---|---|---|---|---|---|
| 1990 Proof | 30,000 | Value: 25.00 | | | | |

**10 YUAN** **Y#251** **Weight:** 27.0000 g. **Composition:** 0.9250 Silver .8031 oz. ASW **Subject:** XI Asian Games **Reverse:** Javelin Thrower

| Date | Mintage | F | VF | XF | Unc | BU |
|---|---|---|---|---|---|---|
| 1990 Proof | 20,000 | Value: 35.00 | | | | |

**10 YUAN** **Y#252** **Weight:** 27.0000 g. **Composition:** 0.9250 Silver .8031 oz. ASW **Subject:** XI Asian Games **Reverse:** Baseball player

| Date | Mintage | F | VF | XF | Unc | BU |
|---|---|---|---|---|---|---|
| 1990 Proof | 20,000 | Value: 35.00 | | | | |

**10 YUAN** **Y#253** **Weight:** 27.0000 g. **Composition:** 0.9250 Silver .8031 oz. ASW **Subject:** XI Asian Games **Reverse:** Gymnast on rings

| Date | Mintage | F | VF | XF | Unc | BU |
|---|---|---|---|---|---|---|
| 1990 Proof | 20,000 | Value: 35.00 | | | | |

**10 YUAN** **Y#254** **Weight:** 27.0000 g. **Composition:** 0.9250 Silver .8031 oz. ASW **Subject:** XI Asian Games **Reverse:** Soccer player

| Date | Mintage | F | VF | XF | Unc | BU |
|---|---|---|---|---|---|---|
| 1990 Proof | 20,000 | Value: 35.00 | | | | |

**10 YUAN** **Y#261** **Weight:** 31.1000 g. **Composition:** 0.9990 Silver 1.0000 oz. ASW **Obverse:** Great Wall **Reverse:** Phoenix and dragon

| Date | Mintage | F | VF | XF | Unc | BU |
|---|---|---|---|---|---|---|
| 1990 Proof | 12,000 | Value: 35.00 | | | | |

**10 YUAN** **Y#267** **Weight:** 3.1100 g. **Composition:** 0.9995 Platinum .1000 oz. APW **Reverse:** Panda with branch

| Date | Mintage | F | VF | XF | Unc | BU |
|---|---|---|---|---|---|---|
| 1990 Proof | 2,500 | Value: 90.00 | | | | |

**10 YUAN** **Y#283** **Weight:** 27.0000 g. **Composition:** 0.9000 Silver .7814 oz. ASW **Series:** Summer Olympics **Subject:** Bicycle Racing

| Date | Mintage | F | VF | XF | Unc | BU |
|---|---|---|---|---|---|---|
| 1990 Proof | 30,000 | Value: 22.50 | | | | |

**10 YUAN** **Y#300** **Weight:** 27.0000 g. **Composition:** 0.9000 Silver .7814 oz. ASW **Series:** Summer Olympics **Subject:** High Jumping

| Date | Mintage | F | VF | XF | Unc | BU |
|---|---|---|---|---|---|---|
| 1990 Proof | 30,000 | Value: 25.00 | | | | |

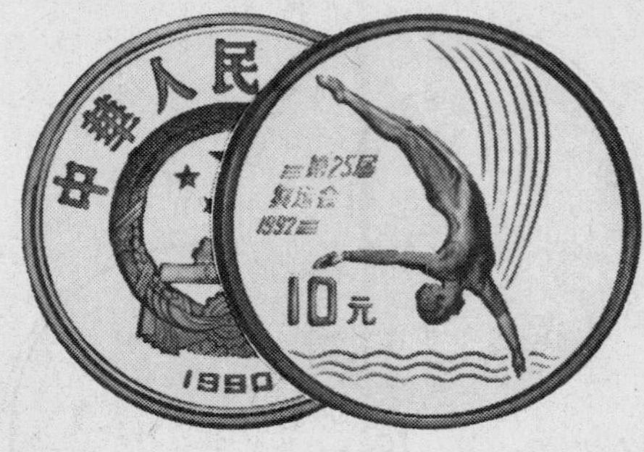


**10 YUAN** **Y#366** **Weight:** 30.0000 g. **Composition:** 0.9000 Silver .8682 oz. ASW **Series:** Olympics **Subject:** Diver

| Date | Mintage | F | VF | XF | Unc | BU |
|---|---|---|---|---|---|---|
| 1990 Proof | 30,000 | Value: 27.50 | | | | |

**10 YUAN** **Y#270** **Weight:** 15.0000 g. **Composition:** 0.9000 Silver .4340 oz. ASW **Subject:** Year of the Goat **Obverse:** Chinese building and legehd

| Date | Mintage | F | VF | XF | Unc | BU |
|---|---|---|---|---|---|---|
| 1991 Proof | 15,000 | Value: 40.00 | | | | |

**10 YUAN** **Y#271** **Weight:** 31.1000 g. **Composition:** 0.9990 Silver 1.0000 oz. ASW **Subject:** Year of the Goat

| Date | Mintage | F | VF | XF | Unc | BU |
|---|---|---|---|---|---|---|
| 1991 Proof | 8,000 | Value: 75.00 | | | | |

**10 YUAN** **Y# 308.1** **Weight:** 31.1000 g. **Composition:** 0.9990 Silver 1.0000 oz. ASW **Obverse:** Date with bottom serifs **Reverse:** Panda - Hind feet in water

| Date | Mintage | F | VF | XF | Unc | BU |
|---|---|---|---|---|---|---|
| 1991 | 100,000 | — | — | — | 20.00 | — |

**10 YUAN** **Y# 308.2** **Weight:** 31.1000 g. **Composition:** 0.9990 Silver 1.0000 oz. ASW **Reverse:** P behind panda

| Date | Mintage | F | VF | XF | Unc | BU |
|---|---|---|---|---|---|---|
| 1991 Proof | 20,000 | Value: 30.00 | | | | |

**10 YUAN** **Y# 308.3** **Weight:** 31.1000 g. **Composition:** 0.9990 Silver 1.0000 oz. ASW **Obverse:** Date without bottom serifs

| Date | Mintage | F | VF | XF | Unc | BU |
|---|---|---|---|---|---|---|
| 1991 | Inc. above | — | — | — | 18.00 | — |

**10 YUAN** **Y#314** **Weight:** 62.2000 g. **Composition:** 0.9990 Silver 2.0000 oz. ASW **Reverse:** Panda - Climbing bamboo branch

| Date | Mintage | F | VF | XF | Unc | BU |
|---|---|---|---|---|---|---|
| 1991 Proof | 10,000 | Value: 50.00 | | | | |

**10 YUAN** **Y#318** **Weight:** 27.0800 g. **Composition:** 0.9250 Silver .8030 oz. ASW **Subject:** 1st World Women's Football Championships **Obverse:** 5 story building **Reverse:** Women's soccer, 2 players

| Date | Mintage | F | VF | XF | Unc | BU |
|---|---|---|---|---|---|---|
| 1991 Proof | 2,800 | Value: 35.00 | | | | |

**10 YUAN** **Y#319** **Weight:** 27.0800 g. **Composition:** 0.9250 Silver .8030 oz. ASW **Subject:** 1st World Women's Football Championships **Obverse:** 5 story building **Reverse:** Women's soccer, 3 players

| Date | Mintage | F | VF | XF | Unc | BU |
|---|---|---|---|---|---|---|
| 1991 Proof | 2,800 | Value: 35.00 | | | | |

**10 YUAN** **Y#347** **Weight:** 27.0800 g. **Composition:** 0.9250 Silver .8030 oz. ASW **Subject:** Mozart

| Date | Mintage | F | VF | XF | Unc | BU |
|---|---|---|---|---|---|---|
| 1991 Proof | — | Value: 25.00 | | | | |

**10 YUAN** **Y#348** **Weight:** 27.0800 g. **Composition:** 0.9250 Silver .8030 oz. ASW **Subject:** Coumbus

| Date | Mintage | F | VF | XF | Unc | BU |
|---|---|---|---|---|---|---|
| 1991 Proof | — | Value: 25.00 | | | | |

**10 YUAN** **Y#349** **Weight:** 27.0800 g. **Composition:** 0.9250 Silver .8030 oz. ASW **Subject:** Einstein

| Date | Mintage | F | VF | XF | Unc | BU |
|---|---|---|---|---|---|---|
| 1991 Proof | — | Value: 28.50 | | | | |

**10 YUAN** **Y#350** **Weight:** 27.0800 g. **Composition:** 0.9250 Silver .8030 oz. ASW **Subject:** Mark Twain

| Date | Mintage | F | VF | XF | Unc | BU |
|---|---|---|---|---|---|---|
| 1991 Proof | — | Value: 25.00 | | | | |

**10 YUAN** **Y#367** **Weight:** 30.0000 g. **Composition:** 0.9000 Silver .8682 oz. ASW **Series:** Olympics **Reverse:** Downhill skier

| Date | Mintage | F | VF | XF | Unc | BU |
|---|---|---|---|---|---|---|
| 1991 Proof | 30,000 | Value: 25.00 | | | | |

**10 YUAN** **Y#456** **Weight:** 30.0000 g. **Composition:** 0.9000 Silver .8682 oz. ASW **Series:** Olympics **Subject:** Women's Table Tennis

| Date | Mintage | F | VF | XF | Unc | BU |
|---|---|---|---|---|---|---|
| 1991 Proof | 30,000 | Value: 35.00 | | | | |

**10 YUAN** **Y#476** **Weight:** 31.1035 g. **Composition:** 0.9990 Silver 1.0000 oz. ASW **Subject:** 80th Anniversary - 1911 Revolution **Obverse:** Sun Yat Sen in civilian clothes

| Date | Mintage | F | VF | XF | Unc | BU |
|---|---|---|---|---|---|---|
| ND(1991) Proof | 2,500 | Value: 50.00 | | | | |

**10 YUAN** **Y# 310** **Weight:** 3.1100 g. **Composition:** 0.9990 Gold .10000 oz. AGW **Note:** Similar to 100 Yuan, KM#313.

| Date | Mintage | F | VF | XF | Unc | BU |
|---|---|---|---|---|---|---|
| 1991 | — | — | — | — | 60.00 | — |
| 1991 Proof | — | Value: 70.00 | | | | |

**10 YUAN** **Y# 342** **Weight:** 3.1103 g. **Composition:** 0.9990 Gold .1000 oz. AGW **Note:** Similar to Y#346.

| Date | Mintage | F | VF | XF | Unc | BU |
|---|---|---|---|---|---|---|
| 1992 | — | — | — | — | 65.00 | — |
| 1992 Proof | — | Value: 75.00 | | | | |

**10 YUAN** **Y#288** **Weight:** 15.0000 g. **Composition:** 0.9000 Silver .4340 oz. ASW **Subject:** Year of the Monkey

| Date | Mintage | F | VF | XF | Unc | BU |
|---|---|---|---|---|---|---|
| 1992 Proof | — | Value: 50.00 | | | | |

**10 YUAN** **Y#294** **Weight:** 31.1000 g. **Composition:** 0.9990 Silver 1.0000 oz. ASW **Subject:** Year of the Monkey

| Date | Mintage | F | VF | XF | Unc | BU |
|---|---|---|---|---|---|---|
| 1992 Proof | 8,000 | Value: 60.00 | | | | |

**10 YUAN** **Y#346** **Weight:** 31.1000 g. **Composition:** 0.9990 Silver 1.0000 oz. ASW **Reverse:** Panda climbing right on eucalyptus branch

| Date | Mintage | F | VF | XF | Unc | BU |
|---|---|---|---|---|---|---|
| 1992 | 100,000 | — | — | — | 20.00 | — |
| 1992 Proof | 5,202 | Value: 35.00 | | | | |

**10 YUAN** **Y#351** **Weight:** 26.8300 g. **Composition:** 0.9000 Silver .7764 oz. ASW **Series:** 1994 Winter Olympics **Subject:** Slalom **Obverse:** State seal

| Date | Mintage | F | VF | XF | Unc | BU |
|---|---|---|---|---|---|---|
| 1992 Proof | 7,500 | Value: 37.50 | | | | |

**10 YUAN** **Y#368** **Weight:** 26.8300 g. **Composition:** 0.9000 Silver .7764 oz. ASW **Series:** 1994 Winter Olympics **Subject:** Cross Country Skiing **Obverse:** State seal

| Date | Mintage | F | VF | XF | Unc | BU |
|---|---|---|---|---|---|---|
| 1992 Proof | 7,500 | Value: 30.00 | | | | |

**10 YUAN** **Y#391** **Weight:** 3.1103 g. **Composition:** 0.9990 Silver .1000 oz. ASW **Reverse:** Panda on branch

| Date | Mintage | F | VF | XF | Unc | BU |
|---|---|---|---|---|---|---|
| 1992 Proof | 30,000 | Value: 120 | | | | |

**10 YUAN** **Y#486** **Weight:** 27.0000 g. **Composition:** 0.9250 Silver .8031 oz. ASW **Subject:** Wildlife **Reverse:** White Storks

| Date | Mintage | F | VF | XF | Unc | BU |
|---|---|---|---|---|---|---|
| 1992 Proof | 7,260 | Value: 38.50 | | | | |

**10 YUAN** **Y#490** **Weight:** 26.9500 g. **Composition:** 0.9000 Silver .7798 oz. ASW **Series:** 1994 Winter Olympics **Reverse:** Ski jumper

| Date | Mintage | F | VF | XF | Unc | BU |
|---|---|---|---|---|---|---|
| 1992 Proof | 30,000 | Value: 30.00 | | | | |

**10 YUAN** **Y#584** **Weight:** 26.9500 g. **Composition:** 0.9000 Silver .7798 oz. ASW **Reverse:** Snow leopard

| Date | Mintage | F | VF | XF | Unc | BU |
|---|---|---|---|---|---|---|
| 1992 Proof | 7,260 | Value: 32.50 | | | | |

**10 YUAN** **Y#709** **Weight:** 27.1100 g. **Composition:** 0.9000 Silver .7844 oz. ASW **Obverse:** State seal **Reverse:** Tschaikovsky leaning against piano

| Date | Mintage | F | VF | XF | Unc | BU |
|---|---|---|---|---|---|---|
| 1992 Proof | — | Value: 32.50 | | | | |

**10 YUAN** **Y#755** **Weight:** 27.0000 g. **Composition:** 0.9250 Silver .8030 oz. ASW **Subject:** International Celebrities **Obverse:** State seal **Reverse:** Leonardo Da Vinci

| Date | Mintage | F | VF | XF | Unc | BU |
|---|---|---|---|---|---|---|
| 1992 Proof | 30,000 | Value: 27.50 | | | | |

**10 YUAN** **Y#756** **Weight:** 27.0000 g. **Composition:** 0.9250 Silver .8030 oz. ASW **Subject:** International Celebrities **Obverse:** State seal **Reverse:** Wolfgang Von Goethe

| Date | Mintage | F | VF | XF | Unc | BU |
|---|---|---|---|---|---|---|
| 1992 Proof | 30,000 | Value: 27.50 | | | | |

**10 YUAN** **Y#757** **Weight:** 27.0000 g. **Composition:** 0.9250 Silver .8030 oz. ASW **Subject:** International Celebrities **Obverse:** State seal **Reverse:** Alfred Nobel

| Date | Mintage | F | VF | XF | Unc | BU |
|---|---|---|---|---|---|---|
| 1992 Proof | 30,000 | Value: 27.50 | | | | |

**10 YUAN** **Y#942** **Weight:** 31.1035 g. **Composition:** 0.9990 Silver 1.0000 oz. ASW **Subject:** Environmental Protection **Obverse:** National arms **Reverse:** Kneeling woman fetching water at stream

| Date | Mintage | F | VF | XF | Unc | BU |
|---|---|---|---|---|---|---|
| 1992 | 60,000 | — | — | — | 30.00 | — |

**10 YUAN** **Y#352** **Weight:** 31.1000 g. **Composition:** 0.9990 Silver 1.0000 oz. ASW **Obverse:** Temple of Heaven **Reverse:** Peacocks

| Date | Mintage | F | VF | XF | Unc | BU |
|---|---|---|---|---|---|---|
| 1992 Proof | — | Value: 40.00 | | | | |

| Date | Mintage | F | VF | XF | Unc | BU |
|---|---|---|---|---|---|---|
| 1993 Proof | 7,000 | Value: 40.00 | | | | |
| 1997 Prooflike | — | — | — | — | — | — |

**10 YUAN** **Y#360** **Weight:** 31.1000 g. **Composition:** 0.9990 Silver 1.0000 oz. ASW **Obverse:** Similar to KM#361 **Reverse:** Mother panda nurturing cub

| Date | Mintage | F | VF | XF | Unc | BU |
|---|---|---|---|---|---|---|
| 1993 Proof | 20,000 | Value: 35.00 | | | | |

**10 YUAN** **Y#361** **Weight:** 31.1000 g. **Composition:** 0.9990 Silver 1.0000 oz. ASW **Reverse:** Panda on flat rock

| Date | Mintage | F | VF | XF | Unc | BU |
|---|---|---|---|---|---|---|
| 1993 | 120,000 | — | — | — | 20.00 | — |

**10 YUAN** **Y# 412.1** **Weight:** 27.0000 g. **Composition:** 0.9250 Silver .8031 oz. ASW **Subject:** Bust of Mao

| Date | Mintage | F | VF | XF | Unc | BU |
|---|---|---|---|---|---|---|
| 1993 | 30,000 | — | — | — | 40.00 | — |

**10 YUAN** **Y# 412.2** **Weight:** 27.0000 g. **Composition:** 0.9250 Silver .8031 oz. ASW **Reverse:** Revised bust of Mao

| Date | Mintage | F | VF | XF | Unc | BU |
|---|---|---|---|---|---|---|
| 1993 | — | — | — | — | 40.00 | — |

**10 YUAN** **Y#418** **Weight:** 24.2550 g. **Composition:** 0.9000 Silver .7799 oz. ASW **Subject:** World Cup Soccer - 1994

| Date | Mintage | F | VF | XF | Unc | BU |
|---|---|---|---|---|---|---|
| 1993 Proof | 30,000 | Value: 35.00 | | | | |

**10 YUAN** **Y#474** **Weight:** 3.1103 g. **Composition:** 0.9990 Gold .1000 oz. AGW **Obverse:** Temple of Harmony **Reverse:** 2 peacocks

| Date | Mintage | F | VF | XF | Unc | BU |
|---|---|---|---|---|---|---|
| 1993 Prooflike | — | — | — | — | 65.00 | — |

**10 YUAN** **Y#480** **Weight:** 20.7500 g. **Composition:** 0.9990 Silver .6640 oz. ASW **Subject:** Year of the Rooster **Shape:** Scalloped

| Date | Mintage | F | VF | XF | Unc | BU |
|---|---|---|---|---|---|---|
| 1993 Proof | 6,800 | Value: 95.00 | | | | |

**10 YUAN** **Y#484** **Weight:** 3.1103 g. **Composition:** 0.9990 Gold .1000 oz. AGW

| Date | Mintage | F | VF | XF | Unc | BU |
|---|---|---|---|---|---|---|
| 1993 | — | — | — | — | 65.00 | — |
| 1993 Proof | — | Value: 75.00 | | | | |

**10 YUAN** **Y#484a** **Weight:** 3.1100 g. **Composition:** 0.9995 Platinum .1000 oz. APW **Reverse:** Panda seated on rock

| Date | Mintage | F | VF | XF | Unc | BU |
|---|---|---|---|---|---|---|
| 1993 | — | — | — | — | 75.00 | — |

**10 YUAN** **Y#492** **Weight:** 30.0000 g. **Composition:** 0.9000 Silver .8682 oz. ASW **Series:** Olympics **Reverse:** Runners

| Date | Mintage | F | VF | XF | Unc | BU |
|---|---|---|---|---|---|---|
| 1993 Proof | 30,000 | Value: 30.00 | | | | |

**10 YUAN** **Y#493** **Weight:** 30.0000 g. **Composition:** 0.9000 Silver .8682 oz. ASW **Subject:** Olympics **Reverse:** Fencing

| Date | Mintage | F | VF | XF | Unc | BU |
|---|---|---|---|---|---|---|
| 1993 Proof | 30,000 | Value: 30.00 | | | | |

**10 YUAN** **Y#499** **Weight:** 3.1103 g. **Composition:** 0.9990 Gold .1000 oz. AGW **Reverse:** Goddess of Mercy - holding flower

| Date | Mintage | F | VF | XF | Unc | BU |
|---|---|---|---|---|---|---|
| 1993 Prooflike | 10,000 | — | — | — | 40.00 | — |

**10 YUAN** **Y#501** **Weight:** 3.1103 g. **Composition:** 0.9990 Gold .1000 oz. AGW **Reverse:** Goddess Guanyin - seated in flowers

| Date | Mintage | F | VF | XF | Unc | BU |
|---|---|---|---|---|---|---|
| 1993 Proof | 1,000 | Value: 60.00 | | | | |

**10 YUAN** **Y#567** **Weight:** 31.1000 g. **Composition:** 0.9990 Silver 1.0000 oz. ASW **Subject:** Year of the Rooster

| Date | Mintage | F | VF | XF | Unc | BU |
|---|---|---|---|---|---|---|
| 1993 Proof | Est. 9,000 | Value: 60.00 | | | | |

**10 YUAN** **Y#758** **Weight:** 30.0000 g. **Composition:** 0.9000 Silver .8681 oz. ASW **Subject:** Song Qingling **Obverse:** National emblem **Reverse:** Seated figure

| Date | Mintage | F | VF | XF | Unc | BU |
|---|---|---|---|---|---|---|
| 1993 Proof | 20,000 | Value: 35.00 | | | | |

**10 YUAN** **Y#759** **Weight:** 30.0000 g. **Composition:** 0.9000 Silver .8681 oz. ASW **Subject:** Song Qingling **Obverse:** National emblem **Reverse:** Standing figure

| Date | Mintage | F | VF | XF | Unc | BU |
|---|---|---|---|---|---|---|
| 1993 Proof | 20,000 | Value: 35.00 | | | | |

**10 YUAN** **Y#774** **Weight:** 3.1030 g. **Composition:** 0.9990 Gold .1000 oz. AGW **Subject:** Mount Heng **Obverse:** Great Wall **Reverse:** Mountain side

| Date | Mintage | F | VF | XF | Unc | BU |
|---|---|---|---|---|---|---|
| 1993 Proof | 8,888 | Value: 40.00 | | | | |

**10 YUAN** **Y#779** **Weight:** 27.0000 g. **Composition:** 0.9250 Silver .8030 oz. ASW **Subject:** World Cup Soccer **Obverse:** National emblem **Reverse:** 3 soccer players

| Date | Mintage | F | VF | XF | Unc | BU |
|---|---|---|---|---|---|---|
| 1993 Proof | 30,000 | Value: 32.50 | | | | |

**10 YUAN** **Y#932** **Weight:** 31.2000 g. **Composition:** 0.9990 Silver 1.0021 oz. ASW **Subject:** Mt. Heng **Obverse:** Great Wall **Reverse:** Large building, islands in background

| Date | Mintage | F | VF | XF | Unc | BU |
|---|---|---|---|---|---|---|
| 1993 Proof | 60,000 | Value: 35.00 | | | | |

**10 YUAN** **Y#933** **Weight:** 31.2000 g. **Composition:** 0.9990 Silver 1.0021 oz. ASW **Subject:** Mt. Tai **Obverse:** Great Wall **Reverse:** Small building with long staircase

| Date | Mintage | F | VF | XF | Unc | BU |
|---|---|---|---|---|---|---|
| 1993 Proof | 60,000 | Value: 35.00 | | | | |

**10 YUAN** **Y#934** **Weight:** 31.2000 g. **Composition:** 0.9990 Silver 1.0021 oz. ASW **Subject:** Mt. Hua **Obverse:** Great Wall **Reverse:** Bird's eye view of mountain tops, shelter

| Date | Mintage | F | VF | XF | Unc | BU |
|---|---|---|---|---|---|---|
| 1993 Proof | 60,000 | Value: 35.00 | | | | |

**10 YUAN** **Y#935** **Weight:** 31.2000 g. **Composition:** 0.9990 Silver 1.0021 oz. ASW **Subject:** Mt. Song **Obverse:** Great Wall **Reverse:** Tail domed building

| Date | Mintage | F | VF | XF | Unc | BU |
|---|---|---|---|---|---|---|
| 1993 Proof | 60,000 | Value: 35.00 | | | | |

**10 YUAN** **Y# 611** **Composition:** Gold **Reverse:** Panda on flat rock

| Date | Mintage | F | VF | XF | Unc | BU |
|---|---|---|---|---|---|---|
| 1993 Proof | — | Value: 65.00 | | | | |

**10 YUAN** **Y# 1077** **Weight:** 30.0000 g. **Composition:** 0.9000 Silver .8681 oz. ASW **Subject:** Yin and Yang Concept **Obverse:** Great Wall blockhouse. **Reverse:** Four men studying the symbol. **Edge:** Reeded. **Size:** 40 mm.

| Date | Mintage | F | VF | XF | Unc | BU |
|---|---|---|---|---|---|---|
| 1993 | — | — | — | — | 50.00 | — |

**Note:** Probably minted at a much later date.

**10 YUAN** **Y#681** **Weight:** 20.7360 g. **Composition:** 0.9000 Silver .6013 oz. ASW **Reverse:** Magpies on branch **Note:** 12-sided.

| Date | Mintage | F | VF | XF | Unc | BU |
|---|---|---|---|---|---|---|
| 1994 Proof | 3,900 | Value: 40.00 | | | | |

**10 YUAN** **Y#432** **Weight:** 3.1103 g. **Composition:** 0.9990 Gold .1000 oz. AGW **Reverse:** Seated panda eating **Note:** Similar to Y#416.

| Date | Mintage | F | VF | XF | Unc | BU |
|---|---|---|---|---|---|---|
| 1994 | — | — | — | — | 55.00 | — |
| 1994 Prof | — | Value: 75.00 | | | | |

**10 YUAN** **Y#421** **Weight:** 3.1103 g. **Composition:** 0.9990 Gold .1000 oz. AGW **Note:** Similar to Y#420.

| Date | Mintage | F | VF | XF | Unc | BU |
|---|---|---|---|---|---|---|
| 1994 Proof | 5,100 | Value: 95.00 | | | | |

**10 YUAN** **Y#494** **Weight:** 31.1035 g. **Composition:** 0.9990 Silver 1.0000 oz. ASW **Series:** Olympics **Subject:** Basketball

| Date | Mintage | F | VF | XF | Unc | BU |
|---|---|---|---|---|---|---|
| 1994 Proof | 30,000 | Value: 32.50 | | | | |

**10 YUAN** **Y#396** **Weight:** 31.1000 g. **Composition:** 0.9990 Silver 1.0000 oz. ASW **Subject:** Year of the Dog

| Date | Mintage | F | VF | XF | Unc | BU |
|---|---|---|---|---|---|---|
| 1994 Proof | 8,000 | Value: 55.00 | | | | |

**10 YUAN** **Y#416** **Weight:** 31.1000 g. **Composition:** 0.9990 Silver 1.0000 oz. ASW **Reverse:** Seated panda eating

| Date | Mintage | F | VF | XF | Unc | BU |
|---|---|---|---|---|---|---|
| 1994 | 120,000 | — | — | — | 22.50 | — |

**10 YUAN** **Y#420** **Weight:** 31.1000 g. **Composition:** 0.9990 Silver 1.0000 oz. ASW **Reverse:** Unicorn

| Date | Mintage | F | VF | XF | Unc | BU |
|---|---|---|---|---|---|---|
| 1994 | 50,000 | — | — | — | 27.50 | — |
| 1994 Proof | 4,000 | Value: 40.00 | | | | |

**10 YUAN** **Y#432a** **Weight:** 3.1103 g. **Composition:** 0.9990 Platinum .1000 oz. APW

| Date | Mintage | F | VF | XF | Unc | BU |
|---|---|---|---|---|---|---|
| 1994 | 2,500 | — | — | — | 125 | — |

**10 YUAN** **Y#437** **Weight:** 31.1000 g. **Composition:** 0.9990 Silver 1.0000 oz. ASW **Reverse:** Panda sitting on branch of tree

| Date | Mintage | F | VF | XF | Unc | BU |
|---|---|---|---|---|---|---|
| 1994 Proof | 20,000 | Value: 35.00 | | | | |

**10 YUAN** **Y#438** **Weight:** 27.0000 g. **Composition:** 0.9250 Silver .8031 oz. ASW **Subject:** 12th Asian Games **Reverse:** Swimming

| Date | Mintage | F | VF | XF | Unc | BU |
|---|---|---|---|---|---|---|
| 1994 Proof | 5,000 | Value: 30.00 | | | | |

**10 YUAN** **Y#439** **Weight:** 27.0000 g. **Composition:** 0.9250 Silver .8031 oz. ASW **Subject:** 12th Asian Games **Reverse:** Runners

| Date | Mintage | F | VF | XF | Unc | BU |
|---|---|---|---|---|---|---|
| 1994 Proof | 5,000 | Value: 30.00 | | | | |

**10 YUAN** **Y#457** **Weight:** 31.1035 g. **Composition:** 0.9990 Silver 1.0000 oz. ASW **Subject:** Children at Play **Reverse:** 2 children and cat

| Date | Mintage | F | VF | XF | Unc | BU |
|---|---|---|---|---|---|---|
| 1994 Proof | 6,000,000 | Value: 30.00 | | | | |

**10 YUAN** **Y#458** **Weight:** 31.1035 g. **Composition:** 0.9990 Silver 1.0000 oz. ASW **Subject:** Children at Play **Reverse:** 3 children and toy boat

| Date | Mintage | F | VF | XF | Unc | BU |
|---|---|---|---|---|---|---|
| 1994 Proof | 6,000,000 | Value: 30.00 | | | | |

**10 YUAN** **Y#463** **Weight:** 3.1103 g. **Composition:** 0.9990 Silver .1000 oz. ASW **Reverse:** Phoenix and dragon

| Date | Mintage | F | VF | XF | Unc | BU |
|---|---|---|---|---|---|---|
| 1994 | 2,500 | — | — | — | 125 | — |

**10 YUAN** **Y#482** **Weight:** 31.1035 g. **Composition:** 0.9990 Silver 1.0000 oz. ASW **Reverse:** Guanyin - Goddess of Mercy - with child

| Date | Mintage | F | VF | XF | Unc | BU |
|---|---|---|---|---|---|---|
| 1994 Proof | 30,000 | Value: 30.00 | | | | |

**10 YUAN** **Y#495** **Weight:** 31.1035 g. **Composition:** 0.9990 Silver 1.0000 oz. ASW **Series:** Olympics **Subject:** Female Archery

| Date | Mintage | F | VF | XF | Unc | BU |
|---|---|---|---|---|---|---|
| 1994 Proof | 30,000 | Value: 32.50 | | | | |

**10 YUAN** **Y#496** **Weight:** 31.1035 g. **Composition:** 0.9990 Silver 1.0000 oz. ASW **Series:** Olympics **Subject:** Boxing

| Date | Mintage | F | VF | XF | Unc | BU |
|---|---|---|---|---|---|---|
| 1994 Proof | 30,000 | Value: 30.00 | | | | |

**10 YUAN** **Y#510** **Weight:** 3.1103 g. **Composition:** 0.9990 Gold .1000 oz. AGW **Reverse:** Guanyin-Goddess of Mercy - with child

| Date | Mintage | F | VF | XF | Unc | BU |
|---|---|---|---|---|---|---|
| 1994 Prooflike | 8,000 | — | — | — | 50.00 | — |

**10 YUAN** **Y#539** **Weight:** 27.0000 g. **Composition:** 0.9250 Silver .8031 oz. ASW **Subject:** Confucius **Obverse:** State emblem

| Date | Mintage | F | VF | XF | Unc | BU |
|---|---|---|---|---|---|---|
| 1994 Proof | — | Value: 30.00 | | | | |

**10 YUAN** **Y#540** **Weight:** 27.0000 g. **Composition:** 0.9250 Silver .8031 oz. ASW **Subject:** Socrates

| Date | Mintage | F | VF | XF | Unc | BU |
|---|---|---|---|---|---|---|
| 1994 Proof | — | Value: 30.00 | | | | |

**10 YUAN** **Y#541** **Weight:** 27.0000 g. **Composition:** 0.9250 Silver .8031 oz. ASW **Subject:** Rembrandt

| Date | Mintage | F | VF | XF | Unc | BU |
|---|---|---|---|---|---|---|
| 1994 Proof | — | Value: 30.00 | | | | |

**10 YUAN** **Y#542** **Weight:** 27.0000 g. **Composition:** 0.9250 Silver .8031 oz. ASW **Subject:** Verdi

| Date | Mintage | F | VF | XF | Unc | BU |
|---|---|---|---|---|---|---|
| 1994 Proof | — | Value: 30.00 | | | | |

**10 YUAN** **Y#579** **Weight:** 27.0000 g. **Composition:** 0.9250 Silver .8031 oz. ASW **Reverse:** 2 Bactrian camels

| Date | Mintage | F | VF | XF | Unc | BU |
|---|---|---|---|---|---|---|
| 1994 Proof | 4,825 | Value: 35.00 | | | | |

**10 YUAN** **Y#580** **Weight:** 27.0000 g. **Composition:** 0.9250 Silver .8031 oz. ASW **Subject:** Pere David Deer

| Date | Mintage | F | VF | XF | Unc | BU |
|---|---|---|---|---|---|---|
| 1994 Proof | 4,825 | Value: 35.00 | | | | |

**10 YUAN** **Y#615** **Weight:** 27.2000 g. **Composition:** 0.9250 Silver .8089 oz. ASW **Obverse:** State emblem **Reverse:** Soccer player

| Date | Mintage | F | VF | XF | Unc | BU |
|---|---|---|---|---|---|---|
| 1994 Prof | — | Value: 40.00 | | | | |

**10 YUAN** **Y#680** **Weight:** 3.1103 g. **Composition:** 0.9990 Silver .1000 oz. ASW **Reverse:** Panda tugging bamboo sprig

| Date | Mintage | F | VF | XF | Unc | BU |
|---|---|---|---|---|---|---|
| 1994 Proof | 2,500 | Value: 125 | | | | |

**10 YUAN** **Y#710** **Weight:** 31.1035 g. **Composition:** 0.9990 Silver 1.0000 oz. ASW **Subject:** Sino - Singapore Friendship **Obverse:** Great Wall **Reverse:** City view of Singapore

| Date | Mintage | F | VF | XF | Unc | BU |
|---|---|---|---|---|---|---|
| 1994 Proof | 30,000 | Value: 40.00 | | | | |

**10 YUAN** **Y#783** **Weight:** 31.1035 g. **Composition:** 0.9990 Silver 1.0000 oz. ASW **Subject:** Children at Play **Obverse:** Imperial Palace, corner building **Reverse:** Three children carrying tray

| Date | Mintage | F | VF | XF | Unc | BU |
|---|---|---|---|---|---|---|
| 1994 Proof | 2,500 | Value: 35.00 | | | | |

**10 YUAN** **Y#784** **Weight:** 31.1035 g. **Composition:** 0.9990 Silver 1.0000 oz. ASW **Subject:** Children at Play **Obverse:** Imperial Palace, corner building **Reverse:** Three children playing on ground

| Date | Mintage | F | VF | XF | Unc | BU |
|---|---|---|---|---|---|---|
| 1994 Proof | 2,500 | Value: 35.00 | | | | |

**10 YUAN** **Y#450** **Weight:** 31.2400 g. **Composition:** 0.9990 Silver 1.0045 oz. ASW **Subject:** Year of the Pig

| Date | Mintage | F | VF | XF | Unc | BU |
|---|---|---|---|---|---|---|
| 1995 Proof | 8,000 | Value: 75.00 | | | | |

**10 YUAN** **Y#452** **Weight:** 20.7500 g. **Composition:** 0.9990 Silver .6640 oz. ASW **Subject:** Year of the Pig **Reverse:** 2 pigs

| Date | Mintage | F | VF | XF | Unc | BU |
|---|---|---|---|---|---|---|
| 1995 Proof | 6,800 | Value: 100 | | | | |

**10 YUAN** **Y#469** **Weight:** 27.0000 g. **Composition:** 0.9250 Silver .8022 oz. ASW **Subject:** Dinosaurs **Reverse:** Pterodactylus

| Date | Mintage | F | VF | XF | Unc | BU |
|---|---|---|---|---|---|---|
| 1995 Proof | Est. 5,000 | Value: 40.00 | | | | |

**10 YUAN** **Y#470** **Weight:** 27.0000 g. **Composition:** 0.9250 Silver .8022 oz. ASW **Subject:** Dinosaurs **Reverse:** Stegosaurus

| Date | Mintage | F | VF | XF | Unc | BU |
|---|---|---|---|---|---|---|
| 1995 Proof | Est. 5,000 | Value: 45.00 | | | | |

**10 YUAN** **Y# 485.1** **Weight:** 31.1035 g. **Composition:** 0.9990 Silver 1.0000 oz. ASW **Subject:** Shanghai Mint **Obverse:** Temple of Heaven **Reverse:** Panda sitting on branch eating large twig

| Date | Mintage | F | VF | XF | Unc | BU |
|---|---|---|---|---|---|---|
| 1995 | — | — | — | — | 20.00 | — |

**10 YUAN** **Y# 485.2** **Weight:** 31.1035 g. **Composition:** 0.9990 Silver 1.0000 oz. ASW **Subject:** Shenyang Mint **Reverse:** Panda eating small twig

| Date | Mintage | F | VF | XF | Unc | BU |
|---|---|---|---|---|---|---|
| 1995 | — | — | — | — | 20.00 | — |

**10 YUAN** **Y# 489** **Weight:** 31.1035 g. **Composition:** 0.9990 Silver 1.0000 oz. ASW **Reverse:** Guanyin - Goddess of Mercy with sceptre

| Date | Mintage | F | VF | XF | Unc | BU |
|---|---|---|---|---|---|---|
| 1995 Prooflike | 30,000 | — | — | — | 30.00 | — |

**10 YUAN** **Y# 520** **Weight:** 3.1103 g. **Composition:** 0.9990 Gold .1000 oz. AGW **Reverse:** Guanyin - Goddess of Mercy with Lotus flower

| Date | Mintage | F | VF | XF | Unc | BU |
|---|---|---|---|---|---|---|
| 1995 Proof | 3,000 | Value: 75.00 | | | | |

**10 YUAN** **Y# 521** **Weight:** 3.1103 g. **Composition:** 0.9990 Gold .1000 oz. AGW **Reverse:** Guanyin - Goddess of Mercy with wheel

| Date | Mintage | F | VF | XF | Unc | BU |
|---|---|---|---|---|---|---|
| 1995 Proof | 3,000 | Value: 75.00 | | | | |

**10 YUAN** **Y# 522** **Weight:** 3.1103 g. **Composition:** 0.9990 Gold .1000 oz. AGW **Reverse:** Guanyin - Goddess of Mercy with sceptre

| Date | Mintage | F | VF | XF | Unc | BU |
|---|---|---|---|---|---|---|
| 1995 Proof | 3,000 | Value: 75.00 | | | | |

**10 YUAN** **Y# 523** **Weight:** 3.1103 g. **Composition:** 0.9990 Gold .1000 oz. AGW **Reverse:** Guanyin - Goddess of Mercy with bowl

| Date | Mintage | F | VF | XF | Unc | BU |
|---|---|---|---|---|---|---|
| 1995 Proof | 3,000 | Value: 75.00 | | | | |

**10 YUAN** **Y# 531** **Weight:** 31.1035 g. **Composition:** 0.9990 Silver 1.0000 oz. ASW **Subject:** Return of Hong Kong to China **Obverse:** Tiananmen **Reverse:** Deng Xiao Ping

| Date | Mintage | F | VF | XF | Unc | BU |
|---|---|---|---|---|---|---|
| 1995 Proof | 88,000 | Value: 80.00 | | | | |

**10 YUAN** **Y# 571** **Ring Weight:** 1.1108 g. **Ring Composition:** 0.9990 Silver .0356 oz. ASW **Center Weight:** 3.1103 g. **Center Composition:** 0.9990 Gold .1000 oz. AGW **Reverse:** Panda at stream

| Date | Mintage | F | VF | XF | Unc | BU |
|---|---|---|---|---|---|---|
| 1995 Proof set | 2,000 | Value: 100 | | | | |

**10 YUAN** **Y# 588** **Weight:** 27.0000 g. **Composition:** 0.9250 Silver .8031 oz. ASW **Obverse:** Dragon in inner circle **Reverse:** Huang Di in chariot

| Date | Mintage | F | VF | XF | Unc | BU |
|---|---|---|---|---|---|---|
| 1995 Proof | 5,000 | Value: 40.00 | | | | |

**10 YUAN** **Y# 589** **Weight:** 27.0000 g. **Composition:** 0.9250 Silver .8031 oz. ASW **Obverse:** Dragon in inner circle **Reverse:** Yan Di, wearing skins

| Date | Mintage | F | VF | XF | Unc | BU |
|---|---|---|---|---|---|---|
| 1995 Proof | 5,000 | Value: 40.00 | | | | |

**10 YUAN** **Y# 590** **Weight:** 27.0000 g. **Composition:** 0.9250 Silver .8031 oz. ASW **Obverse:** Dragon in inner circle **Reverse:** Yao holding feathers

| Date | Mintage | F | VF | XF | Unc | BU |
|---|---|---|---|---|---|---|
| 1995 Proof | 5,000 | Value: 40.00 | | | | |

**10 YUAN** **Y# 591** **Weight:** 27.0000 g. **Composition:** 0.9250 Silver .8031 oz. ASW **Obverse:** Dragon in inner circle **Reverse:** Shun with urn

| Date | Mintage | F | VF | XF | Unc | BU |
|---|---|---|---|---|---|---|
| 1995 Proof | 5,000 | Value: 40.00 | | | | |

**10 YUAN** **Y# 641** **Weight:** 3.1103 g. **Composition:** 0.9990 Gold .1000 oz. AGW **Obverse:** Temple of Heaven **Reverse:** Panda eating bamboo

| Date | Mintage | F | VF | XF | Unc | BU |
|---|---|---|---|---|---|---|
| 1995 | — | — | — | — | 55.00 | — |

**10 YUAN** **Y# 641a** **Weight:** 3.1103 g. **Composition:** 0.9990 Platinum .1000 oz. APW

| Date | Mintage | F | VF | XF | Unc | BU |
|---|---|---|---|---|---|---|
| 1995 Proof | 5,000 | Value: 100 | | | | |

**10 YUAN** **Y# 647** **Weight:** 27.0000 g. **Composition:** 0.9250 Silver .8031 oz. ASW **Reverse:** Dragon boat

| Date | Mintage | F | VF | XF | Unc | BU |
|---|---|---|---|---|---|---|
| 1995 Proof | 10,000 | Value: 75.00 | | | | |

**10 YUAN** **Y#650** **Weight:** 27.0000 g. **Composition:** 0.9250 Silver .8031 oz. ASW **Reverse:** Junk

| Date | Mintage | F | VF | XF | Unc | BU |
|---|---|---|---|---|---|---|
| 1995 Proof | 10,000 | Value: 75.00 | | | | |

**10 YUAN** **Y#682** **Weight:** 27.0000 g. **Composition:** 0.9250 Silver .8031 oz. ASW **Series:** 50th Anniversary - United Nations **Obverse:** UN logo **Reverse:** UN building

| Date | Mintage | F | VF | XF | Unc | BU |
|---|---|---|---|---|---|---|
| 1995 Proof | 115,000 | Value: 30.00 | | | | |

**10 YUAN** **Y#683** **Weight:** 31.1003 g. **Composition:** 0.9990 Silver 1.0001 oz. ASW **Reverse:** Unicorn with offspring

| Date | Mintage | F | VF | XF | Unc | BU |
|---|---|---|---|---|---|---|
| 1995 Proof | — | Value: 30.00 | | | | |

**10 YUAN** **Y#684** **Weight:** 31.1003 g. **Composition:** 0.9990 Silver 1.0001 oz. ASW **Subject:** 50th Anniversary of Anti-Japanese War **Obverse:** State seal **Reverse:** Chou and Mao above soldiers

| Date | Mintage | F | VF | XF | Unc | BU |
|---|---|---|---|---|---|---|
| 1995 Proof | 3,750 | Value: 35.00 | | | | |

**10 YUAN** **Y#685** **Weight:** 31.1003 g. **Composition:** 0.9990 Silver 1.0001 oz. ASW **Obverse:** State seal **Reverse:** Attacking soldiers above bridge guarded by lion

| Date | Mintage | F | VF | XF | Unc | BU |
|---|---|---|---|---|---|---|
| 1995 Proof | 3,750 | Value: 35.00 | | | | |

**10 YUAN** **Y#713** **Weight:** 27.0000 g. **Composition:** 0.9250 Silver .8022 oz. ASW **Series:** 1996 Olympics **Obverse:** State seal **Reverse:** Handball player

| Date | Mintage | F | VF | XF | Unc | BU |
|---|---|---|---|---|---|---|
| 1995 Proof | — | Value: 27.50 | | | | |

**10 YUAN** **Y#714** **Weight:** 27.0000 g. **Composition:** 0.9250 Silver .8022 oz. ASW **Series:** 1996 Olympics **Obverse:** State seal **Reverse:** Kick boxer

| Date | Mintage | F | VF | XF | Unc | BU |
|---|---|---|---|---|---|---|
| 1995 Proof | — | Value: 27.50 | | | | |

**10 YUAN** **Y#737** **Weight:** 3.1100 g. **Composition:** 0.9990 Gold .0999 oz. AGW **Obverse:** Eastern unicorn **Reverse:** Western unicorn with offspring

| Date | Mintage | F | VF | XF | Unc | BU |
|---|---|---|---|---|---|---|
| 1995 Proof | 5,000 | Value: 95.00 | | | | |

**10 YUAN** **Y#787** **Weight:** 31.1035 g. **Composition:** 0.9990 Silver 1.0000 oz. ASW **Obverse:** Temple of Heaven **Reverse:** Panda approaching water from right

| Date | Mintage | F | VF | XF | Unc | BU |
|---|---|---|---|---|---|---|
| 1995 Proof only | — | Value: 40.00 | | | | |

**10 YUAN** **Y#792** **Weight:** 31.1035 g. **Composition:** 0.9990 Silver 1.0000 oz. ASW **Subject:** Beijing Stamp Fair **Obverse:** Temple of Heaven with additional legend below **Reverse:** Similar to Y#787

| Date | Mintage | F | VF | XF | Unc | BU |
|---|---|---|---|---|---|---|
| 1995 Proof | 18,000 | Value: 40.00 | | | | |

**10 YUAN** **Y#799** **Weight:** 3.1103 g. **Composition:** 0.9990 Gold .1000 oz. AGW **Subject:** Chinese Culture Series **Obverse:** Great Wall seen through arch **Reverse:** Pagoda of six harmonies

| Date | Mintage | F | VF | XF | Unc | BU |
|---|---|---|---|---|---|---|
| 1995 Proof | 25,000 | Value: 55.00 | | | | |

**10 YUAN** **Y#800** **Weight:** 3.1103 g. **Composition:** 0.9990 Gold .1000 oz. AGW **Subject:** Chinese Culture Series **Obverse:** Great Wall seen through arch **Reverse:** Mencius seated at table

| Date | Mintage | F | VF | XF | Unc | BU |
|---|---|---|---|---|---|---|
| 1995 Proof | 25,000 | Value: 55.00 | | | | |

**10 YUAN** **Y#801** **Weight:** 3.1103 g. **Composition:** 0.9990 Gold .1000 oz. AGW **Subject:** Chinese Culture Series **Obverse:** Great Wall seen through arch **Reverse:** Tang Taizong seated

| Date | Mintage | F | VF | XF | Unc | BU |
|---|---|---|---|---|---|---|
| 1995 Proof | 25,000 | Value: 55.00 | | | | |

**10 YUAN** **Y#802** **Weight:** 3.1103 g. **Composition:** 0.9990 Gold .1000 oz. AGW **Subject:** Chinese Culture Series **Obverse:** Great Wall seen through arch **Reverse:** Lion dance

| Date | Mintage | F | VF | XF | Unc | BU |
|---|---|---|---|---|---|---|
| 1995 Proof | 25,000 | Value: 55.00 | | | | |

**10 YUAN** **Y#803** **Weight:** 3.1103 g. **Composition:** 0.9990 Gold .1000 oz. AGW **Subject:** Chinese Culture Series **Obverse:** Great Wall seen through arch **Reverse:** Female opera role

| Date | Mintage | F | VF | XF | Unc | BU |
|---|---|---|---|---|---|---|
| 1995 Proof | 25,000 | Value: 55.00 | | | | |

**10 YUAN** **Y#809** **Weight:** 20.7333 g. **Composition:** 0.9000 Silver .5999 oz. ASW **Obverse:** Great Wall **Reverse:** Eagle in flight **Shape:** 12-sided

| Date | Mintage | F | VF | XF | Unc | BU |
|---|---|---|---|---|---|---|
| 1995 Proof | 3,900 | Value: 65.00 | | | | |

**10 YUAN** **Y#811** **Weight:** 31.1035 g. **Composition:** 0.9990 Silver 1.0000 oz. ASW **Subject:** 50th Anniversary - Return of Taiwan to China **Obverse:** Great Wall **Reverse:** Taiwan and China maps

| Date | Mintage | F | VF | XF | Unc | BU |
|---|---|---|---|---|---|---|
| 1995 Proof | 5,000 | Value: 200 | | | | |

**10 YUAN** **Y#812** **Weight:** 31.1035 g. **Composition:** 0.9990 Silver 1.0000 oz. ASW **Subject:** 50th Anniversary - Return of Taiwan to China **Obverse:** Great Wall **Reverse:** Zhongshan Hall

| Date | Mintage | F | VF | XF | Unc | BU |
|---|---|---|---|---|---|---|
| 1995 Proof | 5,000 | Value: 200 | | | | |

**10 YUAN** **Y#819** **Weight:** 27.0000 g. **Composition:** 0.9250 Silver .8030 oz. ASW **Subject:** Painter Zu Beihong **Obverse:** Portrait **Reverse:** Cat stalking

| Date | Mintage | F | VF | XF | Unc | BU |
|---|---|---|---|---|---|---|
| 1995 Proof | 8,000 | Value: 50.00 | | | | |

**10 YUAN** **Y#820** **Weight:** 27.0000 g. **Composition:** 0.9250 Silver .8030 oz. ASW **Subject:** Painter Zu Beihong **Obverse:** Portrait **Reverse:** Horse running

| Date | Mintage | F | VF | XF | Unc | BU |
|---|---|---|---|---|---|---|
| 1995 Proof | 8,000 | Value: 50.00 | | | | |

**10 YUAN** **Y#825** **Weight:** 27.0000 g. **Composition:** 0.9250 Silver .8030 oz. ASW **Subject:** Romance of the Three Kingdoms Series **Obverse:** Luo Guanzhong bust **Reverse:** Liu Bei standing holding rod

| Date | Mintage | F | VF | XF | Unc | BU |
|---|---|---|---|---|---|---|
| 1995 Proof | 7,000 | Value: 60.00 | | | | |

**10 YUAN** **Y#826** **Weight:** 27.0000 g. **Composition:** 0.9250 Silver .8030 oz. ASW **Subject:** Romance of the Three Kingdoms Series **Obverse:** Luo Guanzhong bust **Reverse:** Guan Yo reading

| Date | Mintage | F | VF | XF | Unc | BU |
|---|---|---|---|---|---|---|
| 1995 Proof | 7,000 | Value: 60.00 | | | | |

**10 YUAN** **Y#827** **Weight:** 27.0000 g. **Composition:** 0.9250 Silver .8030 oz. ASW **Subject:** Romance of the Three Kingdoms Series **Obverse:** Luo Guanzhong bust **Reverse:** Zhang Fei on horse

| Date | Mintage | F | VF | XF | Unc | BU |
|---|---|---|---|---|---|---|
| 1995 Proof | 7,000 | Value: 60.00 | | | | |

**10 YUAN** **Y#828** **Weight:** 27.0000 g. **Composition:** 0.9250 Silver .8030 oz. ASW **Subject:** Romance of the Three Kingdoms Series **Obverse:** Luo Guanzhong bust **Reverse:** Zhuge Liang on throne

| Date | Mintage | F | VF | XF | Unc | BU |
|---|---|---|---|---|---|---|
| 1995 Proof | 7,000 | Value: 60.00 | | | | |

**10 YUAN** **Y#836** **Weight:** 31.1035 g. **Composition:** 0.9990 Silver 1.0000 oz. ASW **Subject:** Table Tennis **Obverse:** Tianjing Stadium **Reverse:** Table tennis player

| Date | Mintage | F | VF | XF | Unc | BU |
|---|---|---|---|---|---|---|
| 1995 Proof | 3,000 | Value: 75.00 | | | | |

**10 YUAN** **Y#837** **Weight:** 31.1035 g. **Composition:** 0.9990 Silver 1.0000 oz. ASW **Subject:** Table Tennis **Obverse:** Tianjing Stadium **Reverse:** Two table tennis players

| Date | Mintage | F | VF | XF | Unc | BU |
|---|---|---|---|---|---|---|
| 1995 Proof | 3,000 | Value: 75.00 | | | | |

**10 YUAN** **Weight:** 31.1035 g. **Composition:** 0.9990 Silver 1.0000 oz. ASW **Subject:** 4th UN World Women's Conference **Obverse:** Logo above building **Reverse:** Three women with flowers and birds

| Date | Mintage | F | VF | XF | Unc | BU |
|---|---|---|---|---|---|---|
| 1995 | 30,000 | — | — | — | 50.00 | — |
| 1995 Proof | 500 | Value: 75.00 | | | | |

**10 YUAN** **Y#841** **Weight:** 31.1035 g. **Composition:** 0.9990 Silver 1.0000 oz. ASW **Series:** Olympics **Obverse:** National emblem **Reverse:** Gymnast

| Date | Mintage | F | VF | XF | Unc | BU |
|---|---|---|---|---|---|---|
| 1995 | 30,000 | — | — | — | 27.50 | — |

**10 YUAN** **Y#842** **Weight:** 31.1035 g. **Composition:** 0.9990 Silver 1.0000 oz. ASW **Series:** 1996 Olympics **Obverse:** State seal **Reverse:** Female shooter

| Date | Mintage | F | VF | XF | Unc | BU |
|---|---|---|---|---|---|---|
| 1995 | 30,000 | — | — | — | 27.50 | — |

**10 YUAN** **Y#686** **Weight:** 31.1003 g. **Composition:** 0.9990 Silver 1.0001 oz. ASW **Subject:** 4th UN World Women's Congress **Obverse:** Logo above building. **Reverse:** Three women with flowers and birds. **Note:** Similar to 50 Yuan, Y#691.

| Date | Mintage | F | VF | XF | Unc | BU |
|---|---|---|---|---|---|---|
| 1995 Proof | 30,500 | Value: 35.00 | | | | |

**10 YUAN** **Y#575** **Weight:** 3.1103 g. **Composition:** 0.9990 Gold .1000 oz. AGW **Reverse:** Panda in tree **Note:** Similar to 100 Yuan, Y#578.

| Date | Mintage | F | VF | XF | Unc | BU |
|---|---|---|---|---|---|---|
| 1996 | — | — | — | — | 55.00 | — |

**10 YUAN** **Y#575a** **Weight:** 3.1103 g. **Composition:** 0.9990 Platinum .1000 oz. APW

| Date | Mintage | F | VF | XF | Unc | BU |
|---|---|---|---|---|---|---|
| 1996 | 2,500 | — | — | — | 125 | — |

**10 YUAN** **Y#583** **Weight:** 31.1035 g. **Composition:** 0.9990 Silver 1.0000 oz. ASW **Obverse:** Temple of Heaven **Reverse:** Seated panda mother and cub

| Date | Mintage | F | VF | XF | Unc | BU |
|---|---|---|---|---|---|---|
| 1996 Prooflike | — | — | — | — | 22.50 | — |

**10 YUAN** **Y#585** **Weight:** 31.1035 g. **Composition:** 0.9990 Silver 1.0000 oz. ASW **Subject:** Year of the Rat

| Date | Mintage | F | VF | XF | Unc | BU |
|---|---|---|---|---|---|---|
| 1996 Proof | 8,000 | Value: 65.00 | | | | |

**10 YUAN** **Y#741** **Weight:** 31.1700 g. **Composition:** 0.9990 Silver 1.0011 oz. ASW **Obverse:** Eastern unicorn **Reverse:** Western unicorn in wreath

| Date | Mintage | F | VF | XF | Unc | BU |
|---|---|---|---|---|---|---|
| 1996 Proof | 8,000 | Value: 60.00 | | | | |

**10 YUAN** **Y#742** **Weight:** 3.1100 g. **Composition:** 0.9990 Gold .0999 oz. AGW **Obverse:** Eastern unicorn **Reverse:** Western unicorn in wreath

| Date | Mintage | F | VF | XF | Unc | BU |
|---|---|---|---|---|---|---|
| 1996 Proof | 5,000 | Value: 75.00 | | | | |

**10 YUAN** **Y#845** **Weight:** 27.0000 g. **Composition:** 0.9250 Silver .8030 oz. ASW **Subject:** Ninth Asian Stamp Exhibition **Obverse:** Temple of Heaven with additional legend **Reverse:** Seated panda eating with cub

| Date | Mintage | F | VF | XF | Unc | BU |
|---|---|---|---|---|---|---|
| 1996 Proof | 2,000 | Value: 50.00 | | | | |

**10 YUAN** **Y#846** **Weight:** 27.0000 g. **Composition:** 0.9250 Silver .8030 oz. ASW **Subject:** Beijing Coin Fair **Obverse:** Similar to Y#845 with additional legend **Reverse:** Similar to Y#845 with gold insert

| Date | Mintage | F | VF | XF | Unc | BU |
|---|---|---|---|---|---|---|
| 1996 Proof | 2,000 | Value: 50.00 | | | | |

**10 YUAN** **Y#848** **Weight:** 3.1103 g. **Composition:** 0.9990 Gold .1000 oz. AGW **Subject:** 15th Anniversary - Gold Panda Coins **Obverse:** Temple of Heaven with additional legend **Reverse:** Panda in tree

| Date | Mintage | F | VF | XF | Unc | BU |
|---|---|---|---|---|---|---|
| 1996 Proof | 20,000 | Value: 60.00 | | | | |

**10 YUAN** **Y#851** **Ring Weight:** 1.1108 g. **Ring Composition:** 0.9990 Silver .0357 oz. ASW **Center Weight:** 3.1103 g. **Center Composition:** 0.9990 Gold .1000 oz. AGW **Obverse:** Temple of Heaven **Reverse:** Panda seated in rock

| Date | Mintage | F | VF | XF | Unc | BU |
|---|---|---|---|---|---|---|
| 1996 Proof | 2,500 | Value: 100 | | | | |

**10 YUAN** **Y#854** **Weight:** 23.0375 g. **Composition:** 0.9000 Silver .6666 oz. ASW **Subject:** Year of the Rat **Obverse:** Dengdu Pavilion **Reverse:** Rat and corn

| Date | Mintage | F | VF | XF | Unc | BU |
|---|---|---|---|---|---|---|
| 1996 Proof | 6,800 | Value: 75.00 | | | | |

**10 YUAN** **Y#858** **Weight:** 31.1035 g. **Composition:** 0.9990 Silver 1.0000 oz. ASW **Subject:** Sun Yat-Sen **Obverse:** Building **Reverse:** Portrait

| Date | Mintage | F | VF | XF | Unc | BU |
|---|---|---|---|---|---|---|
| 1996 Proof | 20,000 | Value: 50.00 | | | | |

**10 YUAN** **Y#860** **Weight:** 31.1035 g. **Composition:** 0.9990 Silver 1.0000 oz. ASW **Subject:** Return of Hong Kong to China **Obverse:** Tiananmen Square **Reverse:** Law book above Hong Kong harbor view

| Date | Mintage | F | VF | XF | Unc | BU |
|---|---|---|---|---|---|---|
| 1996 Proof | 88,000 | Value: 75.00 | | | | |

**10 YUAN** **Y#861** **Weight:** 31.1035 g. **Composition:** 0.9990 Silver 1.0000 oz. ASW **Subject:** 45th Anniversary - Chinese Aviation Industry **Obverse:** National emblem **Reverse:** Propeller airplane

| Date | Mintage | F | VF | XF | Unc | BU |
|---|---|---|---|---|---|---|
| 1996 Proof | 20,000 | Value: 50.00 | | | | |

**10 YUAN** **Y#862** **Weight:** 31.1035 g. **Composition:** 0.9990 Silver 1.0000 oz. ASW **Subject:** 45th Anniversary - Chinese Aviation Industry **Obverse:** National emblem **Reverse:** Jet airplane

| Date | Mintage | F | VF | XF | Unc | BU |
|---|---|---|---|---|---|---|
| 1996 Proof | 20,000 | Value: 50.00 | | | | |

**10 YUAN** **Y#863** **Weight:** 31.1035 g. **Composition:** 0.9990 Silver 1.0000 oz. ASW **Subject:** 40th Anniversary - Chinese Aviation Industry **Obverse:** National emblem above Great Wall **Reverse:** Satellites

| Date | Mintage | F | VF | XF | Unc | BU |
|---|---|---|---|---|---|---|
| 1996 Proof | 20,000 | Value: 50.00 | | | | |

**10 YUAN** **Y#864** **Weight:** 31.1035 g. **Composition:** 0.9990 Silver 1.0000 oz. ASW **Subject:** 40th Anniversary - Chinese Aviation Industry **Obverse:** National emblem above Great Wall **Reverse:** Rocket and satellites

| Date | Mintage | F | VF | XF | Unc | BU |
|---|---|---|---|---|---|---|
| 1996 Proof | 20,000 | Value: 50.00 | | | | |

**10 YUAN** **Y#865** **Weight:** 31.1035 g. **Composition:** 0.9990 Silver 1.0000 oz. ASW **Subject:** Centennial of Chinese Post Office **Obverse:** Modern stamp **Reverse:** Imperial stamp

| Date | Mintage | F | VF | XF | Unc | BU |
|---|---|---|---|---|---|---|
| 1996 Proof | 20,000 | Value: 50.00 | | | | |

**10 YUAN** **Y#866** **Weight:** 31.1035 g. **Composition:** 0.9990 Silver 1.0000 oz. ASW **Subject:** 9th Asian Stamp Exhibition **Obverse:** Similar to Y#866 **Reverse:** Similar to Y#866 with additional legend

| Date | Mintage | F | VF | XF | Unc | BU |
|---|---|---|---|---|---|---|
| 1996 Proof | 20,000 | Value: 55.00 | | | | |

**10 YUAN** **Y#868** **Weight:** 31.1035 g. **Composition:** 0.9990 Silver 1.0000 oz. ASW **Subject:** 60th Anniversary - Long March **Obverse:** Flag above building **Reverse:** Chairman Mao on horse

| Date | Mintage | F | VF | XF | Unc | BU |
|---|---|---|---|---|---|---|
| 1996 Proof | 20,000 | Value: 50.00 | | | | |

**10 YUAN** **Y#869** **Weight:** 31.1035 g. **Composition:** 0.9990 Silver 1.0000 oz. ASW **Subject:** 60th Anniversary - Long March **Obverse:** Flag above Baota Mountain **Reverse:** Two armies joining

| Date | Mintage | F | VF | XF | Unc | BU |
|---|---|---|---|---|---|---|
| 1996 Proof | 20,000 | Value: 50.00 | | | | |

**10 YUAN** **Y#876** **Weight:** 27.0000 g. **Composition:** 0.9250 Silver .8030 oz. ASW **Subject:** Romance of the Three Kingdoms Series **Obverse:** Luo Guanzhong portrait **Reverse:** Cao Cao standing with spear

| Date | Mintage | F | VF | XF | Unc | BU |
|---|---|---|---|---|---|---|
| 1996 Proof | 7,000 | Value: 50.00 | | | | |

**10 YUAN** **Y#877** **Weight:** 27.0000 g. **Composition:** 0.9250 Silver .8030 oz. ASW **Subject:** Romance of the Three Kingdoms Series **Obverse:** Luo Guanzhong portrait **Reverse:** Cao Pi seated at desk

| Date | Mintage | F | VF | XF | Unc | BU |
|---|---|---|---|---|---|---|
| 1996 Proof | 7,000 | Value: 50.00 | | | | |

**10 YUAN** **Y#878** **Weight:** 27.0000 g. **Composition:** 0.9250 Silver .8030 oz. ASW **Subject:** Romance of the Three Kingdoms Series **Obverse:** Luo Guanzhong portrait **Reverse:** Cao Zhi standing with scroll and flags

| Date | Mintage | F | VF | XF | Unc | BU |
|---|---|---|---|---|---|---|
| 1996 Proof | 7,000 | Value: 50.00 | | | | |

**10 YUAN** **Y#879** **Weight:** 27.0000 g. **Composition:** 0.9250 Silver .8030 oz. ASW **Subject:** Romance of the Three Kingdoms Series **Obverse:** Luo Guanzhong portrait **Reverse:** Sima Yi on horse with spear

| Date | Mintage | F | VF | XF | Unc | BU |
|---|---|---|---|---|---|---|
| 1996 Proof | 7,000 | Value: 50.00 | | | | |

**10 YUAN Y#886 Weight:** 31.1035 g. **Composition:** 0.9990 Silver 1.0000 oz. ASW **Subject:** Goddess of Mercy - Guanyin **Obverse:** Temple **Reverse:** Goddess holding flower

| Date | Mintage | F | VF | XF | Unc | BU |
|---|---|---|---|---|---|---|
| 1996 Proof | 30,000 | Value: 27.50 | | | | |

**10 YUAN Y#887 Weight:** 3.1101 g. **Composition:** 0.9990 Gold .1000 oz. AGW **Subject:** Goddess Guanyin **Obverse:** Temple **Reverse:** Goddess holding flower

| Date | Mintage | F | VF | XF | Unc | BU |
|---|---|---|---|---|---|---|
| 1996 Proof | — | Value: 75.00 | | | | |

**10 YUAN Y#890 Weight:** 27.0000 g. **Composition:** 0.9250 Silver .8030 oz. ASW **Series:** Olympics **Obverse:** National emblem **Reverse:** Sailboarder

| Date | Mintage | F | VF | XF | Unc | BU |
|---|---|---|---|---|---|---|
| 1996 Proof | 30,000 | Value: 45.00 | | | | |

**10 YUAN Y#711 Weight:** 31.1035 g. **Composition:** 0.9990 Silver 1.0000 oz. ASW **Subject:** Sino - Thailand Friendship **Obverse:** Forbidden City and Thai Royal Palace **Reverse:** 2 Buddha statues

| Date | Mintage | F | VF | XF | Unc | BU |
|---|---|---|---|---|---|---|
| 1997 Proof | 45,000 | Value: 22.50 | | | | |

**10 YUAN Y#715 Weight:** 31.1035 g. **Composition:** 0.9990 Silver 1.0000 oz. ASW **Obverse:** Temple of Heaven **Reverse:** Panda on thick branch

| Date | Mintage | F | VF | XF | Unc | BU |
|---|---|---|---|---|---|---|
| 1997 Prooflike | — | — | — | — | 32.50 | — |

**10 YUAN Y#717a Weight:** 3.1100 g. **Composition:** 0.9990 Platinum .1000 oz. APW

| Date | Mintage | F | VF | XF | Unc | BU |
|---|---|---|---|---|---|---|
| 1997 | 2,500 | — | — | — | 125 | — |

**10 YUAN Y#722 Ring Composition:** Brass **Center Composition:** Copper-Nickel **Subject:** Return of Hong Kong **Obverse:** Stylized flower **Reverse:** City view

| Date | Mintage | F | VF | XF | Unc | BU |
|---|---|---|---|---|---|---|
| 1997 | — | — | — | — | 6.50 | — |

**Note:** 5,000 pieces were struck and issued in boxes with certificates and are valued at $350

**10 YUAN Y#723 Ring Composition:** Copper-Nickel **Center Composition:** Brass **Subject:** Hong Kong - Constitution **Obverse:** Stylized flower **Reverse:** Document with state emblem

| Date | Mintage | F | VF | XF | Unc | BU |
|---|---|---|---|---|---|---|
| 1997 | — | — | — | — | 6.50 | — |

**10 YUAN Y#726 Weight:** 31.2200 g. **Composition:** 0.9990 Silver 1.0027 oz. ASW **Obverse:** Temple of Heaven **Reverse:** Panda on large tree branch

| Date | Mintage | F | VF | XF | Unc | BU |
|---|---|---|---|---|---|---|
| 1997 | 50,000 | — | — | — | 20.00 | — |

**10 YUAN Y#894 Weight:** 31.1035 g. **Composition:** 0.9990 Silver 1.0000 oz. ASW **Obverse:** Temple of Heaven **Reverse:** Panda on branch

| Date | Mintage | F | VF | XF | Unc | BU |
|---|---|---|---|---|---|---|
| 1997 Proof | 50,000 | Value: 45.00 | | | | |

**10 YUAN Y#894a Weight:** 3.1100 g. **Composition:** 0.9995 Platinum .1000 oz. APW **Reverse:** Panda on branch

| Date | Mintage | F | VF | XF | Unc | BU |
|---|---|---|---|---|---|---|
| 1997 Proof | 2,500 | Value: 125 | | | | |

**10 YUAN Y#895 Weight:** 31.1035 g. **Composition:** 0.9990 Silver 1.000 oz. ASW **Obverse:** Similar to Y#894 with legend variety **Reverse:** Similar to Y#8945 with gold insert

| Date | Mintage | F | VF | XF | Unc | BU |
|---|---|---|---|---|---|---|
| 1997 Proof | 30,000 | Value: 30.00 | | | | |

**10 YUAN Y#896 Weight:** 23.0375 g. **Composition:** 0.9000 Silver .6666 oz. ASW **Subject:** Year of the Ox **Obverse:** Mingyuan Pavilion **Reverse:** Bull **Shape:** Scalloped

| Date | Mintage | F | VF | XF | Unc | BU |
|---|---|---|---|---|---|---|
| 1997 Proof | 6,800 | Value: 70.00 | | | | |

**10 YUAN Y# 899.1 Weight:** 31.1035 g. **Composition:** 0.9990 Silver 1.0000 oz. ASW **Subject:** Year of the Ox **Obverse:** State seal **Reverse:** Water buffalo

| Date | Mintage | F | VF | XF | Unc | BU |
|---|---|---|---|---|---|---|
| 1997 Proof | 8,000 | Value: 65.00 | | | | |

**10 YUAN Y# 901 Weight:** 3.1103 g. **Composition:** 0.9990 Gold .1000 oz. AGW **Subject:** Year of the Ox **Obverse:** Mingyuan Pavilion **Reverse:** Calf

| Date | Mintage | F | VF | XF | Unc | BU |
|---|---|---|---|---|---|---|
| 1997 Proof | 48,000 | Value: 90.00 | | | | |

**10 YUAN** **Y#902** **Weight:** 31.1035 g. **Composition:** 0.9990 Silver 1.0000 oz. ASW **Subject:** Return of Hong Kong to China **Obverse:** Tiananmen Square **Reverse:** Flag and fireworks over city

| Date | Mintage | F | VF | XF | Unc | BU |
|---|---|---|---|---|---|---|
| 1997 | 800,000 | — | — | — | 40.00 | — |
| 1997 Proof | 88,000 | Value: 75.00 | | | | |

**10 YUAN** **Y#905** **Weight:** 31.1035 g. **Composition:** 0.9990 Silver 1.0000 oz. ASW **Subject:** Return of Macao to China **Obverse:** Tiananmen Square **Reverse:** Deng Xiaoping viewing Macao

| Date | Mintage | F | VF | XF | Unc | BU |
|---|---|---|---|---|---|---|
| 1997 Proof | — | Value: 60.00 | | | | |

**10 YUAN** **Y#908** **Weight:** 31.1035 g. **Composition:** 0.9990 Silver 1.0000 oz. ASW **Subject:** Peoples Liberation Army **Obverse:** Radiant star above Great Wall **Reverse:** Founding of PLA scene

| Date | Mintage | F | VF | XF | Unc | BU |
|---|---|---|---|---|---|---|
| 1997 Proof | 30,000 | Value: 40.00 | | | | |

**10 YUAN** **Y#909** **Weight:** 31.1035 g. **Composition:** 0.9990 Silver 1.0000 oz. ASW **Obverse:** Radiant star above Great Wall **Reverse:** Three members of the PRC Army, Air Force and Navy. Airplanes, boates and missile in background.

| Date | Mintage | F | VF | XF | Unc | BU |
|---|---|---|---|---|---|---|
| 1997 Proof | 30,000 | Value: 40.00 | | | | |

**10 YUAN** **Y#912** **Weight:** 31.1035 g. **Composition:** 0.9990 Silver 1.0000 oz. ASW **Obverse:** Eastern unicorn **Reverse:** Western unicorn

| Date | Mintage | F | VF | XF | Unc | BU |
|---|---|---|---|---|---|---|
| 1997 Proof | 8,000 | Value: 27.50 | | | | |

**10 YUAN** **Y#912a** **Weight:** 3.1100 g. **Composition:** 0.9990 Gold .1000 oz. AGW **Obverse:** Eastern unicorn **Reverse:** Western unicorn

| Date | Mintage | F | VF | XF | Unc | BU |
|---|---|---|---|---|---|---|
| 1997 Proof | 5,000 | Value: 95.00 | | | | |

**10 YUAN** **Y#913** **Weight:** 3.1100 g. **Composition:** 0.9990 Gold .1000 oz. AGW **Subject:** Goddess Guanyin **Obverse:** Putuo Hill Temple **Reverse:** Goddess holding jug of dew

| Date | Mintage | F | VF | XF | Unc | BU |
|---|---|---|---|---|---|---|
| 1997 Proof | 30,000 | Value: 40.00 | | | | |

**10 YUAN** **Y# 914.1** **Weight:** 31.1035 g. **Composition:** 0.9990 Silver 1.0000 oz. ASW **Subject:** Celebrating Spring **Obverse:** Lantern **Reverse:** Children setting off firecrackers

| Date | Mintage | F | VF | XF | Unc | BU |
|---|---|---|---|---|---|---|
| 1997 | 20,000 | — | — | — | 60.00 | — |
| 1997 Proof | 60,000 | Value: 40.00 | | | | |

**10 YUAN** **Y# 717** **Weight:** 3.1103 g. **Composition:** 0.9990 Gold .1000 oz. AGW **Subject:** Panda Bullion **Note:** Similar to 100 Yuan, Y#720.

| Date | Mintage | F | VF | XF | Unc | BU |
|---|---|---|---|---|---|---|
| 1997 | — | — | — | — | 50.00 | — |

**Note:** Exists in large and small date varieties

**10 YUAN** **Y# 899.2** **Weight:** 31.1035 g. **Composition:** 0.9990 Silver 1.0000 oz. ASW **Subject:** Year of the Ox **Note:** Increased size 40mm.

| Date | Mintage | F | VF | XF | Unc | BU |
|---|---|---|---|---|---|---|
| 1997 | 50,000 | — | — | — | 45.00 | — |

**10 YUAN** **Y# 1060** **Weight:** 31.1035 g. **Composition:** 0.9990 Silver 1.0000 oz. ASW **Subject:** Panda **Obverse:** Temple of Heaven. **Reverse:** Multicolor panda and flora. **Edge:** Reeded. **Size:** 40 mm.

| Date | Mintage | F | VF | XF | Unc | BU |
|---|---|---|---|---|---|---|
| 1997 | — | — | — | — | 35.00 | — |

**10 YUAN** **Y# 983** **Weight:** 3.1103 g. **Composition:** 0.9990 Gold .1000 oz. AGW **Subject:** Celebrating Spring **Obverse:** Lantern **Reverse:** Children setting off firecrackers

| Date | Mintage | F | VF | XF | Unc | BU |
|---|---|---|---|---|---|---|
| 1997 | 100,000 | — | — | — | 40.00 | — |

**10 YUAN** **Y# 917.1** **Weight:** 31.1035 g. **Composition:** 0.9990 Silver 1.0000 oz. ASW **Subject:** Traditional Chinese Mascot **Obverse:** Monument in Tinamen Square, sprays below. **Reverse:** Child holding carp

| Date | Mintage | F | VF | XF | Unc | BU |
|---|---|---|---|---|---|---|
| 1997 Proof | 8,000 | Value: 40.00 | | | | |

**10 YUAN** **Y# 917.2** **Weight:** 31.1035 g. **Composition:** 0.9990 Silver 1.0000 oz. ASW **Subject:** Traditional Chinese Mascot **Obverse:** Monument in Tiananmen Square, sprays below **Reverse:** Multicolor version of child holding carp

| Date | Mintage | F | VF | XF | Unc | BU |
|---|---|---|---|---|---|---|
| 1997 Proof | 100,000 | Value: 35.00 | | | | |
| 1998 Proof | — | Value: 35.00 | | | | |

**10 YUAN** **Y#919 Weight:** 31.1035 g. **Composition:** 0.9990 Silver 1.0000 oz. ASW **Subject:** Wildlife of China **Obverse:** State seal **Reverse:** Two white dolphins

| Date | Mintage | F | VF | XF | Unc | BU |
|---|---|---|---|---|---|---|
| 1997 Proof | 68,000 | Value: 40.00 | | | | |

**10 YUAN** **Y#920 Weight:** 31.1035 g. **Composition:** 0.9990 Silver 1.0000 oz. ASW **Subject:** Wildlife of China **Obverse:** State seal **Reverse:** Swan and signets

| Date | Mintage | F | VF | XF | Unc | BU |
|---|---|---|---|---|---|---|
| 1997 Proof | 68,000 | Value: 40.00 | | | | |

**10 YUAN** **Y#936 Weight:** 31.2000 g. **Composition:** 0.9990 Silver 1.0021 oz. ASW **Subject:** Gesal, King of Tibet **Obverse:** Towered building **Reverse:** King on horseback

| Date | Mintage | F | VF | XF | Unc | BU |
|---|---|---|---|---|---|---|
| 1997 Proof | 28,000 | Value: 37.50 | | | | |

**10 YUAN** **Y#937 Weight:** 31.2000 g. **Composition:** 0.9990 Silver 1.0021 oz. ASW **Subject:** Gadamellin of Mongolia **Obverse:** Towered building **Reverse:** Cavalry attack with swords

| Date | Mintage | F | VF | XF | Unc | BU |
|---|---|---|---|---|---|---|
| 1997 Proof | 28,000 | Value: 37.50 | | | | |

**10 YUAN** **Y#938 Weight:** 31.2000 g. **Composition:** 0.9990 Silver 1.0021 oz. ASW **Subject:** Yi Nationality **Obverse:** Towered building **Reverse:** Madame She Ziang with sword

| Date | Mintage | F | VF | XF | Unc | BU |
|---|---|---|---|---|---|---|
| 1997 Proof | 28,000 | Value: 32.50 | | | | |

**10 YUAN** **Y#939 Weight:** 31.2000 g. **Composition:** 0.9990 Silver 1.0021 oz. ASW **Subject:** Li Nationality **Obverse:** Towered building **Reverse:** Madame Zian reading scroll

| Date | Mintage | F | VF | XF | Unc | BU |
|---|---|---|---|---|---|---|
| 1997 Proof | 28,000 | Value: 32.50 | | | | |

**10 YUAN** **Y#984 Weight:** 3.1103 g. **Composition:** 0.9990 Gold .1000 oz. AGW **Obverse:** Forbidden city **Reverse:** Bronze chinze

| Date | Mintage | F | VF | XF | Unc | BU |
|---|---|---|---|---|---|---|
| 1997 Proof | 11,000 | Value: 65.00 | | | | |

**10 YUAN** **Y#985 Weight:** 3.1103 g. **Composition:** 0.9990 Gold .1000 oz. AGW **Subject:** Goddess of Mercy - Guanyin

| Date | Mintage | F | VF | XF | Unc | BU |
|---|---|---|---|---|---|---|
| 1997 | 10,000 | — | — | — | 55.00 | — |

**10 YUAN** **Y#986 Ring Weight:** 1.5552 g. **Ring Composition:** 0.9990 Silver .0500 oz. ASW **Center Weight:** 3.1103 g. **Center Composition:** 0.9990 Gold .1000 oz. AGW **Reverse:** Panda climbing tree

| Date | Mintage | F | VF | XF | Unc | BU |
|---|---|---|---|---|---|---|
| 1997 Proof | 2,800 | Value: 75.00 | | | | |

**10 YUAN** **Y#963 Weight:** 31.1035 g. **Composition:** 0.9990 Silver 1.0000 oz. ASW **Reverse:** Multicolored panda

| Date | Mintage | F | VF | XF | Unc | BU |
|---|---|---|---|---|---|---|
| 1997 | 100,000 | — | — | — | 35.00 | — |

**10 YUAN** **Y#724 Weight:** 31.0220 g. **Composition:** 0.9990 Silver .9963 oz. ASW **Subject:** 100th Birthday - Zhou Enlai **Obverse:** Zhou Enlai Memorial Hall **Reverse:** Zhou on horseback

| Date | Mintage | F | VF | XF | Unc | BU |
|---|---|---|---|---|---|---|
| 1998 Proof | 38,000 | Value: 40.00 | | | | |

**10 YUAN** **Y#725 Weight:** 31.0220 g. **Composition:** 0.9990 Silver .9963 oz. ASW **Subject:** 100th Birthday - Zhou Enlai **Obverse:** Zhou Enlai Memorial Hall **Reverse:** Zhou standing facing 3/4 right

| Date | Mintage | F | VF | XF | Unc | BU |
|---|---|---|---|---|---|---|
| 1998 Proof | 38,000 | Value: 40.00 | | | | |

**10 YUAN** **Y#727 Weight:** 31.3900 g. **Composition:** 0.9990 Silver 1.0082 oz. ASW **Subject:** Dr. Norman Bethune **Obverse:** State emblem **Reverse:** Portrait with surgery scene

| Date | Mintage | F | VF | XF | Unc | BU |
|---|---|---|---|---|---|---|
| 1998 In Proof sets only | 61,000 | Value: 30.00 | | | | |

**10 YUAN** **Y# 744** **Weight:** 31.4700 g. **Composition:** 0.9990 Silver 1.0110 oz. ASW **Subject:** Celebrating Spring **Obverse:** Radiant lantern **Reverse:** Three children about to fly kites

| Date | Mintage | F | VF | XF | Unc | BU |
|---|---|---|---|---|---|---|
| 1998 Proof | — | Value: 40.00 | | | | |

**10 YUAN** **Y# 922** **Weight:** 31.1035 g. **Composition:** 0.9990 Silver 1.0000 oz. ASW **Subject:** Year of the Tiger **Obverse:** National emblem **Reverse:** Tiger on rock

| Date | Mintage | F | VF | XF | Unc | BU |
|---|---|---|---|---|---|---|
| 1998 | 50,000 | — | — | — | 40.00 | — |

**10 YUAN** **Y# 923** **Weight:** 31.1035 g. **Composition:** 0.9990 Silver 1.0000 oz. ASW **Subject:** Year of the Tiger **Obverse:** Badaling building **Reverse:** Multicolor tiger cub

| Date | Mintage | F | VF | XF | Unc | BU |
|---|---|---|---|---|---|---|
| 1998 | 100,000 | — | — | — | 50.00 | — |

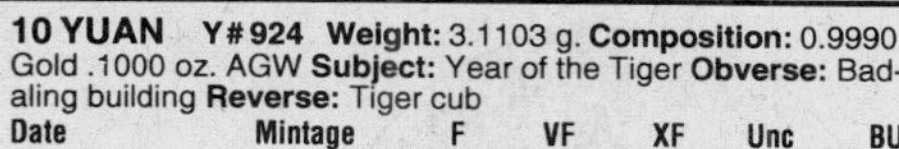

**10 YUAN** **Y# 924** **Weight:** 3.1103 g. **Composition:** 0.9990 Gold .1000 oz. AGW **Subject:** Year of the Tiger **Obverse:** Badaling building **Reverse:** Tiger cub

| Date | Mintage | F | VF | XF | Unc | BU |
|---|---|---|---|---|---|---|
| 1998 Proof | 48,000 | Value: 80.00 | | | | |

**10 YUAN** **Y# 925** **Weight:** 3.1103 g. **Composition:** 0.9990 Gold .1000 oz. AGW **Subject:** Year of the Tiger **Obverse:** Badaling building **Reverse:** Multicolor tiger head

| Date | Mintage | F | VF | XF | Unc | BU |
|---|---|---|---|---|---|---|
| 1998 Proof | 30,000 | Value: 80.00 | | | | |

**10 YUAN** **Y# 926** **Weight:** 23.0375 g. **Composition:** 0.9000 Silver .6666 oz. ASW **Subject:** Year of the Tiger **Obverse:** Badaling building **Reverse:** Tiger

| Date | Mintage | F | VF | XF | Unc | BU |
|---|---|---|---|---|---|---|
| 1998 Proof | 6,800 | Value: 65.00 | | | | |

**10 YUAN** **Y# 969** **Weight:** 31.1035 g. **Composition:** 0.9990 Silver 1.0000 oz. ASW **Reverse:** Panda

| Date | Mintage | F | VF | XF | Unc | BU |
|---|---|---|---|---|---|---|
| 1998 | 250,000 | — | — | — | 25.00 | — |

**10 YUAN** **Y# 970** **Weight:** 31.1035 g. **Composition:** 0.9990 Silver 1.0000 oz. ASW **Reverse:** Multicolor panda

| Date | Mintage | F | VF | XF | Unc | BU |
|---|---|---|---|---|---|---|
| 1998 | 100,000 | — | — | — | 35.00 | — |

**10 YUAN** **Y# 987** **Weight:** 3.1103 g. **Composition:** 0.9990 Gold .1000 oz. AGW **Subject:** Culture of Dragons

| Date | Mintage | F | VF | XF | Unc | BU |
|---|---|---|---|---|---|---|
| 1998 Proof | — | Value: 60.00 | | | | |

**10 YUAN** **Y# 988** **Weight:** 3.1103 g. **Composition:** 0.9990 Gold .1000 oz. AGW **Obverse:** Temple of Heaven **Reverse:** Panda seated on rock

| Date | Mintage | F | VF | XF | Unc | BU |
|---|---|---|---|---|---|---|
| 1998 | — | — | — | — | 55.00 | — |

**Note:** Exists in large and small date varieties

**10 YUAN** **Y# 1063** **Weight:** 31.1035 g. **Composition:** 0.9990 Silver 1.0000 oz. ASW **Subject:** World Wildlife Fund **Obverse:** National arms. **Reverse:** Clouded leopard. **Edge:** Reeded. **Size:** 38 mm.

| Date | Mintage |
|---|---|
| 1998 Proof | — Value: 50.00 |

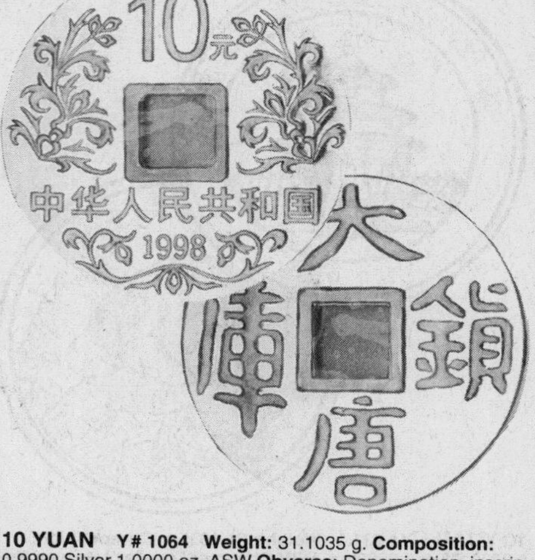


**10 YUAN** **Y# 1064** **Weight:** 31.1035 g. **Composition:** 0.9990 Silver 1.0000 oz. ASW **Obverse:** Denomination, inscription and ornamental design. **Reverse:** Old cash coin characters. **Edge:** Reeded. **Size:** 40 mm. **Note:** Square holed cash coin design.

| Date | Mintage |
|---|---|
| 1998 Proof | — Value: 40.00 |

**10 YUAN** **Y# 1065** **Weight:** 3.1100 g. **Composition:** 0.9990 Gold .0999 oz. AGW **Obverse:** Denomination, inscription and ornamental design. **Reverse:** Old cash coin characters. **Edge:** Reeded. **Size:** 18 mm. **Note:** Square holed cash coin design.

| Date | Mintage |
|---|---|
| 1998 Proof | — Value: 50.00 |

**10 YUAN** **Y# 980** **Weight:** 3.1103 g. **Composition:** 0.9990 Gold .1000 oz. AGW **Subject:** Year of the Rabbit

| Date | Mintage | F | VF | XF | Unc | BU |
|---|---|---|---|---|---|---|
| 1999 Proof | 48,000 | Value: 75.00 | | | | |

**10 YUAN** **Y# 1078** **Weight:** 30.9200 g. **Composition:** 0.9990 Silver .9931 oz. ASW **Subject:** Yin and Yang Concept **Obverse:** Gate. **Reverse:** Gold plated standing goddess. **Edge:** Reeded. **Size:** 40 mm.

| Date | Mintage | F | VF | XF | Unc | BU |
|---|---|---|---|---|---|---|
| 1999 Proof | — | Value: 50.00 | | | | |

**10 YUAN** **Y# 989** **Weight:** 3.1103 g. **Composition:** 0.9990 Gold .1000 oz. AGW **Obverse:** Temple of Heaven **Reverse:** Panda on ledge

| Date | Mintage | F | VF | XF | Unc | BU |
|---|---|---|---|---|---|---|
| 1999 | — | — | — | — | 55.00 | — |

**Note:** Exists in large and small date varieties

**10 YUAN** **Y# 991** **Weight:** 3.1103 g. **Composition:** 0.9990 Gold .1000 oz. AGW **Reverse:** Multicolor rabbit

| Date | Mintage | F | VF | XF | Unc | BU |
|---|---|---|---|---|---|---|
| 1999 Proof | 30,000 | Value: 75.00 | | | | |

**10 YUAN** **Y# 931.1** **Weight:** 31.1035 g. **Composition:** 0.9990 Silver 1.0000 oz. ASW **Obverse:** Temple of Heaven **Reverse:** Panda on rock

| Date | Mintage | F | VF | XF | Unc | BU |
|---|---|---|---|---|---|---|
| 1999 Large date; Proof | — | Value: 50.00 | | | | |

**10 YUAN** **Y# 931.2** **Weight:** 31.1035 g. **Composition:** 0.9990 Silver 1.0000 oz. ASW

| Date | Mintage | F | VF | XF | Unc | BU |
|---|---|---|---|---|---|---|
| 1999 Small date; Proof | — | Value: 50.00 | | | | |

**10 YUAN** **Y# 943** **Weight:** 31.1035 g. **Composition:** 0.9990 Silver 1.0000 oz. ASW **Obverse:** Wan Chun Pavilion **Reverse:** Gold plated Chinese roses

| Date | Mintage | F | VF | XF | Unc | BU |
|---|---|---|---|---|---|---|
| 1999 | 100,000 | — | — | — | 50.00 | — |

**10 YUAN** **Y# 944** **Weight:** 31.1035 g. **Composition:** 0.9990 Silver 1.0000 oz. ASW **Obverse:** Da Guan Tower in Kunming **Reverse:** Multicolored camellias

| Date | Mintage | F | VF | XF | Unc | BU |
|---|---|---|---|---|---|---|
| 1999 Proof | 100,000 | Value: 50.00 | | | | |

**10 YUAN** **Y# 973** **Weight:** 31.1035 g. **Composition:** 0.9990 Silver 1.0000 oz. ASW **Reverse:** Panda

| Date | Mintage | F | VF | XF | Unc | BU |
|---|---|---|---|---|---|---|
| 1999 | 250,000 | — | — | — | 20.00 | — |

**10 YUAN** **Y# 974** **Weight:** 31.1035 g. **Composition:** 0.9990 Silver 1.0000 oz. ASW **Reverse:** Multicolored panda

| Date | Mintage | F | VF | XF | Unc | BU |
|---|---|---|---|---|---|---|
| 1999 | 100,000 | — | — | — | 35.00 | — |

**10 YUAN** **Y# 914.2** **Weight:** 31.2600 g. **Composition:** 0.9990 Silver 1.0040 oz. ASW **Subject:** Celebrating Spring **Obverse:** Radiant lantern **Reverse:** Multicolor, children lighting firecrackers

| Date | Mintage | F | VF | XF | Unc | BU |
|---|---|---|---|---|---|---|
| 1999 Proof | — | Value: 40.00 | | | | |

**10 YUAN** **Y# 978** **Weight:** 23.0375 g. **Composition:** 0.9000 Silver .6666 oz. ASW **Subject:** Year of the Dragon **Obverse:** Building **Reverse:** Dragon **Shape:** Scalloped

| Date | Mintage | F | VF | XF | Unc | BU |
|---|---|---|---|---|---|---|
| 2000 Proof | 6,800 | Value: 65.00 | | | | |

**10 YUAN** **Y# 992** **Weight:** 3.1103 g. **Composition:** 0.9990 Gold .1000 oz. AGW **Subject:** Year of the Dragon

| Date | Mintage | F | VF | XF | Unc | BU |
|---|---|---|---|---|---|---|
| 2000 Proof | 48,000 | Value: 75.00 | | | | |

**10 YUAN** **Y# 993** **Weight:** 23.0375 g. **Composition:** 0.9000 Silver .6666 oz. ASW **Reverse:** Multicolored dragon **Size:** 40 mm.

| Date | Mintage | F | VF | XF | Unc | BU |
|---|---|---|---|---|---|---|
| 2000 | 100,000 | — | — | — | 25.00 | — |
| 2000 Proof | 30,000 | Value: 75.00 | | | | |

**10 YUAN** **Y# 979** **Weight:** 31.1035 g. **Composition:** 0.9990 Silver 1.0000 oz. ASW **Obverse:** Temple of Heaven **Reverse:** Panda seated

| Date | Mintage | F | VF | XF | Unc | BU |
|---|---|---|---|---|---|---|
| 2000 | — | — | — | — | 25.00 | — |

**Note:** Domestic Chinese examples struck with mirror fields, overseas examples struck with frosted fields

**10 YUAN** **Y# 994** **Weight:** 3.1103 g. **Composition:** 0.9990 Gold .1000 oz. AGW **Subject:** Y2K

| Date | Mintage | F | VF | XF | Unc | BU |
|---|---|---|---|---|---|---|
| 2000 | 50,000 | — | — | — | 50.00 | — |

**10 YUAN** **Y# 995** **Weight:** 3.1103 g. **Composition:** 0.9990 Gold .1000 oz. AGW **Subject:** Chinese Grotto Art

| Date | Mintage | F | VF | XF | Unc | BU |
|---|---|---|---|---|---|---|
| 2000 | 50,000 | — | — | — | 50.00 | — |

**10 YUAN** **Y# 996** **Weight:** 3.1103 g. **Composition:** 0.9990 Gold .1000 oz. AGW **Subject:** Goddess Guanyin

| Date | Mintage | F | VF | XF | Unc | BU |
|---|---|---|---|---|---|---|
| 2000 | 33,000 | — | — | — | 50.00 | — |

**10 YUAN** **Y# 1048** **Weight:** 20.7357 g. **Composition:** 0.9000 Silver .6000 oz. ASW **Subject:** Dragons **Note:** Scalloped edge.

| Date | Mintage | F | VF | XF | Unc | BU |
|---|---|---|---|---|---|---|
| 2000 Proof | 6,800 | Value: 75.00 | | | | |

**10 YUAN** **Y# 946** **Weight:** 3.1103 g. **Composition:** 0.9990 Gold .1000 oz. AGW **Obverse:** Temple of Heaven **Reverse:** Panda seated on leaves **Note:** Similar to 100 Yuan, Y#949.

| Date | Mintage | F | VF | XF | Unc | BU |
|---|---|---|---|---|---|---|
| 2000 Proof | — | Value: 60.00 | | | | |

**10 YUAN** **Y# 1041** **Weight:** 30.8400 g. **Composition:** 0.9990 Silver .9905 oz. ASW **Subject:** Year of the Snake **Obverse:** Traditional style building. **Reverse:** Snake. **Edge:** Scalloped. **Size:** 39.9 mm.

| Date | Mintage | F | VF | XF | Unc | BU |
|---|---|---|---|---|---|---|
| 2001 Proof | 6,800,000 | Value: 65.00 | | | | |

**10 YUAN** **Y# 1042** **Weight:** 31.1035 g. **Composition:** 0.9990 Silver 1.0000 oz. ASW **Subject:** Year of the Snake **Shape:** Fan-like

| Date | Mintage | F | VF | XF | Unc | BU |
|---|---|---|---|---|---|---|
| 2001 | 66,000 | — | — | — | 35.00 | — |

**10 YUAN** **Y# 1043** **Weight:** 3.1104 g. **Composition:** 0.9990 Gold .1000 oz. AGW **Subject:** Year of the Snake

| Date | Mintage | F | VF | XF | Unc | BU |
|---|---|---|---|---|---|---|
| 2001 | 48,000 | — | — | — | 60.00 | — |

**15 YUAN** **Y# 745** **Weight:** 10.0000 g. **Composition:** 0.8000 Silver .2572 oz. ASW **Series:** Olympics **Obverse:** State seal **Reverse:** Ancient archers

| Date | Mintage | F | VF | XF | Unc | BU |
|---|---|---|---|---|---|---|
| 1980 | 15,000 | — | — | — | 75.00 | — |

**20 YUAN** **Y# 18** **Weight:** 10.3500 g. **Composition:** 0.8500 Silver .2829 oz. ASW **Series:** 1980 Olympics **Subject:** Wrestling **Obverse:** Similar to 1 Yuan, Y#10

| Date | Mintage | F | VF | XF | Unc | BU |
|---|---|---|---|---|---|---|
| 1980 Proof | 29,000 | Value: 16.50 | | | | |

**20 YUAN** **Y# 38** **Weight:** 15.0000 g. **Composition:** 0.8500 Silver .4099 oz. ASW **Subject:** Year of the Dog **Obverse:** Temple of Heaven **Reverse:** Dog

| Date | Mintage | F | VF | XF | Unc | BU |
|---|---|---|---|---|---|---|
| 1982 Proof | 8,825 | Value: 125 | | | | |

**20 YUAN** **Y# 207** **Weight:** 62.2060 g. **Composition:** 0.9990 Silver 2.0000 oz. ASW **Reverse:** Phoenix and dragon

| Date | Mintage | F | VF | XF | Unc | BU |
|---|---|---|---|---|---|---|
| 1989 Proof | 7,325 | Value: 90.00 | | | | |

**20 YUAN** **Y# 888** **Weight:** 62.2060 g. **Composition:** 0.9990 Silver 2.0000 oz. ASW **Obverse:** Great Wall **Reverse:** Horse and dragon

| Date | Mintage | F | VF | XF | Unc | BU |
|---|---|---|---|---|---|---|
| 1992 Proof | 6,000 | Value: 100 | | | | |

**Note:** Issued in 1996

**20 YUAN** **Y# 595** **Weight:** 62.2060 g. **Composition:** 0.9990 Silver 2.0000 oz. ASW **Obverse:** Bai Di city gate **Reverse:** Yangtze River scene **Shape:** Rectangular

| Date | Mintage | F | VF | XF | Unc | BU |
|---|---|---|---|---|---|---|
| 1996 Proof | 8,000 | Value: 60.00 | | | | |

**20 YUAN** **Y# 596** **Weight:** 62.2060 g. **Composition:** 0.9990 Silver 2.0000 oz. ASW **Obverse:** Qu Yuan Temple **Shape:** Rectangular

| Date | Mintage | F | VF | XF | Unc | BU |
|---|---|---|---|---|---|---|
| 1996 Proof | 8,000 | Value: 60.00 | | | | |

**20 YUAN** **Y# 597** **Weight:** 62.2060 g. **Composition:** 0.9990 Silver 2.0000 oz. ASW **Obverse:** Zhang Fei Temple **Shape:** Rectangular

| Date | Mintage | F | VF | XF | Unc | BU |
|---|---|---|---|---|---|---|
| 1996 Proof | 8,000 | Value: 60.00 | | | | |

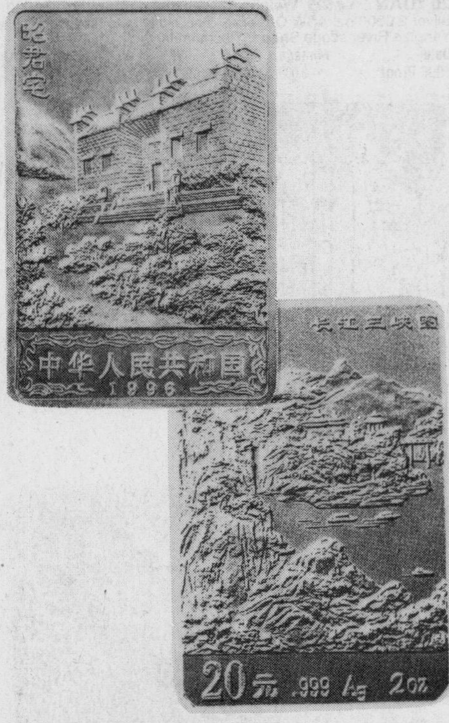

**20 YUAN** **Y# 598** **Weight:** 62.2060 g. **Composition:** 0.9990 Silver 2.0000 oz. ASW **Obverse:** Zhao Jun Temple **Shape:** Rectangular

| Date | Mintage | F | VF | XF | Unc | BU |
|---|---|---|---|---|---|---|
| 1996 Proof | 8,000 | Value: 60.00 | | | | |

**25 YUAN** **Y# 35** **Weight:** 19.4400 g. **Composition:** 0.8000 Silver .5000 oz. ASW **Subject:** World Soccer Cup

| Date | Mintage | F | VF | XF | Unc | BU |
|---|---|---|---|---|---|---|
| 1982 Proof | 40,000 | Value: 27.50 | | | | |

**25 YUAN** **Y# 36** **Weight:** 19.4400 g. **Composition:** 0.8000 Silver .5000 oz. ASW **Subject:** World Soccer Cup

| Date | Mintage | F | VF | XF | Unc | BU |
|---|---|---|---|---|---|---|
| 1982 Proof | 40,000 | Value: 27.50 | | | | |

**25 YUAN** **Y# 50** **Weight:** 7.7758 g. **Composition:** 0.9990 Gold .2500 oz. AGW **Obverse:** Temple of Heaven **Reverse:** Panda walking right in inner circle

| Date | Mintage | F | VF | XF | Unc | BU |
|---|---|---|---|---|---|---|
| 1983 | 39,000 | — | — | — | 150 | — |

**25 YUAN** **Y# 75** **Weight:** 7.7758 g. **Composition:** 0.9990 Gold .2500 oz. AGW **Obverse:** Temple of Heaven **Reverse:** Lounging Panda with bamboo

| Date | Mintage | F | VF | XF | Unc | BU |
|---|---|---|---|---|---|---|
| 1984 | 38,000 | — | — | — | 150 | — |

**25 YUAN** **Y# 82** **Weight:** 7.7758 g. **Composition:** 0.9990 Gold .2500 oz. AGW **Obverse:** Temple of Heaven **Reverse:** Panda hanging onto bamboo branch

| Date | Mintage | F | VF | XF | Unc | BU |
|---|---|---|---|---|---|---|
| 1985 | 95,000 | — | — | — | 175 | — |

**25 YUAN** **Y# 103** **Weight:** 7.7758 g. **Composition:** 0.9990 Gold .2500 oz. AGW **Obverse:** Temple of Heaven **Reverse:** Facing panda standing

| Date | Mintage | F | VF | XF | Unc | BU |
|---|---|---|---|---|---|---|
| 1986 | 33,000 | — | — | — | 95.00 | — |
| 1986 P Proof | 11,000 | Value: 100 | | | | |

**25 YUAN** **Y# 126** **Weight:** 7.7758 g. **Composition:** 0.9990 Gold .2500 oz. AGW **Obverse:** Temple of Heaven **Reverse:** Panda drinking

| Date | Mintage | F | VF | XF | Unc | BU |
|---|---|---|---|---|---|---|
| 1987(s) | 73,000 | — | — | — | 95.00 | — |
| 1987(y) | 31,000 | — | — | — | 95.00 | — |
| 1987 P Proof | 10,000 | Value: 100 | | | | |

**25 YUAN** **Y# 154** **Weight:** 7.7758 g. **Composition:** 0.9990 Gold .2500 oz. AGW **Obverse:** Temple of Heaven **Reverse:** Panda pawing bamboo

| Date | Mintage | F | VF | XF | Unc | BU |
|---|---|---|---|---|---|---|
| 1988 | 122,000 | — | — | — | 125 | — |
| 1988 Proof | 10,000 | Value: 135 | | | | |

**25 YUAN** **Y# 189** **Weight:** 7.7758 g. **Composition:** 0.9990 Gold .2500 oz. AGW **Note:** Similar to 100 Yuan, Y#191.

| Date | Mintage | F | VF | XF | Unc | BU |
|---|---|---|---|---|---|---|
| 1989 | 71,000 | — | — | — | 125 | — |
| 1989 Proof | — | Value: 150 | | | | |

**25 YUAN** **Y# 240** **Weight:** 7.7758 g. **Composition:** 0.9990 Gold .2500 oz. AGW **Reverse:** Panda

| Date | Mintage | F | VF | XF | Unc | BU |
|---|---|---|---|---|---|---|
| 1990 | — | — | — | — | 135 | — |
| 1990 Proof | 5,000 | Value: 150 | | | | |

**25 YUAN** **Y# 268** **Weight:** 7.7758 g. **Composition:** 0.9995 Platinum .2500 oz. APW **Reverse:** Panda climbing tree

| Date | Mintage | F | VF | XF | Unc | BU |
|---|---|---|---|---|---|---|
| 1990 Proof | 2,500 | Value: 185 | | | | |

**25 YUAN** **Y# 301** **Weight:** 11.6700 g. **Composition:** 0.9990 Silver .2500 oz. ASW **Reverse:** Seated panda

| Date | Mintage | F | VF | XF | Unc | BU |
|---|---|---|---|---|---|---|
| 1991 Proof | 2,000 | Value: 175 | | | | |

**25 YUAN** **Y# 311** **Weight:** 7.7758 g. **Composition:** 0.9990 Gold .2500 oz. AGW **Note:** Similar to Y#301 without inner circle.

| Date | Mintage | F | VF | XF | Unc | BU |
|---|---|---|---|---|---|---|
| 1991 | — | — | — | — | 135 | — |
| 1991 Proof | — | Value: 165 | | | | |

**25 YUAN** **Y# 343** **Weight:** 7.7758 g. **Composition:** 0.9990 Gold .2500 oz. AGW **Reverse:** Panda on limb **Note:** Similar to 100 Yuan, Y#345.

| Date | Mintage | F | VF | XF | Unc | BU |
|---|---|---|---|---|---|---|
| 1992 | — | — | — | — | 125 | — |
| 1992 Proof | — | Value: 165 | | | | |

**25 YUAN** **Y# 555** **Weight:** 8.4800 g. **Composition:** 0.9170 Gold .2500 oz. AGW **Subject:** Bronze Age Sculptures **Obverse:** State seal **Reverse:** Ram

| Date | Mintage | F | VF | XF | Unc | BU |
|---|---|---|---|---|---|---|
| 1992 Proof | Est. 500 | Value: 250 | | | | |

**25 YUAN** **Y# 556** **Weight:** 8.4800 g. **Composition:** 0.9170 Gold .2500 oz. AGW **Subject:** Bronze Age Sculptures **Reverse:** Panther

| Date | Mintage | F | VF | XF | Unc | BU |
|---|---|---|---|---|---|---|
| 1992 Proof | Est. 500 | Value: 250 | | | | |

**25 YUAN** **Y# 889** **Weight:** 7.7759 g. **Composition:** 0.9990 Gold .2500 oz. AGW **Obverse:** Great Wall **Reverse:** Horse and dragon

| Date | Mintage | F | VF | XF | Unc | BU |
|---|---|---|---|---|---|---|
| 1992 Proof | 5,000 | Value: 120 | | | | |

**Note:** Issued in 1996

**25 YUAN** **Y# 404** **Weight:** 7.7759 g. **Composition:** 0.9990 Gold .2500 oz. AGW **Reverse:** Chinese Gods Fu, Lu and Shu

| Date | Mintage | F | VF | XF | Unc | BU |
|---|---|---|---|---|---|---|
| 1993 | Est. 3,000 | — | — | — | 175 | — |

**25 YUAN** **Y# 408** **Weight:** 8.4900 g. **Composition:** 0.9170 Gold .2500 oz. AGW **Subject:** Bronze Age Sculptures **Obverse:** State seal **Reverse:** Horse

| Date | Mintage | F | VF | XF | Unc | BU |
|---|---|---|---|---|---|---|
| 1993 Proof | 500 | Value: 175 | | | | |

**25 YUAN** **Y# 409** **Weight:** 8.4900 g. **Composition:** 0.9170 Gold .2500 oz. AGW **Subject:** Bronze Age Sculptures **Obverse:** State seal **Reverse:** Pig

| Date | Mintage | F | VF | XF | Unc | BU |
|---|---|---|---|---|---|---|
| 1993 Proof | 500 | Value: 175 | | | | |

**25 YUAN** **Y# 475** **Weight:** 7.7758 g. **Composition:** 0.9990 Gold .2500 oz. AGW **Obverse:** Temple of Heaven **Reverse:** Two peacocks

| Date | Mintage | F | VF | XF | Unc | BU |
|---|---|---|---|---|---|---|
| 1993 Prooflike | — | — | — | — | 150 | — |

**25 YUAN** **Y# 502** **Weight:** 7.7758 g. **Composition:** 0.9990 Gold .2500 oz. AGW **Reverse:** Koddess Kuan Yin seated in flower

| Date | Mintage | F | VF | XF | Unc | BU |
|---|---|---|---|---|---|---|
| 1993 Proof | 1,000 | Value: 175 | | | | |

**25 YUAN** **Y# 930** **Ring Weight:** 3.3879 g. **Ring Composition:** 0.9990 Silver .1250 oz. ASW **Center Weight:** 7.7758 g. **Center Composition:** 0.9990 Gold .2500 oz. AGW **Reverse:** Panda on rock

| Date | Mintage | F | VF | XF | Unc | BU |
|---|---|---|---|---|---|---|
| 1993 Proof | 2,500 | Value: 200 | | | | |

**25 YUAN** **Y# 775** **Weight:** 7.7758 g. **Composition:** 0.9990 Gold .2500 oz. AGW **Subject:** Mount Heng **Obverse:** Great Wall **Reverse:** Large temple

| Date | Mintage | F | VF | XF | Unc | BU |
|---|---|---|---|---|---|---|
| 1993 Proof | 8,888 | Value: 200 | | | | |

**25 YUAN** **Y# 1072** **Weight:** 7.7758 g. **Composition:** 0.9995 Platinum .2500 oz. APW **Series:** Chinese Inventions and Discoveries **Obverse:** Great Wall. **Reverse:** Stirrup and equestrians. **Edge:** Reeded. **Size:** 21.95 mm.

| Date | Mintage | F | VF | XF | Unc | BU |
|---|---|---|---|---|---|---|
| 1993 Proof | 100 | Value: 375 | | | | |

**25 YUAN** **Y# 1073** **Weight:** 7.7758 g. **Composition:** 0.9995 Platinum .2500 oz. APW **Series:** Chinese Inventions and Discoveries **Obverse:** Great Wall. **Reverse:** Umbrella use and repair scene.

| Date | Mintage | F | VF | XF | Unc | BU |
|---|---|---|---|---|---|---|
| 1993 Proof | 100 | Value: 375 | | | | |

**25 YUAN** **Y# 1074** **Weight:** 7.7758 g. **Composition:** 0.9995 Platinum .2500 oz. APW **Series:** Chinese Inventions and Discoveries **Obverse:** Great Wall. **Reverse:** Mathematicians using an abacus.

| Date | Mintage | F | VF | XF | Unc | BU |
|---|---|---|---|---|---|---|
| 1993 Proof | 100 | Value: 375 | | | | |

**25 YUAN** **Y# 1075** **Weight:** 7.7758 g. **Composition:** 0.9995 Platinum .2500 oz. APW **Series:** Chinese Inventions and Discoveries **Obverse:** Great Wall. **Reverse:** Two men and Yin and Yang symbol.

| Date | Mintage | F | VF | XF | Unc | BU |
|---|---|---|---|---|---|---|
| 1993 Proof | 100 | Value: 375 | | | | |

**25 YUAN** **Y# 1076** **Weight:** 7.7758 g. **Composition:** 0.9995 Platinum .2500 oz. APW **Series:** Chinese Inventions and Discoveries **Obverse:** Great Wall. **Reverse:** Excavating the Terracotta army.

| Date | Mintage | F | VF | XF | Unc | BU |
|---|---|---|---|---|---|---|
| 1993 Proof | 100 | Value: 375 | | | | |

**25 YUAN** **Y# 612** **Weight:** 7.7758 g. **Composition:** 0.9990 Gold .2500 oz. AGW **Note:** Similar to Y#544.

| Date | Mintage | F | VF | XF | Unc | BU |
|---|---|---|---|---|---|---|
| 1993 | — | — | — | — | 125 | — |
| 1993 Proof | — | Value: 150 | | | | |

**25 YUAN** **Y# 422** **Ring Weight:** 3.3879 g. **Ring Composition:** 0.9990 Silver .1250 oz. ASW **Center Weight:** 7.7758 g. **Center Composition:** 0.9990 Gold .2500 oz. AGW **Reverse:** Unicorn **Note:** Similar to 10 Yuan, Y#420.

| Date | Mintage | F | VF | XF | Unc | BU |
|---|---|---|---|---|---|---|
| 1994 Proof | 1,100 | Value: 175 | | | | |

**25 YUAN** **Y# 423** **Weight:** 7.7758 g. **Composition:** 0.9990 Gold .2500 oz. AGW **Reverse:** Unicorn

| Date | Mintage | F | VF | XF | Unc | BU |
|---|---|---|---|---|---|---|
| 1994 Proof | 5,100 | Value: 200 | | | | |

**25 YUAN** **Y# 433** **Weight:** 7.7758 g. **Composition:** 0.9990 Gold .2500 oz. AGW **Reverse:** Panda tugging on bamboo sprig

| Date | Mintage | F | VF | XF | Unc | BU |
|---|---|---|---|---|---|---|
| 1994 | 35,000 | — | — | — | 125 | — |
| 1994 Proof | — | Value: 175 | | | | |

**25 YUAN** **Y# 544** **Ring Weight:** 3.3879 g. **Ring Composition:** 0.9990 Silver .1250 oz. ASW **Center Weight:** 7.7758 g. **Center Composition:** 0.9990 Gold .2500 oz. AGW **Reverse:** Panda tugging on bamboo sprig

| Date | Mintage | F | VF | XF | Unc | BU |
|---|---|---|---|---|---|---|
| 1994 Proof | 2,000 | Value: 200 | | | | |

**25 YUAN** **Y# 511** **Weight:** 3.1103 g. **Composition:** 0.9990 Gold .1000 oz. AGW **Reverse:** Goddess Kuan Yin with child

| Date | Mintage | F | VF | XF | Unc | BU |
|---|---|---|---|---|---|---|
| 1994 Proof | 1,000 | Value: 200 | | | | |

**25 YUAN** **Y# 512** **Weight:** 3.1103 g. **Composition:** 0.9990 Gold .1000 oz. AGW **Reverse:** Goddess Kuan Yin with bottle

| Date | Mintage | F | VF | XF | Unc | BU |
|---|---|---|---|---|---|---|
| 1994 Proof | 1,000 | Value: 200 | | | | |

**25 YUAN** **Y# 513** **Weight:** 3.1103 g. **Composition:** 0.9990 Gold .1000 oz. AGW **Reverse:** Goddess Kuan Yin standing

| Date | Mintage | F | VF | XF | Unc | BU |
|---|---|---|---|---|---|---|
| 1994 Proof | 1,000 | Value: 200 | | | | |

**25 YUAN** **Y# 514** **Weight:** 3.1103 g. **Composition:** 0.9990 Gold .1000 oz. AGW **Reverse:** Goddess Kuan Yin seated

| Date | Mintage | F | VF | XF | Unc | BU |
|---|---|---|---|---|---|---|
| 1994 Proof | 1,000 | Value: 200 | | | | |

**25 YUAN** **Y# 524** **Weight:** 7.7758 g. **Composition:** 0.9990 Gold .2500 oz. AGW **Obverse:** Pu-Tow temple **Reverse:** Goddess of Mercy - with Lotus flower

| Date | Mintage | F | VF | XF | Unc | BU |
|---|---|---|---|---|---|---|
| 1995 Proof | 1,000 | Value: 175 | | | | |

**25 YUAN** **Y# 525** **Weight:** 7.7758 g. **Composition:** 0.9990 Gold .2500 oz. AGW **Reverse:** Goddess of Mercy with wheel

| Date | Mintage | F | VF | XF | Unc | BU |
|---|---|---|---|---|---|---|
| 1995 Proof | 1,000 | Value: 175 | | | | |

**25 YUAN** **Y# 526** **Weight:** 7.7758 g. **Composition:** 0.9990 Gold .2500 oz. AGW **Reverse:** Goddess of Mercy with sceptre

| Date | Mintage | F | VF | XF | Unc | BU |
|---|---|---|---|---|---|---|
| 1995 Proof | 1,000 | Value: 175 | | | | |

**25 YUAN** **Y# 527** **Weight:** 7.7758 g. **Composition:** 0.9990 Gold .2500 oz. AGW **Reverse:** Goddess of Mercy with bowl

| Date | Mintage | F | VF | XF | Unc | BU |
|---|---|---|---|---|---|---|
| 1995 Proof | 1,000 | Value: 175 | | | | |

**25 YUAN** **Y# 572** **Ring Weight:** 3.8879 g. **Ring Composition:** 0.9990 Silver .1250 oz. ASW **Center Weight:** 7.7758 g. **Center Composition:** 0.9990 Gold .2500 oz. AGW **Reverse:** Panda at stream

| Date | Mintage | F | VF | XF | Unc | BU |
|---|---|---|---|---|---|---|
| 1995 Proof set | Est. 2,000 | Value: 210 | | | | |

**25 YUAN** **Y# 687** **Ring Weight:** 3.8879 g. **Ring Composition:** 0.9990 Silver .1250 oz. ASW **Center Weight:** 7.7758 g. **Center Composition:** 0.9990 Gold .2500 oz. AGW **Reverse:** Unicorn with offspring

| Date | Mintage | F | VF | XF | Unc | BU |
|---|---|---|---|---|---|---|
| 1995 Proof | — | Value: 175 | | | | |

**25 YUAN** **Y# 738** **Weight:** 7.8300 g. **Composition:** 0.9990 Gold .2515 oz. AGW **Obverse:** Eastern unicorn **Reverse:** Western unicorn with offspring

| Date | Mintage | F | VF | XF | Unc | BU |
|---|---|---|---|---|---|---|
| 1995 Proof | 5,000 | Value: 250 | | | | |

**25 YUAN** **Y# 835** **Weight:** 7.8300 g. **Composition:** 0.9990 Gold .2515 oz. AGW **Subject:** Sea Goddess Mazhu **Obverse:** Mazhu Temple **Reverse:** Mazhu's portrayal

| Date | Mintage | F | VF | XF | Unc | BU |
|---|---|---|---|---|---|---|
| 1995 Proof | 3,000 | Value: 150 | | | | |

**25 YUAN** **Y# 642** **Weight:** 7.7600 g. **Composition:** 0.9990 Gold .2500 oz. AGW **Reverse:** Panda **Note:** Similar to 10 Yuan, Y#641.

| Date | Mintage | F | VF | XF | Unc | BU |
|---|---|---|---|---|---|---|
| 1995 | — | — | — | — | 120 | — |

**25 YUAN** **Y# 1061** **Ring Weight:** 3.8879 g. **Ring Composition:** 0.9990 Silver .1250 oz. ASW **Center Weight:** 7.7758 g. **Center Composition:** 0.9990 Gold .2500 oz. AGW **Subject:** Unicorn **Obverse:** Eastern unicorn. **Reverse:** Western unicorn with offspring. **Edge:** Reeded. **Size:** 30 mm.

| Date | Mintage | F | VF | XF | Unc | BU |
|---|---|---|---|---|---|---|
| 1995 Proof | — | Value: 220 | | | | |

**25 YUAN** **Y# 955** **Weight:** 7.7758 g. **Composition:** 0.9995 Platinum .2500 oz. APW **Subject:** Unicorn **Obverse:** Eastern unicorn, full body. **Reverse:** Western unicorn head. **Edge:** Reeded. **Size:** 21.9 mm.

| Date | Mintage | F | VF | XF | Unc | BU |
|---|---|---|---|---|---|---|
| 1996 Proof | — | Value: 225 | | | | |

**25 YUAN** **Y# 576** **Weight:** 7.8300 g. **Composition:** 0.9990 Gold .2515 oz. AGW **Reverse:** Panda **Note:** Similar to 100 Yuan, Y#578.

| Date | Mintage | F | VF | XF | Unc | BU |
|---|---|---|---|---|---|---|
| 1996 | — | — | — | — | 140 | — |

**25 YUAN** **Y# 849** **Weight:** 7.7759 g. **Composition:** 0.9990 Gold .2500 oz. AGW **Subject:** 15th Anniversary - Gold Panda Coinage **Obverse:** Temple of Heaven with additional legend **Reverse:** Panda in tree

| Date | Mintage | F | VF | XF | Unc | BU |
|---|---|---|---|---|---|---|
| 1996 Proof | 8,000 | Value: 200 | | | | |

**25 YUAN** Y# 852 **Ring Weight:** 3.8879 g. **Ring Composition:** 0.9990 Silver .1250 oz. ASW **Center Weight:** 7.7759 g. **Center Composition:** 0.9990 Gold .2500 oz. AGW **Obverse:** Temple of Heaven **Reverse:** Panda seated on rock

| Date | Mintage | F | VF | XF | Unc | BU |
|---|---|---|---|---|---|---|
| 1996 Proof | 2,500 | Value: 220 | | | | |

**25 YUAN** Y# 867 **Weight:** 7.7759 g. **Composition:** 0.9990 Gold .2500 oz. AGW **Subject:** Centennial of Chinese Post Office **Obverse:** Modern postal stamp **Reverse:** Imperial postal stamp

| Date | Mintage | F | VF | XF | Unc | BU |
|---|---|---|---|---|---|---|
| 1996 Proof | 3,000 | Value: 125 | | | | |

**25 YUAN** Y# 743 **Weight:** 7.7759 g. **Composition:** 0.9990 Gold .2500 oz. AGW **Obverse:** Eastern unicorn **Reverse:** Western unicorn and maiden

| Date | Mintage | F | VF | XF | Unc | BU |
|---|---|---|---|---|---|---|
| 1996 Proof | 3,000 | Value: 225 | | | | |

**25 YUAN** Y# 743a **Weight:** 7.7759 g. **Composition:** 0.9990 Platinum .2500 oz. APW

| Date | Mintage | F | VF | XF | Unc | BU |
|---|---|---|---|---|---|---|
| 1996 Proof | 500 | Value: 250 | | | | |

**25 YUAN** Y# 915 **Weight:** 7.7759 g. **Composition:** 0.9990 Gold .2500 oz. AGW **Subject:** Celebrating Spring **Obverse:** Radiant lantern **Reverse:** Children setting off firecrackers

| Date | Mintage | F | VF | XF | Unc | BU |
|---|---|---|---|---|---|---|
| 1997 Proof | 10,000 | Value: 100 | | | | |

**25 YUAN** Y# 997 **Weight:** 7.7759 g. **Composition:** 0.9990 Gold .2500 oz. AGW **Subject:** China Palace Museum **Obverse:** Forbidden City **Reverse:** Imperial Gardens

| Date | Mintage | F | VF | XF | Unc | BU |
|---|---|---|---|---|---|---|
| 1997 Proof | 4,000 | Value: 125 | | | | |

**25 YUAN** Y# 998 **Weight:** 7.7759 g. **Composition:** 0.9990 Gold .2500 oz. AGW **Subject:** China Palace Museum **Obverse:** Forbidden City **Reverse:** Jin Shui

| Date | Mintage | F | VF | XF | Unc | BU |
|---|---|---|---|---|---|---|
| 1997 Proof | 4,000 | Value: 125 | | | | |

**25 YUAN** Y# 999 **Weight:** 7.7759 g. **Composition:** 0.9990 Gold .2500 oz. AGW **Subject:** China Palace Museum **Obverse:** Forbidden City **Reverse:** Quan Quin Palace

| Date | Mintage | F | VF | XF | Unc | BU |
|---|---|---|---|---|---|---|
| 1997 Proof | 4,000 | Value: 125 | | | | |

**25 YUAN** Y# 1000 **Weight:** 7.7759 g. **Composition:** 0.9990 Gold .2500 oz. AGW **Subject:** China Palace Museum **Obverse:** Forbidden City **Reverse:** Inner view of palace

| Date | Mintage | F | VF | XF | Unc | BU |
|---|---|---|---|---|---|---|
| 1997 Proof | 4,000 | Value: 125 | | | | |

**25 YUAN** Y# 1001 **Ring Weight:** 3.3879 g. **Ring Composition:** 0.9990 Silver .1250 oz. ASW **Center Weight:** 7.7758 g. **Center Composition:** 0.9990 Gold .2500 oz. AGW **Reverse:** Panda climbing tree

| Date | Mintage | F | VF | XF | Unc | BU |
|---|---|---|---|---|---|---|
| 1997 Proof | 2,800 | Value: 220 | | | | |

**25 YUAN** Y# 718 **Weight:** 7.7759 g. **Composition:** 0.9990 Gold .2500 oz. AGW **Subject:** Panda Bullion **Obverse:** Temple of Heaven **Reverse:** Panda on branch **Note:** Similar to 100 Yuan, Y#720.

| Date | Mintage | F | VF | XF | Unc | BU |
|---|---|---|---|---|---|---|
| 1997 | — | — | — | — | 125 | — |

**Note:** Exists in large and small date varietes

**25 YUAN** Y# 1002 **Weight:** 7.7758 g. **Composition:** 0.9990 Gold .2500 oz. AGW **Obverse:** Temple of Heaven **Reverse:** Panda seated on rock

| Date | Mintage | F | VF | XF | Unc | BU |
|---|---|---|---|---|---|---|
| 1998 | — | — | — | — | 95.00 | — |

**Note:** Exists in both large and small date varieties

**25 YUAN** Y# 1003 **Weight:** 7.7758 g. **Composition:** 0.9990 Gold .2500 oz. AGW **Obverse:** Temple of Heaven **Reverse:** Panda on ledge

| Date | Mintage | F | VF | XF | Unc | BU |
|---|---|---|---|---|---|---|
| 1999 | — | — | — | — | 95.00 | — |

**Note:** Exists in both large and small date varieties

**25 YUAN** Y# 947 **Weight:** 7.7758 g. **Composition:** 0.9990 Gold .2500 oz. AGW **Obverse:** Temple of Heaven **Reverse:** Panda seated on leaves **Note:** Similar to 100 Yuan, Y#949.

| Date | Mintage | F | VF | XF | Unc | BU |
|---|---|---|---|---|---|---|
| 2000 Proof | — | Value: 125 | | | | |

**Note:** Domestic Chinese examples struck with mirror fields, overseas examples struck with frosted fields

**30 YUAN** Y# 19 **Weight:** 15.0000 g. **Composition:** 0.8500 Silver .4099 oz. ASW **Series:** 1980 Olympics **Subject:** Equestrian **Obverse:** State seal **Reverse:** Horse racing

| Date | Mintage | F | VF | XF | Unc | BU |
|---|---|---|---|---|---|---|
| 1980 Proof | 29,000 | Value: 17.50 | | | | |

**30 YUAN** Y# 20 **Weight:** 15.0000 g. **Composition:** 0.8500 Silver .4099 oz. ASW **Series:** 1980 Olympics **Obverse:** State seal **Reverse:** Soccer

| Date | Mintage | F | VF | XF | Unc | BU |
|---|---|---|---|---|---|---|
| 1980 Proof | 29,000 | Value: 17.50 | | | | |

**30 YUAN** Y# 21 **Weight:** 15.0000 g. **Composition:** 0.8500 Silver .4099 oz. ASW **Series:** 1980 Olympics **Obverse:** State seal **Reverse:** Speed Skating

| Date | Mintage | F | VF | XF | Unc | BU |
|---|---|---|---|---|---|---|
| 1980 Proof | 20,000 | Value: 18.50 | | | | |

**30 YUAN** Y# 746 **Weight:** 16.0000 g. **Composition:** Silver .4373 oz. ASW **Series:** 1980 Olympics **Obverse:** State seal **Reverse:** Downhill skier

| Date | Mintage | F | VF | XF | Unc | BU |
|---|---|---|---|---|---|---|
| 1980 Proof | 20,000 | Value: 18.50 | | | | |

**30 YUAN** Y# 747 **Weight:** 16.0000 g. **Composition:** Silver .4373 oz. ASW **Series:** 1980 Olympics **Obverse:** State seal **Reverse:** Figure skater

| Date | Mintage | F | VF | XF | Unc | BU |
|---|---|---|---|---|---|---|
| 1980 Proof | 20,000 | Value: 18.50 | | | | |

**30 YUAN** Y# 748 **Weight:** 16.0000 g. **Composition:** Silver .4373 oz. ASW **Series:** 1980 Olympics **Obverse:** State seal **Reverse:** Biathalon skier

| Date | Mintage | F | VF | XF | Unc | BU |
|---|---|---|---|---|---|---|
| 1980 Proof | 20,000 | Value: 18.50 | | | | |

**30 YUAN** Y# 32 **Weight:** 15.0000 g. **Composition:** 0.8500 Silver .4099 oz. ASW **Subject:** Year of the Rooster **Obverse:** Shoreline temple **Reverse:** Cock

| Date | Mintage | F | VF | XF | Unc | BU |
|---|---|---|---|---|---|---|
| 1981 Proof | 10,000 | Value: 225 | | | | |

**35 YUAN** Y# 8 **Weight:** 19.4400 g. **Composition:** 0.8000 Silver .5000 oz. ASW **Subject:** UNICEF and IYC **Obverse:** State seal above sprays **Reverse:** Children planting a flower

| Date | Mintage | F | VF | XF | Unc | BU |
|---|---|---|---|---|---|---|
| 1979 Matte | 1,000 | — | — | — | 100 | — |
| 1979 Proof | 14,000 | Value: 65.00 | | | | |

**35 YUAN** Y# 46 **Weight:** 33.5800 g. **Composition:** 0.8000 Silver .8638 oz. ASW **Subject:** 70th Anniversary - 1911 Revolution **Obverse:** Staue of Sun Yat-sen **Reverse:** Mausoleum

| Date | Mintage | F | VF | XF | Unc | BU |
|---|---|---|---|---|---|---|
| 1981 Proof | 3,885 | Value: 200 | | | | |

**50 YUAN** Y# 51 **Weight:** 15.5517 g. **Composition:** 0.9990 Gold .5000 oz. AGW **Obverse:** Temple of Heaven **Reverse:** Panda walking right in inner circle

| Date | Mintage | F | VF | XF | Unc | BU |
|---|---|---|---|---|---|---|
| 1983 Proof | 23,000 | Value: 250 | | | | |

**50 YUAN** Y# 76 **Weight:** 15.5517 g. **Composition:** 0.9990 Gold .5000 oz. AGW **Obverse:** Temple of Heaven **Reverse:** Lounging panda with bamboo sprig

| Date | Mintage | F | VF | XF | Unc | BU |
|---|---|---|---|---|---|---|
| 1984 Proof | 17,000 | Value: 275 | | | | |

**50 YUAN** **Y# 83** **Weight:** 15.5517 g. **Composition:** 0.9990 Gold .5000 oz. AGW **Obverse:** Temple of Heaven **Reverse:** Panda hanging onto bamboo branch

| Date | Mintage | F | VF | XF | Unc | BU |
|---|---|---|---|---|---|---|
| 1985 Proof | 76,000 | Value: 250 | | | | |

**50 YUAN** **Y# 104** **Weight:** 15.5517 g. **Composition:** 0.9990 Gold .5000 oz. AGW **Obverse:** Temple of Heaven **Reverse:** Facing panda standing

| Date | Mintage | F | VF | XF | Unc | BU |
|---|---|---|---|---|---|---|
| 1986 | 28,000 | — | — | — | 225 | — |
| 1986 P Proof | 10,000 | Value: 250 | | | | |

**50 YUAN** **Y# 108** **Weight:** 155.5000 g. **Composition:** 0.9990 Silver 5.0000 oz. ASW **Subject:** 120th Anniversary - Birth of Sun Yat-sen **Reverse:** Sun Yat-sen standing facing **Size:** 70 mm. **Note:** Illustration reduced.

| Date | Mintage | F | VF | XF | Unc | BU |
|---|---|---|---|---|---|---|
| 1986 Proof | 3,000 | Value: 175 | | | | |

**50 YUAN** **Y# 134** **Weight:** 155.5000 g. **Composition:** 0.9990 Silver 5.0000 oz. ASW **Obverse:** Temple of Heaven **Reverse:** Panda clinging to tree trunk **Size:** 70 mm. **Note:** Illustration reduced.

| Date | Mintage | F | VF | XF | Unc | BU |
|---|---|---|---|---|---|---|
| 1987 Proof | 8,540 | Value: 80.00 | | | | |

**50 YUAN** **Y# 122** **Weight:** 155.5000 g. **Composition:** 0.9990 Silver 5.0000 oz. ASW **Subject:** Year of the Rabbit **Note:** Similar to 150 Yuan, Y#123.

| Date | Mintage | F | VF | XF | Unc | BU |
|---|---|---|---|---|---|---|
| 1987 Proof | 4,000 | Value: 250 | | | | |

**50 YUAN** **Y# 127** **Weight:** 15.5517 g. **Composition:** 0.9990 Gold .5000 oz. AGW **Obverse:** Temple of Heaven **Reverse:** Panda drinking water

| Date | Mintage | F | VF | XF | Unc | BU |
|---|---|---|---|---|---|---|
| 1987(s) | 78,000 | — | — | — | 225 | — |
| 1987(y) | 17,000 | — | — | — | 225 | — |
| 1987 P Proof | 10,000 | Value: 250 | | | | |

**50 YUAN** **Y# 155** **Weight:** 15.5517 g. **Composition:** 0.9990 Gold .5000 oz. AGW **Reverse:** Panda pawing bamboo

| Date | Mintage | F | VF | XF | Unc | BU |
|---|---|---|---|---|---|---|
| 1988 | 104,000 | — | — | — | 225 | — |
| 1988 Proof | 10,000 | Value: 250 | | | | |

**50 YUAN** **Y# 168** **Weight:** 155.5000 g. **Composition:** 0.9990 Silver 5.0000 oz. ASW **Obverse:** Temple of Heaven **Reverse:** Two pandas in tree

| Date | Mintage | F | VF | XF | Unc | BU |
|---|---|---|---|---|---|---|
| 1988 Proof | 11,000 | Value: 95.00 | | | | |

**50 YUAN** **Y# 142** **Weight:** 155.5000 g. **Composition:** 0.9990 Silver 5.0000 oz. ASW **Subject:** Year of the Dragon **Obverse:** Great Wall **Size:** 70 mm. **Note:** Illustration reduced.

| Date | Mintage | F | VF | XF | Unc | BU |
|---|---|---|---|---|---|---|
| 1988 Proof | 5,000 | Value: 250 | | | | |

**50 YUAN** **Y# 170** **Weight:** 155.5000 g. **Composition:** 0.9990 Silver 5.0000 oz. ASW **Series:** 1988 Summer Olympics **Reverse:** Vollyball **Size:** 70 mm. **Note:** Illustration reduced.

| Date | Mintage | F | VF | XF | Unc | BU |
|---|---|---|---|---|---|---|
| 1988 Proof | 3,898 | Value: 250 | | | | |

**50 YUAN** **Y# 178** **Weight:** 155.5000 g. **Composition:** 0.9990 Silver 5.0000 oz. ASW **Subject:** Year of the Snake **Obverse:** Shanhaiguan Pass Gate **Size:** 70 mm. **Note:** Illustration reduced.

| Date | Mintage | F | VF | XF | Unc | BU |
|---|---|---|---|---|---|---|
| 1989 Proof | 1,000 | Value: 350 | | | | |

**50 YUAN** **Y# 190** **Weight:** 15.5517 g. **Composition:** 0.9990 Gold .5000 oz. AGW **Obverse:** Temple of Heaven **Reverse:** Grid behind panda **Note:** Similar to Y#220.

| Date | Mintage | F | VF | XF | Unc | BU |
|---|---|---|---|---|---|---|
| 1989 | 46,000 | — | — | — | 235 | — |
| 1989 Proof | — | Value: 250 | | | | |

**50 YUAN** **Y# 218** **Weight:** 155.5000 g. **Composition:** 0.9990 Silver 5.0000 oz. ASW **Obverse:** Temple of Heaven **Reverse:** Mother panda with cub

| Date | Mintage | F | VF | XF | Unc | BU |
|---|---|---|---|---|---|---|
| 1989 Proof | 9,599 | Value: 100 | | | | |

**50 YUAN** **Y# 220** **Weight:** 31.1030 g. **Composition:** 0.9990 Palladium 1.0000 oz.

| Date | Mintage | F | VF | XF | Unc | BU |
|---|---|---|---|---|---|---|
| 1989 | 5,000 | — | — | BV+10% | | — |

**50 YUAN** **Y# 241** **Weight:** 15.5517 g. **Composition:** 0.9990 Gold .5000 oz. AGW **Reverse:** Panda

| Date | Mintage | F | VF | XF | Unc | BU |
|---|---|---|---|---|---|---|
| 1990 | — | — | — | — | 250 | — |
| 1990 Proof | 5,000 | Value: 275 | | | | |

**50 YUAN** Y# 262 **Weight:** 155.5000 g. **Composition:** 0.9990 Silver 5.0000 oz. ASW **Obverse:** Temple of Heaven **Reverse:** Two pandas, one in tree

| Date | Mintage | F | VF | XF | Unc | BU |
|---|---|---|---|---|---|---|
| 1990 Proof | 4,000 | Value: 100 | | | | |

**50 YUAN** Y# 266 **Ring Weight:** 6.2207 g. **Ring Composition:** 0.9990 Silver .2000 oz. ASW **Center Weight:** 15.5517 g. **Center Composition:** 0.9990 Gold .5000 oz. AGW **Reverse:** Panda walking

| Date | Mintage | F | VF | XF | Unc | BU |
|---|---|---|---|---|---|---|
| 1990 Proof | 2,000 | Value: 275 | | | | |

**50 YUAN** Y#269 **Weight:** 15.5517 g. **Composition:** 0.9995 Platinum .5000 oz. APW **Reverse:** Panda eating bamboo on rock

| Date | Mintage | F | VF | XF | Unc | BU |
|---|---|---|---|---|---|---|
| 1990 Proof | 2,500 | Value: 370 | | | | |

**50 YUAN** Y#704 **Weight:** 15.5517 g. **Composition:** 0.9990 Gold .5000 oz. AGW **Subject:** Taiwan Scenery Series **Obverse:** Great Wall **Reverse:** Pagoda

| Date | Mintage | F | VF | XF | Unc | BU |
|---|---|---|---|---|---|---|
| 1990 Proof | 2,000 | Value: 250 | | | | |

**50 YUAN** Y#705 **Weight:** 15.5517 g. **Composition:** 0.9990 Gold .5000 oz. AGW **Subject:** Taiwan Scenery Series **Obverse:** Great Wall **Reverse:** Pondside building

| Date | Mintage | F | VF | XF | Unc | BU |
|---|---|---|---|---|---|---|
| 1990 Proof | 2,000 | Value: 250 | | | | |

**50 YUAN** Y#706 **Weight:** 15.5517 g. **Composition:** 0.9990 Gold .5000 oz. AGW **Subject:** Taiwan Scenery Series **Obverse:** Great Wall **Reverse:** Hillside building

| Date | Mintage | F | VF | XF | Unc | BU |
|---|---|---|---|---|---|---|
| 1990 Proof | 2,000 | Value: 250 | | | | |

**50 YUAN** Y#707 **Weight:** 15.5517 g. **Composition:** 0.9990 Gold .5000 oz. AGW **Obverse:** Great Wall **Reverse:** Three buildings joined by docks and bridge

| Date | Mintage | F | VF | XF | Unc | BU |
|---|---|---|---|---|---|---|
| 1990 Proof | 2,000 | Value: 250 | | | | |

**50 YUAN** Y# 321 **Weight:** 155.6800 g. **Composition:** 0.9990 Silver 5.0053 oz. ASW **Series:** 1992 Olympics **Subject:** Speed Skaters **Note:** Illustration reduced.

| Date | Mintage | F | VF | XF | Unc | BU |
|---|---|---|---|---|---|---|
| 1990 Proof | 10,000 | Value: 165 | | | | |

**50 YUAN** Y# 223 **Weight:** 155.5000 g. **Composition:** 0.9990 Silver 5.0000 oz. ASW **Subject:** Year of the Horse **Obverse:** Temple of Confucius **Size:** 70 mm. **Note:** Illustration reduced.

| Date | Mintage | F | VF | XF | Unc | BU |
|---|---|---|---|---|---|---|
| 1990 Proof | 2,000 | Value: 200 | | | | |

**50 YUAN** Y#315 **Weight:** 31.1035 g. **Composition:** 0.9990 Gold 1.0000 oz. AGW **Subject:** 10th Anniversary of Panda Coinage **Reverse:** Panda climing bamboo branch **Note:** Double thick.

| Date | Mintage | F | VF | XF | Unc | BU |
|---|---|---|---|---|---|---|
| 1991 Proof | 2,500 | Value: 375 | | | | |

**50 YUAN** Y# 272 **Weight:** 155.5000 g. **Composition:** 0.9990 Silver 5.0000 oz. ASW **Subject:** Year of the Goat **Obverse:** Chinese building and legend **Size:** 60 mm. **Note:** Illustration reduced.

| Date | Mintage | F | VF | XF | Unc | BU |
|---|---|---|---|---|---|---|
| 1991 Proof | 2,000 | Value: 250 | | | | |

**50 YUAN** Y#312 **Weight:** 15.5517 g. **Composition:** 0.9990 Gold .5000 oz. AGW **Note:** Similar to 100 Yuan, Y#313.

| Date | Mintage | F | VF | XF | Unc | BU |
|---|---|---|---|---|---|---|
| 1991 | — | — | — | — | 250 | — |
| 1991 Proof | — | Value: 275 | | | | |

**50 YUAN** Y# 373 **Weight:** 155.5000 g. **Composition:** 0.9990 Silver 5.0000 oz. ASW **Reverse:** Panda

| Date | Mintage | F | VF | XF | Unc | BU |
|---|---|---|---|---|---|---|
| 1991 Proof | 5,000 | Value: 120 | | | | |

**50 YUAN** Y# 472 **Weight:** 155.5000 g. **Composition:** 0.9990 Silver 5.0000 oz. ASW **Series:** 1992 Olympics **Obverse:** State seal **Reverse:** Female runners

| Date | Mintage | F | VF | XF | Unc | BU |
|---|---|---|---|---|---|---|
| 1991 Proof | 10,000 | Value: 175 | | | | |

**50 YUAN** Y# 477 **Weight:** 155.5000 g. **Composition:** 0.9990 Silver 5.0000 oz. ASW **Subject:** 80th Anniversary - 1911 Revolution **Obverse:** Similar to 10 Yuan, Y#476 **Reverse:** Sun Yat Sen in uniform

| Date | Mintage | F | VF | XF | Unc | BU |
|---|---|---|---|---|---|---|
| 1991 Proof | 1,000 | Value: 350 | | | | |

**50 YUAN** Y# 374 **Weight:** 155.5000 g. **Composition:** 0.9990 Silver 5.0000 oz. ASW **Reverse:** Pandas

| Date | Mintage | F | VF | XF | Unc | BU |
|---|---|---|---|---|---|---|
| 1992 Proof | 4,000 | Value: 120 | | | | |

**50 YUAN** Y#557 **Weight:** 16.9600 g. **Composition:** 0.9170 Gold .5000 oz. AGW **Subject:** Bronze Age Sculptures **Obverse:** State seal **Reverse:** Kneeling figure

| Date | Mintage | F | VF | XF | Unc | BU |
|---|---|---|---|---|---|---|
| 1992 Proof | Est. 500 | Value: 350 | | | | |

**50 YUAN** Y#344 **Weight:** 15.5660 g. **Composition:** 0.9990 Gold .5000 oz. AGW **Reverse:** Panda on tree branch **Note:** Similar to 100 Yuan, Y#345.

| Date | Mintage | F | VF | XF | Unc | BU |
|---|---|---|---|---|---|---|
| 1992 | — | — | — | — | 250 | — |
| 1992 Proof | — | Value: 300 | | | | |

**50 YUAN** Y# 289 **Weight:** 155.5000 g. **Composition:** 0.9990 Silver 5.0000 oz. ASW **Subject:** Year of the Monkey **Obverse:** Building **Reverse:** Monkey **Note:** Similar to 50 Yuan, Y#292.

| Date | Mintage | F | VF | XF | Unc | BU |
|---|---|---|---|---|---|---|
| 1992 Proof | 1,000 | Value: 300 | | | | |

**50 YUAN** Y# 405 **Weight:** 155.5175 g. **Composition:** 0.9990 Silver 5.0000 oz. ASW **Subject:** Chinese Gods, Fu, Lu and Shu **Note:** Similar to 500 Yuan, Y#407.

| Date | Mintage | F | VF | XF | Unc | BU |
|---|---|---|---|---|---|---|
| 1993 Proof | 1,000 | Value: 325 | | | | |

**50 YUAN Y# 413 Weight:** 155.5175 g. **Composition:** 0.9990 Silver 5.0000 oz. ASW **Reverse:** Chairman Mao writing **Size:** 70 mm. **Note:** Illustration reduced.

| Date | Mintage | F | VF | XF | Unc | BU |
|---|---|---|---|---|---|---|
| 1993 | 1,500 | — | — | — | 300 | — |

**50 YUAN Y# 353 Weight:** 155.5000 g. **Composition:** 0.9990 Silver 5.0000 oz. ASW **Obverse:** Temple of Heaven **Reverse:** Two peacocks

| Date | Mintage | F | VF | XF | Unc | BU |
|---|---|---|---|---|---|---|
| 1993 Proof | 888 | Value: 275 | | | | |

**50 YUAN Y#378 Weight:** 15.5517 g. **Composition:** 0.9990 Gold .5000 oz. AGW **Reverse:** Chin with Yin Yang

| Date | Mintage | F | VF | XF | Unc | BU |
|---|---|---|---|---|---|---|
| 1993 Proof | 1,200 | Value: 275 | | | | |

**50 YUAN Y# 379 Weight:** 155.5000 g. **Composition:** 0.9990 Silver 5.0000 oz. ASW **Obverse:** Temple of Heaven **Reverse:** Pandas

| Date | Mintage | F | VF | XF | Unc | BU |
|---|---|---|---|---|---|---|
| 1993 Proof | Est. 3,000 | Value: 135 | | | | |

**50 YUAN Y# 381 Weight:** 155.5000 g. **Composition:** 0.9990 Silver 5.0000 oz. ASW **Subject:** Year of the Rooster

| Date | Mintage | F | VF | XF | Unc | BU |
|---|---|---|---|---|---|---|
| 1993 Proof | 1,000 | Value: 275 | | | | |

**50 YUAN Y# 394 Weight:** 155.5000 g. **Composition:** 0.9990 Silver 5.0000 oz. ASW **Subject:** Marco Polo

| Date | Mintage | F | VF | XF | Unc | BU |
|---|---|---|---|---|---|---|
| 1993 Proof | 500 | Value: 285 | | | | |

**50 YUAN Y#401 Weight:** 15.5517 g. **Composition:** 0.9990 Gold .5000 oz. AGW **Subject:** Invention of the Umbrella **Obverse:** Great Wall

| Date | Mintage | F | VF | XF | Unc | BU |
|---|---|---|---|---|---|---|
| 1993 Proof | 1,200 | Value: 275 | | | | |

**50 YUAN Y#410 Weight:** 16.9800 g. **Composition:** 0.9170 Gold .5000 oz. AGW **Subject:** Bronze Age Sculptures **Obverse:** State seal **Reverse:** Kneeling man lantern

| Date | Mintage | F | VF | XF | Unc | BU |
|---|---|---|---|---|---|---|
| 1993 Proof | 500 | Value: 300 | | | | |

**50 YUAN Y#414 Weight:** 15.5517 g. **Composition:** 0.9990 Gold .5000 oz. AGW **Subject:** Chairman Mao

| Date | Mintage | F | VF | XF | Unc | BU |
|---|---|---|---|---|---|---|
| 1993 | 2,500 | — | — | — | 425 | — |

**50 YUAN Y#445 Weight:** 15.5517 g. **Composition:** 0.9990 Gold .5000 oz. AGW **Subject:** Taiwan Temples **Obverse:** Great Wall **Reverse:** Buddha statue

| Date | Mintage | F | VF | XF | Unc | BU |
|---|---|---|---|---|---|---|
| 1993 Proof | 500 | Value: 250 | | | | |

**50 YUAN Y#446 Weight:** 15.5517 g. **Composition:** 0.9990 Gold .5000 oz. AGW **Subject:** Taiwan Temples **Obverse:** Great Wall **Reverse:** Large temple

| Date | Mintage | F | VF | XF | Unc | BU |
|---|---|---|---|---|---|---|
| 1993 Proof | 500 | Value: 250 | | | | |

**50 YUAN Y#447 Weight:** 15.5517 g. **Composition:** 0.9990 Gold .5000 oz. AGW **Subject:** Taiwan Temples **Obverse:** Great Wall **Reverse:** Small temple

| Date | Mintage | F | VF | XF | Unc | BU |
|---|---|---|---|---|---|---|
| 1993 Proof | 500 | Value: 250 | | | | |

**50 YUAN Y#448 Weight:** 15.5517 g. **Composition:** 0.9990 Gold .5000 oz. AGW **Subject:** Taiwan Temples **Obverse:** Great Wall **Reverse:** Tower temple

| Date | Mintage | F | VF | XF | Unc | BU |
|---|---|---|---|---|---|---|
| 1993 Proof | 500 | Value: 250 | | | | |

**50 YUAN Y#503 Weight:** 15.5517 g. **Composition:** 0.9990 Gold .5000 oz. AGW **Obverse:** Great Wall **Reverse:** Goddess Kuan Yin - seated in flower

| Date | Mintage | F | VF | XF | Unc | BU |
|---|---|---|---|---|---|---|
| 1993 Proof | 1,000 | Value: 275 | | | | |

**50 YUAN Y#613 Weight:** 15.5517 g. **Composition:** 0.9990 Gold .5000 oz. AGW **Obverse:** Temple of Heaven **Reverse:** Pandas

| Date | Mintage | F | VF | XF | Unc | BU |
|---|---|---|---|---|---|---|
| 1993 | — | — | — | — | 250 | — |
| 1993 Proof | — | Value: 300 | | | | |

**50 YUAN Y#765 Weight:** 15.5517 g. **Composition:** 0.9990 Gold .5000 oz. AGW **Subject:** Chinese Inventions and Discoveries **Obverse:** Great Wall **Reverse:** Stirrup

| Date | Mintage | F | VF | XF | Unc | BU |
|---|---|---|---|---|---|---|
| 1993 Proof | 1,200 | Value: 275 | | | | |

**50 YUAN Y#766 Weight:** 15.5517 g. **Composition:** 0.9990 Gold .5000 oz. AGW **Subject:** Chinese Inventions and Discoveries **Obverse:** Great Wall **Reverse:** Excavation of the Terra Cotta Army

| Date | Mintage | F | VF | XF | Unc | BU |
|---|---|---|---|---|---|---|
| 1993 Proof | 1,200 | Value: 275 | | | | |

**50 YUAN Y#767 Weight:** 15.5517 g. **Composition:** 0.9990 Gold .5000 oz. AGW **Subject:** Chinese Inventions and Discoveries **Obverse:** Great Wall **Reverse:** Discovery of mathematical zero

| Date | Mintage | F | VF | XF | Unc | BU |
|---|---|---|---|---|---|---|
| 1993 Proof | 1,200 | Value: 275 | | | | |

**50 YUAN Y# 772 Weight:** 155.5518 g. **Composition:** 0.9990 Silver 5.0000 oz. ASW **Subject:** Chinese Wildlife **Obverse:** State seal **Reverse:** Brown bear and cub

| Date | Mintage | F | VF | XF | Unc | BU |
|---|---|---|---|---|---|---|
| 1993 Proof | 4,500 | Value: 350 | | | | |

**50 YUAN Y# 776 Weight:** 155.5518 g. **Composition:** 0.9990 Silver 5.0000 oz. ASW **Obverse:** Great Wall **Reverse:** Mount Hau and river

| Date | Mintage | F | VF | XF | Unc | BU |
|---|---|---|---|---|---|---|
| 1993 Proof | 8,888 | Value: 275 | | | | |

**50 YUAN Y# 386 Weight:** 155.5000 g. **Composition:** 0.9990 Silver 5.0000 oz. ASW **Subject:** Year of the Dog

| Date | Mintage | F | VF | XF | Unc | BU |
|---|---|---|---|---|---|---|
| 1994 Proof | 1,000 | Value: 225 | | | | |

**50 YUAN Y#460 Weight:** 15.5517 g. **Composition:** 0.9990 Gold .5000 oz. AGW **Subject:** Children At Play **Obverse:** Temple of Heaven **Reverse:** Three children with toy boat

| Date | Mintage | F | VF | XF | Unc | BU |
|---|---|---|---|---|---|---|
| 1994 Proof | 1,888 | Value: 250 | | | | |

**50 YUAN Y# 461 Weight:** 155.5000 g. **Composition:** 0.9990 Silver 5.0000 oz. ASW **Subject:** Children At Play **Obverse:** Temple of Heaven **Reverse:** Two children with cat

| Date | Mintage | F | VF | XF | Unc | BU |
|---|---|---|---|---|---|---|
| 1994 Proof | 500 | Value: 375 | | | | |

**50 YUAN Y#621 Weight:** 15.5517 g. **Composition:** 0.9990 Gold .5000 oz. AGW **Subject:** Oriental Inventions **Obverse:** Great Wall **Reverse:** First tuned bells

| Date | Mintage | F | VF | XF | Unc | BU |
|---|---|---|---|---|---|---|
| 1994 Proof | 1,200 | Value: 275 | | | | |

**50 YUAN Y#623 Weight:** 15.5517 g. **Composition:** 0.9990 Gold .5000 oz. AGW **Subject:** Oriental Inventions - Astronomy **Obverse:** Great Wall **Reverse:** First records of comets

| Date | Mintage | F | VF | XF | Unc | BU |
|---|---|---|---|---|---|---|
| 1994 Proof | 1,200 | Value: 275 | | | | |

**50 YUAN Y#625 Weight:** 15.5517 g. **Composition:** 0.9990 Gold .5000 oz. AGW **Subject:** Oriental Inventions **Obverse:** Great Wall **Reverse:** First chain pumps used to draw water

| Date | Mintage | F | VF | XF | Unc | BU |
|---|---|---|---|---|---|---|
| 1994 Proof | 1,200 | Value: 275 | | | | |

**50 YUAN** **Y# 638** **Weight:** 155.5000 g. **Composition:** 0.9990 Silver 5.0000 oz. ASW **Obverse:** Temple of Heaven **Reverse:** Two pandas, one in tree

| Date | Mintage | F | VF | XF | Unc | BU |
|---|---|---|---|---|---|---|
| 1994 Proof | 3,000 | Value: 175 | | | | |

**50 YUAN** **Y# 708** **Weight:** 155.5175 g. **Composition:** 0.9990 Silver 5.0000 oz. ASW **Reverse:** Taiwan temple

| Date | Mintage | F | VF | XF | Unc | BU |
|---|---|---|---|---|---|---|
| 1994 Proof | 500 | Value: 250 | | | | |

**50 YUAN** **Y# 785** **Weight:** 155.5175 g. **Composition:** 0.9990 Silver 5.0000 oz. ASW **Subject:** Sino-Singapore Friendship **Obverse:** Great Wall **Reverse:** Singapore harbor view

| Date | Mintage | F | VF | XF | Unc | BU |
|---|---|---|---|---|---|---|
| 1994 Proof | 300 | Value: 800 | | | | |

**50 YUAN** **Y#459** **Weight:** 15.5517 g. **Composition:** 0.9990 Gold .5000 oz. AGW **Subject:** Children At Play **Reverse:** Two children with cat **Note:** Similar to 500 Yuan, Y#462.

| Date | Mintage | F | VF | XF | Unc | BU |
|---|---|---|---|---|---|---|
| 1994 Proof | 1,888 | Value: 250 | | | | |

**50 YUAN** **Y#624** **Weight:** 15.5517 g. **Composition:** 0.9990 Gold .5000 oz. AGW **Subject:** Oriental Inventions **Obverse:** Great Wall **Reverse:** First masts for sailing **Note:** Similar to 5 Yuan, Y#619.

| Date | Mintage | F | VF | XF | Unc | BU |
|---|---|---|---|---|---|---|
| 1994 Proof | 1,200 | Value: 275 | | | | |

**50 YUAN** **Y#434** **Weight:** 15.5517 g. **Composition:** 0.9990 Gold .5000 oz. AGW **Obverse:** Temple of Heaven **Reverse:** Panda **Note:** Similar to 100 Yuan, Y#435.

| Date | Mintage | F | VF | XF | Unc | BU |
|---|---|---|---|---|---|---|
| 1994 | 35,000 | — | — | — | 250 | — |
| 1994 Proof | — | Value: 300 | | | | |

**50 YUAN** **Y# 424** **Weight:** 155.5000 g. **Composition:** 0.9990 Silver 5.0000 oz. ASW **Reverse:** Unicorn **Note:** Similar to 10 Yuan, Y#420.

| Date | Mintage | F | VF | XF | Unc | BU |
|---|---|---|---|---|---|---|
| 1994 Proof | 1,100 | Value: 150 | | | | |

**50 YUAN** **Y#425** **Weight:** 15.5517 g. **Composition:** 0.9990 Gold .5000 oz. AGW **Note:** Similar to 10 Yuan, Y#420.

| Date | Mintage | F | VF | XF | Unc | BU |
|---|---|---|---|---|---|---|
| 1994 Proof | 1,100 | Value: 300 | | | | |

**50 YUAN** **Y#648** **Weight:** 15.5517 g. **Composition:** 0.9990 Gold .5000 oz. AGW **Reverse:** Dragon boat **Note:** Similar to 10 Yuan, Y#647.

| Date | Mintage | F | VF | XF | Unc | BU |
|---|---|---|---|---|---|---|
| 1995 Proof | 1,000 | Value: 450 | | | | |

**50 YUAN** **Y#651** **Weight:** 15.5517 g. **Composition:** 0.9990 Gold .5000 oz. AGW **Reverse:** Junk **Note:** Similar to 10 Yuan, Y#650.

| Date | Mintage | F | VF | XF | Unc | BU |
|---|---|---|---|---|---|---|
| 1995 Proof | 1,000 | Value: 450 | | | | |

**50 YUAN** **Y#633** **Weight:** 11.3180 g. **Composition:** 0.9160 Gold .3333 oz. AGW **Subject:** Oriental Inventions **Obverse:** Great Wall **Reverse:** Individual block printing **Note:** Similar to 5 Yuan, Y#629.

| Date | Mintage | F | VF | XF | Unc | BU |
|---|---|---|---|---|---|---|
| 1995 Proof | 1,200 | Value: 275 | | | | |

**50 YUAN** **Y# 592** **Weight:** 1555.5175 g. **Composition:** 0.9990 Silver 5.0000 oz. ASW **Reverse:** Da Yu walking through water **Size:** 70 mm. **Note:** Illustration reduced.

| Date | Mintage | F | VF | XF | Unc | BU |
|---|---|---|---|---|---|---|
| 1995 Proof | 500 | Value: 325 | | | | |

**50 YUAN** **Y# 688** **Weight:** 155.5000 g. **Composition:** 0.9990 Silver 5.0000 oz. ASW **Reverse:** Unicorn with offspring **Size:** 69 mm. **Note:** Illustration reduced.

| Date | Mintage | F | VF | XF | Unc | BU |
|---|---|---|---|---|---|---|
| 1995 Proof | — | Value: 150 | | | | |

**50 YUAN** **Y# 689** **Weight:** 155.5000 g. **Composition:** 0.9990 Silver 5.0000 oz. ASW **Reverse:** Junk **Size:** 70 mm. **Note:** Illustration reduced.

| Date | Mintage | F | VF | XF | Unc | BU |
|---|---|---|---|---|---|---|
| 1995 Proof | 1,000 | Value: 300 | | | | |

**50 YUAN** **Y# 891** **Weight:** 155.5175 g. **Composition:** 0.9990 Silver 5.0000 oz. ASW **Series:** 1996 Summer Olympics **Obverse:** State seal **Reverse:** Table tennis player **Note:** Illustration reduced.

| Date | Mintage | F | VF | XF | Unc | BU |
|---|---|---|---|---|---|---|
| 1995 Proof | — | Value: 110 | | | | |
| 1996 Proof | 3,000 | Value: 125 | | | | |

**50 YUAN** **Y# 464** **Weight:** 155.5175 g. **Composition:** 0.9990 Silver 5.0000 oz. ASW **Subject:** Year of the Pig **Obverse:** Traditional building **Reverse:** Sow and 4 piglets

| Date | Mintage | F | VF | XF | Unc | BU |
|---|---|---|---|---|---|---|
| 1995 Proof | 1,000 | Value: 225 | | | | |

**50 YUAN** **Y#471** **Weight:** 15.5517 g. **Composition:** 0.9990 Gold .5000 oz. AGW **Subject:** Dinosaur **Reverse:** Brontosaurus

| Date | Mintage | F | VF | XF | Unc | BU |
|---|---|---|---|---|---|---|
| 1995 Proof | Est. 2,000 | Value: 250 | | | | |

**50 YUAN** **Y#488** **Weight:** 15.5517 g. **Composition:** 0.9990 Gold .5000 oz. AGW **Series:** 50th Anniversary - United Nations

| Date | Mintage | F | VF | XF | Unc | BU |
|---|---|---|---|---|---|---|
| 1995 Proof | 8,500 | Value: 275 | | | | |

**50 YUAN** **Y#532** **Weight:** 15.5517 g. **Composition:** 0.9990 Gold .5000 oz. AGW **Subject:** Return of Hong Kong to China - Series I **Obverse:** Tiananmen building and monument **Reverse:** Deng Xiaoping's portrait above Hong Kong skyline

| Date | Mintage | F | VF | XF | Unc | BU |
|---|---|---|---|---|---|---|
| 1995 Proof | 12,000 | Value: 300 | | | | |

**50 YUAN** **Y# 573** **Ring Weight:** 6.2207 g. **Ring Composition:** 0.9990 Silver .2000 oz. ASW **Center Weight:** 21.7724 g. **Center Composition:** 0.9990 Gold .5000 oz. AGW **Reverse:** Panda at stream

| Date | Mintage | F | VF | XF | Unc | BU |
|---|---|---|---|---|---|---|
| 1995 Proof set | Est. 2,000 | Value: 300 | | | | |

**50 YUAN** **Y# 593** **Weight:** 15.5517 g. **Composition:** 0.9990 Gold .5000 oz. AGW **Reverse:** Nu Wa Rising

| Date | Mintage | F | VF | XF | Unc | BU |
|---|---|---|---|---|---|---|
| 1995 Proof | 2,500 | Value: 350 | | | | |

**50 YUAN** **Y# 632** **Weight:** 11.3180 g. **Composition:** 0.9160 Gold .3333 oz. AGW **Subject:** Oriental Inventions **Obverse:** Great Wall **Reverse:** Soldiers with cannon and gunpowder

| Date | Mintage | F | VF | XF | Unc | BU |
|---|---|---|---|---|---|---|
| 1995 Proof | 1,200 | Value: 275 | | | | |

**50 YUAN** **Y# 636** **Weight:** 11.3180 g. **Composition:** 0.9160 Gold .3333 oz. AGW **Subject:** Oriental Inventions **Obverse:** Great Wall **Reverse:** Teacher with anatomy chart of human body

| Date | Mintage | F | VF | XF | Unc | BU |
|---|---|---|---|---|---|---|
| 1995 Proof | 1,200 | Value: 275 | | | | |

**50 YUAN** **Y# 643** **Weight:** 15.5517 g. **Composition:** 0.9990 Gold .5000 oz. AGW **Obverse:** Temple of Heaven **Reverse:** Panda eating bamboo

| Date | Mintage | F | VF | XF | Unc | BU |
|---|---|---|---|---|---|---|
| 1995 | — | — | — | — | 250 | — |

**50 YUAN** **Y# 645** **Weight:** 155.5000 g. **Composition:** 0.9990 Silver 5.0000 oz. ASW **Obverse:** Temple of Heaven **Reverse:** 2 pandas on river bank

| Date | Mintage | F | VF | XF | Unc | BU |
|---|---|---|---|---|---|---|
| 1995 Proof | 3,000 | Value: 175 | | | | |

**50 YUAN** **Y# 690** **Weight:** 155.5517 g. **Composition:** 0.9990 Gold .5000 oz. AGW **Subject:** 50th Anniversary - Anti-Japanese War **Obverse:** State seal **Reverse:** Zhou and Mao above soldiers

| Date | Mintage | F | VF | XF | Unc | BU |
|---|---|---|---|---|---|---|
| 1995 Proof | 2,500 | Value: 300 | | | | |

**50 YUAN** **Y# 691** **Ring Weight:** 5.1800 g. **Ring Composition:** 0.9990 Silver .1667 oz. ASW **Center Weight:** 10.3600 g. **Center Composition:** 0.9990 Gold .3335 oz. AGW **Subject:** World Women's Conference

| Date | Mintage | F | VF | XF | Unc | BU |
|---|---|---|---|---|---|---|
| 1995 Proof | 3,000 | Value: 250 | | | | |

**50 YUAN** **Y# 739** **Weight:** 15.5517 g. **Composition:** 0.9990 Gold .5000 oz. AGW **Obverse:** Eastern unicorn **Reverse:** Western unicorn with offspring

| Date | Mintage | F | VF | XF | Unc | BU |
|---|---|---|---|---|---|---|
| 1995 Proof | 2,000 | Value: 300 | | | | |

**50 YUAN** **Y# 739a** **Weight:** 15.5517 g. **Composition:** 0.9995 Platinum .5000 oz. APW **Subject:** Unicorn **Obverse:** Eastern unicorn. **Reverse:** Western unicorn with offspring. **Edge:** Reeded. **Size:** 26.8 mm.

| Date | Mintage | F | VF | XF | Unc | BU |
|---|---|---|---|---|---|---|
| 1995 Proof | — | Value: 525 | | | | |

**50 YUAN** **Y# 789** **Ring Weight:** 6.2207 g. **Ring Composition:** 0.9990 Silver .2000 oz. ASW **Center Weight:** 15.5517 g. **Center Composition:** 9990.0000 Gold .5000 oz. AGW **Obverse:** Temple of Heaven **Reverse:** Panda approaching water from right

| Date | Mintage | F | VF | XF | Unc | BU |
|---|---|---|---|---|---|---|
| 1995 Proof only | — | — | — | — | 300 | — |

**50 YUAN** **Y# 813** **Weight:** 155.5175 g. **Composition:** 0.9990 Silver 5.000 oz. ASW **Subject:** 50th Anniversary - For the return of Taiwan to China **Obverse:** Great Wall **Reverse:** Taiwan and China maps

| Date | Mintage | F | VF | XF | Unc | BU |
|---|---|---|---|---|---|---|
| 1995 Proof | 999 | Value: 575 | | | | |

**50 YUAN** **Y# 814** **Weight:** 15.5517 g. **Composition:** 0.9990 Gold .5000 oz. AGW **Subject:** 50th Anniversary - For the return of Taiwan to China **Obverse:** Great Wall **Reverse:** Taiwan and China maps

| Date | Mintage | F | VF | XF | Unc | BU |
|---|---|---|---|---|---|---|
| 1995 Proof | 3,000 | Value: 250 | | | | |

**50 YUAN** **Y# 815** **Weight:** 15.5517 g. **Composition:** 0.9990 Gold .5000 oz. AGW **Subject:** 50th Anniversary - For the return of Taiwan to China **Obverse:** Great Wall **Reverse:** Zhongshan Hall

| Date | Mintage | F | VF | XF | Unc | BU |
|---|---|---|---|---|---|---|
| 1995 Proof | 3,000 | Value: 250 | | | | |

**50 YUAN** **Y# 821** **Weight:** 7.9020 g. **Composition:** 0.9160 Gold .2327 oz. AGW **Obverse:** Bust of painter Xu Beihong **Reverse:** Lion

| Date | Mintage | F | VF | XF | Unc | BU |
|---|---|---|---|---|---|---|
| 1995 Proof | 3,000 | Value: 150 | | | | |

**50 YUAN** **Y# 822** **Weight:** 155.5175 g. **Composition:** 0.9990 Silver 5.0000 oz. ASW **Obverse:** Chiqian building **Reverse:** Zheng Chenggong standing with flag and ships

| Date | Mintage | F | VF | XF | Unc | BU |
|---|---|---|---|---|---|---|
| 1995 Proof | 250 | Value: 475 | | | | |

**50 YUAN** **Y# 829** **Weight:** 155.5175 g. **Composition:** 0.9990 Silver 5.0000 oz. ASW **Subject:** Three Shu Han Heroes **Obverse:** Luo Guanzhong **Reverse:** Three figures

| Date | Mintage | F | VF | XF | Unc | BU |
|---|---|---|---|---|---|---|
| 1995 Proof | 7,000 | Value: 475 | | | | |

**50 YUAN** **Y# 829a** **Weight:** 155.5517 g. **Composition:** 0.9990 Gold .5000 oz. AGW

| Date | Mintage | F | VF | XF | Unc | BU |
|---|---|---|---|---|---|---|
| 1995 Proof | 2,000 | Value: 275 | | | | |

**50 YUAN** **Y# 838** **Weight:** 10.3678 g. **Composition:** 0.9990 Gold .3333 oz. AGW **Subject:** Table Tennis **Obverse:** Tianjing Stadium **Reverse:** Table tennis player

| Date | Mintage | F | VF | XF | Unc | BU |
|---|---|---|---|---|---|---|
| 1995 Proof | 2,000 | Value: 250 | | | | |

**50 YUAN** **Y# 577** **Weight:** 15.5517 g. **Composition:** 0.9990 Gold .5000 oz. AGW **Reverse:** Panda in tree

| Date | Mintage | F | VF | XF | Unc | BU |
|---|---|---|---|---|---|---|
| 1996 | — | — | — | — | 250 | — |

**50 YUAN** **Y# 599** **Weight:** 15.5517 g. **Composition:** 0.9990 Gold .5000 oz. AGW **Obverse:** Yangtze River scene **Reverse:** Large dam **Shape:** Rectangular

| Date | Mintage | F | VF | XF | Unc | BU |
|---|---|---|---|---|---|---|
| 1996 Proof | 6,000 | Value: 350 | | | | |

**50 YUAN** **Y# 608** **Weight:** 11.3180 g. **Composition:** 0.9160 Gold .3333 oz. AGW **Reverse:** Man riding camel

| Date | Mintage | F | VF | XF | Unc | BU |
|---|---|---|---|---|---|---|
| 1996 Proof | Est. 10,000 | Value: 200 | | | | |

**50 YUAN** **Y# 609** **Weight:** 11.3180 g. **Composition:** 0.9160 Gold .3333 oz. AGW **Reverse:** Water vendor

| Date | Mintage | F | VF | XF | Unc | BU |
|---|---|---|---|---|---|---|
| 1996 Proof | 10,000 | Value: 200 | | | | |

**50 YUAN** **Y# 853** **Ring Weight:** 6.2207 g. **Ring Composition:** 0.9990 Silver .2000 oz. ASW **Center Weight:** 15.5517 g. **Center Composition:** 0.9990 Gold .5000 oz. AGW **Obverse:** Temple of Heaven **Reverse:** Panda seated on rock

| Date | Mintage | F | VF | XF | Unc | BU |
|---|---|---|---|---|---|---|
| 1996 Proof | 2,500 | Value: 325 | | | | |

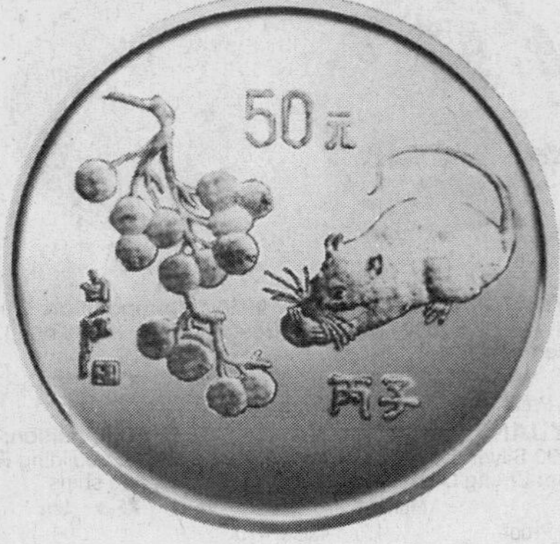


**50 YUAN** **Y# 855** **Weight:** 155.5175 g. **Composition:** 0.9990 Silver 5.0000 oz. ASW **Subject:** Year of the Rat **Obverse:** Dengdu Pavilion **Reverse:** Rat and grapes

| Date | Mintage | F | VF | XF | Unc | BU |
|---|---|---|---|---|---|---|
| 1996 Proof | 1,000 | Value: 240 | | | | |

**50 YUAN** **Y# 859** **Weight:** 15.5517 g. **Composition:** 0.9990 Gold .5000 oz. AGW **Obverse:** Building **Reverse:** Sun Yat-sen bust facing, fan sprays

| Date | Mintage | F | VF | XF | Unc | BU |
|---|---|---|---|---|---|---|
| 1996 Proof | 3,000 | Value: 300 | | | | |

**50 YUAN** **Y# 870** **Weight:** 155.5517 g. **Composition:** 0.9990 Gold .5000 oz. AGW **Subject:** 60th Anniversary - Long March **Obverse:** Flag above building **Reverse:** Chairman Mao portrait

| Date | Mintage | F | VF | XF | Unc | BU |
|---|---|---|---|---|---|---|
| 1996 Proof | 6,000 | Value: 275 | | | | |

**50 YUAN** **Y# 881** **Weight:** 15.5517 g. **Composition:** 0.9990 Gold .5000 oz. AGW **Subject:** Romance of the Three Kingdoms Series **Obverse:** Luo Guanzhong portrait **Reverse:** Guand Du leading his troops

| Date | Mintage | F | VF | XF | Unc | BU |
|---|---|---|---|---|---|---|
| 1996 Proof | 2,000 | Value: 225 | | | | |

**50 YUAN** **Y# 658** **Weight:** 15.5517 g. **Composition:** 0.9990 Gold .5000 oz. AGW **Subject:** Return of Hong Kong to China Series II **Obverse:** Hong Kong Harbor

| Date | Mintage | F | VF | XF | Unc | BU |
|---|---|---|---|---|---|---|
| 1996 Proof | — | Value: 275 | | | | |

**50 YUAN** **Y# 1039** **Weight:** 15.5517 g. **Composition:** 0.9990 Gold .5000 oz. AGW **Subject:** Unicorn **Obverse:** Eastern unicorn, full body. **Reverse:** Western unicorn in wreath. **Edge:** Reeded. **Size:** 27 mm.

| Date | Mintage | F | VF | XF | Unc | BU |
|---|---|---|---|---|---|---|
| 1996 Proof | — | Value: 275 | | | | |

**50 YUAN** **Y# 1038** **Weight:** 155.5175 g. **Composition:** 0.9990 Silver 5.0000 oz. ASW **Subject:** Unicorn **Obverse:** Eastern unicorn, full body. **Reverse:** Western unicorn with maiden. **Edge:** Reeded. **Size:** 70.2 mm. **Note:** Illustration reduced.

| Date | Mintage | F | VF | XF | Unc | BU |
|---|---|---|---|---|---|---|
| 1996 Proof | — | Value: 325 | | | | |

**50 YUAN** **Y# 880** **Weight:** 155.5175 g. **Composition:** 0.9990 Silver 5.0000 oz. ASW **Subject:** Romance of the Three Kingdoms Series **Obverse:** Bust of Luo Guanzhong **Reverse:** Battle scene **Size:** 80 mm. **Note:** Illustration reduced.

| Date | Mintage | F | VF | XF | Unc | BU |
|---|---|---|---|---|---|---|
| 1996 Proof | 500 | Value: 325 | | | | |

**50 YUAN** **Y# 897** **Weight:** 155.5175 g. **Composition:** 0.9990 Silver 5.0000 oz. ASW **Subject:** Year of the Ox **Obverse:** Mingyuan Pavilion **Reverse:** Bull **Size:** 80 mm. **Note:** Illustration reduced.

| Date | Mintage | F | VF | XF | Unc | BU |
|---|---|---|---|---|---|---|
| 1997 Proof | 1,000 | Value: 300 | | | | |

**50 YUAN** **Y# 906** **Weight:** 155.5175 g. **Composition:** 0.9990 Silver 5.0000 oz. ASW **Subject:** Return of Macao to China **Obverse:** Tiananmen Square - Forbidden City **Reverse:** Deng Xiaoping viewing Macao **Size:** 80 mm. **Note:** Illustration reduced.

| Date | Mintage | F | VF | XF | Unc | BU |
|---|---|---|---|---|---|---|
| 1997 Proof | — | Value: 200 | | | | |

**50 YUAN** **Y# 1005** **Weight:** 15.5517 g. **Composition:** 0.9990 Gold .50000 oz. AGW **Obverse:** Portrait of Qi Bashi **Reverse:** Squirrels eating grapes **Note:** Rectangular.

| Date | Mintage | F | VF | XF | Unc | BU |
|---|---|---|---|---|---|---|
| 1997 Proof | 5,000 | Value: 375 | | | | |

**50 YUAN** **Y#719** **Weight:** 15.5517 g. **Composition:** 0.9990 Gold .5000 oz. AGW **Reverse:** Panda on large tree branch **Note:** Similar to 100 Yuan, Y#720.

| Date | Mintage | F | VF | XF | Unc | BU |
|---|---|---|---|---|---|---|
| 1997 | — | — | — | — | 225 | — |

**Note:** Exists in large and small date varieties

**50 YUAN** **Y#903** **Weight:** 15.5517 g. **Composition:** 0.9990 Gold .5000 oz. AGW **Subject:** Return of Hong Kong to China - Series III **Obverse:** Tiananmen Square - Forbidden City **Reverse:** Flag and fireworks above Hong Kong

| Date | Mintage | F | VF | XF | Unc | BU |
|---|---|---|---|---|---|---|
| 1997 Proof | 12,000 | Value: 250 | | | | |

**50 YUAN** **Y# 1004** **Weight:** 15.5517 g. **Composition:** 0.9990 Gold .5000 oz. AGW **Subject:** Huang (Yellow) River Culture **Obverse:** Archer **Reverse:** Dragon

| Date | Mintage | F | VF | XF | Unc | BU |
|---|---|---|---|---|---|---|
| 1997 Proof | 3,000 | Value: 250 | | | | |

**50 YUAN** **Y# 906a** **Weight:** 155.5517 g. **Composition:** 0.9990 Gold .5000 oz. AGW

| Date | Mintage | F | VF | XF | Unc | BU |
|---|---|---|---|---|---|---|
| 1997 Proof | 5,000 | Value: 325 | | | | |

**50 YUAN** **Y# 910** **Weight:** 155.5517 g. **Composition:** 0.9990 Gold .5000 oz. AGW **Subject:** People's Liberation Army **Obverse:** Radiant star above Great Wall **Reverse:** Youthful Chairman Mao standing

| Date | Mintage | F | VF | XF | Unc | BU |
|---|---|---|---|---|---|---|
| 1997 Proof | 12,000 | Value: 250 | | | | |

**50 YUAN** **Y# 918** **Weight:** 155.5175 g. **Composition:** 0.9990 Silver 5.0000 oz. ASW **Subject:** Traditional Chinese Mascot **Obverse:** Ornamental column **Reverse:** Child holding carp

| Date | Mintage | F | VF | XF | Unc | BU |
|---|---|---|---|---|---|---|
| 1997 Proof | 3,800 | Value: 120 | | | | |

**50 YUAN** **Y# 1009** **Ring Weight:** 6.2207 g. **Ring Composition:** 0.9990 Silver .2000 oz. ASW **Center Weight:** 15.5517 g. **Center Composition:** 0.9990 Gold .5000 oz. AGW **Reverse:** Panda climbing tree

| Date | Mintage | F | VF | XF | Unc | BU |
|---|---|---|---|---|---|---|
| 1997 Proof | 2,800 | Value: 325 | | | | |

**50 YUAN** **Y#921** **Weight:** 15.5517 g. **Composition:** 0.9990 Gold .50000 oz. AGW **Subject:** Chinese Wildlife **Obverse:** State seal **Reverse:** Two white dolphins

| Date | Mintage | F | VF | XF | Unc | BU |
|---|---|---|---|---|---|---|
| 1997 Proof | 30,000 | Value: 225 | | | | |

**50 YUAN** **Y# 927** **Weight:** 155.5175 g. **Composition:** 0.9990 Silver 5.0000 oz. ASW **Subject:** Year of the Tiger **Obverse:** Badaling building **Reverse:** Tiger

| Date | Mintage | F | VF | XF | Unc | BU |
|---|---|---|---|---|---|---|
| 1998 Proof | 1,000 | Value: 300 | | | | |

**50 YUAN** **Y# 1007** **Weight:** 15.5517 g. **Composition:** 0.9990 Gold .5000 oz. AGW **Subject:** Zhou Enlai

| Date | Mintage | F | VF | XF | Unc | BU |
|---|---|---|---|---|---|---|
| 1998 Proof | 8,000 | Value: 300 | | | | |

**50 YUAN** **Y# 1010** **Weight:** 15.5517 g. **Composition:** 0.9990 Gold .5000 oz. AGW **Obverse:** Temple of Heaven **Reverse:** Panda seated on rock

| Date | Mintage | F | VF | XF | Unc | BU |
|---|---|---|---|---|---|---|
| 1998 | — | — | — | — | 175 | — |

**Note:** Exists in large and small date varieties

**50 YUAN** **Y# 1011** **Weight:** 15.5517 g. **Composition:** 0.9990 Gold .5000 oz. AGW **Obverse:** Temple of Heaven **Reverse:** Panda on ledge

| Date | Mintage | F | VF | XF | Unc | BU |
|---|---|---|---|---|---|---|
| 1999 | — | — | — | — | 175 | — |

**Note:** Exists in large and small date varieties

**50 YUAN** **Y# 1008** **Weight:** 15.5517 g. **Composition:** 0.9990 Gold .5000 oz. AGW **Subject:** 50th Anniversary of Peoples Republic

| Date | Mintage | F | VF | XF | Unc | BU |
|---|---|---|---|---|---|---|
| 1999 Proof | 22,000 | Value: 300 | | | | |

**50 YUAN** **Y# 1044** **Weight:** 15.5518 g. **Composition:** 0.9990 Gold .5000 oz. AGW **Subject:** Year of the Snake

| Date | Mintage | F | VF | XF | Unc | BU |
|---|---|---|---|---|---|---|
| 2000 | 6,600 | — | — | — | 285 | — |

**50 YUAN** **Y#948** **Weight:** 15.5518 g. **Composition:** 0.9990 Gold .5000 oz. AGW **Obverse:** Temple of Heaven **Reverse:** Panda seated on leaves **Note:** Similar to 100 Yuan, Y#949.

| Date | Mintage | F | VF | XF | Unc | BU |
|---|---|---|---|---|---|---|
| 2000 Proof | — | Value: 215 | | | | |

**Note:** Domestic Chinese examples struck with mirror fields, overseas examples struck with frosted fields

**50 YUAN** **Y# 1006** **Weight:** 15.5518 g. **Composition:** 0.9990 Gold .5000 oz. AGW **Subject:** Year of the Dragon **Note:** Fan shape.

| Date | Mintage | F | VF | XF | Unc | BU |
|---|---|---|---|---|---|---|
| 2000 | 6,600 | — | — | — | 350 | — |

**50 YUAN** **Y# 1050** **Weight:** 15.5518 g. **Composition:** 0.9990 Gold .5000 oz. AGW **Reverse:** Dragons **Note:** Fan shape.

| Date | Mintage | F | VF | XF | Unc | BU |
|---|---|---|---|---|---|---|
| 2000 | 6,600 | — | — | — | 350 | — |

**50 YUAN** **Y# 1049** **Weight:** 155.5175 g. **Composition:** 0.9990 Silver 5.0000 oz. ASW **Reverse:** Dragons **Note:** Rectangle shape.

| Date | Mintage | F | VF | XF | Unc | BU |
|---|---|---|---|---|---|---|
| 2000 Proof | 1,888 | Value: 325 | | | | |

**50 YUAN** **Y# 1040** **Weight:** 155.4400 g. **Composition:** 0.9990 Silver 4.9925 oz. ASW **Subject:** Year of the Snake **Obverse:** Traditional style building. **Reverse:** Snake. **Edge:** Plain. **Size:** 80.6 x 50.5 mm. **Note:** Illustration reduced. Actual size: 80.6 x 50.5 mm.

| Date | Mintage | F | VF | XF | Unc | BU |
|---|---|---|---|---|---|---|
| 2001 Proof | 1,888,000 | Value: 235 | | | | |

**100 YUAN** **Y# 52** **Weight:** 31.1320 g. **Composition:** 0.9990 Gold 1.0000 oz. AGW

| Date | Mintage | F | VF | XF | Unc | BU |
|---|---|---|---|---|---|---|
| 1983 | 22,000 | — | — | — | 500 | — |

**100 YUAN** **Y# 56** **Weight:** 11.0000 g. **Composition:** 0.9000 Goid .3183 oz. AGW **Subject:** Marco Polo

| Date | Mintage | F | VF | XF | Unc | BU |
|---|---|---|---|---|---|---|
| 1983 Proof | 1,030 | Value: 500 | | | | |

**100 YUAN** **Y# 72** **Weight:** 11.3180 g. **Composition:** 0.9170 Gold .3337 oz. AGW **Subject:** Emperor Huang Di

| Date | Mintage | F | VF | XF | Unc | BU |
|---|---|---|---|---|---|---|
| 1984 Proof | 10,000 | Value: 200 | | | | |

**100 YUAN** **Y# 77** **Weight:** 31.1320 g. **Composition:** 0.9990 Gold 1.0000 oz. AGW

| Date | Mintage | F | VF | XF | Unc | BU |
|---|---|---|---|---|---|---|
| 1984 | 23,000 | — | — | — | 450 | — |

**100 YUAN** **Y# 84** **Weight:** 31.1320 g. **Composition:** 0.9990 Gold 1.0000 oz. AGW

| Date | Mintage | F | VF | XF | Unc | BU |
|---|---|---|---|---|---|---|
| 1985 | 164,000 | — | — | — | 375 | — |

**100 YUAN** **Y# 94** **Weight:** 11.3180 g. **Composition:** 0.9170 Gold .3337 oz. AGW **Subject:** Founders of Chinese Culture - Confucius

| Date | Mintage | F | VF | XF | Unc | BU |
|---|---|---|---|---|---|---|
| 1985 Proof | 7,000 | Value: 200 | | | | |

**100 YUAN** **Y# 105** **Weight:** 31.1320 g. **Composition:** 0.9990 Gold 1.0000 oz. AGW

| Date | Mintage | F | VF | XF | Unc | BU |
|---|---|---|---|---|---|---|
| 1986 | 97,000 | — | — | — | 375 | — |
| 1986 P Proof | 10,000 | Value: 400 | | | | |

**100 YUAN** **Y# 107** **Weight:** 11.3180 g. **Composition:** 0.9170 Gold .3337 oz. AGW **Subject:** Wildlife **Reverse:** Wild Yak

| Date | Mintage | F | VF | XF | Unc | BU |
|---|---|---|---|---|---|---|
| 1986 Proof | 3,000 | Value: 250 | | | | |

**100 YUAN** **Y# 117** **Weight:** 11.3180 g. **Composition:** 0.9170 Gold .3337 oz. AGW **Subject:** Chinese Culture - Liu Bang **Reverse:** Revolutionary Soldier

| Date | Mintage | F | VF | XF | Unc | BU |
|---|---|---|---|---|---|---|
| 1986 Proof | 7,000 | Value: 200 | | | | |

**100 YUAN** **Y# 120** **Weight:** 11.3180 g. **Composition:** 0.9170 Gold .3337 oz. AGW **Subject:** Year of Peace **Reverse:** Statue of seated female **Note:** Similar to 5 Yuan, Y#119.

| Date | Mintage | F | VF | XF | Unc | BU |
|---|---|---|---|---|---|---|
| 1986 Proof | — | Value: 475 | | | | |

**100 YUAN** **Y# 158** **Weight:** 31.1030 g. **Composition:** 0.9995 Platinum 1.0000 oz. APW **Note:** Similar to 100 Yuan, Y#128.

| Date | Mintage | F | VF | XF | Unc | BU |
|---|---|---|---|---|---|---|
| | 2,000 | | | | | |

**100 YUAN** **Y# 131** **Weight:** 373.2360 g. **Composition:** 0.9990 Silver 12.0000 oz. ASW **Subject:** 125th Anniversary - Birth of Zhan Tianyou **Obverse:** State seal **Reverse:** Bust of Zhan Tianyou facing above steam locomotive crossing bridge **Size:** 80 mm. **Note:** Illustration reduced.

| Date | Mintage | F | VF | XF | Unc | BU |
|---|---|---|---|---|---|---|
| 1987 Proof | 2,911 | Value: 250 | | | | |

**100 YUAN** **Y# 128** **Weight:** 31.1320 g. **Composition:** 0.9990 Gold 1.0000 oz. AGW

| Date | Mintage | F | VF | XF | Unc | BU |
|---|---|---|---|---|---|---|
| 1987(s) | 84,000 | — | — | — | 375 | — |
| 1987(y) | 47,000 | — | — | — | 375 | — |
| 1987 P Proof | 10,000 | Value: 400 | | | | |

**100 YUAN** **Y# 139** **Weight:** 11.3180 g. **Composition:** 0.9170 Gold .3337 oz. AGW **Obverse:** State seal **Reverse:** Emperor Li Shih on horseback

| Date | Mintage | F | VF | XF | Unc | BU |
|---|---|---|---|---|---|---|
| 1987 Proof | 7,000 | Value: 200 | | | | |

**100 YUAN** **Y# 156** **Weight:** 31.1320 g. **Composition:** 0.9990 Gold 1.0000 oz. AGW **Reverse:** Panda pawing bamboo

| Date | Mintage | F | VF | XF | Unc | BU |
|---|---|---|---|---|---|---|
| 1988 | 167,000 | — | — | — | 375 | — |
| 1988 Proof | 10,000 | Value: 400 | | | | |

**100 YUAN** **Y# 164** **Weight:** 11.3180 g. **Composition:** 0.9170 Gold .3337 oz. AGW **Subject:** Emperor Zhao Kuangyin

| Date | Mintage | F | VF | XF | Unc | BU |
|---|---|---|---|---|---|---|
| 1988 Proof | Est. 7,000 | Value: 250 | | | | |

**100 YUAN** **Y# 167** **Weight:** 8.0000 g. **Composition:** 0.9170 Gold .2359 oz. AGW **Subject:** Rare Animal Protection **Reverse:** Monkey

| Date | Mintage | F | VF | XF | Unc | BU |
|---|---|---|---|---|---|---|
| 1988 Proof | 29,000 | Value: 135 | | | | |

**100 YUAN** **Y# 173** **Weight:** 15.5500 g. **Composition:** 0.9990 Gold .5000 oz. AGW **Series:** Olympics **Reverse:** Sword dancer

| Date | Mintage | F | VF | XF | Unc | BU |
|---|---|---|---|---|---|---|
| 1988 Proof | 5,500 | Value: 250 | | | | |

**100 YUAN** **Y# 175** **Weight:** 31.1320 g. **Composition:** 0.9990 Gold 1.0000 oz. AGW **Subject:** Year of the Dragon **Obverse:** Temple of Heaven **Reverse:** 2 floating dragons

| Date | Mintage | F | VF | XF | Unc | BU |
|---|---|---|---|---|---|---|
| 1988 Proof | 10,000 | Value: 475 | | | | |

**100 YUAN** **Y# 176** **Weight:** 31.1030 g. **Composition:** 0.9995 Platinum 1.0000 oz. APW **Subject:** Year of the Dragon **Obverse:** Temple of Heaven **Reverse:** 2 floating dragons

| Date | Mintage | F | VF | XF | Unc | BU |
|---|---|---|---|---|---|---|
| | 2,000 | | | | | |

**100 YUAN** **Y# 143** **Weight:** 373.2360 g. **Composition:** 0.9990 Silver 12.0000 oz. ASW **Subject:** Year of the Dragon **Obverse:** Similar to 10 Yuan, Y#141 **Reverse:** Two dragons facing **Size:** 80 mm. **Note:** Illustration reduced.

| Date | Mintage | F | VF | XF | Unc | BU |
|---|---|---|---|---|---|---|
| 1988 Proof | 3,000 | Value: 450 | | | | |

**100 YUAN** **Y# 169** **Weight:** 373.2360 g. **Composition:** 0.9990 Silver 12.0000 oz. ASW **Obverse:** Temple of Heaven **Reverse:** Two pandas in tree **Size:** 70 mm. **Note:** Illustration reduced.

| Date | Mintage | F | VF | XF | Unc | BU |
|---|---|---|---|---|---|---|
| 1988 Proof | 5,000 | Value: 190 | | | | |

**100 YUAN** **Y# 159** **Weight:** 31.1030 g. **Composition:** 0.9995 Platinum 1.0000 oz. APW **Obverse:** Temple of Heaven **Reverse:** Panda grasping bamboo shoot **Note:** Similar to 100 Yuan, Y#156.

| Date | Mintage | F | VF | XF | Unc | BU |
|---|---|---|---|---|---|---|
| | 2,000 | | | | | |

**100 YUAN** **Y# 179** **Weight:** 373.2360 g. **Composition:** 0.9990 Silver 12.0000 oz. ASW **Subject:** Year of the Snake **Obverse:** Similar to 10 Yuan, Y#177 **Note:** Illustration reduced.

| Date | Mintage | F | VF | XF | Unc | BU |
|---|---|---|---|---|---|---|
| 1989 Proof | 400 | Value: 800 | | | | |

**100 YUAN** **Y# 184** **Weight:** 31.1320 g. **Composition:** 0.9990 Gold 1.0000 oz. AGW **Subject:** Year of the Snake

| Date | Mintage | F | VF | XF | Unc | BU |
|---|---|---|---|---|---|---|
| 1989 Proof | 3,000 | Value: 575 | | | | |

**100 YUAN** **Y# 185** **Weight:** 31.1030 g. **Composition:** 0.9995 Platinum 1.0000 oz. APW **Subject:** Year of the Snake **Obverse:** State seal

| Date | Mintage | F | VF | XF | Unc | BU |
|---|---|---|---|---|---|---|
| | 1,000 | | | | | |

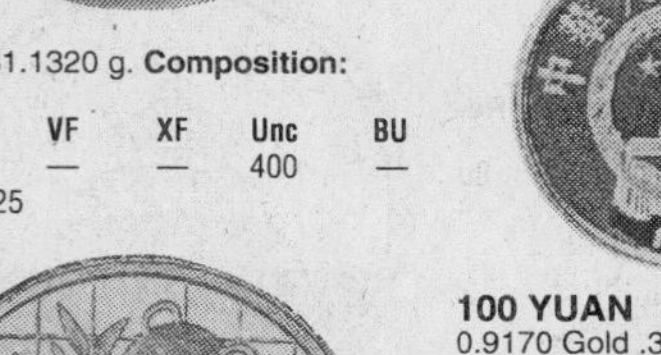

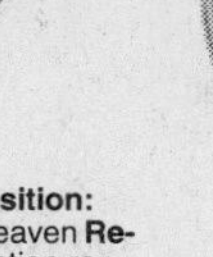

**100 YUAN** **Y# 191** **Weight:** 31.1320 g. **Composition:** 0.9990 Gold 1.0000 oz. AGW

| Date | Mintage | F | VF | XF | Unc | BU |
|---|---|---|---|---|---|---|
| 1989 | — | — | — | — | 400 | — |
| 1989 Proof | — | Value: 425 | | | | |

**100 YUAN** **Y# 191a** **Weight:** 31.1030 g. **Composition:** 0.9995 Platinum 1.0000 oz. APW

| Date | Mintage | F | VF | XF | Unc | BU |
|---|---|---|---|---|---|---|
| | 5,000 | | | | | |

**100 YUAN** **Y# 203** **Weight:** 8.0000 g. **Composition:** 0.9170 Gold .2359 oz. AGW **Subject:** 1990 Asian Games **Reverse:** Ribbon dancer

| Date | Mintage | F | VF | XF | Unc | BU |
|---|---|---|---|---|---|---|
| 1989 Proof | Est. 7,000 | Value: 125 | | | | |

**100 YUAN** **Y# 217** **Weight:** 11.3180 g. **Composition:** 0.9170 Gold .3337 oz. AGW **Obverse:** State seal **Reverse:** Genghis Khan on horseback

| Date | Mintage | F | VF | XF | Unc | BU |
|---|---|---|---|---|---|---|
| 1989 Proof | Est. 7,000 | Value: 250 | | | | |

**100 YUAN** **Y# 219** **Weight:** 373.2360 g. **Composition:** 0.9990 Silver 12.0000 oz. ASW **Reverse:** Pandas

| Date | Mintage | F | VF | XF | Unc | BU |
|---|---|---|---|---|---|---|
| 1989 Proof | 3,670 | Value: 200 | | | | |

**100 YUAN** **Y# 231** **Weight:** 11.3180 g. **Composition:** 0.9170 Gold .3337 oz. AGW **Series:** Save the Children Fund

| Date | Mintage | F | VF | XF | Unc | BU |
|---|---|---|---|---|---|---|
| 1989 Proof | 5,000 | Value: 200 | | | | |

**100 YUAN** **Y# 250** **Weight:** 8.0000 g. **Composition:** 0.9170 Gold .2359 oz. AGW **Series:** Endangered Animals **Obverse:** State seal **Reverse:** Chinese tiger

| Date | Mintage | F | VF | XF | Unc | BU |
|---|---|---|---|---|---|---|
| 1989 Proof | 14,000 | Value: 150 | | | | |

**100 YUAN** **Y# 299** **Weight:** 7.7750 g. **Composition:** 0.9990 Gold .2500 oz. AGW **Subject:** 40th Anniversary of Peoples Republic **Obverse:** State seal **Reverse:** Pair of flying cranes

| Date | Mintage | F | VF | XF | Unc | BU |
|---|---|---|---|---|---|---|
| 1989 Proof | 1,000 | Value: 250 | | | | |

**100 YUAN** **Y# 225** **Weight:** 31.1320 g. **Composition:** 0.9990 Gold 1.0000 oz. AGW **Subject:** Year of the Horse

| Date | Mintage | F | VF | XF | Unc | BU |
|---|---|---|---|---|---|---|
| 1990 Proof | 6,000 | Value: 450 | | | | |

**100 YUAN** **Y# 225a** **Weight:** 31.1030 g. **Composition:** 0.9995 Platinum 1.0000 oz. APW **Subject:** Year of the Horse

| Date | Mintage | F | VF | XF | Unc | BU |
|---|---|---|---|---|---|---|
|  | 2,000 |  |  |  |  |  |

**100 YUAN** **Y# 242** **Weight:** 31.1320 g. **Composition:** 0.9990 Gold 1.0000 oz. AGW **Obverse:** Temple of Heaven **Reverse:** Panda climbing rock

| Date | Mintage | F | VF | XF | Unc | BU |
|---|---|---|---|---|---|---|
| 1990 | 5,000 | — | — | — | 425 | — |
| 1990 Proof | — | Value: 475 |  |  |  |  |

**100 YUAN** **Y# 256** **Weight:** 8.0000 g. **Composition:** 0.9170 Gold .2359 oz. AGW **Subject:** XI Asian Games **Reverse:** Swimmer

| Date | Mintage | F | VF | XF | Unc | BU |
|---|---|---|---|---|---|---|
| 1990 Proof | 10,000 | Value: 125 |  |  |  |  |

**100 YUAN** **Y# 263** **Weight:** 373.2360 g. **Composition:** 0.9990 Silver 12.0000 oz. ASW **Obverse:** Temple of Heaven **Reverse:** Three curious pandas

| Date | Mintage | F | VF | XF | Unc | BU |
|---|---|---|---|---|---|---|
| 1990 Proof | 2,500 | Value: 225 |  |  |  |  |

**100 YUAN** **Y# 287** **Weight:** 10.3700 g. **Composition:** 0.9170 Gold .3054 oz. AGW **Obverse:** State seal **Reverse:** First emperor, Huang Di standing

| Date | Mintage | F | VF | XF | Unc | BU |
|---|---|---|---|---|---|---|
| 1990 Proof | 20,000 | Value: 250 |  |  |  |  |

**100 YUAN** **Y# 306** **Weight:** 11.3180 g. **Composition:** 0.9170 Gold .3333 oz. AGW **Obverse:** State seal **Reverse:** Emperor Zhu Yuanzhang seated

| Date | Mintage | F | VF | XF | Unc | BU |
|---|---|---|---|---|---|---|
| 1990 | Est. 7,000 | — | — | — | 275 | — |

**100 YUAN** **Y# 327** **Weight:** 11.3180 g. **Composition:** 0.9170 Gold .3333 oz. AGW **Series:** 1990 Summer Olympics **Subject:** Women's Basketball **Obverse:** State seal

| Date | Mintage | F | VF | XF | Unc | BU |
|---|---|---|---|---|---|---|
| 1990 | 10,000 | — | — | — | 155 | — |

**100 YUAN** **Y# 735** **Weight:** 31.1400 g. **Composition:** 0.9995 Platinum 1.0077 oz. APW **Obverse:** Temple of Heaven **Reverse:** Panda on rock

| Date | Mintage | F | VF | XF | Unc | BU |
|---|---|---|---|---|---|---|
| 1990 Proof | 778 | Value: 750 |  |  |  |  |

**100 YUAN** **Y# 224** **Weight:** 373.2360 g. **Composition:** 0.9990 Silver 12.0000 oz. ASW **Subject:** Year of the Horse **Obverse:** Temple of Confucius **Size:** 80 mm. **Note:** Illustration reduced.

| Date | Mintage | F | VF | XF | Unc | BU |
|---|---|---|---|---|---|---|
| 1990 Proof | 1,000 | Value: 375 |  |  |  |  |

**100 YUAN** **Y# 273** **Weight:** 373.2360 g. **Composition:** 0.9990 Silver 12.0000 oz. ASW **Subject:** Year of the Goat **Size:** 80 mm. **Note:** Illustration reduced.

| Date | Mintage | F | VF | XF | Unc | BU |
|---|---|---|---|---|---|---|
| 1991 Proof | 1,000 | Value: 375 |  |  |  |  |

**100 YUAN** **Y# 274** **Weight:** 31.1320 g. **Composition:** 0.9990 Gold 1.0000 oz. AGW **Subject:** Year of the Goat

| Date | Mintage | F | VF | XF | Unc | BU |
|---|---|---|---|---|---|---|
| 1991 Proof | 1,800 | Value: 1,000 |  |  |  |  |

**100 YUAN** **Y# 274a** **Weight:** 31.1030 g. **Composition:** 0.9995 Platinum 1.0000 oz. APW **Subject:** Year of the Goat **Obverse:** State seal

| Date | Mintage | F | VF | XF | Unc | BU |
|---|---|---|---|---|---|---|
| 1991 Proof | 500 | Value: 1,100 |  |  |  |  |

**100 YUAN** **Y# 313** **Weight:** 31.1320 g. **Composition:** 0.9990 Gold 1.0000 oz. AGW **Obverse:** Temple of Heaven **Reverse:** Panda with hind feet in water eating bamboo

| Date | Mintage | F | VF | XF | Unc | BU |
|---|---|---|---|---|---|---|
| 1991 | — | — | — | — | 475 | — |
| 1991 Proof | — | Value: 550 |  |  |  |  |

**100 YUAN** **Y# 320** **Weight:** 8.0000 g. **Composition:** 0.9160 Gold .2357 oz. AGW **Subject:** Women's Soccer

| Date | Mintage | F | VF | XF | Unc | BU |
|---|---|---|---|---|---|---|
| 1991 Proof | 1,400 | Value: 150 |  |  |  |  |

**100 YUAN** **Y# 326** **Weight:** 8.0000 g. **Composition:** 0.9160 Gold .2357 oz. AGW **Subject:** Emperor Kang Xi **Obverse:** State seal

| Date | Mintage | F | VF | XF | Unc | BU |
|---|---|---|---|---|---|---|
| 1991 Proof | Est. 7,000 | Value: 275 |  |  |  |  |

**100 YUAN** **Y# 375** **Weight:** 373.2360 g. **Composition:** 0.9990 Silver 12.0000 oz. ASW **Reverse:** Pandas

| Date | Mintage | F | VF | XF | Unc | BU |
|---|---|---|---|---|---|---|
| 1991 Proof | Est. 2,500 | Value: 250 |  |  |  |  |

**100 YUAN** **Y# 473** **Weight:** 11.3180 g. **Composition:** 0.9170 Gold .3334 oz. AGW **Series:** 1992 Olympics **Reverse:** Pairs figure skating

| Date | Mintage | F | VF | XF | Unc | BU |
|---|---|---|---|---|---|---|
| 1991 Proof | 10,000 | Value: 150 | | | | |

**100 YUAN** **Y# 478** **Weight:** 8.6000 g. **Composition:** 0.9170 Gold .2533 oz. AGW **Subject:** 80th Anniversary - 1911 Revolution **Reverse:** Sun Yat-sen writing

| Date | Mintage | F | VF | XF | Unc | BU |
|---|---|---|---|---|---|---|
| 1991 Proof | 2,500 | Value: 285 | | | | |

**100 YUAN** **Y# 479** **Weight:** 31.1035 g. **Composition:** 0.9990 Gold 1.0000 oz. AGW **Reverse:** Sun Yat-sen in uniform

| Date | Mintage | F | VF | XF | Unc | BU |
|---|---|---|---|---|---|---|
| ND(1991) Proof | 1,000 | Value: 800 | | | | |

**100 YUAN** **Y# 545** **Weight:** 11.3180 g. **Composition:** 0.9170 Gold .3337 oz. AGW **Reverse:** Emperor Yan Di

| Date | Mintage | F | VF | XF | Unc | BU |
|---|---|---|---|---|---|---|
| 1991 Proof | — | Value: 285 | | | | |

**100 YUAN** **Y# 295** **Weight:** 31.1035 g. **Composition:** 0.9990 Gold 1.0000 oz. AGW **Subject:** Year of the Monkey

| Date | Mintage | F | VF | XF | Unc | BU |
|---|---|---|---|---|---|---|
| 1992 Proof | 1,800 | Value: 900 | | | | |

**100 YUAN** **Y# 295a** **Weight:** 31.1030 g. **Composition:** 0.9995 Platinum 1.0000 oz. APW **Subject:** Year of the Monkey

| Date | Mintage | F | VF | XF | Unc | BU |
|---|---|---|---|---|---|---|
| 1992 Proof | 300 | Value: 950 | | | | |

**100 YUAN** **Y# 336** **Weight:** 31.1035 g. **Composition:** 0.9990 Gold 1.0000 oz. AGW **Subject:** Chinese inventions **Reverse:** Ancient ships and shipbuilding

| Date | Mintage | F | VF | XF | Unc | BU |
|---|---|---|---|---|---|---|
| 1992 Proof | 1,000 | Value: 500 | | | | |

**100 YUAN** **Y# 337** **Weight:** 31.1035 g. **Composition:** 0.9990 Gold 1.0000 oz. AGW **Subject:** Chinese inventions **Reverse:** Compass

| Date | Mintage | F | VF | XF | Unc | BU |
|---|---|---|---|---|---|---|
| 1992 Proof | 1,000 | Value: 500 | | | | |

**100 YUAN** **Y# 338** **Weight:** 31.1035 g. **Composition:** 0.9990 Gold 1.0000 oz. AGW **Subject:** Chinese inventions **Reverse:** First seismograph

| Date | Mintage | F | VF | XF | Unc | BU |
|---|---|---|---|---|---|---|
| 1992 Proof | 1,000 | Value: 500 | | | | |

**100 YUAN** **Y# 339** **Weight:** 31.1035 g. **Composition:** 0.9990 Gold 1.0000 oz. AGW **Subject:** Chinese inventions **Reverse:** First Kite

| Date | Mintage | F | VF | XF | Unc | BU |
|---|---|---|---|---|---|---|
| 1992 Proof | 1,000 | Value: 500 | | | | |

**100 YUAN** **Y# 340** **Weight:** 31.1035 g. **Composition:** 0.9990 Gold 1.0000 oz. AGW **Reverse:** Bronze Age Metal Working, large urn

| Date | Mintage | F | VF | XF | Unc | BU |
|---|---|---|---|---|---|---|
| 1992 Proof | 1,000 | Value: 500 | | | | |

**100 YUAN** **Y# 345** **Weight:** 31.1035 g. **Composition:** 0.9990 Gold 1.0000 oz. AGW **Reverse:** Panda

| Date | Mintage | F | VF | XF | Unc | BU |
|---|---|---|---|---|---|---|
| 1992 | — | — | — | — | 425 | — |
| 1992 Proof | — | Value: 525 | | | | |

**100 YUAN** **Y# 376** **Weight:** 373.2360 g. **Composition:** 0.9990 Silver 12.0000 oz. ASW **Reverse:** Pandas **Size:** 80 mm.

| Date | Mintage | F | VF | XF | Unc | BU |
|---|---|---|---|---|---|---|
| 1992 Proof | Est. 2,500 | Value: 250 | | | | |

**100 YUAN** **Y# 546** **Weight:** 10.3700 g. **Composition:** 0.9170 Gold .3054 oz. AGW **Subject:** Emperor Da Yu **Obverse:** State seal

| Date | Mintage | F | VF | XF | Unc | BU |
|---|---|---|---|---|---|---|
| 1992 Proof | — | Value: 285 | | | | |

**100 YUAN** **Y# 554** **Weight:** 11.3180 g. **Composition:** 0.9170 Gold .3334 oz. AGW **Subject:** Wu Zetian "The Iron Lady" **Obverse:** State seal

| Date | Mintage | F | VF | XF | Unc | BU |
|---|---|---|---|---|---|---|
| 1992 Proof | Est. 7,000 | Value: 275 | | | | |

**100 YUAN** **Y# 692** **Weight:** 11.3180 g. **Composition:** 0.9170 Gold .3334 oz. AGW **Series:** 1994 Olympics **Reverse:** Male figure skater

| Date | Mintage | F | VF | XF | Unc | BU |
|---|---|---|---|---|---|---|
| 1992 Proof | 10,000 | Value: 150 | | | | |

**100 YUAN** **Y# 693** **Weight:** 8.0000 g. **Composition:** 0.9170 Gold .2356 oz. AGW **Series:** Endangered Wildlife **Reverse:** Mountain sheep

| Date | Mintage | F | VF | XF | Unc | BU |
|---|---|---|---|---|---|---|
| 1992 Proof | 1,500 | Value: 225 | | | | |

**100 YUAN** **Y# 290** **Weight:** 373.2360 g. **Composition:** 0.9990 Silver 12.0000 oz. ASW **Subject:** Year of the Monkey **Note:** Similar to 1000 Yuan, Y#293.

| Date | Mintage | F | VF | XF | Unc | BU |
|---|---|---|---|---|---|---|
| 1992 Proof | 500 | Value: 475 | | | | |

**100 YUAN** **Y# 754** **Weight:** 33.9600 g. **Composition:** 0.9160 Gold .2356 oz. AGW **Subject:** Archeological Finds **Obverse:** State seal **Reverse:** Resting deer with long antlers

| Date | Mintage | F | VF | XF | Unc | BU |
|---|---|---|---|---|---|---|
| 1992 Proof | 500 | Value: 700 | | | | |

**100 YUAN** **Y# 406** **Weight:** 31.1035 g. **Composition:** 0.9990 Gold 1.0000 oz. AGW **Subject:** Chinese Gods Fu, Lu and Shu **Note:** Similar to 500 Yuan, Y#407.

| Date | Mintage | F | VF | XF | Unc | BU |
|---|---|---|---|---|---|---|
| 1993 Proof | 888 | Value: 700 | | | | |

**100 YUAN** **Y# 354** **Weight:** 31.1320 g. **Composition:** 0.9990 Gold 1.0000 oz. AGW **Obverse:** Temple **Reverse:** Two peacocks

| Date | Mintage | F | VF | XF | Unc | BU |
|---|---|---|---|---|---|---|
| 1993 Proof | 1,200 | Value: 625 | | | | |

**100 YUAN** **Y# 380** **Weight:** 373.2360 g. **Composition:** 0.9990 Silver 12.0000 oz. ASW **Reverse:** Pandas

| Date | Mintage | F | VF | XF | Unc | BU |
|---|---|---|---|---|---|---|
| 1993 Proof | Est. 2,500 | Value: 250 | | | | |

**100 YUAN** **Y# 382** **Weight:** 31.1030 g. **Composition:** 0.9995 Platinum 1.0000 oz. APW **Subject:** Year of the Rooster

| Date | Mintage | F | VF | XF | Unc | BU |
|---|---|---|---|---|---|---|
| 1993 Proof | 300 | Value: 950 | | | | |

**100 YUAN** **Y# 383** **Weight:** 373.2360 g. **Composition:** 0.9990 Silver 12.0000 oz. ASW **Subject:** Year of the Rooster

| Date | Mintage | F | VF | XF | Unc | BU |
|---|---|---|---|---|---|---|
| 1993 Proof | 500 | Value: 425 | | | | |

**100 YUAN** **Y# 411** **Weight:** 33.9500 g. **Composition:** 0.9170 Gold 1.0000 oz. AGW **Subject:** Bronze Age Sculptures **Obverse:** State seal **Reverse:** Bull lantern

| Date | Mintage | F | VF | XF | Unc | BU |
|---|---|---|---|---|---|---|
| 1993 Proof | 500 | Value: 700 | | | | |

**100 YUAN** **Y# 491** **Weight:** 10.3600 g. **Composition:** 0.9170 Gold .3053 oz. AGW **Subject:** World Cup Soccer **Obverse:** State seal **Reverse:** Player kicking ball

| Date | Mintage | F | VF | XF | Unc | BU |
|---|---|---|---|---|---|---|
| 1993 Proof | 5,000 | Value: 175 | | | | |

**100 YUAN** **Y# 504** **Weight:** 31.1035 g. **Composition:** 0.9990 Gold 1.0000 oz. AGW **Reverse:** Guanyin - Goddess of Mercy - seated in flower

| Date | Mintage | F | VF | XF | Unc | BU |
|---|---|---|---|---|---|---|
| 1993 Proof | 1,000 | Value: 625 | | | | |

**100 YUAN** **Y# 538** **Weight:** 11.3180 g. **Composition:** 0.9170 Gold .3337 oz. AGW **Obverse:** State seal **Reverse:** Bust of Chairman Mao Zedong

| Date | Mintage | F | VF | XF | Unc | BU |
|---|---|---|---|---|---|---|
| 1993 Proof | Est. 7,000 | Value: 300 | | | | |

**100 YUAN** **Y# 568** **Weight:** 15.5517 g. **Composition:** 0.9170 Gold .5000 oz. AGW **Subject:** Year of the Rooster **Shape:** Scalloped

| Date | Mintage | F | VF | XF | Unc | BU |
|---|---|---|---|---|---|---|
| 1993 Proof | Est. 2,300 | Value: 500 | | | | |

**100 YUAN** **Y# 569** **Weight:** 373.2420 g. **Composition:** 0.9990 Silver 12.0000 oz. ASW **Subject:** Year of the Rooster **Obverse:** State seal

| Date | Mintage | F | VF | XF | Unc | BU |
|---|---|---|---|---|---|---|
| 1993 Proof | Est. 500 | Value: 500 | | | | |

**100 YUAN** **Y# 570** **Weight:** 31.1035 g. **Composition:** 0.9990 Gold 1.0000 oz. AGW **Subject:** Year of the Rooster **Obverse:** State seal **Reverse:** Rooster and hen

| Date | Mintage | F | VF | XF | Unc | BU |
|---|---|---|---|---|---|---|
| 1993 Proof | 19,000 | Value: 700 | | | | |

**100 YUAN** **Y# 614** **Weight:** 31.1035 g. **Composition:** 0.9990 Gold 1.0000 oz. AGW **Reverse:** Panda seated on rock

| Date | Mintage | F | VF | XF | Unc | BU |
|---|---|---|---|---|---|---|
| 1993 | — | — | — | — | 450 | — |

**100 YUAN** **Y# 760** **Weight:** 8.0000 g. **Composition:** 0.9160 Gold .2356 oz. AGW **Obverse:** National seal **Reverse:** Bust of Song Qingling

| Date | Mintage | F | VF | XF | Unc | BU |
|---|---|---|---|---|---|---|
| 1993 Proof | 2,000 | Value: 200 | | | | |

**100 YUAN** **Y# 763** **Weight:** 31.1035 g. **Composition:** 0.9990 Gold 1.0000 oz. AGW **Obverse:** Home of Sun Yat-sen **Reverse:** Bust of Sun Yat-sen

| Date | Mintage | F | VF | XF | Unc | BU |
|---|---|---|---|---|---|---|
| 1993 Proof | 8,888 | Value: 725 | | | | |

**100 YUAN** **Y# 777** **Weight:** 31.1035 g. **Composition:** 0.9990 Gold 1.0000 oz. AGW **Subject:** Mount Tai **Obverse:** Great Wall **Reverse:** Temple

| Date | Mintage | F | VF | XF | Unc | BU |
|---|---|---|---|---|---|---|
| 1993 Proof | 8,888 | Value: 500 | | | | |

**100 YUAN** **Y# 388** **Weight:** 373.2360 g. **Composition:** 0.9990 Silver 12.0000 oz. ASW **Subject:** Year of the Dog

| Date | Mintage | F | VF | XF | Unc | BU |
|---|---|---|---|---|---|---|
| 1994 Proof | 500 | Value: 425 | | | | |

**100 YUAN** **Y# 397** **Weight:** 31.1320 g. **Composition:** 0.9990 Gold 1.0000 oz. AGW **Subject:** Year of the Dog

| Date | Mintage | F | VF | XF | Unc | BU |
|---|---|---|---|---|---|---|
| 1994 Proof | 1,800 | Value: 700 | | | | |

**100 YUAN** **Y# 397a** **Weight:** 31.1030 g. **Composition:** 0.9995 Platinum 1.0000 oz. APW **Subject:** Year of the Dog

| Date | Mintage | F | VF | XF | Unc | BU |
|---|---|---|---|---|---|---|
| 1994 Proof | 300 | Value: 950 | | | | |

**100 YUAN** **Y# 427** **Weight:** 31.1035 g. **Composition:** 0.9990 Gold 1.0000 oz. AGW **Reverse:** Unicorn

| Date | Mintage | F | VF | XF | Unc | BU |
|---|---|---|---|---|---|---|
| 1994 Proof | 1,100 | Value: 525 | | | | |

**100 YUAN** **Y# 435** **Weight:** 31.1035 g. **Composition:** 0.9990 Gold 1.0000 oz. AGW **Reverse:** Panda

| Date | Mintage | F | VF | XF | Unc | BU |
|---|---|---|---|---|---|---|
| 1994 | — | — | — | — | 550 | — |

**100 YUAN** **Y# 440** **Weight:** 8.0000 g. **Composition:** 0.9170 Gold .2356 oz. AGW **Subject:** 12th Asian Games **Reverse:** Gymnast on bars

| Date | Mintage | F | VF | XF | Unc | BU |
|---|---|---|---|---|---|---|
| 1994 Proof | 3,000 | Value: 200 | | | | |

**100 YUAN** **Y# 497** **Weight:** 10.3600 g. **Composition:** 0.9170 Gold .3053 oz. AGW **Series:** 1994 Olympics **Reverse:** Female torch runner

| Date | Mintage | F | VF | XF | Unc | BU |
|---|---|---|---|---|---|---|
| 1994 Proof | 5,000 | Value: 150 | | | | |

**100 YUAN** **Y# 543** **Weight:** 10.3600 g. **Composition:** 0.9170 Gold .3053 oz. AGW **Subject:** Emperor Zhou Wenwang

| Date | Mintage | F | VF | XF | Unc | BU |
|---|---|---|---|---|---|---|
| 1994 Proof | — | Value: 275 | | | | |

**100 YUAN** **Y# 652** **Weight:** 373.2360 g. **Composition:** 0.9990 Silver 12.0000 oz. ASW **Reverse:** Pandas

| Date | Mintage | F | VF | XF | Unc | BU |
|---|---|---|---|---|---|---|
| 1994 Proof | 2,500 | Value: 250 | | | | |

**100 YUAN** **Y# 694** **Weight:** 8.0000 g. **Composition:** 0.9160 Gold .2361 oz. AGW **Reverse:** Panda climbing tree

| Date | Mintage | F | VF | XF | Unc | BU |
|---|---|---|---|---|---|---|
| 1994 Proof | — | Value: 200 | | | | |

**100 YUAN** **Y# 780** **Weight:** 16.3980 g. **Composition:** 0.9160 Gold .5000 oz. AGW **Subject:** Year of the Dog **Obverse:** Phoenix Pavilion **Reverse:** Lap dog **Shape:** Scalloped

| Date | Mintage | F | VF | XF | Unc | BU |
|---|---|---|---|---|---|---|
| 1994 Proof | 2,300 | Value: 375 | | | | |

**100 YUAN** **Y# 781** **Weight:** 373.2420 g. **Composition:** 0.9990 Silver 12.0000 oz. ASW **Subject:** Year of the Dog **Obverse:** Phoenix Pavilion **Reverse:** Large dog

| Date | Mintage | F | VF | XF | Unc | BU |
|---|---|---|---|---|---|---|
| 1994 Proof | 500 | Value: 575 | | | | |

**100 YUAN** **Y# 695** **Weight:** 15.5500 g. **Composition:** 0:9160 Gold .4579 oz. AGW **Reverse:** Black-billed Magpie on branch **Note:** 12-sided.

| Date | Mintage | F | VF | XF | Unc | BU |
|---|---|---|---|---|---|---|
| 1994 Proof | 1,300 | Value: 300 | | | | |

**100 YUAN** **Y# 426** **Weight:** 373.2360 g. **Composition:** 0.9990 Silver 12.0000 oz. ASW **Reverse:** Unicorn with offspring **Size:** 85 mm. **Note:** Illustration reduced.

| Date | Mintage | F | VF | XF | Unc | BU |
|---|---|---|---|---|---|---|
| 1994 Proof | 2,000 | Value: 300 | | | | |

**100 YUAN** **Y# 698** **Weight:** 373.2360 g. **Composition:** 0.9990 Silver 20.0000 oz. ASW **Reverse:** Unicorn with offspring **Size:** 98 mm. **Note:** Illustration reduced.

| Date | Mintage | F | VF | XF | Unc | BU |
|---|---|---|---|---|---|---|
| 1995 Proof | — | Value: 300 | | | | |

**100 YUAN** **Y# 644** **Weight:** 31.1030 g. **Composition:** 0.9990 Gold 1.0000 oz. AGW **Reverse:** Panda **Note:** Similar to 10 Yuan, Y#641.

| Date | Mintage | F | VF | XF | Unc | BU |
|---|---|---|---|---|---|---|
| 1995 | — | — | — | — | 450 | — |

**100 YUAN** **Y# 466** **Weight:** 373.2420 g. **Composition:** 0.9990 Silver 12.0000 oz. ASW **Subject:** Year of the Pig **Reverse:** Sow and five piglets **Size:** 80 mm. **Note:** Illustration reduced.

| Date | Mintage | F | VF | XF | Unc | BU |
|---|---|---|---|---|---|---|
| 1995 Proof | 500 | Value: 400 | | | | |

**100 YUAN** **Y# 646** **Weight:** 373.2360 g. **Composition:** 0.9990 Silver 12.0000 oz. ASW **Obverse:** Temple of Heaven **Reverse:** Panda family

| Date | Mintage | F | VF | XF | Unc | BU |
|---|---|---|---|---|---|---|
| 1995 Proof | 500 | Value: 400 | | | | |

**100 YUAN** **Y# 1062** **Weight:** 31.1035 g. **Composition:** 0.9990 Gold 1.0000 oz. AGW **Subject:** Unicorn **Obverse:** Eastern unicorn. **Reverse:** Western unicorn with offspring. **Edge:** Reeded. **Size:** 32 mm.

| Date | Mintage | F | VF | XF | Unc | BU |
|---|---|---|---|---|---|---|
| 1995 Proof | — | Value: 500 | | | | |

**100 YUAN** **Y# 843** **Weight:** 10.3678 g. **Composition:** 0.9990 Gold .3330 oz. AGW **Series:** Olympics **Obverse:** National emblem **Reverse:** High diver

| Date | Mintage | F | VF | XF | Unc | BU |
|---|---|---|---|---|---|---|
| 1995 Proof | 10,000 | Value: 150 | | | | |

**100 YUAN** **Y# 844** **Weight:** 10.3678 g. **Composition:** 0.9990 Gold .3330 oz. AGW **Series:** Olympics **Obverse:** National emblem **Reverse:** Rhythmic gymnast

| Date | Mintage | F | VF | XF | Unc | BU |
|---|---|---|---|---|---|---|
| 1995 Proof | 10,000 | Value: 150 | | | | |

**100 YUAN** **Y# 451** **Weight:** 31.1030 g. **Composition:** 0.9990 Gold 1.0000 oz. AGW **Subject:** Year of the Pig

| Date | Mintage | F | VF | XF | Unc | BU |
|---|---|---|---|---|---|---|
| 1995 Proof | 1,800 | Value: 700 | | | | |

**100 YUAN** **Y# 453** **Weight:** 15.5557 g. **Composition:** 0.9990 Gold .5000 oz. AGW **Subject:** Year of the Pig **Reverse:** Two pigs **Shape:** Scalloped

| Date | Mintage | F | VF | XF | Unc | BU |
|---|---|---|---|---|---|---|
| 1995 Proof | 2,300 | Value: 375 | | | | |

**100 YUAN** **Y# 465** **Weight:** 31.1030 g. **Composition:** 0.9995 Platinum 1.0000 oz. APW **Subject:** Year of the Pig

| Date | Mintage | F | VF | XF | Unc | BU |
|---|---|---|---|---|---|---|
| 1995 Proof | 300 | Value: 950 | | | | |

**100 YUAN** **Y# 1012** **Weight:** 31.1030 g. **Composition:** 0.9990 Gold 1.0000 oz. AGW **Reverse:** Unicorn

| Date | Mintage | F | VF | XF | Unc | BU |
|---|---|---|---|---|---|---|
| 1995 Proof | 1,500 | Value: 525 | | | | |

**100 YUAN** **Y# 696** **Weight:** 31.1035 g. **Composition:** 0.9990 Gold 1.0000 oz. AGW **Subject:** 50th Anniversary - Anti-Japanese War **Reverse:** People at wall

| Date | Mintage | F | VF | XF | Unc | BU |
|---|---|---|---|---|---|---|
| 1995 Proof | 1,400 | Value: 600 | | | | |

**100 YUAN** **Y# 697** **Weight:** 31.1035 g. **Composition:** 0.9990 Gold 1.0000 oz. AGW **Reverse:** Soldiers above bridge guarded by chinze

| Date | Mintage | F | VF | XF | Unc | BU |
|---|---|---|---|---|---|---|
| 1995 Proof | 1,400 | Value: 600 | | | | |

**100 YUAN** **Y# 790** **Weight:** 31.0103 g. **Composition:** 0.9990 Gold 1.0000 oz. AGW **Obverse:** Temple of Heaven **Reverse:** Panda approaching water from right

| Date | Mintage | F | VF | XF | Unc | BU |
|---|---|---|---|---|---|---|
| 1995 Proof only | 2,000 | Value: 700 | | | | |

**100 YUAN** **Y# 804** **Weight:** 31.0103 g. **Composition:** 0.9990 Gold 1.0000 oz. AGW **Subject:** Chinese Culture Series **Obverse:** Great Wall seen through arch **Reverse:** Pagoda of Six Harmonies

| Date | Mintage | F | VF | XF | Unc | BU |
|---|---|---|---|---|---|---|
| 1995 Proof | 25,000 | Value: 375 | | | | |

**100 YUAN** **Y# 805** **Weight:** 31.0103 g. **Composition:** 0.9990 Gold 1.0000 oz. AGW **Subject:** Chinese Culture Series **Obverse:** Great Wall seen through arch **Reverse:** Mencius seated at table

| Date | Mintage | F | VF | XF | Unc | BU |
|---|---|---|---|---|---|---|
| 1995 Proof | 25,000 | Value: 375 | | | | |

**100 YUAN** **Y# 806** **Weight:** 31.0103 g. **Composition:** 0.9990 Gold 1.0000 oz. AGW **Subject:** Chinese Culture Series **Obverse:** Great Wall seen through arch **Reverse:** Tang Taizong seated

| Date | Mintage | F | VF | XF | Unc | BU |
|---|---|---|---|---|---|---|
| 1995 Proof | 25,000 | Value: 375 | | | | |

**100 YUAN** **Y# 807** **Weight:** 31.0103 g. **Composition:** 0.9990 Gold 1.0000 oz. AGW **Subject:** Chinese Culture Series **Obverse:** Great Wall seen through arch **Reverse:** Lion dance

| Date | Mintage | F | VF | XF | Unc | BU |
|---|---|---|---|---|---|---|
| 1995 Proof | 25,000 | Value: 375 | | | | |

**100 YUAN** **Y# 808** **Weight:** 31.0103 g. **Composition:** 0.9990 Gold 1.0000 oz. AGW **Subject:** Chinese Culture Series **Obverse:** Great Wall seen through arch **Reverse:** Female opera role

| Date | Mintage | F | VF | XF | Unc | BU |
|---|---|---|---|---|---|---|
| 1995 Proof | 25,000 | Value: 375 | | | | |

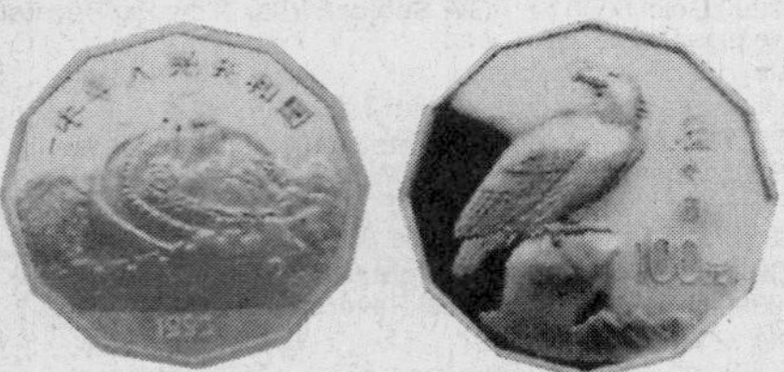

**100 YUAN** **Y# 810** **Weight:** 16.9779 g. **Composition:** 0.9160 Gold .5000 oz. AGW **Obverse:** Great Wall **Reverse:** Perched eagle **Shape:** 12-sided

| Date | Mintage | F | VF | XF | Unc | BU |
|---|---|---|---|---|---|---|
| 1995 Proof | 1,300 | Value: 300 | | | | |

**100 YUAN** **Y# 823** **Weight:** 373.2420 g. **Composition:** 0.9990 Silver 12.0000 oz. ASW **Subject:** Zheng Chenggong **Obverse:** Chiqian building **Reverse:** Standing figure with flag and ships

| Date | Mintage | F | VF | XF | Unc | BU |
|---|---|---|---|---|---|---|
| 1995 Proof | 150 | Value: 900 | | | | |

**100 YUAN** **Y# 830** **Weight:** 373.2420 g. **Composition:** 0.9990 Silver 12.0000 oz. ASW **Subject:** Romance of the Three Kingdoms **Obverse:** Luo Guanzhong **Reverse:** Standing Liu Bei with flags

| Date | Mintage | F | VF | XF | Unc | BU |
|---|---|---|---|---|---|---|
| 1995 Proof | 1,500 | Value: 700 | | | | |

**100 YUAN** **Y# 831** **Weight:** 373.2420 g. **Composition:** 0.9990 Silver 12.0000 oz. ASW **Subject:** Romance of the Three Kingdoms **Obverse:** Luo Guanzhong **Reverse:** Seated Guan Yu reading

| Date | Mintage | F | VF | XF | Unc | BU |
|---|---|---|---|---|---|---|
| 1995 Proof | 1,500 | Value: 700 | | | | |

**100 YUAN** **Y# 832** **Weight:** 373.2420 g. **Composition:** 0.9990 Silver 12.0000 oz. ASW **Subject:** Romance of the Three Kingdoms **Obverse:** Luo Guanzhong **Reverse:** Zhang Fei on horseback

| Date | Mintage | F | VF | XF | Unc | BU |
|---|---|---|---|---|---|---|
| 1995 Proof | 1,500 | Value: 700 | | | | |

**100 YUAN** **Y# 833** **Weight:** 373.2420 g. **Composition:** 0.9990 Silver 12.0000 oz. ASW **Subject:** Romance of the Three Kingdoms **Obverse:** Luo Guanzhong **Reverse:** Zhuge Liang seated on throne

| Date | Mintage | F | VF | XF | Unc | BU |
|---|---|---|---|---|---|---|
| 1995 Proof | 1,500 | Value: 700 | | | | |

**100 YUAN** **Y# 578** **Weight:** 31.1035 g. **Composition:** 0.9990 Gold 1.0000 oz. AGW **Obverse:** Temple of Heaven **Reverse:** Panda in tree

| Date | Mintage | F | VF | XF | Unc | BU |
|---|---|---|---|---|---|---|
| 1996 | — | — | — | — | 425 | — |

**100 YUAN** **Y# 1013** **Weight:** 31.1035 g. **Composition:** 0.9990 Gold 1.0000 oz. AGW **Obverse:** Temple of Heaven **Reverse:** Panda sitting on rock

| Date | Mintage | F | VF | XF | Unc | BU |
|---|---|---|---|---|---|---|
| 1996 Proof | 1,500 | Value: 700 | | | | |

**100 YUAN** **Y# 586** **Weight:** 31.1035 g. **Composition:** 0.9990 Gold 1.0000 oz. AGW **Subject:** Year of the Rat

| Date | Mintage | F | VF | XF | Unc | BU |
|---|---|---|---|---|---|---|
| 1996 Proof | 1,800 | Value: 700 | | | | |

**100 YUAN** **Y# 586a** **Weight:** 31.1035 g. **Composition:** 0.9995 Platinum 1.0000 oz. APW **Subject:** Year of the Rat

| Date | Mintage | F | VF | XF | Unc | BU |
|---|---|---|---|---|---|---|
| 1996 Proof | 300 | Value: 950 | | | | |

**100 YUAN** **Y# 850** **Weight:** 31.1035 g. **Composition:** 0.9990 Gold 1.0000 oz. AGW **Subject:** 15th Anniversary - Gold Panda Coins **Obverse:** Temple of Heaven with additional legend **Reverse:** Panda in tree

| Date | Mintage | F | VF | XF | Unc | BU |
|---|---|---|---|---|---|---|
| 1996 Proof | 1,500 | Value: 550 | | | | |

**100 YUAN** **Y# 956** **Weight:** 31.1035 g. **Composition:** 0.9990 Gold 1.0000 oz. AGW **Obverse:** Eastern unicorn **Reverse:** Western unicorn in wreath

| Date | Mintage | F | VF | XF | Unc | BU |
|---|---|---|---|---|---|---|
| 1996 Proof | 1,250 | Value: 575 | | | | |

**100 YUAN** **Y# 956a** **Weight:** 31.1035 g. **Composition:** 0.9990 Platinum 1.0000 oz. APW **Subject:** Unicorn **Obverse:** Eastern unicorn, full body. **Reverse:** Western unicorn and maiden. **Edge:** Reeded. **Size:** 32 mm.

| Date | Mintage | F | VF | XF | Unc | BU |
|---|---|---|---|---|---|---|
| 1996 Proof | 500 | Value: 850 | | | | |

**100 YUAN** **Y# 856** **Weight:** 16.9779 g. **Composition:** 0.9160 Gold .5000 oz. AGW **Subject:** Year of the Rat **Obverse:** Dengdu Pavilion **Reverse:** Rat on corn cob

| Date | Mintage | F | VF | XF | Unc | BU |
|---|---|---|---|---|---|---|
| 1996 Proof | 2,300 | Value: 400 | | | | |

**100 YUAN** **Y# 1014** **Weight:** 31.1035 g. **Composition:** 0.9990 Gold 1.0000 oz. AGW **Subject:** Unicorn **Obverse:** Eastern unicorn, full body. **Reverse:** Western unicorn. **Edge:** Reeded. **Size:** 32.1 mm.

| Date | Mintage |
|---|---|
| 1996 Proof | — Value: 500 |

**100 YUAN** **Y# 669** **Weight:** 373.2360 g. **Composition:** 0.9990 Silver 12.0000 oz. ASW **Subject:** Year of the Ox

| Date | Mintage | F | VF | XF | Unc | BU |
|---|---|---|---|---|---|---|
| 1997 | 500 | — | — | — | 450 | — |

**100 YUAN** **Y# 670** **Weight:** 15.5557 g. **Composition:** 0.9990 Gold .5000 oz. AGW **Subject:** Year of the Ox **Shape:** Scalloped

| Date | Mintage | F | VF | XF | Unc | BU |
|---|---|---|---|---|---|---|
| 1997 Proof | 2,300 | Value: 400 | | | | |

**100 YUAN** **Y# 720** **Weight:** 31.1035 g. **Composition:** 0.9990 Gold 1.0000 oz. AGW **Obverse:** Temple of Heaven **Reverse:** Panda on branch

| Date | Mintage | F | VF | XF | Unc | BU |
|---|---|---|---|---|---|---|
| 1997 | — | — | — | — | 375 | — |

**Note:** Exists in large and small date varieteis

**100 YUAN** **Y# 898** **Weight:** 373.2420 g. **Composition:** 0.9990 Silver 12.0000 oz. ASW **Subject:** Year of the Ox **Obverse:** Minguan Pavilion **Reverse:** Cow nursing calf

| Date | Mintage | F | VF | XF | Unc | BU |
|---|---|---|---|---|---|---|
| 1997 Proof | 500 | Value: 475 | | | | |

**100 YUAN** **Y# 900** **Weight:** 31.1035 g. **Composition:** 0.9990 Gold 1.0000 oz. AGW **Subject:** Year of the Ox **Obverse:** State seal **Reverse:** Water buffalo

| Date | Mintage | F | VF | XF | Unc | BU |
|---|---|---|---|---|---|---|
| 1997 Proof | 1,600 | Value: 600 | | | | |

**100 YUAN** **Y# 900a** **Weight:** 31.1035 g. **Composition:** 0.9995 Platinum 1.0000 oz. APW

| Date | Mintage | F | VF | XF | Unc | BU |
|---|---|---|---|---|---|---|
| 1997 Proof | 300 | Value: 950 | | | | |

**100 YUAN** **Y# 966** **Weight:** 31.1035 g. **Composition:** 0.9995 Platinum 1.0000 oz. APW **Obverse:** Eastern unicorn **Reverse:** Western unicorn

| Date | Mintage | F | VF | XF | Unc | BU |
|---|---|---|---|---|---|---|
| 1997 Proof | 500 | Value: 800 | | | | |

**100 YUAN** **Y# 928** **Weight:** 373.2420 g. **Composition:** 0.9990 Silver 12.0000 oz. ASW **Subject:** Year of the Tiger **Obverse:** Badaling building **Reverse:** Tiger

| Date | Mintage | F | VF | XF | Unc | BU |
|---|---|---|---|---|---|---|
| 1998 Proof | 500 | Value: 600 | | | | |

**100 YUAN** **Y# 929** **Weight:** 31.1035 g. **Composition:** 0.9990 Gold 1.0000 oz. AGW **Subject:** Year of the Tiger **Obverse:** State seal **Reverse:** Tiger

| Date | Mintage | F | VF | XF | Unc | BU |
|---|---|---|---|---|---|---|
| 1998 Proof | 1,600 | Value: 700 | | | | |

**100 YUAN** **Y# 929a** **Weight:** 31.1035 g. **Composition:** 0.9990 Platinum 1.0000 oz. APW

| Date | Mintage | F | VF | XF | Unc | BU |
|---|---|---|---|---|---|---|
| 1998 Proof | 300 | Value: 1,150 | | | | |

**100 YUAN** **Y# 1015** **Weight:** 15.5557 g. **Composition:** 0.9990 Gold .5000 oz. AGW **Subject:** Year of the Tiger **Shape:** Scalloped

| Date | Mintage | F | VF | XF | Unc | BU |
|---|---|---|---|---|---|---|
| 1998 Proof | 2,300 | Value: 400 | | | | |

**100 YUAN** **Y# 1016** **Weight:** 31.1320 g. **Composition:** 0.9990 Gold 1.0000 oz. AGW **Obverse:** Temple of Heaven **Reverse:** Panda seated on rock

| Date | Mintage | F | VF | XF | Unc | BU |
|---|---|---|---|---|---|---|
| 1998 | — | — | — | — | 350 | — |

**Note:** Exists in large and small date varieties

**100 YUAN** **Y# 1017** **Weight:** 31.1320 g. **Composition:** 0.9990 Gold 1.0000 oz. AGW **Obverse:** Temple of Heaven **Reverse:** Panda on ledge

| Date | Mintage | F | VF | XF | Unc | BU |
|---|---|---|---|---|---|---|
| 1999 | — | — | — | — | 325 | — |

**Note:** Exists in large and small date varieties

**100 YUAN** **Y# 1018** **Weight:** 31.1035 g. **Composition:** 0.9990 Gold 1.0000 oz. AGW **Subject:** Year of the Rabbit

| Date | Mintage | F | VF | XF | Unc | BU |
|---|---|---|---|---|---|---|
| 1999 Proof | — | Value: 600 | | | | |

**100 YUAN** **Y# 1018a** **Weight:** 31.1035 g. **Composition:** 0.9990 Platinum 1.0000 oz. APW

| Date | Mintage | F | VF | XF | Unc | BU |
|---|---|---|---|---|---|---|
| 1999 Proof | — | Value: 1,150 | | | | |

**100 YUAN** **Y# 1019** **Weight:** 15.5551 g. **Composition:** 0.9990 Gold .5000 oz. AGW **Subject:** Year of the Rabbit **Shape:** Scalloped

| Date | Mintage | F | VF | XF | Unc | BU |
|---|---|---|---|---|---|---|
| 1999 Prof | — | Value: 400 | | | | |

**100 YUAN** **Y# 949** **Weight:** 31.1036 g. **Composition:** 0.9990 Gold 1.0000 oz. AGW **Obverse:** Temple of Heaven **Reverse:** Panda seated on leaves

| Date | Mintage | F | VF | XF | Unc | BU |
|---|---|---|---|---|---|---|
| 2000 Proof | — | Value: 420 | | | | |

**Note:** Domestic Chinese examples struck with mirror fields, overseas examples struck with frosted fields

**100 YUAN** **Y# 1051** **Weight:** 15.5518 g. **Composition:** 0.9160 Gold .4580 oz. AGW **Reverse:** Dragons **Shape:** Scalloped

| Date | Mintage | F | VF | XF | Unc | BU |
|---|---|---|---|---|---|---|
| 2000 Proof | 2,300 | Value: 450 | | | | |

**150 YUAN** **Y# 45** **Weight:** 8.0000 g. **Composition:** 0.9170 Gold .2359 oz. AGW **Subject:** Year of the Pig

| Date | Mintage | F | VF | XF | Unc | BU |
|---|---|---|---|---|---|---|
| 1983 Proof | 2,035 | Value: 1,250 | | | | |

**150 YUAN** **Y# 60** **Weight:** 8.0000 g. **Composition:** 0.9170 Gold .2359 oz. AGW **Subject:** Year of the Rat

| Date | Mintage | F | VF | XF | Unc | BU |
|---|---|---|---|---|---|---|
| 1984 Proof | 2,248 | Value: 1,750 | | | | |

**150 YUAN** **Y# 79** **Weight:** 8.0000 g. **Composition:** 0.9170 Gold .2359 oz. AGW **Subject:** Year of the Ox **Obverse:** Houseboat in harbor

| Date | Mintage | F | VF | XF | Unc | BU |
|---|---|---|---|---|---|---|
| 1985 Proof | 16,000 | Value: 185 | | | | |

**Note:** 5,000 pieces were struck and issued in boxes with certificates and are valued at $350

**150 YUAN** **Y# 99** **Weight:** 8.0000 g. **Composition:** 0.9170 Gold .2359 oz. AGW **Subject:** Year of the Tiger **Obverse:** Qing Dynasty Palace

| Date | Mintage | F | VF | XF | Unc | BU |
|---|---|---|---|---|---|---|
| 1986 Proof | 5,480 | Value: 350 | | | | |

**150 YUAN** **Y# 123** **Weight:** 8.0000 g. **Composition:** 0.9170 Gold .2359 oz. AGW **Subject:** Year of the Rabbit

| Date | Mintage | F | VF | XF | Unc | BU |
|---|---|---|---|---|---|---|
| 1987 Proof | 4,780 | Value: 350 | | | | |

**150 YUAN** **Y# 144** **Weight:** 8.0000 g. **Composition:** 0.9170 Gold .2359 oz. AGW **Subject:** Year of the Dragon **Obverse:** Great Wall of China

| Date | Mintage | F | VF | XF | Unc | BU |
|---|---|---|---|---|---|---|
| 1988 Proof | 7,600 | Value: 300 | | | | |

**150 YUAN** **Y# 180** **Weight:** 8.0000 g. **Composition:** 0.9170 Gold .2359 oz. AGW **Subject:** Year of the Snake **Obverse:** Shanhaiguan Pass Gate

| Date | Mintage | F | VF | XF | Unc | BU |
|---|---|---|---|---|---|---|
| 1989 Proof | 7,500 | Value: 165 | | | | |

**150 YUAN** **Y# 208** **Weight:** 622.0400 g. **Composition:** 0.9990 Silver 20.0000 oz. ASW **Reverse:** Phoenix and dragon

| Date | Mintage | F | VF | XF | Unc | BU |
|---|---|---|---|---|---|---|
| 1990 Proof | 1,500 | Value: 650 | | | | |

**150 YUAN** **Y# 227** **Weight:** 8.0000 g. **Composition:** 0.9170 Gold .2359 oz. AGW **Subject:** Year of the Horse **Obverse:** Temple of Confucius

| Date | Mintage | F | VF | XF | Unc | BU |
|---|---|---|---|---|---|---|
| 1990 Proof | 7,500 | Value: 250 | | | | |

**150 YUAN** **Y# 276** **Weight:** 8.0000 g. **Composition:** 0.9170 Gold .2359 oz. AGW **Subject:** Year of the Goat **Obverse:** Chinese building and legend

| Date | Mintage | F | VF | XF | Unc | BU |
|---|---|---|---|---|---|---|
| 1991 Proof | 7,500 | Value: 175 | | | | |

**150 YUAN** **Y# 291** **Weight:** 8.0000 g. **Composition:** 0.9170 Gold .2359 oz. AGW **Subject:** Year of the Monkey **Obverse:** Pavilion of Emperor Teng

| Date | Mintage | F | VF | XF | Unc | BU |
|---|---|---|---|---|---|---|
| 1992 Proof | 5,000 | Value: 250 | | | | |

**150 YUAN** **Y# 355** **Weight:** 373.2360 g. **Composition:** 0.9990 Silver 12.0000 oz. ASW **Obverse:** Temple of Harmony **Reverse:** Two peacocks

| Date | Mintage | F | VF | XF | Unc | BU |
|---|---|---|---|---|---|---|
| 1993 Proof | 500 | Value: 650 | | | | |

**150 YUAN** **Y# 428** **Weight:** 622.0400 g. **Composition:** 0.9990 Silver 20.0000 oz. ASW **Reverse:** Unicorn **Note:** Similar to 10 Yuan, Y#420.

| Date | Mintage | F | VF | XF | Unc | BU |
|---|---|---|---|---|---|---|
| 1994 Proof | 500 | Value: 500 | | | | |

**150 YUAN** **Y# 699** **Weight:** 622.0400 g. **Composition:** 0.9990 Silver 20.0000 oz. ASW **Obverse:** Mythical animal **Reverse:** Unicorn with offspring **Size:** 98 mm. **Note:** Illustration reduced.

| Date | Mintage | F | VF | XF | Unc | BU |
|---|---|---|---|---|---|---|
| 1995 | — | — | — | — | 450 | — |

**150 YUAN** **Y# 884** **Weight:** 622.0400 g. **Composition:** 0.9990 Silver 20.0000 oz. ASW **Obverse:** Eastern unicorn **Reverse:** Western unicorn

| Date | Mintage | F | VF | XF | Unc | BU |
|---|---|---|---|---|---|---|
| 1996 Proof | 500 | Value: 600 | | | | |

**200 YUAN** **Y# 28** **Weight:** 8.4700 g. **Composition:** 0.9170 Gold .2497 oz. AGW **Subject:** Chinese Bronze Age Finds **Obverse:** State seal **Reverse:** Leopard

| Date | Mintage | F | VF | XF | Unc | BU |
|---|---|---|---|---|---|---|
| 1981 Proof | 1,000 | Value: 350 | | | | |

**200 YUAN** **Y# 29** **Weight:** 8.4700 g. **Composition:** 0.9170 Gold .2497 oz. AGW **Subject:** Chinese Bronze Age Finds **Obverse:** State seal **Reverse:** Winged creature

| Date | Mintage | F | VF | XF | Unc | BU |
|---|---|---|---|---|---|---|
| 1981 Proof | 1,000 | Value: 550 | | | | |

**200 YUAN** **Y# 37** **Weight:** 8.4700 g. **Composition:** 0.9170 Gold .2497 oz. AGW **Subject:** World Cup Soccer

| Date | Mintage | F | VF | XF | Unc | BU |
|---|---|---|---|---|---|---|
| 1982 Proof | 1,261 | Value: 350 | | | | |

**200 YUAN** **Y# 39** **Weight:** 8.4700 g. **Composition:** 0.9170 Gold .2497 oz. AGW **Subject:** Year of the Dog

| Date | Mintage | F | VF | XF | Unc | BU |
|---|---|---|---|---|---|---|
| 1982 Proof | 2,500 | Value: 600 | | | | |

**200 YUAN** **Y# 209** **Weight:** 62.2060 g. **Composition:** 0.9990 Gold 2.0000 oz. AGW **Reverse:** Phoenix and dragon

| Date | Mintage | F | VF | XF | Unc | BU |
|---|---|---|---|---|---|---|
| 1989 Proof | 2,538 | Value: 850 | | | | |

**200 YUAN** Y# 700 **Weight:** 1000.0000 g. **Composition:** 0.9990 Silver 32.1895 oz. ASW **Subject:** Completion of 150 Yuan Lunar - Animal Coin Series **Size:** 120 mm. **Note:** Illustration reduced.

| Date | Mintage | F | VF | XF | Unc | BU |
|---|---|---|---|---|---|---|
| 1992 Proof | 185 | Value: 1,250 | | | | |

**200 YUAN** Y# 816 **Weight:** 1000.0000 g. **Composition:** 0.9990 Silver 32.1895 oz. ASW **Subject:** 50th Anniversary - Return of Taiwan to China **Obverse:** Great Wall **Reverse:** Taiwan and China maps **Size:** 100 mm.

| Date | Mintage | F | VF | XF | Unc | BU |
|---|---|---|---|---|---|---|
| 1995 Proof | 100 | Value: 2,100 | | | | |

**200 YUAN** Y# 712 **Weight:** 1000.0000 g. **Composition:** 0.9990 Silver 32.1895 oz. ASW **Subject:** Sino - Thailand Friendship **Obverse:** Forbidden City and Thai Royal Palace **Reverse:** 2 Buddha statues **Note:** Similar to 10 Yuan, Y#711.

| Date | Mintage | F | VF | XF | Unc | BU |
|---|---|---|---|---|---|---|
| 1997 Proof | 880 | Value: 1,000 | | | | |

**200 YUAN** Y# 968 **Weight:** 1000.0000 g. **Composition:** 0.9990 Silver 32.1895 oz. ASW **Reverse:** Panda

| Date | Mintage | F | VF | XF | Unc | BU |
|---|---|---|---|---|---|---|
| 1998 Proof | 1,998 | Value: 650 | | | | |

**200 YUAN** Y# 976 **Weight:** 1000.2108 g. **Composition:** 0.9990 Silver 32.1253 oz. ASW **Subject:** Completion of 12 Year Lunar Cycle

| Date | Mintage | F | VF | XF | Unc | BU |
|---|---|---|---|---|---|---|
| 1999 Proof | 1,000 | Value: 1,200 | | | | |

**200 YUAN** Y# 971 **Weight:** 1000.2108 g. **Composition:** 0.9990 Silver 32.1253 oz. ASW **Obverse:** Temple of Heaven **Reverse:** Panda on rock **Size:** 100 mm. **Note:** Illustration reduced.

| Date | Mintage | F | VF | XF | Unc | BU |
|---|---|---|---|---|---|---|
| 1999 Proof | — | Value: 750 | | | | |

**200 YUAN** Y# 1045 **Weight:** 15.5518 g. **Composition:** 0.9990 Gold .5000 oz. AGW **Subject:** Year of the Snake **Shape:** Scalloped

| Date | Mintage | F | VF | XF | Unc | BU |
|---|---|---|---|---|---|---|
| 2001 Proof | 2,300 | Value: 320 | | | | |

**250 YUAN** Y# 22 **Weight:** 8.0000 g. **Composition:** 0.9170 Gold .2358 oz. AGW **Subject:** 1980 Winter Olympics **Obverse:** State seal **Reverse:** Alpine Skiing

| Date | Mintage | F | VF | XF | Unc | BU |
|---|---|---|---|---|---|---|
| 1980 Proof | 10,000 | Value: 150 | | | | |

**250 YUAN** Y# 33 **Weight:** 8.0000 g. **Composition:** 0.9170 Gold .2358 oz. AGW **Subject:** Year of the Rooster **Obverse:** Monument

| Date | Mintage | F | VF | XF | Unc | BU |
|---|---|---|---|---|---|---|
| 1981 Proof | 5,015 | Value: 375 | | | | |

**300 YUAN** Y# 23 **Weight:** 10.0000 g. **Composition:** 0.9170 Gold .2948 oz. AGW **Series:** 1980 Olympics **Subject:** Archery

| Date | Mintage | F | VF | XF | Unc | BU |
|---|---|---|---|---|---|---|
| 1980 Proof | 15,000 | Value: 200 | | | | |

**300 YUAN** Y# 515 **Weight:** 103.1250 g. **Composition:** 0.9990 Gold 3.3155 oz. AGW **Obverse:** Great Wall **Reverse:** Guanyin - Goddess of Mercy - With Child

| Date | Mintage | F | VF | XF | Unc | BU |
|---|---|---|---|---|---|---|
| 1994 Proof | 128 | Value: 2,800 | | | | |

**300 YUAN** Y# 1071 **Weight:** 999.9775 g. **Composition:** 0.9990 Silver 32.1500 oz. ASW **Subject:** Panda Billion. **Obverse:** Temple of Heaven. **Reverse:** Panda seated on leaves. **Edge:** Plain. **Size:** 100 mm. **Note:** Illustration reduced. Actual size: 100 mm.

| Date | Mintage | F | VF | XF | Unc | BU |
|---|---|---|---|---|---|---|
| 2000 Proof | 2,000 | Value: 750 | | | | |

**400 YUAN** Y# 4 **Weight:** 16.9500 g. **Composition:** 0.9170 Gold .4997 oz. AGW **Reverse:** 30th Anniversary of Peoples Republic - Tienanmen

| Date | Mintage | F | VF | XF | Unc | BU |
|---|---|---|---|---|---|---|
| ND(1979) Proof | 23,000 | Value: 200 | | | | |

**400 YUAN** Y# 5 **Weight:** 16.9500 g. **Composition:** 0.9170 Gold .4997 oz. AGW **Subject:** 30th Anniversary of Peoples Republic **Reverse:** Peoples Heroes Monument

| Date | Mintage | F | VF | XF | Unc | BU |
|---|---|---|---|---|---|---|
| ND(1979) Proof | 23,000 | Value: 200 | | | | |

**400 YUAN** Y# 6 **Weight:** 16.9500 g. **Composition:** 0.9170 Gold .4997 oz. AGW **Subject:** 30th Anniversary of Peoples Republic **Reverse:** Chairman Mao Memorial Hall

| Date | Mintage | F | VF | XF | Unc | BU |
|---|---|---|---|---|---|---|
| ND(1979) Proof | 23,000 | Value: 200 | | | | |

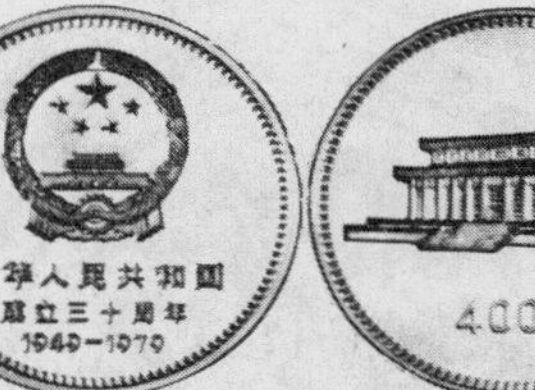


**400 YUAN** Y# 7 **Weight:** 16.9500 g. **Composition:** 0.9170 Gold .4997 oz. AGW **Subject:** 30th Anniversary of Peoples Republic **Reverse:** Great Hall of the People

| Date | Mintage | F | VF | XF | Unc | BU |
|---|---|---|---|---|---|---|
| ND(1979) Proof | 23,000 | Value: 200 | | | | |

**400 YUAN** Y# 30 **Weight:** 16.9500 g. **Composition:** 0.9170 Gold .4997 oz. AGW **Subject:** Chinese Bronze Age Finds **Reverse:** Rhinoceros

| Date | Mintage | F | VF | XF | Unc | BU |
|---|---|---|---|---|---|---|
| 1981 Proof | 1,000 | Value: 650 | | | | |

**400 YUAN** Y# 47 **Weight:** 13.3600 g. **Composition:** 0.9170 Gold .3939 oz. AGW **Subject:** 70th Anniversary of 1911 Revolution

| Date | Mintage | F | VF | XF | Unc | BU |
|---|---|---|---|---|---|---|
| 1981 Proof | 1,338 | Value: 1,150 | | | | |

**450 YUAN** **Y# 9** **Weight:** 17.1700 g. **Composition:** 0.9000 Gold .4968 oz. AGW **Series:** International Year of the Child

| Date | Mintage | F | VF | XF | Unc | BU |
|---|---|---|---|---|---|---|
| 1979 Proof | 12,000 | Value: 250 | | | | |

**500 YUAN** **Y# 147** **Weight:** 155.5150 g. **Composition:** 0.9990 Gold 5.0000 oz. AGW **Subject:** International Year of the Child **Size:** 60 mm. **Note:** Illustration reduced.

| Date | Mintage | F | VF | XF | Unc | BU |
|---|---|---|---|---|---|---|
| 1987 Proof | Est. 3,000 | Value: 2,400 | | | | |

**500 YUAN** **Y# 145** **Weight:** 155.5150 g. **Composition:** 0.9990 Gold 5.0000 oz. AGW **Subject:** Year of the Dragon **Obverse:** Great Wall **Size:** 60 mm. **Note:** Illustration reduced.

| Date | Mintage | F | VF | XF | Unc | BU |
|---|---|---|---|---|---|---|
| 1988 Proof | 3,000 | Value: 3,200 | | | | |

**500 YUAN** **Y# 233** **Weight:** 155.5150 g. **Composition:** 0.9990 Gold 5.0000 oz. AGW

| Date | Mintage | F | VF | XF | Unc | BU |
|---|---|---|---|---|---|---|
| 1988 Proof | 3,000 | Value: 2,500 | | | | |

**500 YUAN** **Y# 181** **Weight:** 155.5150 g. **Composition:** 0.9990 Gold 5.0000 oz. AGW **Subject:** Year of the Snake **Obverse:** State seal **Size:** 60 mm. **Note:** Illustration reduced.

| Date | Mintage | F | VF | XF | Unc | BU |
|---|---|---|---|---|---|---|
| 1989 Proof | 500 | Value: 3,000 | | | | |

**500 YUAN** **Y# 228** **Weight:** 155.5150 g. **Composition:** 0.9990 Gold 5.0000 oz. AGW **Subject:** Year of the Horse **Obverse:** Temple of Confucius **Size:** 60 mm. **Note:** Illustration reduced.

| Date | Mintage | F | VF | XF | Unc | BU |
|---|---|---|---|---|---|---|
| 1990 Proof | 500 | Value: 3,000 | | | | |

**500 YUAN** **Y# 277** **Weight:** 155.5150 g. **Composition:** 0.9990 Gold 5.0000 oz. AGW **Subject:** Year of the Goat **Obverse:** Temple of Heaven **Size:** 60 mm. **Note:** Illustration reduced.

| Date | Mintage | F | VF | XF | Unc | BU |
|---|---|---|---|---|---|---|
| 1991 Proof | 250 | Value: 3,200 | | | | |

**500 YUAN** **Y# 292** **Weight:** 155.5150 g. **Composition:** 0.9990 Gold 5.0000 oz. AGW **Subject:** Year of the Monkey **Obverse:** Chinese building **Size:** 60 mm. **Note:** Illustration reduced.

| Date | Mintage | F | VF | XF | Unc | BU |
|---|---|---|---|---|---|---|
| 1992 Proof | 99 | Value: 4,800 | | | | |

**500 YUAN** **Y# 369** **Weight:** 155.5150 g. **Composition:** 0.9990 Gold 5.0000 oz. AGW **Reverse:** Pandas

| Date | Mintage | F | VF | XF | Unc | BU |
|---|---|---|---|---|---|---|
| 1992 Proof | 99 | Value: 3,500 | | | | |

**500 YUAN** **Y# 384** **Weight:** 155.5150 g. **Composition:** 0.9990 Gold 5.0000 oz. AGW **Subject:** Year of the Rooster

| Date | Mintage | F | VF | XF | Unc | BU |
|---|---|---|---|---|---|---|
| 1993 Proof | 99 | Value: 3,900 | | | | |

**500 YUAN** **Y# 761** **Weight:** 155.5150 g. **Composition:** 0.9990 Gold 5.0000 oz. AGW **Obverse:** Temple of Heaven **Reverse:** Two pandas climbing tree stumps

| Date | Mintage | F | VF | XF | Unc | BU |
|---|---|---|---|---|---|---|
| 1993 Proof | 99 | Value: 3,500 | | | | |

**500 YUAN** **Y# 764** **Weight:** 155.5150 g. **Composition:** 0.9990 Gold 5.0000 oz. AGW **Subject:** Sun Yat-sen **Obverse:** Home of Sun Yat-sen **Reverse:** Portrait

| Date | Mintage | F | VF | XF | Unc | BU |
|---|---|---|---|---|---|---|
| 1993 Proof | 99 | Value: 4,500 | | | | |

**500 YUAN** **Y# 778** **Weight:** 155.5150 g. **Composition:** 0.9990 Gold 5.0000 oz. AGW **Subject:** Tomb of Emperor Huang **Obverse:** Great Wall **Reverse:** Tomb

| Date | Mintage | F | VF | XF | Unc | BU |
|---|---|---|---|---|---|---|
| 1993 Proof | 99 | Value: 3,000 | | | | |

**500 YUAN** **Y# 395** **Weight:** 155.5150 g. **Composition:** 0.9990 Gold 5.0000 oz. AGW **Subject:** Marco Polo **Size:** 60 mm. **Note:** Illustration reduced.

| Date | Mintage | F | VF | XF | Unc | BU |
|---|---|---|---|---|---|---|
| 1993 Proof | 100 | Value: 2,400 | | | | |

**500 YUAN** **Y# 407** **Weight:** 155.5150 g. **Composition:** 0.9990 Gold 5.0000 oz. AGW **Subject:** Chinese Gods Fu, Lu and Shu **Size:** 60 mm. **Note:** Illustration reduced.

| Date | Mintage | F | VF | XF | Unc | BU |
|---|---|---|---|---|---|---|
| 1993 Proof | 99 | Value: 2,900 | | | | |

**500 YUAN** **Y# 415** **Weight:** 155.5150 g. **Composition:** 0.9990 Gold 5.0000 oz. AGW **Subject:** Chairman Mao **Size:** 60 mm. **Note:** Illustration reduced.

| Date | Mintage | F | VF | XF | Unc | BU |
|---|---|---|---|---|---|---|
| 1993 Proof | 100 | Value: 4,250 | | | | |

**500 YUAN** **Y# 417** **Weight:** 155.5150 g. **Composition:** 0.9990 Gold 5.0000 oz. AGW **Subject:** Yandi, Semi-mythical First Emperor **Obverse:** State seal **Size:** 60 mm. **Note:** Illustration reduced.

| Date | Mintage | F | VF | XF | Unc | BU |
|---|---|---|---|---|---|---|
| 1993 Proof | 99 | Value: 2,800 | | | | |

**500 YUAN** **Y# 356** **Weight:** 155.5150 g. **Composition:** 0.9990 Gold 5.0000 oz. AGW **Obverse:** Temple of Harmony **Reverse:** Two peacocks **Note:** Similar to 100 Yuan, Y#356.

| Date | Mintage | F | VF | XF | Unc | BU |
|---|---|---|---|---|---|---|
| 1993 Proof | 99 | Value: 4,000 | | | | |

**500 YUAN** **Y# 429** **Weight:** 155.5150 g. **Composition:** 0.9990 Gold 5.0000 oz. AGW **Reverse:** Unicorn **Note:** Similar to 10 Yuan, Y#420.

| Date | Mintage | F | VF | XF | Unc | BU |
|---|---|---|---|---|---|---|
| 1994 Proof | 99 | Value: 3,900 | | | | |

**500 YUAN** **Y# 449** **Weight:** 155.5150 g. **Composition:** 0.9990 Gold 5.0000 oz. AGW **Obverse:** Taiwan Temple **Reverse:** Buddha Statue **Size:** 60 mm. **Note:** Illustration reduced.

| Date | Mintage | F | VF | XF | Unc | BU |
|---|---|---|---|---|---|---|
| 1994 Proof | 76 | Value: 3,750 | | | | |

**500 YUAN** **Y# 462** **Weight:** 155.5150 g. **Composition:** 0.9990 Gold 5.0000 oz. AGW **Subject:** Children At Play **Reverse:** Two children with cat **Size:** 60 mm. **Note:** Illustration reduced.

| Date | Mintage | F | VF | XF | Unc | BU |
|---|---|---|---|---|---|---|
| 1994 Proof | 99 | Value: 3,200 | | | | |

**500 YUAN** **Y# 701** **Weight:** 155.5150 g. **Composition:** 0.9990 Gold 5.0000 oz. AGW **Subject:** Sino-Singapore Friendship **Note:** Illustration reduced.

| Date | Mintage | F | VF | XF | Unc | BU |
|---|---|---|---|---|---|---|
| 1994 Proof | 91 | Value: 3,250 | | | | |

**500 YUAN** **Y# 389** **Weight:** 155.5150 g. **Composition:** 0.9990 Gold 5.0000 oz. AGW **Subject:** Year of the Dog

| Date | Mintage | F | VF | XF | Unc | BU |
|---|---|---|---|---|---|---|
| 1994 Proof | 99 | Value: 3,900 | | | | |

**500 YUAN** **Y# 639** **Weight:** 155.5150 g. **Composition:** 0.9990 Gold 5.0000 oz. AGW **Obverse:** Temple of Heaven **Reverse:** Two pandas, one in tree

| Date | Mintage | F | VF | XF | Unc | BU |
|---|---|---|---|---|---|---|
| 1994 Proof | 99 | Value: 3,500 | | | | |

**500 YUAN** **Y# 467** **Weight:** 155.5150 g. **Composition:** 0.9990 Gold 5.0000 oz. AGW **Subject:** Year of the Pig

| Date | Mintage | F | VF | XF | Unc | BU |
|---|---|---|---|---|---|---|
| 1995 Proof | 99 | Value: 3,900 | | | | |

**500 YUAN** **Y# 656** **Weight:** 155.5150 g. **Composition:** 0.9990 Gold 5.0000 oz. AGW **Subject:** Unicorn **Obverse:** Eastern unicorn. **Reverse:** Unicorn mother and baby **Edge:** Reeded. **Size:** 60 mm.

| Date | Mintage | F | VF | XF | Unc | BU |
|---|---|---|---|---|---|---|
| 1995 Proof | 99 | Value: 3,900 | | | | |

**500 YUAN** **Y# 793** **Ring Weight:** 62.2070 g. **Ring Composition:** 0.9990 Silver 2.0000 oz. ASW **Center Weight:** 155.5175 g. **Center Composition:** 0.9999 Gold 5.0000 oz. AGW **Obverse:** Temple of Heaven **Reverse:** Two pandas sitting on rock

| Date | Mintage | F | VF | XF | Unc | BU |
|---|---|---|---|---|---|---|
| 1995 Proof | 199 | Value: 2,750 | | | | |

**500 YUAN** **Y# 817** **Weight:** 155.5175 g. **Composition:** 0.9999 Gold 5.0000 oz. AGW **Subject:** 50th Anniversary - Taiwan's Return to China **Obverse:** Great Wall **Reverse:** Taiwan and China maps

| Date | Mintage | F | VF | XF | Unc | BU |
|---|---|---|---|---|---|---|
| 1995 Proof | 99 | Value: 3,000 | | | | |

**500 YUAN** **Y# 824** **Weight:** 155.5175 g. **Composition:** 0.9999 Gold 5.0000 oz. AGW **Subject:** Zheng Chenggong **Obverse:** Chiqian Building **Reverse:** Standing figure with flag and ships

| Date | Mintage | F | VF | XF | Unc | BU |
|---|---|---|---|---|---|---|
| 1995 Proof | 99 | Value: 2,400 | | | | |

**500 YUAN** **Y# 834** **Weight:** 155.5175 g. **Composition:** 0.9999 Gold 5.0000 oz. AGW **Subject:** Romance of the Three Kingdoms Series **Obverse:** Luo Guanzhong **Reverse:** Three heroes of Shu Han

| Date | Mintage | F | VF | XF | Unc | BU |
|---|---|---|---|---|---|---|
| 1995 Proof | 99 | Value: 2,400 | | | | |

**500 YUAN** **Y# 594** **Weight:** 155.5150 g. **Composition:** 0.9990 Gold 5.0000 oz. AGW **Reverse:** Nu Wa Rising **Size:** 60 mm. **Note:** Illustration reduced.

| Date | Mintage | F | VF | XF | Unc | BU |
|---|---|---|---|---|---|---|
| 1995 Proof | 99 | Value: 3,250 | | | | |

**500 YUAN** **Y# 649** **Weight:** 155.5150 g. **Composition:** 0.9990 Gold 5.0000 oz. AGW **Reverse:** Dragon boat **Size:** 60 mm. **Note:** Illustration reduced.

| Date | Mintage | F | VF | XF | Unc | BU |
|---|---|---|---|---|---|---|
| 1995 Proof | 99 | Value: 6,000 | | | | |

**500 YUAN** **Y# 533** **Weight:** 155.5150 g. **Composition:** 0.9990 Gold 5.0000 oz. AGW **Subject:** Return of Hong Kong to China - Series I **Obverse:** Bust of Deng Xiaoping over Hong Kong city view **Note:** Similar to 10 Yuan, Y#531.

| Date | Mintage | F | VF | XF | Unc | BU |
|---|---|---|---|---|---|---|
| 1995 Proof | 228 | Value: 4,250 | | | | |

**500 YUAN** **Y# 657** **Weight:** 155.5175 g. **Composition:** 0.9999 Gold 5.0000 oz. AGW **Obverse:** Western unicorn on hind legs, surrounded by roses **Reverse:** Eastern unicorn standing

| Date | Mintage | F | VF | XF | Unc | BU |
|---|---|---|---|---|---|---|
| 1996 Proof | 108 | Value: 3,900 | | | | |

**500 YUAN** **Y# 659** **Weight:** 155.5175 g. **Composition:** 0.9999 Gold 5.0000 oz. AGW **Subject:** Return of Hong Kong to China - Series II

| Date | Mintage | F | VF | XF | Unc | BU |
|---|---|---|---|---|---|---|
| 1996 Proof | 228 | Value: 3,000 | | | | |

**500 YUAN** **Y# 663** **Weight:** 155.5175 g. **Composition:** 0.9999 Gold 5.0000 oz. AGW **Subject:** Year of the Rat

| Date | Mintage | F | VF | XF | Unc | BU |
|---|---|---|---|---|---|---|
| 1996 Proof | 99 | Value: 4,000 | | | | |

**500 YUAN** **Y# 882** **Weight:** 155.5175 g. **Composition:** 0.9990 Gold 5.0000 oz. AGW **Subject:** Romance of the Three Kingdoms Series **Obverse:** Bust of Luo Guanzhong **Reverse:** Guan Du on horseback leading troops

| Date | Mintage | F | VF | XF | Unc | BU |
|---|---|---|---|---|---|---|
| 1996 Proof | 99 | Value: 2,400 | | | | |

**500 YUAN** **Y# 1020** **Ring Weight:** 62.2070 g. **Ring Composition:** 0.9990 Silver 2.0000 oz. ASW **Center Weight:** 155.5175 g. **Center Composition:** 0.9990 Gold 5.0000 oz. AGW **Reverse:** Panda

| Date | Mintage | F | VF | XF | Unc | BU |
|---|---|---|---|---|---|---|
| 1996 Proof | 199 | Value: 2,750 | | | | |

**500 YUAN** **Y# 672** **Weight:** 155.5175 g. **Composition:** 0.9990 Gold 5.0000 oz. AGW **Subject:** Year of the Ox

| Date | Mintage | F | VF | XF | Unc | BU |
|---|---|---|---|---|---|---|
| 1997 Proof | 99 | Value: 3,900 | | | | |

**500 YUAN** **Y# 904** **Weight:** 155.5175 g. **Composition:** 0.9990 Gold 5.0000 oz. AGW **Subject:** Return of Hong Kong to China - Series III **Obverse:** Tiananmen Square **Reverse:** Bust of Deng Xiaoping above city

| Date | Mintage | F | VF | XF | Unc | BU |
|---|---|---|---|---|---|---|
| 1997 Proof | 228 | Value: 3,500 | | | | |

**500 YUAN** **Y# 907** **Weight:** 155.5175 g. **Composition:** 0.9990 Gold 5.0000 oz. AGW **Subject:** Return of Macao to China **Obverse:** Tiananmen Square **Reverse:** Deng Xiaoping standing viewing Macao

| Date | Mintage | F | VF | XF | Unc | BU |
|---|---|---|---|---|---|---|
| 1997 Proof | 228 | Value: 3,500 | | | | |

**500 YUAN** **Y# 1021** **Ring Weight:** 62.2070 g. **Ring Composition:** 0.9990 Silver 2.0000 oz. ASW **Center Weight:** 155.5175 g. **Center Composition:** 0.9990 Gold 5.0000 oz. AGW **Reverse:** Two pandas resting near stream

| Date | Mintage | F | VF | XF | Unc | BU |
|---|---|---|---|---|---|---|
| 1997 Proof | 199 | Value: 2,750 | | | | |

**500 YUAN** **Y# 1022** **Weight:** 155.5175 g. **Composition:** 0.9990 Gold 5.0000 oz. AGW **Subject:** Greeting Spring **Obverse:** Lantern **Reverse:** Children lighting firecrackers

| Date | Mintage | F | VF | XF | Unc | BU |
|---|---|---|---|---|---|---|
| 1997 Proof | 108 | Value: 2,250 | | | | |

**500 YUAN** **Y# 1029** **Weight:** 155.5175 g. **Composition:** 0.9990 Gold 5.0000 oz. AGW **Obverse:** Bust of Qi Bashi **Reverse:** Squirrels eating grapes

| Date | Mintage | F | VF | XF | Unc | BU |
|---|---|---|---|---|---|---|
| 1997 Proof | 99 | Value: 3,500 | | | | |

**500 YUAN** **Y# 1023** **Weight:** 155.5175 g. **Composition:** 0.9990 Gold 5.0000 oz. AGW **Subject:** Greeting Spring **Obverse:** Lantern **Reverse:** Children making kites

| Date | Mintage | F | VF | XF | Unc | BU |
|---|---|---|---|---|---|---|
| 1998 Proof | 128 | Value: 2,500 | | | | |

**500 YUAN** **Y# 1024** **Weight:** 155.5175 g. **Composition:** 0.9990 Gold 5.0000 oz. AGW **Subject:** Year of the Tiger

| Date | Mintage | F | VF | XF | Unc | BU |
|---|---|---|---|---|---|---|
| 1998 Proof | 99 | Value: 3,900 | | | | |

**500 YUAN** **Y# 1025** **Weight:** 155.5175 g. **Composition:** 0.9990 Gold 5.0000 oz. AGW **Subject:** Year of the Rabbit

| Date | Mintage | F | VF | XF | Unc | BU |
|---|---|---|---|---|---|---|
| 1999 Proof | 99 | Value: 3,900 | | | | |

**500 YUAN** **Y# 1026** **Weight:** 155.5175 g. **Composition:** 0.9990 Gold 5.0000 oz. AGW **Subject:** 50th Anniversary of Peoples Republic Founding Ceremony **Note:** Rectangular.

| Date | Mintage | F | VF | XF | Unc | BU |
|---|---|---|---|---|---|---|
| 1999 Proof | 990 | Value: 3,500 | | | | |

**500 YUAN** **Y# 1027** **Weight:** 155.5175 g. **Composition:** 0.9990 Gold 5.0000 oz. AGW **Subject:** Year of the Dragon **Note:** Rectangular.

| Date | Mintage | F | VF | XF | Unc | BU |
|---|---|---|---|---|---|---|
| 2000 Proof | 108 | Value: 4,500 | | | | |

**500 YUAN** **Y# 1028** **Weight:** 155.5175 g. **Composition:** 0.9990 Gold 5.0000 oz. AGW **Subject:** Y2K

| Date | Mintage | F | VF | XF | Unc | BU |
|---|---|---|---|---|---|---|
| 2000 Proof | Est. 1,000 | — | — | — | — | — |

**800 YUAN** **Y# 31** **Weight:** 33.2000 g. **Composition:** 0.9170 Gold .9789 oz. AGW **Subject:** Chinese Bronze Age Finds **Obverse:** State seal **Reverse:** Elephant

| Date | Mintage | F | VF | XF | Unc | BU |
|---|---|---|---|---|---|---|
| 1981 Proof | 1,000 | Value: 1,000 | | | | |

**1000 YUAN** **Y# 66** **Weight:** 373.2360 g. **Composition:** 0.9990 Gold 12.0000 oz. AGW **Obverse:** Temple of Heaven **Reverse:** Panda seated **Size:** 70 mm. **Note:** Illustration reduced.

| Date | Mintage | F | VF | XF | Unc | BU |
|---|---|---|---|---|---|---|
| 1984 Proof | 250 | Value: 10,000 | | | | |

**Note:** A typical sealed proof exhibits some scuffing and is valued as above, while perfect examples can bring up to a 50% premium

**1000 YUAN** **Y# 118.1** **Weight:** 373.2360 g. **Composition:** 0.9990 Gold 12.0000 oz. AGW **Obverse:** Temple of Heaven **Reverse:** Panda eating bamboo shoot with cub **Size:** 70 mm. **Note:** Illustration reduced.

| Date | Mintage | F | VF | XF | Unc | BU |
|---|---|---|---|---|---|---|
| 1986 Proof | 2,550 | Value: 4,500 | | | | |

**1000 YUAN** **Y# 118.2** **Weight:** 373.2360 g. **Composition:** 0.9990 Gold 12.0000 oz. AGW **Edge:** Plain

| Date | Mintage | F | VF | XF | Unc | BU |
|---|---|---|---|---|---|---|
| 1986 2 known; Proof | — | Value: 45,000 | | | | |

**1000 YUAN** **Y# 157** **Weight:** 373.2360 g. **Composition:** 0.9990 Gold 12.0000 oz. AGW **Shape:** 70 **Note:** Illustration reduced.

| Date | Mintage | F | VF | XF | Unc | BU |
|---|---|---|---|---|---|---|
| 1987 Proof | 2,445 | Value: 4,500 | | | | |

**1000 YUAN** **Y# 146** **Weight:** 373.2360 g. **Composition:** 0.9990 Gold 12.0000 oz. AGW **Subject:** Year of the Dragon **Size:** 70 mm. **Note:** Illustration reduced.

| Date | Mintage | F | VF | XF | Unc | BU |
|---|---|---|---|---|---|---|
| 1988 Proof | 518 | Value: 7,000 | | | | |

**1000 YUAN** **Y# 234** **Weight:** 373.2360 g. **Composition:** 0.9990 Gold 12.0000 oz. AGW **Reverse:** Pandas in tree **Note:** Similar to 500 Yuan, KM#233.

| Date | Mintage | F | VF | XF | Unc | BU |
|---|---|---|---|---|---|---|
| 1988 Proof | 1,650 | Value: 5,000 | | | | |

**1000 YUAN** **Y# 182** **Weight:** 373.2360 g. **Composition:** 0.9990 Gold 12.0000 oz. AGW **Subject:** Year of the Snake **Obverse:** State seal **Size:** 70 mm. **Note:** Illustration reduced.

| Date | Mintage | F | VF | XF | Unc | BU |
|---|---|---|---|---|---|---|
| 1989 Proof | 200 | Value: 6,000 | | | | |

**1000 YUAN** **Y# 229** **Weight:** 373.2360 g. **Composition:** 0.9990 Gold 12.0000 oz. AGW **Subject:** Year of the Horse **Obverse:** Temple of Confucius **Size:** 70 mm. **Note:** Illustration reduced.

| Date | Mintage | F | VF | XF | Unc | BU |
|---|---|---|---|---|---|---|
| 1990 Proof | 500 | Value: 5,500 | | | | |

**1000 YUAN** **Y# 282** **Weight:** 373.2360 g. **Composition:** 0.9990 Gold 12.0000 oz. AGW **Obverse:** Temple of Heaven **Reverse:** Three pandas **Size:** 70 mm.

| Date | Mintage | F | VF | XF | Unc | BU |
|---|---|---|---|---|---|---|
| 1990 Proof | 500 | Value: 5,250 | | | | |

**1000 YUAN** **Y# 371** **Weight:** 373.2360 g. **Composition:** 0.9990 Gold 12.0000 oz. AGW **Reverse:** Pandas

| Date | Mintage | F | VF | XF | Unc | BU |
|---|---|---|---|---|---|---|
| 1991 Proof | 400 | Value: 5,250 | | | | |

**1000 YUAN** **Y# 278** **Weight:** 373.2360 g. **Composition:** 0.9990 Gold 12.0000 oz. AGW **Subject:** Year of the Goat **Obverse:** Chinese building and legend **Note:** Illustration reduced.

| Date | Mintage | F | VF | XF | Unc | BU |
|---|---|---|---|---|---|---|
| 1991 Proof | 200 | Value: 5,500 | | | | |

**1000 YUAN** **Y# 293** **Weight:** 373.2360 g. **Composition:** 0.9990 Gold 12.0000 oz. AGW **Subject:** Year of the Monkey **Obverse:** Chinese building **Note:** Illustration reduced.

| Date | Mintage | F | VF | XF | Unc | BU |
|---|---|---|---|---|---|---|
| 1992 Proof | 99 | Value: 7,000 | | | | |

**1000 YUAN** **Y# 372** **Weight:** 373.2360 g. **Composition:** 0.9990 Gold 12.0000 oz. AGW **Reverse:** Pandas

| Date | Mintage | F | VF | XF | Unc | BU |
|---|---|---|---|---|---|---|
| 1992 Proof | 99 | Value: 5,750 | | | | |

**1000 YUAN** **Y# 385** **Weight:** 373.2360 g. **Composition:** 0.9990 Gold 12.0000 oz. AGW **Subject:** Year of the Rooster

| Date | Mintage | F | VF | XF | Unc | BU |
|---|---|---|---|---|---|---|
| 1993 Proof | 99 | Value: 6,500 | | | | |

**1000 YUAN** **Y# 762** **Weight:** 373.2360 g. **Composition:** 0.9990 Gold 12.0000 oz. AGW **Obverse:** Temple of Heaven **Reverse:** Panda family of three

| Date | Mintage | F | VF | XF | Unc | BU |
|---|---|---|---|---|---|---|
| 1993 Proof | 99 | Value: 5,750 | | | | |

**1000 YUAN** **Y# 390** **Weight:** 373.2360 g. **Composition:** 0.9990 Gold 12.0000 oz. AGW **Subject:** Year of the Dog

| Date | Mintage | F | VF | XF | Unc | BU |
|---|---|---|---|---|---|---|
| 1994 Proof | 99 | Value: 6,500 | | | | |

**1000 YUAN** Y# 468 **Weight:** 373.2360 g. **Composition:** 0.9990 Gold 12.0000 oz. AGW **Subject:** Year of the Pig

| Date | Mintage | F | VF | XF | Unc | BU |
|---|---|---|---|---|---|---|
| 1995 Proof | 99 | Value: 6,500 | | | | |

**1000 YUAN** Y# 664 **Weight:** 373.2360 g. **Composition:** 0.9990 Gold 12.0000 oz. AGW **Subject:** Year of the Rat

| Date | Mintage | F | VF | XF | Unc | BU |
|---|---|---|---|---|---|---|
| 1996 Proof | 99 | Value: 6,500 | | | | |

**1000 YUAN** Y# 673 **Weight:** 373.2360 g. **Composition:** 0.9990 Gold 12.0000 oz. AGW **Subject:** Year of the Ox

| Date | Mintage | F | VF | XF | Unc | BU |
|---|---|---|---|---|---|---|
| 1997 Proof | 99 | Value: 6,500 | | | | |

**1000 YUAN** Y# 1030 **Weight:** 373.2360 g. **Composition:** 0.9990 Gold 12.0000 oz. AGW **Subject:** Year of the Tiger

| Date | Mintage | F | VF | XF | Unc | BU |
|---|---|---|---|---|---|---|
| 1998 Proof | 99 | Value: 6,500 | | | | |

**1000 YUAN** Y# 1031 **Weight:** 373.2360 g. **Composition:** 0.9990 Gold 12.0000 oz. AGW **Subject:** Year of the Rabbit

| Date | Mintage | F | VF | XF | Unc | BU |
|---|---|---|---|---|---|---|
| 1999 Proof | 99 | Value: 6,500 | | | | |

**1500 YUAN** Y# 210 **Weight:** 622.6000 g. **Composition:** 0.9990 Gold 20.0000 oz. AGW **Reverse:** Phoenix and dragon

| Date | Mintage | F | VF | XF | Unc | BU |
|---|---|---|---|---|---|---|
| 1989 Proof | 250 | Value: 11,000 | | | | |

**1500 YUAN** Y# 232 **Weight:** 622.6000 g. **Composition:** 0.9990 Gold 20.0000 oz. AGW **Subject:** Anniversary of Peoples Republic **Obverse:** State seal above city view with fireworks in sky **Size:** 90 mm. **Note:** Illustration reduced.

| Date | Mintage | F | VF | XF | Unc | BU |
|---|---|---|---|---|---|---|
| 1989 Proof | 100 | Value: 30,000 | | | | |

**1500 YUAN** Y# 505 **Weight:** 562.5068 g. **Composition:** 0.9990 Gold 18.0850 oz. AGW **Reverse:** Guanyin - Goddess of Mercy - seated in flower **Size:** 85 mm. **Note:** Illustration reduced.

| Date | Mintage | F | VF | XF | Unc | BU |
|---|---|---|---|---|---|---|
| 1993 Proof | 88 | Value: 12,500 | | | | |

**1500 YUAN** Y# 357 **Weight:** 622.6000 g. **Composition:** 0.9990 Gold 20.0000 oz. AGW **Obverse:** Temple of Harmony **Reverse:** Two peacocks

| Date | Mintage | F | VF | XF | Unc | BU |
|---|---|---|---|---|---|---|
| 1993 Proof | 66 | Value: 12,500 | | | | |

**2000 YUAN** Y# 749 **Weight:** 1000.0000 g. **Composition:** 0.9990 Gold 32.1500 oz. AGW **Subject:** Chinese Inventions and Discoveries **Obverse:** Great Wall **Reverse:** Seismograph, similar to 100 Yuan, KM#338

| Date | Mintage | F | VF | XF | Unc | BU |
|---|---|---|---|---|---|---|
| 1992 Proof | 16 | — | — | — | — | — |

**2000 YUAN** Y# 402 **Weight:** 1000.0000 g. **Composition:** 0.9990 Gold 32.1500 oz. AGW **Subject:** Chinese inventions **Reverse:** First compass **Size:** 100 mm. **Note:** Illustration reduced.

| Date | Mintage | F | VF | XF | Unc | BU |
|---|---|---|---|---|---|---|
| 1992 Proof | 16 | — | — | — | — | — |

**2000 YUAN** Y# 702 **Weight:** 1000.0000 g. **Composition:** 0.9990 Gold 32.1500 oz. AGW **Subject:** Completion of 150 Yuan Lunar Animal Coin Series **Size:** 100 mm. **Note:** Illustration reduced.

| Date | Mintage | F | VF | XF | Unc | BU |
|---|---|---|---|---|---|---|
| 1992 Proof | 21 | — | — | — | — | — |

**2000 YUAN** Y# 703 **Weight:** 1000.0000 g. **Composition:** 0.9990 Gold 32.1500 oz. AGW **Subject:** Sino-Singapore Friendship **Size:** 112 mm. **Note:** Illustration reduced.

| Date | Mintage | F | VF | XF | Unc | BU |
|---|---|---|---|---|---|---|
| 1994 | 15 | — | — | — | 18,000 | — |

**2000 YUAN** Y# 430 **Weight:** 1000.0000 g. **Composition:** 0.9990 Gold 32.1500 oz. AGW **Reverse:** Unicorn **Note:** Similar to 10 Yuan, Y#420.

| Date | Mintage | F | VF | XF | Unc | BU |
|---|---|---|---|---|---|---|
| 1994 Proof | 20 | Value: 25,000 | | | | |

**2000 YUAN** Y# 660 **Weight:** 1000.0000 g. **Composition:** 0.9990 Gold 32.1500 oz. AGW **Subject:** Year of the Pig **Edge:** Scalloped

| Date | Mintage | F | VF | XF | Unc | BU |
|---|---|---|---|---|---|---|
| 1995 Proof | 15 | Value: 25,000 | | | | |

**2000 YUAN** Y# 818 **Weight:** 1000.0000 g. **Composition:** 0.9990 Gold 32.1500 oz. AGW **Subject:** 50th Anniversary - Taiwan's Return to China **Obverse:** Great Wall **Reverse:** Taiwan and China maps

| Date | Mintage | F | VF | XF | Unc | BU |
|---|---|---|---|---|---|---|
| 1995 Proof | 25 | Value: 20,000 | | | | |

**2000 YUAN** Y# 665 **Weight:** 1000.0000 g. **Composition:** 0.9990 Gold 32.1500 oz. AGW **Subject:** Year of the Rat **Shape:** Scalloped

| Date | Mintage | F | VF | XF | Unc | BU |
|---|---|---|---|---|---|---|
| 1996 Proof | 15 | Value: 25,000 | | | | |

**2000 YUAN** Y# 957 **Weight:** 1000.0000 g. **Composition:** 0.9990 Gold 32.1500 oz. AGW **Obverse:** Eastern unicorn **Reverse:** Western unicorn with maiden

| Date | Mintage | F | VF | XF | Unc | BU |
|---|---|---|---|---|---|---|
| 1996 Proof | 18 | Value: 20,000 | | | | |

**2000 YUAN** Y# 961 **Weight:** 1000.0000 g. **Composition:** 0.9990 Gold 32.1500 oz. AGW **Reverse:** Panda

| Date | Mintage | F | VF | XF | Unc | BU |
|---|---|---|---|---|---|---|
| 1997 Proof | 58 | Value: 15,000 | | | | |

**2000 YUAN** Y# 674 **Weight:** 1000.0000 g. **Composition:** 0.9990 Gold 32.1500 oz. AGW **Subject:** Year of the Ox

| Date | Mintage | F | VF | XF | Unc | BU |
|---|---|---|---|---|---|---|
| 1997 Proof | 15 | Value: 25,000 | | | | |

**2000 YUAN** Y# 1036 **Weight:** 1000.0000 g. **Composition:** 0.9990 Gold 32.1500 oz. AGW **Reverse:** Panda

| Date | Mintage | F | VF | XF | Unc | BU |
|---|---|---|---|---|---|---|
| 1998 Proof | 58 | Value: 15,000 | | | | |

**2000 YUAN** Y# 967 **Weight:** 1000.0000 g. **Composition:** 0.9990 Gold 32.1500 oz. AGW **Subject:** Year of the Tiger **Shape:** Scalloped

| Date | Mintage | F | VF | XF | Unc | BU |
|---|---|---|---|---|---|---|
| 1998 Proof | 15 | Value: 25,000 | | | | |

**2000 YUAN** Y# 975 **Weight:** 1000.0000 g. **Composition:** 0.9990 Gold 32.1500 oz. AGW **Subject:** Year of the Rabbit **Shape:** Scalloped

| Date | Mintage | F | VF | XF | Unc | BU |
|---|---|---|---|---|---|---|
| 1999 Proof | 15 | Value: 25,000 | | | | |

**2000 YUAN** Y# 972 **Weight:** 1000.2108 g. **Composition:** 0.9990 Gold 32.1253 oz. AGW **Obverse:** Temple of Heaven **Reverse:** Panda on rock **Note:** Similar to 200 Yuan, KM#971.

| Date | Mintage | F | VF | XF | Unc | BU |
|---|---|---|---|---|---|---|
| 1999 Proof | 68 | Value: 15,000 | | | | |

**2000 YUAN** Y# 977 **Weight:** 1000.2108 g. **Composition:** 0.9990 Gold 32.1253 oz. AGW **Subject:** Year of the Dragon **Size:** Scalloped mm.

| Date | Mintage | F | VF | XF | Unc | BU |
|---|---|---|---|---|---|---|
| 2000 Proof | 15 | Value: 30,000 | | | | |

**2000 YUAN** Y# 1046 **Weight:** 155.5175 g. **Composition:** 0.9990 Gold 5.0000 oz. AGW **Subject:** Year of the Snake **Shape:** Rectangle

| Date | Mintage | F | VF | XF | Unc | BU |
|---|---|---|---|---|---|---|
| 2001 Proof | 118 | Value: 3,500 | | | | |

**10000 YUAN** Y# 358 **Weight:** 4851.6001 g. **Composition:** 0.9990 Gold 156.000 oz. AGW **Subject:** 10th Anniversary of Gold Panda Issue **Obverse:** Temple of Heaven

| Date | Mintage | F | VF | XF | Unc | BU |
|---|---|---|---|---|---|---|
| 1991 Proof | 10 | Value: 120,000 | | | | |

**10000 YUAN** Y# 1052 **Weight:** 1000.2108 g. **Composition:** 0.9990 Gold 32.1575 oz. AGW **Reverse:** Dragons **Shape:** Scalloped

| Date | Mintage | F | VF | XF | Unc | BU |
|---|---|---|---|---|---|---|
| 2000 Proof | 15 | Value: 30,000 | | | | |

**10000 YUAN** Y# 1047 **Weight:** 1000.2108 g. **Composition:** 0.9990 Gold 32.1575 oz. AGW **Subject:** Year of the Snake **Shape:** Scalloped

| Date | Mintage | F | VF | XF | Unc | BU |
|---|---|---|---|---|---|---|
| 2001 Proof | 15 | Value: 25,000 | | | | |

**30000 YUAN** Y# 1070 **Weight:** 8228.4492 g. **Composition:** 0.9999 Gold 264.5506 oz. AGW **Subject:** Third Millennium - House of Borbon - Philip V **Obverse:** China Centenary Altar. **Reverse:** Denominations. **Edge:** Plain. **Size:** 180 mm. **Note:** Illustration reduced. Actual size: 180 mm.

| Date | Mintage | F | VF | XF | Unc | BU |
|---|---|---|---|---|---|---|
| 2000 Proof | 20 | — | — | — | — | — |

## GOLD BULLION COINAGE

**1/10 OUNCE** Y# 40 **Weight:** 3.1103 g. **Composition:** 0.9990 Gold .1000 oz. AGW **Obverse:** Similar to 1 Ounce, Y#43

| Date | Mintage | F | VF | XF | Unc | BU |
|---|---|---|---|---|---|---|
| 1982 | 75,000 | — | — | — | 90.00 | — |

**1/4 OUNCE** Y# 41 **Weight:** 7.7758 g. **Composition:** 0.9990 Gold .2500 oz. AGW **Obverse:** Similar to 1 Ounce, Y#43

| Date | Mintage | F | VF | XF | Unc | BU |
|---|---|---|---|---|---|---|
| 1982 | 40,000 | — | — | — | 165 | — |

**1/2 OUNCE** Y# 42 **Weight:** 15.5517 g. **Composition:** 0.9990 Gold .5000 oz. AGW **Obverse:** Similar to 1 Ounce, Y#43

| Date | Mintage | F | VF | XF | Unc | BU |
|---|---|---|---|---|---|---|
| 1982 | 13,000 | — | — | — | 400 | — |

**OUNCE** Y# 43 **Weight:** 31.1035 g. **Composition:** 0.9990 Gold 1.0000 oz. AGW

| Date | Mintage | F | VF | XF | Unc | BU |
|---|---|---|---|---|---|---|
| 1982 | 16,000 | — | — | — | 950 | — |

## PATTERNS

Including off metal strikes

| KM# | Date | Mintage | Identification | Issue Price | Mkt Val |
|---|---|---|---|---|---|
| Pn1 | 1983 | — | 5 Yuan. (No Composition). Silvered base metal. | — | 600 |
| Pn2 | 1983 | — | 100 Yuan. Gilt Bronze. | — | 600 |
| Pn3 | 1985 | — | 200 Yuan. Gold. Decade for Women, KM#89. | — | — |
| Pn9 | 1991 | — | 10000 Yuan. Gold. Y#358. | — | — |
| Pn4 | 1991 | — | Yuan. Nickel Plated Steel. Raised character "pattern". Y#284. | — | 100 |
| Pn5 | 1991 | — | Yuan. Nickel Plated Steel. Raised character "pattern". Y#285. | — | 100 |
| Pn6 | 1991 | — | Yuan. Nickel Plated Steel. Raised character "pattern". Y#287. | — | 100 |
| Pn7 | 1991 | — | Yuan. Nickel Plated Steel. Raised character "pattern". Y#315. | — | 150 |
| Pn8 | 1991 | — | Yuan. Nickel Plated Steel. Raised character "pattern". Y#317. | — | 150 |

## PIEFORTS

| KM# | Date | Mintage | Identification | Issue Price | Mkt Val |
|---|---|---|---|---|---|
| P1 | 1979 | 3,500 | 35 Yuan. 0.8000 Silver. Y#8. | — | 200 |
| P2 | 1979 | 500 | 450 Yuan. 0.9000 Gold. Y#9. | — | 2,250 |
| P3 | 1980 | 2,500 | Yuan. Copper. Y#10. | — | 15.00 |
| P4 | 1980 | 2,500 | Yuan. Copper. Y#11. | — | 15.00 |
| P5 | 1980 | 2,500 | Yuan. Copper. Y#12. | — | 15.00 |
| P6 | 1980 | 2,500 | Yuan. Copper. Y#13. | — | 15.00 |
| P7 | 1980 | 1,000 | Yuan. Copper. Y#14. | — | 15.00 |
| P8 | 1980 | 1,000 | Yuan. Copper. Y#15. | — | 15.00 |
| P9 | 1980 | 1,000 | Yuan. Copper. Y#16. | — | 15.00 |
| P10 | 1980 | 1,000 | Yuan. Copper. Y#17. | — | 15.00 |
| P11 | 1980 | 2,000 | 15 Yuan. 0.8000 Silver. Archery. | — | 85.00 |
| P12 | 1980 | 2,000 | 20 Yuan. 0.8000 Silver. Y#18, Wrestling. | — | 85.00 |
| P13 | 1980 | 1,000 | 30 Yuan. 0.8000 Silver. Equestrian, Y#19. | 248 | 80.00 |
| P14 | 1980 | 1,000 | 30 Yuan. 0.8000 Silver. Soccer. | 248 | 80.00 |
| P15 | 1980 | 2,000 | 30 Yuan. 0.8000 Silver. Speed skating, Y#21. | 248 | 80.00 |
| P16 | 1980 | 2,000 | 30 Yuan. 0.8000 Silver. Alpine skiing. | — | 80.00 |
| P17 | 1980 | 2,000 | 30 Yuan. 0.8000 Silver. Biathalon. | — | 80.00 |
| P18 | 1980 | 2,000 | 30 Yuan. 0.8000 Silver. Figure skating. | — | 80.00 |
| P19 | 1980 | 360 | 250 Yuan. 0.9170 Gold. Alpine skiing, Y#22. | 1,750 | 850 |
| P20 | 1980 | 500 | 300 Yuan. 0.9170 Gold. Archery, Y#23. | — | 900 |
| P21 | 1992 | — | 5 Yuan. 0.9000 Silver. Ancient ship building, Y#331. | — | 60.00 |
| P22 | 1992 | — | 5 Yuan. 0.9000 Silver. First compass, Y#332. | — | 60.00 |
| P23 | 1992 | — | 5 Yuan. 0.9000 Silver. First seismograph, Y#333. | — | 60.00 |
| P24 | 1992 | — | 5 Yuan. 0.9000 Silver. Ancient kite flying, Y#334. | — | 60.00 |
| P25 | 1992 | — | 5 Yuan. 0.9000 Silver. Bronze metal working, Y#335. | — | 60.00 |
| P26 | 1997 | 80,000 | 5 Yuan. 0.9990 Silver. Y#916. | — | 30.00 |
| P27 | 1998 | — | 10 Yuan. 0.9990 Silver. Y#922. | — | 60.00 |

| KM# | Date | Mintage | Identification | Issue Price | Mkt Val |
|---|---|---|---|---|---|
| P28 | 1998 | 100,000 | 10 Yuan. 0.9990 Silver. Y#917. | — | 40.00 |

## MINT SETS

| KM# | Date | Mintage | Identification | Issue Price | Mkt Val |
|---|---|---|---|---|---|
| MS1 | 1979 (s) (3) | — | Y#1-3 Medal | — | 7.50 |
| MS2 | 1980(b) (7) | — | Y#1-3, 24-27 | — | 8.50 |
| MS3 | 1982 (4) | — | Y#40-43 | 750 | 3,400 |
| MS4 | 1986 (2) | — | KM#151 (2) | — | 12.50 |
| MS5 | 1990 (2) | — | Y#264-265 | — | 8.00 |
| MS7 | 1991 (2) | — | Y#316-317 | — | 5.00 |
| MS6 | 1991 (6) | — | Y#1-3, 328-330 | — | 5.50 |
| MS8 | 1992 (6) | — | Y#1-3, 328-330 | — | 5.50 |
| MS9 | 1993 (6) | — | Y#1-3, 328-330 | — | 5.50 |
| MS10 | 1994 (6) | — | Y#1-3, 328-330 | — | 5.50 |
| MS11 | 1995 (6) | — | Y#1-3, 328-330 | — | 5.50 |
| MS12 | 1996 (6) | — | Y#1-3, 328-330 | — | 5.50 |

## PROOF SETS

| KM# | Date | Mintage | Identification | Issue Price | Mkt Val |
|---|---|---|---|---|---|
| PS36 | 1992 (5) | 2,500 | P#21-25 Piefort | — | 350 |
| PS1 | 1979 (4) | 70,000 | Y#4-7 | 1,695 | 800 |
| PS2 | 1980 (14) | 1,000 | Y#10-23 | 1,750 | 425 |
| PS4 | 1980 (4) | — | Y#10-13 | — | 40.00 |
| PS5 | 1980 (4) | — | Y#14-17 | — | 45.00 |
| PS6 | 1980 (3) | 1,000 | Y#18-20 | — | 50.00 |
| PS3 | 1980 (7) | — | Y#1-3, 24-27 | — | 10.00 |
| PS8 | 1981 (4) | 1,000 | Y#28-31 | 2,950 | 2,550 |
| PS7 | 1981(s) (7) | 10,000 | Y#1-3, 24-27 Medal | — | 12.00 |
| PS9 | 1982(s) (7) | — | Y#1-3, 24-27 Medal | — | 10.00 |
| PS10 | 1983(s) (7) | — | Y#1-3, 24-27 Book | — | 12.50 |
| PS11 | 1983(s) (7) | — | Y#1-3, 24-27 Medal (paper cover) | — | 140 |
| PS13 | 1984 (4) | — | Y#68-71 | — | 90.00 |
| PS12 | 1984(y) (7) | — | Y#1-3, 24-27 Medal | — | 12.50 |
| PS14 | 1984 (3) | — | Y#85-87 | — | 22.50 |
| PS15 | 1985 (2) | — | Y#96-97 | 45.00 | 60.00 |
| PS16 | 1985(y) (7) | — | Y#1-3, 24-27 Medal | — | 12.00 |
| PS17 | 1985 (2) | — | Y#109-110 | 45.00 | 65.00 |
| PS18 | 1985 (4) | — | Y#90-93 | — | 115 |
| PS19 | 1986(y) (7) | — | Y#1-3, 24-27 Medal | 10.00 | 15.00 |
| PS21 | 1986 (4) | — | Y#113-116 | — | 110 |
| PS20 | 1986 (5) | 10,000 | Y#101-105 | — | 800 |
| PS23 | 1987 (2) | — | Y#133-134 | 278 | 115 |
| PS24 | 1987 (4) | — | Y#135-138 | — | 120 |
| PS22 | 1987 (5) | 10,000 | Y#124-128 | — | 800 |
| PS25 | 1988 (4) | — | Y#160-163 | 200 | 110 |
| PS26 | 1988 (5) | 10,000 | Y#152-156 | — | 900 |
| PS28 | 1989 (4) | — | Y#213-216 | — | 130 |
| PS27 | 1989 (5) | 8,000 | Y#187-191 | — | 950 |
| PS30 | 1990 (3) | 2,500 | Y#267-269 | 1,095 | 550 |
| PS31 | 1990 (2) | 2,000 | Y#266 and medal | 995 | 500 |
| PS29 | 1990 (5) | 5,000 | Y#238-242 | — | 1,000 |
| PS33 | 1991 (2) | 2,000 | Y#301 and medal | 575 | 350 |
| PS32 | 1991 (6) | — | Y#1-3, 328-330 | — | 6.50 |
| PS34 | 1991 (5) | 350 | Y#309-313 | — | 1,000 |
| PS37 | 1992 (5) | 1,000 | Y#331-335 | — | 4,500 |
| PS35 | 1992 (6) | — | Y#1-3, 328-330 | — | 6.50 |
| PS38 | 1992 (5) | — | Y#341-345 | — | 1,000 |
| PS39 | 1993 (4) | 2,000 | Y#441-444 | 200 | 140 |
| PS40 | 1993 (4) | 1,000 | Y#445-448 | 1,600 | 1,300 |
| PS41 | 1993 (3) | — | Y#352-354 | — | 925 |
| PS42 | 1993 (5) | — | Y#610-614 | — | 600 |
| PS44 | 1993 (5) | 100 | Y#1072-1076 | 1,875 | 1,875 |
| PS43 | 1993 (6) | — | Y#1-3, 328-330 | — | 8.00 |
| PS45 | 1994 (12) | 50 | Y#419, 420 Unc/Proof, 421-429 | — | 5,860 |
| PS46 | 1994 (11) | 50 | Y#419, 420 Unc/Proof, 421-428 | — | 4,360 |
| PS47 | 1994 (5) | 1,000 | Y#419, 421-423, 425 | — | 1,385 |
| PS48 | 1994 (4) | 2,500 | Y#419-421, 423 | 645 | 655 |
| PS49 | 1994 (3) | 1,000 | Y#420-424, 426 | — | 845 |
| PS50 | 1994 (2) | 400 | Y#420, 428 | — | 1,270 |
| PS51 | 1994 (5) | — | Y#431-434, 544 | — | 600 |
| PS52 | 1994 (6) | — | Y#1-3, 328-330 | — | 8.00 |
| PS53 | 1995 (3) | 2,000 | Y#469-471 | 485 | 500 |
| PS54 | 1995 (3) | 2,000 | Y#571-573 | — | 710 |
| PS55 | 1995 (2) | 3,000 | Y#469-470 | 89.00 | 90.00 |
| PS56 | 1995 (4) | 15,000 | Y#600-603 | — | 150 |
| PS57 | 1995 (4) | 9,000 | Y#588-591 | — | 160 |
| PS59 | 1995 (5) | 1,000 | Y#687, 736-739 | — | 1,385 |
| PS58 | 1995 (6) | — | Y#1-3, 328-330 | — | 8.00 |
| PS60 | 1996 (4) | 15,000 | Y#604-607 | — | 180 |
| PS61 | 1996 (4) | 8,000 | Y#595-598 | — | 240 |
| PS63 | 1996 (4) | 750 | Y#740-743 Plus bottle | — | 625 |
| PS62 | 1996 (6) | — | Y#1-3, 328-330 | — | 8.00 |
| PS64 | 1997 (4) | 28,000 | Y#936-939 | — | 200 |
| PS65 | 1998 (2) | 61,000 | China Y#727 and Canadian KM#316 | 72.50 | 70.00 |

# COLOMBIA

The Republic of Colombia, in the northwestern corner of South America, has an area of 440,831 sq. mi. (1,138,910 sq. km.) and a population of*42.3 million. Capital: Bogota. The economy is primarily agricultural with a mild, rich coffee being the chief crop. Colombia has the world's largest platinum deposits and important reserves of coal, iron ore, petroleum and limestone; other precious metals and emeralds are also mined. Coffee, crude oil, bananas, sugar and emeralds are exported.

The northern coast of present Colombia was one of the first parts of the American continent to be visited by Spanish navigators. At Darien in Panama is the site of the first permanent European settlement on the American mainland in 1510. New Granada, as Colombia was known until 1861, stemmed from the settlement of Santa Marta in 1525. New Granada was established as a Spanish colony in 1549. Independence was declared in 1810, and secured in 1819 when Simon Bolivar united Colombia, Venezuela, Panama and Ecuador as the Republic of Gran Colombia. Venezuela withdrew from the Republic in 1829; Ecuador in 1830; and Panama in 1903.

**MINT MARKS**

A, M – Medellin (capital), Antioquia (state)
B - BOGOTA
(D) Denver, USA
H – Birmingham (Heaton & Sons)
(m) - Medellin, w/o mint mark
(Mo) - Mexico City
NI - Numismatica Italiana, Arezzo, Italy mint marks stylized in wreath
(P) - Philadelphia
(S) - San Francisco, USA.
(W) - Waterbury, CT (USA, Scoville mint)

# REPUBLIC

## DECIMAL COINAGE

**CENTAVO** **KM# 275** **Composition:** Copper-Nickel **Note:** Erratically punched final two digits of date are common on these issues, especially 1935-1948. A very faint "17" is often observable beneath the final two digits on many dates of this type.

| Date | Mintage | F | VF | XF | Unc | BU |
|---|---|---|---|---|---|---|
| 1918 | 430,000 | 4.00 | 12.00 | 20.00 | 40.00 | — |
| 1919 | Inc. above | 15.00 | 25.00 | 37.50 | 65.00 | — |
| 1920(D) | 7,540,000 | 2.50 | 7.50 | 13.50 | 40.00 | — |
| 1921(D) | 12,460,000 | 1.25 | 6.00 | 12.00 | 22.50 | — |
| 1933(P) | 3,000,000 | 0.50 | 2.25 | 3.75 | 8.00 | — |
| 1935(P) | 5,000,000 | 0.50 | 3.00 | 5.00 | 10.00 | — |
| 1936 | 1,540,000 | 1.50 | 5.00 | 7.50 | 13.50 | — |
| 1938(P) | 7,920,000 | 0.15 | 0.25 | 1.00 | 3.00 | — |
| 1941B | 1,000,000 | 0.35 | 0.75 | 2.00 | 6.00 | — |
| 1946B | 2,096,000 | 0.30 | 0.55 | 1.50 | 4.00 | — |
| 1947/17B | 1,835,000 | 1.00 | 3.50 | 6.00 | 12.00 | — |
| 1947/37B | Inc. above | 1.00 | 3.50 | 6.00 | 12.00 | — |
| 1947/6B | Inc. above | 1.00 | 3.50 | 6.00 | 12.00 | — |
| 1947B | Inc. above | 0.35 | 0.75 | 1.50 | 3.75 | — |
| 1948/38B | 1,139,000 | 1.00 | 3.50 | 6.00 | 12.00 | — |
| 1948B | Inc. above | 0.35 | 0.75 | 2.00 | 4.50 | — |

**CENTAVO** **KM# 205** **Composition:** Bronze **Note:** Several date varieties exist.

| Date | Mintage | F | VF | XF | Unc | BU |
|---|---|---|---|---|---|---|
| 1942 | 1,000,000 | 0.20 | 1.00 | 3.00 | 6.50 | — |
| 1942B | Inc. above | 0.25 | 2.00 | 4.50 | 9.00 | — |
| 1943 | — | 0.15 | 0.35 | 1.00 | 3.00 | — |
| 1943B | 4,515,000 | 0.15 | 0.35 | 1.00 | 3.00 | — |
| 1944B | 4,515,000 | 0.15 | 0.35 | 1.00 | 3.00 | — |
| 1945 | 3,769,000 | 0.15 | 0.35 | 1.00 | 3.00 | — |
| 1945B | — | 0.15 | 0.35 | 1.00 | 3.00 | — |
| 1948B | 585,000 | 0.30 | 1.00 | 2.50 | 6.50 | — |
| 1949B | 4,255,000 | 0.15 | 0.35 | 1.00 | 3.50 | — |
| 1950B | 5,827,000 | 0.15 | 0.35 | 1.00 | 3.50 | — |

| Date | Mintage | F | VF | XF | Unc | BU |
|---|---|---|---|---|---|---|
| 1951B | Inc. above | 0.20 | 0.60 | 1.75 | 4.50 | — |
| 1957 | 2,500,000 | — | 0.10 | 0.20 | 1.00 | — |
| 1958 | 590,000 | 0.10 | 0.25 | 0.50 | 2.00 | — |
| 1959 | 2,677,000 | — | 0.10 | 0.20 | 1.00 | — |
| 1960 | 2,500,000 | — | 0.10 | 0.20 | 1.00 | — |
| 1961 Widely spaced date | 3,673,000 | 0.10 | 0.15 | 0.30 | 1.50 | — |
| 1961 Narrowly spaced date | Inc. above | — | 0.10 | 0.20 | 1.00 | — |
| 1962 | 4,065,000 | — | 0.10 | 0.20 | 1.00 | — |
| 1963 | 1,845,000 | 0.10 | 0.15 | 0.30 | 2.00 | — |
| 1964/44 | 3,165,000 | 0.10 | 0.30 | 0.75 | 2.50 | — |
| 1964 | Inc. above | 0.10 | 0.15 | 0.30 | 1.50 | — |
| 1965 Large date | 5,510,000 | — | 0.10 | 0.20 | 1.00 | — |
| 1965 Small date | Inc. above | — | 0.10 | 0.20 | 1.00 | — |
| 1966 | 3,910,000 | 0.10 | 0.15 | 0.30 | 1.50 | — |

**CENTAVO** **KM# 275a** **Composition:** Nickel Clad Steel **Note:** Erratically punched final two digits of date are common on these issues.

| Date | Mintage | F | VF | XF | Unc | BU |
|---|---|---|---|---|---|---|
| 1952B | Inc. above | 0.10 | 0.15 | 0.25 | 1.00 | — |
| 1954B | 5,080,000 | 0.10 | 0.15 | 0.25 | 1.00 | — |
| 1956 | 1,315,000 | 0.10 | 0.15 | 0.40 | 1.50 | — |
| 1957 | 900,000 | 0.15 | 0.25 | 0.50 | 2.50 | — |
| 1958/48 | — | 0.35 | 0.75 | 1.50 | 5.00 | — |
| 1958 | 1,596,000 | 0.10 | 0.15 | 0.40 | 2.00 | — |

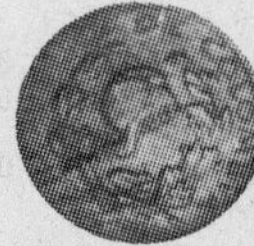

**CENTAVO** **KM# 218** **Composition:** Bronze **Subject:** Uprising Sesqucentennial **Note:** This and the other issues in the uprising commemorative series offer the usual design of the period with the dates 1810-1960 added at the bottom of the obverse.

| Date | Mintage | F | VF | XF | Unc | BU |
|---|---|---|---|---|---|---|
| ND(1960) | 500,000 | 0.60 | 1.50 | 3.00 | 6.50 | — |

**CENTAVO** **KM# 205a** **Composition:** Copper Clad Steel **Note:** Several date varieties exist.

| Date | Mintage | F | VF | XF | Unc | BU |
|---|---|---|---|---|---|---|
| 1967 | 5,730,000 | — | 0.10 | 0.15 | 0.25 | — |
| 1968 | 7,390,000 | — | 0.10 | 0.15 | 0.25 | — |
| 1969 | 6,870,000 | — | 0.10 | 0.15 | 0.25 | — |
| 1970 | 3,839,000 | — | 0.10 | 0.15 | 0.25 | — |
| 1971 | 3,020,000 | — | 0.10 | 0.20 | 0.50 | — |
| 1972 | 3,100,000 | — | 0.10 | 0.15 | 0.25 | — |
| 1973 | — | — | — | 0.10 | 0.20 | — |
| 1974 | 2,000,000 | — | — | 0.10 | 0.20 | — |
| 1975 | 1,000,000 | — | — | 0.10 | 0.20 | — |
| 1976 | 1,000,000 | — | — | 0.10 | 0.20 | — |
| 1977 | 900,000 | — | — | 0.10 | 0.20 | — |
| 1978 | 224,000 | — | 0.10 | 0.20 | 0.40 | — |

**2 CENTAVOS** **KM# 198** **Composition:** Copper-Nickel **Note:** Erratically punched final two digits exist for 1946-1947. A very faint "17" is often observable beneath the final two digits on many dates of this type.

| Date | Mintage | F | VF | XF | Unc | BU |
|---|---|---|---|---|---|---|
| 1918 | 930,000 | 8.00 | 15.00 | 38.00 | 85.00 | — |
| 1919 | Inc. above | 10.00 | 20.00 | 45.00 | 110 | — |
| 1920 | 3,855,000 | 1.00 | 2.25 | 7.50 | 15.00 | — |
| 1921 | 11,145,000 | 0.25 | 0.75 | 2.50 | 9.00 | — |
| 1922 10 pieces known | — | — | — | — | 400 | — |
| 1933(P) | 3,500,000 | 0.25 | 0.75 | 3.00 | 6.00 | — |
| 1935(P) | 2,500,000 | 0.25 | 0.75 | 3.00 | 6.00 | — |
| 1938(P) | 3,872,000 | 0.20 | 0.50 | 2.00 | 5.00 | — |
| 1941B | 500,000 | 0.75 | 1.50 | 2.75 | 6.50 | — |
| 1942B | 500,000 | 1.50 | 2.50 | 3.75 | 7.50 | — |
| 1946/36B | 2,593,000 | 1.25 | 2.50 | 6.00 | 12.00 | — |
| 1946B | Inc. above | 1.25 | 2.50 | 5.75 | 11.50 | — |
| 1947/3B | 1,337,000 | 1.00 | 2.00 | 4.50 | 10.00 | — |
| 1947/36B | Inc. above | 1.00 | 2.00 | 4.50 | 10.00 | — |
| 1947B | Inc. above | 0.50 | 1.00 | 2.50 | 5.50 | — |

**2 CENTAVOS** **KM# 210** **Composition:** Bronze

| Date | Mintage | F | VF | XF | Unc | BU |
|---|---|---|---|---|---|---|
| 1948B | 2,648,000 | 0.50 | 1.00 | 4.00 | 7.50 | — |
| 1949B | 1,278,000 | 0.50 | 1.00 | 4.50 | 8.50 | — |
| 1950B | 2,285,000 | 0.50 | 1.00 | 4.00 | 8.50 | — |

**2 CENTAVOS** **KM# 211** **Composition:** Aluminum-Bronze **Obverse:** Divided legend

| Date | Mintage | F | VF | XF | Unc | BU |
|---|---|---|---|---|---|---|
| 1952B Small date | 5,038,000 | — | 0.10 | 0.25 | 1.00 | — |
| 1965/3 | 1,830,000 | — | 0.15 | 0.20 | 0.35 | — |
| 1965 Large date | Inc. above | — | 0.10 | 0.20 | 0.85 | — |

**2 CENTAVOS** **KM# 214** **Composition:** Aluminum-Bronze **Obverse:** Continuous legend

| Date | Mintage | F | VF | XF | Unc | BU |
|---|---|---|---|---|---|---|
| 1955 Large date | 2,513,000 | 0.10 | 0.20 | 0.75 | 3.00 | — |
| 1955B Large date | Inc. above | — | 0.10 | 0.20 | 0.85 | — |
| 1959 Small date | 4,609,000 | — | 0.10 | 0.15 | 0.50 | — |

**2 CENTAVOS** **KM# 219** **Composition:** Aluminum-Bronze **Subject:** Uprising Sesquicentennial

| Date | Mintage | F | VF | XF | Unc | BU |
|---|---|---|---|---|---|---|
| ND(1960) | 250,000 | 1.00 | 1.65 | 2.25 | 5.00 | — |

**2-1/2 CENTAVOS** **KM# 190** **Composition:** Copper-Nickel

| Date | Mintage | F | VF | XF | Unc | BU |
|---|---|---|---|---|---|---|
| 1902(W) | 400,000 | — | — | 350 | 500 | — |

**5 CENTAVOS** **KM# 184** **Composition:** Copper-Nickel

| Date | Mintage | F | VF | XF | Unc | BU |
|---|---|---|---|---|---|---|
| 1902(W) | 400,000 | — | — | 550 | 700 | — |

**5 CENTAVOS** **KM# 191** **Weight:** 1.2500 g. **Composition:** 0.6660 Silver .0268 oz. ASW **Edge:** Plain

| Date | Mintage | F | VF | XF | Unc | BU |
|---|---|---|---|---|---|---|
| 1902(P) | 400,000 | 0.35 | 1.00 | 2.25 | 5.50 | — |

**5 CENTAVOS** **KM# 199** **Composition:** Copper-Nickel **Note:** Varieties exist. Erratically punched final two digits of date are common on these issues, especially 1935-1950. A very faint "17" is often observable beneath the final two digits on many dates of this type.

| Date | Mintage | F | VF | XF | Unc | BU |
|---|---|---|---|---|---|---|
| 1918 | 767,000 | 6.50 | 10.00 | 15.00 | 35.00 | — |
| 1919 | 1,926,000 | 2.50 | 4.00 | 9.00 | 22.50 | — |
| 1920 | 2,062,000 | 3.50 | 6.00 | 10.00 | 25.00 | — |
| 1920H | — | 3.50 | 6.00 | 10.00 | 25.00 | — |
| 1921 | 1,574,000 | 1.50 | 3.00 | 6.00 | 17.50 | — |
| 1921H | — | 1.50 | 3.00 | 6.00 | 17.50 | — |
| 1922 | 2,623,000 | 3.50 | 5.00 | 10.00 | 20.00 | — |
| 1922H | — | 3.50 | 5.00 | 10.00 | 20.00 | — |
| 1924 | 120,000 | 8.00 | 17.50 | 27.50 | 60.00 | — |
| 1933(P) | 2,000,000 | 0.75 | 1.50 | 2.50 | 5.00 | — |
| 1935/24 | 1,616,000 | — | — | — | — | — |
| 1935(P) | 10,000,000 | 0.50 | 1.50 | 2.00 | 4.00 | — |
| 1936 | — | 4.50 | 7.50 | 12.50 | 27.50 | — |
| 1938B | 2,000,000 | 1.50 | 3.50 | 5.00 | 10.00 | — |
| 1938 | 3,867,000 | 0.50 | 1.35 | 2.00 | 5.00 | — |
| 1938 Large 8 in date | Inc. above | 0.75 | 2.00 | 3.50 | 8.00 | — |
| 1939/5 | 2,000,000 | 0.75 | 1.75 | 3.50 | 8.00 | — |
| 1939 | Inc. above | 0.50 | 1.35 | 2.50 | 5.50 | — |
| 1941 | — | 2.75 | 5.00 | 7.50 | 18.00 | — |
| 1941B | 500,000 | 1.25 | 2.50 | 3.50 | 7.00 | — |
| 1946(P) (S) Small date | 40,000,000 | 0.20 | 0.50 | 0.75 | 2.00 | — |
| 1946 Large date | 3,330,000 | 2.00 | 4.00 | 7.50 | 15.00 | — |
| 1949B | 2,750,000 | 0.45 | 1.00 | 2.00 | 4.00 | — |
| 1949 | — | 1.75 | 3.00 | 4.50 | 10.00 | — |
| 1950B Large 50 in date | 3,611,000 | 0.45 | 1.00 | 2.00 | 4.00 | — |
| 1950B Small 50 in date | Inc. above | 0.45 | 1.00 | 2.00 | 4.00 | — |

**5 CENTAVOS** **KM# 206** **Composition:** Bronze **Note:** Some coins of 1942-1956 have weak "B" mint mark.

| Date | Mintage | F | VF | XF | Unc | BU |
|---|---|---|---|---|---|---|
| 1942 | — | 1.25 | 2.50 | 4.00 | 12.00 | — |
| 1942B | 800,000 | 0.50 | 1.25 | 2.00 | 7.00 | — |
| 1943 | — | 1.00 | 1.75 | 3.50 | 10.00 | — |
| 1943B | 6,053,000 | 0.20 | 0.60 | 1.00 | 4.00 | — |
| 1944 | — | 0.25 | 0.75 | 1.25 | 7.00 | — |
| 1944B | 9,013,000 | 0.25 | 0.75 | 1.50 | 8.00 | — |
| 1945/4 | — | 0.50 | 1.25 | 2.50 | 9.00 | — |
| 1945 | — | 0.50 | 1.25 | 2.50 | 9.00 | — |
| 1945B | 11,101,000 | 0.25 | 0.75 | 1.25 | 4.00 | — |
| 1946/5 | — | 1.25 | 2.50 | 3.50 | 10.00 | — |
| 1946 | — | 0.50 | 1.25 | 2.00 | 7.00 | — |
| 1952 | — | 1.25 | 2.50 | 3.50 | 10.00 | — |
| 1952B | 3,985,000 | 0.15 | 0.40 | 0.75 | 1.25 | — |
| 1953B | 5,180,000 | 0.10 | 0.25 | 0.50 | 1.00 | — |
| 1954B | 1,159,000 | 0.10 | 0.25 | 0.50 | 1.00 | — |
| 1955B | 6,819,000 | 0.10 | 0.25 | 0.50 | 1.00 | — |
| 1956 | 8,772,000 | 0.10 | 0.25 | 0.50 | 1.00 | — |
| 1956B | — | 0.35 | 1.25 | 2.50 | 6.50 | — |
| 1957 | 8,912,000 | 0.10 | 0.25 | 0.50 | 1.00 | — |
| 1958 | 15,016,000 | 0.10 | 0.25 | 0.40 | 0.80 | — |
| 1959 | 14,271,000 | 0.10 | 0.25 | 0.40 | 0.80 | — |
| 1960/660 | 11,716,000 | 0.25 | 0.75 | 1.00 | 2.00 | — |
| 1960/70 | Inc. above | 0.25 | 0.75 | 1.00 | 2.00 | — |
| 1960 | Inc. above | 0.10 | 0.25 | 0.40 | 0.80 | — |
| 1961 | 11,200,000 | 0.10 | 0.25 | 0.40 | 0.65 | — |
| CD1962 | 10,928,000 | — | 0.10 | 0.20 | 0.35 | — |
| 1963/53 | 15,113,000 | — | — | — | — | — |
| 1963 | Inc. above | — | 0.10 | 0.20 | 0.40 | — |
| 1964 | 9,336,000 | — | 0.10 | 0.20 | 0.35 | — |
| 1965 | 6,460,000 | — | 0.10 | 0.20 | 0.40 | — |
| 1966 | 7,170,000 | — | 0.10 | 0.35 | 1.00 | — |

**5 CENTAVOS** **KM# 220** **Composition:** Bronze **Subject:** Uprising Sesquicentennial

| Date | Mintage | F | VF | XF | Unc | BU |
|---|---|---|---|---|---|---|
| ND(1960) | 400,000 | 1.75 | 3.50 | 7.50 | 25.00 | — |

**5 CENTAVOS** **KM# 206a** **Composition:** Bronze **Note:** Varieties exist for 1967, 1970, and 1973.

| Date | Mintage | F | VF | XF | Unc | BU |
|---|---|---|---|---|---|---|
| 1967 | 10,280,000 | — | — | 0.10 | 0.25 | — |
| 1968 | 8,900,000 | — | — | 0.10 | 0.25 | — |
| 1969 | 17,800,000 | — | — | 0.10 | 0.25 | — |
| 1970 | 14,842,000 | — | — | 0.10 | 0.25 | — |
| 1971 | 10,730,000 | — | — | 0.10 | 0.25 | — |
| 1972 | 10,170,000 | — | — | 0.10 | 0.25 | — |
| 1973 | 10,525,000 | — | — | 0.10 | 0.25 | — |
| 1974 | 5,310,000 | — | — | 0.10 | 0.20 | — |
| 1975 | 5,631,000 | — | — | 0.10 | 0.20 | — |
| 1976 | 3,009,000 | — | — | 0.10 | 0.20 | — |
| 1977 | 2,000,000 | — | — | 0.10 | 0.20 | — |
| 1978 | 468,000 | — | 0.10 | 0.15 | 0.30 | — |
| 1979 | 8,087,000 | — | — | 0.10 | 0.20 | — |

**10 CENTAVOS** **KM# 196.1** **Weight:** 2.5000 g. **Composition:** 0.9000 Silver .0723 oz. ASW **Obverse:** Simon Bolivar **Note:** Varieties exist.

| Date | Mintage | F | VF | XF | Unc | BU |
|---|---|---|---|---|---|---|
| 1911 | 5,065,000 | 1.00 | 1.75 | 5.00 | 25.00 | — |
| 1913 | 8,305,000 | 1.00 | 1.75 | 4.00 | 20.00 | — |
| 1914 | 3,840,000 | 1.00 | 1.75 | 5.00 | 25.00 | — |
| 1920 | 2,149,000 | 1.00 | 1.75 | 5.00 | 25.00 | — |
| 1934 B on obverse | 140,000 | 2.50 | 4.00 | 8.00 | 35.00 | — |
| 1934/24 | Inc. above | 2.00 | 3.50 | 7.50 | 35.00 | — |
| 1934 | Inc. above | 15.00 | 25.00 | 35.00 | 75.00 | — |
| 1937 | — | 8.00 | 18.50 | 27.50 | 50.00 | — |
| 1938/7 | 2,055,000 | 1.75 | 3.75 | 6.50 | 20.00 | — |
| 1938 Wide date | Inc. above | 0.75 | 1.25 | 3.00 | 7.50 | — |
| 1938 Narrow date | Inc. above | 0.75 | 1.25 | 3.00 | 7.50 | — |
| 1940 | 450,000 | 1.50 | 2.50 | 4.50 | 15.00 | — |
| 1941 | 4,415,000 | 0.75 | 1.25 | 3.00 | 7.50 | — |
| 1942 | 3,140,000 | 5.00 | 10.00 | 16.50 | 37.50 | — |
| 1942 B on reverse | Inc. above | 0.75 | 1.25 | 3.00 | 7.50 | — |

**10 CENTAVOS** **KM# 196.2** **Weight:** 2.5000 g. **Composition:** 0.9000 Silver .0723 oz. ASW **Obverse:** Simon Bolivar **Reverse:** National arms recut

| Date | Mintage | F | VF | XF | Unc | BU |
|---|---|---|---|---|---|---|
| 1920 | Inc. above | 1.50 | 2.50 | 7.00 | 27.50 | — |

**10 CENTAVOS** **KM# 207.1** **Weight:** 2.5000 g. **Composition:** 0.5000 Silver .0401 oz. ASW **Obverse:** Francisco de Paula Santander **Reverse:** Mint mark at bottom

| Date | Mintage | F | VF | XF | Unc | BU |
|---|---|---|---|---|---|---|
| 1945B | 4,830,000 | 0.50 | 1.25 | 2.50 | 6.00 | — |
| 1945 B-B | — | — | — | — | — | — |
| 1945 Backwards B | — | 1.00 | 2.00 | 4.00 | 9.00 | — |
| 1946/5B | — | 0.60 | 1.50 | 3.00 | 8.00 | — |
| 1946B | — | 0.60 | 1.50 | 3.00 | 8.00 | — |
| 1947/5B | 7,366,000 | 1.50 | 3.00 | 5.00 | 10.00 | — |
| 1947/6B | Inc. above | 1.50 | 3.00 | 5.00 | 10.00 | — |
| 1947B | Inc. above | 1.50 | 3.00 | 5.00 | 10.00 | — |

**10 CENTAVOS** **KM# 207.2** **Weight:** 2.5000 g. **Composition:** 0.5000 Silver .0401 oz. ASW **Obverse:** Francisco de Paula Santander **Reverse:** Mint mark at top **Note:** Varieties exist. Almost all dies for 1946-1951 show at least faint traces of overdating from 1945. Coins with absolutely no underdate, and those with very bold underdate, are generally worth more to advanced specialists.

| Date | Mintage | F | VF | XF | Unc | BU |
|---|---|---|---|---|---|---|
| 1947/5B | Inc. above | 2.00 | 4.00 | 7.50 | 20.00 | — |
| 1947B | Inc. above | 2.00 | 4.00 | 7.50 | 20.00 | — |
| 1948/5B | 3,629,000 | 0.60 | 1.50 | 3.00 | 8.00 | — |
| 1948B | Inc. above | 0.50 | 1.00 | 2.25 | 6.00 | — |
| 1949/5B | 5,923,000 | 2.00 | 4.00 | 7.50 | 20.00 | — |
| 1949B | Inc. above | 0.50 | 1.00 | 2.00 | 5.00 | — |
| 1950B | 6,783,000 | 0.50 | 1.00 | 2.25 | 6.00 | — |
| 1951/5B | 5,185,000 | 0.50 | 1.00 | 2.25 | 6.00 | — |
| 1951B | Inc. above | 0.50 | 1.00 | 2.00 | 5.00 | — |
| 1952B | 1,060,000 | 1.00 | 1.50 | 3.00 | 8.00 | — |

**10 CENTAVOS** **KM# 212.1** **Composition:** Copper-Nickel **Reverse:** Head of Chief Calarca right **Note:** 18mm.

| Date | Mintage | F | VF | XF | Unc | BU |
|---|---|---|---|---|---|---|
| 1952B | 6,035,000 | 0.10 | 0.25 | 0.60 | 2.25 | — |
| 1953B | 6,985,000 | 0.10 | 0.25 | 0.60 | 2.25 | — |

**10 CENTAVOS** **KM# 212.2** **Composition:** Copper-Nickel **Note:** 18.5mm. Varieties exist.

| Date | Mintage | F | VF | XF | Unc | BU |
|---|---|---|---|---|---|---|
| 1954B | 13,006,000 | 0.10 | 0.20 | 0.30 | 2.00 | — |
| 1955B | 9,968,000 | 0.10 | 0.20 | 0.30 | 1.75 | — |

| Date | Mintage | F | VF | XF | Unc | BU |
|---|---|---|---|---|---|---|
| 1956 | 36,010,000 | 0.10 | 0.20 | 0.30 | 1.00 | — |
| 1956B | — | 0.10 | 0.20 | 0.30 | 1.00 | — |
| 1958 | 41,695,000 | 0.20 | 0.50 | 1.00 | 3.00 | — |
| 1959 | 36,653,000 | 0.10 | 0.20 | 0.30 | 1.00 | — |
| 1960 | 32,290,000 | 0.10 | 0.20 | 0.30 | 2.00 | — |
| 1961 | 17,780,000 | 0.10 | 0.20 | 0.30 | 2.00 | — |
| 1962 | 8,930,000 | 0.10 | 0.20 | 0.30 | 1.50 | — |
| 1963 | 37,540,000 | 0.10 | 0.20 | 0.30 | 1.00 | — |
| 1964 | 61,672,000 | 0.10 | 0.20 | 0.30 | 0.75 | — |
| 1965 | 12,804,000 | 0.10 | 0.20 | 0.30 | 1.50 | — |
| 1966 Large date | 23,544,000 | 0.10 | 0.20 | 0.30 | 0.50 | — |

**10 CENTAVOS** **KM# 221** **Composition:** Copper-Nickel **Subject:** Uprising Sesquicentennial

| Date | Mintage | F | VF | XF | Unc | BU |
|---|---|---|---|---|---|---|
| ND(1960) | 1,000,000 | 0.75 | 1.25 | 2.50 | 8.00 | — |

**10 CENTAVOS** **KM# 226** **Composition:** Nickel Clad Steel **Obverse:** Francisco de Paula Santander

| Date | Mintage | F | VF | XF | Unc | BU |
|---|---|---|---|---|---|---|
| 1967 | 26,980,000 | — | 0.10 | 0.15 | 0.50 | — |
| 1968 | 23,670,000 | — | 0.10 | 0.15 | 0.50 | — |
| 1969 | 29,450,000 | — | 0.10 | 0.15 | 0.50 | — |

**10 CENTAVOS** **KM# 236** **Composition:** Nickel Clad Steel **Issuer:** Francisco de Paula Santander **Obverse:** Legend divided after REPUBLICA DE.

| Date | Mintage | F | VF | XF | Unc | BU |
|---|---|---|---|---|---|---|
| 1969 | Inc. above | — | — | 0.10 | 0.15 | — |
| 1970 | 38,935,000 | — | — | 0.10 | 0.15 | — |
| 1971 | 53,314,000 | — | 0.10 | 0.15 | 0.20 | — |

**10 CENTAVOS** **KM# 243** **Composition:** Nickel Clad Steel **Obverse:** Legend divided after REPUBLICA

| Date | Mintage | F | VF | XF | Unc | BU |
|---|---|---|---|---|---|---|
| 1970 | — | — | — | — | — | — |
| 1971 | — | — | — | — | — | — |

**10 CENTAVOS** **KM# 253** **Composition:** Nickel Clad Steel **Obverse:** Continuous legend **Note:** Varieties exist.

| Date | Mintage | F | VF | XF | Unc | BU |
|---|---|---|---|---|---|---|
| 1972 | 58,000,000 | — | 0.10 | 0.15 | 0.20 | — |
| 1973 | 46,549,000 | — | 0.10 | 0.15 | 0.20 | — |
| 1974 | 49,740,000 | — | 0.10 | 0.15 | 0.20 | — |
| 1975 | 46,037,000 | — | 0.10 | 0.15 | 0.20 | — |
| 1976 | 46,084,000 | — | 0.10 | 0.15 | 0.20 | — |
| 1977 | 8,127,000 | — | 0.10 | 0.15 | 0.20 | — |
| 1978 | 97,081,000 | — | 0.10 | 0.15 | 0.20 | — |
| 1980 | 18,929,000 | — | 0.10 | 0.15 | 0.20 | — |

**20 CENTAVOS** **KM# 197** **Weight:** 5.0000 g. **Composition:** 0.9000 Silver .1446 oz. ASW **Obverse:** Bust of Simon Bolivar right **Reverse:** Arms

| Date | Mintage | F | VF | XF | Unc | BU |
|---|---|---|---|---|---|---|
| 1911 | 1,206,000 | 1.50 | 3.50 | 7.50 | 17.50 | — |
| 1913 | 1,630,000 | 1.50 | 3.50 | 7.50 | 22.50 | — |
| 1914 | 2,560,000 | 1.50 | 3.50 | 9.00 | 25.00 | — |
| 1920 Wide date | 1,242,000 | 1.75 | 4.00 | 10.00 | 27.50 | — |
| 1920 Narrow date | Inc. above | 1.75 | 4.00 | 10.00 | 27.50 | — |
| 1921 | 372,000 | 4.00 | 10.00 | 22.50 | 55.00 | — |
| 1922 | 45,000 | 13.50 | 30.00 | 57.50 | 135 | — |
| 1933B Mint mark on obverse | 330,000 | 2.00 | 5.00 | 9.00 | 25.00 | — |
| 1933B Mint mark on reverse | Inc. above | 12.50 | 25.00 | 45.00 | 125 | — |
| 1933B Mint mark on both sides | Inc. above | 3.00 | 6.00 | 10.00 | 30.00 | — |
| 1938/1 | 1,410,000 | — | — | — | — | — |
| 1938 | Inc. above | 1.25 | 2.50 | 5.00 | 15.00 | — |
| 1941 | — | 1.50 | 3.50 | 7.50 | 22.50 | — |
| 1942 | 155,000 | 9.00 | 20.00 | 32.50 | 65.00 | — |
| 1942B Mint mark on reverse | Inc. above | 1.50 | 3.50 | 7.50 | 20.00 | — |

**20 CENTAVOS** **KM# 208.1** **Weight:** 5.0000 g. **Composition:** 0.5000 Silver .0803 oz. ASW **Obverse:** Francisco de Paula Santander **Reverse:** Mint mark in field below CENTAVOS

| Date | Mintage | F | VF | XF | Unc | BU |
|---|---|---|---|---|---|---|
| 1945B | 1,675,000 | 1.00 | 2.50 | 5.00 | 10.00 | — |
| 1945BB | Inc. above | 4.25 | 8.00 | 15.00 | 32.50 | — |

**Note:** 1945BB has extra B on wreath at bottom

| Date | Mintage | F | VF | XF | Unc | BU |
|---|---|---|---|---|---|---|
| 1946/5B | 6,599,000 | 1.00 | 2.50 | 5.00 | 10.00 | — |
| 1946B | Inc. above | 1.50 | 3.00 | 5.50 | 12.00 | — |
| 1947/5B | 9,708,000 | 2.50 | 4.50 | 8.00 | 20.00 | — |
| 1947B | — | 2.50 | 4.50 | 8.00 | 20.00 | — |

**20 CENTAVOS** **KM# 208.3** **Weight:** 5.0000 g. **Composition:** 0.5000 Silver .0803 oz. ASW **Obverse:** Francisco de Paula Santander **Reverse:** Without mint mark

| Date | Mintage | F | VF | XF | Unc | BU |
|---|---|---|---|---|---|---|
| 1946/5(m) | — | 3.75 | 9.50 | 16.50 | 37.50 | — |
| 1946(m) | — | 3.00 | 7.50 | 15.00 | 32.50 | — |
| 1947(m) | 1,748,000 | 5.00 | 8.50 | 15.00 | 35.00 | — |

**20 CENTAVOS** **KM# 208.2** **Weight:** 5.0000 g. **Composition:** 0.5000 Silver .0803 oz. ASW **Obverse:** Francisco de Paula Santander **Reverse:** Mint mark on wreath at top **Note:** Almost all dies for 1946-1951 show at least faint traces of overdating from 1945. Coins with absolutely no underdate, and those with very bold underdate, are generally worth more to advanced specialists. Varieties exist.

| Date | Mintage | F | VF | XF | Unc | BU |
|---|---|---|---|---|---|---|
| 1947/5B | Inc. above | 5.00 | 10.00 | 20.00 | 50.00 | — |
| 1948/5B | Inc. above | 1.00 | 3.00 | 5.00 | 12.00 | — |
| 1948B | Inc. above | 1.50 | 3.00 | 5.00 | 14.00 | — |
| 1949/5B | 403,000 | 3.75 | 8.50 | 17.50 | 45.00 | — |
| 1949B | Inc. above | 2.50 | 5.00 | 10.00 | 32.50 | — |
| 1950/45B | 1,899,000 | 2.75 | 6.75 | 15.00 | 50.00 | — |
| 1950B | Inc. above | 2.75 | 6.00 | 13.50 | 37.50 | — |
| 1951/45B | 7,498,000 | 0.75 | 2.00 | 4.00 | 9.00 | — |
| 1951B | Inc. above | 0.75 | 2.00 | 3.50 | 7.00 | — |

**20 CENTAVOS** **KM# 213** **Weight:** 5.0000 g. **Composition:** 0.3000 Silver .0482 oz. ASW **Obverse:** Arms **Reverse:** Bust of Simon Bolivar left

| Date | Mintage | F | VF | XF | Unc | BU |
|---|---|---|---|---|---|---|
| 1952B Rare | 3,887 | — | — | — | — | — |
| 1953B | 17,819,000 | 0.40 | 0.60 | 1.25 | 3.50 | — |

**20 CENTAVOS** **KM# 215.1** **Composition:** Copper-Nickel **Obverse:** Bust of Simon Bolivar right, small date

| Date | Mintage | F | VF | XF | Unc | BU |
|---|---|---|---|---|---|---|
| 1956 | 39,778,000 | 0.10 | 0.15 | 0.20 | 1.00 | — |
| 1959 | 44,779,000 | 0.10 | 0.15 | 0.20 | 1.00 | — |
| 1961 | 10,740,000 | 0.15 | 0.25 | 0.50 | 2.00 | — |

**20 CENTAVOS** **KM# 222** **Composition:** Copper-Nickel **Subject:** Uprising Sesquicentennial

| Date | Mintage | F | VF | XF | Unc | BU |
|---|---|---|---|---|---|---|
| ND(1960) | 500,000 | 0.75 | 1.50 | 3.00 | 8.00 | — |

**20 CENTAVOS** **KM# 215.2** **Composition:** Copper-Nickel **Obverse:** Bust of Simon Bolivar right, large date

| Date | Mintage | F | VF | XF | Unc | BU |
|---|---|---|---|---|---|---|
| 1963 | 12,035,000 | — | 0.10 | 0.20 | 0.75 | — |
| 1964 | 29,075,000 | — | 0.10 | 0.20 | 0.50 | — |
| 1965 | 19,180,000 | 0.10 | 0.20 | 0.40 | 1.50 | — |

**20 CENTAVOS** **KM# 224** **Composition:** Copper-Nickel **Reverse:** Jorge Eliecer Gaitan

| Date | Mintage | F | VF | XF | Unc | BU |
|---|---|---|---|---|---|---|
| 1965 | 1,000,000 | — | 0.10 | 0.20 | 0.50 | — |

**20 CENTAVOS** **KM# 215.3** **Composition:** Copper-Nickel **Obverse:** Bust of Simon Bolivar right, medium date

| Date | Mintage | F | VF | XF | Unc | BU |
|---|---|---|---|---|---|---|
| 1966 | 23,060,000 | 0.10 | 0.15 | 0.20 | 1.00 | — |

**20 CENTAVOS** **KM# 227** **Composition:** Nickel Clad Steel **Obverse:** Francisco de Paula Santander

| Date | Mintage | F | VF | XF | Unc | BU |
|---|---|---|---|---|---|---|
| 1967 | 15,720,000 | — | 0.10 | 0.20 | 0.75 | — |
| 1968 | 26,680,000 | — | 0.10 | 0.20 | 0.75 | — |
| 1969 | 22,470,000 | — | 0.10 | 0.20 | 0.75 | — |

**20 CENTAVOS** **KM# 237** **Composition:** Nickel Clad Steel **Obverse:** Francisco de Paula Santander, legend divided after REPUBLICA

| Date | Mintage | F | VF | XF | Unc | BU |
|---|---|---|---|---|---|---|
| 1969 | Inc. above | — | — | — | — | — |
| 1970 | 44,358,000 | — | 0.10 | 0.20 | 0.75 | — |

**20 CENTAVOS** **KM# 245** **Composition:** Nickel Clad Steel **Obverse:** Legend divided after REPUBLICA DE

| Date | Mintage | F | VF | XF | Unc | BU |
|---|---|---|---|---|---|---|
| 1971 | 77,526,000 | — | — | 0.10 | 0.20 | — |

**20 CENTAVOS** **KM# 246.1** **Composition:** Nickel Clad Steel **Obverse:** Legend continuous **Note:** Varieties exist with and without dots.

| Date | Mintage | F | VF | XF | Unc | BU |
|---|---|---|---|---|---|---|
| 1971 | Inc. above | — | — | 0.10 | 0.20 | — |
| 1972 | 41,891,000 | — | — | 0.10 | 0.20 | — |
| 1973/1 | 41,440,000 | — | — | 0.10 | 0.20 | — |
| 1973 | Inc. above | — | — | 0.10 | 0.25 | — |
| 1974/1 | 45,941,000 | — | — | 0.35 | 0.85 | — |
| 1974 | Inc. above | — | — | 0.10 | 0.20 | — |
| 1975 | 28,635,000 | — | — | 0.10 | 0.20 | — |
| 1976 | 29,590,000 | — | — | 0.10 | 0.20 | — |
| 1977 | 2,054,000 | — | — | 0.10 | 0.25 | — |
| 1978 | 10,630,000 | — | — | 0.10 | 0.20 | — |

**20 CENTAVOS** **KM# 246.2** **Composition:** Nickel Clad Steel **Obverse:** Smaller letters in legend **Reverse:** Wreath with larger 20 and smaller CENTAVOS

| Date | Mintage | F | VF | XF | Unc | BU |
|---|---|---|---|---|---|---|
| 1979 | 16,655,000 | — | — | 0.10 | 0.20 | — |

**20 CENTAVOS** **KM# 267** **Composition:** Aluminum-Bronze

| Date | Mintage | F | VF | XF | Unc | BU |
|---|---|---|---|---|---|---|
| 1979 | 88,874,000 | — | 0.10 | 0.15 | 0.25 | — |
| 1980 | 46,168,000 | — | 0.10 | 0.15 | 0.25 | — |

**50 CENTAVOS** **KM# 192** **Weight:** 12.5000 g. **Composition:** 0.8350 Silver .3356 oz. ASW **Obverse:** Liberty head **Reverse:** Arms

| Date | Mintage | F | VF | XF | Unc | BU |
|---|---|---|---|---|---|---|
| 1902(P) | 960,000 | 7.00 | 13.50 | 27.50 | 90.00 | — |

**50 CENTAVOS** **KM# 186.2** **Weight:** 12.5000 g. **Composition:** 0.8350 Silver .3356 oz. ASW **Obverse:** Liberty head, incuse lettering on head band **Edge Lettering:** DIOS LEI LIBERTAD **Note:** Similar to KM#186.1a. Struck at the Bogota Mint.

| Date | Mintage | VG | F | VF | XF | Unc |
|---|---|---|---|---|---|---|
| 1906 | 446,000 | 7.00 | 15.00 | 25.00 | 50.00 | — |
| 1907 | 1,126,000 | 5.00 | 10.00 | 18.50 | 40.00 | — |
| 1908/7 | 871,000 | 20.00 | 40.00 | 70.00 | 150 | — |
| 1908 | Inc. above | 10.00 | 17.50 | 27.50 | 75.00 | — |

**50 CENTAVOS** **KM# 193.1** **Weight:** 12.5000 g. **Composition:** 0.9000 Silver .3617 oz. ASW **Obverse:** Simon Bolivar, sharper featured bust **Reverse:** Left wing and flags far from legend **Note:** Struck at Birmingham and Bogota mints. Many date varieties exist.

| Date | Mintage | F | VF | XF | Unc | BU |
|---|---|---|---|---|---|---|
| 1912 | 1,207,000 | 5.00 | 9.00 | 22.50 | 55.00 | — |
| 1912 Proof; rare | — | — | — | — | — | — |
| 1913 | 417,000 | 5.00 | 9.00 | 22.50 | 55.00 | — |
| 1914 Closed 4 | 769,000 | BV | 6.50 | 20.00 | 75.00 | — |
| 1915 Small date | 946,000 | 5.00 | 7.50 | 15.00 | 50.00 | — |
| 1915 Small date; Proof; rare | — | — | — | — | — | — |
| 1915 Large date | Inc. above | 5.00 | 7.50 | 15.00 | 50.00 | — |
| 1915 Proof; rare | — | — | — | — | — | — |
| 1916 Small date | 1,060,000 | 5.00 | 10.00 | 22.50 | 50.00 | — |
| 1917 Normal 7 | 99,000 | 10.00 | 20.00 | 30.00 | 65.00 | — |
| 1917 Foot on 7 | Inc. above | 5.00 | 10.00 | 25.00 | 50.00 | — |
| 1917 Curved top | Inc. above | 5.00 | 10.00 | 25.00 | 50.00 | — |
| 1918 | 400,000 | 5.00 | 10.00 | 25.00 | 50.00 | — |
| 1919 | Inc. above | 15.00 | 25.00 | 35.00 | 80.00 | — |
| 1922 | 150,000 | 10.00 | 15.00 | 30.00 | 75.00 | — |
| 1923 | 150,000 | 10.00 | 15.00 | 30.00 | 75.00 | — |
| 1931/21B | — | BV | 6.00 | 17.50 | 35.00 | — |
| 1931B | 700,000 | BV | 5.00 | 15.00 | 30.00 | — |
| 1931 | Inc. above | 40.00 | 75.00 | 120 | 350 | — |
| 1932/12B | 300,000 | 8.00 | 14.00 | 25.00 | 50.00 | — |
| 1932/22B | Inc. above | BV | 7.00 | 20.00 | 40.00 | — |
| 1932B | Inc. above | BV | 5.00 | 15.00 | 30.00 | — |
| 1932 Flat top 3, no B | Inc. above | 20.00 | 30.00 | 40.00 | 80.00 | — |
| 1933/13B | 1,000,000 | 5.00 | 10.00 | 20.00 | 45.00 | — |
| 1933/23B | Inc. above | 5.00 | 10.00 | 25.00 | 50.00 | — |
| 1933B | Inc. above | BV | 5.00 | 10.00 | 28.00 | — |

**50 CENTAVOS** **KM# 193.2** **Weight:** 12.5000 g. **Composition:** 0.9000 Silver .3617 oz. ASW **Obverse:** Simon Bolivar, sharper featured bust **Reverse:** Larger letters, left wing and flags close to legend **Note:** Many date varieties exist. Struck at the Medellin Mint.

| Date | Mintage | F | VF | XF | Unc | BU |
|---|---|---|---|---|---|---|
| 1914 Open 4 | — | 5.00 | 10.00 | 25.00 | 75.00 | — |
| 1915/4 Large date | — | 25.00 | 55.00 | 85.00 | 175 | — |
| 1915 Large date | — | 35.00 | 65.00 | 95.00 | 175 | — |
| 1918/4 | — | 10.00 | 20.00 | 35.00 | 75.00 | — |
| 1918 | — | 5.00 | 10.00 | 25.00 | 65.00 | — |
| 1919/8 | — | 7.50 | 15.00 | 30.00 | 70.00 | — |
| 1919 | — | 7.50 | 15.00 | 30.00 | 70.00 | — |
| 1921 | 300,000 | 7.50 | 15.00 | 30.00 | 70.00 | — |
| 1922 | — | 5.00 | 10.00 | 25.00 | 65.00 | — |
| 1932/22M | 1,200,000 | 10.00 | 15.00 | 25.00 | 50.00 | — |
| 1932M | Inc. above | BV | 5.00 | 10.00 | 25.00 | — |
| 1932 Round top 3, no M | Inc. above | 20.00 | 35.00 | 60.00 | 125 | — |
| 1933M | 800,000 | BV | 7.50 | 25.00 | 50.00 | — |
| 1933/23 Round top 3s, no M | Inc. above | 15.00 | 25.00 | 35.00 | 75.00 | — |

**50 CENTAVOS** **KM# 274** **Weight:** 12.5000 g. **Composition:** 0.9000 Silver .3617 oz. ASW **Obverse:** Simon Bolivar, rounded featured bust

| Date | Mintage | F | VF | XF | Unc | BU |
|---|---|---|---|---|---|---|
| 1916(P) | 1,300,000 | BV | 7.50 | 25.00 | 50.00 | — |
| 1917(P) | 142,000 | 15.00 | 30.00 | 60.00 | 125 | — |
| 1921(P) | 1,000,000 | BV | 5.00 | 20.00 | 45.00 | — |
| 1922(P) | 3,000,000 | BV | 5.00 | 15.00 | 40.00 | — |
| 1934(S) | 10,000,000 | BV | 5.00 | 15.00 | 40.00 | — |

**50 CENTAVOS** **KM# 209** **Weight:** 12.5000 g. **Composition:** 0.5000 Silver .2009 oz. ASW **Obverse:** Simon Bolivar

| Date | Mintage | F | VF | XF | Unc | BU |
|---|---|---|---|---|---|---|
| 1947/6B | 1,240,000 | 3.00 | 6.00 | 20.00 | 50.00 | — |
| 1947B | Inc. above | 10.00 | 15.00 | 30.00 | 75.00 | — |
| 1948/6B | 707,000 | 3.00 | 6.00 | 20.00 | 50.00 | — |
| 1948B/B | Inc. above | 5.00 | 10.00 | 20.00 | 50.00 | — |
| 1948B | Inc. above | 7.50 | 12.50 | 25.00 | 65.00 | — |

**50 CENTAVOS** **KM# 217** **Composition:** Copper-Nickel **Obverse:** Arms **Reverse:** Simon Bolivar **Note:** Various sizes of date exist.

| Date | Mintage | F | VF | XF | Unc | BU |
|---|---|---|---|---|---|---|
| 1958 | 3,596,000 | 0.15 | 0.30 | 0.50 | 2.00 | — |
| 1959 | 13,466,000 | 0.15 | 0.30 | 0.45 | 1.50 | — |
| 1960 | 4,360,000 | 0.15 | 0.30 | 0.75 | 2.00 | — |
| 1961 | 3,260,000 | 0.15 | 0.30 | 0.75 | 2.00 | — |
| 1962 | 2,336,000 | 0.15 | 0.30 | 0.75 | 2.00 | — |
| 1963 | 4,098,000 | 0.15 | 0.30 | 0.50 | 1.50 | — |
| 1964 | 9,274,000 | 0.10 | 0.20 | 0.40 | 1.50 | — |
| 1965 | 5,800,000 | 0.10 | 0.15 | 0.25 | 1.00 | — |
| 1966 | 2,820,000 | 0.15 | 0.30 | 0.50 | 1.50 | — |

**50 CENTAVOS** **KM# 223** **Composition:** Copper-Nickel **Subject:** Uprising Sesquicentennial

| Date | Mintage | F | VF | XF | Unc | BU |
|---|---|---|---|---|---|---|
| ND(1960) | 200,000 | 1.50 | 3.00 | 7.50 | 15.00 | — |

**50 CENTAVOS** **KM# 225** **Composition:** Copper-Nickel **Reverse:** Jorge Eliecer Gaitan

| Date | Mintage | F | VF | XF | Unc | BU |
|---|---|---|---|---|---|---|
| 1965 | 600,000 | 0.10 | 0.20 | 0.30 | 0.60 | — |

**50 CENTAVOS** **KM# 228** **Composition:** Nickel Clad Steel **Obverse:** Francisco de Paula Santander

| Date | Mintage | F | VF | XF | Unc | BU |
|---|---|---|---|---|---|---|
| 1967 | 3,460,000 | 0.10 | 0.15 | 0.25 | 0.65 | — |
| 1968 | 5,460,000 | 0.10 | 0.15 | 0.25 | 0.65 | — |
| 1969 | 1,590,000 | 0.10 | 0.15 | 0.25 | 0.65 | — |

**50 CENTAVOS** **KM# 244.1** **Composition:** Nickel Clad Steel **Obverse:** Flat truncation **Reverse:** 5 far from wreath **Note:** Date varieties exist.

| Date | Mintage | F | VF | XF | Unc | BU |
|---|---|---|---|---|---|---|
| 1970 | 30,906,000 | — | 0.10 | 0.15 | 0.35 | — |
| 1971 | 32,650,000 | — | 0.10 | 0.15 | 0.30 | — |

| Date | Mintage | F | VF | XF | Unc | BU |
|---|---|---|---|---|---|---|
| 1972 | 25,290,000 | — | 0.10 | 0.15 | 0.30 | — |
| 1973 | 8,060,000 | — | 0.10 | 0.15 | 0.30 | — |
| 1974 | 19,541,000 | — | 0.10 | 0.15 | 0.25 | — |
| 1975 | 4,325,000 | — | 0.10 | 0.15 | 0.30 | — |
| 1976 | 13,181,000 | — | 0.10 | 0.15 | 0.25 | — |
| 1977 | 10,413,000 | — | 0.10 | 0.15 | 0.25 | — |
| 1978 | 10,736,000 | — | 0.10 | 0.15 | 0.25 | — |

**50 CENTAVOS** **KM# 244.2** **Composition:** Nickel Clad Steel **Obverse:** Angled truncation **Reverse:** 5 close to wreath **Note:** Various sizes of dates exist.

| Date | Mintage | F | VF | XF | Unc | BU |
|---|---|---|---|---|---|---|
| 1979 | 22,584,000 | — | 0.10 | 0.15 | 0.25 | — |
| 1980 | 16,433,000 | — | 0.10 | 0.15 | 0.25 | — |
| 1982 | 10,107,000 | — | 0.10 | 0.15 | 0.25 | — |

**50 CENTAVOS** **KM# 244.3** **Composition:** Nickel Clad Steel **Obverse:** 244.2 **Reverse:** 244.1 **Note:** Mule.

| Date | Mintage | F | VF | XF | Unc | BU |
|---|---|---|---|---|---|---|
| 1979 | — | 10.00 | 20.00 | 30.00 | 50.00 | — |

**PESO** **KM# 216** **Weight:** 25.0000 g. **Composition:** 0.9000 Silver .7234 oz. ASW **Subject:** 200th Anniversary of Popayan Mint

| Date | Mintage | F | VF | XF | Unc | BU |
|---|---|---|---|---|---|---|
| ND(1956)(Mo) | 12,000 | 6.00 | 9.00 | 15.00 | 25.00 | — |

**PESO** **KM# 229** **Composition:** Copper-Nickel **Obverse:** Simon Bolivar

| Date | Mintage | F | VF | XF | Unc | BU |
|---|---|---|---|---|---|---|
| 1967 | 4,000,000 | 0.15 | 0.30 | 0.50 | 1.00 | — |

**PESO** **KM# 258.1** **Composition:** Copper-Nickel **Obverse:** Simon Bolivar, small date

| Date | Mintage | F | VF | XF | Unc | BU |
|---|---|---|---|---|---|---|
| 1974 | 56,020,000 | — | 0.10 | 0.15 | 0.40 | — |
| 1975 | 117,714,000 | — | 0.10 | 0.15 | 0.35 | — |
| 1976 | 98,728,000 | — | 0.10 | 0.15 | 0.35 | — |

**PESO** **KM# 258.2** **Composition:** Copper-Nickel **Obverse:** Simon Bolivar, large date

| Date | Mintage | F | VF | XF | Unc | BU |
|---|---|---|---|---|---|---|
| 1976 | Inc. above | — | 0.10 | 0.15 | 0.35 | — |
| 1977 | 62,083,000 | — | 0.10 | 0.15 | 0.35 | — |
| 1978 | 48,624,000 | — | 0.10 | 0.15 | 0.35 | — |
| 1979 | 83,908,000 | — | 0.10 | 0.15 | 0.35 | — |
| 1980 | 93,406,000 | — | 0.10 | 0.15 | 0.35 | — |
| 1981 | 65,219,000 | — | 0.10 | 0.15 | 0.35 | — |

**2 PESOS** **KM# 263** **Composition:** Bronze **Obverse:** Simon Bolivar **Note:** Varieties exist.

| Date | Mintage | F | VF | XF | Unc | BU |
|---|---|---|---|---|---|---|
| 1977 | 76,661,000 | 0.10 | 0.15 | 0.25 | 0.50 | — |
| 1978 | 69,575,000 | 0.10 | 0.15 | 0.25 | 0.50 | — |
| 1979 | 56,537,000 | 0.10 | 0.15 | 0.25 | 0.50 | — |
| 1980 | 108,521,000 | 0.10 | 0.15 | 0.25 | 0.50 | — |
| 1981 | 40,368,000 | 0.10 | 0.15 | 0.25 | 0.50 | — |
| 1983 | 8,358,000 | 0.10 | 0.15 | 0.25 | 0.50 | — |
| 1987 | — | 0.10 | 0.15 | 0.25 | 0.50 | — |
| 1988 | 16,200,000 | 0.10 | 0.15 | 0.25 | 0.50 | — |

**2-1/2 PESOS** **KM# 194** **Weight:** 3.9940 g. **Composition:** 0.9170 Gold .1177 oz. AGW

| Date | Mintage | F | VF | XF | Unc | BU |
|---|---|---|---|---|---|---|
| 1913 | 18,000 | — | BV | 75.00 | 125 | — |

**2-1/2 PESOS** **KM# 200** **Weight:** 3.9940 g. **Composition:** 0.9170 Gold .1177 oz. AGW **Obverse:** Simon Bolivar, large head

| Date | Mintage | F | VF | XF | Unc | BU |
|---|---|---|---|---|---|---|
| 1919A | — | — | BV | 60.00 | 100 | — |
| 1919B | — | — | — | — | — | — |
| 1919 | 34,000 | — | BV | 60.00 | 100 | — |
| 1920/19A | — | — | BV | 60.00 | 100 | — |
| 1920A | — | — | BV | 60.00 | 100 | — |
| 1920 | 34,000 | — | BV | 85.00 | 150 | — |

**2-1/2 PESOS** **KM# 203** **Weight:** 3.9940 g. **Composition:** 0.9170 Gold .1177 oz. AGW **Obverse:** Simon Bolivar, small head, MEDELLIN below bust

| Date | Mintage | F | VF | XF | Unc | BU |
|---|---|---|---|---|---|---|
| 1924 | — | — | BV | 60.00 | 100 | — |
| 1925 Rare | — | — | — | — | — | — |
| 1927 | — | — | BV | 75.00 | 125 | — |
| 1928 | 14,000 | — | BV | 100 | 175 | — |
| 1929 Rare | — | — | — | — | — | — |

**5 PESOS** **KM# 195.2** **Weight:** 7.9881 g. **Composition:** 0.9170 Gold .2355 oz. AGW **Note:** Medallic die rotation.

| Date | Mintage | F | VF | XF | Unc | BU |
|---|---|---|---|---|---|---|
| 1913 | Inc. above | — | BV | 100 | 150 | — |
| 1917 | 43,000 | — | BV | 100 | 150 | — |
| 1918 | Inc. above | — | BV | 100 | 175 | — |
| 1919 | Inc. above | — | BV | 100 | 150 | — |

**5 PESOS** **KM# 195.1** **Weight:** 7.9881 g. **Composition:** 0.9170 Gold .2355 oz. AGW **Note:** Various rotations of dies exist.

| Date | Mintage | F | VF | XF | Unc | BU |
|---|---|---|---|---|---|---|
| 1913 | 17,000 | — | BV | 125 | 200 | — |
| 1918/3 | 423,000 | — | BV | 100 | 175 | — |
| 1918 | Inc. above | — | BV | 100 | 175 | — |
| 1919 | 2,181,000 | — | — | BV | 125 | — |
| 1919 Long-tail 9 | Inc. above | — | — | BV | 130 | — |
| 1919 Dot over 9 | Inc. above | — | BV | 100 | 175 | — |

**5 PESOS** **KM# 201.1** **Weight:** 7.9881 g. **Composition:** 0.9170 Gold .2355 oz. AGW **Obverse:** Simon Bolivar, large head **Note:** 1920A dated coins come with mint mark centered or on right side of coat of arms; 1923B dated coins come with B on the left or right of coat of arms. The 1923B mint mark to right carries a 25% premium in value. Various rotations of dies exist.

| Date | Mintage | F | VF | XF | Unc | BU |
|---|---|---|---|---|---|---|
| 1919 Long-tail 9 | Inc. above | — | BV | 90.00 | 125 | — |
| 1919A | Inc. above | — | BV | 90.00 | 125 | — |
| 1919B | — | — | BV | 100 | 145 | — |
| 1920 | 870,000 | — | BV | 90.00 | 125 | — |
| 1920A | Inc. above | — | BV | 90.00 | 125 | — |
| 1920B | 108,000 | — | BV | 100 | 145 | — |
| 1921A | — | — | — | — | — | — |
| 1922B | 29,000 | — | BV | 90.00 | 125 | — |
| 1923B | 74,000 | — | BV | 90.00 | 125 | — |
| 1924B | 705,000 | — | BV | 90.00 | 125 | — |

**5 PESOS** **KM# 201.2** **Weight:** 7.9881 g. **Composition:** 0.9170 Gold .2355 oz. AGW **Obverse:** Simon Bolivar, large head **Note:** Medallic die rotation.

| Date | Mintage | F | VF | XF | Unc | BU |
|---|---|---|---|---|---|---|
| 1920 | Inc. above | 100 | 145 | — | — | — |

**5 PESOS** **KM# 204** **Weight:** 7.9881 g. **Composition:** 0.9170 Gold .2355 oz. AGW **Obverse:** Simon Bolivar, small head, MEDELLIN below bust **Note:** 1924 dated coins have several varieties in size of 2 and 4. 1925 dated coins exist with an Arabic and a Spanish style 5. 1930 dated coins have three varieties in size and placement of 3.

| Date | Mintage | F | VF | XF | Unc | BU |
|---|---|---|---|---|---|---|
| 1924 Large 2 | 120,000 | — | BV | 100 | 145 | — |
| 1924 Large 4 | Inc. above | — | BV | 85.00 | 115 | — |
| 1924 Small 4 | Inc. above | — | BV | 90.00 | 125 | — |
| 1925/4 | 668,000 | — | BV | 85.00 | 115 | — |
| 1925 | Inc. above | — | BV | 85.00 | 115 | — |
| 1926 | 383,000 | — | BV | 90.00 | 125 | — |

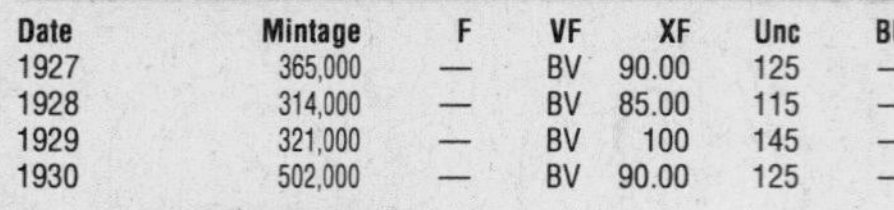

| Date | Mintage | F | VF | XF | Unc | BU |
|---|---|---|---|---|---|---|
| 1927 | 365,000 | — | BV | 90.00 | 125 | — |
| 1928 | 314,000 | — | BV | 85.00 | 115 | — |
| 1929 | 321,000 | — | BV | 100 | 145 | — |
| 1930 | 502,000 | — | BV | 90.00 | 125 | — |

**5 PESOS** **KM# 230** **Composition:** Copper-Nickel **Subject:** International Eucharistic Congress

| Date | Mintage | F | VF | XF | Unc | BU |
|---|---|---|---|---|---|---|
| 1968B | 660,000 | 0.25 | 0.50 | 0.75 | 1.75 | — |

**5 PESOS** **KM# 247** **Composition:** Nickel Clad Steel **Subject:** 6th Pan-American Games

| Date | Mintage | F | VF | XF | Unc | BU |
|---|---|---|---|---|---|---|
| 1971 | 2,000,000 | 0.15 | 0.35 | 0.60 | 1.50 | — |

**5 PESOS** **KM# 268** **Composition:** Bronze

| Date | Mintage | F | VF | XF | Unc | BU |
|---|---|---|---|---|---|---|
| 1980 | 146,268,000 | 0.15 | 0.35 | 0.60 | 1.25 | — |
| 1.981 | 9,148,000 | 0.15 | 0.35 | 0.60 | 1.25 | — |
| 1.982 | — | 0.15 | 0.35 | 0.75 | 1.50 | — |
| 1983 | 84,107,000 | 0.15 | 0.35 | 0.60 | 1.25 | — |
| 1985 | — | 0.15 | 0.35 | 0.60 | 1.25 | — |
| 1986 | 14,700,000 | 0.15 | 0.35 | 0.60 | 1.25 | — |
| 1987 | — | 0.15 | 0.35 | 0.60 | 1.25 | — |
| 1988 Small date | 45,000,000 | 0.15 | 0.35 | 0.60 | 1.25 | — |
| 1988 Large inverted date | Inc. above | 0.15 | 0.35 | 0.60 | 1.25 | — |
| 1989 | — | 0.15 | 0.35 | 0.60 | 1.25 | — |

**5 PESOS** **KM# 280** **Composition:** Copper-Aluminum-Nickel **Note:** Varieties exist, such as 1989 where some have 72 beads on the obverse and reverse and some have 66 beads.

| Date | Mintage | F | VF | XF | Unc | BU |
|---|---|---|---|---|---|---|
| 1989 | — | — | — | — | 0.35 | — |
| 1990 | — | — | — | — | 0.35 | — |
| 1991 | — | — | — | — | 0.35 | — |
| 1992 | — | — | — | — | 0.35 | — |
| 1993 | — | — | — | — | 0.35 | — |

**10 PESOS** **KM# 202** **Weight:** 15.9761 g. **Composition:** 0.9170 Gold .4710 oz. AGW **Obverse:** Simon Bolivar

| Date | Mintage | F | VF | XF | Unc | BU |
|---|---|---|---|---|---|---|
| 1919 | 101,000 | — | BV | 225 | 350 | — |
| 1924B | 55,000 | — | BV | 225 | 350 | — |

**10 PESOS** **KM# 270** **Composition:** Copper-Nickel-Zinc **Reverse:** Map showing San Andreas Island and Providencia. **Note:** Date varieties exist.

| Date | Mintage | F | VF | XF | Unc | BU |
|---|---|---|---|---|---|---|
| 1.981 | 104,554,000 | — | 0.15 | 0.25 | 1.25 | — |
| 1.982 | 83,605,000 | — | 0.15 | 0.25 | 1.25 | — |
| 1983 | 104,051,000 | — | 0.15 | 0.25 | 1.25 | — |
| 1985 | 80,000,000 | — | 0.15 | 0.25 | 1.25 | — |
| 1988 | 50,700,000 | — | 0.15 | 0.25 | 1.25 | — |
| 1989 | — | — | 0.15 | 0.25 | 1.25 | — |

**10 PESOS** **KM# 281.1** **Composition:** Copper-Nickel-Zinc **Obverse:** Flags and arms **Reverse:** Wide 10 (5mm) **Note:** Varieties exist.

| Date | Mintage | F | VF | XF | Unc | BU |
|---|---|---|---|---|---|---|
| 1989 | — | — | — | — | 0.50 | — |
| 1990 | — | — | — | — | 0.50 | — |
| 1991 | — | — | — | — | 0.50 | — |
| 1992 | — | — | — | — | 0.50 | — |
| 1993 | — | — | — | — | 0.50 | — |
| 1994 | — | — | — | — | 0.50 | — |

**10 PESOS** **KM# 281.2** **Composition:** Copper-Nickel-Zinc **Obverse:** Flags and arms **Reverse:** Narrow 10 (4.5mm)

| Date | Mintage | F | VF | XF | Unc | BU |
|---|---|---|---|---|---|---|
| 1993 | — | — | — | 3.00 | 7.00 | — |
| 1994 | — | — | — | 3.00 | 7.00 | — |

**20 PESOS** **KM# 271** **Composition:** Aluminum-Bronze **Note:** 1985 and 1988 coins exist with large and small dates.

| Date | Mintage | F | VF | XF | Unc | BU |
|---|---|---|---|---|---|---|
| 1982 | — | — | 0.15 | 0.20 | 0.30 | — |
| 1984 | 64,066,000 | — | 0.15 | 0.20 | 0.30 | — |
| 1985 | 100,690,000 | — | 0.15 | 0.20 | 0.30 | — |
| 1986 | 18,300,000 | — | 0.15 | 0.20 | 0.30 | — |
| 1987 | — | — | 0.15 | 0.20 | 0.30 | — |
| 1988 | 72,000,000 | — | 0.15 | 0.20 | 0.30 | — |
| 1989 | — | — | 0.15 | 0.20 | 0.30 | — |

**20 PESOS** **KM# 282.1** **Composition:** Copper-Aluminum-Nickel **Obverse:** 72 beads circle around the rim **Note:** Varieties exist.

| Date | Mintage | F | VF | XF | Unc | BU |
|---|---|---|---|---|---|---|
| 1989 | — | — | — | — | 0.50 | — |
| 1990 | — | — | — | — | 0.50 | — |
| 1991 | — | — | — | — | 0.50 | — |
| 1992 | — | — | — | — | 0.50 | — |
| 1993 | — | — | — | — | 0.50 | — |
| 1994 | — | — | — | — | 0.50 | — |

**20 PESOS** **KM# 282.2** **Composition:** Copper-Aluminum-Nickel **Obverse:** 68 beads circle around the rim

| Date | Mintage | F | VF | XF | Unc | BU |
|---|---|---|---|---|---|---|
| 1994 | — | — | — | — | 0.50 | — |

**50 PESOS** **KM# 272** **Composition:** Copper-Nickel **Subject:** National Constitution

| Date | Mintage | F | VF | XF | Unc | BU |
|---|---|---|---|---|---|---|
| 1986 | 14,900,000 | — | — | — | 1.25 | — |
| 1987 Large date | — | — | — | — | 1.25 | — |
| 1988 Small date | 100,000,000 | — | — | — | 1.25 | — |
| 1989 | — | — | — | — | 1.25 | — |

**50 PESOS** **KM# 283.1** **Composition:** Copper-Nickel-Zinc **Reverse:** 66 beads circle around rim. **Note:** Varieties exist.

| Date | Mintage | F | VF | XF | Unc | BU |
|---|---|---|---|---|---|---|
| 1989 | — | — | — | — | 1.00 | — |
| 1990 | — | — | — | — | 1.00 | — |
| 1991 | — | — | — | — | 1.00 | — |
| 1992 | — | — | — | — | 1.00 | — |
| 1993 | — | — | — | — | 1.00 | — |
| 1994 | — | — | — | — | 1.00 | — |

**50 PESOS** **KM# 283.2** **Composition:** Copper-Nickel-Zinc **Reverse:** 72 beads circle around rim.

| Date | Mintage | F | VF | XF | Unc | BU |
|---|---|---|---|---|---|---|
| 1990 | — | — | — | — | 1.00 | — |
| 1994 | — | — | — | — | 1.00 | — |

**100 PESOS** **KM# 231** **Weight:** 4.3000 g. **Composition:** 0.9000 Gold .1244 oz. AGW **Subject:** Interntional Eucharistic Congress

| Date | Mintage | F | VF | XF | Unc | BU |
|---|---|---|---|---|---|---|
| 1968 | 108,000 | — | — | — | 65.00 | — |
| 1968 Proof | 8,000 | Value: 85.00 | | | | |

**100 PESOS** **KM# 238** **Weight:** 4.3000 g. **Composition:** 0.9000 Gold .1244 oz. AGW **Subject:** Battle of Boyaca - Joachim Paris **Obverse:** Bust of Bolivar **Reverse:** Bust of Paris

| Date | Mintage | F | VF | XF | Unc | BU |
|---|---|---|---|---|---|---|
| 1969B Proof | 6,000 | Value: 90.00 | | | | |
| 1969NI Proof | Inc. above | Value: 90.00 | | | | |

**100 PESOS** **KM# 248** **Weight:** 4.3000 g. **Composition:** 0.9000 Gold .1244 oz. AGW **Subject:** 6th Pan-American Games

| Date | Mintage | F | VF | XF | Unc | BU |
|---|---|---|---|---|---|---|
| 1971 Proof | 6,000 | Value: 100 | | | | |

**100 PESOS** **KM# 285.1** **Composition:** Brass **Reverse:** Numerals 4.5mm talll

| Date | Mintage | F | VF | XF | Unc | BU |
|---|---|---|---|---|---|---|
| 1992 | — | — | — | — | 1.75 | — |
| 1993 | — | — | — | — | 1.75 | — |
| 1994 | — | — | — | — | 1.75 | — |
| 1995 | — | — | — | — | 1.75 | — |

**100 PESOS** **KM# 285.2** **Composition:** Brass **Reverse:** Numerals 6mm talll **Note:** Edge varieties exist.

| Date | Mintage | F | VF | XF | Unc | BU |
|---|---|---|---|---|---|---|
| 1994 | — | — | — | — | 1.75 | — |
| 1995 | — | — | — | — | 1.75 | — |

**200 PESOS** **KM# 232** **Weight:** 8.6000 g. **Composition:** 0.9000 Gold .2488 oz. AGW **Subject:** International Eucharistic Congress **Reverse:** Arms and value

| Date | Mintage | F | VF | XF | Unc | BU |
|---|---|---|---|---|---|---|
| 1968 | 108,000 | — | — | — | 130 | — |
| 1968 Proof | 8,000 | Value: 150 | | | | |

**200 PESOS** **KM# 239** **Weight:** 8.6000 g. **Composition:** 0.9000 Gold .2488 oz. AGW **Subject:** Battle of Boyaca - Carlos Soublette **Obverse:** Bust of Bolivar **Reverse:** Bust of Soublette

| Date | Mintage | F | VF | XF | Unc | BU |
|---|---|---|---|---|---|---|
| 1969B Proof | 6,000 | Value: 165 | | | | |
| 1969NI Proof | Inc. above | Value: 165 | | | | |

**200 PESOS** **KM# 249** **Weight:** 8.6000 g. **Composition:** 0.9000 Gold .2488 oz. AGW **Subject:** 6th Pan-American Games

| Date | Mintage | F | VF | XF | Unc | BU |
|---|---|---|---|---|---|---|
| 1971 Proof | 6,000 | Value: 175 | | | | |

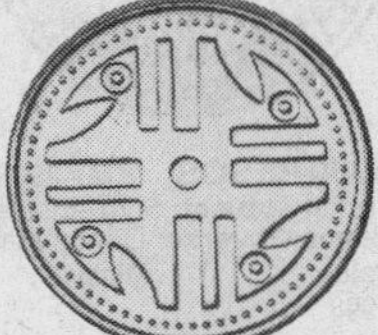

**200 PESOS** **KM# 287** **Composition:** Copper-Zinc-Nickel **Reverse:** Quimbaya artwork

| Date | Mintage | F | VF | XF | Unc | BU |
|---|---|---|---|---|---|---|
| 1994 | — | — | — | — | 1.50 | — |
| 1995 | — | — | — | — | 1.50 | — |
| 1996 | — | — | — | — | 1.50 | — |

**300 PESOS** **KM# 233** **Weight:** 12.9000 g. **Composition:** 0.9000 Gold .3733 oz. AGW **Subject:** International Eucharistic Congress

| Date | Mintage | F | VF | XF | Unc | BU |
|---|---|---|---|---|---|---|
| 1968 | 62,000 | — | — | — | 185 | — |
| 1968 Proof | 8,000 | Value: 225 | | | | |

**300 PESOS** **KM# 240** **Weight:** 12.9000 g. **Composition:** 0.9000 Gold .3733 oz. AGW **Subject:** Battle of Boyaca - Jose Anzoategui **Obverse:** Bust of Bolivar **Reverse:** Bust of Anzoategui

| Date | Mintage | F | VF | XF | Unc | BU |
|---|---|---|---|---|---|---|
| 1969B Proof | 6,000 | Value: 220 | | | | |
| 1969NI Proof | Inc. above | Value: 220 | | | | |

**300 PESOS** **KM# 250** **Weight:** 12.9000 g. **Composition:** 0.9000 Gold .3733 oz. AGW **Subject:** 6th Pan-American Games

| Date | Mintage | F | VF | XF | Unc | BU |
|---|---|---|---|---|---|---|
| 1971 Proof | 6,000 | Value: 245 | | | | |

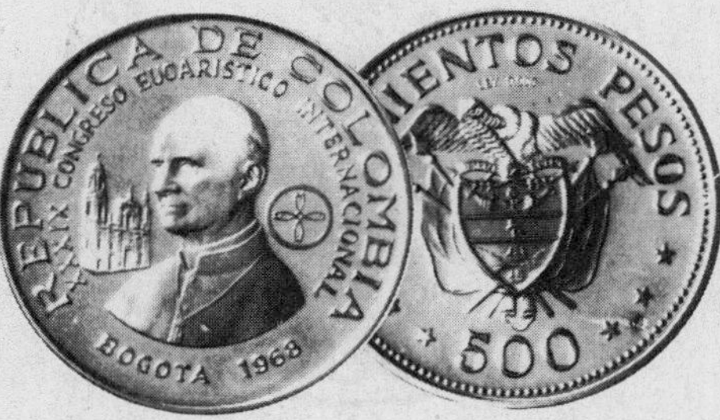

**500 PESOS** **KM# 234** **Weight:** 21.5000 g. **Composition:** 0.9000 Gold .6221 oz. AGW **Subject:** International Eucharistic Congress **Reverse:** Arms and value

| Date | Mintage | F | VF | XF | Unc | BU |
|---|---|---|---|---|---|---|
| 1968 | 14,000 | — | — | — | 325 | — |
| 1968 Proof | 8,000 | Value: 350 | | | | |

**500 PESOS** **KM# 241** **Weight:** 21.5000 g. **Composition:** 0.9000 Gold .6221 oz. AGW **Subject:** Battle of Boyaca **Obverse:** Simon Bolivar **Reverse:** Juan Jose Rondon

| Date | Mintage | F | VF | XF | Unc | BU |
|---|---|---|---|---|---|---|
| ND(1969)B Proof | 6,000 | Value: 350 | | | | |
| ND(1969)NI Proof | Inc. above | Value: 350 | | | | |

**500 PESOS** **KM# 251** **Weight:** 21.5000 g. **Composition:** 0.9000 Gold .6221 oz. AGW **Subject:** 6th Pan-American Games

| Date | Mintage | F | VF | XF | Unc | BU |
|---|---|---|---|---|---|---|
| 1971 Proof | 6,000 | Value: 420 | | | | |

**500 PESOS** **KM# 264** **Weight:** 28.2800 g. **Composition:** 0.9250 Silver .8411 oz. ASW **Subject:** Conservation **Reverse:** Orinoco Crocodile

| Date | Mintage | F | VF | XF | Unc | BU |
|---|---|---|---|---|---|---|
| 1978 | 2,678 | — | — | — | 22.50 | — |
| 1978 Proof | 3,233 | Value: 32.50 | | | | |

**500 PESOS** **KM# 286** **Ring Composition:** Copper-Nickel **Center Composition:** Aluminum-Bronze **Reverse:** Guacari Tree

| Date | Mintage | F | VF | XF | Unc | BU |
|---|---|---|---|---|---|---|
| 1993 | — | — | — | — | 3.25 | — |
| 1994 | — | — | — | — | 3.25 | — |
| 1995 | — | — | — | — | 3.25 | — |
| 1996 | — | — | — | — | 3.25 | — |

**750 PESOS** KM# 265 **Weight:** 35.0000 g. **Composition:** 0.9250 Silver 1.0409 oz. ASW **Subject:** Conservation **Obverse:** Similar to 500 Pesos, KM#264 **Reverse:** Chestnut-bellied Hummingbird

| Date | Mintage | F | VF | XF | Unc | BU |
|---|---|---|---|---|---|---|
| 1978 | 2,656 | — | — | — | 27.50 | — |
| 1978 Proof | 3,100 | Value: 37.50 | | | | |

**1000 PESOS** KM# 254 **Weight:** 4.3000 g. **Composition:** 0.9000 Gold .1244 oz. AGW **Subject:** 100th Anniversary - Birth of Guillermo Valencia

| Date | Mintage | F | VF | XF | Unc | BU |
|---|---|---|---|---|---|---|
| 1973 Proof | 10,003 | Value: 65.00 | | | | |

**1000 PESOS** KM# 259 **Weight:** 4.3000 g. **Composition:** 0.9000 Gold .1244 oz. AGW **Subject:** 450th Anniversary - City of Santa Marta

| Date | Mintage | F | VF | XF | Unc | BU |
|---|---|---|---|---|---|---|
| ND(1975) Proof | 2,500 | Value: 75.00 | | | | |

**1000 PESOS** KM# 260 **Weight:** 4.3000 g. **Composition:** 0.9000 Gold .1244 oz. AGW **Subject:** Tricentennial - City of Medellin

| Date | Mintage | F | VF | XF | Unc | BU |
|---|---|---|---|---|---|---|
| ND(1975) Proof | 4,000 | Value: 75.00 | | | | |

**1000 PESOS** KM# 288 **Composition:** Copper-Aluminum-Nickel **Edge:** Reeded and lettered **Edge Lettering:** CULTURA SINU MIL PESOS

| Date | Mintage | F | VF | XF | Unc | BU |
|---|---|---|---|---|---|---|
| 1996 | — | — | — | — | 3.75 | — |
| 1997 | — | — | — | — | 3.75 | — |
| 1998 | — | — | — | — | 3.75 | — |

**1500 PESOS** KM# 235 **Weight:** 64.5000 g. **Composition:** 0.9000 Gold 1.8664 oz. AGW **Subject:** International Eucharistic Congress **Obverse:** Similar to 300 Pesos, KM#233

| Date | Mintage | F | VF | XF | Unc | BU |
|---|---|---|---|---|---|---|
| 1968 | 5,722 | — | — | — | 1,000 | — |
| 1968 Proof | 8,000 | Value: 1,200 | | | | |

**1500 PESOS** KM# 242 **Weight:** 64.5000 g. **Composition:** 0.9000 Gold 1.8664 oz. AGW **Subject:** Battle of Boyaca **Obverse:** Bust of Bolivar **Reverse:** Portrait of Santander

| Date | Mintage | F | VF | XF | Unc | BU |
|---|---|---|---|---|---|---|
| ND(1969)B Proof | 6,000 | Value: 1,200 | | | | |
| ND(1969)NI Proof | Inc. above | Value: 1,200 | | | | |

**1500 PESOS** KM# 252 **Weight:** 64.5000 g. **Composition:** 0.9000 Gold 1.8664 oz. AGW **Subject:** 6th Pan-American Games **Obverse:** Similar to 300 Pesos, KM#250

| Date | Mintage | F | VF | XF | Unc | BU |
|---|---|---|---|---|---|---|
| 1971 Proof | 6,000 | Value: 1,400 | | | | |

**1500 PESOS** KM# 255 **Weight:** 19.1000 g. **Composition:** 0.9000 Gold .5527 oz. AGW **Subject:** 50th Anniversary - Gold Museum of Central Bank of Bogota

| Date | Mintage | F | VF | XF | Unc | BU |
|---|---|---|---|---|---|---|
| ND(1973) Proof | 4,911 | Value: 275 | | | | |

**2000 PESOS** KM# 257 **Weight:** 12.9000 g. **Composition:** 0.9000 Gold .3733 oz. AGW **Subject:** 100th Anniversary - Birth of Guillermo Valencia

| Date | Mintage | F | VF | XF | Unc | BU |
|---|---|---|---|---|---|---|
| 1973 Proof | 5,003 | Value: 225 | | | | |

**2000 PESOS** KM# 261 **Weight:** 8.6000 g. **Composition:** 0.9000 Gold .2488 oz. AGW **Subject:** 450th Anniversary - City of Santa Marta

| Date | Mintage | F | VF | XF | Unc | BU |
|---|---|---|---|---|---|---|
| ND(1975) Proof | 2,500 | Value: 150 | | | | |

**2000 PESOS** KM# 262 **Weight:** 8.6000 g. **Composition:** 0.9000 Gold .2488 oz. AGW **Subject:** Tricentennial - City of Medellin

| Date | Mintage | F | VF | XF | Unc | BU |
|---|---|---|---|---|---|---|
| ND(1975) Proof | 4,000 | Value: 150 | | | | |

**5000 PESOS** KM# 293 **Weight:** 15.3000 g. **Composition:** Nickel **Subject:** 50th Anniversary - Organization of American States **Obverse:** Denomination **Reverse:** Circle of flags

| Date | Mintage | F | VF | XF | Unc | BU |
|---|---|---|---|---|---|---|
| 1998 | — | — | — | — | 5.50 | — |

**10000 PESOS** KM# 284 **Weight:** 27.0000 g. **Composition:** 0.9250 Silver .8029 oz. ASW **Series:** Ibero - American **Subject:** Bogota Mint

| Date | Mintage | F | VF | XF | Unc | BU |
|---|---|---|---|---|---|---|
| 1991 Proof | 70,000 | Value: 50.00 | | | | |

**15000 PESOS** KM# 266 **Weight:** 33.4370 g. **Composition:** 0.9000 Gold .9676 oz. AGW **Subject:** Conservation **Reverse:** Ocelot

| Date | Mintage | F | VF | XF | Unc | BU |
|---|---|---|---|---|---|---|
| 1978 | 490 | — | — | — | 650 | — |
| 1978 Proof | 148 | Value: 2,000 | | | | |

**15000 PESOS** KM# 276 **Weight:** 17.2900 g. **Composition:** 0.9000 Gold .5000 oz. AGW **Subject:** 150th Anniversary - Death of Antonio Jose De Sucre

| Date | Mintage | F | VF | XF | Unc | BU |
|---|---|---|---|---|---|---|
| 1980 Proof | 250 | Value: 285 | | | | |

**15000 PESOS** KM# 278 **Weight:** 17.2900 g. **Composition:** 0.9000 Gold .5000 oz. AGW **Subject:** 150th Anniversary - Death of Jose Maria Cordova

| Date | Mintage | F | VF | XF | Unc | BU |
|---|---|---|---|---|---|---|
| 1980 Proof | 250 | Value: 285 | | | | |

**20000 PESOS** KM# 289 **Weight:** 8.6400 g. **Composition:** 0.9000 Gold .2500 oz. AGW **Subject:** Birth Centennial **Obverse:** Alfonso Lopez-Pumarejo **Reverse:** Building

| Date | Mintage | F | VF | XF | Unc | BU |
|---|---|---|---|---|---|---|
| ND(1986) Proof | 1,351 | Value: 200 | | | | |

**30000 PESOS** KM# 269 **Weight:** 34.5800 g. **Composition:** 0.9000 Gold 1.0007 oz. AGW **Subject:** Death of Bolivar

| Date | Mintage | F | VF | XF | Unc | BU |
|---|---|---|---|---|---|---|
| 1980 Proof | 500 | Value: 550 | | | | |

**35000 PESOS** KM# 273 **Weight:** 8.6400 g. **Composition:** 0.9000 Gold .2500 oz. AGW **Subject:** 100th Anniversary - Birth of President Santos

| Date | Mintage | F | VF | XF | Unc | BU |
|---|---|---|---|---|---|---|
| ND(1988) Proof | 900 | Value: 200 | | | | |

**40000 PESOS** KM# 292 **Weight:** 17.2800 g. **Composition:** 0.9000 Gold .5000 oz. AGW **Subject:** Centennial - Birthday of Alfonso Lopez-Pumarejo **Note:** Similar to 20,000 Pesos, KM#289

| Date | Mintage | F | VF | XF | Unc | BU |
|---|---|---|---|---|---|---|
| ND(1986) Proof | 1,351 | Value: 400 | | | | |

**50000 PESOS** KM# 290 **Weight:** 8.6400 g. **Composition:** 0.9000 Gold .2500 oz. AGW **Subject:** Centennial - Birthday of Mariano Ospina P **Obverse:** Portrait **Reverse:** Inscription and wreath

| Date | Mintage | F | VF | XF | Unc | BU |
|---|---|---|---|---|---|---|
| ND(1991) Proof | — | Value: 200 | | | | |

**100000 PESOS** KM# 291 **Weight:** 17.2800 g. **Composition:** 0.9000 Gold .5000 oz. AGW **Subject:** Centennial - Birthday of Mariano Ospina P **Obverse:** Portrait **Reverse:** Inscription and wreath

| Date | Mintage | F | VF | XF | Unc | BU |
|---|---|---|---|---|---|---|
| ND(1991) Proof | — | Value: 400 | | | | |

## INFLATIONARY COINAGE

P/M - Papel Moneda

Beginning about 1886, Colombia fell victim to rampant "printing press" inflation and a debased, vanishing coinage. Left without solid backing, the peso gradually fell until it was worth 1 centavo of the old silver-based currency. The copper-nickel 1, 2, and 5 peso p/m coins reflected this inflation, and later circulated at par with the newer 1, 2, and 5 centavo coins.

**PESO (Papel Moneda)** KM# A279 **Composition:** Copper-Nickel

| Date | Mintage | F | VF | XF | Unc | BU |
|---|---|---|---|---|---|---|
| 1907 AM | 2,860,000 | 0.75 | 1.75 | 5.00 | 15.00 | — |
| 1907 AM Proof | — | Value: 80.00 | | | | |
| 1910 AM | 1,205,000 | 1.25 | 2.50 | 7.00 | 25.00 | — |
| 1911 AM | 2,816,000 | 1.75 | 2.50 | 8.00 | 27.50 | — |
| 1912 AM | 6,094,000 | 1.25 | 2.00 | 6.00 | 20.00 | — |
| 1912 H Without crossbar | 2,000,000 | 1.25 | 2.00 | 6.00 | 20.00 | — |
| 1912 H With crossbar | Inc. above | 1.25 | 2.00 | 6.00 | 20.00 | — |
| 1913 AM | 306,000 | 3.00 | 7.50 | 13.50 | 30.00 | — |
| 1914 AM | 552,000 | 3.50 | 8.50 | 20.00 | 47.50 | — |
| 1916/4 AM | 234,000 | 4.25 | 9.00 | 18.50 | 45.00 | — |
| 1916 AM | Inc. above | 4.25 | 9.00 | 18.50 | 45.00 | — |

**2 PESOS (Papel Moneda)** KM# B279 **Composition:** Copper-Nickel **Note:** Date varieties exist.

| Date | Mintage | F | VF | XF | Unc | BU |
|---|---|---|---|---|---|---|
| 1907 AM | 4,161,000 | 1.50 | 2.75 | 8.50 | 27.50 | — |
| 1907 AM Proof | — | Value: 90.00 | | | | |
| 1910/07 AM | 649,000 | 3.25 | 5.75 | 12.50 | 40.00 | — |
| 1910 AM | Inc. above | 3.00 | 5.00 | 9.00 | 32.50 | — |
| 1911 | 458,000 | 3.50 | 8.50 | 16.50 | 55.00 | — |
| 1913 Reported, not confirmed | 82,000 | — | — | — | — | — |
| 1914 AM | 1,000,000 | 3.00 | 6.50 | 15.00 | 50.00 | — |

**5 PESOS (Papel Moneda)** KM# 279 **Composition:** Copper-Nickel

| Date | Mintage | F | VF | XF | Unc | BU |
|---|---|---|---|---|---|---|
| 1907 AM | 6,143,000 | 0.75 | 2.50 | 7.00 | 20.00 | — |
| 1907 AM Proof | — | Value: 110 | | | | |
| 1909 AM | 4,000,000 | 1.00 | 2.75 | 7.50 | 20.00 | — |
| 1912 H | 2,000,000 | 1.00 | 2.75 | 7.50 | 20.00 | — |
| 1912 AM | 1,897,000 | 2.25 | 5.00 | 12.50 | 27.50 | — |
| 1913 AM | Inc. above | 5.00 | 15.00 | 40.00 | — | — |
| 1914 AM | Inc. above | 12.50 | 27.50 | 50.00 | 80.00 | — |

## LEPROSARIUM COINAGE

Bogota Mint

Special coinage for use in the three government leper colonies of Agua de Dios, Cano de Lord, and Contrataction. The hospitals were closed in the late 1950s and patients were allowed to exchange these special coins for regular currency at any bank.

**CENTAVO** KM# L9 **Composition:** Copper-Nickel

| Date | Mintage | Good | VG | F | VF | XF |
|---|---|---|---|---|---|---|
| 1921 RH | 300,000 | 0.75 | 1.50 | 3.50 | 7.00 | — |

**2 CENTAVOS** KM# L10 **Composition:** Copper-Nickel

| Date | Mintage | Good | VG | F | VF | XF |
|---|---|---|---|---|---|---|
| 1921 RH | 350,000 | 0.75 | 1.50 | 4.00 | 8.00 | — |

**2-1/2 CENTAVOS** KM# L1 **Composition:** Brass

| Date | Mintage | Good | VG | F | VF | XF |
|---|---|---|---|---|---|---|
| 1901 Rare | 20,000 | — | — | — | — | — |

**Note:** Only a few examples of this type are currently known to have survived.

**5 CENTAVOS** KM# L2 **Composition:** Brass

| Date | Mintage | Good | VG | F | VF | XF |
|---|---|---|---|---|---|---|
| 1901 B | 15,000 | 6.00 | 12.50 | 22.00 | 45.00 | — |

**5 CENTAVOS** KM# L11 **Composition:** Copper-Nickel

| Date | Mintage | Good | VG | F | VF | XF |
|---|---|---|---|---|---|---|
| 1921 H | 200,000 | 1.00 | 2.00 | 4.50 | 9.00 | — |

**10 CENTAVOS** KM# L3 **Composition:** Brass

| Date | Mintage | Good | VG | F | VF | XF |
|---|---|---|---|---|---|---|
| 1901 B | 10,000 | 10.00 | 15.00 | 28.00 | 50.00 | — |

**10 CENTAVOS** KM# L12 **Composition:** Copper-Nickel

| Date | Mintage | Good | VG | F | VF | XF |
|---|---|---|---|---|---|---|
| 1921 RH | 200,000 | 1.00 | 2.00 | 4.50 | 9.00 | — |

**20 CENTAVOS** KM# L4 **Composition:** Brass

| Date | Mintage | Good | VG | F | VF | XF |
|---|---|---|---|---|---|---|
| 1901 B | 30,000 | 10.00 | 15.00 | 28.00 | 50.00 | — |

**50 CENTAVOS** KM# L5 **Composition:** Brass

| Date | Mintage | Good | VG | F | VF | XF |
|---|---|---|---|---|---|---|
| 1901 B | 26,000 | 13.50 | 20.00 | 35.00 | 65.00 | — |

**50 CENTAVOS** KM# L5a **Composition:** Copper

| Date | Mintage | Good | VG | F | VF | XF |
|---|---|---|---|---|---|---|
| 1901 2 known | — | — | — | — | — | — |

**50 CENTAVOS** KM# L13 **Composition:** Copper-Nickel

| Date | Mintage | Good | VG | F | VF | XF |
|---|---|---|---|---|---|---|
| 1921 RH | 120,000 | 2.00 | 4.00 | 7.50 | 16.00 | — |

**50 CENTAVOS** KM# L14 **Composition:** Brass

| Date | Mintage | Good | VG | F | VF | XF |
|---|---|---|---|---|---|---|
| 1928 RH | 50,000 | 2.00 | 4.50 | 9.00 | 18.00 | — |

**50 CENTAVOS** KM# L14a **Composition:** Copper

| Date | Mintage | Good | VG | F | VF | XF |
|---|---|---|---|---|---|---|
| 1928 Proof; Rare | Inc. above | — | — | — | — | — |

## INFLATIONARY LEPROSARIUM COINAGE

P/M - Papel Moneda

1 Peso was equal in value to 1 Centavo of the old silver currency. It later circulated at par with the newer 1 Centavo coins.

**PESO (Papel Moneda)** KM# L6 **Composition:** Copper-Nickel

| Date | Mintage | Good | VG | F | VF | XF |
|---|---|---|---|---|---|---|
| 1907/0 | 792,000 | — | — | — | — | — |
| 1907 | Inc. above | 5.00 | 10.00 | 20.00 | 45.00 | — |

**5 PESOS (Papel Moneda)** KM# L7 **Composition:** Copper-Nickel

| Date | Mintage | Good | VG | F | VF | XF |
|---|---|---|---|---|---|---|
| 1907 | 159,000 | 30.00 | 60.00 | 100 | 200 | — |

**10 PESOS (Papal Moneda)** KM# L8 **Composition:** Copper-Nickel

| Date | Mintage | Good | VG | F | VF | XF |
|---|---|---|---|---|---|---|
| 1907 | 129,000 | 40.00 | 75.00 | 125 | 250 | — |

# PROVINCE OF SANTANDER

## CIVIL WAR COINAGE

**10 CENTAVOS** KM# A1 **Composition:** Brass **Note:** Uniface.

| Date | Mintage | F | VF | XF | Unc | BU |
|---|---|---|---|---|---|---|
| ND(1902) | — | 20.00 | 30.00 | 55.00 | — | — |

**20 CENTAVOS** KM# A2 **Composition:** Brass **Note:** Uniface.

| Date | Mintage | F | VF | XF | Unc | BU |
|---|---|---|---|---|---|---|
| 1902 | — | 25.00 | 40.00 | 70.00 | — | — |

**50 CENTAVOS** KM# A3 **Composition:** Brass **Note:** Uniface. Varieties exist in shape of "0" in denomination: a fully rounded zero commands double the listed values. Later 20th Century counterfeits are known.

| Date | Mintage | F | VF | XF | Unc | BU |
|---|---|---|---|---|---|---|
| 1902 | — | 4.00 | 8.50 | 20.00 | — | — |

## PATTERNS

Including off metal strikes

| KM# | Date | Mintage | Identification | Mkt Val |
|---|---|---|---|---|
| Pn80 | 1900 | — | 10 Centavos. Silver. Reeded edge. | — |
| Pn81 | 1900 | — | 20 Centavos. Silver. Reeded edge. | — |
| Pn82 | 1900 | — | 50 Centavos. 0.8350 Silver. Plain edge. | — |
| Pn83 | 1900 | — | 50 Centavos. 0.8350 Silver. Reeded edge. | — |
| Pn76 | 1900 | — | 5 Centavos. Copper-Nickel. | 275 |
| Pn77 | 1900 | — | 10 Centavos. Copper-Nickel. | 175 |
| Pn78 | 1900 | — | 10 Centavos. Copper-Nickel. ESSAI MONETAIRE. | 100 |
| Pn79 | 1900 | — | 10 Centavos. Copper-Nickel. Quartefoil. | 100 |
| Pn84 | 1909 | — | 5 Centavos. Copper-Nickel. | — |
| Pn85 | 1913 | — | 5 Decimos. Thin Bolivar head. | — |
| Pn86 | 1913 | — | 5 Decimos. Thin Bolivar head, canceled obverse die. | — |
| Pn87 | 1913 | — | 2-1/2 Pesos. Gold. ENSAYO; KM#194. | — |
| Pn88 | 1913 | — | 5 Pesos. Gold. ENSAYO; KM#195. | — |
| Pn89 | 1915 | — | 2-1/2 Pesos. Gold. ENSAYO; KM#194. | — |
| Pn90 | 1917 | — | 5 Centavos. Copper-Nickel. PAZ on cap band, similar to KM#199. | — |
| Pn91 | 1917 | — | 5 Centavos. Copper-Nickel. KM#199. | — |
| Pn93 | 1923 | — | 2-1/2 Pesos. Silver. ESSAI; KM#203. | — |
| Pn94 | 1923 | — | 5 Pesos. ENSAYO, KM#204. | — |
| Pn95 | 1923 | — | 5 Pesos. Silver. ESSAI; KM#204. | — |
| Pn92 | 1923 | — | 2-1/2 Pesos. ENSAYO; KM#203. | 2,450 |
| Pn96 | 1941 | — | 5 Centavos. Copper-Nickel. KM#199. | — |
| Pn97 | 1946 | — | 50 Centavos. Copper-Nickel. 10-sided planchet. | — |
| Pn98 | 1946 | — | 50 Centavos. 0.5000 Silver. Reeded edge. | — |
| Pn102 | 1950 | — | 50 Centavos. 0.9000 Silver. | — |
| Pn99 | 1950 | — | 20 Centavos. 0.5000 Silver. | 100 |
| Pn100 | 1950 | — | 50 Centavos. 0.9000 Silver. Bolivar military bust, condor over large shield. | 100 |
| Pn101 | 1950 | — | 50 Centavos. 0.9000 Silver. Condor over small shield. | 100 |
| Pn103 | 1951 | — | 50 Centavos. Silver. | 100 |
| Pn104 | 1952 | — | 50 Centavos. Silver. | 100 |
| Pn105 | 1956 | — | 50 Centavos. Copper-Nickel. | 125 |
| Pn106 | 1956 | — | Peso. Gold. | — |
| Pn107 | 1957 | — | 50 Centavos. Copper-Nickel. | 125 |
| Pn108 | 1963 | — | Peso. Copper-Nickel. Previous KM#Pn57. | 125 |
| Pn109 | 1968 | — | Peso. Copper-Nickel. Previous KM#Pn58. | 125 |
| Pn110 | 1969 | — | 50 Centavos. Copper-Nickel. Previous KM#Pn59. | 75.00 |
| Pn111 | 1969 | — | 50 Centavos. Copper-Nickel. Previous KM#Pn60. | 75.00 |
| Pn112 | 1969 | — | Peso. Copper-Nickel. Previous KM#Pn61. | 125 |
| Pn113 | 1969 | — | Peso. Copper-Nickel. Previous KM#Pn62. | 125 |
| Pn114 | 1969 | — | Peso. Copper-Nickel. Previous KM#Pn63. | 125 |
| Pn115 | 1970 | — | Centavo. Aluminum. Previous KM#Pn64. | 25.00 |
| Pn116 | 1970 | — | 5 Centavos. Aluminum. Previous KM#Pn65. | 25.00 |
| Pn117 | 1971 | — | 10 Centavos. Aluminum. Previous KM#Pn66. | 30.00 |
| Pn118 | 1971 | — | 50 Centavos. Copper-Nickel. Previous KM#Pn67. | 65.00 |
| Pn119 | 1974 | — | Peso. Silver. 6.7000 g. Previous KM#Pn68. | 150 |
| Pn120 | 1979 | — | 5 Pesos. Inverted date. Previous KM#Pn69. | — |

## PIEFORTS

| KM# | Date | Mintage | Identification | Mkt Val |
|---|---|---|---|---|
| P3 | 1913 | — | 50 Centavos. 0.9000 Silver. Ensayo | 2,500 |

| KM# | Date | Mintage | Identification | Mkt Val |
|---|---|---|---|---|
| P4 | 1915 | — | 10 Centavos. 0.9000 Silver. Ensayo | — |
| P5 | 1915 | — | 20 Centavos. 0.9000 Silver. Ensayo | — |

## TRIAL STRIKES

| KM# | Date | Mintage | Identification | Mkt Val |
|---|---|---|---|---|
| TS15 | 1911 | — | 10 Centavos. Lead. Uniface. | — |
| TS16 | 1911 | — | 20 Centavos. Lead. Uniface. | — |
| TS14 | ND | — | 50 Centavos. Lead. | — |

## PROOF SETS

| KM# | Date | Mintage | Identification | Issue Price | Mkt Val |
|---|---|---|---|---|---|
| PS7 | 1979 (2) | — | KM#264-265 | — | 75.00 |
| PS1 | 1968 (5) | 8,000 | KM#231-235 | 340 | 1,950 |
| PS2 | 1969 (5) | 6,000 | KM#238-242 | — | 2,000 |
| PS3 | 1971 (5) | 6,000 | KM#248-252 | — | 2,300 |
| PS4 | 1973 (3) | — | KM#254, 256, 257 | — | 450 |
| PS5 | 1975 (2) | 2,500 | KM#260, 262 | 195 | 235 |
| PS6 | 1975 (2) | 4,000 | KM#259, 261 | 195 | 245 |

# COMOROS

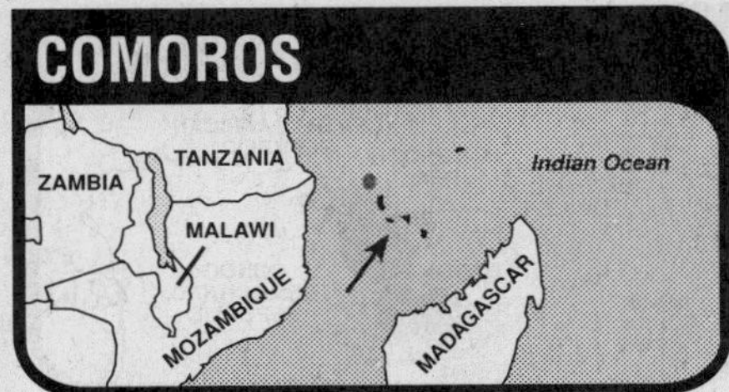


The Federal Islamic Republic of the Comoros, a volcanic archipelago located in the Mozambique Channel of the Indian Ocean 300 miles (483 km.) northwest of Madagascar, has an area of 719 sq. mi. (2,171 sq. km.) and a population of *714,000. Capital: Moroni. The economy of the islands is based on agriculture. There are practically no mineral resources. Vanilla, essence for perfumes, copra, and sisal are exported.

Ancient Phoenician traders were probably the first visitors to the Comoro Islands, but the first detailed knowledge of the area was gathered by Arab sailors. Arab dominion and culture were firmly established when the Portuguese, Dutch, and French arrived in the 16th century. In 1843 a Malagasy ruler ceded the island of Mayotte to France; the other three principal islands of the archipelago-Anjouan, Moheli, and Grand Comore came under French protection in 1886. The islands were joined administratively with Madagascar in 1912. The Comoros became partially autonomous, with the status of a French overseas territory, in 1946, and achieved complete internal autonomy in 1961. On Dec. 31, 1975, after 133 years of French association, the Comoro Islands became the independent Republic of the Comoros.

Mayotte retained the option of determining its future ties and in 1976 voted to remain French. Its present status is that of a French Territorial Collectivity. French currency now circulates there.

**TITLES**

Daulat Anjazanchiyah

**RULERS**

French, 1886-1975

**MINT MARKS**

(a) - Paris, privy marks only
A - Paris

**MONETARY SYSTEM**

100 Centimes = 1 Franc

## FRENCH COLONIAL

### DECIMAL COINAGE

**25 CENTIMES KM# Tn1 Weight:** 1.2000 g. **Composition:** Aluminum **Issuer:** Societe Anonyme

| Date | Mintage | F | VF | XF | Unc | BU |
|---|---|---|---|---|---|---|
| ND(1915) | — | 30.00 | 60.00 | 125 | — | — |

**FRANC KM# 4 Composition:** 0.9000 Aluminum

| Date | Mintage | F | VF | XF | Unc | BU |
|---|---|---|---|---|---|---|
| 1964(a) | 500,000 | 0.15 | 0.25 | 0.40 | 1.25 | — |

**2 FRANCS KM# 5 Composition:** Aluminum

| Date | Mintage | F | VF | XF | Unc | BU |
|---|---|---|---|---|---|---|
| 1964(a) | 600,000 | 0.15 | 0.25 | 0.50 | 1.50 | — |

**5 FRANCS KM# 6 Composition:** Aluminum

| Date | Mintage | F | VF | XF | Unc | BU |
|---|---|---|---|---|---|---|
| 1964(a) | 1,000,000 | 0.20 | 0.40 | 0.65 | 2.00 | — |

**10 FRANCS KM# 7 Composition:** Aluminum-Bronze

| Date | Mintage | F | VF | XF | Unc | BU |
|---|---|---|---|---|---|---|
| 1964(a) | 600,000 | 0.20 | 0.50 | 1.00 | 2.50 | — |

**20 FRANCS KM# 8 Composition:** Aluminum-Bronze

| Date | Mintage | F | VF | XF | Unc | BU |
|---|---|---|---|---|---|---|
| 1964(a) | 500,000 | 0.30 | 0.65 | 1.25 | 3.00 | — |

### TOKEN COINAGE

**25 CENTIMES KM# Tn1a Weight:** 4.6000 g. **Composition:** Brass **Issuer:** Societe Anonyme

| Date | Mintage | F | VF | XF | Unc | BU |
|---|---|---|---|---|---|---|
| ND(1922) | — | — | — | 150 | — | — |

**50 CENTIMES KM# Tn2 Composition:** Aluminum **Note:** Similar to 25 Centimes, Tn#1.

| Date | Mintage | F | VF | XF | Unc | BU |
|---|---|---|---|---|---|---|
| ND(1915) | — | 35.00 | 70.00 | 120 | — | — |

**50 CENTIMES KM# Tn2a Composition:** Brass

| Date | Mintage | F | VF | XF | Unc | BU |
|---|---|---|---|---|---|---|
| ND(1915) | — | — | — | 350 | — | — |

**FRANC KM# Tn3 Weight:** 1.3000 g. **Composition:** Aluminum **Note:** Similar to 25 Centimes, Tn#1.

| Date | Mintage | F | VF | XF | Unc | BU |
|---|---|---|---|---|---|---|
| ND(1915) | — | 40.00 | 80.00 | 135 | — | — |

**FRANC KM# Tn3a Composition:** Brass

| Date | Mintage | F | VF | XF | Unc | BU |
|---|---|---|---|---|---|---|
| ND(1922) | — | — | — | 200 | — | — |

**2 FRANCS KM# Tn4 Composition:** Aluminum 1.7 oz. **Note:** Similar to 25 Centimes, Tn#1.

| Date | Mintage | F | VF | XF | Unc | BU |
|---|---|---|---|---|---|---|
| ND(1915) | — | 50.00 | 90.00 | 155 | — | — |

**2 FRANCS KM# Tn5 Composition:** Aluminum 1.7 oz. **Note:** Uniface.

| Date | Mintage | F | VF | XF | Unc | BU |
|---|---|---|---|---|---|---|
| 1915 | — | 50.00 | 100 | 165 | — | — |

## FEDERAL ISLAMIC REPUBLIC

### STANDARD COINAGE

**5 FRANCS KM# 15 Composition:** Aluminum **Issuer:** Banque Central **Subject:** World Fisheries Conference **Obverse:** Coelacanth fish

| Date | Mintage | F | VF | XF | Unc | BU |
|---|---|---|---|---|---|---|
| 1984(a) | 1,010,000 | 0.25 | 0.50 | 1.00 | 2.50 | — |
| 1992(a) | — | 0.25 | 0.50 | 1.00 | 2.50 | — |

**10 FRANCS KM# 17 Composition:** Aluminum-Bronze **Issuer:** Banque Central

| Date | Mintage | F | VF | XF | Unc | BU |
|---|---|---|---|---|---|---|
| 1992(a) | — | — | — | — | 1.65 | — |

**25 FRANCS KM# 14 Composition:** Nickel **Issuer:** Banque Central **Series:** F.A.O **Obverse:** Chickens

| Date | Mintage | F | VF | XF | Unc | BU |
|---|---|---|---|---|---|---|
| 1981(a) | 1,000,000 | 1.50 | 3.00 | 6.00 | 16.00 | — |
| 1982(a) | 2,007,000 | 0.20 | 0.40 | 0.80 | 1.75 | — |

**50 FRANCS KM# 9 Composition:** Nickel **Issuer:** Institut d' Emmission **Subject:** Independence of Republic

| Date | Mintage | F | VF | XF | Unc | BU |
|---|---|---|---|---|---|---|
| 1975(a) | 1,200,000 | 0.40 | 0.75 | 1.25 | 2.25 | — |

**50 FRANCS KM# 16 Composition:** Nickel Plated Steel **Issuer:** Institut d' Emission

| Date | Mintage | F | VF | XF | Unc | BU |
|---|---|---|---|---|---|---|
| 1990(a) | — | 0.50 | 0.80 | 1.50 | 2.50 | — |
| 1994(a) | — | 0.50 | 0.80 | 1.50 | 2.50 | — |

**100 FRANCS KM# 13 Composition:** Nickel **Issuer:** Institut d' Emmission **Series:** F.A.O

| Date | Mintage | F | VF | XF | Unc | BU |
|---|---|---|---|---|---|---|
| 1977(a) | 1,500,000 | 0.60 | 1.00 | 2.00 | 3.75 | — |

**100 FRANCS KM# 18 Weight:** 10.0000 g. **Composition:** Nickel Plated Steel **Subject:** Circulation Type **Obverse:** Denomination. **Reverse:** Boat and fish. **Edge:** Plain. **Size:** 28 mm.

| Date | Mintage | F | VF | XF | Unc | BU |
|---|---|---|---|---|---|---|
| 1999 | — | — | — | — | 3.00 | — |

**5000 FRANCS** **KM#10** **Weight:** 44.8300 g. **Composition:** 0.9250 Silver 1.3332 oz. ASW **Issuer:** Etat Comorien **Obverse:** Flowers **Reverse:** Similar to 20,000 Francs, KM#12

| Date | Mintage | F | VF | XF | Unc | BU |
|---|---|---|---|---|---|---|
| 1976 | 700 | — | — | — | 70.00 | — |
| 1976 Proof | 1,000 | Value: 90.00 | | | | |

**10000 FRANCS** **KM# 11** **Weight:** 3.0700 g. **Composition:** 0.9000 Gold .0888 oz. AGW **Issuer:** Etat Comorien **Obverse:** Hummingbird, similar to 20,000 Francs, KM#12

| Date | Mintage | F | VF | XF | Unc | BU |
|---|---|---|---|---|---|---|
| 1976 | 500 | — | — | — | 100 | — |
| 1976 Proof | 500 | Value: 125 | | | | |

**20000 FRANCS** **KM# 12** **Weight:** 6.1400 g. **Composition:** 0.9000 Gold .1776 oz. AGW **Issuer:** Etat Comorien **Obverse:** Coelacanth fish **Reverse:** Said Mohamed Cheikh

| Date | Mintage | F | VF | XF | Unc | BU |
|---|---|---|---|---|---|---|
| 1976 | 500 | — | — | — | 200 | — |
| 1976 Proof | 500 | Value: 225 | | | | |

## ESSAIS

Standard metals unless otherwise noted

| KM# | Date | Mintage | Identification | Issue Price | Mkt Val |
|---|---|---|---|---|---|
| E1 | 1964 | 1,700 | Franc. KM4. | — | 15.00 |
| E2 | 1964 | 1,700 | 2 Francs. KM5. | — | 15.00 |
| E3 | 1964 | 1,700 | 5 Francs. KM6. | — | 15.00 |
| E4 | 1964 | 1,700 | 10 Francs. KM7. | — | 15.00 |
| E5 | 1964 | 1,700 | 20 Francs. KM8. | — | 17.50 |
| E6 | 1975 | 1,800 | 50 Francs. KM9. | — | 22.50 |
| E7 | 1977 | 1,900 | 100 Francs. KM13. | — | 25.00 |
| E8 | 1982 | 1,900 | 25 Francs. | — | 20.00 |
| E9 | 1984 | 1,700 | 5 Francs. KM15. | — | 17.50 |

## "FDC" SETS

| KM# | Date | Mintage | Identification | Issue Price | Mkt Val |
|---|---|---|---|---|---|
| SS1 | 1964 (5) | — | KM4-8. Issued with reunion set. | — | 15.00 |

## MINT SETS

| KM# | Date | Mintage | Identification | Issue Price | Mkt Val |
|---|---|---|---|---|---|
| MS1 | 1976 (3) | 500 | KM10-12 | — | 370 |

## PROOF SETS

| KM# | Date | Mintage | Identification | Issue Price | Mkt Val |
|---|---|---|---|---|---|
| PS1 | 1976 (3) | 500 | KM10-12 | 229 | 435 |

# CONGO FREE STATE

## ROYAL DOMAIN

### STANDARD COINAGE

**5 CENTIMES** **KM# 9** **Composition:** Copper-Nickel **Ruler:** Leopold II

| Date | Mintage | F | VF | XF | Unc | BU |
|---|---|---|---|---|---|---|
| 1906 | 100,000 | 5.00 | 10.00 | 25.00 | 60.00 | — |
| 1908 | 180,000 | 4.00 | 8.00 | 20.00 | 50.00 | — |

**10 CENTIMES** **KM# 10** **Composition:** Copper-Nickel **Ruler:** Leopold II

| Date | Mintage | F | VF | XF | Unc | BU |
|---|---|---|---|---|---|---|
| 1906 | 100,000 | 5.00 | 12.00 | 35.00 | 85.00 | — |
| 1908 | 800,000 | 3.00 | 8.00 | 30.00 | 80.00 | — |

**20 CENTIMES** **KM# 11** **Composition:** Copper-Nickel **Ruler:** Leopold II

| Date | Mintage | F | VF | XF | Unc | BU |
|---|---|---|---|---|---|---|
| 1906 | 100,000 | 5.00 | 12.00 | 40.00 | 110 | — |
| 1908 | 400,000 | 4.00 | 8.00 | 35.00 | 95.00 | — |

# CONGO REPUBLIC

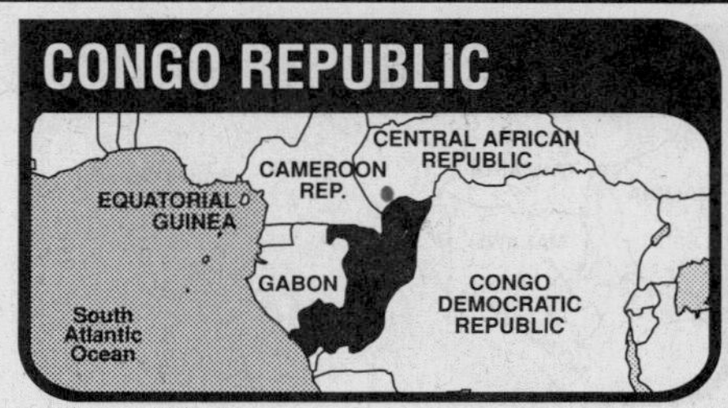


The Republic of the Congo (formerly the Peoples Republic of the Congo), located on the equator in west-central Africa, has an area of 132,047 sq. mi. (342,000 sq. km.) and a population of *2.98 million. Capital: Brazzaville. Agriculture forestry, mining, and food processing are the principal industries. Timber, industrial diamonds, potash, peanuts, and cocoa beans are exported.

The Portuguese were the first Europeans to explore the Congo (Brazzaville) area, 14th century. They conducted a slave trade with the tribal kingdoms of Teke, Loango, and Kongo without attempting developmental colonization. French influence was established in 1883 when the king of Teke signed a treaty with Savorgnan de Brazza, thereby placing his kingdom under the protection of France. While a French protectorate, the area was known as Middle Congo. In 1910 Middle Congo became a part of French Equatorial Africa, which also included Gabon, Ubangi-Shari (now the Central African Republic), and Chad. Following World War II, during which it was an important center of Free French activities, the Middle Congo was given a large measure of internal autonomy, and its inhabitants were made French citizens. Upon approval of the constitution of the Fifth French Republic, 1958, it became a member of the new French Community. On Aug. 15, 1960, Middle Congo became the independent Republic of the Congo-Brazzaville. In Jan. 1970 the country's name was changed to Peoples Republic of the Congo. A new constitution which asserts the government's advocacy of socialism was adopted in 1973.

In June and July of 1992, a new 125-member National Assembly was elected. Later that year a new president, Pascal Lissouba was elected. In November, President Lissouba dismissed the previous government and dissolved the National Assembly. A new 23-member government, including members of the opposition, was formed in December, 1992, and the name was changed to Republique du Congo.

**NOTE:** For earlier and related coinage see French Equatorial Africa and the Equatorial African States. For later coinage see Central African States.

**RULERS**
French until 1960

**MINT MARKS**
(a) - Paris, privy marks only

**MONETARY SYSTEM**
100 Centimes = 1 Franc

## PEOPLE'S REPUBLIC

### Republique Populaire du Congo

### DECIMAL COINAGE

**100 FRANCS** **KM# 1** **Composition:** Nickel

| Date | Mintage | F | VF | XF | Unc | BU |
|---|---|---|---|---|---|---|
| 1971(a) | 2,500,000 | 8.00 | 15.00 | 25.00 | 40.00 | — |
| 1972(a) | — | 8.00 | 15.00 | 25.00 | 40.00 | — |

**100 FRANCS** **KM# 2** **Composition:** Nickel

| Date | Mintage | F | VF | XF | Unc | BU |
|---|---|---|---|---|---|---|
| 1975(a) | — | 4.00 | 8.00 | 16.50 | 30.00 | — |
| 1982(a) | — | 2.50 | 4.50 | 8.00 | 12.50 | — |
| 1983(a) | — | 2.50 | 5.00 | 8.00 | 12.50 | — |
| 1985(a) | — | 2.00 | 3.00 | 6.00 | 10.00 | — |
| 1990(a) | — | 2.00 | 3.00 | 4.00 | 6.00 | — |

**100 FRANCS** **KM# 3** **Composition:** Copper-Nickel **Subject:** International Games **Reverse:** Handball

| Date | Mintage | F | VF | XF | Unc | BU |
|---|---|---|---|---|---|---|
| 1984 Proof | — | Value: 20.00 | | | | |

**100 FRANCS** **KM# 7** **Composition:** Nickel Plated Steel **Subject:** Olympics **Reverse:** Boxing

| Date | Mintage | F | VF | XF | Unc | BU |
|---|---|---|---|---|---|---|
| 1991 | 5,000 | — | — | — | 15.00 | — |

**100 FRANCS** **KM# 8** **Composition:** Nickel Plated Steel **Subject:** Olympics **Reverse:** Hurdler

| Date | Mintage | F | VF | XF | Unc | BU |
|---|---|---|---|---|---|---|
| 1991 | 5,000 | — | — | — | 15.00 | — |

**100 FRANCS** **KM# 10** **Composition:** Nickel Plated Steel **Series:** Old Ships **Reverse:** Spanish galleon

| Date | Mintage | F | VF | XF | Unc | BU |
|---|---|---|---|---|---|---|
| 1991 | — | — | — | — | 12.50 | — |

**100 FRANCS** **KM# 30** **Composition:** Copper **Series:** Old ships **Obverse:** National arms, "Republique Populaire du Congo" in legend **Reverse:** Spanish galleon

| Date | Mintage | F | VF | XF | Unc | BU |
|---|---|---|---|---|---|---|
| 1991 Proof | 100 | Value: 50.00 | | | | |

**100 FRANCS** **KM# 22** **Composition:** Copper **Series:** Protection of nature **Reverse:** Congolese peacock

| Date | Mintage | F | VF | XF | Unc | BU |
|---|---|---|---|---|---|---|
| 1992 | — | — | — | — | 10.00 | — |

**100 FRANCS** **KM# 31** **Composition:** Copper Nickel **Series:** Protection of nature **Obverse:** National arms, "Republic Populaire du Congo" in legend **Reverse:** Congolese peacock

| Date | Mintage | F | VF | XF | Unc | BU |
|---|---|---|---|---|---|---|
| 1992 | 333 | — | — | — | 50.00 | — |

**500 FRANCS** **KM# 4** **Composition:** Copper Nickel

| Date | Mintage | F | VF | XF | Unc | BU |
|---|---|---|---|---|---|---|
| 1985(a) | — | 3.50 | 6.50 | 10.00 | 18.50 | — |
| 1986(a) | — | 3.50 | 6.50 | 10.00 | 18.50 | — |

**500 FRANCS** **KM# 5** **Weight:** 16.0000 g. **Composition:** 0.9990 Silver .5144 oz. ASW **Series:** Old ships **Reverse:** Spanish galleon

| Date | Mintage | F | VF | XF | Unc | BU |
|---|---|---|---|---|---|---|
| 1991 Proof | — | Value: 30.00 | | | | |

**500 FRANCS** **KM# 6** **Weight:** 12.0000 g. **Composition:** 0.9990 Silver .3858 oz. ASW **Subject:** World Cup Soccer

| Date | Mintage | F | VF | XF | Unc | BU |
|---|---|---|---|---|---|---|
| 1991 | — | — | — | — | 27.50 | — |

**500 FRANCS** **KM# 9** **Weight:** 16.0700 g. **Composition:** 0.9990 Silver .517 oz. ASW **Subject:** Olympics **Reverse:** Hurdler

| Date | Mintage | F | VF | XF | Unc | BU |
|---|---|---|---|---|---|---|
| 1991 Proof | — | Value: 25.00 | | | | |

**500 FRANCS** **KM# 9a** **Weight:** 20.0000 g. **Composition:** 0.9990 Silver .6425 oz. ASW **Subject:** Olympics **Reverse:** Hurdler

| Date | Mintage | F | VF | XF | Unc | BU |
|---|---|---|---|---|---|---|
| 1991 | 5,000 | — | — | — | 27.50 | — |

**500 FRANCS** **KM# 11** **Weight:** 20.0000 g. **Composition:** 0.9990 Silver .643 oz. ASW **Subject:** World Cup Soccer **Reverse:** Player and Statue of Liberty

| Date | Mintage | F | VF | XF | Unc | BU |
|---|---|---|---|---|---|---|
| 1992 Proof | — | Value: 25.00 | | | | |

**500 FRANCS** **KM# 12** **Weight:** 19.9500 g. **Composition:** 0.9990 Silver .6415 oz. ASW **Subject:** Protection of nature **Reverse:** Congolese peacock

| Date | Mintage | F | VF | XF | Unc | BU |
|---|---|---|---|---|---|---|
| 1992 Proof | — | Value: 32.50 | | | | |

## REPUBLIC

### Republique du Congo

### DECIMAL COINAGE

**100 FRANCS** **KM# 18** **Composition:** Copper Nickel **Obverse:** Female writing on tablets **Reverse:** 4-masted sailing ship "Herzogin Cecilie"

| Date | Mintage | F | VF | XF | Unc | BU |
|---|---|---|---|---|---|---|
| 1993 | — | — | — | — | 10.00 | — |

**100 FRANCS** **KM# 20** **Composition:** Copper **Subject:** Preservation of nature **Reverse:** 4 elephants

| Date | Mintage | F | VF | XF | Unc | BU |
|---|---|---|---|---|---|---|
| 1993 | — | — | — | — | 10.00 | — |

**100 FRANCS** **KM# 32** **Composition:** Copper **Obverse:** Woman writing on tablets **Reverse:** 4-masted sailing ship "Herzogin Cecilie"

| Date | Mintage | F | VF | XF | Unc | BU |
|---|---|---|---|---|---|---|
| 1993 Proof | 100 | Value: 50.00 | | | | |

**100 FRANCS** **KM# 33** **Composition:** Copper **Subject:** Prehistoric animals **Obverse:** Woman writing on tablets **Reverse:** Brachiosaurus

| Date | Mintage | F | VF | XF | Unc | BU |
|---|---|---|---|---|---|---|
| 1993 Proof | 100 | Value: 50.00 | | | | |

**100 FRANCS** **KM# 16** **Composition:** Copper Nickel **Subject:** Prehistoric animals **Obverse:** Woman writing on tablets **Reverse:** Polacanthus

| Date | Mintage | F | VF | XF | Unc | BU |
|---|---|---|---|---|---|---|
| 1994 | — | — | — | — | 15.00 | — |

**100 FRANCS** **KM# 19** **Composition:** Copper Nickel **Subject:** Prehistoric animals **Obverse:** Woman writing on tablets **Reverse:** Spinosaurus

| Date | Mintage | F | VF | XF | Unc | BU |
|---|---|---|---|---|---|---|
| 1994 | — | — | — | — | 25.00 | — |

**100 FRANCS** **KM# 34** **Composition:** Copper Nickel **Subject:** Prehistoric animals **Obverse:** Woman writing on tablets **Reverse:** Mammuthus

| Date | Mintage | F | VF | XF | Unc | BU |
|---|---|---|---|---|---|---|
| 1994 Proof | 100 | Value: 50.00 | | | | |

**100 FRANCS** **KM# 21** **Composition:** Copper Nickel **Reverse:** Junkers JU52 trimotor airplane **Note:** Multicolored.

| Date | Mintage | F | VF | XF | Unc | BU |
|---|---|---|---|---|---|---|
| 1995 | 25,000 | — | — | — | 25.00 | — |

**100 FRANCS** **KM# 45** **Composition:** Copper Nickel **Subject:** XXVII Olympiade **Obverse:** Woman seated with tablet **Reverse:** Shot putter

| Date | Mintage | F | VF | XF | Unc | BU |
|---|---|---|---|---|---|---|
| 1999 | 10,000 | — | — | — | 7.50 | — |

**1000 FRANCS** **KM# 13** **Weight:** 20.0000 g. **Composition:** 0.9990 Silver .643 oz. ASW **Subject:** Preservation of nature **Reverse:** Elephants

| Date | Mintage | F | VF | XF | Unc | BU |
|---|---|---|---|---|---|---|
| 1993 Proof | — | Value: 35.00 | | | | |

**1000 FRANCS** **KM# 14** **Weight:** 15.9000 g. **Composition:** 0.9990 Silver .5107 oz. ASW **Subject:** Prehistoric animals **Reverse:** Brachiosaurus

| Date | Mintage | F | VF | XF | Unc | BU |
|---|---|---|---|---|---|---|
| 1993 Proof | — | Value: 37.50 | | | | |

**1000 FRANCS** **KM# 15** **Weight:** 20.1000 g. **Composition:** 0.9990 Silver .6456 oz. ASW **Reverse:** 4 masted sailing ship "Herzogin Cecilie"

| Date | Mintage | F | VF | XF | Unc | BU |
|---|---|---|---|---|---|---|
| 1993 | 100 | — | — | — | 100 | — |
| 1993 Proof | — | Value: 35.00 | | | | |

**1000 FRANCS** **KM# 17** **Weight:** 15.8800 g. **Composition:** 0.9990 Silver .5106 oz. ASW **Subject:** Prehistoric animals **Reverse:** Mammoth

| Date | Mintage | F | VF | XF | Unc | BU |
|---|---|---|---|---|---|---|
| 1994 Proof | — | Value: 35.00 | | | | |

**1000 FRANCS** **KM# 23** **Weight:** 20.0000 g. **Composition:** 0.9990 Silver .6430 oz. ASW **Subject:** 1996 Olympics **Reverse:** Discus throwing

| Date | Mintage | F | VF | XF | Unc | BU |
|---|---|---|---|---|---|---|
| 1995 Proof | 15,000 | Value: 30.00 | | | | |

**1000 FRANCS** **KM# 24** **Weight:** 20.0000 g. **Composition:** 0.9990 Silver .6430 oz. ASW **Reverse:** Swiss airliner - Junkers JU 52 **Note:** Multicolored.

| Date | Mintage | F | VF | XF | Unc | BU |
|---|---|---|---|---|---|---|
| 1995 Proof | 15,000 | Value: 60.00 | | | | |

**1000 FRANCS** **KM# 25** **Weight:** 20.0000 g. **Composition:** 0.9990 Silver .6430 oz. ASW **Reverse:** Panther **Note:** Multicolored.

| Date | Mintage | F | VF | XF | Unc | BU |
|---|---|---|---|---|---|---|
| 1996 Proof | — | Value: 60.00 | | | | |

**1000 FRANCS** **KM# 27** **Weight:** 20.0000 g. **Composition:** 0.9990 Silver .6430 oz. ASW **Subject:** World Cup Soccer **Obverse:** Woman writing on tablets **Reverse:** Eiffel Tower, soccer ball, French flag **Note:** Multicolored.

| Date | Mintage | F | VF | XF | Unc | BU |
|---|---|---|---|---|---|---|
| 1996 Proof | — | Value: 45.00 | | | | |

**1000 FRANCS** KM#26 **Weight:** 20.0000 g. **Composition:** 0.9990 Silver .6430 oz. ASW **Subject:** World Cup Soccer **Obverse:** Woman writing on tablets **Reverse:** Two soccer players

| Date | Mintage | F | VF | XF | Unc | BU |
|---|---|---|---|---|---|---|
| 1996 | 100 | — | — | — | 75.00 | — |
| 1996 Proof | — | Value: 45.00 | | | | |

**1000 FRANCS** KM#29 **Weight:** 15.0000 g. **Composition:** 0.9990 Silver .4818 oz. ASW **Obverse:** Woman writing on tablets **Reverse:** Ancient Roman ship

| Date | Mintage | F | VF | XF | Unc | BU |
|---|---|---|---|---|---|---|
| 1997 Proof | 5,000 | Value: 35.00 | | | | |

**1000 FRANCS** KM# 28.1 **Weight:** 20.0000 g. **Composition:** 0.9990 Silver .6430 oz. ASW **Subject:** XXVII Olympiade **Obverse:** Woman writing on tablets **Reverse:** Two boxers **Note:** Multicolored.

| Date | Mintage | F | VF | XF | Unc | BU |
|---|---|---|---|---|---|---|
| 1997 | 100 | — | — | — | 100 | — |
| 1997 Proof | 500 | Value: 55.00 | | | | |

**1000 FRANCS** KM# 28.2 **Weight:** 15.8800 g. **Composition:** 0.9990 Silver .5106 oz. ASW **Subject:** XXVII Olympiade **Obverse:** Woman writing on tablets **Reverse:** Two boxers **Note:** Multicolored.

| Date | Mintage | F | VF | XF | Unc | BU |
|---|---|---|---|---|---|---|
| 1998 | 100 | — | — | — | 100 | — |
| 1998 Proof | 5,000 | Value: 45.00 | | | | |

**1000 FRANCS** KM#46 **Weight:** 20.1000 g. **Composition:** 0.9990 Silver .6456 oz. ASW **Subject:** XXVII Olympiade **Obverse:** Woman seated with tablet **Reverse:** Shot putter

| Date | Mintage | F | VF | XF | Unc | BU |
|---|---|---|---|---|---|---|
| 1999 Proof | 5,000 | Value: 35.00 | | | | |

## ESSAIS

Standard metals unless otherwise noted

| KM# | Date | Mintage | Identification | Mkt Val |
|---|---|---|---|---|
| E1 | 1971 | 1,450 | 100 Francs. | 25.00 |
| E2 | 1971 | 4 | 100 Francs. Gold. | 1,250 |
| E3 | 1975 | 1,700 | 100 Francs. | 20.00 |

| KM# | Date | Mintage | Identification | Mkt Val |
|---|---|---|---|---|
| E5 | 1985 | 1,700 | 500 Francs. KM4. | 35.00 |

## PIEFORTS

| KM# | Date | Mintage | Identification | Mkt Val |
|---|---|---|---|---|
| P1 | 1991 | 110 | 500 Francs. 0.9990 Silver. KM5. | 110 |

## TRIAL STRIKES

| KM# | Date | Mintage | Identification | Mkt Val |
|---|---|---|---|---|
| TS1 | 1984 | 3 | 10 Francs. Silver. Fencing. Uniface. | 750 |
| TS2 | 1984 | 3 | 50 Francs. Silver. Shot put. Uniface | 750 |

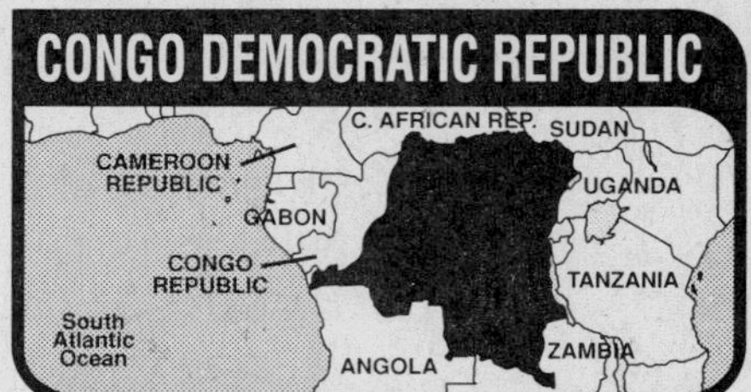


The Democratic Republic of the Congo (formerly the Republic of Zaire, and earlier the Belgian Congo), located in the south-central part of Africa, has an area of 905,568 sq. mi. (2,345,410 sq. km.) and a population of *47.4 million. Capital: Kinshasa. The mineral-rich country produces copper, tin, diamonds, gold, zinc, cobalt and uranium.

In ancient times the territory comprising former Zaire was occupied by Negrito peoples (Pygmies) pushed into the mountains by Bantu and Nilotic invaders. The interior was first explored by the American correspondent Henry Stanley, who was subsequently commissioned by King Leopold II of Belgium to conclude development treaties with the local chiefs. The Berlin conference of 1885 awarded the area to Leopold, who administered and exploited it as his private property until it was annexed to Belgium in 1908. Belgium received the mandate for the German territory of Ruanda-Urundi as a result of the international treaties after WWI. During World War II, Belgian Congolese troops fought on the side of the Allies, notably in Ethiopia. Following the eruption of bloody independence riots in 1959, Belgium granted the Belgian Congo independence as the Republic of the Congo on June 30, 1960. The nation officially changed its name to Zaire on Oct. 27, 1971, and following a Civil War in 1997 changed its name to the "Democratic Republic of the Congo."

# REPUBLIC, 1960-1971

## DECIMAL COINAGE

**10 FRANCS** KM# 1 **Composition:** Aluminum **Note:** Most recalled and melted.

| Date | Mintage | F | VF | XF | Unc | BU |
|---|---|---|---|---|---|---|
| 1965(b) | Est. 100,000,000 | 0.60 | 1.50 | 3.00 | 7.00 | — |

**10 FRANCS** KM# 2 **Weight:** 3.2260 g. **Composition:** 0.9000 Gold .0934 oz. AGW **Subject:** 5th anniversary of independence **Obverse:** Similar to 100 Francs, KM#6 **Note:** Approximately 70 percent melted.

| Date | Mintage | F | VF | XF | Unc | BU |
|---|---|---|---|---|---|---|
| 1965 Proof | Est. 3,000 | Value: 70.00 | | | | |

**20 FRANCS** KM# 3 **Weight:** 6.4520 g. **Composition:** 0.9000 Gold .1867 oz. AGW **Subject:** 5th anniversary of independence **Note:** Approximately 70 percent melted.

| Date | Mintage | F | VF | XF | Unc | BU |
|---|---|---|---|---|---|---|
| 1965 Proof | Est. 3,000 | Value: 125 | | | | |

**25 FRANCS** KM# 4 **Weight:** 8.0640 g. **Composition:** 0.9000 Gold .2334 oz. AGW **Subject:** 5th anniversary of independence **Note:** Approximately 70 percent melted.

| Date | Mintage | F | VF | XF | Unc | BU |
|---|---|---|---|---|---|---|
| 1965 Proof | Est. 3,000 | Value: 160 | | | | |

**25 FRANCS** KM# 4a **Composition:** Silver **Subject:** 5th anniversary of independence

| Date | Mintage | F | VF | XF | Unc | BU |
|---|---|---|---|---|---|---|
| 1965 Proof | — | Value: 60.00 | | | | |

**50 FRANCS** KM# 5 **Weight:** 16.1290 g. **Composition:** 0.9000 Gold .4668 oz. AGW **Subject:** 5th anniversary of independence **Note:** Approximately 70 percent melted.

| Date | Mintage | F | VF | XF | Unc | BU |
|---|---|---|---|---|---|---|
| 1965 Proof | Est. 3,000 | Value: 325 | | | | |

**100 FRANCS** KM# 6 **Weight:** 32.2580 g. **Composition:** 0.9000 Gold .9335 oz. AGW **Subject:** 5th anniversary of independence **Obverse:** President Joseph Kasa-Vubu **Reverse:** Similar to 50 Francs, KM#5 **Note:** Approximately 70 percent melted.

| Date | Mintage | F | VF | XF | Unc | BU |
|---|---|---|---|---|---|---|
| 1965 Proof | Est. 3,000 | Value: 550 | | | | |

**100 FRANCS** KM# 6a **Composition:** Silver **Subject:** 5th anniversary of independence **Obverse:** President Joseph Kasa-Vubu **Reverse:** Similar to 50 Francs, KM#5

| Date | Mintage | F | VF | XF | Unc | BU |
|---|---|---|---|---|---|---|
| 1965 Proof | — | Value: 100 | | | | |

## REFORM COINAGE

100 Sengis = 1 Likuta;
100 Makuta (plural of Likuta) = 1 Zaire

**10 SENGIS** KM# 7 **Composition:** Aluminum

| Date | Mintage | F | VF | XF | Unc | BU |
|---|---|---|---|---|---|---|
| 1967 | 90,996,000 | — | 0.15 | 0.45 | 1.00 | — |

**10 SENGIS** KM# 10 **Weight:** 3.2000 g. **Composition:** 0.9000 Gold .0926 oz. AGW **Subject:** 5th year of Mobutu presidency

| Date | Mintage | F | VF | XF | Unc | BU |
|---|---|---|---|---|---|---|
| 1970 | 1,000 | — | — | — | 55.00 | — |
| 1970 Proof | 1,000 | Value: 85.00 | | | | |

**10 SENGIS** KM# 10a **Composition:** Gilt Brass **Subject:** 5th year of Mobutu presidency

| Date | Mintage | F | VF | XF | Unc | BU |
|---|---|---|---|---|---|---|
| 1970 Proof | — | Value: 70.00 | | | | |

**LIKUTA** KM# 8 **Composition:** Aluminum

| Date | Mintage | F | VF | XF | Unc | BU |
|---|---|---|---|---|---|---|
| 1967 | 49,180,000 | — | 0.15 | 0.50 | 1.25 | — |

**5 MAKUTA** KM# 9 **Composition:** Copper-Nickel **Reverse:** President Mobutu

| Date | Mintage | F | VF | XF | Unc | BU |
|---|---|---|---|---|---|---|
| 1967 | 2,470,000 | 0.25 | 0.50 | 1.00 | 3.00 | — |

**25 MAKUTAS** KM# 11 **Composition:** Gilt Brass **Subject:** 5th year of Mobutu presidency

| Date | Mintage | F | VF | XF | Unc | BU |
|---|---|---|---|---|---|---|
| 1970 Proof | — | Value: 100 | | | | |

**25 MAKUTAS** KM# 11a **Weight:** 8.0000 g. **Composition:** 0.9000 Gold .2315 oz. AGW **Subject:** 5th year of Mobutu presidency

| Date | Mintage | F | VF | XF | Unc | BU |
|---|---|---|---|---|---|---|
| 1970 | 1,000 | — | — | — | 100 | — |
| 1970 Proof | 1,000 | Value: 155 | | | | |

**50 MAKUTAS** KM# 12 **Composition:** Gilt Brass **Subject:** 5th year of Mobutu presidency

| Date | Mintage | F | VF | XF | Unc | BU |
|---|---|---|---|---|---|---|
| 1970 Proof | — | Value: 125 | | | | |

**50 MAKUTAS** KM# 12a **Weight:** 16.0000 g. **Composition:** 0.9000 Gold .4630 oz. AGW **Subject:** 5th year of Mobutu presidency

| Date | Mintage | F | VF | XF | Unc | BU |
|---|---|---|---|---|---|---|
| 1970 | 1,000 | — | — | — | 200 | — |
| 1970 Proof | 1,000 | Value: 275 | | | | |

**ZAIRE** KM# 13 **Composition:** Gilt Brass **Subject:** 5th year of Mobutu presidency

| Date | Mintage | F | VF | XF | Unc | BU |
|---|---|---|---|---|---|---|
| 1970 Proof | — | Value: 150 | | | | |

**ZAIRE** KM# 13a **Weight:** 32.0000 g. **Composition:** 0.9000 Gold .9261 oz. AGW **Subject:** 5th year of Mobutu presidency

| Date | Mintage | F | VF | XF | Unc | BU |
|---|---|---|---|---|---|---|
| 1970 | 1,000 | — | — | — | 400 | — |
| 1970 Proof | 1,000 | Value: 485 | | | | |

# REPUBLIC, 1998-

## REFORM COINAGE

Congo Francs replace Zaire; July 1998

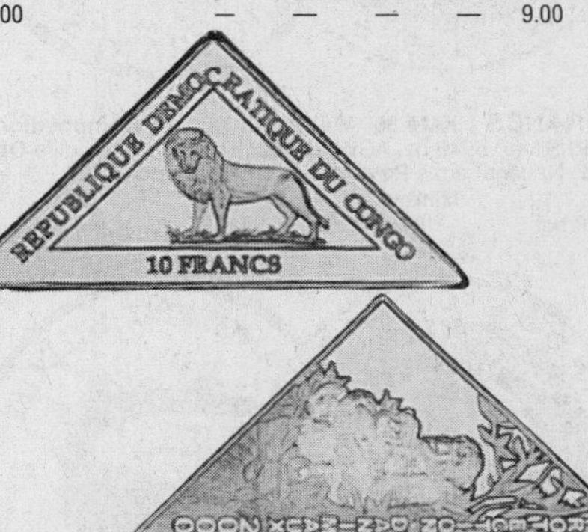

**5 FRANCS** KM# 47 **Composition:** Copper-Nickel **Subject:** Panama Canal **Obverse:** Lion **Reverse:** Sailing ship above map

| Date | Mintage | F | VF | XF | Unc | BU |
|---|---|---|---|---|---|---|
| 2000 | — | — | — | — | 9.00 | — |

**10 FRANCS** KM# 58 **Weight:** 31.2600 g. **Composition:** 0.9990 Silver 1.004 oz. ASW **Subject:** Animal protection **Obverse:** Lion above denomination **Reverse:** Female chimpanzee with young one **Edge:** Plain **Note:** Triangle; 45.1 x 23.4 millimeters.

| Date | Mintage | F | VF | XF | Unc | BU |
|---|---|---|---|---|---|---|
| 2000 Proof | — | Value: 32.50 | | | | |

**10 FRANCS** KM# 38 **Weight:** 20.0000 g. **Composition:** 0.9250 Silver .5948 oz. ASW **Series:** Endangered wildlife **Obverse:** National arms **Reverse:** Water chevrotain

| Date | Mintage | F | VF | XF | Unc | BU |
|---|---|---|---|---|---|---|
| 1999 Proof | 10,000 | Value: 35.00 | | | | |

**10 FRANCS** KM# 35 **Weight:** 20.0000 g. **Composition:** 0.9250 Silver .5948 oz. ASW **Series:** Endangered wildlife **Obverse:** National arms **Reverse:** Bonobos, chimpanzee mother and child

| Date | Mintage | F | VF | XF | Unc | BU |
|---|---|---|---|---|---|---|
| 1999 Proof | 10,000 | Value: 35.00 | | | | |

**10 FRANCS** KM# 36 **Weight:** 20.0000 g. **Composition:** 0.9250 Silver .5948 oz. ASW **Series:** Endangered wildlife **Obverse:** National arms **Reverse:** Pygmy hippopotamus

| Date | Mintage | F | VF | XF | Unc | BU |
|---|---|---|---|---|---|---|
| 1999 Proof | 10,000 | Value: 35.00 | | | | |

**10 FRANCS** KM# 37 **Weight:** 20.0000 g. **Composition:** 0.9250 Silver .5948 oz. ASW **Series:** Endangered wildlife **Obverse:** National arms **Reverse:** Crocodile

| Date | Mintage | F | VF | XF | Unc | BU |
|---|---|---|---|---|---|---|
| 1999 Proof | 10,000 | Value: 35.00 | | | | |

**10 FRANCS** KM# 39 **Weight:** 20.0000 g. **Composition:** 0.9250 Silver .5948 oz. ASW **Series:** Endangered wildlife **Obverse:** National arms **Reverse:** Ground pangolin

| Date | Mintage | F | VF | XF | Unc | BU |
|---|---|---|---|---|---|---|
| 1999 Proof | 10,000 | Value: 35.00 | | | | |

**10 FRANCS** KM# 40 **Weight:** 20.0000 g. **Composition:** 0.9250 Silver .5948 oz. ASW **Series:** Endangered wildlife **Obverse:** National arms **Reverse:** Poto

| Date | Mintage | F | VF | XF | Unc | BU |
|---|---|---|---|---|---|---|
| 1999 Proof | 10,000 | Value: 35.00 | | | | |

**10 FRANCS** KM# 41 **Weight:** 25.3100 g. **Composition:** 0.9250 Silver .7524 oz. ASW **Subject:** Explorers of Africa **Obverse:** National arms **Reverse:** Dr. David Livingstone

| Date | Mintage | F | VF | XF | Unc | BU |
|---|---|---|---|---|---|---|
| 1999 Proof | 10,000 | Value: 37.50 | | | | |

**10 FRANCS** KM# 42 **Weight:** 25.3100 g. **Composition:** 0.9250 Silver .7524 oz. ASW **Subject:** Explorers of Africa **Obverse:** National arms **Reverse:** Sir Henry Morton Stanley

| Date | Mintage | F | VF | XF | Unc | BU |
|---|---|---|---|---|---|---|
| 1999 Proof | 10,000 | Value: 37.50 | | | | |

**10 FRANCS** KM# 43 **Weight:** 25.3100 g. **Composition:** 0.9250 Silver .7524 oz. ASW **Subject:** 30th anniversary of the lunar landing **Obverse:** National arms **Reverse:** First lunar landing scene

| Date | Mintage | F | VF | XF | Unc | BU |
|---|---|---|---|---|---|---|
| 1999 Proof | 10,000 | Value: 37.50 | | | | |

**10 FRANCS** KM# 44 **Weight:** 25.3100 g. **Composition:** 0.9250 Silver .7524 oz. ASW **Subject:** Sydney 2000 **Obverse:** National arms **Reverse:** Diver and opera house

| Date | Mintage | F | VF | XF | Unc | BU |
|---|---|---|---|---|---|---|
| 1999 Proof | 10,000 | Value: 37.50 | | | | |

**10 FRANCS** KM# 48 **Weight:** 25.1300 g. **Composition:** 0.9250 Silver .7474 oz. ASW **Subject:** Panama Canal **Obverse:** Lion **Reverse:** Sailing ship above map

| Date | Mintage | F | VF | XF | Unc | BU |
|---|---|---|---|---|---|---|
| 2000 Proof | — | Value: 35.00 | | | | |

**10 FRANCS** KM# 53 **Weight:** 25.4500 g. **Composition:** 0.9250 Silver .7569 oz. ASW **Subject:** Wildlife protection **Obverse:** Lion above denomination **Reverse:** Parrot with open wings **Edge:** Reeded **Size:** 37.3 mm. **Note:** Multicolored.

| Date | Mintage | F | VF | XF | Unc | BU |
|---|---|---|---|---|---|---|
| 2000 Proof | — | Value: 45.00 | | | | |

**10 FRANCS** **KM# 54** **Weight:** 25.4500 g. **Composition:** 0.9250 Silver .7569 oz. ASW **Subject:** Wildlife protection **Obverse:** Lion above denomination **Reverse:** Parrot with folded wings **Edge:** Reeded **Size:** 37.3 mm. **Note:** Multicolored.

| Date | Mintage | F | VF | XF | Unc | BU |
|---|---|---|---|---|---|---|
| 2000 Proof | — | Value: 45.00 | | | | |

**10 FRANCS** **KM# 55** **Weight:** 31.2600 g. **Composition:** 0.9990 Silver 1.004 oz. ASW **Subject:** Millennium - space travel **Obverse:** Lion above denomination **Reverse:** Footprint on the moon **Edge:** Plain **Note:** Rectangle; 47.7 x 27.1 millimeters.

| Date | Mintage | F | VF | XF | Unc | BU |
|---|---|---|---|---|---|---|
| 2000 Proof | — | Value: 32.50 | | | | |

**10 FRANCS** **KM# 56** **Weight:** 31.2600 g. **Composition:** 0.9990 Silver 1.004 oz. ASW **Subject:** Animal protection **Obverse:** Lion above denomination **Reverse:** Chimpanzee hanging from branches **Edge:** Plain **Note:** Triangle; 45.1 x 23.4 millimeters.

| Date | Mintage | F | VF | XF | Unc | BU |
|---|---|---|---|---|---|---|
| 2000 Proof | — | Value: 32.50 | | | | |

**10 FRANCS** **KM# 57** **Weight:** 31.2600 g. **Composition:** 0.9990 Silver 1.004 oz. ASW **Subject:** Animal protection **Obverse:** Lion above denomination **Reverse:** 2 chimpanzees in trees **Edge:** Plain **Note:** Triangle; 45.1 x 23.4 millimeters.

| Date | Mintage | F | VF | XF | Unc | BU |
|---|---|---|---|---|---|---|
| 2000 Proof | — | Value: 32.50 | | | | |

**10 FRANCS** **KM# 59** **Weight:** 31.2600 g. **Composition:** 0.9990 Silver 1.004 oz. ASW **Subject:** Animal protection **Obverse:** Lion above denomination **Reverse:** 2 chimpanzees on the ground **Edge:** Plain **Note:** Triangle; 45.1 x 23.4 millimeters.

| Date | Mintage | F | VF | XF | Unc | BU |
|---|---|---|---|---|---|---|
| 2000 Proof | — | Value: 32.50 | | | | |

**10 FRANCS** **KM# 49** **Weight:** 25.1300 g. **Composition:** 0.9250 Silver .7474 oz. ASW **Subject:** Panama Canal **Obverse:** Lion **Reverse:** Cargo ship over map of Panama

| Date | Mintage | F | VF | XF | Unc | BU |
|---|---|---|---|---|---|---|
| 2000 Proof | — | Value: 35.00 | | | | |

**10 FRANCS** **KM# 50** **Weight:** 25.1300 g. **Composition:** 0.9250 Silver .7474 oz. ASW **Subject:** 25th anniversary - visit of Pope John Paul II **Obverse:** Lion **Reverse:** Bust right of Pope John Paul II

| Date | Mintage | F | VF | XF | Unc | BU |
|---|---|---|---|---|---|---|
| 2000 Proof | — | Value: 35.00 | | | | |

**10 FRANCS** **KM# 51** **Weight:** 25.1300 g. **Composition:** 0.9250 Silver .7474 oz. ASW **Subject:** 25th anniversary - visit of Pope John Paul II **Obverse:** Lion **Reverse:** Half-length bust of Pope John Paul II facing

| Date | Mintage | F | VF | XF | Unc | BU |
|---|---|---|---|---|---|---|
| 2000 Proof | — | Value: 35.00 | | | | |

**20 FRANCS** **KM# 52** **Weight:** 1.5300 g. **Composition:** 0.9990 Gold .0492 oz. AGW **Subject:** 25th anniversary - visit of Pope John Paul II **Obverse:** Lion **Reverse:** Bust right of Pope John Paul II

| Date | Mintage | F | VF | XF | Unc | BU |
|---|---|---|---|---|---|---|
| 2000 Proof | — | Value: 40.00 | | | | |

## ESSAIS

| KM# | Date | Mintage | Identification | Mkt Val |
|---|---|---|---|---|
| E1 | 1965 | — | 10 Francs. Silver. | — |
| E2 | 1965 | — | 10 Francs. Gold. | — |

**Note:** Aluminum and copper-nickel essais of the 10 Francs are valued at $175 and $250 respectively. These are considered off-metal pieces created as die trials or set-up strikes in the process of producing the official silver and gold coins.

| KM# | Date | Mintage | Identification | Mkt Val |
|---|---|---|---|---|
| E3 | 1970 | — | 50 Makutas. Pewter. KM12. | 250 |
| E4 | 1970 | — | Zaire. Pewter. KM13. | 325 |
| E5 | 1970 | — | Zaire. Silver. KM13. | 165 |
| E6 | 1970 | 10 | Zaire. Gold. ESSAI. | 1,000 |

## PIEFORTS WITH ESSAI

| KM# | Date | Mintage | Identification | Mkt Val |
|---|---|---|---|---|
| PE1 | 1970 | 10 | Zaire. Silver. 2.4 millimeters thick. | 250 |
| PE2 | 1970 | 10 | Zaire. Silver. 4.7 millimeters thick. | 365 |

## MINT SETS

| KM# | Date | Mintage | Identification | Issue Price | Mkt Val |
|---|---|---|---|---|---|
| MS1 | 1970 (4) | 1,000 | KM10-13 | 1,300 | 900 |

## PROOF SETS

| KM# | Date | Mintage | Identification | Issue Price | Mkt Val |
|---|---|---|---|---|---|
| PS1 | 1965 (5) | 3,000 | KM2-6. Approximately 70 percent melted. | 490 | 1,290 |
| PS2 | 1970 (4) | 1,000 | KM10-13 | — | 1,100 |

# COOK ISLANDS

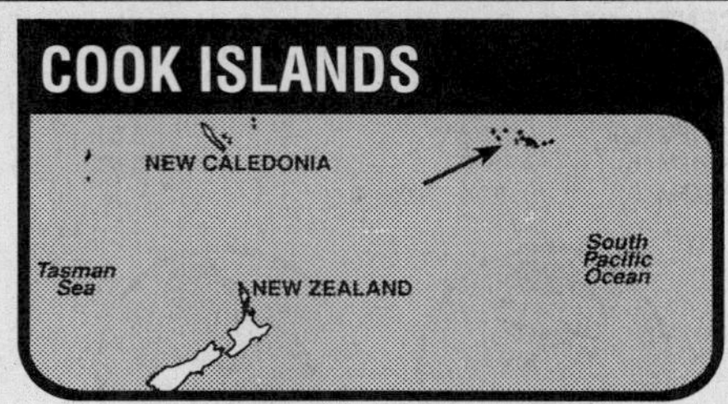


Cook Islands, a political dependency of New Zealand consisting of 15 islands, is located in the South Pacific Ocean about 2,000 miles (3,218 km.) northeast of New Zealand. It has an area of 93 sq. mi. (234 sq. km.) and a population of 17,185. Capital: Avarua. The United States claims the islands of Danger, Manahiki, Penrhyn, and Rakahanga atolls. Citrus and canned fruits and juices, copra, clothing, jewelry, and mother-of-pearl shell are exported.

The islands were first sighted by Spanish navigator Alvaro de Mendada in 1595. Portuguese navigator Pedro Fernandes de Quieros landed on Rakahanga in 1606. English navigator Capt. James Cook sailed to the islands on three occasions: 1773, 1774 and 1777. He named them Hervey Islands, in honor of Augustus John Hervey, a lord of the Admiralty. The islands were declared a British protectorate in 1888, and were annexed to New Zealand in 1901. They were granted internal self-government in 1965. New Zealand provides an annual subsidy and retains responsibility for defense and foreign affairs.

**RULERS**
British

**MINT MARKS**
(b) - British Royal Mint
FM - Franklin Mint, U.S.A. *
PM - Pobjoy Mint

***NOTE**: From 1975-1985 the Franklin Mint produced coinage in up to three different qualities. Qualities of issue are designated in () after each date and are defined as follows:

**(M) MATTE** - Normal circulation strike or a dull finish produced by sandblasting special uncirculated (polish finish) or proof quality dies.

**(U) SPECIAL UNCIRCULATED** - Polished or proof-like in appearance without any frosted features.

**(P) PROOF** - The highest quality obtainable having mirror-like fields and frosted features.

**MONETARY SYSTEM**

**(Until 1967)**

12 Pence = 1 Shilling
20 Shillings = 1 Pound

**(Commencing 1967)**

100 Cents = 1 Dollar

# DEPENDENCY OF NEW ZEALAND

## DECIMAL COINAGE

**CENT** **KM# 1** **Composition:** Bronze **Reverse:** Taro leaf

| Date | Mintage | F | VF | XF | Unc | BU |
|---|---|---|---|---|---|---|
| 1972 | 117,000 | — | — | 0.10 | 0.20 | — |
| 1972 Proof | 17,000 | Value: 0.50 | | | | |
| 1973 | 8,500 | — | — | 0.10 | 0.20 | — |
| 1973 Proof | 13,000 | Value: 0.50 | | | | |
| 1974 | 300,000 | — | — | 0.10 | 0.20 | — |
| 1974 Proof | 7,300 | Value: 0.50 | | | | |
| 1975 | 429,000 | — | — | 0.10 | 0.20 | — |
| 1975FM (M) | 1,000 | — | — | — | 0.50 | — |
| 1975FM (U) | 2,251 | — | — | — | 0.20 | — |
| 1975FM (P) | 21,000 | Value: 0.50 | | | | |
| 1976FM (M) | 1,001 | — | — | — | 0.50 | — |
| 1976FM (U) | 1,066 | — | — | — | 0.20 | — |
| 1976FM (P) | 18,000 | Value: 0.50 | | | | |
| 1977FM (M) | 1,171 | — | — | — | 0.50 | — |
| 1977FM (U) | 1,002 | — | — | — | 0.20 | — |
| 1977FM (P) | 5,986 | Value: 0.50 | | | | |
| 1979FM (M) | 1,000 | — | — | — | 0.50 | — |
| 1979FM (U) | 500 | — | — | — | 1.00 | — |
| 1979FM (P) | 4,058 | Value: 0.50 | | | | |
| 1983 | — | — | — | 0.10 | 0.20 | — |
| 1983 Proof | 10,000 | Value: 0.50 | | | | |

**CENT** **KM# 1a** **Composition:** Bronze **Edge Lettering:** 1728 CAPTAIN COOK 1978

| Date | Mintage | F | VF | XF | Unc | BU |
|---|---|---|---|---|---|---|
| 1978FM (M) | 1,000 | — | — | — | 1.00 | — |
| 1978FM (U) | 767 | — | — | — | 1.00 | — |
| 1978FM (P) | 6,287 | Value: 0.50 | | | | |

**CENT** **KM# 1b** **Composition:** Bronze **Subject:** Wedding of Prince Charles and Lady Diana **Edge Lettering:** THE ROYAL WEDDING 29 JULY 1981

| Date | Mintage | F | VF | XF | Unc | BU |
|---|---|---|---|---|---|---|
| 1981FM (M) | 1,000 | — | — | — | 0.50 | — |
| 1981FM (U) | 1,100 | — | — | — | 0.50 | — |
| 1981FM (P) | 9,205 | Value: 0.40 | | | | |

**2 CENTS** **KM# 2** **Composition:** Bronze **Reverse:** Pineapple

| Date | Mintage | F | VF | XF | Unc | BU |
|---|---|---|---|---|---|---|
| 1972 | 63,000 | — | 0.10 | 0.15 | 0.30 | — |
| 1972 Proof | 17,000 | Value: 0.75 | | | | |
| 1973 | 8,500 | — | 0.15 | 0.20 | 0.40 | — |
| 1973 Proof | 13,000 | Value: 0.75 | | | | |
| 1974 | 120,000 | — | 0.10 | 0.15 | 0.30 | — |
| 1974 Proof | 7,300 | Value: 0.75 | | | | |
| 1975 | 129,000 | — | 0.10 | 0.15 | 0.25 | — |
| 1975FM (M) | 1,000 | — | — | — | 0.75 | — |
| 1975FM (U) | 2,251 | — | — | — | 0.30 | — |
| 1975FM (P) | 21,000 | Value: 0.75 | | | | |
| 1976FM (M) | 1,001 | — | — | — | 0.75 | — |
| 1976FM (U) | 1,066 | — | — | — | 0.30 | — |
| 1976FM (P) | 18,000 | Value: 0.75 | | | | |
| 1977FM (M) | 1,171 | — | — | — | 0.75 | — |
| 1977FM (U) | 1,002 | — | — | — | 0.30 | — |
| 1977FM (P) | 5,986 | Value: 0.75 | | | | |
| 1979FM (M) | 1,000 | — | — | — | 0.75 | — |
| 1979FM (U) | 500 | — | — | — | 0.30 | — |
| 1979FM (P) | 4,058 | Value: 0.75 | | | | |
| 1983 | — | — | 0.10 | 0.15 | 0.25 | — |
| 1983 Proof | 10,000 | Value: 0.75 | | | | |

**2 CENTS** **KM# 2a** **Composition:** Bronze **Edge Lettering:** 1798 CAPTAIN COOK 1978

| Date | Mintage | F | VF | XF | Unc | BU |
|---|---|---|---|---|---|---|
| 1978FM (M) | 1,000 | — | — | — | 0.75 | — |
| 1978FM (U) | 767 | — | — | — | 0.75 | — |
| 1978FM (P) | 6,287 | Value: 0.50 | | | | |

**2 CENTS** **KM# 2b** **Composition:** Bronze **Subject:** Wedding of Prince Charles and Lady Diana **Edge Lettering:** THE ROYAL WEDDING 29 JULY 1981

| Date | Mintage | F | VF | XF | Unc | BU |
|---|---|---|---|---|---|---|
| 1981FM (M) | 1,000 | — | — | — | 0.75 | — |
| 1981FM (U) | 1,100 | — | — | — | 0.75 | — |
| 1981FM (P) | 9,205 | Value: 0.50 | | | | |

**5 CENTS** **KM# 3** **Composition:** Copper-Nickel **Reverse:** Hibiscus

| Date | Mintage | F | VF | XF | Unc | BU |
|---|---|---|---|---|---|---|
| 1972 | 32,000 | — | 0.10 | 0.20 | 0.40 | — |
| 1972 Proof | 17,000 | Value: 1.00 | | | | |
| 1973 | 8,500 | — | 0.15 | 0.25 | 0.50 | — |
| 1973 Proof | 13,000 | Value: 1.00 | | | | |
| 1974 | 80,000 | — | 0.10 | 0.20 | 0.40 | — |
| 1974 Proof | 7,300 | Value: 1.00 | | | | |
| 1975 | 89,000 | — | 0.10 | 0.20 | 0.40 | — |
| 1975FM (M) | 1,000 | — | — | — | 1.00 | — |
| 1975FM (U) | 2,251 | — | — | — | 0.40 | — |
| 1975FM (P) | 21,000 | Value: 1.00 | | | | |
| 1976FM (M) | 1,001 | — | — | — | 1.00 | — |
| 1976FM (U) | 1,066 | — | — | — | 0.40 | — |
| 1976FM (P) | 18,000 | Value: 1.00 | | | | |
| 1977FM (M) | 1,171 | — | — | — | 1.00 | — |
| 1977FM (U) | 1,002 | — | — | — | 0.40 | — |
| 1977FM (P) | 5,986 | Value: 1.00 | | | | |
| 1979FM (M) | 1,000 | — | — | — | 1.00 | — |
| 1979FM (U) | 500 | — | — | — | 0.40 | — |
| 1979FM (P) | 4,058 | Value: 1.00 | | | | |
| 1983 | — | — | 0.10 | 0.20 | 0.40 | — |
| 1983 Proof | 10,000 | Value: 1.00 | | | | |

**5 CENTS** **KM# 3a** **Composition:** Copper-Nickel **Edge Lettering:** 1728 CAPTAIN COOK 1978

| Date | Mintage | F | VF | XF | Unc | BU |
|---|---|---|---|---|---|---|
| 1978FM (M) | 1,000 | — | — | — | 1.00 | — |
| 1978FM (U) | 767 | — | — | — | 0.75 | — |
| 1978FM (P) | 6,287 | Value: 0.50 | | | | |

**5 CENTS** **KM# 3b** **Composition:** Copper-Nickel **Subject:** Wedding of Prince Charles and Lady Diana **Edge Lettering:** THE ROYAL WEDDING 29 JULY 1981

| Date | Mintage | F | VF | XF | Unc | BU |
|---|---|---|---|---|---|---|
| 1981FM (M) | 1,000 | — | — | — | 1.00 | — |
| 1981FM (U) | 1,100 | — | — | — | 1.00 | — |
| 1981FM (P) | 9,205 | Value: 0.50 | | | | |

**5 CENTS** **KM# 33** **Composition:** Copper-Nickel

| Date | Mintage | F | VF | XF | Unc | BU |
|---|---|---|---|---|---|---|
| 1987 | — | — | — | 0.10 | 0.25 | — |
| 1987 Proof | — | Value: 1.25 | | | | |
| 1988 | — | — | — | 0.10 | 0.25 | — |
| 1988 Proof | — | Value: 1.25 | | | | |
| 1992 | — | — | — | 0.10 | 0.25 | — |
| 1992 Proof | — | Value: 1.25 | | | | |
| 1994 | 20,000 | — | — | 0.10 | 0.25 | — |
| 1994 Proof | 200 | Value: 1.50 | | | | |

**5 CENTS** **KM# 369** **Weight:** 4.4300 g. **Composition:** Nickel Clad Steel **Subject:** F.A.O. **Obverse:** Queen's portrait. **Reverse:** Statue of Tangaroa. **Edge:** Plain. **Size:** 24 mm.

| Date | Mintage | F | VF | XF | Unc | BU |
|---|---|---|---|---|---|---|
| 2000 | — | — | — | — | 1.00 | — |

**10 CENTS** **KM# 4** **Composition:** Copper-Nickel **Reverse:** Orange

| Date | Mintage | F | VF | XF | Unc | BU |
|---|---|---|---|---|---|---|
| 1972 | 35,000 | — | 0.10 | 0.20 | 0.50 | — |
| 1972 Proof | 17,000 | Value: 1.25 | | | | |
| 1973 | 59,000 | — | 0.10 | 0.20 | 0.50 | — |
| 1973 Proof | 13,000 | Value: 1.25 | | | | |
| 1974 | 50,000 | — | 0.10 | 0.20 | 0.50 | — |
| 1974 Proof | 7,300 | Value: 1.25 | | | | |
| 1975 | 59,000 | — | 0.10 | 0.20 | 0.50 | — |
| 1975FM (M) | 1,000 | — | — | — | 1.25 | — |
| 1975FM (U) | 2,251 | — | — | — | 0.50 | — |
| 1975FM (P) | 21,000 | Value: 1.25 | | | | |
| 1976FM (M) | 1,001 | — | — | — | 1.25 | — |
| 1976FM (U) | 1,066 | — | — | — | 0.50 | — |
| 1976FM (P) | 18,000 | Value: 1.25 | | | | |
| 1977FM (M) | 1,171 | — | — | — | 1.25 | — |
| 1977FM (U) | 1,002 | — | — | — | 0.50 | — |
| 1977FM (P) | 5,986 | Value: 1.25 | | | | |
| 1983 | — | — | 0.10 | 0.20 | 0.50 | — |
| 1983 Proof | 10,000 | Value: 1.25 | | | | |

**10 CENTS** **KM# 4a** **Composition:** Copper-Nickel **Edge Lettering:** 1728 CAPTAIN COOK 1978

| Date | Mintage | F | VF | XF | Unc | BU |
|---|---|---|---|---|---|---|
| 1978FM (M) | 1,000 | — | — | — | 1.25 | — |
| 1978FM (U) | 767 | — | — | — | 1.25 | — |
| 1978FM (P) | 6,287 | Value: 1.00 | | | | |

**10 CENTS** **KM# 4b** **Composition:** Copper-Nickel **Series:** F.A.O

| Date | Mintage | F | VF | XF | Unc | BU |
|---|---|---|---|---|---|---|
| 1979FM (M) | 9,000 | — | — | — | 1.00 | — |
| 1979FM (U) | 500 | — | — | — | 1.50 | — |
| 1979FM (P) | 4,058 | Value: 1.25 | | | | |

**10 CENTS** **KM# 4c** **Composition:** Copper-Nickel **Subject:** Wedding of Prince Charles and Lady Diana **Edge Lettering:** THE ROYAL WEDDING 29 JULY 1981

| Date | Mintage | F | VF | XF | Unc | BU |
|---|---|---|---|---|---|---|
| 1981FM (M) | 1,000 | — | — | — | 1.25 | — |
| 1981FM (U) | 1,100 | — | — | — | 1.25 | — |
| 1981FM (P) | 9,205 | Value: 0.75 | | | | |

**10 CENTS** **KM# 34** **Composition:** Copper-Nickel

| Date | Mintage | F | VF | XF | Unc | BU |
|---|---|---|---|---|---|---|
| 1987 | — | — | — | 0.15 | 0.25 | — |
| 1987 Proof | — | Value: 1.25 | | | | |
| 1988 | — | — | — | 0.15 | 0.25 | — |
| 1988 Proof | — | Value: 1.25 | | | | |
| 1992 | — | — | — | 0.15 | 0.25 | — |
| 1992 Proof | — | Value: 1.25 | | | | |
| 1994 | 20,000 | — | — | 0.15 | 0.25 | — |
| 1994 Proof | 200 | Value: 1.50 | | | | |

**20 CENTS** **KM# 5** **Composition:** Copper-Nickel **Reverse:** Fairy Tern

| Date | Mintage | F | VF | XF | Unc | BU |
|---|---|---|---|---|---|---|
| 1972 | 31,000 | — | 0.20 | 0.40 | 0.75 | — |
| 1972 Proof | 17,000 | Value: 1.50 | | | | |
| 1973 | 49,000 | — | 0.20 | 0.40 | 0.75 | — |
| 1973 Proof | 13,000 | Value: 1.50 | | | | |
| 1974 | 5,500 | — | 0.20 | 0.45 | 0.85 | — |
| 1974 Proof | 7,300 | Value: 1.50 | | | | |
| 1975 | 60,000 | — | 0.20 | 0.40 | 0.75 | — |
| 1975FM (M) | 1,000 | — | — | — | 1.50 | — |
| 1975FM (U) | 2,251 | — | — | — | 0.85 | — |
| 1975FM (P) | 21,000 | Value: 1.50 | | | | |
| 1983 | — | — | 0.20 | 0.40 | 0.85 | — |
| 1983 Proof | 10,000 | Value: 1.50 | | | | |

**20 CENTS** **KM# 14** **Composition:** Copper-Nickel **Reverse:** Pacific Triton Shell

| Date | Mintage | F | VF | XF | Unc | BU |
|---|---|---|---|---|---|---|
| 1976FM (M) | 1,001 | — | — | — | 1.50 | — |
| 1976FM (U) | 1,066 | — | — | — | 1.00 | — |
| 1976FM (P) | 18,000 | Value: 1.50 | | | | |
| 1977FM (M) | 1,171 | — | — | — | 1.50 | — |
| 1977FM (U) | 1,002 | — | — | — | 1.00 | — |
| 1977FM (P) | 5,986 | Value: 1.50 | | | | |
| 1979FM (M) | 1,000 | — | — | — | 1.50 | — |
| 1979FM (U) | 500 | — | — | — | 2.00 | — |
| 1979FM (P) | 4,058 | Value: 1.50 | | | | |

**20 CENTS** **KM# 14a** **Composition:** Copper-Nickel **Edge Lettering:** 1728 CAPTAIN COOK 1978

| Date | Mintage | F | VF | XF | Unc | BU |
|---|---|---|---|---|---|---|
| 1978FM (M) | 1,000 | — | — | — | 1.50 | — |
| 1978FM (U) | 767 | — | — | — | 2.00 | — |
| 1978FM (P) | 6,287 | Value: 1.00 | | | | |

**20 CENTS** **KM# 14b** **Composition:** Copper-Nickel **Subject:** Wedding of Prince Charles and Lady Diana **Edge Lettering:** THE ROYAL WEDDING 29 JULY 1981

| Date | Mintage | F | VF | XF | Unc | BU |
|---|---|---|---|---|---|---|
| 1981FM (M) | 1,000 | — | — | — | 1.50 | — |
| 1981FM (U) | 1,100 | — | — | — | 1.50 | — |
| 1981FM (P) | 9,205 | Value: 1.00 | | | | |

**20 CENTS** **KM# 35** **Composition:** Copper-Nickel

| Date | Mintage | F | VF | XF | Unc | BU |
|---|---|---|---|---|---|---|
| 1987 | — | — | — | 0.25 | 0.35 | — |
| 1987 Proof | — | Value: 1.50 | | | | |
| 1988 | — | — | — | 0.25 | 0.35 | — |
| 1988 Proof | — | Value: 1.50 | | | | |
| 1992 | — | — | — | 0.25 | 0.35 | — |
| 1992 Proof | — | Value: 1.50 | | | | |
| 1994 | 20,000 | — | — | 0.25 | 0.35 | — |
| 1994 Proof | 200 | Value: 2.00 | | | | |

**50 CENTS** **KM# 6.1** **Composition:** Copper-Nickel **Obverse:** Machin bust of Queen Elizabeth II **Reverse:** Bonito fish, denomination

| Date | Mintage | F | VF | XF | Unc | BU |
|---|---|---|---|---|---|---|
| 1972 | 31,000 | — | 0.40 | 0.75 | 1.50 | — |
| 1972 Proof | 17,000 | Value: 3.00 | | | | |
| 1973 | 19,000 | — | 0.40 | 0.75 | 1.50 | — |
| 1973 Proof | 13,000 | Value: 3.00 | | | | |
| 1974 | 10,000 | — | 0.40 | 0.75 | 1.50 | — |
| 1974 Proof | 7,300 | Value: 3.00 | | | | |
| 1975 | 19,000 | — | 0.40 | 0.75 | 1.50 | — |
| 1975FM (M) | 1,000 | — | — | — | 2.00 | — |
| 1975FM (U) | 2,251 | — | — | — | 1.50 | — |
| 1975FM (P) | 21,000 | Value: 3.00 | | | | |
| 1976FM (M) | 1,001 | — | — | — | 2.00 | — |
| 1976FM (U) | 1,066 | — | — | — | 1.50 | — |
| 1976FM (P) | 18,000 | Value: 3.00 | | | | |
| 1977FM (M) | 1,171 | — | — | — | 2.00 | — |
| 1977FM (U) | 1,002 | — | — | — | 1.50 | — |
| 1977FM (P) | 5,986 | Value: 3.00 | | | | |
| 1983 | — | — | 0.40 | 0.75 | 1.50 | — |
| 1983 Proof | 10,000 | Value: 3.50 | | | | |

**50 CENTS** **KM# 6.2** **Composition:** Copper-Nickel **Edge Lettering:** 1728 CAPTAIN COOK 1978

| Date | Mintage | F | VF | XF | Unc | BU |
|---|---|---|---|---|---|---|
| 1978FM (M) | 1,000 | — | — | — | 2.00 | — |
| 1978FM (U) | 767 | — | — | — | 2.00 | — |
| 1978FM (P) | 6,287 | Value: 2.00 | | | | |

**50 CENTS** **KM# 6.3** **Composition:** Copper-Nickel **Series:** F.A.O **Reverse:** FAO logo, fish, denomination

| Date | Mintage | F | VF | XF | Unc | BU |
|---|---|---|---|---|---|---|
| 1979FM (M) | 9,000 | — | 0.50 | 1.00 | 2.00 | — |
| 1979FM (U) | 500 | — | — | — | 2.50 | — |
| 1979FM (P) | 4,058 | Value: 2.25 | | | | |

**50 CENTS** **KM# 6.4** **Composition:** Copper-Nickel **Subject:** Wedding of Prince Charles and Lady Diana **Edge Lettering:** THE ROYAL WEDDING 29 JULY 1981

| Date | Mintage | F | VF | XF | Unc | BU |
|---|---|---|---|---|---|---|
| 1981FM (M) | 1,000 | — | — | — | 2.00 | — |
| 1981 (U) | 1,100 | — | — | — | 2.00 | — |
| 1981FM (P) | 9,205 | Value: 1.50 | | | | |

**50 CENTS** **KM# 36** **Composition:** Copper-Nickel **Obverse:** Mature portrait of Queen Elizabeth **Reverse:** Fish, denomination

| Date | Mintage | F | VF | XF | Unc | BU |
|---|---|---|---|---|---|---|
| 1987 | — | — | 0.40 | 0.75 | 1.50 | — |
| 1987 Proof | — | Value: 2.00 | | | | |
| 1992 | — | — | 0.40 | 0.75 | 1.50 | — |

**50 CENTS** **KM# 307** **Composition:** Copper-Nickel **Obverse:** Queen's portrait **Reverse:** Princeness Diana's portrait, dates

| Date | Mintage | F | VF | XF | Unc | BU |
|---|---|---|---|---|---|---|
| 1997 Proof | — | Value: 12.00 | | | | |

**50 CENTS** **KM# 338** **Weight:** 26.9000 g. **Composition:** Copper-Nickel **Obverse:** Queen's head right **Reverse:** Cartoon cat "Garfield" **Edge:** Reeded **Note:** Multicolored.

| Date | Mintage | F | VF | XF | Unc | BU |
|---|---|---|---|---|---|---|
| 1999 Proof | — | Value: 17.50 | | | | |

**50 TENE** **KM# 41** **Composition:** Copper-Nickel **Reverse:** Turtle

| Date | Mintage | F | VF | XF | Unc | BU |
|---|---|---|---|---|---|---|
| 1988 | 60,000 | — | — | — | 1.50 | — |
| 1988 Proof | 1,000 | Value: 2.50 | | | | |
| 1992 | — | — | — | — | 1.50 | — |
| 1992 Proof | — | Value: 2.50 | | | | |
| 1994 | 20,000 | — | — | — | 1.50 | — |
| 1994 Proof | 200 | Value: 3.00 | | | | |

**DOLLAR** **KM# 7** **Composition:** Copper-Nickel **Reverse:** Tangaroa, Polynesian God of Creation

| Date | Mintage | F | VF | XF | Unc | BU |
|---|---|---|---|---|---|---|
| 1972 | 31,000 | — | 1.25 | 2.00 | 4.00 | — |
| 1972 Proof | 27,000 | Value: 5.00 | | | | |
| 1973 | 49,000 | — | 1.25 | 2.00 | 4.00 | — |
| 1973 Proof | 13,000 | Value: 6.00 | | | | |
| 1974 | 20,000 | — | 1.25 | 2.00 | 4.00 | — |
| 1974 Proof | 7,300 | Value: 6.00 | | | | |
| 1975 | 29,000 | — | 1.25 | 2.00 | 4.00 | — |
| 1975FM (M) | 1,000 | — | — | — | 5.00 | — |
| 1975FM (U) | 2,251 | — | — | — | 4.00 | — |
| 1975FM (P) | 21,000 | Value: 6.00 | | | | |
| 1976FM (M) | 1,001 | — | — | — | 5.00 | — |
| 1976FM (U) | 1,066 | — | — | — | 5.00 | — |
| 1976FM (P) | 18,000 | Value: 6.00 | | | | |
| 1977FM (M) | 1,171 | — | — | — | 5.00 | — |
| 1977FM (U) | 1,002 | — | — | — | 5.00 | — |
| 1977FM (P) | 5,986 | Value: 8.00 | | | | |
| 1979FM (M) | 1,000 | — | — | — | 5.00 | — |
| 1979FM (U) | 500 | — | — | — | 6.00 | — |
| 1979FM (P) | 4,058 | Value: 8.00 | | | | |
| 1983 | — | — | 1.25 | 2.00 | 4.00 | — |
| 1983 Proof | 10,000 | Value: 6.00 | | | | |

**DOLLAR** **KM# 7a** **Composition:** Copper-Nickel **Edge Lettering:** 1728 CAPTAIN COOK 1978

| Date | Mintage | F | VF | XF | Unc | BU |
|---|---|---|---|---|---|---|
| 1978FM (M) | 1,000 | — | — | — | 6.00 | — |
| 1978FM (U) | 767 | — | — | — | 6.00 | — |
| 1978FM (P) | 6,287 | Value: 5.00 | | | | |

**DOLLAR** **KM# 7b** **Composition:** Copper-Nickel **Subject:** Wedding of Prince Charles and Lady Diana **Edge Lettering:** THE ROYAL WEDDING 29 JULY 1981

| Date | Mintage | F | VF | XF | Unc | BU |
|---|---|---|---|---|---|---|
| 1981FM (M) | 1,000 | — | — | — | 6.00 | — |
| 1981FM (U) | 1,100 | — | — | — | 6.00 | — |
| 1981FM (P) | 9,205 | Value: 5.00 | | | | |

**DOLLAR** **KM# 30** **Composition:** Copper-Nickel **Subject:** 16th Forum, 2nd P.I.C. and Mini Games **Reverse:** Tangaroa, Polynesian God of Creation

| Date | Mintage | F | VF | XF | Unc | BU |
|---|---|---|---|---|---|---|
| 1985 | — | — | — | — | 4.50 | — |

**DOLLAR** **KM# 30a** **Weight:** 27.2200 g. **Composition:** 0.9250 Silver .8096 oz. ASW **Subject:** 16th Forum, 2nd P.I.C. and Mini Games **Reverse:** Tangarpa, Polynesian God of Creation

| Date | Mintage | F | VF | XF | Unc | BU |
|---|---|---|---|---|---|---|
| 1985 Proof | Est. 2,500 | Value: 40.00 | | | | |

**DOLLAR** **KM# 30b** **Weight:** 39.8000 g. **Composition:** 0.9170 Gold 1.1735 oz. AGW **Subject:** 16th Forum, 2nd P.I.C. and Mini Games **Reverse:** Tangaroa, Polynesian God of Creation

| Date | Mintage | F | VF | XF | Unc | BU |
|---|---|---|---|---|---|---|
| 1985 Proof | Est. 25 | Value: 3,000 | | | | |

**DOLLAR** **KM# 31** **Composition:** Copper-Nickel **Subject:** 60th Birthday of Queen Elizabeth II

| Date | Mintage | F | VF | XF | Unc | BU |
|---|---|---|---|---|---|---|
| 1986 | 20,000 | — | — | — | 4.50 | — |

**DOLLAR** KM# 32 **Composition:** Copper-Nickel **Subject:** Prince Andrew's Wedding

| Date | Mintage | F | VF | XF | Unc | BU |
|---|---|---|---|---|---|---|
| 1986 | Est. 20,000 | — | — | — | 4.50 | — |

**DOLLAR** KM# 31a **Weight:** 27.2200 g. **Composition:** 0.9250 Silver .8096 oz. ASW **Subject:** 60th Birthday of Queen Elizabeth II

| Date | Mintage | F | VF | XF | Unc | BU |
|---|---|---|---|---|---|---|
| 1986 Proof | Est. 2,500 | Value: 16.50 | | | | |

**DOLLAR** KM# 32a **Weight:** 27.2200 g. **Composition:** 0.9250 Silver .8096 oz. ASW

| Date | Mintage | F | VF | XF | Unc | BU |
|---|---|---|---|---|---|---|
| 1986 Proof | Est. 2,500 | Value: 13.50 | | | | |

**DOLLAR** KM# 31b **Weight:** 44.0000 g. **Composition:** 0.9170 Gold 1.2969 oz. AGW **Subject:** 60th Birthday of Queen Elizabeth II

| Date | Mintage | F | VF | XF | Unc | BU |
|---|---|---|---|---|---|---|
| 1986 Proof | Est. 60 | Value: 1,500 | | | | |

**DOLLAR** KM# 32b **Weight:** 44.0000 g. **Composition:** 0.9170 Gold 1.2969 oz. AGW **Subject:** Prince Andrew's Wedding

| Date | Mintage | F | VF | XF | Unc | BU |
|---|---|---|---|---|---|---|
| 1986 Proof | Est. 75 | Value: 825 | | | | |

**DOLLAR** KM# 37 **Composition:** Copper-Nickel

| Date | Mintage | F | VF | XF | Unc | BU |
|---|---|---|---|---|---|---|
| 1987 | — | — | — | 1.50 | 3.50 | — |
| 1987 Proof | — | Value: 5.00 | | | | |
| 1988 | — | — | — | 1.50 | 3.50 | — |
| 1988 Proof | — | Value: 5.00 | | | | |
| 1992 | — | — | — | 1.50 | 3.50 | — |
| 1992 Proof | — | Value: 5.00 | | | | |
| 1994 | 20,000 | — | — | 1.50 | 3.50 | — |
| 1994 Proof | 200 | Value: 6.00 | | | | |

**DOLLAR** KM# 147 **Composition:** Copper-Nickel **Obverse:** Portrait of Queen Elizabeth **Reverse:** Tangaroa, Polynesian God of Fertility

| Date | Mintage | F | VF | XF | Unc | BU |
|---|---|---|---|---|---|---|
| 1992 | — | — | — | — | 4.00 | — |

**DOLLAR** KM#266 **Composition:** Copper-Nickel **Reverse:** Queen Mother and Daughters

| Date | Mintage | F | VF | XF | Unc | BU |
|---|---|---|---|---|---|---|
| 1995 Proof | Est. 30,000 | Value: 8.00 | | | | |

**DOLLAR** KM#268 **Composition:** Copper-Nickel **Reverse:** Sir Francis Drake and Sailing Ship

| Date | Mintage | F | VF | XF | Unc | BU |
|---|---|---|---|---|---|---|
| 1996 Proof | Est. 25,000 | Value: 11.50 | | | | |

**DOLLAR** KM# 277 **Composition:** Copper-Nickel **Subject:** Yellowstone National Park **Reverse:** Multicolored Grizzly Bear and cub

| Date | Mintage | F | VF | XF | Unc | BU |
|---|---|---|---|---|---|---|
| 1996 | — | — | — | — | 7.50 | — |

**DOLLAR** KM# 278 **Composition:** Copper-Nickel **Subject:** Olympic National Park **Reverse:** Multicolored Bald Eagle in flight

| Date | Mintage | F | VF | XF | Unc | BU |
|---|---|---|---|---|---|---|
| 1996 | — | — | — | — | 7.50 | — |

**DOLLAR** KM# 341 **Composition:** Copper-Nickel **Subject:** Endangered Wildlife **Reverse:** Senegalese lion

| Date | Mintage | F | VF | XF | Unc | BU |
|---|---|---|---|---|---|---|
| 1996 | — | — | — | — | 10.00 | — |

**DOLLAR** KM# 267 **Weight:** 10.0000 g. **Composition:** 0.5000 Silver .1607 oz. ASW **Subject:** 1996 Summer Olympics **Reverse:** Horse jumping

| Date | Mintage | F | VF | XF | Unc | BU |
|---|---|---|---|---|---|---|
| 1996 Proof | Est. 10,000 | Value: 14.50 | | | | |

**DOLLAR** KM# 311 **Weight:** 9.9700 g. **Composition:** 0.5000 Silver .1603 oz. ASW **Subject:** Endangered Wildlife **Obverse:** Queen's portrait **Reverse:** Mother elephant w/calf

| Date | Mintage | F | VF | XF | Unc | BU |
|---|---|---|---|---|---|---|
| 1996 Proof | — | Value: 13.50 | | | | |

**DOLLAR** KM# 326 **Weight:** 31.1035 g. **Composition:** 0.9990 Silver 1.0000 oz. ASW **Subject:** Lunar Year of the Mouse **Obverse:** Queen's portrait **Reverse:** Mouse in basket

| Date | Mintage | F | VF | XF | Unc | BU |
|---|---|---|---|---|---|---|
| 1996 Proof | — | Value: 35.00 | | | | |

**DOLLAR** KM# 327 **Weight:** 31.1035 g. **Composition:** 0.9990 Silver 1.0000 oz. ASW **Obverse:** Queen's portrait **Reverse:** Carnation **Note:** Multicolor.

| Date | Mintage | F | VF | XF | Unc | BU |
|---|---|---|---|---|---|---|
| 1996 Proof | — | Value: 45.00 | | | | |

**DOLLAR** KM# 342 **Composition:** Copper-Nickel **Subject:** Endangered Wildlife **Obverse:** Queen's portrait right **Reverse:** European otters

| Date | Mintage | F | VF | XF | Unc | BU |
|---|---|---|---|---|---|---|
| 1996 | — | — | — | — | 10.00 | — |

**DOLLAR** KM# 343 **Composition:** Copper-Nickel **Subject:** Endangered Wildlife **Obverse:** Queen's portrait right **Reverse:** Jackass penguins

| Date | Mintage | F | VF | XF | Unc | BU |
|---|---|---|---|---|---|---|
| 1996 | — | — | — | — | 10.00 | — |

**DOLLAR** KM# 344 **Composition:** Copper-Nickel **Subject:** Endangered Wildlife **Obverse:** Queen's portrait right **Reverse:** Fallow deer

| Date | Mintage | F | VF | XF | Unc | BU |
|---|---|---|---|---|---|---|
| 1996 | — | — | — | — | 10.00 | — |

**DOLLAR** KM# 345 **Composition:** Copper-Nickel **Subject:** Endangered Wildlife **Obverse:** Queen's portrait right **Reverse:** Heaviside's dolphins

| Date | Mintage | F | VF | XF | Unc | BU |
|---|---|---|---|---|---|---|
| 1996 | — | — | — | — | 10.00 | — |

**DOLLAR** KM# 346 **Composition:** Copper-Nickel **Subject:** Endangered Wildlife **Obverse:** Queen's portrait right **Reverse:** Cougar and cub

| Date | Mintage | F | VF | XF | Unc | BU |
|---|---|---|---|---|---|---|
| 1996 | — | — | — | — | 10.00 | — |

**DOLLAR** KM# 347 **Composition:** Copper-Nickel **Subject:** Endangered Wildlife **Obverse:** Queen's portrait right **Reverse:** Lowland gorilla

| Date | Mintage | F | VF | XF | Unc | BU |
|---|---|---|---|---|---|---|
| 1996 | — | — | — | — | 10.00 | — |

**DOLLAR** KM# 348 **Composition:** Copper-Nickel **Subject:** Endangered Wildlife **Obverse:** Queen's portrait right **Reverse:** Peregrine falcon

| Date | Mintage | F | VF | XF | Unc | BU |
|---|---|---|---|---|---|---|
| 1996 | — | — | — | — | 10.00 | — |

**DOLLAR** KM# 349 **Composition:** Copper-Nickel **Subject:** Endangered Wildlife **Obverse:** Queen's portrait right **Reverse:** Kangaroo

| Date | Mintage | F | VF | XF | Unc | BU |
|---|---|---|---|---|---|---|
| 1996 | — | — | — | — | 10.00 | — |

**DOLLAR** KM# 350 **Composition:** Copper-Nickel **Subject:** Endangered Wildlife **Obverse:** Queen's portrait right **Reverse:** Bee hummingbird

| Date | Mintage | F | VF | XF | Unc | BU |
|---|---|---|---|---|---|---|
| 1996 | — | — | — | — | 10.00 | — |

**DOLLAR** KM# 351 **Composition:** Copper-Nickel **Subject:** Endangered Wildlife **Obverse:** Queen's portrait right **Reverse:** Butterfly and thistle

| Date | Mintage | F | VF | XF | Unc | BU |
|---|---|---|---|---|---|---|
| 1996 | — | — | — | — | 10.00 | — |

**DOLLAR** KM# 352 **Composition:** Copper-Nickel **Subject:** Endangered Wildlife **Obverse:** Queen's portrait right **Reverse:** Ring-tailed lemurs

| Date | Mintage | F | VF | XF | Unc | BU |
|---|---|---|---|---|---|---|
| 1996 | — | — | — | — | 10.00 | — |

**DOLLAR** **KM# 353** **Composition:** Copper-Nickel **Subject:** Endangered Wildlife **Obverse:** Queen's portrait right **Reverse:** Szechuan takins

| Date | Mintage | F | VF | XF | Unc | BU |
|---|---|---|---|---|---|---|
| 1996 | — | — | — | — | 10.00 | — |

**DOLLAR** **KM# 354** **Composition:** Copper-Nickel **Subject:** Endangered Wildlife **Obverse:** Queen's portrait right **Reverse:** Eagle owl

| Date | Mintage | F | VF | XF | Unc | BU |
|---|---|---|---|---|---|---|
| 1996 | — | — | — | — | 10.00 | — |

**DOLLAR** **KM# 355** **Composition:** Copper-Nickel **Subject:** Endangered Wildlife **Obverse:** Queen's portrait right **Reverse:** White-tailed deer

| Date | Mintage | F | VF | XF | Unc | BU |
|---|---|---|---|---|---|---|
| 1996 | — | — | — | — | 10.00 | — |

**DOLLAR** **KM# 356** **Composition:** Copper-Nickel **Subject:** Endangered Wildlife **Obverse:** Queen's portrait right **Reverse:** Drill

| Date | Mintage | F | VF | XF | Unc | BU |
|---|---|---|---|---|---|---|
| 1996 | — | — | — | — | 10.00 | — |

**DOLLAR** **KM# 308.2** **Weight:** 34.4600 g. **Composition:** 0.9990 Silver 1.0104 oz. ASW **Note:** Matte fields with polished portraits.

| Date | Mintage | F | VF | XF | Unc | BU |
|---|---|---|---|---|---|---|
| 1997 Matte Proof | — | — | — | — | 22.50 | — |

**DOLLAR** **KM# 308.1** **Weight:** 31.4600 g. **Composition:** 0.9990 Silver 1.0104 oz. ASW **Obverse:** Queen's portrait right **Reverse:** Princess Diana's portrait, dates **Note:** Polished fields with matte portraits.

| Date | Mintage | F | VF | XF | Unc | BU |
|---|---|---|---|---|---|---|
| 1997 Proof | — | Value: 32.50 | | | | |

**DOLLAR** **KM# 314** **Weight:** 31.6350 g. **Composition:** 0.9990 Silver 1.0160 oz. ASW **Subject:** Australian Fauna Series **Obverse:** Queen's portrait right **Reverse:** Multicolor ring-tailed gecko

| Date | Mintage | F | VF | XF | Unc | BU |
|---|---|---|---|---|---|---|
| 1998 Proof | Est. 4,000 | Value: 45.00 | | | | |

**DOLLAR** **KM# 315** **Weight:** 31.6350 g. **Composition:** 0.9990 Silver 1.0160 oz. ASW **Subject:** Australian Fauna Series **Obverse:** Queen's portrait right **Reverse:** Multicolor bilby (mouse)

| Date | Mintage | F | VF | XF | Unc | BU |
|---|---|---|---|---|---|---|
| 1998 Proof | Est. 4,000 | Value: 45.00 | | | | |

**DOLLAR** **KM# 316** **Weight:** 31.6350 g. **Composition:** 0.9990 Silver 1.0160 oz. ASW **Subject:** Australian Fauna Series **Obverse:** Queen's portrait right **Reverse:** Multicolor platypus

| Date | Mintage | F | VF | XF | Unc | BU |
|---|---|---|---|---|---|---|
| 1998 Proof | Est. 4,000 | Value: 45.00 | | | | |

**DOLLAR** **KM# 317** **Weight:** 31.6350 g. **Composition:** 0.9990 Silver 1.0160 oz. ASW **Subject:** Australian Fauna Series **Obverse:** Queen's portrait right **Reverse:** Multicolor ghost bat

| Date | Mintage | F | VF | XF | Unc | BU |
|---|---|---|---|---|---|---|
| 1998 Proof | Est. 4,000 | Value: 45.00 | | | | |

**DOLLAR** **KM# 318** **Weight:** 31.6350 g. **Composition:** 0.9990 Silver 1.0160 oz. ASW **Subject:** Australian Fauna Series **Obverse:** Queen's portrait right **Reverse:** Multicolor hatback turtle

| Date | Mintage | F | VF | XF | Unc | BU |
|---|---|---|---|---|---|---|
| 1998 Proof | Est. 4,000 | Value: 45.00 | | | | |

**DOLLAR** **KM# 361** **Weight:** 31.6800 g. **Composition:** 0.9990 Silver 1.0000 oz. ASW **Subject:** Tropical Fish Series **Obverse:** Queens portrait right **Reverse:** Multicolor Lemonpeel angelfish **Edge:** Reeded

| Date | Mintage | F | VF | XF | Unc | BU |
|---|---|---|---|---|---|---|
| 1999 Proof | — | Value: 45.00 | | | | |

**DOLLAR** **KM# 362** **Weight:** 31.6800 g. **Composition:** 0.9990 Silver 1.0000 oz. ASW **Subject:** Tropical Fish Series **Obverse:** Queen's portrait right **Reverse:** Multicolor Clown triggerfish **Edge:** Reeded

| Date | Mintage | F | VF | XF | Unc | BU |
|---|---|---|---|---|---|---|
| 1999 Proof | — | Value: 45.00 | | | | |

**DOLLAR** **KM# 364** **Center Weight:** 31.6800 g. **Center Composition:** 0.9990 Silver 1.0000 oz. ASW **Subject:** Tropical Fish Series **Obverse:** Queens portrait right **Reverse:** Multicolor serpent starfish **Edge:** Reeded

| Date | Mintage | F | VF | XF | Unc | BU |
|---|---|---|---|---|---|---|
| 1999 Proof | — | Value: 45.00 | | | | |

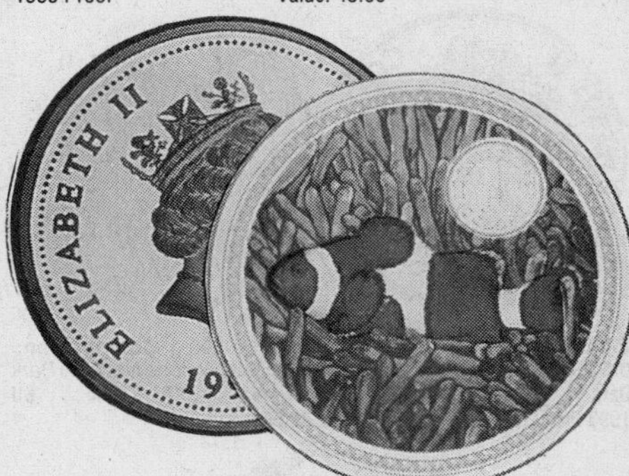


**DOLLAR** **KM# 365** **Weight:** 31.6800 g. **Composition:** 0.9990 Silver 1.0000 oz. ASW **Subject:** Tropical Fish Series **Obverse:** Queen's portrait right **Reverse:** Multicolor cloun anemone fish **Edge:** Reeded

| Date | Mintage | F | VF | XF | Unc | BU |
|---|---|---|---|---|---|---|
| 1999 Proof | — | Value: 45.00 | | | | |

**DOLLAR** **KM# 363** **Weight:** 31.6800 g. **Composition:** 0.9990 Silver 1.0000 oz. ASW **Subject:** Tropical Fish Series **Ob-**

verse: Queen's portrait right **Reverse:** Regal angelfish **Edge:** Reeded **Note:** Multicolored.

| Date | Mintage | F | VF | XF | Unc | BU |
|---|---|---|---|---|---|---|
| 1999 Proof | — | Value: 45.00 | | | | |

**2 DOLLARS** **KM# 8** **Weight:** 25.7000 g. **Composition:** 0.9250 Silver .7646 oz. ASW **Subject:** 20th Anniversary of Coronation **Obverse:** Queen's portrait right

| Date | Mintage | F | VF | XF | Unc | BU |
|---|---|---|---|---|---|---|
| 1973 | 16,000 | — | — | — | 8.00 | — |
| 1973 Proof | 46,000 | Value: 8.00 | | | | |

**2 DOLLARS** **KM# 38** **Composition:** Copper-Nickel

| Date | Mintage | F | VF | XF | Unc | BU |
|---|---|---|---|---|---|---|
| 1987 | — | — | — | 2.25 | 3.75 | — |
| 1987 Proof | — | Value: 7.50 | | | | |
| 1988 | — | — | — | 2.25 | 3.75 | — |
| 1988 Proof | — | Value: 7.50 | | | | |
| 1992 | — | — | — | 2.25 | 3.75 | — |
| 1992 Proof | — | Value: 7.50 | | | | |
| 1994 | 20,000 | — | — | 2.25 | 3.75 | — |
| 1994 Proof | 200 | Value: 8.50 | | | | |

**2 DOLLARS** **KM# 279** **Weight:** 10.0000 g. **Composition:** 0.5000 Silver .1607 oz. ASW **Subject:** Yellowstone National Park

| Date | Mintage | F | VF | XF | Unc | BU |
|---|---|---|---|---|---|---|
| 1996 Proof | — | Value: 13.50 | | | | |

**2 DOLLARS** **KM# 280** **Weight:** 10.0000 g. **Composition:** 0.5000 Silver .1607 oz. ASW **Subject:** Olympic National Park

| Date | Mintage | F | VF | XF | Unc | BU |
|---|---|---|---|---|---|---|
| 1996 Proof | — | Value: 13.50 | | | | |

**2 DOLLARS** **KM# 376** **Weight:** 15.8400 g. **Composition:** 0.9990 Silver 14.3400 oz. ASW **Subject:** British Queen Mother **Obverse:** Obv: Queen's portrait. **Reverse:** Queen Mother and daughters circa 1936. **Edge:** Reeded. **Size:** 28.3 mm.

| Date | Mintage | F | VF | XF | Unc | BU |
|---|---|---|---|---|---|---|
| 1997 Proof | — | Value: 25.00 | | | | |

**2 DOLLARS** **KM# 371** **Weight:** 10.0000 g. **Composition:** 0.5000 Silver .1608 oz. ASW **Subject:** Great Smoky Mountains National Park **Obverse:** Queen's portrait. **Reverse:** Red wolf and two cubs. **Edge:** Reeded. **Size:** 30 mm.

| Date | Mintage | F | VF | XF | Unc | BU |
|---|---|---|---|---|---|---|
| 1997 Proof | — | Value: 15.00 | | | | |

**2 DOLLARS** **KM# 372** **Weight:** 10.0000 g. **Composition:** 0.5000 Silver .1608 oz. ASW **Subject:** Theodore Roosevelt National Park **Obverse:** Queen's portrait. **Reverse:** Bison. **Edge:** Reeded. **Size:** 30 mm.

| Date | Mintage | F | VF | XF | Unc | BU |
|---|---|---|---|---|---|---|
| 1997 Proof | — | Value: 15.00 | | | | |

**2 DOLLARS** **KM# 373** **Weight:** 10.0000 g. **Composition:** 0.5000 Silver .1608 oz. ASW **Subject:** Yosemite National Park **Obverse:** Queen's portrait. **Reverse:** Peregrine falcon. **Edge:** Reeded. **Size:** 30 mm.

| Date | Mintage | F | VF | XF | Unc | BU |
|---|---|---|---|---|---|---|
| 1997 Proof | — | Value: 15.00 | | | | |

**2 DOLLARS** **KM# 374** **Weight:** 10.0000 g. **Composition:** 0.5000 Silver .1608 oz. ASW **Subject:** North Cascades National Park **Obverse:** Queen's portrait. **Reverse:** Spotted owl. **Edge:** Reeded. **Size:** 30 mm.

| Date | Mintage | F | VF | XF | Unc | BU |
|---|---|---|---|---|---|---|
| 1998 Proof | — | Value: 15.00 | | | | |

**2 DOLLARS** **KM# 321** **Weight:** 42.4139 g. **Composition:** 0.9250 Silver 1.3636 oz. ASW **Obverse:** Queen's portrait right **Reverse:** Denomination, Cook Islands attractions and features

| Date | Mintage | F | VF | XF | Unc | BU |
|---|---|---|---|---|---|---|
| 1998 Proof | Est. 20,000 | Value: 65.00 | | | | |

**Note:** This coin is part of a tri-national, three coin matching set with Fiji and Western Samoa

**2 DOLLARS** **KM# 328** **Weight:** 10.0000 g. **Composition:** 0.5000 Silver .160736 oz. ASW **Subject:** Petrified Forest National Park **Obverse:** Queen's portrait right **Reverse:** Pronghorn

| Date | Mintage | F | VF | XF | Unc | BU |
|---|---|---|---|---|---|---|
| 1998 Proof | — | Value: 13.50 | | | | |

**2 DOLLARS** **KM# 329** **Weight:** 10.0000 g. **Composition:** 0.5000 Silver .160736 oz. ASW **Subject:** Crater Lake National Park **Obverse:** Queen's portrait right **Reverse:** White-tailed deer

| Date | Mintage | F | VF | XF | Unc | BU |
|---|---|---|---|---|---|---|
| 1998 Proof | — | Value: 13.50 | | | | |

**2 DOLLARS** **KM# 339** **Weight:** 31.1035 g. **Composition:** 0.9990 Silver 1.0000 oz. ASW **Subject:** Garfield **Obverse:** Queen's portrait right **Reverse:** Multicolor Garfield flipping coin cartoon **Edge:** Reeded

| Date | Mintage | F | VF | XF | Unc | BU |
|---|---|---|---|---|---|---|
| 1999 Proof | — | Value: 45.00 | | | | |

**2 DOLLARS** **KM# 340** **Weight:** 31.1035 g. **Composition:** 0.9990 Silver 1.0000 oz. ASW **Obverse:** Queen's portrait right **Reverse:** Garfield tricking Odie **Edge:** Reeded **Note:** Multicolored.

| Date | Mintage | F | VF | XF | Unc | BU |
|---|---|---|---|---|---|---|
| 1999 Proof | — | Value: 45.00 | | | | |

**2-1/2 DOLLARS** **KM# 9** **Weight:** 27.3500 g. **Composition:** 0.9250 Silver .8133 oz. ASW **Subject:** Captain James Cook's 2nd Pacific Voyage **Obverse:** Queen's portrait right

| Date | Mintage | F | VF | XF | Unc | BU |
|---|---|---|---|---|---|---|
| 1973 | 6,000 | — | — | — | 12.50 | — |
| 1973 Proof | 12,000 | Value: 10.00 | | | | |
| 1974 | 2,000 | — | — | — | 20.00 | — |
| 1974 Proof | 12,000 | Value: 10.00 | | | | |

**5 DOLLARS** **KM# 15** **Weight:** 27.3000 g. **Composition:** 0.5000 Silver .4388 oz. ASW **Subject:** Wildlife Conservation **Obverse:** Queen's portrait right **Reverse:** Mangara kingfisher

| Date | Mintage | F | VF | XF | Unc | BU |
|---|---|---|---|---|---|---|
| 1976FM (M) | 251 | — | — | — | 25.00 | — |
| 1976FM (U) | 2,192 | — | — | — | 12.50 | — |
| 1976FM (P) | 28,000 | Value: 10.50 | | | | |

**5 DOLLARS** **KM# 17** **Weight:** 27.3000 g. **Composition:** 0.5000 Silver .4388 oz. ASW **Obverse:** Queen's portrait right **Reverse:** Atiu swiftlet **Edge Lettering:** Woldlife Conservation

| Date | Mintage | F | VF | XF | Unc | BU |
|---|---|---|---|---|---|---|
| 1977FM (M) | 252 | — | — | — | 35.00 | — |
| 1977FM (U) | 4,032 | — | — | — | 12.50 | — |
| 1977FM (P) | 11,000 | Value: 10.00 | | | | |

**5 DOLLARS** **KM# 20** **Weight:** 27.3000 g. **Composition:** 0.5000 Silver .4388 oz. ASW **Subject:** Wildlife Conservation **Obverse:** Queen's portrait right **Reverse:** Polynesian warbler

| Date | Mintage | F | VF | XF | Unc | BU |
|---|---|---|---|---|---|---|
| 1978FM (M) | 250 | — | — | — | 25.00 | — |
| 1978FM (U) | 3,659 | — | — | — | 12.50 | — |
| 1978FM (P) | 11,000 | Value: 10.00 | | | | |

**5 DOLLARS** **KM# 24** **Weight:** 27.3000 g. **Composition:** 0.5000 Silver .4388 oz. ASW **Subject:** Wildlife Conservation **Obverse:** Queen's portrait right **Reverse:** Rarotongan fruit dove

| Date | Mintage | F | VF | XF | Unc | BU |
|---|---|---|---|---|---|---|
| 1979FM (U) | 2,500 | — | — | — | 16.50 | — |
| 1979FM (P) | 8,612 | Value: 18.50 | | | | |

**5 DOLLARS** **KM# 39** **Composition:** Aluminum-Bronze **Reverse:** Counch shell

| Date | Mintage | F | VF | XF | Unc | BU |
|---|---|---|---|---|---|---|
| 1987 | — | — | — | 5.00 | 10.00 | — |
| 1987 Proof | — | Value: 15.00 | | | | |
| 1988 | — | — | — | 5.00 | 10.00 | — |
| 1988 Proof | — | Value: 15.00 | | | | |
| 1992 | — | — | — | 5.00 | 10.00 | — |
| 1992 Proof | — | Value: 15.00 | | | | |
| 1994 | 20,000 | — | — | 5.00 | 10.00 | — |
| 1994 Proof | 200 | Value: 16.00 | | | | |

**5 DOLLARS** **KM# 39a** **Composition:** Copper-Nickel **Note:** Mint error, struck on Australian 50 cents planchet.

| Date | Mintage | F | VF | XF | Unc | BU |
|---|---|---|---|---|---|---|
| 1988 | — | — | — | — | — | — |

**5 DOLLARS** **KM# 181** **Composition:** Copper-Nickel **Subject:** Endangered World Wildlife **Reverse:** Tiger

| Date | Mintage | F | VF | XF | Unc | BU |
|---|---|---|---|---|---|---|
| 1990 | — | — | — | — | 12.00 | — |

**5 DOLLARS** **KM# 149** **Weight:** 9.9500 g. **Composition:** 0.5000 Silver .1600 oz. ASW **Subject:** World Cup Soccer **Reverse:** 3 soccer players

| Date | Mintage | F | VF | XF | Unc | BU |
|---|---|---|---|---|---|---|
| 1991 Proof | 150,000 | Value: 7.50 | | | | |

**5 DOLLARS** **KM# 217** **Weight:** 9.8500 g. **Composition:** 0.5000 Silver .1600 oz. ASW **Obverse:** Queen's portrait **Reverse:** Christopher Columbus

| Date | Mintage | F | VF | XF | Unc | BU |
|---|---|---|---|---|---|---|
| 1991 | Est. 50,000 | — | — | — | 12.50 | — |

**5 DOLLARS** **KM# 218** **Weight:** 9.9500 g. **Composition:** 500.0000 Silver .1600 oz. ASW **Subject:** Endangered Wildlife **Obverse:** Queen's portrait **Reverse:** European Otters

| Date | Mintage | F | VF | XF | Unc | BU |
|---|---|---|---|---|---|---|
| 1991 | Est. 100,000 | — | — | — | 11.50 | — |

**5 DOLLARS** **KM# 219** **Weight:** 9.9500 g. **Composition:** 0.5000 Silver .1600 oz. ASW **Subject:** Endangered Wildlife **Obverse:** Queen's portrait **Reverse:** Penguins

| Date | Mintage | F | VF | XF | Unc | BU |
|---|---|---|---|---|---|---|
| 1991 | Est. 100,000 | — | — | — | 11.50 | — |

**5 DOLLARS** **KM# 220** **Weight:** 9.9500 g. **Composition:** 0.5000 Silver .1600 oz. ASW **Subject:** Endangered Wildlife **Obverse:** Queen's portrait **Reverse:** Deer

| Date | Mintage | F | VF | XF | Unc | BU |
|---|---|---|---|---|---|---|
| 1991 | Est. 100,000 | — | — | — | 11.50 | — |

**5 DOLLARS** **KM# 221** **Weight:** 9.9500 g. **Composition:** 0.5000 Silver .1600 oz. ASW **Subject:** Endangered Wildlife **Obverse:** Queen's portrait **Reverse:** Cape dolphins

| Date | Mintage | F | VF | XF | Unc | BU |
|---|---|---|---|---|---|---|
| 1991 | Est. 100,000 | — | — | — | 11.50 | — |

**5 DOLLARS** **KM# 222** **Weight:** 9.9500 g. **Composition:** 0.5000 Silver .1600 oz. ASW **Subject:** Endangered Wildlife **Obverse:** Queen's portrait **Reverse:** Cougar

| Date | Mintage | F | VF | XF | Unc | BU |
|---|---|---|---|---|---|---|
| 1991 | Est. 100,000 | — | — | — | 11.50 | — |

**5 DOLLARS** **KM# 223** **Weight:** 9.9500 g. **Composition:** 0.5000 Silver .1600 oz. ASW **Subject:** Endangered Wildlife **Obverse:** Queen's portrait **Reverse:** Ibex

| Date | Mintage | F | VF | XF | Unc | BU |
|---|---|---|---|---|---|---|
| 1991 | Est. 100,000 | — | — | — | 11.50 | — |

**5 DOLLARS** **KM# 224** **Weight:** 9.9500 g. **Composition:** 0.5000 Silver .1600 oz. ASW **Subject:** Endangered Wildlife **Obverse:** Queen's portrait **Reverse:** Eagle owl

| Date | Mintage | F | VF | XF | Unc | BU |
|---|---|---|---|---|---|---|
| 1991 | Est. 100,000 | — | — | — | 11.50 | — |

**5 DOLLARS** **KM# 225** **Weight:** 9.9500 g. **Composition:** 0.5000 Silver .1600 oz. ASW **Subject:** Endangered Wildlife **Obverse:** Queen's portrait **Reverse:** Peregrine falcon

| Date | Mintage | F | VF | XF | Unc | BU |
|---|---|---|---|---|---|---|
| 1991 | Est. 100,000 | — | — | — | 11.50 | — |

**5 DOLLARS** **KM# 226** **Weight:** 9.9500 g. **Composition:** 0.5000 Silver .1600 oz. ASW **Subject:** Endangered Wildlife **Obverse:** Queen's portrait **Reverse:** African lion

| Date | Mintage | F | VF | XF | Unc | BU |
|---|---|---|---|---|---|---|
| 1991 | Est. 100,000 | — | — | — | 11.50 | — |

**5 DOLLARS** **KM# 227** **Weight:** 9.9500 g. **Composition:** 0.5000 Silver .1600 oz. ASW **Subject:** Endangered Wildlife **Obverse:** Queen's portrait **Reverse:** Bee hummingbird

| Date | Mintage | F | VF | XF | Unc | BU |
|---|---|---|---|---|---|---|
| 1991 | Est. 100,000 | — | — | — | 11.50 | — |

**5 DOLLARS** **KM# 228** **Weight:** 9.9500 g. **Composition:** 0.5000 Silver .1600 oz. ASW **Subject:** Endangered Wildlife **Obverse:** Queen's portrait **Reverse:** Kangaroo

| Date | Mintage | F | VF | XF | Unc | BU |
|---|---|---|---|---|---|---|
| 1991 | Est. 100,000 | — | — | — | 11.50 | — |

**5 DOLLARS** **KM# 229** **Weight:** 9.9500 g. **Composition:** 0.5000 Silver .1600 oz. ASW **Subject:** Endangered Wildlife **Obverse:** Queen's portrait **Reverse:** Persian fallow deer

| Date | Mintage | F | VF | XF | Unc | BU |
|---|---|---|---|---|---|---|
| 1991 | Est. 100,000 | — | — | — | 11.50 | — |

**5 DOLLARS** **KM# 230** **Weight:** 9.9500 g. **Composition:** 0.5000 Silver .1600 oz. ASW **Subject:** Endangered Wildlife **Obverse:** Queen's portrait **Reverse:** Lowland gorilla

| Date | Mintage | F | VF | XF | Unc | BU |
|---|---|---|---|---|---|---|
| 1991 | Est. 100,000 | — | — | — | 11.50 | — |

**5 DOLLARS** **KM# 253** **Weight:** 10.1300 g. **Composition:** 0.5000 Silver .1628 oz. ASW **Obverse:** Queen's portrait **Reverse:** First man on the moon

| Date | Mintage | F | VF | XF | Unc | BU |
|---|---|---|---|---|---|---|
| 1991 Proof | — | Value: 10.00 | | | | |

**5 DOLLARS** **KM# 137** **Weight:** 10.0000 g. **Composition:** 0.5000 Silver .1607 oz. ASW **Subject:** Environmental Protection **Obverse:** Queen's portrait **Reverse:** Child watching butterfly

| Date | Mintage | F | VF | XF | Unc | BU |
|---|---|---|---|---|---|---|
| 1992 Proof | Est. 25,000 | Value: 8.00 | | | | |

**5 DOLLARS** **KM# 150** **Weight:** 10.0000 g. **Composition:** 0.5000 Silver .1607 oz. ASW **Obverse:** Queen's portrait **Reverse:** John Sebastian Bach

| Date | Mintage | F | VF | XF | Unc | BU |
|---|---|---|---|---|---|---|
| 1992 Proof | — | Value: 10.00 | | | | |

**5 DOLLARS** **KM# 160** **Weight:** 10.0000 g. **Composition:** 0.5000 Silver .1607 oz. ASW **Obverse:** Queen's portrait **Reverse:** Sailing ship and astrolab

| Date | Mintage | F | VF | XF | Unc | BU |
|---|---|---|---|---|---|---|
| 1992 Proof | — | Value: 10.00 | | | | |

**5 DOLLARS** **KM# 231** **Weight:** 10.0000 g. **Composition:** 0.5000 Silver .1607 oz. ASW **Subject:** Endangered Wildlife **Obverse:** Queen's portrait **Reverse:** Drill

| Date | Mintage | F | VF | XF | Unc | BU |
|---|---|---|---|---|---|---|
| 1992 | Est. 100,000 | — | — | — | 13.50 | — |

**5 DOLLARS** **KM# 232** **Weight:** 10.0000 g. **Composition:** 0.5000 Silver .1607 oz. ASW **Subject:** Endangered Wildlife **Obverse:** Queen's portrait **Reverse:** Butterfly

| Date | Mintage | F | VF | XF | Unc | BU |
|---|---|---|---|---|---|---|
| 1992 | Est. 100,000 | — | — | — | 13.50 | — |

**5 DOLLARS** **KM# 233** **Weight:** 10.0000 g. **Composition:** 0.5000 Silver .1607 oz. ASW **Subject:** Endangered Wildlife **Obverse:** Queen's portrait **Reverse:** Takin

| Date | Mintage | F | VF | XF | Unc | BU |
|---|---|---|---|---|---|---|
| 1992 | Est. 100,000 | — | — | — | 13.50 | — |

**5 DOLLARS** **KM# 252** **Weight:** 9.9500 g. **Composition:** 0.5000 Silver .1600 oz. ASW **Subject:** 1992 Oly;mpic **Obverse:** Queen's portrait **Reverse:** High jumb

| Date | Mintage | F | VF | XF | Unc | BU |
|---|---|---|---|---|---|---|
| 1992 Proof | 150,000 | Value: 12.50 | | | | |

**5 DOLLARS** **KM# 255** **Weight:** 31.4700 g. **Composition:** 0.9250 Silver .9359 oz. ASW **Obverse:** Queen's portrait **Reverse:** St. Paul's Cathedral

| Date | Mintage | F | VF | XF | Unc | BU |
|---|---|---|---|---|---|---|
| 1995 Proof | Est. 30,000 | Value: 21.50 | | | | |

**5 DOLLARS** **KM# 234** **Weight:** 10.0000 g. **Composition:** 0.5000 Silver .1607 oz. ASW **Subject:** Endangered Wildlife **Obverse:** Queen's portrait **Reverse:** African elephant

| Date | Mintage | F | VF | XF | Unc | BU |
|---|---|---|---|---|---|---|
| 1995 Proof | Est. 25,000 | Value: 15.00 | | | | |

**5 DOLLARS** **KM# 269** **Weight:** 31.4700 g. **Composition:** 0.9250 Silver .9359 oz. ASW **Subject:** Endangered Wildlife **Obverse:** Queen's portrait **Reverse:** Cheetah

| Date | Mintage | F | VF | XF | Unc | BU |
|---|---|---|---|---|---|---|
| 1996 Proof | Est. 15,000 | Value: 25.00 | | | | |

**5 DOLLARS** **KM# 281** **Weight:** 28.0000 g. **Composition:** 0.9250 Silver .8327 oz. ASW **Subject:** Yellowstone National Park **Obverse:** Queen's portrait **Reverse:** Multicolored grizzly bear and cub

| Date | Mintage | F | VF | XF | Unc | BU |
|---|---|---|---|---|---|---|
| 1996 Proof | 25,000 | Value: 22.50 | | | | |

**5 DOLLARS** **KM# 282** **Weight:** 28.0000 g. **Composition:** 0.9250 Silver .8327 oz. ASW **Subject:** Olympic National Park **Obverse:** Queen's portrait **Reverse:** Multicolored bald eagle in flight

| Date | Mintage | F | VF | XF | Unc | BU |
|---|---|---|---|---|---|---|
| 1996 Proof | 25,000 | Value: 22.50 | | | | |

**5 DOLLARS** **KM# 301** **Weight:** 28.0000 g. **Composition:** 0.9250 Silver .8327 oz. ASW **Subject:** Endangered Wildlife Series **Obverse:** Queen's portrait **Reverse:** Crocodile on river bank

| Date | Mintage | F | VF | XF | Unc | BU |
|---|---|---|---|---|---|---|
| 1996 Proof | — | Value: 40.00 | | | | |

**5 DOLLARS** **KM# 302** **Weight:** 28.0000 g. **Composition:** 0.9250 Silver .8327 oz. ASW **Subject:** Endangered Wildlife Series **Obverse:** Queen's portrait **Reverse:** Lion, lioness and cubs

| Date | Mintage | F | VF | XF | Unc | BU |
|---|---|---|---|---|---|---|
| 1996 Proof | — | Value: 25.00 | | | | |

**5 DOLLARS** **KM# 303** **Weight:** 28.0000 g. **Composition:** 0.9250 Silver .8327 oz. ASW **Subject:** Endangered Wildlife Series **Obverse:** Queen's portrait **Reverse:** Femaile gorilla and offspring

| Date | Mintage | F | VF | XF | Unc | BU |
|---|---|---|---|---|---|---|
| 1996 Proof | — | Value: 25.00 | | | | |

**5 DOLLARS** **KM# 304** **Weight:** 28.0000 g. **Composition:** 0.9250 Silver .8327 oz. ASW **Subject:** Endangered Wildlife Series **Obverse:** Queen's portrait **Reverse:** Penquin family

| Date | Mintage | F | VF | XF | Unc | BU |
|---|---|---|---|---|---|---|
| 1996 Proof | — | Value: 40.00 | | | | |

**5 DOLLARS** **KM# 368** **Weight:** 28.0000 g. **Composition:** 0.9250 Silver .8327 oz. ASW **Subject:** Great Smoky Mountains National Park **Obverse:** Queen's head right **Reverse:** Red wolf and 2 cubs **Edge:** Reeded

| Date | Mintage | F | VF | XF | Unc | BU |
|---|---|---|---|---|---|---|
| 1996 Proof | — | — | — | — | — | — |

**5 DOLLARS** **KM# 366** **Weight:** 31.4700 g. **Composition:** 0.9250 Silver .9353 oz. ASW **Subject:** Protect Our World **Obverse:** Queen's head right **Reverse:** Charles Darwin bust at right, map and tortoise **Edge:** Reeded

| Date | Mintage | F | VF | XF | Unc | BU |
|---|---|---|---|---|---|---|
| 1996 Proof | — | Value: 45.00 | | | | |

**5 DOLLARS** **KM# 370** **Weight:** 31.5000 g. **Composition:** 0.9250 Silver .9368 oz. ASW **Subject:** Olympics **Obverse:** Queen's portrait. **Reverse:** Pole vaulter and runner. **Edge:** Reeded. **Size:** 38.6 mm.

| Date | Mintage | F | VF | XF | Unc | BU |
|---|---|---|---|---|---|---|
| 1996 Proof | — | Value: 35.00 | | | | |

**5 DOLLARS** **KM# 335** **Weight:** 15.5200 g. **Composition:** 0.9990 Silver .4985 oz. ASW **Subject:** Japanese Samurai **Obverse:** Queen's head right **Reverse:** 3/4 bust Yoshinobu Tokugawa facing **Edge:** Reeded

| Date | Mintage | F | VF | XF | Unc | BU |
|---|---|---|---|---|---|---|
| 1997FM Proof | — | Value: 25.00 | | | | |

**5 DOLLARS** **KM# 312** **Weight:** 1.2441 g. **Composition:** 0.9999 Gold .400 oz. AGW **Obverse:** Queen's portrait **Reverse:** Portrait of Princess Diana, dates

| Date | Mintage | F | VF | XF | Unc | BU |
|---|---|---|---|---|---|---|
| 1997 Proof | — | Value: 40.00 | | | | |

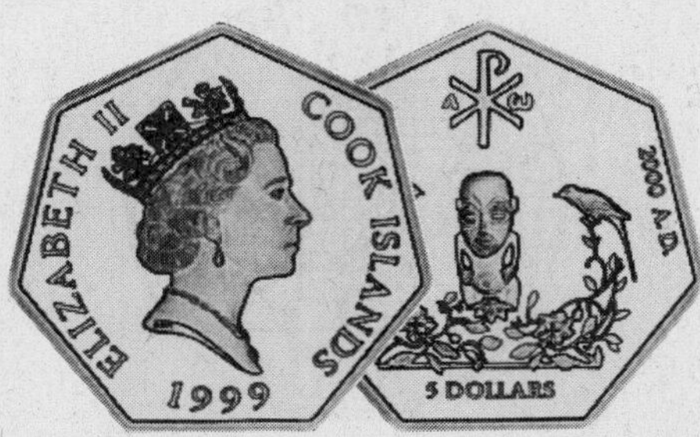


**5 DOLLARS** **KM# 367** **Weight:** 31.4500 g. **Composition:** 0.9250 Silver .9353 oz. ASW **Subject:** Millennium - 2000 A.D. **Obverse:** Queen's head right **Reverse:** Christian symbol above Tangaroa, Pagon God of Creation **Edge:** Plain **Note:** 7-sided.

| Date | Mintage | F | VF | XF | Unc | BU |
|---|---|---|---|---|---|---|
| 1999 Proof | — | Value: 30.00 | | | | |

**5 DOLLARS** **KM# 375** **Weight:** 28.1000 g. **Composition:** 0.9250 Silver .8357 oz. ASW **Subject:** Queen Mother's 100th Birthday **Obverse:** Queen's portrait. **Reverse:** Queen Mother and daughters circa 1980. **Edge:** Reeded. **Size:** 38.6 mm. **Note:** Gold plated outer ring.

| Date | Mintage | F | VF | XF | Unc | BU |
|---|---|---|---|---|---|---|
| 2000 Proof | 1,000 | Value: 60.00 | | | | |

**7-1/2 DOLLARS** **KM# 10** **Weight:** 33.8000 g. **Composition:** 0.9250 Silver 1.0052 oz. ASW **Subject:** Capt. James Cook's 2nd Pacific Voyage **Obverse:** Queen's portrait right

| Date | Mintage | F | VF | XF | Unc | BU |
|---|---|---|---|---|---|---|
| 1973 | 6,000 | — | — | — | 18.50 | — |
| 1973 Proof | 12,000 | Value: 13.50 | | | | |
| 1974 | 2,000 | — | — | — | 25.00 | — |
| 1974 Proof | 13,000 | Value: 13.50 | | | | |

**10 DOLLARS** **KM# 21** **Weight:** 27.9000 g. **Composition:** 0.9250 Silver .8297 oz. ASW **Subject:** 25th Anniversary of Coronation **Obverse:** Queen's portrait right

| Date | Mintage | F | VF | XF | Unc | BU |
|---|---|---|---|---|---|---|
| 1978 | 5,350 | — | — | — | 17.50 | — |
| 1978 Proof | 11,000 | Value: 13.50 | | | | |

**10 DOLLARS** **KM# 72** **Weight:** 10.0000 g. **Composition:** 0.9250 Silver .2974 oz. ASW **Subject:** Endangered World Wildlife **Obverse:** Queen's portrait right **Reverse:** Elephant

| Date | Mintage | F | VF | XF | Unc | BU |
|---|---|---|---|---|---|---|
| 1990 Proof | 25,000 | Value: 15.00 | | | | |

**10 DOLLARS** KM# 73 **Weight:** 10.0000 g. **Composition:** 0.9250 Silver .2974 oz. ASW **Subject:** Endangered World Wildlife **Obverse:** Queen's portrait right **Reverse:** Tiger

| Date | Mintage | F | VF | XF | Unc | BU |
|---|---|---|---|---|---|---|
| 1990 Proof | Est. 25,000 | Value: 15.00 | | | | |

**10 DOLLARS** KM# 79 **Weight:** 10.0000 g. **Composition:** 0.9250 Silver .2974 oz. ASW **Subject:** Olympics **Obverse:** Queen's portrait right **Reverse:** Runner

| Date | Mintage | F | VF | XF | Unc | BU |
|---|---|---|---|---|---|---|
| 1990 Proof | 150,000 | Value: 6.50 | | | | |

**10 DOLLARS** KM# 80 **Weight:** 10.0000 g. **Composition:** 0.9250 Silver .2974 oz. ASW **Subject:** Endangered World Wildlife **Obverse:** Queen's portrait right **Reverse:** African elephants

| Date | Mintage | F | VF | XF | Unc | BU |
|---|---|---|---|---|---|---|
| 1990 Proof | Est. 25,000 | Value: 15.00 | | | | |

**10 DOLLARS** KM# 81 **Weight:** 28.0000 g. **Composition:** 0.9250 Silver .8327 oz. ASW **Subject:** Save the Children **Obverse:** Queen's portrait right

| Date | Mintage | F | VF | XF | Unc | BU |
|---|---|---|---|---|---|---|
| 1990 Proof | 20,000 | Value: 22.50 | | | | |

**10 DOLLARS** KM# 90 **Weight:** 10.0000 g. **Composition:** 0.9250 Silver .2974 oz. ASW **Subject:** 500 Years of America **Obverse:** Queen's portrait right

| Date | Mintage | F | VF | XF | Unc | BU |
|---|---|---|---|---|---|---|
| 1990 Proof | Est. 150,000 | Value: 7.50 | | | | |

**10 DOLLARS** KM# 91 **Weight:** 10.0000 g. **Composition:** 0.9250 Silver .2974 oz. ASW **Subject:** 1991 Winter Olympics **Obverse:** Queen's portrait right **Reverse:** Cross country skier

| Date | Mintage | F | VF | XF | Unc | BU |
|---|---|---|---|---|---|---|
| 1990 Proof | 150,000 | Value: 15.00 | | | | |

**10 DOLLARS** KM# 121 **Weight:** 10.0000 g. **Composition:** 0.9250 Silver .2974 oz. ASW **Subject:** 500 Years of America **Obverse:** Queen's portrait right **Reverse:** Columbus and ship

| Date | Mintage | F | VF | XF | Unc | BU |
|---|---|---|---|---|---|---|
| 1990 Proof | Est. 150,000 | Value: 7.50 | | | | |

**10 DOLLARS** KM# 136 **Weight:** 31.4700 g. **Composition:** 0.9250 Silver .9359 oz. ASW **Obverse:** Queen's portrait right **Reverse:** Nicolaus Copernicus

| Date | Mintage | F | VF | XF | Unc | BU |
|---|---|---|---|---|---|---|
| 1992 Proof | — | Value: 22.50 | | | | |

**10 DOLLARS** KM# 254 **Weight:** 31.4700 g. **Composition:** 0.9250 Silver .9359 oz. ASW **Subject:** Soccer **Obverse:** Queen's portrait right **Reverse:** Goalie catching ball

| Date | Mintage | F | VF | XF | Unc | BU |
|---|---|---|---|---|---|---|
| 1992 Proof | Est. 20,000 | Value: 25.00 | | | | |

**10 DOLLARS** KM# 358 **Weight:** 14.8000 g. **Composition:** 0.9250 Silver .4401 oz. ASW **Subject:** Captian Cook **Obverse:** Queen's portrait right **Reverse:** Captain Cook wading ashore **Edge:** Reeded

| Date | Mintage | F | VF | XF | Unc | BU |
|---|---|---|---|---|---|---|
| 1994FM Proof | — | Value: 17.50 | | | | |

**10 DOLLARS** KM# 285 **Weight:** 1.2441 g. **Composition:** 0.9990 Gold .0399 oz. AGW **Subject:** Olympic National Park

| Date | Mintage | F | VF | XF | Unc | BU |
|---|---|---|---|---|---|---|
| 1996 Proof | — | Value: 42.50 | | | | |

**10 DOLLARS** KM# 286 **Weight:** 1.2441 g. **Composition:** 0.9990 Gold .0399 oz. AGW **Subject:** Yellowstone National Park

| Date | Mintage | F | VF | XF | Unc | BU |
|---|---|---|---|---|---|---|
| 1996 Proof | — | Value: 42.50 | | | | |

**10 DOLLARS** KM# 283 **Weight:** 28.0000 g. **Composition:** 0.9250 Silver .8327 oz. ASW **Subject:** Olympic National Park **Obverse:** Queen's portrait right **Reverse:** Bald eagle in flight **Note:** Multicolored.

| Date | Mintage | F | VF | XF | Unc | BU |
|---|---|---|---|---|---|---|
| 1996 Proof | 10,000 | Value: 30.00 | | | | |

**10 DOLLARS** KM# 284 **Weight:** 28.0000 g. **Composition:** 0.9250 Silver .8327 oz. ASW **Subject:** Yellowstone National Park **Obverse:** Queen's portrait right **Reverse:** Grizzly bear and cub **Note:** Multicolored.

| Date | Mintage | F | VF | XF | Unc | BU |
|---|---|---|---|---|---|---|
| 1996 Proof | 10,000 | Value: 30.00 | | | | |

**10 DOLLARS** KM# 359 **Weight:** 28.0000 g. **Composition:** 0.9250 Silver .8327 oz. ASW **Subject:** Theodore Roosevelt National Park **Obverse:** Queen's portrait right **Reverse:** Bison **Edge:** Reeded **Note:** Multicolored.

| Date | Mintage | F | VF | XF | Unc | BU |
|---|---|---|---|---|---|---|
| 1996 Proof | — | Value: 32.50 | | | | |

**10 DOLLARS** KM# 330 **Weight:** 28.0000 g. **Composition:** 0.9250 Silver .8327 oz. ASW **Subject:** Great Smoky Mountains National Park **Obverse:** Queen's portrait right **Reverse:** Red wolf w/2 cubs **Note:** Multicolored.

| Date | Mintage | F | VF | XF | Unc | BU |
|---|---|---|---|---|---|---|
| 1997 Proof | — | Value: 35.00 | | | | |

**10 DOLLARS** **KM# 331** **Weight:** 28.0000 g. **Composition:** 0.9250 Silver .8327 oz. ASW **Subject:** Yosemite National Park **Obverse:** Queen's portrait right **Reverse:** Peregrine falcon **Note:** Multicolored.

| Date | Mintage | F | VF | XF | Unc | BU |
|---|---|---|---|---|---|---|
| 1997 Proof | — | Value: 35.00 | | | | |

**10 DOLLARS** **KM# 360** **Weight:** 28.0000 g. **Composition:** 0.9250 Silver .8327 oz. ASW **Subject:** Glacier Bay National Park **Obverse:** Queen's portrait right **Reverse:** Humpback whale **Note:** Multicolored.

| Date | Mintage | F | VF | XF | Unc | BU |
|---|---|---|---|---|---|---|
| 1997 Proof | — | Value: 32.50 | | | | |

**10 DOLLARS** **KM# 332** **Weight:** 28.0000 g. **Composition:** 0.9250 Silver .8327 oz. ASW **Subject:** Grand Teton National park **Obverse:** Queen's portrait right **Reverse:** Whooping crane **Note:** Multicolored.

| Date | Mintage | F | VF | XF | Unc | BU |
|---|---|---|---|---|---|---|
| 1998 Proof | — | Value: 35.00 | | | | |

**10 DOLLARS** **KM# 333** **Weight:** 28.0000 g. **Composition:** 0.9250 Silver .8327 oz. ASW **Subject:** Grand Canyon National Park **Obverse:** Queen's portrait right **Reverse:** California condor **Note:** Multicolored.

| Date | Mintage | F | VF | XF | Unc | BU |
|---|---|---|---|---|---|---|
| 1998 Proof | — | Value: 35.00 | | | | |

**20 DOLLARS** **KM# 28** **Weight:** 28.2800 g. **Composition:** 0.9250 Silver .8411 oz. ASW **Subject:** International Year of the Scout **Obverse:** Queen's portrait right

| Date | Mintage | F | VF | XF | Unc | BU |
|---|---|---|---|---|---|---|
| 1983 | 10,000 | — | — | — | 45.00 | — |
| 1983 Proof | 10,000 | Value: 50.00 | | | | |

**20 DOLLARS** **KM# 151** **Weight:** 31.4700 g. **Composition:** 0.9250 Silver .9359 oz. ASW **Obverse:** Queen's portrait right **Reverse:** Friedrich von Schiller

| Date | Mintage | F | VF | XF | Unc | BU |
|---|---|---|---|---|---|---|
| 1993 Proof | — | Value: 35.00 | | | | |

**20 DOLLARS** **KM# 152** **Weight:** 31.4700 g. **Composition:** 0.9250 Silver .9359 oz. ASW **Obverse:** Queen's portrait right **Reverse:** Charles Darwin

| Date | Mintage | F | VF | XF | Unc | BU |
|---|---|---|---|---|---|---|
| 1993 Proof | 10,000 | Value: 35.00 | | | | |

**20 DOLLARS** **KM# 161** **Weight:** 31.4700 g. **Composition:** 0.9250 Silver .9359 oz. ASW **Subject:** 1996 Olympics **Obverse:** Queen's portrait right **Reverse:** Pole valut and sprinter

| Date | Mintage | F | VF | XF | Unc | BU |
|---|---|---|---|---|---|---|
| 1993 Proof | 50,000 | Value: 25.00 | | | | |

**20 DOLLARS** **KM# 235** **Weight:** 31.4700 g. **Composition:** 0.9250 Silver .9359 oz. ASW **Obverse:** Queen's portrait right **Reverse:** Catamaran

| Date | Mintage | F | VF | XF | Unc | BU |
|---|---|---|---|---|---|---|
| 1995 Proof | Est. 15,000 | Value: 30.00 | | | | |

**20 DOLLARS** **KM# 236** **Weight:** 1.2441 g. **Composition:** 0.9990 Gold .400 oz. AGW **Subject:** 500 Years of America **Obverse:** Queen's portrait right **Reverse:** Columbus claims the New World

| Date | Mintage | F | VF | XF | Unc | BU |
|---|---|---|---|---|---|---|
| 1995 | Est. 25,000 | — | — | — | 40.00 | — |

**20 DOLLARS** **KM# 237** **Weight:** 1.2441 g. **Composition:** 0.9990 Gilt Silver .400 oz. **Subject:** 500 Years of America **Obverse:** Queen's portrait right **Reverse:** Washinton crossing the Delaware

| Date | Mintage | F | VF | XF | Unc | BU |
|---|---|---|---|---|---|---|
| 1995 | Est. 25,000 | — | — | — | 40.00 | — |

**20 DOLLARS** **KM# 256** **Weight:** 31.4700 g. **Composition:** 0.9250 Silver .9359 oz. ASW **Obverse:** Queen's portrait right **Reverse:** Queen Mother and daughters

| Date | Mintage | F | VF | XF | Unc | BU |
|---|---|---|---|---|---|---|
| 1995 Proof | Est. 30,000 | Value: 30.00 | | | | |

**20 DOLLARS** **KM# 257** **Weight:** 1.2441 g. **Composition:** 0.9999 Gold .0400 oz. AGW **Subject:** 500 Years of America **Obverse:** Queen's portrait right **Reverse:** Stature of Liberty

| Date | Mintage | F | VF | XF | Unc | BU |
|---|---|---|---|---|---|---|
| 1995 | Est. 25,000 | — | — | — | 40.00 | — |

**20 DOLLARS** **KM# 258** **Weight:** 1.2441 g. **Composition:** 0.9999 Gold .0400 oz. AGW **Subject:** 500 Years of America **Obverse:** Queen's portrait right **Reverse:** Capt. James Cook

| Date | Mintage | F | VF | XF | Unc | BU |
|---|---|---|---|---|---|---|
| 1995 Proof | Est. 25,000 | Value: 40.00 | | | | |

**20 DOLLARS** KM# 270 **Weight:** 1.2441 g. **Composition:** 0.9999 Gold .0400 oz. AGW **Subject:** 500 Years of America **Obverse:** Queen's portrait right **Reverse:** Astronaut on moon

| Date | Mintage | F | VF | XF | Unc | BU |
|---|---|---|---|---|---|---|
| 1995 Proof | Est. 25,000 | Value: 40.00 | | | | |

**20 DOLLARS** KM# 287 **Weight:** 155.5175 g. **Composition:** 0.9990 Silver 4.9950 oz. ASW **Subject:** Olympic National Park **Obverse:** Queen's portrait right **Reverse:** Bald eagle

| Date | Mintage | F | VF | XF | Unc | BU |
|---|---|---|---|---|---|---|
| 1996 Proof | 1,000 | Value: 85.00 | | | | |

**20 DOLLARS** KM# 288 **Weight:** 155.5175 g. **Composition:** 0.9990 Silver 4.9950 oz. ASW **Subject:** Yellowstone National Park **Obverse:** Queen's portrait right **Reverse:** Girzzly bear

| Date | Mintage | F | VF | XF | Unc | BU |
|---|---|---|---|---|---|---|
| 1996 Proof | 1,000 | Value: 85.00 | | | | |

**20 DOLLARS** KM# 298 **Weight:** 3.0000 g. **Composition:** 0.9999 Gold .0964 oz. AGW **Subject:** Year of the Mouse **Obverse:** Queen's portrait right **Reverse:** Mickey Mouse portrait **Note:** Multicolored.

| Date | Mintage | F | VF | XF | Unc | BU |
|---|---|---|---|---|---|---|
| 1996 Proof | — | Value: 70.00 | | | | |

**20 DOLLARS** KM# 334 **Weight:** 32.0200 g. **Composition:** 0.9250 Silver .9517 oz. ASW **Subject:** 12th Centuray **Obverse:** Queen's portrait right **Reverse:** Genghis Khan

| Date | Mintage | F | VF | XF | Unc | BU |
|---|---|---|---|---|---|---|
| 1997 Proof | — | Value: 20.00 | | | | |

**20 DOLLARS** KM# 336 **Weight:** 31.8800 g. **Composition:** 0.9250 Silver .9481 oz. ASW **Subject:** 18th Century **Obverse:** Queen's portrait right **Reverse:** Signing of the Declaration of Independence **Edge:** Reeded

| Date | Mintage | F | VF | XF | Unc | BU |
|---|---|---|---|---|---|---|
| 1997FM Proof | — | Value: 20.00 | | | | |

**20 DOLLARS** KM# 337 **Weight:** 31.8800 g. **Composition:** 0.9250 Silver .9481 oz. ASW **Subject:** 19th Century **Obverse:** Queen's portrait right **Reverse:** Waving driver w/2 passengers in horseless carriage, bicycle at right in back **Edge:** Reeded

| Date | Mintage | F | VF | XF | Unc | BU |
|---|---|---|---|---|---|---|
| 1997FM Proof | — | Value: 20.00 | | | | |

**25 DOLLARS** KM# 18 **Weight:** 48.8500 g. **Composition:** 0.9250 Silver 1.4527 oz. ASW **Subject:** Queen's Silver Jubilee **Obverse:** Queen's portrait right **Reverse:** Similar to 50 cents, KM#6

| Date | Mintage | F | VF | XF | Unc | BU |
|---|---|---|---|---|---|---|
| 1977 | 100 | — | — | — | 75.00 | — |
| 1977 | 4,068 | — | — | — | 27.50 | — |
| 1977 Proof | 17,000 | Value: 16.50 | | | | |

**25 DOLLARS** KM# 42 **Weight:** 37.0000 g. **Composition:** 0.9250 Silver 1.1005 oz. ASW **Subject:** 100th Anniversary of British Rule **Obverse:** Queen's portrait right

| Date | Mintage | F | VF | XF | Unc | BU |
|---|---|---|---|---|---|---|
| 1988 Proof | 3,000 | Value: 37.50 | | | | |

**25 DOLLARS** KM# 83 **Weight:** 1.2144 g. **Composition:** 0.9990 Gold .0400 oz. AGW **Subject:** Endangered Wildlife **Obverse:** Queen's portrait right **Reverse:** Bison

| Date | Mintage | F | VF | XF | Unc | BU |
|---|---|---|---|---|---|---|
| 1990 Proof | 100,000 | Value: 42.50 | | | | |

**25 DOLLARS** KM# 84 **Weight:** 1.2144 g. **Composition:** 0.9990 Gold .0400 oz. AGW **Subject:** Endangered Wildlife **Obverse:** Queen's portrait right **Reverse:** Longhorn sheep

| Date | Mintage | F | VF | XF | Unc | BU |
|---|---|---|---|---|---|---|
| 1990 Proof | Est. 100,000 | Value: 42.50 | | | | |

**25 DOLLARS** KM# 85 **Weight:** 1.2144 g. **Composition:** 0.9990 Gold .0400 oz. AGW **Subject:** Endangered Wildlife **Obverse:** Queen's portrait right **Reverse:** Tiger

| Date | Mintage | F | VF | XF | Unc | BU |
|---|---|---|---|---|---|---|
| 1990 Proof | — | Value: 42.50 | | | | |

**25 DOLLARS** KM# 86 **Weight:** 1.2144 g. **Composition:** 0.9990 Gold .0400 oz. AGW **Subject:** Endangered Wildlife **Obverse:** Queen's portrait right **Reverse:** Eagle

| Date | Mintage | F | VF | XF | Unc | BU |
|---|---|---|---|---|---|---|
| 1990 Proof | Est. 100,000 | Value: 42.50 | | | | |

**25 DOLLARS** KM# 87 **Weight:** 1.2144 g. **Composition:** 0.9990 Gold .0400 oz. AGW **Subject:** Endangered Wildlife **Obverse:** Queen's portrait right **Reverse:** Elephant

| Date | Mintage | F | VF | XF | Unc | BU |
|---|---|---|---|---|---|---|
| 1990 Proof | Est. 100,000 | Value: 42.50 | | | | |

**25 DOLLARS** KM# 88 **Weight:** 1.2144 g. **Composition:** 0.9990 Gold .0400 oz. AGW **Subject:** Endangered Wildlife **Obverse:** Queen's portrait right **Reverse:** Lynx

| Date | Mintage | F | VF | XF | Unc | BU |
|---|---|---|---|---|---|---|
| 1990 Proof | Est. 100,000 | Value: 42.50 | | | | |

**25 DOLLARS** KM# 239 **Weight:** 1.2144 g. **Composition:** 0.9990 Gold .0400 oz. AGW **Subject:** Endangered Wildlife **Obverse:** Queen's portrait right **Reverse:** Bee hummingbird

| Date | Mintage | F | VF | XF | Unc | BU |
|---|---|---|---|---|---|---|
| 1990 Proof | Est. 100,000 | Value: 42.50 | | | | |

**25 DOLLARS** KM# 240 **Weight:** 1.2144 g. **Composition:** 0.9990 Gold .0400 oz. AGW **Subject:** Endangered Wildlife **Obverse:** Queen's portrait right **Reverse:** Koala

| Date | Mintage | F | VF | XF | Unc | BU |
|---|---|---|---|---|---|---|
| 1991 Proof | Est. 100,000 | Value: 42.50 | | | | |

**25 DOLLARS** KM# 241 **Weight:** 1.2144 g. **Composition:** 0.9990 Gold .0400 oz. AGW **Subject:** Endangered Wildlife **Obverse:** Queen's portrait right **Reverse:** Panda

| Date | Mintage | F | VF | XF | Unc | BU |
|---|---|---|---|---|---|---|
| 1991 Proof | Est. 100,000 | Value: 42.50 | | | | |

**25 DOLLARS** KM# 138 **Weight:** 1.2144 g. **Composition:** 0.9990 Gold .0400 oz. AGW **Subject:** Endangered Wildlife **Obverse:** Queen's portrait right **Reverse:** Przewalski's horse

| Date | Mintage | F | VF | XF | Unc | BU |
|---|---|---|---|---|---|---|
| 1992 Proof-like | — | — | — | — | — | — |

**25 DOLLARS** KM# 242 **Weight:** 1.2144 g. **Composition:** 0.9990 Gold .0400 oz. AGW **Subject:** Endangered Wildlife **Obverse:** Queen's portrait right **Reverse:** African lion

| Date | Mintage | F | VF | XF | Unc | BU |
|---|---|---|---|---|---|---|
| 1992 Proof | Est. 100,000 | Value: 42.50 | | | | |

**25 DOLLARS** KM# 243 **Weight:** 1.2144 g. **Composition:** 0.9990 Gold .0400 oz. AGW **Subject:** Endangered Wildlife **Obverse:** Queen's portrait right **Reverse:** Butterfly

| Date | Mintage | F | VF | XF | Unc | BU |
|---|---|---|---|---|---|---|
| 1992 Proof | Est. 100,000 | Value: 42.50 | | | | |

**25 DOLLARS** **KM# 238** **Weight:** 6.2200 g. **Composition:** 0.5830 Gold .1166 oz. AGW **Subject:** 1996 Olympics **Obverse:** Queen's portrait right **Reverse:** Ancient archer

| Date | Mintage | F | VF | XF | Unc | BU |
|---|---|---|---|---|---|---|
| 1995 Proof | Est. 5,000 | Value: 65.00 | | | | |

**25 DOLLARS** **KM# 271** **Weight:** 155.5175 g. **Composition:** 0.9990 Silver 5.000 oz. ASW **Subject:** Endangered Wildlife **Obverse:** Queen's portrait right **Reverse:** Koala and baby

| Date | Mintage | F | VF | XF | Unc | BU |
|---|---|---|---|---|---|---|
| 1996 Proof | Est. 10,000 | Value: 85.00 | | | | |

**25 DOLLARS** **KM# 272** **Weight:** 155.5175 g. **Composition:** 0.9990 Silver 5.000 oz. ASW **Subject:** Endangered Wildlife **Obverse:** Queen's portrait right **Reverse:** Family of chimpanzees

| Date | Mintage | F | VF | XF | Unc | BU |
|---|---|---|---|---|---|---|
| 1996 Proof | Est. 10,000 | Value: 85.00 | | | | |

**25 DOLLARS** **KM# 273** **Weight:** 155.5175 g. **Composition:** 0.9990 Silver 5.000 oz. ASW **Subject:** Endangered Wildlife **Obverse:** Queen's portrait right **Reverse:** Family of elephants

| Date | Mintage | F | VF | XF | Unc | BU |
|---|---|---|---|---|---|---|
| 1996 Proof | Est. 10,000 | Value: 85.00 | | | | |

**25 DOLLARS** **KM# 274** **Weight:** 155.5175 g. **Composition:** 0.9990 Silver 5.000 oz. ASW **Subject:** Endangered Wildlife **Obverse:** Queen's portrait right **Reverse:** Family of whooping cranes

| Date | Mintage | F | VF | XF | Unc | BU |
|---|---|---|---|---|---|---|
| 1996 Proof | Est. 10,000 | Value: 85.00 | | | | |

**25 DOLLARS** **KM# 289** **Weight:** 155.5175 g. **Composition:** 0.9990 Silver 5.000 oz. ASW **Subject:** Olympic National Park **Obverse:** Queen's portrait right **Reverse:** Multicolored bald eagle in flight

| Date | Mintage | F | VF | XF | Unc | BU |
|---|---|---|---|---|---|---|
| 1996 Proof | 1,000 | Value: 100 | | | | |

**25 DOLLARS** **KM# 290** **Weight:** 155.5175 g. **Composition:** 0.9990 Silver 5.000 oz. ASW **Subject:** Yellowstone Natonal Park **Obverse:** Queen's portrait right **Reverse:** Multicolored grizzly bear and cub

| Date | Mintage | F | VF | XF | Unc | BU |
|---|---|---|---|---|---|---|
| 1996 Proof | 1,000 | Value: 100 | | | | |

**25 DOLLARS** **KM# 291** **Weight:** 3.1103 g. **Composition:** 0.9990 Gold .1000 oz. AGW **Subject:** Olympic National Park **Obverse:** Queen's portrait right **Reverse:** Bald eagle

| Date | Mintage | F | VF | XF | Unc | BU |
|---|---|---|---|---|---|---|
| 1996 Proof | — | Value: 85.00 | | | | |

**25 DOLLARS** **KM# 292** **Weight:** 3.1103 g. **Composition:** 0.9990 Gold .1000 oz. AGW **Subject:** Yellowstone National Park **Obverse:** Queen's portrait right **Reverse:** Girzzly bear

| Date | Mintage | F | VF | XF | Unc | BU |
|---|---|---|---|---|---|---|
| 1996 Proof | — | Value: 85.00 | | | | |

**25 DOLLARS** **KM# 309** **Weight:** 10000.0996 g. **Composition:** 0.9990 Silver 32.1218 oz. ASW **Obverse:** Queen's portrait right **Reverse:** Princess Diana's portrait, dates

| Date | Mintage | F | VF | XF | Unc | BU |
|---|---|---|---|---|---|---|
| 1997 Matte Proof | — | Value: 400 | | | | |

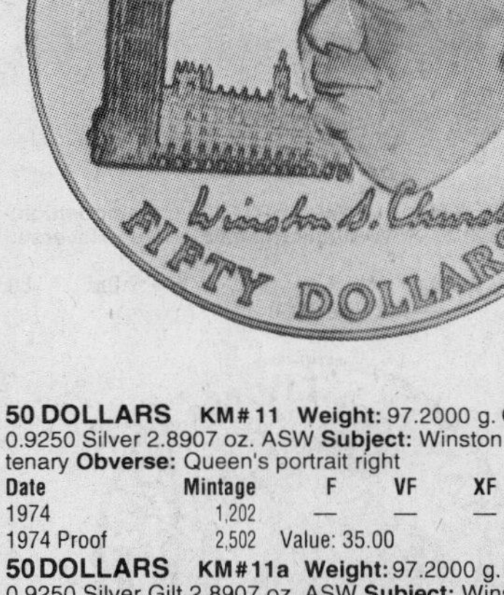


**50 DOLLARS** **KM# 11** **Weight:** 97.2000 g. **Composition:** 0.9250 Silver 2.8907 oz. ASW **Subject:** Winston Churchill Centenary **Obverse:** Queen's portrait right

| Date | Mintage | F | VF | XF | Unc | BU |
|---|---|---|---|---|---|---|
| 1974 | 1,202 | — | — | — | 30.00 | — |
| 1974 Proof | 2,502 | Value: 35.00 | | | | |

**50 DOLLARS** **KM# 11a** **Weight:** 97.2000 g. **Composition:** 0.9250 Silver Gilt 2.8907 oz. ASW **Subject:** Winston Churchill Centenary **Obverse:** Queen's portrait right

| Date | Mintage | F | VF | XF | Unc | BU |
|---|---|---|---|---|---|---|
| 1974 Proof | 2,002 | Value: 50.00 | | | | |

**50 DOLLARS** **KM# 203** **Weight:** 3.9450 g. **Composition:** 0.5000 Gold 0.634 oz. AGW **Obverse:** Queen's portrait right

| Date | Mintage | F | VF | XF | Unc | BU |
|---|---|---|---|---|---|---|
| 1980 Proof | — | Value: 90.00 | | | | |

**50 DOLLARS** **KM# 27** **Weight:** 3.9450 g. **Composition:** 0.5000 Gold 0.634 oz. AGW **Subject:** Wedding of Prince Charles and Lady Diana **Obverse:** Queen's portrait right

| Date | Mintage | F | VF | XF | Unc | BU |
|---|---|---|---|---|---|---|
| 1981 | 220 | — | — | — | 75.00 | — |
| 1981 Proof | 1,309 | Value: 90.00 | | | | |

**50 DOLLARS** **KM# 40** **Weight:** 28.2800 g. **Composition:** 0.9250 Silver .8411 oz. ASW **Subject:** 1988 Olympics **Obverse:** Queen's portrait right **Reverse:** Tourch bearer

| Date | Mintage | F | VF | XF | Unc | BU |
|---|---|---|---|---|---|---|
| 1987PM Proof | 20,000 | Value: 27.50 | | | | |

**50 DOLLARS** **KM# 111** **Weight:** 20.9400 g. **Composition:** 0.9250 Silver .6228 oz. ASW **Subject:** Great Explorers **Reverse:** Richard Byrd

| Date | Mintage | F | VF | XF | Unc | BU |
|---|---|---|---|---|---|---|
| 1988FM (P) | — | Value: 27.50 | | | | |

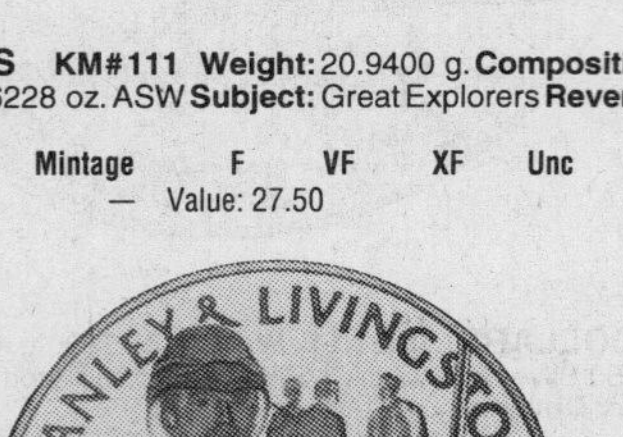


**50 DOLLARS** **KM# 61** **Weight:** 20.9400 g. **Composition:** 0.9250 Silver .6228 oz. ASW **Subject:** Great Explorers **Obverse:** Queen's portrait right **Reverse:** Stanley and Livingstone

| Date | Mintage | F | VF | XF | Unc | BU |
|---|---|---|---|---|---|---|
| 1988FM (P) | — | Value: 25.00 | | | | |

**50 DOLLARS** **KM# 62** **Weight:** 20.9400 g. **Composition:** 0.9250 Silver .6228 oz. ASW **Subject:** Great Explorers **Obverse:** Queen's portrait right **Reverse:** Capt. James Cook

| Date | Mintage | F | VF | XF | Unc | BU |
|---|---|---|---|---|---|---|
| 1988FM (P) | — | Value: 27.50 | | | | |

**50 DOLLARS** **KM# 63** **Weight:** 20.9400 g. **Composition:** 0.9250 Silver .6228 oz. ASW **Subject:** Great Explorers **Obverse:** Queen's portrait right **Reverse:** Vasco Nunez de Balboa

| Date | Mintage | F | VF | XF | Unc | BU |
|---|---|---|---|---|---|---|
| 1988FM (P) | — | Value: 22.50 | | | | |

**50 DOLLARS** **KM# 64** **Weight:** 20.9400 g. **Composition:** 0.9250 Silver .6228 oz. ASW **Subject:** Great Explorers **Obverse:** Queen's portrait right **Reverse:** Ferdinand Magellan

| Date | Mintage | F | VF | XF | Unc | BU |
|---|---|---|---|---|---|---|
| 1988FM (P) | — | Value: 20.00 | | | | |

**50 DOLLARS** **KM# 65** **Weight:** 20.9400 g. **Composition:** 0.9250 Silver .6228 oz. ASW **Subject:** Great Explorers **Obverse:** Queen's portrait right **Reverse:** Marco Polo

| Date | Mintage | F | VF | XF | Unc | BU |
|---|---|---|---|---|---|---|
| 1988FM (P) | — | Value: 20.00 | | | | |

**50 DOLLARS** **KM# 66** **Weight:** 20.9400 g. **Composition:** 0.9250 Silver .6228 oz. ASW **Subject:** Great Explorers **Obverse:** Queen's portrait right **Reverse:** Vasco da Gama

| Date | Mintage | F | VF | XF | Unc | BU |
|---|---|---|---|---|---|---|
| 1988FM (P) | — | Value: 20.00 | | | | |

**50 DOLLARS** **KM# 67** **Weight:** 20.9400 g. **Composition:** 0.9250 Silver .6228 oz. ASW **Subject:** Great Explorers **Obverse:** Queen's portrait right **Reverse:** Christopher Columbus

| Date | Mintage | F | VF | XF | Unc | BU |
|---|---|---|---|---|---|---|
| 1988FM (P) | — | Value: 20.00 | | | | |

**50 DOLLARS** **KM# 68** **Weight:** 20.9400 g. **Composition:** 0.9250 Silver .6228 oz. ASW **Subject:** Great Explorers **Obverse:** Queen's portrait right **Reverse:** Sir Francis Drake

| Date | Mintage | F | VF | XF | Unc | BU |
|---|---|---|---|---|---|---|
| 1988FM (P) | — | Value: 22.50 | | | | |

**50 DOLLARS** **KM# 69** **Weight:** 20.9400 g. **Composition:** 0.9250 Silver .6228 oz. ASW **Subject:** Great Explorers **Obverse:** Queen's portrait right **Reverse:** Sieur de la Salle

| Date | Mintage | F | VF | XF | Unc | BU |
|---|---|---|---|---|---|---|
| 1988FM (P) | — | Value: 22.50 | | | | |

**50 DOLLARS** **KM# 96** **Weight:** 20.9400 g. **Composition:** 0.9250 Silver .6228 oz. ASW **Subject:** Great Explorers **Obverse:** Queen's portrait right **Reverse:** Alexander the Great

| Date | Mintage | F | VF | XF | Unc | BU |
|---|---|---|---|---|---|---|
| 1988FM (P) | — | Value: 22.50 | | | | |

**50 DOLLARS** **KM# 97** **Weight:** 20.9400 g. **Composition:** 0.9250 Silver .6228 oz. ASW **Subject:** Great Explorers **Obverse:** Queen's portrait right **Reverse:** Leif Ericson

| Date | Mintage | F | VF | XF | Unc | BU |
|---|---|---|---|---|---|---|
| 1988FM (P) | — | Value: 22.50 | | | | |

**50 DOLLARS** **KM# 98** **Weight:** 20.9400 g. **Composition:** 0.9250 Silver .6228 oz. ASW **Subject:** Great Explorers **Obverse:** Queen's portrait right **Reverse:** Amerigo Vespucci

| Date | Mintage | F | VF | XF | Unc | BU |
|---|---|---|---|---|---|---|
| 1988FM (P) | — | Value: 20.00 | | | | |

**50 DOLLARS** **KM# 99** **Weight:** 20.9400 g. **Composition:** 0.9250 Silver .6228 oz. ASW **Subject:** Great Explorers **Obverse:** Queen's portrait right **Reverse:** Bartolomeu Diaz

| Date | Mintage | F | VF | XF | Unc | BU |
|---|---|---|---|---|---|---|
| 1988FM (P) | — | Value: 25.00 | | | | |

**50 DOLLARS** **KM# 100** **Weight:** 20.9400 g. **Composition:** 0.9250 Silver .6228 oz. ASW **Subject:** Great Explorers **Obverse:** Queen's portrait right **Reverse:** Juan Ponce de Leon

| Date | Mintage | F | VF | XF | Unc | BU |
|---|---|---|---|---|---|---|
| 1988FM (P) | — | Value: 27.50 | | | | |

**50 DOLLARS** **KM# 101** **Weight:** 20.9400 g. **Composition:** 0.9250 Silver .6228 oz. ASW **Subject:** Great Explorers **Obverse:** Queen's portrait right **Reverse:** Hernando Cortes

| Date | Mintage | F | VF | XF | Unc | BU |
|---|---|---|---|---|---|---|
| 1988FM (P) | — | Value: 20.00 | | | | |

**50 DOLLARS** **KM# 102** **Weight:** 20.9400 g. **Composition:** 0.9250 Silver .6228 oz. ASW **Subject:** Great Explorers **Obverse:** Queen's portrait right **Reverse:** Francisco Coronado

| Date | Mintage | F | VF | XF | Unc | BU |
|---|---|---|---|---|---|---|
| 1988FM (P) | — | Value: 22.50 | | | | |

**50 DOLLARS** **KM# 103** **Weight:** 20.9400 g. **Composition:** 0.9250 Silver .6228 oz. ASW **Subject:** Great Explorers **Obverse:** Queen's portrait right **Reverse:** Francisco Pizarro

| Date | Mintage | F | VF | XF | Unc | BU |
|---|---|---|---|---|---|---|
| 1988FM (P) | — | Value: 20.00 | | | | |

**50 DOLLARS** **KM# 104** **Weight:** 20.9400 g. **Composition:** 0.9250 Silver .6228 oz. ASW **Subject:** Great Explorers **Obverse:** Queen's portrait right **Reverse:** Samuel de Champlain

| Date | Mintage | F | VF | XF | Unc | BU |
|---|---|---|---|---|---|---|
| 1988FM (P) | — | Value: 22.50 | | | | |

**50 DOLLARS** **KM# 105** **Weight:** 20.9400 g. **Composition:** 0.9250 Silver .6228 oz. ASW **Subject:** Great Explorers **Obverse:** Queen's portrait right **Reverse:** John Cabot

| Date | Mintage | F | VF | XF | Unc | BU |
|---|---|---|---|---|---|---|
| 1988FM (P) | — | Value: 20.00 | | | | |

**50 DOLLARS** **KM# 106** **Weight:** 20.9400 g. **Composition:** 0.9250 Silver .6228 oz. ASW **Subject:** Great Explorers **Obverse:** Queen's portrait right **Reverse:** Abel Janszoon Tasman

| Date | Mintage | F | VF | XF | Unc | BU |
|---|---|---|---|---|---|---|
| 1988FM (P) | — | Value: 22.50 | | | | |

**50 DOLLARS** **KM# 107** **Weight:** 20.9400 g. **Composition:** 0.9250 Silver .6228 oz. ASW **Subject:** Great Explorers **Obverse:** Queen's portrait right **Reverse:** Lewis and Clark

| Date | Mintage | F | VF | XF | Unc | BU |
|---|---|---|---|---|---|---|
| 1988FM (P) | — | Value: 22.50 | | | | |

**50 DOLLARS** **KM# 108** **Weight:** 20.9400 g. **Composition:** 0.9250 Silver .6228 oz. ASW **Subject:** Great Explorers **Obverse:** Queen's portrait right **Reverse:** Fridtjof Nansen

| Date | Mintage | F | VF | XF | Unc | BU |
|---|---|---|---|---|---|---|
| 1988FM (P) | — | Value: 27.50 | | | | |

**50 DOLLARS** **KM# 109** **Weight:** 20.9400 g. **Composition:** 0.9250 Silver .6228 oz. ASW **Subject:** Great Explorers **Obverse:** Queen's portrait right **Reverse:** Robert Peary

| Date | Mintage | F | VF | XF | Unc | BU |
|---|---|---|---|---|---|---|
| 1988FM (P) | — | Value: 20.00 | | | | |

**50 DOLLARS** **KM#110** **Weight:** 20.9400 g. **Composition:** 0.9250 Silver .6228 oz. ASW **Subject:** Great Explorers **Obverse:** Queen's portrait right **Reverse:** Roald Amundsen

| Date | Mintage | F | VF | XF | Unc | BU |
|---|---|---|---|---|---|---|
| 1988FM (P); Proof | — | Value: 20.00 | | | | |

**50 DOLLARS** **KM# 47** **Weight:** 29.9000 g. **Composition:** 0.9250 Silver .8892 oz. ASW **Subject:** 500 Years of America **Obverse:** Queen's portrait right **Reverse:** Christopher Columbus **Edge Lettering:** CHRISTOPHER COLUMBUS WITH THE SANTA MARIA

| Date | Mintage | F | VF | XF | Unc | BU |
|---|---|---|---|---|---|---|
| 1989 Proof | Est. 15,000 | Value: 30.00 | | | | |

**Note:** Prior to the 27th edition, the illustration for KM#47 was incorrect. Please see KM182 for correct listing

**50 DOLLARS** **KM# 49** **Weight:** 31.1000 g. **Composition:** 0.9250 Silver .9250 oz. ASW **Subject:** 500 Years of America **Obverse:** Queen's portrait right **Reverse:** Ferdinand Magellan

| Date | Mintage | F | VF | XF | Unc | BU |
|---|---|---|---|---|---|---|
| 1989 Proof | 15,000 | Value: 22.50 | | | | |
| 1991 Proof | Est. 60,000 | Value: 22.50 | | | | |

**50 DOLLARS** **KM# 60** **Weight:** 28.2800 g. **Composition:** 0.9250 Silver .8411 oz. ASW **Subject:** 1990 Olympics **Obverse:** Queen's portrait right **Reverse:** Runners and biathalon

| Date | Mintage | F | VF | XF | Unc | BU |
|---|---|---|---|---|---|---|
| 1989 Proof | 40,000 | — | — | — | 25.00 | — |

**50 DOLLARS** **KM# 70** **Weight:** 28.2800 g. **Composition:** 0.9250 Silver .8411 oz. ASW **Subject:** Soccer World championship **Obverse:** Queen's portrait right

| Date | Mintage | F | VF | XF | Unc | BU |
|---|---|---|---|---|---|---|
| 1989 Proof | — | Value: 22.50 | | | | |

**50 DOLLARS** **KM# 45** **Weight:** 19.4000 g. **Composition:** 0.9250 Silver .5770 oz. ASW **Subject:** 500 Years of America **Obverse:** Queen's portrait right **Reverse:** Sir Francis Drake

| Date | Mintage | F | VF | XF | Unc | BU |
|---|---|---|---|---|---|---|
| 1989 Proof | 15,000 | Value: 30.00 | | | | |
| 1990 Proof | — | Value: 22.50 | | | | |

**50 DOLLARS** **KM# 46** **Weight:** 31.1000 g. **Composition:** 0.9990 Silver 1.0000 oz. ASW **Subject:** 500 Years of America **Obverse:** Queen's portrait right **Reverse:** Capt. James Cook

| Date | Mintage | F | VF | XF | Unc | BU |
|---|---|---|---|---|---|---|
| 1989 Proof | 15,000 | Value: 22.50 | | | | |

**50 DOLLARS** **KM# 43** **Weight:** 31.1000 g. **Composition:** 0.9250 Silver .9250 oz. ASW **Subject:** 500 Years of America **Obverse:** Queen's portrait right **Reverse:** Jacques Cartier

| Date | Mintage | F | VF | XF | Unc | BU |
|---|---|---|---|---|---|---|
| 1990 Proof | 60,000 | Value: 20.00 | | | | |
| 1991 Proof | — | Value: 25.00 | | | | |

**50 DOLLARS** **KM# 44** **Weight:** 31.1000 g. **Composition:** 0.9990 Silver 1.0000 oz. ASW **Subject:** 500 Years of America **Obverse:** Queen's portrait right **Reverse:** Vasco Nunez de Balboa

| Date | Mintage | F | VF | XF | Unc | BU |
|---|---|---|---|---|---|---|
| 1990 Proof | 15,000 | Value: 20.00 | | | | |
| 1991 Proof | — | Value: 20.00 | | | | |

**50 DOLLARS** **KM# 265** **Weight:** 28.3000 g. **Composition:** 0.9250 Silver .8416 oz. ASW **Subject:** World Cup Soccer

| Date | Mintage | F | VF | XF | Unc | BU |
|---|---|---|---|---|---|---|
| 1990 Proof | — | Value: 22.50 | | | | |

**50 DOLLARS** **KM# 52** **Weight:** 19.4000 g. **Composition:** 0.9250 Silver .5770 oz. ASW **Subject:** Endangered World Wildlife **Obverse:** Queen's portrait right **Reverse:** Grizzly Bear

| Date | Mintage | F | VF | XF | Unc | BU |
|---|---|---|---|---|---|---|
| 1990PM Matte | 550 | Value: 75.00 | | | | |
| 1990PM Proof | 2,500 | Value: 22.50 | | | | |

**50 DOLLARS** **KM# 48** **Weight:** 31.1000 g. **Composition:** 0.9990 Silver 1.0000 oz. ASW **Subject:** 500 Years of America **Obverse:** Queen's portrait right **Reverse:** President Abraham Lincoln

| Date | Mintage | F | VF | XF | Unc | BU |
|---|---|---|---|---|---|---|
| 1990 Proof | 15,000 | Value: 20.00 | | | | |
| 1991 Proof | — | Value: 20.00 | | | | |

**50 DOLLARS** **KM# 53** **Weight:** 19.4000 g. **Composition:** 0.9250 Silver 5770 oz. ASW **Subject:** Endangered World Wildlife **Obverse:** Queen's portrait right **Reverse:** African elephant

| Date | Mintage | F | VF | XF | Unc | BU |
|---|---|---|---|---|---|---|
| 1990 Matte | 1,000 | Value: 55.00 | | | | |
| 1990 Proof | 25,000 | Value: 22.50 | | | | |

**50 DOLLARS** **KM# 54** **Weight:** 19.4000 g. **Composition:** 0.9250 Silver 5770 oz. ASW **Subject:** Endangered World Wildlife **Obverse:** Queen's portrait right **Reverse:** Lynx

| Date | Mintage | F | VF | XF | Unc | BU |
|---|---|---|---|---|---|---|
| 1990 Proof | 25,000 | Value: 22.50 | | | | |

**50 DOLLARS** **KM# 55** **Weight:** 19.4000 g. **Composition:** 0.9250 Silver 5770 oz. ASW **Subject:** Endangered World Wildlife **Obverse:** Queen's portrait right **Reverse:** Black rhinoceros

| Date | Mintage | F | VF | XF | Unc | BU |
|---|---|---|---|---|---|---|
| 1990 Proof | Est. 25,000 | Value: 22.50 | | | | |

**50 DOLLARS** **KM# 56** **Weight:** 19.4000 g. **Composition:** 0.9250 Silver 5770 oz. ASW **Subject:** Endangered World Wildlife **Obverse:** Queen's portrait right **Reverse:** Big horn sheep

| Date | Mintage | F | VF | XF | Unc | BU |
|---|---|---|---|---|---|---|
| 1990 Proof | Est. 25,000 | Value: 22.50 | | | | |

**50 DOLLARS** **KM# 57** **Weight:** 19.4000 g. **Composition:** 0.9250 Silver 5770 oz. ASW **Subject:** Endangered World Wildlife **Obverse:** Queen's portrait right **Reverse:** Koala

| Date | Mintage | F | VF | XF | Unc | BU |
|---|---|---|---|---|---|---|
| 1990 Proof | Est. 25,000 | Value: 25.00 | | | | |

**50 DOLLARS** **KM# 58** **Weight:** 19.4000 g. **Composition:** 0.9250 Silver 5770 oz. ASW **Subject:** Endangered World Wildlife **Obverse:** Queen's portrait right **Reverse:** Buffalo

| Date | Mintage | F | VF | XF | Unc | BU |
|---|---|---|---|---|---|---|
| 1990 | 600 | — | — | — | 60.00 | — |
| 1990 Proof | 25,000 | Value: 22.50 | | | | |

**50 DOLLARS** **KM# 59** **Weight:** 19.4000 g. **Composition:** 0.9250 Silver 5770 oz. ASW **Subject:** Endangered World Wildlife **Obverse:** Queen's portrait right **Reverse:** Chimpanzee

| Date | Mintage | F | VF | XF | Unc | BU |
|---|---|---|---|---|---|---|
| 1990 Proof | Est. 25,000 | Value: 22.50 | | | | |

**50 DOLLARS** **KM# 89** **Weight:** 31.1000 g. **Composition:** 0.9250 Silver .9250 oz. ASW **Subject:** 500 Years of America **Obverse:** Queen's portrait right **Reverse:** Henry Hudson

| Date | Mintage | F | VF | XF | Unc | BU |
|---|---|---|---|---|---|---|
| 1990 Proof | 60,000 | Value: 25.00 | | | | |

**50 DOLLARS** **KM# 134** **Weight:** 31.1000 g. **Composition:** 0.9250 Silver .9250 oz. ASW **Subject:** 500 Years of America **Obverse:** Queen's portrait right **Reverse:** Cabral

| Date | Mintage | F | VF | XF | Unc | BU |
|---|---|---|---|---|---|---|
| 1990 Proof | Est. 60,000 | Value: 20.00 | | | | |

**50 DOLLARS** **KM# 135** **Weight:** 31.1000 g. **Composition:** 0.9250 Silver .9250 oz. ASW **Subject:** 500 Years of America **Obverse:** Queen's portrait right **Reverse:** Bolivar

| Date | Mintage | F | VF | XF | Unc | BU |
|---|---|---|---|---|---|---|
| 1990 Proof | Est. 60,000 | Value: 22.50 | | | | |

**50 DOLLARS** **KM# 139** **Weight:** 31.2600 g. **Composition:** 0.9250 Silver .9296 oz. ASW **Subject:** 500 Years of America **Obverse:** Queen's portrait right **Reverse:** Samuel Clemens

| Date | Mintage | F | VF | XF | Unc | BU |
|---|---|---|---|---|---|---|
| 1990 Proof | Est. 60,000 | Value: 25.00 | | | | |

**50 DOLLARS** **KM# 182** **Weight:** 31.3500 g. **Composition:** 0.9250 Silver .9324 oz. ASW **Subject:** 500 Years of America **Obverse:** Queen's portrait right **Reverse:** Arms above Columbus' portrait w/Santa Maria in background

| Date | Mintage | F | VF | XF | Unc | BU |
|---|---|---|---|---|---|---|
| 1990 Proof | — | Value: 27.50 | | | | |

**50 DOLLARS** **KM# 184** **Weight:** 31.3500 g. **Composition:** 0.9250 Silver .9324 oz. ASW **Subject:** 500 Years of America **Obverse:** Queen's portrait right **Reverse:** Inca Prince

| Date | Mintage | F | VF | XF | Unc | BU |
|---|---|---|---|---|---|---|
| 1990 Proof | Est. 60,000 | Value: 22.50 | | | | |

**50 DOLLARS** **KM#185** **Weight:** 31.3500 g. **Composition:** 0.9250 Silver .9324 oz. ASW **Subject:** 500 Years of America **Obverse:** Queen's portrait right **Reverse:** Cortez and Montezuma

| Date | Mintage | F | VF | XF | Unc | BU |
|---|---|---|---|---|---|---|
| 1990 Proof | Est. 60,000 | Value: 22.50 | | | | |

**50 DOLLARS** **KM#186** **Weight:** 31.3500 g. **Composition:** 0.9250 Silver .9324 oz. ASW **Subject:** 500 Years of America **Obverse:** Queen's portrait right **Reverse:** Samuel de Champalin

| Date | Mintage | F | VF | XF | Unc | BU |
|---|---|---|---|---|---|---|
| 1990 Proof | Est. 60,000 | Value: 20.00 | | | | |

**50 DOLLARS** **KM#188** **Weight:** 31.3500 g. **Composition:** 0.9250 Silver .9324 oz. ASW **Subject:** 500 Years of America **Obverse:** Queen's portrait right **Reverse:** Sir Walter Raleigh

| Date | Mintage | F | VF | XF | Unc | BU |
|---|---|---|---|---|---|---|
| 1990 Proof | Est. 60,000 | Value: 25.00 | | | | |

**50 DOLLARS** **KM#112** **Weight:** 19.2000 g. **Composition:** 0.9250 Silver .5768 oz. ASW **Subject:** 1992 Olympics **Obverse:** Queen's portrait right **Reverse:** Runer

| Date | Mintage | F | VF | XF | Unc | BU |
|---|---|---|---|---|---|---|
| 1990 Proof | 40,000 | Value: 27.50 | | | | |

**50 DOLLARS** **KM#115** **Weight:** 19.8000 g. **Composition:** 0.9250 Silver .5888 oz. ASW **Subject:** Endangered World Wildlife **Obverse:** Queen's portrait right **Reverse:** Blackbuck

| Date | Mintage | F | VF | XF | Unc | BU |
|---|---|---|---|---|---|---|
| 1990 Proof | — | Value: 27.50 | | | | |

**50 DOLLARS** **KM#116** **Weight:** 19.8000 g. **Composition:** 0.9250 Silver .5888 oz. ASW **Subject:** Endangered World Wildlife **Obverse:** Queen's portrait right **Reverse:** European mouflon

| Date | Mintage | F | VF | XF | Unc | BU |
|---|---|---|---|---|---|---|
| 1990 Proof | — | Value: 27.50 | | | | |

**50 DOLLARS** **KM#117** **Weight:** 19.8000 g. **Composition:** 0.9250 Silver .5888 oz. ASW **Subject:** Endangered World Wildlife **Obverse:** Queen's portrait right **Reverse:** Whooping crane

| Date | Mintage | F | VF | XF | Unc | BU |
|---|---|---|---|---|---|---|
| 1990 Proof | — | Value: 27.50 | | | | |

**50 DOLLARS** **KM#144** **Weight:** 19.4000 g. **Composition:** 0.9250 Silver .5768 oz. ASW **Subject:** Endangered World Wildlife **Obverse:** Queen's portrait right **Reverse:** European hedgehog

| Date | Mintage | F | VF | XF | Unc | BU |
|---|---|---|---|---|---|---|
| 1990 Proof | Est. 25,000 | Value: 27.50 | | | | |

**50 DOLLARS** **KM#205** **Weight:** 19.2000 g. **Composition:** 0.9250 Silver .5768 oz. ASW **Subject:** Endangered World Wildlife **Obverse:** PM mint mark below truncaton **Reverse:** European bison and calf

| Date | Mintage | F | VF | XF | Unc | BU |
|---|---|---|---|---|---|---|
| 1990PM Proof | Est. 25,000 | Value: 35.00 | | | | |

**50 DOLLARS** **KM#206** **Weight:** 19.2000 g. **Composition:** 0.9250 Silver .5768 oz. ASW **Subject:** Endangered World Wildlife **Obverse:** Queen's portrait right **Reverse:** Tiger

| Date | Mintage | F | VF | XF | Unc | BU |
|---|---|---|---|---|---|---|
| 1990 Proof | Est. 25,000 | Value: 25.00 | | | | |

**50 DOLLARS** **KM#207** **Weight:** 19.2000 g. **Composition:** 0.9250 Silver .5768 oz. ASW **Subject:** Endangered World Wildlife **Obverse:** Queen's portrait right **Reverse:** Dama gazelles

| Date | Mintage | F | VF | XF | Unc | BU |
|---|---|---|---|---|---|---|
| 1990 Proof | Est. 25,000 | Value: 22.50 | | | | |

**50 DOLLARS** **KM#208** **Weight:** 19.2000 g. **Composition:** 0.9250 Silver .5768 oz. ASW **Subject:** Endangered World Wildlife **Obverse:** Queen's portrait right **Reverse:** Cougars

| Date | Mintage | F | VF | XF | Unc | BU |
|---|---|---|---|---|---|---|
| 1990PM Proof | — | Value: 42.50 | | | | |

**50 DOLLARS** **KM#209** **Weight:** 19.2000 g. **Composition:** 0.9250 Silver .5768 oz. ASW **Subject:** Endangered World Wildlife **Obverse:** Queen's portrait right **Reverse:** Eagle Owl

| Date | Mintage | F | VF | XF | Unc | BU |
|---|---|---|---|---|---|---|
| 1990(b) Proof | — | Value: 42.50 | | | | |

**50 DOLLARS** **KM#212** **Weight:** 19.2000 g. **Composition:** 0.9250 Silver .5768 oz. ASW **Subject:** Endangered World Wildlife **Obverse:** Queen's portrait right **Reverse:** Alpine ibex

| Date | Mintage | F | VF | XF | Unc | BU |
|---|---|---|---|---|---|---|
| 1990 Proof | — | Value: 37.50 | | | | |

**50 DOLLARS** **KM#216** **Weight:** 19.2000 g. **Composition:** 0.9250 Silver .5768 oz. ASW **Subject:** Endangered World Wildlife **Obverse:** Queen's portrait right **Reverse:** Jackass penquins

| Date | Mintage | F | VF | XF | Unc | BU |
|---|---|---|---|---|---|---|
| 1990 Proof | — | Value: 37.50 | | | | |

**50 DOLLARS** **KM#210** **Weight:** 19.2000 g. **Composition:** 0.9250 Silver .5768 oz. ASW **Subject:** Endangered World Wildlife **Obverse:** Queen's portrait right **Reverse:** Heaviside's dolphins

| Date | Mintage | F | VF | XF | Unc | BU |
|---|---|---|---|---|---|---|
| 1990(b) Proof | — | Value: 45.00 | | | | |

**50 DOLLARS** **KM#213** **Weight:** 19.2000 g. **Composition:** 0.9250 Silver .5768 oz. ASW **Subject:** Endangered World Wildlife **Obverse:** Queen's portrait right **Reverse:** Senegalese lion

| Date | Mintage | F | VF | XF | Unc | BU |
|---|---|---|---|---|---|---|
| 1990 Proof | — | Value: 42.50 | | | | |

**50 DOLLARS** **KM# 93** **Weight:** 19.8000 g. **Composition:** 0.9250 Silver .5888 oz. ASW **Subject:** Endangered World Wildlife **Obverse:** Queen's portrait right **Reverse:** Eagle owl

| Date | Mintage | F | VF | XF | Unc | BU |
|---|---|---|---|---|---|---|
| 1991 Proof | Est. 25,000 | Value: 22.50 | | | | |

**50 DOLLARS** **KM#211** **Weight:** 19.2000 g. **Composition:** 0.9250 Silver .5768 oz. ASW **Subject:** Endangered World Wildlife **Obverse:** Queen's portrait right **Reverse:** European otters

| Date | Mintage | F | VF | XF | Unc | BU |
|---|---|---|---|---|---|---|
| 1990 Proof | — | Value: 42.50 | | | | |

**50 DOLLARS** **KM#214** **Weight:** 19.2000 g. **Composition:** 0.9250 Silver .5768 oz. ASW **Subject:** Endangered World Wildlife **Obverse:** Queen's portrait right **Reverse:** Fallow deer

| Date | Mintage | F | VF | XF | Unc | BU |
|---|---|---|---|---|---|---|
| 1990 Proof | — | Value: 40.00 | | | | |

**50 DOLLARS** **KM# 95** **Weight:** 19.2000 g. **Composition:** 0.9250 Silver .5768 oz. ASW **Subject:** Endangered World Wildlife **Obverse:** Queen's portrait right **Reverse:** Heavisdie's dolphins

| Date | Mintage | F | VF | XF | Unc | BU |
|---|---|---|---|---|---|---|
| 1991 Proof | Est. 25,000 | Value: 22.50 | | | | |

**50 DOLLARS** **KM#357** **Weight:** 19.2000 g. **Composition:** 0.9250 Silver .5768 oz. ASW **Subject:** Endangered World Wildlife **Obverse:** Queen's portrait right **Reverse:** Peregrine falcon

| Date | Mintage | F | VF | XF | Unc | BU |
|---|---|---|---|---|---|---|
| 1990 Proof | — | Value: 42.50 | | | | |

**50 DOLLARS** **KM#215** **Weight:** 19.2000 g. **Composition:** 0.9250 Silver .5768 oz. ASW **Subject:** Endangered World Wildlife **Obverse:** Queen's portrait right **Reverse:** Bee hunningbird

| Date | Mintage | F | VF | XF | Unc | BU |
|---|---|---|---|---|---|---|
| 1990 Proof | — | Value: 42.50 | | | | |

**50 DOLLARS** **KM#118** **Weight:** 19.2000 g. **Composition:** 0.9250 Silver .5768 oz. ASW **Subject:** Endangered World Wildlife **Obverse:** Queen's portrait right **Reverse:** European otters

| Date | Mintage | F | VF | XF | Unc | BU |
|---|---|---|---|---|---|---|
| 1991 Proof | — | Value: 22.50 | | | | |

**50 DOLLARS** **KM# 119** **Weight:** 19.2000 g. **Composition:** 0.9250 Silver .5768 oz. ASW **Subject:** Endangered World Wildlife **Obverse:** Queen's portrait right **Reverse:** Peregrine falcon

| Date | Mintage | F | VF | XF | Unc | BU |
|---|---|---|---|---|---|---|
| 1991 Proof | Est. 25,000 | Value: 22.50 | | | | |

**50 DOLLARS** **KM# 124** **Weight:** 19.2000 g. **Composition:** 0.9250 Silver .5768 oz. ASW **Subject:** Endangered World Wildlife **Obverse:** Queen's portrait right **Reverse:** Kangaroo

| Date | Mintage | F | VF | XF | Unc | BU |
|---|---|---|---|---|---|---|
| 1991 Proof | Est. 25,000 | Value: 22.50 | | | | |

**50 DOLLARS** **KM# 128** **Weight:** 19.2000 g. **Composition:** 0.9250 Silver .5768 oz. ASW **Subject:** Endangered World Wildlife **Obverse:** Queen's portrait right **Reverse:** Jackass penquins

| Date | Mintage | F | VF | XF | Unc | BU |
|---|---|---|---|---|---|---|
| 1991 Proof | Est. 25,000 | Value: 22.50 | | | | |

**50 DOLLARS** **KM# 120** **Weight:** 19.2000 g. **Composition:** 0.9250 Silver .5768 oz. ASW **Subject:** Endangered World Wildlife **Obverse:** Queen's portrait right **Reverse:** Alpine ibex

| Date | Mintage | F | VF | XF | Unc | BU |
|---|---|---|---|---|---|---|
| 1991 Proof | Est. 25,000 | Value: 25.00 | | | | |

**50 DOLLARS** **KM# 125** **Weight:** 19.2000 g. **Composition:** 0.9250 Silver .5768 oz. ASW **Subject:** Endangered World Wildlife **Obverse:** Queen's portrait right **Reverse:** Cougar and cub

| Date | Mintage | F | VF | XF | Unc | BU |
|---|---|---|---|---|---|---|
| 1991 Proof | Est. 25,000 | Value: 25.00 | | | | |

**50 DOLLARS** **KM# 94** **Weight:** 31.1000 g. **Composition:** 0.9250 Silver .9250 oz. ASW **Subject:** 500 Years of America **Obverse:** Queen's portrait right **Reverse:** Sitting Bull

| Date | Mintage | F | VF | XF | Unc | BU |
|---|---|---|---|---|---|---|
| 1991 Proof | Est. 15,000 | Value: 27.50 | | | | |

**50 DOLLARS** **KM# 122** **Weight:** 19.2000 g. **Composition:** 0.9250 Silver .5768 oz. ASW **Subject:** Endangered World Wildlife **Obverse:** Queen's portrait right **Reverse:** Senegalese lion

| Date | Mintage | F | VF | XF | Unc | BU |
|---|---|---|---|---|---|---|
| 1991 Proof | Est. 25,000 | Value: 30.00 | | | | |

**50 DOLLARS** **KM# 126** **Weight:** 19.2000 g. **Composition:** 0.9250 Silver .5768 oz. ASW **Subject:** Endangered World Wildlife **Obverse:** Queen's portrait right **Reverse:** Fallow deer

| Date | Mintage | F | VF | XF | Unc | BU |
|---|---|---|---|---|---|---|
| 1991 Proof | Est. 25,000 | Value: 22.50 | | | | |

**50 DOLLARS** **KM# 140** **Weight:** 31.2600 g. **Composition:** 0.9250 Silver .9296 oz. ASW **Subject:** 500 Years of America **Obverse:** Queen's portrait right **Reverse:** Mayflower and pilgrims

| Date | Mintage | F | VF | XF | Unc | BU |
|---|---|---|---|---|---|---|
| 1991 Proof | — | Value: 20.00 | | | | |
| 1992 Proof | 60,000 | Value: 20.00 | | | | |

**50 DOLLARS** **KM# 123** **Weight:** 19.2000 g. **Composition:** 0.9250 Silver .5768 oz. ASW **Subject:** Endangered World Wildlife **Obverse:** Queen's portrait right **Reverse:** White-tailed deer

| Date | Mintage | F | VF | XF | Unc | BU |
|---|---|---|---|---|---|---|
| 1991 Proof | Est. 25,000 | Value: 30.00 | | | | |

**50 DOLLARS** **KM# 127** **Weight:** 19.2000 g. **Composition:** 0.9250 Silver .5768 oz. ASW **Subject:** Endangered World Wildlife **Obverse:** Queen's portrait right **Reverse:** Bee hummingbird

| Date | Mintage | F | VF | XF | Unc | BU |
|---|---|---|---|---|---|---|
| 1991 Proof | Est. 25,000 | Value: 22.50 | | | | |

**50 DOLLARS** **KM# 141** **Weight:** 31.2600 g. **Composition:** 0.9250 Silver .9296 oz. ASW **Subject:** 500 Years of America **Obverse:** Queen's portrait right **Reverse:** Alexander Mackenzie

| Date | Mintage | F | VF | XF | Unc | BU |
|---|---|---|---|---|---|---|
| 1991 Proof | 60,000 | Value: 20.00 | | | | |

**50 DOLLARS KM# 145 Weight:** 7.7750 g. **Composition:** 0.5833 Gold .1458 oz. AGW **Subject:** 500 Years of America **Obverse:** Queen's portrait right **Reverse:** Columbus kneeling

| Date | Mintage | F | VF | XF | Unc | BU |
|---|---|---|---|---|---|---|
| 1991 Proof | Est. 60,000 | Value: 85.00 | | | | |

**50 DOLLARS KM# 148 Weight:** 31.1000 g. **Composition:** 0.9250 Silver .9250 oz. ASW **Subject:** 500 Years of America **Obverse:** Queen's portrait right **Reverse:** Aztec Priest

| Date | Mintage | F | VF | XF | Unc | BU |
|---|---|---|---|---|---|---|
| 1991 Proof | Est. 15,000 | Value: 20.00 | | | | |

**50 DOLLARS KM# 189 Weight:** 31.1000 g. **Composition:** 0.9250 Silver .9250 oz. ASW **Subject:** 500 Years of America **Obverse:** Queen's portrait right **Reverse:** Franicsco Pizarro

| Date | Mintage | F | VF | XF | Unc | BU |
|---|---|---|---|---|---|---|
| 1991 Proof | Est. 60,000 | Value: 20.00 | | | | |

**50 DOLLARS KM# 190 Weight:** 31.1000 g. **Composition:** 0.9250 Silver .9250 oz. ASW **Subject:** 500 Years of America **Obverse:** Queen's portrait right **Reverse:** Jusuit Church in Cuzco

| Date | Mintage | F | VF | XF | Unc | BU |
|---|---|---|---|---|---|---|
| 1991 Proof | Est. 60,000 | Value: 20.00 | | | | |

**50 DOLLARS KM# 191 Weight:** 31.1000 g. **Composition:** 0.9250 Silver .9250 oz. ASW **Subject:** 500 Years of America **Obverse:** Queen's portrait right **Reverse:** Peter Minuit's purchase of Manhattan Island

| Date | Mintage | F | VF | XF | Unc | BU |
|---|---|---|---|---|---|---|
| 1991 Proof | Est. 60,000 | Value: 20.00 | | | | |

**50 DOLLARS KM# 192 Weight:** 31.1000 g. **Composition:** 0.9250 Silver .9250 oz. ASW **Subject:** 500 Years of America **Obverse:** Queen's portrait right **Reverse:** Boston Tea Party

| Date | Mintage | F | VF | XF | Unc | BU |
|---|---|---|---|---|---|---|
| 1991 Proof | Est. 60,000 | Value: 20.00 | | | | |

**50 DOLLARS KM# 193 Weight:** 31.1000 g. **Composition:** 0.9250 Silver .9250 oz. ASW **Subject:** 500 Years of America **Obverse:** Queen's portrait right **Reverse:** Marquis de Lafayette

| Date | Mintage | F | VF | XF | Unc | BU |
|---|---|---|---|---|---|---|
| 1991 Proof | Est. 60,000 | Value: 20.00 | | | | |

**50 DOLLARS KM# 194 Weight:** 31.1000 g. **Composition:** 0.9250 Silver .9250 oz. ASW **Subject:** 500 Years of America **Obverse:** Queen's portrait right **Reverse:** Robert Fulton

| Date | Mintage | F | VF | XF | Unc | BU |
|---|---|---|---|---|---|---|
| 1991 Proof | Est. 60,000 | Value: 20.00 | | | | |

**50 DOLLARS KM# 195 Weight:** 31.1000 g. **Composition:** 0.9250 Silver .9250 oz. ASW **Subject:** 500 Years of America **Obverse:** Queen's portrait right **Reverse:** First U.S. transcontinental railroad

| Date | Mintage | F | VF | XF | Unc | BU |
|---|---|---|---|---|---|---|
| 1991 Proof | Est. 60,000 | Value: 20.00 | | | | |

**50 DOLLARS KM# 196 Weight:** 31.1000 g. **Composition:** 0.9250 Silver .9250 oz. ASW **Subject:** 500 Years of America **Obverse:** Queen's portrait right **Reverse:** Emperior Maximilian of Mexico

| Date | Mintage | F | VF | XF | Unc | BU |
|---|---|---|---|---|---|---|
| 1991 Proof | Est. 60,000 | Value: 20.00 | | | | |

**50 DOLLARS KM# 305 Weight:** 31.1000 g. **Composition:** 0.9250 Silver .9250 oz. ASW **Subject:** 500 Years of America **Obverse:** Queen's portrait right **Reverse:** Capt. James Cook

| Date | Mintage | F | VF | XF | Unc | BU |
|---|---|---|---|---|---|---|
| 1991 Proof | Est. 60,000 | Value: 20.00 | | | | |

**50 DOLLARS KM# 44a Weight:** 31.1000 g. **Composition:** 0.9250 Silver .9250 oz. ASW **Subject:** 500 Years of America **Obverse:** Queen's portrait right **Reverse:** Vasco Nunez de Balboa

| Date | Mintage | F | VF | XF | Unc | BU |
|---|---|---|---|---|---|---|
| 1991 Proof | 60,000 | Value: 35.00 | | | | |

**50 DOLLARS KM# 46a Weight:** 31.1000 g. **Composition:** 0.9250 Silver .9250 oz. ASW **Subject:** 500 Years of America **Obverse:** Queen's portrait right **Reverse:** Capt. James Cook

| Date | Mintage | F | VF | XF | Unc | BU |
|---|---|---|---|---|---|---|
| 1991 Proof | Est. 60,000 | Value: 25.00 | | | | |

**50 DOLLARS KM# 244 Weight:** 19.2000 g. **Composition:** 0.9250 Silver .5768 oz. ASW **Note:** Poplar Admiral Butterfly and Thistle

| Date | Mintage | F | VF | XF | Unc | BU |
|---|---|---|---|---|---|---|
| 1992 Proof | Est. 25,000 | Value: 35.00 | | | | |

**50 DOLLARS KM# 261 Weight:** 19.2000 g. **Composition:** 0.9250 Silver .5768 oz. ASW **Subject:** Endangered Wildlife **Obverse:** Queen's portrait right **Reverse:** Szechuan Takins

| Date | Mintage | F | VF | XF | Unc | BU |
|---|---|---|---|---|---|---|
| 1992 Proof | 25,000 | Value: 25.00 | | | | |

**50 DOLLARS** **KM# 262** **Weight:** 19.2000 g. **Composition:** 0.9250 Silver .5768 oz. ASW **Subject:** Endangered Wildlife **Obverse:** Queen's portrait right **Reverse:** Ring-tailed lemurs

| Date | Mintage | F | VF | XF | Unc | BU |
|---|---|---|---|---|---|---|
| 1992 Proof | 25,000 | Value: 25.00 | | | | |

**50 DOLLARS** **KM# 263** **Weight:** 19.2000 g. **Composition:** 0.9250 Silver .5768 oz. ASW **Subject:** Endangered Wildlife **Obverse:** Queen's portrait right **Reverse:** Drill

| Date | Mintage | F | VF | XF | Unc | BU |
|---|---|---|---|---|---|---|
| 1992 Proof | 25,000 | Value: 25.00 | | | | |

**50 DOLLARS** **KM# 264** **Weight:** 19.2000 g. **Composition:** 0.9250 Silver .5768 oz. ASW **Subject:** Endangered Wildlife **Obverse:** Queen's portrait right **Reverse:** Lowland gorilla

| Date | Mintage | F | VF | XF | Unc | BU |
|---|---|---|---|---|---|---|
| 1992 Proof | 25,000 | Value: 25.00 | | | | |

**50 DOLLARS** **KM# 310** **Weight:** 31.0000 g. **Composition:** 0.9250 Silver .9219 oz. ASW **Obverse:** Queen's portrait right **Reverse:** Aztec kneels before Alvarado **Edge Lettering:** PEDRO DE ALVARADO CONQUEROR of the AZTEC EMPIRE

| Date | Mintage | F | VF | XF | Unc | BU |
|---|---|---|---|---|---|---|
| 1992 Proof | — | Value: 22.50 | | | | |

**50 DOLLARS** **KM# 114** **Weight:** 31.1000 g. **Composition:** 0.9250 Silver .9250 oz. ASW **Subject:** 500 Years of America **Obverse:** Queen's portrait right **Reverse:** Coronado's discovery of the Grand Canyon

| Date | Mintage | F | VF | XF | Unc | BU |
|---|---|---|---|---|---|---|
| 1992 Proof | Est. 15,000 | Value: 27.50 | | | | |

**50 DOLLARS** **KM# 129** **Weight:** 7.7760 g. **Composition:** 0.5830 Gold .1458 oz. AGW **Subject:** Endangered Wildlife **Obverse:** Queen's portrait right **Reverse:** Eagle head

| Date | Mintage | F | VF | XF | Unc | BU |
|---|---|---|---|---|---|---|
| 1992 Proof | — | Value: 85.00 | | | | |

**50 DOLLARS** **KM# 131** **Weight:** 7.7760 g. **Composition:** 0.5830 Gold .1458 oz. AGW **Subject:** Endangered Wildlife **Obverse:** Queen's portrait right **Reverse:** Elephant head

| Date | Mintage | F | VF | XF | Unc | BU |
|---|---|---|---|---|---|---|
| 1992 Proof | — | Value: 85.00 | | | | |

**50 DOLLARS** **KM# 132** **Weight:** 7.7760 g. **Composition:** 0.5830 Gold .1458 oz. AGW **Subject:** Endangered Wildlife **Obverse:** Queen's portrait right **Reverse:** Tiger head

| Date | Mintage | F | VF | XF | Unc | BU |
|---|---|---|---|---|---|---|
| 1992 Proof | — | Value: 85.00 | | | | |

**50 DOLLARS** **KM# 142** **Weight:** 31.2600 g. **Composition:** 0.9250 Silver .9296 oz. ASW **Subject:** 500 Years of America **Obverse:** Queen's portrait right **Reverse:** John Davis

| Date | Mintage | F | VF | XF | Unc | BU |
|---|---|---|---|---|---|---|
| 1992 Proof | Est. 60,000 | Value: 20.00 | | | | |

**50 DOLLARS** **KM# 143** **Weight:** 31.2600 g. **Composition:** 0.9250 Silver .9296 oz. ASW **Subject:** 500 Years of America **Obverse:** Queen's portrait right **Reverse:** Vitus Bering

| Date | Mintage | F | VF | XF | Unc | BU |
|---|---|---|---|---|---|---|
| 1992 Proof | Est. 60,000 | Value: 20.00 | | | | |

**50 DOLLARS** **KM# 156** **Weight:** 31.1035 g. **Composition:** 0.9250 Silver .9250 oz. ASW **Subject:** 500 Years of America **Obverse:** Queen's portrait right **Reverse:** Pedro de Valdivia

| Date | Mintage | F | VF | XF | Unc | BU |
|---|---|---|---|---|---|---|
| 1992 Proof | — | Value: 20.00 | | | | |

**50 DOLLARS** **KM# 157** **Weight:** 31.1035 g. **Composition:** 0.9250 Silver .9250 oz. ASW **Subject:** 500 Years of America **Obverse:** Queen's portrait right **Reverse:** Diego de Almagro

| Date | Mintage | F | VF | XF | Unc | BU |
|---|---|---|---|---|---|---|
| 1992 Proof | — | Value: 20.00 | | | | |

**50 DOLLARS** **KM# 162** **Weight:** 31.1035 g. **Composition:** 0.9250 Silver .9250 oz. ASW **Subject:** 500 Years of America **Obverse:** Queen's portrait right **Reverse:** Francisco de Coronado

| Date | Mintage | F | VF | XF | Unc | BU |
|---|---|---|---|---|---|---|
| 1992 Proof | — | Value: 20.00 | | | | |

**50 DOLLARS** **KM# 176** **Weight:** 7.7760 g. **Composition:** 0.5833 Gold .1458 oz. AGW **Subject:** 500 Years of America **Obverse:** Queen's portrait right **Reverse:** Robert de La Salle

| Date | Mintage | F | VF | XF | Unc | BU |
|---|---|---|---|---|---|---|
| 1992 Proof | — | Value: 85.00 | | | | |

**50 DOLLARS** **KM# 183** **Weight:** 31.1035 g. **Composition:** 0.9250 Silver .9250 oz. ASW **Subject:** 500 Years of America **Obverse:** Queen's portrait right **Reverse:** Giovanni da Verrazano

| Date | Mintage | F | VF | XF | Unc | BU |
|---|---|---|---|---|---|---|
| 1992 Proof | Est. 60,000 | Value: 20.00 | | | | |

**50 DOLLARS** **KM# 197** **Weight:** 31.1035 g. **Composition:** 0.9250 Silver .9250 oz. ASW **Subject:** 500 Years of America **Obverse:** Queen's portrait right **Reverse:** Juan Ponce de Leon

| Date | Mintage | F | VF | XF | Unc | BU |
|---|---|---|---|---|---|---|
| 1992 Proof | Est. 60,000 | Value: 20.00 | | | | |

**50 DOLLARS** **KM# 198** **Weight:** 31.1035 g. **Composition:** 0.9250 Silver .9250 oz. ASW **Subject:** 500 Years of America **Obverse:** Queen's portrait right **Reverse:** Pedro de Mendoza

| Date | Mintage | F | VF | XF | Unc | BU |
|---|---|---|---|---|---|---|
| 1992 Proof | Est. 60,000 | Value: 20.00 | | | | |

**50 DOLLARS** **KM# 199** **Weight:** 31.1035 g. **Composition:** 0.9250 Silver .9250 oz. ASW **Subject:** 500 Years of America **Obverse:** Queen's portrait right **Reverse:** Pedro Menendez de Aviles

| Date | Mintage | F | VF | XF | Unc | BU |
|---|---|---|---|---|---|---|
| 1992 Proof | — | Value: 20.00 | | | | |

**50 DOLLARS** **KM# 200** **Weight:** 31.1035 g. **Composition:** 0.9250 Silver .9250 oz. ASW **Subject:** 500 Years of America **Obverse:** Queen's portrait right **Reverse:** Independence Hall

| Date | Mintage | F | VF | XF | Unc | BU |
|---|---|---|---|---|---|---|
| 1992 Proof | — | Value: 20.00 | | | | |

**50 DOLLARS** **KM# 201** **Weight:** 31.1035 g. **Composition:** 0.9250 Silver .9250 oz. ASW **Subject:** 500 Years of America **Obverse:** Queen's portrait right **Reverse:** Sacagawea guiding Lewis and Clark

| Date | Mintage | F | VF | XF | Unc | BU |
|---|---|---|---|---|---|---|
| 1992 Proof | Est. 60,000 | Value: 20.00 | | | | |

**50 DOLLARS** **KM# 202** **Weight:** 31.1035 g. **Composition:** 0.9250 Silver .9250 oz. ASW **Subject:** 500 Years of America **Obverse:** Queen's portrait right **Reverse:** Oregon Trail

| Date | Mintage | F | VF | XF | Unc | BU |
|---|---|---|---|---|---|---|
| 1992 Proof | Est. 60,000 | Value: 20.00 | | | | |

**50 DOLLARS** **KM# 204** **Weight:** 7.7760 g. **Composition:** 0.5833 Gold .1458 oz. AGW **Subject:** 500 Years of America **Obverse:** Queen's portrait right **Reverse:** John Cabot

| Date | Mintage | F | VF | XF | Unc | BU |
|---|---|---|---|---|---|---|
| 1992 Proof | 5,000 | Value: 85.00 | | | | |

**50 DOLLARS** **KM# 249** **Weight:** 7.7760 g. **Composition:** 0.5830 Gold .1458 oz. AGW **Subject:** 500 Years of America **Obverse:** Queen's portrait right **Reverse:** Ferdinand and Isabella

| Date | Mintage | F | VF | XF | Unc | BU |
|---|---|---|---|---|---|---|
| 1992 Proof | Est. 5,000 | Value: 85.00 | | | | |

**50 DOLLARS** **KM# 259** **Weight:** 7.7760 g. **Composition:** 0.5830 Gold .1458 oz. AGW **Subject:** 500 Years of America **Obverse:** Queen's portrait right **Reverse:** Paul de Maisonneuve, map and city view

| Date | Mintage | F | VF | XF | Unc | BU |
|---|---|---|---|---|---|---|
| 1992 Proof | Est. 5,000 | Value: 85.00 | | | | |

**50 DOLLARS** **KM# 260** **Weight:** 7.7760 g. **Composition:** 0.5830 Gold .1458 oz. AGW **Subject:** 500 Years of America **Obverse:** Queen's portrait right **Reverse:** Jakob le Maire, ship and map

| Date | Mintage | F | VF | XF | Unc | BU |
|---|---|---|---|---|---|---|
| 1992 Proof | Est. 5,000 | Value: 85.00 | | | | |

**50 DOLLARS** **KM# 155** **Weight:** 31.1035 g. **Composition:** 0.9250 Silver .9250 oz. ASW **Subject:** 500 Years of America **Obverse:** Queen's portrait right **Reverse:** Father Jacques Marquette

| Date | Mintage | F | VF | XF | Unc | BU |
|---|---|---|---|---|---|---|
| 1993 Proof | — | Value: 22.50 | | | | |

**50 DOLLARS** **KM# 163** **Weight:** 31.1035 g. **Composition:** 0.9250 Silver .9250 oz. ASW **Subject:** 500 Years of America **Obverse:** Queen's portrait right **Reverse:** Francisco de Orellana

| Date | Mintage | F | VF | XF | Unc | BU |
|---|---|---|---|---|---|---|
| 1993 Proof | — | Value: 22.50 | | | | |

**50 DOLLARS** **KM# 153** **Weight:** 7.7760 g. **Composition:** 0.5833 Gold .1453 oz. AGW **Subject:** Endangered Wildlife **Obverse:** Queen's portrait right **Reverse:** Ibex

| Date | Mintage | F | VF | XF | Unc | BU |
|---|---|---|---|---|---|---|
| 1993 Proof | — | Value: 85.00 | | | | |

**50 DOLLARS** **KM# 154** **Weight:** 7.7760 g. **Composition:** 0.5833 Gold .1453 oz. AGW **Subject:** Endangered Wildlife **Obverse:** Queen's portrait right **Reverse:** Owl and parrot

| Date | Mintage | F | VF | XF | Unc | BU |
|---|---|---|---|---|---|---|
| 1993 Proof | — | Value: 85.00 | | | | |

**50 DOLLARS** **KM# 164** **Weight:** 31.1035 g. **Composition:** 0.9250 Silver .9250 oz. ASW **Subject:** 500 Years of America **Obverse:** Queen's portrait right **Reverse:** Pinzon Brothers

| Date | Mintage | F | VF | XF | Unc | BU |
|---|---|---|---|---|---|---|
| 1993 Proof | — | Value: 22.50 | | | | |

**50 DOLLARS** **KM# 165** **Weight:** 31.1035 g. **Composition:** 0.9250 Silver .9250 oz. ASW **Subject:** 500 Years of America **Obverse:** Queen's portrait right **Reverse:** Juan de la Cosa

| Date | Mintage | F | VF | XF | Unc | BU |
|---|---|---|---|---|---|---|
| 1993 Proof | — | Value: 22.50 | | | | |

**50 DOLLARS** **KM# 166** **Weight:** 31.1035 g. **Composition:** 0.9250 Silver .9250 oz. ASW **Subject:** 500 Years of America **Obverse:** Queen's portrait right **Reverse:** William Penn

| Date | Mintage | F | VF | XF | Unc | BU |
|---|---|---|---|---|---|---|
| 1993 Proof | — | Value: 22.50 | | | | |

**50 DOLLARS** **KM# 167** **Weight:** 31.1035 g. **Composition:** 0.9250 Silver .9250 oz. ASW **Subject:** 500 Years of America **Obverse:** Queen's portrait right **Reverse:** Diego de Velasquez

| Date | Mintage | F | VF | XF | Unc | BU |
|---|---|---|---|---|---|---|
| 1993 Proof | — | Value: 22.50 | | | | |

**50 DOLLARS** **KM# 168** **Weight:** 31.1035 g. **Composition:** 0.9250 Silver .9250 oz. ASW **Subject:** 500 Years of America **Obverse:** Queen's portrait right **Reverse:** Miner panning for gold

| Date | Mintage | F | VF | XF | Unc | BU |
|---|---|---|---|---|---|---|
| 1993 Proof | — | Value: 22.50 | | | | |

**50 DOLLARS** **KM# 169** **Weight:** 31.1035 g. **Composition:** 0.9250 Silver .9250 oz. ASW **Subject:** 500 Years of America **Obverse:** Queen's portrait right **Reverse:** Sir Martin Frobisher

| Date | Mintage | F | VF | XF | Unc | BU |
|---|---|---|---|---|---|---|
| 1993 Proof | — | Value: 22.50 | | | | |

**50 DOLLARS** **KM# 170** **Weight:** 31.1035 g. **Composition:** 0.9250 Silver .9250 oz. ASW **Subject:** 500 Years of America **Obverse:** Queen's portrait right **Reverse:** George Vancouver

| Date | Mintage | F | VF | XF | Unc | BU |
|---|---|---|---|---|---|---|
| 1993 Proof | — | Value: 22.50 | | | | |

**50 DOLLARS** **KM# 171** **Weight:** 31.1035 g. **Composition:** 0.9250 Silver .9250 oz. ASW **Subject:** 500 Years of America **Obverse:** Queen's portrait right **Reverse:** John Hawkins

| Date | Mintage | F | VF | XF | Unc | BU |
|---|---|---|---|---|---|---|
| 1993 Proof | — | Value: 22.50 | | | | |

**50 DOLLARS** **KM# 172** **Weight:** 31.1035 g. **Composition:** 0.9250 Silver .9250 oz. ASW **Subject:** 500 Years of America **Obverse:** Queen's portrait right **Reverse:** Amerigo Vespucci

| Date | Mintage | F | VF | XF | Unc | BU |
|---|---|---|---|---|---|---|
| 1993 Proof | — | Value: 22.50 | | | | |

**50 DOLLARS** **KM# 173** **Weight:** 7.7760 g. **Composition:** 0.5833 Gold .1458 oz. AGW **Subject:** 500 Years of America **Obverse:** Queen's portrait right **Reverse:** George Washington

| Date | Mintage | F | VF | XF | Unc | BU |
|---|---|---|---|---|---|---|
| 1993 Proof | — | Value: 85.00 | | | | |

**50 DOLLARS** **KM# 174** **Weight:** 7.7760 g. **Composition:** 0.5833 Gold .1458 oz. AGW **Subject:** 500 Years of America **Obverse:** Queen's portrait right **Reverse:** Alonso de Hojeda

| Date | Mintage | F | VF | XF | Unc | BU |
|---|---|---|---|---|---|---|
| 1993 Proof | — | Value: 85.00 | | | | |

**50 DOLLARS** **KM# 175** **Weight:** 7.7760 g. **Composition:** 0.5833 Gold .1458 oz. AGW **Subject:** 500 Years of America **Obverse:** Queen's portrait right **Reverse:** Thomas Jefferson

| Date | Mintage | F | VF | XF | Unc | BU |
|---|---|---|---|---|---|---|
| 1993 Proof | — | Value: 85.00 | | | | |

**50 DOLLARS** **KM# 177** **Weight:** 7.7760 g. **Composition:** 0.5833 Gold .1458 oz. AGW **Subject:** 500 Years of America **Obverse:** Queen's portrait right **Reverse:** Capt. James Cook

| Date | Mintage | F | VF | XF | Unc | BU |
|---|---|---|---|---|---|---|
| 1993 Proof | — | Value: 85.00 | | | | |

**50 DOLLARS** **KM# 178** **Weight:** 7.7760 g. **Composition:** 0.5833 Gold .1458 oz. AGW **Subject:** 500 Years of America **Obverse:** Queen's portrait right **Reverse:** Christopher Columbus

| Date | Mintage | F | VF | XF | Unc | BU |
|---|---|---|---|---|---|---|
| 1993 Proof | — | Value: 85.00 | | | | |

**50 DOLLARS** **KM# 179** **Weight:** 7.7760 g. **Composition:** 0.5833 Gold .1458 oz. AGW **Subject:** 500 Years of America **Obverse:** Queen's portrait right **Reverse:** Statue of Liberty

| Date | Mintage | F | VF | XF | Unc | BU |
|---|---|---|---|---|---|---|
| 1993 Proof | — | Value: 85.00 | | | | |

**50 DOLLARS** **KM# 180** **Weight:** 7.7760 g. **Composition:** 0.5833 Gold .1458 oz. AGW **Subject:** 1996 Olympics **Obverse:** Queen's portrait right **Reverse:** Gymnastics

| Date | Mintage | F | VF | XF | Unc | BU |
|---|---|---|---|---|---|---|
| 1993 Proof | Est. 5,000 | Value: 85.00 | | | | |

**50 DOLLARS** **KM# 245** **Weight:** 7.7760 g. **Composition:** 0.5833 Gold .1458 oz. AGW **Subject:** Endangered Wildlife **Obverse:** Queen's portrait right **Reverse:** African lion

| Date | Mintage | F | VF | XF | Unc | BU |
|---|---|---|---|---|---|---|
| 1993 Proof | Est. 10,000 | Value: 85.00 | | | | |

**50 DOLLARS** **KM# 248** **Weight:** 31.1035 g. **Composition:** 0.9250 Silver .9250 oz. ASW **Subject:** 500 Years of America **Obverse:** Queen's portrait right **Reverse:** Jose de San Martin

| Date | Mintage | F | VF | XF | Unc | BU |
|---|---|---|---|---|---|---|
| 1993 Proof | Est. 60,000 | Value: 32.50 | | | | |

**50 DOLLARS** **KM# 246** **Weight:** 7.7760 g. **Composition:** 0.5830 Gold .1458 oz. AGW **Subject:** Endangered Wildlife **Obverse:** Queen's portrait right **Reverse:** Sea otter

| Date | Mintage | F | VF | XF | Unc | BU |
|---|---|---|---|---|---|---|
| 1994 Proof | Est. 10,000 | Value: 75.00 | | | | |

**50 DOLLARS** **KM# 247** **Weight:** 7.7760 g. **Composition:** 0.5830 Gold .1458 oz. AGW **Subject:** Endangered Wildlife **Obverse:** Queen's portrait right **Reverse:** Przewalski's horse

| Date | Mintage | F | VF | XF | Unc | BU |
|---|---|---|---|---|---|---|
| 1994 Proof | Est. 10,000 | Value: 75.00 | | | | |

**50 DOLLARS** **KM# 275** **Weight:** 7.7760 g. **Composition:** 0.5830 Gold .1458 oz. AGW **Subject:** Endangered Wildlife **Obverse:** Queen's portrait right **Reverse:** Poplar admiral butterflies

| Date | Mintage | F | VF | XF | Unc | BU |
|---|---|---|---|---|---|---|
| 1994 Proof | Est. 10,000 | Value: 80.00 | | | | |

**50 DOLLARS** **KM# 276** **Weight:** 7.7760 g. **Composition:** 0.5830 Gold .1458 oz. AGW **Obverse:** Queen's portrait right **Reverse:** The Queen Mother and daughters

| Date | Mintage | F | VF | XF | Unc | BU |
|---|---|---|---|---|---|---|
| 1995 Proof | Est. 5,000 | Value: 85.00 | | | | |

**50 DOLLARS** **KM# 299** **Weight:** 8.0000 g. **Composition:** 0.9999 Gold .2572 oz. AGW **Subject:** Year of the Mouse **Obverse:** Queen's portrait right **Reverse:** Mickey and Minnie Mouse portrait

| Date | Mintage | F | VF | XF | Unc | BU |
|---|---|---|---|---|---|---|
| 1996 Proof | — | Value: 185 | | | | |

**50 DOLLARS** **KM# 322** **Weight:** 32.2225 g. **Composition:** 0.9250 Silver .9583 oz. ASW **Subject:** 2nd Century **Obverse:** Queen's portrait right **Reverse:** Chinese paper maker

| Date | Mintage | F | VF | XF | Unc | BU |
|---|---|---|---|---|---|---|
| 1997 Proof | — | Value: 47.50 | | | | |

**50 DOLLARS** **KM# 323** **Weight:** 32.2225 g. **Composition:** 0.9250 Silver .9583 oz. ASW **Subject:** 8th Century **Obverse:** Queen's portrait right **Reverse:** Coronation of Charlemagne

| Date | Mintage | F | VF | XF | Unc | BU |
|---|---|---|---|---|---|---|
| 1997 Proof | — | Value: 47.50 | | | | |

**50 DOLLARS** **KM# 324** **Weight:** 32.2225 g. **Composition:** 0.9250 Silver .9583 oz. ASW **Subject:** 12th Century **Obverse:** Queen's portrait right **Reverse:** Genghis Khan

| Date | Mintage | F | VF | XF | Unc | BU |
|---|---|---|---|---|---|---|
| 1997 Proof | — | Value: 47.50 | | | | |

**50 DOLLARS** **KM# 325** **Weight:** 32.2225 g. **Composition:** 0.9250 Silver .9583 oz. ASW **Subject:** 13th Century **Obverse:** Queen's portrait right **Reverse:** Marco Polo and Kublai Khan

| Date | Mintage | F | VF | XF | Unc | BU |
|---|---|---|---|---|---|---|
| 1997 Proof | — | Value: 47.50 | | | | |

**50 DOLLARS** **KM# 306** **Ring Weight:** 3.8879 g. **Ring Composition:** 0.9999 Gold .1250 oz. AGW **Center Weight:** 3.8879 g. **Center Composition:** 0.9995 Platinum .1250 oz. APW **Obverse:** Queen's portrait right **Reverse:** Mother seal w/pup

| Date | Mintage | F | VF | XF | Unc | BU |
|---|---|---|---|---|---|---|
| 1997 Proof | — | Value: 200 | | | | |

**100 DOLLARS** **KM# 12** **Weight:** 16.7185 g. **Composition:** 0.9170 Gold .4929 oz. AGW **Subject:** Winston Churchill Centenary

| Date | Mintage | F | VF | XF | Unc | BU |
|---|---|---|---|---|---|---|
| 1974 | 368 | — | — | — | 325 | — |
| 1974 Proof | 1,453 | Value: 250 | | | | |

**100 DOLLARS** **KM# 13** **Weight:** 9.6000 g. **Composition:** 0.9000 Gold .2778 oz. AGW **Subject:** Bicentennial - Return of Capt. James Cook from 2nd pacific Voyage

| Date | Mintage | F | VF | XF | Unc | BU |
|---|---|---|---|---|---|---|
| 1975 | 100 | — | — | — | 400 | — |
| 1975 | 7,447 | — | — | — | 125 | — |
| 1975 Proof | 17,000 | Value: 150 | | | | |

**100 DOLLARS** **KM# 16** **Weight:** 9.6000 g. **Composition:** 0.9000 Gold .2778 oz. AGW **Subject:** U.S. Bicentennial

| Date | Mintage | F | VF | XF | Unc | BU |
|---|---|---|---|---|---|---|
| 1976 | 50 | — | — | — | 350 | — |
| 1976 | 852 | — | — | — | 150 | — |
| 1976 Proof | 9,373 | Value: 180 | | | | |

**100 DOLLARS** **KM# 19** **Weight:** 9.6000 g. **Composition:** 0.9000 Gold .2778 oz. AGW **Subject:** Queen's Silver Jubilee

| Date | Mintage | F | VF | XF | Unc | BU |
|---|---|---|---|---|---|---|
| 1977 | 50 | — | — | — | 350 | — |
| 1977 | 562 | — | — | — | 150 | — |
| 1977 Proof | 9,364 | Value: 200 | | | | |

**100 DOLLARS** **KM# 25** **Weight:** 9.6000 g. **Composition:** 0.9000 Gold .2778 oz. AGW **Subject:** Membership in Commonwealth of Natons

| Date | Mintage | F | VF | XF | Unc | BU |
|---|---|---|---|---|---|---|
| 1979 | 400 | — | — | — | 175 | — |
| 1979 Proof | 3,367 | Value: 165 | | | | |

**100 DOLLARS** **KM# 74** **Weight:** 1.2441 g. **Composition:** 0.9990 Gold .0400 oz. AGW **Subject:** Endangered World Wildlife **Obverse:** Queen's portrait right **Reverse:** American bald eagale

| Date | Mintage | F | VF | XF | Unc | BU |
|---|---|---|---|---|---|---|
| 1990 Proof Like | 1,320 | — | — | — | — | — |

**100 DOLLARS** **KM# 75** **Weight:** 1.2441 g. **Composition:** 0.9990 Gold .0400 oz. AGW **Subject:** Endangered World Wildlife **Obverse:** Queen's portrait right **Reverse:** Bison

| Date | Mintage | F | VF | XF | Unc | BU |
|---|---|---|---|---|---|---|
| 1990 Proof Like | 320 | — | — | — | — | — |

**100 DOLLARS** **KM# 76** **Weight:** 1.2441 g. **Composition:** 0.9990 Gold .0400 oz. AGW **Subject:** Endangered World Wildlife **Obverse:** Queen's portrait right **Reverse:** Elephant

| Date | Mintage | F | VF | XF | Unc | BU |
|---|---|---|---|---|---|---|
| 1990 Proof Like | 720 | — | — | — | — | — |

**100 DOLLARS** **KM# 77** **Weight:** 1.2441 g. **Composition:** 0.9990 Gold .0400 oz. AGW **Subject:** Endangered World Wildlife **Obverse:** Queen's portrait right **Reverse:** Tiger

| Date | Mintage | F | VF | XF | Unc | BU |
|---|---|---|---|---|---|---|
| 1990 Proof Like | 420 | — | — | — | — | — |

**100 DOLLARS** **KM# 78** **Weight:** 1.2441 g. **Composition:** 0.9990 Gold .0400 oz. AGW **Subject:** Endangered World Wildlife **Obverse:** Queen's portrait right **Reverse:** Mouflon

| Date | Mintage | F | VF | XF | Unc | BU |
|---|---|---|---|---|---|---|
| 1990 Proof Like | 320 | — | — | — | — | — |

**100 DOLLARS** **KM# 92** **Weight:** 3.4550 g. **Composition:** 0.9000 Gold .09999 oz. AGW **Subject:** 1992 Summer Olympics **Obverse:** Queens' portrait right **Reverse:** Bicyclists

| Date | Mintage | F | VF | XF | Unc | BU |
|---|---|---|---|---|---|---|
| 1990 Proof | Est. 5,000 | Value: 100 | | | | |

**100 DOLLARS** **KM# 113** **Weight:** 172.1100 g. **Composition:** Silver **Subject:** 500 Years of America **Obverse:** Queen's portrait right **Reverse:** Ferdinand Magellan

| Date | Mintage | F | VF | XF | Unc | BU |
|---|---|---|---|---|---|---|
| 1990 Proof | Est. 3,000 | Value: 120 | | | | |

**100 DOLLARS** **KM# 319** **Weight:** 170.6000 g. **Composition:** 0.9250 Silver 5.0735 oz. ASW **Subject:** 500 Years of America **Obverse:** Queen's portrait right **Reverse:** Mt. Rushmore

| Date | Mintage | F | VF | XF | Unc | BU |
|---|---|---|---|---|---|---|
| 1991 Proof | — | Value: 115 | | | | |

**100 DOLLARS** **KM# 297** **Weight:** 155.6500 g. **Composition:** 0.9990 Silver 4.992 oz. ASW **Subject:** Endangered Wildlife **Reverse:** Three elephants

| Date | Mintage | F | VF | XF | Unc | BU |
|---|---|---|---|---|---|---|
| 1991 Proof | — | Value: 130 | | | | |

**100 DOLLARS** **KM# 320** **Weight:** 170.6000 g. **Composition:** 0.9250 Silver 5.0735 oz. ASW **Subject:** 500 Years of America **Obverse:** Queen's portrait right **Reverse:** Columbus portrait w/three ships

| Date | Mintage | F | VF | XF | Unc | BU |
|---|---|---|---|---|---|---|
| 1992 Proof | — | Value: 125 | | | | |

**100 DOLLARS** **KM# 159** **Weight:** 155.5175 g. **Composition:** 0.9990 Silver 5.0000 oz. ASW **Subject:** 500 Years of America **Obverse:** Queens' portrait right **Reverse:** Hudson's "Half Moon" and New York City skyline

| Date | Mintage | F | VF | XF | Unc | BU |
|---|---|---|---|---|---|---|
| 1993 Proof | — | Value: 125 | | | | |

**100 DOLLARS** **KM# 158** **Weight:** 155.5176 g. **Composition:** 0.9990 Silver 5.0000 oz. ASW **Subject:** Endangered Wildlife **Obverse:** Queen's portrait right **Reverse:** Manchurian cranes

| Date | Mintage | F | VF | XF | Unc | BU |
|---|---|---|---|---|---|---|
| 1993 Proof | — | Value: 200 | | | | |

**100 DOLLARS** **KM# 250** **Weight:** 7.7761 g. **Composition:** 0.9990 Platinum .1458 oz. APW **Obverse:** Queen's portrait right **Reverse:** Javelin throwing

| Date | Mintage | F | VF | XF | Unc | BU |
|---|---|---|---|---|---|---|
| 1995 Proof | Est. 1,000 | Value: 150 | | | | |

**100 DOLLARS** **KM# 300** **Weight:** 15.0000 g. **Composition:** 0.9999 Gold .4822 oz. AGW **Subject:** Year of the Mouse **Obverse:** Queen's portrait right **Reverse:** Mickey Mouse sailboarding

| Date | Mintage | F | VF | XF | Unc | BU |
|---|---|---|---|---|---|---|
| 1996 Proof | — | Value: 350 | | | | |

**100 DOLLARS** **KM# 293** **Weight:** 7.7800 g. **Composition:** 0.9990 Gold .2501 oz. AGW **Obverse:** Queen's portrait right **Note:** Olympic National Park.

| Date | Mintage | F | VF | XF | Unc | BU |
|---|---|---|---|---|---|---|
| 1996 Proof | — | Value: 165 | | | | |

**100 DOLLARS** **KM# 294** **Weight:** 7.7800 g. **Composition:** 0.9990 Gold .2501 oz. AGW **Obverse:** Queen's portrait right **Note:** Yellowstone National Park.

| Date | Mintage | F | VF | XF | Unc | BU |
|---|---|---|---|---|---|---|
| 1996 Proof | — | Value: 165 | | | | |

**200 DOLLARS** **KM# 22** **Weight:** 16.6000 g. **Composition:** 0.9000 Gold .4803 oz. AGW **Subject:** Bicentennial - Discovery of Hawaii by Capt. James Cook **Obverse:** Queen's portrait right

| Date | Mintage | F | VF | XF | Unc | BU |
|---|---|---|---|---|---|---|
| 1978 | 26 | — | — | — | 600 | — |
| 1978 | 621 | — | — | — | 275 | — |
| 1978 Proof | 3,216 | Value: 225 | | | | |

**200 DOLLARS** **KM# 26** **Weight:** 16.6000 g. **Composition:** 0.9000 Gold .4803 oz. AGW **Subject:** Legacy of Capt. James Cook **Obverse:** Queen's portrait right

| Date | Mintage | F | VF | XF | Unc | BU |
|---|---|---|---|---|---|---|
| 1979 | 271 | — | — | — | 290 | — |
| 1979 Proof | 1,939 | Value: 275 | | | | |

**200 DOLLARS** **KM# 29** **Weight:** 15.9800 g. **Composition:** 0.9170 Gold .4712 oz. AGW **Subject:** International Year of the Scout **Obverse:** Queen's portrait right

| Date | Mintage | F | VF | XF | Unc | BU |
|---|---|---|---|---|---|---|
| 1983 Proof | — | Value: 450 | | | | |

**200 DOLLARS** **KM# 251** **Weight:** 15.5520 g. **Composition:** 0.9990 Platinum .2916 oz. APW **Obverse:** Queen's portrait right **Reverse:** Wrestling

| Date | Mintage | F | VF | XF | Unc | BU |
|---|---|---|---|---|---|---|
| 1995 Proof | 1,000 | Value: 300 | | | | |

**250 DOLLARS** KM# 23 **Weight:** 17.9000 g. **Composition:** 0.9000 Gold .5180 oz. AGW **Subject:** 250th Anniversary - Birth of James Cook **Obverse:** Queen's portrait right

| Date | Mintage | F | VF | XF | Unc | BU |
|---|---|---|---|---|---|---|
| 1978 | 25 | — | — | — | 600 | — |
| 1978 | 200 | — | — | — | 275 | — |
| 1978 Proof | 1,757 | Value: 250 | | | | |

**250 DOLLARS** KM# 50 **Weight:** 7.7750 g. **Composition:** 0.9990 Gold .2500 oz. AGW **Subject:** 500 Years of America **Obverse:** Queen's portrait right **Reverse:** Captain James Cook and Benjamin Franklin

| Date | Mintage | F | VF | XF | Unc | BU |
|---|---|---|---|---|---|---|
| 1989 Proof | 3,000 | Value: 225 | | | | |

**250 DOLLARS** KM# 51 **Weight:** 7.7750 g. **Composition:** 0.9990 Gold .2500 oz. AGW **Subject:** 500 Years of America **Obverse:** Queen's portrait right **Reverse:** Amerigo Vespucci

| Date | Mintage | F | VF | XF | Unc | BU |
|---|---|---|---|---|---|---|
| 1990 Proof | Est. 3,000 | Value: 225 | | | | |

**250 DOLLARS** KM# 82 **Weight:** 9.6000 g. **Composition:** 0.9000 Gold .2778 oz. AGW **Subject:** Save the Children **Obverse:** Queen's portrait right

| Date | Mintage | F | VF | XF | Unc | BU |
|---|---|---|---|---|---|---|
| 1990 Proof | 3,000 | Value: 265 | | | | |

**250 DOLLARS** KM# 71 **Weight:** 7.7750 g. **Composition:** 0.9990 Gold .2500 oz. AGW **Subject:** 1992 Olympics **Obverse:** Queen's portrait right **Reverse:** Torch

| Date | Mintage | F | VF | XF | Unc | BU |
|---|---|---|---|---|---|---|
| 1991 Proof | Est. 5,000 | Value: 225 | | | | |

**250 DOLLARS** KM# 296 **Weight:** 31.1035 g. **Composition:** 0.9990 Gold 1.0000 oz. AGW **Subject:** Yellowstone National Park **Obverse:** Queen's portrait right **Reverse:** Multicolored grizzly bear and cub

| Date | Mintage | F | VF | XF | Unc | BU |
|---|---|---|---|---|---|---|
| 1996 Proof | 1,000 | Value: 525 | | | | |

**250 DOLLARS** KM# 295 **Weight:** 31.1035 g. **Composition:** 0.9990 Gold 1.0000 oz. AGW **Subject:** Olympic National Park **Obverse:** Queen's portrait right **Reverse:** Bald eagle in flight **Note:** Multicolored.

| Date | Mintage | F | VF | XF | Unc | BU |
|---|---|---|---|---|---|---|
| 1996 Proof | 1,000 | Value: 525 | | | | |

**500 DOLLARS** KM# 313 **Weight:** 14.7400 g. **Composition:** 0.9990 Platinum .4734 oz. APW **Obverse:** Queen's portrait right **Reverse:** Marco Polo, oriental building in background

| Date | Mintage | F | VF | XF | Unc | BU |
|---|---|---|---|---|---|---|
| 1995 Proof | Est. 1,000 | Value: 500 | | | | |

## PIEFORTS

| KM# | Date | Mintage | Identification | Mkt Val |
|---|---|---|---|---|
| P1 | 1985 | 250 | Dollar. 0.9250 Silver. | 200 |
| P3 | 1986 | 500 | Dollar. 0.9250 Silver. | 40.00 |
| P2 | 1986 | 500 | Dollar. 0.9250 Silver. | 55.00 |

## TRIAL STRIKES

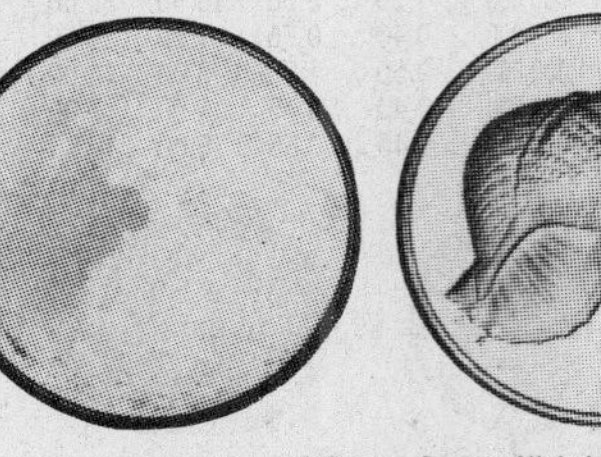

| KM# | Date | Mintage | Identification | Mkt Val |
|---|---|---|---|---|
| TS1 | | — | 20 Cents. Copper Nickel. KM#14. Reverse of KM#14 | — |

## MINT SETS

| KM# | Date | Mintage | Identification | Issue Price | Mkt Val |
|---|---|---|---|---|---|
| MS2 | 1973 (9) | 3,652 | KM1-5, 6.1,7, 9, 10 | 52.50 | 40.00 |
| MS1 | 1972 (7) | 11,045 | KM1-5, 6.1, 7 | 7.50 | 5.00 |
| MS3 | 1973 (7) | 3,023 | KM1-5, 6.1, 7 | 10.00 | 8.00 |
| MS4 | 1973 (2) | 2,348 | KM9, 10 | 45.00 | 35.00 |
| MS5 | 1974 (9) | 913 | KM1-5, 6.1, 7. 9. 10 | 5,250 | 50.00 |
| MS6 | 1974 (7) | 2,087 | KM1-5, 6.1, 7 | 10.00 | 6.00 |
| MS7 | 1974 (2) | 587 | KM9, 10 | 45.00 | 45.00 |
| MS8 | 1975 (7) | 2,251 | KM1-5, 6.1, 7 | 10.00 | 6.00 |
| MS9 | 1976 (8) | 1,066 | KM1-4, 6.1,7, 14, 15 | 20.00 | 25.00 |
| MS10 | 1977 (8) | 1,171 | KM1-4, 6.1, 7, 14, 17 | 20.00 | 25.00 |
| MS11 | 1978 (8) | 767 | KM1a-4a, 6.2, 7a, 14a, 20 | 20.00 | 30.00 |
| MS12 | 1979 (8) | 500 | KM1-3, 4b, 6.3 7, 14, 24 | — | 30.00 |
| MS13 | 1981 (7) | 1,100 | KM1b-3b, 4c, 6.4, 7b, 14b | — | 1,500 |
| MS14 | 1983 | — | KM1-5, 6.1, 7 | — | 6.00 |
| MS15 | 1987 (7) | — | KM33-39 | — | 15.00 |
| MS16 | 1988 (7) | — | KM33-35, 37-39, 41 | — | 16.00 |
| MS17 | 1992 (7) | — | KM33-35, 37-39, 41 | — | 16.00 |

## PROOF SETS

| KM# | Date | Mintage | Identification | Issue Price | Mkt Val |
|---|---|---|---|---|---|
| PS1 | 1972 (7) | 17,101 | KM1-5, 6.1, 7 | 20.00 | 9.00 |
| PS2 | 1973 (9) | 7,395 | KM1-5, 6.1, 7, 9-10 | 89.50 | 45.00 |
| PS3 | 1973 (7) | 5,136 | KM1-5, 6.1, 7 | 29.50 | 10.00 |
| PS4 | 1973 (2) | 4,754 | KM9-10 | 60.00 | 35.00 |
| PS5 | 1974 (9) | 4,444 | KM1-5, 6.1, 7, 9-10 | 95.00 | 50.00 |
| PS6 | 1974 (7) | 5,300 | KM1-5, 6.1, 7 | 32.50 | 10.00 |
| PS7 | 1974 (2) | 2,856 | KM9-10 | 65.00 | 35.00 |
| PS8 | 1975 (7) | 21,290 | KM-15, 6.1, 7 | 31.50 | 10.00 |
| PS9 | 1976 (8) | 17,658 | KM1-4, 6.1, 7, 14-15 | 40.00 | 22.50 |
| PS10 | 1977 (8) | 5,986 | KM1-4, 6.1, 7, 14, 17 | 42.00 | 25.00 |
| PS11 | 1978 (8) | 6,287 | KM1a-4a, 6.2, 7a, 14a, 20 | 42.00 | 25.00 |
| PS12 | 1979 (8) | 4,058 | KM1-3,4b, 6.3, 7, 14, 24 | 44.00 | 25.00 |
| PS13 | 1981 (7) | 9,205 | KM1b-3b, 4c, 6.4, 7b, 14b | 39.50 | 12.50 |
| PS14 | 1983 (7) | 10,000 | KM1-5, 6.1, 7 | 29.95 | 10.00 |
| PS15 | 1987 (7) | — | KM33-39 | — | 32.50 |
| PS16 | 1988 (7) | — | KM33-35, 37-39, 41 | — | 32.50 |
| PS17 | 1991 (12) | 1,000 | KM93, 95, 118-120, 122-128 | — | 300 |
| PS18 | 1992 (7) | — | KM33-35, 37-39, 41 | — | 32.50 |
| PS19 | 1994 (7) | 200 | KM33-35, 37-39, 41 | — | 37.50 |
| PS20 | 1996 (3) | — | KM298-300 | — | 600 |
| PS21 | 1996 (6) | — | KM284, 286, 288, 292, 294, 296 | — | 935 |
| PS22 | 1998 (5) | 4,000 | KM314-318 | 185 | 225 |
| PS23 | 1999 (3) | — | KM338-340 | 98.00 | 110 |
| PS24 | 1999 (5) | 4,000 | KM361-365 | 122 | 225 |

## PROOF-LIKE SETS (PL)

| KM# | Date | Mintage | Identification | Issue Price | Mkt Val |
|---|---|---|---|---|---|
| PLS1 | 1990 (5) | — | KM74-78 | 325 | 350 |

# COSTA RICA

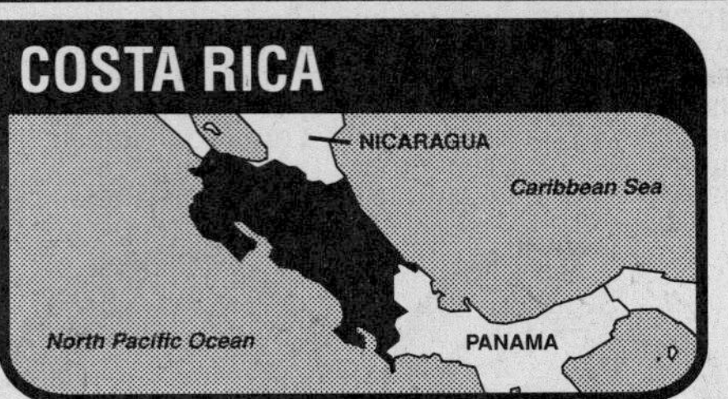


The Republic of Costa Rica, located in southern Central America between Nicaragua and Panama, has an area of 19,730 sq. mi. (51,100 sq. km.) and a population of 3.4 million. Capital: San Jose. Agriculture predominates; tourism and coffee, bananas, beef and sugar contribute heavily to the country's export earnings.

Costa Rica was discovered by Christopher Columbus in 1502, during his last voyage to the New World, and was a colony of Spain from 1522 until independence in 1821. Columbus named the territory Nueva Cartago; the name Costa Rica wasn't generally applied until 1540. Bartholomew Columbus attempted the first settlement but was driven off by Indian attacks and the country wasn't subdued until 1530. After centuries, as part of the Spanish Captaincy-General of Guatemala, Costa Rica was absorbed into the Mexican Empire of Augustin de Iturbide from 1821-1823. From 1823 to 1848, it was a constituent state of the Central American Republic (q.v.). Established as a republic in 1848, Costa Rica adopted democratic reforms in the 1870's and 80's. Today, Costa Rica remains a model of orderly democracy in Latin America, although, like most of the hemisphere - its economy is in stress.

NOTE: Also see Central American Republic.

**MINT MARKS**

CR - San Jose 1825-1947
HEATON - Heaton, Birmingham, England, 1889-93
BIRMm - Heaton, Birmingham, England, 1889-93

**ISSUING BANK INITIALS - MINTS**

BCCR - Philadelphia 1951-1958,1961
BICR - Philadelphia 1935
BNCR - London 1937,1948
BNCR - San Jose 1942-1947
GCR - Philadelphia 1905-1914,1929
GCR - San Jose 1917-1941

**ASSAYERS INITIALS**

MM – Miguel Mora, 1842
JB – Juan Barth, 1847-1864
GW – Guillermo Witting, 1854-1890
CB – Carlos Blanco, 1889
CY – Carlos Iglesias, 1902
JCV – Jesus Cubero Vargas, 1903

**MONETARY SYSTEM**

8 Reales = 1 Peso
16 Pesos = 8 Escudos = 1 Onza

## REPUBLIC

### REFORM COINAGE

1897, 100 Centimos = 1 Colon

**2 CENTIMOS** KM# 144 **Weight:** 1.0000 g. **Composition:** Copper-Nickel **Edge:** Plain

| Date | Mintage | F | VF | XF | Unc | BU |
|---|---|---|---|---|---|---|
| 1903 | 360,000 | 0.50 | 1.00 | 2.25 | 5.00 | — |

**5 CENTIMOS** KM# 145 **Weight:** 1.0000 g. **Composition:** 0.9000 Silver .0289 oz. ASW **Obverse:** Ornate arms **Edge:** Reeded

| Date | Mintage | F | VF | XF | Unc | BU |
|---|---|---|---|---|---|---|
| 1905(P) | 500,000 | BV | 0.75 | 2.00 | 6.00 | — |
| 1910(P) | 400,000 | BV | 0.75 | 2.00 | 7.50 | — |
| 1912(P) | 540,000 | BV | 0.75 | 1.50 | 5.00 | — |
| 1914(P) | 510,000 | BV | 0.75 | 1.50 | 5.50 | — |

**10 CENTIMOS** KM# 146 **Weight:** 2.0000 g. **Composition:** 0.9000 Silver .0578 oz. ASW **Obverse:** Ornate arms

| Date | Mintage | F | VF | XF | Unc | BU |
|---|---|---|---|---|---|---|
| 1905(P) | 400,000 | BV | 1.00 | 3.00 | 10.00 | — |
| 1910(P) | 400,000 | BV | 1.00 | 3.00 | 10.00 | — |
| 1912(P) | 270,000 | BV | 1.00 | 3.00 | 10.00 | — |
| 1914(P) | 150,000 | BV | 1.25 | 4.00 | 13.50 | — |

**50 CENTIMOS** KM# 143 **Weight:** 10.0000 g. **Composition:** 0.9000 Silver .2893 oz. ASW **Obverse:** Ornate arms

| Date | Mintage | F | VF | XF | Unc | BU |
|---|---|---|---|---|---|---|
| 1902 CY | 120,000 | 15.00 | 27.50 | 45.00 | 110 | — |
| 1903 JCV | 380,000 | 10.00 | 18.00 | 32.50 | 75.00 | — |
| 1914(P) GCR | 200,000 | 300 | 500 | 850 | 1,200 | — |

**Note:** Most coins dated 1914 were later counterstamped UN COLON/ 1923. See KM#164

**2 COLONES** KM# 139 **Weight:** 1.5560 g. **Composition:** 0.9000 Gold .4560 oz. AGW **Obverse:** Ornate arms **Reverse:** Bust of Christopher Colombus

| Date | Mintage | F | VF | XF | Unc | BU |
|---|---|---|---|---|---|---|
| 1897 Proof | 500 | Value: 750 | | | | |
| 1915 | 5,000 | 40.00 | 60.00 | 75.00 | 100 | — |
| 1916 | 5,000 | 40.00 | 60.00 | 75.00 | 100 | — |
| 1921 | 3,000 | 50.00 | 75.00 | 100 | 140 | — |
| 1922 | 13,000 | 30.00 | 40.00 | 60.00 | 80.00 | — |
| 1926 | 15,000 | 30.00 | 40.00 | 60.00 | 80.00 | — |
| 1928 | 25,000 | 25.00 | 37.50 | 60.00 | 80.00 | — |

## REFORM COINAGE

1917, 100 Centavos = 1 Colon

**5 CENTAVOS** KM# 147 **Weight:** 1.0000 g. **Composition:** Brass **Obverse:** Ornate arms **Edge:** Plain

| Date | Mintage | F | VF | XF | Unc | BU |
|---|---|---|---|---|---|---|
| 1917 | 400,000 | 2.00 | 4.50 | 12.50 | 32.50 | — |
| 1918 | 1,000,000 | 1.25 | 4.00 | 10.00 | 28.50 | — |
| 1919 | 500,000 | 2.00 | 4.50 | 11.00 | 32.50 | — |

**10 CENTAVOS** KM# 148 **Weight:** 2.0000 g. **Composition:** 0.5000 Silver .0321 oz. ASW **Obverse:** Ornate arms **Edge:** Reeded

| Date | Mintage | F | VF | XF | Unc | BU |
|---|---|---|---|---|---|---|
| 1917 | 100,000 | 1.00 | 2.00 | 3.00 | 6.50 | — |

**10 CENTAVOS** KM# 149.1 **Weight:** 2.0000 g. **Composition:** Brass **Obverse:** Ornate arms **Reverse:** GCR at lower right

| Date | Mintage | F | VF | XF | Unc | BU |
|---|---|---|---|---|---|---|
| 1917 GCR | 500,000 | 1.50 | 3.50 | 8.50 | 30.00 | — |

**10 CENTAVOS** KM# 149.2 **Weight:** 2.0000 g. **Composition:** Brass **Obverse:** Ornate arms **Reverse:** GCR at bottom center

| Date | Mintage | F | VF | XF | Unc | BU |
|---|---|---|---|---|---|---|
| 1917 GCR | Inc. above | 2.75 | 5.00 | 15.00 | 38.50 | — |
| 1918 GCR | 900,000 | 1.25 | 3.00 | 8.00 | 27.50 | — |
| 1919 GCR | 250,000 | 1.75 | 5.00 | 13.50 | 35.00 | — |

**50 CENTAVOS** KM# 150 **Weight:** 10.0000 g. **Composition:** 0.5000 Silver .1607 oz. ASW **Obverse:** Ornate arms **Note:** All but 10 examples of the 1917 issue and the complete 1918 mintage were counterstamped UN COLON/1923. See KM#165.

| Date | Mintage | F | VF | XF | Unc | BU |
|---|---|---|---|---|---|---|
| 1917 GCR | 9,400 | — | — | 800 | 1,000 | — |
| 1918 GCR | 30,000 | — | — | — | — | — |

## REFORM COINAGE

1920, 100 Centimos = 1 Colon

**5 CENTIMOS** KM# 151 **Weight:** 1.0000 g. **Composition:** Brass **Edge:** Plain

| Date | Mintage | F | VF | XF | Unc | BU |
|---|---|---|---|---|---|---|
| 1920 | 500,000 | 1.25 | 4.00 | 12.50 | 25.00 | — |
| 1921 | 500,000 | 1.25 | 4.00 | 10.00 | 27.50 | — |
| 1922 | 500,000 | 1.75 | 5.00 | 13.50 | 35.00 | — |
| 1936 | 1,500,000 | 0.40 | 0.75 | 1.50 | 6.50 | — |
| 1938 | 1,000,000 | 0.50 | 1.25 | 3.00 | 10.00 | — |
| 1940 | 1,300,000 | 0.40 | 0.75 | 1.50 | 7.00 | — |
| 1941 | 1,000,000 | 0.40 | 0.85 | 5.00 | 12.50 | — |

**5 CENTIMOS** KM# 169 **Composition:** Bronze **Obverse:** Ornate arms

| Date | Mintage | F | VF | XF | Unc | BU |
|---|---|---|---|---|---|---|
| 1929 | 1,500,000 | 0.60 | 1.25 | 3.25 | 7.50 | — |

**5 CENTIMOS** KM# 178 **Composition:** Copper-Nickel **Obverse:** Ornate arms

| Date | Mintage | F | VF | XF | Unc | BU |
|---|---|---|---|---|---|---|
| 1942 | 274,000 | 0.55 | 1.25 | 3.50 | 10.00 | — |

**Note:** Struck over 2 Centimos, KM#144. Overstrikes with clear evidence of the undertype command a 10-15% premium

**5 CENTIMOS** KM# 179 **Composition:** Brass **Obverse:** Ornate arms

| Date | Mintage | F | VF | XF | Unc | BU |
|---|---|---|---|---|---|---|
| 1942 | 1,730,000 | 0.20 | 0.60 | 1.25 | 4.50 | — |
| 1942 Prooflike | — | Value: 22.50 | | | | |
| 1943 | 1,000,000 | 0.20 | 0.60 | 2.00 | 6.00 | — |
| 1946 | 1,000,000 | 0.35 | 0.90 | 2.25 | 6.50 | — |
| 1946 Proof | — | Value: 60.00 | | | | |
| 1947 | 3,000,000 | 0.15 | 0.45 | 1.00 | 3.50 | — |

**5 CENTIMOS** KM# A184 (KM184.1) **Composition:** Copper-Nickel **Obverse:** Ornate arms **Reverse:** Large lettering B.C. - C.R. divided at bottom

| Date | Mintage | F | VF | XF | Unc | BU |
|---|---|---|---|---|---|---|
| 1951 | 3,000,000 | 0.35 | 0.75 | 1.50 | 4.50 | — |

**5 CENTIMOS** KM# 184.1 (KM184.2) **Composition:** Copper-Nickel **Obverse:** Ornate arms **Reverse:** Small lettering B.C.C.R. not divided

| Date | Mintage | F | VF | XF | Unc | BU |
|---|---|---|---|---|---|---|
| 1951 | 7,000,000 | 0.10 | 0.15 | 0.40 | 1.00 | — |

**5 CENTIMOS** KM# 184.1a (KM184.2a) **Composition:** Stainless Steel **Obverse:** Ornate arms

| Date | Mintage | F | VF | XF | Unc | BU |
|---|---|---|---|---|---|---|
| 1953 | 9,040,000 | — | — | 0.10 | 0.25 | — |
| 1958 | 19,940,000 | — | — | 0.10 | 0.15 | — |
| 1967 | 6,020,000 | — | — | 0.10 | 0.20 | — |

**5 CENTIMOS** KM# 184.2 (KM184.3) **Composition:** Copper-Nickel **Obverse:** Small ships, 7 stars on arms, no flag on near ship **Note:** Varieties exist for shields of each date.

| Date | Mintage | F | VF | XF | Unc | BU |
|---|---|---|---|---|---|---|
| 1969 | 20,000,000 | — | — | 0.10 | 0.15 | — |
| 1976 | — | — | — | 0.10 | 0.15 | — |
| 1976 Proof | — | Value: 0.75 | | | | |
| 1978 | 7,520,000 | — | — | 0.10 | 0.15 | — |

**5 CENTIMOS** KM# 184.3 (KM184.4) **Composition:** Copper-Nickel **Obverse:** Large ships, 7 stars on arms, flag on near ship **Note:** Dies vary for each date.

| Date | Mintage | F | VF | XF | Unc | BU |
|---|---|---|---|---|---|---|
| 1972 | 12,550,000 | — | — | 0.10 | 0.15 | — |
| 1973 | 20,000,000 | — | — | 0.10 | 0.15 | — |
| 1976 | 33,270,000 | — | — | 0.10 | 0.15 | — |

**5 CENTIMOS** KM# 184.3a (KM184.4a) **Composition:** Brass **Obverse:** Large date, flag, no sun

| Date | Mintage | F | VF | XF | Unc | BU |
|---|---|---|---|---|---|---|
| 1979 | 3,060,000 | — | — | 0.10 | 0.15 | — |

**10 CENTIMOS** KM# 152 **Composition:** Brass **Obverse:** Ornate arms **Reverse:** GCR at lower right

| Date | Mintage | F | VF | XF | Unc | BU |
|---|---|---|---|---|---|---|
| 1920 GCR | 850,000 | 0.75 | 2.00 | 6.50 | 28.50 | — |
| 1921 GCR | 750,000 | 1.00 | 2.50 | 8.00 | 35.00 | — |
| 1922 GCR | 750,000 | 0.75 | 2.00 | 6.50 | 27.50 | — |

**10 CENTIMOS** KM# 170 **Composition:** Bronze **Obverse:** Ornate arms **Reverse:** GCR at bottom

| Date | Mintage | F | VF | XF | Unc | BU |
|---|---|---|---|---|---|---|
| 1929 GCR | 500,000 | 1.25 | 2.75 | 6.00 | 17.50 | — |

**10 CENTIMOS** KM# 174 **Composition:** Brass **Obverse:** Ornate arms

| Date | Mintage | F | VF | XF | Unc | BU |
|---|---|---|---|---|---|---|
| 1936 | 750,000 | 0.35 | 0.65 | 2.50 | 10.00 | — |
| 1941 | 500,000 | 0.50 | 1.25 | 3.50 | 13.50 | — |

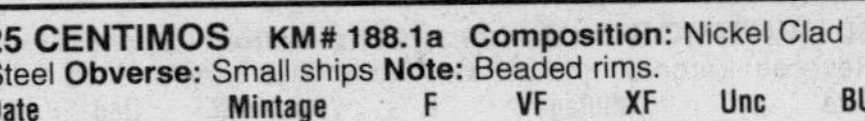

**10 CENTIMOS** **KM# 180** **Composition:** Brass **Obverse:** Ornate arms **Reverse:** B.N. - C.R. divided at bottom

| Date | Mintage | F | VF | XF | Unc | BU |
|---|---|---|---|---|---|---|
| 1942 | 1,000,000 | 0.30 | 0.60 | 2.00 | 6.50 | — |
| 1943 | 500,000 | 0.35 | 0.75 | 3.50 | 9.00 | — |
| 1946 | 500,000 | 0.50 | 1.00 | 3.50 | 10.00 | — |
| 1947 | 1,500,000 | 0.25 | 0.50 | 1.50 | 5.50 | — |

**Note:** Edge varieties exist on 1947 strikes

**10 CENTIMOS** **KM# 185.1** **Composition:** Copper-Nickel **Obverse:** Small ships, 5 stars in shield **Reverse:** B.C.C.R. at bottom

| Date | Mintage | F | VF | XF | Unc | BU |
|---|---|---|---|---|---|---|
| 1951 | 2,500,000 | 0.10 | 0.20 | 0.70 | 1.25 | — |

**10 CENTIMOS** **KM# 185.1a** **Composition:** Stainless Steel **Obverse:** Ornate arms

| Date | Mintage | F | VF | XF | Unc | BU |
|---|---|---|---|---|---|---|
| 1953 | 5,290,000 | — | — | 0.10 | 0.75 | — |
| 1958 | 10,470,000 | — | — | 0.10 | 0.25 | — |
| 1967 | 5,500,000 | — | — | 0.10 | 0.25 | — |

**10 CENTIMOS** **KM# 185.2** **Composition:** Copper-Nickel **Obverse:** Small ships, 7 stars in field **Reverse:** Small 10 **Note:** Dies vary for each date

| Date | Mintage | F | VF | XF | Unc | BU |
|---|---|---|---|---|---|---|
| 1969 | 10,000,000 | — | — | 0.10 | 0.15 | — |
| 1976 | 40,000,000 | — | — | 0.10 | 0.15 | — |
| 1976 Proof | — | Value: 0.75 | | | | |

**10 CENTIMOS** **KM# 185.3** **Composition:** Copper-Nickel **Obverse:** Large ships, 7 stars in field **Reverse:** Large 10

| Date | Mintage | F | VF | XF | Unc | BU |
|---|---|---|---|---|---|---|
| 1972 | 20,000,000 | — | — | 0.10 | 0.15 | — |
| 1975 | 5,000,000 | — | — | 0.10 | 0.15 | — |

**10 CENTIMOS** **KM# 185.2b** **Composition:** Nickel Clad Steel

| Date | Mintage | F | VF | XF | Unc | BU |
|---|---|---|---|---|---|---|
| 1979 | 10,000,000 | — | — | 0.10 | 0.15 | — |

**10 CENTIMOS** **KM# 185.2a** **Composition:** Aluminum **Obverse:** Small ships, 7 stars in field

| Date | Mintage | F | VF | XF | Unc | BU |
|---|---|---|---|---|---|---|
| 1982 | 40,000,000 | — | — | 0.10 | 0.15 | — |

**25 CENTIMOS** **KM# 168** **Weight:** 3.4500 g. **Composition:** 0.6500 Silver .0721 oz. ASW **Obverse:** Ornate arms **Edge:** Reeded

| Date | Mintage | F | VF | XF | Unc | BU |
|---|---|---|---|---|---|---|
| 1924 | 1,340,000 | 1.25 | 2.25 | 5.00 | 15.00 | — |

**Note:** Typical examples of KM#168 are weak at centers, fully struck up XF and Unc pieces command a 50% premium

**25 CENTIMOS** **KM# 171** **Composition:** Copper-Nickel **Obverse:** Ornate arms **Reverse:** BICR at bottom **Edge:** Incuse lettered

| Date | Mintage | F | VF | XF | Unc | BU |
|---|---|---|---|---|---|---|
| 1935 | 1,200,000 | 0.25 | 0.75 | 2.50 | 15.00 | — |

**25 CENTIMOS** **KM# 175** **Composition:** Copper-Nickel **Obverse:** Ornate arms **Reverse:** B.N.C.R. at bottom

| Date | Mintage | F | VF | XF | Unc | BU |
|---|---|---|---|---|---|---|
| 1937 | 1,600,000 | 0.25 | 0.75 | 1.75 | 8.00 | — |
| 1937 Proof | — | Value: 100 | | | | |
| 1948 | 9,200,000 | 0.10 | 0.20 | 0.40 | 1.25 | — |
| 1948 Proof | — | — | — | — | — | — |

**25 CENTIMOS** **KM# 181** **Composition:** Yellow Brass **Obverse:** Ornate arms **Reverse:** B.N. * C.R. at bottom **Edge:** Reeded

| Date | Mintage | F | VF | XF | Unc | BU |
|---|---|---|---|---|---|---|
| 1944 | 800,000 | 0.50 | 1.25 | 3.50 | 14.50 | — |
| 1945 | 1,200,000 | 0.50 | 1.00 | 2.75 | 12.50 | — |
| 1946 | 1,200,000 | 0.50 | 1.00 | 2.50 | 10.00 | — |

**25 CENTIMOS** **KM# 181a** **Composition:** Red Brass **Edge:** Reeded

| Date | Mintage | F | VF | XF | Unc | BU |
|---|---|---|---|---|---|---|
| 1945 | Inc. above | 1.00 | 2.00 | 4.00 | 20.00 | — |

**25 CENTIMOS** **KM# 188.1** **Composition:** Copper-Nickel **Obverse:** Small ships, 7 stars on arms **Reverse:** B.C.C.R. at bottom **Note:** Dies vary for each date.

| Date | Mintage | F | VF | XF | Unc | BU |
|---|---|---|---|---|---|---|
| 1967 | 4,000,000 | — | — | 0.10 | 0.50 | — |
| 1969 | 4,000,000 | — | — | 0.10 | 0.50 | — |
| 1974 | — | — | — | 0.10 | 0.30 | — |
| 1976 | 12,000,000 | — | — | 0.10 | 0.30 | — |
| 1978 | — | — | — | 0.10 | 0.30 | — |

**25 CENTIMOS** **KM# 188.2** **Composition:** Aluminum **Obverse:** Large ships, 7 stars on arms, flag

| Date | Mintage | F | VF | XF | Unc | BU |
|---|---|---|---|---|---|---|
| 1972 | 8,000,000 | — | — | 0.10 | 0.25 | — |

**25 CENTIMOS** **KM# 188.1a** **Composition:** Nickel Clad Steel **Obverse:** Small ships **Note:** Beaded rims.

| Date | Mintage | F | VF | XF | Unc | BU |
|---|---|---|---|---|---|---|
| 1980 | 30,000,000 | — | — | 0.10 | 0.25 | — |

**25 CENTIMOS** **KM# 188.1b** **Composition:** Aluminum **Edge:** Plain

| Date | Mintage | F | VF | XF | Unc | BU |
|---|---|---|---|---|---|---|
| 1982 | 30,000,000 | — | — | 0.10 | 0.25 | — |

**25 CENTIMOS** **KM# 188.3** **Composition:** Aluminum **Edge:** Reeded **Note:** Reduced size, 17 millimeters. Dies vary for each date.

| Date | Mintage | F | VF | XF | Unc | BU |
|---|---|---|---|---|---|---|
| 1983 | — | — | — | 0.10 | 0.20 | — |
| 1986 | — | — | — | 0.10 | 0.20 | — |
| 1989 | — | — | — | 0.10 | 0.20 | — |

**50 CENTIMOS** **KM# 172** **Composition:** Copper-Nickel **Obverse:** Ornate arms **Reverse:** B.I.C.R. at bottom

| Date | Mintage | F | VF | XF | Unc | BU |
|---|---|---|---|---|---|---|
| 1935 | 700,000 | 0.50 | 1.25 | 5.00 | 25.00 | — |

**50 CENTIMOS** **KM# 176** **Composition:** Copper-Nickel **Obverse:** Ornate arms **Reverse:** B.N.C.R. at bottom

| Date | Mintage | F | VF | XF | Unc | BU |
|---|---|---|---|---|---|---|
| 1937 | 600,000 | 0.30 | 1.00 | 3.00 | 14.00 | — |
| 1937 Proof | — | Value: 125 | | | | |

**50 CENTIMOS** **KM# 182** **Composition:** Copper-Nickel **Obverse:** Ornate arms

| Date | Mintage | F | VF | XF | Unc | BU |
|---|---|---|---|---|---|---|
| 1948 | 4,000,000 | 0.15 | 0.25 | 0.50 | 2.00 | — |
| 1948 Proof | — | — | — | — | — | — |

**50 CENTIMOS** **KM# 189.1** **Composition:** Copper-Nickel **Obverse:** Small ships, 7 stars in shield, small 50

| Date | Mintage | F | VF | XF | Unc | BU |
|---|---|---|---|---|---|---|
| 1965 | 1,000,000 | — | 0.10 | 0.25 | 1.00 | — |

**50 CENTIMOS** **KM# 189.3** **Composition:** Copper-Nickel **Reverse:** Large 50 and B.C.C.R **Note:** Dies vary for each date.

| Date | Mintage | F | VF | XF | Unc | BU |
|---|---|---|---|---|---|---|
| 1968 | 2,000,000 | — | 0.10 | 0.15 | 0.50 | — |
| 1970 | 4,000,000 | — | 0.10 | 0.15 | 0.35 | — |
| 1976 | 6,000,000 | — | 0.10 | 0.15 | 0.35 | — |
| 1976 Proof | — | Value: 1.50 | | | | |
| 1978 | — | — | 0.10 | 0.15 | 0.35 | — |

**50 CENTIMOS** **KM# 189.2** **Composition:** Copper-Nickel **Obverse:** Large ships, 7 stars in shield

| Date | Mintage | F | VF | XF | Unc | BU |
|---|---|---|---|---|---|---|
| 1972 Large date | 4,000,000 | — | 0.10 | 0.15 | 0.35 | — |
| 1972 Small date | Inc. above | — | 0.10 | 0.15 | 0.35 | — |
| 1975 Large date | 524,000 | — | 0.10 | 0.15 | 0.35 | — |
| 1975 Small date | Inc. above | — | 0.10 | 0.15 | 0.35 | — |

**50 CENTIMOS** **KM# 209.1** **Composition:** Stainless Steel **Obverse:** Large ships, letters incuse on ribbon

| Date | Mintage | F | VF | XF | Unc | BU |
|---|---|---|---|---|---|---|
| 1982 | 12,000,000 | — | — | 0.10 | 0.25 | — |
| 1983 | — | — | — | 0.10 | 0.25 | — |
| 1990 | — | — | — | 0.10 | 0.25 | — |

**50 CENTIMOS** **KM# 209.2** **Composition:** Stainless Steel **Obverse:** Small ships, letters in relief on ribbon

| Date | Mintage | F | VF | XF | Unc | BU |
|---|---|---|---|---|---|---|
| 1984 | — | — | — | 0.10 | 0.25 | — |

**COLON** **KM# 173** **Composition:** Copper-Nickel **Obverse:** Ornate arms **Reverse:** B.I.C.R at bottom **Edge:** Incuse BICR; plain **Note:** Beaded rims.

| Date | Mintage | F | VF | XF | Unc | BU |
|---|---|---|---|---|---|---|
| 1935 | 350,000 | 0.75 | 2.00 | 7.00 | 37.50 | — |

**COLON** **KM# 177** **Composition:** Copper-Nickel **Obverse:** Ornate arms **Reverse:** B.N.C.R. at bottom

| Date | Mintage | F | VF | XF | Unc | BU |
|---|---|---|---|---|---|---|
| 1937 | 300,000 | 0.50 | 1.25 | 4.50 | 20.00 | — |
| 1937 Proof | — | Value: 150 | | | | |
| 1948 | 1,350,000 | 0.20 | 0.40 | 0.75 | 2.00 | — |
| 1948 Proof | — | — | — | — | — | — |

**COLON** **KM# 186.1** **Composition:** Stainless Steel **Obverse:** Small ships, 5 stars in shield

| Date | Mintage | F | VF | XF | Unc | BU |
|---|---|---|---|---|---|---|
| 1954 | 990,000 | 0.20 | 0.35 | 1.00 | 7.50 | — |

**COLON** **KM# 186.1a** **Composition:** Copper-Nickel

| Date | Mintage | F | VF | XF | Unc | BU |
|---|---|---|---|---|---|---|
| 1961 | 1,000,000 | 0.10 | 0.20 | 0.50 | 2.00 | — |

**COLON** **KM# 186.2** **Composition:** Copper-Nickel **Obverse:** Small ships, 7 stars in shield **Reverse:** Small 1

| Date | Mintage | F | VF | XF | Unc | BU |
|---|---|---|---|---|---|---|
| 1965 | 1,000,000 | 0.10 | 0.20 | 0.40 | 1.00 | — |
| 1968 | 2,000,000 | 0.10 | 0.20 | 0.30 | 0.65 | — |
| 1970 | 2,000,000 | 0.10 | 0.20 | 0.30 | 0.65 | — |
| 1974 | — | 0.10 | 0.20 | 0.30 | 0.65 | — |
| 1978 | — | 0.10 | 0.20 | 0.30 | 0.65 | — |

**COLON** **KM# 186.3** **Composition:** Copper-Nickel **Obverse:** Large ships, 7 stars in shield

| Date | Mintage | F | VF | XF | Unc | BU |
|---|---|---|---|---|---|---|
| 1972 | 2,000,000 | 0.10 | 0.20 | 0.30 | 0.65 | — |
| 1975 | 1,028,000 | 0.10 | 0.20 | 0.30 | 0.65 | — |

**COLON** **KM# 186.4** **Composition:** Copper-Nickel **Obverse:** Small ships, 7 stars in shield **Reverse:** Large 1 **Note:** Dies vary for each date.

| Date | Mintage | F | VF | XF | Unc | BU |
|---|---|---|---|---|---|---|
| 1976 | 12,000,000 | 0.10 | 0.20 | 0.30 | 0.65 | — |
| 1976 Proof | — | Value: 2.50 | | | | |
| 1977 | 22,000,000 | 0.10 | 0.20 | 0.30 | 0.65 | — |

**COLON** **KM# 210.1** **Composition:** Stainless Steel **Obverse:** Large ships, letters incuse on ribbon

| Date | Mintage | F | VF | XF | Unc | BU |
|---|---|---|---|---|---|---|
| 1982 | 12,000,000 | — | — | 0.15 | 0.35 | — |
| 1983 | — | — | — | 0.15 | 0.35 | — |
| 1984 | — | — | — | 0.15 | 0.35 | — |
| 1991 | — | — | — | 0.15 | 0.35 | — |

**COLON** **KM# 210.2** **Composition:** Stainless Steel **Obverse:** Small ships, letters in relief on ribbon

| Date | Mintage | F | VF | XF | Unc | BU |
|---|---|---|---|---|---|---|
| 1984 | — | — | — | 0.15 | 0.35 | — |
| 1989 | — | — | — | 0.15 | 0.35 | — |
| 1993 | — | — | — | 0.15 | 0.35 | — |
| 1994 | — | — | — | 0.15 | 0.35 | — |

**COLON** **KM# 233** **Composition:** Brass **Obverse:** National arms **Reverse:** Denomination

| Date | Mintage | F | VF | XF | Unc | BU |
|---|---|---|---|---|---|---|
| 1998 | — | — | — | 0.10 | 0.35 | — |

**2 COLONES** **KM# 183** **Composition:** Copper-Nickel **Obverse:** Ornate arms

| Date | Mintage | F | VF | XF | Unc | BU |
|---|---|---|---|---|---|---|
| 1948 | 1,380,000 | 0.50 | 0.75 | 1.25 | 3.00 | — |
| 1948 Proof | — | — | — | — | — | — |

**2 COLONES** **KM# 187.1** **Composition:** Stainless Steel **Obverse:** Ornate arms with small ships, 5 stars in shield

| Date | Mintage | F | VF | XF | Unc | BU |
|---|---|---|---|---|---|---|
| 1954 | 1,030,000 | 0.25 | 0.50 | 2.00 | 10.00 | — |

**2 COLONES** **KM# 187.1a** **Composition:** Copper-Nickel

| Date | Mintage | F | VF | XF | Unc | BU |
|---|---|---|---|---|---|---|
| 1961 | 1,000,000 | 0.15 | 0.30 | 0.50 | 1.25 | — |

**2 COLONES** **KM# 187.2** **Composition:** Copper-Nickel **Obverse:** Small ships, 7 stars in shield **Note:** Dies vary for each date.

| Date | Mintage | F | VF | XF | Unc | BU |
|---|---|---|---|---|---|---|
| 1968 | 2,000,000 | 0.15 | 0.30 | 0.45 | 1.00 | — |
| 1970 | 1,000,000 | 0.15 | 0.30 | 0.45 | 1.25 | — |
| 1972 | 2,000,000 | 0.15 | 0.30 | 0.45 | 1.00 | — |
| 1976 | — | 0.15 | 0.30 | 0.45 | 1.00 | — |
| 1978 | — | 0.15 | 0.30 | 0.45 | 1.00 | — |

**2 COLONES** **KM# 190** **Weight:** 4.3000 g. **Composition:** 0.9990 Silver .1381 oz. ASW **Subject:** 20th Anniversary of the Central Bank

| Date | Mintage | F | VF | XF | Unc | BU |
|---|---|---|---|---|---|---|
| 1970 Proof | 5,157 | Value: 7.50 | | | | |

**Note:** Also exists with a small oval with 1000 inside above the S in COLONES

**2 COLONES** **KM# 211.1** **Composition:** Stainless Steel **Obverse:** Large ships, letters incuse on ribbon

| Date | Mintage | F | VF | XF | Unc | BU |
|---|---|---|---|---|---|---|
| 1982 | 12,000,000 | — | — | 0.20 | 0.60 | — |
| 1983 | — | — | — | 0.20 | 0.60 | — |

**2 COLONES** **KM# 211.2** **Composition:** Stainless Steel **Obverse:** Small ship, letters in relief on ribbon

| Date | Mintage | F | VF | XF | Unc | BU |
|---|---|---|---|---|---|---|
| 1984 | — | — | — | 0.20 | 0.60 | — |

**5 COLONES** **KM# 191** **Weight:** 10.7800 g. **Composition:** 0.9990 Silver .3463 oz. ASW **Subject:** 400th Year - The Founding of New Carthage **Reverse:** Raised 1000 hallmark in oval below '0' of 'Cartago' **Edge:** Reeded

| Date | Mintage | F | VF | XF | Unc | BU |
|---|---|---|---|---|---|---|
| 1970 Proof | 5,157 | Value: 12.50 | | | | |

**5 COLONES** **KM# 203** **Composition:** Nickel **Subject:** 25th Anniversary of the Central Bank

| Date | Mintage | F | VF | XF | Unc | BU |
|---|---|---|---|---|---|---|
| ND(1975) | 2,000,000 | — | 0.15 | 0.35 | 1.25 | — |
| ND(1975) Proof | 5,000,000 | Value: 2.00 | | | | |

**5 COLONES** **KM# 214.1** **Composition:** Stainless Steel **Obverse:** Small ship, letters in relief on ribbon

| Date | Mintage | F | VF | XF | Unc | BU |
|---|---|---|---|---|---|---|
| 1983 | — | — | 0.10 | 0.25 | 0.75 | — |
| 1989 | — | — | 0.10 | 0.25 | 0.75 | — |
| 1993 | — | — | 0.10 | 0.25 | 0.75 | — |

**5 COLONES** **KM# 214.2** **Composition:** Stainless Steel **Obverse:** Large ship, letters incuse on ribbon

| Date | Mintage | F | VF | XF | Unc | BU |
|---|---|---|---|---|---|---|
| 1985 | — | — | 0.10 | 0.25 | 0.75 | — |

**5 COLONES** **KM# 227** **Composition:** Brass Plated Steel **Obverse:** National arms **Reverse:** Denomination

| Date | Mintage | F | VF | XF | Unc | BU |
|---|---|---|---|---|---|---|
| 1995 | — | — | — | 0.25 | 0.75 | — |
| 1997 | — | — | — | 0.25 | 0.75 | — |
| 1999 | — | — | — | 0.25 | 0.75 | — |

**10 COLONES** **KM# 192** **Weight:** 21.7000 g. **Composition:** 0.9990 Silver .6976 oz. ASW **Subject:** Attempt of Unification of Middle America **Obverse:** Similar to 5 Colones, KM#191

| Date | Mintage | F | VF | XF | Unc | BU |
|---|---|---|---|---|---|---|
| 1970 Proof | 5,157 | Value: 22.00 | | | | |

**10 COLONES** **KM# 204** **Composition:** Nickel **Subject:** 25th Anniversary of the Central Bank

| Date | Mintage | F | VF | XF | Unc | BU |
|---|---|---|---|---|---|---|
| ND(1975) | 500,000 | 0.25 | 0.50 | 1.00 | 2.00 | — |
| ND(1975) Proof | 5,000 | Value: 4.00 | | | | |

**10 COLONES** **KM# 215.1** **Composition:** Stainless Steel **Obverse:** Small ship, letters in relief on ribbon

| Date | Mintage | F | VF | XF | Unc | BU |
|---|---|---|---|---|---|---|
| 1983 | — | — | 0.20 | 0.35 | 1.25 | — |
| 1992 | — | — | 0.20 | 0.35 | 1.25 | — |

**10 COLONES** **KM# 215.2** **Composition:** Stainless Steel **Obverse:** Large ship, letters incuse on ribbon

| Date | Mintage | F | VF | XF | Unc | BU |
|---|---|---|---|---|---|---|
| 1985 | — | — | 0.20 | 0.35 | 1.25 | — |

**10 COLONES** **KM# 228** **Composition:** Brass Plated Steel **Obverse:** National arms **Reverse:** Denomination

| Date | Mintage | F | VF | XF | Unc | BU |
|---|---|---|---|---|---|---|
| 1995 | — | — | — | 0.35 | 1.25 | — |
| 1996 | — | — | — | 0.35 | 1.25 | — |
| 1997 | — | — | — | 0.35 | 1.25 | — |

**20 COLONES** **KM# 193** **Weight:** 43.7000 g. **Composition:** 0.9990 Silver 1.4050 oz. ASW **Reverse:** Venus de Milo statue

| Date | Mintage | F | VF | XF | Unc | BU |
|---|---|---|---|---|---|---|
| 1970 Proof | 7,500 | Value: 37.50 | | | | |

**20 COLONES** **KM# 205** **Composition:** Nickel **Subject:** 25th Anniversary of the Central Bank

| Date | Mintage | F | VF | XF | Unc | BU |
|---|---|---|---|---|---|---|
| ND(1975) | 250,000 | 0.50 | 1.00 | 2.00 | 4.00 | — |
| ND(1975) Proof | 5,000 | Value: 9.00 | | | | |

**20 COLONES** **KM# 216.1** **Composition:** Stainless Steel **Obverse:** Letters in relief on ribbon

| Date | Mintage | F | VF | XF | Unc | BU |
|---|---|---|---|---|---|---|
| 1983 | — | — | 0.35 | 0.65 | 1.75 | — |
| 1989 | — | — | 0.35 | 0.65 | 1.75 | — |
| 1994 | — | — | 0.35 | 0.65 | 1.75 | — |

**20 COLONES** **KM# 216.2** **Composition:** Stainless Steel **Obverse:** Letters incuse on ribbon

| Date | Mintage | F | VF | XF | Unc | BU |
|---|---|---|---|---|---|---|
| 1985 | — | — | 0.35 | 0.65 | 1.75 | — |
| 1994 | — | — | 0.35 | 0.65 | 1.75 | — |
| 1996 | — | — | 0.35 | 0.65 | 1.75 | — |

**25 COLONES** **KM# 194** **Weight:** 53.9000 g. **Composition:** 0.9990 Silver 1.7312 oz. ASW **Subject:** 25 Years of Social Legislation **Obverse:** Similar to 5 Colones, KM#191 **Reverse:** "Materidad" Sculpture by F. Zuniga.

| Date | Mintage | F | VF | XF | Unc | BU |
|---|---|---|---|---|---|---|
| 1970 Proof | 6,800 | Value: 45.00 | | | | |

**25 COLONES** **KM# 229** **Composition:** Brass Plated Steel **Obverse:** National arms **Reverse:** Denomination

| Date | Mintage | F | VF | XF | Unc | BU |
|---|---|---|---|---|---|---|
| 1995 | — | — | — | — | 2.50 | — |

**50 COLONES** **KM# 195.1** **Weight:** 7.4500 g. **Composition:** 0.9000 Gold .2155 oz. AGW **Subject:** Inter-American Human Rights Convention

| Date | Mintage | F | VF | XF | Unc | BU |
|---|---|---|---|---|---|---|
| 1970 Proof | 3,507 | Value: 125 | | | | |

**50 COLONES** **KM# 195.2** **Weight:** 7.4500 g. **Composition:** 0.9000 Gold .2155 oz. AGW **Reverse:** '1 AR' countermark above fineness statement

| Date | Mintage | F | VF | XF | Unc | BU |
|---|---|---|---|---|---|---|
| 1970 Proof | Inc. above | Value: 150 | | | | |

**50 COLONES** **KM# 200** **Weight:** 25.5500 g. **Composition:** 0.5000 Silver .4107 oz. ASW **Subject:** Conservation **Reverse:** Green Turtle

| Date | Mintage | F | VF | XF | Unc | BU |
|---|---|---|---|---|---|---|
| 1974 | 7,599 | — | — | — | 16.50 | — |

**50 COLONES** **KM# 200a** **Weight:** 28.2800 g. **Composition:** 0.9250 Silver .8411 oz. ASW **Subject:** Conservation **Obv. Legend:** Green Turtle

| Date | Mintage | F | VF | XF | Unc | BU |
|---|---|---|---|---|---|---|
| 1974 Proof | 11,000 | Value: 20.00 | | | | |

**50 COLONES** **KM# 231** **Composition:** Brass **Obverse:** National arms **Reverse:** Denomination

| Date | Mintage | F | VF | XF | Unc | BU |
|---|---|---|---|---|---|---|
| 1997 | — | — | — | — | 3.00 | — |
| 1999 | — | — | — | — | 3.00 | — |

**100 COLONES** **KM# 196** **Weight:** 14.9000 g. **Composition:** 0.9000 Gold .4311 oz. AGW

| Date | Mintage | F | VF | XF | Unc | BU |
|---|---|---|---|---|---|---|
| 1970 Proof | 3,507 | Value: 245 | | | | |

**100 COLONES** **KM# 201** **Weight:** 32.1000 g. **Composition:** 0.5000 Silver .5160 oz. ASW **Subject:** Conservation **Obverse:** Similar to 1500 Colones, KM#202 **Reverse:** Manatee

| Date | Mintage | F | VF | XF | Unc | BU |
|---|---|---|---|---|---|---|
| 1974 | 7,599 | — | — | — | 22.50 | — |

**100 COLONES** **KM# 201a** **Weight:** 35.0000 g. **Composition:** 0.9250 Silver 1.0409 oz. ASW **Subject:** Conservation **Reverse:** Manatee

| Date | Mintage | F | VF | XF | Unc | BU |
|---|---|---|---|---|---|---|
| 1974 Proof | 11,000 | Value: 30.00 | | | | |

**100 COLONES** **KM# 206** **Weight:** 35.0000 g. **Composition:** 0.9250 Silver 1.0409 oz. ASW **Subject:** International Year of the Child

| Date | Mintage | F | VF | XF | Unc | BU |
|---|---|---|---|---|---|---|
| 1979 | 9,500 | — | — | — | 10.00 | — |
| 1979 Proof | 5,000 | Value: 27.50 | | | | |

**100 COLONES** **KM# 224** **Composition:** Nickel **Reverse:** President Dr. Oscar Arias S.

| Date | Mintage | F | VF | XF | Unc | BU |
|---|---|---|---|---|---|---|
| 1987 | 25,000 | — | — | — | 7.50 | — |

**100 COLONES** **KM# 230** **Composition:** Brass Plated Steel **Obverse:** National arms **Reverse:** Denomination

| Date | Mintage | F | VF | XF | Unc | BU |
|---|---|---|---|---|---|---|
| 1995 | — | — | — | — | 4.50 | — |

**100 COLONES** **KM# 230a** **Composition:** Brass

| Date | Mintage | F | VF | XF | Unc | BU |
|---|---|---|---|---|---|---|
| 1997 | — | — | — | — | 4.50 | — |
| 1998 | — | — | — | — | 4.50 | — |
| 1999 | — | — | — | — | 4.50 | — |

**200 COLONES** **KM# 197** **Weight:** 29.8000 g. **Composition:** 0.9000 Gold .8623 oz. AGW **Reverse:** Juan Santamaria and canon

| Date | Mintage | F | VF | XF | Unc | BU |
|---|---|---|---|---|---|---|
| 1970 Proof | 3,507 | Value: 500 | | | | |

**250 COLONES** **KM# 212** **Weight:** 30.3300 g. **Composition:** 0.9250 Silver .9020 oz. ASW **Subject:** Conservation **Reverse:** Jaguar

| Date | Mintage | F | VF | XF | Unc | BU |
|---|---|---|---|---|---|---|
| 1982(P) FM Proof | 1,109 | Value: 95.00 | | | | |

**250 COLONES** **KM# 217** **Weight:** 30.3300 g. **Composition:** 0.9250 Silver .9020 oz. ASW **Reverse:** National Flower

| Date | Mintage | F | VF | XF | Unc | BU |
|---|---|---|---|---|---|---|
| 1983(P) FM Proof | 393 | Value: 75.00 | | | | |

**300 COLONES** **KM# 207** **Weight:** 10.9700 g. **Composition:** 0.9250 Silver .3262 oz. ASW **Subject:** 125th Anniversary - Death of Juan Santamaria **Reverse:** Juan Santamaria standing with flag and rifle

| Date | Mintage | F | VF | XF | Unc | BU |
|---|---|---|---|---|---|---|
| 1981 Proof | 10,000 | Value: 12.50 | | | | |

**300 COLONES** **KM# 223** **Weight:** 10.9700 g. **Composition:** 0.9250 Silver .3262 oz. ASW **Subject:** 200th Anniversary - Founding of Alajuela

| Date | Mintage | F | VF | XF | Unc | BU |
|---|---|---|---|---|---|---|
| 1981 Proof | — | Value: 12.50 | | | | |

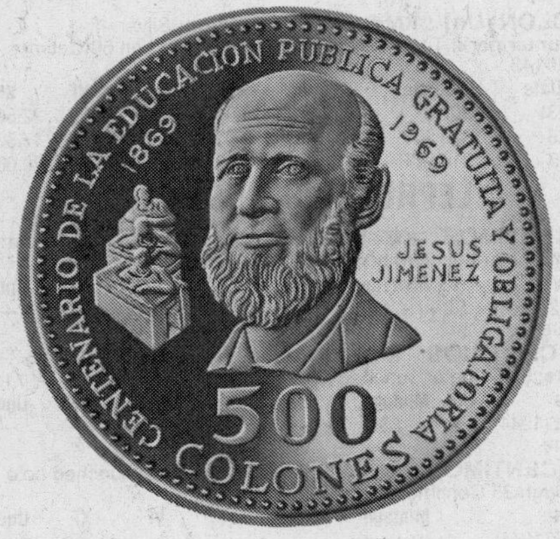

**500 COLONES** **KM# 198** **Weight:** 74.5200 g. **Composition:** 0.9000 Gold 2.1565 oz. AGW **Subject:** 100th Anniversary of Public Education **Obverse:** Similar to 100 Colones, KM#196 **Reverse:** Jesus Jimenes and students at desks

| Date | Mintage | F | VF | XF | Unc | BU |
|---|---|---|---|---|---|---|
| 1970 Proof | 3,507 | Value: 1,200 | | | | |

**500 COLONES** **KM# 236** **Composition:** Brass **Subject:** 50 Years - Central Bank **Obverse:** National arms **Reverse:** Bank building

| Date | Mintage | F | VF | XF | Unc | BU |
|---|---|---|---|---|---|---|
| 2000 | 5,000 | — | — | — | 2.50 | — |

**1000 COLONES** **KM# 199** **Weight:** 149.0400 g. **Composition:** 0.9000 Gold 4.3126 oz. AGW **Subject:** 150th Anniversary of Central American Independence **Obverse:** Similar to 100 Colones, KM#196

| Date | Mintage | F | VF | XF | Unc | BU |
|---|---|---|---|---|---|---|
| 1970 Proof | 3,507 | Value: 3,150 | | | | |

**1000 COLONES** **KM# 225** **Weight:** 10.9700 g. **Composition:** 0.9250 Silver .3272 oz. ASW **Reverse:** President Dr. Oscar Arias S.

| Date | Mintage | F | VF | XF | Unc | BU |
|---|---|---|---|---|---|---|
| 1987 | 10,000 | — | — | — | 30.00 | — |

**1500 COLONES** **KM# 202** **Weight:** 33.4370 g. **Composition:** 0.9000 Gold .9676 oz. AGW **Subject:** Conservation **Reverse:** Giant Anteater

| Date | Mintage | F | VF | XF | Unc | BU |
|---|---|---|---|---|---|---|
| 1974 | 2,418 | — | — | — | 420 | — |
| 1974 Proof | 726 | Value: 650 | | | | |

**1500 COLONES** **KM# 213** **Weight:** 6.9800 g. **Composition:** 0.5000 Gold .1122 oz. AGW **Reverse:** Francisco Coronado and Christopher Columbus

| Date | Mintage | F | VF | XF | Unc | BU |
|---|---|---|---|---|---|---|
| 1982FM (P) | 724 | Value: 125 | | | | |

**1500 COLONES** **KM# 218** **Weight:** 6.9800 g. **Composition:** 0.5000 Gold .1122 oz. AGW

| Date | Mintage | F | VF | XF | Unc | BU |
|---|---|---|---|---|---|---|
| 1983FM (P) | 272 | Value: 275 | | | | |

**3000 COLONES** **KM# 234** **Weight:** 25.3600 g. **Composition:** 0.9250 Silver .7542 oz. ASW **Subject:** 150th Anniversary San Juan de Dios Hospital **Obverse:** National arms **Reverse:** Hospital building

| Date | Mintage | F | VF | XF | Unc | BU |
|---|---|---|---|---|---|---|
| 1994 Proof | — | — | — | — | — | — |

**5000 COLONES** **KM# 208** **Weight:** 15.0000 g. **Composition:** 0.9000 Gold .4341 oz. AGW **Subject:** 125th Anniversary - Death of Juan Santamaria

| Date | Mintage | F | VF | XF | Unc | BU |
|---|---|---|---|---|---|---|
| 1981 | | — | — | — | 185 | — |
| 1981 Proof | 2,000 | Value: 225 | | | | |

**5000 COLONES** **KM# 232** **Weight:** 15.0000 g. **Composition:** 0.9000 Gold .4341 oz. AGW **Subject:** Founding of Alajuela **Obverse:** National arms **Reverse:** Portrait of Ramirez

| Date | Mintage | F | VF | XF | Unc | BU |
|---|---|---|---|---|---|---|
| 1981 Proof | 2,000 | Value: 235 | | | | |

**5000 COLONES** **KM# 235** **Weight:** 25.0600 g. **Composition:** 0.9250 Silver .7453 oz. ASW **Subject:** Centennial of the Colon **Obverse:** National arms **Reverse:** Portrait of Columbus

| Date | Mintage | F | VF | XF | Unc | BU |
|---|---|---|---|---|---|---|
| 1997 Proof | — | Value: 50.00 | | | | |

**5000 COLONES** KM# 237 **Weight:** 31.1000 g. **Composition:** 0.9250 Silver .9429 oz. ASW **Subject:** 50 Years - Central Bank **Obverse:** National arms **Reverse:** Man working screw press

| Date | Mintage | F | VF | XF | Unc | BU |
|---|---|---|---|---|---|---|
| 2000 Proof | 7,500 | Value: 30.00 | | | | |

**25000 COLONES** KM# 226 **Weight:** 15.0000 g. **Composition:** 0.9000 Gold .4341 oz. AGW **Reverse:** President Dr. Oscar Arias S.

| Date | Mintage | F | VF | XF | Unc | BU |
|---|---|---|---|---|---|---|
| 1987 Proof | 5,000 | Value: 225 | | | | |

**100000 COLONES** KM# 238 **Weight:** 15.5500 g. **Composition:** 0.9000 Gold .4499 oz. AGW **Subject:** 50 Years - Central Bank **Obverse:** National arms **Reverse:** 3 standing citizens

| Date | Mintage | F | VF | XF | Unc | BU |
|---|---|---|---|---|---|---|
| 2000 Proof | 2,500 | Value: 350 | | | | |

## COUNTERSTAMPED COINAGE

Type VIII • 1923

Obverse counterstamp: 1923 in 11mm circle.
Reverse counterstamp: 50/CENTIMOS in 11mm circle.
NOTE: The total mintage for KM#154-159 was 1,866,000 pieces

**50 CENTIMOS** KM# 156 **Composition:** Silver
**Countermark:** Type VIII **Note:** Counterstamped on 25 Centavos, KM#106.

| CS Date | Host Date | Good | VG | F | VF | XF |
|---|---|---|---|---|---|---|
| 1923 | 1864 GW | — | 225 | 400 | 650 | — |
| 1923 | 1865 GW | — | 35.00 | 58.00 | 80.00 | 125 |
| 1923 | 1875 GW | — | 22.50 | 42.00 | 65.00 | 100 |

**50 CENTIMOS** KM# 157 **Composition:** Silver
**Countermark:** Type VIII **Note:** Counterstamped on 25 Centavos, KM#127.1.

| CS Date | Host Date | Good | VG | F | VF | XF |
|---|---|---|---|---|---|---|
| 1923 | 1886 GW | — | 3.00 | 5.00 | 9.00 | 15.00 |
| 1923 | 1887 GW | — | 3.00 | 5.00 | 9.00 | 15.00 |

**50 CENTIMOS** KM# 158 **Composition:** Silver
**Countermark:** Type VIII **Reverse:** 9Ds GW **Note:** Counterstamped on 25 Centavos, KM#127.2.

| CS Date | Host Date | Good | VG | F | VF | XF |
|---|---|---|---|---|---|---|
| 1923 | 1886 GW | — | 4.00 | 8.00 | 15.00 | 25.00 |
| 1923 | 1887 GW | — | 3.00 | 5.00 | 9.00 | 15.00 |

**50 CENTIMOS** KM# 159 **Composition:** Silver
**Countermark:** Type VIII **Note:** Counterstamped on 25 Centavos, KM#130.

| CS Date | Host Date | Good | VG | F | VF | XF |
|---|---|---|---|---|---|---|
| 1923 | 1889HEATON | — | 1.50 | 2.75 | 5.00 | 8.50 |
| 1923 | 1890/80HEATON | — | 2.50 | 3.75 | 7.00 | 10.00 |
| 1923 | 1890HEATON | — | 1.50 | 2.75 | 5.00 | 8.50 |
| 1923 | 1892HEATON | — | 1.50 | 2.75 | 5.00 | 8.50 |
| 1923 | 1893HEATON | — | 1.25 | 2.50 | 4.50 | 7.50 |

**50 CENTIMOS** KM# 154 **Composition:** Silver
**Countermark:** Type VIII **Note:** Counterstamped on 1/4 Peso, KM#103.

| CS Date | Host Date | Good | VG | F | VF | XF |
|---|---|---|---|---|---|---|
| 1923 | 1850 JB | — | 500 | 700 | 1,000 | 1,250 |

**50 CENTIMOS** KM# 155 **Composition:** Silver
**Countermark:** Type VIII **Note:** Counterstamped on 25 Centavos, KM#105.

| CS Date | Host Date | Good | VG | F | VF | XF |
|---|---|---|---|---|---|---|
| 1923 | 1864 GW | — | 325 | 550 | 900 | — |

## COUNTERSTAMPED COINAGE

Type IX • 1923

Obverse counterstamp: 1923 in 14mm circle
Reverse counterstamp: UN/COLON in 14 mm circle

**COLON** KM# 162 **Composition:** Silver
**Countermark:** Type IX **Note:** Counterstamped on 50 Centavos, KM#112. The total mintage for KM#162-164 was 421,810 pieces. Host dates of 1867 GW, 1870 GW and 1872 GW are listed, but no examples are currently known to exist

| CS Date | Host Date | Good | VG | F | VF | XF |
|---|---|---|---|---|---|---|
| 1923 | 1865 GW | — | 35.00 | 50.00 | 75.00 | 125 |
| 1923 | 1866/5 GW | — | 37.50 | 55.00 | 85.00 | 150 |
| 1923 | 1867 GW | — | — | — | — | — |
| 1923 | 1870 GW | — | — | — | — | — |
| 1923 | 1872 GW | — | — | — | — | — |
| 1923 | 1875 GW | — | 32.50 | 45.00 | 70.00 | 125 |

**COLON** KM# 165 **Composition:** Silver
**Countermark:** Type IX **Note:** Counterstamped on 50 Cetimos, KM#150. For KM#165 the mintage were: 1917 host 9,390 pieces; 1918 host 28,800 pieces.

| CS Date | Host Date | Good | VG | F | VF | XF |
|---|---|---|---|---|---|---|
| 1923 | 1917 GCR | — | 6.00 | 12.00 | 17.50 | 25.00 |
| 1923 | 1918 GCR | — | 4.50 | 8.50 | 13.50 | 20.00 |

**COLON (Un)** KM# 163 **Composition:** Silver
**Countermark:** Type IX **Note:** Counterstamped on 50 Centavos, KM#124.

| CS Date | Host Date | Good | VG | F | VF | XF |
|---|---|---|---|---|---|---|
| 1923 | 1880 GW | — | 6.50 | 10.00 | 25.00 | 50.00 |
| 1923 | 1885 GW | — | 6.50 | 10.00 | 25.00 | 50.00 |
| 1923 | 1886 GW | — | 9.00 | 17.50 | 30.00 | 60.00 |
| 1923 | 1887 GW | — | 6.50 | 10.00 | 27.50 | 55.00 |
| 1923 | 1890 GW | — | 6.50 | 10.00 | 27.50 | 55.00 |

**COLON (Un)** KM# 164 **Composition:** Silver
**Countermark:** Type IX **Note:** Counterstamped on 50 Cetimos, KM#143.

| CS Date | Host Date | Good | VG | F | VF | XF |
|---|---|---|---|---|---|---|
| 1923 | 1902 CY | — | 4.00 | 8.00 | 13.50 | 22.50 |
| 1923 | 1903 JCV | — | 3.00 | 6.00 | 10.00 | 17.50 |
| 1923 | 1914 GCR | — | 4.00 | 8.00 | 13.50 | 20.00 |

## LEPROSARIUM COINAGE

**5 CENTIMOS** KM# L1 **Composition:** Copper Nickel **Note:** 4 millimeter punched hole through 5 Centimos, KM#178.

| Date | Mintage | VG | F | VF | XF | Unc |
|---|---|---|---|---|---|---|
| 1942(1944) Rare | 2,000 | — | — | — | — | — |

**25 CENTIMOS** KM# L2 **Composition:** Copper Nickel **Note:** 6 millimeter punched hole through 25 Centimos, KM#171.

| Date | Mintage | VG | F | VF | XF | Unc |
|---|---|---|---|---|---|---|
| 1935(1944) Rare | 2,000 | — | — | — | — | — |

**25 CENTIMOS** KM# L3 **Note:** 6 millimeter punched hole through 25 Centimos, KM#175.

| Date | Mintage | VG | F | VF | XF | Unc |
|---|---|---|---|---|---|---|
| 1937(1944) Rare | Inc. above | — | — | — | — | — |

**50 CENTIMOS** KM# L4 **Composition:** Copper Nickel **Note:** 8 millimeter punched hole through 50 Centimos, KM#172.

| Date | Mintage | VG | F | VF | XF | Unc |
|---|---|---|---|---|---|---|
| 1935(1944) Rare | 800 | — | — | — | — | — |

**50 CENTIMOS** KM# L5 **Composition:** Copper Nickel **Note:** 8 millimeter punched hole throuth 50 Centimos, KM#176.

| Date | Mintage | VG | F | VF | XF | Unc |
|---|---|---|---|---|---|---|
| 1937(1944) Rare | Inc. above | — | — | — | — | — |

**COLON** KM# L6 **Composition:** Copper Nickel **Note:** 9 millimeter punched hole through 1 Colon, KM#173.

| Date | Mintage | VG | F | VF | XF | Unc |
|---|---|---|---|---|---|---|
| 1935(1944) Rare | 1,000 | — | — | — | — | — |

**COLON** KM# L7 **Composition:** Copper Nickel **Note:** 9 millimeter punched hole through 1 Colon, KM#177.

| Date | Mintage | VG | F | VF | XF | Unc |
|---|---|---|---|---|---|---|
| 1937(1944) Rare | Inc. above | — | — | — | — | — |

## PATTERNS

| KM# | Date | Mintage | Identification | Mkt Val |
|---|---|---|---|---|
| Pn11 | 1917 | — | 10 Centavos. Silver. Similar to KM#129. As KM#148. | — |
| Pn12 | 1924 | — | 25 Centimos. Brass. KM#168. | — |
| Pn14 | 19xx | — | 5 Centimos. Brass. Similar to 1929 issues. | — |

| KM# | Date | Mintage | Identification | Mkt Val |
|---|---|---|---|---|
| Pn13 | 19xx | — | 5 Centimos. Copper Nickel. Similar to 1929 issue | 50.00 |

| KM# | Date | Mintage | Identification | Mkt Val |
|---|---|---|---|---|

| KM# | Date | Mintage | Identification | Mkt Val |
|---|---|---|---|---|
| Pn15 | 19xx | — | 10 Centimos. Copper-Nickel. Similar to 1929 issue. | 60.00 |
| Pn16 | 1944 | — | 25 Centimos. Silver. | — |
| Pn17 | 1944 | — | 25 Centimos. Brass. Polished dies. | — |

## PIEFORTS

| KM# | Date | Mintage | Identification | Mkt Val |
|---|---|---|---|---|
| P5 | 1946 | — | 25 Centimos. Brass. | — |
| P6 | 1946 | — | 25 Centimos. Nickel. | — |

## MINT SETS

| KM# | Date | Mintage | Identification | Issue Price | Mkt Val |
|---|---|---|---|---|---|
| MS1 | 1972 (6) | — | KM#184.4, 185.3-186.3, 187.2, 188.2-189.2 | — | 10.00 |
| MS2 | 1975 (3) | — | KM#203-205 | — | 7.50 |

## PROOF SETS

| KM# | Date | Mintage | Identification | Issue Price | Mkt Val |
|---|---|---|---|---|---|
| PS1 | 1889 (4) | — | KM#128-131 | — | — |
| PS2 | 1937 (3) | — | KM#175-177 | — | 375 |
| PS3 | 1970 (10) | 570 | KM#190-199 | — | 5,350 |
| PS4 | 1970 (5) | 4,650 | KM#190-194 | 52.00 | 125 |
| PS5 | 1970 (5) | 3,000 | KM#195-199 | 832 | 5,225 |
| PS6 | 1974 (2) | 30,000 | KM#200a-201a | 50.00 | 50.00 |
| PS7 | 1975 (3) | — | KM#203-205 | — | 15.00 |
| PS8 | 1976 (5) | 5,000 | KM#184.3, 185.2, 186.4, 188.1, 189.1 | 10.00 | 7.50 |

# CRETE

The island of Crete (Kriti), located 60 miles southeast of the Peloponnesus, was the center of a brilliant civilization that flourished before the advent of Greek culture. After being conquered by the Romans, Byzantines, Moslems and Venetians, Crete became part of the Turkish Empire in 1669. As a consequence of the Greek Revolution of the1820s, it was ceded to Egypt. Egypt returned the island to the Turks in 1840, and they ceded it to Greece in 1913, after the Second Balkan War.

**RULERS**
Prince George, 1898-1906

**MINT MARKS**
A - Paris
(a) - Paris (privy marks only)

## TURKISH EMPIRE

### STANDARD COINAGE

**LEPTON KM# 1.1 Composition:** Bronze

| Date | Mintage | F | VF | XF | Unc | BU |
|---|---|---|---|---|---|---|
| 1901A | 1,711,000 | 3.00 | 7.00 | 16.50 | 45.00 | — |

**LEPTON KM# 1.2 Composition:** Bronze

| Date | Mintage | F | VF | XF | Unc | BU |
|---|---|---|---|---|---|---|
| 1901A | Inc. above | 4.00 | 8.00 | 17.50 | 50.00 | — |

**2 LEPTA KM# 2 Composition:** Bronze

| Date | Mintage | F | VF | XF | Unc | BU |
|---|---|---|---|---|---|---|
| 1901A | 707,000 | 5.00 | 10.00 | 22.50 | 55.00 | — |

**50 LEPTA KM# 6 Weight:** 2.5000 g. **Composition:** 0.8350 Silver .0671 oz. ASW

| Date | Mintage | F | VF | XF | Unc | BU |
|---|---|---|---|---|---|---|
| 1901(a) | 600,000 | 20.00 | 50.00 | 100 | 250 | — |

**DRACHMA KM# 7 Weight:** 5.0000 g. **Composition:** 0.8350 Silver .1342 oz. ASW

| Date | Mintage | F | VF | XF | Unc | BU |
|---|---|---|---|---|---|---|
| 1901(a) | 500,000 | 30.00 | 50.00 | 150 | 500 | — |

**2 DRACHMAI KM# 8 Weight:** 10.0000 g. **Composition:** 0.8350 Silver .2685 oz. ASW

| Date | Mintage | F | VF | XF | Unc | BU |
|---|---|---|---|---|---|---|
| 1901(a) | 175,000 | 50.00 | 100 | 300 | 1,000 | — |

**5 DRACHMAI KM# 9 Weight:** 25.0000 g. **Composition:** 0.9000 Silver .7234 oz. ASW

| Date | Mintage | F | VF | XF | Unc | BU |
|---|---|---|---|---|---|---|
| 1901(a) | 150,000 | 75.00 | 150 | 650 | 3,500 | — |

The Republic of Croatia, (Hrvatska) bordered on the west by the Adriatic Sea and the northeast by Hungary, has an area of 21,829 sq. mi. (56,538 sq. km.) and a population of 4.7 million. Capital: Zagreb.

The country was attached to the Kingdom of Hungary until Dec. 1, 1918, when it joined with the Serbs and Slovenes to form the Kingdom of the Serbs, Croats and Slovenes, which changed its name to the Kingdom of Yugoslavia on Oct. 3, 1929. On April 6, 1941, Hitler, angered by the coup d'etat that overthrew the pro-Nazi regime of regent Prince Paul, sent the Nazi armies crashing across the Yugoslav borders from Germany, Hungary, Romania and Bulgaria. Within a week the army of the Balkan Kingdom was prostrate and broken. Yugoslavia was dismembered to reward Hitler's Balkan allies. Croatia, reconstituted as a nominal kingdom, was given to the administration of an Italian princeling, who wisely decided to remain in Italy. By 1947 it was again totally part of the 6 Yugoslav Socialist Republics.

Croatia proclaimed their independence from Yugoslavia on Oct. 8, 1991.

Local Serbian forces, supported by the Yugoslav Federal Army, had developed a military stronghold and proclaimed an independent "SRPSKEKRAJINA" State in the area around Knin, located in southern Croatia having an estimated population of 350,000 Croat Serbs. In September, 1995, Croat forces overwhelmed Croat Serb forces ending the short life of their proclaimed Serbian Republic.

**MONETARY SYSTEM**

100 Banica = 1 Kuna

The word kunas', derived from the Russian Icunica' which means marten, reflects the use of furs for money in medieval eastern Europe.

# KINGDOM

## DECIMAL COINAGE

**KUNA** **KM# 1** **Composition:** Zinc **Note:** Similar to 2 Kune, KM#2.

| Date | Mintage | F | VF | XF | Unc | BU |
|---|---|---|---|---|---|---|
| 1941 Rare | — | — | — | — | — | — |

**2 KUNE** **KM# 2** **Composition:** Zinc

| Date | Mintage | F | VF | XF | Unc | BU |
|---|---|---|---|---|---|---|
| 1941 | — | 3.00 | 7.00 | 15.00 | 35.00 | — |
| 1941 Proof | — | Value: 80.00 | | | | |

**500 KUNA** **KM# B3** **Weight:** 9.9500 g. **Composition:** 0.9000 Gold .2821 oz. AGW

| Date | Mintage | F | VF | XF | Unc | BU |
|---|---|---|---|---|---|---|
| 1941 | — | — | — | — | 3,000 | — |

**500 KUNA** **KM# A3** **Weight:** 9.9500 g. **Composition:** 0.9000 Gold .2821 oz. AGW

| Date | Mintage | F | VF | XF | Unc | BU |
|---|---|---|---|---|---|---|
| 1941 | 170 | — | 1,750 | 2,250 | 3,000 | — |

# REPUBLIC

## REFORM COINAGE

1000 Dinara = 1 Kuna;
100 Lipa = 1 Kuna

**LIPA** **KM# 3** **Composition:** Aluminum **Reverse:** Ears of corn

| Date | Mintage | F | VF | XF | Unc | BU |
|---|---|---|---|---|---|---|
| 1993 | — | — | — | 0.20 | 0.50 | — |
| 1993 Proof | 17,000 | Value: 1.00 | | | | |
| 1995 With dot | — | — | — | 0.20 | 0.50 | — |
| 1995 With dot, proof | 4,000 | Value: 1.00 | | | | |
| 1999 | — | — | — | 0.20 | 0.50 | — |

**LIPA** **KM# 3a** **Composition:** Silver **Reverse:** Ears of corn

| Date | Mintage | F | VF | XF | Unc | BU |
|---|---|---|---|---|---|---|
| 1993 Proof, rare | 10 | — | — | — | — | — |

**LIPA** **KM# 3b** **Composition:** Gold **Reverse:** Ears of corn

| Date | Mintage | F | VF | XF | Unc | BU |
|---|---|---|---|---|---|---|
| 1993 Proof, rare | 5 | — | — | — | — | — |

**LIPA** **KM# 12** **Composition:** Aluminum **Reverse:** Ears of corn **Rev. Legend:** ZEA MAYS

| Date | Mintage | F | VF | XF | Unc | BU |
|---|---|---|---|---|---|---|
| 1994 | — | — | — | 0.30 | 0.60 | — |
| 1994 Proof | 4,000 | Value: 1.00 | | | | |
| 1996 | — | — | — | 0.30 | 0.60 | — |
| 1996 Proof | 5,000 | Value: 1.00 | | | | |

**LIPA** **KM# 13** **Composition:** Aluminum **Reverse:** Ears of corn **Rev. Legend:** FAO

| Date | Mintage | F | VF | XF | Unc | BU |
|---|---|---|---|---|---|---|
| ND(1995) | 1,000,000 | — | — | 0.30 | 1.00 | — |
| ND(1995) Proof | 5,000 | Value: 1.50 | | | | |

**2 LIPE** **KM# 4** **Composition:** Aluminum **Reverse:** Grape vine

| Date | Mintage | F | VF | XF | Unc | BU |
|---|---|---|---|---|---|---|
| 1993 | — | — | — | 0.40 | 1.00 | — |
| 1993 Proof | 17,000 | Value: 2.00 | | | | |
| 1995 With dot | — | — | — | 0.40 | 1.00 | — |
| 1995 With dot, proof | 4,000 | Value: 2.00 | | | | |
| 1999 | — | — | — | 0.40 | 1.00 | — |

**2 LIPE** **KM# 4a** **Composition:** Silver **Reverse:** Grape vine

| Date | Mintage | F | VF | XF | Unc | BU |
|---|---|---|---|---|---|---|
| 1993 Proof, rare | 10 | — | — | — | — | — |

**2 LIPE** **KM# 4b** **Composition:** Gold **Reverse:** Grape vine

| Date | Mintage | F | VF | XF | Unc | BU |
|---|---|---|---|---|---|---|
| 1993 Proof, rare | 5 | — | — | — | — | — |

**2 LIPE** **KM# 14** **Composition:** Aluminum **Reverse:** Grape vine **Rev. Legend:** VIIIS VINIFERA

| Date | Mintage | F | VF | XF | Unc | BU |
|---|---|---|---|---|---|---|
| 1994 | — | — | — | 0.50 | 1.50 | — |
| 1994 Proof | 4,000 | Value: 2.00 | | | | |
| 1996 | — | — | — | 0.50 | 1.50 | — |
| 1996 Proof | 5,000 | Value: 2.00 | | | | |

**2 LIPE** **KM# 36** **Composition:** Aluminum **Subject:** Olympics **Obverse:** Denomination **Reverse:** Olympic rings, flame

| Date | Mintage | F | VF | XF | Unc | BU |
|---|---|---|---|---|---|---|
| 1996 | — | — | — | 0.30 | 0.60 | — |
| 1996 Proof | 5,000 | Value: 1.00 | | | | |

**5 LIPA** **KM# 5** **Composition:** Brass Plated Steel **Reverse:** Oak leaves

| Date | Mintage | F | VF | XF | Unc | BU |
|---|---|---|---|---|---|---|
| 1993 | — | — | — | 0.40 | 1.50 | — |
| 1993 Proof | 17,000 | Value: 2.00 | | | | |
| 1995 With dot | — | — | — | 0.40 | 1.00 | — |
| 1995 Proof | 4,000 | Value: 3.00 | | | | |
| 1999 | — | — | — | 0.40 | 1.00 | — |

**5 LIPA** **KM# 5a** **Composition:** Silver **Reverse:** Oak leaves

| Date | Mintage | F | VF | XF | Unc | BU |
|---|---|---|---|---|---|---|
| 1993 Proof, rare | 10 | — | — | — | — | — |

**5 LIPA** **KM# 5b** **Composition:** Gold **Reverse:** Oak leaves

| Date | Mintage | F | VF | XF | Unc | BU |
|---|---|---|---|---|---|---|
| 1993 Proof, rare | 5 | — | — | — | — | — |

**5 LIPA** **KM# 15** **Composition:** Brass Plated Steel **Reverse:** Oak leaves **Rev. Legend:** QUERCUS ROBUR

| Date | Mintage | F | VF | XF | Unc | BU |
|---|---|---|---|---|---|---|
| 1994 | — | — | — | 0.30 | 1.00 | — |
| 1994 Proof | 4,000 | Value: 2.00 | | | | |
| 1996 | — | — | — | 0.30 | 1.00 | — |
| 1996 Proof | 5,000 | Value: 2.50 | | | | |
| 1997 | — | — | — | 0.30 | 1.00 | — |

**5 LIPA** **KM# 37** **Composition:** Brass Plated Steel **Subject:** Olympics **Obverse:** Denomination **Reverse:** Olympic rings, flame

| Date | Mintage | F | VF | XF | Unc | BU |
|---|---|---|---|---|---|---|
| 1996 | — | — | — | 0.60 | 1.20 | — |
| 1996 Proof | 5,000 | Value: 2.00 | | | | |

**10 LIPA** **KM# 6** **Composition:** Brass Plated Steel **Reverse:** Tobacco plant

| Date | Mintage | F | VF | XF | Unc | BU |
|---|---|---|---|---|---|---|
| 1993 | — | — | — | 0.40 | 1.50 | — |
| 1993 Proof | 17,000 | Value: 3.00 | | | | |
| 1995 With dot | — | — | — | 0.40 | 1.50 | — |
| 1995 With dot, proof | 4,000 | Value: 4.00 | | | | |
| 1997 | — | — | — | 0.40 | 1.50 | — |
| 1999 | — | — | — | 0.40 | 1.50 | — |

**10 LIPA** **KM# 6a** **Composition:** Silver **Reverse:** Tobacco plant

| Date | Mintage | F | VF | XF | Unc | BU |
|---|---|---|---|---|---|---|
| 1993 Proof, rare | 10 | — | — | — | — | — |

**10 LIPA** **KM# 6b** **Composition:** Gold **Reverse:** Oak leaves

| Date | Mintage | F | VF | XF | Unc | BU |
|---|---|---|---|---|---|---|
| 1993 Proof, rare | 5 | — | — | — | — | — |

**10 LIPA** **KM# 16** **Composition:** Brass Plated Steel **Reverse:** Tobacco plant **Rev. Legend:** NICOLIANA TABAUUM

| Date | Mintage | F | VF | XF | Unc | BU |
|---|---|---|---|---|---|---|
| 1994 | — | — | — | 0.35 | 1.50 | — |
| 1994 Proof | 4,000 | Value: 4.00 | | | | |
| 1996 | — | — | — | 0.30 | 1.50 | — |
| 1996 Proof | 5,000 | Value: 3.50 | | | | |

**10 LIPA** **KM# 38** **Composition:** Brass **Subject:** 50th Anniversary - UN **Obverse:** Denomination **Reverse:** UN logo

| Date | Mintage | F | VF | XF | Unc | BU |
|---|---|---|---|---|---|---|
| ND(1995) | — | — | — | 0.50 | 1.00 | — |
| ND(1995) | 5,000 | Value: 4.00 | | | | |

**20 LIPA** **KM# 7** **Composition:** Nickel Plated Steel **Reverse:** Olive branch

| Date | Mintage | F | VF | XF | Unc | BU |
|---|---|---|---|---|---|---|
| 1993 | — | — | — | 0.50 | 1.50 | — |
| 1993 Proof | 17,000 | Value: 3.00 | | | | |
| 1995 With dot | — | — | — | 0.50 | 1.50 | — |
| 1995 Proof | 4,000 | Value: 4.00 | | | | |
| 1996 | — | — | — | 0.45 | 1.50 | — |
| 2001 | — | — | — | 0.45 | 1.50 | — |

**20 LIPA** **KM# 7a** **Composition:** Silver **Reverse:** Olive branch

| Date | Mintage | F | VF | XF | Unc | BU |
|---|---|---|---|---|---|---|
| 1993 Proof, rare | 10 | — | — | — | — | — |

**20 LIPA** **KM# 7b** **Composition:** Gold **Reverse:** Olive branch

| Date | Mintage | F | VF | XF | Unc | BU |
|---|---|---|---|---|---|---|
| 1993 Proof, rare | 5 | — | — | — | — | — |

**20 LIPA** **KM# 17** **Composition:** Nickel Plated Steel **Reverse:** Olive branch **Rev. Legend:** OLEA EUROPAEA

| Date | Mintage | F | VF | XF | Unc | BU |
|---|---|---|---|---|---|---|
| 1994 | — | — | — | 0.50 | 1.50 | — |
| 1994 Proof | 4,000 | Value: 3.00 | | | | |
| 1996 | — | — | — | 0.45 | 1.50 | — |
| 1996 Proof | 5,000 | Value: 4.00 | | | | |

**20 LIPA** **KM# 18** **Composition:** Nickel Plated Steel **Reverse:** Olive branch **Rev. Legend:** FAO

| Date | Mintage | F | VF | XF | Unc | BU |
|---|---|---|---|---|---|---|
| ND(1995) | 1,000,000 | — | — | 0.50 | 1.50 | — |
| ND(1995) Proof | 5,000 | Value: 4.50 | | | | |

**50 LIPA** **KM# 8** **Composition:** Nickel Plated Steel **Reverse:** Flowers

| Date | Mintage | F | VF | XF | Unc | BU |
|---|---|---|---|---|---|---|
| 1993 | — | — | — | 0.60 | 1.50 | — |
| 1993 Proof | 17,000 | Value: 4.00 | | | | |
| 1995 With dot | — | — | — | 0.60 | 1.50 | — |
| 1995 With dot, proof | 4,000 | Value: 4.50 | | | | |
| 1999 | — | — | — | 0.60 | 1.50 | — |

**50 LIPA** **KM# 8a** **Composition:** Silver **Reverse:** Flowers

| Date | Mintage | F | VF | XF | Unc | BU |
|---|---|---|---|---|---|---|
| 1993 Proof, rare | 10 | — | — | — | — | — |

**50 LIPA** **KM# 8b** **Composition:** Gold **Reverse:** Flowers

| Date | Mintage | F | VF | XF | Unc | BU |
|---|---|---|---|---|---|---|
| 1993 Proof, rare | 5 | — | — | — | — | — |

**50 LIPA** **KM# 19** **Composition:** Nickel Plated Steel **Reverse:** Flowers **Rev. Legend:** DEGENIA VELEBITICA

| Date | Mintage | F | VF | XF | Unc | BU |
|---|---|---|---|---|---|---|
| 1994 | — | — | — | 0.60 | 1.60 | — |
| 1994 Proof | 4,000 | Value: 4.00 | | | | |
| 1996 | — | — | — | 0.60 | 1.50 | — |
| 1996 Proof | 5,000 | Value: 4.00 | | | | |

**50 LIPA** **KM# 39** **Composition:** Nickel Plated Steel **Subject:** European soccer **Obverse:** Denomination **Reverse:** Checkered shield, soccer ball

| Date | Mintage | F | VF | XF | Unc | BU |
|---|---|---|---|---|---|---|
| 1996 | — | — | — | 0.40 | 1.50 | — |
| 1996 Proof | 5,000 | Value: 4.00 | | | | |

**KUNA** **KM# 9.1** **Composition:** Copper Nickel **Reverse:** Nightingale

| Date | Mintage | F | VF | XF | Unc | BU |
|---|---|---|---|---|---|---|
| 1993 | — | — | — | 0.75 | 1.50 | — |
| 1993 Proof | 17,000 | Value: 3.00 | | | | |
| 1995 With dot | — | — | — | 0.75 | 1.50 | — |
| 1995 With dot, proof | 5,000 | Value: 3.50 | | | | |

**KUNA** **KM# 9.1a** **Composition:** Silver **Reverse:** Nightingale

| Date | Mintage | F | VF | XF | Unc | BU |
|---|---|---|---|---|---|---|
| 1993 Proof, rare | 10 | — | — | — | — | — |

**KUNA** **KM# 9.1b** **Composition:** Gold **Reverse:** Nightingale

| Date | Mintage | F | VF | XF | Unc | BU |
|---|---|---|---|---|---|---|
| 1993 Proof, rare | 5 | — | — | — | — | — |

**KUNA** **KM# 20** **Composition:** Copper Nickel **Reverse:** Nightingale **Rev. Legend:** LUSCINNIA MEGARHYNCHOS

| Date | Mintage | F | VF | XF | Unc | BU |
|---|---|---|---|---|---|---|
| 1994 | — | — | — | 0.50 | 1.75 | — |
| 1994 Proof | 4,000 | Value: 4.00 | | | | |
| 1996 | — | — | — | 0.50 | 1.50 | — |
| 1996 Proof | 5,000 | Value: 3.00 | | | | |
| 1997 | — | — | — | 0.50 | 1.50 | — |
| 1998 | — | — | — | 0.50 | 1.50 | — |

**KUNA** **KM# 40** **Composition:** Copper-Nickel **Subject:** Olympics **Obverse:** Denomination **Reverse:** Olympic flame, rings

| Date | Mintage | F | VF | XF | Unc | BU |
|---|---|---|---|---|---|---|
| 1996 | — | — | — | 0.40 | 1.50 | — |
| 1996 Proof | 5,000 | Value: 3.00 | | | | |

**KUNA** **KM# 9.2** **Weight:** 4.9300 g. **Composition:** Copper Nickel **Obverse:** Denomination **Reverse:** "1994" above bird in field **Edge:** Reeded **Size:** 22.5 mm.

| Date | Mintage | F | VF | XF | Unc | BU |
|---|---|---|---|---|---|---|
| 1999 | — | — | — | 0.75 | 1.50 | — |

**2 KUNE** **KM# 10** **Composition:** Copper-Nickel **Reverse:** Tuna

| Date | Mintage | F | VF | XF | Unc | BU |
|---|---|---|---|---|---|---|
| 1993 | — | — | — | 1.00 | 2.00 | — |
| 1993 Proof | 17,000 | Value: 4.50 | | | | |
| 1995 With dot | — | — | — | 1.00 | 2.00 | — |
| 1995 With dot, proof | 4,000 | Value: 5.50 | | | | |
| 1997 | — | — | — | 1.00 | 2.00 | — |

**2 KUNE** **KM# 10a** **Composition:** Silver **Reverse:** Tuna

| Date | Mintage | F | VF | XF | Unc | BU |
|---|---|---|---|---|---|---|
| 1993 Proof, rare | 10 | — | — | — | — | — |

**2 KUNE** **KM# 10b** **Composition:** Gold **Reverse:** Tuna

| Date | Mintage | F | VF | XF | Unc | BU |
|---|---|---|---|---|---|---|
| 1993 Proof, rare | 5 | — | — | — | — | — |

**2 KUNE** **KM# 21** **Composition:** Copper Nickel **Reverse:** Tuna **Rev. Legend:** THUNNUS - THYNNUS

| Date | Mintage | F | VF | XF | Unc | BU |
|---|---|---|---|---|---|---|
| 1994 | 500,000 | — | — | 0.75 | 2.00 | — |
| 1994 Proof | 4,000 | Value: 5.00 | | | | |
| 1996 | — | — | — | 0.70 | 2.00 | — |
| 1996 Proof | 5,000 | Value: 4.50 | | | | |

**2 KUNE** **KM# 22** **Composition:** Copper Nickel **Reverse:** Tuna **Rev. Legend:** FAO

| Date | Mintage | F | VF | XF | Unc | BU |
|---|---|---|---|---|---|---|
| ND(1995) | — | — | — | 0.60 | 2.00 | — |
| ND(1995) Proof | 5,000 | Value: 5.50 | | | | |

**5 KUNA** KM# 11 **Composition:** Copper Nickel **Reverse:** Bear

| Date | Mintage | F | VF | XF | Unc | BU |
|---|---|---|---|---|---|---|
| 1993 | — | — | — | 1.50 | 3.00 | — |
| 1993 Proof | 17,000 | Value: 6.50 | | | | |
| 1995 With dot | — | — | — | 1.50 | 3.00 | — |
| 1995 With dot, proof | 4,000 | Value: 7.00 | | | | |

**5 KUNA** KM# 11a **Composition:** Silver **Reverse:** Bear

| Date | Mintage | F | VF | XF | Unc | BU |
|---|---|---|---|---|---|---|
| 1993 Proof, rare | 10 | — | — | — | — | — |

**5 KUNA** KM# 11b **Composition:** Gold **Reverse:** Bear

| Date | Mintage | F | VF | XF | Unc | BU |
|---|---|---|---|---|---|---|
| 1993 Proof, rare | 5 | — | — | — | — | — |

**5 KUNA** KM# 23 **Composition:** Copper Nickel **Reverse:** Bear **Rev. Legend:** URSUS ARCTOS

| Date | Mintage | F | VF | XF | Unc | BU |
|---|---|---|---|---|---|---|
| 1994 | — | — | — | 1.00 | 3.50 | — |
| 1994 Proof | 4,000 | Value: 7.50 | | | | |
| 1996 | — | — | — | 1.00 | 3.50 | — |
| 1996 Proof | 5,000 | Value: 7.50 | | | | |

**5 KUNA** KM# 24a **Composition:** Silver **Subject:** 500th Anniversary - Senj

| Date | Mintage | F | VF | XF | Unc | BU |
|---|---|---|---|---|---|---|
| 1994 Proof | 500 | Value: 270 | | | | |

**5 KUNA** KM# 24b **Composition:** Gold **Subject:** 500th Anniversary - Senj

| Date | Mintage | F | VF | XF | Unc | BU |
|---|---|---|---|---|---|---|
| 1994 Proof | 250 | Value: 390 | | | | |

**5 KUNA** KM# 24 **Composition:** Copper Nickel **Subject:** 500th Anniversary - Senj

| Date | Mintage | F | VF | XF | Unc | BU |
|---|---|---|---|---|---|---|
| 1994 | — | — | — | — | 3.50 | — |
| 1994 Proof | 5,000 | Value: 8.00 | | | | |

**25 KUNA** KM# 47 **Ring Composition:** Copper Nickel **Center Composition:** Brass **Subject:** Danube Border Region **Obverse:** Denomination in inner circle **Reverse:** Regional map

| Date | Mintage | F | VF | XF | Unc | BU |
|---|---|---|---|---|---|---|
| 1997 | — | — | — | — | 9.00 | — |

**25 KUNA** KM# 48 **Ring Composition:** Copper Nickel **Center Composition:** Brass **Subject:** 5th Anniversary - UN Membership **Obverse:** National arms **Reverse:** UN emblem

| Date | Mintage | F | VF | XF | Unc | BU |
|---|---|---|---|---|---|---|
| 1997 | — | — | — | — | 8.50 | — |

**25 KUNA** KM# 49 **Ring Composition:** Copper Nickel **Center Composition:** Brass **Subject:** First Croatian Esperanto Congress **Obverse:** Denomination **Reverse:** Logo

| Date | Mintage | F | VF | XF | Unc | BU |
|---|---|---|---|---|---|---|
| 1997 | — | — | — | — | 10.00 | — |

**25 KUNA** KM# 63 **Ring Composition:** Copper Nickel **Center Composition:** Brass **Subject:** Lisbon Expo **Obverse:** Denomination **Reverse:** Sailboat

| Date | Mintage | F | VF | XF | Unc | BU |
|---|---|---|---|---|---|---|
| 1998 | — | — | — | — | 10.00 | — |

**25 KUNA** KM# 64 **Ring Composition:** Copper Nickel **Center Weight:** 12.5600 g. **Center Composition:** Brass **Subject:** European Union **Obverse:** Denomination **Reverse:** 12 stars on a large "E" **Edge:** Plain **Size:** 31 mm. **Note:** 12-sided.

| Date | Mintage | F | VF | XF | Unc | BU |
|---|---|---|---|---|---|---|
| 1999 | — | — | — | — | 10.00 | — |

**25 KUNA** KM# 65 **Ring Composition:** Copper-Nickel **Center Weight:** 12.6500 g. **Center Composition:** Brass **Obverse:** Denomination. **Reverse:** Human fetus. **Edge:** Plain, 12-sided. **Size:** 31 mm.

| Date | Mintage | F | VF | XF | Unc | BU |
|---|---|---|---|---|---|---|
| 2000 | — | — | — | — | 10.00 | — |

**100 KUNA** KM# 25.1 **Weight:** 15.0000 g. **Composition:** Silver **Subject:** 900th Anniversary - St. Blaza Church **Reverse:** Altar at St. Blaza

| Date | Mintage | F | VF | XF | Unc | BU |
|---|---|---|---|---|---|---|
| ND(1994) Proof | 3,000 | Value: 47.50 | | | | |

**100 KUNA** KM# 25.2 **Weight:** 15.0000 g. **Composition:** Silver **Subject:** 900th Anniversary - St. Blaza Church **Obverse:** Series II mark added **Reverse:** Altar at St. Blaza

| Date | Mintage | F | VF | XF | Unc | BU |
|---|---|---|---|---|---|---|
| ND(1994) Proof | 1,000 | Value: 75.00 | | | | |

**100 KUNA** KM# 26 **Weight:** 33.6300 g. **Composition:** Silver **Subject:** Pope John Paul II

| Date | Mintage | F | VF | XF | Unc | BU |
|---|---|---|---|---|---|---|
| 1994 Proof | 10,000 | Value: 65.00 | | | | |

**100 KUNA** KM# 27 **Weight:** 20.0000 g. **Composition:** 0.9250 Silver .5947 oz. ASW **Subject:** 5th Anniversary of Independence

| Date | Mintage | F | VF | XF | Unc | BU |
|---|---|---|---|---|---|---|
| ND(1995) Proof | 6,000 | Value: 35.00 | | | | |

**100 KUNA** KM# 50 **Weight:** 20.0000 g. **Composition:** 0.9250 Silver .5947 oz. ASW **Subject:** City of Split **Obverse:** Towered building **Reverse:** Ancient depiction of king on throne

| Date | Mintage | F | VF | XF | Unc | BU |
|---|---|---|---|---|---|---|
| ND(1995) Proof | 5,000 | Value: 32.00 | | | | |

**100 KUNA** KM# 41 **Weight:** 20.0000 g. **Composition:** 0.9250 Silver .5947 oz. ASW **Subject:** Olympics **Obverse:** Sailboat racing **Reverse:** Wheelchair-bound javelin thrower

| Date | Mintage | F | VF | XF | Unc | BU |
|---|---|---|---|---|---|---|
| 1996 Proof | 2,000 | Value: 40.00 | | | | |

**100 KUNA** KM# 42 **Weight:** 20.0000 g. **Composition:** 0.9250 Silver .5947 oz. ASW **Subject:** Olympics **Obverse:** Rowing **Reverse:** Water-polo player

| Date | Mintage | F | VF | XF | Unc | BU |
|---|---|---|---|---|---|---|
| 1996 Proof | 2,000 | Value: 40.00 | | | | |

**150 KUNA** KM# 28 **Weight:** 24.0000 g. **Composition:** 0.9250 Silver .7136 oz. ASW **Subject:** 5th Anniversary of Independence

| Date | Mintage | F | VF | XF | Unc | BU |
|---|---|---|---|---|---|---|
| 1995 Proof | 5,000 | Value: 42.50 | | | | |

**150 KUNA** KM# 43 **Weight:** 24.0000 g. **Composition:** 0.9250 Silver .7136 oz. ASW **Subject:** Olympics **Obverse:** Gymnast **Reverse:** Basketball players

| Date | Mintage | F | VF | XF | Unc | BU |
|---|---|---|---|---|---|---|
| 1996 Proof | 2,000 | Value: 42.50 | | | | |

**150 KUNA** KM# 44 **Weight:** 24.0000 g. **Composition:** 0.9250 Silver .7136 oz. ASW **Subject:** Olympics **Obverse:** Table tennis and paddle **Reverse:** Marksmanship eye design

| Date | Mintage | F | VF | XF | Unc | BU |
|---|---|---|---|---|---|---|
| 1996 | 2,000 | Value: 42.50 | | | | |

**150 KUNA** KM# 56 **Weight:** 24.0000 g. **Composition:** 0.9250 Silver .7136 oz. ASW **Subject:** 800th Anniversary - City of Osijek **Obverse:** National arms above denomination **Reverse:** City view

| Date | Mintage | F | VF | XF | Unc | BU |
|---|---|---|---|---|---|---|
| ND(1996) Proof | 1,000 | Value: 40.00 | | | | |

**150 KUNA** KM# 59 **Weight:** 24.0000 g. **Composition:** 0.9250 Silver .7136 oz. ASW **Subject:** President Tudman **Obverse:** Denomination above national arms **Reverse:** Portrait

| Date | Mintage | F | VF | XF | Unc | BU |
|---|---|---|---|---|---|---|
| 1997 Proof | 10,000 | Value: 40.00 | | | | |

**200 KUNA** KM# 29.1 **Weight:** 33.6300 g. **Composition:** 0.9250 Silver .9999 oz. ASW **Obverse:** St. Marka Church **Reverse:** Portal of St. Marka Church

| Date | Mintage | F | VF | XF | Unc | BU |
|---|---|---|---|---|---|---|
| ND(1994) Proof | 3,000 | Value: 75.00 | | | | |

**200 KUNA** KM# 29.2 **Weight:** 33.6300 g. **Composition:** 0.9250 Silver .9999 oz. ASW **Obverse:** St. Marka Church, series II mark added **Reverse:** Portal of St. Marka Church

| Date | Mintage | F | VF | XF | Unc | BU |
|---|---|---|---|---|---|---|
| ND(1994) Proof | 1,000 | Value: 90.00 | | | | |

**200 KUNA** KM# 30 **Weight:** 33.6300 g. **Composition:** 0.9250 Silver .9999 oz. ASW **Subject:** 5th Anniversary of Independence

| Date | Mintage | F | VF | XF | Unc | BU |
|---|---|---|---|---|---|---|
| ND(1995) Proof | 4,000 | Value: 75.00 | | | | |

**200 KUNA** KM# 51 **Weight:** 33.6300 g. **Composition:** 0.9250 Silver .9999 oz. ASW **Subject:** Spalatum **Obverse:** Diocletian's palace **Reverse:** Sarcophagus

| Date | Mintage | F | VF | XF | Unc | BU |
|---|---|---|---|---|---|---|
| ND(1995) Proof | 5,000 | Value: 45.00 | | | | |

**200 KUNA** KM# 45 **Weight:** 33.6300 g. **Composition:** 0.9250 Silver .9999 oz. ASW **Subject:** Olympics **Obverse:** High jumper **Reverse:** Tennis player

| Date | Mintage | F | VF | XF | Unc | BU |
|---|---|---|---|---|---|---|
| ND Proof | 2,000 | Value: 45.00 | | | | |

**200 KUNA** KM# 46 **Weight:** 33.6300 g. **Composition:** 0.9250 Silver .9999 oz. ASW **Subject:** Olympics **Obverse:** Diving swimmers **Reverse:** Basketball game

| Date | Mintage | F | VF | XF | Unc | BU |
|---|---|---|---|---|---|---|
| 1996 Proof | 2,000 | Value: 45.00 | | | | |

**200 KUNA** KM# 54 **Weight:** 33.6300 g. **Composition:** 0.9250 Silver .9999 oz. ASW **Subject:** University in Zadar **Obverse:** Circle of arches **Reverse:** Saint reading

| Date | Mintage | F | VF | XF | Unc | BU |
|---|---|---|---|---|---|---|
| ND(1996) Proof | 1,000 | Value: 55.00 | | | | |

**200 KUNA** KM# 57 **Weight:** 33.6300 g. **Composition:** 0.9250 Silver .9999 oz. ASW **Subject:** 500th Anniversary - City of Osijek **Obverse:** National arms above denomination **Reverse:** City view

| Date | Mintage | F | VF | XF | Unc | BU |
|---|---|---|---|---|---|---|
| ND(1996) Proof | 1,000 | Value: 52.00 | | | | |

**200 KUNA** KM# 60 **Weight:** 33.6300 g. **Composition:** 0.9250 Silver .9999 oz. ASW **Subject:** President Tudman **Obverse:** Denomination above national arms **Reverse:** Portrait

| Date | Mintage | F | VF | XF | Unc | BU |
|---|---|---|---|---|---|---|
| 1997 Proof | 5,000 | Value: 45.00 | | | | |

**500 KUNA** KM# 31.1 **Weight:** 3.5000 g. **Composition:** 0.9860 Gold .1109 oz. AGW **Obverse:** Izborna Cathedral

| Date | Mintage | F | VF | XF | Unc | BU |
|---|---|---|---|---|---|---|
| 1994 Proof | 1,000 | Value: 200 | | | | |

**500 KUNA** KM# 31.2 **Weight:** 3.5000 g. **Composition:** 0.9860 Gold .1109 oz. AGW **Obverse:** Izborna Cathedral, series II added

| Date | Mintage | F | VF | XF | Unc | BU |
|---|---|---|---|---|---|---|
| 1994 Proof | 1,000 | Value: 175 | | | | |

**500 KUNA** KM# 32 **Weight:** 3.5000 g. **Composition:** 0.9860 Gold .1109 oz. AGW **Subject:** 5th Anniversary of Independence

| Date | Mintage | F | VF | XF | Unc | BU |
|---|---|---|---|---|---|---|
| 1995 Proof | 4,000 | Value: 175 | | | | |

**500 KUNA** KM# 52 **Weight:** 3.5000 g. **Composition:** 0.9860 Gold .1109 oz. AGW **Subject:** City of Split **Obverse:** Towered building **Reverse:** Ancient depiction of king on throne

| Date | Mintage | F | VF | XF | Unc | BU |
|---|---|---|---|---|---|---|
| ND(1995) Proof | 6,000 | Value: 150 | | | | |

**500 KUNA** KM# 55 **Weight:** 3.5000 g. **Composition:** 0.9860 Gold .1109 oz. AGW **Subject:** University of Zadar **Obverse:** Circle of arches **Reverse:** Saint reading

| Date | Mintage | F | VF | XF | Unc | BU |
|---|---|---|---|---|---|---|
| ND(1996) Proof | 1,000 | Value: 175 | | | | |

**500 KUNA** KM# 58 **Weight:** 3.5000 g. **Composition:** 0.9860 Gold .1109 oz. AGW **Subject:** 800th Anniversary - City of Osijek **Obverse:** National arms **Reverse:** City view

| Date | Mintage | F | VF | XF | Unc | BU |
|---|---|---|---|---|---|---|
| ND(1996) Proof | 1,000 | Value: 175 | | | | |

**1000 KUNA** KM# 33 **Weight:** 7.0000 g. **Composition:** 0.9860 Gold .2218 oz. AGW **Subject:** Pope John Paul II

| Date | Mintage | F | VF | XF | Unc | BU |
|---|---|---|---|---|---|---|
| 1994 Proof | 4,000 | Value: 285 | | | | |

**1000 KUNA** KM# 34 **Weight:** 7.0000 g. **Composition:** 0.9860 Gold .2218 oz. AGW **Subject:** 5th Anniversary of Independence

| Date | Mintage | F | VF | XF | Unc | BU |
|---|---|---|---|---|---|---|
| ND(1995) Proof | 3,000 | Value: 285 | | | | |

**1000 KUNA** KM# 53 **Weight:** 7.0000 g. **Composition:** 0.9860 Gold .2218 oz. AGW **Subject:** Spalatum **Obverse:** Diocletian's palace **Reverse:** Sarcophagus

| Date | Mintage | F | VF | XF | Unc | BU |
|---|---|---|---|---|---|---|
| ND(1995) Proof | 3,000 | Value: 285 | | | | |

## TRADE COINAGE

**DUCAT** KM# 35 **Weight:** 3.5000 g. **Composition:** 0.9860 Gold .1109 oz. AGW **Reverse:** Ruder Boskovic

| Date | Mintage | F | VF | XF | Unc | BU |
|---|---|---|---|---|---|---|
| 1994 Proof | 5,000 | Value: 150 | | | | |

**DUCAT** KM# 62 **Weight:** 3.5000 g. **Composition:** 0.9860 Gold .1109 oz. AGW **Subject:** Liberation of Knin **Obverse:** Crowned arms **Reverse:** Regional view

| Date | Mintage | F | VF | XF | Unc | BU |
|---|---|---|---|---|---|---|
| ND(1995) | 3,000 | — | — | — | 145 | — |

## PATTERNS

Including off metal strikes

| KM# | Date | Mintage | Identification | Mkt Val |
|---|---|---|---|---|
| Pn5 | 1934 | — | 5 Kuna. Bronze. | 350 |
| Pn6 | 1934 | — | 5 Kuna. Copper Nickel. | 400 |
| Pn7 | 1934 | — | 5 Kuna. 0.9000 Silver. | 450 |
| Pn8 | 1934 | — | 5 Kuna. Zinc. | — |
| Pn9 | 1941 | — | 25 Banica. Zinc. With initials. 16 or 17 mm. | — |
| Pn10 | 1941 | — | 25 Banica. Zinc. Without initials. 16 or 17 mm. | — |
| Pn11 | 1941 | — | 25 Banica. Nickel. 16 or 17 mm. | — |
| Pn12 | 1941 | — | 25 Banica. Gold. 16 or 17 mm. | 3,500 |
| Pn13 | 1941 | — | 50 Banica. Nickel. | — |
| Pn14 | 1941 | — | 50 Banica. Zinc. | — |
| Pn15 | 1941 | — | 50 Banica. Silver. | — |
| Pn16 | 1941 | — | 50 Banica. Gold. | 4,500 |
| Pn17 | 1941 | — | Kuna. Zinc. | — |
| Pn18 | 1941 | — | Kuna. Copper. | — |
| Pn19 | 1941 | — | Kuna. Aluminum. | 175 |
| Pn20 | 1941 | — | Kuna. Nickel. | — |
| Pn21 | 1941 | — | Kuna. Silver. | 450 |
| Pn22 | 1941 | — | Kuna. Gold. | 3,500 |
| Pn23 | 1941 | — | Kuna. Silver. 4.3800 g. 20 mm. Without undulating background. | — |
| Pn24 | 1941 | — | 2 Kune. Aluminum. | — |
| Pn25 | 1941 | — | 2 Kune. Nickel. | — |
| Pn26 | 1941 | — | 2 Kune. Silver. 4.8900 g. 22 mm. | — |
| Pn27 | 1941 | — | 2 Kune. Gold. | 4,500 |
| Pn28 | 1941 | — | 10 Kuna. Similar to Pn 19. 10 Kuna above shield within wheat border. Reported, not confirmed. | — |
| Pn29 | 1941 | — | 500 Kuna. Aluminum. Pn 26. Similar to B3. | — |
| Pn30 | 1941 | — | 500 Kuna. Copper Nickel. Pn 26. Similar to B3. | — |
| Pn31 | 1941 | — | 500 Kuna. Aluminum. Chain. | — |
| Pn32 | 1941 | — | 500 Kuna. Aluminum-Bronze. | — |
| Pn33 | 1941 | — | 500 Kuna. Copper. | — |
| Pn34 | 1941 | — | 500 Kuna. Copper Nickel. | — |

| KM# | Date | Mintage | Identification | Mkt Val |
|---|---|---|---|---|
| Pn35 | 1941 | — | 500 Kuna. Silver. | — |
| Pn36 | 1941 | — | 500 Kuna. Aluminum. 1.6700 g. 22 mm. Wheat chain. Similar to KMA3. | 600 |
| Pn37 | 1941 | — | 500 Kuna. Gold. 27 mm. Chain. KMA3. | — |
| Pn38 | 1941 | — | 500 Kuna. Nickel. 22 mm. KMA3. | — |
| Pn39 | 1941 | — | 500 Kuna. Aluminum. KMA3. | — |
| Pn40 | 1941 | — | 500 Kuna. Brass. 7.1100 g. 23 mm. KMA3. | 400 |
| Pn41 | 1943 | — | 5 Kuna. | — |
| Pn42 | 1943 | — | 10 Kuna. | — |

## MINT SETS

| KM# | Date | Mintage | Identification | Issue Price | Mkt Val |
|---|---|---|---|---|---|
| MS1 | 1993 (9) | 50,000 | KM3-11 | 8.00 | 14.00 |

## PROOF SETS

| KM# | Date | Mintage | Identification | Issue Price | Mkt Val |
|---|---|---|---|---|---|
| PS1 | 1993 (9) | 17,000 | KM3-11 | 15.20 | 28.50 |
| PS2 | 1993 (9) | 10 | KM3a-11a, rare | — | — |
| PS3 | 1993 (9) | 5 | KM3b-11b, rare | — | — |
| PS7 | 1994 (2) | 1,000 | KM26, 33 | 240 | 350 |
| PS8 | ND (1994) (3) | 250 | KM25.1, 29.1, 31.1 | 154 | 325 |
| PS10 | 1994-95 (2) | 1,000 | KM22, 25.2 | — | 85.00 |
| PS11 | 1994-95 (4) | — | KM13, 18, 22, 24 | — | 40.00 |
| PS12 | 1994-96 (9) | 5,000 | KM13, 18, 22, 24, 36-40 | 8.00 | 33.50 |
| PS4 | 1994 (9) | 4,000 | KM12, 14-17, 19-21, 23 | 15.20 | 32.50 |
| PS9 | ND (1994) (3) | 500 | KM25.2, 29.2, 31.2 | 154 | 340 |
| PS5 | 1994 (3) | 500 | KM21, 23, 24a | — | 280 |
| PS6 | 1994 (3) | 250 | KM21, 23, 24b | — | 400 |
| PS14 | 1995 (5) | — | KM27, 28, 30, 32, 34 | — | 550 |
| PS20 | ND (1995) (5) | 1,000 | KM 27, 28, 30, 32, 34 | 406 | 620 |
| PS21 | ND (1995) (3) | 2,000 | KM 27, 30, 34 | 270 | 400 |
| PS22 | 1995 (2) | 2,000 | KM28, 32 | 135 | 225 |
| PS13 | 1995 (9) | 4,000 | KM3-11 | 15.20 | 34.50 |
| PS15 | ND (1995) (4) | 1,000 | KM50-53 | 375 | 500 |
| PS16 | ND (1995) (2) | 1,000 | KM50, 51 | 62.50 | 75.00 |
| PS17 | ND (1995) (2) | 1,000 | KM50, 52 | 125 | 180 |
| PS18 | ND (1995) (2) | 1,000 | KM51, 53 | 250 | 325 |
| PS19 | ND (1995) (2) | 1,000 | KM52, 53 | 312 | 430 |
| PS23 | 1996 (6) | 1,000 | KM41-46 | 187 | 265 |
| PS24 | 1996 (9) | 5,000 | KM12, 14-17, 19-21, 23 | 8.00 | 32.00 |
| PS25 | ND (1996) (2) | 500 | KM54-55 | 146 | 230 |
| PS26 | ND (1996) (3) | 300 | KM56-58 | 177 | 265 |
| PS27 | 1997 (3) | 300 | KM59-61 | 281 | 370 |

# CUBA

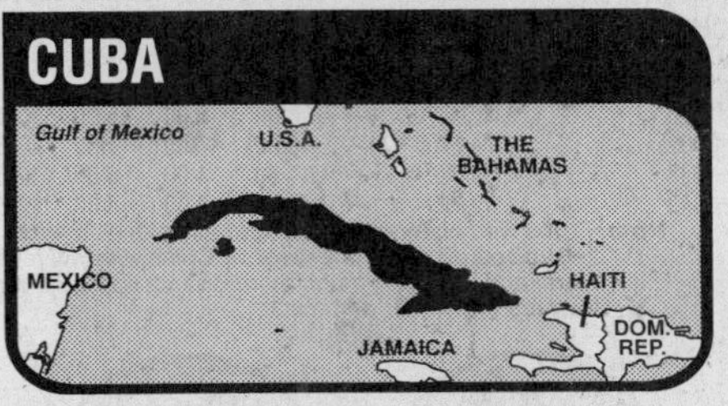


The Republic of Cuba, situated at the northern edge of the Caribbean Sea about 90 miles (145 km.) south of Florida, has an area of 42,804 sq. mi. (110,860 sq. km.) and a population of *11.2 million. Capital: Havana. The Cuban economy is based on the cultivation and refining of sugar, which provides 80 percent of export earnings.

Discovered by Columbus in 1492 and settled by Diego Velasquez in the early 1500s, Cuba remained a Spanish possession until 1898, except for a brief British occupancy of Havana in 1762-63. Cuban attempts to gain freedom were crushed, even while Spain was granting independence to its other American possessions. Ten years of warfare, 1868-78, between Spanish troops and Cuban rebels exacted guarantees of rights which were never implemented. The final revolt, begun in 1895, evoked American sympathy, and with the aid of U.S. troops independence was proclaimed on May 20, 1902. Fulgencio Batista seized the government in 1952 and established a dictatorship. Opposition to Batista, led by Fidel Castro, drove him into exile on Jan. 1, 1959. A communist-type, 25-member collective leadership headed by Castro was inaugurated in March, 1962.

**RULERS**
Spanish, until 1898

**MINT MARKS**
Key - Havana, 1977--

**MONETARY SYSTEM**
100 Centavos = 1 Peso

# REPUBLIC

## DECIMAL COINAGE

**CENTAVO** KM# 9.1 **Composition:** Copper-Nickel **Reverse:** 2.5 G

| Date | Mintage | F | VF | XF | Unc | BU |
|---|---|---|---|---|---|---|
| 1915 | 9,396,000 | — | 1.00 | 2.00 | 30.00 | 70.00 |
| 1915 Proof | 200 | Value: 175 | | | | |
| 1916 | 9,318,000 | — | 1.00 | 2.00 | 40.00 | 90.00 |
| 1916 Proof | 104 | Value: 750 | | | | |
| 1920 | 19,378,000 | — | 1.50 | 3.00 | 40.00 | 100 |
| 1938 | 2,000,000 | — | 2.50 | 6.00 | 55.00 | 130 |

**CENTAVO** KM# 9.2a **Composition:** Brass **Reverse:** 2.5 GR

| Date | Mintage | F | VF | XF | Unc | BU |
|---|---|---|---|---|---|---|
| 1943 | 20,000,000 | — | 0.40 | 1.25 | 7.00 | 15.00 |

**CENTAVO** KM# 9.2 **Composition:** Copper-Nickel **Reverse:** 2.5 GR

| Date | Mintage | F | VF | XF | Unc | BU |
|---|---|---|---|---|---|---|
| 1946 | 50,000,000 | — | 0.20 | 1.00 | 4.00 | 12.50 |
| 1961 | 100,000,000 | — | 0.25 | 0.60 | 1.50 | 2.50 |

**CENTAVO** KM# 26 **Composition:** Brass **Subject:** Birth of Jose Marti Centennial

| Date | Mintage | F | VF | XF | Unc | BU |
|---|---|---|---|---|---|---|
| 1953 | 50,000,000 | — | 0.15 | 0.75 | 10.00 | 25.00 |
| 1953 Proof; Rare | 100 | — | — | — | — | — |

**CENTAVO** KM# 30 **Composition:** Copper-Nickel **Reverse:** Bust of Jose Marti

| Date | Mintage | F | VF | XF | Unc | BU |
|---|---|---|---|---|---|---|
| 1958 | 50,000,000 | — | 0.15 | 0.75 | 45.00 | 75.00 |

**CENTAVO** KM# 33.1 **Composition:** Aluminum
**Rev. Legend:** PATRIA Y LIBERTAD

| Date | Mintage | F | VF | XF | Unc | BU |
|---|---|---|---|---|---|---|
| 1963 | 200,020,000 | — | 0.10 | 0.30 | 0.60 | 1.25 |
| 1966 | 50,000,000 | — | 0.10 | 0.40 | 0.80 | 1.75 |
| 1967 | — | — | — | — | — | — |
| 1969 | 50,000,000 | — | 0.10 | 0.40 | 0.80 | 1.75 |
| 1970 | 50,000,000 | — | 0.10 | 0.40 | 0.80 | 1.75 |
| 1971 | 49,960,000 | — | 0.40 | 0.80 | 1.50 | 3.00 |
| 1972 | 100,000,000 | — | 0.10 | 0.40 | 0.80 | 1.75 |
| 1978 | 50,000,000 | — | 0.10 | 0.40 | 0.80 | 1.75 |
| 1979 | 100,000,000 | — | 0.10 | 0.40 | 0.80 | 1.75 |
| 1981 | — | — | 0.10 | 0.40 | 0.80 | 1.75 |
| 1982 | — | — | 0.10 | 0.40 | 0.80 | 1.75 |

**CENTAVO** KM# 33.2 **Composition:** Aluminum
**Rev. Legend:** PATRIA O MUERTE

| Date | Mintage | F | VF | XF | Unc | BU |
|---|---|---|---|---|---|---|
| 1983 | — | — | 0.10 | 0.40 | 0.80 | 1.75 |
| 1984 | — | — | 0.10 | 0.40 | 0.80 | 1.75 |
| 1985 | — | — | 0.10 | 0.40 | 0.80 | 1.75 |
| 1986 | — | — | 0.10 | 0.40 | 0.80 | 1.75 |
| 1987 | — | — | 0.10 | 0.40 | 0.80 | 1.75 |
| 1988 | — | — | 0.10 | 0.40 | 0.80 | 1.75 |

**CENTAVO** KM# 33.3 **Composition:** Aluminum **Obverse:** Cuban arms **Reverse:** Wide "1" in star

| Date | Mintage | F | VF | XF | Unc | BU |
|---|---|---|---|---|---|---|
| 1998 | — | — | 0.10 | 0.40 | 0.80 | 1.75 |

**2 CENTAVOS** KM# A10 (KM10.1) **Composition:** Copper-Nickel

| Date | Mintage | F | VF | XF | Unc | BU |
|---|---|---|---|---|---|---|
| 1915 | 6,090,000 | — | 1.25 | 3.00 | 35.00 | 90.00 |
| 1915 Proof | 150 | Value: 150 | | | | |
| 1916 | 5,322,000 | — | 1.25 | 3.50 | 40.00 | 100 |
| 1916 Proof | 100 | Value: 750 | | | | |

**2 CENTAVOS** KM# 104.1 **Composition:** Aluminum **Obverse:** Small lettered legends, long edge denticles **Reverse:** Small lettered legends, long edge denticles

| Date | Mintage | F | VF | XF | Unc | BU |
|---|---|---|---|---|---|---|
| 1983 | 3,996,000 | — | 0.10 | 0.25 | 1.00 | 2.00 |

**2 CENTAVOS** KM# 104.2 **Composition:** Aluminum **Obverse:** Large lettered legends, short edge denticles **Reverse:** Large lettered legends, short edge denticles

| Date | Mintage | F | VF | XF | Unc | BU |
|---|---|---|---|---|---|---|
| 1983 | Inc. above | — | 0.10 | 0.20 | 0.50 | 1.00 |
| 1984 | — | — | 0.10 | 0.25 | 1.00 | 2.00 |
| 1985 | — | — | 0.10 | 0.20 | 0.50 | 1.00 |
| 1986 | — | — | 0.10 | 0.20 | 0.50 | 1.00 |

**5 CENTAVOS** KM# 11.1 **Composition:** Copper-Nickel **Reverse:** 5.0 G

| Date | Mintage | F | VF | XF | Unc | BU |
|---|---|---|---|---|---|---|
| 1915 | 5,096,000 | — | 1.50 | 4.00 | 40.00 | 100 |
| 1915 Proof | 150 | Value: 175 | | | | |
| 1916 | 1,714,000 | — | 1.50 | 5.00 | 45.00 | 135 |
| 1916 Proof | 100 | Value: 800 | | | | |
| 1920 | 10,000,000 | — | 1.50 | 4.50 | 55.00 | 125 |

**5 CENTAVOS** KM# 11.2 **Reverse:** 5.0 G

| Date | Mintage | F | VF | XF | Unc | BU |
|---|---|---|---|---|---|---|
| 1920 | — | — | 1.75 | 5.00 | 75.00 | 150 |

**5 CENTAVOS** KM# 11.3a (KM11.2a) **Composition:** Brass **Reverse:** 5.0 GR

| Date | Mintage | F | VF | XF | Unc | BU |
|---|---|---|---|---|---|---|
| 1943 | 6,000,000 | — | 1.00 | 3.50 | 15.00 | 25.00 |

**5 CENTAVOS** KM# 11.3 (KM11.2) **Composition:** Copper-Nickel **Reverse:** 5.0 GR

| Date | Mintage | F | VF | XF | Unc | BU |
|---|---|---|---|---|---|---|
| 1946 | 40,000,000 | — | 0.50 | 0.75 | 5.00 | 8.50 |
| 1960 | 20,000,000 | — | 0.75 | 1.25 | 15.00 | 40.00 |
| 1961 | 70,000,000 | — | 0.15 | 0.40 | 1.00 | 2.00 |

**5 CENTAVOS** KM# 34 **Composition:** Aluminum

| Date | Mintage | F | VF | XF | Unc | BU |
|---|---|---|---|---|---|---|
| 1963 | 80,000,000 | — | 0.10 | 0.25 | 0.75 | 1.50 |
| 1966 | 50,000,000 | — | 0.15 | 0.35 | 1.50 | 3.00 |
| 1968 | — | — | 0.15 | 0.35 | 1.50 | 3.00 |
| 1969 | — | — | 0.25 | 0.50 | 2.50 | 5.00 |
| 1971 | 100,020,000 | — | 0.10 | 0.25 | 0.75 | 1.50 |
| 1972 | 100,000,000 | — | 0.10 | 0.25 | 0.75 | 1.50 |

**10 CENTAVOS** KM# A12 (KM12.1) **Weight:** 2.5000 g. **Composition:** 0.9000 Silver .723 oz. ASW

| Date | Mintage | F | VF | XF | Unc | BU |
|---|---|---|---|---|---|---|
| 1915 | 5,690,000 | — | 4.00 | 12.00 | 75.00 | 175 |
| 1915 Proof | 125 | Value: 850 | | | | |
| 1916 | 560,000 | — | 20.00 | 75.00 | 450 | 1,750 |
| 1916 Proof | 50 | Value: 1,350 | | | | |
| 1920 | 3,090,000 | — | 6.00 | 20.00 | 175 | 425 |
| 1948 | 5,120,000 | — | 1.25 | 2.00 | 4.00 | 10.00 |
| 1949 | 9,880,000 | — | 1.25 | 1.75 | 4.00 | 10.00 |

**10 CENTAVOS** KM# 23 **Weight:** 2.5000 g. **Composition:** 0.9000 Silver .0723 oz. ASW **Subject:** 50th Year of Republic

| Date | Mintage | F | VF | XF | Unc | BU |
|---|---|---|---|---|---|---|
| 1952 | 10,000,000 | — | 0.50 | 1.00 | 4.00 | 10.00 |

**20 CENTAVOS** KM# 13.1 **Weight:** 5.0000 g. **Composition:** 0.9000 Silver .1446 oz. ASW **Reverse:** High relief star

| Date | Mintage | F | VF | XF | Unc | BU |
|---|---|---|---|---|---|---|
| 1915- fine reeding | — | — | 8.00 | 35.00 | 200 | 450 |
| 1915 Proof | 125 | Value: 825 | | | | |
| 1915- coarse reeding | Inc. above | — | 225 | 450 | — | — |

**20 CENTAVOS** KM# 13.2 **Weight:** 5.0000 g. **Composition:** 0.9000 Silver .1446 oz. ASW **Reverse:** Low relief star

| Date | Mintage | F | VF | XF | Unc | BU |
|---|---|---|---|---|---|---|
| 1915- fine reeding | Inc. above | — | 50.00 | 175 | 1,000 | 1,500 |
| 1915- course reeding | Inc. above | — | 5.00 | 15.00 | 60.00 | 100 |
| 1916 | 2,535,000 | — | 6.50 | 18.00 | 200 | 450 |
| 1916 Proof | 50 | Value: 1,750 | | | | |
| 1920 | 6,130,000 | — | 3.00 | 8.00 | 45.00 | 90.00 |
| 1932 | 184,000 | — | 75.00 | 300 | 850 | 1,450 |
| 1948 | 6,830,000 | — | 1.50 | 3.00 | 6.00 | 12.50 |
| 1949 | 13,170,000 | — | 1.50 | 3.00 | 6.00 | 12.50 |

**Note:** Coins with high relief stars normally exhibit a weak key and palm tree on the reverse. Coins with low relief stars tend to exhibit much more distinct lines running towards the center of the star

**20 CENTAVOS** KM# 24 **Weight:** 5.0000 g. **Composition:** 0.9000 Silver .1446 oz. ASW **Subject:** 50th Year of Republic

| Date | Mintage | F | VF | XF | Unc | BU |
|---|---|---|---|---|---|---|
| 1952 | 8,700,000 | — | 1.00 | 2.50 | 6.50 | 17.50 |

**20 CENTAVOS** KM# 31 **Composition:** Copper Nickel **Subject:** Jose Marti

| Date | Mintage | F | VF | XF | Unc | BU |
|---|---|---|---|---|---|---|
| 1962 | 83,860,000 | — | 1.00 | 1.50 | 3.00 | 6.00 |
| 1968 | 25,750,000 | — | 1.25 | 2.00 | 4.00 | 8.00 |

**20 CENTAVOS** KM# 35 **Composition:** Aluminum

| Date | Mintage | F | VF | XF | Unc | BU |
|---|---|---|---|---|---|---|
| 1969 | 25,000,000 | — | 1.00 | 1.50 | 2.50 | 5.00 |
| 1970 | 29,560,000 | 0.35 | 1.25 | 1.75 | 4.00 | — |
| 1971 | 25,000,000 | — | 1.00 | 1.50 | 2.50 | 5.00 |
| 1972 | — | — | 1.00 | 1.50 | 2.50 | 5.00 |

**25 CENTAVOS** KM# 27 **Weight:** 6.2500 g. **Composition:** 0.9000 Silver .1808 oz. ASW **Subject:** Centennial - Birth of Jose Marti

| Date | Mintage | F | VF | XF | Unc | BU |
|---|---|---|---|---|---|---|
| 1953 | 19,000,000 | — | 1.75 | 3.50 | 7.00 | 15.00 |
| 1953 Proof; Rare | — | — | — | — | — | — |

**25 CENTAVOS** KM# 360 **Composition:** Copper Nickel **Subject:** Carlos Finlay

| Date | Mintage | F | VF | XF | Unc | BU |
|---|---|---|---|---|---|---|
| ND | — | — | — | 3.00 | 6.00 | 9.00 |

**25 CENTAVOS** KM# 361 **Composition:** Copper Nickel **Subject:** Alexander von Humboldt

| Date | Mintage | F | VF | XF | Unc | BU |
|---|---|---|---|---|---|---|
| 1989 | — | — | — | 3.00 | 6.00 | 9.00 |

**40 CENTAVOS** KM# 14.1 **Weight:** 10.0000 g. **Composition:** 0.9000 Silver .2893 oz. ASW **Reverse:** High relief star

| Date | Mintage | F | VF | XF | Unc | BU |
|---|---|---|---|---|---|---|
| 1915 | 2,633,000 | — | 12.00 | 25.00 | 200 | 350 |
| 1915 Proof | 100 | Value: 850 | | | | |
| 1920 | 540,000 | — | 45.00 | 100 | 450 | 1,250 |
| 1920 Proof; Rare | — | — | — | — | — | — |

**40 CENTAVOS** KM# 14.2 **Weight:** 10.0000 g. **Composition:** 0.9000 Silver .2893 oz. ASW **Reverse:** Medium relief star

| Date | Mintage | F | VF | XF | Unc | BU |
|---|---|---|---|---|---|---|
| 1915 | Inc. above | — | 100 | 275 | 1,250 | 1,750 |

**40 CENTAVOS** KM# 14.3 **Weight:** 10.0000 g. **Composition:** 0.9000 Silver .2893 oz. ASW **Reverse:** Low relief star

| Date | Mintage | F | VF | XF | Unc | BU |
|---|---|---|---|---|---|---|
| 1915 | Inc. above | — | 15.00 | 35.00 | 145 | 300 |
| 1916 | 188,000 | — | 65.00 | 350 | 1,250 | 2,500 |
| 1916 Proof | 50 | Value: 2,500 | | | | |
| 1920 | Inc. above | — | 75.00 | 175 | 575 | 1,150 |

**Note:** Coins with high relief stars normally exhibit a weak key and palm tree on the reverse. Coins with low relief stars tend to exhibit much more distinct lines running towards the center of the star

**40 CENTAVOS** KM# 25 **Weight:** 10.0000 g. **Composition:** 0.9000 Silver .2893 oz. ASW **Subject:** 50th Year of Republic

| Date | Mintage | F | VF | XF | Unc | BU |
|---|---|---|---|---|---|---|
| 1952 | 1,250,000 | — | 2.50 | 5.00 | 25.00 | 55.00 |

**40 CENTAVOS** KM# 32 **Composition:** Copper Nickel **Subject:** Camilo Cienfuegos Gornaran

| Date | Mintage | F | VF | XF | Unc | BU |
|---|---|---|---|---|---|---|
| 1962 | 15,250,000 | — | 3.00 | 5.00 | 7.00 | 12.00 |

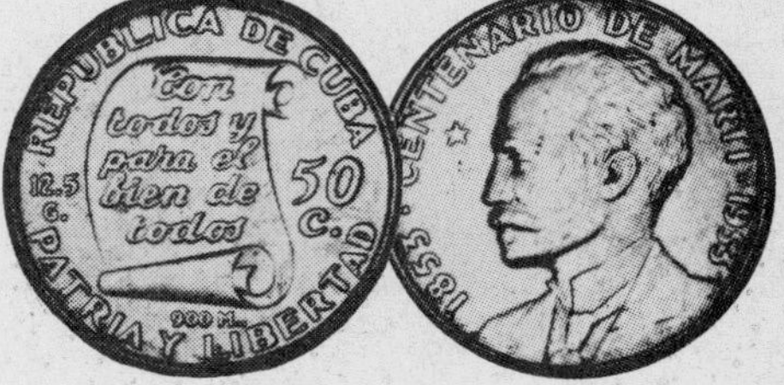

**50 CENTAVOS** **KM# 28** **Weight:** 12.5000 g. **Composition:** 0.9000 Silver .3617 oz. ASW **Subject:** Centennial - Birth of Jose Marti

| Date | Mintage | F | VF | XF | Unc | BU |
|---|---|---|---|---|---|---|
| ND(1953) | 2,000,000 | — | 3.50 | 7.50 | 20.00 | 35.00 |
| ND(1953)Proof; Rare | — | — | — | — | — | — |

**PESO** **KM# 15.1** **Weight:** 26.7295 g. **Composition:** 0.9000 Silver .7735 oz. ASW **Reverse:** High relief star

| Date | Mintage | F | VF | XF | Unc | BU |
|---|---|---|---|---|---|---|
| 1915 | 1,976,000 | — | 20.00 | 60.00 | 300 | 650 |
| 1915 Proof | 100 | Value: 2,000 | | | | |

**PESO** **KM# 15.2** **Weight:** 26.7295 g. **Composition:** 0.9000 Silver .7735 oz. ASW **Reverse:** Low relief star

| Date | Mintage | F | VF | XF | Unc | BU |
|---|---|---|---|---|---|---|
| 1915 | Inc. above | — | 225 | 550 | 1,850 | 3,500 |
| 1916 | 843,000 | — | 20.00 | 70.00 | 1,000 | 1,750 |
| 1916 Proof | 50 | Value: 3,000 | | | | |
| 1932 | 3,550,000 | — | 9.00 | 28.00 | 175 | 450 |
| 1933 | 6,000,000 | — | 9.00 | 20.00 | 125 | 200 |
| 1934 | 3,000,000 | — | 9.00 | 20.00 | 100 | 175 |

**Note:** Coins with high relief stars normally exhibit a weak key and palm tree on the reverse. Coins with low relief stars tend to exhibit much more distinct lines running towards the center of the star

**PESO** **KM# 16** **Weight:** 1.6718 g. **Composition:** 0.9000 Gold .0483 oz. AGW **Obverse:** Arms **Reverse:** Bust of Jose Marti

| Date | Mintage | F | VF | XF | Unc | BU |
|---|---|---|---|---|---|---|
| 1915 | 6,850 | 50.00 | 100 | 150 | 250 | — |
| 1915 Proof | 140 | Value: 1,500 | | | | |
| 1916 | 11,000 | 50.00 | 100 | 150 | 250 | — |
| 1916 Proof | 100 | Value: 1,700 | | | | |

**PESO** **KM# 22** **Weight:** 26.7295 g. **Composition:** 0.9000 Silver .7735 oz. ASW **Note:** Known as the "ABC" Peso.

| Date | Mintage | F | VF | XF | Unc | BU |
|---|---|---|---|---|---|---|
| 1934 | 7,000,000 | — | 25.00 | 60.00 | 175 | 325 |
| 1934- Matte Proof | — | Value: 5,250 | | | | |
| 1935 | 12,500,000 | — | 25.00 | 55.00 | 175 | 285 |
| 1936 | 16,000,000 | — | 25.00 | 65.00 | 250 | 475 |
| 1937 | 11,500,000 | — | 250 | 550 | 1,000 | 1,750 |
| 1938 | 10,800,000 | — | 22.50 | 45.00 | 120 | 200 |
| 1939 | 9,200,000 | — | 22.50 | 40.00 | 90.00 | 140 |

**PESO** **KM# 29** **Weight:** 26.7295 g. **Composition:** 0.9000 Silver .7735 oz. ASW **Subject:** Centennial of Jose Marti

| Date | Mintage | F | VF | XF | Unc | BU |
|---|---|---|---|---|---|---|
| ND(1953) | 1,000,000 | — | 4.50 | 7.00 | 25.00 | 55.00 |
| ND(1953) Proof; Rare | — | — | — | — | — | — |

**PESO** **KM# 186** **Composition:** Copper Nickel **Subject:** Carlos Manuel de Cespedes

| Date | Mintage | F | VF | XF | Unc | BU |
|---|---|---|---|---|---|---|
| ND(1977) | 3,000 | — | — | — | 7.00 | — |

**PESO** **KM# 187** **Composition:** Copper Nickel **Subject:** Ignacio Agramonte

| Date | Mintage | F | VF | XF | Unc | BU |
|---|---|---|---|---|---|---|
| 1977 | 3,000 | — | — | — | 7.00 | — |

**PESO** **KM# 188** **Composition:** Copper Nickel **Subject:** Maximo Gomez

| Date | Mintage | F | VF | XF | Unc | BU |
|---|---|---|---|---|---|---|
| 1977 | 3,000 | — | — | — | 7.00 | — |

**PESO** **KM# 189** **Composition:** Copper Nickel **Subject:** Antonio Maceo

| Date | Mintage | F | VF | XF | Unc | BU |
|---|---|---|---|---|---|---|
| 1977 | 3,000 | — | — | — | 7.00 | — |

**PESO** **KM# 190** **Composition:** Copper Nickel **Subject:** 60th Anniversary of Socialist Revolution - Lenin

| Date | Mintage | F | VF | XF | Unc | BU |
|---|---|---|---|---|---|---|
| ND | 6,000 | — | — | — | 15.00 | — |

**PESO** **KM# 191** **Composition:** Copper-Nickel **Subject:** Nonaligned Nations Conference

| Date | Mintage | F | VF | XF | Unc | BU |
|---|---|---|---|---|---|---|
| 1979 | 3,000 | — | — | — | 7.00 | — |

**PESO** **KM# 46** **Composition:** Copper Nickel **Subject:** Cuban Flower - Mariposa

| Date | Mintage | F | VF | XF | Unc | BU |
|---|---|---|---|---|---|---|
| 1980 | 3,000 | — | — | — | 8.00 | — |

**PESO** **KM# 192** **Composition:** Copper Nickel **Subject:** Olympics - Athletes in Frames

| Date | Mintage | F | VF | XF | Unc | BU |
|---|---|---|---|---|---|---|
| 1980 | 3,000 | — | — | — | 5.50 | — |

**PESO** **KM# 193** **Composition:** Copper Nickel **Subject:** Olympics - 3 Athletic Figures

| Date | Mintage | F | VF | XF | Unc | BU |
|---|---|---|---|---|---|---|
| 1980 | 3,000 | — | — | — | 5.50 | — |

**PESO** **KM# 194** **Composition:** Copper Nickel **Subject:** Soviet - Cuban Space Flight

| Date | Mintage | F | VF | XF | Unc | BU |
|---|---|---|---|---|---|---|
| 1980 | 3,000 | — | — | — | 7.50 | — |

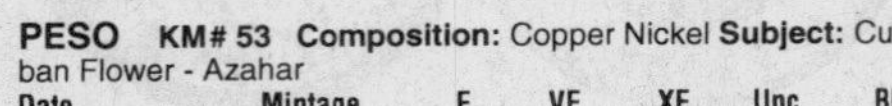

**PESO** **KM# 53** **Composition:** Copper Nickel **Subject:** Cuban Flower - Azahar

| Date | Mintage | F | VF | XF | Unc | BU |
|---|---|---|---|---|---|---|
| 1981 | 3,000 | — | — | — | 8.00 | — |

**PESO** **KM# 54** **Composition:** Copper Nickel **Subject:** Cuban Flower - Orquidea

| Date | Mintage | F | VF | XF | Unc | BU |
|---|---|---|---|---|---|---|
| 1981 | 3,000 | — | — | — | 8.00 | — |

**PESO** **KM# 55** **Composition:** Copper Nickel **Subject:** Cuban Fauna - Cuban Crocodile **Obverse:** Similar to KM#58

| Date | Mintage | F | VF | XF | Unc | BU |
|---|---|---|---|---|---|---|
| 1981 | 5,000 | — | — | — | 9.00 | — |

**PESO** **KM# 56** **Composition:** Copper Nickel **Subject:** Cuban Fauna - Emerald Hummingbird **Obverse:** Similar to KM#58

| Date | Mintage | F | VF | XF | Unc | BU |
|---|---|---|---|---|---|---|
| 1981 | 5,000 | — | — | — | 8.00 | — |

**PESO** **KM# 57** **Composition:** Copper Nickel **Subject:** Cuban Fauna - Bee Humingbird **Obverse:** Similar to KM#58

| Date | Mintage | F | VF | XF | Unc | BU |
|---|---|---|---|---|---|---|
| 1981 | 5,000 | — | — | — | 8.00 | — |

**PESO** **KM# 59** **Composition:** Copper Nickel **Subject:** World Food Day - Sugar Production

| Date | Mintage | F | VF | XF | Unc | BU |
|---|---|---|---|---|---|---|
| 1981 | 10,000 | — | — | — | 8.00 | — |

**PESO** **KM# 60** **Composition:** Copper Nickel **Subject:** XIV Central American and Caribbean Games **Reverse:** Symbols

| Date | Mintage | F | VF | XF | Unc | BU |
|---|---|---|---|---|---|---|
| 1981 | 5,000 | — | — | — | 6.00 | — |

**PESO** **KM# 61** **Composition:** Copper Nickel **Subject:** XIV Central American and Caribbean Games **Reverse:** 3 athletes

| Date | Mintage | F | VF | XF | Unc | BU |
|---|---|---|---|---|---|---|
| 1981 | 5,000 | — | — | — | 9.00 | — |

**PESO** **KM# 62** **Composition:** Copper Nickel **Subject:** XIV Central American and Caribbean Games **Reverse:** Boxers

| Date | Mintage | F | VF | XF | Unc | BU |
|---|---|---|---|---|---|---|
| 1981 | 5,000 | — | — | — | 9.00 | — |

**PESO** **KM# 63** **Composition:** Copper Nickel **Subject:** Cuban Fauna - Cuban Trogon **Obverse:** Siimilar to KM#60

| Date | Mintage | F | VF | XF | Unc | BU |
|---|---|---|---|---|---|---|
| 1981 | 5,000 | — | — | — | 8.00 | — |

**PESO** **KM# 64** **Composition:** Copper Nickel **Subject:** Cuban Fauna - Cuban Solendodon **Obverse:** Siimilar to KM#60

| Date | Mintage | F | VF | XF | Unc | BU |
|---|---|---|---|---|---|---|
| 1981 | 5,000 | — | — | — | 8.00 | — |

**PESO** **KM# 65** **Composition:** Copper Nickel **Subject:** Cuban Fauna - Giant Gar Fish **Obverse:** Siimilar to KM#60

| Date | Mintage | F | VF | XF | Unc | BU |
|---|---|---|---|---|---|---|
| 1981 | 5,000 | — | — | — | 8.00 | — |

**PESO** **KM# 66** **Composition:** Copper Nickel **Subject:** Columbus' Ship - Nina

| Date | Mintage | F | VF | XF | Unc | BU |
|---|---|---|---|---|---|---|
| 1981 | 10,000 | — | — | — | 12.00 | — |

**PESO** **KM# 67** **Composition:** Copper Nickel **Subject:** Columbus' Ship - Pinta

| Date | Mintage | F | VF | XF | Unc | BU |
|---|---|---|---|---|---|---|
| 1981 | 10,000 | — | — | — | 12.00 | — |

**PESO** **KM# 68** **Composition:** Copper Nickel **Subject:** Columbus' Ship - Santa Maria

| Date | Mintage | F | VF | XF | Unc | BU |
|---|---|---|---|---|---|---|
| 1981 | 10,000 | — | — | — | 12.00 | — |

**PESO** **KM# 58** **Composition:** Copper Nickel **Subject:** Soccer World Championship - Spain 1982 **Note:** Soccer Gmaes Spain 1982

| Date | Mintage | F | VF | XF | Unc | BU |
|---|---|---|---|---|---|---|
| 1981 | 10,000 | — | — | — | 8.00 | — |

**PESO** **KM# 88** **Composition:** Copper Nickel **Subject:** Ernest Hemingway - Portrait

| Date | Mintage | F | VF | XF | Unc | BU |
|---|---|---|---|---|---|---|
| 1982 | 7,000 | — | — | — | 15.00 | — |

**PESO** **KM# 89** **Composition:** Copper Nickel **Subject:** Ernest Hemingway - Fishing Yacht

| Date | Mintage | F | VF | XF | Unc | BU |
|---|---|---|---|---|---|---|
| 1982 | 7,000 | — | — | — | 15.00 | — |

**PESO** **KM# 90** **Composition:** Copper Nickel **Subject:** Ernest Hemingway - Small Boat

| Date | Mintage | F | VF | XF | Unc | BU |
|---|---|---|---|---|---|---|
| ND | 7,000 | — | — | — | 15.00 | — |

**PESO** **KM# 91** **Composition:** Copper Nickel **Subject:** Miquel De Cervantes

| Date | Mintage | F | VF | XF | Unc | BU |
|---|---|---|---|---|---|---|
| 1982 | 7,000 | — | — | — | 6.50 | — |

**PESO** **KM# 92** **Composition:** Copper Nickel **Subject:** Hidalgo Don Quijote

| Date | Mintage | F | VF | XF | Unc | BU |
|---|---|---|---|---|---|---|
| 1982 | 7,000 | — | — | — | 6.50 | — |

**PESO** **KM# 93** **Composition:** Copper Nickel **Subject:** Hidalgo Don Quijote and Sancho Panza

| Date | Mintage | F | VF | XF | Unc | BU |
|---|---|---|---|---|---|---|
| 1982 | 7,000 | — | — | — | 6.50 | — |

**PESO** **KM# 94** **Composition:** Copper Nickel **Series:** F.A.O. **Reverse:** Citrus fruit

| Date | Mintage | F | VF | XF | Unc | BU |
|---|---|---|---|---|---|---|
| 1982 | 6,609 | — | — | — | 6.50 | — |

**PESO** **KM# 95** **Composition:** Copper Nickel **Series:** F.A.O. **Reverse:** Cow

| Date | Mintage | F | VF | XF | Unc | BU |
|---|---|---|---|---|---|---|
| 1982 | 5,684 | — | — | — | 7.00 | — |

**PESO** **KM# 105** **Composition:** Brass

| Date | Mintage | F | VF | XF | Unc | BU |
|---|---|---|---|---|---|---|
| 1983 | 10,000,000 | 0.25 | 0.50 | 1.00 | 2.50 | — |
| 1984 | — | 0.25 | 0.50 | 1.00 | 2.50 | — |
| 1985 | — | 0.25 | 0.50 | 1.00 | 2.50 | — |
| 1986 | — | 0.25 | 0.50 | 1.00 | 2.50 | — |
| 1987 | — | 0.25 | 0.50 | 1.00 | 2.50 | — |
| 1988 | — | 0.25 | 0.50 | 1.00 | 2.50 | — |
| 1989 | — | 0.25 | 0.50 | 1.00 | 2.50 | — |

**PESO** **KM# 106** **Composition:** Copper Nickel **Subject:** Railroad

| Date | Mintage | F | VF | XF | Unc | BU |
|---|---|---|---|---|---|---|
| 1983 | 7,000 | — | — | — | 7.50 | — |

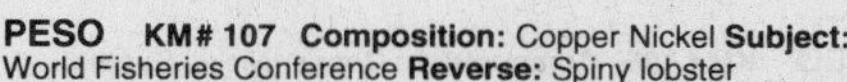

**PESO** **KM# 107** **Composition:** Copper Nickel **Subject:** World Fisheries Conference **Reverse:** Spiny lobster

| Date | Mintage | F | VF | XF | Unc | BU |
|---|---|---|---|---|---|---|
| 1983 | 5,000 | — | — | — | 6.50 | — |

**PESO** **KM# 173** **Composition:** Copper Nickel **Subject:** 1984 Olympics - Runner

| Date | Mintage | F | VF | XF | Unc | BU |
|---|---|---|---|---|---|---|
| 1983 | 3,000 | — | — | — | 4.50 | — |

**PESO** **KM# 174** **Composition:** Copper Nickel **Subject:** 1984 Olympics - Discus Thrower

| Date | Mintage | F | VF | XF | Unc | BU |
|---|---|---|---|---|---|---|
| 1983 | 3,000 | — | — | — | 4.50 | — |

**PESO** **KM# 175** **Composition:** Copper Nickel **Subject:** 1984 Olympics - Judo

| Date | Mintage | F | VF | XF | Unc | BU |
|---|---|---|---|---|---|---|
| 1983 | 3,000 | — | — | — | 4.50 | — |

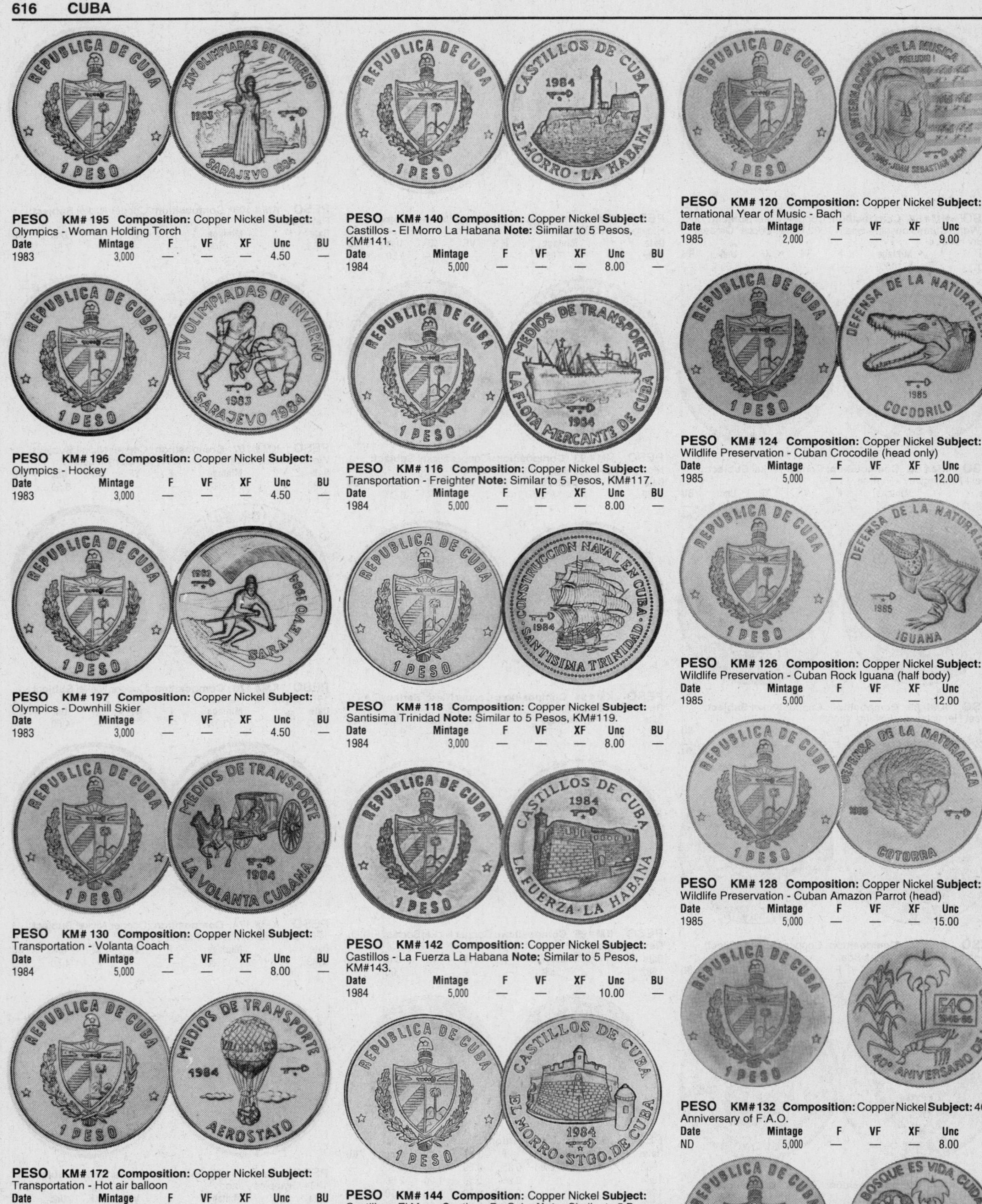


**PESO KM# 195 Composition:** Copper Nickel **Subject:** Olympics - Woman Holding Torch

| Date | Mintage | F | VF | XF | Unc | BU |
|---|---|---|---|---|---|---|
| 1983 | 3,000 | — | — | — | 4.50 | — |

**PESO KM# 196 Composition:** Copper Nickel **Subject:** Olympics - Hockey

| Date | Mintage | F | VF | XF | Unc | BU |
|---|---|---|---|---|---|---|
| 1983 | 3,000 | — | — | — | 4.50 | — |

**PESO KM# 197 Composition:** Copper Nickel **Subject:** Olympics - Downhill Skier

| Date | Mintage | F | VF | XF | Unc | BU |
|---|---|---|---|---|---|---|
| 1983 | 3,000 | — | — | — | 4.50 | — |

**PESO KM# 130 Composition:** Copper Nickel **Subject:** Transportation - Volanta Coach

| Date | Mintage | F | VF | XF | Unc | BU |
|---|---|---|---|---|---|---|
| 1984 | 5,000 | — | — | — | 8.00 | — |

**PESO KM# 172 Composition:** Copper Nickel **Subject:** Transportation - Hot air balloon

| Date | Mintage | F | VF | XF | Unc | BU |
|---|---|---|---|---|---|---|
| 1984 | 23 | — | — | — | 1,400 | — |

**PESO KM# 140 Composition:** Copper Nickel **Subject:** Castillos - El Morro La Habana **Note:** Siimilar to 5 Pesos, KM#141.

| Date | Mintage | F | VF | XF | Unc | BU |
|---|---|---|---|---|---|---|
| 1984 | 5,000 | — | — | — | 8.00 | — |

**PESO KM# 116 Composition:** Copper Nickel **Subject:** Transportation - Freighter **Note:** Similar to 5 Pesos, KM#117.

| Date | Mintage | F | VF | XF | Unc | BU |
|---|---|---|---|---|---|---|
| 1984 | 5,000 | — | — | — | 8.00 | — |

**PESO KM# 118 Composition:** Copper Nickel **Subject:** Santisima Trinidad **Note:** Similar to 5 Pesos, KM#119.

| Date | Mintage | F | VF | XF | Unc | BU |
|---|---|---|---|---|---|---|
| 1984 | 3,000 | — | — | — | 8.00 | — |

**PESO KM# 142 Composition:** Copper Nickel **Subject:** Castillos - La Fuerza La Habana **Note;** Similar to 5 Pesos, KM#143.

| Date | Mintage | F | VF | XF | Unc | BU |
|---|---|---|---|---|---|---|
| 1984 | 5,000 | — | — | — | 10.00 | — |

**PESO KM# 144 Composition:** Copper Nickel **Subject:** Castillos - El Morro Santiago De Cuba **Note:** Similar to 5 Pesos, KM#145.

| Date | Mintage | F | VF | XF | Unc | BU |
|---|---|---|---|---|---|---|
| 1984 | 5,000 | — | — | — | 8.00 | — |

**PESO KM# 120 Composition:** Copper Nickel **Subject:** International Year of Music - Bach

| Date | Mintage | F | VF | XF | Unc | BU |
|---|---|---|---|---|---|---|
| 1985 | 2,000 | — | — | — | 9.00 | — |

**PESO KM# 124 Composition:** Copper Nickel **Subject:** Wildlife Preservation - Cuban Crocodile (head only)

| Date | Mintage | F | VF | XF | Unc | BU |
|---|---|---|---|---|---|---|
| 1985 | 5,000 | — | — | — | 12.00 | — |

**PESO KM# 126 Composition:** Copper Nickel **Subject:** Wildlife Preservation - Cuban Rock Iguana (half body)

| Date | Mintage | F | VF | XF | Unc | BU |
|---|---|---|---|---|---|---|
| 1985 | 5,000 | — | — | — | 12.00 | — |

**PESO KM# 128 Composition:** Copper Nickel **Subject:** Wildlife Preservation - Cuban Amazon Parrot (head)

| Date | Mintage | F | VF | XF | Unc | BU |
|---|---|---|---|---|---|---|
| 1985 | 5,000 | — | — | — | 15.00 | — |

**PESO KM#132 Composition:** Copper Nickel **Subject:** 40th Anniversary of F.A.O.

| Date | Mintage | F | VF | XF | Unc | BU |
|---|---|---|---|---|---|---|
| ND | 5,000 | — | — | — | 8.00 | — |

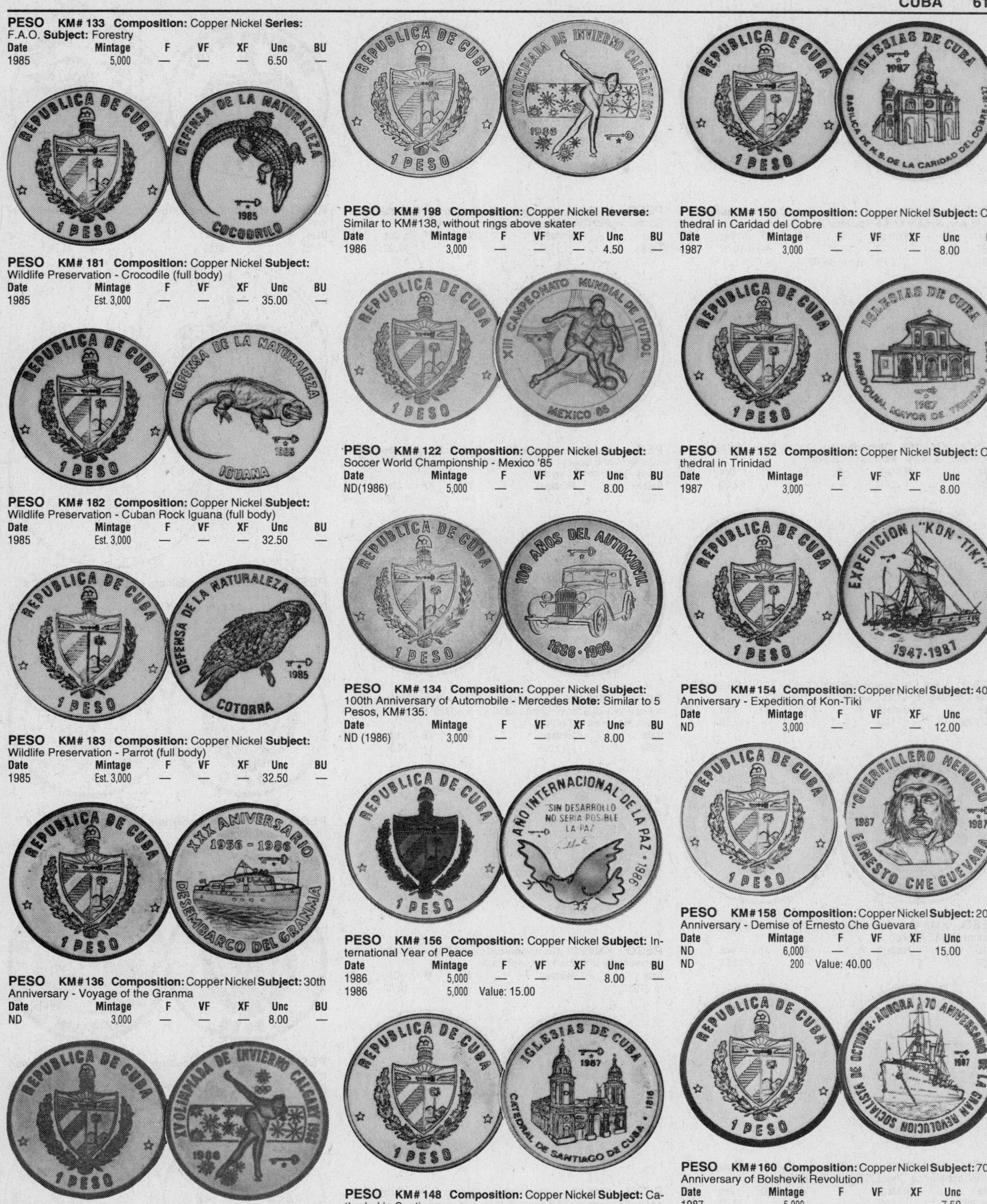

**PESO KM# 133 Composition:** Copper Nickel **Series:** F.A.O. **Subject:** Forestry

| Date | Mintage | F | VF | XF | Unc | BU |
|---|---|---|---|---|---|---|
| 1985 | 5,000 | — | — | — | 6.50 | — |

**PESO KM# 181 Composition:** Copper Nickel **Subject:** Wildlife Preservation - Crocodile (full body)

| Date | Mintage | F | VF | XF | Unc | BU |
|---|---|---|---|---|---|---|
| 1985 | Est. 3,000 | — | — | — | 35.00 | — |

**PESO KM# 182 Composition:** Copper Nickel **Subject:** Wildlife Preservation - Cuban Rock Iguana (full body)

| Date | Mintage | F | VF | XF | Unc | BU |
|---|---|---|---|---|---|---|
| 1985 | Est. 3,000 | — | — | — | 32.50 | — |

**PESO KM# 183 Composition:** Copper Nickel **Subject:** Wildlife Preservation - Parrot (full body)

| Date | Mintage | F | VF | XF | Unc | BU |
|---|---|---|---|---|---|---|
| 1985 | Est. 3,000 | — | — | — | 32.50 | — |

**PESO KM# 136 Composition:** Copper Nickel **Subject:** 30th Anniversary - Voyage of the Granma

| Date | Mintage | F | VF | XF | Unc | BU |
|---|---|---|---|---|---|---|
| ND | 3,000 | — | — | — | 8.00 | — |

**PESO KM# 138 Composition:** Copper Nickel **Subject:** Olympics - Speed Skater

| Date | Mintage | F | VF | XF | Unc | BU |
|---|---|---|---|---|---|---|
| 1986 | 1,000 | — | — | — | 12.50 | — |

**PESO KM# 198 Composition:** Copper Nickel **Reverse:** Similar to KM#138, without rings above skater

| Date | Mintage | F | VF | XF | Unc | BU |
|---|---|---|---|---|---|---|
| 1986 | 3,000 | — | — | — | 4.50 | — |

**PESO KM# 122 Composition:** Copper Nickel **Subject:** Soccer World Championship - Mexico '85

| Date | Mintage | F | VF | XF | Unc | BU |
|---|---|---|---|---|---|---|
| ND(1986) | 5,000 | — | — | — | 8.00 | — |

**PESO KM# 134 Composition:** Copper Nickel **Subject:** 100th Anniversary of Automobile - Mercedes **Note:** Similar to 5 Pesos, KM#135.

| Date | Mintage | F | VF | XF | Unc | BU |
|---|---|---|---|---|---|---|
| ND (1986) | 3,000 | — | — | — | 8.00 | — |

**PESO KM# 156 Composition:** Copper Nickel **Subject:** International Year of Peace

| Date | Mintage | F | VF | XF | Unc | BU |
|---|---|---|---|---|---|---|
| 1986 | 5,000 | — | — | — | 8.00 | — |
| 1986 | 5,000 | Value: 15.00 | | | | |

**PESO KM# 148 Composition:** Copper Nickel **Subject:** Cathedral in Santiago

| Date | Mintage | F | VF | XF | Unc | BU |
|---|---|---|---|---|---|---|
| 1987 | 3,000 | — | — | — | 8.00 | — |

**PESO KM# 150 Composition:** Copper Nickel **Subject:** Cathedral in Caridad del Cobre

| Date | Mintage | F | VF | XF | Unc | BU |
|---|---|---|---|---|---|---|
| 1987 | 3,000 | — | — | — | 8.00 | — |

**PESO KM# 152 Composition:** Copper Nickel **Subject:** Cathedral in Trinidad

| Date | Mintage | F | VF | XF | Unc | BU |
|---|---|---|---|---|---|---|
| 1987 | 3,000 | — | — | — | 8.00 | — |

**PESO KM# 154 Composition:** Copper Nickel **Subject:** 40th Anniversary - Expedition of Kon-Tiki

| Date | Mintage | F | VF | XF | Unc | BU |
|---|---|---|---|---|---|---|
| ND | 3,000 | — | — | — | 12.00 | — |

**PESO KM# 158 Composition:** Copper Nickel **Subject:** 20th Anniversary - Demise of Ernesto Che Guevara

| Date | Mintage | F | VF | XF | Unc | BU |
|---|---|---|---|---|---|---|
| ND | 6,000 | — | — | — | 15.00 | — |
| ND | 200 | Value: 40.00 | | | | |

**PESO KM# 160 Composition:** Copper Nickel **Subject:** 70th Anniversary of Bolshevik Revolution

| Date | Mintage | F | VF | XF | Unc | BU |
|---|---|---|---|---|---|---|
| 1987 | 5,000 | — | — | — | 7.50 | — |

**PESO** **KM# 165** **Composition:** Copper Nickel **Subject:** 100th Anniversary of the Souvenir Peso

| Date | Mintage | F | VF | XF | Unc | BU |
|---|---|---|---|---|---|---|
| 1987 | 3,000 | — | — | — | 10.00 | — |
| 1987 | 3,000 | Value: 45.00 | | | | |

**PESO** **KM# 167** **Composition:** Copper Nickel **Subject:** 100th Anniversary - Aboliton of Slavery

| Date | Mintage | F | VF | XF | Unc | BU |
|---|---|---|---|---|---|---|
| 1987 | 2,000 | — | — | — | 12.50 | — |

**PESO** **KM# 179** **Composition:** Copper Nickel **Subject:** Jose Capablanca Chess Centennial - Player

| Date | Mintage | F | VF | XF | Unc | BU |
|---|---|---|---|---|---|---|
| ND(1988) | 1,000 | — | — | — | 13.50 | — |

**PESO** **KM# 184** **Composition:** Copper Nickel **Subject:** Soccer - 1986 Mexico

| Date | Mintage | F | VF | XF | Unc | BU |
|---|---|---|---|---|---|---|
| 1988 | 1,000 | — | — | — | 13.50 | — |

**PESO** **KM# 200** **Composition:** Copper Nickel **Subject:** Jose Capablanca Chess Centennial - Chess Pieces

| Date | Mintage | F | VF | XF | Unc | BU |
|---|---|---|---|---|---|---|
| ND(1988) | 6,000 | — | — | — | 10.00 | — |

**PESO** **KM# 244** **Composition:** Copper Nickel **Subject:** Soccer World Championship - Italy 1990

| Date | Mintage | F | VF | XF | Unc | BU |
|---|---|---|---|---|---|---|
| 1988 | 2,000 | — | — | — | 12.00 | — |

**PESO** **KM# 245** **Composition:** Copper Nickel **Subject:** European World Soccer Championship - Federal Republic of Germany **Reverse:** 3 players

| Date | Mintage | F | VF | XF | Unc | BU |
|---|---|---|---|---|---|---|
| 1988 | 2,000 | — | — | — | 12.00 | — |

**PESO** **KM# 246** **Composition:** Copper Nickel **Subject:** European World Soccer Championship - Federal Republic of Germany **Reverse:** 4 players

| Date | Mintage | F | VF | XF | Unc | BU |
|---|---|---|---|---|---|---|
| 1988 | 2,000 | — | — | — | 14.50 | — |

**PESO** **KM# 276** **Composition:** Copper Nickel **Subject:** 40th Anniversary of Cuban National Ballet

| Date | Mintage | F | VF | XF | Unc | BU |
|---|---|---|---|---|---|---|
| ND(1988) | 2,000 | — | — | — | 10.00 | — |

**PESO** **KM# 277** **Composition:** Copper Nickel **Subject:** 150th Anniversary of Havana Grand Theater

| Date | Mintage | F | VF | XF | Unc | BU |
|---|---|---|---|---|---|---|
| ND(1977) | 2,000 | — | — | — | 10.00 | — |

**PESO** **KM# 282** **Composition:** Copper Nickel **Subject:** Carlos J. Finlay

| Date | Mintage | F | VF | XF | Unc | BU |
|---|---|---|---|---|---|---|
| 1988 | 2,000 | — | — | — | 11.50 | — |

**PESO** **KM# 512** **Composition:** Copper **Subject:** Carlos J. Finlay

| Date | Mintage | F | VF | XF | Unc | BU |
|---|---|---|---|---|---|---|
| ND(1988) | 2,500 | — | — | — | 6.00 | — |

**PESO** **KM# 258** **Composition:** Copper **Subject:** World Health Organization

| Date | Mintage | F | VF | XF | Unc | BU |
|---|---|---|---|---|---|---|
| 1988 | 2,000 | — | — | — | 10.00 | — |

**PESO** **KM# 269** **Composition:** Copper **Subject:** Transportation - Zeppelin

| Date | Mintage | F | VF | XF | Unc | BU |
|---|---|---|---|---|---|---|
| 1988 | 1,000 | — | — | — | 25.00 | — |

**PESO** **KM# 324** **Composition:** Copper Nickel **Subject:** Assault of the Moncada Garrison

| Date | Mintage | F | VF | XF | Unc | BU |
|---|---|---|---|---|---|---|
| 1988 | 2,000 | — | — | — | 10.00 | — |

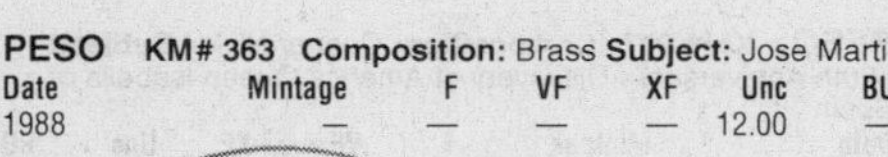

**PESO** **KM# 363** **Composition:** Brass **Subject:** Jose Marti

| Date | Mintage | F | VF | XF | Unc | BU |
|---|---|---|---|---|---|---|
| 1988 | — | — | — | — | 12.00 | — |

**PESO** **KM# 513** **Composition:** Copper **Subject:** Transportation - Zeppelin

| Date | Mintage | F | VF | XF | Unc | BU |
|---|---|---|---|---|---|---|
| 1988 | 2,500 | — | — | — | 10.00 | — |

**PESO** **KM# 247** **Composition:** Copper Nickel **Subject:** World Soccer Championship - Italy 1990 **Reverse:** 3 players

| Date | Mintage | F | VF | XF | Unc | BU |
|---|---|---|---|---|---|---|
| 1989 | 4,000 | — | — | — | 12.00 | — |

**PESO** **KM# 248** **Composition:** Copper Nickel **Subject:** World Championship - Italy 1990 **Reverse:** Colosseum

| Date | Mintage | F | VF | XF | Unc | BU |
|---|---|---|---|---|---|---|
| 1989 | 2,000 | — | — | — | 12.00 | — |

**PESO** **KM# 253** **Composition:** Copper Nickel **Subject:** 30th Anniversary of Revolution - Castro

| Date | Mintage | F | VF | XF | Unc | BU |
|---|---|---|---|---|---|---|
| ND(1989) | 5,000 | — | — | — | 10.00 | — |

**PESO** **KM# 254** **Composition:** Copper Nickel **Subject:** 30th Anniversary of Revolution - Jose Marti and Castro

| Date | Mintage | F | VF | XF | Unc | BU |
|---|---|---|---|---|---|---|
| 1989 | 5,000 | — | — | — | 12.00 | — |

**PESO** **KM# 255** **Composition:** Copper Nickel **Subject:** 30th Anniversary of Revolution - Cienfuegos and Castro

| Date | Mintage | F | VF | XF | Unc | BU |
|---|---|---|---|---|---|---|
| ND(1989) | 5,000 | — | — | — | 10.00 | — |

**PESO** **KM# 257** **Composition:** Copper Nickel **Subject:** Triumph of the Revolution

| Date | Mintage | F | VF | XF | Unc | BU |
|---|---|---|---|---|---|---|
| 1989 | 2,000 | — | — | — | 12.00 | — |

**PESO** **KM# 259** **Composition:** Copper Nickel **Subject:** Cuban Tobacco

| Date | Mintage | F | VF | XF | Unc | BU |
|---|---|---|---|---|---|---|
| 1989 | 1,000 | — | — | — | 14.00 | — |

**PESO** **KM# 260** **Composition:** Copper Nickel **Subject:** 160th Anniversary of First Railroad in England

| Date | Mintage | F | VF | XF | Unc | BU |
|---|---|---|---|---|---|---|
| 1989 | 2,000 | — | — | — | 12.00 | — |

**PESO** **KM# 261** **Composition:** Copper Nickel **Subject:** 500th Anniversary - Discovery of America

| Date | Mintage | F | VF | XF | Unc | BU |
|---|---|---|---|---|---|---|
| 1989 | 3,145 | — | — | — | 12.00 | — |

**PESO** **KM# 270** **Composition:** Copper Nickel **Subject:** 30th Anniversary - The March to Victory

| Date | Mintage | F | VF | XF | Unc | BU |
|---|---|---|---|---|---|---|
| 1989 | 2,000 | — | — | — | 10.00 | — |

**PESO** **KM# 271** **Composition:** Copper Nickel **Subject:** 200th Anniversary of French Revolution - Female Allegory of Revolution

| Date | Mintage | F | VF | XF | Unc | BU |
|---|---|---|---|---|---|---|
| ND(1989) | 2,000 | — | — | — | 10.00 | — |

**PESO** **KM# 272** **Composition:** Copper Nickel **Subject:** 200th Anniversary of French Revolution - Bastille

| Date | Mintage | F | VF | XF | Unc | BU |
|---|---|---|---|---|---|---|
| ND(1989) | 2,000 | — | — | — | 8.00 | — |

**PESO** **KM# 274** **Composition:** Copper Nickel **Subject:** First Spanish Railroad

| Date | Mintage | F | VF | XF | Unc | BU |
|---|---|---|---|---|---|---|
| 1989 | 2,000 | — | — | — | 10.00 | — |

**PESO** **KM# 275** **Composition:** Copper Nickel **Subject:** First Cuban Railroad

| Date | Mintage | F | VF | XF | Unc | BU |
|---|---|---|---|---|---|---|
| 1989 | 2,000 | — | — | — | 15.00 | — |

**PESO** KM# 278 **Composition:** Copper Nickel **Subject:** 5th Centennial - Discovery of America

| Date | Mintage | F | VF | XF | Unc | BU |
|---|---|---|---|---|---|---|
| 1989 | 2,000 | — | — | — | 10.00 | — |

**PESO** KM# 283 **Composition:** Copper Nickel **Subject:** Alexander von Humboldt

| Date | Mintage | F | VF | XF | Unc | BU |
|---|---|---|---|---|---|---|
| 1989 | 2,000 | — | — | — | 12.50 | — |

**PESO** KM# 284 **Composition:** Copper Nickel **Subject:** 1992 Olympics - Boxing

| Date | Mintage | F | VF | XF | Unc | BU |
|---|---|---|---|---|---|---|
| 1989 | 1,000 | — | — | — | 13.50 | — |

**PESO** KM# 285 **Composition:** Copper Nickel **Subject:** Camilo Cienfuegos

| Date | Mintage | F | VF | XF | Unc | BU |
|---|---|---|---|---|---|---|
| 1989 | 2,000 | — | — | — | 10.00 | — |

**PESO** KM# 286 **Composition:** Copper Nickel **Subject:** Ernesto Che Guevara

| Date | Mintage | F | VF | XF | Unc | BU |
|---|---|---|---|---|---|---|
| 1989 | 2,000 | — | — | — | 18.00 | — |

**PESO** KM# 287 **Composition:** Copper Nickel **Subject:** Tania La Guerrillera

| Date | Mintage | F | VF | XF | Unc | BU |
|---|---|---|---|---|---|---|
| 1989 | 2,000 | — | — | — | 10.00 | — |

**PES** KM# 436 **Composition:** Copper **Subject:** Alexander von ... oldt

| Date | Mintage | F | VF | XF | Unc | BU |
|---|---|---|---|---|---|---|
| 198. | — | — | — | — | 10.00 | — |

**PESO** KM# 250 **Composition:** Copper **Subject:** Esperanto

| Date | Mintage | F | VF | XF | Unc | BU |
|---|---|---|---|---|---|---|
| 1990 | 6,000 | — | — | — | 10.00 | — |

**PESO** KM# 273 **Composition:** Copper **Subject:** Discovery of America - Columbus departing from Spain

| Date | Mintage | F | VF | XF | Unc | BU |
|---|---|---|---|---|---|---|
| 1990 | 12,000 | — | — | — | 15.00 | — |

**PESO** KM# 279 **Composition:** Copper Nickel **Subject:** 5th Centennial of Columbus' arrival in Cuba

| Date | Mintage | F | VF | XF | Unc | BU |
|---|---|---|---|---|---|---|
| 1990 | 2,000 | — | — | — | 12.00 | — |

**PESO** KM# 288 **Composition:** Copper Nickel **Subject:** Columbus meeting natives

| Date | Mintage | F | VF | XF | Unc | BU |
|---|---|---|---|---|---|---|
| 1990 | 2,000 | — | — | — | 12.00 | — |

**PESO** KM# 289 **Composition:** Copper Nickel **Subject:** Soccer

| Date | Mintage | F | VF | XF | Unc | BU |
|---|---|---|---|---|---|---|
| 1990 | — | — | — | — | 12.00 | — |

**PESO** KM# 306 **Composition:** Copper Nickel **Subject:** 500th Anniversary - Discovery of America King Ferdinand of Spain

| Date | Mintage | F | VF | XF | Unc | BU |
|---|---|---|---|---|---|---|
| 1990 | 3,000 | — | — | — | 9.00 | — |

**PESO** KM# 307 **Composition:** Copper Nickel **Subject:** 500th Anniversary - Discovery of America Queen Isabella of Spain

| Date | Mintage | F | VF | XF | Unc | BU |
|---|---|---|---|---|---|---|
| 1990 | 3,000 | — | — | — | 9.00 | — |

**PESO** KM# 308 **Composition:** Copper Nickel **Subject:** 500th Anniversary - Discovery of American Christopher Columbus

| Date | Mintage | F | VF | XF | Unc | BU |
|---|---|---|---|---|---|---|
| 1990 | 3,000 | — | — | — | 6.50 | — |

**PESO** KM# 309 **Composition:** Copper Nickel **Subject:** 500th Anniversary - Discovery of America Juan de la Cosa

| Date | Mintage | F | VF | XF | Unc | BU |
|---|---|---|---|---|---|---|
| 1990 | 3,000 | — | — | — | 6.50 | — |

**PESO** KM# 310 **Composition:** Copper Nickel **Subject:** Pan American Games - High Jump

| Date | Mintage | F | VF | XF | Unc | BU |
|---|---|---|---|---|---|---|
| 1990 | 5,000 | — | — | — | 8.00 | — |

**PESO** KM# 311 **Composition:** Copper Nickel **Subject:** Pan American Games - Volleyball

| Date | Mintage | F | VF | XF | Unc | BU |
|---|---|---|---|---|---|---|
| 1990 | 5,000 | — | — | — | 10.00 | — |

**PESO** **KM# 312** **Composition:** Copper Nickel **Subject:** Pan American Games - Baseball

| Date | Mintage | F | VF | XF | Unc | BU |
|---|---|---|---|---|---|---|
| 1990 | 5,000 | — | — | — | 10.00 | — |

**PESO** **KM# 325** **Composition:** Copper Nickel **Subject:** Columbus' Ships Sailing West

| Date | Mintage | F | VF | XF | Unc | BU |
|---|---|---|---|---|---|---|
| 1990 | 12,000 | — | — | — | 7.50 | — |

**PESO** **KM# 340** **Composition:** Copper Nickel **Subject:** Celia Sanchez Manduley

| Date | Mintage | F | VF | XF | Unc | BU |
|---|---|---|---|---|---|---|
| 1990 | — | — | — | — | 8.00 | — |

**PESO** **KM# 387** **Composition:** Copper Nickel **Subject:** Route of first voyage of Columbus

| Date | Mintage | F | VF | XF | Unc | BU |
|---|---|---|---|---|---|---|
| 1990 | 2,000 | — | — | — | 12.00 | — |

**PESO** **KM# 471** **Composition:** Copper **Subject:** Columbus meeting natives

| Date | Mintage | F | VF | XF | Unc | BU |
|---|---|---|---|---|---|---|
| 1990 | — | — | — | — | 10.00 | — |

**PESO** **KM# 514** **Composition:** Copper Nickel **Subject:** Simon Bolivar - Libertador

| Date | Mintage | F | VF | XF | Unc | BU |
|---|---|---|---|---|---|---|
| 1990 | 2,000 | — | — | — | 6.50 | — |

**PESO** **KM# 364** **Composition:** Nickel Bonded Steel **Subject:** Hatuey Tribesman

| Date | Mintage | F | VF | XF | Unc | BU |
|---|---|---|---|---|---|---|
| 1991 | 3,000 | — | — | — | 9.00 | — |

**PESO** **KM# 365** **Composition:** Nickel Bonded Steel **Subject:** Pinzon Brothers

| Date | Mintage | F | VF | XF | Unc | BU |
|---|---|---|---|---|---|---|
| 1991 | 3,000 | — | — | — | 9.00 | — |

**PESO** **KM# 366** **Composition:** Nickel Bonded Steel **Subject:** Queen Joanna

| Date | Mintage | F | VF | XF | Unc | BU |
|---|---|---|---|---|---|---|
| 1991 | 3,000 | — | — | — | 9.00 | — |

**PESO** **KM# 367** **Composition:** Nickel Bonded Steel **Subject:** Diego Velazquez

| Date | Mintage | F | VF | XF | Unc | BU |
|---|---|---|---|---|---|---|
| 1991 | 3,000 | — | — | — | 9.00 | — |

**PESO** **KM# 388** **Composition:** Nickel Bonded Steel **Subject:** Madrid - Alcala Gate

| Date | Mintage | F | VF | XF | Unc | BU |
|---|---|---|---|---|---|---|
| 1991 | 10,000 | — | — | — | 9.00 | — |

**PESO** **KM# 389** **Composition:** Nickel Bonded Steel **Subject:** Barcelona - Olympic Stadium

| Date | Mintage | F | VF | XF | Unc | BU |
|---|---|---|---|---|---|---|
| 1991 | — | — | — | — | 5.00 | — |

**PESO** **KM# 390** **Composition:** Nickel Bonded Steel **Subject:** Seville - La Giralda Tower

| Date | Mintage | F | VF | XF | Unc | BU |
|---|---|---|---|---|---|---|
| 1991 | — | — | — | — | 9.00 | — |

**PESO** **KM# 347** **Composition:** Brass Plated Steel **Subject:** Jose Marti

| Date | Mintage | F | VF | XF | Unc | BU |
|---|---|---|---|---|---|---|
| 1992 | — | — | — | 1.00 | 2.00 | — |
| 1994 | — | — | — | 1.00 | 2.00 | — |

**PESO** **KM# 368** **Composition:** Copper Nickel **Subject:** Postal Ship

| Date | Mintage | F | VF | XF | Unc | BU |
|---|---|---|---|---|---|---|
| 1992 | — | — | — | — | 12.00 | — |

**PESO** **KM# 391** **Composition:** Nickel Bonded Steel **Subject:** 25th Anniversary - Death of Ernesto Che Guevara

| Date | Mintage | F | VF | XF | Unc | BU |
|---|---|---|---|---|---|---|
| 1992 | — | — | — | — | 9.00 | — |

**PESO** **KM# 392** **Composition:** Nickel Bonded Steel **Subject:** Bartolome de Las Casas

| Date | Mintage | F | VF | XF | Unc | BU |
|---|---|---|---|---|---|---|
| 1992 | 3,000 | — | — | — | 9.00 | — |

**PESO** **KM# 393** **Composition:** Nickel Bonded Steel **Subject:** Chief Guama

| Date | Mintage | F | VF | XF | Unc | BU |
|---|---|---|---|---|---|---|
| 1992 | 3,000 | — | — | — | 9.00 | — |

**PESO** **KM# 394** **Composition:** Nickel Bonded Steel **Subject:** King Philipp of Spain

| Date | Mintage | F | VF | XF | Unc | BU |
|---|---|---|---|---|---|---|
| 1992 | 3,000 | — | — | — | 9.00 | — |

**PESO** **KM# 395** **Composition:** Nickel Bonded Steel **Subject:** Spanish Royalty

| Date | Mintage | F | VF | XF | Unc | BU |
|---|---|---|---|---|---|---|
| ND(1992) | 3,000 | — | — | — | 9.00 | — |

**PESO** **KM# 401** **Composition:** Copper Nickel **Subject:** Seville Tower of Gold

| Date | Mintage | F | VF | XF | Unc | BU |
|---|---|---|---|---|---|---|
| 1992 | — | — | — | — | 5.00 | — |

**PESO** **KM# 402** **Composition:** Copper Nickel **Subject:** El Escorial

| Date | Mintage | F | VF | XF | Unc | BU |
|---|---|---|---|---|---|---|
| 1992 | — | — | — | — | 5.00 | — |

**PESO** **KM# 403** **Composition:** Copper Nickel **Subject:** St. Jorge Palace

| Date | Mintage | F | VF | XF | Unc | BU |
|---|---|---|---|---|---|---|
| 1992 | 10,000 | — | — | — | 5.00 | — |

**PESO** **KM# 437** **Composition:** Copper **Subject:** 25th Anniversary - Death of Ernesto Che Guevara

| Date | Mintage | F | VF | XF | Unc | BU |
|---|---|---|---|---|---|---|
| ND(1992) | — | — | — | — | 6.50 | — |

**PESO** **KM# 462** **Composition:** Nickel Bonded Steel **Subject:** Introduction of Africans to America

| Date | Mintage | F | VF | XF | Unc | BU |
|---|---|---|---|---|---|---|
| 1992 | — | — | — | — | 11.50 | — |

**PESO** **KM#396** **Composition:** Copper **Subject:** Millennium of St. Jacobi

| Date | Mintage | F | VF | XF | Unc | BU |
|---|---|---|---|---|---|---|
| 1993 | — | — | — | — | 6.00 | — |

**PESO** **KM# 397** **Composition:** Copper **Subject:** 40th Anniversary of Moncada

| Date | Mintage | F | VF | XF | Unc | BU |
|---|---|---|---|---|---|---|
| 1993 | — | — | — | — | 6.00 | — |

**PESO** **KM# 404** **Composition:** Copper Nickel **Subject:** Prehistoric Animals - Chalicotherium

| Date | Mintage | F | VF | XF | Unc | BU |
|---|---|---|---|---|---|---|
| 1993 | — | — | — | — | 20.00 | — |

**PESO** **KM# 429** **Composition:** Copper Nickel **Subject:** Federico Garcia Lorca

| Date | Mintage | F | VF | XF | Unc | BU |
|---|---|---|---|---|---|---|
| 1993 | — | — | — | — | 10.00 | — |

**PESO** **KM# 509** **Composition:** Copper **Subject:** President Abraham Lincoln

| Date | Mintage | F | VF | XF | Unc | BU |
|---|---|---|---|---|---|---|
| 1993 | — | — | — | — | 7.50 | — |

**PESO** **KM# 515** **Composition:** Copper **Subject:** Bolivar and Marti

| Date | Mintage | F | VF | XF | Unc | BU |
|---|---|---|---|---|---|---|
| 1993- Antiqued finish | — | — | — | — | 9.00 | — |
| 1993- Plain finish | — | — | — | — | 9.00 | — |

**PESO** **KM# 438** **Composition:** Copper-Nickel Plated Steel **Subject:** Prehistoric Animals - Stegosaurus

| Date | Mintage | F | VF | XF | Unc | BU |
|---|---|---|---|---|---|---|
| 1994 | — | — | — | — | 22.50 | — |

**PESO** **KM# 439** **Composition:** Copper-Nickel **Subject:** Caribbean Fauna - Multicolor Bottle-nosed Dolphins

| Date | Mintage | F | VF | XF | Unc | BU |
|---|---|---|---|---|---|---|
| 1994 | 25,000 | — | — | — | 37.00 | — |

**PESO** **KM# 460** **Composition:** Copper-Nickel **Subject:** Caribbean Fauna - Multicolor Spotted Eagle Ray

| Date | Mintage | F | VF | XF | Unc | BU |
|---|---|---|---|---|---|---|
| 1994 | 25,000 | — | — | — | 37.00 | — |

**PESO** **KM# 463** **Composition:** Nickel Bonded Steel **Subject:** Isla del Evangelista - Parrot, ship and sea chest

| Date | Mintage | F | VF | XF | Unc | BU |
|---|---|---|---|---|---|---|
| 1994 | — | — | — | — | 6.50 | — |

**PESO** **KM# 464** **Composition:** Nickel Bonded Steel **Subject:** Sailing Ship - NAO VICTORIA

| Date | Mintage | F | VF | XF | Unc | BU |
|---|---|---|---|---|---|---|
| 1994 | — | — | — | — | 9.00 | — |

**PESO** **KM# 465** **Composition:** Nickel Bonded Steel **Subject:** Sailing Ship - LA INDIA

| Date | Mintage | F | VF | XF | Unc | BU |
|---|---|---|---|---|---|---|
| 1994 | — | — | — | — | 9.00 | — |

**PESO** **KM# 466** **Composition:** Copper Nickel **Subject:** Caribbean Fauna - Multicolor Yellow Sea Bass (Coney)

| Date | Mintage | F | VF | XF | Unc | BU |
|---|---|---|---|---|---|---|
| 1994 | 25,000 | — | — | — | 32.50 | — |

**PESO** **KM# 467** **Composition:** Copper Nickel **Subject:** Caribbean Fauna - Multicolor Sword Fish

| Date | Mintage | F | VF | XF | Unc | BU |
|---|---|---|---|---|---|---|
| 1994 | 25,000 | — | — | — | 37.00 | — |

**PESO** **KM# 497** **Composition:** Copper Nickel **Subject:** Caribbean Fauna - Multicolor Pelican

| Date | Mintage | F | VF | XF | Unc | BU |
|---|---|---|---|---|---|---|
| 1994 | 25,000 | — | — | — | 40.00 | — |

**PESO** **KM# 498** **Composition:** Copper Nickel **Subject:** Caribbean Fauna - Multicolor Flamingos

| Date | Mintage | F | VF | XF | Unc | BU |
|---|---|---|---|---|---|---|
| 1994 | 25,000 | — | — | — | 32.50 | — |

**PESO** **KM# 517** **Composition:** Copper **Subject:** Nao Victoria

| Date | Mintage | F | VF | XF | Unc | BU |
|---|---|---|---|---|---|---|
| 1994 | 2,500 | — | — | — | 12.00 | — |

**PESO** **KM# 518** **Composition:** Nickel Bonded Steel **Subject:** Multicolor Fokker Dr. I

| Date | Mintage | F | VF | XF | Unc | BU |
|---|---|---|---|---|---|---|
| 1994 | — | — | — | — | 18.50 | — |

**PESO** **KM# 547** **Composition:** Nickel Bonded Steel **Subject:** Multicolor Fighter Plane - Albatross DII

| Date | Mintage | F | VF | XF | Unc | BU |
|---|---|---|---|---|---|---|
| 1994 | 25,000 | — | — | — | 18.50 | — |

**PESO** **KM# 606** **Composition:** Copper **Subject:** 500th Anniversary - Discovery of Evangelista Island **Obverse:** Cuban arms **Reverse:** Parrot, chest and ship

| Date | Mintage | F | VF | XF | Unc | BU |
|---|---|---|---|---|---|---|
| 1994 | — | — | — | — | 8.00 | — |

**PESO** **KM# 516** **Composition:** Copper **Subject:** Monticristi Manifesto **Note:** Antique finish

| Date | Mintage | F | VF | XF | Unc | BU |
|---|---|---|---|---|---|---|
| 1994 | — | — | — | — | 12.00 | — |

**PESO** **KM# 516a** **Composition:** Copper **Note:** Brilliant finish

| Date | Mintage | F | VF | XF | Unc | BU |
|---|---|---|---|---|---|---|
| 1994 | — | — | — | — | 15.00 | — |

**PESO** **KM# 519a** **Composition:** Copper **Subject:** Centennial - Death of Jose Marti in Combat **Note:** Brilliant finish

| Date | Mintage | F | VF | XF | Unc | BU |
|---|---|---|---|---|---|---|
| 1995 | — | — | — | — | 15.00 | — |

**PESO** **KM# 519** **Composition:** Copper **Subject:** Centennial - Death of Jose Marti in combat **Note:** Antique finish

| Date | Mintage | F | VF | XF | Unc | BU |
|---|---|---|---|---|---|---|
| 1995- Antiqued finish | 3,000 | — | — | — | 12.00 | — |
| 1995- Plain finish | — | — | — | — | 12.00 | — |

**PESO** **KM# 520** **Composition:** Copper **Subject:** Centennial 1895-1995 **Note:** Antique finish

| Date | Mintage | F | VF | XF | Unc | BU |
|---|---|---|---|---|---|---|
| ND | 2,000 | — | — | — | 12.00 | — |

**PESO** **KM# 473** **Composition:** Copper-Nickel **Subject:** Pirates of the Caribbean **Reverse:** Sir Henry Morgan

| Date | Mintage | F | VF | XF | Unc | BU |
|---|---|---|---|---|---|---|
| 1995 | 25,000 | — | — | — | 10.00 | — |

**PESO** **KM# 472** **Composition:** Copper Nickel **Subject:** Pirates of the Caribbean - Blackbeard

| Date | Mintage | F | VF | XF | Unc | BU |
|---|---|---|---|---|---|---|
| 1995 | Est. 25,000 | — | — | — | 10.00 | — |

**PESO** **KM# 477** **Composition:** Copper Nickel **Subject:** Pirates of the Caribbean - Piet Heyn

| Date | Mintage | F | VF | XF | Unc | BU |
|---|---|---|---|---|---|---|
| 1995 | Est. 25,000 | — | — | — | 10.00 | — |

**PESO** **KM# 474** **Composition:** Copper Nickel **Subject:** Pirates of the Caribbean - Anny Bonny

| Date | Mintage | F | VF | XF | Unc | BU |
|---|---|---|---|---|---|---|
| 1995 | Est. 25,000 | — | — | — | 10.00 | — |

**PESO** **KM# 475** **Composition:** Copper Nickel **Subject:** Pirates of the Caribbean - Mary Read

| Date | Mintage | F | VF | XF | Unc | BU |
|---|---|---|---|---|---|---|
| 1995 | Est. 25,000 | — | — | — | 10.00 | — |

**PESO** **KM# 476** **Composition:** Copper Nickel **Subject:** Pirates of the Caribbean - Captain Kidd

| Date | Mintage | F | VF | XF | Unc | BU |
|---|---|---|---|---|---|---|
| 1995 | Est. 25,000 | — | — | — | 10.00 | — |

**PESO** **KM# 521** **Composition:** Nickel Bonded Steel **Subject:** Jose Marti

| Date | Mintage | F | VF | XF | Unc | BU |
|---|---|---|---|---|---|---|
| 1995 | — | — | — | — | 7.50 | — |

**PESO KM# 522 Composition:** Nickel-Bonded Steel And Enamel **Subject:** SIAI Marchetti Seaplane

| Date | Mintage | F | VF | XF | Unc | BU |
|---|---|---|---|---|---|---|
| 1995 | — | — | — | — | 18.50 | — |

**PESO KM# 523 Composition:** Copper Nickel **Subject:** 50th Anniversary - United Nations

| Date | Mintage | F | VF | XF | Unc | BU |
|---|---|---|---|---|---|---|
| ND(1995) | — | — | — | — | 15.00 | — |

**PESO KM# 607 Composition:** Nickel Bonded Steel **Subject:** 50th Anniversary - F.A.O. **Obverse:** Cuban arms **Reverse:** Farmer plowing behind two oxen

| Date | Mintage | F | VF | XF | Unc | BU |
|---|---|---|---|---|---|---|
| ND(1995) | — | — | — | — | 7.50 | — |

**PESO KM# 549 Composition:** Nickel Bonded Steel **Subject:** Caribbean Fauna - Multicolor Ruby Throated Hummingbird

| Date | Mintage | F | VF | XF | Unc | BU |
|---|---|---|---|---|---|---|
| 1996 | 10,000 | — | — | — | 22.50 | — |

**PESO KM# 550 Composition:** Nickel Bonded Steel **Subject:** Caribbean Fauna - Multicolor Yellow Perch

| Date | Mintage | F | VF | XF | Unc | BU |
|---|---|---|---|---|---|---|
| 1996 | 10,000 | — | — | — | 22.50 | — |

**PESO KM# 551 Composition:** Nickel Bonded Steel **Subject:** Caribbean Fauna - Multicolor Cuban Tody Bird

| Date | Mintage | F | VF | XF | Unc | BU |
|---|---|---|---|---|---|---|
| 1996 | 10,000 | — | — | — | 25.00 | — |

**PESO KM# 552 Composition:** Nickel Bonded Steel **Subject:** Caribbean Fauna - Multicolor Wood Duck

| Date | Mintage | F | VF | XF | Unc | BU |
|---|---|---|---|---|---|---|
| 1996 | 10,000 | — | — | — | 22.50 | — |

**PESO KM# 565 Composition:** Nickel Bonded Steel **Subject:** Caribbean Fauna **Reverse:** Multicolor Papilio butterfly

| Date | Mintage | F | VF | XF | Unc | BU |
|---|---|---|---|---|---|---|
| 1996 | 10,000 | — | — | — | 32.50 | — |

**PESO KM# 614 Composition:** 25.9100 Copper Nickel **Subject:** 40th Anniversary of the "Granma" Landing **Obverse:** National arms. **Reverse:** Portrait above ship. **Edge:** Plain. **Size:** 37.9 mm.

| Date | Mintage | F | VF | XF | Unc | BU |
|---|---|---|---|---|---|---|
| ND(1996) | — | Value: 15.00 | | | | |

**PESO KM# 562 Composition:** Nickel Bonded Steel **Subject:** Caribbean Fauna - Multicolor Vaca Anil Fish **Note:** Similar to 10 Pesos, KM#563.

| Date | Mintage | F | VF | XF | Unc | BU |
|---|---|---|---|---|---|---|
| 1996 | 10,000 | — | — | — | 27.50 | — |

**PESO KM# 722 Composition:** Copper Nickel 12.9 oz. **Subject:** Hibiscus Elatus **Obverse:** National arms. **Reverse:** Multicolor flower. **Size:** 32.5 mm.

| Date | Mintage | F | VF | XF | Unc | BU |
|---|---|---|---|---|---|---|
| 1997 | 5,000 | Value: 10.00 | | | | |

**PESO KM# 617 Composition:** Copper-Nickel **Subject:** 30th Anniversary - Death of Ernesto Che Guevara **Reverse:** Full

figure of Guevara with rifle walking down road between anniversary dates, mountains behind. **Size:** 37 mm.

| Date | Mintage | F | VF | XF | Unc | BU |
|---|---|---|---|---|---|---|
| 1997 | — | — | — | — | 15.00 | — |

**PESO** **KM# 612** **Composition:** Copper Nickel **Subject:** Fidel Castro's visit to the Vatican **Obverse:** Cuban arms **Reverse:** Pope and Castro meeting

| Date | Mintage | F | VF | XF | Unc | BU |
|---|---|---|---|---|---|---|
| 1997 | — | — | — | — | 15.00 | — |

**PESO** **Composition:** Copper Nickel **Subject:** Fidel Castro's visit to the Vatican **Obverse:** Cuban arms **Reverse:** Pope and Castro meeting

| Date | Mintage | F | VF | XF | Unc | BU |
|---|---|---|---|---|---|---|
| 1997 | — | — | — | — | 15.00 | — |

**PESO** **KM# 622** **Composition:** Copper Nickel **Subject:** AIDS **Obverse:** Cuban arms **Reverse:** AIDS ribbon on silhouette before world map

| Date | Mintage | F | VF | XF | Unc | BU |
|---|---|---|---|---|---|---|
| 1998 | 50,000 | — | — | — | 15.00 | — |

**PESO** **KM# 662** **Composition:** Copper Nickel **Subject:** 40th Anniversary - The Triumph of the Revolution

| Date | Mintage | F | VF | XF | Unc | BU |
|---|---|---|---|---|---|---|
| 1999 | — | — | — | — | 15.00 | — |

**2 PESOS** **KM# 17** **Weight:** 3.3436 g. **Composition:** 0.9000 Gold .0967 oz. AGW **Obverse:** Arms **Reverse:** Bust of Jose Marti

| Date | Mintage | F | VF | XF | Unc | BU |
|---|---|---|---|---|---|---|
| 1915 | 10,000 | 65.00 | 85.00 | 115 | 200 | — |
| 1915 Proof | 100 | Value: 2,000 | | | | |
| 1916 | 150,000 | 60.00 | 70.00 | 85.00 | 120 | — |
| 1916 Proof; Rare | 8 | — | — | — | — | — |

**3 PESOS** **KM# 346** **Composition:** Copper Nickel **Subject:** Ernesto Che Guevara

| Date | Mintage | F | VF | XF | Unc | BU |
|---|---|---|---|---|---|---|
| 1990 | 4,050,000 | — | — | 3.00 | 6.00 | — |

**3 PESOS** **KM# 346a** **Composition:** Nickel Clad Steel

| Date | Mintage | F | VF | XF | Unc | BU |
|---|---|---|---|---|---|---|
| 1992 | — | — | — | 3.00 | 6.00 | — |
| 1992 | 500 | Value: 12.50 | | | | |
| 1993 | — | — | — | 3.00 | 6.00 | — |
| 1995 | — | — | — | 3.00 | 6.00 | — |

**4 PESOS** **KM# 18** **Weight:** 6.6872 g. **Composition:** 0.9000 Gold .1935 oz. AGW **Obverse:** Arms **Reverse:** Bust of Jose Marti

| Date | Mintage | F | VF | XF | Unc | BU |
|---|---|---|---|---|---|---|
| 1915 | 6,300 | 125 | 175 | 275 | 600 | — |
| 1915 Proof | 100 | Value: 3,000 | | | | |
| 1916 | 129,000 | 100 | 120 | 150 | 250 | — |
| 1916 Proof | 90 | Value: 4,500 | | | | |

**5 PESOS** **KM# 19** **Weight:** 8.3592 g. **Composition:** 0.9000 Gold .2419 oz. AGW **Obverse:** Arms **Reverse:** Bust of Jose Marti

| Date | Mintage | F | VF | XF | Unc | BU |
|---|---|---|---|---|---|---|
| 1915 | 696,000 | — | BV | 125 | 165 | — |
| 1915 Proof | — | Value: 3,200 | | | | |
| 1916 | 1,132,000 | — | BV | 125 | 150 | — |
| 1916 Proof | — | Value: 6,500 | | | | |

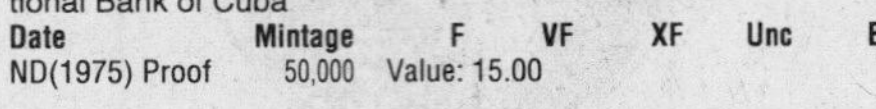

**5 PESOS** **KM# 36** **Weight:** 13.3300 g. **Composition:** 0.9000 Silver .3857 oz. ASW **Subject:** 25th Anniversary - National Bank of Cuba

| Date | Mintage | F | VF | XF | Unc | BU |
|---|---|---|---|---|---|---|
| ND(1975) Proof | 50,000 | Value: 15.00 | | | | |

**5 PESOS** **KM# 47** **Weight:** 12.0000 g. **Composition:** 0.9990 Silver .3855 oz. ASW **Subject:** First Soviet-Cuban Space Flight

| Date | Mintage | F | VF | XF | Unc | BU |
|---|---|---|---|---|---|---|
| 1980 | 10,000 | — | — | — | 11.50 | — |
| 1980 Proof | 5,000 | Value: 50.00 | | | | |

**5 PESOS** **KM# 48** **Weight:** 12.0000 g. **Composition:** 0.9990 Silver .3855 oz. ASW **Subject:** Moscow Olympics

| Date | Mintage | F | VF | XF | Unc | BU |
|---|---|---|---|---|---|---|
| 1980 | 10,000 | — | — | — | 10.00 | — |

**5 PESOS** **KM# 49** **Weight:** 12.0000 g. **Composition:** 0.9990 Silver .3855 oz. ASW **Subject:** Cuban flower - Mariposa

| Date | Mintage | F | VF | XF | Unc | BU |
|---|---|---|---|---|---|---|
| 1980 | 10,000 | — | — | — | 12.50 | — |
| 1980 Proof | 2,000 | Value: 25.00 | | | | |

**5 PESOS** **KM# 69** **Weight:** 12.0000 g. **Composition:** 0.9990 Silver .3855 oz. ASW **Subject:** Cuban flower = Azahar

| Date | Mintage | F | VF | XF | Unc | BU |
|---|---|---|---|---|---|---|
| 1981 | 10,000 | — | — | — | 12.50 | — |
| 1981 Proof | 2,000 | Value: 25.00 | | | | |

**5 PESOS** **KM# 70** **Weight:** 12.0000 g. **Composition:** 0.9990 Silver .3855 oz. ASW **Subject:** Cuban flower - Orquidea

| Date | Mintage | F | VF | XF | Unc | BU |
|---|---|---|---|---|---|---|
| 1981 | 10,000 | — | — | — | 12.50 | — |
| 1981 Proof | 2,000 | Value: 25.00 | | | | |

**5 PESOS** **KM# 71** **Weight:** 12.0000 g. **Composition:** 0.9990 Silver .3855 oz. ASW **Subject:** Columbus' Ship - Nina

| Date | Mintage | F | VF | XF | Unc | BU |
|---|---|---|---|---|---|---|
| 1981 | 10,000 | — | — | — | 22.50 | — |
| 1981 Proof | 1,000 | Value: 37.50 | | | | |

**5 PESOS** **KM# 72** **Weight:** 12.0000 g. **Composition:** 0.9990 Silver .3855 oz. ASW **Subject:** Columbus' Ship - Pinta

| Date | Mintage | F | VF | XF | Unc | BU |
|---|---|---|---|---|---|---|
| 1981 | 10,000 | — | — | — | 22.50 | — |
| 1981 Proof | 1,000 | Value: 37.50 | | | | |

**5 PESOS** **KM# 73** **Weight:** 12.0000 g. **Composition:** 0.9990 Silver .3855 oz. ASW **Subject:** Columbus' Ship - Santa Maria

| Date | Mintage | F | VF | XF | Unc | BU |
|---|---|---|---|---|---|---|
| 1981 | 10,000 | — | — | — | 22.50 | — |
| 1981 Proof | 1,000 | Value: 37.50 | | | | |

**5 PESOS** **KM# 74** **Weight:** 12.0000 g. **Composition:** 0.9990 Silver .3855 oz. ASW **Subject:** Cuban Fauna - Crocodile

| Date | Mintage | F | VF | XF | Unc | BU |
|---|---|---|---|---|---|---|
| 1981 | 5,000 | — | — | — | 18.50 | — |
| 1981 Proof | 1,000 | Value: 35.00 | | | | |

**5 PESOS** **KM# 75** **Weight:** 12.0000 g. **Composition:** 0.9990 Silver .3855 oz. ASW **Subject:** Cuban Fauna - Emerald Hummingbird

| Date | Mintage | F | VF | XF | Unc | BU |
|---|---|---|---|---|---|---|
| 1981 | 5,000 | — | — | — | 18.50 | — |
| 1981 Proof | 1,000 | Value: 35.00 | | | | |

**5 PESOS** **KM# 76** **Weight:** 12.0000 g. **Composition:** 0.9990 Silver .3855 oz. ASW **Subject:** Cuban Fauna - Bee Hummingbird

| Date | Mintage | F | VF | XF | Unc | BU |
|---|---|---|---|---|---|---|
| 1981 | 5,000 | — | — | — | 18.50 | — |
| 1981 Proof | 1,000 | Value: 35.00 | | | | |

**5 PESOS** **KM# 77** **Weight:** 12.0000 g. **Composition:** 0.9990 Silver .3855 oz. ASW **Subject:** Soccer Games - Spain 1982

| Date | Mintage | F | VF | XF | Unc | BU |
|---|---|---|---|---|---|---|
| 1981 Proof | 4,000 | Value: 22.50 | | | | |

**5 PESOS** **KM# 78** **Weight:** 12.0000 g. **Composition:** 0.9990 Silver .3855 oz. ASW **Subject:** World Food Day - Sugar Production

| Date | Mintage | F | VF | XF | Unc | BU |
|---|---|---|---|---|---|---|
| 1981 | 7,000 | — | — | — | 20.00 | — |
| 1981 Proof | 1,560 | Value: 25.00 | | | | |

**5 PESOS** **KM# 79** **Weight:** 12.0000 g. **Composition:** 0.9990 Silver .3855 oz. ASW **Subject:** XIV Central American and Caribbean Games - Animated Mascot

| Date | Mintage | F | VF | XF | Unc | BU |
|---|---|---|---|---|---|---|
| 1981 | 5,000 | — | — | — | 12.50 | — |
| 1981 Proof | 2,000 | Value: 32.50 | | | | |

**5 PESOS** **KM# 80** **Weight:** 12.0000 g. **Composition:** 0.9990 Silver .3855 oz. ASW **Subject:** XIV Central American and Caribbean Games - 3 Athletes

| Date | Mintage | F | VF | XF | Unc | BU |
|---|---|---|---|---|---|---|
| 1981 | 5,000 | — | — | — | 11.50 | — |
| 1981 Proof | 2,000 | Value: 35.00 | | | | |

**5 PESOS** **KM# 81** **Weight:** 12.0000 g. **Composition:** 0.9990 Silver .3855 oz. ASW **Subject:** XIV Central American and Caribbean Games - Boxers

| Date | Mintage | F | VF | XF | Unc | BU |
|---|---|---|---|---|---|---|
| 1981 | 5,000 | — | — | — | 11.50 | — |
| 1981 Proof | 2,000 | Value: 35.00 | | | | |

**5 PESOS** **KM# 82** **Weight:** 12.0000 g. **Composition:** 0.9990 Silver .3855 oz. ASW **Subject:** Cuban Fauna - Cugan Trogon

| Date | Mintage | F | VF | XF | Unc | BU |
|---|---|---|---|---|---|---|
| 1981 | 5,000 | — | — | — | 12.50 | — |
| 1981 Proof | 1,000 | Value: 30.00 | | | | |

**5 PESOS** **KM# 83** **Weight:** 12.0000 g. **Composition:** 0.9990 Silver .3855 oz. ASW **Subject:** Cuban Fauna - Cuban Solenodon

| Date | Mintage | F | VF | XF | Unc | BU |
|---|---|---|---|---|---|---|
| 1981 | 5,000 | — | — | — | 12.50 | — |
| 1981 Proof | 1,000 | Value: 28.00 | | | | |

**5 PESOS** **KM# 84** **Weight:** 12.0000 g. **Composition:** 0.9990 Silver .3855 oz. ASW **Subject:** Cuban Fauna - Giant Gar Fish

| Date | Mintage | F | VF | XF | Unc | BU |
|---|---|---|---|---|---|---|
| 1981 | 5,000 | — | — | — | 12.50 | — |
| 1981 Proof | 1,000 | Value: 30.00 | | | | |

**5 PESOS** **KM# 96** **Weight:** 12.0000 g. **Composition:** 0.9990 Silver .3855 oz. ASW **Subject:** Ernest Hemingway - Portrait

| Date | Mintage | F | VF | XF | Unc | BU |
|---|---|---|---|---|---|---|
| 1982 | 5,000 | — | — | — | 20.00 | — |
| 1982 Proof | 1,000 | Value: 40.00 | | | | |

**5 PESOS** **KM# 97** **Weight:** 12.0000 g. **Composition:** 0.9990 Silver .3855 oz. ASW **Subject:** Ernestr Hemingway - Fishing yacht

| Date | Mintage | F | VF | XF | Unc | BU |
|---|---|---|---|---|---|---|
| 1982 | 5,000 | — | — | — | 20.00 | — |
| 1982 Proof | 1,000 | Value: 40.00 | | | | |

**5 PESOS** **KM# 98** **Weight:** 12.0000 g. **Composition:** 0.9990 Silver .3855 oz. ASW **Subject:** Ernest Hemingway Small boat

| Date | Mintage | F | VF | XF | Unc | BU |
|---|---|---|---|---|---|---|
| 1982 | 5,000 | — | — | — | 20.00 | — |
| 1982 Proof | 1,000 | Value: 40.00 | | | | |

**5 PESOS** **KM# 99** **Weight:** 12.0000 g. **Composition:** 0.9990 Silver .3855 oz. ASW **Subject:** Miguel De Cervantes

| Date | Mintage | F | VF | XF | Unc | BU |
|---|---|---|---|---|---|---|
| 1982 | 7,000 | — | — | — | 11.50 | — |
| 1982 Proof | 2,000 | Value: 30.00 | | | | |

**5 PESOS** **KM# 100** **Weight:** 12.0000 g. **Composition:** 0.9990 Silver .3855 oz. ASW **Subject:** Hidalgo Don Quijote

| Date | Mintage | F | VF | XF | Unc | BU |
|---|---|---|---|---|---|---|
| 1982 | 7,000 | — | — | — | 11.50 | — |
| 1982 Proof | 2,000 | Value: 30.00 | | | | |

**5 PESOS** **KM# 101** **Weight:** 12.0000 g. **Composition:** 0.9990 Silver .3855 oz. ASW **Subject:** Hidalgo Don Quijote and Sancho Panza

| Date | Mintage | F | VF | XF | Unc | BU |
|---|---|---|---|---|---|---|
| 1982 | 7,000 | — | — | — | 11.50 | — |
| 1982 Proof | 2,000 | Value: 30.00 | | | | |

**5 PESOS** **KM# 102** **Weight:** 12.0000 g. **Composition:** 0.9990 Silver .3855 oz. ASW **Series:** F.A.O. **Subject:** Citrus fruit **Note:** Similar to 1 Peso, KM$94.

| Date | Mintage | F | VF | XF | Unc | BU |
|---|---|---|---|---|---|---|
| 1982 | 3,125 | — | — | — | 22.00 | — |
| 1982 Proof | 1,040 | Value: 32.50 | | | | |

**5 PESOS** **KM# 103** **Weight:** 12.0000 g. **Composition:** 0.9990 Silver .3855 oz. ASW **Series:** F.A.O. **Subject:** Cow **Note:** Similar to 1 Peso, KM$95.

| Date | Mintage | F | VF | XF | Unc | BU |
|---|---|---|---|---|---|---|
| 1982 | 4,177 | — | — | — | 22.00 | — |
| 1982 Proof | 1,000 | Value: 32.50 | | | | |

**5 PESOS** **KM# 108** **Weight:** 12.0000 g. **Composition:** 0.9990 Silver .3855 oz. ASW **Subject:** 1984 Winter Olympics Hockey **Obverse:** Similar to KM$99

| Date | Mintage | F | VF | XF | Unc | BU |
|---|---|---|---|---|---|---|
| 1983 Proof | 5,000 | Value: 13.50 | | | | |

**5 PESOS** **KM# 109** **Weight:** 12.0000 g. **Composition:** 0.9990 Silver .3855 oz. ASW **Subject:** 1984 Summer Olympics - Runner **Obverse:** Similar to KM$99

| Date | Mintage | F | VF | XF | Unc | BU |
|---|---|---|---|---|---|---|
| 1983 Proof | 5,000 | Value: 13.50 | | | | |

**5 PESOS** **KM# 110** **Weight:** 12.0000 g. **Composition:** 0.9990 Silver .3855 oz. ASW **Subject:** Railroad

| Date | Mintage | F | VF | XF | Unc | BU |
|---|---|---|---|---|---|---|
| 1983 | 5,000 | — | — | — | 15.00 | — |
| 1983 Proof | 2,000 | Value: 30.00 | | | | |

**5 PESOS** **KM# 111** **Weight:** 12.0000 g. **Composition:** 0.9990 Silver .3855 oz. ASW **Subject:** World Fisheries - Spiny lobster

| Date | Mintage | F | VF | XF | Unc | BU |
|---|---|---|---|---|---|---|
| 1983 | 5,000 | — | — | — | 22.50 | — |
| 1983 Proof | 1,000 | Value: 45.00 | | | | |

**5 PESOS** **KM# 112** **Weight:** 12.0000 g. **Composition:** 0.9990 Silver .3855 oz. ASW **Subject:** Winter Olympics - Woman holding torch **Obverse:** Similar to KM#114

| Date | Mintage | F | VF | XF | Unc | BU |
|---|---|---|---|---|---|---|
| 1983 Proof | 5,000 | Value: 13.50 | | | | |

**5 PESOS** **KM# 113** **Weight:** 12.0000 g. **Composition:** 0.9990 Silver .3855 oz. ASW **Subject:** Winter Olympics - Downhill skier **Obverse:** Similar to KM#114

| Date | Mintage | F | VF | XF | Unc | BU |
|---|---|---|---|---|---|---|
| 1983 Proof | 5,000 | Value: 13.50 | | | | |

**5 PESOS** **KM# 114** **Weight:** 12.0000 g. **Composition:** 0.9990 Silver .3855 oz. ASW **Subject:** Summer Olympics - Discus Thrower

| Date | Mintage | F | VF | XF | Unc | BU |
|---|---|---|---|---|---|---|
| 1983 Proof | 5,000 | Value: 12.50 | | | | |

**5 PESOS** **KM# 115** **Weight:** 12.0000 g. **Composition:** 0.9990 Silver .3855 oz. ASW **Subject:** Summer Olympics - Judo

| Date | Mintage | F | VF | XF | Unc | BU |
|---|---|---|---|---|---|---|
| 1983 Proof | 5,000 | Value: 15.00 | | | | |

**5 PESOS** **KM# 117** **Weight:** 12.0000 g. **Composition:** 0.9990 Silver .3855 oz. ASW **Subject:** Transportation - Freighter

| Date | Mintage | F | VF | XF | Unc | BU |
|---|---|---|---|---|---|---|
| 1984 | 5,000 | — | — | — | 20.00 | — |
| 1984 Proof | 1,000 | Value: 40.00 | | | | |

**5 PESOS** **KM# 119** **Weight:** 12.0000 g. **Composition:** 0.9990 Silver .3855 oz. ASW **Subject:** Santisimo Trinidad

| Date | Mintage | F | VF | XF | Unc | BU |
|---|---|---|---|---|---|---|
| 1984 | 5,000 | — | — | — | 16.50 | — |

**5 PESOS** **KM# 131** **Weight:** 12.0000 g. **Composition:** 0.9990 Silver .3855 oz. ASW **Subject:** Transportation - Volanta Coach

| Date | Mintage | F | VF | XF | Unc | BU |
|---|---|---|---|---|---|---|
| 1984 | 5,000 | — | — | — | 11.50 | — |
| 1984 Proof | 1,000 | Value: 40.00 | | | | |

**5 PESOS** **KM# 666** **Weight:** 12.0000 g. **Composition:** 0.9990 Silver .3855 oz. ASW **Subject:** Transportation - Hot air balloon

| Date | Mintage | F | VF | XF | Unc | BU |
|---|---|---|---|---|---|---|
| 1984 | 2 | — | — | — | 4,000 | — |

**5 PESOS** **KM# 141** **Weight:** 12.0000 g. **Composition:** 0.9990 Silver .3855 oz. ASW **Subject:** Fortress - El Morro La Habana

| Date | Mintage | F | VF | XF | Unc | BU |
|---|---|---|---|---|---|---|
| 1984 | 5,000 | — | — | — | 11.50 | — |
| 1984 Proof | 1,000 | Value: 45.00 | | | | |

**5 PESOS** **KM# 143** **Weight:** 12.0000 g. **Composition:** 0.9990 Silver .3855 oz. ASW **Subject:** Fortress - La Fuerza La Habana

| Date | Mintage | F | VF | XF | Unc | BU |
|---|---|---|---|---|---|---|
| 1984 | 5,000 | — | — | — | 11.50 | — |
| 1984 Proof | 1,000 | Value: 45.00 | | | | |

**5 PESOS** **KM# 145** **Weight:** 12.0000 g. **Composition:** 0.9990 Silver .3855 oz. ASW **Subject:** Fortress - El Morro Santiago De Cuba

| Date | Mintage | F | VF | XF | Unc | BU |
|---|---|---|---|---|---|---|
| 1984 | 5,000 | — | — | — | 11.50 | — |
| 1984 Proof | 1,000 | Value: 45.00 | | | | |

**5 PESOS** **KM# 121** **Weight:** 12.0000 g. **Composition:** 0.9990 Silver .3855 oz. ASW **Subject:** International Year of Music - Bach

| Date | Mintage | F | VF | XF | Unc | BU |
|---|---|---|---|---|---|---|
| 1985 | 2,000 | — | — | — | 32.50 | — |
| 1985 Proof | — | Value: 45.00 | | | | |

**5 PESOS** **KM# 125** **Weight:** 12.0000 g. **Composition:** 0.9990 Silver .3855 oz. ASW **Subject:** Wildlife Preservation - Cuban Crocodile

| Date | Mintage | F | VF | XF | Unc | BU |
|---|---|---|---|---|---|---|
| 1985 | 5,000 | — | — | — | 45.00 | — |

**5 PESOS** **KM# 127** **Weight:** 12.0000 g. **Composition:** 0.9990 Silver .3855 oz. ASW **Subject:** Wildlife Preservation - Cuban Rock Iquana

| Date | Mintage | F | VF | XF | Unc | BU |
|---|---|---|---|---|---|---|
| 1985 | 5,000 | — | — | — | 32.50 | — |

**5 PESOS** **KM# 129** **Weight:** 12.0000 g. **Composition:** 0.9990 Silver .3855 oz. ASW **Subject:** Wildlife Preservation - Cuban Amazon Parrot

| Date | Mintage | F | VF | XF | Unc | BU |
|---|---|---|---|---|---|---|
| 1985 | 5,000 | — | — | — | 27.50 | — |

**5 PESOS** **KM# 146** **Weight:** 12.0000 g. **Composition:** 0.9990 Silver .3855 oz. ASW **Subject:** 40th Anniversary of F.A.O. **Obverse:** Similar to KM#129 **Reverse:** Lobster, palm tree & sugar cane

| Date | Mintage | F | VF | XF | Unc | BU |
|---|---|---|---|---|---|---|
| ND(1985) | 4,500 | — | — | — | 11.50 | — |
| ND(1985) Proof | 500 | Value: 45.00 | | | | |

**5 PESOS** **KM# 147** **Weight:** 12.0000 g. **Composition:** 0.9990 Silver .3855 oz. ASW **Series:** F.A.O. **Subject:** Forestry **Obverse:** Similar to KM#129 **Reverse:** Stylized forest

| Date | Mintage | F | VF | XF | Unc | BU |
|---|---|---|---|---|---|---|
| ND(1985) | 4,500 | — | — | — | 22.50 | — |
| ND(1985) Proof | 500 | Value: 40.00 | | | | |

**5 PESOS** **KM# 123** **Weight:** 12.0000 g. **Composition:** 0.9990 Silver .3855 oz. ASW **Subject:** Soccer **Note:** Similar to 1 Peso, KM#122.

| Date | Mintage | F | VF | XF | Unc | BU |
|---|---|---|---|---|---|---|
| 1985 | 5,000 | — | — | — | 22.00 | — |
| 1985 Proof | — | Value: 35.00 | | | | |

**5 PESOS** **KM# 135** **Weight:** 12.0000 g. **Composition:** 0.9990 Silver .3855 oz. ASW **Subject:** 100th Anniversary of the Automobile

| Date | Mintage | F | VF | XF | Unc | BU |
|---|---|---|---|---|---|---|
| ND(1986) | 2,500 | — | — | — | 22.50 | — |

**5 PESOS** **KM# 137** **Weight:** 12.0000 g. **Composition:** 0.9990 Silver .3855 oz. ASW **Subject:** 30th Anniversary - Voyage of the Granma

| Date | Mintage | F | VF | XF | Unc | BU |
|---|---|---|---|---|---|---|
| ND(1986) | 2,500 | — | — | — | 20.00 | — |

**5 PESOS** **KM# 139** **Weight:** 12.0000 g. **Composition:** 0.9990 Silver .3855 oz. ASW **Subject:** Olympics - Skater

| Date | Mintage | F | VF | XF | Unc | BU |
|---|---|---|---|---|---|---|
| 1986 | 2,500 | — | — | — | 25.00 | — |

**5 PESOS** **KM# 157** **Weight:** 12.0000 g. **Composition:** 0.9990 Silver .3855 oz. ASW **Series:** F.A.O. **Subject:** Internaticanl Year of Peace

| Date | Mintage | F | VF | XF | Unc | BU |
|---|---|---|---|---|---|---|
| 1986 | 10,000 | — | — | — | 22.50 | — |
| 1986 Proof | 2,000 | Value: 32.50 | | | | |

**5 PESOS** **KM# 199** **Weight:** 12.0000 g. **Composition:** 0.9990 Silver .3855 oz. ASW **Subject:** Olympics - Skater **Reverse:** Without rings above skater

| Date | Mintage | F | VF | XF | Unc | BU |
|---|---|---|---|---|---|---|
| 1986 | 10,000 | — | — | — | 10.00 | — |

**5 PESOS** **KM# 149** **Weight:** 12.0000 g. **Composition:** 0.9990 Silver .3855 oz. ASW **Subject:** Cathedral in Santiago

| Date | Mintage | F | VF | XF | Unc | BU |
|---|---|---|---|---|---|---|
| 1987 | 2,500 | — | — | — | 25.00 | — |

**5 PESOS** **KM# 151** **Weight:** 12.0000 g. **Composition:** 0.9990 Silver .3855 oz. ASW **Subject:** Cathedral in Caridad del Cobre

| Date | Mintage | F | VF | XF | Unc | BU |
|---|---|---|---|---|---|---|
| 1987 | 2,500 | — | — | — | 25.00 | — |

**5 PESOS** **KM# 153** **Weight:** 12.0000 g. **Composition:** 0.9990 Silver .3855 oz. ASW **Subject:** Cathedral in Trinidad

| Date | Mintage | F | VF | XF | Unc | BU |
|---|---|---|---|---|---|---|
| 1987 | 2,500 | — | — | — | 25.00 | — |

**5 PESOS** **KM# 155** **Weight:** 12.0000 g. **Composition:** 0.9990 Silver .3855 oz. ASW **Subject:** 40th Anniversary - Expedition of Kon-Tiki

| Date | Mintage | F | VF | XF | Unc | BU |
|---|---|---|---|---|---|---|
| ND(1987) | 5,000 | — | — | — | 20.00 | — |

**5 PESOS** **KM# 159** **Weight:** 12.0000 g. **Composition:** 0.9990 Silver .3855 oz. ASW **Subject:** 20th Anniversary - Demise of Ernesto Che Guevara

| Date | Mintage | F | VF | XF | Unc | BU |
|---|---|---|---|---|---|---|
| ND(1987) | 5,000 | — | — | — | 30.00 | — |
| ND(1987) Proof | 200 | Value: 75.00 | | | | |

**5 PESOS** **KM# 161** **Weight:** 12.0000 g. **Composition:** 0.9990 Silver .3855 oz. ASW **Subject:** 70th Anniversary - Bolshevik Revolution

| Date | Mintage | F | VF | XF | Unc | BU |
|---|---|---|---|---|---|---|
| 1987 | 3,000 | — | — | — | 22.50 | — |
| 1987 Proof | 1,000 | Value: 45.00 | | | | |

**5 PESOS** **KM# 166** **Weight:** 12.0000 g. **Composition:** 0.9990 Silver .3855 oz. ASW **Subject:** 100th Anniversary - Souvenir Peso

| Date | Mintage | F | VF | XF | Unc | BU |
|---|---|---|---|---|---|---|
| 1987 | 3,000 | — | — | — | 25.00 | — |

**5 PESOS** **KM# 326** **Weight:** 12.0000 g. **Composition:** 0.9990 Silver .3855 oz. ASW **Subject:** Abolition of Slavery

| Date | Mintage | F | VF | XF | Unc | BU |
|---|---|---|---|---|---|---|
| 1987 | 2,000 | — | — | — | 32.50 | — |

**5 PESOS** **KM# 180** **Weight:** 12.0000 g. **Composition:** 0.9990 Silver .3855 oz. ASW **Subject:** Jose Capablanca Chess Championship - Player

| Date | Mintage | F | VF | XF | Unc | BU |
|---|---|---|---|---|---|---|
| ND | 5,000 | — | — | — | 22.50 | — |

**5 PESOS** **KM# 185** **Weight:** 12.0000 g. **Composition:** 0.9990 Silver .3855 oz. ASW **Subject:** Soccer - Mexico 1986

| Date | Mintage | F | VF | XF | Unc | BU |
|---|---|---|---|---|---|---|
| 1988 | 5,000 | — | — | — | 16.50 | — |
| 1988 Proof | — | Value: 30.00 | | | | |

**5 PESOS** **KM# 216** **Weight:** 6.0000 g. **Composition:** 0.9990 Silver .1927 oz. ASW **Subject:** Soccer - Italy 1990

| Date | Mintage | F | VF | XF | Unc | BU |
|---|---|---|---|---|---|---|
| 1988 | — | — | — | — | 16.50 | — |

**5 PESOS** **KM# 216a** **Weight:** 12.0000 g. **Composition:** 0.9990 Silver .3855 oz. ASW **Subject:** Soccer - Italy 1990

| Date | Mintage | F | VF | XF | Unc | BU |
|---|---|---|---|---|---|---|
| 1988 | 5,000 | — | — | — | 20.00 | — |

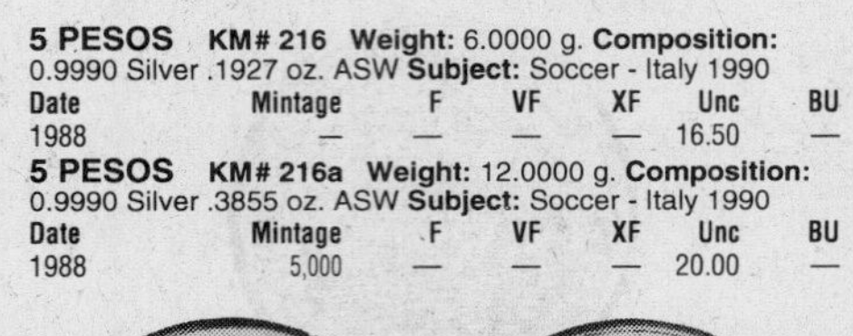

**5 PESOS** **KM# 217** **Weight:** 12.0000 g. **Composition:** 0.9990 Silver .3855 oz. ASW **Subject:** Soccer - West Germany - 3 players

| Date | Mintage | F | VF | XF | Unc | BU |
|---|---|---|---|---|---|---|
| 1988 | 5,000 | — | — | — | 18.50 | — |

**5 PESOS** **KM# 218** **Weight:** 12.0000 g. **Composition:** 0.9990 Silver .3855 oz. ASW **Subject:** Soccer - West Germany - 4 players

| Date | Mintage | F | VF | XF | Unc | BU |
|---|---|---|---|---|---|---|
| 1988 | 5,000 | — | — | — | 18.50 | — |

**5 PESOS** **KM# 219** **Weight:** 16.0000 g. **Composition:** 0.9990 Silver .5145 oz. ASW **Subject:** 40th Anniversary - Cuban National Ballet

| Date | Mintage | F | VF | XF | Unc | BU |
|---|---|---|---|---|---|---|
| ND(1988) Proof | 2,000 | Value: 47.50 | | | | |

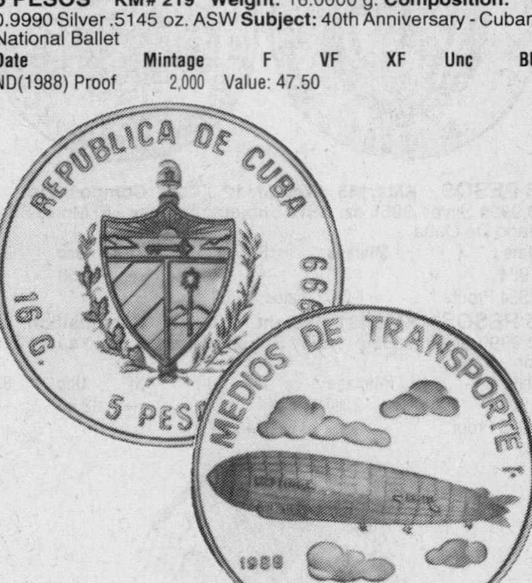


**5 PESOS** **KM# 220.1** **Weight:** 16.0000 g. **Composition:** 0.9990 Silver .5145 oz. ASW **Subject:** Graf Zeppelin

| Date | Mintage | F | VF | XF | Unc | BU |
|---|---|---|---|---|---|---|
| 1988 Proof | 3,000 | Value: 250 | | | | |

**5 PESOS** **KM# 220.2** **Weight:** 15.9400 g. **Composition:** 0.9990 Silver .5119 oz. ASW **Obverse:** Thicker wreath

| Date | Mintage | F | VF | XF | Unc | BU |
|---|---|---|---|---|---|---|
| 1988 Proof | — | Value: 37.50 | | | | |

**5 PESOS** **KM# 221** **Weight:** 16.0000 g. **Composition:** 0.9990 Silver .5119 oz. ASW **Subject:** Carlos J. Finlay

| Date | Mintage | F | VF | XF | Unc | BU |
|---|---|---|---|---|---|---|
| ND(1988) Proof | 2,000 | Value: 47.50 | | | | |

**5 PESOS** **KM# 222** **Weight:** 16.0000 g. **Composition:** 0.9990 Silver .5119 oz. ASW **Subject:** World Health Organization

| Date | Mintage | F | VF | XF | Unc | BU |
|---|---|---|---|---|---|---|
| ND(1988) Proof | 2,000 | Value: 47.50 | | | | |

**5 PESOS** **KM# 223** **Weight:** 16.0000 g. **Composition:** 0.9990 Silver .5119 oz. ASW **Subject:** 150th Anniversary - Grand National Theater in Havana

| Date | Mintage | F | VF | XF | Unc | BU |
|---|---|---|---|---|---|---|
| ND(1988) Proof | 2,000 | Value: 55.00 | | | | |

**5 PESOS** **KM# 224** **Weight:** 16.0000 g. **Composition:** 0.9990 Silver .5119 oz. ASW **Series:** Olympics **Subject:** Barcelona **Reverse:** Boxing

| Date | Mintage | F | VF | XF | Unc | BU |
|---|---|---|---|---|---|---|
| 1989 Proof | 10,000 | Value: 25.00 | | | | |

**5 PESOS** **KM# 225** **Weight:** 16.0000 g. **Composition:** 0.9990 Silver .5119 oz. ASW **Series:** Olympics **Subject:** Italy **Reverse:** 3 players

| Date | Mintage | F | VF | XF | Unc | BU |
|---|---|---|---|---|---|---|
| 1989 Proof | 10,000 | Value: 52.50 | | | | |

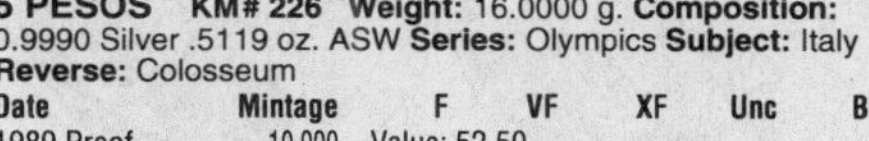

**5 PESOS** **KM# 226** **Weight:** 16.0000 g. **Composition:** 0.9990 Silver .5119 oz. ASW **Series:** Olympics **Subject:** Italy **Reverse:** Colosseum

| Date | Mintage | F | VF | XF | Unc | BU |
|---|---|---|---|---|---|---|
| 1989 Proof | 10,000 | Value: 52.50 | | | | |

**5 PESOS** **KM# 227** **Weight:** 16.0000 g. **Composition:** 0.9990 Silver .5119 oz. ASW **Subject:** Cuban tobacco

| Date | Mintage | F | VF | XF | Unc | BU |
|---|---|---|---|---|---|---|
| 1989 Proof | 2,000 | Value: 52.50 | | | | |

**5 PESOS** **KM# 231** **Weight:** 16.0000 g. **Composition:** 0.9990 Silver .5119 oz. ASW **Subject:** Alexander von Humboldt

| Date | Mintage | F | VF | XF | Unc | BU |
|---|---|---|---|---|---|---|
| 1989 Proof | 3,000 | Value: 50.00 | | | | |

**5 PESOS** **KM# 251** **Weight:** 16.0000 g. **Composition:** 0.9990 Silver .5119 oz. ASW **Subject:** Universal Congress of Esperanto

| Date | Mintage | F | VF | XF | Unc | BU |
|---|---|---|---|---|---|---|
| 1990 Proof | 6,000 | Value: 45.00 | | | | |

**5 PESOS** **KM# 290** **Weight:** 16.0000 g. **Composition:** 0.9990 Silver .5119 oz. ASW **Subject:** Soccer - Map of Italy and soccer balls

| Date | Mintage | F | VF | XF | Unc | BU |
|---|---|---|---|---|---|---|
| 1990 Proof | 10,000 | Value: 55.00 | | | | |

**5 PESOS** **KM# 338** **Weight:** 12.0000 g. **Composition:** 0.9990 Silver .3855 oz. ASW **Subject:** Soccer Championship

| Date | Mintage | F | VF | XF | Unc | BU |
|---|---|---|---|---|---|---|
| 1991 Proof | 10,000 | — | — | — | 52.50 | — |

**5 PESOS** **KM# 405** **Weight:** 6.0000 g. **Composition:** 0.9990 Silver .1927 oz. ASW **Subject:** Prehistoric Animals - Apatosaurus

| Date | Mintage | F | VF | XF | Unc | BU |
|---|---|---|---|---|---|---|
| 1993 Proof | 30,000 | Value: 22.50 | | | | |

**5 PESOS** **KM# 524** **Weight:** 15.0000 g. **Composition:** 0.9990 Silver .4818 oz. ASW **Subject:** Historia Postal de Cuba Steamship

| Date | Mintage | F | VF | XF | Unc | BU |
|---|---|---|---|---|---|---|
| 1993 Proof | 25,000 | Value: 16.50 | | | | |

**5 PESOS** **KM# 440** **Weight:** 16.0000 g. **Composition:** 0.9990 Silver .5145 oz. ASW **Subject:** Prehistoric Animals Triceratops

| Date | Mintage | F | VF | XF | Unc | BU |
|---|---|---|---|---|---|---|
| 1994 Proof | 10,000 | Value: 50.00 | | | | |

**5 PESOS** **KM# 573** **Weight:** 16.0000 g. **Composition:** 0.9990 Silver .5145 oz. ASW **Subject:** Prehistoric Animals - Maiasaura

| Date | Mintage | F | VF | XF | Unc | BU |
|---|---|---|---|---|---|---|
| 1994 Proof | — | Value: 50.00 | | | | |

**5 PESOS** **KM# 581** **Weight:** 7.0000 g. **Composition:** 0.9990 Silver .2248 oz. ASW **Subject:** Hibiscus Elatus Flower **Obverse:** Cuban arms **Reverse:** Multicolro hibiscus

| Date | Mintage | F | VF | XF | Unc | BU |
|---|---|---|---|---|---|---|
| 1997 Proof | — | Value: 20.00 | | | | |

**5 PESOS** **KM# 623** **Weight:** 11.3000 g. **Composition:** 0.9990 Silver .3633 oz. ASW **Subject:** AIDS **Obverse:** Cuban arms **Reverse:** AIDS ribbon on silhouette before world map

| Date | Mintage | F | VF | XF | Unc | BU |
|---|---|---|---|---|---|---|
| 1998 Proof | 50,000 | Value: 18.50 | | | | |

**5 PESOS** **KM# 655** **Weight:** 11.3000 g. **Composition:** 0.9990 Silver .3633 oz. ASW **Subject:** Expo 2000 - Philadelphia **Obverse:** Cuban arms **Reverse:** Cartoon above building

| Date | Mintage | F | VF | XF | Unc | BU |
|---|---|---|---|---|---|---|
| 1999 Proof | 31,000 | Value: 16.50 | | | | |

**5 PESOS** **KM# 656** **Weight:** 11.3000 g. **Composition:** 0.9990 Silver .3633 oz. ASW **Subject:** Expo 2000 - Hannover **Obverse:** Cuban arms **Reverse:** Cartoon above city hall

| Date | Mintage | F | VF | XF | Unc | BU |
|---|---|---|---|---|---|---|
| 1999 Proof | 31,000 | Value: 16.50 | | | | |

**5 PESOS** **KM# 657** **Weight:** 11.3000 g. **Composition:** 0.9990 Silver .3633 oz. ASW **Subject:** Expo 2000 - Osaka **Obverse:** Cuban arms **Reverse:** Cartoon above city view

| Date | Mintage | F | VF | XF | Unc | BU |
|---|---|---|---|---|---|---|
| 1999 Proof | 31,000 | Value: 16.50 | | | | |

**5 PESOS** **KM# 658** **Weight:** 11.3000 g. **Composition:** 0.9990 Silver .3633 oz. ASW **Subject:** Expo 2000 - Montreal **Obverse:** Cuban arms **Reverse:** Cartoon above sports buildings

| Date | Mintage | F | VF | XF | Unc | BU |
|---|---|---|---|---|---|---|
| 1999 Proof | 31,000 | Value: 16.50 | | | | |

**5 PESOS** **KM# 660** **Weight:** 11.3000 g. **Composition:** 0.9990 Silver .3633 oz. ASW **Subject:** Expo 2000 **Obverse:** Cuban arms **Reverse:** World map with logo center square

| Date | Mintage | F | VF | XF | Unc | BU |
|---|---|---|---|---|---|---|
| 1999 Proof | 31,000 | Value: 16.50 | | | | |

**5 PESOS** **KM# 673** **Composition:** 0.9990 Gold .0500 oz. AGW **Subject:** Zunzuncita **Reverse:** Hummingbird

| Date | Mintage | F | VF | XF | Unc | BU |
|---|---|---|---|---|---|---|
| 1999 Proof | — | Value: 75.00 | | | | |

**5 PESOS** **KM# 659** **Weight:** 11.3000 g. **Composition:** 0.9990 Silver .3633 oz. ASW **Subject:** Expo 2000 - Twipsy **Obverse:** Cuban arms **Reverse:** "Twipsy" in square **Note:** Similar to 50 Pesos, KM#654

| Date | Mintage | F | VF | XF | Unc | BU |
|---|---|---|---|---|---|---|
| 1999 Proof | 31,000 | Value: 16.50 | | | | |

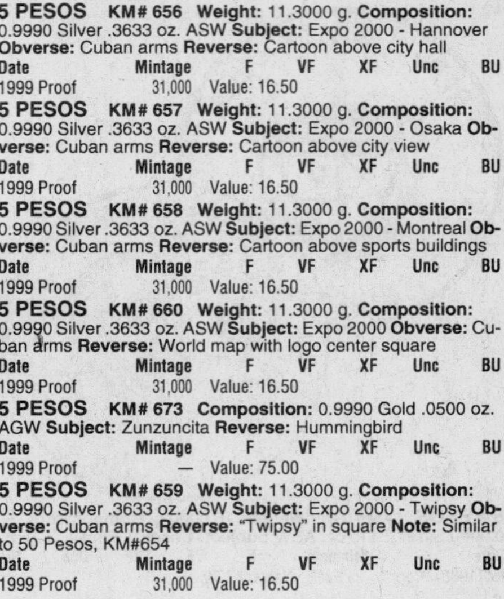

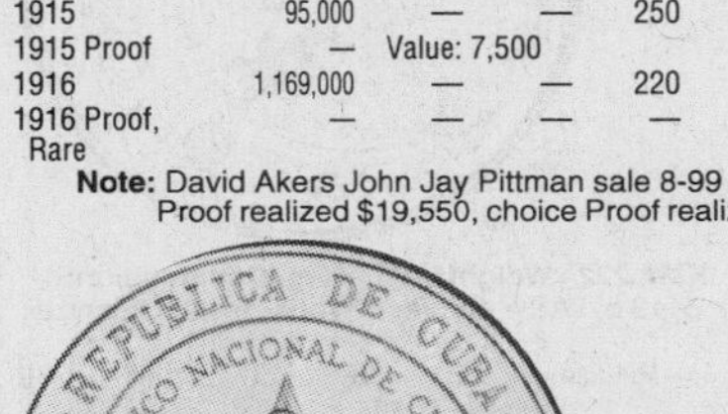

**10 PESOS** **KM# 20** **Weight:** 16.7185 g. **Composition:** 0.9000 Gold .4838 oz. AGW **Obverse:** Arms **Reverse:** Bust of Jose Marti

| Date | Mintage | F | VF | XF | Unc | BU |
|---|---|---|---|---|---|---|
| 1915 | 95,000 | — | — | 250 | 300 | — |
| 1915 Proof | — | Value: 7,500 | | | | |
| 1916 | 1,169,000 | — | — | 220 | 275 | — |
| 1916 Proof, Rare | — | — | — | — | — | — |

**Note:** David Akers John Jay Pittman sale 8-99 very choice Proof realized $19,550, choice Proof realized $14,950

**10 PESOS** **KM# 37** **Weight:** 26.6600 g. **Composition:** 0.9000 Silver .7715 oz. ASW **Subject:** 25th Anniversary - National Bank of Cuba

| Date | Mintage | F | VF | XF | Unc | BU |
|---|---|---|---|---|---|---|
| 1975 Proof | 55,000 | Value: 40.00 | | | | |

**10 PESOS** **KM# 50** **Weight:** 18.0000 g. **Composition:** 0.9990 Silver .5782 oz. ASW **Subject:** First Soviet-Cuban Space Flight

| Date | Mintage | F | VF | XF | Unc | BU |
|---|---|---|---|---|---|---|
| 1980 | 10,000 | — | — | — | 20.00 | — |
| 1980 Proof | 5,000 | Value: 35.00 | | | | |
| 1980- Matte proof | — | — | — | — | 45.00 | — |

**10 PESOS** **KM# 51** **Weight:** 18.0000 g. **Composition:** 0.9990 Silver .5782 oz. ASW **Subject:** Moscow Olympics

| Date | Mintage | F | VF | XF | Unc | BU |
|---|---|---|---|---|---|---|
| 1980 | 10,000 | — | — | — | 12.50 | — |
| 1980- Matte proof | — | Value: 65.00 | | | | |

**10 PESOS** **KM# 162** **Weight:** 31.1000 g. **Composition:** 0.9990 Silver 1.0000 oz. ASW **Subject:** Triumph of the Revolution

| Date | Mintage | F | VF | XF | Unc | BU |
|---|---|---|---|---|---|---|
| 1987 Proof | 2,000 | Value: 47.50 | | | | |
| 1988 Proof | 4,000 | Value: 37.50 | | | | |
| 1989 Proof | 2,000 | Value: 47.50 | | | | |

**10 PESOS** **KM# 163** **Weight:** 31.1000 g. **Composition:** 0.9990 Silver 1.0000 oz. ASW **Subject:** 60th Anniversary - Birth of Ernesto Che Guevara

| Date | Mintage | F | VF | XF | Unc | BU |
|---|---|---|---|---|---|---|
| 1987 Proof | 2,000 | Value: 47.50 | | | | |
| 1988 Proof | 4,000 | Value: 37.50 | | | | |
| 1989 Proof | 2,000 | Value: 47.50 | | | | |

**10 PESOS** **KM# 164** **Weight:** 31.1000 g. **Composition:** 0.9990 Silver 1.0000 oz. ASW **Subject:** 30th Anniversary - The March to Victory

| Date | Mintage | F | VF | XF | Unc | BU |
|---|---|---|---|---|---|---|
| 1987 Proof | 2,000 | Value: 47.50 | | | | |
| 1988 Proof | 4,000 | Value: 37.50 | | | | |
| 1989 Proof | 2,000 | Value: 47.50 | | | | |

**10 PESOS** **KM# 205** **Weight:** 31.1000 g. **Composition:** 0.9990 Silver 1.0000 oz. ASW **Subject:** 150th Anniversary - First Railroad in Spanish Cuba

| Date | Mintage | F | VF | XF | Unc | BU |
|---|---|---|---|---|---|---|
| 1988 Proof | 5,000 | Value: 37.50 | | | | |

**10 PESOS** **KM# 206** **Weight:** 31.1000 g. **Composition:** 0.9990 Silver 1.0000 oz. ASW **Subject:** 140th Anniversary - First Railroad in Spain

| Date | Mintage | F | VF | XF | Unc | BU |
|---|---|---|---|---|---|---|
| 1988 Proof | 5,000 | Value: 37.50 | | | | |

**10 PESOS** **KM# 207** **Weight:** 31.1000 g. **Composition:** 0.9990 Silver 1.0000 oz. ASW **Subject:** 160th Anniversary - First Railroad in England

| Date | Mintage | F | VF | XF | Unc | BU |
|---|---|---|---|---|---|---|
| 1988 Proof | 5,000 | Value: 37.50 | | | | |

**10 PESOS** **KM# 211** **Weight:** 3.1100 g. **Composition:** 0.9990 Gold .1000 oz. AGW **Subject:** Jose Marti

| Date | Mintage | F | VF | XF | Unc | BU |
|---|---|---|---|---|---|---|
| 1988 | 50 | — | — | — | 75.00 | — |
| 1988 Proof | 10 | Value: 125 | | | | |
| 1989 | 2,250 | — | — | — | 60.00 | — |
| 1989 Proof | 15 | Value: 125 | | | | |
| 1990 | 15 | — | — | — | 100 | — |
| 1990 Proof | 12 | Value: 125 | | | | |

**10 PESOS** **KM# 228** **Weight:** 31.1000 g. **Composition:** 0.9990 Silver 1.0000 oz. ASW **Subject:** Tania La Guerrillera

| Date | Mintage | F | VF | XF | Unc | BU |
|---|---|---|---|---|---|---|
| 1988 Proof | 5,000 | Value: 42.50 | | | | |

**10 PESOS** **KM# 229** **Weight:** 31.1000 g. **Composition:** 0.9990 Silver 1.0000 oz. ASW **Subject:** Camilo Cienfuegos

| Date | Mintage | F | VF | XF | Unc | BU |
|---|---|---|---|---|---|---|
| 1988 Proof | 5,000 | Value: 42.50 | | | | |

**10 PESOS** **KM# 230** **Weight:** 31.1000 g. **Composition:** 0.9990 Silver 1.0000 oz. ASW **Subject:** 35th Anniversary - Assault of the Moncada Garrison

| Date | Mintage | F | VF | XF | Unc | BU |
|---|---|---|---|---|---|---|
| ND(1988) Proof | 5,000 | Value: 42.50 | | | | |

**10 PESOS** **KM# 238** **Weight:** 20.0000 g. **Composition:** 0.9990 Silver .6431 oz. ASW **Subject:** 5th Centennial - Discovery of America

| Date | Mintage | F | VF | XF | Unc | BU |
|---|---|---|---|---|---|---|
| 1989 | 3,145 | — | — | — | 47.50 | — |

**10 PESOS** **KM# 239** **Weight:** 26.7200 g. **Composition:** 0.9990 Silver .8592 oz. ASW **Subject:** 200th Anniversary of French Revolution - Lady Justice

| Date | Mintage | F | VF | XF | Unc | BU |
|---|---|---|---|---|---|---|
| ND(1989) | 500 | — | — | — | 40.00 | — |
| ND(1989) Proof | 2,000 | Value: 60.00 | | | | |

**10 PESOS** **KM# 240** **Weight:** 26.7200 g. **Composition:** 0.9990 Silver .8592 oz. ASW **Subject:** 200th Anniversary of French Revolution - Bastille

| Date | Mintage | F | VF | XF | Unc | BU |
|---|---|---|---|---|---|---|
| ND(1989) | 500 | — | — | — | 45.00 | — |
| ND(1989) Proof | 2,000 | Value: 65.00 | | | | |

**10 PESOS** **KM# 241** **Weight:** 31.1000 g. **Composition:** 0.9990 Silver 1.0000 oz. ASW **Subject:** 30th Anniversary of Revolution - Castro

| Date | Mintage | F | VF | XF | Unc | BU |
|---|---|---|---|---|---|---|
| ND(1989) | 5,000 | — | — | — | 35.00 | — |
| ND(1989) Proof | 5,000 | Value: 45.00 | | | | |

**10 PESOS** **KM# 242** **Weight:** 31.1000 g. **Composition:** 0.9990 Silver 1.0000 oz. ASW **Subject:** 30th Anniversary of Revolution - Jose Marti and Castro

| Date | Mintage | F | VF | XF | Unc | BU |
|---|---|---|---|---|---|---|
| 1989 | 5,000 | — | — | — | 30.00 | — |
| 1989 Proof | 5,000 | Value: 40.00 | | | | |

**10 PESOS** **KM# 243** **Weight:** 31.1000 g. **Composition:** 0.9990 Silver 1.0000 oz. ASW **Subject:** 30th Anniversary of Revolution - Camilo Cienfuegos and Fidel Castro

| Date | Mintage | F | VF | XF | Unc | BU |
|---|---|---|---|---|---|---|
| ND | 5,000 | — | — | — | 35.00 | — |
| ND Proof | 5,000 | Value: 45.00 | | | | |

**10 PESOS** **KM# 249** **Weight:** 20.0000 g. **Composition:** 0.9990 Silver .6431 oz. ASW **Subject:** Discovery of America - 3 sailing ships

| Date | Mintage | F | VF | XF | Unc | BU |
|---|---|---|---|---|---|---|
| 1989 Proof | 8,855 | Value: 32.50 | | | | |

**10 PESOS** **KM# 383** **Weight:** 3.1100 g. **Composition:** 0.9990 Gold .1000 oz. AGW **Subject:** Alexander von Humboldt

| Date | Mintage | F | VF | XF | Unc | BU |
|---|---|---|---|---|---|---|
| 1989 | 500 | — | — | — | 50.00 | — |
| 1989 Proof | — | Value: 55.00 | | | | |

**10 PESOS** **KM# 252** **Weight:** 20.0000 g. **Composition:** 0.9990 Silver .6431 oz. ASW **Subject:** Discovery of America Ship and Cuba

| Date | Mintage | F | VF | XF | Unc | BU |
|---|---|---|---|---|---|---|
| 1990 Proof | 10,000 | Value: 32.50 | | | | |

**10 PESOS** **KM# 256** **Weight:** 20.0000 g. **Composition:** 0.9990 Silver .6431 oz. ASW **Subject:** 500th Anniversary of Columbus Meeting Native Americans

| Date | Mintage | F | VF | XF | Unc | BU |
|---|---|---|---|---|---|---|
| 1990 Proof | 10,000 | Value: 32.50 | | | | |

**10 PESOS** **KM# 262** **Weight:** 31.1030 g. **Composition:** 0.9990 Silver 1.0000 oz. ASW **Subject:** Celia Sanchez Manduley

| Date | Mintage | F | VF | XF | Unc | BU |
|---|---|---|---|---|---|---|
| 1990 Proof | 2,000 | Value: 55.00 | | | | |

**10 PESOS** **KM# 263** **Weight:** 31.1030 g. **Composition:** 0.9990 Silver 1.0000 oz. ASW **Subject:** Discovery of America King Ferdinand

| Date | Mintage | F | VF | XF | Unc | BU |
|---|---|---|---|---|---|---|
| 1990 Proof | 5,000 | Value: 50.00 | | | | |

**10 PESOS** **KM# 264** **Weight:** 31.1030 g. **Composition:** 0.9990 Silver 1.0000 oz. ASW **Subject:** Discovery of America Queen Isabella

| Date | Mintage | F | VF | XF | Unc | BU |
|---|---|---|---|---|---|---|
| 1990 Proof | 5,000 | Value: 50.00 | | | | |

**10 PESOS** **KM# 265** **Weight:** 31.1030 g. **Composition:** 0.9990 Silver 1.0000 oz. ASW **Subject:** Discovery of America Christopher Columbus

| Date | Mintage | F | VF | XF | Unc | BU |
|---|---|---|---|---|---|---|
| 1990 Proof | 5,000 | Value: 50.00 | | | | |

**10 PESOS** **KM# 266** **Weight:** 31.1030 g. **Composition:** 0.9990 Silver 1.0000 oz. ASW **Subject:** Discovery of America Juan de la Casa

| Date | Mintage | F | VF | XF | Unc | BU |
|---|---|---|---|---|---|---|
| 1990 Proof | 5,000 | Value: 50.00 | | | | |

**10 PESOS** **KM# 267** **Weight:** 20.0000 g. **Composition:** 0.9990 Silver .6438 oz. ASW **Subject:** Discovery of America Map of Columbus' route

| Date | Mintage | F | VF | XF | Unc | BU |
|---|---|---|---|---|---|---|
| 1990 Proof | 10,000 | Value: 32.50 | | | | |

**10 PESOS** **KM# 280** **Weight:** 25.0000 g. **Composition:** 0.9990 Silver .9037 oz. ASW **Subject:** Simon Bolivar

| Date | Mintage | F | VF | XF | Unc | BU |
|---|---|---|---|---|---|---|
| 1990 Proof | 3,300 | Value: 47.50 | | | | |

**10 PESOS** **KM# 291** **Weight:** 31.1000 g. **Composition:** 0.9990 Silver 1.0000 oz. ASW **Subject:** Pan American Games High Jumper

| Date | Mintage | F | VF | XF | Unc | BU |
|---|---|---|---|---|---|---|
| 1990 Proof | 3,000 | Value: 55.00 | | | | |

**10 PESOS** **KM# 292** **Weight:** 31.1000 g. **Composition:** 0.9990 Silver 1.0000 oz. ASW **Subject:** Pan American Games Volleyball

| Date | Mintage | F | VF | XF | Unc | BU |
|---|---|---|---|---|---|---|
| 1990 Proof | 3,000 | Value: 55.00 | | | | |

**10 PESOS** **KM# 293** **Weight:** 31.1000 g. **Composition:** 0.9990 Silver 1.0000 oz. ASW **Subject:** Pan American Games Baseball

| Date | Mintage | F | VF | XF | Unc | BU |
|---|---|---|---|---|---|---|
| 1990 Proof | 3,000 | Value: 57.50 | | | | |

**10 PESOS** **KM# 336** **Weight:** 28.0000 g. **Composition:** 0.9250 Silver .8327 oz. ASW **Subject:** Summer Olympics - Hurdler

| Date | Mintage | F | VF | XF | Unc | BU |
|---|---|---|---|---|---|---|
| 1990 Proof | 25,000 | Value: 25.00 | | | | |

**10 PESOS** **KM# 342** **Weight:** 3.1100 g. **Composition:** 0.9990 Gold .1000 oz. AGW **Subject:** Olympics - Basketball

| Date | Mintage | F | VF | XF | Unc | BU |
|---|---|---|---|---|---|---|
| 1990 Proof | Est. 5,000 | Value: 75.00 | | | | |

**10 PESOS** **KM# 344** **Weight:** 28.0000 g. **Composition:** 0.9250 Silver .8327 oz. ASW **Subject:** Summer Olympics - Volleyball

| Date | Mintage | F | VF | XF | Unc | BU |
|---|---|---|---|---|---|---|
| 1990 Proof | 25,000 | Value: 25.00 | | | | |

**10 PESOS** **KM# 345** **Weight:** 28.0000 g. **Composition:** 0.9250 Silver .8327 oz. ASW **Subject:** Summer Olympics - High Jumper

| Date | Mintage | F | VF | XF | Unc | BU |
|---|---|---|---|---|---|---|
| 1990 Proof | 25,000 | Value: 27.50 | | | | |

**10 PESOS** **KM# 362** **Weight:** 28.0000 g. **Composition:** 0.9250 Silver .8327 oz. ASW **Subject:** Olympics - Basketball

| Date | Mintage | F | VF | XF | Unc | BU |
|---|---|---|---|---|---|---|
| 1990 Proof | 25,000 | Value: 25.00 | | | | |

**10 PESOS** **KM# 369** **Weight:** 28.0000 g. **Composition:** 0.9990 Silver .8994 oz. ASW **Subject:** Olympics - Pommel Morse

| Date | Mintage | F | VF | XF | Unc | BU |
|---|---|---|---|---|---|---|
| 1990 Proof | Est. 25,000 | Value: 25.00 | | | | |

**10 PESOS** **KM# 327** **Weight:** 31.1000 g. **Composition:** 0.9990 Silver 1.0000 oz. ASW **Subject:** Vicente and Martin Pinzon

| Date | Mintage | F | VF | XF | Unc | BU |
|---|---|---|---|---|---|---|
| 1991 Proof | 3,000 | Value: 55.00 | | | | |

**10 PESOS** **KM# 328** **Weight:** 31.1000 g. **Composition:** 0.9990 Silver 1.0000 oz. ASW **Subject:** Hatuey Tribesman

| Date | Mintage | F | VF | XF | Unc | BU |
|---|---|---|---|---|---|---|
| 1991 Proof | 3,000 | Value: 55.00 | | | | |

**10 PESOS** **KM# 329** **Weight:** 25.0000 g. **Composition:** 0.9990 Silver .8031 oz. ASW **Subject:** American International Monetary Conference

| Date | Mintage | F | VF | XF | Unc | BU |
|---|---|---|---|---|---|---|
| ND(1991) Proof | 3,300 | Value: 55.00 | | | | |

**10 PESOS** **KM# 337** **Weight:** 27.0000 g. **Composition:** 0.9990 Silver .8673 oz. ASW **Subject:** Ibero - American - Columbus at Gardenas

| Date | Mintage | F | VF | XF | Unc | BU |
|---|---|---|---|---|---|---|
| 1991 Proof | 51,000 | Value: 40.00 | | | | |

**10 PESOS** **KM# 348** **Weight:** 31.1000 g. **Composition:** 0.9990 Silver 1.0000 oz. ASW **Subject:** Madrid - Alcala Gate

| Date | Mintage | F | VF | XF | Unc | BU |
|---|---|---|---|---|---|---|
| 1991 Proof | Est. 3,250 | Value: 55.00 | | | | |

**10 PESOS** **KM# 349** **Weight:** 31.1000 g. **Composition:** 0.9990 Silver 1.0000 oz. ASW **Subject:** Seville - La Giralda Tower

| Date | Mintage | F | VF | XF | Unc | BU |
|---|---|---|---|---|---|---|
| 1991 Proof | Est. 3,250 | Value: 55.00 | | | | |

**10 PESOS** **KM# 350** **Weight:** 31.1000 g. **Composition:** 0.9990 Silver 1.0000 oz. ASW **Subject:** Barcelona - Olympic Stadium

| Date | Mintage | F | VF | XF | Unc | BU |
|---|---|---|---|---|---|---|
| 1991 Proof | 3,250 | Value: 42.50 | | | | |

**10 PESOS** **KM# 525** **Weight:** 31.1000 g. **Composition:** 0.9990 Silver 1.0000 oz. ASW **Subject:** Diego Velazquez

| Date | Mintage | F | VF | XF | Unc | BU |
|---|---|---|---|---|---|---|
| 1991 Proof | 3,000 | Value: 55.00 | | | | |

**10 PESOS** **KM# 526** **Weight:** 31.1000 g. **Composition:** 0.9990 Silver 1.0000 oz. ASW **Subject:** Queen Joanna

| Date | Mintage | F | VF | XF | Unc | BU |
|---|---|---|---|---|---|---|
| 1991 Proof | 3,000 | Value: 55.00 | | | | |

**10 PESOS** **KM# 341.1** **Weight:** 20.0000 g. **Composition:** 0.9990 Silver .6430 oz. ASW **Subject:** Postal History of Cuba **Obverse:** 1992 style national arms **Reverse:** Spanish galleon sailship, 1765 date

| Date | Mintage | F | VF | XF | Unc | BU |
|---|---|---|---|---|---|---|
| 1992 Proof | 10,000 | Value: 35.00 | | | | |

**10 PESOS** **KM# 341.2** **Weight:** 20.0000 g. **Composition:** 0.9990 Silver .6430 oz. ASW **Obverse:** Pre 1990 detailed, styled arms

| Date | Mintage | F | VF | XF | Unc | BU |
|---|---|---|---|---|---|---|
| 1992 Proof | — | Value: 32.50 | | | | |

**10 PESOS** **KM# 351** **Weight:** 31.1000 g. **Composition:** 0.9990 Silver 1.0000 oz. ASW **Subject:** Seville - Tower of Gold

| Date | Mintage | F | VF | XF | Unc | BU |
|---|---|---|---|---|---|---|
| 1992 Proof | 2,050 | Value: 55.00 | | | | |

**10 PESOS** **KM# 352** **Weight:** 31.1000 g. **Composition:** 0.9990 Silver 1.0000 oz. ASW **Subject:** El Escorial

| Date | Mintage | F | VF | XF | Unc | BU |
|---|---|---|---|---|---|---|
| 1992 Proof | 2,050 | Value: 55.00 | | | | |

**10 PESOS** **KM# 353** **Weight:** 31.1000 g. **Composition:** 0.9990 Silver 1.0000 oz. ASW **Subject:** Philip I

| Date | Mintage | F | VF | XF | Unc | BU |
|---|---|---|---|---|---|---|
| 1992 Proof | 3,000 | Value: 55.00 | | | | |

**10 PESOS** **KM# 354.1** **Weight:** 20.0000 g. **Composition:** 0.9990 Silver .6430 oz. ASW **Subject:** Ptolomeo and Toscanelli

| Date | Mintage | F | VF | XF | Unc | BU |
|---|---|---|---|---|---|---|
| 1992 Proof | — | Value: 37.50 | | | | |

**10 PESOS** **KM# 354.2** **Weight:** 20.0000 g. **Composition:** 0.9990 Silver .6430 oz. ASW **Obverse:** Arms with thick wreath of the pre-1990 style

| Date | Mintage | F | VF | XF | Unc | BU |
|---|---|---|---|---|---|---|
| 1992 Proof | — | Value: 35.00 | | | | |

**10 PESOS** **KM# 355** **Weight:** 31.1000 g. **Composition:** 0.9990 Silver 1.0000 oz. ASW **Subject:** Guama Tribesman

| Date | Mintage | F | VF | XF | Unc | BU |
|---|---|---|---|---|---|---|
| 1992 Proof | 2,050 | Value: 55.00 | | | | |

**10 PESOS** **KM# 370** **Weight:** 20.0000 g. **Composition:** 0.9990 Silver .6430 oz. ASW **Subject:** Postal History - Steam powered sailing ship

| Date | Mintage | F | VF | XF | Unc | BU |
|---|---|---|---|---|---|---|
| 1992 Proof | 10,000 | Value: 32.50 | | | | |

**10 PESOS** **KM# 372** **Weight:** 31.0000 g. **Composition:** 0.9990 Silver 1.0000 oz. ASW **Subject:** Bartolome de Las Casas

| Date | Mintage | F | VF | XF | Unc | BU |
|---|---|---|---|---|---|---|
| 1992 Proof | 2,050 | Value: 50.00 | | | | |

**10 PESOS** **KM# 373** **Weight:** 31.0000 g. **Composition:** 0.9990 Silver 1.0000 oz. ASW **Subject:** Spanish Kings and Queens **Obverse:** Coat of arms

| Date | Mintage | F | VF | XF | Unc | BU |
|---|---|---|---|---|---|---|
| ND(1992) Proof | 2,050 | Value: 55.00 | | | | |

**10 PESOS** **KM# 374** **Weight:** 31.0000 g. **Composition:** 0.9990 Silver 1.0000 oz. ASW **Subject:** San Jorge Palace

| Date | Mintage | F | VF | XF | Unc | BU |
|---|---|---|---|---|---|---|
| 1992 Proof | 2,050 | Value: 40.00 | | | | |

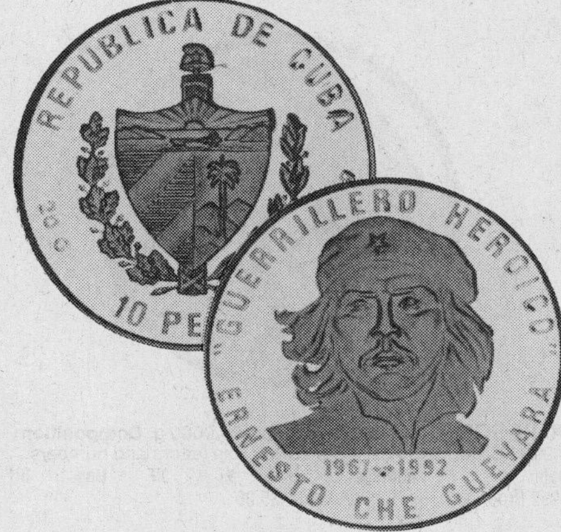


**10 PESOS** **KM# 527** **Weight:** 20.0000 g. **Composition:** 0.9990 Silver .6430 oz. ASW **Subject:** 25th Anniversary - Death of Ernesto Che Guevara

| Date | Mintage | F | VF | XF | Unc | BU |
|---|---|---|---|---|---|---|
| ND(1992) Proof | 10,000 | Value: 35.00 | | | | |

**10 PESOS** **KM# 561** **Weight:** 20.0000 g. **Composition:** 0.9990 Silver .6430 oz. ASW **Subject:** Cuban Postal History **Reverse:** Old steam and sail ship

| Date | Mintage | F | VF | XF | Unc | BU |
|---|---|---|---|---|---|---|
| 1992 Proof | — | Value: 32.50 | | | | |

**10 PESOS** **KM# 458.1** **Weight:** 20.0000 g. **Composition:** 0.9990 Silver .6430 oz. ASW **Subject:** World Cup Soccer **Note:** Thick letters and numbers.

| Date | Mintage | F | VF | XF | Unc | BU |
|---|---|---|---|---|---|---|
| 1992 Proof | — | Value: 35.00 | | | | |

**10 PESOS** **KM# 371.2** **Weight:** 20.0000 g. **Composition:** 0.9990 Silver .6430 oz. ASW **Note:** Thick wreath.

| Date | Mintage | F | VF | XF | Unc | BU |
|---|---|---|---|---|---|---|
| 1992 Proof | — | Value: 42.50 | | | | |

**10 PESOS** **KM# 458.2** **Weight:** 20.0000 g. **Composition:** 0.9990 Silver .6430 oz. ASW **Note:** Thin letters and numbers.

| Date | Mintage | F | VF | XF | Unc | BU |
|---|---|---|---|---|---|---|
| 1992 Proof | — | Value: 35.00 | | | | |

**10 PESOS** **KM# 371.1** **Weight:** 20.0000 g. **Composition:** 0.9990 Silver .6430 oz. ASW **Subject:** Introduction of Africans into America **Note:** Thin wreath.

| Date | Mintage | F | VF | XF | Unc | BU |
|---|---|---|---|---|---|---|
| 1992 Proof | 10,000 | Value: 42.50 | | | | |

**10 PESOS** **KM# 406.1** **Weight:** 31.1035 g. **Composition:** 0.9990 Silver 1.0000 oz. ASW **Subject:** Bolivar and Mari **Obverse:** Lower left division of the arms has two slanting bars on a solid field.

| Date | Mintage | F | VF | XF | Unc | BU |
|---|---|---|---|---|---|---|
| 1993 Proof | — | Value: 40.00 | | | | |

**10 PESOS** **KM# 406.2** **Weight:** 31.1035 g. **Composition:** 0.9990 Silver 1.0000 oz. ASW **Subject:** Bolivar and Marti **Obverse:** Lower left division of the arms has two slanting bars on a horizontally lined field.

| Date | Mintage | F | VF | XF | Unc | BU |
|---|---|---|---|---|---|---|
| 1993 Proof | — | Value: 60.00 | | | | |

**10 PESOS** **KM# 375** **Weight:** 20.0000 g. **Composition:** 0.9990 Silver .6430 oz. ASW **Subject:** President Abraham Lincoln

| Date | Mintage | F | VF | XF | Unc | BU |
|---|---|---|---|---|---|---|
| 1993 Proof | — | Value: 32.50 | | | | |

**10 PESOS** **KM# 398.1** **Weight:** 31.1000 g. **Composition:** 0.9990 Silver 1.0000 oz. ASW **Subject:** Fidel Castro **Reverse:** Frosted portrait

| Date | Mintage | F | VF | XF | Unc | BU |
|---|---|---|---|---|---|---|
| 1993 Proof | 5,000 | Value: 45.00 | | | | |

**10 PESOS** **KM# 398.2** **Weight:** 31.1000 g. **Composition:** 0.9990 Silver 1.0000 oz. ASW **Reverse:** Polished portrait

| Date | Mintage | F | VF | XF | Unc | BU |
|---|---|---|---|---|---|---|
| 1993 Proof | Inc. above | Value: 45.00 | | | | |

**10 PESOS** **KM# 399** **Weight:** 31.1000 g. **Composition:** 0.9990 Silver 1.0000 oz. ASW **Subject:** St. Jacobi

| Date | Mintage | F | VF | XF | Unc | BU |
|---|---|---|---|---|---|---|
| 1993 Proof | 5,000 | Value: 50.00 | | | | |

**10 PESOS** **KM# 406** **Weight:** 31.1000 g. **Composition:** 0.9990 Silver 1.0000 oz. ASW **Subject:** Bolivar and Marti

| Date | Mintage | F | VF | XF | Unc | BU |
|---|---|---|---|---|---|---|
| 1993 Proof | 3,000 | Value: 40.00 | | | | |

**10 PESOS** **KM# 407** **Weight:** 31.1000 g. **Composition:** 0.9990 Silver 1.0000 oz. ASW **Subject:** Frederico Garcia Lorca

| Date | Mintage | F | VF | XF | Unc | BU |
|---|---|---|---|---|---|---|
| 1993 Proof | 3,300 | Value: 45.00 | | | | |

**10 PESOS** **KM# 496** **Weight:** 19.9600 g. **Composition:** 0.9990 Silver .6411 oz. ASW **Subject:** Postal History - Steamship Almen Dares

| Date | Mintage | F | VF | XF | Unc | BU |
|---|---|---|---|---|---|---|
| 1993 Proof | — | Value: 45.00 | | | | |

**10 PESOS** **KM# 408** **Weight:** 19.9600 g. **Composition:** 0.9990 Silver .6411 oz. ASW **Subject:** Monticristi Manifesto

| Date | Mintage | F | VF | XF | Unc | BU |
|---|---|---|---|---|---|---|
| 1994 Proof | 3,300 | Value: 45.00 | | | | |

**10 PESOS** **KM# 427** **Weight:** 20.0000 g. **Composition:** 0.9990 Silver .6430 oz. ASW **Subject:** Sailing Ship - LA INDIA

| Date | Mintage | F | VF | XF | Unc | BU |
|---|---|---|---|---|---|---|
| 1994 Proof | 10,000 | Value: 32.50 | | | | |

**10 PESOS** **KM# 428** **Weight:** 20.0000 g. **Composition:** 0.9990 Silver .6430 oz. ASW **Subject:** Sailing Ship - NAO VICTORIA

| Date | Mintage | F | VF | XF | Unc | BU |
|---|---|---|---|---|---|---|
| 1994 Proof | 10,000 | Value: 32.50 | | | | |

**10 PESOS** **KM# 441** **Weight:** 20.0000 g. **Composition:** 0.9990 Silver .6430 oz. ASW **Subject:** Evangelista Island

| Date | Mintage | F | VF | XF | Unc | BU |
|---|---|---|---|---|---|---|
| 1994 Proof | — | Value: 32.50 | | | | |

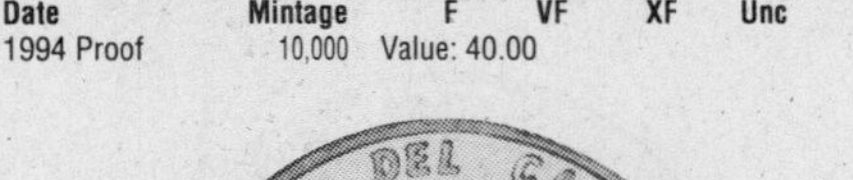

**10 PESOS** **KM# 442** **Weight:** 20.0000 g. **Composition:** 0.9990 Silver .6430 oz. ASW **Subject:** Caribbean Fauna - Multicolor Flamingos

| Date | Mintage | F | VF | XF | Unc | BU |
|---|---|---|---|---|---|---|
| 1994 Proof | 10,000 | Value: 40.00 | | | | |

**10 PESOS** **KM# 443** **Weight:** 20.0000 g. **Composition:** 0.9990 Silver .6430 oz. ASW **Subject:** Caribbean Fauna - Multicolor Yellow Sea Bass (Coney)

| Date | Mintage | F | VF | XF | Unc | BU |
|---|---|---|---|---|---|---|
| 1994 Proof | 10,000 | Value: 50.00 | | | | |

**10 PESOS** **KM# 468** **Weight:** 20.0000 g. **Composition:** 0.9990 Silver .6430 oz. ASW **Subject:** Environmental Protection - Scale

| Date | Mintage | F | VF | XF | Unc | BU |
|---|---|---|---|---|---|---|
| 1994 Proof | Est. 5,000 | Value: 45.00 | | | | |

**10 PESOS** **KM# 469** **Weight:** 20.0000 g. **Composition:** 0.9990 Silver .6430 oz. ASW **Subject:** 1996 Olympics - Boxers

| Date | Mintage | F | VF | XF | Unc | BU |
|---|---|---|---|---|---|---|
| 1994 Proof | Est. 30,000 | Value: 27.50 | | | | |

**10 PESOS** **KM# 470** **Weight:** 20.0000 g. **Composition:** 0.9990 Silver .6430 oz. ASW **Subject:** Red Baron Plane - Multicolor Fokker Dr. I

| Date | Mintage | F | VF | XF | Unc | BU |
|---|---|---|---|---|---|---|
| 1994 Proof | — | Value: 55.00 | | | | |

**10 PESOS** **KM# 499** **Weight:** 20.0000 g. **Composition:** 0.9990 Silver .6424 oz. ASW **Subject:** Caribbean Fauna - Multicolor Bottle-nosed Dolphins

| Date | Mintage | F | VF | XF | Unc | BU |
|---|---|---|---|---|---|---|
| 1994 Proof | Est. 10,000 | Value: 50.00 | | | | |

**10 PESOS** **KM# 500** **Weight:** 20.0000 g. **Composition:** 0.9990 Silver .6424 oz. ASW **Subject:** Caribbean Fauna - Multicolor Swordfish

| Date | Mintage | F | VF | XF | Unc | BU |
|---|---|---|---|---|---|---|
| 1994 Proof | 10,000 | Value: 40.00 | | | | |

**10 PESOS** **KM# 501** **Weight:** 20.0000 g. **Composition:** 0.9990 Silver .6424 oz. ASW **Subject:** Caribbean Fauna - Multicolor Brown Pelican

| Date | Mintage | F | VF | XF | Unc | BU |
|---|---|---|---|---|---|---|
| 1994 Proof | 10,000 | Value: 50.00 | | | | |

**10 PESOS** **KM# 502** **Weight:** 20.0000 g. **Composition:** 0.9990 Silver .6424 oz. ASW **Subject:** Caribbean Fauna - Multicolor Spotted Eagle Ray

| Date | Mintage | F | VF | XF | Unc | BU |
|---|---|---|---|---|---|---|
| 1994 Proof | 10,000 | Value: 60.00 | | | | |

**10 PESOS** **KM# 510.1** **Weight:** 20.0000 g. **Composition:** 0.9990 Silver .6424 oz. ASW **Subject:** World Cup Soccer - Football and Bridge **Obverse:** Thin letters **Reverse:** Thick letters and date

| Date | Mintage | F | VF | XF | Unc | BU |
|---|---|---|---|---|---|---|
| 1994 Proof | Est. 10,000 | Value: 50.00 | | | | |

**10 PESOS** **KM# 510.2** **Weight:** 20.0000 g. **Composition:** 0.9990 Silver .6424 oz. ASW **Obverse:** Thick letters **Reverse:** Thin letters and date

| Date | Mintage | F | VF | XF | Unc | BU |
|---|---|---|---|---|---|---|
| 1994 Proof | Inc. above | Value: 350 | | | | |

**10 PESOS** **KM# 528** **Weight:** 20.0000 g. **Composition:** 0.9990 Silver .6424 oz. ASW **Subject:** Albatross DII Fighter

| Date | Mintage | F | VF | XF | Unc | BU |
|---|---|---|---|---|---|---|
| 1994 Proof | — | Value: 42.50 | | | | |

**10 PESOS** **KM# 541** **Weight:** 27.0000 g. **Composition:** 0.9250 Silver .8030 oz. ASW **Subject:** Environmental Protection - Ivory-billed Woodpecker

| Date | Mintage | F | VF | XF | Unc | BU |
|---|---|---|---|---|---|---|
| 1994 Proof | 20,000 | Value: 45.00 | | | | |

**10 PESOS** **KM# 478** **Weight:** 20.0000 g. **Composition:** 0.9990 Silver .6430 oz. ASW **Subject:** Pirates of the Caribbean - Blackbeard

| Date | Mintage | F | VF | XF | Unc | BU |
|---|---|---|---|---|---|---|
| 1995 Proof | Est. 10,000 | Value: 60.00 | | | | |

**10 PESOS** **KM# 479** **Weight:** 20.0000 g. **Composition:** 0.9990 Silver .6430 oz. ASW **Subject:** Pirates of the Caribbean - Sir Henry Morgan

| Date | Mintage | F | VF | XF | Unc | BU |
|---|---|---|---|---|---|---|
| 1995 Proof | Est. 10,000 | Value: 60.00 | | | | |

**10 PESOS** **KM# 480** **Weight:** 20.0000 g. **Composition:** 0.9990 Silver .6430 oz. ASW **Subject:** Pirates of the Caribbean - Anne Bonny

| Date | Mintage | F | VF | XF | Unc | BU |
|---|---|---|---|---|---|---|
| 1995 Proof | Est. 10,000 | Value: 60.00 | | | | |

**10 PESOS** **KM# 481** **Weight:** 20.0000 g. **Composition:** 0.9990 Silver .6430 oz. ASW **Subject:** Pirates of the Caribbean - Mary Read

| Date | Mintage | F | VF | XF | Unc | BU |
|---|---|---|---|---|---|---|
| 1995 Proof | Est. 10,000 | Value: 60.00 | | | | |

**10 PESOS** **KM# 482** **Weight:** 20.0000 g. **Composition:** 0.9990 Silver .6430 oz. ASW **Subject:** Pirates of the Caribbean - Captain Kidd

| Date | Mintage | F | VF | XF | Unc | BU |
|---|---|---|---|---|---|---|
| 1995 Proof | Est. 10,000 | Value: 60.00 | | | | |

**10 PESOS** **KM# 483** **Weight:** 20.0000 g. **Composition:** 0.9990 Silver .6430 oz. ASW **Subject:** Pirates of the Caribbean - Piet Heyn

| Date | Mintage | F | VF | XF | Unc | BU |
|---|---|---|---|---|---|---|
| 1995 Proof | Est. 10,000 | Value: 60.00 | | | | |

**10 PESOS** **KM# 511** **Weight:** 20.0000 g. **Composition:** 0.9990 Silver .6430 oz. ASW **Subject:** Arnaldo Tamayo Mendez

| Date | Mintage | F | VF | XF | Unc | BU |
|---|---|---|---|---|---|---|
| 1995 Proof | Est. 5,000 | Value: 45.00 | | | | |

**10 PESOS** **KM# 529** **Weight:** 20.0000 g. **Composition:** 0.9990 Silver .6430 oz. ASW **Subject:** F.A.O. 50th Anniversary

| Date | Mintage | F | VF | XF | Unc | BU |
|---|---|---|---|---|---|---|
| ND(1995) Proof | 3,000 | Value: 40.00 | | | | |

**10 PESOS** **KM# 530** **Weight:** 31.1000 g. **Composition:** 0.9990 Silver 1.0000 oz. ASW **Subject:** Centennial 1895-1995

| Date | Mintage | F | VF | XF | Unc | BU |
|---|---|---|---|---|---|---|
| ND(1995) Proof | 500 | Value: 60.00 | | | | |

**10 PESOS** **KM# 540** **Weight:** 28.2800 g. **Composition:** 0.9250 Silver .8411 oz. ASW **Subject:** 50th Anniversary - United Nations

| Date | Mintage | F | VF | XF | Unc | BU |
|---|---|---|---|---|---|---|
| ND(1995) Proof | Est. 105,000 | Value: 40.00 | | | | |

**10 PESOS** **KM# 548** **Composition:** Silver And Enamel **Subject:** Seaplane - SIAI Marchetti S55

| Date | Mintage | F | VF | XF | Unc | BU |
|---|---|---|---|---|---|---|
| 1995 Proof | 15,000 | Value: 45.00 | | | | |

**10 PESOS** **KM# 574** **Weight:** 20.0000 g. **Composition:** 0.9990 Silver .6430 oz. ASW **Subject:** Death of Jose Marti

| Date | Mintage | F | VF | XF | Unc | BU |
|---|---|---|---|---|---|---|
| 1995 | — | — | — | — | 45.00 | — |

**10 PESOS** **KM# 600** **Weight:** 15.0000 g. **Composition:** 0.9990 Silver .6423 oz. ASW **Subject:** Caribbean Flora **Obverse:** Cuban arms **Reverse:** Multicolor flower, Ruelia tuberosa

| Date | Mintage | F | VF | XF | Unc | BU |
|---|---|---|---|---|---|---|
| ND(1995) Proof | 3,000 | Value: 40.00 | | | | |

**10 PESOS** **KM# 553** **Weight:** 20.0000 g. **Composition:** 0.9990 Silver And Multi-Color Enamel .6430 oz. **Subject:** Caribbean Fauna - Ruby Throaded Hummingbird

| Date | Mintage | F | VF | XF | Unc | BU |
|---|---|---|---|---|---|---|
| 1996 Proof | 5,000 | Value: 50.00 | | | | |

**10 PESOS** **KM# 554** **Composition:** Silver And Multi-Color Enamel **Subject:** Caribbean Fauna - Yellow Perch

| Date | Mintage | F | VF | XF | Unc | BU |
|---|---|---|---|---|---|---|
| 1996 Proof | 5,000 | Value: 40.00 | | | | |

**10 PESOS** **KM# 555** **Weight:** 20.0000 g. **Composition:** 0.9990 Silver And Multi-Color Enamel .6430 oz. **Subject:** Caribbean Fauna - Cuban Tody Bird

| Date | Mintage | F | VF | XF | Unc | BU |
|---|---|---|---|---|---|---|
| 1996 Proof | 5,000 | Value: 50.00 | | | | |

**10 PESOS** **KM# 556** **Weight:** 20.0000 g. **Composition:** 0.9990 Silver And Multi-Color Enamel .6430 oz. **Subject:** Caribbean Fauna - Wood Duck

| Date | Mintage | F | VF | XF | Unc | BU |
|---|---|---|---|---|---|---|
| 1996 Proof | 5,000 | — | — | — | 50.00 | — |

**10 PESOS** **KM# 566** **Weight:** 20.0000 g. **Composition:** 0.9990 Silver And Multi-Color Enamel .6430 oz. **Subject:** Caribbean Fauna - Papilio Butterfly

| Date | Mintage | F | VF | XF | Unc | BU |
|---|---|---|---|---|---|---|
| 1996 | 5,000 | Value: 75.00 | | | | |

**10 PESOS** **KM# 563.1** **Weight:** 20.0000 g. **Composition:** 0.9990 Silver And Multi-Color Enamel .6430 oz. **Subject:** Caribbean Fauna - Vaca Anil Fish

| Date | Mintage | F | VF | XF | Unc | BU |
|---|---|---|---|---|---|---|
| 1996 Proof | 5,000 | Value: 50.00 | | | | |

**10 PESOS** **KM# 582** **Weight:** 15.0000 g. **Composition:** 0.9990 Silver .6423 oz. ASW **Subject:** First Railroads - Germany **Obverse:** Cuban arms **Reverse:** First German locomotive, date 1835-1996

| Date | Mintage | F | VF | XF | Unc | BU |
|---|---|---|---|---|---|---|
| 1996 Proof | — | Value: 32.50 | | | | |

**10 PESOS** **KM# 583** **Weight:** 15.0000 g. **Composition:** 0.9990 Silver .6423 oz. ASW **Subject:** First Railroads - Austria **Obverse:** Cuban arms **Reverse:** First Austrian locomotive, date 1848-1996

| Date | Mintage | F | VF | XF | Unc | BU |
|---|---|---|---|---|---|---|
| 1996 Proof | — | Value: 32.50 | | | | |

**10 PESOS** **KM# 584** **Weight:** 15.0000 g. **Composition:** 0.9990 Silver .6423 oz. ASW **Subject:** First Railroads - Switzerland **Obverse:** Cuban arms **Reverse:** First Swiss locomotive, date 1847-1997

| Date | Mintage | F | VF | XF | Unc | BU |
|---|---|---|---|---|---|---|
| 1996 Proof | — | Value: 32.50 | | | | |

**10 PESOS** **KM# 585** **Weight:** 15.0000 g. **Composition:** 0.9990 Silver .6423 oz. ASW **Subject:** El Mundo de la Aventura **Obverse:** Cuban arms **Reverse:** Multicolor submarine and cameo portrait of Capt. Nemo

| Date | Mintage | F | VF | XF | Unc | BU |
|---|---|---|---|---|---|---|
| 1996 Proof | — | Value: 40.00 | | | | |

**10 PESOS** **KM# 586** **Weight:** 20.0000 g. **Composition:** 0.9990 Silver .6430 oz. ASW **Subject:** Campeonato Mundial de Futbol - Francia **Obverse:** Cuban arms **Reverse:** Joan of Arc with France's flag before soccer ball

| Date | Mintage | F | VF | XF | Unc | BU |
|---|---|---|---|---|---|---|
| 1996 Proof | — | Value: 45.00 | | | | |

**10 PESOS** **KM# 587** **Weight:** 20.0000 g. **Composition:** 0.9990 Silver .6430 oz. ASW **Subject:** America - El Nuevo Mundo **Obverse:** Cuban arms **Reverse:** Ship and cameo portrait of America Vespucci

| Date | Mintage | F | VF | XF | Unc | BU |
|---|---|---|---|---|---|---|
| 1996 Proof | — | Value: 35.00 | | | | |

**10 PESOS** **KM# 588** **Weight:** 20.0000 g. **Composition:** 0.9990 Silver .6430 oz. ASW **Subject:** World Food Summit **Obverse:** Cuban arms **Reverse:** Woman picking fruit, F.A.O. logo, dates

| Date | Mintage | F | VF | XF | Unc | BU |
|---|---|---|---|---|---|---|
| 1996 Proof | — | Value: 45.00 | | | | |

**10 PESOS** **KM# 589** **Weight:** 31.1035 g. **Composition:** 0.9990 Silver 1.0000 oz. ASW **Subject:** 40th Anniversary of the Granma's Landing **Obverse:** Cuban arms **Reverse:** Castro's portrait above ship

| Date | Mintage | F | VF | XF | Unc | BU |
|---|---|---|---|---|---|---|
| 1996 Proof | — | Value: 50.00 | | | | |

**10 PESOS** **KM# 590** **Weight:** 20.0000 g. **Composition:** 0.9990 Silver .6430 oz. ASW **Subject:** Circumnavigation of Cuba - Pinzon **Obverse:** Cuban arms **Reverse:** Sailship and cameo portrait of Vincente Pizon

| Date | Mintage | F | VF | XF | Unc | BU |
|---|---|---|---|---|---|---|
| 1997 Proof | — | Value: 35.00 | | | | |

**10 PESOS** **KM# 591** **Weight:** 15.0000 g. **Composition:** 0.9990 Silver .6423 oz. ASW **Subject:** XXVII Olimpiada **Obverse:** Cuban arms **Reverse:** Two fencers

| Date | Mintage | F | VF | XF | Unc | BU |
|---|---|---|---|---|---|---|
| 1997 Proof | — | Value: 35.00 | | | | |

**10 PESOS** **KM# 592** **Weight:** 15.0000 g. **Composition:** 0.9990 Silver .6423 oz. ASW **Subject:** XXVII Olimpiada **Obverse:** Cuban arms **Reverse:** Multicolor baseballl player at bat

| Date | Mintage | F | VF | XF | Unc | BU |
|---|---|---|---|---|---|---|
| 1997 Proof | — | Value: 40.00 | | | | |

**10 PESOS** **KM# 593** **Weight:** 15.0000 g. **Composition:** 0.9990 Silver .6423 oz. ASW **Subject:** Wonders of the Ancient World - Hanging Gardens of Babylon **Obverse:** Cuban arms **Reverse:** Street scene with terraced building

| Date | Mintage | F | VF | XF | Unc | BU |
|---|---|---|---|---|---|---|
| 1997 Proof | — | Value: 32.50 | | | | |

**10 PESOS** **KM# 594** **Weight:** 15.0000 g. **Composition:** 0.9990 Silver .6423 oz. ASW **Subject:** Wonders of the Ancient World - Temple of Artemis **Obverse:** Cuban arms **Reverse:** Large classic Greek building

| Date | Mintage | F | VF | XF | Unc | BU |
|---|---|---|---|---|---|---|
| 1997 Proof | — | Value: 32.50 | | | | |

**10 PESOS** **KM# 595** **Weight:** 15.0000 g. **Composition:** 0.9990 Silver .6423 oz. ASW **Subject:** Wonders of the Ancient

World - Lighthouse of Alexandria **Obverse:** Cuban arms **Reverse:** Ancient lighthouse

| Date | Mintage | F | VF | XF | Unc | BU |
|---|---|---|---|---|---|---|
| 1997 Proof | — | Value: 32.50 | | | | |

**10 PESOS** **KM# 596** **Weight:** 15.0000 g. **Composition:** 0.9990 Silver .6423 oz. ASW **Subject:** Wonders of the Ancient World - Colossus of Rhodes **Obverse:** Cuban arms **Reverse:** Statue of Colossus over break water

| Date | Mintage | F | VF | XF | Unc | BU |
|---|---|---|---|---|---|---|
| 1997 Proof | — | Value: 32.50 | | | | |

**10 PESOS** **KM# 597** **Weight:** 15.0000 g. **Composition:** 0.9990 Silver .6423 oz. ASW **Subject:** Wonders of the Ancient World - Egyptian Pyramids **Obverse:** Cuban arms **Reverse:** Painting above pyramids and excavation

| Date | Mintage | F | VF | XF | Unc | BU |
|---|---|---|---|---|---|---|
| 1997 Proof | — | Value: 32.50 | | | | |

**10 PESOS** **KM# 598** **Weight:** 15.0000 g. **Composition:** 0.9990 Silver .6423 oz. ASW **Subject:** Wonders of the Ancient World - Temple of Jupiter **Obverse:** Cuban arms **Reverse:** Statue of Jupiter inside temple

| Date | Mintage | F | VF | XF | Unc | BU |
|---|---|---|---|---|---|---|
| 1997 Proof | — | Value: 32.50 | | | | |

**10 PESOS** **KM# 601** **Weight:** 15.0000 g. **Composition:** 0.9990 Silver .6423 oz. ASW **Subject:** Caribbean FLora Sebestena **Obverse:** Cuban arms **Reverse:** Multicolor flower, "Cordia sebestena"

| Date | Mintage | F | VF | XF | Unc | BU |
|---|---|---|---|---|---|---|
| 1997 Proof | — | Value: 32.50 | | | | |

**10 PESOS** **KM# 602** **Weight:** 15.0000 g. **Composition:** 0.9990 Silver .6423 oz. ASW **Subject:** Caribbean FLora - Rosea **Obverse:** Cuban arms **Reverse:** Multicolor flower, "Lochnera rosea"

| Date | Mintage | F | VF | XF | Unc | BU |
|---|---|---|---|---|---|---|
| 1997 Proof | — | Value: 32.50 | | | | |

**10 PESOS** **KM# 603** **Weight:** 15.0000 g. **Composition:** 0.9990 Silver .6423 oz. ASW **Subject:** Caribbena Flora - Ulmifolia **Obverse:** Cuban arms **Reverse:** Multicolor flower, "Turnera ulmifolia"

| Date | Mintage | F | VF | XF | Unc | BU |
|---|---|---|---|---|---|---|
| 1997 Proof | — | Value: 32.50 | | | | |

**10 PESOS** **KM# 604** **Weight:** 15.0000 g. **Composition:** 0.9990 Silver .6423 oz. ASW **Subject:** Caribbean Flora - Pilosa **Obverse:** Cuban arms **Reverse:** Multicolor flower, "Bidens pilosa"

| Date | Mintage | F | VF | XF | Unc | BU |
|---|---|---|---|---|---|---|
| 1997 Proof | — | Value: 32.50 | | | | |

**10 PESOS** **KM# 609** **Weight:** 15.0000 g. **Composition:** 0.9990 Silver .4818 oz. ASW **Subject:** Sesqyucentennial of First Stearn/Sail Powered Ship **Obverse:** Cuban arms **Reverse:** Ship, date

| Date | Mintage | F | VF | XF | Unc | BU |
|---|---|---|---|---|---|---|
| 1997 Proof | 5,000 | Value: 42.50 | | | | |

**10 PESOS** **KM# 613** **Weight:** 31.1035 g. **Composition:** 0.9990 Silver 1.0000 oz. ASW **Subject:** Castro Visit to Vatican **Obverse:** Cuban arms **Reverse:** Pope and Castro meeting

| Date | Mintage | F | VF | XF | Unc | BU |
|---|---|---|---|---|---|---|
| 1997 | — | — | — | — | 55.00 | — |

**10 PESOS** **KM# 667** **Weight:** 15.0000 g. **Composition:** 0.9990 Silver .4818 oz. ASW **Subject:** 450th Anniversary - Birth of Cervantes

| Date | Mintage | F | VF | XF | Unc | BU |
|---|---|---|---|---|---|---|
| 1997 Proof | — | Value: 50.00 | | | | |

**10 PESOS** **KM# 625** **Weight:** 27.0000 g. **Composition:** 0.9250 Silver .8030 oz. ASW **Subject:** Ibero - American **Reverse:** 2 rumba dancers

| Date | Mintage | F | VF | XF | Unc | BU |
|---|---|---|---|---|---|---|
| 1997 | — | — | — | — | 50.00 | — |

**10 PESOS** **KM# 723** **Weight:** 31.1035 g. **Composition:** 0.9990 Silver 1.0000 oz. ASW **Subject:** 25th Anniversary Ernesto Che Guevara's Death **Obverse:** National arms and inscription. **Reverse:** Ernesto Che Guevara walking. **Edge:** Edge. **Size:** 42 mm.

| Date | Mintage | F | VF | XF | Unc | BU |
|---|---|---|---|---|---|---|
| ND(1997) Proof | 10,000 | Value: 50.00 | | | | |

**10 PESOS** **KM# 724** **Weight:** 31.1035 g. **Composition:** 0.9990 Silver 1.0000 oz. ASW **Subject:** 25th Anniversary - Ernesto Che Guevara's Death **Reverse:** Ernest Cheo Guevara's portrait. **Edge:** Reeded. **Size:** 42 mm.

| Date | Mintage | F | VF | XF | Unc | BU |
|---|---|---|---|---|---|---|
| ND(1997) Proof | 10,000 | Value: 50.00 | | | | |

**10 PESOS** **KM# 599** **Weight:** 15.0000 g. **Composition:** 0.9990 Silver .6423 oz. ASW **Subject:** Wonders of the Ancient World **Obverse:** Cuban Arms **Reverse:** Mausoleum of Halicarnas

| Date | Mintage | F | VF | XF | Unc | BU |
|---|---|---|---|---|---|---|
| 1997 Proof | — | Value: 32.50 | | | | |

**10 PESOS** **KM# 668** **Weight:** 31.1035 g. **Composition:** 0.9990 Silver 1.0015 oz. ASW **Subject:** Havana Puzzle - Frigate

Oquendo **Obverse:** Cuban arms. **Reverse:** Two sailing ships. **Edge:** Plain. **Size:** 45.2 x 35.1 mm. **Note:** Rectangular shaped.

| Date | Mintage | F | VF | XF | Unc | BU |
|---|---|---|---|---|---|---|
| 1998 Proof | — | Value: 50.00 | | | | |

**10 PESOS** **KM# 669** **Weight:** 31.1035 g. **Composition:** 0.9990 Silver 1.0015 oz. ASW **Subject:** Havana Puzzle - City of Havana **Obverse:** Cuban arms. **Reverse:** Havana city view. **Edge:** Plain. **Size:** 45.2 x 35.1 mm. **Note:** Rectangular shaped.

| Date | Mintage | F | VF | XF | Unc | BU |
|---|---|---|---|---|---|---|
| 1998 Proof | 3,000 | Value: 50.00 | | | | |

**10 PESOS** **KM# 670** **Weight:** 31.1800 g. **Composition:** 0.9990 Silver 1.0015 oz. ASW **Subject:** Havana Puzzle - Sailing Ship San Genaro **Obverse:** Cuban arms. **Reverse:** Three sailing ships. **Edge:** Plain. **Size:** 45.2 x 35.1 mm. **Note:** Rectangular shaped.

| Date | Mintage | F | VF | XF | Unc | BU |
|---|---|---|---|---|---|---|
| 1998 Proof | 3,000 | Value: 50.00 | | | | |

**10 PESOS** **KM# 671** **Weight:** 31.1800 g. **Composition:** 0.9990 Silver 1.0015 oz. ASW **Subject:** Hava Puzzle - El Morro **Obverse:** Cuban arms. **Reverse:** Light house and sailing ships. **Edge:** Plain. **Size:** 45.2 x 35.1 mm. **Note:** Rectangular shaped.

| Date | Mintage | F | VF | XF | Unc | BU |
|---|---|---|---|---|---|---|
| 1998 Proof | 3,000 | Value: 50.00 | | | | |

**10 PESOS** **KM# 648** **Weight:** 31.1035 g. **Composition:** 0.9990 Silver 1.0000 oz. ASW **Subject:** Expo 2000 - Twipsy **Obverse:** Cuban arms **Reverse:** "Twipsy" cartoon logo **Note:** Similar to 50 Pesos, KM$654.

| Date | Mintage | F | VF | XF | Unc | BU |
|---|---|---|---|---|---|---|
| 1998 Proof | 19,000 | Value: 35.00 | | | | |

**10 PESOS** **KM# 610** **Weight:** 15.0000 g. **Composition:** 0.9990 Silver .4818 oz. ASW **Subject:** Mississippi **Obverse:** Cuban arms **Reverse:** River boat

| Date | Mintage | F | VF | XF | Unc | BU |
|---|---|---|---|---|---|---|
| 1998 Proof | 5,000 | Value: 37.50 | | | | |

**10 PESOS** **KM# 611** **Weight:** 15.0000 g. **Composition:** 0.9990 Silver .4818 oz. ASW **Subject:** Rio Bravo **Obverse:** Cuban arms **Reverse:** Ship

| Date | Mintage | F | VF | XF | Unc | BU |
|---|---|---|---|---|---|---|
| 1998 Proof | — | Value: 35.00 | | | | |

**10 PESOS** **KM# 644** **Weight:** 31.1035 g. **Composition:** 0.9990 Silver 1.0000 oz. ASW **Subject:** Centenario - Explosion del Maine **Obverse:** Cuban arms **Reverse:** Exploding ship

| Date | Mintage | F | VF | XF | Unc | BU |
|---|---|---|---|---|---|---|
| 1998 Proof | 5,000 | Value: 65.00 | | | | |

**10 PESOS** **KM# 645** **Weight:** 31.1035 g. **Composition:** 0.9990 Silver 1.0000 oz. ASW **Subject:** Centenario - Battalla Naval de Santiago de Cuba **Obverse:** Cuban arms **Reverse:** Portrait of Admiral Cervera and burning ship

| Date | Mintage | F | VF | XF | Unc | BU |
|---|---|---|---|---|---|---|
| 1998 Proof | 5,000 | Value: 65.00 | | | | |

**10 PESOS** **KM# 646** **Weight:** 31.1035 g. **Composition:** 0.9990 Silver 1.0000 oz. ASW **Subject:** Centenario - Calixto Garcia - Combate en Oriente **Obverse:** Cuban arms **Reverse:** Portrait above three Cuban cavalry troopers

| Date | Mintage | F | VF | XF | Unc | BU |
|---|---|---|---|---|---|---|
| 1998 Proof | 5,000 | Value: 65.00 | | | | |

**10 PESOS** **KM# 647** **Weight:** 31.1035 g. **Composition:** 0.9990 Silver 1.0000 oz. ASW **Subject:** Leonor Molina **Reverse:** Souvenir peso design

| Date | Mintage | F | VF | XF | Unc | BU |
|---|---|---|---|---|---|---|
| 1998 Proof | 5,000 | Value: 55.00 | | | | |

**10 PESOS** **KM# 649** **Weight:** 31.1035 g. **Composition:** 0.9990 Silver 1.0000 oz. ASW **Subject:** Expo 2000 - Germany **Obverse:** Cuban arms **Reverse:** German map

| Date | Mintage | F | VF | XF | Unc | BU |
|---|---|---|---|---|---|---|
| 1998 Proof | 19,000 | Value: 35.00 | | | | |

**10 PESOS** **KM# 650** **Weight:** 31.1035 g. **Composition:** 0.9990 Silver 1.0000 oz. ASW **Subject:** Expo 2000 - London **Obverse:** Cuban arms **Reverse:** Cartoon over exhibit hall

| Date | Mintage | F | VF | XF | Unc | BU |
|---|---|---|---|---|---|---|
| 1998 Proof | 19,000 | Value: 35.00 | | | | |

**10 PESOS** **KM# 651** **Weight:** 31.1035 g. **Composition:** 0.9990 Silver 1.0000 oz. ASW **Subject:** Expo 2000 - Paris **Obverse:** Cuban arms **Reverse:** Cartoon and Eiffel Tower

| Date | Mintage | F | VF | XF | Unc | BU |
|---|---|---|---|---|---|---|
| 1998 Proof | 19,000 | Value: 35.00 | | | | |

**10 PESOS** **KM# 652** **Weight:** 31.1035 g. **Composition:** 0.9990 Silver 1.0000 oz. ASW **Subject:** Expo 2000 - Brussels **Obverse:** Cuban arms **Reverse:** Cartoon and Atomium structure

| Date | Mintage | F | VF | XF | Unc | BU |
|---|---|---|---|---|---|---|
| 1998 Proof | 19,000 | Value: 35.00 | | | | |

**10 PESOS** **KM# 653** **Weight:** 31.1035 g. **Composition:** 0.9990 Silver 1.0000 oz. ASW **Subject:** Expo 2000 - Postrimerias **Obverse:** Cuban arms **Reverse:** Cartoon on tree bearing world globe

| Date | Mintage | F | VF | XF | Unc | BU |
|---|---|---|---|---|---|---|
| 1998 Proof | 19,000 | Value: 35.00 | | | | |

**10 PESOS** **KM# 672** **Weight:** 31.1035 g. **Composition:** 0.9990 Silver 1.0000 oz. ASW **Subject:** 40th Anniversary - Triumph of the Revolution

| Date | Mintage | F | VF | XF | Unc | BU |
|---|---|---|---|---|---|---|
| 1999 Proof | — | Value: 45.00 | | | | |

**10 PESOS** **KM# 674** **Weight:** 31.1035 g. **Composition:** 0.9990 Silver 1.0000 oz. ASW **Subject:** Spanish Royal Visit Fidel Castro receives King Juan Carlos I

| Date | Mintage | F | VF | XF | Unc | BU |
|---|---|---|---|---|---|---|
| 1999 Proof | — | Value: 75.00 | | | | |

**10 PESOS** **KM# 676** **Weight:** 31.1035 g. **Composition:** 0.9990 Silver 1.0000 oz. ASW **Subject:** Spanish Royal Visit - 2 Peoples United

| Date | Mintage | F | VF | XF | Unc | BU |
|---|---|---|---|---|---|---|
| 1999 Proof | — | Value: 75.00 | | | | |

**10 PESOS** **KM# 677** **Weight:** 31.1035 g. **Composition:** 0.9990 Silver 1.0000 oz. ASW **Subject:** Spanish Royal Visit - Homage to the Spanish Soldier

| Date | Mintage | F | VF | XF | Unc | BU |
|---|---|---|---|---|---|---|
| 1999 Proof | — | Value: 75.00 | | | | |

**10 PESOS** **KM# 661** **Weight:** 31.1035 g. **Composition:** 0.9990 Silver 1.0000 oz. ASW **Subject:** Zunzuncito **Obverse:** National arms **Reverse:** Hummingbird **Edge:** Plain

| Date | Mintage | F | VF | XF | Unc | BU |
|---|---|---|---|---|---|---|
| 1999 Proof | — | Value: 50.00 | | | | |

**10 PESOS** **Composition:** 0.9990 Gold .1000 oz. AGW **Subject:** Zunzuncito **Edge:** Plain

| Date | Mintage | F | VF | XF | Unc | BU |
|---|---|---|---|---|---|---|
| 1999 Proof | — | — | — | — | 100 | — |

**10 PESOS** **Y# 725** **Weight:** 3.1100 g. **Composition:** 0.9990 Gold .1000 oz. AGW **Subject:** Zunzuncito **Obverse:** National arms. **Reverse:** Hummingbird. **Edge:** Reeded. **Size:** 18 mm.

| Date | Mintage | F | VF | XF | Unc | BU |
|---|---|---|---|---|---|---|
| 1999 Proof | 1,000 | Value: 100 | | | | |

**15 PESOS** **KM# 212** **Weight:** 3.8800 g. **Composition:** 0.9990 Gold .1250 oz. AGW **Subject:** Jose Marti

| Date | Mintage | F | VF | XF | Unc | BU |
|---|---|---|---|---|---|---|
| 1988 | 50 | — | — | — | 100 | — |
| 1988 Proof | 15 | Value: 150 | | | | |
| 1989 | 50 | — | — | — | 100 | — |
| 1989 Proof | 15 | Value: 150 | | | | |
| 1990 | 15 | — | — | — | 125 | — |
| 1990 Proof | 12 | Value: 150 | | | | |

**20 PESOS** **KM# 21** **Weight:** 33.4370 g. **Composition:** 0.9000 Gold .9676 oz. AGW **Subject:** Jose Marti

| Date | Mintage | F | VF | XF | Unc | BU |
|---|---|---|---|---|---|---|
| 1915 | 57,000 | BV | 475 | 550 | 750 | — |
| 1915 Proof; Rare | — | — | — | — | — | — |

**Note:** David Akers John Jay Pittman sale 8-99 very choice proof 1915 realized $11,500

| Date | Mintage | F | VF | XF | Unc | BU |
|---|---|---|---|---|---|---|
| 1916 Proof; Rare | 10 | — | — | — | — | — |

**Note:** David Akers John Jay Pittman sale 8-99 nearly choice Proof 1916 realized $43,125

**20 PESOS** **KM# 38** **Weight:** 26.0000 g. **Composition:** 0.9250 Silver .7732 oz. ASW **Subject:** Ignacio Agramonte

| Date | Mintage | F | VF | XF | Unc | BU |
|---|---|---|---|---|---|---|
| 1977 Proof | 25,000 | Value: 32.50 | | | | |

**20 PESOS** **KM# 39** **Weight:** 26.0000 g. **Composition:** 0.9250 Silver .7732 oz. ASW **Subject:** Maximo Gomez

| Date | Mintage | F | VF | XF | Unc | BU |
|---|---|---|---|---|---|---|
| 1977 Proof | 75,000 | Value: 28.00 | | | | |

**20 PESOS** **KM# 40** **Weight:** 26.0000 g. **Composition:** 0.9250 Silver .7732 oz. ASW **Subject:** Antonio Maceo

| Date | Mintage | F | VF | XF | Unc | BU |
|---|---|---|---|---|---|---|
| 1977 Proof | 75,000 | Value: 28.00 | | | | |

**20 PESOS** **KM# 41** **Weight:** 26.0000 g. **Composition:** 0.9250 Silver .7732 oz. ASW **Subject:** 60th Anniversary Socialist Revolution - Lenin

| Date | Mintage | F | VF | XF | Unc | BU |
|---|---|---|---|---|---|---|
| 1977 Proof | 100 | Value: 1,400 | | | | |

**20 PESOS** **KM# 44** **Weight:** 26.0000 g. **Composition:** 0.9250 Silver .7732 oz. ASW **Subject:** Nonaligned Nations Conference

| Date | Mintage | F | VF | XF | Unc | BU |
|---|---|---|---|---|---|---|
| 1979 | 20,000 | — | — | — | 12.50 | — |
| 1979 Proof | — | Value: 60.00 | | | | |
| 1980- Matte Proof | — | Value: 100 | | | | |

**20 PESOS** **KM# 169** **Weight:** 62.2000 g. **Composition:** 0.9990 Silver 2.0000 oz. ASW **Subject:** Triumph of the Revolution

| Date | Mintage | F | VF | XF | Unc | BU |
|---|---|---|---|---|---|---|
| 1987 Proof | 500 | Value: 85.00 | | | | |
| 1988 Proof | 1,000 | Value: 75.00 | | | | |
| 1989 Proof | 500 | Value: 85.00 | | | | |

**20 PESOS** **KM# 170** **Weight:** 62.2000 g. **Composition:** 0.9990 Silver 2.0000 oz. ASW **Subject:** 60th Anniversary - Birth of Ernesto Che Guevara

| Date | Mintage | F | VF | XF | Unc | BU |
|---|---|---|---|---|---|---|
| 1987 Proof | 500 | Value: 85.00 | | | | |
| 1988 Proof | 1,000 | Value: 75.00 | | | | |
| 1989 Proof | 500 | Value: 85.00 | | | | |

**20 PESOS** **KM# 171** **Weight:** 62.2000 g. **Composition:** 0.9990 Silver 2.0000 oz. ASW **Subject:** 30th Anniversary - The March to Victory

| Date | Mintage | F | VF | XF | Unc | BU |
|---|---|---|---|---|---|---|
| 1987 Proof | 333 | Value: 85.00 | | | | |
| 1988 Proof | 1,000 | Value: 75.00 | | | | |
| 1989 Proof | 500 | Value: 85.00 | | | | |

**20 PESOS** **KM# 232** **Weight:** 62.2000 g. **Composition:** 0.9990 Silver 2.0000 oz. ASW **Subject:** 150th Anniversary - Railroad in Cuba

| Date | Mintage | F | VF | XF | Unc | BU |
|---|---|---|---|---|---|---|
| 1988 Proof | Est. 1,000 | Value: 80.00 | | | | |

**20 PESOS** **KM# 233** **Weight:** 62.2000 g. **Composition:** 0.9990 Silver 2.0000 oz. ASW **Subject:** 140th Anniversary - Railroad in Spain

| Date | Mintage | F | VF | XF | Unc | BU |
|---|---|---|---|---|---|---|
| ND(1988) Proof | Est. 1,000 | Value: 80.00 | | | | |

**20 PESOS** **KM# 234** **Weight:** 62.2000 g. **Composition:** 0.9990 Silver 2.0000 oz. ASW **Subject:** 160th Anniversary - Railroad in England

| Date | Mintage | F | VF | XF | Unc | BU |
|---|---|---|---|---|---|---|
| 1988 Proof | Est. 1,000 | Value: 80.00 | | | | |

**20 PESOS** **KM# 235** **Weight:** 62.2000 g. **Composition:** 0.9990 Silver 2.0000 oz. ASW **Subject:** Tania La Guerrillera

| Date | Mintage | F | VF | XF | Unc | BU |
|---|---|---|---|---|---|---|
| 1988 Proof | 1,000 | Value: 75.00 | | | | |

**20 PESOS** **KM# 236** **Weight:** 62.2000 g. **Composition:** 0.9990 Silver 2.0000 oz. ASW **Subject:** Camilo Cienfuegos

| Date | Mintage | F | VF | XF | Unc | BU |
|---|---|---|---|---|---|---|
| 1988 Proof | 1,000 | Value: 75.00 | | | | |

**20 PESOS** **KM# 237** **Weight:** 62.2000 g. **Composition:** 0.9990 Silver 2.0000 oz. ASW **Subject:** 35th Anniversary - Assault of the Moncada Garrison

| Date | Mintage | F | VF | XF | Unc | BU |
|---|---|---|---|---|---|---|
| ND(1988) Proof | 1,000 | Value: 75.00 | | | | |

**20 PESOS** **KM# 531** **Weight:** 62.2000 g. **Composition:** 0.9990 Silver 2.0000 oz. ASW **Subject:** Jose Raul Capablanca

| Date | Mintage | F | VF | XF | Unc | BU |
|---|---|---|---|---|---|---|
| ND(1988) Proof | 1,000 | Value: 90.00 | | | | |

**20 PESOS** **KM# 532** **Weight:** 62.2000 g. **Composition:** 0.9990 Silver 2.0000 oz. ASW **Subject:** 25th Anniversary - Death of Ernesto Che Guevara

| Date | Mintage | F | VF | XF | Unc | BU |
|---|---|---|---|---|---|---|
| ND(1992) Proof | 1,000 | Value: 80.00 | | | | |

**20 PESOS** **KM# 471.1** **Weight:** 62.2000 g. **Composition:** 0.9990 Silver 2.0000 oz. ASW **Subject:** Fidel Castro - 40th Anniversary of Moncada

| Date | Mintage | F | VF | XF | Unc | BU |
|---|---|---|---|---|---|---|
| 1993 Proof | — | Value: 90.00 | | | | |

**20 PESOS** **KM# 459** **Weight:** 62.2000 g. **Composition:** 0.9990 Silver 2.0000 oz. ASW **Subject:** Cuban Railroad

| Date | Mintage | F | VF | XF | Unc | BU |
|---|---|---|---|---|---|---|
| 1994 Proof | — | Value: 90.00 | | | | |

**20 PESOS** **KM# 533** **Weight:** 62.2000 g. **Composition:** 0.9990 Silver 2.0000 oz. ASW **Subject:** Transportation - Zeppelin

| Date | Mintage | F | VF | XF | Unc | BU |
|---|---|---|---|---|---|---|
| 1995 Proof | 1,000 | Value: 95.00 | | | | |

**25 PESOS** **KM# 213** **Weight:** 7.7700 g. **Composition:** 0.9990 Gold .2500 oz. AGW **Subject:** Jose Marti

| Date | Mintage | F | VF | XF | Unc | BU |
|---|---|---|---|---|---|---|
| 1988 | 50 | — | — | — | 200 | — |
| 1988 Proof | 15 | Value: 300 | | | | |
| 1989 | 50 | — | — | — | 200 | — |
| 1989 Proof | 15 | Value: 300 | | | | |
| 1990 | 12 | — | — | — | 250 | — |
| 1990 Proof | 12 | Value: 300 | | | | |

**25 PESOS** **Y# 726** **Weight:** 7.7759 g. **Composition:** 0.9990 Gold .2500 oz. AGW **Subject:** Zunzuncito **Obverse:** National arms. **Reverse:** Hummingbird. **Edge:** Reeded. **Size:** 20 mm.

| Date | Mintage | F | VF | XF | Unc | BU |
|---|---|---|---|---|---|---|
| 1999 Proof | 1,000 | Value: 135 | | | | |

**30 PESOS** **KM# 431** **Weight:** 93.3000 g. **Composition:** 0.9990 Silver 2.9970 oz. ASW **Subject:** Diego Velazquez

| Date | Mintage | F | VF | XF | Unc | BU |
|---|---|---|---|---|---|---|
| 1991 Proof | 1,000 | Value: 165 | | | | |

**30 PESOS** **KM# 422** **Weight:** 93.2500 g. **Composition:** 0.9990 Silver 2.9951 oz. ASW **Subject:** Vincente and Martin Pinzon **Note:** Similar to 10 Pesos, KM#327.

| Date | Mintage | F | VF | XF | Unc | BU |
|---|---|---|---|---|---|---|
| 1991 Proof | 1,000 | Value: 125 | | | | |

**30 PESOS** **KM# 423** **Weight:** 93.2500 g. **Composition:** 0.9990 Silver 2.9951 oz. ASW **Subject:** Hatuey People **Note:** Similar to 10 Pesos, KM#328.

| Date | Mintage | F | VF | XF | Unc | BU |
|---|---|---|---|---|---|---|
| 1991 Proof | 1,000 | Value: 125 | | | | |

**30 PESOS** **KM# 430** **Weight:** 93.3000 g. **Composition:** 0.9990 Silver 2.9970 oz. ASW **Subject:** Queen Joanna **Note:** Similar to 10 Pesos, KM#328.

| Date | Mintage | F | VF | XF | Unc | BU |
|---|---|---|---|---|---|---|
| 1991 Proof | 1,000 | Value: 165 | | | | |

**30 PESOS** **KM# 376** **Weight:** 93.2500 g. **Composition:** 0.9990 Silver 2.9951 oz. ASW **Subject:** Guama Native

| Date | Mintage | F | VF | XF | Unc | BU |
|---|---|---|---|---|---|---|
| 1992 Proof | 550 | Value: 125 | | | | |

**30 PESOS** **KM# 377** **Weight:** 93.2500 g. **Composition:** 0.9990 Silver 2.9951 oz. ASW **Subject:** Bartolome de Las Casas

| Date | Mintage | F | VF | XF | Unc | BU |
|---|---|---|---|---|---|---|
| 1992 Proof | 550 | Value: 125 | | | | |

**30 PESOS** **KM# 378** **Weight:** 93.2500 g. **Composition:** 0.9990 Silver 2.9951 oz. ASW **Subject:** King Philipp

| Date | Mintage | F | VF | XF | Unc | BU |
|---|---|---|---|---|---|---|
| 1992 Proof | 550 | Value: 125 | | | | |

**30 PESOS** **KM# 379** **Weight:** 93.2500 g. **Composition:** 0.9990 Silver 2.9951 oz. ASW **Subject:** Spanish Kings and Queens

| Date | Mintage | F | VF | XF | Unc | BU |
|---|---|---|---|---|---|---|
| ND(1992) Proof | 550 | Value: 125 | | | | |

**50 PESOS** **KM# 208** **Weight:** 15.5500 g. **Composition:** 0.9990 Gold .5000 oz. AGW **Subject:** 30th Anniversary - The March to Victory

| Date | Mintage | F | VF | XF | Unc | BU |
|---|---|---|---|---|---|---|
| 1988 Proof | 150 | Value: 300 | | | | |

**50 PESOS** **KM# 209** **Weight:** 15.5500 g. **Composition:** 0.9990 Gold .5000 oz. AGW **Subject:** 60th Anniversary - Birth of Ernesto Che Guevara

| Date | Mintage | F | VF | XF | Unc | BU |
|---|---|---|---|---|---|---|
| 1988 Proof | 150 | Value: 300 | | | | |

**50 PESOS** **KM# 210** **Weight:** 15.5500 g. **Composition:** 0.9990 Gold .5000 oz. AGW **Subject:** Triumph of the Revolutionary

| Date | Mintage | F | VF | XF | Unc | BU |
|---|---|---|---|---|---|---|
| 1988 Proof | 150 | Value: 300 | | | | |

**50 PESOS** **KM# 214** **Weight:** 15.5500 g. **Composition:** 0.9990 Gold .5000 oz. AGW **Subject:** Jose Marti

| Date | Mintage | F | VF | XF | Unc | BU |
|---|---|---|---|---|---|---|
| 1988 | 12 | — | — | — | 450 | — |
| 1988 Proof | 15 | Value: 600 | | | | |
| 1989 | 150 | — | — | — | 300 | — |
| 1989 Proof | 15 | Value: 600 | | | | |
| 1990 | 15 | — | — | — | 450 | — |
| 1990 Proof | 12 | Value: 600 | | | | |

**50 PESOS** **KM# 314** **Weight:** 15.5500 g. **Composition:** 0.9990 Gold .5000 oz. AGW **Subject:** 150th Anniversary - First Train in Spanish America **Reverse:** Train **Rev. Legend:** HABANA-BEJUCAL **Note:** Similar to 10 Pesos, KM#205.

| Date | Mintage | F | VF | XF | Unc | BU |
|---|---|---|---|---|---|---|
| 1989 Proof | 150 | Value: 260 | | | | |

**50 PESOS** **KM# 315** **Weight:** 15.5500 g. **Composition:** 0.9990 Gold .5000 oz. AGW **Subject:** 140th Anniversary - First Train in Spain **Reverse:** Train **Rev. Legend:** BARCELONA-MATARD **Note:** Similar to 10 Pesos, KM#206.

| Date | Mintage | F | VF | XF | Unc | BU |
|---|---|---|---|---|---|---|
| 1989 Proof | 150 | Value: 260 | | | | |

**50 PESOS** **KM# 313** **Weight:** 15.5500 g. **Composition:** 0.9990 Gold .5000 oz. AGW **Subject:** 160th Anniversary - First Train in England **Reverse:** Train, Liverpool - Manchester **Note:** Similar to 10 Pesos, KM#207.

| Date | Mintage | F | VF | XF | Unc | BU |
|---|---|---|---|---|---|---|
| 1989 Proof | 150 | Value: 260 | | | | |

**50 PESOS** **KM# 330** **Weight:** 15.5500 g. **Composition:** 0.9990 Gold .5000 oz. AGW **Subject:** Tania La Guerrillera **Reverse:** Portrait of female guerilla fighter **Note:** Similar to 10 Pesos, KM#228.

| Date | Mintage | F | VF | XF | Unc | BU |
|---|---|---|---|---|---|---|
| 1989 Proof | 150 | Value: 375 | | | | |

**50 PESOS** **KM# 331** **Weight:** 15.5500 g. **Composition:** 0.9990 Gold .5000 oz. AGW **Subject:** Camilo Cienfuegos Gornaran **Reverse:** Portrait of Camilo Cienfuegos **Note:** Similar to 10 Pesos, KM#229

| Date | Mintage | F | VF | XF | Unc | BU |
|---|---|---|---|---|---|---|
| 1989 Proof | 150 | Value: 375 | | | | |

**50 PESOS** **KM# 332** **Weight:** 15.5500 g. **Composition:** 0.9990 Gold .5000 oz. AGW **Subject:** Assualt of the Moncada Garrison **Reverse:** Battle scene **Note:** Similar to 10 Pesos, KM#230.

| Date | Mintage | F | VF | XF | Unc | BU |
|---|---|---|---|---|---|---|
| 1989 Proof | 150 | Value: 375 | | | | |

**50 PESOS** **KM# 295** **Weight:** 155.5150 g. **Composition:** 0.9990 Silver 5.0000 oz. ASW **Subject:** 500th Anniversary - Discovery of America **Reverse:** King Ferdinand of Spain **Note:** Similar to 10 Pesos, KM#263.

| Date | Mintage | F | VF | XF | Unc | BU |
|---|---|---|---|---|---|---|
| 1990 Proof | 2,000 | Value: 110 | | | | |

**50 PESOS** **KM# 299** **Weight:** 15.5500 g. **Composition:** 0.9990 Gold .5000 oz. AGW **Subject:** 500th Anniversary - Discovery of America **Reverse:** Portrait of King Ferdinand V **Note:** Similar to 10 Pesos, KM#263.

| Date | Mintage | F | VF | XF | Unc | BU |
|---|---|---|---|---|---|---|
| 1990 Proof | 250 | Value: 300 | | | | |

**50 PESOS** **KM# 296** **Weight:** 155.5150 g. **Composition:** 0.9990 Silver 5.0000 oz. ASW **Subject:** 500th Anniversary - Discovery of America **Reverse:** Queen Isabella of Spain **Note:** Similar to 10 Pesos, KM#264.

| Date | Mintage | F | VF | XF | Unc | BU |
|---|---|---|---|---|---|---|
| 1990 Proof | 2,000 | Value: 110 | | | | |

**50 PESOS** **KM# 300** **Weight:** 15.5500 g. **Composition:** 0.9990 Gold .5000 oz. AGW **Subject:** 500th Anniversary - Discovery of America **Reverse:** Portrait of Queen Isabella of Spain **Note:** Similar to 10 Pesos, KM#264.

| Date | Mintage | F | VF | XF | Unc | BU |
|---|---|---|---|---|---|---|
| 1990 Proof | 250 | Value: 300 | | | | |

**50 PESOS** **KM# 298** **Weight:** 15.5500 g. **Composition:** 0.9990 Gold .5000 oz. AGW **Subject:** 500th Anniversary - Discovery of America **Reverse:** Portrait of Christopher Columbus **Note:** Similar to 10 Pesos, KM#265.

| Date | Mintage | F | VF | XF | Unc | BU |
|---|---|---|---|---|---|---|
| 1990 Proof | 250 | Value: 300 | | | | |

**50 PESOS** **KM# 301** **Weight:** 15.5500 g. **Composition:** 0.9990 Gold .5000 oz. AGW **Subject:** 500th Anniversary - Discovery of America **Reverse:** Portrait of Juan de la Cosa **Note:** Similar to 10 Pesos, KM#266.

| Date | Mintage | F | VF | XF | Unc | BU |
|---|---|---|---|---|---|---|
| 1990 Proof | 250 | Value: 300 | | | | |

**50 PESOS** **KM# 281** **Weight:** 15.5500 g. **Composition:** 0.9990 Gold .5000 oz. AGW **Subject:** Simon Bolivar **Reverse:** Portrait of Simon Bolivar **Note:** Similar to 10 Pesos, KM#280.

| Date | Mintage | F | VF | XF | Unc | BU |
|---|---|---|---|---|---|---|
| 1990 Proof | 50 | Value: 325 | | | | |

**50 PESOS** **KM# 322** **Weight:** 15.5500 g. **Composition:** 0.9990 Gold .5000 oz. AGW **Subject:** Pan American Games -

High Jump **Reverse:** High jumper clearing pole **Note:** Similar to 10 Pesos, KM#291.

| Date | Mintage | F | VF | XF | Unc | BU |
|---|---|---|---|---|---|---|
| 1990 Proof | 15 | Value: 400 | | | | |

**50 PESOS** **KM# 323** **Weight:** 15.5500 g. **Composition:** 0.9990 Gold .5000 oz. AGW **Subject:** Pan American Games - Volleyball **Reverse:** Volleyball players **Note:** Similar to 10 Pesos, KM#292

| Date | Mintage | F | VF | XF | Unc | BU |
|---|---|---|---|---|---|---|
| 1990 Proof | 15 | Value: 400 | | | | |

**50 PESOS** **KM# 321** **Weight:** 15.5500 g. **Composition:** 0.9990 Gold .5000 oz. AGW **Subject:** Pan American Games - Baseball **Reverse:** Baseball players **Note:** Similar to 10 Pesos, KM#293.

| Date | Mintage | F | VF | XF | Unc | BU |
|---|---|---|---|---|---|---|
| 1990 Proof | 15 | Value: 400 | | | | |

**50 PESOS** **KM# 297** **Weight:** 155.5150 g. **Composition:** 0.9990 Silver 5.0000 oz. ASW **Subject:** 500th Anniversary - Discovery of America **Reverse:** Juan de la Cosa **Note:** Similar to10 Pesos, KM#266.

| Date | Mintage | F | VF | XF | Unc | BU |
|---|---|---|---|---|---|---|
| 1990 Proof | 2,000 | Value: 110 | | | | |

**50 PESOS** **KM# 294** **Weight:** 155.5150 g. **Composition:** 0.9990 Silver 5.0000 oz. ASW **Subject:** 500th Anniversary - Discovery of America **Reverse:** Christopher Columbus

| Date | Mintage | F | VF | XF | Unc | BU |
|---|---|---|---|---|---|---|
| 1990 Proof | 2,000 | Value: 110 | | | | |

**50 PESOS** **KM# 339** **Weight:** 15.5500 g. **Composition:** 0.9990 Gold .5000 oz. AGW **Subject:** Hatuey Tribesman

| Date | Mintage | F | VF | XF | Unc | BU |
|---|---|---|---|---|---|---|
| 1991 Proof | 200 | Value: 300 | | | | |

**50 PESOS** **KM# 343** **Weight:** 155.5000 g. **Composition:** 0.9990 Silver 5.0000 oz. ASW **Subject:** Olympics - Stadium **Obverse:** Simlar to 30 Pesos, KM#376

| Date | Mintage | F | VF | XF | Unc | BU |
|---|---|---|---|---|---|---|
| 1991 Proof | 1,050 | Value: 240 | | | | |

**50 PESOS** **KM# 432** **Weight:** 155.5000 g. **Composition:** 0.9990 Silver 5.0000 oz. ASW **Subject:** 500th Anniversary - Queen Joanna

| Date | Mintage | F | VF | XF | Unc | BU |
|---|---|---|---|---|---|---|
| 1991 | 1,000 | — | — | — | — | — |

**50 PESOS** **KM# 433** **Weight:** 155.5000 g. **Composition:** 0.9990 Silver 5.0000 oz. ASW **Subject:** 500th Anniversary - Diego Valezquez

| Date | Mintage | F | VF | XF | Unc | BU |
|---|---|---|---|---|---|---|
| 1991 | 1,000 | — | — | — | — | — |

**50 PESOS** **KM# 434** **Weight:** 155.5000 g. **Composition:** 0.9990 Silver 5.0000 oz. ASW **Subject:** 500th Anniversary - Pinzon Brothers

| Date | Mintage | F | VF | XF | Unc | BU |
|---|---|---|---|---|---|---|
| 1991 Proof | 1,000 | Value: 165 | | | | |

**50 PESOS** **KM# 435** **Weight:** 155.5000 g. **Composition:** 0.9990 Silver 5.0000 oz. ASW **Subject:** 500th Anniversary - Hatuey Tribesman

| Date | Mintage | F | VF | XF | Unc | BU |
|---|---|---|---|---|---|---|
| 1991 Proof | 1,000 | Value: 165 | | | | |

**50 PESOS** **KM# 444** **Weight:** 15.5500 g. **Composition:** 0.9990 Gold .5000 oz. AGW **Subject:** Queen Joanna **Note:** Similar to KM#432.

| Date | Mintage | F | VF | XF | Unc | BU |
|---|---|---|---|---|---|---|
| 1991 Proof | 200 | Value: 300 | | | | |

**50 PESOS** **KM# 445** **Weight:** 15.5500 g. **Composition:** 0.9990 Gold .5000 oz. AGW **Subject:** Diego Valezquez **Note:** Similar to KM#433.

| Date | Mintage | F | VF | XF | Unc | BU |
|---|---|---|---|---|---|---|
| 1991 Proof | 200 | Value: 300 | | | | |

**50 PESOS** **KM# 446** **Weight:** 15.5500 g. **Composition:** 0.9990 Gold .5000 oz. AGW **Subject:** Pinzon Brothers **Note:** Similar to KM#434.

| Date | Mintage | F | VF | XF | Unc | BU |
|---|---|---|---|---|---|---|
| 1991 Proof | 200 | Value: 300 | | | | |

**50 PESOS** **KM# 356** **Weight:** 155.5000 g. **Composition:** 0.9990 Silver 5.0000 oz. ASW **Subject:** Madrid - Alcala Gate **Note:** Similar to 10 Pesos, KM#348.

| Date | Mintage | F | VF | XF | Unc | BU |
|---|---|---|---|---|---|---|
| 1991 Proof | 550 | Value: 285 | | | | |

**50 PESOS** **KM# 357** **Weight:** 155.5000 g. **Composition:** 0.9990 Silver 5.0000 oz. ASW **Subject:** Seville - La Giralda Tower **Note:** Similar to 10 Pesos, KM#349.

| Date | Mintage | F | VF | XF | Unc | BU |
|---|---|---|---|---|---|---|
| 1991 Proof | 550 | Value: 285 | | | | |

**50 PESOS** **KM# 568** **Weight:** 155.7300 g. **Composition:** 0.9990 Silver 5.0019 oz. ASW **Subject:** El Escorial **Note:** Similar to 10 Pesos, KM#352.

| Date | Mintage | F | VF | XF | Unc | BU |
|---|---|---|---|---|---|---|
| 1992 Proof | — | Value: 175 | | | | |

**50 PESOS** **KM# 359** **Weight:** 155.5000 g. **Composition:** 0.9990 Silver 5.0000 oz. ASW **Subject:** Chief Guama **Note:** Similar to 10 Pesos, KM#355.

| Date | Mintage | F | VF | XF | Unc | BU |
|---|---|---|---|---|---|---|
| 1992 Proof | 550 | Value: 185 | | | | |

**50 PESOS** **KM# 382** **Weight:** 155.7300 g. **Composition:** 0.9990 Silver 5.0019 oz. ASW **Subject:** San Jorge Palace **Note:** Similar to 10 Pesos, KM#374.

| Date | Mintage | F | VF | XF | Unc | BU |
|---|---|---|---|---|---|---|
| 1992 Proof | 550 | Value: 185 | | | | |

**50 PESOS** **KM# 380** **Weight:** 155.7300 g. **Composition:** 0.9990 Silver 5.0019 oz. ASW **Subject:** Bartolome de Las Casas **Note:** Similar to 10 Pesos, KM#392.

| Date | Mintage | F | VF | XF | Unc | BU |
|---|---|---|---|---|---|---|
| 1992 Proof | 550 | Value: 185 | | | | |

**50 PESOS** **KM# 381** **Weight:** 155.7300 g. **Composition:** 0.9990 Silver 5.0019 oz. ASW **Subject:** Spanish Kings and Queens **Note:** Similar to 10 Pesos, KM#395.

| Date | Mintage | F | VF | XF | Unc | BU |
|---|---|---|---|---|---|---|
| ND(1992) Proof | 550 | Value: 185 | | | | |

**50 PESOS** **KM# 358** **Weight:** 155.5000 g. **Composition:** 0.9990 Silver 5.0000 oz. ASW **Subject:** Philip I **Note:** Similar to 10 Pesos, KM#533.

| Date | Mintage | F | VF | XF | Unc | BU |
|---|---|---|---|---|---|---|
| 1992 Proof | 550 | Value: 185 | | | | |

**50 PESOS** **KM# 641** **Weight:** 155.7300 g. **Composition:** 0.9990 Silver 5.0019 oz. ASW **Subject:** 1982 - Ano de Espana **Obverse:** Cuban arms **Reverse:** Seville's Tower of Gold

| Date | Mintage | F | VF | XF | Unc | BU |
|---|---|---|---|---|---|---|
| 1992 Proof | — | Value: 200 | | | | |

**50 PESOS** **KM# 693** **Weight:** 15.5518 g. **Composition:** 0.9990 Gold .4990 oz. AGW **Subject:** 40th Anniversary - Assault on Moncada Garrison

| Date | Mintage | F | VF | XF | Unc | BU |
|---|---|---|---|---|---|---|
| 1993 Proof | — | Value: 350 | | | | |

**50 PESOS** **KM# 400** **Weight:** 155.5150 g. **Composition:** 0.9990 Silver 5.0000 oz. ASW **Subject:** St. Jacobi **Note:** Similar to 10 Pesos, KM#399.

| Date | Mintage | F | VF | XF | Unc | BU |
|---|---|---|---|---|---|---|
| 1993 Proof | 1,000 | Value: 175 | | | | |

**50 PESOS** **KM# 503** **Weight:** 155.5150 g. **Composition:** 0.9990 Silver 5.0000 oz. ASW **Subject:** Caribbean Fauna - Bottle-nosed dophins **Edge:** Reeded

| Date | Mintage | F | VF | XF | Unc | BU |
|---|---|---|---|---|---|---|
| 1994 Proof | 2,500 | Value: 225 | | | | |

**50 PESOS** **KM# 504** **Weight:** 155.5150 g. **Composition:** 0.9990 Silver 5.0000 oz. ASW **Subject:** Caribbean Fauna - Swordfish

| Date | Mintage | F | VF | XF | Unc | BU |
|---|---|---|---|---|---|---|
| 1994 Proof | 2,500 | Value: 200 | | | | |

**50 PESOS** **KM# 507** **Weight:** 155.5150 g. **Composition:** 0.9990 Silver 5.0000 oz. ASW **Subject:** Caribbean Fauna - yellow sea bass (Coney)

| Date | Mintage | F | VF | XF | Unc | BU |
|---|---|---|---|---|---|---|
| 1994 Proof | 2,500 | Value: 200 | | | | |

**50 PESOS** **KM# 505** **Weight:** 155.5150 g. **Composition:** 0.9990 Silver 5.0000 oz. ASW **Subject:** Caribbean Fauna - brown pelican

| Date | Mintage | F | VF | XF | Unc | BU |
|---|---|---|---|---|---|---|
| 1994 Proof | 2,500 | Value: 225 | | | | |

**50 PESOS** **KM# 508** **Weight:** 155.5150 g. **Composition:** 0.9990 Silver 5.0000 oz. ASW **Subject:** Caribbean Fauna - spotted eagle ray

| Date | Mintage | F | VF | XF | Unc | BU |
|---|---|---|---|---|---|---|
| 1994 Proof | 2,500 | Value: 250 | | | | |

**50 PESOS** **KM# 506** **Weight:** 155.5150 g. **Composition:** 0.9990 Silver 5.0000 oz. ASW **Subject:** Caribbean Fauna - flamingos

| Date | Mintage | F | VF | XF | Unc | BU |
|---|---|---|---|---|---|---|
| 1994 Proof | 2,500 | Value: 200 | | | | |

**50 PESOS** **KM# 484** **Weight:** 155.5150 g. **Composition:** 0.9990 Silver 5.0000 oz. ASW **Subject:** Pirate of the Caribbean - Blackbeard

| Date | Mintage | F | VF | XF | Unc | BU |
|---|---|---|---|---|---|---|
| 1995 Proof | Est. 3,000 | Value: 265 | | | | |

**50 PESOS** **KM# 485** **Weight:** 155.5150 g. **Composition:** 0.9990 Silver 5.0000 oz. ASW **Subject:** Pirates of the Caribbean - Sir Henry Morgan

| Date | Mintage | F | VF | XF | Unc | BU |
|---|---|---|---|---|---|---|
| 1995 Proof | Est. 3,000 | Value: 265 | | | | |

**50 PESOS** **KM# 486** **Weight:** 155.5150 g. **Composition:** 0.9990 Silver 5.0000 oz. ASW **Subject:** Pirates of the Caribbean - Anne Bonny

| Date | Mintage | F | VF | XF | Unc | BU |
|---|---|---|---|---|---|---|
| 1995 Proof | Est. 3,000 | Value: 265 | | | | |

**50 PESOS** **KM# 487** **Weight:** 155.5150 g. **Composition:** 0.9990 Silver 5.0000 oz. ASW **Subject:** Pirates of the Caribbean - Mary Read

| Date | Mintage | F | VF | XF | Unc | BU |
|---|---|---|---|---|---|---|
| 1995 Proof | Est. 3,000 | Value: 265 | | | | |

**50 PESOS** **KM# 488** **Weight:** 155.5150 g. **Composition:** 0.9990 Silver 5.0000 oz. ASW **Subject:** Pirates of the Caribbean - Captain Kidd

| Date | Mintage | F | VF | XF | Unc | BU |
|---|---|---|---|---|---|---|
| 1995 Proof | Est. 3,000 | Value: 265 | | | | |

**50 PESOS** **KM# 489** **Weight:** 155.5150 g. **Composition:** 0.9990 Silver 5.0000 oz. ASW **Subject:** Pirates of the Caribbean - Piet Heyn

| Date | Mintage | F | VF | XF | Unc | BU |
|---|---|---|---|---|---|---|
| 1995 Proof | Est. 3,000 | Value: 265 | | | | |

**50 PESOS** **KM# 490** **Weight:** 13.0000 g. **Composition:** 0.9170 Gold .3829 oz. AGW **Subject:** Pirates of the Caribbean - Blackbeard

| Date | Mintage | F | VF | XF | Unc | BU |
|---|---|---|---|---|---|---|
| 1995 Proof | Est. 1,000 | Value: 275 | | | | |

**50 PESOS** **KM# 491** **Weight:** 13.0000 g. **Composition:** 0.9170 Gold .3829 oz. AGW **Subject:** Pirates of the Caribbean - Sir Henry Morgan

| Date | Mintage | F | VF | XF | Unc | BU |
|---|---|---|---|---|---|---|
| 1995 Proof | Est. 1,000 | Value: 275 | | | | |

**50 PESOS** **KM# 492** **Weight:** 13.0000 g. **Composition:** 0.9170 Gold .3829 oz. AGW **Subject:** Pirates of the Caribbean - Anne Bonny

| Date | Mintage | F | VF | XF | Unc | BU |
|---|---|---|---|---|---|---|
| 1995 Proof | Est. 1,000 | Value: 275 | | | | |

**50 PESOS** **KM# 493** **Weight:** 13.0000 g. **Composition:** 0.9170 Gold .3829 oz. AGW **Subject:** Pirates of the Caribbean - Mary Read

| Date | Mintage | F | VF | XF | Unc | BU |
|---|---|---|---|---|---|---|
| 1995 Proof | Est. 1,000 | Value: 275 | | | | |

**50 PESOS** **KM# 494** **Weight:** 13.0000 g. **Composition:** 0.9170 Gold .3829 oz. AGW **Subject:** Pirates of the Caribbean - Captain Kidd

| Date | Mintage | F | VF | XF | Unc | BU |
|---|---|---|---|---|---|---|
| 1995 Proof | Est. 1,000 | Value: 275 | | | | |

**50 PESOS** **KM# 495** **Weight:** 13.0000 g. **Composition:** 0.9170 Gold .3829 oz. AGW **Subject:** Pirates of the Caribbean - Piet Heyn

| Date | Mintage | F | VF | XF | Unc | BU |
|---|---|---|---|---|---|---|
| 1995 Proof | Est. 1,000 | Value: 275 | | | | |

**50 PESOS** **KM# 564** **Weight:** 155.0000 g. **Composition:** 0.9990 Silver 4.9944 oz. ASW **Subject:** Caribbean Fauna - Vaca anil fish **Note:** Similar to 10 Pesos, KM#563.

| Date | Mintage | F | VF | XF | Unc | BU |
|---|---|---|---|---|---|---|
| 1996 Proof | 950 | Value: 300 | | | | |

**50 PESOS** **KM# 557** **Weight:** 155.0000 g. **Composition:** 0.9990 Silver 4.9944 oz. ASW **Subject:** Caribbean Fauna - Ruby throated hummingbird **Note:** Similar to 1 Peso, KM#549.

| Date | Mintage | F | VF | XF | Unc | BU |
|---|---|---|---|---|---|---|
| 1996 Proof | 950 | Value: 300 | | | | |

**50 PESOS** **KM# 558** **Weight:** 155.0000 g. **Composition:** 0.9990 Silver 4.9944 oz. ASW **Subject:** Caribbean Fauna - yellow perch **Note:** Similar to 1 Peso, KM#550.

| Date | Mintage | F | VF | XF | Unc | BU |
|---|---|---|---|---|---|---|
| 1996 Proof | 950 | Value: 300 | | | | |

**50 PESOS** **KM# 559** **Weight:** 155.0000 g. **Composition:** 0.9990 Silver 4.9944 oz. ASW **Subject:** Caribbean Fauna - Cuban tody bird **Note:** Similar to 1 Peso, KM#551.

| Date | Mintage | F | VF | XF | Unc | BU |
|---|---|---|---|---|---|---|
| 1996 Proof | 950 | Value: 300 | | | | |

**50 PESOS** **KM# 560** **Weight:** 155.0000 g. **Composition:** 0.9990 Silver 4.9944 oz. ASW **Subject:** Caribbean Fauna - shy duck **Note:** Similar to 1 Peso, KM#552.

| Date | Mintage | F | VF | XF | Unc | BU |
|---|---|---|---|---|---|---|
| 1996 Proof | 950 | Value: 300 | | | | |

**50 PESOS** **KM# 567** **Weight:** 155.0000 g. **Composition:** 0.9990 Silver 4.9944 oz. ASW **Subject:** Caribbean Fauna - papilio butterfly **Note:** Similar to 10 Pesos, IM#566.

| Date | Mintage | F | VF | XF | Unc | BU |
|---|---|---|---|---|---|---|
| 1996 Proof | 950 | Value: 300 | | | | |

**50 PESOS** **KM# 694** **Weight:** 155.0000 g. **Composition:** 0.9990 Silver 4.9944 oz. ASW **Subject:** Caribbean Flora - bidens **Reverse:** Multicolor flower, "Bidens Romerillo"

| Date | Mintage | F | VF | XF | Unc | BU |
|---|---|---|---|---|---|---|
| 1997 Proof | — | Value: 300 | | | | |

**50 PESOS** **KM# 695** **Weight:** 155.0000 g. **Composition:** 0.9990 Silver 4.9944 oz. ASW **Subject:** Caribbean Flora - cordia **Reverse:** Multicolor flower, "Cordia Vomitel"

| Date | Mintage | F | VF | XF | Unc | BU |
|---|---|---|---|---|---|---|
| 1997 Proof | — | Value: 300 | | | | |

**50 PESOS** **KM# 697** **Weight:** 155.0000 g. **Composition:** 0.9990 Silver 4.9944 oz. ASW **Subject:** Wonders of the Ancient World - Temple of Artemisa

| Date | Mintage | F | VF | XF | Unc | BU |
|---|---|---|---|---|---|---|
| 1997 Proof | — | Value: 250 | | | | |

**50 PESOS** **KM# 698** **Weight:** 155.0000 g. **Composition:** 0.9990 Silver 4.9944 oz. ASW **Subject:** Wonders of the Ancient World - Pyramids

| Date | Mintage | F | VF | XF | Unc | BU |
|---|---|---|---|---|---|---|
| 1997 Proof | — | Value: 250 | | | | |

**50 PESOS** **KM# 699** **Weight:** 155.0000 g. **Composition:** 0.9990 Silver 4.9944 oz. ASW **Subject:** Wonders of the Ancient World - Hanging Gardesn of Babylon

| Date | Mintage | F | VF | XF | Unc | BU |
|---|---|---|---|---|---|---|
| 1997 Proof | — | Value: 250 | | | | |

**50 PESOS** **KM# 700** **Weight:** 155.0000 g. **Composition:** 0.9990 Silver 4.9944 oz. ASW **Subject:** Wonders of teh Ancient World - Statue of Jupiter at Olympus

| Date | Mintage | F | VF | XF | Unc | BU |
|---|---|---|---|---|---|---|
| 1997 Proof | — | Value: 250 | | | | |

**50 PESOS** **KM# 701** **Weight:** 155.0000 g. **Composition:** 0.9990 Silver 4.9944 oz. ASW **Subject:** Wonders of the Ancient World - Colossus of Rhodes

| Date | Mintage | F | VF | XF | Unc | BU |
|---|---|---|---|---|---|---|
| 1997 Proof | — | Value: 250 | | | | |

**50 PESOS** **KM# 702** **Weight:** 155.0000 g. **Composition:** 0.9990 Silver 4.9944 oz. ASW **Subject:** Wonders of the Ancient World - Mausoleum at Halicarnasos

| Date | Mintage | F | VF | XF | Unc | BU |
|---|---|---|---|---|---|---|
| 1997 Proof | — | Value: 250 | | | | |

**50 PESOS** **KM# 654** **Weight:** 15.5500 g. **Composition:** 0.9990 Gold .4999 oz. AGW **Subject:** Expo 2000 **Obverse:** Cuban arms **Reverse:** Twipsy cartoon logo

| Date | Mintage | F | VF | XF | Unc | BU |
|---|---|---|---|---|---|---|
| 1998 Proof | 3,125 | Value: 275 | | | | |

**50 PESOS** **KM# 638** **Weight:** 15.5500 g. **Composition:** 0.9990 Gold .4999 oz. AGW **Subject:** AIDS **Obverse:** Cuban arms **Reverse:** AIDS ribbon on silhouette before world map

| Date | Mintage | F | VF | XF | Unc | BU |
|---|---|---|---|---|---|---|
| 1998 Proof | 2,000 | Value: 320 | | | | |

**50 PESOS** **KM# 703** **Weight:** 15.5500 g. **Composition:** 0.9990 Gold .4999 oz. AGW **Subject:** 40th Anniversary - Triumph of the Revolution

| Date | Mintage | F | VF | XF | Unc | BU |
|---|---|---|---|---|---|---|
| 1999 Proof | — | Value: 450 | | | | |

**50 PESOS** **KM# 704** **Weight:** 15.5500 g. **Composition:** 0.9990 Gold .4999 oz. AGW **Subject:** Zunzuncito **Reverse:** Hummingbird

| Date | Mintage | F | VF | XF | Unc | BU |
|---|---|---|---|---|---|---|
| 1999 Proof | — | Value: 400 | | | | |

**50 PESOS** **Y# 727** **Weight:** 15.5518 g. **Composition:** 0.9990 Gold .5000 oz. AGW **Subject:** Zunzuncito **Obverse:** National arms. **Reverse:** Hummingbird. **Edge:** Reeded. **Size:** 32.5 mm.

| Date | Mintage | F | VF | XF | Unc | BU |
|---|---|---|---|---|---|---|
| 1999 Proof | 1,000 | Value: 200 | | | | |

**100 PESOS** **KM# 42** **Weight:** 12.0000 g. **Composition:** 0.9170 Gold .3538 oz. AGW **Subject:** 60th Anniversary of Socialist Revolution Lenin

| Date | Mintage | F | VF | XF | Unc | BU |
|---|---|---|---|---|---|---|
| ND(1977) Proof | 10 | Value: 10,000 | | | | |

**100 PESOS** **KM# 43** **Weight:** 12.0000 g. **Composition:** 0.9170 Gold .3538 oz. AGW **Subject:** Carlos Manuel de Cespedes

| Date | Mintage | F | VF | XF | Unc | BU |
|---|---|---|---|---|---|---|
| ND(1977) Proof | 25,000 | Value: 200 | | | | |

**100 PESOS** **KM# 45** **Weight:** 12.0000 g. **Composition:** 0.9170 Gold .3538 oz. AGW **Subject:** Nonaligned Nations Conference

| Date | Mintage | F | VF | XF | Unc | BU |
|---|---|---|---|---|---|---|
| 1979 | 2,000 | — | — | — | 350 | — |
| 1979 Proof | 20,000 | Value: 275 | | | | |

**100 PESOS** **KM# 52** **Weight:** 12.0000 g. **Composition:** 0.9170 Gold .3538 oz. AGW **Subject:** First Soviet-Cuban space flight

| Date | Mintage | F | VF | XF | Unc | BU |
|---|---|---|---|---|---|---|
| 1980 | 1,000 | — | — | — | 350 | — |

**100 PESOS** **KM# 85** **Weight:** 12.0000 g. **Composition:** 0.9170 Gold .3538 oz. AGW **Subject:** Columbus' Ship - Nina **Obverse:** Similar to KM#45

| Date | Mintage | F | VF | XF | Unc | BU |
|---|---|---|---|---|---|---|
| 1981 | 2,000 | — | — | — | 200 | — |

**100 PESOS** **KM# 86** **Weight:** 12.0000 g. **Composition:** 0.9170 Gold .3538 oz. AGW **Subject:** Columbus' Ship - Pinta **Obverse:** Similar to KM#45

| Date | Mintage | F | VF | XF | Unc | BU |
|---|---|---|---|---|---|---|
| 1981 | 2,000 | — | — | — | 200 | — |

**100 PESOS** **KM# 87** **Weight:** 12.0000 g. **Composition:** 0.9170 Gold .3538 oz. AGW **Subject:** Columbus' Ship - Santa Maria **Obverse:** Similar to KM#45

| Date | Mintage | F | VF | XF | Unc | BU |
|---|---|---|---|---|---|---|
| 1981 | 2,000 | — | — | — | 200 | — |

**100 PESOS** **KM# 202** **Weight:** 31.1030 g. **Composition:** 0.9990 Gold 1.0000 oz. AGW **Subject:** 30th Anniversary of Revolution

| Date | Mintage | F | VF | XF | Unc | BU |
|---|---|---|---|---|---|---|
| 1988 Proof | 100 | Value: 650 | | | | |

**100 PESOS** **KM# 203** **Weight:** 31.1030 g. **Composition:** 0.9990 Gold 1.0000 oz. AGW **Subject:** 60th Anniversary - Birth of Ernesto Che Guevara

| Date | Mintage | F | VF | XF | Unc | BU |
|---|---|---|---|---|---|---|
| 1988 Proof | 100 | Value: 650 | | | | |

**100 PESOS** **KM# 204** **Weight:** 31.1030 g. **Composition:** 0.9990 Gold 1.0000 oz. AGW **Subject:** 30th Anniversary - Triumph of the Revolution

| Date | Mintage | F | VF | XF | Unc | BU |
|---|---|---|---|---|---|---|
| 1988 Proof | 100 | Value: 650 | | | | |

**100 PESOS** **KM# 215** **Weight:** 31.1030 g. **Composition:** 0.9990 Gold 1.0000 oz. AGW **Subject:** Jose Marti

| Date | Mintage | F | VF | XF | Unc | BU |
|---|---|---|---|---|---|---|
| 1988 | 50 | — | — | — | 800 | — |
| 1988 Proof | 15 | Value: 1,200 | | | | |
| 1989 | 150 | — | — | — | 650 | — |
| 1989 Proof | 15 | Value: 1,200 | | | | |
| 1990 | 15 | — | — | — | 1,000 | — |
| 1990 Proof | 12 | Value: 1,250 | | | | |

**100 PESOS** **KM# 447** **Weight:** 31.1030 g. **Composition:** 0.9990 Gold 1.0000 oz. AGW **Subject:** 30th Anniversary of Revolution

| Date | Mintage | F | VF | XF | Unc | BU |
|---|---|---|---|---|---|---|
| 1989 Proof | 250 | Value: 700 | | | | |

**100 PESOS** **KM# 317** **Weight:** 31.1030 g. **Composition:** 0.9990 Gold 1.0000 oz. AGW **Subject:** 150th Anniversary - First train in Spanish America **Reverse:** Train **Rev. Legend:** HABANA-BEJUCAL **Note:** Similar to 10 Pesos, KM#205.

| Date | Mintage | F | VF | XF | Unc | BU |
|---|---|---|---|---|---|---|
| 1989 Proof | 150 | Value: 650 | | | | |

**100 PESOS** **KM# 318** **Weight:** 31.1030 g. **Composition:** 0.9990 Gold 1.0000 oz. AGW **Subject:** 140th Anniversary - First train in Spain **Reverse:** Train **Rev. Legend:** BARCELONA-MATARO **Note:** Similar to 10 Pesos, KM#206.

| Date | Mintage | F | VF | XF | Unc | BU |
|---|---|---|---|---|---|---|
| 1989 Proof | 150 | Value: 650 | | | | |

**100 PESOS** **KM# 316** **Weight:** 31.1030 g. **Composition:** 0.9990 Gold 1.0000 oz. AGW **Subject:** 160th Anniversary - First train in England **Reverse:** Train **Rev. Legend:** LIVERPOOL-MANCHESTER **Note:** Similar to 10 Pesos, KM#207.

| Date | Mintage | F | VF | XF | Unc | BU |
|---|---|---|---|---|---|---|
| 1989 Proof | 150 | Value: 650 | | | | |

**100 PESOS** **KM# 333** **Weight:** 31.1030 g. **Composition:** 0.9990 Gold 1.0000 oz. AGW **Subject:** Tania La Guerrillera **Reverse:** Portrait of female guerilla fighter **Note:** Similar to 10 Pesos, KM#228.

| Date | Mintage | F | VF | XF | Unc | BU |
|---|---|---|---|---|---|---|
| 1989 Proof | 150 | Value: 800 | | | | |

**100 PESOS** **KM# 334** **Weight:** 31.1030 g. **Composition:** 0.9990 Gold 1.0000 oz. AGW **Subject:** Camilo Cienfuegos Gornaran **Reverse:** Portrait of Camilo Cienfuegos **Note:** Similar to 10 Pesos, KM#229.

| Date | Mintage | F | VF | XF | Unc | BU |
|---|---|---|---|---|---|---|
| 1989 Proof | 150 | Value: 800 | | | | |

**100 PESOS** **KM# 335** **Weight:** 31.1030 g. **Composition:** 0.9990 Gold 1.0000 oz. AGW **Subject:** 35th Anniversary - Assault of the Moncada Garrison **Reverse:** Battle scene **Note:** Similar to 10 Pesos, KM#230.

| Date | Mintage | F | VF | XF | Unc | BU |
|---|---|---|---|---|---|---|
| 1989 Proof | 150 | Value: 800 | | | | |

**100 PESOS** **KM# 319** **Weight:** 31.1030 g. **Composition:** 0.9990 Gold 1.0000 oz. AGW **Subject:** 200th Anniversary of French Revolution - Lady Justice **Reverse:** Female revolutionary raising flag **Note:** Similar to 10 Pesos, KM#239.

| Date | Mintage | F | VF | XF | Unc | BU |
|---|---|---|---|---|---|---|
| 1989 Proof | 150 | Value: 800 | | | | |

**100 PESOS** **KM# 320** **Weight:** 31.1030 g. **Composition:** 0.9990 Gold 1.0000 oz. AGW **Subject:** 200th Anniversary of French Revolution - Bastille **Reverse:** Bastille, soldiers in foreground **Note:** Similar to 10 Pesos, KM#240.

| Date | Mintage | F | VF | XF | Unc | BU |
|---|---|---|---|---|---|---|
| 1989 | 150 | — | — | — | 800 | — |

**100 PESOS** **KM# 449** **Weight:** 31.1030 g. **Composition:** 0.9990 Gold 1.0000 oz. AGW **Subject:** 30th Anniversary of Revolution **Note:** Similar to 10 Pesos, KM#243.

| Date | Mintage | F | VF | XF | Unc | BU |
|---|---|---|---|---|---|---|
| 1989 Proof | 250 | Value: 700 | | | | |

**100 PESOS** **KM# 448** **Weight:** 31.1030 g. **Composition:** 0.9990 Gold 1.0000 oz. AGW **Subject:** 30th Anniversary of Revolution **Note:** Similar of 10 Pesos, KM#242.

| Date | Mintage | F | VF | XF | Unc | BU |
|---|---|---|---|---|---|---|
| 1989 Proof | 250 | Value: 700 | | | | |

**100 PESOS** **KM# 303** **Weight:** 31.1030 g. **Composition:** 0.9990 Gold 1.0000 oz. AGW **Subject:** 500th Anniversary - Discovery of America **Reverse:** Portrait of King Ferdinand V **Note:** Simlar to 10 Pesos, KM#263.

| Date | Mintage | F | VF | XF | Unc | BU |
|---|---|---|---|---|---|---|
| 1990 Proof | 250 | Value: 825 | | | | |

**100 PESOS** **KM# 304** **Weight:** 31.1030 g. **Composition:** 0.9990 Gold 1.0000 oz. AGW **Subject:** 500th Anniversary - Discovery of America **Reverse:** Portrait of Queen Isabella **Note:** Similar to 10 Pesos, KM#264.

| Date | Mintage | F | VF | XF | Unc | BU |
|---|---|---|---|---|---|---|
| 1990 Proof | 250 | Value: 825 | | | | |

**100 PESOS** **KM# 305** **Weight:** 31.1030 g. **Composition:** 0.9990 Gold 1.0000 oz. AGW **Subject:** 500th Anniversary - Discovery of America **Reverse:** Portrait of Juan de la Cosa **Note:** Similar to 10 Pesos, KM#264.

| Date | Mintage | F | VF | XF | Unc | BU |
|---|---|---|---|---|---|---|
| 1990 Proof | 250 | Value: 825 | | | | |

**100 PESOS** **KM# 302** **Weight:** 31.1030 g. **Composition:** 0.9990 Gold 1.0000 oz. AGW **Subject:** 500th Anniversary - Discovery of America **Reverse:** Portrait of Columbus **Note:** Similar to 10 Pesos, KM#265.

| Date | Mintage | F | VF | XF | Unc | BU |
|---|---|---|---|---|---|---|
| 1990 Proof | 250 | Value: 825 | | | | |

**100 PESOS** **KM# 569** **Weight:** 31.1030 g. **Composition:** 0.9990 Gold 1.0000 oz. AGW **Subject:** Hatuey People **Note:** Similar to 10 Pesos, KM#328.

| Date | Mintage | F | VF | XF | Unc | BU |
|---|---|---|---|---|---|---|
| 1991 Proof | — | Value: 800 | | | | |

**100 PESOS** **KM# 534** **Weight:** 31.1030 g. **Composition:** 0.9990 Gold 1.0000 oz. AGW **Subject:** Olympic - Stadium

| Date | Mintage | F | VF | XF | Unc | BU |
|---|---|---|---|---|---|---|
| 1991 Proof | 225 | Value: 800 | | | | |

**100 PESOS** **KM# 535** **Weight:** 31.1030 g. **Composition:** 0.9990 Gold 1.0000 oz. AGW **Subject:** Madrid - Alcala Gate

| Date | Mintage | F | VF | XF | Unc | BU |
|---|---|---|---|---|---|---|
| 1991 Proof | 225 | Value: 800 | | | | |

**100 PESOS** **KM# 450** **Weight:** 31.1030 g. **Composition:** 0.9990 Gold 1.0000 oz. AGW **Subject:** Pinson Brothers **Note:** Simlar to 50 Pesos, KM#434.

| Date | Mintage | F | VF | XF | Unc | BU |
|---|---|---|---|---|---|---|
| 1991 Proof | 200 | Value: 750 | | | | |

**100 PESOS** **KM# 451** **Weight:** 31.1030 g. **Composition:** 0.9990 Gold 1.0000 oz. AGW **Subject:** Queen Joanna **Note:** Similar to 50 Pesos, KM#432.

| Date | Mintage | F | VF | XF | Unc | BU |
|---|---|---|---|---|---|---|
| 1991 Proof | 200 | Value: 750 | | | | |

**100 PESOS** **KM# 452** **Weight:** 31.1030 g. **Composition:** 0.9990 Gold 1.0000 oz. AGW **Subject:** Diego Velazquez **Note:** Similar to 50 Pesos, KM#433.

| Date | Mintage | F | VF | XF | Unc | BU |
|---|---|---|---|---|---|---|
| 1991 Proof | 200 | Value: 750 | | | | |

**100 PESOS** **KM# 454** **Weight:** 31.1030 g. **Composition:** 0.9990 Gold 1.0000 oz. AGW **Subject:** Guama Tribesman **Note:** Similar to 30 Pesos, KM#376.

| Date | Mintage | F | VF | XF | Unc | BU |
|---|---|---|---|---|---|---|
| 1992 Proof | 100 | Value: 750 | | | | |

**100 PESOS** **KM# 453** **Weight:** 31.1030 g. **Composition:** 0.9990 Gold 1.0000 oz. AGW **Subject:** Bartolome de las Casas **Note:** Similar to 30 Pesos, KM#377.

| Date | Mintage | F | VF | XF | Unc | BU |
|---|---|---|---|---|---|---|
| 1992 Proof | 100 | Value: 750 | | | | |

**100 PESOS** **KM# 455** **Weight:** 31.1030 g. **Composition:** 0.9990 Gold 1.0000 oz. AGW **Subject:** King Philipp **Note:** Similar to 30 Pesos, KM#378.

| Date | Mintage | F | VF | XF | Unc | BU |
|---|---|---|---|---|---|---|
| 1992 Proof | 100 | Value: 750 | | | | |

**100 PESOS** **KM# 456** **Weight:** 31.1030 g. **Composition:** 0.9990 Gold 1.0000 oz. AGW **Subject:** Spanish Kings and Queens **Note:** Similar to 30 Pesos, KM#379.

| Date | Mintage | F | VF | XF | Unc | BU |
|---|---|---|---|---|---|---|
| 1992 Proof | 100 | Value: 750 | | | | |

**100 PESOS** **KM# 536** **Weight:** 31.1030 g. **Composition:** 0.9990 Gold 1.0000 oz. AGW **Subject:** San Jorge Palace

| Date | Mintage | F | VF | XF | Unc | BU |
|---|---|---|---|---|---|---|
| 1992 Proof | 225 | Value: 800 | | | | |

**100 PESOS** **KM# 384** **Weight:** 31.1030 g. **Composition:** 0.9990 Gold 1.0000 oz. AGW **Subject:** Seville - Tower of Gold **Reverse:** Tower of Gold in Seville **Note:** Similar to 10 Pesos, KM#351.

| Date | Mintage | F | VF | XF | Unc | BU |
|---|---|---|---|---|---|---|
| 1992 Proof | 225 | Value: 825 | | | | |

**100 PESOS** **KM# 385** **Weight:** 31.1030 g. **Composition:** 0.9990 Gold 1.0000 oz. AGW **Subject:** El Escorial **Reverse:** El Escorial palace **Note:** Similar to 10 Pesos, KM#352.

| Date | Mintage | F | VF | XF | Unc | BU |
|---|---|---|---|---|---|---|
| 1992 Proof | 225 | Value: 825 | | | | |

**100 PESOS** **KM# 570** **Weight:** 31.1030 g. **Composition:** 0.9990 Gold 1.0000 oz. AGW **Subject:** Ernesto Che Guevara **Note:** Similar to 10 Pesos, KM#527.

| Date | Mintage | F | VF | XF | Unc | BU |
|---|---|---|---|---|---|---|
| 1992 Proof | — | Value: 700 | | | | |

**100 PESOS** **KM# 537** **Weight:** 31.1030 g. **Composition:** 0.9990 Gold 1.0000 oz. AGW **Subject:** Fidel Castro - 40th Anniversary of Moncada

| Date | Mintage | F | VF | XF | Unc | BU |
|---|---|---|---|---|---|---|
| 1993 Proof | 100 | Value: 775 | | | | |

**100 PESOS** **KM# 538** **Weight:** 31.1030 g. **Composition:** 0.9990 Gold 1.0000 oz. AGW **Subject:** St. Jacobi

| Date | Mintage | F | VF | XF | Unc | BU |
|---|---|---|---|---|---|---|
| 1993 Proof | 100 | Value: 775 | | | | |

**100 PESOS** **KM# 539** **Weight:** 31.1030 g. **Composition:** 0.9990 Gold 1.0000 oz. AGW **Subject:** Federico Garcia Lorca

| Date | Mintage | F | VF | XF | Unc | BU |
|---|---|---|---|---|---|---|
| 1993 Proof | 100 | Value: 775 | | | | |

**100 PESOS** **KM# 571** **Weight:** 31.1030 g. **Composition:** 0.9990 Gold 1.0000 oz. AGW **Subject:** Jose Marti **Note:** Similar to 1 Peso, KM#519.

| Date | Mintage | F | VF | XF | Unc | BU |
|---|---|---|---|---|---|---|
| 1994 Proof | — | Value: 650 | | | | |

**100 PESOS** **KM# 572** **Weight:** 31.1030 g. **Composition:** 0.9990 Gold 1.0000 oz. AGW **Subject:** Centennial of the Necessary War **Note:** Similar to 10 Pesos, KM#530.

| Date | Mintage | F | VF | XF | Unc | BU |
|---|---|---|---|---|---|---|
| 1995 Proof | — | Value: 650 | | | | |

**100 PESOS** **KM# 708** **Weight:** 31.1030 g. **Composition:** 0.9990 Gold 1.0000 oz. AGW **Subject:** Meeting of Fidel Castro and Pope John Paul II in the Vatican

| Date | Mintage | F | VF | XF | Unc | BU |
|---|---|---|---|---|---|---|
| 1997 Proof | — | Value: 800 | | | | |

**100 PESOS** **KM# 709** **Weight:** 31.1030 g. **Composition:** 0.9990 Gold 1.0000 oz. AGW **Subject:** Papal visit to Cuba

| Date | Mintage | F | VF | XF | Unc | BU |
|---|---|---|---|---|---|---|
| 1997 Proof | — | Value: 800 | | | | |

**100 PESOS** **KM# 710** **Weight:** 31.1030 g. **Composition:** 0.9990 Gold 1.0000 oz. AGW **Subject:** 90th Anniversary - Triumph of the Revolution

| Date | Mintage | F | VF | XF | Unc | BU |
|---|---|---|---|---|---|---|
| 1999 Proof | — | Value: 700 | | | | |

**100 PESOS** **KM# 719** **Weight:** 31.1030 g. **Composition:** 0.9990 Gold 1.0000 oz. AGW **Subject:** Zunzuncito **Reverse:** Hummingbird

| Date | Mintage | F | VF | XF | Unc | BU |
|---|---|---|---|---|---|---|
| 1999 Proof | — | Value: 800 | | | | |

**100 PESOS** **Y# 728** **Weight:** 31.1035 g. **Composition:** 0.9990 Gold 1.0000 oz. AGW **Subject:** Zunzuncito **Obverse:** National arms. **Reverse:** Hummingbird. **Edge:** Reeded. **Size:** 38 mm.

| Date | Mintage | F | VF | XF | Unc | BU |
|---|---|---|---|---|---|---|
| 1999 Proof | 1,000 | Value: 450 | | | | |

**150 PESOS** **KM# 642** **Weight:** 411.4225 g. **Composition:** 0.9990 Silver 13.2275 oz. ASW **Subject:** Tocororo **Obverse:** Cuban arms **Reverse:** Multicolor Tocororo bird

| Date | Mintage | F | VF | XF | Unc | BU |
|---|---|---|---|---|---|---|
| 1996 Proof | Est. 420 | Value: 600 | | | | |

**200 PESOS** **KM# 542** **Weight:** 31.1000 g. **Composition:** Gold **Subject:** Bolivar and Marti

| Date | Mintage | F | VF | XF | Unc | BU |
|---|---|---|---|---|---|---|
| 1993 | 100 | — | — | — | 750 | — |
| 1993 Proof | 100 | Value: 800 | | | | |

**200 PESOS** **KM# 543** **Weight:** 31.1000 g. **Composition:** Gold **Subject:** Prehistoric animals - Apatosaurus

| Date | Mintage | F | VF | XF | Unc | BU |
|---|---|---|---|---|---|---|
| 1993 Proof | 100 | Value: 900 | | | | |

**200 PESOS** **KM# 544** **Weight:** 31.1000 g. **Composition:** Gold **Subject:** Prehistoric animals - Chalicotherium

| Date | Mintage | F | VF | XF | Unc | BU |
|---|---|---|---|---|---|---|
| 1993 Proof | 100 | Value: 900 | | | | |

**200 PESOS** **KM# 545** **Weight:** 31.1000 g. **Composition:** Gold **Subject:** Montecristi Manifesto

| Date | Mintage | F | VF | XF | Unc | BU |
|---|---|---|---|---|---|---|
| 1994 Proof | 100 | Value: 800 | | | | |

**300 PESOS** **KM# 643** **Weight:** 822.8449 g. **Composition:** 0.9990 Silver 27.5661 oz. ASW **Subject:** Mariposa **Obverse:** Cuban arms **Reverse:** Multicolor Mariposa butterfly

| Date | Mintage | F | VF | XF | Unc | BU |
|---|---|---|---|---|---|---|
| 1996 Proof | Est. 420 | Value: 975 | | | | |

**500 PESOS** **KM# 457** **Weight:** 155.5500 g. **Composition:** 0.9990 Gold 5,0000 oz. AGW **Subject:** Christopher Columbus **Note:** Similar to 10 Pesos, KM#265.

| Date | Mintage | F | VF | XF | Unc | BU |
|---|---|---|---|---|---|---|
| 1990 Proof | 15 | Value: 4,000 | | | | |

**500 PESOS** **KM# 386** **Weight:** 155.5500 g. **Composition:** 0.9990 Gold 5,0000 oz. AGW **Subject:** Spanish Kings and Queens **Obverse:** Coat of arms **Reverse:** 4 portraits of royalty **Note:** Similar to 10 Pesos, KM#373.

| Date | Mintage | F | VF | XF | Unc | BU |
|---|---|---|---|---|---|---|
| ND(1992) Proof | 15 | Value: 4,000 | | | | |

**500 PESOS** **KM# 605** **Weight:** 155.5500 g. **Composition:** 0.9990 Platinum 5,0000 oz. APW **Note:** Similar to 10 Pesos, KM#398.

| Date | Mintage | F | VF | XF | Unc | BU |
|---|---|---|---|---|---|---|
| 1993 Proof | — | — | — | — | — | — |

## MEDALLIC COINAGE

**ONZA** **KM# MB4** **Weight:** 31.1000 g. **Composition:** 0.9990 Silver 1.0000 oz. ASW

| Date | Mintage | F | VF | XF | Unc | BU |
|---|---|---|---|---|---|---|
| 1986 | 2,000 | — | — | — | 25.00 | — |

**ONZA** **KM# MB5** **Weight:** 31.1000 g. **Composition:** 0.9990 Silver 1.0000 oz. ASW **Subject:** Discorvery of America

| Date | Mintage | F | VF | XF | Unc | BU |
|---|---|---|---|---|---|---|
| 1987 | — | — | — | — | 20.00 | — |

**ONZA** **KM# 721** **Weight:** 31.1000 g. **Composition:** 0.9990 Silver 1.0000 oz. ASW **Subject:** Zunzuncito - Hummingbird

| Date | Mintage | F | VF | XF | Unc | BU |
|---|---|---|---|---|---|---|
| 1999 | 12 | — | — | — | 300 | — |
| 1999 Proof | — | Value: 30.00 | | | | |

## VISITOR'S COINAGE

**CENTAVO** **KM# 409** **Composition:** Copper Nickel

| Date | Mintage | F | VF | XF | Unc | BU |
|---|---|---|---|---|---|---|
| 1988 | — | — | 0.50 | 1.50 | 3.00 | — |

**CENTAVO** **KM# 410** **Composition:** Aluminum

| Date | Mintage | F | VF | XF | Unc | BU |
|---|---|---|---|---|---|---|
| 1988 | — | — | 0.50 | 1.50 | 5.00 | — |

**5 CENTAVOS** **KM# 411** **Composition:** Copper Nickel

| Date | Mintage | F | VF | XF | Unc | BU |
|---|---|---|---|---|---|---|
| 1981 | — | 0.45 | 0.75 | 2.00 | 4.00 | — |

**5 CENTAVOS** KM# 412.1 **Composition:** Copper Nickel **Reverse:** Large, thick 5

| Date | Mintage | F | VF | XF | Unc | BU |
|---|---|---|---|---|---|---|
| 1981 | — | 0.45 | 0.75 | 2.00 | 4.00 | — |

**5 CENTAVOS** KM# 412.2 **Composition:** Copper Nickel **Reverse:** Large, thin 5

| Date | Mintage | F | VF | XF | Unc | BU |
|---|---|---|---|---|---|---|
| 1981 | — | 0.45 | 0.75 | 2.00 | 4.00 | — |

**5 CENTAVOS** KM# 413 **Composition:** Aluminum

| Date | Mintage | F | VF | XF | Unc | BU |
|---|---|---|---|---|---|---|
| 1988 | — | 0.50 | 1.00 | 3.00 | 5.00 | — |

**5 CENTAVOS** KM# 412.3 **Composition:** Copper Nickel **Reverse:** Small 5

| Date | Mintage | F | VF | XF | Unc | BU |
|---|---|---|---|---|---|---|
| 1989 | — | 0.35 | 0.50 | 1.50 | 3.00 | — |

**5 CENTAVOS** KM# 412.3a **Composition:** Stainless Steel

| Date | Mintage | F | VF | XF | Unc | BU |
|---|---|---|---|---|---|---|
| 1989 | — | — | 1.00 | 3.00 | 6.00 | — |

**10 CENTAVOS** KM# 414 **Composition:** Copper Nickel

| Date | Mintage | F | VF | XF | Unc | BU |
|---|---|---|---|---|---|---|
| 1981 | — | — | 0.65 | 2.00 | 4.00 | — |

**10 CENTAVOS** KM# 416 **Composition:** Aluminum

| Date | Mintage | F | VF | XF | Unc | BU |
|---|---|---|---|---|---|---|
| 1988 | — | — | 0.65 | 2.00 | 4.00 | — |

**10 CENTAVOS** KM# 415.1 **Composition:** Copper Nickel **Note:** Large 10

| Date | Mintage | F | VF | XF | Unc | BU |
|---|---|---|---|---|---|---|
| 1989 | — | 0.50 | 1.00 | 3.00 | 5.00 | — |

**10 CENTAVOS** KM# 415.3 **Composition:** Copper **Note:** Reduced size.

| Date | Mintage | F | VF | XF | Unc | BU |
|---|---|---|---|---|---|---|
| 1989 | — | — | 1.25 | 4.50 | 10.00 | — |

**10 CENTAVOS** KM# 415.2 **Composition:** Copper Nickel **Note:** Small 10

| Date | Mintage | F | VF | XF | Unc | BU |
|---|---|---|---|---|---|---|
| 1989 | — | — | 0.65 | 2.00 | 4.00 | — |

**10 CENTAVOS** KM# 415.2a **Composition:** Stainless Steel **Note:** Small 10.

| Date | Mintage | F | VF | XF | Unc | BU |
|---|---|---|---|---|---|---|
| 1989 | — | — | 1.25 | 4.00 | 9.00 | — |

**25 CENTAVOS** KM# 417 **Composition:** Copper Nickel

| Date | Mintage | F | VF | XF | Unc | BU |
|---|---|---|---|---|---|---|
| 1981 | — | 0.50 | 1.00 | 2.50 | 6.00 | — |

**25 CENTAVOS** KM# 418.1 **Composition:** Copper Nickel **Reverse:** Large 25

| Date | Mintage | F | VF | XF | Unc | BU |
|---|---|---|---|---|---|---|
| 1981 | — | — | 1.00 | 3.00 | 7.00 | — |

**25 CENTAVOS** KM# 419 **Composition:** Aluminum

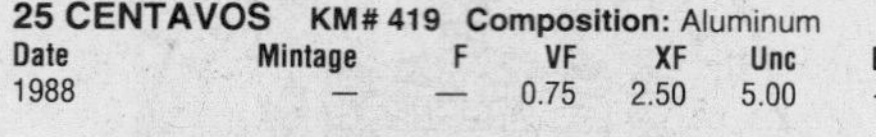

| Date | Mintage | F | VF | XF | Unc | BU |
|---|---|---|---|---|---|---|
| 1988 | — | — | 0.75 | 2.50 | 5.00 | — |

**25 CENTAVOS** KM# 418.2 **Composition:** Copper Nickel **Reverse:** Small 25

| Date | Mintage | F | VF | XF | Unc | BU |
|---|---|---|---|---|---|---|
| 1989 | — | — | 1.00 | 3.00 | 7.00 | — |

**25 CENTAVOS** KM# 418.2a **Composition:** Stainless Steel

| Date | Mintage | F | VF | XF | Unc | BU |
|---|---|---|---|---|---|---|
| 1989 | — | — | 2.00 | 5.50 | 12.00 | — |

**50 CENTAVOS** KM# 420 **Composition:** Copper Nickel

| Date | Mintage | F | VF | XF | Unc | BU |
|---|---|---|---|---|---|---|
| 1981 | — | — | 2.50 | 7.50 | 15.00 | — |

**Note:** Varieties exist in the number of lines below the palm tree

**50 CENTAVOS** KM# 461 **Composition:** Copper Nickel **Obverse:** Palm tree **Reverse:** Denomination and logo

| Date | Mintage | F | VF | XF | Unc | BU |
|---|---|---|---|---|---|---|
| 1989 | — | — | 2.00 | 7.00 | 14.00 | — |

**PESO** KM# 421 **Composition:** Copper Nickel

| Date | Mintage | F | VF | XF | Unc | BU |
|---|---|---|---|---|---|---|
| 1981 | — | — | 4.00 | 12.00 | 24.00 | — |

**PESO** KM# 580 **Composition:** Copper Nickel **Obverse:** Lighthouse **Reverse:** Denomination and logo

| Date | Mintage | F | VF | XF | Unc | BU |
|---|---|---|---|---|---|---|
| 1989 | — | — | 4.00 | 12.00 | 24.00 | — |

## PESO CONVERTIBLE SERIES

**5 CENTAVOS** KM# 575 **Composition:** Stainless Steel **Obverse:** National arms **Reverse:** Casa Colonial

| Date | Mintage | F | VF | XF | Unc | BU |
|---|---|---|---|---|---|---|
| 1994 | — | — | — | — | 1.00 | — |
| 1996 | — | — | — | — | 1.00 | — |
| 1998 | — | — | — | — | 1.00 | — |
| 1999 | — | — | — | — | 1.00 | — |

**10 CENTAVOS** KM# 576 **Composition:** Stainless Steel **Obverse:** National arms **Reverse:** Castillo de la Fuerza

| Date | Mintage | F | VF | XF | Unc | BU |
|---|---|---|---|---|---|---|
| 1994 | — | — | — | — | 2.00 | — |
| 1996 | — | — | — | — | 2.00 | — |

**25 CENTAVOS** KM# 577 **Composition:** Stainless Steel **Obverse:** National arms **Reverse:** Trinidad

| Date | Mintage | F | VF | XF | Unc | BU |
|---|---|---|---|---|---|---|
| 1994 | — | — | — | — | 3.00 | — |
| 1998 | — | — | — | — | 3.00 | — |
| 2000 | — | — | — | — | 3.00 | — |

**50 CENTAVOS** KM# 578 **Composition:** Stainless Steel **Obverse:** Cuban arms **Reverse:** Cathedral of Havana

| Date | Mintage | F | VF | XF | Unc | BU |
|---|---|---|---|---|---|---|
| 1994 | — | — | — | — | 5.00 | — |

**PESO** KM# 579 **Composition:** Stainless Steel **Obverse:** National arms **Reverse:** Guama

| Date | Mintage | F | VF | XF | Unc | BU |
|---|---|---|---|---|---|---|
| 1994 | — | — | — | — | 7.00 | — |

## TRIAL STRIKES

| KM# | Date | Mintage | Identification | Mkt Val |
|---|---|---|---|---|
| TS3 | 1994 | 1 | 50 Pesos. Silver. KM503; dolphins green and red. | — |
| TS4 | 1994 | 1 | 50 Pesos. Silver. KM503, dolphins green and red. | — |
| TS2 | 1994 | 10 | 100 Pesos. Gold. Reverse of KM467, uniface. | 2,000 |
| TS5 | 1977 | — | 20 Pesos. Brass. Antonio Maceo, KM40. | 300 |
| TS6 | 1977 | — | 20 Pesos. Brass. Maximo Gomez, KM39. | 300 |
| TS7 | 1977 | — | 20 Pesos. Brass. Ignacio Aramonte, KM38. | 300 |
| TS8 | 1977 | — | 20 Pesos. Copper-Nickel. Antonio Maceo, KM40. | 500 |
| TS9 | 1977 | — | 100 Pesos. Brass. de Cespedes, KM43. | 300 |

## PIEFORTS

| KM# | Date | Mintage | Identification | Mkt Val |
|---|---|---|---|---|
| P22 | 1989 | 10 | 50 Pesos. Gold. KM214. | 2,000 |
| P23 | 1989 | 15 | 50 Pesos. Gold. KM214. | 2,000 |
| P24 | 1989 | 12 | 50 Pesos. Gold. KM313. | 1,650 |
| P25 | 1989 | 12 | 50 Pesos. Gold. KM314. | 1,650 |
| P26 | 1989 | 12 | 50 Pesos. Gold. KM315. | 1,650 |
| P28 | 1989 | 10 | 100 Pesos. Gold. KM215. | 2,000 |
| P29 | 1989 | 15 | 100 Pesos. Gold. KM215. | 2,000 |
| P30 | 1989 | 12 | 100 Pesos. Gold. KM316. | 1,500 |
| P31 | 1989 | 12 | 100 Pesos. Gold. KM317. | 1,600 |
| P32 | 1989 | 12 | 100 Pesos. Gold. KM318. | 1,600 |
| P33 | 1989 | 12 | 100 Pesos. Gold. KM319. | 2,000 |
| P34 | 1989 | 12 | 100 Pesos. Gold. KM320. | 2,000 |
| P27 | 1989 | 15 | 100 Pesos. Silver. KM215. | — |
| P35 | 1990 | 50 | 10 Pesos. Silver. Ship and Cub; KM252. | — |
| P44 | 1990 | 12 | 25 Pesos. Gold. 15.5400 g. KM213. | — |
| P45 | 1990 | 12 | 25 Pesos. Gold. 15.5400 g. KM213. | — |
| P36 | 1990 | 15 | 10 Pesos. Silver. KM280. | 160 |
| P37 | 1990 | 100 | 10 Pesos. Silver. KM291. | 160 |
| P38 | 1990 | 100 | 10 Pesos. Silver. KM292. | 160 |
| P39 | 1990 | 100 | 10 Pesos. Silver. KM293. | 160 |
| P40 | 1990 | 12 | 10 Pesos. Gold. KM211. | 1,000 |
| P41 | 1990 | 12 | 10 Pesos. Gold. KM211. | 1,000 |
| P42 | 1990 | 12 | 15 Pesos. Gold. KM212. | 1,000 |
| P43 | 1990 | 12 | 15 Pesos. Gold. KM212. | 1,000 |
| P46 | 1990 | 12 | 50 Pesos. Gold. KM214. | 2,000 |
| P47 | 1990 | 12 | 50 Pesos. Gold. KM214. | 2,000 |
| P48 | 1990 | 12 | 50 Pesos. Gold. KM321. | 2,000 |
| P49 | 1990 | 12 | 50 Pesos. Gold. KM322. | 2,000 |
| P50 | 1990 | 12 | 50 Pesos. Gold. KM323. | 2,000 |
| P51 | 1990 | 12 | 100 Pesos. Gold. KM215. | 2,000 |
| P52 | 1990 | 15 | 100 Pesos. Gold. KM215. | 2,000 |
| P53 | 1992 | 50 | 10 Pesos. Silver. KM341. | 150 |
| P54 | 1993 | 150 | 5 Pesos. Silver. KM405. | 150 |
| P55 | 1993 | — | 10 Pesos. Silver. KM406. | 150 |
| P56 | 1993 | 15 | 200 Pesos. Gold. KM542. | 2,000 |

| KM# | Date | Mintage | Identification | Mkt Val |
|---|---|---|---|---|
| P58 | 1993 | — | 100 Pesos. Gold. Similar to 200 Pesos; KM542. | — |
| P57 | 1994 | 10 | 100 Pesos. Gold. KM545. | 1,600 |
| P65 | 1999 | — | 10 Pesos. Silver. KM672. | 200 |

| KM# | Date | Mintage | Identification | Mkt Val |
|---|---|---|---|---|
| PA65 | | 100 | 50 Pesos. Gold Plated Brass. | — |

## PATTERNS

Including off metal strikes

| KM# | Date | Mintage | Identification | Mkt Val |
|---|---|---|---|---|
| PnB10 | 1915 | — | 2 Centavos. Bronze. | 2,000 |
| Pn10 | 1915 | — | Centavo. Bronze. | — |
| PnA11 | 1970 | — | Peso. 0.9990 Silver. KM158. | 500 |
| PnB11 | 1970 | — | Peso. 0.9990 Silver. KM158. | 500 |
| PnC11 | 1986 | — | 5 Pesos. 0.9000 Copper. KM326. | — |
| PnD11 | 1986 | — | 5 Pesos. 0.0500 Silver. KM326. | — |
| PnE11 | 1986 | — | 5 Pesos. 0.0500 Gold. KM326. | — |
| PnF11 | 1987 | — | 5 Pesos. Copper. KM166. | — |
| PnG11 | 1987 | — | 5 Pesos. Copper. .900 Copper, 050 Silver, .050 Gold, KM#26. | — |
| Pn11 | 1987 | 3 | 5 Pesos. 0.9990 Gold. KM159. | 6,000 |
| PnA12 | 1988 | 6 | 5 Pesos. 0.9990 Silver. | 1,150 |
| Pn12 | 1988 | 6 | 5 Pesos. Silver. | 1,150 |
| PnA13 | 1988 | 6 | 100 Pesos. 0.9990 Gold. | 5,000 |
| PnB13 | 1988 | — | 100 Pesos. 0.9990 Gold. | 5,000 |
| Pn13 | 1988 | 6 | 100 Pesos. Gold. | — |
| Pn14 | 1993 | 34 | 10 Pesos. Silver. Mirror bust with frosted field. KM398. | 500 |
| Pn15 | 1994 | 25 | 10 Pesos. Silver. KM510. | 385 |
| Pn16 | 1995 | 22 | 10 Pesos. Silver. Date, mint mark, in proof relief. | 385 |
| Pn17 | 1995 | 100 | Peso. Copper Nickel. Pirates del Carib, Sir Francis Drake, proof. | 50.00 |
| Pn22 | (1995) | 100 | 10 Pesos. Brass. Similar to Pn25 Proof. | 65.00 |
| Pn25 | (1995) | 100 | 10 Pesos. Brass In Silver. Proof. | 65.00 |
| Pn38 | 1995 | 50 | 10 Pesos. Brass In Silver. Mariposas del Caribe, green background; Proof. | 80.00 |
| Pn105 | 1995 | 50 | 10 Pesos. Aluminum. Mariposas del Caribe, pink bckground, Proof. | 65.00 |
| Pn106 | 1999 | — | Peso. Copper-Nickel. KM662. | 100 |
| Pn107 | 1999 | — | 10 Pesos. Silver. KM672. | 200 |
| Pn108 | 1999 | — | 100 Pesos. Gold. KM710. | 1,200 |

## MINT SETS

| KM# | Date | Mintage | Identification | Issue Price | Mkt Val |
|---|---|---|---|---|---|
| MS1 | 1953 (4) | — | KM#26-29 | — | 125 |
| MS2 | 1994 (5) | — | KM#575-579 | — | 35.00 |

## PROOF SETS

| KM# | Date | Mintage | Identification | Issue Price | Mkt Val |
|---|---|---|---|---|---|
| PS1 | 1915 (7) | 20 | KM#9-15 | — | 3,600 |
| PS2 | 1915 (6) | 24 | KM#16-21; Rare | — | — |
| PS4 | 1916 (6) | — | KM#16-21; Rare | — | — |
| PS3 | 1916 (7) | 20 | KM#9-15 | — | 6,250 |
| PS5 | 1953 (4) | — | KM#26-29; Rare | — | — |
| PS6 | 1975 (2) | — | KM#36, 37 | — | 30.00 |
| PS7 | 1977 (4) | — | KM#38-40, 43 | 290 | 335 |
| PSA7 | 1977 (3) | — | KM#38-40 | — | 110 |
| PS8 | 1979 (2) | — | KM#44, 45 | 240 | 260 |
| PS9 | 1988 (5) | 15 | KM#211-215 | — | 1,650 |
| PS10 | 1998 (4) | — | KM#668-671 | — | 200 |
| PS11 | 1999 (5) | — | KM#671, 673, 692, 704, 719 | — | 1,250 |

# CURACAO

The island of Curacao, the largest of the Netherlands Antilles, which is an autonomous part of the Kingdom of the Netherlands located in the Caribbean Sea 40 miles off the coast of Venezuela, has an area of 173 sq. mi. (472 sq. km.) and a population of 127,900. Capital: Willemstad. The chief industries are banking and tourism. Salt, phosphates and cattle are exported.

Curacao was discovered by Spanish navigator Alonsode Ojeda in 1499 and was settled by Spain in 1527. The Dutch West India Company took the island from Spain in 1634 and administered it until 1787, when it was surrendered to the United Netherlands. The Dutch held it there-after except for two periods during the Napoleonic Wars, 1800-1803 and 1807-16, when it was occupied by the British. During World War II, Curacao refined 60 percent of the oil used by the Allies; the refineries were protected by U.S. troops after Germany invaded the Netherlands in1940.

During the second occupation of the Napoleonic period, the British created an emergency coinage for Curacao by cutting the Spanish dollar into 5 equal segments and countermarking each piece with a rosette indent.

**MINT MARKS**
D - Denver
P - Philadelphia
(u) - Utrecht

# NETHERLANDS RESTORED

## MODERN COINAGE

100 Cents = 1 Gulden

**CENT** **KM# 39** **Composition:** Bronze

| Date | Mintage | F | VF | XF | Unc | BU |
|---|---|---|---|---|---|---|
| 1942P | 2,500,000 | 1.25 | 2.50 | 5.00 | 10.00 | — |

**Note:** This coin was also circulated in Surinam. For similar coins dated 1943P & 1957-1960, see Surinam

**CENT** **KM# 41** **Composition:** Bronze

| Date | Mintage | F | VF | XF | Unc | BU |
|---|---|---|---|---|---|---|
| 1944D | 3,000,000 | 0.75 | 1.50 | 3.00 | 6.50 | — |
| 1947 (u) | 1,500,000 | 1.25 | 2.50 | 4.00 | 8.50 | — |
| 1947 (u) Proof | 80 | Value: 25.00 | | | | |

**2-1/2 CENTS** **KM# 42** **Composition:** Bronze

| Date | Mintage | F | VF | XF | Unc | BU |
|---|---|---|---|---|---|---|
| 1944D | 1,000,000 | 1.00 | 1.50 | 3.00 | 6.50 | — |
| 1947 (u) | 500,000 | 1.25 | 2.50 | 5.00 | 10.00 | — |
| 1947 (u) Proof | 80 | Value: 25.00 | | | | |
| 1948 (u) | 1,000,000 | 0.75 | 1.50 | 3.00 | 6.50 | — |
| 1948 (u) Proof | 75 | Value: 25.00 | | | | |

**5 CENTS** **KM# 40** **Composition:** Copper-Nickel

| Date | Mintage | F | VF | XF | Unc | BU |
|---|---|---|---|---|---|---|
| 1943 | 8,595,000 | 1.25 | 2.50 | 4.00 | 8.50 | — |

**Note:** The above piece does not bear either a palm tree privy mark or a mint mark, but it was struck expressly for use in Curacao and Surinam. This homeland type of KM#153 was last issued in the Netherlands in 1940

**5 CENTS** **KM# 47** **Composition:** Copper-Nickel

| Date | Mintage | F | VF | XF | Unc | BU |
|---|---|---|---|---|---|---|
| 1948 | 1,000,000 | 1.00 | 2.00 | 4.00 | 8.50 | — |
| 1948 Proof | 75 | Value: 45.00 | | | | |

**10 CENTS** **KM# 37** **Weight:** 1.4000 g. **Composition:** 0.6400 Silver .0288 oz. ASW

| Date | Mintage | F | VF | XF | Unc | BU |
|---|---|---|---|---|---|---|
| 1941P | 800,000 | 3.75 | 8.00 | 17.50 | 35.00 | — |
| 1943P | 4,500,000 | 2.50 | 6.00 | 15.00 | 30.00 | — |

**Note:** Both these coins were also circulated in Surinam. For coins dated 1942P, see Surinam

**25 CENTS** **KM# 38** **Weight:** 3.5800 g. **Composition:** 0.6400 Silver .0736 oz. ASW

| Date | Mintage | F | VF | XF | Unc | BU |
|---|---|---|---|---|---|---|
| 1941P | 1,100,000 | 2.50 | 5.50 | 12.00 | 25.00 | — |
| 1943/1P | 2,500,000 | 4.00 | 8.00 | 17.50 | 35.00 | — |
| 1943P | Inc. above | 1.50 | 4.00 | 8.50 | 17.50 | — |

**Note:** Both coins were also circulated in Surinam. For similar coins dated 1943, 1944 & 1945-P with acorn mint mark see Netherlands

**1/10 GULDEN** **KM# 36** **Weight:** 1.4000 g. **Composition:** 0.6400 Silver .0288 oz. ASW

| Date | Mintage | F | VF | XF | Unc | BU |
|---|---|---|---|---|---|---|
| 1901 | 300,000 | 10.00 | 20.00 | 40.00 | 90.00 | — |
| 1901 Proof | 40 | Value: 250 | | | | |

**1/10 GULDEN** **KM# 43** **Weight:** 1.4000 g. **Composition:** 0.6400 Silver .0288 oz. ASW

| Date | Mintage | F | VF | XF | Unc | BU |
|---|---|---|---|---|---|---|
| 1944D | 1,500,000 | 1.00 | 1.50 | 3.00 | 6.50 | — |
| 1947 | 1,000,000 | 1.00 | 1.50 | 3.00 | 6.50 | — |
| 1947 Proof | 80 | Value: 60.00 | | | | |

**1/10 GULDEN** **KM# 48** **Weight:** 1.4000 g. **Composition:** 0.6400 Silver .0288 oz. ASW

| Date | Mintage | F | VF | XF | Unc | BU |
|---|---|---|---|---|---|---|
| 1948 | 1,000,000 | 1.00 | 1.50 | 3.00 | 6.50 | — |
| 1948 Proof | 75 | Value: 60.00 | | | | |

**1/4 GULDEN** **KM# 35** **Weight:** 3.5800 g. **Composition:** 0.6400 Silver .0736 oz. ASW

| Date | Mintage | F | VF | XF | Unc | BU |
|---|---|---|---|---|---|---|
| 1900 (u) | 480,000 | 12.00 | 20.00 | 35.00 | 65.00 | — |
| 1900 (u) Proof | 40 | Value: 200 | | | | |

**1/4 GULDEN** **KM# 44** **Weight:** 3.5800 g. **Composition:** 0.6400 Silver .0736 oz. ASW

| Date | Mintage | F | VF | XF | Unc | BU |
|---|---|---|---|---|---|---|
| 1944D | 1,500,000 | 1.00 | 2.00 | 3.50 | 7.50 | — |
| 1947 (u) | 1,000,000 | 1.00 | 2.00 | 3.50 | 7.50 | — |
| 1947 (u) Proof | 80 | Value: 80.00 | | | | |

**GULDEN** **KM# 45** **Weight:** 10.0000 g. **Composition:** 0.7200 Silver .2315 oz. ASW

| Date | Mintage | F | VF | XF | Unc | BU |
|---|---|---|---|---|---|---|
| 1944D | 500,000 | 2.50 | 5.00 | 11.50 | 25.00 | — |

**2-1/2 GULDEN** **KM# 46** **Weight:** 25.0000 g. **Composition:** 0.7200 Silver .5787 oz. ASW

| Date | Mintage | F | VF | XF | Unc | BU |
|---|---|---|---|---|---|---|
| 1944D | 200,000 | — | — | 4.50 | 10.00 | — |

## PROOF SETS

| KM# | Date | Mintage | Identification | Issue Price | Mkt Val |
|---|---|---|---|---|---|
| PS1 | 1901 (2) | 40 | KM36(1901), KM35(1900) | — | 400 |
| PS2 | 1947 (4) | 80 | KM41-44 | — | 185 |
| PS3 | 1948 (3) | 75 | KM42, 47-48 | — | 125 |

The Republic of Cyprus, a member of the British Commonwealth, lies in the eastern Mediterranean Sea 44 miles (71 km.) south of Turkey and 60 miles (97 km.) west of Syria. It is the third largest island in the Mediterranean Sea, having an area of 3,572 sq. mi. (9,251 sq. km.) and a population of 736,636. Capital: Nicosia. Agriculture, light manufacturing and tourism are the chief industries. Citrus fruit, potatoes, footwear and clothing are exported

The importance of Cyprus dates from the Bronze Age when it was desired as a principal source of copper (from which the island derived its name) and as a strategic trading center. It was during this period that large numbers of Greeks settled on the island and gave it the predominantly Greek character. Its role as an international marketplace made it a prime disseminator of the then prevalent cultures, a role that still influences the civilization of Western man. Because of its fortuitous position and influential role, Cyprus was conquered by a succession of empires: the Assyrian, Egyptian, Persian, Macedonian, Ptolemaic, Roman and Byzantine. It was taken from Isaac Comnenus by Richard the Lion-Heart in 1191, sold to the Templar Knights and for the following 7 centuries was ruled by the Franks, the Venetians and the Ottomans. During the Ottoman period Cyprus acquired its Turkish community (18 percent of its population). In 1878 the island fell into British hands and was made a crown colony of Britain in 1925. Finally, on Aug. 16, 1960, it became an independent republic.

In 1964, the ethnic Turks withdrew from active participation in the government. Turkish forces invaded Cyprus in 1974, gained control of 40 percent of the island and forcibly separated the Greek and Turkish communities. In 1983, Turkish Cypriots proclaimed their own state in northern Cyprus, which remains without international recognition.

Cyprus is a member of the Commonwealth of Nations. The president is Chief of State and Head of Government.

**RULERS**
British, until 1960

**MINT MARKS**
no mint mark - Royal Mint, London, England
H - Birmingham, England

**MONETARY SYSTEM**
9 Piastres = 1 Shilling
20 Shillings = 1 Pound

# BRITISH COLONY

## PIASTRE COINAGE

**1/4 PIASTRE** **KM# 1.2** **Composition:** Bronze **Size:** 21 mm.

| Date | Mintage | F | VF | XF | Unc | BU |
|---|---|---|---|---|---|---|
| 1901 | 72,000 | 10.00 | 25.00 | 60.00 | 140 | — |

**1/4 PIASTRE** **KM# 8** **Composition:** Bronze

| Date | Mintage | F | VF | XF | Unc | BU |
|---|---|---|---|---|---|---|
| 1902 | 72,000 | 5.00 | 12.50 | 30.00 | 125 | — |
| 1905 | 422,000 | 4.00 | 12.50 | 27.50 | 100 | — |
| 1908 | 36,000 | 35.00 | 100 | 150 | 350 | — |

**1/4 PIASTRE** **KM# 16** **Composition:** Bronze

| Date | Mintage | F | VF | XF | Unc | BU |
|---|---|---|---|---|---|---|
| 1922 | 72,000 | 5.00 | 15.00 | 30.00 | 80.00 | — |
| 1926 | 360,000 | 3.50 | 7.50 | 15.00 | 65.00 | — |
| 1926 Proof | — | Value: 365 | | | | |

**1/2 PIASTRE** **KM# 11** **Composition:** Bronze

| Date | Mintage | F | VF | XF | Unc | BU |
|---|---|---|---|---|---|---|
| 1908 | 36,000 | 50.00 | 150 | 350 | 600 | — |

**1/2 PIASTRE** **KM# 17** **Composition:** Bronze

| Date | Mintage | F | VF | XF | Unc | BU |
|---|---|---|---|---|---|---|
| 1922 | 36,000 | 20.00 | 50.00 | 125 | 250 | — |
| 1927 | 108,000 | 3.50 | 10.00 | 35.00 | 80.00 | — |
| 1927 Proof | — | Value: 375 | | | | |
| 1930 | 180,000 | 3.00 | 8.00 | 30.00 | 75.00 | — |
| 1930 Proof | — | Value: 365 | | | | |
| 1931 | 90,000 | 5.00 | 15.00 | 40.00 | 100 | — |
| 1931 Proof | — | Value: 425 | | | | |

**1/2 PIASTRE** **KM# 20** **Composition:** Copper-Nickel

| Date | Mintage | F | VF | XF | Unc | BU |
|---|---|---|---|---|---|---|
| 1934 | 1,440,000 | 0.75 | 2.50 | 6.50 | 16.50 | — |
| 1934 Proof | — | Value: 325 | | | | |

**1/2 PIASTRE** **KM# 22** **Composition:** Copper-Nickel

| Date | Mintage | F | VF | XF | Unc | BU |
|---|---|---|---|---|---|---|
| 1938 | 1,080,000 | 0.35 | 1.00 | 4.00 | 12.50 | — |
| 1938 Proof | — | Value: 325 | | | | |

**1/2 PIASTRE** **KM# 22a** **Composition:** Bronze

| Date | Mintage | F | VF | XF | Unc | BU |
|---|---|---|---|---|---|---|
| 1942 | 1,080,000 | 0.25 | 1.00 | 2.50 | 12.50 | — |
| 1942 Proof | — | Value: 200 | | | | |
| 1943 | 1,620,000 | 0.25 | 1.00 | 2.50 | 12.50 | — |
| 1944 | 2,160,000 | 0.25 | 1.00 | 2.50 | 12.50 | — |
| 1945 | 1,080,000 | 0.25 | 1.00 | 2.50 | 12.50 | — |
| 1945 Proof | — | Value: 200 | | | | |

**1/2 PIASTRE** **KM# 29** **Composition:** Bronze

| Date | Mintage | F | VF | XF | Unc | BU |
|---|---|---|---|---|---|---|
| 1949 | 1,080,000 | 0.15 | 0.35 | 1.00 | 3.50 | — |
| 1949 Proof | — | Value: 150 | | | | |

**PIASTRE** **KM# 3.2** **Composition:** Bronze **Reverse:** Thick "1"

| Date | Mintage | F | VF | XF | Unc | BU |
|---|---|---|---|---|---|---|
| 1881 Proof | Inc. above | Value: 1,000 | | | | |
| 1881H Proof | — | Value: 900 | | | | |
| 1882H | 18,000 | 135 | 225 | 450 | 1,250 | — |
| 1882H Proof | — | Value: 2,000 | | | | |
| 1884 | 18,000 | 135 | 225 | 450 | 1,250 | — |
| 1884 Proof | — | Value: 1,800 | | | | |
| 1885 | 54,000 | 25.00 | 70.00 | 115 | 275 | — |
| 1885 Proof | — | Value: 1,220 | | | | |
| 1886 | 227,000 | 10.00 | 30.00 | 85.00 | 175 | — |
| 1887 | 45,000 | 10.00 | 32.50 | 100 | 200 | — |
| 1889 | 27,000 | 30.00 | 90.00 | 250 | 500 | — |
| 1890 | 90,000 | 20.00 | 70.00 | 150 | 350 | — |
| 1891 | 54,000 | 25.00 | 80.00 | 200 | 400 | — |
| 1891 Proof | — | Value: 780 | | | | |
| 1895 | 54,000 | 25.00 | 80.00 | 200 | 400 | — |
| 1896 | 54,000 | 25.00 | 80.00 | 200 | 400 | — |
| 1900 | 27,000 | 35.00 | 100 | 250 | 500 | — |
| 1900 Proof | — | Value: 1,900 | | | | |

**PIASTRE** **KM# 12** **Composition:** Bronze

| Date | Mintage | F | VF | XF | Unc | BU |
|---|---|---|---|---|---|---|
| 1908 | 27,000 | 100 | 200 | 350 | 700 | — |

**PIASTRE** **KM# 18** **Composition:** Bronze

| Date | Mintage | F | VF | XF | Unc | BU |
|---|---|---|---|---|---|---|
| 1922 | 54,000 | 10.00 | 35.00 | 125 | 250 | — |
| 1927 | 127,000 | 5.00 | 20.00 | 60.00 | 150 | — |
| 1927 Proof | — | Value: 400 | | | | |
| 1930 | 96,000 | 6.00 | 22.50 | 70.00 | 175 | — |
| 1930 Proof | — | Value: 400 | | | | |
| 1931 | 45,000 | 15.00 | 35.00 | 75.00 | 200 | — |
| 1931 Proof | — | Value: 725 | | | | |

**PIASTRE** **KM# 21** **Composition:** Copper-Nickel

| Date | Mintage | F | VF | XF | Unc | BU |
|---|---|---|---|---|---|---|
| 1934 | 1,440,000 | 1.00 | 2.50 | 6.50 | 16.50 | — |
| 1934 Proof | — | Value: 325 | | | | |

**PIASTRE** **KM# 23** **Composition:** Copper-Nickel

| Date | Mintage | F | VF | XF | Unc | BU |
|---|---|---|---|---|---|---|
| 1938 | 2,700,000 | 0.60 | 1.50 | 3.00 | 12.50 | — |
| 1938 Proof | — | Value: 325 | | | | |

**PIASTRE** **KM# 23a** **Composition:** Bronze

| Date | Mintage | F | VF | XF | Unc | BU |
|---|---|---|---|---|---|---|
| 1942 | 1,260,000 | 0.50 | 1.00 | 2.50 | 10.00 | — |
| 1942 Proof | — | Value: 225 | | | | |
| 1943 | 2,520,000 | 0.50 | 1.00 | 2.50 | 10.00 | — |
| 1944 | 3,240,000 | 0.50 | 1.00 | 2.50 | 10.00 | — |
| 1945 | 1,080,000 | 0.60 | 1.50 | 3.00 | 12.00 | — |
| 1945 Proof | — | Value: 200 | | | | |
| 1946 | 1,080,000 | 0.60 | 1.50 | 3.00 | 12.00 | — |
| 1946 Proof | — | Value: 200 | | | | |

**PIASTRE** **KM# 30** **Composition:** Bronze **Obv. Legend:** ends ...DEI GRATIA REX

| Date | Mintage | F | VF | XF | Unc | BU |
|---|---|---|---|---|---|---|
| 1949 | 1,080,000 | 0.25 | 0.75 | 2.00 | 4.00 | — |
| 1949 Proof | — | Value: 150 | | | | |

**3 PIASTRES** **KM# 4** **Weight:** 1.8851 g. **Composition:** 0.9250 Silver .0561 oz. ASW

| Date | Mintage | F | VF | XF | Unc | BU |
|---|---|---|---|---|---|---|
| 1901 | 300,000 | 8.00 | 20.00 | 40.00 | 100 | — |
| 1901 Proof | — | Value: 800 | | | | |

**4-1/2 PIASTRES** **KM# 5** **Weight:** 2.8276 g. **Composition:** 0.9250 Silver .0841 oz. ASW

| Date | Mintage | F | VF | XF | Unc | BU |
|---|---|---|---|---|---|---|
| 1901 | 400,000 | 5.00 | 15.00 | 40.00 | 100 | — |
| 1901 Proof | — | Value: 950 | | | | |

**4-1/2 PIASTRES** **KM# 15** **Weight:** 2.8276 g. **Composition:** 0.9250 Silver .0841 oz. ASW

| Date | Mintage | F | VF | XF | Unc | BU |
|---|---|---|---|---|---|---|
| 1921 | 600,000 | 3.50 | 10.00 | 30.00 | 80.00 | — |

**4-1/2 PIASTRES** **KM# 24** **Weight:** 2.8276 g. **Composition:** 0.9250 Silver .0841 oz. ASW

| Date | Mintage | F | VF | XF | Unc | BU |
|---|---|---|---|---|---|---|
| 1938 | 192,000 | 2.00 | 4.00 | 12.00 | 30.00 | — |
| 1938 Proof | — | Value: 400 | | | | |

**9 PIASTRES** **KM# 6** **Weight:** 5.6552 g. **Composition:** 0.9250 Silver .1682 oz. ASW

| Date | Mintage | F | VF | XF | Unc | BU |
|---|---|---|---|---|---|---|
| 1901 | 600,000 | 15.00 | 40.00 | 100 | 200 | — |
| 1901 Proof | — | Value: 1,250 | | | | |

**9 PIASTRES** **KM# 9** **Weight:** 5.6552 g. **Composition:** 0.9250 Silver .1682 oz. ASW

| Date | Mintage | F | VF | XF | Unc | BU |
|---|---|---|---|---|---|---|
| 1907 | 60,000 | 35.00 | 100 | 275 | 500 | — |

**9 PIASTRES** **KM# 13** **Weight:** 5.6552 g. **Composition:** 0.9250 Silver .1682 oz. ASW

| Date | Mintage | F | VF | XF | Unc | BU |
|---|---|---|---|---|---|---|
| 1913 | 50,000 | 40.00 | 125 | 300 | 600 | — |
| 1919 | 400,000 | 2.50 | 10.00 | 30.00 | 100 | — |
| 1921 | 490,000 | 2.50 | 10.00 | 30.00 | 100 | — |

**9 PIASTRES** **KM# 25** **Weight:** 5.6552 g. **Composition:** 0.9250 Silver .1682 oz. ASW

| Date | Mintage | F | VF | XF | Unc | BU |
|---|---|---|---|---|---|---|
| 1938 | 504,000 | 2.00 | 3.50 | 8.00 | 30.00 | — |
| 1938 Proof | — | Value: 400 | | | | |
| 1940 | 800,000 | 1.50 | 3.00 | 7.00 | 27.50 | — |
| 1940 Proof | — | Value: 400 | | | | |

**SHILLING** **KM# 27** **Composition:** Copper-Nickel

| Date | Mintage | F | VF | XF | Unc | BU |
|---|---|---|---|---|---|---|
| 1947 | 1,440,000 | 0.50 | 1.00 | 5.00 | 30.00 | — |
| 1947 Proof | — | Value: 300 | | | | |

**SHILLING** **KM# 31** **Composition:** Copper-Nickel **Obv. Legend:** ends ... DEI GRATIA REX

| Date | Mintage | F | VF | XF | Unc | BU |
|---|---|---|---|---|---|---|
| 1949 | 1,440,000 | 0.50 | 1.00 | 5.00 | 30.00 | — |
| 1949 Proof | — | Value: 300 | | | | |

**18 PIASTRES** **KM# 7** **Weight:** 11.3104 g. **Composition:** 0.9250 Silver .3364 oz. ASW

| Date | Mintage | F | VF | XF | Unc | BU |
|---|---|---|---|---|---|---|
| 1901 | 200,000 | 40.00 | 150 | 300 | 500 | — |
| 1901 Proof | — | Value: 2,500 | | | | |

**18 PIASTRES** **KM# 10** **Weight:** 11.3104 g. **Composition:** 0.9250 Silver .3364 oz. ASW

| Date | Mintage | F | VF | XF | Unc | BU |
|---|---|---|---|---|---|---|
| 1907 | 20,000 | 55.00 | 225 | 485 | 1,250 | — |

**18 PIASTRES** **KM# 14** **Weight:** 11.3104 g. **Composition:** 0.9250 Silver .3364 oz. ASW

| Date | Mintage | F | VF | XF | Unc | BU |
|---|---|---|---|---|---|---|
| 1913 | 25,000 | 35.00 | 140 | 350 | 650 | — |
| 1921 | 155,000 | 25.00 | 60.00 | 150 | 350 | — |

**18 PIASTRES** **KM# 26** **Weight:** 11.3104 g. **Composition:** 0.9250 Silver .3364 oz. ASW

| Date | Mintage | F | VF | XF | Unc | BU |
|---|---|---|---|---|---|---|
| 1938 | 200,000 | 3.50 | 5.00 | 10.00 | 40.00 | — |
| 1938 Proof | — | Value: 450 | | | | |
| 1940 | 100,000 | 4.00 | 6.50 | 15.00 | 50.00 | — |
| 1940 Proof | — | Value: 450 | | | | |

**2 SHILLING** **KM# 28** **Weight:** 4.0000 g. **Composition:** Copper-Nickel

| Date | Mintage | F | VF | XF | Unc | BU |
|---|---|---|---|---|---|---|
| 1947 | 720,000 | 1.00 | 2.50 | 7.50 | 35.00 | — |
| 1947 Proof | — | Value: 400 | | | | |

**2 SHILLING** **KM# 32** **Composition:** Copper-Nickel **Obverse:** ends ...DEI GRATIA REX

| Date | Mintage | F | VF | XF | Unc | BU |
|---|---|---|---|---|---|---|
| 1949 | 720,000 | 1.00 | 2.50 | 7.50 | 35.00 | — |
| 1949 Proof | — | Value: 400 | | | | |

**45 PIASTRES** **KM# 19** **Weight:** 28.2759 g. **Composition:** 0.9250 Silver .8409 oz. ASW **Subject:** 50th Anniversary of British Rule

| Date | Mintage | F | VF | XF | Unc | BU |
|---|---|---|---|---|---|---|
| ND | 80,000 | 15.00 | 25.00 | 50.00 | 150 | — |
| ND(1928) | 517 | Value: 600 | | | | |

## DECIMAL COINAGE

50 Mils = 1 Shilling; 20 Shillings = 1 Pound; 1000 Mils = 1 Pound

**3 MILS** **KM# 33** **Composition:** Bronze **Reverse:** Flying Fish

| Date | Mintage | F | VF | XF | Unc | BU |
|---|---|---|---|---|---|---|
| 1955 | 6,250,000 | — | — | 0.10 | 0.20 | — |
| 1955 Proof | 2,000 | Value: 2.50 | | | | |

**5 MILS** **KM# 34** **Composition:** Bronze

| Date | Mintage | F | VF | XF | Unc | BU |
|---|---|---|---|---|---|---|
| 1955 | 10,000,000 | — | 0.15 | 0.25 | 0.40 | — |
| 1955 Proof | 2,000 | Value: 3.00 | | | | |
| 1956 | 2,950,000 | — | 0.15 | 0.30 | 0.50 | — |
| 1956 Proof | — | Value: 300 | | | | |

**25 MILS** **KM# 35** **Composition:** Copper-Nickel **Reverse:** Head of Bull

| Date | Mintage | F | VF | XF | Unc | BU |
|---|---|---|---|---|---|---|
| 1955 | 2,500,000 | — | 0.25 | 0.35 | 0.50 | — |
| 1955 Proof | 2,000 | Value: 3.00 | | | | |

**100 MILS** **KM# 37** **Composition:** Copper-Nickel

| Date | Mintage | F | VF | XF | Unc | BU |
|---|---|---|---|---|---|---|
| 1955 | 2,500,000 | — | 0.50 | 0.75 | 1.50 | — |
| 1955 Proof | 2,000 | Value: 4.50 | | | | |
| 1957 | Est. 500,000 | — | 10.00 | 15.00 | 50.00 | — |
| 1957 Proof | — | Value: 440 | | | | |

**Note:** All but 10,000 of 1957 issue were melted down

**50 MILS** **KM# 36** **Composition:** Copper-Nickel **Reverse:** Fern Leaves

| Date | Mintage | F | VF | XF | Unc | BU |
|---|---|---|---|---|---|---|
| 1955 | 4,000,000 | — | 0.35 | 0.50 | 1.00 | — |
| 1955 Proof | 2,000 | Value: 3.00 | | | | |

# REPUBLIC

## MIL COINAGE

**MIL** **KM# 38** **Composition:** Aluminum

| Date | Mintage | F | VF | XF | Unc | BU |
|---|---|---|---|---|---|---|
| 1963 | 5,000,000 | — | — | — | 0.15 | — |
| 1963 Proof | 25,000 | Value: 1.00 | | | | |
| 1971 | 500,000 | — | — | 0.10 | 0.25 | — |
| 1972 | 500,000 | — | — | 0.10 | 0.25 | — |
| 1972 Proof | — | Value: 2.00 | | | | |

**5 MILS** **KM# 39** **Composition:** Bronze

| Date | Mintage | F | VF | XF | Unc | BU |
|---|---|---|---|---|---|---|
| 1963 | 12,000,000 | — | — | 0.10 | 0.35 | — |
| 1963 Proof | 25,000 | Value: 1.25 | | | | |
| 1970 | 2,500,000 | — | — | 0.10 | 0.35 | — |
| 1971 | 2,500,000 | — | — | 0.10 | 0.35 | — |
| 1972 | 2,500,000 | — | — | 0.10 | 0.35 | — |
| 1973 | 5,000,000 | — | — | 0.10 | 0.35 | — |
| 1974 | 2,500,000 | — | — | 0.10 | 0.35 | — |
| 1976 | 2,000,000 | — | — | 0.10 | 0.35 | — |
| 1977 | 2,000,000 | — | — | 0.10 | 0.35 | — |
| 1978 | 2,000,000 | — | — | 0.10 | 0.35 | — |
| 1979 | 2,000,000 | — | — | 0.10 | 0.35 | — |
| 1980 | 4,000,000 | — | — | 0.10 | 0.35 | — |
| 1980 Proof | — | Value: 2.50 | | | | |

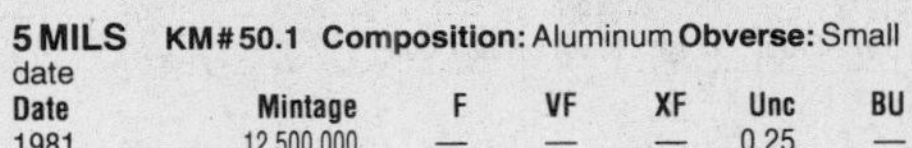

**5 MILS** **KM# 50.1** **Composition:** Aluminum **Obverse:** Small date

| Date | Mintage | F | VF | XF | Unc | BU |
|---|---|---|---|---|---|---|
| 1981 | 12,500,000 | — | — | — | 0.25 | — |

**5 MILS** **KM# 50.2** **Composition:** Aluminum **Obverse:** Large date and legends

| Date | Mintage | F | VF | XF | Unc | BU |
|---|---|---|---|---|---|---|
| 1982 | 15,000,000 | — | — | — | 0.25 | — |
| 1982 Proof | — | Value: 2.00 | | | | |

**25 MILS** **KM# 40** **Composition:** Copper-Nickel **Note:** Cedar of Lebanon.

| Date | Mintage | F | VF | XF | Unc | BU |
|---|---|---|---|---|---|---|
| 1963 | 2,500,000 | — | 0.10 | 0.15 | 0.45 | — |
| 1963 Proof | 25,000 | Value: 1.50 | | | | |
| 1968 | 1,500,000 | — | 0.10 | 0.15 | 0.45 | — |
| 1971 | 1,000,000 | — | 0.10 | 0.15 | 0.45 | — |
| 1972 | 500,000 | — | 0.10 | 0.15 | 0.50 | — |
| 1973 | 1,000,000 | — | 0.10 | 0.15 | 0.45 | — |
| 1974 | 1,000,000 | — | 0.10 | 0.15 | 0.45 | — |
| 1976 | 2,000,000 | — | 0.10 | 0.15 | 0.45 | — |
| 1977 | 500,000 | — | 0.10 | 0.15 | 0.45 | — |
| 1978 | 500,000 | — | 0.10 | 0.15 | 0.45 | — |
| 1979 | 1,000,000 | — | 0.10 | 0.15 | 0.45 | — |
| 1980 | 2,000,000 | — | 0.10 | 0.15 | 0.45 | — |
| 1981 | 3,000,000 | — | 0.10 | 0.15 | 0.45 | — |
| 1982 | 1,000,000 | — | 0.10 | 0.15 | 0.45 | — |
| 1982 Proof | — | Value: 3.00 | | | | |

**100 MILS** **KM# 42** **Composition:** Copper-Nickel **Reverse:** Cyprus Mouflon

| Date | Mintage | F | VF | XF | Unc | BU |
|---|---|---|---|---|---|---|
| 1963 | 1,750,000 | — | 0.40 | 0.70 | 2.00 | — |
| 1963 Proof | 25,000 | Value: 2.50 | | | | |
| 1971 | 500,000 | — | 0.50 | 0.75 | 2.00 | — |
| 1973 | 750,000 | — | 0.40 | 0.70 | 2.00 | — |
| 1974 | 1,000,000 | — | 0.50 | 0.75 | 2.00 | — |
| 1976 | 1,500,000 | — | 0.40 | 0.70 | 2.00 | — |
| 1977 | 500,000 | — | 0.50 | 0.75 | 2.00 | — |
| 1978 | 1,000,000 | — | 0.50 | 0.75 | 2.00 | — |
| 1979 | 1,000,000 | — | 0.40 | 0.70 | 2.00 | — |
| 1980 | 1,000,000 | — | 0.40 | 0.70 | 2.00 | — |
| 1981 | 2,000,000 | — | 0.40 | 0.70 | 2.00 | — |
| 1982 | 2,000,000 | — | 0.40 | 0.70 | 2.00 | — |
| 1982 Proof | — | Value: 5.00 | | | | |

**50 MILS** **KM# 41** **Composition:** Copper-Nickel **Reverse:** Bunch of grapes

| Date | Mintage | F | VF | XF | Unc | BU |
|---|---|---|---|---|---|---|
| 1963 | 2,800,000 | — | 0.20 | 0.30 | 1.00 | — |
| 1963 Proof | 25,000 | Value: 1.75 | | | | |
| 1970 | 500,000 | — | 0.20 | 0.35 | 1.25 | — |
| 1971 | 500,000 | — | 0.20 | 0.35 | 1.25 | — |
| 1972 | 750,000 | — | 0.20 | 0.30 | 1.00 | — |
| 1973 | 750,000 | — | 0.20 | 0.30 | 1.00 | — |
| 1974 | 1,500,000 | — | 0.20 | 0.30 | 1.00 | — |
| 1976 | 1,500,000 | — | 0.20 | 0.30 | 1.00 | — |
| 1977 | 500,000 | — | 0.20 | 0.30 | 1.00 | — |
| 1978 | 500,000 | — | 0.20 | 0.30 | 1.00 | — |
| 1979 | 1,000,000 | — | 0.20 | 0.30 | 1.00 | — |
| 1980 | 3,000,000 | — | 0.20 | 0.30 | 1.00 | — |
| 1981 | 4,000,000 | — | 0.20 | 0.30 | 1.00 | — |
| 1982 | 2,000,000 | — | 0.20 | 0.30 | 1.00 | — |
| 1982 Proof | — | Value: 3.50 | | | | |

**500 MILS** KM# 43 **Composition:** Copper-Nickel **Series:** F.A.O.

| Date | Mintage | F | VF | XF | Unc | BU |
|---|---|---|---|---|---|---|
| 1970 | 80,000 | — | 1.25 | 2.75 | 7.50 | — |

**500 MILS** KM# 43a **Weight:** 22.6200 g. **Composition:** 0.8000 Silver .5818 oz. ASW **Series:** F.A.O

| Date | Mintage | F | VF | XF | Unc | BU |
|---|---|---|---|---|---|---|
| 1970 Proof | 5,000 | Value: 55.00 | | | | |

**500 MILS** KM# 44 **Composition:** Copper-Nickel **Series:** F.A.O **Reverse:** Hercules

| Date | Mintage | F | VF | XF | Unc | BU |
|---|---|---|---|---|---|---|
| 1975 | 500,000 | — | 1.25 | 1.75 | 3.50 | — |
| 1977 | 300,000 | — | 1.25 | 1.75 | 3.50 | — |
| 1977 Proof | — | Value: 15.00 | | | | |

**500 MILS** KM# 44a **Weight:** 14.1400 g. **Composition:** 0.8000 Silver .3637 oz. ASW **Series:** F.A.O.

| Date | Mintage | F | VF | XF | Unc | BU |
|---|---|---|---|---|---|---|
| 1975 Proof | 10,000 | Value: 22.50 | | | | |

**500 MILS** KM# 45 **Composition:** Copper-Nickel **Series:** F.A.O. **Subject:** Refugees

| Date | Mintage | F | VF | XF | Unc | BU |
|---|---|---|---|---|---|---|
| 1976 | 25,000 | — | 1.25 | 2.00 | 4.00 | — |

**500 MILS** KM# 45a **Weight:** 14.1400 g. **Composition:** 0.9250 Silver .4205 oz. ASW **Series:** F.A.O.

| Date | Mintage | F | VF | XF | Unc | BU |
|---|---|---|---|---|---|---|
| 1976 Proof | 25,000 | Value: 25.00 | | | | |

**500 MILS** KM# 48 **Composition:** Copper-Nickel **Series:** F.A.O. **Subject:** Human Rights

| Date | Mintage | F | VF | XF | Unc | BU |
|---|---|---|---|---|---|---|
| ND(1978) | 50,000 | — | 1.25 | 2.00 | 4.00 | — |

**500 MILS** KM# 48a **Weight:** 14.1400 g. **Composition:** 0.9250 Silver .4205 oz. ASW

| Date | Mintage | F | VF | XF | Unc | BU |
|---|---|---|---|---|---|---|
| ND Proof | 5,000 | Value: 65.00 | | | | |

**500 MILS** KM# 49a **Weight:** 14.1400 g. **Composition:** 0.9250 Silver .4205 oz. ASW

| Date | Mintage | F | VF | XF | Unc | BU |
|---|---|---|---|---|---|---|
| 1980 Proof | 7,500 | Value: 50.00 | | | | |

**500 MILS** KM# 49 **Composition:** Copper-Nickel **Series:** F.A.O **Subject:** Summer Olympic Games

| Date | Mintage | F | VF | XF | Unc | BU |
|---|---|---|---|---|---|---|
| 1980 | 50,000 | — | 1.25 | 2.50 | 6.50 | — |

**500 MILS** KM# 51 **Composition:** Copper-Nickel **Subject:** World Food Day **Reverse:** Swordfish

| Date | Mintage | F | VF | XF | Unc | BU |
|---|---|---|---|---|---|---|
| ND(1978) | 50 | — | 1.25 | 2.00 | 5.00 | — |

**500 MILS** KM# 51a **Weight:** 14.1400 g. **Composition:** 0.9250 Silver .4205 oz. ASW

| Date | Mintage | F | VF | XF | Unc | BU |
|---|---|---|---|---|---|---|
| ND(1978) Proof | 7,500 | Value: 45.00 | | | | |

**POUND** KM# 46a **Weight:** 28.2800 g. **Composition:** 0.9250 Silver .8411 oz. ASW

| Date | Mintage | F | VF | XF | Unc | BU |
|---|---|---|---|---|---|---|
| 1976 Proof | 25,000 | Value: 42.50 | | | | |

**POUND** KM# 46 **Composition:** Copper-Nickel **Note:** Refugee Commemorataive.

| Date | Mintage | F | VF | XF | Unc | BU |
|---|---|---|---|---|---|---|
| 1976 | 25,000 | — | 2.00 | 2.50 | 5.50 | — |

**50 POUNDS** KM# 47 **Weight:** 15.9800 g. **Composition:** 0.9170 Gold .4711 oz. AGW **Reverse:** Archbishop Makarios

| Date | Mintage | F | VF | XF | Unc | BU |
|---|---|---|---|---|---|---|
| 1977 | 39,000 | — | — | — | 275 | — |
| 1977 Proof | 51,000 | Value: 300 | | | | |

## REFORM COINAGE

100 Cents = 1 Pound

**HALF CENT** KM# 52 **Composition:** Aluminum **Reverse:** Cyclamen

| Date | Mintage | F | VF | XF | Unc | BU |
|---|---|---|---|---|---|---|
| 1983 | 10,000,000 | — | — | 0.10 | 0.15 | — |
| 1983 Proof | 6,250 | Value: 1.50 | | | | |

**CENT** KM# 53.1 **Composition:** Nickel-Brass **Reverse:** Stylized bird on a branch; value number surrounded by single line

| Date | Mintage | F | VF | XF | Unc | BU |
|---|---|---|---|---|---|---|
| 1983 | 15,000,000 | — | — | 0.10 | 0.20 | — |
| 1983 Proof | 6,250 | Value: 1.50 | | | | |

**CENT** KM# 53.2 **Composition:** Nickel-Brass **Reverse:** Stylized bird on a branch; value number surrounded by double line

| Date | Mintage | F | VF | XF | Unc | BU |
|---|---|---|---|---|---|---|
| 1985 | 5,000,000 | — | — | 0.10 | 0.20 | — |
| 1987 | 5,000,000 | — | — | 0.10 | 0.20 | — |
| 1988 | 5,000,000 | — | — | 0.10 | 0.20 | — |
| 1989 | — | — | — | 0.10 | 0.20 | — |
| 1990 | — | — | — | 0.10 | 0.20 | — |
| 1994 | — | — | — | 0.10 | 0.20 | — |

**CENT** KM# 53.3 **Composition:** Nickel-Brass **Obverse:** Stylized bird on a bronch; altered wreath around arms

| Date | Mintage | F | VF | XF | Unc | BU |
|---|---|---|---|---|---|---|
| 1991 | — | — | — | 0.10 | 0.20 | — |
| 1992 | — | — | — | 0.10 | 0.20 | — |
| 1993 | — | — | — | 0.10 | 0.20 | — |
| 1994 | — | — | — | 0.10 | 0.20 | — |
| 1996 | — | — | — | 0.10 | 0.20 | — |
| 1998 | — | — | — | 0.10 | 0.20 | — |

**2 CENTS** KM# 54.1 **Composition:** Nickel-Brass **Reverse:** Stylized goats; value number surrounded by single line

| Date | Mintage | F | VF | XF | Unc | BU |
|---|---|---|---|---|---|---|
| 1983 | 12,000,000 | — | — | 0.15 | 0.25 | — |
| 1983 Proof | 6,250 | Value: 1.50 | | | | |

**2 CENTS** KM# 54.2 **Composition:** Nickel-Brass **Reverse:** Stylized goats; value number surrounded by double line

| Date | Mintage | F | VF | XF | Unc | BU |
|---|---|---|---|---|---|---|
| 1985 | 8,000,000 | — | — | 0.15 | 0.25 | — |
| 1987 | — | — | — | 0.15 | 0.25 | — |
| 1988 | 5,150,000 | — | — | 0.15 | 0.25 | — |
| 1989 | — | — | — | 0.15 | 0.25 | — |
| 1990 | — | — | — | 0.15 | 0.25 | — |

**2 CENTS** KM# 54.3 **Composition:** Nickel-Brass **Obverse:** Stylized goats, altered wereath around arms

| Date | Mintage | F | VF | XF | Unc | BU |
|---|---|---|---|---|---|---|
| 1991 | — | — | — | 0.15 | 0.25 | — |
| 1992 | — | — | — | 0.15 | 0.25 | — |
| 1993 | — | — | — | 0.15 | 0.25 | — |
| 1994 | — | — | — | 0.15 | 0.25 | — |
| 1996 | — | — | — | 0.15 | 0.25 | — |

**5 CENTS** **KM# 55.1** **Composition:** Nickel-Brass **Reverse:** Value number surrounded by single line

| Date | Mintage | F | VF | XF | Unc | BU |
|---|---|---|---|---|---|---|
| 1983 | 15,000,000 | — | — | 0.20 | 0.50 | — |
| 1983 Proof | 6,250 | Value: 2.00 | | | | |

**5 CENTS** **KM# 55.2** **Composition:** Nickel-Brass **Reverse:** Value number surrounded by double line

| Date | Mintage | F | VF | XF | Unc | BU |
|---|---|---|---|---|---|---|
| 1985 | 5,000,000 | — | — | 0.20 | 0.50 | — |
| 1987 | 5,000,000 | — | — | 0.20 | 0.50 | — |
| 1988 | 5,060,000 | — | — | 0.20 | 0.50 | — |
| 1989 | — | — | — | 0.20 | 0.50 | — |
| 1990 | — | — | — | 0.20 | 0.50 | — |

**5 CENTS** **KM# 55.3** **Composition:** Nickel-Brass **Obverse:** Altered wreath around arms

| Date | Mintage | F | VF | XF | Unc | BU |
|---|---|---|---|---|---|---|
| 1991 | — | — | — | 0.20 | 0.50 | — |
| 1992 | — | — | — | 0.20 | 0.50 | — |
| 1993 | — | — | — | 0.20 | 0.50 | — |
| 1994 | — | — | — | 0.20 | 0.50 | — |
| 1998 | — | — | — | 0.20 | 0.50 | — |

**10 CENTS** **KM# 56.1** **Composition:** Nickel-Brass **Reverse:** Value number surrounded by single line

| Date | Mintage | F | VF | XF | Unc | BU |
|---|---|---|---|---|---|---|
| 1983 | 10,000,000 | — | — | 0.35 | 0.75 | — |
| 1983 Proof | 6,250 | Value: 3.00 | | | | |

**10 CENTS** **KM# 56.2** **Composition:** Nickel-Brass **Reverse:** Value number surrounded by double line

| Date | Mintage | F | VF | XF | Unc | BU |
|---|---|---|---|---|---|---|
| 1985 | 5,000,000 | — | — | 0.35 | 0.75 | — |
| 1987 | — | — | — | 0.35 | 0.75 | — |
| 1988 | 5,035,000 | — | — | 0.35 | 0.75 | — |
| 1989 | — | — | — | 0.35 | 0.75 | — |
| 1990 | — | — | — | 0.35 | 0.75 | — |

**10 CENTS** **KM# 56.3** **Composition:** Nickel-Brass **Obverse:** Altered wreath around arms

| Date | Mintage | F | VF | XF | Unc | BU |
|---|---|---|---|---|---|---|
| 1991 | — | — | — | 0.35 | 0.75 | — |
| 1992 | — | — | — | 0.35 | 0.75 | — |
| 1993 | — | — | — | 0.35 | 0.75 | — |
| 1994 | — | — | — | 0.35 | 0.75 | — |

**20 CENTS** **KM# 57.1** **Composition:** Nickel-Brass **Reverse:** Value number framed by single line

| Date | Mintage | F | VF | XF | Unc | BU |
|---|---|---|---|---|---|---|
| 1983 | 10,000,000 | — | — | 0.50 | 1.50 | — |
| 1983 Proof | 6,200 | Value: 5.00 | | | | |

**20 CENTS** **KM# 57.2** **Composition:** Nickel-Brass **Reverse:** Value number framed by double line

| Date | Mintage | F | VF | XF | Unc | BU |
|---|---|---|---|---|---|---|
| 1985 | 5,040,000 | — | — | 0.50 | 1.50 | — |
| 1987 | — | — | — | 0.50 | 1.50 | — |
| 1988 | 1,000,000 | — | — | 0.50 | 1.50 | — |

**20 CENTS** **KM# 62.1** **Composition:** Bronze **Reverse:** Zamon D. Keteus head left

| Date | Mintage | F | VF | XF | Unc | BU |
|---|---|---|---|---|---|---|
| 1989 | — | — | — | — | 1.00 | — |
| 1989 Proof | — | Value: 18.00 | | | | |
| 1990 | — | — | — | — | 1.00 | — |

**20 CENTS** **KM# 62.2** **Composition:** Nickel-Brass **Obverse:** Zamon D. Keteus head left, altered wreath around arms

| Date | Mintage | F | VF | XF | Unc | BU |
|---|---|---|---|---|---|---|
| 1991 | — | — | — | — | 1.00 | — |
| 1992 | — | — | — | — | 1.00 | — |
| 1993 | — | — | — | — | 1.00 | — |
| 1994 | — | — | — | — | 1.00 | — |

**50 CENTS** **KM# 58** **Composition:** Copper-Nickel **Series:** F.A.O. **Subject:** Forestry

| Date | Mintage | F | VF | XF | Unc | BU |
|---|---|---|---|---|---|---|
| 1985 | 33,000 | — | 1.50 | 3.50 | 9.00 | — |

**50 CENTS** **KM# 58a** **Weight:** 14.1400 g. **Composition:** 0.9250 Silver .4205 oz. ASW **Series:** F.A.O.

| Date | Mintage | F | VF | XF | Unc | BU |
|---|---|---|---|---|---|---|
| 1985 Proof | 4,000 | Value: 50.00 | | | | |

**50 CENTS** **KM# 60a** **Weight:** 14.1400 g. **Composition:** 0.9250 Silver .4205 oz. ASW

| Date | Mintage | F | VF | XF | Unc | BU |
|---|---|---|---|---|---|---|
| 1988 Proof | 4,000 | Value: 45.00 | | | | |

**50 CENTS** **KM# 60** **Composition:** Copper-Nickel **Subject:** Olympics **Reverse:** Symbols

| Date | Mintage | F | VF | XF | Unc | BU |
|---|---|---|---|---|---|---|
| 1988 | 14,000 | — | — | — | 3.50 | — |

**50 CENTS** **KM# 66** **Composition:** Copper-Nickel **Subject:** Abduction of Europe

| Date | Mintage | F | VF | XF | Unc | BU |
|---|---|---|---|---|---|---|
| 1991 | 3,005,000 | — | — | — | 2.50 | — |
| 1993 | — | — | — | — | 2.50 | — |
| 1994 | — | — | — | — | 2.50 | — |
| 1996 | — | — | — | — | 2.50 | — |

**50 CENTS** **KM# 66a** **Weight:** 7.0000 g. **Composition:** 0.9250 Silver .2082 oz. ASW

| Date | Mintage | F | VF | XF | Unc | BU |
|---|---|---|---|---|---|---|
| 1991 Proof | 5,000 | Value: 35.00 | | | | |

**POUND** **KM# 59** **Composition:** Copper-Nickel **Subject:** World Wildlife Fund **Obverse:** National arms **Reverse:** Cyprian wild sheep

| Date | Mintage | F | VF | XF | Unc | BU |
|---|---|---|---|---|---|---|
| 1986 | 39,000 | — | — | — | 5.50 | — |

**POUND** **KM# 59a** **Composition:** 0.9250 Silver

| Date | Mintage | F | VF | XF | Unc | BU |
|---|---|---|---|---|---|---|
| 1986 Proof | 13,000 | Value: 37.50 | | | | |

**POUND** **KM# 61a** **Weight:** 28.2800 g. **Composition:** 0.9250 Silver .8411 oz. ASW

| Date | Mintage | F | VF | XF | Unc | BU |
|---|---|---|---|---|---|---|
| 1988 Proof | 4,000 | Value: 55.00 | | | | |

**POUND** **KM# 61** **Composition:** Copper-Nickel **Subject:** Olympics **Reverse:** Symbols

| Date | Mintage | F | VF | XF | Unc | BU |
|---|---|---|---|---|---|---|
| 1988 | 14,000 | — | — | — | 6.50 | — |

**POUND** **KM# 63** **Composition:** Copper-Nickel **Subject:** Small European States Games

| Date | Mintage | F | VF | XF | Unc | BU |
|---|---|---|---|---|---|---|
| 1989 | — | — | — | — | 5.50 | — |

**POUND** **KM# 64** **Composition:** Copper-Nickel **Subject:** Save the Children Fund

| Date | Mintage | F | VF | XF | Unc | BU |
|---|---|---|---|---|---|---|
| 1989 | — | — | — | — | 5.50 | — |

**POUND** **KM# 63a** **Weight:** 28.2800 g. **Composition:** 0.9250 Silver .8411 oz. ASW

| Date | Mintage | F | VF | XF | Unc | BU |
|---|---|---|---|---|---|---|
| 1989 Proof | 4,000 | Value: 50.00 | | | | |

**POUND** **KM# 64a** **Weight:** 28.2800 g. **Composition:** 0.9250 Silver .8411 oz. ASW

| Date | Mintage | F | VF | XF | Unc | BU |
|---|---|---|---|---|---|---|
| 1989 Proof | 4,000 | Value: 42.50 | | | | |

**POUND** **KM# 67a** **Weight:** 28.2800 g. **Composition:** 0.9250 Silver .8411 oz. ASW

| Date | Mintage | F | VF | XF | Unc | BU |
|---|---|---|---|---|---|---|
| 1992 Proof | 4,000 | Value: 55.00 | | | | |

**POUND** **KM# 67** **Composition:** Copper-Nickel **Subject:** Olympics **Reverse:** Relay Racing

| Date | Mintage | F | VF | XF | Unc | BU |
|---|---|---|---|---|---|---|
| 1992 | 8,000 | — | — | — | 8.50 | — |

**POUND** **KM# 69** **Composition:** Copper-Nickel **Subject:** 50th Anniversary - United Nations **Obverse:** National arms **Reverse:** Tree of flag shields, denomination and logo

| Date | Mintage | F | VF | XF | Unc | BU |
|---|---|---|---|---|---|---|
| 1995 | Est. 100,000 | — | — | — | 8.50 | — |

**POUND** **KM# 70** **Composition:** Copper-Nickel **Series:** F.A.O. **Subject:** 50th Anniversary - United Nations **Obverse:** National arms **Reverse:** Bovine portrait, wheat and denominaton

| Date | Mintage | F | VF | XF | Unc | BU |
|---|---|---|---|---|---|---|
| 1995 | — | — | — | — | 12.50 | — |

**POUND** **KM# 69a** **Weight:** 28.2800 g. **Composition:** 0.9250 Silver .8411 oz. ASW **Series:** 50th Anniversary - United Nations **Obverse:** National Arms **Reverse:** Tree of flags, denomination amd logo

| Date | Mintage | F | VF | XF | Unc | BU |
|---|---|---|---|---|---|---|
| 1995 | Est. 100,000 | Value: 40.00 | | | | |

**POUND** **KM# 70a** **Weight:** 28.2800 g. **Composition:** 0.9250 Silver .8411 oz. ASW **Series:** 50th Anniversary - F.A.O. **Obverse:** National Arms **Reverse:** Bovine Portrait, wheat and denomination

| Date | Mintage | F | VF | XF | Unc | BU |
|---|---|---|---|---|---|---|
| 1995 | 4,000 | Value: 55.00 | | | | |

**POUND** **KM# 71a** **Series:** 1996 Olympics **Obverse:** National Arms **Reverse:** Olympic rings, stylized flames, olive branch

| Date | Mintage | F | VF | XF | Unc | BU |
|---|---|---|---|---|---|---|
| 1996 | 4,000 | Value: 40.00 | | | | |

**POUND** **KM# 71** **Composition:** Copper-Nickel **Subject:** 1996 Olympics **Obverse:** National arms **Reverse:** Olympic rings, stylized flames, olive branch

| Date | Mintage | F | VF | XF | Unc | BU |
|---|---|---|---|---|---|---|
| 1996 Proof | 2,000 | Value: 45.00 | | | | |

**POUND** **KM# 72** **Composition:** Copper-Nickel **Subject:** World Wildlife Fund - Conserving Nature **Obverse:** National arms **Reverse:** Green turtle

| Date | Mintage | F | VF | XF | Unc | BU |
|---|---|---|---|---|---|---|
| 1997 | — | — | — | — | 14.50 | — |

**POUND** **KM# 72a** **Weight:** 28.2800 g. **Composition:** 0.9250 Silver .8411 oz. ASW

| Date | Mintage | F | VF | XF | Unc | BU |
|---|---|---|---|---|---|---|
| 1997 Proof | Est. 15,000 | Value: 50.00 | | | | |

**2 POUNDS** **KM# 73** **Composition:** Bronze **Subject:** Millennium. **Obverse:** National arms and denomination. **Reverse:** Three line inscription. **Shape:** Ox hide shaped or ancient ingot. **Size:** 44.5 x 25 mm.

| Date | Mintage | F | VF | XF | Unc | BU |
|---|---|---|---|---|---|---|
| 1999 | — | — | — | — | 20.00 | — |

**2 POUNDS** **KM# 73a** **Weight:** 15.0000 g. **Composition:** 0.9250 Silver .4461 oz. ASW **Subject:** Millennium **Obverse:** National arms and denomination. **Reverse:** Three line inscription. **Edge:** Plain. **Shape:** Ox hide shape, or like ancient ingots. **Size:** 44.5 x 25 mm.

| Date | Mintage | F | VF | XF | Unc | BU |
|---|---|---|---|---|---|---|
| 2000 | 32,000 | — | — | — | 50.00 | — |

**20 POUNDS** **KM# 65** **Weight:** 7.9881 g. **Composition:** 0.9170 Silver .2354 oz. ASW **Subject:** 30th Anniversary of the Republic **Obverse:** State emblem **Reverse:** Value superimposed on stylized bird

| Date | Mintage | F | VF | XF | Unc | BU |
|---|---|---|---|---|---|---|
| 1990 Proof | 5,000 | Value: 250 | | | | |

**20 POUNDS** **KM# 68** **Weight:** 7.9881 g. **Composition:** 0.9170 Silver .2354 oz. ASW **Subject:** Museum Building Fund

| Date | Mintage | F | VF | XF | Unc | BU |
|---|---|---|---|---|---|---|
| 1992 Proof | 5,000 | Value: 225 | | | | |

**100 POUNDS** **KM# 74** **Composition:** Gold **Subject:** Millennium **Obverse:** National arms and denomination. **Reverse:** Three line inscription. **Shape:** Ox hide shaped or ancient ingot.

| Date | Mintage | F | VF | XF | Unc | BU |
|---|---|---|---|---|---|---|
| 2000 | 750 | — | — | — | 400 | — |

## MEDALLIC COINAGE

**1/2 SOVEREIGN** **KM# M1** **Weight:** 4.0000 g. **Composition:** 0.9170 Gold .1179 oz. AGW **Series:** Archbishop Makarios Fund **Obverse:** Archbishop Makarios III

| Date | Mintage | F | VF | XF | Unc | BU |
|---|---|---|---|---|---|---|
| 1966 Proof | 25,000 | Value: 115 | | | | |

**SOVEREIGN** **KM# M2** **Weight:** 8.0000 g. **Composition:** 0.9170 Gold .2359 oz. AGW **Series:** Archbishop Makarios Fund **Obverse:** Archbishop Makarios III

| Date | Mintage | F | VF | XF | Unc | BU |
|---|---|---|---|---|---|---|
| 1966 Proof | 50,000 | Value: 175 | | | | |

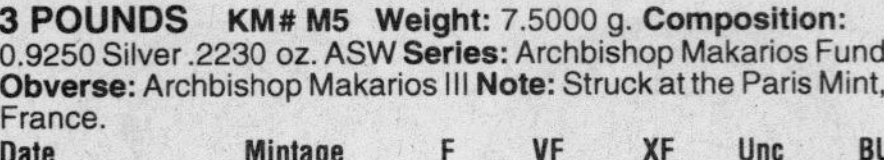

**3 POUNDS** KM# M5 **Weight:** 7.5000 g. **Composition:** 0.9250 Silver .2230 oz. ASW **Series:** Archbishop Makarios Fund **Obverse:** Archbishop Makarios III **Note:** Struck at the Paris Mint, France.

| Date | Mintage | F | VF | XF | Unc | BU |
|---|---|---|---|---|---|---|
| 1974 | — | — | — | — | 15.00 | — |

**5 POUNDS** KM# M3 **Weight:** 40.0000 g. **Composition:** 0.9170 Gold 1.1793 oz. AGW **Series:** Archbishop Makarios Fund **Obverse:** Archbishop Makarios III

| Date | Mintage | F | VF | XF | Unc | BU |
|---|---|---|---|---|---|---|
| 1966 | 1,500 | — | — | 1,200 | 1,750 | — |

**5 POUNDS** KM# M4 **Weight:** 40.0000 g. **Composition:** 0.9170 Gold **Series:** Archbishop Makarios Fund **Edge:** Plain **Note:** Modified design.

| Date | Mintage | F | VF | XF | Unc | BU |
|---|---|---|---|---|---|---|
| 1966 | — | — | — | 2,500 | 3,500 | — |

**6 POUNDS** KM# M6 **Weight:** 15.0000 g. **Composition:** 0.9250 Silver .4461 oz. ASW **Series:** Archbishop Makarios Fund **Obverse:** Archbishop Makarios III

| Date | Mintage | F | VF | XF | Unc | BU |
|---|---|---|---|---|---|---|
| 1974 | — | — | — | — | 25.00 | — |

**12 POUNDS** KM# M7 **Weight:** 30.0000 g. **Composition:** 0.9250 Silver .8922 oz. ASW **Series:** Archbishop Makarios Fund **Obverse:** Archbishop Makarios III

| Date | Mintage | F | VF | XF | Unc | BU |
|---|---|---|---|---|---|---|
| 1974 | — | — | — | — | 45.00 | — |

## TRIAL STRIKES

| KM# | Date | Mintage | Identification | Mkt Val |
|---|---|---|---|---|
| TS1 | 1879 | — | Piastre. 0.9170 Gold. 40.0000 g. Uniface. | 2,500 |

| KM# | Date | Mintage | Identification | Mkt Val |
|---|---|---|---|---|
| TS2 | | — | 45 Piastres. 0.9170 Gold. 40.0000 g. Uniface. | 3,000 |

**Note:** 1 known

## MINT SETS

| KM# | Date | Mintage | Identification | Issue Price | Mkt Val |
|---|---|---|---|---|---|
| MS1 | 1955 (5) | 2,550 | KM33-37 | 2.20 | 6.50 |
| MS2 | 1963 (5) | 8,050 | KM38-42 | 1.95 | 5.00 |
| MS3 | 1971 (5) | 3,000 | KM38-42 | 1.65 | 5.00 |
| MS4 | 1972 (4) | 30,000 | KM38-41 | 2.35 | 5.00 |
| MS5 | 1973 (4) | 5,000 | KM39-42 | 2.75 | 5.00 |
| MS6 | 1974 (4) | 5,000 | KM39-42 | 3.25 | 5.00 |
| MS7 | 1976 (3) | 5,000 | KM40-42 | 1.25 | 4.50 |
| MS8 | 1976 (2) | 25,000 | KM45-46 | 6.50 | 6.00 |
| MS9 | 1977 (5) | 10,000 | KM39-42, 44 | — | 6.50 |
| MS10 | 1978 (5) | — | KM39-42, 48 | 5.50 | 6.50 |
| MS11 | 1979 (4) | — | KM39-42 | — | 6.50 |
| MS12 | 1980 (4) | — | KM39-42 | — | 6.50 |
| MS13 | 1981 (5) | — | KM40-42, 50.1, 51 | 5.00 | 6.50 |
| MS14 | 1981 (4) | — | KM40-42, 50.1 | 5.00 | 6.50 |
| MS15 | 1982 (4) | 5,000 | KM40-42, 50.2 | 5.00 | 6.50 |
| MS16 | 1983 (6) | 11,400 | KM52,53.1-57.1 | 15.00 | 10.00 |
| MS17 | 1988 (5) | — | KM53.2-57.2 | — | 10.00 |
| MS18 | 1989 (5) | — | KM53.2-56.2, 62.1 | — | 10.00 |
| MS19 | 1990 (5) | — | KM53.2-56.2, 62.1 | 10.00 | 10.00 |

## PROOF SETS

| KM# | Date | Mintage | Identification | Issue Price | Mkt Val |
|---|---|---|---|---|---|
| PS1 | 1879 (3) | — | KM1.1, 2, 3.1 | — | 3,000 |
| PS2 | 1881 (3) | — | KM1.1, 2, 3.1 | — | 1,800 |
| PS3 | 1900 (3) | — | KM1.1, 2, 3.2 | — | 3,500 |
| PS4 | 1901 (4) | — | KM4-7 | — | 5,500 |
| PS5 | 1931 (2) | — | KM17-18 | — | 1,175 |
| PS6 | 1934 (2) | — | KM20-21 | — | 650 |
| PS7 | 1938 (5) | — | KM-22-26 | — | 2,000 |
| PS8 | 1947 (2) | — | KM27-28 | — | 700 |
| PS10 | 1949 (4) | — | KM29-32 | — | 950 |
| PS9 | 1949 (2) | — | KM31-32 | — | 700 |
| PS11 | 1955 (5) | 2,000 | KM33-37 | 5.50 | 16.00 |
| PS12 | 1963 (5) | 24,501 | KM38-42 | 9.00 | 8.50 |
| PS13 | 1963 (5) | 500 | KM38-42 | 8.70 | 8.00 |
| PS15 | (7) | — | KM38(72), 39(80), 40-42(82), 50.2(82) | 30.00 | 30.00 |
| PS14 | 1976 (2) | 25,000 | KM45a-46a | 50.00 | 35.00 |
| PS16 | 1983 (6) | 6,250 | KM52, 53.1-57.1 | 40.00 | 15.00 |

# CZECH REPUBLIC

The Czech Republic was formerly united with Slovakia as Czechoslovakia. It is bordered in the west by Germany, to the north by Poland, to the east by Slovakia and to the south by Austria. It consists of 3 major regions: Bohemia, Moravia and Silesia and has an area of 30,450 sq. mi. (78,864 sq. km.) and a population of 10.4 million. Capital: Prague (Praha). Agriculture and livestock are chief occupations while coal deposits are the main mineral resources.

The Czech lands were united with the Slovaks to form the Czechoslovak State, which came into existence on Oct. 28, 1918 upon the dissolution of the Austrian-Hungarian Empire. In 1938, this territory was broken up for the benefit of Germany, Poland, and Hungary by the Munich (Munchen) Agreement. In March 1939 the German influenced Slovak government proclaimed Slovakia independent. Germany incorporated the Czech lands into the Third Reich as the "Protectorate of Bohemia and Moravia." A Czech government-in-exile was set up in London in July 1940. The Soviets and USA forces liberated the area by May 1945. Communist influence increased steadily while pressure for liberalization culminated in the overthrow of the Stalinist leader Antonin Novotny and his associates in 1968. The Communist Party then introduced far reaching reforms which resulted in warnings from Moscow (Moskva), followed by occupation and stationing of Soviet forces. Mass demonstrations for reform began again in Nov. 1989 and the Federal Assembly abolished the Communist Party's sole right to govern. The new government formed was the Czech and Slovak Federal Republic. A movement for Democratic Slovakia was apparent in the June 1992 elections and on December 31, 1992, the CSFR was dissolved and the two new republics came into being on Jan. 1, 1993.

**NOTE**: For earlier issues see Czechoslovakia, Bohemia and Moravia or Slovakia listings.

**MINT MARKS**

(c) - castle = Hamburg
(cr) - cross = British Royal Mint
(l) - leaf = Royal Canadian
(m) - crowned *b* and *CM* = Jablonec nad Nisou
(mk) - *MK* in circle = Kremnica
(o) - broken circle = Vienna (Wien)

**MONETARY SYSTEM**

1 Czechoslovak Koruna (Kcs) = 1 Czech Koruna (Kc)
1 Koruna = 100 Haleru

# REPUBLIC

## STANDARD COINAGE

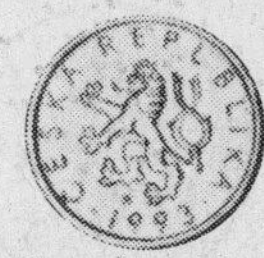

**10 HALERU** KM# 6 **Composition:** Aluminum **Note:** Two varieties of mint marks exist for 1994.

| Date | Mintage | F | VF | XF | Unc | BU |
|---|---|---|---|---|---|---|
| 1993(c) | 100,000,000 | — | — | — | 0.20 | — |
| 1993(m) | 94,902,000 | — | — | — | 0.20 | — |
| 1994(c) | — | — | — | — | 0.20 | — |
| 1994(m) | 53,127,000 | — | — | — | 0.20 | — |
| 1994(m) Proof | 2,000 | — | — | — | — | — |
| 1995(m) | 100,000 | — | — | — | 0.20 | — |
| 1996(m) | — | — | — | — | 0.20 | — |
| 1997(m) | — | — | — | — | 0.20 | — |
| 1997(m) Proof | — | Value: 3.50 | | | | |
| 1998(m) | — | — | — | — | 0.20 | — |
| 1998(m) Proof | — | Value: 2.00 | | | | |
| 1999(m) | — | — | — | — | 0.20 | — |
| 1999(m) Proof | — | Value: 2.00 | | | | |
| 2001(m) | — | — | — | — | 0.20 | — |
| 2001(m) Proof | — | Value: 2.00 | | | | |

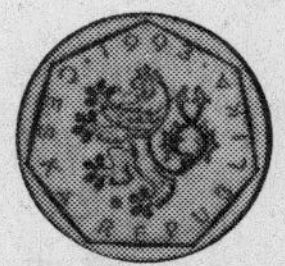

**20 HALERU** KM# 2.1 **Composition:** Aluminum **Reverse:** Closed 2 in denomination, "h" above flat line **Note:** Medallic coin alignment.

| Date | Mintage | F | VF | XF | Unc | BU |
|---|---|---|---|---|---|---|
| 1993(c) | 80,000,000 | — | — | — | 0.30 | — |
| 1993(m) | 30,558,000 | — | — | — | 0.30 | — |
| 1994(c) | 9,310,000 | — | — | — | 0.30 | — |

| Date | Mintage | F | VF | XF | Unc | BU |
|---|---|---|---|---|---|---|
| 1994(m) | 81,291,000 | — | — | — | 0.30 | — |
| 1994(m) Proof | 2,000 | — | — | — | — | — |
| 1995(c) Proof | — | — | — | — | — | — |
| 1995(m) | — | — | — | — | 0.30 | — |
| 1996(m) | — | — | — | — | 0.30 | — |
| 1997(m) | — | — | — | — | 0.30 | — |
| 1997(m) Proof | — | Value: 5.00 | | | | |

**20 HALERU** **KM# 2.3** **Composition:** Aluminum **Reverse:** Open 2 in denomination, "h" above angle line **Note:** Medallic coin alignment.

| Date | Mintage | F | VF | XF | Unc | BU |
|---|---|---|---|---|---|---|
| 1998(m) | — | — | — | — | 0.30 | — |
| 1998(m) Proof | — | Value: 3.00 | | | | |
| 1999(m) | — | — | — | — | 0.30 | — |
| 1999(m) Proof | — | Value: 3.00 | | | | |
| 2001(m) | — | — | — | — | 0.30 | — |
| 2001(m) Proof | — | Value: 3.00 | | | | |

**20 HALERU** **(KM2.2)** **Composition:** Aluminum **Reverse:** %h" above flat line

| Date | Mintage | F | VF | XF | Unc | BU |
|---|---|---|---|---|---|---|
| 1998 | — | — | — | — | 0.30 | — |
| 1998 Proof | — | Value: 3.00 | | | | |
| 1999 | — | — | — | — | 0.30 | — |
| 1999 Proof | — | Value: 3.00 | | | | |

**50 HALERU** **KM# 3** **Composition:** Aluminum **Note:** Two styles of "9" exist for 1994.

| Date | Mintage | F | VF | XF | Unc | BU |
|---|---|---|---|---|---|---|
| 1993(c) | 70,003,000 | — | — | — | 0.50 | — |
| 1993(m) | 30,474,000 | — | — | — | 0.50 | — |
| 1994(c) | — | — | — | — | 0.50 | — |
| 1994(m) | 21,109,000 | — | — | — | 0.50 | — |
| 1994(m) Proof | Est. 2,000 | — | — | — | — | — |
| 1995(m) | 30,000 | — | — | — | 0.50 | — |
| 1996(m) | — | — | — | — | 0.50 | — |
| 1997(m) | — | — | — | — | 0.50 | — |
| 1997(m) Proof | — | Value: 5.00 | | | | |
| 1998(m) | — | — | — | — | 0.50 | — |
| 1998(m) Proof | — | Value: 3.00 | | | | |
| 1999(m) | — | — | — | — | 0.50 | — |
| 1999(m) Proof | — | Value: 3.00 | | | | |
| 2000(m) | — | — | — | — | 0.50 | — |
| 2001(m) | — | — | — | — | 0.50 | — |
| 2001(m) Proof | — | Value: 3.00 | | | | |

**KORUNA** **KM# 7** **Composition:** Nickel Clad Steel **Note:** Two varieties of mint marks exist for 1996.

| Date | Mintage | F | VF | XF | Unc | BU |
|---|---|---|---|---|---|---|
| 1993(l) | 102,431,000 | — | — | — | 0.60 | — |
| 1993(m) | — | — | — | — | 0.60 | — |
| 1994(m) | 52,162,000 | — | — | — | 0.60 | — |
| 1994(l) | — | — | — | — | 0.60 | — |
| 1995(m) | 40,000 | — | — | — | 0.60 | — |
| 1996(m) | — | — | — | — | 0.60 | — |
| 1997(m) | — | — | — | — | 0.60 | — |
| 1997(m) Proof | — | Value: 6.50 | | | | |
| 1998(m) | — | — | — | — | 0.60 | — |
| 1998(m) Proof | — | Value: 4.00 | | | | |
| 1999(m) | — | — | — | — | 0.60 | — |
| 1999(m) Proof | — | Value: 4.00 | | | | |
| 2000(m) | — | — | — | — | 0.60 | — |
| 2001(m) | — | — | — | — | 0.60 | — |
| 2001(m) Proof | — | Value: 4.00 | | | | |

**2 KORUN** **KM# 9** **Composition:** Nickel Clad Steel

| Date | Mintage | F | VF | XF | Unc | BU |
|---|---|---|---|---|---|---|
| 1993(l) | 80,001,000 | — | — | — | 0.65 | — |
| 1994(m) | 30,310,000 | — | — | — | 0.65 | — |
| 1994(l) | 18,360,000 | — | — | — | 0.65 | — |
| 1995(m) | 30,000,000 | — | — | — | 0.65 | — |
| 1996(m) | — | — | — | — | 0.65 | — |
| 1997(m) | — | — | — | — | 0.65 | — |
| 1997(m) Proof | — | Value: 8.50 | | | | |
| 1998(m) | 10,426,000 | — | — | — | 0.65 | — |
| 1998(m) Proof | — | Value: 5.00 | | | | |
| 1999(m) | — | — | — | — | 0.65 | — |
| 1999(m) Proof | — | Value: 5.00 | | | | |
| 2000 | — | — | — | — | 0.65 | — |
| 2001(m) | — | — | — | — | 0.65 | — |
| 2001(m) Proof | — | Value: 5.00 | | | | |

**5 KORUN** **KM# 8** **Composition:** Nickel Plated Steel

| Date | Mintage | F | VF | XF | Unc | BU |
|---|---|---|---|---|---|---|
| 1993(l) | 70,001,000 | — | — | — | 1.00 | — |
| 1994(m) | 30,475,000 | — | — | — | 1.00 | — |
| 1994(l) | 14,400,000 | — | — | — | 1.00 | — |
| 1995(m) | 20,000,000 | — | — | — | 1.00 | — |
| 1996(m) | 52,162,000 | — | — | — | 1.00 | — |
| 1997(m) | — | — | — | — | 1.00 | — |
| 1997(m) Proof | — | Value: 10.00 | | | | |
| 1998(m) | — | — | — | — | 1.00 | — |
| 1998(m) Proof | — | Value: 6.00 | | | | |
| 1999(m) | — | — | — | — | 1.00 | — |
| 1999(m) Proof | — | Value: 6.00 | | | | |
| 2000 | — | — | — | — | 1.00 | — |
| 2001(m) | — | — | — | — | 1.00 | — |
| 2001(m) Proof | — | Value: 6.00 | | | | |

**10 KORUN** **KM# 4** **Composition:** Copper Plated Steel **Reverse:** Brno Cathedral **Note:** Position of designer's initials on reverse change with the 1996 strike.

| Date | Mintage | F | VF | XF | Unc | BU |
|---|---|---|---|---|---|---|
| 1993(c) | 70,001,000 | — | — | — | 2.00 | — |
| 1993(c) Small 10 | 1,000 | — | — | — | 5.00 | — |
| 1994(c) | — | — | — | — | 2.00 | — |
| 1994(m) | 20,677,000 | — | — | — | 1.50 | — |
| 1995(m) | — | — | — | — | 1.50 | — |
| 1996(m) | — | — | — | — | 1.50 | — |
| 1997(m) | — | — | — | — | 1.50 | — |
| 1997(m) Proof | — | Value: 12.00 | | | | |
| 1998(m) | — | — | — | — | 1.50 | — |
| 1998(m) Proof | — | Value: 7.00 | | | | |
| 1999(m) | — | — | — | — | 1.50 | — |
| 1999(m) Proof | — | Value: 7.00 | | | | |
| 2001(m) | — | — | — | — | 1.50 | — |
| 2001(m) Proof | — | Value: 7.00 | | | | |

**10 KORUN** **KM# 42** **Weight:** 7.5200 g. **Composition:** Copper Plated Steel **Subject:** Year 2000 **Obverse:** Rampant lion left **Reverse:** Clock works above denomination **Edge:** Reeded

| Date | Mintage | F | VF | XF | Unc | BU |
|---|---|---|---|---|---|---|
| 2000 | 10,000 | — | — | — | 1.50 | — |
| 2000 Proof | 5,000 | Value: 7.50 | | | | |

**20 KORUN** **KM# 5** **Composition:** Brass Plated Steel **Reverse:** St. Wenceslas (Duke Vaclav) on horse **Note:** Two varieties of mint marks and style of 9s exist for 1997.

| Date | Mintage | F | VF | XF | Unc | BU |
|---|---|---|---|---|---|---|
| 1993(c) | 55,001,000 | — | — | 1.00 | 3.00 | — |
| 1993(m) | — | — | — | — | — | — |
| 1994(m) | — | — | — | — | — | — |
| 1994(c) In sets only | 100,000 | — | — | — | 3.50 | — |
| 1995(m) In sets only | 100,000 | — | — | — | 2.50 | — |
| 1996(m) In sets only | 100,000 | — | — | — | 2.50 | — |
| 1997(m) | — | — | — | — | 2.50 | — |
| 1997(m) Proof | — | Value: 16.50 | | | | |
| 1998(m) | — | — | — | — | 2.50 | — |
| 1998(m) Proof | — | Value: 10.00 | | | | |
| 1999(m) | — | — | — | — | 2.50 | — |
| 1999(m) Proof | — | Value: 10.00 | | | | |
| 2001(m) | — | — | — | — | 2.50 | — |
| 2001(m) Proof | — | Value: 10.00 | | | | |

**20 KORUN** **KM# 43** **Weight:** 8.6000 g. **Composition:** Brass Plated Steel **Subject:** Year 2000 **Obverse:** Rampant lion left **Reverse:** Astrolab and denomination **Edge:** Plain **Note:** 13-sided.

| Date | Mintage | F | VF | XF | Unc | BU |
|---|---|---|---|---|---|---|
| 2000 | 10,000 | — | — | — | 2.50 | — |
| 2000 Proof | 5,000 | Value: 10.00 | | | | |

**50 KORUN** **KM# 1** **Ring Composition:** Copper Plated Steel **Reverse:** Prague city view

| Date | Mintage | F | VF | XF | Unc | BU |
|---|---|---|---|---|---|---|
| 1993(c) | 35,021,000 | — | — | 2.50 | 7.50 | — |
| 1993(m) | — | — | — | — | — | — |
| 1994(m) | — | — | — | — | — | — |
| 1994(c) In sets only | 100,000 | — | — | — | 9.00 | — |
| 1995(m) In sets only | 100,000 | — | — | — | 9.00 | — |
| 1996(m) In sets only | 100,000 | — | — | — | 9.00 | — |
| 1997(m) In sets only | 100,000 | — | — | — | 9.00 | — |
| 1997(m) Proof | 100,000 | Value: 35.00 | | | | |
| 1998(m) | 100,000 | — | — | — | 9.00 | — |
| 1998(m) Proof | — | Value: 20.00 | | | | |
| 1999(m) | 100,000 | — | — | — | 9.00 | — |
| 1999(m) Proof | — | Value: 20.00 | | | | |
| 2001(m) | — | — | — | — | 9.00 | — |
| 2001(m) Proof | — | Value: 20.00 | | | | |

**200 KORUN** **KM# 10** **Weight:** 13.0000 g. **Composition:** 0.9000 Silver .3440 oz. ASW **Subject:** 1st Anniversary of Constitution **Note:** 22 pieces, Unc and Proof, were melted by the Czech National Bank in 1977.

| Date | Mintage | F | VF | XF | Unc | BU |
|---|---|---|---|---|---|---|
| 1993(o) | 30,000 | — | — | — | 13.50 | — |
| 1993(o) Proof | 5,000 | Value: 30.00 | | | | |

**200 KORUN** **KM# 14** **Weight:** 13.0000 g. **Composition:** 0.9000 Silver .3440 oz. ASW **Subject:** Environmental Protection **Note:** 22 pieces, Unc and Proof, were melted by the Czech National Bank in 1997.

| Date | Mintage | F | VF | XF | Unc | BU |
|---|---|---|---|---|---|---|
| 1994(m) | 25,000 | — | — | — | 15.00 | — |
| 1994(m) Proof | 2,000 | Value: 45.00 | | | | |

**200 KORUN** **KM# 13.2** **Weight:** 13.0000 g. **Composition:** 0.9000 Silver .3440 oz. ASW **Subject:** 125th Anniversary **Edge:** Plain **Note:** 22 pieces, Unc and Proof, were melted by the Czech National Bank in 1997. Beginning with KM#14, all 200 Korun strikes come either reeded, or plain edges with the inscription, "CESKA NARODNI BANKA".

| Date | Mintage | F | VF | XF | Unc | BU |
|---|---|---|---|---|---|---|
| 1994 | Est. 2,000 | Value: 35.00 | | | | |

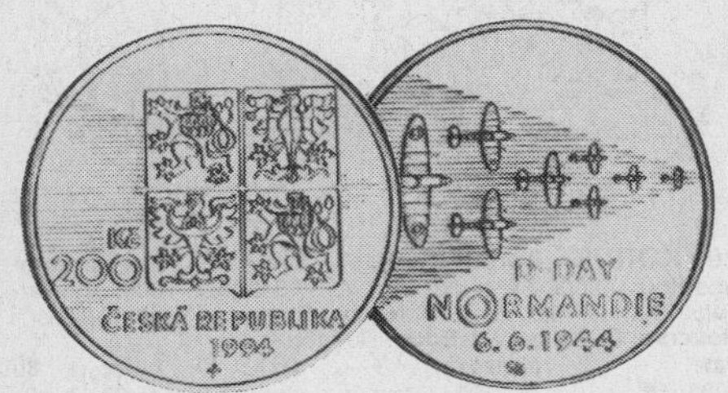


**200 KORUN** **KM# 12** **Weight:** 13.0000 g. **Composition:** 0.9000 Silver .3440 oz. ASW **Subject:** 50th Anniversary - Normandy Invasion **Reverse:** Spitfires **Note:** 6,445 pieces, Unc and Proof, were melted by the Czech National Bank in 1997.

| Date | Mintage | F | VF | XF | Unc | BU |
|---|---|---|---|---|---|---|
| 1994(cr) | 30,000 | — | — | — | 17.50 | — |
| 1994(cr) | Est. 2,000 | Value: 45.00 | | | | |

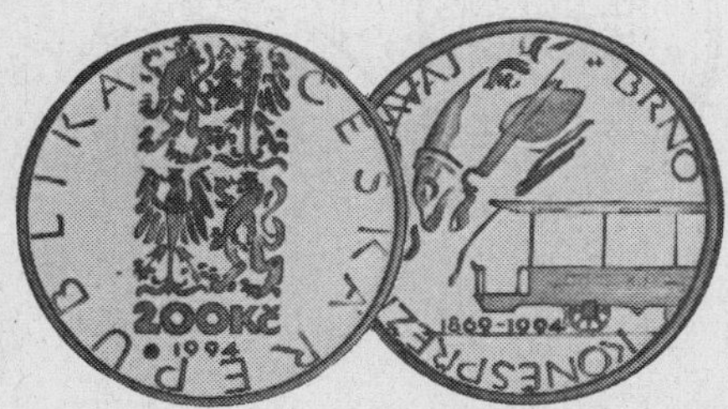


**200 KORUN** **KM# 13.1** **Weight:** 13.0000 g. **Composition:** 0.9000 Silver .3440 oz. ASW **Subject:** 125th Anniversary **Reverse:** Horse-drawn tram in Brno **Edge:** Reeded **Note:** See not ewith KM#13.2.

| Date | Mintage | F | VF | XF | Unc | BU |
|---|---|---|---|---|---|---|
| 1994(mk) | Est. 25,000 | — | — | — | 15.00 | — |

**200 KORUN** **KM# 11.1** **Weight:** 13.0000 g. **Composition:** 0.9000 Silver .3440 oz. ASW **Subject:** 650th Anniversary **Reverse:** Prague Archbishopric and St. Vitus Cathedral **Edge:** Reeded **Note:** See note with KM#11.2.

| Date | Mintage | F | VF | XF | Unc | BU |
|---|---|---|---|---|---|---|
| ND (1994)(o) | 28,000 | — | — | — | 13.50 | — |

**200 KORUN** **KM# 11.2** **Weight:** 13.0000 g. **Composition:** 0.9000 Silver .3440 oz. ASW **Subject:** 650th Anniversary **Reverse:** Prague Archbishopric and St. Vitus Cathedral **Edge:** Plain **Note:** 22 pieces, Unc and Proof of KM#11.1 and 11.2, were melted by the Czech National Bank in 1997.

| Date | Mintage | F | VF | XF | Unc | BU |
|---|---|---|---|---|---|---|
| ND (1994)(o) | Est. 2,500 | Value: 50.00 | | | | |

**200 KORUN** **KM# 17** **Weight:** 13.0000 g. **Composition:** 0.9000 Silver .3440 oz. ASW **Subject:** 50th Anniversary - United Nations **Note:** 25 pieces, Unc and Proof, were melted by the Czech National Bank in 1997.

| Date | Mintage | F | VF | XF | Unc | BU |
|---|---|---|---|---|---|---|
| ND (1995) | 25,000 | — | — | — | 15.00 | — |
| ND (1995) Proof | 2,500 | Value: 40.00 | | | | |

**200 KORUN** **KM# 15** **Weight:** 13.0000 g. **Composition:** 0.9000 Silver .3440 oz. ASW **Subject:** 50th Anniversary - Victory Over Fascism **Note:** 22 pieces, Unc and Proof, were melted by the Czech National Bank in 1997.

| Date | Mintage | F | VF | XF | Unc | BU |
|---|---|---|---|---|---|---|
| ND (1995) | 25,000 | — | — | — | 15.00 | — |
| ND (1995) Proof | 2,000 | Value: 55.00 | | | | |

**200 KORUN** **KM# 16** **Weight:** 13.0000 g. **Composition:** 0.9000 Silver .3440 oz. ASW **Subject:** 200th Anniversary - Birth of Pavel Josef Safarik **Note:** 22 pieces, Unc and Proof, were melted by the Czech National Bank in 1997.

| Date | Mintage | F | VF | XF | Unc | BU |
|---|---|---|---|---|---|---|
| 1995 | 25,000 | — | — | — | 15.00 | — |
| 1995 Proof | 2,000 | Value: 42.00 | | | | |

**200 KORUN** **KM# 22** **Weight:** 13.0000 g. **Composition:** 0.9000 Silver .3440 oz. ASW **Subject:** Czech Philharmonic **Reverse:** Building and musical instruments **Note:** 25 pieces, Unc and Proof, were melted by the Czech National Bank in 1997.

| Date | Mintage | F | VF | XF | Unc | BU |
|---|---|---|---|---|---|---|
| 1996 | 25,000 | — | — | — | 15.00 | — |
| 1996 Proof | 2,500 | Value: 45.00 | | | | |

**200 KORUN** **KM# 23** **Weight:** 13.0000 g. **Composition:** 0.9000 Silver .3440 oz. ASW **Subject:** Karel Svolinsky **Note:** 25 pieces, Unc and Proof, were melted by the Czech National Bank in 1997.

| Date | Mintage | F | VF | XF | Unc | BU |
|---|---|---|---|---|---|---|
| ND (1996) | 25,000 | — | — | — | 15.00 | — |
| ND (1996) Proof | 2,000 | Value: 45.00 | | | | |

**200 KORUN** **KM# 24** **Weight:** 13.0000 g. **Composition:** 0.9000 Silver .3440 oz. ASW **Subject:** Jean-Baptiste Gaspard Deburau

| Date | Mintage | F | VF | XF | Unc | BU |
|---|---|---|---|---|---|---|
| 1996 | 25,000 | — | — | — | 15.00 | — |
| 1996 Proof | 2,000 | Value: 35.00 | | | | |

**200 KORUN** **KM# 25** **Weight:** 13.0000 g. **Composition:** 0.9000 Silver .3761 oz. ASW **Subject:** 200th Anniversary - Czech Christmas Mass by Jakub J. Ryba

| Date | Mintage | F | VF | XF | Unc | BU |
|---|---|---|---|---|---|---|
| ND (1996) | 25,000 | — | — | — | 15.00 | — |
| ND (1996) Proof | 2,500 | Value: 40.00 | | | | |

**200 KORUN** **KM# 26** **Weight:** 13.0000 g. **Composition:** 0.9000 Silver .3761 oz. ASW **Subject:** Centennial - First Automobile in Bohemia **Obverse:** National arms **Reverse:** Sideview of antique automobile

| Date | Mintage | F | VF | XF | Unc | BU |
|---|---|---|---|---|---|---|
| ND (1997) | 23,000 | — | — | — | 15.00 | — |
| ND (1997) Proof | 3,000 | Value: 32.00 | | | | |

**200 KORUN** **KM# 27** **Weight:** 13.0000 g. **Composition:** 0.9000 Silver .3761 oz. ASW **Subject:** Millenium - St. Adalbert's Death **Obverse:** Unbordered arms **Reverse:** Bishop's portrait

| Date | Mintage | F | VF | XF | Unc | BU |
|---|---|---|---|---|---|---|
| ND (1997) | 23,000 | — | — | — | 15.00 | — |
| ND (1997) Proof | 3,000 | Value: 32.00 | | | | |

**200 KORUN** **KM# 28** **Weight:** 13.0000 g. **Composition:** 0.9000 Silver .3761 oz. ASW **Subject:** Czech Amateur Athletic Union **Obverse:** Unbordered arms **Reverse:** Runners

| Date | Mintage | F | VF | XF | Unc | BU |
|---|---|---|---|---|---|---|
| ND (1997) | 23,000 | — | — | — | 15.00 | — |
| ND (1997) Proof | 3,000 | Value: 35.00 | | | | |

**200 KORUN** **KM# 29** **Weight:** 13.0000 g. **Composition:** 0.9000 Silver .3761 oz. ASW **Subject:** 650th Anniversary - Na Slovanech-Emauzy Monastery **Obverse:** National arms **Reverse:** Seated saintly figure

| Date | Mintage | F | VF | XF | Unc | BU |
|---|---|---|---|---|---|---|
| ND (1997) | 23,000 | — | — | — | 15.00 | — |
| ND (1997) Proof | 3,000 | Value: 32.00 | | | | |

**200 KORUN** **KM# 30** **Weight:** 13.0000 g. **Composition:** 0.9000 Silver .3761 oz. ASW **Subject:** 650th Anniversary - Charles University in Prague **Obverse:** National arms **Reverse:** Charles IV portrait and document seal

| Date | Mintage | F | VF | XF | Unc | BU |
|---|---|---|---|---|---|---|
| ND (1998) | 27,000 | — | — | — | 15.00 | — |
| ND (1998) Proof | — | Value: 35.00 | | | | |

**200 KORUN** **KM# 31** **Weight:** 13.0000 g. **Composition:** 0.9000 Silver .3761 oz. ASW **Subject:** 200th Aniversary - Birth of Frantisek Palacky **Obverse:** National arms **Reverse:** Portrait

| Date | Mintage | F | VF | XF | Unc | BU |
|---|---|---|---|---|---|---|
| ND (1998) | 20,000 | — | — | — | 15.00 | — |
| ND (1998) Proof | — | Value: 30.00 | | | | |

**200 KORUN** **KM# 32** **Weight:** 13.0000 g. **Composition:** 0.9000 Silver .3761 oz. ASW **Subject:** 800th Anniversary - Coronation of King Premysl I. Otakar **Obverse:** National arms **Reverse:** Portrait and coin design

| Date | Mintage | F | VF | XF | Unc | BU |
|---|---|---|---|---|---|---|
| ND (1998)(m) | 20,000 | — | — | — | 15.00 | — |
| ND (1998) Proof | — | Value: 30.00 | | | | |

**200 KORUN** **KM# 33** **Weight:** 13.0000 g. **Composition:** 0.9000 Silver .3761 oz. ASW **Subject:** 200th Anniversary - Birth of Frantisek Kmoch **Obverse:** National arms **Reverse:** Portrait, dates

| Date | Mintage | F | VF | XF | Unc | BU |
|---|---|---|---|---|---|---|
| ND (1998)(m) | 20,000 | — | — | — | 12.50 | — |
| ND (1998)(m) | 3,000 | — | — | — | 28.00 | — |

**200 KORUN** **KM# 34** **Weight:** 13.0000 g. **Composition:** 0.9000 Silver .3761 oz. ASW **Subject:** 50th Anniversary - NATO **Obverse:** Undivided national arms **Reverse:** NATO style cross **Edge Lettering:** CESKA REPUBLIKA CLENSKA ZEME NATO 1996

| Date | Mintage | F | VF | XF | Unc | BU |
|---|---|---|---|---|---|---|
| ND (1999) | 20,000 | — | — | — | 15.00 | — |
| ND (1999) Proof | 3,000 | Value: 30.00 | | | | |

**200 KORUN** **KM# 35** **Weight:** 13.0000 g. **Composition:** 0.9000 Silver .3761 oz. ASW **Subject:** 200 Years - Prague Fine Arts Academy **Obverse:** Stylized national arms **Reverse:** Stylized design **Edge:** Reeded

| Date | Mintage | F | VF | XF | Unc | BU |
|---|---|---|---|---|---|---|
| ND (1999) | 20,000 | — | — | — | 15.00 | — |
| ND (1999) Proof | 3,000 | Value: 28.00 | | | | |

**200 KORUN** **KM# 36** **Weight:** 13.0000 g. **Composition:** 0.9000 Silver .3761 oz. ASW **Subject:** 100 Years - Brno University of Technology **Obverse:** Undivided national arms **Reverse:** Stylized design

| Date | Mintage | F | VF | XF | Unc | BU |
|---|---|---|---|---|---|---|
| ND (1999) | 20,000 | — | — | — | 15.00 | — |
| ND (1999) Proof | 3,200 | Value: 28.00 | | | | |

**200 KORUN** **KM# 37** **Weight:** 13.0000 g. **Composition:** 0.9000 Silver .3761 oz. ASW **Subject:** 100th Birthday - Ondrei Sekora **Obverse:** National arms **Reverse:** Bee holding flowers

| Date | Mintage | F | VF | XF | Unc | BU |
|---|---|---|---|---|---|---|
| ND (1999) | — | — | — | — | 15.00 | — |
| ND (1999) Proof | — | Value: 28.00 | | | | |

**200 KORUN** **KM# 46.1 (KM46)** **Weight:** 13.0000 g. **Composition:** 0.9000 Silver .3762 oz. ASW **Subject:** 700th Anniversary - Prague Groschen - Currency Reform **Obverse:** National arms above coin design **Reverse:** Seated king between two coin designs **Edge:** Reeded

| Date | Mintage | F | VF | XF | Unc | BU |
|---|---|---|---|---|---|---|
| 2000 | 20,000 | — | — | — | 15.00 | — |
| 2000 Proof | 3,500 | Value: 28.00 | | | | |

**200 KORUN** **KM# 47.1 (KM47)** **Weight:** 13.0000 g. **Composition:** 0.9000 Silver .3762 oz. ASW **Subject:** 100th Anniversary - Birth of Poet Vitezslav Nedbal **Obverse:** National arms **Reverse:** Facial portrait **Edge:** Reeded

| Date | Mintage | F | VF | XF | Unc | BU |
|---|---|---|---|---|---|---|
| 2000 | 20,000 | — | — | — | 15.00 | — |
| 2000 Proof | 3,200 | Value: 28.00 | | | | |

**200 KORUN** **KM# 48** **Weight:** 13.0000 g. **Composition:** 0.9000 Silver .3762 oz. ASW **Subject:** 150th Anniversary - Birth of Zdenek Fibich, Musical Composer **Obverse:** National arms **Reverse:** Portrait **Edge:** Reeded

| Date | Mintage | F | VF | XF | Unc | BU |
|---|---|---|---|---|---|---|
| 2000 | 17,000 | — | — | — | 15.00 | — |
| 2000 Proof | 3,200 | Value: 28.00 | | | | |

**200 KORUN** **KM# 49** **Weight:** 13.0000 g. **Composition:** 0.9000 Silver .3762 oz. ASW **Subject:** International Monetary

Fund and Prague World Bank Group **Obverse:** Crowned lion in swirling dots **Reverse:** Circle of swirling dots **Edge:** Reeded

| Date | Mintage | F | VF | XF | Unc | BU |
|---|---|---|---|---|---|---|
| 2000 | 18,000 | — | — | — | 15.00 | — |
| 2000 Proof | 5,000 | Value: 28.00 | | | | |

**200 KORUN** **KM# 50** **Weight:** 13.0000 g. **Composition:** 0.9000 Silver .3762 oz. ASW **Subject:** New Millennium **Obverse:** National arms **Reverse:** Stylized phoenix design **Edge:** Reeded

| Date | Mintage | F | VF | XF | Unc | BU |
|---|---|---|---|---|---|---|
| 2000 | — | — | — | — | 15.00 | — |
| 2000 Proof | — | Value: 28.00 | | | | |

**200 KORUN** **KM# 46.2** **Weight:** 13.0000 g. **Composition:** 0.9000 Silver .3762 oz. ASW **Subject:** 700th Anniversary - Prague Groschen **Obverse:** National arms above coin design **Reverse:** Seated king between two coin designs **Edge:** Reeded **Edge Lettering:** "CESKA NARODNI BANK"

| Date | Mintage | F | VF | XF | Unc | BU |
|---|---|---|---|---|---|---|
| ND(2000) Proof | 3,500 | Value: 30.00 | | | | |

**200 KORUN** **KM# 47.2** **Weight:** 13.0000 g. **Composition:** 0.9000 Silver .3762 oz. ASW **Subject:** Vitezslava Nezvala **Obverse:** National arms **Reverse:** Facial portrait **Edge:** Reeded **Edge Lettering:** "CESKA NARODNI BANK"

| Date | Mintage | F | VF | XF | Unc | BU |
|---|---|---|---|---|---|---|
| ND(2000) Proof | 3,500 | Value: 30.00 | | | | |

**1000 KORUN** **KM# 18** **Weight:** 3.1103 g. **Composition:** 0.9999 Gold .1000 oz. AGW **Subject:** Historic Coins **Note:** Silesian Tolar of Silesian Moravian Estates 12-1/2 Toler (tolaru) of 1620.

| Date | Mintage | F | VF | XF | Unc | BU |
|---|---|---|---|---|---|---|
| 1995 | 2,000 | — | — | — | 100 | — |
| 1996 | 3,256 | — | — | — | 100 | — |
| 1996 Proof | 744 | Value: 145 | | | | |
| 1997 Proof | 3,000 | Value: 120 | | | | |

**1000 KORUN** **KM# 38** **Weight:** 3.1103 g. **Composition:** 0.9999 Gold .1000 oz. AGW **Note:** Karlstein Castle.

| Date | Mintage | F | VF | XF | Unc | BU |
|---|---|---|---|---|---|---|
| 1998 | — | — | — | — | 75.00 | — |
| 1998 Proof | — | Value: 80.00 | | | | |
| 1999 Proof | — | Value: 80.00 | | | | |

**2000 KORUN** **KM# 44** **Weight:** 31.1030 g. **Composition:** 0.9990 Silver .9990 oz. ASW **Subject:** Millennium **Obverse:** National arm hologram on gold inlay **Reverse:** Stylized 2000 **Edge Lettering:** *CNB* Ag 0.999* 31.103 g *CNB* AU 999.9 *3. 111 g* **Note:** With a 3.1110 gram, .999 gold, .0999 ounce actual gold weight gold inlay.

| Date | Mintage | F | VF | XF | Unc | BU |
|---|---|---|---|---|---|---|
| ND (1999)(m) | 17,000 | — | — | — | 85.00 | — |
| ND (1999)(m) | 3,000 | Value: 150 | | | | |

**2500 KORUN** **KM# 19** **Weight:** 7.7759 g. **Composition:** 0.9999 Gold .2500 oz. AGW **Subject:** Historic Coins - 1620 Toler of Silesian Estates

| Date | Mintage | F | VF | XF | Unc | BU |
|---|---|---|---|---|---|---|
| 1995 | 2,000 | — | — | — | 250 | — |
| 1996 | 1,256 | — | — | — | 250 | — |
| 1996 Proof | 744 | Value: 300 | | | | |
| 1997 Proof | 3,000 | Value: 265 | | | | |

**2500 KORUN** **KM# 39** **Weight:** 7.7759 g. **Composition:** 0.9999 Gold .2500 oz. AGW **Reverse:** Seal of Karel IV

| Date | Mintage | F | VF | XF | Unc | BU |
|---|---|---|---|---|---|---|
| 1998 | — | — | — | — | 160 | — |
| 1998 Proof | — | Value: 200 | | | | |
| 1999 Proof | — | Value: 160 | | | | |

**5000 KORUN** **KM# 20** **Weight:** 15.5517 g. **Composition:** 0.9999 Gold .5000 oz. AGW **Subject:** Historic Coins **Reverse:** Bohemian Maley Gros of 1587

| Date | Mintage | F | VF | XF | Unc | BU |
|---|---|---|---|---|---|---|
| 1995 | 1,000 | — | — | — | 550 | — |
| 1996 | 1,256 | — | — | — | 550 | — |
| 1996 Proof | 744 | Value: 625 | | | | |
| 1997 Proof | 2,000 | Value: 575 | | | | |

**5000 KORUN** **KM# 40** **Weight:** 15.5517 g. **Composition:** 0.9999 Gold .5000 oz. AGW **Reverse:** Karel IV teaching

| Date | Mintage | F | VF | XF | Unc | BU |
|---|---|---|---|---|---|---|
| 1998 | — | — | — | — | 300 | — |
| 1998 Proof | — | Value: 350 | | | | |
| 1999 Proof | — | Value: 275 | | | | |

**10000 KORUN** **KM# 21** **Weight:** 31.1035 g. **Composition:** 0.9999 Gold 1.0000 oz. AGW **Subject:** Historic Coins **Reverse:** Lion holding Prague Gros

| Date | Mintage | F | VF | XF | Unc | BU |
|---|---|---|---|---|---|---|
| 1995 | 1,000 | — | — | — | 950 | — |
| 1996 | 1,256 | — | — | — | 950 | — |
| 1996 Proof | 744 | Value: 1,100 | | | | |
| 1997 Proof | 2,000 | Value: 1,000 | | | | |

**10000 KORUN** **KM# 41** **Weight:** 31.1035 g. **Composition:** 0.9999 Gold 1.0000 oz. AGW **Reverse:** Karel IV and seals

| Date | Mintage | F | VF | XF | Unc | BU |
|---|---|---|---|---|---|---|
| 1998 | — | — | — | — | 575 | — |
| 1998 Proof | — | Value: 650 | | | | |
| 1999 Proof | — | Value: 525 | | | | |

## MINT SETS

| KM# | Date | Mintage | Identification | Issue Price | Mkt Val |
|---|---|---|---|---|---|
| MS1 | 1993 (9) | 35,000 | KM1, 2.1, 3-9 | — | 14.00 |
| MS2 | 1994 (9) | 30,000 | KM1, 2.1, 3-9 | — | 14.00 |
| MS3 | 1995 (9) | 30,000 | KM1, 2.1, 3-9 | — | 14.00 |
| MS4 | 1996 (9) | 15,000 | KM1, 2.1, 3-9 | — | 14.00 |
| MS5 | 1996 (9) | 15,000 | KM1, 2.1, 3-9 w/EURO 96 medal | — | 15.50 |
| MS6 | 1997 (9) | 15,000 | KM1, 2.1, 3-9 | — | 14.00 |
| MS7 | 1998 (9) | — | KM1, 2.3, 3-9, Olympic Hockey Folder | — | 14.00 |
| MS10 | 1999 (9) | — | KM1, 2.3, 3-9, Childrens Motif Folder | — | 14.00 |
| MS8 | 1999 (9) | 2,000 | KM1, 2.3, 3-9, Parler Folder | — | 14.00 |
| MS9 | 1999 (9) | — | KM1, 2.3, 3-9, Nato Folder | — | 14.00 |
| MS11 | 2001 (9) | — | KM#1, 2.3, 3-9 | — | 14.00 |

## PROOF SETS

| KM# | Date | Mintage | Identification | Issue Price | Mkt Val |
|---|---|---|---|---|---|
| PS1 | 1994 (3) | 2,000 | KM2.1, 3, 6 | — | — |
| PS2 | 1997 (9) | 1,500 | KM1, 2.1, 3-9, plus silver medal | — | 100 |
| PS3 | 1998 (9) | 2,500 | KM1, 2.3, 3-9, plus silver medal | — | 60.00 |
| PS4 | 1999 (9) | — | KM1, 2.3, 3-9, plus silver medal | — | 60.00 |
| PS5 | 2001 (9) | — | KM#1, 2.3, 3-9 | — | 50.00 |

The Republic of Czechoslovakia, founded at the end of World War I, was part of the old Austrian-Hungarian Empire. It had an area of 49,371 sq. mi. (127,870 sq. km.) and a population of 15.6 million. Capital: Prague (Praha).

Czechoslovakia proclaimed itself a republic on Oct. 28, 1918, with Tomas G. Masaryk as President. Hitler's rise to power in Germany provoked Czechoslovakia's German minority in the Sudetenland to agitate for autonomy. At Munich (Munchen) in Sept. of 1938, France and Britain, seeking to avoid World War II, forced the cession of the Sudetenland to Germany. In March, 1939, Germany invaded Czechoslovakia and established the "protectorate of Bohemia and Moravia". Bohemia is a historic province in northwest Czechoslovakia that includes the city of Prague, one of the oldest continually occupied sites in Europe. Moravia is an area of considerable mineral wealth in central Czechoslovakia. Slovakia, a province in southeastern Czechoslovakia under Nazi influence was constituted as a republic. The end of World War II saw the re-established independence of Czechoslovakia, while bringing it within the Russian sphere of influence. On Feb. 23-25, 1948, the Communists seized control of the government in a coup d'etat, and adopted a constitution making the country a 'people's republic'. A new constitution adopted June 11, 1960, converted the country into a 'socialist republic', which lasted until 1989. On Nov. 11, 1989, demonstrations against the communist government began and in Dec. of that same year, communism was overthrown, and the Czech and Slovak Federal Republic was formed. In 1993 the CSFR split into the Czech Republic and The Republic of Slovakia.

**NOTE**: For additional listings see Bohemia and Moravia, Czech Republic and Slovakia.

**MINT MARKS**

(k) - Kremnica

(l) - Leningrad

**MONETARY SYSTEM**

100 Haleru = 1 Koruna

# REPUBLIC

## DECIMAL COINAGE

### 2 HALERE KM# 5 Composition: Zinc

| Date | Mintage | F | VF | XF | Unc | BU |
|---|---|---|---|---|---|---|
| 1923 | 2,700,000 | 3.00 | 5.00 | 10.00 | 16.00 | — |
| 1924 | 17,300,000 | 2.25 | 3.50 | 5.00 | 9.00 | — |
| 1925 | 2,000,000 | 3.00 | 5.00 | 7.50 | 17.00 | — |

### 5 HALERU KM# 6 Composition: Bronze

| Date | Mintage | F | VF | XF | Unc | BU |
|---|---|---|---|---|---|---|
| 1923 | 37,800,000 | 0.20 | 0.30 | 0.50 | 2.00 | — |
| 1924 | 10 | — | — | — | 1,500 | — |
| Note: There are two varieteis of the number 4 in 1924 dated coins: w/ and w/out seraphs | | | | | | |
| 1925 | 12,000,000 | 0.20 | 0.30 | 0.50 | 2.50 | — |
| 1926 | 1,084,000 | 1.50 | 3.25 | 6.00 | 12.00 | — |
| 1927 | 8,916,000 | 0.25 | 0.35 | 0.75 | 2.50 | — |
| 1928 | 5,320,000 | 0.30 | 0.45 | 0.75 | 2.50 | — |
| 1929 | 12,680,000 | 0.25 | 0.35 | 0.75 | 2.50 | — |
| 1930 | 5,000,000 | 0.25 | 0.35 | 0.75 | 2.50 | — |
| 1931 | 7,448,000 | 0.25 | 0.35 | 0.75 | 2.50 | — |
| 1932 | 3,556,000 | 0.60 | 1.00 | 2.00 | 5.00 | — |
| 1938 | 14,244,000 | 0.25 | 0.35 | 0.75 | 2.00 | — |

### 10 HALERU KM# 3 Composition: Bronze

| Date | Mintage | F | VF | XF | Unc | BU |
|---|---|---|---|---|---|---|
| 1922 | 6,000,000 | 0.30 | 0.45 | 1.00 | 2.75 | — |
| 1923 | 24,000,000 | 0.25 | 0.35 | 0.75 | 2.00 | — |
| 1924 | 5,320,000 | 0.30 | 0.45 | 1.00 | 3.00 | — |
| 1925 | 24,680,000 | 0.25 | 0.35 | 0.60 | 2.25 | — |
| 1926 | 10,000,000 | 0.25 | 0.35 | 0.75 | 2.25 | — |
| 1927 | 10,000,000 | 0.25 | 0.35 | 0.75 | 2.25 | — |
| 1928 | 14,290,000 | 0.25 | 0.35 | 0.75 | 2.25 | — |
| 1929 | 5,710,000 | 1.25 | 2.00 | 3.50 | 7.00 | — |
| 1930 | 6,980,000 | 0.30 | 0.45 | 1.00 | 2.50 | — |
| 1931 | 6,740,000 | 0.30 | 0.45 | 1.00 | 2.50 | — |
| 1932 | 11,280,000 | 0.25 | 0.35 | 0.75 | 2.00 | — |
| 1933 | 4,190,000 | 0.35 | 0.60 | 1.25 | 5.00 | — |
| 1934 | 13,200,000 | 0.25 | 0.35 | 0.75 | 2.00 | — |
| 1935 | 3,420,000 | 0.50 | 0.75 | 1.50 | 5.00 | — |
| 1936 | 8,560,000 | 0.25 | 0.35 | 0.75 | 2.00 | — |
| 1937 | 20,200,000 | 0.25 | 0.35 | 0.75 | 2.00 | — |
| 1938 | 21,400,000 | 0.25 | 0.35 | 0.75 | 2.00 | — |

### 20 HALERU KM# 1 Composition: Copper-Nickel

| Date | Mintage | F | VF | XF | Unc | BU |
|---|---|---|---|---|---|---|
| 1921 | 40,000,000 | 0.25 | 0.35 | 0.60 | 2.50 | — |
| 1922 | 9,100 | 0.25 | 0.35 | 0.60 | 2.50 | — |
| 1924 | 20,931,000 | 0.25 | 0.35 | 0.60 | 2.50 | — |
| 1925 | 4,244,000 | 0.60 | 1.00 | 2.00 | 6.00 | — |
| 1926 | 14,825,000 | 0.25 | 0.35 | 0.60 | 2.50 | — |
| 1927 | 11,757,000 | 0.25 | 0.35 | 0.60 | 2.50 | — |
| 1928 | 14,018,000 | 0.25 | 0.35 | 0.60 | 2.50 | — |
| 1929 | 4,225,000 | 0.30 | 0.50 | 1.25 | 3.50 | — |
| 1930 | — | 0.30 | 0.40 | 0.75 | 3.00 | — |
| 1931 | 5,000,000 | 0.30 | 0.40 | 0.75 | 3.00 | — |
| 1933 | Inc. above | 9.00 | 18.00 | 35.00 | 75.00 | — |
| 1937 | 8,208,000 | 0.25 | 0.35 | 0.60 | 2.50 | — |
| 1938 | 18,787,000 | 0.25 | 0.35 | 0.60 | 2.50 | — |

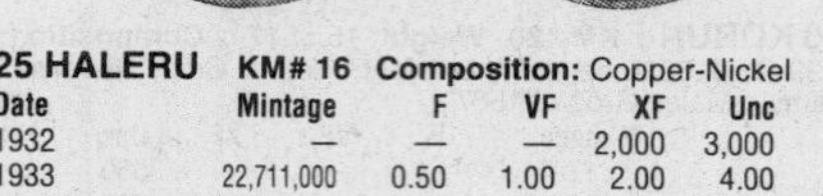

### 25 HALERU KM# 16 Composition: Copper-Nickel

| Date | Mintage | F | VF | XF | Unc | BU |
|---|---|---|---|---|---|---|
| 1932 | — | — | — | 2,000 | 3,000 | — |
| 1933 | 22,711,000 | 0.50 | 1.00 | 2.00 | 4.00 | — |

### 50 HALERU KM# 2 Composition: Copper-Nickel

| Date | Mintage | F | VF | XF | Unc | BU |
|---|---|---|---|---|---|---|
| 1921 | 3,000,000 | 0.25 | 0.50 | 1.00 | 3.00 | — |
| 1922 | 37,000,000 | 0.20 | 0.40 | 0.60 | 2.50 | — |
| 1924 | 10,000,000 | 0.20 | 0.40 | 0.60 | 3.00 | — |
| 1925 | 1,415,000 | 0.50 | 1.00 | 2.00 | 9.00 | — |
| 1926 | 1,585,000 | 3.50 | 7.00 | 15.00 | 35.00 | — |
| 1927 | 2,000,000 | 0.50 | 1.00 | 2.00 | 9.00 | — |
| 1931 | 6,000,000 | 0.25 | 0.50 | 1.00 | 2.50 | — |

### KORUNA KM# 4 Composition: Copper-Nickel

| Date | Mintage | F | VF | XF | Unc | BU |
|---|---|---|---|---|---|---|
| 1922 | 50,000,000 | 0.30 | 0.50 | 0.75 | 2.00 | — |
| 1923 | 15,385,000 | 0.30 | 0.50 | 0.75 | 2.00 | — |
| 1924 | 21,041,000 | 0.30 | 0.50 | 0.75 | 2.00 | — |
| 1925 | 8,574,000 | 0.40 | 0.60 | 1.00 | 4.00 | — |
| 1929 | 5,000,000 | 0.50 | 0.75 | 1.25 | 3.50 | — |
| 1930 | 5,000,000 | 0.40 | 0.60 | 1.00 | 4.00 | — |
| 1937 | 3,806,000 | 0.40 | 0.60 | 1.00 | 3.00 | — |
| 1938 | 8,582,000 | 0.40 | 0.60 | 1.00 | 3.00 | — |

### 5 KORUN KM# 10 Composition: Copper-Nickel

| Date | Mintage | F | VF | XF | Unc | BU |
|---|---|---|---|---|---|---|
| 1925 | 16,475,000 | 1.50 | 2.50 | 3.50 | 9.00 | — |
| 1926 | 8,912,000 | 1.75 | 2.75 | 4.00 | 10.00 | — |
| 1927 | 4,614,000 | 2.50 | 4.00 | 5.75 | 24.00 | — |

### 5 KORUN KM# 11 Weight: 7.0000 g. Composition: 0.5000 Silver .125 oz. ASW

| Date | Mintage | F | VF | XF | Unc | BU |
|---|---|---|---|---|---|---|
| 1928 | 1,710,000 | 2.00 | 3.00 | 5.00 | 10.00 | — |
| Note: Edge varieties exist for 1928 | | | | | | |
| 1929 | 12,861,000 | 1.00 | 2.00 | 4.00 | 8.50 | — |
| 1930 | 10,429,000 | 1.00 | 2.00 | 4.00 | 8.50 | — |
| 1931 | 2,000,000 | 2.00 | 3.00 | 5.00 | 12.00 | — |
| 1932 | 1,000,000 | 5.00 | 7.50 | 10.00 | 35.00 | — |

### 5 KORUN KM# 11a Weight: 7.0000 g. Composition: 0.5000 Nickel .125 oz.

| Date | Mintage | F | VF | XF | Unc | BU |
|---|---|---|---|---|---|---|
| 1937 | 36,000 | 100 | 175 | 300 | 500 | — |
| 1938 | 17,200,000 | 1.25 | 2.50 | 4.00 | 6.50 | — |

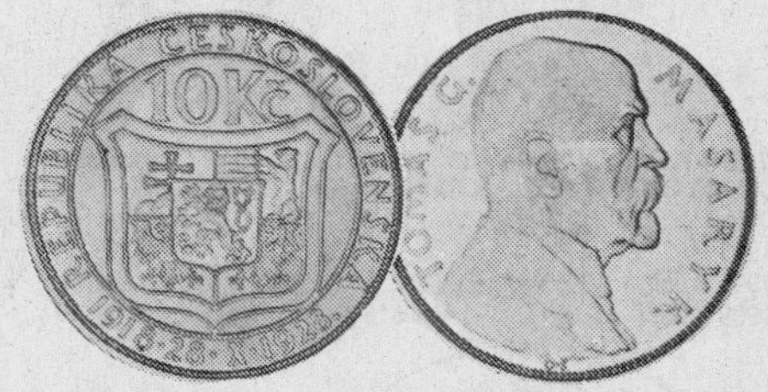

### 10 KORUN KM# 12 Weight: 10.0000 g. Composition: 0.7000 Silver .2250 oz. ASW Subject: 10th Anniversary of Independence

| Date | Mintage | F | VF | XF | Unc | BU |
|---|---|---|---|---|---|---|
| ND (1928) | 1,000,000 | 2.50 | 4.50 | 6.50 | 11.00 | — |

### 10 KORUN KM# 15 Weight: 10.0000 g. Composition: 0.7000 Silver .2250 oz. ASW

| Date | Mintage | F | VF | XF | Unc | BU |
|---|---|---|---|---|---|---|
| 1930 | 4,949,000 | 2.50 | 4.00 | 7.00 | 11.50 | — |
| 1931 | 6,689,000 | 2.50 | 3.75 | 6.00 | 10.00 | — |
| 1932 | 11,448,000 | 2.00 | 3.50 | 5.00 | 9.00 | — |
| 1933 | 915,000 | 10.00 | 20.00 | 60.00 | 250 | — |

**20 KORUN** KM# 17 **Weight:** 12.0000 g. **Composition:** 0.7000 Silver .2700 oz. ASW

| Date | Mintage | F | VF | XF | Unc | BU |
|---|---|---|---|---|---|---|
| 1933 | 2,280,000 | — | 4.00 | 7.50 | 14.00 | — |
| 1934 | 3,280,000 | — | 4.00 | 7.50 | 14.00 | — |

**20 KORUN** KM# 18 **Weight:** 12.0000 g. **Composition:** 0.7000 Silver .2700 oz. ASW **Subject:** Death of President Masaryk

| Date | Mintage | F | VF | XF | Unc | BU |
|---|---|---|---|---|---|---|
| ND (1937) | 1,000,000 | — | 3.50 | 6.50 | 11.00 | — |

## TRADE COINAGE

**DUKAT** KM# 7 **Weight:** 3.4900 g. **Composition:** 0.9860 Gold .1106 oz. AGW **Subject:** 5th Anniversary of the Republic **Obverse:** Coat of arms **Reverse:** Duke Wenceslas (Vaclav)

| Date | Mintage | F | VF | XF | Unc | BU |
|---|---|---|---|---|---|---|
| 1923 | 1,000 | — | 250 | 600 | 1,000 | — |

**Note:** The above coins are serially numbered below the duke

**DUKAT** KM# 8 **Weight:** 3.4900 g. **Composition:** 0.9860 Gold .1106 oz. AGW **Note:** Similar to KM#7 but w/o serial numbers.

| Date | Mintage | F | VF | XF | Unc | BU |
|---|---|---|---|---|---|---|
| 1923 | 62,000 | — | 55.00 | 75.00 | 125 | — |
| 1924 | 33,000 | — | 55.00 | 75.00 | 125 | — |
| 1925 | 66,000 | — | 55.00 | 75.00 | 125 | — |
| 1926 | 59,000 | — | 55.00 | 75.00 | 125 | — |
| 1927 | 26,000 | — | 55.00 | 75.00 | 125 | — |
| 1928 | 19,000 | — | 55.00 | 75.00 | 135 | — |
| 1929 | 10,000 | — | 60.00 | 80.00 | 165 | — |
| 1930 | 11,000 | — | 60.00 | 80.00 | 165 | — |
| 1931 | 43,000 | — | 55.00 | 75.00 | 125 | — |
| 1932 | 27,000 | — | 55.00 | 75.00 | 125 | — |
| 1933 | 58,000 | — | 55.00 | 75.00 | 125 | — |
| 1934 | 9,729 | — | 80.00 | 100 | 175 | — |
| 1935 | 13,000 | — | 55.00 | 75.00 | 135 | — |
| 1936 | 15,000 | — | 55.00 | 75.00 | 135 | — |
| 1937 | 324 | — | 200 | 500 | 1,000 | — |
| 1938 | 56 | — | 600 | 1,000 | 2,000 | — |
| 1939 | 276 | — | 200 | 500 | 1,000 | — |

**Note:** Czech reports show mintage of 20 for Czechoslovakia and 256 for state of Slovakia

| Date | Mintage | F | VF | XF | Unc | BU |
|---|---|---|---|---|---|---|
| 1951 | 500 | — | 150 | 450 | 1,000 | — |

**2 DUKATY** KM# 9 **Weight:** 6.9800 g. **Composition:** 0.9860 Gold .2212 oz. AGW **Reverse:** Duke Wenceslas (Vaclav)

| Date | Mintage | F | VF | XF | Unc | BU |
|---|---|---|---|---|---|---|
| 1923 | 4,000 | — | 150 | 225 | 350 | — |
| 1929 | 3,262 | — | 150 | 225 | 350 | — |
| 1930 | Inc. above | — | 150 | 250 | 400 | — |
| 1931 | 2,994 | — | 150 | 225 | 350 | — |
| 1932 | 5,496 | — | 150 | 225 | 350 | — |
| 1933 | 4,671 | — | 150 | 225 | 350 | — |
| 1934 | 2,403 | — | 150 | 225 | 350 | — |
| 1935 | 2,577 | — | 150 | 225 | 350 | — |
| 1936 | 819 | — | 300 | 400 | 750 | — |
| 1937 | 8 | — | 1,500 | 2,000 | 5,000 | — |
| 1938 | 186 | — | 600 | 800 | 1,500 | — |

**Note:** Czech reports show mintage of 14 for Czechoslovakia and 172 for state of Slovakia

| Date | Mintage | F | VF | XF | Unc | BU |
|---|---|---|---|---|---|---|
| 1951 | 200 | — | 300 | 500 | 1,500 | — |

**5 DUKATU** KM# 13 **Weight:** 17.4500 g. **Composition:** 0.9860 Gold .5532 oz. AGW **Reverse:** Duke Wenceslas

| Date | Mintage | F | VF | XF | Unc | BU |
|---|---|---|---|---|---|---|
| 1929 | 1,827 | — | 350 | 450 | 725 | — |
| 1930 | 543 | — | 500 | 700 | 1,250 | — |
| 1931 | 1,528 | — | 350 | 450 | 725 | — |
| 1932 | 1,827 | — | 350 | 450 | 725 | — |
| 1933 | 1,752 | — | 350 | 450 | 725 | — |
| 1934 | 1,101 | — | 350 | 450 | 725 | — |
| 1935 | 1,037 | — | 350 | 450 | 725 | — |
| 1936 | 728 | — | 500 | 700 | 1,000 | — |
| 1937 | 4 | — | — | — | 7,500 | — |
| 1938 | 56 | — | 1,000 | 2,000 | 3,000 | — |

**Note:** Czech reports show mintage of 12 for Czechoslovakia and 44 for state of Slovakia

| Date | Mintage | F | VF | XF | Unc | BU |
|---|---|---|---|---|---|---|
| 1951 | 100 | — | 400 | 800 | 2,800 | — |

**10 DUKATU** KM# 14 **Weight:** 34.9000 g. **Composition:** 0.9860 Gold 1.1064 oz. AGW **Reverse:** Duke Wenceslas

| Date | Mintage | F | VF | XF | Unc | BU |
|---|---|---|---|---|---|---|
| 1929 | 1,564 | — | 700 | 1,100 | 1,650 | — |
| 1930 | 394 | — | 1,000 | 1,900 | 3,000 | — |
| 1931 | 1,239 | — | 700 | 1,100 | 1,750 | — |
| 1932 | 1,035 | — | 700 | 1,100 | 1,750 | — |
| 1933 | 1,780 | — | 700 | 1,100 | 1,750 | — |
| 1934 | 1,298 | — | 700 | 1,100 | 1,750 | — |
| 1935 | 600 | — | 750 | 1,350 | 2,100 | — |
| 1936 | 633 | — | 750 | 1,350 | 2,100 | — |
| 1937 | 34 | — | — | — | 12,000 | — |
| 1938 | 192 | — | 2,000 | 2,800 | 5,000 | — |
| 1951 | 100 | — | 2,000 | 3,500 | 7,500 | — |

**Note:** Czech reports show mintage of 20 for Czechoslo- vakia and 172 for state of Slovakia.

## POST WAR COINAGE

**20 HALERU** KM# 20 **Composition:** Bronze

| Date | Mintage | F | VF | XF | Unc | BU |
|---|---|---|---|---|---|---|
| 1947 | — | 65.00 | 125 | 200 | 300 | — |
| 1948 | 24,340,000 | 0.10 | 0.15 | 0.40 | 1.50 | — |
| 1949 | 25,660,000 | 0.10 | 0.15 | 0.40 | 1.50 | — |
| 1950 | 11,132,000 | 0.10 | 0.15 | 0.40 | 2.00 | — |

**20 HALERU** KM# 31 **Composition:** Aluminum

| Date | Mintage | F | VF | XF | Unc | BU |
|---|---|---|---|---|---|---|
| 1951 | 46,800,000 | 0.10 | 0.15 | 0.25 | 1.00 | — |
| 1952 | 80,340,000 | 0.10 | 0.15 | 0.25 | 1.00 | — |

**50 HALERU** KM# 21 **Composition:** Bronze

| Date | Mintage | F | VF | XF | Unc | BU |
|---|---|---|---|---|---|---|
| 1947 | 50,000,000 | 0.15 | 0.25 | 0.40 | 1.00 | — |
| 1948 | 20,000,000 | 0.15 | 0.25 | 0.40 | 1.50 | — |
| 1949 | 12,715,000 | 0.15 | 0.25 | 0.40 | 2.00 | — |
| 1950 | 17,415,000 | 0.15 | 0.25 | 0.40 | 1.80 | — |

**50 HALERU** KM# 32 **Composition:** Aluminum

| Date | Mintage | F | VF | XF | Unc | BU |
|---|---|---|---|---|---|---|
| 1951 | 60,000,000 | 0.15 | 0.35 | 0.50 | 0.75 | — |
| 1952 | 60,000,000 | 0.25 | 0.45 | 0.60 | 1.00 | — |
| 1953 | 34,920,000 | 1.00 | 2.50 | 6.00 | 10.00 | — |

**KORUNA** KM# 19 **Composition:** Copper-Nickel

| Date | Mintage | F | VF | XF | Unc | BU |
|---|---|---|---|---|---|---|
| 1946 | 88,000,000 | 0.15 | 0.25 | 0.50 | 1.00 | — |
| 1947 | 12,550,000 | 1.50 | 2.50 | 3.75 | 6.50 | — |

**Note:** Varieties exist for "4" in 1946 strikes

**KORUNA** KM# 22 **Composition:** Aluminum

| Date | Mintage | F | VF | XF | Unc | BU |
|---|---|---|---|---|---|---|
| 1947 | — | 50.00 | 120 | 200 | 350 | — |
| 1950 | 62,190,000 | 0.20 | 0.35 | 0.45 | 1.00 | — |
| 1951 | 61,395,000 | 0.20 | 0.35 | 0.45 | 1.25 | — |
| 1952 | 101,105,000 | 0.20 | 0.30 | 0.40 | 0.80 | — |
| 1953 | 73,905,000 | 0.40 | 0.75 | 1.75 | 4.50 | — |

**2 KORUNY** KM# 23 **Composition:** Copper-Nickel

| Date | Mintage | F | VF | XF | Unc | BU |
|---|---|---|---|---|---|---|
| 1947 | 20,000,000 | 0.20 | 0.40 | 0.60 | 1.25 | — |
| 1948 | 20,476,000 | 0.20 | 0.40 | 0.60 | 1.50 | — |

**5 KORUN** KM# 34 **Composition:** Aluminum

| Date | Mintage | F | VF | XF | Unc | BU |
|---|---|---|---|---|---|---|
| 1951 | — | — | — | — | 1,500 | — |

**Note:** Not released for circulation. Almost the entire mintage was melted

| Date | Mintage | F | VF | XF | Unc | BU |
|---|---|---|---|---|---|---|
| 1952 | 40,715,000 | 17.50 | 25.00 | 40.00 | 75.00 | — |

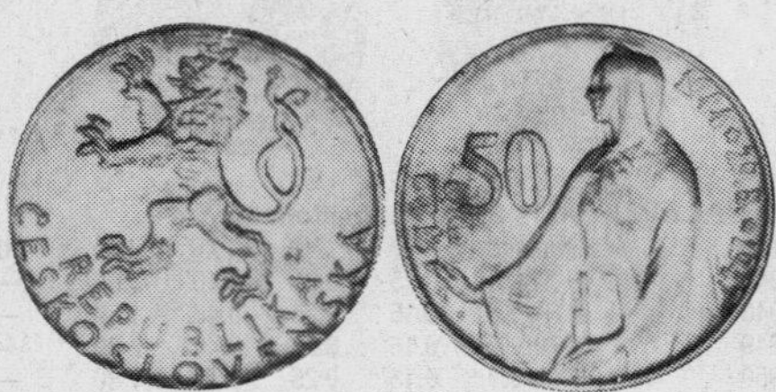

**50 KORUN** KM# 24 **Weight:** 10.0000 g. **Composition:** 0.5000 Silver .1607 oz. ASW **Subject:** 1944 Slovak Uprising

| Date | Mintage | F | VF | XF | Unc | BU |
|---|---|---|---|---|---|---|
| ND (1947) | 1,000,000 | — | 2.75 | 4.50 | 6.50 | — |

**50 KORUN** KM# 25 **Weight:** 10.0000 g. **Composition:** 0.5000 Silver .1607 oz. ASW **Subject:** 3rd Anniverary - Prague Uprising

| Date | Mintage | F | VF | XF | Unc | BU |
|---|---|---|---|---|---|---|
| ND (1948) | 1,000,000 | — | 2.75 | 4.50 | 6.50 | — |

**50 KORUN** KM# 28 **Weight:** 10.0000 g. **Composition:** 0.5000 Silver .1607 oz. ASW **Subject:** 70th Birthday - Josef Stalin

| Date | Mintage | F | VF | XF | Unc | BU |
|---|---|---|---|---|---|---|
| ND (1949) | 1,000,000 | — | 2.75 | 4.50 | 7.00 | — |

**100 KORUN** KM# 26 **Weight:** 14.0000 g. **Composition:** 0.5000 Silver .2250 oz. ASW **Subject:** 600th Anniversary - Charles University

| Date | Mintage | F | VF | XF | Unc | BU |
|---|---|---|---|---|---|---|
| 1948 | 1,000,000 | — | 2.75 | 4.50 | 7.00 | — |

**100 KORUN** KM# 27 **Weight:** 14.0000 g. **Composition:** 0.5000 Silver .2250 oz. ASW **Subject:** 30th Anniversary of Independence

| Date | Mintage | F | VF | XF | Unc | BU |
|---|---|---|---|---|---|---|
| ND (1948) | 1,000,000 | — | 2.75 | 4.50 | 7.00 | — |

**100 KORUN** KM# 29 **Weight:** 14.0000 g. **Composition:** 0.5000 Silver .2250 oz. ASW **Subject:** 700th Anniversary - Jihlava Mining Privileges

| Date | Mintage | F | VF | XF | Unc | BU |
|---|---|---|---|---|---|---|
| 1949 | 1,000,000 | — | 2.75 | 4.50 | 7.00 | — |

**100 KORUN** KM# 30 **Weight:** 14.0000 g. **Composition:** 0.5000 Silver .2250 oz. ASW **Subject:** 70th Birthday - Stalin

| Date | Mintage | F | VF | XF | Unc | BU |
|---|---|---|---|---|---|---|
| ND (1949) | 1,000,000 | — | 2.75 | 4.50 | 7.00 | — |

**100 KORUN** KM# 33 **Weight:** 14.0000 g. **Composition:** 0.5000 Silver .2250 oz. ASW **Subject:** 30th Anniversary - Communist party **Reverse:** Bust right of Kelment Gottwald

| Date | Mintage | F | VF | XF | Unc | BU |
|---|---|---|---|---|---|---|
| ND (1951) | 1,000,000 | — | 2.75 | 4.50 | 7.00 | — |

# PEOPLES REPUBLIC

## DECIMAL COINAGE

**HALER** KM# 35 **Composition:** Aluminum

| Date | Mintage | F | VF | XF | Unc | BU |
|---|---|---|---|---|---|---|
| 1953 | 188,885,000 | — | — | 0.10 | 0.25 | — |
| 1954 | — | — | — | 0.10 | 0.25 | — |
| 1955 | — | — | — | 0.10 | 0.25 | — |
| 1956 | — | — | — | 0.10 | 0.25 | — |
| 1957 | — | — | — | 0.10 | 0.25 | — |
| 1958 | — | 0.10 | 0.25 | 0.35 | 0.75 | — |
| 1959 | — | — | — | 0.10 | 0.25 | — |
| 1960 | — | — | — | 0.10 | 0.25 | — |

**3 HALERE** KM# 36 **Composition:** Aluminum

| Date | Mintage | F | VF | XF | Unc | BU |
|---|---|---|---|---|---|---|
| 1953 | 90,001,000 | — | 0.10 | 0.15 | 0.30 | — |
| 1954 | Inc. above | — | 0.10 | 0.15 | 0.30 | — |

**5 HALERU** KM# 37 **Composition:** Aluminum

| Date | Mintage | F | VF | XF | Unc | BU |
|---|---|---|---|---|---|---|
| 1953 | 160,233,000 | 0.10 | 0.15 | 0.25 | 0.50 | — |
| 1954 | Inc. above | 0.10 | 0.15 | 0.25 | 0.50 | — |
| 1955 | Inc. above | 0.30 | 0.50 | 0.75 | 2.00 | — |

**10 HALERU** KM# 38 **Composition:** Aluminum

| Date | Mintage | F | VF | XF | Unc | BU |
|---|---|---|---|---|---|---|
| 1953 | — | 0.10 | 0.15 | 0.30 | 0.80 | — |

**Note:** Unknown Mint-125 notches in milled edge

| Date | Mintage | F | VF | XF | Unc | BU |
|---|---|---|---|---|---|---|
| 1953 | 160,000 | 0.10 | 0.15 | 0.30 | 0.80 | — |

**Note:** Leningrad Mint-133 notches in milled edge

| Date | Mintage | F | VF | XF | Unc | BU |
|---|---|---|---|---|---|---|
| 1953 | — | 0.25 | 0.50 | 0.75 | 2.00 | — |

**Note:** Unknown Mint-125 notches in milled edge

| Date | Mintage | F | VF | XF | Unc | BU |
|---|---|---|---|---|---|---|
| 1954 | — | 0.25 | 0.50 | 0.75 | 2.00 | — |
| 1955 | — | 0.50 | 0.75 | 1.25 | 3.00 | — |
| 1956 | — | 0.10 | 0.15 | 0.30 | 0.80 | — |
| 1958 | — | 0.50 | 0.75 | — | 4.00 | — |

**25 HALERU** KM# 39 **Composition:** Aluminum

| Date | Mintage | F | VF | XF | Unc | BU |
|---|---|---|---|---|---|---|
| 1953 | 215,002,000 | 0.10 | 0.20 | 0.30 | 0.80 | — |

**Note:** Kremnica Mint-134 notches in milled edge

| Date | Mintage | F | VF | XF | Unc | BU |
|---|---|---|---|---|---|---|
| 1953 | Inc. above | 0.30 | 0.50 | 0.60 | 1.50 | — |

**Note:** Leningrad Mint-145 notches in milled edge

| Date | Mintage | F | VF | XF | Unc | BU |
|---|---|---|---|---|---|---|
| 1954 | Inc. above | 4.00 | 8.00 | 16.00 | 38.00 | — |

**KORUNA** KM# 46 **Composition:** Aluminum-Bronze

| Date | Mintage | F | VF | XF | Unc | BU |
|---|---|---|---|---|---|---|
| 1957 | 137,000,000 | 0.20 | 0.30 | 0.45 | 2.50 | — |
| 1958 | Inc. above | 0.20 | 0.30 | 0.45 | 2.50 | — |
| 1959 | Inc. above | 0.15 | 0.25 | 0.35 | 1.50 | — |
| 1960 | Inc. above | 0.15 | 0.25 | 0.35 | 1.50 | — |

**10 KORUN** **KM# 40** **Weight:** 12.0000 g. **Composition:** 0.5000 Silver .1929 oz. ASW **Subject:** 10th Anniversary - Slovak Uprising **Note:** 61,010 pieces, Unc and Proof, were melted by the Czech National Bank in 1997.

| Date | Mintage | F | VF | XF | Unc | BU |
|---|---|---|---|---|---|---|
| ND (1954) | 250 | — | 2.00 | 3.00 | 5.00 | — |
| ND (1954) Proof | 5,000 | Value: 8.00 | | | | |

**10 KORUN** **KM# 42** **Weight:** 12.0000 g. **Composition:** 0.5000 Silver .1929 oz. ASW **Subject:** 10th Anniversary - Liberation from Germany **Note:** 90,552 pieces Unc and Proof, were melted by the Czech National Bank in 1997.

| Date | Mintage | F | VF | XF | Unc | BU |
|---|---|---|---|---|---|---|
| ND (1955) | 300 | — | 2.50 | 3.50 | 6.00 | — |
| ND (1955) Proof | 5,000 | Value: 11.50 | | | | |

**10 KORUN** **KM# 47.2** **Weight:** 12.0000 g. **Composition:** 0.5000 Silver .1929 oz. ASW **Note:** Incuse designer initials.

| Date | Mintage | F | VF | XF | Unc | BU |
|---|---|---|---|---|---|---|
| 1957 Proof | Est. 5,000 | Value: 11.50 | | | | |

**Note:** 138 pieces, Unc and Proof, were melted by the Czech National Bank in 1997

**10 KORUN** **KM# 47.1** **Weight:** 12.0000 g. **Composition:** 0.5000 Silver .1929 oz. ASW **Subject:** 250th Anniversary - Technical College **Note:** Raised designer initials.

| Date | Mintage | F | VF | XF | Unc | BU |
|---|---|---|---|---|---|---|
| 1957 | 75,000 | — | 2.50 | 3.50 | 7.50 | — |

**Note:** See note below KM#47.2

**10 KORUN** **KM# 48** **Weight:** 12.0000 g. **Composition:** 0.5000 Silver .1929 oz. ASW **Reverse:** J. A. Komensky **Note:** 6,454 pieces, 4,654 Unc and 1,800 Proof, were melted by the Czech National Bank in 1997.

| Date | Mintage | F | VF | XF | Unc | BU |
|---|---|---|---|---|---|---|
| 1957 | 150 | — | 2.50 | 3.50 | 6.50 | — |
| 1957 Proof | 5,000 | Value: 11.50 | | | | |

**25 KORUN** **KM# 41** **Weight:** 16.0000 g. **Composition:** 0.5000 Silver .2572 oz. ASW **Subject:** 10th Anniversary - Slovak Unprising **Note:** 106,433 pieces, 105,633 Unc and 800 Proof, were melted by the Czech National Bank in 1997.

| Date | Mintage | F | VF | XF | Unc | BU |
|---|---|---|---|---|---|---|
| ND (1954) | 250 | — | — | 5.00 | 7.50 | — |
| ND (1954) | Est. 5,000 | Value: 20.00 | | | | |

**25 KORUN** **KM# 43** **Weight:** 16.0000 g. **Composition:** 0.5000 Silver .2572 oz. ASW **Subject:** 10th Anniversary - Liberation from Germany **Note:** 76,143 pieces, Unc and Proof, were melted by the Czech National Bank in 1997.

| Date | Mintage | F | VF | XF | Unc | BU |
|---|---|---|---|---|---|---|
| ND (1955) | 200 | — | — | 5.00 | 7.50 | — |
| ND (1955) Ptoof | 5,000 | Value: 18.50 | | | | |

**50 KORUN** **KM# 44** **Weight:** 20.0000 g. **Composition:** 0.9000 Silver .5787 oz. ASW **Subject:** 10th Anniversary - Liberation from Germany **Note:** 36,050 pieces were melted by the Czech National Bank in 1997.

| Date | Mintage | F | VF | XF | Unc | BU |
|---|---|---|---|---|---|---|
| 1955 | 120,000 | — | 5.00 | 9.00 | 16.50 | — |

**100 KORUN** **KM# 45** **Weight:** 24.0000 g. **Composition:** 0.9000 Silver .6945 oz. ASW **Subject:** 10th Anniversary - Liberation from Germany

| Date | Mintage | F | VF | XF | Unc | BU |
|---|---|---|---|---|---|---|
| ND | Est. 75,000 | — | 10.00 | 18.50 | 36.50 | — |

**Note:** 22,044 pieces were melted by the Czech National Bank in 1997

# SOCIALIST REPUBLIC

## DECIMAL COINAGE

**HALER** **KM# 51** **Composition:** Aluminum

| Date | Mintage | F | VF | XF | Unc | BU |
|---|---|---|---|---|---|---|
| 1962 | 20,056,000 | — | — | 0.10 | 0.15 | — |
| 1963 | Inc. above | — | — | 0.10 | 0.15 | — |
| 1986 | 3,360 | — | — | — | 1.00 | — |

**3 HALERE** **KM# 52** **Composition:** Aluminum

| Date | Mintage | F | VF | XF | Unc | BU |
|---|---|---|---|---|---|---|
| 1962 | | 100 | 150 | 200 | 280 | — |
| 1963 | 5,130,000 | — | — | 0.10 | 0.15 | — |

**5 HALERU** **KM# 53** **Composition:** Aluminum

| Date | Mintage | F | VF | XF | Unc | BU |
|---|---|---|---|---|---|---|
| 1962 | 55,150,000 | — | 0.10 | 0.15 | 0.25 | — |
| 1963 | Inc. above | — | 0.10 | 0.15 | 0.25 | — |
| 1966 | Inc. above | — | 0.10 | 0.15 | 0.25 | — |
| 1967 | 20,770,000 | — | 0.10 | 0.15 | 0.25 | — |
| 1970 | 5,090,000 | — | 0.10 | 0.15 | 0.20 | — |
| 1972 | 10,090,000 | — | 0.10 | 0.15 | 0.20 | — |
| 1973 | 10,140,000 | — | 0.10 | 0.15 | 0.20 | — |
| 1974 | 15,510,000 | — | 0.10 | 0.15 | 0.20 | — |
| 1975 | 15,510,000 | — | 0.10 | 0.15 | 0.20 | — |
| 1976 | 15,550,000 | — | 0.10 | 0.15 | 0.20 | — |

**5 HALERU** **KM# 86** **Composition:** Aluminum

| Date | Mintage | F | VF | XF | Unc | BU |
|---|---|---|---|---|---|---|
| 1977 | 26,710,000 | — | — | 0.10 | 0.25 | — |
| 1978 | 51,110,000 | — | — | 0.10 | 0.25 | — |
| 1979 | 72,380,000 | — | — | 0.10 | 0.25 | — |
| 1980 In mint set only | 51,000 | — | — | — | 0.25 | — |
| 1981 In mint set only | 66,000 | — | — | — | 0.25 | — |
| 1982 In mint set only | 54,000 | — | — | — | 0.50 | — |
| 1983 In mint set only | 60,000 | — | — | — | 0.25 | — |
| 1984 In mint set only | 40,000 | — | — | — | 0.50 | — |
| 1985 In mint set only | 40,000 | — | — | — | 0.50 | — |
| 1986 | 20,020,000 | — | — | 0.10 | 0.25 | — |
| 1987 | 520,000 | — | — | 0.10 | 0.25 | — |
| 1988 | 8,030,000 | — | — | 0.10 | 0.25 | — |
| 1989 | 110,000 | — | — | 0.10 | 0.25 | — |
| 1990 | 13,950,000 | — | — | 0.10 | 0.25 | — |

**10 HALERU** KM# 49.1 **Composition:** Aluminum

| Date | Mintage | F | VF | XF | Unc | BU |
|---|---|---|---|---|---|---|
| 1961 | 314,480,000 | — | 0.10 | 0.20 | 0.35 | — |
| 1962 | Inc. above | — | 0.10 | 0.20 | 0.35 | — |
| 1963 | Inc. above | — | 0.10 | 0.20 | 0.35 | — |
| 1964 | Inc. above | — | 0.10 | 0.20 | 0.35 | — |
| 1965 | Inc. above | — | 0.10 | 0.20 | 0.35 | — |
| 1966 | Inc. above | — | 0.10 | 0.20 | 0.35 | — |
| 1967 | 46,990,000 | — | 0.10 | 0.20 | 0.35 | — |
| 1968 | 37,275,000 | — | 0.10 | 0.20 | 0.35 | — |
| 1969 | 80,000,000 | — | 0.10 | 0.15 | 0.35 | — |
| 1970 | 50,005,000 | — | 0.10 | 0.20 | 0.35 | — |
| 1971 | 30,450,000 | — | 0.10 | 0.20 | 0.35 | — |

**10 HALERU** KM# 49.2 **Composition:** Aluminum **Obverse:** Flat top 3 in date

| Date | Mintage | F | VF | XF | Unc | BU |
|---|---|---|---|---|---|---|
| 1963 | Est. 3,600 | 12.50 | 25.00 | 37.50 | 65.00 | — |

**10 HALERU** KM# 80 **Composition:** Aluminum **Note:** Varieties exist.

| Date | Mintage | F | VF | XF | Unc | BU |
|---|---|---|---|---|---|---|
| 1974 | 11,470,000 | — | — | 0.10 | 0.25 | — |
| 1975 | 41,002,000 | — | — | 0.10 | 0.25 | — |
| 1976 | 182,000,000 | — | — | 0.10 | 0.25 | — |
| 1977 | 151,760,000 | — | — | 0.10 | 0.25 | — |
| 1978 | 62,620,000 | — | — | 0.10 | 0.25 | — |
| 1979 | 30,240,000 | — | — | 0.10 | 0.25 | — |
| 1980 | 31,280,000 | — | — | 0.10 | 0.25 | — |
| 1981 | 43,616,000 | — | — | 0.10 | 0.25 | — |
| 1982 | 74,564,000 | — | — | 0.10 | 0.25 | — |
| 1983 | 50,560,000 | — | — | 0.10 | 0.25 | — |
| 1984 | 40,370,000 | — | — | 0.10 | 0.25 | — |
| 1985 | 92,930,000 | — | — | 0.10 | 0.25 | — |
| 1986 | 87,260,000 | — | — | 0.10 | 0.25 | — |
| 1987 | 30,030,000 | — | — | 0.10 | 0.25 | — |
| 1988 | 47,480,000 | — | — | 0.10 | 0.25 | — |
| 1989 | 50,300,000 | — | — | 0.10 | 0.25 | — |
| 1990 | 25,220,000 | — | — | 0.10 | 0.25 | — |

**20 HALERU** KM# 74 **Composition:** Brass **Note:** Varieties exist.

| Date | Mintage | F | VF | XF | Unc | BU |
|---|---|---|---|---|---|---|
| 1972 | 25,820,000 | — | 0.10 | 0.20 | 0.40 | — |
| 1973 | 39,095,000 | — | 0.10 | 0.20 | 0.40 | — |
| 1974 | 24,795,000 | — | 0.10 | 0.20 | 0.40 | — |
| 1975 | 30,025,000 | — | 0.10 | 0.20 | 0.40 | — |
| 1976 | 30,540,000 | — | 0.10 | 0.20 | 0.40 | — |
| 1977 | 30,655,000 | — | 0.10 | 0.20 | 0.40 | — |
| 1978 | 30,095,000 | — | 0.10 | 0.20 | 0.40 | — |
| 1979 | 12,120,000 | — | 0.10 | 0.20 | 0.40 | — |
| 1980 | 52,301,000 | — | 0.10 | 0.15 | 0.30 | — |
| 1981 | 35,126,000 | — | 0.10 | 0.15 | 0.30 | — |
| 1982 | 41,239,000 | — | 0.10 | 0.15 | 0.30 | — |
| 1983 | 50,160,000 | — | 0.10 | 0.15 | 0.30 | — |
| 1984 | 33,685,000 | — | 0.10 | 0.15 | 0.30 | — |
| 1985 | 40,455,000 | — | 0.10 | 0.15 | 0.30 | — |
| 1986 | 37,055,000 | — | 0.10 | 0.15 | 0.30 | — |
| 1987 | 26,975,000 | — | 0.10 | 0.15 | 0.30 | — |
| 1988 | 18,260,000 | — | 0.10 | 0.15 | 0.30 | — |
| 1989 | 29,980,000 | — | 0.10 | 0.15 | 0.30 | — |
| 1990 | 15,030,000 | — | 0.10 | 0.15 | 0.30 | — |

**25 HALERU** KM# 54 **Composition:** Aluminum **Note:** Haleru ceased to be legal tender.

| Date | Mintage | F | VF | XF | Unc | BU |
|---|---|---|---|---|---|---|
| 1962 | 69,880,000 | 0.10 | 0.15 | 0.20 | 0.35 | — |
| 1963 | Inc. above | 0.10 | 0.15 | 0.20 | 0.35 | — |
| 1964 | Inc. above | 0.10 | 0.15 | 0.20 | 0.35 | — |

**50 HALERU** KM# 55.1 **Composition:** Bronze

| Date | Mintage | F | VF | XF | Unc | BU |
|---|---|---|---|---|---|---|
| 1963 | 80,560,000 | 0.10 | 0.20 | 0.30 | 0.45 | — |
| 1964 | Inc. above | 0.10 | 0.20 | 0.30 | 0.45 | — |
| 1965 | Inc. above | 0.10 | 0.20 | 0.30 | 0.45 | — |
| 1969 | 9,876,000 | 0.10 | 0.20 | 0.30 | 0.45 | — |
| 1970 | 31,536,000 | 0.10 | 0.20 | 0.30 | 0.40 | — |
| 1971 | 20,800,000 | 0.10 | 0.20 | 0.30 | 0.40 | — |

**50 HALERU** KM# 55.2 **Composition:** Bronze **Obv. Legend:** Small date, without dots

| Date | Mintage | F | VF | XF | Unc | BU |
|---|---|---|---|---|---|---|
| 1969 | — | 12.50 | 22.50 | 40.00 | 75.00 | — |

**50 HALERU** KM# 89 **Composition:** Copper-Nickel **Note:** Date varieties exist.

| Date | Mintage | F | VF | XF | Unc | BU |
|---|---|---|---|---|---|---|
| 1978 | 40,480,000 | — | — | 0.10 | 0.50 | — |
| 1979 | 76,116,000 | — | — | 0.10 | 0.50 | — |
| 1980 In mint sets only | 51,000 | — | — | — | 1.00 | — |
| 1981 In mint sets only | 66,000 | — | — | — | 1.00 | — |
| 1982 | 14,262,000 | — | — | 0.10 | 0.50 | — |
| 1983 | 16,168,000 | — | — | 0.10 | 0.50 | — |
| 1984 | 16,208,000 | — | — | 0.10 | 0.50 | — |
| 1985 | 10,468,000 | — | — | 0.10 | 0.50 | — |
| 1986 | 10,020,000 | — | — | 0.10 | 0.50 | — |
| 1987 | 5,138,000 | — | — | 0.10 | 0.50 | — |
| 1988 | 5,090,000 | — | — | 0.10 | 0.50 | — |
| 1989 | 13,030,000 | — | — | 0.10 | 0.50 | — |
| 1990 | 7,742,000 | — | — | 0.10 | 0.50 | — |

**KORUNA** KM# 50 **Composition:** Aluminum-Bronze **Note:** Date varieties exist.

| Date | Mintage | F | VF | XF | Unc | BU |
|---|---|---|---|---|---|---|
| 1961 | 146,964,000 | — | 0.15 | 0.30 | 0.60 | — |
| 1962 | Inc. above | — | 0.15 | 0.30 | 0.60 | — |
| 1963 | Inc. above | — | 0.15 | 0.30 | 0.60 | — |
| 1964 | Inc. above | — | 0.15 | 0.30 | 0.60 | — |
| 1965 | Inc. above | — | 0.15 | 0.30 | 0.60 | — |
| 1966 | Inc. above | 0.40 | 0.65 | 0.90 | 1.25 | — |
| 1967 | 7,924,000 | — | 0.15 | 0.30 | 0.60 | — |
| 1968 | 10,696,000 | — | 0.15 | 0.30 | 0.60 | — |
| 1969 | 21,820,000 | — | 0.15 | 0.30 | 0.60 | — |
| 1970 | 31,036,000 | — | 0.15 | 0.30 | 0.60 | — |
| 1971 | 10,152,000 | — | 0.15 | 0.30 | 0.60 | — |
| 1975 | 6,657,000 | — | 0.15 | 0.30 | 0.60 | — |
| 1976 | 14,211,000 | — | 0.15 | 0.30 | 0.60 | — |
| 1977 | 10,434,000 | — | 0.15 | 0.30 | 0.75 | — |
| 1979 | | — | 0.15 | 0.30 | 0.75 | — |
| 1980 | 24,513,000 | — | 0.15 | 0.30 | 0.75 | — |
| 1981 | 7,179,000 | — | 0.15 | 0.30 | 0.75 | — |
| 1982 | 17,163,000 | — | 0.15 | 0.30 | 0.75 | — |
| 1983 | 4,758,000 | — | 0.15 | 0.30 | 0.75 | — |
| 1984 | 9,733,000 | — | 0.15 | 0.30 | 0.75 | — |
| 1985 | 10,546,000 | — | 0.15 | 0.30 | 0.75 | — |
| 1986 | 2,789,000 | — | 0.15 | 0.30 | 0.75 | — |
| 1987 In mint sets only | 30,000 | — | — | — | 1.50 | — |
| 1988 In mint sets only | 30,000 | — | — | — | 1.50 | — |
| 1989 | 1,038,000 | — | 0.15 | 0.30 | 0.75 | — |
| 1990 | 19,368,000 | — | 0.15 | 0.30 | 0.75 | — |

**2 KORUNY** KM# 75 **Composition:** Copper-Nickel

| Date | Mintage | F | VF | XF | Unc | BU |
|---|---|---|---|---|---|---|
| 1972 | 20,344,000 | — | 0.25 | 0.45 | 1.00 | — |
| 1973 | 21,087,000 | — | 0.25 | 0.45 | 1.00 | — |
| **Note:** 1973 date exists with edge of KM#60 | | | | | | |
| 1974 | 27,957,000 | — | 0.25 | 0.45 | 1.00 | — |
| 1975 | 35,094,000 | — | 0.25 | 0.45 | 1.00 | — |
| 1976 | 1,100,000 | — | 0.25 | 0.45 | 1.00 | — |
| 1977 | 4,201,000 | — | 0.25 | 0.65 | 1.50 | — |
| 1980 | 14,943,000 | — | 0.25 | 0.35 | 0.75 | — |
| 1981 | 17,264,000 | — | 0.25 | 0.35 | 0.75 | — |
| 1982 | 8,108,000 | — | 0.25 | 0.35 | 0.75 | — |
| 1983 | 10,190,000 | — | 0.25 | 0.35 | 0.75 | — |
| 1984 | 8,634,000 | — | 0.25 | 0.35 | 0.75 | — |
| 1985 | 6,772,000 | — | 0.25 | 0.35 | 0.75 | — |
| 1986 | 10,262,000 | — | 0.25 | 0.35 | 0.75 | — |
| 1987 In mint sets only | 30,000 | — | — | — | 1.50 | — |
| 1988 In mint sets only | 30,000 | — | — | — | 1.50 | — |
| 1989 | 9,092,000 | — | 0.25 | 0.35 | 0.75 | — |
| 1990 | 10,672,000 | — | 0.25 | 0.35 | 0.75 | — |

**3 KORUNY** KM# 57 **Composition:** Copper-Nickel

| Date | Mintage | F | VF | XF | Unc | BU |
|---|---|---|---|---|---|---|
| 1965 | 15,000,000 | — | 0.50 | 1.00 | 2.50 | — |
| 1966 | Inc. above | — | 0.50 | 1.00 | 2.50 | — |
| 1968 | 7,000,000 | — | 0.45 | 0.85 | 2.00 | — |
| 1969 | 10,080,000 | — | 0.40 | 0.75 | 1.50 | — |

**5 KORUN** KM# 60 **Composition:** Copper-Nickel

| Date | Mintage | F | VF | XF | Unc | BU |
|---|---|---|---|---|---|---|
| 1966 | 6,383,000 | — | 0.75 | 1.00 | 2.00 | — |
| **Note:** 1966 varieties on obverse of coin: large date: no space between letter B in REPUBLIC and coat of arms; small date: space between letter B in REPUBLIC and coat of arms; plain edge: no ornamental inscription on edge (error coin). So far there has been no indication of any of the varieties as being scarce | | | | | | |
| 1967 | 4,544,000 | — | — | 0.75 | 1.50 | — |
| 1968 | 14,120,000 | — | — | 0.75 | 1.50 | — |
| 1969 Straight date | 5,486,000 | — | — | 0.75 | 1.50 | — |
| 1969 Date in semi-circle | Inc. above | 0.75 | 1.25 | 2.00 | 3.00 | — |
| 1970 | 10,073,000 | — | — | 0.75 | 1.50 | — |
| 1973 (2 vars. in 3 of date) | 15,620,000 | — | — | 0.75 | 1.25 | — |
| 1974 (3 vars. in 4 of date) | 20,053,000 | — | — | 0.75 | 1.25 | — |
| 1975 | 17,158,000 | — | — | 0.75 | 1.25 | — |
| 1978 | 5,317,000 | — | — | 0.75 | 1.25 | — |
| 1979 | 9,219,000 | — | — | 0.75 | 1.25 | — |
| 1980 | 12,559,000 | — | — | 0.75 | 1.25 | — |
| 1981 | 8,620,000 | — | — | 0.75 | 1.25 | — |
| 1982 | 6,904,000 | — | — | 0.75 | 1.25 | — |
| 1983 | 6,704,000 | — | — | 0.75 | 1.25 | — |
| 1984 | 6,857,000 | — | — | 0.75 | 1.25 | — |
| 1985 | 6,764,000 | — | — | 0.75 | 1.25 | — |
| 1986 In mint sets only | 20,000 | — | — | — | 5.00 | — |
| 1987 In mint sets only | 30,000 | — | — | — | 2.50 | — |
| 1988 | 30,000 | — | — | — | 2.50 | — |
| 1989 | 5,039,000 | — | — | 0.75 | 1.25 | — |
| 1990 | 2,783,000 | — | — | 0.75 | 1.25 | — |

**10 KORUN** **KM# 56** **Weight:** 12.0000 g. **Composition:** 0.5000 Silver .1929 oz. ASW **Subject:** 20th Anniversary - 1994 Slovak Uprising **Note:** 7,976 pieces were melted by the Czech National Bank in 1997.

| Date | Mintage | F | VF | XF | Unc | BU |
|---|---|---|---|---|---|---|
| ND (1964) | Est. 120,000 | — | — | 3.00 | 5.00 | — |

**10 KORUN** **KM# 58** **Weight:** 12.0000 g. **Composition:** 0.5000 Silver .1929 oz. ASW **Subject:** 550th Anniversary - Death of Jan Hus **Note:** 80 pieces, Unc and Proof, were melted by the Czech National Bank in 1997.

| Date | Mintage | F | VF | XF | Unc | BU |
|---|---|---|---|---|---|---|
| ND (1965) | 55,000 | — | — | 7.00 | 15.00 | — |
| CDND (1965) Proof | 5,000 | Value: 20.00 | | | | |

**10 KORUN** **KM# 61** **Weight:** 12.0000 g. **Composition:** 0.5000 Silver .1929 oz. ASW **Subject:** 1100th Anniversary of Great Moravia **Note:** 3,146 pieces, Unc and Proof, were melted by the Czech National Bank in 1997.

| Date | Mintage | F | VF | XF | Unc | BU |
|---|---|---|---|---|---|---|
| 1966 | 115,000 | — | — | 4.00 | 6.50 | — |
| 1966 Proof | 5,000 | Value: 12.50 | | | | |

**10 KORUN** **KM# 62** **Weight:** 12.0000 g. **Composition:** 0.5000 Silver .1929 oz. ASW **Subject:** 500th Anniversary - Bratislava University **Note:** 103 pieces, Unc and Proof, were melted by the Czech National Bank in 1997.

| Date | Mintage | F | VF | XF | Unc | BU |
|---|---|---|---|---|---|---|
| ND (1967) | 45,000 | — | — | 10.00 | 20.00 | — |
| ND (1967) Proof | 500 | Value: 22.50 | | | | |

**10 KORUN** **KM# 63** **Weight:** 12.0000 g. **Composition:** 0.5000 Silver .1929 oz. ASW **Subject:** Centennial - Prague (Praha) National Theater **Note:** 50 pieces, Unc and Proof, were melted by the Czech National Bank in 1997.

| Date | Mintage | F | VF | XF | Unc | BU |
|---|---|---|---|---|---|---|
| ND (1968) | 55,000 | — | — | 15.00 | 20.00 | — |
| ND (1968) Proof | 5,000 | Value: 40.00 | | | | |

**20 KORUN** **KM# 76** **Weight:** 9.0000 g. **Composition:** 0.5000 Silver .1446 oz. ASW **Subject:** Centennial - Death of Andrej Sladkovic **Note:** 2,642 pieces, 2,600 Unc and 42 Proof, were melted by the Czech National Bank in 1997.

| Date | Mintage | F | VF | XF | Unc | BU |
|---|---|---|---|---|---|---|
| CDND (1972) | 55,000 | — | — | 3.00 | 5.00 | — |
| ND (1972) Proof | 5,000 | Value: 12.50 | | | | |

**25 KORUN** **KM# 59** **Weight:** 16.0000 g. **Composition:** 0.5000 Silver .2572 oz. ASW **Subject:** 20th Anniversary - Czechoslovakian Liberation **Note:** 21,114 pieces, Unc and Proof, were melted by the Czech National Bank in 1997.

| Date | Mintage | F | VF | XF | Unc | BU |
|---|---|---|---|---|---|---|
| ND (1965) | 150,000 | — | — | 4.00 | 6.50 | — |
| ND (1965) Proof | 5,000 | Value: 12.50 | | | | |

**25 KORUN** **KM# 64** **Weight:** 16.0000 g. **Composition:** 0.5000 Silver .2572 oz. ASW **Subject:** Sesquicentennial - Prague (Praha) National Museum **Note:** 51 pieces, Unc and Proof, were melted by the Czech National Bank in 1997.

| Date | Mintage | F | VF | XF | Unc | BU |
|---|---|---|---|---|---|---|
| ND (1968) | 51,000 | — | — | 4.50 | 9.00 | — |
| ND (1968) Proof | 5,000 | Value: 40.00 | | | | |

**25 KORUN** **KM# 66** **Weight:** 16.0000 g. **Composition:** 0.5000 Silver .2572 oz. ASW **Subject:** 100th Anniversary - Death of J. E. Purkyne **Note:** Edge varieties exist; 40 pieces, Unc and Proof, were melted by the Czech National Bank in 1997.

| Date | Mintage | F | VF | XF | Unc | BU |
|---|---|---|---|---|---|---|
| ND (1969) | 45,000 | — | — | 4.00 | 8.00 | — |
| ND (1969) Proof | 5,000 | Value: 28.00 | | | | |

**25 KORUN** **KM# 67** **Weight:** 16.0000 g. **Composition:** 0.5000 Silver .2572 oz. ASW **Subject:** 25th Anniversary - 1944 Slovak Uprising **Note:** Edge varieties exist; 40 pieces, Unc and Proof, were melted by the Czech National Bank in 1997.

| Date | Mintage | F | VF | XF | Unc | BU |
|---|---|---|---|---|---|---|
| ND (1969) | 25,000 | — | — | 20.00 | 40.00 | — |
| ND (1969) Proof | 5,000 | Value: 50.00 | | | | |

**25 KORUN** **KM# 69** **Weight:** 10.0000 g. **Composition:** 0.5000 Silver .1607 oz. ASW **Subject:** 25th Anniversary of Liberation **Note:** 18,052 pieces, Unc and Proof, were melted by the Czech National Bank in 1997.

| Date | Mintage | F | VF | XF | Unc | BU |
|---|---|---|---|---|---|---|
| ND (1970) | 95,000 | — | — | 4.00 | 6.00 | — |
| ND (1970) Proof | 5,000 | Value: 15.00 | | | | |

**25 KORUN** **KM# 68** **Weight:** 10.0000 g. **Composition:** 0.5000 Silver .1607 oz. ASW **Subject:** 50th Anniversary - Slovak National Theater **Note:** 2,323 pieces, Unc and Proof, were melted by the Czech National Bank in 1997.

| Date | Mintage | F | VF | XF | Unc | BU |
|---|---|---|---|---|---|---|
| ND (1970) | 45,000 | — | — | 5.00 | 10.00 | — |
| ND (1970) Proof | 5,000 | Value: 60.00 | | | | |

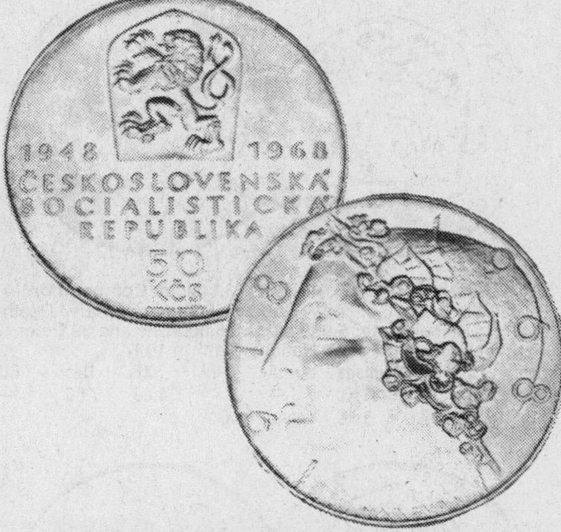


**50 KORUN** **KM# 65** **Weight:** 20.0000 g. **Composition:** 0.9000 Silver .5787 oz. ASW **Subject:** 50th Anniversary of Czechoslovakia 20th Anniversary - People's Republic **Note:** 50 pieces, Unc and Proof, were melted by the Czech National Bank in 1997.

| Date | Mintage | F | VF | XF | Unc | BU |
|---|---|---|---|---|---|---|
| ND (1968) | 58,000 | — | — | 18.00 | 32.00 | — |
| ND (1968) Proof | 2,000 | Value: 75.00 | | | | |

**50 KORUN** **KM# 70** **Weight:** 13.0000 g. **Composition:** 0.7000 Silver .2926 oz. ASW **Subject:** Centennial - Birch of Lenin **Note:** 51 pieces, Unc and Proof, were melted by the Czech National Bank in 1997.

| Date | Mintage | F | VF | XF | Unc | BU |
|---|---|---|---|---|---|---|
| ND (1970) | 44,000 | — | — | 4.00 | 8.00 | — |
| ND (1970) Proof | 6,200 | Value: 30.00 | | | | |

**50 KORUN** **KM# 72** **Weight:** 13.0000 g. **Composition:** 0.7000 Silver .2926 oz. ASW **Subject:** 50th Anniversary - Death of Pavol Orsagh-Hviezdoslav **Note:** 3,900 pieces, 3,800 Unc and 100 Proof, were melted by the Czech National Bank in 1997.

| Date | Mintage | F | VF | XF | Unc | BU |
|---|---|---|---|---|---|---|
| ND (1971) | 45,000 | — | — | 4.00 | 7.00 | — |
| ND (1971) Proof | 5,000 | Value: 20.00 | | | | |

**50 KORUN** **KM# 71** **Weight:** 13.0000 g. **Composition:** 0.7000 Silver .2926 oz. ASW **Subject:** 50th Anniversary - Czechoslovak Communist Party **Note:** 4,450 pieces, 4,400 Unc and 50 Proof, were melted by the Czech National Bank in 1997.

| Date | Mintage | F | VF | XF | Unc | BU |
|---|---|---|---|---|---|---|
| ND (1971) | 45,000 | — | — | 4.00 | 8.00 | — |
| ND (1971) Proof | 5,000 | Value: 22.00 | | | | |

**50 KORUN** **KM# 77** **Weight:** 13.0000 g. **Composition:** 0.7000 Silver .2926 oz. ASW **Subject:** 50th Anniversary - Death of J. V. Myslbek **Note:** 6,039 pieces, 6,000 Unc and 39 Proof, were melted by the Czech National Bank in 1997.

| Date | Mintage | F | VF | XF | Unc | BU |
|---|---|---|---|---|---|---|
| ND (1972) | 45,000 | — | — | 4.00 | 7.00 | — |
| ND (1972) Proof | 5,000 | Value: 20.00 | | | | |

**50 KORUN** **KM# 78** **Weight:** 13.0000 g. **Composition:** 0.7000 Silver .2926 oz. ASW **Subject:** 25th Anniversary - Victory of Communist Party **Note:** 4,740 pieces, 4,637 Unc and 103 Proof, were melted by the Czech National Bank in 1997.

| Date | Mintage | F | VF | XF | Unc | BU |
|---|---|---|---|---|---|---|
| ND (1973) | 55,000 | — | — | 4.00 | 7.00 | — |
| ND (1973) Proof | 5,000 | Value: 20.00 | | | | |

**50 KORUN** **KM# 79** **Weight:** 13.0000 g. **Composition:** 0.7000 Silver .2926 oz. ASW **Subject:** 200th Anniversary - Birth of Josef Jungmann **Note:** 1,584 pieces, 1,500 Unc and 84 Proof, were melted by the Czech National Bank in 1997.

| Date | Mintage | F | VF | XF | Unc | BU |
|---|---|---|---|---|---|---|
| ND (1973) | 45,000 | — | — | 4.00 | 7.00 | — |
| ND (1973) Proof | 5,000 | Value: 11.50 | | | | |

**50 KORUN** **KM# 81** **Weight:** 13.0000 g. **Composition:** 0.7000 Silver .2926 oz. ASW **Subject:** Centennial - Birth of Janko Jesensky **Note:** 10,738 pieces, 9,700 Unc and 1,038 Proof, were melted by the Czech National Bank in 1997.

| Date | Mintage | F | VF | XF | Unc | BU |
|---|---|---|---|---|---|---|
| ND (1974) | 55,000 | — | — | 4.00 | 6.50 | — |
| ND (1974) Proof | 5,000 | Value: 11.50 | | | | |

**50 KORUN** **KM# 83** **Weight:** 13.0000 g. **Composition:** 0.7000 Silver .2926 oz. ASW **Subject:** Centennial - Birth of S. K. Neumann **Note:** 11,037 pieces, 9,000 Unc and 2,037 Proof, were melted by the Czech National Bank in 1997.

| Date | Mintage | F | VF | XF | Unc | BU |
|---|---|---|---|---|---|---|
| ND (1975) | 55,000 | — | — | 4.00 | 6.50 | — |
| ND (1975) Proof | 5,000 | Value: 11.50 | | | | |

**50 KORUN** **KM# 87** **Weight:** 13.0000 g. **Composition:** 0.7000 Silver .2926 oz. ASW **Subject:** 125th Anniversary - Death of Jan Kollar **Note:** 19,043 pieces, 18,143 Unc and 900 Proof, were melted by the Czech National Bank in 1997.

| Date | Mintage | F | VF | XF | Unc | BU |
|---|---|---|---|---|---|---|
| ND (1977) | 75,000 | — | — | 4.00 | 6.50 | — |
| ND (1977) Proof | 5,000 | Value: 11.50 | | | | |

**50 KORUN** **KM# 91** **Weight:** 13.0000 g. **Composition:** 0.7000 Silver .2926 oz. ASW **Subject:** 650th Anniversary of Kremnica Mint **Note:** 21,537 pieces, 19,837 Unc and 1,700 Proof, were melted by the Czech National Bank in 1997.

| Date | Mintage | F | VF | XF | Unc | BU |
|---|---|---|---|---|---|---|
| ND (1978) | 93,000 | — | — | 4.00 | 6.50 | — |
| ND (1978) Proof | 7,000 | Value: 11.50 | | | | |

**50 KORUN** **KM# 90** **Weight:** 13.0000 g. **Composition:** 0.7000 Silver .2926 oz. ASW **Subject:** Centennial - Birth of Zdenek Nejedly **Note:** 18,938 pieces, Unc and 1,100 Proof, were melted by the Czech National Bank in 1997.

| Date | Mintage | F | VF | XF | Unc | BU |
|---|---|---|---|---|---|---|
| ND (1978) | 75,000 | — | — | 4.00 | 6.50 | — |
| ND (1978) Proof | 5,000 | Value: 11.50 | | | | |

**50 KORUN** **KM# 98** **Weight:** 13.0000 g. **Composition:** 0.7000 Silver .2926 oz. ASW **Subject:** 30th Anniversary of 9th Congress **Note:** 26,239 pieces, 24,039 Unc and 2,200 Proof, were melted by the Czech National Bank in 1997.

| Date | Mintage | F | VF | XF | Unc | BU |
|---|---|---|---|---|---|---|
| ND (1979) | 94,000 | — | — | 4.00 | 6.50 | — |
| ND (1979) Proof | 6,000 | Value: 11.50 | | | | |

**50 KORUN** **KM# 121** **Weight:** 7.0000 g. **Composition:** 0.5000 Silver .1125 oz. ASW **Reverse:** Prague **Note:** 3,738 pieces, 3,700 Unc and 38 Proof, were melted by the Czech National Bank in 1997.

| Date | Mintage | F | VF | XF | Unc | BU |
|---|---|---|---|---|---|---|
| 1986 | 90,000 | — | — | — | 6.00 | — |
| 1986 Proof | 10,000 | Value: 12.50 | | | | |

**50 KORUN** **KM# 125** **Weight:** 7.0000 g. **Composition:** 0.5000 Silver .1125 oz. ASW **Reverse:** Bratislava **Note:** 5,738 pieces 5,700 Unc and 38 Proof, were melted by the Czech National Bank in 1997.

| Date | Mintage | F | VF | XF | Unc | BU |
|---|---|---|---|---|---|---|
| 1986 | 69,000 | — | — | — | 6.00 | — |
| 1986 Proof | 10,000 | Value: 11.50 | | | | |

**50 KORUN** KM# 124 **Weight:** 7.0000 g. **Composition:** 0.5000 Silver .1125 oz. ASW **Reverse:** Telc **Note:** 5,938 pieces 5,900 Unc and 38 Proof, were melted by the Czech National Bank in 1997.

| Date | Mintage | F | VF | XF | Unc | BU |
|---|---|---|---|---|---|---|
| 1986 | 69,000 | — | — | — | 6.00 | — |
| 1986 Proof | 10,000 | Value: 11.50 | | | | |

**50 KORUN** KM# 126 **Weight:** 7.0000 g. **Composition:** 0.5000 Silver .1125 oz. ASW **Reverse:** Cesky Krumlov **Note:** 4,538 pieces 4,500 Unc and 38 Proof, were melted by the Czech National Bank in 1997.

| Date | Mintage | F | VF | XF | Unc | BU |
|---|---|---|---|---|---|---|
| 1986 | 69,000 | — | — | — | 6.00 | — |
| 1986 Proof | 10,000 | Value: 11.50 | | | | |

**50 KORUN** KM# 122 **Weight:** 7.0000 g. **Composition:** 0.5000 Silver .1125 oz. ASW **Reverse:** Levoca **Note:** 4,338 pieces 4,300 Unc and 38 Proof, were melted by the Czech National Bank in 1997.

| Date | Mintage | F | VF | XF | Unc | BU |
|---|---|---|---|---|---|---|
| 1986 | 69,000 | — | — | — | 6.00 | — |
| 1986 Proof | 10,000 | Value: 11.50 | | | | |

**50 KORUN** KM# 127 **Weight:** 7.0000 g. **Composition:** 0.5000 Silver .1125 oz. ASW **Subject:** Environmental Protection **Reverse:** Przewalski's horses **Note:** 38 pieces Unc and Proof, were melted by the Czech National Bank in 1997.

| Date | Mintage | F | VF | XF | Unc | BU |
|---|---|---|---|---|---|---|
| 1987 | 55,000 | — | — | — | 10.00 | — |
| 1987 Proof | 5,000 | Value: 20.00 | | | | |

**50 KORUN** KM# 129 **Weight:** 7.0000 g. **Composition:** 0.5000 Silver .1125 oz. ASW **Subject:** 300th Anniversary - Birth of Juraj Janosik **Note:** 35 pieces Unc and Proof, were melted by the Czech National Bank in 1997.

| Date | Mintage | F | VF | XF | Unc | BU |
|---|---|---|---|---|---|---|
| ND (1988) | 53,000 | — | — | — | 7.00 | — |
| ND (1988) Proof | 5,000 | Value: 15.00 | | | | |

**50 KORUN** KM# 133 **Weight:** 7.0000 g. **Composition:** 0.5000 Silver .1125 oz. ASW **Subject:** 150th Anniversary - Breclav to Brno Railroad **Note:** 35 pieces Unc and Proof, were melted by the Czech National Bank in 1997.

| Date | Mintage | F | VF | XF | Unc | BU |
|---|---|---|---|---|---|---|
| ND (1989) | 67,000 | — | — | — | 7.00 | — |
| ND (1989) Proof | 3,000 | Value: 16.00 | | | | |

**100 KORUN** KM# 73 **Weight:** 15.0000 g. **Composition:** 0.7000 Silver .3376 oz. ASW **Subject:** Centennial - Death of Josef Manes **Note:** 6,403 pieces 6,300 Unc and 103 Proof, were melted by the Czech National Bank in 1997.

| Date | Mintage | F | VF | XF | Unc | BU |
|---|---|---|---|---|---|---|
| ND (1971) | 45,000 | — | — | 10.00 | 13.50 | — |
| ND (1971) Proof | 5,000 | Value: 17.50 | | | | |

**100 KORUN** KM# 82 **Weight:** 15.0000 g. **Composition:** 0.7000 Silver .3376 oz. ASW **Subject:** Sesquicentennial - Birth of Bedrich Smetana **Note:** 5,061 pieces 3,561 Unc and 1,500 Proof, were melted by the Czech National Bank in 1997.

| Date | Mintage | F | VF | XF | Unc | BU |
|---|---|---|---|---|---|---|
| ND (1974) | 75,000 | — | — | 10.00 | 12.00 | — |
| ND (1974) Proof | 5,000 | Value: 17.50 | | | | |

**100 KORUN** KM# 84 **Weight:** 15.0000 g. **Composition:** 0.7000 Silver .3376 oz. ASW **Subject:** Centennial - Death of Janko Kral **Note:** 19,039 pieces 13,500 Unc and 5,539 Proof, were melted by the Czech National Bank in 1997.

| Date | Mintage | F | VF | XF | Unc | BU |
|---|---|---|---|---|---|---|
| ND (1976) | 75,000 | — | — | 10.00 | 12.00 | — |
| ND (1976) Proof | 5,000 | Value: 17.50 | | | | |

**100 KORUN** KM# 85 **Weight:** 15.0000 g. **Composition:** 0.7000 Silver .3376 oz. ASW **Subject:** Centennial - Birth of Viktor Kaplan **Note:** 21,339 pieces 19,638 Unc and 1,7019 Proof, were melted by the Czech National Bank in 1997.

| Date | Mintage | F | VF | XF | Unc | BU |
|---|---|---|---|---|---|---|
| ND (1976) | 75,000 | — | — | 10.00 | 12.00 | — |
| ND (1976) Proof | 5,000 | Value: 17.50 | | | | |

**100 KORUN** KM# 88 **Weight:** 15.0000 g. **Composition:** 0.7000 Silver .3376 oz. ASW **Subject:** 300th Anniversary - Death of Wenceslas **Note:** 29,739 pieces, 27,240 Unc and 2,499 Proof, were melted by the Czech National Bank in 1997.

| Date | Mintage | F | VF | XF | Unc | BU |
|---|---|---|---|---|---|---|
| ND (1977) | 95,000 | — | — | 10.00 | 12.00 | — |
| ND (1977) Proof | 5,000 | Value: 17.50 | | | | |

**100 KORUN** KM# 93 **Weight:** 15.0000 g. **Composition:** 0.7000 Silver .3376 oz. ASW **Subject:** 600th Anniversary - Death of King Karel IV **Note:** 32,238 pieces, 32,238 Unc and 27,038 Proof, were melted by the Czech National Bank in 1997.

| Date | Mintage | F | VF | XF | Unc | BU |
|---|---|---|---|---|---|---|
| 1978 | 90,000 | — | — | 10.00 | 12.00 | — |
| 1978 Proof | 10,000 | Value: 17.50 | | | | |

**100 KORUN** KM# 92 **Weight:** 15.0000 g. **Composition:** 0.7000 Silver .3376 oz. ASW **Subject:** 75th Anniversary - Birth of Julius Fucik **Note:** 24,240 pieces, 22,040 Unc and 2,200 Proof, were melted by the Czech National Bank in 1997.

| Date | Mintage | F | VF | XF | Unc | BU |
|---|---|---|---|---|---|---|
| ND (1978) | 75,000 | — | — | 10.00 | 12.00 | — |
| ND (1978) Proof | 5,000 | Value: 17.50 | | | | |

**100 KORUN** KM# 99 **Weight:** 15.0000 g. **Composition:** 0.7000 Silver .3376 oz. ASW **Subject:** 150th Anniversary - Birth of Jan Botto **Note:** 24,240 pieces, 22,540 Unc and 1,800 Proof, were melted by the Czech National Bank in 1997.

| Date | Mintage | F | VF | XF | Unc | BU |
|---|---|---|---|---|---|---|
| ND (1979) | 75,000 | — | — | 10.00 | 12.00 | — |
| ND (1979) Proof | 5,000 | Value: 17.50 | | | | |

**100 KORUN** **KM# 102** **Weight:** 9.0000 g. **Composition:** 0.5000 Silver .1446 oz. ASW **Subject:** Centennial - Birth of Bohumir Smeral **Note:** 26,443 pieces, 23,443 Unc and 3,000 Proof, were melted by the Czech National Bank in 1997.

| Date | Mintage | F | VF | XF | Unc | BU |
|---|---|---|---|---|---|---|
| ND (1980) | 74,000 | — | — | — | 12.00 | — |
| ND (1980) Proof | 6,000 | Value: 17.50 | | | | |

**100 KORUN** **KM# 100** **Weight:** 15.0000 g. **Composition:** 0.7000 Silver .3376 oz. ASW **Subject:** 150th Anniversary - Birth of Peter Parler **Note:** 54,738 pieces, 50,038 Unc and 4,600 Proof, were melted by the Czech National Bank in 1997.

| Date | Mintage | F | VF | XF | Unc | BU |
|---|---|---|---|---|---|---|
| ND (1980) | 91,000 | — | — | 10.00 | 12.00 | — |
| ND (1980) Proof | 9,000 | Value: 17.50 | | | | |

**100 KORUN** **KM# 101** **Weight:** 9.0000 g. **Composition:** 0.5000 Silver .1446 oz. ASW **Subject:** Fifth Spartakiade Games **Note:** 45,541 pieces, 39,541 Unc and 6,000 Proof, were melted by the Czech National Bank in 1997.

| Date | Mintage | F | VF | XF | Unc | BU |
|---|---|---|---|---|---|---|
| 1980 | 110,000 | — | — | — | 12.00 | — |
| 1980 Proof | 10,000 | Value: 18.50 | | | | |

**100 KORUN** **KM# 104** **Weight:** 9.0000 g. **Composition:** 0.5000 Silver .1446 oz. ASW **Subject:** Centennial - Birth of Prof. Otakar Spaniel **Note:** 45,139 pieces, 42,239 Unc and 2,900 Proof, were melted by the Czech National Bank in 1997.

| Date | Mintage | F | VF | XF | Unc | BU |
|---|---|---|---|---|---|---|
| ND (1981) | 115,000 | — | — | — | 9.00 | — |
| ND (1981) Proof | 5,000 | Value: 17.50 | | | | |

**100 KORUN** **KM# 103** **Weight:** 9.0000 g. **Composition:** 0.5000 Silver .1446 oz. ASW **Subject:** 20th Anniversary - Manned Space Flight **Note:** 24,739 pieces, 24,539 Unc and 200 Proof, were melted by the Czech National Bank in 1997.

| Date | Mintage | F | VF | XF | Unc | BU |
|---|---|---|---|---|---|---|
| ND (1981) | 95,000 | — | — | — | 9.00 | — |
| ND (1981) Proof | 5,000 | Value: 17.50 | | | | |

**100 KORUN** **KM# 106** **Weight:** 9.0000 g. **Composition:** 0.5000 Silver .1446 oz. ASW **Subject:** Centennial - Birth of Ivan Olbracht **Note:** 16,140 pieces, 15,340 Unc and 800 Proof, were melted by the Czech National Bank in 1997.

| Date | Mintage | F | VF | XF | Unc | BU |
|---|---|---|---|---|---|---|
| ND (1982) | 76,000 | — | — | — | 12.00 | — |
| ND (1982) Proof | 4,000 | Value: 20.00 | | | | |

**100 KORUN** **KM# 107** **Weight:** 9.0000 g. **Composition:** 0.5000 Silver .1446 oz. ASW **Subject:** 150th Anniversary - Horse Drawn Railway **Note:** 9,139 pieces, 6,739 Unc and 2,400 Proof, were melted by the Czech National Bank in 1997.

| Date | Mintage | F | VF | XF | Unc | BU |
|---|---|---|---|---|---|---|
| ND (1982) | 76,000 | — | — | — | 12.00 | — |
| ND (1982) Proof | 7,000 | Value: 17.50 | | | | |

**100 KORUN** **KM# 110** **Weight:** 9.0000 g. **Composition:** 0.5000 Silver .1446 oz. ASW **Subject:** Centennial - Death of Samo Chalupka **Note:** 21,538 pieces, 19,938 Unc and 1,600 Proof, were melted by the Czech National Bank in 1997.

| Date | Mintage | F | VF | XF | Unc | BU |
|---|---|---|---|---|---|---|
| ND (1983) | 76,000 | — | — | — | 12.00 | — |
| ND (1983) Proof | 4,000 | Value: 20.00 | | | | |

**100 KORUN** **KM# 111** **Weight:** 9.0000 g. **Composition:** 0.5000 Silver .1446 oz. ASW **Subject:** 100th Anniversary of National Theater of Prague **Note:** 13,338 pieces, 7,738 Unc and 5,600 Proof, were melted by the Czech National Bank in 1997.

| Date | Mintage | F | VF | XF | Unc | BU |
|---|---|---|---|---|---|---|
| ND (1983) | 140,000 | — | — | — | 9.00 | — |
| ND (1983) Proof | 10,000 | Value: 17.50 | | | | |

**100 KORUN** **KM# 108** **Weight:** 9.0000 g. **Composition:** 0.5000 Silver .1446 oz. ASW **Subject:** 100th Anniversary - Death of Karl Marx **Note:** 15,343 pieces, 14,543 Unc and 800 Proof, were melted by the Czech National Bank in 1997.

| Date | Mintage | F | VF | XF | Unc | BU |
|---|---|---|---|---|---|---|
| ND (1983) | 76,000 | — | — | — | 12.00 | — |
| ND (1983) Proof | 4,000 | Value: 20.00 | | | | |

**100 KORUN** **KM# 109** **Weight:** 9.0000 g. **Composition:** 0.5000 Silver .1446 oz. ASW **Subject:** Centennial - Birth of Jaroslav Hasek **Note:** 15,638 pieces, 14,838 Unc and 800 Proof, were melted by the Czech National Bank in 1997.

| Date | Mintage | F | VF | XF | Unc | BU |
|---|---|---|---|---|---|---|
| ND (1983) | 76,000 | — | — | — | 12.00 | — |
| ND (1983) Proof | 4,000 | Value: 20.00 | | | | |

**100 KORUN** **KM# 115** **Weight:** 9.0000 g. **Composition:** 0.5000 Silver .1446 oz. ASW **Subject:** Centennial - Birth of Antonin Zapotocky **Note:** 13,038 pieces, 12,238 Unc and 800 Proof, were melted by the Czech National Bank in 1997.

| Date | Mintage | F | VF | XF | Unc | BU |
|---|---|---|---|---|---|---|
| ND (1984) | 76,000 | — | — | — | 12.00 | — |
| ND (1984) Proof | 4,000 | Value: 20.00 | | | | |

**100 KORUN** **KM# 113** **Weight:** 9.0000 g. **Composition:** 0.5000 Silver .1446 oz. ASW **Subject:** 300th Anniversary - Birth of Matej Bel **Note:** 438 pieces, 400 Unc and 38 Proof, were melted by the Czech National Bank in 1997.

| Date | Mintage | F | VF | XF | Unc | BU |
|---|---|---|---|---|---|---|
| ND (1984) | 57,000 | — | — | — | 12.00 | — |
| ND (1984) Proof | 3,000 | Value: 20.00 | | | | |

**100 KORUN** **KM# 114** **Weight:** 9.0000 g. **Composition:** 0.5000 Silver .1446 oz. ASW **Subject:** 150th Anniversary - Birth of Jan Neruda **Note:** 3,539 pieces, 2,739 Unc and 800 Proof, were melted by the Czech National Bank in 1997.

| Date | Mintage | F | VF | XF | Unc | BU |
|---|---|---|---|---|---|---|
| ND (1984) | 76,000 | — | — | — | 12.00 | — |
| ND (1984) Proof | 4,000 | Value: 20.00 | | | | |

**100 KORUN** **KM# 116** **Weight:** 9.0000 g. **Composition:** 0.5000 Silver .1446 oz. ASW **Subject:** 200th Anniversary - Birth of Jan Holly **Note:** 4,438 pieces, 4,400 Unc and 38 Proof, were melted by the Czech National Bank in 1997.

| Date | Mintage | F | VF | XF | Unc | BU |
|---|---|---|---|---|---|---|
| ND (1985) | 62,000 | — | — | — | 12.00 | — |
| ND (1985) Proof | 3,000 | Value: 20.00 | | | | |

**100 KORUN** **KM# 117** **Weight:** 9.0000 g. **Composition:** 0.5000 Silver .1446 oz. ASW **Subject:** 1985 Ice Hockey Championships **Note:** 38 pieces, Unc and Proof, were melted by the Czech National Bank in 1997.

| Date | Mintage | F | VF | XF | Unc | BU |
|---|---|---|---|---|---|---|
| 1985 | 66,000 | — | — | — | 12.00 | — |
| 1985 Proof | 4,000 | Value: 20.00 | | | | |

**100 KORUN** **KM# 118** **Weight:** 9.0000 g. **Composition:** 0.5000 Silver .1446 oz. ASW **Subject:** 125th Anniversary - Birth of Martin Kukucin **Note:** 6,238 pieces, 5,438 Unc and 800 Proof, were melted by the Czech National Bank in 1997.

| Date | Mintage | F | VF | XF | Unc | BU |
|---|---|---|---|---|---|---|
| ND (1985) | 62,000 | — | — | — | 12.00 | — |
| ND (1985) Proof | 3,000 | Value: 20.00 | | | | |

**100 KORUN** **KM# 120** **Weight:** 9.0000 g. **Composition:** 0.5000 Silver .1446 oz. ASW **Subject:** 250th Anniversary - Death of Petr Brandl **Note:** 8,938 pieces, 8,900 Unc and 38 Proof, were melted by the Czech National Bank in 1997.

| Date | Mintage | F | VF | XF | Unc | BU |
|---|---|---|---|---|---|---|
| ND (1985) | 71,000 | — | — | — | 10.00 | — |
| ND (1985) Proof | 4,000 | Value: 20.00 | | | | |

**100 KORUN** **KM# 119** **Weight:** 9.0000 g. **Composition:** 0.5000 Silver .1446 oz. ASW **Subject:** 10th Anniversary of Helsinki Conference **Note:** 11,938 pieces, 9,538 Unc and 2,400 Proof, were melted by the Czech National Bank in 1997.

| Date | Mintage | F | VF | XF | Unc | BU |
|---|---|---|---|---|---|---|
| ND (1985) | 75,000 | — | — | — | 10.00 | — |
| ND (1985) Proof | 5,000 | Value: 20.00 | | | | |

**100 KORUN** **KM# 123** **Weight:** 13.0000 g. **Composition:** 0.5000 Silver .2090 oz. ASW **Subject:** 150th Anniversary - Death of Karel Hynek Macha **Note:** 4,338 pieces, 4,300 Unc and 38 Proof, were melted by the Czech National Bank in 1997.

| Date | Mintage | F | VF | XF | Unc | BU |
|---|---|---|---|---|---|---|
| ND (1986) | 63,000 | — | — | — | 10.00 | — |
| ND (1986) Proof | 5,000 | Value: 20.00 | | | | |

**100 KORUN** **KM# 128** **Weight:** 13.0000 g. **Composition:** 0.5000 Silver .2090 oz. ASW **Subject:** 225th Anniversary of Mining Academy **Note:** 2,438 pieces, 2,400 Unc and 38 Proof, were melted by the Czech National Bank in 1997.

| Date | Mintage | F | VF | XF | Unc | BU |
|---|---|---|---|---|---|---|
| ND (1987) | 55,000 | — | — | — | 12.00 | — |
| ND (1987) Proof | 5,000 | Value: 22.50 | | | | |

**100 KORUN** **KM# 130** **Weight:** 13.0000 g. **Composition:** 0.5000 Silver .2090 oz. ASW **Subject:** Prague Philatelic Exposition **Note:** 7,035 pieces, 7,000 Unc and 35 Proof, were melted by the Czech National Bank in 1997.

| Date | Mintage | F | VF | XF | Unc | BU |
|---|---|---|---|---|---|---|
| 1988 | 66,000 | — | — | — | 12.00 | — |
| 1988 Proof | 5,000 | Value: 25.00 | | | | |

**100 KORUN** **KM# 132** **Weight:** 13.0000 g. **Composition:** 0.5000 Silver .2090 oz. ASW **Subject:** Centennial - Birth of Martin Benka **Note:** 7,035 pieces, 7,000 Unc and 35 Proof, were melted by the Czech National Bank in 1997.

| Date | Mintage | F | VF | XF | Unc | BU |
|---|---|---|---|---|---|---|
| ND (1988) | 55,000 | — | — | — | 12.00 | — |
| ND (1988) Proof | 5,000 | Value: 28.00 | | | | |

**100 KORUN** **KM# 135** **Weight:** 13.0000 g. **Composition:** 0.5000 Silver .2090 oz. ASW **Subject:** 50th Anniversary of Student Organization Against Occupation and Fascism **Note:** 35 pieces, Unc and Proof, were melted by the Czech National Bank in 1997.

| Date | Mintage | F | VF | XF | Unc | BU |
|---|---|---|---|---|---|---|
| ND (1989) | 67,000 | — | — | — | 14.00 | — |
| ND (1989) Proof | Est. 3,000 | Value: 25.00 | | | | |

**100 KORUN** **KM# 137** **Weight:** 13.0000 g. **Composition:** 0.5000 Silver .2090 oz. ASW **Subject:** 100th Anniversary - Birth of Karel Capek **Note:** 3,020 pieces, 2,020 Unc and 1,000 Proof, were melted by the Czech National Bank in 1997.

| Date | Mintage | F | VF | XF | Unc | BU |
|---|---|---|---|---|---|---|
| ND (1990) | 67,000 | — | — | — | 14.00 | — |
| ND (1990) Proof | 3,500 | Value: 25.00 | | | | |

**100 KORUN** **KM# 138** **Weight:** 13.0000 g. **Composition:** 0.5000 Silver .2090 oz. ASW **Subject:** 250th Anniversary - Death of Jan Kupecky **Note:** 3,020 pieces, 4,000 Unc and 20 Proof, were melted by the Czech National Bank in 1997.

| Date | Mintage | F | VF | XF | Unc | BU |
|---|---|---|---|---|---|---|
| ND (1990) | 58,000 | — | — | — | 14.00 | — |
| ND (1990) Proof | 2,500 | Value: 28.00 | | | | |

**Note:** KM#165-166 previously listed here were sold by the National Bank as medals and have been removed

**500 KORUN** **KM# 105** **Weight:** 24.0000 g. **Composition:** 0.9000 Silver .6944 oz. ASW **Subject:** 125th Anniversary - Death of Ludovit Stur **Note:** 5,657 pieces, 4,057 Unc and 1,600 Proof, were melted by the Czech National Bank in 1997.

| Date | Mintage | F | VF | XF | Unc | BU |
|---|---|---|---|---|---|---|
| ND (1981) | 51,000 | — | — | — | 35.00 | — |
| ND (1981) Proof | 4,000 | Value: 65.00 | | | | |

**500 KORUN** **KM# 112** **Weight:** 24.0000 g. **Composition:** 0.9000 Silver .6944 oz. ASW **Subject:** 100th Anniversary of Prague Theaster **Note:** 3,640 pieces, 2,040 Unc and 1,600 Proof, were melted by the Czech National Bank in 1997.

| Date | Mintage | F | VF | XF | Unc | BU |
|---|---|---|---|---|---|---|
| ND (1983) | 55,000 | — | — | — | 40.00 | — |
| ND (1983) Proof | 5,000 | Value: 75.00 | | | | |

**500 KORUN** **KM# 136** **Weight:** 24.0000 g. **Composition:** 0.9000 Silver .6944 oz. ASW **Subject:** 100th Anniversary - Birth of Josef Lada **Note:** 838 pieces, 800 Unc and 38 Proof, were melted by the Czech National Bank in 1997.

| Date | Mintage | F | VF | XF | Unc | BU |
|---|---|---|---|---|---|---|
| ND (1987) | 45,000 | — | — | — | 45.00 | — |
| ND (1987) Proof | 5,000 | Value: 70.00 | | | | |

**500 KORUN** **KM# 131** **Weight:** 24.0000 g. **Composition:** 0.9000 Silver .6944 oz. ASW **Subject:** 20th Anniversary of National Federation **Note:** 5,035 pieces, 5,000 Unc and 35 Proof, were melted by the Czech National Bank in 1997.

| Date | Mintage | F | VF | XF | Unc | BU |
|---|---|---|---|---|---|---|
| ND (1988) | 46,000 | — | — | — | 40.00 | — |
| ND (1988) Proof | 3,000 | Value: 75.00 | | | | |

**500 KORUN** **KM# 134** **Weight:** 24.0000 g. **Composition:** 0.9000 Silver .6944 oz. ASW **Subject:** 125th Anniversary of Matica Slovenska Institute **Note:** 5,038 pieces, 5,000 Unc and 38 Proof, were melted by the Czech National Bank in 1997.

| Date | Mintage | F | VF | XF | Unc | BU |
|---|---|---|---|---|---|---|
| ND (1988) | 44,000 | — | — | — | 40.00 | — |
| ND (1988) Proof | 5,000 | Value: 70.00 | | | | |

# CZECH SLOVAK FEDERAL REPUBLIC

## DECIMAL COINAGE

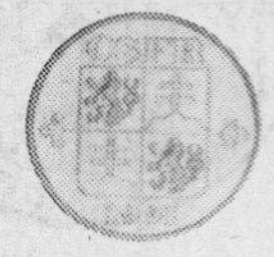

**HALER** **KM# 149** **Composition:** Aluminum

| Date | Mintage | F | VF | XF | Unc | BU |
|---|---|---|---|---|---|---|
| 1991 | 55,000 | — | — | — | 0.10 | — |
| 1992 | 50,000 | — | — | — | 0.10 | — |

**5 HALERU** **KM# 150** **Composition:** Aluminum

| Date | Mintage | F | VF | XF | Unc | BU |
|---|---|---|---|---|---|---|
| 1991 | 10,055,000 | — | — | 0.10 | 0.25 | — |
| 1992 In mint set only | 50,000 | — | — | — | 0.25 | — |

**10 HALERU** **KM# 146** **Composition:** Aluminum

| Date | Mintage | F | VF | XF | Unc | BU |
|---|---|---|---|---|---|---|
| 1991 In mint sets only | 55,000 | — | — | — | 0.50 | — |
| 1992 In mint sets only | 50,000 | — | — | — | 0.50 | — |

**20 HALERU** **KM# 143** **Composition:** Aluminum-Bronze

| Date | Mintage | F | VF | XF | Unc | BU |
|---|---|---|---|---|---|---|
| 1991 | 41,105,000 | — | — | 0.20 | 0.50 | — |
| 1992 | 35,050,000 | — | — | 0.20 | 0.50 | — |

**50 HALERU** **KM# 144** **Composition:** Copper-Nickel

| Date | Mintage | F | VF | XF | Unc | BU |
|---|---|---|---|---|---|---|
| 1991 | 24,463,000 | — | — | 0.35 | 0.75 | — |
| 1992 | 15,062,000 | — | — | 0.35 | 0.75 | — |

**KORUNA** **KM# 151** **Composition:** Copper-Aluminum

| Date | Mintage | F | VF | XF | Unc | BU |
|---|---|---|---|---|---|---|
| 1991 | 20,056,000 | — | — | 0.50 | 1.00 | — |
| 1992 | 20,387,000 | — | — | 0.50 | 1.00 | — |

**2 KORUNY** **KM# 148** **Composition:** Copper-Nickel

| Date | Mintage | F | VF | XF | Unc | BU |
|---|---|---|---|---|---|---|
| 1991(k) | 25,201,000 | — | — | 0.60 | 1.25 | — |
| 1991(l) | 20,000,000 | — | — | 0.60 | 1.25 | — |
| 1992 | 1,051,000 | — | — | — | 1.25 | — |

**5 KORUN** **KM# 152** **Composition:** Copper-Nickel

| Date | Mintage | F | VF | XF | Unc | BU |
|---|---|---|---|---|---|---|
| 1991(l) | 10,000,750 | — | — | — | — | — |
| 1991(k) | 18,564,000 | — | — | 0.75 | 2.00 | — |
| 1992 In mint sets only | 50,000 | — | — | 0.75 | 2.00 | — |

**10 KORUN** **KM# 139.1** **Composition:** Nickel-Bronze **Reverse:** Tomas G. Masaryk **Note:** Designer initials below bust, varieties exist.

| Date | Mintage | F | VF | XF | Unc | BU |
|---|---|---|---|---|---|---|
| 1990 | 9,990,000 | — | — | 2.00 | 5.00 | — |
| 1992 In sets only | — | — | — | — | — | — |
| 1993 | 2,500,000 | — | — | 2.50 | 7.00 | — |

**10 KORUN** **KM# 139.2** **Composition:** Nickel-Bronze **Obverse:** Tomas G. Masaryk **Note:** Designer name below bust: RONAI.

| Date | Mintage | F | VF | XF | Unc | BU |
|---|---|---|---|---|---|---|
| 1990 | Inc. above | — | 2.00 | 5.00 | 10.00 | — |

**10 KORUN** **KM# 153** **Composition:** Nickel-Bronze **Reverse:** M. R. Stefanik

| Date | Mintage | F | VF | XF | Unc | BU |
|---|---|---|---|---|---|---|
| 1991 | 10,036,000 | — | — | 2.00 | 5.00 | — |
| 1993 | 2,500,000 | — | — | 2.50 | 7.00 | — |

**10 KORUN** **KM# 159** **Composition:** Nickel-Bronze **Reverse:** A. Rasin

| Date | Mintage | F | VF | XF | Unc | BU |
|---|---|---|---|---|---|---|
| 1992 | 5,050,000 | — | — | 2.00 | 5.00 | — |

**50 KORUN** **KM# 140.2** **Weight:** 7.0200 g. **Composition:** 0.5000 Silver .1125 oz. ASW **Reverse:** W/o LK (designer initials) **Note:** 20 pieces, Unc and Proof of either KM#140.1 or 140.2, were melted by the Czech National Bank in 1977.

| Date | Mintage | F | VF | XF | Unc | BU |
|---|---|---|---|---|---|---|
| 1990 | Inc. above | — | — | — | 10.00 | — |

**50 KORUN** **KM# 140.1** **Weight:** 7.0200 g. **Composition:** 0.5000 Silver .1125 oz. ASW **Reverse:** St. Agnes (Anezka) **Note:** See note with KM#140.2. Designer emblem exists with and without initials.

| Date | Mintage | F | VF | XF | Unc | BU |
|---|---|---|---|---|---|---|
| 1990 | 147,000 | — | — | — | 7.00 | — |
| 1990 Proof | 3,000 | Value: 18.00 | | | | |

**50 KORUN** **KM# 145** **Weight:** 7.0200 g. **Composition:** 0.5000 Silver .1125 oz. ASW **Reverse:** Steamship Bohemia **Note:** 20 pieces, Unc and Proof, were melted by the Czech National Bank in 1977.

| Date | Mintage | F | VF | XF | Unc | BU |
|---|---|---|---|---|---|---|
| CDND (1991) | 77,000 | — | — | — | 7.00 | — |
| ND (1991) Proof | 3,000 | Value: 18.00 | | | | |

**50 KORUN** **KM# 157** **Weight:** 7.0000 g. **Composition:** 0.7000 Silver .1575 oz. ASW **Reverse:** Karlovy Vary S pa **Note:** 11,020, pieces, 10,020 Unc and 1,000 Proof, were melted by the Czech National Bank in 1977.

| Date | Mintage | F | VF | XF | Unc | BU |
|---|---|---|---|---|---|---|
| 1991 | 75,000 | — | — | — | 7.50 | — |
| 1991 Proof | 5,000 | Value: 16.50 | | | | |

**50 KORUN** **KM# 156** **Weight:** 7.0000 g. **Composition:** 0.7000 Silver .1575 oz. ASW **Reverse:** Marianske Lazne Spa **Note:** 13,520 pieces, 12,020 Unc and 1,500 Proof, were melted by the Czech National Bank in 1977.

| Date | Mintage | F | VF | XF | Unc | BU |
|---|---|---|---|---|---|---|
| 1991 | 75,000 | — | — | — | 7.50 | — |
| 1991 Proof | 5,000 | Value: 16.50 | | | | |

**50 KORUN** **KM# 155** **Weight:** 7.0000 g. **Composition:** 0.7000 Silver .1575 oz. ASW **Reverse:** Piestany Spa **Note:** 13,520 pieces, 12,020 Unc and 2,000 Proof, were melted by the Czech National Bank in 1977.

| Date | Mintage | F | VF | XF | Unc | BU |
|---|---|---|---|---|---|---|
| 1991 | 75,000 | — | — | — | 7.50 | — |
| 1991 | Est. 5,000 | Value: 16.50 | | | | |

**Note:** @06*NOTE: @0513,520 pieces, 12,020 Unc and 2,000 Proof, were melted by the Czech National Bank in 1997.

**100 KORUN** **KM# 141** **Weight:** 13.0000 g. **Composition:** 0.5000 Silver .2090 oz. ASW **Subject:** Steeple Chase in Pardubice **Note:** 20 pieces, Unc and Proof, were melted by the Czech National Bank in 1977.

| Date | Mintage | F | VF | XF | Unc | BU |
|---|---|---|---|---|---|---|
| 1990 | 67,000 | — | — | — | 15.00 | — |
| 1990 Proof | 3,000 | Value: 25.00 | | | | |

**100 KORUN** **KM# 142** **Weight:** 13.0000 g. **Composition:** 0.5000 Silver .2090 oz. ASW **Reverse:** Bohuslav Martinu **Note:** 20 pieces, Unc and Proof, were melted by the Czech National Bank in 1977.

| Date | Mintage | F | VF | XF | Unc | BU |
|---|---|---|---|---|---|---|
| ND (1990) | 53,000 | — | — | — | 15.00 | — |
| ND (1990) Proof | 2,000 | Value: 22.00 | | | | |

**100 KORUN** **KM# 154** **Weight:** 13.0000 g. **Composition:** 0.5000 Silver .2926 oz. ASW **Reverse:** Mozart **Note:** 1,020 pieces, 1,000 Unc and 20 Proof, were melted by the Czech National Bank in 1977.

| Date | Mintage | F | VF | XF | Unc | BU |
|---|---|---|---|---|---|---|
| ND (1991) | 75,000 | — | — | — | 12.00 | — |
| ND (1991) Proof | 5,000 | Value: 20.00 | | | | |

**100 KORUN** **KM# 147** **Weight:** 13.0000 g. **Composition:** 0.5000 Silver .2926 oz. ASW **Reverse:** Antonin Dvorak **Note:** 12,020 pieces, 10,029 Unc and 2,000 Proof, were melted by the Czech National Bank in 1977.

| Date | Mintage | F | VF | XF | Unc | BU |
|---|---|---|---|---|---|---|
| 1991 | 75,000 | — | — | — | 12.00 | — |
| 1991 Proof | Est. 5,000 | Value: 20.00 | | | | |

**100 KORUN** **KM# 161** **Weight:** 13.0000 g. **Composition:** 0.5000 Silver .2926 oz. ASW **Subject:** Nazi Massacres at Lidice and Lezaky **Note:** 22,020 pieces, 22,000 Unc and 20 Proof, were melted by the Czech National Bank in 1977.

| Date | Mintage | F | VF | XF | Unc | BU |
|---|---|---|---|---|---|---|
| 1992 | 70,000 | — | — | — | 10.00 | — |
| 1992 Proof | 3,000 | Value: 22.00 | | | | |

**100 KORUN** **KM# 160** **Weight:** 13.0000 g. **Composition:** 0.5000 Silver .2926 oz. ASW **Reverse:** Moravian Museum **Note:** 23,877 pieces, Unc and Proof, were melted by the Czech National Bank in 1977.

| Date | Mintage | F | VF | XF | Unc | BU |
|---|---|---|---|---|---|---|
| 1992 | 73,000 | — | — | — | 10.00 | — |
| 1992 Proof | 5,000 | Value: 22.00 | | | | |

**100 KORUN** **KM# 162** **Weight:** 13.0000 g. **Composition:** 0.5000 Silver .2926 oz. ASW **Subject:** 1000 Years of Brevnovsky Monastery **Note:** 24,132 pieces, 24,000 Unc and 132 Proof, were melted by the Czech National Bank in 1977.

| Date | Mintage | F | VF | XF | Unc | BU |
|---|---|---|---|---|---|---|
| ND (1993) | 70,000 | — | — | — | 8.00 | — |
| ND (1993) Proof | 3,000 | Value: 22.00 | | | | |

**100 KORUN** **KM# 163** **Weight:** 13.0000 g. **Composition:** 0.5000 Silver .2926 oz. ASW **Subject:** Society for Slovakian Museum **Note:** 30,132 pieces, 30,000 Unc and 132 Proof, were melted by the Czech National Bank in 1977.

| Date | Mintage | F | VF | XF | Unc | BU |
|---|---|---|---|---|---|---|
| ND (1993) | 70,000 | — | — | — | 8.00 | — |
| ND (1993) Proof | 3,000 | Value: 22.00 | | | | |

**500 KORUN** KM# 158 **Weight:** 24.0000 g. **Composition:** 0.9000 Silver .6944 oz. ASW **Subject:** 400th Anniversary - Birth of J. A. Komensky **Note:** 12,020 pieces, 10,020 Unc and 2000 Proof, were melted by the Czech National Bank in 1977.

| Date | Mintage | F | VF | XF | Unc | BU |
|---|---|---|---|---|---|---|
| 1992 | 60,000 | — | — | — | 32.50 | — |
| 1992 Proof | 5,000 | Value: 55.00 | | | | |

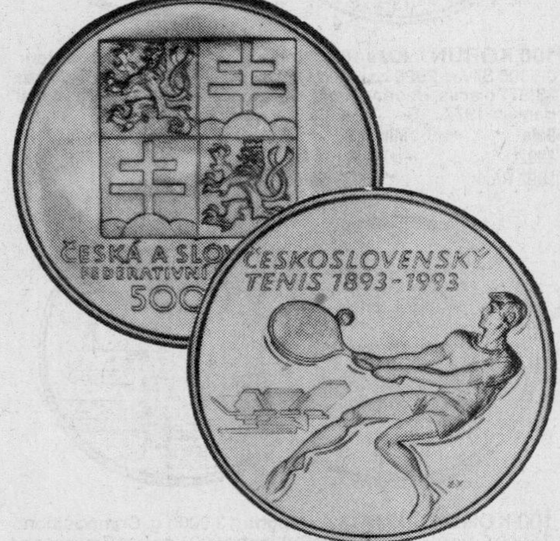


**500 KORUN** KM# 164 **Weight:** 24.0000 g. **Composition:** 0.9000 Silver .6944 oz. ASW **Subject:** 100th year of Czech Tennis **Note:** 18,174 pieces, 18,042 Unc and 132 Proof, were melted by the Czech National Bank in 1977.

| Date | Mintage | F | VF | XF | Unc | BU |
|---|---|---|---|---|---|---|
| ND (1993) | 62,000 | — | — | — | 35.00 | — |
| ND (1993) Proof | 3,000 | Value: 65.00 | | | | |

## PROBA

| KM# | Date | Mintage | Identification | Mkt Val |
|---|---|---|---|---|
| Pr1 | 1922 | — | Koruna. Aluminum. | — |
| Pr2 | 1922 | — | Koruna. Copper-Nickel. | — |
| Pr4 | 1932 | 2 | 25 Haleru. Copper-Nickel. W/dense notches. | — |
| Pr5 | 1932 | 2 | 25 Haleru. Copper-Nickel. Thin notches. | — |
| Pr6 | 1932 | 10 | 25 Haleru. Copper-Nickel. | — |
| Pr3 | 1951 | — | 5 Koruna. Aluminum-Copper Magnesium. | — |
| Pr7 | 1976 | — | 3 Koruny. | — |
| Pr8 | | 2,500 | 100 Korun. | 100 |

## MINT SETS

| KM# | Date | Mintage | Identification | Issue Price | Mkt Val |
|---|---|---|---|---|---|
| MS2 | 1981 (7) | 66,000 | KM50, 60, 74-75, 80, 86, 89 | — | 3.50 |
| MS1 | 1980 (7) | 50,000 | KM50, 60, 74-75, 80, 86, 89 | 5.00 | 3.50 |
| MS3 | 1982 (7) | 53,000 | KM50, 60, 74-75, 80, 86, 89 | — | 6.50 |
| MS4 | 1983 (7) | 50,000 | KM50, 60, 74-75, 80, 86, 89 | — | 3.50 |
| MS5 | 1984 (7) | 39,000 | KM50, 60, 74-75, 80, 86, 89 | — | 6.50 |
| MS6 | 1985 (7) | 39,000 | KM50, 60, 74-75, 80, 86, 89 | — | 6.50 |
| MS7 | 1986 (7) | 20,000 | KM50, 60, 74-75, 80, 86, 89 | — | 10.00 |
| MS8 | 1987 (7) | 30,000 | km50, 60, 74-75, 80, 86, 89 | — | 10.00 |
| MS9 | 1988 (7) | 29,000 | KM50, 60, 74-75, 80, 86, 89 | — | 10.00 |
| MS10 | 1989 (7) | 30,000 | KM50, 60, 74-75, 80, 86, 89 | — | 10.00 |
| MS11 | 1990 (7) | 30,000 | KM50, 60, 74-75, 80, 86, 89 | — | 10.00 |
| MS12 | 1991 (9) | 25,000 | KM143-144, 146, 148-153 | — | 10.00 |
| MS13 | 1991 (8) | 30,000 | KM143-144, 146, 148-152 | — | 6.00 |
| MS14 | 1992 (9) | 49,000 | KM143-144, 146, 148-152, 159 | — | 10.00 |
| MS15 | 1992 (8) | 49,000 | KM143-144,146, 148-152 | — | 6.00 |

## PROOF SETS

| KM# | Date | Mintage | Identification | Issue Price | Mkt Val |
|---|---|---|---|---|---|
| PS1 | 1966 (4) | — | KM49.1, 53, 57, 60 | — | — |
| PS2 | 1981 (7) | — | KM50, 60, 74-75, 80, 86, 89 | — | — |

# DAHOMEY

Porto-Novo, on the Bight of Benin, was founded as a trading post by the Portuguese in the 17th century. At that time, Dahomey (Benin) was composed of an aggregation of mutually suspicious tribes, the majority of which were tributary to the powerful northern Kingdom of Abomey. In 1863, the King of Porto-Novo petitioned France for protection from Abomey. The French subjugated other militant tribes as well, and in 1892 organized the area as a protectorate of France; in 1904 it was incorporated into French West Africa as the Territory of Dahomey. After the establishment of the Fifth French Republic, the Territory at Dahomey became an autonomous state within the French community. On Aug. 1, 1960, it became the fully independent Republic of Dahomey. In 1974, the republic began a transition to a socialist society with Marxism-Leninism as its revolutionary philosophy under Col. Ahmed Kerekou. On Nov. 30, 1975, the name of the Republic of Dahomey was changed to the Peoples Republic of Benin. As a result of Benin's first free presidential election in 30 years, Nicephore Soglo defeated Colonel Kerekou.

**MINT MARKS**

1 AR - Uno-A-Erre, Arezzo, Italy

## REPUBLIC

### STANDARD COINAGE

**100 FRANCS** KM# 1.1 **Weight:** 5.1000 g. **Composition:** 0.9990 Silver .1638 oz. ASW **Subject:** 10th Anniversary of Independence **Obverse:** Hallmark "999.9" above denomination

| Date | Mintage | F | VF | XF | Unc | BU |
|---|---|---|---|---|---|---|
| 1971 Proof | 4,650 | Value: 17.50 | | | | |

**100 FRANCS** KM# 1.2 **Weight:** 5.1000 g. **Composition:** 0.9990 Silver .1638 oz. ASW **Obverse:** Hallmark "999.9" right of denomination

| Date | Mintage | F | VF | XF | Unc | BU |
|---|---|---|---|---|---|---|
| 1971 Proof | Inc. above | Value: 17.50 | | | | |

**100 FRANCS** KM# 1.3 **Weight:** 5.1000 g. **Composition:** 0.9990 Silver .1638 oz. ASW **Obverse:** Hallmark "1000" lower right S in FRANCS

| Date | Mintage | F | VF | XF | Unc | BU |
|---|---|---|---|---|---|---|
| 1971 Proof | Inc. above | Value: 17.50 | | | | |

**200 FRANCS** KM# 2.1 **Weight:** 10.2500 g. **Composition:** 0.9990 Silver .3292 oz. ASW **Subject:** 10th Anniversary of Independence **Obverse:** Hallmark "999.9" between 200 and FRANCS

| Date | Mintage | F | VF | XF | Unc | BU |
|---|---|---|---|---|---|---|
| 1971 Proof | 5,150 | Value: 27.50 | | | | |

**200 FRANCS** KM# 2.2 **Weight:** 10.2500 g. **Composition:** 0.9990 Silver .3292 oz. ASW **Obverse:** Hallmark "1000" lower right of S in FRANCS

| Date | Mintage | F | VF | XF | Unc | BU |
|---|---|---|---|---|---|---|
| 1971 Proof | Inc. above | Value: 27.50 | | | | |

**200 FRANCS** KM# 2.3 **Weight:** 10.2500 g. **Composition:** 0.9990 Silver .3292 oz. ASW **Obverse:** Hallmark "999.9" lower right of S in FRANCS

| Date | Mintage | F | VF | XF | Unc | BU |
|---|---|---|---|---|---|---|
| 1971 Proof | Inc. above | Value: 27.50 | | | | |

**200 FRANCS** KM# 2.4 **Weight:** 10.2500 g. **Composition:** 0.9990 Silver .3292 oz. ASW **Obverse:** Hallmark "999.9" in oval below "F" in "CFA".

| Date | Mintage | F | VF | XF | Unc | BU |
|---|---|---|---|---|---|---|
| 1971 Proof | Inc. above | Value: 50.00 | | | | |

**500 FRANCS** KM# 3.1 **Weight:** 25.2000 g. **Composition:** 0.9990 Silver .8094 oz. ASW **Subject:** 10th Anniversary of Independence **Obverse:** "1000" in oval below "S" in FRANCS

| Date | Mintage | F | VF | XF | Unc | BU |
|---|---|---|---|---|---|---|
| 1971 Proof | 5,550 | Value: 75.00 | | | | |

**500 FRANCS** **KM# 3.2** **Weight:** 25.2000 g. **Composition:** 0.9990 Silver .8094 oz. ASW **Obverse:** "1 AR" and "1000" to right of CFA

| Date | Mintage | F | VF | XF | Unc | BU |
|---|---|---|---|---|---|---|
| 1971 Proof | Inc. above | Value: 75.00 | | | | |

**1000 FRANCS** **KM# 4.1** **Weight:** 51.5000 g. **Composition:** 0.9990 Silver 1.6542 oz. ASW **Subject:** 10th Anniversary of Independence **Obverse:** Similar to 500 Francs, KM#3.1

| Date | Mintage | F | VF | XF | Unc | BU |
|---|---|---|---|---|---|---|
| 1971 Proof | 6,500 | Value: 125 | | | | |

**1000 FRANCS** **KM# 4.2** **Weight:** 51.5000 g. **Composition:** 0.9990 Silver 1.6542 oz. ASW **Obverse:** Similar to 500 Francs, KM#3.2

| Date | Mintage | F | VF | XF | Unc | BU |
|---|---|---|---|---|---|---|
| 1971 Proof | Inc. above | Value: 125 | | | | |

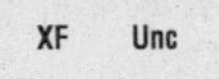

**2500 FRANCS** **KM# 6** **Weight:** 8.8800 g. **Composition:** 0.9000 Gold .2569 oz. AGW **Subject:** 10th Anniversary of Independence **Reverse:** Dancers

| Date | Mintage | F | VF | XF | Unc | BU |
|---|---|---|---|---|---|---|
| 1971 Proof | 960 | Value: 220 | | | | |

**5000 FRANCS** **KM# 7** **Weight:** 17.7700 g. **Composition:** 0.9000 Gold .5142 oz. AGW **Subject:** 10th Anniversary of Independence **Obverse:** Similar to 2500 Francs, KM#6 **Reverse:** Water Buffalos

| Date | Mintage | F | VF | XF | Unc | BU |
|---|---|---|---|---|---|---|
| 1971 Proof | 610 | Value: 425 | | | | |

**10000 FRANCS** **KM# 8** **Weight:** 35.5500 g. **Composition:** 0.9000 Gold 1.0287 oz. AGW **Subject:** 10th Anniversary of Independence **Obverse:** Similar to 2500 Francs, KM#6 **Reverse:** Hippopotamuses

| Date | Mintage | F | VF | XF | Unc | BU |
|---|---|---|---|---|---|---|
| 1971 Proof | 470 | Value: 825 | | | | |

**25000 FRANCS** **KM# 9** **Weight:** 88.8800 g. **Composition:** 0.9000 Gold 2.5720 oz. AGW **Subject:** 10th Anniversary of Independence **Obverse:** Similar to 2500 Francs, KM#6 **Reverse:** Presidents

| Date | Mintage | F | VF | XF | Unc | BU |
|---|---|---|---|---|---|---|
| 1971 Proof | 380 | Value: 1,450 | | | | |

## PROOF SETS

| KM# | Date | Mintage | Identification | Issue Price | Mkt Val |
|---|---|---|---|---|---|
| PS1 | 1971 (8) | 380 | KM#1-4, 6-9 | — | 3,175 |
| PS2 | 1971 (4) | 4,270 | KM1-4 | 36.00 | 250 |

# DANISH WEST INDIES

The Danish West Indies (now the U.S. organized unincorporated territory of the Virgin Islands of the United States) consisted of the islands of St. Thomas, St. John, St. Croix, and 62 islets in the Caribbean Sea roughly 40 miles (64 km.) east of Puerto Rico. The islands have a combined area of 133 sq. mi. (352 sq. km.) and a population of *106,000. Capital: Charlotte Amalie. Tourism is the principal industry. Watch movements, costume jewelry, pharmaceuticals, and rum are exported.

The Virgin Islands were discovered by Columbus, in 1493, during his second voyage to America. During the 17th century, individual islands, actually the peaks of a submerged mountain range, were held by Spain, Holland, England, France and Denmark. These islands were also the favorite resorts of the buccaneers operating in the Caribbean and the coastal waters of eastern North America. Control of most of the 100-island group finally passed to Denmark, with England securing the easterly remainder. The Danish islands had their own coinage from the early 18th century, based on but unequal to, Denmark's homeland system. In the late 18th and early 19th centuries, Danish minor copper and silver coinage augmented the islands currency. The Danish islands were purchased by the United States in 1917 for $25 million, mainly to forestall their acquisition by Germany and because they command the Anegada Passage into the Caribbean Sea, a strategic point on the defense perimeter of the Panama Canal.

**RULERS**
Danish, until 1917

**MINTMASTERS INITIALS**
See Denmark

**MONETARY SYSTEM**

(From 1904)
5 Bit = 1 Cent
5 Francs = 1 Daler

## DANISH COLONY

### DECIMAL COINAGE

20 Cents = 1 Franc

**1/2 CENT (2-1/2 Bit)** **KM# 74** **Composition:** Bronze **Note:** Mintmaster's initial: P. Moneyer's initials: GJ.

| Date | Mintage | VG | F | VF | XF | Unc |
|---|---|---|---|---|---|---|
| 1905(h) | 190,000 | — | 3.50 | 5.50 | 12.50 | 22.50 |
| 1905(h) Prooflike, rare | — | — | — | — | — | — |

**CENT (5 Bit)** **KM# 75** **Composition:** Bronze **Note:** Mintmaster's initial: P. Moneyer's initials: GJ.

| Date | Mintage | VG | F | VF | XF | Unc |
|---|---|---|---|---|---|---|
| 1905(h) | 500,000 | — | 3.50 | 7.50 | 18.50 | 36.50 |

**CENT (5 Bit)** **KM# 83** **Composition:** Bronze **Note:** Mintmaster's initials: VBP. Moneyer's initials: AH-GJ.

| Date | Mintage | VG | F | VF | XF | Unc |
|---|---|---|---|---|---|---|
| 1913(h) | 200,000 | — | 10.00 | 17.50 | 37.50 | 60.00 |

**2 CENTS (10 Bit)** **KM# 76** **Composition:** Bronze **Note:** Mintmaster's initial: P. Moneyer's initials: GJ.

| Date | Mintage | VG | F | VF | XF | Unc |
|---|---|---|---|---|---|---|
| 1905(h) | 150,000 | — | 5.00 | 13.50 | 28.50 | 50.00 |
| 1905(h) Prooflike, rare | 20 | — | — | — | — | — |

**5 CENTS (25 Bit)** **KM# 77** **Composition:** Nickel **Note:** Mintmaster's initial: P. Moneyer's initials: GJ.

| Date | Mintage | VG | F | VF | XF | Unc |
|---|---|---|---|---|---|---|
| 1905(h) | 199,000 | — | 2.50 | 7.00 | 18.50 | 47.50 |
| 1905(h) Prooflike, rare | 20 | — | — | — | — | — |

**10 CENTS (50 Bit)** **KM# 78** **Weight:** 2.5000 g. **Composition:** 0.8000 Silver .0643 oz. ASW **Note:** Mintmaster's initial: P. Moneyer's initials: GJ.

| Date | Mintage | VG | F | VF | XF | Unc |
|---|---|---|---|---|---|---|
| 1905(h) | 175,000 | — | 3.50 | 8.50 | 18.50 | 47.50 |
| 1905(h) Prooflike, rare | 20 | — | — | — | — | — |

**20 CENTS (1 Franc)** **KM# 79** **Weight:** 5.0000 g. **Composition:** 0.8000 Silver .1286 oz. ASW **Note:** Mintmaster's initial: P. Moneyer's initials: GJ.

| Date | Mintage | VG | F | VF | XF | Unc |
|---|---|---|---|---|---|---|
| 1905(h) | 150,000 | — | 12.50 | 30.00 | 65.00 | 110 |
| 1905(h) Prooflike, rare | 20 | — | — | — | — | — |

**20 CENTS (1 Franc)** **KM# 81** **Weight:** 5.0000 g. **Composition:** 0.8000 Silver .1286 oz. ASW **Note:** Mintmaster's initial: P. Moneyer's initials: GJ.

| Date | Mintage | VG | F | VF | XF | Unc |
|---|---|---|---|---|---|---|
| 1907(h) | 101,000 | — | 15.00 | 32.50 | 80.00 | 135 |
| 1907(h) Prooflike, rare | 10 | — | — | — | — | — |

**40 CENTS (2 Francs)** **KM# 80** **Weight:** 10.0000 g. **Composition:** 0.8000 Silver .2572 oz. ASW **Note:** Mintmaster's initial: P. Moneyer's initials: GJ.

| Date | Mintage | VG | F | VF | XF | Unc |
|---|---|---|---|---|---|---|
| 1905(h) | 38,000 | — | 30.00 | 60.00 | 135 | 235 |
| 1905(h) Prooflike, rare | 20 | — | — | — | — | — |

**40 CENTS (2 Francs)** **KM# 82** **Weight:** 10.0000 g. **Composition:** 0.8000 Silver .2572 oz. ASW **Note:** Mintmaster's initial: P. Moneyer's initials: GJ.

| Date | Mintage | VG | F | VF | XF | Unc |
|---|---|---|---|---|---|---|
| 1907(h) | 25,000 | — | 50.00 | 115 | 185 | 300 |
| 1907(h) | 10 | — | — | — | — | — |

**4 DALER (20 Francs)** **KM# 72** **Weight:** 6.4516 g. **Composition:** 0.9000 Gold .1867 oz. AGW **Note:** Mintmaster's initial: P. Moneyer's initials: GJ.

| Date | Mintage | F | VF | XF | Unc | BU |
|---|---|---|---|---|---|---|
| 1904(h) | 121,000 | 150 | 250 | 350 | 575 | — |
| 1905(h) | Inc. above | 150 | 275 | 400 | 675 | — |

**10 DALER (50 Francs)** **KM# 73** **Weight:** 16.1290 g. **Composition:** 0.9000 Gold .4667 oz. AGW **Note:** Mintmaster's initial: P. Moneyer's initials: GJ.

| Date | Mintage | F | VF | XF | Unc | BU |
|---|---|---|---|---|---|---|
| 1904(h) | 2,005 | 1,250 | 2,000 | 4,200 | 6,750 | — |

## TRIAL STRIKES

| KM# | Date | Mintage | Identification | Mkt Val |
|---|---|---|---|---|
| TS1 | 1904 | — | 20 Francs. Copper. 10.8000 g. KM#72. | — |
| TS2 | 1904 | — | 20 Francs. Copper. 10.8000 g. KM#72. | — |

## PROOF-LIKE SETS (PL)

| KM# | Date | Mintage | Identification | Issue Price | Mkt Val |
|---|---|---|---|---|---|
| PL2 | 1862 (2) | — | | — | — |
| PL3 | 1878 | — | | — | — |
| PL1 | 1859 (5) | 10 | KM#63-67 | — | — |
| PL4 | 1905 (5) | 20 | KM#76-80 | — | — |
| PL5 | 1907 (2) | 10 | KM#81-82 | — | — |

The Kingdom of Denmark (Danmark), a constitutional monarchy located at the mouth of the Baltic Sea, has an area of 16,639 sq. mi. (43,070 sq. km.) and a population of 5.2 million. Capital: Copenhagen. Most of the country is arable. Agriculture, is conducted by large farms served by cooperatives. The largest industries are food processing, iron and metal, and fishing. Machinery, meats (chiefly bacon), dairy products and chemicals are exported.

Denmark, a great power during the Viking period of the 9th-11th centuries, conducted raids on western Europe and England, and in the 11th century united England, Denmark and Norway under the rule of King Canute. Despite a struggle between the crown and the nobility (13th-14th centuries) which forced the King to grant a written constitution, Queen Margaret (Margrethe) (1387-1412) succeeded in uniting Denmark, Norway, Sweden, Finland and Greenland under the Danish crown, placing all of Scandinavia under the rule of Denmark. An unwise alliance with Napoleon contributed to the dismembering of the empire and fostered a liberal movement which succeeded in making Denmark a constitutional monarchy in 1849.

In 1864, Denmark lost Schleswig and Holstein to Prussia. In 1920, Denmark regained North-Schleswig by plebiscite.

The present decimal system of coinage was introduced in 1874.

**RULERS**

Christian IX, 1863-1906
Frederik VIII, 1906-1912
Christian X, 1912-1947
Frederik IX, 1947-1972
Margrethe II, 1972—

**MINT MARKS**

(h) - Copenhagen, heart

**MINTMASTERS INITIALS**

**Copenhagen**

| Letter | Date | Name |
|---|---|---|
| *P, VBP | 1893-1918 | Vilhelm Buchard Poulsen |
| HCN | 1919-1927 | Hans Christian Nielsen |
| N | 1927-1955 | Niels Peter Nielsen |
| C | 1956-1971 | Alfred Frederik Christiansen |
| S | 1971-1978 | Vagn Sorensen |
| B | 1978-1981 | Peter M Bjarno |
| R, NR | 1982-1989 | N. Norregaard Rasmussen |
| LG | 1989- | Laust Grove |

**NOTE**: The letter P was only used on Danish West Indies coins.

**MONEYERS INITIALS**

**Copenhagen**

| Letter | Date | Name |
|---|---|---|
| GI, GJ | 1901-1933 | Knud Gunnar Jensen |
| AH | 1908-1924 | Andreas Frederik Vilhelm Hansen |
| HS, S | 1933-1968 | Harald Salomon |
| B | 1968-1983 | Frode Bahnsen |
| A | 1986- | Johan Alkjaer (designer) |
| HV | 1986- | Hanne Varming (sculptor) |
| JP | 1989- | Jan Petersen |

**MONETARY SYSTEM**

100 Øre = 1 Krone

# KINGDOM

## DECIMAL COINAGE

100 Ore = 1 Krone

**ORE** **KM# 792.2** **Composition:** Bronze **Ruler:** Christian IX

| Date | Mintage | F | VF | XF | Unc | BU |
|---|---|---|---|---|---|---|
| 1902/802(h) VBP | 2,977,000 | 2.75 | 4.50 | 10.00 | 25.00 | — |
| 1902(h) VBP | Inc. above | 1.75 | 2.75 | 6.50 | 20.00 | — |
| 1904/804(h) VBP | 4,962,000 | 1.75 | 3.50 | 6.00 | 17.50 | — |
| 1904(h) VBP | Inc. above | 1.25 | 2.25 | 3.50 | 12.50 | — |

**ORE** **KM# 804** **Composition:** Bronze **Ruler:** Frederik VIII

| Date | Mintage | F | VF | XF | Unc | BU |
|---|---|---|---|---|---|---|
| 1907(h) VBP, GJ | 5,975,000 | 1.25 | 2.75 | 5.50 | 14.00 | — |
| 1909(h) VBP, GJ | 2,985,000 | 1.25 | 2.75 | 5.50 | 15.00 | — |
| 1910(h) VBP; GJ | 2,994,000 | 1.75 | 4.50 | 10.00 | 22.00 | — |
| 1912(h) VBP; GJ | 3,006,000 | 1.25 | 3.75 | 7.00 | 18.50 | — |

**ORE** **KM# 812.1** **Composition:** Bronze **Ruler:** Christian X

| Date | Mintage | F | VF | XF | Unc | BU |
|---|---|---|---|---|---|---|
| 1913(h) VBP; GJ | 5,011,000 | 1.00 | 1.50 | 2.00 | 6.00 | — |
| 1915(h) VBP; GJ | 4,940,000 | 1.35 | 2.25 | 3.75 | 8.00 | — |
| 1916(h) VBP; GJ | 2,439,000 | 1.35 | 2.75 | 4.50 | 11.00 | — |
| 1917(h) VBP; GJ | 4,564,000 | 16.00 | 25.00 | 37.50 | 70.00 | — |

**ORE** **KM# 812.1a** **Composition:** Iron **Ruler:** Christian X

| Date | Mintage | F | VF | XF | Unc | BU |
|---|---|---|---|---|---|---|
| 1918(h) VBP; GJ | 6,776,000 | 1.75 | 3.75 | 11.50 | 37.50 | — |

**ORE** **KM# 812.2** **Composition:** Bronze **Ruler:** Christian X

| Date | Mintage | F | VF | XF | Unc | BU |
|---|---|---|---|---|---|---|
| 1919(h) HCN; GJ | 4,586,000 | 1.00 | 1.75 | 4.00 | 8.50 | — |
| 1920(h) HCN; GJ | 2,367,000 | 6.00 | 12.00 | 22.50 | 50.00 | — |
| 1921(h) HCN; GJ | 3,121,000 | 1.35 | 2.25 | 3.25 | 8.50 | — |
| 1922(h) HCN; GJ | 3,267,000 | 1.75 | 2.50 | 4.00 | 9.50 | — |
| 1923(h) HCN; GJ | 2,938,000 | 1.75 | 2.50 | 3.75 | 8.50 | — |

**ORE** **KM# 812.2a** **Composition:** Iron **Ruler:** Christian X

| Date | Mintage | F | VF | XF | Unc | BU |
|---|---|---|---|---|---|---|
| 1919(h) HCN; GJ | 931,000 | 4.50 | 14.00 | 32.00 | 65.00 | — |

**ORE** **KM# 826.1** **Composition:** Bronze **Ruler:** Christian X

| Date | Mintage | F | VF | XF | Unc | BU |
|---|---|---|---|---|---|---|
| 1926(h) HCN; GJ | 1,572,000 | 2.75 | 5.50 | 18.50 | 50.00 | — |
| 1927(h) HCN; GJ | Inc. above | 0.10 | 0.30 | 3.50 | 17.50 | — |

**ORE** **KM# 826.2** **Composition:** Bronze **Ruler:** Christian X
**Note:** For coins dated 1941 refer to Faeroe Islands listings at the end of Denmark.

| Date | Mintage | F | VF | XF | Unc | BU |
|---|---|---|---|---|---|---|
| 1927(h) N; GJ | Inc. above | 3.75 | 9.50 | 25.00 | 80.00 | — |
| 1928(h) N; GJ | 29,691,000 | 0.10 | 0.25 | 2.75 | 12.50 | — |
| 1929(h) N; GJ | 5,172,000 | 0.10 | 0.25 | 2.75 | 16.50 | — |
| 1930(h) N; GJ | 5,306,000 | 0.10 | 0.20 | 2.75 | 19.50 | — |
| 1932(h) N; GJ | 5,089,000 | 0.10 | 0.20 | 2.75 | 16.50 | — |
| 1933(h) N; GJ | 2,095,000 | 0.25 | 1.00 | 4.00 | 27.50 | — |
| 1934(h) N; GJ | 3,665,000 | — | 0.10 | 1.00 | 9.00 | — |
| 1935(h) N; GJ | 5,668,000 | — | 0.10 | 1.00 | 6.50 | — |
| 1936(h) N; GJ | 5,584,000 | — | 0.10 | 0.50 | 3.50 | — |
| 1937(h) N; GJ | 6,877,000 | — | 0.10 | 0.50 | 2.75 | — |
| 1938(h) N; GJ | 3,850,000 | — | 0.10 | 0.50 | 2.25 | — |
| 1939(h) N; GJ | 5,662,000 | — | 0.10 | 0.35 | 2.25 | — |
| 1940(h) N; GJ | 1,965,000 | — | 0.10 | 0.35 | 1.75 | — |

**ORE** **KM# 832** **Composition:** Zinc **Ruler:** Christian X

| Date | Mintage | F | VF | XF | Unc | BU |
|---|---|---|---|---|---|---|
| 1941(h) N; S | 21,570,000 | 0.10 | 0.35 | 6.50 | 28.00 | — |
| 1942(h) N; S | 6,997,000 | 0.10 | 0.35 | 6.50 | 28.00 | — |
| 1943(h) N; S | 15,082,000 | 0.10 | 0.35 | 6.50 | 28.00 | — |
| 1944(h) N; S | 11,981,000 | 0.10 | 0.35 | 6.50 | 28.00 | — |
| 1945(h) N; S | 916,000 | 1.00 | 2.00 | 13.50 | 37.50 | — |
| 1946(h) N; S | 712,000 | 3.00 | 6.50 | 18.50 | 50.00 | — |

**ORE** **KM# 839.1** **Composition:** Zinc **Ruler:** Frederik IX

| Date | Mintage | F | VF | XF | Unc | BU |
|---|---|---|---|---|---|---|
| 1948(h) N; S | 460,000 | 1.25 | 2.25 | 9.50 | 40.00 | — |
| 1949(h) N; S | 2,513,000 | 0.35 | 1.00 | 3.50 | 40.00 | — |
| 1950(h) N; S | 9,453,000 | 0.25 | 0.50 | 3.25 | 30.00 | — |
| 1951(h) N; S | 2,931,000 | 0.35 | 1.00 | 3.50 | 40.00 | — |
| 1952(h) N; S | 7,626,000 | 0.10 | 0.35 | 2.25 | 20.00 | — |
| 1953(h) N; S | 11,994,000 | 0.10 | 0.25 | 2.25 | 20.00 | — |
| 1954(h) N; S | 12,642,000 | 0.10 | 0.25 | 2.25 | 18.00 | — |
| 1955(h) N; S | 14,177,000 | 0.10 | 0.25 | 1.75 | 18.00 | — |

**ORE** **KM# 839.2** **Composition:** Zinc **Ruler:** Frederik IX

| Date | Mintage | F | VF | XF | Unc | BU |
|---|---|---|---|---|---|---|
| 1956(h) C; S | 20,211,000 | 0.10 | 0.25 | 1.00 | 4.50 | — |
| 1957(h) C; S | 20,900,000 | 0.10 | 0.25 | 1.00 | 4.50 | — |
| 1958(h) C; S | 16,021,000 | — | 0.10 | 0.75 | 3.75 | — |
| 1959(h) C; S | 15,929,000 | — | 0.10 | 0.75 | 3.75 | — |
| 1960(h) C; S | 23,982,000 | — | 0.10 | 0.75 | 2.75 | — |
| 1961(h) C; S | 18,986,000 | — | 0.10 | 0.60 | 2.25 | — |
| 1962(h) C; S | 16,992,000 | — | 0.10 | 0.50 | 1.50 | — |
| 1963(h) C; S | 28,986,000 | — | 0.10 | 0.50 | 1.50 | — |
| 1964(h) C; S | 21,971,000 | — | 0.10 | 0.35 | 1.50 | — |
| 1965(h) C; S | 29,943,000 | — | 0.10 | 0.25 | 1.50 | — |
| 1966(h) C; S | 35,907,000 | — | 0.10 | 0.25 | 1.50 | — |
| 1967(h) C; S | 32,959,000 | — | 0.10 | 0.25 | 1.50 | — |
| 1968(h) C; S | 21,889,000 | — | — | 0.10 | 0.85 | — |
| 1969(h) C; S | 29,243,000 | — | — | 0.10 | 0.88 | — |
| 1970(h) C; S | 22,970,000 | — | — | 0.10 | 0.50 | — |
| 1971(h) C; S | 21,983,000 | — | — | 0.10 | 0.50 | — |

**ORE** **KM# 846** **Composition:** Bronze **Ruler:** Frederik IX
**Note:** Never released for circulation, see note 2 Ore, KM#847.

| Date | Mintage | F | VF | XF | Unc | BU |
|---|---|---|---|---|---|---|
| 1960(h) C; S | 8,990,000 | — | — | — | 3.00 | — |
| 1962(h) C; S | Inc. above | — | — | — | 3.00 | — |
| 1963(h) C; S | 9,980,000 | — | — | — | 3.00 | — |
| 1964(h) C; S | 2,990,000 | — | — | — | 3.00 | — |

**ORE** **KM# 839.3** **Composition:** Zinc **Ruler:** Frederik IX

| Date | Mintage | F | VF | XF | Unc | BU |
|---|---|---|---|---|---|---|
| 1972(h) S; S | 13,000,000 | — | — | 0.10 | 0.60 | — |

**2 ORE** **KM# 793.2** **Composition:** Bronze **Ruler:** Christian IX

| Date | Mintage | F | VF | XF | Unc | BU |
|---|---|---|---|---|---|---|
| 1902/802(h) VBP | 3,502,000 | 1.75 | 4.00 | 6.50 | 42.00 | — |
| 1902(h) VBP | Inc. above | 1.35 | 2.75 | 5.00 | 32.00 | — |
| 1906(h) VBP | 2,498,000 | 3.25 | 7.00 | 11.50 | 42.00 | — |

**2 ORE** **KM# 805** **Composition:** Bronze **Ruler:** Frederik VIII

| Date | Mintage | F | VF | XF | Unc | BU |
|---|---|---|---|---|---|---|
| 1907(h) VBP; GJ | 2,502,000 | 1.50 | 3.00 | 7.50 | 22.00 | — |
| 1909(h) VBP; GJ | 2,485,000 | 2.00 | 4.00 | 16.50 | 50.00 | — |
| 1912(h) VBP; GJ | 2,480,000 | 2.00 | 4.00 | 10.00 | 30.00 | — |

**2 ORE** **KM# 813.1** **Composition:** Bronze **Ruler:** Christian X

| Date | Mintage | F | VF | XF | Unc | BU |
|---|---|---|---|---|---|---|
| 1913(h) VBP; GJ | 373,000 | 27.50 | 45.00 | 72.50 | 145 | — |
| 1914(h) VBP; GJ | 2,126,000 | 2.25 | 4.00 | 6.50 | 25.00 | — |
| 1915(h) VBP; GJ | 2,485,000 | 1.75 | 4.00 | 6.50 | 22.50 | — |
| 1916(h) VBP; GJ | 1,383,000 | 2.75 | 4.00 | 7.50 | 27.50 | — |
| 1917(h) VBP; GJ | 1,837,000 | 14.00 | 27.50 | 45.00 | 80.00 | — |

**2 ORE** **KM# 813.1a** **Composition:** Iron **Ruler:** Christian X

| Date | Mintage | F | VF | XF | Unc | BU |
|---|---|---|---|---|---|---|
| 1918(h) VBP; GJ | 4,160,999 | 2.00 | 4.00 | 14.00 | 55.00 | — |

**2 ORE** **KM# 813.2** **Composition:** Bronze **Ruler:** Christian X

| Date | Mintage | F | VF | XF | Unc | BU |
|---|---|---|---|---|---|---|
| 1919(h) HCN; GJ | 5,503,000 | 5.50 | 10.00 | 22.50 | 50.00 | — |
| 1920(h) HCN; GJ | 2,528,000 | 1.00 | 1.50 | 3.50 | 20.00 | — |
| 1921(h) HCN; GJ | 2,158,000 | 3.25 | 5.00 | 7.50 | 17.50 | — |
| 1923(h) HCN; GJ | 2,625,000 | 2.25 | 4.00 | 6.00 | 17.50 | — |

**2 ORE** **KM# 813.2a** **Composition:** Iron **Ruler:** Christian X

| Date | Mintage | F | VF | XF | Unc | BU |
|---|---|---|---|---|---|---|
| 1919(h) HCN; GJ | 1,944,000 | 16.50 | 37.50 | 70.00 | 175 | — |

**2 ORE** **KM# 827.1** **Composition:** Bronze **Ruler:** Christian X

| Date | Mintage | F | VF | XF | Unc | BU |
|---|---|---|---|---|---|---|
| 1926(h) HCN; GJ | 301,000 | 37.50 | 55.00 | 180 | 550 | — |
| 1927(h) HCN; GJ | 15,359,000 | 0.10 | 0.20 | 2.75 | 18.50 | — |

**2 ORE** **KM# 827.2** **Composition:** Bronze **Ruler:** Christian X **Note:** For coins dated 1941 refer to Faeore Islands listings at the end of Denmark.

| Date | Mintage | F | VF | XF | Unc | BU |
|---|---|---|---|---|---|---|
| 1927(h) N; GJ | Inc. above | 1.25 | 2.25 | 37.50 | 150 | — |
| 1928(h) N; GJ | 5,758,000 | 0.10 | 0.20 | 2.25 | 16.00 | — |
| 1929(h) N; GJ | 6,817,000 | 0.10 | 0.20 | 2.25 | 32.00 | — |
| 1930(h) N; GJ | 2,327,000 | 0.60 | 1.25 | 5.50 | 60.00 | — |
| 1931(h) N; GJ | 5,135,000 | 0.10 | 0.20 | 2.25 | 25.00 | — |
| 1932(h) N; GJ | Inc. above | 1.25 | 2.25 | 18.50 | 90.00 | — |
| 1934(h) N; GJ | 756,000 | 0.50 | 1.00 | 7.00 | 37.50 | — |
| 1935(h) N; GJ | 1,391,000 | 0.10 | 0.20 | 1.50 | 18.50 | — |
| 1936(h) N; GJ | 2,973,000 | 0.10 | 0.20 | 1.00 | 18.50 | — |
| 1937(h) N; GJ | 3,437,000 | 0.10 | 0.20 | 1.00 | 9.50 | — |
| 1938(h) N; GJ | 2,177,000 | — | 0.10 | 0.55 | 4.50 | — |
| 1939(h) N; GJ | 3,165,000 | — | 0.10 | 0.55 | 2.75 | — |
| 1940(h) N; GJ | 1,582,000 | — | 0.10 | 0.50 | 2.00 | — |

**2 ORE** **KM# 833** **Composition:** Aluminum **Ruler:** Christian X

| Date | Mintage | F | VF | XF | Unc | BU |
|---|---|---|---|---|---|---|
| 1941(h) N; S | 26,205,000 | 0.10 | 0.60 | 2.25 | 12.50 | — |

**2 ORE** **KM# 833a** **Composition:** Zinc **Ruler:** Christian X

| Date | Mintage | F | VF | XF | Unc | BU |
|---|---|---|---|---|---|---|
| 1942(h) N; S | 12,934,000 | 0.10 | 0.50 | 5.50 | 35.00 | — |
| 1943(h) N; S | 9,603,000 | 0.10 | 0.50 | 5.50 | 35.00 | — |
| 1944(h) N; S | 6,069,000 | 0.10 | 0.50 | 5.50 | 35.00 | — |
| 1945(h) N; S | 329,000 | 3.75 | 7.50 | 27.50 | 90.00 | — |
| 1947(h) N; S | 589,000 | 1.35 | 2.25 | 14.00 | 70.00 | — |

**2 ORE** **KM# 840.1** **Composition:** Zinc **Ruler:** Frederik IX

| Date | Mintage | F | VF | XF | Unc | BU |
|---|---|---|---|---|---|---|
| 1948(h) N; S | 1,927,000 | 0.40 | 1.00 | 4.50 | 27.50 | — |
| 1949(h) N; S | 1,603,000 | 3.75 | 14.50 | 40.00 | 165 | — |
| 1950(h) N; S | 4,544,000 | 0.75 | 1.35 | 4.50 | 32.00 | — |
| 1951(h) N; S | 3,766,000 | 1.50 | 2.50 | 9.50 | 55.00 | — |
| 1952(h) N; S | 4,874,000 | 0.10 | 0.20 | 2.25 | 27.50 | — |
| 1953(h) N; S | 8,112,000 | 0.10 | 0.20 | 2.25 | 20.00 | — |
| 1954(h) N; S | 6,497,000 | 0.10 | 0.20 | 2.25 | 18.00 | — |
| 1955(h) N; S | 6,968,000 | — | 0.10 | 1.50 | 11.50 | — |

**2 ORE** **KM# 840.2** **Composition:** Zinc **Ruler:** Frederik IX

| Date | Mintage | F | VF | XF | Unc | BU |
|---|---|---|---|---|---|---|
| 1956(h) C; S | 10,004,000 | — | 0.10 | 1.25 | 5.50 | — |
| 1957(h) C; S | 15,329,000 | — | 0.10 | 1.00 | 4.50 | — |
| 1958(h) C; S | 8,119,999 | — | 0.10 | 1.00 | 4.00 | — |
| 1959(h) C; S | 10,462,000 | — | 0.10 | 1.00 | 3.75 | — |
| 1960(h) C; S | 16,504,000 | — | 0.10 | 0.80 | 2.75 | — |
| 1961(h) C; S | 15,504,000 | — | 0.10 | 0.80 | 2.25 | — |
| 1962(h) C; S | 10,980,000 | — | 0.10 | 0.80 | 2.25 | — |
| 1963(h) C; S | 19,470,000 | — | 0.10 | 0.35 | 1.50 | — |
| 1964(h) C; S | 15,411,000 | — | 0.10 | 0.35 | 1.25 | — |
| 1965(h) C; S | 20,173,000 | — | 0.10 | 0.20 | 1.00 | — |
| 1966(h) C; S | 21,949,000 | — | 0.10 | 0.20 | 1.00 | — |
| 1967(h) C; S | 22,439,000 | — | 0.10 | 0.20 | 1.00 | — |
| 1968(h) C; S | 17,632,000 | — | — | 0.10 | 0.80 | — |
| 1969(h) C; S | 29,276,000 | — | — | 0.10 | 0.80 | — |
| 1970(h) C; S | 23,864,000 | — | — | 0.10 | 0.50 | — |
| 1971(h) C; S | 35,811,000 | — | — | 0.10 | 0.50 | — |

**2 ORE** **KM# 847** **Composition:** Bronze **Ruler:** Frederik IX
**Note:** KM#847 was never released for circulation. Together with the 4 dates of 1 Ore, KM#846, they were sold as a 10 coin set to collectors by the mint. Approximately 100,000 sets were sold, remaining coins were melted.

| Date | Mintage | F | VF | XF | Unc | BU |
|---|---|---|---|---|---|---|
| 1960(h) C; S | Inc. above | — | — | — | 3.00 | — |
| 1962(h) C; S | Inc. above | — | — | — | 3.00 | — |
| 1963(h) C; S | 100,000 | — | — | — | 3.00 | — |
| 1964(h) C; S | 3,990,000 | — | — | — | 3.00 | — |
| 1965(h) C; S | 11,980,000 | — | — | — | 3.00 | — |
| 1966(h) C; S | 12,000,000 | — | — | — | 3.00 | — |

**2 ORE** **KM# 840.3** **Composition:** Zinc **Ruler:** Frederik IX

| Date | Mintage | F | VF | XF | Unc | BU |
|---|---|---|---|---|---|---|
| 1972(h) S; S | 6,496,000 | — | 0.15 | 0.35 | 0.85 | — |

**5 ORE** KM# 794.2 **Composition:** Bronze **Ruler:** Frederik IX

| Date | Mintage | F | VF | XF | Unc | BU |
|---|---|---|---|---|---|---|
| 1902(h) VBP | 601,000 | 10.00 | 17.50 | 37.50 | 125 | — |
| 1904(h) VBP | 397,000 | 20.00 | 37.50 | 75.00 | 210 | — |
| 1906(h) VBP | 1,000,000 | 10.00 | 17.50 | 37.50 | 110 | — |

**5 ORE** KM# 806 **Composition:** Bronze **Ruler:** Frederik VIII

| Date | Mintage | F | VF | XF | Unc | BU |
|---|---|---|---|---|---|---|
| 1907(h) VBP; GJ | 1,000,000 | 5.50 | 10.00 | 18.00 | 45.00 | — |
| 1908(h) VBP; GJ | 1,198,000 | 6.00 | 12.00 | 20.00 | 50.00 | — |
| 1912(h) VBP; GJ | 999,000 | 6.50 | 13.00 | 22.50 | 55.00 | — |

**5 ORE** KM# 814.1 **Composition:** Bronze **Ruler:** Christian X

| Date | Mintage | F | VF | XF | Unc | BU |
|---|---|---|---|---|---|---|
| 1913(h) VBP; GJ | 216,000 | 60.00 | 100 | 165 | 285 | — |
| 1914(h) VBP; GJ | 785,000 | 7.00 | 13.50 | 18.50 | 40.00 | — |
| 1916(h) VBP; GJ | 887,000 | 8.50 | 17.50 | 25.00 | 50.00 | — |
| 1917(h) VBP; GJ | 494,000 | 9.00 | 18.00 | 35.00 | 70.00 | — |

**5 ORE** KM# 814.1a **Composition:** Iron **Ruler:** Christian X

| Date | Mintage | F | VF | XF | Unc | BU |
|---|---|---|---|---|---|---|
| 1918(h) VBP; GJ | 1,918,000 | 5.50 | 9.50 | 22.50 | 70.00 | — |

**5 ORE** KM# 814.2 **Composition:** Bronze **Ruler:** Christian X

| Date | Mintage | F | VF | XF | Unc | BU |
|---|---|---|---|---|---|---|
| 1919(h) HCN; GJ | 994,000 | 3.25 | 5.50 | 8.50 | 18.50 | — |
| 1920(h) HCN; GJ | 2,618,000 | 7.00 | 13.50 | 22.50 | 40.00 | — |
| 1921(h) HCN; GJ | 3,248,000 | 4.50 | 8.00 | 11.50 | 22.50 | — |
| 1923(h) HCN; GJ | 369,000 | 85.00 | 175 | 235 | 375 | — |

**5 ORE** KM# 814.2a **Composition:** Iron **Ruler:** Christian X

| Date | Mintage | F | VF | XF | Unc | BU |
|---|---|---|---|---|---|---|
| 1919(h) HCN; GJ | 1,034,999 | 15.00 | 30.00 | 55.00 | 160 | — |

**5 ORE** KM# 828.1 **Composition:** Bronze **Ruler:** Christian X

| Date | Mintage | F | VF | XF | Unc | BU |
|---|---|---|---|---|---|---|
| 1926(h) HCN; GJ Unique | — | — | — | — | — | — |

**Note:** Thomas Hoiland Sale 11-00 $8,600. Beware of counterfeits

| Date | Mintage | F | VF | XF | Unc | BU |
|---|---|---|---|---|---|---|
| 1927(h) HCN; GJ | 7,129,000 | 0.10 | 0.20 | 2.75 | 20.00 | — |

**5 ORE** KM# 828.2 **Composition:** Bronze **Ruler:** Christian X **Note:** For coins dated 1941 refer to Faeroe Islands listings at the end of Denmark.

| Date | Mintage | F | VF | XF | Unc | BU |
|---|---|---|---|---|---|---|
| 1927(h) N; GJ | Inc. above | 3.75 | 7.00 | 70.00 | 375 | — |
| 1928(h) N; GJ | 4,685,000 | 0.10 | 0.50 | 3.25 | 22.50 | — |
| 1929(h) N; GJ | 1,387,000 | 0.35 | 0.75 | 4.50 | 65.00 | — |
| 1930(h) N; GJ | 1,339,000 | 0.45 | 0.80 | 10.00 | 70.00 | — |
| 1932(h) N; GJ | 1,010,999 | 0.35 | 0.75 | 8.50 | 65.00 | — |
| 1934(h) N; GJ | 524,000 | 0.35 | 0.75 | 7.00 | 60.00 | — |
| 1935(h) N; GJ | 1,124,000 | 1.75 | 3.75 | 20.00 | 100 | — |
| 1936(h) N; GJ | 1,091,000 | 0.25 | 0.50 | 2.75 | 27.50 | — |
| 1937(h) N; GJ | 1,209,000 | 0.25 | 0.50 | 1.35 | 20.00 | — |
| 1938(h) N; GJ | 1,093,000 | 0.45 | 0.80 | 1.75 | 10.00 | — |
| 1939(h) N; GJ | 1,402,000 | 0.15 | 0.25 | 0.50 | 3.75 | — |
| 1940(h) N; GJ | 2,735,000 | 0.15 | 0.25 | 0.50 | 3.75 | — |

**5 ORE** KM# 834 **Composition:** Aluminum **Ruler:** Christian X

| Date | Mintage | F | VF | XF | Unc | BU |
|---|---|---|---|---|---|---|
| 1941(h) N; S | 16,984,000 | 0.10 | 1.00 | 3.75 | 16.50 | — |

**5 ORE** KM# 834a **Composition:** Zinc **Ruler:** Christian X

| Date | Mintage | F | VF | XF | Unc | BU |
|---|---|---|---|---|---|---|
| 1942(h) N; S | 2,963,000 | 1.25 | 2.50 | 18.50 | 60.00 | — |
| 1943(h) N; S | 4,522,000 | 0.50 | 1.50 | 11.50 | 50.00 | — |
| 1944(h) N; S | 3,744,000 | 0.60 | 1.75 | 11.50 | 50.00 | — |
| 1945(h) N; S | 864,000 | 3.50 | 8.50 | 27.50 | 87.50 | — |

**5 ORE** KM# 843.1 **Composition:** Zinc **Ruler:** Frederik IX

| Date | Mintage | F | VF | XF | Unc | BU |
|---|---|---|---|---|---|---|
| 1950(h) N; S | 657,000 | 6.00 | 10.00 | 32.50 | 87.50 | — |
| 1951(h) N; S Straight 5 | 1,858,000 | 1.25 | 2.50 | 10.00 | 40.00 | — |
| 1951(h) N; S Slant 5 | Inc. above | 1.25 | 2.25 | 9.50 | 37.50 | — |
| 1952(h) N; S | 3,562,000 | 0.60 | 1.25 | 4.50 | 25.00 | — |
| 1953(h) N; S | 5,944,000 | 0.60 | 1.25 | 3.75 | 20.00 | — |
| 1954(h) N; S | 3,060,000 | 0.40 | 1.00 | 2.75 | 16.50 | — |
| 1955(h) N; S | 2,314,000 | 1.00 | 1.75 | 4.00 | 16.50 | — |

**5 ORE** KM# 843.2 **Composition:** Zinc **Ruler:** Frederik IX

| Date | Mintage | F | VF | XF | Unc | BU |
|---|---|---|---|---|---|---|
| 1956(h) C; S | 5,888,000 | 0.50 | 1.00 | 2.25 | 9.50 | — |
| 1957(h) C; S | 8,606,000 | 0.25 | 0.50 | 1.50 | 5.50 | — |
| 1958(h) C; S | 9,598,000 | 0.25 | 0.50 | 1.50 | 4.50 | — |
| 1959(h) C; S | 6,110,000 | 0.10 | 0.25 | 1.00 | 4.50 | — |
| 1960(h) C; S | 11,800,000 | 0.10 | 0.25 | 1.00 | 2.75 | — |
| 1961(h) C; S | 8,995,000 | 0.20 | 0.45 | 1.00 | 2.25 | — |
| 1962(h) C; S | 9,729,000 | 0.10 | 0.25 | 0.80 | 2.25 | — |
| 1963(h) C; S | 8,980,000 | 0.10 | 0.25 | 0.80 | 2.25 | — |
| 1964(h) C; S | 6,738,000 | 0.75 | 1.25 | 2.75 | 5.50 | — |

**5 ORE** KM# 848.1 **Composition:** Bronze **Ruler:** Frederik IX

| Date | Mintage | F | VF | XF | Unc | BU |
|---|---|---|---|---|---|---|
| 1960(h) C; S | 3,760,000 | 0.10 | 0.25 | 1.00 | 4.50 | — |
| 1962(h) C; S | 5,873,000 | 0.25 | 0.50 | 1.75 | 11.50 | — |
| 1963(h) C; S | 23,287,000 | — | 0.10 | 0.60 | 2.75 | — |
| 1964(h) C; S | 41,521,000 | — | 0.10 | 0.60 | 2.75 | — |
| 1965(h) C; S | 14,229,000 | — | 0.10 | 0.60 | 2.75 | — |
| 1966(h) C; S | 23,410,000 | — | 0.10 | 0.60 | 2.75 | — |
| 1967(h) C; S | 15,094,000 | — | 0.10 | 0.60 | 2.75 | — |
| 1968(h) C; S | 16,105,000 | — | 0.10 | 0.50 | 1.75 | — |
| 1969(h) C; S | 23,594,000 | — | 0.10 | 0.35 | 1.00 | — |
| 1970(h) C; S | 26,176,000 | — | — | 0.10 | 1.00 | — |
| 1971(h) C; S | 10,076,000 | — | — | 0.10 | 1.00 | — |

**5 ORE** KM# 848.2 **Composition:** Bronze **Ruler:** Frederik IX

| Date | Mintage | F | VF | XF | Unc | BU |
|---|---|---|---|---|---|---|
| 1972(h) S; S | 27,938,000 | — | — | 0.10 | 1.00 | — |

**5 ORE** KM# 859.1 **Composition:** Copper Clad Iron **Ruler:** Margrethe II

| Date | Mintage | F | VF | XF | Unc | BU |
|---|---|---|---|---|---|---|
| 1973(h) S; B | 75,138,000 | — | — | 0.10 | 0.70 | — |
| 1974(h) S; B | 71,796,000 | — | — | 0.10 | 0.70 | — |
| 1975(h) S; B | 45,004,000 | — | — | 0.10 | 0.70 | — |
| 1976(h) S; B | 73,296,000 | — | — | 0.10 | 0.70 | — |
| 1977(h) S; B | 74,066,000 | — | — | 0.10 | 0.70 | — |
| 1978(h) S; B | 52,425,000 | — | — | 0.10 | 0.70 | — |

**5 ORE** KM# 859.2 **Composition:** Copper Clad Iron **Ruler:** Margrethe II

| Date | Mintage | F | VF | XF | Unc | BU |
|---|---|---|---|---|---|---|
| 1979(h) B; B | 58,953,000 | — | — | 0.10 | 0.70 | — |
| 1980(h) B; B | 54,362,000 | — | — | 0.10 | 0.70 | — |
| 1981(h) B; B | 52,201,000 | — | — | 0.10 | 0.35 | — |

**5 ORE** KM# 859.3 **Composition:** Copper Clad Iron **Ruler:** Margrethe II

| Date | Mintage | F | VF | XF | Unc | BU |
|---|---|---|---|---|---|---|
| 1982(h) R; B | 74,296,000 | — | — | 0.10 | 0.35 | — |
| 1983(h) R; B | 70,655,000 | — | — | 0.10 | 0.35 | — |
| 1984(h) R; B | 27,599,000 | — | — | 0.10 | 0.35 | — |
| 1985(h) R; B | 56,676,000 | — | — | 0.10 | 0.35 | — |
| 1986(h) R; B | 62,496,000 | — | — | 0.10 | 0.35 | — |
| 1987(h) R; B | 71,798,000 | — | — | 0.10 | 0.35 | — |
| 1988(h) R; B | 48,925,000 | — | — | 0.10 | 0.35 | — |

**10 ORE** KM# 795.2 **Weight:** 1.4500 g. **Composition:** 0.4000 Silver .0186 oz. ASW **Ruler:** Christian IX

| Date | Mintage | F | VF | XF | Unc | BU |
|---|---|---|---|---|---|---|
| 1903/803(h) VBP | 3,007,000 | 3.75 | 6.00 | 10.00 | 32.00 | — |
| 1903(h) VBP | Inc. above | 2.25 | 4.50 | 9.00 | 22.50 | — |
| 1904(h) VBP | 2,449,000 | 16.00 | 27.50 | 35.00 | 70.00 | — |
| 1905(h) VBP | 1,571,000 | 2.00 | 4.00 | 8.00 | 18.50 | — |

**10 ORE** KM# 807 **Weight:** 1.4500 g. **Composition:** 0.4000 Silver .0186 oz. ASW **Ruler:** Frederik VIII

| Date | Mintage | F | VF | XF | Unc | BU |
|---|---|---|---|---|---|---|
| 1907(h) VBP; GJ | 3,068,000 | 2.75 | 4.50 | 9.00 | 18.50 | — |
| 1910(h) VBP; GJ | 2,530,000 | 3.25 | 5.50 | 10.00 | 21.50 | — |
| 1911(h) VBP; GJ | 579,000 | 27.50 | 45.00 | 67.50 | 100 | — |
| 1912(h) VBP; GJ | 1,951,000 | 3.75 | 6.50 | 10.00 | 21.50 | — |

**10 ORE** KM# 818.1 **Weight:** 1.4500 g. **Composition:** 0.4000 Silver .0186 oz. ASW **Ruler:** Christian X

| Date | Mintage | F | VF | XF | Unc | BU |
|---|---|---|---|---|---|---|
| 1914(h) VBP; GJ | 2,128,000 | 4.00 | 6.00 | 9.00 | 16.50 | — |
| 1915(h) VBP; GJ | 915,000 | 5.50 | 9.00 | 13.50 | 20.00 | — |
| 1916(h) VBP; GJ | 2,699,000 | 4.00 | 6.50 | 10.00 | 16.50 | — |
| 1917(h) VBP; GJ | 6,003,000 | 2.25 | 3.50 | 5.50 | 9.00 | — |
| 1918(h) VBP; GJ | 5,042,000 | 1.35 | 2.25 | 3.75 | 6.00 | — |

**10 ORE** KM# 818.2 **Weight:** 1.4500 g. **Composition:** 0.4000 Silver .0186 oz. ASW **Ruler:** Christian X

| Date | Mintage | F | VF | XF | Unc | BU |
|---|---|---|---|---|---|---|
| 1919(h) HCN; GJ | 10,184,000 | 1.00 | 1.50 | 2.25 | 3.50 | — |

**10 ORE** KM# 818.2a **Composition:** Copper-Nickel **Ruler:** Christian X

| Date | Mintage | F | VF | XF | Unc | BU |
|---|---|---|---|---|---|---|
| 1920(h) HCN; GJ | 10,234,000 | 2.75 | 4.00 | 9.50 | 32.50 | — |
| 1921(h) HCN; GJ | 8,064,000 | 2.75 | 3.75 | 8.00 | 28.00 | — |
| 1922(h) HCN; GJ | 3,065,000 | 18.50 | 27.50 | 36.00 | 65.00 | — |
| 1923(h) HCN; GJ | 1,790,000 | 250 | 385 | 500 | 700 | — |

**10 ORE** **KM# 822.1** **Composition:** Copper-Nickel **Ruler:** Christian X

| Date | Mintage | F | VF | XF | Unc | BU |
|---|---|---|---|---|---|---|
| 1924(h) HCN; GJ | 14,661,000 | 0.20 | 0.75 | 2.25 | 11.50 | — |
| 1925(h) HCN; G | 8,678,000 | 0.25 | 0.75 | 7.00 | 27.50 | — |
| 1926(h) HCN; GJ | 4,107,000 | 0.25 | 0.75 | 7.00 | 32.50 | — |

**10 ORE** **KM# 822.2** **Composition:** Copper-Nickel **Ruler:** Christian X **Note:** For coins dated 1941 without mintmint or initials refer to Faeroe Islands listings.

| Date | Mintage | F | VF | XF | Unc | BU |
|---|---|---|---|---|---|---|
| 1929(h) N; GJ | 5,037,000 | 0.75 | 1.25 | 7.00 | 36.50 | — |
| 1931(h) N; GJ | 3,054,000 | 1.35 | 2.25 | 9.50 | 45.00 | — |
| 1933(h) N; GJ | 1,274,000 | 6.50 | 12.00 | 27.00 | 75.00 | — |
| 1934(h) N; GJ | 2,013,000 | 1.25 | 2.25 | 7.00 | 25.00 | — |
| 1935(h) N; GJ | 2,848,000 | 1.35 | 2.25 | 6.00 | 22.50 | — |
| 1936(h) N; GJ | 3,320,000 | 1.35 | 2.25 | 5.50 | 36.50 | — |
| 1937(h) N; GJ | 2,234,000 | 1.00 | 1.50 | 5.50 | 18.50 | — |
| 1938(h) N; GJ | 2,991,000 | 1.75 | 2.75 | 4.50 | 16.50 | — |
| 1939(h) N; GJ | 2,973,000 | 1.00 | 1.75 | 4.50 | 16.50 | — |
| 1940(h) N; GJ | 2,998,000 | 0.60 | 1.25 | 2.00 | 10.00 | — |
| 1941(h) N; GJ | 748,000 | 2.75 | 4.50 | 7.00 | 20.00 | — |
| 1946(h) N; GJ | 460,000 | 2.00 | 3.75 | 5.00 | 8.50 | — |
| 1947(h) N; GJ | 1,292,000 | 85.00 | 110 | 165 | 220 | — |

**10 ORE** **KM# 822.2a** **Composition:** Zinc **Ruler:** Christian X

| Date | Mintage | F | VF | XF | Unc | BU |
|---|---|---|---|---|---|---|
| 1941(h) N; GJ | 7,706,000 | 1.00 | 2.00 | 9.00 | 30.00 | — |
| 1942(h) N; GJ | 8,676,000 | 1.00 | 2.00 | 9.00 | 30.00 | — |
| 1943(h) N; GJ | 2,181,000 | 1.75 | 3.25 | 11.50 | 32.50 | — |
| 1944(h) N; GJ | 7,994,000 | 1.35 | 2.50 | 7.50 | 23.50 | — |
| 1945(h) N; GJ | 1,280,000 | 40.00 | 60.00 | 90.00 | 185 | — |

**10 ORE** **KM# 841.1** **Composition:** Copper-Nickel **Ruler:** Frederik IX

| Date | Mintage | F | VF | XF | Unc | BU |
|---|---|---|---|---|---|---|
| 1948(h) N; S | 5,317,000 | 0.25 | 0.75 | 3.25 | 16.50 | — |
| 1949(h) N; S | 7,595,000 | 0.10 | 0.25 | 2.75 | 14.50 | — |
| 1950(h) N; S | 6,886,000 | 0.10 | 0.25 | 2.75 | 14.50 | — |
| 1951(h) N; S | 8,763,000 | 0.10 | 0.25 | 3.25 | 22.50 | — |
| 1952(h) N; S | 6,810,000 | 0.10 | 0.25 | 2.75 | 14.50 | — |
| 1953(h) N; S | 11,946,000 | 0.10 | 0.25 | 2.75 | 13.50 | — |
| 1954(h) N; S | 19,739,000 | — | 0.10 | 1.50 | 8.50 | — |
| 1955(h) N; S | 17,623,000 | — | 0.10 | 1.50 | 8.50 | — |

**10 ORE** **KM# 841.2** **Composition:** Copper-Nickel **Ruler:** Frederik IX

| Date | Mintage | F | VF | XF | Unc | BU |
|---|---|---|---|---|---|---|
| 1956(h) C; S | 12,323,000 | — | 0.10 | 2.25 | 11.50 | — |
| 1957(h) C; S | 13,227,000 | — | 0.10 | 1.00 | 5.50 | — |
| 1958(h) C; S | 10,870,000 | — | 0.10 | 1.00 | 5.50 | — |
| 1959(h) C; S | 1,255,000 | 27.50 | 40.00 | 55.00 | 115 | — |
| 1960(h) C; S | 5,107,000 | 0.10 | 0.30 | 1.00 | 3.75 | — |

**10 ORE** **KM# 849.1** **Composition:** Copper-Nickel **Ruler:** Frederik IX

| Date | Mintage | F | VF | XF | Unc | BU |
|---|---|---|---|---|---|---|
| 1960(h) C; S | Inc. above | 0.10 | 0.30 | 0.75 | 3.75 | — |
| 1961(h) C; S | 20,258,000 | — | 0.15 | 0.50 | 4.50 | — |
| 1962(h) C; S | 12,785,000 | — | 0.15 | 0.50 | 4.50 | — |
| 1963(h) C; S | 17,171,000 | — | 0.15 | 0.50 | 3.75 | — |
| 1964(h) C; S | 14,282,000 | — | 0.15 | 0.50 | 3.25 | — |
| 1965(h) C; S | 21,857,000 | — | 0.15 | 0.50 | 3.25 | — |
| 1966(h) C; S | 24,160,000 | — | 0.15 | 0.25 | 2.75 | — |
| 1967(h) C; S | 21,544,000 | — | 0.15 | 0.25 | 1.75 | — |
| 1968(h) C; S | 7,586,000 | — | 0.15 | 0.25 | 1.50 | — |
| 1969(h) C; S | 31,534,000 | — | — | 0.10 | 1.00 | — |
| 1970(h) C; S | 37,813,000 | — | — | 0.10 | 0.35 | — |
| 1971(h) C; S | 17,719,000 | — | — | 0.10 | 0.35 | — |

**10 ORE** **KM# 849.2** **Composition:** Copper-Nickel **Ruler:** Frederik IX

| Date | Mintage | F | VF | XF | Unc | BU |
|---|---|---|---|---|---|---|
| 1972(h) S; S | 46,959,000 | — | — | 0.10 | 0.35 | — |

**10 ORE** **KM# 860.1** **Composition:** Copper-Nickel **Ruler:** Margrethe II

| Date | Mintage | F | VF | XF | Unc | BU |
|---|---|---|---|---|---|---|
| 1973(h) S; B | 37,538,000 | — | — | 0.10 | 0.35 | — |
| 1974(h) S; B | 38,570,000 | — | — | 0.10 | 0.35 | — |
| 1975(h) S; B | 62,633,000 | — | — | 0.10 | 0.35 | — |
| 1976(h) S; B | 64,358,999 | — | — | 0.10 | 0.35 | — |
| 1977(h) S; B | 61,994,000 | — | — | 0.10 | 0.35 | — |
| 1978(h) S; B | 30,302,000 | — | — | 0.10 | 0.35 | — |

**10 ORE** **KM# 860.2** **Composition:** Copper-Nickel **Ruler:** Margrethe II

| Date | Mintage | F | VF | XF | Unc | BU |
|---|---|---|---|---|---|---|
| 1979(h) B; B | 10,224,000 | — | — | 0.10 | 0.35 | — |
| 1980(h) B; B | 37,233,000 | — | — | 0.10 | 0.35 | — |
| 1981(h) B; B | 51,565,000 | — | — | 0.10 | 0.25 | — |

**10 ORE** **KM# 860.3** **Composition:** Copper-Nickel **Ruler:** Margrethe II

| Date | Mintage | F | VF | XF | Unc | BU |
|---|---|---|---|---|---|---|
| 1982(h) R; B | 40,195,000 | — | — | 0.10 | 0.25 | — |
| 1983(h) R; B | 35,634,000 | — | — | 0.10 | 0.25 | — |
| 1984(h) R; B | 17,828,000 | — | — | 0.10 | 0.25 | — |
| 1985(h) R; B | 29,317,000 | — | — | 0.10 | 0.25 | — |
| 1986(h) R; B | 46,254,000 | — | — | 0.10 | 0.25 | — |
| 1987(h) R; B | 27,898,000 | — | — | 0.10 | 0.25 | — |
| 1988(h) R; B | 29,400,000 | — | — | 0.10 | 0.25 | — |

**25 ORE** **KM# 796.2** **Weight:** 2.4200 g. **Composition:** 0.6000 Silver .0467 oz. ASW **Ruler:** Christian IX

| Date | Mintage | F | VF | XF | Unc | BU |
|---|---|---|---|---|---|---|
| 1900/800(h) VBP | 1,206,000 | 15.00 | 30.00 | 40.00 | 90.00 | — |
| 1900(h) VBP | Inc. above | 13.00 | 27.50 | 37.50 | 85.00 | — |
| 1904(h) VBP | 1,922,000 | 14.00 | 25.00 | 37.50 | 82.50 | — |
| 1905/805(h) VBP | 1,722,000 | 7.00 | 12.00 | 27.50 | 50.00 | — |
| 1905(h) VBP | Inc. above | 5.50 | 10.00 | 22.50 | 45.00 | — |

**25 ORE** **KM# 808** **Weight:** 2.4200 g. **Composition:** 0.6000 Silver .0467 oz. ASW **Ruler:** Frederik VIII

| Date | Mintage | F | VF | XF | Unc | BU |
|---|---|---|---|---|---|---|
| 1907(h) VBP; GJ | 2,009,000 | 5.50 | 10.00 | 16.50 | 32.50 | — |
| 1911(h) VBP; GJ | 2,015,000 | 5.50 | 10.00 | 16.50 | 32.50 | — |

**25 ORE** **KM# 815.1** **Weight:** 2.4200 g. **Composition:** 0.6000 Silver .0467 oz. ASW **Ruler:** Frederik VIII

| Date | Mintage | F | VF | XF | Unc | BU |
|---|---|---|---|---|---|---|
| 1913(h) VBP; GJ | 2,016,000 | 4.00 | 7.50 | 11.50 | 22.50 | — |
| 1914(h) VBP; GJ | 347,000 | 85.00 | 135 | 175 | 245 | — |
| 1915(h) VBP; GJ | 2,862,000 | 3.25 | 6.00 | 9.00 | 16.50 | — |
| 1916(h) VBP; GJ | 938,000 | 10.00 | 16.00 | 22.50 | 37.50 | — |
| 1917(h) VBP; GJ | 1,354,000 | 40.00 | 65.00 | 85.00 | 135 | — |
| 1918(h) VBP; GJ | 2,089,999 | 6.00 | 9.50 | 14.50 | 23.50 | — |

**25 ORE** **KM# 815.2** **Weight:** 2.4200 g. **Composition:** 0.6000 Silver .0467 oz. ASW **Ruler:** Christian X

| Date | Mintage | F | VF | XF | Unc | BU |
|---|---|---|---|---|---|---|
| 1919(h) HCN; GJ | 9,295,000 | 1.25 | 1.75 | 2.75 | 5.00 | — |

**25 ORE** **KM# 815.2a** **Composition:** Copper-Nickel **Ruler:** Christian X

| Date | Mintage | F | VF | XF | Unc | BU |
|---|---|---|---|---|---|---|
| 1920(h) HCN; GJ | 12,288,000 | 2.75 | 4.50 | 13.50 | 38.00 | — |
| 1921(h) HCN; GJ | 9,444,000 | 2.25 | 3.75 | 13.50 | 38.00 | — |
| 1922(h) HCN; GJ | 5,701,000 | 25.00 | 35.00 | 50.00 | 90.00 | — |

**25 ORE** **KM# 823.1** **Composition:** Copper-Nickel **Ruler:** Christian X

| Date | Mintage | F | VF | XF | Unc | BU |
|---|---|---|---|---|---|---|
| 1924(h) HCN; GJ | 8,035,000 | 0.35 | 1.75 | 4.00 | 16.50 | — |
| 1925(h) HCN; GJ | 1,906,000 | 4.50 | 8.00 | 18.50 | 60.00 | — |
| 1926(h) HCN; GJ | 2,659,000 | 1.75 | 2.75 | 7.50 | 42.50 | — |

**25 ORE** **KM# 823.2** **Composition:** Copper-Nickel **Ruler:** Christian X **Note:** For coins dated 1941 refer to Faeroe Islands listings.

| Date | Mintage | F | VF | XF | Unc | BU |
|---|---|---|---|---|---|---|
| 1929(h) N; GJ | 886,000 | 1.75 | 3.75 | 9.50 | 45.00 | — |
| 1930(h) N; GJ | 3,423,000 | 2.25 | 4.50 | 14.00 | 55.00 | — |
| 1932(h) N; GJ | 846,000 | 8.50 | 12.50 | 22.50 | 65.00 | — |
| 1933(h) N; GJ | 479,000 | 25.00 | 36.50 | 52.50 | 120 | — |
| 1934(h) N; GJ | 1,660,000 | 2.25 | 3.75 | 9.50 | 37.50 | — |
| 1935(h) N; GJ | 1,032,000 | 11.00 | 20.00 | 37.50 | 85.00 | — |
| 1936(h) N; GJ | 1,453,000 | 1.75 | 2.75 | 7.50 | 32.50 | — |
| 1937(h) N; GJ | 1,612,000 | 3.25 | 5.50 | 9.50 | 22.50 | — |
| 1938(h) N; GJ | 1,794,000 | 2.75 | 4.00 | 8.00 | 25.00 | — |
| 1939(h) N; GJ | 1,972,000 | 11.00 | 18.50 | 30.00 | 60.00 | — |
| 1940(h) N; GJ | 1,356,000 | 1.35 | 2.25 | 4.00 | 11.50 | — |
| 1946(h) N; GJ | 2,323,000 | 1.25 | 2.75 | 4.00 | 9.50 | — |
| 1947(h) N; GJ | 1,751,000 | 4.00 | 7.00 | 9.00 | 14.00 | — |

**25 ORE** **KM# 823.2a** **Composition:** Zinc **Ruler:** Christian X

| Date | Mintage | F | VF | XF | Unc | BU |
|---|---|---|---|---|---|---|
| 1941(h) N; GJ | 15,332,000 | 3.75 | 7.00 | 12.50 | 32.50 | — |
| 1942(h) N; GJ | 997,000 | 1.35 | 2.75 | 6.50 | 27.50 | — |
| 1943(h) N; GJ | 5,784,000 | 3.75 | 7.50 | 14.00 | 35.00 | — |
| 1944(h) N; GJ | 10,665,000 | 1.35 | 3.25 | 6.50 | 25.00 | — |
| 1945(h) N; GJ | 4,543,000 | 2.25 | 4.00 | 7.50 | 25.00 | — |

**25 ORE** **KM# 842.1** **Composition:** Copper-Nickel **Ruler:** Frederik IX

| Date | Mintage | F | VF | XF | Unc | BU |
|---|---|---|---|---|---|---|
| 1948(h) N; S | 1,853,000 | 2.25 | 5.00 | 10.00 | 37.50 | — |
| 1949(h) N; S | 15,000,000 | 0.10 | 0.35 | 2.25 | 11.50 | — |
| 1950(h) N; S | 13,771,000 | 0.10 | 0.35 | 3.75 | 20.00 | — |
| 1951(h) N; S | 5,045,000 | 0.10 | 0.35 | 4.50 | 22.50 | — |
| 1952(h) N; S | 2,017,999 | 0.75 | 1.50 | 11.50 | 35.00 | — |
| 1953(h) N; S | 9,553,000 | 0.10 | 0.35 | 2.25 | 8.50 | — |
| 1954(h) N; S | 11,337,000 | 0.10 | 0.30 | 1.50 | 5.50 | — |
| 1955(h) N; S | 6,385,000 | 0.20 | 0.35 | 1.50 | 5.50 | — |

**25 ORE** **KM# 842.2** **Composition:** Copper-Nickel **Ruler:** Frederik IX

| Date | Mintage | F | VF | XF | Unc | BU |
|---|---|---|---|---|---|---|
| 1956(h) C; S | 10,228,000 | 0.10 | 0.25 | 1.00 | 4.50 | — |
| 1957(h) C; S | 7,421,000 | 0.10 | 0.25 | 0.75 | 3.75 | — |
| 1958(h) C; S | 3,600,000 | 0.30 | 0.50 | 1.00 | 4.00 | — |
| 1959(h) C; S | 2,211,000 | 1.75 | 3.75 | 6.00 | 9.50 | — |
| 1960(h) C; S | 3,453,000 | 0.30 | 0.50 | 1.25 | 4.50 | — |

**25 ORE** **KM# 850** **Composition:** Copper-Nickel **Ruler:** Frederik IX

| Date | Mintage | F | VF | XF | Unc | BU |
|---|---|---|---|---|---|---|
| 1960(h) C; S | Inc. above | 5.50 | 9.50 | 13.50 | 20.00 | — |
| 1961(h) C; S | 20,860,000 | 0.10 | 0.25 | 0.75 | 4.00 | — |
| 1962(h) C; S | 12,563,000 | 0.10 | 0.25 | 0.75 | 3.25 | — |
| 1964(h) C; S | 6,175,000 | 0.10 | 0.25 | 0.75 | 3.25 | — |
| 1965(h) C; S | 13,492,000 | 0.10 | 0.25 | 0.75 | 3.25 | — |
| 1966(h) C; S | 50,220,000 | 0.10 | 0.25 | 0.75 | 3.25 | — |
| 1967(h) C; S | 87,468,000 | 4.50 | 9.50 | 13.50 | 20.00 | — |

**25 ORE** **KM# 855.1** **Composition:** Copper-Nickel **Ruler:** Frederik IX

| Date | Mintage | F | VF | XF | Unc | BU |
|---|---|---|---|---|---|---|
| 1966(h) C; S | Inc. above | — | 0.10 | 0.40 | 2.25 | — |
| 1967(h) C; S | Inc. above | — | 0.10 | 0.40 | 1.75 | — |
| 1968(h) C; S | 39,142,000 | — | 0.10 | 0.40 | 1.35 | — |
| 1969(h) C; S | 16,974,000 | — | 0.10 | 0.40 | 1.00 | — |

| Date | Mintage | F | VF | XF | Unc | BU |
|---|---|---|---|---|---|---|
| 1970(h) C; S | 5,393,000 | — | — | 0.15 | 0.75 | — |
| 1971(h) C; S | 12,725,000 | — | — | 0.15 | 0.60 | — |

**25 ORE** **KM# 855.2** **Composition:** Copper-Nickel **Ruler:** Frederik IX

| Date | Mintage | F | VF | XF | Unc | BU |
|---|---|---|---|---|---|---|
| 1972(h) S; S | 31,422,000 | — | — | 0.10 | 0.45 | — |

**25 ORE** **KM# 861.1** **Composition:** Copper-Nickel **Ruler:** Margrethe II

| Date | Mintage | F | VF | XF | Unc | BU |
|---|---|---|---|---|---|---|
| 1973(h) S; B | 30,834,000 | — | — | 0.10 | 0.45 | — |
| 1974(h) S; B | 22,178,000 | — | — | 0.10 | 0.45 | — |
| 1975(h) S; B | 28,798,000 | — | — | 0.10 | 0.45 | — |
| 1976(h) S; B | 48,388,000 | — | — | 0.10 | 0.45 | — |
| 1977(h) S; B | 32,238,999 | — | — | 0.10 | 0.45 | — |
| 1978(h) S; B | 17,444,000 | — | — | 0.10 | 0.35 | — |

**25 ORE** **KM# 861.2** **Composition:** Copper-Nickel **Ruler:** Margrethe II

| Date | Mintage | F | VF | XF | Unc | BU |
|---|---|---|---|---|---|---|
| 1979(h) B; B | 24,261,000 | — | — | 0.10 | 0.35 | — |
| 1980(h) B; B | 30,448,000 | — | — | 0.10 | 0.35 | — |
| 1981(h) B; B | 1,427,000 | — | — | 0.10 | 0.35 | — |

**25 ORE** **KM# 861.3** **Composition:** Copper-Nickel **Ruler:** Margrethe II

| Date | Mintage | F | VF | XF | Unc | BU |
|---|---|---|---|---|---|---|
| 1982(h) R; B | 24,671,000 | — | — | 0.10 | 0.35 | — |
| 1983(h) R; B | 32,706,000 | — | — | 0.10 | 0.35 | — |
| 1984(h) R; B | 22,882,000 | — | — | 0.10 | 0.35 | — |
| 1985(h) R; B | 29,048,000 | — | — | 0.10 | 0.35 | — |
| 1986(h) R; B | 53,496,000 | — | — | 0.10 | 0.35 | — |
| 1987(h) R; B | 30,575,000 | — | — | 0.10 | 0.35 | — |
| 1988(h) R; B | 23,370,000 | — | — | 0.10 | 0.35 | — |

**25 ORE** **KM# 868** **Composition:** Bronze **Ruler:** Margrethe II **Note:** Beginning in 1996 and ending with 1998, the words "DANMARK" and "ORE" have raised edges. Heart mint mark under "ORE".

| Date | Mintage | F | VF | XF | Unc | BU |
|---|---|---|---|---|---|---|
| 1990 LG; JP and A | 109,084,000 | — | — | — | 0.15 | — |
| 1991 LG; JP and A | 102,162,000 | — | — | — | 0.15 | — |
| 1992 LG; JP and A | 6,293,000 | — | — | — | 0.15 | — |
| 1993 LG; JP and A | 14,756,000 | — | — | — | 0.15 | — |
| 1994 LG; JP and A | 35,750,000 | — | — | — | 0.15 | — |
| 1995 LG; JP and A | 40,000,000 | — | — | — | 0.15 | — |
| 1996 LG; JP and A | 46,760,000 | — | — | — | 0.15 | — |
| 1997 LG; JP and A | 30,306,000 | — | — | — | 0.15 | — |
| 1998 LG; JP and A | 17,200,000 | — | — | — | 0.15 | — |
| 1999 LG; JP and A | 18,748,000 | — | — | — | 0.15 | — |
| 2000 | 14,500,000 | — | — | — | 0.15 | — |
| 2001 | Inc. above | — | — | — | 0.15 | — |

**50 ORE** **KM# 866.1** **Composition:** Bronze **Ruler:** Margrethe II **Note:** Heart mint mark under the word "Ore". Mintmasters initials: NR. Moneyers initials: JP and A.

| Date | Mintage | F | VF | XF | Unc | BU |
|---|---|---|---|---|---|---|
| 1989 NR; JP and A | 92,236,000 | — | — | — | 0.20 | — |
| 1989 | 92,236,000 | — | — | — | 0.20 | — |

**50 ORE** **KM# 866.2** **Composition:** Bronze **Ruler:** Margrethe II **Note:** Beginning in 1996 and ending with 1998, the words "DANMARK" and "ORE" have raised edges. Heart mint mark under the word "ORE". Mintmasters initials: LG. Moneyers initials: JP and A.

| Date | Mintage | F | VF | XF | Unc | BU |
|---|---|---|---|---|---|---|
| 1990 LG; JP and A | 63,518,000 | — | — | — | 0.20 | — |
| 1991 LG; JP and A | 11,115,000 | — | — | — | 0.20 | — |
| 1992 LG; JP and A | 14,397,000 | — | — | — | 0.20 | — |
| 1993 LG; JP and A | 14,328,000 | — | — | — | 0.20 | — |
| 1994 LG; JP and A | 25,055,000 | — | — | — | 0.20 | — |
| 1995 LG; JP and A | 15,988,000 | — | — | — | 0.20 | — |
| 1996 LG; JP and A | 11,536,000 | — | — | — | 0.20 | — |
| 1997 LG; JP and A | 15,574,000 | — | — | — | 0.20 | — |
| 1998 LG; JP and A | 13,120,000 | — | — | — | 0.20 | — |
| 1999 LG; JP and A | 14,186,000 | — | — | — | 0.20 | — |
| 2000 | 15,500,000 | — | — | — | 0.20 | — |
| 2001 | Inc. above | — | — | — | 0.20 | — |

**1/2 KRONE** **KM# 831.1** **Composition:** Aluminum-Bronze **Ruler:** Christian X

| Date | Mintage | F | VF | XF | Unc | BU |
|---|---|---|---|---|---|---|
| 1924(h) HCN; GJ | 2,150,000 | 4.00 | 8.00 | 14.50 | 42.50 | — |
| 1925(h) HCN; GJ | 3,432,000 | 4.00 | 8.00 | 16.50 | 47.50 | — |
| 1926(h) HCN; GJ | 716,000 | 11.50 | 20.00 | 32.00 | 65.00 | — |

**1/2 KRONE** **KM# 831.2** **Composition:** Aluminum-Bronze **Ruler:** Christian X

| Date | Mintage | F | VF | XF | Unc | BU |
|---|---|---|---|---|---|---|
| 1939(h) N; GJ | 226,000 | 60.00 | 85.00 | 115 | 150 | — |
| 1940(h) N; GJ | 1,871,000 | 4.00 | 8.00 | 11.00 | 17.50 | — |

**KRONE** **KM# 819** **Weight:** 7.5000 g. **Composition:** 0.8000 Silver .1929 oz. ASW **Ruler:** Christian X

| Date | Mintage | F | VF | XF | Unc | BU |
|---|---|---|---|---|---|---|
| 1915(h) VBP; AH | 1,410,000 | 2.25 | 4.50 | 7.50 | 18.50 | — |
| 1916(h) VBP; AH | 992,000 | 3.75 | 8.00 | 14.00 | 22.00 | — |

**KRONE** **KM# 824.1** **Composition:** Aluminum-Bronze **Ruler:** Christian X

| Date | Mintage | F | VF | XF | Unc | BU |
|---|---|---|---|---|---|---|
| 1924(h) HCN; GJ | 999,000 | 135 | 285 | 750 | 2,000 | — |
| 1925(h) HCN; GJ | 6,314,000 | 1.50 | 7.00 | 30.00 | 82.00 | — |
| 1926(h) HCN; GJ | 2,706,000 | 1.50 | 7.00 | 32.50 | 90.00 | — |

**KRONE** **KM# 824.2** **Composition:** Aluminum-Bronze **Ruler:** Christian X

| Date | Mintage | F | VF | XF | Unc | BU |
|---|---|---|---|---|---|---|
| 1929(h) N; GJ | 501,000 | 5.50 | 12.50 | 60.00 | 185 | — |
| 1930(h) N; GJ | 540,000 | 16.00 | 27.50 | 80.00 | 290 | — |
| 1931(h) N; GJ | 540,000 | 5.50 | 12.00 | 45.00 | 155 | — |
| 1934(h) N; GJ | 529,000 | 3.75 | 8.00 | 35.00 | 125 | — |
| 1935(h) N; GJ | 505,000 | 25.00 | 40.00 | 72.50 | 185 | — |
| 1936(h) N; GJ | 558,000 | 8.00 | 15.00 | 36.50 | 135 | — |
| 1938(h) N; GJ | 407,000 | 14.00 | 22.00 | 36.50 | 130 | — |
| 1939(h) N; GJ | 1,517,000 | 1.75 | 2.75 | 8.50 | 40.00 | — |
| 1940(h) N; GJ | 1,496,000 | 1.75 | 3.25 | 8.00 | 42.50 | — |
| 1941(h) N; GJ | 661,000 | 7.00 | 14.00 | 36.50 | 185 | — |

**KRONE** **KM# 835** **Composition:** Aluminum-Bronze **Ruler:** Christian X

| Date | Mintage | F | VF | XF | Unc | BU |
|---|---|---|---|---|---|---|
| 1942(h) N; S | 3,952,000 | 1.00 | 2.75 | 8.50 | 36.00 | — |
| 1943(h) N; S | 798,000 | 7.00 | 16.00 | 82.50 | 285 | — |
| 1944(h) N; S | 1,760,000 | 1.35 | 2.25 | 14.00 | 47.50 | — |
| 1945(h) N; S | 2,581,000 | 1.35 | 2.25 | 7.00 | 35.00 | — |
| 1946(h) N; S | 4,321,000 | 1.00 | 1.75 | 4.50 | 20.00 | — |
| 1947(h) N; S | 5,060,000 | 1.00 | 1.50 | 2.25 | 9.50 | — |

**KRONE** **KM# 837.1** **Composition:** Aluminum-Bronze **Ruler:** Frederik IX

| Date | Mintage | F | VF | XF | Unc | BU |
|---|---|---|---|---|---|---|
| 1947(h) N; S | Inc. above | 2.00 | 3.75 | 6.50 | 16.00 | — |
| 1948(h) N; S | 4,248,000 | 1.00 | 2.00 | 3.75 | 10.00 | — |
| 1949(h) N; S | 1,300,000 | 3.25 | 6.00 | 12.50 | 30.00 | — |
| 1952(h) N; S | 2,124,000 | 1.75 | 3.25 | 6.50 | 16.00 | — |
| 1953(h) N; S | 573,000 | 2.75 | 5.50 | 93.50 | 18.50 | — |
| 1954(h) N; S | 584,000 | 11.50 | 20.00 | 28.00 | 45.00 | — |
| 1955(h) N; S | 1,359,000 | 4.00 | 7.00 | 10.00 | 18.50 | — |

**KRONE** **KM# 837.2** **Composition:** Aluminum-Bronze **Ruler:** Frederik IX

| Date | Mintage | F | VF | XF | Unc | BU |
|---|---|---|---|---|---|---|
| 1956(h) C; S | 2,858,000 | 1.75 | 2.75 | 4.00 | 6.50 | — |
| 1957(h) C; S | 10,896,000 | 0.65 | 1.00 | 1.50 | 3.25 | — |
| 1958(h) C; S | 1,507,000 | 1.00 | 1.75 | 2.25 | 3.75 | — |
| 1959(h) C; S | 243,000 | 14.00 | 22.50 | 27.50 | 37.50 | — |
| 1960(h) C; S | 100 | — | — | 2,900 | 3,250 | — |

**Note:** 1960 dated coins were not released into circulation until 1969

**KRONE** **KM# 851.1** **Composition:** Copper-Nickel **Ruler:** Frederik IX

| Date | Mintage | F | VF | XF | Unc | BU |
|---|---|---|---|---|---|---|
| 1960(h) C; S | 1,000,000 | 0.75 | 1.35 | 2.75 | 7.00 | — |
| 1961(h) C; S | 10,348,000 | — | 0.35 | 1.75 | 11.50 | — |
| 1962(h) C; S | 27,068,000 | — | 0.25 | 1.75 | 10.00 | — |
| 1963(h) C; S | 32,083,000 | — | 0.25 | 1.35 | 5.00 | — |
| 1964(h) C; S | 5,984,000 | — | 0.25 | 1.35 | 5.00 | — |
| 1965(h) C; S | 13,799,000 | — | 0.25 | 1.00 | 5.50 | — |
| 1966(h) C; S | 10,890,000 | — | 0.25 | 1.00 | 4.50 | — |
| 1967(h) C; S | 18,304,000 | — | 0.25 | 1.00 | 4.50 | — |
| 1968(h) C; S | 8,212,999 | — | 0.25 | 0.75 | 3.75 | — |
| 1969(h) C; S | 9,597,000 | — | 0.25 | 0.65 | 1.75 | — |
| 1970(h) C; S | 9,460,000 | — | — | 0.45 | 1.35 | — |
| 1971(h) C; S | 13,985,000 | — | — | 0.25 | 0.75 | — |

**KRONE** **KM# 851.2** **Composition:** Copper-Nickel **Ruler:** Frederik IX

| Date | Mintage | F | VF | XF | Unc | BU |
|---|---|---|---|---|---|---|
| 1972(h) S; S | 21,019,000 | — | — | 0.25 | 0.50 | — |

**KRONE** **KM# 862.1** **Composition:** Copper-Nickel **Ruler:** Margrethe II

| Date | Mintage | F | VF | XF | Unc | BU |
|---|---|---|---|---|---|---|
| 1973(h) S; B Narrow rim (0.7mm) | 18,268,000 | — | — | 0.25 | 0.75 | — |
| 1973(h) S; B Wide rim (1.1mm) | Inc. above | — | — | 0.30 | 0.75 | — |
| 1974(h) S; B | 17,742,000 | — | — | 0.30 | 0.75 | — |
| 1975(h) S; B | 20,136,000 | — | — | 0.30 | 0.75 | — |
| 1976(h) S; B | 28,049,000 | — | — | 0.30 | 0.75 | — |
| 1977(h) S; B | 25,685,000 | — | — | 0.30 | 0.75 | — |
| 1978(h) S; B | 11,286,000 | — | — | 0.30 | 0.75 | — |

**KRONE** **KM# 862.2** **Composition:** Copper-Nickel **Ruler:** Margrethe II

| Date | Mintage | F | VF | XF | Unc | BU |
|---|---|---|---|---|---|---|
| 1979(h) B; B | 25,216,000 | — | — | 0.25 | 0.75 | — |
| 1980(h) B; B | 25,825,000 | — | — | 0.25 | 0.75 | — |
| 1981(h) B; B | 8,889,000 | — | — | 0.25 | 0.75 | — |

**KRONE** **KM# 862.3** **Composition:** Copper-Nickel **Ruler:** Margrethe II

| Date | Mintage | F | VF | XF | Unc | BU |
|---|---|---|---|---|---|---|
| 1982(h) R; B | 5,011,000 | — | — | 0.25 | 0.50 | — |
| 1983(h) R; B | 13,946,000 | — | — | 0.20 | 0.50 | — |
| 1984(h) R; B | 36,439,000 | — | — | 0.20 | 0.40 | — |
| 1985(h) R; B | 10,843,000 | — | — | 0.20 | 0.40 | — |
| 1986(h) R; B | 12,556,000 | — | — | 0.20 | 0.40 | — |
| 1987(h) R; B | 20,120,000 | — | — | 0.20 | 0.40 | — |

| Date | Mintage | F | VF | XF | Unc | BU |
|---|---|---|---|---|---|---|
| 1988(h) R; B | 32,073,999 | — | — | 0.20 | 0.40 | — |
| 1989(h) R; B | 15,704,000 | — | — | 0.20 | 0.40 | — |

**KRONE** **KM# 873** **Composition:** Copper-Nickel **Ruler:** Margrethe II **Reverse:** Crowned MII monograms

| Date | Mintage | F | VF | XF | Unc | BU |
|---|---|---|---|---|---|---|
| 1992 LG; JP and A | 81,621,000 | — | — | — | 0.35 | — |
| 1993 LG; JP and A | 15,844,000 | — | — | — | 0.35 | — |
| 1994 LG; JP and A | 23,658,000 | — | — | — | 0.35 | — |
| 1995 LG; JP and A | 34,966,000 | — | — | — | 0.35 | — |
| 1996 LG; JP and A | 10,081,000 | — | — | — | 0.35 | — |
| 1997 LG; JP and A | 10,121,000 | — | — | — | 0.35 | — |
| 1998 LG; JP and A | 13,080,000 | — | — | — | 0.35 | — |
| 1999 LG; JP and A | 6,479,000 | — | — | — | 0.35 | — |
| 2000 | 21,500,000 | — | — | — | 0.35 | — |
| 2001 | Inc. above | — | — | — | 0.35 | — |

**2 KRONER** **KM# 802** **Weight:** 15.0000 g. **Composition:** 0.8000 Silver .3858 oz. ASW **Ruler:** Christian IX **Subject:** 40th Anniversary of Reign

| Date | Mintage | F | VF | XF | Unc | BU |
|---|---|---|---|---|---|---|
| 1903(h) P; GJ | 103,000 | 5.50 | 14.00 | 25.00 | 40.00 | — |

**2 KRONER** **KM# 803** **Weight:** 15.0000 g. **Composition:** 0.8000 Silver .3858 oz. ASW **Ruler:** Christian IX **Subject:** Death of Christian IX and Accession of Frederik VIII

| Date | Mintage | F | VF | XF | Unc | BU |
|---|---|---|---|---|---|---|
| 1906(h) VBP GJ | 151,000 | 3.00 | 7.00 | 16.00 | 27.50 | — |

**2 KRONER** **KM# 811** **Weight:** 15.0000 g. **Composition:** 0.8000 Silver .3858 oz. ASW **Ruler:** Frederik VIII **Subject:** Death of Frederik VIII and Accession of Christian X

| Date | Mintage | F | VF | XF | Unc | BU |
|---|---|---|---|---|---|---|
| 1912(h) VBP; AH | 102,000 | 5.50 | 14.00 | 25.00 | 45.00 | — |

**2 KRONER** **KM# 820** **Weight:** 15.0000 g. **Composition:** 0.8000 Silver .3858 oz. ASW **Ruler:** Christian X

| Date | Mintage | F | VF | XF | Unc | BU |
|---|---|---|---|---|---|---|
| 1915(h) AH | 657,000 | 9.50 | 20.00 | 32.00 | 55.00 | — |
| 1916(h) AH | 402,000 | 5.50 | 11.50 | 16.50 | 32.50 | — |

**2 KRONER** **KM# 821** **Weight:** 15.0000 g. **Composition:** 0.8000 Silver .3858 oz. ASW **Ruler:** Christian X **Subject:** Silver Wedding Anniversary

| Date | Mintage | F | VF | XF | Unc | BU |
|---|---|---|---|---|---|---|
| 1923(h) HCN; GJ | 203,000 | — | — | 11.50 | 20.00 | — |

**2 KRONER** **KM# 825.1** **Composition:** Aluminum-Bronze **Ruler:** Christian X

| Date | Mintage | F | VF | XF | Unc | BU |
|---|---|---|---|---|---|---|
| 1924(h) HCN; GJ | 1,138,000 | 18.50 | 90.00 | 430 | 1,500 | — |
| 1925(h) HCN; GJ | 3,248,000 | 1.35 | 9.50 | 27.50 | 87.50 | — |
| 1926(h) HCN; GJ | 1,126,000 | 1.35 | 9.50 | 35.00 | 120 | — |

**2 KRONER** **KM# 829** **Weight:** 15.0000 g. **Composition:** 0.8000 Silver .3858 oz. ASW **Ruler:** Christian X **Subject:** King's 60th Birthday

| Date | Mintage | F | VF | XF | Unc | BU |
|---|---|---|---|---|---|---|
| 1930(h) N; AH/HS | 303,000 | — | — | 5.00 | 9.50 | — |

**2 KRONER** **KM# 825.2** **Composition:** Aluminum-Bronze **Ruler:** Christian X

| Date | Mintage | F | VF | XF | Unc | BU |
|---|---|---|---|---|---|---|
| 1936(h) N; GJ | 400,000 | 5.50 | 13.00 | 60.00 | 290 | — |
| 1938(h) N; GJ | 191,000 | 14.00 | 22.50 | 67.50 | 200 | — |
| 1939(h) N; GJ | 723,000 | 2.00 | 3.75 | 9.50 | 35.00 | — |
| 1940(h) N; GJ | 743,000 | 6.00 | 10.00 | 20.00 | 55.00 | — |
| 1941(h) N; GJ | 129,000 | 35.00 | 50.00 | 160 | 375 | — |

**2 KRONER** **KM# 830** **Weight:** 15.0000 g. **Composition:** 0.8000 Silver .3858 oz. ASW **Ruler:** Christian X **Subject:** 25th Anniversary of Reign

| Date | Mintage | F | VF | XF | Unc | BU |
|---|---|---|---|---|---|---|
| ND(1937)(h) N; S | 209,000 | — | — | 6.50 | 14.00 | — |

**2 KRONER** **KM# 836** **Weight:** 15.0000 g. **Composition:** 0.8000 Silver .3858 oz. ASW **Ruler:** Christian X **Subject:** King's 75th Birthday

| Date | Mintage | F | VF | XF | Unc | BU |
|---|---|---|---|---|---|---|
| ND(1945)(h) N; S | 157,000 | — | — | 8.50 | 16.00 | — |

**2 KRONER** **KM# 838.1** **Composition:** Aluminum-Bronze **Ruler:** Frederik IX

| Date | Mintage | F | VF | XF | Unc | BU |
|---|---|---|---|---|---|---|
| 1947(h) N; S | 1,151,000 | 2.25 | 4.00 | 10.00 | 20.00 | — |
| 1948(h) N; S | 857,000 | 1.75 | 2.75 | 6.50 | 14.50 | — |
| 1949(h) N; S | 272,000 | 4.50 | 9.50 | 18.50 | 36.00 | — |
| 1951(h) N; S | 1,576,000 | 1.35 | 2.25 | 4.50 | 15.00 | — |
| 1952(h) N; S | 1,958,000 | 1.00 | 2.00 | 4.00 | 11.50 | — |
| 1953(h) N; S | 432,000 | 2.25 | 4.50 | 9.50 | 25.00 | — |
| 1954(h) N; S | 716,000 | 2.25 | 4.00 | 8.00 | 16.50 | — |
| 1955(h) N; S | 457,000 | 3.75 | 6.50 | 9.50 | 17.50 | — |

**2 KRONER** **KM# 844** **Weight:** 15.0000 g. **Composition:** 0.8000 Silver .3858 oz. ASW **Ruler:** Frederik IX **Note:** Greenland Commemorative.

| Date | Mintage | F | VF | XF | Unc | BU |
|---|---|---|---|---|---|---|
| 1953(h) N; S | 152,000 | — | 4.50 | 14.00 | 25.00 | — |

**2 KRONER** **KM# 838.2** **Composition:** Aluminum-Bronze **Ruler:** Frederik IX

| Date | Mintage | F | VF | XF | Unc | BU |
|---|---|---|---|---|---|---|
| 1956(h) C; S | 1,444,000 | 1.75 | 2.75 | 4.50 | 8.50 | — |
| 1957(h) C; S | 2,610,000 | 1.00 | 1.65 | 2.25 | 4.50 | — |
| 1958(h) C; S | 2,605,000 | 1.25 | 1.85 | 2.75 | 5.50 | — |
| 1959(h) C; S | 192,000 | 14.50 | 21.50 | 28.00 | 42.50 | — |

**2 KRONER** **KM# 845** **Weight:** 15.0000 g. **Composition:** 0.8000 Silver .3858 oz. ASW **Ruler:** Frederik IX **Subject:** Princess Margrethe's 18th Birthday

| Date | Mintage | F | VF | XF | Unc | BU |
|---|---|---|---|---|---|---|
| ND(1958)(h) C; S | 301,000 | — | — | 7.00 | 11.50 | — |

**2 KRONER** KM# 874 **Composition:** Copper-Nickel **Ruler:** Margrethe II **Reverse:** Crowned MII monograms

| Date | Mintage | F | VF | XF | Unc | BU |
|---|---|---|---|---|---|---|
| 1992 LG; JP and A | 41,648,000 | — | — | — | 0.60 | — |
| 1993 LG; JP and A | 43,864,000 | — | — | — | 0.60 | — |
| 1994 LG; JP and A | 27,629,000 | — | — | — | 0.60 | — |
| 1995 LG; JP and A | 19,850,000 | — | — | — | 0.60 | — |
| 1996 LG; JP and A | 2,884,000 | — | — | — | 0.60 | — |
| 1997 LG; JP and A | 25,874,000 | — | — | — | 0.60 | — |
| 1998 LG; JP and A | 4,360,000 | — | — | — | 0.60 | — |
| 1999 LG; JP and A | 20,608,000 | — | — | — | 0.60 | — |
| 2000 | 10,400,000 | — | — | — | 0.60 | — |
| 2001 | Inc. above | — | — | — | 0.60 | — |

**5 KRONER** KM# 852 **Weight:** 17.0000 g. **Composition:** 0.8000 Silver .4372 oz. ASW **Ruler:** Frederik IX **Subject:** Silver Wedding Anniversary

| Date | Mintage | F | VF | XF | Unc | BU |
|---|---|---|---|---|---|---|
| ND(1960)(h) C; S | 410,000 | — | 3.50 | 5.50 | 9.50 | — |

**5 KRONER** KM# 853.1 **Composition:** Copper-Nickel **Ruler:** Frederik IX

| Date | Mintage | F | VF | XF | Unc | BU |
|---|---|---|---|---|---|---|
| 1960(h) C; S | 6,418,000 | — | 1.50 | 2.50 | 9.50 | — |
| 1961(h) C; S | 9,744,000 | — | 1.50 | 3.25 | 15.00 | — |
| 1962(h) C; S | 2,073,999 | — | 2.50 | 4.00 | 15.00 | — |
| 1963(h) C; S | 709,000 | — | 2.00 | 3.00 | 18.50 | — |
| 1964(h) C; S | 1,443,000 | — | 1.50 | 4.00 | 16.00 | — |
| 1965(h) C; S | 2,574,000 | — | 1.50 | 2.50 | 14.00 | — |
| 1966(h) C; S | 4,370,000 | — | 1.35 | 1.85 | 8.50 | — |
| 1967(h) C; S | 1,864,000 | — | 1.35 | 1.85 | 5.50 | — |
| 1968(h) C; S | 4,131,999 | — | 1.35 | 1.85 | 4.50 | — |
| 1969(h) C; S | 72,000 | 2.00 | 4.50 | 7.50 | 10.00 | — |
| 1970(h) C; S | 2,246,000 | — | — | 1.35 | 2.25 | — |
| 1971(h) C; S | 4,767,000 | — | — | 1.35 | 1.85 | — |

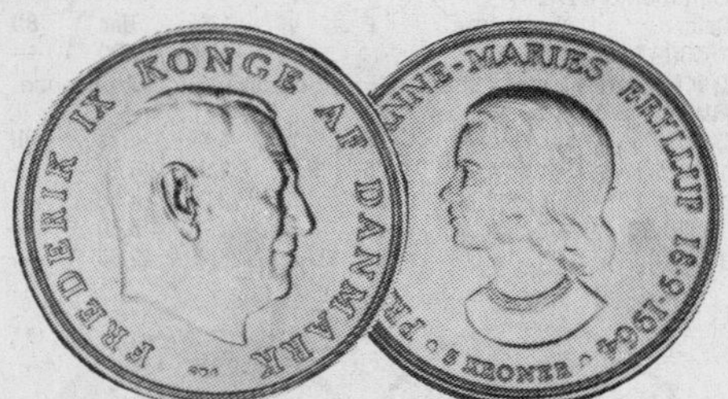


**5 KRONER** KM# 854 **Weight:** 17.0000 g. **Composition:** 0.8000 Silver .4372 oz. ASW **Ruler:** Frederik IX **Subject:** Wedding of Princess Anne Marie

| Date | Mintage | F | VF | XF | Unc | BU |
|---|---|---|---|---|---|---|
| 1964(h) C; S | 359,000 | — | — | 5.50 | 9.50 | — |

**5 KRONER** KM# 853.2 **Composition:** Copper-Nickel **Ruler:** Frederik IX

| Date | Mintage | F | VF | XF | Unc | BU |
|---|---|---|---|---|---|---|
| 1972(h) S; S | 2,599,000 | — | — | 1.25 | 1.75 | — |

**5 KRONER** KM# 863.1 **Composition:** Copper-Nickel **Ruler:** Margrethe II

| Date | Mintage | F | VF | XF | Unc | BU |
|---|---|---|---|---|---|---|
| 1973(h) S; B Narrow rim (1.0mm) | 3,774,000 | — | — | 1.25 | 2.25 | — |
| 1973(h) S; B Wide rim (1.5mm) | Inc. above | — | — | 1.25 | 2.25 | — |
| 1974(h) S; B | 5,239,000 | — | — | 1.25 | 2.25 | — |
| 1975(h) S; B | 5,810,000 | — | — | 2.25 | 5.50 | — |
| 1976(h) S; B | 7,651,000 | — | — | 1.35 | 2.75 | — |
| 1977(h) S; B | 6,885,000 | — | — | 1.35 | 2.75 | — |
| 1978(h) S; B | 2,984,000 | — | — | 1.35 | 2.75 | — |

**5 KRONER** KM# 863.2 **Composition:** Copper-Nickel **Ruler:** Margrethe II

| Date | Mintage | F | VF | XF | Unc | BU |
|---|---|---|---|---|---|---|
| 1979(h) B; B | 2,861,000 | — | — | 1.35 | 2.25 | — |
| 1980(h) B; B | 3,622,000 | — | — | 2.25 | 4.00 | — |
| 1981(h) B; B | 1,057,000 | — | — | 1.35 | 2.25 | — |

**5 KRONER** KM# 863.3 **Composition:** Copper-Nickel **Ruler:** Margrethe II

| Date | Mintage | F | VF | XF | Unc | BU |
|---|---|---|---|---|---|---|
| 1982(h) R; B | 1,002,000 | — | — | 2.25 | 4.00 | — |
| 1983(h) R; B | 1,044,000 | — | — | 1.25 | 2.25 | — |
| 1984(h) R; B | 713,000 | — | — | 1.25 | 2.25 | — |
| 1985(h) R; B | 621,000 | — | — | 1.25 | 2.25 | — |
| 1986(h) R; B | 1,042,000 | — | — | 1.25 | 2.25 | — |
| 1987(h) R; B | 611,000 | — | — | 1.25 | 2.25 | — |
| 1988(h) R; B | 648,000 | — | — | 1.25 | 2.25 | — |

**5 KRONER** KM# 869 **Composition:** Copper-Nickel **Ruler:** Margrethe II

| Date | Mintage | F | VF | XF | Unc | BU |
|---|---|---|---|---|---|---|
| 1990 LG; JP and A | 46,745,000 | — | — | — | 1.25 | — |
| 1991 LG; JP and A | 3,752,000 | — | — | — | 1.25 | — |
| 1992 LG; JP and A | 2,426,000 | — | — | — | 1.25 | — |
| 1993 LG; JP and A | 1,538,000 | — | — | — | 1.25 | — |
| 1994 LG; JP and A | 7,920,000 | — | — | — | 1.25 | — |
| 1995 LG; JP and A | 5,850,000 | — | — | — | 1.25 | — |
| 1997 LG; JP and A | 5,258,000 | — | — | — | 1.25 | — |
| 1998 LG; JP and A | 6,450,000 | — | — | — | 1.25 | — |
| 1999 LG; JP and A | 4,786,000 | — | — | — | 1.25 | — |
| 2000 | 2,800,000 | — | — | — | 1.25 | — |
| 2001 | Inc. above | — | — | — | 1.25 | — |

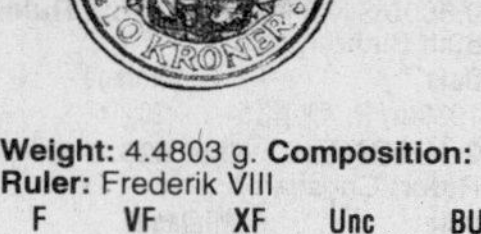


**10 KRONER** KM# 809 **Weight:** 4.4803 g. **Composition:** 0.9000 Gold .1296 oz. AGW **Ruler:** Frederik VIII

| Date | Mintage | F | VF | XF | Unc | BU |
|---|---|---|---|---|---|---|
| 1908(h) VBP; GJ | 308,000 | — | BV | 50.00 | 80.00 | — |
| 1909(h) VBP; GJ | 153,000 | — | BV | 55.00 | 85.00 | — |

**10 KRONER** KM# 816 **Weight:** 4.4803 g. **Composition:** 0.9000 Gold .1296 oz. AGW **Ruler:** Christian X

| Date | Mintage | F | VF | XF | Unc | BU |
|---|---|---|---|---|---|---|
| 1913(h) AH/ GJ | 312,000 | — | BV | 50.00 | 80.00 | — |
| 1917(h) AH/ GJ | 132,000 | — | BV | 60.00 | 90.00 | — |

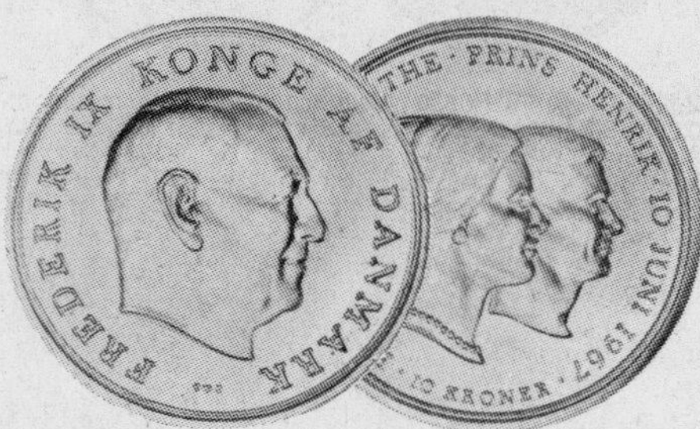


**10 KRONER** KM# 856 **Weight:** 20.4000 g. **Composition:** 0.8000 Silver .5247 oz. ASW **Ruler:** Frederik IX **Subject:** Wedding of Princess Margrethe

| Date | Mintage | F | VF | XF | Unc | BU |
|---|---|---|---|---|---|---|
| ND(1967)(h) C; S | 419,000 | — | — | 5.50 | 9.50 | — |

**Note:** 78,383 were melted

**10 KRONER** KM# 857 **Weight:** 20.4000 g. **Composition:** 0.8000 Silver .5247 oz. ASW **Ruler:** Frederik IX **Subject:** Wedding of Princess Benedikte

| Date | Mintage | F | VF | XF | Unc | BU |
|---|---|---|---|---|---|---|
| ND(1968)(h) C; S | 254,000 | — | — | 6.00 | 11.50 | — |

**Note:** 42,923 were melted

**10 KRONER** KM# 858 **Weight:** 20.4000 g. **Composition:** 0.8000 Silver .5247 oz. ASW **Ruler:** Frederik IX **Subject:** Death of Frederik IX and Accession of Margrethe II

| Date | Mintage | F | VF | XF | Unc | BU |
|---|---|---|---|---|---|---|
| 1972(h) S; S | 402,000 | — | — | 5.50 | 7.50 | — |

**10 KRONER** KM# 864.1 **Composition:** Copper-Nickel **Ruler:** Margrethe II

| Date | Mintage | F | VF | XF | Unc | BU |
|---|---|---|---|---|---|---|
| 1979(h) B; B | 76,801,000 | — | — | 1.35 | 2.75 | — |
| 1981(h) B; B | 10,520,000 | — | 2.00 | 4.00 | 9.50 | — |

**10 KRONER** KM# 864.2 **Composition:** Copper-Nickel **Ruler:** Margrethe II

| Date | Mintage | F | VF | XF | Unc | BU |
|---|---|---|---|---|---|---|
| 1982(h) R; B | 1,065,000 | — | 2.00 | 4.00 | 9.50 | — |
| 1983(h) R; B | 1,123,000 | — | 2.00 | 4.00 | 9.50 | — |
| 1984(h) R; B | 748,000 | — | 2.00 | 3.25 | 9.50 | — |
| 1985(h) R; B | 720,000 | — | 2.00 | 3.25 | 11.50 | — |
| 1987(h) R; B | 719,000 | — | 2.00 | 3.25 | 9.50 | — |
| 1988(h) R; B | 718,000 | — | 2.00 | 3.25 | 8.50 | — |

**10 KRONER** **KM# 865** **Composition:** Copper-Nickel **Ruler:** Margrethe II **Subject:** Crown Prince's 18th Birthday

| Date | Mintage | F | VF | XF | Unc | BU |
|---|---|---|---|---|---|---|
| ND(1986)(h) R; A | 1,090,000 | — | — | — | 2.75 | — |
| ND(1986)(h) R; A Proof | 2,000 | Value: 200 | | | | |

**10 KRONER** **KM# 865a** **Weight:** 14.3000 g. **Composition:** 0.8000 Silver .3678 oz. ASW **Ruler:** Margrethe II

| Date | Mintage | F | VF | XF | Unc | BU |
|---|---|---|---|---|---|---|
| 1986(h) R; A Proof | 24,000 | Value: 52.50 | | | | |

**10 KRONER** **KM# 867.1** **Composition:** Aluminum-Bronze **Ruler:** Margrethe II

| Date | Mintage | F | VF | XF | Unc | BU |
|---|---|---|---|---|---|---|
| 1989 NR; JP and A | 38,346,000 | — | — | — | 2.00 | — |

**10 KRONER** **KM# 867.2** **Composition:** Aluminum-Bronze **Ruler:** Margrethe II

| Date | Mintage | F | VF | XF | Unc | BU |
|---|---|---|---|---|---|---|
| 1990 LG; JP and A | 12,193,000 | — | — | — | 2.00 | — |
| 1991 LG; JP and A | 1,065,000 | — | — | — | 2.00 | — |
| 1992 LG; JP and A | 484,000 | — | — | — | 3.25 | — |
| 1993 LG; JP and A | 1,069,000 | — | — | — | 2.00 | — |

**10 KRONER** **KM# 877** **Composition:** Aluminum-Bronze **Ruler:** Margrethe II **Obverse:** New portrait of Queen Margrethe **Edge:** Plain **Note:** Beginning with strikes in 1995 and ending in 1998, letters and numbers on reverse have raised edges.

| Date | Mintage | F | VF | XF | Unc | BU |
|---|---|---|---|---|---|---|
| 1994 LG; JP and A | 4,058,000 | — | — | — | 2.00 | — |
| 1995 LG; JP and A | 9,461,000 | — | — | — | 2.00 | — |
| 1997 LG; JP and A | 3,725,000 | — | — | — | 2.00 | — |
| 1998 LG; JP and A | 6,000,000 | — | — | — | 2.00 | — |
| 1999 LG; JP and A | — | — | — | — | 2.00 | — |

**10 KRONER** **KM# 887** **Weight:** 7.0000 g. **Composition:** Copper-Aluminum-Nickel **Ruler:** Margrethe II **Obverse:** Queen's new portrait **Reverse:** Crowned arms above denomination **Edge:** Plain

| Date | Mintage | F | VF | XF | Unc | BU |
|---|---|---|---|---|---|---|
| 2001 | — | — | — | — | 3.50 | — |

**20 KRONER** **KM# 810** **Weight:** 8.9606 g. **Composition:** 0.9000 Gold .2592 oz. AGW **Ruler:** Frederik VIII

| Date | Mintage | F | VF | XF | Unc | BU |
|---|---|---|---|---|---|---|
| 1908(h) VBP; GJ | 243,000 | BV | 85.00 | 110 | 170 | — |
| 1909(h) VBP; GJ | 365,000 | BV | 95.00 | 120 | 180 | — |
| 1910(h) VBP; GJ | 200,000 | BV | 100 | 125 | 190 | — |
| 1911(h) VBP; GJ | 183,000 | BV | 90.00 | 115 | 170 | — |
| 1912(h) VBP; GJ | 184,000 | BV | 90.00 | 115 | 170 | — |

**20 KRONER** **KM# 817.1** **Weight:** 8.9606 g. **Composition:** 0.9000 Gold .2592 oz. AGW **Ruler:** Frederik VIII

| Date | Mintage | F | VF | XF | Unc | BU |
|---|---|---|---|---|---|---|
| 1913(h) AH/GJ | 815,000 | BV | 85.00 | 110 | 150 | — |
| 1914(h) AH/GJ | 920,000 | BV | 85.00 | 110 | 150 | — |
| 1915(h) AH/GJ | 532,000 | BV | 85.00 | 115 | 155 | — |
| 1916(h) AH/GJ | 1,401,000 | BV | 90.00 | 120 | 170 | — |
| 1917(h) AH/GJ | Inc. above | BV | 90.00 | 115 | 160 | — |

**20 KRONER** **KM# 817.2** **Weight:** 8.9606 g. **Composition:** 0.9000 Gold .2592 oz. AGW **Ruler:** Christian X **Note:** 1926-1931 dated 20 Kroners were not released for circulation.

| Date | Mintage | F | VF | XF | Unc | BU |
|---|---|---|---|---|---|---|
| 1926(h) HCN | 358,000 | — | — | 2,750 | 4,500 | — |
| 1927(h) HCN | Inc. above | — | — | 2,750 | 4,500 | — |

**20 KRONER** **KM# 817.3** **Weight:** 8.9606 g. **Composition:** 0.9000 Gold .2592 oz. AGW **Ruler:** Christian X **Note:** The 1926-1931 dated 20 Kroners were not released for circulation.

| Date | Mintage | F | VF | XF | Unc | BU |
|---|---|---|---|---|---|---|
| 1930(h) N | 1,285,000 | — | — | 2,750 | 4,500 | — |
| 1931(h) N | Inc. above | — | — | 2,750 | 4,500 | — |

**20 KRONER** **KM# 871** **Composition:** Aluminum-Bronze **Ruler:** Margrethe II **Note:** Date varieties exist.

| Date | Mintage | F | VF | XF | Unc | BU |
|---|---|---|---|---|---|---|
| 1990(h) LG; JP and A | 34,368,000 | — | — | — | 4.00 | — |
| 1991(h) LG; JP and A | 11,563,000 | — | — | — | 4.00 | — |
| 1993(h) LG; JP and A | 674,000 | — | — | — | 4.00 | — |

**20 KRONER** **KM# 870** **Composition:** Aluminum-Bronze **Ruler:** Margrethe II **Subject:** 50th Birthday of Queen Margarethe

| Date | Mintage | F | VF | XF | Unc | BU |
|---|---|---|---|---|---|---|
| ND(1990)(h) LG | 1,101,000 | — | — | 4.00 | 5.50 | — |

**20 KRONER** **KM# 875** **Composition:** Aluminum-Bronze **Ruler:** Margrethe II **Subject:** Silver Wedding Anniversary

| Date | Mintage | F | VF | XF | Unc | BU |
|---|---|---|---|---|---|---|
| ND(1992)(h) LG | 994,000 | — | — | 4.00 | 5.50 | — |

**20 KRONER** **KM# 878** **Composition:** Aluminum-Bronze **Ruler:** Margrethe II **Obverse:** New portrait of Queen Margrethe **Edge:** Alternating reeded and plain sections **Note:** Strikes dated 1996 and 1998 have letters and numbers on reverse with raised edges.

| Date | Mintage | F | VF | XF | Unc | BU |
|---|---|---|---|---|---|---|
| 1994(h) LG, JP and A | 2,565,000 | — | — | — | 4.50 | — |
| 1996(h) LG, JP and A | 8,651,000 | — | — | — | 4.50 | — |
| 1998(h) LG, JP and A | 3,980,000 | — | — | — | 4.50 | — |
| 1999(h) LG, JP and A | — | — | — | — | 4.50 | — |

**20 KRONER** **KM# 879** **Composition:** Aluminum-Bronze **Ruler:** Margrethe II **Subject:** 1000 Years of Danish Coinage

| Date | Mintage | F | VF | XF | Unc | BU |
|---|---|---|---|---|---|---|
| ND(1995)(h) LG, JP and A | 1,000,000 | — | — | 4.00 | 5.50 | — |

**20 KRONER** **KM# 881** **Composition:** Aluminum-Bronze **Ruler:** Margrethe II **Subject:** Wedding of Prince Joachim

| Date | Mintage | F | VF | XF | Unc | BU |
|---|---|---|---|---|---|---|
| 1995(h) LJ, JP and A | 1,000,000 | — | — | 4.00 | 5.50 | — |

**Note:** Although dated 1995, minted at the end of the year and included in a 1996 mint set

**20 KRONER** **KM# 883** **Composition:** Aluminum-Bronze **Ruler:** Margrethe II **Subject:** 25th Anniversary - Queen's Reign **Obverse:** Full-length portrait **Reverse:** Crowned arms

| Date | Mintage | F | VF | XF | Unc | BU |
|---|---|---|---|---|---|---|
| ND(1997)(h) LG, JP and A | — | — | — | 4.00 | 5.50 | — |

**20 KRONER** **KM# 885** **Weight:** 9.3600 g. **Composition:** Brass **Ruler:** Margrethe II **Subject:** 60th Birthday of Queen Margrethe II **Obverse:** Bust of Queen Margrethe II right **Reverse:** Crown above flowers **Edge:** Alternating reeded and plain sections

| Date | Mintage | F | VF | XF | Unc | BU |
|---|---|---|---|---|---|---|
| ND(2000) | — | — | — | 4.00 | 5.50 | — |

**20 KRONER** **KM# 888** **Weight:** 9.3000 g. **Composition:** Copper-Aluminum-Nickel **Ruler:** Margrethe II **Obverse:** Queen's new portrait **Reverse:** Crowned arms above denomination **Edge:** Alternating reeded and plain sections

| Date | Mintage | F | VF | XF | Unc | BU |
|---|---|---|---|---|---|---|
| 2001 | — | — | — | — | 5.00 | — |

**200 KRONER** **KM# 872** **Weight:** 31.1000 g. **Composition:** 0.8000 Silver .8000 oz. ASW **Ruler:** Margrethe II **Subject:** 50th Birthday of Queen Margrethe

| Date | Mintage | F | VF | XF | Unc | BU |
|---|---|---|---|---|---|---|
| ND(1990) | 128,000 | — | — | — | 37.50 | — |

**200 KRONER** **KM# 876** **Weight:** 31.1000 g. **Composition:** 0.9990 Silver 1.0000 oz. ASW **Ruler:** Margrethe II **Subject:** Silver Wedding Anniversary

| Date | Mintage | F | VF | XF | Unc | BU |
|---|---|---|---|---|---|---|
| ND(1992) | 58,000 | — | — | — | 37.50 | — |

**200 KRONER** **KM# 880** **Weight:** 31.1000 g. **Composition:** 0.9990 Silver 1.0000 oz. ASW **Ruler:** Margrethe II **Subject:** 1000 Year of Danish Coinage

| Date | Mintage | F | VF | XF | Unc | BU |
|---|---|---|---|---|---|---|
| ND(1995) | 27,000 | — | — | — | 42.50 | — |

**200 KRONER** **KM# 882** **Weight:** 31.1000 g. **Composition:** 0.9990 Silver 1.0000 oz. ASW **Ruler:** Margrethe II **Subject:** Wedding of Prince Joachim **Reverse:** Palace

| Date | Mintage | F | VF | XF | Unc | BU |
|---|---|---|---|---|---|---|
| 1995 | 55,000 | — | — | — | 37.50 | — |

**200 KRONER** **KM# 884** **Weight:** 31.1000 g. **Composition:** 0.9990 Silver 1.0000 oz. ASW **Ruler:** Margrethe II **Subject:** 25th Anniversary - Queen's Reign

| Date | Mintage | F | VF | XF | Unc | BU |
|---|---|---|---|---|---|---|
| ND(1997) | 60,000 | — | — | — | 45.00 | — |

**200 KRONER** **KM# 886** **Weight:** 31.1000 g. **Composition:** 0.9990 Silver 1.0000 oz. ASW **Ruler:** Margrethe II **Subject:** 60th Birthday of Queen Margrethe II **Obverse:** Bust of Queen Margrethe II right **Reverse:** Crown above flowers **Edge:** Plain. **Size:** 38 mm.

| Date | Mintage | F | VF | XF | Unc | BU |
|---|---|---|---|---|---|---|
| ND(2000) | 60,000 | — | — | — | 45.00 | — |

## MEDALLIC COINAGE

The Medallic Issues are similar to circulation coinage except they are without a denomination

**2 KRONER** **KM# M1** **Weight:** 15.0000 g. **Composition:** 0.8000 Silver .3858 oz. ASW **Ruler:** Christian IX **Subject:** 40th Anniversary of Reign

| Date | Mintage | F | VF | XF | Unc | BU |
|---|---|---|---|---|---|---|
| 1903(h) P Proof | — | Value: 1,875 | | | | |

**2 KRONER** **KM# M2** **Weight:** 15.0000 g. **Composition:** 0.8000 Silver .3858 oz. ASW **Ruler:** Christian X **Subject:** Silver Wedding Anniversary

| Date | Mintage | F | VF | XF | Unc | BU |
|---|---|---|---|---|---|---|
| 1923(h) HCN Proof | — | Value: 3,000 | | | | |

**2 KRONER** **KM# M3** **Weight:** 15.0000 g. **Composition:** 0.8000 Silver .3858 oz. ASW **Ruler:** Christian X **Subject:** King's 60th Birthday

| Date | Mintage | F | VF | XF | Unc | BU |
|---|---|---|---|---|---|---|
| 1930(h) N Proof | — | Value: 2,700 | | | | |

**2 KRONER** **KM# M4** **Weight:** 15.0000 g. **Composition:** 0.8000 Silver .3858 oz. ASW **Ruler:** Christian X **Subject:** 25th Anniversary of Reign

| Date | Mintage | F | VF | XF | Unc | BU |
|---|---|---|---|---|---|---|
| 1937(h) N; S Proof | — | Value: 3,450 | | | | |

**2 KRONER** **KM# M5** **Weight:** 15.0000 g. **Composition:** 0.8000 Silver .3858 oz. ASW **Ruler:** Christian X **Subject:** King's 75th Birthday

| Date | Mintage | F | VF | XF | Unc | BU |
|---|---|---|---|---|---|---|
| ND(1945)(h) N; S Proof | — | Value: 1,275 | | | | |

**2 KRONER** **KM# M6** **Weight:** 15.0000 g. **Composition:** 0.8000 Silver .3858 oz. ASW **Ruler:** Frederik IX **Note:** Greenland Commemorative.

| Date | Mintage | F | VF | XF | Unc | BU |
|---|---|---|---|---|---|---|
| 1953(h) N; S Proof | — | Value: 3,150 | | | | |

**2 KRONER** **KM# M7** **Weight:** 15.0000 g. **Composition:** 0.8000 Silver .3858 oz. ASW **Ruler:** Frederik IX **Subject:** Princess Margrethe's 18th Birthday

| Date | Mintage | F | VF | XF | Unc | BU |
|---|---|---|---|---|---|---|
| ND(1958)(h) C; S Proof | 110 | Value: 350 | | | | |

**5 KRONER** **KM# M8** **Weight:** 17.0000 g. **Composition:** 0.8000 Silver .4372 oz. ASW **Ruler:** Frederik IX **Subject:** Silver Wedding Anniversary

| Date | Mintage | F | VF | XF | Unc | BU |
|---|---|---|---|---|---|---|
| ND(1960)(h) C; S Proof | 250 | Value: 245 | | | | |

**5 KRONER** **KM# M9** **Weight:** 17.0000 g. **Composition:** 0.8000 Silver .4372 oz. ASW **Ruler:** Frederik IX **Subject:** Wedding of Princess Anne Marie

| Date | Mintage | F | VF | XF | Unc | BU |
|---|---|---|---|---|---|---|
| ND(1964)(h) C; S Proof | 100 | Value: 365 | | | | |

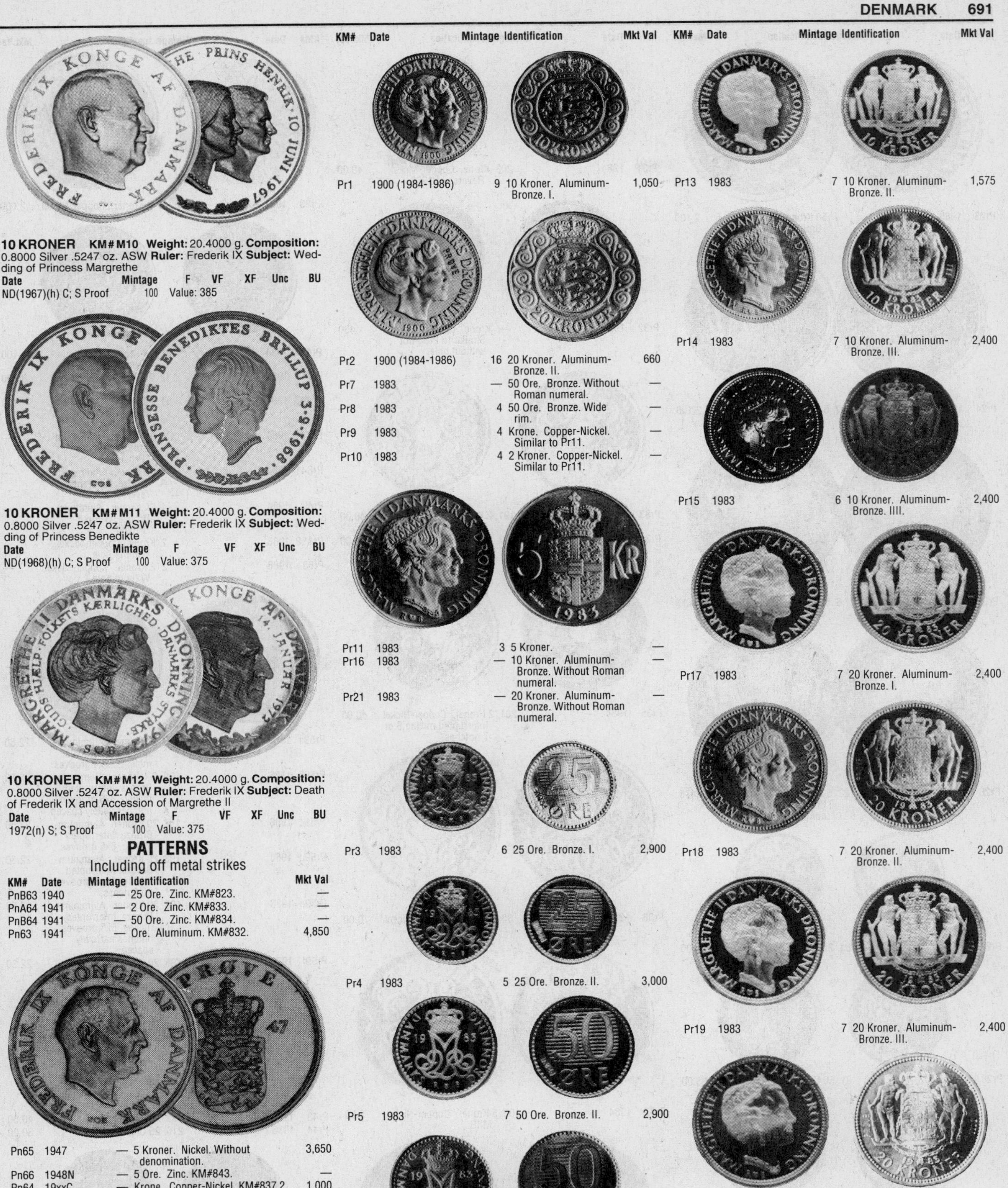

**10 KRONER** **KM# M10** **Weight:** 20.4000 g. **Composition:** 0.8000 Silver .5247 oz. ASW **Ruler:** Frederik IX **Subject:** Wedding of Princess Margrethe

| Date | Mintage | F | VF | XF | Unc | BU |
|---|---|---|---|---|---|---|
| ND(1967)(h) C; S Proof | 100 | Value: 385 | | | | |

**10 KRONER** **KM# M11** **Weight:** 20.4000 g. **Composition:** 0.8000 Silver .5247 oz. ASW **Ruler:** Frederik IX **Subject:** Wedding of Princess Benedikte

| Date | Mintage | F | VF | XF | Unc | BU |
|---|---|---|---|---|---|---|
| ND(1968)(h) C; S Proof | 100 | Value: 375 | | | | |

**10 KRONER** **KM# M12** **Weight:** 20.4000 g. **Composition:** 0.8000 Silver .5247 oz. ASW **Ruler:** Frederik IX **Subject:** Death of Frederik IX and Accession of Margrethe II

| Date | Mintage | F | VF | XF | Unc | BU |
|---|---|---|---|---|---|---|
| 1972(n) S; S Proof | 100 | Value: 375 | | | | |

## PATTERNS

Including off metal strikes

| KM# | Date | Mintage | Identification | Mkt Val |
|---|---|---|---|---|
| PnB63 | 1940 | — | 25 Ore. Zinc. KM#823. | — |
| PnA64 | 1941 | — | 2 Ore. Zinc. KM#833. | — |
| PnB64 | 1941 | — | 50 Ore. Zinc. KM#834. | — |
| Pn63 | 1941 | — | Ore. Aluminum. KM#832. | 4,850 |
| Pn65 | 1947 | — | 5 Kroner. Nickel. Without denomination. | 3,650 |
| Pn66 | 1948N | — | 5 Ore. Zinc. KM#843. | — |
| Pn64 | 19xxC | — | Krone. Copper-Nickel. KM#837.2. | 1,000 |

## PROVAS

| KM# | Date | Mintage | Identification | Mkt Val |
|---|---|---|---|---|
| Pr69 | 1990 LG-JP | — | Krone. Copper-Nickel. | 5.50 |
| Pr70 | 1990 LG-JP | — | 2 Kroner. Copper-Nickel. | 5.50 |
| Pr1 | 1900 (1984-1986) | 9 | 10 Kroner. Aluminum-Bronze. I. | 1,050 |
| Pr2 | 1900 (1984-1986) | 16 | 20 Kroner. Aluminum-Bronze. II. | 660 |
| Pr7 | 1983 | — | 50 Ore. Bronze. Without Roman numeral. | — |
| Pr8 | 1983 | 4 | 50 Ore. Bronze. Wide rim. | — |
| Pr9 | 1983 | 4 | Krone. Copper-Nickel. Similar to Pr11. | — |
| Pr10 | 1983 | 4 | 2 Kroner. Copper-Nickel. Similar to Pr11. | — |
| Pr11 | 1983 | 3 | 5 Kroner. | — |
| Pr16 | 1983 | — | 10 Kroner. Aluminum-Bronze. Without Roman numeral. | — |
| Pr21 | 1983 | — | 20 Kroner. Aluminum-Bronze. Without Roman numeral. | — |
| Pr3 | 1983 | 6 | 25 Ore. Bronze. I. | 2,900 |
| Pr4 | 1983 | 5 | 25 Ore. Bronze. II. | 3,000 |
| Pr5 | 1983 | 7 | 50 Ore. Bronze. II. | 2,900 |
| Pr6 | 1983 | 6 | 50 Ore. Bronze. II. | 2,900 |
| PrA11 | 1983 | 4 | 5 Kroner. | 1,800 |
| PrB11 | 1983 | 6 | 5 Kroner. | 1,500 |
| Pr12 | 1983 | 6 | 10 Kroner. Aluminum-Bronze. I. | 2,000 |
| Pr13 | 1983 | 7 | 10 Kroner. Aluminum-Bronze. II. | 1,575 |
| Pr14 | 1983 | 7 | 10 Kroner. Aluminum-Bronze. III. | 2,400 |
| Pr15 | 1983 | 6 | 10 Kroner. Aluminum-Bronze. IIII. | 2,400 |
| Pr17 | 1983 | 7 | 20 Kroner. Aluminum-Bronze. I. | 2,400 |
| Pr18 | 1983 | 7 | 20 Kroner. Aluminum-Bronze. II. | 2,400 |
| Pr19 | 1983 | 7 | 20 Kroner. Aluminum-Bronze. III. | 2,400 |
| Pr20 | 1983 | 6 | 20 Kroner. Aluminum-Bronze. IIII. | 2,650 |

| KM# | Date | Mintage | Identification | Mkt Val |
|---|---|---|---|---|
| Pr23 | 1983 | 7 | 50 Kroner. Aluminum-Bronze. II. | 2,100 |
| Pr24 | 1983 | 7 | 50 Kroner. Aluminum-Bronze. III. | 2,100 |
| Pr25 | 1983 | 6 | 50 Kroner. Aluminum-Bronze. IIII. | 2,400 |
| Pr26 | 1983 | 22 | 50 Kroner. Aluminum-Bronze. Without Roman numeral. | 1,475 |
| Pr27 | 1984 | 81 | 25 Ore. Bronze. | 85.00 |
| Pr28 | 1984 | 81 | 50 Ore. Bronze. | 85.00 |
| Pr29 | 1984 | 99 | Krone. Copper-Nickel. | 70.00 |
| Pr30 | 1984 | 118 | Krone. Copper-Nickel. | 50.00 |

| KM# | Date | Mintage | Identification | Mkt Val |
|---|---|---|---|---|
| Pr31 | 1984 | 203 | Krone. Copper-Nickel. Reverse of 1988. | 40.00 |
| Pr32 | 1984 | — | Krone. Copper-Nickel. Similar to Pr30 but without hole. | 450 |
| Pr33 | 1984 | 191 | 2 Kroner. Copper-Nickel. Triple monogram. | 40.00 |
| Pr34 | 1984 | 103 | 2 Kroner. Copper-Nickel. MIIR. | 75.00 |
| Pr35 | 1984 | 201 | 2 Kroner. Copper-Nickel. Interrupted milling 6 or 7 notches. | 40.00 |
| Pr36 | 1984 | 85 | 5 Kroner. Copper-Nickel. Triple monogram. | 70.00 |
| Pr37 | 1984 | 108 | 5 Kroner. Copper-Nickel. MIIR. | 75.00 |
| Pr38 | 1984 | 202 | 5 Kroner. Copper-Nickel. Reverse of 1988. | 40.00 |

| KM# | Date | Mintage | Identification | Mkt Val |
|---|---|---|---|---|
| Pr39 | 1984 | 6 | 5 Kroner. Copper-Nickel. | 2,000 |
| Pr40 | 1984 | 85 | 10 Kroner. Aluminum-Bronze. | 100 |
| Pr41 | 1984 | 112 | 20 Kroner. Aluminum-Bronze. | 80.00 |
| PrA43 | 1984 | 51 | 20 Kroner. Aluminum-Bronze. Different reverse. | 150 |
| PrA41 | 1984 | 4 | 10 Kroner. Aluminum-Bronze. Without "Prove". | — |
| PrB41 | 1984 | 3 | 10 Kroner. Aluminum-Bronze. Different reverse. | — |
| Pr42 | 1984 | 4 | 20 Kroner. Aluminum-Bronze. Without "PROVE". | — |
| PrA52 | 1986 | 2 | Krone. Copper-Nickel. Without hole. | — |
| Pr53 | 1986 | 2 | 2 Kroner. Copper-Nickel. Without hole. | — |
| Pr59a | 1986 | 198 | 20 Kroner. Aluminum-Bronze. Interrupted milling, 12x4 grooves. | 22.50 |
| Pr59b | 1986 | 198 | 20 Kroner. Aluminum-Bronze. Interrupted milling, 8x8 grooves, notches widely spaced. | 22.50 |
| Pr59c | 1986 | 198 | 20 Kroner. Aluminum-Bronze. Interrupted milling, 8x6 grooves. | 22.50 |
| Pr59d | 1986 | 198 | 20 Kroner. Aluminum-Bronze. Interrupted milling, 16x3 grooves, no notches. | 22.50 |
| Pr59e | 1986 | 198 | 20 Kroner. Aluminum-Bronze. Interrupted milling, 8x8 grooves, notches narrowly spaced. | 22.50 |
| Pr59f | 1986 | 198 | 20 Kroner. Aluminum-Bronze. Interrupted milling, 8x8 grooves. | 22.50 |
| Pr43 | 1986 | 183 | 25 Ore. Bronze. | 40.00 |
| Pr44 | 1986 | 210 | 25 Ore. Bronze. | 30.00 |
| Pr45 | 19(86) | 23 | 50 Ore. Bronze. | 215 |

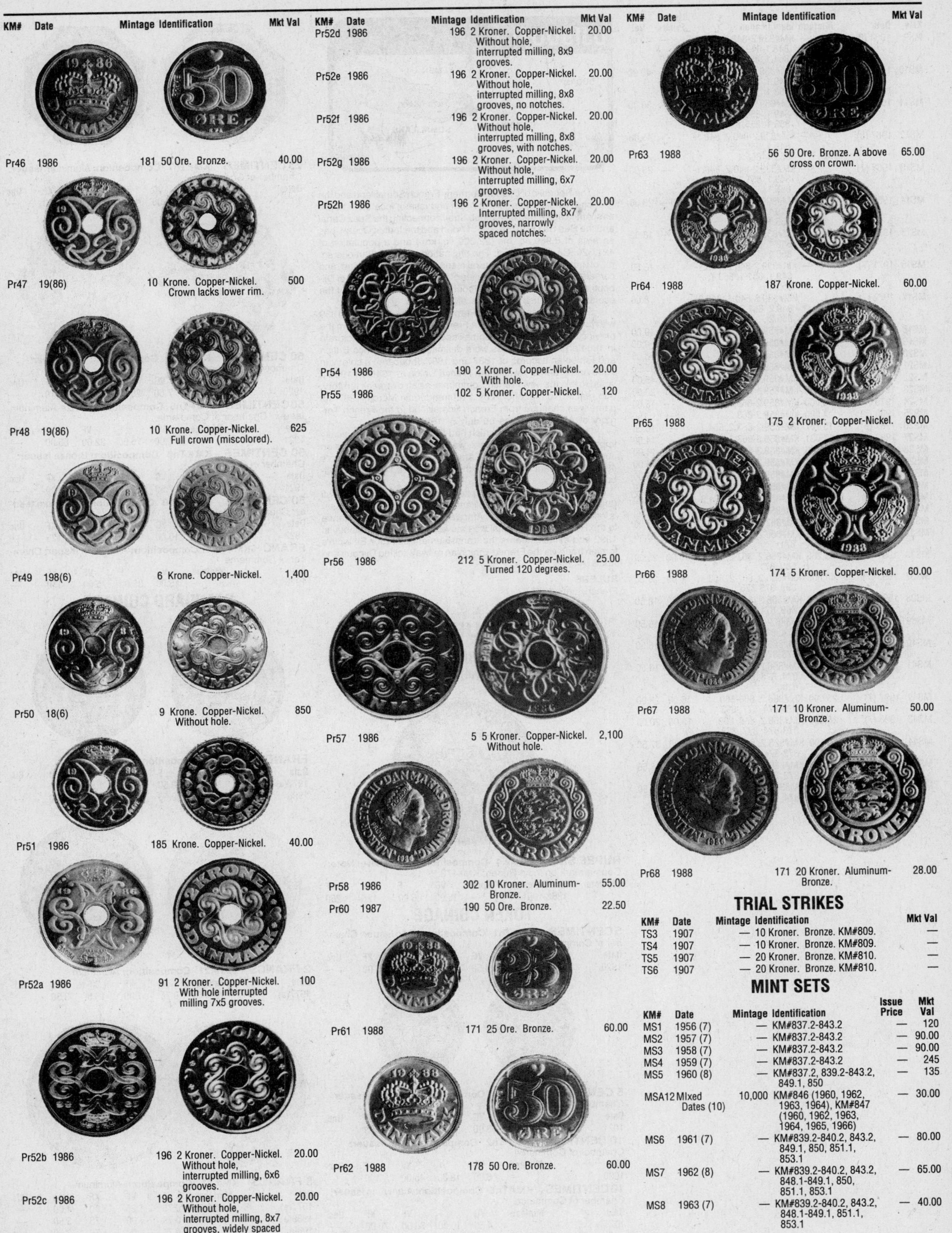

| KM# | Date | Mintage | Identification | Mkt Val |
|---|---|---|---|---|
| Pr46 | 1986 | 181 | 50 Ore. Bronze. | 40.00 |
| Pr47 | 19(86) | 10 | Krone. Copper-Nickel. Crown lacks lower rim. | 500 |
| Pr48 | 19(86) | 10 | Krone. Copper-Nickel. Full crown (miscolored). | 625 |
| Pr49 | 198(6) | 6 | Krone. Copper-Nickel. | 1,400 |
| Pr50 | 18(6) | 9 | Krone. Copper-Nickel. Without hole. | 850 |
| Pr51 | 1986 | 185 | Krone. Copper-Nickel. | 40.00 |
| Pr52a | 1986 | 91 | 2 Kroner. Copper-Nickel. With hole interrupted milling 7x5 grooves. | 100 |
| Pr52b | 1986 | 196 | 2 Kroner. Copper-Nickel. Without hole, interrupted milling, 6x6 grooves. | 20.00 |
| Pr52c | 1986 | 196 | 2 Kroner. Copper-Nickel. Without hole, interrupted milling, 8x7 grooves, widely spaced notches. | 20.00 |
| Pr52d | 1986 | 196 | 2 Kroner. Copper-Nickel. Without hole, interrupted milling, 8x9 grooves. | 20.00 |
| Pr52e | 1986 | 196 | 2 Kroner. Copper-Nickel. Without hole, interrupted milling, 8x8 grooves, no notches. | 20.00 |
| Pr52f | 1986 | 196 | 2 Kroner. Copper-Nickel. Without hole, interrupted milling, 8x8 grooves, with notches. | 20.00 |
| Pr52g | 1986 | 196 | 2 Kroner. Copper-Nickel. Without hole, interrupted milling, 6x7 grooves. | 20.00 |
| Pr52h | 1986 | 196 | 2 Kroner. Copper-Nickel. Interrupted milling, 8x7 grooves, narrowly spaced notches. | 20.00 |
| Pr54 | 1986 | 190 | 2 Kroner. Copper-Nickel. With hole. | 20.00 |
| Pr55 | 1986 | 102 | 5 Kroner. Copper-Nickel. | 120 |
| Pr56 | 1986 | 212 | 5 Kroner. Copper-Nickel. Turned 120 degrees. | 25.00 |
| Pr57 | 1986 | 5 | 5 Kroner. Copper-Nickel. Without hole. | 2,100 |
| Pr58 | 1986 | 302 | 10 Kroner. Aluminum-Bronze. | 55.00 |
| Pr60 | 1987 | 190 | 50 Ore. Bronze. | 22.50 |
| Pr61 | 1988 | 171 | 25 Ore. Bronze. | 60.00 |
| Pr62 | 1988 | 178 | 50 Ore. Bronze. | 60.00 |
| Pr63 | 1988 | 56 | 50 Ore. Bronze. A above cross on crown. | 65.00 |
| Pr64 | 1988 | 187 | Krone. Copper-Nickel. | 60.00 |
| Pr65 | 1988 | 175 | 2 Kroner. Copper-Nickel. | 60.00 |
| Pr66 | 1988 | 174 | 5 Kroner. Copper-Nickel. | 60.00 |
| Pr67 | 1988 | 171 | 10 Kroner. Aluminum-Bronze. | 50.00 |
| Pr68 | 1988 | 171 | 20 Kroner. Aluminum-Bronze. | 28.00 |

## TRIAL STRIKES

| KM# | Date | Mintage | Identification | Mkt Val |
|---|---|---|---|---|
| TS3 | 1907 | — | 10 Kroner. Bronze. KM#809. | — |
| TS4 | 1907 | — | 10 Kroner. Bronze. KM#809. | — |
| TS5 | 1907 | — | 20 Kroner. Bronze. KM#810. | — |
| TS6 | 1907 | — | 20 Kroner. Bronze. KM#810. | — |

## MINT SETS

| KM# | Date | Mintage | Identification | Issue Price | Mkt Val |
|---|---|---|---|---|---|
| MS1 | 1956 (7) | — | KM#837.2-843.2 | — | 120 |
| MS2 | 1957 (7) | — | KM#837.2-843.2 | — | 90.00 |
| MS3 | 1958 (7) | — | KM#837.2-843.2 | — | 90.00 |
| MS4 | 1959 (7) | — | KM#837.2-843.2 | — | 245 |
| MS5 | 1960 (8) | — | KM#837.2, 839.2-843.2, 849.1, 850 | — | 135 |
| MSA12 | MIxed Dates (10) | 10,000 | KM#846 (1960, 1962, 1963, 1964), KM#847 (1960, 1962, 1963, 1964, 1965, 1966) | — | 30.00 |
| MS6 | 1961 (7) | — | KM#839.2-840.2, 843.2, 849.1, 850, 851.1, 853.1 | — | 80.00 |
| MS7 | 1962 (8) | — | KM#839.2-840.2, 843.2, 848.1-849.1, 850, 851.1, 853.1 | — | 65.00 |
| MS8 | 1963 (7) | — | KM#839.2-840.2, 843.2, 848.1-849.1, 851.1, 853.1 | — | 40.00 |

| KM# | Date | Mintage | Identification | Issue Price | Mkt Val |
|---|---|---|---|---|---|
| MS9 | 1964 (8) | — | KM#839.2-840.2, 843.2, 848.1-849.1, 850, 851.1, 853.1 | — | 40.00 |
| MS10 | 1965 (7) | — | KM#839.2-840.2, 848.1-849.1, 850, 851.1, 853.1 | — | 40.00 |
| MS11 | 1966 (8) | — | KM#839.2-840.2, 848.1-849.1, 850, 851.1, 853.1, 855.1 | — | 30.00 |
| MS12 | 1967 (8) | — | KM#839.2-840.2, 848.1-849.1, 850, 851.1, 853.1, 855.1 | — | 45.00 |
| MS13 | 1968 (7) | — | KM#839.2-840.2, 848.1-849.1, 851.1, 853.1, 855.1 | — | 28.00 |
| MS14 | 1969 (7) | — | KM#839.2-840.2, 848.1-849.1, 851.1, 853.1, 855.1 | — | 28.00 |
| MS15 | 1970 (7) | — | KM#839.2-840.2, 848.1-849.1, 851.1, 853.1, 855.1 | — | 13.50 |
| MS16 | 1971 (7) | — | KM#839.2-840.2, 848.1-849.1, 851.1, 853.1, 855.1 | — | 13.50 |
| MS17 | 1972 (7) | — | KM#839.3-840.3, 848.2-849.2, 851.2, 853.2, 855.2 | — | 8.00 |
| MS18 | 1973 (5) | — | KM#859.1-863.1 | — | 10.00 |
| MS19 | 1974 (5) | — | KM#859.1-863.1 | 6.00 | 8.00 |
| MS20 | 1975 (5) | 4,300 | KM#859.1-863.1 | 6.00 | 90.00 |
| MS21 | 1976 (5) | 6,000 | KM#859.1-863.1 | 3.55 | 45.00 |
| MS22 | 1977 (5) | 6,000 | KM#859.1-863.1 | — | 45.00 |
| MS23 | 1978 (5) | 6,000 | KM#859.1-863.1 | — | 20.00 |
| MS24 | 1979 (6) | 6,000 | KM#859.2-863.2, 864.1 | — | 18.00 |
| MS25 | 1980 (5) | 4,000 | KM#859.2-863.2 | — | 150 |
| MS26 | 1981 (6) | 15,767 | KM#859.2-863.2, 864.1 | — | 16.50 |
| MS27 | 1982 (6) | 17,031 | KM#859.3-863.3, 864.2 | — | 14.00 |
| MS28 | 1983 (6) | 14,595 | KM#859.3-863.3, 864.2 | — | 14.00 |
| MS29 | 1984 (6) | 14,041 | KM#859.3-863.3, 864.2 | — | 14.00 |
| MS30 | 1985 (6) | 14,000 | KM#859.3-863.3, 864.2 | — | 14.00 |
| MS31 | 1986 (6) | 20,000 | KM#859.3-863.3, 865 | — | 25.00 |
| MS32 | 1987 (6) | 15,000 | KM#859.3-863.3, 864.2 | — | 25.00 |
| MS33 | 1988 (6) | 19,692 | KM#859.3-863.3, 864.2 | — | 14.00 |
| MS34 | 1989 (3) | 27,123 | KM#862.3, 866.1, 867.1 | 12.00 | 10.00 |
| MS35 | 1990 (6) | 39,258 | KM#866.2, 867.2, 868-871 | 15.00 | 16.50 |
| MS36 | 1991 (5) | 33,258 | KM#866.2, 867.2, 868-869, 871 | 15.00 | 25.00 |
| MS37 | 1992 (7) | 40,000 | KM#866.2, 867.2, 868-869, 873-875 | 15.00 | 25.00 |
| MS38 | 1993 (7) | 35,000 | KM#866.2, 867.2, 868-869, 871, 873-874 | 15.00 | 18.50 |
| MS39 | 1994 (7) | 30,000 | K#866.2, 868-869, 873-874, 877-878 | 15.00 | 16.50 |
| MS40 | 1995 (7) | 25,000 | KM#866.2, 868-869, 873-874, 877, 879 | 15.00 | 16.50 |
| MS41 | 1996 (6) | 25,000 | KM#866.2, 868, 873-874, 878, 881 (1995 date) | 15.00 | 16.50 |
| MS42 | 1997 (7) | 25,000 | KM#866.2, 868-869, 873-874, 877, 883 | 15.00 | 25.00 |
| MS43 | 1998 (7) | 28,000 | KM#866.2, 868, 869, 873-874, 877, 878 | 15.00 | 20.00 |
| MS44 | 1999 (7) | 30,100 | KM#866.2, 868-869, 873-874, 877, 878 | 15.00 | 37.50 |
| MS45 | 2000 (6) | 28,000 | KM#866.2, 868, 869, 873, 874, 885 | 15.00 | 18.50 |
| MS46 | 2001 (7) | — | KM866.2, 868, 869, 873, 874, 887, 888 | 15.00 | 16.50 |

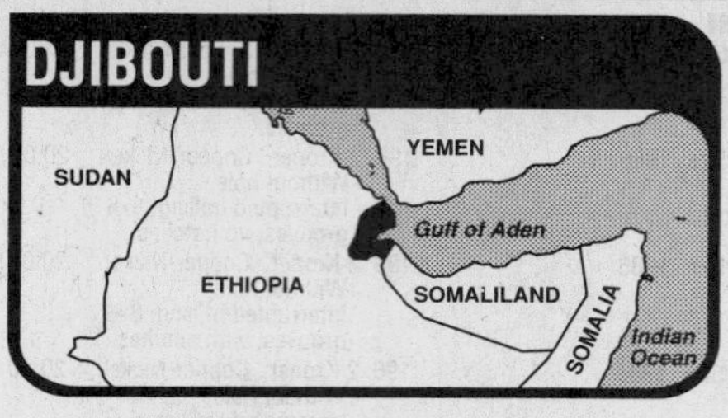


The Republic of Djibouti (formerly French Somaliland and the French Overseas Territory of Afars and Issas), located in northeast Africa at the Bab el Mandeb Strait connecting the Suez Canal and the Red Sea with the Gulf of Aden and the Indian Ocean, has an area of 8,950 sq. mi. (22,000 sq. km.) and a population of 421,320. Capital: Djibouti. The tiny nation has less than one sq. mi. of arable land, and no natural resources except salt, sand, and camels. The commercial activities of the transshipment port of Djibouti and the Addis Abada-Djibouti railroad are the basis of the economy. Salt, fish and hides are exported.

French interest in former French Somaliland began in 1839 with concessions obtained by a French naval lieutenant from the provincial sultans. French Somaliland was made a protectorate in 1884 and its boundaries were delimited by the Franco-British and Ethiopian accords of 1887 and 1897. It became a colony in 1896 and a territory within the French Union in 1946. In 1958 it voted to join the new French Community as an overseas territory, and reaffirmed that choice by a referendum in March, 1967. Its name was changed from French Somaliland to the French Territory of Afars and Issas on July 5, 1967.

The French Tricolor, which had flown over the strategically important territory for 115 years, was lowered for the last time on June 27, 1977, when French Afars and Issas became Africa's 49th independent state, under the name of the Republic of Djibouti.

Djibouti, a seaportand capitalcity of the Republic of Djibouti (and formerly of French Somaliland and French Afars and Issas) is located on the east coast of Africa at the southernmost entrance to the Red Sea. The capital was moved from Obok to Djibouti in 1892 and established as the transshipment point for Ethiopia's foreign trade via the Franco-Ethiopian railway linking Djibouti and Addis Ababa.

**RULERS**

French, until 1977

# REPUBLIC

## COUNTERMARKED COINAGE

Rupee-Taler (Riyal) Coinage Series

**RUPEE SIZE** **KM# 2.4** **Composition:** 0.9170 Silver **Note:** Countermark on India Rupee, KM#473.

| CM Date | Host Date | Good | VG | F | VF | XF |
|---|---|---|---|---|---|---|
| | 1862-1901 | — | 35.00 | 65.00 | 125 | 250 |

## TOKEN COINAGE

**5 CENTIMES** **KM# Tn1** **Composition:** Zinc **Issuer:** Chamber of Commerce

| Date | Mintage | VG | F | VF | XF | Unc |
|---|---|---|---|---|---|---|
| 1920 | — | 4.50 | 10.00 | 35.00 | 85.00 | — |

**5 CENTIMES** **KM# Tn5** **Composition:** Aluminum **Issuer:** Chamber of Commerce

| Date | Mintage | VG | F | VF | XF | Unc |
|---|---|---|---|---|---|---|
| 1921 | — | 3.00 | 7.50 | 28.00 | 65.00 | — |

**10 CENTIMES** **KM# Tn2** **Composition:** Zinc **Issuer:** Chamber of Commerce

| Date | Mintage | VG | F | VF | XF | Unc |
|---|---|---|---|---|---|---|
| 1920 | — | 6.00 | 18.00 | 45.00 | 100 | — |

**10 CENTIMES** **KM# Tn6** **Composition:** Aluminum **Issuer:** Chamber of Commerce

| Date | Mintage | VG | F | VF | XF | Unc |
|---|---|---|---|---|---|---|
| 1921 | — | 4.50 | 10.00 | 30.00 | 70.00 | — |

**25 CENTIMES** **KM# Tn7** **Composition:** Aluminum **Issuer:** Chamber of Commerce

| Date | Mintage | VG | F | VF | XF | Unc |
|---|---|---|---|---|---|---|
| 1921 | — | 6.00 | 12.00 | 38.00 | 90.00 | — |

**50 CENTIMES** **KM# Tn3** **Composition:** Zinc **Issuer:** Chamber of Commerce

| Date | Mintage | VG | F | VF | XF | Unc |
|---|---|---|---|---|---|---|
| 1920 | — | 7.50 | 20.00 | 55.00 | 110 | — |

**50 CENTIMES** **KM# Tn8** **Composition:** Bronze-Aluminum **Issuer:** Chamber of Commerce

| Date | Mintage | VG | F | VF | XF | Unc |
|---|---|---|---|---|---|---|
| 1921 | — | 6.00 | 15.00 | 32.00 | 85.00 | — |

**50 CENTIMES** **KM# Tn9** **Composition:** Bronze **Issuer:** Chamber of Commerce

| Date | Mintage | VG | F | VF | XF | Unc |
|---|---|---|---|---|---|---|
| 1921 | — | 7.50 | 20.00 | 48.00 | 100 | — |

**50 CENTIMES** **KM# Tn10** **Composition:** Aluminum **Issuer:** Chamber of Commerce

| Date | Mintage | VG | F | VF | XF | Unc |
|---|---|---|---|---|---|---|
| 1922 | — | 10.00 | 28.00 | 65.00 | 125 | — |

**FRANC** **KM# Tn4** **Composition:** Aluminum **Issuer:** Chamber of Commerce

| Date | Mintage | VG | F | VF | XF | Unc |
|---|---|---|---|---|---|---|
| 1920 | — | 15.00 | 35.00 | 75.00 | 150 | — |

## STANDARD COINAGE

**FRANC** **KM# 20** **Composition:** Aluminum

| Date | Mintage | F | VF | XF | Unc | BU |
|---|---|---|---|---|---|---|
| 1977(a) | 300,000 | 0.50 | 0.75 | 1.50 | 3.00 | — |
| 1996 | — | 0.50 | 0.75 | 1.50 | 3.00 | — |

**2 FRANCS** **KM# 21** **Composition:** Aluminum

| Date | Mintage | F | VF | XF | Unc | BU |
|---|---|---|---|---|---|---|
| 1977(a) | 200,000 | 0.75 | 1.00 | 1.75 | 3.50 | — |

**5 FRANCS** **KM# 22** **Composition:** Aluminum

| Date | Mintage | F | VF | XF | Unc | BU |
|---|---|---|---|---|---|---|
| 1977(a) | 400,000 | 0.75 | 1.25 | 2.00 | 4.00 | — |
| 1986(a) | — | 0.75 | 1.00 | 1.75 | 3.50 | — |
| 1989(a) | — | 0.75 | 1.00 | 1.75 | 3.50 | — |
| 1991(a) | — | 0.75 | 1.00 | 1.75 | 3.50 | — |

**10 FRANCS** KM# 23 **Composition:** Aluminum-Bronze
**Note:** Varieties exist.

| Date | Mintage | F | VF | XF | Unc | BU |
|---|---|---|---|---|---|---|
| 1977(a) | 600,000 | 0.45 | 0.85 | 1.50 | 3.00 | — |
| 1983(a) | — | 0.50 | 1.00 | 1.75 | 3.50 | — |
| 1989(a) | — | 0.45 | 0.75 | 1.25 | 2.50 | — |
| 1991(a) | — | 0.45 | 0.75 | 1.25 | 2.50 | — |
| 1996(a) | — | 0.45 | 0.75 | 1.25 | 2.50 | — |

**20 FRANCS** KM# 24 **Composition:** Aluminum-Bronze
**Note:** Varieties exist.

| Date | Mintage | F | VF | XF | Unc | BU |
|---|---|---|---|---|---|---|
| 1977(a) | 700,000 | 0.50 | 1.00 | 1.50 | 3.00 | — |
| 1982(a) | — | 0.50 | 1.00 | 1.75 | 3.50 | — |
| 1983(a) | — | 0.50 | 1.00 | 1.50 | 3.00 | — |
| 1986(a) | — | 0.45 | 0.75 | 1.25 | 2.50 | — |
| 1991(a) | — | 0.45 | 0.75 | 1.25 | 2.50 | — |
| 1996(a) | — | 0.45 | 0.75 | 1.25 | 2.50 | — |

**50 FRANCS** KM# 25 **Composition:** Copper-Nickel **Reverse:** Pair of dromedary camels, denomination

| Date | Mintage | F | VF | XF | Unc | BU |
|---|---|---|---|---|---|---|
| 1977(a) | 1,500,000 | 0.75 | 1.50 | 3.00 | 6.00 | — |
| 1982(a) | — | 0.75 | 1.50 | 3.00 | 6.00 | — |
| 1983(a) | — | 0.50 | 1.00 | 2.25 | 4.50 | — |
| 1986(a) | — | 0.50 | 1.00 | 2.25 | 4.50 | — |
| 1989(a) | — | 0.50 | 1.00 | 2.25 | 4.50 | — |
| 1991(a) | — | 0.50 | 1.00 | 2.25 | 4.50 | — |

**100 FRANCS** KM# 26 **Composition:** Copper-Nickel **Reverse:** Pair of dromedary camels, denomination

| Date | Mintage | F | VF | XF | Unc | BU |
|---|---|---|---|---|---|---|
| 1977(a) | 1,500,000 | 1.00 | 2.00 | 3.00 | 6.50 | — |
| 1983(a) | — | 1.00 | 2.50 | 3.50 | 7.00 | — |
| 1991(a) | — | 1.00 | 1.75 | 2.75 | 5.50 | — |

**100 FRANCS** KM# 29 **Weight:** 31.4700 g. **Composition:** 0.9250 Silver **Subject:** World Cup Soccer

| Date | Mintage | F | VF | XF | Unc | BU |
|---|---|---|---|---|---|---|
| 1994 Proof | Est. 15,000 | Value: 35.00 | | | | |

**100 FRANCS** KM# 30 **Weight:** 31.4700 g. **Composition:** 0.9250 Silver **Subject:** 1996 Olympic Games **Reverse:** Runner

| Date | Mintage | F | VF | XF | Unc | BU |
|---|---|---|---|---|---|---|
| 1994 Proof | Est. 30,000 | Value: 32.50 | | | | |

**100 FRANCS** KM# 31 **Weight:** 31.4700 g. **Composition:** 0.9250 Silver **Reverse:** Frigate "Bateau"

| Date | Mintage | F | VF | XF | Unc | BU |
|---|---|---|---|---|---|---|
| 1994 Proof | Est. 15,000 | Value: 40.00 | | | | |

**100 FRANCS** KM# 32 **Weight:** 31.4700 g. **Composition:** 0.9250 Silver **Subject:** Endangered Wildlife **Reverse:** Grevy zebras

| Date | Mintage | F | VF | XF | Unc | BU |
|---|---|---|---|---|---|---|
| 1994 Proof | Est. 15,000 | Value: 42.50 | | | | |

**100 FRANCS** KM# 33 **Weight:** 31.4700 g. **Composition:** 0.9250 Silver **Reverse:** Portuguese "Nao" ship

| Date | Mintage | F | VF | XF | Unc | BU |
|---|---|---|---|---|---|---|
| 1996 Proof | Est. 15,000 | Value: 40.00 | | | | |

**500 FRANCS** KM# 27 **Composition:** Aluminum-Bronze

| Date | Mintage | F | VF | XF | Unc | BU |
|---|---|---|---|---|---|---|
| 1989(a) | — | 3.00 | 4.00 | 6.00 | 10.00 | — |
| 1991(a) | — | 3.00 | 4.00 | 6.00 | 10.00 | — |

**15000 FRANCS** **KM# 28** **Weight:** 24.3000 g. **Composition:** 0.9990 Silver .7710 oz. ASW **Note:** Republic of Djibouti.

| Date | Mintage | F | VF | XF | Unc | BU |
|---|---|---|---|---|---|---|
| 1991 | Est. 10,000 | — | — | — | 125 | — |

## ESSAIS

Standard metals unless otherwise noted

| KM# | Date | Mintage | Identification | Issue Price | Mkt Val |
|---|---|---|---|---|---|
| E4 | 1977 | — | 10 Francs. KM23. | — | 14.50 |
| E1 | 1977 | — | Franc. KM20. | — | 12.50 |
| E2 | 1977 | — | 2 Francs. KM21. | — | 12.50 |
| E3 | 1977 | — | 5 Francs. KM22. | — | 12.50 |
| E5 | 1977 | — | 20 Francs. KM24. | — | 14.50 |
| E6 | 1977 | — | 50 Francs. KM25. | — | 16.50 |
| E7 | 1977 | — | 100 Francs. KM26. | — | 17.50 |

The Commonwealth of Dominica, situated in the Lesser Antilles midway between Guadeloupe to the north and Martinique to the south, has an area of 290 sq. mi. (750 sq. km.) and a population of 82,608. Capital: Roseau. Agriculture is the chief economic activity of the mountainous island. Bananas are the chief export.

Columbus discovered and named the island on Nov. 3, 1493. Spain neglected it and it was finally colonized by the French in 1632. The British drove the French from the island in 1756. Thereafter it changed hands between the French and British a dozen or more times before becoming permanently British in 1805. Around 1761, pierced or mutilated silver from Martinique was used on the island. A council in 1798 acknowledged and established value for these mutilated coins and ordered other cut and countermarked to be made in Dominica. These remained in use until 1862, when they were demonetized and sterling became the standard. Throughout the greater part of its British history, Dominica was a presidency of the Leeward Islands. In 1940 its administration was transferred to the Windward Islands and it was established as a separate colony with considerable local autonomy. From 1955, Dominica was a member of the currency board of the British Caribbean Territories (Eastern Group), which issued its own coins until 1965. Dominica became a West Indies associated state with a built in option for independence in 1967. Full independence was attained on Nov. 3, 1978. Dominica, which has a republican form of government, is a member of the Commonwealth of Nations.

**RULERS**

British, until 1978

**MINT MARKS**

CHI in circle - Valcambi, Chiasso, Italy
(ml) - maple leaf - Canadian Royal Mint

**MONETARY SYSTEM**

(Commencing 1813)
16 Bits = 12 Shillings = 1 Dollar (Spanish)
100 Cents = 10 Shillings = 1 Dollar (Dominican)

# COMMONWEALTH

## MODERN COINAGE

**4 DOLLARS** **KM# 11** **Composition:** Copper-Nickel **Series:** F.A.O **Obverse:** Arms **Reverse:** Sugar cane and banana tree branch **Note:** This 4-dollar F.A.O. commemorative coin is part of a group. The others are listed individually under their respective country names: Antigua, Barbados, Dominica, Grenada, Montserrat, St. Kitts, St. Lucia, and St. Vincent.

| Date | Mintage | F | VF | XF | Unc | BU |
|---|---|---|---|---|---|---|
| 1970 | 13,000 | — | 4.00 | 6.50 | 12.00 | — |
| 1970 Proof | 2,000 | Value: 17.50 | | | | |

**10 DOLLARS** **KM# 12.1** **Weight:** 20.5000 g. **Composition:** 0.9250 Silver .6097 oz. ASW **Subject:** Independence - History of Carnival **Obverse:** Queen Elizabeth **Reverse:** With mint mark

| Date | Mintage | F | VF | XF | Unc | BU |
|---|---|---|---|---|---|---|
| ND(1978)CHI | 1,500 | — | — | 7.50 | 18.50 | — |
| ND(1978)CHI Proof | 2,000 | Value: 25.00 | | | | |

**10 DOLLARS** **KM# 12.2** **Weight:** 20.5000 g. **Composition:** 0.9250 Silver .6097 oz. ASW **Subject:** Independence - History of Carnival **Obverse:** Queen Elizabeth **Reverse:** Without mint mark

| Date | Mintage | F | VF | XF | Unc | BU |
|---|---|---|---|---|---|---|
| ND(1978) | — | — | — | 7.50 | 18.50 | — |

**10 DOLLARS** **KM# 12.3** **Weight:** 20.5000 g. **Composition:** 0.9250 Silver .6097 oz. ASW **Subject:** Independence - History of Carnival **Obverse:** Queen Elizabeth **Reverse:** Canadian mint mark and fineness

| Date | Mintage | F | VF | XF | Unc | BU |
|---|---|---|---|---|---|---|
| ND(1978)(ml) | 18 | — | — | — | — | — |
| ND(1978)(ml) Proof | 233 | — | — | — | — | — |

**10 DOLLARS** **KM# 16** **Weight:** 20.5000 g. **Composition:** 0.9250 Silver .6097 oz. ASW **Subject:** Visit of Pope John Paul II **Obverse:** Queen Elizabeth II **Reverse:** Pope John Paul II

| Date | Mintage | F | VF | XF | Unc | BU |
|---|---|---|---|---|---|---|
| ND(1979) | 1,150 | — | — | 7.50 | 20.00 | — |
| ND(1979) Proof | 3,450 | Value: 25.00 | | | | |

**10 DOLLARS** **KM# 20** **Composition:** Copper Nickel **Subject:** Royal Visit **Obverse:** Mature portrait of Queen Elizabeth II **Reverse:** Arms in inner circle

| Date | Mintage | F | VF | XF | Unc | BU |
|---|---|---|---|---|---|---|
| 1985 | Est. 100,000 | — | — | 5.00 | 8.00 | — |

**10 DOLLARS** **KM# 20a** **Weight:** 28.2800 g. **Composition:** 0.9250 Silver .8409 oz. ASW **Subject:** Royal Visit **Obverse:** Mature portrait of Queen Elizabeth II **Reverse:** Arms in inner circle

| Date | Mintage | F | VF | XF | Unc | BU |
|---|---|---|---|---|---|---|
| 1985 Proof | Est. 5,000 | Value: 27.50 | | | | |

**10 DOLLARS** **KM# 20b** **Weight:** 47.5400 g. **Composition:** 0.9170 Gold 1.4013 oz. AGW **Subject:** Royal Visit **Obverse:** Mature portrait of Queen Elizabeth II **Reverse:** Arms in inner circle

| Date | Mintage | F | VF | XF | Unc | BU |
|---|---|---|---|---|---|---|
| 1985 Proof | Est. 250 | Value: 850 | | | | |

**20 DOLLARS** **KM# 13.1** **Weight:** 40.9100 g. **Composition:** 0.9250 Silver 1.2167 oz. ASW **Subject:** Independence and 50th Anniversary of Graf Zeppelin **Obverse:** Similar to 300 Dollars, KM#15 **Reverse:** Blimp

| Date | Mintage | F | VF | XF | Unc | BU |
|---|---|---|---|---|---|---|
| ND(1978)CHI | 500 | — | — | 30.00 | 65.00 | — |
| ND(1978)CHI Proof | 1,000 | Value: 80.00 | | | | |

**20 DOLLARS** **KM# 13.2** **Weight:** 40.9100 g. **Composition:** 0.9250 Silver 1.2167 oz. ASW **Subject:** Independence and 50th Anniversary of Graf Zeppelin **Obverse:** Similar to 300 Dollars, KM#15 **Reverse:** Blimp; Canadian mint mark and .925 fineness stamp added

| Date | Mintage | F | VF | XF | Unc | BU |
|---|---|---|---|---|---|---|
| ND(1978)(ml) | — | — | — | — | — | — |
| ND(1978)(ml) Proof | 233 | — | — | — | — | — |

**20 DOLLARS** **KM# 17** **Weight:** 40.9100 g. **Composition:** 0.9250 Silver 1.2167 oz. ASW **Subject:** Israel and Egypt Peace Treaty **Obverse:** Queen Elizabeth II **Reverse:** Portrait of Sadat, Begin, and Carter

| Date | Mintage | F | VF | XF | Unc | BU |
|---|---|---|---|---|---|---|
| ND(1979) | 200 | — | — | 35.00 | 75.00 | — |
| ND(1979) Proof | 200 | Value: 95.00 | | | | |

**100 DOLLARS** **KM# 21** **Weight:** 129.5900 g. **Composition:** 0.9250 Silver 3.8543 oz. ASW **Subject:** Tropical Birds - Imperial Parrots **Obverse:** Arms in inner circle **Reverse:** Parrots in trees **Size:** 63 mm. **Note:** Illustration reduced.

| Date | Mintage | F | VF | XF | Unc | BU |
|---|---|---|---|---|---|---|
| 1988 Proof | Est. 10,000 | Value: 150 | | | | |

**150 DOLLARS** **KM# 14.1** **Weight:** 9.6000 g. **Composition:** 0.9000 Gold .2778 oz. AGW **Subject:** Independence - Imperial Parrot **Obverse:** Queen Elizabeth II **Reverse:** Map of Dominica and parrot, without fineness

| Date | Mintage | F | VF | XF | Unc | BU |
|---|---|---|---|---|---|---|
| ND(1978) | 300 | — | — | — | 200 | — |
| ND(1978) Proof | 400 | Value: 240 | | | | |

**150 DOLLARS** **KM# 14.2** **Weight:** 9.6000 g. **Composition:** 0.9000 Gold .2778 oz. AGW **Subject:** Independence - Imperial Parrot **Obverse:** Queen Elizabeth II **Reverse:** Canadian mint mark and .900 fineness added

| Date | Mintage | F | VF | XF | Unc | BU |
|---|---|---|---|---|---|---|
| ND(1978) | 18 | — | — | — | — | — |
| ND(1978) Proof | 116 | Value: 265 | | | | |

**150 DOLLARS** **KM# 18** **Weight:** 9.6000 g. **Composition:** 0.9000 Gold .2778 oz. AGW **Subject:** Israel and Egypt Peace Treaty

| Date | Mintage | F | VF | XF | Unc | BU |
|---|---|---|---|---|---|---|
| ND(1979)(ml) | 100 | — | — | — | 500 | — |
| ND(1979)(ml) Proof | 100 | Value: 550 | | | | |

**300 DOLLARS** **KM# 15.1** **Weight:** 19.2000 g. **Composition:** 0.9000 Gold .5556 oz. AGW **Subject:** Independence - Arms **Obverse:** Queen Elizabeth II **Reverse:** Dominican arms and parrots, without fineness

| Date | Mintage | F | VF | XF | Unc | BU |
|---|---|---|---|---|---|---|
| ND(1978) | 500 | — | — | — | 350 | — |
| ND(1978) Proof | 800 | Value: 400 | | | | |

**300 DOLLARS** **KM# 15.2** **Weight:** 19.2000 g. **Composition:** 0.9000 Gold .5556 oz. AGW **Subject:** Independence - Arms **Obverse:** Queen Elizabeth II **Reverse:** Canadian mint mark and .900 fineness added

| Date | Mintage | F | VF | XF | Unc | BU |
|---|---|---|---|---|---|---|
| ND(1978)(ml) | 18 | — | — | — | — | — |
| ND(1978)(ml) Proof | 82 | Value: 450 | | | | |

**300 DOLLARS** **KM# 19** **Weight:** 19.2000 g. **Composition:** 0.9000 Gold .5556 oz. AGW **Subject:** Visit of Pope John Paul II

| Date | Mintage | F | VF | XF | Unc | BU |
|---|---|---|---|---|---|---|
| ND(1979) | 5,000 | — | — | — | 300 | — |
| ND(1979) | 300 | — | — | — | 525 | — |

## TOKEN COINAGE

**10 CENTS** **KM# Tn1** **Composition:** Brass **Obverse:** Denomination **Reverse:** Denomination

| Date | Mintage | VG | F | VF | XF | Unc |
|---|---|---|---|---|---|---|
| ND | — | 7.00 | 15.00 | 30.00 | 50.00 | — |

# DOMINICAN REPUBLIC

North Atlantic Ocean
CUBA
HAITI
JAMAICA
PUERTO RICO
Caribbean Sea

The Dominican Republic, which occupies the eastern two-thirds of the island of Hispaniola, has an area of 18,704 sq. mi. (48,734 sq. km.) and a population of 7.9 million. Capital: Santo Domingo. The largely agricultural economy produces sugar, coffee, tobacco and cocoa. Tourism and casino gaming are also a rising source of revenue.

Columbus discovered Hispaniola in 1492, and named it La Isla Espanola - 'the Spanish Island'. Santo Domingo, the oldest white settlement in the Western Hemisphere, was the base from which Spain conducted its exploration of the New World. Later, French buccaneers settled the western third of Hispaniola, naming the colony St. Dominique, which in 1697, was ceded to France by Spain. In 1804, following a bloody revolt by former slaves, the French colony became the Republic of Haiti - mountainous country'. The Spanish called their part of Hispaniola Santo Domingo. In 1822, the Haitians conquered the entire island and held it until 1844, when Juan Pablo Duarte, the national hero of the Dominican Republic, drove them out of Santo Domingo and established an independent Dominican Republic. The republic returned voluntarily to Spanish dominion from 1861 to 1865, after being rejected by France, Britain and the United States. Independence was reclaimed in 1866.

**MINT MARKS**

(c) - Stylized maple leaf, Royal Canadian Mint
Mo – Mexico City
(o) - CHI in oval - Valcambi, Chiasso, Italy
(t) - Tower, Tower Mint, London

**MONETARY SYSTEM**

100 Centavos = 1 Peso Oro

## REPUBLIC

### DECIMAL COINAGE

1937

100 Centavos = 1 Peso Oro

**CENTAVO** **KM# 17** **Composition:** Bronze **Obverse:** Banner over national arms **Reverse:** Palm tree, denomination

| Date | Mintage | F | VF | XF | Unc | BU |
|---|---|---|---|---|---|---|
| 1937 | 1,000,000 | 0.50 | 1.50 | 7.50 | 75.00 | — |
| 1937 | — | Value: 350 | | | | |
| 1939 | 2,000,000 | 0.50 | 1.25 | 5.00 | 40.00 | — |
| 1941 | 2,000,000 | 0.25 | 0.50 | 3.00 | 12.00 | — |
| 1942 | 2,000,000 | 0.25 | 0.50 | 3.00 | 15.00 | — |
| 1944 | 5,000,000 | 0.20 | 0.50 | 1.50 | 10.00 | — |
| 1947 | 3,000,000 | 0.20 | 0.50 | 1.00 | 8.00 | — |
| 1949 | 3,000,000 | 0.20 | 0.40 | 1.00 | 8.00 | — |
| 1951 | 3,000,000 | 0.20 | 0.35 | 0.75 | 8.00 | — |
| 1952 | 3,000,000 | 0.20 | 0.35 | 0.75 | 8.00 | — |
| 1955 | 3,000,000 | 0.15 | 0.35 | 0.75 | 6.00 | — |
| 1956 | 3,000,000 | 0.15 | 0.35 | 0.75 | 6.00 | — |
| 1957 | 5,000,000 | 0.10 | 0.25 | 0.75 | 5.00 | — |
| 1959 | 5,000,000 | 0.10 | 0.25 | 0.75 | 5.00 | — |
| 1961 | 5,000,000 | 0.10 | 0.20 | 0.50 | 2.00 | — |

**CENTAVO** **KM# 25** **Composition:** Bronze **Subject:** 100th Anniversary - Restoration of the Republic **Obverse:** Banner over national arms **Reverse:** Profile of native princess

| Date | Mintage | F | VF | XF | Unc | BU |
|---|---|---|---|---|---|---|
| 1963 | 13,000,000 | — | — | 0.10 | 0.40 | — |

**CENTAVO** **KM# 31** **Composition:** Bronze **Obverse:** Banner over national arms **Reverse:** Profile of native princess

| Date | Mintage | F | VF | XF | Unc | BU |
|---|---|---|---|---|---|---|
| 1968 | 5,000,000 | — | — | 0.10 | 0.20 | — |
| 1971 | 6,000,000 | — | — | 0.10 | 0.20 | — |
| 1972 | 3,000,000 | — | — | 0.10 | 0.20 | — |
| 1972 Proof | 500 | Value: 15.00 | | | | |
| 1975 | 500,000 | — | — | 0.10 | 0.20 | — |

**CENTAVO** **KM# 32** **Composition:** Bronze **Series:** F.A.O. **Obverse:** Banner over national arms **Reverse:** Profile of native princess

| Date | Mintage | F | VF | XF | Unc | BU |
|---|---|---|---|---|---|---|
| 1969 | 5,000,000 | — | — | 0.10 | 0.30 | — |

**CENTAVO** **KM# 40** **Composition:** Bronze **Subject:** Centennial - Death of Juan Pablo Duarte **Obverse:** Banner over national arms **Reverse:** Portrait of Duarte

| Date | Mintage | F | VF | XF | Unc | BU |
|---|---|---|---|---|---|---|
| 1976 | 3,995,000 | — | — | 0.10 | 0.20 | — |
| 1976 Proof | 5,000 | Value: 1.00 | | | | |

**CENTAVO** **KM# 48** **Composition:** Bronze **Obverse:** Without memorial legend

| Date | Mintage | F | VF | XF | Unc | BU |
|---|---|---|---|---|---|---|
| 1978 | 2,995,000 | — | — | 0.10 | 0.15 | — |
| 1978 Proof | 5,000 | Value: 2.00 | | | | |
| 1979 | 2,985,000 | — | — | 0.10 | 0.15 | — |
| 1979 Proof | 500 | Value: 15.00 | | | | |
| 1980 | 200,000 | — | — | 0.10 | 0.15 | — |
| 1980 Proof | 3,000 | Value: 1.00 | | | | |
| 1981 Proof | 3,000 | Value: 1.00 | | | | |

**CENTAVO** **KM# 48a** **Weight:** 3.5800 g. **Composition:** 0.9000 Silver .1036 oz. ASW

| Date | Mintage | F | VF | XF | Unc | BU |
|---|---|---|---|---|---|---|
| 1978 Proof | 15 | Value: 125 | | | | |
| 1979 Proof | 15 | Value: 125 | | | | |
| 1980 Proof | 15 | Value: 125 | | | | |
| 1981 Proof | 15 | Value: 125 | | | | |

**CENTAVO** **KM# 64** **Composition:** Copper Plated Zinc **Subject:** Human Rights **Obverse:** Banner over national arms **Reverse:** Bust of Coanabo

| Date | Mintage | F | VF | XF | Unc | BU |
|---|---|---|---|---|---|---|
| 1984Mo | 10,000,000 | — | — | — | 0.25 | — |
| 1984Mo Proof | 1,600 | Value: 1.50 | | | | |
| 1986 | 18,067,000 | — | — | — | 0.25 | — |
| 1986 Proof | 1,600 | Value: 1.50 | | | | |
| 1987 | 15,000,000 | — | — | — | 0.25 | — |
| 1987 Proof | 1,600 | Value: 1.50 | | | | |

**CENTAVO** **KM# 64a** **Weight:** 2.0000 g. **Composition:** 0.9000 Silver .0578 oz. ASW **Subject:** Human Rights **Obverse:** Banner over national arms **Reverse:** Bust of Coanabo

| Date | Mintage | F | VF | XF | Unc | BU |
|---|---|---|---|---|---|---|
| 1984Mo Proof | 100 | Value: 20.00 | | | | |
| 1986 Proof | 100 | Value: 20.00 | | | | |

**CENTAVO** **KM# 72** **Composition:** Copper Plated Zinc **Obverse:** Banner over national arms **Reverse:** Triangular artifact

| Date | Mintage | F | VF | XF | Unc | BU |
|---|---|---|---|---|---|---|
| 1989 | 1,115 | — | — | — | 1.25 | — |

**CENTAVO** **KM# 72a** **Weight:** 3.7000 g. **Composition:** 0.9250 Silver .1100 oz. ASW **Obverse:** Banner over national arms **Reverse:** Triangular artifact

| Date | Mintage | F | VF | XF | Unc | BU |
|---|---|---|---|---|---|---|
| 1989 Proof | 2,600 | — | — | — | — | — |

**5 CENTAVOS** **KM# 18** **Composition:** Copper-Nickel **Obverse:** Banner over national arms **Reverse:** Profile of native princess

| Date | Mintage | F | VF | XF | Unc | BU |
|---|---|---|---|---|---|---|
| 1937 | 2,000,000 | 1.00 | 1.75 | 5.00 | 50.00 | — |
| 1937 Proof | — | Value: 450 | | | | |
| 1939 | 200,000 | 3.50 | 8.00 | 40.00 | 350 | — |
| 1951 | 2,000,000 | 0.75 | 1.25 | 2.00 | 20.00 | — |
| 1956 | 1,000,000 | 0.20 | 0.50 | 0.80 | 3.50 | — |
| 1959 | 1,000,000 | 0.20 | 0.50 | 0.80 | 3.50 | — |
| 1961 | 4,000,000 | 0.10 | 0.20 | 0.35 | 0.75 | — |
| 1971 | 440,000 | 0.10 | 0.15 | 0.20 | 0.50 | — |
| 1972 | 2,000,000 | 0.10 | 0.15 | 0.20 | 0.40 | — |
| 1972 Proof | 500 | Value: 15.00 | | | | |
| 1974 | 5,000,000 | — | — | 0.10 | 0.40 | — |
| 1974 Proof | 500 | Value: 15.00 | | | | |

**5 CENTAVOS** **KM# 18a** **Weight:** 5.0000 g. **Composition:** 0.3500 Silver .0563 oz. ASW **Obverse:** Banner over national arms **Reverse:** Profile of native princess

| Date | Mintage | F | VF | XF | Unc | BU |
|---|---|---|---|---|---|---|
| 1944 | 2,000,000 | 1.50 | 3.50 | 7.50 | 30.00 | — |

**5 CENTAVOS** **KM# 26** **Composition:** Copper-Nickel **Subject:** 100th Anniversary - Restoration of the Republic **Obverse:** Banner over national arms **Reverse:** Profile of native princess

| Date | Mintage | F | VF | XF | Unc | BU |
|---|---|---|---|---|---|---|
| 1963 | 4,000,000 | — | 0.10 | 0.15 | 0.60 | — |

**5 CENTAVOS** **KM# 41** **Composition:** Copper-Nickel **Subject:** Centennial - Death of Juan Pablo Duarte **Obverse:** Banner over national arms **Reverse:** Portrait of Duarte

| Date | Mintage | F | VF | XF | Unc | BU |
|---|---|---|---|---|---|---|
| 1976 | 5,595,000 | — | — | 0.10 | 0.50 | — |
| 1976 Proof | 5,000 | Value: 2.00 | | | | |

**5 CENTAVOS** **KM# 49** **Composition:** Copper-Nickel **Reverse:** Without memorial legend

| Date | Mintage | F | VF | XF | Unc | BU |
|---|---|---|---|---|---|---|
| 1978 | 1,996,000 | — | — | 0.10 | 0.35 | — |
| 1978 Proof | 5,000 | Value: 1.50 | | | | |
| 1979 | 2,988,000 | — | — | 0.10 | 0.35 | — |
| 1979 Proof | 500 | Value: 15.00 | | | | |
| 1980 | 5,300,000 | — | — | 0.10 | 0.35 | — |
| 1980 Proof | 3,000 | Value: 2.00 | | | | |

| Date | Mintage | F | VF | XF | Unc | BU |
|---|---|---|---|---|---|---|
| 1981 | 4,500,000 | — | — | 0.10 | 0.35 | — |
| 1981 Proof | 3,000 | Value: 2.00 | | | | |

**5 CENTAVOS** **KM# 49a** **Weight:** 5.8600 g. **Composition:** 0.9000 Silver .1696 oz. ASW **Reverse:** Without memorial legend

| Date | Mintage | F | VF | XF | Unc | BU |
|---|---|---|---|---|---|---|
| 1978 Proof | 15 | Value: 125 | | | | |
| 1979 Proof | 15 | Value: 125 | | | | |
| 1980 Proof | 15 | Value: 125 | | | | |
| 1981 Proof | 15 | Value: 125 | | | | |

**5 CENTAVOS** **KM# 59** **Composition:** Copper Nickel **Subject:** Human Rights **Obverse:** Banner over national arms **Reverse:** Conjoined busts of Sanchez and Mello

| Date | Mintage | F | VF | XF | Unc | BU |
|---|---|---|---|---|---|---|
| 1983 | 3,998,000 | — | — | 0.10 | 0.30 | — |
| 1983(t) Proof | 1,600 | Value: 2.00 | | | | |
| 1984Mo | 10,000,000 | — | — | 0.10 | 0.30 | — |
| 1984Mo Proof | 1,600 | Value: 2.00 | | | | |
| 1986 | 12,898,000 | — | — | 0.10 | 0.30 | — |
| 1986 Proof | 1,600 | Value: 2.00 | | | | |
| 1987 | 10,000,000 | — | — | 0.10 | 0.30 | — |
| 1987 Proof | 1,700 | Value: 2.00 | | | | |

**5 CENTAVOS** **KM# 59a** **Weight:** 5.0000 g. **Composition:** 0.9000 Silver .1447 oz. ASW **Subject:** Human Rights **Obverse:** Banner over national arms **Reverse:** Conjoined busts of Sanchez and Mello

| Date | Mintage | F | VF | XF | Unc | BU |
|---|---|---|---|---|---|---|
| 1983 Proof | 100 | Value: 30.00 | | | | |
| 1984Mo Proof | 100 | Value: 30.00 | | | | |
| 1986 Proof | 100 | Value: 30.00 | | | | |

**5 CENTAVOS** **KM# 69** **Composition:** Nickel Clad Steel **Subject:** Native Culture **Obverse:** Banner over national arms **Reverse:** Native drummer

| Date | Mintage | F | VF | XF | Unc | BU |
|---|---|---|---|---|---|---|
| 1989 | 50,000,000 | — | — | — | 0.35 | — |

**5 CENTAVOS** **KM# 69a** **Weight:** 5.8300 g. **Composition:** 0.9250 Silver .1734 oz. ASW **Subject:** Native Culture **Obverse:** Banner over national arms **Reverse:** Native drummer

| Date | Mintage | F | VF | XF | Unc | BU |
|---|---|---|---|---|---|---|
| 1989 Proof | 2,600 | — | — | — | — | — |

**10 CENTAVOS** **KM# 19** **Weight:** 2.5000 g. **Composition:** 0.9000 Silver .0723 oz. ASW **Obverse:** Banner over national arms **Reverse:** Profile of native princess

| Date | Mintage | F | VF | XF | Unc | BU |
|---|---|---|---|---|---|---|
| 1937 | 1,000,000 | BV | 2.00 | 5.00 | 40.00 | — |
| 1937 Proof | — | Value: 550 | | | | |
| 1939 | 150,000 | 3.00 | 6.00 | 20.00 | 300 | — |
| 1942 | 2,000,000 | 1.00 | 2.00 | 3.00 | 30.00 | — |
| 1944 | 1,000,000 | 1.00 | 2.00 | 4.00 | 50.00 | — |
| 1951 | 500,000 | 1.00 | 2.00 | 3.00 | 10.00 | — |
| 1952 | 500,000 | 1.00 | 2.00 | 3.00 | 10.00 | — |
| 1953 | 750,000 | 1.00 | 2.00 | 3.00 | 8.00 | — |
| 1956 | 1,000,000 | 0.75 | 1.50 | 2.50 | 8.00 | — |
| 1959 | 2,000,000 | BV | 1.25 | 2.25 | 7.00 | — |
| 1961 | 2,000,000 | BV | 1.00 | 2.00 | 6.00 | — |

**10 CENTAVOS** **KM# 27** **Weight:** 2.5000 g. **Composition:** 0.6500 Silver .0522 oz. ASW **Subject:** 100th Anniversary - Restoration of the Republic **Obverse:** Banner over national arms **Reverse:** Profile of native princess

| Date | Mintage | F | VF | XF | Unc | BU |
|---|---|---|---|---|---|---|
| 1963 | 4,000,000 | — | BV | 1.00 | 2.00 | — |

**10 CENTAVOS** **KM# 19a** **Composition:** Copper-Nickel **Obverse:** Banner over national arms **Reverse:** Profile of native princess **Edge:** Plain

| Date | Mintage | F | VF | XF | Unc | BU |
|---|---|---|---|---|---|---|
| 1967 | 10,000,000 | — | — | 0.15 | 0.50 | — |
| 1973 | 8,000,000 | — | — | 0.15 | 0.50 | — |
| 1973 Proof | 500 | Value: 20.00 | | | | |
| 1975 | 8,000,000 | — | — | 0.15 | 0.50 | — |

**10 CENTAVOS** **KM# 42** **Composition:** Copper-Nickel **Subject:** Centennial - Death of Juan Pablo Duarte **Obverse:** Banner over national arms **Reverse:** Portrait of Duarte

| Date | Mintage | F | VF | XF | Unc | BU |
|---|---|---|---|---|---|---|
| 1976 | 5,595,000 | — | — | 0.10 | 0.75 | — |
| 1976 Proof | 5,000 | Value: 2.00 | | | | |

**10 CENTAVOS** **KM# 50** **Composition:** Copper-Nickel

| Date | Mintage | F | VF | XF | Unc | BU |
|---|---|---|---|---|---|---|
| 1978 | 3,000,000 | — | — | 0.10 | 0.50 | — |
| 1978 Proof | 5,000 | Value: 2.00 | | | | |
| 1979 | 4,020,000 | — | — | 0.10 | 0.50 | — |
| 1979 Proof | 500 | Value: 20.00 | | | | |
| 1980 | 4,400,000 | — | — | 0.10 | 0.35 | — |
| 1980 Proof | 3,000 | Value: 3.00 | | | | |
| 1981 | 6,000,000 | — | — | 0.10 | 0.35 | — |
| 1981 Proof | 3,000 | Value: 3.00 | | | | |

**10 CENTAVOS** **KM# 50a** **Weight:** 2.9500 g. **Composition:** 0.9000 Silver .0854 oz. ASW **Obverse:** Without memorial legend

| Date | Mintage | F | VF | XF | Unc | BU |
|---|---|---|---|---|---|---|
| 1978 Proof | 15 | Value: 125 | | | | |
| 1979 Proof | 15 | Value: 125 | | | | |
| 1980 Proof | 15 | Value: 125 | | | | |
| 1981 Proof | 15 | Value: 125 | | | | |

**10 CENTAVOS** **KM# 60** **Composition:** Copper-Nickel **Subject:** Human Rights **Obverse:** Banner over national arms **Reverse:** Profile of Duarte

| Date | Mintage | F | VF | XF | Unc | BU |
|---|---|---|---|---|---|---|
| 1983 | 4,998,000 | — | — | 0.10 | 0.35 | — |
| 1983(t) | 4,000,000 | — | — | 0.10 | 0.35 | — |
| 1983(t) Proof | 1,600 | Value: 2.50 | | | | |
| 1984Mo | 15,000,000 | — | — | 0.10 | 0.25 | — |
| 1984Mo Proof | 1,600 | Value: 2.50 | | | | |
| 1986 | 15,515,000 | — | — | 0.10 | 0.25 | — |
| 1986 Proof | 1,600 | Value: 2.50 | | | | |
| 1987 | 20,000,000 | — | — | 0.10 | 0.25 | — |
| 1987 Proof | 1,700 | Value: 2.50 | | | | |

**10 CENTAVOS** **KM# 60a** **Weight:** 2.5000 g. **Composition:** 0.9000 Silver .0723 oz. ASW **Subject:** Human Rights **Obverse:** Banner over national arms **Reverse:** Profile of Duarte

| Date | Mintage | F | VF | XF | Unc | BU |
|---|---|---|---|---|---|---|
| 1983(t) Proof | 100 | Value: 30.00 | | | | |
| 1984 Proof | 100 | Value: 30.00 | | | | |
| 1986 Proof | 100 | Value: 30.00 | | | | |

**10 CENTAVOS** **KM# 70** **Composition:** Nickel Clad Steel **Obverse:** Banner over national arms **Reverse:** Indigenous fruits and vegetables

| Date | Mintage | F | VF | XF | Unc | BU |
|---|---|---|---|---|---|---|
| 1989 | 40,000,000 | — | — | — | 0.40 | — |
| 1991 | 3,500,000 | — | — | — | 0.40 | — |

**10 CENTAVOS** **KM# 70a** **Weight:** 2.9000 g. **Composition:** 925.0000 Silver .0863 oz. ASW **Obverse:** Banner over national arms **Reverse:** Indigenous fruits and vegetables

| Date | Mintage | F | VF | XF | Unc | BU |
|---|---|---|---|---|---|---|
| 1989 Proof | 2,600 | — | — | — | — | — |

**25 CENTAVOS** **KM# 20** **Weight:** 6.2500 g. **Composition:** 0.9000 Silver .1808 oz. ASW **Obverse:** Banner over national arms **Reverse:** Profile of native princess

| Date | Mintage | F | VF | XF | Unc | BU |
|---|---|---|---|---|---|---|
| 1937 | 560,000 | BV | 5.00 | 15.00 | 65.00 | — |
| 1937 Proof | — | Value: 650 | | | | |
| 1939 | 160,000 | 4.00 | 8.00 | 25.00 | 500 | — |
| 1942 | 560,000 | 2.00 | 4.00 | 10.00 | 100 | — |
| 1944 | 400,000 | 2.00 | 4.00 | 8.00 | 80.00 | — |
| 1947 | 400,000 | 2.00 | 4.00 | 8.00 | 80.00 | — |
| 1951 | 400,000 | 2.00 | 4.00 | 8.00 | 80.00 | — |
| 1952 | 400,000 | 2.00 | 3.00 | 5.00 | 12.50 | — |
| 1956 | 400,000 | 2.00 | 2.50 | 4.00 | 10.00 | — |
| 1960 | 600,000 | 2.00 | 2.50 | 4.00 | 10.00 | — |
| 1961 | 800,000 | 2.00 | 2.50 | 4.00 | 10.00 | — |

**25 CENTAVOS** **KM# 28** **Weight:** 6.2500 g. **Composition:** 0.6500 Silver .1306 oz. ASW **Subject:** 100th Anniversary - Restoration of the Republic **Obverse:** Banner over national arms **Reverse:** Profile of native princess

| Date | Mintage | F | VF | XF | Unc | BU |
|---|---|---|---|---|---|---|
| 1963 | 2,400,000 | — | BV | 1.50 | 3.00 | — |

**25 CENTAVOS** **KM# 20a.1** **Composition:** Copper Nickel **Obverse:** Banner over national arms **Reverse:** Profile of native princess **Edge:** Plain

| Date | Mintage | F | VF | XF | Unc | BU |
|---|---|---|---|---|---|---|
| 1967 | 5,000,000 | — | 0.10 | 0.20 | 0.75 | — |
| 1972 | 800,000 | — | 0.10 | 0.40 | 1.00 | — |
| 1972 Proof | 500 | Value: 20.00 | | | | |

**25 CENTAVOS** **KM# 20a.2** **Composition:** Copper-Nickel **Obverse:** Banner over national arms **Reverse:** Profile of native princess **Edge:** Reeded

| Date | Mintage | F | VF | XF | Unc | BU |
|---|---|---|---|---|---|---|
| 1974 | 2,000,000 | — | 0.10 | 0.40 | 1.00 | — |
| 1974 Proof | 500 | Value: 20.00 | | | | |

**25 CENTAVOS** **KM# 43** **Composition:** Copper-Nickel **Subject:** Centennial - Death of Juan Pablo Duarte **Obverse:** Banner over national arms **Reverse:** Portrait of Duarte

| Date | Mintage | F | VF | XF | Unc | BU |
|---|---|---|---|---|---|---|
| 1976 | 3,195,000 | — | 0.10 | 0.40 | 1.00 | — |
| 1976 Proof | 5,000 | Value: 2.50 | | | | |

**25 CENTAVOS** **KM# 51** **Composition:** Copper-Nickel **Reverse:** Without memorial legend

| Date | Mintage | F | VF | XF | Unc | BU |
|---|---|---|---|---|---|---|
| 1978 | 996,000 | — | — | 0.35 | 0.75 | — |
| 1978 Proof | 5,000 | Value: 3.00 | | | | |
| 1979 | 2,089,000 | — | — | 0.15 | 0.50 | — |
| 1979 Proof | 500 | Value: 25.00 | | | | |
| 1980 | 2,600,000 | — | — | 0.15 | 0.50 | — |
| 1980 Proof | 3,000 | Value: 3.00 | | | | |
| 1981 | 3,200,000 | — | — | 0.15 | 0.50 | — |
| 1981 Proof | 3,000 | Value: 3.00 | | | | |

**25 CENTAVOS** **KM# 51a** **Weight:** 7.3200 g. **Composition:** 0.9000 Silver .2118 oz. ASW **Reverse:** Without memorial legend

| Date | Mintage | F | VF | XF | Unc | BU |
|---|---|---|---|---|---|---|
| 1978 Proof | 15 | Value: 150 | | | | |
| 1979 Proof | 15 | Value: 150 | | | | |
| 1980 Proof | 15 | Value: 150 | | | | |
| 1981 Proof | 15 | Value: 150 | | | | |

**25 CENTAVOS** **KM# 61a** **Weight:** 6.2500 g. **Composition:** 0.9000 Silver .1808 oz. ASW **Subject:** Human Rights **Obverse:** Banner over national arms **Reverse:** Profile of the Mirabel sisters

| Date | Mintage | F | VF | XF | Unc | BU |
|---|---|---|---|---|---|---|
| 1983(t) Proof | 100 | Value: 40.00 | | | | |
| 1984Mo Proof | 100 | Value: 40.00 | | | | |
| 1986 Proof | 100 | Value: 40.00 | | | | |

**25 CENTAVOS** **KM# 61** **Composition:** Copper-Nickel **Subject:** Human Rights **Obverse:** Banner over national arms **Reverse:** Profile of the Mirabel sisters **Note:** Coin and medal rotations and edge-reeding varieties exist.

| Date | Mintage | F | VF | XF | Unc | BU |
|---|---|---|---|---|---|---|
| 1983 | 793,000 | — | 0.10 | 0.20 | 0.50 | — |
| 1983(t) | 5,000 | — | — | — | 2.50 | — |
| 1983(t) Proof | 1,600 | Value: 8.00 | | | | |
| 1984Mo | 6,400,000 | — | — | 0.15 | 0.40 | — |
| 1984Mo Proof | 1,600 | Value: 8.00 | | | | |
| 1986 | 10,132,000 | — | — | 0.15 | 0.40 | — |
| 1986 Proof | 1,600 | Value: 8.00 | | | | |
| 1987 | 6,000,000 | — | — | 0.15 | 0.40 | — |
| 1987 Proof | 1,700 | Value: 8.00 | | | | |

**25 CENTAVOS** **KM# 71.2** **Composition:** Nickel Clad Steel **Subject:** Native Culture **Obverse:** Banner over national arms. **Reverse:** Two oxen pulling cart **Note:** Obverse and reverse legends and designs in beaded circle. Varieties exist.

| Date | Mintage | F | VF | XF | Unc | BU |
|---|---|---|---|---|---|---|
| 1989 | Inc. above | — | — | — | 0.60 | — |
| 1990 | 20,000,000 | — | — | — | 0.60 | — |

**25 CENTAVOS** **KM# 71.1** **Composition:** Nickel Clad Steel **Subject:** Native Culture **Obverse:** Banner over national arms **Reverse:** Two oxen pulling cart

| Date | Mintage | F | VF | XF | Unc | BU |
|---|---|---|---|---|---|---|
| 1989 | 16,000,000 | — | — | — | 0.60 | — |
| 1991 | 38,000,000 | — | — | — | 0.60 | — |

**25 CENTAVOS** **KM# 71.1a** **Weight:** 6.7400 g. **Composition:** 0.9250 Silver .2005 oz. ASW **Subject:** Native Culture **Obverse:** Banner over national arms. **Reverse:** Two oxen pulling cart

| Date | Mintage | F | VF | XF | Unc | BU |
|---|---|---|---|---|---|---|
| 1989 Proof | 2,600 | — | — | — | — | — |

**1/2 PESO** **KM# 21** **Weight:** 12.5000 g. **Composition:** 0.9000 Silver .3617 oz. ASW **Obverse:** Banner over national arms. **Reverse:** Profile of native princess

| Date | Mintage | F | VF | XF | Unc | BU |
|---|---|---|---|---|---|---|
| 1937 | 500,000 | BV | 7.50 | 12.50 | 70.00 | — |
| 1937 Proof | — | Value: 750 | | | | |
| 1944 | 100,000 | BV | 10.00 | 25.00 | 300 | — |
| 1947 | 200,000 | BV | 7.50 | 15.00 | 200 | — |
| 1951 | 200,000 | BV | 7.50 | 15.00 | 150 | — |
| 1952 | 140,000 | BV | 7.50 | 12.50 | 70.00 | — |
| 1959 | 100,000 | BV | 6.00 | 10.00 | 40.00 | — |
| 1960 | 100,000 | BV | 6.00 | 9.00 | 30.00 | — |
| 1961 | 400,000 | BV | 4.00 | 6.00 | 25.00 | — |

**1/2 PESO** **KM# 29** **Weight:** 12.5000 g. **Composition:** 0.6500 Silver .2612 oz. ASW **Subject:** 100th Anniversary - Restoration of the Republic **Obverse:** Banner over national arms **Reverse:** Profile of native princess

| Date | Mintage | F | VF | XF | Unc | BU |
|---|---|---|---|---|---|---|
| 1963 | 300,000 | — | BV | 4.00 | 7.50 | — |

**1/2 PESO** **KM# 21a.1** **Composition:** Copper-Nickel **Obverse:** Banner over national arms **Reverse:** Profile of native princess **Edge:** Plain

| Date | Mintage | F | VF | XF | Unc | BU |
|---|---|---|---|---|---|---|
| 1967 | 1,500,000 | — | 0.20 | 0.40 | 1.50 | — |
| 1968 | 600,000 | — | 0.30 | 0.50 | 2.50 | — |

**1/2 PESO** **KM# 21a.2** **Composition:** Copper-Nickel **Obverse:** Banner over national arms **Reverse:** Profile of native princess **Edge:** Reeded

| Date | Mintage | F | VF | XF | Unc | BU |
|---|---|---|---|---|---|---|
| 1973 | 600,000 | — | 0.20 | 0.40 | 1.50 | — |
| 1973 Proof | 500 | Value: 30.00 | | | | |
| 1975 | 600,000 | — | 0.20 | 0.40 | 1.50 | — |

**1/2 PESO** **KM# 44** **Composition:** Copper-Nickel **Subject:** Centennial - Death of Juan Pablo Duarte **Obverse:** Banner over national arms **Reverse:** Portrait of Duarte

| Date | Mintage | F | VF | XF | Unc | BU |
|---|---|---|---|---|---|---|
| 1976 | 195,000 | — | 0.20 | 0.40 | 1.50 | — |
| 1976 Proof | 5,000 | Value: 3.00 | | | | |

**1/2 PESO** **KM# 52** **Composition:** Copper-Nickel **Reverse:** Without memorial legend

| Date | Mintage | F | VF | XF | Unc | BU |
|---|---|---|---|---|---|---|
| 1978 | 296,000 | — | 0.20 | 0.40 | 1.50 | — |
| 1978 Proof | 5,000 | Value: 4.00 | | | | |
| 1979 | 967,000 | — | 0.20 | 0.40 | 1.50 | — |
| 1979 Proof | 500 | Value: 30.00 | | | | |
| 1980 | 1,000,000 | — | 0.20 | 0.40 | 1.50 | — |
| 1980 Proof | 3,000 | Value: 5.00 | | | | |
| 1981 | 1,300,000 | — | 0.20 | 0.40 | 1.50 | — |
| 1981 Proof | 3,000 | Value: 5.00 | | | | |

**1/2 PESO** **KM# 52a** **Weight:** 14.5500 g. **Composition:** 0.9000 Silver .4210 oz. ASW **Reverse:** Without memorial legend

| Date | Mintage | F | VF | XF | Unc | BU |
|---|---|---|---|---|---|---|
| 1978 Proof | 15 | Value: 150 | | | | |
| 1979 Proof | 15 | Value: 150 | | | | |
| 1980 Proof | 15 | Value: 150 | | | | |
| 1981 Proof | 15 | Value: 150 | | | | |

**1/2 PESO** **KM# 62a** **Weight:** 12.5000 g. **Composition:** 0.9000 Silver .3617 oz. ASW **Subject:** Human Rights **Obverse:** Banner over national arms **Reverse:** Profiles of Bono, Espaillat and Rojas

| Date | Mintage | F | VF | XF | Unc | BU |
|---|---|---|---|---|---|---|
| 1983(t) Proof | 100 | Value: 50.00 | | | | |
| 1984Mo Proof | 100 | Value: 50.00 | | | | |
| 1986 Proof | 100 | Value: 50.00 | | | | |

**1/2 PESO** **KM# 62** **Composition:** Copper-Nickel **Subject:** Human Rights **Obverse:** Banner over national arms **Reverse:** Profiles of Bono, Espaillat and Rojas **Note:** Coin and medal rotations exist.

| Date | Mintage | F | VF | XF | Unc | BU |
|---|---|---|---|---|---|---|
| 1983 | 393,000 | — | 0.20 | 0.40 | 1.50 | — |
| 1983(t) | 5,000 | — | — | — | 4.00 | — |
| 1983(t) Proof | 1,600 | Value: 15.00 | | | | |
| 1984Mo | 3,200,000 | — | 0.20 | 0.40 | 1.50 | — |
| 1984Mo Proof | 1,600 | Value: 15.00 | | | | |
| 1986 | 5,225,000 | — | 0.20 | 0.40 | 1.50 | — |
| 1986 Proof | 1,600 | Value: 15.00 | | | | |
| 1987 | 3,000,000 | — | 0.20 | 0.40 | 1.50 | — |
| 1987 Proof | 1,700 | Value: 15.00 | | | | |

**1/2 PESO** **KM# 73.1a** **Weight:** 14.6500 g. **Composition:** 0.9250 Silver .4357 oz. ASW **Subject:** National Culture **Obverse:** Banner over national arms **Reverse:** Beacon at Colon

| Date | Mintage | F | VF | XF | Unc | BU |
|---|---|---|---|---|---|---|
| 1989 Proof | 2,600 | — | — | — | — | — |

**1/2 PESO** **KM# 73.1** **Composition:** Nickel Clad Steel **Subject:** National Culture **Obverse:** Banner over national arms **Reverse:** Beacon at Colon

| Date | Mintage | F | VF | XF | Unc | BU |
|---|---|---|---|---|---|---|
| 1989 | 8,000,000 | — | — | — | 2.00 | — |

**1/2 PESO** **KM# 73.2** **Composition:** Nickel-Clad Steel **Subject:** National Culture **Obverse:** Banner over national arms, legend and design in inner circle **Reverse:** Beacon at Colon

| Date | Mintage | F | VF | XF | Unc | BU |
|---|---|---|---|---|---|---|
| 1990 | 1,500,000 | — | — | — | 2.00 | — |

**PESO KM# 22 Weight:** 26.7000 g. **Composition:** 0.9000 Silver .7725 oz. ASW **Obverse:** Banner over national arms **Reverse:** HP below bust of native princess

| Date | Mintage | F | VF | XF | Unc | BU |
|---|---|---|---|---|---|---|
| 1939 | 15,000 | 15.00 | 20.00 | 45.00 | 750 | — |
| 1939 Proof | — | Value: 2,250 | | | | |
| 1952 | 20,000 | BV | 7.00 | 10.00 | 15.00 | — |

**PESO KM# 23 Weight:** 26.7000 g. **Composition:** 0.9000 Silver .7725 oz. ASW **Subject:** 25th Anniversary of Trujullo Regime **Obverse:** Banner over national arms **Reverse:** Profile bust of Trujillo **Note:** 30,550 officially melted following Trujillo's assassination in 1961.

| Date | Mintage | F | VF | XF | Unc | BU |
|---|---|---|---|---|---|---|
| 1955 | 50,000 | 7.50 | 10.00 | 15.00 | 25.00 | — |

**PESO KM# 30 Weight:** 26.7000 g. **Composition:** 0.6500 Silver .5579 oz. ASW **Subject:** 100th Anniversary - Restoration of the Republic **Obverse:** Memorial legend around national arms **Reverse:** Profile of native princess

| Date | Mintage | F | VF | XF | Unc | BU |
|---|---|---|---|---|---|---|
| 1963 | 20,000 | — | — | 5.00 | 9.00 | — |
| 1963 Proof | — | — | — | — | — | — |

**PESO KM# 33 Composition:** Copper-Nickel **Subject:** 125th Anniversary of the Republic **Obverse:** Memorial legend around national arms **Reverse:** Pueblo entrance

| Date | Mintage | F | VF | XF | Unc | BU |
|---|---|---|---|---|---|---|
| 1969 | 30,000 | — | — | 2.00 | 4.50 | — |

**PESO KM# 34 Weight:** 26.7000 g. **Composition:** 0.9000 Silver .7725 oz. ASW **Subject:** 25th Anniversary - Central Bank **Obverse:** Memorial legend around national arms **Reverse:** Bank door in inner circle

| Date | Mintage | F | VF | XF | Unc | BU |
|---|---|---|---|---|---|---|
| 1972 | 27,000 | — | — | — | 9.00 | — |
| 1972 Proof | 3,000 | Value: 15.00 | | | | |

**PESO KM# 35 Weight:** 26.7000 g. **Composition:** 0.9000 Silver .7725 oz. ASW **Subject:** 12th Central American and Caribbean Games **Obverse:** Without memorial legend **Reverse:** Map and coat of arms

| Date | Mintage | F | VF | XF | Unc | BU |
|---|---|---|---|---|---|---|
| 1974 | 50,000 | — | — | — | 9.00 | — |
| 1974 Proof | 5,000 | Value: 15.00 | | | | |

**PESO KM# 45 Composition:** Copper-Nickel **Subject:** Centennial - Death of Juan Pablo Duarte **Obverse:** Banner over national arms **Reverse:** Portrait of Duarte

| Date | Mintage | F | VF | XF | Unc | BU |
|---|---|---|---|---|---|---|
| 1976 | 25,000 | — | — | 1.00 | 2.00 | — |
| 1976 Proof | 5,000 | Value: 7.50 | | | | |

**PESO KM# 53 Composition:** Copper-Nickel **Obverse:** Without memorial legend **Reverse:** Portrait of Duarte

| Date | Mintage | F | VF | XF | Unc | BU |
|---|---|---|---|---|---|---|
| 1978 | 35,000 | — | — | 1.00 | 2.00 | — |
| 1978 Proof | 5,000 | Value: 7.50 | | | | |
| 1979 | 45,000 | — | — | 1.00 | 2.00 | — |
| 1979 Proof | 500 | Value: 35.00 | | | | |
| 1980 | 20,000 | — | — | 1.00 | 2.00 | — |
| 1980 Proof | 3,000 | Value: 6.00 | | | | |
| 1981 Proof | 3,000 | Value: 6.00 | | | | |

**PESO KM# 53a Weight:** 30.9200 g. **Composition:** 0.9000 Silver .8947 oz. ASW **Subject:** Centennial - Death of Juan Pablo Duarte **Obverse:** Without memorial legend **Reverse:** Portrait of Duarte

| Date | Mintage | F | VF | XF | Unc | BU |
|---|---|---|---|---|---|---|
| 1978 Proof | 15 | Value: 300 | | | | |
| 1979 Proof | 15 | Value: 300 | | | | |
| 1980 Proof | 15 | Value: 300 | | | | |
| 1981 Proof | 15 | Value: 300 | | | | |

**PESO** **KM# 63** **Composition:** Copper Nickel **Subject:** Human Rights - Montesinos, Enriquillo and Lemba **Obverse:** Denomination, national arms **Reverse:** Profile portraits of Montesinos, Enriquillo and Lemba **Shape:** 10 sided **Note:** Coin and medal rotations exist.

| Date | Mintage | F | VF | XF | Unc | BU |
|---|---|---|---|---|---|---|
| 1983(t) | 93,000 | — | — | 1.00 | 2.50 | — |
| 1983 | 5,000 | — | — | — | 6.00 | — |
| 1983(t) Proof | 1,600 | Value: 15.00 | | | | |
| 1984Mo | 120,000 | — | — | 1.00 | 2.50 | — |
| 1984Mo Proof | 1,600 | Value: 15.00 | | | | |
| 1986 | — | — | — | 1.00 | 2.50 | — |

**PESO** **KM# 63a** **Weight:** 17.0000 g. **Composition:** 0.9000 Silver .4919 oz. ASW **Subject:** Human Rights **Obverse:** Denomination, national arms **Reverse:** Profile portraits of Montesinos, Enriquillo and Lemba **Shape:** 10 sided **Note:** 10-sided.

| Date | Mintage | F | VF | XF | Unc | BU |
|---|---|---|---|---|---|---|
| 1983 Proof | 100 | Value: 100 | | | | |
| 1984 Proof | 100 | Value: 100 | | | | |

**PESO** **KM# 65** **Composition:** Nickel Bonded Steel **Subject:** 15th Central American and Caribbean Games **Obverse:** Denomination, national arms **Reverse:** St. George, coat of arms **Shape:** Round

| Date | Mintage | F | VF | XF | Unc | BU |
|---|---|---|---|---|---|---|
| 1986 | 100,000 | — | — | 1.00 | 3.00 | — |
| 1986 Proof | 1,700 | Value: 15.00 | | | | |

**PESO** **KM# 65a** **Weight:** 6.5000 g. **Composition:** Copper-Nickel **Subject:** 15th Central American and Caribbean Games **Obverse:** Denomination, national arms **Reverse:** St. George, coat of arms **Shape:** Round

| Date | Mintage | F | VF | XF | Unc | BU |
|---|---|---|---|---|---|---|
| 1986 Proof | 48 | — | — | — | — | — |
| 1986 | 548 | — | — | — | 40.00 | — |

**PESO** **KM# 65b** **Weight:** 10.0000 g. **Composition:** Copper-Nickel **Subject:** 15th Central American and Caribbean Games **Obverse:** Denomination, national arms **Reverse:** St. George, coat of arms **Shape:** Round

| Date | Mintage | F | VF | XF | Unc | BU |
|---|---|---|---|---|---|---|
| 1986 | 550 | — | — | — | 40.00 | — |
| 1986 Proof | 50 | — | — | — | — | — |

**PESO** **KM# 66** **Weight:** 19.8400 g. **Composition:** Copper-Nickel **Subject:** 500th Anniversary - Discovery and Evangelization **Obverse:** Denomination, national arms **Reverse:** 3 ships at sea

| Date | Mintage | F | VF | XF | Unc | BU |
|---|---|---|---|---|---|---|
| 1988(c) | 150,000 | — | — | — | 2.50 | — |
| 1988(c) Proof | 1,500 | Value: 12.50 | | | | |

**PESO** **KM# 66a** **Weight:** 21.1035 g. **Composition:** 0.9990 Silver 1 oz. ASW **Subject:** 500th Anniversary - Discovery and Evangelization **Obverse:** Denomination, national arms **Reverse:** 3 ships at sea

| Date | Mintage | F | VF | XF | Unc | BU |
|---|---|---|---|---|---|---|
| 1988 Proof | 10,000 | Value: 18.50 | | | | |

**PESO** **KM# 66b** **Weight:** 31.1035 g. **Composition:** 0.9990 Gold 1 oz. AGW **Subject:** 500th Anniversary - Discovery and Evangelization **Obverse:** Denomination, national arms **Reverse:** 3 ships at sea

| Date | Mintage | F | VF | XF | Unc | BU |
|---|---|---|---|---|---|---|
| 1988 Proof | — | Value: 1,250 | | | | |

**PESO** **KM# 74** **Composition:** Copper-Nickel **Subject:** 500th Anniversary - Discovery and Evangelization **Obverse:** Denomination, national arms **Reverse:** Sailship landing

| Date | Mintage | F | VF | XF | Unc | BU |
|---|---|---|---|---|---|---|
| 1989(c) | — | — | — | — | 2.50 | — |

**PESO** **KM# 74a** **Weight:** 31.1035 g. **Composition:** 0.9990 Silver 1 oz. ASW **Subject:** 500th Anniversary - Discovery and Evangelization **Obverse:** Denomination, national arms **Reverse:** Sailship landing

| Date | Mintage | F | VF | XF | Unc | BU |
|---|---|---|---|---|---|---|
| 1989 Proof | 10,000 | Value: 18.50 | | | | |

**PESO** **KM# 74b** **Weight:** 31.1035 g. **Composition:** 0.9990 Gold 1 oz. AGW **Subject:** 500th Anniversary - Discovery and Evangelization **Obverse:** Denomination, national arms **Reverse:** Sailship landing

| Date | Mintage | F | VF | XF | Unc | BU |
|---|---|---|---|---|---|---|
| 1989(c) Proof | 30 | Value: 1,250 | | | | |

**PESO** **KM# 77** **Composition:** Copper-Nickel **Subject:** 500th Anniversary - Discovery and Evangelization

| Date | Mintage | F | VF | XF | Unc | BU |
|---|---|---|---|---|---|---|
| 1990(c) | 30,000 | — | — | — | 2.50 | — |

**PESO** **KM# 77a** **Weight:** 31.1035 g. **Composition:** 0.9990 Silver 1 oz. ASW **Subject:** 500th Anniversary - Discovery and Evangelization

| Date | Mintage | F | VF | XF | Unc | BU |
|---|---|---|---|---|---|---|
| 1990 Proof | 10,000 | Value: 18.00 | | | | |

**PESO** **KM# 77b** **Weight:** 31.1035 g. **Composition:** 0.9990 Gold 1 oz. AGW **Subject:** 500th Anniversary - Discovery and Evangelization

| Date | Mintage | F | VF | XF | Unc | BU |
|---|---|---|---|---|---|---|
| 1990 Proof | 50 | — | — | — | 1,000 | — |

**PESO** **KM# 80.1** **Composition:** Copper-Zinc **Subject:** Juan Pablo Duarte **Obverse:** Denomination, national arms **Reverse:** DUARTE on bust

| Date | Mintage | F | VF | XF | Unc | BU |
|---|---|---|---|---|---|---|
| 1991 | 40,000,000 | — | — | — | 2.00 | — |
| 1992 | 35,000,000 | — | — | — | 2.00 | — |

**PESO** **KM# 81** **Composition:** Copper-Nickel **Obverse:** Denomination, national arms **Reverse:** Pinzon brothers on ship at sea

| Date | Mintage | F | VF | XF | Unc | BU |
|---|---|---|---|---|---|---|
| 1991(c) | 50,000 | — | — | — | 2.50 | — |

**PESO** **KM# 81a** **Weight:** 31.1035 g. **Composition:** 999.0000 Silver 1 oz. ASW **Obverse:** Denomination, national arms **Reverse:** Pinzon Brothers on ship at sea

| Date | Mintage | F | VF | XF | Unc | BU |
|---|---|---|---|---|---|---|
| 1991 Proof | 10,000 | Value: 20.00 | | | | |

**PESO** **KM# 81b** **Weight:** 31.1035 g. **Composition:** 999.0000 Gold 1 oz. AGW **Obverse:** Denomination, national arms **Reverse:** Pinzon Brothers on ship at sea

| Date | Mintage | F | VF | XF | Unc | BU |
|---|---|---|---|---|---|---|
| 1991 Proof | 35 | Value: 1,150 | | | | |

**PESO** **KM# 82** **Composition:** Copper-Nickel **Subject:** Christopher Columbus **Obverse:** Denomination, national arms **Reverse:** Portrait of Columbus

| Date | Mintage | F | VF | XF | Unc | BU |
|---|---|---|---|---|---|---|
| 1992(c) | 50,000 | — | — | — | 2.50 | — |

**PESO** **KM# 82a** **Weight:** 31.1035 g. **Composition:** 0.9990 Silver 1 oz. ASW **Subject:** Christopher Columbus **Obverse:** Denomination, national arms **Reverse:** Portrait of Columbus

| Date | Mintage | F | VF | XF | Unc | BU |
|---|---|---|---|---|---|---|
| 1992 Proof | 10,000 | Value: 20.00 | | | | |

**PESO** **KM# 82b** **Weight:** 31.1035 g. **Composition:** 0.9990 Gold 1 oz. AGW **Subject:** Christopher Columbus **Obverse:** Denomination, national arms **Reverse:** Portrait of Columbus

| Date | Mintage | F | VF | XF | Unc | BU |
|---|---|---|---|---|---|---|
| 1992(c) Proof | 35 | Value: 1,150 | | | | |

**PESO** **KM# 80.2** **Composition:** Copper-Zinc **Subject:** Juan Pablo Duarte **Obverse:** Denomination, national arms **Reverse:** DUARTE below bust

| Date | Mintage | F | VF | XF | Unc | BU |
|---|---|---|---|---|---|---|
| 1992 | 35,000,000 | — | — | — | 2.00 | — |
| 1993 | 40,000,000 | — | — | — | 2.00 | — |
| 1997 | — | — | — | — | 2.00 | — |

**PESO** **KM# 87** **Composition:** Copper-Nickel **Subject:** UN - Peace **Obverse:** Denomination, arms, stars **Reverse:** UN logo, two doves

| Date | Mintage | F | VF | XF | Unc | BU |
|---|---|---|---|---|---|---|
| 1995 | — | — | — | — | 8.00 | — |

**PESO** **KM# 87a** **Weight:** 28.4400 g. **Composition:** 0.9250 Silver .8458 oz. ASW **Subject:** UN - Peace **Obverse:** Denomination, arms, stars **Reverse:** UN logo, two doves

| Date | Mintage | F | VF | XF | Unc | BU |
|---|---|---|---|---|---|---|
| 1995 Proof | — | Value: 35.00 | | | | |

**5 PESOS** **KM# 88** **Ring Composition:** Brass **Center Composition:** Stainless Steel **Subject:** 50th Anniversary - Central Bank **Obverse:** Denomination and national arms **Reverse:** Portrait, dates

| Date | Mintage | F | VF | XF | Unc | BU |
|---|---|---|---|---|---|---|
| 1997 | — | — | — | — | 2.00 | — |

**10 PESOS** **KM# 37** **Weight:** 28.0000 g. **Composition:** 0.9000 Silver .8102 oz. ASW **Subject:** International Bankers' Conference - First Hispaniola Coinage of Carlos and Johanna **Obverse:** National arms, denomination **Reverse:** Arms of Castille in inner ring

| Date | Mintage | F | VF | XF | Unc | BU |
|---|---|---|---|---|---|---|
| 1975 | 26,000 | — | — | — | 10.00 | — |
| 1975 Proof | 4,000 | Value: 17.50 | | | | |

**10 PESOS** **KM# 38** **Weight:** 30.0000 g. **Composition:** 0.9000 Silver .8681 oz. ASW **Subject:** Taino Art **Obverse:** National arms **Reverse:** Ancient figurine "Pueblo Viejo Mine"

| Date | Mintage | F | VF | XF | Unc | BU |
|---|---|---|---|---|---|---|
| 1975 | 45,000 | — | — | — | 8.50 | — |
| 1975 Proof | 5,000 | Value: 13.50 | | | | |

**10 PESOS** **KM# 57** **Weight:** 23.3300 g. **Composition:** 0.9250 Silver .6938 oz. ASW **Subject:** International Year of the Child **Obverse:** Banner over national arms

| Date | Mintage | F | VF | XF | Unc | BU |
|---|---|---|---|---|---|---|
| 1982(o) Proof | 8,712 | Value: 12.50 | | | | |

**25 PESOS** **KM# 54** **Weight:** 65.0000 g. **Composition:** 0.9250 Silver .9332 oz. ASW **Subject:** Pope John Paul II's Visit

| Date | Mintage | F | VF | XF | Unc | BU |
|---|---|---|---|---|---|---|
| ND(1979) | 3,000 | — | — | — | 37.50 | — |
| ND(1979) Proof | 6,000 | Value: 45.00 | | | | |

**30 PESOS** **KM# 24** **Weight:** 29.6220 g. **Composition:** 0.9000 Gold .8572 oz. AGW **Subject:** 25th Anniversary of Trujillo regime

| Date | Mintage | F | VF | XF | Unc | BU |
|---|---|---|---|---|---|---|
| 1955 | 33,000 | — | — | BV | 385 | — |

**30 PESOS** **KM# 36** **Weight:** 11.7000 g. **Composition:** 0.9000 Gold .3385 oz. AGW **Subject:** 12th Central American and Caribbean Games

| Date | Mintage | F | VF | XF | Unc | BU |
|---|---|---|---|---|---|---|
| 1974 | 25,000 | — | — | — | 150 | — |
| 1974 Proof | 5,000 | Value: 175 | | | | |

**30 PESOS** **KM# 46** **Weight:** 78.0000 g. **Composition:** 0.9250 Silver 2.3199 oz. ASW **Subject:** 30th Anniversary of Central Bank

| Date | Mintage | F | VF | XF | Unc | BU |
|---|---|---|---|---|---|---|
| 1977 | 5,000 | — | — | — | 27.50 | — |
| 1977 Proof | 2,000 | Value: 40.00 | | | | |

**100 PESOS** **KM# 39** **Weight:** 10.0000 g. **Composition:** 0.9000 Gold .2893 oz. AGW **Subject:** Taino Art

| Date | Mintage | F | VF | XF | Unc | BU |
|---|---|---|---|---|---|---|
| 1975 | 18,000 | — | — | — | 125 | — |
| 1975 Proof | 2,000 | Value: 150 | | | | |

**100 PESOS** **KM# 55** **Weight:** 12.0000 g. **Composition:** 0.9000 Gold .3472 oz. AGW **Subject:** Pope John Paul II's Visit

| Date | Mintage | F | VF | XF | Unc | BU |
|---|---|---|---|---|---|---|
| ND(1979) | 1,000 | — | — | — | 155 | — |
| ND(1979) Proof | 3,000 | Value: 175 | | | | |

**100 PESOS** KM# 67 **Weight:** 155.5000 g. **Composition:** 0.9990 Silver 5 oz. ASW **Subject:** Discovery of America - Native Americans **Size:** 65 mm. **Note:** Illustration reduced.

| Date | Mintage | F | VF | XF | Unc | BU |
|---|---|---|---|---|---|---|
| 1988 Proof | 5,300 | Value: 85.00 | | | | |

**100 PESOS** KM# 75 **Weight:** 155.5000 g. **Composition:** 0.9990 Silver 5 oz. ASW **Subject:** 500th Anniversary of Discovery and Evangelization of America - Columbus and Crew **Obverse:** Arms

| Date | Mintage | F | VF | XF | Unc | BU |
|---|---|---|---|---|---|---|
| 1989(c) (c) Proof | 1,500 | Value: 125 | | | | |

**100 PESOS** KM# 75a **Weight:** 155.5000 g. **Composition:** 0.9990 Gold 5 oz. AGW **Subject:** 500th Anniversary of Discovery and Evangelization of America - Columbus and Crew **Obverse:** Arms

| Date | Mintage | F | VF | XF | Unc | BU |
|---|---|---|---|---|---|---|
| 1989 Proof | 30 | Value: 3,500 | | | | |

**100 PESOS** KM# 78 **Weight:** 155.5000 g. **Composition:** 0.9990 Silver 5 oz. ASW **Subject:** 500th Anniversary of Discovery and Evangelization of America - Building a Stockade **Size:** 65 mm. **Note:** Illustration reduced.

| Date | Mintage | F | VF | XF | Unc | BU |
|---|---|---|---|---|---|---|
| 1990 Proof | 1,000 | Value: 145 | | | | |

**100 PESOS** KM# 78a **Weight:** 155.5300 g. **Composition:** 0.9990 Gold 5 oz. AGW **Subject:** 500th Anniversary of Discovery and Evangelization of America - Building a Stockade **Size:** 65 mm. **Note:** Illustration reduced.

| Date | Mintage | F | VF | XF | Unc | BU |
|---|---|---|---|---|---|---|
| 1990 Proof | 50 | Value: 3,000 | | | | |

**100 PESOS** KM# 83 **Weight:** 155.5300 g. **Composition:** 0.9990 Silver 5 oz. ASW **Subject:** 500th Anniversary of Discovery and Evangelization of America - Columbus Presenting Native American to Court **Obverse:** Similar to KM#78 **Size:** 65 mm. **Note:** Illustration reduced.

| Date | Mintage | F | VF | XF | Unc | BU |
|---|---|---|---|---|---|---|
| 1991 Proof | 1,500 | Value: 125 | | | | |

**100 PESOS** KM# 83a **Weight:** 155.5300 g. **Composition:** 0.9990 Gold 5 oz. AGW **Subject:** 500th Anniversary of Discovery and Evangelization of America - Columbus Presenting Native American to Court **Size:** 65 mm. **Note:** Illustration reduced.

| Date | Mintage | F | VF | XF | Unc | BU |
|---|---|---|---|---|---|---|
| 1991 Proof | 35 | Value: 3,200 | | | | |

**100 PESOS** KM# 84 **Weight:** 155.5300 g. **Composition:** 0.9990 Silver 5 oz. ASW **Subject:** 500th Anniversary - Discovery and Evangelization of America - Columbus and Anchored Ship **Obverse:** Similar to KM#78 **Size:** 65 mm. **Note:** Illustration reduced.

| Date | Mintage | F | VF | XF | Unc | BU |
|---|---|---|---|---|---|---|
| 1992 Proof | 1,500 | Value: 135 | | | | |

**100 PESOS** KM# 84a **Weight:** 155.5300 g. **Composition:** 0.9990 Gold 5 oz. AGW **Subject:** 500th Anniversary - Discovery and Evangelization of America - Columbus and Anchored Ship **Obverse:** Similar to KM#78 **Size:** 65 mm. **Note:** Illustration reduced.

| Date | Mintage | F | VF | XF | Unc | BU |
|---|---|---|---|---|---|---|
| 1992 Proof | 35 | Value: 3,200 | | | | |

**200 PESOS** KM# 47 **Weight:** 31.0000 g. **Composition:** 0.8000 Gold .7974 oz. AGW **Subject:** Centennial - Death of Juan Pablo Duarte **Note:** Large quantities of both varieties were melted for bullion.

| Date | Mintage | F | VF | XF | Unc | BU |
|---|---|---|---|---|---|---|
| 1977 | 1,000 | — | — | — | 450 | — |
| 1977 Proof | 2,000 | Value: 500 | | | | |

**200 PESOS** KM# 58 **Weight:** 17.1700 g. **Composition:** 0.9000 Gold .4969 oz. AGW **Subject:** International Year of the Child

| Date | Mintage | F | VF | XF | Unc | BU |
|---|---|---|---|---|---|---|
| 1982 Proof | 4,303 | Value: 250 | | | | |

**250 PESOS** KM# 56 **Weight:** 31.1000 g. **Composition:** 0.9000 Gold .9000 oz. AGW **Subject:** Visit of Pope John Paul II

| Date | Mintage | F | VF | XF | Unc | BU |
|---|---|---|---|---|---|---|
| 1979 | 1,000 | — | — | — | 475 | — |
| 1979 Proof | 3,000 | Value: 525 | | | | |

**500 PESOS** KM# 68 **Weight:** 31.1000 g. **Composition:** 0.9990 Gold .9989 oz. AGW **Subject:** Discovery of America - Columbus

| Date | Mintage | F | VF | XF | Unc | BU |
|---|---|---|---|---|---|---|
| 1988 Proof | 2,600 | Value: 650 | | | | |

**500 PESOS** KM# 76 **Weight:** 31.1000 g. **Composition:** 0.9990 Gold .9989 oz. AGW **Subject:** 500th Anniversary - Discovery and Evangelization of America **Obverse:** National arms **Reverse:** Portraits of Ferdinand and Isabella

| Date | Mintage | F | VF | XF | Unc | BU |
|---|---|---|---|---|---|---|
| 1989 Proof | 600 | Value: 825 | | | | |

**500 PESOS** **KM# 76a** **Weight:** 31.1000 g. **Composition:** 0.9990 Platinum .9989 oz. APW **Subject:** 500th Anniversary - Discovery and Evangelization of America **Obverse:** National arms **Reverse:** Portraits of Ferdinand and Isabella

| Date | Mintage | F | VF | XF | Unc | BU |
|---|---|---|---|---|---|---|
| 1989 Proof | — | Value: 850 | | | | |

**500 PESOS** **KM# 79** **Weight:** 16.9600 g. **Composition:** 0.9170 Gold .5 oz. AGW **Subject:** 500th Anniversary - Discovery and Evangelization of America **Obverse:** National arms **Reverse:** Santa Maria and landing crew

| Date | Mintage | F | VF | XF | Unc | BU |
|---|---|---|---|---|---|---|
| 1990 Proof | 1,500 | Value: 350 | | | | |

**500 PESOS** **KM# 79a** **Weight:** 15.5500 g. **Composition:** 0.9990 Platinum .5 oz. APW **Subject:** 500th Anniversary - Discovery and Evangelization of America **Obverse:** National arms **Reverse:** Santa Maria and landing crew

| Date | Mintage | F | VF | XF | Unc | BU |
|---|---|---|---|---|---|---|
| 1990 Proof | 50 | Value: 650 | | | | |

**500 PESOS** **KM# 85** **Weight:** 16.9600 g. **Composition:** 0.9170 Gold .5 oz. AGW **Subject:** 500th Anniversary - Discovery and Evangelization of America **Obverse:** National arms **Reverse:** American fruits

| Date | Mintage | F | VF | XF | Unc | BU |
|---|---|---|---|---|---|---|
| 1991 Proof | 1,500 | Value: 350 | | | | |

**500 PESOS** **KM# 85a** **Weight:** 15.5500 g. **Composition:** 0.9990 Platinum .5 oz. APW **Subject:** 500th Anniversary - Discovery and Evangelization of America **Obverse:** National arms **Reverse:** American fruits

| Date | Mintage | F | VF | XF | Unc | BU |
|---|---|---|---|---|---|---|
| 1991 Proof | 35 | Value: 700 | | | | |

**500 PESOS** **KM# 86** **Weight:** 16.9600 g. **Composition:** 0.9170 Gold .5 oz. AGW **Subject:** 500th Anniversary - Discovery and Evangelization of America **Obverse:** National arms **Reverse:** Enshrined tomb of Christopher Columbus

| Date | Mintage | F | VF | XF | Unc | BU |
|---|---|---|---|---|---|---|
| 1992 Proof | 2,000 | Value: 325 | | | | |

**500 PESOS** **KM# 86a** **Weight:** 15.5000 g. **Composition:** 0.9990 Platinum .5 oz. APW **Subject:** 500th Anniversary - Discovery and Evangelization of America **Obverse:** National arms **Reverse:** Enshrined tomb of Christopher Columbus

| Date | Mintage | F | VF | XF | Unc | BU |
|---|---|---|---|---|---|---|
| 1992 Proof | 35 | Value: 700 | | | | |

## PATTERNS

Including off metal strikes

| KM# | Date | Mintage | Identification | Mkt Val |
|---|---|---|---|---|
| Pn7 | 1937 | — | 50 Centavos. Copper. Obverse only. | — |
| Pn8 | 1937 | — | 50 Centavos. Silver. Reverse only. | — |
| Pn9 | 1961 | — | 5 Centavos. Copper-Bonded Steel. | — |
| Pn11 | 1961 | — | 5 Centavos. Copper-Bonded Steel. Same design both sides. | — |
| Pn12 | 1961 | — | 10 Centavos. Copper-Bonded Steel. | — |
| Pn13 | 1961 | — | 25 Centavos. Chrome Plated Steel. | — |
| Pn10 | 1961 | — | 5 Centavos. Copper-Bonded Steel. | — |
| Pn14 | 1968 | 3 | 50 Centavos. Reeded edge. | — |
| Pn15 | 1972 | 1 | 25 Centavos. Reeded edge. | — |
| Pn16 | 1975 | 1 | 10 Pesos. Silver. | — |
| Pn17 | 1975 | 11 | 10 Pesos. 0.5000 Gold. | — |
| Pn18 | 1975 | 1 | 10 Pesos. 0.2940 Gold. | — |
| Pn19 | 1975 | 1 | 10 Pesos. 0.4000 Gold. | — |
| Pn20 | 1975 | 1 | 10 Pesos. 0.8000 Gold. | — |
| Pn21 | 1975 | 1 | 100 Pesos. 0.9000 Gold. without matte details. | — |
| Pn22 | 1975 | 1 | 100 Pesos. 0.8000 Gold. alloyed with .050 Silver and .150 Copper. | — |
| Pn23 | 1975 | 5 | 100 Pesos. 0.8000 Gold. alloyed with .150 Silver. | — |
| Pn24 | 1975 | 5 | 100 Pesos. 0.8000 Gold. alloyed with .150 Silver and .050 Copper, Proof. | — |
| Pn25 | 1976 | 3 | 10 Centavos. Plain rim. | — |
| Pn26 | 1977 | 5 | 30 Pesos. Gold. Proof. | — |
| Pn27 | 1978 | 3 | Centavo. Aluminum. | — |
| Pn29 | 1978 | 3 | 25 Centavos. 6-1/2 Gramos. | — |
| Pn28 | 1978 | 3 | Centavo. Copper And Zinc. | 100 |
| Pn30 | 1979 | 3 | 25 Centavos. 6-1/2 Gramos. | — |
| Pn31 | 1982 | 80 | 10 Pesos. KM#57. | — |
| Pn32 | 1983 | 15 | 25 Centavos. Nickel Bonded Steel. | 200 |
| Pn33 | 1984 | 3 | 25 Centavos. Nickel Bonded Steel. | 200 |
| Pn34 | 1984 | 5 | Peso. Nickel Bonded Steel. | — |
| Pn35 | 1986 | 500 | Peso. Copper-Nickel. | — |

**Note:** Several issues previously listed under Patterns have now been correctly identified as commercially inspired, privately contracted Medallic Issues and have been moved to that section. The remaining patterns have been renumbered

## ESSAIS

| KM# | Date | Mintage | Identification | Mkt Val |
|---|---|---|---|---|
| E13 | 1878 | — | 2 Centavos. Nickel. | — |

## PIEFORTS

| KM# | Date | Mintage | Identification | Mkt Val |
|---|---|---|---|---|
| P1 | 1977 | 5 | 30 Pesos. Gold. Piefort. | — |
| P2 | 1982 | 262 | 10 Pesos. | 150 |
| P3 | 1982 | 42 | 200 Pesos. | 2,250 |
| P4 | 1983 | 300 | 5 Centavos. | 20.00 |
| P5 | 1983 | 300 | 10 Centavos. Nickel Bonded Steel. | 30.00 |
| P6 | 1983 | 300 | 25 Centavos. KM#61. | 35.00 |
| P7 | 1983 | 300 | 25 Centavos. Copper-Nickel. | 35.00 |
| P8 | 1983 | 300 | 1/2 Peso. KM#62. | 40.00 |
| P9 | 1983 | 300 | Peso. KM#63. | 50.00 |
| P10 | 1984 | 300 | Centavo. | 5.00 |
| P11 | 1984 | 300 | 5 Centavos. | 5.00 |
| P12 | 1984 | 300 | 10 Centavos. | 5.00 |
| P13 | 1984 | 300 | 25 Centavos. | 8.00 |
| P14 | 1984 | 300 | 1/2 Peso. | 10.00 |
| P15 | 1984 | 300 | Peso. | 12.00 |
| P16 | 1986 | 300 | Peso. Nickel Bonded Steel. | 15.00 |
| P18 | 1986 | 300 | Centavo. Copper Plated Zinc. | 5.00 |
| P19 | 1986 | 300 | 5 Centavos. Copper-Nickel. | 5.00 |
| P20 | 1986 | 300 | 10 Centavos. Copper-Nickel. | 8.00 |
| P21 | 1986 | 300 | 25 Centavos. Copper-Nickel. | 10.00 |
| P22 | 1986 | 300 | 1/2 Peso. Copper-Nickel. | 12.00 |
| P17 | 1986 | 50 | Peso. Copper Nickel. 20.0000 g. | — |
| P23 | 1987 | 300 | Centavo. 0.9250 Silver. | — |
| P24 | 1987 | 300 | 5 Centavos. 0.9250 Silver. | — |
| P25 | 1987 | 300 | 10 Centavos. 0.9250 Silver. | — |
| P26 | 1987 | 300 | 25 Centavos. 0.9250 Silver. | — |
| P27 | 1987 | 300 | 1/2 Peso. 0.9250 Silver. | — |
| P28 | 1988 | 100 | Peso. 0.9990 Silver. KM#67. | 50.00 |
| P29 | 1988 | 100 | 100 Pesos. 0.9990 Silver. KM#67. | 325 |
| P35 | 1989 | 10,000 | Peso. 0.9990 Silver. KM#74. | 40.00 |
| P36 | 1989 | 200 | 100 Pesos. 0.9990 Silver. KM#75. | 375 |
| P30 | 1989 | 300 | Centavo. 0.9250 Silver. KM#72a. | — |
| P31 | 1989 | 300 | 5 Centavos. 0.9250 Silver. KM#69a. | — |
| P32 | 1989 | 300 | 10 Centavos. 0.9250 Silver. KM#70a. | — |
| P33 | 1989 | 300 | 25 Centavos. 0.9250 Silver. KM#71a. | — |
| P34 | 1989 | 300 | 1/2 Peso. 0.9250 Silver. KM#73a. | — |
| P37 | 1990 | 10,000 | Peso. 0.9990 Silver. KM#77. | 40.00 |
| P38 | 1990 | 200 | 100 Pesos. 0.9990 Silver. KM#78. | 300 |

| KM# | Date | Mintage | Identification | Mkt Val |
|---|---|---|---|---|
| P39 | 1991 | 10,000 | Peso. 0.9990 Silver. KM#81. | 40.00 |
| P40 | 1992 | 10,000 | Peso. 0.9990 Silver. KM#82. | 40.00 |

## MINT SETS

| KM# | Date | Mintage | Identification | Issue Price | Mkt Val |
|---|---|---|---|---|---|
| MS1 | 1983 (5) | 2,000 | KM#59-63 | 10.00 | 15.00 |
| MS2 | 1984 | 2,000 | KM#59-64 | — | 15.00 |
| MS3 | 1986 (5) | 2,000 | KM#59-62, 64 | 10.00 | 14.00 |
| MS4 | 1987 (5) | 1,000 | KM#59-62, 64 | 10.00 | 14.00 |
| MS5 | 1989 (5) | 1,000 | KM#69-73 | — | 14.00 |

## PROOF SETS

| KM# | Date | Mintage | Identification | Issue Price | Mkt Val |
|---|---|---|---|---|---|
| PS1 | 1937 (5) | — | KM#17-21 | — | 2,750 |
| PS2 | 1972 (4) | 500 | KM#18, 20a.1, 31, 34 | 20.00 | 65.00 |
| PS3 | 1973 (2) | 500 | KM#19a, 21a.2 | 5.00 | 50.00 |
| PS4 | 1974 (2) | 500 | KM#18, 20a.2 | 5.00 | 35.00 |
| PS5 | 1974 (2) | 500 | KM#35-36 | 120 | 190 |
| PS6 | 1975 (2) | 500 | KM#38-39 | 200 | 165 |
| PS7 | 1976 (6) | 5,000 | KM#40-45 | 10.00 | 20.00 |
| PS9 | 1978 (6) | 15 | KM#48a-53a | 175 | 900 |
| PS8 | 1978 (6) | 5,000 | KM#48-53 | 10.00 | 20.00 |
| PS11 | 1979 (6) | 15 | KM#48a-53a | 255 | 900 |
| PS1- | 1979 (6) | 500 | KM#48-53 | 15.00 | 135 |
| PS13 | 1980 (6) | 15 | KM#48a-53a | 255 | 900 |
| PS12 | 1980 (6) | 3,000 | KM#48-53 | 15.00 | 20.00 |
| PS14 | 1981 (6) | 3,000 | KM#48-53 | 15.00 | 20.00 |
| PS15 | 1981 (6) | 15 | KM#48a-53a | 300 | 900 |
| PS17 | 1983 (2) | 300 | KM-P4, P5 | 25.00 | 50.00 |
| PS18 | 1983 (2) | 100 | KM#59a, 60a | 45.00 | 45.00 |
| PS20 | 1983 (3) | 270 | KM-P7, 8, 9 | 45.00 | 115 |
| PS21 | 1983 (3) | 70 | KM#61a-63a | 125 | 125 |
| PS16 | 1983 (2) | 1,600 | KM#59-60 | 10.00 | 10.00 |
| PS19 | 1983 (3) | 1,570 | KM#61-63 | 20.00 | 20.00 |
| PS23 | 1984 (6) | 270 | KM-P10, 11, 12, 13, 14, 15 | 30.00 | 30.00 |
| PS24 | 1984 (6) | 70 | KM#59a-64a | 250 | 250 |
| PS22 | 1984 (6) | 1,570 | KM#59-64 | 20.00 | 45.00 |
| PS26 | 1986 (5) | 270 | KM-P17, 19, 20, 21, 22 | 40.00 | 40.00 |
| PS27 | 1986 (5) | 70 | KM#59a-62a, 64a | 150 | 150 |
| PS25 | 1986 (5) | 1,570 | KM#59-62, 64 | 30.00 | 20.00 |
| PS29 | 1987 (5) | 300 | KM-P23, 24, 25, 26, 27 | — | 75.00 |
| PS28 | 1987 (5) | 1,600 | KM#59-62, 64 | — | 30.00 |
| PS30 | 1989 (5) | 2,500 | KM#69a-70a, 71.1a, 72a, 73.1a | — | — |
| PS31 | 1989 (5) | 300 | KM-P30, 31, 32, 33, 34 | — | — |

## SPECIAL SETS

| KM# | Date | Mintage | Identification | Issue Price | Mkt Val |
|---|---|---|---|---|---|
| SS1 | 1983 (15) | 30 | KM#61-63, 61a-63a, all mint marks, including Piefiorts | 200 | 200 |
| SS2 | 1984 (24) | 30 | KM#59-64, including Piefiorts | 400 | 400 |
| SS3 | 1986 (20) | 30 | KM#59-64 | 300 | 300 |
| SS4 | 1986 (2) | 1,700 | KM65 | 35.00 | 25.00 |
| SS5 | 1986 (3) | 300 | KM#65, KM-P16 | 75.00 | 75.00 |
| SS6 | 1986 (2) | 23 | KM#65a | — | — |
| SS7 | 1986 (3) | 25 | KM#65a, KM-P17 | — | — |
| SS8 | 1986 (2) | 25 | KM#65b | — | — |
| SS9 | 1986 (3) | 25 | KM#65b, KM-P17 | — | — |
| SS10 | 1987 (15) | 100 | KM#59-62, 64, KM-P23, 24, 25, 26, 27 | — | 125 |
| SS11 | 1989 (15) | 100 | KM#69-73, KM-P31, 32, 33, 34, 35 | — | — |

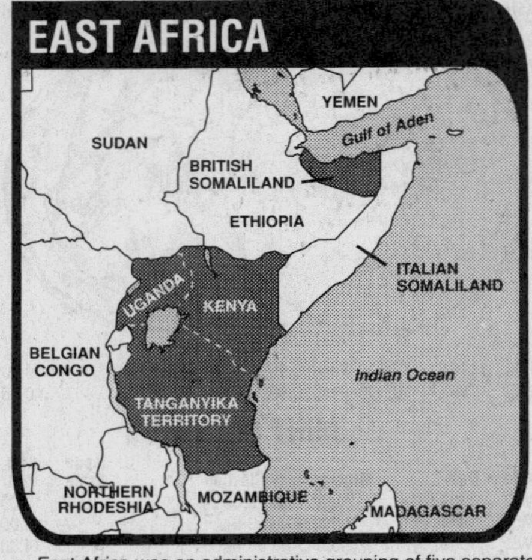


East Africa was an administrative grouping of five separate British territories: Kenya, Tanganyika (now part of Tanzania), the Sultanate of Zanzibar and Pemba (now part of Tanzania), Uganda and British Somaliland (now part of Somalia). See individual entries for specific statistics and history.

The common interest of Kenya, Tanganyika and Uganda invited cooperation in economic matters and consideration of political union. The territorial governors, organized as the East Africa High Commission, met periodically to administer such common activities as taxation, industrial development and education. The authority of the Commission did not infringe upon the constitution and internal autonomy of the individual colonies. A common coinage and banknotes, which were also legal tender in Aden, were provided for use of the member colonies by the East Africa Currency Board. The coinage through 1919 had the legend "East Africa and Uganda Protectorate". From 1920 on, the legend has read, "East Africa". The East African coinage includes two denominations of 1936 which bear the style and titles of Edward VIII.

**NOTE**: For later coinage see Kenya, Tanzania and Uganda.

**RULERS**
British

**MINT MARKS**
A - Ackroyd & Best, Morley
I - Bombay Mint
H - Heaton Mint, Birmingham, England
K, KN - King's Norton Mint, Birmingham, England
SA - Pretoria Mint, South Africa
no mint mark – British Royal Mint, London

# EAST AFRICA AND UGANDA PROTECTORATES

## 100 Cents = 1 Rupee.

## DECIMAL COINAGE

**1/2 CENT** **KM# 6** **Composition:** Aluminum **Ruler:** Edward VII

| Date | Mintage | F | VF | XF | Unc | BU |
|---|---|---|---|---|---|---|
| 1907 | 5 | 400 | 750 | 1,500 | 3,000 | — |
| 1908 | 900,000 | 15.00 | 25.00 | 50.00 | 90.00 | — |

**1/2 CENT** **KM# 6a** **Composition:** Copper-Nickel **Ruler:** Edward VII

| Date | Mintage | F | VF | XF | Unc | BU |
|---|---|---|---|---|---|---|
| 1909 | 900,000 | 6.00 | 12.00 | 25.00 | 60.00 | — |

**CENT** **KM# 5** **Composition:** Aluminum **Ruler:** Edward VII

| Date | Mintage | F | VF | XF | Unc | BU |
|---|---|---|---|---|---|---|
| 1906 | — | 500 | 750 | 1,500 | 2,000 | — |
| 1907 | 6,948,000 | 5.00 | 10.00 | 30.00 | 50.00 | — |
| 1907 Proof | — | Value: 200 | | | | |
| 1908 | 2,871,000 | 8.00 | 16.00 | 30.00 | 60.00 | — |

**CENT** **KM# 5a** **Composition:** Copper-Nickel **Ruler:** Edward VII

| Date | Mintage | F | VF | XF | Unc | BU |
|---|---|---|---|---|---|---|
| 1908 Unique | — | — | — | — | — | — |
| 1909 | 25,000,000 | 0.50 | 1.25 | 3.00 | 7.00 | — |
| 1910 | 6,000,000 | 0.50 | 1.25 | 4.00 | 12.00 | — |

**CENT** **KM# 7** **Composition:** Copper-Nickel **Ruler:** George V

| Date | Mintage | F | VF | XF | Unc | BU |
|---|---|---|---|---|---|---|
| 1911H | 25,000,000 | 0.25 | 1.00 | 2.50 | 15.00 | — |
| 1912H | 20,000,000 | 0.25 | 1.00 | 2.00 | 8.00 | — |
| 1913 | 4,529,000 | 0.75 | 1.50 | 3.75 | 20.00 | — |
| 1914 | 6,000,000 | 0.75 | 1.75 | 5.00 | 15.00 | — |
| 1914H | 2,500,000 | 1.00 | 3.00 | 7.50 | 20.00 | — |
| 1916H | 1,824,000 | 1.25 | 4.00 | 6.00 | 25.00 | — |
| 1917H | 3,176,000 | 0.75 | 2.00 | 5.00 | 15.00 | — |
| 1918H | 10,000,000 | 0.50 | 1.00 | 3.25 | 12.00 | — |

**5 CENTS** **KM# A11** **Composition:** Copper-Nickel **Ruler:** Edward VII

| Date | Mintage | F | VF | XF | Unc | BU |
|---|---|---|---|---|---|---|
| 1907 Rare | — | — | — | — | — | — |

**5 CENTS** **KM# 11** **Composition:** Copper-Nickel **Ruler:** George V

| Date | Mintage | F | VF | XF | Unc | BU |
|---|---|---|---|---|---|---|
| 1913H | 300,000 | 1.50 | 4.00 | 15.00 | 35.00 | — |
| 1914K | 1,240,000 | 0.75 | 3.25 | 6.00 | 22.50 | — |
| 1914K Proof | — | Value: 200 | | | | |
| 1919H | 200,000 | 10.00 | 15.00 | 40.00 | 120 | — |

**Note:** The 1914K was issued with British West Africa KM#8 in a double (4 pieces) Specimen Set

**10 CENTS** **KM# 2** **Composition:** Copper-Nickel **Ruler:** Edward VII

| Date | Mintage | F | VF | XF | Unc | BU |
|---|---|---|---|---|---|---|
| 1906 | — | 1,000 | 1,500 | 2,000 | 3,000 | — |
| 1907 | 1,000,000 | 1.50 | 4.00 | 10.00 | 30.00 | — |
| 1910 | 500,000 | 4.00 | 8.00 | 25.00 | 60.00 | — |

**10 CENTS** **KM# 8** **Composition:** Copper-Nickel **Ruler:** George V

| Date | Mintage | F | VF | XF | Unc | BU |
|---|---|---|---|---|---|---|
| 1911H | 1,250,000 | 2.00 | 5.00 | 10.00 | 40.00 | — |
| 1912H | 1,050,000 | 2.00 | 5.00 | 12.50 | 55.00 | — |
| 1913 | 50,000 | 75.00 | 150 | 250 | 500 | — |
| 1918H | 400,000 | 10.00 | 20.00 | 50.00 | 150 | — |

**25 CENTS** **KM# 3** **Weight:** 2.9160 g. **Composition:** 0.8000 Silver .0750 oz. ASW **Ruler:** Edward VII

| Date | Mintage | F | VF | XF | Unc | BU |
|---|---|---|---|---|---|---|
| 1906 | 400,000 | 3.00 | 7.00 | 22.00 | 60.00 | — |
| 1910H | 200,000 | 4.00 | 8.00 | 30.00 | 90.00 | — |

**25 CENTS** **KM# 10** **Weight:** 2.9160 g. **Composition:** 0.8000 Silver .0750 oz. ASW **Ruler:** George V

| Date | Mintage | F | VF | XF | Unc | BU |
|---|---|---|---|---|---|---|
| 1912 | 180,000 | 4.00 | 8.00 | 25.00 | 80.00 | — |
| 1913 | 300,000 | 3.50 | 7.50 | 22.50 | 60.00 | — |
| 1914H | 80,000 | 20.00 | 35.00 | 60.00 | 100 | — |
| 1914H Proof | — | Value: 400 | | | | |
| 1918H | 40,000 | 150 | 300 | 500 | 900 | — |

**50 CENTS** **KM# 4** **Weight:** 5.8319 g. **Composition:** 0.8000 Silver .1500 oz. ASW **Ruler:** Edward VII

| Date | Mintage | F | VF | XF | Unc | BU |
|---|---|---|---|---|---|---|
| 1906 | 200,000 | 4.50 | 12.50 | 30.00 | 140 | — |
| 1906 Proof | — | Value: 400 | | | | |
| 1909 | 100,000 | 15.00 | 30.00 | 85.00 | 300 | — |
| 1910 | 100,000 | 10.00 | 22.00 | 60.00 | 225 | — |

**50 CENTS** **KM# 9** **Weight:** 5.8319 g. **Composition:** 0.8000 Silver .1500 oz. ASW **Ruler:** George V

| Date | Mintage | F | VF | XF | Unc | BU |
|---|---|---|---|---|---|---|
| 1911 | 150,000 | 7.50 | 15.00 | 35.00 | 140 | — |
| 1911 Proof | — | Value: 250 | | | | |
| 1912 | 100,000 | 8.00 | 20.00 | 60.00 | 200 | — |
| 1913 | 200,000 | 5.00 | 12.50 | 30.00 | 135 | — |
| 1914H | 180,000 | 5.00 | 12.50 | 30.00 | 135 | — |
| 1918H | 60,000 | 60.00 | 150 | 250 | 500 | — |
| 1919 | 100,000 | 250 | 350 | 600 | 1,500 | — |

# BRITISH COLONY

## DECIMAL COINAGE

**CENT** **KM# 12** **Composition:** Copper-Nickel **Ruler:** Edward VII

| Date | Mintage | F | VF | XF | Unc | BU |
|---|---|---|---|---|---|---|
| 1920H | Est. 2,908,000 | 30.00 | 60.00 | 100 | 225 | — |
| 1920H Proof | 20-30 pcs | Value: 300 | | | | |

**Note:** Only about 30% of the total mintage was released into circulation

| Date | Mintage | F | VF | XF | Unc | BU |
|---|---|---|---|---|---|---|
| 1920 | — | — | — | — | 750 | — |
| 1921 | — | — | — | — | 3,000 | — |

**Note:** Not released for circulation

**5 CENTS** **KM# 13** **Composition:** Copper-Nickel **Ruler:** Edward VII

| Date | Mintage | F | VF | XF | Unc | BU |
|---|---|---|---|---|---|---|
| 1920H Proof | Est. 550,000 | 75.00 | 150 | 200 | 400 | — |

**Note:** Only about 30% of the total mintage was released into circulation

| Date | Mintage | F | VF | XF | Unc | BU |
|---|---|---|---|---|---|---|
| 1920H Proof | 20-30 pcs | Value: 450 | | | | |

**10 CENTS** **KM# 14** **Composition:** Copper-Nickel **Ruler:** Edward VII

| Date | Mintage | F | VF | XF | Unc | BU |
|---|---|---|---|---|---|---|
| 1920H | Est. 700,000 | 120 | 150 | 225 | 375 | — |
| 1920HProof | 20-30pcs | Value: 600 | | | | |

**25 CENTS** **KM# 15** **Weight:** 2.9160 g. **Composition:** 0.5000 Silver .0469 oz. ASW **Ruler:** Edward VII

| Date | Mintage | F | VF | XF | Unc | BU |
|---|---|---|---|---|---|---|
| 1920H | 748,000 | 25.00 | 35.00 | 75.00 | 150 | — |
| 1920H 20-30 pieces; Proof | — | Value: 250 | | | | |

**50 CENTS** **KM# 16** **Weight:** 5.8319 g. **Composition:** 0.5000 Silver .0937 oz. ASW **Ruler:** Edward VII **Note:** Not released for circulation.

| Date | Mintage | F | VF | XF | Unc | BU |
|---|---|---|---|---|---|---|
| 1920A | 12,000 | 1,500 | 2,000 | 3,000 | 4,000 | — |
| 1920H | 62,000 | 500 | 1,000 | 1,500 | 2,000 | — |
| 1920H 20-30 pieces; Proof | — | Value: 600 | | | | |

**FLORIN** **KM# 17** **Weight:** 11.6638 g. **Composition:** 0.5000 Silver .1875 oz. ASW **Ruler:** Edward VII

| Date | Mintage | F | VF | XF | Unc | BU |
|---|---|---|---|---|---|---|
| 1920 | 1,479,000 | 15.00 | 35.00 | 100 | 325 | — |
| 1920A | 542,000 | 200 | 300 | 600 | 2,000 | — |
| 1920H | 9,689,000 | 12.50 | 25.00 | 75.00 | 275 | — |
| 1920H 20-30 pieces; Proof | — | Value: 800 | | | | |
| 1921 | 2 | — | — | — | 4,500 | — |

## REFORM COINAGE

Commencing May 1921

100 Cents = 1 Shilling

**CENT** **KM# 22** **Composition:** Bronze **Ruler:** Edward VII

| Date | Mintage | F | VF | XF | Unc | BU |
|---|---|---|---|---|---|---|
| 1922 | 8,250,000 | 0.25 | 1.00 | 3.00 | 15.00 | — |
| 1922H | 43,750,000 | 0.25 | 0.50 | 1.50 | 6.50 | — |
| 1923 | 50,000,000 | 0.25 | 0.50 | 1.50 | 6.50 | — |
| 1924 | Inc. above | 0.25 | 0.75 | 3.25 | 10.00 | — |
| 1924H | 17,500,000 | 0.25 | 0.75 | 3.25 | 8.00 | — |
| 1924KN | 10,720,000 | 0.25 | 0.75 | 3.25 | 8.00 | — |
| 1924KN Proof | — | Value: 125 | | | | |
| 1925 | 6,000,000 | 50.00 | 100 | 175 | 350 | — |
| 1925KN | 6,780,000 | 2.00 | 4.00 | 15.00 | 35.00 | — |
| 1927 | 10,000,000 | 0.25 | 0.75 | 3.00 | 10.00 | — |
| 1927 Proof | — | Value: 125 | | | | |
| 1928H | 12,000,000 | 0.25 | 0.75 | 3.25 | 8.00 | — |
| 1928KN | 11,764,000 | 0.50 | 2.00 | 5.00 | 12.00 | — |
| 1928KN Proof | — | Value: 125 | | | | |
| 1930 | 15,000,000 | 0.25 | 0.75 | 2.00 | 5.00 | — |
| 1930 Proof | — | Value: 125 | | | | |
| 1935 | 10,000,000 | 0.25 | 0.50 | 1.25 | 3.50 | — |

**CENT** **KM# 29** **Composition:** Bronze **Ruler:** Edward VII

| Date | Mintage | F | VF | XF | Unc | BU |
|---|---|---|---|---|---|---|
| 1942 | 25,000,000 | 0.10 | 0.25 | 0.85 | 2.50 | — |
| 1942I | 15,000,000 | 0.15 | 0.30 | 1.00 | 3.00 | — |

**CENT** **KM# 32** **Composition:** Bronze **Ruler:** Edward VII **Obv. Legend:** ET IND. IMP. dropped

| Date | Mintage | F | VF | XF | Unc | BU |
|---|---|---|---|---|---|---|
| 1949 | 4,000,000 | 0.35 | 0.75 | 2.00 | 4.00 | — |
| 1949 Proof | — | Value: 125 | | | | |
| 1950 | 16,000,000 | 0.10 | 0.25 | 0.85 | 2.50 | — |
| 1950 Proof | — | Value: 150 | | | | |
| 1951H | 9,000,000 | 0.10 | 0.25 | 0.85 | 2.50 | — |
| 1951H Proof | — | Value: 125 | | | | |
| 1951KN | 11,140,000 | 0.10 | 0.25 | 0.85 | 2.50 | — |
| 1951KN Proof | — | Value: 125 | | | | |
| 1952 | 7,000,000 | 0.10 | 0.25 | 0.85 | 2.50 | — |
| 1952 Proof | — | Value: 150 | | | | |
| 1952H | 13,000,000 | 0.10 | 0.25 | 0.85 | 2.50 | — |
| 1952H Proof | — | Value: 125 | | | | |
| 1952KN | 5,230,000 | 0.10 | 0.35 | 1.25 | 5.00 | — |

**CENT** **KM# 35** **Composition:** Bronze **Ruler:** Edward VII

| Date | Mintage | F | VF | XF | Unc | BU |
|---|---|---|---|---|---|---|
| 1954 | 8,000,000 | 0.10 | 0.25 | 0.85 | 2.50 | — |
| 1954 Proof | — | Value: 150 | | | | |
| 1955 | 5,000,000 | 0.10 | 0.25 | 0.50 | 1.75 | — |
| 1955H | 6,384,000 | 0.10 | 0.20 | 0.65 | 1.75 | — |
| 1955KN | 4,000,000 | 0.10 | 0.20 | 0.65 | 1.75 | — |
| 1956H | 15,616,000 | 0.10 | 0.15 | 0.30 | 1.25 | — |
| 1956KN | 9,680,000 | 0.10 | 0.20 | 0.40 | 1.25 | — |
| 1957 | 15,000,000 | 0.10 | 0.20 | 0.65 | 1.75 | — |
| 1957H | 5,000,000 | 1.50 | 3.00 | 6.00 | 15.00 | — |
| 1957KN | Inc. above | 0.10 | 0.20 | 0.65 | 1.75 | — |
| 1959H | 10,000,000 | 0.10 | 0.20 | 0.40 | 1.25 | — |
| 1959KN | 10,000,000 | 0.10 | 0.20 | 0.40 | 1.25 | — |
| 1961 | 1,800,000 | 0.15 | 0.40 | 2.00 | 3.50 | — |
| 1961 Proof | — | Value: 100 | | | | |
| 1961H | 1,800,000 | 0.15 | 0.40 | 2.00 | 3.50 | — |
| 1962H | 10,320,000 | 0.10 | 0.20 | 0.40 | 1.25 | — |

**5 CENTS** **KM# 18** **Composition:** Bronze **Ruler:** Edward VII

| Date | Mintage | F | VF | XF | Unc | BU |
|---|---|---|---|---|---|---|
| 1921 | 1,000,000 | 2.00 | 4.00 | 10.00 | 32.00 | — |
| 1922 | 2,500,000 | 0.50 | 1.25 | 4.50 | 12.50 | — |
| 1923 | 2,400,000 | 0.50 | 1.25 | 4.50 | 12.50 | — |
| 1923 Proof | — | Value: 150 | | | | |
| 1924 | 4,800,000 | 0.50 | 1.00 | 3.00 | 15.00 | — |
| 1925 | 6,600,000 | 0.50 | 1.00 | 3.00 | 10.00 | — |
| 1925 Proof | — | Value: 125 | | | | |
| 1928 | 1,200,000 | 1.50 | 3.00 | 5.00 | 25.00 | — |
| 1928 Proof | — | Value: 150 | | | | |
| 1933 | 5,000,000 | 0.50 | 1.00 | 2.50 | 10.00 | — |
| 1934 | 3,910,000 | 0.50 | 1.00 | 3.50 | 15.00 | — |
| 1934 Proof | — | Value: 150 | | | | |
| 1935 | 5,800,000 | 0.50 | 1.00 | 3.00 | 10.00 | — |
| 1935 Proof | — | Value: 150 | | | | |
| 1936 | 1,000,000 | 2.00 | 6.00 | 10.00 | 50.00 | — |

**5 CENTS** **KM# 23** **Composition:** Bronze **Ruler:** Edward VII

| Date | Mintage | F | VF | XF | Unc | BU |
|---|---|---|---|---|---|---|
| 1936H | 3,500,000 | 0.25 | 0.50 | 1.00 | 5.50 | — |
| 1936H Proof | — | Value: 150 | | | | |
| 1936KN | 2,150,000 | 0.25 | 0.50 | 1.00 | 5.50 | — |
| 1936KN Proof | — | Value: 150 | | | | |

**5 CENTS** **KM# 25.1** **Composition:** Bronze **Ruler:** Edward VII **Note:** Thick flan.

| Date | Mintage | F | VF | XF | Unc | BU |
|---|---|---|---|---|---|---|
| 1937H | 3,000,000 | 0.50 | 1.00 | 2.00 | 4.00 | — |
| 1937KN | 3,000,000 | 0.50 | 1.00 | 2.00 | 6.00 | — |
| 1939H | 2,000,000 | 0.50 | 1.00 | 3.00 | 13.50 | — |
| 1939KN | 2,000,000 | 0.50 | 1.00 | 3.00 | 13.50 | — |
| 1941 | — | 3.00 | 7.50 | 15.00 | 40.00 | — |
| 1941I | 20,000,000 | 0.50 | 1.00 | 2.00 | 5.00 | — |

**5 CENTS** **KM# 25.2** **Composition:** Bronze **Ruler:** Edward VII **Note:** Thin flan, reduced weight.

| Date | Mintage | F | VF | XF | Unc | BU |
|---|---|---|---|---|---|---|
| 1941I | Inc. above | 0.50 | 1.00 | 2.00 | 5.00 | — |
| 1942 | 16,000,000 | 0.50 | 1.00 | 2.00 | 4.00 | — |
| 1942SA | 4,120,000 | 1.00 | 2.00 | 10.00 | 30.00 | — |
| 1943SA | 17,880,000 | 0.50 | 1.00 | 5.00 | 10.00 | — |

**5 CENTS** **KM# 25.3** **Composition:** Bronze **Ruler:** Edward VII **Note:** Similar to KM#25.2, but hole not punched.

| Date | Mintage | F | VF | XF | Unc | BU |
|---|---|---|---|---|---|---|
| 1942 | — | — | — | — | 100 | — |

**5 CENTS** **KM# 33** **Composition:** Bronze **Ruler:** Edward VII **Obv. Legend:** ET IND. IMP. dropped

| Date | Mintage | F | VF | XF | Unc | BU |
|---|---|---|---|---|---|---|
| 1949 | 4,000,000 | 0.25 | 0.50 | 3.00 | 6.00 | — |
| 1949 Proof | — | Value: 175 | | | | |
| 1951H | 6,000,000 | 0.25 | 0.50 | 2.00 | 5.00 | — |
| 1951H Proof | — | Value: 175 | | | | |
| 1952 | 11,200,000 | 0.20 | 0.40 | 1.00 | 3.00 | — |
| 1952 Proof | — | Value: 200 | | | | |

**5 CENTS** **KM# 37** **Composition:** Bronze **Ruler:** Edward VII

| Date | Mintage | F | VF | XF | Unc | BU |
|---|---|---|---|---|---|---|
| 1955 | 2,000,000 | 0.10 | 0.25 | 0.75 | 2.00 | — |
| 1955 Proof | — | Value: 150 | | | | |
| 1955H | 4,000,000 | 0.20 | 0.50 | 1.25 | 3.50 | — |
| 1955H Proof | — | Value: 150 | | | | |
| 1955KN | 2,000,000 | 0.35 | 0.80 | 2.50 | 5.00 | — |
| 1956H | 3,000,000 | 0.15 | 0.35 | 1.00 | 3.00 | — |
| 1956KN | 3,000,000 | 3.00 | 5.00 | 8.00 | 10.00 | — |
| 1956KN Proof | — | Value: 125 | | | | |
| 1957H | 5,000,000 | 0.10 | 0.25 | 0.75 | 2.00 | — |
| 1957KN | 5,000,000 | 0.10 | 0.25 | 0.75 | 2.00 | — |
| 1961H | 4,000,000 | 0.15 | 0.35 | 1.00 | 3.00 | — |
| 1963 | 12,600,000 | — | 0.10 | 0.30 | 0.75 | — |
| 1963 Proof | — | Value: 150 | | | | |

**5 CENTS** **KM# 39** **Composition:** Bronze **Ruler:** Edward VII **Note:** Post-Independence Issue

| Date | Mintage | F | VF | XF | Unc | BU |
|---|---|---|---|---|---|---|
| 1964 | 7,600,000 | — | 0.10 | 0.20 | 0.50 | — |

**10 CENTS** **KM# 19** **Composition:** Bronze **Ruler:** Edward VII

| Date | Mintage | F | VF | XF | Unc | BU |
|---|---|---|---|---|---|---|
| 1921 | 130,000 | 5.00 | 10.00 | 25.00 | 80.00 | — |
| 1922 | 7,120,000 | 1.00 | 3.00 | 8.00 | 20.00 | — |
| 1923 | 1,200,000 | 1.25 | 4.00 | 12.50 | 40.00 | — |
| 1924 | 4,900,000 | 0.65 | 2.25 | 6.00 | 25.00 | — |
| 1925 | 4,800,000 | 0.65 | 2.25 | 6.00 | 25.00 | — |
| 1927 | 2,000,000 | 0.75 | 2.50 | 6.50 | 20.00 | — |
| 1928 | 3,800,000 | 0.75 | 2.50 | 6.50 | 30.00 | — |
| 1928 Proof | — | Value: 175 | | | | |
| 1933 | 6,260,000 | 0.75 | 2.50 | 6.50 | 17.50 | — |
| 1934 | 3,649,000 | 0.75 | 2.50 | 6.50 | 30.00 | — |
| 1935 | 7,300,000 | 0.65 | 2.00 | 5.00 | 18.00 | — |
| 1936 | 500,000 | 1.50 | 5.00 | 15.00 | 50.00 | — |

**10 CENTS** **KM# 24a** **Composition:** Copper-Nickel **Ruler:** Edward VII

| Date | Mintage | F | VF | XF | Unc | BU |
|---|---|---|---|---|---|---|
| 1936KN | — | — | — | — | — | — |

**10 CENTS** **KM# 24** **Composition:** Bronze **Ruler:** Edward VII **Note:** For listing of mule dated 1936H with obverse of KM#24 and reverse of British West Africa KM#16 refer to British West Africa listings.

| Date | Mintage | F | VF | XF | Unc | BU |
|---|---|---|---|---|---|---|
| 1936 | 2,000,000 | 1.00 | 3.50 | 8.00 | 25.00 | — |
| 1936 Proof | — | Value: 200 | | | | |
| 1936H | 4,330,000 | 0.25 | 0.50 | 1.50 | 6.50 | — |
| 1936H Proof | — | Value: 325 | | | | |
| 1936KN | 4,142,000 | 0.25 | 0.50 | 1.50 | 6.50 | — |
| 1936KN Proof | — | Value: 145 | | | | |

**10 CENTS** **KM# 26.1** **Composition:** Bronze **Ruler:** Edward VII **Note:** Thick flan.

| Date | Mintage | F | VF | XF | Unc | BU |
|---|---|---|---|---|---|---|
| 1937 | 2,000,000 | 0.25 | 0.75 | 2.50 | 6.00 | — |
| 1937 Proof | — | Value: 175 | | | | |
| 1937H | 2,500,000 | 0.25 | 0.75 | 2.50 | 8.00 | — |
| 1937H Proof | — | Value: 175 | | | | |
| 1937KN | 2,500,000 | 0.25 | 0.75 | 2.50 | 8.00 | — |
| 1937KN Proof | — | Value: 175 | | | | |
| 1939H | 2,000,000 | 0.25 | 0.70 | 3.50 | 15.00 | — |
| 1939KN | 2,029,999 | 0.25 | 0.70 | 3.50 | 12.50 | — |
| 1939KN Proof | — | Value: 175 | | | | |
| 1941I | 15,682,000 | 0.35 | 1.00 | 4.00 | 15.00 | — |
| 1941I Proof | — | Value: 175 | | | | |
| 1941 | — | 0.50 | 1.50 | 4.50 | 16.00 | — |
| 1941 Proof | — | Value: 175 | | | | |

**10 CENTS** **KM# 26.2** **Composition:** Bronze **Ruler:** Edward VII **Note:** Thin flan, reduced weight.

| Date | Mintage | F | VF | XF | Unc | BU |
|---|---|---|---|---|---|---|
| 1942 | 12,000,000 | 0.20 | 0.50 | 1.75 | 4.00 | — |
| 1942 Proof | — | Value: 175 | | | | |
| 1942I | 4,317,000 | 3.00 | 5.00 | 10.00 | 20.00 | — |
| 1943SA | 14,093,000 | 0.25 | 0.50 | 4.50 | 10.00 | — |
| 1945SA | 5,000,000 | 0.25 | 0.50 | 3.00 | 12.50 | — |

**10 CENTS** **KM# 34** **Composition:** Bronze **Ruler:** Edward VII **Obv. Legend:** ET IND. IMP. dropped

| Date | Mintage | F | VF | XF | Unc | BU |
|---|---|---|---|---|---|---|
| 1949 | 4,000,000 | 0.25 | 0.50 | 2.00 | 5.00 | — |
| 1949 Proof | — | Value: 175 | | | | |
| 1950 | 8,000,000 | 0.20 | 0.40 | 1.75 | 4.00 | — |
| 1950 Proof | — | Value: 200 | | | | |
| 1951 | 14,500,000 | 0.20 | 0.40 | 1.25 | 3.00 | — |
| 1951 Proof | — | Value: 175 | | | | |
| 1952 | 15,800,000 | 0.20 | 0.40 | 1.25 | 3.00 | — |
| 1952 Proof | — | Value: 250 | | | | |
| 1952H | 2,000,000 | 3.00 | 5.00 | 10.00 | 20.00 | — |

**10 CENTS** **KM# 38** **Composition:** Bronze **Ruler:** Edward VII

| Date | Mintage | F | VF | XF | Unc | BU |
|---|---|---|---|---|---|---|
| 1956 | 6,001,000 | 0.35 | 1.00 | 2.50 | 10.00 | — |
| 1956 Proof | — | Value: 175 | | | | |
| 1964H | — | — | — | — | 1,250 | — |

**10 CENTS** **KM# 40** **Composition:** Bronze **Ruler:** Edward VII **Note:** Post-Independence Issue.

| Date | Mintage | F | VF | XF | Unc | BU |
|---|---|---|---|---|---|---|
| 1964H | 10,002,000 | 0.10 | 0.15 | 0.30 | 1.00 | — |

**50 CENTS** **KM# 20** **Weight:** 3.8879 g. **Composition:** 0.2500 Silver .0312 oz. ASW **Ruler:** Edward VII **Reverse:** Fifty Cents - Half Shilling

| Date | Mintage | F | VF | XF | Unc | BU |
|---|---|---|---|---|---|---|
| 1921 | 6,200,000 | 1.00 | 2.00 | 7.50 | 30.00 | — |
| 1922 | Inc. above | 1.00 | 2.00 | 6.00 | 27.50 | — |
| 1923 | 396,000 | 5.00 | 8.00 | 40.00 | 80.00 | — |
| 1924 | 1,000,000 | 2.00 | 4.00 | 10.00 | 40.00 | — |

**50 CENTS** **KM# 27** **Weight:** 3.8879 g. **Composition:** 0.2500 Silver .0312 oz. ASW **Ruler:** Edward VII

| Date | Mintage | F | VF | XF | Unc | BU |
|---|---|---|---|---|---|---|
| 1937H | 4,000,000 | 0.75 | 1.25 | 3.50 | 12.50 | — |
| 1937H Proof | — | Value: 275 | | | | |
| 1942H | 5,000,000 | 0.75 | 1.25 | 4.00 | 20.00 | — |
| 1943I | 2,000,000 | 1.50 | 3.00 | 7.50 | 30.00 | — |
| 1944SA | 1,000,000 | 2.00 | 4.00 | 9.00 | 32.50 | — |

**50 CENTS** **KM# 30** **Composition:** Copper-Nickel **Ruler:** Edward VII **Obv. Legend:** ET INDIA IMPERATOR dropped

| Date | Mintage | F | VF | XF | Unc | BU |
|---|---|---|---|---|---|---|
| 1948 | 7,290,000 | 0.20 | 0.40 | 1.75 | 6.00 | — |
| 1948 Proof | — | Value: 250 | | | | |
| 1949 | 12,960,000 | 0.15 | 0.30 | 1.25 | 4.00 | — |
| 1949 Proof | — | Value: 325 | | | | |
| 1952KN | 2,000,000 | 0.20 | 0.40 | 1.75 | 7.50 | — |

**50 CENTS** **KM# 36** **Composition:** Copper-Nickel **Ruler:** Edward VII **Note:** The KHN mint marks above exist because the master dies were produced with both the KN and H mint marks for use at either mint. Each mint was required to remove the others mint mark before striking, but this was not always meticulously done. When one or the other mint mark was not fully removed a weak trace would remain creating the appearance of a wide space K N with a weak H in the middle or an H flanked by a weak K and N, in the field below the lion.

| Date | Mintage | F | VF | XF | Unc | BU |
|---|---|---|---|---|---|---|
| 1954 | 3,700,000 | 0.15 | 0.35 | 1.00 | 3.00 | — |
| 1954 Proof | — | Value: 225 | | | | |
| 1955H | 1,600,000 | 1.00 | 3.00 | 6.00 | 15.00 | — |
| 1955H Proof | — | Value: 225 | | | | |
| 1955KHN | — | 10.00 | 20.00 | 35.00 | 65.00 | — |
| 1955KN | — | 0.15 | 0.35 | 1.75 | 4.50 | — |
| 1956H | 2,000,000 | 0.15 | 0.25 | 1.25 | 3.00 | — |
| 1956H Proof | — | Value: 225 | | | | |
| 1956KHN | — | 10.00 | 20.00 | 35.00 | 65.00 | — |
| 1956KN | 2,000,000 | 0.15 | 0.35 | 1.75 | 4.00 | — |
| 1958H | 2,600,000 | 0.15 | 0.40 | 2.00 | 5.00 | — |
| 1960 | 4,000,000 | 0.10 | 0.25 | 1.25 | 3.25 | — |
| 1962KN | 4,000,000 | 0.15 | 0.35 | 1.75 | 4.50 | — |
| 1963 | 6,000,000 | 0.10 | 0.25 | 1.25 | 3.00 | — |

**SHILLING** **KM# 21** **Weight:** 7.7759 g. **Composition:** 0.2500 Silver .0625 oz. ASW **Ruler:** Edward VII

| Date | Mintage | F | VF | XF | Unc | BU |
|---|---|---|---|---|---|---|
| 1921 | 6,141,000 | 1.50 | 2.75 | 10.00 | 30.00 | — |
| 1921H | 4,240,000 | 1.75 | 3.00 | 15.00 | 40.00 | — |
| 1922 | 18,858,000 | 1.25 | 2.25 | 9.00 | 28.00 | — |
| 1922H | 20,052,000 | 1.25 | 2.25 | 9.00 | 28.00 | — |
| 1923 | 4,000,000 | 5.00 | 10.00 | 25.00 | 45.00 | — |
| 1924 | 44,604,000 | 1.00 | 2.00 | 7.00 | 18.00 | — |
| 1925 | 28,405,000 | 1.00 | 2.00 | 7.00 | 20.00 | — |
| 1925 Proof | — | Value: 250 | | | | |

**SHILLING** **KM# 28.1** **Weight:** 7.7759 g. **Composition:** 0.2500 Silver .0625 oz. ASW **Ruler:** Edward VII **Obverse:** Bust of King George VI **Reverse:** Type I, thin rim and short milling, EAST AFRICA further from edge than Type II, larger loop on right side of coin below diamond in legend. Edge reeding spaced out

| Date | Mintage | F | VF | XF | Unc | BU |
|---|---|---|---|---|---|---|
| 1937H | 7,672,000 | 1.00 | 2.00 | 6.00 | 20.00 | — |
| 1937H Proof | — | Value: 300 | | | | |
| 1941I | 7,000,000 | 1.25 | 2.00 | 8.00 | 28.00 | — |
| 1942H | 4,430,000 | 1.25 | 2.00 | 8.00 | 28.00 | — |
| 1942H Proof | — | Value: 300 | | | | |
| 1944H | 10,000,000 | 1.25 | 2.00 | 10.00 | 32.00 | — |

**SHILLING** **KM# 28.2** **Weight:** 7.7759 g. **Composition:** 0.2500 Silver .0625 oz. ASW **Ruler:** Edward VII **Reverse:** Type II, thicker rim and larger milling, EAST AFRICA and leaves very near the edge, small leaf (loop) under diamond on right side

| Date | Mintage | F | VF | XF | Unc | BU |
|---|---|---|---|---|---|---|
| 1941I Rare | — | — | — | — | — | — |

**SHILLING** **KM# 28.3** **Weight:** 7.7759 g. **Composition:** 0.2500 Silver .0625 oz. ASW **Ruler:** Edward VII **Reverse:** Type III, retouched central image, especially tuft of grass in front of lion

| Date | Mintage | F | VF | XF | Unc | BU |
|---|---|---|---|---|---|---|
| 1942I | 3,900,000 | 1.00 | 2.00 | 7.00 | 25.00 | — |
| 1943I 25-50 pieces | — | 500 | 750 | 1,000 | 1,500 | — |

**SHILLING** **KM# 28.4** **Weight:** 7.7759 g. **Composition:** 0.2500 Silver .0625 oz. ASW **Ruler:** Edward VII **Note:** Obverse and reverse as KM#28.1, edge reeding close. For more in-depth comparison of these reverse variety types, see The Guidebook and Catalogue of British Commonwealth Coins, 1649-1971, 3rd Edition, Remick, J. Winnipeg, Regency Coin and Stamp, 1971.

| Date | Mintage | F | VF | XF | Unc | BU |
|---|---|---|---|---|---|---|
| 1944SA | 5,820,000 | 1.25 | 2.00 | 7.00 | 30.00 | — |
| 1945SA | 10,080,000 | 1.25 | 2.00 | 7.00 | 27.50 | — |
| 1946SA | 18,260,000 | 1.25 | 2.00 | 5.00 | 20.00 | — |

**SHILLING** **KM# 31** **Composition:** Copper-Nickel **Ruler:** Edward VII **Obv. Legend:** ET INDIA IMPERATOR dropped

| Date | Mintage | F | VF | XF | Unc | BU |
|---|---|---|---|---|---|---|
| 1948 | 19,704,000 | 0.50 | 0.90 | 1.50 | 6.50 | — |
| 1949 | 38,318,000 | 0.50 | 0.90 | 1.50 | 6.50 | — |
| 1949 Proof | — | Value: 250 | | | | |
| 1949H | 12,584,000 | 0.50 | 0.90 | 1.50 | 7.50 | — |
| 1949KN | 15,060,000 | 0.50 | 0.90 | 1.50 | 7.50 | — |
| 1950 | 56,362,000 | 0.35 | 0.60 | 1.00 | 3.00 | — |
| 1950 Proof | — | Value: 250 | | | | |
| 1950H | 12,416,000 | 0.50 | 0.90 | 2.25 | 6.00 | — |
| 1950KN | 10,040,000 | 0.40 | 0.70 | 2.00 | 5.00 | — |
| 1952 | 55,605,000 | 0.35 | 0.60 | 1.00 | 3.00 | — |
| 1952 Proof | — | Value: 175 | | | | |
| 1952H | 8,023,999 | 0.35 | 0.60 | 1.25 | 3.50 | — |
| 1952KN | 9,360,000 | 0.35 | 0.60 | 1.25 | 3.50 | — |

## PATTERNS

Including off metal strikes

| KM# | Date | Mintage | Identification | Mkt Val |
|---|---|---|---|---|
| Pn6 | 1906 | — | Cent. Aluminum. KM#5. | 1,500 |
| Pn7 | 1907 | — | 1/2 Cent. Aluminum. KM#6. | 2,000 |
| Pn8 | 1907 | — | 5 Cents. Copper-Nickel. KM#11. | 2,500 |
| Pn9 | 1908 | — | Cent. Copper-Nickel. KM#5. | — |
| Pn10 | 1920 | — | 50 Cents. Aluminum. KM#16. | 3,000 |
| Pn11 | 1920 | — | Florin. Aluminum. KM#17. | 2,000 |

## MINT SETS

| KM# | Date | Mintage | Identification | Issue Price | Mkt Val |
|---|---|---|---|---|---|
| MS1 | 1921-1922 (5) | — | KM#18-22. The 5 cent coin is dated 1921, all others are 1922. | — | 2,000 |

## PROOF SETS

| KM# | Date | Mintage | Identification | Issue Price | Mkt Val |
|---|---|---|---|---|---|
| PS1 | 1906-1907 (4) | — | KM#2-5, Pn7-8; Rare | — | — |
| PSA1 | 1920H (6) | — | KM#12-17; 20-30 pieces | — | 3,000 |
| PS2 | 1949 (5) | — | KM#30-34 | — | 1,000 |
| PS3 | 1950 (3) | — | KM#31, 32, 34 | — | 600 |
| PS4 | 1952 (3) | — | KM#32, 33, 34 | — | 600 |

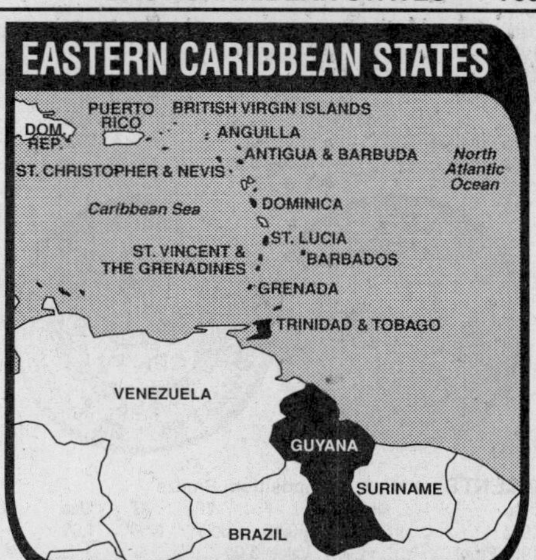


The East Caribbean States, formerly the British Caribbean Territories (Eastern group), formed a currency board in 1950 to provide the constituent territories of Trinidad & Tobago, Barbados, British Guiana (now Guyana), British Virgin Islands, Anguilla, St. Kitts, Nevis, Antigua, Dominica, St. Lucia, St. Vincent and Grenada with a common currency, thereby permitting withdrawal of the regular British Pound currency. This was dissolved in 1965 and after the breakup, the East Caribbean Territories, a grouping including Barbados, the Leeward and Windward Islands, came into being. Coinage of the dissolved 'Eastern Group' continues to circulate. Paper currency of the East Caribbean Authority was first issued in 1965 and although Barbados withdrew from the group they continued using them prior to 1973 when Barbados issued a decimal coinage.

A series of 4-dollar coins tied to the FAO coinage program were released in 1970 under the name of the Caribbean Development Bank by eight loosely federated island groupings in the eastern Caribbean. These issues are listed individually in this volume under Antigua, Barbados, Dominica, Grenada, Montserrat, St. Kitts, St. Lucia and St. Vincent.

**RULERS**
British

# BRITISH EAST CARIBBEAN TERRITORIES

## STANDARD COINAGE

100 Cents = 1 British West Indies Dollar

**1/2 CENT** **KM# 1** **Composition:** Bronze

| Date | Mintage | F | VF | XF | Unc | BU |
|---|---|---|---|---|---|---|
| 1955 | 500,000 | 0.30 | 0.50 | 1.00 | 2.50 | — |
| 1955 Proof | 2,000 | Value: 3.00 | | | | |
| 1958 | 200 | 0.50 | 0.75 | 1.50 | 3.00 | — |
| 1958 Proof | 20 | Value: 145 | | | | |

**CENT** **KM# 2** **Composition:** Bronze

| Date | Mintage | F | VF | XF | Unc | BU |
|---|---|---|---|---|---|---|
| 1955 | 8,000,000 | 0.15 | 0.25 | 0.60 | 1.00 | — |
| 1955 Proof | 2,000 | Value: 3.00 | | | | |
| 1957 | 3,000,000 | 0.15 | 0.25 | 1.75 | 3.00 | — |
| 1957 Proof | — | Value: 100 | | | | |
| 1958 | 1,500,000 | 0.35 | 0.50 | 4.50 | 7.50 | — |
| 1958 Proof | 20 | Value: 165 | | | | |
| 1959 | 500,000 | 0.40 | 0.60 | 6.00 | 20.00 | — |
| 1959 Proof | — | Value: 100 | | | | |
| 1960 | 2,500,000 | 0.15 | 0.25 | 0.60 | 1.25 | — |
| 1960 Proof | — | Value: 100 | | | | |
| 1961 | 2,280,000 | 0.25 | 0.35 | 0.75 | 1.25 | — |
| 1961 Proof | — | Value: 100 | | | | |
| 1962 | 2,000,000 | 0.15 | 0.25 | 0.50 | 1.25 | — |
| 1962 Proof | — | Value: 100 | | | | |
| 1963 | 750,000 | 0.45 | 0.70 | 1.20 | 2.50 | — |

| Date | Mintage | F | VF | XF | Unc | BU |
|---|---|---|---|---|---|---|
| 1963 Proof | — | Value: 100 | | | | |
| 1964 | 2,500,000 | — | — | 0.20 | 0.35 | — |
| 1964 Proof | — | Value: 100 | | | | |
| 1965 | 4,800,000 | — | — | 0.20 | 0.35 | — |
| 1965 Prooflike | — | — | — | — | 0.75 | — |
| 1965 Proof | — | Value: 5.00 | | | | |

**2 CENTS** **KM# 3** **Composition:** Bronze

| Date | Mintage | F | VF | XF | Unc | BU |
|---|---|---|---|---|---|---|
| 1955 | 5,500,000 | 0.15 | 0.25 | 0.50 | 1.00 | — |
| 1955 Proof | 2,000 | Value: 3.00 | | | | |
| 1957 | 1,250,000 | 0.15 | 0.25 | 1.25 | 2.50 | — |
| 1957 Proof | — | Value: 110 | | | | |
| 1958 | 1,250,000 | 0.15 | 0.25 | 2.50 | 5.00 | — |
| 1958 Proof | 20 | Value: 185 | | | | |
| 1960 | 750,000 | 0.15 | 0.25 | 1.75 | 3.50 | — |
| 1960 Proof | — | Value: 110 | | | | |
| 1961 | 788,000 | 0.15 | 0.25 | 1.75 | 3.50 | — |
| 1961 Proof | — | Value: 110 | | | | |
| 1962 | 1,060,000 | 0.10 | 0.20 | 0.30 | 0.85 | — |
| 1962 Proof | — | Value: 110 | | | | |
| 1963 | 250,000 | 0.50 | 0.75 | 1.50 | 5.00 | — |
| 1963 Proof | — | Value: 110 | | | | |
| 1964 | 1,188,000 | 0.10 | 0.20 | 0.30 | 0.75 | — |
| 1964 Proof | — | Value: 110 | | | | |
| 1965 | 2,001,000 | — | 0.10 | 0.20 | 0.45 | — |
| 1965 Prooflike | — | — | — | — | 0.75 | — |
| 1965 Proof | — | Value: 5.00 | | | | |

**5 CENTS** **KM# 4** **Composition:** Nickel-Brass

| Date | Mintage | F | VF | XF | Unc | BU |
|---|---|---|---|---|---|---|
| 1955 | 8,600,000 | 0.15 | 0.25 | 0.60 | 1.25 | — |
| 1955 Proof | 2,000 | Value: 4.50 | | | | |
| 1956 | 2,000,000 | 0.15 | 0.25 | 0.60 | 1.00 | — |
| 1956 Proof | — | Value: 300 | | | | |
| 1960 | 1,000,000 | 0.20 | 0.30 | 0.90 | 1.50 | — |
| 1960 Proof | — | Value: 150 | | | | |
| 1962 | 1,300,000 | 0.15 | 0.25 | 0.50 | 1.00 | — |
| 1962 Proof | — | Value: 150 | | | | |
| 1963 | 200,000 | 0.25 | 0.35 | 1.20 | 2.00 | — |
| 1963 Proof | — | Value: 150 | | | | |
| 1964 | 1,350,000 | — | 0.10 | 0.30 | 0.75 | — |
| 1964 Proof | — | Value: 150 | | | | |
| 1965 | 2,400,000 | — | 0.10 | 0.20 | 0.50 | — |
| 1965 Prooflike | — | — | — | — | 0.75 | — |
| 1965 Proof | — | Value: 5.00 | | | | |

**10 CENTS** **KM# 5** **Composition:** Copper-Nickel

| Date | Mintage | F | VF | XF | Unc | BU |
|---|---|---|---|---|---|---|
| 1955 | 5,000,000 | 0.15 | 0.25 | 0.45 | 0.75 | — |
| 1955 Proof | 2,000 | Value: 4.50 | | | | |
| 1956 | 4,000,000 | 0.15 | 0.25 | 0.45 | 0.75 | — |
| 1956 Proof | — | Value: 175 | | | | |
| 1959 | 2,000,000 | 0.15 | 0.25 | 0.60 | 1.00 | — |
| 1959 Proof | — | Value: 175 | | | | |
| 1961 | 1,260,000 | 0.20 | 0.30 | 0.50 | 1.00 | — |
| 1961 Proof | — | Value: 175 | | | | |
| 1962 | 1,200,000 | 0.15 | 0.25 | 0.50 | 1.00 | — |
| 1962 Proof | — | Value: 175 | | | | |
| 1964 | 1,400,000 | 0.10 | 0.20 | 0.35 | 0.65 | — |
| 1965 | 3,200,000 | 0.10 | 0.20 | 0.30 | 0.50 | — |
| 1965 Prooflike | — | — | — | — | 0.75 | — |
| 1965 Proof | — | Value: 5.00 | | | | |

**25 CENTS** **KM# 6** **Composition:** Copper-Nickel

| Date | Mintage | F | VF | XF | Unc | BU |
|---|---|---|---|---|---|---|
| 1955 | 7,000,000 | 0.35 | 0.50 | 0.70 | 1.00 | — |
| 1955 Proof | 2,000 | Value: 6.50 | | | | |
| 1957 | 800,000 | 0.75 | 1.00 | 2.25 | 4.50 | — |
| 1957 Proof | — | Value: 225 | | | | |
| 1959 | 1,000,000 | 0.35 | 0.50 | 1.25 | 2.25 | — |
| 1959 Proof | — | Value: 225 | | | | |
| 1961 | 744,000 | 0.50 | 0.75 | 2.50 | 5.00 | — |
| 1961 Proof | — | Value: 225 | | | | |
| 1962 | 480,000 | 0.25 | 0.50 | 1.25 | 2.50 | — |
| 1962 Proof | — | Value: 225 | | | | |
| 1963 | 480,000 | 0.25 | 0.50 | 1.25 | 2.50 | — |
| 1963 Proof | — | Value: 225 | | | | |
| 1964 | 480,000 | 0.25 | 0.50 | 1.00 | 1.75 | — |
| 1964 Proof | — | Value: 225 | | | | |
| 1965 | 1,280,000 | 0.25 | 0.50 | 0.75 | 1.00 | — |
| 1965 Prooflike | — | — | — | — | 1.50 | — |
| 1965 Proof | — | Value: 7.50 | | | | |

**50 CENTS** **KM# 7** **Composition:** Copper-Nickel

| Date | Mintage | F | VF | XF | Unc | BU |
|---|---|---|---|---|---|---|
| 1955 | 1,500,000 | 1.00 | 1.50 | 2.00 | 3.50 | — |
| 1955 Proof | 2,000 | Value: 12.50 | | | | |
| 1965 | 100,000 | 2.00 | 5.00 | 7.50 | 15.00 | — |
| 1965 Prooflike | — | — | — | — | 7.50 | — |
| 1965 Proof | — | Value: 10.00 | | | | |

## EAST CARIBBEAN TERRITORIES

### 100 Cents = 1 Dollar.

### STANDARD COINAGE

100 Cents = 1 Dollar

**10 DOLLARS** **KM# 8** **Composition:** Copper-Nickel **Subject:** 10th Anniversary of Caribbean Development Bank **Note:** Previous KM#1

| Date | Mintage | F | VF | XF | Unc | BU |
|---|---|---|---|---|---|---|
| 1980 | — | — | — | — | 7.00 | — |

**10 DOLLARS** **KM# 8a** **Weight:** 28.2800 g. **Composition:** 0.9250 Silver .8411 oz. ASW **Note:** Previous KM#1a

| Date | Mintage | F | VF | XF | Unc | BU |
|---|---|---|---|---|---|---|
| 1980 Proof | 10,000 | Value: 45.00 | | | | |

**10 DOLLARS** **KM# 9** **Composition:** Copper-Nickel **Subject:** Wedding of Prince Charles and Lady Diana **Note:** Previous KM#2.

| Date | Mintage | F | VF | XF | Unc | BU |
|---|---|---|---|---|---|---|
| 1981 | 50,000 | — | — | — | 7.00 | — |

**10 DOLLARS** **KM# 9a** **Weight:** 28.2800 g. **Composition:** 0.9250 Silver .8411 oz. ASW **Note:** Previous KM#2a.

| Date | Mintage | F | VF | XF | Unc | BU |
|---|---|---|---|---|---|---|
| 1981 Proof | 30,000 | Value: 30.00 | | | | |

## EAST CARIBBEAN STATES

### British Administration.

### STANDARD COINAGE

100 Cents = 1 Dollar

**1/2 CENT** **KM# 10** **Composition:** Bronze **Note:** Previous KM#1.

| Date | Mintage | F | VF | XF | Unc | BU |
|---|---|---|---|---|---|---|
| 1981 | — | — | — | — | 0.20 | |
| 1981 Proof | 5,000 | Value: 1.25 | | | | |
| 1983 | — | — | — | — | 0.20 | — |
| 1984 | — | — | — | — | 0.20 | — |
| 1986 | — | — | — | — | 0.20 | — |
| 1986 Proof | 2,500 | Value: 1.25 | | | | |
| 1987 | — | — | — | — | 0.20 | — |
| 1989 | — | — | — | — | 0.20 | — |
| 1991 | — | — | — | — | 0.20 | — |
| 1992 | — | — | — | — | 0.20 | — |
| 1993 | — | — | — | — | 0.20 | — |
| 1994 | — | — | — | — | 0.20 | — |
| 1995 | — | — | — | — | 0.20 | — |
| 1996 | — | — | — | — | 0.20 | — |
| 1997 | — | — | — | — | 0.20 | — |
| 1998 | — | — | — | — | 0.20 | — |
| 1999 | — | — | — | — | 0.20 | — |
| 2000 | — | — | — | — | 0.20 | — |

**2 CENTS** **KM# 11** **Composition:** Aluminum **Shape:** Square **Note:** Previous KM#2.

| Date | Mintage | F | VF | XF | Unc | BU |
|---|---|---|---|---|---|---|
| 1981 | — | — | — | 0.10 | 0.25 | |
| 1981 Proof | 5,000 | Value: 1.50 | | | | |
| 1984 | — | — | — | 0.10 | 0.25 | — |
| 1986 | — | — | — | 0.10 | 0.25 | — |
| 1986 Proof | 2,500 | Value: 1.50 | | | | |
| 1987 | — | — | — | 0.10 | 0.25 | — |
| 1989 | — | — | — | 0.10 | 0.25 | — |
| 1991 | — | — | — | 0.10 | 0.25 | — |
| 1992 | — | — | — | 0.10 | 0.25 | — |
| 1993 | — | — | — | 0.10 | 0.25 | — |
| 1994 | — | — | — | 0.10 | 0.25 | — |
| 1995 | — | — | — | 0.10 | 0.25 | — |
| 1996 | — | — | — | 0.10 | 0.25 | — |
| 1997 | — | — | — | 0.10 | 0.25 | — |
| 1999 | — | — | — | 0.10 | 0.25 | — |
| 2000 | — | — | — | 0.10 | 0.25 | — |

**5 CENTS** **KM# 12** **Composition:** Aluminum **Shape:** Scalloped **Note:** Previous KM#3.

| Date | Mintage | F | VF | XF | Unc | BU |
|---|---|---|---|---|---|---|
| 1981 | — | — | — | 0.10 | 0.30 | — |
| 1981 Proof | 5,000 | Value: 2.25 | | | | |
| 1984 | — | — | — | 0.10 | 0.30 | — |
| 1986 | — | — | — | 0.10 | 0.30 | — |
| 1986 Proof | 2,500 | Value: 2.25 | | | | |
| 1987 | — | — | — | 0.10 | 0.30 | — |
| 1989 | — | — | — | 0.10 | 0.30 | — |
| 1991 | — | — | — | 0.10 | 0.30 | — |
| 1992 | — | — | — | 0.10 | 0.30 | — |
| 1993 | — | — | — | 0.10 | 0.30 | — |
| 1994 | — | — | — | 0.10 | 0.30 | — |
| 1995 | — | — | — | 0.10 | 0.30 | — |
| 1996 | — | — | — | 0.10 | 0.30 | — |
| 1997 | — | — | — | 0.10 | 0.30 | — |
| 1998 | — | — | — | 0.10 | 0.30 | — |
| 1999 | — | — | — | 0.10 | 0.30 | — |
| 2000 | — | — | — | 0.10 | 0.30 | — |

**10 CENTS** **KM# 13** **Composition:** Copper-Nickel **Note:** Previous KM#4.

| Date | Mintage | F | VF | XF | Unc | BU |
|---|---|---|---|---|---|---|
| 1981 | — | — | 0.10 | 0.15 | 0.40 | — |
| 1981 Proof | 5,000 | Value: 3.00 | | | | |
| 1986 | — | — | 0.10 | 0.15 | 0.40 | — |
| 1986 Proof | 2,500 | Value: 3.00 | | | | |
| 1987 | — | — | 0.10 | 0.15 | 0.40 | — |
| 1989 | — | — | 0.10 | 0.15 | 0.40 | — |
| 1991 | — | — | 0.10 | 0.15 | 0.40 | — |
| 1992 | — | — | 0.10 | 0.15 | 0.35 | — |
| 1993 | — | — | 0.10 | 0.15 | 0.40 | — |
| 1994 | — | — | 0.10 | 0.15 | 0.40 | — |
| 1995 | — | — | 0.10 | 0.15 | 0.40 | — |
| 1996 | — | — | 0.10 | 0.15 | 0.40 | — |
| 1997 | — | — | 0.10 | 0.15 | 0.40 | — |
| 1998 | — | — | 0.10 | 0.15 | 0.40 | — |
| 1999 | — | — | 0.10 | 0.15 | 0.40 | — |
| 2000 | — | — | 0.10 | 0.15 | 0.40 | — |

**25 CENTS** **KM# 14** **Composition:** Copper-Nickel **Note:** Previous KM#5.

| Date | Mintage | F | VF | XF | Unc | BU |
|---|---|---|---|---|---|---|
| 1981 | — | — | 0.15 | 0.20 | 0.50 | — |
| 1981 Proof | 5,000 | Value: 4.00 | | | | |
| 1986 | — | — | 0.15 | 0.20 | 0.50 | — |
| 1986 Proof | 2,500 | Value: 4.00 | | | | |
| 1987 | — | — | 0.15 | 0.20 | 0.50 | — |
| 1989 | — | — | 0.15 | 0.20 | 0.50 | — |
| 1991 | — | — | 0.15 | 0.20 | 0.50 | — |
| 1992 | — | — | 0.15 | 0.20 | 0.50 | — |
| 1993 | — | — | 0.15 | 0.20 | 0.50 | — |
| 1994 | — | — | 0.15 | 0.20 | 0.50 | — |
| 1995 | — | — | 0.15 | 0.20 | 0.50 | — |
| 1996 | — | — | 0.15 | 0.20 | 0.50 | — |
| 1997 | — | — | 0.15 | 0.20 | 0.50 | — |
| 1998 | — | — | 0.15 | 0.20 | 0.50 | — |
| 1999 | — | — | 0.15 | 0.20 | 0.50 | — |
| 2000 | — | — | 0.15 | 0.20 | 0.50 | — |

**DOLLAR** **KM# 15** **Composition:** Aluminum-Bronze **Note:** Previous KM#6.

| Date | Mintage | F | VF | XF | Unc | BU |
|---|---|---|---|---|---|---|
| 1981 | — | — | 0.50 | 0.75 | 1.50 | — |
| 1981 Proof | 5,000 | Value: 8.00 | | | | |
| 1986 | — | — | 0.50 | 0.75 | 1.50 | — |
| 1986 Proof | 2,500 | Value: 8.00 | | | | |

**DOLLAR** **KM# 20** **Composition:** Copper-Nickel **Shape:** 10-sided **Note:** Previous KM#11.

| Date | Mintage | F | VF | XF | Unc | BU |
|---|---|---|---|---|---|---|
| 1989 | — | — | — | — | 2.25 | — |
| 1991 | — | — | — | — | 2.25 | — |
| 1992 | — | — | — | — | 2.25 | — |
| 1993 | — | — | — | — | 2.25 | — |
| 1994 | — | — | — | — | 2.25 | — |
| 1995 | — | — | — | — | 2.25 | — |
| 1996 | — | — | — | — | 2.25 | — |
| 1997 | — | — | — | — | 2.00 | — |
| 1998 | — | — | — | — | 2.00 | — |
| 1999 | — | — | — | — | 2.00 | — |
| 2000 | — | — | — | — | 2.00 | — |

**2 DOLLARS** **KM# 24** **Composition:** Copper-Nickel **Subject:** 10th Anniversary of Central Bank **Note:** Previous KM#15.

| Date | Mintage | F | VF | XF | Unc | BU |
|---|---|---|---|---|---|---|
| ND(1993) | — | — | — | — | 9.50 | — |

**10 DOLLARS** **(KM7a)** **Weight:** 28.2800 g. **Composition:** 0.5000 Silver .4546 oz. ASW

| Date | Mintage | F | VF | XF | Unc | BU |
|---|---|---|---|---|---|---|
| 1981 | 10,000 | — | — | — | 13.50 | — |
| 1981 Proof | 5,000 | Value: 37.50 | | | | |

**10 DOLLARS** **KM# 16** **Composition:** Copper-Nickel **Series:** F.A.O. **Subject:** World Food Day **Note:** Previous KM#7.

| Date | Mintage | F | VF | XF | Unc | BU |
|---|---|---|---|---|---|---|
| 1981 | — | — | — | — | 14.50 | — |

**10 DOLLARS** **KM# 16a** **Weight:** 28.2800 g. **Composition:** 0.5000 Silver .4546 oz. ASW **Note:** Previous KM#7a.

| Date | Mintage | F | VF | XF | Unc | BU |
|---|---|---|---|---|---|---|
| 1981 | 10,000 | — | — | — | 17.50 | — |
| 1981 Proof | 5,000 | Value: 47.50 | | | | |

**10 DOLLARS** **KM# 22** **Weight:** 28.2800 g. **Composition:** 0.9250 Silver .8411 oz. ASW **Subject:** Queen Mother's 90th Birthday **Note:** Previous KM#13.

| Date | Mintage | F | VF | XF | Unc | BU |
|---|---|---|---|---|---|---|
| ND(1990) Proof | — | Value: 50.00 | | | | |

**10 DOLLARS** **KM# 23** **Weight:** 28.2800 g. **Composition:** 0.9250 Silver .8411 oz. ASW **Subject:** 40th Anniversary - Coronation of Queen Elizabeth **Note:** Previous KM#14.

| Date | Mintage | F | VF | XF | Unc | BU |
|---|---|---|---|---|---|---|
| ND(1993) Proof | 10,000 | Value: 47.50 | | | | |

**10 DOLLARS** **KM# 25** **Weight:** 28.2800 g. **Composition:** 0.9250 Silver .8411 oz. ASW **Subject:** 10th Anniversary of Central Bank **Note:** Previous KM#16.

| Date | Mintage | F | VF | XF | Unc | BU |
|---|---|---|---|---|---|---|
| ND(1993) Proof | 2,500 | Value: 55.00 | | | | |

**10 DOLLARS** **KM# 27** **Weight:** 31.4700 g. **Composition:** 0.9250 Silver .9359 oz. ASW **Subject:** World Cup Soccer **Note:** Previous KM#18.

| Date | Mintage | F | VF | XF | Unc | BU |
|---|---|---|---|---|---|---|
| 1994 Proof | 10,000 | Value: 45.00 | | | | |

**10 DOLLARS** **KM# 30** **Weight:** 28.2800 g. **Composition:** 0.9250 Silver .8410 oz. ASW **Subject:** Montserrat Volcano Appeal Fund **Obverse:** Queen Elizabeth II **Reverse:** Multicolor rainbow and volcano **Note:** Previous KM#30.

| Date | Mintage | F | VF | XF | Unc | BU |
|---|---|---|---|---|---|---|
| 1998 Proof | 10,000 | Value: 60.00 | | | | |

**10 DOLLARS** **KM# 28** **Weight:** 28.2800 g. **Composition:** 0.9250 Silver .8410 oz. ASW **Subject:** 50th Anniversary - University of the West Indies **Obverse:** Portrait **Reverse:** University arms **Note:** Previous KM#19.

| Date | Mintage | F | VF | XF | Unc | BU |
|---|---|---|---|---|---|---|
| ND(1999) Proof | 1,000 | Value: 60.00 | | | | |

**2000 CENTS** **KM# 31** **Weight:** 7.9800 g. **Composition:** 0.9170 Gold .2353 oz. AGW **Series:** Millennium **Subject:** British Royal Mint **Obverse:** Queen's head right **Reverse:** Ship, palm trees and radiant sun **Edge:** Reeded **Note:** Previous KM#22.

| Date | Mintage | F | VF | XF | Unc | BU |
|---|---|---|---|---|---|---|
| 2000 | — | — | — | — | 115 | — |

**50 DOLLARS** **KM# 19** **Weight:** 28.2800 g. **Composition:** 0.9250 Silver .8411 oz. ASW **Series:** International Year of Disabled Persons **Note:** Previous KM#10.

| Date | Mintage | F | VF | XF | Unc | BU |
|---|---|---|---|---|---|---|
| 1981 | 10,000 | — | — | — | 30.00 | — |
| 1981 Proof | 10,000 | Value: 45.00 | | | | |

**50 DOLLARS** **KM# 17** **Weight:** 28.2800 g. **Composition:** 0.9250 Silver .8411 oz. ASW **Series:** International Year of the Scout **Note:** Previous KM#8.

| Date | Mintage | F | VF | XF | Unc | BU |
|---|---|---|---|---|---|---|
| ND(1983) | 10,000 | — | — | — | 30.00 | — |
| ND(1983) Proof | 10,000 | Value: 47.50 | | | | |

**100 DOLLARS** **KM# 26** **Weight:** 15.9760 g. **Composition:** 0.9170 Gold .4708 oz. AGW **Subject:** 10th Anniversary of Central Bank **Obverse:** Bank **Reverse:** Portrait of Sir Arthur Lewis **Note:** Similar to 10 Dollars, KM#25; Previous KM#17.

| Date | Mintage | F | VF | XF | Unc | BU |
|---|---|---|---|---|---|---|
| 1993 Proof | 150 | Value: 500 | | | | |

**100 DOLLARS** **KM# 29** **Weight:** 15.9760 g. **Composition:** 0.9170 Gold .4708 oz. AGW **Subject:** 50th Anniversary - University of West Indies **Obverse:** Portrait **Reverse:** University arms **Note:** Similar to 10 Dollars, KM#28; Previous KM#20.

| Date | Mintage | F | VF | XF | Unc | BU |
|---|---|---|---|---|---|---|
| ND(1999) Proof | 300 | Value: 530 | | | | |

**500 DOLLARS** **KM# 21** **Weight:** 15.9800 g. **Composition:** 0.9170 Gold .4712 oz. AGW **Series:** International Year of Disabled Persons **Note:** Previous KM#12.

| Date | Mintage | F | VF | XF | Unc | BU |
|---|---|---|---|---|---|---|
| 1981 | — | — | — | — | 500 | — |
| 1981 Proof | — | Value: 750 | | | | |

**500 DOLLARS** **KM# 18** **Weight:** 15.9800 g. **Composition:** 0.9170 Gold .4712 oz. AGW **Series:** International Year of the Scout **Obverse:** Bust of Elizabeth II right **Reverse:** One scout standing, pointing; one scout kneeling with map **Note:** Previous KM#9.

| Date | Mintage | F | VF | XF | Unc | BU |
|---|---|---|---|---|---|---|
| ND(1983) | 2,000 | — | — | — | 375 | — |
| ND(1983) Proof | 2,000 | Value: 550 | | | | |

## PIEFORTS

| KM# | Date | Mintage | Identification | Mkt Val |
|---|---|---|---|---|
| P1 | 1981 | 1,000 | 50 Dollars. KM#10. | 65.00 |
| P2 | 1981 | — | 500 Dollars. KM#12. | 1,600 |

## MINT SETS

| KM# | Date | Mintage | Identification | Issue Price | Mkt Val |
|---|---|---|---|---|---|
| MS1 | 1986 (6) | — | KM#10-15 | — | 7.50 |
| MS2 | 1991 (6) | — | KM#10-14, 20 | 19.95 | 20.00 |
| MS3 | 1992 (6) | — | KM#10-14, 20 | — | 15.00 |
| MS4 | 1995-97 (6) | — | KM#10-11 (1995), 12-14, 20 (1997) | 25.00 | 25.00 |
| MS5 | 1999 (6) | — | KM#10-14, 20 | 25.00 | 25.00 |
| MS6 | 2000 (7) | — | KM#10-14, 20, 31 | 139 | 145 |

## PROOF SETS

| KM# | Date | Mintage | Identification | Issue Price | Mkt Val |
|---|---|---|---|---|---|
| PS1 | 1955 (7) | 2,000 | KM#1-7 | — | 30.00 |
| PS2 | 1958 (3) | 20 | KM#1-3 | — | 500 |
| PS3 | 1965 (6) | — | KM#2-7 | — | 35.00 |
| PS5 | 1981 (6) | 5,000 | KM#10-15 | 29.00 | 20.00 |
| PS6 | 1986 (6) | 2,500 | KM#10-15 | 30.75 | 20.00 |

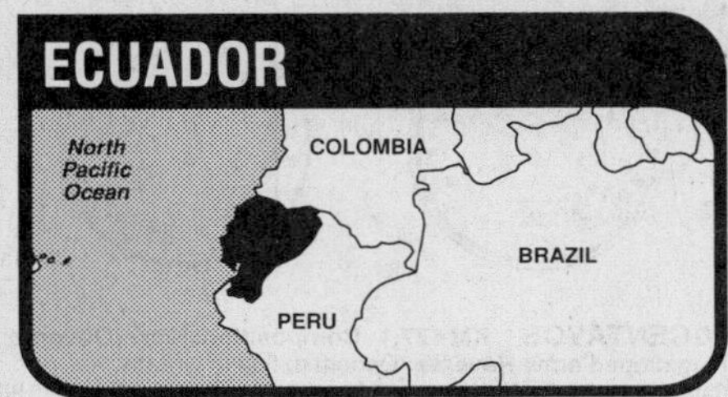


The Republic of Ecuador, located astride the equator on the Pacific Coast of South America, has an area of 105,037 sq. mi. (283,560 sq. km.) and a population of 10.9 million. Capital: Quito. Agriculture is the mainstay of the economy but there are appreciable deposits of minerals and petroleum. It is one of the world's largest exporters of bananas and balsa wood. Coffee, cacao, sugar and petroleum are also valuable exports.

Ecuador was first sighted in 1526 by Francisco Pizarro. Conquest was undertaken by Sebastian de Benalcazar, who founded Quito in 1534. Ecuador was part of the Viceroyalty of New Granada through the 16th and 17th centuries. After previous attempts to attain independence were crushed, Antonio Sucre, the able lieutenant of Bolivar, secured Ecuador's freedom in the Battle of Pinchincha, May 24, 1822. It then joined Venezuela and Colombia in a confederation known as Gran Colombia, and became an independent republic when it left the confederacy in 1830.

**MINT MARKS**

BIRMm - Birmingham, Heaton
Birmingham - Birmingham
D - Denver
H - Heaton, Birmingham
HF - LeLocle (Swiss)
LIMA - Lima
Mo - Mexico
PHILA.U.S.A. - Philadelphia
PHILADELPHIA - Philadelphia
PHILA - Philadelphia

**MONETARY SYSTEM**

10 Centavos = 1 Decimo
10 Decimos = 1 Sucre
25 Sucres = 1 Condor

# REPUBLIC

## DECIMAL COINAGE

10 Centavos = 1 Decimo; 10 Decimos = 1 Sucre; 25 Sucres = 1 Condor

**1/2 CENTAVO (Medio)** **KM# 57** **Composition:** Copper-Nickel **Obverse:** Flag draped arms **Reverse:** Denomination in laurels

| Date | Mintage | F | VF | XF | Unc | BU |
|---|---|---|---|---|---|---|
| 1909H | 4,000,000 | 3.00 | 7.00 | 15.00 | 30.00 | — |

**CENTAVO (Un)** **KM# 58** **Composition:** Copper-Nickel **Obverse:** Flag draped arms

| Date | Mintage | F | VF | XF | Unc | BU |
|---|---|---|---|---|---|---|
| 1909H | 3,000,000 | 3.50 | 7.50 | 15.00 | 35.00 | — |

**CENTAVO (Un)** **KM# 67** **Composition:** Bronze **Obverse:** Flag draped arms **Reverse:** Denomination in laurels

| Date | Mintage | F | VF | XF | Unc | BU |
|---|---|---|---|---|---|---|
| 1928 | 2,016,000 | 1.00 | 2.00 | 7.50 | 15.00 | — |

**CENTAVO (Un)** **KM# 104** **Weight:** 2.5200 g. **Composition:** Brass **Obverse:** Map of the Americas **Reverse:** Denomination **Edge:** Plain **Size:** 19 mm.

| Date | Mintage | F | VF | XF | Unc | BU |
|---|---|---|---|---|---|---|
| 2000 | — | — | — | — | 0.20 | — |

**2 CENTAVOS (Dos)** **KM# 59** **Composition:** Copper-Nickel **Obverse:** Flag draped arms **Reverse:** Denomination in laurels

| Date | Mintage | F | VF | XF | Unc | BU |
|---|---|---|---|---|---|---|
| 1909H | 2,500,000 | 2.00 | 5.00 | 20.00 | 50.00 | — |
| 1909H Proof | — | Value: 175 | | | | |

**2-1/2 CENTAVOS** **KM# 61** **Composition:** Copper-Nickel **Obverse:** Flag draped arms **Reverse:** Denomination in laurels

| Date | Mintage | F | VF | XF | Unc | BU |
|---|---|---|---|---|---|---|
| 1917 | 1,600,000 | 3.00 | 10.00 | 35.00 | 150 | — |

**2-1/2 CENTAVOS** **KM# 68** **Composition:** Nickel **Obverse:** Flag draped arms **Reverse:** Denomination in laurels

| Date | Mintage | F | VF | XF | Unc | BU |
|---|---|---|---|---|---|---|
| 1928 | 4,000,000 | 2.00 | 4.00 | 15.00 | 30.00 | — |

**1/2 DECIMO (Medio)** **KM# 55.1** **Weight:** 1.2500 g. **Composition:** 0.9000 Silver .0361 oz. ASW **Obverse:** Denomination in laurels **Reverse:** Flag draped arm

| Date | Mintage | F | VF | XF | Unc | BU |
|---|---|---|---|---|---|---|
| 1902/892LIMA JF | 1,000,000 | 1.00 | 2.00 | 7.50 | 15.00 | — |
| 1902/802LIMA JF | Inc. above | 1.00 | 2.00 | 7.50 | 15.00 | — |
| 1902LIMA JF | Inc. above | 0.75 | 1.25 | 5.00 | 10.00 | — |
| 1905/805LIMA JF | 500,000 | 3.00 | 5.00 | 15.00 | 40.00 | — |
| 1905/2LIMA JF | Inc. above | 3.50 | 6.00 | 18.00 | 50.00 | — |
| 1905LIMA JF | Inc. above | 0.75 | 1.25 | 5.00 | 10.00 | — |
| 1912/05LIMA FG | 20,000 | 3.00 | 6.00 | 18.00 | 50.00 | — |
| 1912LIMA FG | Inc. above | 0.75 | 1.25 | 5.00 | 10.00 | — |
| 1912LIMA FG | Inc. above | 2.00 | 3.00 | 7.50 | 15.00 | — |

**Note:** FCUADOR (obverse error)

**1/2 DECIMO (Medio)** **KM# 55.2** **Weight:** 1.2500 g. **Composition:** 0.9000 Silver .0361 oz. ASW **Obverse:** Head of Sucre **Reverse:** Modified flag draped arm

| Date | Mintage | F | VF | XF | Unc | BU |
|---|---|---|---|---|---|---|
| 1915BIRMm | 2,000,000 | 0.75 | 1.25 | 3.00 | 8.00 | — |
| 1915BIRMm Proof | — | Value: 150 | | | | |

**5 CENTAVOS (Cinco)** **KM# 60.1** **Composition:** Copper-Nickel **Obverse:** Flag draped arms with tails on flagpoles pointing outward **Reverse:** Denomination in laurels

| Date | Mintage | F | VF | XF | Unc | BU |
|---|---|---|---|---|---|---|
| 1909H | 2,000,000 | 4.50 | 10.00 | 30.00 | 80.00 | — |

**5 CENTAVOS (Cinco)** **KM# 60.2** **Composition:** Copper-Nickel **Obverse:** Flag draped arms with tails on flagpoles pointing downward **Reverse:** Denomination in laurels **Note:** Thin planchet.

| Date | Mintage | F | VF | XF | Unc | BU |
|---|---|---|---|---|---|---|
| 1917 | 1,200,000 | 5.50 | 12.50 | 35.00 | 150 | — |
| 1918 | 7,980,000 | 2.00 | 4.00 | 10.00 | 45.00 | — |

**5 CENTAVOS (Cinco)** **KM# 63** **Composition:** Copper-Nickel **Obverse:** Flag draped arms **Reverse:** Denomination in laurels

| Date | Mintage | F | VF | XF | Unc | BU |
|---|---|---|---|---|---|---|
| 1919 | 12,000,000 | 1.00 | 2.00 | 8.00 | 15.00 | — |
| **Note:** 3 berries to left of "C" on reverse | | | | | | |
| 1919 | Inc. above | 1.25 | 2.50 | 10.00 | 20.00 | — |
| **Note:** 4 berries loose to left of "C" on reverse | | | | | | |
| 1919 | Inc. above | 1.25 | 2.50 | 10.00 | 20.00 | — |
| **Note:** 4 berries tight to left of "C" on reverse | | | | | | |

**5 CENTAVOS (Cinco)** **KM# 65** **Composition:** Copper-Nickel

| Date | Mintage | F | VF | XF | Unc | BU |
|---|---|---|---|---|---|---|
| 1924H | 10,000,000 | 1.00 | 1.75 | 4.00 | 22.00 | — |

**5 CENTAVOS (Cinco)** **KM# 69** **Composition:** Nickel

| Date | Mintage | F | VF | XF | Unc | BU |
|---|---|---|---|---|---|---|
| 1928 | 16,000,000 | 0.75 | 1.00 | 2.00 | 4.50 | — |

**5 CENTAVOS (Cinco)** **KM# 75** **Composition:** Nickel **Obverse:** Flag draped arms **Reverse:** Denomination in wreath

| Date | Mintage | F | VF | XF | Unc | BU |
|---|---|---|---|---|---|---|
| 1937HF | 15,000,000 | 0.10 | 0.20 | 0.75 | 2.00 | — |

**5 CENTAVOS (Cinco)** **KM# 75a** **Composition:** Brass **Obverse:** Flag draped arms **Reverse:** Denomination in wreath

| Date | Mintage | F | VF | XF | Unc | BU |
|---|---|---|---|---|---|---|
| 1942 | 2,000,000 | 1.00 | 2.00 | 6.00 | 15.00 | — |
| 1944D | 3,000,000 | 1.00 | 2.00 | 5.00 | 10.00 | — |

**5 CENTAVOS (Cinco)** **KM# 75b** **Composition:** Copper-Nickel **Obverse:** Flag draped arms **Reverse:** Denomination in wreath

| Date | Mintage | F | VF | XF | Unc | BU |
|---|---|---|---|---|---|---|
| 1946 | 40,000,000 | — | — | 0.40 | 1.00 | — |

**5 CENTAVOS (Cinco)** **KM# 75c** **Composition:** Nickel Clad Steel

| Date | Mintage | F | VF | XF | Unc | BU |
|---|---|---|---|---|---|---|
| 1970 | — | — | — | 0.15 | 0.50 | — |
| 1970 | — | — | — | — | — | — |

**Note:** ECADOR (obverse legend error)

**5 CENTAVOS (Cinco)** **KM# 105** **Weight:** 5.0000 g. **Composition:** Steel **Subject:** Juan Montalvo **Obverse:** Portrait and arms **Reverse:** Denomination **Edge:** Plain **Size:** 21.2 mm.

| Date | Mintage | F | VF | XF | Unc | BU |
|---|---|---|---|---|---|---|
| 2000 | — | — | — | — | 0.50 | — |

**DECIMO (Un)** **KM# 50.3** **Weight:** 2.5000 g. **Composition:** 0.9000 Silver .0723 oz. ASW **Obverse:** Head of Sucre left, legend without LEY **Rev. Legend:** Flag draped arms

| Date | Mintage | VG | F | VF | XF | Unc |
|---|---|---|---|---|---|---|
| 1902LIMA JF | 519,000 | — | 1.00 | 2.50 | 5.00 | 10.00 |
| **Note:** With JR below fasces on reverse | | | | | | |
| 1902LIMA JF | Inc. above | — | 1.00 | 2.50 | 5.00 | 10.00 |
| **Note:** Without JR below fasces on reverse | | | | | | |
| 1902LIMA JF/TF | — | — | 1.00 | 2.50 | 5.00 | 10.00 |
| 1905LIMA JF | 250,000 | — | 1.00 | 2.50 | 5.00 | 10.00 |
| 1912LIMA FG | 30,000 | — | 2.00 | 3.00 | 6.00 | 15.00 |

**DECIMO (Un)** **KM# 50.4** **Weight:** 2.5000 g. **Composition:** 0.9000 Silver .0723 oz. ASW **Obverse:** Head of Sucre left **Reverse:** Flag draped arms

| Date | Mintage | VG | F | VF | XF | Unc |
|---|---|---|---|---|---|---|
| 1915BIRMm | 1,000,000 | — | BV | 1.25 | 2.00 | 7.00 |
| 1915BIRMm Proof | — | Value: 200 | | | | |

**DECIMO (Un)** **KM# 50.5** **Weight:** 2.5000 g. **Composition:** 0.9000 Silver .0723 oz. ASW **Obverse:** Head of Sucre left **Reverse:** Flag draped arms

| Date | Mintage | VG | F | VF | XF | Unc |
|---|---|---|---|---|---|---|
| 1916PHILA | 2,000,000 | — | BV | 1.25 | 2.00 | 5.00 |

**10 CENTAVOS (Diez)** **KM# 62** **Composition:** Copper-Nickel **Obverse:** Flag draped arms **Reverse:** Denomination in wreath

| Date | Mintage | F | VF | XF | Unc | BU |
|---|---|---|---|---|---|---|
| 1918 | 1,000,000 | 5.50 | 11.00 | 25.00 | 65.00 | — |

**10 CENTAVOS (Diez)** **KM# 64** **Composition:** Copper-Nickel **Obverse:** Flag draped arms **Reverse:** Denomination in wreath

| Date | Mintage | F | VF | XF | Unc | BU |
|---|---|---|---|---|---|---|
| 1919 | 2,000,000 | 1.00 | 2.00 | 7.50 | 18.00 | — |
| 1919 Proof | — | Value: 200 | | | | |

**10 CENTAVOS (Diez)** **KM# 66** **Composition:** Copper-Nickel **Obverse:** Flag draped arms **Reverse:** Bust of Bolivar **Note:** The H mint mark is very small and is located above the date.

| Date | Mintage | F | VF | XF | Unc | BU |
|---|---|---|---|---|---|---|
| 1924H | 5,000,000 | 0.75 | 1.50 | 5.00 | 15.00 | — |
| 1924H Proof | — | Value: 80.00 | | | | |

**10 CENTAVOS (Diez)** **KM# 70** **Composition:** Nickel **Obverse:** Flag draped arms **Reverse:** Bolivar head right

| Date | Mintage | F | VF | XF | Unc | BU |
|---|---|---|---|---|---|---|
| 1928 | 16,000,000 | 0.50 | 1.00 | 4.00 | 15.00 | — |

**10 CENTAVOS (Diez)** **KM# 76** **Composition:** Nickel **Obverse:** Flag draped arms **Reverse:** Denomination in wreath

| Date | Mintage | F | VF | XF | Unc | BU |
|---|---|---|---|---|---|---|

**10 CENTAVOS (Diez)** **KM# 76a** **Composition:** Brass **Obverse:** Flag draped arms **Reverse:** Denomination in wreath

| Date | Mintage | F | VF | XF | Unc | BU |
|---|---|---|---|---|---|---|
| 1942 | 5,000,000 | 0.60 | 1.00 | 5.00 | 15.00 | — |

**10 CENTAVOS (Diez)** **KM# 76b** **Composition:** Copper-Nickel **Obverse:** Flag draped arms **Reverse:** Denomination in wreath

| Date | Mintage | F | VF | XF | Unc | BU |
|---|---|---|---|---|---|---|
| 1946 | 40,000,000 | 0.10 | 0.15 | 0.25 | 1.00 | — |

**10 CENTAVOS (Diez)** **KM# 76c** **Composition:** Nickel Clad Steel **Note:** Varieties exist.

| Date | Mintage | F | VF | XF | Unc | BU |
|---|---|---|---|---|---|---|
| 1964 | 20,000,000 | — | — | 0.15 | 0.50 | — |
| 1968 | 15,000,000 | — | — | 0.15 | 0.50 | — |
| 1972 | 20,000,000 | — | — | 0.15 | 0.40 | — |

**10 CENTAVOS (Diez)** **KM# 76d** **Composition:** Copper-Nickel Clad Steel

| Date | Mintage | F | VF | XF | Unc | BU |
|---|---|---|---|---|---|---|
| 1976 | 10,000,000 | — | — | 0.15 | 0.40 | — |

**10 CENTAVOS (Diez)** **KM# 106** **Weight:** 2.2400 g. **Composition:** Steel **Subject:** Eugenio Espejo **Obverse:** Portrait and arms **Reverse:** Denomination **Edge:** Plain **Size:** 17.9 mm.

| Date | Mintage | F | VF | XF | Unc | BU |
|---|---|---|---|---|---|---|
| 2000 | — | — | — | — | 0.75 | — |

**2 DECIMOS (Dos)** **KM# 51.3** **Weight:** 5.0000 g. **Composition:** 0.9000 Silver .1446 oz. ASW **Obverse:** Head of Sucre left **Reverse:** Flag draped arms; legend without LEY

| Date | Mintage | F | VF | XF | Unc | BU |
|---|---|---|---|---|---|---|
| 1912/18 FG | 50,000 | 5.00 | 7.50 | 10.00 | 25.00 | — |
| 1912 FG | Inc. above | 2.00 | 4.00 | 7.00 | 15.00 | — |
| 1914 FG LIMA. | 110,000 | 3.00 | 5.00 | 10.00 | 20.00 | — |
| 1914 FG LIMA | Inc. above | 2.00 | 4.00 | 7.00 | 15.00 | — |
| 1915 FG | 157,000 | 3.00 | 5.00 | 10.00 | 20.00 | — |
| **Note:** Small "R" below fasces on reverse | | | | | | |

**2 DECIMOS (Dos)** **KM# 51.4** **Weight:** 5.0000 g. **Composition:** 0.9000 Silver .1446 oz. ASW **Obverse:** Head of Sucre **Reverse:** Flag draped arms

| Date | Mintage | F | VF | XF | Unc | BU |
|---|---|---|---|---|---|---|
| 1914PHILADELPHIA TF | 2,500,000 | 1.50 | 3.00 | 5.00 | 10.00 | — |
| 1916PHILADELPHIA TF | 1,000,000 | 1.50 | 3.00 | 5.00 | 10.00 | — |

**20 CENTAVOS** **KM# 77.1** **Composition:** Nickel **Obverse:** Flag draped arms **Reverse:** Denomination in wreath

| Date | Mintage | F | VF | XF | Unc | BU |
|---|---|---|---|---|---|---|
| 1937HF | 7,500,000 | 0.25 | 0.50 | 1.00 | 3.50 | — |

**20 CENTAVOS** **KM# 77.1a** **Composition:** Brass **Obverse:** Flag draped arms **Reverse:** Denomination in wreath

| Date | Mintage | F | VF | XF | Unc | BU |
|---|---|---|---|---|---|---|
| 1942 | 5,000,000 | 0.60 | 1.00 | 6.00 | 15.00 | — |
| 1944 D | 15,000,000 | 0.40 | 0.75 | 4.00 | 10.00 | — |

**20 CENTAVOS** **KM# 77.1b** **Composition:** Copper Nickel **Obverse:** Flag draped arms **Reverse:** Denomination in wreath

| Date | Mintage | F | VF | XF | Unc | BU |
|---|---|---|---|---|---|---|
| 1946 | 30,000,000 | 0.10 | 0.20 | 0.35 | 1.25 | — |

**20 CENTAVOS** **KM# 77.1c** **Composition:** Nickel Clad Steel **Obverse:** Flag draped arms **Reverse:** Denomination in wreath

| Date | Mintage | F | VF | XF | Unc | BU |
|---|---|---|---|---|---|---|
| 1959 | 14,400,000 | — | — | 0.15 | 0.50 | — |
| 1962 | 14,400,000 | — | — | 0.15 | 0.50 | — |
| 1966 | 24,000,000 | — | — | 0.15 | 0.50 | — |
| 1969 | 24,000,000 | — | — | 0.15 | 0.50 | — |
| 1971 | 12,000,000 | — | — | 0.15 | 0.50 | — |
| 1972 | 48,432,000 | — | — | 0.15 | 0.50 | — |

**20 CENTAVOS** **KM# 77.2** **Composition:** Copper-Nickel **Obverse:** Modified coat of arms

| Date | Mintage | F | VF | XF | Unc | BU |
|---|---|---|---|---|---|---|
| 1974 | 19,562,000 | — | — | 0.15 | 0.50 | — |

**20 CENTAVOS** **KM# 77.2a** **Composition:** Nickel Coated Steel

| Date | Mintage | F | VF | XF | Unc | BU |
|---|---|---|---|---|---|---|
| 1975 | 52,437,000 | — | — | — | — | — |
| 1978 | 37,500,000 | — | — | 0.15 | 0.35 | — |
| 1980 | 18,000,000 | — | — | 0.15 | 0.35 | — |
| 1981 | 21,000,000 | — | — | 0.15 | 0.35 | — |

**25 CENTAVOS** **KM# 107** **Weight:** 5.6500 g. **Composition:** Steel **Subject:** Jose Joaquin De Olmedo **Obverse:** Portrait and arms **Reverse:** Denomination **Edge:** Reeded **Size:** 24.2 mm.

| Date | Mintage | F | VF | XF | Unc | BU |
|---|---|---|---|---|---|---|
| 2000 | — | — | — | — | 1.00 | — |

**50 CENTAVOS (Cinquenta)** **KM# 71** **Weight:** 2.5000 g. **Composition:** 0.7200 Silver .0579 oz. ASW **Obverse:** Head of Sucre left **Reverse:** Flag draped arms

| Date | Mintage | F | VF | XF | Unc | BU |
|---|---|---|---|---|---|---|
| 1928PHILA•U•S•A. | 1,000,000 | BV | 2.00 | 7.00 | 25.00 | — |
| 1930PHILA•U•S•A. | 155,000 | BV | 5.00 | 15.00 | 35.00 | — |

**50 CENTAVOS (Cinquenta)** **KM# 81** **Composition:** Nickel Clad Steel

| Date | Mintage | F | VF | XF | Unc | BU |
|---|---|---|---|---|---|---|
| 1963 | 20,000,000 | — | 0.15 | 0.25 | 0.60 | — |
| 1971 | 5,000,000 | — | 0.15 | 0.25 | 0.60 | — |
| 1974 | — | — | 0.15 | 0.25 | 0.60 | — |
| 1975 | — | — | 0.15 | 0.25 | 0.60 | — |
| 1977 | 40,000,000 | — | 0.10 | 0.20 | 0.50 | — |
| 1979 | 25,000,000 | — | 0.10 | 0.20 | 0.50 | — |
| 1982 | 20,000,000 | — | 0.10 | 0.20 | 0.50 | — |

**50 CENTAVOS (Cinquenta)** **KM# 87** **Composition:** Nickel Clad Steel **Obverse:** Modified coat of arms

| Date | Mintage | F | VF | XF | Unc | BU |
|---|---|---|---|---|---|---|
| 1985 | 30,000,000 | — | 0.10 | 0.20 | 0.40 | — |

**50 CENTAVOS (Cinquenta)** **KM# 90** **Composition:** Nickel Clad Steel **Note:** The circulation strikes were withdrawn from circulation and remelted. Approximately 100,000 pieces were released.

| Date | Mintage | F | VF | XF | Unc | BU |
|---|---|---|---|---|---|---|
| 1988 | — | — | — | — | 0.30 | — |
| 1988 Proof | 25 | — | — | — | — | — |

**50 CENTAVOS (Cinquenta)** **KM# 108** **Weight:** 11.3200 g. **Composition:** Steel **Subject:** Eloy Alfaro **Obverse:** Portrait and arms **Reverse:** Denomination **Edge:** Reeded **Size:** 30.6 mm.

| Date | Mintage | F | VF | XF | Unc | BU |
|---|---|---|---|---|---|---|
| 2000 | — | — | — | — | 2.00 | — |

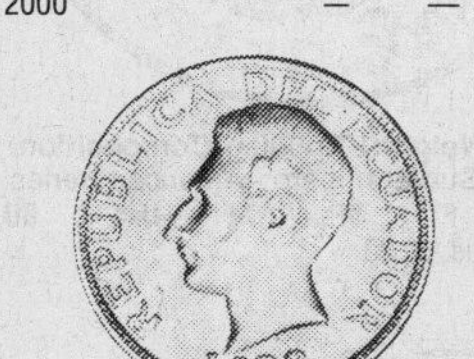

**SUCRE (Un)** **KM# 72** **Weight:** 5.0000 g. **Composition:** 0.7200 Silver .1157 oz. ASW **Obverse:** Head of Sucre left **Reverse:** Flag draped arms

| Date | Mintage | F | VF | XF | Unc | BU |
|---|---|---|---|---|---|---|
| 1928PHILA•U•S•A. | 3,000,000 | BV | 2.50 | 10.00 | 25.00 | — |
| 1930PHILA•U•S•A. | 400,000 | 2.00 | 8.00 | 20.00 | 50.00 | — |
| 1934PHILA•U•S•A. | 2,000,000 | BV | 2.00 | 5.00 | 15.00 | — |

**SUCRE (Un)** **KM# 78.1** **Composition:** Nickel **Obverse:** Flag draped arms **Reverse:** Head of Sucre left **Size:** 26.5 mm.

| Date | Mintage | F | VF | XF | Unc | BU |
|---|---|---|---|---|---|---|
| 1937 HF | 9,000,000 | 0.50 | 1.00 | 2.00 | 7.00 | — |

**SUCRE (Un)** **KM# 78.2** **Composition:** Nickel **Obverse:** Flag draped arms **Reverse:** Head of Sucre left **Size:** 25.9 mm.

| Date | Mintage | F | VF | XF | Unc | BU |
|---|---|---|---|---|---|---|
| 1946 | 18,000,000 | 0.40 | 0.60 | 0.80 | 2.00 | — |

**SUCRE (Un)** **KM# 78a** **Composition:** Copper-Nickel **Obverse:** Flag draped arms **Reverse:** Head of Sucre left

| Date | Mintage | F | VF | XF | Unc | BU |
|---|---|---|---|---|---|---|
| 1959 | 8,400,000 | 0.25 | 0.50 | 0.65 | 1.00 | — |
| 1959 Proof | — | Value: 250 | | | | |

**SUCRE (Un)** **KM# 78b** **Composition:** Nickel Clad Steel **Obverse:** Ship in arms similar to KM#78

| Date | Mintage | F | VF | XF | Unc | BU |
|---|---|---|---|---|---|---|
| 1964 | 20,000,000 | — | 0.10 | 0.25 | 0.50 | — |
| 1970 | 24,000,000 | — | 0.10 | 0.25 | 0.50 | — |
| 1971 | 8,092,000 | — | 0.10 | 0.25 | 0.50 | — |
| 1974 | 40,308,000 | — | 0.10 | 0.25 | 0.50 | — |
| 1978 | 32,000,000 | — | 0.10 | 0.25 | 0.50 | — |
| 1979 | 32,000,000 | — | 0.10 | 0.25 | 0.50 | — |
| 1980 | 110,000,000 | — | 0.10 | 0.25 | 0.50 | — |
| 1981 | 70,000,000 | — | 0.10 | 0.25 | 0.50 | — |

**SUCRE (Un)** **KM# 83** **Composition:** Nickel Clad Steel **Obverse:** Modified coat of arms, ship similar to KM#78a

| Date | Mintage | F | VF | XF | Unc | BU |
|---|---|---|---|---|---|---|
| 1974 | 32,000,000 | — | 0.10 | 0.20 | 0.40 | — |
| 1975 | 32,000,000 | — | 0.10 | 0.20 | 0.40 | — |
| 1975 Proof | — | Value: 150 | | | | |
| 1977 | 32,000,000 | — | 0.10 | 0.20 | 0.35 | — |

**SUCRE (Un)** **KM# 85.1** **Composition:** Nickel Clad Steel **Obverse:** Modified coat of arms **Reverse:** Large head

| Date | Mintage | F | VF | XF | Unc | BU |
|---|---|---|---|---|---|---|
| 1985 | — | — | — | — | 0.50 | — |

**SUCRE (Un)** **KM# 85.2** **Composition:** Nickel Clad Steel **Reverse:** Small head

| Date | Mintage | F | VF | XF | Unc | BU |
|---|---|---|---|---|---|---|
| 1986 | — | — | — | — | 0.50 | — |

**SUCRE (Un)** **KM# 89** **Composition:** Nickel Clad Steel **Note:** The 1988 circulation strikes were reportedly withdrawn from circulation and remelted. Approximately 100,000 pieces were released.

| Date | Mintage | F | VF | XF | Unc | BU |
|---|---|---|---|---|---|---|
| 1988 | — | — | — | — | 0.40 | — |
| 1988 Proof | 25 | — | — | — | — | — |
| 1990 | — | — | — | — | 0.40 | — |
| 1992 | — | — | — | — | 0.40 | — |

**2 SUCRES (Dos)** **KM# 73** **Weight:** 10.0000 g. **Composition:** 0.7200 Silver .2315 oz. ASW **Obverse:** Head of Sucre **Reverse:** Flag draped arms

| Date | Mintage | F | VF | XF | Unc | BU |
|---|---|---|---|---|---|---|
| 1928PHILA•U•S•A. | 500,000 | 2.50 | 7.50 | 22.50 | 45.00 | — |
| 1930PHILA•U•S•A. | 100,000 | 4.00 | 15.00 | 35.00 | 65.00 | — |

**2 SUCRES (Dos)** **KM# 80** **Weight:** 10.0000 g. **Composition:** 0.7200 Silver .2315 oz. ASW **Obverse:** Head of Sucre **Reverse:** Flag draped arms

| Date | Mintage | F | VF | XF | Unc | BU |
|---|---|---|---|---|---|---|
| 1944Mo | 1,000,000 | 2.50 | 3.50 | 5.00 | 10.00 | — |

**2 SUCRES (Dos)** **KM# 82** **Composition:** Copper-Nickel **Note:** Not released to circulation. All but approximately 35 pieces were remelted.

| Date | Mintage | F | VF | XF | Unc | BU |
|---|---|---|---|---|---|---|
| 1973 | 2,000,000 | — | — | 200 | 300 | — |

**5 SUCRES (Cinco)** **KM# 79** **Weight:** 25.0000 g. **Composition:** 0.7200 Silver .5787 oz. ASW **Obverse:** Head of Sucre left **Reverse:** Flag draped arms

| Date | Mintage | F | VF | XF | Unc | BU |
|---|---|---|---|---|---|---|
| 1943Mo | 1,000,000 | — | BV | 6.00 | 10.00 | — |
| 1944Mo | 2,600,000 | — | BV | 5.00 | 8.00 | — |

**5 SUCRES (Cinco)** **KM# 84** **Composition:** Copper-Nickel **Note:** Only 7 pieces were distributed to Ecuadorian government officials. Eight pieces (5 of them canceled) reside in the Central Bank Collection. The remaining 485 have been remelted.

| Date | Mintage | F | VF | XF | Unc | BU |
|---|---|---|---|---|---|---|
| 1973 | 500 | — | — | — | 1,200 | — |

**5 SUCRES (Cinco)** **KM# 91** **Composition:** Nickel Clad Steel **Note:** The 1988 circulation strikes were reportedly withdrawn from circulation and remelted. Approximately 100,000 pieces released.

| Date | Mintage | F | VF | XF | Unc | BU |
|---|---|---|---|---|---|---|
| 1988 | — | — | — | — | 0.50 | — |
| 1988 Proof | 25 | — | — | — | — | — |
| 1991 | — | — | — | — | 0.50 | — |

**10 SUCRES (Diez)** **KM# 92.1** **Composition:** Nickel Clad Steel **Note:** Similar to KM#92.2 but small arms and letters. The circulation strikes were withdrawn from circulation and remelted. Approximately 100,000 pieces were released.

| Date | Mintage | F | VF | XF | Unc | BU |
|---|---|---|---|---|---|---|
| 1988 | — | — | — | — | 1.00 | — |
| 1988 Proof | 25 | — | — | — | — | — |

**10 SUCRES (Diez)** **KM# 92.2** **Composition:** Nickel Clad Steel **Obverse:** Large arms and letters

| Date | Mintage | F | VF | XF | Unc | BU |
|---|---|---|---|---|---|---|
| 1991 | — | — | — | — | 1.00 | — |

**20 SUCRES** **KM# 94.1** **Composition:** Nickel Clad Steel **Note:** The circulation strikes were withdrawn from circulation and remelted. Approximately 100,000 pieces released.

| Date | Mintage | F | VF | XF | Unc | BU |
|---|---|---|---|---|---|---|
| 1988 | — | — | — | — | 1.75 | — |
| 1988 Proof | 25 | — | — | — | — | — |

**20 SUCRES** **KM# 94.2** **Composition:** Nickel Clad Steel **Obverse:** Modified coat of arms

| Date | Mintage | F | VF | XF | Unc | BU |
|---|---|---|---|---|---|---|
| 1991 | — | — | — | — | 1.75 | — |

**50 SUCRES** **KM# 93** **Composition:** Nickel Clad Steel **Note:** The 1988 circulation strikes were withdrawn from circulation and remelted. Approximately 100,000 pieces released.

| Date | Mintage | F | VF | XF | Unc | BU |
|---|---|---|---|---|---|---|
| 1988 | — | — | — | — | 3.00 | — |
| 1988 Proof | 25 | — | — | — | — | — |
| 1991 wide date | — | — | — | — | 3.00 | — |
| 1991 narrow date | — | — | — | — | 3.00 | — |

**100 SUCRES** **KM# 96** **Ring Composition:** Nickel Plated Steel **Center Composition:** Bronze Plated Steel **Subject:** National Bicentennial

| Date | Mintage | F | VF | XF | Unc | BU |
|---|---|---|---|---|---|---|
| 1995 | — | — | 0.35 | 0.55 | 1.25 | — |

**100 SUCRES** **KM# 101** **Ring Composition:** Stainless Steel **Center Composition:** Brass Clad Steel **Subject:** 70th Anniversary - Central Bank **Obverse:** Portrait of Antonio Jose de Sucre left **Reverse:** Denomination

| Date | Mintage | F | VF | XF | Unc | BU |
|---|---|---|---|---|---|---|
| ND(1997) | — | — | 0.25 | 0.50 | 1.00 | — |

**500 SUCRES** **KM# 97** **Ring Composition:** Nickel Plated Steel **Center Composition:** Bronze Plated Steel **Subject:** State Reform **Reverse:** Isidro Ayora

| Date | Mintage | F | VF | XF | Unc | BU |
|---|---|---|---|---|---|---|
| 1995 | — | — | — | — | 1.75 | — |

**500 SUCRES** **KM# 102** **Ring Composition:** Copper-Nickel **Center Composition:** Aluminum-Bronze **Subject:** 70th Anniversary - Central Bank **Obverse:** Portrait of Isidro Ayora **Reverse:** Denomination

| Date | Mintage | F | VF | XF | Unc | BU |
|---|---|---|---|---|---|---|
| ND(1997) | — | — | — | — | 1.50 | — |

**1000 SUCRES** **KM# 86** **Weight:** 23.3300 g. **Composition:** 0.9250 Silver .6938 oz. ASW **Subject:** Championship Soccer

| Date | Mintage | F | VF | XF | Unc | BU |
|---|---|---|---|---|---|---|
| 1986 Proof | 8,125 | Value: 30.00 | | | | |

**1000 SUCRES** **KM# 88** **Weight:** 23.3300 g. **Composition:** 0.9250 Silver .6938 oz. ASW **Subject:** Championship Soccer

| Date | Mintage | F | VF | XF | Unc | BU |
|---|---|---|---|---|---|---|
| 1986 Proof | Est. 10,000 | Value: 30.00 | | | | |

**1000 SUCRES** **KM# 99** **Ring Composition:** Stainless Steel **Center Composition:** Brass **Reverse:** Portrait of Eugenio Espejo right

| Date | Mintage | F | VF | XF | Unc | BU |
|---|---|---|---|---|---|---|
| 1996 | — | — | — | — | 2.50 | — |

**1000 SUCRES** **KM# 103** **Ring Composition:** Copper-Nickel **Center Composition:** Aluminum-Bronze **Subject:** 70th Anniversary - Central Bank **Reverse:** Portrait of Eugenio Espejo right

| Date | Mintage | F | VF | XF | Unc | BU |
|---|---|---|---|---|---|---|
| ND(1997) | — | — | — | — | 2.25 | — |

**5000 SUCRES** **KM# 95** **Weight:** 27.0000 g. **Composition:** 0.9250 Silver .8029 oz. ASW **Subject:** Ibero - American Series

| Date | Mintage | F | VF | XF | Unc | BU |
|---|---|---|---|---|---|---|
| 1991 Proof | 50,000 | Value: 50.00 | | | | |

**5000 SUCRES** **KM# 98** **Weight:** 27.0000 g. **Composition:** 0.9250 Silver .8029 oz. ASW **Subject:** Environmental Protection - Galapagos Penguins

| Date | Mintage | F | VF | XF | Unc | BU |
|---|---|---|---|---|---|---|
| 1994 Proof | 20,000 | Value: 70.00 | | | | |

**5000 SUCRES** **KM# 100** **Weight:** 27.0000 g. **Composition:** 0.9250 Silver .8029 oz. ASW **Subject:** Ibero-American Series - Native Costumes

| Date | Mintage | F | VF | XF | Unc | BU |
|---|---|---|---|---|---|---|
| 1997 Proof | 20,000 | Value: 60.00 | | | | |

**CONDOR (Un)** **KM# 74** **Weight:** 8.3592 g. **Composition:** 0.9000 Gold .2419 oz. AGW **Obverse:** Head of Bolivar **Reverse:** Flag draped arms **Note:** 5,000 were released into circulation; the remainder are held as the Central Bank gold reserve.

| Date | Mintage | F | VF | XF | Unc | BU |
|---|---|---|---|---|---|---|
| 1928Birmingham | 20,000 | 90.00 | 140 | 200 | 350 | — |

## PATTERNS

Including off metal strikes

| KM# | Date | Mintage | Identification | Mkt Val |
|---|---|---|---|---|
| Pn11 | 1928 | — | Condor. Copper-Nickel. KM#74. | — |
| Pn12 | 1928 | — | Condor. Copper. KM#74. | — |
| Pn13 | 1974 | — | 20 Centavos. Brass. 3.6000 g. KM#77.2 | 150 |
| Pn14 | 1975 | — | 50 Centavos. Brass. 5.2100 g. KM#81. | 150 |
| Pn15 | 1975 | — | Sucre. Brass. 6.7900 g. KM#83. | 150 |
| Pn16 | 1976 | — | 10 Centavos. Brass. 2.9100 g. KM#76d. | 150 |

## PIEFORTS

| KM# | Date | Mintage | Identification | Mkt Val |
|---|---|---|---|---|
| P1 | 1915 | — | 1/2 Decimo. Copper Nickel. | — |
| P2 | 1915 | — | Decimo. Copper Nickel. | — |

## PROOF SETS

| KM# | Date | Mintage | Identification | Issue Price | Mkt Val |
|---|---|---|---|---|---|
| PS1 | 1884 (8) | — | Unique. KM#50.1, 51.1, 52, 53.1 (2 of each) | — | — |
| PS2 | 1988 (6) | 25 | KM#89-94 | — | — |

# EGYPT

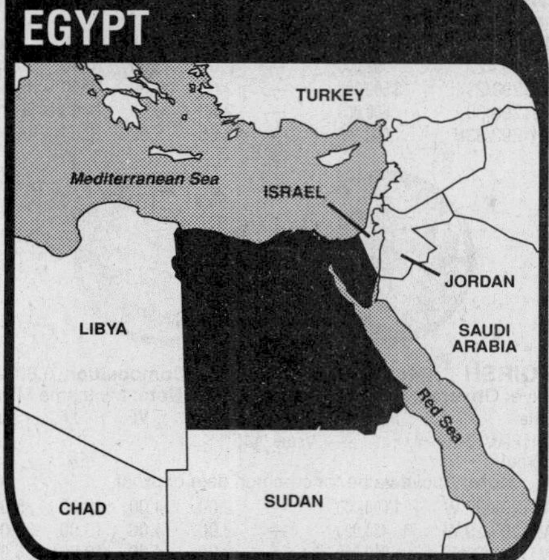


The Arab Republic of Egypt, located on the northeastern corner of Africa, has an area of 385,229 sq. mi. (1,1001,450 sq. km.) and a population of 62.4 million. Capital: Cairo. Although Egypt is an almost rainless expanse of desert, its economy is predominantly agricultural. Cotton, rice and petroleum are exported. Other main sources of income are revenues from the Suez Canal, remittances of Egyptian workers abroad and tourism.

Egyptian history dates back to about 3000 B.C. when the empire was established by uniting the upper and lower kingdoms. Following its 'Golden Age' (16th to 13th centuries B.C.), Egypt was conquered by Persia (525 B.C.) and Alexander the Great (332 B.C.). The Ptolemies, descended from one of Alexander's generals, ruled until the suicide of Cleopatra (30 B.C.) when Egypt became the private domain of the Roman emperor, and subsequently part of the Byzantine world. Various Muslim dynasties ruled Egypt from 641 on, including Ayyubid Sultans to 1250 and Mamluks to 1517, when it was conquered by the Ottoman Turks, interrupted by the occupation of Napoleon (1798-1801). A semi-independent dynasty was founded by Muhammad Ali in 1805 which lasted until 1952. Turkish rule became increasingly casual, permitting Great Britain to inject its influence by purchasing shares in the Suez Canal. British troops occupied Egypt in 1882, becoming the de facto rulers. On Dec. 14, 1914, Egypt was made a protectorate of Britain. British occupation ended on Feb. 28, 1922, when Egypt became a sovereign, independent kingdom. The monarchy was abolished and a republic proclaimed on July 23, 1953.

On Feb. 1, 1958, Egypt and Syria formed the United Arab Republic. Yemen joined on March 8 in an association known as the United Arab States. Syria withdrew from the United Arab Republic on Sept. 29, 1961, and on Dec. 26 Egypt dissolved its ties with Yemen in the United Arab States. On Sept. 2, 1971, Egypt finally shed the name United Arab Republic in favor of the Arab Republic of Egypt.

### RULERS

British, 1882-1922

**Local Khedives**

Mohammed Tewfik Pasha, 1882--
Abbas II Hilmi, 1892-1914

**Local Sultans**

Hussein Kamil, 1914-1917
Ahmed Fuad I, 1917-1922

**Kingdom, 1922-1952**

Ahmed Fuad I, 1922-1936
Farouk, 1936-1952
Fuad II, 1952-1953

**Republic, 1952-**

### MONETARY SYSTEM

**(1885-1916)**

10 Ushr-al-Qirsh = 1 Piastre

**(Commencing 1916)**

10 Milliemes = 1 Piastre (Qirsh)
100 Piastres = 1 Pound (Gunayh)

### MINT MARKS

Egyptian coins issued prior to the advent of the British Protectorate series of Sultan Hussein Kamil introduced in 1916 were very similar to Turkish coins of the same period. They can best be distinguished by the presence of the Arabic word *Misr* Egypt) on the reverse, which generally appears immediately above the Muslim accession date of the ruler, which is presented in Arabic numerals. Each coin is individually dated according to the regnal years.

BP - Budapest, Hungary
H - Birmingham, England
KN - King's Norton, England

### ENGRAVER

W - Emil Weigand, Berlin

### INITIAL LETTERS

Letters, symbols and numerals were placed on coins during the reigns of Mustafa II (1695) until Selim III (1789). They have been observed in various positions but the most common position being over *bin* in the third row of the obverse. In Egypt these letters and others used on the Paras (Medins) above the word *duribe* on the reverse during this period.

### REGNAL YEAR IDENTIFICATION

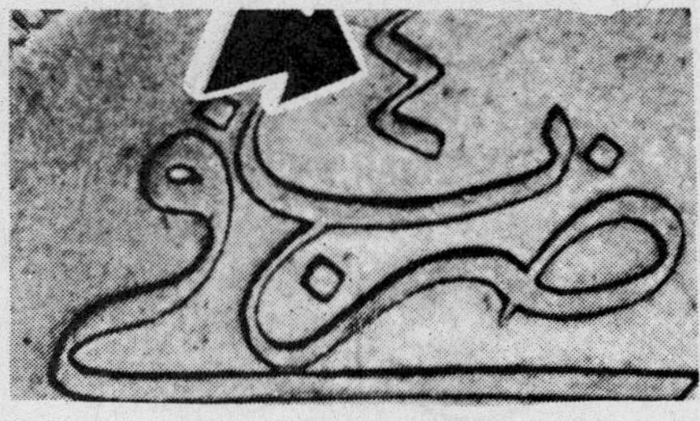

4
Duriba fi

*Misr* + Accession Date

### DENOMINATIONS

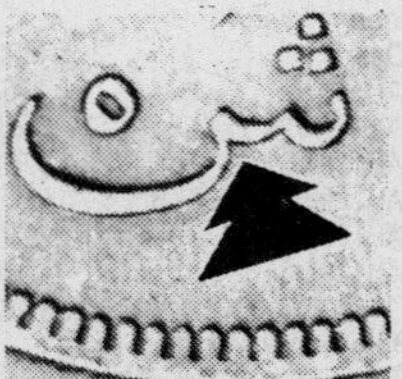

Para + Qirsh

**NOTE**: The unit of value on coins of this period is generally presented on the obverse immediately below the toughra, as shown in the illustrations above.

*Piastres* 1916-1933

*Milliemes* + *Piastres* 1934 –

### TITLES

المملكة المصرية

al-Mamlaka + al-Misriya
(The Kingdom of Egypt)

### U.A.R. EGYPT

The legend illustrated is *Jumhuriyat Misr al-Arabiyya* which translates to 'The Arab Republic of Egypt'. Similar legends are found on the modern issues of Syria.

# OTTOMAN EMPIRE

## Abdul Hamid II

### AH1293-1327/1876-1909AD

### OTTOMAN COINAGE

**1/40 QIRSH** KM# 287 **Composition:** Bronze **Note:** Mintname Misr.

| Date | Mintage | VG | F | VF | XF | Unc |
|---|---|---|---|---|---|---|
| AH1293/27 | 1,200,000 | — | 1.50 | 3.00 | 7.00 | 18.00 |
| AH1293/29 | 2,000,000 | — | 1.00 | 2.00 | 4.00 | 15.00 |
| AH1293/31H | 2,400,000 | — | 1.00 | 2.00 | 4.00 | 15.00 |
| AH1293/32H | | — | 1.00 | 2.00 | 4.00 | 15.00 |
| AH1293/33H | 1,200,000 | — | 1.00 | 2.00 | 4.00 | 12.00 |
| AH1293/35H | 1,200,000 | — | 2.00 | 5.00 | 7.00 | 15.00 |

**1/20 QIRSH** KM# 288 **Composition:** Bronze **Note:** Mintname Misr.

| Date | Mintage | VG | F | VF | XF | Unc |
|---|---|---|---|---|---|---|
| AH1293/27 | 1,402,000 | — | 1.00 | 2.00 | 3.00 | 12.00 |
| AH1293/29 | 3,200,000 | — | 1.00 | 2.00 | 3.00 | 12.00 |
| AH1293/31H | 3,000,000 | — | 1.00 | 2.00 | 3.00 | 10.00 |
| AH1293/32(1906) H | | | | | | |
| AH1293/33H | 1,400,000 | — | 2.00 | 3.00 | 5.00 | 15.00 |
| AH1293/35H | 1,400,000 | — | 3.00 | 6.00 | 10.00 | 20.00 |

**1/20 QIRSH** KM# 288 **Composition:** Bronze **Note:** Mintname Misr.

| Date | Mintage | F | VF | XF | Unc |
|---|---|---|---|---|---|
| AH1293/27 | 1,402,000 | | | | |
| AH1293/29 | 3,200,000 | | | | |
| AH1293/31H | 3,000,000 | | | | |
| AH1293/32(1906) H | | 1.00 | 2.00 | 3.00 | 10.00 |
| AH1293/33H | 1,400,000 | | | | |
| AH1293/35H | 1,400,000 | | | | |

**1/10 QIRSH** KM# 289 **Composition:** Copper-Nickel **Note:** Mintname Misr.

| Date | Mintage | VG | F | VF | XF | Unc |
|---|---|---|---|---|---|---|
| AH1293/27-35 Proof | — | Value: 100 | | | | |

**Note:** Above value for common date proof

| Date | Mintage | VG | F | VF | XF | Unc |
|---|---|---|---|---|---|---|
| AH1293/27 | 3,010,000 | — | 1.00 | 1.50 | 3.00 | 10.00 |
| AH1293/28 | 6,000,000 | — | 1.00 | 1.50 | 3.00 | 10.00 |
| AH1293/29 | 1,500,000 | — | 1.00 | 2.00 | 4.00 | 15.00 |
| AH1293/30 | 1,000,000 | — | 1.00 | 1.50 | 3.00 | 12.50 |
| AH1293/31H | 3,000,000 | — | 1.00 | 1.50 | 4.00 | 15.00 |
| AH1293/32H | | — | 1.00 | 1.50 | 3.00 | 12.50 |
| AH1293/33H | 2,000,000 | — | 1.00 | 1.50 | 2.50 | 8.50 |
| AH1293/35H | 2,000,000 | — | 1.25 | 3.00 | 6.00 | 20.00 |

**2/10 QIRSH** KM# 290 **Composition:** Copper-Nickel **Note:** Mintname Misr.

| Date | Mintage | VG | F | VF | XF | Unc |
|---|---|---|---|---|---|---|
| AH1293/27 | 1,002,000 | — | 1.00 | 3.00 | 6.00 | 20.00 |
| AH1293/28 | 2,000,000 | — | 1.00 | 3.00 | 6.00 | 20.00 |
| AH1293/29 | 1,500,000 | — | 1.00 | 3.00 | 6.00 | 20.00 |
| AH1293/30 | — | — | 3.00 | 6.00 | 12.00 | 40.00 |
| AH1293/31H | 1,000,000 | — | 1.00 | 3.00 | 6.00 | 20.00 |
| AH1293/33H | 1,500,000 | — | 1.00 | 3.00 | 6.00 | 20.00 |
| AH1293/35H | 750,000 | — | 2.00 | 6.00 | 10.00 | 35.00 |

**5/10 QIRSH** KM# 291 **Composition:** Copper-Nickel **Note:** Mintname Misr.

| Date | Mintage | VG | F | VF | XF | Unc |
|---|---|---|---|---|---|---|
| AH1293/27-33 Proof | — | Value: 145 | | | | |

**Note:** Above value for common date proof

| Date | Mintage | VG | F | VF | XF | Unc |
|---|---|---|---|---|---|---|
| AH1293/27 | 4,999,000 | — | 0.30 | 1.50 | 5.00 | 20.00 |
| AH1293/29 | 12,000,000 | — | 0.30 | 1.50 | 5.00 | 20.00 |
| AH1293/30 | 2,000,000 | — | 0.50 | 2.00 | 6.00 | 25.00 |
| AH1293/33H | 1,000,000 | — | 2.00 | 6.00 | 12.50 | 40.00 |

**QIRSH** KM# 292 **Weight:** 1.4000 g. **Composition:** 0.8330 Silver .0375 oz. ASW ASW **Note:** Mintname Misr.

| Date | Mintage | VG | F | VF | XF | Unc |
|---|---|---|---|---|---|---|
| AH1293/27-33 Proof | — | Value: 135 | | | | |

**Note:** Above value for common date proof

| Date | Mintage | VG | F | VF | XF | Unc |
|---|---|---|---|---|---|---|
| AH1293/27 W | 200,000 | — | 1.25 | 4.00 | 10.00 | 27.50 |
| AH1293/29 W | 100,000 | — | 1.50 | 4.00 | 10.00 | 30.00 |
| AH1293/29H | 100,000 | — | 1.25 | 3.00 | 7.50 | 25.00 |
| AH1293/33H | 100,000 | — | 1.25 | 3.00 | 7.50 | 25.00 |

**QIRSH** KM# 299 **Composition:** Copper-Nickel **Note:** Mintname Misr.

| Date | Mintage | VG | F | VF | XF | Unc |
|---|---|---|---|---|---|---|
| AH1293/27 | 999,000 | — | 2.00 | 6.00 | 20.00 | 50.00 |
| AH1293/29 | 3,500,000 | — | 2.00 | 5.00 | 15.00 | 40.00 |
| AH1293/30 | 500,000 | — | 2.50 | 6.00 | 20.00 | 55.00 |
| AH1293/33H | 1,000,000 | — | 2.00 | 5.00 | 15.00 | 40.00 |

**2 QIRSH** KM# 293 **Weight:** 2.8000 g. **Composition:** 0.8330 Silver **Obverse:** Flower to right of toughra **Note:** Mintname Misr.

| Date | Mintage | VG | F | VF | XF | Unc |
|---|---|---|---|---|---|---|
| AH1293/17-33 Proof | — | Value: 145 | | | | |

**Note:** Above value for common date of proof

| Date | Mintage | VG | F | VF | XF | Unc |
|---|---|---|---|---|---|---|
| AH1293/27 W | 1,000,000 | — | 2.00 | 4.00 | 10.00 | 35.00 |
| AH1293/29 W | 450,000 | — | 2.00 | 4.00 | 10.00 | 35.00 |
| AH1293/29H | 1,250,000 | — | 2.00 | 4.00 | 10.00 | 35.00 |
| AH1293/30H | 500,000 | — | 3.00 | 6.00 | 15.00 | 40.00 |
| AH1293/31H | Inc. above | — | 3.00 | 6.00 | 15.00 | 40.00 |
| AH1293/33H | 450,000 | — | 2.00 | 4.00 | 10.00 | 35.00 |

**5 QIRSH** KM# 294 **Weight:** 7.0000 g. **Composition:** 0.8330 Silver .1875 oz. ASW ASW **Obverse:** Flower at right of toughra **Note:** Mintname Misr.

| Date | Mintage | VG | F | VF | XF | Unc |
|---|---|---|---|---|---|---|
| AH1293/27-33 Proof | — | Value: 285 | | | | |

**Note:** Above value for common date of proof

| Date | Mintage | VG | F | VF | XF | Unc |
|---|---|---|---|---|---|---|
| AH1293/27 W | 448,000 | — | 5.00 | 12.50 | 20.00 | 50.00 |
| AH1293/29 W | 600,000 | — | 5.00 | 10.00 | 20.00 | 50.00 |
| AH1293/29H | 3,465,000 | — | 5.00 | 10.00 | 20.00 | 50.00 |
| AH1293/30H | 1,213,000 | — | 5.00 | 10.00 | 22.50 | 60.00 |
| AH1293/31H | 1,959,000 | — | 5.00 | 10.00 | 22.50 | 60.00 |
| AH1293/32H | | — | 5.00 | 10.00 | 20.00 | 50.00 |
| AH1293/33H | 2,800,000 | — | 3.00 | 7.50 | 20.00 | 50.00 |

**5 QIRSH** KM# 298 **Weight:** 0.4200 g. **Composition:** 0.8750 Gold .0118 oz. AGW **Obverse:** "Al Ghazi" at right of toughra **Note:** Mintname Misr.

| Date | Mintage | VG | F | VF | XF | Unc |
|---|---|---|---|---|---|---|
| AH1293/24(1898) | — | 25.00 | 50.00 | 90.00 | 145 | — |
| AH1293/26(1900) | — | 25.00 | 50.00 | 90.00 | 145 | — |
| AH1293/27-33 Proof | — | — | — | — | — | — |
| AH1293/34 | 8,000 | — | 35.00 | 60.00 | 80.00 | — |

**5 QIRSH** KM# 294 **Weight:** 7.0000 g. **Composition:** 0.8330 Silver .1875 oz. ASW ASW **Obverse:** Flower at right of toughra **Note:** Mintname Misr.

| Date | Mintage | VG | F | VF | XF | Unc |
|---|---|---|---|---|---|---|
| | 600,000 | | | | | |
| | 1,205,000 | | | | | |
| AH1293/27-33 Proof | — | Value: 285 | | | | |

**Note:** Above value for common date of proof

| Date | Mintage | VG | F | VF | XF | Unc |
|---|---|---|---|---|---|---|
| AH1293/27 W | 448,000 | — | 5.00 | 12.50 | 20.00 | 50.00 |
| AH1293/29 W | 600,000 | — | 5.00 | 10.00 | 20.00 | 50.00 |
| AH1293/29H | 3,465,000 | — | 5.00 | 10.00 | 20.00 | 50.00 |
| AH1293/30H | 1,213,000 | — | 5.00 | 10.00 | 22.50 | 60.00 |
| AH1293/31H | 1,959,000 | — | 5.00 | 10.00 | 22.50 | 60.00 |
| AH1293/32H | | — | 5.00 | 10.00 | 20.00 | 50.00 |
| AH1293/33H | 2,800,000 | — | 3.00 | 7.50 | 20.00 | 50.00 |

**5 QIRSH** KM# 298 **Weight:** 0.4200 g. **Composition:** 0.8750 Gold .0118 oz. AGW **Obverse:** "Al Ghazi" at right of toughra **Note:** Mintname Misr.

| Date | Mintage | VG | F | VF | XF | Unc |
|---|---|---|---|---|---|---|
| AH1293/24(1898) | — | 25.00 | 50.00 | 90.00 | 145 | — |
| AH1293/26(1900) | — | 25.00 | 50.00 | 90.00 | 145 | — |
| AH1293/27-33 Proof | — | — | — | — | — | — |
| AH1293/34 | 8,000 | — | 35.00 | 60.00 | 80.00 | — |

**10 QIRSH** KM# 295 **Weight:** 14.0000 g. **Composition:** 0.8330 Silver .3749 oz. ASW ASW **Obverse:** Flower at right of toughra **Note:** Mintname Misr.

| Date | Mintage | VG | F | VF | XF | Unc |
|---|---|---|---|---|---|---|
| AH1293/27-33 Proof | — | Value: 435 | | | | |

**Note:** Above value for common date of proof

| Date | Mintage | VG | F | VF | XF | Unc |
|---|---|---|---|---|---|---|
| AH1293/27 W | 250,000 | — | 15.00 | 25.00 | 60.00 | 150 |
| AH1293/29 W | Est. 2,450,000 | — | 8.00 | 15.00 | 40.00 | 100 |
| AH1293/29H | 2,950,000 | — | 8.00 | 15.00 | 35.00 | 100 |
| AH1293/30H | 1,000,000 | — | 8.00 | 15.00 | 35.00 | 100 |
| AH1293/31H | 1,250,000 | — | 10.00 | 20.00 | 45.00 | 150 |
| AH1293/32H | | — | 8.00 | 15.00 | 35.00 | 100 |
| AH1293/33H | 2,400,000 | — | 8.00 | 12.50 | 35.00 | 100 |

**10 QIRSH** KM# 282 **Weight:** 0.8544 g. **Composition:** 0.8750 Gold .0240 oz. AGW **Obverse:** Al-Ghazi at right of toughra **Note:** Mintname Misr.

| Date | Mintage | VG | F | VF | XF | Unc |
|---|---|---|---|---|---|---|
| AH1293/34 | 5,000 | — | 40.00 | 70.00 | 110 | — |

**20 QIRSH** KM# 296 **Weight:** 28.0000 g. **Composition:** 0.8330 Silver .7499 oz. ASW ASW **Note:** Mintname Misr.

| Date | Mintage | VG | F | VF | XF | Unc |
|---|---|---|---|---|---|---|
| AH1293/27-33 Proof | — | Value: 825 | | | | |

**Note:** Above value for common date of proof

| Date | Mintage | VG | F | VF | XF | Unc |
|---|---|---|---|---|---|---|
| AH1293/27 W | 25,000 | — | 17.50 | 50.00 | 150 | 500 |
| AH1293/29 W | 50,000 | — | 15.00 | 40.00 | 100 | 425 |
| AH1293/29H | 425,000 | — | 12.00 | 30.00 | 80.00 | 400 |
| AH1293/30H | 200,000 | — | 12.00 | 30.00 | 80.00 | 400 |
| AH1293/31H | 250,000 | — | 12.00 | 30.00 | 80.00 | 400 |
| AH1293/32H | | — | 12.00 | 30.00 | 85.00 | 400 |
| AH1293/33H | 300,000 | — | 12.00 | 30.00 | 85.00 | 400 |

**20 QIRSH** KM# 296 **Weight:** 28.0000 g. **Composition:** 0.8330 Silver .7499 oz. ASW ASW **Note:** Mintname Misr.

| Date | Mintage | F | VF | XF | Unc |
|---|---|---|---|---|---|
| AH1293/27-33(1901) Proof | — | Value: 825 | | | |

**Note:** Above value for common date of proof

| Date | Mintage | F | VF | XF | Unc |
|---|---|---|---|---|---|
| AH1293/27 W | 25,000 | | | | |
| AH1293/29 W | 50,000 | | | | |
| AH1293/29H | 425,000 | | | | |
| AH1293/30H | 200,000 | | | | |
| AH1293/31H | 250,000 | | | | |
| AH1293/32H | | | | | |
| AH1293/33H | 300,000 | | | | |

## Muhammad V

### AH1327-1332/1909-1914AD

### OTTOMAN COINAGE

**1/40 QIRSH** KM# 300 **Composition:** Bronze **Note:** Mintname Misr.

| Date | Mintage | VG | F | VF | XF | Unc |
|---|---|---|---|---|---|---|
| AH1327/2H | 2,000,000 | — | 1.50 | 3.00 | 7.50 | 25.00 |
| AH1327/3H | 2,000,000 | — | 1.50 | 3.00 | 7.50 | 25.00 |
| AH1327/4H | 1,200,000 | — | 1.50 | 3.00 | 7.50 | 25.00 |
| AH1327/6H | 1,200,000 | — | 1.00 | 2.00 | 5.00 | 20.00 |

**1/20 QIRSH** KM# 301 **Composition:** Bronze **Note:** Mintname Misr.

| Date | Mintage | VG | F | VF | XF | Unc |
|---|---|---|---|---|---|---|
| AH1327/2H | 2,000,000 | — | 1.00 | 3.00 | 6.00 | 18.00 |
| AH1327/3H | 2,000,000 | — | 1.50 | 4.00 | 8.00 | 25.00 |
| AH1327/4H | 2,400,000 | — | 1.00 | 3.00 | 6.00 | 18.00 |
| AH1327/6H | 1,400,000 | — | 0.75 | 2.00 | 6.00 | 18.00 |

**1/10 QIRSH** KM# 302 **Composition:** Copper-Nickel **Note:** Mintname Misr.

| Date | Mintage | VG | F | VF | XF | Unc |
|---|---|---|---|---|---|---|
| AH1327/2-6H Proof | — | Value: 110 | | | | |

**Note:** Above value for common date of proof

| Date | Mintage | VG | F | VF | XF | Unc |
|---|---|---|---|---|---|---|
| AH1327/2H | 3,000,000 | — | 3.00 | 6.00 | 10.00 | 25.00 |
| AH1327/3 | 1,000,000 | — | 5.00 | 12.00 | 20.00 | 50.00 |
| AH1327/4H | 3,000,000 | — | 1.00 | 2.00 | 4.00 | 12.50 |
| AH1327/6H | 3,000,000 | — | 0.75 | 1.50 | 3.00 | 12.50 |

**2/10 QIRSH** KM# 303 **Composition:** Copper-Nickel **Note:** Mintname Misr

| Date | Mintage | F | VF | XF | Unc |
|---|---|---|---|---|---|
| AH1327/2(1910) H | 1,000,000 | 2.00 | 4.00 | 7.00 | 25.00 |
| AH1327/3(1911) | 500,000 | 3.00 | 10.00 | 15.00 | 35.00 |
| AH1327/4(1911) H | 1,000,000 | 2.00 | 4.00 | 7.00 | 25.00 |
| AH1327/6(1913) H | 1,000,000 | 1.25 | 3.00 | 7.00 | 25.00 |
| AH1327/2-6(1914) H Proof | — | Value: 120 | | | |

**Note:** Above value for common date proof

**5/10 QIRSH** KM# 304 **Composition:** Copper-Nickel **Note:** Mintname Misr.

| Date | Mintage | VG | F | VF | XF | Unc |
|---|---|---|---|---|---|---|
| AH1327/2H | 2,131,000 | — | 2.50 | 6.00 | 15.00 | 50.00 |
| AH1327/3 | 1,000,000 | — | 5.00 | 15.00 | 35.00 | 75.00 |
| AH1327/4H | 3,327,000 | — | 1.00 | 2.50 | 6.00 | 25.00 |
| AH1327/6H | 3,000,000 | — | 1.00 | 2.50 | 6.00 | 25.00 |

**QIRSH** KM# 305 **Weight:** 1.4000 g. **Composition:** 0.8330 Silver .0375 oz. ASW **Note:** Mintname Misr.

| Date | Mintage | VG | F | VF | XF | Unc |
|---|---|---|---|---|---|---|
| AH1327/2H | 251,000 | — | 2.00 | 4.00 | 15.00 | 28.00 |
| AH1327/3H | 171,000 | — | 2.25 | 4.50 | 16.00 | 35.00 |

**QIRSH** KM# 306 **Composition:** Copper-Nickel **Note:** Mintname Misr.

| Date | Mintage | VG | F | VF | XF | Unc |
|---|---|---|---|---|---|---|
| AH1327/2H | 1,000,000 | — | 2.00 | 5.00 | 12.00 | 35.00 |
| AH1327/3 | 300,000 | — | 20.00 | 40.00 | 75.00 | 150 |
| AH1327/4H | 500,000 | — | 4.00 | 8.00 | 22.50 | 65.00 |
| AH1327/6H | 2,500,000 | — | 2.00 | 4.00 | 8.00 | 28.00 |

**2 QIRSH** KM# 307 **Weight:** 2.8000 g. **Composition:** 0.8330 Silver .0750 oz. ASW **Note:** Mintname Misr.

| Date | Mintage | F | VF | XF | Unc |
|---|---|---|---|---|---|
| AH1327/2H | 250,000 | 5.00 | 12.50 | 28.00 | 90.00 |
| AH1327/3H | 300,000 | 5.00 | 12.50 | 28.00 | 90.00 |

**5 QIRSH** KM# 308 **Weight:** 7.0000 g. **Composition:** 0.8330 Silver .1875 oz. ASW ASW **Note:** Mintname Misr.

| Date | Mintage | F | VF | XF | Unc |
|---|---|---|---|---|---|
| AH1327/2-6H Proof | — | Value: 350 | | | |

**Note:** Above value for common date proof

| Date | Mintage | F | VF | XF | Unc |
|---|---|---|---|---|---|
| AH1327/2H | 574,000 | 10.00 | 30.00 | 60.00 | 150 |
| AH1327/3H | 2,400,000 | 5.00 | 12.50 | 30.00 | 70.00 |
| AH1327/4H | 1,351,000 | 6.00 | 15.00 | 35.00 | 85.00 |
| AH1327/6H | 7,400,000 | 4.00 | 10.00 | 20.00 | 55.00 |

**10 QIRSH** KM# 309 **Weight:** 14.0000 g. **Composition:** 0.8330 Silver .3749 oz. ASW ASW **Note:** Mintname Misr.

| Date | Mintage | F | VF | XF | Unc |
|---|---|---|---|---|---|
| AH1327/2-6H Proof | — | Value: 475 | | | |

**Note:** Above value for common date proof

| Date | Mintage | F | VF | XF | Unc |
|---|---|---|---|---|---|
| AH1327/2H | 300,000 | 20.00 | 30.00 | 60.00 | 200 |
| AH1327/3H | 1,300,000 | 8.00 | 15.00 | 30.00 | 115 |
| AH1327/4H | 300,000 | 10.00 | 25.00 | 40.00 | 200 |
| AH1327/6H | 4,212,000 | 6.00 | 12.50 | 25.00 | 100 |

**20 QIRSH** KM# 310 **Weight:** 28.0000 g. **Composition:** 0.8330 Silver .7499 oz. ASW ASW **Note:** Mintname Misr.

| Date | Mintage | F | VF | XF | Unc |
|---|---|---|---|---|---|
| AH1327/2-6H Proof | — | Value: 950 | | | |

**Note:** Above value for common date proof

| Date | Mintage | F | VF | XF | Unc |
|---|---|---|---|---|---|
| AH1327/2H | 75,000 | 25.00 | 45.00 | 160 | 500 |
| AH1327/3(1911) H | 600,000 | 12.50 | 25.00 | 75.00 | 325 |
| AH1327/4(1911) H | 100,000 | 20.00 | 35.00 | 90.00 | 425 |
| AH1327/6(1913) H | 875,000 | 11.50 | 22.50 | 60.00 | 300 |

# BRITISH OCCUPATION
## AH1333-1341/1914-1922AD.

# Hussein Kamil
### As Sultan, AH1333-1336/1914-1917AD

## OCCUPATION COINAGE
British

**1/2 MILLIEME** KM# 312 **Composition:** Bronze **Note:** Accession date, AH1333.

| Date | Mintage | F | VF | XF | Unc |
|---|---|---|---|---|---|
| AH1335-1917 | 4,000,000 | 1.35 | 3.50 | 7.50 | 25.00 |

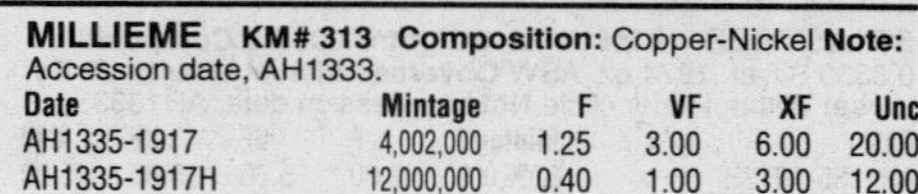

**MILLIEME** KM# 313 **Composition:** Copper-Nickel **Note:** Accession date, AH1333.

| Date | Mintage | F | VF | XF | Unc |
|---|---|---|---|---|---|
| AH1335-1917 | 4,002,000 | 1.25 | 3.00 | 6.00 | 20.00 |
| AH1335-1917H | 12,000,000 | 0.40 | 1.00 | 3.00 | 12.00 |

**2 MILLIEMES** KM# 314 **Composition:** Copper-Nickel **Note:** Accession date, AH1333.

| Date | Mintage | F | VF | XF | Unc |
|---|---|---|---|---|---|
| AH1335-1916H | 300,000 | 1.25 | 3.00 | 7.50 | 30.00 |
| AH1335-1917 | 3,006,000 | 1.00 | 2.50 | 6.50 | 22.00 |
| AH1335-1917H | 9,000,000 | 0.40 | 1.00 | 3.00 | 14.00 |

**5 MILLIEMES** KM# 315 **Composition:** Copper-Nickel **Note:** Accession date, AH1333.

| Date | Mintage | F | VF | XF | Unc |
|---|---|---|---|---|---|
| AH1335-1916 | 3,000,000 | 2.00 | 5.00 | 10.00 | 25.00 |
| AH1335-1916H | 3,000,000 | 1.35 | 3.50 | 8.00 | 20.00 |
| AH1335-1917 | 6,776,000 | 1.00 | 2.50 | 6.00 | 15.00 |
| AH1335-1917H | 37,000,000 | 0.60 | 1.50 | 2.50 | 8.00 |

**10 MILLIEMES** KM# 316 **Composition:** Copper-Nickel **Note:** Accession date, AH1333.

| Date | Mintage | F | VF | XF | Unc |
|---|---|---|---|---|---|
| AH1335-1916 | 1,006,999 | 2.00 | 5.00 | 10.00 | 35.00 |
| AH1335-1916H | 1,000,000 | 1.50 | 4.00 | 8.00 | 25.00 |
| AH1335-1917 | 1,010,999 | 2.00 | 5.00 | 15.00 | 40.00 |
| AH1335-1917H | 6,000,000 | 0.75 | 2.00 | 4.00 | 15.00 |
| AH1335-1917KN | 4,000,000 | 1.25 | 3.00 | 6.00 | 20.00 |

**2 PIASTRES** KM# 317.1 **Weight:** 2.8000 g. **Composition:** 0.8330 Silver .0749 oz. ASW **Note:** Accession date, AH1333.

| Date | Mintage | F | VF | XF | Unc |
|---|---|---|---|---|---|
| AH1335-1916 | 2,505,000 | 1.50 | 4.00 | 10.00 | 30.00 |
| AH1335-1917 | 4,461,000 | 1.00 | 2.50 | 5.00 | 20.00 |

**2 PIASTRES** KM# 317.2 **Weight:** 2.8000 g. **Composition:** 0.8330 Silver .0749 oz. ASW **Obverse:** Without inner circle **Reverse:** Without inner circle **Note:** Accession date, AH1333.

| Date | Mintage | F | VF | XF | Unc |
|---|---|---|---|---|---|
| AH1335-1917H | 2,180,000 | 1.00 | 2.50 | 5.00 | 15.00 |

**5 PIASTRES** KM# 318.1 **Weight:** 7.0000 g. **Composition:** 0.8330 Silver .1874 oz. ASW **Note:** Accession date, AH1333.

| Date | Mintage | F | VF | XF | Unc |
|---|---|---|---|---|---|
| AH1335-1916 | 6,000,000 | 2.00 | 5.00 | 15.00 | 35.00 |
| AH1335-1917 | 9,218,000 | 1.50 | 4.00 | 12.50 | 32.00 |

**5 PIASTRES** KM# 318.2 **Weight:** 7.0000 g. **Composition:** 0.8330 Silver .1874 oz. ASW **Obverse:** Without inner circle **Reverse:** Without inner circle **Note:** Accession date, AH1333.

| Date | Mintage | F | VF | XF | Unc |
|---|---|---|---|---|---|
| AH1335-1917H | 5,036,000 | 2.00 | 5.00 | 15.00 | 45.00 |
| AH1335-1917H Proof | — | Value: 325 | | | |

**10 PIASTRES** KM# 319 **Weight:** 14.0000 g. **Composition:** 0.8330 Silver .3749 oz. ASW **Note:** Accession date, AH1333.

| Date | Mintage | F | VF | XF | Unc |
|---|---|---|---|---|---|
| AH1335-1916 | 2,900,000 | 4.00 | 10.00 | 25.00 | 95.00 |
| AH1335-1917 | 4,859,000 | 4.00 | 10.00 | 20.00 | 85.00 |

**10 PIASTRES** KM# 320 **Weight:** 14.0000 g. **Composition:** 0.8330 Silver .3749 oz. ASW **Obverse:** Without inner circle **Reverse:** Without inner circle **Note:** Accession date, AH1333.

| Date | Mintage | F | VF | XF | Unc |
|---|---|---|---|---|---|
| AH1335-1917H | 2,000,000 | 4.00 | 10.00 | 28.00 | 100 |

**20 PIASTRES** KM# 321 **Weight:** 28.0000 g. **Composition:** 0.8330 Silver .7499 oz. ASW **Note:** Accession date, AH1333.

| Date | Mintage | F | VF | XF | Unc |
|---|---|---|---|---|---|
| AH1335-1916 | 1,500,000 | 6.50 | 16.00 | 35.00 | 160 |
| AH1335-1917 | 840,000 | 6.50 | 16.00 | 35.00 | 180 |
| AH1335-1917 Proof | — | Value: 750 | | | |

**20 PIASTRES** KM# 322 **Weight:** 28.0000 g. **Composition:** 0.8330 Silver .7499 oz. ASW **Obverse:** Without inner circle **Reverse:** Without inner circle **Note:** Accession date, AH1333.

| Date | Mintage | F | VF | XF | Unc |
|---|---|---|---|---|---|
| AH1335-1917H | 250,000 | 20.00 | 40.00 | 70.00 | 300 |

**100 PIASTRES** KM# 324 **Weight:** 8.5000 g. **Composition:** 0.8750 Gold .2391 oz. AGW **Note:** Accession date, AH1333.

| Date | Mintage | F | VF | XF | Unc |
|---|---|---|---|---|---|
| AH1335-1916 | 10,000 | 50.00 | 100 | 150 | 300 |
| AH1335-1916 Proof | — | Value: 1,500 | | | |

**Note:** Restrikes may exist

# Fuad I

## As Sultan, AH1335-1341/1917-1922AD

## OCCUPATION COINAGE

British

**2 PIASTRES** KM# 325 **Weight:** 2.8000 g. **Composition:** 0.8330 Silver .0749 oz. ASW **Note:** Accession date, AH1335.

| Date | Mintage | F | VF | XF | Unc |
|---|---|---|---|---|---|
| AH1338-1920H | 2,820,000 | 37.50 | 75.00 | 150 | 365 |

**5 PIASTRES** KM# 326 **Weight:** 7.0000 g. **Composition:** 0.8330 Silver .1874 oz. ASW **Note:** Accession date, AH1335.

| Date | Mintage | F | VF | XF | Unc |
|---|---|---|---|---|---|
| AH1338-1920H | 1,000,000 | 17.50 | 35.00 | 80.00 | 340 |

**10 PIASTRES** KM# 327 **Weight:** 14.0000 g. **Composition:** 0.8330 Silver .3749 oz. ASW **Note:** Accession date, AH1335.

| Date | Mintage | F | VF | XF | Unc |
|---|---|---|---|---|---|
| AH1338-1920H | 500,000 | 17.50 | 35.00 | 85.00 | 350 |

**20 PIASTRES** KM# 328 **Weight:** 28.0000 g. **Composition:** 0.8330 Silver .7499 oz. ASW **Note:** Accession date, AH1335.

| Date | Mintage | F | VF | XF | Unc |
|---|---|---|---|---|---|
| AH1338-1920H Rare | 2 | — | — | — | — |

# KINGDOM

## AH1341-1372/1922-1952AD.

# Fuad I

## As King, AH1341-1355/1922-1936AD

## DECIMAL COINAGE

**1/2 MILLIEME** KM# 330 **Composition:** Bronze

| Date | Mintage | F | VF | XF | Unc |
|---|---|---|---|---|---|
| AH1342-1924H | 3,000,000 | 2.00 | 5.00 | 10.00 | 25.00 |
| AH1342-1924H Proof | — | Value: 120 | | | |

**1/2 MILLIEME** KM# 343 **Composition:** Bronze

| Date | Mintage | F | VF | XF | Unc |
|---|---|---|---|---|---|
| AH1348-1929BP | 1,000,000 | 6.00 | 15.00 | 25.00 | 50.00 |
| AH1351-1932H | 1,000,000 | 3.00 | 7.50 | 15.00 | 30.00 |
| AH1351-1932H Proof | — | Value: 160 | | | |

**MILLIEME** KM# 331 **Composition:** Bronze

| Date | Mintage | F | VF | XF | Unc |
|---|---|---|---|---|---|
| AH1342-1924H | 6,500,000 | 1.25 | 3.00 | 6.00 | 15.00 |

**MILLIEME** KM# 344 **Composition:** Bronze

| Date | Mintage | F | VF | XF | Unc |
|---|---|---|---|---|---|
| AH1348-1929BP | 4,500,000 | 1.50 | 4.00 | 8.00 | 20.00 |
| AH1351-1932H | 2,500,000 | 0.50 | 1.25 | 3.00 | 15.00 |
| AH1351-1932H Proof | — | Value: 120 | | | |
| AH1352-1933H | 5,110,000 | 1.25 | 3.00 | 6.00 | 15.00 |
| AH1354-1935H | 18,000,000 | 0.20 | 0.50 | 2.00 | 8.00 |

**2 MILLIEMES** KM# 332 **Composition:** Copper-Nickel

| Date | Mintage | F | VF | XF | Unc |
|---|---|---|---|---|---|
| AH1342-1924H | 4,500,000 | 1.25 | 3.00 | 8.00 | 20.00 |
| AH1342-1924H Proof | — | Value: 120 | | | |

**2 MILLIEMES** KM# 345 **Composition:** Copper-Nickel

| Date | Mintage | F | VF | XF | Unc |
|---|---|---|---|---|---|
| AH1348-1929BP | Est. 3,500,000 | 0.40 | 1.00 | 3.00 | 10.00 |

**2-1/2 MILLIEMES** **KM# 356** **Composition:** Copper-Nickel

| Date | Mintage | F | VF | XF | Unc |
|---|---|---|---|---|---|
| AH1352-1933 | 4,000,000 | 1.25 | 3.00 | 8.00 | 30.00 |

**5 MILLIEMES** **KM# 333** **Composition:** Copper-Nickel

| Date | Mintage | F | VF | XF | Unc |
|---|---|---|---|---|---|
| AH1342-1924 | 6,000,000 | 1.25 | 3.00 | 7.50 | 28.00 |

**5 MILLIEMES** **KM# 346** **Composition:** Copper-Nickel

| Date | Mintage | F | VF | XF | Unc |
|---|---|---|---|---|---|
| AH1348-1929BP | 4,000,000 | 0.75 | 2.00 | 8.00 | 25.00 |
| AH1352-1933H | 3,000,000 | 1.50 | 4.00 | 12.00 | 35.00 |
| AH1354-1935H | 8,000,000 | 0.80 | 1.00 | 5.00 | 12.50 |
| AH1354-1935H Proof | — | Value: 120 | | | |

**10 MILLIEMES** **KM# 334** **Composition:** Copper-Nickel

| Date | Mintage | F | VF | XF | Unc |
|---|---|---|---|---|---|
| AH1342-1924 | 2,000,000 | 2.00 | 5.00 | 15.00 | 50.00 |

**10 MILLIEMES** **KM# 347** **Composition:** Copper-Nickel

| Date | Mintage | F | VF | XF | Unc |
|---|---|---|---|---|---|
| AH1348-1929BP | 1,500,000 | 1.35 | 3.50 | 10.00 | 38.00 |
| AH1352-1933H | 1,500,000 | 1.35 | 3.50 | 10.00 | 45.00 |
| AH1354-1935H | 4,000,000 | 0.75 | 2.00 | 7.50 | 20.00 |

**2 PIASTRES** **KM# 335** **Weight:** 2.8000 g. **Composition:** 0.8330 Silver .0749 oz. ASW ASW

| Date | Mintage | F | VF | XF | Unc |
|---|---|---|---|---|---|
| AH1342-1923H | 2,500,000 | 1.75 | 4.50 | 11.50 | 35.00 |

**2 PIASTRES** **KM# 348** **Weight:** 2.8000 g. **Composition:** 0.8330 Silver .0749 oz. ASW ASW

| Date | Mintage | F | VF | XF | Unc |
|---|---|---|---|---|---|
| AH1348-1929BP | 500,000 | 1.75 | 2.00 | 6.00 | 20.00 |

**Note:** Edge varieties exist

**5 PIASTRES** **KM# 336** **Weight:** 7.0000 g. **Composition:** 0.8330 Silver .1874 oz. ASW ASW

| Date | Mintage | F | VF | XF | Unc |
|---|---|---|---|---|---|
| AH1341-1923 | 800,000 | 4.00 | 10.00 | 27.00 | 60.00 |
| AH1341-1923H | 1,800,000 | 2.50 | 6.00 | 25.00 | 60.00 |
| AH1341-1923H Proof | — | Value: 250 | | | |

**5 PIASTRES** **KM# 349** **Weight:** 7.0000 g. **Composition:** 0.8330 Silver .1874 oz. ASW ASW

| Date | Mintage | F | VF | XF | Unc |
|---|---|---|---|---|---|
| AH1348-1929BP | 800,000 | 4.00 | 10.00 | 35.00 | 65.00 |
| AH1352-1933 | 1,300,000 | 3.00 | 7.50 | 25.00 | 55.00 |
| AH1352-1933 Proof | — | Value: 250 | | | |

**10 PIASTRES** **KM# 337** **Weight:** 14.0000 g. **Composition:** 0.8330 Silver .3749 oz. ASW ASW

| Date | Mintage | F | VF | XF | Unc |
|---|---|---|---|---|---|
| AH1341-1923 | 400,000 | 5.00 | 12.50 | 40.00 | 120 |
| AH1341-1923H | 1,000,000 | 5.00 | 12.50 | 40.00 | 120 |
| AH1341-1923H Proof | — | Value: 450 | | | |

**10 PIASTRES** **KM# 350** **Weight:** 14.0000 g. **Composition:** 0.8330 Silver .3749 oz. ASW ASW

| Date | Mintage | F | VF | XF | Unc |
|---|---|---|---|---|---|
| AH1348-1929BP | 400,000 | 5.00 | 12.50 | 35.00 | 100 |
| AH1352-1933 | Est. 350,000 | 5.00 | 12.50 | 35.00 | 100 |
| AH1352-1933 Proof | — | Value: 475 | | | |

**20 PIASTRES** **KM# 338** **Weight:** 28.0000 g. **Composition:** 0.8330 Silver .7499 oz. ASW ASW

| Date | Mintage | F | VF | XF | Unc |
|---|---|---|---|---|---|
| AH1341-1923 | 100,000 | 20.00 | 40.00 | 90.00 | 425 |
| AH1341-1923H | 50,000 | 20.00 | 40.00 | 90.00 | 425 |
| AH1341-1923H Proof | — | Value: 875 | | | |

**20 PIASTRES** **KM# 339** **Weight:** 1.7000 g. **Composition:** 0.8750 Gold .0478 oz. AGW

| Date | Mintage | F | VF | XF | Unc |
|---|---|---|---|---|---|
| AH1341-1923 | 65,000 | 25.00 | 40.00 | 60.00 | 115 |

**20 PIASTRES** **KM# 351** **Weight:** 1.7000 g. **Composition:** 0.8750 Gold .0478 oz. AGW **Obverse:** Bust left

| Date | Mintage | F | VF | XF | Unc |
|---|---|---|---|---|---|
| AH1348 Proof | — | — | — | — | — |
| AH1348-1929 | — | 25.00 | 40.00 | 55.00 | 110 |
| AH1349-1930 | — | 25.00 | 40.00 | 55.00 | 110 |
| AH1349-1930 Proof | — | — | — | — | — |

**20 PIASTRES** **KM# 352** **Weight:** 28.0000 g. **Composition:** 0.8330 Silver .7499 oz. ASW ASW

| Date | Mintage | F | VF | XF | Unc |
|---|---|---|---|---|---|
| AH1348-1929BP | 50,000 | 15.00 | 30.00 | 65.00 | 350 |
| AH1352-1933 | 25,000 | 12.50 | 25.00 | 50.00 | 300 |
| AH1352-1933 Proof | — | — | — | — | — |

**50 PIASTRES** KM# 340 **Weight:** 4.2500 g. **Composition:** 0.8750 Gold .1195 oz. AGW

| Date | Mintage | F | VF | XF | Unc |
|---|---|---|---|---|---|
| AH1341-1923 | 18,000 | 40.00 | 70.00 | 90.00 | 145 |

**50 PIASTRES** KM# 353 **Weight:** 4.2500 g. **Composition:** 0.8750 Gold .1195 oz. AGW

| Date | Mintage | F | VF | XF | Unc |
|---|---|---|---|---|---|
| AH1348-1929 | — | 47.50 | 80.00 | 100 | 160 |
| AH1348-1929 Proof | — | — | — | — | — |
| AH1349-1930 | — | 42.50 | 70.00 | 80.00 | 130 |
| AH1349-1930 Proof | — | — | — | — | — |

**100 PIASTRES** KM# 341 **Weight:** 8.5000 g. **Composition:** 0.8750 Gold .2391 oz. AGW

| Date | Mintage | F | VF | XF | Unc |
|---|---|---|---|---|---|
| AH1340-1922 | 25,000 | BV | 115 | 135 | 245 |

**100 PIASTRES** KM# 354 **Weight:** 8.5000 g. **Composition:** 0.8750 Gold .2391 oz. AGW **Obverse:** Bust of Fuad I left

| Date | Mintage | F | VF | XF | Unc |
|---|---|---|---|---|---|
| AH1348-1929 | — | BV | 120 | 140 | 255 |
| AH1349-1930 | — | BV | 115 | 135 | 245 |
| AH1349-1930 Proof | — | — | — | — | — |

**500 PIASTRES** KM# 342 **Weight:** 42.5000 g. **Composition:** 0.8750 Gold 1.1957 oz. AGW

| Date | Mintage | F | VF | XF | Unc |
|---|---|---|---|---|---|
| AH1340-1922 | 1,800 | — | — | 800 | 1,500 |
| AH1340-1922 Proof | — | Value: 1,650 | | | |

**Note:** Circulation coins were struck in both red and yellow gold

**500 PIASTRES** KM# 355 **Weight:** 42.5000 g. **Composition:** 0.8750 Gold 1.1957 oz. AGW

| Date | Mintage | F | VF | XF | Unc |
|---|---|---|---|---|---|
| AH1348-1929 | — | — | — | 675 | 1,250 |
| AH1349-1930 | — | — | — | 675 | 1,250 |
| AH1351-1932 | — | — | — | 675 | 1,250 |
| AH1351-1932 Proof | — | Value: 1,450 | | | |

## Farouk
## AH1355-1372/1936-1952AD

### DECIMAL COINAGE

**1/2 MILLIEME** KM# 357 **Composition:** Bronze

| Date | Mintage | F | VF | XF | Unc |
|---|---|---|---|---|---|
| AH1357-1938 | 4,000,000 | 1.50 | 4.00 | 6.00 | 18.00 |
| AH1357-1938 Proof | — | Value: 100 | | | |

**MILLIEME** KM# 358 **Composition:** Bronze

| Date | Mintage | F | VF | XF | Unc |
|---|---|---|---|---|---|
| AH1357-1938 | 26,240,000 | 0.20 | 0.50 | 2.00 | 7.00 |
| AH1357-1938 Proof | — | Value: 120 | | | |
| AH1364-1945 | 10,000,000 | 1.25 | 3.00 | 10.00 | 50.00 |
| AH1366-1947 | — | 1.25 | 3.00 | 10.00 | 50.00 |
| AH1369-1950 | 5,000,000 | 0.40 | 1.00 | 3.00 | 10.00 |
| AH1369-1950 Proof | — | Value: 85.00 | | | |

**MILLIEME** KM# 362 **Composition:** Copper-Nickel

| Date | Mintage | F | VF | XF | Unc |
|---|---|---|---|---|---|
| AH1357-1938 | 3,500,000 | 1.00 | 2.50 | 5.00 | 15.00 |

**2 MILLIEMES** KM# 359 **Composition:** Copper-Nickel

| Date | Mintage | F | VF | XF | Unc |
|---|---|---|---|---|---|
| AH1357-1938 | 2,500,000 | 1.50 | 4.00 | 10.00 | 25.00 |
| AH1357-1938 Proof | — | Value: 140 | | | |

**5 MILLIEMES** KM# 360 **Composition:** Bronze

| Date | Mintage | F | VF | XF | Unc |
|---|---|---|---|---|---|
| AH1357-1938 | — | 0.40 | 1.00 | 3.00 | 10.00 |
| AH1357-1938 Proof | — | Value: 65.00 | | | |
| AH1362-1943 | — | 0.40 | 1.00 | 3.00 | 10.00 |

**5 MILLIEMES** KM# 363 **Composition:** Copper-Nickel

| Date | Mintage | F | VF | XF | Unc |
|---|---|---|---|---|---|
| AH1357-1938 | 7,000,000 | 0.40 | 1.00 | 3.00 | 10.00 |
| AH1357-1938 Proof | — | Value: 75.00 | | | |
| AH1360-1941 | 11,500,000 | 0.20 | 0.50 | 2.50 | 8.00 |

**10 MILLIEMES** KM# 361 **Composition:** Bronze

| Date | Mintage | F | VF | XF | Unc |
|---|---|---|---|---|---|
| AH1357-1938 | — | 0.40 | 1.00 | 3.00 | 10.00 |
| AH1357-1938 Proof | — | Value: 140 | | | |
| AH1362-1943 | — | — | 0.75 | 3.00 | 10.00 |

**10 MILLIEMES** KM# 364 **Composition:** Copper-Nickel

| Date | Mintage | F | VF | XF | Unc |
|---|---|---|---|---|---|
| AH1357-1938 | 3,500,000 | 0.40 | 1.00 | 3.00 | 12.50 |
| AH1357-1938 Proof | — | Value: 85.00 | | | |
| AH1360-1941 | 5,322,000 | 0.40 | 1.00 | 3.00 | 12.50 |

**2 PIASTRES** KM# 365 **Weight:** 2.8000 g. **Composition:** 0.8330 Silver .0749 oz. ASW ASW

| Date | Mintage | F | VF | XF | Unc |
|---|---|---|---|---|---|
| AH1356-1937 | 500,000 | 0.60 | 1.50 | 3.00 | 8.00 |
| AH1356-1937 Proof | — | Value: 300 | | | |
| AH1358-1939 | 500,000 | 1.50 | 4.00 | 10.00 | 75.00 |
| AH1358-1939 Proof | — | Value: 200 | | | |
| AH1361-1942 | 10,000,000 | 0.60 | 1.50 | 4.00 | 10.00 |

**Note:** Normal and flat rim varieties exist for AH1361 coins

**2 PIASTRES** KM# 369 **Weight:** 2.8000 g. **Composition:** 0.5000 Silver .0450 oz. ASW ASW

| Date | Mintage | F | VF | XF | Unc |
|---|---|---|---|---|---|
| AH1363-1944 | 32,000 | 0.40 | 1.00 | 2.00 | 4.50 |

**5 PIASTRES** KM# 366 **Weight:** 7.0000 g. **Composition:** 0.8330 Silver .1874 oz. ASW ASW

| Date | Mintage | F | VF | XF | Unc |
|---|---|---|---|---|---|
| AH1356-1937 | — | 1.25 | 3.00 | 6.00 | 15.00 |
| AH1356-1937 Proof | — | Value: 275 | | | |
| AH1358-1939 | 8,000,000 | 1.25 | 3.00 | 6.00 | 15.00 |
| AH1358-1939 Proof | — | Value: 275 | | | |

**10 PIASTRES** KM# 367 **Weight:** 14.0000 g. **Composition:** 0.8330 Silver .3749 oz. ASW ASW

| Date | Mintage | F | VF | XF | Unc |
|---|---|---|---|---|---|
| AH1356-1937 | 2,800,000 | 3.00 | 7.50 | 10.00 | 32.00 |
| AH1356-1937 Proof | — | Value: 375 | | | |
| AH1358-1939 | 2,850,000 | 3.00 | 7.50 | 10.00 | 32.00 |
| AH1358-1939 Proof | — | Value: 300 | | | |

**20 PIASTRES** KM# 368 **Weight:** 28.0000 g. **Composition:** 0.8330 Silver .7499 oz. ASW ASW

| Date | Mintage | F | VF | XF | Unc |
|---|---|---|---|---|---|
| AH1356-1937 | — | 6.00 | 15.00 | 35.00 | 85.00 |
| AH1356-1937 Proof | — | Value: 1,000 | | | |

| Date | Mintage | F | VF | XF | Unc |
|---|---|---|---|---|---|
| AH1358-1939 | — | 6.00 | 15.00 | 35.00 | 85.00 |
| AH1358-1939 Proof | — | Value: 1,200 | | | |

**20 PIASTRES** **KM# 370** **Weight:** 1.7000 g. **Composition:** 0.8750 Gold .0478 oz. AGW **Subject:** Royal Wedding

| Date | Mintage | F | VF | XF | Unc |
|---|---|---|---|---|---|
| AH1357-1938 | 20,000 | — | 28.00 | 40.00 | 85.00 |

**50 PIASTRES** **KM# 371** **Weight:** 4.2500 g. **Composition:** 0.8750 Gold .1195 oz. AGW **Subject:** Royal Wedding

| Date | Mintage | F | VF | XF | Unc |
|---|---|---|---|---|---|
| AH1357-1938 | 10,000 | — | 75.00 | 125 | 215 |

**100 PIASTRES** **KM# 372** **Weight:** 8.5000 g. **Composition:** 0.8750 Gold .2391 oz. AGW **Subject:** Royal Wedding

| Date | Mintage | F | VF | XF | Unc |
|---|---|---|---|---|---|
| AH1357-1938 | 5,000 | — | 135 | 185 | 320 |

**Note:** Circulation coins were struck in both red and yellow gold

**500 PIASTRES** **KM# 373** **Weight:** 42.5000 g. **Composition:** 0.8750 Gold 1.1957 oz. AGW **Subject:** Royal Wedding

| Date | Mintage | F | VF | XF | Unc |
|---|---|---|---|---|---|
| AH1357-1938 | — | — | — | 1,250 | 2,000 |
| AH1357-1938 Proof | — | Value: 2,250 | | | |

# REPUBLIC
## AH1373-1378/1953-1958AD.
## DECIMAL COINAGE

**MILLIEME** **KM# 375** **Composition:** Aluminum-Bronze **Reverse:** Small sphinx with outlined base

| Date | Mintage | F | VF | XF | Unc |
|---|---|---|---|---|---|
| AH1373-1954 | — | — | 50.00 | 100 | 200 |
| AH1374-1954 | — | — | 3.00 | 6.00 | 25.00 |
| AH1374-1955 | — | — | 2.00 | 5.00 | 15.00 |
| AH1375-1955 | — | — | 2.00 | 5.00 | 15.00 |
| AH1375-1956 | — | — | 2.00 | 5.00 | 15.00 |

**MILLIEME** **KM# 376** **Composition:** Aluminum-Bronze **Reverse:** Small sphinx without base outlined

| Date | Mintage | F | VF | XF | Unc |
|---|---|---|---|---|---|
| AH1374-1954 | — | — | 2.00 | 5.00 | 15.00 |
| AH1373-1954 | — | — | — | — | — |
| AH1374-1955 | — | — | 1.00 | 2.00 | 5.00 |
| AH1375-1955 | — | — | 1.00 | 2.00 | 5.00 |
| AH1375-1956 | — | — | 1.50 | 2.50 | 10.00 |
| AH1376-1957 | — | — | — | — | — |

**MILLIEME** **KM# 377** **Composition:** Aluminum-Bronze **Reverse:** Large sphinx

| Date | Mintage | F | VF | XF | Unc |
|---|---|---|---|---|---|
| AH1375-1956 | — | — | 0.50 | 1.00 | 4.00 |
| AH1376-1957 | — | — | 0.75 | 1.50 | 5.00 |
| AH1377-1958 | — | — | 0.75 | 1.50 | 5.00 |

**5 MILLIEMES** **KM# 378** **Composition:** Aluminum-Bronze **Reverse:** Small sphinx with outlined base

| Date | Mintage | F | VF | XF | Unc |
|---|---|---|---|---|---|
| AH1373-1954 | — | — | 5.00 | 10.00 | 35.00 |
| AH1374-1954 | — | — | 4.00 | 8.00 | 25.00 |
| AH1374-1955 | — | — | 10.00 | 20.00 | 50.00 |
| AH1375-1956 | — | — | 3.00 | 6.00 | 15.00 |

**5 MILLIEMES** **KM# 379** **Composition:** Aluminum-Bronze **Reverse:** Large sphinx

| Date | Mintage | F | VF | XF | Unc |
|---|---|---|---|---|---|
| AH1376-1957 | — | — | 2.00 | 4.00 | 10.00 |
| AH1377-1957 | — | — | 2.00 | 4.00 | 10.00 |
| AH1377-1958 | — | — | 2.00 | 4.00 | 10.00 |

Thin *milliemes*

Thick *milliemes*

**10 MILLIEMES** **KM# 380** **Composition:** Aluminum-Bronze **Reverse:** Small sphinx without base outlined

| Date | Mintage | F | VF | XF | Unc |
|---|---|---|---|---|---|
| AH1373-1954 | — | — | 5.00 | 10.00 | 25.00 |
| **Note:** Thin milliemes | | | | | |
| AH1374-1954 | — | — | 4.00 | 8.00 | 20.00 |

| Date | Mintage | F | VF | XF | Unc |
|---|---|---|---|---|---|
| AH1374-1955 | — | — | 3.00 | 6.00 | 15.00 |

**Note:** Thick milliemes

**10 MILLIEMES** **KM# 381** **Composition:** Aluminum-Bronze **Reverse:** Large sphinx

| Date | Mintage | F | VF | XF | Unc |
|---|---|---|---|---|---|
| AH1374-1955 | — | — | 50.00 | 85.00 | 150 |
| AH1375-1956 | — | — | 3.00 | 6.00 | 15.00 |
| AH1376-1957 | — | — | 2.00 | 5.00 | 12.00 |
| AH1377-1958 | — | — | 2.00 | 5.00 | 12.00 |

**5 PIASTRES** **KM# 382** **Weight:** 3.5000 g. **Composition:** 0.7200 Silver .0810 oz. ASW ASW

| Date | Mintage | F | VF | XF | Unc |
|---|---|---|---|---|---|
| AH1375-1956 | — | — | 1.50 | 3.00 | 8.00 |
| AH1376-1956 | — | — | 3.00 | 5.00 | 10.00 |
| AH1376-1957 | — | — | 1.50 | 3.00 | 8.00 |

**10 PIASTRES** **KM# 383** **Weight:** 7.0000 g. **Composition:** 0.6250 Silver .1406 oz. ASW ASW

| Date | Mintage | F | VF | XF | Unc |
|---|---|---|---|---|---|
| AH1374-1955 | 1,408,000 | — | 3.50 | 7.00 | 18.00 |

**Note:** Varieties in date sizes exist

**10 PIASTRES** **KM# 383a** **Weight:** 7.0000 g. **Composition:** 0.7200 Silver .1620 oz. ASW ASW

| Date | Mintage | F | VF | XF | Unc |
|---|---|---|---|---|---|
| AH1375-1956 | — | — | 3.50 | 7.00 | 15.00 |
| AH1376-1957 | — | — | 3.50 | 6.00 | 12.00 |

**20 PIASTRES** **KM# 384** **Weight:** 14.0000 g. **Composition:** 0.7200 Silver .3241 oz. ASW ASW

| Date | Mintage | F | VF | XF | Unc |
|---|---|---|---|---|---|
| AH1375-1956 | — | — | 5.00 | 9.00 | 18.00 |

**25 PIASTRES** **KM# 385** **Weight:** 17.5000 g. **Composition:** 0.7200 Silver .4051 oz. ASW **Subject:** Suez Canal Nationalization

| Date | Mintage | F | VF | XF | Unc |
|---|---|---|---|---|---|
| AH1375-1956 | 258,000 | — | 6.00 | 10.00 | 20.00 |

**25 PIASTRES** **KM# 389** **Weight:** 17.5000 g. **Composition:** 0.7200 Silver .4051 oz. ASW **Subject:** National Assembly Inauguration

| Date | Mintage | F | VF | XF | Unc |
|---|---|---|---|---|---|
| AH1376-1957 | 246,000 | — | 6.00 | 9.00 | 17.00 |

**50 PIASTRES** **KM# 386** **Weight:** 28.0000 g. **Composition:** 0.9000 Silver .8102 oz. ASW **Subject:** Evacuation of the British

| Date | Mintage | F | VF | XF | Unc |
|---|---|---|---|---|---|
| AH1375-1956 | 250,000 | — | 7.50 | 13.50 | 22.00 |

**POUND** **KM# 387** **Weight:** 8.5000 g. **Composition:** 0.8750 Gold .2391 oz. AGW **Subject:** 3rd and 5th Anniversaries of Revolution **Reverse:** Horse, chariot, and archer

| Date | Mintage | F | VF | XF | Unc |
|---|---|---|---|---|---|
| AH1374-1955 | 16,000 | — | — | 130 | 210 |
| AH1377-1957 | 10,000 | — | — | 140 | 220 |

**Note:** Struck in red and yellow gold

**5 POUNDS** **KM# 388** **Weight:** 42.5000 g. **Composition:** 0.8750 Gold 1.1957 oz. AGW **Subject:** 3rd and 5th Anniversaries of Revolution **Reverse:** Horse, chariot, and archer

| Date | Mintage | F | VF | XF | Unc |
|---|---|---|---|---|---|
| AH1374-1955 | — | — | — | 650 | 1,200 |
| AH1377-1957 | — | — | — | 650 | 1,200 |

**Note:** Struck in red and yellow gold

# UNITED ARAB REPUBLIC

## AH1378-1391/1958-1971AD.

## DECIMAL COINAGE

**MILLIEME** **KM# 393** **Composition:** Aluminum-Bronze

| Date | Mintage | F | VF | XF | Unc |
|---|---|---|---|---|---|
| AH1380-1960 | — | — | 0.10 | 0.15 | 0.30 |
| AH1386-1966 Proof | — | Value: 3.00 | | | |

**2 MILLIEMES** **KM# 403** **Composition:** Aluminum-Bronze

| Date | Mintage | F | VF | XF | Unc |
|---|---|---|---|---|---|
| AH1381-1962 | — | — | 0.15 | 0.35 | 0.60 |
| AH1386-1966 Proof | — | Value: 3.00 | | | |

**5 MILLIEMES** **KM# 394** **Composition:** Aluminum-Bronze

| Date | Mintage | F | VF | XF | Unc |
|---|---|---|---|---|---|
| AH1380-1960 | — | — | 0.15 | 0.45 | 0.80 |
| AH1386-1966 Proof | — | Value: 3.00 | | | |

**5 MILLIEMES** **KM# 410** **Composition:** Aluminum

| Date | Mintage | F | VF | XF | Unc |
|---|---|---|---|---|---|
| AH1386-1967 | — | — | 0.15 | 0.40 | 0.65 |

**10 MILLIEMES** **KM# 395** **Composition:** Aluminum-Bronze **Obverse:** Legend above denomination **Obv. Legend:** Misr

| Date | Mintage | F | VF | XF | Unc |
|---|---|---|---|---|---|
| AH1377-1958 | — | — | 15.00 | 20.00 | 40.00 |
| AH1380-1960 | 16,079,999 | — | 0.80 | 1.20 | 2.25 |
| AH1386-1966 Proof | — | Value: 4.00 | | | |

**10 MILLIEMES** **KM# 396** **Composition:** Aluminum-Bronze **Obverse:** Without Misr above denomination

| Date | Mintage | F | VF | XF | Unc |
|---|---|---|---|---|---|
| AH1377-1958 | — | — | 15.00 | 20.00 | 40.00 |

**10 MILLIEMES** **KM# 411** **Composition:** Aluminum

| Date | Mintage | F | VF | XF | Unc |
|---|---|---|---|---|---|
| AH1386-1967 | — | — | 0.10 | 0.25 | 0.65 |

**20 MILLIEMES** **KM# 390** **Composition:** Aluminum-Bronze **Subject:** Agriculture and Industrial Fair

| Date | Mintage | F | VF | XF | Unc |
|---|---|---|---|---|---|
| AH1378-1958 | — | — | 0.75 | 1.50 | 5.00 |

**5 PIASTRES** **KM# 397** **Weight:** 3.5000 g. **Composition:** 0.7200 Silver .810 oz. ASW ASW

| Date | Mintage | F | VF | XF | Unc |
|---|---|---|---|---|---|
| AH1380-1960 | — | — | 1.75 | 3.00 | 5.00 |
| AH1386-1966 | — | Value: 8.00 | | | |

**5 PIASTRES** **KM# 404** **Weight:** 2.5000 g. **Composition:** 0.7200 Silver .0578 oz. ASW **Subject:** Diversion of the Nile **Reverse:** Nile River basin scene

| Date | Mintage | F | VF | XF | Unc |
|---|---|---|---|---|---|
| AH1384-1964 | 500,000 | — | 1.25 | 2.50 | 4.00 |
| AH1384-1964 Proof | 2,000 | Value: 8.00 | | | |

**5 PIASTRES** **KM# 412** **Composition:** Copper-Nickel

| Date | Mintage | F | VF | XF | Unc |
|---|---|---|---|---|---|
| AH1387-1967 | 10,800,000 | — | 0.50 | 0.75 | 1.50 |

**Note:** Edge varieties, narrow and gapped milling, exist

**5 PIASTRES** **KM# 414** **Composition:** Copper-Nickel **Subject:** International Industrial Fair **Reverse:** Globe with cogwheel section around

| Date | Mintage | F | VF | XF | Unc |
|---|---|---|---|---|---|
| AH1388-1968 | 500,000 | — | 0.75 | 1.00 | 2.50 |

**5 PIASTRES** **KM# 417** **Composition:** Copper-Nickel **Subject:** 50th Anniversary - International Labor Organization **Reverse:** Hands holding open-ended wrenches

| Date | Mintage | F | VF | XF | Unc |
|---|---|---|---|---|---|
| AH1389-1969 | 500,000 | — | 0.75 | 1.00 | 2.50 |

**10 PIASTRES** **KM# 392** **Weight:** 7.0000 g. **Composition:** 0.7200 Silver .1620 oz. ASW **Subject:** First Anniversary of U.A.R. Founding

| Date | Mintage | F | VF | XF | Unc |
|---|---|---|---|---|---|
| AH1378-1959 | — | — | 3.25 | 6.00 | 17.50 |

**10 PIASTRES** **KM# 398** **Weight:** 7.0000 g. **Composition:** 0.7200 Silver .1620 oz. ASW ASW

| Date | Mintage | F | VF | XF | Unc |
|---|---|---|---|---|---|
| AH1380-1960 | 500,000 | — | 3.00 | 4.50 | 7.50 |
| AH1386-1966 Proof | — | Value: 12.50 | | | |

**10 PIASTRES** **KM# 405** **Weight:** 5.0000 g. **Composition:** 0.7200 Silver .1157 oz. ASW **Subject:** Diversion of the Nile **Reverse:** Nile River basin scene

| Date | Mintage | F | VF | XF | Unc |
|---|---|---|---|---|---|
| AH1384-1964 | 500,000 | — | 2.50 | 3.50 | 5.50 |
| AH1384-1964 Proof | 2,000 | Value: 12.50 | | | |

**10 PIASTRES** **KM# 413** **Composition:** Copper-Nickel

| Date | Mintage | F | VF | XF | Unc |
|---|---|---|---|---|---|
| AH1387-1967 | 13,200,000 | — | 0.60 | 0.90 | 2.00 |

**10 PIASTRES** **KM# 419** **Composition:** Copper-Nickel **Subject:** Cairo International Agricultural Fair

| Date | Mintage | F | VF | XF | Unc |
|---|---|---|---|---|---|
| AH1389-1969 | 1,000,000 | — | 0.75 | 1.25 | 3.00 |

**10 PIASTRES** **KM# 418** **Composition:** Copper-Nickel **Series:** F.A.O.

| Date | Mintage | F | VF | XF | Unc |
|---|---|---|---|---|---|
| ND(1970) | 500,000 | — | 0.75 | 1.25 | 3.50 |

**10 PIASTRES** **KM# 420** **Composition:** Copper-Nickel **Subject:** 50 Years - Banque Misr

| Date | Mintage | F | VF | XF | Unc |
|---|---|---|---|---|---|
| AH1390-1970 | 500,000 | — | 0.60 | 1.00 | 2.00 |

**10 PIASTRES** **KM# 421.1** **Composition:** Copper-Nickel **Subject:** Cairo International Industrial Fair

| Date | Mintage | F | VF | XF | Unc |
|---|---|---|---|---|---|
| AH1390-1970 | 500,000 | — | 0.60 | 1.00 | 3.25 |

**10 PIASTRES** **KM# 421.2** **Composition:** Copper-Nickel **Subject:** Cairo International Industrial Fair **Obverse:** New shorter Arabic inscriptions

| Date | Mintage | F | VF | XF | Unc |
|---|---|---|---|---|---|
| AH1391-1971 | 500,000 | — | 0.60 | 1.00 | 2.75 |

**20 PIASTRES** **KM# 399** **Weight:** 14.0000 g. **Composition:** 0.7200 Silver .3241 oz. ASW ASW

| Date | Mintage | F | VF | XF | Unc |
|---|---|---|---|---|---|
| AH1380-1960 | 400,000 | — | 6.00 | 10.00 | 25.00 |
| AH1386-1966 Proof | — | Value: 32.50 | | | |

**25 PIASTRES** **KM# 400** **Weight:** 17.5000 g. **Composition:** 0.7200 Silver .4051 oz. ASW **Subject:** 3rd Year of National Assembly

| Date | Mintage | F | VF | XF | Unc |
|---|---|---|---|---|---|
| AH1380-1960 | 250,000 | — | 5.00 | 8.00 | 18.00 |

**25 PIASTRES** **KM# 406** **Weight:** 10.0000 g. **Composition:** 0.7200 Silver .2315 oz. ASW **Subject:** Diversion of the Nile **Reverse:** Nile River basin scene

| Date | Mintage | F | VF | XF | Unc |
|---|---|---|---|---|---|
| AH1384-1964 | 250,000 | — | 3.00 | 4.50 | 7.00 |
| AH1384-1964 Proof | 2,000 | Value: 20.00 | | | |

**25 PIASTRES** **KM# 422** **Weight:** 6.0000 g. **Composition:** 0.7200 Silver .1388 oz. ASW **Subject:** President Nasser **Obverse:** Head of President Nasser right

| Date | Mintage | F | VF | XF | Unc |
|---|---|---|---|---|---|
| AH1390-1970 | 700,000 | — | 2.50 | 4.00 | 6.50 |

**50 PIASTRES** **KM# 407** **Weight:** 20.0000 g. **Composition:** 0.7200 Silver .4630 oz. ASW **Subject:** Diversion of the Nile **Reverse:** Nile River basin scene

| Date | Mintage | F | VF | XF | Unc |
|---|---|---|---|---|---|
| AH1384-1964 | 250,000 | — | 4.50 | 5.50 | 8.00 |
| AH1384-1964 Proof | 2,000 | Value: 40.00 | | | |

**50 PIASTRES** **KM# 423** **Weight:** 12.5000 g. **Composition:** 0.7200 Silver .2893 oz. ASW **Subject:** President Nasser **Obverse:** Head of President Nasser right

| Date | Mintage | F | VF | XF | Unc |
|---|---|---|---|---|---|
| AH1390-1970 | 400,000 | — | 3.00 | 5.00 | 7.50 |

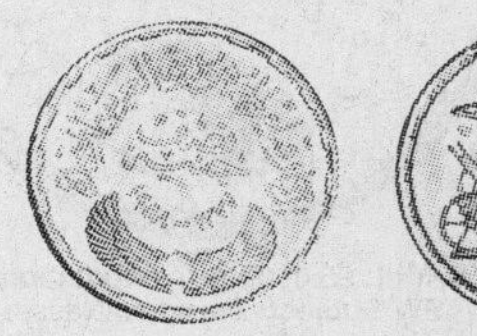

**1/2 POUND** **KM# 391** **Weight:** 4.2500 g. **Composition:** 0.8750 Gold .1195 oz. AGW **Subject:** U.A.R. Founding

| Date | Mintage | F | VF | XF | Unc |
|---|---|---|---|---|---|
| AH1377-1958 | 30,000 | — | — | — | 185 |

**POUND** **KM# 401** **Weight:** 8.5000 g. **Composition:** 0.8750 Gold .2391 oz. AGW **Subject:** Aswan Dam **Reverse:** Aswan Dam

| Date | Mintage | F | VF | XF | Unc |
|---|---|---|---|---|---|
| AH1379-1960 | 252,000 | — | — | — | 140 |

**POUND** **KM# 415** **Weight:** 25.0000 g. **Composition:** 0.7200 Silver .5787 oz. ASW **Subject:** Power Station for Aswan Dam **Reverse:** Power station for Aswan Dam

| Date | Mintage | F | VF | XF | Unc |
|---|---|---|---|---|---|
| AH1387-1968 | 100,000 | — | 5.00 | 6.00 | 8.50 |

**POUND** **KM# 424** **Weight:** 25.0000 g. **Composition:** 0.7200 Silver .5787 oz. ASW **Subject:** 1000th Anniversary - Al Azhar Mosque **Reverse:** Al Azhar Mosque

| Date | Mintage | F | VF | XF | Unc |
|---|---|---|---|---|---|
| AH1359-1361 - 1970-1972 | 100,000 | — | 6.00 | 7.50 | 11.50 |

**POUND** **KM# 425** **Weight:** 25.0000 g. **Composition:** 0.7200 Silver .5787 oz. ASW **Subject:** President Nasser **Reverse:** Head of President Nasser right

| Date | Mintage | F | VF | XF | Unc |
|---|---|---|---|---|---|
| AH1390-1970 | 400,000 | — | 5.00 | 6.50 | 9.00 |

**POUND** **KM# 426** **Weight:** 8.0000 g. **Composition:** 0.8750 Gold .2251 oz. AGW **Subject:** President Nasser **Reverse:** Head of President Nasser right

| Date | Mintage | F | VF | XF | Unc |
|---|---|---|---|---|---|
| AH1390-1970 | 10,000 | — | — | — | 140 |

**5 POUNDS** **KM# 402** **Weight:** 42.5000 g. **Composition:** 0.8750 Gold 1.1957 oz. AGW **Subject:** Aswan Dam **Reverse:** Aswan Dam

| Date | Mintage | F | VF | XF | Unc |
|---|---|---|---|---|---|
| AH1379-1960 | 5,000 | — | — | — | 600 |

**5 POUNDS** **KM# 408** **Weight:** 26.0000 g. **Composition:** 0.8750 Gold .7315 oz. AGW **Subject:** Diversion of the Nile **Reverse:** Nile River basin scene

| Date | Mintage | F | VF | XF | Unc |
|---|---|---|---|---|---|
| AH1384-1964 | — | — | — | — | 375 |

**5 POUNDS** **KM# 416** **Weight:** 26.0000 g. **Composition:** 0.8750 Gold .7315 oz. AGW **Subject:** 1400th Anniversary of the Koran **Reverse:** Open Koran book above globe with radiant sun in back

| Date | Mintage | F | VF | XF | Unc |
|---|---|---|---|---|---|
| AH1388-1968 | 10,000 | — | — | — | 335 |

**5 POUNDS** **KM# 427** **Weight:** 26.0000 g. **Composition:** 0.8750 Gold .7315 oz. AGW **Subject:** 1000th Anniversary - Al Azhar Mosque **Reverse:** Al Azhar Mosque

| Date | Mintage | F | VF | XF | Unc |
|---|---|---|---|---|---|
| AH1390-1970 | — | — | — | — | 350 |

**5 POUNDS** **KM# 428** **Weight:** 26.0000 g. **Composition:** 0.8750 Gold .7315 oz. AGW **Subject:** President Nasser **Reverse:** Head of President Nasser right

| Date | Mintage | F | VF | XF | Unc |
|---|---|---|---|---|---|
| AH1390-1970 | 3,000 | — | — | — | 335 |

**10 POUNDS** **KM# 409** **Weight:** 52.0000 g. **Composition:** 0.8750 Gold 1.4630 oz. AGW **Subject:** Diversion of the Nile **Reverse:** Nile River basin scene

| Date | Mintage | F | VF | XF | Unc |
|---|---|---|---|---|---|
| AH1384-1964 | 2,000 | — | — | — | 675 |

# ARAB REPUBLIC
## AH1391- /1971- AD.

## DECIMAL COINAGE

**MILLIEME** **KM# A423** **Composition:** Aluminum

| Date | Mintage | F | VF | XF | Unc |
|---|---|---|---|---|---|
| AH1392-1972 | — | — | 0.10 | 0.30 | 0.50 |

**5 MILLIEMES** **KM# A425** **Composition:** Aluminum

| Date | Mintage | F | VF | XF | Unc |
|---|---|---|---|---|---|
| AH1392-1972 | 16,000,000 | — | 0.20 | 0.50 | 2.50 |

**5 MILLIEMES** **KM# A424** **Composition:** Aluminum **Obverse:** KM#A425 **Reverse:** KM#433 **Note:** Mule.

| Date | Mintage | F | VF | XF | Unc |
|---|---|---|---|---|---|
| AH1392-1972 | — | — | 10.00 | 20.00 | 45.00 |

**5 MILLIEMES** **KM# A433** **Composition:** Aluminum **Obverse:** KM#433 **Reverse:** KM#A425 **Note:** Mule.

| Date | Mintage | F | VF | XF | Unc |
|---|---|---|---|---|---|
| AH1393-1973 | — | — | 10.00 | 20.00 | 45.00 |

**5 MILLIEMES** **KM# 434** **Composition:** Brass **Obverse:** KM#432 **Reverse:** KM#445 **Note:** Mule

| Date | Mintage | F | VF | XF | Unc |
|---|---|---|---|---|---|
| AH1393-1973 | — | — | 5.00 | 10.00 | 20.00 |

**5 MILLIEMES** **KM# 432** **Composition:** Brass

| Date | Mintage | F | VF | XF | Unc |
|---|---|---|---|---|---|
| AH1393-1973 | — | — | 0.10 | 0.15 | 0.30 |

**5 MILLIEMES** **KM# 433** **Composition:** Aluminum **Series:** F.A.O.

| Date | Mintage | F | VF | XF | Unc |
|---|---|---|---|---|---|
| AH1393-1973 | 10,000,000 | — | 0.10 | 0.20 | 0.35 |

**5 MILLIEMES** **KM# 445** **Composition:** Brass **Series:** International Women's Year

| Date | Mintage | F | VF | XF | Unc |
|---|---|---|---|---|---|
| AH1395-1975 | 10,000,000 | — | 0.10 | 0.15 | 0.30 |

**5 MILLIEMES** **KM# 462** **Composition:** Brass **Series:** F.A.O.

| Date | Mintage | F | VF | XF | Unc |
|---|---|---|---|---|---|
| AH1397-1977 | 5,000,000 | — | 0.10 | 0.20 | 0.50 |

**5 MILLIEMES** **KM# 463** **Composition:** Brass **Subject:** 1971 Corrective Revolution

| Date | Mintage | F | VF | XF | Unc |
|---|---|---|---|---|---|
| AH1397-1977 | 2,500,000 | — | 0.10 | 0.20 | 0.50 |
| AH1399-1979 | 2,500,000 | — | 0.10 | 0.20 | 0.50 |

**PIASTRE** **KM# 553.1** **Composition:** Aluminum-Bronze **Obverse:** Christian date left of denomination

| Date | Mintage | F | VF | XF | Unc |
|---|---|---|---|---|---|
| AH1404-1984 | — | — | — | 0.15 | 0.35 |

**PIASTRE** **KM# 553.2** **Composition:** Aluminum-Bronze **Obverse:** Islamic date left of denomination

| Date | Mintage | F | VF | XF | Unc |
|---|---|---|---|---|---|
| AH1404-1984 | — | — | — | 0.15 | 0.35 |

**10 MILLIEMES** **KM# A426** **Composition:** Aluminum

| Date | Mintage | F | VF | XF | Unc |
|---|---|---|---|---|---|
| AH1392-1972 | 20,000,000 | — | 0.50 | 2.00 | 6.00 |

**Note:** 2 varieties of edge letterings exist

**10 MILLIEMES** **KM# 435** **Composition:** Brass

| Date | Mintage | F | VF | XF | Unc |
|---|---|---|---|---|---|
| AH1393-1973 | — | — | 0.10 | 0.25 | 0.50 |
| AH1396-1976 | — | — | 0.75 | 1.50 | 3.00 |

**10 MILLIEMES** **KM# 446** **Composition:** Brass **Series:** F.A.O.

| Date | Mintage | F | VF | XF | Unc |
|---|---|---|---|---|---|
| AH1395-1975 | 10,000,000 | — | 0.10 | 0.20 | 0.35 |

**10 MILLIEMES** **KM# 449** **Composition:** Brass **Series:** F.A.O.

| Date | Mintage | F | VF | XF | Unc |
|---|---|---|---|---|---|
| AH1396-1976 | 10,000,000 | — | 0.10 | 0.20 | 0.30 |

**10 MILLIEMES** **KM# 464** **Composition:** Brass **Series:** F.A.O.

| Date | Mintage | F | VF | XF | Unc |
|---|---|---|---|---|---|
| AH1397-1977 | 10,000,000 | — | 0.10 | 0.20 | 0.85 |

**10 MILLIEMES** **KM# 465** **Composition:** Brass **Subject:** 1971 Corrective Revolution

| Date | Mintage | F | VF | XF | Unc |
|---|---|---|---|---|---|
| AH1397-1977 | 2,500,000 | — | 0.10 | 0.20 | 0.65 |
| AH1399-1979 | 2,500,000 | — | 0.20 | 0.40 | 1.00 |

**10 MILLIEMES** **KM# 476** **Composition:** Brass **Series:** F.A.O.

| Date | Mintage | F | VF | XF | Unc |
|---|---|---|---|---|---|
| AH1398-1978 | 2,000,000 | — | 0.10 | 0.20 | 0.80 |

**10 MILLIEMES** **KM# 483** **Composition:** Brass **Series:** International Year of the Child

| Date | Mintage | F | VF | XF | Unc |
|---|---|---|---|---|---|
| AH1399-1979 | 2,000,000 | — | 0.10 | 0.20 | 0.65 |

**10 MILLIEMES** **KM# 498** **Composition:** Aluminum-Bronze **Subject:** Sadat's Corrective Revolution

| Date | Mintage | F | VF | XF | Unc |
|---|---|---|---|---|---|
| AH1400-1980 | 2,500,000 | — | 0.10 | 0.25 | 1.00 |

**10 MILLIEMES** **KM# 499** **Composition:** Aluminum-Bronze **Series:** F.A.O.

| Date | Mintage | F | VF | XF | Unc |
|---|---|---|---|---|---|
| AH1400-1980 | 2,000,000 | — | 0.10 | 0.20 | 0.60 |

**2 PIASTRES** **KM# 500** **Composition:** Aluminum-Bronze

| Date | Mintage | F | VF | XF | Unc |
|---|---|---|---|---|---|
| AH1400-1980 | — | — | 0.20 | 0.30 | 0.60 |

**2 PIASTRES** **KM# 554.1** **Composition:** Aluminum-Bronze **Obverse:** Christian date left of denomination

| Date | Mintage | F | VF | XF | Unc |
|---|---|---|---|---|---|
| AH1404-1984 | — | — | — | 0.20 | 0.50 |

**2 PIASTRES** **KM# 554.2** **Composition:** Aluminum-Bronze **Obverse:** Islamic date left of denomination

| Date | Mintage | F | VF | XF | Unc |
|---|---|---|---|---|---|
| AH1404-1984 | — | — | — | 0.20 | 0.50 |

**5 PIASTRES** **KM# A427** **Composition:** Copper-Nickel **Subject:** 25th Anniversary of UNICEF

| Date | Mintage | F | VF | XF | Unc |
|---|---|---|---|---|---|
| AH1392-1972 | 500,000 | — | 0.75 | 1.00 | 3.00 |

**Note:** Error in spelling "UNICFE".

**5 PIASTRES** **KM# A428** **Composition:** Copper-Nickel **Reverse:** Islamic falcon

| Date | Mintage | F | VF | XF | Unc |
|---|---|---|---|---|---|
| AH1392-1972 | — | — | 0.50 | 0.75 | 2.00 |

**5 PIASTRES KM# 436 Composition:** Copper-Nickel **Subject:** Cairo State Fair

| Date | Mintage | F | VF | XF | Unc |
|---|---|---|---|---|---|
| AH1393-1973 | 500,000 | — | 0.60 | 0.75 | 2.25 |

**5 PIASTRES KM# 437 Composition:** Copper-Nickel **Subject:** 75th Anniversary - National Bank of Egypt **Reverse:** Bank building in front of globe at left

| Date | Mintage | F | VF | XF | Unc |
|---|---|---|---|---|---|
| AH1393-1973 | 1,000,000 | — | 0.60 | 0.75 | 2.00 |

**5 PIASTRES KM# A441 Composition:** Copper-Nickel **Subject:** First Anniversary - October War **Reverse:** Soldier with gun facing right

| Date | Mintage | F | VF | XF | Unc |
|---|---|---|---|---|---|
| AH1394-1974 | 2,000,000 | — | 0.60 | 0.75 | 2.00 |

**5 PIASTRES KM# 447 Composition:** Copper-Nickel **Series:** International Women's Year **Reverse:** Bust of Nefertiti right, sheaf of grain at left

| Date | Mintage | F | VF | XF | Unc |
|---|---|---|---|---|---|
| AH1395-1975 | 2,000,000 | — | 0.50 | 0.65 | 1.25 |

**5 PIASTRES KM# 451 Composition:** Copper-Nickel **Subject:** 1976 Cairo Trade Fair

| Date | Mintage | F | VF | XF | Unc |
|---|---|---|---|---|---|
| AH1396-1976 | 500,000 | — | 0.60 | 0.75 | 2.00 |

**5 PIASTRES KM# 450 Composition:** Copper-Nickel **Obverse:** KM#451 **Reverse:** KM#A428 **Note:** Mule

| Date | Mintage | F | VF | XF | Unc |
|---|---|---|---|---|---|
| AH1396-1976 | — | — | 5.00 | 10.00 | 20.00 |

**5 PIASTRES KM# 466 Composition:** Copper-Nickel **Subject:** 1971 Corrective Revolution

| Date | Mintage | F | VF | XF | Unc |
|---|---|---|---|---|---|
| AH1397-1977 | 1,000,000 | — | 0.50 | 0.60 | 1.50 |
| AH1399-1979 | — | — | 0.50 | 0.60 | 1.25 |

**5 PIASTRES KM# 467 Composition:** Copper-Nickel **Subject:** 50th Anniversary - Textile Industry

| Date | Mintage | F | VF | XF | Unc |
|---|---|---|---|---|---|
| AH1397-1977 | 1,000,000 | — | 0.50 | 0.75 | 1.65 |

**5 PIASTRES KM# 468 Composition:** Copper-Nickel **Series:** F.A.O.

| Date | Mintage | F | VF | XF | Unc |
|---|---|---|---|---|---|
| AH1397-1977 | — | — | 0.50 | 0.75 | 1.65 |

**Note:** Edge varieties exist

**5 PIASTRES KM# 477 Composition:** Copper-Nickel **Subject:** Portland Cement

| Date | Mintage | F | VF | XF | Unc |
|---|---|---|---|---|---|
| AH1398-1978 | 500,000 | — | 0.50 | 0.75 | 1.65 |

**5 PIASTRES KM# 478 Composition:** Copper-Nickel **Series:** F.A.O.

| Date | Mintage | F | VF | XF | Unc |
|---|---|---|---|---|---|
| AH1398-1978 | 1,000,000 | — | 0.50 | 0.75 | 1.65 |

**5 PIASTRES KM# 484 Composition:** Copper-Nickel **Series:** International Year of the Child

| Date | Mintage | F | VF | XF | Unc |
|---|---|---|---|---|---|
| AH1399-1979 | 1,000,000 | — | 0.50 | 0.75 | 1.65 |

**5 PIASTRES KM# 501 Composition:** Copper-Nickel **Subject:** Applied Professions

| Date | Mintage | F | VF | XF | Unc |
|---|---|---|---|---|---|
| AH1400-1980 | 500,000 | — | 0.50 | 0.75 | 1.35 |

**5 PIASTRES KM# 502 Composition:** Copper-Nickel **Subject:** Sadat's Corrective Revolution of May 15, 1971 **Reverse:** Raised clenched fist holding stalk of grain

| Date | Mintage | F | VF | XF | Unc |
|---|---|---|---|---|---|
| AH1400-1980 | 1,000,000 | — | 0.50 | 0.75 | 1.75 |

**5 PIASTRES KM# 555.1 Composition:** Aluminum-Bronze **Obverse:** Christian date left of denomination

| Date | Mintage | F | VF | XF | Unc |
|---|---|---|---|---|---|
| AH1404-1984 | — | — | — | 0.25 | 0.75 |

**Note:** Varieties exist with wide and narrow rims

**5 PIASTRES KM# 555.2 Composition:** Aluminum-Bronze **Obverse:** Islamic date left of denomination

| Date | Mintage | F | VF | XF | Unc |
|---|---|---|---|---|---|
| AH1404-1984 | — | — | — | 0.25 | 0.75 |

**5 PIASTRES KM# 622.1 Composition:** Aluminum-Bronze **Obverse:** Denomination not shaded

| Date | Mintage | F | VF | XF | Unc |
|---|---|---|---|---|---|
| AH1404-1984 | — | — | — | 0.25 | 0.85 |

**5 PIASTRES KM# 622.2 Composition:** Aluminum-Bronze **Obverse:** Denomination shaded

| Date | Mintage | F | VF | XF | Unc |
|---|---|---|---|---|---|
| AH1404-1984 | — | — | — | 0.25 | 0.85 |

**5 PIASTRES KM# 731 Composition:** Brass **Reverse:** Decorated vase

| Date | Mintage | F | VF | XF | Unc |
|---|---|---|---|---|---|
| AH1413-1992 | — | — | — | — | 0.85 |

**10 PIASTRES KM# 429 Composition:** Copper-Nickel **Subject:** Cairo International Fair

| Date | Mintage | F | VF | XF | Unc |
|---|---|---|---|---|---|
| AH1392-1972 | 500,000 | — | 0.60 | 1.00 | 2.50 |

**10 PIASTRES** **KM# 430** **Composition:** Copper-Nickel **Reverse:** Islamic falcon

| Date | Mintage | F | VF | XF | Unc |
|---|---|---|---|---|---|
| AH1392-1972 | — | — | 0.60 | 1.00 | 2.50 |

**10 PIASTRES** **KM# 431** **Composition:** Copper-Nickel **Obverse:** KM#452 **Reverse:** KM#430 **Note:** Mule.

| Date | Mintage | F | VF | XF | Unc |
|---|---|---|---|---|---|
| AH1392-1972 | — | — | 5.50 | 12.50 | 27.50 |

**Note:** Wide and narrow inscriptions exist for obverse

**10 PIASTRES** **KM# 442** **Composition:** Copper-Nickel **Subject:** First Anniversary - October War

| Date | Mintage | F | VF | XF | Unc |
|---|---|---|---|---|---|
| AH1394-1974 | 2,000,000 | — | 0.60 | 1.00 | 3.50 |

**10 PIASTRES** **KM# 448** **Composition:** Copper-Nickel **Series:** F.A.O.

| Date | Mintage | F | VF | XF | Unc |
|---|---|---|---|---|---|
| AH1395-1975 | 2,000,000 | — | 0.60 | 1.00 | 3.50 |

**10 PIASTRES** **KM# 452** **Composition:** Copper-Nickel **Subject:** Reopening of the Suez Canal

| Date | Mintage | F | VF | XF | Unc |
|---|---|---|---|---|---|
| AH1396-1976 | 5,000,000 | — | 0.60 | 1.00 | 3.50 |

**Note:** Wide and narrow inscriptions exist for the obverse

**10 PIASTRES** **KM# 469** **Composition:** Copper-Nickel **Series:** F.A.O.

| Date | Mintage | F | VF | XF | Unc |
|---|---|---|---|---|---|
| AH1397-1977 | 1,000,000 | — | 0.60 | 1.00 | 2.25 |

**10 PIASTRES** **KM# 470** **Composition:** Copper-Nickel **Subject:** 1971 Corrective Revolution

| Date | Mintage | F | VF | XF | Unc |
|---|---|---|---|---|---|
| AH1397-1977 | 1,000,000 | — | 0.50 | 0.85 | 2.50 |
| AH1399-1979 | 1,000,000 | — | 0.50 | 0.85 | 2.50 |

**10 PIASTRES** **KM# 471** **Composition:** Copper-Nickel **Subject:** 20th Anniversary - Economic Union

| Date | Mintage | F | VF | XF | Unc |
|---|---|---|---|---|---|
| AH1397-1977 | 1,000,000 | — | 0.50 | 0.85 | 2.25 |

**10 PIASTRES** **KM# 479** **Composition:** Copper-Nickel **Subject:** Cairo International Fair

| Date | Mintage | F | VF | XF | Unc |
|---|---|---|---|---|---|
| AH1398-1978 | — | — | 0.50 | 0.85 | 2.75 |

**10 PIASTRES** **KM# 485** **Composition:** Copper-Nickel **Subject:** 25th Anniversary of Abbasia Mint

| Date | Mintage | F | VF | XF | Unc |
|---|---|---|---|---|---|
| AH1399-1979 | 1,000,000 | — | 0.50 | 0.85 | 2.25 |

**10 PIASTRES** **KM# 486** **Composition:** Copper-Nickel **Subject:** National Education Day

| Date | Mintage | F | VF | XF | Unc |
|---|---|---|---|---|---|
| AH1399-1979 | 1,000,000 | — | 0.50 | 0.85 | 2.25 |

**10 PIASTRES** **KM# 503** **Composition:** Copper-Nickel **Subject:** Doctor's Day **Reverse:** Seated Egyptian healer with staff left

| Date | Mintage | F | VF | XF | Unc |
|---|---|---|---|---|---|
| AH1400-1980 | 1,000,000 | — | 0.50 | 0.85 | 2.50 |

**10 PIASTRES** **KM# 504** **Composition:** Copper-Nickel **Subject:** Egyptian-Israeli Peace Treaty **Reverse:** Anwar Sadat facing left at right, dove of peace, hand with quill signing treaty

| Date | Mintage | F | VF | XF | Unc |
|---|---|---|---|---|---|
| AH1400-1980 | 1,000,000 | — | 1.00 | 2.00 | 3.50 |

**10 PIASTRES** **KM# 505** **Composition:** Copper-Nickel **Series:** F.A.O.

| Date | Mintage | F | VF | XF | Unc |
|---|---|---|---|---|---|
| AH1400-1980 | 1,000,000 | — | 0.50 | 0.85 | 2.25 |

**10 PIASTRES** **KM# 506** **Composition:** Copper-Nickel **Series:** F.A.O. **Subject:** Sadat's Corrective Revolution of May 15, 1971

| Date | Mintage | F | VF | XF | Unc |
|---|---|---|---|---|---|
| AH1400-1980 | 1,000,000 | — | 0.50 | 0.85 | 2.25 |
| AH1401-1981 | — | — | 0.60 | 1.20 | 3.50 |

**10 PIASTRES** **KM# 520** **Composition:** Copper-Nickel **Subject:** Scientist's Day

| Date | Mintage | F | VF | XF | Unc |
|---|---|---|---|---|---|
| AH1401-1981 | — | — | 0.50 | 0.85 | 2.25 |

**10 PIASTRES** **KM# 521** **Composition:** Copper-Nickel **Subject:** 25th Anniversary - Trade Unions

| Date | Mintage | F | VF | XF | Unc |
|---|---|---|---|---|---|
| AH1402-1981 | — | — | 1.00 | 2.00 | 3.50 |

**10 PIASTRES** **KM# 599** **Composition:** Copper-Nickel **Subject:** 50th Anniversary of Egyptian Products Co.

| Date | Mintage | F | VF | XF | Unc |
|---|---|---|---|---|---|
| AH1402-1982 | — | — | 0.50 | 0.85 | 2.25 |

**10 PIASTRES** **KM# 556** **Composition:** Copper-Nickel
**Subject:** Circulation Coinage

| Date | Mintage | F | VF | XF | Unc |
|---|---|---|---|---|---|
| AH1404-1984 | — | — | — | 0.50 | 0.85 |

**10 PIASTRES** **KM# 570** **Composition:** Copper-Nickel
**Subject:** 25th Anniversary - National Planning Institute

| Date | Mintage | F | VF | XF | Unc |
|---|---|---|---|---|---|
| AH1405-1985 | 100,000 | — | — | — | 1.75 |

**10 PIASTRES** **KM# 573** **Composition:** Copper-Nickel
**Subject:** 60th Anniversary - Egyptian Parliament

| Date | Mintage | F | VF | XF | Unc |
|---|---|---|---|---|---|
| AH1405-1985 | 250,000 | — | — | — | 1.75 |

**10 PIASTRES** **KM# 675** **Composition:** Copper-Nickel
**Subject:** 1973 October War

| Date | Mintage | F | VF | XF | Unc |
|---|---|---|---|---|---|
| AH1410-1989 | 250,000 | — | — | — | 1.75 |

**10 PIASTRES** **KM# 732** **Composition:** Brass

| Date | Mintage | F | VF | XF | Unc |
|---|---|---|---|---|---|
| AH1413-1992 | — | — | — | — | 1.25 |

**20 PIASTRES** **KM# 507** **Composition:** Copper-Nickel

| Date | Mintage | F | VF | XF | Unc |
|---|---|---|---|---|---|
| AH1400-1980 | — | — | 0.75 | 1.00 | 2.35 |

**20 PIASTRES** **KM# 557** **Composition:** Copper-Nickel
**Subject:** Circulation Coinage

| Date | Mintage | F | VF | XF | Unc |
|---|---|---|---|---|---|
| AH1404-1984 | — | — | — | 0.70 | 1.65 |

**20 PIASTRES** **KM# 596** **Composition:** Copper-Nickel
**Subject:** 25th Anniversary - Cairo International Airport

| Date | Mintage | F | VF | XF | Unc |
|---|---|---|---|---|---|
| AH1405-1985 | 50,000 | — | — | — | 2.25 |

**20 PIASTRES** **KM# 597** **Composition:** Copper-Nickel
**Subject:** Professions

| Date | Mintage | F | VF | XF | Unc |
|---|---|---|---|---|---|
| AH1406-1985 | 100,000 | — | — | — | 2.50 |

**20 PIASTRES** **KM# 606** **Composition:** Copper-Nickel
**Subject:** Soldiers

| Date | Mintage | F | VF | XF | Unc |
|---|---|---|---|---|---|
| AH1406-1986 | 50,000 | — | — | — | 2.50 |

**20 PIASTRES** **KM# 607** **Composition:** Copper-Nickel
**Subject:** Census

| Date | Mintage | F | VF | XF | Unc |
|---|---|---|---|---|---|
| AH1407-1986 | 500,000 | — | — | — | 2.25 |

**20 PIASTRES** **KM# 652** **Composition:** Copper-Nickel
**Subject:** Investment Bank

| Date | Mintage | F | VF | XF | Unc |
|---|---|---|---|---|---|
| AH1407-1987 | 250,000 | — | — | — | 2.50 |

**20 PIASTRES** **KM# 646** **Composition:** Copper-Nickel
**Subject:** Police Day

| Date | Mintage | F | VF | XF | Unc |
|---|---|---|---|---|---|
| AH1408-1988 | 250,000 | — | — | — | 2.75 |

**20 PIASTRES** **KM# 650** **Composition:** Copper-Nickel
**Subject:** Dedication of Cairo Opera House

| Date | Mintage | F | VF | XF | Unc |
|---|---|---|---|---|---|
| AH1409-1988 | 250,000 | — | — | — | 2.50 |

**20 PIASTRES** **KM# 676** **Composition:** Copper-Nickel
**Subject:** 1973 October War

| Date | Mintage | F | VF | XF | Unc |
|---|---|---|---|---|---|
| AH1410-1989 | 250,000 | — | — | — | 2.50 |

**20 PIASTRES** **KM# 685** **Composition:** Copper-Nickel
**Subject:** National Health Insurance

| Date | Mintage | F | VF | XF | Unc |
|---|---|---|---|---|---|
| AH1409-1989 | 250,000 | — | — | — | 2.50 |

**20 PIASTRES** **KM# 690** **Composition:** Copper-Nickel
**Subject:** Cairo Subway

| Date | Mintage | F | VF | XF | Unc |
|---|---|---|---|---|---|
| AH1409-1989 | 250,000 | — | — | — | 2.75 |

**20 PIASTRES** **KM# 733** **Composition:** Copper-Nickel
**Subject:** Mosque

| Date | Mintage | F | VF | XF | Unc |
|---|---|---|---|---|---|
| AH1413-1992 | — | — | — | — | 2.50 |

**25 PIASTRES** KM# 438 **Weight:** 6.0000 g. **Composition:** 0.7200 Silver .1388 oz. ASW **Subject:** 75th Anniversary - National Bank of Egypt **Reverse:** National Bank building at right, globe at left in back

| Date | Mintage | F | VF | XF | Unc |
|---|---|---|---|---|---|
| AH1393-1973 | 100,000 | — | 4.00 | 6.00 | 9.00 |

**25 PIASTRES** KM# 734 **Composition:** Copper-Nickel

| Date | Mintage | F | VF | XF | Unc |
|---|---|---|---|---|---|
| AH1413-1993 | — | — | — | — | 2.75 |

**1/2 POUND** KM# 834 **Weight:** 4.0000 g. **Composition:** 0.8750 Gold .1125 oz. AGW **Subject:** El Akkad **Obverse:** Legend and vase **Reverse:** Portrait

| Date | Mintage | F | VF | XF | Unc |
|---|---|---|---|---|---|
| AH1413-1992 | 600 | — | — | — | 250 |

**1/2 POUND** KM# 809 **Weight:** 4.0000 g. **Composition:** 0.8750 Gold .1125 oz. AGW **Subject:** 20th Anniversary - October War **Obverse:** Smoking chimney text **Reverse:** Soldier with flag

| Date | Mintage | F | VF | XF | Unc |
|---|---|---|---|---|---|
| AH1414-1993 | Est. 5,000 | — | — | — | 250 |

**1/2 POUND** KM# 760 **Weight:** 4.0000 g. **Composition:** 0.8750 Gold .1125 oz. AGW **Subject:** Salah El Din El-Ayubi **Obverse:** Denomination **Reverse:** Portrait

| Date | Mintage | F | VF | XF | Unc |
|---|---|---|---|---|---|
| AH1414-1994 | 500 | — | — | — | 250 |

**POUND** KM# 439 **Weight:** 25.0000 g. **Composition:** 0.7200 Silver .5787 oz. ASW **Series:** F.A.O. **Reverse:** Aswan Dam

| Date | Mintage | F | VF | XF | Unc |
|---|---|---|---|---|---|
| AH1393-1973 | 50,000 | — | 5.00 | 6.00 | 9.00 |

**POUND** KM# 440 **Weight:** 8.0000 g. **Composition:** 0.8750 Gold .2250 oz. AGW **Subject:** 75th Anniversary - National Bank of Egypt **Reverse:** National Bank of Egypt building

| Date | Mintage | F | VF | XF | Unc |
|---|---|---|---|---|---|
| AH1393-1973 | 7,000 | — | — | — | 125 |

**POUND** KM# 443 **Weight:** 15.0000 g. **Composition:** 0.7200 Silver .3472 oz. ASW **Subject:** First Anniversary - October War

| Date | Mintage | F | VF | XF | Unc |
|---|---|---|---|---|---|
| AH1394-1974 | 50,000 | — | — | — | 7.50 |

**POUND** KM# 453 **Weight:** 15.0000 g. **Composition:** 0.7200 Silver .3472 oz. ASW **Series:** F.A.O.

| Date | Mintage | F | VF | XF | Unc |
|---|---|---|---|---|---|
| AH1396-1976 | 50,000 | — | — | — | 7.50 |

**POUND** KM# 454 **Weight:** 15.0000 g. **Composition:** 0.7200 Silver .3472 oz. ASW **Subject:** Reopening of Suez Canal

| Date | Mintage | F | VF | XF | Unc |
|---|---|---|---|---|---|
| AH1396-1976 | 250,000 | — | — | — | 7.50 |

**POUND** KM# 455 **Weight:** 15.0000 g. **Composition:** 0.7200 Silver .3472 oz. ASW **Reverse:** Om Kalsoum right

| Date | Mintage | F | VF | XF | Unc |
|---|---|---|---|---|---|
| AH1396-1976 | 250,000 | — | — | — | 7.50 |

**POUND** KM# 456 **Weight:** 8.0000 g. **Composition:** 0.8750 Gold .2250 oz. AGW **Reverse:** Om Kalsoum right

| Date | Mintage | F | VF | XF | Unc |
|---|---|---|---|---|---|
| AH1396-1976 | 5,000 | — | — | — | 150 |

**POUND** KM# 457 **Weight:** 15.0000 g. **Composition:** 0.7200 Silver .3472 oz. ASW **Reverse:** Bust of King Faisal half right

| Date | Mintage | F | VF | XF | Unc |
|---|---|---|---|---|---|
| AH1396-1976 | 100,000 | — | — | — | 7.50 |

**POUND** KM# 458 **Weight:** 8.0000 g. **Composition:** 0.8750 Gold .2250 oz. AGW **Reverse:** Bust of King Faisal half right

| Date | Mintage | F | VF | XF | Unc |
|---|---|---|---|---|---|
| AH1396-1976 | 8,000 | — | — | — | 145 |

**POUND** KM# 472 **Weight:** 15.0000 g. **Composition:** 0.7200 Silver .3472 oz. ASW **Series:** F.A.O.

| Date | Mintage | F | VF | XF | Unc |
|---|---|---|---|---|---|
| AH1397-1977 | 50,000 | — | — | — | 7.50 |

**POUND** KM# 473 **Weight:** 15.0000 g. **Composition:** 0.7200 Silver .3472 oz. ASW **Subject:** 1971 Corrective Revolution

| Date | Mintage | F | VF | XF | Unc |
|---|---|---|---|---|---|
| AH1397-1977 | 50,000 | — | — | — | 7.50 |
| AH1399-1979 | 49,000 | — | — | — | 7.50 |
| AH1399-1979 Proof | 1,500 | Value: 11.50 | | | |

**POUND** KM# 474 **Weight:** 15.0000 g. **Composition:** 0.7200 Silver .3472 oz. ASW **Subject:** 20th Anniversary - Economic Union

| Date | Mintage | F | VF | XF | Unc |
|---|---|---|---|---|---|
| AH1397-1977 | 50,000 | — | — | — | 7.50 |

**POUND** KM# 475 **Weight:** 8.0000 g. **Composition:** 0.8750 Gold .2250 oz. AGW **Subject:** 20th Anniversary - Economic Union

| Date | Mintage | F | VF | XF | Unc |
|---|---|---|---|---|---|
| AH1397-1977 | 5,000 | — | — | — | 150 |

**POUND** KM# 480 **Weight:** 15.0000 g. **Composition:** 0.7200 Silver .3472 oz. ASW **Subject:** Portland Cement

| Date | Mintage | F | VF | XF | Unc |
|---|---|---|---|---|---|
| AH1398-1978 | 50,000 | — | — | — | 7.50 |

**POUND KM# 481 Weight:** 15.0000 g. **Composition:** 0.7200 Silver .3472 oz. ASW **Subject:** 25th Anniversary - Ain Shams University

| Date | Mintage | F | VF | XF | Unc |
|---|---|---|---|---|---|
| AH1398-1978 | 50,000 | — | — | — | 7.50 |

**POUND KM# 482 Weight:** 15.0000 g. **Composition:** 0.7200 Silver .3472 oz. ASW **Series:** F.A.O.

| Date | Mintage | F | VF | XF | Unc |
|---|---|---|---|---|---|
| AH1398-1978 | 50,000 | — | — | — | 7.50 |

**POUND KM# 488 Weight:** 15.0000 g. **Composition:** 0.7200 Silver .3472 oz. ASW **Subject:** 25th Anniversary - Abbasia Mint

| Date | Mintage | F | VF | XF | Unc |
|---|---|---|---|---|---|
| AH1399-1979 | 23,000 | — | — | — | 7.50 |
| AH1399-1979 Proof | 2,000 | Value: 10.00 | | | |

**POUND KM# 489 Weight:** 15.0000 g. **Composition:** 0.7200 Silver .3472 oz. ASW **Series:** F.A.O. and I.Y.C.

| Date | Mintage | F | VF | XF | Unc |
|---|---|---|---|---|---|
| AH1399-1979 | 48,000 | — | — | — | 7.50 |
| AH1399-1979 Proof | 2,500 | Value: 10.00 | | | |

**POUND KM# 490 Weight:** 15.0000 g. **Composition:** 0.7200 Silver .3472 oz. ASW **Subject:** National Education Day

| Date | Mintage | F | VF | XF | Unc |
|---|---|---|---|---|---|
| AH1399-1979 | 98,000 | — | — | — | 7.50 |
| AH1399-1979 Proof | 2,000 | Value: 10.00 | | | |

**POUND KM# 491 Weight:** 15.0000 g. **Composition:** 0.7200 Silver .3472 oz. ASW **Subject:** 100th Anniversary - Bank of Land Reform

| Date | Mintage | F | VF | XF | Unc |
|---|---|---|---|---|---|
| AH1399-1979 | 98,000 | — | — | — | 7.50 |
| AH1399-1979 Proof | 2,000 | Value: 10.00 | | | |

**POUND KM# 492 Weight:** 8.0000 g. **Composition:** 0.8750 Gold .2250 oz. AGW **Subject:** 100th Anniversary - Bank of Land Reform

| Date | Mintage | F | VF | XF | Unc |
|---|---|---|---|---|---|
| AH1399-1979 | 4,200 | — | — | — | 145 |
| AH1399-1979 Proof | 800 | Value: 225 | | | |

**POUND KM# 493 Weight:** 15.0000 g. **Composition:** 0.7200 Silver .3472 oz. ASW **Subject:** 1400th Anniversary - Mohammed's Flight

| Date | Mintage | F | VF | XF | Unc |
|---|---|---|---|---|---|
| AH1400-1979 | 97,000 | — | — | — | 7.50 |
| AH1400-1979 Proof | 3,000 | Value: 10.00 | | | |

**POUND KM# 494 Weight:** 8.0000 g. **Composition:** 0.8750 Gold .2250 oz. AGW **Subject:** 1400th Anniversary - Mohammed's Flight

| Date | Mintage | F | VF | XF | Unc |
|---|---|---|---|---|---|
| AH1400-1979 | 2,000 | — | — | — | 150 |
| AH1400-1979 Proof | 2,000 | Value: 200 | | | |

**POUND KM# 508 Weight:** 15.0000 g. **Composition:** 0.7200 Silver .3472 oz. ASW **Subject:** Egyptian-Israeli Peace Treaty **Reverse:** Head of Anwar Sadat at right facing left with dove of peace at left

| Date | Mintage | F | VF | XF | Unc |
|---|---|---|---|---|---|
| AH1400-1980 | 95,000 | — | — | — | 7.50 |
| AH1400-1980 | 5,000 | Value: 11.50 | | | |

**POUND KM# 509 Weight:** 8.0000 g. **Composition:** 0.8750 Gold .2250 oz. AGW **Subject:** Egyptian-Israeli Peace Treaty **Reverse:** Head of Anwar Sadat left with dove of peace at right

| Date | Mintage | F | VF | XF | Unc |
|---|---|---|---|---|---|
| AH1400-1980 | 9,500 | — | — | — | 110 |
| AH1400-1980 Proof | 500 | Value: 185 | | | |

**POUND KM# 510 Weight:** 15.0000 g. **Composition:** 0.7200 Silver .3472 oz. ASW **Subject:** Applied Professions in Egypt **Reverse:** Different professions depicted

| Date | Mintage | F | VF | XF | Unc |
|---|---|---|---|---|---|
| AH1400-1980 | 22,000 | — | — | — | 6.50 |
| AH1400-1980 Proof | 3,000 | Value: 9.00 | | | |

**POUND KM# 511 Weight:** 15.0000 g. **Composition:** 0.7200 Silver .3472 oz. ASW **Subject:** Doctor's Day **Reverse:** Seated healer with staff facing left

| Date | Mintage | F | VF | XF | Unc |
|---|---|---|---|---|---|
| AH1400-1980 | 97,000 | — | — | — | 6.50 |
| AH1400-1980 Proof | 3,000 | Value: 9.00 | | | |

**POUND KM# 512 Weight:** 8.0000 g. **Composition:** 0.8750 Gold .2250 oz. AGW **Subject:** Doctor's Day **Reverse:** Seated healer with staff facing left

| Date | Mintage | F | VF | XF | Unc |
|---|---|---|---|---|---|
| AH1400-1980 Proof | 5,000 | Value: 185 | | | |

**POUND KM# 513 Weight:** 15.0000 g. **Composition:** 0.7200 Silver .3472 oz. ASW **Series:** F.A.O.

| Date | Mintage | F | VF | XF | Unc |
|---|---|---|---|---|---|
| AH1400-1980 | 97,000 | — | — | — | 6.50 |
| AH1400-1980 Proof | 3,000 | Value: 9.00 | | | |

**POUND KM# 514 Weight:** 15.0000 g. **Composition:** 0.7200 Silver .3472 oz. ASW **Subject:** Sadat's Corrective Revolution of May 15, 1971 **Reverse:** Raised clenched fist holding grain sprig

| Date | Mintage | F | VF | XF | Unc |
|---|---|---|---|---|---|
| AH1400-1980 | 47,000 | — | — | — | 8.00 |
| AH1400-1980 Proof | 3,000 | Value: 14.00 | | | |

**POUND KM# 515 Weight:** 15.0000 g. **Composition:** 0.7200 Silver .3472 oz. ASW **Reverse:** Cairo University Law facility

| Date | Mintage | F | VF | XF | Unc |
|---|---|---|---|---|---|
| AH1400-1980 | 47,000 | — | — | — | 8.00 |
| AH1400-1980 Proof | 3,000 | Value: 14.00 | | | |

**POUND KM# 516 Weight:** 8.0000 g. **Composition:** 0.8750 Gold .2250 oz. AGW **Reverse:** Cairo University Law facility

| Date | Mintage | F | VF | XF | Unc |
|---|---|---|---|---|---|
| AH1400-1980 | 2,000 | — | — | — | 150 |
| AH1400-1980 Proof | — | Value: 225 | | | |

**POUND** **KM# 522** **Weight:** 15.0000 g. **Composition:** 0.7200 Silver .3472 oz. ASW **Subject:** Scientist's Day

| Date | Mintage | F | VF | XF | Unc |
|---|---|---|---|---|---|
| AH1401-1981 | 25,000 | — | — | — | 9.00 |

**POUND** **KM# 523** **Weight:** 15.0000 g. **Composition:** 0.7200 Silver .3472 oz. ASW **Series:** World Food Day

| Date | Mintage | F | VF | XF | Unc |
|---|---|---|---|---|---|
| AH1401-1981 | 50,000 | — | — | — | 7.50 |
| AH1401-1981 Proof | 1,500 | Value: 16.00 | | | |

**POUND** **KM# 524** **Weight:** 15.0000 g. **Composition:** 0.7200 Silver .3472 oz. ASW **Subject:** 3rd Anniversary - Suez Canal Reopening

| Date | Mintage | F | VF | XF | Unc |
|---|---|---|---|---|---|
| AH1401-1981 | 50,000 | — | — | — | 9.00 |
| AH1401-1981 Proof | 2,000 | Value: 13.50 | | | |

**POUND** **KM# 525** **Weight:** 8.0000 g. **Composition:** 0.8750 Gold .2250 oz. AGW **Subject:** 3rd Anniversary - Suez Canal Reopening

| Date | Mintage | F | VF | XF | Unc |
|---|---|---|---|---|---|
| AH1401-1981 Proof | 150 | Value: 250 | | | |

**POUND** **KM# 528** **Weight:** 15.0000 g. **Composition:** 0.7200 Silver .3472 oz. ASW **Subject:** 25th Anniversary - Nationalization of Suez Canal

| Date | Mintage | F | VF | XF | Unc |
|---|---|---|---|---|---|
| AH1401-1981 | 25,000 | — | — | — | 10.00 |
| AH1401-1981 Proof | 1,500 | Value: 25.00 | | | |

**POUND** **KM# 529** **Weight:** 8.0000 g. **Composition:** 0.8750 Gold .2250 oz. AGW **Subject:** 25th Anniversary - Nationalization of Suez Canal

| Date | Mintage | F | VF | XF | Unc |
|---|---|---|---|---|---|
| AH1401-1981 | 3,000 | — | — | — | 175 |

**POUND** **KM# 532** **Weight:** 15.0000 g. **Composition:** 0.7200 Silver .3472 oz. ASW **Series:** F.A.O.

| Date | Mintage | F | VF | XF | Unc |
|---|---|---|---|---|---|
| AH1401-1981 | 50,000 | — | — | — | 7.50 |

**POUND** **KM# 526** **Weight:** 15.0000 g. **Composition:** 0.7200 Silver .3472 oz. ASW **Subject:** 25th Anniversary - Egyptian Industry

| Date | Mintage | F | VF | XF | Unc |
|---|---|---|---|---|---|
| AH1402-1981 | 25,000 | — | — | — | 8.50 |

**POUND** **KM# 527** **Weight:** 15.0000 g. **Composition:** 0.7200 Silver .3472 oz. ASW **Subject:** 25th Anniversary - Trade Unions

| Date | Mintage | F | VF | XF | Unc |
|---|---|---|---|---|---|
| AH1402-1981 | 25,000 | — | — | — | 8.50 |

**POUND** **KM# 530** **Weight:** 15.0000 g. **Composition:** 0.7200 Silver .3472 oz. ASW **Subject:** 100th Anniversary - Revolt by Arabi Pasha **Reverse:** Pasha mounted on horse in front of his followers

| Date | Mintage | F | VF | XF | Unc |
|---|---|---|---|---|---|
| AH1402-1981 | 50,000 | — | — | — | 10.00 |
| AH1402-1981 Proof | 1,500 | Value: 25.00 | | | |

**POUND** **KM# 531** **Weight:** 8.0000 g. **Composition:** 0.8750 Gold .2250 oz. AGW **Subject:** 100th Anniversary - Revolt by Arabi Pasha **Reverse:** Pasha mounted on horse in front of his followers

| Date | Mintage | F | VF | XF | Unc |
|---|---|---|---|---|---|
| AH1402-1981 | 3,000 | — | — | — | 175 |

**POUND** **KM# 539** **Weight:** 15.0000 g. **Composition:** 0.7200 Silver .3472 oz. ASW **Subject:** Golden Jubilee - Egypt Air

| Date | Mintage | F | VF | XF | Unc |
|---|---|---|---|---|---|
| AH1402-1982 | 20,000 | — | — | — | 12.00 |

**POUND** **KM# 540** **Weight:** 15.0000 g. **Composition:** 0.7200 Silver .3472 oz. ASW **Subject:** 1000th Anniversary - Al Azhar Mosque **Reverse:** Mosque

| Date | Mintage | F | VF | XF | Unc |
|---|---|---|---|---|---|
| AH1402-1982 | 23,000 | — | — | — | 10.00 |
| AH1402-1982 Proof | 4,000 | Value: 15.00 | | | |

**POUND** **KM# 541** **Weight:** 8.0000 g. **Composition:** 0.8750 Gold .2250 oz. AGW **Subject:** 1000th Anniversary - Al Azhar Mosque **Reverse:** Mosque

| Date | Mintage | F | VF | XF | Unc |
|---|---|---|---|---|---|
| AH1402-1982 Proof | 2,000 | Value: 175 | | | |

**POUND** **KM# 544** **Weight:** 15.0000 g. **Composition:** 0.7200 Silver .3472 oz. ASW **Subject:** 50th Anniversary - Egyptian Products Co.

| Date | Mintage | F | VF | XF | Unc |
|---|---|---|---|---|---|
| AH1402-1982 | 5,000 | — | — | — | 20.00 |
| AH1402-1982 Proof | 2,000 | Value: 25.00 | | | |

**POUND** **KM# 545** **Weight:** 15.0000 g. **Composition:** 0.7200 Silver .3472 oz. ASW **Subject:** Return of Sinai to Egypt

| Date | Mintage | F | VF | XF | Unc |
|---|---|---|---|---|---|
| AH1402-1982(1983) | 50,000 | — | — | — | 10.00 |
| AH1402-1982(1983) Proof | 2,000 | Value: 20.00 | | | |

**POUND** **KM# 542** **Weight:** 15.0000 g. **Composition:** 0.7200 Silver .3472 oz. ASW **Subject:** 50th Anniversary of Air Force **Reverse:** Air Force insignia within wreath

| Date | Mintage | F | VF | XF | Unc |
|---|---|---|---|---|---|
| AH1403-1982 | 10,000 | — | — | — | 13.50 |
| AH1403-1982 Proof | 2,260 | Value: 25.00 | | | |

**POUND** **KM# 543** **Weight:** 8.0000 g. **Composition:** 0.8750 Gold .2250 oz. AGW **Subject:** 50th Anniversary of Air Force **Reverse:** Air Force insignia within wreath

| Date | Mintage | F | VF | XF | Unc |
|---|---|---|---|---|---|
| AH1403-1982 Proof | 2,000 | Value: 175 | | | |

**POUND** **KM# 549** **Weight:** 15.0000 g. **Composition:** 0.7200 Silver .3472 oz. ASW **Subject:** 50th Anniversary - Deaths of Shawky and Hafez

| Date | Mintage | F | VF | XF | Unc |
|---|---|---|---|---|---|
| AH1403-1983 | 25,000 | — | — | — | 12.00 |

**POUND** **KM# 551** **Weight:** 15.0000 g. **Composition:** 0.7200 Silver .3472 oz. ASW **Subject:** Misr Insurance Company

| Date | Mintage | F | VF | XF | Unc |
|---|---|---|---|---|---|
| AH1404-1984 | 20,000 | — | — | — | 12.00 |

**POUND** **KM# 559** **Weight:** 15.0000 g. **Composition:** 0.7200 Silver .3472 oz. ASW **Subject:** Helwan University Faculty of Fine Arts

| Date | Mintage | F | VF | XF | Unc |
|---|---|---|---|---|---|
| AH1404-1984 | 25,000 | — | — | — | 12.00 |
| AH1404-1984 Proof | 25 | Value: 80.00 | | | |

**POUND** **KM# 583** **Weight:** 8.0000 g. **Composition:** 0.8750 Gold .2250 oz. AGW **Subject:** 50th Anniversary - Egyptian Radio Broadcasting

| Date | Mintage | F | VF | XF | Unc |
|---|---|---|---|---|---|
| AH1404-1984 | 2,000 | — | — | — | 175 |

**POUND** **KM# 571** **Weight:** 8.0000 g. **Composition:** 0.8750 Gold .2250 oz. AGW **Subject:** 25th Anniversary - National Planning Institute

| Date | Mintage | F | VF | XF | Unc |
|---|---|---|---|---|---|
| AH1405-1985 | 200 | — | — | — | 275 |

**POUND** **KM# 574** **Weight:** 8.0000 g. **Composition:** 0.8750 Gold .2250 oz. AGW **Subject:** 60th Anniversary - Egyptian Parliament **Reverse:** Parliament building

| Date | Mintage | F | VF | XF | Unc |
|---|---|---|---|---|---|
| AH1405-1985 | 1,000 | — | — | — | 200 |

**POUND** **KM# 577** **Weight:** 8.0000 g. **Composition:** 0.8750 Gold .2250 oz. AGW **Subject:** 25th Anniversary - Cairo Stadium **Reverse:** Stadium

| Date | Mintage | F | VF | XF | Unc |
|---|---|---|---|---|---|
| AH1405-1985 | 300 | — | — | — | 250 |

**POUND** **KM# 580** **Weight:** 8.0000 g. **Composition:** 0.8750 Gold .2250 oz. AGW **Subject:** 25th Anniversary - Egyptian Television

| Date | Mintage | F | VF | XF | Unc |
|---|---|---|---|---|---|
| AH1405-1985 | 150 | — | — | — | 275 |

**POUND** **KM# 604** **Weight:** 8.0000 g. **Composition:** 0.8750 Gold .2250 oz. AGW **Subject:** Commerce Day **Reverse:** Stylized depictions of commercial activity

| Date | Mintage | F | VF | XF | Unc |
|---|---|---|---|---|---|
| AH1405-1985 Proof | 2,000 | Value: 175 | | | |

**POUND** **KM# 605** **Weight:** 8.0000 g. **Composition:** 0.8750 Gold .2250 oz. AGW **Subject:** Faculty of Economics and Political Science **Obverse:** Arabic legends, seals, and date **Reverse:** Graph within wreath, partial gear wheel

| Date | Mintage | F | VF | XF | Unc |
|---|---|---|---|---|---|
| AH1405-1985 Proof | 250 | Value: 250 | | | |

**POUND** **KM# 635** **Weight:** 8.0000 g. **Composition:** 0.8750 Gold .2250 oz. AGW **Subject:** 25th Anniversary - Cairo International Airport **Obverse:** Stylized legend above dates, dividing 2 seals **Reverse:** 2 circling vultures within Arabic and English legends

| Date | Mintage | F | VF | XF | Unc |
|---|---|---|---|---|---|
| AH1405-1985 | 200 | — | — | — | 250 |

**POUND** **KM# 632** **Weight:** 8.0000 g. **Composition:** 0.8750 Gold .2250 oz. AGW **Subject:** Prophet's Mosque **Obverse:** Minaret, globe, denomination, legends **Reverse:** Crescent, mosque, minaret below legend arch

| Date | Mintage | F | VF | XF | Unc |
|---|---|---|---|---|---|
| AH1406-1985 | 800 | — | — | — | 175 |

**POUND** **KM# 636** **Weight:** 8.0000 g. **Composition:** 0.8750 Gold .2250 oz. AGW **Subject:** Cairo University Faculty of Commerce **Obverse:** Stylized legend above dates, dividing 2 seals **Reverse:** Ancient Egyptian commerce related scenes

| Date | Mintage | F | VF | XF | Unc |
|---|---|---|---|---|---|
| AH1406-1986 | 200 | — | — | — | 250 |

**POUND** **KM# 637** **Weight:** 8.0000 g. **Composition:** 0.8750 Gold .2250 oz. AGW **Subject:** 25th Anniversary - Egyptian Central Bank **Obverse:** Stylized flowers, gear wheel and cotton within legend **Reverse:** Ancient Egyptian sculptures, legends above and below within ornamental border

| Date | Mintage | F | VF | XF | Unc |
|---|---|---|---|---|---|
| AH1406-1986 | 200 | — | — | — | 275 |

**POUND** **KM# 638** **Weight:** 8.0000 g. **Composition:** 0.8750 Gold .2250 oz. AGW **Subject:** 100th Anniversary - Petroleum Industry **Obverse:** Stylized legend above dates, dividing 2 seals **Reverse:** Oil well and landscape within ornamental circle

| Date | Mintage | F | VF | XF | Unc |
|---|---|---|---|---|---|
| AH1406-1986 | 800 | — | — | — | 175 |

**POUND** **KM# 640** **Weight:** 8.0000 g. **Composition:** 0.8750 Gold .2250 oz. AGW **Subject:** 50th Anniversary - National Theater **Obverse:** Stylized stage curtain, legend within **Reverse:** Large building, 2 masks in foreground, legend above

| Date | Mintage | F | VF | XF | Unc |
|---|---|---|---|---|---|
| AH1406-1986 | 250 | — | — | — | 225 |

**POUND** **KM# 644** **Weight:** 8.0000 g. **Composition:** 0.8750 Gold .2250 oz. AGW **Subject:** Restoration of Parliament Building **Obverse:** Arabic legends **Reverse:** Dome and tower with scaffolding

| Date | Mintage | F | VF | XF | Unc |
|---|---|---|---|---|---|
| AH1406-1986 | 400 | — | — | — | 175 |

**POUND** **KM# 639** **Weight:** 8.0000 g. **Composition:** 0.8750 Gold .2250 oz. AGW **Subject:** Census **Obverse:** Arabic legends, seals, date **Reverse:** City view with paper doll cutout human figures

| Date | Mintage | F | VF | XF | Unc |
|---|---|---|---|---|---|
| AH1407-1986 | 200 | — | — | — | 200 |

**POUND** **KM# 643** **Weight:** 8.0000 g. **Composition:** 0.8750 Gold .2250 oz. AGW **Subject:** 40th Anniversary - Engineer's Syndicate **Obverse:** Arabic legends, seals, dates **Reverse:** 3 triangles, legend, ornamentation

| Date | Mintage | F | VF | XF | Unc |
|---|---|---|---|---|---|
| AH1407-1986 | 400 | — | — | — | 175 |

**POUND** **KM# 645** **Weight:** 8.0000 g. **Composition:** 0.8750 Gold .2250 oz. AGW **Subject:** Parliament Museum **Obverse:** Arabic legends, seals, dates **Reverse:** Documents, quill, carriage, building with national emblem

| Date | Mintage | F | VF | XF | Unc |
|---|---|---|---|---|---|
| AH1407-1987 | 400 | — | — | — | 175 |

**POUND** **KM# 653** **Weight:** 8.0000 g. **Composition:** 0.8750 Gold .2250 oz. AGW **Subject:** Investment Bank **Obverse:** Toughra, legends above and below, dates **Reverse:** Symbol within stylized circle, legend around

| Date | Mintage | F | VF | XF | Unc |
|---|---|---|---|---|---|
| AH1407-1987 | 600 | — | — | — | 175 |

**POUND** **KM# 673** **Weight:** 8.0000 g. **Composition:** 0.8750 Gold .2250 oz. AGW **Subject:** First African Subway **Obverse:** Stylized legends and denomination **Reverse:** Subway emerging from tunnel emerging from tunnel with legend around rim

| Date | Mintage | F | VF | XF | Unc |
|---|---|---|---|---|---|
| AH1408-1987 Proof | 500 | Value: 225 | | | |

**POUND** **KM# 647** **Weight:** 8.0000 g. **Composition:** 0.8750 Gold .2250 oz. AGW **Subject:** Police Day **Obverse:** Arabic and English legends, seals, dates **Reverse:** Police emblem - eagle in wreath, legends

| Date | Mintage | F | VF | XF | Unc |
|---|---|---|---|---|---|
| AH1408-1988 | 500 | — | — | — | 175 |

**POUND** **KM# 654** **Weight:** 8.0000 g. **Composition:** 0.8750 Gold .2250 oz. AGW **Subject:** Dedication of Cairo Opera House **Obverse:** Arabic legends, seals, dates **Reverse:** Opera house, legends above and below

| Date | Mintage | F | VF | XF | Unc |
|---|---|---|---|---|---|
| AH1409-1988 | 1,500 | — | — | — | 225 |

**POUND** **KM# 661** **Weight:** 8.0000 g. **Composition:** 0.8750 Gold .2250 oz. AGW **Subject:** Naquib Mahfouz, Nobel Laureate **Obverse:** Stylized quill ink and paper design with legend above **Reverse:** Head of Mahfouz left

| Date | Mintage | F | VF | XF | Unc |
|---|---|---|---|---|---|
| AH1409-1988 Proof | 1,000 | Value: 175 | | | |

**POUND** **KM# 664** **Weight:** 8.0000 g. **Composition:** 0.8750 Gold .2250 oz. AGW **Subject:** United Parliamentary Union **Obverse:** Kufic legend above denomination and dates **Reverse:** Anniversary dates, map in wreath above domed building, and legend

| Date | Mintage | F | VF | XF | Unc |
|---|---|---|---|---|---|
| AH1409-1989 Proof | 200 | Value: 275 | | | |

**POUND** **KM# 666** **Weight:** 8.0000 g. **Composition:** 0.8750 Gold .2250 oz. AGW **Subject:** First Arab Olympics **Obverse:** Kufic legend above denomination and dates **Reverse:** 5 Olympic rings and map as part of torch held by hand within wreath and legend

| Date | Mintage | F | VF | XF | Unc |
|---|---|---|---|---|---|
| AH1409-1989 Proof | 300 | Value: 250 | | | |

**POUND** **KM# 668** **Weight:** 8.0000 g. **Composition:** 0.8750 Gold .2250 oz. AGW **Subject:** National Research Center **Obverse:** Kufic legend above denomination and dates **Reverse:** Stylized ancient and modern research elements

| Date | Mintage | F | VF | XF | Unc |
|---|---|---|---|---|---|
| AH1409-1989 Proof | 250 | Value: 250 | | | |

**POUND** **KM# 677** **Weight:** 8.0000 g. **Composition:** 0.8750 Gold .2250 oz. AGW **Subject:** University of Cairo, School of Agriculture **Obverse:** Denomination between wheat ears above legend **Reverse:** Ancient farming scene and coat of arms, building in background

| Date | Mintage | F | VF | XF | Unc |
|---|---|---|---|---|---|
| AH1410-1989 Proof | 200 | Value: 275 | | | |

**POUND** **KM# 695** **Weight:** 8.0000 g. **Composition:** 0.8750 Gold .2250 oz. AGW **Subject:** Export Trade Show **Obverse:** Toughra, inscription above **Reverse:** Display of symbols

| Date | Mintage | F | VF | XF | Unc |
|---|---|---|---|---|---|
| AH1410-1989 Proof | 200 | Value: 275 | | | |

**POUND** **KM# 696** **Weight:** 8.0000 g. **Composition:** 0.8750 Gold .2250 oz. AGW **Subject:** Union of African Parliament **Obverse:** Toughra, denomination, date within circle and legend **Reverse:** Map of Africa, laurel branch and Parliament building

| Date | Mintage | F | VF | XF | Unc |
|---|---|---|---|---|---|
| AH1410-1990 Proof | 200 | Value: 275 | | | |

**POUND** **KM# 699** **Weight:** 8.0000 g. **Composition:** 0.8750 Gold .2250 oz. AGW **Subject:** 5th African Games - Cairo **Obverse:** Torch with legend and inscription **Reverse:** Logo above rings within legend

| Date | Mintage | F | VF | XF | Unc |
|---|---|---|---|---|---|
| AH1411-1991 Proof | 200 | Value: 275 | | | |

**POUND** **KM# 832** **Weight:** 8.0000 g. **Composition:** 0.8750 Gold .2250 oz. AGW **Subject:** Library of Alexandria **Obverse:** Legend and inscription **Reverse:** Waterfront building with tower

| Date | Mintage | F | VF | XF | Unc |
|---|---|---|---|---|---|
| AH1411-1991 | 300 | — | — | — | 400 |

**POUND** **KM# 726** **Weight:** 8.0000 g. **Composition:** 0.8750 Gold .2250 oz. AGW **Subject:** Mohamed Abdel Wahab **Reverse:** Bust of Mohamed Abdel Wahab left with music sheet in background

| Date | Mintage | F | VF | XF | Unc |
|---|---|---|---|---|---|
| AH1412-1991 | 1,000 | — | — | — | 175 |

**POUND** **KM# 835** **Weight:** 15.0000 g. **Composition:** 0.7200 Silver .3472 oz. ASW **Subject:** Gorgui Zidane **Obverse:** Legend and vase **Reverse:** Portrait **Edge:** Reeded

| Date | Mintage | F | VF | XF | Unc |
|---|---|---|---|---|---|
| AH1413-1992 | 3,000 | — | — | — | 20.00 |

**POUND** **KM# 836** **Weight:** 8.0000 g. **Composition:** 0.8750 Gold .2250 oz. AGW **Subject:** Rifa'a El Tahtaoui **Obverse:** Legend and vase **Reverse:** Portrait

| Date | Mintage | F | VF | XF | Unc |
|---|---|---|---|---|---|
| AH1413-1992 | 800 | — | — | — | 400 |

**POUND** **KM# 810** **Weight:** 15.0000 g. **Composition:** 0.7200 Silver .3472 oz. ASW **Subject:** 20th Anniversary - October War **Obverse:** Smoking chimney text **Reverse:** Soldier with flag

| Date | Mintage | F | VF | XF | Unc |
|---|---|---|---|---|---|
| AH1414-1993 | Est. 25,000 | — | — | — | 30.00 |

**POUND** **KM# 811** **Weight:** 8.0000 g. **Composition:** 0.8750 Gold .2250 oz. AGW **Subject:** 20th Anniversary - October War **Obverse:** Smoking chimney text **Reverse:** Soldier with flag

| Date | Mintage | F | VF | XF | Unc |
|---|---|---|---|---|---|
| AH1414-1993 | Est. 3,000 | — | — | — | 400 |

**POUND** **KM# 761** **Weight:** 15.0000 g. **Composition:** 0.7200 Silver .3472 oz. ASW **Subject:** Salah El Din El-Ayubi **Obverse:** Denomination **Reverse:** Portrait

| Date | Mintage | F | VF | XF | Unc |
|---|---|---|---|---|---|
| AH1414-1994 | 5,000 | — | — | — | 25.00 |

**POUND** KM# 762 **Weight:** 8.0000 g. **Composition:** 0.8750 Gold .2250 oz. AGW **Subject:** Salah El Din El-Ayubi **Obverse:** Denomination **Reverse:** Portrait

| Date | Mintage | F | VF | XF | Unc |
|---|---|---|---|---|---|
| AH1414-1994 | 300 | — | — | — | 400 |

**POUND** KM# 764 **Weight:** 15.0000 g. **Composition:** 0.7200 Silver .3472 oz. ASW **Subject:** 125 Years - Suez Canal **Obverse:** Toughra **Reverse:** Building and canal scenes

| Date | Mintage | F | VF | XF | Unc |
|---|---|---|---|---|---|
| AH1415-1994 | 3,000 | — | — | — | 20.00 |

**POUND** KM# 766 **Weight:** 15.0000 g. **Composition:** 0.7200 Silver .3472 oz. ASW **Subject:** 75 Years - Bank of Misr **Obverse:** Inscription **Reverse:** Bank building and emblem

| Date | Mintage | F | VF | XF | Unc |
|---|---|---|---|---|---|
| AH1415-1994 | 2,500 | — | — | — | 30.00 |

**POUND** KM# 839 **Weight:** 15.0000 g. **Composition:** 0.7200 Silver .3472 oz. ASW **Subject:** Abd Al Halem Hafez **Obverse:** Denomination **Reverse:** Portrait

| Date | Mintage | F | VF | XF | Unc |
|---|---|---|---|---|---|
| AH1416-1995 | 3,000 | — | — | — | 20.00 |

**POUND** KM# 767 **Weight:** 8.0000 g. **Composition:** 0.8750 Gold .2250 oz. AGW **Subject:** 75 Years - Bank of Misr

| Date | Mintage | F | VF | XF | Unc |
|---|---|---|---|---|---|
| AH1415-1995 | 1,000 | — | — | — | 400 |

**POUND** KM# 769 **Weight:** 15.0000 g. **Composition:** 0.7200 Silver .3472 oz. ASW **Series:** F.A.O. **Reverse:** Workers

| Date | Mintage | F | VF | XF | Unc |
|---|---|---|---|---|---|
| AH1415-1995 | 3,000 | — | — | — | 40.00 |

**POUND** KM# 771 **Weight:** 8.0000 g. **Composition:** 0.8750 Gold .2250 oz. AGW **Subject:** Pediatrics International Conference

| Date | Mintage | F | VF | XF | Unc |
|---|---|---|---|---|---|
| AH1416-1995 | 300 | — | — | — | 400 |

**POUND** KM# 840 **Weight:** 8.0000 g. **Composition:** 0.8750 Gold .2250 oz. AGW **Subject:** Abd Al Halem Hafez **Obverse:** Denomination **Reverse:** Abd Al Halem Hafez

| Date | Mintage | F | VF | XF | Unc |
|---|---|---|---|---|---|
| AH1416-1995 | 500 | — | — | — | 400 |

**POUND** KM# 844 **Weight:** 15.0000 g. **Composition:** 0.7200 Silver .3472 oz. ASW **Subject:** Centennial - Electrification **Obverse:** Legend and inscription **Reverse:** Electric bolt on Pyramid

| Date | Mintage | F | VF | XF | Unc |
|---|---|---|---|---|---|
| AH1417-1996 | 3,000 | — | — | — | 15.00 |

**POUND** KM# 845 **Weight:** 15.0000 g. **Composition:** 0.7200 Silver .3472 oz. ASW **Subject:** 65 Years - Egyptian Air Force **Obverse:** Denomination **Reverse:** Flying eagle in wreath

| Date | Mintage | F | VF | XF | Unc |
|---|---|---|---|---|---|
| AH1418-1997 | 226 | — | — | — | 85.00 |

**POUND** KM# 847 **Weight:** 15.0000 g. **Composition:** 0.7200 Silver .3472 oz. ASW **Subject:** 50 Years Arab Land Bank **Obverse:** Denomination **Reverse:** Domed building

| Date | Mintage | F | VF | XF | Unc |
|---|---|---|---|---|---|
| AH1418-1997 | — | — | — | — | 35.00 |

**POUND** KM# 849 **Weight:** 15.0000 g. **Composition:** 0.7200 Silver .3472 oz. ASW **Subject:** 95th Interparliamentary Union Conference **Obverse:** Circular design above inscription **Reverse:** Pyramids in wreath

| Date | Mintage | F | VF | XF | Unc |
|---|---|---|---|---|---|
| AH1418-1997 | 375 | — | — | — | 85.00 |

**POUND** KM# 851 **Weight:** 15.0000 g. **Composition:** 0.7200 Silver .3472 oz. ASW **Series:** Centennial - Chemical Office **Obverse:** Denomination **Reverse:** Symbolic design

| Date | Mintage | F | VF | XF | Unc |
|---|---|---|---|---|---|
| AH1419-1998 | — | — | — | — | 35.00 |

**POUND** KM# 855 **Weight:** 15.0000 g. **Composition:** 0.7200 Silver .3472 oz. ASW **Series:** Centennial - National Bank **Obverse:** Denomination **Reverse:** Large "100"

| Date | Mintage | F | VF | XF | Unc |
|---|---|---|---|---|---|
| AH1419-1998 | 200 | — | — | — | 85.00 |

**POUND** KM# 857 **Weight:** 15.0000 g. **Composition:** 0.7200 Silver .3472 oz. ASW **Subject:** 25th Anniversary - October War **Obverse:** Denomination **Reverse:** Symbolic design

| Date | Mintage | F | VF | XF | Unc |
|---|---|---|---|---|---|
| AH1419-1998 | — | — | — | — | 40.00 |

**POUND** KM# 859 **Weight:** 15.0000 g. **Composition:** 0.7200 Silver .3472 oz. ASW **Subject:** Imam Metwaly El Sharawi **Obverse:** Open book **Reverse:** Portrait

| Date | Mintage | F | VF | XF | Unc |
|---|---|---|---|---|---|
| AH1419-1998 | — | — | — | — | 40.00 |

**POUND** KM# 861 **Weight:** 15.0000 g. **Composition:** 0.7200 Silver .3472 oz. ASW **Series:** Centennial - Land Surveying **Obverse:** Denomination **Reverse:** "100" above ancient surveyors

| Date | Mintage | F | VF | XF | Unc |
|---|---|---|---|---|---|
| AH1419-1998 | — | — | — | — | 35.00 |

**POUND** KM# 863 **Weight:** 15.0000 g. **Composition:** 0.7200 Silver .3472 oz. ASW **Series:** Centennial - Solidarity **Obverse:** Denomination **Reverse:** Symbolic design

| Date | Mintage | F | VF | XF | Unc |
|---|---|---|---|---|---|
| AH1419-1998 | — | — | — | — | 35.00 |

**POUND** KM# 865 **Weight:** 15.0000 g. **Composition:** 0.7200 Silver .3472 oz. ASW **Subject:** Golden Jubilee of Ash Shanns University **Obverse:** Denomination **Reverse:** Monument

| Date | Mintage | F | VF | XF | Unc |
|---|---|---|---|---|---|
| AH1420-1999 | — | — | — | — | 35.00 |

**POUND** **Weight:** 15.0000 g. **Composition:** 0.7200 Silver .3472 oz. ASW **Subject:** Cairo Metropolitan Mass Transit System **Obverse:** Legend and inscription **Reverse:** Water above subway train

| Date | Mintage | F | VF | XF | Unc |
|---|---|---|---|---|---|
| AH1420-1999 | — | — | — | — | 35.00 |

**5 POUNDS** KM# 441 **Weight:** 26.0000 g. **Composition:** 0.8750 Gold .7315 oz. AGW **Subject:** 75th Anniveresary - National Bank of Egypt **Reverse:** World globe with bank building at right

| Date | Mintage | F | VF | XF | Unc |
|---|---|---|---|---|---|
| AH1393-1973 | 1,000 | — | — | — | 400 |
| AH1393-1973 Proof | — | Value: 600 | | | |

**5 POUNDS** KM# 444 **Weight:** 26.0000 g. **Composition:** 0.8750 Gold .7315 oz. AGW **Subject:** 1973 October War

| Date | Mintage | F | VF | XF | Unc |
|---|---|---|---|---|---|
| AH1394-1974 | 1,000 | — | — | — | 420 |

**5 POUNDS** KM# 459 **Weight:** 26.0000 g. **Composition:** 0.8750 Gold .7315 oz. AGW **Subject:** King Faisal of Saudi Arabia **Reverse:** Head of King Faisal half right

| Date | Mintage | F | VF | XF | Unc |
|---|---|---|---|---|---|
| AH1396-1976 | 2,500 | — | — | — | 550 |

**5 POUNDS** KM# 460 **Weight:** 26.0000 g. **Composition:** 0.8750 Gold .7315 oz. AGW **Subject:** Reopening of Suez Canal

| Date | Mintage | F | VF | XF | Unc |
|---|---|---|---|---|---|
| AH1396-1976 | 2,000 | — | — | — | 400 |

**5 POUNDS** KM# 461 **Weight:** 26.0000 g. **Composition:** 0.8750 Gold .7315 oz. AGW **Subject:** Om Kalsoum **Reverse:** Head of Om Kalsoum right

| Date | Mintage | F | VF | XF | Unc |
|---|---|---|---|---|---|
| AH1396-1976 | 1,000 | — | — | — | 800 |

**5 POUNDS** KM# 495 **Weight:** 26.0000 g. **Composition:** 0.8750 Gold .7315 oz. AGW **Subject:** 100th Anniversary - Bank of Land Reform **Reverse:** Seated man, farmer tilling soil with 3 oxen behind, mural showing workers cutting grain sheaves

| Date | Mintage | F | VF | XF | Unc |
|---|---|---|---|---|---|
| AH1399-1979 | 1,750 | — | — | — | 400 |
| AH1399-1979 Proof | 250 | Value: 550 | | | |

**5 POUNDS** KM# 496 **Weight:** 26.0000 g. **Composition:** 0.8750 Gold .7315 oz. AGW **Subject:** 1400th Anniversary - Mohammed's Flight **Reverse:** 2 doves with eggs in front of spider web

| Date | Mintage | F | VF | XF | Unc |
|---|---|---|---|---|---|
| AH1400-1979 | 2,000 | — | — | — | 400 |

**5 POUNDS** KM# 517 **Weight:** 26.0000 g. **Composition:** 0.8750 Gold .7315 oz. AGW **Subject:** Egyptian-Israeli Peace

Treaty **Reverse:** Head of Anwar Sadat at right facing left, dove of peace at right behind

| Date | Mintage | F | VF | XF | Unc |
|---|---|---|---|---|---|
| AH1400-1980 | 2,375 | — | — | — | 375 |
| AH1400-1980 Proof | 125 | Value: 625 | | | |

**5 POUNDS** **KM# 518** **Weight:** 26.0000 g. **Composition:** 0.8750 Gold .7315 oz. AGW **Subject:** Doctor's Day

| Date | Mintage | F | VF | XF | Unc |
|---|---|---|---|---|---|
| AH1400-1980 | 1,000 | — | — | — | 550 |

**5 POUNDS** **KM# 533** **Weight:** 24.0000 g. **Composition:** 0.9250 Silver .7138 oz. ASW **Series:** International Year of the Child **Reverse:** Children holding hands and dancing around stylistic globe

| Date | Mintage | F | VF | XF | Unc |
|---|---|---|---|---|---|
| AH1401-1981 Proof | 10,000 | Value: 30.00 | | | |

**5 POUNDS** **KM# 537** **Weight:** 26.0000 g. **Composition:** 0.8750 Gold .7315 oz. AGW **Subject:** 25th Anniversary - Nationalization of Suez Canal

| Date | Mintage | F | VF | XF | Unc |
|---|---|---|---|---|---|
| AH1401-1981 | 1,000 | — | — | — | 400 |

**5 POUNDS** **KM# 535** **Weight:** 26.0000 g. **Composition:** 0.8750 Gold .7315 oz. AGW **Subject:** 25th Anniversary - Ministry of Industry

| Date | Mintage | F | VF | XF | Unc |
|---|---|---|---|---|---|
| AH1402-1981 Proof | 1,500 | Value: 400 | | | |

**5 POUNDS** **KM# 536** **Weight:** 26.0000 g. **Composition:** 0.8750 Gold .7315 oz. AGW **Subject:** 100th Anniversary - Revolt by Arabi Pasha **Reverse:** Pasha mounted on horse in front of his followers

| Date | Mintage | F | VF | XF | Unc |
|---|---|---|---|---|---|
| AH1402-1981 | 1,000 | — | — | — | 400 |

**5 POUNDS** **KM# 534** **Weight:** 26.0000 g. **Composition:** 0.8750 Gold .7315 oz. AGW **Subject:** 3rd Anniversary - Suez Canal Reopening

| Date | Mintage | F | VF | XF | Unc |
|---|---|---|---|---|---|
| AH1401-1981 | 925 | — | — | — | 400 |
| AH1401-1981 Proof | 75 | Value: 650 | | | |

**5 POUNDS** **KM# 546** **Weight:** 26.0000 g. **Composition:** 0.8750 Gold .7315 oz. AGW **Subject:** 1000th Anniversary - Al Azhar Mosque **Reverse:** Mosque

| Date | Mintage | F | VF | XF | Unc |
|---|---|---|---|---|---|
| AH1402-1982 | 1,500 | — | — | — | 400 |

**5 POUNDS** **KM# 547** **Weight:** 26.0000 g. **Composition:** 0.8750 Gold .7315 oz. AGW **Subject:** 50th Anniversary - Air Force **Reverse:** Air Force insignia within wreath

| Date | Mintage | F | VF | XF | Unc |
|---|---|---|---|---|---|
| AH1403-1982 | 1,000 | — | — | — | 400 |

**5 POUNDS** **KM# 552** **Weight:** 17.5000 g. **Composition:** 0.7200 Silver .4051 oz. ASW **Subject:** 75th Anniversary - Cairo University

| Date | Mintage | F | VF | XF | Unc |
|---|---|---|---|---|---|
| AH1404-1983 | 25,000 | — | — | — | 18.00 |

**5 POUNDS** **KM# 558** **Weight:** 17.5000 g. **Composition:** 0.7200 Silver .4051 oz. ASW **Subject:** Los Angeles Olympics

| Date | Mintage | F | VF | XF | Unc |
|---|---|---|---|---|---|
| AH1404-1984 | 20,000 | — | — | — | 13.50 |

**5 POUNDS** **KM# 560** **Weight:** 17.5000 g. **Composition:** 0.7200 Silver .4051 oz. ASW **Subject:** Academy of Arabic Languages

| Date | Mintage | F | VF | XF | Unc |
|---|---|---|---|---|---|
| AH1404-1984 | 25,000 | — | — | — | 13.50 |

**5 POUNDS** **KM# 561** **Weight:** 17.5000 g. **Composition:** 0.7200 Silver .4051 oz. ASW **Subject:** 50th Anniversary - Egyptian Radio Broadcasting

| Date | Mintage | F | VF | XF | Unc |
|---|---|---|---|---|---|
| AH1404-1984 | 25,000 | — | — | — | 13.50 |

**5 POUNDS** **KM# 565** **Weight:** 17.5000 g. **Composition:** 0.7200 Silver .4051 oz. ASW **Subject:** Sculptor Mahmoud Mokhtar **Reverse:** Bust of Mokhtar left

| Date | Mintage | F | VF | XF | Unc |
|---|---|---|---|---|---|
| AH1404-1984 | 10,000 | — | — | — | 12.50 |

**5 POUNDS** **KM# 566** **Weight:** 17.5000 g. **Composition:** 0.7200 Silver .4051 oz. ASW **Subject:** Golden Jubilee of Petroleum Industry

| Date | Mintage | F | VF | XF | Unc |
|---|---|---|---|---|---|
| AH1404-1984 | 10,000 | — | — | — | 13.50 |

**5 POUNDS** **KM# 567** **Weight:** 17.5000 g. **Composition:** 0.7200 Silver .4051 oz. ASW **Subject:** Diamond Jubilee of Cooperation **Reverse:** Seven joined hexagons with different scenes

| Date | Mintage | F | VF | XF | Unc |
|---|---|---|---|---|---|
| AH1404-1984 | 10,000 | — | — | — | 12.50 |

**5 POUNDS** **KM# 671** **Weight:** 26.0000 g. **Composition:** 0.8750 Gold .7315 oz. AGW **Subject:** 50th Anniversary - Egyptian Radio **Obverse:** Arabic legends **Reverse:** Tall buildings with transmitter

| Date | Mintage | F | VF | XF | Unc |
|---|---|---|---|---|---|
| AH1404-1984 Proof | 500 | Value: 450 | | | |

**5 POUNDS** **KM# 563** **Weight:** 17.5000 g. **Composition:** 0.7205 Silver .4051 oz. ASW **Subject:** 100th Anniversary - Moharram Printing Press Co.

| Date | Mintage | F | VF | XF | Unc |
|---|---|---|---|---|---|
| AH1405-1985 | 20,000 | — | — | — | 14.50 |

**5 POUNDS** **KM# 564** **Weight:** 40.0000 g. **Composition:** 0.8750 Gold 1.1253 oz. AGW **Subject:** 100th Anniversary - Moharram Printing Press Co.

| Date | Mintage | F | VF | XF | Unc |
|---|---|---|---|---|---|
| AH1405-1985 | 200 | — | — | — | 1,850 |

**5 POUNDS** **KM# 572** **Weight:** 17.5000 g. **Composition:** 0.7200 Silver .4051 oz. ASW **Subject:** 25th Anniversary - National Planning Institute

| Date | Mintage | F | VF | XF | Unc |
|---|---|---|---|---|---|
| AH1405-1985 | 15,000 | — | — | — | 12.50 |

**5 POUNDS** **KM# 575** **Weight:** 17.5000 g. **Composition:** 0.7200 Silver .4051 oz. ASW **Subject:** 60th Anniversary - Egyptian Parliament **Reverse:** Parliament building

| Date | Mintage | F | VF | XF | Unc |
|---|---|---|---|---|---|
| AH1405-1985 | 25,000 | — | — | — | 12.50 |

**5 POUNDS** **KM# 576** **Weight:** 26.0000 g. **Composition:** 0.8750 Gold .7315 oz. AGW **Subject:** 60th Anniversary - Egyptian Parliament **Reverse:** Parliament building

| Date | Mintage | F | VF | XF | Unc |
|---|---|---|---|---|---|
| AH1405-1985 | 500 | — | — | — | 1,750 |

**5 POUNDS** **KM# 578** **Weight:** 17.5000 g. **Composition:** 0.7200 Silver .4051 oz. ASW **Subject:** 25th Anniversary - Cairo Stadium **Reverse:** Stadium

| Date | Mintage | F | VF | XF | Unc |
|---|---|---|---|---|---|
| AH1405-1985 | 25,000 | — | — | — | 12.50 |

**5 POUNDS** **KM# 581** **Weight:** 17.5000 g. **Composition:** 0.7200 Silver .4051 oz. ASW **Subject:** 25th Anniversary - Egyptian Television

| Date | Mintage | F | VF | XF | Unc |
|---|---|---|---|---|---|
| AH1405-1985 | 5,000 | — | — | — | 12.50 |

**5 POUNDS** **KM# 585** **Weight:** 17.5000 g. **Composition:** 0.7200 Silver .4051 oz. ASW **Subject:** 25th Anniversary - Cairo International Airport

| Date | Mintage | F | VF | XF | Unc |
|---|---|---|---|---|---|
| AH1405-1985 | 20,000 | — | — | — | 12.50 |

**5 POUNDS** **KM# 592** **Weight:** 17.5000 g. **Composition:** 0.7200 Silver .4051 oz. ASW **Subject:** Tutankhamen **Reverse:** Bust of Tutankhamen left

| Date | Mintage | F | VF | XF | Unc |
|---|---|---|---|---|---|
| AH1405-1985 | 6,000 | — | — | — | 18.00 |
| AH1405-1985 Proof | 2,000 | Value: 30.00 | | | |

**5 POUNDS** **KM# 593** **Weight:** 17.5000 g. **Composition:** 0.7200 Silver .4051 oz. ASW **Subject:** XV UIA Congress **Reverse:** Pyramid

| Date | Mintage | F | VF | XF | Unc |
|---|---|---|---|---|---|
| AH1405-1985 | 10,000 | — | — | — | 13.50 |
| AH1405-1985 Proof | Est. 500 | Value: 25.00 | | | |

**5 POUNDS** **KM# 598** **Weight:** 17.5000 g. **Composition:** 0.7200 Silver .4051 oz. ASW **Subject:** Faculty of Economics and Political Science

| Date | Mintage | F | VF | XF | Unc |
|---|---|---|---|---|---|
| AH1405-1985 | 8,000 | — | — | — | 14.00 |

**5 POUNDS** **KM# 600** **Weight:** 17.5000 g. **Composition:** 0.7200 Silver .4051 oz. ASW **Subject:** Commerce Day

| Date | Mintage | F | VF | XF | Unc |
|---|---|---|---|---|---|
| AH1405-1985 | 20,000 | — | — | — | 11.50 |
| AH1405-1985 Proof | 1,000 | Value: 21.50 | | | |

**5 POUNDS** **KM# 584** **Weight:** 17.5000 g. **Composition:** 0.7200 Silver .4051 oz. ASW **Subject:** The Prophet's Mosque **Reverse:** Mosque

| Date | Mintage | F | VF | XF | Unc |
|---|---|---|---|---|---|
| AH1406-1985 | 25,000 | — | — | — | 11.50 |
| AH1406-1985 Proof | 1,000 | Value: 21.50 | | | |

**5 POUNDS** **KM# 587** **Weight:** 17.5000 g. **Composition:** 0.7200 Silver .4051 oz. ASW **Subject:** Professions **Reverse:** Different professions illustrated on coin

| Date | Mintage | F | VF | XF | Unc |
|---|---|---|---|---|---|
| AH1406-1985 | 8,000 | — | — | — | 13.50 |

**5 POUNDS** **KM# 633** **Weight:** 26.0000 g. **Composition:** 0.8750 Gold .7315 oz. AGW **Subject:** Prophet's Mosque **Obverse:** Minaret, globe, denomination, legends **Reverse:** Crescent, mosque, minaret below legend arch

| Date | Mintage | F | VF | XF | Unc |
|---|---|---|---|---|---|
| AH1406-1985 | 400 | — | — | — | 450 |

**5 POUNDS** **KM# 579** **Weight:** 26.0000 g. **Composition:** 0.8750 Gold .7315 oz. AGW **Subject:** 25th Anniversary - Cairo Stadium **Reverse:** Stadium

| Date | Mintage | F | VF | XF | Unc |
|---|---|---|---|---|---|
| AH1405-1985 | 200 | — | — | — | 1,800 |

**5 POUNDS** **KM# 582** **Weight:** 26.0000 g. **Composition:** 0.8750 Gold .7315 oz. AGW **Subject:** 25th Anniversary - Egyptian Television

| Date | Mintage | F | VF | XF | Unc |
|---|---|---|---|---|---|
| AH1405-1985 | 100 | — | — | — | 1,100 |

**5 POUNDS** **KM# 609a** **Weight:** 26.0000 g. **Composition:** 0.8750 Gold .7315 oz. AGW **Subject:** Mecca

| Date | Mintage | F | VF | XF | Unc |
|---|---|---|---|---|---|
| AH1406-1986 Proof | 1,400 | Value: 400 | | | |

**5 POUNDS** **KM# 615** **Weight:** 17.5000 g. **Composition:** 0.7200 Silver .4051 oz. ASW **Subject:** 30th Anniversary - Atomic Energy Organization

| Date | Mintage | F | VF | XF | Unc |
|---|---|---|---|---|---|
| AH1406-1986 | 5,000 | — | — | — | 15.00 |

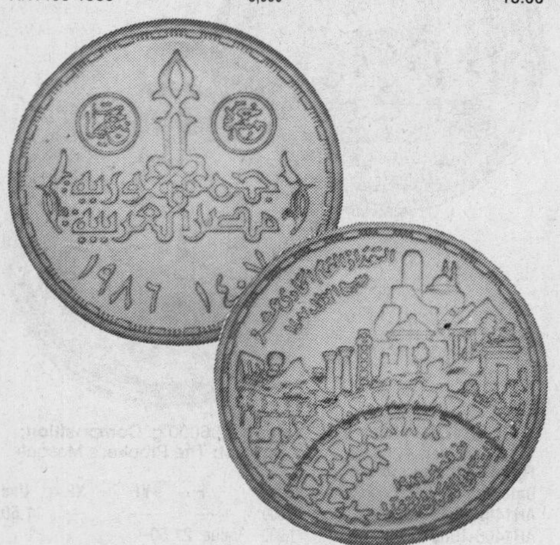

**5 POUNDS** **KM# 603** **Weight:** 17.5000 g. **Composition:** 0.7200 Silver .4051 oz. ASW **Subject:** Census

| Date | Mintage | F | VF | XF | Unc |
|---|---|---|---|---|---|
| AH1407-1986 | 6,000 | — | — | — | 15.00 |

**5 POUNDS** **KM# 610** **Weight:** 17.5000 g. **Composition:** 0.7200 Silver .4051 oz. ASW **Subject:** 40th Anniversary - Engineer's Syndicate

| Date | Mintage | F | VF | XF | Unc |
|---|---|---|---|---|---|
| AH1407-1986 | 6,000 | — | — | — | 15.00 |

**5 POUNDS** **KM# 616** **Weight:** 17.5000 g. **Composition:** 0.7200 Silver .4051 oz. ASW **Subject:** 30th Anniversary - Egyptian Industry

| Date | Mintage | F | VF | XF | Unc |
|---|---|---|---|---|---|
| AH1407-1986 | 5,000 | — | — | — | 15.00 |

**5 POUNDS** **KM# 586** **Weight:** 17.5000 g. **Composition:** 0.7200 Silver .4051 oz. ASW **Subject:** Cairo University Faculty of Commerce

| Date | Mintage | F | VF | XF | Unc |
|---|---|---|---|---|---|
| AH1406-1986 | 20,000 | — | — | — | 13.50 |

**5 POUNDS** **KM# 588** **Weight:** 17.5000 g. **Composition:** 0.7200 Silver .4051 oz. ASW **Subject:** 25th Anniversary - Egyptian National Bank

| Date | Mintage | F | VF | XF | Unc |
|---|---|---|---|---|---|
| AH1406-1986 | 6,000 | — | — | — | 13.50 |

**5 POUNDS** **KM# 589** **Weight:** 17.6800 g. **Composition:** 0.7200 Silver .4093 oz. ASW **Subject:** World Soccer Championships **Reverse:** Soccer ball, 3 pyramids

| Date | Mintage | F | VF | XF | Unc |
|---|---|---|---|---|---|
| AH1406-1986 Proflike | 5,000 | — | — | — | 15.00 |
| AH1406-1986 Proof | 2,150 | Value: 30.00 | | | |

**5 POUNDS** **KM# 590** **Weight:** 17.5000 g. **Composition:** 0.7200 Silver .4051 oz. ASW **Subject:** African Soccer Championship Games **Reverse:** Two soccer players at right

| Date | Mintage | F | VF | XF | Unc |
|---|---|---|---|---|---|
| AH1406-1986 | 15,000 | — | — | — | 14.00 |
| AH1406-1986 Proof | 2,000 | Value: 30.00 | | | |

**5 POUNDS** **KM# 594** **Weight:** 17.5000 g. **Composition:** 0.7200 Silver .4051 oz. ASW **Subject:** 50th Anniversary - Ministry of Health

| Date | Mintage | F | VF | XF | Unc |
|---|---|---|---|---|---|
| AH1406-1986 | 10,000 | — | — | — | 14.00 |
| AH1406-1986 Proof | Est. 500 | Value: 30.00 | | | |

**5 POUNDS** **KM# 601** **Weight:** 17.5000 g. **Composition:** 0.7200 Silver .4051 oz. ASW **Subject:** Crossed Swords **Reverse:** Crossed swords within wreath

| Date | Mintage | F | VF | XF | Unc |
|---|---|---|---|---|---|
| AH1406-1986 | 16,000 | — | — | — | 13.50 |

**5 POUNDS** **KM# 602** **Weight:** 17.5000 g. **Composition:** 0.7200 Silver .4051 oz. ASW **Subject:** 100th Anniversary - Petroleum Industry **Reverse:** Oil derrick with building behind

| Date | Mintage | F | VF | XF | Unc |
|---|---|---|---|---|---|
| AH1406-1986 | 6,000 | — | — | — | 15.00 |

**5 POUNDS** **KM# 608** **Weight:** 17.5000 g. **Composition:** 0.7200 Silver .4051 oz. ASW **Subject:** 50th Anniversary - National Theater

| Date | Mintage | F | VF | XF | Unc |
|---|---|---|---|---|---|
| AH1406-1986 | 6,000 | — | — | — | 15.00 |

**5 POUNDS** **KM# 609** **Weight:** 17.5000 g. **Composition:** 0.7200 Silver .4051 oz. ASW **Subject:** Mecca

| Date | Mintage | F | VF | XF | Unc |
|---|---|---|---|---|---|
| AH1406-1986 | 30,000 | — | — | — | 12.50 |
| AH1406-1986 Proof | — | Value: 22.50 | | | |

**5 POUNDS** **KM# 614** **Weight:** 17.5000 g. **Composition:** 0.7200 Silver .4051 oz. ASW **Subject:** Restoration of Parliament Building **Obverse:** Arabic legends **Reverse:** Dome and tower with scaffolding

| Date | Mintage | F | VF | XF | Unc |
|---|---|---|---|---|---|
| AH1406-1986 | 5,000 | — | — | — | 15.00 |

**5 POUNDS** **KM# 614a** **Weight:** 26.0000 g. **Composition:** 0.8750 Gold .7315 oz. AGW **Subject:** Restoration of Parliament Building **Obverse:** Arabic legends **Reverse:** Dome and tower with scaffolding

| Date | Mintage | F | VF | XF | Unc |
|---|---|---|---|---|---|
| AH1406-1986 | 300 | — | — | — | 350 |

**5 POUNDS** **KM# 611** **Weight:** 17.5000 g. **Composition:** 0.7200 Silver .4051 oz. ASW **Subject:** Aida Opera

| Date | Mintage | F | VF | XF | Unc |
|---|---|---|---|---|---|
| ND(1407-1987) | 25,000 | — | — | — | 35.00 |

**5 POUNDS** **KM# 617** **Weight:** 17.5000 g. **Composition:** 0.7200 Silver .4051 oz. ASW **Subject:** Parliament Museum **Obverse:** Arabic legends, seals and dates **Reverse:** Documents, quill, carriage, building with national emblem

| Date | Mintage | F | VF | XF | Unc |
|---|---|---|---|---|---|
| AH1407-1987 | 5,000 | — | — | — | 15.00 |

**5 POUNDS** **KM# 618** **Weight:** 17.5000 g. **Composition:** 0.7200 Silver .4051 oz. ASW **Subject:** Veterinarian Day

| Date | Mintage | F | VF | XF | Unc |
|---|---|---|---|---|---|
| AH1407-1987 | 5,000 | — | — | — | 12.50 |

**5 POUNDS** **KM# 619** **Weight:** 17.5000 g. **Composition:** 0.7200 Silver .4051 oz. ASW **Subject:** 75th Anniversary - Misr Petroleum Company

| Date | Mintage | F | VF | XF | Unc |
|---|---|---|---|---|---|
| AH1407-1987 | 10,000 | — | — | — | 13.50 |

**5 POUNDS** **KM# 630** **Weight:** 17.5000 g. **Composition:** 0.7200 Silver .4051 oz. ASW **Subject:** Faculty of Fine Arts

| Date | Mintage | F | VF | XF | Unc |
|---|---|---|---|---|---|
| AH1407-1987 | 5,000 | — | — | — | 13.50 |

**5 POUNDS** KM# 651 **Weight:** 17.7800 g. **Composition:** 0.7200 Silver .4052 oz. ASW **Subject:** Investment Bank

| Date | Mintage | F | VF | XF | Unc |
|---|---|---|---|---|---|
| AH1407-1987 | 8,000 | — | — | — | 12.50 |

**5 POUNDS** KM# 620 **Weight:** 17.5000 g. **Composition:** 0.7200 Silver .4051 oz. ASW **Subject:** First African Subway

| Date | Mintage | F | VF | XF | Unc |
|---|---|---|---|---|---|
| AH1408-1987 | 15,000 | — | — | — | 12.50 |

**5 POUNDS** KM# 623 **Weight:** 17.5000 g. **Composition:** 0.7200 Silver .4051 oz. ASW **Subject:** 25th Anniversary - Hellwan Company

| Date | Mintage | F | VF | XF | Unc |
|---|---|---|---|---|---|
| AH1408-1987 | 8,000 | — | — | — | 13.50 |

**5 POUNDS** KM# 617a **Weight:** 26.0000 g. **Composition:** 0.8750 Gold .7315 oz. AGW **Subject:** Parliament Museum **Obverse:** Arabic legends, seals and dates **Reverse:** Documents, quill, carriage, building with national emblem

| Date | Mintage | F | VF | XF | Unc |
|---|---|---|---|---|---|
| AH1407-1987 | 300 | — | — | — | 350 |

**5 POUNDS** KM# 674 **Weight:** 26.0000 g. **Composition:** 0.8750 Gold .7315 oz. AGW **Subject:** First African Subway **Obverse:** Stylized legends and denomination **Reverse:** Subway emerging from tunnel with legend around rim

| Date | Mintage | F | VF | XF | Unc |
|---|---|---|---|---|---|
| AH1408-1987 Proof | 200 | Value: 550 | | | |

**5 POUNDS** KM# 670 **Weight:** 26.0000 g. **Composition:** 0.8750 Gold .7315 oz. AGW **Subject:** National Research Center **Obverse:** Kufic legend above denomination and date **Reverse:** Stylized ancient and modern research elements

| Date | Mintage | F | VF | XF | Unc |
|---|---|---|---|---|---|
| AH1408-1988 | — | Value: 550 | | | |
| AH1409-1989 Proof | 200 | Value: 550 | | | |

**5 POUNDS** KM# 655 **Weight:** 26.0000 g. **Composition:** 0.8750 Gold .7315 oz. AGW **Subject:** Dedication of Cairo Opera House **Obverse:** Arabic legends, seals, dates **Reverse:** Opera house, legends above and below

| Date | Mintage | F | VF | XF | Unc |
|---|---|---|---|---|---|
| AH1409-1988 | 200 | — | — | — | 525 |

**5 POUNDS** KM# 621 **Weight:** 17.5000 g. **Composition:** 0.7200 Silver .4051 oz. ASW **Subject:** Police Day

| Date | Mintage | F | VF | XF | Unc |
|---|---|---|---|---|---|
| AH1408-1988 | 35,000 | — | — | — | 13.50 |

**5 POUNDS** KM# 624 **Weight:** 17.5000 g. **Composition:** 0.7200 Silver .4051 oz. ASW **Series:** Summer Olympics **Reverse:** Pharoah and athletes

| Date | Mintage | F | VF | XF | Unc |
|---|---|---|---|---|---|
| AH1408-1988 | 30,000 | — | — | — | 13.50 |
| AH1408-1988 Matte | — | — | — | — | 55.00 |
| AH1408-1988 Proof | 2,000 | Value: 27.50 | | | |

**5 POUNDS** KM# 626 **Weight:** 17.5000 g. **Composition:** 0.7200 Silver .4051 oz. ASW **Series:** Summer Olympics **Reverse:** Athletes and mythological figures

| Date | Mintage | F | VF | XF | Unc |
|---|---|---|---|---|---|
| AH1408-1988 | 24,000 | — | — | — | 13.50 |
| AH1408-1988 Matte | — | — | — | — | 55.00 |
| AH1408-1988 Proof | 5,000 | Value: 30.00 | | | |

**5 POUNDS** KM# 628 **Weight:** 17.5000 g. **Composition:** 0.7200 Silver .4051 oz. ASW **Series:** Winter Olympics **Reverse:** Ski jumper and figure skater

| Date | Mintage | F | VF | XF | Unc |
|---|---|---|---|---|---|
| AH1408-1988 | 8,000 | — | — | — | 13.50 |
| AH1408-1988 Matte | — | — | — | — | 55.00 |
| AH1408-1988 Proof | 2,000 | Value: 30.00 | | | |

**5 POUNDS** KM# 631 **Weight:** 17.5000 g. **Composition:** 0.7200 Silver .4051 oz. ASW **Subject:** 50th Anniversary of Air Travel

| Date | Mintage | F | VF | XF | Unc |
|---|---|---|---|---|---|
| AH1408-1988 | 5,000 | — | — | — | 13.50 |

**5 POUNDS** KM# 649 **Weight:** 17.5000 g. **Composition:** 0.7200 Silver .4051 oz. ASW **Subject:** Dedication of Cairo Opera House

| Date | Mintage | F | VF | XF | Unc |
|---|---|---|---|---|---|
| AH1409-1988 | 30,000 | — | — | — | 12.50 |

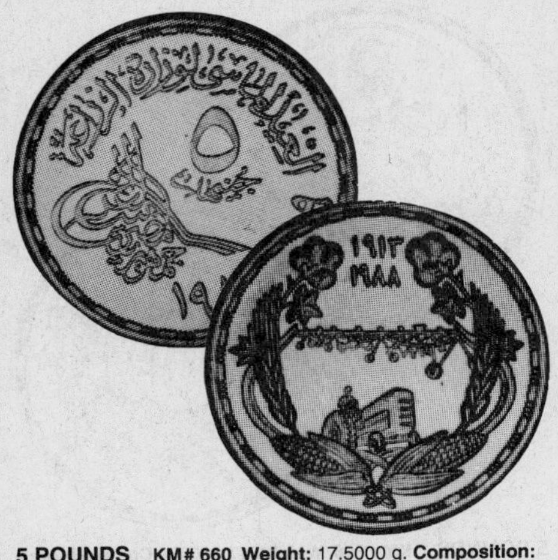

**5 POUNDS** **KM# 660** **Weight:** 17.5000 g. **Composition:** 0.7200 Silver .4051 oz. ASW **Subject:** Ministry of Agriculture

| Date | Mintage | F | VF | XF | Unc |
|---|---|---|---|---|---|
| AH1409-1988 | 5,000 | — | — | — | 12.50 |

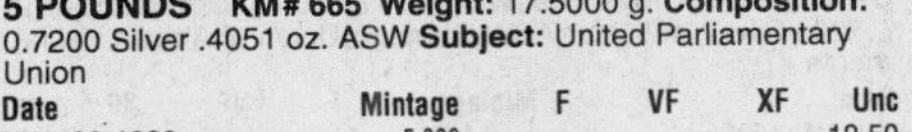

**5 POUNDS** **KM# 665** **Weight:** 17.5000 g. **Composition:** 0.7200 Silver .4051 oz. ASW **Subject:** United Parliamentary Union

| Date | Mintage | F | VF | XF | Unc |
|---|---|---|---|---|---|
| AH1409-1989 | 5,000 | — | — | — | 12.50 |

**5 POUNDS** **KM# 686** **Weight:** 17.5000 g. **Composition:** 0.7200 Silver .4051 oz. ASW **Subject:** National Health Insurance

| Date | Mintage | F | VF | XF | Unc |
|---|---|---|---|---|---|
| AH1409-1989 | 3,000 | — | — | — | 15.00 |

**5 POUNDS** **KM# 662** **Weight:** 17.5000 g. **Composition:** 0.7200 Silver .4051 oz. ASW **Subject:** Naguib Mahfouz, Nobel Laureate **Reverse:** Head of Mahfouz left

| Date | Mintage | F | VF | XF | Unc |
|---|---|---|---|---|---|
| AH1409-1988 | 15,000 | — | — | — | 12.50 |

**5 POUNDS** **KM# 667** **Weight:** 17.5000 g. **Composition:** 0.7200 Silver .4051 oz. ASW **Subject:** First Arab Olympics **Obverse:** Kufic legend above denomination and date

| Date | Mintage | F | VF | XF | Unc |
|---|---|---|---|---|---|
| AH1409-1989 | 8,000 | — | — | — | 12.50 |

**5 POUNDS** **KM# 678** **Weight:** 17.5000 g. **Composition:** 0.7200 Silver .4051 oz. ASW **Subject:** University of Cairo - School of Agriculture

| Date | Mintage | F | VF | XF | Unc |
|---|---|---|---|---|---|
| AH1410-1989 | 4,000 | — | — | — | 22.00 |

**5 POUNDS** **KM# 663** **Weight:** 17.5000 g. **Composition:** 0.7200 Silver .4051 oz. ASW **Subject:** Advista Arabia II

| Date | Mintage | F | VF | XF | Unc |
|---|---|---|---|---|---|
| AH1409-1989 | 5,000 | — | — | — | 12.50 |

**5 POUNDS** **KM# 669** **Weight:** 17.5000 g. **Composition:** 0.7200 Silver .4051 oz. ASW **Subject:** National Research Center **Reverse:** Stylized ancient and modern research elements

| Date | Mintage | F | VF | XF | Unc |
|---|---|---|---|---|---|
| AH1409-1989 | 5,000 | — | — | — | 12.50 |

**5 POUNDS** **KM# 679** **Weight:** 17.5000 g. **Composition:** 0.7200 Silver .4051 oz. ASW **Series:** Soccer World Championship - Italy **Reverse:** Ancient Gods in front of pyramid with soccer ball above

| Date | Mintage | F | VF | XF | Unc |
|---|---|---|---|---|---|
| AH1410-1990 | 600 | — | — | — | 35.00 |
| AH1410-1990 Proof | 8,000 | Value: 25.00 | | | |

**5 POUNDS** **KM# 682** **Weight:** 17.5000 g. **Composition:** 0.7200 Silver .4051 oz. ASW **Series:** Soccer World Championship - Italy **Reverse:** Player chasing ball

| Date | Mintage | F | VF | XF | Unc |
|---|---|---|---|---|---|
| AH1410-1990 Matte | 400 | — | — | — | 40.00 |
| AH1410-1990 Proof | 4,000 | Value: 30.00 | | | |

**5 POUNDS** **KM# 689** **Weight:** 17.5000 g. **Composition:** 0.7200 Silver .4051 oz. ASW **Subject:** Union of African Parliaments

| Date | Mintage | F | VF | XF | Unc |
|---|---|---|---|---|---|
| AH1410-1990 | 5,000 | — | — | — | 13.50 |

**5 POUNDS** **KM# 698** **Weight:** 17.5000 g. **Composition:** 0.7200 Silver .4051 oz. ASW **Subject:** Alexandria Sports Club

| Date | Mintage | F | VF | XF | Unc |
|---|---|---|---|---|---|
| AH1411-1990 | 5,000 | — | — | — | 20.00 |

**5 POUNDS** **KM# 687** **Weight:** 17.5000 g. **Composition:** 0.7200 Silver .4051 oz. ASW **Subject:** Export Drive

| Date | Mintage | F | VF | XF | Unc |
|---|---|---|---|---|---|
| AH1410-1990 | 4,000 | — | — | — | 15.00 |

**5 POUNDS** **KM# 691** **Weight:** 17.8200 g. **Composition:** 0.9000 Silver .5156 oz. ASW **Subject:** Dar-el-Eloun Faculty

| Date | Mintage | F | VF | XF | Unc |
|---|---|---|---|---|---|
| AH1410-1990 | 5,000 | — | — | — | 13.50 |

**5 POUNDS** **KM# 692** **Weight:** 17.8200 g. **Composition:** 0.9000 Silver .5156 oz. ASW **Subject:** Islamic Development Bank

| Date | Mintage | F | VF | XF | Unc |
|---|---|---|---|---|---|
| AH1411-1991 | 5,000 | — | — | — | 13.50 |

**5 POUNDS** **KM# 688** **Weight:** 17.5000 g. **Composition:** 0.7200 Silver .4051 oz. ASW **Subject:** National Population Center

| Date | Mintage | F | VF | XF | Unc |
|---|---|---|---|---|---|
| AH1410-1990 | 5,000 | — | — | — | 13.50 |

**5 POUNDS** **KM# 697** **Weight:** 17.5000 g. **Composition:** 0.7200 Silver .4051 oz. ASW **Subject:** Newly Populated Areas Organization

| Date | Mintage | F | VF | XF | Unc |
|---|---|---|---|---|---|
| AH1410-1990 | 2,000 | — | — | — | 45.00 |

**5 POUNDS** **KM# 700** **Weight:** 17.8200 g. **Composition:** 0.9000 Silver .5156 oz. ASW **Subject:** 5th African Games - Cairo

| Date | Mintage | F | VF | XF | Unc |
|---|---|---|---|---|---|
| AH1411-1991 | 3,000 | — | — | — | 30.00 |

**5 POUNDS** **KM# 791** **Weight:** 17.4200 g. **Composition:** 0.7200 Silver .4032 oz. ASW **Subject:** National Zoo **Obverse:** Zoo entrance, dates **Reverse:** Zoo animals

| Date | Mintage | F | VF | XF | Unc |
|---|---|---|---|---|---|
| AH1411-1991 | — | — | — | — | 25.00 |

**5 POUNDS** **KM# 804** **Weight:** 17.5000 g. **Composition:** 0.7200 Silver .4051 oz. ASW **Subject:** Atomic Energy **Obverse:** Denomination **Reverse:** Ancient statue and pyramid within rings

| Date | Mintage | F | VF | XF | Unc |
|---|---|---|---|---|---|
| AH1411-1991 | Est. 5,000 | — | — | — | 15.00 |

**5 POUNDS** **KM# 805** **Weight:** 17.5000 g. **Composition:** 0.7200 Silver .4051 oz. ASW **Subject:** Library of Alexandria **Obverse:** Arabic inscription **Reverse:** Library building complex

| Date | Mintage | F | VF | XF | Unc |
|---|---|---|---|---|---|
| AH1411-1991 | Est. 8,000 | — | — | — | 15.00 |

**5 POUNDS** **KM# 728** **Weight:** 26.0000 g. **Composition:** 0.8750 Gold .7314 oz. AGW **Subject:** Muhamed Abdel Wahab **Obverse:** Arabic legends and inscriptions **Reverse:** Bust of Wahab left with music sheet in background

| Date | Mintage | F | VF | XF | Unc |
|---|---|---|---|---|---|
| AH1412-1991 Proof | 400 | — | — | — | 500 |

**5 POUNDS** **KM# 727** **Weight:** 17.5000 g. **Composition:** 0.7200 Silver .4051 oz. ASW **Subject:** Muhamed Abdel Wahab **Obverse:** Arabic legends and inscriptions **Reverse:** Bust of Wahab left with music sheet in background

| Date | Mintage | F | VF | XF | Unc |
|---|---|---|---|---|---|
| AH1412-1991 | 30,000 | — | — | — | 13.50 |

**5 POUNDS** **KM# 833** **Weight:** 26.0000 g. **Composition:** 0.8750 Gold .7315 oz. AGW **Subject:** Library of Alexandria **Obverse:** Legend and inscription **Reverse:** Waterfront building with tower

| Date | Mintage | F | VF | XF | Unc |
|---|---|---|---|---|---|
| AH1411-1991 | 200 | — | — | — | 500 |

**5 POUNDS** **KM# 805a** **Weight:** 26.0000 g. **Composition:** 0.8750 Gold .7314 oz. AGW **Subject:** Library of Alexandria **Obverse:** Arabic inscription **Reverse:** Library building complex **Edge:** Reeded **Note:** Struck at Cairo

| Date | Mintage | F | VF | XF | Unc |
|---|---|---|---|---|---|
| AH1411-1991 Proof | 200 | — | — | — | 500 |

**5 POUNDS** **KM# 701** **Weight:** 17.5000 g. **Composition:** 0.7200 Silver .4051 oz. ASW **Series:** Summer Olympics **Reverse:** Two men fencing

| Date | Mintage | F | VF | XF | Unc |
|---|---|---|---|---|---|
| AH1412-1992 | 999 | — | — | — | 45.00 |
| AH1412-1992 Proof | 2,999 | Value: 40.00 | | | |

**5 POUNDS** **KM# 702** **Weight:** 17.5000 g. **Composition:** 0.7200 Silver .4051 oz. ASW **Series:** Summer Olympics **Reverse:** Two men wrestling

| Date | Mintage | F | VF | XF | Unc |
|---|---|---|---|---|---|
| AH1412-1992 | 999 | — | — | — | 45.00 |
| AH1412-1992 Proof | 2,999 | Value: 40.00 | | | |

**5 POUNDS** **KM# 703** **Weight:** 17.5000 g. **Composition:** 0.7200 Silver .4051 oz. ASW **Series:** Summer Olympics **Reverse:** Archery demonstrated

| Date | Mintage | F | VF | XF | Unc |
|---|---|---|---|---|---|
| AH1412-1992 | 999 | — | — | — | 45.00 |
| AH1412-1992 Proof | 2,999 | Value: 40.00 | | | |

**5 POUNDS** **KM# 704** **Weight:** 17.5000 g. **Composition:** 0.7200 Silver .4051 oz. ASW **Series:** Summer Olympics **Reverse:** Many men wrestling an ox

| Date | Mintage | F | VF | XF | Unc |
|---|---|---|---|---|---|
| AH1412-1992 | 999 | — | — | — | 45.00 |
| AH1412-1992 Proof | 2,999 | Value: 40.00 | | | |

**5 POUNDS** **KM# 705** **Weight:** 17.5000 g. **Composition:** 0.7200 Silver .4051 oz. ASW **Series:** Summer Olympics **Reverse:** Swimmer stalking a duck

| Date | Mintage | F | VF | XF | Unc |
|---|---|---|---|---|---|
| AH1412-1992 | 999 | — | — | — | 45.00 |
| AH1412-1992 Proof | 2,999 | Value: 40.00 | | | |

**5 POUNDS** **KM# 706** **Weight:** 17.5000 g. **Composition:** 0.7200 Silver .4051 oz. ASW **Series:** Summer Olympics **Reverse:** Handball player

| Date | Mintage | F | VF | XF | Unc |
|---|---|---|---|---|---|
| AH1412-1992 | 999 | — | — | — | 45.00 |
| AH1412-1992 Proof | 25,000 | Value: 22.50 | | | |

**5 POUNDS** **KM# 707** **Weight:** 17.5000 g. **Composition:** 0.7200 Silver .4051 oz. ASW **Series:** Summer Olympics **Reverse:** Field hockey player

| Date | Mintage | F | VF | XF | Unc |
|---|---|---|---|---|---|
| AH1412-1992 | 999 | — | — | — | 45.00 |
| AH1412-1992 Proof | 25,000 | Value: 22.50 | | | |

**5 POUNDS** **KM# 708** **Weight:** 17.5000 g. **Composition:** 0.7200 Silver .4051 oz. ASW **Series:** Summer Olympics **Reverse:** Soccer player

| Date | Mintage | F | VF | XF | Unc |
|---|---|---|---|---|---|
| AH1412-1992 | 999 | — | — | — | 45.00 |
| AH1412-1992 Proof | 25,000 | Value: 22.50 | | | |

**5 POUNDS** **KM# 806** **Weight:** 17.5000 g. **Composition:** 0.7200 Silver .4051 oz. ASW **Subject:** Lighthouse of Alexandria **Obverse:** Denomination **Reverse:** Ancient tower and Egyptian

| Date | Mintage | F | VF | XF | Unc |
|---|---|---|---|---|---|
| AH1412-1992 | Est. 3,000 | — | — | — | 17.50 |

**5 POUNDS** **KM# 807** **Weight:** 17.5000 g. **Composition:** 0.7200 Silver .4051 oz. ASW **Subject:** 50 Years - University of Alexandria **Obverse:** Arabic inscription **Reverse:** University emblem

| Date | Mintage | F | VF | XF | Unc |
|---|---|---|---|---|---|
| AH1413-1992 | Est. 3,000 | — | — | — | 18.50 |

**5 POUNDS** **KM# 808** **Weight:** 17.5000 g. **Composition:** 0.7200 Silver .4051 oz. ASW **Subject:** Naguib Mahfouz, Nobel Laureate **Obverse:** Vase and inscriptions **Reverse:** Bust of Naguib Mahfouz right

| Date | Mintage | F | VF | XF | Unc |
|---|---|---|---|---|---|
| AH1413-1992 | Est. 6,000 | — | — | — | 15.00 |

**5 POUNDS** **KM# 735** **Weight:** 22.5000 g. **Composition:** 0.9990 Silver .7227 oz. ASW **Subject:** Cleopatra **Reverse:** Bust of Cleopatra left

| Date | Mintage | F | VF | XF | Unc |
|---|---|---|---|---|---|
| AH1413-1993 Proof | 50,000 | Value: 36.50 | | | |

**5 POUNDS** **KM# 759** **Weight:** 17.5000 g. **Composition:** 0.7200 Silver .4051 oz. ASW **Subject:** Beram El Tunsi, Poet **Reverse:** Bust of Beram El Tunsi facing left

| Date | Mintage | F | VF | XF | Unc |
|---|---|---|---|---|---|
| AH1413-1993 | 3,000 | — | — | — | 25.00 |

**5 POUNDS** **KM# 740** **Weight:** 22.5000 g. **Composition:** 0.9990 Silver .7227 oz. ASW **Subject:** Pyramids **Reverse:** Three pyramids

| Date | Mintage | F | VF | XF | Unc |
|---|---|---|---|---|---|
| AH1414-1993 Proof | 50,000 | Value: 36.50 | | | |

**5 POUNDS** **KM# 741** **Weight:** 22.5000 g. **Composition:** 0.9990 Silver .7227 oz. ASW **Subject:** Sphinx

| Date | Mintage | F | VF | XF | Unc |
|---|---|---|---|---|---|
| AH1414-1993 Proof | 50,000 | Value: 36.50 | | | |

**5 POUNDS** **KM# 742** **Weight:** 22.5000 g. **Composition:** 0.9990 Silver .7227 oz. ASW **Subject:** King Narmur Smiting a Foe

| Date | Mintage | F | VF | XF | Unc |
|---|---|---|---|---|---|
| AH1414-1993 Proof | 50,000 | Value: 31.50 | | | |

**5 POUNDS** **KM# 743** **Weight:** 22.5000 g. **Composition:** 0.9990 Silver .7227 oz. ASW **Subject:** Guardian Goddess Serket

| Date | Mintage | F | VF | XF | Unc |
|---|---|---|---|---|---|
| AH1414-1993 Proof | 50,000 | Value: 31.50 | | | |

**5 POUNDS** **KM# 744** **Weight:** 22.5000 g. **Composition:** 0.9990 Silver .7227 oz. ASW **Subject:** Amulet of Hathor

| Date | Mintage | F | VF | XF | Unc |
|---|---|---|---|---|---|
| AH1414-1993 Proof | 50,000 | Value: 31.50 | | | |

**5 POUNDS** **KM# 745** **Weight:** 22.5000 g. **Composition:** 0.9990 Silver .7227 oz. ASW **Subject:** Standing Ramses II

| Date | Mintage | F | VF | XF | Unc |
|---|---|---|---|---|---|
| AH1414-1993 Proof | 50,000 | Value: 31.50 | | | |

**5 POUNDS** **KM# 746** **Weight:** 22.5000 g. **Composition:** 0.9990 Silver .7227 oz. ASW **Subject:** Menkaure Triad

| Date | Mintage | F | VF | XF | Unc |
|---|---|---|---|---|---|
| AH1414-1993 Proof | 50,000 | Value: 31.50 | | | |

**5 POUNDS** **KM# 747** **Weight:** 22.5000 g. **Composition:** 0.9990 Silver .7227 oz. ASW **Subject:** Symbol of Unification **Reverse:** Two females representing the upper & lower Nile

| Date | Mintage | F | VF | XF | Unc |
|---|---|---|---|---|---|
| AH1414-1993 Proof | 50,000 | Value: 31.50 | | | |

**5 POUNDS** **KM# 793** **Weight:** 22.5000 g. **Composition:** 0.9990 Silver .7227 oz. ASW **Obverse:** Vulture **Reverse:** Tutankhamen's burial mask

| Date | Mintage | F | VF | XF | Unc |
|---|---|---|---|---|---|
| AH1414-1993 Proof | — | Value: 37.50 | | | |

**5 POUNDS** **KM# 812** **Weight:** 17.5000 g. **Composition:** 0.7200 Silver .4051 oz. ASW **Subject:** 20th Anniversary - October War **Obverse:** Smoking chimney text **Reverse:** Soldier with flag

| Date | Mintage | F | VF | XF | Unc |
|---|---|---|---|---|---|
| AH1414-1993 | Est. 5,000 | — | — | — | 15.00 |

**5 POUNDS** **KM# 837** **Weight:** 17.5000 g. **Composition:** 0.7200 Silver .4051 oz. ASW **Subject:** 125th Anniversary of Taalat Harb Birth **Obverse:** Denomination and date in circle above inscription **Reverse:** Taalat Harb wearing fez **Edge:** Reeded

| Date | Mintage | F | VF | XF | Unc |
|---|---|---|---|---|---|
| AH1413-1993 | 5,000 | — | — | — | 25.00 |

**5 POUNDS** **KM# 869** **Weight:** 22.5500 g. **Composition:** 0.9990 Silver .7243 oz. ASW **Subject:** King Kha-Sekhem **Obverse:** Vulture **Reverse:** Seated figure **Edge:** Reeded

| Date | Mintage | F | VF | XF | Unc |
|---|---|---|---|---|---|
| AH1414-1993 Proof | 15,000 | — | — | — | 45.00 |

**5 POUNDS** **KM# 748** **Weight:** 22.5000 g. **Composition:** 0.9990 Silver .7227 oz. ASW **Series:** World Cup Soccer **Reverse:** Kneeling King Pepi I facing

| Date | Mintage | F | VF | XF | Unc |
|---|---|---|---|---|---|
| AH1414-1993 Proof | — | Value: 31.50 | | | |
| AH1415-1994 Proof | 50,000 | Value: 31.50 | | | |

**5 POUNDS** **KM# 879** **Weight:** 26.0000 g. **Composition:** 0.8750 Gold .7315 oz. AGW **Subject:** Symbol of Unification **Reverse:** Two females representing the upper & lower Nile

| Date | Mintage | F | VF | XF | Unc |
|---|---|---|---|---|---|
| AH1414-1993 Proof | 3,000 | — | — | — | 275 |

**5 POUNDS** **KM# 880** **Weight:** 26.0000 g. **Composition:** 0.8750 Gold .7315 oz. AGW **Reverse:** Kneeling King Pepi I facing

| Date | Mintage | F | VF | XF | Unc |
|---|---|---|---|---|---|
| AH1415-1994 Proof | 3,000 | — | — | — | 275 |

**5 POUNDS** **KM# 881** **Weight:** 26.0000 g. **Composition:** 0.8750 Gold .7315 oz. AGW **Reverse:** Statue of King Amenemhat III

| Date | Mintage | F | VF | XF | Unc |
|---|---|---|---|---|---|
| AH1415-1994 Proof | 3,000 | — | — | — | 275 |

**5 POUNDS** **KM# 785** **Weight:** 22.5000 g. **Composition:** 0.9990 Silver .7227 oz. ASW **Obverse:** Ancient style vulture **Reverse:** Five birds

| Date | Mintage | F | VF | XF | Unc |
|---|---|---|---|---|---|
| AH1415-1994 Proof | 50,000 | Value: 40.00 | | | |

**5 POUNDS** **KM# 786** **Weight:** 22.5000 g. **Composition:** 0.9990 Silver .7227 oz. ASW **Obverse:** Ancient style vulture **Reverse:** Hippopotamus right

| Date | Mintage | F | VF | XF | Unc |
|---|---|---|---|---|---|
| AH1415-1994 Proof | 50,000 | Value: 40.00 | | | |

**5 POUNDS** **KM# 787** **Weight:** 22.5000 g. **Composition:** 0.9990 Silver .7227 oz. ASW **Obverse:** Ancient style vulture **Reverse:** Ruins of Karnak

| Date | Mintage | F | VF | XF | Unc |
|---|---|---|---|---|---|
| AH1415-1994 Proof | 50,000 | Value: 31.50 | | | |

**5 POUNDS** **KM# 788** **Weight:** 22.5000 g. **Composition:** 0.9990 Silver .7227 oz. ASW **Obverse:** Ancient style vulture **Reverse:** Standing goddess Neith wearing the Red Crown

| Date | Mintage | F | VF | XF | Unc |
|---|---|---|---|---|---|
| AH1415-1994 Proof | 50,000 | Value: 31.50 | | | |

**5 POUNDS** **KM# 789** **Weight:** 22.5000 g. **Composition:** 0.9990 Silver .7227 oz. ASW **Obverse:** Ancient style vulture **Reverse:** Statue of King Amenemhat III

| Date | Mintage | F | VF | XF | Unc |
|---|---|---|---|---|---|
| AH1415-1994 Proof | 50,000 | Value: 31.50 | | | |

**5 POUNDS** **KM# 790** **Weight:** 22.5000 g. **Composition:** 0.9990 Silver .7227 oz. ASW **Obverse:** Ancient style vulture **Reverse:** Ritual mask of Queen Hatshepsut

| Date | Mintage | F | VF | XF | Unc |
|---|---|---|---|---|---|
| AH1415-1994 Proof | 50,000 | Value: 31.50 | | | |

**5 POUNDS** **KM# 792** **Weight:** 15.0000 g. **Composition:** 0.7200 Silver .3472 oz. ASW **Subject:** ICPD Cairo **Obverse:** Inscription and seals **Reverse:** Stylized design

| Date | Mintage | F | VF | XF | Unc |
|---|---|---|---|---|---|
| AH1415-1994 | — | — | — | — | 17.50 |

**5 POUNDS** **KM# 794** **Weight:** 22.5950 g. **Composition:** 0.9990 Silver .7264 oz. ASW **Obverse:** Ancient style vulture **Reverse:** Seated, jeweled cat

| Date | Mintage | F | VF | XF | Unc |
|---|---|---|---|---|---|
| AH1415-1994 Proof | — | Value: 40.00 | | | |

**5 POUNDS** **KM# 795** **Weight:** 22.5950 g. **Composition:** 0.9990 Silver .7264 oz. ASW **Obverse:** Ancient style vulture **Reverse:** Sacred falcon at Edfu

| Date | Mintage | F | VF | XF | Unc |
|---|---|---|---|---|---|
| AH1415-1994 Proof | — | Value: 40.00 | | | |

**5 POUNDS** **KM# 797** **Weight:** 22.5950 g. **Composition:** 0.9990 Silver .7264 oz. ASW **Obverse:** Ancient style vulture **Reverse:** Tutankhamon's throne

| Date | Mintage | F | VF | XF | Unc |
|---|---|---|---|---|---|
| AH1415-1994 Proof | — | Value: 31.50 | | | |

**5 POUNDS** **KM# 798** **Weight:** 22.5950 g. **Composition:** 0.9990 Silver .7264 oz. ASW **Obverse:** Ancient style vulture **Reverse:** King Au as high priest

| Date | Mintage | F | VF | XF | Unc |
|---|---|---|---|---|---|
| AH1415-1994 Proof | — | Value: 31.50 | | | |

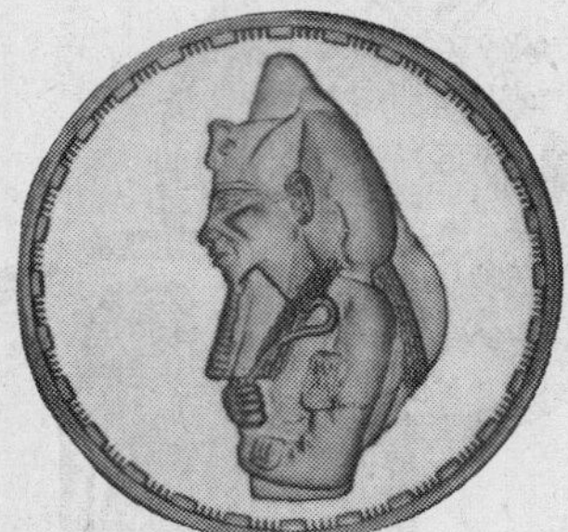

**5 POUNDS** **KM# 799** **Weight:** 22.5950 g. **Composition:** 0.9990 Silver .7264 oz. ASW **Obverse:** Ancient style vulture **Reverse:** Akhnaton

| Date | Mintage | F | VF | XF | Unc |
|---|---|---|---|---|---|
| AH1415-1994 Proof | — | Value: 40.00 | | | |

**5 POUNDS** **KM# 800** **Weight:** 22.5950 g. **Composition:** 0.9990 Silver .7264 oz. ASW **Obverse:** Ancient style vulture **Reverse:** Osiris seated right

| Date | Mintage | F | VF | XF | Unc |
|---|---|---|---|---|---|
| AH1415-1994 Proof | — | Value: 31.50 | | | |

**5 POUNDS** **KM# 801** **Weight:** 22.5950 g. **Composition:** 0.9990 Silver .7264 oz. ASW **Obverse:** Ancient style vulture **Reverse:** RE, the sun god walking left

| Date | Mintage | F | VF | XF | Unc |
|---|---|---|---|---|---|
| AH1415-1994 Proof | — | Value: 31.50 | | | |

**5 POUNDS** **KM# 802** **Weight:** 22.5950 g. **Composition:** 0.9990 Silver .7264 oz. ASW **Obverse:** Ancient style vulture **Reverse:** The god Khnoum walking right

| Date | Mintage | F | VF | XF | Unc |
|---|---|---|---|---|---|
| AH1415-1994 Proof | — | Value: 37.50 | | | |

**5 POUNDS** **KM# 803** **Weight:** 22.5950 g. **Composition:** 0.9990 Silver .7264 oz. ASW **Obverse:** Ancient style vulture **Reverse:** Sobek, crocodile god, walking left

| Date | Mintage | F | VF | XF | Unc |
|---|---|---|---|---|---|
| AH1415-1994 Proof | — | Value: 37.50 | | | |

**5 POUNDS** **KM# 813** **Weight:** 22.5500 g. **Composition:** 0.9990 Silver .7243 oz. ASW **Obverse:** Ancient style vulture, denomination **Reverse:** Seated ancient scribe **Edge:** Reeded

| Date | Mintage | F | VF | XF | Unc |
|---|---|---|---|---|---|
| AH1415-1994 Proof | — | Value: 37.50 | | | |

**5 POUNDS** **KM# 826** **Weight:** 22.5000 g. **Composition:** 0.9990 Silver .7227 oz. ASW **Obverse:** Ancient style vulture, denomination **Reverse:** King Thoutmosis III kneeling left

| Date | Mintage | F | VF | XF | Unc |
|---|---|---|---|---|---|
| AH1415-1994 Proof | — | Value: 31.50 | | | |

**5 POUNDS** **KM# 830** **Weight:** 22.5000 g. **Composition:** 0.9990 Silver .7227 oz. ASW **Obverse:** Ancient style vulture, denomination **Reverse:** Seated goddess Isis nursing child

| Date | Mintage | F | VF | XF | Unc |
|---|---|---|---|---|---|
| AH1415-1994 Proof | — | Value: 31.50 | | | |

**5 POUNDS** **KM# 823** **Weight:** 22.5000 g. **Composition:** 0.9990 Silver .7227 oz. ASW **Obverse:** Ancient style vulture, denomination **Reverse:** Temple of Ramses II

| Date | Mintage | F | VF | XF | Unc |
|---|---|---|---|---|---|
| AH1415-1994 Proof | — | Value: 36.50 | | | |

**5 POUNDS** **KM# 827** **Weight:** 22.5000 g. **Composition:** 0.9990 Silver .7227 oz. ASW **Obverse:** Ancient style vulture, denomination **Reverse:** Seated King Khufu

| Date | Mintage | F | VF | XF | Unc |
|---|---|---|---|---|---|
| AH1415-1994 Proof | — | Value: 31.50 | | | |

**5 POUNDS** **KM# 831** **Weight:** 22.5000 g. **Composition:** 0.9990 Silver .7227 oz. ASW **Obverse:** Ancient style vulture, denomination **Reverse:** Dwarf Seneb and family

| Date | Mintage | F | VF | XF | Unc |
|---|---|---|---|---|---|
| AH1415-1994 Proof | — | Value: 31.50 | | | |

**5 POUNDS** **KM# 878** **Weight:** 26.0000 g. **Composition:** 0.8750 Gold .7315 oz. AGW **Obverse:** Ancient style vulture, denomination **Reverse:** Dwarf Seneb and family

| Date | Mintage | F | VF | XF | Unc |
|---|---|---|---|---|---|
| AH1415-1994 Proof | 3,000 | — | — | — | 275 |

**5 POUNDS** **KM# 874** **Weight:** 26.0000 g. **Composition:** 0.8750 Gold .7315 oz. AGW **Reverse:** Sphinx and pyramids

| Date | Mintage | F | VF | XF | Unc |
|---|---|---|---|---|---|
| AH1415-1994 Proof | 5,000 | — | — | — | 275 |

**5 POUNDS** **KM# 824** **Weight:** 22.5000 g. **Composition:** 0.9990 Silver .7227 oz. ASW **Obverse:** Ancient style vulture, denomination **Reverse:** Ancient ruins

| Date | Mintage | F | VF | XF | Unc |
|---|---|---|---|---|---|
| AH1415-1994 Proof | — | Value: 31.50 | | | |

**5 POUNDS** **KM# 828** **Weight:** 22.5000 g. **Composition:** 0.9990 Silver .7227 oz. ASW **Obverse:** Ancient style vulture, denomination **Reverse:** Standing goddess Hathor left

| Date | Mintage | F | VF | XF | Unc |
|---|---|---|---|---|---|
| AH1415-1994 Proof | — | Value: 31.50 | | | |

**5 POUNDS** **KM# 877** **Weight:** 26.0000 g. **Composition:** 0.8750 Gold .7315 oz. AGW **Reverse:** Seated scribe

| Date | Mintage | F | VF | XF | Unc |
|---|---|---|---|---|---|
| AH1415-1994 Proof | 3,000 | Value: 275 | | | |

**5 POUNDS** **KM# 876** **Weight:** 26.0000 g. **Composition:** 0.8750 Gold .7315 oz. AGW **Reverse:** 3/4 length standing Sheikh El Balad

| Date | Mintage | F | VF | XF | Unc |
|---|---|---|---|---|---|
| AH1415-1994 Proof | 3,000 | Value: 275 | | | |

**5 POUNDS** **KM# 825** **Weight:** 22.5000 g. **Composition:** 0.9990 Silver .7227 oz. ASW **Obverse:** Ancient style vulture, denomination **Reverse:** Goat right

| Date | Mintage | F | VF | XF | Unc |
|---|---|---|---|---|---|
| AH1415-1994 Proof | — | Value: 36.50 | | | |

**5 POUNDS** **KM# 829** **Weight:** 22.5000 g. **Composition:** 0.9990 Silver .7227 oz. ASW **Obverse:** Ancient style vulture, denomination **Reverse:** Standing god Ptah of Memphis right

| Date | Mintage | F | VF | XF | Unc |
|---|---|---|---|---|---|
| AH1415-1994 Proof | — | Value: 31.50 | | | |

**5 POUNDS** **KM# 750** **Weight:** 22.5000 g. **Composition:** 0.9990 Silver .7227 oz. ASW **Reverse:** King Djoser wearing the Red Crown right

| Date | Mintage | F | VF | XF | Unc |
|---|---|---|---|---|---|
| AH1415-1994 Proof | 50,000 | Value: 31.50 | | | |

**5 POUNDS** **KM# 751** **Weight:** 22.5000 g. **Composition:** 0.9990 Silver .7227 oz. ASW **Reverse:** King Khonsu facing

| Date | Mintage | F | VF | XF | Unc |
|---|---|---|---|---|---|
| AH1415-1994 Proof | 50,000 | Value: 31.50 | | | |

**5 POUNDS** **KM# 752** **Weight:** 22.5000 g. **Composition:** 0.9990 Silver .7227 oz. ASW **Reverse:** Re (Sun God) presenting the Ankh (Symbol of Life) to Sesostris I wearing Double Crown

| Date | Mintage | F | VF | XF | Unc |
|---|---|---|---|---|---|
| AH1415-1994 Proof | 50,000 | Value: 31.50 | | | |

**5 POUNDS** **KM# 753** **Weight:** 22.5000 g. **Composition:** 0.9990 Silver .7227 oz. ASW **Reverse:** God Horus wearing Double Crown

| Date | Mintage | F | VF | XF | Unc |
|---|---|---|---|---|---|
| AH1415-1994 Proof | 50,000 | Value: 31.50 | | | |

**5 POUNDS** **KM# 754** **Weight:** 22.5000 g. **Composition:** 0.9990 Silver .7227 oz. ASW **Reverse:** Standing god Seth left

| Date | Mintage | F | VF | XF | Unc |
|---|---|---|---|---|---|
| AH1415-1994 Proof | 50,000 | Value: 31.50 | | | |

**5 POUNDS** **KM# 757** **Weight:** 22.5000 g. **Composition:** 0.9990 Silver .7227 oz. ASW **Reverse:** Queen Nofretari, wife of Ramses II kneeling right

| Date | Mintage | F | VF | XF | Unc |
|---|---|---|---|---|---|
| AH1415-1994 Proof | Est. 25,000 | Value: 37.50 | | | |

**5 POUNDS** **KM# 783** **Weight:** 22.5000 g. **Composition:** 0.9990 Silver .7227 oz. ASW **Obverse:** Ancient style vulture **Reverse:** Bust of Nefertiti right

| Date | Mintage | F | VF | XF | Unc |
|---|---|---|---|---|---|
| AH1415-1994 Proof | 50,000 | Value: 36.50 | | | |

**5 POUNDS** **KM# 784** **Weight:** 22.5000 g. **Composition:** 0.9990 Silver .7227 oz. ASW **Obverse:** Ancient style vulture **Reverse:** Archer in chariot

| Date | Mintage | F | VF | XF | Unc |
|---|---|---|---|---|---|
| AH1415-1994 Proof | 50,000 | Value: 37.50 | | | |

**5 POUNDS** **KM# 749** **Weight:** 22.5000 g. **Composition:** 0.9990 Silver .7227 oz. ASW **Reverse:** Sphinx and pyramids

| Date | Mintage | F | VF | XF | Unc |
|---|---|---|---|---|---|
| AH1414-1994 Proof | 50,000 | Value: 31.50 | | | |

**5 POUNDS** **KM# 763** **Weight:** 17.5000 g. **Composition:** 0.7200 Silver .4051 oz. ASW **Subject:** Salah El Din El-Ayubi **Reverse:** Bust of El-Ayubi center, mosque behind at left, mounted rider with sword at right

| Date | Mintage | F | VF | XF | Unc |
|---|---|---|---|---|---|
| AH1414-1994 | 5,000 | — | — | — | 25.00 |

**5 POUNDS** **KM# 736** **Weight:** 17.5000 g. **Composition:** 0.9250 Silver .5205 oz. ASW **Series:** World Cup Soccer **Reverse:** Two players, pyramid with Statue of Liberty at left

| Date | Mintage | F | VF | XF | Unc |
|---|---|---|---|---|---|
| AH1415-1994 | 499 | — | — | — | 45.00 |
| AH1415-1994 Proof | 15,000 | Value: 40.00 | | | |

**5 POUNDS** **KM# 738** **Weight:** 17.5000 g. **Composition:** 0.9250 Silver .5205 oz. ASW **Series:** World Cup Soccer **Reverse:** Stylized player

| Date | Mintage | F | VF | XF | Unc |
|---|---|---|---|---|---|
| AH1415-1994 | 499 | — | — | — | 45.00 |
| AH1415-1994 Proof | 15,000 | Value: 40.00 | | | |

**5 POUNDS** **KM# 875** **Weight:** 22.5000 g. **Composition:** 0.9990 Silver .7227 oz. ASW **Reverse:** 3/4-length standing Sheikh El Balad

| Date | Mintage | F | VF | XF | Unc |
|---|---|---|---|---|---|
| AH1415-1994 Proof | 15,000 | Value: 40.00 | | | |

**5 POUNDS** **KM# 883** **Weight:** 22.5000 g. **Composition:** 0.9990 Silver .7227 oz. ASW **Reverse:** Seated King Horemheb

| Date | Mintage | F | VF | XF | Unc |
|---|---|---|---|---|---|
| AH1415-1994 Proof | 15,000 | Value: 40.00 | | | |

**5 POUNDS** **KM# 889** **Weight:** 22.5000 g. **Composition:** 0.9990 Silver .7227 oz. ASW **Reverse:** Akhnaton and family

| Date | Mintage | F | VF | XF | Unc |
|---|---|---|---|---|---|
| AH1415-1994 Proof | 15,000 | Value: 40.00 | | | |

**5 POUNDS** **KM# 894** **Weight:** 22.5000 g. **Composition:** 0.9990 Silver .7227 oz. ASW **Reverse:** Bust amulet of Hathor

| Date | Mintage | F | VF | XF | Unc |
|---|---|---|---|---|---|
| AH1415-1994 Proof | 15,000 | Value: 40.00 | | | |

**5 POUNDS** **KM# 896** **Weight:** 22.5000 g. **Composition:** 0.9990 Silver .7227 oz. ASW **Reverse:** Pair of geese

| Date | Mintage | F | VF | XF | Unc |
|---|---|---|---|---|---|
| AH1415-1994 Proof | 15,000 | Value: 40.00 | | | |

**5 POUNDS** **KM# 765** **Weight:** 17.5000 g. **Composition:** 0.7200 Silver .4051 oz. ASW **Subject:** 50 Years - Arab League

| Date | Mintage | F | VF | XF | Unc |
|---|---|---|---|---|---|
| AH1415-1995 | 5,000 | — | — | — | 25.00 |

**5 POUNDS** **KM# 768** **Weight:** 17.5000 g. **Composition:** 0.7200 Silver .4051 oz. ASW **Subject:** 75 Years - Bank of Misr

| Date | Mintage | F | VF | XF | Unc |
|---|---|---|---|---|---|
| AH1415-1995 | 2,500 | — | — | — | 28.00 |

**5 POUNDS** **KM# 770** **Weight:** 17.5000 g. **Composition:** 0.7200 Silver .4051 oz. ASW **Series:** F.A.O. **Reverse:** People working

| Date | Mintage | F | VF | XF | Unc |
|---|---|---|---|---|---|
| AH1415-1995 | 5,000 | — | — | — | 50.00 |

**5 POUNDS** **KM# 772** **Weight:** 17.5000 g. **Composition:** 0.7200 Silver .4051 oz. ASW **Subject:** Pediatrics International Conference

| Date | Mintage | F | VF | XF | Unc |
|---|---|---|---|---|---|
| AH1416-1995 | 4,000 | — | — | — | 22.00 |

**5 POUNDS** **KM# 773** **Weight:** 17.5000 g. **Composition:** 0.7200 Silver .4051 oz. ASW **Subject:** 75 Years - Architects Association

| Date | Mintage | F | VF | XF | Unc |
|---|---|---|---|---|---|
| AH1416-1995 | 3,000 | — | — | — | 50.00 |

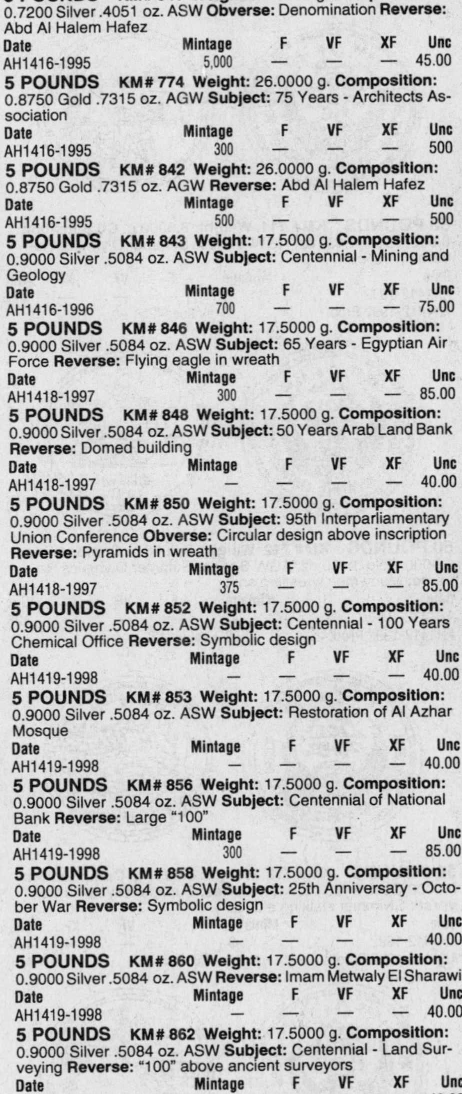

**5 POUNDS** **KM# 838** **Weight:** 17.5000 g. **Composition:** 0.7200 Silver .4051 oz. ASW **Subject:** 75 Years - American University in Cairo

| Date | Mintage | F | VF | XF | Unc |
|---|---|---|---|---|---|
| AH1415-1995 | 3,000 | — | — | — | 28.00 |

**5 POUNDS** **KM# 841** **Weight:** 17.5000 g. **Composition:** 0.7200 Silver .4051 oz. ASW **Obverse:** Denomination **Reverse:** Abd Al Halem Hafez

| Date | Mintage | F | VF | XF | Unc |
|---|---|---|---|---|---|
| AH1416-1995 | 5,000 | — | — | — | 45.00 |

**5 POUNDS** **KM# 774** **Weight:** 26.0000 g. **Composition:** 0.8750 Gold .7315 oz. AGW **Subject:** 75 Years - Architects Association

| Date | Mintage | F | VF | XF | Unc |
|---|---|---|---|---|---|
| AH1416-1995 | 300 | — | — | — | 500 |

**5 POUNDS** **KM# 842** **Weight:** 26.0000 g. **Composition:** 0.8750 Gold .7315 oz. AGW **Reverse:** Abd Al Halem Hafez

| Date | Mintage | F | VF | XF | Unc |
|---|---|---|---|---|---|
| AH1416-1995 | 500 | — | — | — | 500 |

**5 POUNDS** **KM# 843** **Weight:** 17.5000 g. **Composition:** 0.9000 Silver .5084 oz. ASW **Subject:** Centennial - Mining and Geology

| Date | Mintage | F | VF | XF | Unc |
|---|---|---|---|---|---|
| AH1416-1996 | 700 | — | — | — | 75.00 |

**5 POUNDS** **KM# 846** **Weight:** 17.5000 g. **Composition:** 0.9000 Silver .5084 oz. ASW **Subject:** 65 Years - Egyptian Air Force **Reverse:** Flying eagle in wreath

| Date | Mintage | F | VF | XF | Unc |
|---|---|---|---|---|---|
| AH1418-1997 | 300 | — | — | — | 85.00 |

**5 POUNDS** **KM# 848** **Weight:** 17.5000 g. **Composition:** 0.9000 Silver .5084 oz. ASW **Subject:** 50 Years Arab Land Bank **Reverse:** Domed building

| Date | Mintage | F | VF | XF | Unc |
|---|---|---|---|---|---|
| AH1418-1997 | — | — | — | — | 40.00 |

**5 POUNDS** **KM# 850** **Weight:** 17.5000 g. **Composition:** 0.9000 Silver .5084 oz. ASW **Subject:** 95th Interparliamentary Union Conference **Obverse:** Circular design above inscription **Reverse:** Pyramids in wreath

| Date | Mintage | F | VF | XF | Unc |
|---|---|---|---|---|---|
| AH1418-1997 | 375 | — | — | — | 85.00 |

**5 POUNDS** **KM# 852** **Weight:** 17.5000 g. **Composition:** 0.9000 Silver .5084 oz. ASW **Subject:** Centennial - 100 Years Chemical Office **Reverse:** Symbolic design

| Date | Mintage | F | VF | XF | Unc |
|---|---|---|---|---|---|
| AH1419-1998 | — | — | — | — | 40.00 |

**5 POUNDS** **KM# 853** **Weight:** 17.5000 g. **Composition:** 0.9000 Silver .5084 oz. ASW **Subject:** Restoration of Al Azhar Mosque

| Date | Mintage | F | VF | XF | Unc |
|---|---|---|---|---|---|
| AH1419-1998 | — | — | — | — | 40.00 |

**5 POUNDS** **KM# 856** **Weight:** 17.5000 g. **Composition:** 0.9000 Silver .5084 oz. ASW **Subject:** Centennial of National Bank **Reverse:** Large "100"

| Date | Mintage | F | VF | XF | Unc |
|---|---|---|---|---|---|
| AH1419-1998 | 300 | — | — | — | 85.00 |

**5 POUNDS** **KM# 858** **Weight:** 17.5000 g. **Composition:** 0.9000 Silver .5084 oz. ASW **Subject:** 25th Anniversary - October War **Reverse:** Symbolic design

| Date | Mintage | F | VF | XF | Unc |
|---|---|---|---|---|---|
| AH1419-1998 | — | — | — | — | 40.00 |

**5 POUNDS** **KM# 860** **Weight:** 17.5000 g. **Composition:** 0.9000 Silver .5084 oz. ASW **Reverse:** Imam Metwaly El Sharawi

| Date | Mintage | F | VF | XF | Unc |
|---|---|---|---|---|---|
| AH1419-1998 | — | — | — | — | 40.00 |

**5 POUNDS** **KM# 862** **Weight:** 17.5000 g. **Composition:** 0.9000 Silver .5084 oz. ASW **Subject:** Centennial - Land Surveying **Reverse:** "100" above ancient surveyors

| Date | Mintage | F | VF | XF | Unc |
|---|---|---|---|---|---|
| AH1419-1998 | — | — | — | — | 40.00 |

**5 POUNDS** **KM# 864** **Weight:** 17.5000 g. **Composition:** 0.9000 Silver .5084 oz. ASW **Subject:** Centennial - Solidarity **Reverse:** Symbolic design

| Date | Mintage | F | VF | XF | Unc |
|---|---|---|---|---|---|
| AH1419-1998 | — | — | — | — | 40.00 |

**5 POUNDS** **KM# 854** **Weight:** 17.5000 g. **Composition:** 0.9000 Silver .5084 oz. ASW **Subject:** 16th Men's World Handball Championship

| Date | Mintage | F | VF | XF | Unc |
|---|---|---|---|---|---|
| AH1420-1999 | — | — | — | — | 45.00 |

**5 POUNDS** **KM# 867** **Weight:** 17.5000 g. **Composition:** 0.9000 Silver .5084 oz. ASW **Subject:** 50 Years Cairo Metropolitan Mass Transit System **Reverse:** Water above subway train

| Date | Mintage | F | VF | XF | Unc |
|---|---|---|---|---|---|
| AH1420-1999 | — | — | — | — | 40.00 |

**5 POUNDS** **KM# 897** **Weight:** 17.5000 g. **Composition:** 0.9000 Silver .5084 oz. ASW **Subject:** 75 Years - Dar El-Eloum University

| Date | Mintage | F | VF | XF | Unc |
|---|---|---|---|---|---|
| AH1420-1999 | — | — | — | — | 40.00 |

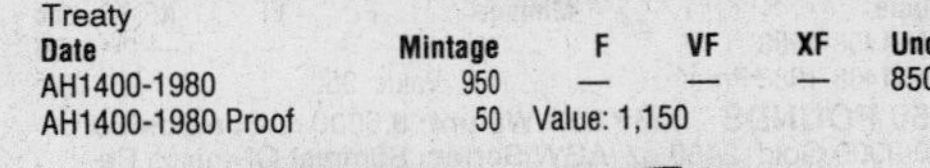

**10 POUNDS** **KM# 519** **Weight:** 40.0000 g. **Composition:** 0.8750 Gold 1.1254 oz. AGW **Subject:** Egyptian-Israeli Peace Treaty

| Date | Mintage | F | VF | XF | Unc |
|---|---|---|---|---|---|
| AH1400-1980 | 950 | — | — | — | 850 |
| AH1400-1980 Proof | 50 | Value: 1,150 | | | |

**10 POUNDS** **KM# 538** **Weight:** 40.0000 g. **Composition:** 0.8750 Gold 1.1254 oz. AGW **Subject:** 25th Anniversary - Ministry of Industry

| Date | Mintage | F | VF | XF | Unc |
|---|---|---|---|---|---|
| AH1402-1981 | 18 | — | — | — | 1,500 |
| AH1402-1981 Proof | 1,000 | Value: 700 | | | |

**10 POUNDS** KM# 548 **Weight:** 40.0000 g. **Composition:** 0.8750 Gold 1.1254 oz. AGW **Subject:** 1000th Anniversary - Al Azhar Mosque

| Date | Mintage | F | VF | XF | Unc |
|---|---|---|---|---|---|
| AH1402-1982 Proof | 1,322 | Value: 700 | | | |

**10 POUNDS** KM# 634 **Weight:** 40.0000 g. **Composition:** 0.8750 Gold 1.1254 oz. AGW **Subject:** Prophet's Mosque **Obverse:** Minaret, globe, denomination, legends **Reverse:** Crescent, mosque, minaret below legend arch

| Date | Mintage | F | VF | XF | Unc |
|---|---|---|---|---|---|
| AH1406-1985 Proof | 300 | Value: 600 | | | |

**50 POUNDS** KM# 672 **Weight:** 8.5000 g. **Composition:** 0.9000 Gold .2460 oz. AGW **Series:** World Soccer Championships **Obverse:** Stylized flowers, denomination, date and legends **Reverse:** Soccer ball on road between Mexican and Egyptian pyramids

| Date | Mintage | F | VF | XF | Unc |
|---|---|---|---|---|---|
| AH1406-1986 | 250 | — | — | — | 250 |
| AH1406-1986 Proof | 250 | Value: 300 | | | |

**50 POUNDS** KM# 641 **Weight:** 8.5000 g. **Composition:** 0.9000 Gold .2460 oz. AGW **Subject:** Mecca **Obverse:** Arabic legend, ornamentation **Reverse:** Interior view of the Kaaba

| Date | Mintage | F | VF | XF | Unc |
|---|---|---|---|---|---|
| AH1406-1986 | 14,000 | — | — | — | 200 |

**50 POUNDS** KM# 612 **Weight:** 8.5000 g. **Composition:** 0.9000 Gold .2460 oz. AGW **Subject:** Aida Opera **Obverse:** Radiant sun, pillars and inscriptions **Reverse:** Ancient figures among ruins

| Date | Mintage | F | VF | XF | Unc |
|---|---|---|---|---|---|
| AH1407-1987 | 40,000 | — | — | — | 225 |

**50 POUNDS** KM# 625 **Weight:** 8.5000 g. **Composition:** 0.9000 Gold .2460 oz. AGW **Series:** Summer Olympics **Obverse:** Arabic legend and ornamentation within English legend **Reverse:** Pharoah and athletes

| Date | Mintage | F | VF | XF | Unc |
|---|---|---|---|---|---|
| AH1408-1988 | 150 | — | — | — | 300 |
| AH1408-1988 Proof | 50 | Value: 350 | | | |

**50 POUNDS** KM# 627 **Weight:** 8.5000 g. **Composition:** 0.9000 Gold .2460 oz. AGW **Series:** Summer Olympics **Reverse:** Athletes and mythological figures

| Date | Mintage | F | VF | XF | Unc |
|---|---|---|---|---|---|
| AH1408-1988 | 750 | — | — | — | 250 |
| AH1408-1988 Proof | 250 | Value: 275 | | | |

**50 POUNDS** KM# 629 **Weight:** 8.5000 g. **Composition:** 0.9000 Gold .2460 oz. AGW **Series:** Winter Olympics **Obverse:** Winged design, English legend, Arabic inscription **Reverse:** Ski jumper and figure skater within Arabic legend

| Date | Mintage | F | VF | XF | Unc |
|---|---|---|---|---|---|
| AH1408-1988 | 150 | — | — | — | 300 |
| AH1408-1988 Proof | 50 | Value: 350 | | | |

**50 POUNDS** KM# 680 **Weight:** 8.5000 g. **Composition:** 0.9000 Gold .2460 oz. AGW **Subject:** Soccer World Championship - Italy **Reverse:** Ancient gods

| Date | Mintage | F | VF | XF | Unc |
|---|---|---|---|---|---|
| AH1410-1990 Proof | 225 | Value: 450 | | | |

**50 POUNDS** KM# 683 **Weight:** 8.5000 g. **Composition:** 0.9000 Gold .2460 oz. AGW **Subject:** Soccer World Championship **Reverse:** Player chasing ball

| Date | Mintage | F | VF | XF | Unc |
|---|---|---|---|---|---|
| AH1410-1990 Proof | 75 | Value: 500 | | | |

**50 POUNDS** KM# 709 **Weight:** 8.5000 g. **Composition:** 0.9000 Gold .2460 oz. AGW **Series:** Summer Olympics **Reverse:** Fencing

| Date | Mintage | F | VF | XF | Unc |
|---|---|---|---|---|---|
| AH1412-1992 | 49 | — | — | — | 425 |
| AH1412-1992 Proof | 99 | Value: 425 | | | |

**50 POUNDS** KM# 710 **Weight:** 8.5000 g. **Composition:** 0.9000 Gold .2460 oz. AGW **Series:** Summer Olympics **Reverse:** Wrestling

| Date | Mintage | F | VF | XF | Unc |
|---|---|---|---|---|---|
| AH1412-1992 | 49 | — | — | — | 425 |
| AH1412-1992 Proof | 99 | Value: 425 | | | |

**50 POUNDS** KM# 711 **Weight:** 8.5000 g. **Composition:** 0.9000 Gold .2460 oz. AGW **Series:** Summer Olympics **Reverse:** Archery

| Date | Mintage | F | VF | XF | Unc |
|---|---|---|---|---|---|
| AH1412-1992 | 49 | — | — | — | 425 |
| AH1412-1992 Proof | 99 | Value: 425 | | | |

**50 POUNDS** KM# 712 **Weight:** 8.5000 g. **Composition:** 0.9000 Gold .2460 oz. AGW **Series:** Summer Olympics **Reverse:** Many men wrestling an ox

| Date | Mintage | F | VF | XF | Unc |
|---|---|---|---|---|---|
| AH1412-1992 | 49 | — | — | — | 425 |
| AH1412-1992 Proof | 99 | Value: 425 | | | |

**50 POUNDS** KM# 713 **Weight:** 8.5000 g. **Composition:** 0.9000 Gold .2460 oz. AGW **Series:** Summer Olympics **Reverse:** Swimmer stalking a duck

| Date | Mintage | F | VF | XF | Unc |
|---|---|---|---|---|---|
| AH1412-1992 | 49 | — | — | — | 425 |
| AH1412-1992 Proof | 99 | Value: 425 | | | |

**50 POUNDS** KM# 714 **Weight:** 8.5000 g. **Composition:** 0.9000 Gold .2460 oz. AGW **Series:** Summer Olympics **Reverse:** Handball player

| Date | Mintage | F | VF | XF | Unc |
|---|---|---|---|---|---|
| AH1412-1992 | 49 | — | — | — | 425 |
| AH1412-1992 Proof | 99 | Value: 425 | | | |

**50 POUNDS** KM# 715 **Weight:** 8.5000 g. **Composition:** 0.9000 Gold .2460 oz. AGW **Series:** Summer Olympics **Reverse:** Field hockey player

| Date | Mintage | F | VF | XF | Unc |
|---|---|---|---|---|---|
| AH1412-1992 | 49 | — | — | — | 425 |
| AH1412-1992 Proof | 99 | Value: 425 | | | |

**50 POUNDS** KM# 716 **Weight:** 8.5000 g. **Composition:** 0.9000 Gold .2460 oz. AGW **Series:** Summer Olympics **Reverse:** Soccer player

| Date | Mintage | F | VF | XF | Unc |
|---|---|---|---|---|---|
| AH1412-1992 | 49 | — | — | — | 425 |
| AH1412-1992 Proof | 115 | Value: 425 | | | |

**50 POUNDS** KM# 755 **Weight:** 8.5000 g. **Composition:** 0.9000 Gold .2460 oz. AGW **Reverse:** King Tutankhamen's Burial Mask

| Date | Mintage | F | VF | XF | Unc |
|---|---|---|---|---|---|
| AH1414-1993 Proof | — | Value: 260 | | | |

**50 POUNDS** KM# 756 **Weight:** 8.5000 g. **Composition:** 0.9000 Gold .2460 oz. AGW **Subject:** Cleopatra **Reverse:** Bust of Cleopatra left

| Date | Mintage | F | VF | XF | Unc |
|---|---|---|---|---|---|
| AH1414-1993 Proof | — | Value: 240 | | | |

**50 POUNDS** KM# 776 **Weight:** 8.5000 g. **Composition:** 0.9000 Gold .2460 oz. AGW **Reverse:** Sphinx head

| Date | Mintage | F | VF | XF | Unc |
|---|---|---|---|---|---|
| AH1414-1993 Proof | — | Value: 200 | | | |

**50 POUNDS** **KM# 777** **Weight:** 8.5000 g. **Composition:** 0.9000 Gold .2460 oz. AGW **Reverse:** Standing Ramses II

| Date | Mintage | F | VF | XF | Unc |
|---|---|---|---|---|---|
| AH1414-1993 Proof | — | Value: 200 | | | |

**50 POUNDS** **KM# 778** **Weight:** 8.5000 g. **Composition:** 0.9000 Gold .2460 oz. AGW **Reverse:** Crowned falcon left

| Date | Mintage | F | VF | XF | Unc |
|---|---|---|---|---|---|
| AH1414-1993 Proof | — | Value: 220 | | | |

**50 POUNDS** **KM# 868** **Weight:** 8.5000 g. **Composition:** 0.9000 Gold .2460 oz. AGW **Subject:** King Narmer Palette **Obverse:** Vulture **Reverse:** King Narmer killing a wounded foe

| Date | Mintage | F | VF | XF | Unc |
|---|---|---|---|---|---|
| AH1414-1993 Proof | 3,000 | Value: 250 | | | |

**50 POUNDS** **KM# 870** **Weight:** 8.5000 g. **Composition:** 0.9000 Gold .2460 oz. AGW **Subject:** King Kna-Sekhem **Reverse:** Seated king

| Date | Mintage | F | VF | XF | Unc |
|---|---|---|---|---|---|
| AH1414-1993 Proof | 3,000 | Value: 250 | | | |

**50 POUNDS** **KM# 873** **Weight:** 8.5000 g. **Composition:** 0.9000 Gold .2460 oz. AGW **Subject:** Menkaure Triad **Reverse:** Three carved figurines

| Date | Mintage | F | VF | XF | Unc |
|---|---|---|---|---|---|
| AH1414-1993 Proof | 3,000 | Value: 250 | | | |

**50 POUNDS** **KM# 885** **Weight:** 8.5000 g. **Composition:** 0.9000 Gold .2460 oz. AGW **Subject:** Thoutmosis III **Reverse:** Kneeling figure holding jar

| Date | Mintage | F | VF | XF | Unc |
|---|---|---|---|---|---|
| AH1414-1993 Proof | 3,000 | Value: 250 | | | |

**50 POUNDS** **KM# 775** **Weight:** 8.5000 g. **Composition:** 0.9000 Gold .2460 oz. AGW **Reverse:** Three pyramids

| Date | Mintage | F | VF | XF | Unc |
|---|---|---|---|---|---|
| AH1414-1993 Proof | — | Value: 200 | | | |

**50 POUNDS** **KM# 737** **Weight:** 8.5000 g. **Composition:** 0.9000 Gold .2460 oz. AGW **Series:** World Cup Soccer **Reverse:** Two players, pyramid and Statue of Liberty

| Date | Mintage | F | VF | XF | Unc |
|---|---|---|---|---|---|
| AH1415-1994 | 99 | — | — | — | 300 |
| AH1415-1994 Proof | 99 | Value: 300 | | | |

**50 POUNDS** **KM# 739** **Weight:** 8.5000 g. **Composition:** 0.9000 Gold .2460 oz. AGW **Series:** World Cup Soccer **Reverse:** Stylized player

| Date | Mintage | F | VF | XF | Unc |
|---|---|---|---|---|---|
| AH1415-1994 | 99 | — | — | — | 300 |
| AH1415-1994 Proof | 99 | Value: 300 | | | |

**50 POUNDS** **KM# 779** **Weight:** 8.5000 g. **Composition:** 0.9000 Gold .2460 oz. AGW **Subject:** Queen Nefertiti **Reverse:** Bust of Queen Nefertiti right

| Date | Mintage | F | VF | XF | Unc |
|---|---|---|---|---|---|
| AH1415-1994 Proof | — | Value: 200 | | | |

**50 POUNDS** **KM# 780** **Weight:** 8.5000 g. **Composition:** 0.9000 Gold .2460 oz. AGW **Reverse:** Seated cat right

| Date | Mintage | F | VF | XF | Unc |
|---|---|---|---|---|---|
| AH1415-1994 Proof | — | Value: 200 | | | |

**50 POUNDS** **KM# 781** **Weight:** 8.5000 g. **Composition:** 0.9000 Gold .2460 oz. AGW **Reverse:** Archer in chariot

| Date | Mintage | F | VF | XF | Unc |
|---|---|---|---|---|---|
| AH1415-1994 Proof | — | Value: 220 | | | |

**50 POUNDS** **KM# 782** **Weight:** 8.5000 g. **Composition:** 0.9000 Gold .2460 oz. AGW **Reverse:** Standing god Seth left

| Date | Mintage | F | VF | XF | Unc |
|---|---|---|---|---|---|
| AH1415-1994 Proof | — | Value: 165 | | | |

**50 POUNDS** **KM# 814** **Weight:** 8.5000 g. **Composition:** 0.9000 Gold .2460 oz. AGW **Reverse:** Hippopotamus

| Date | Mintage | F | VF | XF | Unc |
|---|---|---|---|---|---|
| AH1415-1994 Proof | — | Value: 165 | | | |

**50 POUNDS** **KM# 815** **Weight:** 8.5000 g. **Composition:** 0.9000 Gold .2460 oz. AGW **Reverse:** Egyptian gazelle

| Date | Mintage | F | VF | XF | Unc |
|---|---|---|---|---|---|
| AH1415-1994 Proof | — | Value: 165 | | | |

**50 POUNDS** **KM# 816** **Weight:** 8.5000 g. **Composition:** 0.9000 Gold .2460 oz. AGW **Reverse:** Phoenix birds

| Date | Mintage | F | VF | XF | Unc |
|---|---|---|---|---|---|
| AH1415-1994 Proof | — | Value: 165 | | | |

**50 POUNDS** **KM# 817** **Weight:** 8.5000 g. **Composition:** 0.9000 Gold .2460 oz. AGW **Reverse:** Egyptian geese

| Date | Mintage | F | VF | XF | Unc |
|---|---|---|---|---|---|
| AH1415-1994 Proof | — | Value: 165 | | | |

**50 POUNDS** **KM# 818** **Weight:** 8.5000 g. **Composition:** 0.9000 Gold .2460 oz. AGW **Reverse:** King Taharqa

| Date | Mintage | F | VF | XF | Unc |
|---|---|---|---|---|---|
| AH1415-1994 Proof | — | Value: 165 | | | |

**50 POUNDS** **KM# 819** **Weight:** 8.5000 g. **Composition:** 0.9000 Gold .2460 oz. AGW **Reverse:** Amenhotep Temple

| Date | Mintage | F | VF | XF | Unc |
|---|---|---|---|---|---|
| AH1415-1994 Proof | — | Value: 165 | | | |

**50 POUNDS** **KM# 820** **Weight:** 8.5000 g. **Composition:** 0.9000 Gold .2460 oz. AGW **Reverse:** Karnak Temple

| Date | Mintage | F | VF | XF | Unc |
|---|---|---|---|---|---|
| AH1415-1994 Proof | — | Value: 165 | | | |

**50 POUNDS** **KM# 821** **Weight:** 8.5000 g. **Composition:** 0.9000 Gold .2460 oz. AGW **Reverse:** Philae Temple

| Date | Mintage | F | VF | XF | Unc |
|---|---|---|---|---|---|
| AH1415-1994 Proof | — | Value: 165 | | | |

**50 POUNDS** **KM# 822** **Weight:** 8.5000 g. **Composition:** 0.9000 Gold .2460 oz. AGW **Reverse:** Khonsu Temple

| Date | Mintage | F | VF | XF | Unc |
|---|---|---|---|---|---|
| AH1415-1994 Proof | — | Value: 165 | | | |

**50 POUNDS** **KM# 871** **Weight:** 8.5000 g. **Composition:** 0.9000 Gold .2460 oz. AGW **Reverse:** King Djoser wearing the red crown

| Date | Mintage | F | VF | XF | Unc |
|---|---|---|---|---|---|
| AH1415-1994 Proof | 3,000 | Value: 250 | | | |

**50 POUNDS** **KM# 872** **Weight:** 8.5000 g. **Composition:** 0.9000 Gold .2460 oz. AGW **Reverse:** Seated King Khufu with flat-top hat

| Date | Mintage | F | VF | XF | Unc |
|---|---|---|---|---|---|
| AH1415-1994 Proof | 3,000 | Value: 250 | | | |

**50 POUNDS** **KM# 882** **Weight:** 8.5000 g. **Composition:** 0.9000 Gold .2460 oz. AGW **Subject:** King Sesostris I **Reverse:** RE (sun god) presenting the ANKH (symbol of life) to the king wearing the double crown

| Date | Mintage | F | VF | XF | Unc |
|---|---|---|---|---|---|
| AH1415-1994 Proof | 3,000 | Value: 275 | | | |

**50 POUNDS** **KM# 884** **Weight:** 8.5000 g. **Composition:** 0.9000 Gold .2460 oz. AGW **Subject:** King Horemheb **Reverse:** Seated King Horemheb

| Date | Mintage | F | VF | XF | Unc |
|---|---|---|---|---|---|
| AH1415-1994 Proof | 3,000 | Value: 275 | | | |

**50 POUNDS** **KM# 886** **Weight:** 8.5000 g. **Composition:** 0.9000 Gold .2460 oz. AGW **Subject:** King Khonsu **Reverse:** 1/2-length King Khonsu

| Date | Mintage | F | VF | XF | Unc |
|---|---|---|---|---|---|
| AH1415-1994 Proof | 3,000 | Value: 275 | | | |

**50 POUNDS** **KM# 887** **Weight:** 8.5000 g. **Composition:** 0.9000 Gold .2460 oz. AGW **Subject:** Tutankhamon's Throne **Reverse:** King Tut seated on throne with servant

| Date | Mintage | F | VF | XF | Unc |
|---|---|---|---|---|---|
| AH1415-1994 Proof | 3,000 | Value: 300 | | | |

**50 POUNDS** **KM# 888** **Weight:** 8.5000 g. **Composition:** 0.9000 Gold .2460 oz. AGW **Subject:** Queen Hatshepsut **Reverse:** Queen's facial sculpture

| Date | Mintage | F | VF | XF | Unc |
|---|---|---|---|---|---|
| AH1415-1994 Proof | 3,000 | Value: 275 | | | |

**50 POUNDS** **KM# 890** **Weight:** 8.5000 g. **Composition:** 0.9000 Gold .2460 oz. AGW **Subject:** Akhnaton and Family **Reverse:** Family scene

| Date | Mintage | F | VF | XF | Unc |
|---|---|---|---|---|---|
| AH1415-1994 Proof | 3,000 | Value: 275 | | | |

**50 POUNDS** **KM# 891** **Weight:** 8.5000 g. **Composition:** 0.9000 Gold .2460 oz. AGW **Reverse:** Akhnaton

| Date | Mintage | F | VF | XF | Unc |
|---|---|---|---|---|---|
| AH1415-1994 Proof | 3,000 | Value: 275 | | | |

**50 POUNDS** **KM# 892** **Weight:** 8.5000 g. **Composition:** 0.9000 Gold .2460 oz. AGW **Subject:** Queen Nefertarl **Reverse:** Kneeling Queen Nefertarl

| Date | Mintage | F | VF | XF | Unc |
|---|---|---|---|---|---|
| AH1415-1994 Proof | 5,000 | Value: 275 | | | |

**50 POUNDS** **KM# 893** **Weight:** 8.5000 g. **Composition:** 0.9000 Gold .2460 oz. AGW **Subject:** Ramses III **Reverse:** 3/4-length Ramses III

| Date | Mintage | F | VF | XF | Unc |
|---|---|---|---|---|---|
| AH1415-1994 Proof | 3,000 | Value: 300 | | | |

**50 POUNDS** **KM# 895** **Weight:** 8.5000 g. **Composition:** 0.9000 Gold .2460 oz. AGW **Reverse:** Amulet of Hathor

| Date | Mintage | F | VF | XF | Unc |
|---|---|---|---|---|---|
| AH1415-1994 Proof | 3,000 | Value: 275 | | | |

**100 POUNDS** **KM# 550** **Weight:** 17.1500 g. **Composition:** 0.9000 Gold .4963 oz. AGW **Reverse:** Queen Nefertiti

| Date | Mintage | F | VF | XF | Unc |
|---|---|---|---|---|---|
| 1983 Proof | 16,000 | Value: 600 | | | |

**100 POUNDS** **KM# 562** **Weight:** 17.1500 g. **Composition:** 0.9000 Gold .4963 oz. AGW **Reverse:** Cleopatra VII

| Date | Mintage | F | VF | XF | Unc |
|---|---|---|---|---|---|
| 1984 Proof | 2,121 | Value: 675 | | | |

**100 POUNDS** **KM# 569** **Weight:** 17.1500 g. **Composition:** 0.9000 Gold .4963 oz. AGW **Reverse:** The golden falcon

| Date | Mintage | F | VF | XF | Unc |
|---|---|---|---|---|---|
| 1985 Proof | 1,800 | Value: 425 | | | |

**100 POUNDS** KM# 591 **Weight:** 17.1500 g. **Composition:** 0.9000 Gold .4963 oz. AGW **Reverse:** Tutankhamen

| Date | Mintage | F | VF | XF | Unc |
|---|---|---|---|---|---|
| 1986 Proof | 7,500 | Value: 600 | | | |

**100 POUNDS** KM# 642 **Weight:** 17.0000 g. **Composition:** 0.9000 Gold .4918 oz. AGW **Subject:** Mecca **Obverse:** Arabic legend, ornamentation **Reverse:** Interior view of the Kaaba

| Date | Mintage | F | VF | XF | Unc |
|---|---|---|---|---|---|
| AH1406-1986 | 700 | — | — | — | 350 |

**100 POUNDS** KM# 613 **Weight:** 17.0000 g. **Composition:** 0.9000 Gold .4918 oz. AGW **Reverse:** The golden ram

| Date | Mintage | F | VF | XF | Unc |
|---|---|---|---|---|---|
| 1987 Proof | 7,500 | Value: 400 | | | |

**100 POUNDS** KM# 648 **Weight:** 17.0000 g. **Composition:** 0.9000 Gold .4918 oz. AGW **Reverse:** The golden warrior

| Date | Mintage | F | VF | XF | Unc |
|---|---|---|---|---|---|
| 1988 Proof | 5,500 | Value: 450 | | | |

**100 POUNDS** KM# 656 **Weight:** 17.1500 g. **Composition:** 0.9000 Gold .4963 oz. AGW **Reverse:** The golden cat

**100 POUNDS** KM# 681 **Weight:** 17.0000 g. **Composition:** 0.9000 Gold .4918 oz. AGW **Series:** World Soccer Championship - Italy **Reverse:** Ancient gods

**100 POUNDS** KM# 684 **Weight:** 17.0000 g. **Composition:** 0.9000 Gold .4918 oz. AGW **Series:** World Soccer Championship - Italy **Reverse:** Player chasing ball

| Date | Mintage | F | VF | XF | Unc |
|---|---|---|---|---|---|
| AH1410-1990 Proof | 75 | Value: 800 | | | |

**100 POUNDS** KM# 693 **Weight:** 17.0000 g. **Composition:** 0.9000 Gold .4918 oz. AGW **Series:** Ancient Egyptian Culture **Reverse:** Sphinx

| Date | Mintage | F | VF | XF | Unc |
|---|---|---|---|---|---|
| 1990 FM Proof | Est. 5,000 | Value: 500 | | | |

**100 POUNDS** KM# 729 **Weight:** 17.0000 g. **Composition:** 0.9000 Gold .4918 oz. AGW **Series:** Ancient Egyptian Culture **Reverse:** Pyramids of Giza

| Date | Mintage | F | VF | XF | Unc |
|---|---|---|---|---|---|
| 1991 Proof | Est. 5,000 | Value: 500 | | | |

**100 POUNDS** KM# 717 **Weight:** 17.0000 g. **Composition:** 0.9000 Gold .4918 oz. AGW **Series:** Summer Olympics **Reverse:** Fencing

| Date | Mintage | F | VF | XF | Unc |
|---|---|---|---|---|---|
| AH1412-1992 | 49 | — | — | — | 800 |
| AH1412-1992 Proof | 99 | Value: 800 | | | |

**100 POUNDS** KM# 718 **Weight:** 17.0000 g. **Composition:** 0.9000 Gold .4918 oz. AGW **Series:** Summer Olympics **Reverse:** Two men wrestling

| Date | Mintage | F | VF | XF | Unc |
|---|---|---|---|---|---|
| AH1412-1992 | 49 | — | — | — | 800 |
| AH1412-1992 Proof | 99 | Value: 800 | | | |

**100 POUNDS** KM# 720 **Weight:** 17.0000 g. **Composition:** 0.9000 Gold .4918 oz. AGW **Series:** Summer Olympics **Reverse:** Many men wrestling an ox

| Date | Mintage | F | VF | XF | Unc |
|---|---|---|---|---|---|
| AH1412-1992 | 49 | — | — | — | 800 |
| AH1412-1992(1992) Proof | 99 | Value: 800 | | | |

**100 POUNDS** KM# 721 **Weight:** 17.0000 g. **Composition:** 0.9000 Gold .4918 oz. AGW **Series:** Summer Olympics **Reverse:** Swimmer stalking a duck

| Date | Mintage | F | VF | XF | Unc |
|---|---|---|---|---|---|
| AH1412-1992 | 49 | — | — | — | 800 |
| AH1412-1992(1992) Proof | 99 | Value: 800 | | | |

**100 POUNDS** KM# 723 **Weight:** 17.0000 g. **Composition:** 0.9000 Gold .4918 oz. AGW **Series:** Summer Olympics **Reverse:** Field hockey player

| Date | Mintage | F | VF | XF | Unc |
|---|---|---|---|---|---|
| AH1412-1992 | 49 | — | — | — | 800 |
| AH1412-1992 Proof | 99 | Value: 800 | | | |

**100 POUNDS** KM# 724 **Weight:** 17.0000 g. **Composition:** 0.9000 Gold .4918 oz. AGW **Series:** Summer Olympics **Reverse:** Soccer player

| Date | Mintage | F | VF | XF | Unc |
|---|---|---|---|---|---|
| AH1412-1992 | 49 | — | — | — | 800 |
| AH1412-1992 Proof | 115 | Value: 800 | | | |

**100 POUNDS** KM# 730 **Weight:** 17.1500 g. **Composition:** 0.9000 Gold .4963 oz. AGW **Subject:** The Golden Guardians

| Date | Mintage | F | VF | XF | Unc |
|---|---|---|---|---|---|
| 1992 Proof | Est. 5,000 | Value: 500 | | | |

**100 POUNDS** KM# 719 **Weight:** 17.0000 g. **Composition:** 0.9000 Gold .4918 oz. AGW **Series:** Summer Olympics **Reverse:** Archery demonstration

| Date | Mintage | F | VF | XF | Unc |
|---|---|---|---|---|---|
| AH1412-1992 | 49 | — | — | — | 800 |
| AH1412-1992 Proof | 99 | Value: 800 | | | |

**100 POUNDS** **KM# 720** **Weight:** 17.0000 g. **Composition:** 0.9000 Gold .4918 oz. AGW **Series:** Summer Olympics **Reverse:** Many men wrestling an ox

| Date | Mintage | F | VF | XF | Unc |
|---|---|---|---|---|---|
| AH1412-1992 | 49 | — | — | — | 800 |
| AH1412-1992(1992) Proof | 99 | Value: 800 | | | |

**100 POUNDS** **KM# 721** **Weight:** 17.0000 g. **Composition:** 0.9000 Gold .4918 oz. AGW **Series:** Summer Olympics **Reverse:** Swimmer stalking a duck

| Date | Mintage | F | VF | XF | Unc |
|---|---|---|---|---|---|
| AH1412-1992 | 49 | — | — | — | 800 |
| AH1412-1992(1992) Proof | 99 | Value: 800 | | | |

**100 POUNDS** **KM# 722** **Weight:** 17.0000 g. **Composition:** 0.9000 Gold .4918 oz. AGW **Series:** Summer Olympics **Reverse:** Handball player

| Date | Mintage | F | VF | XF | Unc |
|---|---|---|---|---|---|
| AH1412-1992(1992) | 49 | — | — | — | 800 |
| AH1412-1992(1992) Proof | 99 | Value: 800 | | | |

## PATTERNS

Including off metal strikes

| KM# | Date | Mintage | Identification | Mkt Val |
|---|---|---|---|---|
| Pn26 | 1917 | — | 1/2 Millieme. Copper-Nickel. | 125 |
| Pn27 | 1361-1942 | — | 2 Piastres. Platinum. KM#365 | — |
| Pn28 | 1960 | — | 25 Piastres. Silver. KM#400 but with hand pointing to right | — |
| Pn29 | 1962 | — | 5 Piastres. Bronze. ESSAY | — |
| Pn30 | 1382-1962 | — | 5 Piastres. Brass Or Aluminum-Bronze. 7.3400 g. | 1,600 |
| Pn31 | 1964 | — | 10 Piastres. Copper-Nickel. | — |

## PIEFORTS

| KM# | Date | Mintage | Identification | Mkt Val |
|---|---|---|---|---|
| P1 | 1981 | 152 | 5 Pounds. 0.9000 Gold. KM533 | 165 |

## PROOF SETS

| KM# | Date | Mintage | Identification | Issue Price | Mkt Val |
|---|---|---|---|---|---|
| PS1 | 1938 (4) | — | KM#370, 371, 372, 373 | 4,200 | 4,500 |
| PS3 | 1966 (7) | 2,500 | KM#393, 394, 395, 397, 398, 399, 403 | 9.00 | 75.00 |
| PS2 | 1964 (4) | 2,000 | KM#404, 405, 406, 407 | 18.00 | 90.00 |
| PS4 | 1980 (4) | — | KM#508, 509, 517, 519 | — | 1,875 |
| PS5 | 1980 (3) | — | KM#509, 517, 519 | — | 1,850 |

## SPECIMEN SETS (SS)

| KM# | Date | Mintage | Identification | Issue Price | Mkt Val |
|---|---|---|---|---|---|
| SS1 | 1916/7 (10) | — | KM#312-316, 317.1, 318.1, 319, 321, 324 | — | 1,700 |

# EL SALVADOR

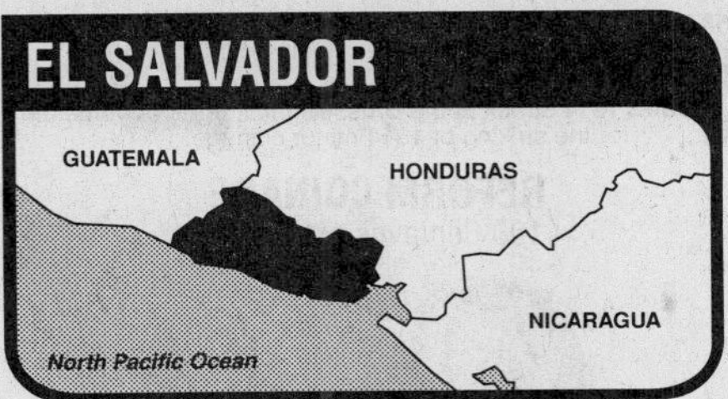


The Republic of El Salvador, a Central American country bordered by Guatemala, Honduras and the Pacific Ocean, has an area of 8,124 sq. mi. (21,040 sq. km.) and a population of 6.0 million. Capital: San Salvador. This most intensely cultivated of Latin America countries produces coffee (the major crop), sugar and balsam for export. Gold, silver and other metals are largely unexploited.

The first Spanish attempt to subjugate the area was undertaken in 1523 by Pedro de Alvarado, Cortes' lieutenant. He was forced to retreat by Indian forces, but returned in 1525 and succeeded in bringing the region under control of the Captaincy General of Guatemala. In 1821, El Salvador and the other Central American provinces jointly declared independence from Spain. In 1823, the Republic of Central America was formed by the five Central American states; this federation dissolved in 1839. El Salvador then became an independent republic in 1841.

Since 1960, El Salvador has been a part of the Central American Common Market. During the 1980's El Salvador went through a 12 year Civil War that ended in 1992 with the signing of a United Nations-sponsored Peace Accord. Free elections, with full participation of all political parties, were held in 1994, 1997 and 1999. Armando Calderon-Sol was elected president in 1994 for a 5-year term and Francisco Flores was elected in 1999 for a 5-year term as well.

**MINT MARKS**

C.A.M. - Central American Mint, San Salvador
H - Heaton Mint, Birmingham
S - San Francisco
Mo - Mexico
(a) - British Royal Mint, England
(b) - Denver Mint, USA
(c) - Deutsche Nickel A.G., Germany
(d) - Guatemala City Mint, Guatemala
(e) - Mexico City Mint, Mexico
(f) - San Francisco Mint, USA
(g) - Sherrit Mint, Canada
(h) - Vereingte Deutsche Metall, Germany
(i) - Royal Canadian Mint, Canada

# REPUBLIC OF EL SALVADOR

## DECIMAL COINAGE

100 Centavos = 1 Peso

**1/4 REAL** **KM# 120** **Composition:** Bronze **Note:** The decimal value of this coin was about 3 Centavos. It was apparently struck in response to the continuing use of the Reales monetary system in rural areas.

| Date | Mintage | F | VF | XF | Unc | BU |
|---|---|---|---|---|---|---|
| 1909 | — | 20.00 | 30.00 | 45.00 | 60.00 | — |

**CENTAVO** **KM# 106** **Composition:** Copper-Nickel **Obverse:** Francisco Morazan

| Date | Mintage | F | VF | XF | Unc | BU |
|---|---|---|---|---|---|---|
| 1889H | 1,500,000 | 1.00 | 2.50 | 4.50 | 13.50 | — |
| 1913H | 2,500,000 | 1.50 | 3.50 | 6.00 | 35.00 | — |

**CENTAVO** **KM# 127** **Composition:** Copper **Obverse:** Francisco Morazan **Reverse:** Denomination

| Date | Mintage | F | VF | XF | Unc | BU |
|---|---|---|---|---|---|---|
| 1915 | 5,000,000 | 0.75 | 2.50 | 7.00 | 20.00 | — |
| 1919 | 1,000,000 | 1.50 | 4.00 | 10.00 | 40.00 | — |
| 1920 | 1,490,000 | 1.00 | 3.00 | 8.00 | 25.00 | — |

| Date | Mintage | F | VF | XF | Unc | BU |
|---|---|---|---|---|---|---|
| 1925 | 200,000 | 4.00 | 8.00 | 15.00 | 50.00 | — |
| 1926 | 400,000 | 3.00 | 6.00 | 12.00 | 45.00 | — |
| 1928S | 5,000,000 | 0.75 | 2.00 | 6.00 | 35.00 | — |
| 1936 | 2,500,000 | 0.75 | 2.00 | 6.00 | 22.50 | — |

**3 CENTAVOS** **KM# 107** **Composition:** Copper-Nickel **Obverse:** Francisco Morazan

| Date | Mintage | F | VF | XF | Unc | BU |
|---|---|---|---|---|---|---|
| 1913H | 1,000,000 | 2.00 | 6.00 | 14.00 | 50.00 | — |

**3 CENTAVOS** **KM# 128** **Composition:** Copper Nickel **Obverse:** Francisco Morazan **Reverse:** Denomination

| Date | Mintage | F | VF | XF | Unc | BU |
|---|---|---|---|---|---|---|
| 1915 | 2,700,000 | 2.00 | 5.00 | 15.00 | 50.00 | — |

**5 CENTAVOS** **KM# 121** **Weight:** 1.2500 g. **Composition:** 0.8350 Silver .0336 oz. ASW

| Date | Mintage | F | VF | XF | Unc | BU |
|---|---|---|---|---|---|---|
| 1911 | 1,000,000 | 2.00 | 4.00 | 8.00 | 30.00 | — |

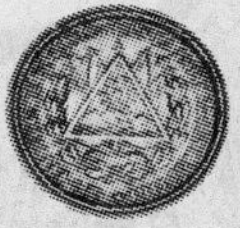

**5 CENTAVOS** **KM# 124** **Weight:** 1.2500 g. **Composition:** 0.8350 Silver .0336 oz. ASW

| Date | Mintage | F | VF | XF | Unc | BU |
|---|---|---|---|---|---|---|
| 1914 | 2,000,000 | 1.50 | 3.00 | 6.00 | 22.50 | — |
| 1914 Proof | 20 | Value: 200 | | | | |

**5 CENTAVOS** **KM# 129** **Composition:** Copper-Nickel **Obverse:** Francisco Morazan **Reverse:** Denomination

| Date | Mintage | F | VF | XF | Unc | BU |
|---|---|---|---|---|---|---|
| 1915 | 2,500,000 | 0.75 | 2.00 | 6.00 | 35.00 | — |
| 1916 | 1,500,000 | 1.25 | 3.50 | 8.00 | 35.00 | — |
| 1917 | 1,000,000 | 1.50 | 4.00 | 10.00 | 45.00 | — |
| 1918/7 | 1,000,000 | 1.25 | 3.50 | 8.00 | 30.00 | — |
| 1918 | Inc. above | 1.25 | 3.50 | 8.00 | 40.00 | — |
| 1919 | 2,000,000 | 1.00 | 3.00 | 8.00 | 25.00 | — |
| 1920 | 2,000,000 | 0.75 | 2.00 | 6.00 | 20.00 | — |
| 1921 | 1,780,000 | 1.00 | 2.50 | 7.00 | 30.00 | — |
| 1925 | 4,000,000 | 0.50 | 1.50 | 5.00 | 17.50 | — |

**10 CENTAVOS** **KM# 122** **Composition:** Silver **Obverse:** Arms **Reverse:** Denomination

| Date | Mintage | F | VF | XF | Unc | BU |
|---|---|---|---|---|---|---|
| 1911 | 1,000,000 | 2.25 | 4.00 | 8.00 | 45.00 | — |

**10 CENTAVOS** KM# 125 **Composition:** Silver **Obverse:** Triangular arms **Reverse:** Denomination

| Date | Mintage | F | VF | XF | Unc | BU |
|---|---|---|---|---|---|---|
| 1914 | 1,500,000 | 2.00 | 3.50 | 6.00 | 30.00 | — |
| 1914 Proof | 20 | Value: 250 | | | | |

**25 CENTAVOS** KM# 123 **Weight:** 6.2500 g. **Composition:** 0.8350 Silver .1678 oz. ASW **Obverse:** Arms **Reverse:** Denomination

| Date | Mintage | F | VF | XF | Unc | BU |
|---|---|---|---|---|---|---|
| 1911 | 600,000 | 4.75 | 6.00 | 8.50 | 35.00 | — |

**25 CENTAVOS** KM# 126 **Weight:** 6.2500 g. **Composition:** 0.8350 Silver .1678 oz. ASW **Obverse:** Triangular arms **Reverse:** Denomination

| Date | Mintage | F | VF | XF | Unc | BU |
|---|---|---|---|---|---|---|
| 1914 15 DE SEPT DE 1821 | 1,400,000 | 5.50 | 6.50 | 10.00 | 25.00 | — |
| 1914 15 SET DE 1821 | Inc. above | 5.50 | 6.50 | 10.00 | 25.00 | — |
| 1914 Proof | 20 | Value: 500 | | | | |

**PESO (Colon)** KM# 115.2 **Weight:** 25.0000 g. **Composition:** 0.9000 Silver .7234 oz. ASW **Reverse:** Heavier portrait (wider right shoulder) **Note:** Struck at United States mints.

| Date | Mintage | F | VF | XF | Unc | BU |
|---|---|---|---|---|---|---|
| 1904C.A.M. | 400,000 | 8.00 | 15.00 | 35.00 | 125 | — |
| 1909C.A.M. | 690,000 | 6.50 | 12.00 | 20.00 | 100 | — |
| 1911C.A.M. | 1,020,000 | 6.50 | 12.00 | 20.00 | 100 | — |
| 1914C.A.M. | 2,100,000 | 6.50 | 12.00 | 20.00 | 100 | — |
| 1914C.A.M. Est. 20; Proof | — | Value: 1,800 | | | | |

**PESO (Colon)** KM# 115.1 **Weight:** 25.0000 g. **Composition:** 0.9000 Silver .7234 oz. ASW **Obverse:** Arms **Reverse:** Columbus **Note:** Struck in San Salvador and European mints.

| Date | Mintage | F | VF | XF | Unc | BU |
|---|---|---|---|---|---|---|
| 1904C.A.M. | 600,000 | 6.50 | 12.00 | 20.00 | 125 | — |
| 1908C.A.M. | 1,600,000 | 6.50 | 10.00 | 18.00 | 100 | — |
| 1911C.A.M. | 500,000 | 6.50 | 12.00 | 20.00 | 100 | — |
| 1914C.A.M. | 700,000 | — | — | — | 575 | — |

**Note:** 1914 struck at the Brussels mint, but then remelted for the striking of 1914 minor coinage.

## REFORM COINAGE

100 Centavos = 1 Colon

**CENTAVO** KM# 133 **Composition:** Copper-Nickel **Obverse:** Francisco Morazan **Reverse:** Denomination

| Date | Mintage | F | VF | XF | Unc | BU |
|---|---|---|---|---|---|---|
| 1940 | 1,000,000 | 1.25 | 3.50 | 7.00 | 30.00 | — |

**CENTAVO** KM# 135.1 (135) **Composition:** Bronze **Obverse:** Francisco Morazan **Reverse:** Denomination

| Date | Mintage | F | VF | XF | Unc | BU |
|---|---|---|---|---|---|---|
| 1942 | 5,000,000 | 0.20 | 0.50 | 1.00 | 4.00 | — |
| 1943 | 5,000,000 | 0.20 | 0.50 | 1.00 | 4.00 | — |
| 1945 | 5,000,000 | 0.20 | 0.40 | 0.75 | 2.50 | — |
| 1947 | 5,000,000 | 0.20 | 0.50 | 1.00 | 3.00 | — |
| 1951 | 10,000,000 | 0.10 | 0.30 | 0.75 | 2.00 | — |
| 1952 | 10,000,000 | 0.10 | 0.20 | 0.40 | 1.25 | — |
| 1956 | 10,000,000 | 0.10 | 0.20 | 0.40 | 1.00 | — |
| 1966 | 5,000,000 | — | — | 0.10 | 0.50 | — |
| 1968 (f) | 5,000,000 | — | — | 0.10 | 0.50 | — |
| 1969 (b) | 5,000,000 | — | — | 0.10 | 0.50 | — |
| 1972 (f) | 20,000,000 | — | — | 0.10 | 0.30 | — |

**CENTAVO** KM# 135.2 **Composition:** Brass **Obverse:** Jose Francisco Morazan **Reverse:** Denomination **Note:** Previously KM#135a.

| Date | Mintage | F | VF | XF | Unc | BU |
|---|---|---|---|---|---|---|
| 1976(g) | 20,000,000 | — | — | 0.10 | 0.20 | — |
| 1977(g) | 40,000,000 | — | — | 0.10 | 0.20 | — |

**CENTAVO** KM# 135.2a **Composition:** Copper-Zinc **Obverse:** DH monogram at truncation, smaller Morazan portrait **Reverse:** Denomination in wreath, SM at right base of 1 **Note:** Previously KM#135c.

| Date | Mintage | F | VF | XF | Unc | BU |
|---|---|---|---|---|---|---|
| 1981(d) | 50,000,000 | — | — | 0.10 | 0.20 | — |

**CENTAVO** KM# 135.2b **Composition:** Copper Clad Steel **Obverse:** DH monogram at truncation, smaller Morazan portrait **Reverse:** Denomination in wreath, SM at right base of 1 **Note:** Previously KM#135b.

| Date | Mintage | F | VF | XF | Unc | BU |
|---|---|---|---|---|---|---|
| 1986 (a) | 30,000,000 | — | — | 0.10 | 0.20 | — |

**CENTAVO** KM# 135.1a **Composition:** Bronze Clad Steel **Obverse:** Jose Francisco Morazan **Reverse:** Denomination **Note:** Previously KM#135d.

| Date | Mintage | F | VF | XF | Unc | BU |
|---|---|---|---|---|---|---|
| 1989(h) | 36,000,000 | — | — | 0.10 | 0.20 | — |
| 1992(h) | — | — | — | 0.10 | 0.20 | — |

**CENTAVO** KM# 135.2c **Composition:** Brass Clad Steel **Obverse:** DH monogram at truncation, smaller portrait **Reverse:** Denomination in wreath, SM at right base of 1

| Date | Mintage | F | VF | XF | Unc | BU |
|---|---|---|---|---|---|---|
| 1995(a) | — | — | — | 0.10 | 0.20 | — |

**2 CENTAVOS** KM# 147 **Composition:** Nickel-Brass **Obverse:** Francisco Morazan **Reverse:** Denomination

| Date | Mintage | F | VF | XF | Unc | BU |
|---|---|---|---|---|---|---|
| 1974(a) | 10,002,000 | — | 0.10 | 0.15 | 0.20 | — |
| 1974(a) In proof sets only | 2,000 | Value: 30.00 | | | | |

**3 CENTAVOS** KM# 148 **Composition:** Nickel-Brass **Obverse:** Francisco Morazan **Reverse:** Denomination

| Date | Mintage | F | VF | XF | Unc | BU |
|---|---|---|---|---|---|---|
| 1974(a) | 10,002,000 | 0.10 | 0.15 | 0.20 | 0.40 | — |
| 1974(a) In proof sets only | 2,000 | Value: 35.00 | | | | |

**5 CENTAVOS** KM# 134 **Composition:** Copper-Nickel **Obverse:** Francisco Morazan **Reverse:** Denomination

| Date | Mintage | F | VF | XF | Unc | BU |
|---|---|---|---|---|---|---|
| 1940 | 800,000 | 0.50 | 1.00 | 3.50 | 20.00 | — |
| 1951 | 2,000,000 | 0.25 | 0.50 | 1.25 | 7.00 | — |
| 1956 | 8,000,000 | 0.10 | 0.15 | 0.25 | 0.75 | — |
| 1959 | 6,000,000 | 0.10 | 0.15 | 0.25 | 0.75 | — |
| 1963 | 10,000,000 | — | 0.10 | 0.15 | 0.30 | — |
| 1966 | 6,000,000 | 0.10 | 0.15 | 0.25 | 0.50 | — |
| 1967 (f) | 10,000,000 | — | 0.10 | 0.15 | 0.30 | — |
| 1972 (f) | 10,000,000 | — | 0.10 | 0.15 | 0.30 | — |
| 1974 (g) | 10,002,000 | — | 0.10 | 0.15 | 0.30 | — |
| 1974 (g) In proof sets only | 2,000 | Value: 35.00 | | | | |

**5 CENTAVOS** KM# 134a **Composition:** Copper-Nickel-Zinc **Obverse:** Jose Francisco Morazan **Reverse:** Denomination

| Date | Mintage | F | VF | XF | Unc | BU |
|---|---|---|---|---|---|---|
| 1944 | 5,000,000 | 0.25 | 0.50 | 1.50 | 5.00 | — |
| 1948 | 3,000,000 | 0.25 | 0.50 | 1.00 | 2.50 | — |
| 1950 | 2,000,000 | 0.25 | 0.50 | 1.50 | 5.00 | — |
| 1952 | 4,000,000 | 0.20 | 0.35 | 0.75 | 4.00 | — |

**5 CENTAVOS** KM# 149 (149.1) **Composition:** Copper-Nickel Clad Steel **Obverse:** Francisco Morazan **Reverse:** Denomination

| Date | Mintage | F | VF | XF | Unc | BU |
|---|---|---|---|---|---|---|
| 1975 (a) | 15,000,000 | — | 0.10 | 0.15 | 0.30 | — |
| 1975 In proof sets only | 2,000 | Value: 35.00 | | | | |
| 1986 (h) | 30,000,000 | — | 0.10 | 0.15 | 0.30 | — |
| 1986 | — | — | 0.10 | 0.15 | 0.30 | — |

**5 CENTAVOS** KM# 149.a (149.2) **Composition:** Nickel Clad Steel **Obverse:** Jose Francisco Morazan **Reverse:** Denomination

| Date | Mintage | F | VF | XF | Unc | BU |
|---|---|---|---|---|---|---|
| 1976 (g) | 15,000,000 | — | 0.10 | 0.15 | 0.30 | — |
| 1984 (a) | 15,000,000 | — | 0.10 | 0.15 | 0.30 | — |

**5 CENTAVOS** KM# 149b **Composition:** Copper-Nickel-Zinc **Obverse:** Jose Francisco Morazan **Reverse:** Denomination **Note:** Previously KM#149a.

| Date | Mintage | F | VF | XF | Unc | BU |
|---|---|---|---|---|---|---|
| 1977(h) | 26,000,000 | — | 0.10 | 0.15 | 0.30 | — |

**5 CENTAVOS** KM# 154 **Composition:** Stainless Steel **Obverse:** Jose Francisco Morazan

| Date | Mintage | F | VF | XF | Unc | BU |
|---|---|---|---|---|---|---|
| 1987(h) | 30,000,000 | — | 0.10 | 0.15 | 0.30 | — |
| 1999(h) | — | — | 0.10 | 0.15 | 0.30 | — |

**5 CENTAVOS** KM# 154a **Composition:** Copper-Nickel Clad Steel **Obverse:** Jose Francisco Morazan

| Date | Mintage | F | VF | XF | Unc | BU |
|---|---|---|---|---|---|---|
| 1991 (h) | — | — | 0.10 | 0.15 | 0.30 | — |
| 1998 (c) | — | — | 0.10 | 0.15 | 0.30 | — |

**5 CENTAVOS** KM# 154b **Composition:** Nickel Clad Steel **Obverse:** Jose Francisco Morazan

| Date | Mintage | F | VF | XF | Unc | BU |
|---|---|---|---|---|---|---|
| 1992 (g) | — | — | 0.10 | 0.15 | 0.30 | — |
| 1993 (g) | — | — | 0.10 | 0.15 | 0.30 | — |
| 1994 (h) | — | — | 0.10 | 0.15 | 0.30 | — |
| 1995 (g) | — | — | 0.10 | 0.15 | 0.30 | — |
| 1998 | — | — | 0.10 | 0.15 | 0.30 | — |
| 1999 | — | — | 0.10 | 0.15 | 0.30 | — |

**10 CENTAVOS** **KM# 130** **Composition:** Copper-Nickel **Obverse:** Francisco Morazan **Reverse:** Denomination

| Date | Mintage | F | VF | XF | Unc | BU |
|---|---|---|---|---|---|---|
| 1921 | 2,000,000 | 1.50 | 5.00 | 12.00 | 30.00 | — |
| 1925 | 2,000,000 | 2.00 | 6.00 | 14.00 | 35.00 | — |
| 1940 | 500,000 | 3.50 | 9.00 | 20.00 | 55.00 | — |
| 1951 | 1,000,000 | 0.50 | 1.50 | 3.00 | 8.00 | — |
| 1967 (f) | 2,000,000 | — | 0.10 | 0.50 | 2.00 | — |
| 1968 (b) | 3,000,000 | — | 0.10 | 0.40 | 1.00 | — |
| 1969 (b) | 3,000,000 | — | 0.10 | 0.40 | 1.00 | — |
| 1972 (f) | 7,000,000 | — | 0.10 | 0.25 | 0.75 | — |

**10 CENTAVOS** **KM# 130a** **Composition:** Copper-Nickel-Zinc

| Date | Mintage | F | VF | XF | Unc | BU |
|---|---|---|---|---|---|---|
| 1952 | 2,000,000 | 0.15 | 0.25 | 0.75 | 4.00 | — |
| 1985 Mo | 15,000,000 | — | 0.10 | 0.15 | 0.30 | — |

**10 CENTAVOS** **KM# 150** **Composition:** Copper-Nickel Clad Steel **Obverse:** Francisco Morazan **Reverse:** Denomination

| Date | Mintage | F | VF | XF | Unc | BU |
|---|---|---|---|---|---|---|
| 1975(a) | 15,000,000 | — | 0.15 | 0.25 | 0.50 | — |
| 1975(a) Proof sets only | 2,000 | Value: 35.00 | | | | |

**10 CENTAVOS** **KM# 150a** **Composition:** Copper-Nickel-Zinc **Obverse:** Jose Francisco Morazan **Reverse:** Denomination

| Date | Mintage | F | VF | XF | Unc | BU |
|---|---|---|---|---|---|---|
| 1977(h) | 24,000,000 | — | 0.10 | 0.20 | 0.45 | — |

**10 CENTAVOS** **KM# 155** **Composition:** Stainless Steel **Obverse:** Jose Francisco Morazan

| Date | Mintage | F | VF | XF | Unc | BU |
|---|---|---|---|---|---|---|
| 1987 (h) | 30,000,000 | — | 0.10 | 0.20 | 0.40 | — |
| 1999 (i) | — | — | 0.10 | 0.20 | 0.40 | — |

**10 CENTAVOS** **KM# 155a** **Composition:** Nickel Clad Steel

| Date | Mintage | F | VF | XF | Unc | BU |
|---|---|---|---|---|---|---|
| 1992 (a) | — | — | 0.10 | 0.20 | 0.40 | — |
| 1993 (g) | — | — | 0.10 | 0.20 | 0.40 | — |
| 1994 (h) | — | — | 0.10 | 0.20 | 0.40 | — |
| 1994 Proof | — | — | — | — | — | — |

**10 CENTAVOS** **KM# 155b** **Composition:** Copper-Nickel Clad Steel

| Date | Mintage | F | VF | XF | Unc | BU |
|---|---|---|---|---|---|---|
| 1995 (c) | — | — | 0.10 | 0.20 | 0.40 | — |
| 1998 (c) | — | — | 0.10 | 0.20 | 0.40 | — |
| 1999 | — | — | 0.10 | 0.20 | 0.40 | — |

**25 CENTAVOS** **KM# 136** **Weight:** 7.5000 g. **Composition:** 0.9000 Silver .217 oz. ASW **Obverse:** Francisco Morazan **Reverse:** Denomination

| Date | Mintage | F | VF | XF | Unc | BU |
|---|---|---|---|---|---|---|
| 1943 | 1,000,000 | 1.50 | 2.50 | 5.00 | 9.00 | — |
| 1944 | 1,000,000 | 1.50 | 2.50 | 5.00 | 9.00 | — |

**25 CENTAVOS** **KM# 137** **Weight:** 2.5000 g. **Composition:** 0.9000 Silver .0723 oz. ASW **Obverse:** Jose Francisco Morazan **Reverse:** Denomination

| Date | Mintage | F | VF | XF | Unc | BU |
|---|---|---|---|---|---|---|
| 1953 | 14,000,000 | 0.50 | 1.00 | 1.50 | 3.00 | — |

**25 CENTAVOS** **KM# 139** **Composition:** Nickel **Obverse:** Jose Francisco Morazan **Reverse:** Denomination

| Date | Mintage | F | VF | XF | Unc | BU |
|---|---|---|---|---|---|---|
| 1970 (a) | 14,000,000 | — | 0.10 | 0.20 | 0.60 | — |
| 1973 (g) | 28,000,000 | — | 0.10 | 0.20 | 0.50 | — |
| 1975 (g) | 20,000,000 | — | 0.10 | 0.20 | 0.50 | — |
| 1977 (a) | 22,400,000 | — | 0.10 | 0.20 | 0.50 | — |

**25 CENTAVOS** **KM# 139a** **Composition:** Copper-Nickel **Obverse:** Jose Francisco Morazan **Reverse:** Denomination

| Date | Mintage | F | VF | XF | Unc | BU |
|---|---|---|---|---|---|---|
| 1986Mo | 21,000,000 | — | 0.10 | 0.20 | 0.50 | — |

**25 CENTAVOS** **KM# 157** **Composition:** Stainless Steel **Obverse:** Jose Francisco Morazan **Reverse:** Denomination

| Date | Mintage | F | VF | XF | Unc | BU |
|---|---|---|---|---|---|---|
| 1988 (h) | 20,000,000 | — | 0.10 | 0.20 | 0.50 | — |
| 1999 (i) | — | — | 0.10 | 0.20 | 0.50 | — |

**25 CENTAVOS** **KM# 157a** **Composition:** Copper-Nickel Clad Steel **Obverse:** Jose Francisco Morazan **Reverse:** Denomination

| Date | Mintage | F | VF | XF | Unc | BU |
|---|---|---|---|---|---|---|
| 1992(c) | — | — | 0.10 | 0.20 | 0.50 | — |
| 1995(c) | — | — | 0.10 | 0.20 | 0.50 | — |

**25 CENTAVOS** **KM# 157b** **Composition:** Nickel Clad Steel **Obverse:** Jose Francisco Morazan **Reverse:** Denomination

| Date | Mintage | F | VF | XF | Unc | BU |
|---|---|---|---|---|---|---|
| 1993 (a) | — | — | 0.10 | 0.20 | 0.50 | — |
| 1994 (g) | — | — | 0.10 | 0.20 | 0.50 | — |
| 1998 | — | — | 0.10 | 0.20 | 0.50 | — |
| 1999 | — | — | 0.10 | 0.20 | 0.50 | — |

**50 CENTAVOS** **KM# 138** **Weight:** 5.0000 g. **Composition:** 0.9000 Silver .1446 oz. ASW

| Date | Mintage | F | VF | XF | Unc | BU |
|---|---|---|---|---|---|---|
| 1953 | 3,000,000 | 1.00 | 2.00 | 3.00 | 5.00 | — |

**50 CENTAVOS** **KM# 140.1** **Composition:** Nickel **Note:** 1.65 millimeters thick.

| Date | Mintage | F | VF | XF | Unc | BU |
|---|---|---|---|---|---|---|
| 1970(a) | 3,000,000 | — | 0.20 | 0.30 | 0.60 | — |

**50 CENTAVOS** **KM# 140.2** **Composition:** Nickel **Note:** 2 millimeters thick.

| Date | Mintage | F | VF | XF | Unc | BU |
|---|---|---|---|---|---|---|
| 1977(a) | 1,500,000 | — | 0.20 | 0.30 | 0.60 | — |

**COLON** **KM# 131** **Weight:** 25.0000 g. **Composition:** 0.9000 Silver .7234 oz. ASW **Subject:** 400th Anniversary - San Salvador

| Date | Mintage | F | VF | XF | Unc | BU |
|---|---|---|---|---|---|---|
| ND(1925)Mo | 2,000 | 50.00 | 90.00 | 125 | 200 | — |

**COLON** **KM# 141** **Weight:** 2.3000 g. **Composition:** 0.9990 Silver .0738 oz. ASW **Subject:** 150th Anniversary of Independence

| Date | Mintage | F | VF | XF | Unc | BU |
|---|---|---|---|---|---|---|
| 1971 Proof | 21,000 | Value: 7.50 | | | | |

**COLON** **KM# 153** **Composition:** Copper-Nickel **Obverse:** Christopher Columbus

| Date | Mintage | F | VF | XF | Unc | BU |
|---|---|---|---|---|---|---|
| 1984Mo | 10,000,000 | — | 0.50 | 1.00 | 2.50 | — |
| 1984Mo Proof | — | Value: 125 | | | | |
| 1985Mo | 20,000,000 | — | 0.50 | 1.00 | 2.50 | — |
| 1985Mo Proof | — | Value: 200 | | | | |

**COLON** **KM# 156** **Composition:** Stainless Steel **Obverse:** Christopher Columbus

| Date | Mintage | F | VF | XF | Unc | BU |
|---|---|---|---|---|---|---|
| 1988 (h) | 30,000,000 | — | 0.40 | 0.80 | 2.25 | — |
| 1988 Proof | — | — | — | — | — | — |
| 1999 (i) | — | — | — | 0.80 | 2.25 | — |

**COLON** **KM# 156a** **Composition:** Copper-Nickel Clad Steel **Obverse:** Christopher Columbus

| Date | Mintage | F | VF | XF | Unc | BU |
|---|---|---|---|---|---|---|
| 1991(h) | — | — | 0.40 | 0.80 | 2.25 | — |

**COLON** **KM# 156b** **Composition:** Nickel Clad Steel **Obverse:** Christopher Columbus

| Date | Mintage | F | VF | XF | Unc | BU |
|---|---|---|---|---|---|---|
| 1993 (a) | — | — | 0.40 | 0.80 | 2.25 | — |
| 1994 (g) | — | — | 0.40 | 0.80 | 2.25 | — |
| 1995 (h) | — | — | 0.40 | 0.80 | 2.25 | — |
| 1998 | — | — | 0.40 | 0.80 | 2.25 | — |
| 1999 | — | — | 0.40 | 0.80 | 2.25 | — |

**5 COLONES** **KM# 142** **Weight:** 11.5000 g. **Composition:** 0.9990 Silver .3694 oz. ASW **Subject:** 150th Anniversary of Indepedence

| Date | Mintage | F | VF | XF | Unc | BU |
|---|---|---|---|---|---|---|
| 1971 Proof | 18,000 | Value: 12.50 | | | | |

**20 COLONES** **KM# 132** **Weight:** 15.5600 g. **Composition:** 0.9000 Gold .4502 oz. AGW **Subject:** 400th Anniversary - San Salvador

| Date | Mintage | F | VF | XF | Unc | BU |
|---|---|---|---|---|---|---|
| ND(1925)Mo | 100 | — | 800 | 1,600 | 2,500 | — |

**25 COLONES** **KM# 143** **Weight:** 2.9400 g. **Composition:** 0.9000 Gold .0850 oz. AGW **Subject:** 150th Anniversary of Independence

| Date | Mintage | F | VF | XF | Unc | BU |
|---|---|---|---|---|---|---|
| 1971 Proof | 7,650 | Value: 75.00 | | | | |

**25 COLONES** **KM# 151** **Weight:** 25.0000 g. **Composition:** 0.9000 Silver .7234 oz. ASW **Subject:** 18th Annual Governors' Assembly

| Date | Mintage | F | VF | XF | Unc | BU |
|---|---|---|---|---|---|---|
| 1977 | 2,000 | — | — | — | 27.50 | — |
| 1977 Proof | 20,000 | Value: 36.00 | | | | |

**50 COLONES** **KM# 144** **Weight:** 5.9000 g. **Composition:** 0.9000 Gold .1707 oz. AGW **Subject:** 150th Anniversary of Independence

| Date | Mintage | F | VF | XF | Unc | BU |
|---|---|---|---|---|---|---|
| 1971 Proof | 3,530 | Value: 100 | | | | |

**100 COLONES** **KM# 145** **Weight:** 11.8000 g. **Composition:** 0.9000 Gold .3414 oz. AGW **Subject:** 150th Anniversary of Independence

| Date | Mintage | F | VF | XF | Unc | BU |
|---|---|---|---|---|---|---|
| 1971 Proof | 2,750 | Value: 200 | | | | |

**150 COLONES** **KM# 158** **Weight:** 25.0000 g. **Composition:** 0.9000 Silver .7235 oz. ASW **Subject:** Union for Peace **Obverse:** Four clasped hands

| Date | Mintage | F | VF | XF | Unc | BU |
|---|---|---|---|---|---|---|
| 1992 | — | — | — | — | 42.50 | — |

**150 COLONES** **KM# 160** **Weight:** 25.0000 g. **Composition:** 0.9000 Silver .7235 oz. ASW **Subject:** Discovery of America **Obverse:** Columbus' ships and world map

| Date | Mintage | F | VF | XF | Unc | BU |
|---|---|---|---|---|---|---|
| 1992 | — | — | — | — | 47.50 | — |

**200 COLONES** **KM# 146** **Weight:** 23.6000 g. **Composition:** 0.9000 Gold .6829 oz. AGW **Subject:** 150th Anniversary of Independence

| Date | Mintage | F | VF | XF | Unc | BU |
|---|---|---|---|---|---|---|
| 1971 Proof | 2,245 | Value: 375 | | | | |

**250 COLONES** **KM# 152** **Weight:** 16.0000 g. **Composition:** 0.9170 Gold .4717 oz. AGW **Subject:** 18th Annual Governors' Assembly

| Date | Mintage | F | VF | XF | Unc | BU |
|---|---|---|---|---|---|---|
| 1977 | 4,000 | — | — | — | 225 | — |
| 1977 Proof | 400 | Value: 350 | | | | |

**2500 COLONES** **KM# 159** **Weight:** 16.0000 g. **Composition:** 0.9170 Gold .4715 oz. AGW **Subject:** Union for Peace **Obverse:** Four clasped hands

| Date | Mintage | F | VF | XF | Unc | BU |
|---|---|---|---|---|---|---|
| 1992 | — | — | — | — | 350 | — |

**2500 COLONES** **KM# 161** **Weight:** 16.0000 g. **Composition:** 0.9170 Gold .4715 oz. AGW **Subject:** Discovery of America **Obverse:** Columbus' ships and world map

| Date | Mintage | F | VF | XF | Unc | BU |
|---|---|---|---|---|---|---|
| 1992 | — | — | — | — | 350 | — |

## PROOF SETS

| KM# | Date | Mintage | Identification | Issue Price | Mkt Val |
|---|---|---|---|---|---|
| PS1 | 1889H (2) | — | KM#106-107 | — | 350 |
| PS2 | 1892 (10) | — | KM#108-112, 114, 116-119 | — | 16,000 |
| PS3 | 1914 (4) | — | KM#115.2, 124-126 | — | 4,000 |
| PS4 | 1971 (6) | — | KM#141-146 | — | 770 |
| PS5 | 1971 (4) | — | KM#143-146 | 250 | 750 |
| PS6 | 1971 (2) | — | KM#141-142 | 6.00 | 20.00 |
| PS7 | 1974 (3) | 2,000 | KM#134, 147-148 | — | 100 |
| PS8 | 1975 (2) | 2,000 | KM#149.1, 150 | — | 70.00 |

# EQUATORIAL AFRICAN STATES

**For historical background, see the introduction to Central African States.**

## CURRENCY UNION

### DECIMAL COINAGE

100 Centimes = 1 Franc

**FRANC KM# 6 Composition:** Aluminum **Obverse:** Three giant eland **Reverse:** Denomination

| Date | Mintage | F | VF | XF | Unc | BU |
|---|---|---|---|---|---|---|
| 1969(a) | 2,500,000 | 0.25 | 0.65 | 1.00 | 2.25 | — |
| 1971(a) | 3,000,000 | 0.25 | 0.65 | 1.00 | 2.25 | — |

**5 FRANCS KM# 24 Composition:** Aluminum-Bronze **Obverse:** Three giant eland **Reverse:** Denomination

| Date | Mintage | F | VF | XF | Unc | BU |
|---|---|---|---|---|---|---|
| 1958(a) | 30,000,000 | 0.25 | 0.50 | 1.00 | 3.00 | — |

**5 FRANCS KM# 1 Composition:** Aluminum-Bronze **Obverse:** Three giant eland **Reverse:** Denomination

| Date | Mintage | F | VF | XF | Unc | BU |
|---|---|---|---|---|---|---|
| 1961(a) | 10,000,000 | 0.35 | 1.00 | 1.50 | 2.50 | — |
| 1962(a) | 5,000,000 | 0.35 | 1.00 | 1.50 | 2.50 | — |

**5 FRANCS KM# 1a Composition:** Aluminum-Nickel-Bronze **Obverse:** Three giant eland **Reverse:** Denomination

| Date | Mintage | F | VF | XF | Unc | BU |
|---|---|---|---|---|---|---|
| 1965(a) | 2,010,000 | 0.35 | 1.00 | 1.50 | 3.00 | — |
| 1967(a) | 5,795,000 | 0.35 | 1.00 | 1.25 | 2.50 | — |
| 1968(a) | 5,000,000 | 0.35 | 1.00 | 1.25 | 2.50 | — |
| 1969(a) | — | 0.35 | 1.00 | 1.25 | 2.50 | — |
| 1970(a) | 9,000,000 | 0.35 | 1.00 | 1.25 | 2.50 | — |
| 1972(a) | 31,010,000 | 0.35 | 1.00 | 1.25 | 2.50 | — |
| 1973(a) | 5,010,000 | 0.35 | 1.00 | 1.25 | 2.50 | — |

**10 FRANCS KM# 25 Composition:** Aluminum-Bronze **Obverse:** Three giant eland **Reverse:** Denomination

| Date | Mintage | F | VF | XF | Unc | BU |
|---|---|---|---|---|---|---|
| 1958(a) | 25,000,000 | 0.25 | 0.50 | 1.50 | 4.00 | — |

**10 FRANCS KM# 2 Composition:** Aluminum-Bronze **Obverse:** Three giant eland **Reverse:** Denomination

| Date | Mintage | F | VF | XF | Unc | BU |
|---|---|---|---|---|---|---|
| 1961(a) | 10,000,000 | 0.40 | 1.00 | 1.75 | 3.00 | — |
| 1962(a) | 5,000,000 | 0.40 | 1.00 | 1.75 | 3.00 | — |

**10 FRANCS KM# 2a Composition:** Aluminum-Nickel-Bronze **Obverse:** Three giant eland **Reverse:** Denomination

| Date | Mintage | F | VF | XF | Unc | BU |
|---|---|---|---|---|---|---|
| 1965(a) | 7,000,000 | 1.00 | 1.75 | 2.75 | 5.00 | — |
| 1967(a) | 8,000,000 | 0.40 | 1.00 | 1.75 | 3.00 | — |
| 1968(a) | 2,000,000 | 1.50 | 2.25 | 3.50 | 6.00 | — |
| 1969(a) | 10,000,000 | 0.40 | 1.00 | 1.75 | 3.00 | — |
| 1972(a) | 23,500,000 | 0.40 | 1.00 | 1.75 | 3.00 | — |
| 1973(a) | 5,000,000 | 0.75 | 1.50 | 2.50 | 4.50 | — |

**25 FRANCS KM# 26 Composition:** Aluminum-Bronze **Obverse:** Three giant eland **Reverse:** Denomination

| Date | Mintage | F | VF | XF | Unc | BU |
|---|---|---|---|---|---|---|
| 1958(a) | 12,000,000 | 0.50 | 1.00 | 2.00 | 6.00 | — |

**25 FRANCS KM# 4 Composition:** Aluminum-Bronze **Obverse:** Three giant eland **Reverse:** Denomination

| Date | Mintage | F | VF | XF | Unc | BU |
|---|---|---|---|---|---|---|
| 1962(a) | 6,000,000 | 0.50 | 1.25 | 2.25 | 4.00 | — |

**25 FRANCS KM# 4a Composition:** Aluminum-Nickel-Bronze **Obverse:** Three giant eland **Reverse:** Denomination

| Date | Mintage | F | VF | XF | Unc | BU |
|---|---|---|---|---|---|---|
| 1968(a) | — | 1.25 | 2.50 | 4.00 | 7.50 | — |
| 1969(a) | — | 1.25 | 2.50 | 4.00 | 7.50 | — |
| 1970(a) | 3,019,000 | 0.50 | 1.25 | 2.25 | 4.00 | — |
| 1972(a) | 18,516,000 | 0.50 | 1.25 | 2.00 | 3.00 | — |
| 1973(a) | — | 1.25 | 2.50 | 4.00 | 7.50 | — |

**50 FRANCS KM# 3 Composition:** Copper-Nickel **Obverse:** Three giant eland **Reverse:** Denomination

| Date | Mintage | F | VF | XF | Unc | BU |
|---|---|---|---|---|---|---|
| 1961(a) | 5,000,000 | 2.00 | 4.00 | 6.00 | 10.00 | — |
| 1963(a) | 5,000,000 | 2.00 | 4.00 | 6.00 | 10.00 | — |

**100 FRANCS KM# 5 Composition:** Nickel **Obverse:** Three giant eland **Reverse:** Denomination

| Date | Mintage | F | VF | XF | Unc | BU |
|---|---|---|---|---|---|---|
| 1966(a) | 9,948,000 | 2.00 | 4.00 | 7.00 | 12.00 | — |
| 1967(a) | 11,000,000 | 2.00 | 4.00 | 7.00 | 12.00 | — |
| 1968(a) | — | 2.00 | 4.00 | 7.00 | 12.00 | — |

### ESSAIS

Standard metals unless otherwise noted

| KM | Date | Mintage | Identification | Mkt Val |
|---|---|---|---|---|
| E1 | 1961 | — | 5 Francs. KM#1. | 10.00 |
| E2 | 1961 | — | 10 Francs. KM#2. | 15.00 |
| E3 | 1961 | — | 50 Francs. KM#3. | 30.00 |
| E4 | 1961 | — | 50 Francs. Gold. KM#4. | 1,100 |
| E5 | 1962 | — | 25 Francs. KM#4. This is a mule, having an old reverse die with a wing privy mark. | 15.00 |
| E6 | 1966 | — | 100 Francs. KM#5. | 20.00 |
| E7 | 1969 | — | Franc. KM#6. | 12.00 |

### PIEFORTS

| KM# | Date | Mintage | Identification | Mkt Val |
|---|---|---|---|---|
| P1 | 1965 | — | 100 Francs. Gold. 23.4800 g. KM#5. With ESSAI. | 775 |

# EQUATORIAL GUINEA

GHANA
TOGO
BENIN
NIGERIA
CAMEROON REPUBLIC
CENTRAL AFRICAN REPUBLIC
CONGO DEMOCRATIC REPUBLIC
South Atlantic Ocean
GABON
CONGO REPUBLIC

The Republic of Equatorial Guinea (formerly Spanish Guinea) consists of Rio Muni, located on the coast of west- - Central Africa between Cameroon and Gabon, and the off-shore islands of Fernando Po, Annobon, Corisco, Elobey Grande and Elobey Chico. The equatorial country has an area of 10,831 sq. mi. (28,050 sq. km.) and a population of 420,293. Capital: Malabo. The economy is based on agriculture and forestry. Cacao, wood and coffee are exported.

Fernando Po was discovered between 1474 and 1496 by Portuguese navigators charting a route to the spice islands of the Far East. Portugal retained control of it and the adjacent islands until 1778 when they, together with trading rights to the African coast between the Ogooue and Niger Rivers, were ceded to Spain. Fernando Po was administered, with Spanish consent, by the British from 1827 to 1844 when it was reclaimed by Spain. Mainland Rio Muni was granted to Spain by the Berlin Conference of 1885. The name of the colony was changed from Spanish Guinea to Equatorial Guinea in Dec. of 1963. Independence was attained on Oct. 12, 1968.

Equatorial Guinea converted to the CFA currency system as issued for the Central African States issuing its first 100 Franc denomination in 1985.

**NOTE**: The 1969 coinage carries the actual minting date in the stars at the sides of the large date.

**MINT MARKS**

(a) - Paris, privy marks only

## REPUBLIC

### PESETA COINAGE

**PESETA KM# 1 Composition:** Aluminum-Bronze

| Date | Mintage | F | VF | XF | Unc | BU |
|---|---|---|---|---|---|---|
| 1969(69) | — | 0.35 | 0.75 | 1.25 | 2.00 | — |

**5 PESETAS KM# 2 Composition:** Copper-Nickel

| Date | Mintage | F | VF | XF | Unc | BU |
|---|---|---|---|---|---|---|
| 1969(69) | — | 0.75 | 1.50 | 2.50 | 8.00 | — |

**25 PESETAS KM# 3 Composition:** Copper-Nickel

| Date | Mintage | F | VF | XF | Unc | BU |
|---|---|---|---|---|---|---|
| 1969(69) | — | 1.50 | 2.50 | 6.50 | 12.00 | — |

**25 PESETAS KM# 5 Weight:** 5.0000 g. **Composition:** 0.9990 Silver .1606 oz. ASW **Subject:** World Bank

| Date | Mintage | F | VF | XF | Unc | BU |
|---|---|---|---|---|---|---|
| 1970 Proof | 2,475 | Value: 9.00 | | | | |

**25 PESETAS** **KM# 6** **Weight:** 5.0000 g. **Composition:** 0.9990 Silver .1606 oz. ASW **Subject:** United Nations

| Date | Mintage | F | VF | XF | Unc | BU |
|---|---|---|---|---|---|---|
| 1970 Proof | 2,475 | Value: 9.00 | | | | |

**50 PESETAS** **KM# 4** **Composition:** Copper-Nickel

| Date | Mintage | F | VF | XF | Unc | BU |
|---|---|---|---|---|---|---|
| 1969(69) | — | 2.00 | 3.00 | 7.50 | 15.00 | — |

**50 PESETAS** **KM# 7** **Weight:** 10.0000 g. **Composition:** 0.9990 Silver .3212 oz. ASW **Reverse:** Durer's Praying Hands

| Date | Mintage | F | VF | XF | Unc | BU |
|---|---|---|---|---|---|---|
| 1970 Proof | 3,840 | Value: 12.00 | | | | |

**75 PESETAS** **KM# 8** **Weight:** 15.0000 g. **Composition:** 0.9990 Silver .4818 oz. ASW **Obverse:** Similar to KM#10 **Reverse:** Pope John XXIII

| Date | Mintage | F | VF | XF | Unc | BU |
|---|---|---|---|---|---|---|
| 1970 Proof | 4,000 | Value: 21.50 | | | | |

**75 PESETAS** **KM# 9** **Weight:** 15.0000 g. **Composition:** 0.9990 Silver .4818 oz. ASW **Subject:** Centennial - Birth of Vladimir Ilyich Lenin **Reverse:** Portrait of Lenin

| Date | Mintage | F | VF | XF | Unc | BU |
|---|---|---|---|---|---|---|
| 1970 Proof | 4,000 | Value: 21.50 | | | | |

**75 PESETAS** **KM# 10.1** **Weight:** 15.0000 g. **Composition:** 0.9990 Silver .4818 oz. ASW **Obverse:** Hallmark "1000" in oval at left tusk base **Reverse:** President Abraham Lincoln

| Date | Mintage | F | VF | XF | Unc | BU |
|---|---|---|---|---|---|---|
| 1970 Proof | 4,390 | Value: 16.50 | | | | |

**75 PESETAS** **KM# 10.2** **Weight:** 15.0000 g. **Composition:** 0.9990 Silver .4818 oz. ASW **Obverse:** "1 AR" Hallmark above "E" in "Pesetas"

| Date | Mintage | F | VF | XF | Unc | BU |
|---|---|---|---|---|---|---|
| 1970 Proof | Inc. above | Value: 30.00 | | | | |

**75 PESETAS** **KM# 11** **Weight:** 15.0000 g. **Composition:** 0.9990 Silver .4818 oz. ASW **Subject:** Centennial - Birth of Mahatma Gandhi **Obverse:** Similar to KM#10 **Reverse:** Portrait of Gandhi

| Date | Mintage | F | VF | XF | Unc | BU |
|---|---|---|---|---|---|---|
| 1970 Proof | 4,000 | Value: 21.50 | | | | |

**100 PESETAS** **KM# 12.1** **Weight:** 20.0000 g. **Composition:** 0.9990 Silver .6430 oz. ASW **Obverse:** Similar to KM#13.1 **Reverse:** Durer's Praying Hands

| Date | Mintage | F | VF | XF | Unc | BU |
|---|---|---|---|---|---|---|
| 1970 Proof | 4,000 | Value: 16.50 | | | | |

**100 PESETAS** **KM# 12.2** **Weight:** 20.0000 g. **Composition:** 0.9990 Silver .6430 oz. ASW **Obverse:** "1 AR" hallmark **Reverse:** Durer's Praying Hands

| Date | Mintage | F | VF | XF | Unc | BU |
|---|---|---|---|---|---|---|
| 1970 Proof | Inc. above | Value: 27.50 | | | | |

**100 PESETAS** **KM# 13.1** **Weight:** 20.0000 g. **Composition:** 0.9990 Silver .6430 oz. ASW **Reverse:** Goya's Naked Maja

| Date | Mintage | F | VF | XF | Unc | BU |
|---|---|---|---|---|---|---|
| 1970 Proof | 30,000 | Value: 35.00 | | | | |

**100 PESETAS** **KM# 13.2** **Weight:** 20.0000 g. **Composition:** 0.9990 Silver .6430 oz. ASW **Obverse:** Fineness stamp at base of right tusk **Reverse:** Goya's Naked Maja

| Date | Mintage | F | VF | XF | Unc | BU |
|---|---|---|---|---|---|---|
| 1970 Proof | Inc. above | Value: 35.00 | | | | |

**100 PESETAS** **KM# 13.3** **Weight:** 20.0000 g. **Composition:** 0.9990 Silver .6430 oz. ASW **Obverse:** Fineness stamp below base of right tusk **Reverse:** Goya's Naked Maja

| Date | Mintage | F | VF | XF | Unc | BU |
|---|---|---|---|---|---|---|
| 1970 Proof | Inc. above | Value: 35.00 | | | | |

**100 PESETAS** **KM# 13.4** **Weight:** 20.0000 g. **Composition:** 0.9990 Silver .6430 oz. ASW **Obverse:** Fineness stamp above letters AN **Reverse:** Goya's Naked Maja

| Date | Mintage | F | VF | XF | Unc | BU |
|---|---|---|---|---|---|---|
| 1970 Proof | Inc. above | Value: 35.00 | | | | |

**100 PESETAS** **KM# 13.5** **Weight:** 20.0000 g. **Composition:** 0.9990 Silver .6430 oz. ASW **Obverse:** 1000 in oval counterstamp at base of right tusk **Reverse:** Goya's Naked Maja

| Date | Mintage | F | VF | XF | Unc | BU |
|---|---|---|---|---|---|---|
| 1970 Proof | Inc. above | Value: 35.00 | | | | |

**150 PESETAS** **KM#14** **Weight:** 30.0000 g. **Composition:** 0.9990 Silver .9636 oz. ASW **Subject:** Centennial of the Capital Rome **Reverse:** Roma

| Date | Mintage | F | VF | XF | Unc | BU |
|---|---|---|---|---|---|---|
| 1970 Proof | 3,520 | Value: 27.50 | | | | |

**150 PESETAS** **KM#15** **Weight:** 30.0000 g. **Composition:** 0.9990 Silver .9636 oz. ASW **Subject:** Centennial of the Capital Rome **Reverse:** Colisseum

| Date | Mintage | F | VF | XF | Unc | BU |
|---|---|---|---|---|---|---|
| 1970 Proof | 3,520 | Value: 27.50 | | | | |

**150 PESETAS** **KM#16** **Weight:** 30.0000 g. **Composition:** 0.9990 Silver .9636 oz. ASW **Subject:** Centennial of the Capital Rome **Reverse:** Athena

| Date | Mintage | F | VF | XF | Unc | BU |
|---|---|---|---|---|---|---|
| 1970 Proof | 3,520 | Value: 27.50 | | | | |

**150 PESETAS** **KM#17** **Weight:** 30.0000 g. **Composition:** 0.9990 Silver .9636 oz. ASW **Subject:** Centennial of the Capital Rome **Reverse:** Mercury

| Date | Mintage | F | VF | XF | Unc | BU |
|---|---|---|---|---|---|---|
| 1970 Proof | 3,520 | Value: 27.50 | | | | |

**200 PESETAS** **KM# 18.1** **Weight:** 40.0000 g. **Composition:** 0.9990 Silver 1.2848 oz. ASW **Subject:** World Soccer Championship in Mexico **Obverse:** Similar to 100 Pesetas, KM#13

| Date | Mintage | F | VF | XF | Unc | BU |
|---|---|---|---|---|---|---|
| 1970 Proof | 4,200 | Value: 45.00 | | | | |

**200 PESETAS** **KM# 18.2** **Weight:** 40.0000 g. **Composition:** 0.9990 Silver 1.2848 oz. ASW **Subject:** World Soccer Championship in Mexico **Obverse:** Similar to 100 Pesetas, KM#13 **Reverse:** Fineness stamp in oval at base of right tusk; mint mark stamp "1 AR" at base of left tusk; incuse serial number below denomination

| Date | Mintage | F | VF | XF | Unc | BU |
|---|---|---|---|---|---|---|
| 1970 Proof | Inc. above | Value: 75.00 | | | | |

**200 PESETAS** **KM#19** **Weight:** 40.0000 g. **Composition:** 0.9990 Silver 1.2848 oz. ASW **Subject:** First President Francisco Macias

| Date | Mintage | F | VF | XF | Unc | BU |
|---|---|---|---|---|---|---|
| 1970 Proof | 4,000 | Value: 37.50 | | | | |

**250 PESETAS** **KM# 20** **Weight:** 3.5200 g. **Composition:** 0.9000 Gold .1018 oz. AGW **Reverse:** Goya's Naked Maja

| Date | Mintage | F | VF | XF | Unc | BU |
|---|---|---|---|---|---|---|
| 1970 Proof | 3,500 | Value: 120 | | | | |

**250 PESETAS** **KM# 21** **Weight:** 3.5200 g. **Composition:** 0.9000 Gold .1018 oz. AGW **Reverse:** Durer's Praying Hands **Note:** Similar to 100 pesetas, KM#12.

| Date | Mintage | F | VF | XF | Unc | BU |
|---|---|---|---|---|---|---|
| 1970 Proof | 2,000 | Value: 65.00 | | | | |

**500 PESETAS** **KM# 23** **Weight:** 7.0500 g. **Composition:** 0.9000 Gold .2040 oz. AGW **Reverse:** Vladimir Illyich Lenin **Note:** Similar to 75 Pesetas, KM#9.

| Date | Mintage | F | VF | XF | Unc | BU |
|---|---|---|---|---|---|---|
| 1970 Proof | 1,680 | Value: 135 | | | | |

**500 PESETAS** **KM# 22** **Weight:** 7.0500 g. **Composition:** 0.9000 Gold .2040 oz. AGW **Reverse:** Bust of Pope John XXIII

| Date | Mintage | F | VF | XF | Unc | BU |
|---|---|---|---|---|---|---|
| 1970 Proof | 1,680 | Value: 130 | | | | |

**500 PESETAS** **KM# 24** **Weight:** 7.0500 g. **Composition:** 0.9000 Gold .2040 oz. AGW **Reverse:** President Abraham Lincoln

| Date | Mintage | F | VF | XF | Unc | BU |
|---|---|---|---|---|---|---|
| 1970 Proof | 1,700 | Value: 125 | | | | |

**500 PESETAS** **KM# 25** **Weight:** 7.0500 g. **Composition:** 0.9000 Gold .2040 oz. AGW **Subject:** Centennial - Birth of Mahatma Gandhi **Reverse:** Portrait of Gandhi

| Date | Mintage | F | VF | XF | Unc | BU |
|---|---|---|---|---|---|---|
| 1970 Proof | 1,680 | Value: 135 | | | | |

**750 PESETAS** **KM#26** **Weight:** 10.5700 g. **Composition:** 0.9000 Gold .3058 oz. AGW **Subject:** Centennial of the Capital Rome - Roma **Note:** Similar to 150 Pesetas, KM#14.

| Date | Mintage | F | VF | XF | Unc | BU |
|---|---|---|---|---|---|---|
| 1970 Proof | 1,650 | Value: 185 | | | | |

**750 PESETAS** **KM#27** **Weight:** 10.5700 g. **Composition:** 0.9000 Gold .3058 oz. AGW **Subject:** Centennial of the Capital Rome - Colisseum **Note:** Similar to 150 Pesetas, KM#15.

| Date | Mintage | F | VF | XF | Unc | BU |
|---|---|---|---|---|---|---|
| 1970 Proof | 1,550 | Value: 185 | | | | |

**750 PESETAS** **KM#28** **Weight:** 10.5700 g. **Composition:** 0.9000 Gold .3058 oz. AGW **Subject:** Centennial of the Capital Rome - Athena **Note:** Similar to 150 Pesetas, KM#16.

| Date | Mintage | F | VF | XF | Unc | BU |
|---|---|---|---|---|---|---|
| 1970 Proof | 1,550 | Value: 185 | | | | |

**750 PESETAS** **KM#29** **Weight:** 10.5700 g. **Composition:** 0.9000 Gold .3058 oz. AGW **Subject:** Centennial of the Capital Rome - Mercury **Note:** Similar to 150 Pesetas, KM#17.

| Date | Mintage | F | VF | XF | Unc | BU |
|---|---|---|---|---|---|---|
| 1970 Proof | 1,550 | Value: 185 | | | | |

**1000 PESETAS** **KM# 30** **Weight:** 14.1000 g. **Composition:** 0.9000 Gold .4080 oz. AGW **Subject:** World Soccer Championship in Mexico **Note:** Similar to 200 Pesetas, KM#18.

| Date | Mintage | F | VF | XF | Unc | BU |
|---|---|---|---|---|---|---|
| 1970 Proof | 1,190 | Value: 250 | | | | |

**5000 PESETAS** **KM# 31** **Weight:** 70.5200 g. **Composition:** 0.9000 Gold 2.0407 oz. AGW **Subject:** First President - Francisco Macias **Note:** Similar to 200 Pesetas, KM#19.

| Date | Mintage | F | VF | XF | Unc | BU |
|---|---|---|---|---|---|---|
| 1970 Proof | 330 | Value: 1,350 | | | | |

## REFORM COINAGE

1975-1980

**EKUELE** **KM# 32** **Composition:** Brass **Note:** Withdrawn from circulation.

| Date | Mintage | F | VF | XF | Unc | BU |
|---|---|---|---|---|---|---|
| 1975 | 3,000,000 | 1.00 | 2.00 | 3.00 | 5.00 | — |

**5 EKUELE** **KM# 33** **Composition:** Copper-Nickel **Note:** Withdrawn from circulation.

| Date | Mintage | F | VF | XF | Unc | BU |
|---|---|---|---|---|---|---|
| 1975 | 2,800,000 | 1.00 | 2.00 | 3.50 | 6.00 | — |

**10 EKUELE** **KM# 34** **Composition:** Copper-Nickel **Note:** Withdrawn from circulation.

| Date | Mintage | F | VF | XF | Unc | BU |
|---|---|---|---|---|---|---|
| 1975 | 1,300,000 | 1.50 | 2.50 | 4.50 | 9.00 | — |

**1000 EKUELE** **KM#35** **Weight:** 21.4300 g. **Composition:** 0.9250 Silver .6373 oz. ASW **Reverse:** President Masie Nguema Biyogo

| Date | Mintage | F | VF | XF | Unc | BU |
|---|---|---|---|---|---|---|
| 1978 Proof | 31,000 | Value: 17.50 | | | | |

**2000 EKUELE** **KM#55** **Weight:** 31.0000 g. **Composition:** 0.9270 Silver .9270 oz. ASW **Reverse:** Burchell's zebra

| Date | Mintage | F | VF | XF | Unc | BU |
|---|---|---|---|---|---|---|
| 1980 (1983) Proof | 1,000 | Value: 30.00 | | | | |

**2000 EKUELE** **KM#56** **Weight:** 31.0000 g. **Composition:** 0.9270 Silver .9270 oz. ASW **Reverse:** Impalas

| Date | Mintage | F | VF | XF | Unc | BU |
|---|---|---|---|---|---|---|
| 1980 (1983) Proof | 1,000 | Value: 28.00 | | | | |

**2000 EKUELE** **KM#38** **Weight:** 42.8700 g. **Composition:** 0.9250 Silver 1.2749 oz. ASW **Subject:** Soccer Games - Argentina 1978

| Date | Mintage | F | VF | XF | Unc | BU |
|---|---|---|---|---|---|---|
| ND(1979) Proof | 195 | Value: 80.00 | | | | |

**2000 EKUELE** **KM#36** **Weight:** 42.8700 g. **Composition:** 0.9250 Silver 1.2749 oz. ASW **Reverse:** President Masie Nguema Biyogo

| Date | Mintage | F | VF | XF | Unc | BU |
|---|---|---|---|---|---|---|
| 1978 Proof | 31,000 | Value: 30.00 | | | | |

**2000 EKUELE** **KM#37** **Weight:** 31.1000 g. **Composition:** 0.9270 Silver .9270 oz. ASW **Subject:** XXII Olympics

| Date | Mintage | F | VF | XF | Unc | BU |
|---|---|---|---|---|---|---|
| ND(1979) Proof | 11,000 | Value: 18.50 | | | | |

**2000 EKUELE** **KM#57** **Weight:** 31.0000 g. **Composition:** 0.9270 Silver .9270 oz. ASW **Reverse:** Tiger

| Date | Mintage | F | VF | XF | Unc | BU |
|---|---|---|---|---|---|---|
| 1980 (1983) Proof | 1,000 | Value: 35.00 | | | | |

**2000 EKUELE** **KM#58** **Weight:** 31.0000 g. **Composition:** 0.9270 Silver .9270 oz. ASW **Reverse:** Cheetah

| Date | Mintage | F | VF | XF | Unc | BU |
|---|---|---|---|---|---|---|
| 1980 (1983) Proof | 1,000 | Value: 30.00 | | | | |

**5000 EKUELE** **KM# 39** **Weight:** 6.9600 g. **Composition:** 0.9170 Gold .2052 oz. AGW **Reverse:** President Nguema Biyogo

| Date | Mintage | F | VF | XF | Unc | BU |
|---|---|---|---|---|---|---|
| 1978 Proof | 31,000 | Value: 150 | | | | |

**10000 EKUELE** **KM# 40** **Weight:** 13.9200 g. **Composition:** 0.9170 Gold .4104 oz. AGW **Reverse:** President Nguema Biyogo

| Date | Mintage | F | VF | XF | Unc | BU |
|---|---|---|---|---|---|---|
| 1978 Proof | 31,000 | Value: 300 | | | | |

**10000 EKUELE** **KM# 41** **Weight:** 13.9200 g. **Composition:** 0.9170 Gold .4104 oz. AGW **Subject:** Soccer Games - Argentina 1978

| Date | Mintage | F | VF | XF | Unc | BU |
|---|---|---|---|---|---|---|
| ND(1979) Proof | 121 | Value: 500 | | | | |

## REFORM COINAGE

1980-1982

**EKUELE** **KM# 50** **Composition:** Aluminum-Bronze **Obverse:** T.E. Nkogo

| Date | Mintage | F | VF | XF | Unc | BU |
|---|---|---|---|---|---|---|
| 1980 | Est. 200,000 | — | — | — | 55.00 | — |

**EKUELE** **KM# 54** **Weight:** 62.2900 g. **Composition:** 0.9990 Gold 2.0009 oz. AGW **Obverse:** Coat of arms **Reverse:** Pope John Paul II

| Date | Mintage | F | VF | XF | Unc | BU |
|---|---|---|---|---|---|---|
| 1982 | — | — | — | — | 1,200 | — |

**5 BIPKWELE** **KM# 51** **Composition:** Copper Nickel **Obverse:** T.E. Nkogo right **Reverse:** Value and arms

| Date | Mintage | F | VF | XF | Unc | BU |
|---|---|---|---|---|---|---|
| 1980 | Est. 200,000 | — | 60.00 | 100 | 150 | — |

**25 BIPKWELE** **KM# 52** **Composition:** Copper Nickel **Obverse:** T.E. Nkogo

| Date | Mintage | F | VF | XF | Unc | BU |
|---|---|---|---|---|---|---|
| 1980 | Est. 200,000 | — | 12.00 | 18.00 | 30.00 | — |
| 1981 | Est. 800,000 | — | — | — | — | — |

**50 BIPKWELE** **KM# 53** **Composition:** Copper Nickel **Obverse:** T.E. Nkogo right **Reverse:** Value and arms

| Date | Mintage | F | VF | XF | Unc | BU |
|---|---|---|---|---|---|---|
| 1980 | Est. 200,000 | — | — | — | 37.50 | — |
| 1981 | Est. 500,000 | — | — | — | — | — |

**7000 FRANCOS** **KM# 114** **Weight:** 9.9300 g. **Composition:** 0.7400 Silver .2362 oz. ASW **Subject:** Endangered Wildlife **Obverse:** National arms **Reverse:** Giraffe family **Edge:** Reeded **Size:** 34.8 mm.

| Date | Mintage | F | VF | XF | Unc | BU |
|---|---|---|---|---|---|---|
| 1993 Proof | — | Value: 50.00 | | | | |

**30000 FRANCOS** **KM# 107** **Weight:** 33.9300 g. **Composition:** 0.9170 Gold 1.0003 oz. AGW **Subject:** Elephant Protection **Obverse:** National arms **Reverse:** Elephant **Edge:** Reeded **Size:** 32.8 mm.

| Date | Mintage | F | VF | XF | Unc | BU |
|---|---|---|---|---|---|---|
| 1993 Proof | 700 | Value: 600 | | | | |

**Note:** 400 pieces remelted at mint

## REFORM COINAGE

1985-

**5 FRANCOS** **KM# 62** **Composition:** Aluminum-Bronze

| Date | Mintage | F | VF | XF | Unc | BU |
|---|---|---|---|---|---|---|
| 1985(a) | — | — | 2.50 | 4.50 | 8.00 | — |

**25 FRANCOS** **KM# 60** **Composition:** Aluminum-Bronze

| Date | Mintage | F | VF | XF | Unc | BU |
|---|---|---|---|---|---|---|
| 1985(a) | — | — | 3.50 | 7.00 | 15.00 | — |

**50 FRANCOS** **KM# 64** **Composition:** Nickel

| Date | Mintage | F | VF | XF | Unc | BU |
|---|---|---|---|---|---|---|
| 1985(a) | — | — | 8.00 | 16.00 | 28.00 | — |
| 1986(a) | — | — | 6.00 | 12.00 | 20.00 | — |

**100 FRANCOS** **KM# 59** **Composition:** Nickel

| Date | Mintage | F | VF | XF | Unc | BU |
|---|---|---|---|---|---|---|
| 1985(a) | — | — | 10.00 | 20.00 | 35.00 | — |
| 1986(a) | — | — | 7.00 | 14.00 | 25.00 | — |

**1000 FRANCOS** **KM# 68** **Composition:** Copper-Nickel **Reverse:** Brandenburg Gate

| Date | Mintage | F | VF | XF | Unc | BU |
|---|---|---|---|---|---|---|
| 1991 Proof | 6,000 | Value: 10.00 | | | | |

**1000 FRANCOS** **KM# 81** **Composition:** Copper-Nickel **Subject:** Jurassic Dinosaurs **Reverse:** Diplodocus **Note:** Multi-colored.

| Date | Mintage | F | VF | XF | Unc | BU |
|---|---|---|---|---|---|---|
| 1993 | — | — | — | — | 27.50 | — |

**1000 FRANCOS** **KM# 82** **Composition:** Copper-Nickel **Subject:** Jurassic Dinosaurs **Reverse:** Styracosaurus

| Date | Mintage | F | VF | XF | Unc | BU |
|---|---|---|---|---|---|---|
| 1993 | — | — | — | — | 25.00 | — |

**1000 FRANCOS** **KM# 83** **Composition:** Copper-Nickel **Subject:** Jurassic Dinosaurs **Reverse:** Tyrannosaurus

| Date | Mintage | F | VF | XF | Unc | BU |
|---|---|---|---|---|---|---|
| 1993 | — | — | — | — | 32.50 | — |

**1000 FRANCOS** **KM# 87** **Composition:** Copper-Nickel **Subject:** Jurassic Dinosaurs **Reverse:** Allosaurus

| Date | Mintage | F | VF | XF | Unc | BU |
|---|---|---|---|---|---|---|
| 1993 | — | — | — | — | 27.50 | — |

**1000 FRANCOS** **KM# 88** **Composition:** Copper-Nickel **Subject:** Jurassic Dinosaurs **Reverse:** Plateosaurus

| Date | Mintage | F | VF | XF | Unc | BU |
|---|---|---|---|---|---|---|
| 1993 | — | — | — | — | 27.50 | — |

**1000 FRANCOS** KM# 90 **Composition:** Copper-Nickel **Subject:** World Soccer Championship - 1994

| Date | Mintage | F | VF | XF | Unc | BU |
|---|---|---|---|---|---|---|
| 1994 | — | — | — | — | 27.50 | — |

**1000 FRANCOS** KM# 89 **Composition:** Copper-Nickel **Subject:** African Bird Wildlife - Kingfisher **Note:** Similar to 7000 Francos, KM#98.

| Date | Mintage | F | VF | XF | Unc | BU |
|---|---|---|---|---|---|---|
| 1994 | — | — | — | — | 25.00 | — |

**1000 FRANCOS** KM# 91 **Composition:** Copper-Nickel **Subject:** World's Famous Dogs - St. Bernard **Note:** Multicolored.

| Date | Mintage | F | VF | XF | Unc | BU |
|---|---|---|---|---|---|---|
| 1994 | — | — | — | — | 22.50 | — |

**1000 FRANCOS** KM# 92 **Composition:** Copper-Nickel **Subject:** 25th Anniversary - Moon Landing

| Date | Mintage | F | VF | XF | Unc | BU |
|---|---|---|---|---|---|---|
| 1994 | — | — | — | — | 22.50 | — |

**1000 FRANCOS** KM# 93 **Composition:** Copper-Nickel **Subject:** Famous Stamps of the World - Swiss

| Date | Mintage | F | VF | XF | Unc | BU |
|---|---|---|---|---|---|---|
| 1994 | — | — | — | — | 20.00 | — |

**1000 FRANCOS** KM# 84.1 **Composition:** Copper-Nickel **Subject:** 150th Anniversary - Basel "Taube" Stamp **Note:** Multicolored.

| Date | Mintage | F | VF | XF | Unc | BU |
|---|---|---|---|---|---|---|
| 1995 | 15,000 | — | — | — | 20.00 | — |

**1000 FRANCOS** KM# 84.2 **Composition:** Copper-Nickel **Subject:** 150th Anniversary - Basel "Taube" Stamp **Rev. Legend:** Error, "TAUBER" **Note:** Multicolored.

| Date | Mintage | F | VF | XF | Unc | BU |
|---|---|---|---|---|---|---|
| 1995 | Inc. above | — | — | — | 35.00 | — |

**1000 FRANCOS** KM# 95 **Composition:** Copper-Nickel **Subject:** Famous Places in the World - Altdorf-Wilhelm Tell **Obverse:** State arms **Reverse:** Multicolored applique of Wilhelm Tell

| Date | Mintage | F | VF | XF | Unc | BU |
|---|---|---|---|---|---|---|
| 1996 Proof | — | Value: 27.50 | | | | |

**1000 FRANCOS** KM# 96 **Composition:** Copper-Nickel **Subject:** Famous Stamps of the World - Pintores Famosos dei Mundo - Rolf Knie **Obverse:** State arms **Reverse:** Multicolored applique of Swiss circus stamp design

| Date | Mintage | F | VF | XF | Unc | BU |
|---|---|---|---|---|---|---|
| 1996 Proof | — | Value: 35.00 | | | | |

**1000 FRANCOS** KM# 97 **Composition:** Copper-Nickel **Subject:** Famous Stamps of the World - XXVI Juegos Olimpicos de Verano **Obverse:** State arms **Reverse:** Stamp with downhill skier

| Date | Mintage | F | VF | XF | Unc | BU |
|---|---|---|---|---|---|---|
| 1996 Proof | — | Value: 35.00 | | | | |

**7000 FRANCOS** KM# 66 **Weight:** 26.3000 g. **Composition:** 0.9990 Silver .8455 oz. ASW **Reverse:** President Mbasogo bust above three shields

| Date | Mintage | F | VF | XF | Unc | BU |
|---|---|---|---|---|---|---|
| 1991 Proof | — | Value: 42.50 | | | | |

**7000 FRANCOS** KM# 67 **Weight:** 25.7000 g. **Composition:** 0.9990 Silver .8263 oz. ASW **Subject:** Soccer - Italy 1990

| Date | Mintage | F | VF | XF | Unc | BU |
|---|---|---|---|---|---|---|
| 1991 Proof | 6,000 | Value: 45.00 | | | | |

**7000 FRANCOS** KM# 69 **Weight:** 20.0000 g. **Composition:** 0.9990 Silver .6430 oz. ASW **Subject:** Discovery of America **Reverse:** Santa Maria

| Date | Mintage | F | VF | XF | Unc | BU |
|---|---|---|---|---|---|---|
| 1991 Proof | 15,000 | Value: 40.00 | | | | |

**7000 FRANCOS** **KM# 70** **Weight:** 20.0000 g. **Composition:** 0.9990 Silver .6430 oz. ASW **Subject:** Seville Expo

| Date | Mintage | F | VF | XF | Unc | BU |
|---|---|---|---|---|---|---|
| 1991 Proof | 15,000 | Value: 40.00 | | | | |

**7000 FRANCOS** **KM# 71** **Weight:** 20.0000 g. **Composition:** 0.9990 Silver .6430 oz. ASW **Subject:** Barcelona Olympics **Reverse:** Athletes on rings

| Date | Mintage | F | VF | XF | Unc | BU |
|---|---|---|---|---|---|---|
| 1991 Proof | 15,000 | Value: 42.50 | | | | |

**7000 FRANCOS** **KM# 76** **Weight:** 510.3000 g. **Composition:** 0.9990 Silver 16.4062 oz. ASW **Subject:** Endangered Wildlife **Reverse:** Lions **Size:** 75.1 mm. **Note:** Illustration reduced.

| Date | Mintage | F | VF | XF | Unc | BU |
|---|---|---|---|---|---|---|
| 1992 Proof | — | Value: 225 | | | | |

**7000 FRANCOS** **KM# 105** **Weight:** 7.7700 g. **Composition:** 0.9000 Gold .2248 oz. AGW **Subject:** Endangered Wildlife **Reverse:** Lions

| Date | Mintage | F | VF | XF | Unc | BU |
|---|---|---|---|---|---|---|
| 1992 Proof | 450 | Value: 200 | | | | |

**7000 FRANCOS** **KM# 80** **Weight:** 10.4800 g. **Composition:** 0.9990 Silver .3366 oz. ASW **Subject:** Barcelona Olympics **Reverse:** Female runner

| Date | Mintage | F | VF | XF | Unc | BU |
|---|---|---|---|---|---|---|
| 1992 Proof | 25,000 | Value: 27.50 | | | | |

**7000 FRANCOS** **KM# 77** **Weight:** 10.5100 g. **Composition:** 0.9990 Silver .3379 oz. ASW **Subject:** African Elephant Protection

| Date | Mintage | F | VF | XF | Unc | BU |
|---|---|---|---|---|---|---|
| 1993 Proof | Est. 25,000 | Value: 27.50 | | | | |

**7000 FRANCOS** **KM# 78** **Weight:** 20.0000 g. **Composition:** 0.9990 Silver .6430 oz. ASW **Subject:** Barcelona Olympics **Reverse:** Athletes on Olympic rings

| Date | Mintage | F | VF | XF | Unc | BU |
|---|---|---|---|---|---|---|
| 1993 Proof | — | Value: 65.00 | | | | |

**7000 FRANCOS** **KM# 94** **Weight:** 20.1700 g. **Composition:** 0.9990 Silver .6478 oz. ASW **Subject:** Jurassic Dinosaurs **Obverse:** National arms **Reverse:** Multicolored stegosaurus scene applique

| Date | Mintage | F | VF | XF | Unc | BU |
|---|---|---|---|---|---|---|
| 1993 Proof | — | Value: 65.00 | | | | |

**7000 FRANCOS** **KM# 86** **Weight:** 20.1700 g. **Composition:** 0.9990 Silver .6651 oz. ASW **Subject:** World Cup Soccer

| Date | Mintage | F | VF | XF | Unc | BU |
|---|---|---|---|---|---|---|
| 1994 Proof | — | Value: 40.00 | | | | |

**7000 FRANCOS** **KM# 98** **Weight:** 20.3500 g. **Composition:** 0.9990 Silver .6536 oz. ASW **Subject:** African Bird Wildlife - Kingfisher **Obverse:** National arms **Reverse:** Pair of multicolored kingfishers

| Date | Mintage | F | VF | XF | Unc | BU |
|---|---|---|---|---|---|---|
| 1994 Proof | — | Value: 42.50 | | | | |

**7000 FRANCOS** **KM# 99** **Weight:** 20.3500 g. **Composition:** 0.9990 Silver .6536 oz. ASW **Subject:** World Famous Dogs - St. Bernard **Obverse:** National arms **Reverse:** Pair of multicolored St. Bernards

| Date | Mintage | F | VF | XF | Unc | BU |
|---|---|---|---|---|---|---|
| 1994 Proof | — | Value: 42.50 | | | | |

**7000 FRANCOS** **KM# 108** **Weight:** 20.3500 g. **Composition:** 0.9990 Silver .6536 oz. ASW **Subject:** 25th Anniversary - Moon Landing **Reverse:** Multicolored moon-landing scene

| Date | Mintage | F | VF | XF | Unc | BU |
|---|---|---|---|---|---|---|
| 1994 Proof | — | Value: 42.50 | | | | |

**7000 FRANCOS** **KM# 109** **Weight:** 20.3500 g. **Composition:** 0.9990 Silver .6536 oz. ASW **Subject:** 150th Anniversary - Basel "Taube" Stamp **Reverse:** Multicolored stamp

| Date | Mintage | F | VF | XF | Unc | BU |
|---|---|---|---|---|---|---|
| 1995 Proof | — | Value: 35.00 | | | | |

**7000 FRANCOS** **KM# 85** **Weight:** 21.0000 g. **Composition:** 0.9990 Silver .6752 oz. ASW **Subject:** 50th Anniversary - United Nations

| Date | Mintage | F | VF | XF | Unc | BU |
|---|---|---|---|---|---|---|
| 1995 Proof | — | Value: 37.50 | | | | |

**7000 FRANCOS** **KM# 100** **Weight:** 157.5500 g. **Composition:** 0.9990 Silver 5.0603 oz. ASW **Subject:** Endangered wildlife **Obverse:** Topical map of Africa, similar to KM#76 **Reverse:** Elephant head **Size:** 64.9 mm. **Note:** Illustration reduced.

| Date | Mintage | F | VF | XF | Unc | BU |
|---|---|---|---|---|---|---|
| 1995 Proof | 555 | Value: 100 | | | | |

**7000 FRANCOS** **KM# 101** **Weight:** 157.5500 g. **Composition:** 0.9990 Silver 5.0603 oz. ASW **Subject:** Endangered wildlife **Obverse:** Topical map of Africa **Reverse:** Mother elephant with calf

| Date | Mintage | F | VF | XF | Unc | BU |
|---|---|---|---|---|---|---|
| 1995 Proof | 555 | Value: 100 | | | | |

**7000 FRANCOS** **KM# 102** **Weight:** 157.5500 g. **Composition:** 0.9990 Silver 5.0603 oz. ASW **Subject:** Endangered wildlife **Obverse:** Topical map of Africa **Reverse:** Elephant at watering hole

| Date | Mintage | F | VF | XF | Unc | BU |
|---|---|---|---|---|---|---|
| 1995 Proof | 555 | Value: 100 | | | | |

**7000 FRANCOS** **KM# 103** **Weight:** 157.5500 g. **Composition:** 0.9990 Silver 5.0603 oz. ASW **Subject:** Endangered wildlife **Obverse:** Topical map of Africa **Reverse:** Elephant family

| Date | Mintage | F | VF | XF | Unc | BU |
|---|---|---|---|---|---|---|
| 1995 Proof | 555 | Value: 100 | | | | |

**7000 FRANCOS** **KM# 104** **Weight:** 157.5500 g. **Composition:** 0.9990 Silver 5.0603 oz. ASW **Subject:** Endangered wildlife **Obverse:** Topical map of Africa **Reverse:** Adolescent elephant with adult

| Date | Mintage | F | VF | XF | Unc | BU |
|---|---|---|---|---|---|---|
| 1995 Proof | 555 | Value: 100 | | | | |

**15000 FRANCOS** **KM# 72** **Weight:** 7.0000 g. **Composition:** 0.9170 Gold .2063 oz. AGW **Subject:** Discovery of America - Columbus **Obverse:** Coat of arms above denomination

| Date | Mintage | F | VF | XF | Unc | BU |
|---|---|---|---|---|---|---|
| 1991 Proof | 1,500 | Value: 155 | | | | |

**15000 FRANCOS** **KM# 73** **Weight:** 7.0000 g. **Composition:** 0.9170 Gold .2063 oz. AGW **Subject:** Expo Seville - Ship and Space Shuttle **Obverse:** Coat of arms above denomination

| Date | Mintage | F | VF | XF | Unc | BU |
|---|---|---|---|---|---|---|
| 1991 Proof | 1,500 | Value: 155 | | | | |

**15000 FRANCOS** **KM# 74** **Weight:** 7.0000 g. **Composition:** 0.9170 Gold .2063 oz. AGW **Subject:** Barcelona Olympics - Equestrian Jumping **Obverse:** Coat of arms above denomination

| Date | Mintage | F | VF | XF | Unc | BU |
|---|---|---|---|---|---|---|
| 1991 Proof | 1,500 | Value: 165 | | | | |

**15000 FRANCOS** **KM# 74a** **Weight:** 20.3300 g. **Composition:** 0.9990 Silver .6350 oz. ASW **Subject:** Barcelona Olympics - Equestrian Jumping **Obverse:** Coat of arms above denomination

| Date | Mintage | F | VF | XF | Unc | BU |
|---|---|---|---|---|---|---|
| 1992 Proof | — | Value: 50.00 | | | | |

**15000 FRANCOS** **KM# 79** **Weight:** 855.3422 g. **Composition:** 0.9990 Silver 27.49 oz. ASW **Subject:** Endangered wildlife **Obverse:** Similar to KM#76 **Reverse:** Elephant **Size:** 106 mm. **Note:** Illustration reduced.

| Date | Mintage | F | VF | XF | Unc | BU |
|---|---|---|---|---|---|---|
| 1992 Proof | — | Value: 275 | | | | |

**15000 FRANCOS** **KM# 106** **Weight:** 15.5500 g. **Composition:** 0.9000 Gold .4499 oz. AGW **Subject:** Endangered wildlife **Reverse:** Elephant

| Date | Mintage | F | VF | XF | Unc | BU |
|---|---|---|---|---|---|---|
| 1992 Proof | 450 | Value: 300 | | | | |

## MEDALLIC COINAGE

**1000 BIPKWELE** **KM# M1** **Weight:** 12.5000 g. **Composition:** 0.9250 Silver .3717 oz. ASW **Subject:** Royal Couple Visit

| Date | Mintage | F | VF | XF | Unc | BU |
|---|---|---|---|---|---|---|
| ND(1980) Proof | 3,000 | Value: 25.00 | | | | |
| ND(1980) | 5,125 | — | — | — | 17.50 | — |

**1000 BIPKWELE** **KM# M5** **Weight:** 12.5000 g. **Composition:** 0.9250 Silver .3717 oz. ASW **Subject:** Visit by Juan Carlo I **Reverse:** Similar to 2000 Bipkwele, KM#45

| Date | Mintage | F | VF | XF | Unc | BU |
|---|---|---|---|---|---|---|
| ND(1980) | 5,125 | — | — | — | 17.50 | — |
| ND(1980) Proof | 3,000 | Value: 25.00 | | | | |

**2000 BIPKWELE** **KM# M2** **Weight:** 25.0000 g. **Composition:** 0.9250 Silver .7435 oz. ASW **Subject:** Royal Couple Visit

| Date | Mintage | F | VF | XF | Unc | BU |
|---|---|---|---|---|---|---|
| ND(1980) | 5,125 | — | — | — | 27.50 | — |
| ND(1980) Proof | 3,000 | Value: 40.00 | | | | |

**2000 BIPKWELE** **KM# M6** **Weight:** 25.0000 g. **Composition:** 0.9250 Silver .7435 oz. ASW **Subject:** Visit by Juan Carlos I

| Date | Mintage | F | VF | XF | Unc | BU |
|---|---|---|---|---|---|---|
| ND(1980) | 5,125 | — | — | — | 27.50 | — |
| ND(1980) Proof | 3,000 | Value: 40.00 | | | | |

**5000 BIPKWELE** **KM# M3** **Weight:** 4.0000 g. **Composition:** 0.9170 Gold .1179 oz. AGW **Subject:** Royal Couple Visit

| Date | Mintage | F | VF | XF | Unc | BU |
|---|---|---|---|---|---|---|
| ND(1980) | 4,250 | — | — | — | 70.00 | — |
| ND(1980) Proof | 2,000 | Value: 100 | | | | |

**5000 BIPKWELE** **KM# M7** **Weight:** 4.0000 g. **Composition:** 0.9170 Gold .1179 oz. AGW **Subject:** Visit by Juan Carlos I

| Date | Mintage | F | VF | XF | Unc | BU |
|---|---|---|---|---|---|---|
| ND(1980) | 4,250 | — | — | — | 70.00 | — |
| ND(1980) Proof | 2,000 | Value: 100 | | | | |

**10000 BIPKWELE** **KM# M8** **Weight:** 8.0000 g. **Composition:** 0.9170 Gold .2358 oz. AGW **Subject:** Visit by Juan Carlos I

| Date | Mintage | F | VF | XF | Unc | BU |
|---|---|---|---|---|---|---|
| ND(1980) Proof | 2,000 | Value: 175 | | | | |
| ND(1980) | 4,250 | — | — | — | 140 | — |

**10000 BIPKWELE** **KM# M4** **Weight:** 8.0000 g. **Composition:** 0.9170 Gold .2358 oz. AGW **Subject:** Royal Couple Visit

| Date | Mintage | F | VF | XF | Unc | BU |
|---|---|---|---|---|---|---|
| ND(1980) | 4,250 | — | — | — | 140 | — |
| ND(1980) Proof | 2,000 | Value: 175 | | | | |

## ESSAIS

| KM# | Date | Mintage | Identification | Issue Price | Mkt Val |
|---|---|---|---|---|---|
| E14 | 1980 | — | 1000 Bipkwele. Copper. M5. | — | 18.00 |
| E1 | 1978 | 25 | 1000 Ekuele. Aluminum. KM#35. | — | 45.00 |
| E2 | 1978 | 20 | 1000 Ekuele. Copper. KM#35. | — | 50.00 |
| E3 | 1978 | 25 | 2000 Ekuele. Aluminum. KM#36. | — | 55.00 |
| E4 | 1978 | — | 2000 Ekuele. Copper. KM#36. | — | 60.00 |
| E5 | 1978 | — | 5000 Ekuele. Aluminum. KM#39. | — | 35.00 |
| E6 | 1978 | — | 5000 Ekuele. Copper. KM#39. | — | 40.00 |
| E7 | 1978 | — | 10000 Ekuele. Aluminum. KM#40. | — | 45.00 |
| E8 | 1978 | — | 10000 Ekuele. Copper. KM#40. | — | 50.00 |
| E9 | (1979) | — | 2000 Ekuele. Aluminum. KM#38. | — | 25.00 |
| E10 | (1979) | — | 2000 Ekuele. Copper. KM#38. | — | 90.00 |
| E11 | (1979) | — | 10000 Ekuele. Aluminum. KM#41. | — | 25.00 |
| E12 | (1979) | — | 10000 Ekuele. Copper. KM#41. | — | 60.00 |
| E13 | 1980 | — | Bipkwele. Copper. M1. | — | 20.00 |
| E15 | 1980 | — | 2000 Bipkwele. Aluminum. M2. | — | 20.00 |
| E16 | 1980 | — | 2000 Bipkwele. Copper. M2. | — | 30.00 |
| E17 | 1980 | — | 2000 Bipkwele. Aluminum. M6. | — | 17.50 |
| E18 | 1980 | — | 2000 Bipkwele. Copper. M6. | — | 27.50 |
| E19 | 1980 | — | 5000 Bipkwele. Aluminum. M3. | — | 12.50 |
| E20 | 1980 | — | 5000 Bipkwele. Copper. M3. | — | 16.50 |
| E21 | 1980 | — | 5000 Bipkwele. Aluminum. M7. | — | 10.00 |
| E22 | 1980 | — | 5000 Bipkwele. Copper. M7. | — | 14.50 |
| E23 | 1980 | — | 10000 Bipkwele. Aluminum. KM#48. | — | 18.50 |
| E24 | 1980 | — | 10000 Bipkwele. Copper. M4. | — | 22.50 |
| E25 | 1980 | — | 10000 Bipkwele. 0.9250 Silver. M4. | — | 65.00 |
| E26 | 1980 | — | 10000 Bipkwele. Aluminum. M8. | — | 14.50 |
| E27 | 1980 | — | 10000 Bipkwele. Copper. M8. | — | 18.50 |

| KM# | Date | Mintage | Identification | Issue Price | Mkt Val |
|---|---|---|---|---|---|
| E28 | 1985 | — | 5 Francos. Aluminum-Bronze. KM#62. | — | 17.50 |

| KM# | Date | Mintage | Identification | Issue Price | Mkt Val |
|---|---|---|---|---|---|
| E29 | 1985 | — | 25 Francos. KM#60. | — | 22.50 |

| KM# | Date | Mintage | Identification | Issue Price | Mkt Val |
|---|---|---|---|---|---|
| E31 | 1985 | — | 100 Francos. KM#59. | — | 27.50 |
| E30 | 1985 | — | 50 Francos. KM#64. | — | 25.00 |

## PATTERNS

| KM# | Date | Mintage | Identification | Mkt Val |
|---|---|---|---|---|
| Pn1 | 1980 | — | 5000 Bipkwele. Silver. Similar to M1. | 55.00 |
| Pn2 | 1980 | — | 5000 Bipkwele. Goldine. Similar to M1. | 45.00 |
| Pn3 | 1980 | — | 5000 Bipkwele. Silver. Similar to M5. | 50.00 |
| Pn4 | 1980 | — | 5000 Bipkwele. Goldine. Similar to M5. | 40.00 |
| Pn5 | 1980 | — | 10000 Bipkwele. Silver. Reeded edge. Similar to M2. | 110 |
| Pn6 | 1980 | — | 10000 Bipkwele. Silver. Plain edge. Similar to M2. | 110 |
| Pn7 | 1980 | — | 10000 Bipkwele. Goldine. Plain edge. Similar to M2. | 85.00 |
| Pn8 | 1980 | — | 10000 Bipkwele. Silver. Reeded edge. Similar to M6. | 100 |
| Pn9 | 1980 | — | 10000 Bipkwele. Silver. Plain edge. Similar to M6. | 100 |
| Pn10 | 1980 | — | 10000 Bipkwele. Goldine. Plain edge. Similar to M6. | 75.00 |
| Pn11 | 1992 | — | 15000 Francos. 0.9990 Gold Plated Silver. 12.6700 g. | — |
| Pn12 | 1993 | — | 1000 Francos. Copper Nickel. Soccer scene. | 45.00 |
| Pn13 | 1993 | — | 1000 Francos. Copper Nickel. Soccer players through net. | 45.00 |
| Pn14 | 1994 | — | 1000 Francos. Copper Nickel. Hands holding FIFA cup. | 35.00 |
| Pn15 | 1994 | — | 1000 Francos. Copper Nickel. Three players holding cup. | 35.00 |
| Pn16 | 1994 | — | 7000 Francos. 0.9990 Silver. 19.9100 g. | — |

## PIEFORTS

| KM# | Date | Mintage | Identification | Issue Price | Mkt Val |
|---|---|---|---|---|---|
| P1 | 1978 | — | 1000 Ekuele. Copper. KM#35. | — | 200 |
| P2 | 1978 | — | 1000 Ekuele. 0.9250 Silver. KM#35. | — | 250 |
| P3 | 1978 | — | 2000 Ekuele. Copper. 6.8 mm. Plain edge. KM#36. | — | 300 |
| P4 | 1978 | — | 5000 Ekuele. Copper. 2.6 mm. Milled edge. KM#39. | — | 175 |
| P5 | 1978 | — | 5000 Ekuele. Copper. 4.1 mm. Plain edge. | — | 150 |

| KM# | Date | Mintage | Identification | Issue Price | Mkt Val |
|---|---|---|---|---|---|
| P6 | 1978 | — | 10000 Ekuele. Copper. 3.4 mm. Milled edge. KM#41. | — | 110 |
| P7 | (1979) | — | 2000 Ekuele. Copper. KM#38. | — | 215 |
| P11 | (1979) | — | 10000 Ekuele. Gold. KM#41. | — | 1,200 |
| P8 | (1979) | — | 2000 Ekuele. 0.9250 Silver. KM#38. | — | 300 |
| P9 | (1979) | — | 2000 Ekuele. Gilt Copper. | — | 215 |
| P10 | (1979) | — | 10000 Ekuele. Copper. KM#41. | — | 225 |
| P12 | (1979) | — | 10000 Ekuele. Gilt Copper. KM#41. | — | 200 |
| P13 | 1980 | — | 1000 Bipkwele. Gilt Copper. M1. | — | 45.00 |
| P33 | 1980 | 750 | 10000 Bipkwele. M4. | — | 400 |
| P35 | 1980 | 750 | 10000 Bipkwele. M8. | — | 400 |
| P14 | 1980 | — | 1000 Bipkwele. 0.9250 Silver. 25.4900 g. M1. | — | 65.00 |
| P25 | 1980 | 750 | 5000 Bipkwele. M3. | — | 200 |
| P27 | 1980 | 750 | 5000 Bipkwele. M7. | — | 200 |
| P29 | 1980 | — | 5000 Bipkwele. Goldine. Plain edge. Similar to M1. | — | 85.00 |
| P15 | 1980 | — | 1000 Bipkwele. Gold. 25.5000 g. | — | 475 |
| P16 | 1980 | — | 1000 Bipkwele. Copper. M5. | — | 35.00 |
| P17 | 1980 | — | 1000 Bipkwele. Silver. M5. | — | 55.00 |
| P18 | 1980 | — | 2000 Bipkwele. Copper. Plain edge. M2. | — | 65.00 |
| P19 | 1980 | — | 2000 Bipkwele. Silver. Reeded edge. M2. | — | 125 |
| P20 | 1980 | — | 2000 Bipkwele. Silver. Plain edge. M2. | — | 125 |
| P21 | 1980 | — | 2000 Bipkwele. Copper. Plain edge. M6. | — | 55.00 |
| P22 | 1980 | — | 2000 Bipkwele. Silver. Reeded edge. M6. | — | 115 |
| P23 | 1980 | — | 2000 Bipkwele. Silver. Plain edge. M6. | — | 115 |
| P24 | 1980 | — | 5000 Bipkwele. Copper. M3. | — | 45.00 |
| P26 | 1980 | — | 5000 Bipkwele. Copper. M7. | — | 40.00 |
| P28 | 1980 | — | 5000 Bipkwele. Silver. Plain edge. Similar to M1. | — | 110 |
| P30 | 1980 | — | 5000 Bipkwele. Silver. Plain edge. Similar to M5. | — | 100 |
| P31 | 1980 | — | 5000 Bipkwele. Goldine. Plain edge. Similar to M5. | — | 75.00 |
| P32 | 1980 | — | 10000 Bipkwele. Copper. M4. | — | 65.00 |
| P34 | 1980 | — | 10000 Bipkwele. Copper. M8. | — | 65.00 |

## TRIAL STRIKES

| KM# | Date | Mintage | Identification | Issue Price | Mkt Val |
|---|---|---|---|---|---|
| TS8 | 1978(80) | — | 2000 Bipkwele. 0.9250 Silver. 25.2100 g. PRUEBA. M3. | — | 150 |
| TS5 | 1978 | — | 10000 Ekuele. Copper. 3.6 mm. KM40. PRUEBA. | — | 75.00 |
| TS1 | 1978 | — | 2000 Ekuele. Copper. 3.9 mm. KM#36. PRUEBA. | — | 150 |
| TS2 | 1978 | — | 2000 Ekuele. Copper. 3.9 mm. PRUEBA. KM#36. | — | 150 |

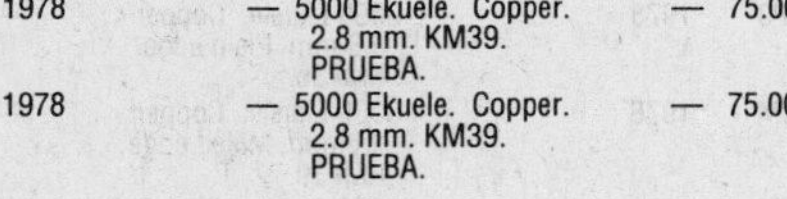

| KM# | Date | Mintage | Identification | Issue Price | Mkt Val |
|---|---|---|---|---|---|
| TS3 | 1978 | — | 5000 Ekuele. Copper. 2.8 mm. KM39. PRUEBA. | — | 75.00 |
| TS4 | 1978 | — | 5000 Ekuele. Copper. 2.8 mm. KM39. PRUEBA. | — | 75.00 |

| KM# | Date | Mintage | Identification | Issue Price | Mkt Val |
|---|---|---|---|---|---|
| TS6 | 1978 | — | 10000 Ekuele. Copper. PRUEBA. KM#40. | — | 75.00 |
| TS7 | 1978(80) | — | 2000 Bipkwele. 0.9250 Silver. 25.2100 g. M3. PRUEBA. | — | 150 |

## MINT SETS

| KM# | Date | Mintage | Identification | Issue Price | Mkt Val |
|---|---|---|---|---|---|
| MS1 | 1975 (3) | — | KM#32-34 | — | 22.00 |

## PROOF SETS

| KM# | Date | Mintage | Identification | Issue Price | Mkt Val |
|---|---|---|---|---|---|
| PS1 | 1970 (27) | 330 | KM#5-31 | — | 3,500 |
| PS2 | 1970 (15) | 2,475 | KM#5-19 | 126 | 350 |
| PS3 | 1970 (12) | 330 | KM#20-31 | — | 3,150 |

# ERITREA

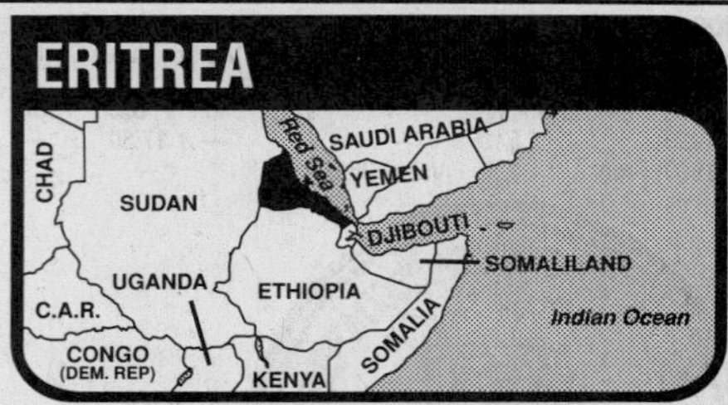


The State of Eritrea, a former Ethiopian province fronting on the Red Sea, has an area of 45,300 sq. mi. (117,600 sq. km.) and a population of 3.6 million. It was an Italian colony from 1889 until its incorporation into Italian East Africa in 1936. It was under the British Military Administration from 1941 to Sept. 15, 1952, when the United Nations designated it an autonomous unit within the federation of Ethiopia and Eritrea. On Nov. 14, 1962, it was annexed with Ethiopia. In 1991 the Eritrean Peoples Liberation Front extended its control over the entire territory of Eritrea. Following 2 years of provisional government, Eritrea held a referendum on independence in May 1993. Overwhelming popular approval led to the proclamation of an independent Republic of Eritrea on May 24.

**RULERS**

Umberto I, 1889-1900
Vittorio Emanuele III, 1900-1945

**MINT MARKS**

M - Milan
PM - Pobjoy
R – Rome

**MONETARY SYSTEM**

100 Centesimi = 1 Lira
5 Lire = 1 Tallero

## ITALIAN COLONY

### COLONIAL COINAGE

**TALLERO** KM# 5 **Weight:** 28.0668 g. **Composition:** 0.8350 Silver .7535 oz. ASW

| Date | Mintage | F | VF | XF | Unc | BU |
|---|---|---|---|---|---|---|
| 1918R | 510,000 | 25.00 | 55.00 | 125 | 425 | — |

## REPUBLIC

### DECIMAL COINAGE

**CENT** KM# 43 **Composition:** Nickel Clad Steel **Obverse:** Antelope **Reverse:** Soldiers with flag

| Date | Mintage | F | VF | XF | Unc | BU |
|---|---|---|---|---|---|---|
| 1997 | — | — | — | — | 0.25 | — |

**5 CENTS** KM# 44 **Composition:** Nickel Clad Steel **Obverse:** Leopard on log **Reverse:** Soldiers with flag

| Date | Mintage | F | VF | XF | Unc | BU |
|---|---|---|---|---|---|---|
| 1997 | — | — | — | — | 0.50 | — |

**10 CENTS** KM# 45 **Composition:** Nickel Clad Steel **Obverse:** Ostrich **Reverse:** Soldiers with flag

| Date | Mintage | F | VF | XF | Unc | BU |
|---|---|---|---|---|---|---|
| 1997 | — | — | — | — | 0.75 | — |

**25 CENTS** KM# 46 **Composition:** Nickel Clad Steel **Obverse:** Grevy's zebra **Reverse:** Soldiers with flag

| Date | Mintage | F | VF | XF | Unc | BU |
|---|---|---|---|---|---|---|
| 1997 | — | — | — | — | 1.25 | — |

**50 CENTS** KM# 47 **Composition:** Nickel Clad Steel **Obverse:** Antelope **Reverse:** Soldiers with flag

| Date | Mintage | F | VF | XF | Unc | BU |
|---|---|---|---|---|---|---|
| 1997 | — | — | — | — | 1.50 | — |

**100 CENTS** KM# 48 **Composition:** Nickel Clad Steel **Obverse:** Elephant and calf **Reverse:** Soldiers with flag

| Date | Mintage | F | VF | XF | Unc | BU |
|---|---|---|---|---|---|---|
| 1997 | — | — | — | — | 1.75 | — |

**DOLLAR** KM# 6 **Composition:** Copper-Nickel **Subject:** Independence Day

| Date | Mintage | F | VF | XF | Unc | BU |
|---|---|---|---|---|---|---|
| 1993 | — | — | — | — | 8.50 | — |

**DOLLAR** KM# 10 **Composition:** Copper-Nickel **Subject:** Preserve Planet Earth **Reverse:** Triceratops

| Date | Mintage | F | VF | XF | Unc | BU |
|---|---|---|---|---|---|---|
| 1993 | — | — | — | — | 9.00 | — |

**DOLLAR** KM# 13 **Composition:** Copper-Nickel **Subject:** Preserve Planet Earth **Reverse:** Ankylosaurus

| Date | Mintage | F | VF | XF | Unc | BU |
|---|---|---|---|---|---|---|
| 1993 | — | — | — | — | 9.00 | — |

**DOLLAR** KM# 14 **Composition:** Copper-Nickel **Subject:** Preserve Planet Earth **Reverse:** Pteranodon

| Date | Mintage | F | VF | XF | Unc | BU |
|---|---|---|---|---|---|---|
| 1993 | — | — | — | — | 9.00 | — |

**DOLLAR** KM# 15 **Composition:** Copper-Nickel **Subject:** Preserve Planet Earth **Reverse:** Cheetah

| Date | Mintage | F | VF | XF | Unc | BU |
|---|---|---|---|---|---|---|
| 1994 | — | — | — | — | 8.50 | — |

**DOLLAR** KM# 16 **Composition:** Copper-Nickel **Subject:** Preserve Planet Earth **Reverse:** Black Rhinoceros

| Date | Mintage | F | VF | XF | Unc | BU |
|---|---|---|---|---|---|---|
| 1994 | — | — | — | — | 8.50 | — |

**DOLLAR** KM# 17 **Composition:** Copper-Nickel **Subject:** Preserve Planet Earth **Reverse:** Black and White Colobus Monkey

| Date | Mintage | F | VF | XF | Unc | BU |
|---|---|---|---|---|---|---|
| 1994 | — | — | — | — | 8.50 | — |

**DOLLAR** KM# 28 **Composition:** Copper-Nickel **Subject:** Preserve Planet Earth **Reverse:** Lions **Note:** Similar to 10 Dollars, KM#29.

| Date | Mintage | F | VF | XF | Unc | BU |
|---|---|---|---|---|---|---|
| 1995PM | — | — | — | — | 8.50 | — |

**DOLLAR** KM# 31 **Composition:** Copper-Nickel **Subject:** Preserve Planet Earth **Reverse:** Cape Eagle owl **Note:** Similar to 10 Dollars, KM#32.

| Date | Mintage | F | VF | XF | Unc | BU |
|---|---|---|---|---|---|---|
| 1995PM | — | — | — | — | 8.50 | — |

**DOLLAR** KM# 34 **Composition:** Copper-Nickel **Subject:** Preserve Planet Earth **Reverse:** Wattled Cranes **Note:** Similar to 10 Dollars, KM#35.

| Date | Mintage | F | VF | XF | Unc | BU |
|---|---|---|---|---|---|---|
| 1996 | — | — | — | — | 8.50 | — |

**DOLLAR** KM# 37 **Composition:** Copper-Nickel **Subject:** Preserve Planet Earth **Reverse:** Laner falcon **Note:** Similar to 10 Dollars, KM#38.

| Date | Mintage | F | VF | XF | Unc | BU |
|---|---|---|---|---|---|---|
| 1996 | — | — | — | — | 8.50 | — |

**DOLLAR** KM# 40 **Composition:** Copper-Nickel **Subject:** Jurassic Park **Obverse:** National emblem **Reverse:** Triceratops, Jurassic Park logo **Note:** Similar to 10 Dollars, KM#41

| Date | Mintage | F | VF | XF | Unc | BU |
|---|---|---|---|---|---|---|
| 1997 | — | — | — | — | 9.00 | — |

**10 DOLLARS** KM# 7 **Weight:** 31.1030 g. **Composition:** 0.9999 Silver 1.0000 oz. ASW **Subject:** Independence Day

| Date | Mintage | F | VF | XF | Unc | BU |
|---|---|---|---|---|---|---|
| 1993 Proof | Est. 30,000 | Value: 45.00 | | | | |

**10 DOLLARS** KM# 11 **Weight:** 28.2800 g. **Composition:** 0.9250 Silver .8411 oz. ASW **Subject:** Preserve Planet Earth **Reverse:** Triceratops

| Date | Mintage | F | VF | XF | Unc | BU |
|---|---|---|---|---|---|---|
| 1993 Proof | Est. 30,000 | Value: 42.50 | | | | |

**10 DOLLARS** KM# 24 **Weight:** 28.2800 g. **Composition:** 0.9250 Silver .8411 oz. ASW **Subject:** Preserve Planet Earth **Reverse:** Ankylosaurus **Note:** Similar to 1 Dollar, KM#13.

| Date | Mintage | F | VF | XF | Unc | BU |
|---|---|---|---|---|---|---|
| 1993 Proof | Est. 30,000 | Value: 42.50 | | | | |

**10 DOLLARS** KM# 25 **Weight:** 28.2800 g. **Composition:** 0.9250 Silver .8411 oz. ASW **Subject:** Preserve Planet Earth **Reverse:** Pteranodon **Note:** Similar to 1 Dollar, KM#14.

| Date | Mintage | F | VF | XF | Unc | BU |
|---|---|---|---|---|---|---|
| 1993 Proof | Est. 30,000 | Value: 42.50 | | | | |

**10 DOLLARS** KM# 18 **Weight:** 28.2800 g. **Composition:** 0.9250 Silver .8411 oz. ASW **Subject:** Preserve Planet Earth **Reverse:** Cheetah

| Date | Mintage | F | VF | XF | Unc | BU |
|---|---|---|---|---|---|---|
| 1994 Proof | Est. 30,000 | Value: 42.50 | | | | |

**10 DOLLARS** KM# 19 **Weight:** 28.2800 g. **Composition:** 0.9250 Silver .8411 oz. ASW **Subject:** Preserve Planet Earth **Reverse:** Black rhinoceros

| Date | Mintage | F | VF | XF | Unc | BU |
|---|---|---|---|---|---|---|
| 1994 Proof | Est. 30,000 | Value: 42.50 | | | | |

**10 DOLLARS** KM# 20 **Weight:** 28.2800 g. **Composition:** 0.9250 Silver .8411 oz. ASW **Subject:** Preserve Planet Earth **Reverse:** Colobus monkey

| Date | Mintage | F | VF | XF | Unc | BU |
|---|---|---|---|---|---|---|
| 1994 Proof | Est. 30,000 | Value: 42.50 | | | | |

**10 DOLLARS** KM# 29 **Weight:** 28.2800 g. **Composition:** 0.9250 Silver .8411 oz. ASW **Subject:** Preserve Planet Earth **Reverse:** Lions

| Date | Mintage | F | VF | XF | Unc | BU |
|---|---|---|---|---|---|---|
| 1995PM Proof | 5,000 | Value: 42.50 | | | | |

**10 DOLLARS** KM# 32 **Weight:** 28.2800 g. **Composition:** 0.9250 Silver .8411 oz. ASW **Subject:** Preserve Planet Earth **Reverse:** Cape Eagle owl

| Date | Mintage | F | VF | XF | Unc | BU |
|---|---|---|---|---|---|---|
| 1995PM Proof | Est. 30,000 | Value: 42.50 | | | | |

**10 DOLLARS** KM# 35 **Weight:** 28.2800 g. **Composition:** 0.9250 Silver .8411 oz. ASW **Subject:** Preserve Planet Earth **Reverse:** Wattled cranes

| Date | Mintage | F | VF | XF | Unc | BU |
|---|---|---|---|---|---|---|
| 1996 Proof | Est. 30,000 | Value: 42.50 | | | | |

**10 DOLLARS** KM# 38 **Weight:** 28.2800 g. **Composition:** 0.9250 Silver .8411 oz. ASW **Subject:** Preserve Planet Earth **Reverse:** Laner falcon

| Date | Mintage | F | VF | XF | Unc | BU |
|---|---|---|---|---|---|---|
| 1996 Proof | Est. 30,000 | Value: 42.50 | | | | |

**10 DOLLARS** KM# 41 **Weight:** 28.2800 g. **Composition:** 0.9250 Silver .8411 oz. ASW **Subject:** Jurassic Park **Obverse:** National emblem **Reverse:** Triceratops, Jurassic Park logo

| Date | Mintage | F | VF | XF | Unc | BU |
|---|---|---|---|---|---|---|
| 1997 Proof | Est. 10,000 | Value: 47.50 | | | | |

**50 DOLLARS** KM# 8 **Weight:** 3.1100 g. **Composition:** 0.9990 Gold .1000 oz. AGW **Subject:** Independence Day **Note:** Similar to 1 Dollar, KM#6.

| Date | Mintage | F | VF | XF | Unc | BU |
|---|---|---|---|---|---|---|
| 1993 Proof | Est. 20,000 | Value: 100 | | | | |

**100 DOLLARS** KM# 26 **Weight:** 6.2200 g. **Composition:** 0.9990 Gold .2000 oz. AGW **Subject:** Preserve Planet Earth **Reverse:** Ankylosaurus **Note:** Similar to 1 Dollar KM#13.

| Date | Mintage | F | VF | XF | Unc | BU |
|---|---|---|---|---|---|---|
| 1993 Proof | Est. 5,000 | Value: 175 | | | | |

**100 DOLLARS** KM# 27 **Weight:** 6.2200 g. **Composition:** 0.9990 Gold .2000 oz. AGW **Subject:** Preserve Planet Earth **Reverse:** Pteranodon **Note:** Similar to 1 Dollar KM#14.

| Date | Mintage | F | VF | XF | Unc | BU |
|---|---|---|---|---|---|---|
| 1993 Proof | Est. 5,000 | Value: 175 | | | | |

**100 DOLLARS** KM# 9 **Weight:** 6.2200 g. **Composition:** 0.9990 Gold .2000 oz. AGW **Subject:** Independence Day

| Date | Mintage | F | VF | XF | Unc | BU |
|---|---|---|---|---|---|---|
| 1993 Proof | Est. 5,000 | Value: 200 | | | | |

**100 DOLLARS** KM# 12 **Weight:** 6.2200 g. **Composition:** 0.9990 Gold .2000 oz. AGW **Subject:** Preserve Planet Earth **Reverse:** Triceratops

| Date | Mintage | F | VF | XF | Unc | BU |
|---|---|---|---|---|---|---|
| 1993 Proof | Est. 5,000 | Value: 175 | | | | |

**100 DOLLARS** KM# 21 **Weight:** 6.2200 g. **Composition:** 0.9990 Gold .2000 oz. AGW **Subject:** Preserve Planet Earth **Obverse:** State emblem **Reverse:** Mother and by cheetah **Note:** Similar to 1 Dollar KM#18.

| Date | Mintage | F | VF | XF | Unc | BU |
|---|---|---|---|---|---|---|
| 1994 Proof | 5,000 | Value: 175 | | | | |

**100 DOLLARS** KM# 22 **Weight:** 6.2200 g. **Composition:** 0.9990 Gold .2000 oz. AGW **Subject:** Preserve Planet Earth **Obverse:** State emblem **Reverse:** Rhinoceros head right **Note:** Similar to 1 Dollar KM#19.

| Date | Mintage | F | VF | XF | Unc | BU |
|---|---|---|---|---|---|---|
| 1994 Proof | 5,000 | Value: 175 | | | | |

**100 DOLLARS** KM# 23 **Weight:** 6.2200 g. **Composition:** 0.9990 Gold .2000 oz. AGW **Subject:** Preserve Planet Earth **Obverse:** State emblem **Reverse:** Colobus monkey **Note:** Similar to 1 Dollar, KM#20.

| Date | Mintage | F | VF | XF | Unc | BU |
|---|---|---|---|---|---|---|
| 1994 Proof | 5,000 | Value: 175 | | | | |

**100 DOLLARS** KM# 30 **Weight:** 6.2200 g. **Composition:** 0.9990 Gold .2000 oz. AGW **Subject:** Preserve Planet Earth **Obverse:** State emblem **Reverse:** Female lion and cub **Note:** Similar to 1 Dollar, KM#29.

| Date | Mintage | F | VF | XF | Unc | BU |
|---|---|---|---|---|---|---|
| 1995 Proof | Est. 5,000 | Value: 185 | | | | |

**100 DOLLARS** KM# 33 **Weight:** 6.2200 g. **Composition:** 0.9990 Gold .2000 oz. AGW **Subject:** Preserve Planet Earth **Obverse:** State emblem **Reverse:** Cape eagle owl **Note:** Similar to 1 Dollar, KM#32.

| Date | Mintage | F | VF | XF | Unc | BU |
|---|---|---|---|---|---|---|
| 1995 Proof | Est. 5,000 | Value: 175 | | | | |

**100 DOLLARS** KM# 36 **Weight:** 6.2200 g. **Composition:** 0.9990 Gold .2000 oz. AGW **Subject:** Preserve Planet Earth **Reverse:** Wattled cranes **Note:** Similar to 1 Dollar, KM#35.

| Date | Mintage | F | VF | XF | Unc | BU |
|---|---|---|---|---|---|---|
| 1996 Proof | Est. 5,000 | Value: 175 | | | | |

**100 DOLLARS** KM# 39 **Weight:** 6.2200 g. **Composition:** 0.9990 Gold .2000 oz. AGW **Subject:** Preserve Planet Earth **Reverse:** Laner falcon **Note:** Similar to 1 Dollar, KM#38.

| Date | Mintage | F | VF | XF | Unc | BU |
|---|---|---|---|---|---|---|
| 1996 Proof | Est. 5,000 | Value: 175 | | | | |

**100 DOLLARS** KM# 42 **Weight:** 6.2200 g. **Composition:** 0.9990 Gold .2000 oz. AGW **Subject:** Jurassic Park **Obverse:** National emblem **Reverse:** Triceratops, Jurassic Park logo

| Date | Mintage | F | VF | XF | Unc | BU |
|---|---|---|---|---|---|---|
| 1997 Proof | Est. 2,500 | Value: 185 | | | | |

## PROVAS

| KM# | Date | Mintage | Identification | Mkt Val |
|---|---|---|---|---|
| PR1 | 1918 | — | Tallero. KM5. | 550 |

# ESTONIA

The Republic of Estonia (formerly the Estonian Soviet Socialist Republic of the U.S.S.R.) is the northernmost of the three Baltic States in Eastern Europe. It has an area of 17,462 sq. mi. (45,100 sq. km.) and a population of 1.6 million. Capital: Tallinn. Agriculture and dairy farming are the principal industries. Butter, eggs, bacon, timber and petroleum are exported.

This small and ancient Baltic state had enjoyed but two decades of independence since the 13th century until the present time. After having been conquered by the Danes, the Livonian Knights, the Teutonic Knights of Germany (who reduced the people to serfdom), the Swedes, the Poles and Russia, Estonia declared itself an independent republic on Feb. 24, 1918 but was not freed until Feb. 1919. The peace treaty was signed Feb. 2, 1920. Shortly after the start of World War II, it was again occupied by Russia and incorporated as the 16th state of the U.S.S.R Germany occupied the tiny state from 1941 to 1944, after which it was retaken by Russia. Most of the nations of the world, including the United States and Great Britain, did not recognize Estonia's incorporation into the Soviet Union.

The coinage, issued during the country's brief independence, is obsolete.

On August 20, 1991, the Parliament of the Estonian Soviet Socialist Republic voted to reassert the republic's independence.

## REPUBLIC
### 1918-1941

### REPUBLIC COINAGE

**MARK** KM# 1 **Composition:** Copper-Nickel

| Date | Mintage | F | VF | XF | Unc | BU |
|---|---|---|---|---|---|---|
| 1922 | 5,025,000 | 1.50 | 2.50 | 5.50 | 12.50 | — |

**MARK** KM# 1a **Composition:** Nickel-Bronze

| Date | Mintage | F | VF | XF | Unc | BU |
|---|---|---|---|---|---|---|
| 1924 | 1,985,000 | 2.00 | 4.00 | 7.50 | 15.00 | — |

**MARK** KM# 5 **Composition:** Nickel-Bronze

| Date | Mintage | F | VF | XF | Unc | BU |
|---|---|---|---|---|---|---|
| 1926 | 3,979,000 | 3.50 | 6.50 | 12.00 | 30.00 | — |

**3 MARKA** KM# 2 **Composition:** Copper-Nickel

| Date | Mintage | F | VF | XF | Unc | BU |
|---|---|---|---|---|---|---|
| 1922 | 2,089,000 | 2.00 | 4.00 | 6.00 | 12.50 | — |

**3 MARKA** KM# 2a **Composition:** Nickel-Bronze

| Date | Mintage | F | VF | XF | Unc | BU |
|---|---|---|---|---|---|---|
| 1925 | 1,134,000 | 4.00 | 7.00 | 12.50 | 30.00 | — |

**3 MARKA** KM# 6 **Composition:** Nickel-Bronze

| Date | Mintage | F | VF | XF | Unc | BU |
|---|---|---|---|---|---|---|
| 1926 | 903,000 | 25.00 | 50.00 | 80.00 | 150 | — |

**5 MARKA** KM# 3 **Composition:** Copper-Nickel

| Date | Mintage | F | VF | XF | Unc | BU |
|---|---|---|---|---|---|---|
| 1922 | 3,983,000 | 3.00 | 5.00 | 8.00 | 20.00 | — |

**5 MARKA** KM# 3a **Composition:** Nickel-Bronze

| Date | Mintage | F | VF | XF | Unc | BU |
|---|---|---|---|---|---|---|
| 1924 | 1,335,000 | 3.50 | 6.00 | 9.00 | 25.00 | — |

**5 MARKA** KM# 7 **Composition:** Nickel-Bronze

| Date | Mintage | F | VF | XF | Unc | BU |
|---|---|---|---|---|---|---|
| 1926 | 1,038,000 | 75.00 | 150 | 200 | 350 | — |

**10 MARKA** KM# 4 **Composition:** Nickel-Bronze

| Date | Mintage | F | VF | XF | Unc | BU |
|---|---|---|---|---|---|---|
| 1925 | 2,200,000 | 3.50 | 7.50 | 12.50 | 37.50 | — |

**10 MARKA** KM# 8 **Composition:** Nickel-Bronze

| Date | Mintage | F | VF | XF | Unc | BU |
|---|---|---|---|---|---|---|
| 1926 | 2,789,000 | 650 | 1,000 | 1,500 | 2,000 | — |

**Note:** Most of this issue were melted down. Not released to circulation

### REFORM COINAGE

100 Senti = 1 Kroon

**SENT** KM# 10 **Composition:** Bronze

| Date | Mintage | F | VF | XF | Unc | BU |
|---|---|---|---|---|---|---|
| 1929 | 23,553,000 | 0.50 | 1.00 | 2.00 | 4.00 | — |

**SENT** KM# 19.2 **Composition:** Bronze **Note:** 0.9 millimeter thick planchet.

| Date | Mintage | F | VF | XF | Unc | BU |
|---|---|---|---|---|---|---|
| 1939 | Inc. above | 4.00 | 8.00 | 15.00 | 35.00 | — |

**SENT** KM# 19.1 **Composition:** Bronze **Note:** 1 millimeter thick planchet.

| Date | Mintage | F | VF | XF | Unc | BU |
|---|---|---|---|---|---|---|
| 1939 | 5,000,000 | 4.00 | 8.00 | 15.00 | 35.00 | — |

**2 SENTI** KM# 15 **Composition:** Bronze

| Date | Mintage | F | VF | XF | Unc | BU |
|---|---|---|---|---|---|---|
| 1934 | 5,838,000 | 1.50 | 2.50 | 4.50 | 10.00 | — |

**5 SENTI** **KM# 11** **Composition:** Bronze

| Date | Mintage | F | VF | XF | Unc | BU |
|---|---|---|---|---|---|---|
| 1931 | 11,000,000 | 1.50 | 2.50 | 4.50 | 10.00 | — |

**10 SENTI** **KM# 12** **Composition:** Nickel-Bronze

| Date | Mintage | F | VF | XF | Unc | BU |
|---|---|---|---|---|---|---|
| 1931 | 4,089,000 | 1.50 | 2.50 | 4.50 | 12.00 | — |

**20 SENTI** **KM# 17** **Composition:** Nickel-Bronze

| Date | Mintage | F | VF | XF | Unc | BU |
|---|---|---|---|---|---|---|
| 1935 | 4,250,000 | 2.00 | 3.50 | 5.50 | 15.00 | — |

**25 SENTI** **KM# 9** **Composition:** Nickel-Bronze

| Date | Mintage | F | VF | XF | Unc | BU |
|---|---|---|---|---|---|---|
| 1928 | 2,025,000 | 3.00 | 6.00 | 10.00 | 25.00 | — |

**25 SENTI** **KM# 18** **Composition:** Nickel-Bronze

| Date | Mintage | F | VF | XF | Unc | BU |
|---|---|---|---|---|---|---|
| 1936 | 1,256,000 | 3.00 | 6.00 | 12.00 | 30.00 | — |

**KROON** **KM# 14** **Weight:** 6.0000 g. **Composition:** 0.5000 Silver .0965 oz. ASW **Subject:** 10th Singing Festival

| Date | Mintage | F | VF | XF | Unc | BU |
|---|---|---|---|---|---|---|
| 1933 | 350,000 | 7.00 | 14.00 | 30.00 | 55.00 | — |

**KROON** **KM# 16** **Composition:** Aluminum-Bronze **Note:** 1990 restrikes which exist are private issues.

| Date | Mintage | F | VF | XF | Unc | BU |
|---|---|---|---|---|---|---|
| 1934 | 3,304,000 | 3.50 | 6.00 | 14.00 | 40.00 | — |

**2 KROONI** **KM# 20** **Weight:** 12.0000 g. **Composition:** 0.50 Silver .1929 oz. ASW **Subject:** Toompea Fortress at Tallinn

| Date | Mintage | F | VF | XF | Unc | BU |
|---|---|---|---|---|---|---|
| 1930 | 1,276,000 | 3.50 | 6.50 | 13.50 | 38.00 | — |

**2 KROONI** **KM# 13** **Weight:** 12.0000 g. **Composition:** 0.5000 Silver .1929 oz. ASW **Subject:** Tercentenary - University of Tartu

| Date | Mintage | F | VF | XF | Unc | BU |
|---|---|---|---|---|---|---|
| 1932 | 100,000 | 10.00 | 20.00 | 30.00 | 50.00 | — |

## NEW REPUBLIC
### 1991 - present
### STANDARD COINAGE

**5 SENTI** **KM# 21** **Composition:** Brass

| Date | Mintage | F | VF | XF | Unc | BU |
|---|---|---|---|---|---|---|
| 1991 | — | — | — | — | 0.25 | — |
| 1992 | — | — | — | — | 0.25 | — |
| 1995 | — | — | — | — | 0.25 | — |

**10 SENTI** **KM# 22** **Composition:** Brass

| Date | Mintage | F | VF | XF | Unc | BU |
|---|---|---|---|---|---|---|
| 1991 | — | — | — | — | 0.50 | — |
| 1992 | — | — | — | — | 0.50 | — |
| 1994 | — | — | — | — | 0.50 | — |
| 1996 | — | — | — | — | 0.50 | — |
| 1997 | — | — | — | — | 0.50 | — |
| 1998 | — | — | — | — | 0.50 | — |

**20 SENTI** **KM# 23** **Composition:** Brass

| Date | Mintage | F | VF | XF | Unc | BU |
|---|---|---|---|---|---|---|
| 1992 | — | — | — | — | 0.75 | — |
| 1996 | — | — | — | — | 0.75 | — |

**20 SENTI** **KM# 23a** **Composition:** Nickel Plated Steel

| Date | Mintage | F | VF | XF | Unc | BU |
|---|---|---|---|---|---|---|
| 1997 | — | — | — | — | 0.75 | — |

**50 SENTI** **KM# 24** **Composition:** Brass

| Date | Mintage | F | VF | XF | Unc | BU |
|---|---|---|---|---|---|---|
| 1992 | — | — | — | — | 1.00 | — |

**KROON** **KM# 28** **Composition:** Copper-Nickel

| Date | Mintage | F | VF | XF | Unc | BU |
|---|---|---|---|---|---|---|
| 1992 In sets only | 20,000 | — | — | — | — | — |
| 1993 | — | — | — | — | 1.50 | — |
| 1995 | — | — | — | — | 1.50 | — |

**KROON** **KM# 35** **Composition:** Brass

| Date | Mintage | F | VF | XF | Unc | BU |
|---|---|---|---|---|---|---|
| 1998 | — | — | — | — | 1.25 | — |

**KROON** **KM#36** **Composition:** Brass **Obverse:** Bird above date **Reverse:** Festival building and denomination

| Date | Mintage | F | VF | XF | Unc | BU |
|---|---|---|---|---|---|---|
| 1999 | 100,000 | — | — | — | 5.00 | — |

**5 KROONI** **KM# 29** **Composition:** Brass **Subject:** 75th Anniversary - Declaration of Independence

| Date | Mintage | F | VF | XF | Unc | BU |
|---|---|---|---|---|---|---|
| 1993 | — | — | — | — | 2.25 | — |
| 1993 Prooflike | — | Value: 4.50 | | | | |

**5 KROONI** **KM# 30** **Composition:** Brass **Subject:** 75th Anniversary - Estonian National Bank

| Date | Mintage | F | VF | XF | Unc | BU |
|---|---|---|---|---|---|---|
| 1994 | — | — | — | — | 2.00 | — |

**10 KROONI** **KM# 25** **Weight:** 28.2800 g. **Composition:** 0.9250 Silver .8411 oz. ASW **Reverse:** Olympics - 2 Sail Boats

| Date | Mintage | F | VF | XF | Unc | BU |
|---|---|---|---|---|---|---|
| 1992 Proof | Est. 20,000 | Value: 47.50 | | | | |

**10 KROONI** **KM# 26** **Weight:** 28.2800 g. **Composition:** 0.9250 Silver .8411 oz. ASW **Reverse:** Barn Swallow

| Date | Mintage | F | VF | XF | Unc | BU |
|---|---|---|---|---|---|---|
| 1992 Proof | Est. 10,000 | Value: 50.00 | | | | |

**10 KROONI** **KM# 32** **Weight:** 16.0000 g. **Composition:** 0.9250 Silver .4758 oz. ASW **Subject:** 80th Anniversary of Nation **Obverse:** Framed dates **Reverse:** Farmer plowing field

| Date | Mintage | F | VF | XF | Unc | BU |
|---|---|---|---|---|---|---|
| ND(1998) Prooflike | Est. 15,000 | — | — | — | 20.00 | — |

**15.65 KROONI** **KM# 37** **Weight:** 1.7300 g. **Composition:** 0.9000 Gold .0501 oz. AGW **Subject:** Estonia's Euro Equivalent **Obverse:** National arms **Reverse:** Cross and stars design

| Date | Mintage | F | VF | XF | Unc | BU |
|---|---|---|---|---|---|---|
| 1999 Proof | Est. 5,000 | Value: 37.50 | | | | |

**100 KROONI** **KM# 27** **Weight:** 24.0000 g. **Composition:** 0.9250 Silver .7135 oz. ASW **Reverse:** Barn Swallows

| Date | Mintage | F | VF | XF | Unc | BU |
|---|---|---|---|---|---|---|
| 1992 Proof | Est. 50,000 | Value: 30.00 | | | | |

**100 KROONI** **KM# 31** **Weight:** 28.28 g. **Composition:** 0.9250 Silver .8411 oz. ASW **Reverse:** Olympics-Nike crowning Wrestler

| Date | Mintage | F | VF | XF | Unc | BU |
|---|---|---|---|---|---|---|
| 1996 | — | — | — | — | 30.00 | — |
| 1996 Proof | 10,000 | Value: 40.00 | | | | |

**100 KROONI** **KM# 33** **Weight:** 27.0000 g. **Composition:** 0.9250 Silver .8030 oz. ASW **Subject:** 80th Ann. of Nation **Obverse:** Framed dates **Reverse:** Male figure and stylized eagle head

| Date | Mintage | F | VF | XF | Unc | BU |
|---|---|---|---|---|---|---|
| ND(1998) Proof | Est. 12,000 | Value: 42.50 | | | | |

**500 KROONI** **KM# 34** **Weight:** 8.6400 g. **Composition:** 0.9000 Gold .2500 oz. AGW **Subject:** 80th Anniversary of Nation **Obverse:** Framed dates **Reverse:** Male figure on horse

| Date | Mintage | F | VF | XF | Unc | BU |
|---|---|---|---|---|---|---|
| ND(1998) Proof | Est. 3,000 | Value: 185 | | | | |

## MINT SETS

| KM# | Date | Mintage | Identification | Issue Price | Mkt Val |
|---|---|---|---|---|---|
| MS1 | 1992 (5) | 20,000 | KM#21-24, 28 | — | 38.50 |

# ETHIOPIA

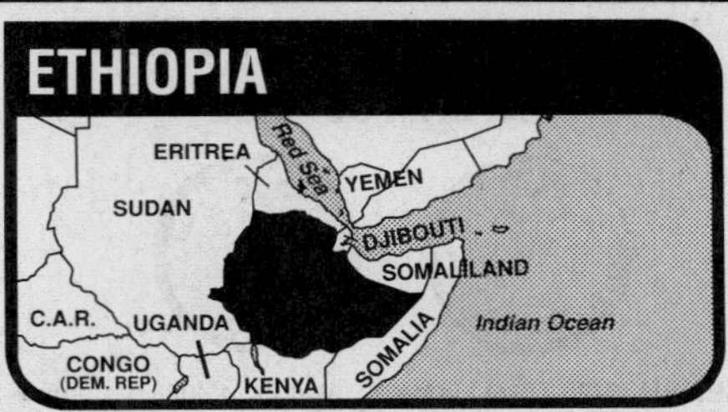


The People's Federal Republic of Ethiopia (formerly the Peoples Democratic Republic and the Empire of Ethiopia), Africa's oldest independent nation, faces the Red Sea in East-Central Africa. The country has an area of 424,214 sq. mi. (1,004,390 sq. km.) and a population of 56 million people who are divided among 40 tribes that speak some 270 languages and dialects. Capital: Addis Ababa. The economy is predominantly agricultural and pastoral. Gold and platinum are mined and petroleum fields are being developed. Coffee, oilseeds, hides and cereals are exported.

Legend claims that Menelik I, the son born to Solomon, King of Israel, by the Queen of Sheba, settled in Axum in North Ethiopia to establish the dynasty, which reigned with only brief interruptions until 1974. Modern Ethiopian history began with the reign of Emperor Menelik II (1889-1913) under whose guidance the country emerged from medieval isolation. Progress continued throughout the reigns of Menelik's daughter, Empress Zauditu, and her successor Emperor Haile Selassie I who was coronated in 1930. Ethiopia was invaded by Italy in 1935, and together with Italian Somaliland and Eritrea became part of Italian East Africa. Victor Emmanuel III, as declared by Mussolini, would be Ethiopia's emperor as well as a king of Italy. Liberated by British and Ethiopian troops in 1941, Ethiopia reinstated Haile Selassie I to the throne. The 225th consecutive Solomonic ruler was deposed by a military committee on Sept 12, 1974. In July 1976 Ethiopia's military provisional government referred to the country as Socialist Ethiopia. After establishing a new regime in 1991, Ethiopia became a federated state and is now the Federal Republic of Ethiopia. Following 2 years of provisional government, the province of Eritrea held a referendum on independence in May 1993 leading to the proclamation of its independence on May 24.

No coins, patterns or presentation pieces are known bearing Emperor Lij Yasu's likeness or titles. Coins of Menelik II were struck during this period with dates frozen.

**RULERS**

Menelik II, 1889-1913
Lij Yasu, 1913-1916
Zauditu, Empress, 1916-1930
Haile Selassie I
1930-36, 1941-1974
Victor Emmanuel III, of Italy
1936-1941

**MINT MARKS**

A - Paris
- Paris, privy marks only

**Coinage of Menelik II, 1889-1913**

**NOTE:** The first national issue coinage, dated 1887 and 1888 E.E., carried a cornucopia, A, and fasces on the reverse. Subsequent dates have a torch substituted for the fasces, the A being dropped. All issues bearing these marks were struck at the Paris Mint. Coins without mint marks were struck in Addis Ababa.

**MONETARY SYSTEM**

**(Until about 1903)**

40 Besa = 20 Gersh = 1 Birr

**(After 1903)**

32 Besa = 16 Gersh = 1 Birr

**DATING**

Ethiopian coinage is dated by the Ethiopian Era calendar (E.E.), which commenced 7 years and 8 months after the advent of A.D. dating.

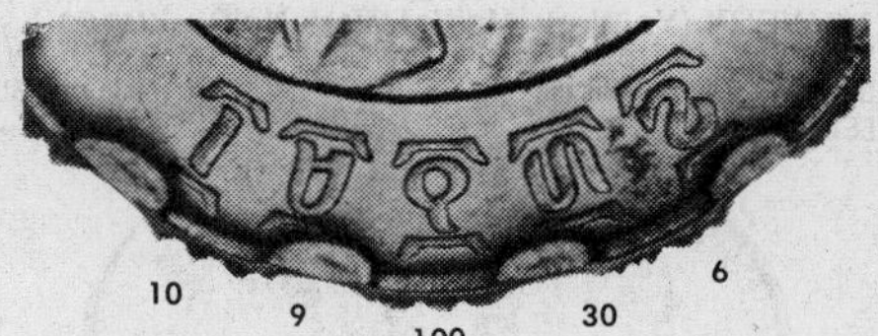

10 9 100 30 6

**EXAMPLE**

1900 (10 and 9 = 19 x 100)
36 (Add 30 and 6)
1936 E.E.
8 (Add)
1943/4 AD

# KINGDOM OF ABYSSINIA

## REFORM COINAGE

**GERSH (1/20 Birr)** **KM# 12** **Weight:** 1.4038 g. **Composition:** 0.8350 Silver .0377 oz. ASW **Reverse:** Lion's left foreleg raised

| Date | Mintage | F | VF | XF | Unc | BU |
|---|---|---|---|---|---|---|
| EE1895A (1903) | 44,789,000 | 2.00 | 3.50 | 6.00 | 15.00 | — |

**Note:** Struck between 1903-1928

**1/4 BIRR (Ya Birr Rub/of Birr Fourth)** **KM# 3** **Weight:** 7.1088 g. **Composition:** 0.8350 Silver .1884 oz. ASW **Reverse:** Lion's left foreleg raised

| Date | Mintage | F | VF | XF | Unc | BU |
|---|---|---|---|---|---|---|
| EE1895A (1903) | 821,000 | 4.00 | 8.00 | 20.00 | 80.00 | — |

**Note:** Struck between 1903 and 1925

**BIRR** **KM# 19** **Weight:** 28.0750 g. **Composition:** 0.8350 Silver .7537 oz. ASW **Reverse:** Lion's right foreleg raised

| Date | Mintage | F | VF | XF | Unc | BU |
|---|---|---|---|---|---|---|
| EE1895 (1903) | 459,000 | 12.50 | 25.00 | 85.00 | 250 | — |
| EE1895 (1903) | Proof | Value:500.00 | | | | |

**Note:** Struck in 1901, 1903 and 1904

**1/2 WERK (Ya Werk Alad/of Werk Half)** **KM# 20** **Weight:** 3.5000 g. **Composition:** 0.9000 Gold .1012 oz. AGW

| Date | Mintage | F | VF | XF | Unc | BU |
|---|---|---|---|---|---|---|
| EE1923 (1931) | — | 175 | 325 | 500 | 850 | — |

**WERK** **KM# 21** **Weight:** 7.0000 g. **Composition:** 0.9000 Gold .2025 oz. AGW

| Date | Mintage | F | VF | XF | Unc | BU |
|---|---|---|---|---|---|---|
| EE1923 (1931) | — | 225 | 450 | 700 | 1,200 | — |

# EMPIRE OF ETHIOPIA

## New Monetary System

## DECIMAL COINAGE

100 Matonas = 100 Santeems
100 Santeems = (Cents)
1 Birr (Dollar)

**MATONA** **KM# 27** **Composition:** Copper

| Date | Mintage | F | VF | XF | Unc | BU |
|---|---|---|---|---|---|---|
| EE1923 (1931) | 1,250,000 | 1.50 | 2.50 | 5.00 | 15.00 | — |

**Note:** Struck by ICI in Birmingham, England. Other denominations in the Matona series were struck in Addis Ababa

**CENT (Ande Santeem)** **KM# 32** **Composition:** Copper

| Date | Mintage | F | VF | XF | Unc | BU |
|---|---|---|---|---|---|---|
| EE19360 (1944) | 20,000 | — | 0.10 | 0.20 | 0.50 | — |

**Note:** Coins in the one cent to fifty cent denominations were struck at Philadelphia, Birmingham and the Royal Mint, London between 1944 and 1975 with the date EE1936 frozen

**5 MATONAS** **KM# 28.1** **Composition:** Copper **Edge:** Plain

| Date | Mintage | F | VF | XF | Unc | BU |
|---|---|---|---|---|---|---|
| EE1923 (1931) | 1,363,000 | 2.00 | 3.50 | 6.00 | 20.00 | — |

**5 MATONAS** **KM# 28.2** **Composition:** Copper **Edge:** Reeded

| Date | Mintage | F | VF | XF | Unc | BU |
|---|---|---|---|---|---|---|
| EE1923 (1931) | Inc. above | 2.00 | 3.50 | 7.00 | 25.00 | — |

**5 CENTS (Amist Santeem)** **KM# 33** **Composition:** Copper

| Date | Mintage | F | VF | XF | Unc | BU |
|---|---|---|---|---|---|---|
| EE1936 (1944) | 219,000,000 | — | 0.10 | 0.20 | 0.50 | — |

**Note:** Struck between 1944-1962 in Philadelphia and 1964-1966 in Birmingham

**10 MATONAS** **KM# 29** **Composition:** Nickel

| Date | Mintage | F | VF | XF | Unc | BU |
|---|---|---|---|---|---|---|
| EE1923 (1931) | 936,000 | 1.50 | 2.50 | 4.50 | 12.50 | — |

**10 CENTS (Assir Santeem)** **KM# 34** **Composition:** Copper

| Date | Mintage | F | VF | XF | Unc | BU |
|---|---|---|---|---|---|---|
| EE1936 (1944) | 348,998,000 | — | 0.10 | 0.25 | 0.75 | — |

**Note:** Struck between 1945-1963 in Philadelphia, 1964-1966 in Birmingham and 1974-1975 in London

**25 MATONAS** **KM# 30** **Composition:** Nickel

| Date | Mintage | F | VF | XF | Unc | BU |
|---|---|---|---|---|---|---|
| EE1923 (1931) | 2,742,000 | 1.25 | 2.00 | 3.25 | 10.00 | — |

**25 CENTS (Haya Amist Santeem)** **KM# 35** **Composition:** Copper

| Date | Mintage | F | VF | XF | Unc | BU |
|---|---|---|---|---|---|---|
| EE1936 (1944) | 10,000,000 | 5.00 | 10.00 | 20.00 | 45.00 | — |

**Note:** 421,500 issued and 1952 withdrawn and replaced by KM#36

**25 CENTS (Haya Amist Santeem)** **KM# 36** **Composition:** Copper

| Date | Mintage | F | VF | XF | Unc | BU |
|---|---|---|---|---|---|---|
| EE1936 (1944) | 30,000,000 | 0.25 | 0.50 | 1.00 | 3.00 | — |

**Note:** Issued in 1952 and 1953. Crude and refined edges

**50 MATONAS** **KM# 31** **Composition:** Nickel

| Date | Mintage | F | VF | XF | Unc | BU |
|---|---|---|---|---|---|---|
| EE1923 (1931) | 1,621,000 | 1.50 | 2.50 | 4.50 | 11.50 | — |

**50 CENTS (Hamsa Santeem)** **KM# 37** **Weight:** 7.0307 g. **Composition:** 0.8000 Silver .1808 oz. ASW

| Date | Mintage | F | VF | XF | Unc | BU |
|---|---|---|---|---|---|---|
| EE1936 (1944) | 30,000,000 | 2.00 | 3.50 | 7.50 | 15.00 | — |

**Note:** Struck in 1944-1945

**50 CENTS (Hamsa Santeem)** **KM# 37a** **Weight:** 7.0307 g. **Composition:** 0.7000 Silver .1582 oz. ASW

| Date | Mintage | F | VF | XF | Unc | BU |
|---|---|---|---|---|---|---|
| EE1936 (1944) | 20,434,000 | 2.00 | 3.50 | 7.50 | 15.00 | — |

**Note:** Struck in 1947

**5 DOLLARS** **KM# 48** **Weight:** 20.0000 g. **Composition:** 0.9250 Silver .5948 oz. ASW **Obverse:** Theodros II

| Date | Mintage | F | VF | XF | Unc | BU |
|---|---|---|---|---|---|---|
| EE1964(1972) F-NI | — | — | — | — | 75.00 | — |
| EE1964(1972) NI Proof | 55,000 | Value: 35.00 | | | | |

**5 DOLLARS** **KM# 49** **Weight:** 20.0000 g. **Composition:** 0.9250 Silver .5948 oz. ASW **Obverse:** Yohannes Iv **Reverse:** Similar to KM#50

| Date | Mintage | F | VF | XF | Unc | BU |
|---|---|---|---|---|---|---|
| EE1964(1972) F-NI | — | — | — | — | 75.00 | — |
| EE1964(1972) NI Proof | 55,000 | Value: 35.00 | | | | |

**5 DOLLARS** **KM# 50** **Weight:** 20.0000 g. **Composition:** 0.9250 Silver .5948 oz. ASW **Obverse:** Menelik II

| Date | Mintage | F | VF | XF | Unc | BU |
|---|---|---|---|---|---|---|
| EE1964(1972) F-NI | — | — | — | — | 85.00 | — |
| EE1964(1972) NI Proof | 60,000 | Value: 35.00 | | | | |

**5 DOLLARS** **KM# 51** **Weight:** 20.0000 g. **Composition:** 0.9250 Silver .5948 oz. ASW **Obverse:** Zauditu bust veiled left

| Date | Mintage | F | VF | XF | Unc | BU |
|---|---|---|---|---|---|---|
| EE1964(1972) F-NI | — | — | — | — | 90.00 | — |
| EE1964(1972) NI Proof | 60,000 | Value: 40.00 | | | | |

**5 DOLLARS** **KM# 52** **Weight:** 25.0000 g. **Composition:** 0.9999 Silver .8030 oz. ASW **Obverse:** Haile Selassie bust right

| Date | Mintage | F | VF | XF | Unc | BU |
|---|---|---|---|---|---|---|
| EE1972(1972) HF Proof | 100,000 | Value: 15.00 | | | | |

**10 DOLLARS** **KM# 38** **Weight:** 4.0000 g. **Composition:** 0.9000 Gold .1157 oz. AGW **Subject:** 75th Anniverary of Birth and 50th Jubilee of Reign of Emperor Haile Selassie I

| Date | Mintage | F | VF | XF | Unc | BU |
|---|---|---|---|---|---|---|
| EE1958(1966) NI Proof | 28,000 | Value: 95.00 | | | | |

**10 DOLLARS** **KM# 53** **Weight:** 40.0000 g. **Composition:** 0.9250 Silver 1.1895 oz. ASW **Obverse:** Emperor Haile Selassie I

| Date | Mintage | F | VF | XF | Unc | BU |
|---|---|---|---|---|---|---|
| EE1964(1972) F-NI | — | — | — | — | 175 | — |
| EE1964(1972) NI Proof | 50,000 | Value: 85.00 | | | | |

**20 DOLLARS** **KM# 39** **Weight:** 8.0000 g. **Composition:** 0.9000 Gold .2315 oz. AGW **Subject:** 75th Anniversary of Birth and 50th Jubilee of Reign of Emperor Haile Selassie I

| Date | Mintage | F | VF | XF | Unc | BU |
|---|---|---|---|---|---|---|
| EE1958(1966) NI Proof | 25,000 | Value: 145 | | | | |

**50 DOLLARS** **KM# 40** **Weight:** 20.0000 g. **Composition:** 0.9000 Gold .5787 oz. AGW **Subject:** 75th Anniversary of Birth and 50th Jubilee of Reign of Emperor Haile Selassie I

| Date | Mintage | F | VF | XF | Unc | BU |
|---|---|---|---|---|---|---|
| EE1958(1966) NI Proof | 15,000 | Value: 300 | | | | |

**50 DOLLARS** **KM# 55** **Weight:** 20.0000 g. **Composition:** 0.9000 Gold .5787 oz. AGW **Obverse:** Bust of Theodros II **Reverse:** Lion

| Date | Mintage | F | VF | XF | Unc | BU |
|---|---|---|---|---|---|---|
| EE1964(1972) NI Proof | 12,000 | Value: 375 | | | | |

**50 DOLLARS** **KM# 56** **Weight:** 20.0000 g. **Composition:** 0.9000 Gold .5787 oz. AGW **Obverse:** Bust of Yohannes IV

| Date | Mintage | F | VF | XF | Unc | BU |
|---|---|---|---|---|---|---|
| EE1964(1972) NI Proof | 12,000 | Value: 375 | | | | |

**50 DOLLARS** **KM# 57** **Weight:** 20.0000 g. **Composition:** 0.9000 Gold .5787 oz. AGW **Obverse:** Bust of Menelik II

| Date | Mintage | F | VF | XF | Unc | BU |
|---|---|---|---|---|---|---|
| EE1964(1972) NI Proof | 20,000 | Value: 375 | | | | |

**50 DOLLARS** **KM# 58** **Weight:** 20.0000 g. **Composition:** 0.9000 Gold .5787 oz. AGW **Obverse:** Bust of Empress Zauditu

| Date | Mintage | F | VF | XF | Unc | BU |
|---|---|---|---|---|---|---|
| EE1964(1972) NI Proof | 16,000 | Value: 375 | | | | |

**100 DOLLARS** **KM# 41** **Weight:** 40.0000 g. **Composition:** 0.9000 Gold 1.1575 oz. AGW **Subject:** 75th Anniversary of Birth and 50th Jubilee of Reign of Emperor Haile Selassie I

| Date | Mintage | F | VF | XF | Unc | BU |
|---|---|---|---|---|---|---|
| EE1958(1966) NI Proof | 11,000 | Value: 550 | | | | |

**100 DOLLARS** **KM# 59** **Weight:** 40.0000 g. **Composition:** 0.9000 Gold 1.1575 oz. AGW **Obverse:** Emperor Haile Selassie I **Note:** Similar to 10 Dollars, KM#53

| Date | Mintage | F | VF | XF | Unc | BU |
|---|---|---|---|---|---|---|
| EE1964(1972) NI Proof | 10,000 | Value: 750 | | | | |

**200 DOLLARS** KM# 42 **Weight:** 80.0000 g. **Composition:** 0.9000 Gold 2.3151 oz. AGW **Subject:** 75th Anniversary of Birth and 50th Jubilee of Reign of Emperor Haile Selassie I

| Date | Mintage | F | VF | XF | Unc | BU |
|---|---|---|---|---|---|---|
| EE1958(1966) NI Proof | 8,823 | Value: 1,175 | | | | |

## MEDALLIC COINAGE

**1/8 BIRR** KM# M1.1 **Composition:** Gold **Obverse:** Empress Zauditu **Reverse:** Denomination obliterated

| Date | Mintage | F | VF | XF | Unc | BU |
|---|---|---|---|---|---|---|
| EE1917 (1925) | — | — | 500 | 900 | 1,800 | — |

**1/8 BIRR** KM# M1.2 **Composition:** Gold **Reverse:** Denomination clear

| Date | Mintage | F | VF | XF | Unc | BU |
|---|---|---|---|---|---|---|
| EE1917 (1925) | — | — | — | 1,250 | — | — |

**1/4 BIRR** KM# M2.1 **Composition:** Gold **Obverse:** Empress Zauditu **Reverse:** Denomination obliterated

| Date | Mintage | F | VF | XF | Unc | BU |
|---|---|---|---|---|---|---|
| EE1917 (1925) | — | — | 750 | 1,500 | 2,500 | — |

**1/4 BIRR** KM# M2.2 **Composition:** Gold **Reverse:** Denomination clear

| Date | Mintage | F | VF | XF | Unc | BU |
|---|---|---|---|---|---|---|
| EE1917 (1925) | — | — | — | 1,750 | 2,800 | — |

**1/2 BIRR** KM# M3 **Composition:** Gold **Obverse:** Empress Zauditu **Reverse:** Denomination obliterated

| Date | Mintage | F | VF | XF | Unc | BU |
|---|---|---|---|---|---|---|
| EE1917 (1925) | — | — | 2,500 | 3,500 | 5,500 | — |

**1/2 BIRR** KM# M3a.1 **Composition:** Silver **Reverse:** Denomination obliterated

| Date | Mintage | F | VF | XF | Unc | BU |
|---|---|---|---|---|---|---|
| EE1917 (1925) | — | — | 1,500 | 2,250 | 3,000 | — |

**1/2 BIRR** KM# M3a.2 **Composition:** Silver **Reverse:** Denomination clear

| Date | Mintage | F | VF | XF | Unc | BU |
|---|---|---|---|---|---|---|
| EE1917 (1925) | — | — | 2,000 | 2,800 | 3,900 | — |

**BIRR** KM# M4 **Composition:** Gold **Obverse:** Empress Zauditu **Reverse:** Denomination obliterated

| Date | Mintage | F | VF | XF | Unc | BU |
|---|---|---|---|---|---|---|
| EE1917 Rare (1925) | 2 | — | — | — | — | — |

**Note:** Bowers and Merena Guia sale 3-88 AU realized $15,400

## TOKEN COINAGE

**PIASTRE (1/16 Thaler)** KM# Tn1 **Composition:** Aluminum

| Date | Mintage | VG | F | VF | XF | Unc |
|---|---|---|---|---|---|---|
| 1922 | — | 12.00 | 25.00 | 40.00 | 60.00 | — |

**Note:** Issued by a commercial syndicate in Dire Dawa

**PIASTRE (1/16 Thaler)** KM# Tn2 **Composition:** Aluminum

| Date | Mintage | VG | F | VF | XF | Unc |
|---|---|---|---|---|---|---|
| ND | — | 10.00 | 20.00 | 35.00 | 55.00 | — |

**Note:** Issued by P. P. Trohalis in Addis Ababa

**PIASTRE (1/16 Thaler)** KM# Tn3 **Composition:** Copper-Nickel-Zinc

| Date | Mintage | VG | F | VF | XF | Unc |
|---|---|---|---|---|---|---|
| ND | — | 25.00 | 40.00 | 65.00 | 85.00 | — |

**Note:** Issued by Magdalinos Freres in Addis Ababa

**PIASTRE (1/16 Thaler)** KM# Tn4 **Composition:** Aluminum

| Date | Mintage | VG | F | VF | XF | Unc |
|---|---|---|---|---|---|---|
| ND | — | 20.00 | 35.00 | 60.00 | 80.00 | — |

**Note:** Issued by Prasso Concessions En Abyssinie

**PIASTRE (1/16 Thaler)** KM# Tn5 **Composition:** Aluminum **Note:** Uniface

| Date | Mintage | VG | F | VF | XF | Unc |
|---|---|---|---|---|---|---|
| ND | — | 25.00 | 45.00 | 75.00 | 90.00 | — |

**Note:** Issued by F. L. in Addis Abada

# PEOPLES DEMOCRATIC REPUBLIC

## DECIMAL COINAGE

**CENT** KM# 43.1 **Composition:** Aluminum **Series:** F.A.O **Obverse:** Small lion head

| Date | Mintage | F | VF | XF | Unc | BU |
|---|---|---|---|---|---|---|
| EE1969 (1977) | 35,034,000 | 0.20 | 0.30 | 0.50 | 1.00 | — |

**CENT** KM# 43.2 **Composition:** Aluminum **Obverse:** Large lion head

| Date | Mintage | F | VF | XF | Unc | BU |
|---|---|---|---|---|---|---|
| EE1969 FM Proof (1977) | 12,000 | Value: 2.50 | | | | |

**5 CENTS** KM# 44.1 **Composition:** Copper-Zinc **Obverse:** Small lion head

| Date | Mintage | F | VF | XF | Unc | BU |
|---|---|---|---|---|---|---|
| EE1969 (1977) | 201,275,000 | 0.20 | 0.30 | 0.50 | 1.00 | — |

**5 CENTS** KM# 44.2 **Composition:** Copper-Zinc **Obverse:** Larage lion head

| Date | Mintage | F | VF | XF | Unc | BU |
|---|---|---|---|---|---|---|
| EE1969 FM Proof (1977) | 12,000 | Value: 2.50 | | | | |

**10 CENTS** **KM# 45.1** **Composition:** Copper-Zinc **Obverse:** Small lion head **Reverse:** Mountain Nyala

| Date | Mintage | F | VF | XF | Unc | BU |
|---|---|---|---|---|---|---|
| EE1969 | 202,722,000 | 0.20 | 0.35 | 0.60 | 1.50 | — |

**10 CENTS** **KM# 45.2** **Composition:** Copper-Zinc **Obverse:** Large lion head

| Date | Mintage | F | VF | XF | Unc | BU |
|---|---|---|---|---|---|---|
| EE1969 FM | — | — | — | — | 1.25 | — |
| EE1969 FM Proof | 12,000 | Value: 4.00 | | | | |

**25 CENTS** **KM# 46.2** **Composition:** Copper-Nickel **Obverse:** Large lion head

| Date | Mintage | F | VF | XF | Unc | BU |
|---|---|---|---|---|---|---|
| EE1969 FM Proof | 12,000 | Value: 4.50 | | | | |

**25 CENTS** **KM# 46.1** **Composition:** Copper-Nickel **Obverse:** Small lion head

| Date | Mintage | F | VF | XF | Unc | BU |
|---|---|---|---|---|---|---|
| EE1969 FM | 44,983,000 | 0.20 | 0.30 | 0.60 | 1.25 | — |

**50 CENTS** **KM# 47.1** **Composition:** Copper-Nickel **Obverse:** Small lion head

| Date | Mintage | F | VF | XF | Unc | BU |
|---|---|---|---|---|---|---|
| EE1969 FM | 27,772,000 | 0.40 | 0.75 | 1.25 | 2.50 | — |

**50 CENTS** **KM# 47.2** **Composition:** Copper-Nickel **Obverse:** Large lion head

| Date | Mintage | F | VF | XF | Unc | BU |
|---|---|---|---|---|---|---|
| EE1969 FM Proof | 12,000 | Value: 7.50 | | | | |

**2 BIRR** **KM# 64** **Composition:** Copper-Nickel **Subject:** World Soccer Games 1982

| Date | Mintage | F | VF | XF | Unc | BU |
|---|---|---|---|---|---|---|
| EE1964 (error) | 7 | — | — | — | 145 | — |
| EE1974 | — | — | — | — | 7.00 | — |

**10 BIRR** **KM# 61** **Weight:** 25.3100 g. **Composition:** 0.9250 Silver .7527 oz. ASW **Subject:** Conservation **Reverse:** Bearded Vulture

| Date | Mintage | F | VF | XF | Unc | BU |
|---|---|---|---|---|---|---|
| EE1970 | 4,002 | — | — | — | 25.00 | — |

**10 BIRR** **KM# 61a** **Weight:** 28.2800 g. **Composition:** 0.9250 Silver .8411 oz. ASW

| Date | Mintage | F | VF | XF | Unc | BU |
|---|---|---|---|---|---|---|
| EE1970 Proof | 3,460 | Value: 35.00 | | | | |

**20 BIRR** **KM# 54** **Weight:** 23.3300 g. **Composition:** 0.9250 Silver .6938 oz. ASW **Subject:** International Year of the Child

| Date | Mintage | F | VF | XF | Unc | BU |
|---|---|---|---|---|---|---|
| EE1972 Proof | 16,000 | Value: 20.00 | | | | |

**20 BIRR** **KM# 65** **Weight:** 23.3300 g. **Composition:** 0.9250 Silver .6938 oz. ASW **Subject:** World Soccer Games 1982 **Obverse:** Similar to 2 Birr, KM#64

| Date | Mintage | F | VF | XF | Unc | BU |
|---|---|---|---|---|---|---|
| EE1974 Proof | 10,000 | Value: 40.00 | | | | |

**20 BIRR** **KM# 73** **Weight:** 23.3300 g. **Composition:** 0.9250 Silver .6938 oz. ASW **Subject:** Decade for Women

| Date | Mintage | F | VF | XF | Unc | BU |
|---|---|---|---|---|---|---|
| 1984 Proof | 372 | Value: 85.00 | | | | |

**20 BIRR** **KM# 74** **Weight:** 23.3300 g. **Composition:** 0.9250 Silver .6938 oz. ASW **Subject:** 50th Anniversary Unicef - Folk Dance

| Date | Mintage | F | VF | XF | Unc | BU |
|---|---|---|---|---|---|---|
| 1998 Proof | — | Value: 28.00 | | | | |

**25 BIRR** **KM# 62** **Weight:** 31.6500 g. **Composition:** 0.9250 Silver .9413 oz. ASW **Subject:** Conservation **Obverse:** Similar to 10 Birr, KM#61 **Reverse:** Mountain nyala

| Date | Mintage | F | VF | XF | Unc | BU |
|---|---|---|---|---|---|---|
| EE1970 | 4,002 | — | — | — | 30.00 | — |

**25 BIRR** **KM# 62a** **Weight:** 35.0000 g. **Composition:** 0.9250 Silver 1.0409 oz. ASW

| Date | Mintage | F | VF | XF | Unc | BU |
|---|---|---|---|---|---|---|
| EE1970 Proof | 3,295 | Value: 40.00 | | | | |

**50 BIRR** **KM# 66** **Weight:** 28.2800 g. **Composition:** 0.9250 Silver .8411 oz. ASW **Subject:** International Year of Disabled Persons

| Date | Mintage | F | VF | XF | Unc | BU |
|---|---|---|---|---|---|---|
| EE1974 (1981) | 11,000 | — | — | — | 32.50 | — |
| EE1974 (1981) Proof | 10,000 | Value: 45.00 | | | | |

**200 BIRR** **KM# 67** **Weight:** 7.1300 g. **Composition:** 0.9000 Gold .2063 oz. AGW **Subject:** World Soccer Games 1982

| Date | Mintage | F | VF | XF | Unc | BU |
|---|---|---|---|---|---|---|
| 1982 Proof | 1,310 | Value: 175 | | | | |

**200 BIRR** **KM# 72** **Weight:** 7.1300 g. **Composition:** 0.9000 Gold .2063 oz. AGW **Subject:** Decade for Women

| Date | Mintage | F | VF | XF | Unc | BU |
|---|---|---|---|---|---|---|
| 1984 Proof | 298 | Value: 250 | | | | |

**400 BIRR** **KM# 60** **Weight:** 17.1700 g. **Composition:** 0.9000 Gold .4968 oz. AGW **Subject:** International Year of the Child

| Date | Mintage | F | VF | XF | Unc | BU |
|---|---|---|---|---|---|---|
| EE1972 (1980) Proof | 3,387 | Value: 185 | | | | |

**500 BIRR** **KM# 68** **Weight:** 15.9800 g. **Composition:** 0.9170 Gold .5006 oz. AGW **Subject:** International Year of Disabled Persons

| Date | Mintage | F | VF | XF | Unc | BU |
|---|---|---|---|---|---|---|
| EE1974 (1981) | 2,007 | — | — | — | 245 | — |
| EE1974 (1981) Proof | 2,042 | Value: 275 | | | | |

**600 BIRR** **KM# 63** **Weight:** 33.4370 g. **Composition:** 0.9000 Gold .9676 oz. AGW **Subject:** Conservation **Reverse:** Walia Ibex

| Date | Mintage | F | VF | XF | Unc | BU |
|---|---|---|---|---|---|---|
| EE1970 (1978) | 547 | — | — | — | 450 | — |
| EE1970 (1978) Proof | 160 | Value: 750 | | | | |

## PATTERNS

Including off metal strikes

| KM# | Date | Mintage | Identification | Mkt Val |
|---|---|---|---|---|
| Pn7 | 1921 | — | 1/2 Werk. Gold. Similar to KM20 (proof) | — |
| Pn8 | 1921 | — | Werk. Gold. Similar to KM21 (proof) | — |

## TRIAL STRIKES

| KM# | Date | Mintage | Identification | Mkt Val |
|---|---|---|---|---|
| TS9 | 1917 | — | 1/2 Birr. Pewter. KM M3. (thin) | 300 |
| TS10 | 1917 | — | Birr. Pewter. KM M4. (thin) | 500 |
| TS11 | 1966 | — | 10 Dollars. Gilt Bronze. KM38 | 50.00 |
| TS12 | 1966 | — | 20 Dollars. Gilt Bronze. KM39 | 80.00 |
| TS13 | 1966 | — | 50 Dollars. Gilt Bronze. KM40 | 130 |
| TS14 | 1966 | — | 100 Dollars. Gilt Bronze. KM41 | 240 |
| TS15 | 1966 | — | 200 Dollars. Gilt Bronze. KM42 | 450 |

**Note:** Issued in cased set of five pieces

## PIEFORTS

| KM# | Date | Mintage | Identification | Issue Price | Mkt Val |
|---|---|---|---|---|---|
| P1 | 1980 | 39 | 20 Birr. KM54 | — | 115 |
| P2 | 1980 | 8 | 400 Birr. KM60 | — | 775 |
| P3 | 1981 | 1,100 | 50 Birr. KM66 | — | 65.00 |
| P4 | 1982 | 520 | 500 Birr. KM68 | — | 1,000 |

## MINT SETS

| KM# | Date | Mintage | Identification | Issue Price | Mkt Val |
|---|---|---|---|---|---|
| MS1 | 1972 (5) | — | KM48-51, 53 | — | 475 |

## PROOF SETS

| KM# | Date | Mintage | Identification | Issue Price | Mkt Val |
|---|---|---|---|---|---|
| PS1 | 1894 (4) | — | KM2-5 | — | 2,600 |
| PS2 | 1966 (5) | 8,823 | KM38-42 | — | 2,250 |
| PS3 | 1972 (10) | — | KM48-51, 53, 55-59 | — | 2,500 |
| PS5 | 1972 (5) | 10,000 | KM55-59 | — | 2,250 |
| PS6 | 1972 (5) | 50,000 | KM48-51, 53 | 46.00 | 220 |
| PS7 | 1977 (5) | 11,724 | KM43.2-47.2 | 25.00 | 21.50 |
| PS8 | 1979 (2) | — | KM61a-62a | — | 75.00 |

# FAEROE ISLANDS

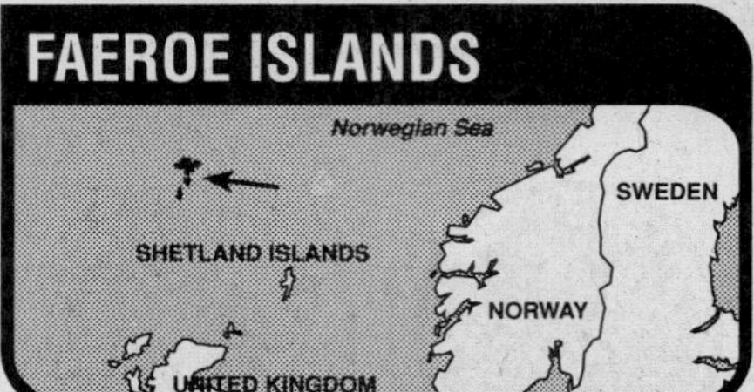


The Faeroe Islands, a self-governing community within the kingdom of Denmark, are situated in the North Atlantic between Iceland and the Shetland Islands. The 17 inhabited islands and numerous islets and reefs have an area of 540 sq. mi. (1,400 sq. km.)and a population of 46,000. Capital: Thorshavn. The principal industries are fishing and livestock. Fish and fish products are exported.

While it is thought that Irish hermits lived on the islands in the 7th and 8th centuries, the present inhabitants are descended from 6th century Norse settlers. The Faeroe Islands became a Norwegian fief in 1035 and became Danish in 1380 when Norway and Denmark were united. They have ever since remained in Danish possession and were granted self-gpvernment (except for an appointed governor-general) with their own legislature, executive and flag in 1948.

The islands were occupied by British troops during World War II, after the German occupation of Denmark. The Faeroe island coinage was struck in London during World War II.

**RULER**
Danish

**MONETARY SYSTEM**
100 Øre = 1 Krone

## DANISH COLONY

### DECIMAL COINAGE

**ORE** **KM# 1** **Composition:** Bronze

| Date | Mintage | F | VF | XF | Unc | BU |
|---|---|---|---|---|---|---|
| 1941 | Est. 200,000 | 20.00 | 40.00 | 60.00 | 85.00 | — |

**Note:** Also struck in 1942 with 1941 dies

| 1941 Proof | — | Value: 550 |
|---|---|---|

**2 ORE** **KM# 2** **Composition:** Bronze

| Date | Mintage | F | VF | XF | Unc | BU |
|---|---|---|---|---|---|---|
| 1941 | Est. 200,000 | 5.00 | 10.00 | 22.50 | 50.00 | — |

**Note:** Also struck in 1942 with 1941 dies

| 1941 Proof | — | Value: 550 |
|---|---|---|

**5 ORE** **KM# 3** **Composition:** Bronze

| Date | Mintage | F | VF | XF | Unc | BU |
|---|---|---|---|---|---|---|
| 1941 | Est. 200,000 | 4.00 | 8.00 | 18.50 | 50.00 | — |

**Note:** Also struck in 1942 with 1941 dies

| 1941 Proof | — | Value: 550 |
|---|---|---|

**10 ORE** **KM# 4** **Composition:** Copper-Nickel

| Date | Mintage | F | VF | XF | Unc | BU |
|---|---|---|---|---|---|---|
| 1941 | Est. 300,000 | 5.50 | 11.00 | 27.50 | 75.00 | — |

**Note:** Also struck in 1942 with 1941 dies

| 1941 Proof | — | Value: 575 |
|---|---|---|

**25 ORE** **KM# 5** **Composition:** Copper-Nickel

| Date | Mintage | F | VF | XF | Unc | BU |
|---|---|---|---|---|---|---|
| 1941 | Est. 250,000 | 7.00 | 12.50 | 30.00 | 85.00 | — |

**Note:** Also struck in 1942 with 1941 dies

| 1941 Proof | — | Value: 575 |
|---|---|---|

## PROOF SETS

| KM# | Date | Mintage | Identification | Issue Price | Mkt Val |
|---|---|---|---|---|---|
| PS1 | 1941 (5) | — | KM1-5 | — | 2,800 |

# FALKLAND ISLANDS

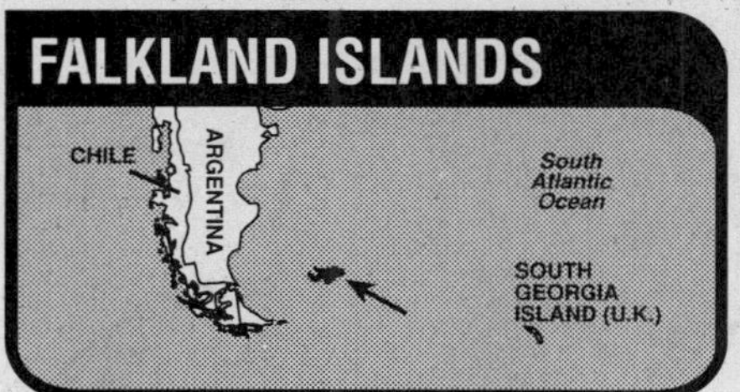


The Colony of the Falkland Islands and Dependencies, a British colony located in the South Atlantic about 500 miles northeast of Cape Horn, has an area of 4,700 sq. mi. (12,170 sq. km.) and a population of 2,121. East Falkland, West Falkland, South Georgia, and South Sandwich are the largest of the 200 islands. Capital: Stanley. Sheep grazing is the main industry. Wool, whale oil, and seal oil are exported.

The Falklands were discovered by British navigator John Davis (Davys) in 1592, and named by Capt. John Strong - for Viscount Falkland, treasurer of the British navy - in 1690. French navigator Louis De Bougainville established the first settlement, at Port Louis, in 1764. The following year Capt. John Byron claimed the islands for Britain and left a small party at Saunders Island. Spain later forced the French and British to abandon their settlements but did not implement its claim to the islands. In 1829 the Republic of Buenos Aires, which claimed to have inherited the Spanish rights, sent Louis Vernet to develop a colony on the islands. In 1831 he seized three American sealing vessels, whereupon the men of the corvette, the U.S.S. Lexington, destroyed his settlement and proclaimed the Falklands to be 'free of all governance'. Britain, which had never renounced its claim, then re-established its settlement in 1833.

**RULERS**
British

**MONETARY SYSTEM**
100 Pence = 1 Pound

# BRITISH COLONY

## DECIMAL COINAGE

**1/2 PENNY** **KM# 1** **Composition:** Bronze **Reverse:** Salmon

| Date | Mintage | F | VF | XF | Unc | BU |
|---|---|---|---|---|---|---|
| 1974 | 140,000 | — | — | 0.10 | 0.25 | — |
| 1974 Proof | 23,000 | Value: 1.50 | | | | |
| 1980 | — | — | — | 0.10 | 0.15 | — |
| 1980 Proof | 10,000 | Value: 1.50 | | | | |
| 1982 | — | — | — | 0.10 | 0.15 | — |
| 1982 Proof | — | Value: 1.50 | | | | |
| 1983 | — | — | — | 0.10 | 0.15 | — |

**PENNY** **KM# 2** **Composition:** Bronze **Reverse:** Gentee penguins

| Date | Mintage | F | VF | XF | Unc | BU |
|---|---|---|---|---|---|---|
| 1974 | 96,000 | — | 0.10 | 0.20 | 0.60 | — |
| 1974 Proof | 23,000 | Value: 2.00 | | | | |
| 1980 | — | — | 0.10 | 0.20 | 0.60 | — |
| 1980 Proof | 10,000 | Value: 2.00 | | | | |
| 1982 | — | — | 0.10 | 0.20 | 0.60 | — |
| 1982 Proof | — | Value: 2.00 | | | | |
| 1983 | — | — | 0.10 | 0.20 | 0.60 | — |
| 1985 | — | — | 0.10 | 0.20 | 0.45 | — |
| 1987 | 111,000 | — | — | 0.20 | 0.45 | — |
| 1987 Proof | — | Value: 2.50 | | | | |
| 1992 | — | — | 0.10 | 0.20 | 0.45 | — |
| 1992 Proof | — | Value: 2.50 | | | | |

**PENNY** **KM# 2a** **Composition:** Copper Plated Steel

| Date | Mintage | F | VF | XF | Unc | BU |
|---|---|---|---|---|---|---|
| 1998 | 2,500 | — | — | — | 0.40 | — |
| 1999 | — | — | — | — | 0.40 | — |
| 1999 Proof | 2,500 | Value: 2.00 | | | | |

**2 PENCE** **KM# 3** **Composition:** Bronze **Reverse:** Upland goose

| Date | Mintage | F | VF | XF | Unc | BU |
|---|---|---|---|---|---|---|
| 1974 | 72,000 | — | 0.10 | 0.15 | 0.50 | — |
| 1974 Proof | 23,000 | Value: 3.00 | | | | |
| 1980 | — | — | 0.10 | 0.15 | 0.40 | — |
| 1980 Proof | 10,000 | Value: 3.00 | | | | |
| 1982 | — | — | 0.10 | 0.15 | 0.40 | — |
| 1982 Proof | — | Value: 3.00 | | | | |
| 1983 | — | — | 0.10 | 0.15 | 0.40 | — |
| 1985 | — | — | 0.10 | 0.15 | 0.40 | — |
| 1987 | 106,000 | — | — | 0.15 | 0.40 | — |
| 1987 Proof | — | Value: 3.50 | | | | |
| 1992 | — | — | 0.10 | 0.15 | 0.40 | — |
| 1992 Proof | — | Value: 3.50 | | | | |

**2 PENCE** **KM# 3a** **Composition:** Copper Plated Steel

| Date | Mintage | F | VF | XF | Unc | BU |
|---|---|---|---|---|---|---|
| 1998 | — | — | — | — | 0.35 | — |
| 1999 | — | — | — | — | 0.35 | — |
| 1999 Proof | 2,500 | Value: 3.00 | | | | |

**5 PENCE** **KM# 4.1** **Composition:** Copper-Nickel **Reverse:** Blackbrowed albatross

| Date | Mintage | F | VF | XF | Unc | BU |
|---|---|---|---|---|---|---|
| 1974 | 67,000 | — | 0.10 | 0.25 | 0.65 | — |
| 1974 Proof | 23,000 | Value: 3.50 | | | | |
| 1980 | — | — | 0.10 | 0.25 | 0.65 | — |
| 1980 Proof | 10,000 | Value: 4.00 | | | | |
| 1982 | — | — | 0.10 | 0.25 | 0.65 | — |
| 1982 Proof | — | Value: 4.00 | | | | |
| 1983 | — | — | 0.10 | 0.25 | 0.65 | — |
| 1985 | — | — | 0.10 | 0.20 | 0.65 | — |
| 1987 | 5,000 | — | — | 0.25 | 0.65 | — |
| 1987 Proof | — | Value: 4.50 | | | | |
| 1992 | — | — | 0.10 | 0.25 | 0.65 | — |
| 1992 Proof | — | Value: 4.50 | | | | |

**5 PENCE** **KM# 4.2** **Composition:** Copper-Nickel

| Date | Mintage | F | VF | XF | Unc | BU |
|---|---|---|---|---|---|---|
| 1998 | — | — | — | — | 0.60 | — |
| 1999 | — | — | — | — | 0.60 | — |
| 1999 Proof | 2,500 | Value: 4.00 | | | | |

**10 PENCE** **KM# 5.1** **Composition:** Copper-Nickel **Reverse:** Ursine seal

| Date | Mintage | F | VF | XF | Unc | BU |
|---|---|---|---|---|---|---|
| 1974 | 87,000 | — | 0.20 | 0.40 | 1.50 | — |
| 1974 Proof | 23,000 | Value: 4.50 | | | | |
| 1980 | — | — | 0.20 | 0.40 | 1.50 | — |
| 1980 Proof | 10,000 | Value: 5.00 | | | | |
| 1982 | — | — | 0.20 | 0.40 | 1.50 | — |
| 1982 Proof | — | Value: 5.00 | | | | |
| 1983 | — | — | 0.20 | 0.40 | 1.50 | — |
| 1985 | — | — | 0.20 | 0.40 | 1.50 | — |
| 1987 | 4,000 | — | — | 0.40 | 1.50 | — |
| 1987 Proof | — | Value: 5.50 | | | | |
| 1992 | — | — | 0.20 | 0.40 | 1.50 | — |
| 1992 Proof | — | Value: 5.50 | | | | |

**10 PENCE KM# 5.2 Composition:** Copper-Nickel

| Date | Mintage | F | VF | XF | Unc | BU |
|---|---|---|---|---|---|---|
| 1998 | — | — | — | — | 1.00 | — |
| 1999 | — | — | — | — | 1.00 | — |
| 1999 Proof | 2,500 | Value: 5.00 | | | | |

**20 PENCE KM# 17 Composition:** Copper-Nickel **Reverse:** Romney marsh sheep

| Date | Mintage | F | VF | XF | Unc | BU |
|---|---|---|---|---|---|---|
| 1982 | — | — | 0.40 | 0.65 | 2.00 | — |
| 1982 Proof | — | Value: 5.00 | | | | |
| 1983 | — | — | 0.40 | 0.65 | 2.00 | — |
| 1985 | — | — | 0.40 | 0.65 | 2.00 | — |
| 1987 | 4,250 | — | 0.40 | 0.65 | 2.00 | — |
| 1987 Proof | — | Value: 5.50 | | | | |
| 1992 | — | — | 0.40 | 0.65 | 2.00 | — |
| 1992 Proof | — | Value: 5.50 | | | | |
| 1999 | — | — | — | — | 2.00 | — |
| 1999 Proof | 2,500 | Value: 5.00 | | | | |

**50 PENCE KM# 10 Composition:** Copper-Nickel **Subject:** Queen's Silver Jubilee

| Date | Mintage | F | VF | XF | Unc | BU |
|---|---|---|---|---|---|---|
| ND (1977) | 100,000 | — | 1.00 | 1.50 | 3.00 | — |

**50 PENCE KM# 10a Weight:** 28.2800 g. **Composition:** 0.9250 Silver .8411 oz. ASW

| Date | Mintage | F | VF | XF | Unc | BU |
|---|---|---|---|---|---|---|
| ND (1977) Proof | 22,000 | Value: 13.50 | | | | |

**50 PENCE KM# 14 Composition:** Copper-Nickel **Reverse:** Falkland Island fox (extinct)

| Date | Mintage | F | VF | XF | Unc | BU |
|---|---|---|---|---|---|---|
| 1980 | — | — | 1.00 | 2.00 | 5.00 | — |
| 1980 Proof | — | Value: 6.00 | | | | |
| 1982 | — | — | 1.00 | 2.00 | 5.00 | — |
| 1982 Proof | — | Value: 6.00 | | | | |
| 1983 | — | — | 1.00 | 2.00 | 5.00 | — |
| 1985 | — | — | 1.00 | 2.00 | 5.00 | — |
| 1987 | 4,000 | — | 1.00 | 2.00 | 5.00 | — |
| 1987 Proof | — | Value: 6.50 | | | | |
| 1992 | — | — | 1.00 | 2.00 | 5.00 | — |
| 1992 Proof | — | Value: 6.50 | | | | |
| 1995 | — | — | — | 2.00 | 5.00 | — |
| 1999 | — | — | — | 2.00 | 5.00 | — |
| 1999 Proof | 2,500 | Value: 6.00 | | | | |

**50 PENCE KM# 15 Composition:** Copper-Nickel **Subject:** 80th Anniversary - Birth of Queen Mother

| Date | Mintage | F | VF | XF | Unc | BU |
|---|---|---|---|---|---|---|
| ND (1980) | — | — | 1.00 | 1.50 | 3.00 | — |

**50 PENCE KM# 15A Weight:** 28.2800 g. **Composition:** 0.9250 Silver .8411 oz. ASW

| Date | Mintage | F | VF | XF | Unc | BU |
|---|---|---|---|---|---|---|
| ND (1980) Proof | — | Value: 13.50 | | | | |

**50 PENCE KM# 16 Composition:** Copper-Nickel **Subject:** Wedding of Prince Charles and Lady Diana

| Date | Mintage | F | VF | XF | Unc | BU |
|---|---|---|---|---|---|---|
| 1981 | — | — | 1.00 | 1.50 | 3.00 | — |

**50 PENCE KM# 16a Weight:** 28.2800 g. **Composition:** 0.9250 Silver .8411 oz. ASW

| Date | Mintage | F | VF | XF | Unc | BU |
|---|---|---|---|---|---|---|
| 1981 Proof | 40,000 | Value: 20.00 | | | | |

**50 PENCE KM# 18a Weight:** 28.2800 g. **Composition:** 0.9250 Silver .8411 oz. ASW

| Date | Mintage | F | VF | XF | Unc | BU |
|---|---|---|---|---|---|---|
| ND (1982) Proof | Est. 25,000 | Value: 15.00 | | | | |

**50 PENCE KM# 18b Weight:** 47.5000 g. **Composition:** 0.9170 Gold 1.4005 oz. AGW **Subject:** Liberation From Argentina Forces

| Date | Mintage | F | VF | XF | Unc | BU |
|---|---|---|---|---|---|---|
| ND (1982) Proof | 25 | Value: 5,500 | | | | |

**50 PENCE KM# 18 Composition:** Copper-Nickel **Subject:** Liberation From Argentina Forces

| Date | Mintage | F | VF | XF | Unc | BU |
|---|---|---|---|---|---|---|
| ND (1982) | — | — | 1.00 | 1.50 | 3.00 | — |

**50 PENCE KM# 19 Composition:** Copper-Nickel **Subject:** 150th Anniversary of British Rule

| Date | Mintage | F | VF | XF | Unc | BU |
|---|---|---|---|---|---|---|
| ND (1983) | Est. 50,000 | — | 1.00 | 2.00 | 5.00 | — |

**50 PENCE KM# 19b Weight:** 47.5400 g. **Composition:** 0.9170 Gold 1.4017 oz. AGW **Subject:** 150th Anniversary of British Rule

| Date | Mintage | F | VF | XF | Unc | BU |
|---|---|---|---|---|---|---|
| ND (1983) Proof | 150 | Value: 1,350 | | | | |

**50 PENCE KM# 19a Weight:** 28.2800 g. **Composition:** 0.9250 Silver .8411 oz. ASW

| Date | Mintage | F | VF | XF | Unc | BU |
|---|---|---|---|---|---|---|
| ND (1983) Proof | Est. 10,000 | Value: 18.50 | | | | |

**50 PENCE KM# 21a Weight:** 28.2750 g. **Composition:** 0.9250 Silver .8410 oz. ASW

| Date | Mintage | F | VF | XF | Unc | BU |
|---|---|---|---|---|---|---|
| ND (1985) Proof | Est. 5,000 | Value: 17.50 | | | | |

**50 PENCE KM# 21 Composition:** Copper-Nickel **Subject:** Opening of Mount Pleasant Airport

| Date | Mintage | F | VF | XF | Unc | BU |
|---|---|---|---|---|---|---|
| ND (1985) | — | — | — | — | 3.00 | — |

**50 PENCE KM# 25 Composition:** Copper-Nickel **Subject:** World Wildlife Fund **Reverse:** King penguins

| Date | Mintage | F | VF | XF | Unc | BU |
|---|---|---|---|---|---|---|
| 1987 | — | — | — | — | 6.00 | — |

**50 PENCE KM# 25a Weight:** 28.2800 g. **Composition:** 0.9250 Silver .8411 oz. ASW

| Date | Mintage | F | VF | XF | Unc | BU |
|---|---|---|---|---|---|---|
| 1987 Proof | Est. 25,000 | Value: 32.50 | | | | |

**50 PENCE KM# 26a Weight:** 28.2800 g. **Composition:** 0.9250 Silver .8411 oz. ASW

| Date | Mintage | F | VF | XF | Unc | BU |
|---|---|---|---|---|---|---|
| 1990 Proof | — | Value: 37.50 | | | | |

**50 PENCE** **KM# 26** **Composition:** Copper-Nickel **Subject:** Children's Fund

| Date | Mintage | F | VF | XF | Unc | BU |
|---|---|---|---|---|---|---|
| 1990 | Est. 20,000 | — | — | — | 4.50 | — |

**50 PENCE** **KM# 34** **Composition:** Copper-Nickel **Subject:** 40th Anniversary - Reign of Queen Elizabeth II

| Date | Mintage | F | VF | XF | Unc | BU |
|---|---|---|---|---|---|---|
| ND (1992) | — | — | — | — | 4.50 | — |

**50 PENCE** **KM# 34a** **Weight:** 28.2800 g. **Composition:** 0.9250 Silver .8411 oz. ASW

| Date | Mintage | F | VF | XF | Unc | BU |
|---|---|---|---|---|---|---|
| ND (1992) Proof | 5,000 | Value: 50.00 | | | | |

**50 PENCE** **KM# 34b** **Weight:** 47.5400 g. **Composition:** 0.9170 Gold 1.4011 oz. AGW **Subject:** 40th Aniversary - Reign of Queen Elizabeth

| Date | Mintage | F | VF | XF | Unc | BU |
|---|---|---|---|---|---|---|
| ND (1992) Proof | 150 | Value: 950 | | | | |

**50 PENCE** **KM# 43a** **Weight:** 28.2800 g. **Composition:** 0.9250 Silver .8411 oz. ASW

| Date | Mintage | F | VF | XF | Unc | BU |
|---|---|---|---|---|---|---|
| ND (1993) Proof | Est. 10,000 | Value: 55.00 | | | | |

**50 PENCE** **KM# 43** **Composition:** Copper-Nickel **Subject:** 40th Anniversary - Coronation of Queen Elizabeth II

| Date | Mintage | F | VF | XF | Unc | BU |
|---|---|---|---|---|---|---|
| ND (1993) | — | — | — | — | 6.50 | — |

**50 PENCE** **KM# 45** **Composition:** Copper-Nickel **Subject:** V. E.-Day 50th Anniversary

| Date | Mintage | F | VF | XF | Unc | BU |
|---|---|---|---|---|---|---|
| 1995 | — | — | — | — | 5.50 | — |

**50 PENCE** **KM# 45a** **Weight:** 28.2800 g. **Composition:** 0.9250 Silver .8411 oz. ASW

| Date | Mintage | F | VF | XF | Unc | BU |
|---|---|---|---|---|---|---|
| 1995 Proof | Est. 10,000 | Value: 50.00 | | | | |

**50 PENCE** **KM# 45b** **Weight:** 47.5400 g. **Composition:** 0.9170 Gold 1.4011 oz. AGW **Subject:** V.E. -Day 50th Anniversary

| Date | Mintage | F | VF | XF | Unc | BU |
|---|---|---|---|---|---|---|
| 1995 Proof | Est. 100 | Value: 1,100 | | | | |

**50 PENCE** **KM# 46a** **Weight:** 28.2800 g. **Composition:** 0.9250 Silver .8411 oz. ASW

| Date | Mintage | F | VF | XF | Unc | BU |
|---|---|---|---|---|---|---|
| 1996 Proof | — | Value: 50.00 | | | | |

**50 PENCE** **KM# 46** **Composition:** Copper-Nickel **Subject:** Queen Elizabeth II's 70th Birthday **Obverse:** Queen's portrait **Reverse:** Queen and Prince Philip as young adults

| Date | Mintage | F | VF | XF | Unc | BU |
|---|---|---|---|---|---|---|
| 1996 | — | — | — | — | 8.00 | — |

**50 PENCE** **KM# 59** **Composition:** Copper-Nickel **Subject:** WWF - Conserving Nature **Obverse:** Queen's portrait **Reverse:** Pair of Black-browed Albatross

| Date | Mintage | F | VF | XF | Unc | BU |
|---|---|---|---|---|---|---|
| 1997 | — | — | — | — | 8.00 | — |

**50 PENCE** **KM# 59a** **Weight:** 28.2800 g. **Composition:** 0.9250 Silver .8410 oz. ASW

| Date | Mintage | F | VF | XF | Unc | BU |
|---|---|---|---|---|---|---|
| 1997 Proof | Est. 15,000 | Value: 40.00 | | | | |

**50 PENCE** **KM# 60** **Composition:** Copper-Nickel **Subject:** WWF - Conserving Nature **Obverse:** Queen's portrait **Reverse:** Peale's dolphin

| Date | Mintage | F | VF | XF | Unc | BU |
|---|---|---|---|---|---|---|
| 1998 | — | — | — | — | 8.00 | — |

**50 PENCE** **KM# 66a** **Weight:** 28.2800 g. **Composition:** 0.9250 Silver .8410 oz. ASW

| Date | Mintage | F | VF | XF | Unc | BU |
|---|---|---|---|---|---|---|
| 1999 Proof | 2,500 | Value: 50.00 | | | | |

**50 PENCE** **KM# 66b** **Weight:** 47.5400 g. **Composition:** 0.9160 Gold 1.4010 oz. AGW

| Date | Mintage | F | VF | XF | Unc | BU |
|---|---|---|---|---|---|---|
| 1999 Proof | 125 | Value: 1,500 | | | | |

**50 PENCE** **KM# 66** **Weight:** 28.2800 g. **Composition:** Copper-Nickel **Subject:** Winston Churchill **Obverse:** Queen's head right **Reverse:** Churchill in Admiral's uniform

| Date | Mintage | F | VF | XF | Unc | BU |
|---|---|---|---|---|---|---|
| 1999 | — | — | — | — | 8.00 | — |

**1/2 POUND** **KM# 6** **Weight:** 3.9900 g. **Composition:** 0.9170 Gold .1176 oz. AGW **Reverse:** Romney marsh sheep

| Date | Mintage | F | VF | XF | Unc | BU |
|---|---|---|---|---|---|---|
| 1974 Proof | 2,673 | Value: 150 | | | | |

**POUND** **KM# 7** **Weight:** 7.9900 g. **Composition:** 0.9170 Gold .2356 oz. AGW **Reverse:** Romney marsh sheep

| Date | Mintage | F | VF | XF | Unc | BU |
|---|---|---|---|---|---|---|
| 1974 Proof | 2,675 | Value: 250 | | | | |

**POUND** **KM# 24** **Composition:** Nickel-Brass

| Date | Mintage | F | VF | XF | Unc | BU |
|---|---|---|---|---|---|---|
| 1987 | — | — | — | — | 3.50 | — |
| 1987 Proof | 2,500 | Value: 12.50 | | | | |
| 1992 | — | — | — | — | 3.50 | — |
| 1992 Proof | — | Value: 12.50 | | | | |
| 1999 | — | — | — | — | 3.50 | — |
| 1999 Proof | 2,500 | Value: 12.50 | | | | |

**POUND** **KM# 24a** **Weight:** 9.5000 g. **Composition:** 0.9250 Silver .2825 oz. ASW

| Date | Mintage | F | VF | XF | Unc | BU |
|---|---|---|---|---|---|---|
| 1987 Proof | Est. 5,000 | Value: 22.50 | | | | |

**POUND** **KM# 24b** **Weight:** 19.6500 g. **Composition:** 0.9170 Gold .5791 oz. AGW **Reverse:** Romney marsh sheep

| Date | Mintage | F | VF | XF | Unc | BU |
|---|---|---|---|---|---|---|
| 1987 Proof | Est. 200 | Value: 600 | | | | |

**2 POUNDS** **KM# 8** **Weight:** 15.9800 g. **Composition:** 0.9170 Gold .4712 oz. AGW **Reverse:** Romney marsh sheep

| Date | Mintage | F | VF | XF | Unc | BU |
|---|---|---|---|---|---|---|
| 1974 Proof | 2,158 | Value: 500 | | | | |

**2 POUNDS** **KM# 22** **Weight:** 28.2800 g. **Composition:** 0.5000 Silver .4546 oz. ASW **Subject:** Commonwealth Games

| Date | Mintage | F | VF | XF | Unc | BU |
|---|---|---|---|---|---|---|
| 1986 | Est. 50,000 | — | — | — | 32.00 | — |

**2 POUNDS** **KM# 22a** **Weight:** 28.2800 g. **Composition:** 0.9250 Silver .8411 oz. ASW

| Date | Mintage | F | VF | XF | Unc | BU |
|---|---|---|---|---|---|---|
| 1986 | Est. 20,000 | Value: 45.00 | | | | |

**2 POUNDS** **KM# 32** **Weight:** 28.2800 g. **Composition:** 0.9250 Silver .8411 oz. ASW **Subject:** 10th Wedding Anniversary - Prince Charles and Lady Diana

| Date | Mintage | F | VF | XF | Unc | BU |
|---|---|---|---|---|---|---|
| 1991 Proof | Est. 10,000 | Value: 40.00 | | | | |

**2 POUNDS** **KM# 35a** **Weight:** 28.2800 g. **Composition:** 0.9250 Silver .8411 oz. ASW

| Date | Mintage | F | VF | XF | Unc | BU |
|---|---|---|---|---|---|---|
| 1992 Proof | Est. 7,500 | Value: 37.50 | | | | |

**2 POUNDS** **KM# 35** **Composition:** Copper-Nickel **Subject:** Heritage Year

| Date | Mintage | F | VF | XF | Unc | BU |
|---|---|---|---|---|---|---|
| 1992 | — | — | — | — | 11.50 | — |

**2 POUNDS** **KM# 47** **Composition:** Copper-Nickel **Subject:** Royal Heritage - Egbert of Wessex **Obverse:** Queen's portrait **Reverse:** Egbert in archway, dates

| Date | Mintage | F | VF | XF | Unc | BU |
|---|---|---|---|---|---|---|
| 1996 | — | — | — | — | 11.50 | — |

**2 POUNDS** **KM# 48** **Composition:** Copper-Nickel **Subject:** Royal Heritage - Alfred the Great **Obverse:** Queen's portrait **Reverse:** Alfred w/axe, scroll, ancient coin, dates

| Date | Mintage | F | VF | XF | Unc | BU |
|---|---|---|---|---|---|---|
| 1996 | — | — | — | — | 11.50 | — |

**2 POUNDS** **KM# 49** **Composition:** Copper-Nickel **Subject:** Royal Heritage -Edward the Confessor **Obverse:** Queen's portrait **Reverse:** Edward with halo offering miniature church; dates

| Date | Mintage | F | VF | XF | Unc | BU |
|---|---|---|---|---|---|---|
| 1996 | — | — | — | — | 11.50 | — |

**2 POUNDS** **KM# 50** **Composition:** Copper-Nickel **Subject:** Royal Heritage - William I **Obverse:** Queen's portrait **Reverse:** Seated William w/shield, minature church, Domesday Book, dates

| Date | Mintage | F | VF | XF | Unc | BU |
|---|---|---|---|---|---|---|
| 1996 | — | — | — | — | 11.50 | — |

**2 POUNDS** **KM# 51** **Composition:** Copper-Nickel **Subject:** Royal Heritage - Henry II **Obverse:** Queen's portrait **Reverse:** Crowned bust of Henry II; dates

| Date | Mintage | F | VF | XF | Unc | BU |
|---|---|---|---|---|---|---|
| 1996 | — | — | — | — | 11.50 | — |

**2 POUNDS** **KM# 52** **Composition:** Copper-Nickel **Subject:** Royal Heritage - Richard I The Lionheart **Obverse:** Queen's portrait **Reverse:** Seated Richard flanked by sun and crescent moon; dates

| Date | Mintage | F | VF | XF | Unc | BU |
|---|---|---|---|---|---|---|
| 1996 | — | — | — | — | 11.50 | — |

**2 POUNDS** **KM# 53** **Composition:** Copper-Nickel **Subject:** Royal Heritage - Henry IV **Obverse:** Queen's portrait **Reverse:** Portrait of Henry in crown and cape; dates

| Date | Mintage | F | VF | XF | Unc | BU |
|---|---|---|---|---|---|---|
| 1996 | — | — | — | — | 11.50 | — |

**2 POUNDS** **KM# 54** **Composition:** Copper-Nickel **Subject:** Royal Heritage - Edward IV **Obverse:** Queen's portrait **Reverse:** Youthful Edward portrait

| Date | Mintage | F | VF | XF | Unc | BU |
|---|---|---|---|---|---|---|
| 1996 | — | — | — | — | 11.50 | — |

**2 POUNDS** **KM# 55** **Composition:** Copper-Nickel **Subject:** Royal Heritage - Henry VIII **Obverse:** Queen's portrait **Reverse:** Standing Henry w/shield; dates

| Date | Mintage | F | VF | XF | Unc | BU |
|---|---|---|---|---|---|---|
| 1996 | — | — | — | — | 11.50 | — |

**2 POUNDS** **KM# 56** **Composition:** Copper-Nickel **Subject:** Royal Heritage - Elizabeth I **Obverse:** Queen Elizabeth II's portrait **Reverse:** Bust of Queen Elizabeth I; dates

| Date | Mintage | F | VF | XF | Unc | BU |
|---|---|---|---|---|---|---|
| 1996 | — | — | — | — | 11.50 | — |

**2 POUNDS** **KM# 57** **Composition:** Copper-Nickel **Subject:** Royal Heritage - Charles I **Obverse:** Queen's portrait **Reverse:** Smiling portrait of Charles, shield, dates

| Date | Mintage | F | VF | XF | Unc | BU |
|---|---|---|---|---|---|---|
| 1996 | — | — | — | — | 11.50 | — |

**2 POUNDS** **KM# 58** **Composition:** Copper-Nickel **Subject:** Royal Heritage - Victoria **Obverse:** Queen Elizabeth II's portrait **Reverse:** Seated Queen Victoria w/sceptre, shield

| Date | Mintage | F | VF | XF | Unc | BU |
|---|---|---|---|---|---|---|
| 1996 | — | — | — | — | 11.50 | — |

**2 POUNDS** **KM# 47a** **Weight:** 28.2800 g. **Composition:** 0.9250 Silver .8411 oz. ASW

| Date | Mintage | F | VF | XF | Unc | BU |
|---|---|---|---|---|---|---|
| 1996 Proof | Est. 10,000 | Value: 50.00 | | | | |

**2 POUNDS** **KM# 48a** **Center Weight:** 28.2800 g. **Center Composition:** 0.9250 Silver .8411 oz. ASW

| Date | Mintage | F | VF | XF | Unc | BU |
|---|---|---|---|---|---|---|
| 1996 Proof | Est. 10,000 | Value: 45.00 | | | | |

**2 POUNDS** **KM# 49a** **Center Weight:** 28.2800 g. **Center Composition:** 0.9250 Silver .8411 oz. ASW

| Date | Mintage | F | VF | XF | Unc | BU |
|---|---|---|---|---|---|---|
| 1996 Proof | Est. 10,000 | Value: 45.00 | | | | |

**2 POUNDS** **KM# 50a** **Center Weight:** 28.2800 g. **Center Composition:** 0.9250 Silver .8411 oz. ASW

| Date | Mintage | F | VF | XF | Unc | BU |
|---|---|---|---|---|---|---|
| 1996 Proof | Est. 10,000 | Value: 45.00 | | | | |

**2 POUNDS** **KM# 51a** **Center Weight:** 28.2800 g. **Center Composition:** 0.9250 Silver .8411 oz. ASW

| Date | Mintage | F | VF | XF | Unc | BU |
|---|---|---|---|---|---|---|
| 1996 Proof | Est. 10,000 | Value: 45.00 | | | | |

**2 POUNDS** **KM# 52a** **Center Weight:** 28.2800 g. **Center Composition:** 0.9250 Silver .8411 oz. ASW

| Date | Mintage | F | VF | XF | Unc | BU |
|---|---|---|---|---|---|---|
| 1996 Proof | Est. 10,000 | Value: 45.00 | | | | |

**2 POUNDS** **KM# 53a** **Center Weight:** 28.2800 g. **Center Composition:** 0.9250 Silver .8411 oz. ASW

| Date | Mintage | F | VF | XF | Unc | BU |
|---|---|---|---|---|---|---|
| 1996 Proof | Est. 10,000 | Value: 45.00 | | | | |

**2 POUNDS** **KM# 54a** **Center Weight:** 28.2800 g. **Center Composition:** 0.9250 Silver .8411 oz. ASW

| Date | Mintage | F | VF | XF | Unc | BU |
|---|---|---|---|---|---|---|
| 1996 Proof | Est. 10,000 | Value: 45.00 | | | | |

**2 POUNDS** **KM# 55a** **Center Weight:** 28.2800 g. **Center Composition:** 0.9250 Silver .8411 oz. ASW

| Date | Mintage | F | VF | XF | Unc | BU |
|---|---|---|---|---|---|---|
| 1996 Proof | Est. 10,000 | Value: 45.00 | | | | |

**2 POUNDS** **KM# 56a** **Center Weight:** 28.2800 g. **Center Composition:** 0.9250 Silver .8411 oz. ASW

| Date | Mintage | F | VF | XF | Unc | BU |
|---|---|---|---|---|---|---|
| 1996 Proof | Est. 10,000 | Value: 45.00 | | | | |

**2 POUNDS** **KM# 57a** **Center Weight:** 28.2800 g. **Center Composition:** 0.9250 Silver .8411 oz. ASW

| Date | Mintage | F | VF | XF | Unc | BU |
|---|---|---|---|---|---|---|
| 1996 Proof | Est. 10,000 | Value: 45.00 | | | | |

**2 POUNDS** **KM# 58a** **Center Weight:** 28.2800 g. **Center Composition:** 0.9250 Silver .8411 oz. ASW

| Date | Mintage | F | VF | XF | Unc | BU |
|---|---|---|---|---|---|---|
| 1996 Proof | Est. 10,000 | Value: 45.00 | | | | |

**2 POUNDS** **KM# 61a** **Center Weight:** 28.2800 g. **Center Composition:** 0.9250 Silver .8411 oz. ASW

| Date | Mintage | F | VF | XF | Unc | BU |
|---|---|---|---|---|---|---|
| 1998 Proof | Est. 10,000 | Value: 50.00 | | | | |

**2 POUNDS** **KM# 61** **Composition:** Copper-Nickel **Subject:** Flying Doctyor Service **Obverse:** Queen's portrait **Reverse:** Two airplanes in flight

| Date | Mintage | F | VF | XF | Unc | BU |
|---|---|---|---|---|---|---|
| 1998 | — | — | — | — | 8.50 | — |

**2 POUNDS** **KM# 64** **Composition:** Copper-Nickel **Subject:** Sir Ernest Henry Shackleton **Obverse:** Queen's portrait **Reverse:** Cameo portrait and icebound ship "Endurance"

| Date | Mintage | F | VF | XF | Unc | BU |
|---|---|---|---|---|---|---|
| 1999 | — | — | — | — | 8.50 | — |

**2 POUNDS** **KM# 64a** **Center Weight:** 28.2800 g. **Center Composition:** 0.9250 Silver .8411 oz. ASW

| Date | Mintage | F | VF | XF | Unc | BU |
|---|---|---|---|---|---|---|
| 1999 Proof | Est. 10,000 | Value: 50.00 | | | | |

**2 POUNDS** **KM# 69** **Ring Composition:** Nickel-Brass **Center Weight:** 28.2800 g. **Center Composition:** Copper-Nickel **Obverse:** Queen's head right **Reverse:** Island map, radiant sun in circle of wildlife **Edge:** Plain

| Date | Mintage | F | VF | XF | Unc | BU |
|---|---|---|---|---|---|---|
| 1999 | — | — | — | — | 10.00 | — |
| 1999 Proof | 2,500 | Value: 20.00 | | | | |

**2 POUNDS** **KM# 67a** **Center Weight:** 28.2800 g. **Center Composition:** 0.9250 Silver .8411 oz. ASW

| Date | Mintage | F | VF | XF | Unc | BU |
|---|---|---|---|---|---|---|
| 2000 Proof | 10,000 | Value: 47.50 | | | | |

**2 POUNDS** **KM# 67** **Weight:** 28.2800 g. **Composition:** Copper-Nickel **Subject:** The Gold Rush - "Vicar of Bray" Ship **Obverse:** Queen's head right **Reverse:** "Vicar of Bray" in harbar **Edge:** Reeded

| Date | Mintage | F | VF | XF | Unc | BU |
|---|---|---|---|---|---|---|
| 2000 | — | — | — | — | 8.50 | — |

**5 POUNDS** **KM# 9** **Weight:** 39.9400 g. **Composition:** 0.9170 Gold 1.1773 oz. AGW **Obverse:** Queen's portrait **Rev. Legend:** Romney marsh sheep

| Date | Mintage | F | VF | XF | Unc | BU |
|---|---|---|---|---|---|---|
| 1974 Proof | 2,158 | Value: 1,100 | | | | |

**5 POUNDS** **KM# 11** **Weight:** 28.2800 g. **Composition:** 0.9250 Silver .8411 oz. ASW **Subject:** Conservation **Obverse:** Portrait of Queen Elizabeth II **Obv. Legend:** Humpback whale

| Date | Mintage | F | VF | XF | Unc | BU |
|---|---|---|---|---|---|---|
| 1979 | 3,998 | — | — | — | 30.00 | — |
| 1979 Proof | 3,432 | Value: 45.00 | | | | |

**5 POUNDS** **KM# 27a** **Weight:** 28.2800 g. **Composition:** 0.9250 Silver .8411 oz. ASW

| Date | Mintage | F | VF | XF | Unc | BU |
|---|---|---|---|---|---|---|
| 1990 Proof | Est. 10,000 | Value: 37.50 | | | | |

**5 POUNDS** **KM# 27** **Composition:** Copper-Nickel **Subject:** 90th Birthday of Queen Mother

| Date | Mintage | F | VF | XF | Unc | BU |
|---|---|---|---|---|---|---|
| 1990 | — | — | — | — | 17.50 | — |

**5 POUNDS** **KM# 33** **Weight:** 39.9400 g. **Composition:** 0.9170 Gold 1.1773 oz. AGW **Subject:** 10th Wedding Anniversary - Prince Charles and Lady Diana **Obverse:** Portrait of Queen

**Reverse:** Facing cameo portraits of Prince Charles and Princess Diana **Note:** Similar to 2 Pounds, KM#32

| Date | Mintage | F | VF | XF | Unc | BU |
|---|---|---|---|---|---|---|
| 1991 Proof | Est. 200 | Value: 850 | | | | |

**5 POUNDS** **KM# 36** **Composition:** Copper-Nickel **Subject:** 10th Anniversary of Liberation

| Date | Mintage | F | VF | XF | Unc | BU |
|---|---|---|---|---|---|---|
| 1992 | — | — | — | — | 15.00 | — |

**5 POUNDS** **KM# 36b** **Weight:** 39.9400 g. **Composition:** 0.9170 Gold 1.1773 oz. AGW **Subject:** 10th Anniversary of Liberation

| Date | Mintage | F | VF | XF | Unc | BU |
|---|---|---|---|---|---|---|
| 1992 Proof | 100 | Value: 1,000 | | | | |

**5 POUNDS** **KM# 36a** **Weight:** 28.2800 g. **Composition:** 0.9250 Silver .8411 oz. ASW

| Date | Mintage | F | VF | XF | Unc | BU |
|---|---|---|---|---|---|---|
| 1992 Proof | Est. 5,000 | Value: 50.00 | | | | |

**5 POUNDS** **KM# 37** **Weight:** 28.2800 g. **Composition:** 0.9250 Silver .8411 oz. ASW **Subject:** 400th Anniversary of Discovery - Ship "Desire"

| Date | Mintage | F | VF | XF | Unc | BU |
|---|---|---|---|---|---|---|
| ND (1992) Proof | Est. 20,000 | Value: 40.00 | | | | |

**5 POUNDS** **KM# 63** **Composition:** Copper-Nickel **Subject:** Queen's Golden Wedding Anniversary **Obverse:** Queen's portrait **Reverse:** Royal couple

| Date | Mintage | F | VF | XF | Unc | BU |
|---|---|---|---|---|---|---|
| 1997 | — | — | — | — | 20.00 | — |

**10 POUNDS** **KM# 12** **Weight:** 35.0000 g. **Composition:** 0.9250 Silver 1.0409 oz. ASW **Subject:** Conservation **Obverse:** Portrait of Queen Elizabeth II **Reverse:** Flightless steamer duck

| Date | Mintage | F | VF | XF | Unc | BU |
|---|---|---|---|---|---|---|
| 1979 | 3,996 | — | — | — | 35.00 | — |
| 1979 Proof | 3,247 | Value: 50.00 | | | | |

**10 POUNDS** **KM# 28** **Weight:** 3.1300 g. **Composition:** 0.9990 Gold .1000 oz. AGW **Subject:** 90th Birthday of Queen Mother **Obverse:** Portrait of Queen Elizabeth

| Date | Mintage | F | VF | XF | Unc | BU |
|---|---|---|---|---|---|---|
| ND (1990) Proof | Est. 750 | Value: 75.00 | | | | |

**10 POUNDS** **KM# 38** **Weight:** 3.1300 g. **Composition:** 0.9990 Gold .1000 oz. AGW **Subject:** 400th Anniversary of Discovery - Ship "Desire" **Note:** Similar to 5 Pounds, KM#37.

| Date | Mintage | F | VF | XF | Unc | BU |
|---|---|---|---|---|---|---|
| ND (1992) Proof | Est. 400 | Value: 65.00 | | | | |

**20 POUNDS** **KM# 62** **Weight:** 6.2200 g. **Composition:** 0.9990 Gold .2000 oz. AGW **Subject:** Flying Doctor Service **Obverse:** Queen's portrait **Reverse:** Two airplanes in flight **Note:** Similar to 2 Pounds, KM#61.

| Date | Mintage | F | VF | XF | Unc | BU |
|---|---|---|---|---|---|---|
| 1998 Proof | Est. 1,000 | Value: 175 | | | | |

**20 POUNDS** **KM# 65** **Weight:** 6.2200 g. **Composition:** 0.9990 Gold .2000 oz. AGW **Subject:** Sir Ernest H. Shackleton **Obverse:** Queen's portrait **Reverse:** Cameo portrait and ice-bound ship **Note:** Similar to 2 Pounds, KM#64.

| Date | Mintage | F | VF | XF | Unc | BU |
|---|---|---|---|---|---|---|
| 1999 Proof | Est. 1,000 | Value: 175 | | | | |

**20 POUNDS** **KM# 68** **Weight:** 6.2200 g. **Composition:** 0.9990 Gold .2000 oz. AGW **Subject:** The Gold Rush - "Vicar of Bray" Ship **Obverse:** Queen's head right **Reverse:** "Vicar of Bray" in harbor **Edge:** Reeded

| Date | Mintage | F | VF | XF | Unc | BU |
|---|---|---|---|---|---|---|
| 2000 Proof | 1,000 | Value: 175 | | | | |

**25 POUNDS** **KM# 20** **Weight:** 150.0000 g. **Composition:** 0.9250 Silver 4.4614 oz. ASW **Subject:** 100 Years of Self Sufficiency

| Date | Mintage | F | VF | XF | Unc | BU |
|---|---|---|---|---|---|---|
| ND (1985) Proof | Est. 20,000 | Value: 55.00 | | | | |

**25 POUNDS** **KM# 23** **Weight:** 150.0000 g. **Composition:** 0.9250 Silver 4.4614 oz. ASW **Subject:** Prince Andrew's Wedding

| Date | Mintage | F | VF | XF | Unc | BU |
|---|---|---|---|---|---|---|
| 1986 Proof | Est. 20,000 | Value: 45.00 | | | | |

**25 POUNDS** **KM# 29** **Weight:** 7.8100 g. **Composition:** 0.9990 Gold .2500 oz. AGW **Subject:** 90th Birthday of Queen Mother **Obverse:** Portrait of Queen Elizabeth

| Date | Mintage | F | VF | XF | Unc | BU |
|---|---|---|---|---|---|---|
| ND (1990) Proof | Est. 750 | Value: 200 | | | | |

**25 POUNDS** **KM# 40** **Weight:** 7.8100 g. **Composition:** 0.9990 Gold .2500 oz. AGW **Subject:** 100th Anniversary of Christchurch Cathedral **Reverse:** Cathedral and cross

| Date | Mintage | F | VF | XF | Unc | BU |
|---|---|---|---|---|---|---|
| 1992 Proof | Est. 400 | Value: 160 | | | | |

**25 POUNDS** **KM# 39** **Weight:** 155.5800 g. **Composition:** 0.9990 Silver 4.9970 oz. ASW **Subject:** 400th Anniversary - First Sighting of Falkland Islands

| Date | Mintage | F | VF | XF | Unc | BU |
|---|---|---|---|---|---|---|
| ND (1992) Proof | Est. 3,000 | Value: 200 | | | | |

**50 POUNDS** **KM# 30** **Weight:** 15.6100 g. **Composition:** 0.9990 Gold .5000 oz. AGW **Subject:** 90th Birthday of Queen Mother **Obverse:** Portrait of Queen Elizabeth

| Date | Mintage | F | VF | XF | Unc | BU |
|---|---|---|---|---|---|---|
| ND (1990) Proof | Est. 750 | Value: 325 | | | | |

**50 POUNDS** **KM# 41** **Weight:** 15.6100 g. **Composition:** 0.9990 Gold .5000 oz. AGW **Subject:** 100th Anniversary of Defense **Reverse:** Soldier

| Date | Mintage | F | VF | XF | Unc | BU |
|---|---|---|---|---|---|---|
| ND (1992) Proof | Est. 400 | Value: 300 | | | | |

**50 POUNDS** **KM# 44** **Weight:** 47.5400 g. **Composition:** 0.9170 Gold 1.4013 oz. AGW **Subject:** 40th Anniverary - Coronation of Queen Elizabeth II

| Date | Mintage | F | VF | XF | Unc | BU |
|---|---|---|---|---|---|---|
| ND (1993) Proof | Est. 100 | Value: 1,150 | | | | |

**100 POUNDS** **KM# 31** **Weight:** 31.2100 g. **Composition:** 0.9990 Gold 1.0000 oz. AGW **Subject:** 90th Birthday of Queen Mother **Obverse:** Portrait of Queen Elizabeth

| Date | Mintage | F | VF | XF | Unc | BU |
|---|---|---|---|---|---|---|
| ND (1990) Proof | Est. 750 | Value: 550 | | | | |

**100 POUNDS** **KM# 42** **Weight:** 31.2100 g. **Composition:** 0.9990 Gold 1.0000 oz. AGW **Subject:** 400th Anniversary of Discovery - SHip "Desire' **Note:** Similar to 5 Pounds, KM#37.

| Date | Mintage | F | VF | XF | Unc | BU |
|---|---|---|---|---|---|---|
| CDND (1992) Proof | Est. 400 | Value: 525 | | | | |

**150 POUNDS** **KM# 13** **Weight:** 33.4370 g. **Composition:** 0.9000 Gold .9676 oz. AGW **Subject:** Conservation **Obverse:** Portrait of Queen Elizabeth II **Reverse:** Falkland Fur Seal

| Date | Mintage | F | VF | XF | Unc | BU |
|---|---|---|---|---|---|---|
| 1979 | 488 | — | — | — | 625 | — |
| 1979 Proof | 164 | Value: 1,350 | | | | |

## PIEFORTS

| KM# | Date | Mintage | Identification | Mkt Val |
|---|---|---|---|---|
| P1 | 1987 | 2,500 | Pound. 0.9250 Silver. KM24a. | 55.00 |
| P2 | 1992 | 750 | 50 Pence. 0.9250 Silver. KM34a | 65.00 |
| P3 | 1995 | — | 50 Pence. 0.9250 Silver. KM48a | 100 |

## MINT SETS

| KM# | Date | Mintage | Identification | Issue Price | Mkt Val |
|---|---|---|---|---|---|
| MS1 | 1987 (7) | — | KM2-3, 4.1-5.1, 14, 17, 24 | 10.00 | 12.00 |
| MS2 | 1992 (8) | — | KM2-3, 4.1-5.1, 14, 17, 24, 35 | 24.50 | 25.00 |
| MS3 | 1999 (8) | — | KM2a-3a, 4.2-5.2, 14, 17, 24, 69 | 20.00 | 22.50 |

## PROOF SETS

| KM# | Date | Mintage | Identification | Issue Price | Mkt Val |
|---|---|---|---|---|---|
| PS1 | 1974 (5) | 20,000 | KM1-3, 4.1-5.1 | 12.00 | 15.50 |
| PS2 | 1974 (4) | 2,000 | KM6-9 | 1,100 | 2,000 |
| PS3 | 1979 (2) | 10,000 | KM11-12 | — | 115 |
| PS4 | 1980 (6) | 10,000 | KM1-3, 4.1-5.1, 14 | 35.00 | 20.00 |
| PS5 | 1982 (8) | 5,000 | KM1-3, 4.1-5.1, 14, 17, 18a | — | 45.00 |
| PS6 | 1982 (7) | 5,000 | KM1-3, 4.1-5.1, 14, 17 | — | 26.50 |
| PS7 | 1987 (7) | 2,500 | KM2-3, 4.1-5.1, 14, 17, 24 | 35.00 | 40.00 |
| PS8 | 1990 (4) | 750 | KM28-31 | 1,595 | 1,150 |
| PS10 | 1992 (4) | 400 | KM38, 40-42 | 1,595 | 1,075 |
| PS9 | 1992 (8) | 2,500 | KM2-3, 4.1-5.1, 14, 17, 24, 35a | 89.50 | 90.00 |
| PS11 | 1999 (8) | 2,500 | KM2a-3a, 4.2-5.2, 14, 17, 24, 69 | 50.00 | 55.00 |

# FIJI ISLANDS

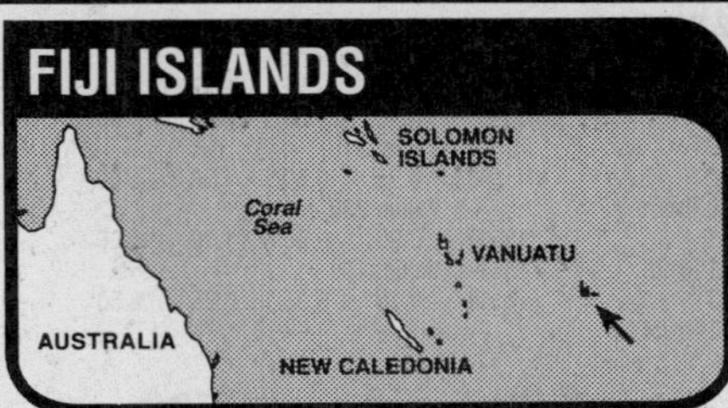


The Republic of Fiji, consists of about 320 islands located in the southwestern Pacific 1,100 miles (1,770 km.) north of New Zealand. The islands have a combined area of 7,056 sq. mi. (18,274 sq. km.) and a population of 772,891. Capital: Suva. Fiji's economy is based on agriculture and mining. Sugar, coconut products, manganese, and gold are exported.

The first European to sight Fiji was the Dutch navigator Abel Tasman in 1643 and the islands were visited by British naval captain James Cook in 1774. The first complete survey of the island was conducted by the United States in 1840. Settlement by mercenaries from Tonga, and traders attracted by the sandalwood trade, began in 1801. Following a lengthy period of intertribal warfare, the islands were unconditionally ceded to Great Britain in 1874 by King Cakobau. Fiji became a sovereign and independent nation on Oct. 10, 1970, the 96th anniversary of the cession of the islands to Queen Victoria.

Fiji was declared a Republic in 1987 following two military coups. It left the British Commonwealth and Queen Elizabeth ceased to be the Head of State. A new constitution was introduced in 1991. The country returned to the Commonwealth in 1997 with a revised constitution.

**RULERS**

British until 1970

**MINT MARKS**

(c) - Australian Mint, Canberra
(o) - Royal Canadian Mint, Ottawa
S - San Francisco, U.S.A.

**MONETARY SYSTEM**

12 Pence = 1 Shilling
2 Shillings = 1 Florin
20 Shillings = 1 Pound

# COLONY AND REPUBLIC

## POUND STERLING COINAGE

**1/2 PENNY** **KM# 1** **Composition:** Copper-Nickel

| Date | Mintage | F | VF | XF | Unc | BU |
|---|---|---|---|---|---|---|
| 1934 | 96,000 | 1.00 | 3.00 | 6.00 | 17.50 | — |
| 1934 Proof | — | — | — | — | — | — |

**1/2 PENNY** **KM# 14** **Composition:** Copper-Nickel

| Date | Mintage | F | VF | XF | Unc | BU |
|---|---|---|---|---|---|---|
| 1940 | 24,000 | 5.00 | 10.00 | 20.00 | 30.00 | — |
| 1940 Proof | — | Value: 350 | | | | |
| 1941 | 96,000 | 0.75 | 1.50 | 4.00 | 12.50 | — |
| 1941 Proof | — | Value: 200 | | | | |

**1/2 PENNY** **KM# 14a** **Composition:** Brass

| Date | Mintage | F | VF | XF | Unc | BU |
|---|---|---|---|---|---|---|
| 1942S | 250,000 | 0.25 | 0.50 | 3.50 | 15.00 | — |
| 1943S | 250,000 | 0.25 | 0.50 | 3.50 | 17.50 | — |

**1/2 PENNY KM# 16 Composition:** Copper-Nickel **Obverse:** EMPEROR dropped from legend

| Date | Mintage | F | VF | XF | Unc | BU |
|---|---|---|---|---|---|---|
| 1949 | 96,000 | 0.50 | 1.00 | 2.00 | 6.00 | — |
| 1949 | — | Value: 210 | | | | |
| 1950 | 115,000 | 0.25 | 0.50 | 1.50 | 5.00 | — |
| 1950 Proof | — | Value: 230 | | | | |
| 1951 | 115,000 | 0.25 | 0.50 | 1.50 | 5.00 | — |
| 1951 Proof | — | Value: 190 | | | | |
| 1952 | 228,000 | 0.15 | 0.35 | 0.75 | 2.50 | — |
| 1952 Proof | — | — | — | — | — | — |

**1/2 PENNY KM# 20 Composition:** Copper-Nickel

| Date | Mintage | F | VF | XF | Unc | BU |
|---|---|---|---|---|---|---|
| 1954 | 228,000 | 0.15 | 0.25 | 0.50 | 1.00 | — |
| 1954 Proof | — | Value: 180 | | | | |

**PENNY KM# 2 Composition:** Copper-Nickel

| Date | Mintage | F | VF | XF | Unc | BU |
|---|---|---|---|---|---|---|
| 1934 Proof | — | — | — | — | — | — |
| 1934 | 480,000 | 0.50 | 1.00 | 5.00 | 15.00 | — |
| 1935 | 240,000 | 0.65 | 1.25 | 5.50 | 17.50 | — |
| 1935 Proof | — | — | — | — | — | — |
| 1936 Proof | — | — | — | — | — | — |
| 1936 | 240,000 | 0.65 | 1.25 | 5.50 | 28.00 | — |

**PENNY KM# 6 Composition:** Copper-Nickel

| Date | Mintage | F | VF | XF | Unc | BU |
|---|---|---|---|---|---|---|
| 1936 | 120,000 | 0.50 | 1.00 | 2.00 | 4.00 | — |
| 1936 Proof | — | Value: 225 | | | | |

**PENNY KM# 7 Composition:** Copper-Nickel

| Date | Mintage | F | VF | XF | Unc | BU |
|---|---|---|---|---|---|---|
| 1937 | 360,000 | 0.50 | 1.00 | 3.00 | 8.50 | — |
| 1937 Proof | — | Value: 225 | | | | |
| 1940 | 144,000 | 2.00 | 3.00 | 15.00 | 40.00 | — |
| 1940 Proof | — | Value: 225 | | | | |
| 1941 | 228,000 | 0.50 | 1.00 | 2.00 | 9.00 | — |
| 1941 Proof | — | Value: 225 | | | | |
| 1945 | 240,000 | 2.00 | 3.00 | 8.00 | 25.00 | — |
| 1945 Proof | — | Value: 225 | | | | |

**PENNY KM# 7a Composition:** Brass

| Date | Mintage | F | VF | XF | Unc | BU |
|---|---|---|---|---|---|---|
| 1942S | 1,000,000 | 0.50 | 1.00 | 3.50 | 17.50 | — |
| 1943S | 1,000,000 | 0.50 | 1.00 | 3.50 | 20.00 | — |

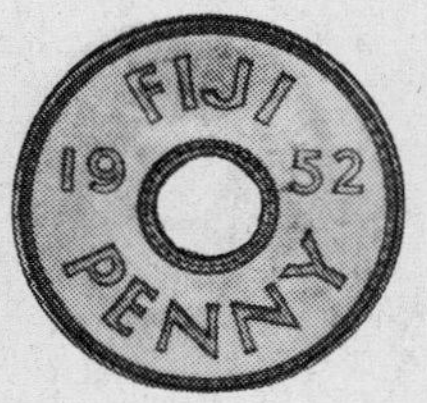

**PENNY KM# 17 Composition:** Copper-Nickel **Obverse:** EMPEROR dropped from legend

| Date | Mintage | F | VF | XF | Unc | BU |
|---|---|---|---|---|---|---|
| 1949 | 120,000 | 0.25 | 0.50 | 1.00 | 6.00 | — |
| 1949 Proof | — | Value: 325 | | | | |
| 1950 | 58,000 | 2.00 | 4.50 | 12.50 | 55.00 | — |
| 1950 Proof | — | Value: 200 | | | | |
| 1952 | 230,000 | 0.25 | 0.50 | 1.00 | 5.00 | — |
| 1952 Proof | — | Value: 175 | | | | |

**PENNY KM# 21 Composition:** Copper-Nickel

| Date | Mintage | F | VF | XF | Unc | BU |
|---|---|---|---|---|---|---|
| 1954 | 511,000 | 0.20 | 0.50 | 1.00 | 3.00 | — |
| 1954 Proof | — | Value: 175 | | | | |
| 1955 | 230,000 | 0.25 | 0.50 | 1.25 | 7.50 | — |
| 1955 Proof | — | Value: 175 | | | | |
| 1956 | 230,000 | 0.25 | 0.50 | 1.25 | 5.00 | — |
| 1956 Proof | — | Value: 175 | | | | |
| 1957 | 360,000 | 0.10 | 0.25 | 0.75 | 4.00 | — |
| 1957 Proof | — | Value: 175 | | | | |
| 1959 | 864,000 | 0.10 | 0.20 | 0.35 | 2.00 | — |
| 1959 Proof | — | Value: 175 | | | | |
| 1961 | 432,000 | 0.20 | 0.35 | 0.50 | 1.25 | — |
| 1961 Proof | — | Value: 175 | | | | |
| 1963 | 432,000 | 0.20 | 0.35 | 0.50 | 1.25 | — |
| 1963 Proof | — | Value: 175 | | | | |
| 1964 | 864,000 | 0.10 | 0.15 | 0.25 | 0.85 | — |
| 1964 Proof | — | Value: 150 | | | | |
| 1965 | 1,440,000 | 0.10 | 0.15 | 0.25 | 0.75 | — |
| 1966 | 720,000 | 0.10 | 0.15 | 0.25 | 0.85 | — |
| 1967 | 720,000 | 0.10 | 0.15 | 0.25 | 0.75 | — |
| 1968 | 720,000 | 0.10 | 0.15 | 0.25 | 0.75 | — |

**THREEPENCE KM# 15 Composition:** Nickel-Brass **Reverse:** Natiave dwelling

| Date | Mintage | F | VF | XF | Unc | BU |
|---|---|---|---|---|---|---|
| 1947 | 450,000 | 1.50 | 2.50 | 6.00 | 20.00 | — |
| 1947 Proof | — | Value: 190 | | | | |

**THREEPENCE KM# 18 Composition:** Nickel-Brass **Obverse:** EMPEROR dropped from legend

| Date | Mintage | F | VF | XF | Unc | BU |
|---|---|---|---|---|---|---|
| 1950 | 450,000 | 0.50 | 1.00 | 4.00 | 12.50 | — |
| 1950 Proof | — | Value: 190 | | | | |
| 1952 | 400,000 | 0.50 | 1.00 | 5.00 | 20.00 | — |
| 1952 Proof | — | Value: 190 | | | | |

**THREEPENCE KM# 22 Composition:** Nickel-Brass

| Date | Mintage | F | VF | XF | Unc | BU |
|---|---|---|---|---|---|---|
| 1955 | 400,000 | 0.50 | 1.00 | 4.00 | 12.50 | — |
| 1955 | — | Value: 130 | | | | |
| 1956 | 200,000 | 0.50 | 1.00 | 5.00 | 25.00 | — |
| 1956 Proof | — | Value: 155 | | | | |
| 1958 | 200,000 | 0.50 | 1.00 | 4.00 | 20.00 | — |
| 1958 Proof | — | Value: 140 | | | | |
| 1960 | 240,000 | 0.25 | 0.50 | 3.00 | 10.00 | — |
| 1960 Proof | — | Value: 125 | | | | |
| 1961 | 240,000 | 0.25 | 0.50 | 1.25 | 5.00 | — |
| 1961 Proof | — | Value: 125 | | | | |
| 1963 | 240,000 | 0.15 | 0.30 | 0.75 | 4.00 | — |
| 1963 Proof | — | Value: 115 | | | | |
| 1964 | 240,000 | 0.15 | 0.30 | 0.50 | 2.00 | — |

| Date | Mintage | F | VF | XF | Unc | BU |
|---|---|---|---|---|---|---|
| 1965 | 800,000 | 0.10 | 0.15 | 0.25 | 1.50 | — |
| 1967 | 800,000 | 0.10 | 0.15 | 0.25 | 1.50 | — |

**SIXPENCE KM# 3 Weight:** 2.8276 g. **Composition:** 0.5000 Silver .0455 oz. ASW **Reverse:** Sea turtle

| Date | Mintage | F | VF | XF | Unc | BU |
|---|---|---|---|---|---|---|
| 1934 | 160,000 | 1.00 | 2.50 | 10.00 | 35.00 | — |
| 1934 Proof | — | Value: 450 | | | | |
| 1935 | 120,000 | 1.50 | 3.50 | 12.50 | 47.50 | — |
| 1935 Proof | — | — | — | — | — | — |
| 1936 | 40,000 | 2.00 | 4.00 | 15.00 | 55.00 | — |
| 1936 Proof | — | — | — | — | — | — |

**SIXPENCE KM# 8 Weight:** 2.8276 g. **Composition:** 0.5000 Silver .0455 oz. ASW

| Date | Mintage | F | VF | XF | Unc | BU |
|---|---|---|---|---|---|---|
| 1937 | 40,000 | 2.00 | 4.00 | 16.00 | 60.00 | — |
| 1937 Proof | — | Value: 400 | | | | |

**SIXPENCE KM# 11 Weight:** 2.8276 g. **Composition:** 0.5000 Silver .0455 oz. ASW **Obverse:** Smaller head

| Date | Mintage | F | VF | XF | Unc | BU |
|---|---|---|---|---|---|---|
| 1938 | 40,000 | 2.00 | 4.00 | 13.50 | 50.00 | — |
| 1938 Proof | — | — | — | — | — | — |
| 1940 | 40,000 | 2.00 | 4.00 | 13.50 | 50.00 | — |
| 1940 Proof | — | — | — | — | — | — |
| 1941 | 40,000 | 3.00 | 8.00 | 20.00 | 75.00 | — |
| 1941 Proof | — | — | — | — | — | — |

**SIXPENCE KM# 11a Weight:** 2.8276 g. **Composition:** 0.9000 Silver .0818 oz. ASW

| Date | Mintage | F | VF | XF | Unc | BU |
|---|---|---|---|---|---|---|
| 1942 | 400,000 | — | 1.00 | 2.50 | 6.50 | — |
| 1943 | 400,000 | — | 1.00 | 2.50 | 6.50 | — |

**SIXPENCE KM# 19 Composition:** Copper-Nickel

| Date | Mintage | F | VF | XF | Unc | BU |
|---|---|---|---|---|---|---|
| 1953 | 800,000 | 0.15 | 0.30 | 1.00 | 3.00 | — |
| 1953 Proof | — | Value: 210 | | | | |
| 1958 | 400,000 | 0.25 | 0.50 | 1.50 | 4.50 | — |
| 1958 Proof | — | Value: 200 | | | | |
| 1961 | 400,000 | 0.25 | 0.50 | 1.00 | 3.50 | — |
| 1961 Proof | — | Value: 200 | | | | |
| 1962 | 400,000 | 0.25 | 0.50 | 1.00 | 3.00 | — |
| 1962 Proof | — | Value: 200 | | | | |
| 1965 | 800,000 | 0.15 | 0.30 | 0.75 | 2.50 | — |
| 1967 | 800,000 | 0.15 | 0.30 | 0.75 | 2.50 | — |

**SHILLING KM# 4 Weight:** 5.6552 g. **Composition:** 0.5000 Silver .0909 oz. ASW **Reverse:** Outrigger

| Date | Mintage | F | VF | XF | Unc | BU |
|---|---|---|---|---|---|---|
| 1934 | 360,000 | 1.50 | 4.00 | 14.50 | 60.00 | — |
| 1934 Proof | — | Value: 650 | | | | |
| 1935 | 180,000 | 1.50 | 4.00 | 14.50 | 80.00 | — |
| 1935 Proof | — | — | — | — | — | — |
| 1936 | 140,000 | 1.50 | 6.00 | 15.50 | 80.00 | — |
| 1936 Proof | — | — | — | — | — | — |

**SHILLING** KM#9 **Weight:** 5.6552 g. **Composition:** 0.5000 Silver .0909 oz. ASW

| Date | Mintage | F | VF | XF | Unc | BU |
|---|---|---|---|---|---|---|
| 1937 | 40,000 | 1.50 | 7.00 | 17.50 | 90.00 | — |
| 1937 Proof | — | Value: 500 | | | | |

**SHILLING** KM# 12 **Weight:** 5.6552 g. **Composition:** 0.5000 Silver .0909 oz. ASW **Obverse:** Smaller head

| Date | Mintage | F | VF | XF | Unc | BU |
|---|---|---|---|---|---|---|
| 1938 | 40,000 | 1.50 | 7.00 | 17.50 | 85.00 | — |
| 1938 Proof | — | — | — | — | — | — |
| 1941 | 40,000 | 1.50 | 7.00 | 17.50 | 80.00 | — |
| 1941 Proof | — | — | — | — | — | — |

**SHILLING** KM# 12a **Weight:** 5.6552 g. **Composition:** 0.9000 Silver .1636 oz. ASW

| Date | Mintage | F | VF | XF | Unc | BU |
|---|---|---|---|---|---|---|
| 1942 | 500,000 | — | 1.25 | 3.00 | 7.50 | — |
| 1943 | 500,000 | — | 1.25 | 3.00 | 7.50 | — |

**SHILLING** KM# 23 **Composition:** Copper-Nickel

| Date | Mintage | F | VF | XF | Unc | BU |
|---|---|---|---|---|---|---|
| 1957 | 400,000 | 0.50 | 0.75 | 2.00 | 8.50 | — |
| 1957 Proof | — | — | — | — | — | — |
| 1958 | 400,000 | 0.50 | 0.75 | 2.25 | 9.00 | — |
| 1958 Proof | — | — | — | — | — | — |
| 1961 | 200,000 | 0.75 | 1.00 | 2.25 | 7.50 | — |
| 1961 Proof | — | Value: 275 | | | | |
| 1962 | 400,000 | 0.35 | 0.75 | 1.25 | 4.50 | — |
| 1962 Proof | — | Value: 250 | | | | |
| 1965 | 800,000 | 0.25 | 0.50 | 0.75 | 2.00 | — |

**FLORIN** KM# 5 **Weight:** 11.3104 g. **Composition:** 0.5000 Silver .1818 oz. ASW

| Date | Mintage | F | VF | XF | Unc | BU |
|---|---|---|---|---|---|---|
| 1934 | 200,000 | 1.50 | 4.50 | 17.50 | 125 | — |
| 1934 Proof | — | Value: 750 | | | | |
| 1935 | 50,000 | 2.00 | 9.00 | 20.00 | 190 | — |
| 1935 Proof | — | — | — | — | — | — |
| 1936 | 65,000 | 2.00 | 9.00 | 20.00 | 170 | — |
| 1936 Proof | — | — | — | — | — | — |

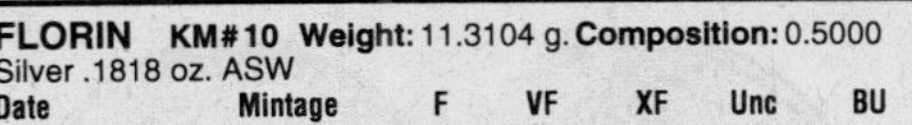

**FLORIN** KM# 10 **Weight:** 11.3104 g. **Composition:** 0.5000 Silver .1818 oz. ASW

| Date | Mintage | F | VF | XF | Unc | BU |
|---|---|---|---|---|---|---|
| 1937 | 30,000 | 2.50 | 7.00 | 17.50 | 150 | — |
| 1937 Proof | — | Value: 750 | | | | |

**FLORIN** KM# 13 **Weight:** 11.3104 g. **Composition:** 0.5000 Silver .1818 oz. ASW **Obverse:** Smaller head

| Date | Mintage | F | VF | XF | Unc | BU |
|---|---|---|---|---|---|---|
| 1938 | 20,000 | 4.00 | 12.00 | 25.00 | 170 | — |
| 1938 Proof | — | — | — | — | — | — |
| 1941 | 20,000 | 4.00 | 12.00 | 25.00 | 170 | — |
| 1941 Proof | — | — | — | — | — | — |
| 1945 | 100,000 | 9.00 | 20.00 | 35.00 | 210 | — |
| 1945 Proof | — | — | — | — | — | — |

**FLORIN** KM# 13a **Weight:** 11.3104 g. **Composition:** 0.9000 Silver .3273 oz. ASW

| Date | Mintage | F | VF | XF | Unc | BU |
|---|---|---|---|---|---|---|
| 1942 | 250,000 | — | 2.50 | 5.00 | 15.00 | — |
| 1943 | 250,000 | — | 2.50 | 5.00 | 17.50 | — |

**FLORIN** KM# 24 **Composition:** Copper-Nickel

| Date | Mintage | F | VF | XF | Unc | BU |
|---|---|---|---|---|---|---|
| 1957 | 300,000 | 0.50 | 1.00 | 4.00 | 15.00 | — |
| 1957 Proof | — | Value: 375 | | | | |
| 1958 | 220,000 | 0.50 | 1.00 | 4.00 | 15.00 | — |
| 1958 Proof | — | Value: 375 | | | | |
| 1962 | 200,000 | 0.25 | 0.50 | 2.00 | 10.00 | — |
| 1962 Proof | — | Value: 375 | | | | |
| 1964 | 200,000 | 0.25 | 0.50 | 1.50 | 5.00 | — |
| 1964 Proof | — | Value: 400 | | | | |
| 1965 | 400,000 | 0.25 | 0.50 | 1.00 | 3.00 | — |

## DECIMAL COINAGE

100 Cents = 1 Dollar

**CENT** KM# 27 **Composition:** Bronze **Reverse:** Tanoa kava dish

| Date | Mintage | F | VF | XF | Unc | BU |
|---|---|---|---|---|---|---|
| 1969 | 11,000,000 | — | — | 0.10 | 0.20 | — |
| 1969 Proof | 10,000 | Value: 0.50 | | | | |
| 1973 | 3,000,000 | — | — | 0.10 | 1.00 | — |
| 1975 | 2,064,000 | — | — | 0.10 | 0.50 | — |
| 1976 | 2,005,000 | — | — | 0.10 | 0.50 | — |
| 1983 | — | — | — | 0.10 | 0.50 | — |
| 1983 Proof | 3,000 | Value: 1.00 | | | | |
| 1984 | 2,295,000 | — | — | 0.10 | 0.35 | — |
| 1985 | — | — | — | 0.10 | 0.35 | — |

**CENT** KM# 27a **Weight:** 2.2600 g. **Composition:** 0.9250 Silver .0672 oz. ASW

| Date | Mintage | F | VF | XF | Unc | BU |
|---|---|---|---|---|---|---|
| 1976 Proof | 3,012 | Value: 3.50 | | | | |

**CENT** KM# 39 **Composition:** Bronze **Series:** F.A.O **Reverse:** Rice

| Date | Mintage | F | VF | XF | Unc | BU |
|---|---|---|---|---|---|---|
| 1977 | 3,000,000 | — | — | 0.10 | 0.50 | — |
| 1978 | 3,032,000 | — | — | 0.10 | 0.50 | — |
| 1978 Proof | 2,000 | Value: 2.50 | | | | |
| 1979 | 2,500,000 | — | — | 0.15 | 1.00 | — |
| 1980 | 314,000 | — | — | 0.10 | 0.50 | — |
| 1980 Proof | 2,500 | Value: 1.50 | | | | |
| 1981 | 4,040,000 | — | — | 0.10 | 0.50 | — |
| 1982 | 5,000,000 | — | — | 0.10 | 0.50 | — |
| 1982 Proof | 3,000 | Value: 1.00 | | | | |

**CENT** KM# 49 **Composition:** Bronze

| Date | Mintage | F | VF | XF | Unc | BU |
|---|---|---|---|---|---|---|
| 1986(c) | 3,400,000 | — | — | 0.10 | 0.50 | — |
| 1987(c) | 3,400,000 | — | — | 0.15 | 1.00 | — |

**CENT** KM# 49a **Composition:** Copper Plated Zinc

| Date | Mintage | F | VF | XF | Unc | BU |
|---|---|---|---|---|---|---|
| 1990 | 8,500,000 | — | — | — | 0.25 | — |
| 1992 | — | — | — | — | 0.25 | — |
| 1994 | — | — | — | — | 0.25 | — |
| 1995 | — | — | — | — | 0.25 | — |

**2 CENTS** KM# 28 **Composition:** Bronze **Reverse:** Palm fan

| Date | Mintage | F | VF | XF | Unc | BU |
|---|---|---|---|---|---|---|
| 1969 | 8,000,000 | — | — | 0.10 | 0.50 | — |
| 1969 Proof | 10,000 | Value: 0.75 | | | | |
| 1973 | 2,110,000 | — | 0.10 | 0.15 | 0.75 | — |
| 1975 | 1,500,000 | — | 0.10 | 0.15 | 0.50 | — |
| 1976 | 1,004,999 | — | 0.10 | 0.15 | 0.50 | — |
| 1977 | 1,250,000 | — | — | 0.10 | 0.50 | — |
| 1978 | 1,502,000 | — | — | 0.10 | 0.50 | — |
| 1978 Proof | 2,000 | Value: 3.50 | | | | |
| 1979 | 500,000 | — | 0.10 | 0.20 | 1.50 | — |
| 1980 | 4,019,999 | — | — | 0.10 | 0.50 | — |
| 1980 Proof | 2,500 | Value: 2.50 | | | | |
| 1981 | 3,250,000 | — | — | 0.10 | 0.50 | — |
| 1982 | 4,000,000 | — | — | 0.10 | 0.50 | — |
| 1982 Proof | 3,000 | Value: 2.00 | | | | |
| 1983 | — | — | — | 0.10 | 0.50 | — |
| 1983 Proof | 3,000 | Value: 1.50 | | | | |
| 1984 | 1,845,000 | — | — | 0.10 | 0.40 | — |
| 1985 | 1,700,000 | — | — | 0.10 | 0.40 | — |

**2 CENTS** KM# 28a **Weight:** 4.5300 g. **Composition:** 0.9250 Silver .1347 oz. ASW

| Date | Mintage | F | VF | XF | Unc | BU |
|---|---|---|---|---|---|---|
| 1976 Proof | 3,012 | Value: 4.50 | | | | |

**2 CENTS** KM# 50 **Composition:** Bronze

| Date | Mintage | F | VF | XF | Unc | BU |
|---|---|---|---|---|---|---|
| 1986(c) | 1,700,000 | — | — | 0.15 | 0.75 | — |
| 1987(c) | 1,700,000 | — | — | 0.15 | 1.00 | — |

**2 CENTS** KM# 50a **Composition:** Copper Plated Zinc

| Date | Mintage | F | VF | XF | Unc | BU |
|---|---|---|---|---|---|---|
| 1990(o) | 5,500,000 | — | — | — | 0.35 | — |
| 1992(o) | — | — | — | — | 0.35 | — |
| 1994 | — | — | — | — | 0.35 | — |

**5 CENTS** KM# 29 **Composition:** Copper-Nickel **Reverse:** Fijian drum

| Date | Mintage | F | VF | XF | Unc | BU |
|---|---|---|---|---|---|---|
| 1969 | 9,200,000 | — | 0.10 | 0.20 | 0.75 | — |
| 1969 Proof | 10,000 | Value: 0.75 | | | | |
| 1973 | 600,000 | — | 0.10 | 0.30 | 1.50 | — |
| 1974 | 608,000 | — | 0.10 | 0.30 | 1.25 | — |
| 1975 | 1,008,000 | — | 0.10 | 0.20 | 0.75 | — |
| 1976 | 1,205,000 | — | 0.10 | 0.20 | 0.75 | — |
| 1977 | 960,000 | — | 0.10 | 0.20 | 0.75 | — |
| 1978 | 880,000 | — | 0.10 | 0.20 | 0.75 | — |
| 1978 Proof | 2,000 | Value: 5.00 | | | | |
| 1979 | 1,500,000 | — | 0.10 | 0.25 | 1.50 | — |
| 1980 | 2,506,000 | — | 0.10 | 0.15 | 0.75 | — |

| Date | Mintage | F | VF | XF | Unc | BU |
|---|---|---|---|---|---|---|
| 1980 Proof | 2,500 | Value: 3.50 | | | | |
| 1981 | 1,980,000 | — | 0.10 | 0.15 | 0.50 | — |
| 1982 | 2,700,000 | — | 0.10 | 0.15 | 0.50 | — |
| 1982 Proof | 3,000 | Value: 3.00 | | | | |
| 1983 | — | — | 0.10 | 0.15 | 0.50 | — |
| 1983 Proof | 3,000 | Value: 2.00 | | | | |
| 1984 | 5,000 | — | 0.10 | 0.20 | 0.75 | — |

**5 CENTS** **KM# 29a** **Weight:** 3.2800 g. **Composition:** 0.9250 Silver .0975 oz. ASW **Series:** F.A.O.

| Date | Mintage | F | VF | XF | Unc | BU |
|---|---|---|---|---|---|---|
| 1976 Proof | 3,012 | Value: 6.00 | | | | |

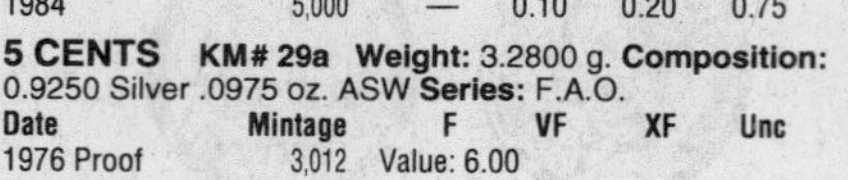

**5 CENTS** **KM# 51** **Composition:** Copper-Nickel

| Date | Mintage | F | VF | XF | Unc | BU |
|---|---|---|---|---|---|---|
| 1986(c) | 1,200,000 | — | 0.10 | 0.20 | 0.75 | — |
| 1987(c) | 1,200,000 | — | 0.10 | 0.20 | 0.75 | — |

**5 CENTS** **KM# 51a** **Composition:** Nickel Bonded Steel

| Date | Mintage | F | VF | XF | Unc | BU |
|---|---|---|---|---|---|---|
| 1990 | 4,000,000 | — | — | — | 0.35 | — |
| 1992 | — | — | — | — | 0.35 | — |
| 1994 | — | — | — | — | 0.35 | — |

**5 CENTS** **KM# 77** **Composition:** Nickel Bonded Steel **Series:** F.A.O. **Subject:** Harvest from the Sea **Obverse:** Queen's portrait **Reverse:** Fish, F.A.O. logo

| Date | Mintage | F | VF | XF | Unc | BU |
|---|---|---|---|---|---|---|
| 1995 | — | — | — | — | 0.50 | — |

**10 CENTS** **KM# 30** **Composition:** Copper-Nickel **Reverse:** Throwing club

| Date | Mintage | F | VF | XF | Unc | BU |
|---|---|---|---|---|---|---|
| 1969 | 3,500,000 | — | 0.20 | 0.40 | 1.00 | — |
| 1969 Proof | 10,000 | Value: 1.00 | | | | |
| 1973 | 750,000 | — | 0.25 | 0.65 | 2.00 | — |
| 1975 | 752,000 | — | 0.20 | 0.50 | 1.25 | — |
| 1976 | 805,000 | — | 0.20 | 0.50 | 1.25 | — |
| 1977 | 240,000 | — | 0.25 | 0.65 | 1.25 | — |
| 1978 | 664,000 | — | 0.20 | 0.50 | 1.25 | — |
| 1978 Proof | 2,000 | Value: 6.00 | | | | |
| 1979 | 702,000 | — | 0.25 | 0.65 | 2.00 | — |
| 1980 | 1,000,000 | — | 0.15 | 0.30 | 1.25 | — |
| 1980 Proof | 2,500 | Value: 4.50 | | | | |
| 1981 | 1,200,000 | — | 0.20 | 0.50 | 1.25 | — |
| 1982 | 1,500,000 | — | 0.20 | 0.50 | 1.25 | — |
| 1982 Proof | 3,000 | Value: 4.00 | | | | |
| 1983 | 3,000 | — | 0.25 | 0.65 | 2.00 | — |
| 1983 Proof | 3,000 | Value: 3.00 | | | | |
| 1984 | 5,000 | — | 0.25 | 0.65 | 1.75 | — |
| 1985 | 660,000 | — | 0.20 | 0.50 | 1.00 | — |

**10 CENTS** **KM# 30a** **Weight:** 6.5500 g. **Composition:** 0.9250 Silver .1948 oz. ASW

| Date | Mintage | F | VF | XF | Unc | BU |
|---|---|---|---|---|---|---|
| 1976 Proof | 3,012 | Value: 6.50 | | | | |

**10 CENTS** **KM# 52** **Composition:** Copper-Nickel

| Date | Mintage | F | VF | XF | Unc | BU |
|---|---|---|---|---|---|---|
| 1986(c) | 740,000 | — | 0.20 | 0.40 | 1.25 | — |
| 1987(c) | 740,000 | — | 0.20 | 0.40 | 1.00 | — |

**10 CENTS** **KM# 52a** **Composition:** Nickel Bonded Steel

| Date | Mintage | F | VF | XF | Unc | BU |
|---|---|---|---|---|---|---|
| 1990 | 2,000,000 | — | — | — | 0.60 | — |
| 1992 | — | — | — | — | 0.60 | — |
| 1994 | — | — | — | — | 0.60 | — |
| 1996 | — | — | — | — | 0.60 | — |

**20 CENTS** **KM# 31** **Composition:** Copper-Nickel **Reverse:** Tabua on braided sennit cord

| Date | Mintage | F | VF | XF | Unc | BU |
|---|---|---|---|---|---|---|
| 1969 | 2,000,000 | — | 0.30 | 0.80 | 1.50 | — |
| 1969 Proof | 10,000 | Value: 1.75 | | | | |
| 1973 | 250,000 | — | 0.35 | 1.00 | 2.25 | — |
| 1974 | 252,000 | — | 0.35 | 0.75 | 1.75 | — |
| 1975 | 352,000 | — | 0.35 | 0.75 | 1.75 | — |
| 1976 | 405,000 | — | 0.25 | 0.65 | 1.75 | — |
| 1977 | 200,000 | — | 0.35 | 0.75 | 2.50 | — |
| 1978 | 406,000 | — | 0.25 | 0.50 | 1.75 | — |
| 1978 Proof | 2,000 | Value: 8.00 | | | | |
| 1979 | 500,000 | — | 0.25 | 0.60 | 1.75 | — |
| 1980 | 1,014,000 | — | 0.25 | 0.60 | 1.50 | — |
| 1980 Proof | 2,500 | Value: 6.50 | | | | |
| 1981 | 1,200,000 | — | 0.25 | 0.60 | 1.50 | — |
| 1982 | 1,500,000 | — | 0.25 | 0.60 | 1.50 | — |
| 1982 Proof | 3,000 | Value: 6.00 | | | | |
| 1983 | 3,000 | — | 0.35 | 0.75 | 2.50 | — |
| 1983 Proof | 3,000 | Value: 5.00 | | | | |
| 1984 | 5,000 | — | 0.35 | 0.75 | 2.25 | — |
| 1985 | 240,000 | — | 0.20 | 0.35 | 0.70 | — |

**20 CENTS** **KM# 31a** **Weight:** 13.0900 g. **Composition:** 0.9250 Silver .3893 oz. ASW

| Date | Mintage | F | VF | XF | Unc | BU |
|---|---|---|---|---|---|---|
| 1976 Proof | 3,012 | Value: 8.50 | | | | |

**20 CENTS** **KM# 53** **Composition:** Copper-Nickel

| Date | Mintage | F | VF | XF | Unc | BU |
|---|---|---|---|---|---|---|
| 1986(c) | 360,000 | — | 0.25 | 0.60 | 1.50 | — |
| 1987(c) | 360,000 | — | 0.25 | 0.60 | 1.25 | — |

**20 CENTS** **KM# 53a** **Composition:** Nickel Bonded Steel

| Date | Mintage | F | VF | XF | Unc | BU |
|---|---|---|---|---|---|---|
| 1990 | 1,500,000 | — | 0.20 | 0.35 | 0.85 | — |
| 1992 | — | — | 0.20 | 0.35 | 0.85 | — |
| 1994 | — | — | 0.20 | 0.35 | 0.85 | — |
| 1995 | — | — | 0.20 | 0.35 | 0.85 | — |

**50 CENTS** **KM# 36** **Composition:** Copper-Nickel **Reverse:** Sailing canoe - Takia

| Date | Mintage | F | VF | XF | Unc | BU |
|---|---|---|---|---|---|---|
| 1975 | 1,000,000 | — | 0.75 | 1.50 | 5.00 | — |
| 1976 | 805,000 | — | 0.75 | 1.00 | 3.00 | — |
| 1978 | 4,006 | — | 1.25 | 2.50 | 6.00 | — |
| 1978 Proof | 2,000 | Value: 13.00 | | | | |
| 1980 | 316,000 | — | 0.75 | 1.00 | 3.00 | — |
| 1980 Proof | 2,500 | Value: 11.50 | | | | |
| 1981 | 511,000 | — | 0.75 | 1.00 | 3.00 | — |
| 1982 | 1,000,000 | — | 0.75 | 1.00 | 3.00 | — |
| 1982 Proof | 3,000 | Value: 10.00 | | | | |
| 1983 | 3,000 | — | 0.65 | 1.00 | 3.50 | — |
| 1983 Proof | 3,000 | Value: 9.00 | | | | |
| 1984 | 5,000 | — | 0.65 | 1.00 | 3.25 | — |

**50 CENTS** **KM# 36a** **Weight:** 18.0000 g. **Composition:** 0.9250 Silver .5353 oz. ASW

| Date | Mintage | F | VF | XF | Unc | BU |
|---|---|---|---|---|---|---|
| 1976 Proof | 3,012 | Value: 13.50 | | | | |

**50 CENTS** **KM# 44** **Composition:** Copper-Nickel **Series:** F.A.O. **Subject:** First Indians in Fiji Centennial

| Date | Mintage | F | VF | XF | Unc | BU |
|---|---|---|---|---|---|---|
| 1979 | 258,000 | — | — | — | 2.50 | — |
| 1979 Proof | 6,004 | Value: 7.50 | | | | |

**50 CENTS** **KM# 45** **Composition:** Copper-Nickel **Subject:** 10th Anniversary of Independence **Reverse:** Prince Charles

| Date | Mintage | F | VF | XF | Unc | BU |
|---|---|---|---|---|---|---|
| 1980 | 10,000 | — | — | — | 2.50 | — |

**50 CENTS** **KM# 54** **Composition:** Copper-Nickel

| Date | Mintage | F | VF | XF | Unc | BU |
|---|---|---|---|---|---|---|
| 1986(c) | 160,000 | — | 0.75 | 1.00 | 3.00 | — |
| 1987(c) | 160,000 | — | 0.50 | 0.75 | 1.75 | — |

**50 CENTS** **KM# 54a** **Composition:** Nickel Bonded Steel

| Date | Mintage | F | VF | XF | Unc | BU |
|---|---|---|---|---|---|---|
| 1990(o) | 800,000 | — | — | 0.60 | 1.25 | — |
| 1992(o) | — | — | — | 0.60 | 1.25 | — |
| 1994(o) | — | — | — | 0.60 | 1.25 | — |

**DOLLAR** **KM# 32** **Composition:** Copper-Nickel

| Date | Mintage | F | VF | XF | Unc | BU |
|---|---|---|---|---|---|---|
| 1969 | 70,000 | — | 1.00 | 2.00 | 4.50 | — |
| 1969 Proof | 10,000 | Value: 5.00 | | | | |
| 1976 | 5,007 | — | 1.50 | 3.00 | 6.50 | — |

**DOLLAR** KM# 33 **Composition:** Copper-Nickel **Subject:** Independence Commemorative

| Date | Mintage | F | VF | XF | Unc | BU |
|---|---|---|---|---|---|---|
| 1970 | 15,000 | — | — | — | 5.00 | — |
| 1970 Proof | 15,000 | Value: 6.00 | | | | |

**Note:** Variety w/medallic alignment exists. Value: $100.+

**DOLLAR** KM# 33a **Weight:** 28.2800 g. **Composition:** 0.9250 Silver .8411 oz. ASW

| Date | Mintage | F | VF | XF | Unc | BU |
|---|---|---|---|---|---|---|
| 1970 Proof | 1,000 | Value: 50.00 | | | | |

**DOLLAR** KM# 32a **Weight:** 28.2800 g. **Composition:** 0.9250 Silver .8411 oz. ASW

| Date | Mintage | F | VF | XF | Unc | BU |
|---|---|---|---|---|---|---|
| 1976 Proof | 3,012 | Value: 20.00 | | | | |

**DOLLAR** KM# 71 **Composition:** Copper-Nickel **Subject:** Move to Buckingham Palace **Reverse:** Buckingham Palace and soldier

| Date | Mintage | F | VF | XF | Unc | BU |
|---|---|---|---|---|---|---|
| 1995 | Est. 300,000 | — | — | — | 10.00 | — |

**DOLLAR** KM# 73 **Composition:** Brass **Reverse:** Native rattle

| Date | Mintage | F | VF | XF | Unc | BU |
|---|---|---|---|---|---|---|
| 1995 | — | — | — | — | 3.00 | — |

**2 DOLLARS** KM# 78 **Weight:** 42.4139 g. **Composition:** 0.9250 Silver 1.3636 oz. ASW **Subject:** Soft Coral Capital of the World **Obverse:** Queen's portrait **Reverse:** Denominatoin, coral industry scenes

| Date | Mintage | F | VF | XF | Unc | BU |
|---|---|---|---|---|---|---|
| 1998 Proof | Est. 20,000 | Value: 35.00 | | | | |

**Note:** Part of a tri-nation, three coin matching set w/Cook Islands and Western Samoa

**5 DOLLARS** KM# 81 **Weight:** 20.0000 g. **Composition:** 0.5000 Silver .3215 oz. ASW **Subject:** Protect Our World **Obverse:** Queen's portrait **Reverse:** Heron, fish and tree **Edge:** Reeded

| Date | Mintage | F | VF | XF | Unc | BU |
|---|---|---|---|---|---|---|
| 1993 Proof | 25,000 | Value: 17.50 | | | | |

**5 DOLLARS** KM# 69 **Weight:** 20.0000 g. **Composition:** 0.5000 Silver .3215 oz. ASW **Subject:** Queen Mother's London House **Obverse:** Queen's portrait **Reverse:** Clarence House

| Date | Mintage | F | VF | XF | Unc | BU |
|---|---|---|---|---|---|---|
| 1994 Proof | Est. 50,000 | Value: 17.50 | | | | |

**5 DOLLARS** KM# 80 **Weight:** 31.4400 g. **Composition:** 0.9250 Silver .9350 oz. ASW **Subject:** Millennium 2000 **Obverse:** Queen's portrait **Reverse:** Native, map and branch

| Date | Mintage | F | VF | XF | Unc | BU |
|---|---|---|---|---|---|---|
| 1999 Proof | — | Value: 30.00 | | | | |

**10 DOLLARS** KM# 40 **Weight:** 30.3000 g. **Composition:** 0.9250 Silver .9012 oz. ASW **Subject:** Queen's Silver Jubilee

| Date | Mintage | F | VF | XF | Unc | BU |
|---|---|---|---|---|---|---|
| 1977 Proof | 3,010 | Value: 18.50 | | | | |

**10 DOLLARS** KM# 41 **Weight:** 28.2800 g. **Composition:** 0.5000 Silver .4547 oz. ASW **Subject:** Conservation **Reverse:** Pink-billed parrot finch

| Date | Mintage | F | VF | XF | Unc | BU |
|---|---|---|---|---|---|---|
| 1978 | 3,582 | — | — | — | 22.50 | — |

**10 DOLLARS** KM#41a **Weight:** 28.2800 g. **Composition:** 0.9250 Silver .8411 oz. ASW

| Date | Mintage | F | VF | XF | Unc | BU |
|---|---|---|---|---|---|---|
| 1978 Proof | 4,026 | Value: 30.00 | | | | |

**10 DOLLARS** KM# 46 **Weight:** 28.4400 g. **Composition:** 0.5000 Silver .4572 oz. ASW **Subject:** 10th Anniversary of Independence **Reverse:** Prince Charles

| Date | Mintage | F | VF | XF | Unc | BU |
|---|---|---|---|---|---|---|
| 1980 | 5,001 | — | — | — | 12.50 | — |

**10 DOLLARS** KM#46a **Weight:** 30.4800 g. **Composition:** 0.9250 Silver .9066 oz. ASW

| Date | Mintage | F | VF | XF | Unc | BU |
|---|---|---|---|---|---|---|
| 1980 Proof | 3,001 | Value: 20.00 | | | | |

**10 DOLLARS** KM# 48 **Weight:** 30.0000 g. **Composition:** 0.9250 Silver .8922 oz. ASW **Subject:** Wedding of Prince Charles and Lady Diana **Obverse:** Queen's portrait right

| Date | Mintage | F | VF | XF | Unc | BU |
|---|---|---|---|---|---|---|
| 1981 Proof | 5,000 | Value: 21.50 | | | | |

**10 DOLLARS** **KM# 55** **Weight:** 28.2800 g. **Composition:** 0.9250 Silver .8411 oz. ASW **Subject:** 25th Anniversary - World Wildlife Fund **Obverse:** Queen's portrait right **Reverse:** Fijian ground frog

| Date | Mintage | F | VF | XF | Unc | BU |
|---|---|---|---|---|---|---|
| 1986 Proof | Est. 25,000 | Value: 27.50 | | | | |

**10 DOLLARS** **KM# 60** **Weight:** 28.2800 g. **Composition:** 0.9250 Silver .8411 oz. ASW **Subject:** Save the Children Fund

| Date | Mintage | F | VF | XF | Unc | BU |
|---|---|---|---|---|---|---|
| 1991 Proof | 20,000 | Value: 22.50 | | | | |

**10 DOLLARS** **KM# 62** **Weight:** 28.2800 g. **Composition:** 0.9250 Silver .8411 oz. ASW **Subject:** 40th Anniversary - Coronation of Queen Elizabeth II

| Date | Mintage | F | VF | XF | Unc | BU |
|---|---|---|---|---|---|---|
| 1993 Proof | Est. 10,000 | Value: 22.50 | | | | |

**10 DOLLARS** **KM# 63** **Weight:** 31.1035 g. **Composition:** 0.9250 Silver .9250 oz. ASW **Subject:** Discovery of Fiji **Reverse:** Abel J. Tasman

| Date | Mintage | F | VF | XF | Unc | BU |
|---|---|---|---|---|---|---|
| 1993 Proof | 10,000 | Value: 22.50 | | | | |

**10 DOLLARS** **KM# 64** **Weight:** 31.1035 g. **Composition:** 0.9250 Silver .9250 oz. ASW **Subject:** Discovery of Fiji **Reverse:** William Bligh

| Date | Mintage | F | VF | XF | Unc | BU |
|---|---|---|---|---|---|---|
| 1993 Proof | 10,000 | Value: 22.50 | | | | |

**10 DOLLARS** **KM# 66** **Weight:** 31.4600 g. **Composition:** 0.9250 Silver .9357 oz. ASW **Subject:** Protect Our World

| Date | Mintage | F | VF | XF | Unc | BU |
|---|---|---|---|---|---|---|
| 1993 Proof | — | Value: 22.50 | | | | |

**10 DOLLARS** **KM# 67** **Weight:** 31.4600 g. **Composition:** 0.9250 Silver .9357 oz. ASW **Subject:** 1996 Olympics **Reverse:** Judo

| Date | Mintage | F | VF | XF | Unc | BU |
|---|---|---|---|---|---|---|
| 1993 Proof | 20,000 | Value: 20.00 | | | | |

**10 DOLLARS** **KM# 68** **Weight:** 31.6400 g. **Composition:** 0.9250 Silver .9409 oz. ASW **Subject:** World Cup Soccer

| Date | Mintage | F | VF | XF | Unc | BU |
|---|---|---|---|---|---|---|
| 1993 Proof | — | Value: 25.00 | | | | |

**10 DOLLARS** **KM# 70** **Weight:** 31.4700 g. **Composition:** 0.9250 Silver .9359 oz. ASW **Subject:** Lunar Module "Eagle" **Obverse:** Queen's portrait right **Reverse:** Lunar module on moon

| Date | Mintage | F | VF | XF | Unc | BU |
|---|---|---|---|---|---|---|
| 1994 Proof | Est. 10,000 | Value: 35.00 | | | | |

**10 DOLLARS** **KM# 74** **Weight:** 31.3700 g. **Composition:** 0.9250 Silver .9329 oz. ASW **Subject:** Endangered Wildlife **Obverse:** Queen's portrait right **Reverse:** Fantail on branch

| Date | Mintage | F | VF | XF | Unc | BU |
|---|---|---|---|---|---|---|
| 1995 Proof | — | Value: 32.50 | | | | |

**10 DOLLARS** **KM# 75** **Weight:** 34.4600 g. **Composition:** 0.9250 Silver .9357 oz. ASW **Subject:** Silver Jubilee of Independence **Obverse:** Queen's portrait right **Reverse:** Cost of arms

| Date | Mintage | F | VF | XF | Unc | BU |
|---|---|---|---|---|---|---|
| 1995 Proof | — | Value: 30.00 | | | | |

**10 DOLLARS** **KM# 79** **Weight:** 31.5200 g. **Composition:** 0.9250 Silver .9368 oz. ASW **Subject:** Olympic Games 1996 **Obverse:** Queen's portrait right **Reverse:** Two sailboarders

| Date | Mintage | F | VF | XF | Unc | BU |
|---|---|---|---|---|---|---|
| 1995 Proof | — | Value: 32.50 | | | | |

**10 DOLLARS** **KM# 76** **Weight:** 31.3300 g. **Composition:** 0.9250 Silver .9317 oz. ASW **Subject:** Endangered Wildlife **Obverse:** Queen's portrait right **Reverse:** Banded iguana

| Date | Mintage | F | VF | XF | Unc | BU |
|---|---|---|---|---|---|---|
| 1997 Proof | — | Value: 32.50 | | | | |

**10 DOLLARS** **KM# 82** **Weight:** 31.6200 g. **Composition:** 0.9250 Silver .9404 oz. ASW **Subject:** HMS Providence **Ob-**

verse: Queen's portrait **Reverse:** Sail powered war ship **Edge:** Reeded **Size:** 38.6 mm.

| Date | Mintage | F | VF | XF | Unc | BU |
|---|---|---|---|---|---|---|
| 2001 Proof | — | Value: 50.00 | | | | |

**20 DOLLARS** **KM# 42** **Weight:** 35.0000 g. **Composition:** 0.5000 Silver .5627 oz. ASW **Subject:** Conservation **Obverse:** Queen's portrait right **Reverse:** Golden cowrie

| Date | Mintage | F | VF | XF | Unc | BU |
|---|---|---|---|---|---|---|
| 1978 | 3,584 | — | — | — | 30.00 | — |

**20 DOLLARS** **KM# 42a** **Weight:** 35.0000 g. **Composition:** 0.9250 Silver 1.0409 oz. ASW

| Date | Mintage | F | VF | XF | Unc | BU |
|---|---|---|---|---|---|---|
| 1978 Proof | 3,869 | Value: 35.00 | | | | |

**25 DOLLARS** **KM# 34** **Weight:** 48.6000 g. **Composition:** 0.9250 Silver 1.4455 oz. ASW **Subject:** 100th Anniversary - Cession to Great Britian **Obverse:** Queen's portrait right

| Date | Mintage | F | VF | XF | Unc | BU |
|---|---|---|---|---|---|---|
| 1974 | 2,400 | — | — | — | 35.00 | — |
| 1974 Proof | 8,299 | Value: 20.00 | | | | |

**25 DOLLARS** **KM# 37** **Weight:** 48.6000 g. **Composition:** 0.9250 Silver 1.4455 oz. ASW **Obverse:** Queen's portrait right **Reverse:** King Cakobau

| Date | Mintage | F | VF | XF | Unc | BU |
|---|---|---|---|---|---|---|
| 1975 | 836 | — | — | — | 50.00 | — |
| 1975 Proof | 5,157 | Value: 27.50 | | | | |

**25 DOLLARS** **KM# 57** **Weight:** 7.7750 g. **Composition:** 0.7500 Gold .1875 oz. AGW **Reverse:** Balikula mint mark of Pacific Sovereign Mint, Fijian thatched temple **Note:** Dates are privy marks; 1990 - Boar Tusks; 1991 - War Fan; 1992 - ?.

| Date | Mintage | F | VF | XF | Unc | BU |
|---|---|---|---|---|---|---|
| ND (1990) | 443 | — | — | — | 150 | — |
| ND (1991) | 512 | — | — | — | 150 | — |
| ND (1992) | 50 | — | — | — | 200 | — |

**50 DOLLARS** **KM# 58** **Weight:** 15.5500 g. **Composition:** 0.7500 Gold .3750 oz. AGW **Reverse:** Balikula mint mark of Pacific Sovereign Mint, Fijian warrior **Note:** Dates are privy marks; 1990 - Boar Tusks; 1991 - War Fan; 1992 - ?.

| Date | Mintage | F | VF | XF | Unc | BU |
|---|---|---|---|---|---|---|
| ND (1990) | 168 | — | — | — | 275 | — |
| ND (1991) | 141 | — | — | — | 275 | — |
| ND (1992) | 43 | — | — | — | 350 | — |

**50 DOLLARS** **KM# 72** **Weight:** 7.7760 g. **Composition:** 0.5833 Gold .1458 oz. AGW **Subject:** Olympics **Reverse:** Two field hockey players

| Date | Mintage | F | VF | XF | Unc | BU |
|---|---|---|---|---|---|---|
| 1996 | Est. 3,000 | — | — | — | 80.00 | — |

**100 DOLLARS** **KM# 35** **Weight:** 31.3600 g. **Composition:** 0.5000 Gold .5042 oz. AGW **Subject:** 100th Anniversary - Cession to Great Britain **Obverse:** Similar to 250 Dollars KM#43

| Date | Mintage | F | VF | XF | Unc | BU |
|---|---|---|---|---|---|---|
| 1974 | 1,109 | — | — | — | 200 | — |
| 1974 Proof | 2,321 | Value: 235 | | | | |

**100 DOLLARS** **KM# 38** **Weight:** 31.3000 g. **Composition:** 0.5000 Gold .5032 oz. AGW **Obverse:** Similar to 250 Dollars KM#43 **Reverse:** King Cakobau

| Date | Mintage | F | VF | XF | Unc | BU |
|---|---|---|---|---|---|---|
| 1975 | 593 | — | — | — | 240 | — |
| 1975 Proof | 3,197 | Value: 255 | | | | |

**100 DOLLARS** **KM# 59** **Weight:** 31.1000 g. **Composition:** 0.7500 Gold .7500 oz. AGW **Reverse:** Balikula mint mark of Pacific Sovereign Mint **Note:** Dates are privy marks; 1990 - Boar Tusks; 1991 - War Fan; 1992 - ?.

| Date | Mintage | F | VF | XF | Unc | BU |
|---|---|---|---|---|---|---|
| ND (1990) | 161 | — | — | — | 550 | — |
| ND (1991) | 131 | — | — | — | 550 | — |
| ND (1992) | 41 | — | — | — | 650 | — |

**100 DOLLARS** **KM# 65** **Weight:** 7.5000 g. **Composition:** 0.9170 Gold .2209 oz. AGW **Subject:** Discovery of Fiji **Reverse:** James Cook

| Date | Mintage | F | VF | XF | Unc | BU |
|---|---|---|---|---|---|---|
| 1993 Proof | 3,000 | Value: 150 | | | | |

**200 DOLLARS** **KM# 47** **Weight:** 15.9800 g. **Composition:** 0.9170 Gold .4712 oz. AGW **Subject:** 10th Anniversary of Independence **Reverse:** Prince Charles

| Date | Mintage | F | VF | XF | Unc | BU |
|---|---|---|---|---|---|---|
| 1980 | 500 | — | — | — | 245 | — |
| 1980 Proof | 1,166 | Value: 200 | | | | |

**200 DOLLARS** **KM# 56** **Weight:** 15.9800 g. **Composition:** 0.9170 Gold .4712 oz. AGW **Subject:** 25th Anniversary - World Wildlife Fund **Obverse:** Similar to 10 cents, KM#31 **Reverse:** Ogmodon

| Date | Mintage | F | VF | XF | Unc | BU |
|---|---|---|---|---|---|---|
| 1986 Proof | 5,000 | Value: 285 | | | | |

**200 DOLLARS** **KM# 61** **Weight:** 10.0000 g. **Composition:** 0.9170 Gold .2948 oz. AGW **Subject:** Save the Children Fund

| Date | Mintage | F | VF | XF | Unc | BU |
|---|---|---|---|---|---|---|
| 1991 Proof | 32,000 | Value: 200 | | | | |

**250 DOLLARS** **KM# 43** **Weight:** 33.4370 g. **Composition:** 0.9000 Gold .9676 oz. AGW **Subject:** Conservation **Reverse:** Banded iguana

| Date | Mintage | F | VF | XF | Unc | BU |
|---|---|---|---|---|---|---|
| 1978 | 810 | — | — | — | 500 | — |
| 1978 Proof | 252 | Value: 800 | | | | |

## TRIAL STRIKES

| KM# | Date | Mintage | Identification | Mkt Val |
|---|---|---|---|---|
| TS2 | 1974 | — | Cent. Bronze. Fijian planting taro. | 200 |
| TS3 | 1974 | — | Cent. Copper-Nickel. Fijian planting taro. | 250 |
| TS1 | 1974 | — | 100 Dollars. Bronze. KM35. | 750 |

## MINT SETS

| KM# | Date | Mintage | Identification | Issue Price | Mkt Val |
|---|---|---|---|---|---|
| MSA1 | 1934 (3) | — | KM3-5 | — | 500 |
| MSB1 | 1969 (6) | — | KM27-32 | — | 8.00 |
| MS1 | 1976 (7) | 5,001 | KM27-32, 36 | 9.00 | 12.50 |
| MS2 | 1976 (6) | — | KM27-31, 36 | — | 6.50 |
| MS3 | 1978 (6) | 4,006 | KM28-31, 36, 39 | 4.50 | 8.00 |
| MS4 | 1978 (3) | — | KM41-43 | 444 | 550 |
| MS5 | 1978 (2) | — | KM41-42 | 44.00 | 50.00 |
| MS6 | 1983 (6) | 3,000 | KM27-31, 36 | 5.00 | 4.50 |
| MS7 | 1984 (6) | 5,000 | KM27-31, 36 | 3.60 | 4.50 |
| MS8 | 1990 (8) | — | KM49a-54a | — | 5.00 |
| MS9 | 1990 (3) | — | KM57-59 | 905 | 975 |

## PROOF SETS

| KM# | Date | Mintage | Identification | Issue Price | Mkt Val |
|---|---|---|---|---|---|
| PS1 | 1969 (6) | 10,000 | KM#27-32 | 7.20 | 8.00 |
| PS2 | 1976 (7) | 3,023 | KM#27a-32a, 36a | 87.50 | 45.00 |
| PS3 | 1978 (6) | 2,000 | KM#28-31, 36, 39 | 31.00 | 20.00 |
| PS4 | 1978 (2) | — | KM#41a, 42a | 76.00 | 65.00 |
| PS5 | 1978 (3) | — | KM#41a, 42a, 43 | 726 | 865 |
| PS6 | 1980 (6) | 2,500 | KM#28-31, 36, 39 | 45.00 | 20.00 |
| PS7 | 1982 (6) | 3,000 | KM#28-31, 36, 39 | 32.00 | 22.50 |
| PS8 | 1983 (6) | 3,000 | KM#27-31, 36 | 27.00 | 22.50 |
| PS9 | 1993 (3) | — | KM#63-65 | 370 | 25.00 |

# FINLAND

The Republic of Finland, the third most northerly state of the European continent, has an area of 130,559 sq. mi. (338,127 sq. km.) and a population of 5.1 million. Capital: Helsinki. Lumbering, shipbuilding, metal and woodworking are the leading industries. Paper, timber, woodpulp, plywood and metal products are exported.

The Finns, who probably originated in the Volga region of Russia, took Finland from the Lapps late in the 7th century. They were conquered in the 12th century by Eric IX of Sweden, and brought into contact with Western Christendom. In 1809, Sweden was conquered by Alexander I of Russia, and the peace terms gave Finland to Russia which became a grand duchy within the Russian Empire until Dec. 6, 1917, when, shortly after the Bolshevik revolution it declared its independence. After a brief but bitter civil war between the Russian sympathizers and Finnish nationalists in which the Whites (nationalists) were victorious, a new constitution was adopted, and on Dec. 6, 1917 Finland was established as a republic. In 1939 Soviet troops invaded Finland over disputed territorial concessions which were later granted in the peace treaty of 1940. When the Germans invaded Russia, Finland became involved and in the Armistice of 1944 lost the Petsamo area to the Soviets.

**RULERS**

Alexander II, 1855-1881
Alexander III, 1881-1894
**Nicholas II, 1894-1917**

**MONETARY SYSTEM**

100 Pennia = 1 Markka

**Commencing 1963**

100 Old Markka = 1 New Markka

**MINT MARKS**

H - Birmingham 1921
Heart (h) - Copenhagen 1922
No mm – Helsinki

**MINTMASTERS INITIALS**

| Letter | Date | Name |
|---|---|---|
| H | 1948-1958 | Peippo Uolevi Helle |
| H-M | 1990` | Raimo Heino & Raimo Makkonen |
| K | 1976-1983 | Timo Koivuranta |
| K-H | 1977, 1979 | Timo Koivuranta & Heikki Haivaoja (Designer) |
| K-M | 1983 | Timo Koivuranta & Pertti Makinen |
| K-N | 1978 | Timo Koivuranta & Antti Neuvonen |
| K-T | 1982 | Timo Koivuranta & Erja Tielinen |
| L | 1885-1912 | Johan Conrad Lihr |
| L | 1948 | Vesa Uolevi Liuhto |
| L-M | 1991 | Arto Lappalainen & Raimo Makkonen |
| L-M | 2000 | Maija Lavonen & Raimo Makkonen |
| M | 1987 | Raimo Makkonen |
| M-G | 1998 | Raimo Makkonen & Henrik Gummerus |
| M-L | 1997 | Raimo Makkonen & Tero Lounas |
| M-L-L | 1995 | Raimo Makkonen & Arto Lappalainen & Marita Lappalainen |
| M-L-M | 1989 | Marjo Lahtinen & Raimo Makkonen |
| M-O | 1998 | Raimo Makkonen & Harri Ojala |
| M-S | 1992, 1997 | Raimo Makkonen & Erkki Salmela |
| N | 1983-1987 | Tapio Nevalainen |
| P-M | 1989-1991, 1994-1995, 1997, 2000 | Reijo Paavilainen & Raimo Makkonen |
| P-N | 1985 | Reijo Paavilainen & Tapio Nevalainen |
| P-V-M | 1999 | Juhani Pallasmaa, Jukka Veistola & Raimo Makkonen |
| R-M | 1999 | Jarkko Roth & Raimo Makkonen |
| S | 1912-1947 | Isak Gustaf Sundell |
| S | 1958-1975 | Allan Alarik Soiniemi |
| S-H | 1967-1971 | Allan Alarik Soiniemi & Heikki Haivaoja (Designer) |
| S-J | 1960 | Allan Alarik Soiniemi & Toivo Jaatinen |
| S-M | 1995 | Terho Sakki & Raimo Makkonen |
| T-M | 1996, 2000 | Erja Tielinen & Raimo Makkonen |

# GRAND DUCHY

## DECIMAL COINAGE

**PENNI** **KM# 13** **Composition:** Copper

| Date | Mintage | F | VF | XF | Unc | BU |
|---|---|---|---|---|---|---|
| 1901 | 1,520,000 | 0.75 | 1.25 | 2.50 | 5.00 | — |
| 1902 | 1,000,000 | 0.75 | 1.25 | 2.50 | 7.50 | — |
| 1903 Small 3 | 1,145,000 | 0.75 | 1.25 | 2.50 | 7.50 | — |
| 1903 Large 3 | Inc. above | 1.00 | 2.00 | 5.00 | 12.00 | — |
| 1904 | 500,000 | 2.50 | 5.00 | 10.00 | 20.00 | — |
| 1905 | 1,390,000 | 0.50 | 1.00 | 2.00 | 4.00 | — |
| 1906 | 1,020,000 | 0.50 | 1.00 | 2.00 | 4.00 | — |
| 1907 Normal 7 | 2,490,000 | 0.75 | 1.25 | 2.50 | 4.00 | — |
| 1907 Without serif on 7 arm | Inc. above | 0.30 | 0.75 | 1.75 | 4.00 | — |
| 1908 | 950,000 | 0.50 | 1.00 | 2.00 | 5.00 | — |
| 1909 | 3,060,000 | 0.25 | 0.65 | 1.25 | 2.50 | — |
| 1911 | 2,550,000 | 0.25 | 0.65 | 1.25 | 2.50 | — |
| 1912 | 2,450,000 | 0.25 | 0.65 | 1.25 | 2.50 | — |
| 1913 | 1,650,000 | 0.25 | 0.65 | 1.25 | 3.00 | — |
| 1914 | 1,900,000 | 0.25 | 0.65 | 1.25 | 3.50 | — |
| 1915 | 2,250,000 | 0.25 | 0.65 | 1.25 | 2.50 | — |
| 1916 | 3,040,000 | 0.25 | 0.50 | 1.00 | 2.00 | — |

**5 PENNIA** **KM# 15** **Composition:** Copper

| Date | Mintage | F | VF | XF | Unc | BU |
|---|---|---|---|---|---|---|
| 1901 | 990,000 | 1.00 | 4.00 | 10.00 | 60.00 | — |
| 1905 | 620,000 | 1.00 | 5.00 | 20.00 | 80.00 | — |
| 1906 | 960,000 | 0.75 | 2.50 | 10.00 | 60.00 | — |
| 1907 | 770,000 | 1.00 | 5.00 | 20.00 | 75.00 | — |
| 1908 | 1,660,000 | 0.75 | 2.50 | 10.00 | 40.00 | — |
| 1910 | 60,000 | 20.00 | 35.00 | 75.00 | 175 | — |
| 1911 | 1,050,000 | 0.75 | 2.50 | 6.00 | 30.00 | — |
| 1912 | 460,000 | 1.50 | 5.00 | 15.00 | 60.00 | — |
| 1913 | 1,060,000 | 0.65 | 1.25 | 4.00 | 15.00 | — |
| 1914 | 820,000 | 0.65 | 1.25 | 3.00 | 15.00 | — |
| 1915 | 2,080,000 | 0.30 | 0.75 | 3.00 | 10.00 | — |
| 1916 | 4,470,000 | 0.30 | 0.75 | 3.00 | 10.00 | — |
| 1917 | 4,070,000 | 0.30 | 0.75 | 3.00 | 10.00 | — |

**10 PENNIA** **KM# 14** **Composition:** Copper

| Date | Mintage | F | VF | XF | Unc | BU |
|---|---|---|---|---|---|---|
| 1905 | 500,000 | 1.25 | 5.00 | 30.00 | 110 | — |
| 1907 | 503,000 | 1.25 | 5.00 | 30.00 | 110 | — |
| 1908 | 320,000 | 1.50 | 7.50 | 25.00 | 90.00 | — |
| 1909 | 180,000 | 2.00 | 10.00 | 35.00 | 110 | — |
| 1910 | 241,000 | 1.50 | 7.50 | 25.00 | 80.00 | — |
| 1911 | 370,000 | 1.00 | 5.00 | 15.00 | 50.00 | — |
| 1912 | 191,000 | 1.50 | 7.50 | 20.00 | 80.00 | — |
| 1913 | 150,000 | 2.50 | 7.50 | 40.00 | 110 | — |
| 1914 | 605,000 | 0.75 | 1.50 | 10.00 | 30.00 | — |
| 1915 | 420,000 | 0.50 | 1.00 | 5.00 | 15.00 | — |
| 1916 | 1,952,000 | 0.50 | 1.00 | 3.00 | 10.00 | — |
| 1917 | 1,600,000 | 0.75 | 1.50 | 4.00 | 12.00 | — |

**25 PENNIA** **KM# 6.2** **Weight:** 1.2747 g. **Composition:** 0.7500 Silver .0307 oz. ASW **Note:** Dentilated border.

| Date | Mintage | F | VF | XF | Unc | BU |
|---|---|---|---|---|---|---|
| 1901 L | 993,000 | 1.00 | 2.00 | 8.00 | 35.00 | — |
| 1902 L | 210,000 | 3.00 | 7.00 | 20.00 | 75.00 | — |
| 1906 L | 281,000 | 2.00 | 5.00 | 10.00 | 50.00 | — |
| 1907 L | 590,000 | 1.00 | 2.00 | 5.00 | 25.00 | — |
| 1908 L | 340,000 | 1.00 | 2.50 | 15.00 | 40.00 | — |
| 1909 L | 1,099,000 | 0.75 | 1.50 | 5.00 | 15.00 | — |
| 1910 L | 392,000 | 2.50 | 5.00 | 15.00 | 50.00 | — |
| 1913 S | 832,000 | 0.50 | 1.00 | 1.50 | 3.00 | — |
| 1915 S | 2,400,000 | 0.50 | 0.75 | 1.00 | 1.50 | — |
| 1916 S | 6,392,000 | 0.50 | 0.75 | 1.00 | 1.50 | — |
| 1917 S | 5,820,000 | 0.50 | 0.75 | 1.00 | 1.50 | — |

**50 PENNIA** KM# 2.2 **Weight:** 2.5494 g. **Composition:** 0.7500 Silver .0615 oz. ASW **Note:** Dentilated border.

| Date | Mintage | F | VF | XF | Unc | BU |
|---|---|---|---|---|---|---|
| 1907 L | 260,000 | 1.00 | 3.00 | 30.00 | 90.00 | — |
| 1908 L | 353,000 | 0.75 | 2.00 | 10.00 | 30.00 | — |
| 1911 L | 616,000 | 0.75 | 1.25 | 2.50 | 5.00 | — |
| 1914 S | 600,000 | 0.75 | 1.00 | 1.50 | 4.00 | — |
| 1915 S | 1,000,000 | 0.75 | 1.00 | 1.50 | 2.50 | — |
| 1916 S | 4,752,000 | 0.75 | 1.00 | 1.50 | 2.50 | — |
| 1917 S | 3,972,000 | 0.75 | 1.00 | 1.50 | 2.50 | — |

**MARKKA** KM# 3.2 **Weight:** 5.1828 g. **Composition:** 0.8680 Silver .1446 oz. ASW **Note:** Dentilated border.

| Date | Mintage | F | VF | XF | Unc | BU |
|---|---|---|---|---|---|---|
| 1907 L | 350,000 | 2.00 | 3.00 | 8.00 | 25.00 | — |
| 1908 L | 153,000 | 4.00 | 10.00 | 25.00 | 50.00 | — |
| 1915 S | 1,212,000 | 2.00 | 3.00 | 6.00 | 10.00 | — |

**MARKKA** KM# 95 **Weight:** 8.6400 g. **Composition:** 0.7500 Gold .2083 oz. AGW **Subject:** Last Markka Coin **Obverse:** National arms **Reverse:** Symbolic design **Edge:** Reeded **Size:** 22 mm.

| Date | Mintage | F | VF | XF | Unc | BU |
|---|---|---|---|---|---|---|
| 2001 Proof | 55,000 | Value: 254 | | | | |

**2 MARKKAA** KM# 7.2 **Weight:** 10.3657 g. **Composition:** 0.8680 Silver .2893 oz. ASW **Note:** Dentilated border.

| Date | Mintage | F | VF | XF | Unc | BU |
|---|---|---|---|---|---|---|
| 1905 L | 24,000 | 60.00 | 100 | 300 | 850 | — |
| 1906 L | 225,000 | 5.00 | 8.00 | 40.00 | 80.00 | — |
| 1907 L | 125,000 | 10.00 | 20.00 | 60.00 | 100 | — |
| 1908 L | 124,000 | 5.00 | 15.00 | 30.00 | 60.00 | — |

**10 MARKKAA** KM# 8.2 **Weight:** 3.2258 g. **Composition:** 0.9000 Gold .0933 oz. AGW **Obverse:** Wide eagle **Note:** Regal issues; similar to 20 Markkaa, KM#9.2.

| Date | Mintage | F | VF | XF | Unc | BU |
|---|---|---|---|---|---|---|
| 1904 L | 102,000 | 225 | 250 | 300 | 350 | — |
| 1904 L | 102,000 | 225 | 250 | 300 | 350 | — |
| 1905 L | 43,000 | 1,000 | 1,200 | 1,400 | 1,700 | — |
| 1913 L | 396,000 | 50.00 | 60.00 | 70.00 | 85.00 | — |

**20 MARKKAA** KM# 9.2 **Weight:** 6.4516 g. **Composition:** 0.9000 Gold .1867 oz. AGW **Obverse:** Wide eagle **Note:** Regal issues.

| Date | Mintage | F | VF | XF | Unc | BU |
|---|---|---|---|---|---|---|
| 1903 L | 112,000 | 75.00 | 85.00 | 110 | 140 | — |
| 1903 L | 112,000 | 75.00 | 85.00 | 110 | 140 | — |
| 1904 L | 188,000 | 75.00 | 85.00 | 110 | 130 | — |
| 1910 L | 201,000 | 75.00 | 85.00 | 110 | 130 | — |
| 1911 L | 161,000 | 75.00 | 85.00 | 110 | 140 | — |
| 1912 L | 881,000 | 1,000 | 1,500 | 2,500 | 4,000 | — |
| 1912 S | Inc. above | 70.00 | 80.00 | 100 | 115 | — |
| 1913 S | 214,000 | 70.00 | 80.00 | 100 | 115 | — |

## CIVIL WAR COINAGE

Kerenski Government Issue

**PENNI** KM# 16 **Composition:** Copper

| Date | Mintage | F | VF | XF | Unc | BU |
|---|---|---|---|---|---|---|
| 1917 | 1,650,000 | 0.25 | 0.75 | 1.00 | 1.50 | — |

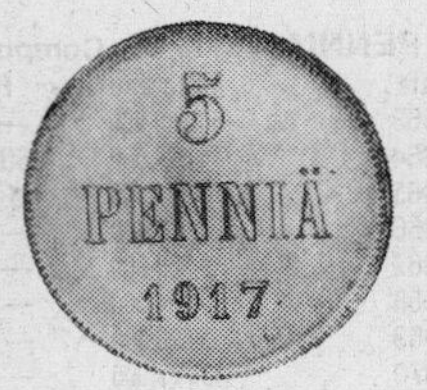


**5 PENNIA** KM# 17 **Composition:** Copper

| Date | Mintage | F | VF | XF | Unc | BU |
|---|---|---|---|---|---|---|
| 1917 | Inc. above | 0.30 | 0.75 | 2.50 | 5.00 | — |

**10 PENNIA** KM# 18 **Composition:** Copper

| Date | Mintage | F | VF | XF | Unc | BU |
|---|---|---|---|---|---|---|
| 1917 | Inc. above | 0.50 | 1.00 | 2.50 | 7.50 | — |

**25 PENNIA** KM# 19 **Weight:** 1.2747 g. **Composition:** 0.7500 Silver .0307 oz. ASW **Obverse:** Crown above eagle removed

| Date | Mintage | F | VF | XF | Unc | BU |
|---|---|---|---|---|---|---|
| 1917 S | 2,310,000 | — | BV | 1.00 | 1.50 | — |

**50 PENNIA** KM# 20 **Weight:** 2.5494 g. **Composition:** 0.7500 Silver .0615 oz. ASW **Obverse:** Crown above eagle removed

| Date | Mintage | F | VF | XF | Unc | BU |
|---|---|---|---|---|---|---|
| 1917 S | 570,000 | — | BV | 1.25 | 2.00 | — |

## CIVIL WAR COINAGE

Liberated Finnish Government Issue

**5 PENNIA** KM# 21.1 **Composition:** Copper **Obverse:** Wreath knot centered between 9 and 1 of date

| Date | Mintage | F | VF | XF | Unc | BU |
|---|---|---|---|---|---|---|
| 1918 | 35,000 | 20.00 | 30.00 | 45.00 | 60.00 | — |

**5 PENNIA** KM# 21.2 **Composition:** Copper **Obverse:** Wreath knot above second 1 in 1918

| Date | Mintage | F | VF | XF | Unc | BU |
|---|---|---|---|---|---|---|
| 1918 | — | 50.00 | 100 | 175 | 350 | — |

**Note:** This type was unofficially struck outside of Finland in the early 1920's

# REPUBLIC

## DECIMAL COINAGE

**MARKKAA** KM# 49 **Weight:** 6.4000 g. **Composition:** 0.3500 Silver .0720 oz. ASW

| Date | Mintage | F | VF | XF | Unc | BU |
|---|---|---|---|---|---|---|
| 1964 S | 9,999,000 | — | BV | 1.50 | 5.00 | — |
| 1965 S | 15,107,000 | — | BV | 1.00 | 3.00 | — |
| 1966 S | 15,183,000 | — | BV | 0.75 | 2.00 | — |
| 1967 S | 6,249,000 | — | BV | 0.75 | 2.00 | — |
| 1968 S | 3,063,000 | — | BV | 0.75 | 2.00 | — |

**MARKKAA** KM# 49A **Composition:** Copper-Nickel

| Date | Mintage | F | VF | XF | Unc | BU |
|---|---|---|---|---|---|---|
| 1969 S | 1,308,000 | 0.35 | 0.45 | 0.60 | 1.50 | — |
| 1970 S | 12,255,000 | — | 0.35 | 0.50 | 1.00 | — |
| 1971 S | 19,676,000 | — | 0.35 | 0.50 | 1.00 | — |
| 1972 S | 19,885,000 | — | 0.35 | 0.50 | 1.00 | — |
| 1973 S | 17,060,000 | — | 0.35 | 0.50 | 1.00 | — |
| 1974 S | 18,065,000 | — | 0.35 | 0.50 | 1.00 | — |
| 1975 S | 11,523,000 | — | 0.35 | 0.50 | 1.00 | — |
| 1976 K | 12,048,000 | — | 0.35 | 0.50 | 1.00 | — |
| 1977 K | 10,077,000 | — | 0.35 | 0.50 | 1.00 | — |
| 1978 K | 10,022,000 | — | 0.35 | 0.50 | 1.00 | — |
| 1979 K | 11,311,000 | — | 0.35 | 0.50 | 1.00 | — |
| 1980 K | 19,306,000 | — | — | 0.35 | 0.75 | — |
| 1981 K | 32,003,000 | — | — | 0.35 | 0.75 | — |
| 1982 K | 30,001,000 | — | — | 0.35 | 0.75 | — |
| 1983 K | 8,074,999 | — | — | 0.35 | 0.75 | — |
| 1983 N | 11,927,000 | — | — | 0.35 | 0.75 | — |
| 1984 N | 15,000,000 | — | — | 0.35 | 0.75 | — |
| 1985 N | 19,001,000 | — | — | 0.35 | 0.75 | — |
| 1986 N | 10,000,000 | — | — | 0.35 | 0.75 | — |
| 1987 N | 700,000 | — | — | 1.00 | 2.00 | — |
| 1987 M | 9,303,000 | — | — | 0.35 | 0.75 | — |
| 1988 M | 27,535,000 | — | — | 0.35 | 0.75 | — |
| 1989 M | 37,520,000 | — | — | 0.35 | 0.75 | — |
| 1990 M | 50,305,000 | — | — | 0.35 | 0.75 | — |
| 1991 M | 15,026,000 | — | — | 0.35 | 0.75 | — |
| 1992 M | 3,628,000 | — | — | 0.35 | 0.75 | — |
| 1993 M | 1,036,000 | — | — | 0.50 | 1.00 | — |

**MARKKAA** KM# 76 **Composition:** Aluminum-Bronze

| Date | Mintage | F | VF | XF | Unc | BU |
|---|---|---|---|---|---|---|
| 1993 M | 91,588,000 | — | — | 0.35 | 0.75 | — |
| 1994 M | 152,011,000 | — | — | 0.35 | 0.75 | — |
| 1994 M Proof | 5,000 | Value: 10.00 | | | | |
| 1995 M | 40,008,000 | — | — | 0.35 | 0.75 | — |
| 1995 M Proof | 3,000 | Value: 10.00 | | | | |
| 1996 M | 21,000,000 | — | — | 0.35 | 0.75 | — |
| 1996 M Proof | 1,200 | Value: 10.00 | | | | |
| 1997 M | — | — | — | 0.35 | 0.75 | — |
| 1997 M Proof | 2,000 | Value: 10.00 | | | | |
| 1998 M | — | — | — | 0.35 | 0.75 | — |
| 1998 M Proof | 2,000 | Value: 10.00 | | | | |
| 1999 M | — | — | — | 0.35 | 0.75 | — |
| 1999 M Proof | — | Value: 10.00 | | | | |
| 2000 M | — | — | — | 0.35 | 0.75 | — |
| 2000 M Proof | — | Value: 10.00 | | | | |
| 2001 M | Inc. above | — | — | 0.35 | 0.75 | — |
| 2001 M | Inc. above | Value: 10.00 | | | | |

**MARKKAA** KM# 76a **Composition:** Copper-Nickel

| Date | Mintage | F | VF | XF | Unc | BU |
|---|---|---|---|---|---|---|
| 1993 M In sets only | 100,000 | — | — | — | — | — |

**PENNI** **KM# 23** **Composition:** Copper

| Date | Mintage | F | VF | XF | Unc | BU |
|---|---|---|---|---|---|---|
| 1919 | 1,200,000 | 0.25 | 0.65 | 1.75 | 3.00 | — |
| 1920 | 720,000 | 0.25 | 0.65 | 1.75 | 3.00 | — |
| 1921 | 510,000 | 0.35 | 1.00 | 2.00 | 4.00 | — |
| 1922 | 1,060,000 | 0.25 | 0.65 | 1.75 | 3.00 | — |
| 1923 | 990,000 | 0.25 | 0.65 | 1.75 | 3.00 | — |
| 1924 | 2,180,000 | 0.25 | 0.65 | 1.75 | 3.00 | — |

**PENNI** **KM# 44** **Composition:** Copper

| Date | Mintage | F | VF | XF | Unc | BU |
|---|---|---|---|---|---|---|
| 1963 Square edge | 62,460 | — | 0.10 | 0.40 | 1.00 | — |
| 1963 Round edge | 108,870 | — | 0.10 | 0.20 | 0.50 | — |
| 1964 | 49,300 | — | 0.10 | 0.40 | 1.00 | — |
| 1965 | 43,112 | — | 0.10 | 0.40 | 1.00 | — |
| 1966 | 36,880 | — | 0.10 | 0.40 | 1.00 | — |
| 1967 | 62,792 | — | 0.10 | 0.40 | 1.00 | — |
| 1968 | 73,416 | — | — | 0.40 | 1.00 | — |
| 1969 | 51,748 | — | — | 0.40 | 1.00 | — |

**PENNI** **KM# 44a** **Composition:** Aluminum

| Date | Mintage | F | VF | XF | Unc | BU |
|---|---|---|---|---|---|---|
| 1969 | 28,524,000 | — | — | 0.40 | 1.00 | — |
| 1970 | 85,140,000 | — | — | 0.10 | 0.50 | — |
| 1971 | 70,240,000 | — | — | 0.10 | 0.50 | — |
| 1972 | 95,096,000 | — | — | 0.10 | 0.50 | — |
| 1973 | 115,532,000 | — | — | 0.10 | 0.25 | — |
| 1974 | 100,132,000 | — | — | 0.10 | 0.25 | — |
| 1975 | 111,906,000 | — | — | 0.10 | 0.25 | — |
| 1976 | 34,965,000 | — | — | 0.10 | 0.50 | — |
| 1977 | 61,393,000 | — | — | 0.10 | 0.25 | — |
| 1978 | 90,132,000 | — | — | 0.10 | 0.25 | — |
| 1979 | 33,388,000 | — | — | 0.10 | 0.25 | — |

**5 PENNIA** **KM# 22** **Composition:** Copper

| Date | Mintage | F | VF | XF | Unc | BU |
|---|---|---|---|---|---|---|
| 1918 | 4,270,000 | 0.10 | 0.25 | 1.00 | 4.00 | — |
| 1919 | 4,640,000 | 0.10 | 0.25 | 1.00 | 4.00 | — |
| 1920 | 7,710,000 | 0.10 | 0.25 | 1.00 | 3.00 | — |
| 1921 | 5,910,000 | 0.10 | 0.25 | 1.00 | 3.00 | — |
| 1922 | 8,540,000 | 0.10 | 0.25 | 1.00 | 3.00 | — |
| 1927 | 1,520,000 | 0.75 | 1.50 | 3.50 | 15.00 | — |
| 1928 | 2,110,000 | 0.25 | 0.50 | 1.50 | 8.00 | — |
| 1929 | 1,500,000 | 0.25 | 0.50 | 1.50 | 8.00 | — |
| 1930 | 2,140,000 | 0.75 | 1.25 | 3.00 | 12.00 | — |
| 1932 | 2,130,000 | 0.15 | 0.50 | 1.00 | 4.00 | — |
| 1934 | 2,180,000 | 0.15 | 0.50 | 1.00 | 4.00 | — |
| 1935 | 1,610,000 | 0.15 | 0.35 | 1.00 | 3.00 | — |
| 1936 | 2,610,000 | 0.15 | 0.35 | 1.00 | 3.00 | — |
| 1937 | 3,830,000 | 0.10 | 0.25 | 1.00 | 3.00 | — |
| 1938 | 4,300,000 | 0.10 | 0.25 | 1.00 | 3.00 | — |
| 1939 | 2,270,000 | 0.10 | 0.25 | 1.00 | 3.00 | — |
| 1940 | 1,610,000 | 0.25 | 0.50 | 1.50 | 5.00 | — |

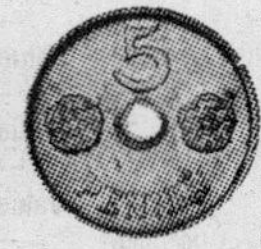

**5 PENNIA** **KM# 64.1** **Composition:** Copper **Note:** Punched center hole.

| Date | Mintage | F | VF | XF | Unc | BU |
|---|---|---|---|---|---|---|
| 1941 | 5,950,000 | 0.10 | 0.20 | 0.50 | 1.25 | — |
| 1942 | 4,280,000 | 0.10 | 0.20 | 0.50 | 1.25 | — |
| 1943 | 1,530,000 | 0.10 | 0.50 | 1.25 | 2.50 | — |

**5 PENNIA** **KM# 64.2** **Composition:** Copper **Note:** Without punched center hole. These issues were not authorized by the government and any that exist were illegally removed from the mint.

| Date | Mintage | F | VF | XF | Unc | BU |
|---|---|---|---|---|---|---|
| 1941 | Inc. above | 25.00 | 30.00 | 70.00 | 100 | — |
| 1942 | Inc. above | 25.00 | 30.00 | 70.00 | 100 | — |
| 1943 | Inc. above | 50.00 | 70.00 | 100 | 125 | — |

**5 PENNIA** **KM# 45** **Composition:** Copper

| Date | Mintage | F | VF | XF | Unc | BU |
|---|---|---|---|---|---|---|
| 1963 | 60,320,000 | — | 0.10 | 0.50 | 1.50 | — |
| 1964 | 4,634,000 | 0.50 | 1.00 | 2.00 | 7.50 | — |
| 1965 | 10,264,000 | — | 0.10 | 0.50 | 1.50 | — |
| 1966 | 8,064,000 | — | 0.10 | 0.50 | 1.50 | — |
| 1967 | 9,968,000 | — | 0.10 | 0.50 | 1.50 | — |
| 1968 | 6,144,000 | — | 0.10 | 0.50 | 1.50 | — |
| 1969 | 3,598,000 | — | 0.15 | 0.50 | 2.00 | — |
| 1970 | 13,772,000 | — | 0.10 | 0.25 | 1.00 | — |
| 1971 | 20,010,000 | — | — | 0.25 | 1.00 | — |
| 1972 | 24,122,000 | — | — | 0.25 | 1.00 | — |
| 1973 | 25,644,000 | — | — | 0.25 | 1.00 | — |
| 1974 | 21,530,000 | — | — | 0.25 | 1.00 | — |
| 1975 | 25,010,000 | — | — | 0.25 | 1.00 | — |
| 1976 | 25,551,000 | — | — | 0.25 | 1.00 | — |
| 1977 | 1,489,000 | — | 0.10 | 0.50 | 1.50 | — |

**5 PENNIA** **KM# 45a** **Composition:** Aluminum

| Date | Mintage | F | VF | XF | Unc | BU |
|---|---|---|---|---|---|---|
| 1977 | 30,552,000 | — | — | 0.15 | 0.50 | — |
| 1978 | 26,112,000 | — | — | 0.15 | 0.50 | — |
| 1979 | 40,042,000 | — | — | 0.15 | 0.50 | — |
| 1980 | 60,026,000 | — | — | 0.15 | 0.50 | — |
| 1981 | 2,044,000 | — | 0.20 | 0.40 | 1.00 | — |
| 1982 | 10,012,000 | — | — | 0.25 | 0.75 | — |
| 1983 | 33,885,000 | — | — | — | 0.25 | — |
| 1984 | 25,001,000 | — | — | — | 0.25 | — |
| 1985 | 25,000,000 | — | — | — | 0.25 | — |
| 1986 | 20,000,000 | — | — | — | 0.25 | — |
| 1987 | 2,020,000 | — | — | — | 0.25 | — |
| 1988 | 33,005,000 | — | — | — | 0.15 | — |
| 1989 | 2,200,000 | — | — | — | 0.25 | — |
| 1990 | 2,506,000 | — | — | — | 0.25 | — |

**10 PENNIA** **KM# 24** **Composition:** Copper

| Date | Mintage | F | VF | XF | Unc | BU |
|---|---|---|---|---|---|---|
| 1919 | 3,670,000 | 0.10 | 0.25 | 1.00 | 5.00 | — |
| 1920 | 2,380,000 | 0.10 | 0.25 | 1.00 | 5.00 | — |
| 1921 | 3,970,000 | 0.10 | 0.25 | 1.00 | 5.00 | — |
| 1922 | 2,180,000 | 0.10 | 0.25 | 2.00 | 7.00 | — |
| 1923 | 910,000 | 0.75 | 1.50 | 7.00 | 20.00 | — |
| 1924 | 1,350,000 | 0.25 | 0.50 | 3.00 | 12.00 | — |
| 1926 | 1,690,000 | 0.25 | 0.50 | 2.00 | 10.00 | — |
| 1927 | 1,330,000 | 0.50 | 1.00 | 3.00 | 12.00 | — |
| 1928 | 1,006,000 | 0.50 | 1.00 | 2.50 | 10.00 | — |
| 1929 | 1,560,000 | 0.35 | 0.85 | 2.00 | 7.00 | — |
| 1930 | 650,000 | 0.75 | 1.50 | 7.00 | 15.00 | — |
| 1931 | 1,040,000 | 1.00 | 2.00 | 7.00 | 20.00 | — |
| 1934 | 1,680,000 | 0.35 | 0.85 | 2.00 | 7.00 | — |
| 1935 | 1,690,000 | 0.15 | 0.25 | 1.00 | 5.00 | — |
| 1936 | 2,009,999 | 0.15 | 0.25 | 1.00 | 5.00 | — |
| 1937 | 2,420,000 | 0.10 | 0.25 | 0.50 | 3.50 | — |
| 1938 | 2,940,000 | 0.10 | 0.25 | 0.50 | 3.50 | — |
| 1939 | 2,100,000 | 0.10 | 0.25 | 0.50 | 3.50 | — |
| 1940 | 2,009,999 | 0.25 | 0.50 | 1.00 | 5.00 | — |

**10 PENNIA** **KM# 33.1** **Composition:** Copper

| Date | Mintage | F | VF | XF | Unc | BU |
|---|---|---|---|---|---|---|
| 1941 | 3,610,000 | 0.10 | 0.25 | 0.50 | 1.25 | — |
| 1942 | 4,970,000 | 0.10 | 0.25 | 0.50 | 1.25 | — |
| 1943 | 1,860,000 | 0.25 | 0.75 | 1.50 | 2.50 | — |

**10 PENNIA** **KM# 33.2** **Composition:** Copper **Note:** Without punched center hole. These issues were not authorized by the government and any that exist were illegally removed from the mint.

| Date | Mintage | F | VF | XF | Unc | BU |
|---|---|---|---|---|---|---|
| 1941 | Inc. above | 20.00 | 30.00 | 50.00 | 75.00 | — |
| 1942 | Inc. above | 20.00 | 30.00 | 50.00 | 75.00 | — |
| 1943 | Inc. above | 30.00 | 50.00 | 70.00 | 100 | — |

**10 PENNIA** **KM# 34.2** **Composition:** Iron **Note:** Without punched center hole. These issues were not authorized by the government and any that exist were illegally removed from the mint.

| Date | Mintage | F | VF | XF | Unc | BU |
|---|---|---|---|---|---|---|
| 1943 | Inc. above | 30.00 | 50.00 | 70.00 | 100 | — |
| 1944 | Inc. above | 30.00 | 50.00 | 70.00 | 100 | — |
| 1945 | Inc. above | 50.00 | 70.00 | 100 | 150 | — |

**10 PENNIA** **KM# 34.1** **Composition:** Iron **Note:** Reduced planchet size.

| Date | Mintage | F | VF | XF | Unc | BU |
|---|---|---|---|---|---|---|
| 1943 | 1,430,000 | 0.10 | 0.25 | 1.00 | 5.00 | — |
| 1944 | 3,040,000 | 0.10 | 0.25 | 1.00 | 5.00 | — |
| 1945 | 1,810,000 | 0.25 | 0.50 | 2.00 | 10.00 | — |

**10 PENNIA** **KM# 46** **Composition:** Aluminum-Bronze

| Date | Mintage | F | VF | XF | Unc | BU |
|---|---|---|---|---|---|---|
| 1963 S | 38,420,000 | — | 0.10 | 0.25 | 1.50 | — |
| 1964 S | 6,926,000 | — | 0.10 | 0.50 | 2.00 | — |
| 1965 S | 4,524,000 | — | 0.10 | 0.25 | 1.50 | — |
| 1966 S | 3,094,000 | — | 0.10 | 0.25 | 1.50 | — |
| 1967 S | 1,050,000 | 0.10 | 0.20 | 2.00 | 5.00 | — |
| 1968 S | 3,004,000 | — | 0.10 | 0.20 | 1.50 | — |
| 1969 S | 5,046,000 | — | — | 0.20 | 1.50 | — |
| 1970 S | 3,996,000 | — | — | 0.20 | 1.50 | — |
| 1971 S | 15,026,000 | — | — | 0.10 | 1.00 | — |
| 1972 S | 19,900,000 | — | — | 0.10 | 1.00 | — |
| 1973 S | 9,196,000 | — | — | 0.10 | 1.00 | — |
| 1974 S | 8,930,000 | — | — | 0.10 | 1.00 | — |
| 1975 S | 15,064,000 | — | — | 0.10 | 0.50 | — |
| 1976 K | 10,063,000 | — | — | 0.10 | 0.50 | — |
| 1977 K | 10,043,000 | — | — | 0.10 | 0.50 | — |
| 1978 K | 10,062,000 | — | — | 0.10 | 0.50 | — |
| 1979 K | 13,072,000 | — | — | 0.10 | 0.50 | — |
| 1980 K | 23,654,000 | — | — | 0.10 | 0.50 | — |
| 1981 K | 30,036,000 | — | — | 0.10 | 0.50 | — |
| 1982 K | 35,548,000 | — | — | 0.10 | 0.50 | — |

**10 PENNIA** **KM# 46a** **Composition:** Aluminum

| Date | Mintage | F | VF | XF | Unc | BU |
|---|---|---|---|---|---|---|
| 1983 K | 6,320,000 | — | — | 0.25 | 1.00 | — |
| 1983 N | 4,191,000 | — | — | 0.25 | 1.00 | — |
| 1984 N | 20,061,000 | — | — | 0.10 | 0.50 | — |
| 1985 N | 20,000,000 | — | — | 0.10 | 0.50 | — |
| 1986 N | 15,000,000 | — | — | 0.10 | 0.50 | — |
| 1987 N | 1,400,000 | — | — | 0.25 | 1.00 | — |
| 1987 M | 8,654,000 | — | — | 0.25 | 1.00 | — |
| 1988 M | 23,197,000 | — | — | 0.10 | 0.50 | — |
| 1989 M | 2,400,000 | — | — | 0.25 | 0.50 | — |
| 1990 M | 2,254,000 | — | — | 0.25 | 0.50 | — |

**10 PENNIA** **KM# 65** **Composition:** Copper-Nickel **Obverse:** Flower pods and stems

| Date | Mintage | F | VF | XF | Unc | BU |
|---|---|---|---|---|---|---|
| 1990 M | 338,100,000 | — | — | 0.10 | 0.15 | — |
| 1991 M | 263,899,000 | — | — | 0.10 | 0.15 | — |
| 1992 M | 136,131,000 | — | — | 0.10 | 0.15 | — |
| 1993 M | 56,206,000 | — | — | 0.10 | 0.15 | — |
| 1994 M | 59,946,000 | — | — | 0.10 | 0.15 | — |
| 1994 M Proof | 5,000 | Value: 7.00 | | | | |
| 1995 M | 85,000,000 | — | — | 0.10 | 0.15 | — |
| 1995 M Proof | 3,000 | Value: 7.00 | | | | |
| 1996 M | 123,000,000 | — | — | 0.10 | 0.15 | — |
| 1996 M Proof | 1,200 | Value: 7.00 | | | | |
| 1997 M | — | — | — | 0.10 | 0.15 | — |
| 1997 M Proof | 2,000 | Value: 7.00 | | | | |
| 1998 M | — | — | — | 0.10 | 0.15 | — |
| 1998 M Proof | 2,000 | Value: 7.00 | | | | |
| 1999 M | — | — | — | 0.10 | 0.15 | — |
| 1999 M Proof | — | Value: 7.00 | | | | |
| 2000 M | — | — | — | — | 0.15 | — |
| 2000 M Proof | — | Value: 7.00 | | | | |
| 2001 M | Inc. above | — | — | — | 0.15 | — |
| 2001 M | Inc. above | Value: 7.00 | | | | |

**20 PENNIA** KM# 47 **Composition:** Aluminum-Bronze

| Date | Mintage | F | VF | XF | Unc | BU |
|---|---|---|---|---|---|---|
| 1963 S | 39,970,000 | — | 0.10 | 0.20 | 1.50 | — |
| 1964 S | 4,248,000 | 0.10 | 0.25 | 1.00 | 3.00 | — |
| 1965 S | 5,704,000 | — | 0.10 | 0.20 | 1.50 | — |
| 1966 S | 4,085,000 | — | 0.10 | 0.20 | 1.50 | — |
| 1967 S | 1,716,000 | — | 0.10 | 0.20 | 1.50 | — |
| 1968 S | 1,330,000 | — | 0.10 | 0.20 | 1.50 | — |
| 1969 S | 201,000 | 0.50 | 1.00 | 1.50 | 3.50 | — |
| 1970 S | 230,000 | 0.50 | 1.00 | 1.50 | 3.50 | — |
| 1971 S | 5,150,000 | — | 0.25 | 0.50 | 1.00 | — |

**Note:** Some coins dated 1971 are magnetic and command a higher premium

| Date | Mintage | F | VF | XF | Unc | BU |
|---|---|---|---|---|---|---|
| 1972 S | 10,001,000 | — | 0.10 | 0.25 | 0.50 | — |
| 1973 S | 9,462,000 | — | 0.10 | 0.25 | 0.50 | — |
| 1974 S | 12,705,000 | — | 0.10 | 0.25 | 0.50 | — |
| 1975 S | 12,068,000 | — | — | 0.10 | 0.50 | — |
| 1976 K | 20,058,000 | — | — | 0.10 | 0.50 | — |
| 1977 K | 10,063,000 | — | — | 0.10 | 0.50 | — |
| 1978 K | 10,014,000 | — | — | 0.10 | 0.50 | — |
| 1979 K | 7,513,000 | — | — | 0.10 | 0.50 | — |
| 1980 K | 20,047,000 | — | — | 0.10 | 0.25 | — |
| 1981 K | 30,002,000 | — | — | 0.10 | 0.25 | — |
| 1982 K | 35,050,000 | — | — | 0.10 | 0.25 | — |
| 1983 K | 7,113,000 | — | — | 0.10 | 0.25 | — |
| 1983 N | 12,889,000 | — | — | 0.10 | 0.25 | — |
| 1984 N | 20,029,000 | — | — | 0.10 | 0.25 | — |
| 1985 N | 15,004,000 | — | — | 0.10 | 0.25 | — |
| 1986 N | 20,001,000 | — | — | 0.10 | 0.25 | — |
| 1987 N | 1,200,000 | — | 0.25 | 0.50 | 1.00 | — |
| 1987 M | 25,670,000 | — | — | 0.10 | 0.25 | — |
| 1988 M | 13,853,000 | — | — | 0.10 | 0.25 | — |
| 1989 M | 40,695,000 | — | — | 0.10 | 0.25 | — |
| 1990 M | 9,168,000 | — | — | 0.10 | 0.25 | — |

**25 PENNIA** KM# 25 **Composition:** Copper-Nickel

| Date | Mintage | F | VF | XF | Unc | BU |
|---|---|---|---|---|---|---|
| 1921 H | 20,096,000 | 0.10 | 0.25 | 1.00 | 3.00 | — |
| 1925 S | 1,250,000 | 0.50 | 1.50 | 10.00 | 20.00 | — |
| 1926 S | 2,820,000 | 0.40 | 1.25 | 5.00 | 12.00 | — |
| 1927 S | 1,120,000 | 0.50 | 1.50 | 10.00 | 20.00 | — |
| 1928 S | 2,920,000 | 0.40 | 1.00 | 5.00 | 12.00 | — |
| 1929 S | 200,000 | 2.00 | 4.00 | 20.00 | 40.00 | — |
| 1930 S | 1,090,000 | 0.50 | 1.50 | 5.00 | 15.00 | — |
| 1934 S | 1,260,000 | 0.40 | 0.75 | 2.00 | 7.00 | — |
| 1935 S | 2,190,000 | 0.30 | 0.50 | 1.50 | 6.00 | — |
| 1936 S | 2,300,000 | 0.20 | 0.40 | 1.00 | 3.00 | — |
| 1937 S | 4,019,999 | 0.20 | 0.40 | 1.00 | 3.00 | — |
| 1938 S | 4,500,000 | 0.20 | 0.40 | 1.00 | 3.00 | — |
| 1939 S | 2,712,000 | 0.20 | 0.40 | 1.00 | 3.00 | — |
| 1940 S | 4,840,000 | 0.15 | 0.30 | 0.75 | 2.00 | — |

**25 PENNIA** KM# 25A **Composition:** Copper

| Date | Mintage | F | VF | XF | Unc | BU |
|---|---|---|---|---|---|---|
| 1940 S | 72,000 | 0.50 | 1.00 | 3.00 | 12.00 | — |
| 1941 S | 5,980,000 | 0.10 | 0.35 | 2.00 | 5.00 | — |
| 1942 S | 6,464,000 | 0.10 | 0.35 | 2.00 | 5.00 | — |
| 1943 S | 4,912,000 | 0.25 | 0.50 | 2.00 | 7.00 | — |

**25 PENNIA** KM# 25b **Composition:** Iron

| Date | Mintage | F | VF | XF | Unc | BU |
|---|---|---|---|---|---|---|
| 1943 S | 2,700,000 | 0.15 | 0.50 | 2.00 | 10.00 | — |
| 1943 S Small closed 4's | 5,480,000 | 0.15 | 0.50 | 1.50 | 7.00 | — |
| 1943 S Large open 4's | Inc. above | 0.15 | 0.50 | 1.50 | 7.00 | — |
| 1945 S | 6,810,000 | 0.25 | 0.75 | 2.00 | 8.00 | — |

**50 PENNIA** KM# 26 **Composition:** Copper-Nickel

| Date | Mintage | F | VF | XF | Unc | BU |
|---|---|---|---|---|---|---|
| 1921 H | 10,072,000 | 0.15 | 0.30 | 1.00 | 3.00 | — |
| 1923 S | 6,000,000 | 0.25 | 1.00 | 3.00 | 12.00 | — |
| 1929 S | 984,000 | 0.75 | 1.50 | 10.00 | 35.00 | — |
| 1934 S | 612,000 | 1.00 | 2.50 | 10.00 | 35.00 | — |
| 1935 S | 610,000 | 1.00 | 2.50 | 7.50 | 30.00 | — |
| 1936 S | 1,520,000 | 0.30 | 0.50 | 2.00 | 7.50 | — |
| 1937 S | 2,350,000 | 0.15 | 0.25 | 1.00 | 5.00 | — |
| 1938 S | 2,330,000 | 0.15 | 0.25 | 1.00 | 5.00 | — |
| 1939 S | 1,280,000 | 0.15 | 0.25 | 1.00 | 5.00 | — |
| 1940 S | 3,152,000 | 0.15 | 0.25 | 1.00 | 3.00 | — |

**50 PENNIA** KM# 26a **Composition:** Copper

| Date | Mintage | F | VF | XF | Unc | BU |
|---|---|---|---|---|---|---|
| 1940 S | 480,000 | 1.25 | 2.50 | 5.00 | 12.00 | — |
| 1941 S | 3,860,000 | 0.15 | 0.40 | 2.00 | 5.00 | — |
| 1942 S | 5,900,000 | 0.15 | 0.40 | 2.00 | 5.00 | — |
| 1943 S | 3,140,000 | 0.25 | 0.50 | 2.00 | 5.00 | — |

**50 PENNIA** KM# 26b **Composition:** Iron

| Date | Mintage | F | VF | XF | Unc | BU |
|---|---|---|---|---|---|---|
| 1943 S | 1,580,000 | 0.25 | 0.50 | 2.50 | 15.00 | — |
| 1944 S | 7,600,000 | 0.15 | 0.40 | 2.00 | 12.00 | — |
| 1945 S | 4,700,000 | 0.15 | 0.40 | 2.00 | 12.00 | — |
| 1946 S | 2,632,000 | 0.30 | 0.50 | 2.00 | 12.00 | — |
| 1947 S | 1,748,000 | 0.50 | 1.50 | 5.00 | 20.00 | — |
| 1948 L | 1,112,000 | 3.00 | 5.00 | 12.00 | 25.00 | — |

**50 PENNIA** KM# 48 **Composition:** Aluminum-Bronze

| Date | Mintage | F | VF | XF | Unc | BU |
|---|---|---|---|---|---|---|
| 1963 S | 17,316,000 | — | 0.20 | 0.50 | 2.00 | — |
| 1964 S | 3,101,000 | — | 0.25 | 2.00 | 5.00 | — |
| 1965 S | 1,667,000 | — | 0.20 | 1.00 | 3.00 | — |
| 1966 S | 1,051,000 | — | 0.20 | 1.00 | 3.00 | — |
| 1967 S | 400,000 | 0.25 | 0.50 | 2.00 | 4.00 | — |
| 1968 S | 816,000 | — | 0.25 | 1.00 | 2.50 | — |
| 1969 S | 1,341,000 | — | 0.20 | 0.50 | 2.00 | — |
| 1970 S | 2,250,000 | — | 0.20 | 0.30 | 1.50 | — |
| 1971 S | 10,003,000 | — | — | 0.25 | 1.00 | — |

**Note:** Some coins dated 1971 are magnetic and command a higher premium

| Date | Mintage | F | VF | XF | Unc | BU |
|---|---|---|---|---|---|---|
| 1972 S | 7,892,000 | — | — | 0.25 | 1.00 | — |
| 1973 S | 5,428,000 | — | — | 0.25 | 1.00 | — |
| 1974 S | 5,049,000 | — | — | 0.25 | 1.00 | — |
| 1975 S | 4,305,000 | — | — | 0.25 | 1.00 | — |
| 1976 K | 7,022,000 | — | — | 0.25 | 1.00 | — |
| 1977 K | 8,077,000 | — | — | 0.25 | 1.00 | — |
| 1978 K | 8,048,000 | — | — | 0.25 | 1.00 | — |
| 1979 K | 8,004,000 | — | — | 0.25 | 1.00 | — |
| 1980 K | 5,349,000 | — | — | 0.25 | 1.00 | — |
| 1981 K | 20,031,000 | — | — | 0.25 | 0.50 | — |
| 1982 K | 5,042,000 | — | — | 0.25 | 1.00 | — |
| 1983 K | 4,043,999 | — | — | 0.25 | 1.00 | — |
| 1983 N | 1,016,000 | — | 0.20 | 0.50 | 1.50 | — |
| 1984 N | 3,006,000 | — | — | 0.25 | 1.00 | — |
| 1985 N | 10,000,000 | — | — | 0.25 | 1.00 | — |
| 1986 N | 9,002,000 | — | — | 0.25 | 1.00 | — |
| 1987 N | 700,000 | — | 0.30 | 0.75 | 1.50 | — |
| 1987 M | 4,305,000 | — | — | 0.25 | 1.00 | — |
| 1988 M | 14,735,000 | — | — | 0.25 | 1.00 | — |
| 1989 M | 10,651,000 | — | — | 0.25 | 1.00 | — |
| 1990 M | 5,391,000 | — | — | 0.50 | 2.00 | — |

**50 PENNIA** KM# 66 **Composition:** Copper-Nickel **Obverse:** Polar bear

| Date | Mintage | F | VF | XF | Unc | BU |
|---|---|---|---|---|---|---|
| 1990 M | 70,459,000 | — | — | 0.20 | 0.50 | — |
| 1991 M | 90,480,000 | — | — | 0.20 | 0.50 | — |
| 1992 M | 58,996,000 | — | — | 0.20 | 0.50 | — |
| 1993 M | 10,066,000 | — | — | 0.20 | 0.50 | — |
| 1994 M | 3,005,000 | — | — | 0.20 | 0.50 | — |
| 1994 M Proof | 5,000 | Value: 8.00 | | | | |
| 1995 M | 1,048,000 | — | — | 0.20 | 0.50 | — |
| 1995 M Proof | 3,000 | Value: 8.00 | | | | |
| 1996 M | 17,000,000 | — | — | 0.20 | 0.50 | — |
| 1996 M Proof | 1,200 | Value: 8.00 | | | | |
| 1997 M | — | — | — | 0.20 | 0.50 | — |
| 1997 M Proof | 2,000 | Value: 8.00 | | | | |
| 1998 M | — | — | — | 0.20 | 0.50 | — |
| 1998 M Proof | 2,000 | Value: 8.00 | | | | |
| 1999 M | — | — | — | 0.20 | 0.50 | — |
| 1999 M Proof | — | Value: 8.00 | | | | |
| 2000 M | — | — | — | 0.20 | 0.50 | — |
| 2000 M Proof | — | Value: 8.00 | | | | |
| 2001 M | Inc. above | — | — | 0.20 | 0.50 | — |
| 2001 M Proof | Inc. above | Value: 8.00 | | | | |

**MARKKA** KM# 27 **Composition:** Copper-Nickel

| Date | Mintage | F | VF | XF | Unc | BU |
|---|---|---|---|---|---|---|
| 1921 H | 10,048,000 | 0.50 | 1.00 | 2.50 | 5.00 | — |
| 1922 Heart | 10,000,000 | 0.75 | 1.50 | 3.50 | 10.00 | — |
| 1922 | — | — | — | — | — | — |
| 1923 S | 1,780,000 | 7.50 | 15.00 | 25.00 | 50.00 | — |
| 1924 S | 3,270,000 | 3.00 | 7.00 | 15.00 | 30.00 | — |

**MARKKA** KM# 30 **Composition:** Copper-Nickel **Note:** Reduced size.

| Date | Mintage | F | VF | XF | Unc | BU |
|---|---|---|---|---|---|---|
| 1928 S | 3,000,000 | 0.15 | 0.30 | 3.00 | 20.00 | — |
| 1929 S | 3,862,000 | 0.15 | 0.30 | 3.00 | 20.00 | — |
| 1930 S | 10,284,000 | 0.15 | 0.30 | 1.00 | 12.00 | — |
| 1931 S | 2,830,000 | 0.15 | 0.30 | 1.00 | 12.00 | — |
| 1932 S | 4,140,000 | 0.15 | 0.30 | 1.00 | 10.00 | — |
| 1933 S | 4,032,000 | 0.15 | 0.30 | 1.00 | 10.00 | — |
| 1936 S | 562,000 | 0.50 | 1.50 | 7.00 | 30.00 | — |
| 1937 S | 4,930,000 | 0.15 | 0.30 | 1.00 | 6.00 | — |
| 1938 S | 4,410,000 | 0.15 | 0.25 | 1.00 | 6.00 | — |
| 1939 S | 3,070,000 | 0.15 | 0.25 | 1.00 | 6.00 | — |
| 1940 S | 3,372,000 | 0.15 | 0.25 | 1.00 | 6.00 | — |

**Note:** Coins dated 1928S, 1929S and 1930S are known to be restruck on 1921-24, KM#27 coins. (1928S: 2 or 3 known

**MARKKA** KM# 30a **Composition:** Copper

| Date | Mintage | F | VF | XF | Unc | BU |
|---|---|---|---|---|---|---|
| 1940 S | 84,000 | 1.50 | 3.50 | 8.00 | 20.00 | — |
| 1941 S | 8,970,000 | 0.15 | 0.50 | 1.25 | 6.00 | — |
| 1942 S | 11,200,000 | 0.15 | 0.50 | 1.00 | 4.00 | — |
| 1943 S | 7,460,000 | 0.15 | 0.50 | 1.25 | 5.00 | — |
| 1949 H | 250 | 1,500 | 2,500 | 3,500 | 5,000 | — |
| 1950 H | 320,000 | 0.50 | 1.00 | 2.00 | 10.00 | — |
| 1951 H | 4,630,000 | 0.25 | 0.50 | 1.00 | 6.00 | — |

**MARKKA** KM# 30b **Composition:** Iron

| Date | Mintage | F | VF | XF | Unc | BU |
|---|---|---|---|---|---|---|
| 1943 S | 7,460,000 | 0.15 | 0.25 | 2.00 | 12.00 | — |
| 1944 S | 12,830,000 | 0.15 | 0.25 | 2.00 | 10.00 | — |
| 1945 S | 21,950,000 | 0.15 | 0.25 | 2.00 | 10.00 | — |
| 1946 S | 2,630,000 | 0.15 | 0.30 | 2.00 | 12.00 | — |
| 1947 S | 1,750,000 | 0.25 | 0.50 | 2.00 | 17.00 | — |
| 1948 L | 20,500,000 | 0.15 | 0.25 | 1.00 | 8.00 | — |
| 1949 H | 17,358,000 | 0.15 | 0.25 | 0.75 | 7.00 | — |
| 1950 H | 14,654,000 | 0.15 | 0.25 | 0.75 | 7.00 | — |
| 1951 H | 21,414,000 | 0.15 | 0.25 | 0.75 | 7.00 | — |
| 1952 H | 5,410,000 | 0.25 | 0.50 | 2.00 | 12.00 | — |

**MARKKA** KM# 36 **Composition:** Iron

| Date | Mintage | F | VF | XF | Unc | BU |
|---|---|---|---|---|---|---|
| 1952 | 22,050,000 | 0.15 | 0.35 | 1.00 | 7.00 | — |
| 1953 | 28,618,000 | 0.15 | 0.35 | 1.00 | 7.00 | — |

**MARKKA** KM# 36a **Composition:** Nickel Plated Iron

| Date | Mintage | F | VF | XF | Unc | BU |
|---|---|---|---|---|---|---|
| 1953 | 6,000,000 | 5.00 | 8.00 | 12.50 | 20.00 | — |
| 1954 | 36,400,000 | — | 0.10 | 0.25 | 0.50 | — |
| 1955 | 38,100,000 | — | 0.10 | 0.25 | 0.50 | — |
| 1956 | 35,600,000 | — | 0.10 | 0.25 | 0.50 | — |
| 1957 | 29,100,000 | — | 0.10 | 0.25 | 0.50 | — |
| 1958 | 19,940,000 | 0.10 | 0.20 | 0.35 | 0.70 | — |
| 1959 Thick letters | 23,920,000 | — | 0.10 | 0.25 | 0.50 | — |
| 1959 Thin letters | Inc. above | — | 0.10 | 0.25 | 0.50 | — |
| 1960 | 22,020,000 | — | 0.10 | 0.25 | 0.50 | — |
| 1961 | 32,220,000 | — | 0.10 | 0.25 | 0.50 | — |
| 1962 | 29,040,000 | — | 0.10 | 0.25 | 0.50 | — |

**5 MARKKAA** **KM# 31** **Composition:** Aluminum-Bronze

| Date | Mintage | F | VF | XF | Unc | BU |
|---|---|---|---|---|---|---|
| 1928 S | 580,000 | 30.00 | 50.00 | 100 | 250 | — |
| 1929 S | Inc. above | 30.00 | 50.00 | 90.00 | 220 | — |
| 1930 S | 592,000 | 0.75 | 1.75 | 10.00 | 50.00 | — |
| 1931 S | 3,090,000 | 0.50 | 1.00 | 6.00 | 30.00 | — |
| 1932 S | 964,000 | 5.00 | 10.00 | 60.00 | 150 | — |
| 1933 S | 1,050,000 | 0.50 | 1.00 | 10.00 | 40.00 | — |
| 1935 S | 440,000 | 1.50 | 3.00 | 12.00 | 50.00 | — |
| 1936 S | 470,000 | 1.50 | 3.00 | 12.00 | 50.00 | — |
| 1937 S | 1,032,000 | 0.50 | 1.00 | 6.00 | 20.00 | — |
| 1938 S | 912,000 | 0.50 | 1.00 | 6.00 | 20.00 | — |
| 1939 S | 752,000 | 0.50 | 1.00 | 6.00 | 20.00 | — |
| 1940 S | 820,000 | 1.25 | 2.75 | 10.00 | 30.00 | — |
| 1941 S | 1,452,000 | 0.50 | 1.00 | 5.00 | 12.00 | — |
| 1942 S | 1,390,000 | 0.50 | 1.00 | 7.00 | 15.00 | — |
| 1946 S | 618,000 | 3.50 | 7.00 | 20.00 | 60.00 | — |

**5 MARKKAA** **KM# 31a** **Composition:** Brass

| Date | Mintage | F | VF | XF | Unc | BU |
|---|---|---|---|---|---|---|
| 1946 S | 5,538,000 | 0.20 | 0.50 | 1.50 | 3.50 | — |
| 1947 S | 6,550,000 | 0.25 | 0.75 | 2.00 | 6.00 | — |
| 1948 L | 8,210,000 | 0.25 | 0.50 | 1.50 | 5.00 | — |
| 1949 H Thin H | 11,014,000 | 0.50 | 1.00 | 3.00 | 5.00 | — |
| 1949 H Wide H | Inc. above | 0.20 | 0.50 | 1.50 | 3.50 | — |
| 1950 H | 4,760,000 | 0.20 | 0.50 | 1.50 | 3.50 | — |
| 1951 H | 7,800,000 | 0.20 | 0.50 | 1.50 | 3.50 | — |
| 1952 H | 1,210,000 | 2.50 | 6.00 | 12.00 | 25.00 | — |

**5 MARKKAA** **KM# 37** **Composition:** Iron

| Date | Mintage | F | VF | XF | Unc | BU |
|---|---|---|---|---|---|---|
| 1952 | 10,820,000 | 0.20 | 0.35 | 2.00 | 8.00 | — |
| 1953 | 9,772,000 | 0.20 | 0.35 | 3.00 | 10.00 | — |

**5 MARKKAA** **KM# 37a** **Composition:** Nickel Plated Iron

| Date | Mintage | F | VF | XF | Unc | BU |
|---|---|---|---|---|---|---|
| 1953 | Inc. above | 35.00 | 60.00 | 80.00 | 125 | — |
| 1954 | 6,696,000 | — | 0.20 | 0.35 | 1.50 | — |
| 1955 | 9,894,000 | — | 0.20 | 0.35 | 1.50 | — |
| 1956 | 8,220,000 | — | 0.20 | 0.35 | 1.00 | — |
| 1957 | 4,276,000 | — | 0.20 | 0.35 | 1.00 | — |
| 1958 | 3,300,000 | — | 0.20 | 0.35 | 1.50 | — |
| 1959 | 5,874,000 | — | 0.20 | 0.35 | 1.00 | — |
| 1960 | 3,066,000 | 0.10 | 0.25 | 0.35 | 1.50 | — |
| 1961 | 7,254,000 | 0.10 | 0.25 | 0.35 | 1.50 | — |
| 1962 | 4,542,000 | 0.50 | 1.00 | 3.00 | 6.00 | — |

**5 MARKKAA** **KM# 53** **Composition:** Aluminum-Bronze **Obverse:** Icebreaker "Varma"

| Date | Mintage | F | VF | XF | Unc | BU |
|---|---|---|---|---|---|---|
| 1972 S | 400,000 | 1.50 | 2.00 | 2.50 | 4.00 | — |
| 1973 S | 2,188,000 | — | 1.25 | 2.00 | 3.00 | — |
| 1974 S | 300,000 | — | 1.25 | 2.00 | 3.00 | — |
| 1975 S | 300,000 | — | 1.25 | 2.00 | 3.00 | — |
| 1976 K | 400,000 | — | 1.25 | 2.00 | 3.00 | — |
| 1977 K | 300,000 | — | 1.25 | 2.00 | 3.00 | — |
| 1978 K | 300,000 | — | 1.25 | 2.00 | 3.00 | — |

**5 MARKKAA** **KM# 57** **Composition:** Aluminum-Bronze **Obverse:** Icebreaker "Urho"

| Date | Mintage | F | VF | XF | Unc | BU |
|---|---|---|---|---|---|---|
| 1979 K | 2,005,000 | — | — | 1.50 | 2.25 | — |
| 1980 K | 501,000 | — | 1.50 | 2.00 | 3.00 | — |
| 1981 K | 1,009,000 | — | — | 1.50 | 2.25 | — |
| 1982 K | 3,004,000 | — | — | 1.50 | 2.25 | — |
| 1983 K | 8,776,000 | — | — | 1.50 | 2.25 | — |
| 1983 N | 11,230,000 | — | — | 1.50 | 2.25 | — |
| 1984 N | 15,001,000 | — | — | 1.50 | 2.25 | — |
| 1985 N | 8,005,000 | — | — | 1.50 | 2.25 | — |
| 1986 N | 5,006,000 | — | — | 1.50 | 2.25 | — |
| 1987 N | 660,000 | — | 1.50 | 2.00 | 3.00 | — |
| 1987 M | 2,348,000 | — | — | 1.50 | 2.25 | — |
| 1988 M | 3,042,000 | — | — | 1.50 | 2.25 | — |
| 1989 M | 10,175,000 | — | — | 1.50 | 2.25 | — |
| 1990 M | 9,925,000 | — | — | 1.50 | 2.25 | — |
| 1991 M | 9,910,000 | — | — | 2.00 | 3.00 | — |
| 1992 M | 547,000 | — | — | 2.00 | 3.00 | — |
| 1993 M | 911,000 | — | — | 2.00 | 3.00 | — |

**5 MARKKAA** **KM# 73** **Composition:** Copper-Aluminum-Nickel **Obverse:** Lake Saimaa ringed seal

| Date | Mintage | F | VF | XF | Unc | BU |
|---|---|---|---|---|---|---|
| 1992 M | 800,000 | — | — | — | 3.50 | — |
| 1993 M | 46,034,000 | — | — | — | 2.00 | — |
| 1994 M | 19,003,000 | — | — | — | 2.00 | — |
| 1994 M Proof | 5,000 | Value: 12.00 | | | | |
| 1995 M | 9,016,000 | — | — | — | 2.50 | — |
| 1995 M Proof | 3,000 | Value: 12.00 | | | | |
| 1996 M | 7,000,000 | — | — | — | 2.50 | — |
| 1996 M Proof | 1,200 | Value: 12.00 | | | | |
| 1997 M | — | — | — | — | 2.50 | — |
| 1997 M Proof | 2,000 | Value: 12.00 | | | | |
| 1998 M | — | — | — | — | 2.50 | — |
| 1998 M Proof | 2,000 | Value: 12.00 | | | | |
| 1999 M | — | — | — | — | 2.50 | — |
| 1999 M Proof | — | Value: 12.00 | | | | |
| 2000 M | — | — | — | — | 2.50 | — |
| 2000 M Proof | — | Value: 12.00 | | | | |
| 2001 M | Inc. above | — | — | — | 2.50 | — |
| 2001 M | Inc. above | Value: 12.00 | | | | |

**10 MARKKAA** **KM# 63** **Composition:** Aluminum-Bronze

| Date | Mintage | F | VF | XF | Unc | BU |
|---|---|---|---|---|---|---|
| 1928 S | 730,000 | 2.50 | 5.00 | 25.00 | 130 | — |
| 1929 S | Inc. above | 2.00 | 4.00 | 20.00 | 100 | — |
| 1930 S | 260,000 | 1.00 | 2.50 | 15.00 | 80.00 | — |
| 1931 S | 1,530,000 | 1.00 | 2.50 | 10.00 | 70.00 | — |
| 1932 S | 1,010,000 | 1.00 | 2.50 | 8.00 | 55.00 | — |
| 1934 S | 154,000 | 1.50 | 3.00 | 20.00 | 100 | — |
| 1935 S | 81,000 | 3.00 | 5.00 | 20.00 | 100 | — |
| 1936 S | 304,000 | 2.00 | 4.00 | 20.00 | 80.00 | — |
| 1937 S | 181,000 | 1.50 | 2.50 | 10.00 | 70.00 | — |
| 1938 S | 631,000 | 0.75 | 1.50 | 10.00 | 60.00 | — |
| 1939 S | 133,000 | 4.00 | 8.00 | 15.00 | 60.00 | — |

**10 MARKKAA** **KM# 38** **Composition:** Aluminum-Bronze

| Date | Mintage | F | VF | XF | Unc | BU |
|---|---|---|---|---|---|---|
| 1952 H | 6,390,000 | 0.20 | 0.50 | 2.00 | 7.00 | — |
| 1953 H | 22,650,000 | 0.15 | 0.35 | 1.00 | 5.00 | — |
| 1954 H | 2,452,000 | 0.50 | 1.00 | 5.00 | 15.00 | — |
| 1955 H | 2,342,000 | 0.20 | 0.50 | 3.00 | 10.00 | — |
| 1956 H | 4,240,000 | 0.20 | 0.40 | 2.00 | 7.00 | — |
| 1958 H Thin 1 | 3,292,000 | 2.00 | 5.00 | 12.00 | 30.00 | — |
| 1958 H Wide 1 | Inc. above | 0.20 | 0.40 | 1.00 | 5.00 | — |
| 1960 S | 740,000 | 1.00 | 2.00 | 7.00 | 15.00 | — |
| 1961 S | 3,580,000 | 0.20 | 0.50 | 1.50 | 5.00 | — |
| 1961 S Wide 1 | Inc. above | 2.00 | 4.00 | 10.00 | 20.00 | — |
| 1962 S | 1,852,000 | 0.30 | 0.60 | 1.75 | 5.00 | — |

**Note:** The "1" in the denomination on all 1952 to 1956 issues is the thin variety. 1960 issues are the wide variety, and 1962's are thin. Varieties exist in root length of tree

**10 MARKKAA** **KM# 50** **Weight:** 23.7500 g. **Composition:** 0.9000 Silver .6872 oz. ASW **Subject:** 50th Anniversary of Independence

| Date | Mintage | F | VF | XF | Unc | BU |
|---|---|---|---|---|---|---|
| 1967 S-H | 1,000,000 | — | — | 4.00 | 7.00 | — |

**10 MARKKAA** **KM# 51** **Weight:** 22.7500 g. **Composition:** 0.5000 Silver .3657 oz. ASW **Subject:** Centennial - Birth of President Paasikivi

| Date | Mintage | F | VF | XF | Unc | BU |
|---|---|---|---|---|---|---|
| 1970 S-H | 600,000 | — | — | 3.00 | 5.00 | — |

**10 MARKKAA** **KM# 52** **Weight:** 24.2000 g. **Composition:** 0.5000 Silver .3890 oz. ASW **Subject:** 10th European Athletic Championships

| Date | Mintage | F | VF | XF | Unc | BU |
|---|---|---|---|---|---|---|
| 1971 S-H | 1,000,000 | — | — | 3.00 | 5.00 | — |

**10 MARKKAA** **KM# 54** **Weight:** 23.5000 g. **Composition:** 0.5000 Silver .3778 oz. ASW **Subject:** 75th Birthday of President Kekkonen

| Date | Mintage | F | VF | XF | Unc | BU |
|---|---|---|---|---|---|---|
| 1975 S-H | 1,000,000 | — | — | 3.00 | 5.00 | — |

**10 MARKKAA** **KM# 55** **Weight:** 21.7800 g. **Composition:** 0.5000 Silver .3501 oz. ASW **Subject:** 60th Anniversary of Independence

| Date | Mintage | F | VF | XF | Unc | BU |
|---|---|---|---|---|---|---|
| 1977 K-H | 400,000 | — | — | 3.00 | 5.00 | — |

**10 MARKKAA** **KM# 77** **Ring Composition:** Copper-Nickel **Center Composition:** Bi-Metallic Brass **Obverse:** Capercaillie bird

| Date | Mintage | F | VF | XF | Unc | BU |
|---|---|---|---|---|---|---|
| 1993 M | 30,002,000 | — | — | — | 4.50 | — |
| 1994 M | 19,979,000 | — | — | — | 4.50 | — |
| 1994 M Proof | 5,000 | Value: 18.00 | | | | |
| 1995 M | 4,008,000 | — | — | — | 5.00 | — |
| 1995 M Proof | 3,000 | Value: 18.00 | | | | |
| 1996 M | 3,300,000 | — | — | — | 5.50 | — |
| 1996 M Proof | 1,200 | Value: 18.00 | | | | |
| 1997 M | — | — | — | — | 5.50 | — |
| 1997 M Proof | 2,000 | Value: 18.00 | | | | |
| 1998 M | — | — | — | — | 5.50 | — |
| 1998 M Proof | 2,000 | Value: 18.00 | | | | |
| 1999 M | — | — | — | — | 5.50 | — |
| 1999 M Proof | — | Value: 18.00 | | | | |
| 2000 M | — | — | — | — | 5.50 | — |
| 2000 M Proof | — | Value: 18.00 | | | | |
| 2001 M | Inc. above | — | — | — | 5.50 | — |
| 2001 M | Inc. above | Value: 18.00 | | | | |

**10 MARKKAA** **KM# 82** **Ring Composition:** Copper-Nickel **Center Composition:** Bi-Metallic Brass **Subject:** European Unity **Obverse:** Swan in flight

| Date | Mintage | F | VF | XF | Unc | BU |
|---|---|---|---|---|---|---|
| 1995 M | 500,000 | — | — | — | 5.00 | — |

**10 MARKKAA** **KM# 82a** **Ring Composition:** 0.9250 Silver **Center Composition:** 0.5850 Gold **Subject:** European Unity **Obverse:** Swan in flight

| Date | Mintage | F | VF | XF | Unc | BU |
|---|---|---|---|---|---|---|
| 1995 M Proof | 2,000 | Value: 600 | | | | |

**10 MARKKAA** **KM# 91** **Ring Composition:** Copper-Nickel **Center Weight:** 8.8200 g. **Center Composition:** Brass **Obverse:** Fire breathing face **Reverse:** Denomination, pine branch **Note:** Finnish Presidency of the EU.

| Date | Mintage | F | VF | XF | Unc | BU |
|---|---|---|---|---|---|---|
| 1999 | 100,000 | — | — | — | 5.00 | — |

**10 MARKKAA** **KM# 91a** **Ring Composition:** 0.7500 Gold **Center Weight:** 13.2000 g. **Center Composition:** 0.9250 Silver **Edge:** Lettered

| Date | Mintage | F | VF | XF | Unc | BU |
|---|---|---|---|---|---|---|
| 1999 Proof | 3,000 | Value: 400 | | | | |

**20 MARKKAA** **KM# 32** **Composition:** Aluminum-Bronze

| Date | Mintage | F | VF | XF | Unc | BU |
|---|---|---|---|---|---|---|
| 1931 S | 16,000 | 25.00 | 35.00 | 50.00 | 80.00 | — |
| 1932 S | 14,000 | 30.00 | 40.00 | 60.00 | 100 | — |
| 1934 S | 390,000 | 2.00 | 10.00 | 25.00 | 80.00 | — |
| 1935 S | 250,000 | 2.00 | 10.00 | 25.00 | 80.00 | — |
| 1936 S | 110,000 | 3.00 | 10.00 | 30.00 | 120 | — |
| 1937 S | 510,000 | 1.50 | 2.00 | 15.00 | 50.00 | — |
| 1938 S | 360,000 | 1.50 | 2.00 | 15.00 | 50.00 | — |
| 1939 S | 960,000 | 1.00 | 2.00 | 6.00 | 20.00 | — |

**20 MARKKAA** **KM# 39** **Composition:** Aluminum-Bronze

| Date | Mintage | F | VF | XF | Unc | BU |
|---|---|---|---|---|---|---|
| 1952 H | 83,000 | 7.00 | 10.00 | 20.00 | 40.00 | — |
| 1953 H | 2,880,000 | 0.25 | 0.50 | 3.00 | 15.00 | — |
| 1954 H | 17,034,000 | 0.15 | 0.50 | 2.00 | 10.00 | — |
| 1955 H | 2,800,000 | 0.25 | 0.50 | 3.00 | 15.00 | — |
| 1956 H | 2,540,000 | 0.25 | 0.50 | 3.00 | 15.00 | — |
| 1957 H | 1,050,000 | 0.50 | 1.00 | 5.00 | 17.00 | — |
| 1958 H | 515,000 | 2.50 | 5.00 | 15.00 | 30.00 | — |
| 1959 S | 1,580,000 | 0.25 | 0.50 | 3.00 | 15.00 | — |
| 1960 S | 3,850,000 | 0.15 | 0.50 | 2.00 | 8.00 | — |
| 1961 S | 4,430,000 | 0.15 | 0.50 | 2.00 | 8.00 | — |
| 1962 S | 2,280,000 | 0.15 | 0.50 | 1.50 | 6.00 | — |

**25 MARKKAA** **KM# 56** **Weight:** 26.3000 g. **Composition:** 0.5000 Silver .4228 oz. ASW **Subject:** Winter Games in Lahti

| Date | Mintage | F | VF | XF | Unc | BU |
|---|---|---|---|---|---|---|
| 1978 K-N | 500,000 | — | — | 6.00 | 8.00 | — |

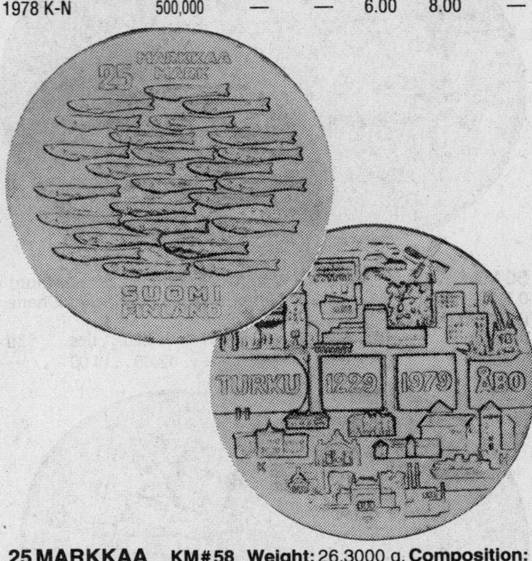


**25 MARKKAA** **KM# 58** **Weight:** 26.3000 g. **Composition:** 0.5000 Silver .4228 oz. ASW **Subject:** 750th Anniversary of Turku

| Date | Mintage | F | VF | XF | Unc | BU |
|---|---|---|---|---|---|---|
| 1979 K-H | 300,000 | — | — | 6.00 | 8.00 | — |

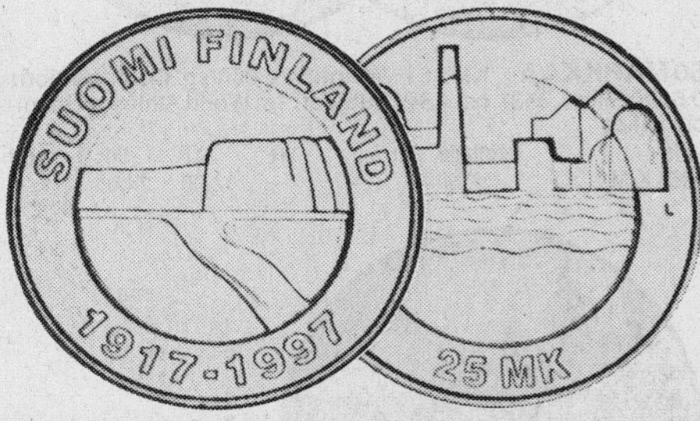


**25 MARKKAA** **KM# 85** **Ring Composition:** Copper-Nickel **Center Composition:** Brass **Subject:** 80th Anniversary of Independenceersary of Turku **Obverse:** Stylized landscape **Reverse:** Stylized city view

| Date | Mintage | F | VF | XF | Unc | BU |
|---|---|---|---|---|---|---|
| ND M-L | 100,000 | — | — | — | 10.00 | — |
| ND M-L Proof | 2,000 | Value: 15.00 | | | | |

**50 MARKKAA** **KM# 40** **Composition:** Aluminum-Bronze

| Date | Mintage | F | VF | XF | Unc | BU |
|---|---|---|---|---|---|---|
| 1952 H | 991,000 | 1.00 | 3.00 | 10.00 | 20.00 | — |
| 1953 H | 10,300,000 | 0.25 | 0.50 | 3.00 | 10.00 | — |
| 1954 H | 1,170,000 | 1.00 | 3.00 | 10.00 | 20.00 | — |
| 1955 H | 583,000 | 2.50 | 5.00 | 20.00 | 35.00 | — |
| 1956 H | 792,000 | 1.00 | 3.00 | 10.00 | 20.00 | — |
| 1958 H | 242,000 | 20.00 | 25.00 | 35.00 | 50.00 | — |
| 1960 S | 110,000 | 20.00 | 30.00 | 45.00 | 70.00 | — |
| 1961 S | 1,811,000 | 1.00 | 2.00 | 5.00 | 10.00 | — |
| 1962 S | 405,000 | 2.00 | 4.00 | 10.00 | 17.00 | — |

**50 MARKKAA** **KM# 59** **Weight:** 20.0000 g. **Composition:** 0.5000 Silver .3216 oz. ASW **Subject:** 80th Birthday of President Kekkonen

| Date | Mintage | F | VF | XF | Unc | BU |
|---|---|---|---|---|---|---|
| 1981 K | 500,000 | — | — | 11.50 | 13.50 | — |

**50 MARKKAA** **KM# 60** **Weight:** 23.0000 g. **Composition:** 0.5000 Silver .3698 oz. ASW **Subject:** World Ice Hockey Championship Games

| Date | Mintage | F | VF | XF | Unc | BU |
|---|---|---|---|---|---|---|
| 1982 K-T | 400,000 | — | — | 12.00 | 14.00 | — |

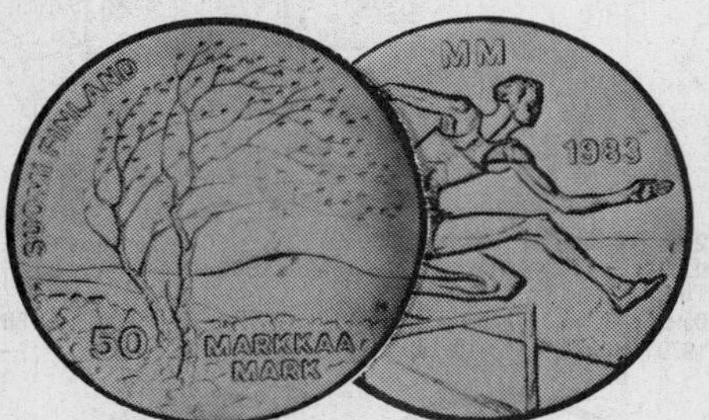


**50 MARKKAA** **KM# 61** **Weight:** 22.0000 g. **Composition:** 0.5000 Silver .3537 oz. ASW **Subject:** 1st World Athletics Championships

| Date | Mintage | F | VF | XF | Unc | BU |
|---|---|---|---|---|---|---|
| 1983 K-M | 450,000 | — | — | 12.00 | 14.00 | — |

**50 MARKKAA** **KM# 62** **Weight:** 20.0000 g. **Composition:** 0.5000 Silver .3216 oz. ASW **Subject:** National Epic - The Kalevala

| Date | Mintage | F | VF | XF | Unc | BU |
|---|---|---|---|---|---|---|
| 1985 P-N | 300,000 | — | — | 13.50 | 17.50 | — |

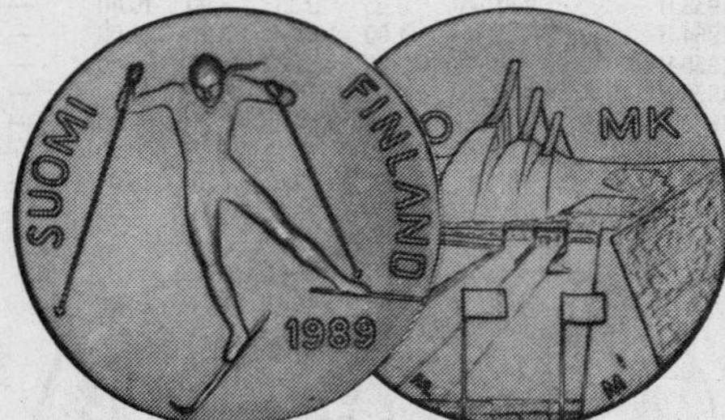


**100 MARKKAA** **KM# 74** **Weight:** 24.0000 g. **Composition:** 0.8300 Silver .6405 oz. ASW **Subject:** World Ski Championship

| Date | Mintage | F | VF | XF | Unc | BU |
|---|---|---|---|---|---|---|
| 1989 M-L-M | 100,000 | — | — | 25.00 | 35.00 | — |

**100 MARKKAA** **KM# 28** **Weight:** 4.2105 g. **Composition:** 0.9000 Gold .1218 oz. AGW

| Date | Mintage | F | VF | XF | Unc | BU |
|---|---|---|---|---|---|---|
| 1926 S | 50,000 | — | 450 | 650 | 850 | — |

**100 MARKKAA** **KM# 41** **Weight:** 5.2000 g. **Composition:** 0.5000 Silver .0836 oz. ASW

| Date | Mintage | F | VF | XF | Unc | BU |
|---|---|---|---|---|---|---|
| 1956 H | 3,012,000 | — | BV | 1.50 | 3.00 | — |
| 1957 H | 3,012,000 | — | BV | 1.50 | 3.00 | — |
| 1958 H | 1,704,000 | BV | 1.50 | 2.50 | 4.00 | — |
| 1959 H | 1,270,000 | 3.00 | 5.00 | 10.00 | 15.00 | — |
| 1960 S | 290,000 | 3.50 | 5.50 | 8.00 | 12.00 | — |

**100 MARKKAA** **KM# 75** **Weight:** 24.0000 g. **Composition:** 0.8300 Silver .6405 oz. ASW **Subject:** Pictorial Arts of Finland

| Date | Mintage | F | VF | XF | Unc | BU |
|---|---|---|---|---|---|---|
| 1989 P-M | 100,000 | — | — | 25.00 | 35.00 | — |

**100 MARKKAA** **KM# 67** **Weight:** 24.0000 g. **Composition:** 0.8300 Silver .6405 oz. ASW **Subject:** 50th Anniversary of Disabled War Veterans Association

| Date | Mintage | F | VF | XF | Unc | BU |
|---|---|---|---|---|---|---|
| 1990 P-M | 100,000 | — | — | 25.00 | 35.00 | — |

**100 MARKKAA** **KM# 68** **Weight:** 24.0000 g. **Composition:** 0.8300 Silver .6405 oz. ASW **Subject:** 350th Anniversary - University of Helsinki

| Date | Mintage | F | VF | XF | Unc | BU |
|---|---|---|---|---|---|---|
| 1990 H-M | 150,000 | — | — | 25.00 | 35.00 | — |

**100 MARKKAA** **KM# 69** **Weight:** 24.0000 g. **Composition:** 0.8300 Silver .6405 oz. ASW **Subject:** Ice Hockey World Championship Games

| Date | Mintage | F | VF | XF | Unc | BU |
|---|---|---|---|---|---|---|
| 1991 L-M | 150,000 | — | — | 25.00 | 35.00 | — |
| 1991 L-M | 200 | Value: 350 | | | | |

**Note:** Struck w/polished dies to prooflike quality and encapsulated in hard plastic 60 mm x 83 mm square. These pieces were given out as business gifts to selected mint visitors

**100 MARKKAA** **KM# 70** **Weight:** 24.0000 g. **Composition:** 0.9250 Silver .7137 oz. ASW **Subject:** 70th Anniversary - Autonomy of Aland

| Date | Mintage | F | VF | XF | Unc | BU |
|---|---|---|---|---|---|---|
| 1991 P-M | 100,000 | — | — | 25.00 | 35.00 | — |
| 1991 P-M | Est. 700 | Value: 300 | | | | |

**Note:** Encapsulated as KM#69 above, but struck to higher prooflike quality

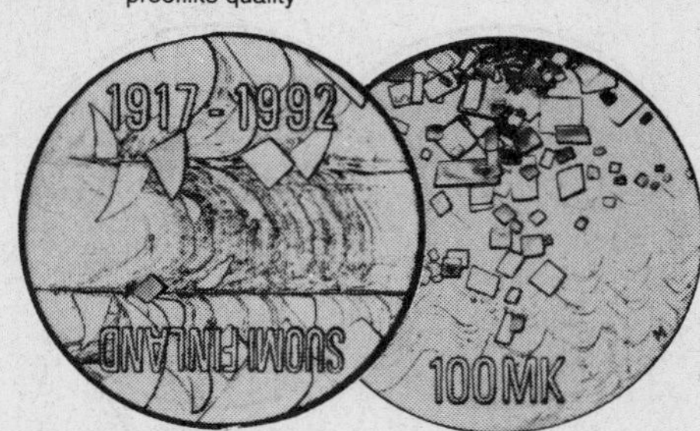


**100 MARKKAA** **KM# 71** **Weight:** 24.0000 g. **Composition:** 0.9250 Silver .7137 oz. ASW **Subject:** 75th Anniversary of Independence

| Date | Mintage | F | VF | XF | Unc | BU |
|---|---|---|---|---|---|---|
| 1992 M-S | 300,000 | — | — | 25.00 | 35.00 | — |

**100 MARKKAA** **KM# 78** **Weight:** 24.0000 g. **Composition:** 0.9250 Silver .7137 oz. ASW **Subject:** Stadium of Friendship

| Date | Mintage | F | VF | XF | Unc | BU |
|---|---|---|---|---|---|---|
| 1994 P-M | 80,000 | — | — | — | 35.00 | — |

**Note:** Encapsulated as KM#69 above, but struck to higher proof quality

| Date | Mintage | F | VF | XF | Unc | BU |
|---|---|---|---|---|---|---|
| 1994 P-M Proof | 15,000 | Value: 65.00 | | | | |

**100 MARKKAA** **KM# 80** **Weight:** 24.0000 g. **Composition:** 0.9250 Silver .7137 oz. ASW **Subject:** 100th Birthday - Arturi Ilmari Virtanen

| Date | Mintage | F | VF | XF | Unc | BU |
|---|---|---|---|---|---|---|
| 1995 S-M | 40,000 | — | — | — | 35.00 | — |
| 1995 S-M Proof | 3,000 | Value: 65.00 | | | | |

**100 MARKKAA** **KM# 81** **Weight:** 24.0000 g. **Composition:** 0.9250 Silver .7137 oz. ASW **Subject:** 50th Anniversary - United Nations

| Date | Mintage | F | VF | XF | Unc | BU |
|---|---|---|---|---|---|---|
| 1995 P-M | 40,000 | — | — | — | 35.00 | — |
| 1995 P-M Proof | 3,000 | Value: 65.00 | | | | |

**100 MARKKAA** **KM# 83** **Weight:** 24.0000 g. **Composition:** 0.9250 Silver .7137 oz. ASW **Subject:** Helene Schjerfbeck - Painter

| Date | Mintage | F | VF | XF | Unc | BU |
|---|---|---|---|---|---|---|
| 1996 T-M | 300,000 | — | — | — | 35.00 | — |
| 1996 T-M Proof | 3,000 | Value: 65.00 | | | | |

**100 MARKKAA** **KM# 84** **Weight:** 22.0000 g. **Composition:** 0.9250 Silver .6543 oz. ASW **Subject:** 100th Birthday - Paavo Nurmi **Obverse:** Two gymnasts **Reverse:** Facial portrait and runner

| Date | Mintage | F | VF | XF | Unc | BU |
|---|---|---|---|---|---|---|
| 1997 M-S | 45,000 | — | — | — | 35.00 | — |
| 1997 M-S Proof | 6,500 | Value: 65.00 | | | | |

**100 MARKKAA** **KM# 87** **Weight:** 22.0000 g. **Composition:** 0.9250 Silver .6543 oz. ASW **Subject:** 100th Birthday - Alvar Aalto **Obverse:** Walls above cliffs and denominations **Reverse:** Mature rye plants

| Date | Mintage | F | VF | XF | Unc | BU |
|---|---|---|---|---|---|---|
| 1998 M-G | Est. 44,000 | — | — | — | 35.00 | — |
| 1998 M-G Proof | 4,000 | Value: 65.00 | | | | |

**100 MARKKAA** **KM# 88** **Weight:** 22.0000 g. **Composition:** 0.9250 Silver .6543 oz. ASW **Subject:** Suomenlinna Fortress **Obverse:** Stylized island view **Reverse:** Sailship and fortress gate

| Date | Mintage | F | VF | XF | Unc | BU |
|---|---|---|---|---|---|---|
| 1998 M-O | 30,000 | — | — | — | 35.00 | — |
| 1998 M-O Proof | 3,300 | Value: 65.00 | | | | |

**100 MARKKAA** **KM# 89** **Weight:** 22.0000 g. **Composition:** 0.9250 Silver .6543 oz. ASW **Subject:** Jean Sibelius - Composer **Obverse:** Finlandia musical score **Reverse:** Sibelius head left

| Date | Mintage | F | VF | XF | Unc | BU |
|---|---|---|---|---|---|---|
| 1999 P-V-M | 30,000 | — | — | — | 35.00 | — |
| 1999 P-V-M Proof | 6,000 | Value: 65.00 | | | | |

**100 MARKKAA** **KM# 92** **Weight:** 22.0000 g. **Composition:** 0.9250 Silver .6543 oz. ASW **Subject:** Jubilee Year 2000 **Obverse:** Turku Cathedral vault ceiling design **Reverse:** Leaf **Edge:** Plain

| Date | Mintage | F | VF | XF | Unc | BU |
|---|---|---|---|---|---|---|
| 2000 L-M | 15,000 | — | — | — | 35.00 | — |
| 2000 L-M Proof | 3,000 | Value: 65.00 | | | | |

**100 MARKKAA** **KM# 93** **Weight:** 22.0000 g. **Composition:** 0.9250 Silver .6543 oz. ASW **Subject:** 450th Anniversary - Helsinki Cultural Capital **Obverse:** Symbolic column design **Reverse:** Carved city view **Edge:** Plain

| Date | Mintage | F | VF | XF | Unc | BU |
|---|---|---|---|---|---|---|
| 2000 P-M | 10,000 | — | — | — | 35.00 | — |
| 2000 P-M Proof | 8,000 | Value: 65.00 | | | | |

**100 MARKKAA** **KM# 94** **Weight:** 22.0000 g. **Composition:** 0.9250 Silver .6543 oz. ASW **Subject:** Aleksis Kivi **Obverse:** Books on shelves **Reverse:** Portrait on partial disc **Edge:** Plain **Size:** 35 mm.

| Date | Mintage | F | VF | XF | Unc | BU |
|---|---|---|---|---|---|---|
| 2000 Proof | 12,000 | Value: 30.00 | | | | |

**200 MARKKAA** **KM# 29** **Weight:** 8.4210 g. **Composition:** 0.9000 Gold .2436 oz. AGW

| Date | Mintage | F | VF | XF | Unc | BU |
|---|---|---|---|---|---|---|
| 1926 S | 50,000 | — | 650 | 900 | 1,100 | — |

**200 MARKKAA** **KM# 42** **Weight:** 8.3000 g. **Composition:** 0.5000 Silver .1334 oz. ASW

| Date | Mintage | F | VF | XF | Unc | BU |
|---|---|---|---|---|---|---|
| 1956 H | 1,552,000 | — | BV | 2.50 | 5.00 | — |
| 1957 H | 2,157,000 | — | BV | 2.50 | 5.00 | — |
| 1958 H | 1,477,000 | BV | 2.50 | 4.00 | 7.00 | — |
| 1958 S | 34,000 | 300 | 400 | 500 | 600 | — |
| 1959 S | 70,000 | 25.00 | 30.00 | 40.00 | 60.00 | — |

**500 MARKKAA** **KM# 35** **Weight:** 12.0000 g. **Composition:** 0.5000 Silver .1929 oz. ASW

| Date | Mintage | F | VF | XF | Unc | BU |
|---|---|---|---|---|---|---|
| 1951 H | 19,000 | 200 | 250 | 325 | 400 | — |
| 1952 H | 586,000 | 15.00 | 18.00 | 28.00 | 38.00 | — |

**1000 MARKKAA** **KM# 43** **Weight:** 14.0000 g. **Composition:** 0.8750 Silver .3938 oz. ASW **Subject:** Markka Currency System Centennial - Snellman

| Date | Mintage | F | VF | XF | Unc | BU |
|---|---|---|---|---|---|---|
| 1960 S-J | 201,000 | 7.00 | 10.00 | 15.00 | 20.00 | — |

**1000 MARKKAA** **KM# 72** **Weight:** 9.0000 g. **Composition:** 0.9000 Gold .2604 oz. AGW **Subject:** 75th Anniversary of Independence

| Date | Mintage | F | VF | XF | Unc | BU |
|---|---|---|---|---|---|---|
| 1992 M-S Proof | 35,000 | Value: 275 | | | | |

**1000 MARKKAA** **KM# 86** **Weight:** 8.6400 g. **Composition:** 0.9000 Gold .2500 oz. AGW **Subject:** 80th Anniversary of Independence **Obverse:** New shoot growing from tree stump **Reverse:** Symbolic design separating dates

| Date | Mintage | F | VF | XF | Unc | BU |
|---|---|---|---|---|---|---|
| ND (1997) M-P Proof | 20,000 | Value: 285 | | | | |

**1000 MARKKAA** **KM# 90** **Weight:** 8.6400 g. **Composition:** 0.9000 Gold .2500 oz. AGW **Subject:** Jean Sibelius - Composer **Obverse:** Sibelius head left **Reverse:** Finlandia musical score, denomination above, date below

| Date | Mintage | F | VF | XF | Unc | BU |
|---|---|---|---|---|---|---|
| 1999 P-V-M Proof | 25,000 | Value: 275 | | | | |

**2000 MARKKAA** **KM# 79** **Weight:** 16.9700 g. **Composition:** 0.9000 Gold .4910 oz. AGW **Subject:** 50 Years of Peace

| Date | Mintage | F | VF | XF | Unc | BU |
|---|---|---|---|---|---|---|
| 1995 M-L-L Proof | 6,900 | Value: 450 | | | | |

## MEDALLIC COINAGE

Ecu Series

**5 ECU** **KM# M1** **Composition:** Copper-Nickel **Subject:** CSCE Conference

| Date | Mintage | F | VF | XF | Unc | BU |
|---|---|---|---|---|---|---|
| 1992 | 10,000 | — | — | — | 10.00 | — |

**20 ECU** **KM# M2** **Weight:** 25.0000 g. **Composition:** 0.9250 Silver .7435 oz. ASW **Subject:** CSCE Conference **Note:** Similar to 5 Ecu, KM#M1.

| Date | Mintage | F | VF | XF | Unc | BU |
|---|---|---|---|---|---|---|
| 1992 Proof | 7,500 | Value: 35.00 | | | | |

**20 ECU** **KM# M4** **Weight:** 27.0000 g. **Composition:** 0.9250 Silver .8029 oz. ASW **Reverse:** Castle of Turku

| Date | Mintage | F | VF | XF | Unc | BU |
|---|---|---|---|---|---|---|
| 1996 Proof | 25,000 | Value: 35.00 | | | | |

**20 ECU** **KM# M7** **Weight:** 27.0000 g. **Composition:** 0.9250 Silver .8029 oz. ASW **Reverse:** Aurora Borealis

| Date | Mintage | F | VF | XF | Unc | BU |
|---|---|---|---|---|---|---|
| 1997 Proof | 20,000 | Value: 35.00 | | | | |

**20 ECU** **KM# M8** **Weight:** 27.0000 g. **Composition:** 0.9250 Silver .8029 oz. ASW **Reverse:** Castle of Hume and Ingeborg Aakentytar Tott **Note:** Castle of Hame

| Date | Mintage | F | VF | XF | Unc | BU |
|---|---|---|---|---|---|---|
| 1997 Proof | 20,000 | Value: 35.00 | | | | |

**20 ECU** **KM# M11** **Weight:** 27.0000 g. **Composition:** 0.9250 Silver .8029 oz. ASW **Note:** Zacharius Topelius.

| Date | Mintage | F | VF | XF | Unc | BU |
|---|---|---|---|---|---|---|
| 1998 Proof | 20,000 | Value: 35.00 | | | | |

**150 ECU** **KM# M3** **Weight:** 6.7200 g. **Composition:** 0.7500 Gold .1620 oz. AGW **Subject:** CSCE Conference **Obverse:** Human head on strange shape **Reverse:** Building complex **Note:** Similar to 5 Ecu, KM#M1.

| Date | Mintage | F | VF | XF | Unc | BU |
|---|---|---|---|---|---|---|
| 1992 Proof | 1,000 | Value: 150 | | | | |

## MEDALLIC COINAGE

Euro Series

**10 EURO** **KM# M5** **Weight:** 14.4000 g. **Composition:** 0.9250 Silver .4282 oz. ASW **Reverse:** Castle of Olavi

| Date | Mintage | F | VF | XF | Unc | BU |
|---|---|---|---|---|---|---|
| 1996 | 25,000 | — | — | — | 15.00 | — |

**10 EURO** **KM# M6** **Weight:** 27.0000 g. **Composition:** 0.9250 Silver .8029 oz. ASW **Subject:** 75 Years of Aland Self-government

| Date | Mintage | F | VF | XF | Unc | BU |
|---|---|---|---|---|---|---|
| 1997 | 10,000 | — | — | — | 20.00 | — |

**10 EURO** **KM# M9** **Weight:** 27.0000 g. **Composition:** 0.9250 Silver .8029 oz. ASW **Subject:** Nagano Games **Reverse:** Cross Country Skiing

| Date | Mintage | F | VF | XF | Unc | BU |
|---|---|---|---|---|---|---|
| 1998 Proof | 30,000 | Value: 20.00 | | | | |

**10 EURO** **KM# M10** **Weight:** 27.0000 g. **Composition:** 0.9250 Silver .8029 oz. ASW **Subject:** Nagano Games **Reverse:** Alpine skiing

| Date | Mintage | F | VF | XF | Unc | BU |
|---|---|---|---|---|---|---|
| 1998 Proof | 30,000 | Value: 20.00 | | | | |

**50 EURO** **KM# M12** **Weight:** 8.6400 g. **Composition:** 0.9000 Gold .2500 oz. AGW **Subject:** Nagano Games **Reverse:** Cross country skiing

| Date | Mintage | F | VF | XF | Unc | BU |
|---|---|---|---|---|---|---|
| 1998 Proof | 5,000 | Value: 120 | | | | |

## PATTERNS

Including off metal strikes

| KM# | Date | Mintage | Identification | Mkt Val |
|---|---|---|---|---|
| Pn42 | 1953 | — | Markka. Aluminum. With pearls. | — |
| Pn53 | 1956 | — | 500 Markkaa. Silver. With waves. | — |
| Pn54 | 1956 | — | 500 Markkaa. Silver. With plain field. | — |
| Pn48 | 1954 | — | Markkaa. Iron. With pearls. | 1,700 |
| Pn11 | 1918 | — | 5 Pennia. Silver. | 3,500 |
| Pn12 | 1919 | — | Penni. Nickel. | — |
| Pn13 | 1921 | — | 10 Pennia. Iron. | — |
| Pn14 | 1922 | — | 5 Pennia. Silver. | — |
| Pn15 | 1923 | — | 50 Pennia. Copper. | — |
| Pn16 | 1923 | — | Markkaa. Copper. | — |
| Pn17 | 1924 | — | 10 Pennia. Nickel. | — |
| Pn18 | 1926 | — | 200 Markkaa. Copper. | — |
| Pn19 | 1927 | — | 10 Pennia. Copper. | — |
| Pn20 | 1936 | — | 25 Pennia. Copper. | — |
| Pn21 | 1936 | — | Markkaa. Iron. | — |
| Pn22 | 1941 | — | 10 Pennia. Iron. | 250 |
| Pn23 | 1942 | — | 25 Pennia. Aluminum. | — |
| Pn24 | 1942 | — | 50 Pennia. Aluminum. | — |
| Pn25 | 1942 | — | Markkaa. Aluminum. | — |
| Pn26 | 1942 | — | Markka. Iron - Blued. | — |
| Pn27 | 1942 | — | 5 Markkaa. Brass. | — |
| Pn28 | 1945 | — | Markkaa. Brass. | 3,000 |
| Pn29 | 1946 | — | 5 Markkaa. Nickel. | — |
| Pn30 | 1947 | — | 5 Markkaa. Iron. | — |
| Pn31 | 1948 | — | Markkaa. Aluminum. | — |
| Pn32 | 1948 | — | Markkaa. Bronze. | — |
| Pn33 | 1948 | — | 5 Markkaa. Nickel. | — |
| Pn35 | 1949 | — | 5 Markkaa. Iron. | — |
| Pn34 | 1949 | — | Markkaa. Copper. | 5,000 |
| Pn36 | 1950 H | — | Markkaa. Brass. | 2,500 |
| Pn37 | 1951 | — | 500 Markkaa. Aluminum - Blued. | — |
| Pn38 | 1952 | — | Markkaa. Iron - Blued. | — |
| Pn39 | 1952 | — | 5 Markkaa. Iron - Blued. | — |
| Pn41 | 1952 | — | 10 Markkaa. Copper. | — |
| Pn40 | 1952 | — | 10 Markkaa. Iron. | 500 |
| Pn43 | 1953 | — | Markka. Iron. Lion head. | — |
| Pn44 | 1953 | — | Markka. Iron. With pearls. | — |
| Pn45 | 1953 | — | 5 Markkaa. Iron - Blued. | — |
| Pn46 | 1953 | — | 50 Markkaa. Nickel. | — |
| Pn48 | 1954 | — | Markkaa. Iron. With pearls. | — |
| Pn49 | 1954 | — | 5 Markkaa. Iron. With pearls. | — |
| Pn50 | 1954 | — | 20 Markkaa. Nickel. | — |
| Pn47 | 1954 | — | Markkaa. Nickel Plated Iron. | 1,000 |
| Pn51 | 1956 | — | 20 Markkaa. Nickel. | — |
| Pn52 | 1956 | — | 20 Markkaa. Silver. | — |
| Pn55 | 1969 | — | 5 Markkaa. Copper-Nickel. | — |

## TRIAL STRIKES

| KM# | Date | Mintage | Identification | Mkt Val |
|---|---|---|---|---|
| TS6 | 1918 | — | 5 Pennia. Iron. | 2,000 |
| TS7 | 1960 | — | (1000 Markkaa). Brass. | — |
| TS8 | 1960 | — | (1000 Markkaa). Brass. | — |

## MINT SETS

| KM# | Date | Mintage | Identification | Issue Price | Mkt Val |
|---|---|---|---|---|---|
| MS1 | 1973 (7) | 10,029 | KM44a, 45-48, 49a, 53 | 5.00 | 25.00 |
| MS2 | 1973 (7) | 9,978 | KM44a, 45-48, 49a, 53 | 10.00 | 60.00 |
| MS3 | 1974 | 79,258 | KM44a, 45-48, 49a, 53 | 3.75 | 8.00 |
| MS4 | 1975 (7) | 58,820 | KM44a, 45-48, 49a, 53 | 3.75 | 8.00 |
| MS5 | 1976 (7) | 45,263 | KM44a, 45-48, 49a, 53 | 3.75 | 8.00 |
| MS6 | 1977 (7) | 40,392 | KM44a, 45-48, 49a, 53 | 4.00 | 10.00 |
| MS7 | 1978 (7) | 39,745 | KM44a-45a, 46-48, 49a, 53 | 4.45 | 8.00 |
| MS8 | 1979 (7) | 36,000 | KM44a-45a, 46-48, 49a, 57 | 4.85 | 10.00 |
| MS9 | 1980 (6) | 33,805 | KM45a, 46-48, 49a, 57 | 5.00 | 8.00 |
| MS10 | 1981 (6) | 63,100 | KM45a, 46-48, 49a, 57 | 5.25 | 8.00 |
| MS11 | 1982 (6) | 35,500 | KM45a, 46-48, 49a, 57 | 5.50 | 8.00 |
| MS12 | 1983 (6) | 30,100 | KM45a-46a, 47-48, 49a, 57 | 3.25 | 8.00 |
| MS13 | 1983 (6) | 9,250 | KM45a-46a, 47-48, 49a, 57 | 3.25 | 20.00 |
| MS14 | 1984 (6) | 30,500 | KM45a-46a, 47-48, 49a, 57 | 3.25 | 6.00 |
| MS15 | 1984 (6) | 600 | KM45a-46a, 47-48, 49a, 57 | 3.75 | 50.00 |
| MA16 | 1985 (6) | 38,385 | KM45a-46a, 47-48, 49a, 57 | 3.25 | 6.00 |
| MS17 | 1985 (6) | 1,500 | KM45a-46a, 47-48, 49a, 57 | 4.65 | 20.00 |
| MS18 | 1985 (6) | 1,560 | KM45a-46a, 47-48, 49a, 57 | 3.75 | 20.00 |
| MS19 | 1986 (6) | 37,100 | KM45a-46a, 47-48, 49a, 57 | 3.25 | 6.00 |
| MS20 | 1986 (6) | 1,300 | KM45a-46a, 47-48, 49a, 57 | 5.00 | 20.00 |
| MS21 | 1986 (6) | 1,780 | KM45a-46a, 47-48, 49a, 57 | 4.25 | 20.00 |
| MS22 | 1987 (6) | 34,300 | KM45a-46a, 47-48, 49a, 57 | — | 6.00 |
| MS23 | 1987 (6) | 1,120 | KM45a-46a, 47-48, 49a, 57 | — | 20.00 |
| MS24 | 1987 (6) | 1,400 | KM45a-46a, 47-48, 49a, 57 | — | 20.00 |
| MS25 | 1987 (6) | 15,900 | KM45a-46a, 47-48, 49a, 57 | — | 10.00 |
| MS26 | 1987 (6) | 300 | KM45a-46a, 47-48, 57 | — | 50.00 |
| MS27 | 1987 (6) | 180 | KM45a-46a, 47-48, 49a, 57 | — | 50.00 |
| MS28 | 1988 (6) | 35,750 | KM45a-46a, 47-48, 49a, 57 | — | 6.00 |
| MS29 | 1988 (6) | 1,450 | KM45a-46a, 47-48, 49a, 57 | — | 15.00 |
| MS30 | 1988 (6) | 1,220 | KM45a-46a, 47-48, 49a, 57 | — | 15.00 |
| MS31 | 1989 (6) | 33,000 | KM45a-46a, 47-48, 49a, 57 | — | 6.00 |
| MS32 | 1989 (6) | 1,450 | KM45a-46a, 47-48, 49a, 57 | — | 10.00 |
| MS33 | 1989 (6) | 1,700 | KM45a-46a, 47-48, 49a, 57 | — | 10.00 |
| MS34 | 1989 (6) | 15,982 | KM45a-46a, 47-48, 49a, 57 | — | 22.00 |
| MS35 | 1989 (6) | 1,000 | KM45a-46a, 47-48, 49a, 57 | — | 35.00 |
| MS36 | 1989 (6) | 1,150 | KM45a-46a, 47-48, 49a, 57 | — | 35.00 |
| MS37 | 1990 (6) | 29,400 | KM45a-46a, 47-48, 49a, 57 | — | 6.00 |
| MS38 | 1990 (6) | 1,000 | KM45a-46a, 47-48, 49a, 57 | — | 10.00 |
| MS39 | 1990 (6) | 1,000 | KM45a-46a, 47-48, 49a, 57 | — | 10.00 |
| MS40 | 1990 (4) | 41,750 | KM49a, 57, 65-66 | — | 9.00 |
| MS41 | 1990 (4) | 3,500 | KM49a, 57, 65-66 | — | 10.00 |
| MS42 | 1991 (4) | 30,000 | KM49a, 57, 65-66 | — | 10.00 |
| MS43 | 1991 (4) | 5,000 | KM49a, 57, 65-66 | — | 10.00 |
| MS44 | 1992 (5) | 28,000 | KM49a, 57, 65-55, 73 | — | 12.50 |
| MS45 | 1993 (6) | 100,000 | KM49a, 65-66, 73, 76a, 77 | — | 21.50 |
| MS46 | 1993 (5) | — | Km65-66, 73, 76-77 | 13.30 | 13.50 |
| MS47 | 1993 (4) | 20,000 | Km49a, 65-66, 73 | — | 15.00 |
| MS48 | 1994 (5) | 25,000 | Km65-66, 73, 76-77 | — | 18.00 |
| MS49 | 1995 (5) | 23,190 | KM65-66, 73, 76-77 | — | 20.00 |
| MS50 | 1995 (5) | 15,000 | KM65-66, 73, 76-77 | — | 20.00 |
| MS51 | 1996 (5) | 16,300 | KM65-66, 73, 76-77 | — | 20.00 |
| MS52 | 1997 (5) | 18,000 | KM65-66, 73, 76-77 | — | 20.00 |
| MS56 | 2000 (5) | — | KM65-66, 73, 76-77 | 12.50 | 20.00 |
| MS53 | 1998 (5) | 18,000 | KM65-66, 73, 76-77 | — | 20.00 |
| MS54 | 1999 (5) | — | KM65-66, 73, 76-77 | — | 20.00 |
| MS55 | 1999 (5) | — | KM65-66, 73, 76-77 | 12.50 | 20.00 |
| MS57 | 2000 (5) | — | KM65-66, 73, 76-77 | 12.50 | 20.00 |
| MS58 | 2001 (5) | 20,000 | KM#65, 66, 73, 76, 77 | 18.00 | 20.00 |

## PROOF SETS

| KM# | Date | Mintage | Identification | Issue Price | Mkt Val |
|---|---|---|---|---|---|
| PS1 | 1994 (5) | 1,000 | KM65-66, 73, 76-77 | — | 150 |
| PS2 | 1995 (2) | 500 | KM80, 80a | 802 | 700 |
| PS3 | 1995 (5) | 1,810 | KM65-66, 73, 76-77 | — | 55.00 |
| PS4 | 1996 (5) | 1,200 | KM65-66, 73, 76-77 | — | 55.00 |
| PS5 | 1997 (6) | 2,000 | KM65-66, 73, 76-77, 85 | 67.50 | 70.00 |
| PS6 | 1998 (5) | 1,600 | KM65-66, 73, 76-77 | — | 55.00 |
| PS7 | 1999 (5) | — | KM65-66, 73, 76-77 | — | 55.00 |
| PS8 | 2000 (5) | — | KM65-66, 73, 76-77 | — | 55.00 |

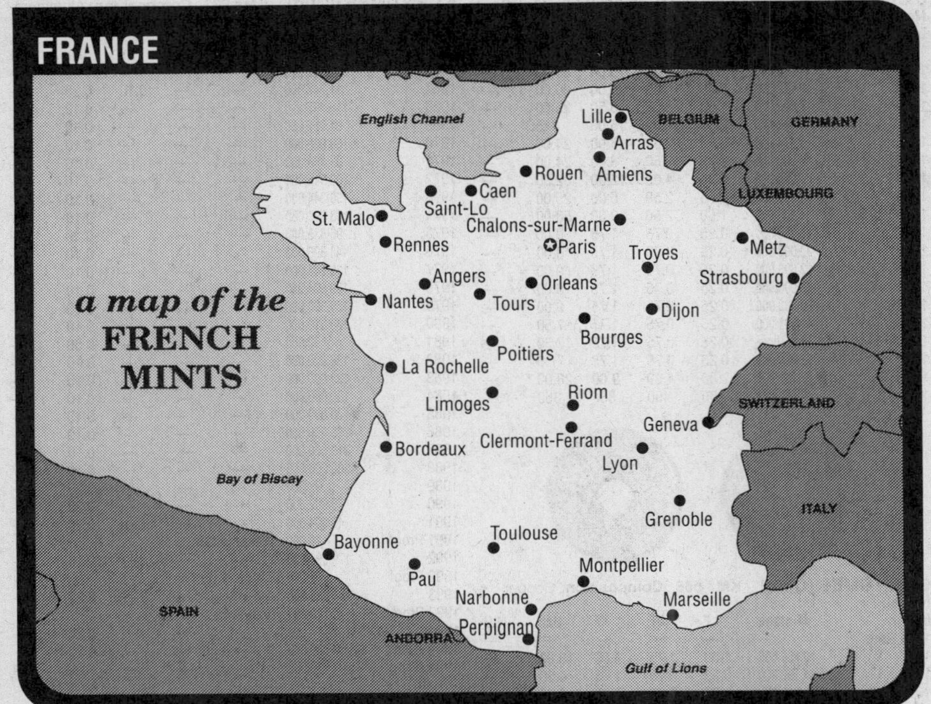


The French Republic, largest of the West European nations, has an area of 210,026 sq. mi. (547,030 sq. km.) and a population of 58.1 million. Capital: Paris. Agriculture, manufacturing, tourist industry and financial services are the most important elements of France's diversified economy. Textiles and clothing, steel products, machinery and transportation equipment, chemicals, pharmaceuticals, nuclear electricity, agricultural products and wine are exported.

France, the Gaul of ancient times, emerged from the Renaissance as a modern centralized national state which reached its zenith during the reign of Louis XIV (1643-1715) when it became an absolute monarchy and the foremost power in Europe. Although his reign marks the golden age of French culture, the domestic abuses and extravagance of Louis XIV plunged France into a series of costly wars. This, along with a system of special privileges granted the nobility and other favored groups, weakened the monarchy and brought France to bankruptcy. This laid the way for the French Revolution of 1789-99 that shook Europe and affected the whole world.

The monarchy was abolished and the First Republic formed in 1793. The new government fell in 1799 to a coup led by Napoleon Bonaparte who, after declaring himself First Consul for life, in 1804 had himself proclaimed Emperor of France and King of Italy.

Napoleon's military victories made him master of much of Europe, but his disastrous Russian campaign of 1812 initiated a series of defeats that led to his abdication in 1814 and exile to the island of Elba. The monarchy was briefly restored under Louis XVIII. Napoleon returned to France in March 1815, but his efforts to uphold his power were totally crushed at the battle of Waterloo. He was exiled to the island of St. Helena where he died in 1821.

The monarchy under Louis XVIII was again restored in 1815, but the ultra reactionary regime of Charles X (1824-30) was overthrown by a liberal revolution and Louis Philippe of Orleans replaced him as monarch. The monarchy was ousted by the Revolution of 1848 and the Second Republic proclaimed. Louis Napoleon Bonaparte (nephew of Napoleon I) was elected president of the Second Republic. He was proclaimed emperor in 1852. As Napoleon III, he gave France two decades of prosperity under a stable, autocratic regime, but led it to defeat in the Franco-Prussian War of 1870, after which the Third Republic was established.

The Third Republic endured until 1940 and the capitulation of France to the swiftly maneuvering German forces. Marshal Philippe Petain formed a puppet government that sued for peace and ruled unoccupied France until 1942 from Vichy. Meanwhile, General Charles de Gaulle escaped to London where he formed a wartime government in exile and the Free French army. De Gaulle's provisional exile government was officially recognized by the Allies after the liberation of Paris in 1944, and De Gaulle, who had been serving as head of the provisional government, tacitly maintained that position. In October 1945, the people overwhelmingly rejected a return to the prewar government, thus paving the way for the formation of the Fourth Republic in 1947 just after the dismissal of De Gaulle, at grips with a coalition of rival parties, the Communists especially.

In actual operation, the Fourth Republic was remarkably like the Third, with the National Assembly the focus of power causing a constant governmental instability. The later years of the Fourth Republic were marked by a burst of industrial expansion unmatched in modern French history. The growth rate, however, was marred by a two colonial wars, nagging inflationary trend that weakened the franc and undermined the betterment of the people's buying power. This and the Algerian conflict led to the recall of De Gaulle to power, the adoption of a new constitution vesting strong powers in the executive, and the establishment in 1959 of the current Fifth Republic.

**RULERS**

Third Republic, 1871-1940
Vichy State, 1940-1944
De Gaulle's Provisional Govt., 1944-1946
Fourth Republic, 1947-1958
Fifth Republic, 1959—

**MINT MARKS AND PRIVY MARKS**

In addition to the date and mint mark which are customary on western civilization coinage, most coins manufactured by the French Mints contain two or three small 'Marks or Differents' as the French call them. These privy marks represent the men responsible for the dies which struck the coins. One privy mark is sometimes for the Engraver General (since 1880 the title is Chief Engraver). The other privy mark is the signature of the Mint Director of each mint; another one is the different' of the local engraver. Three other marks appeared at the end of Louis XIV's reign: one for the Director General of Mints, one for the General Engineer of Mechanical edge-marking, one identifying over struck coins in 1690-1705 and in 1715-1723. Equally amazing and unique is that sometimes the local assayer's or Judge-custody's 'different' or 'secret pellet' appears. Since 1880 this privy mark has represented the office rather than the personage of both the Administration of Coins & Medals and the Mint Director, and a standard privy mark has been used (cornucopia).

For most dates these privy marks are important though minor features for advanced collectors or local researchers. During some issue dates, however, the marks changed. To be even more accurate sometimes the marks changed when the date didn't, even though it should have. These coins can be attributed to the proper mintage report only by considering the privy marks. Previous references (before G. Sobin and F. Droulers) have by and large ignored these privy marks. It is entirely possible that unattributed varieties may exist for any privy mark transition. All transition years which may have two or three varieties or combinations of privy marks have the known attribution indicated after the date (if it has been confirmed).

**ENGRAVER GENERAL'S PRIVY MARKS**

| Mark | Date | Name |
|---|---|---|
| | Torch, 1896-1926 | |
| | Wing, 1927-58 | |
| | Owl, 1958-74 | |
| | Fish, 1974-94 | |
| | Bee, 1994- | |

**MINT DIRECTOR'S PRIVY MARKS**

Some modern coins struck from dies produced at the Paris Mint have the 'A' mint mark. In the absence of a mint mark, the cornucopia privy mark serves to attribute a coin to Paris design.

**A – Paris, Central Mint**

**B – Beaumont – Le Roger**

| Mark | Date | Name |
|---|---|---|
| | Cornucopia, 1943-58 | |

**(b) – Brussels**

| Mark | Date | Name |
|---|---|---|
| | None, (1939) | |

**Legend ending BD, see PAU**

**C - Castelsarrasin**

| Date | Mark | Name |
|---|---|---|
| C | | |
| C | Cornucopia, 1914, 1943-46 | |

**Thunderbolt (tb) - Poissy**

| Mark | Date | Name |
|---|---|---|
| | Cornucopia, 1922-24 | |

**Star (s) - Madrid**

| Date | Mark | Name |
|---|---|---|
| * | 1916 | |

**MONETARY SYSTEM**
**(Commencing 1960)**

1 Old Franc = 1 New Centime
100 New Centimes = 1 New Franc

# MODERN REPUBLICS

## DECIMAL COINAGE

**CENTIME** **KM# 928a** **Weight:** 2.5000 g. **Composition:** 0.7500 Gold .0603 oz. AGW **Obverse:** Medallic alignment **Reverse:** Medallic alignment **Edge:** Plain **Note:** Last Centime. Struck at Paris Mint.

| Date | Mintage | F | VF | XF | Unc | BU |
|---|---|---|---|---|---|---|
| 2000 | 25,000 | — | — | — | 45.00 | — |
| 2001 | Est. 25,000 | — | — | — | 65.00 | — |

**CENTIME (Un)** **KM# 840** **Composition:** Bronze **Note:** Without mint mark or privy mark. Struck at Paris Mint.

| Date | Mintage | F | VF | XF | Unc | BU |
|---|---|---|---|---|---|---|
| 1901 | 1,000,000 | 1.00 | 2.00 | 15.00 | 35.00 | — |
| 1902 | 1,000,000 | 0.75 | 1.50 | 4.00 | 15.00 | — |
| 1903 | 2,000,000 | 0.50 | 1.50 | 3.00 | 15.00 | — |
| 1904 | 1,000,000 | 0.75 | 1.50 | 4.00 | 15.00 | — |
| 1908 | 4,500,000 | 2.00 | 4.00 | 10.00 | 20.00 | — |
| 1909 | 1,500,000 | 3.00 | 5.00 | 12.00 | 30.00 | — |
| 1910 | 1,500,000 | 10.00 | 20.00 | 40.00 | 80.00 | — |
| 1911 | 5,000,000 | 0.25 | 0.75 | 1.50 | 5.00 | — |
| 1912 | 2,000,000 | 0.50 | 1.00 | 2.00 | 7.00 | — |
| 1913 | 1,500,000 | 0.50 | 1.00 | 2.00 | 7.00 | — |
| 1914 | 1,000,000 | 0.75 | 1.50 | 3.00 | 9.50 | — |
| 1916 | 1,996,000 | 0.50 | 1.00 | 2.00 | 6.50 | — |
| 1919 | 2,407,000 | 0.25 | 0.75 | 1.50 | 4.00 | — |
| 1920 | 2,594,000 | 0.25 | 0.75 | 1.50 | 4.00 | — |

**CENTIME (Un)** **KM# 928** **Composition:** Chrome-Steel **Note:** 1991-1993 dated coins, non-Proof, exist in both coin and medal alignment. Values given here are for medal alignment examples. Pieces struck in coin alignment have been traded for as much as $50.00. Struck at Paris Mint.

| Date | Mintage | F | VF | XF | Unc | BU |
|---|---|---|---|---|---|---|
| 1962 | 34,200,000 | — | — | 0.10 | 0.25 | — |
| 1963 | 16,811,000 | — | 0.10 | 0.15 | 0.35 | — |
| 1964 | 22,654,000 | — | — | 0.10 | 0.25 | — |
| 1965 | 47,799,000 | — | — | 0.10 | 0.25 | — |
| 1966 | 19,688,000 | — | — | 0.10 | 0.25 | — |
| 1967 | 52,308,000 | — | — | 0.10 | 0.25 | — |
| 1968 | 40,890,000 | — | — | 0.10 | 0.25 | — |
| 1969 | 35,430,000 | — | — | 0.10 | 0.25 | — |
| 1970 | 29,600,000 | — | — | 0.10 | 0.25 | — |
| 1971 | 3,082,000 | — | — | 0.10 | 0.25 | — |
| 1972 | 1,014,999 | — | 0.10 | 0.15 | 0.35 | — |
| 1973 | 1,806,000 | — | 0.10 | 0.15 | 0.35 | — |
| 1974 | 7,949,000 | — | — | 0.10 | 0.25 | — |
| 1975 | 771,000 | — | 0.10 | 0.25 | 1.00 | — |
| 1976 | 4,482,000 | — | — | 0.10 | 0.25 | — |
| 1977 | 6,425,000 | — | — | 0.10 | 0.25 | — |
| 1978 | 1,236,000 | — | 0.10 | 0.15 | 0.35 | — |
| 1979 | 2,213,000 | — | — | 0.10 | 0.25 | — |
| 1980 | 60,000 | — | — | — | 1.00 | — |
| 1981 | 50,000 | — | — | — | 1.00 | — |
| 1982 | 69,000 | — | — | — | 1.00 | — |
| 1983 | 101,000 | — | — | — | 1.00 | — |
| 1984 | 50,000 | — | — | — | 1.00 | — |
| 1985 In sets only | 20,000 | — | — | — | 1.00 | — |
| 1986 In sets only | 48,000 | — | — | — | 1.00 | — |
| 1987 | 100,000 | — | — | — | 1.00 | — |
| 1988 | 100,000 | — | — | — | 1.00 | — |
| 1989 | 83,000 | — | — | — | 1.00 | — |
| 1990 | 15,000 | — | — | — | 1.00 | — |
| 1991 | 5,000 | — | — | — | 1.00 | — |
| 1991 Proof | 10,000 | Value: 2.00 | | | | |
| 1992 | 85,000 | — | — | — | 1.00 | — |
| 1992 Proof | 15,000 | Value: 2.00 | | | | |
| 1993 | 40,000 | — | — | — | 1.00 | — |
| 1993 Proof | 10,000 | Value: 2.00 | | | | |
| 1994 (bee) | 20,000 | — | — | — | — | — |
| 1994 (fish) | 10,000 | — | — | — | — | — |
| 1995 | 25,000 | — | — | — | 1.00 | — |
| 1995 Proof | 10,000 | Value: 2.00 | | | | |
| 1996 | 17,000 | — | — | — | 1.00 | — |
| 1996 Proof | 8,000 | Value: 2.00 | | | | |
| 1997 | 15,000 | — | — | — | 1.00 | — |
| 1997 Proof | 10,000 | Value: 2.00 | | | | |
| 1998 | — | — | — | — | 1.00 | — |
| 1998 Proof | — | Value: 2.00 | | | | |
| 1999 | — | — | — | — | 1.00 | — |
| 1999 Proof | — | Value: 2.00 | | | | |
| 2000 | — | — | — | — | 1.00 | — |
| 2000 Proof | — | Value: 2.00 | | | | |

**2 CENTIMES KM# 841 Composition:** Bronze **Note:** Without mark mark or privy mark. Struck at Paris Mint.

| Date | Mintage | F | VF | XF | Unc | BU |
|---|---|---|---|---|---|---|
| 1901 | 1,000,000 | 1.00 | 2.50 | 4.00 | 11.50 | — |
| 1902 | 750,000 | 1.50 | 3.50 | 5.50 | 15.00 | — |
| 1903 | 750,000 | 1.50 | 3.50 | 5.50 | 16.50 | — |
| 1904 | 500,000 | 2.00 | 4.50 | 7.50 | 18.50 | — |
| 1907 | 250,000 | 10.00 | 25.00 | 55.00 | 130 | — |
| 1908 | 3,500,000 | 0.35 | 0.75 | 2.00 | 6.00 | — |
| 1909 | 1,750,000 | 6.00 | 12.00 | 30.00 | 50.00 | — |
| 1910 | 1,750,000 | 0.50 | 1.00 | 5.00 | 12.50 | — |
| 1911 | 5,000,000 | 0.15 | 0.50 | 1.25 | 5.00 | — |
| 1912 | 1,500,000 | 0.25 | 1.00 | 2.00 | 7.00 | — |
| 1913 | 1,750,000 | 0.25 | 1.00 | 2.00 | 7.00 | — |
| 1914 | 2,000,000 | 0.15 | 0.50 | 1.25 | 5.00 | — |
| 1916 | 500,000 | 0.75 | 1.50 | 3.00 | 9.00 | — |
| 1919 | 902,000 | 0.50 | 1.00 | 2.00 | 6.00 | — |
| 1920 | 598,000 | 0.75 | 1.50 | 3.00 | 8.00 | — |

**5 CENTIMES (Cinq) KM# 875a Weight:** 1.5000 g. **Composition:** Nickel-Bronze

| Date | Mintage | F | VF | XF | Unc | BU |
|---|---|---|---|---|---|---|
| .1938. | 26,330,000 | 0.15 | 0.50 | 1.00 | 3.00 | — |
| .1938. star | Inc. above | 100 | 200 | 300 | 425 | — |
| .1939. | 52,673,000 | 0.10 | 0.25 | 0.75 | 2.00 | — |

**5 CENTIMES (Cinq) KM# 842 Composition:** Bronze **Note:** Without mint mark. Struck at Paris Mint.

| Date | Mintage | F | VF | XF | Unc | BU |
|---|---|---|---|---|---|---|
| 1901 (c) | 6,000,000 | 1.75 | 3.50 | 15.00 | 60.00 | — |
| 1902 | 7,900,000 | 1.75 | 3.50 | 10.00 | 50.00 | — |
| 1903 | 2,879,000 | 5.00 | 10.00 | 25.00 | 80.00 | — |
| 1904 | 8,000,000 | 1.00 | 3.00 | 6.50 | 25.00 | — |
| 1905 | 2,100,000 | 6.00 | 16.00 | 45.00 | 115 | — |
| 1906 | 8,394,000 | 0.75 | 2.50 | 6.00 | 24.00 | — |
| 1907 | 7,900,000 | 0.75 | 2.50 | 6.00 | 24.00 | — |
| 1908 | 6,090,000 | 2.00 | 4.00 | 12.00 | 32.00 | — |
| 1909 | 8,000,000 | 0.75 | 2.50 | 6.00 | 25.00 | — |
| 1910 | 4,000,000 | 1.50 | 2.50 | 9.00 | 50.00 | — |
| 1911 | 15,386,000 | 0.25 | 0.75 | 1.75 | 9.00 | — |
| 1912 | 20,000,000 | 0.25 | 0.75 | 1.75 | 9.00 | — |
| 1913 | 12,603,000 | 0.25 | 0.75 | 1.75 | 9.00 | — |
| 1914 | 7,000,000 | 0.25 | 0.75 | 1.75 | 9.00 | — |
| 1915 | 6,032,000 | 0.25 | 0.75 | 1.75 | 9.00 | — |
| 1916 | 41,531,000 | 0.25 | 0.75 | 1.75 | 7.50 | — |
| 1916 (s) | Inc. above | 0.25 | 0.75 | 1.75 | 7.50 | — |
| 1917 | 16,963,000 | 0.25 | 0.75 | 1.75 | 7.50 | — |
| 1920 | 8,151,999 | 2.00 | 4.00 | 9.00 | 28.00 | — |
| 1921 | 142,000 | 250 | 450 | 850 | 1,350 | — |

**5 CENTIMES (Cinq) KM# 865 Composition:** Copper-Nickel

| Date | Mintage | F | VF | XF | Unc | BU |
|---|---|---|---|---|---|---|
| 1914 Rare | — | — | — | — | — | — |
| 1917 | 10,458,000 | 1.00 | 1.75 | 4.00 | 18.00 | — |
| 1918 | 35,592,000 | 0.25 | 0.75 | 1.75 | 4.50 | — |
| 1919 | 43,848,000 | 0.25 | 0.75 | 1.75 | 4.00 | — |
| 1920 | 51,321,000 | 0.25 | 0.50 | 1.75 | 3.50 | — |

**5 CENTIMES (Cinq) KM# 875 Weight:** 2.0000 g. **Composition:** Copper-Nickel

| Date | Mintage | F | VF | XF | Unc | BU |
|---|---|---|---|---|---|---|
| 1920 | Inc. above | 5.00 | 15.00 | 28.00 | 75.00 | — |
| 1921 | 32,908,000 | 0.25 | 0.50 | 1.75 | 4.00 | — |
| 1922 | 31,700,000 | 0.25 | 0.50 | 1.75 | 4.00 | — |
| 1922 (t) | 17,717,000 | 1.50 | 2.50 | 5.00 | 13.50 | — |
| 1923 | 23,322,000 | 0.50 | 1.50 | 2.00 | 6.50 | — |
| 1923 (t) | 45,097,000 | 0.25 | 0.50 | 1.00 | 3.50 | — |
| 1924 | 47,018,000 | 0.25 | 0.50 | 1.00 | 3.50 | — |
| 1924 (t) | 21,210,000 | 0.50 | 1.50 | 2.00 | 5.50 | — |
| 1925 | 66,837,999 | 0.25 | 0.50 | 1.00 | 2.50 | — |
| 1926 | 19,820,000 | 0.25 | 1.50 | 2.00 | 5.50 | — |
| 1927 | 6,066,000 | 2.50 | 8.50 | 25.00 | 70.00 | — |
| 1930 | 31,902,000 | 0.20 | 0.50 | 1.00 | 2.25 | — |
| 1931 | 34,711,000 | 0.20 | 0.50 | 1.00 | 2.25 | — |
| 1932 | 31,112,000 | 0.20 | 0.50 | 1.00 | 2.25 | — |
| 1933 | 12,970,000 | 1.00 | 1.75 | 4.00 | 10.00 | — |
| 1934 | 27,144,000 | 0.30 | 0.65 | 2.00 | 5.00 | — |
| 1935 | 57,221,000 | 0.25 | 0.50 | 1.00 | 2.25 | — |
| 1936 | 64,340,999 | 0.15 | 0.25 | 0.75 | 2.25 | — |
| 1937 | 26,329,000 | 0.15 | 0.25 | 0.75 | 2.25 | — |
| 1938 | 21,614,000 | 0.15 | 0.25 | 0.75 | 2.25 | — |

**5 CENTIMES (Cinq) KM# 927 Composition:** Chrome-Steel **Note:** Struck at Paris Mint.

| Date | Mintage | F | VF | XF | Unc | BU |
|---|---|---|---|---|---|---|
| 1961 | 39,000,000 | 0.10 | 0.20 | 0.50 | 2.00 | — |
| 1962 | 166,360,000 | 0.10 | 0.15 | 0.20 | 0.75 | — |
| 1963 | 71,900,000 | 0.10 | 0.20 | 0.40 | 1.00 | — |
| 1964 | 126,480,000 | 0.10 | 0.15 | 0.30 | 0.75 | — |

**5 CENTIMES (Cinq) KM# 933 Composition:** Aluminum-Bronze **Note:** 1991-1993 dated coins, non-Proof exist in both coin and medal alignment.

| Date | Mintage | F | VF | XF | Unc | BU |
|---|---|---|---|---|---|---|
| 1966 | 502,512,000 | — | — | — | 0.10 | — |
| 1967 | 11,747,000 | — | — | 0.10 | 0.25 | — |
| 1968 | 110,395,000 | — | — | — | 0.10 | — |
| 1969 | 94,955,000 | — | — | — | 0.10 | — |
| 1970 | 58,900,000 | — | — | — | 0.10 | — |
| 1971 | 93,190,000 | — | — | — | 0.10 | — |
| 1972 | 100,515,000 | — | — | — | 0.10 | — |
| 1973 | 100,344,000 | — | — | — | 0.10 | — |
| 1974 | 103,890,000 | — | — | — | 0.10 | — |
| 1975 | 95,835,000 | — | — | — | 0.10 | — |
| 1976 | 148,395,000 | — | — | — | 0.10 | — |
| 1977 | 115,285,000 | — | — | — | 0.10 | — |
| 1978 | 189,804,000 | — | — | — | 0.10 | — |
| 1979 | 180,000,000 | — | — | — | 0.10 | — |
| 1980 | 180,010,000 | — | — | — | 0.10 | — |
| 1981 | 50,000 | — | — | — | 0.50 | — |
| 1982 | 138,000,000 | — | — | — | 0.10 | — |
| 1983 | 132,000,000 | — | — | — | 0.10 | — |
| 1984 | 150,000,000 | — | — | — | 0.10 | — |
| 1985 | 170,000,000 | — | — | — | 0.10 | — |
| 1986 | 280,000,000 | — | — | — | 0.10 | — |
| 1987 | 310,000,000 | — | — | — | 0.10 | — |
| 1988 | 200,000,000 | — | — | — | 0.10 | — |
| 1989 | 72,000 | — | — | — | 0.20 | — |
| 1990 | 79,992,000 | — | — | — | 0.20 | — |
| 1991 | 49,994,000 | — | — | — | 0.20 | — |
| 1991 Proof | 10,000 | Value: 1.00 | | | | |
| 1992 | 179,996,000 | — | — | — | 0.20 | — |
| 1992 Proof | 15,000 | Value: 1.00 | | | | |
| 1993 | 154,988,000 | — | — | — | 0.20 | — |
| 1993 Proof | 10,000 | Value: 1.00 | | | | |
| 1994 | — | — | — | — | 0.20 | — |
| 1994 (Fish) | 60,000,000 | — | — | — | 0.20 | — |
| 1994 (Fish) Proof | 10,000 | — | — | — | — | — |
| 1994 (Bee) | 59,996,000 | — | — | — | 0.20 | — |
| 1995 | 129,991,999 | — | — | — | 0.20 | — |
| 1995 Proof | 10,000 | Value: 1.00 | | | | |
| 1996 | 139,990,000 | — | — | — | 0.20 | — |
| 1996 Proof | 8,000 | Value: 1.00 | | | | |
| 1997 | 199,995,000 | — | — | — | 0.20 | — |
| 1997 Proof | 10,000 | Value: 1.00 | | | | |
| 1998 | — | — | — | — | 0.20 | — |
| 1998 Proof | — | Value: 1.00 | | | | |
| 1999 | — | — | — | — | 0.20 | — |
| 1999 Proof | — | Value: 1.00 | | | | |
| 2000 | — | — | — | — | 0.20 | — |
| 2000 Proof | — | Value: 1.00 | | | | |

**10 CENTIMES (Dix) KM# 897 Composition:** Zinc **Reverse:** Dot before and after date, or just after

| Date | Mintage | F | VF | XF | Unc | BU |
|---|---|---|---|---|---|---|
| .1941. | Inc. above | 0.25 | 0.50 | 1.00 | 4.00 | — |
| 1941. | Inc. above | 0.25 | 0.50 | 1.00 | 4.00 | — |

**10 CENTIMES (Dix) KM# 843 Composition:** Bronze **Note:** Without mint mark. Struck at Paris Mint.

| Date | Mintage | F | VF | XF | Unc | BU |
|---|---|---|---|---|---|---|
| 1898 | 4,000,000 | 1.00 | 3.00 | 8.00 | 20.00 | — |
| 1898 Matte Proof | — | Value: 450 | | | | |
| 1899 | 4,000,000 | 1.00 | 3.00 | 8.00 | 20.00 | — |
| 1900 (n) | 5,000,000 | 1.00 | 3.00 | 8.00 | 20.00 | — |
| 1900 (n) Proof | — | Value: 425 | | | | |
| 1901 (c) | 2,700,000 | 1.50 | 3.00 | 20.00 | 55.00 | — |
| 1902 | 3,800,000 | 0.75 | 1.75 | 6.50 | 25.00 | — |
| 1903 | 3,650,000 | 0.75 | 1.75 | 6.50 | 25.00 | — |
| 1904 | 3,800,000 | 0.75 | 1.75 | 6.50 | 25.00 | — |
| 1905 | 950,000 | 25.00 | 50.00 | 125 | 275 | — |
| 1906 | 3,000,000 | 2.00 | 5.00 | 12.00 | 40.00 | — |
| 1907 | 4,000,000 | 0.75 | 1.75 | 4.50 | 20.00 | — |
| 1908 | 3,500,000 | 0.75 | 1.75 | 4.50 | 20.00 | — |
| 1909 | 2,933,000 | 0.75 | 1.75 | 4.50 | 25.00 | — |
| 1910 | 3,567,000 | 0.75 | 1.75 | 4.50 | 20.00 | — |
| 1911 | 7,903,000 | 0.50 | 1.25 | 2.75 | 12.00 | — |
| 1912 | 9,500,000 | 0.50 | 1.25 | 2.75 | 12.00 | — |

| Date | Mintage | F | VF | XF | Unc | BU |
|---|---|---|---|---|---|---|
| 1913 | 9,000,000 | 0.50 | 1.25 | 2.75 | 12.00 | — |
| 1914 | 6,000,000 | 0.75 | 1.75 | 3.50 | 14.00 | — |
| 1915 | 4,362,000 | 0.50 | 1.25 | 2.75 | 12.00 | — |
| 1916 | 22,477,000 | 0.25 | 0.75 | 1.50 | 7.00 | — |
| 1916 (s) | Inc. above | 0.25 | 0.75 | 1.50 | 7.00 | — |
| 1917 | 11,914,000 | 0.25 | 0.75 | 1.50 | 7.00 | — |
| 1920 | 4,119,000 | 1.50 | 3.00 | 10.00 | 40.00 | — |
| 1921 | 1,896,000 | 8.00 | 16.00 | 40.00 | 85.00 | — |

**10 CENTIMES (Dix)** **KM# 866** **Composition:** Nickel

| Date | Mintage | F | VF | XF | Unc | BU |
|---|---|---|---|---|---|---|
| 1914 dash | 3,972 | 400 | 700 | 1,000 | 1,600 | — |

**10 CENTIMES (Dix)** **KM# 866a** **Composition:** Copper-Nickel

| Date | Mintage | F | VF | XF | Unc | BU |
|---|---|---|---|---|---|---|
| 1917 | 8,170,999 | 0.75 | 1.50 | 3.50 | 20.00 | — |
| 1918 | 30,605,000 | 0.25 | 0.50 | 1.00 | 3.50 | — |
| 1919 | 33,488,999 | 0.25 | 0.50 | 1.00 | 3.50 | — |
| 1920 | 38,845,000 | 0.25 | 0.50 | 1.00 | 3.50 | — |
| 1921 | 42,768,000 | 0.10 | 0.35 | 0.75 | 2.50 | — |
| 1922 | 23,033,000 | 0.35 | 0.75 | 1.25 | 4.00 | — |
| 1922 (t) | 12,412,000 | 0.75 | 1.50 | 2.50 | 6.50 | — |
| 1923 | 18,701,000 | 0.50 | 1.00 | 2.00 | 4.50 | — |
| 1923 (t) | 30,016,000 | 0.25 | 0.50 | 1.00 | 3.00 | — |
| 1924 | 43,949,000 | 0.10 | 0.35 | 0.75 | 2.00 | — |
| 1924 (t) | 13,591,000 | 1.50 | 4.50 | 12.50 | 38.00 | — |
| 1925 | 46,266,000 | 0.10 | 0.35 | 0.75 | 2.00 | — |
| 1926 | 25,660,000 | 0.25 | 0.50 | 1.00 | 3.00 | — |
| 1927 | 16,203,000 | 0.40 | 0.75 | 1.25 | 4.00 | — |
| 1928 | 6,967,000 | 1.00 | 2.50 | 8.00 | 28.00 | — |
| 1929 | 24,531,000 | 0.10 | 0.35 | 1.00 | 2.00 | — |
| 1930 | 22,146,000 | 0.10 | 0.35 | 1.00 | 2.00 | — |
| 1931 | 49,107,000 | 0.10 | 0.35 | 1.00 | 2.00 | — |
| 1932 | 30,317,000 | 0.10 | 0.35 | 1.00 | 2.00 | — |
| 1933 | 13,042,000 | 0.35 | 0.75 | 1.50 | 4.00 | — |
| 1934 | 24,067,000 | 0.10 | 0.50 | 1.00 | 2.00 | — |
| 1935 | 47,487,000 | 0.10 | 0.50 | 1.00 | 2.00 | — |
| 1936 | 57,738,000 | 0.10 | 0.50 | 1.00 | 2.00 | — |
| 1937 | 25,308,000 | 0.10 | 0.50 | 1.00 | 2.00 | — |
| 1938 | 17,063,000 | 0.25 | 0.75 | 1.75 | 4.50 | — |

**10 CENTIMES (Dix)** **KM# 889.1** **Composition:** Nickel-Bronze

| Date | Mintage | F | VF | XF | Unc | BU |
|---|---|---|---|---|---|---|
| .1938. | 24,151,000 | 0.25 | 0.50 | 1.00 | 2.00 | — |
| 1.938. | Inc. above | — | — | — | — | — |
| .1939. | 62,269,000 | 0.15 | 0.30 | 0.65 | 1.75 | — |

**10 CENTIMES (Dix)** **KM# 889.2** **Composition:** Nickel-Bronze **Note:** Thin flan.

| Date | Mintage | F | VF | XF | Unc | BU |
|---|---|---|---|---|---|---|
| .1939. | Inc. above | 0.10 | 0.20 | 0.50 | 1.25 | — |

**10 CENTIMES (Dix)** **KM# 898.1** **Composition:** Zinc **Note:** Issued for Vichy French State, thickness 1.5mm.

| Date | Mintage | F | VF | XF | Unc | BU |
|---|---|---|---|---|---|---|
| 1941 | 70,860,000 | 0.35 | 0.65 | 1.50 | 5.00 | — |
| 1942 | 139,598,000 | 0.30 | 0.60 | 1.25 | 2.50 | — |
| 1943 | 21,520,000 | 1.00 | 2.00 | 4.00 | 12.00 | — |

**10 CENTIMES (Dix)** **KM# 898.2** **Composition:** Zinc **Note:** Without mint mark. Thin flan, 1.3mm. Struck at Paris Mint.

| Date | Mintage | F | VF | XF | Unc | BU |
|---|---|---|---|---|---|---|
| 1941 | Inc. above | 0.25 | 0.50 | 1.25 | 3.00 | — |
| 1942 | Inc. above | 0.20 | 0.40 | 1.00 | 2.25 | — |
| 1943 | Inc. above | 0.75 | 1.50 | 2.75 | 6.00 | — |

**10 CENTIMES (Dix)** **KM# 895** **Composition:** Zinc **Reverse:** Without dash below MES in C MES

| Date | Mintage | F | VF | XF | Unc | BU |
|---|---|---|---|---|---|---|
| 1941 | 235,875,000 | 1.00 | 2.00 | 6.00 | 15.00 | — |

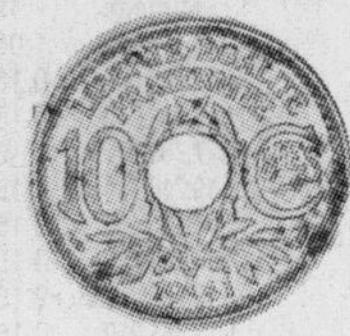

**10 CENTIMES (Dix)** **KM# 896** **Composition:** Zinc **Reverse:** Dash below MES in C MES

| Date | Mintage | F | VF | XF | Unc | BU |
|---|---|---|---|---|---|---|
| 1941 | Inc. above | 0.75 | 1.25 | 4.00 | 10.00 | — |

**10 CENTIMES (Dix)** **KM# 903** **Composition:** Zinc

| Date | Mintage | F | VF | XF | Unc | BU |
|---|---|---|---|---|---|---|
| 1943 | 22,008,000 | 0.25 | 0.75 | 2.50 | 7.00 | — |
| 1944 | 58,463,000 | 0.25 | 0.50 | 2.00 | 5.00 | — |

**10 CENTIMES (Dix)** **KM# 906.1** **Composition:** Zinc

| Date | Mintage | F | VF | XF | Unc | BU |
|---|---|---|---|---|---|---|
| 1945 | 38,174,000 | 1.00 | 1.75 | 3.25 | 12.00 | — |
| 1946 Rare | — | — | — | — | — | — |

**10 CENTIMES (Dix)** **KM# 906.2** **Composition:** Zinc

| Date | Mintage | F | VF | XF | Unc | BU |
|---|---|---|---|---|---|---|
| 1945B | 7,246,000 | 1.50 | 3.00 | 6.00 | 16.00 | — |
| 1946B | 10,566,000 | 2.50 | 5.00 | 10.00 | 25.00 | — |

**10 CENTIMES (Dix)** **KM# 906.3** **Composition:** Zinc

| Date | Mintage | F | VF | XF | Unc | BU |
|---|---|---|---|---|---|---|
| 1945C | 8,379,000 | 2.00 | 4.00 | 8.00 | 20.00 | — |

**10 CENTIMES (Dix)** **KM# 929** **Composition:** Aluminum-Bronze **Note:** Without mint mark. Struck at Paris Mint. 1991-1993 dated coins, non-Proof, exist in both coinand medal alignment.

| Date | Mintage | F | VF | XF | Unc | BU |
|---|---|---|---|---|---|---|
| 1962 | 29,100,000 | — | — | 0.10 | 0.40 | — |
| 1963 | 217,601,000 | — | — | — | 0.10 | — |
| 1964 | 93,409,000 | — | — | 0.10 | 0.20 | — |
| 1965 | 41,220,000 | — | — | 0.10 | 0.30 | — |
| 1966 | 16,428,999 | — | 0.10 | 0.15 | 0.40 | — |
| 1967 | 196,728,000 | — | — | — | 0.10 | — |
| 1968 | 111,700,000 | — | — | — | 0.10 | — |
| 1969 | 129,530,000 | — | — | — | 0.10 | — |
| 1970 | 77,020,000 | — | — | — | 0.10 | — |
| 1971 | 26,280,000 | — | — | — | 0.10 | — |
| 1972 | 45,700,000 | — | — | — | 0.10 | — |
| 1973 | 58,000,000 | — | — | — | 0.10 | — |
| 1974 | 91,990,000 | — | — | — | 0.10 | — |
| 1975 | 74,450,000 | — | — | — | 0.10 | — |
| 1976 | 137,320,000 | — | — | — | 0.10 | — |
| 1977 | 140,110,000 | — | — | — | 0.10 | — |
| 1978 | 154,360,000 | — | — | — | 0.10 | — |
| 1979 | 140,000,000 | — | — | — | 0.10 | — |
| 1980 | 140,010,000 | — | — | — | 0.10 | — |
| 1981 | 135,000,000 | — | — | — | 0.10 | — |
| 1982 | 110,000,000 | — | — | — | 0.10 | — |
| 1983 | 150,000,000 | — | — | — | 0.10 | — |
| 1984 | 200,000,000 | — | — | — | 0.10 | — |
| 1985 | 170,000,000 | — | — | — | 0.10 | — |
| 1986 | 150,000,000 | — | — | — | 0.10 | — |
| 1987 | 150,000,000 | — | — | — | 0.10 | — |
| 1988 | 145,000,000 | — | — | — | 0.10 | — |
| 1989 | 179,984,000 | — | — | — | 0.10 | — |
| 1990 | 179,992,000 | — | — | — | 0.10 | — |
| 1991 | 179,986,000 | — | — | — | 0.10 | — |
| 1991 Proof | 10,000 | Value: 1.00 | | | | |
| 1992 | 179,996,000 | — | — | — | 0.10 | — |
| 1992 Proof | 15,000 | Value: 1.00 | | | | |
| 1993 | 154,988,000 | — | — | — | 0.10 | — |
| 1993 Proof | 10,000 | Value: 1.00 | | | | |
| 1994 | — | — | — | — | 0.10 | — |
| 1994 (Fish) | 103,000,000 | — | — | — | 0.10 | — |
| 1994 (Fish) Proof | 10,000 | Value: 1.00 | | | | |
| 1994 (Bee) | 76,988,000 | — | — | — | 0.10 | — |
| 1995 | 169,996,000 | — | — | — | 0.10 | — |
| 1995 Proof | 10,000 | Value: 1.00 | | | | |
| 1996 | 179,981,000 | — | — | — | 0.10 | — |
| 1996 Proof | 8,000 | Value: 1.00 | | | | |
| 1997 | 551,991,000 | — | — | — | 0.10 | — |
| 1997 Proof | 10,000 | Value: 1.00 | | | | |
| 1998 | — | — | — | — | 0.10 | — |
| 1998 Proof | — | Value: 1.00 | | | | |
| 1999 | — | — | — | — | 0.10 | — |
| 1999 Proof | — | Value: 1.00 | | | | |
| 2000 | — | — | — | — | 0.10 | — |
| 2000 Proof | — | Value: 1.00 | | | | |

**20 CENTIMES (Vingt)** **KM# 899** **Composition:** Zinc **Note:** Issued for Vichy French State.

| Date | Mintage | F | VF | XF | Unc | BU |
|---|---|---|---|---|---|---|
| 1941 | 54,044,000 | 1.00 | 2.00 | 4.00 | 15.00 | — |

**20 CENTIMES (Vingt)** **KM# 900.1** **Weight:** 3.5000 g. **Composition:** Zinc **Note:** Thick flan.

| Date | Mintage | F | VF | XF | Unc | BU |
|---|---|---|---|---|---|---|
| 1941 | 31,397,000 | 1.00 | 2.00 | 4.00 | 15.00 | — |
| 1942 | 112,868,000 | 0.50 | 1.00 | 2.00 | 7.00 | — |
| 1943 | 64,138,000 | 0.75 | 1.50 | 2.50 | 8.50 | — |

**20 CENTIMES (Vingt)** **KM# 900.2** **Weight:** 3.0000 g. **Composition:** Zinc **Note:** Without mint mark. Thin flan. Struck at Paris Mint.

| Date | Mintage | F | VF | XF | Unc | BU |
|---|---|---|---|---|---|---|
| 1941 | Inc. above | 0.50 | 0.75 | 2.00 | 8.50 | — |
| 1943 | Inc. above | 0.50 | 0.75 | 2.00 | 6.50 | — |
| 1944 | 5,250,000 | 15.00 | 30.00 | 80.00 | 165 | — |

**20 CENTIMES (Vingt)** **KM# 900.2a** **Composition:** Iron

| Date | Mintage | F | VF | XF | Unc | BU |
|---|---|---|---|---|---|---|
| 1944 | 695,000 | 25.00 | 50.00 | 150 | 185 | — |

**20 CENTIMES (Vingt)** **KM# 907.2** **Composition:** Zinc

| Date | Mintage | F | VF | XF | Unc | BU |
|---|---|---|---|---|---|---|
| 1945B | 100,000 | 85.00 | 165 | 285 | 470 | — |
| 1946B | 5,525,000 | 75.00 | 150 | 260 | 450 | — |

**20 CENTIMES (Vingt)** **KM# 907.3** **Composition:** Zinc

| Date | Mintage | F | VF | XF | Unc | BU |
|---|---|---|---|---|---|---|
| 1945C | 299,000 | 20.00 | 40.00 | 85.00 | 150 | |

**20 CENTIMES (Vingt)** **KM# 907.1** **Composition:** Zinc **Note:** Fourth Republic.

| Date | Mintage | F | VF | XF | Unc | BU |
|---|---|---|---|---|---|---|
| 1945 | 6,003,000 | 2.00 | 4.00 | 9.00 | 22.00 | — |
| 1946 | 2,662,000 | 8.00 | 18.00 | 35.00 | 70.00 | — |

**20 CENTIMES (Vingt)** **KM# 930** **Composition:** Aluminum-Bronze **Note:** Without mint mark. Struck at Paris Mint. 1991-1993 dated coins, non-Proof, exist in both coin and medal alignment.

| Date | Mintage | F | VF | XF | Unc | BU |
|---|---|---|---|---|---|---|
| 1962 | 48,200,000 | — | — | 0.10 | 0.40 | — |
| 1963 | 190,330,000 | — | — | 0.10 | 0.30 | — |
| 1964 | 127,521,000 | — | — | 0.10 | 0.30 | — |
| 1965 | 27,024,000 | — | 0.10 | 0.20 | 0.40 | — |
| 1966 | 21,762,000 | — | 0.10 | 0.20 | 0.40 | — |
| 1967 | 138,780,000 | — | — | 0.10 | 0.15 | — |
| 1968 | 77,408,000 | — | — | 0.10 | 0.20 | — |
| 1969 | 50,570,000 | — | — | 0.10 | 0.20 | — |
| 1970 | 70,040,000 | — | — | 0.10 | 0.15 | — |
| 1971 | 31,080,000 | — | — | 0.10 | 0.15 | — |
| 1972 | 39,740,000 | — | — | 0.10 | 0.15 | — |
| 1973 | 45,240,000 | — | — | 0.10 | 0.15 | — |
| 1974 | 54,250,000 | — | — | 0.10 | 0.15 | — |
| 1975 | 40,570,000 | — | — | 0.10 | 0.15 | — |
| 1976 | 117,610,000 | — | — | — | 0.10 | — |
| 1977 | 100,340,000 | — | — | — | 0.10 | — |
| 1978 | 125,015,000 | — | — | — | 0.10 | — |
| 1979 | 70,000,000 | — | — | — | 0.10 | — |

| Date | Mintage | F | VF | XF | Unc | BU |
|---|---|---|---|---|---|---|
| 1980 | 20,010,000 | — | — | 0.10 | 0.15 | — |
| 1981 | 125,000,000 | — | — | — | 0.10 | — |
| 1982 | 150,000,000 | — | — | — | 0.10 | — |
| 1983 | 110,000,000 | — | — | — | 0.10 | — |
| 1984 | 200,000,000 | — | — | — | 0.10 | — |
| 1985 | 150,000,000 | — | — | — | 0.10 | — |
| 1986 | 40,000,000 | — | — | — | 0.10 | — |
| 1987 | 60,000,000 | — | — | — | 0.10 | — |
| 1988 | 220,000,000 | — | — | — | 0.10 | — |
| 1989 | 139,985,000 | — | — | — | 0.10 | — |
| 1990 | 49,990,000 | — | — | — | 0.10 | — |
| 1991 | 39,992,000 | — | — | — | 0.10 | — |
| 1991 1 Proof | 10,000 | Value: 1.00 | | | | |
| 1992 | 89,985,000 | — | — | — | 0.10 | — |
| 1992 1 Proof | 15,000 | Value: 1.00 | | | | |
| 1993 | 10,990,000 | — | — | — | 0.10 | — |
| 1993 1 Proof | 10,000 | Value: 1.00 | | | | |
| 1994 | — | — | — | — | 0.10 | — |
| 1994 (Fish) | 60,000,000 | — | — | — | 0.10 | — |
| 1994 (Fish) Proof | 10,000 | Value: 1.00 | | | | |
| 1994 (Bee) | 79,900,000 | — | — | — | 0.10 | — |
| 1995 | 109,995,000 | — | — | — | 0.10 | — |
| 1995 Proof | 10,000 | Value: 1.00 | | | | |
| 1996 | 139,987,000 | — | — | — | 0.10 | — |
| 1996 Proof | 8,000 | Value: 1.00 | | | | |
| 1997 | 435,990,000 | — | — | — | 0.10 | — |
| 1997 Proof | 10,000 | Value: 1.00 | | | | |
| 1998 | — | — | — | — | 0.10 | — |
| 1998 Proof | — | Value: 1.00 | | | | |
| 1999 | — | — | — | — | 0.10 | — |
| 1999 Proof | — | Value: 1.00 | | | | |
| 2000 | — | — | — | — | 0.10 | — |
| 2000 Proof | — | Value: 1.00 | | | | |

**25 CENTIMES** **KM# 855** **Composition:** Nickel **Note:** Without mint mark. Struck at Paris Mint.

| Date | Mintage | F | VF | XF | Unc | BU |
|---|---|---|---|---|---|---|
| 1903 | 16,000,000 | 0.25 | 1.00 | 2.00 | 11.50 | — |

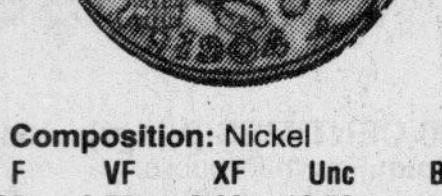

**25 CENTIMES** **KM# 856** **Composition:** Nickel

| Date | Mintage | F | VF | XF | Unc | BU |
|---|---|---|---|---|---|---|
| 1904 | 16,000,000 | 0.25 | 0.75 | 2.00 | 13.50 | — |
| 1905 | 8,000,000 | 0.50 | 1.50 | 3.50 | 20.00 | — |

**25 CENTIMES** **KM# 867** **Composition:** Nickel **Reverse:** Dash under MES in denomination

| Date | Mintage | F | VF | XF | Unc | BU |
|---|---|---|---|---|---|---|
| 1914 | 941,000 | 1.50 | 3.00 | 7.00 | 22.50 | — |
| 1915 | 535,000 | 2.50 | 4.00 | 8.00 | 32.00 | — |
| 1916 | 100,000 | 15.00 | 30.00 | 60.00 | 120 | — |
| 1917 | 65,000 | 30.00 | 50.00 | 85.00 | 185 | — |

**25 CENTIMES** **KM# 867a** **Composition:** Copper-Nickel **Reverse:** Without dash under MES in denomination

| Date | Mintage | F | VF | XF | Unc | BU |
|---|---|---|---|---|---|---|
| 1917 | 3,085,000 | 2.00 | 4.00 | 12.00 | 22.00 | — |
| 1918 | 18,330,000 | 0.25 | 0.50 | 1.50 | 3.50 | — |

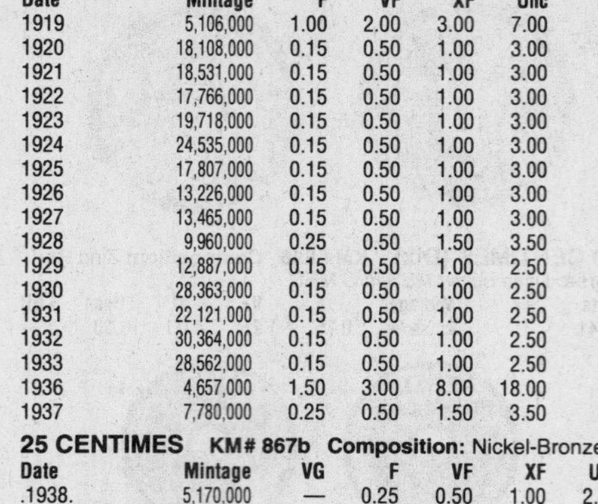

| Date | Mintage | F | VF | XF | Unc | BU |
|---|---|---|---|---|---|---|
| 1919 | 5,106,000 | 1.00 | 2.00 | 3.00 | 7.00 | — |
| 1920 | 18,108,000 | 0.15 | 0.50 | 1.00 | 3.00 | — |
| 1921 | 18,531,000 | 0.15 | 0.50 | 1.00 | 3.00 | — |
| 1922 | 17,766,000 | 0.15 | 0.50 | 1.00 | 3.00 | — |
| 1923 | 19,718,000 | 0.15 | 0.50 | 1.00 | 3.00 | — |
| 1924 | 24,535,000 | 0.15 | 0.50 | 1.00 | 3.00 | — |
| 1925 | 17,807,000 | 0.15 | 0.50 | 1.00 | 3.00 | — |
| 1926 | 13,226,000 | 0.15 | 0.50 | 1.00 | 3.00 | — |
| 1927 | 13,465,000 | 0.15 | 0.50 | 1.00 | 3.00 | — |
| 1928 | 9,960,000 | 0.25 | 0.50 | 1.50 | 3.50 | — |
| 1929 | 12,887,000 | 0.15 | 0.50 | 1.00 | 2.50 | — |
| 1930 | 28,363,000 | 0.15 | 0.50 | 1.00 | 2.50 | — |
| 1931 | 22,121,000 | 0.15 | 0.50 | 1.00 | 2.50 | — |
| 1932 | 30,364,000 | 0.15 | 0.50 | 1.00 | 2.50 | — |
| 1933 | 28,562,000 | 0.15 | 0.50 | 1.00 | 2.50 | — |
| 1936 | 4,657,000 | 1.50 | 3.00 | 8.00 | 18.00 | — |
| 1937 | 7,780,000 | 0.25 | 0.50 | 1.50 | 3.50 | — |

**25 CENTIMES** **KM# 867b** **Composition:** Nickel-Bronze

| Date | Mintage | VG | F | VF | XF | Unc |
|---|---|---|---|---|---|---|
| .1938. | 5,170,000 | — | 0.25 | 0.50 | 1.00 | 2.50 |
| .1939. Thick flan (1.55mm) | 42,964,000 | — | 0.15 | 0.35 | 0.75 | 1.50 |
| .1939. Thin flan (1.35mm) | Inc. above | — | 0.15 | 0.35 | 0.75 | 1.50 |
| .1940. | 3,446,000 | — | 6.00 | 12.00 | 18.00 | 35.00 |

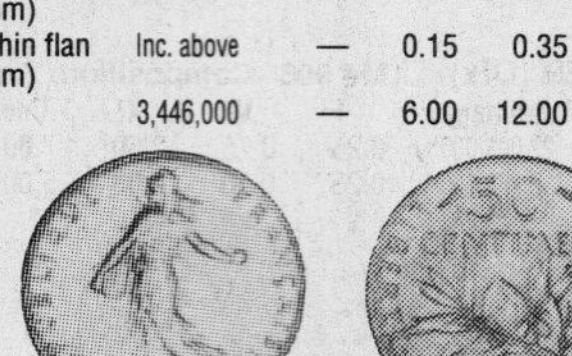

**50 CENTIMES** **KM# 854** **Weight:** 2.5000 g. **Composition:** 0.8350 Silver .0671 oz. ASW **Note:** Without mint mark. Struck at Paris Mint.

| Date | Mintage | F | VF | XF | Unc | BU |
|---|---|---|---|---|---|---|
| 1897 | 88,000 | 30.00 | 75.00 | 125 | 200 | — |
| 1897 Proof | — | Value: 300 | | | | |
| 1898 | 30,000,000 | 1.00 | 2.00 | 10.00 | 20.00 | — |
| 1898 Proof | — | Value: 300 | | | | |
| 1899 | 18,000,000 | 1.50 | 3.00 | 8.00 | 35.00 | — |
| 1900 | 9,195,000 | 3.00 | 6.00 | 15.00 | 45.00 | — |
| 1900 Proof | — | Value: 300 | | | | |
| 1901 | 4,960,000 | 2.00 | 4.00 | 12.00 | 45.00 | — |
| 1902 | 3,778,000 | 2.50 | 5.00 | 15.00 | 55.00 | — |
| 1903 | 2,222,000 | 12.00 | 25.00 | 50.00 | 150 | — |
| 1904 | 4,000,000 | 1.50 | 3.50 | 10.00 | 45.00 | — |
| 1905 | 2,381,000 | 5.00 | 9.00 | 20.00 | 100 | — |
| 1906 | 2,679,000 | 2.50 | 5.00 | 15.00 | 55.00 | — |
| 1907 | 7,332,000 | 1.50 | 3.50 | 10.00 | 30.00 | — |
| 1908 | 14,304,000 | 0.75 | 1.50 | 4.00 | 15.00 | — |
| 1909 | 9,900,000 | 0.75 | 1.50 | 4.00 | 15.00 | — |
| 1910 | 15,923,000 | BV | 1.00 | 3.00 | 10.00 | — |
| 1911 | 1,330,000 | 20.00 | 50.00 | 110 | 200 | — |
| 1912 | 16,000,000 | BV | 0.75 | 1.50 | 5.00 | — |
| 1913 | 14,000,000 | BV | 0.75 | 1.50 | 5.00 | — |
| 1914 | 9,657,000 | BV | 0.75 | 1.50 | 6.00 | — |
| 1915 | 20,893,000 | BV | 0.75 | 1.25 | 3.00 | — |
| 1916 | 52,963,000 | BV | 0.75 | 1.25 | 2.50 | — |
| 1917 | 48,629,000 | BV | 0.75 | 1.25 | 2.50 | — |
| 1918 | 36,492,000 | BV | 0.75 | 1.25 | 2.50 | — |
| 1919 | 24,299,000 | BV | 0.75 | 1.25 | 2.50 | — |
| 1920 | 8,509,000 | 0.75 | 1.50 | 3.00 | 6.00 | — |

**50 CENTIMES** **KM# 884** **Composition:** Aluminum-Bronze

| Date | Mintage | F | VF | XF | Unc | BU |
|---|---|---|---|---|---|---|
| 1921 | 8,692,000 | 0.75 | 2.00 | 6.00 | 18.00 | — |
| 1922 | 86,226,000 | 0.15 | 0.25 | 1.00 | 4.00 | — |
| 1923 | 119,584,000 | 0.15 | 0.25 | 0.75 | 2.50 | — |
| 1924 | 97,036,000 | 0.15 | 0.25 | 1.00 | 3.00 | — |
| 1925 | 48,017,000 | 0.25 | 0.50 | 1.25 | 5.00 | — |
| 1926 | 46,447,000 | 0.25 | 0.50 | 1.25 | 5.00 | — |
| 1927 | 23,703,000 | 0.75 | 1.50 | 3.00 | 8.50 | — |
| 1928 | 10,329,000 | 0.75 | 2.00 | 5.00 | 16.00 | — |
| 1929 | 6,669,000 | 2.50 | 6.00 | 12.50 | 25.00 | — |

**50 CENTIMES** **KM# 894.1** **Composition:** Aluminum-Bronze

| Date | Mintage | F | VF | XF | Unc | BU |
|---|---|---|---|---|---|---|
| 1931 | 62,775,000 | 0.15 | 0.25 | 1.00 | 3.00 | — |
| 1932 | 108,839,000 | 0.15 | 0.25 | 0.50 | 2.00 | — |
| 1932 Closed date | Inc. above | 0.15 | 0.25 | 0.50 | 2.00 | — |
| 1933 | 41,937,000 | 0.15 | 0.25 | 0.75 | 3.00 | — |
| 1933 Closed date | Inc. above | 0.15 | 0.25 | 0.75 | 3.00 | — |
| 1936 | 16,602,000 | 0.50 | 1.00 | 2.00 | 5.00 | — |
| 1937 | 43,950,000 | 0.15 | 0.25 | 0.75 | 3.00 | — |
| 1938 | 55,707,000 | 0.15 | 0.25 | 0.75 | 3.00 | — |
| 1939 | 96,594,000 | 0.15 | 0.25 | 0.50 | 2.00 | — |
| 1940 | 10,854,000 | 0.50 | 1.00 | 2.00 | 5.00 | — |
| 1941 | 82,958,000 | 0.15 | 0.25 | 1.00 | 3.00 | — |
| 1947 | Est. 2,170,000 | 60.00 | 125 | 225 | 350 | — |

**Note:** 1947 date was struck for colonial use in Africa

**50 CENTIMES** **KM# 894.2** **Composition:** Aluminum-Bronze

| Date | Mintage | F | VF | XF | Unc | BU |
|---|---|---|---|---|---|---|
| 1939B | 6,200,000 | 0.50 | 1.00 | 2.50 | 10.00 | — |

**50 CENTIMES** **KM# 894.1a** **Composition:** Aluminum **Note:** Without mint mark. Struck at Paris Mint. Thick and think planchets exist.

| Date | Mintage | F | VF | XF | Unc | BU |
|---|---|---|---|---|---|---|
| 1941 | 129,758,000 | 0.15 | 0.25 | 0.50 | 2.00 | — |
| 1944 | 9,898,000 | 0.50 | 1.00 | 2.50 | 6.00 | — |
| 1945 | 26,224,000 | 0.15 | 0.25 | 1.00 | 3.00 | — |
| 1946 | 24,605,000 | 0.15 | 0.25 | 1.00 | 3.00 | — |
| 1947 | 51,744,000 | 0.15 | 0.25 | 0.60 | 2.00 | — |

**50 CENTIMES** **KM# 914.4** **Composition:** Aluminum **Note:** Without mint mark. Thin flan. Struck at Paris Mint.

| Date | Mintage | F | VF | XF | Unc | BU |
|---|---|---|---|---|---|---|
| 1942 | — | 0.15 | 0.25 | 1.00 | 2.50 | — |
| 1943 | — | 0.15 | 0.25 | 0.50 | 1.25 | — |

**50 CENTIMES** **KM# 914.1** **Composition:** Aluminum **Note:** Without mint mark. Vichy French State. Struck at Paris Mint. Thick and thin planchets exist.

| Date | Mintage | F | VF | XF | Unc | BU |
|---|---|---|---|---|---|---|
| 1942 | 50,134,000 | 0.15 | 0.25 | 0.75 | 2.00 | — |
| 1943 | 84,462,000 | 0.15 | 0.25 | 0.75 | 1.50 | — |
| 1944 | 57,410,000 | 1.50 | 3.00 | 6.00 | 14.00 | — |

**50 CENTIMES** **KM# 914.2** **Composition:** Aluminum

| Date | Mintage | F | VF | XF | Unc | BU |
|---|---|---|---|---|---|---|
| 1943B | 21,916,000 | 5.00 | 10.00 | 28.00 | 50.00 | — |
| 1944B | 27,334,000 | 1.50 | 3.00 | 7.00 | 15.00 | — |

**50 CENTIMES** **KM# 894.2a** **Composition:** Aluminum

| Date | Mintage | F | VF | XF | Unc | BU |
|---|---|---|---|---|---|---|
| 1944B Reported, not confirmed | 20,000 | — | — | — | — | — |
| 1945B | 6,357,000 | 0.50 | 1.00 | 3.00 | 8.00 | — |
| 1946B | 29,344,000 | 0.15 | 0.25 | 1.00 | 4.00 | — |
| 1947B | 18,504,000 | 2.00 | 5.00 | 10.00 | 20.00 | — |

**50 CENTIMES** **KM# 894.3a** **Composition:** Aluminum

| Date | Mintage | F | VF | XF | Unc | BU |
|---|---|---|---|---|---|---|
| 1944C Reported, not confirmed | 17,220,000 | — | — | — | — | — |
| 1945C | 2,968,000 | 1.00 | 3.00 | 6.00 | 12.00 | — |

**50 CENTIMES** **KM# 939.1** **Composition:** Aluminum-Bronze **Obverse:** 3 folds in collar

| Date | Mintage | F | VF | XF | Unc | BU |
|---|---|---|---|---|---|---|
| 1962 | 37,560,000 | 0.30 | 0.60 | 1.50 | 3.00 | — |
| 1963 | 62,482,000 | 0.20 | 0.40 | 1.00 | 2.00 | — |

**50 CENTIMES** **KM# 939.2** **Composition:** Aluminum-Bronze **Obverse:** 4 folds in collar

| Date | Mintage | F | VF | XF | Unc | BU |
|---|---|---|---|---|---|---|
| 1962 | Inc. above | 30.00 | 70.00 | 120 | 160 | — |
| 1963 | Inc. above | 0.20 | 0.40 | 1.00 | 2.00 | — |
| 1964 | 41,471,000 | 0.45 | 0.90 | 2.00 | 6.00 | — |

**50 CENTIMES** **KM# 914.3** **Composition:** Aluminum

| Date | Mintage | F | VF | XF | Unc | BU |
|---|---|---|---|---|---|---|
| 1944C Large C | Inc. above | — | — | — | — | — |
| 1944C Small C | 27,213,000 | 2.00 | 4.00 | 8.00 | 26.00 | — |

**1/2 FRANC KM# 931.1 Composition:** Nickel **Note:** Without mint mark. Struck at Paris Mint.

| Date | Mintage | F | VF | XF | Unc | BU |
|---|---|---|---|---|---|---|
| 1965 Small legends | 184,834,000 | — | — | 0.15 | 0.30 | — |
| 1965 Large legends | Inc. above | — | — | 0.15 | 0.30 | — |
| 1966 Without O. ROTY | 88,890,000 | — | — | 0.15 | 0.30 | — |
| 1967 | 28,394,000 | — | — | 0.15 | 0.40 | — |
| 1968 Without O. ROTY | 57,548,000 | — | — | 0.15 | 0.30 | — |
| 1969 | 47,144,000 | — | — | 0.15 | 0.30 | — |
| 1970 | 42,298,000 | — | — | 0.15 | 0.30 | — |
| 1971 | 36,068,000 | — | — | 0.15 | 0.30 | — |
| 1972 | 42,302,000 | — | — | 0.15 | 0.30 | — |
| 1972 Without O. ROTY | Inc. above | 25.00 | 50.00 | 100 | 150 | — |
| 1973 Without O. ROTY | 48,372,000 | — | — | 0.15 | 0.30 | — |
| 1974 | 37,072,000 | — | — | 0.15 | 0.30 | — |
| 1975 | 22,803,000 | — | — | 0.15 | 0.40 | — |
| 1976 | 115,314,000 | — | — | 0.15 | 0.30 | — |
| 1977 | 131,644,000 | — | — | 0.15 | 0.30 | — |
| 1978 | 63,360,000 | — | — | 0.15 | 0.30 | — |
| 1979 | 51,000 | — | — | — | 0.50 | — |
| 1980 In sets only | 60,000 | — | — | — | 0.50 | — |
| 1981 | 50,000 | — | — | — | 0.50 | — |
| 1982 | 78,000 | — | — | — | 0.50 | — |
| 1983 | 50,000,000 | — | — | 0.15 | 0.30 | — |
| 1984 | 80,000,000 | — | — | 0.15 | 0.30 | — |
| 1985 | 50,000,000 | — | — | — | 1.50 | — |
| 1986 | 110,000,000 | — | — | — | 1.50 | — |
| 1987 | 50,000,000 | — | — | — | 0.30 | — |
| 1988 | 100,000 | — | — | — | 0.40 | — |
| 1989 | 83,000 | — | — | — | 0.40 | — |
| 1990 | 15,000 | — | — | — | 0.40 | — |
| 1991 | — | — | — | — | 0.40 | — |
| **Note:** Exists in both coin and medal alignment | | | | | | |
| 1992 | — | — | — | — | 0.40 | — |
| **Note:** Exists in both coin and medal alignment | | | | | | |
| 1993 | — | — | — | — | 0.40 | — |
| 1994 | — | — | — | — | 0.40 | — |
| 1995 | — | — | — | — | 0.40 | — |
| 1996 | — | — | — | — | 0.40 | — |
| 1997 | — | — | — | — | 0.40 | — |
| 1998 | — | — | — | — | 0.40 | — |
| 1999 | — | — | — | — | 0.40 | — |

**1/2 FRANC KM# 931.2 Composition:** Nickel **Obverse:** Modified sower, engraver's signature. O. ROTY preceded by D'AP **Edge:** Plain

| Date | Mintage | F | VF | XF | Unc | BU |
|---|---|---|---|---|---|---|
| 1991 | 49,990,000 | — | — | — | 0.40 | — |
| 1991 Proof | 10,000 | Value: 1.50 | | | | |
| 1992 | 29,988,000 | — | — | — | 0.40 | — |
| 1992 Proof | 15,000 | Value: 1.50 | | | | |
| 1993 | 24,992,000 | — | — | — | 0.40 | — |
| 1993 Proof | 10,000 | Value: 1.50 | | | | |
| 1994 (Fish) | 10,000,000 | — | — | — | 0.40 | — |
| 1994 (Fish) Proof | 10,000 | Value: 1.50 | | | | |
| 1994 (Bee) | 29,992,000 | — | — | — | 0.40 | — |
| 1995 | 29,996,000 | — | — | — | 0.40 | — |
| 1995 Proof | 10,000 | Value: 1.50 | | | | |
| 1996 | 55,983,000 | — | — | — | 0.40 | — |
| 1996 Proof | 8,000 | Value: 1.50 | | | | |
| 1997 | 99,991,000 | — | — | — | 0.40 | — |
| 1997 Proof | 10,000 | Value: 1.50 | | | | |
| 1998 Proof | — | Value: 1.50 | | | | |
| 1999 Proof | — | Value: 1.50 | | | | |
| 2000 | — | — | — | — | 0.40 | — |
| 2000 Proof | — | Value: 1.50 | | | | |

**FRANC KM# 844.1 Weight:** 5.0000 g. **Composition:** 0.8350 Silver .1342 oz. ASW **Note:** Without mint mark. Struck at Paris Mint.

| Date | Mintage | F | VF | XF | Unc | BU |
|---|---|---|---|---|---|---|
| 1898 | 15,000,000 | 1.50 | 2.50 | 5.00 | 30.00 | — |
| 1898 Proof | — | Value: 400 | | | | |
| 1899 | 11,000,000 | 1.50 | 3.00 | 7.00 | 35.00 | — |
| 1900 | 99,000 | 125 | 225 | 450 | 850 | — |
| 1900 Proof | — | Value: 425 | | | | |
| 1901 | 6,200,000 | 2.00 | 4.00 | 20.00 | 75.00 | — |
| 1902 | 6,000,000 | 2.00 | 4.00 | 20.00 | 75.00 | — |
| 1903 | 472,000 | 40.00 | 80.00 | 325 | 650 | — |
| 1904 | 7,000,000 | 2.00 | 4.00 | 17.50 | 75.00 | — |
| 1905 | 6,004,000 | 2.00 | 4.00 | 15.00 | 65.00 | — |
| 1906 | 1,908,000 | 6.00 | 20.00 | 40.00 | 100 | — |
| 1907 | 2,563,000 | 4.00 | 9.00 | 30.00 | 90.00 | — |
| 1908 | 3,961,000 | 2.50 | 5.00 | 20.00 | 65.00 | — |
| 1909 | 10,924,000 | 1.25 | 2.50 | 5.00 | 22.00 | — |
| 1910 | 7,725,000 | 1.25 | 2.50 | 5.00 | 22.00 | — |
| 1911 | 5,542,000 | 1.75 | 3.00 | 12.00 | 45.00 | — |
| 1912 | 10,001,000 | 1.25 | 2.50 | 5.00 | 22.00 | — |
| 1913 | 13,654,000 | 1.25 | 2.50 | 4.00 | 18.00 | — |
| 1914 | 14,361,000 | 1.25 | 2.50 | 3.50 | 15.00 | — |
| 1915 | 47,955,000 | BV | 1.25 | 2.00 | 5.50 | — |
| 1916 | 92,029,000 | BV | 1.00 | 1.50 | 3.50 | — |
| 1917 | 57,153,000 | BV | 1.00 | 1.50 | 3.50 | — |
| 1918 | 50,112,000 | BV | 1.00 | 1.50 | 3.50 | — |
| 1919 | 46,112,000 | BV | 1.00 | 1.50 | 3.50 | — |
| 1920 | 19,322,000 | BV | 1.50 | 2.50 | 5.50 | — |

**FRANC KM# 844.2 Weight:** 5.0000 g. **Composition:** 0.8350 Silver .1342 oz. ASW

| Date | Mintage | F | VF | XF | Unc | BU |
|---|---|---|---|---|---|---|
| 1914C | 43,000 | 135 | 250 | 325 | 450 | — |

**FRANC KM# 876 Composition:** Aluminum-Bronze **Note:** Without mint mark. Chamber of Commerce. Struck at Paris Mint.

| Date | Mintage | F | VF | XF | Unc | BU |
|---|---|---|---|---|---|---|
| 1920 | 590,000 | 3.00 | 5.00 | 12.50 | 32.00 | — |
| 1921 | 54,572,000 | 0.25 | 0.50 | 1.50 | 5.50 | — |
| 1922 | 111,343,000 | 0.15 | 0.25 | 1.00 | 4.50 | — |
| 1923 | 140,138,000 | 0.15 | 0.25 | 1.00 | 3.50 | — |
| 1924 Open 4 | 87,715,000 | 0.15 | 0.25 | 1.00 | 4.50 | — |
| 1924 Closed 4 | Inc. above | 0.35 | 0.60 | 2.00 | 6.50 | — |
| 1925 | 36,523,000 | 0.25 | 0.50 | 1.50 | 5.50 | — |
| 1926 | 1,580,000 | 3.00 | 8.00 | 20.00 | 45.00 | — |
| 1927 | 11,330,000 | 0.50 | 1.50 | 3.50 | 8.50 | — |

**FRANC KM# 885 Composition:** Aluminum-Bronze

| Date | Mintage | F | VF | XF | Unc | BU |
|---|---|---|---|---|---|---|
| 1931 | 15,504,000 | 0.25 | 0.50 | 2.00 | 6.50 | — |
| 1932 | 29,768,000 | 0.15 | 0.25 | 1.00 | 4.00 | — |
| 1933 | 15,356,000 | 0.25 | 0.50 | 2.00 | 6.50 | — |
| 1934 | 17,286,000 | 0.25 | 0.50 | 2.00 | 5.00 | — |
| 1935 | 1,166,000 | 6.00 | 15.00 | 25.00 | 60.00 | — |
| 1936 | 23,817,000 | 0.15 | 0.25 | 1.00 | 4.00 | — |
| 1937 | 30,940,000 | 0.15 | 0.25 | 1.00 | 3.00 | — |
| 1938 | 66,165,000 | 0.15 | 0.25 | 1.00 | 2.50 | — |
| 1939 | 48,434,000 | 0.15 | 0.25 | 1.00 | 3.00 | — |
| 1940 | 25,525,000 | 0.15 | 0.25 | 1.00 | 3.50 | — |
| 1941 | 34,705,000 | 0.15 | 0.25 | 1.00 | 3.00 | — |

**FRANC KM# 885a.1 Composition:** Aluminum **Note:** Thick and thin planchets exist.

| Date | Mintage | F | VF | XF | Unc | BU |
|---|---|---|---|---|---|---|
| 1941 | 60,877,000 | 0.10 | 0.20 | 1.00 | 4.00 | — |
| 1943 | 4,400 | 1,200 | 1,500 | 2,250 | 4,000 | — |
| 1944 | 22,608,000 | 0.10 | 0.20 | 1.50 | 5.00 | — |
| 1945 | 61,780,000 | 0.10 | 0.15 | 0.50 | 2.00 | — |
| 1946 | 52,516,000 | 0.10 | 0.15 | 0.25 | 2.00 | — |
| 1947 | 110,448,000 | 0.10 | 0.15 | 0.25 | 2.00 | — |
| 1948 | 96,092,000 | 0.10 | 0.15 | 0.25 | 2.00 | — |
| 1949 | 41,090,000 | 0.10 | 0.15 | 0.25 | 2.00 | — |
| 1950 | 27,882,000 | 0.10 | 0.15 | 0.50 | 2.50 | — |
| 1957 | 16,497,000 | 0.10 | 0.15 | 0.75 | 3.00 | — |
| 1958 | 21,197,000 | 0.10 | 0.15 | 0.75 | 3.00 | — |
| 1959 | 41,985,000 | 0.10 | 0.15 | 0.25 | 1.25 | — |

**FRANC KM# 902.1 Composition:** Aluminum **Note:** Without mint mark. Vichy French State Issues. Struck at Paris Mint.

| Date | Mintage | F | VF | XF | Unc | BU |
|---|---|---|---|---|---|---|
| 1942 | 152,144,000 | 0.25 | 0.50 | 1.50 | 4.00 | — |
| 1942 Without LB | Inc. above | — | — | — | — | — |
| 1943 | 205,564,000 | 0.10 | 0.25 | 1.00 | 2.50 | — |
| 1943 Thin flan | Inc. above | 0.10 | 0.25 | 1.00 | 2.50 | — |
| 1944 | 50,605,000 | 0.50 | 1.25 | 2.00 | 8.00 | — |

**FRANC KM# 902.2 Composition:** Aluminum

| Date | Mintage | F | VF | XF | Unc | BU |
|---|---|---|---|---|---|---|
| 1943B | 68,082,000 | 5.00 | 9.00 | 28.00 | 80.00 | — |
| 1944B | 13,622,000 | 1.50 | 3.00 | 12.00 | 25.00 | — |

**FRANC KM# 885b Composition:** Zinc **Note:** Struck for colonial use in Africa.

| Date | Mintage | F | VF | XF | Unc | BU |
|---|---|---|---|---|---|---|
| 1943A | Est. 17,000 | 750 | 1,100 | 1,700 | 3,200 | — |

**FRANC KM# 885a.3 Composition:** Aluminum

| Date | Mintage | F | VF | XF | Unc | BU |
|---|---|---|---|---|---|---|
| 1944C | 33,600,000 | 0.50 | 1.50 | 3.50 | 12.00 | — |
| 1945C | 5,220,000 | 1.50 | 3.50 | 9.00 | 25.00 | — |

**FRANC KM# 885a.2 Composition:** Aluminum

| Date | Mintage | F | VF | XF | Unc | BU |
|---|---|---|---|---|---|---|
| 1945B | 4,251,000 | 1.00 | 3.50 | 9.00 | 28.00 | — |
| 1946B | 26,493,000 | 0.10 | 0.20 | 1.50 | 5.00 | — |
| 1947B | 51,562,000 | 0.10 | 0.20 | 1.00 | 4.00 | — |
| 1948B | 45,481,000 | 0.10 | 0.20 | 1.00 | 3.50 | — |
| 1949B | 35,840,000 | 0.10 | 0.20 | 1.00 | 4.00 | — |
| 1950B | 18,800,000 | 1.00 | 2.00 | 3.50 | 15.00 | — |
| 1957B | 63,976,000 | 0.10 | 0.20 | 1.00 | 4.00 | — |
| 1958B | 13,412,000 | 0.25 | 0.75 | 2.00 | 5.50 | — |

**FRANC KM# 925.1 Composition:** Nickel **Note:** Without mint mark. Struck at Paris Mint.

| Date | Mintage | F | VF | XF | Unc | BU |
|---|---|---|---|---|---|---|
| 1960 | 406,375,000 | — | — | 0.20 | 0.40 | — |
| 1961 | 119,611,000 | — | — | 0.20 | 0.40 | — |
| 1962 | 14,014,000 | — | — | 0.20 | 0.50 | — |
| 1964 | 77,425,000 | — | — | 0.20 | 0.40 | — |
| 1965 | 44,252,000 | — | — | 0.20 | 0.40 | — |
| 1966 | 38,038,000 | — | — | 0.20 | 0.40 | — |
| 1967 | 11,322,000 | — | — | 0.20 | 0.50 | — |
| 1968 | 51,550,000 | — | — | 0.20 | 0.40 | — |
| 1969 | 70,595,000 | — | — | 0.20 | 0.40 | — |
| 1970 | 42,560,000 | — | — | 0.20 | 0.40 | — |
| 1971 | 42,475,000 | — | — | 0.20 | 0.40 | — |
| 1972 | 48,250,000 | — | — | 0.20 | 0.40 | — |
| 1973 | 70,000,000 | — | — | 0.20 | 0.40 | — |
| 1974 | 82,235,000 | — | — | 0.20 | 0.40 | — |
| 1975 | 101,685,000 | — | — | 0.20 | 0.40 | — |
| 1976 | 192,520,000 | — | — | 0.20 | 0.40 | — |
| 1977 | 230,085,000 | — | — | 0.20 | 0.40 | — |
| 1978 | 136,580,000 | — | — | 0.20 | 0.40 | — |
| 1979 | 51,000 | — | — | — | 0.60 | — |
| 1980 In set only | 60,000 | — | — | — | 0.60 | — |
| 1981 | 50,000 | — | — | — | 0.60 | — |
| 1982 | 92,000 | — | — | — | 0.60 | — |
| 1983 | 101,000 | — | — | — | 0.60 | — |
| 1984 | 50,000 | — | — | — | 0.60 | — |
| 1985 | 7,002,000 | — | — | — | 2.00 | — |
| 1986 | 48,000 | — | — | — | 2.00 | — |
| 1987 | 100,000 | — | — | — | 0.40 | — |
| 1988 | 100,000 | — | — | — | 0.40 | — |
| 1989 | 83,000 | — | — | — | 0.40 | — |
| 1990 | 15,000 | — | — | — | 0.40 | — |
| 1991 | — | — | — | — | 0.40 | — |
| **Note:** Exists in both coin and medal alignment | | | | | | |
| 1992 | 30,000,000 | — | — | — | 0.40 | — |
| **Note:** Exists in both coin and medal alignment | | | | | | |
| 1994 (Bee) | — | — | — | — | 0.40 | — |
| 1995 | — | — | — | — | 0.40 | — |
| 1996 | — | — | — | — | 0.40 | — |
| 1997 | — | — | — | — | 0.40 | — |
| 1998 | — | — | — | — | 0.40 | — |
| 1999 | — | — | — | — | 0.40 | — |

**FRANC KM# 963 Composition:** Nickel **Subject:** 30th Anniversary of Fifth Republic

| Date | Mintage | F | VF | XF | Unc | BU |
|---|---|---|---|---|---|---|
| 1988 | 49,921,000 | — | — | — | 1.00 | — |

**FRANC KM# 978 Weight:** 22.2000 g. **Composition:** 0.9000 Silver .6424 oz. ASW **Subject:** 30th Anniversary of Fifth Republic

| Date | Mintage | F | VF | XF | Unc | BU |
|---|---|---|---|---|---|---|
| 1988 Proof | 60,000 | Value: 30.00 | | | | |

**FRANC KM# 979 Weight:** 9.0000 g. **Composition:** 0.9250 Gold .2662 oz. AGW **Subject:** 30th Anniversary of Fifth Republic

| Date | Mintage | F | VF | XF | Unc | BU |
|---|---|---|---|---|---|---|
| 1988 Proof | 20,000 | Value: 200 | | | | |

**FRANCE KM# 967 Composition:** Nickel **Subject:** 200th Anniversary of Estates General

| Date | Mintage | F | VF | XF | Unc | BU |
|---|---|---|---|---|---|---|
| 1989 | 5,010,000 | — | — | — | 2.50 | — |

**FRANC KM# 925.2 Composition:** Nickel **Obverse:** Modified sower, engraver's signature: O. ROTY, preceded by D'AP **Edge:** Plain

| Date | Mintage | F | VF | XF | Unc | BU |
|---|---|---|---|---|---|---|
| 1991 | 54,990,000 | — | — | — | 0.40 | — |
| 1991 Proof | 10,000 | Value: 2.50 | | | | |
| 1992 | 29,983,000 | — | — | — | 0.40 | — |
| 1992 Proof | 15,000 | Value: 2.50 | | | | |
| 1993 | 40,000 | — | — | — | 0.40 | — |
| 1993 Proof | 10,000 | Value: 2.50 | | | | |
| 1994 (Bee) | 4,812,000 | — | — | — | 0.40 | — |
| 1994 (Fish) Proof | 10,000 | Value: 2.50 | | | | |
| 1995 | 35,000 | — | — | — | 0.40 | — |
| 1995 Proof | 10,000 | Value: 2.50 | | | | |
| 1996 | 5,000 | — | — | — | 0.40 | — |
| 1996 Proof | 8,000 | Value: 2.50 | | | | |
| 1997 | 15,000 | — | — | — | 0.40 | — |
| 1997 Proof | — | Value: 2.50 | | | | |
| 1998 Proof | — | Value: 2.50 | | | | |
| 1999 Proof | — | Value: 2.50 | | | | |
| 2000 | — | — | — | — | 0.40 | — |
| 2000 Proof | — | Value: 2.50 | | | | |

**FRANC KM# 1004.1 Composition:** Nickel **Subject:** 200th Anniversary of French Republic

| Date | Mintage | F | VF | XF | Unc | BU |
|---|---|---|---|---|---|---|
| 1992 | 30,000,000 | — | — | — | 1.25 | — |

**FRANC KM# 1004.1a Weight:** 9.0000 g. **Composition:** 0.9200 Gold .2662 oz. AGW **Subject:** 200th Anniversary of the French Republic

| Date | Mintage | F | VF | XF | Unc | BU |
|---|---|---|---|---|---|---|
| 1992 Proof | 5,000 | Value: 200 | | | | |

**FRANC KM# 1004.1b Weight:** 11.0000 g. **Composition:** 0.9990 Platinum .3537 oz. APW

| Date | Mintage | F | VF | XF | Unc | BU |
|---|---|---|---|---|---|---|
| 1992 Proof | 2,000 | Value: 325 | | | | |

**FRANC KM# 1005 Weight:** 15.5500 g. **Composition:** 0.9000 Silver .4500 oz. ASW

| Date | Mintage | F | VF | XF | Unc | BU |
|---|---|---|---|---|---|---|
| 1992 | — | — | — | — | 17.50 | — |
| 1992 Proof | 30,000 | Value: 35.00 | | | | |

**FRANC KM# 1014 Weight:** 22.2000 g. **Composition:** 0.9000 Silver .6424 oz. ASW **Obverse:** Soldiers storming Omaha Beach **Reverse:** Statue of Liberty

| Date | Mintage | F | VF | XF | Unc | BU |
|---|---|---|---|---|---|---|
| 1993 | 1,000,000 | — | — | — | 14.00 | — |
| 1993 Proof | 150,000 | Value: 30.00 | | | | |

**FRANC KM# 1015 Weight:** 17.0000 g. **Composition:** 0.9250 Gold .5028 oz. AGW **Subject:** Normand Invasion **Obverse:** Soldiers storming Omaha beach **Reverse:** Statue of Liberty

| Date | Mintage | F | VF | XF | Unc | BU |
|---|---|---|---|---|---|---|
| 1993 Proof | Est. 20,000 | Value: 275 | | | | |

**FRANC KM# 902.3 Composition:** Aluminum

| Date | Mintage | F | VF | XF | Unc | BU |
|---|---|---|---|---|---|---|
| 1944 Large C | 74,859,000 | 0.25 | 0.75 | 1.50 | 5.50 | — |
| 1944 Small C | Inc. above | 15.00 | 30.00 | 70.00 | 325 | — |

**FRANC KM# 1133 Composition:** Nickel **Subject:** 200th Anniversary of Institute of France **Obverse:** Institut de France building

| Date | Mintage | F | VF | XF | Unc | BU |
|---|---|---|---|---|---|---|
| 1995 | 4,976,000 | — | — | — | 1.50 | — |

**FRANC KM# 1160 Composition:** Nickel Clad Steel **Subject:** 100th Anniversary - Birth of Jacques Rueff **Obverse:** Head of Rueff at right facing

| Date | Mintage | F | VF | XF | Unc | BU |
|---|---|---|---|---|---|---|
| 1996 | 2,976,000 | — | — | — | 1.50 | — |

**FRANC KM# 1211 Weight:** 12.0000 g. **Composition:** 0.9000 Silver .3472 oz. ASW **Subject:** 1998 World Cup Soccer Games **Obverse:** Games logo above denomination **Reverse:** Soccer ball on world globe

| Date | Mintage | F | VF | XF | Unc | BU |
|---|---|---|---|---|---|---|
| 1998 | 250,000 | — | — | — | 25.00 | — |

**FRANC KM# 1214 Weight:** 11.9400 g. **Composition:** 0.9000 Silver .3455 oz. ASW **Subject:** 125th Anniversary - Universal Postal Union **Obverse:** Partial stamp design **Reverse:** Stamp design **Edge:** Reeded

| Date | Mintage | F | VF | XF | Unc | BU |
|---|---|---|---|---|---|---|
| ND(1999) | — | — | — | — | 20.00 | — |

**FRANC KM# 1262 Weight:** 13.0000 g. **Composition:** 0.9000 Silver .3762 oz. ASW **Subject:** World Soccer Championship **Obverse:** Soccer ball design **Reverse:** Soccer player **Edge:** Reeded

| Date | Mintage | F | VF | XF | Unc | BU |
|---|---|---|---|---|---|---|
| 2000 | 10,000 | — | — | — | 25.00 | — |

**FRANC KM# 925.1a Weight:** 8.0000 g. **Composition:** 0.7500 Gold .1929 oz. AGW **Obverse:** Medallic alignment **Reverse:** Medallic alignment **Edge:** Reeded **Note:** Struck at Paris Mint.

| Date | Mintage | F | VF | XF | Unc | BU |
|---|---|---|---|---|---|---|
| 2000 | 5,000 | — | — | — | 100 | — |
| 2001 | Est. 10,000 | — | — | — | 135 | — |

**FRANC KM# 1290a Weight:** 26.1000 g. **Composition:** 0.7500 Gold .6294 oz. AGW **Subject:** The Last Franc **Obv. Legend:** UN ULTIME FRANC **Reverse:** Number 1 **Edge Lettering:** REPUBLIQUE FRANCAISE.STARCK.LIBERTE.EGALITE.FRATERNITE (cornucopia) 2001 **Note:** This coin has an intentionally warped surface and the edge inscription is very weak.

| Date | Mintage | F | VF | XF | Unc | BU |
|---|---|---|---|---|---|---|
| 2001 Matte | 5,000 | — | — | — | 400 | — |

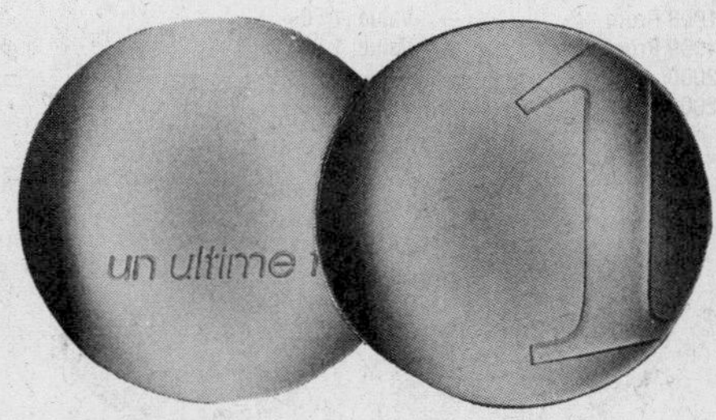

**FRANC KM# 1290 Weight:** 17.7700 g. **Composition:** 0.9800 Silver .5599 oz. ASW **Subject:** The Last Franc **Obv. Legend:** UN ULTIME FRANC **Reverse:** Number "1" **Note:** Edge inscription reads "REPUBLIQUE FRANCAISE STARCK LIBERTE EGALITE FRATERNITE (2001). The coin is intentionally warped and the edge inscription is very faint. Struck at Paris Mint.

| Date | Mintage | F | VF | XF | Unc | BU |
|---|---|---|---|---|---|---|
| 2001 Matte | — | Value: 30.00 | | | | |

**2 FRANCS** **KM# 845.1** **Weight:** 10.0000 g. **Composition:** 0.8250 Silver .2684 oz. ASW **Note:** Without mint mark. Struck at Paris Mint.

| Date | Mintage | F | VF | XF | Unc | BU |
|---|---|---|---|---|---|---|
| 1898 | 5,000,000 | 3.00 | 5.00 | 20.00 | 45.00 | — |
| 1898 Proof | — | Value: 425 | | | | |
| 1899 | 3,500,000 | 4.00 | 7.00 | 25.00 | 50.00 | — |
| 1900 | 500,000 | 30.00 | 80.00 | 200 | 450 | — |
| 1900 Proof | — | Value: 400 | | | | |
| 1901 | 1,860,000 | 6.50 | 18.00 | 50.00 | 150 | — |
| 1902 | 2,000,000 | 6.50 | 18.00 | 50.00 | 125 | — |
| 1904 | 1,500,000 | 7.50 | 18.00 | 40.00 | 175 | — |
| 1905 | 2,000,000 | 6.50 | 18.00 | 50.00 | 150 | — |
| 1908 | 2,502,000 | 3.50 | 6.00 | 20.00 | 75.00 | — |
| 1909 | 1,000,000 | 8.00 | 18.00 | 40.00 | 175 | — |
| 1910 | 2,190,000 | 3.50 | 6.00 | 20.00 | 75.00 | — |
| 1912 | 1,000,000 | 7.00 | 18.00 | 40.00 | 125 | — |
| 1913 | 500,000 | 15.00 | 25.00 | 50.00 | 150 | — |
| 1914 | 5,719,000 | 1.50 | 2.50 | 7.00 | 25.00 | — |
| 1915 | 13,963,000 | BV | 1.50 | 4.00 | 18.00 | — |
| 1916 | 17,887,000 | BV | 1.50 | 4.00 | 18.00 | — |
| 1917 | 16,555,000 | BV | 1.50 | 4.00 | 18.00 | — |
| 1918 | 12,026,000 | BV | 1.50 | 4.00 | 18.00 | — |
| 1919 | 9,261,000 | 1.50 | 2.50 | 4.50 | 15.00 | — |
| 1920 | 3,014,000 | 2.00 | 4.00 | 7.00 | 25.00 | — |

**2 FRANCS** **KM# 845.2** **Weight:** 10.0000 g. **Composition:** 0.8352 Silver .2684 oz. ASW

| Date | Mintage | F | VF | XF | Unc | BU |
|---|---|---|---|---|---|---|
| 1914C | 462,000 | 7.50 | 15.00 | 30.00 | 50.00 | — |
| 1914C Matte Proof | — | Value: 625 | | | | |

**2 FRANCS** **KM# 877** **Composition:** Aluminum-Bronze **Subject:** French Chamber of Commerce **Reverse:** Seated allegorical chamber of commerce figure **Note:** Without mint mark. Struck at Paris Mint.

| Date | Mintage | F | VF | XF | Unc | BU |
|---|---|---|---|---|---|---|
| 1920 | 14,363,000 | 6.00 | 15.00 | 40.00 | 90.00 | — |
| 1921 | Inc. above | 0.75 | 1.50 | 3.00 | 12.50 | — |
| 1922 | 29,463,000 | 0.50 | 1.00 | 2.00 | 7.50 | — |
| 1923 | 43,960,000 | 0.50 | 1.00 | 2.00 | 7.50 | — |
| 1924 Open 4 | 29,631,000 | 0.50 | 1.00 | 2.00 | 7.50 | — |
| 1924 | — | — | — | — | — | — |
| 1924 | — | — | — | — | — | — |
| 1924 Closed 4 | Inc. above | 0.65 | 1.50 | 3.00 | 10.00 | — |
| 1925/3 | 31,607,000 | 0.75 | 1.75 | 4.00 | 12.50 | — |
| 1925 | Inc. above | 0.50 | 1.00 | 2.00 | 8.00 | — |
| 1926 | 2,962,000 | 7.00 | 18.00 | 50.00 | 100 | — |
| 1927 | 1,678,000 | 100 | 150 | 300 | 700 | — |

**2 FRANCS** **KM# 886** **Composition:** Aluminum-Bronze

| Date | Mintage | F | VF | XF | Unc | BU |
|---|---|---|---|---|---|---|
| 1931 | 1,717,000 | 3.00 | 6.00 | 12.00 | 35.00 | — |
| 1932 | 8,943,000 | 0.75 | 1.50 | 3.00 | 10.00 | — |
| 1933 | 8,413,000 | 0.75 | 1.50 | 3.00 | 10.00 | — |
| 1934 | 6,896,000 | 1.25 | 2.50 | 6.00 | 12.00 | — |
| 1935 | 298,000 | 12.00 | 20.00 | 40.00 | 90.00 | — |
| 1936 | 12,394,000 | 0.25 | 1.00 | 2.00 | 6.00 | — |
| 1937 | 11,055,000 | 0.25 | 1.00 | 2.00 | 6.00 | — |
| 1938 | 28,072,000 | 0.20 | 0.50 | 1.00 | 5.00 | — |
| 1939 | 25,403,000 | 0.20 | 0.50 | 1.00 | 5.00 | — |
| 1940 | 9,716,000 | 1.00 | 2.00 | 3.50 | 10.00 | — |
| 1941 | 16,684,000 | 0.25 | 1.00 | 2.00 | 6.00 | — |

**2 FRANCS** **KM# 886a.1** **Composition:** Aluminum

| Date | Mintage | F | VF | XF | Unc | BU |
|---|---|---|---|---|---|---|
| 1941 | Inc. above | 0.25 | 0.50 | 1.00 | 3.00 | — |
| 1944 | 7,224,000 | 0.75 | 1.50 | 4.00 | 12.00 | — |
| 1945 | 16,636,000 | 0.50 | 1.00 | 2.50 | 7.00 | — |
| 1946 | 34,930,000 | 0.20 | 0.50 | 1.00 | 3.50 | — |
| 1947 | 78,984,000 | 0.20 | 0.30 | 1.00 | 2.50 | — |
| 1948 | 32,354,000 | 0.20 | 0.50 | 1.00 | 3.50 | — |
| 1949 | 13,683,000 | 0.25 | 0.50 | 1.00 | 2.50 | — |
| 1950 | 12,191,000 | 0.25 | 0.50 | 1.00 | 2.50 | — |
| 1958 | 9,906,000 | 0.20 | 0.50 | 1.00 | 3.50 | — |
| 1959 | 17,774,000 | 0.20 | 0.50 | 1.00 | 3.50 | — |

**2 FRANCS** **KM# 904.1** **Composition:** Aluminum **Note:** Without mint mark. Issued for Vichy French State. Struck at Paris Mint.

| Date | Mintage | F | VF | XF | Unc | BU |
|---|---|---|---|---|---|---|
| 1943 | 106,997,000 | 0.20 | 0.50 | 1.00 | 5.00 | — |
| 1944 | 25,546,000 | 0.75 | 1.50 | 3.50 | 7.00 | — |

**2 FRANCS** **KM# 904.2** **Composition:** Aluminum

| Date | Mintage | F | VF | XF | Unc | BU |
|---|---|---|---|---|---|---|
| 1943B | 34,131,000 | 3.50 | 7.00 | 18.00 | 30.00 | — |
| 1944B | 10,298,000 | 1.50 | 3.00 | 6.00 | 18.00 | — |

**2 FRANCS** **KM# 904.3** **Composition:** Aluminum

| Date | Mintage | F | VF | XF | Unc | BU |
|---|---|---|---|---|---|---|
| 1944C | 19,470,000 | 1.25 | 2.50 | 5.00 | 18.00 | — |

**2 FRANCS** **KM# 905** **Composition:** Brass **Note:** Without mint mark. Issued during Allied Occupation.

| Date | Mintage | F | VF | XF | Unc | BU |
|---|---|---|---|---|---|---|
| 1944 | 50,000,000 | 1.00 | 2.00 | 5.00 | 25.00 | — |

**2 FRANCS** **KM# 886a.2** **Composition:** Aluminum

| Date | Mintage | F | VF | XF | Unc | BU |
|---|---|---|---|---|---|---|
| 1944B | 170,000 | — | — | — | — | — |
| 1945B | 1,726,000 | 3.00 | 7.00 | 15.00 | 40.00 | — |
| 1946B | 6,018,000 | 2.00 | 4.00 | 8.00 | 25.00 | — |
| 1947B | 26,220,000 | 0.20 | 0.50 | 1.00 | 3.50 | — |
| 1948B | 39,090,000 | 0.20 | 0.50 | 1.00 | 3.00 | — |
| 1949B | 23,955,000 | 0.20 | 0.50 | 1.00 | 3.50 | — |
| 1950B | 18,185,000 | 0.50 | 1.00 | 3.00 | 5.00 | — |

**2 FRANCS** **KM# 886a.3** **Composition:** Aluminum

| Date | Mintage | F | VF | XF | Unc | BU |
|---|---|---|---|---|---|---|
| 1945C | 1,165,000 | 5.00 | 10.00 | 25.00 | 65.00 | — |

**2 FRANCS** **KM# 942.1** **Composition:** Nickel

| Date | Mintage | F | VF | XF | Unc | BU |
|---|---|---|---|---|---|---|
| 1979 | 130,000,000 | — | — | 0.40 | 0.65 | — |
| 1980 | 100,010,000 | — | — | 0.40 | 0.65 | — |
| 1981 | 120,000,000 | — | — | 0.40 | 0.65 | — |
| 1982 | 90,000,000 | — | — | 0.40 | 0.65 | — |
| 1983 | 90,000,000 | — | — | 0.40 | 0.65 | — |
| 1984 | 50,000 | — | — | — | 0.75 | — |
| 1985 | 20,000 | — | — | — | 2.00 | — |
| 1986 | 48,000 | — | — | — | 2.00 | — |
| 1987 | 100,000 | — | — | — | 0.75 | — |
| 1988 | 100,000 | — | — | — | 0.75 | — |
| 1989 | 83,000 | — | — | — | 0.75 | — |
| 1990 | 15,000 | — | — | — | 0.75 | — |
| 1994 (Fish) | — | — | — | — | 0.75 | — |
| 1994 (Bee) | — | — | — | — | 14.00 | — |
| 1995 | — | — | — | — | 0.75 | — |
| 1996 | — | — | — | — | 0.75 | — |
| 1997 | — | — | — | — | 0.75 | — |
| 1998 | — | — | — | — | 0.75 | — |
| 1999 | — | — | — | — | 0.75 | — |

**2 FRANCS** **KM# 942.2** **Composition:** Nickel **Edge:** Plain

| Date | Mintage | F | VF | XF | Unc | BU |
|---|---|---|---|---|---|---|
| 1991 | 5,000 | — | — | — | — | — |
| 1991 Proof | 10,000 | Value: 3.50 | | | | |
| 1992 | 15,000 | — | — | — | 0.75 | — |
| 1992 Proof | 85,000 | Value: 3.50 | | | | |
| 1993 | 40,000 | — | — | — | 0.75 | — |
| 1993 Proof | 10,000 | Value: 3.50 | | | | |
| 1994 (Fish) | 9,870,000 | — | — | — | 0.75 | — |
| 1994 (Fish) Proof | 10,000 | Value: 3.50 | | | | |
| 1994 (Bee) | 20,000 | — | — | — | 0.75 | — |
| 1995 | 20,000 | — | — | — | 0.75 | — |
| 1995 Proof | 10,000 | Value: 3.50 | | | | |
| 1996 | 11,980,000 | — | — | — | 0.75 | — |
| 1996 Proof | 8,000 | Value: 3.50 | | | | |
| 1997 | 9,990,000 | — | — | — | 0.75 | — |
| 1997 Proof | 10,000 | Value: 3.50 | | | | |
| 1998 | — | — | — | — | 0.75 | — |
| 1998 Proof | — | Value: 3.50 | | | | |
| 1999 Proof | — | Value: 3.50 | | | | |
| 2000 | — | — | — | — | 0.75 | — |
| 2000 Proof | — | Value: 3.50 | | | | |

**2 FRANCS** **KM# 1062** **Composition:** Nickel **Obverse:** Jean Moulin facing

| Date | Mintage | F | VF | XF | Unc | BU |
|---|---|---|---|---|---|---|
| 1993 | 30,000,000 | — | — | — | 1.00 | — |

**2 FRANCS** **KM# 1119** **Composition:** Nickel **Obverse:** Head of Louis Pasteur facing

| Date | Mintage | F | VF | XF | Unc | BU |
|---|---|---|---|---|---|---|
| 1995 | 9,975,000 | — | — | — | 2.00 | — |

**2 FRANCS** **KM# 1187** **Composition:** Nickel **Obverse:** Georges Guynemer, WWI fighter pilot ace facing **Reverse:** Guynemer's stork emblem

| Date | Mintage | F | VF | XF | Unc | BU |
|---|---|---|---|---|---|---|
| 1997 | — | — | — | — | 2.25 | — |

**2 FRANCS** **KM# 1213** **Composition:** Nickel **Subject:** 50th Anniversary- Declaration of Human Rights **Obverse:** Head right **Reverse:** Denomination on world globe

| Date | Mintage | F | VF | XF | Unc | BU |
|---|---|---|---|---|---|---|
| 1998 | — | — | — | — | 2.25 | — |

**5 FRANCS** **KM# 887** **Composition:** Nickel **Note:** Without mint mark. Struck at Paris Mint.

| Date | Mintage | F | VF | XF | Unc | BU |
|---|---|---|---|---|---|---|
| 1933 (a) | 160,078,000 | 0.75 | 1.50 | 3.50 | 9.00 | — |

**5 FRANCS** **KM# 888** **Composition:** Nickel **Note:** Without mint mark. Struck at Paris Mint.

| Date | Mintage | F | VF | XF | Unc | BU |
|---|---|---|---|---|---|---|
| 1933 (a) | 56,686,000 | 0.25 | 0.75 | 2.50 | 8.00 | — |
| 1935 (a) | 54,164,000 | 0.25 | 0.75 | 2.50 | 8.00 | — |
| 1936 (a) | 117,000 | 400 | 700 | 1,200 | 1,850 | — |
| 1937 (a) | 157,000 | 35.00 | 60.00 | 120 | 225 | — |
| 1938 (a) | 4,977,000 | 12.00 | 25.00 | 50.00 | 120 | — |
| 1939 (a) | — | 700 | 1,200 | 2,000 | 4,000 | — |

**5 FRANCS** **KM# 888a.1** **Composition:** Aluminum-Bronze **Note:** Struck for colonial use in Algeria

| Date | Mintage | F | VF | XF | Unc | BU |
|---|---|---|---|---|---|---|
| 1938 (a) | 10,144,000 | 6.00 | 10.00 | 18.00 | 85.00 | — |
| 1939 (a) | Inc. above | 2.50 | 5.00 | 12.00 | 30.00 | — |
| 1940 (a) | 38,758,000 | 1.00 | 2.00 | 3.50 | 10.00 | — |

**5 FRANCS** **KM# 901** **Composition:** Copper-Nickel **Note:** Without mint mark. Struck at Paris Mint.

| Date | Mintage | F | VF | XF | Unc | BU |
|---|---|---|---|---|---|---|
| 1941 (a) | 13,782,000 | 65.00 | 100 | 150 | 250 | — |

**Note:** Never released for circulation

**5 FRANCS** **KM# 888a.2** **Composition:** Aluminum-Bronze **Note:** Struck for colonial use in Africa.

| Date | Mintage | F | VF | XF | Unc | BU |
|---|---|---|---|---|---|---|
| 1945 (a) Open 9 | 13,044,000 | 1.00 | 2.00 | 4.00 | 11.00 | — |
| 1946 (a) Open 9 | 21,790,000 | 1.00 | 2.00 | 4.00 | 11.00 | — |
| 1947 (a) | 2,662,000 | 150 | 350 | 550 | 1,000 | — |

**Note:** Date exists with both open and closed 9's

**5 FRANCS** **KM# 888b.1** **Composition:** Aluminum **Note:** Without mint mark. Struck at Paris Mint.

| Date | Mintage | F | VF | XF | Unc | BU |
|---|---|---|---|---|---|---|
| 1945 (a) Open 9 | 95,399,000 | 0.20 | 0.35 | 1.50 | 6.00 | — |
| 1946 (a) Open 9 | 61,332,000 | 0.20 | 0.35 | 1.50 | 6.00 | — |
| 1947 (a) Open & closed 9 | 46,576,000 | 0.20 | 0.35 | 1.50 | 6.00 | — |

**5 FRANCS** **KM# 888a.3** **Composition:** Aluminum-Bronze

| Date | Mintage | F | VF | XF | Unc | BU |
|---|---|---|---|---|---|---|
| 1945C Open 9 | Inc. above | 3.00 | 7.00 | 15.00 | 30.00 | — |
| 1946C Open 9 | Inc. above | 5.00 | 15.00 | 30.00 | 60.00 | — |

**5 FRANCS** **KM# 888b.2** **Composition:** Aluminum

| Date | Mintage | F | VF | XF | Unc | BU |
|---|---|---|---|---|---|---|
| 1945B Open 9 | 6,043,000 | 1.50 | 3.00 | 5.00 | 15.00 | — |
| 1946B Open 9 | 13,360,000 | 0.75 | 1.50 | 3.00 | 12.00 | — |
| 1947B Open & closed 9 | 30,839,000 | 0.50 | 1.00 | 2.50 | 8.00 | — |
| 1948B Open & closed 9 | 28,047,000 | 20.00 | 40.00 | 100 | 175 | — |
| 1949B Closed 9 | 48,414,000 | 0.50 | 1.00 | 2.50 | 8.00 | — |
| 1950B Closed 9 | 28,952,000 | 0.75 | 1.50 | 3.50 | 9.00 | — |

**5 FRANCS** **KM# 888b.3** **Composition:** Aluminum

| Date | Mintage | F | VF | XF | Unc | BU |
|---|---|---|---|---|---|---|
| 1945C Open 9 | 2,208,000 | 7.00 | 15.00 | 28.00 | 60.00 | — |
| 1946C Open 9 | 1,269,000 | 8.00 | 18.00 | 38.00 | 75.00 | — |

**5 FRANCS** **KM# 926** **Weight:** 12.0000 g. **Composition:** 0.8350 Silver .3221 oz. ASW

| Date | Mintage | F | VF | XF | Unc | BU |
|---|---|---|---|---|---|---|
| 1960 | 55,182,000 | — | — | BV | 3.50 | — |
| 1961 | 15,630,000 | — | — | BV | 3.50 | — |
| 1962 | 42,500,000 | — | — | BV | 3.50 | — |
| 1963 | 37,936,000 | — | — | BV | 3.50 | — |
| 1964 | 32,378,000 | — | — | BV | 3.50 | — |
| 1965 | 5,156,000 | — | — | BV | 5.50 | — |
| 1966 | 5,017,000 | — | — | BV | 5.50 | — |
| 1967 | 502,000 | — | BV | 4.00 | 12.00 | — |
| 1968 | 557,000 | — | BV | 3.00 | 10.00 | — |
| 1969 | 504,000 | — | BV | 3.00 | 10.00 | — |

**5 FRANCS** **KM# 926a.1** **Composition:** Nickel Clad Copper-Nickel

| Date | Mintage | F | VF | XF | Unc | BU |
|---|---|---|---|---|---|---|
| 1970 | 57,890,000 | — | — | 1.00 | 1.25 | — |
| 1971 | 142,204,000 | — | — | 1.00 | 1.25 | — |
| 1972 | 45,492,000 | — | — | 1.00 | 1.50 | — |
| 1973 | 45,079,000 | — | — | 1.00 | 1.25 | — |
| 1974 | 26,888,000 | — | — | 1.00 | 1.25 | — |
| 1975 | 16,712,000 | — | — | 1.00 | 1.25 | — |
| 1976 | 1,662,000 | — | 1.00 | 1.25 | 2.00 | — |
| 1977 | 485,000 | — | 1.00 | 1.50 | 2.25 | — |
| 1978 | 30,022,000 | — | — | 1.00 | 1.25 | — |
| 1979 | 51,000 | — | — | 1.75 | 3.50 | — |
| 1980 In sets only | 60,000 | — | — | — | 1.65 | — |
| 1981 | 50,000 | — | — | — | 1.65 | — |
| 1982 | 60,000 | — | — | — | 1.65 | — |
| 1983 | 101,000 | — | — | — | 1.65 | — |
| 1984 | 49,000 | — | — | — | 4.50 | — |
| 1985 In sets only | 20,000 | — | — | — | 6.00 | — |
| 1986 In sets only | 48,000 | — | — | — | 5.00 | — |
| 1987 | 20,000,000 | — | — | — | 1.65 | — |
| 1988 | 100,000 | — | — | — | 1.65 | — |
| 1989 | 83,000 | — | — | — | 1.65 | — |
| 1990 | 15,000 | — | — | — | 1.65 | — |
| 1991 | — | — | — | — | 1.65 | — |
| 1993 | — | — | — | — | 1.65 | — |
| 1994 (Bee) | — | — | — | — | 1.65 | — |
| 1994 (Fish) | — | — | — | — | 1.65 | — |
| 1995 | — | — | — | — | 1.65 | — |
| 1996 | — | — | — | — | 1.65 | — |
| 1997 | — | — | — | — | 1.65 | — |
| 1998 | — | — | — | — | 1.65 | — |
| 1999 | — | — | — | — | 1.65 | — |

**5 FRANCS** **KM# 968** **Composition:** Copper-Nickel **Subject:** Centennial - Erection of Eiffel Tower

| Date | Mintage | F | VF | XF | Unc | BU |
|---|---|---|---|---|---|---|
| 1989 | 9,910,000 | — | — | — | 6.00 | — |

**5 FRANCS** **KM# 968a** **Weight:** 12.0000 g. **Composition:** 0.9000 Silver .3473 oz. ASW **Subject:** Centennial - Erection of Eiffel Tower

| Date | Mintage | F | VF | XF | Unc | BU |
|---|---|---|---|---|---|---|
| 1989 Proof | 80,000 | Value: 28.00 | | | | |

**5 FRANCS** **KM# 968b** **Weight:** 14.0000 g. **Composition:** 0.9250 Gold .4141 oz. AGW **Subject:** Centennial - Erection of Eiffel Tower

| Date | Mintage | F | VF | XF | Unc | BU |
|---|---|---|---|---|---|---|
| 1989 Proof | 30,000 | Value: 225 | | | | |

**5 FRANCS** **KM# 968c** **Weight:** 16.0000 g. **Composition:** 0.9990 Platinum .5145 oz. APW **Subject:** Centennial - Erection of Eiffel Tower

| Date | Mintage | F | VF | XF | Unc | BU |
|---|---|---|---|---|---|---|
| 1989 Proof | Est. 3,000 | Value: 350 | | | | |

**Note:** 1,800 pieces were melted by MTB Banking

**5 FRANCS** **KM# 926a.2** **Composition:** Nickel Clad Copper-Nickel **Obverse:** Modified sower, engraver's signature: O. ROTY preceded by D'AP **Edge:** Plain

| Date | Mintage | F | VF | XF | Unc | BU |
|---|---|---|---|---|---|---|
| 1991 | 7,490,000 | — | — | — | 1.65 | — |
| 1991 Proof | 10,000 | Value: 6.50 | | | | |
| 1992 | 9,986,000 | — | — | — | 1.65 | — |
| 1992 Proof | 15,000 | Value: 6.50 | | | | |
| 1992 | — | — | — | — | 1.65 | — |
| 1993 | 14,990,000 | — | — | — | 1.65 | — |
| 1993 Proof | 10,000 | Value: 6.50 | | | | |
| 1994 (Fish) | 6,000,000 | — | — | — | 1.65 | — |
| 1994 (Fish) Proof | 10,000 | Value: 6.50 | | | | |
| 1994 (Bee) | 3,990,000 | — | — | — | 1.65 | — |
| 1995 | 20,006,000 | — | — | — | 6.50 | — |
| 1995 Proof | — | Value: 1.65 | | | | |
| 1996 | 17,000 | — | — | — | 1.65 | — |
| 1996 Proof | 8,000 | Value: 6.50 | | | | |
| 1997 | 15,000 | — | — | — | 1.65 | — |
| 1997 Proof | — | Value: 6.50 | | | | |
| 1998 Proof | — | Value: 6.50 | | | | |
| 1999 Proof | — | Value: 6.50 | | | | |
| 2000 | — | — | — | — | 1.65 | — |
| 2000 Proof | — | Value: 6.50 | | | | |

**5 FRANCS** **KM# 1006** **Composition:** Copper-Nickel **Reverse:** Bust of Pierre Mendes facing

| Date | Mintage | F | VF | XF | Unc | BU |
|---|---|---|---|---|---|---|
| 1992 | 10,000,000 | — | — | — | 4.00 | — |

**5 FRANCS** **KM# 1006a** **Weight:** 12.0000 g. **Composition:** 0.9000 Silver .3473 oz. ASW **Reverse:** Bust of Pierre Mendes facing

| Date | Mintage | F | VF | XF | Unc | BU |
|---|---|---|---|---|---|---|
| 1992 Proof | 10,000 | Value: 30.00 | | | | |

**5 FRANCS** **KM# 1006b** **Weight:** 14.0000 g. **Composition:** 0.9200 Gold .4141 oz. AGW **Reverse:** Bust of Pierre Mendes facing

| Date | Mintage | F | VF | XF | Unc | BU |
|---|---|---|---|---|---|---|
| 1992 Proof | 1,000 | Value: 265 | | | | |

**5 FRANCS** **KM# 1007** **Weight:** 12.0000 g. **Composition:** 0.9000 Silver .3473 oz. ASW **Subject:** French Antarctic Territories **Reverse:** 3 Albatross in flight

| Date | Mintage | F | VF | XF | Unc | BU |
|---|---|---|---|---|---|---|
| 1992 Proof | 15,000 | Value: 45.00 | | | | |

**5 FRANCS** **KM# 1063** **Composition:** Nickel Clad Copper-Nickel **Obverse:** Head of Voltaire, the poet 1/2 right

| Date | Mintage | F | VF | XF | Unc | BU |
|---|---|---|---|---|---|---|
| 1994 | 15,000,000 | — | — | — | 4.00 | — |

**5 FRANCS** **KM# 1118** **Weight:** 12.0000 g. **Composition:** 0.9000 Silver .3473 oz. ASW **Subject:** 50th Anniversary - United Nations

| Date | Mintage | F | VF | XF | Unc | BU |
|---|---|---|---|---|---|---|
| 1995 Proof | 250,000 | Value: 26.50 | | | | |

**5 FRANCS** **KM# 1118a** **Weight:** 14.0000 g. **Composition:** 0.9200 Gold .4141 oz. AGW

| Date | Mintage | F | VF | XF | Unc | BU |
|---|---|---|---|---|---|---|
| 1995 Proof | 125,000 | Value: 26.50 | | | | |

**5 FRANCS** **KM# 1155** **Composition:** Nickel Clad Steel **Reverse:** Hercules group design

| Date | Mintage | F | VF | XF | Unc | BU |
|---|---|---|---|---|---|---|
| 1996 | 4,976,000 | — | — | — | 4.50 | — |

**5 FRANCS** **KM# 1212** **Weight:** 12.0000 g. **Composition:** 0.9000 Silver .3472 oz. ASW **Subject:** 1998 World Cup Soccer Games: French Victory **Obverse:** Game logo above denomination **Reverse:** Hand held trophy with stadium in background

| Date | Mintage | F | VF | XF | Unc | BU |
|---|---|---|---|---|---|---|
| 1998 Proof | Est. 100,000 | Value: 45.00 | | | | |

**5 FRANCS** **KM# 1215** **Weight:** 12.0000 g. **Composition:** 0.9000 Silver .3472 oz. ASW **Subject:** Yves St. Laurent **Obverse:** RF monogram **Reverse:** Fashion show scene **Note:** Struck at Paris Mint.

| Date | Mintage | F | VF | XF | Unc | BU |
|---|---|---|---|---|---|---|
| 2000 | — | — | — | — | 30.00 | — |

**5 FRANCS** **KM# 1222** **Weight:** 10.0000 g. **Composition:** Copper-Nickel Plated Nickel **Subject:** 2000 Years of French Coinage **Obverse:** Denomination in wreath **Reverse:** 1st century B.C. Celtic Parisii Stater coin design **Edge:** Reeded **Note:** Struck at Paris Mint.

| Date | Mintage | F | VF | XF | Unc | BU |
|---|---|---|---|---|---|---|
| 2000 | 50,000 | — | — | — | 9.50 | — |

**5 FRANCS** **KM# 1223** **Weight:** 10.0000 g. **Composition:** Copper-Nickel Plated Nickel **Subject:** 2000 Years of French Coinage **Obverse:** Denomination in wreath **Reverse:** Charlemagne Denar coin design **Edge:** Reeded **Note:** Struck at Paris Mint.

| Date | Mintage | F | VF | XF | Unc | BU |
|---|---|---|---|---|---|---|
| 2000 | 50,000 | — | — | — | 9.50 | — |

**5 FRANCS** **KM# 1224** **Weight:** 10.0000 g. **Composition:** Copper-Nickel Plated Nickel **Subject:** 2000 Years of French Coinage **Obverse:** Denomination in wreath **Reverse:** Louis IX Gold Ecu design **Edge:** Reeded **Note:** Struck at Paris Mint.

| Date | Mintage | F | VF | XF | Unc | BU |
|---|---|---|---|---|---|---|
| 2000 | 50,000 | — | — | — | 9.50 | — |

**6.55957 FRANCS** **KM# 1255** **Weight:** 22.2000 g. **Composition:** 0.9000 Silver .6424 oz. ASW **Obverse:** Europa allegorical portrait **Reverse:** Country names and euro-currency equivalents around RF and denomination in center plus French coin designs **Edge:** Plain

| Date | Mintage | F | VF | XF | Unc | BU |
|---|---|---|---|---|---|---|
| 1999 Proof | 25,000 | Value: 40.00 | | | | |

**6.55957 FRANCS** **KM# 1254** **Weight:** 13.0000 g. **Composition:** 0.9000 Silver .3762 oz. ASW **Subject:** Euro Conversion Series **Obverse:** Europa allegorical portrait **Reverse:** Country names and euro-currency equivalents around RF and denomination in center **Edge:** Plain **Note:** Struck at Paris Mint.

| Date | Mintage | F | VF | XF | Unc | BU |
|---|---|---|---|---|---|---|
| 1999 | 200,000 | — | — | — | 30.00 | — |

**6.55957 FRANCS** **KM# 1226** **Weight:** 22.2000 g. **Composition:** 0.9000 Silver .6424 oz. ASW **Series:** European Art Styles - Renaissance Classic and Baroque **Note:** Struck at Paris Mint.

| Date | Mintage | F | VF | XF | Unc | BU |
|---|---|---|---|---|---|---|
| 2000 Proof | 15,000 | Value: 35.00 | | | | |

**6.55957 FRANCS** **KM# 1227** **Weight:** 22.2000 g. **Composition:** 0.9000 Silver .6424 oz. ASW **Series:** European Art Styles Renaissance - Art Nouveau **Note:** Struck at Paris Mint.

| Date | Mintage | F | VF | XF | Unc | BU |
|---|---|---|---|---|---|---|
| 2000 Proof | 15,000 | Value: 35.00 | | | | |

**6.55957 FRANCS** **KM# 1228** **Weight:** 22.2000 g. **Composition:** 0.9000 Silver .6424 oz. ASW **Series:** European Art Styles Renaissance - Modern **Note:** Struck at Paris Mint.

| Date | Mintage | F | VF | XF | Unc | BU |
|---|---|---|---|---|---|---|
| 2000 Proof | 15,000 | Value: 35.00 | | | | |

**6.55957 FRANCS** **KM# 1244** **Weight:** 22.2000 g. **Composition:** 0.9000 Silver .6424 oz. ASW **Series:** European Art Styles Renaissance - Greek and Roman **Note:** Struck at Paris Mint.

| Date | Mintage | F | VF | XF | Unc | BU |
|---|---|---|---|---|---|---|
| 2000 Proof | 15,000 | Value: 35.00 | | | | |

**6.55957 FRANCS** **KM# 1245** **Weight:** 22.2000 g. **Composition:** 0.9000 Silver .6424 oz. ASW **Series:** European Art Styles Renaissance - Roman Art and Structures **Note:** Struck at Paris Mint.

| Date | Mintage | F | VF | XF | Unc | BU |
|---|---|---|---|---|---|---|
| 2000 Proof | 15,000 | Value: 35.00 | | | | |

**6.55957 FRANCS** **KM# 1246** **Weight:** 22.2000 g. **Composition:** 0.9000 Silver .6424 oz. ASW **Series:** European Art Styles Renaissance - Gothic **Note:** Struck at Paris Mint.

| Date | Mintage | F | VF | XF | Unc | BU |
|---|---|---|---|---|---|---|
| 2000 Proof | 15,000 | Value: 35.00 | | | | |

**6.55957 FRANCS** **KM# 1225** **Weight:** 22.2000 g. **Composition:** 0.9000 Silver .6424 oz. ASW **Subject:** European Art Styles Renaissance **Obverse:** Denomination and partial portrait **Reverse:** Renaissance style buildings **Edge Lettering:** Europa repeated four times

| Date | Mintage | F | VF | XF | Unc | BU |
|---|---|---|---|---|---|---|
| 2000 Proof | 15,000 | Value: 35.00 | | | | |

**6.55957 FRANCS** **KM# 1258** **Weight:** 13.0000 g. **Composition:** 0.9000 Silver .3762 oz. ASW **Obverse:** Country names and euro-currency equivalents around RF and denomination **Reverse:** Europa allegorical portrait **Edge:** Plain

| Date | Mintage | F | VF | XF | Unc | BU |
|---|---|---|---|---|---|---|
| 2000 | 200,000 | — | — | — | 30.00 | — |

**6.55957 FRANCS** **KM# 1259** **Weight:** 13.0000 g. **Composition:** 0.9000 Silver .3762 oz. ASW **Obverse:** Country names and euro-currency equivalents around RF, denomination and French euro cion designs **Edge:** Plain

| Date | Mintage | F | VF | XF | Unc | BU |
|---|---|---|---|---|---|---|
| 2000 Proof | 10,000 | Value: 40.00 | | | | |

**6.55957 FRANCS** **KM# 1265** **Weight:** 13.0000 g. **Composition:** 0.9000 Silver .3762 oz. ASW **Subject:** Last Year of the French Franc **Obverse:** French and other European euro currency equivalents **Reverse:** Similar to KM#1258 but with addition of "last year of the franc" logo after the date **Edge:** Reeded

| Date | Mintage | F | VF | XF | Unc | BU |
|---|---|---|---|---|---|---|
| 2001 | Est. 20,000 | — | — | — | 18.00 | — |

**6.55957 FRANCS** **KM# 1265.1** **Weight:** 22.2000 g. **Composition:** 0.9000 Silver .6424 oz. ASW **Edge:** Plain

| Date | Mintage | F | VF | XF | Unc | BU |
|---|---|---|---|---|---|---|
| 2001 Proof only | Est. 10,000 | Value: 35.00 | | | | |

**6.55957 FRANCS** **KM# 1276** **Weight:** 22.2000 g. **Composition:** 0.9000 Silver .6424 oz. ASW **Subject:** Motto Series Mottos **Obverse:** Denomination **Reverse:** FRATERNITE in red letters **Edge:** Reeded

| Date | Mintage | F | VF | XF | Unc | BU |
|---|---|---|---|---|---|---|
| 2001 Proof | 20,000 | Value: 38.50 | | | | |

**6.55957 FRANCS** **KM# 1277** **Weight:** 22.2000 g. **Composition:** 0.9000 Silver .6424 oz. ASW **Subject:** Motto Series **Reverse:** EGALITE in white letters

| Date | Mintage | F | VF | XF | Unc | BU |
|---|---|---|---|---|---|---|
| 2001 Proof | 20,000 | Value: 38.50 | | | | |

**6.55957 FRANCS** **KM# 1278** **Weight:** 22.2000 g. **Composition:** 0.9000 Silver .6424 oz. ASW **Subject:** Motto Series **Reverse:** LIBERTE in white letters

| Date | Mintage | F | VF | XF | Unc | BU |
|---|---|---|---|---|---|---|
| 2001 Proof | 20,000 | Value: 38.50 | | | | |

**10 FRANCS** **KM# 846** **Weight:** 3.2258 g. **Composition:** 0.9000 Gold .0933 oz. AGW **Note:** Without mint mark. Struck at Paris Mint.

| Date | Mintage | F | VF | XF | Unc | BU |
|---|---|---|---|---|---|---|
| 1901 | 2,100,000 | BV | 42.00 | 52.00 | 75.00 | — |
| 1901 | 2,100,000 | BV | 42.00 | 52.00 | 75.00 | — |
| 1905 | 1,426,000 | BV | 42.00 | 52.00 | 75.00 | — |
| 1905 | 1,426,000 | BV | 42.00 | 52.00 | 75.00 | — |
| 1906 | 3,665,000 | BV | 42.00 | 52.00 | 75.00 | — |
| 1907 | 3,364,000 | BV | 42.00 | 52.00 | 75.00 | — |
| 1908 | 1,650,000 | BV | 42.00 | 52.00 | 75.00 | — |
| 1909 | 599,000 | BV | 50.00 | 65.00 | 110 | — |
| 1910 | 2,110,000 | BV | 42.00 | 52.00 | 75.00 | — |
| 1911 | 1,881,000 | BV | 42.00 | 52.00 | 75.00 | — |
| 1912 | 1,756,000 | BV | 42.00 | 52.00 | 75.00 | — |
| 1914 | 3,041,000 | BV | 42.00 | 52.00 | 75.00 | — |

**10 FRANCS** **KM# 878** **Weight:** 10.0000 g. **Composition:** 0.6800 Silver .2186 oz. ASW **Note:** Without mint mark. Struck at Paris Mint.

| Date | Mintage | F | VF | XF | Unc | BU |
|---|---|---|---|---|---|---|
| 1929 | 16,292,000 | BV | 2.25 | 5.50 | 12.00 | — |
| 1930 | 36,986,000 | BV | 1.75 | 4.25 | 9.00 | — |
| 1931 | 35,468,000 | BV | 1.75 | 4.25 | 9.00 | — |
| 1932 | 40,288,000 | BV | 1.75 | 3.00 | 7.00 | — |
| 1933 | 31,146,000 | BV | 1.75 | 3.00 | 7.00 | — |
| 1934 | 52,001,000 | BV | 1.75 | 3.00 | 7.00 | — |
| 1936 | — | — | — | — | — | — |
| 1937 | 52,000 | 65.00 | 125 | 250 | 360 | — |
| 1938 | 14,090,000 | BV | 2.00 | 6.00 | 12.50 | — |
| 1939 | 8,298,999 | 2.50 | 3.50 | 8.00 | 17.50 | — |

**10 FRANCS** **KM# 908.1** **Weight:** 10.0000 g. **Composition:** 0.6800 Silver .2186 oz. ASW **Reverse:** Long Leaves & Short Leaves

| Date | Mintage | F | VF | XF | Unc | BU |
|---|---|---|---|---|---|---|
| 1945 (ll) | 6,557,000 | 0.25 | 0.75 | 2.00 | 6.00 | — |
| 1945 (sl) | Inc. above | 15.00 | 30.00 | 50.00 | 90.00 | — |
| 1946 (ll) | 24,409,000 | 185 | 300 | 400 | — | — |
| 1946 (sl) | Inc. above | 0.25 | 0.50 | 2.00 | 5.00 | — |
| 1947 | 41,627,000 | 0.25 | 0.50 | 1.00 | 3.00 | — |

**10 FRANCS** **KM# 908.2** **Weight:** 10.0000 g. **Composition:** 0.6800 Silver .2186 oz. ASW

| Date | Mintage | F | VF | XF | Unc | BU |
|---|---|---|---|---|---|---|
| 1946B (ll) | 8,452,000 | 20.00 | 35.00 | 50.00 | 85.00 | — |
| 1946B (sl) | Inc. above | 0.25 | 0.75 | 2.00 | 6.00 | — |
| 1947B | 17,188,000 | 0.25 | 0.50 | 2.00 | 5.00 | — |

**10 FRANCS** **KM# 909.2** **Weight:** 10.0000 g. **Composition:** 0.6800 Silver .2186 oz. ASW

| Date | Mintage | F | VF | XF | Unc | BU |
|---|---|---|---|---|---|---|
| 1947B | Inc. above | 1.00 | 2.50 | 6.00 | 17.00 | — |
| 1948B | 40,500,000 | 0.35 | 0.75 | 2.00 | 4.00 | — |
| 1949B | 29,518,000 | 0.35 | 0.75 | 2.00 | 4.00 | — |

**10 FRANCS** **KM# 909.1** **Weight:** 10.0000 g. **Composition:** 0.6800 Silver .2186 oz. ASW **Obverse:** Small head **Note:** Without mint mark. Struck at Paris Mint.

| Date | Mintage | F | VF | XF | Unc | BU |
|---|---|---|---|---|---|---|
| 1947 | Inc. above | 0.30 | 0.75 | 1.50 | 3.50 | — |
| 1948 | 155,945,000 | 0.20 | 0.35 | 0.75 | 2.00 | — |
| 1949 | 118,149,000 | 0.20 | 0.35 | 0.75 | 2.00 | — |

**10 FRANCS** **KM# 915.1** **Composition:** Aluminum-Bronze **Note:** Without mint mark. Struck at Paris Mint.

| Date | Mintage | F | VF | XF | Unc | BU |
|---|---|---|---|---|---|---|
| 1950 | 13,534,000 | 0.35 | 0.65 | 1.50 | 5.00 | — |
| 1951 | 153,689,000 | 0.20 | 0.35 | 0.75 | 2.00 | — |
| 1952 | 76,810,000 | 0.20 | 0.35 | 0.75 | 2.00 | — |
| 1953 | 46,272,000 | 0.25 | 0.50 | 0.75 | 2.50 | — |
| 1954 | 2,207,000 | 5.00 | 15.00 | 30.00 | 50.00 | — |
| 1955 | 47,466,000 | 0.20 | 0.35 | 0.75 | 2.50 | — |
| 1956 Reported, not confirmed | 2,570,000 | — | — | — | — | — |
| 1957 | 26,351,000 | 0.50 | 1.00 | 2.00 | 4.50 | — |
| 1958 (w) | 27,213,000 | 0.50 | 1.00 | 2.00 | 4.50 | — |
| 1959 Reported, not confirmed | 125,000 | — | — | — | — | — |

**10 FRANCS** **KM# 915.2** **Composition:** Aluminum-Bronze

| Date | Mintage | F | VF | XF | Unc | BU |
|---|---|---|---|---|---|---|
| 1950B | 4,808,000 | 1.00 | 3.00 | 6.00 | 17.50 | — |
| 1951B | 106,866,000 | 0.20 | 0.35 | 0.75 | 2.00 | — |
| 1952B | 72,346,000 | 0.20 | 0.35 | 0.75 | 2.00 | — |
| 1953B | 36,466,000 | 0.25 | 0.50 | 1.00 | 3.00 | — |
| 1954B | 21,634,000 | 0.75 | 1.50 | 3.50 | 7.00 | — |
| 1958B Reported, not confirmed | 1,500,000 | — | — | — | — | — |

**10 FRANCS** KM# 932 **Weight:** 25.0000 g. **Composition:** 0.9000 Silver .7234 oz. ASW **Note:** Without mint mark. Struck at Paris Mint.

| Date | Mintage | F | VF | XF | Unc | BU |
|---|---|---|---|---|---|---|
| 1965 | 8,051,000 | — | BV | 6.00 | 10.00 | — |
| 1966 | 9,800,000 | — | BV | 6.00 | 10.00 | — |
| 1967 | 10,100,000 | — | BV | 6.00 | 10.00 | — |
| 1968 | 3,887,000 | — | BV | 8.00 | 12.00 | — |
| 1969 | 761,000 | — | BV | 10.00 | 15.00 | — |
| 1970 | 5,013,000 | — | BV | 6.00 | 10.00 | — |
| 1971 | 513,000 | — | BV | 10.00 | 17.50 | — |
| 1972 | 915,000 | — | BV | 8.00 | 12.00 | — |
| 1973 | 207,000 | — | BV | 10.00 | 20.00 | — |

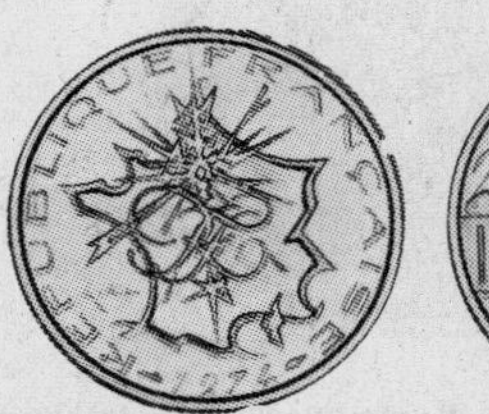

**10 FRANCS** KM# 940 **Composition:** Nickel-Brass

| Date | Mintage | F | VF | XF | Unc | BU |
|---|---|---|---|---|---|---|
| 1974 | 22,447,000 | — | — | 2.00 | 2.50 | — |
| 1975 | 59,013,000 | — | — | 2.00 | 2.50 | — |
| 1976 | 104,093,000 | — | — | 2.00 | 2.50 | — |
| 1977 | 100,028,000 | — | — | 2.00 | 2.50 | — |
| 1978 | 97,590,000 | — | — | 2.00 | 2.50 | — |
| 1979 | 110,000,000 | — | — | 2.00 | 2.50 | — |
| 1980 | 80,010,000 | — | — | 2.00 | 2.50 | — |
| 1981 | 50,000 | — | — | — | 2.75 | — |
| 1982 | 74,000 | — | — | — | 2.75 | — |
| 1983 | 101,000 | — | — | — | 2.75 | — |
| 1984 | 39,988,000 | — | — | 2.00 | 2.50 | — |
| 1985 | 30,000,000 | — | — | 2.00 | 2.50 | — |
| 1987 | Est. 50,000,000 | — | — | — | 2.50 | — |

**10 FRANCS** KM# 950 **Composition:** Nickel-Bronze **Subject:** 100th Anniversary - Death of Leon Gambetta **Reverse:** Head of Gambetta left

| Date | Mintage | F | VF | XF | Unc | BU |
|---|---|---|---|---|---|---|
| 1982 | 3,045,000 | — | — | 2.50 | 4.00 | — |

**10 FRANCS** KM# 952 **Composition:** Nickel-Bronze **Subject:** 200th Anniversary - Montgolfier Balloon **Reverse:** Balloon

| Date | Mintage | F | VF | XF | Unc | BU |
|---|---|---|---|---|---|---|
| 1983 | 3,001,000 | — | — | 2.50 | 4.00 | — |

**10 FRANCS** KM# 953 **Composition:** Nickel-Bronze **Subject:** 200th Anniversary - Birth of Stendhal **Obverse:** Head of Stendhal facing

| Date | Mintage | F | VF | XF | Unc | BU |
|---|---|---|---|---|---|---|
| 1983 | 2,951,000 | — | — | 2.50 | 4.00 | — |

**10 FRANCS** KM# 954 **Composition:** Nickel-Bronze **Subject:** 200th Anniversary - Birth of Francois Rude **Obverse:** Head of Francois Rude 1/2 right

| Date | Mintage | F | VF | XF | Unc | BU |
|---|---|---|---|---|---|---|
| 1984 | 10,000,000 | — | — | 2.50 | 3.50 | — |

**10 FRANCS** KM# 956 **Composition:** Nickel-Bronze **Subject:** Centennial - Death of Victor Hugo **Reverse:** Head of Hugo facing

| Date | Mintage | F | VF | XF | Unc | BU |
|---|---|---|---|---|---|---|
| 1985 | 10,000,000 | — | — | 2.50 | 3.50 | — |

**10 FRANCS** KM# 956a **Weight:** 12.0000 g. **Composition:** 0.9000 Silver .3472 oz. ASW **Subject:** Centennial - Death of Victor Hugo **Reverse:** Head of Hugo facing

| Date | Mintage | F | VF | XF | Unc | BU |
|---|---|---|---|---|---|---|
| 1985 | 20,000 | — | — | — | 20.00 | — |

**10 FRANCS** KM# 956b **Weight:** 12.0000 g. **Composition:** 0.9990 Silver .3854 oz. ASW **Subject:** Centennial - Death of Victor Hugo **Reverse:** Head of Hugo facing

| Date | Mintage | F | VF | XF | Unc | BU |
|---|---|---|---|---|---|---|
| 1985 Proof | 8,000 | Value: 40.00 | | | | |

**10 FRANCS** KM# 958 **Composition:** Nickel **Subject:** 100th Anniversary - Birth of Robert Schuman **Obverse:** Rooster at left, denomination right **Reverse:** Half head of Schuman right

| Date | Mintage | F | VF | XF | Unc | BU |
|---|---|---|---|---|---|---|
| 1986 | 9,961,000 | — | — | 3.00 | 6.50 | — |

**10 FRANCS** KM# 958a **Weight:** 7.0000 g. **Composition:** 0.9000 Silver .2025 oz. ASW **Obverse:** Rooster at left, denomination right **Reverse:** Half head of Schuman right

| Date | Mintage | F | VF | XF | Unc | BU |
|---|---|---|---|---|---|---|
| 1986 | 20,000 | — | — | — | 18.50 | — |

**10 FRANCS** KM# 958b **Weight:** 7.0000 g. **Composition:** 0.9500 Silver .2138 oz. ASW **Obverse:** Rooster at left, denomination right **Reverse:** Half head of Schuman right

| Date | Mintage | F | VF | XF | Unc | BU |
|---|---|---|---|---|---|---|
| 1986 Proof | 6,000 | Value: 45.00 | | | | |

**10 FRANCS** KM# 958c **Weight:** 7.0000 g. **Composition:** 0.9200 Gold .2071 oz. AGW **Subject:** 100th Anniversary - Birth of Robert Schuman **Obverse:** Rooster at left, denomination right **Reverse:** Half head of Schuman right

| Date | Mintage | F | VF | XF | Unc | BU |
|---|---|---|---|---|---|---|
| 1986 Proof | 5,000 | Value: 150 | | | | |

**10 FRANCS** KM# 959 **Composition:** Nickel **Reverse:** Madam Republic

| Date | Mintage | F | VF | XF | Unc | BU |
|---|---|---|---|---|---|---|
| 1986 | 110,015,000 | — | — | 3.00 | 8.00 | — |

**Note:** Recalled and melted, no longer legal tender

**10 FRANCS** KM# 961 **Weight:** 12.0000 g. **Composition:** 0.9000 Silver .3473 oz. ASW **Subject:** Millennium of King Capet and France

| Date | Mintage | F | VF | XF | Unc | BU |
|---|---|---|---|---|---|---|
| 1987 | 20,000 | — | — | — | 18.50 | — |

**10 FRANCS** KM# 961a **Weight:** 12.0000 g. **Composition:** 0.9500 Silver .3665 oz. ASW **Subject:** Millennium of King Capet and France

| Date | Mintage | F | VF | XF | Unc | BU |
|---|---|---|---|---|---|---|
| 1987 Proof | 10,000 | Value: 40.00 | | | | |

**10 FRANCS** KM# 961b **Weight:** 12.0000 g. **Composition:** 0.9200 Gold .3549 oz. AGW **Subject:** Millennium of King Capet and France

| Date | Mintage | F | VF | XF | Unc | BU |
|---|---|---|---|---|---|---|
| 1987 Proof | 6,000 | Value: 200 | | | | |

**10 FRANCS** KM# 961c **Weight:** 14.0000 g. **Composition:** 0.9990 Platinum .4497 oz. APW **Subject:** Millennium of King Capet and France

| Date | Mintage | F | VF | XF | Unc | BU |
|---|---|---|---|---|---|---|
| 1987 Proof | 1,000 | Value: 340 | | | | |

**10 FRANCS** KM# 961d **Composition:** Nickel-Bronze **Subject:** Millennium of King Capet and France

| Date | Mintage | F | VF | XF | Unc | BU |
|---|---|---|---|---|---|---|
| 1987 | 70,000,000 | — | — | 3.00 | 6.50 | — |

**10 FRANCS** KM# 964.1 **Ring Composition:** Aluminum-Bronze **Center Composition:** Steel **Subject:** Spirit of Bastille

| Date | Mintage | F | VF | XF | Unc | BU |
|---|---|---|---|---|---|---|
| 1988 | 100,000,000 | — | — | 2.50 | 6.00 | — |
| 1989 | 249,980,000 | — | — | 2.50 | 6.00 | — |
| 1990 | 250,000,000 | — | — | 2.50 | 6.00 | — |
| 1991 | — | — | — | 2.50 | 6.50 | — |

**Note:** Exist in both medal and coin alignment

| Date | Mintage | F | VF | XF | Unc | BU |
|---|---|---|---|---|---|---|
| 1992 | — | — | — | 2.50 | 6.50 | — |

**Note:** Exists in both medal and coin alignment

**10 FRANCS** KM# 964.1a **Ring Composition:** 0.9200 Gold **Center Composition:** Gold With Palladium And Silver Alloys **Subject:** Spirit of Bastille

| Date | Mintage | F | VF | XF | Unc | BU |
|---|---|---|---|---|---|---|
| 1988 Proof | 5,000 | Value: 325 | | | | |

**10 FRANCS** KM# 965 **Composition:** Aluminum-Bronze **Subject:** 100th Anniversary - Birth of Roland Garros

| Date | Mintage | F | VF | XF | Unc | BU |
|---|---|---|---|---|---|---|
| 1988 | 30,000,000 | — | — | 2.50 | 4.00 | — |

**10 FRANCS** KM# 965a **Weight:** 12.0000 g. **Composition:** 0.9000 Silver .3472 oz. ASW

| Date | Mintage | F | VF | XF | Unc | BU |
|---|---|---|---|---|---|---|
| 1988 | 10,000 | — | — | — | 18.50 | — |

**10 FRANCS** KM# 965b **Weight:** 12.0000 g. **Composition:** 0.9500 Silver .3665 oz. ASW

| Date | Mintage | F | VF | XF | Unc | BU |
|---|---|---|---|---|---|---|
| 1988 Proof | 10,000 | Value: 35.00 | | | | |

**10 FRANCS KM# 965c Weight:** 12.0000 g. **Composition:** 0.9200 Gold .3550 oz. AGW **Subject:** 100th Anniversary - Birth of Roland Garros

| Date | Mintage | F | VF | XF | Unc | BU |
|---|---|---|---|---|---|---|
| 1988 Proof | 3,000 | Value: 210 | | | | |

**10 FRANCS KM# 969 Ring Composition:** Aluminum-Bronze **Center Composition:** Steel **Subject:** 300th Anniversary - Birth of Montesquieu **Obverse:** Bust of Montesquieu right

| Date | Mintage | F | VF | XF | Unc | BU |
|---|---|---|---|---|---|---|
| 1989 | 15,000 | — | — | 6.50 | 17.50 | — |

**Note:** As of 8/99, still not released

**10 FRANCS KM# 969a Ring Composition:** 0.9200 Gold **Center Composition:** Gold With Palladium And Silver Alloys **Subject:** 300th Anniversary - Birth of Montesquieu **Obverse:** Bust of Montesquieu right

| Date | Mintage | F | VF | XF | Unc | BU |
|---|---|---|---|---|---|---|
| 1989 Proof | 5,000 | Value: 325 | | | | |

**Note:** As of 8/99, still not released

**10 FRANCS KM# 964.2 Composition:** Aluminum-Bronze **Edge:** Plain

| Date | Mintage | F | VF | XF | Unc | BU |
|---|---|---|---|---|---|---|
| 1991 | 249,989,000 | — | — | — | — | — |
| **Note:** Exist in both medal and coin alignment | | | | | | |
| 1991 Proof | 10,000 | Value: 15.00 | | | | |
| 1992 | 99,986,000 | — | — | — | 6.00 | — |
| **Note:** Exist in both medal and coin alignment | | | | | | |
| 1992 Proof | 15,000 | Value: 15.00 | | | | |
| 1993 | 20,000 | — | — | — | 6.00 | — |
| 1993 Proof | 10,000 | Value: 15.00 | | | | |
| 1994 (Bee) | 20,000 | — | — | — | 6.00 | — |
| 1994 (Fish) Proof | 10,000 | Value: 15.00 | | | | |
| 1995 | 25,000 | — | — | — | 6.00 | — |
| 1995 Proof | 10,000 | Value: 15.00 | | | | |
| 1996 | 17,000 | — | — | — | 6.00 | — |
| 1996 Proof | 8,000 | Value: 15.00 | | | | |
| 1997 | 15,000 | — | — | — | 6.00 | — |
| 1997 Proof | 10,000 | Value: 15.00 | | | | |
| 1998 | — | — | — | — | 6.00 | — |
| 1998 Proof | — | Value: 15.00 | | | | |
| 1999 | — | — | — | — | 6.00 | — |
| 1999 Proof | — | Value: 15.00 | | | | |
| 2000 | — | — | — | — | 6.00 | — |
| 2000 Proof | — | Value: 15.00 | | | | |

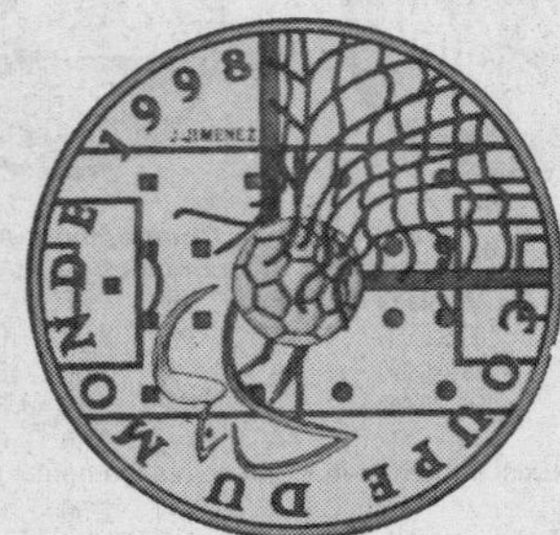


**10 FRANCS KM# 1144 Weight:** 21.1600 g. **Composition:** 0.9000 Silver .6412 oz. ASW **Subject:** World Cup - Coupe du Monde 1998 **Obverse:** World Cup 1998 logo above denomination **Reverse:** Soccer ball breaking net, stylized dove

| Date | Mintage | F | VF | XF | Unc | BU |
|---|---|---|---|---|---|---|
| 1996 Proof | Est. 40,000 | Value: 40.00 | | | | |

**10 FRANCS KM# 1166 Weight:** 21.1600 g. **Composition:** 0.9000 Silver .6412 oz. ASW **Subject:** World Cup - Uruguay 1930 1958 **Obverse:** World Cup 1998 logo above denoomination **Reverse:** Stylized gaucho and soccer player

| Date | Mintage | F | VF | XF | Unc | BU |
|---|---|---|---|---|---|---|
| 1996 Proof | 100,000 | Value: 35.00 | | | | |

**10 FRANCS KM# 1161 Weight:** 21.1600 g. **Composition:** 0.9000 Silver .6412 oz. ASW **Subject:** World Cup - Argentina 1978 1986 **Obverse:** World Cup 1998 logo above denoomination **Reverse:** Stylized bull and soccer player

| Date | Mintage | F | VF | XF | Unc | BU |
|---|---|---|---|---|---|---|
| 1997 Proof | 100,000 | Value: 35.00 | | | | |

**10 FRANCS KM# 1163 Weight:** 21.1600 g. **Composition:** 0.9000 Silver .6412 oz. ASW **Subject:** World Cup - England 1966 **Obverse:** World Cup 1998 logo above denomination **Reverse:** Big Ben and soccer player

| Date | Mintage | F | VF | XF | Unc | BU |
|---|---|---|---|---|---|---|
| 1997 Proof | 100,000 | Value: 35.00 | | | | |

**10 FRANCS KM# 1164 Weight:** 21.1600 g. **Composition:** 0.9000 Silver .6412 oz. ASW **Subject:** World Cup - Germany 1954 1974 1990 **Obverse:** World Cup 1998 logo above denoomination **Reverse:** Brandenburg gate, soccer player

| Date | Mintage | F | VF | XF | Unc | BU |
|---|---|---|---|---|---|---|
| 1997 Proof | 100,000 | Value: 35.00 | | | | |

**10 FRANCS KM# 1165 Weight:** 21.1600 g. **Composition:** 0.9000 Silver .6412 oz. ASW **Subject:** World Cup - Italy 1934 1938 1982 **Obverse:** World Cup 1998 logo above denomination **Reverse:** Colosseum and soccer player

| Date | Mintage | F | VF | XF | Unc | BU |
|---|---|---|---|---|---|---|
| 1997 Proof | 100,000 | Value: 35.00 | | | | |

**10 FRANCS KM# 1162 Weight:** 21.1600 g. **Composition:** 0.9000 Silver .6412 oz. ASW **Subject:** World Cup - Brazil 1958 1968 1970 1994 **Obverse:** World Cup 1998 logo above denoomination **Reverse:** Pavilion and soccer player

| Date | Mintage | F | VF | XF | Unc | BU |
|---|---|---|---|---|---|---|
| 1998 Proof | 100,000 | Value: 35.00 | | | | |

**10 FRANCS KM# 1167 Weight:** 21.1600 g. **Composition:** 0.9000 Silver .6412 oz. ASW **Subject:** World Cup - Coupe du Monte **Obverse:** World Cup 1998 logo above denoomination **Reverse:** World Cup trophy and 11 French city arms

| Date | Mintage | F | VF | XF | Unc | BU |
|---|---|---|---|---|---|---|
| 1998 Proof | 100,000 | Value: 35.00 | | | | |

**10 FRANCS KM# 1205 Weight:** 22.2000 g. **Composition:** 0.9000 Silver .6424 oz. ASW **Series:** Treasures of the Nile - J.F. Champollion **Obverse:** Portrait and obelisk **Reverse:** Sphinx and pyramids

| Date | Mintage | F | VF | XF | Unc | BU |
|---|---|---|---|---|---|---|
| 1998 Proof | 15,000 | Value: 38.50 | | | | |

**10 FRANCS KM# 1206 Weight:** 22.2000 g. **Composition:** 0.9000 Silver .6424 oz. ASW **Series:** Treasures of the Nile - Nefertiti **Obverse:** Crowned bust **Reverse:** Sphinx and pyramids

| Date | Mintage | F | VF | XF | Unc | BU |
|---|---|---|---|---|---|---|
| 1998 Proof | 15,000 | Value: 38.50 | | | | |

**10 FRANCS KM# 1207 Weight:** 22.2000 g. **Composition:** 0.9000 Silver .6424 oz. ASW **Series:** Treasures of the Nile - Ramses II **Obverse:** Seated figure **Reverse:** Sphinx and pyramids

| Date | Mintage | F | VF | XF | Unc | BU |
|---|---|---|---|---|---|---|
| 1998 Proof | 15,000 | Value: 38.50 | | | | |

**10 FRANCS KM# 1216 Weight:** 22.2300 g. **Composition:** 0.9000 Silver .6432 oz. ASW **Series:** XXth Century - Biology and Medicine **Obverse:** Double X design **Reverse:** Parents, fetus, hands **Edge:** Plain **Note:** Struck at Paris Mint.

| Date | Mintage | F | VF | XF | Unc | BU |
|---|---|---|---|---|---|---|
| 2000 Proof | 10,000 | Value: 40.00 | | | | |

**10 FRANCS KM# 1217 Weight:** 22.2300 g. **Composition:** 0.9000 Silver .6432 oz. ASW **Series:** XXth Century - Physical Sciences **Obverse:** Einstein's portrait, atom and planets **Note:** Struck at Paris Mint.

| Date | Mintage | F | VF | XF | Unc | BU |
|---|---|---|---|---|---|---|
| 2000 Proof | 10,000 | Value: 40.00 | | | | |

**10 FRANCS KM# 1218 Weight:** 22.2300 g. **Composition:** 0.9000 Silver .6432 oz. ASW **Series:** XXth Century - Communications **Obverse:** World, satellites and keyboard **Note:** Struck at Paris Mint.

| Date | Mintage | F | VF | XF | Unc | BU |
|---|---|---|---|---|---|---|
| 2000 Proof | 10,000 | Value: 40.00 | | | | |

**10 FRANCS KM# 1219 Weight:** 22.2300 g. **Composition:** 0.9000 Silver .6432 oz. ASW **Series:** XXth Century - The Automobile **Obverse:** Race cars above horse **Note:** Struck at Paris Mint.

| Date | Mintage | F | VF | XF | Unc | BU |
|---|---|---|---|---|---|---|
| 2000 Proof | 10,000 | Value: 40.00 | | | | |

**10 FRANCS KM# 1220 Weight:** 22.2300 g. **Composition:** 0.9000 Silver .6432 oz. ASW **Series:** XXth Century - Flight **Obverse:** Icarus in flight above Bleriot monoplane **Note:** Struck at Paris Mint.

| Date | Mintage | F | VF | XF | Unc | BU |
|---|---|---|---|---|---|---|
| 2000 Proof | 10,000 | Value: 40.00 | | | | |

**10 FRANCS KM# 1221 Weight:** 22.2300 g. **Composition:** 0.9000 Silver .6432 oz. ASW **Series:** XXth Century - Space Travel **Reverse:** Astronaut weightless in space amidst planets **Note:** Struck at Paris Mint.

| Date | Mintage | F | VF | XF | Unc | BU |
|---|---|---|---|---|---|---|
| 2000 Proof | 10,000 | Value: 40.00 | | | | |

**10 FRANCS KM# 1229 Weight:** 22.2000 g. **Composition:** 0.9000 Silver .6424 oz. ASW **Subject:** 2000 Years - French Coinage **Obverse:** Denomination **Reverse:** 1st century B.C. Celtic Parisii Stater coin design **Edge:** Plain **Note:** Struck at Paris Mint.

| Date | Mintage | F | VF | XF | Unc | BU |
|---|---|---|---|---|---|---|
| 2000 Proof | 10,000 | Value: 37.50 | | | | |

**10 FRANCS KM# 1230 Weight:** 22.2000 g. **Composition:** 0.9000 Silver .6424 oz. ASW **Reverse:** Charlemagne Denar coin design **Note:** Struck at Paris Mint.

| Date | Mintage | F | VF | XF | Unc | BU |
|---|---|---|---|---|---|---|
| 2000 Proof | 10,000 | Value: 37.50 | | | | |

**10 FRANCS KM# 1231 Weight:** 22.2000 g. **Composition:** 0.9000 Silver .6424 oz. ASW **Subject:** 2000 Years of French Coinage **Obverse:** Denomination **Reverse:** Louis IX gold ecu coin design **Edge:** Plain **Note:** Struck at Paris Mint.

| Date | Mintage | F | VF | XF | Unc | BU |
|---|---|---|---|---|---|---|
| 2000 Proof | 10,000 | Value: 37.50 | | | | |

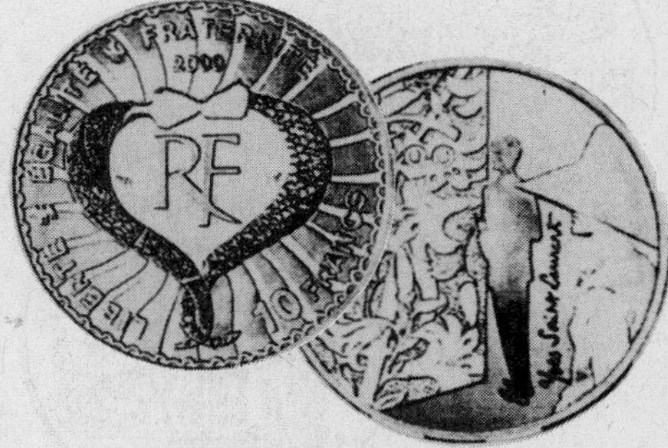

**10 FRANCS KM# 1235 Weight:** 22.2000 g. **Composition:** 0.9000 Silver .6424 oz. ASW **Subject:** Yves St. Laurent **Obverse:** RF monogram **Reverse:** Fashion show scene **Note:** Struck at Paris Mint.

| Date | Mintage | F | VF | XF | Unc | BU |
|---|---|---|---|---|---|---|
| 2000 Proof | 30,000 | Value: 37.50 | | | | |

**10 FRANCS KM# 1263 Weight:** 22.2000 g. **Composition:** 0.9000 Silver .6424 oz. ASW **Subject:** Antoine de St. Exupery **Obverse:** RF Monogram, portrait and bi-plane **Reverse:** Multicolor "Little Prince" character and denomination **Note:** Struck at Paris Mint.

| Date | Mintage | F | VF | XF | Unc | BU |
|---|---|---|---|---|---|---|
| 2000 Proof | 10,000 | Value: 47.50 | | | | |

**10 FRANCS** **KM# 1268** **Weight:** 22.2000 g. **Composition:** 0.9000 Silver .6424 oz. ASW **Subject:** Palace of Versailles **Obverse:** Stylized French map **Reverse:** Louis XIV with internal and external palace views **Edge:** Plain

| Date | Mintage | F | VF | XF | Unc | BU |
|---|---|---|---|---|---|---|
| 2001 Proof | Est. 20,000 | Value: 35.00 | | | | |

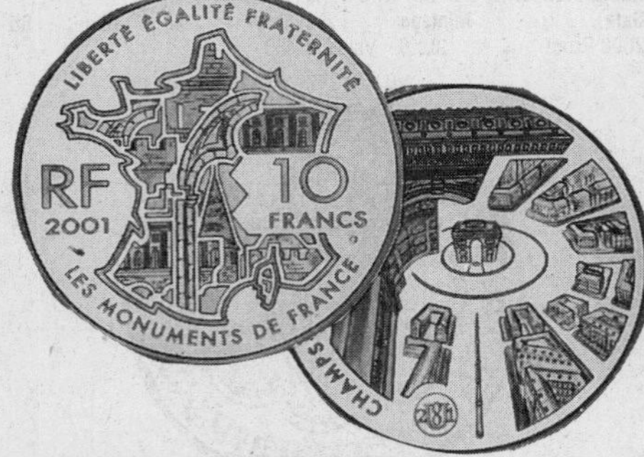


**10 FRANCS** **KM# 1270** **Weight:** 22.2000 g. **Composition:** 0.9000 Silver .6424 oz. ASW **Obverse:** Champs-Elysees **Reverse:** Arch of Triumph partial close up and aerial views

| Date | Mintage | F | VF | XF | Unc | BU |
|---|---|---|---|---|---|---|
| 2001 Proof | Est. 20,000 | Value: 35.00 | | | | |

**10 FRANCS** **KM# 1272** **Weight:** 22.2000 g. **Composition:** 0.9000 Silver .6424 oz. ASW **Obverse:** Notre-Dame Cathedral **Reverse:** Gargoyle and cathedral views

| Date | Mintage | F | VF | XF | Unc | BU |
|---|---|---|---|---|---|---|
| 2001 Proof | Est. 20,000 | Value: 35.00 | | | | |

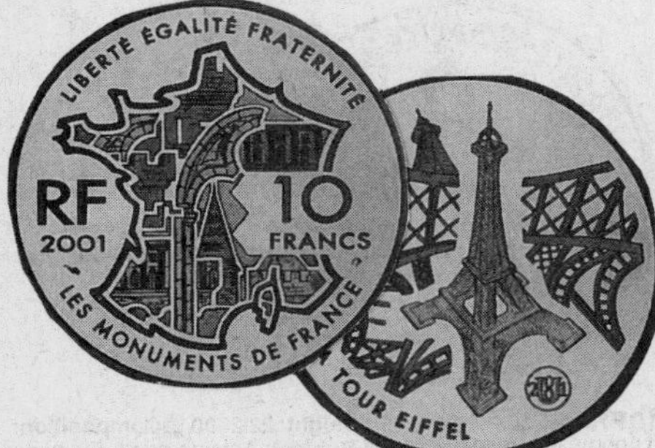


**10 FRANCS** **KM# 1274** **Weight:** 22.2000 g. **Composition:** 0.9000 Silver .6424 oz. ASW **Obverse:** Eiffel Tower **Reverse:** Two tower views

| Date | Mintage | F | VF | XF | Unc | BU |
|---|---|---|---|---|---|---|
| 2001 Proof | Est. 20,000 | Value: 35.00 | | | | |

**20 FRANCS** **KM# 847** **Weight:** 6.4516 g. **Composition:** 0.9000 Gold .1867 oz. AGW **Edge Lettering:** DIEU PROTEGE LA FRANCE

| Date | Mintage | F | VF | XF | Unc | BU |
|---|---|---|---|---|---|---|
| 1901 | 2,643,000 | BV | 70.00 | 80.00 | 125 | — |
| 1901 | 2,643,000 | BV | 70.00 | 80.00 | 125 | — |
| 1902 | 2,394,000 | BV | 70.00 | 80.00 | 125 | — |
| 1902 | 2,394,000 | BV | 70.00 | 80.00 | 125 | — |
| 1903 | 4,405,000 | BV | 70.00 | 80.00 | 125 | — |
| 1904 | 7,706,000 | BV | 70.00 | 80.00 | 125 | — |
| 1905 | 9,158,000 | BV | 70.00 | 80.00 | 125 | — |
| 1906 | 14,613,000 | BV | 70.00 | 80.00 | 125 | — |

**20 FRANCS** **KM# 857** **Weight:** 6.4516 g. **Composition:** 0.9000 Gold .1867 oz. AGW **Edge Lettering:** LIBERTE EGALITE FRATERNITE **Note:** ALl dates from 1907-1914 have been officially restruck.

| Date | Mintage | F | VF | XF | Unc | BU |
|---|---|---|---|---|---|---|
| 1906 | — | BV | 65.00 | 75.00 | 115 | — |
| 1907 | 17,716,000 | BV | 65.00 | 75.00 | 115 | — |
| 1908 | 6,721,000 | BV | 65.00 | 75.00 | 115 | — |
| 1909 | 9,637,000 | BV | 65.00 | 75.00 | 115 | — |
| 1910 | 5,779,000 | BV | 65.00 | 75.00 | 115 | — |
| 1911 | 5,346,000 | BV | 65.00 | 75.00 | 115 | — |
| 1912 | 10,332,000 | BV | 65.00 | 75.00 | 115 | — |
| 1913 | 12,163,000 | BV | 65.00 | 75.00 | 115 | — |
| 1914 | 6,518,000 | BV | 65.00 | 75.00 | 115 | — |

**20 FRANCS** **KM# 879** **Weight:** 20.0000 g. **Composition:** 0.6800 Silver .4372 oz. ASW **Reverse:** Long Leaves & Short Leaves **Note:** Without mint mark. Struck at Paris Mint.

| Date | Mintage | F | VF | XF | Unc | BU |
|---|---|---|---|---|---|---|
| 1929 (ll) | 3,234,000 | BV | 6.00 | 9.00 | 35.00 | — |
| 1933 (sl) | — | BV | 4.50 | 5.50 | 18.00 | — |

**Note:** Counterfeits exist in bronze-aluminum with thin silver sheath

| Date | Mintage | F | VF | XF | Unc | BU |
|---|---|---|---|---|---|---|
| 1933 (ll) | Inc. above | BV | 4.50 | 5.50 | 18.00 | — |
| 1934 (sl) | 11,785,000 | BV | 4.50 | 10.00 | 30.00 | — |
| 1936 (sl) | 48,000 | 200 | 300 | 450 | — | — |
| 1937 (sl) | 1,189,000 | 10.00 | 15.00 | 25.00 | 50.00 | — |
| 1938 (sl) | 10,910,000 | BV | 4.50 | 7.00 | 20.00 | — |
| 1939 (sl) | 3,918 | 1,000 | 2,000 | 2,750 | 4,500 | — |

**20 FRANCS** **KM# 917.1** **Composition:** Aluminum-Bronze **Obverse:** G. GUIRAUD behind head **Note:** Without mint mark. Struck at Paris Mint.

| Date | Mintage | F | VF | XF | Unc | BU |
|---|---|---|---|---|---|---|
| 1950 (3 plumes) | 120,656,000 | 2.00 | 6.00 | 12.00 | 40.00 | — |
| 1950 (4 plumes) | Inc. above | 0.25 | 0.40 | 1.00 | 2.50 | — |
| 1951 (4 plumes) | 97,922,000 | 0.25 | 0.40 | 1.00 | 2.50 | — |
| 1952 (4 plumes) | 130,281,000 | 0.25 | 0.40 | 1.00 | 2.50 | — |
| 1953 (4 plumes) | 60,158,000 | 0.30 | 0.50 | 1.00 | 2.50 | — |

**20 FRANCS** **KM# 916.1** **Composition:** Aluminum-Bronze **Obverse:** GEORGES GUIRAUD behind head

| Date | Mintage | F | VF | XF | Unc | BU |
|---|---|---|---|---|---|---|
| 1950 (3 plumes) | 5,779,000 | 0.50 | 1.00 | 2.50 | 7.00 | — |
| 1950 (4 plumes) | — | 125 | 200 | 350 | 700 | — |

**20 FRANCS** **KM# 916.2** **Composition:** Aluminum-Bronze

| Date | Mintage | F | VF | XF | Unc | BU |
|---|---|---|---|---|---|---|
| 1950B (3 plumes) | — | 1.50 | 3.00 | 7.00 | 20.00 | — |
| 1950B (4 plumes) | — | 40.00 | 85.00 | 150 | 225 | — |

**20 FRANCS** **KM# 917.2** **Composition:** Aluminum-Bronze

| Date | Mintage | F | VF | XF | Unc | BU |
|---|---|---|---|---|---|---|
| 1950B (3 plumes) | 43,355,000 | 25.00 | 35.00 | 50.00 | 135 | — |
| 1950B (4 plumes) | Inc. above | 0.50 | 1.00 | 3.00 | 6.50 | — |
| 1951B (4 plumes) | 46,815,000 | 0.30 | 0.50 | 1.75 | 3.50 | — |
| 1952B (4 plumes) | 54,381,000 | 0.30 | 0.50 | 1.75 | 3.50 | — |
| 1953B (4 plumes) | 42,410,000 | 0.30 | 0.50 | 1.75 | 3.50 | — |
| 1954B (4 plumes) | 1,573,000 | 125 | 200 | 350 | 900 | — |

**20 FRANCS** **KM# 1008.2b** **Note:** .920 Gold center plug, .750 Gold inner ring, .920 Gold outer ring.

| Date | Mintage | F | VF | XF | Unc | BU |
|---|---|---|---|---|---|---|
| 1992 Proof | 5,000 | Value: 375 | | | | |

**20 FRANCS** **KM# 1008.2a** **Obverse:** Mont St. Michel; 5 bands of stripes in outer ring **Note:** 12.6600 g, .720 Gold center plug, .950 Silver inner ring, .750 Gold outer ring.

| Date | Mintage | F | VF | XF | Unc | BU |
|---|---|---|---|---|---|---|
| 1992 Proof | 15,000 | Value: 200 | | | | |

**20 FRANCS** **KM# 1008.1** **Obverse:** Mont St. Michel **Edge:** 4 milled bands **Note:** Copper-Aluminum-Nickel center plug, Nickel inner ring, Copper-Aluminum-Nickel outer ring.

| Date | Mintage | F | VF | XF | Unc | BU |
|---|---|---|---|---|---|---|
| 1992 closed V in outer ring | 60,000,000 | — | — | — | 15.00 | — |
| 1992 open V in outer ring | Inc. above | — | — | — | 15.00 | — |

**20 FRANCS** **KM# 1008.2** **Edge:** 5 milled bands **Note:** Copper-Aluminum-Nickel center plug, Nickel inner ring, Copper-Aluminum-Nickel outer ring.

| Date | Mintage | F | VF | XF | Unc | BU |
|---|---|---|---|---|---|---|
| 1992 closed V in outer ring | 59,986,000 | — | — | — | 6.50 | — |
| 1992 open V in outer ring | Inc. above | — | — | — | 6.50 | — |
| 1992 Proof | 15,000 | Value: 25.00 | | | | |
| **Note:** Non-Proof, exist in both coin and medal alignment | | | | | | |
| 1993 | 54,990,000 | — | — | — | 7.00 | — |
| **Note:** Non-Proof, exist in both coin and medal alignment | | | | | | |
| 1993 Proof | 10,000 | Value: 25.00 | | | | |
| **Note:** Non-Proof, exist in both coin and medal alignment | | | | | | |
| 1994 | — | — | — | — | 8.00 | — |
| 1994 Proof | — | Value: 25.00 | | | | |
| 1994 (Fish) | 5,000,000 | — | — | — | 10.00 | — |
| 1994 (Fish) Proof | 10,000 | Value: 25.00 | | | | |
| 1994 (Bee) | 9,990,000 | — | — | — | 9.00 | — |
| 1995 | 9,996,000 | — | — | — | 9.00 | — |
| 1995 Proof | 10,000 | Value: 25.00 | | | | |
| 1996 | 17,000 | — | — | — | 6.50 | — |
| 1996 Proof | 8,000 | Value: 25.00 | | | | |
| 1997 | 15,000 | — | — | — | 8.00 | — |
| 1997 Proof | 10,000 | Value: 25.00 | | | | |
| 1998 | — | — | — | — | 8.00 | — |
| 1998 Proof | — | Value: 25.00 | | | | |
| 1999 | — | — | — | — | 8.00 | — |

| Date | Mintage | F | VF | XF | Unc | BU |
|---|---|---|---|---|---|---|
| 1999 Proof | — | Value: 25.00 | | | | |
| 2000 | — | — | — | — | 8.00 | — |
| 2000 Proof | — | Value: 25.00 | | | | |

**20 FRANCS** KM# 1016 **Subject:** Mediterranean Games **Note:** Aluminum-Bronze center plug, Nickel inner ring, Copper-Aluminum-Nickel outer ring.

| Date | Mintage | F | VF | XF | Unc | BU |
|---|---|---|---|---|---|---|
| 1993 | 5,001,000 | — | — | — | 10.00 | — |

**20 FRANCS** KM# 1036 **Subject:** Founder of Modern Day Olympics - Pierre de Coubertin **Obverse:** Head of Coubertin left **Note:** Aluminum-Bronze center plug, Nickel inner ring, Copper-Aluminum-Nickel outer ring.

| Date | Mintage | F | VF | XF | Unc | BU |
|---|---|---|---|---|---|---|
| 1994 | 15,000,000 | — | — | — | 10.00 | — |

**50 FRANCS** KM# 831 **Weight:** 16.1290 g. **Composition:** 0.9000 Gold .4467 oz. AGW

| Date | Mintage | F | VF | XF | Unc | BU |
|---|---|---|---|---|---|---|
| 1904A | 20,000 | 300 | 550 | 900 | 1,600 | — |
| 1904A | 20,000 | 300 | 550 | 900 | 1,600 | — |

**50 FRANCS** KM# 918.1 **Composition:** Aluminum-Bronze **Note:** Without mint mark. Struck at Paris Mint.

| Date | Mintage | F | VF | XF | Unc | BU |
|---|---|---|---|---|---|---|
| 1950 | 600,000 | 75.00 | 150 | 350 | 625 | — |
| 1951 | 68,630,000 | 0.50 | 1.00 | 2.25 | 5.50 | — |
| 1952 | 74,212,000 | 0.50 | 1.00 | 2.25 | 5.50 | — |
| 1953 | 63,172,000 | 0.50 | 1.00 | 2.25 | 5.50 | — |
| 1954 | 997,000 | 15.00 | 35.00 | 65.00 | 110 | — |
| 1958 (w) | 501,000 | 25.00 | 60.00 | 110 | 240 | — |

**50 FRANCS** KM# 918.2 **Composition:** Aluminum-Bronze

| Date | Mintage | F | VF | XF | Unc | BU |
|---|---|---|---|---|---|---|
| 1951B | 11,829,000 | 0.75 | 1.50 | 3.00 | 9.00 | — |
| 1952B | 13,432,000 | 1.00 | 2.00 | 5.00 | 15.00 | — |
| 1953B | 23,376,000 | 0.65 | 1.25 | 2.50 | 8.00 | — |
| 1954B | 6,531,000 | 3.00 | 5.50 | 11.50 | 30.00 | — |

**50 FRANCS** KM# 941.2 **Weight:** 30.0000 g. **Composition:** 0.9000 Silver .8682 oz. ASW **Reverse:** Legend begins at the level of the beltline of the boddess of Hercules' left

| Date | Mintage | F | VF | XF | Unc | BU |
|---|---|---|---|---|---|---|
| 1974 | — | 15.00 | 25.00 | 40.00 | 65.00 | — |

**50 FRANCS** KM# 941.1 **Weight:** 30.0000 g. **Composition:** 0.9000 Silver .8682 oz. ASW **Note:** Without mint mark. Struck at Paris Mint.

| Date | Mintage | F | VF | XF | Unc | BU |
|---|---|---|---|---|---|---|
| 1974 | 4,299,000 | — | — | — | 10.00 | — |
| 1975 | 4,551,000 | — | — | — | 12.50 | — |
| 1976 | 7,739,000 | — | — | — | 11.50 | — |
| 1977 | 7,884,000 | — | — | — | 10.00 | — |
| 1978 | 12,028,000 | — | — | — | 10.00 | — |
| 1979 | 12,041,000 | — | — | — | 10.00 | — |
| 1980 In sets only | 60,000 | — | — | — | 50.00 | — |

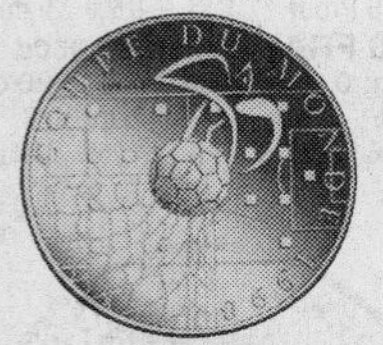

**50 FRANCS** KM# 1145 **Weight:** 8.4521 g. **Composition:** 0.9200 Gold .2500 oz. AGW **Subject:** World Class Soccer **Obverse:** Soccer ball, denomination **Reverse:** Stylized dove, soccer ball

| Date | Mintage | F | VF | XF | Unc | BU |
|---|---|---|---|---|---|---|
| 1996 Proof | Est. 10,000 | Value: 175 | | | | |

**50 FRANCS** KM# 1208 **Weight:** 8.4521 g. **Composition:** 0.9200 Gold .2500 oz. AGW **Subject:** Treasures of the Nile **Obverse:** Portrait and obelisk **Reverse:** Sphinx and pyramids

| Date | Mintage | F | VF | XF | Unc | BU |
|---|---|---|---|---|---|---|
| 1998 Proof | 3,000 | Value: 260 | | | | |

**50 FRANCS** KM# 1236 **Weight:** 8.4521 g. **Composition:** 0.9200 Gold .2500 oz. AGW **Subject:** Yves St. Laurent **Obverse:** RF monogram, denomination **Reverse:** Fashion show scene **Edge:** Plain

| Date | Mintage | F | VF | XF | Unc | BU |
|---|---|---|---|---|---|---|
| 2000 Proof | 2,000 | Value: 250 | | | | |

**65.5997 FRANCS** KM# 1256 **Weight:** 8.4500 g. **Composition:** 0.9250 Gold .2499 oz. AGW **Series:** Euro Conversion Series **Obverse:** Country names with euro currency equivalents around RF, denomination and French coin designs **Reverse:** Europa allegorical portrait **Edge:** Plain

| Date | Mintage | F | VF | XF | Unc | BU |
|---|---|---|---|---|---|---|
| 1999 Proof | 10,000 | Value: 250 | | | | |

**65.5997 FRANCS** KM# 1260 **Weight:** 8.4500 g. **Composition:** 0.9250 Gold .2499 oz. AGW **Obverse:** Country names with euro-currency equivalents around RF, denomination and French euro coin designs

| Date | Mintage | F | VF | XF | Unc | BU |
|---|---|---|---|---|---|---|
| 2000 Proof | 3,000 | Value: 265 | | | | |

**65.5997 FRANCS** KM# 1266 **Weight:** 8.4500 g. **Composition:** 0.9200 Gold .2499 oz. AGW **Subject:** Last Year of the French Franc **Obverse:** French and other European euro currency equivalents **Reverse:** Similar to KM#1258 but with addition of "last year of the franc" logo after the date **Edge:** Reeded

| Date | Mintage | F | VF | XF | Unc | BU |
|---|---|---|---|---|---|---|
| 2001 Proof | 3,000 | Value: 185 | | | | |

**100 FRANCS** KM# 832 **Weight:** 32.2581 g. **Composition:** 0.9000 Gold .9335 oz. AGW **Edge Lettering:** DIEU PROTEGE LA FRANCE

| Date | Mintage | F | VF | XF | Unc | BU |
|---|---|---|---|---|---|---|
| 1900A | 20,000 | 450 | 475 | 525 | 675 | — |
| 1900A Proof | — | Value: 5,000 | | | | |
| 1901A | 10,000 | 450 | 475 | 525 | 675 | — |
| 1901A | 10,000 | 450 | 475 | 525 | 675 | — |
| 1902A | 10,000 | 450 | 475 | 525 | 675 | — |
| 1902A | 10,000 | 450 | 475 | 525 | 675 | — |
| 1903A | 10,000 | 450 | 475 | 525 | 675 | — |
| 1904A | 20,000 | 450 | 475 | 525 | 675 | — |
| 1905A | 10,000 | 450 | 475 | 525 | 675 | — |
| 1906A | 30,000 | 450 | 475 | 525 | 675 | — |

**100 FRANCS** KM# 858 **Weight:** 32.2581 g. **Composition:** 0.9000 Gold .9335 oz. AGW **Edge Lettering:** LIBERTE EGALITE FRATERNITE

| Date | Mintage | F | VF | XF | Unc | BU |
|---|---|---|---|---|---|---|
| 1907 | 20,000 | 350 | 375 | 400 | 550 | — |
| 1908 | 23,000 | 350 | 375 | 400 | 550 | — |
| 1909 | 20,000 | 350 | 375 | 400 | 550 | — |
| 1910 | 20,000 | 350 | 375 | 400 | 550 | — |
| 1911 | 30,000 | 350 | 375 | 400 | 550 | — |
| 1912 | 20,000 | 350 | 375 | 400 | 550 | — |
| 1913 | 30,000 | 350 | 375 | 400 | 550 | — |
| 1914 Rare | 1,281 | — | — | — | — | — |

**100 FRANCS** KM# 880 **Weight:** 6.5500 g. **Composition:** 0.9000 Gold .1895 oz. AGW **Note:** Without mint mark. Struck at Paris Mint.

| Date | Mintage | F | VF | XF | Unc | BU |
|---|---|---|---|---|---|---|
| 1929 | 50 | — | — | 2,500 | 4,000 | — |
| 1932 | Est. 50 | — | — | 3,100 | 4,600 | — |
| 1933 | Est. 300 | — | — | 1,650 | 2,250 | — |
| 1934 Rare | — | — | — | — | — | — |
| 1935 | 6,102,000 | — | — | 500 | 800 | — |
| 1936 | 7,689,000 | — | — | 500 | 800 | — |

**100 FRANCS** KM# 919.1 **Composition:** Copper-Nickel

| Date | Mintage | F | VF | XF | Unc | BU |
|---|---|---|---|---|---|---|
| 1954 | 97,285,000 | 0.50 | 1.00 | 2.50 | 7.00 | — |
| 1955 | 152,517,000 | 0.25 | 0.75 | 1.50 | 4.50 | — |
| 1956 | 7,578,000 | 3.50 | 7.50 | 15.00 | 40.00 | — |
| 1957 | 11,312,000 | 1.50 | 3.00 | 6.00 | 18.00 | — |
| 1958 (w) | 3,256,000 | 2.50 | 5.50 | 12.50 | 35.00 | — |
| 1958 (o) | Inc. above | 20.00 | 40.00 | 90.00 | 175 | — |

**100 FRANCS** KM# 919.2 **Composition:** Copper-Nickel

| Date | Mintage | F | VF | XF | Unc | BU |
|---|---|---|---|---|---|---|
| 1954B | 86,261,000 | 0.50 | 1.25 | 2.50 | 5.00 | — |
| 1955B | 136,585,000 | 0.25 | 0.75 | 1.50 | 3.50 | — |
| 1956B | 19,154,000 | 1.00 | 2.00 | 4.50 | 10.00 | — |
| 1957B | 25,702,000 | 1.00 | 2.00 | 4.50 | 12.50 | — |
| 1958B | 54,072,000 | 1.00 | 2.00 | 4.50 | 11.50 | — |

**100 FRANCS** **KM# 951.1** **Weight:** 15.0000 g. **Composition:** 0.9000 Silver .4340 oz. ASW **Obverse:** Pantheon **Note:** Without mint mark. Struck at Paris Mint.

| Date | Mintage | F | VF | XF | Unc | BU |
|---|---|---|---|---|---|---|
| 1982 | 3,030,000 | — | — | — | 27.50 | — |
| 1982 Proof | 25,000 | Value: 45.00 | | | | |
| 1983 | 5,001,000 | — | — | — | 27.50 | — |
| 1983 Proof | 17,000 | Value: 45.00 | | | | |
| 1984 | 5,000,000 | — | — | — | 27.50 | — |
| 1985 | 999,000 | — | — | — | 30.00 | — |
| 1985 Proof | 13,000 | Value: 45.00 | | | | |
| 1986 | 519,000 | — | — | — | 30.00 | — |
| 1987 | 100,000 | — | — | — | 30.00 | — |
| 1988 | 100,000 | — | — | — | 30.00 | — |
| 1989 | 83,000 | — | — | — | 30.00 | — |
| 1990 | 15,000 | — | — | — | 35.00 | — |
| 1991 | 5,000 | — | — | — | 35.00 | — |
| 1991 Proof | 10,000 | Value: 55.00 | | | | |
| 1992 Proof | 15,000 | Value: 45.00 | | | | |
| 1993 Proof | 15,000 | Value: 45.00 | | | | |
| 1994 Proof | 15,000 | Value: 45.00 | | | | |
| 1995 | 4,011 | — | — | — | 32.00 | — |
| 1995 Proof | 10,000 | Value: 45.00 | | | | |
| 1996 | 2,013 | — | — | — | 40.00 | — |
| 1996 Proof | 8,000 | Value: 50.00 | | | | |
| 1997 | — | — | — | — | 40.00 | — |
| 1997 Proof | — | Value: 50.00 | | | | |
| 1998 | — | — | — | — | 40.00 | — |
| 1998 Proof | — | Value: 50.00 | | | | |
| 1999 | — | — | — | — | 40.00 | — |
| 1999 Proof | — | Value: 50.00 | | | | |
| 2000 | — | — | — | — | 40.00 | — |
| 2000 Proof | — | Value: 50.00 | | | | |

**100 FRANCS** **KM# 955** **Weight:** 15.0000 g. **Composition:** 0.9000 Silver .4340 oz. ASW **Subject:** 50th Anniversary - Death of Marie Curie **Reverse:** Head of Marie Curie right

| Date | Mintage | F | VF | XF | Unc | BU |
|---|---|---|---|---|---|---|
| 1984 | 3,964,000 | — | — | — | 25.00 | — |

**100 FRANCS** **KM# 955a** **Weight:** 15.0000 g. **Composition:** 0.9500 Silver .4582 oz. ASW **Reverse:** Head of Marie Curie right

| Date | Mintage | F | VF | XF | Unc | BU |
|---|---|---|---|---|---|---|
| 1984 Proof | 1,000 | Value: 200 | | | | |

**100 FRANCS** **KM# 955b** **Weight:** 17.0000 g. **Composition:** 0.9200 Gold .5028 oz. AGW **Subject:** 50th Anniversary - Death of Marie Curie **Reverse:** Head of Marie Curie right

| Date | Mintage | F | VF | XF | Unc | BU |
|---|---|---|---|---|---|---|
| 1984 Proof | 5,000 | Value: 400 | | | | |

**100 FRANCS** **KM# 957** **Weight:** 15.0000 g. **Composition:** 0.9000 Silver .4340 oz. ASW **Subject:** Centennial of Emile Zola's Novel **Reverse:** Head of Emile Zola right

| Date | Mintage | F | VF | XF | Unc | BU |
|---|---|---|---|---|---|---|
| 1985 | 3,980,000 | — | — | — | 28.00 | — |
| 1985 Proof | 13,000 | Value: 55.00 | | | | |

**100 FRANCS** **KM# 957a** **Weight:** 15.0000 g. **Composition:** 0.9500 Silver .4582 oz. ASW **Reverse:** Head of Emile Zola right

| Date | Mintage | F | VF | XF | Unc | BU |
|---|---|---|---|---|---|---|
| 1985 Proof | 5,000 | Value: 115 | | | | |

**100 FRANCS** **KM# 957b** **Weight:** 17.0000 g. **Composition:** 0.9200 Gold .5028 oz. AGW **Subject:** Centennial of Emile Zola's Novel **Reverse:** Head of Emile Zola right

| Date | Mintage | F | VF | XF | Unc | BU |
|---|---|---|---|---|---|---|
| 1985 Proof | 5,000 | Value: 400 | | | | |

**100 FRANCS** **KM# 960** **Weight:** 15.0000 g. **Composition:** 0.9000 Silver .4340 oz. ASW **Subject:** Centennial - Statue of Liberty **Obverse:** Statue of Liberty

| Date | Mintage | F | VF | XF | Unc | BU |
|---|---|---|---|---|---|---|
| 1986 | 4,427,000 | — | — | — | 11.50 | — |

**100 FRANCS** **KM# 960a** **Weight:** 15.0000 g. **Composition:** 0.9500 Silver .4582 oz. ASW **Obverse:** Statue of Liberty

| Date | Mintage | F | VF | XF | Unc | BU |
|---|---|---|---|---|---|---|
| 1986 Proof | 18,000 | Value: 45.00 | | | | |

**100 FRANCS** **KM# 960b** **Weight:** 17.0000 g. **Composition:** 0.9200 Gold .5028 oz. AGW **Subject:** Centennial - Statue of Liberty **Obverse:** Statue of Liberty

| Date | Mintage | F | VF | XF | Unc | BU |
|---|---|---|---|---|---|---|
| 1986 | 13,000 | — | — | — | 200 | — |
| 1986 Proof | 17,000 | Value: 225 | | | | |

**100 FRANCS** **KM# 960c** **Weight:** 20.0000 g. **Composition:** 0.9990 Platinum .6430 oz. APW **Obverse:** Statue of Liberty

| Date | Mintage | F | VF | XF | Unc | BU |
|---|---|---|---|---|---|---|
| 1986 Proof | 9,500 | Value: 435 | | | | |

**100 FRANCS** **KM# 960d** **Weight:** 17.0000 g. **Composition:** 0.9000 Palladium .4920 oz. **Obverse:** Statue of Liberty

| Date | Mintage | F | VF | XF | Unc | BU |
|---|---|---|---|---|---|---|
| 1986 Proof | 1,250 | Value: 585 | | | | |

**100 FRANCS** **KM# 962** **Weight:** 15.0000 g. **Composition:** 0.9000 Silver .4340 oz. ASW **Subject:** 230th Anniversary - Birth of General Lafayette **Obverse:** Bust of Lafayette left

| Date | Mintage | F | VF | XF | Unc | BU |
|---|---|---|---|---|---|---|
| 1987 | 4,801,000 | — | — | — | 20.00 | — |

**100 FRANCS** **KM# 962a** **Weight:** 15.0000 g. **Composition:** 0.9500 Silver .4582 oz. ASW **Obverse:** Bust of Lafayette left

| Date | Mintage | F | VF | XF | Unc | BU |
|---|---|---|---|---|---|---|
| 1987 Proof | 30,000 | Value: 30.00 | | | | |

**100 FRANCS** **KM# 962b** **Weight:** 17.0000 g. **Composition:** 0.9200 Gold .5028 oz. AGW **Subject:** 230th Anniversary - Birth of General Lafayette **Obverse:** Bust of Lafayette left

| Date | Mintage | F | VF | XF | Unc | BU |
|---|---|---|---|---|---|---|
| 1987 | 10,000 | — | — | — | 200 | — |
| 1987 Proof | 20,000 | Value: 215 | | | | |

**100 FRANCS** **KM# 962c** **Weight:** 20.0000 g. **Composition:** 0.9990 Platinum .6430 oz. APW **Obverse:** Bust of Lafayette left

| Date | Mintage | F | VF | XF | Unc | BU |
|---|---|---|---|---|---|---|
| 1987 Proof | 8,500 | Value: 450 | | | | |

**100 FRANCS** **KM# 962d** **Weight:** 17.0000 g. **Composition:** 0.9000 Palladium .4920 oz. **Obverse:** Bust of Lafayette left

| Date | Mintage | F | VF | XF | Unc | BU |
|---|---|---|---|---|---|---|
| 1987 Proof | 7,000 | Value: 585 | | | | |

**100 FRANCS** **KM# 966** **Weight:** 15.0000 g. **Composition:** 0.9000 Silver .4340 oz. ASW **Subject:** Fraternity

| Date | Mintage | F | VF | XF | Unc | BU |
|---|---|---|---|---|---|---|
| 1988 | 4,853,000 | — | — | — | 26.50 | — |

**100 FRANCS** **KM# 966a** **Weight:** 15.0000 g. **Composition:** 0.9500 Silver .4582 oz. ASW **Subject:** Fraternity

| Date | Mintage | F | VF | XF | Unc | BU |
|---|---|---|---|---|---|---|
| 1988 Proof | 20,000 | Value: 37.50 | | | | |

**100 FRANCS** **KM# 966b** **Weight:** 17.0000 g. **Composition:** 0.9200 Gold .5028 oz. AGW **Subject:** Fraternity

| Date | Mintage | F | VF | XF | Unc | BU |
|---|---|---|---|---|---|---|
| 1988 | 3,000 | — | — | — | 450 | — |
| 1988 Proof | 12,000 | Value: 300 | | | | |

**100 FRANCS** **KM# 966c** **Weight:** 20.0000 g. **Composition:** 0.9990 Platinum .6430 oz. APW **Subject:** Fraternity

| Date | Mintage | F | VF | XF | Unc | BU |
|---|---|---|---|---|---|---|
| 1988 Proof | 5,000 | Value: 550 | | | | |

**100 FRANCS** **KM# 966d** **Weight:** 17.0000 g. **Composition:** 0.9000 Palladium .4920 oz. **Subject:** Fraternity

| Date | Mintage | F | VF | XF | Unc | BU |
|---|---|---|---|---|---|---|
| 1988 Proof | 7,000 | Value: 565 | | | | |

**100 FRANCS** **KM# 970** **Weight:** 15.0000 g. **Composition:** 0.9000 Silver .4340 oz. ASW **Subject:** Human Rights

| Date | Mintage | F | VF | XF | Unc | BU |
|---|---|---|---|---|---|---|
| 1989 | 4,823,000 | — | — | — | 32.50 | — |

**100 FRANCS** **KM# 970a** **Weight:** 15.0000 g. **Composition:** 0.9500 Silver .4582 oz. ASW **Subject:** Human Rights

| Date | Mintage | F | VF | XF | Unc | BU |
|---|---|---|---|---|---|---|
| 1989 Proof | 40,000 | Value: 47.50 | | | | |

**100 FRANCS** **KM# 970b** **Weight:** 17.0000 g. **Composition:** 0.9200 Gold .5028 oz. AGW **Subject:** Human Rights

| Date | Mintage | F | VF | XF | Unc | BU |
|---|---|---|---|---|---|---|
| 1989 | 1,000 | — | — | — | 600 | — |
| 1989 Proof | 20,000 | Value: 300 | | | | |

**100 FRANCS** **KM# 970c** **Weight:** 20.0000 g. **Composition:** 0.9990 Platinum .6430 oz. APW **Subject:** Human Rights

| Date | Mintage | F | VF | XF | Unc | BU |
|---|---|---|---|---|---|---|
| 1989 Proof | 1,000 | Value: 800 | | | | |

**100 FRANCS** **KM# 970d** **Weight:** 17.0000 g. **Composition:** 0.9000 Palladium .4920 oz. **Subject:** Human Rights

| Date | Mintage | F | VF | XF | Unc | BU |
|---|---|---|---|---|---|---|
| 1989 Proof | 1,250 | Value: 585 | | | | |

**100 FRANCS** **KM# 971** **Weight:** 22.2000 g. **Composition:** 0.9000 Silver .6424 oz. ASW **Subject:** 1992 Olympics **Note:** Similar to 500 Francs, KM#973.

| Date | Mintage | F | VF | XF | Unc | BU |
|---|---|---|---|---|---|---|
| 1989 Proof | 136,000 | Value: 30.00 | | | | |

**100 FRANCS** **KM# 972** **Weight:** 22.2000 g. **Composition:** 0.9000 Silver .6424 oz. ASW **Subject:** 1992 Olympics **Obverse:** Ice Skating Couple **Note:** Similar to 500 Francs, KM#974.

| Date | Mintage | F | VF | XF | Unc | BU |
|---|---|---|---|---|---|---|
| 1989 Proof | 179,000 | Value: 30.00 | | | | |

**100 FRANCS** **KM# 980** **Weight:** 22.2000 g. **Composition:** 0.9000 Silver .6424 oz. ASW **Subject:** 1992 Olympics **Obverse:** Speed Skating

| Date | Mintage | F | VF | XF | Unc | BU |
|---|---|---|---|---|---|---|
| 1990 Proof | 137,000 | Value: 32.50 | | | | |

**100 FRANCS** **KM# 981** **Weight:** 22.2000 g. **Composition:** 0.9000 Silver .6424 oz. ASW **Subject:** 1992 Olympics **Obverse:** Bobsledding **Reverse:** Games logo, value and legend

| Date | Mintage | F | VF | XF | Unc | BU |
|---|---|---|---|---|---|---|
| 1990 Proof | 127,000 | Value: 32.50 | | | | |

**100 FRANCS** **KM# 982** **Weight:** 15.0100 g. **Composition:** 0.9000 Silver .4340 oz. ASW **Subject:** Charlemagne

| Date | Mintage | F | VF | XF | Unc | BU |
|---|---|---|---|---|---|---|
| 1990 | 4,950,000 | — | — | — | 37.50 | — |

**100 FRANCS** **KM# 983** **Weight:** 22.2000 g. **Composition:** 0.9000 Silver .6423 oz. ASW **Subject:** 1992 Olympics **Obverse:** Free Style Skier

| Date | Mintage | F | VF | XF | Unc | BU |
|---|---|---|---|---|---|---|
| 1990 Proof | 110,000 | Value: 35.00 | | | | |

**100 FRANCS** **KM# 984** **Weight:** 22.2000 g. **Composition:** 0.9000 Silver .6423 oz. ASW **Subject:** 1992 Olympics **Obverse:** Slalom Skiers

| Date | Mintage | F | VF | XF | Unc | BU |
|---|---|---|---|---|---|---|
| 1990 Proof | 110,000 | Value: 35.00 | | | | |

**100 FRANCS** **KM# 991** **Weight:** 22.2000 g. **Composition:** 0.9000 Silver .6423 oz. ASW **Subject:** 100th Anniversary of Basketball **Obverse:** 2 players

| Date | Mintage | F | VF | XF | Unc | BU |
|---|---|---|---|---|---|---|
| 1991 Proof | 13,000 | Value: 65.00 | | | | |

**100 FRANCS** **KM# 992** **Weight:** 22.2000 g. **Composition:** 0.9000 Silver .6423 oz. ASW **Subject:** 100th Anniversary of Basketball **Obverse:** 1 player

| Date | Mintage | F | VF | XF | Unc | BU |
|---|---|---|---|---|---|---|
| 1991 Proof | 13,000 | Value: 65.00 | | | | |

**100 FRANCS** **KM# 993** **Weight:** 22.2000 g. **Composition:** 0.9000 Silver .6423 oz. ASW **Subject:** 1992 Olympics **Obverse:** Hockey Players

| Date | Mintage | F | VF | XF | Unc | BU |
|---|---|---|---|---|---|---|
| 1991 Proof | 93,000 | Value: 37.50 | | | | |

**100 FRANCS** **KM# 994** **Weight:** 22.2000 g. **Composition:** 0.9000 Silver .6423 oz. ASW **Subject:** 1992 Olympics **Obverse:** Cross Country Skier

| Date | Mintage | F | VF | XF | Unc | BU |
|---|---|---|---|---|---|---|
| 1991 Proof | 93,000 | Value: 37.50 | | | | |

**100 FRANCS** **KM# 995** **Weight:** 22.2000 g. **Composition:** 0.9000 Silver .6423 oz. ASW **Subject:** 1992 Olympics **Obverse:** Ski Jumpers

| Date | Mintage | F | VF | XF | Unc | BU |
|---|---|---|---|---|---|---|
| 1991 Proof | 90,000 | Value: 37.50 | | | | |

**100 FRANCS** **KM# 996** **Weight:** 15.0100 g. **Composition:** 0.9000 Silver .4340 oz. ASW **Reverse:** Head of Descartes 1/2 right

| Date | Mintage | F | VF | XF | Unc | BU |
|---|---|---|---|---|---|---|
| 1991 | 3,985,000 | — | — | — | 32.50 | — |

**100 FRANCS** **KM# 1009** **Weight:** 22.2000 g. **Composition:** 0.9000 Silver .6423 oz. ASW **Subject:** Paralympics **Obverse:** Segmented Flying Birds

| Date | Mintage | F | VF | XF | Unc | BU |
|---|---|---|---|---|---|---|
| 1992 Proof | 5,000 | Value: 95.00 | | | | |

**100 FRANCS** **KM# 1010** **Weight:** 22.2000 g. **Composition:** 0.9000 Silver .6423 oz. ASW **Subject:** French Antarctic Territories - Sea Lions

| Date | Mintage | F | VF | XF | Unc | BU |
|---|---|---|---|---|---|---|
| 1992 Proof | 15,000 | Value: 70.00 | | | | |

**100 FRANCS** **KM# 1011** **Weight:** 22.2000 g. **Composition:** 0.9000 Silver .6423 oz. ASW **Subject:** French Antarctic Territories - Penguins

| Date | Mintage | F | VF | XF | Unc | BU |
|---|---|---|---|---|---|---|
| 1992 Proof | 15,000 | Value: 70.00 | | | | |

**100 FRANCS** **KM# 1120** **Weight:** 15.0100 g. **Composition:** 0.9000 Silver .4340 oz. ASW **Subject:** Jean Monet

| Date | Mintage | F | VF | XF | Unc | BU |
|---|---|---|---|---|---|---|
| 1992 | 3,925,000 | — | — | — | 35.00 | — |

**100 FRANCS** **KM# 1017** **Weight:** 22.2000 g. **Composition:** 0.9000 Silver .6423 oz. ASW **Series:** Bicentennial of the Louvre **Obverse:** Mona Lisa

| Date | Mintage | F | VF | XF | Unc | BU |
|---|---|---|---|---|---|---|
| 1993 | — | — | — | — | — | — |
| 1993 Proof | 200,000 | Value: 40.00 | | | | |

**100 FRANCS** **KM# 1018.1** **Weight:** 15.0000 g. **Composition:** 0.9000 Silver .4340 oz. ASW **Series:** Bicentennial of the Louvre **Obverse:** Liberty

| Date | Mintage | F | VF | XF | Unc | BU |
|---|---|---|---|---|---|---|
| 1993 | — | — | — | — | 35.00 | — |

**100 FRANCS** **KM# 1018.2** **Weight:** 22.2000 g. **Composition:** 0.9000 Silver .6423 oz. ASW **Series:** Bicentennial of the Louvre **Obverse:** Liberty

| Date | Mintage | F | VF | XF | Unc | BU |
|---|---|---|---|---|---|---|
| 1993 | — | — | — | — | — | — |
| 1993 Proof | 20,000 | Value: 37.50 | | | | |

**100 FRANCS** **KM# 1018.2a** **Weight:** 17.0000 g. **Composition:** 0.9200 Gold .5028 oz. AGW **Series:** Bicentennial of the Louvre **Obverse:** Liberty

| Date | Mintage | F | VF | XF | Unc | BU |
|---|---|---|---|---|---|---|
| 1993 | — | — | — | — | — | — |
| 1993 Proof | 5,000 | Value: 400 | | | | |

**100 FRANCS** **KM# 1019** **Weight:** 22.2000 g. **Composition:** 0.9000 Silver .6420 oz. ASW **Series:** Bicentennial of the Louvre **Obverse:** Victory

| Date | Mintage | F | VF | XF | Unc | BU |
|---|---|---|---|---|---|---|
| 1993 | — | — | — | — | — | — |
| 1993 Proof | 20,000 | Value: 37.50 | | | | |

**100 FRANCS** **KM# 1019a** **Weight:** 17.0000 g. **Composition:** 0.9200 Gold .5028 oz. AGW **Series:** Bicentennial of the Louvre **Obverse:** Victory

| Date | Mintage | F | VF | XF | Unc | BU |
|---|---|---|---|---|---|---|
| 1993 | — | — | — | — | — | — |
| 1993 Proof | 5,000 | Value: 400 | | | | |

**100 FRANCS** **KM# 1020** **Weight:** 22.2600 g. **Composition:** 0.9000 Silver .6420 oz. ASW **Series:** Bicentennial of the Louvre **Obverse:** Venus de Milo

| Date | Mintage | F | VF | XF | Unc | BU |
|---|---|---|---|---|---|---|
| 1993 | — | — | — | — | — | — |
| 1993 Proof | 20,000 | Value: 40.00 | | | | |

**100 FRANCS** **KM# 1021** **Weight:** 22.2600 g. **Composition:** 0.9000 Silver .6420 oz. ASW **Series:** Bicentennial of the Louvre **Obverse:** Marie-Marguerite

| Date | Mintage | F | VF | XF | Unc | BU |
|---|---|---|---|---|---|---|
| 1993 | — | — | — | — | — | — |
| 1993 Proof | 20,000 | Value: 35.00 | | | | |

**100 FRANCS** **KM# 1021a** **Weight:** 17.0000 g. **Composition:** 0.9200 Gold .5028 oz. AGW **Series:** Bicentennial of the Louvre **Obverse:** Marie-Marguerite

| Date | Mintage | F | VF | XF | Unc | BU |
|---|---|---|---|---|---|---|
| 1993 | — | — | — | — | — | — |
| 1993 Proof | 5,000 | Value: 400 | | | | |

**100 FRANCS** **KM# 1022** **Weight:** 22.2600 g. **Composition:** 0.9000 Silver .6420 oz. ASW **Series:** Bicentennial of the Louvre **Obverse:** Napoleon Crowning Josephine

| Date | Mintage | F | VF | XF | Unc | BU |
|---|---|---|---|---|---|---|
| 1993 | — | — | — | — | — | — |
| 1993 Proof | 20,000 | Value: 42.50 | | | | |

**100 FRANCS** **KM# 1022a** **Weight:** 17.0000 g. **Composition:** 0.9200 Gold .5028 oz. AGW **Series:** Bicentennial of the Louvre **Obverse:** Napoleon Crowning Josephine

| Date | Mintage | F | VF | XF | Unc | BU |
|---|---|---|---|---|---|---|
| 1993 | — | — | — | — | — | — |
| 1993 Proof | 5,000 | Value: 400 | | | | |

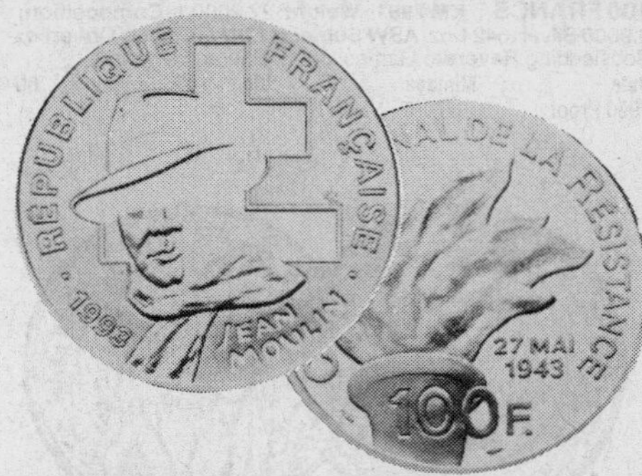

**100 FRANCS** **KM# 1023** **Weight:** 22.2000 g. **Composition:** 0.9000 Silver .6424 oz. ASW **Obverse:** Head of Jean Moulin facing

| Date | Mintage | F | VF | XF | Unc | BU |
|---|---|---|---|---|---|---|
| 1993 | 100,000 | — | — | — | 25.00 | — |
| 1993 Proof | 50,000 | Value: 40.00 | | | | |

**100 FRANCS** **KM# 1037** **Weight:** 22.2000 g. **Composition:** 0.9000 Silver .6424 oz. ASW **Subject:** Winston Churchill

| Date | Mintage | F | VF | XF | Unc | BU |
|---|---|---|---|---|---|---|
| 1994 Proof | Est. 30,000 | Value: 42.50 | | | | |

**100 FRANCS** **KM# 1038** **Weight:** 22.2000 g. **Composition:** 0.9000 Silver .6424 oz. ASW **Obverse:** Bust of General de Gaulle right **Reverse:** Map of France, inscription overlay

| Date | Mintage | F | VF | XF | Unc | BU |
|---|---|---|---|---|---|---|
| 1994 Proof | Est. 30,000 | Value: 42.50 | | | | |

**100 FRANCS** **KM# 1039** **Weight:** 22.2000 g. **Composition:** 0.9000 Silver .6424 oz. ASW **Obverse:** Bust of General Leclerc facing **Reverse:** Flag, inscription, fort, denomination

| Date | Mintage | F | VF | XF | Unc | BU |
|---|---|---|---|---|---|---|
| 1994 Proof | Est. 30,000 | Value: 42.50 | | | | |

**100 FRANCS** **KM# 1040** **Weight:** 22.2000 g. **Composition:** 0.9000 Silver .6424 oz. ASW **Obverse:** Bust of General Marie Pierre Koenig facing 1/2 left **Reverse:** Battle scene

| Date | Mintage | F | VF | XF | Unc | BU |
|---|---|---|---|---|---|---|
| 1994 Proof | Est. 30,000 | Value: 42.50 | | | | |

**100 FRANCS** **KM# 1041** **Weight:** 22.2000 g. **Composition:** 0.9000 Silver .6424 oz. ASW **Obverse:** Profile bust of General Juin right, map of Italy at right. Mountaintop building

| Date | Mintage | F | VF | XF | Unc | BU |
|---|---|---|---|---|---|---|
| 1994 Proof | Est. 30,000 | Value: 42.50 | | | | |

**100 FRANCS** **KM# 1042** **Weight:** 22.2000 g. **Composition:** 0.9000 Silver .6424 oz. ASW **Obverse:** Bust of General Dwight David Eisenhower facing 1/2 left **Reverse:** Flags representing allied countries under Supreme Commander Eisenhower

| Date | Mintage | F | VF | XF | Unc | BU |
|---|---|---|---|---|---|---|
| 1994 Proof | Est. 30,000 | Value: 42.50 | | | | |

**100 FRANCS** **KM# 1043** **Weight:** 22.2000 g. **Composition:** 0.9000 Silver .6424 oz. ASW **Subject:** Sainte - Mere - Eglise **Obverse:** Church, parachute behind

| Date | Mintage | F | VF | XF | Unc | BU |
|---|---|---|---|---|---|---|
| 1994 Proof | Est. 30,000 | Value: 42.50 | | | | |

**100 FRANCS** **KM# 1044** **Weight:** 22.2000 g. **Composition:** 0.9000 Silver .6424 oz. ASW **Obverse:** Face in profile of General de Lattre de Tassigny right **Reverse:** Waving flags below denomination

| Date | Mintage | F | VF | XF | Unc | BU |
|---|---|---|---|---|---|---|
| 1994 Proof | Est. 30,000 | Value: 42.50 | | | | |

**100 FRANCS** **KM# 1045.2** **Weight:** 22.2000 g. **Composition:** 0.9000 Silver .6424 oz. ASW

| Date | Mintage | F | VF | XF | Unc | BU |
|---|---|---|---|---|---|---|
| 1994 | — | — | — | — | 30.00 | — |
| 1994 Proof | Est. 30,000 | Value: 42.50 | | | | |

**100 FRANCS** **KM# 1046** **Weight:** 22.2000 g. **Composition:** 0.9000 Silver .6424 oz. ASW **Obverse:** Facing busts of de Gaulle and Adenauer **Reverse:** Two hands joined in handshake

| Date | Mintage | F | VF | XF | Unc | BU |
|---|---|---|---|---|---|---|
| 1994 Proof | Est. 30,000 | Value: 42.50 | | | | |

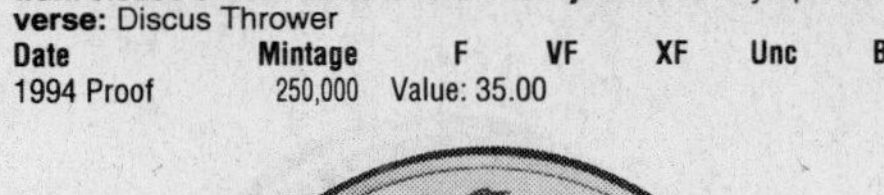

**100 FRANCS** **KM# 1047** **Weight:** 33.6300 g. **Composition:** 0.9250 Silver 1.0000 oz. ASW **Subject:** 1996 Olympics **Reverse:** Discus Thrower

| Date | Mintage | F | VF | XF | Unc | BU |
|---|---|---|---|---|---|---|
| 1994 Proof | 250,000 | Value: 35.00 | | | | |

**100 FRANCS** **KM# 1048** **Weight:** 33.6300 g. **Composition:** 0.9250 Silver 1.0000 oz. ASW **Subject:** 1996 Olympics **Reverse:** Javelin Thrower

| Date | Mintage | F | VF | XF | Unc | BU |
|---|---|---|---|---|---|---|
| 1994 Proof | 250,000 | Value: 35.00 | | | | |

**100 FRANCS** **KM# 1072** **Weight:** 22.2000 g. **Composition:** 0.9000 Silver .6424 oz. ASW **Series:** Centennial of Cinema **Obverse:** Antique moive camera **Reverse:** Conjoined busts of the Lumiere Brothers right

| Date | Mintage | F | VF | XF | Unc | BU |
|---|---|---|---|---|---|---|
| 1994 Proof | 15,000 | Value: 32.50 | | | | |

**100 FRANCS** **KM# 1073** **Weight:** 17.0000 g. **Composition:** 0.9200 Gold .5028 oz. AGW **Series:** Centennial of Cinema **Obverse:** Antique moive camera **Reverse:** Conjoined busts of the Lumiere Brothers right

| Date | Mintage | F | VF | XF | Unc | BU |
|---|---|---|---|---|---|---|
| 1994 Proof | 5,000 | Value: 400 | | | | |

**100 FRANCS** **KM# 1076** **Weight:** 22.2000 g. **Composition:** 0.9000 Silver .6424 oz. ASW **Series:** Centennial of Cinema **Reverse:** Head of Charlie Chaplin facing

| Date | Mintage | F | VF | XF | Unc | BU |
|---|---|---|---|---|---|---|
| 1994 Proof | 15,000 | Value: 42.00 | | | | |

**100 FRANCS** **KM# 1077** **Weight:** 17.0000 g. **Composition:** 0.9200 Gold .5028 oz. AGW **Series:** Centennial of Cinema **Reverse:** Head of Charlie Chaplin facing

| Date | Mintage | F | VF | XF | Unc | BU |
|---|---|---|---|---|---|---|
| 1994 Proof | 5,000 | Value: 425 | | | | |

**100 FRANCS** **KM# 1182** **Weight:** 22.2000 g. **Composition:** 0.9000 Silver .6424 oz. ASW **Reverse:** Voltaire

| Date | Mintage | F | VF | XF | Unc | BU |
|---|---|---|---|---|---|---|
| 1994 Proof | 3,000 | Value: 50.00 | | | | |

**100 FRANCS** **KM# 1045.1** **Weight:** 15.0000 g. **Composition:** 0.9000 Silver .4340 oz. ASW **Subject:** Liberation of Paris **Obverse:** Battle scene **Reverse:** Triumphant troops marching down Champs Elysees **Note:** Smaller size.

| Date | Mintage | F | VF | XF | Unc | BU |
|---|---|---|---|---|---|---|
| 1994 | 1,598,000 | — | — | — | 35.00 | — |

**100 FRANCS** **KM# 1080** **Weight:** 22.2000 g. **Composition:** 0.9000 Silver .6424 oz. ASW **Series:** Centennial of Cinema **Reverse:** Head of Leon Gaumont facing

| Date | Mintage | F | VF | XF | Unc | BU |
|---|---|---|---|---|---|---|
| 1995 Proof | 15,000 | Value: 40.00 | | | | |

**100 FRANCS** **KM# 1081** **Weight:** 17.0000 g. **Composition:** 0.9200 Gold .5028 oz. AGW **Series:** Centennial of Cinema **Reverse:** Head of Leon Gaumont facing

| Date | Mintage | F | VF | XF | Unc | BU |
|---|---|---|---|---|---|---|
| 1995 Proof | 5,000 | Value: 425 | | | | |

**100 FRANCS** **KM# 1084** **Weight:** 22.2000 g. **Composition:** 0.9000 Silver .6424 oz. ASW **Series:** Centennial of Cinema **Reverse:** Head of Jean Renoir right

| Date | Mintage | F | VF | XF | Unc | BU |
|---|---|---|---|---|---|---|
| 1995 Proof | 15,000 | Value: 30.00 | | | | |

**100 FRANCS** **KM# 1085** **Weight:** 17.0000 g. **Composition:** 0.9200 Gold .5028 oz. AGW **Series:** Centennial of Cinema **Reverse:** Head of Jean Renoir right

| Date | Mintage | F | VF | XF | Unc | BU |
|---|---|---|---|---|---|---|
| 1995 Proof | 5,000 | Value: 400 | | | | |

**100 FRANCS** **KM# 1088** **Weight:** 22.2000 g. **Composition:** 0.9000 Silver .6424 oz. ASW **Series:** Centennial of Cinema **Reverse:** Head of Alfred Hitchcock 1/2 left

| Date | Mintage | F | VF | XF | Unc | BU |
|---|---|---|---|---|---|---|
| 1995 Proof | 15,000 | Value: 40.00 | | | | |

**100 FRANCS** **KM# 1089** **Weight:** 17.0000 g. **Composition:** 0.9200 Gold .5028 oz. AGW **Series:** Centennial of Cinema **Reverse:** Head of Alfred Hitchcock 1/2 left

| Date | Mintage | F | VF | XF | Unc | BU |
|---|---|---|---|---|---|---|
| 1995 Proof | 5,000 | Value: 475 | | | | |

**100 FRANCS** **KM# 1092** **Weight:** 22.2000 g. **Composition:** 0.9000 Silver .6424 oz. ASW **Series:** Centennial of Cinema **Obverse:** Antique movie camera **Reverse:** Head of Greta Garbo in profile right

| Date | Mintage | F | VF | XF | Unc | BU |
|---|---|---|---|---|---|---|
| 1995 Proof | 15,000 | Value: 37.50 | | | | |

**100 FRANCS** **KM# 1093** **Weight:** 17.0000 g. **Composition:** 0.9200 Gold .5028 oz. AGW **Series:** Centennial of Cinema **Obverse:** Antique movie camera **Reverse:** Head of Greta Garbo in profile right

| Date | Mintage | F | VF | XF | Unc | BU |
|---|---|---|---|---|---|---|
| 1995 Proof | 5,000 | Value: 475 | | | | |

**100 FRANCS** **KM# 1096** **Weight:** 22.2000 g. **Composition:** 0.9000 Silver .6424 oz. ASW **Series:** Centennial of Cinema **Obverse:** Antique movie camera **Reverse:** Head of Audrey Hepburn 1/2 left

| Date | Mintage | F | VF | XF | Unc | BU |
|---|---|---|---|---|---|---|
| 1995 Proof | 15,000 | Value: 37.50 | | | | |

**100 FRANCS** **KM# 1097** **Weight:** 17.0000 g. **Composition:** 0.9200 Gold .5028 oz. AGW **Series:** Centennial of Cinema **Obverse:** Antique movie camera **Reverse:** Head of Audrey Hepburn 1/2 left

| Date | Mintage | F | VF | XF | Unc | BU |
|---|---|---|---|---|---|---|
| 1995 Proof | 5,000 | Value: 400 | | | | |

**100 FRANCS** **KM# 1100** **Weight:** 22.2000 g. **Composition:** 0.9000 Silver .6424 oz. ASW **Series:** Centennial of Cinema **Obverse:** Antique movie camera **Reverse:** Bust of Federico Fellini 1/2 right

| Date | Mintage | F | VF | XF | Unc | BU |
|---|---|---|---|---|---|---|
| 1995 Proof | 15,000 | Value: 30.00 | | | | |

**100 FRANCS** **KM# 1101** **Weight:** 17.0000 g. **Composition:** 0.9200 Gold .5028 oz. AGW **Series:** Centennial of Cinema **Obverse:** Antique movie camera **Reverse:** Bust of Federico Fellini 1/2 right

| Date | Mintage | F | VF | XF | Unc | BU |
|---|---|---|---|---|---|---|
| 1995 Proof | 5,000 | Value: 450 | | | | |

**100 FRANCS** **KM# 1104** **Weight:** 22.2000 g. **Composition:** 0.9000 Silver .6424 oz. ASW **Series:** Centennial of Cinema **Obverse:** Antique movie camera **Reverse:** Bust of Yves Montand facing

| Date | Mintage | F | VF | XF | Unc | BU |
|---|---|---|---|---|---|---|
| 1995 Proof | 15,000 | Value: 30.00 | | | | |

**100 FRANCS** **KM# 1105** **Weight:** 17.0000 g. **Composition:** 0.9200 Gold .5028 oz. AGW **Series:** Centennial of Cinema **Obverse:** Antique movie camera **Reverse:** Bust of Yves Montand facing

| Date | Mintage | F | VF | XF | Unc | BU |
|---|---|---|---|---|---|---|
| 1995 Proof | 5,000 | Value: 450 | | | | |

**100 FRANCS** **KM# 1108** **Weight:** 22.2000 g. **Composition:** 0.9000 Silver .6424 oz. ASW **Series:** Centennial of Cinema **Obverse:** Antique movie camera **Reverse:** Bust of Romy Schneider 1/2 left

| Date | Mintage | F | VF | XF | Unc | BU |
|---|---|---|---|---|---|---|
| 1995 Proof | 15,000 | Value: 30.00 | | | | |

**100 FRANCS** **KM# 1109** **Weight:** 17.0000 g. **Composition:** 0.9200 Gold .5028 oz. AGW **Series:** Centennial of Cinema **Obverse:** Antique movie camera **Reverse:** Bust of Romy Schneider 1/2 left

| Date | Mintage | F | VF | XF | Unc | BU |
|---|---|---|---|---|---|---|
| 1995 Proof | 5,000 | Value: 400 | | | | |

**100 FRANCS** **KM# 1116.1** **Weight:** 15.0000 g. **Composition:** 0.9000 Silver .4340 oz. ASW **Subject:** V.E. Day **Obverse:** Victory in Europe date, May 8, 1945

| Date | Mintage | F | VF | XF | Unc | BU |
|---|---|---|---|---|---|---|
| 1995 | 1,990,000 | — | — | — | 40.00 | — |

**100 FRANCS** **KM# 1116.2** **Weight:** 22.2000 g. **Composition:** 0.9000 Silver .6424 oz. ASW

| Date | Mintage | F | VF | XF | Unc | BU |
|---|---|---|---|---|---|---|
| 1995 Proof | 30,000 | Value: 45.00 | | | | |

**100 FRANCS** **KM# 1134** **Weight:** 22.2000 g. **Composition:** 0.9000 Silver .6424 oz. ASW **Obverse:** Bust of Louis Pasteur facing **Reverse:** Lab bottles, denomination

| Date | Mintage | F | VF | XF | Unc | BU |
|---|---|---|---|---|---|---|
| 1995 Proof | 10,000 | Value: 45.00 | | | | |

**100 FRANCS** **KM# 1136** **Weight:** 22.2000 g. **Composition:** 0.9000 Silver .6424 oz. ASW **Obverse:** Bust of Jean de la Fontaine 1/2 left

| Date | Mintage | F | VF | XF | Unc | BU |
|---|---|---|---|---|---|---|
| 1995 Proof | 10,000 | Value: 45.00 | | | | |

**100 FRANCS** **KM# 1138** **Weight:** 22.2000 g. **Composition:** 0.9000 Silver .6424 oz. ASW **Obverse:** Bust of Madame de Sevigne 1/2 left

| Date | Mintage | F | VF | XF | Unc | BU |
|---|---|---|---|---|---|---|
| 1996 Proof | 5,000 | Value: 65.00 | | | | |

**100 FRANCS** **KM# 1180** **Weight:** 15.0500 g. **Composition:** 0.9000 Silver .4340 oz. ASW **Obverse:** Bust of King Clovis I facing **Reverse:** Baptism scene

| Date | Mintage | F | VF | XF | Unc | BU |
|---|---|---|---|---|---|---|
| 1996 | 2,000,000 | — | — | — | 32.50 | — |
| 1996 Proof | — | Value: 60.00 | | | | |

**100 FRANCS** **KM# 1172** **Weight:** 17.0000 g. **Composition:** 0.9200 Gold .5028 oz. AGW **Subject:** Coupe du Monde 1998 - France **Obverse:** World Cup 1998 logo above denomination **Reverse:** Segment of Eiffel tower, soccer player

| Date | Mintage | F | VF | XF | Unc | BU |
|---|---|---|---|---|---|---|
| 1996 Proof | 25,000 | Value: 375 | | | | |

**100 FRANCS** **KM# 1168** **Weight:** 17.0000 g. **Composition:** 0.9200 Gold .5028 oz. AGW **Subject:** Coupe du Monde 1998 - Africa **Reverse:** Soccer player and map of Africa

| Date | Mintage | F | VF | XF | Unc | BU |
|---|---|---|---|---|---|---|
| 1997 Proof | 25,000 | Value: 400 | | | | |

**100 FRANCS** **KM# 1169** **Weight:** 17.0000 g. **Composition:** 0.9200 Gold .5028 oz. AGW **Subject:** Coupe du Monde 1998 - America **Reverse:** Soccer player and map of North & South America

| Date | Mintage | F | VF | XF | Unc | BU |
|---|---|---|---|---|---|---|
| 1997 Proof | 25,000 | Value: 400 | | | | |

**100 FRANCS** **KM# 1170** **Weight:** 17.0000 g. **Composition:** 0.9200 Gold .5028 oz. AGW **Subject:** Coupe du Monde 1998 - Asia **Reverse:** Soccer player and map of Asia

| Date | Mintage | F | VF | XF | Unc | BU |
|---|---|---|---|---|---|---|
| 1997 Proof | 25,000 | Value: 400 | | | | |

**100 FRANCS** **KM# 1173** **Weight:** 17.0000 g. **Composition:** 0.9200 Gold .5028 oz. AGW **Subject:** Coupe du Monde 1998 - Oceania **Reverse:** Soccer player and map of Australia

| Date | Mintage | F | VF | XF | Unc | BU |
|---|---|---|---|---|---|---|
| 1997 Proof | 25,000 | Value: 400 | | | | |

**100 FRANCS** **KM# 1188** **Weight:** 15.1500 g. **Composition:** 0.9000 Silver .4384 oz. ASW **Obverse:** Head of Andre Malraux facing **Reverse:** Two cats flank denomination

| Date | Mintage | F | VF | XF | Unc | BU |
|---|---|---|---|---|---|---|
| 1997 Proof | 3,000 | Value: 50.00 | | | | |

**100 FRANCS** **KM# 1195** **Weight:** 8.4500 g. **Composition:** 0.9200 Gold .2499 oz. AGW **Obverse:** Pantheon **Reverse:** Denomination and tree design

| Date | Mintage | F | VF | XF | Unc | BU |
|---|---|---|---|---|---|---|
| 1997 Proof | 500 | Value: 350 | | | | |

**100 FRANCS** **KM# 1196** **Weight:** 22.2000 g. **Composition:** 0.9000 Silver .6424 oz. ASW **Obverse:** Bust of Georges Guynemer 1/2 left **Reverse:** Guynemer's stork and denomination

| Date | Mintage | F | VF | XF | Unc | BU |
|---|---|---|---|---|---|---|
| 1997 Proof | 3,000 | Value: 50.00 | | | | |

**100 FRANCS** **KM# 1198** **Weight:** 22.2000 g. **Composition:** 0.9000 Silver .6424 oz. ASW **Obverse:** Conjoined busts of Pierre and Marie Curie left **Reverse:** Denomination

| Date | Mintage | F | VF | XF | Unc | BU |
|---|---|---|---|---|---|---|
| 1997 Proof | 3,000 | Value: 50.00 | | | | |

**100 FRANCS** **KM# 1171** **Weight:** 17.0000 g. **Composition:** 0.9200 Gold .5028 oz. AGW **Subject:** Coupe du Monte 1998 - Europe **Reverse:** Soccer player and map of Europe

| Date | Mintage | F | VF | XF | Unc | BU |
|---|---|---|---|---|---|---|
| 1998 Proof | 25,000 | Value: 400 | | | | |

**100 FRANCS** **KM# 1201** **Weight:** 22.2000 g. **Composition:** 0.9000 Silver .6424 oz. ASW **Obverse:** Bust of Marie Caritat Marquis de Condorcet 1/2 right **Reverse:** Denomination

| Date | Mintage | F | VF | XF | Unc | BU |
|---|---|---|---|---|---|---|
| 1998 Proof | 3,000 | Value: 50.00 | | | | |

**100 FRANCS** **KM# 1203** **Weight:** 22.2000 g. **Composition:** 0.9000 Silver .6424 oz. ASW **Obverse:** 3/4 bust of Gaspard Monge right **Reverse:** Denomination

| Date | Mintage | F | VF | XF | Unc | BU |
|---|---|---|---|---|---|---|
| 1998 Proof | 3,000 | Value: 50.00 | | | | |

**100 FRANCS** **KM# 1209** **Weight:** 17.0000 g. **Composition:** 0.9200 Gold .5028 oz. AGW **Subject:** Treasures of the Nile - King Tutankhamon **Obverse:** Burial mask and dog **Reverse:** Sphinx and pyramids

| Date | Mintage | F | VF | XF | Unc | BU |
|---|---|---|---|---|---|---|
| 1998 Proof | 2,000 | Value: 475 | | | | |

**100 FRANCS** **KM# 1210** **Weight:** 17.0000 g. **Composition:** 0.9200 Gold .5028 oz. AGW **Subject:** Treasures of the Nile - The Scribe Accroupi **Obverse:** Seated scribe **Reverse:** Denomination

| Date | Mintage | F | VF | XF | Unc | BU |
|---|---|---|---|---|---|---|
| 1998 Proof | 2,000 | Value: 475 | | | | |

**100 FRANCS** **KM# 1232** **Weight:** 17.0000 g. **Composition:** 0.9200 Gold .5028 oz. AGW **Subject:** 2000 Years - French Coinage **Obverse:** Denomination **Reverse:** 1st century B.C. Celtic Parisii Stater coin design **Edge:** Plain **Note:** Struck at Paris Mint.

| Date | Mintage | F | VF | XF | Unc | BU |
|---|---|---|---|---|---|---|
| 2000 Prof | 1,000 | Value: 485 | | | | |

**100 FRANCS** **KM# 1233** **Weight:** 17.0000 g. **Composition:** 0.9200 Gold .5028 oz. AGW **Subject:** 2000 Years - French Coinage **Reverse:** Charlemagne Denar coin design **Note:** Struck at Paris Mint.

| Date | Mintage | F | VF | XF | Unc | BU |
|---|---|---|---|---|---|---|
| 2000 Proof | 1,000 | Value: 485 | | | | |

**100 FRANCS** **KM# 1234** **Weight:** 17.0000 g. **Composition:** 0.9200 Gold .5028 oz. AGW **Subject:** 2000 Years - French Coinage **Reverse:** Louis IX gold Ecu coin design **Note:** Struck at Paris Mint.

| Date | Mintage | F | VF | XF | Unc | BU |
|---|---|---|---|---|---|---|
| 2000 Proof | 1,000 | Value: 485 | | | | |

**100 FRANCS** **KM# 1238** **Weight:** 17.0000 g. **Composition:** 0.9200 Gold .5028 oz. AGW **Series:** XXth Century **Subject:** Biology and Medicine **Obverse:** Double X design **Reverse:** Parents, fetus, hands **Note:** Struck at Paris Mint.

| Date | Mintage | F | VF | XF | Unc | BU |
|---|---|---|---|---|---|---|
| 2000 Proof | 1,000 | Value: 475 | | | | |

**100 FRANCS** **KM# 1239** **Weight:** 17.0000 g. **Composition:** 0.9200 Gold .5028 oz. AGW **Series:** XXth Century **Subject:** Physics **Reverse:** Einstein's portrait, atom and formula **Note:** Struck at Paris Mint.

| Date | Mintage | F | VF | XF | Unc | BU |
|---|---|---|---|---|---|---|
| 2000 Proof | 1,000 | Value: 475 | | | | |

**100 FRANCS** **KM# 1240** **Weight:** 17.0000 g. **Composition:** 0.9200 Gold .5028 oz. AGW **Series:** XXth Century **Subject:** Communications **Reverse:** World, satellites, keyboard **Note:** Struck at Paris Mint.

| Date | Mintage | F | VF | XF | Unc | BU |
|---|---|---|---|---|---|---|
| 2000 Proof | 1,000 | Value: 475 | | | | |

**100 FRANCS** **KM# 1241** **Weight:** 17.0000 g. **Composition:** 0.9200 Gold .5028 oz. AGW **Series:** XXth Century **Subject:** Automobile **Reverse:** Race cars above horse **Note:** Struck at Paris Mint.

| Date | Mintage | F | VF | XF | Unc | BU |
|---|---|---|---|---|---|---|
| 2000 Proof | 1,000 | Value: 475 | | | | |

**100 FRANCS** **KM# 1242** **Weight:** 17.0000 g. **Composition:** 0.9200 Gold .5028 oz. AGW **Series:** XXth Century **Subject:** Flight **Reverse:** Icarus in flight above Bleriot monoplane **Note:** Struck at Paris Mint.

| Date | Mintage | F | VF | XF | Unc | BU |
|---|---|---|---|---|---|---|
| 2000 Proof | 1,000 | Value: 475 | | | | |

**100 FRANCS** **KM# 1243** **Weight:** 17.0000 g. **Composition:** 0.9200 Gold .5028 oz. AGW **Series:** XXth Century **Subject:** Space Travel **Reverse:** Astronaut, footprint on moon, planets **Note:** Struck at Paris Mint.

| Date | Mintage | F | VF | XF | Unc | BU |
|---|---|---|---|---|---|---|
| 2000 Proof | 1,000 | Value: 475 | | | | |

**100 FRANCS** **KM# 1264** **Weight:** 17.0000 g. **Composition:** 0.9200 Gold .5028 oz. AGW **Subject:** Antoine de St. Exupery **Obverse:** Portrait, bi-plane **Reverse:** The "Little Prince" standing on a small planet **Note:** Struck at Paris Mint.

| Date | Mintage | F | VF | XF | Unc | BU |
|---|---|---|---|---|---|---|
| 2000 Proof | 1,000 | Value: 450 | | | | |

**100 FRANCS** **KM# 1269** **Weight:** 17.0000 g. **Composition:** 0.9200 Gold .5028 oz. AGW **Subject:** Palace of Versailles **Obverse:** Stylized French map **Reverse:** Louis XIV with internal and exteral palace views **Edge:** Plain

| Date | Mintage | F | VF | XF | Unc | BU |
|---|---|---|---|---|---|---|
| 2001 Proof | 2,000 | Value: 365 | | | | |

**100 FRANCS** **KM# 1271** **Weight:** 17.0000 g. **Composition:** 0.9200 Gold .5028 oz. AGW **Obverse:** Champs-Elysees **Reverse:** Arch of Triumph partial close up and aerial views

| Date | Mintage | F | VF | XF | Unc | BU |
|---|---|---|---|---|---|---|
| 2001 Proof | 2,000 | — | — | — | — | — |

**100 FRANCS** **KM# 1273** **Weight:** 17.0000 g. **Composition:** 0.9200 Gold .5028 oz. AGW **Obverse:** Notre-Dame Cathedral **Reverse:** Gargoyle and cathedral views

| Date | Mintage | F | VF | XF | Unc | BU |
|---|---|---|---|---|---|---|
| 2001 Proof | 2,000 | Value: 365 | | | | |

**100 FRANCS** **KM# 1275** **Weight:** 17.0000 g. **Composition:** 0.9200 Gold .5028 oz. AGW **Obverse:** Eiffel Tower **Reverse:** Two tower views

| Date | Mintage | F | VF | XF | Unc | BU |
|---|---|---|---|---|---|---|
| 2001 Proof | 2,000 | Value: 365 | | | | |

**500 FRANCS** **KM# 974** **Weight:** 17.0000 g. **Composition:** 0.9200 Gold .5029 oz. AGW **Subject:** 1992 Olympics **Obverse:** Ice Skating Couple **Note:** Struck at Paris Mint.

| Date | Mintage | F | VF | XF | Unc | BU |
|---|---|---|---|---|---|---|
| 1989 Proof | Est. 17,000 | Value: 210 | | | | |

**500 FRANCS** **KM# 973** **Weight:** 17.0000 g. **Composition:** 0.9200 Gold .5029 oz. AGW **Subject:** 1992 Olympics **Obverse:** Alpine Skiing **Note:** Without mint mark. Struck at Paris Mint.

| Date | Mintage | F | VF | XF | Unc | BU |
|---|---|---|---|---|---|---|
| 1989 Proof | 19,000 | Value: 210 | | | | |

**500 FRANCS** **KM# 988** **Weight:** 17.0000 g. **Composition:** 0.9200 Gold .5029 oz. AGW **Subject:** 1992 Olympics **Obverse:** Slalom Skiers. Modern and old style slalom skiers **Note:** Struck at Paris Mint. Similar to 100 Francs, KM#284.

| Date | Mintage | F | VF | XF | Unc | BU |
|---|---|---|---|---|---|---|
| 1990 Proof | 8,000 | Value: 235 | | | | |

**500 FRANCS** **KM# 985** **Weight:** 17.0000 g. **Composition:** 0.9200 Gold .5029 oz. AGW **Subject:** 1992 Olympics **Obverse:** Speed Skating **Note:** Struck at Paris Mint. Similar to 100 Francs, KM#980.

| Date | Mintage | F | VF | XF | Unc | BU |
|---|---|---|---|---|---|---|
| 1990 Proof | 13,000 | Value: 210 | | | | |

**500 FRANCS** **KM# 986** **Weight:** 17.0000 g. **Composition:** 0.9200 Gold .5029 oz. AGW **Subject:** 1992 Olympics **Obverse:** Bobsledding **Note:** Struck at Paris Mint. Similar to 100 Francs, KM#981.

| Date | Mintage | F | VF | XF | Unc | BU |
|---|---|---|---|---|---|---|
| 1990 Proof | 13,000 | Value: 210 | | | | |

**500 FRANCS** **KM# 987** **Weight:** 17.0000 g. **Composition:** 0.9200 Gold .5029 oz. AGW **Subject:** 1992 Olympics **Obverse:** Free Style Skier. Free style skier watched by chamois **Reverse:** Similar to KM#1000 obverse **Note:** Struck at Paris Mint. Similar to 100 Francs, KM#983.

| Date | Mintage | F | VF | XF | Unc | BU |
|---|---|---|---|---|---|---|
| 1990 Proof | 8,000 | Value: 235 | | | | |

**500 FRANCS** **KM# 977** **Weight:** 17.0000 g. **Composition:** 0.9200 Gold .5029 oz. AGW **Subject:** 100th Anniversary of Basketball **Obverse:** Player jumping for lay up shot, hoop behind **Note:** Struck at Paris Mint.

| Date | Mintage | F | VF | XF | Unc | BU |
|---|---|---|---|---|---|---|
| 1991 Proof | 5,000 | Value: 325 | | | | |

**500 FRANCS** **KM# 997** **Weight:** 17.0000 g. **Composition:** 0.9200 Gold .5029 oz. AGW **Subject:** 1992 Olympics - Hockey Players **Obverse:** 2 Hockey players and large Ibex ram **Note:** Struck at Paris Mint.

| Date | Mintage | F | VF | XF | Unc | BU |
|---|---|---|---|---|---|---|
| 1991 Proof | 8,000 | Value: 235 | | | | |

**500 FRANCS** **KM# 998** **Weight:** 17.0000 g. **Composition:** 0.9200 Gold .5029 oz. AGW **Note:** Struck at Paris Mint.

| Date | Mintage | F | VF | XF | Unc | BU |
|---|---|---|---|---|---|---|
| 1991 Proof | 8,000 | Value: 275 | | | | |

**500 FRANCS** **KM# 999** **Weight:** 17.0000 g. **Composition:** 0.9200 Gold .5029 oz. AGW **Subject:** 1992 Olympics - Ski Jumpers **Obverse:** Old style and modern ski jumpers **Note:** Struck at Paris Mint.

| Date | Mintage | F | VF | XF | Unc | BU |
|---|---|---|---|---|---|---|
| 1991 Proof | 8,000 | Value: 275 | | | | |

**500 FRANCS** **KM# 1000** **Weight:** 17.0000 g. **Composition:** 0.9200 Gold .5029 oz. AGW **Subject:** 1992 Olympics **Obverse:** Head of Pierre de Coubertin facing **Note:** Struck at Paris Mint.

| Date | Mintage | F | VF | XF | Unc | BU |
|---|---|---|---|---|---|---|
| 1991 Proof | 28,000 | Value: 275 | | | | |

**500 FRANCS** **KM# 1001** **Weight:** 17.0000 g. **Composition:** 0.9200 Gold .5029 oz. AGW **Subject:** 1992 Olympics **Reverse:** Mozart in Paris at piano **Note:** Struck at Paris Mint.

| Date | Mintage | F | VF | XF | Unc | BU |
|---|---|---|---|---|---|---|
| 1991 Proof | Est. 5,000 | Value: 300 | | | | |

**500 FRANCS** **KM# 1024** **Weight:** 31.1040 g. **Composition:** 0.9990 Gold 1.0000 oz. AGW **Series:** Bicentennial of the Louvre **Obverse:** Mona Lisa **Note:** Struck at Paris Mint.

| Date | Mintage | F | VF | XF | Unc | BU |
|---|---|---|---|---|---|---|
| 1993 | — | — | — | — | — | — |
| 1993 Proof | 5,000 | Value: 750 | | | | |
| 1994 Proof | 5,000 | Value: 800 | | | | |

**500 FRANCS** **KM# 1026** **Weight:** 155.5175 g. **Composition:** 0.9990 Gold 5.0000 oz. AGW **Series:** Bicentennial of the Louvre **Obverse:** Liberty **Note:** Struck at Paris Mint.

| Date | Mintage | F | VF | XF | Unc | BU |
|---|---|---|---|---|---|---|
| 1993 Proof | 99 | Value: 3,000 | | | | |
| 1994 Proof | 99 | Value: 3,500 | | | | |

**500 FRANCS** **KM# 1027** **Weight:** 155.5175 g. **Composition:** 0.9990 Gold 5.0000 oz. AGW **Series:** Bicentennial of the Louvre **Obverse:** Mona Lisa **Note:** Struck at Paris Mint.

| Date | Mintage | F | VF | XF | Unc | BU |
|---|---|---|---|---|---|---|
| 1993 Proof | 99 | Value: 3,000 | | | | |
| 1994 Proof | 99 | Value: 3,500 | | | | |

**500 FRANCS** **KM# 1028** **Weight:** 17.0000 g. **Composition:** 0.9200 Gold .5028 oz. AGW **Obverse:** Head of Jean Moulin facing **Note:** Struck at Paris Mint.

| Date | Mintage | F | VF | XF | Unc | BU |
|---|---|---|---|---|---|---|
| 1993 Proof | 5,000 | Value: 325 | | | | |

**500 FRANCS** **KM# 1183** **Weight:** 155.5175 g. **Composition:** 0.9990 Gold 5.0000 oz. AGW **Series:** Bicentennial of the Louvre **Obverse:** Victory **Note:** Struck at Paris Mint.

| Date | Mintage | F | VF | XF | Unc | BU |
|---|---|---|---|---|---|---|
| 1993 Proof | 99 | Value: 4,200 | | | | |
| 1994 Proof | 99 | Value: 4,200 | | | | |

**500 FRANCS** **KM# 1184** **Weight:** 155.5175 g. **Composition:** 0.9990 Gold 5.0000 oz. AGW **Series:** Bicentennial of the Louvre **Obverse:** Napoleon and Josephine **Note:** Struck at Paris Mint.

| Date | Mintage | F | VF | XF | Unc | BU |
|---|---|---|---|---|---|---|
| 1993 Proof | 99 | Value: 3,750 | | | | |
| 1994 Proof | 99 | Value: 3,750 | | | | |

**500 FRANCS** **KM# 1185** **Weight:** 155.5175 g. **Composition:** 0.9990 Gold 5.0000 oz. AGW **Series:** Bicentennial of the Louvre **Obverse:** Marie Marguerite **Note:** Struck at Paris Mint.

| Date | Mintage | F | VF | XF | Unc | BU |
|---|---|---|---|---|---|---|
| 1993 Proof | 99 | Value: 3,750 | | | | |
| 1994 Proof | 99 | Value: 3,750 | | | | |

**500 FRANCS** **KM# 1025** **Weight:** 31.1040 g. **Composition:** 0.9990 Gold 1.0000 oz. AGW **Series:** Bicentennial of the Louvre **Obverse:** Venus de Milo **Note:** Struck at Paris Mint. Similar to 100 Francs, KM#1020.

| Date | Mintage | F | VF | XF | Unc | BU |
|---|---|---|---|---|---|---|
| 1993 | — | — | — | — | — | — |
| 1993 Proof | 5,000 | Value: 750 | | | | |

**500 FRANCS** **KM# 1049** **Weight:** 17.0000 g. **Composition:** 0.9200 Gold .5028 oz. AGW **Obverse:** Bust of Winston Churchill right **Note:** Struck at Paris Mint.

| Date | Mintage | F | VF | XF | Unc | BU |
|---|---|---|---|---|---|---|
| 1994 Proof | Est. 2,000 | Value: 325 | | | | |

**500 FRANCS** **KM# 1051** **Weight:** 17.0000 g. **Composition:** 0.9200 Gold .5028 oz. AGW **Obverse:** Bust of General Leclerc facing **Note:** Struck at Paris Mint.

| Date | Mintage | F | VF | XF | Unc | BU |
|---|---|---|---|---|---|---|
| 1994 Proof | Est. 2,000 | Value: 325 | | | | |

**500 FRANCS** **KM# 1050** **Weight:** 17.0000 g. **Composition:** 0.9200 Gold .5028 oz. AGW **Obverse:** 3/4 bust of General de Gaulle in front of microphone **Note:** Struck at Paris Mint.

| Date | Mintage | F | VF | XF | Unc | BU |
|---|---|---|---|---|---|---|
| 1994 Proof | Est. 5,000 | Value: 325 | | | | |

**500 FRANCS** **KM# 1052** **Weight:** 17.0000 g. **Composition:** 0.9200 Gold .5028 oz. AGW **Obverse:** Bust of General Marie Pierre Koenig 1/2 left **Note:** Struck at Paris Mint.

| Date | Mintage | F | VF | XF | Unc | BU |
|---|---|---|---|---|---|---|
| 1994 Proof | Est. 2,000 | Value: 325 | | | | |

**500 FRANCS** **KM# 1053** **Weight:** 17.0000 g. **Composition:** 0.9200 Gold .5028 oz. AGW **Obverse:** Bust of General Juin right, map of Italy at right **Note:** Struck at Paris Mint.

| Date | Mintage | F | VF | XF | Unc | BU |
|---|---|---|---|---|---|---|
| 1994 Proof | Est. 2,000 | Value: 325 | | | | |

**500 FRANCS** KM# 1054 **Weight:** 17.0000 g. **Composition:** 0.9200 Gold .5028 oz. AGW **Obverse:** Bust of General Dwight David Eisenhower left **Note:** Struck at Paris Mint.

| Date | Mintage | F | VF | XF | Unc | BU |
|---|---|---|---|---|---|---|
| 1994 Proof | Est. 2,000 | Value: 325 | | | | |

**500 FRANCS** KM# 1055 **Weight:** 17.0000 g. **Composition:** 0.9200 Gold .5028 oz. AGW **Obverse:** Church of Sainte - Mere - Eglise, parachute behind **Note:** Struck at Paris Mint.

| Date | Mintage | F | VF | XF | Unc | BU |
|---|---|---|---|---|---|---|
| 1994 Proof | Est. 2,000 | Value: 325 | | | | |

**500 FRANCS** KM# 1056 **Weight:** 17.0000 g. **Composition:** 0.9200 Gold .5028 oz. AGW **Obverse:** Head of General de Lattre de Tassigny right **Note:** Struck at Paris Mint.

| Date | Mintage | F | VF | XF | Unc | BU |
|---|---|---|---|---|---|---|
| 1994 Proof | Est. 2,000 | Value: 325 | | | | |

**500 FRANCS** KM# 1057 **Weight:** 17.0000 g. **Composition:** 0.9200 Gold .5028 oz. AGW **Subject:** Liberation of Paris **Obverse:** Triumphant troops marching down Champs Elysees **Note:** Struck at Paris Mint.

| Date | Mintage | F | VF | XF | Unc | BU |
|---|---|---|---|---|---|---|
| 1994 Proof | Est. 5,000 | Value: 325 | | | | |

**500 FRANCS** KM# 1058 **Weight:** 17.0000 g. **Composition:** 0.9200 Gold .5028 oz. AGW **Obverse:** Heads of de Gaulle and Adenauer facing the center **Note:** Struck at Paris Mint.

| Date | Mintage | F | VF | XF | Unc | BU |
|---|---|---|---|---|---|---|
| 1994 Proof | Est. 2,000 | Value: 320 | | | | |

**500 FRANCS** KM# 1059 **Weight:** 16.9700 g. **Composition:** 0.9170 Gold .5000 oz. AGW **Subject:** 1996 Olympics **Reverse:** Archer in front of Eiffel Tower **Note:** Struck at Paris Mint.

| Date | Mintage | F | VF | XF | Unc | BU |
|---|---|---|---|---|---|---|
| 1994 Proof | 60,000 | Value: 265 | | | | |

**500 FRANCS** KM# 1074 **Weight:** 31.0350 g. **Composition:** 0.9990 Gold 1.0000 oz. AGW **Series:** Centennial of Cinema **Obverse:** Antique camera **Reverse:** Conjoined busts of the Lumiere Brothers right **Note:** Struck at Paris Mint.

| Date | Mintage | F | VF | XF | Unc | BU |
|---|---|---|---|---|---|---|
| 1994 Proof | 3,000 | Value: 900 | | | | |

**500 FRANCS** KM# 1078 **Weight:** 31.0350 g. **Composition:** 0.9990 Gold 1.0000 oz. AGW **Series:** Centennial of Cinema **Reverse:** Head of Charlie Chaplin facing **Note:** Struck at Paris Mint.

| Date | Mintage | F | VF | XF | Unc | BU |
|---|---|---|---|---|---|---|
| 1994 Proof | 3,000 | Value: 900 | | | | |

**500 FRANCS** KM# 1079 **Weight:** 155.5175 g. **Composition:** 0.9990 Gold 5.0000 oz. AGW **Series:** Centennial of Cinema **Reverse:** Head of Charlie Chaplin facing **Note:** Struck at Paris Mint.

| Date | Mintage | F | VF | XF | Unc | BU |
|---|---|---|---|---|---|---|
| 1994 Proof | 99 | Value: 3,500 | | | | |

**500 FRANCS** KM# 1186 **Weight:** 17.0000 g. **Composition:** 0.9200 Gold .5028 oz. AGW **Series:** Centennial of Cinema **Reverse:** Voltaire **Note:** Struck at Paris Mint.

| Date | Mintage | F | VF | XF | Unc | BU |
|---|---|---|---|---|---|---|
| 1994 Proof | 350 | Value: 350 | | | | |

**500 FRANCS** KM# 1082 **Weight:** 31.0350 g. **Composition:** 0.9990 Gold 1.0000 oz. AGW **Series:** Centennial of Cinema **Reverse:** Leon Gaumont **Note:** Struck at Paris Mint.

| Date | Mintage | F | VF | XF | Unc | BU |
|---|---|---|---|---|---|---|
| 1995 Proof | 3,000 | Value: 900 | | | | |

**500 FRANCS** KM# 1083 **Weight:** 155.5175 g. **Composition:** 0.9990 Gold 5.0000 oz. AGW **Series:** Centennial of Cinema **Reverse:** Leon Gaumont **Note:** Struck at Paris Mint.

| Date | Mintage | F | VF | XF | Unc | BU |
|---|---|---|---|---|---|---|
| 1995 Proof | 99 | Value: 3,200 | | | | |

**500 FRANCS** KM# 1086 **Weight:** 31.0350 g. **Composition:** 0.9990 Gold 1.0000 oz. AGW **Series:** Centennial of Cinema **Reverse:** Jean Renoir **Note:** Struck at Paris Mint.

| Date | Mintage | F | VF | XF | Unc | BU |
|---|---|---|---|---|---|---|
| 1995 Proof | 3,000 | Value: 900 | | | | |

**500 FRANCS** KM# 1087 **Weight:** 155.5175 g. **Composition:** 0.9990 Gold 5.0000 oz. AGW **Series:** Centennial of Cinema **Reverse:** Jean Renoir **Note:** Struck at Paris Mint.

| Date | Mintage | F | VF | XF | Unc | BU |
|---|---|---|---|---|---|---|
| 1995 Proof | 99 | Value: 3,700 | | | | |

**500 FRANCS** KM# 1090 **Weight:** 31.0350 g. **Composition:** 0.9990 Gold 1.0000 oz. AGW **Series:** Centennial of Cinema **Reverse:** Alfred Hitchcock **Note:** Struck at Paris Mint.

| Date | Mintage | F | VF | XF | Unc | BU |
|---|---|---|---|---|---|---|
| 1995 Proof | 3,000 | Value: 900 | | | | |

**500 FRANCS** KM# 1091 **Weight:** 155.5175 g. **Composition:** 0.9990 Gold 5.0000 oz. AGW **Series:** Centennial of Cinema **Reverse:** Alfred Hitchcock **Note:** Struck at Paris Mint.

| Date | Mintage | F | VF | XF | Unc | BU |
|---|---|---|---|---|---|---|
| 1995 Proof | 99 | Value: 3,200 | | | | |

**500 FRANCS** KM# 1094 **Weight:** 31.0350 g. **Composition:** 0.9990 Gold 1.0000 oz. AGW **Series:** Centennial of Cinema **Reverse:** Greta Garbo **Note:** Struck at Paris Mint.

| Date | Mintage | F | VF | XF | Unc | BU |
|---|---|---|---|---|---|---|
| 1995 Proof | 3,000 | Value: 900 | | | | |

**500 FRANCS** KM# 1095 **Weight:** 155.5175 g. **Composition:** 0.9990 Gold 5.0000 oz. AGW **Series:** Centennial of Cinema **Reverse:** Greta Garbo **Note:** Struck at Paris Mint.

| Date | Mintage | F | VF | XF | Unc | BU |
|---|---|---|---|---|---|---|
| 1995 Proof | 99 | Value: 3,200 | | | | |

**500 FRANCS** KM# 1098 **Weight:** 31.0350 g. **Composition:** 0.9990 Gold 1.0000 oz. AGW **Series:** Centennial of Cinema **Reverse:** Audrey Hepburn **Note:** Struck at Paris Mint.

| Date | Mintage | F | VF | XF | Unc | BU |
|---|---|---|---|---|---|---|
| 1995 Proof | 3,000 | Value: 900 | | | | |

**500 FRANCS** KM# 1099 **Weight:** 155.5175 g. **Composition:** 0.9990 Gold 5.0000 oz. AGW **Series:** Centennial of Cinema **Reverse:** Audrey Hepburn **Note:** Struck at Paris Mint.

| Date | Mintage | F | VF | XF | Unc | BU |
|---|---|---|---|---|---|---|
| 1995 Proof | 99 | Value: 3,200 | | | | |

**500 FRANCS** KM# 1102 **Weight:** 31.0350 g. **Composition:** 0.9990 Gold 1.0000 oz. AGW **Series:** Centennial of Cinema **Reverse:** Federico Fellini **Note:** Struck at Paris Mint.

| Date | Mintage | F | VF | XF | Unc | BU |
|---|---|---|---|---|---|---|
| 1995 Proof | 3,000 | Value: 900 | | | | |

**500 FRANCS** KM# 1103 **Weight:** 155.5175 g. **Composition:** 0.9990 Gold 5.0000 oz. AGW **Series:** Centennial of Cinema **Reverse:** Federico Fellini **Note:** Struck at Paris Mint.

| Date | Mintage | F | VF | XF | Unc | BU |
|---|---|---|---|---|---|---|
| 1995 Proof | 99 | Value: 3,200 | | | | |

**500 FRANCS** KM# 1106 **Weight:** 31.0350 g. **Composition:** 0.9990 Gold 1.0000 oz. AGW **Series:** Centennial of Cinema **Reverse:** Yves Montand **Note:** Struck at Paris Mint.

| Date | Mintage | F | VF | XF | Unc | BU |
|---|---|---|---|---|---|---|
| 1995 Proof | 3,000 | Value: 900 | | | | |

**500 FRANCS** KM# 1107 **Weight:** 155.5175 g. **Composition:** 0.9990 Gold 5.0000 oz. AGW **Series:** Centennial of Cinema **Reverse:** Yves Montand **Note:** Struck at Paris Mint.

| Date | Mintage | F | VF | XF | Unc | BU |
|---|---|---|---|---|---|---|
| 1995 Proof | 99 | Value: 3,200 | | | | |

**500 FRANCS** KM# 1110 **Weight:** 31.0350 g. **Composition:** 0.9990 Gold 1.0000 oz. AGW **Series:** Centennial of Cinema **Reverse:** Romy Schneider **Note:** Struck at Paris Mint.

| Date | Mintage | F | VF | XF | Unc | BU |
|---|---|---|---|---|---|---|
| 1995 Proof | 3,000 | Value: 900 | | | | |

**500 FRANCS** KM# 1111 **Weight:** 155.5175 g. **Composition:** 0.9990 Gold 5.0000 oz. AGW **Series:** Centennial of Cinema **Reverse:** Romy Schneider **Note:** Struck at Paris Mint.

| Date | Mintage | F | VF | XF | Unc | BU |
|---|---|---|---|---|---|---|
| 1995 Proof | 99 | Value: 3,200 | | | | |

**500 FRANCS** KM# 1117 **Weight:** 17.0000 g. **Composition:** 0.9200 Gold .5028 oz. AGW **Subject:** V.E. Day **Obverse:** Victory in Europe date, May 8, 1945 **Note:** Struck at Paris Mint.

| Date | Mintage | F | VF | XF | Unc | BU |
|---|---|---|---|---|---|---|
| 1995 Proof | 5,000 | Value: 350 | | | | |

**500 FRANCS** KM# 1135 **Weight:** 17.0000 g. **Composition:** 0.9200 Gold .5028 oz. AGW **Obverse:** Louis Pasteur **Note:** Struck at Paris Mint.

| Date | Mintage | F | VF | XF | Unc | BU |
|---|---|---|---|---|---|---|
| 1995 Proof | 1,000 | Value: 365 | | | | |

**500 FRANCS** KM# 1137 **Weight:** 17.0000 g. **Composition:** 0.9200 Gold .5028 oz. AGW **Obverse:** Jean de la Fountain **Note:** Struck at Paris Mint.

| Date | Mintage | F | VF | XF | Unc | BU |
|---|---|---|---|---|---|---|
| 1995 Proof | 1,000 | Value: 365 | | | | |

**500 FRANCS** KM# 1139 **Weight:** 17.0000 g. **Composition:** 0.9200 Gold .5028 oz. AGW **Obverse:** Madame de Sevigne **Note:** Struck at Paris Mint.

| Date | Mintage | F | VF | XF | Unc | BU |
|---|---|---|---|---|---|---|
| 1996 Proof | 500 | Value: 675 | | | | |

**500 FRANCS** KM# 1181 **Weight:** 17.0000 g. **Composition:** 0.9200 Gold .5028 oz. AGW **Obverse:** King Clovis I **Note:** Struck at Paris Mint.

| Date | Mintage | F | VF | XF | Unc | BU |
|---|---|---|---|---|---|---|
| 1996 Proof | 250 | Value: 700 | | | | |

**500 FRANCS** KM# 1197 **Weight:** 17.0000 g. **Composition:** 0.9200 Gold .5028 oz. AGW **Obverse:** Bust of Georges Guynemer facing, dates **Reverse:** Stork emblem and denomination **Note:** Struck at Paris Mint.

| Date | Mintage | F | VF | XF | Unc | BU |
|---|---|---|---|---|---|---|
| 1997 Proof | 300 | Value: 700 | | | | |

**500 FRANCS** KM# 1199 **Weight:** 17.0000 g. **Composition:** 0.9200 Gold .5028 oz. AGW **Obverse:** Conjoined busts of

Pierre and Marie Curie **Reverse:** Denomination **Note:** Struck at Paris Mint.

| Date | Mintage | F | VF | XF | Unc | BU |
|---|---|---|---|---|---|---|
| 1997 Proof | 300 | Value: 700 | | | | |

**500 FRANCS** KM# 1200 **Weight:** 17.0000 g. **Composition:** 0.9200 Gold .5028 oz. AGW **Obverse:** Head of Andre Malraux facing **Reverse:** Cats flanking denomination **Note:** Struck at Paris Mint.

| Date | Mintage | F | VF | XF | Unc | BU |
|---|---|---|---|---|---|---|
| 1997 Proof | 300 | Value: 700 | | | | |

**500 FRANCS** KM# 1202 **Weight:** 17.0000 g. **Composition:** 0.9200 Gold .5028 oz. AGW **Obverse:** Head of Marquis de Condorcet right **Reverse:** Denomination **Note:** Struck at Paris Mint.

| Date | Mintage | F | VF | XF | Unc | BU |
|---|---|---|---|---|---|---|
| 1998 Proof | 300 | Value: 700 | | | | |

**500 FRANCS** KM# 1204 **Weight:** 17.0000 g. **Composition:** 0.9200 Gold .5028 oz. AGW **Obverse:** Head of Gaspard Monge 1/2 right **Reverse:** Denomination **Note:** Struck at Paris Mint.

| Date | Mintage | F | VF | XF | Unc | BU |
|---|---|---|---|---|---|---|
| 1998 Proof | 300 | Value: 700 | | | | |

**500 FRANCS** KM# 1237 **Weight:** 31.1040 g. **Composition:** 0.9990 Gold .9990 oz. AGW **Subject:** Yves St. Laurent **Obverse:** RF monogram, denomination **Reverse:** Fashion show scene **Edge:** Plain **Note:** Struck at Paris Mint.

| Date | Mintage | F | VF | XF | Unc | BU |
|---|---|---|---|---|---|---|
| 2000 Proof | 1,000 | Value: 850 | | | | |

**655.957 FRANCS** KM# 1257 **Weight:** 31.1040 g. **Composition:** 0.9990 Gold .9990 oz. AGW **Obverse:** Country names with euro-currency equivalents around RF, denomination and French coin designs **Reverse:** Europa allegorical portrait **Edge:** Plain **Note:** Euro Conversion Series. Struck at Paris Mint.

| Date | Mintage | F | VF | XF | Unc | BU |
|---|---|---|---|---|---|---|
| 1999 Proof | 2,000 | Value: 750 | | | | |

**655.957 FRANCS** KM# 1261 **Weight:** 31.1040 g. **Composition:** 0.9990 Gold .9990 oz. AGW **Obverse:** Country names with euro-currency equivalents around RF, denomination and French euro coin design **Note:** Struck at Paris Mint.

| Date | Mintage | F | VF | XF | Unc | BU |
|---|---|---|---|---|---|---|
| 2000 Proof | 2,000 | Value: 750 | | | | |

**655.957 FRANCS** KM# 1247 **Weight:** 15.5520 g. **Composition:** 0.9990 Gold .4995 oz. AGW **Series:** European Art Styles - Renaissance **Obverse:** Europe allegorical portrait **Reverse:** Greek and Roman style buildings **Note:** Struck at Paris Mint.

| Date | Mintage | F | VF | XF | Unc | BU |
|---|---|---|---|---|---|---|
| 2000 Proof | 2,000 | Value: 485 | | | | |

**655.957 FRANCS** KM# 1248 **Weight:** 15.5520 g. **Composition:** 0.9990 Gold .4995 oz. AGW **Series:** European Art Styles - Roman **Reverse:** Roman sculpture and ancient buildings **Note:** Struck at Paris Mint.

| Date | Mintage | F | VF | XF | Unc | BU |
|---|---|---|---|---|---|---|
| 2000 Proof | 2,000 | Value: 485 | | | | |

**655.957 FRANCS** KM# 1249 **Weight:** 15.5520 g. **Composition:** 0.9990 Gold .4995 oz. AGW **Series:** European Art Styles - Gothic **Reverse:** Gothic sculpture and buildings **Note:** Struck at Paris Mint.

| Date | Mintage | F | VF | XF | Unc | BU |
|---|---|---|---|---|---|---|
| 2000 Proof | 2,000 | Value: 485 | | | | |

**655.957 FRANCS** KM# 1250 **Weight:** 15.5520 g. **Composition:** 0.9990 Gold .4995 oz. AGW **Series:** European Art Styles - Renaissance **Reverse:** Renaissance buildings **Note:** Struck at Paris Mint.

| Date | Mintage | F | VF | XF | Unc | BU |
|---|---|---|---|---|---|---|
| 2000 Proof | 2,000 | Value: 485 | | | | |

**655.957 FRANCS** KM# 1251 **Weight:** 15.5520 g. **Composition:** 0.9990 Gold .4995 oz. AGW **Series:** European Art Styles - Classic and Baroque **Note:** Struck at Paris Mint.

| Date | Mintage | F | VF | XF | Unc | BU |
|---|---|---|---|---|---|---|
| 2000 Proof | 2,000 | Value: 485 | | | | |

**655.957 FRANCS** KM# 1252 **Weight:** 15.5520 g. **Composition:** 0.9990 Gold .4995 oz. AGW **Series:** European Art Styles - Art Nouveau **Reverse:** Arches and scrollwork **Note:** Struck at Paris Mint.

| Date | Mintage | F | VF | XF | Unc | BU |
|---|---|---|---|---|---|---|
| 2000 Proof | 2,000 | Value: 485 | | | | |

**655.957 FRANCS** KM# 1253 **Weight:** 15.5520 g. **Composition:** 0.9990 Gold .4995 oz. AGW **Series:** European Art Styles - Modern **Reverse:** Similar to 5 Francs, KM#1228 **Note:** Struck at Paris Mint.

| Date | Mintage | F | VF | XF | Unc | BU |
|---|---|---|---|---|---|---|
| 2000 Proof | 2,000 | Value: 485 | | | | |

**655.957 FRANCS** KM# 1267 **Weight:** 31.1035 g. **Composition:** 0.9990 Gold 1.0000 oz. AGW **Subject:** Last Year of the French Franc **Obverse:** French and other European euro currency equivalents **Reverse:** Similar to KM#1258 but with addition of "last year of the franc" logo after the date **Edge:** Plain

| Date | Mintage | F | VF | XF | Unc | BU |
|---|---|---|---|---|---|---|
| 2001 Proof | 2,000 | Value: 635 | | | | |

**655.957 FRANCS** KM# 1267.1 **Weight:** 155.5175 g. **Composition:** 0.9990 Gold 5.0000 oz. AGW **Edge:** Plain

| Date | Mintage | F | VF | XF | Unc | BU |
|---|---|---|---|---|---|---|
| 2001 Proof | 99 | Value: 4,000 | | | | |

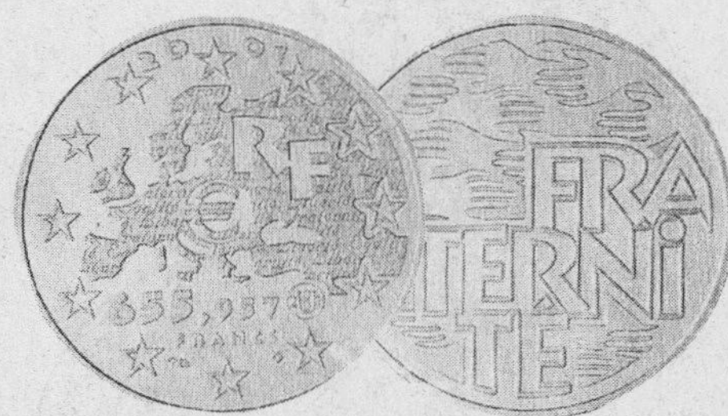

**655.957 FRANCS** KM# 1279 **Weight:** 17.0000 g. **Composition:** 0.9200 Gold .5028 oz. AGW **Subject:** Motto Series **Obverse:** Denomination **Reverse:** FRATERNITE **Edge:** Reeded

| Date | Mintage | F | VF | XF | Unc | BU |
|---|---|---|---|---|---|---|
| 2001 Proof | 2,000 | Value: 365 | | | | |

**655.957 FRANCS** KM# 1280 **Weight:** 17.0000 g. **Composition:** 0.9200 Gold .5028 oz. AGW **Subject:** Motto Series **Obverse:** Denomination **Reverse:** EGALITE

| Date | Mintage | F | VF | XF | Unc | BU |
|---|---|---|---|---|---|---|
| 2001 Proof | 2,000 | Value: 365 | | | | |

**655.957 FRANCS** **KM# 1281** **Weight:** 17.0000 g. **Composition:** 0.9200 Gold .5028 oz. AGW **Subject:** Motto Series **Obverse:** Denomination **Reverse:** LIBERTE

| Date | Mintage | F | VF | XF | Unc | BU |
|---|---|---|---|---|---|---|
| 2001 Proof | 2,000 | Value: 365 | | | | |

## ECU / FRANCS COINAGE

European Currency Units

**100 FRANCS - 15 ECUS** **KM# 989** **Weight:** 22.2000 g. **Composition:** 0.9000 Silver .6424 oz. ASW **Reverse:** Charlemagne

| Date | Mintage | F | VF | XF | Unc | BU |
|---|---|---|---|---|---|---|
| 1990 Proof | 30,000 | Value: 95.00 | | | | |

**100 FRANCS - 15 ECUS** **KM# 1002** **Weight:** 22.2000 g. **Composition:** 0.9000 Silver .6424 oz. ASW **Reverse:** Descartes

| Date | Mintage | F | VF | XF | Unc | BU |
|---|---|---|---|---|---|---|
| 1991 Proof | 20,000 | Value: 65.00 | | | | |

**100 FRANCS - 15 ECUS** **KM# 1012** **Weight:** 22.2000 g. **Composition:** 0.9000 Silver .6424 oz. ASW **Obverse:** Denomination in center within legend and chain above RF **Reverse:** Jean Monnet

| Date | Mintage | F | VF | XF | Unc | BU |
|---|---|---|---|---|---|---|
| 1992 Proof | 30,000 | Value: 55.00 | | | | |

**100 FRANCS - 15 ECUS** **KM# 1029** **Weight:** 22.2000 g. **Composition:** 0.9000 Silver .6424 oz. ASW **Subject:** Mediterranean Games **Reverse:** Swimming

| Date | Mintage | F | VF | XF | Unc | BU |
|---|---|---|---|---|---|---|
| 1993 Proof | 15,000 | Value: 47.50 | | | | |

**100 FRANCS - 15 ECUS** **KM# 1030** **Weight:** 22.2000 g. **Composition:** 0.9000 Silver .6424 oz. ASW **Subject:** Mediterranean Games **Reverse:** Soccer

| Date | Mintage | F | VF | XF | Unc | BU |
|---|---|---|---|---|---|---|
| 1993 Proof | 15,000 | Value: 47.50 | | | | |

**100 FRANCS - 15 ECUS** **KM# 1031** **Weight:** 22.2000 g. **Composition:** 0.9000 Silver .6424 oz. ASW **Reverse:** Arc de Triumph

| Date | Mintage | F | VF | XF | Unc | BU |
|---|---|---|---|---|---|---|
| 1993 Proof | 20,000 | Value: 42.50 | | | | |

**100 FRANCS - 15 ECUS** **KM# 1032** **Weight:** 22.2000 g. **Composition:** 0.9000 Silver .6424 oz. ASW **Reverse:** Brandenburg Gate

| Date | Mintage | F | VF | XF | Unc | BU |
|---|---|---|---|---|---|---|
| 1993 Proof | 20,000 | Value: 42.50 | | | | |

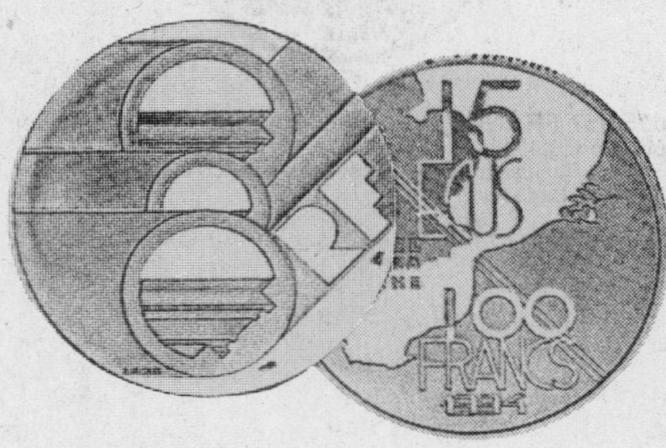


**100 FRANCS - 15 ECUS** **KM# 1060** **Weight:** 22.2000 g. **Composition:** 0.9000 Silver .6424 oz. ASW **Reverse:** Stylized Tunnel View - Map

| Date | Mintage | F | VF | XF | Unc | BU |
|---|---|---|---|---|---|---|
| 1994 Proof | 20,000 | Value: 30.00 | | | | |

**100 FRANCS - 15 ECUS** **KM# 1068** **Weight:** 22.2000 g. **Composition:** 0.9000 Silver .6424 oz. ASW **Reverse:** St. Mark's Cathedral, Venice

| Date | Mintage | F | VF | XF | Unc | BU |
|---|---|---|---|---|---|---|
| 1994 Proof | 20,000 | Value: 32.50 | | | | |

**100 FRANCS - 15 ECUS** **KM# 1070** **Weight:** 22.2000 g. **Composition:** 0.9000 Silver .6424 oz. ASW **Reverse:** Big Ben, London

| Date | Mintage | F | VF | XF | Unc | BU |
|---|---|---|---|---|---|---|
| 1994 Proof | 20,000 | Value: 32.50 | | | | |

**100 FRANCS - 15 ECUS** **KM# 1112** **Weight:** 22.2000 g. **Composition:** 0.9000 Silver .6424 oz. ASW **Reverse:** The Alhambra, Granada

| Date | Mintage | F | VF | XF | Unc | BU |
|---|---|---|---|---|---|---|
| 1995 Proof | 20,000 | Value: 35.00 | | | | |

**100 FRANCS - 15 ECUS** **KM# 1114** **Weight:** 22.2000 g. **Composition:** 0.9000 Silver .6424 oz. ASW **Reverse:** The Parthenon, Greece

| Date | Mintage | F | VF | XF | Unc | BU |
|---|---|---|---|---|---|---|
| 1995 Proof | 20,000 | Value: 35.00 | | | | |

**500 FRANCS - 70 ECUS** **KM# 990** **Weight:** 17.0000 g. **Composition:** 0.9200 Gold .5029 oz. AGW **Reverse:** Charlemagne

| Date | Mintage | F | VF | XF | Unc | BU |
|---|---|---|---|---|---|---|
| 1990 Proof | 5,000 | Value: 350 | | | | |

**500 FRANCS - 70 ECUS** **KM# 990a** **Weight:** 20.0000 g. **Composition:** 0.9990 Platinum .6431 oz. APW

| Date | Mintage | F | VF | XF | Unc | BU |
|---|---|---|---|---|---|---|
| 1990 Proof | 2,000 | Value: 450 | | | | |

**500 FRANCS - 70 ECUS** **KM# 1003** **Weight:** 17.0000 g. **Composition:** 0.9200 Gold .5029 oz. AGW **Reverse:** Descartes

| Date | Mintage | F | VF | XF | Unc | BU |
|---|---|---|---|---|---|---|
| 1991 Proof | 3,000 | Value: 425 | | | | |

**500 FRANCS - 70 ECUS** **KM# 1003a** **Weight:** 20.0000 g. **Composition:** 0.9990 Platinum .6431 oz. APW

| Date | Mintage | F | VF | XF | Unc | BU |
|---|---|---|---|---|---|---|
| 1991 Proof | 1,000 | Value: 500 | | | | |

**500 FRANCS - 70 ECUS** **KM# 1013** **Weight:** 17.0000 g. **Composition:** 0.9200 Gold .5029 oz. AGW **Reverse:** Jean Monet

| Date | Mintage | F | VF | XF | Unc | BU |
|---|---|---|---|---|---|---|
| 1992 Proof | 5,000 | Value: 400 | | | | |

**500 FRANCS - 70 ECUS** **KM# 1013a** **Weight:** 20.0000 g. **Composition:** 0.9990 Platinum .6431 oz. APW

| Date | Mintage | F | VF | XF | Unc | BU |
|---|---|---|---|---|---|---|
| 1992 Proof | 2,000 | Value: 450 | | | | |

**500 FRANCS - 70 ECUS** **KM# 1033** **Weight:** 17.0000 g. **Composition:** 0.9200 Gold .5029 oz. AGW **Subject:** Mediterranean Games

| Date | Mintage | F | VF | XF | Unc | BU |
|---|---|---|---|---|---|---|
| 1993 Proof | 3,000 | Value: 400 | | | | |

**500 FRANCS - 70 ECUS** **KM# 1034** **Weight:** 17.0000 g. **Composition:** 0.9200 Gold .5029 oz. AGW **Reverse:** Arc de Triumph

| Date | Mintage | F | VF | XF | Unc | BU |
|---|---|---|---|---|---|---|
| 1993 Proof | 5,000 | Value: 375 | | | | |

**500 FRANCS - 70 ECUS** **KM# 1034a** **Weight:** 19.8000 g. **Composition:** 0.9900 Platinum .6303 oz. APW **Reverse:** Arc de Triumph

| Date | Mintage | F | VF | XF | Unc | BU |
|---|---|---|---|---|---|---|
| 1993 Proof | 2,000 | Value: 425 | | | | |

**500 FRANCS - 70 ECUS** **KM# 1035** **Weight:** 17.0000 g. **Composition:** 0.9200 Gold .5029 oz. AGW **Reverse:** Brandenburg Gate

| Date | Mintage | F | VF | XF | Unc | BU |
|---|---|---|---|---|---|---|
| 1993 Proof | 5,000 | Value: 375 | | | | |

**500 FRANCS - 70 ECUS** **KM# 1035a** **Weight:** 19.8000 g. **Composition:** 0.9900 Platinum .6303 oz. APW **Reverse:** Brandenburg Gate

| Date | Mintage | F | VF | XF | Unc | BU |
|---|---|---|---|---|---|---|
| 1993 Proof | 2,000 | Value: 450 | | | | |

**500 FRANCS - 70 ECUS** **KM# 1061** **Weight:** 17.0000 g. **Composition:** 0.9200 Gold .5029 oz. AGW **Reverse:** Channel Tunnel

| Date | Mintage | F | VF | XF | Unc | BU |
|---|---|---|---|---|---|---|
| 1994 Proof | 5,000 | Value: 335 | | | | |

**500 FRANCS - 70 ECUS** **KM# 1069** **Weight:** 17.0000 g. **Composition:** 0.9200 Gold .5028 oz. AGW **Reverse:** St. Mark's Cathedral, Venice

| Date | Mintage | F | VF | XF | Unc | BU |
|---|---|---|---|---|---|---|
| 1994 Proof | 5,000 | Value: 375 | | | | |

**500 FRANCS - 70 ECUS** **KM# 1069a** **Weight:** 20.0000 g. **Composition:** 0.9990 Platinum .6431 oz. APW **Reverse:** St. Mark's Cathedral, Venice

| Date | Mintage | F | VF | XF | Unc | BU |
|---|---|---|---|---|---|---|
| 1994 Proof | 2,000 | Value: 425 | | | | |

**500 FRANCS - 70 ECUS** **KM# 1071** **Weight:** 17.0000 g. **Composition:** 0.9200 Gold .5028 oz. AGW **Reverse:** Big Ben, London

| Date | Mintage | F | VF | XF | Unc | BU |
|---|---|---|---|---|---|---|
| 1994 Proof | 5,000 | Value: 375 | | | | |

**500 FRANCS - 70 ECUS** **KM# 1071a** **Weight:** 20.0000 g. **Composition:** 0.9990 Platinum .6431 oz. APW **Reverse:** Big Ben, London

| Date | Mintage | F | VF | XF | Unc | BU |
|---|---|---|---|---|---|---|
| 1994 Proof | 2,000 | Value: 425 | | | | |

**500 FRANCS - 70 ECUS** **KM# 1113** **Weight:** 17.0000 g. **Composition:** 0.9200 Gold .5028 oz. AGW **Reverse:** The Alhambra, Granada

| Date | Mintage | F | VF | XF | Unc | BU |
|---|---|---|---|---|---|---|
| 1995 Proof | 5,000 | Value: 375 | | | | |

**500 FRANCS - 70 ECUS** **KM# 1113a** **Weight:** 20.0000 g. **Composition:** 0.9990 Platinum .6431 oz. APW **Reverse:** The Alhambra, Granada

| Date | Mintage | F | VF | XF | Unc | BU |
|---|---|---|---|---|---|---|
| 1995 Proof | 2,000 | Value: 425 | | | | |

**500 FRANCS - 70 ECUS** **KM# 1115** **Weight:** 17.0000 g. **Composition:** 0.9200 Gold .5028 oz. AGW **Reverse:** The Parthenon, Athens

| Date | Mintage | F | VF | XF | Unc | BU |
|---|---|---|---|---|---|---|
| 1995 Proof | 5,000 | Value: 375 | | | | |

**500 FRANCS - 70 ECUS** **KM# 1115a** **Weight:** 20.0000 g. **Composition:** 0.9990 Platinum .6431 oz. APW **Reverse:** The Parthenon, Athens

| Date | Mintage | F | VF | XF | Unc | BU |
|---|---|---|---|---|---|---|
| 1995 Proof | 2,000 | Value: 425 | | | | |

## MEDALLIC COINAGE

**20 FRANCS** **KM# M27** **Composition:** Silver **Subject:** President of Rene Coty Visit **Obverse:** Head of Republic **Reverse:** Coin press

| Date | Mintage | F | VF | XF | Unc | BU |
|---|---|---|---|---|---|---|
| 1955 | — | — | 50.00 | 100 | 200 | — |

**20 FRANCS** **KM# M27a** **Composition:** Gold **Subject:** President of Rene Coty Visit **Obverse:** Head of Republic **Reverse:** Coin press

| Date | Mintage | F | VF | XF | Unc | BU |
|---|---|---|---|---|---|---|
| 1955 | — | — | 200 | 250 | 400 | — |

**20 FRANCS** **KM# M28** **Composition:** Silver **Subject:** Visit by President of Rene Coty **Obverse:** Head of Republic **Reverse:** Coin press

| Date | Mintage | F | VF | XF | Unc | BU |
|---|---|---|---|---|---|---|
| 1955 | — | — | 50.00 | 100 | 200 | — |

**20 FRANCS** **KM# M28a** **Composition:** Gold **Subject:** Visit by President of Rene Coty **Obverse:** Head of Republic **Reverse:** Coin press

| Date | Mintage | F | VF | XF | Unc | BU |
|---|---|---|---|---|---|---|
| 1955 | — | — | 200 | 250 | 400 | — |

## EURO / FRANCS COINAGE

**10 FRANCS - 1.5 EURO** **KM# 1121** **Weight:** 22.2000 g. **Composition:** 0.9000 Silver .6424 oz. ASW **Series:** Museum Treasures **Obverse:** La Source

| Date | Mintage | F | VF | XF | Unc | BU |
|---|---|---|---|---|---|---|
| 1996 Proof | 15,000 | Value: 35.00 | | | | |

**10 FRANCS - 1.5 EURO** **KM# 1122** **Weight:** 22.2000 g. **Composition:** 0.9000 Silver .6424 oz. ASW **Series:** Museum Treasures **Obverse:** Fife Player

| Date | Mintage | F | VF | XF | Unc | BU |
|---|---|---|---|---|---|---|
| 1996 Proof | 15,000 | Value: 35.00 | | | | |

**10 FRANCS - 1.5 EURO** KM# 1123 **Weight:** 22.2000 g. **Composition:** 0.9000 Silver .6424 oz. ASW **Series:** Museum Treasures **Obverse:** Shang Dynasty Elephant

| Date | Mintage | F | VF | XF | Unc | BU |
|---|---|---|---|---|---|---|
| 1996 Proof | 15,000 | Value: 35.00 | | | | |

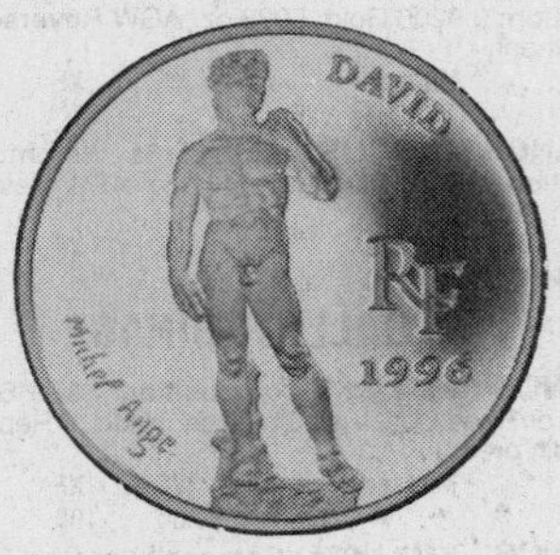


**10 FRANCS - 1.5 EURO** KM# 1146 **Weight:** 22.2000 g. **Composition:** 0.9000 Silver .6424 oz. ASW **Series:** Museum Treasures **Obverse:** David

| Date | Mintage | F | VF | XF | Unc | BU |
|---|---|---|---|---|---|---|
| 1996 Proof | 15,000 | Value: 32.50 | | | | |

**10 FRANCS - 1.5 EURO** KM# 1147 **Weight:** 22.2000 g. **Composition:** 0.9000 Silver .6424 oz. ASW **Series:** Museum Treasures **Obverse:** Van Gogh

| Date | Mintage | F | VF | XF | Unc | BU |
|---|---|---|---|---|---|---|
| 1996 Proof | 15,000 | Value: 35.00 | | | | |

**10 FRANCS - 1.5 EURO** KM# 1148 **Weight:** 22.2000 g. **Composition:** 0.9000 Silver .6424 oz. ASW **Series:** Museum Treasures **Obverse:** Clothed Maya

| Date | Mintage | F | VF | XF | Unc | BU |
|---|---|---|---|---|---|---|
| 1996 Proof | 15,000 | Value: 32.50 | | | | |

**10 FRANCS - 1.5 EURO** KM# 1158 **Weight:** 22.2000 g. **Composition:** 0.9000 Silver .6424 oz. ASW **Series:** Museum Treasures **Obverse:** Chinese Horseman

| Date | Mintage | F | VF | XF | Unc | BU |
|---|---|---|---|---|---|---|
| 1996 Proof | 15,000 | Value: 32.50 | | | | |

**10 FRANCS - 1.5 EURO** KM# 1124 **Weight:** 22.2000 g. **Composition:** 0.9000 Silver .6424 oz. ASW **Series:** Museum Treasures **Obverse:** The Thinker **Note:** Silver coins sold as a set only.

| Date | Mintage | F | VF | XF | Unc | BU |
|---|---|---|---|---|---|---|
| 1996 Proof | 15,000 | Value: 35.00 | | | | |

**100 FRANCS - 15 EURO** KM# 1140 **Weight:** 22.2000 g. **Composition:** 0.9000 Silver .6424 oz. ASW **Reverse:** St. Stephen's Cathedral, Vienna

| Date | Mintage | F | VF | XF | Unc | BU |
|---|---|---|---|---|---|---|
| 1996 Proof | 20,000 | Value: 50.00 | | | | |

**100 FRANCS - 15 EURO** KM# 1142 **Weight:** 22.2000 g. **Composition:** 0.9000 Silver .6424 oz. ASW **Reverse:** Grand Place, Bruxelles

| Date | Mintage | F | VF | XF | Unc | BU |
|---|---|---|---|---|---|---|
| 1996 Proof | 20,000 | Value: 37.50 | | | | |

**100 FRANCS - 15 EURO** KM# 1149 **Weight:** 17.0000 g. **Composition:** 0.9200 Gold .5028 oz. AGW **Series:** Museum Treasures **Obverse:** Van Gogh

| Date | Mintage | F | VF | XF | Unc | BU |
|---|---|---|---|---|---|---|
| 1996 Proof | 5,000 | Value: 375 | | | | |

**100 FRANCS - 15 EURO** KM# 1150 **Weight:** 17.0000 g. **Composition:** 0.9200 Gold .5028 oz. AGW **Series:** Museum Treasures **Obverse:** Clothed Maya

| Date | Mintage | F | VF | XF | Unc | BU |
|---|---|---|---|---|---|---|
| 1996 Proof | 5,000 | Value: 375 | | | | |

**100 FRANCS - 15 EURO** KM# 1156 **Weight:** 22.2000 g. **Composition:** 0.9000 Silver .6424 oz. ASW **Subject:** Amsterdam - Magere Brug **Reverse:** Bridge

| Date | Mintage | F | VF | XF | Unc | BU |
|---|---|---|---|---|---|---|
| 1996 Proof | 20,000 | Value: 37.50 | | | | |

**100 FRANCS - 15 EURO** KM# 1159 **Weight:** 17.0000 g. **Composition:** 0.9200 Gold .5028 oz. AGW **Series:** Museum Treasures **Reverse:** Chinese Horseman **Note:** Similar to 10 Francs / 1-1/2 Euro, KM#1158.

| Date | Mintage | F | VF | XF | Unc | BU |
|---|---|---|---|---|---|---|
| 1996 Proof | 5,000 | Value: 375 | | | | |

**100 FRANCS - 15 EURO** KM# 1125 **Weight:** 17.0000 g. **Composition:** 0.9200 Gold .5028 oz. AGW **Series:** Museum Treasures **Obverse:** La Source **Note:** Similar to 10 Francs / 1.5 Euro, KM#1121.

| Date | Mintage | F | VF | XF | Unc | BU |
|---|---|---|---|---|---|---|
| 1996 Proof | 5,000 | Value: 375 | | | | |

**100 FRANCS - 15 EURO** KM# 1126 **Weight:** 17.0000 g. **Composition:** 0.9200 Gold .5028 oz. AGW **Series:** Museum Treasures **Obverse:** Fife Player **Note:** Similar to 10 Francs / 1.5 Euro, KM#1122.

| Date | Mintage | F | VF | XF | Unc | BU |
|---|---|---|---|---|---|---|
| 1996 Proof | 5,000 | Value: 375 | | | | |

**100 FRANCS - 15 EURO** KM# 1127 **Weight:** 17.0000 g. **Composition:** 0.9200 Gold .5028 oz. AGW **Series:** Museum Treasures **Obverse:** Shang Dynasty Elephant **Note:** Similar to 10 Francs / 1.5 Euro, KM#1123.

| Date | Mintage | F | VF | XF | Unc | BU |
|---|---|---|---|---|---|---|
| 1996 Proof | 5,000 | Value: 375 | | | | |

**100 FRANCS - 15 EURO** KM# 1174 **Weight:** 22.2000 g. **Composition:** 0.9000 Silver .6424 oz. ASW **Subject:** Lisbon **Obverse:** Denominations **Reverse:** Castle-like building Tour de Belem

| Date | Mintage | F | VF | XF | Unc | BU |
|---|---|---|---|---|---|---|
| 1997 Proof | 20,000 | Value: 50.00 | | | | |

**100 FRANCS - 15 EURO** KM# 1176 **Weight:** 22.2000 g. **Composition:** 0.9000 Silver .6424 oz. ASW **Subject:** Helsinki **Obverse:** Denominations **Reverse:** Cathedral, Cathedrale Saint - Nicolas

| Date | Mintage | F | VF | XF | Unc | BU |
|---|---|---|---|---|---|---|
| 1997 Proof | 20,000 | Value: 50.00 | | | | |

**100 FRANCS - 15 EURO** KM# 1178 **Weight:** 22.2000 g. **Composition:** 0.9000 Silver .6424 oz. ASW **Subject:** Copenhagen **Obverse:** Denominations **Reverse:** Statue of the Copenhagen mermaid, Petite Sirene

| Date | Mintage | F | VF | XF | Unc | BU |
|---|---|---|---|---|---|---|
| 1997 Proof | 20,000 | Value: 50.00 | | | | |

**100 FRANCS - 15 EURO** **KM# 1189** **Weight:** 22.2000 g. **Composition:** 0.9000 Silver .6424 oz. ASW **Subject:** Irlande - Rock of Cashel **Obverse:** Denomination **Reverse:** Celtic cross and castle

| Date | Mintage | F | VF | XF | Unc | BU |
|---|---|---|---|---|---|---|
| 1997 Proof | 20,000 | Value: 50.00 | | | | |

**100 FRANCS - 15 EURO** **KM# 1191** **Weight:** 22.2000 g. **Composition:** 0.9000 Silver .6424 oz. ASW **Subject:** Luxembourg - Wenceslaus Wall **Obverse:** Denomination **Reverse:** Walled palace

| Date | Mintage | F | VF | XF | Unc | BU |
|---|---|---|---|---|---|---|
| 1997 Proof | 20,000 | Value: 50.00 | | | | |

**100 FRANCS - 15 EURO** **KM# 1193** **Weight:** 22.2000 g. **Composition:** 0.9000 Silver .6424 oz. ASW **Subject:** Stockholm - Hotel de Ville **Obverse:** Denomination **Reverse:** Tower and building

| Date | Mintage | F | VF | XF | Unc | BU |
|---|---|---|---|---|---|---|
| 1997 Proof | 20,000 | Value: 50.00 | | | | |

**500 FRANCS - 75 EURO** **KM# 1128** **Weight:** 31.1035 g. **Composition:** 0.9990 Gold 1.0000 oz. AGW **Series:** Museum Treasures **Obverse:** The Thinker

| Date | Mintage | F | VF | XF | Unc | BU |
|---|---|---|---|---|---|---|
| 1996 Proof | 5,000 | Value: 575 | | | | |

**500 FRANCS - 75 EURO** **KM# 1129** **Weight:** 155.5175 g. **Composition:** 0.9990 Gold 5.0000 oz. AGW **Series:** Museum Treasures **Obverse:** La Source

| Date | Mintage | F | VF | XF | Unc | BU |
|---|---|---|---|---|---|---|
| 1996 Prof | 99 | Value: 3,250 | | | | |

**500 FRANCS - 75 EURO** **KM# 1130** **Weight:** 155.5175 g. **Composition:** 0.9990 Gold 5.0000 oz. AGW **Series:** Museum Treasures **Obverse:** Fife Player

| Date | Mintage | F | VF | XF | Unc | BU |
|---|---|---|---|---|---|---|
| 1996 Proof | 99 | Value: 3,250 | | | | |

**500 FRANCS - 75 EURO** **KM# 1131** **Weight:** 155.5175 g. **Composition:** 0.9990 Gold 5.0000 oz. AGW **Series:** Museum Treasures **Obverse:** Shang Dynasty Elephant

| Date | Mintage | F | VF | XF | Unc | BU |
|---|---|---|---|---|---|---|
| 1996 Proof | 99 | Value: 3,500 | | | | |

**500 FRANCS - 75 EURO** **KM# 1141** **Weight:** 17.0000 g. **Composition:** 0.9200 Gold .5028 oz. AGW **Subject:** St. Stephen's Cathedral, Vienna

| Date | Mintage | F | VF | XF | Unc | BU |
|---|---|---|---|---|---|---|
| 1996 Proof | 5,000 | Value: 375 | | | | |

**500 FRANCS - 75 EURO** **KM# 1141a** **Weight:** 20.0000 g. **Composition:** 0.9990 Platinum .6431 oz. APW **Subject:** St. Stephen's Cathedral, Vienna

| Date | Mintage | F | VF | XF | Unc | BU |
|---|---|---|---|---|---|---|
| 1996 Prof | 2,000 | Value: 450 | | | | |

**500 FRANCS - 75 EURO** **KM# 1143** **Weight:** 17.0000 g. **Composition:** 0.9200 Gold .5028 oz. AGW **Subject:** Grand Place, Bruxelles

| Date | Mintage | F | VF | XF | Unc | BU |
|---|---|---|---|---|---|---|
| 1996 Proof | 5,000 | Value: 375 | | | | |

**500 FRANCS - 75 EURO** **KM# 1143a** **Weight:** 20.0000 g. **Composition:** 0.9990 Platinum .6431 oz. APW **Subject:** Grand Place, Bruxelles

| Date | Mintage | F | VF | XF | Unc | BU |
|---|---|---|---|---|---|---|
| 1996 Proof | 2,000 | Value: 450 | | | | |

**500 FRANCS - 75 EURO** **KM# 1151** **Weight:** 31.1035 g. **Composition:** 0.9990 Gold 1.0000 oz. AGW **Series:** Museum Treasures **Obverse:** David

| Date | Mintage | F | VF | XF | Unc | BU |
|---|---|---|---|---|---|---|
| 1996 Proof | 5,000 | Value: 575 | | | | |

**500 FRANCS - 75 EURO** **KM# 1153** **Weight:** 155.5175 g. **Composition:** 0.9990 Gold 5.0000 oz. AGW **Series:** Museum Treasures **Obverse:** Van Gogh **Reverse:** Similar to KM#1151

| Date | Mintage | F | VF | XF | Unc | BU |
|---|---|---|---|---|---|---|
| 1996 Proof | 99 | Value: 3,250 | | | | |

**500 FRANCS - 75 EURO** **KM# 1154** **Weight:** 155.5175 g. **Composition:** 0.9990 Gold 5.0000 oz. AGW **Series:** Museum Treasures **Obverse:** Clothed Maya **Reverse:** Similar to KM#1151

| Date | Mintage | F | VF | XF | Unc | BU |
|---|---|---|---|---|---|---|
| 1996 Proof | 99 | Value: 3,250 | | | | |

**500 FRANCS - 75 EURO** **KM# 1157** **Weight:** 17.0000 g. **Composition:** 0.9200 Gold .5028 oz. AGW **Subject:** Amsterdam Magere Brug

| Date | Mintage | F | VF | XF | Unc | BU |
|---|---|---|---|---|---|---|
| 1996 Proof | 5,000 | Value: 375 | | | | |

**500 FRANCS - 75 EURO** **KM# 1157a** **Weight:** 20.0000 g. **Composition:** 0.9990 Platinum .6431 oz. APW **Subject:** Amsterdam Magere Brug

| Date | Mintage | F | VF | XF | Unc | BU |
|---|---|---|---|---|---|---|
| 1996 Proof | 2,000 | Value: 500 | | | | |

**500 FRANCS - 75 EURO** **KM# 1152** **Weight:** 155.5175 g. **Composition:** 0.9990 Gold 5.0000 oz. AGW **Series:** Museum Treasures **Obverse:** David **Note:** Similar to KM#1151.

| Date | Mintage | F | VF | XF | Unc | BU |
|---|---|---|---|---|---|---|
| 1996 Proof | 99 | Value: 3,250 | | | | |

**500 FRANCS - 75 EURO** **KM# 1175** **Weight:** 17.0000 g. **Composition:** 0.9200 Gold .5028 oz. AGW **Subject:** Lisbon **Obverse:** Denominations **Reverse:** Castle-like building Tour de Belem

| Date | Mintage | F | VF | XF | Unc | BU |
|---|---|---|---|---|---|---|
| 1997 Proof | 5,000 | Value: 385 | | | | |

**500 FRANCS - 75 EURO** **KM# 1175a** **Weight:** 20.0000 g. **Composition:** 0.9990 Platinum .6431 oz. APW **Subject:** Lisbon **Obverse:** Denominations **Reverse:** Castle-like building Tour de Belem

| Date | Mintage | F | VF | XF | Unc | BU |
|---|---|---|---|---|---|---|
| 1997 Proof | 2,000 | Value: 485 | | | | |

**500 FRANCS - 75 EURO** **KM# 1177** **Weight:** 17.0000 g. **Composition:** 0.9200 Gold .5028 oz. AGW **Subject:** Helsinki **Obverse:** Denominations **Reverse:** Cathedral, Cathedrale Saint Nicholas

| Date | Mintage | F | VF | XF | Unc | BU |
|---|---|---|---|---|---|---|
| 1997 Proof | 5,000 | Value: 385 | | | | |

**500 FRANCS - 75 EURO** **KM# 1177a** **Weight:** 20.0000 g. **Composition:** 0.9990 Platinum .6431 oz. APW **Subject:** Helsinki **Obverse:** Denominations **Reverse:** Cathedral, Cathedrale Saint Nicholas

| Date | Mintage | F | VF | XF | Unc | BU |
|---|---|---|---|---|---|---|
| 1997 Proof | 2,000 | Value: 485 | | | | |

**500 FRANCS - 75 EURO** **KM# 1179** **Weight:** 17.0000 g. **Composition:** 0.9200 Gold .5028 oz. AGW **Subject:** Copenhagen **Obverse:** Denominations **Reverse:** Statue of Copenhagen's Little Mermaid, Petite Siren

| Date | Mintage | F | VF | XF | Unc | BU |
|---|---|---|---|---|---|---|
| 1997 Proof | 5,000 | Value: 500 | | | | |

**500 FRANCS - 75 EURO** **KM# 1179a** **Weight:** 20.0000 g. **Composition:** 0.9990 Platinum .6431 oz. APW **Subject:** Copenhagen **Obverse:** Denominations **Reverse:** Statue of Copenhagen's Little Mermaid, Petite Siren

| Date | Mintage | F | VF | XF | Unc | BU |
|---|---|---|---|---|---|---|
| 1997 Proof | 2,000 | Value: 600 | | | | |

**500 FRANCS - 75 EURO** **KM# 1190** **Weight:** 17.0000 g. **Composition:** 0.9200 Gold .5028 oz. AGW **Subject:** Ireland - Rock of Cashel **Obverse:** Denomination **Reverse:** Celtic cross and castle

| Date | Mintage | F | VF | XF | Unc | BU |
|---|---|---|---|---|---|---|
| 1997 Proof | 5,000 | Value: 450 | | | | |

**500 FRANCS - 75 EURO** **KM# 1190a** **Weight:** 20.0000 g. **Composition:** 0.9990 Platinum .6431 oz. APW **Subject:** Ireland - Rock of Cashel **Obverse:** Denomination **Reverse:** Celtic cross and castle

| Date | Mintage | F | VF | XF | Unc | BU |
|---|---|---|---|---|---|---|
| 1997 Proof | 2,000 | Value: 500 | | | | |

**500 FRANCS - 75 EURO** **KM# 1192** **Weight:** 17.0000 g. **Composition:** 0.9200 Gold .5028 oz. AGW **Subject:** Luxembourg - Wenceslas Wall **Obverse:** Denomination **Reverse:** Walled palace

| Date | Mintage | F | VF | XF | Unc | BU |
|---|---|---|---|---|---|---|
| 1997 Proof | 5,000 | Value: 450 | | | | |

**500 FRANCS - 75 EURO** **KM# 1192a** **Weight:** 20.0000 g. **Composition:** 0.9990 Platinum .6431 oz. APW

| Date | Mintage | F | VF | XF | Unc | BU |
|---|---|---|---|---|---|---|
| 1997 Proof | 2,000 | Value: 500 | | | | |

**500 FRANCS - 75 EURO** **KM# 1194** **Weight:** 17.0000 g. **Composition:** 0.9990 Gold .5028 oz. AGW **Subject:** Stockholm - Hotel de Ville **Obverse:** Denomination **Reverse:** Tower and building

| Date | Mintage | F | VF | XF | Unc | BU |
|---|---|---|---|---|---|---|
| 1997 Proof | 5,000 | Value: 450 | | | | |

**500 FRANCS - 75 EURO** **KM# 1194a** **Weight:** 20.0000 g. **Composition:** 0.9990 Platinum .5028 oz. APW **Subject:** Stockholm - Hotel de Ville **Obverse:** Denomination **Reverse:** Tower and building

| Date | Mintage | F | VF | XF | Unc | BU |
|---|---|---|---|---|---|---|
| 1997 Proof | 2,000 | Value: 500 | | | | |

## EURO COINAGE

European Economic Community Issues

**EURO CENT** **KM# 1282** **Weight:** 2.2700 g. **Composition:** Copper Plated Steel **Obverse:** Human face **Reverse:** Denomination and globe **Edge:** Plain **Note:** Struck at Paris Mint.

| Date | Mintage | F | VF | XF | Unc | BU |
|---|---|---|---|---|---|---|
| 1999 | — | — | — | — | 0.10 | — |
| 1999 Proof | — | Value: 0.15 | | | | |
| 2000 | — | — | — | — | 0.10 | — |
| 2000 Proof | Est. 15,000 | Value: 0.15 | | | | |
| 2001 | — | — | — | — | 0.10 | — |
| 2001 Proof | Est. 15,000 | Value: 0.15 | | | | |
| 2002 | — | — | — | — | 0.10 | — |
| 2002 Proof | Est. 40,000 | Value: 0.15 | | | | |

**2 EURO CENTS** **KM# 1283** **Weight:** 3.0300 g. **Composition:** Copper-Plated-Steel **Obverse:** Human face **Reverse:** Denomination and globe **Edge:** Grooved **Note:** Struck at Paris Mint.

| Date | Mintage | F | VF | XF | Unc | BU |
|---|---|---|---|---|---|---|
| 1999 | — | — | — | — | 0.20 | — |
| 1999 Proof | Est. 15,000 | Value: 0.30 | | | | |
| 2000 | — | — | — | — | 0.20 | — |
| 2000 Proof | Est. 15,000 | Value: 0.30 | | | | |
| 2001 | — | — | — | — | 0.20 | — |
| 2001 Proof | Est. 15,000 | Value: 0.30 | | | | |
| 2002 | — | — | — | — | 0.20 | — |
| 2002 Proof | Est. 40,000 | Value: 0.30 | | | | |

**5 EURO CENTS** **KM# 1284** **Weight:** 3.8600 g. **Composition:** Copper-Plated-Steel **Note:** Struck at Paris Mint.

| Date | Mintage | F | VF | XF | Unc | BU |
|---|---|---|---|---|---|---|
| 1999 | — | — | — | — | 0.25 | — |
| 1999 Proof | Est. 15,000 | Value: 0.75 | | | | |
| 2000 | — | — | — | — | 0.25 | — |
| 2000 Proof | Est. 15,000 | Value: 0.75 | | | | |
| 2001 | — | — | — | — | 0.25 | — |
| 2001 Proof | Est. 15,000 | Value: 0.75 | | | | |
| 2002 | — | — | — | — | 0.25 | — |
| 2002 Proof | Est. 40,000 | Value: 0.75 | | | | |

**10 EURO CENTS** **KM# 1285** **Weight:** 4.0700 g. **Composition:** Brass **Obverse:** Woman sowing seeds **Reverse:** Denomination and map **Edge:** Reeded **Note:** Struck at Paris Mint.

| Date | Mintage | F | VF | XF | Unc | BU |
|---|---|---|---|---|---|---|
| 1999 | — | — | — | — | 0.35 | — |
| 1999 Proof | Est. 15,000 | Value: 1.50 | | | | |
| 2000 | — | — | — | — | 0.35 | — |
| 2000 Proof | Est. 15,000 | Value: 1.50 | | | | |
| 2001 | — | — | — | — | 0.35 | — |
| 2001 Proof | Est. 15,000 | Value: 1.50 | | | | |
| 2002 | — | — | — | — | 0.35 | — |
| 2002 Proof | Est. 40,000 | Value: 1.50 | | | | |

**20 EURO CENTS** **KM# 1286** **Weight:** 5.7300 g. **Composition:** Brass **Edge:** Notched **Note:** Struck at Paris Mint.

| Date | Mintage | F | VF | XF | Unc | BU |
|---|---|---|---|---|---|---|
| 1999 | — | — | — | — | 0.40 | — |

**50 EURO CENTS** **KM# 1287** **Weight:** 7.8100 g. **Composition:** Brass **Edge:** Reeded **Note:** Struck at Paris Mint.

| Date | Mintage | F | VF | XF | Unc | BU |
|---|---|---|---|---|---|---|
| 1999 | — | — | — | — | 0.75 | — |
| 1999 Proof | Est. 15,000 | Value: 7.50 | | | | |
| 2000 | — | — | — | — | 0.75 | — |
| 2000 Proof | Est. 15,000 | Value: 7.50 | | | | |
| 2001 | — | — | — | — | 0.75 | — |
| 2001 Proof | Est. 15,000 | Value: 7.50 | | | | |
| 2002 | — | — | — | — | 0.75 | — |
| 2002 Proof | Est. 40,000 | Value: 7.50 | | | | |

**EURO** **KM# 1288** **Ring Composition:** Brass **Center Weight:** 7.5000 g. **Center Composition:** Copper-Nickel **Obverse:** Stylized tree **Reverse:** Denomination and map **Edge:** Reeded and plain sections **Note:** Struck at Paris Mint.

| Date | Mintage | F | VF | XF | Unc | BU |
|---|---|---|---|---|---|---|
| 1999 | — | — | — | — | 1.50 | — |
| 1999 Proof | Est. 15,000 | Value: 15.25 | | | | |
| 2000 | — | — | — | — | 1.50 | — |
| 2000 Proof | Est. 15,000 | Value: 15.25 | | | | |
| 2001 | — | — | — | — | 1.50 | — |
| 2001 Proof | Est. 15,000 | Value: 15.25 | | | | |
| 2002 | — | — | — | — | 1.50 | — |
| 2002 Proof | Est. 40,000 | Value: 15.25 | | | | |

**2 EUROS** **KM# 1289** **Ring Composition:** Copper-Nickel **Center Weight:** 8.5200 g. **Center Composition:** Brass **Edge:** Reeding with 2's and stars

| Date | Mintage | F | VF | XF | Unc | BU |
|---|---|---|---|---|---|---|
| 1999 | — | — | — | — | 3.00 | — |
| 1999 Proof | Est. 15,000 | Value: 30.50 | | | | |
| 2000 | — | — | — | — | 3.00 | — |
| 2000 Proof | Est. 15,000 | Value: 30.50 | | | | |
| 2001 | — | — | — | — | 3.00 | — |
| 2001 Proof | Est. 15,000 | Value: 30.50 | | | | |
| 2002 | — | — | — | — | 3.00 | — |
| 2002 Proof | Est. 40,000 | Value: 30.50 | | | | |

## ESSAIS

Standard metals unless otherwise noted

| KM# | Date | Mintage | Identification | Mkt Val |
|---|---|---|---|---|
| E38 | 1903 | — | 25 Centimes. Nickel. KM#855. | 150 |

| KM# | Date | Mintage | Identification | Mkt Val |
|---|---|---|---|---|
| E-A39 | 1904 | — | 25 Centimes. Nickel. Without square around denomination, 22 sided flan. | 140 |
| E39 | 1904 | — | 25 Centimes. Nickel. KM#856. | 140 |
| E-A40 | 1904 | — | 25 Centimes. Nickel. 22 sided flan, KM#856. | 140 |
| E-B40 | 1904 | — | 25 Centimes. Nickel. 18 sided flan, KM#856. | 140 |
| E40 | 1908 | — | 10 Centimes. Aluminum. KM#843. | 150 |
| E-C40 | 1908 | — | 5 Centimes. KM#842. | — |
| E41 | 1910 | — | 5 Centimes. KM#842. | 150 |
| E42 | 1913 | — | 25 Centimes. KM#867. | 100 |
| E43 | 1914 | 104 | 5 Centimes. KM#865. | 500 |
| E44 | 1914 | — | 25 Centimes. KM#867. | 100 |

| KM# | Date | Mintage | Identification | Mkt Val |
|---|---|---|---|---|
| E45 | 1929 | — | 10 Francs. Silver. Delannoy. | 650 |

| KM# | Date | Mintage | Identification | Mkt Val |
|---|---|---|---|---|
| E46 | 1929 | — | 10 Francs. Aluminum-Bronze. | 50.00 |

| KM# | Date | Mintage | Identification | Mkt Val |
|---|---|---|---|---|
| E47 | 1929 | — | 10 Francs. Aluminum-Bronze. | 50.00 |
| E48 | 1929 | — | 10 Francs. KM#878. | 60.00 |
| E49 | 1929 | — | 20 Francs. Silver. KM#879. | 900 |
| E50 | 1929 | — | 20 Francs. Aluminum-Bronze. KM#879. | 100 |

| KM# | Date | Mintage | Identification | Mkt Val |
|---|---|---|---|---|
| E51 | 1929 | 15 | 100 Francs. Gold. | 3,500 |
| E52 | 1929 | 15 | 100 Francs. Gold. | 3,500 |
| E53 | 1929 | 15 | 100 Francs. Gold. | 3,500 |
| E54 | 1929 | 15 | 100 Francs. Gold. | 3,500 |
| E55 | 1929 | 15 | 100 Francs. Gold. | 3,500 |
| E56 | 1929 | 15 | 100 Francs. Gold. | 3,500 |
| E57 | 1929 | 15 | 100 Francs. Gold. | 3,500 |
| E58 | 1929 | 15 | 100 Francs. Gold. | 3,500 |
| E59 | 1929 | 15 | 100 Francs. Gold. | 3,500 |
| E60 | 1929 | 15 | 100 Francs. Gold. | 3,500 |
| E62 | 1929 | 15 | 100 Francs. With Essai, KM#880. | 4,000 |
| E-A64 | 1931 | — | 50 Centimes. Aluminum-Bronze. KM#894.1, Morlon. | 45.00 |
| E-B64 | 1931 | — | Franc. Aluminum-Bronze. KM#885, Morlon. | 65.00 |
| E64 | 1931 | — | 2 Francs. KM#886. | 85.00 |
| E-A65 | 1933 | — | 5 Francs. Nickel. KM#887, Bazor. | 175 |
| E65 | 1933 | — | 5 Francs. KM#888. | 90.00 |
| E-A67 | 1933 | — | 5 Francs. Silver. Turin. | 750 |
| E66 | 1933 | — | 5 Francs. Seated Liberty, date below. 5 FRANCS at center, legend and wheat spears around. | — |
| E67 | 1934 | — | 5 Francs. KM#888. | — |
| E68 | 1938 | — | 25 Centimes. KM#867b. | 150 |
| E69 | 1938 | — | 10 Francs. Nickel. KM#908. | 300 |
| E70 | 1938 | — | 20 Francs. Nickel. KM#879. | 300 |
| E71 | 1938 | — | 20 Francs. Aluminum. KM#879. | 250 |
| E72 | 1939 | — | 20 Francs. Copper-Nickel. KM#879. | 250 |
| E73 | 1940 | — | 25 Centimes. Zinc. KM#867b. | 100 |
| E74 | 1941 | — | 10 Centimes. KM#898. | 100 |
| E75 | 1941 | — | 20 Centimes. KM#899. | 100 |
| E76 | 1941 | — | 20 Centimes. KM#900. | 125 |
| E-A77 | 1941 | — | 2 Francs. Iron. KM#886, Morlon. | 275 |
| E77 | 1941 | — | 5 Francs. Copper-Nickel. Bazor. | 200 |
| E78 | 1941 | — | 10 Francs. Aluminum. Delannoy. | 300 |
| E79 | 1941 | — | 10 Francs. Nickel. | 450 |
| E-A80 | 1941 | — | 10 Francs. Aluminum. Simon. | 300 |
| E80 | 1941 | — | 10 Francs. Nickel. | 500 |
| E81 | 1941 | — | 10 Francs. Copper-Nickel. Galle. | 315 |
| E82 | 1941 | — | 20 Francs. Aluminum. Cochet. | 260 |
| E-A92 | 1941 | — | 20 Francs. Aluminum. Bouchard. | 350 |
| E83 | 1942 | — | Franc. Aluminum. KM#902.1. | — |
| E84 | 1943 | 300 | 10 Centimes. KM#903. | 150 |
| E85 | 1943 | 300 | 2 Francs. KM#904. | 200 |
| E86 | 1943 | — | 10 Francs. Copper-Nickel. Bazor. | 250 |

| KM# | Date | Mintage | Identification | Mkt Val |
|---|---|---|---|---|
| E86a | 1943 | — | 10 Francs. Aluminum. Bazor. | 325 |
| E87 | 1944 | 300 | 10 Centimes. KM#906. | 150 |
| E88 | 1945 | 40 | 20 Centimes. KM#907. | 325 |
| E89 | 1945 | 1,100 | 5 Francs. KM#888b. | 90.00 |
| E90 | 1945 | 1,100 | 10 Francs. KM#909. | 90.00 |
| E91 | 1950 | 1,700 | 10 Francs. KM#915. | 25.00 |
| E92 | 1950 | 25 | 20 Francs. Georges Guiraud, KM#916. | 450 |
| E93 | 1950 | 1,700 | 20 Francs. G. Guiraud, KM#971. | 25.00 |
| E94 | 1950 | 1,700 | 50 Francs. KM#918. | 100 |
| E95 | 1950 | 50 | 100 Francs. | 250 |
| E-A96 | 1950 | — | 100 Francs. Copper-Nickel. KM#919.1. | 4,000 |
| E96 | 1951 | 28 | 20 Francs. KM#917. | 600 |
| E97 | 1954 | 1,200 | 100 Francs. KM#919. | 75.00 |
| E98 | 1959 | 4,000 | Franc. KM#925. | 50.00 |
| E99 | 1959 | 4,000 | Franc. KM#925. | 50.00 |
| E100 | 1959 | — | 2 Francs. Silver. KM#845.1. | 950 |
| E101 | 1959 | 4,000 | 5 Francs. KM#926. | 75.00 |
| E102 | 1959 | I.A. | 5 Francs. Small 5 in date, KM#926. | 75.00 |
| E103 | 1961 | 3,500 | Centime. KM#928. | 20.00 |
| E104 | 1961 | 3,500 | 5 Centimes. KM#927. | 20.00 |
| E105 | 1961 | — | 20 Centimes. KM#930. | — |
| E106 | 1961 | — | 20 Centimes. Laureate bust with short hair. | — |
| E107 | 1961 | — | 20 Centimes. Laureate bust with long hair. | — |
| E108 | 1962 | 3,500 | 10 Centimes. KM#929. | 20.00 |
| E109 | 1962 | 3,500 | 20 Centimes. KM#930. | 20.00 |
| E110 | 1962 | 3,500 | 50 Centimes. KM#939. | 20.00 |
| E111 | 1964 | 3,500 | 10 Francs. KM#932. | 125 |
| E112 | 1965 | 4,700 | 1/2 Franc. KM#931. | 25.00 |
| E113 | 1966 | 4,128 | 5 Centimes. KM#933. | 20.00 |
| E114 | 1970 | 5,000 | 5 Francs. KM#926a. | 40.00 |
| E115 | 1974 | 7,300 | 10 Francs. Nickel-Brass. KM#940. | 40.00 |
| E116 | 1974 | 9 | 10 Francs. Gold. KM#940. | 2,200 |
| E117 | 1974 | 13,800 | 50 Francs. Silver. KM#941. | 75.00 |
| E118 | 1974 | 5 | 50 Francs. Gold. KM#941. | 2,200 |
| E119 | 1978 | 6,000 | 2 Francs. Nickel. KM#942. | 50.00 |
| E120 | 1978 | 22 | 2 Francs. Silver. KM#942. | 400 |
| E121 | 1978 | 12 | 2 Francs. Gold. KM#942. | 1,250 |
| E122 | 1982 | — | 10 Francs. Copper-Nickel. Gambetta, KM#950. | 55.00 |
| E123 | 1982 | — | 100 Francs. Silver. KM#951. | 75.00 |
| E124 | 1983 | 4,000 | 10 Francs. Nickel-Bronze. Baloon, KM#952. | 40.00 |
| E125 | 1983 | 9 | 10 Francs. Gold. Baloon, KM#952. | 1,600 |
| E126 | 1983 | 4,000 | 10 Francs. Nickel-Bronze. Standhal, KM#953. | 40.00 |
| E127 | 1983 | 9 | 10 Francs. Gold. Standhal, KM#953. | 1,500 |
| E128 | 1984 | — | 10 Francs. Nickel-Bronze. Rude, KM#954. | 40.00 |
| E129 | 1984 | — | 100 Francs. Silver. Curie, KM#955. | 70.00 |
| E130 | 1985 | 1,700 | 10 Francs. Nickel-Bronze. Hugo, KM#956. | 40.00 |
| E131 | 1985 | 1,700 | 100 Francs. Silver. Zola, KM#957. | 55.00 |
| E132 | 1986 | 1,750 | 10 Francs. Nickel. KM#959. | 40.00 |
| E133 | 1986 | 9 | 10 Francs. Gold. KM#959. | 1,500 |
| E134 | 1986 | 1,750 | 10 Francs. Nickel. Schuman, KM#958d. | 50.00 |
| E135 | 1986 | 1,750 | 100 Francs. Silver. Liberty, KM#960. | 65.00 |
| E136 | 1987 | 1,850 | 10 Francs. Nickel-Bronze. Capet, KM#916d. | 40.00 |
| E137 | 1987 | 1,850 | 100 Francs. Silver. Lafayette, KM#962. | 85.00 |
| E138 | 1988 | 1,850 | Franc. Nickel. KM#963. | 80.00 |
| E139 | 1988 | 1,850 | 10 Francs. Aluminum-Bronze. Garros, KM#965. | 32.50 |
| E140 | 1988 | 1,850 | 10 Francs. Steel center. Aluminum-Bronze ring. Bastille, KM#964. | 45.00 |
| E141 | 1988 | 1,850 | 100 Francs. Silver. Fraternity, KM#966. | 50.00 |
| E142 | 1989 | — | Franc. Nickel. KM#967. | 40.00 |
| E143 | 1989 | — | 5 Francs. Nickel. Eiffel TOwer, KM#968. | 45.00 |
| E144 | 1989 | — | 10 Francs. Steel center. Aluminum-Bronze ring. Montesquien, KM#969. | 40.00 |
| E145 | 1989 | — | 100 Francs. Silver. Human Rights, KM#970. | 65.00 |
| E146 | 1994 | — | 20 Francs. Aluminum-Bronze center. Nickel inner ring, Copper-Aluminum-Nickel outer ring, KM#1036. | 70.00 |

## PATTERNS

Including off metal strikes

| KM# | Date | Mintage | Identification | Mkt Val |
|---|---|---|---|---|
| Pn102 | 1929 | — | 100 Francs. Aluminum-Bronze. Bust left. Date. CENT FRANCS. | 120 |
| Pn103 | 1933 | — | 5 Francs. Liberty bust left. Legend above, date below. CENT FRANCS. | 200 |
| Pn104 | 1939 | — | 20 Francs. Copper-Nickel. Y#87. | 750 |
| Pn105 | 1941 | — | 10 Francs. Copper-Nickel. Petain bust left, legend in front. People working at sides. TRAVAIL/FAMILLE/PATRIE/10/FRANCS/1941 | 400 |
| Pn106 | 1941 | — | 20 Francs. Copper-Nickel. Petain bust left. Sheaves of wheat bent outward, legend above, 20-FRS below. | 400 |
| Pn107 | 1941 | — | 20 Francs. Copper-Nickel. Petain bust left. Family group above FAMILLE divide 20-FR. | 400 |
| Pn108 | 1941 | — | 20 Francs. Nickel. Petain bust left. 3 figures, 2 standing, 1 sitting. | 400 |
| Pn109 | 1942 | — | 5 Francs. Copper-Nickel. Petain bust left. TRAVAIL/FAMILLE/PATRIE/5/FRANCS/1942 | 400 |
| Pn110 | 1943 | — | 10 Francs. Copper-Nickel. Petain bust left. 3 figures, 2 standing, 1 sitting. | 350 |
| Pn111 | 1950 | — | 20 Francs. Liberty left. 20-FR divided by symbol. | 80.00 |
| Pn112 | 1950 | — | 20 Francs. Liberty left. Inscription above 20 dividing flowers, FRANCS and date below. | 80.00 |
| Pn113 | 1950 | — | 20 Francs. Liberty bust left. 20 over branch at left, FRANCS in center at right, date below. | 80.00 |
| Pn114 | 1950 | — | 20 Francs. Liberty bust left. 20 in small circle of branches, 4 branches to edge of coin. | 80.00 |
| Pn115 | 1950 | — | 100 Francs. Copper-Nickel. | — |
| Pn116 | 1964 | 131 | 10 Francs. Silver. KM#756. KM#932. | 320 |
| Pn117 | 1964 | 3,500 | 10 Francs. Silver. KM#932. | 120 |
| Pn118 | 1977 | 253 | 2 Francs. Nickel. KM#942. | 70.00 |

## PIEFORTS

Standard metals unless otherwise noted

| KM# | Date | Mintage | Identification | Mkt Val |
|---|---|---|---|---|
| P251 | 1903 | — | 25 Centimes. Copper-Nickel-Zinc. | 135 |
| P270 | 1914 | — | 10 Centimes. KM#866. | 100 |
| P272 | 1914 | — | 25 Centimes. KM#867. | 165 |
| P-A297 | 1920 | — | 2 Francs. Aluminum-Bronze. KM#877. | 115 |
| P280 | 1920 | — | 5 Centimes. KM#875. | — |
| P297 | 1928 | — | 2 Francs. KM#845. | 300 |
| P300 | 1929 | — | 100 Francs. KM#880. | 3,500 |
| P305 | 1941 | — | 10 Centimes. KM#895. | 200 |
| P341 | 1962 | 500 | Centime. KM#928. | 20.00 |
| P342 | 1962 | 50 | Centime. Silver. KM#928. | 65.00 |
| P343 | 1962 | 20 | Centime. Gold. KM#928. | 225 |
| P344 | 1962 | 500 | 10 Centimes. KM#929. | 15.00 |
| P345 | 1962 | 50 | 10 Centimes. Silver. KM#929. | 100 |
| P346 | 1962 | 20 | 10 Centimes. Gold. KM#929. | 320 |
| P347 | 1962 | 500 | 20 Centimes. KM#930. | 20.00 |
| P348 | 1962 | 50 | 20 Centimes. Silver. KM#930. | 120 |
| P349 | 1962 | 20 | 20 Centimes. Gold. KM#930. | 365 |
| P350 | 1962 | 500 | 50 Centimes. KM#939. | 25.00 |
| P351 | 1962 | 50 | 50 Centimes. Silver. KM#939. | 120 |
| P352 | 1962 | 20 | 50 Centimes. Gold. KM#939. | 500 |
| P353 | 1965 | 500 | 1/2 Franc. KM#931. | 25.00 |
| P354 | 1965 | 50 | 1/2 Franc. Silver. KM#931. | 75.00 |
| P355 | 1965 | 20 | 1/2 Franc. Gold. KM#931. | 365 |
| P356 | 1965 | 500 | 10 Francs. KM#932. | 75.00 |
| P357 | 1965 | 50 | 10 Francs. Gold. KM#932. | 1,350 |
| P358 | 1966 | 500 | 5 Centimes. KM#933. | 15.00 |
| P359 | 1966 | 50 | 5 Centimes. Silver. KM#933. | 100 |
| P360 | 1966 | 20 | 5 Centimes. Gold. KM#933. | 320 |
| P361 | 1967 | 500 | Centime. KM#928. | 15.00 |
| P362 | 1967 | 50 | Centime. Silver. KM#928. | 28.00 |
| P363 | 1967 | 20 | Centime. Gold. KM#928. | 275 |
| P364 | 1967 | 500 | 5 Centimes. KM#933. | 15.00 |
| P365 | 1967 | 50 | 5 Centimes. Silver. KM#933. | 50.00 |
| P366 | 1967 | 20 | 5 Centimes. Gold. KM#933. | 320 |
| P367 | 1967 | 500 | 10 Centimes. KM#929. | 15.00 |
| P368 | 1967 | 50 | 10 Centimes. Silver. KM#929. | 70.00 |
| P369 | 1967 | 20 | 10 Centimes. Gold. KM#929. | 320 |
| P370 | 1967 | 500 | 20 Centimes. KM#930. | 15.00 |
| P371 | 1967 | 50 | 20 Centimes. Silver. KM#930. | 320 |
| P372 | 1967 | 20 | 20 Centimes. Gold. KM#930. | 365 |
| P373 | 1967 | 500 | 25 Centimes. KM#939. | 15.00 |
| P374 | 1967 | 50 | 50 Centimes. Silver. KM#939. | 100 |
| P375 | 1967 | 20 | 50 Centimes. Gold. KM#939. | 450 |
| P376 | 1967 | 500 | 1/2 Franc. KM#931. | 20.00 |
| P377 | 1967 | 50 | 1/2 Franc. Silver. KM#931. | 75.00 |
| P378 | 1967 | 20 | 1/2 Franc. Gold. KM#931. | 400 |
| P379 | 1967 | 500 | Franc. KM#925. | 15.00 |
| P380 | 1967 | 50 | Franc. Silver. KM#925. | 75.00 |
| P381 | 1967 | 20 | Franc. Gold. KM#925. | 550 |
| P382 | 1967 | 500 | 5 Francs. KM#926. | 50.00 |
| P383 | 1967 | 50 | 5 Francs. Gold. KM#926. | 720 |
| P384 | 1967 | 500 | 10 Francs. KM#932. | 75.00 |
| P385 | 1967 | 50 | 10 Francs. Gold. KM#932. | 1,450 |
| P386 | 1968 | 500 | Centime. KM#928. | 15.00 |
| P387 | 1968 | 50 | Centime. Silver. KM#928. | 28.00 |
| P388 | 1968 | 20 | Centime. Gold. KM#928. | 185 |
| P389 | 1968 | 500 | 5 Centimes. KM#933. | 15.00 |
| P390 | 1968 | 50 | 5 Centimes. Silver. KM#933. | 50.00 |
| P391 | 1968 | 20 | 5 Centimes. Gold. KM#933. | 275 |
| P392 | 1968 | 500 | 10 Centimes. KM#929. | 15.00 |
| P393 | 1968 | 50 | 10 Centimes. Silver. KM#929. | 50.00 |
| P394 | 1968 | 20 | 10 Centimes. Gold. KM#929. | 275 |
| P395 | 1968 | 500 | 20 Centimes. KM#930. | 15.00 |
| P396 | 1968 | 50 | 20 Centimes. Silver. KM#930. | 50.00 |
| P397 | 1968 | 20 | 20 Centimes. Gold. KM#930. | 365 |
| P398 | 1968 | 500 | 1/2 Franc. KM#931. | 15.00 |
| P399 | 1968 | 50 | 1/2 Franc. Silver. KM#931. | 70.00 |
| P400 | 1968 | 20 | 1/2 Franc. Gold. KM#931. | 365 |
| P401 | 1968 | 500 | Franc. KM#925. | 20.00 |
| P402 | 1968 | 50 | Franc. Silver. KM#925. | 75.00 |
| P403 | 1968 | 20 | Franc. Gold. KM#925. | 550 |
| P404 | 1968 | 500 | 5 Francs. KM#926. | 60.00 |
| P405 | 1968 | 50 | 5 Francs. Gold. KM#926. | 725 |
| P406 | 1968 | 500 | 10 Francs. KM#932. | 75.00 |
| P407 | 1968 | 50 | 10 Francs. Gold. KM#932. | 1,350 |
| P408 | 1970 | 500 | 5 Francs. KM#926a. | 20.00 |
| P409 | 1970 | 200 | 5 Francs. Silver. KM#926a. | 70.00 |
| P410 | 1970 | 100 | 5 Francs. Gold. KM#926a. | 500 |
| P411 | 1970 | 100 | 5 Francs. Platinum. KM#926a. | 1,400 |
| P412 | 1971 | 500 | Centime. KM#928. | 15.00 |
| P413 | 1971 | 250 | Centime. Silver. KM#928. | 20.00 |
| P414 | 1971 | 100 | Centime. Gold. KM#928. | 155 |
| P415 | 1971 | 500 | 5 Centimes. KM#933. | 15.00 |
| P416 | 1971 | 250 | 5 Centimes. Silver. KM#933. | 20.00 |
| P417 | 1971 | 100 | 5 Centimes. Gold. KM#933. | 180 |
| P418 | 1971 | 500 | 10 Centimes. KM#929. | 15.00 |
| P419 | 1971 | 250 | 10 Centimes. Silver. KM#929. | 25.00 |
| P420 | 1971 | 100 | 10 Centimes. Gold. KM#929. | 225 |
| P421 | 1971 | 500 | 20 Centimes. KM#930. | 15.00 |
| P422 | 1971 | 250 | 20 Centimes. Silver. KM#930. | 25.00 |
| P423 | 1971 | 100 | 20 Centimes. Gold. KM#930. | 300 |
| P424 | 1971 | 500 | 1/2 Franc. KM#931. | 20.00 |
| P425 | 1971 | 250 | 1/2 Franc. Silver. KM#931. | 25.00 |
| P426 | 1971 | 100 | 1/2 Franc. Gold. KM#931. | 320 |
| P427 | 1971 | 500 | Franc. KM#925. | 20.00 |
| P428 | 1971 | 250 | Franc. Silver. KM#925. | 28.00 |
| P429 | 1971 | 100 | Franc. Gold. KM#925. | 400 |
| P430 | 1971 | 1,000 | 5 Francs. KM#926a. | 16.00 |
| P431 | 1971 | 500 | 5 Francs. Silver. KM#926a. | 52.00 |
| P432 | 1971 | 250 | 5 Francs. Gold. KM#926a. | 585 |
| P433 | 1971 | 100 | 5 Francs. Platinum. KM#926a. | 1,250 |
| P435 | 1971 | 500 | 10 Francs. KM#932. | 100 |
| P436 | 1971 | 250 | 10 Francs. Gold. KM#932. | 1,250 |
| P437 | 1972 | 250 | Centime. KM#928. | 16.00 |
| P438 | 1972 | 150 | Centime. Silver. KM#928. | 25.00 |
| P439 | 1972 | 75 | Centime. Gold. KM#928. | 165 |
| P440 | 1972 | 250 | 5 Centimes. KM#933. | 16.00 |
| P441 | 1972 | 150 | 5 Centimes. Silver. KM#933. | 28.00 |
| P442 | 1972 | 75 | 5 Centimes. Gold. KM#933. | 180 |
| P443 | 1972 | 250 | 10 Centimes. KM#929. | 20.00 |
| P444 | 1972 | 150 | 10 Centimes. Silver. KM#929. | 35.00 |
| P445 | 1972 | 75 | 10 Centimes. Gold. KM#929. | 290 |

| KM# | Date | Mintage | Identification | Mkt Val |
|---|---|---|---|---|
| P446 | 1972 | 250 | 20 Centimes. KM#930. | 20.00 |
| P447 | 1972 | 150 | 20 Centimes. Silver. KM#930. | 40.00 |
| P448 | 1972 | 75 | 20 Centimes. Gold. KM#930. | 320 |
| P449 | 1972 | 250 | 1/2 Franc. KM#931. | 25.00 |
| P450 | 1972 | 150 | 1/2 Franc. Silver. KM#931. | 40.00 |
| P451 | 1972 | 75 | 1/2 Franc. Gold. KM#931. | 385 |
| P452 | 1972 | 250 | Franc. KM#925. | 25.00 |
| P453 | 1972 | 150 | Franc. Silver. KM#925. | 40.00 |
| P454 | 1972 | 75 | Franc. Gold. KM#925. | 360 |
| P455 | 1972 | 500 | 5 Francs. KM#926a. | 16.00 |
| P456 | 1972 | 250 | 5 Francs. Silver. KM#926a. | 55.00 |
| P457 | 1972 | 200 | 5 Francs. Gold. KM#926a. | 520 |
| P458 | 1972 | 500 | 10 Francs. KM#932. | 80.00 |
| P459 | 1972 | 200 | 10 Francs. Gold. KM#932. | 1,100 |
| P460 | 1972 | 20 | 10 Francs. Platinum. KM#932. | 1,850 |
| P461 | 1973 | 250 | Centime. KM#928. | 15.00 |
| P462 | 1973 | 150 | Centime. Silver. KM#928. | 20.00 |
| P463 | 1973 | 75 | Centime. Gold. KM#928. | 165 |
| P464 | 1973 | 250 | 5 Centimes. KM#933. | 15.00 |
| P465 | 1973 | 150 | 5 Centimes. Silver. KM#933. | 20.00 |
| P466 | 1973 | 75 | 5 Centimes. Gold. KM#933. | 180 |
| P467 | 1973 | 250 | 10 Centimes. KM#929. | 15.00 |
| P468 | 1973 | 150 | 10 Centimes. Silver. KM#929. | 25.00 |
| P469 | 1973 | 75 | 10 Centimes. Gold. KM#929. | 225 |
| P470 | 1973 | 250 | 20 Centimes. KM#930. | 16.00 |
| P471 | 1973 | 150 | 20 Centimes. Silver. KM#930. | 25.00 |
| P472 | 1973 | 75 | 20 Centimes. Gold. KM#930. | 290 |
| P473 | 1973 | 250 | 1/2 Franc. KM#931. | 16.00 |
| P474 | 1973 | 150 | 1/2 Franc. Silver. KM#931. | 25.00 |
| P475 | 1973 | 75 | 1/2 Franc. Gold. KM#931. | 320 |
| P476 | 1973 | 250 | Franc. KM#925. | 20.00 |
| P477 | 1973 | 150 | Franc. Silver. KM#925. | 28.00 |
| P478 | 1973 | 75 | Franc. Gold. KM#925. | 385 |
| P479 | 1973 | 500 | 5 Francs. KM#926a. | 16.00 |
| P480 | 1973 | 250 | 5 Francs. Silver. KM#926a. | 40.00 |
| P481 | 1973 | 200 | 5 Francs. Gold. KM#926a. | 520 |
| P482 | 1973 | 500 | 10 Francs. KM#932. | 65.00 |
| P483 | 1973 | 200 | 10 Francs. Gold. KM#932. | 1,050 |
| P484 | 1973 | 20 | 10 Francs. Platinum. KM#932. | 1,750 |
| P485 | 1974 | 127 | Centime. KM#928. | 16.00 |
| P486 | 1974 | 242 | Centime. Silver. KM#928. | 20.00 |
| P487 | 1974 | 96 | Centime. Gold. KM#928. | 135 |
| P488 | 1974 | 98 | 5 Centimes. KM#933. | 16.00 |
| P489 | 1974 | 247 | 5 Centimes. Silver. KM#933. | 20.00 |
| P490 | 1974 | 96 | 5 Centimes. Gold. KM#933. | 165 |
| P491 | 1974 | 97 | 10 Centimes. KM#929. | 16.00 |
| P492 | 1974 | 246 | 10 Centimes. Silver. KM#929. | 20.00 |
| P493 | 1974 | 94 | 10 Centimes. Gold. KM#929. | 200 |
| P494 | 1974 | 101 | 20 Centimes. KM#930. | 16.00 |
| P495 | 1974 | 247 | 20 Centimes. Silver. KM#930. | 20.00 |
| P496 | 1974 | 98 | 20 Centimes. Gold. KM#930. | 270 |
| P497 | 1974 | 102 | 1/2 Franc. KM#931. | 16.00 |
| P498 | 1974 | 241 | 1/2 Franc. Silver. KM#931. | 25.00 |
| P499 | 1974 | 91 | 1/2 Franc. Gold. KM#931. | 290 |
| P500 | 1974 | 118 | Franc. KM#925. | 20.00 |
| P501 | 1974 | 246 | Franc. Silver. KM#925. | 35.00 |
| P502 | 1974 | 95 | Franc. Gold. KM#925. | 360 |
| P503 | 1974 | 162 | 5 Francs. KM#926a. | 16.00 |
| P504 | 1974 | 245 | 5 Francs. Silver. KM#926a. | 55.00 |
| P505 | 1974 | 107 | 5 Francs. Gold. KM#926a. | 520 |
| P506 | 1974 | 493 | 10 Francs. KM#940. | 18.00 |
| P507 | 1974 | 491 | 10 Francs. Silver. KM#940. | 40.00 |
| P508 | 1974 | 172 | 10 Francs. Gold. KM#940. | 450 |
| P509 | 1974 | 982 | 50 Francs. KM#941. | 65.00 |
| P510 | 1974 | 241 | 50 Francs. Gold. KM#941. | 1,600 |
| P511 | 1974 | 18 | 50 Francs. Platinum. KM#941. | 3,800 |
| P512 | 1975 | 147 | Centime. KM#928. | 15.00 |
| P513 | 1975 | 228 | Centime. Silver. KM#928. | 25.00 |
| P514 | 1975 | 67 | Centime. Gold. KM#928. | 135 |
| P515 | 1975 | 129 | 5 Centimes. KM#933. | 15.00 |
| P516 | 1975 | 203 | 5 Centimes. Silver. KM#933. | 20.00 |
| P517 | 1975 | 44 | 5 Centimes. Gold. KM#933. | 165 |
| P518 | 1975 | 127 | 10 Centimes. KM#929. | 15.00 |
| P519 | 1975 | 198 | 10 Centimes. Silver. KM#929. | 20.00 |
| P520 | 1975 | 39 | 10 Centimes. Gold. KM#929. | 200 |
| P521 | 1975 | 133 | 20 Centimes. KM#930. | 15.00 |
| P522 | 1975 | 212 | 20 Centimes. Silver. KM#930. | 20.00 |
| P523 | 1975 | 42 | 20 Centimes. Gold. KM#930. | 270 |
| P524 | 1975 | 131 | 1/2 Franc. KM#931. | 16.00 |
| P525 | 1975 | 213 | 1/2 Franc. Silver. KM#931. | 25.00 |
| P526 | 1975 | 40 | 1/2 Franc. Gold. KM#931. | 290 |
| P527 | 1975 | 145 | Franc. KM#925. | 16.00 |
| P528 | 1975 | 250 | Franc. Silver. KM#925. | 25.00 |
| P529 | 1975 | 51 | Franc. Gold. KM#925. | 360 |
| P530 | 1975 | 202 | 5 Francs. KM#926a. | 15.00 |
| P531 | 1975 | 250 | 5 Francs. Silver. KM#926a. | 55.00 |
| P532 | 1975 | 60 | 5 Francs. Gold. KM#926a. | 520 |
| P533 | 1975 | 356 | 10 Francs. KM#940. | 15.00 |
| P534 | 1975 | 500 | 10 Francs. Silver. KM#940. | 40.00 |
| P535 | 1975 | 62 | 10 Francs. Gold. KM#940. | 520 |
| P536 | 1975 | 955 | 50 Francs. KM#941. | 55.00 |
| P537 | 1975 | 74 | 50 Francs. Gold. KM#941. | 1,650 |
| P538 | 1975 | 10 | 50 Francs. Platinum. KM#941. | 4,000 |
| P539 | 1976 | 200 | Centime. KM#928. | 15.00 |
| P540 | 1976 | 300 | Centime. Silver. KM#928. | 16.00 |
| P541 | 1976 | 100 | Centime. Gold. KM#928. | 135 |
| P542 | 1976 | 200 | 5 Centimes. KM#933. | 15.00 |
| P543 | 1976 | 300 | 5 Centimes. Silver. KM#933. | 16.00 |
| P544 | 1976 | 100 | 5 Centimes. Gold. KM#933. | 165 |
| P545 | 1976 | 200 | 10 Centimes. KM#929. | 15.00 |
| P546 | 1976 | 300 | 10 Centimes. Silver. KM#929. | 16.00 |
| P547 | 1976 | 100 | 10 Centimes. Gold. KM#929. | 200 |
| P548 | 1976 | 200 | 20 Centimes. KM#930. | 15.00 |
| P549 | 1976 | 300 | 20 Centimes. Silver. KM#930. | 25.00 |
| P550 | 1976 | 100 | 20 Centimes. Gold. KM#930. | 270 |
| P551 | 1976 | 200 | 1/2 Franc. KM#931. | 16.00 |
| P552 | 1976 | 250 | 1/2 Franc. Silver. KM#931. | 20.00 |
| P553 | 1976 | 100 | 1/2 Franc. Gold. KM#931. | 290 |
| P554 | 1976 | 126 | Franc. KM#925. | 16.00 |
| P555 | 1976 | 88 | Franc. Silver. KM#925. | 28.00 |
| P556 | 1976 | 38 | Franc. Gold. KM#925. | 360 |
| P557 | 1976 | 178 | 5 Francs. KM#926a. | 16.00 |
| P558 | 1976 | 104 | 5 Francs. Silver. KM#926a. | 40.00 |
| P559 | 1976 | 26 | 5 Francs. Gold. KM#926a. | 520 |
| P560 | 1976 | 175 | 10 Francs. KM#940. | 16.00 |
| P561 | 1976 | 121 | 10 Francs. Silver. KM#940. | 28.00 |
| P562 | 1976 | 36 | 10 Francs. Gold. KM#940. | 565 |
| P563 | 1976 | 213 | 50 Francs. KM#941. | 65.00 |
| P564 | 1976 | 54 | 50 Francs. Gold. KM#941. | 1,500 |
| P565 | 1976 | 6 | 50 Francs. Platinum. KM#941. | 7,000 |
| P566 | 1977 | 118 | Centime. KM#928. | 15.00 |
| P567 | 1977 | 247 | Centime. Silver. KM#928. | 16.00 |
| P568 | 1977 | 53 | Centime. Gold. KM#928. | 135 |
| P569 | 1977 | 89 | 5 Centimes. KM#933. | 16.00 |
| P570 | 1977 | 232 | 5 Centimes. Silver. KM#933. | 20.00 |
| P571 | 1977 | 41 | 5 Centimes. Gold. KM#933. | 165 |
| P572 | 1977 | 85 | 10 Centimes. KM#929. | 20.00 |
| P573 | 1977 | 231 | 10 Centimes. Silver. KM#929. | 16.00 |
| P574 | 1977 | 32 | 10 Centimes. Gold. KM#929. | 200 |
| P575 | 1977 | 88 | 20 Centimes. KM#930. | 20.00 |
| P576 | 1977 | 243 | 20 Centimes. Silver. KM#930. | 20.00 |
| P577 | 1977 | 32 | 20 Centimes. Gold. KM#930. | 270 |
| P578 | 1977 | 89 | 1/2 Franc. KM#931. | 25.00 |
| P579 | 1977 | 234 | 1/2 Franc. Silver. KM#931. | 28.00 |
| P580 | 1977 | 32 | 1/2 Franc. Gold. KM#931. | 290 |
| P581 | 1977 | 100 | Franc. KM#925. | 25.00 |
| P582 | 1977 | 259 | Franc. Silver. KM#925. | 32.00 |
| P583 | 1977 | 42 | Franc. Gold. KM#925. | 360 |
| P584 | 1977 | 139 | 5 Francs. KM#926a. | 25.00 |
| P585 | 1977 | 282 | 5 Francs. Silver. KM#926a. | 35.00 |
| P586 | 1977 | 35 | 5 Francs. Gold. KM#926a. | 520 |
| P587 | 1977 | 146 | 10 Francs. KM#940. | 25.00 |
| P588 | 1977 | 296 | 10 Francs. Silver. KM#940. | 55.00 |
| P589 | 1977 | 43 | 10 Francs. Gold. KM#940. | 565 |
| P590 | 1977 | 465 | 50 Francs. KM#941. | 75.00 |
| P591 | 1977 | 50 | 50 Francs. Gold. KM#941. | 1,500 |
| P592 | 1977 | 19 | 50 Francs. Platinum. KM#941. | 3,800 |
| P593 | 1978 | 150 | Centime. KM#928. | 15.00 |
| P594 | 1978 | 294 | Centime. Silver. KM#928. | 16.00 |
| P595 | 1978 | 144 | Centime. Gold. KM#928. | 115 |
| P596 | 1978 | 148 | 5 Centimes. KM#933. | 15.00 |
| P597 | 1978 | 295 | 5 Centimes. Silver. KM#933. | 16.00 |
| P598 | 1978 | 144 | 5 Centimes. Gold. KM#933. | 135 |
| P599 | 1978 | 147 | 10 Centimes. KM#929. | 15.00 |
| P600 | 1978 | 290 | 10 Centimes. Silver. KM#929. | 16.00 |
| P601 | 1978 | 139 | 10 Centimes. Gold. KM#929. | 180 |
| P602 | 1978 | 148 | 20 Centimes. KM#930. | 15.00 |
| P603 | 1978 | 296 | 20 Centimes. Silver. KM#930. | 25.00 |
| P604 | 1978 | 141 | 20 Centimes. Gold. KM#930. | 225 |
| P605 | 1978 | 149 | 1/2 Franc. KM#931. | 16.00 |
| P606 | 1978 | 296 | 1/2 Franc. Silver. KM#931. | 20.00 |
| P607 | 1978 | 141 | 1/2 Franc. Gold. KM#931. | 245 |
| P608 | 1978 | 149 | Franc. KM#925. | 16.00 |
| P609 | 1978 | 297 | Franc. Silver. KM#925. | 25.00 |
| P610 | 1978 | 142 | Franc. Gold. KM#925. | 300 |
| P611 | 1978 | 350 | 2 Francs. Silver. KM#942. | 35.00 |
| P612 | 1978 | — | 2 Francs. Nickel. KM#942. | 100 |
| P613 | 1978 | 150 | 5 Francs. KM#926a. | 16.00 |
| P614 | 1978 | 306 | 5 Francs. Silver. KM#926a. | 35.00 |
| P615 | 1978 | 143 | 5 Francs. Gold. KM#926a. | 500 |
| P616 | 1978 | 174 | 10 Francs. KM#940. | 16.00 |
| P617 | 1978 | 345 | 10 Francs. Silver. KM#940. | 35.00 |
| P618 | 1978 | 144 | 10 Francs. Gold. KM#940. | 565 |
| P619 | 1978 | 599 | 50 Francs. KM#941. | 75.00 |
| P620 | 1978 | 149 | 50 Francs. Gold. KM#941. | 1,700 |
| P621 | 1978 | 25 | 50 Francs. Platinum. KM#941. | 3,750 |
| P622 | 1979 | 300 | Centime. KM#928. | 15.00 |
| P623 | 1979 | 600 | Centime. Silver. KM#928. | 15.00 |
| P624 | 1979 | 300 | Centime. Gold. KM#928. | 115 |
| P625 | 1979 | 299 | 5 Centimes. KM#935. | 15.00 |
| P626 | 1979 | 600 | 5 Centimes. Silver. KM#933. | 15.00 |
| P627 | 1979 | 300 | 5 Centimes. Gold. KM#933. | 135 |
| P628 | 1979 | 300 | 10 Centimes. KM#929. | 15.00 |
| P629 | 1979 | 600 | 10 Centimes. Silver. KM#929. | 16.00 |
| P630 | 1979 | 300 | 10 Centimes. Gold. KM#929. | 180 |
| P631 | 1979 | 300 | 20 Centimes. KM#930. | 15.00 |
| P632 | 1979 | 600 | 20 Centimes. Silver. KM#930. | 16.00 |
| P633 | 1979 | 300 | 20 Centimes. Gold. KM#930. | 225 |
| P634 | 1979 | 300 | 1/2 Franc. KM#931. | 15.00 |
| P635 | 1979 | 600 | 1/2 Franc. Silver. KM#931. | 16.00 |
| P636 | 1979 | 300 | 1/2 Franc. Gold. KM#931. | 245 |
| P637 | 1979 | 500 | Franc. KM#925. | 15.00 |
| P638 | 1979 | 1,250 | Franc. Silver. KM#925. | 16.00 |
| P639 | 1979 | 600 | Franc. Gold. KM#925. | 290 |
| P640 | 1979 | 500 | 2 Francs. KM#942. | 16.00 |
| P641 | 1979 | 1,250 | 2 Francs. Silver. KM#942. | 25.00 |
| P642 | 1979 | 600 | 2 Francs. Gold. KM#942. | 360 |
| P643 | 1979 | 40 | 2 Francs. Platinum. KM#942. | 900 |
| P644 | 1979 | 300 | 5 Francs. KM#926a. | 16.00 |
| P645 | 1979 | 600 | 5 Francs. Silver. KM#926a. | 25.00 |
| P646 | 1979 | 300 | 5 Francs. Gold. KM#926a. | 450 |
| P647 | 1979 | 349 | 10 Francs. KM#940. | 16.00 |
| P648 | 1979 | 700 | 10 Francs. Silver. KM#940. | 35.00 |
| P649 | 1979 | 300 | 10 Francs. Gold. KM#940. | 500 |
| P650 | 1979 | 2,250 | 50 Francs. KM#941. | 52.00 |
| P651 | 1979 | 400 | 50 Francs. Gold. KM#941. | 1,500 |
| P652 | 1979 | 30 | 50 Francs. Platinum. KM#941. | 3,700 |
| P653 | 1980 | 155 | Centime. KM#928. | 15.00 |
| P654 | 1980 | 570 | Centime. Silver. KM#928. | 16.00 |
| P655 | 1980 | 176 | Centime. Gold. KM#928. | 115 |
| P656 | 1980 | 142 | 5 Centimes. KM#933. | 15.00 |
| P657 | 1980 | 547 | 5 Centimes. Silver. KM#933. | 16.00 |
| P658 | 1980 | 137 | 5 Centimes. Gold. KM#933. | 135 |
| P659 | 1980 | 148 | 10 Centimes. KM#929. | 15.00 |
| P660 | 1980 | 528 | 10 Centimes. Silver. KM#929. | 20.00 |
| P661 | 1980 | 127 | 10 Centimes. Gold. KM#929. | 180 |
| P662 | 1980 | 140 | 20 Centimes. KM#930. | 15.00 |
| P663 | 1980 | 569 | 20 Centimes. Silver. KM#930. | 25.00 |
| P664 | 1980 | 136 | 20 Centimes. Gold. KM#930. | 300 |
| P665 | 1980 | 156 | 1/2 Franc. KM#931. | 16.00 |
| P666 | 1980 | 537 | 1/2 Franc. Silver. KM#931. | 25.00 |
| P667 | 1980 | 118 | 1/2 Franc. Gold. KM#931. | 300 |
| P668 | 1980 | 132 | Franc. KM#925. | 16.00 |
| P669 | 1980 | 563 | Franc. Silver. KM#925. | 25.00 |
| P670 | 1980 | 193 | Franc. Gold. KM#925. | 360 |
| P671 | 1980 | 194 | 2 Francs. KM#942. | 16.00 |
| P672 | 1980 | 772 | 2 Francs. Silver. KM#942. | 35.00 |
| P673 | 1980 | 130 | 2 Francs. Gold. KM#942. | 520 |
| P674 | 1980 | 271 | 5 Francs. KM#926a. | 16.00 |
| P675 | 1980 | 580 | 5 Francs. Silver. KM#926a. | 50.00 |
| P676 | 1980 | 213 | 5 Francs. Gold. KM#926a. | 600 |
| P677 | 1980 | 148 | 10 Francs. KM#940. | 16.00 |
| P678 | 1980 | 730 | 10 Francs. Silver. KM#940. | 50.00 |
| P679 | 1980 | 157 | 10 Francs. Gold. KM#940. | 520 |
| P680 | 1980 | 2,500 | 50 Francs. KM#941. | 52.00 |
| P681 | 1980 | 500 | 50 Francs. Gold. KM#941. | 1,800 |
| P682 | 1980 | 34 | 50 Francs. Platinum. KM#941. | 3,750 |
| P683 | 1981 | 150 | Centime. KM#928. | 15.00 |
| P684 | 1981 | 362 | Centime. Silver. KM#928. | 25.00 |
| P685 | 1981 | 69 | Centime. Gold. KM#928. | 180 |
| P686 | 1981 | 105 | 5 Centimes. KM#933. | 16.00 |
| P687 | 1981 | 358 | 5 Centimes. Silver. KM#933. | 25.00 |
| P688 | 1981 | 42 | 5 Centimes. Gold. KM#933. | 200 |
| P689 | 1981 | 104 | 10 Centimes. KM#929. | 15.00 |
| P690 | 1981 | 357 | 10 Centimes. Silver. KM#929. | 25.00 |
| P691 | 1981 | 32 | 10 Centimes. Gold. KM#929. | 270 |
| P692 | 1981 | 106 | 20 Centimes. KM#930. | 16.00 |
| P693 | 1981 | 359 | 20 Centimes. Silver. KM#930. | 25.00 |
| P694 | 1981 | 30 | 20 Centimes. Gold. KM#930. | 315 |
| P695 | 1981 | 110 | 1/2 Franc. KM#931. | 16.00 |
| P696 | 1981 | 358 | 1/2 Franc. Silver. KM#931. | 25.00 |
| P697 | 1981 | 33 | 1/2 Franc. Gold. KM#931. | 340 |
| P699 | 1981 | 122 | Franc. KM#925. | 16.00 |
| P700 | 1981 | 358 | Franc. Silver. KM#925. | 35.00 |
| P701 | 1981 | 42 | Franc. Gold. KM#925. | 400 |
| P702 | 1981 | 16 | Franc. Platinum. KM#925. | 800 |
| P703 | 1981 | 131 | 2 Francs. KM#942. | 16.00 |
| P704 | 1981 | 359 | 2 Francs. Silver. KM#942. | 35.00 |
| P705 | 1981 | 37 | 2 Francs. Gold. KM#942. | 520 |
| P706 | 1981 | 16 | 2 Francs. Platinum. KM#942. | 900 |
| P707 | 1981 | 150 | 5 Francs. KM#926a. | 16.00 |
| P708 | 1981 | 261 | 5 Francs. Silver. KM#926a. | 65.00 |
| P709 | 1981 | 52 | 5 Francs. Gold. KM#926a. | 650 |
| P710 | 1981 | 16 | 5 Francs. Platinum. KM#926a. | 1,450 |
| P711 | 1981 | 150 | 10 Francs. KM#940. | 16.00 |
| P712 | 1981 | 365 | 10 Francs. Silver. KM#940. | 65.00 |
| P713 | 1981 | 52 | 10 Francs. Gold. KM#940. | 765 |
| P714 | 1981 | 17 | 10 Francs. Platinum. KM#940. | 1,850 |
| P698 | 1981 | 16 | 1/2 Franc. Platinum. KM#931. | — |
| P715 | 1982 | 70 | Centime. Steel. KM#928. | 15.00 |
| P716 | 1982 | 195 | Centime. Silver. KM#928. | 25.00 |
| P717 | 1982 | 36 | Centime. Gold. KM#928. | 200 |
| P718 | 1982 | 53 | 5 Centimes. KM#933. | 15.00 |
| P719 | 1982 | 164 | 5 Centimes. Silver. KM#933. | 25.00 |
| P720 | 1982 | 26 | 5 Centimes. Gold. KM#933. | 225 |
| P721 | 1982 | 53 | 10 Centimes. KM#929. | 15.00 |
| P722 | 1982 | 163 | 10 Centimes. Silver. KM#929. | 25.00 |
| P723 | 1982 | 29 | 10 Centimes. Gold. KM#929. | 180 |
| P724 | 1982 | 53 | 20 Centimes. KM#930. | 16.00 |
| P725 | 1982 | 171 | 20 Centimes. Silver. KM#930. | 25.00 |
| P726 | 1982 | 26 | 20 Centimes. Gold. KM#930. | 350 |
| P727 | 1982 | 54 | 1/2 Franc. KM#931. | 16.00 |
| P728 | 1982 | 165 | 1/2 Franc. Silver. KM#931. | 25.00 |
| P729 | 1982 | 26 | 1/2 Franc. Gold. KM#931. | 335 |
| P730 | 1982 | 4 | 1/2 Franc. Platinum. KM#931. | 2,500 |
| P731 | 1982 | 57 | Franc. KM#925. | 16.00 |
| P732 | 1982 | 252 | Franc. Silver. KM#925. | 25.00 |
| P733 | 1982 | 29 | Franc. Gold. KM#925. | 400 |
| P734 | 1982 | 6 | Franc. Platinum. KM#925. | 1,350 |
| P735 | 1982 | 62 | 2 Francs. KM#942. | 16.00 |
| P736 | 1982 | 203 | 2 Francs. Silver. KM#942. | 35.00 |
| P737 | 1982 | 27 | 2 Francs. Gold. KM#942. | 1,800 |
| P738 | 1982 | 4 | 2 Francs. Platinum. KM#942. | 3,000 |
| P739 | 1982 | 69 | 5 Francs. KM#926a. | 16.00 |
| P740 | 1982 | 188 | 5 Francs. Silver. KM#926a. | 55.00 |
| P741 | 1982 | 27 | 5 Francs. Gold. KM#926a. | 720 |
| P742 | 1982 | 4 | 5 Francs. Platinum. KM#926a. | 3,500 |
| P743 | 1982 | 80 | 10 Francs. KM#940. | 16.00 |
| P744 | 1982 | 239 | 10 Francs. Silver. KM#940. | 55.00 |
| P745 | 1982 | 33 | 10 Francs. Gold. KM#940. | 720 |
| P746 | 1982 | 4 | 10 Francs. Platinum. KM#940. | 3,500 |
| P747 | 1982 | 326 | 10 Francs. KM#950. | 25.00 |
| P748 | 1982 | 812 | 10 Francs. Silver. KM#950. | 50.00 |
| P749 | 1982 | 87 | 10 Francs. Gold. KM#950. | 720 |
| P750 | 1982 | 14 | 10 Francs. Platinum. KM#950. | 1,200 |
| P751 | 1982 | 999 | 100 Francs. Silver. KM#951. | 65.00 |

| KM# | Date | Mintage | Identification | Mkt Val |
|---|---|---|---|---|
| P752 | 1982 | 93 | 100 Francs. Gold. KM#951. | 1,050 |
| P753 | 1982 | 16 | 100 Francs. Platinum. KM#951. | 1,650 |
| P754 | 1983 | 50 | Centime. Steel. KM#928. | 15.00 |
| P755 | 1983 | 98 | Centime. Silver. KM#928. | 25.00 |
| P756 | 1983 | 17 | Centime. Gold. KM#928. | 200 |
| P757 | 1983 | 42 | Centime. KM#933. | 15.00 |
| P758 | 1983 | 90 | 5 Centimes. Silver. KM#933. | 25.00 |
| P759 | 1983 | 7 | 5 Centimes. Gold. KM#933. | 600 |
| P760 | 1983 | 42 | 10 Centimes. KM#929. | 15.00 |
| P761 | 1983 | 90 | 10 Centimes. Silver. KM#929. | 20.00 |
| P762 | 1983 | 6 | 10 Centimes. Gold. KM#929. | 700 |
| P763 | 1983 | 44 | 20 Centimes. KM#930. | 15.00 |
| P764 | 1983 | 95 | 20 Centimes. Silver. KM#930. | 28.00 |
| P765 | 1983 | 5 | 20 Centimes. Gold. KM#930. | 650 |
| P766 | 1983 | 43 | 1/2 Franc. KM#931. | 20.00 |
| P767 | 1983 | 89 | 1/2 Franc. Silver. KM#931. | 35.00 |
| P768 | 1983 | 5 | 1/2 Franc. Gold. KM#931. | 585 |
| P769 | 1983 | 3 | 1/2 Franc. Platinum. KM#931. | 7,000 |
| P770 | 1983 | 46 | Franc. KM#925. | 20.00 |
| P771 | 1983 | 98 | Franc. Silver. KM#925. | 35.00 |
| P772 | 1983 | 11 | Franc. Gold. KM#925. | 450 |
| P773 | 1983 | 3 | Franc. Platinum. KM#925. | 7,000 |
| P774 | 1983 | 51 | 2 Francs. KM#942. | 20.00 |
| P775 | 1983 | 121 | 2 Francs. Silver. KM#942. | 35.00 |
| P776 | 1983 | 9 | 2 Francs. Gold. KM#942. | 600 |
| P777 | 1983 | 3 | 2 Francs. Platinum. KM#942. | 7,000 |
| P778 | 1983 | 58 | 5 Francs. KM#926a. | 20.00 |
| P779 | 1983 | 97 | 5 Francs. Silver. KM#926a. | 65.00 |
| P780 | 1983 | 8 | 5 Francs. Gold. KM#926a. | 720 |
| P781 | 1983 | 3 | 5 Francs. Platinum. KM#926a. | 7,000 |
| P782 | 1983 | 286 | 10 Francs. KM#952. | 15.00 |
| P783 | 1983 | 454 | 10 Francs. Silver. KM#952. | 55.00 |
| P784 | 1983 | 34 | 10 Francs. Gold. KM#952. | 765 |
| P785 | 1983 | 13 | 10 Francs. Platinum. KM#952. | 1,950 |
| P786 | 1983 | 74 | 10 Francs. KM#940. | 20.00 |
| P787 | 1983 | 118 | 10 Francs. Silver. KM#940. | 60.00 |
| P788 | 1983 | 12 | 10 Francs. Gold. KM#940. | 720 |
| P789 | 1983 | 5 | 10 Francs. Platinum. KM#940. | 2,000 |
| P790 | 1983 | 206 | 10 Francs. KM#953. | 15.00 |
| P791 | 1983 | 314 | 10 Francs. Silver. KM#953. | 65.00 |
| P792 | 1983 | 29 | 10 Francs. Gold. KM#953. | 720 |
| P793 | 1983 | 5 | 10 Francs. Platinum. KM#953. | 2,000 |
| P794 | 1983 | 242 | 100 Francs. Silver. KM#951. | 65.00 |
| P795 | 1983 | 14 | 100 Francs. Gold. KM#951. | 1,050 |
| P796 | 1983 | 7 | 100 Francs. Platinum. KM#951. | 2,350 |
| P797 | 1984 | 56 | Centime. Steel. KM#928. | 15.00 |
| P798 | 1984 | 64 | Centime. Silver. KM#928. | 25.00 |
| P799 | 1984 | 10 | Centime. Gold. KM#928. | 200 |
| P800 | 1984 | 36 | 5 Centimes. Copper-Nickel. KM#933. | 15.00 |
| P801 | 1984 | 49 | 5 Centimes. Silver. KM#933. | 28.00 |
| P802 | 1984 | 6 | 5 Centimes. Gold. KM#933. | 450 |
| P803 | 1984 | 34 | 10 Centimes. Copper-Nickel. KM#929. | 15.00 |
| P804 | 1984 | 54 | 10 Centimes. Silver. KM#929. | 28.00 |
| P805 | 1984 | 4 | 10 Centimes. Gold. KM#929. | 700 |
| P806 | 1984 | 34 | 20 Centimes. Copper-Nickel. KM#930. | 16.00 |
| P807 | 1984 | 60 | 20 Centimes. Silver. KM#930. | 20.00 |
| P808 | 1984 | 4 | 20 Centimes. Gold. KM#930. | 850 |
| P809 | 1984 | 34 | 1/2 Franc. Nickel. KM#931. | 16.00 |
| P900 | 1984 | 59 | 1/2 Franc. Silver. KM#931. | 28.00 |
| P901 | 1984 | 8 | 1/2 Franc. Gold. KM#931. | 495 |
| P902 | 1984 | 5 | 1/2 Franc. Platinum. KM#931. | 1,400 |
| P903 | 1984 | 40 | Franc. Nickel. KM#925. | 16.00 |
| P904 | 1984 | 69 | Franc. Silver. KM#925. | 35.00 |
| P905 | 1984 | 6 | Franc. Gold. KM#925. | 645 |
| P906 | 1984 | 5 | Franc. Platinum. KM#925. | 2,500 |
| P907 | 1984 | 42 | 2 Francs. Nickel. KM#942. | 16.00 |
| P908 | 1984 | 79 | 2 Francs. Silver. KM#942. | 35.00 |
| P909 | 1984 | 9 | 2 Francs. Gold. KM#942. | 565 |
| P910 | 1984 | 5 | 2 Francs. Platinum. KM#942. | 1,750 |
| P911 | 1984 | 55 | 5 Francs. Nickel Clad Copper-Nickel. KM#926a. | 20.00 |
| P912 | 1984 | 59 | 5 Francs. Silver. KM#926a. | 65.00 |
| P913 | 1984 | 4 | 5 Francs. Gold. KM#926a. | 1,400 |
| P914 | 1984 | 5 | 5 Francs. Platinum. KM#926a. | 2,400 |
| P915 | 1984 | 50 | 10 Francs. Copper-Nickel-Aluminum. KM#940. | 20.00 |
| P916 | 1984 | 79 | 10 Francs. Silver. KM#940. | 65.00 |
| P917 | 1984 | 6 | 10 Francs. Gold. KM#940. | 720 |
| P918 | 1984 | 5 | 10 Francs. Platinum. KM#940. | 2,000 |
| P919 | 1984 | 184 | 10 Francs. Copper-Nickel-Aluminum. KM#954. | 40.00 |
| P920 | 1984 | 244 | 10 Francs. Silver. KM#954. | 65.00 |
| P921 | 1984 | 18 | 10 Francs. Gold. KM#954. | 720 |
| P922 | 1984 | 5 | 10 Francs. Platinum. KM#954. | 2,000 |
| P923 | 1984 | 500 | 100 Francs. Silver. KM#955. | 55.00 |
| P924 | 1984 | 34 | 100 Francs. Gold. KM#955. | 1,150 |
| P925 | 1984 | 9 | 100 Francs. Platinum. KM#955. | 1,900 |
| P926 | 1984 | 100 | 100 Francs. Silver. KM#951. | 75.00 |
| P927 | 1984 | 10 | 100 Francs. Gold. KM#951. | 1,150 |
| P928 | 1984 | 5 | 100 Francs. Platinum. KM#951. | 2,800 |
| P929 | 1985 | 100 | Centime. 0.9250 Silver. KM#928. | 20.00 |
| P930 | 1985 | 18 | Centime. 0.9200 Gold. KM#928. | 200 |
| P931 | 1985 | 60 | 5 Centimes. 0.9250 Silver. KM#933. | 28.00 |
| P932 | 1985 | 6 | 5 Centimes. 0.9200 Gold. KM#933. | 450 |
| P933 | 1985 | 65 | 10 Centimes. 0.9250 Silver. KM#929. | 28.00 |
| P934 | 1985 | 4 | 10 Centimes. 0.9200 Gold. KM#929. | 650 |
| P935 | 1985 | 85 | 20 Centimes. 0.9250 Silver. KM#930. | 25.00 |
| P936 | 1985 | 4 | 20 Centimes. 0.9200 Gold. KM#930. | 700 |
| P937 | 1985 | 80 | 1/2 Franc. 0.9250 Silver. KM#931. | 28.00 |
| P938 | 1985 | 16 | 1/2 Franc. 0.9200 Gold. KM#931. | 450 |
| P939 | 1985 | 5 | 1/2 Franc. Platinum. KM#931. | 2,000 |
| P940 | 1985 | 90 | Franc. 0.9250 Silver. KM#925. | 35.00 |
| P941 | 1985 | 5 | Franc. 0.9200 Gold. KM#925. | 550 |
| P942 | 1985 | 5 | Franc. Platinum. KM#925. | 1,500 |
| P943 | 1985 | 90 | 2 Francs. 0.9250 Silver. KM#942. | 35.00 |
| P944 | 1985 | 17 | 2 Francs. 0.9200 Gold. KM#942. | 565 |
| P945 | 1985 | 5 | 2 Francs. Platinum. KM#942. | 1,400 |
| P946 | 1985 | 70 | 5 Francs. 0.9250 Silver. KM#926a. | 55.00 |
| P947 | 1985 | 4 | 5 Francs. 0.9200 Gold. KM#926a. | 1,100 |
| P948 | 1985 | 5 | 5 Francs. Platinum. KM#926a. | 2,150 |
| P949 | 1985 | 120 | 10 Francs. 0.9250 Silver. KM#940. | 55.00 |
| P950 | 1985 | 12 | 10 Francs. 0.9200 Gold. KM#940. | 720 |
| P951 | 1985 | 5 | 10 Francs. Platinum. KM#940. | 2,150 |
| P952 | 1985 | 8 | 10 Francs. 0.9200 Gold. KM#952. | 720 |
| P953 | 1985 | 8 | 10 Francs. 0.9200 Gold. KM#953. | 720 |
| P954 | 1985 | 45 | 10 Francs. 0.9250 Silver. KM#954. | 55.00 |
| P955 | 1985 | 8 | 10 Francs. 0.9200 Gold. KM#954. | 720 |
| P956 | 1985 | 215 | 10 Francs. 0.9250 Silver. KM#956. | 55.00 |
| P957 | 1985 | 17 | 10 Francs. 0.9200 Gold. KM#956. | 720 |
| P959 | 1985 | 100 | 100 Francs. 0.9250 Silver. KM#951. | 65.00 |
| P960 | 1985 | 18 | 100 Francs. 0.9200 Gold. KM#951. | 1,150 |
| P961 | 1985 | 10 | 100 Francs. Platinum. KM#951. | 2,850 |
| P962 | 1985 | 200 | 100 Francs. 0.9250 Silver. KM#955a. | 65.00 |
| P963 | 1985 | 8 | 100 Francs. 0.9200 Gold. KM#955b. | 1,400 |
| P964 | 1985 | 440 | 100 Francs. 0.9250 Silver. KM#957. | 65.00 |
| P965 | 1985 | 30 | 100 Francs. 0.9200 Gold. KM#957. | 1,150 |
| P966 | 1985 | 15 | 100 Francs. Platinum. KM#957. | 1,950 |
| P958 | 1985 | 15 | 10 Francs. Platinum. KM#956. | — |
| P967 | 1986 | 10 | 10 Francs. Platinum. KM#958. | 1,500 |
| P968 | 1986 | 200 | 10 Francs. 0.9500 Silver. KM#959. | 60.00 |
| P969 | 1986 | 5 | 10 Francs. Platinum. KM#959. | 2,150 |
| P970 | 1986 | 5 | 100 Francs. Platinum. KM#951. | 3,000 |
| P971 | 1986 | 250 | 100 Francs. Silver. KM#951. | 65.00 |
| P972 | 1986 | 5,000 | 100 Francs. 0.9000 Silver. KM#960. | 15.00 |
| P973 | 1986 | 15 | 100 Francs. Platinum. KM#960. | 2,150 |
| P973b | 1986 | 50 | 100 Francs. Gold. KM#960b. | 1,250 |
| P974 | 1987 | 50 | Centime. 0.9500 Silver. KM#928. | 35.00 |
| P975 | 1987 | 50 | 5 Centimes. 0.9500 Silver. KM#933. | 35.00 |
| P976 | 1987 | 50 | 10 Centimes. 0.9500 Silver. KM#929. | 35.00 |
| P977 | 1987 | 50 | 20 Centimes. 0.9500 Silver. KM#930. | 35.00 |
| P978 | 1987 | 50 | 1/2 Franc. 0.9500 Silver. KM#931. | 40.00 |
| P979 | 1987 | 50 | Franc. 0.9500 Silver. KM#925. | 40.00 |
| P980 | 1987 | 50 | 2 Francs. 0.9500 Silver. KM#942. | 60.00 |
| P981 | 1987 | 50 | 5 Francs. 0.9500 Silver. KM#926a. | 65.00 |
| P982 | 1987 | 50 | 10 Francs. 0.9500 Silver. KM#940. | 100 |
| P983 | 1987 | 15 | 10 Francs. 0.9200 Gold. KM#940. | 765 |
| P984 | 1987 | 5 | 10 Francs. 0.9990 Platinum. KM#940. | 2,000 |
| P985 | 1987 | 1,000 | 10 Francs. 0.9500 Silver. KM#961. | 55.00 |
| P986 | 1987 | 25 | 10 Francs. 0.9200 Gold. KM#961. | 765 |
| P987 | 1987 | 10 | 10 Francs. 0.9990 Platinum. KM#961. | 1,650 |
| P988 | 1987 | 30 | 100 Francs. 0.9000 Silver. KM#951. | 65.00 |
| P989 | 1987 | 15 | 100 Francs. 0.9200 Gold. KM#951. | 1,150 |
| P990 | 1987 | 5 | 100 Francs. 0.9990 Platinum. KM#951. | 2,850 |
| P991 | 1987 | 51,000 | 100 Francs. 0.9500 Silver. KM#962, Proof. | 16.00 |
| P991a | 1987 | 100,000 | 100 Francs. 0.9000 Silver. KM#962, Unc. | 12.50 |
| P992 | 1987 | 50 | 100 Francs. 0.9200 Gold. KM#962. | 1,150 |
| P993 | 1987 | 15 | 100 Francs. 0.9990 Platinum. KM#962. | 2,150 |
| P994 | 1988 | 5 | Centime. Platinum. KM#928. | 375 |
| P995 | 1988 | — | 10 Francs. 0.9000 Silver. KM#965a, Proof. | 100 |
| P996 | 1988 | — | 10 Francs. Gold. KM#965c, Proof. | 1,150 |
| P997 | 1988 | 10 | 10 Francs. Platinum. KM#965. | 1,700 |
| P998 | 1988 | 5 | 100 Francs. Platinum. KM#951. | 2,100 |
| PSA999 | 1988 | — | 100 Francs. 0.9000 Silver. KM#966, Proof. | 2,200 |
| P999 | 1988 | 20,000 | 100 Francs. 0.9000 Silver. KM#966, Unc. | 16.00 |
| P1000 | 1988 | 10 | 10 Francs. Platinum. KM#966. | 2,150 |
| P1001 | 1989 | 5 | Centime. Platinum. KM#928. | 350 |
| P1002 | 1989 | 10 | Franc. Platinum. KM#925. | 1,250 |
| P1003 | 1989 | 300 | Franc. Silver. KM#967. | 35.00 |
| P1004 | 1989 | 25 | Franc. Gold. KM#967. | 720 |
| P1005 | 1989 | 10 | Franc. Platinum. KM#967. | 1,250 |
| P1006 | 1989 | 10 | 5 Francs. Platinum. KM#968. | 1,850 |
| P1007 | 1989 | 5 | 100 Francs. Platinum. KM#951. | 2,150 |
| PA1008 | 1989 | — | 100 Francs. 0.9000 Silver. KM#970, Proof. | 25.00 |
| P1008 | 1989 | 10,000 | 100 Francs. 0.9000 Silver. KM#970, Unc. | 20.00 |
| P1009 | 1989 | 10 | 100 Francs. Platinum. KM#970. | 2,150 |
| P1012 | 1990 | 5 | Centime. Platinum. KM#928. | 350 |
| P1025 | 1990 | 5 | 100 Francs. Platinum. KM#951. | 2,000 |
| P1028 | 1990 | 5 | 100 Francs. Platinum. KM#982. | 2,000 |
| P1010 | 1990 | 50 | Centime. Silver. KM#928. | — |
| P1011 | 1990 | 10 | Centime. Gold. KM#928. | — |
| P1013 | 1990 | 50 | 5 Centimes. Silver. KM#933. | — |
| P1014 | 1990 | 50 | 10 Centimes. Silver. KM#929. | — |
| P1015 | 1990 | 50 | 20 Centimes. Silver. KM#930. | — |
| P1016 | 1990 | 5 | 20 Centimes. Gold. KM#930. | — |
| P1017 | 1990 | 50 | 1/2 Franc. Silver. KM#931. | — |
| P1018 | 1990 | 50 | Franc. Silver. KM#925. | — |
| P1019 | 1990 | 50 | 2 Francs. Silver. KM#942. | — |
| P1020 | 1990 | 5 | 2 Francs. Gold. KM#942. | — |
| P1021 | 1990 | 50 | 5 Francs. Silver. KM#926a. | — |
| P1022 | 1990 | 10 | 10 Francs. Gold. Gold Alloy Spirit of Bastille. | — |
| P1023 | 1990 | 50 | 100 Francs. Silver. KM#951. | — |
| P1024 | 1990 | 10 | 100 Francs. Gold. KM#951. | — |
| P1026 | 1990 | 100 | 100 Francs. Silver. KM#982. | — |
| P1027 | 1990 | 10 | 100 Francs. Gold. KM#982. | — |
| P1029 | 1991 | — | 100 Francs. Silver. KM#951. | 170 |
| P1030 | 1991 | — | 100 Francs. Silver. KM#996. | 160 |

## PIEFORTS WITH ESSAI

Double thickness; standard metals unless otherwise noted

| KM# | Date | Mintage | Identification | Mkt Val |
|---|---|---|---|---|
| PE271 | 1914 | — | 10 Centimes. Nickel. KM#866. | 550 |
| PE272 | 1914 | — | 25 Centimes. KM#867. | 500 |
| PE-A281 | 1920 | — | 5 Centimes. Copper-Nickel. KM#875. | 100 |
| PE281 | 1920 | — | 50 Centimes. Aluminum-Bronze. KM#875. | 100 |
| PE282 | 1920 | — | Franc. Bronze-Aluminum. | 100 |
| PE298 | 1929 | — | 10 Francs. KM#878. | 300 |
| PE299 | 1929 | — | 20 Francs. KM#879. | 375 |
| PE301 | 1931 | — | 50 Centimes. KM#894.1. | — |
| PE302 | 1931 | — | Franc. KM#885. | — |
| PE303 | 1931 | — | 2 Francs. KM#886. | — |
| PE304 | 1941 | — | 20 Centimes. KM#899. | — |
| PE306 | 1941 | — | 10 Centimes. KM#898. | 100 |
| PE307 | 1941 | — | 20 Centimes. KM#900. | 100 |
| PE308 | 1941 | — | 5 Francs. KM#901. | 400 |
| PE309 | 1943 | — | 2 Francs. KM#904. | 120 |
| PE310 | 1945 | 104 | 20 Centimes. KM#907. | 140 |
| PE311 | 1945 | 104 | 5 Francs. KM#888. | 100 |

| KM# | Date | Mintage | Identification | Mkt Val |
|---|---|---|---|---|
| PE312 | 1945 | 104 | 20 Francs. Copper-Nickel. KM#879. | 175 |
| PE313 | 1946 | 104 | 50 Centimes. KM#894.1a. | 75.00 |
| PE314 | 1946 | 104 | Franc. KM#885a. | 75.00 |
| PE315 | 1946 | 104 | 2 Francs. KM#886a. | 100 |
| PE316 | 1946 | 104 | 10 Francs. KM#909. | 160 |
| PE317 | 1950 | — | 10 Francs. KM#915. | 60.00 |
| PE318 | 1950 | — | 20 Francs. KM#916. | 75.00 |
| PE319 | 1950 | — | 50 Francs. KM#918. | 120 |
| PE320 | 1952 | 104 | 10 Francs. KM#915. | 60.00 |
| PE321 | 1952 | 104 | 20 Francs. KM#917. | 75.00 |
| PE322 | 1952 | 104 | 50 Francs. KM#918. | 100 |
| PE323 | 1954 | 104 | 100 Francs. KM#919. | 100 |
| PE324 | 1958 | 65 | 100 Francs. Silver. KM#919. | 500 |
| PE325 | 1959 | 104 | Franc. KM#925. | 75.00 |
| PE326 | 1959 | 104 | 5 Francs. KM#926. | 120 |
| PE327 | 1959 | 104 | 5 Francs. Silver. KM#926. | 350 |
| PE328 | 1960 | 50 | Franc. Silver. KM#925. | 145 |
| PE329 | 1960 | 20 | Franc. Gold. KM#925. | 500 |
| PE330 | 1960 | 500 | Franc. KM#925. | 35.00 |
| PE331 | 1960 | 500 | 5 Francs. Silver. KM#926. | 100 |
| PE332 | 1960 | 50 | 5 Francs. Gold. KM#926. | 725 |
| PE333 | 1961 | 104 | Centime. KM#928. | 55.00 |
| PE334 | 1961 | 104 | 5 Centimes. KM#927. | 55.00 |
| PE335 | 1961 | 500 | 5 Centimes. KM#927. | 20.00 |
| PE336 | 1961 | 50 | 5 Centimes. Silver. KM#927. | 100 |
| PE337 | 1961 | 20 | 5 Centimes. Gold. KM#927. | 320 |
| PE338 | 1962 | 104 | 10 Centimes. KM#929. | 40.00 |
| PE339 | 1962 | 104 | 20 Centimes. KM#930. | 40.00 |
| PE340 | 1962 | 104 | 50 Centimes. KM#939. | 75.00 |
| PE434 | 1971 | 100 | 5 Francs. Platinum. KM#926a. | 1,250 |

## MINT SETS

| KM# | Date | Mintage | Identification | Issue Price | Mkt Val |
|---|---|---|---|---|---|
| MS1 | 1986 (10) | 20,000 | KM#925.1, 926a, 928-931, 933, 942, 951.1, 959 | — | 130 |
| MS2 | 1987 (10) | 4,000 | KM#925.1, 926a, 928-931, 933, 940, 942, 961d | — | 60.00 |
| MS3 | 1988 (10) | 2,000 | KM#925.1, 926a, 928-931, 933, 942, 964-965 | — | 60.00 |
| MS4 | 1989 (10) | 2,000 | KM#925.1, 926a, 928-931, 933, 942, 964, 969 | — | 60.00 |
| MS6 | 1991 (9) | 2,500 | KM#925.1, 926a.1, 928-930, 931.1, 933, 942.1, 964.1, medal rotation | 50.00 | 40.00 |
| MS7 | 1992 (10) | 20,000 | KM#925.1, 926a.1, 928-930, 931.1, 933, 942.1, 964.1, 1008.2, medal rotation | — | 45.00 |
| MS8 | 1993 (10) | 20,000 | KM#925.1, 926a.1, 928-930, 931.1, 933, 942.1, 964.1, 1008.2, medal rotation | — | 40.00 |
| MS9 | 1994 (10) | 20,000 | KM#925.1, 926a.1, 928-930, 931.1, 933, 942.1, 964.2, 1008.2 bee privy mark | — | 50.00 |
| MS10 | 1995 (10) | 20,000 | KM#925.1, 926a.1, 928, 930, 931.1, 933, 942.1, 964.2, 1008.2 | — | 50.00 |
| MS11 | 1996 (10) | 5,000 | KM#925.1, 926a.1, 928-930, 931.1, 933, 942.1, 964.2, 1008.2 | — | 60.00 |
| MS12 | 1996 (3) | 2,500 | KM#1155, 1160, 1180 | — | 35.00 |
| MS13 | 1997 (10) | 15,000 | KM#925.1, 926a.1, 928-930, 931.1, 933, 942.1, 964.2, 1008.2 | — | 50.00 |
| MS14 | 1998 (10) | — | KM#925.1, 926a.1, 928-930, 931.1, 933, 942.1, 964.2, 1008.2 | — | 50.00 |
| MS15 | 1999 (10) | — | KM#925.1, 926a.1, 928-930, 931.1, 933, 942.1, 964.2, 1008.2 | — | 50.00 |
| MS18 | 1999 (8) | 35,000 | KM#1282-1289 | 20.25 | 25.00 |
| MS16 | 2000 (3) | — | KM#1222-1224 | — | 30.00 |
| MS17 | 2000 (10) | 50,000 | KM#925, 926a, 928-931, 933, 942, 964.2, 1008.2 | — | 50.00 |
| MS19 | 2000 (8) | 35,000 | KM#1282-1289 | 20.25 | 25.00 |
| MS20 | 2001 (2) | 10,000 | KM#925.1a, 928a | — | 190 |
| MS21 | 2001 (8) | 35,000 | KM#1282-1289 | 20.25 | 25.00 |
| MS22 | 2002 (8) | 35,000 | KM#1282-1289 | 20.25 | 25.00 |

## PROOF SETS

| KM# | Date | Mintage | Identification | Issue Price | Mkt Val |
|---|---|---|---|---|---|
| PS6 | 1990-91 (9) | — | KM#971-972, 980-981, 983-984, 993-995 | — | 450 |
| PS7 | 1991 (10) | 10,000 | KM#925.2, 926a.2, 928-930, 931.2, 933, 942.2, 951.2, 964.2 | 160 | 145 |
| PS8 | 1991 (3) | 15,000 | KM#977, 991-992 | — | 500 |
| PS10 | 1992 (3) | 2,000 | KM#1007, 1010-1011 | — | 200 |
| PS9 | 1992 (11) | 15,000 | KM#925.2, 926a.2, 928-930, 931-2, 933, 942.2, 951.1, 964.2, 1008.2 | — | 125 |
| PS11 | 1993 (11) | 10,000 | KM#925.1, 926a.1, 928-930, 931.2, 933, 942.1, 964.1, 961.1, 1008.2 | — | 135 |
| PS12 | 1994 (11) | 10,000 | KM#925.2, 926a.2, 928-930, 931.2, 933, 942.2, 951.1, 964.2, 1008.2, fish privy mark | — | 135 |
| PS13 | 1995 (11) | 10,000 | KM#925.2, 926a.2, 928-930, 931.2, 933, 942.2, 951.1, 964.2, 1008.2 | — | 135 |
| PS14 | 1996 (11) | 8,000 | KM#925.2, 926a.2, 928-930, 931.2, 933, 942.2, 951.1, 964.2, 1008.2 | — | 135 |
| PS15 | 1997 (11) | 10,000 | KM#925.2, 926a.2, 928, 930, 931.2, 933, 942.2, 951.1, 964.2, 1008.2 | — | 135 |
| PS16 | 1998 (11) | — | KM#925.2, 926a.2, 928, 930, 931.2, 933, 942.2, 951.1, 964.2, 1008.2 | — | 135 |
| PS17 | 1999 (11) | — | KM#925.2, 926a.2, 928, 930, 941.2, 933, 942.2, 951.1, 964.2, 1008.2 | — | 135 |
| PS19 | 1999 (8) | 15,000 | KM#1282-1289 | 59.00 | 60.00 |
| PS18 | 2000 (11) | — | KM#925.2, 926a.2, 928, 930, 931.2, 933, 942.2, 951.1, 964.2, 1008.2 | — | 135 |
| PS20 | 2000 (8) | 15,000 | KM#1282-1289 | 59.00 | 60.00 |
| PS21 | 2001 (8) | 15,000 | KM#1282-1289 | 59.00 | 60.00 |
| PS22 | 2002 (8) | 40,000 | KM#1282-1289 | 59.00 | 60.00 |

## SPECIMEN FDC SETS (FLEUR DE COIN)

| KM# | Date | Mintage | Identification | Issue Price | Mkt Val |
|---|---|---|---|---|---|
| SS1 | 1964 (7) | 25,600 | KM#925-930, 939 | 4.00 | 7.00 |
| SS2 | 1965 (7) | 35,000 | KM#925-926, 928-932 | 7.60 | 12.00 |
| SS3 | 1966 (8) | 7,171 | KM#925-926, 928-933 | 9.00 | 45.00 |
| SS4 | 1967 (8) | 2,305 | KM#925-926, 928-933 | 10.00 | 150 |
| SS5 | 1968 (8) | 3,000 | With box KM#925-926, 928-933 | 10.00 | 350 |
| SS5A | 1968 (8) | I.A. | KM#925-926, 928-933 without box | — | 75.00 |
| SS6 | 1969 (8) | 6,050 | KM#925-926, 928-933 | 10.00 | 75.00 |
| SS7 | 1970 (8) | 10,000 | KM#925, 926a, 928-933 | 9.00 | 20.00 |
| SS8 | 1971 (8) | 12,000 | KM#925, 926a, 928-933 | 9.00 | 20.00 |
| SS9 | 1972 (8) | 15,000 | KM#925, 926a, 928-933 | 9.00 | 20.00 |
| SS10 | 1973 (8) | 79,000 | KM#925, 926a, 928-933 | 12.00 | 17.00 |
| SS11 | 1974 (9) | 98,800 | KM#925, 926a, 928-931, 933, 940-941 | 31.00 | 15.00 |
| SS12 | 1975 (9) | 52,000 | KM#925, 926a, 928-931, 933, 940-941 | 35.00 | 20.00 |
| SS13 | 1976 (9) | 35,700 | KM#925, 926a, 928-931, 933, 940-941 | 35.00 | 20.00 |
| SS14 | 1977 (9) | 25,000 | KM#925, 926a, 928-931, 933, 940-941 | 36.00 | 25.00 |
| SS15 | 1978 (9) | 24,000 | KM#925, 926a, 928-931, 933, 940-941 | 39.00 | 30.00 |
| SS16 | 1979 (10) | 40,500 | KM#925, 926a, 928-931, 933, 940--942 | 55.00 | 45.00 |
| SS17 | 1980 (10) | 60,000 | KM#925, 926a, 928-931, 933, 940-942 | 90.00 | 40.00 |
| SS18 | 1981 (9) | 26,000 | KM#925, 926a, 928-931, 933, 940, 942 | — | 35.00 |
| SS19 | 1982 (11) | 27,500 | KM#925, 926a, 928-931, 933, 940, 942, 950-951 | — | 60.00 |
| SS20 | 1983 (12) | 16,561 | KM#925, 926a, 928-931, 933, 940, 942, 951-953 | — | 75.00 |
| SS21 | 1984 (12) | 13,388 | KM#825, 926a, 928-931, 933, 940, 942, 951, 954, 955 | — | 125 |
| SS22 | 1985 (12) | 12,224 | KM#925, 926a, 928-931, 933, 940, 942, 951, 956-957 | — | 100 |
| SS23 | 1986 (12) | 13,000 | KM#925.1, 926a.1, 928-931.1, 933, 942.1, 951, 958, 959, 960 | — | 110 |
| SS24 | 1987 (12) | 15,000 | KM#925.1, 926a.1, 928-931.1, 933, 940, 942.1, 951, 961, 962 | 68.00 | 110 |
| SS25 | 1987 (2) | — | KMP991-991a, Proof and BU | 120 | 35.00 |
| SS26 | 1988 (13) | 13,000 | KM#925.1, 926a.1, 928-931.1, 933, 941.1, 951, 963-966 | — | 120 |
| SS27 | 1989 (14) | 10,000 | KM#925.1, 926a.1, 928-931.1, 933, 942.1, 951, 964, 967-970 | — | 130 |
| SS28 | 1990 (13) | 10,000 | KM#925.1, 926a.1, 928-931.1, 933, 942.1, 951, 964, 980-982 | — | 120 |
| SS29 | 1990 (11) | 10,000 | KM#925.1, 926a.1, 928-931.1, 933, 942.1, 951, 964, 982 | — | 110 |

# FRENCH AFARS & ISSAS

**MINT MARKS**
- Paris (privy marks only)

**MONETARY SYSTEM**
100 Centimes = 1 Franc

## FRENCH COLONY

### DECIMAL COINAGE

**FRANC** KM# 16 **Composition:** Aluminum

| Date | Mintage | F | VF | XF | Unc | BU |
|---|---|---|---|---|---|---|
| 1969(a) | 100,000 | 1.00 | 2.00 | 3.50 | 6.00 | — |
| 1971(a) | 100,000 | 1.00 | 2.00 | 3.50 | 6.00 | — |
| 1975(a) | 300,000 | 0.75 | 1.25 | 2.00 | 3.00 | — |

**2 FRANCS** KM# 13 **Composition:** Aluminum

| Date | Mintage | F | VF | XF | Unc | BU |
|---|---|---|---|---|---|---|
| 1968 | 100,000 | 1.00 | 2.00 | 3.50 | 6.00 | — |
| 1975 | 180,000 | 0.75 | 1.50 | 2.50 | 5.00 | — |

**5 FRANCS** KM# 14 **Composition:** Aluminum

| Date | Mintage | F | VF | XF | Unc | BU |
|---|---|---|---|---|---|---|
| 1968(a) | 100,000 | 1.00 | 2.00 | 3.50 | 6.00 | — |
| 1975(a) | 300,000 | 0.75 | 1.25 | 2.00 | 4.00 | — |

**10 FRANCS** KM# 17 **Composition:** Aluminum-Bronze

| Date | Mintage | F | VF | XF | Unc | BU |
|---|---|---|---|---|---|---|
| 1969(a) | 100,000 | 1.50 | 3.00 | 6.00 | 9.00 | — |
| 1970(a) | 300,000 | 1.00 | 2.00 | 4.00 | 7.00 | — |
| 1975(a) | 360,000 | 0.75 | 1.50 | 3.00 | 5.00 | — |

**20 FRANCS** KM# 15 **Composition:** Aluminum-Bronze

| Date | Mintage | F | VF | XF | Unc | BU |
|---|---|---|---|---|---|---|
| 1968(a) | 300,000 | 1.50 | 2.50 | 4.50 | 8.00 | — |
| 1975(a) | 300,000 | 1.25 | 2.00 | 4.00 | 7.00 | — |

**50 FRANCS** KM# 18 **Composition:** Copper Nickel **Reverse:** Pair of dromedary camels, denomination

| Date | Mintage | F | VF | XF | Unc | BU |
|---|---|---|---|---|---|---|
| 1970(a) | 300,000 | 1.50 | 3.00 | 6.00 | 10.00 | — |
| 1975(a) | 180,000 | 1.50 | 3.00 | 6.00 | 10.00 | — |

**100 FRANCS** KM# 19 **Composition:** Copper-Nickel **Reverse:** Pair of dromedary camels, denomination

| Date | Mintage | F | VF | XF | Unc | BU |
|---|---|---|---|---|---|---|
| 1970(a) | 600,000 | 2.50 | 4.50 | 7.50 | 12.50 | — |
| 1975(a) | 400,000 | 2.50 | 4.50 | 7.50 | 12.50 | — |

## ESSAIS

Standard metals unless otherwise noted.

| KM# | Date | Mintage | Identification | Issue Price | Mkt Val |
|---|---|---|---|---|---|
| E1 | 1968 | 1,700 | 2 Francs. KM13. | — | 10.00 |
| E2 | 1968 | 1,700 | 5 Francs. KM14. | — | 10.00 |
| E3 | 1968 | 1,700 | 20 Francs. KM15. | — | 12.50 |
| E4 | 1969 | 1,700 | Franc. KM16. | — | 10.00 |
| E5 | 1969 | 1,700 | 10 Francs. KM17. | — | 12.50 |
| E6 | 1970 | 1,700 | 50 Francs. KM18. | — | 12.50 |
| E7 | 1970 | 1,700 | 100 Francs. KM19. | — | 20.00 |

# FRENCH EQUATORIAL AFRICA

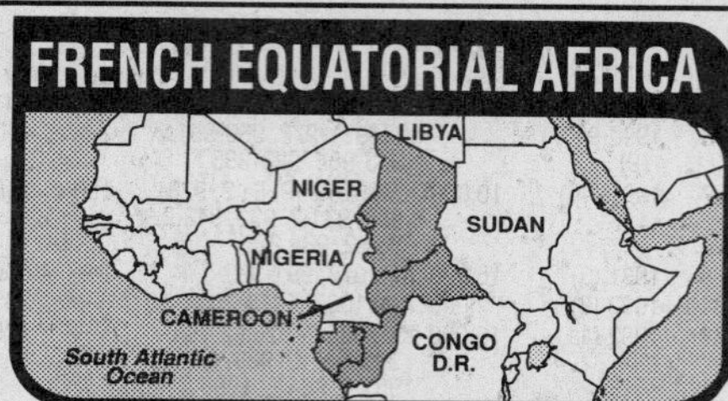


French Equatorial Africa, an area consisting of four self governing dependencies (Middle Congo, Ubangi-Shari, Chad and Gabon) in West-Central Africa, had an area of 969,111 sq. mi. (2,509,987 sq. km.). Capital: Brazzaville. The area, rich in natural resources, exported cotton, timber, coffee, cacao, diamonds and gold.

Little is known of the history of these parts of Africa prior to French occupation - which began with no thought of territorial acquisition. France's initial intent was simply to establish a few supply stations along the west coast of Africa to service the warships assigned to combat the slave trade in the early part of the 19th century. French settlement began in 1839. Gabon (then Gabun) and the Middle Congo were secured between 1885 and 1891; Chad and Ubangi-Shari between 1894 and 1897. The four colonies were joined to form French Equatorial Africa in 1910. The dependencies were changed from colonies to territories within the French Union in 1946, and all the inhabitants were made French citizens. In 1958 they voted to become autonomous republics within the new French Community, and attained full independence in 1960.

For later coinage see Central African States, Congo Peoples Republic, Gabon and Chad.

**RULERS**

French, until 1960

**MINT MARKS**

(a) - Paris, privy marks only
(t) - Poissy, privy marks only, thunderbolt
SA - Pretoria (1942-1943)

**ENGRAVERS INITIALS**

GLS – Steynberg

**MONETARY SYSTEM**

100 Centimes = 1 Franc

# FRENCH COLONY

## DECIMAL COINAGE

**5 CENTIMES** KM# 3 **Composition:** Aluminum-Bronze
**Note:** Similar to 10 Centimes, KM#4.

| Date | Mintage | F | VF | XF | Unc | BU |
|---|---|---|---|---|---|---|
| 1943 | Est. 44,000,000 | 90.00 | 150 | 275 | 625 | — |

**Note:** Not released for circulation

**10 CENTIMES** KM# 4 **Composition:** Aluminum-Bronze

| Date | Mintage | F | VF | XF | Unc | BU |
|---|---|---|---|---|---|---|
| 1943 | Est. 13,000,000 | 75.00 | 100 | 160 | 375 | — |

**Note:** Not released for circulation

**25 CENTIMES** KM# 5 **Composition:** Aluminum-Bronze
**Note:** Similar to 10 Centimes, KM#4.

| Date | Mintage | F | VF | XF | Unc | BU |
|---|---|---|---|---|---|---|
| 1943 | Est. 4,160,000 | 175 | 300 | 500 | 825 | — |

**Note:** Not released for circulation

**50 CENTIMES** KM# 1 **Composition:** Brass

| Date | Mintage | F | VF | XF | Unc | BU |
|---|---|---|---|---|---|---|
| 1942SA | 8,000,000 | 1.50 | 3.00 | 8.00 | 20.00 | — |

**50 CENTIMES** KM# 1a **Composition:** Bronze

| Date | Mintage | F | VF | XF | Unc | BU |
|---|---|---|---|---|---|---|
| 1943SA | 16,000,000 | 1.25 | 2.50 | 7.00 | 18.00 | — |

**FRANC** KM# 2 **Composition:** Brass

| Date | Mintage | F | VF | XF | Unc | BU |
|---|---|---|---|---|---|---|
| 1942SA | 3,000,000 | 2.00 | 3.50 | 10.00 | 30.00 | — |

**FRANC** KM# 2a **Composition:** Bronze

| Date | Mintage | F | VF | XF | Unc | BU |
|---|---|---|---|---|---|---|
| 1943SA | 6,000,000 | 1.75 | 2.75 | 9.00 | 28.00 | — |

**FRANC** KM# 6 **Composition:** Aluminum

| Date | Mintage | F | VF | XF | Unc | BU |
|---|---|---|---|---|---|---|
| 1948(a) | 15,000,000 | 0.15 | 0.25 | 0.50 | 2.00 | — |

**2 FRANCS** KM# 7 **Composition:** Aluminum

| Date | Mintage | F | VF | XF | Unc | BU |
|---|---|---|---|---|---|---|
| 1948(a) | 5,040,000 | 0.25 | 0.50 | 1.50 | 4.00 | — |

## TOKEN COINAGE

Middle Congo

**(NO DENOMINATION)** KM# Tn1 **Composition:** Aluminum **Reverse:** Elephant walking left

| Date | Mintage | F | VF | XF | Unc | BU |
|---|---|---|---|---|---|---|
| 1925(t) | — | 35.00 | 65.00 | 115 | 300 | — |

**(NO DENOMINATION)** KM# Tn2 **Composition:** Aluminum **Reverse:** Leopard walking left

| Date | Mintage | F | VF | XF | Unc | BU |
|---|---|---|---|---|---|---|
| 1926 | — | 40.00 | 75.00 | 150 | 325 | — |

## ESSAIS

Standard metals unless otherwise noted

| KM# | Date | Mintage | Identification | Mkt Val |
|---|---|---|---|---|
| E1 | 1948 | 2,000 | Franc. Copper-Nickel. KM#7 | 20.00 |
| E2 | 1948 | 2,000 | 2 Francs. Copper-Nickel. KM#7 | 25.00 |

## PIEFORTS WITH ESSAI

Standard metals unless otherwise noted

| KM# | Date | Mintage | Identification | Mkt Val |
|---|---|---|---|---|
| PE1 | 1948 | 104 | Franc. KM#6 | 70.00 |
| PE2 | 1948 | 104 | 2 Francs. KM#7 | 90.00 |

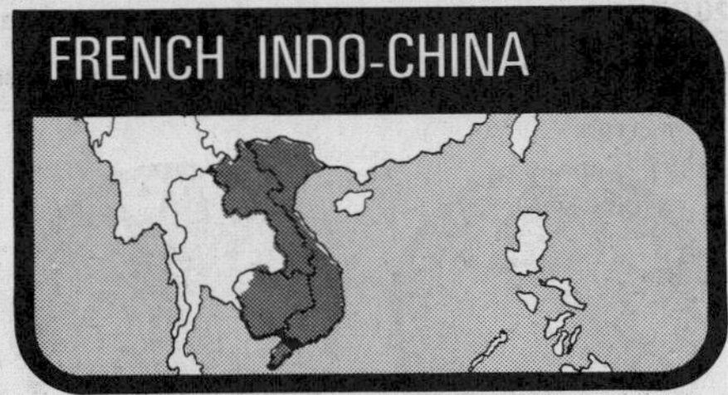


French Indo-China, made up of the protectorates of Annam, Tonkin, Cambodia and Laos and the colony of Cochin-China was located on the Indo-Chinese peninsula of Southeast Asia. The colony had an area of 286,194 sq. mi. (741,242 sq. km.). and a population of 30 million. Principal cities: Saigon, Haiphong, Vientiane, Pnom-Penh and Hanoi.

The forebears of the modern Indo-Chinese people originated in the Yellow River Valley of Northern China. From there, they were driven into the Indo-Chinese peninsula by the Han Chinese. The Chinese followed southward in the second century B.C., conquering the peninsula and ruling it until 938, leaving a lingering heritage of Chinese learning and culture. Indo-Chinese independence was basically maintained until the arrival of the French in the mid-19th century who established control over all of Vietnam, Laos and Cambodia. Activities directed toward obtaining self-determination accelerated during the Japanese occupation of World War II. The dependencies were changed from colonies to territories within the French Union in 1946, and all the inhabitants were made French citizens.

In Aug. of 1945, an uprising erupted involving the French and Vietnamese Nationalists, culminated in the French military disaster at Dien Bien Phu (May, 1954) and the subsequent Geneva Conference that brought an end to French colonial rule in Indo-China.

For later coinage see Kampuchea, Laos and Vietnam.

**RULERS**

French, until 1954

**MINT MARKS**

A - Paris
(a) - Paris, privy marks only
B - Beaumont-le-Roger
C - Castlesarrasin
H - Heaton, Birmingham
(p) - Thunderbolt - Poissy
S - San Francisco, U.S.A.
None - Osaka, Japan
None - Hanoi, Tonkin

**MONETARY SYSTEM**

5 Sapeques = 1 Cent
100 Cents = 1 Piastre

# FRENCH COLONY

## STANDARD COINAGE

**SAPEQUE KM# 6 Composition:** Bronze

| Date | Mintage | F | VF | XF | Unc | BU |
|---|---|---|---|---|---|---|
| 1901A | 4,843,000 | 2.50 | 7.50 | 15.00 | 70.00 | — |
| 1902A | 2,500,000 | 7.50 | 20.00 | 40.00 | 125 | — |

**1/4 CENT KM# 25 Composition:** Zinc **Note:** Lead counterfeits dated 1941 and 1942 are known.

| Date | Mintage | F | VF | XF | Unc | BU |
|---|---|---|---|---|---|---|
| 1942 | 221,800,000 | 8.00 | 15.00 | 35.00 | 75.00 | — |
| 1943 | 279,450,000 | 15.00 | 35.00 | 55.00 | 125 | — |
| 1944 | 46,122,000 | 150 | 250 | 400 | 1,000 | — |

**1/2 CENT KM# 20 Composition:** Bronze

| Date | Mintage | F | VF | XF | Unc | BU |
|---|---|---|---|---|---|---|
| 1935(a) | 26,365,000 | 0.25 | 0.50 | 2.00 | 10.00 | — |
| 1936(a) | 23,635,000 | 0.25 | 0.50 | 2.00 | 10.00 | — |
| 1937(a) | 10,244,000 | 0.50 | 1.50 | 5.00 | 15.00 | — |
| 1938(a) | 16,665,000 | 0.25 | 0.75 | 2.50 | 12.00 | — |
| 1939(a) | 17,305,000 | 0.25 | 0.75 | 2.50 | 12.00 | — |
| 1940(a) | 11,218,000 | 4.00 | 8.00 | 20.00 | 40.00 | — |

**1/2 CENT KM# 20a Composition:** Zinc

| Date | Mintage | F | VF | XF | Unc | BU |
|---|---|---|---|---|---|---|
| 1939(a) | 185,000 | 100 | 200 | 300 | 600 | — |
| 1940(a) | — | 200 | 300 | 400 | 700 | — |

**CENT KM# 8 Composition:** Bronze

| Date | Mintage | F | VF | XF | Unc | BU |
|---|---|---|---|---|---|---|
| 1901 | 9,750,000 | 2.00 | 3.00 | 7.50 | 25.00 | — |
| 1902 | 5,050,000 | 3.00 | 5.00 | 10.00 | 40.00 | — |
| 1903 | 8,000,000 | 2.50 | 4.00 | 8.00 | 30.00 | — |
| 1906 | 2,000,000 | 5.00 | 8.00 | 25.00 | 80.00 | — |

**CENT KM# 12.1 Composition:** Bronze

| Date | Mintage | F | VF | XF | Unc | BU |
|---|---|---|---|---|---|---|
| 1908 | 3,000,000 | 10.00 | 20.00 | 55.00 | 235 | — |
| 1909 | 5,000,000 | 20.00 | 40.00 | 80.00 | 275 | — |
| 1910 | 7,703,000 | 1.00 | 4.00 | 10.00 | 25.00 | — |
| 1911 | 15,234,000 | 0.75 | 3.00 | 10.00 | 20.00 | — |
| 1912 | 17,027,000 | 0.75 | 3.00 | 10.00 | 20.00 | — |
| 1913 | 3,945,000 | 2.00 | 7.00 | 18.00 | 45.00 | — |
| 1914 | 11,027,000 | 0.75 | 3.00 | 15.00 | 30.00 | — |
| 1916 | 1,312,000 | 8.00 | 15.00 | 28.00 | 50.00 | — |
| 1917 | 9,762,000 | 1.00 | 4.00 | 10.00 | 20.00 | — |
| 1918 | 2,372,000 | 6.00 | 12.50 | 25.00 | 50.00 | — |
| 1919 | 9,148,000 | 1.00 | 4.00 | 7.50 | 20.00 | — |
| 1920 | 18,305,000 | 0.75 | 3.00 | 5.00 | 12.50 | — |
| 1921 | 14,722,000 | 0.75 | 2.00 | 3.00 | 10.00 | — |
| 1922 | 8,850,000 | 1.00 | 3.00 | 5.00 | 20.00 | — |
| 1923 | 1,079,000 | 20.00 | 40.00 | 65.00 | 175 | — |
| 1926 | 11,672,000 | 0.75 | 2.00 | 4.00 | 10.00 | — |
| 1927 | 3,328,000 | 5.00 | 10.00 | 25.00 | 50.00 | — |
| 1930 | 4,682,000 | 1.25 | 2.75 | 5.00 | 10.00 | — |
| 1931 Torch privy mark | 5,318,000 | 20.00 | 35.00 | 100 | 350 | — |
| 1931 Wing privy mark | Inc. above | 30.00 | 60.00 | 150 | 450 | — |
| 1937 | 8,902,000 | 0.25 | 0.50 | 1.50 | 8.00 | — |
| 1938 | 15,499,000 | 0.25 | 0.50 | 1.00 | 6.00 | — |
| 1939 | 15,599,000 | 0.25 | 0.50 | 1.00 | 6.00 | — |

**CENT KM# 12.2 Composition:** Bronze **Note:** Without mint mark.

| Date | Mintage | F | VF | XF | Unc | BU |
|---|---|---|---|---|---|---|
| 1920 | 13,290,000 | 1.00 | 2.50 | 5.00 | 17.50 | — |
| 1921 | 1,610,000 | 35.00 | 70.00 | 225 | 450 | — |

**CENT KM# 12.3 Composition:** Bronze

| Date | Mintage | F | VF | XF | Unc | BU |
|---|---|---|---|---|---|---|
| 1922(p) | 9,476,000 | 1.00 | 1.75 | 5.00 | 12.00 | — |
| 1923(p) | 27,891,000 | 0.50 | 0.75 | 1.50 | 7.50 | — |

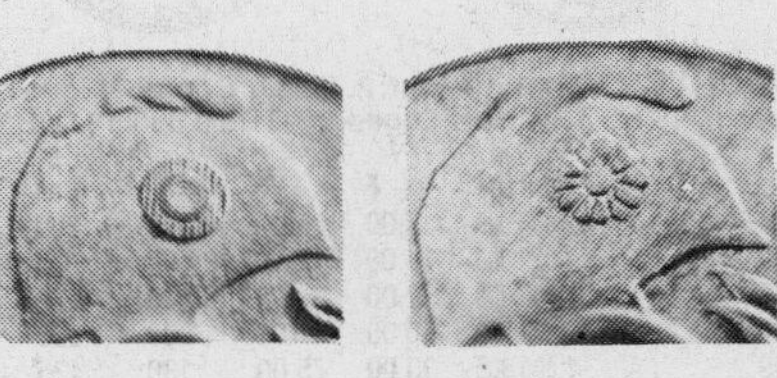

**CENT KM# 24.1 Composition:** Zinc **Note:** Vichy Government issue, circles and rosette. Type 1: Circles on Phrygian cap.

| Date | Mintage | F | VF | XF | Unc | BU |
|---|---|---|---|---|---|---|
| 1940 | 1,990,000 | 5.00 | 8.00 | 20.00 | 45.00 | — |

**CENT KM# 24.2 Composition:** Zinc **Note:** Vichy Government issue. Type 2: Rosette on Phrygian cap. Variety 1: 12 petals.

| Date | Mintage | F | VF | XF | Unc | BU |
|---|---|---|---|---|---|---|
| 1940 | — | 5.00 | 8.00 | 20.00 | 50.00 | — |

**CENT KM# 24.3 Composition:** Zinc **Note:** Vichy Government issue. Type 2: Rosette on Phrygian cap. Variety 2: 11 petals.

| Date | Mintage | F | VF | XF | Unc | BU |
|---|---|---|---|---|---|---|
| 1940 | — | 5.00 | 12.00 | 25.00 | 60.00 | — |
| 1941 | — | 2.00 | 5.00 | 12.00 | 40.00 | — |

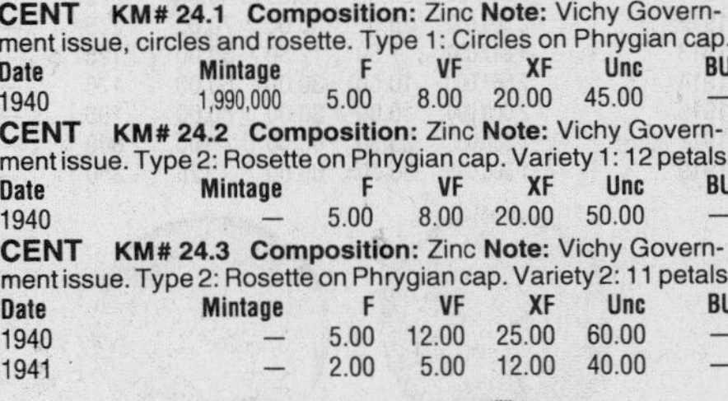

**CENT KM# 26 Composition:** Aluminum **Note:** Edge varieties exist - plain, grooved and partially grooved.

| Date | Mintage | F | VF | XF | Unc | BU |
|---|---|---|---|---|---|---|
| 1943 | — | 0.25 | 0.50 | 1.00 | 3.00 | — |

**5 CENTS KM# 18 (KM18.1) Weight:** 5.0000 g. **Composition:** Copper-Nickel **Note:** 1.6 milimeters thick.

| Date | Mintage | F | VF | XF | Unc | BU |
|---|---|---|---|---|---|---|
| 1923(a) | 1,611,000 | 3.00 | 5.00 | 15.00 | 40.00 | — |
| 1924(a) | 3,389,000 | 1.00 | 3.00 | 12.00 | 35.00 | — |
| 1925(a) | 6,000,000 | 1.00 | 1.75 | 7.00 | 20.00 | — |
| 1930(a) | 4,000,000 | 1.00 | 2.00 | 8.00 | 25.00 | — |
| 1937(a) | 10,000,000 | 0.50 | 1.00 | 4.00 | 15.00 | — |
| 1938(a) | — | 10.00 | 25.00 | 75.00 | 175 | — |
| 1938(a) Proof | — | Value: 275 | | | | |

**5 CENTS KM# 18.1a Weight:** 4.0000 g. **Composition:** Nickel-Brass **Note:** 1.3 milimeters thick.

| Date | Mintage | F | VF | XF | Unc | BU |
|---|---|---|---|---|---|---|
| 1938(a) | 50,569,000 | 0.25 | 0.50 | 1.00 | 5.00 | — |
| 1939(a) | 38,501,000 | 0.25 | 0.50 | 1.00 | 5.00 | — |

**5 CENTS KM# 27 Composition:** Aluminum **Note:** Vichy Government issue. Edge varieties exist: reeded - rare, plain, grooved, and partially grooved.

| Date | Mintage | F | VF | XF | Unc | BU |
|---|---|---|---|---|---|---|
| 1943A | — | 0.25 | 0.50 | 1.50 | 4.00 | — |

**5 CENTS** **KM# 30.1** **Composition:** Aluminum

| Date | Mintage | F | VF | XF | Unc | BU |
|---|---|---|---|---|---|---|
| 1946(a) | 28,000,000 | 0.25 | 0.60 | 1.00 | 5.00 | — |

**5 CENTS** **KM# 30.2** **Composition:** Aluminum

| Date | Mintage | F | VF | XF | Unc | BU |
|---|---|---|---|---|---|---|
| 1946B | 22,000,000 | 0.25 | 0.60 | 1.00 | 5.00 | — |

**10 CENTS** **KM#9** **Weight:** 2.7000 g. **Composition:** 0.8350 Silver .0725 oz. ASW **Rev. Legend:** TITRE 0.835. POIDS 2 GR. 7

| Date | Mintage | F | VF | XF | Unc | BU |
|---|---|---|---|---|---|---|
| 1901 | 2,950,000 | 7.00 | 25.00 | 60.00 | 200 | — |
| 1902 | 7,050,000 | 4.00 | 12.00 | 30.00 | 125 | — |
| 1903 | 1,300,000 | 12.00 | 30.00 | 80.00 | 325 | — |
| 1908 | 1,000,000 | 50.00 | 100 | 200 | 550 | — |
| 1909 | 1,000,000 | 30.00 | 75.00 | 130 | 425 | — |
| 1910 | 2,689,000 | 25.00 | 60.00 | 100 | 350 | — |
| 1911 | 2,311,000 | 25.00 | 40.00 | 80.00 | 325 | — |
| 1912 | 2,500,000 | 25.00 | 35.00 | 70.00 | 275 | — |
| 1913 | 4,847,000 | 7.50 | 12.50 | 30.00 | 125 | — |
| 1914 | 2,667,000 | 10.00 | 30.00 | 60.00 | 175 | — |
| 1916 | 2,000,000 | 10.00 | 30.00 | 60.00 | 185 | — |
| 1917 | 1,500,000 | 25.00 | 50.00 | 100 | 300 | — |
| 1919 | 1,500,000 | 30.00 | 60.00 | 125 | 350 | — |

**10 CENTS** **KM# 14** **Weight:** 3.0000 g. **Composition:** 0.4000 Silver .0386 oz. ASW **Reverse:** Without fineness indicated **Note:** Without mint mark.

| Date | Mintage | F | VF | XF | Unc | BU |
|---|---|---|---|---|---|---|
| 1920 | 10,000,000 | 10.00 | 15.00 | 40.00 | 100 | — |

**10 CENTS** **KM# 16.1** **Weight:** 2.7000 g. **Composition:** 0.6800 Silver .0590 oz. ASW **Rev. Legend:** TITRE 0.680 POIDS 2 GR. 7

| Date | Mintage | F | VF | XF | Unc | BU |
|---|---|---|---|---|---|---|
| 1921A | 12,516,000 | 1.50 | 3.00 | 9.00 | 25.00 | — |
| 1922A | 22,381,000 | 1.50 | 3.00 | 9.00 | 25.00 | — |
| 1923A | 21,755,000 | 1.50 | 3.00 | 9.00 | 25.00 | — |
| 1924A | 2,816,000 | 2.00 | 5.00 | 16.50 | 45.00 | — |
| 1925A | 4,909,000 | 1.75 | 3.50 | 15.00 | 35.00 | — |
| 1927A | 6,471,000 | 2.50 | 7.00 | 17.50 | 40.00 | — |
| 1928A | 1,593,000 | 25.00 | 70.00 | 150 | 450 | — |
| 1929A | 5,831,000 | 1.50 | 3.00 | 10.00 | 30.00 | — |
| 1930A | 6,608,000 | 1.50 | 3.00 | 10.00 | 30.00 | — |
| 1931A Proof | 100 | Value: 325 | | | | |

**10 CENTS** **KM# 16.2** **Weight:** 2.7000 g. **Composition:** 0.6800 Silver .0590 oz. ASW **Rev. Legend:** TITRE 0.680 POIDS 2 GR. 7

| Date | Mintage | F | VF | XF | Unc | BU |
|---|---|---|---|---|---|---|
| 1937(a) | 25,000,000 | 1.00 | 1.50 | 3.00 | 8.00 | — |

**10 CENTS** **KM# 21.1** **Weight:** 2.7000 g. **Composition:** 0.6800 Silver .0590 oz. ASW **Note:** These coins have no dots left and right of date and are magnetic.

| Date | Mintage | F | VF | XF | Unc | BU |
|---|---|---|---|---|---|---|
| 1939(a) | 16,841,000 | 0.25 | 0.50 | 1.00 | 5.00 | — |
| 1940(a) | 25,505,000 | 0.25 | 0.50 | 1.00 | 5.00 | — |

**10 CENTS** **KM# 21.2** **Composition:** Copper-Nickel **Obverse:** Date between two dots

| Date | Mintage | F | VF | XF | Unc | BU |
|---|---|---|---|---|---|---|
| 1939(a) | 2,237,000 | 8.00 | 15.00 | 30.00 | 75.00 | — |
| 1941S | 50,000,000 | 0.20 | 0.40 | 0.75 | 5.00 | — |

**10 CENTS** **KM# 21.1a** **Composition:** Copper-Nickel **Obverse:** Date without dots

| Date | Mintage | F | VF | XF | Unc | BU |
|---|---|---|---|---|---|---|
| 1941S | 50,000,000 | 0.20 | 0.40 | 0.75 | 5.00 | — |

**10 CENTS** **KM# 28.1** **Composition:** Aluminum

| Date | Mintage | F | VF | XF | Unc | BU |
|---|---|---|---|---|---|---|
| 1945(a) | 40,170,000 | 0.25 | 0.50 | 1.00 | 4.50 | — |

**10 CENTS** **KM# 28.2** **Composition:** Aluminum

| Date | Mintage | F | VF | XF | Unc | BU |
|---|---|---|---|---|---|---|
| 1945B | 9,830,000 | 0.50 | 1.50 | 3.00 | 12.50 | — |

**20 CENTS** **KM# 10** **Weight:** 5.4000 g. **Composition:** 0.8350 Silver .1450 oz. ASW

| Date | Mintage | F | VF | XF | Unc | BU |
|---|---|---|---|---|---|---|
| 1901 | 1,375,000 | 20.00 | 50.00 | 100 | 300 | — |
| 1902 | 3,525,000 | 7.50 | 15.00 | 40.00 | 175 | — |
| 1903 | 675,000 | 50.00 | 100 | 150 | 600 | — |
| 1908 | 500,000 | 100 | 250 | 400 | 850 | — |
| 1909 | 200,000 | 100 | 200 | 350 | 850 | — |
| 1911 | 2,340,000 | 7.50 | 15.00 | 35.00 | 120 | — |
| 1912 | 160,000 | 100 | 200 | 400 | 950 | — |
| 1913 | 1,252,000 | 50.00 | 100 | 150 | 400 | — |
| 1914 | 2,500,000 | 7.50 | 15.00 | 25.00 | 120 | — |
| 1916 | 1,000,000 | 12.50 | 35.00 | 100 | 225 | — |

**20 CENTS** **KM# 13** **Composition:** 0.8350 Silver **Obverse:** KM#10 **Reverse:** KM#3a **Note:** Mule.

| Date | Mintage | F | VF | XF | Unc | BU |
|---|---|---|---|---|---|---|
| 1909 | — | 100 | 250 | 650 | 1,200 | — |

**20 CENTS** **KM# 15** **Weight:** 6.0000 g. **Composition:** 0.4000 Silver .0772 oz. ASW **Reverse:** Without fineness indicated **Note:** Without mint mark.

| Date | Mintage | F | VF | XF | Unc | BU |
|---|---|---|---|---|---|---|
| 1920 | 4,000,000 | 12.50 | 25.00 | 50.00 | 125 | — |

**20 CENTS** **KM# 17.1** **Weight:** 5.4000 g. **Composition:** 0.6800 Silver .1181 oz. ASW **Rev. Legend:** TITRE O.680 POIDS 5 GR. 4

| Date | Mintage | F | VF | XF | Unc | BU |
|---|---|---|---|---|---|---|
| 1921A | 3,663,000 | 2.00 | 4.00 | 10.00 | 30.00 | — |
| 1922A | 5,812,000 | 2.00 | 4.00 | 8.00 | 30.00 | — |
| 1923A | 7,109,000 | 2.00 | 4.00 | 8.00 | 30.00 | — |
| 1924A | 1,400,000 | 6.00 | 12.50 | 28.50 | 75.00 | — |
| 1925A | 2,556,000 | 4.00 | 10.00 | 22.50 | 60.00 | — |
| 1927A | 3,245,000 | 3.00 | 7.50 | 15.00 | 30.00 | — |
| 1928A | 794,000 | 10.00 | 20.00 | 60.00 | 200 | — |
| 1929A | 644,000 | 15.00 | 30.00 | 80.00 | 225 | — |
| 1930A | 5,576,000 | 1.50 | 3.00 | 5.00 | 15.00 | — |

**20 CENTS** **KM# 17.2** **Weight:** 5.4000 g. **Composition:** 0.6800 Silver .1181 oz. ASW **Rev. Legend:** TITRE O.680 POIDS 5 GR. 4

| Date | Mintage | F | VF | XF | Unc | BU |
|---|---|---|---|---|---|---|
| 1937(a) | 17,500,000 | 1.00 | 1.50 | 3.00 | 10.00 | — |

**20 CENTS** **KM# 23a.1** **Composition:** Copper-Nickel **Edge:** Reeded

| Date | Mintage | F | VF | XF | Unc | BU |
|---|---|---|---|---|---|---|
| 1939(a) Date between dots | 14,676,000 | 0.25 | 0.50 | 1.00 | 6.00 | — |

**20 CENTS** **KM# 23** **Composition:** Nickel **Note:** Security edge.

| Date | Mintage | F | VF | XF | Unc | BU |
|---|---|---|---|---|---|---|
| 1939(a) | 318,000 | 15.00 | 30.00 | 70.00 | 125 | — |

**20 CENTS** **KM# 23a.2** **Composition:** Copper-Nickel **Edge:** Reeded

| Date | Mintage | F | VF | XF | Unc | BU |
|---|---|---|---|---|---|---|
| 1941S Date between dots | 25,000,000 | 0.25 | 0.50 | 1.00 | 5.00 | — |

**20 CENTS** **KM# 29.1** **Composition:** Aluminum

| Date | Mintage | F | VF | XF | Unc | BU |
|---|---|---|---|---|---|---|
| 1945(a) | 15,412,000 | 0.50 | 1.00 | 2.50 | 10.00 | — |

**20 CENTS** **KM# 29.2** **Composition:** Aluminum

| Date | Mintage | F | VF | XF | Unc | BU |
|---|---|---|---|---|---|---|
| 1945B | 6,665,000 | 2.00 | 4.00 | 8.00 | 25.00 | — |

**20 CENTS** **KM# 29.3** **Composition:** Aluminum

| Date | Mintage | F | VF | XF | Unc | BU |
|---|---|---|---|---|---|---|
| 1945C | 22,423,000 | 0.50 | 1.00 | 3.00 | 15.00 | — |

**50 CENTS** **KM# 4a.2** **Weight:** 13.5000 g. **Composition:** 0.9000 Silver .3906 oz. ASW **Rev. Legend:** TITRE 0.900. POIDS 13 GR. 5

| Date | Mintage | F | VF | XF | Unc | BU |
|---|---|---|---|---|---|---|
| 1936(a) | 4,000,000 | 3.00 | 4.00 | 8.00 | 20.00 | — |

**50 CENTS** **KM# 31** **Composition:** Copper-Nickel **Rev. Legend:** BRONZE DE NICKEL

| Date | Mintage | F | VF | XF | Unc | BU |
|---|---|---|---|---|---|---|
| 1946(a) | 32,292,000 | 2.00 | 4.00 | 9.00 | 25.00 | — |

**PIASTRE** **KM# 5a.1** **Weight:** 27.0000 g. **Composition:** 0.9000 Silver .7812 oz. ASW **Rev. Legend:** TITRE 0.900 POIDS 27 GR.

| Date | Mintage | F | VF | XF | Unc | BU |
|---|---|---|---|---|---|---|
| 1901A | 3,150,000 | 10.00 | 15.00 | 25.00 | 150 | — |
| 1902A | 3,327,000 | 10.00 | 15.00 | 25.00 | 150 | — |
| 1903A | 10,077,000 | 10.00 | 12.50 | 20.00 | 110 | — |
| 1904A | 5,751,000 | 10.00 | 15.00 | 20.00 | 130 | — |
| 1905A | 3,561,000 | 10.00 | 15.00 | 20.00 | 130 | — |
| 1906A | 10,194,000 | 10.00 | 12.50 | 20.00 | 100 | — |
| 1907A | 14,062,000 | 10.00 | 12.50 | 20.00 | 100 | — |
| 1908A | 13,986,000 | 10.00 | 12.50 | 20.00 | 100 | — |
| 1909A | 9,201,000 | 10.00 | 12.50 | 20.00 | 95.00 | — |
| 1910A | 761,000 | 25.00 | 55.00 | 120 | 320 | — |
| 1913A | 3,244,000 | 10.00 | 15.00 | 22.50 | 125 | — |
| 1924A | 2,831,000 | 10.00 | 12.50 | 22.50 | 150 | — |
| 1925A | 2,882,000 | 10.00 | 12.50 | 22.50 | 150 | — |

| Date | Mintage | F | VF | XF | Unc | BU |
|---|---|---|---|---|---|---|
| 1926A | 6,383,000 | 10.00 | 12.50 | 20.00 | 100 | — |
| 1927A | 8,183,999 | 10.00 | 12.50 | 20.00 | 100 | — |
| 1928A | 5,290,000 | 10.00 | 12.50 | 20.00 | 100 | — |

**PIASTRE** **KM# 5a.3** **Weight:** 27.0000 g. **Composition:** 0.9000 Silver .7812 oz. ASW

| Date | Mintage | F | VF | XF | Unc | BU |
|---|---|---|---|---|---|---|
| 1921H | 8,430,000 | 10.00 | 12.50 | 20.00 | 100 | — |
| 1922H | 8,570,000 | 10.00 | 12.50 | 20.00 | 100 | — |

**PIASTRE** **KM# 5a.2** **Weight:** 27.0000 g. **Composition:** 0.9000 Silver .7812 oz. ASW **Note:** Without mint mark

| Date | Mintage | F | VF | XF | Unc | BU |
|---|---|---|---|---|---|---|
| 1921 | 4,850,000 | 10.00 | 12.50 | 25.00 | 150 | — |
| 1922 | 1,150,000 | 12.50 | 20.00 | 40.00 | 200 | — |

**PIASTRE** **KM# 19** **Weight:** 20.0000 g. **Composition:** 0.9000 Silver .5787 oz. ASW

| Date | Mintage | F | VF | XF | Unc | BU |
|---|---|---|---|---|---|---|
| 1931(a) | 16,000,000 | 9.00 | 12.00 | 17.50 | 47.50 | — |

## BULLION COINAGE WWII

Previously listed under Laos and China-Yunnan-Burma. KM#1-2 were originally struck in Hanoi under official direction of the Colonial Vichy Finance Department for payments in the flourishing opium trade in Laos and Tonkin. The origins of KM#3-4 still remain speculative.

**1/2 TAEL (Liang)** **KM# A1.1 (KM1.1)** **Weight:** 19.2000 g. **Composition:** Silver **Obverse:** Chinese character "Fu" (wealth) **Reverse:** Laotian and Chinese denomination **Edge:** Milled **Note:** Struck in Hanoi.

| Date | Mintage | F | VF | XF | Unc | BU |
|---|---|---|---|---|---|---|
| ND(1943-4) | — | — | — | 400 | 550 | — |

**1/2 TAEL (Liang)** **KM# A1.2 (KM1.2)** **Composition:** Silver **Note:** 18.75-18.86 grams.

| Date | Mintage | F | VF | XF | Unc | BU |
|---|---|---|---|---|---|---|
| ND(1943-4) | — | 15.00 | 30.00 | 50.00 | 100 | — |

**TAEL** **KM# A2** **Weight:** 34.0000 g. **Composition:** Silver **Edge:** Milled **Note:** Previous KM#2.

| Date | Mintage | F | VF | XF | Unc | BU |
|---|---|---|---|---|---|---|
| ND(1943-4) | — | 20.00 | 40.00 | 60.00 | 125 | — |

**TAEL** **KM# A2a** **Weight:** 38.2000 g. **Composition:** Silver **Edge:** Milled **Note:** Previous KM#2a.

| Date | Mintage | F | VF | XF | Unc | BU |
|---|---|---|---|---|---|---|
| ND(1943-4) | — | 20.00 | 40.00 | 60.00 | 125 | — |

**TAEL** **KM# A3** **Weight:** 38.2000 g. **Composition:** Silver **Obverse:** Small stag's head with short antlers **Reverse:** Laotian and Chinese denomination **Note:** Previous KM#3.

| Date | Mintage | F | VF | XF | Unc | BU |
|---|---|---|---|---|---|---|
| ND(1943-4) | — | 25.00 | 45.00 | 85.00 | 150 | — |

**TAEL** **KM# A4** **Weight:** 38.2000 g. **Composition:** Silver **Obverse:** Larger stag's head with longer antlers **Reverse:** Smaller Chinese denomination **Edge:** Plain **Note:** Previous KM#4.

| Date | Mintage | F | VF | XF | Unc | BU |
|---|---|---|---|---|---|---|
| ND(1943-4) | — | — | — | 650 | 900 | — |

# FEDERATED STATES

## French Union.

## STANDARD COINAGE

**PIASTRE** **KM# 32.1** **Composition:** Copper-Nickel **Note:** Security edge.

| Date | Mintage | F | VF | XF | Unc | BU |
|---|---|---|---|---|---|---|
| 1946(a) | 2,520,000 | 7.50 | 12.50 | 20.00 | 85.00 | — |
| 1947(a) | 261,000 | 10.00 | 17.50 | 35.00 | 135 | — |

**PIASTRE** **KM# 32.2** **Composition:** Copper-Nickel **Edge:** Reeded **Note:** Similar coins dated 1946 with reverse legend: INDOCHINE - FRANCAISE are Essais.

| Date | Mintage | F | VF | XF | Unc | BU |
|---|---|---|---|---|---|---|
| 1947(a) | 41,958,000 | 1.00 | 3.00 | 7.50 | 15.00 | — |

## ESSAIS

Standard metals unless otherwise noted

| KM# | Date | Mintage | Identification | Mkt Val |
|---|---|---|---|---|
| E7 | 1910 | — | Cent. Copper-Nickel. ESSAI. KM#12.1 | — |
| E8 | 1919 | — | 10 Cents. Fineness 0.700/0.835 incuse plus 0.700 incuse on field on reverse; KM#9. | 225 |
| E9 | ND | — | 20 Cents. Mule. Two reverses. KM#3. | — |
| E10 | 1923 | — | Cent. ESSAI in field; KM#12.1. | 150 |
| E11 | 1923 | — | Cent. ESSAI at rim; KM#12.1. | 150 |

| KM# | Date | Mintage | Identification | Mkt Val |
|---|---|---|---|---|
| E12 | 1923 | — | 5 Cents. KM#18.1 | 125 |
| E14 | 1928 | — | 20 Cents. Bronze. KM#17.1 | 185 |
| E13 | 1928 | — | 20 Cents. Brass. Plain edge. KM#17.1 | — |
| E15 | 19(30a) | — | Cent. Silver. KM#12.1 | 675 |
| E16 | 19(30a) | — | Cent. Aluminum-Bronze. KM#12.1 | 125 |
| E17 | 1930 | — | Piastre. Silver. Uniface. | 4,000 |

| KM# | Date | Mintage | Identification | Mkt Val |
|---|---|---|---|---|
| E26 | 1931 | — | Piastre. Silver. KM#19 | 350 |
| E19 | 19(31a) | — | 10 Cents. Silver-Bronze. KM#16.1 | 325 |
| E20 | 19(31) | — | 20 Cents. Silver-Bronze. | 1,150 |
| E21 | 19(31a) | — | 20 Cents. Silver-Bronze. KM#17.1 | 350 |

| KM# | Date | Mintage | Identification | Mkt Val |
|---|---|---|---|---|
| E23 | 1(931a) | — | 50 Cents. Silver-Bronze. | 400 |
| E24 | 19(31a) | — | Piastre. Silver. KM#19 | 9,775 |
| E25 | 19(31a) | — | Piastre. Silver-Bronze. KM#19 | 350 |
| E18 | 19(31) | — | 10 Cents. Medallic alignment. | — |
| E22 | 1(931) | — | 50 Cents. Medallic alignment. | — |
| E27 | 1935 | — | 1/2 Cent. KM#20 | 70.00 |
| E28 | 1936 | — | 50 Cents. Aluminum. KM#4a.2. | 200 |
| E29 | 1937 | — | 10 Cents. Nickel. KM#16.2 | 125 |
| E30 | 1937 | — | 20 Cents. Silver. KM#17.2 | 250 |
| E31 | 1937 | — | 20 Cents. Nickel. KM#17.2 | 225 |

| KM# | Date | Mintage | Identification | Mkt Val |
|---|---|---|---|---|
| E32 | 1939 | — | 10 Cents. KM#21 | 60.00 |
| E33 | 1939 | — | 20 Cents. Plain edge. KM#23 | 235 |
| E34 | 1939 | — | 20 Cents. Security edge; KM#23 | 165 |
| E35 | 1939 | — | 20 Cents. Reeded edge. KM#23a.1 | 145 |
| E36 | 1940 | — | Cent. Zinc. KM#24.1 | 125 |
| E37 | 1940 | — | Cent. Aluminum-Bronze. KM#24.1 | 100 |
| E45 | ND(1943) | — | Tael. Silver. KM#2. | — |
| E46 | ND(1943) | — | 1/2 Tael. Silver. KM#1 | — |

| KM# | Date | Mintage | Identification | Mkt Val |
|---|---|---|---|---|
| E38 | 1945 | 1,100 | 10 Cents. KM#28.1 | 30.00 |
| E39 | 1945 | 1,100 | 20 Cents. KM#29 | 35.00 |
| E40 | 1946 | 1,100 | 5 Cents. KM#30.1 | 25.00 |

| KM# | Date | Mintage | Identification | Mkt Val |
|---|---|---|---|---|
| E41 | 1946 | 1,100 | 50 Cents. KM#31 | 80.00 |

| KM# | Date | Mintage | Identification | Mkt Val |
|---|---|---|---|---|
| E42 | 1946 | 1,100 | Piastre. Federation. | 150 |

| KM# | Date | Mintage | Identification | Mkt Val |
|---|---|---|---|---|
| E43 | 1946 | 1,100 | Piastre. Indochina. KM#32.1. | 200 |

| KM# | Date | Mintage | Identification | Mkt Val |
|---|---|---|---|---|
| E44 | 1947 | 104 | Piastre. Federation. | 250 |

## PIEFORTS

| KM# | Date | Mintage | Identification | Mkt Val |
|---|---|---|---|---|
| P2 | 1908 | — | Cent. Bronze. KM#12.1 | 245 |
| P3 | 1920 | — | 20 Cents. Brass. Reeded edge. Medallic alignment. KM#15. | — |
| P4 | 1923 | — | Cent. Filled center hole. KM#12.1. | — |
| P5 | 19(30) | — | Cent. Bronze. France Y#81. Filled center hole; KM#12.1. | — |
| P6 | 19(30) | — | Cent. Aluminum-Bronze. France Y#81. Filled center hole; KM#12.1. | — |
| P7 | 19(31) | — | 20 Cents. Medallic alignment. | — |
| P8 | 1939 | — | 1/2 Cent. Zinc. KM#20a. | 300 |

## PIEFORTS WITH ESSAI

Double thickness - Standard metals unless otherwise noted

| KM# | Date | Mintage | Identification | Mkt Val |
|---|---|---|---|---|
| PE1 | 1908 | — | Cent. KM#12.1. | 235 |
| PE2 | 1923 | — | 5 Cents. KM#18.1. | 175 |

| KM# | Date | Mintage | Identification | Mkt Val |
|---|---|---|---|---|
| PE3 | 1931 | — | Piastre. KM#19. | 2,000 |
| PE4 | 1945 | 104 | 10 Cents. KM#28.1. | 100 |
| PE5 | 1945 | 104 | 20 Cents. KM#29.1. | 140 |
| PE6 | 1946 | 104 | 5 Cents. KM#30.1. | 100 |
| PE7 | 1946 | 104 | 50 Cents. KM#31. | 150 |
| PE8 | 1947 | 104 | Piastre. KM#32. | 200 |

## TRIAL STRIKES

| KM# | Date | Mintage | Identification | Mkt Val |
|---|---|---|---|---|
| TS1 | 1921 | — | Piastre. 0.9000 Silver. Without collar. | — |
| TS2 | ND(1931) | — | Piastre. Uniface. | 850 |

| KM# | Date | Mintage | Identification | Mkt Val |
|---|---|---|---|---|
| TS3 | 1931 | — | Piastre. Uniface. | 750 |

## PROOF SETS

| KM# | Date | Mintage | Identification | Issue Price | Mkt Val |
|---|---|---|---|---|---|
| PS1 | 1889 (6) | 100 | KM#1-6 | — | 12,300 |
| PS2 | 1900 (6) | 100 | KM#4a.1-5a.1, 6, 8-10 | — | 19,450 |

The Colony of French Oceania (now the Territory of French Polynesia), comprising 130 basalt and coral islands scattered among five archipelagoes in the South Pacific, had an area of 1,544 sq. mi. (3,999 sq. km.). Capital: Papeete. The colony produced phosphates, copra and vanilla.

Tahiti of the Society Islands, the hub of French Oceania, was visited by Capt. Cook in 1769 and by Capt. Bligh in the Bounty 1788-89. The Society Islands were claimed by France in 1768, and in 1903 grouped with the Marquesas Islands, the Tuamotu Archipelago, the Gambier Islands and the Austral Islands under a single administrative head located at Papeete, Tahiti, to form the colony of French Oceania.

**RULERS**
French

**MINT MARKS**
- Paris, privy marks only

**MONETARY SYSTEM**
100 Centimes = 1 Franc

# FRENCH COLONY

## DECIMAL COINAGE

**50 CENTIMES** KM# 1 **Composition:** Aluminum

| Date | Mintage | F | VF | XF | Unc | BU |
|---|---|---|---|---|---|---|
| 1949(a) | 795,000 | 0.50 | 0.75 | 1.50 | 3.50 | — |

**FRANC** KM# 2 **Composition:** Aluminum

| Date | Mintage | F | VF | XF | Unc | BU |
|---|---|---|---|---|---|---|
| 1949(a) | 2,000,000 | 0.20 | 0.35 | 1.00 | 2.50 | — |

**2 FRANCS** KM# 3 **Composition:** Aluminum

| Date | Mintage | F | VF | XF | Unc | BU |
|---|---|---|---|---|---|---|
| 1949(a) | 1,000,000 | 0.40 | 0.60 | 1.50 | 3.50 | — |

**5 FRANCS** KM# 4 **Composition:** Aluminum

| Date | Mintage | F | VF | XF | Unc | BU |
|---|---|---|---|---|---|---|
| 1952 | 2,000,000 | 0.50 | 0.75 | 1.50 | 4.50 | — |

## ESSAIS

Standard metals unless otherwise noted

| KM# | Date | Mintage | Identification | Issue Price | Mkt Val |
|---|---|---|---|---|---|
| E1 | 1948 | 1,100 | 50 Centimes. | — | 20.00 |
| E2 | 1948 | 1,100 | 50 Centimes. | — | 20.00 |
| E3 | 1948 | 1,100 | Franc. | — | 20.00 |
| E4 | 1948 | 1,100 | Franc. | — | 20.00 |

| KM# | Date | Mintage | Identification | Issue Price | Mkt Val |
|---|---|---|---|---|---|
| E5 | 1948 | 1,100 | 2 Francs. | — | 25.00 |
| E6 | 1948 | 1,100 | 2 Francs. | — | 25.00 |
| E7 | 1949 | 2,000 | 50 Centimes. Copper-Nickel. KM1 | — | 16.00 |
| E8 | 1949 | 2,000 | Franc. Copper-Nickel. KM2 | — | 17.00 |
| E9 | 1949 | 2,000 | 2 Francs. Copper-Nickel. KM3 | — | 20.00 |
| E10 | 1952 | 1,200 | 5 Francs. Copper-Nickel. KM4. | — | 25.00 |

## PIEFORTS WITH ESSAI

Double thickness - Standard metals unless otherwise noted

| KM# | Date | Mintage | Identification | Issue Price | Mkt Val |
|---|---|---|---|---|---|
| PE1 | 1949 | 104 | 50 Centimes. | — | 55.00 |
| PE2 | 1949 | 104 | Franc. | — | 65.00 |
| PE3 | 1949 | 104 | 2 Francs. | — | 85.00 |
| PE4 | 1952 | 104 | 5 Francs. | — | 95.00 |

# FRENCH POLYNESIA

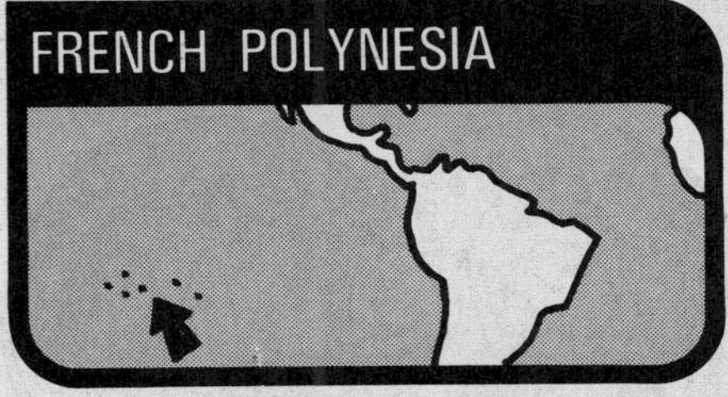


The Territory of French Polynesia (formerly French Oceania) has an area of 1,544 sq. mi. (3,941 sq. km.) and a population of 220,000. It is comprised of the same five archipelagoes that were grouped administratively to form French Oceania.

The colony of French Oceania became the Territory of French Polynesia by act of the French National Assembly in March, 1957. In Sept. of 1958 it voted in favor of the new constitution of the Fifth Republic, thereby electing to remain within the new French Community.

Picturesque, mountainous Tahiti, the setting of many tales of adventure and romance, is one of the most inspiringly beautiful islands in the world. Robert Louis Stevenson called it 'God's sweetest works'. It was there that Paul Gaugin, one of the pioneers of the Impressionist movement, painted the brilliant, exotic pictures that later made him famous. The arid coral atolls of Tuamotu comprise the most economically valuable area of French Polynesia. Pearl oysters thrive in the warm, limpid lagoons, and extensive portions of the atolls are valuable phosphate rock.

**RULERS**
French

**MINT MARKS**
- Paris, privy marks only

**MONETARY SYSTEM**
100 Centimes = 1 Franc

## FRENCH COLONY

### DECIMAL COINAGE

**50 CENTIMES** KM# 1 **Composition:** Aluminum

| Date | Mintage | F | VF | XF | Unc | BU |
|---|---|---|---|---|---|---|
| 1965(a) | 895,000 | 0.10 | 0.25 | 0.50 | 1.50 | — |

**FRANC** KM# 2 **Composition:** Aluminum

| Date | Mintage | F | VF | XF | Unc | BU |
|---|---|---|---|---|---|---|
| 1965(a) | 5,300,000 | — | 0.10 | 0.20 | 0.75 | — |

**FRANC** KM# 11 **Composition:** Aluminum **Obv. Legend:** I. E. O. M. added flanking figure's feet

| Date | Mintage | F | VF | XF | Unc | BU |
|---|---|---|---|---|---|---|
| 1975(a) | 2,000,000 | — | 0.10 | 0.15 | 0.45 | — |
| 1977(a) | 1,000,000 | — | 0.10 | 0.15 | 0.45 | — |
| 1979(a) | 1,500,000 | — | 0.10 | 0.15 | 0.45 | — |
| 1981(a) | 1,000,000 | — | 0.10 | 0.15 | 0.45 | — |
| 1982(a) | 2,000,000 | — | 0.10 | 0.15 | 0.45 | — |
| 1983(a) | 2,200,000 | — | 0.10 | 0.15 | 0.45 | — |
| 1984(a) | 1,500,000 | — | 0.10 | 0.15 | 0.45 | — |
| 1985(a) | 2,000,000 | — | 0.10 | 0.15 | 0.45 | — |
| 1986(a) | 2,000,000 | — | 0.10 | 0.15 | 0.45 | — |
| 1987(a) | 2,000,000 | — | 0.10 | 0.15 | 0.45 | — |
| 1989(a) | 1,000,000 | — | 0.10 | 0.15 | 0.45 | — |
| 1990(a) | — | — | 0.10 | 0.15 | 0.45 | — |

| Date | Mintage | F | VF | XF | Unc | BU |
|---|---|---|---|---|---|---|
| 1991(a) | — | — | 0.10 | 0.15 | 0.35 | — |
| 1992(a) | — | — | 0.10 | 0.15 | 0.35 | — |
| 1993(a) | — | — | 0.10 | 0.15 | 0.35 | — |
| 1994(a) | — | — | 0.10 | 0.15 | 0.35 | — |
| 1995(a) | — | — | 0.10 | 0.15 | 0.35 | — |
| 1996(a) | — | — | 0.10 | 0.15 | 0.35 | — |

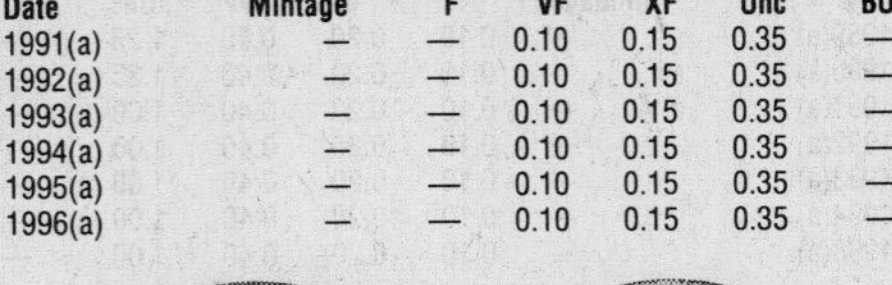

**2 FRANCS** KM# 3 **Composition:** Aluminum

| Date | Mintage | F | VF | XF | Unc | BU |
|---|---|---|---|---|---|---|
| 1965(a) | 2,250,000 | — | 0.10 | 0.25 | 1.00 | — |

**2 FRANCS** KM# 10 **Composition:** Aluminum
**Obv. Legend:** I. E. O. M. added flanking figure's feet

| Date | Mintage | F | VF | XF | Unc | BU |
|---|---|---|---|---|---|---|
| 1973(a) | 400,000 | — | 0.10 | 0.25 | 0.75 | — |
| 1975(a) | 1,000,000 | — | 0.10 | 0.25 | 0.75 | — |
| 1977(a) | 1,000,000 | — | 0.10 | 0.25 | 0.75 | — |
| 1979(a) | 2,000,000 | — | 0.10 | 0.25 | 0.75 | — |
| 1982(a) | 1,000,000 | — | 0.10 | 0.25 | 0.75 | — |
| 1983(a) | 1,500,000 | — | 0.10 | 0.25 | 0.75 | — |
| 1984(a) | 1,200,000 | — | 0.10 | 0.25 | 0.75 | — |
| 1985(a) | 1,400,000 | — | 0.10 | 0.25 | 0.75 | — |
| 1986(a) | 1,500,000 | — | 0.10 | 0.25 | 0.75 | — |
| 1987(a) | 1,000,000 | — | 0.10 | 0.25 | 0.75 | — |
| 1988(a) | 500,000 | — | 0.10 | 0.25 | 0.75 | — |
| 1989(a) | 1,000,000 | — | 0.10 | 0.25 | 0.75 | — |
| 1990(a) | — | — | 0.10 | 0.25 | 0.75 | — |
| 1991(a) | — | — | 0.10 | 0.25 | 0.60 | — |
| 1992(a) | — | — | 0.10 | 0.25 | 0.60 | — |
| 1993(a) | — | — | 0.10 | 0.25 | 0.60 | — |
| 1995(a) | — | — | 0.10 | 0.25 | 0.60 | — |
| 1996(a) | — | — | 0.10 | 0.25 | 0.60 | — |

**5 FRANCS** KM# 4 **Composition:** Aluminum

| Date | Mintage | F | VF | XF | Unc | BU |
|---|---|---|---|---|---|---|
| 1965(a) | 1,520,000 | 0.10 | 0.25 | 0.50 | 1.75 | — |

**5 FRANCS** KM# 12 **Composition:** Aluminum
**Obv. Legend:** I. E. O. M. added flanking figure's feet

| Date | Mintage | F | VF | XF | Unc | BU |
|---|---|---|---|---|---|---|
| 1975(a) | 500,000 | 0.10 | 0.20 | 0.40 | 1.25 | — |
| 1977(a) | 500,000 | 0.10 | 0.20 | 0.40 | 1.25 | — |
| 1979(a) | — | 0.10 | 0.20 | 0.40 | 1.25 | — |
| 1982(a) | 500,000 | 0.10 | 0.20 | 0.40 | 1.25 | — |
| 1983(a) | 800,000 | 0.10 | 0.20 | 0.40 | 1.25 | — |
| 1984(a) | 600,000 | 0.10 | 0.20 | 0.40 | 1.25 | — |
| 1985(a) | — | 0.10 | 0.20 | 0.40 | 1.25 | — |
| 1986(a) | 600,000 | 0.10 | 0.20 | 0.40 | 1.25 | — |
| 1987(a) | 400,000 | 0.10 | 0.20 | 0.40 | 1.25 | — |
| 1988(a) | 400,000 | 0.10 | 0.20 | 0.40 | 1.25 | — |

| Date | Mintage | F | VF | XF | Unc | BU |
|---|---|---|---|---|---|---|
| 1989(a) | — | 0.10 | 0.20 | 0.40 | 1.25 | — |
| 1990(a) | — | 0.10 | 0.20 | 0.40 | 1.25 | — |
| 1991(a) | — | 0.10 | 0.20 | 0.40 | 1.00 | — |
| 1992(a) | — | 0.10 | 0.20 | 0.40 | 1.00 | — |
| 1993(a) | — | 0.10 | 0.20 | 0.40 | 1.00 | — |
| 1994(a) | — | 0.10 | 0.20 | 0.40 | 1.00 | — |
| 1998(a) | — | 0.10 | 0.20 | 0.40 | 1.00 | — |

### 10 FRANCS KM# 5 Composition: Nickel

| Date | Mintage | F | VF | XF | Unc | BU |
|---|---|---|---|---|---|---|
| 1967(a) | 1,000,000 | 0.25 | 0.50 | 0.75 | 1.75 | — |

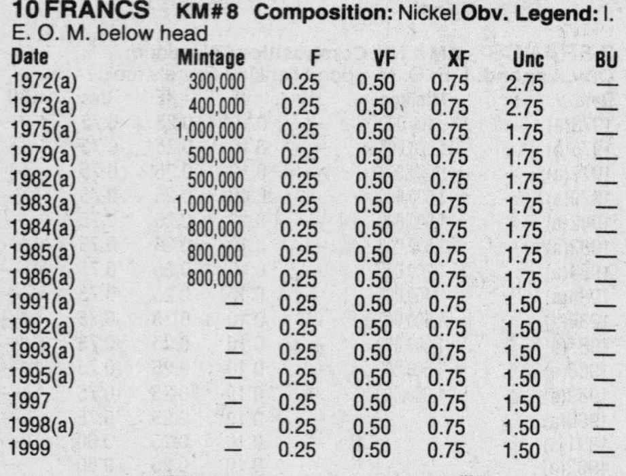

### 10 FRANCS KM# 8 Composition: Nickel Obv. Legend: I. E. O. M. below head

| Date | Mintage | F | VF | XF | Unc | BU |
|---|---|---|---|---|---|---|
| 1972(a) | 300,000 | 0.25 | 0.50 | 0.75 | 2.75 | — |
| 1973(a) | 400,000 | 0.25 | 0.50 | 0.75 | 2.75 | — |
| 1975(a) | 1,000,000 | 0.25 | 0.50 | 0.75 | 1.75 | — |
| 1979(a) | 500,000 | 0.25 | 0.50 | 0.75 | 1.75 | — |
| 1982(a) | 500,000 | 0.25 | 0.50 | 0.75 | 1.75 | — |
| 1983(a) | 1,000,000 | 0.25 | 0.50 | 0.75 | 1.75 | — |
| 1984(a) | 800,000 | 0.25 | 0.50 | 0.75 | 1.75 | — |
| 1985(a) | 800,000 | 0.25 | 0.50 | 0.75 | 1.75 | — |
| 1986(a) | 800,000 | 0.25 | 0.50 | 0.75 | 1.75 | — |
| 1991(a) | — | 0.25 | 0.50 | 0.75 | 1.50 | — |
| 1992(a) | — | 0.25 | 0.50 | 0.75 | 1.50 | — |
| 1993(a) | — | 0.25 | 0.50 | 0.75 | 1.50 | — |
| 1995(a) | — | 0.25 | 0.50 | 0.75 | 1.50 | — |
| 1997 | — | 0.25 | 0.50 | 0.75 | 1.50 | — |
| 1998(a) | — | 0.25 | 0.50 | 0.75 | 1.50 | — |
| 1999 | — | 0.25 | 0.50 | 0.75 | 1.50 | — |

### 20 FRANCS KM# 6 Composition: Nickel

| Date | Mintage | F | VF | XF | Unc | BU |
|---|---|---|---|---|---|---|
| 1967(a) | 750,000 | 0.35 | 0.75 | 1.25 | 3.00 | — |
| 1969(a) | 250,000 | 0.35 | 1.00 | 2.00 | 7.00 | — |
| 1970(a) | 500,000 | 0.35 | 0.75 | 1.25 | 3.25 | — |

### 20 FRANCS KM# 9 Composition: Nickel Obv. Legend: I. E. O. M. below head

| Date | Mintage | F | VF | XF | Unc | BU |
|---|---|---|---|---|---|---|
| 1972(a) | 300,000 | 0.30 | 0.50 | 1.00 | 3.00 | — |
| 1973(a) | 300,000 | 0.30 | 0.50 | 1.00 | 3.00 | — |
| 1975(a) | 700,000 | 0.30 | 0.50 | 1.00 | 2.25 | — |
| 1977(a) | 150,000 | 0.35 | 0.75 | 1.50 | 4.50 | — |
| 1979(a) | 500,000 | 0.30 | 0.50 | 1.00 | 2.25 | — |
| 1983(a) | 800,000 | 0.30 | 0.50 | 1.00 | 2.25 | — |
| 1984(a) | 600,000 | 0.30 | 0.50 | 1.00 | 2.25 | — |
| 1986(a) | 400,000 | 0.30 | 0.50 | 1.00 | 2.25 | — |
| 1988(a) | 250,000 | 0.30 | 0.50 | 1.00 | 2.25 | — |
| 1991(a) | — | 0.30 | 0.50 | 1.00 | 2.00 | — |
| 1992(a) | — | 0.30 | 0.50 | 1.00 | 2.00 | — |
| 1993(a) | — | 0.30 | 0.50 | 1.00 | 2.00 | — |

| Date | Mintage | F | VF | XF | Unc | BU |
|---|---|---|---|---|---|---|
| 1995(a) | — | 0.30 | 0.50 | 1.00 | 2.00 | — |
| 1998(a) | — | 0.30 | 0.50 | 1.00 | 2.00 | — |

### 50 FRANCS KM# 7 Composition: Nickel

| Date | Mintage | F | VF | XF | Unc | BU |
|---|---|---|---|---|---|---|
| 1967(a) | 600,000 | 0.60 | 1.00 | 2.00 | 5.00 | — |

### 50 FRANCS KM# 13 Composition: Nickel Obv. Legend: I. E. O. M. below head

| Date | Mintage | F | VF | XF | Unc | BU |
|---|---|---|---|---|---|---|
| 1975(a) | 500,000 | 0.60 | 0.80 | 1.25 | 4.00 | — |
| 1979(a) | — | 0.60 | 0.80 | 1.25 | 4.00 | — |
| 1982(a) | 500,000 | 0.60 | 0.80 | 1.25 | 4.00 | — |
| 1984(a) | 500,000 | 0.60 | 0.80 | 1.25 | 4.00 | — |
| 1985(a) | Inc. above | 0.60 | 0.80 | 1.25 | 4.00 | — |
| 1988(a) | 125,000 | 0.60 | 0.80 | 1.25 | 4.00 | — |
| 1991(a) | — | 0.60 | 0.80 | 1.25 | 4.00 | — |
| 1993(a) | — | 0.60 | 0.80 | 1.25 | 4.00 | — |
| 1995(a) | — | 0.60 | 0.80 | 1.25 | 4.00 | — |
| 1998(a) | — | 0.60 | 0.80 | 1.25 | 4.00 | — |

### 100 FRANCS KM# 14 Composition: Nickel-Bronze

| Date | Mintage | F | VF | XF | Unc | BU |
|---|---|---|---|---|---|---|
| 1976(a) | 2,000,000 | 1.20 | 1.50 | 2.00 | 4.00 | — |
| 1979(a) | — | 1.20 | 1.50 | 2.25 | 5.00 | — |
| 1982(a) | 1,000,000 | 1.20 | 1.50 | 2.25 | 5.00 | — |
| 1984(a) | 500,000 | 1.20 | 1.50 | 2.25 | 5.00 | — |
| 1986(a) | 400,000 | 1.20 | 1.50 | 2.25 | 5.00 | — |
| 1987(a) | 500,000 | 1.20 | 1.50 | 2.25 | 5.00 | — |
| 1988(a) | 500,000 | 1.20 | 1.50 | 2.25 | 5.00 | — |
| 1991(a) | — | 1.20 | 1.50 | 2.25 | 5.00 | — |
| 1992(a) | — | 1.20 | 1.50 | 2.25 | 5.00 | — |
| 1995(a) | — | 1.20 | 1.50 | 2.25 | 5.00 | — |
| 1998(a) | — | 1.20 | 1.50 | 2.25 | 5.00 | — |

## ESSAIS

Standard metals unless otherwise noted

| KM# | Date | Mintage | Identification | Issue Price | Mkt Val |
|---|---|---|---|---|---|
| E1 | 1967 | 1,700 | 10 Francs. KM5. | — | 18.00 |
| E2 | 1967 | 1,700 | 20 Francs. KM6. | — | 20.00 |
| E3 | 1967 | 1,700 | 50 Francs. KM7. | — | 25.00 |
| E4 | 1976 | — | 100 Francs. KM14. | — | 30.00 |

## PIEFORTS

| KM# | Date | Mintage | Identification | Issue Price | Mkt Val |
|---|---|---|---|---|---|
| P1 | 1967 | 500 | 10 Francs. KM5. | — | 20.00 |
| P2 | 1967 | 50 | 10 Francs. 0.9500 Silver. KM5. | — | 110 |
| P3 | 1967 | 20 | 10 Francs. 0.9200 Gold. KM5. | — | 750 |
| P6 | 1967 | 20 | 20 Francs. 0.9200 Gold. KM6. | — | 1,000 |
| P5 | 1967 | 50 | 20 Francs. 0.9500 Silver. KM6. | — | 140 |
| P4 | 1967 | 500 | 20 Francs. KM6. | — | 25.00 |
| P7 | 1967 | 500 | 50 Francs. KM7. | — | 30.00 |
| P8 | 1967 | 50 | 50 Francs. 0.9500 Silver. KM7. | — | 180 |
| P9 | 1967 | 20 | 50 Francs. 0.9200 Gold. KM7. | — | 1,250 |
| P12 | 1979 | 93 | 50 Centimes. 0.9200 Gold. KM11. | — | 450 |
| P11 | 1979 | 250 | 50 Centimes. 0.9250 Silver. KM11. | — | 75.00 |
| P10 | 1979 | 150 | 50 Centimes. KM11. | — | 20.00 |
| P13 | 1979 | 150 | 2 Francs. KM10. | — | 30.00 |
| P14 | 1979 | 250 | 2 Francs. 0.9250 Silver. KM10. | — | 85.00 |
| P15 | 1979 | 94 | 2 Francs. 0.9200 Gold. KM10. | — | 650 |
| P18 | 1979 | 95 | 5 Francs. 0.9200 Gold. KM12. | — | 900 |
| P17 | 1979 | 250 | 5 Francs. 0.9250 Silver. KM12. | — | 90.00 |
| P16 | 1979 | 150 | 5 Francs. KM12. | — | 40.00 |
| P19 | 1979 | 150 | 5 Francs. KM8. | — | 50.00 |
| P20 | 1979 | 250 | 5 Francs. 0.9250 Silver. KM8. | — | 90.00 |
| P21 | 1979 | 94 | 5 Francs. 0.9200 Gold. KM8. | — | 650 |
| P24 | 1979 | 93 | 20 Francs. 0.9200 Gold. KM9. | — | 850 |
| P23 | 1979 | 250 | 20 Francs. 0.9250 Silver. KM9. | — | 110 |
| P22 | 1979 | 150 | 20 Francs. KM9. | — | 55.00 |
| P25 | 1979 | 150 | 50 Francs. KM13. | — | 60.00 |
| P26 | 1979 | 250 | 50 Francs. 0.9250 Silver. KM13. | — | 130 |
| P27 | 1979 | 94 | 50 Francs. 0.9200 Gold. KM13. | — | 925 |
| P30 | 1979 | 98 | 100 Francs. 0.9200 Gold. KM14. | — | 1,250 |
| P29 | 1979 | 350 | 100 Francs. 0.9250 Silver. KM14. | — | 150 |
| P28 | 1979 | 150 | 100 Francs. KM14. | — | 80.00 |

## "FDC" SETS

| KM# | Date | Mintage | Identification | Issue Price | Mkt Val |
|---|---|---|---|---|---|
| SS1 | 1965 (4) | 2,200 | KM1-4 | — | 7.00 |
| SS2 | 1967 (3) | 2,200 | K5-7 | 10.00 | 15.00 |

# FRENCH SOMALILAND

**MINT MARKS**
- Paris (privy marks only)

**MONETARY SYSTEM**
100 Centimes = 1 Franc

## FRENCH COLONY

### DECIMAL COINAGE

**FRANC** **KM# 4** **Composition:** Aluminum

| Date | Mintage | F | VF | XF | Unc | BU |
|---|---|---|---|---|---|---|
| 1948(a) | 200,000 | 6.50 | 12.50 | 25.00 | 50.00 | — |
| 1949(a) | Inc. above | 8.00 | 15.00 | 30.00 | 60.00 | — |

**FRANC** **KM# 8** **Composition:** Aluminum

| Date | Mintage | F | VF | XF | Unc | BU |
|---|---|---|---|---|---|---|
| 1959(a) | 500,000 | 0.25 | 0.50 | 1.50 | 3.00 | — |
| 1965(a) | 200,000 | 0.35 | 0.60 | 2.00 | 4.00 | — |

**2 FRANCS** **KM# 5** **Composition:** Aluminum

| Date | Mintage | F | VF | XF | Unc | BU |
|---|---|---|---|---|---|---|
| 1948(a) | 200,000 | 6.50 | 12.50 | 25.00 | 60.00 | — |
| 1949(a) | Inc. above | 8.00 | 15.00 | 30.00 | 70.00 | — |

**2 FRANCS** **KM# 9** **Composition:** Aluminum

| Date | Mintage | F | VF | XF | Unc | BU |
|---|---|---|---|---|---|---|
| 1959(a) | 200,000 | 0.25 | 0.75 | 2.50 | 5.00 | — |
| 1965(a) | 240,000 | 0.25 | 0.75 | 2.50 | 5.00 | — |

**5 FRANCS** **KM# 6** **Composition:** Aluminum

| Date | Mintage | F | VF | XF | Unc | BU |
|---|---|---|---|---|---|---|
| 1948(a) | 500,000 | 5.00 | 10.00 | 25.00 | 40.00 | — |

**5 FRANCS** **KM# 10** **Composition:** Aluminum

| Date | Mintage | F | VF | XF | Unc | BU |
|---|---|---|---|---|---|---|
| 1959(a) | 500,000 | 0.25 | 0.75 | 2.50 | 5.50 | — |
| 1965(a) | 200,000 | 0.25 | 0.75 | 3.00 | 6.50 | — |

**10 FRANCS** **KM# 11** **Composition:** Aluminum-Bronze

| Date | Mintage | F | VF | XF | Unc | BU |
|---|---|---|---|---|---|---|
| 1965(a) | 250,000 | 0.50 | 1.00 | 3.00 | 6.00 | — |

**20 FRANCS** **KM# 7** **Composition:** Aluminum-Bronze

| Date | Mintage | F | VF | XF | Unc | BU |
|---|---|---|---|---|---|---|
| 1952(a) | 500,000 | 1.25 | 2.50 | 4.50 | 10.00 | — |

**20 FRANCS** **KM# 12** **Composition:** Aluminum-Bronze

| Date | Mintage | F | VF | XF | Unc | BU |
|---|---|---|---|---|---|---|
| 1965(a) | 200,000 | 1.00 | 2.00 | 4.00 | 8.00 | — |

### ESSAIS

Standard metals unless otherwise noted

| KM# | Date | Mintage | Identification | Issue Price | Mkt Val |
|---|---|---|---|---|---|
| E1 | 1948 | 2,000 | Franc. Copper-Nickel. KM4. | — | 15.00 |
| E2 | 1948 | 2,000 | 2 Francs. Copper-Nickel. KM5. | — | 18.00 |
| E3 | 1948 | 2,000 | 5 Francs. Copper-Nickel. KM6 | — | 20.00 |
| E4 | 1952 | 1,200 | 20 Francs. (No Composition). KM7 | — | 20.00 |
| E5 | 1965 | 2,000 | 10 Francs. (No Composition). KM11 | — | 10.00 |

### PIEFORTS WITH ESSAI

Standard metals unless otherwise noted

| KM# | Date | Mintage | Identification | Issue Price | Mkt Val |
|---|---|---|---|---|---|
| PE1 | 1948 | 104 | Franc. (No Composition). | — | 100 |
| PE2 | 1948 | 104 | 2 Francs. (No Composition). | — | 100 |
| PE3 | 1948 | 104 | 5 Francs. (No Composition). | — | 125 |
| PE4 | 1952 | 104 | 20 Francs. (No Composition). | — | 125 |

### "FDC" SETS

| KM# | Date | Mintage | Identification | Issue Price | Mkt Val |
|---|---|---|---|---|---|
| SS1 | 1965 (5) | 1,898 | KM#8-12; Issued with French Polynesia | — | 30.00 |

# FRENCH WEST AFRICA

French West Africa (Afrique Occidentale Francaise), a former federation of French colonial territories on the northwest coast of Africa, had an area of 1,831,079 sq. mi. (4,742,495 sq. km.) and a population of about 17.4 million. Capital: Dakar. The constituent territories were Mauritania, Senegal, Dahomey, French Sudan, Ivory Coast, Upper Volta, Niger, French Guinea, and later on the mandated area of Togo. Peanuts, palm kernels, cacao, coffee and bananas were exported.

Prior to the mid-19th century, France, as the other European states, maintained establishments on the west coast of Africa for the purpose of trading in slaves and gum, but made no serious attempt at colonization. From 1854 onward, the coastal settlements were gradually extended into the interior until, by the opening of the 20th century, acquisition ended and organization and development began. French West Africa was formed in 1895 by grouping the several colonies under one administration (at Dakar) while retaining a large measure of autonomy to each of the constituent territories. The inhabitants of French West Africa were made French citizens in 1946. With the exception of French Guinea, all of the colonies voted in 1958 to become autonomous members of the new French Community. French Guinea voted to become the fully independent Republic of Guinea. The present-day independent states are members of the "Union Monetaire Ouest-Africaine".<For later coinage see West African States.

**RULERS**
French

**MINT MARKS**
(a) - Paris, privy marks only
(L) – London

**MONETARY SYSTEM**
100 Centimes = 1 Franc
5 Francs = 1 Unit

## FRENCH COLONY

### COLONIAL COINAGE

**50 CENTIMES** **KM# 1** **Composition:** Aluminum-Bronze

| Date | Mintage | F | VF | XF | Unc | BU |
|---|---|---|---|---|---|---|
| 1944(L) | 10,000,000 | 2.00 | 4.00 | 10.00 | 25.00 | — |
| 1944(L) Proof | — | Value: 175 | | | | |

**FRANC** **KM# 2** **Composition:** Aluminum-Bronze

| Date | Mintage | F | VF | XF | Unc | BU |
|---|---|---|---|---|---|---|
| 1944(L) | 15,000,000 | 1.00 | 2.00 | 5.00 | 20.00 | — |
| 1944(L) Proof | — | Value: 200 | | | | |

**FRANC** **KM# 3** **Composition:** Aluminum **Reverse:** Rhim gazelle facing

| Date | Mintage | F | VF | XF | Unc | BU |
|---|---|---|---|---|---|---|
| 1948(a) | 30,110,000 | 0.15 | 0.20 | 0.35 | 1.00 | — |
| 1955(a) | 5,200,000 | 0.20 | 0.35 | 0.50 | 1.50 | — |

**2 FRANCS** KM# 4 **Composition:** Aluminum **Reverse:** Rhim gazelle facing

| Date | Mintage | F | VF | XF | Unc | BU |
|---|---|---|---|---|---|---|
| 1948(a) | 12,665,000 | 0.20 | 0.30 | 0.50 | 1.75 | — |
| 1955(a) | 1,400,000 | 0.25 | 0.40 | 0.75 | 2.00 | — |

**5 FRANCS** KM# 5 **Composition:** Aluminum-Bronze **Reverse:** Rhim gazelle facing

| Date | Mintage | F | VF | XF | Unc | BU |
|---|---|---|---|---|---|---|
| 1956(a) | 85,000,000 | 0.35 | 0.50 | 1.00 | 2.50 | — |

**10 FRANCS** KM# 6 **Composition:** Aluminum-Bronze **Reverse:** Rhim gazelle facing

| Date | Mintage | F | VF | XF | Unc | BU |
|---|---|---|---|---|---|---|
| 1956(a) | 64,133,000 | 0.50 | 1.00 | 1.50 | 3.50 | — |

**10 FRANCS** KM# 8 **Composition:** Aluminum-Bronze

| Date | Mintage | F | VF | XF | Unc | BU |
|---|---|---|---|---|---|---|
| 1957(a) | 30,000,000 | 0.50 | 1.00 | 1.50 | 3.00 | — |

**Note:** Issued for circulation in French West Africa, including Togo

**25 FRANCS** KM# 7 **Composition:** Aluminum-Bronze **Reverse:** Rhim gazelle facing

| Date | Mintage | F | VF | XF | Unc | BU |
|---|---|---|---|---|---|---|
| 1956(a) | 37,877,000 | 0.50 | 1.00 | 2.00 | 5.50 | — |

**25 FRANCS** KM# 9 **Composition:** Aluminum-Bronze

| Date | Mintage | F | VF | XF | Unc | BU |
|---|---|---|---|---|---|---|
| 1957(a) | 30,000,000 | 0.50 | 1.00 | 2.00 | 5.00 | — |

**Note:** Issued for circulation in French West Africa, including Togo

## ESSAIS

Standard metals unless otherwise noted

| KM# | Date | Mintage | Identification | Issue Price | Mkt Val |
|---|---|---|---|---|---|
| E1 | 1948 | 2,000 | Franc. Copper-Nickel. KM3. | — | 15.00 |
| E2 | 1948 | 2,000 | 2 Francs. Copper-Nickel. KM4. | — | 17.50 |
| E3 | 1956 | 2,300 | 5 Francs. KM5 | — | 10.00 |
| E4 | 1956 | 2,300 | 10 Francs. KM6. | — | 15.00 |
| E5 | 1956 | 2,300 | 25 Francs. KM7 | — | 20.00 |
| E6 | 1957 | 2,300 | 10 Francs. KM8. | — | 12.50 |
| E7 | 1957 | 2,300 | 25 Francs. KM9. | — | 15.00 |

## PIEFORTS WITH ESSAI

Double thickness - Standard metals unless otherwise noted

| KM# | Date | Mintage | Identification | Issue Price | Mkt Val |
|---|---|---|---|---|---|
| PE1 | 1948 | 104 | Franc. KM3 | — | 65.00 |
| PE2 | 1948 | 104 | 2 Francs. KM4. | — | 75.00 |

# AL FUJAIRAH

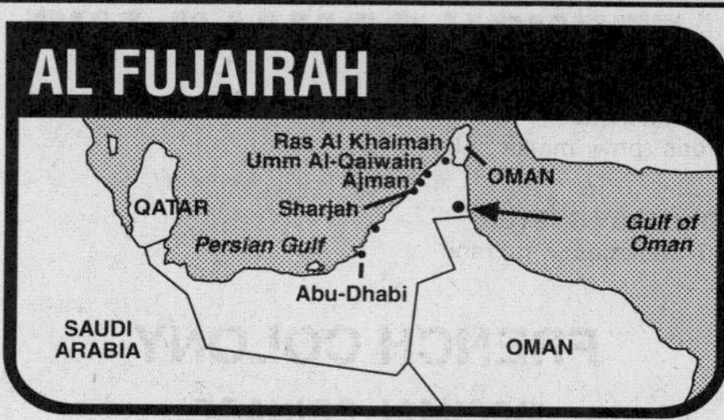


An original member of the United Arab Emirates, al-Fujairah is the only emirate that does not have territory on the Persian Gulf. It is on the eastern side of the "horn" of Oman. It has an estimated area of 450 sq. mi. (1200 sq. km.) and a population of 27,000. Al-Fujairah has been, historically a frequent rival of Sharjah. As recently as 1952 Great Britain recognized al-Fujairah as an autonomous state.

**TITLES**

al Fujaira(t) الفجيرة

**RULERS**

Muhammad bin Hamad al-Sharqi, 1952-74
Hamad bin Muhammad al-Sharqi, 1974--

## UNITED ARAB EMIRAT

### NON-CIRCULATING LEGAL TENDER COINAGE

**RIYAL** KM# 1 **Weight:** 3.0000 g. **Composition:** 1.0000 Silver .0964 oz. ASW **Ruler:** Muhammad bin Hamad al-Sharqi **Subject:** Desert Fort **Obverse:** Similar to KM#2

| Date | Mintage | F | VF | XF | Unc | BU |
|---|---|---|---|---|---|---|
| AH1388(1969) Proof | 4,050 | Value: 22.50 | | | | |
| AH1389(1970) Proof | Inc. above | Value: 22.50 | | | | |

**2 RIYALS** KM# 2 **Weight:** 6.0000 g. **Composition:** 1.0000 Silver .1928 oz. ASW **Ruler:** Muhammad bin Hamad al-Sharqi **Subject:** President Richard Nixon

| Date | Mintage | F | VF | XF | Unc | BU |
|---|---|---|---|---|---|---|
| AH1388(1969) Proof | 6,250 | Value: 28.50 | | | | |
| AH1389(1970) Proof | Inc. above | Value: 28.50 | | | | |

**5 RIYALS** KM# 3 **Weight:** 15.0000 g. **Composition:** 1.0000 Silver .4823 oz. ASW **Ruler:** Muhammad bin Hamad al-Sharqi **Series:** 1972 Munich Olympics

| Date | Mintage | F | VF | XF | Unc | BU |
|---|---|---|---|---|---|---|
| AH1388(1969) Proof | 3,550 | Value: 50.00 | | | | |
| AH1389(1970) Proof | 1,300 | Value: 52.50 | | | | |

**10 RIYALS** **KM# 5** **Weight:** 30.0000 g. **Composition:** 1.0000 Silver .9645 oz. ASW **Ruler:** Muhammad bin Hamad al-Sharqi **Subject:** Apollo XII

| Date | Mintage | F | VF | XF | Unc | BU |
|---|---|---|---|---|---|---|
| AH1388(1969) Proof | 15,000 | Value: 47.50 | | | | |
| AH1389(1970) Proof | 15,000 | Value: 47.50 | | | | |

**10 RIYALS** **KM# 4.1** **Weight:** 30.0000 g. **Composition:** 1.0000 Silver .9645 oz. ASW **Ruler:** Muhammad bin Hamad al-Sharqi **Subject:** Apollo XI **Obverse:** Fineness in oval at lower left, mintage figure at lower right

| Date | Mintage | F | VF | XF | Unc | BU |
|---|---|---|---|---|---|---|
| AH1388(1969) Proof | 14,000 | Value: 55.00 | | | | |

**10 RIYALS** **KM# 4.2** **Weight:** 30.0000 g. **Composition:** 1.0000 Silver .9645 oz. ASW **Ruler:** Muhammad bin Hamad al-Sharqi **Obverse:** Mintage figure stamped at lower left, fineness in oval at lower right

| Date | Mintage | F | VF | XF | Unc | BU |
|---|---|---|---|---|---|---|
| AH1389(1970) Proof | — | Value: 55.00 | | | | |

**10 RIYALS** **KM# 19** **Weight:** 30.0000 g. **Composition:** 1.0000 Silver .9645 oz. ASW **Ruler:** Muhammad bin Hamad al-Sharqi **Subject:** Apollo XIII

| Date | Mintage | F | VF | XF | Unc | BU |
|---|---|---|---|---|---|---|
| AH1389(1970) Proof | 15,000 | Value: 50.00 | | | | |

**10 RIYALS** **KM# 20** **Weight:** 30.0000 g. **Composition:** 1.0000 Silver .9645 oz. ASW **Ruler:** Muhammad bin Hamad al-Sharqi **Subject:** Visit of Pope Paul VI to Philippines **Obverse:** Similar to 10 Riyals, KM#4.1

| Date | Mintage | F | VF | XF | Unc | BU |
|---|---|---|---|---|---|---|
| AH1389(1970) Proof | 300 | Value: 85.00 | | | | |

**10 RIYALS** **KM# 21** **Weight:** 30.0000 g. **Composition:** 1.0000 Silver .9645 oz. ASW **Ruler:** Muhammad bin Hamad al-Sharqi **Subject:** Visit of Pope Paul VI to Australia **Obverse:** Similar to 10 Riyals, KM#4.1

| Date | Mintage | F | VF | XF | Unc | BU |
|---|---|---|---|---|---|---|
| AH1389(1970) Proof | 12,000 | Value: 85.00 | | | | |

**10 RIYALS** **KM# 22** **Weight:** 30.0000 g. **Composition:** 1.0000 Silver .9645 oz. ASW **Ruler:** Muhammad bin Hamad al-Sharqi **Subject:** Apollo XIV **Obverse:** Similar to 10 Riyals, KM#4.1

| Date | Mintage | F | VF | XF | Unc | BU |
|---|---|---|---|---|---|---|
| AH1389(1971) Proof | 14,000 | Value: 75.00 | | | | |

**25 RIYALS** **KM# 7** **Weight:** 5.1800 g. **Composition:** 0.9000 Gold .1499 oz. AGW **Ruler:** Muhammad bin Hamad al-Sharqi **Subject:** U.S. President Richard Nixon **Obverse:** Similar to 10 Riyals, KM#4.1 **Note:** The 1969 issue has the fineness incuse, the 1970 issue has the fineness both raised and incuse.

| Date | Mintage | F | VF | XF | Unc | BU |
|---|---|---|---|---|---|---|
| AH1388(1969) Proof | 3,280 | Value: 125 | | | | |
| AH1389(1970) Proof | Inc. above | Value: 125 | | | | |

**50 RIYALS** **KM# 8** **Weight:** 10.3600 g. **Composition:** 0.9000 Gold .2998 oz. AGW **Ruler:** Muhammad bin Hamad al-Sharqi **Series:** 1972 Munich Olympics

| Date | Mintage | F | VF | XF | Unc | BU |
|---|---|---|---|---|---|---|
| AH1388(1969) Proof | 1,230 | Value: 235 | | | | |
| AH1389(1970) Proof | 400 | Value: 250 | | | | |

**100 RIYALS** **KM# 9** **Weight:** 20.7300 g. **Composition:** 0.9000 Gold .5999 oz. AGW **Ruler:** Muhammad bin Hamad al-Sharqi **Subject:** Apollo X **Obverse:** Similar to KM#24

| Date | Mintage | F | VF | XF | Unc | BU |
|---|---|---|---|---|---|---|
| AH1388(1969) Proof | 2,140 | Value: 385 | | | | |

**100 RIYALS** **KM# 10** **Weight:** 20.7300 g. **Composition:** 0.9000 Gold .5999 oz. AGW **Ruler:** Muhammad bin Hamad al-Sharqi **Subject:** Apollo XII **Obverse:** Similar to KM#24

| Date | Mintage | F | VF | XF | Unc | BU |
|---|---|---|---|---|---|---|
| AH1388(1969) Proof | 3,040 | Value: 375 | | | | |
| AH1389(1970) Proof | — | Value: 375 | | | | |

**100 RIYALS** **KM# 23** **Weight:** 20.7300 g. **Composition:** 0.9000 Gold .5999 oz. AGW **Ruler:** Muhammad bin Hamad al-Sharqi **Subject:** Apollo XIII **Obverse:** Similar to KM#24 **Reverse:** Similar to 10 Riyals, KM#19

| Date | Mintage | F | VF | XF | Unc | BU |
|---|---|---|---|---|---|---|
| AH1389(1970) Proof | 600 | Value: 400 | | | | |

**100 RIYALS** **KM# 24** **Weight:** 20.7300 g. **Composition:** 0.9000 Gold .5999 oz. AGW **Ruler:** Muhammad bin Hamad al-Sharqi **Subject:** Visit of Pope Paul VI to Philippines

| Date | Mintage | F | VF | XF | Unc | BU |
|---|---|---|---|---|---|---|
| AH1389(1970) Proof | 290 | Value: 500 | | | | |

**100 RIYALS** **KM# 26** **Weight:** 20.7300 g. **Composition:** 0.9000 Gold .5999 oz. AGW **Ruler:** Muhammad bin Hamad al-Sharqi **Subject:** Visit of Pope Paul VI to Australia **Obverse:** Similar to KM#24 **Reverse:** Pope facing right, map of Australia **Note:** Similar to 10 Riyals, KM#21.

| Date | Mintage | F | VF | XF | Unc | BU |
|---|---|---|---|---|---|---|
| AH1389(1970) Proof | 250 | Value: 500 | | | | |

**100 RIYALS** **KM# 25** **Weight:** 20.7300 g. **Composition:** 0.9000 Gold .5999 oz. AGW **Ruler:** Muhammad bin Hamad al-Sharqi **Subject:** Apollo XIV **Obverse:** Similar to KM#24

| Date | Mintage | F | VF | XF | Unc | BU |
|---|---|---|---|---|---|---|
| AH1389(1971) Proof | 550 | Value: 375 | | | | |

**200 RIYALS** **KM# 11** **Weight:** 41.4600 g. **Composition:** 0.9000 Gold 1.1998 oz. AGW **Ruler:** Muhammad bin Hamad al-Sharqi **Subject:** Mohamad bin Hamad al-Sharqi **Obverse:** Arms

| Date | Mintage | F | VF | XF | Unc | BU |
|---|---|---|---|---|---|---|
| AH1388(1969) Proof | 680 | Value: 700 | | | | |

**Note:** Serially numbered on the obverse

## PATTERNS

| KM# | Date | Mintage | Identification | Mkt Val |
|---|---|---|---|---|
| Pn1 | 1968 | 15 | 250 Fils. Silver. | 350 |
| Pn2 | 1968 | 15 | 500 Fils. Silver. | 400 |
| Pn3 | 1968 | 15 | 750 Fils. Silver. | 500 |

| KM# | Date | Mintage | Identification | Mkt Val |
|---|---|---|---|---|
| Pn4 | 1968 | 50 | Dinar. Silver. | 600 |
| Pn5 | 1968 | 1 | Dinar. Silver. Matte proof. | 1,000 |

## TRIAL STRIKES

| KM# | Date | Mintage | Identification | Mkt Val |
|---|---|---|---|---|
| TS1 | 1968 | 1 | 500 Fils. Silver. Uniface. | 300 |
| TS2 | 1968 | 1 | 750 Fils. Silver. Uniface. | 300 |
| TS3 | 1968 | 1 | Dinar. Silver. Uniface. | 350 |
| TS4 | 1968 | 1 | Dinar. Silver. Uniface. | 350 |

## PROOF SETS

| KM# | Date | Mintage | Identification | Issue Price | Mkt Val |
|---|---|---|---|---|---|
| PS1 | Mixed 1969-71 (18) | — | 0 | — | — |
| PS3 | Mixed 1969-71 (8) | — | KM#4.2, 5, 19, 22, 9, 10, 23, 25 | — | 1,700 |
| PS4 | 1969 (8) | — | KM#1-4.2, 7-9, 11 | — | 1,600 |
| PS5 | 1969 (5) | 2,550 | KM#1-4.2, 5 | 40.00 | 220 |
| PS6 | 1969 (5) | 5,000 | KM#7-11 | 280 | 1,750 |
| PS7 | 1969 (4) | — | KM#1-4.2 | — | 170 |
| PS2 | Mixed 1969-71 (9) | — | KM#1-4.2, 5, 19-22 | — | 475 |
| PS8 | 1970 (5) | 200 | KM#1-4.2, 5 | 40.00 | 220 |

# GABON

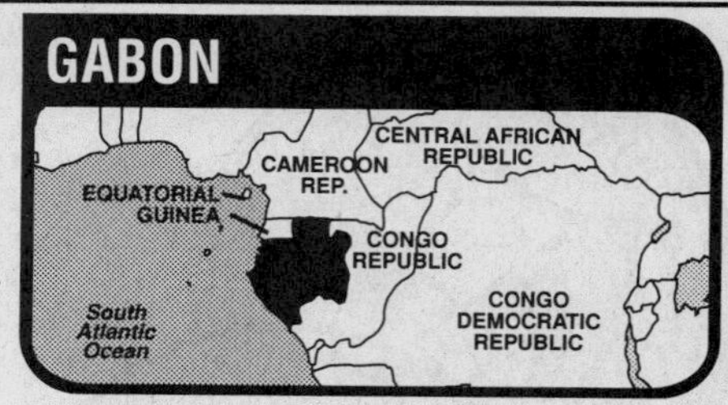


The Gabonese Republic, a member of the French Community, straddles the equator on the west coast of Africa. The hot and humid rain forest country has an area of 103,347 sq. mi. (267,670 sq. km.) and a population of 1.2 million, almost all of Bantu origin. Capital: Libreville. Extravagantly rich in resources, Gabon exports crude oil, manganese ore, gold and timbers.

Gabon was first visited by Portuguese navigator Diego Cam in the 15th century. Dutch, French and British traders, lured by the rich stands of hard woods and oil palms, quickly followed. The French founded their first settlement on the left bank of the Gabon River in 1839 and established their presence by signing treaties with the tribal chiefs. After gradually extending their influence into the interior during the last half of the 19th century, France occupied Gabon in 1885 and, in 1910, organized it as one of the four territories of French Equatorial Africa. It became an autonomous republic within the French Union in 1946, and on Aug. 17, 1960, became a completely independent republic within the new French Community.

For earlier coinage see French Equatorial Africa, Central African States and the Equatorial African States.

**MINT MARKS**

(a) - Paris, privy marks only

(t) - Poissy, privy marks only, thunderbolt

## REPUBLIC

### DECIMAL COINAGE

**10 FRANCS** **KM# 1** **Weight:** 4.2000 g. **Composition:** 0.9000 Gold .1215 oz. AGW **Subject:** Independence **Obverse:** President Mba

| Date | Mintage | F | VF | XF | Unc | BU |
|---|---|---|---|---|---|---|
| 1960 Proof | 500 | Value: 75.00 | | | | |

**25 FRANCS** **KM# 2** **Weight:** 8.0000 g. **Composition:** 0.9000 Gold .2315 oz. AGW **Subject:** Independence **Obverse:** President Mba

| Date | Mintage | F | VF | XF | Unc | BU |
|---|---|---|---|---|---|---|
| 1960 | 10,000 | — | — | — | 100 | — |
| 1960 Proof | 500 | Value: 125 | | | | |

**50 FRANCS** **KM# 3** **Weight:** 16.0000 g. **Composition:** 0.9000 Gold .4630 oz. AGW **Subject:** Independence **Obverse:** President Mba

| Date | Mintage | F | VF | XF | Unc | BU |
|---|---|---|---|---|---|---|
| 1960 Proof | 500 | Value: 225 | | | | |

**100 FRANCS** KM# 4 **Weight:** 32.0000 g. **Composition:** 0.9000 Gold .9260 oz. AGW **Subject:** Independence **Obverse:** President Mba

| Date | Mintage | F | VF | XF | Unc | BU |
|---|---|---|---|---|---|---|
| 1960 Proof | 500 | Value: 425 | | | | |

**100 FRANCS** KM# 12 **Composition:** Nickel

| Date | Mintage | F | VF | XF | Unc | BU |
|---|---|---|---|---|---|---|
| 1971(a) | 1,300,000 | 3.50 | 7.00 | 15.00 | 25.00 | — |
| 1972(a) | 2,000,000 | 3.50 | 7.00 | 15.00 | 25.00 | — |

**100 FRANCS** KM# 13 **Composition:** Nickel

| Date | Mintage | F | VF | XF | Unc | BU |
|---|---|---|---|---|---|---|
| 1975(a) | — | 2.00 | 4.00 | 7.50 | 15.00 | — |
| 1977(a) | — | 3.00 | 6.50 | 12.50 | 22.50 | — |
| 1978(a) | — | 2.50 | 4.50 | 9.00 | 17.50 | — |
| 1982(a) | — | 1.25 | 2.50 | 4.50 | 9.00 | — |
| 1983(a) | — | 1.25 | 2.50 | 4.50 | 9.00 | — |
| 1984(a) | — | 1.00 | 2.00 | 4.00 | 8.00 | — |
| 1985(a) | — | 1.00 | 2.00 | 4.00 | 8.00 | — |

**500 FRANCS** KM# 14 **Composition:** Copper-Nickel

| Date | Mintage | F | VF | XF | Unc | BU |
|---|---|---|---|---|---|---|
| 1985(a) | — | 3.00 | 5.00 | 8.00 | 16.00 | — |

**1000 FRANCS** KM# 6 **Weight:** 3.5000 g. **Composition:** 0.9000 Gold .1012 oz. AGW **Obverse:** Albert Bernard Bongo **Reverse:** Stump of okume tree

| Date | Mintage | F | VF | XF | Unc | BU |
|---|---|---|---|---|---|---|
| 1969 Proof | 4,000 | Value: 65.00 | | | | |

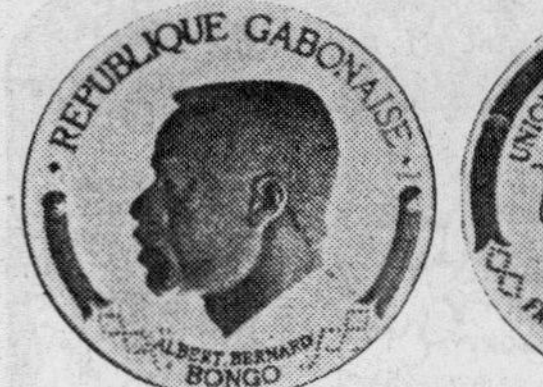

**3000 FRANCS** KM# 7 **Weight:** 10.5000 g. **Composition:** 0.9000 Gold .3038 oz. AGW **Obverse:** Albert Bernard Bongo **Reverse:** Arms

| Date | Mintage | F | VF | XF | Unc | BU |
|---|---|---|---|---|---|---|
| 1969 Proof | 4,000 | Value: 175 | | | | |

**5000 FRANCS** KM# 8 **Weight:** 17.5000 g. **Composition:** 0.9000 Gold .5064 oz. AGW **Obverse:** Albert Bernard Bongo **Reverse:** Reliquary figure of Bakota

| Date | Mintage | F | VF | XF | Unc | BU |
|---|---|---|---|---|---|---|
| 1969 Proof | 4,000 | Value: 275 | | | | |

**5000 FRANCS** KM# 11 **Weight:** 17.5000 g. **Composition:** 0.9000 Gold .5064 oz. AGW **Subject:** Visit of French President Georges Pompidou

| Date | Mintage | F | VF | XF | Unc | BU |
|---|---|---|---|---|---|---|
| 1971 Proof | — | Value: 500 | | | | |

**10000 FRANCS** KM# 9 **Weight:** 35.0000 g. **Composition:** 0.9000 Gold 1.0128 oz. AGW **Subject:** 1st Moon landing **Obverse:** Albert Bernard Bongo **Reverse:** Lunar module

| Date | Mintage | F | VF | XF | Unc | BU |
|---|---|---|---|---|---|---|
| 1969 Proof | 4,000 | Value: 500 | | | | |

**20000 FRANCS** KM# 10 **Weight:** 70.0000 g. **Composition:** 0.9000 Gold 2.0257 oz. AGW **Subject:** 1st Moon landing - Cape Kennedy **Obverse:** Albert Bernard Bongo **Reverse:** Apollo XI at launching pad

| Date | Mintage | F | VF | XF | Unc | BU |
|---|---|---|---|---|---|---|
| 1969 Proof | 4,000 | Value: 1,000 | | | | |

## TOKEN COINAGE

Believed to be initially used for payment of taxes. These tokens do not show a denomination, but circulated until 1930 with varying values corresponding to the animals shown. All have center hole.

**(NO DENOMINATION)** KM# Tn1 **Composition:** Aluminum **Reverse:** Elephant walking left

| Date | Mintage | F | VF | XF | Unc | BU |
|---|---|---|---|---|---|---|
| 1925(t) | — | 35.00 | 60.00 | 120 | 250 | — |

**(NO DENOMINATION)** KM# Tn2 **Composition:** Aluminum **Reverse:** Leopard walking left

| Date | Mintage | F | VF | XF | Unc | BU |
|---|---|---|---|---|---|---|
| 1926 | — | 55.00 | 110 | 225 | 425 | — |

**(NO DENOMINATION)** **KM# Tn3** **Composition:** Aluminum **Reverse:** Ox head facing

| Date | Mintage | F | VF | XF | Unc | BU |
|---|---|---|---|---|---|---|
| 1927(t) | — | 45.00 | 90.00 | 175 | 375 | — |

**(NO DENOMINATION)** **KM# Tn4** **Composition:** Aluminum **Reverse:** Pelican facing right

| Date | Mintage | F | VF | XF | Unc | BU |
|---|---|---|---|---|---|---|
| 1928 | — | 75.00 | 150 | 285 | 550 | — |

**(NO DENOMINATION)** **KM# Tn5** **Composition:** Aluminum **Obverse:** "Gabon" above center hole, date below **Reverse:** Rhinoceros walking left

| Date | Mintage | F | VF | XF | Unc | BU |
|---|---|---|---|---|---|---|
| 1929 | — | 65.00 | 125 | 250 | 500 | — |

## ESSAIS

Standard metals unless otherwise noted

| KM# | Date | Mintage | Identification | Issue Price | Mkt Val |
|---|---|---|---|---|---|
| E1 | 1960 | 10 | 25 Francs. KM2. | — | 500 |
| E2 | 1960 | — | 25 Francs. Silver. KM2. | — | 250 |
| E3 | 1971 | 1,450 | 100 Francs. KM12. | — | 15.00 |
| E5 | 1971 | — | 5000 Francs. Copper-Aluminum-Nickel. KM11. | — | 175 |
| E4 | 1971 | 4 | 100 Francs. Gold. KM12. | — | 1,600 |

| KM# | Date | Mintage | Identification | Issue Price | Mkt Val |
|---|---|---|---|---|---|
| E6 | 1975 | 1,700 | 100 Francs. KM13. | — | 15.00 |

| KM# | Date | Mintage | Identification | Issue Price | Mkt Val |
|---|---|---|---|---|---|
| E7 | 1985 | 1,700 | 500 Francs. KM14. | — | 25.00 |

## PROOF SETS

| KM# | Date | Mintage | Identification | Issue Price | Mkt Val |
|---|---|---|---|---|---|
| PS1 | 1960 (4) | 500 | KM1-4 | — | 850 |
| PS2 | 1969 (5) | 4,000 | KM6-10 | — | 2,150 |

# GAMBIA

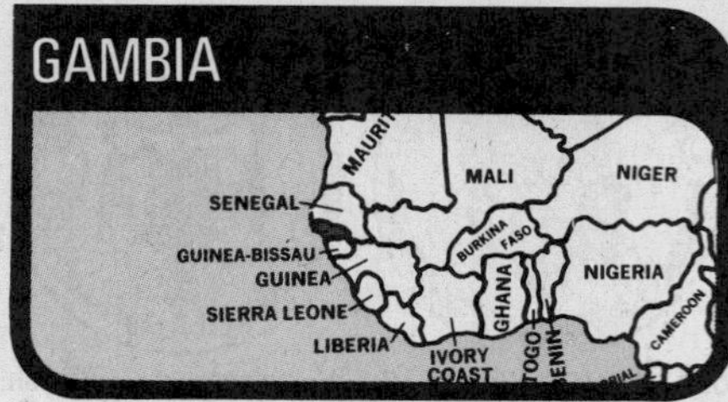


The Republic of The Gambia, an independent member of the British Commonwealth, occupies a strip of land 7 miles (11km.) to 20 miles (32 km.) wide and 200 miles (322 km.) long encompassing both sides of West Africa's Gambia River, and completely surrounded by Senegal. The republic, one of Africa's smallest countries, has an area of 4,127 sq. mi. (11,300 sq. km.) and a population of 989,273. Capital: Banjul. Agriculture and tourism are the principal industries. Peanuts constitute 95 per cent of export earnings.

The Gambia was once part of the great empires of Ghana and Songhay. When Portuguese gold seekers and slave traders visited The Gambia in the 15th century, it was part of the Kingdom of Mali. In 1588 the territory became, through purchase, the first British colony in Africa. English slavers established Fort James, the first settlement, on a small island a dozen miles up the Gambia River in 1664. After alternate periods of union with Sierra Leone and existence as a separate colony The Gambia became a British colony in 1888. On Feb. 18, 1965, The Gambia achieved independence as a constitutional monarchy within the Commonwealth of Nations, with Elizabeth II as Head of State as Queen of The Gambia. It became a republic on April 24, 1970, remaining a member of the Common- wealth, but with the president as Chief of State and Head of Government.

Together with Senegal, The Gambia formed a confederation on February 1, 1982. This confederation was officially dissolved on September 21, 1989. In July, 1994 a military junta took control of The Gambia and disbanded its elected government.

Gambia's 8 Shillings coin is a unique denomination in world coinage.

For earlier coinage see British West Africa.

**RULERS**

British until 1970

**MONETARY SYSTEM**

12 Pence = 1 Shilling
4 Shillings = 1 Dirham
20 Shillings = 1 Pound

## BRITISH COMMONWEALTH

### STERLING COINAGE

**PENNY** **KM# 1** **Composition:** Bronze **Reverse:** Sailing vessel

| Date | Mintage | F | VF | XF | Unc | BU |
|---|---|---|---|---|---|---|
| 1966 | 3,600,000 | — | 0.20 | 0.40 | 1.00 | — |
| 1966 Proof | 6,600 | Value: 1.00 | | | | |

**3 PENCE** **KM# 2** **Composition:** Nickel-Brass **Reverse:** Double-spurred francolin

| Date | Mintage | F | VF | XF | Unc | BU |
|---|---|---|---|---|---|---|
| 1966 | 2,000,000 | — | 0.30 | 0.50 | 1.50 | — |
| 1966 Proof | 6,600 | Value: 1.50 | | | | |

**6 PENCE** **KM# 3** **Composition:** Copper-Nickel **Reverse:** Peanuts

| Date | Mintage | F | VF | XF | Unc | BU |
|---|---|---|---|---|---|---|
| 1966 | 1,500,000 | — | 0.30 | 0.50 | 1.75 | — |
| 1966 Proof | 6,600 | Value: 1.75 | | | | |

**SHILLING** **KM# 4** **Composition:** Copper-Nickel **Reverse:** Oil palm

| Date | Mintage | F | VF | XF | Unc | BU |
|---|---|---|---|---|---|---|
| 1966 | 2,500,000 | — | 0.50 | 0.80 | 2.00 | — |
| 1966 Proof | 6,600 | Value: 2.00 | | | | |

**2 SHILLING** **KM# 5** **Composition:** Copper-Nickel **Reverse:** African domestic ox

| Date | Mintage | F | VF | XF | Unc | BU |
|---|---|---|---|---|---|---|
| 1966 | 1,600,000 | — | 0.75 | 1.50 | 2.50 | — |
| 1966 Proof | 6,600 | Value: 2.50 | | | | |

**4 SHILLINGS** **KM# 6** **Composition:** Copper-Nickel **Reverse:** Slender-snouted crocodile

| Date | Mintage | F | VF | XF | Unc | BU |
|---|---|---|---|---|---|---|
| 1966 | 800,000 | — | 1.50 | 2.50 | 5.50 | — |
| 1966 Proof | 6,600 | Value: 7.50 | | | | |

**8 SHILLINGS** **KM# 7** **Composition:** Copper-Nickel **Reverse:** Hippopotamus

| Date | Mintage | F | VF | XF | Unc | BU |
|---|---|---|---|---|---|---|
| 1970 | 25,000 | — | 2.00 | 4.00 | 8.50 | — |

**8 SHILLINGS** **KM# 7a** **Weight:** 32.4000 g. **Composition:** 0.9250 Silver .9635 oz. ASW **Reverse:** Hippopotamus

| Date | Mintage | F | VF | XF | Unc | BU |
|---|---|---|---|---|---|---|
| 1970 Proof | 4,500 | Value: 28.50 | | | | |

**Note:** VIP issued proofs have a frosted relief, value: $175.00.

# REPUBLIC

## DECIMAL COINAGE

100 Bututs = 1 Dalasi

**BUTUT** **KM# 8** **Composition:** Bronze **Reverse:** Peanuts

| Date | Mintage | F | VF | XF | Unc | BU |
|---|---|---|---|---|---|---|
| 1971 | 12,449,000 | — | — | 0.10 | 0.20 | — |
| 1971 Proof | 32,000 | Value: 0.50 | | | | |
| 1973 | 3,000,000 | — | — | 0.10 | 0.25 | — |
| 1974 | — | — | — | 0.10 | 0.25 | — |
| 1975 | — | — | — | 0.10 | 0.25 | — |

**BUTUT** **KM# 14** **Composition:** Bronze **Series:** F.A.O.

| Date | Mintage | F | VF | XF | Unc | BU |
|---|---|---|---|---|---|---|
| 1974 | 26,062,000 | — | — | 0.10 | 0.20 | — |
| 1985 | 4,500,000 | — | — | 0.15 | 0.25 | — |

**BUTUT** **KM# 54** **Composition:** Copper Plated Steel **Obverse:** National arms **Reverse:** Peanuts

| Date | Mintage | F | VF | XF | Unc | BU |
|---|---|---|---|---|---|---|
| 1998 | — | — | — | — | 0.20 | — |

**5 BUTUTS** **KM# 9** **Composition:** Bronze **Reverse:** Sailing vessel

| Date | Mintage | F | VF | XF | Unc | BU |
|---|---|---|---|---|---|---|
| 1971 | 5,400,000 | — | — | 0.10 | 0.35 | — |
| 1971 Proof | 32,000 | Value: 0.50 | | | | |
| 1977 | 1,506,000 | — | — | 0.10 | 0.35 | — |

**5 BUTUTS** **KM# 55** **Composition:** Bronze **Obverse:** National arms **Reverse:** Sailboat

| Date | Mintage | F | VF | XF | Unc | BU |
|---|---|---|---|---|---|---|
| 1998 | — | — | — | — | 0.35 | — |

**10 BUTUTS** **KM# 10** **Composition:** Nickel-Brass **Reverse:** Double-spurred francolin

| Date | Mintage | F | VF | XF | Unc | BU |
|---|---|---|---|---|---|---|
| 1971 | 3,000,000 | — | 0.15 | 0.35 | 1.50 | — |
| 1971 Proof | 32,000 | Value: 2.00 | | | | |
| 1977 | 750,000 | — | 0.15 | 0.35 | 1.50 | — |

**10 BUTUTS** **KM# 56** **Composition:** Brass Plated Steel **Obverse:** National arms **Reverse:** Double-spurred francolin

| Date | Mintage | F | VF | XF | Unc | BU |
|---|---|---|---|---|---|---|
| 1998 | — | — | — | — | 1.00 | — |

**25 BUTUTS** **KM# 11** **Composition:** Copper-Nickel **Reverse:** Oil palm

| Date | Mintage | F | VF | XF | Unc | BU |
|---|---|---|---|---|---|---|
| 1971 | 3,040,000 | — | 0.15 | 0.30 | 0.75 | — |
| 1971 Proof | 32,000 | Value: 1.25 | | | | |

**25 BUTUTS** **KM# 57** **Composition:** Copper-Nickel **Obverse:** National arms **Reverse:** Oil palm

| Date | Mintage | F | VF | XF | Unc | BU |
|---|---|---|---|---|---|---|
| 1998 | — | — | — | — | 1.00 | — |

**50 BUTUTS** **KM# 12** **Composition:** Copper-Nickel **Reverse:** African domestic ox

| Date | Mintage | F | VF | XF | Unc | BU |
|---|---|---|---|---|---|---|
| 1971 | 1,700,000 | — | 0.35 | 0.65 | 1.50 | — |
| 1971 Proof | 32,000 | Value: 1.75 | | | | |

**50 BUTUTS** **KM# 60** **Weight:** 24.9700 g. **Composition:** 0.9800 Silver .7867 oz. ASW **Subject:** Marine life protection **Obverse:** National arms **Reverse:** Pair of multicolored fish

| Date | Mintage | F | VF | XF | Unc | BU |
|---|---|---|---|---|---|---|
| 1997 Proof | — | Value: 40.00 | | | | |

**50 BUTUTS** **KM# 58** **Composition:** Copper-Nickel **Obverse:** National arms **Reverse:** African domestic ox

| Date | Mintage | F | VF | XF | Unc | BU |
|---|---|---|---|---|---|---|
| 1998 | — | — | — | — | 1.50 | — |

**2000 BUTUTS** **KM# 62** **Weight:** 0.9250 g. **Composition:** Silver **Subject:** Millennium **Obverse:** National arms **Reverse:** Gambian map on radiant sun **Edge:** Reeded, 10-sided **Size:** 37.5 mm. **Note:** Struck at British Royal Mint.

| Date | Mintage | F | VF | XF | Unc | BU |
|---|---|---|---|---|---|---|
| ND(1999) Proof | 30,000 | Value: 60.00 | | | | |

**DALASI** **KM# 13** **Composition:** Copper-Nickel **Reverse:** Slender-snouted crocodile

| Date | Mintage | F | VF | XF | Unc | BU |
|---|---|---|---|---|---|---|
| 1971 | 1,300,000 | — | 2.00 | 3.50 | 6.50 | — |
| 1971 Proof | 32,000 | Value: 5.00 | | | | |

**DALASI** **KM# 29** **Composition:** Copper-Nickel **Shape:** 7-sided

| Date | Mintage | F | VF | XF | Unc | BU |
|---|---|---|---|---|---|---|
| 1987 | — | — | 1.75 | 2.75 | 5.50 | — |

**DALASI** **KM# 59** **Composition:** Copper Nickel **Obverse:** National arms **Reverse:** Slender-snouted crocodile **Shape:** 7-sided

| Date | Mintage | F | VF | XF | Unc | BU |
|---|---|---|---|---|---|---|
| 1998 | — | — | 1.75 | 2.75 | 5.50 | — |

**2 DALASIS** **KM# 46** **Weight:** 9.9200 g. **Composition:** 0.5000 Silver .1595 oz. ASW **Subject:** Olympic Games 1996 **Obverse:** National arms **Reverse:** Two runners crossing a finish line

| Date | Mintage | F | VF | XF | Unc | BU |
|---|---|---|---|---|---|---|
| 1996 Proof | Est. 10,000 | Value: 15.00 | | | | |

**2 DALASIS** **KM# 49** **Composition:** Copper-Nickel **Subject:** 70th birthday of Queen Elizabeth II **Obverse:** National arms

| Date | Mintage | F | VF | XF | Unc | BU |
|---|---|---|---|---|---|---|
| 1996 | 5,000 | — | — | — | 10.00 | — |

**10 DALASIS** **KM# 16** **Weight:** 28.2800 g. **Composition:** 0.5000 Silver .4546 oz. ASW **Subject:** 10th anniversary of independence

| Date | Mintage | F | VF | XF | Unc | BU |
|---|---|---|---|---|---|---|
| 1975 | 50,000 | — | — | — | 8.00 | — |

**10 DALASIS** **KM# 16a** **Weight:** 28.2800 g. **Composition:** 0.9250 Silver .8411 oz. ASW **Subject:** 10th anniversary of independence

| Date | Mintage | F | VF | XF | Unc | BU |
|---|---|---|---|---|---|---|
| 1975 Proof | 20,000 | Value: 15.00 | | | | |

**10 DALASIS** **KM# 23** **Weight:** 28.2800 g. **Composition:** 0.5000 Silver .4546 oz. ASW **Subject:** Commonwealth Games **Reverse:** Hurdlers

| Date | Mintage | F | VF | XF | Unc | BU |
|---|---|---|---|---|---|---|
| 1986 | Est. 50,000 | — | — | — | 12.50 | — |

**10 DALASIS** **KM# 23a** **Weight:** 28.2800 g. **Composition:** 0.9250 Silver .8411 oz. ASW **Subject:** Commonwealth Games **Reverse:** Hurdlers

| Date | Mintage | F | VF | XF | Unc | BU |
|---|---|---|---|---|---|---|
| 1986 Proof | Est. 20,000 | Value: 22.50 | | | | |

**10 DALASIS** **KM# 28** **Weight:** 28.2800 g. **Composition:** 0.9250 Silver .8411 oz. ASW **Subject:** Silver jubilee of independence

| Date | Mintage | F | VF | XF | Unc | BU |
|---|---|---|---|---|---|---|
| 1990 Proof | 2,000 | Value: 42.50 | | | | |

**10 DALASIS** **KM# 30** **Composition:** Copper-Nickel **Subject:** Papal visit

| Date | Mintage | F | VF | XF | Unc | BU |
|---|---|---|---|---|---|---|
| 1992 | — | — | — | — | 6.50 | — |

**10 DALASIS** **KM# 30a** **Weight:** 28.2800 g. **Composition:** 0.9250 Silver .8411 oz. ASW **Subject:** Papal visit

| Date | Mintage | F | VF | XF | Unc | BU |
|---|---|---|---|---|---|---|
| 1992 Proof | 5,000 | Value: 55.00 | | | | |

**10 DALASIS** **KM# 50** **Composition:** Copper Nickel **Subject:** 70th birthday of H.M. Queen Elizabeth II

| Date | Mintage | F | VF | XF | Unc | BU |
|---|---|---|---|---|---|---|
| 1996 | — | — | — | — | 8.00 | — |

**10 DALASIS** **KM# 50a** **Weight:** 28.2800 g. **Composition:** 0.9250 Silver .8411 oz. ASW **Subject:** 70th birthday of H.M. Queen Elizabeth II

| Date | Mintage | F | VF | XF | Unc | BU |
|---|---|---|---|---|---|---|
| 1996 Proof | 70,000 | Value: 40.00 | | | | |

**20 DALASIS** **KM# 17** **Weight:** 28.6300 g. **Composition:** 0.9250 Silver .8514 oz. ASW **Subject:** Conservation **Reverse:** Spur-winged goose

| Date | Mintage | F | VF | XF | Unc | BU |
|---|---|---|---|---|---|---|
| 1977 | 4,302 | — | — | — | 17.50 | — |

**20 DALASIS** **KM# 17a** **Weight:** 28.2800 g. **Composition:** 0.9250 Silver .8411 oz. ASW **Subject:** Conservation **Reverse:** Spur-winged goose

| Date | Mintage | F | VF | XF | Unc | BU |
|---|---|---|---|---|---|---|
| 1977 Proof | 4,404 | Value: 22.50 | | | | |

**20 DALASIS** **KM# 20** **Weight:** 28.2800 g. **Composition:** 0.9250 Silver .8411 oz. ASW **Subject:** World Food Day **Obverse:** Similar to KM#17

| Date | Mintage | F | VF | XF | Unc | BU |
|---|---|---|---|---|---|---|
| 1981 | 10,000 | — | — | — | 20.00 | — |
| 1981 Proof | 5,000 | Value: 30.00 | | | | |

**20 DALASIS** **KM# 21** **Weight:** 28.2800 g. **Composition:** 0.9250 Silver .8411 oz. ASW **Subject:** Year of the Scout

| Date | Mintage | F | VF | XF | Unc | BU |
|---|---|---|---|---|---|---|
| 1983 | Est. 10,000 | — | — | — | 23.50 | — |
| 1983 Proof | Inc. above | Value: 32.50 | | | | |

**20 DALASIS** **KM# 24** **Weight:** 28.2800 g. **Composition:** 0.9250 Silver .8411 oz. ASW **Subject:** World Wildlife Fund **Reverse:** Temminck's colobus monkey

| Date | Mintage | F | VF | XF | Unc | BU |
|---|---|---|---|---|---|---|
| 1987 Proof | Est. 25,000 | Value: 27.50 | | | | |

**20 DALASIS** **KM# 26** **Weight:** 28.2800 g. **Composition:** 0.9250 Silver .8411 oz. ASW **Subject:** Save the Children Fund **Obverse:** Bust of President Alhaji Sir Dawda Dairaba Jawara **Reverse:** Girls playing "akara" (rythmic clapping and dancing game)

| Date | Mintage | F | VF | XF | Unc | BU |
|---|---|---|---|---|---|---|
| 1989 | Est. 20,000 | Value: 26.50 | | | | |

**20 DALASIS** **KM# 32** **Weight:** 31.4700 g. **Composition:** 0.9250 Silver .9359 oz. ASW **Subject:** 40th anniversary - coronation of Queen Elizabeth II

| Date | Mintage | F | VF | XF | Unc | BU |
|---|---|---|---|---|---|---|
| 1993 Proof | Est. 10,000 | Value: 45.00 | | | | |

**20 DALASIS** **KM# 33** **Weight:** 31.2600 g. **Composition:** 0.9250 Silver .9296 oz. ASW **Subject:** Olympics **Reverse:** Wrestling

| Date | Mintage | F | VF | XF | Unc | BU |
|---|---|---|---|---|---|---|
| 1993 Proof | Est. 40,000 | Value: 22.50 | | | | |

**20 DALASIS** **KM# 34** **Weight:** 31.4700 g. **Composition:** 0.9250 Silver .9359 oz. ASW **Subject:** Prince Henry the Navigator

| Date | Mintage | F | VF | XF | Unc | BU |
|---|---|---|---|---|---|---|
| 1993 Proof | Est. 15,000 | Value: 22.50 | | | | |

**20 DALASIS** **KM# 36** **Weight:** 31.4700 g. **Composition:** 0.9250 Silver .9359 oz. ASW **Subject:** Rendezvous in space

| Date | Mintage | F | VF | XF | Unc | BU |
|---|---|---|---|---|---|---|
| 1993 Proof | Est. 10,000 | Value: 30.00 | | | | |

**20 DALASIS** **KM# 35** **Weight:** 31.4700 g. **Composition:** 0.9250 Silver .9359 oz. ASW **Subject:** Soccer - World Cup 1994

| Date | Mintage | F | VF | XF | Unc | BU |
|---|---|---|---|---|---|---|
| 1994 Proof | Est. 15,000 | Value: 30.00 | | | | |

**20 DALASIS** **KM# 40** **Weight:** 31.4700 g. **Composition:** 0.9250 Silver .9359 oz. ASW **Subject:** Elizabeth, the Queen Mother

| Date | Mintage | F | VF | XF | Unc | BU |
|---|---|---|---|---|---|---|
| 1994 Proof | Est. 30,000 | Value: 45.00 | | | | |

**20 DALASIS** **KM# 38** **Weight:** 31.4700 g. **Composition:** 0.9250 Silver .9359 oz. ASW **Subject:** Endangered wildlife **Reverse:** Chimpanzee

| Date | Mintage | F | VF | XF | Unc | BU |
|---|---|---|---|---|---|---|
| 1994 Proof | Est. 15,000 | Value: 32.50 | | | | |

**20 DALASIS** **KM# 39** **Weight:** 31.4700 g. **Composition:** 0.9250 Silver .9359 oz. ASW **Subject:** Mungo Park

| Date | Mintage | F | VF | XF | Unc | BU |
|---|---|---|---|---|---|---|
| 1994 Proof | Est. 10,000 | Value: 32.50 | | | | |

**20 DALASIS** **KM# 47** **Weight:** 31.4700 g. **Composition:** 0.9250 Silver .9359 oz. ASW **Subject:** Olympic Games 1996 **Obverse:** National arms **Reverse:** Two runners crossing a finish line

| Date | Mintage | F | VF | XF | Unc | BU |
|---|---|---|---|---|---|---|
| 1994 Proof | — | Value: 22.50 | | | | |

**20 DALASIS** **KM# 37** **Composition:** Copper-Nickel **Subject:** 50th anniversary - United Nations

| Date | Mintage | F | VF | XF | Unc | BU |
|---|---|---|---|---|---|---|
| 1995 | — | — | — | — | 8.00 | — |

**20 DALASIS** **KM# 37a** **Weight:** 28.2800 g. **Composition:** 0.9250 Silver .8411 oz. ASW **Subject:** 50th anniversary - United Nations

| Date | Mintage | F | VF | XF | Unc | BU |
|---|---|---|---|---|---|---|
| 1995 Proof | — | Value: 35.00 | | | | |

**20 DALASIS** **KM# 41** **Weight:** 31.4700 g. **Composition:** 0.9250 Silver .9359 oz. ASW **Subject:** Protect our world

| Date | Mintage | F | VF | XF | Unc | BU |
|---|---|---|---|---|---|---|
| 1995 Proof | Est. 10,000 | Value: 40.00 | | | | |

**20 DALASIS** **KM# 42** **Weight:** 7.7760 g. **Composition:** 0.5833 Gold .1458 oz. AGW **Subject:** Endangered wildife **Reverse:** Black rhinoceros

| Date | Mintage | F | VF | XF | Unc | BU |
|---|---|---|---|---|---|---|
| 1995 | Est. 2,000 | — | — | — | 100 | — |

**20 DALASIS** **KM# 43** **Weight:** 7.7760 g. **Composition:** 0.5833 Gold .1458 oz. AGW **Subject:** Endangered wildife **Reverse:** African elephant

| Date | Mintage | F | VF | XF | Unc | BU |
|---|---|---|---|---|---|---|
| 1995 | Est. 2,000 | — | — | — | 100 | — |

**20 DALASIS** **KM# 44** **Weight:** 31.4700 g. **Composition:** 0.9250 Silver .9359 oz. ASW **Subject:** Victorian Age **Reverse:** Queen Victoria with first steam locomotive

| Date | Mintage | F | VF | XF | Unc | BU |
|---|---|---|---|---|---|---|
| 1996 | Est. 10,000 | — | — | — | 42.50 | — |

**20 DALASIS** **KM# 51** **Weight:** 31.4700 g. **Composition:** 0.9990 Silver 1.0108 oz. ASW **Subject:** World Cup 1998 **Obverse:** National arms **Reverse:** Two soccer players

| Date | Mintage | F | VF | XF | Unc | BU |
|---|---|---|---|---|---|---|
| 1996 Proof | 10,000 | Value: 40.00 | | | | |

**40 DALASIS** **KM# 18** **Weight:** 35.2900 g. **Composition:** 0.9250 Silver 1.0495 oz. ASW **Subject:** Conservation **Reverse:** Aardvark

| Date | Mintage | F | VF | XF | Unc | BU |
|---|---|---|---|---|---|---|
| 1977 | 4,304 | — | — | — | 22.50 | — |

**40 DALASIS** **KM# 18a** **Weight:** 35.0000 g. **Composition:** 0.9250 Silver 1.0409 oz. ASW **Subject:** Conservation **Reverse:** Aardvark

| Date | Mintage | F | VF | XF | Unc | BU |
|---|---|---|---|---|---|---|
| 1977 Proof | 4,183 | Value: 32.50 | | | | |

**50 DALASIS** **KM# 52** **Weight:** 1.2441 g. **Composition:** 0.9990 Gold .0400 oz. AGW **Subject:** Kankan Manga Musa **Obverse:** National arms **Reverse:** Seated king and supplicant

| Date | Mintage | F | VF | XF | Unc | BU |
|---|---|---|---|---|---|---|
| 1997 Proof | — | Value: 40.00 | | | | |

**100 DALASIS** **KM# 45** **Weight:** 1000.0000 g. **Composition:** 0.9990 Silver 32.1186 oz. ASW **Subject:** Endangered wildlife **Obverse:** National arms **Reverse:** Lion family **Size:** 100 mm. **Note:** Illustration reduced.

| Date | Mintage | F | VF | XF | Unc | BU |
|---|---|---|---|---|---|---|
| 1996 Proof | 1,000 | Value: 500 | | | | |

**100 DALASIS** **KM# 53** **Weight:** 3.1100 g. **Composition:** 0.5833 Gold .0583 oz. AGW **Subject:** Olympic Games 2000 **Obverse:** National arms **Reverse:** Silhouette of three runners

| Date | Mintage | F | VF | XF | Unc | BU |
|---|---|---|---|---|---|---|
| 1997 Proof | 5,000 | Value: 50.00 | | | | |

**150 DALASIS** **KM# 61** **Weight:** 7.7760 g. **Composition:** 0.5830 Gold .1458 oz. AGW **Subject:** British year of 3 kings and Queen Mother **Obverse:** National arms **Reverse:** Busts of Edward VIII, George V and George VI facing within circles

| Date | Mintage | F | VF | XF | Unc | BU |
|---|---|---|---|---|---|---|
| 1996 Proof | — | Value: 145 | | | | |

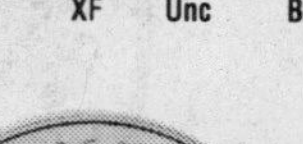


**200 DALASIS** **KM# 48** **Weight:** 31.1035 g. **Composition:** 0.9990 Gold 1 oz. AGW **Subject:** Endangered wildlife **Reverse:** Lion

| Date | Mintage | F | VF | XF | Unc | BU |
|---|---|---|---|---|---|---|
| 1996 Proof | 1,000 | Value: 500 | | | | |

**250 DALASIS** **KM# 22** **Weight:** 15.9800 g. **Composition:** 0.9170 Gold .4712 oz. AGW **Subject:** Year of the Scout

| Date | Mintage | F | VF | XF | Unc | BU |
|---|---|---|---|---|---|---|
| 1983 | 2,000 | — | — | — | 250 | — |
| 1983 Proof | 2,000 | Value: 325 | | | | |

**250 DALASIS** **KM# 31** **Weight:** 47.5400 g. **Composition:** 0.9170 Gold 1.4011 oz. AGW **Subject:** Papal visit **Obverse:** National coat of arms **Reverse:** Pope John Paul II giving a blessing

| Date | Mintage | F | VF | XF | Unc | BU |
|---|---|---|---|---|---|---|
| 1992 Proof | 100 | Value: 1,200 | | | | |

**500 DALASIS** KM# 19 **Weight:** 33.4370 g. **Composition:** 0.9000 Gold .9676 oz. AGW **Subject:** Conservation **Reverse:** Sitatunga

| Date | Mintage | F | VF | XF | Unc | BU |
|---|---|---|---|---|---|---|
| 1977 | 699 | — | — | — | 500 | — |
| 1977 Proof | 285 | Value: 750 | | | | |

**1000 DALASIS** KM# 25 **Weight:** 10.0000 g. **Composition:** 0.9170 Gold .2948 oz. AGW **Subject:** World Wildlife Fund **Reverse:** Gambian puffback bird

| Date | Mintage | F | VF | XF | Unc | BU |
|---|---|---|---|---|---|---|
| 1987 Proof | Est. 5,000 | Value: 185 | | | | |

**1000 DALASIS** KM# 27 **Weight:** 10.0000 g. **Composition:** 0.9170 Gold .2948 oz. AGW **Subject:** Save the Children Fund

| Date | Mintage | F | VF | XF | Unc | BU |
|---|---|---|---|---|---|---|
| 1989 Proof | Est. 3,000 | Value: 225 | | | | |

## PROOF SETS

| KM# | Date | Mintage | Identification | Issue Price | Mkt Val |
|---|---|---|---|---|---|
| PS1 | 1966 (6) | 5,100 | KM1-6 | 13.00 | 16.50 |
| PS2 | 1966 and 1970 (7) | 1,500 | KM1-6, 7a | 25.00 | 42.50 |
| PS3 | 1971 (6) | 26,249 | KM8-13 | — | 9.00 |
| PS4 | 1977 (2) | — | KM17a, 18a | 60.00 | 55.00 |

# GEORGIA

Georgia (formerly the Georgian Social Democratic Republic under the U.S.S.R.), is bounded by the Black Sea to the west and by Turkey, Armenia and Azerbaijan. It occupies the western part of Transcaucasia covering an area of 26,900 sq. mi. (69,700 sq. km.) and a population of 5.7 million. Capitol: Tbilisi. Hydro-electricity, minerals, forestry and agriculture are the chief industries.

After the Russian Revolution the Georgians, Armenians, and Azerbaijanis formed the short-lived Transcaucasian Federal Republic on Sept. 20, 1917, which broke up into three independent republics on May 26, 1918. A Germano-- Georgian treaty was signed on May 28, 1918, followed by a Turko-Georgian peace treaty on June 4. The end of WW I and the collapse of the central powers allowed free elections.

On May 20, 1920, Soviet Russia concluded a peace treaty, recognizing its independence, but later invaded on Feb. 11, 1921 and a soviet republic was proclaimed. On March 12, 1922 Stalin included Georgia in a newly formed Transcaucasian Soviet Federated Socialist Republic. On Dec. 5, 1936 the T.S.F.S.R. was dissolved and Georgia became a direct member of the U.S.S.R. The collapse of the U.S.S.R. allowed full transition to independence and on April 9, 1991 a unanimous vote declared the republic an independent state based on its original treaty of independence of May 1918.

## REPUBLIC (C.I.S.)

### 100 Thetri = 1 Lari.

**THETRI** KM# 76 **Composition:** Stainless Steel

| Date | Mintage | F | VF | XF | Unc | BU |
|---|---|---|---|---|---|---|
| 1993 | — | — | — | — | 0.25 | — |

**2 THETRI** KM# 77 **Composition:** Stainless Steel

| Date | Mintage | F | VF | XF | Unc | BU |
|---|---|---|---|---|---|---|
| 1993 | — | — | — | — | 0.35 | — |

**5 THETRI** KM# 78 **Composition:** Stainless Steel

| Date | Mintage | F | VF | XF | Unc | BU |
|---|---|---|---|---|---|---|
| 1993 | — | — | — | — | 0.80 | — |

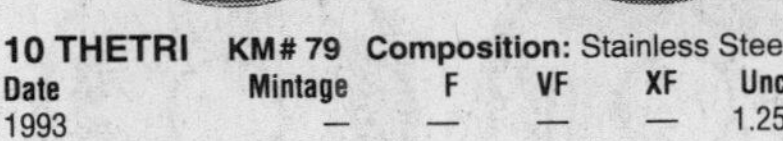

**10 THETRI** KM# 79 **Composition:** Stainless Steel

| Date | Mintage | F | VF | XF | Unc | BU |
|---|---|---|---|---|---|---|
| 1993 | — | — | — | — | 1.25 | — |

**20 THETRI** KM# 80 **Composition:** Stainless Steel

| Date | Mintage | F | VF | XF | Unc | BU |
|---|---|---|---|---|---|---|
| 1993 | — | — | — | — | 1.50 | — |

**50 THETRI** KM# 81 **Composition:** Brass

| Date | Mintage | F | VF | XF | Unc | BU |
|---|---|---|---|---|---|---|
| 1993 | — | — | — | — | 2.00 | — |

**10 LARI** KM# 83 **Weight:** 28.2800 g. **Composition:** 0.9250 Silver .8410 oz. ASW **Subject:** State System 3,000 Years **Obverse:** Denomination **Reverse:** Eagle and lion **Edge:** Reeded **Size:** 38.6 mm.

| Date | Mintage | F | VF | XF | Unc | BU |
|---|---|---|---|---|---|---|
| 2000 Proof | 1,000 | Value: 55.00 | | | | |

**10 LARI** KM# 84 **Weight:** 28.2800 g. **Composition:** 0.9250 Silver .8410 oz. ASW **Subject:** Birth of Jesus 2,000th Anniversary **Obverse:** Denomination **Reverse:** Holy robe in center of arms

| Date | Mintage | F | VF | XF | Unc | BU |
|---|---|---|---|---|---|---|
| 2000 Proof | 1,000 | Value: 55.00 | | | | |

**500 LARI** KM# 82 **Weight:** 17.0000 g. **Composition:** 0.9170 Gold .5010 oz. AGW **Subject:** 50th anniversary - defeat of Fascism **Reverse:** Profiles of Stalin, Roosevelt, Churchill and de Gaulle

| Date | Mintage | F | VF | XF | Unc | BU |
|---|---|---|---|---|---|---|
| 1995 Proof | 2,000 | Value: 500 | | | | |

## MINT SETS

| KM# | Date | Mintage | Identification | Issue Price | Mkt Val |
|---|---|---|---|---|---|
| MS1 | 1993 (6) | — | KM76-81 | — | 7.50 |

# GERMAN EAST AFRICA

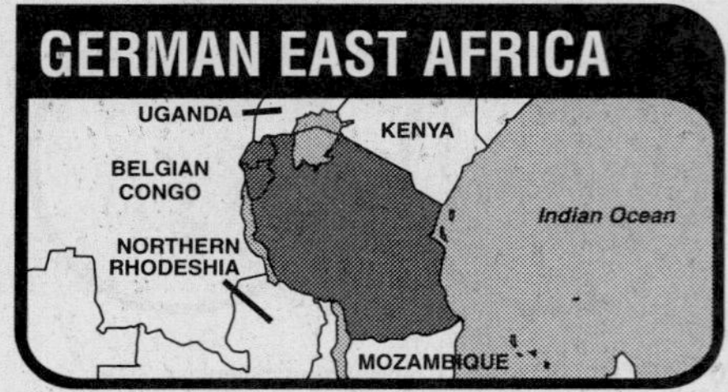


German East Africa (Tanganyika), located on the coast of east-central Africa between British East Africa (nowKenya) and Portuguese East Africa (now Mozambique),had an area of 362,284 sq. mi. (938,216 sq. km.) and apopulation of about 6 million. Capital: Dar es Salaam.Chief products prior to German control were ivory andslaves; after German control, sisal, coffee, and rubber.

Germany acquired control of the area by treaties with coastal chiefs in 1884, established it as a protectorate in1891, and proclaimed it the Colony of German East Africain 1897. After World War I, Tanganyika was entrusted toGreat Britain as a League of Nations mandate, and after World War II as a United Nations trust territory.Tanganyika became an independent nation within the-British Commonwealth on Dec. 9, 1961.Coins dated up until 1901 were issued by theGerman East Africa Company. From 1904 onwards,coins were issued by the government.

**TITLES**

Sharaka(t) Almania شراكتة المانيا

**RULERS**

Wilhelm II, 1888-1918

**MINT MARKS**

A - Berlin
J - Hamburg
T - Tabora

**MONETARY SYSTEM**

Until 1904
64 Pesa = 1 Rupie
Commencing 1904
100 Heller = 1 Rupie

## COLONIAL

### STANDARD COINAGE

64 Pesa = 1 Rupee until 1904; 100 Heller = 1 Rupie commencing 1904

**1/2 HELLER** **KM# 6** **Composition:** Bronze

| Date | Mintage | F | VF | XF | Unc | BU |
|---|---|---|---|---|---|---|
| 1904A | 1,201,000 | 1.25 | 3.50 | 6.50 | 28.00 | — |
| 1905A | 7,192,000 | 2.25 | 5.25 | 9.00 | 32.50 | — |
| 1905J | 4,000,000 | 2.25 | 5.25 | 9.00 | 32.50 | — |
| 1906J | 6,000,000 | 1.25 | 3.50 | 6.50 | 28.00 | — |
| 1906J Proof | — | Value: 250 | | | | |

**HELLER** **KM# 7** **Composition:** Bronze

| Date | Mintage | F | VF | XF | Unc | BU |
|---|---|---|---|---|---|---|
| 1904A | 10,256,000 | 0.75 | 2.25 | 4.00 | 20.00 | — |
| 1904A Proof | — | Value: 125 | | | | |
| 1904J | 2,500,000 | 0.75 | 2.25 | 7.00 | 25.00 | — |
| 1905A | 3,760,000 | 0.75 | 2.25 | 7.00 | 25.00 | — |
| 1905A Proof | — | Value: 125 | | | | |
| 1905J | 7,556,000 | 0.75 | 2.25 | 4.00 | 20.00 | — |
| 1906A | 3,004,000 | 0.75 | 2.25 | 7.00 | 25.00 | — |
| 1906A Proof | — | Value: 125 | | | | |
| 1906J | 1,962,000 | 0.75 | 2.25 | 7.00 | 25.00 | — |
| 1907J | 17,790,000 | 0.75 | 1.50 | 4.00 | 20.00 | — |
| 1908J | 12,205,000 | 0.75 | 1.50 | 4.00 | 20.00 | — |
| 1908J Proof | — | Value: 135 | | | | |
| 1909J | 1,698,000 | 2.50 | 7.50 | 15.00 | 35.00 | — |
| 1909J Proof | — | Value: 135 | | | | |
| 1910J | 5,096,000 | 0.75 | 1.50 | 4.00 | 20.00 | — |
| 1910J Proof | — | Value: 135 | | | | |
| 1911J | 6,420,000 | 0.75 | 1.50 | 4.00 | 20.00 | — |
| 1911J Proof | — | Value: 135 | | | | |
| 1912J | 7,012,000 | 0.75 | 1.50 | 4.00 | 20.00 | — |
| 1912J Proof | — | Value: 135 | | | | |

| Date | Mintage | F | VF | XF | Unc | BU |
|---|---|---|---|---|---|---|
| 1913A | — | 0.75 | 1.50 | 4.00 | 20.00 | — |
| 1913A Proof | — | Value: 135 | | | | |
| 1913J | 5,186,000 | 0.75 | 1.50 | 4.00 | 20.00 | — |
| 1913J Proof | — | Value: 150 | | | | |

**5 HELLER** **KM# 11** **Composition:** Bronze

| Date | Mintage | F | VF | XF | Unc | BU |
|---|---|---|---|---|---|---|
| 1908J | 600,000 | 15.00 | 30.00 | 70.00 | 550 | — |
| 1908J Proof | — | Value: 975 | | | | |
| 1909J | 756,000 | 15.00 | 30.00 | 70.00 | 550 | — |
| 1909J Proof | 60 | Value: 975 | | | | |

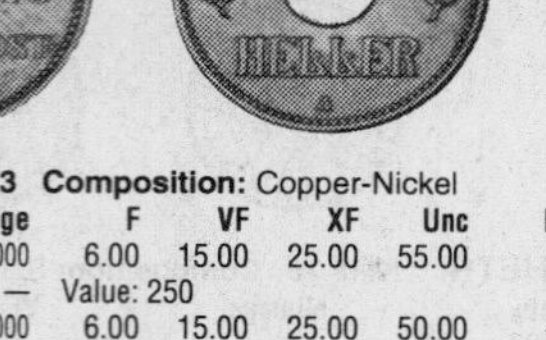

**5 HELLER** **KM# 13** **Composition:** Copper-Nickel

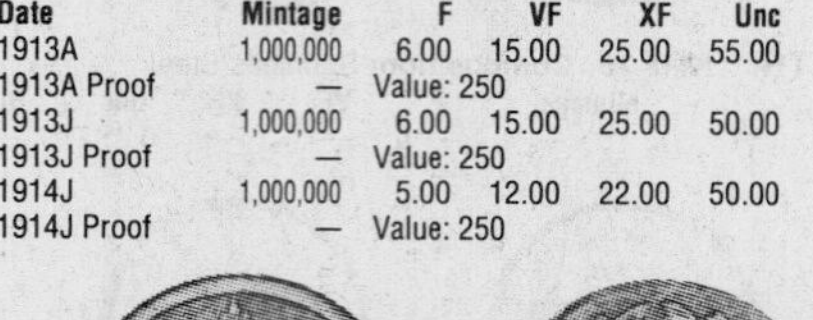

| Date | Mintage | F | VF | XF | Unc | BU |
|---|---|---|---|---|---|---|
| 1913A | 1,000,000 | 6.00 | 15.00 | 25.00 | 55.00 | — |
| 1913A Proof | — | Value: 250 | | | | |
| 1913J | 1,000,000 | 6.00 | 15.00 | 25.00 | 50.00 | — |
| 1913J Proof | — | Value: 250 | | | | |
| 1914J | 1,000,000 | 5.00 | 12.00 | 22.00 | 50.00 | — |
| 1914J Proof | — | Value: 250 | | | | |

**5 HELLER** **KM# 14.1** **Composition:** Brass **Obverse:** Oval base on crown **Note:** 1-1/2 - 2 milimeters thick.

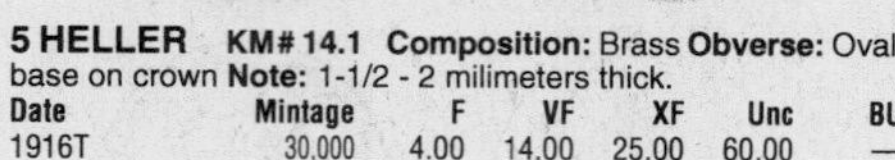

| Date | Mintage | F | VF | XF | Unc | BU |
|---|---|---|---|---|---|---|
| 1916T | 30,000 | 4.00 | 14.00 | 25.00 | 60.00 | — |

**5 HELLER** **KM# 14.2** **Composition:** Brass **Obverse:** Flat base on crown **Note:** 1 milimeter or less thick.

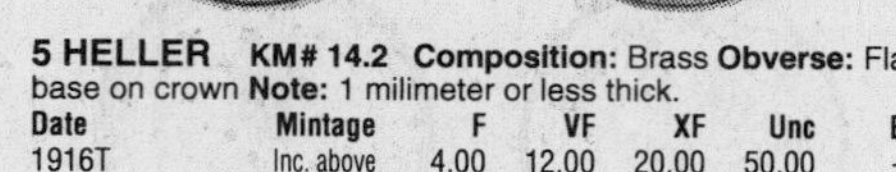

| Date | Mintage | F | VF | XF | Unc | BU |
|---|---|---|---|---|---|---|
| 1916T | Inc. above | 4.00 | 12.00 | 20.00 | 50.00 | — |

**10 HELLER** **KM# 12** **Composition:** Copper-Nickel

| Date | Mintage | F | VF | XF | Unc | BU |
|---|---|---|---|---|---|---|
| 1908J | — | 5.00 | 15.00 | 30.00 | 90.00 | — |
| 1908J Proof | — | Value: 350 | | | | |
| 1909J | 1,990,000 | 3.00 | 10.00 | 20.00 | 60.00 | — |
| 1909J Proof | — | Value: 275 | | | | |
| 1910J | 500,000 | 3.00 | 10.00 | 20.00 | 60.00 | — |
| 1910J Proof | — | Value: 275 | | | | |
| 1911A | 500,000 | 5.00 | 15.00 | 35.00 | 90.00 | — |
| 1911A Proof | — | Value: 300 | | | | |
| 1914J | 200,000 | 5.00 | 15.00 | 35.00 | 90.00 | — |
| 1914 Proof | — | Value: 285 | | | | |

Obverse A
Large Crown

Obverse B
Small Crown

Reverse A
Curled Tip On Second L

Reverse B
Pointed Tips On L's

Reverse C
Curled Tips On L's

**20 HELLER** **KM# 15** **Composition:** Copper **Note:** Obverse A and reverse A.

| Date | Mintage | F | VF | XF | Unc | BU |
|---|---|---|---|---|---|---|
| 1916T | 300,000 | 6.00 | 10.00 | 20.00 | 85.00 | — |
| **Note:** Obverse A and reverse A | | | | | | |
| 1916T | Inc. above | 125 | 200 | 350 | — | — |
| **Note:** Obverse A and reverse B | | | | | | |
| 1916T | Inc. above | 60.00 | 85.00 | 140 | — | — |
| **Note:** Obverse B and reverse A | | | | | | |
| 1916T | Inc. above | 6.00 | 10.00 | 20.00 | 60.00 | — |
| **Note:** Obverse B and reverse B | | | | | | |
| 1916T Rare | Inc. above | — | — | — | — | — |
| **Note:** Obverse A and reverse C | | | | | | |
| 1916T Rare | Inc. above | — | — | — | — | — |
| **Note:** Obverse B and reverse C | | | | | | |

**20 HELLER** **KM# 15a** **Composition:** Brass

| Date | Mintage | F | VF | XF | Unc | BU |
|---|---|---|---|---|---|---|
| 1916T | 1,600,000 | 6.00 | 10.00 | 20.00 | 75.00 | — |
| **Note:** Obverse A and reverse A | | | | | | |
| 1916T | Inc. above | 7.00 | 12.50 | 25.00 | 85.00 | — |
| **Note:** Obverse A and reverse B | | | | | | |
| 1916T | Inc. above | 7.00 | 12.50 | 25.00 | 85.00 | — |
| **Note:** Obverse B and reverse A | | | | | | |
| 1916T | Inc. above | 6.00 | 10.00 | 20.00 | 65.00 | — |
| **Note:** Obverse B and reverse B | | | | | | |
| 1916T | Inc. above | 10.00 | 30.00 | 45.00 | 125 | — |
| **Note:** Obverse A and reverse C | | | | | | |
| 1916T | Inc. above | 12.00 | 35.00 | 50.00 | 135 | — |
| **Note:** Obverse B and reverse C | | | | | | |

**1/4 RUPIE** **KM# 3** **Weight:** 2.9160 g. **Composition:** 0.9170 Silver .0859 oz. ASW

| Date | Mintage | F | VF | XF | Unc | BU |
|---|---|---|---|---|---|---|
| 1901 | 350,000 | 6.00 | 18.00 | 45.00 | 140 | — |

**1/4 RUPIE** **KM# 8** **Weight:** 2.9160 g. **Composition:** 0.9170 Silver .0859 oz. ASW

| Date | Mintage | F | VF | XF | Unc | BU |
|---|---|---|---|---|---|---|
| 1904A | 300,000 | 5.00 | 12.00 | 37.50 | 110 | — |
| 1904A Proof | — | Value: 300 | | | | |
| 1906A | 300,000 | 5.00 | 12.00 | 37.50 | 110 | — |
| 1906A Proof | — | Value: 300 | | | | |
| 1906J | 100,000 | 10.00 | 35.00 | 75.00 | 250 | — |
| 1907J | 200,000 | 7.00 | 18.00 | 50.00 | 175 | — |
| 1907J Proof | — | Value: 375 | | | | |
| 1909A | 300,000 | 6.00 | 13.50 | 40.00 | 150 | — |
| 1910J | 600,000 | 5.00 | 12.00 | 37.50 | 110 | — |
| 1910J Proof | — | Value: 350 | | | | |
| 1912J | 400,000 | 6.00 | 13.50 | 40.00 | 120 | — |
| 1912J Proof | — | Value: 350 | | | | |
| 1913A | 200,000 | 6.50 | 14.50 | 42.50 | 135 | — |
| 1913A Proof | — | Value: 350 | | | | |
| 1913J | 400,000 | 5.00 | 12.00 | 37.50 | 110 | — |
| 1913J Proof | — | Value: 300 | | | | |
| 1914J | 200,000 | 6.50 | 14.50 | 42.50 | 125 | — |
| 1914J Proof | — | Value: 300 | | | | |

**1/2 RUPIE** **KM# 4** **Weight:** 5.8319 g. **Composition:** 0.9170 Silver .1719 oz. ASW

| Date | Mintage | F | VF | XF | Unc | BU |
|---|---|---|---|---|---|---|
| 1901 | 215,000 | 15.00 | 40.00 | 100 | 300 | — |

**1/2 RUPIE** **KM# 9** **Weight:** 5.8319 g. **Composition:** 0.9170 Silver .1719 oz. ASW

| Date | Mintage | F | VF | XF | Unc | BU |
|---|---|---|---|---|---|---|
| 1904A | 400,000 | 15.00 | 40.00 | 95.00 | 275 | — |
| 1904A Proof | — | Value: 450 | | | | |
| 1906A | 50,000 | 75.00 | 150 | 350 | 750 | — |
| 1906A Proof | — | Value: 1,000 | | | | |
| 1906J | 50,000 | 75.00 | 150 | 350 | 750 | — |
| 1907J | 140,000 | 20.00 | 50.00 | 125 | 325 | — |
| 1907J Proof | — | Value: 550 | | | | |
| 1909A | 100,000 | 30.00 | 65.00 | 150 | 400 | — |
| 1910J | 300,000 | 20.00 | 40.00 | 100 | 300 | — |
| 1910J Proof | — | Value: 450 | | | | |
| 1912J | 200,000 | 15.00 | 40.00 | 95.00 | 275 | — |
| 1913A | 100,000 | 20.00 | 45.00 | 110 | 290 | — |
| 1913J | 200,000 | 15.00 | 40.00 | 95.00 | 265 | — |
| 1914J | 100,000 | 20.00 | 45.00 | 100 | 285 | — |

**RUPIE** **KM# 2** **Weight:** 11.6638 g. **Composition:** 0.9170 Silver .3437 oz. ASW

| Date | Mintage | F | VF | XF | Unc | BU |
|---|---|---|---|---|---|---|
| 1901 | 319,000 | 12.50 | 25.00 | 75.00 | 225 | — |
| 1902 | 151,000 | 20.00 | 40.00 | 125 | 450 | — |

**RUPIE** **KM# 10** **Weight:** 11.6638 g. **Composition:** 0.9170 Silver .3437 oz. ASW

| Date | Mintage | F | VF | XF | Unc | BU |
|---|---|---|---|---|---|---|
| 1904A | 1,000,000 | 11.50 | 22.50 | 45.00 | 165 | — |
| 1904A Proof | — | Value: 425 | | | | |
| 1905A | 300,000 | 15.00 | 27.50 | 60.00 | 185 | — |
| 1905A Proof | — | Value: 450 | | | | |
| 1905J | 1,000,000 | 11.50 | 22.50 | 45.00 | 150 | — |
| 1905J Proof | — | Value: 400 | | | | |
| 1906A | 950,000 | 11.50 | 22.50 | 45.00 | 160 | — |
| 1906J | 700,000 | 15.00 | 27.50 | 65.00 | 175 | — |
| 1907J | 880,000 | 9.00 | 15.00 | 35.00 | 180 | — |
| 1908J | 500,000 | 12.50 | 25.00 | 50.00 | 190 | — |
| 1908J Proof | — | Value: 450 | | | | |
| 1909A | 200,000 | 15.00 | 27.50 | 60.00 | 275 | — |
| 1910J | 270,000 | 9.00 | 15.00 | 35.00 | 200 | — |

| Date | Mintage | F | VF | XF | Unc | BU |
|---|---|---|---|---|---|---|
| 1911A | 300,000 | 12.50 | 25.00 | 50.00 | 175 | — |
| 1911A Proof | — | Value: 450 | | | | |
| 1911J | 1,400,000 | 9.00 | 15.00 | 35.00 | 150 | — |
| 1911J Proof | — | Value: 400 | | | | |
| 1912J | 300,000 | 12.50 | 25.00 | 50.00 | 165 | — |
| 1912J Proof | — | Value: 450 | | | | |
| 1913A | 400,000 | 12.50 | 25.00 | 50.00 | 160 | — |
| 1913J | 1,400,000 | 9.00 | 15.00 | 35.00 | 150 | — |
| 1913J Proof | — | Value: 400 | | | | |
| 1914J | 500,000 | 11.50 | 22.50 | 45.00 | 150 | — |

**15 RUPIEN** **KM# 16.1** **Weight:** 7.1680 g. **Composition:** 0.7500 Gold .1728 oz. AGW **Obverse:** Right arabesque ends below T of OSTAFRIKA

| Date | Mintage | F | VF | XF | Unc | BU |
|---|---|---|---|---|---|---|
| 1916T | 9,803 | 425 | 800 | 1,200 | 1,750 | — |

**15 RUPIEN** **KM# 16.2** **Weight:** 7.1680 g. **Composition:** 0.7500 Gold .1728 oz. AGW **Obverse:** Right arabesque ends below first A of OSTAFRIKA

| Date | Mintage | F | VF | XF | Unc | BU |
|---|---|---|---|---|---|---|
| 1916T | 6,395 | 450 | 850 | 1,250 | 1,800 | — |

## PATTERNS

Including off metal strikes

| KM# | Date | Mintage | Identification | Mkt Val |
|---|---|---|---|---|
| Pn4 | 1908 | — | 25 Pfennig. Nickel. With sprigs. | — |
| Pn1 | 1908 | — | 5 Heller. Bronze. | 650 |

| KM# | Date | Mintage | Identification | Mkt Val |
|---|---|---|---|---|
| Pn2 | 1908 | — | 10 Heller. Nickel. Without sprigs | 275 |
| Pn2a | 1908/1908 | — | 10 Heller. Nickel. Two obverses. | 300 |
| Pn3 | 1908 | — | 25 Pfennig. Nickel. With sprigs. | 175 |
| Pn5 | | — | 5 Rupien. White Metal. Uniface. | 260 |

# GERMAN STATES

Although the origin of the German Empire can be traced to the Treaty of Verdun that ceded Charlemagne's lands east of the Rhine to German Prince Louis, it was for centuries little more than a geographic expression, con- sisting of hundreds of effectively autonomous big and little states. Nominally the states owed their allegiance to the Holy Roman Emperor, who was also a German king, but as the Emperors exhibited less and less concern for Germany the actual power devolved on the lords of the individual states. The fragmentation of the empire climaxed with the tragic denouement of the Thirty Years War, 1618-48, which devastated much of Germany, destroyed its agriculture and medieval commercial eminence and ended the attempt of the Hapsburgs to unify Germany. Deprived of administrative capacity by a lack of resources, the imperial authority became utterly powerless. At this time Germany contained an estimated 1,800 individual states, some with a population of as little as 300. The German Empire of recent history (the creation of Bis- marck) was formed on April 14, 1871, when the king of Prussia became German Emperor William I. The new empire comprised 4 kingdoms, 6 grand duchies, 12 duchies and principalities, 3 free cities and the nonautonomous province of Alsace-Lorraine. The states had the right to issue gold and silver coins of higher value than 1 Mark; coins of 1 Mark and under were general issues of the empire.

**MINT MARKS**

A - Berlin, 1750-date
D - Munich (Germany), 1872-date
E - Muldenhutten (Germany), 1887-1953
F - Stuttgart (Germany) 1872-date
G - Karlsruhe (Germany) 1872-date
J - Hamburg (Germany) 1873-date

**MONETARY SYSTEM**

After the German unification in 1871 when the old Thaler system was abandoned in favor of the Mark system (100 Pfennig = 1 Mark) the Vereinsthaler continued to circulate as a legal tender 3 Mark coin, and the double Thaler as a 6 Mark coin until 1908. In 1908 the Vereinsthalers were officially demonetized and the Thaler coinage was replaced by the new 3 Mark coin which had the same specifications as the old Vereinsthaler. The double Thaler coinage was not replaced as there was no great demand for a 6 Mark coin. Until the 1930's the German public continued to refer to the 3 Mark piece as a "Thaler".<

**Commencing 1871**

100 Pfennig = 1 Mark

**VERRECHNUNGS & GUTSCHRIFTS TOKENS**

These were metallic indebtedness receipts used for commercial and banking purposes due to the lack of available subsidiary coinage. These tokens could be redeemed in sufficient quantities.

## ANHALT-DESSAU

Anhalt-Dessau was part of the 1252 division that included Zerbst and Köthen. In 1396, Anhalt-Zerbst was divided into Anhalt-Zerbst and Anhalt-Dessau. In 1508, Anhalt-Zerbst was absorbed into Anhalt-Dessau. The latter was given to the eldest son of Joachim Ernst in the division of 1603. As other lines became extinct, they fell to Anhalt-Dessau, which united all territories of the dynasty in 1863. The last ruler was forced to give up power at the end of World War I.

**RULERS**

Friedrich I, 1871-1904
Friedrich II, 1904-1918

**MINT MARK**

A – Berlin Mint, 1839-1914

## DUCHY

**2 MARK** **KM#27** **Weight:** 11.1110 g. **Composition:** 0.9000 Silver .3215 oz. ASW **Ruler:** Friedrich II

| Date | Mintage | F | VF | XF | Unc | BU |
|---|---|---|---|---|---|---|
| 1904A | 50,000 | 150 | 300 | 500 | 1,000 | — |
| 1904A Proof | 150 | Value: 1,100 | | | | |

**3 MARK** **KM#29** **Weight:** 16.6670 g. **Composition:** 0.9000 Silver .4823 oz. ASW **Ruler:** Friedrich II

| Date | Mintage | F | VF | XF | Unc | BU |
|---|---|---|---|---|---|---|
| 1909A | 100,000 | 35.00 | 75.00 | 150 | 285 | — |
| 1911A | 100,000 | 35.00 | 75.00 | 150 | 285 | — |
| Common dat Proof | — | Value: 400 | | | | |

**3 MARK** **KM#30** **Weight:** 16.6670 g. **Composition:** 0.9000 Silver .4823 oz. ASW **Ruler:** Friedrich II **Subject:** Silver wedding anniversary

| Date | Mintage | F | VF | XF | Unc | BU |
|---|---|---|---|---|---|---|
| 1914A | 200,000 | 25.00 | 50.00 | 85.00 | 165 | — |
| 1914A Proof | 1,000 | Value: 275 | | | | |

**5 MARK** **KM#31** **Weight:** 27.7770 g. **Composition:** 0.9000 Silver .8038 oz. ASW **Ruler:** Friedrich II **Subject:** Silver wedding anniversary

| Date | Mintage | F | VF | XF | Unc | BU |
|---|---|---|---|---|---|---|
| 1914A | 30,000 | 65.00 | 180 | 285 | 450 | — |
| 1914A Proof | 1,000 | Value: 600 | | | | |

**10 MARK** **KM#25** **Weight:** 3.9820 g. **Composition:** 0.9000 Gold .1152 oz. AGW **Ruler:** Friedrich I **Obverse:** Bust right

| Date | Mintage | F | VF | XF | Unc | BU |
|---|---|---|---|---|---|---|
| 1901A | 20,000 | 400 | 700 | 1,000 | 1,500 | — |
| 1901A Proof | 200 | Value: 1,800 | | | | |

**20 MARK** **KM#26** **Weight:** 7.9650 g. **Composition:** 0.9000 Gold .2304 oz. AGW **Ruler:** Friedrich I **Obverse:** Bust right

| Date | Mintage | F | VF | XF | Unc | BU |
|---|---|---|---|---|---|---|
| 1901A | 15,000 | 425 | 725 | 1,100 | 1,400 | — |
| 1901A Proof | 200 | Value: 2,200 | | | | |

**20 MARK** **KM#28** **Weight:** 7.9650 g. **Composition:** 0.9000 Gold .2304 oz. AGW **Ruler:** Friedrich II **Obverse:** Bust left

| Date | Mintage | F | VF | XF | Unc | BU |
|---|---|---|---|---|---|---|
| 1904A | 25,000 | 400 | 700 | 1,000 | 2,000 | — |
| 1904A Proof | 200 | Value: 2,600 | | | | |

### PATTERNS

Including off metal strikes

| KM# | Date | Mintage | Identification | Mkt Val |
|---|---|---|---|---|
| Pn1 | 1901 | — | 2 Mark. Silver. KM23. | — |
| Pn2 | 1901 | — | 5 Mark. Silver. KM24. | — |
| Pn3 | 1914 | — | 3 Mark. Silver. Wreath around rim. KM30. | — |
| Pn4 | 1914 | — | 3 Mark. Brass. | — |
| Pn5 | 1914 | — | 5 Mark. Silver. Pn6. KM31. | — |
| Pn6 | 1914 | — | 5 Mark. Silver. Lettered edge. | — |
| Pn7 | 1914 | — | 5 Mark. Silver. Plain edge. | — |

# BADEN

Although Baden-Durlach was founded upon the division of Baden in 1515, the youngest son of Christoph I did not begin ruling in his own right until the demise of his father. This part of Baden was called Pforzheim until 1565, when the margrave moved his seat from the former to Durlach, located to the west and nearer the Rhine. After the male line of Baden-Baden failed in 1771 and the two parts of Baden were reunited, the fortunes of the margraviate continued to grow. Karlsruhe, near Durlach, was developed into a well-planned capital city. The ruler was given the rank of elector in 1803, only to be raised to grand duke three years later. The monarchy came to an end in 1918, but had by this time become one of the largest states in Germany.

**RULERS**

Friedrich I, Prince Regent 1852-1856, Grand Duke 1856-1907
Friedrich II, 1907-1918

## GRAND DUCHY

### Durlach Line.

**2 MARK** **KM# 269** **Weight:** 11.1110 g. **Composition:** 0.9000 Silver .3215 oz. ASW **Ruler:** Friedrich I as Grand Duke **Obverse:** Head left

| Date | Mintage | F | VF | XF | Unc | BU |
|---|---|---|---|---|---|---|
| 1901G | 451,000 | 25.00 | 75.00 | 250 | 750 | — |
| 1901G Proof | — | Value: 2,500 | | | | |
| 1902G | 5,368 | 250 | 750 | 1,400 | 3,000 | — |
| 1902G Proof | — | Value: 3,500 | | | | |

**2 MARK** **KM# 271** **Weight:** 11.1110 g. **Composition:** 0.9000 Silver .3215 oz. ASW **Ruler:** Friedrich I as Grand Duke **Subject:** 50th year of reign

| Date | Mintage | F | VF | XF | Unc | BU |
|---|---|---|---|---|---|---|
| 1902 | 375,000 | 12.00 | 22.00 | 32.00 | 60.00 | — |

**2 MARK** **KM# 272** **Weight:** 11.1110 g. **Composition:** 0.9000 Silver .3215 oz. ASW **Ruler:** Friedrich I as Grand Duke

| Date | Mintage | F | VF | XF | Unc | BU |
|---|---|---|---|---|---|---|
| 1902G | 198,000 | 25.00 | 60.00 | 120 | 300 | — |
| 1903G | 494,000 | 20.00 | 45.00 | 110 | 200 | — |
| 1904G | 1,122,000 | 20.00 | 40.00 | 70.00 | 200 | — |
| 1905G | 610,000 | 20.00 | 45.00 | 60.00 | 200 | — |
| 1906G | 108,000 | 45.00 | 90.00 | 180 | 500 | — |
| 1907G | 913,000 | 20.00 | 40.00 | 55.00 | 200 | — |

**2 MARK** **KM# 276** **Weight:** 11.1110 g. **Composition:** 0.9000 Silver .3215 oz. ASW **Ruler:** Friedrich I as Grand Duke **Subject:** Golden wedding anniversary

| Date | Mintage | F | VF | XF | Unc | BU |
|---|---|---|---|---|---|---|
| 1906 | 350,000 | 15.00 | 30.00 | 40.00 | 65.00 | — |
| 1906 Matte proof | — | — | — | — | — | — |

**2 MARK** **KM# 278** **Weight:** 11.1110 g. **Composition:** 0.9000 Silver .3215 oz. ASW **Ruler:** Friedrich I as Grand Duke **Subject:** Death of Friedrich

| Date | Mintage | F | VF | XF | Unc | BU |
|---|---|---|---|---|---|---|
| 1907 | 350,000 | 20.00 | 40.00 | 50.00 | 80.00 | — |
| 1907 Proof | — | Value: 150 | | | | |

**2 MARK** **KM# 283** **Weight:** 11.1110 g. **Composition:** 0.9000 Silver .3215 oz. ASW **Ruler:** Friedrich II **Subject:** Head left

| Date | Mintage | F | VF | XF | Unc | BU |
|---|---|---|---|---|---|---|
| 1911G | 80,000 | 125 | 300 | 425 | 850 | — |
| 1913G | 140,000 | 100 | 225 | 375 | 750 | — |
| (1911-1913) Proof | — | Value: 1,200 | | | | |

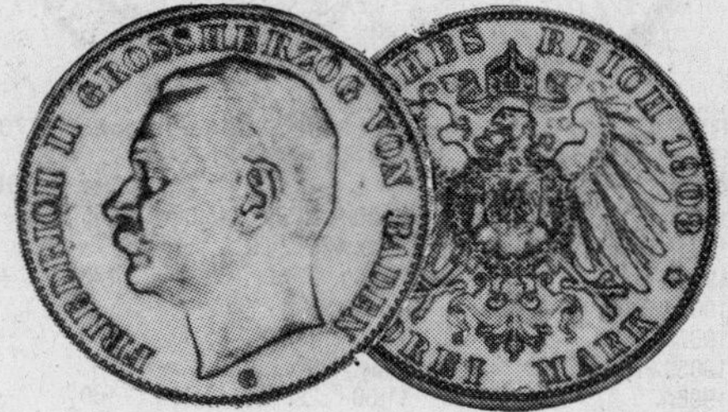

**3 MARK** **KM# 280** **Weight:** 16.6670 g. **Composition:** 0.9000 Silver .4823 oz. ASW **Ruler:** Friedrich II **Obverse:** Head left

| Date | Mintage | F | VF | XF | Unc | BU |
|---|---|---|---|---|---|---|
| 1908G | 300,000 | 10.00 | 22.00 | 35.00 | 75.00 | — |
| 1909G | 760,000 | 10.00 | 22.00 | 35.00 | 75.00 | — |
| 1910G | 670,000 | 10.00 | 22.00 | 35.00 | 75.00 | — |
| 1911G | 380,000 | 10.00 | 22.00 | 35.00 | 75.00 | — |
| 1912G | 840,000 | 10.00 | 22.00 | 35.00 | 75.00 | — |
| 1914G | 410,000 | 10.00 | 22.00 | 30.00 | 70.00 | — |
| 1915G | 170,000 | 20.00 | 60.00 | 90.00 | 200 | — |
| (1908-1915)G Proof | — | Value: 225 | | | | |

**5 MARK** **KM# 268** **Weight:** 27.7770 g. **Composition:** 0.9000 Silver .8038 oz. ASW **Ruler:** Friedrich I as Grand Duke

| Date | Mintage | F | VF | XF | Unc | BU |
|---|---|---|---|---|---|---|
| 1901G | 128,000 | 25.00 | 70.00 | 275 | 1,500 | — |
| 1902G | 43,000 | 35.00 | 85.00 | 250 | 2,000 | — |
| (1891-1902)G Proof | — | Value: 2,500 | | | | |

**5 MARK** **KM# 273** **Weight:** 27.7770 g. **Composition:** 0.9000 Silver .8038 oz. ASW **Ruler:** Friedrich I as Grand Duke **Subject:** 50th year of reign

| Date | Mintage | F | VF | XF | Unc | BU |
|---|---|---|---|---|---|---|
| 1902 | 50,000 | 35.00 | 75.00 | 135 | 185 | — |
| 1902 Proof | — | Value: 625 | | | | |

**5 MARK** **KM# 274** **Weight:** 27.7770 g. **Composition:** 0.9000 Silver .8038 oz. ASW **Ruler:** Friedrich I as Grand Duke

| Date | Mintage | F | VF | XF | Unc | BU |
|---|---|---|---|---|---|---|
| 1902G | 128,000 | 35.00 | 65.00 | 225 | 600 | — |
| 1903G | 439,000 | 20.00 | 45.00 | 165 | 585 | — |
| 1904G | 238,000 | 20.00 | 45.00 | 165 | 585 | — |
| 1907G | 244,000 | 20.00 | 45.00 | 165 | 585 | — |
| (1902-1907G Proof | — | Value: 800 | | | | |

**5 MARK** **KM# 277** **Weight:** 27.7770 g. **Composition:** 0.9000 Silver .8038 oz. ASW **Ruler:** Friedrich I as Grand Duke **Subject:** Golden wedding anniversary

| Date | Mintage | F | VF | XF | Unc | BU |
|---|---|---|---|---|---|---|
| 1906 | 60,000 | 35.00 | 75.00 | 125 | 175 | — |
| 1906 Proof | — | Value: 275 | | | | |

**5 MARK** **KM# 279** **Weight:** 27.7770 g. **Composition:** 0.9000 Silver .8038 oz. ASW **Ruler:** Friedrich I as Grand Duke **Subject:** Death of Friedrich

| Date | Mintage | F | VF | XF | Unc | BU |
|---|---|---|---|---|---|---|
| 1907 | 60,000 | 55.00 | 110 | 145 | 200 | — |
| 1907 Proof | — | Value: 275 | | | | |

**5 MARK** **KM# 281** **Weight:** 27.7770 g. **Composition:** 0.9000 Silver .8038 oz. ASW **Ruler:** Friedrich II **Subject:** Head left

| Date | Mintage | F | VF | XF | Unc | BU |
|---|---|---|---|---|---|---|
| 1908G | 180,000 | 40.00 | 60.00 | 175 | 700 | — |
| 1913G | 240,000 | 30.00 | 50.00 | 165 | 500 | — |
| (1908-1913G Proof | — | Value: 1,000 | | | | |

**10 MARK** **KM# 267** **Weight:** 3.9820 g. **Composition:** 0.9000 Gold .1152 oz. AGW **Ruler:** Friedrich I as Grand Duke **Subject:** Head left

| Date | Mintage | F | VF | XF | Unc | BU |
|---|---|---|---|---|---|---|
| 1901G | 91,000 | 125 | 165 | 225 | 350 | — |
| 1901G Proof | — | Value: 1,300 | | | | |

**10 MARK** **KM# 275** **Weight:** 3.9820 g. **Composition:** 0.9000 Gold .1152 oz. AGW **Ruler:** Friedrich I as Grand Duke

| Date | Mintage | F | VF | XF | Unc | BU |
|---|---|---|---|---|---|---|
| 1902G | 30,000 | 175 | 300 | 450 | 675 | — |
| 1903G | 110,000 | 125 | 200 | 250 | 375 | — |
| 1904G | 150,000 | 110 | 150 | 225 | 350 | — |
| 1905G | 96,000 | 125 | 200 | 250 | 375 | — |
| 1906G | 120,000 | 125 | 150 | 225 | 350 | — |
| 1907G | 120,000 | 110 | 150 | 225 | 350 | — |
| (1902-1907)G Proof | — | Value: 1,500 | | | | |

**10 MARK** **KM# 282** **Weight:** 3.9820 g. **Composition:** 0.9000 Gold .1152 oz. AGW **Ruler:** Friedrich II **Obverse:** Head right

| Date | Mintage | F | VF | XF | Unc | BU |
|---|---|---|---|---|---|---|
| 1909G | 86,000 | 225 | 500 | 650 | 950 | — |
| 1910G | 61,000 | 225 | 500 | 650 | 950 | — |
| 1911G | 29,000 | 2,000 | 4,500 | 6,500 | 8,500 | — |
| 1912G | 26,000 | 700 | 1,200 | 2,200 | 3,250 | — |
| 1913G | 42,000 | 500 | 800 | 1,150 | 2,000 | — |
| (1909-1913)G Proof | — | Value: 2,000 | | | | |

**20 MARK** **KM# 284** **Weight:** 7.9650 g. **Composition:** 0.9000 Gold .2304 oz. AGW **Ruler:** Friedrich II **Obverse:** Head left

| Date | Mintage | F | VF | XF | Unc | BU |
|---|---|---|---|---|---|---|
| 1911G | 190,000 | 125 | 150 | 200 | 300 | — |
| 1912G | 310,000 | 125 | 140 | 200 | 300 | — |
| 1913G | 85,000 | 125 | 150 | 225 | 350 | — |
| 1914G | 280,000 | 125 | 150 | 200 | 300 | — |
| (1911-1914)G Proof | — | Value: 800 | | | | |

## BAVARIA

**(Bayern)**

Located in south Germany. In 1180 the Duchy of Bavaria was given to the Count of Wittelsbach by the emperor. He is the ancestor of all who ruled in Bavaria until 1918. Primogeniture was proclaimed in 1506 and in 1623 the dukes of Bavaria were given the electoral right. Bavaria, which had been divided for the various heirs, was reunited in 1799. The title of king was granted to Bavaria in 1805.

**RULERS**

Otto, 1886-1913, Prince Regent Luitpold, 1886-1912
Ludwig III, 1913-1918

**MINT MARKS**

D - Munich

## KINGDOM

**2 MARK** KM# 511.1 **Weight:** 11.1110 g. **Composition:** 0.9000 Silver .3215 oz. ASW **Ruler:** Otto Prince Regent Luitpold **Obverse:** Closed curl

| Date | Mintage | F | VF | XF | Unc | BU |
|---|---|---|---|---|---|---|
| 1901D | 809,000 | 12.00 | 25.00 | 55.00 | 135 | — |
| 1902D | 1,321,000 | 10.00 | 22.00 | 45.00 | 120 | — |
| 1903D | 1,406,000 | 10.00 | 22.00 | 45.00 | 110 | — |
| 1904D | 2,320,000 | 8.00 | 20.00 | 35.00 | 100 | — |
| 1905D | 1,406,000 | 10.00 | 22.00 | 45.00 | 95.00 | — |
| 1906D | 1,055,000 | 10.00 | 22.00 | 55.00 | 120 | — |
| 1907D | 2,106,000 | 8.00 | 20.00 | 35.00 | 85.00 | — |
| 1908D | 633,000 | 10.00 | 22.00 | 45.00 | 95.00 | — |
| 1912D | 214,000 | 10.00 | 22.00 | 45.00 | 110 | — |
| 1913D | 98,000 | 40.00 | 80.00 | 160 | 250 | — |

**2 MARK** KM# 516 **Weight:** 11.1110 g. **Composition:** 0.9000 Silver .3215 oz. ASW **Ruler:** Otto Prince Regent Luitpold **Subject:** 90th birthday of Prince Regent Luitpold

| Date | Mintage | F | VF | XF | Unc | BU |
|---|---|---|---|---|---|---|
| 1911D | 640,000 | 12.00 | 20.00 | 30.00 | 50.00 | — |
| 1911D Proof | — | Value: 100 | | | | |

**2 MARK** KM# 519 **Weight:** 11.1110 g. **Composition:** 0.9000 Silver .3215 oz. ASW **Ruler:** Ludwig III **Obverse:** Head left

| Date | Mintage | F | VF | XF | Unc | BU |
|---|---|---|---|---|---|---|
| 1914D | 574,000 | 30.00 | 60.00 | 100 | 185 | — |

**3 MARK** KM# 515 **Weight:** 16.6670 g. **Composition:** 0.9000 Silver .4823 oz. ASW **Ruler:** Otto Prince Regent Luitpold **Obverse:** Head left

| Date | Mintage | F | VF | XF | Unc | BU |
|---|---|---|---|---|---|---|
| 1908D | 681,000 | 12.00 | 20.00 | 35.00 | 70.00 | — |
| 1909D | 1,827,000 | 10.00 | 18.00 | 30.00 | 65.00 | — |
| 1910D | 1,496,000 | 10.00 | 18.00 | 30.00 | 65.00 | — |
| 1911D | 843,000 | 12.00 | 20.00 | 35.00 | 70.00 | — |
| 1912D | 1,014,000 | 12.00 | 20.00 | 35.00 | 70.00 | — |
| 1913D | 731,000 | 12.00 | 20.00 | 35.00 | 70.00 | — |
| 1913D Proof | — | Value: 100 | | | | |

**3 MARK** KM# 517 **Weight:** 16.6670 g. **Composition:** 0.9000 Silver .4823 oz. ASW **Ruler:** Otto Prince Regent Luitpold **Subject:** 90th birthday of Prince Regent Luitpold

| Date | Mintage | F | VF | XF | Unc | BU |
|---|---|---|---|---|---|---|
| 1911D | 640,000 | 12.00 | 20.00 | 32.00 | 65.00 | — |
| 1911D Proof | — | Value: 100 | | | | |

**3 MARK** KM# 520 **Weight:** 16.6670 g. **Composition:** 0.9000 Silver .4823 oz. ASW **Ruler:** Ludwig III **Obverse:** Head left

| Date | Mintage | F | VF | XF | Unc | BU |
|---|---|---|---|---|---|---|
| 1914D | 717,000 | 17.50 | 32.50 | 50.00 | 90.00 | — |
| 1914D Proof | — | Value: 150 | | | | |

**3 MARK** KM# 523 **Weight:** 16.6670 g. **Composition:** 0.9000 Silver .4823 oz. ASW **Ruler:** Ludwig III **Subject:** Golden wedding anniversary

| Date | Mintage | F | VF | XF | Unc | BU |
|---|---|---|---|---|---|---|
| 1918D | 130 | — | 15,000 | 28,000 | 40,000 | — |

**5 MARK** KM# 512.3 **Weight:** 27.7770 g. **Composition:** 0.9000 Silver .8038 oz. ASW **Ruler:** Otto **Obverse:** Many locks of hair above ear, closed curl

| Date | Mintage | F | VF | XF | Unc | BU |
|---|---|---|---|---|---|---|
| 1891D | Inc. above | 17.50 | 25.00 | 100 | 400 | — |
| 1893D | Inc. above | 25.00 | 50.00 | 120 | 400 | — |
| 1894D | Inc. above | 17.50 | 35.00 | 120 | 400 | — |
| 1898D | Inc. above | 15.00 | 30.00 | 60.00 | 250 | — |
| 1899D | Inc. above | 25.00 | 50.00 | 90.00 | 325 | — |
| 1913D | Inc. above | 15.00 | 25.00 | 45.00 | 120 | — |

**5 MARK** KM# 512.1 **Weight:** 27.7770 g. **Composition:** 0.9000 Silver .8038 oz. ASW **Ruler:** Otto **Obverse:** Closed curl

| Date | Mintage | F | VF | XF | Unc | BU |
|---|---|---|---|---|---|---|
| 1891D | 98,000 | 17.50 | 35.00 | 100 | 400 | — |
| 1893D | 98,000 | 25.00 | 50.00 | 120 | 400 | — |
| 1894D | 141,000 | 17.50 | 35.00 | 120 | 400 | — |
| 1895D | 141,000 | 22.50 | 45.00 | 110 | 400 | — |
| 1896D | 28,000 | 55.00 | 125 | 600 | 1,250 | — |
| 1898D | 303,000 | 15.00 | 30.00 | 65.00 | 250 | — |
| 1899D | 141,000 | 25.00 | 50.00 | 90.00 | 325 | — |
| 1900D | 295,000 | 15.00 | 30.00 | 80.00 | 300 | — |
| (1891-1900)D Proof | — | Value: 1,000 | | | | |
| 1901D | 275,000 | 12.00 | 25.00 | 80.00 | 300 | — |
| 1902D | 486,000 | 12.00 | 25.00 | 60.00 | 250 | — |
| 1903D | 1,012,000 | 12.00 | 25.00 | 60.00 | 250 | — |
| 1904D | 548,000 | 15.00 | 30.00 | 70.00 | 250 | — |
| 1906D | 70,000 | 35.00 | 75.00 | 200 | 1,000 | — |
| 1907D | 753,000 | 12.00 | 20.00 | 45.00 | 200 | — |
| 1908D | 537,000 | 12.00 | 20.00 | 45.00 | 200 | — |
| 1913D | 420,000 | 12.00 | 20.00 | 35.00 | 120 | — |
| (1901-1913)D Proof | — | Value: 650 | | | | |

**5 MARK** KM# 512.4 **Weight:** 27.7770 g. **Composition:** 0.9000 Silver .8038 oz. ASW **Ruler:** Otto **Obverse:** Large lock of hair above ear, closed curl

| Date | Mintage | F | VF | XF | Unc | BU |
|---|---|---|---|---|---|---|
| 1895D | Inc. above | 22.50 | 45.00 | 110 | 400 | — |
| 1896D | Inc. above | 55.00 | 125 | 600 | 1,250 | — |
| 1898D | Inc. above | 12.00 | 20.00 | 60.00 | 250 | — |
| 1899D | Inc. above | 25.00 | 50.00 | 90.00 | 325 | — |
| 1900D | Inc. above | 15.00 | 30.00 | 80.00 | 300 | — |
| 1901D | Inc. above | 15.00 | 30.00 | 80.00 | 300 | — |
| 1902D | Inc. above | 12.00 | 28.00 | 65.00 | 300 | — |
| 1903D | Inc. above | 12.00 | 28.00 | 65.00 | 300 | — |
| 1904D | Inc. above | 15.00 | 30.00 | 70.00 | 300 | — |
| 1906D | Inc. above | 35.00 | 75.00 | 200 | 800 | — |
| 1907D | Inc. above | 12.00 | 20.00 | 45.00 | 200 | — |
| 1908D | Inc. above | 12.00 | 20.00 | 45.00 | 200 | — |
| 1913D | Inc. above | 12.00 | 20.00 | 35.00 | 120 | — |

**5 MARK** KM# 512.2 **Weight:** 27.7770 g. **Composition:** 0.9000 Silver .8038 oz. ASW **Ruler:** Otto **Obverse:** Open curl

| Date | Mintage | F | VF | XF | Unc | BU |
|---|---|---|---|---|---|---|
| 1898D | Inc. above | 12.00 | 25.00 | 70.00 | 300 | — |
| 1901D | Inc. above | 12.00 | 25.00 | 70.00 | 300 | — |
| 1902D | Inc. above | 12.00 | 25.00 | 70.00 | 300 | — |
| 1906D | Inc. above | 35.00 | 75.00 | 200 | 800 | — |
| 1907D | Inc. above | 12.00 | 20.00 | 45.00 | 200 | — |
| 1908D | Inc. above | 12.00 | 20.00 | 45.00 | 200 | — |
| 1913D | Inc. above | 12.00 | 20.00 | 35.00 | 120 | — |

**5 MARK** KM# 518 **Weight:** 27.7770 g. **Composition:** 0.9000 Silver .8038 oz. ASW **Ruler:** Otto Prince Regent Luitpold **Subject:** 90th birthday of Prince Regent Luitpold

| Date | Mintage | F | VF | XF | Unc | BU |
|---|---|---|---|---|---|---|
| 1911D | 160,000 | 25.00 | 60.00 | 85.00 | 160 | — |
| 1911D Proof | — | Value: 200 | | | | |

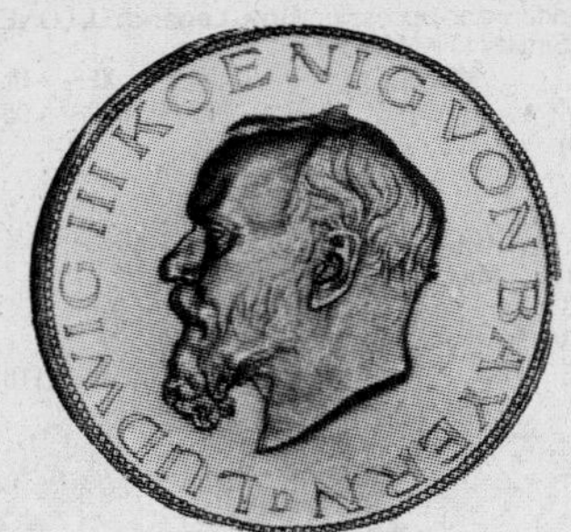

**5 MARK** **KM# 521** **Weight:** 27.7770 g. **Composition:** 0.9000 Silver .8038 oz. ASW **Ruler:** Ludwig III **Obverse:** Head left

| Date | Mintage | F | VF | XF | Unc | BU |
|---|---|---|---|---|---|---|
| 1914D | 142,000 | 40.00 | 75.00 | 125 | 190 | — |

**10 MARK** **KM# 514** **Weight:** 3.9820 g. **Composition:** 0.9000 Gold .1152 oz. AGW **Ruler:** Otto **Obv. Legend:** ... V. BAYERN

| Date | Mintage | F | VF | XF | Unc | BU |
|---|---|---|---|---|---|---|
| 1900D | Inc. above | 65.00 | 140 | 225 | 325 | — |
| 1900D Proof | — | Value: 800 | | | | |
| 1901D | 141,000 | 65.00 | 125 | 200 | 300 | — |
| 1902D | 68,000 | 65.00 | 125 | 200 | 300 | — |
| 1903D | 534,000 | 65.00 | 120 | 180 | 250 | — |
| 1904D | 211,000 | 65.00 | 120 | 180 | 250 | — |
| 1905D | 281,000 | 65.00 | 120 | 180 | 250 | — |
| 1906D | 141,000 | 65.00 | 125 | 190 | 250 | — |
| 1907D | 211,000 | 65.00 | 120 | 190 | 250 | — |
| 1909D | 209,000 | 65.00 | 120 | 190 | 250 | — |
| 1910D | 141,000 | 65.00 | 120 | 190 | 250 | — |
| 1911D | 72,000 | 65.00 | 125 | 200 | 300 | — |
| 1912D | 141,000 | 65.00 | 125 | 190 | 250 | — |
| (1901-1912)D Proof | — | Value: 1,000 | | | | |

**20 MARK** **KM# 513** **Weight:** 7.9650 g. **Composition:** 0.9000 Gold .2304 oz. AGW **Ruler:** Otto **Obverse:** Head left **Reverse:** Type III

| Date | Mintage | F | VF | XF | Unc | BU |
|---|---|---|---|---|---|---|
| 1895D | 501,000 | 125 | 140 | 160 | 250 | — |
| 1895D Proof | — | Value: 800 | | | | |
| 1900D | 501,000 | 125 | 140 | 160 | 250 | — |
| 1905D | 501,000 | 125 | 140 | 160 | 250 | — |
| 1905D Proof | — | Value: 1,100 | | | | |
| 1913D | 311,000 | — | 17,500 | 22,500 | 25,000 | — |
| 1913D Proof | — | Value: 35,000 | | | | |

**20 MARK** **KM# 522** **Weight:** 7.9650 g. **Composition:** 0.9000 Gold .2304 oz. AGW **Ruler:** Ludwig III **Obverse:** Head left **Note:** Never officially released.

| Date | Mintage | F | VF | XF | Unc | BU |
|---|---|---|---|---|---|---|
| 1914D | 533,000 | — | 2,000 | 2,500 | 3,000 | — |
| 1914D Proof | — | Value: 3,650 | | | | |

## PATTERNS

Including off metal strikes

| KM# | Date | Mintage | Identification | Mkt Val |
|---|---|---|---|---|
| Pn14 | 1904 | — | 5 Mark. Silver. Eagle in ring. Reeded edge. | — |
| Pn15 | 1904 | — | 5 Mark. Silver. Eagle in ring. Lettered edge. | — |
| Pn16 | 1904 | — | 5 Mark. Silver. Without inner circle. | — |
| Pn17 | 1905 | — | 5 Mark. Copper. Pn6. KM512. | — |
| Pn18 | 1911 | — | 3 Mark. Silver. | — |
| Pn19 | 1911 | — | 3 Mark. Copper. | — |
| Pn25 | 1913 | — | 3 Mark. Silver. Plain edge. | — |
| Pn35 | 1914 | — | 3 Mark. Silver. Bust faces right. | — |
| Pn36 | 1914 | — | 5 Mark. Silver. Larger lettering, KM521. | — |
| Pn38 | 1914 | — | 20 Mark. Gold. Lettered edge. | — |
| Pn44 | 1914 | — | 20 Mark. Silver Gilt. 18-millimeter bust. KM522. Hallmarked, plain edge. | — |
| Pn37 | 1914 | — | 5 Mark. Silver. Plain edge. KM521. | — |
| Pn39 | 1914 | — | 20 Mark. Silver Gilt. Hallmarked, plain edge. | 150 |
| Pn40 | 1914 | — | 20 Mark. Silver Gilt. Hallmarked, plain edge. KM522. | — |
| Pn41 | 1914 | — | 20 Mark. Gold. Denticled rim. KM522. Plain edge. | — |
| Pn42 | 1914 | — | 20 Mark. Silver Gilt. Denticled rim. KM522. Hallmarked, plain edge. | — |
| Pn43 | 1914 | — | 20 Mark. Gold. 18-millimeter bust. KM522. Lettered edge. | 8,000 |
| Pn45 | 1914 | — | 20 Mark. Gold. Plain rim. KM522. Plain edge. | — |
| Pn46 | 1914 | — | 20 Mark. Gold. Plain rim. KM522. Lettered edge. | — |
| Pn47 | 1914 | — | 20 Mark. Gold. Round "O" in KOENIG. Lettered edge. | — |
| Pn48 | 1914 | — | 20 Mark. Silver Gilt. Round "O" in KOENIG. KM522. Hallmarked, plain edge. | — |
| Pn49 | | — | Gulden. Gold. Bust of Ludwig III in uniform. Main bridge of Wurzburger. | — |

# BREMEN

Established at about the same time as the bishopric in 787, Bremen was under the control of the bishops and archbishops until joining the Hanseatic League in 1276. Archbishop Albrecht II granted the mint right to the city in 1369, but this was not formalized by imperial decree until 1541. In 1646, Bremen was raised to free imperial status and continued to strike its own coins into the early 20th century. The city lost its free imperial status in 1803 and was controlled by France from 1806 until 1813. Regaining it independence in 1815, Bremen joined the North German Confederation in 1867 and the German Empire in 1871. Since 1369, there was practically continuous coinage until 1907.

## FREE CITY

**2 MARK** **KM# 250** **Weight:** 11.1110 g. **Composition:** 0.9000 Silver .3215 oz. ASW

| Date | Mintage | F | VF | XF | Unc | BU |
|---|---|---|---|---|---|---|
| 1904 J | 100,000 | 20.00 | 40.00 | 80.00 | 175 | — |
| 1904 J Proof | 200 | Value: 400 | | | | |

**5 MARK** **KM# 251** **Weight:** 27.7770 g. **Composition:** 0.9000 Silver .8038 oz. ASW

| Date | Mintage | F | VF | XF | Unc | BU |
|---|---|---|---|---|---|---|
| 1906 J | 41,000 | 75.00 | 185 | 285 | 450 | — |
| 1906 J Proof | 600 | Value: 750 | | | | |

**10 MARK** **KM# 253** **Weight:** 3.9820 g. **Composition:** 0.9000 Gold .1152 oz. AGW

| Date | Mintage | F | VF | XF | Unc | BU |
|---|---|---|---|---|---|---|
| 1907 J | 20,000 | 400 | 500 | 900 | 1,600 | — |
| 1907 J Proof | — | Value: 2,000 | | | | |

**20 MARK** **KM# 252** **Weight:** 7.9650 g. **Composition:** 0.9000 Gold .2304 oz. AGW

| Date | Mintage | F | VF | XF | Unc | BU |
|---|---|---|---|---|---|---|
| 1906 J | 20,000 | 400 | 550 | 950 | 1,650 | — |
| 1906 J Proof | — | Value: 2,750 | | | | |

## TOKEN COINAGE

Reckoning Tokens

These vouchers, issued March 18, 1924, were based on the American dollar. Issued in conjunction with Bremens issue of treasury. Due to monies being held to purchase Bremens 5% Dollar Bond, they rarely circulated. The tokens were withdrawn September 30 of that same year.

**2 VERRECHNUNGS-PFENNIG** **KM# Tn1** **Composition:** Brass **Obverse:** State arms **Reverse:** Denomination **Note:** Struck at Nurnberg.

| Date | Mintage | F | VF | XF | Unc | BU |
|---|---|---|---|---|---|---|
| ND(1924) | 501,000 | 10.00 | 25.00 | 45.00 | 85.00 | — |

**5 VERRECHNUNGS-PFENNIG** **KM# Tn2** **Composition:** Aluminum **Obverse:** State arms **Reverse:** Denomination **Note:** Struck at Nurnberg.

| Date | Mintage | F | VF | XF | Unc | BU |
|---|---|---|---|---|---|---|
| ND(1924) | 669,000 | 9.00 | 18.00 | 30.00 | 70.00 | — |

**10 VERRECHNUNGS-PFENNIG** **KM# Tn3** **Composition:** Aluminum **Obverse:** State arms **Reverse:** Denomination **Note:** Struck at Nurnberg.

| Date | Mintage | F | VF | XF | Unc | BU |
|---|---|---|---|---|---|---|
| ND(1924) | 695,000 | 10.00 | 20.00 | 35.00 | 75.00 | — |

**20 VERRECHNUNGS-PFENNIG** **KM# Tn4** **Composition:** Aluminum **Obverse:** State arms **Reverse:** Denomination **Note:** Struck at Nurnberg.

| Date | Mintage | F | VF | XF | Unc | BU |
|---|---|---|---|---|---|---|
| ND(1924) | 382,000 | 17.00 | 35.00 | 60.00 | 120 | — |

**50 VERRECHNUNGS-PFENNIG** **KM# Tn5** **Composition:** Aluminum **Obverse:** Lions supporting crowned arms **Reverse:** Denomination **Note:** Struck at Hamburg.

| Date | Mintage | F | VF | XF | Unc | BU |
|---|---|---|---|---|---|---|
| ND(1924) | 483,000 | 30.00 | 55.00 | 100 | 200 | — |

**VERRECHNUNGSMARK** **KM# Tn6** **Composition:** Aluminum **Obverse:** Lions support crowned arms on pedestal **Reverse:** Denomination **Note:** Struck at Menden. This coin is listed in Jaeger & Funck as struck in aluminum. Kunker has listed it as having an iron core but doesn't indicate what metal clads or plates the piece.

| Date | Mintage | F | VF | XF | Unc | BU |
|---|---|---|---|---|---|---|
| ND(1924) | 382,000 | 75.00 | 150 | 275 | 500 | — |

## PATTERNS

Including off metal strikes

| KM# | Date | Mintage | Identification | Mkt Val |
|---|---|---|---|---|
| Pn40 | 1904 | — | 5 Mark. KM251. | — |
| Pn41 | 1905 | — | 2 Mark. KM250. | — |
| Pn43 | 1905 | — | 5 Mark. Tin. | — |
| Pn42 | 1905 | — | 5 Mark. Silver. Larger lettering without beaded rim. KM251. | 15,000 |
| Pn44 | 1906 | — | 5 Mark. Bronze. | — |
| Pn45 | 1906 | — | 5 Mark. Silver. | — |
| Pn46 | 1906 | — | 5 Mark. Tin. | — |

| KM# | Date | Mintage | Identification | Mkt Val |
|---|---|---|---|---|
| Pn47 | | — | S.M. Copper. | — |

# BRUNSWICK-WOLFENBUTTEL

**(Braunschweig-Wolfenbüttel)**

Located in north-central Germany. Wolfenbüttel was annexed to Brunswick in 1257. One of the five surviving sons of Albrecht II founded the first line in Wolfenbüttel in 1318. A further division in Wolfenbüttel and Lüneburg was undertaken in 1373. Another division occurred in 1495, but the Wolfenbüttel duchy survived in the younger line. Heinrich IX was forced out of his territory during the religious wars of the mid-sixteenth century by Duke Johann Friedrich I of Saxony and Landgrave Philipp of Hessen in 1542, but was restored to his possessions in 1547. Duke Friedrich Ulrich was forced to cede the Grubenhagen lands, which had been acquired by Wolfenbüttel in 1596, to Lüneburg in 1617. When the succession died out in 1634, the lands and titles fell to the cadet line in Dannenberg. The line became extinct once again and passed to Brunswick-Bevern in 1735 from which a new succession of Wolfenbüttel dukes descended. The ducal family was beset by continual personal and political tragedy during the nineteenth century. Two of the dukes were killed in battles with Napoleon, the territories were occupied by the French and became part of the Kingdom of Westphalia, another duke was forced out by a revolt in 1823. From 1884 until 1913, Brunswick-Wolfenbüttel was governed by Prussia and then turned over to a younger prince of Brunswick who married a daughter of Kaiser Wilhelm II. His reign was short, however, as he was forced to abdicate at the end of World War I.

**RULERS**

Prussian rule, 1884-1913
Ernst August, 1913-1918

## DUCHY

**3 MARK** **KM# 1161** **Weight:** 16.6670 g. **Composition:** 0.9000 Silver .4823 oz. ASW **Ruler:** Ernst August **Subject:** Ernst August wedding and accession

| Date | Mintage | F | VF | XF | Unc | BU |
|---|---|---|---|---|---|---|
| 1915A | 1,700 | 600 | 1,150 | 1,850 | 2,900 | — |
| 1915A Proof | — | Value: 3,200 | | | | |

**3 MARK** **KM# 1162** **Weight:** 16.6670 g. **Composition:** 0.9000 Silver .4823 oz. ASW **Ruler:** Ernst August **Subject:** Ernst August wedding and accession **Obv. Legend:** U LUNEB added

| Date | Mintage | F | VF | XF | Unc | BU |
|---|---|---|---|---|---|---|
| 1915A | 32,000 | 50.00 | 110 | 175 | 300 | — |
| 1915A Proof | — | Value: 400 | | | | |

**5 MARK** **KM# 1163** **Weight:** 27.7770 g. **Composition:** 0.9000 Silver .8038 oz. ASW **Ruler:** Ernst August **Subject:** Ernst August wedding and accession

| Date | Mintage | F | VF | XF | Unc | BU |
|---|---|---|---|---|---|---|
| 1915A | 1,400 | 700 | 1,350 | 2,250 | 3,500 | — |
| 1915A Proof | — | Value: 4,000 | | | | |

**5 MARK** **KM# 1164** **Weight:** 27.7770 g. **Composition:** 0.9000 Silver .8038 oz. ASW **Ruler:** Ernst August **Subject:** Ernst August wedding and accession **Obv. Legend:** U. LUNEB added **Reverse:** Similar to KM#1163

| Date | Mintage | F | VF | XF | Unc | BU |
|---|---|---|---|---|---|---|
| 1915A | 8,600 | 165 | 350 | 600 | 950 | — |
| 1915A Proof | — | Value: 1,000 | | | | |

## PATTERNS

Including off metal strikes

| KM# | Date | Mintage | Identification | Mkt Val |
|---|---|---|---|---|
| Pn54 | 1913 | — | 3 Mark. Silver. | — |
| Pn55 | 1913 | — | 5 Mark. Silver. | — |
| Pn56 | 1915 | — | 3 Mark. Silver. Plain edge. KM1161. | — |

| KM# | Date | Mintage | Identification | Mkt Val |
|---|---|---|---|---|
| Pn57 | 1915 | — | 3 Mark. Silver. Beaded rim. Weak 5 in date. Plain edge. KM1162. | — |
| Pn58 | 191x | — | 5 Mark. Silver. Beaded rim, wedding portraits facing left. Partial date. Plain edge. | — |

# HAMBURG

The city of Hamburg is located on the Elbe River about 75 miles (125 kilometers) from the North Sea. Tradition states that it was founded by Charlemagne in the early 9th century. At first, the town was controlled by the archbishopric of Bremen and Hamburg (see Bremen). In 1110, Hamburg and the territory of Holstein came under the rule of Count Adolf I of Schauenburg (Schaumburg, ruled 1106-1128), which inaugurated a period stretching for four centuries in which the Holstein dynasty exercised authority over the city. Hamburg joined with Lübeck in 1241 to form the first partnership in what was to become the Hanseatic League. Count Adolf VI of Schauenburg (1290-1315) gave civic autonomy to Hamburg in 1292 and leased the mint right to the citizens the next year. Local *hohlpfennige* had already been struck fifty years previous. From this early time, the city struck an almost continuous series of coins throughout the centuries up to World War I. In 1510, Hamburg was granted the status of a Free City of the Empire, although it had actually been free for about 250 years. It was occupied by the French during the period of the Napoleonic Wars. In 1866, Hamburg joined the North German Confederation and became a part of the German Empire in 1871.

## FREE CITY

**2 MARK** **KM# 294** **Weight:** 11.1110 g. **Composition:** 0.9000 Silver .3215 oz. ASW

| Date | Mintage | F | VF | XF | Unc | BU |
|---|---|---|---|---|---|---|
| Common dateJ Proof | — | Value: 350 | | | | |
| 1901J | 482,000 | 12.50 | 20.00 | 50.00 | 200 | — |
| 1902J | 779,000 | 12.50 | 20.00 | 50.00 | 200 | — |
| 1903J | 817,000 | 12.50 | 20.00 | 40.00 | 200 | — |
| 1904J | 1,248,000 | 12.50 | 20.00 | 40.00 | 200 | — |
| 1905J | 204,000 | 25.00 | 40.00 | 75.00 | 450 | — |
| 1906J | 1,225,000 | 12.50 | 20.00 | 40.00 | 200 | — |
| 1907J | 1,226,000 | 12.50 | 20.00 | 40.00 | 200 | — |
| 1908J | 368,000 | 12.50 | 25.00 | 45.00 | 200 | — |
| 1911J | 204,000 | 12.50 | 25.00 | 45.00 | 200 | — |
| 1912J | 79,000 | 15.00 | 40.00 | 95.00 | 400 | — |
| 1913J | 105,000 | 12.50 | 25.00 | 55.00 | 200 | — |
| 1914J | 328,000 | 10.00 | 20.00 | 40.00 | 150 | — |
| Common dateJ Proof | — | Value: 350 | | | | |

**3 MARK** **KM# 296** **Weight:** 16.6670 g. **Composition:** 0.9000 Silver .4823 oz. ASW

| Date | Mintage | F | VF | XF | Unc | BU |
|---|---|---|---|---|---|---|
| 1908J | 408,000 | 12.50 | 25.00 | 40.00 | 80.00 | — |
| 1909J | 1,389,000 | 12.50 | 25.00 | 40.00 | 80.00 | — |
| 1910J | 526,000 | 12.50 | 25.00 | 40.00 | 80.00 | — |
| 1911J | 922,000 | 12.50 | 25.00 | 40.00 | 80.00 | — |
| 1912J | 491,000 | 12.50 | 25.00 | 40.00 | 80.00 | — |
| 1913J | 344,000 | 12.50 | 25.00 | 40.00 | 80.00 | — |
| 1914J | 575,000 | 12.50 | 25.00 | 40.00 | 80.00 | — |
| Common dateJ Proof | — | Value: 250 | | | | |

**5 MARK** **KM# 293** **Weight:** 27.7770 g. **Composition:** 0.9000 Silver .8038 oz. ASW

| Date | Mintage | F | VF | XF | Unc | BU |
|---|---|---|---|---|---|---|
| Common dateJ Proof | — | Value: 1,500 | | | | |
| 1901J | 172,000 | 17.50 | 40.00 | 100 | 500 | — |
| 1902J | 294,000 | 17.50 | 35.00 | 80.00 | 400 | — |
| 1903J | 588,000 | 17.50 | 35.00 | 75.00 | 275 | — |
| 1904J | 319,000 | 15.00 | 32.00 | 75.00 | 275 | — |
| 1907J | 326,000 | 15.00 | 32.00 | 75.00 | 275 | — |
| 1908J | 458,000 | 15.00 | 32.00 | 75.00 | 220 | — |
| 1913J | 327,000 | 15.00 | 32.00 | 60.00 | 165 | — |
| Common dateJ Proof | — | Value: 1,500 | | | | |

**10 MARK** **KM# 292** **Weight:** 3.9820 g. **Composition:** 0.9000 Gold .1152 oz. AGW **Reverse:** Type II

| Date | Mintage | F | VF | XF | Unc | BU |
|---|---|---|---|---|---|---|
| 1901J | 82,000 | 70.00 | 110 | 160 | 285 | — |
| 1902J | 41,000 | 150 | 250 | 350 | 550 | — |
| 1903J | 310,000 | 65.00 | 110 | 160 | 240 | — |
| 1905J | 164,000 | 65.00 | 110 | 160 | 240 | — |
| 1906J | 164,000 | 65.00 | 110 | 160 | 240 | — |
| 1907J | 111,000 | 65.00 | 110 | 160 | 240 | — |
| 1908J | 32,000 | 150 | 250 | 350 | 650 | — |
| 1909J | 122,000 | 65.00 | 110 | 160 | 240 | — |
| 1909J Proof | — | Value: 650 | | | | |
| 1910J | 41,000 | 150 | 250 | 350 | 500 | — |
| 1911J | 75,000 | 70.00 | 150 | 200 | 325 | — |
| 1911J Proof | — | Value: 650 | | | | |
| 1912J | 48,000 | 150 | 250 | 350 | 475 | — |
| 1912J Proof | — | Value: 750 | | | | |
| 1913J | 41,000 | 150 | 200 | 300 | 400 | — |
| 1913J Proof | — | Value: 750 | | | | |

**20 MARK** **KM# 295** **Weight:** 7.9650 g. **Composition:** 0.9000 Gold .2304 oz. AGW **Reverse:** Type III

| Date | Mintage | F | VF | XF | Unc | BU |
|---|---|---|---|---|---|---|
| 1900J | 501,000 | 115 | 135 | 160 | 225 | — |
| 1908J Rare | 14 | — | — | — | — | — |
| 1913J | 491,000 | 100 | 120 | 140 | 200 | — |
| 1913J Proof | — | Value: 700 | | | | |

## TOKEN COINAGE

Reckoning Tokens

**1/100 VERRECHNUNGSMARKE** **KM# Tn1** **Composition:** Aluminum **Issuer:** Hamburg Bank **Obverse:** City arms **Reverse:** Denomination **Size:** 20.5 mm.

| Date | Mintage | F | VF | XF | Unc | BU |
|---|---|---|---|---|---|---|
| 1923 | 9,128,000 | 3.00 | 6.00 | 12.50 | 25.00 | — |

**5/100 VERRECHNUNGSMARKE** **KM# Tn2** **Composition:** Aluminum **Issuer:** Hamburg Bank **Obverse:** City arms **Reverse:** Denomination **Size:** 23 mm.

| Date | Mintage | F | VF | XF | Unc | BU |
|---|---|---|---|---|---|---|
| 1923 | 8,100,000 | 2.75 | 4.50 | 9.00 | 18.00 | — |

**1/10 VERRECHNUNGSMARKE** **KM# Tn3** **Composition:** Aluminum **Issuer:** Hamburg Bank **Obverse:** City arms **Reverse:** Denomination **Size:** 26.5 mm.

| Date | Mintage | F | VF | XF | Unc | BU |
|---|---|---|---|---|---|---|
| 1923 | 8,600,000 | 2.75 | 4.50 | 10.00 | 20.00 | — |

## PATTERNS

Including off metal strikes

| KM# | Date | Mintage | Identification | Mkt Val |
|---|---|---|---|---|
| Pn20 | 1906 | — | 5 Mark. Copper. Plain edge. KM293. | — |
| Pn21 | 1913 | — | 5 Mark. Plain edge. KM293. | 1,100 |
| Pn22 | 1913 | — | 5 Mark. Plain edge. KM293. | — |
| Pn23 | 1914 | — | 3 Mark. Silver. Plain edge. KM296. | — |
| Pn24 | 1922 | — | 1/2 Mark. Aluminum. Plain edge. | — |
| Pn28 | 1922 | — | Mark. Aluminum. Plain edge. | — |
| Pn32 | 1922 | — | 2 Mark. Nickel. Plain edge. | — |
| Pn35 | 1922 | — | 3 Mark. Iron. Plain edge. Copper-nickel plated. | — |

| KM# | Date | Mintage | Identification | Mkt Val |
|---|---|---|---|---|
| Pn38 | 1922 | — | 5 Mark. Nickel Plated Iron. Plain edge. | — |
| Pn39 | 1922 | — | 5 Mark. Aluminum. Plain edge. | — |
| Pn36 | 1922 | — | 3 Mark. Aluminum. Plain edge. | — |
| Pn33 | 1922 | — | 2 Mark. Aluminum. Plain edge. | — |
| Pn29 | 1922 | — | Mark. Copper. Plain edge. | — |
| Pn25 | 1922 | — | 1/2 Mark. Iron. Plain edge. | — |
| Pn30 | 1922 | — | Mark. Nickel. Plain edge. | — |
| Pn26 | 1922 | — | 1/2 Mark. Nickel. Plain edge. | — |
| Pn34 | 1922 | — | 2 Mark. Zinc. Plain edge. | — |
| Pn37 | 1922 | — | 3 Mark. Nickel. Plain edge. | — |
| Pn40 | 1922 | — | 5 Mark. Nickel. Plain edge. | — |
| Pn41 | 1922 | — | 5 Mark. Zinc. Plain edge. | — |
| Pn31 | 1922 | — | Mark. Iron. Plain edge. | — |
| Pn27 | 1922 | — | 1/2 Mark. Copper. Plain edge. | 225 |

# HESSE-DARMSTADT

**(Hessen-Darmstadt)**

Founded by the youngest of Philipp I's four sons upon the death of their father in 1567, Hesse-Darmstadt was one of the two main branches of the family which survived past the beginning of the 17th century. The Countship of Hanau-Lichtenberg was through marriage when the male line failed in 1736. Ludwig X was forced to cede that territory to France in 1801. In 1803, Darmstadt acquired part of the Palatinate, the city of Friedberg, part of the city of Mainz, and the Duchy of Westphalia in a general settlement with France. The Landgrave was elevated to the status of Grand Duke in 1806 and reacquired Hesse-Homburg. In 1815 the Congress of Vienna awarded Hesse-Darmstadt the city of Worms and all of Mainz. These were relinquished, along with Hesse-Homburg, to Prussia in 1866 and Hesse-Darmstadt was called just Hesse from 1867 onwards. Hesse became part of the German Empire in 1871, but ceased to exist as a semi-sovereign state at the end of World War I.

**RULERS**

Ernst Ludwig, 1892-1918

## GRAND DUCHY

**2 MARK** **KM# 372** **Weight:** 11.1110 g. **Composition:** 0.9000 Silver .3215 oz. ASW **Subject:** 40th birthday of Philipp the Magnanimous

| Date | Mintage | F | VF | XF | Unc | BU |
|---|---|---|---|---|---|---|
| 1904 | 100,000 | 20.00 | 40.00 | 65.00 | 90.00 | — |
| 1904 Proof | 2,250 | Value: 135 | | | | |

**Note:** Obverse matte, reverse polished.

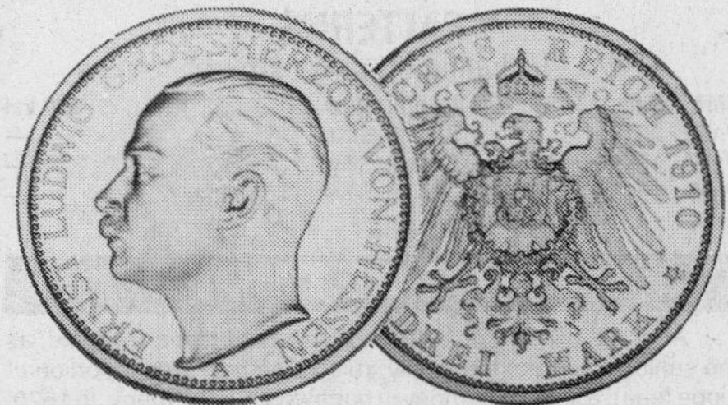

**3 MARK** **KM# 375** **Weight:** 16.6670 g. **Composition:** 0.9000 Silver .4823 oz. ASW **Ruler:** Ernst Ludwig

| Date | Mintage | F | VF | XF | Unc | BU |
|---|---|---|---|---|---|---|
| 1910A | 200,000 | 30.00 | 60.00 | 95.00 | 165 | — |
| 1910A Proof | — | Value: 325 | | | | |

**3 MARK** **KM# 376** **Weight:** 16.6670 g. **Composition:** 0.9000 Silver .4823 oz. ASW **Ruler:** Ernst Ludwig **Subject:** 25-Year Jubilee

| Date | Mintage | F | VF | XF | Unc | BU |
|---|---|---|---|---|---|---|
| 1917A | 1,333 | — | 1,750 | 2,750 | 4,000 | — |
| 1917A Proof | Inc. above | Value: 6,000 | | | | |

**5 MARK** **KM# 373** **Weight:** 27.7770 g. **Composition:** 0.9000 Silver .8038 oz. ASW **Ruler:** Ernst Ludwig **Subject:** 400th birthday of Philipp the Magnanimous

| Date | Mintage | F | VF | XF | Unc | BU |
|---|---|---|---|---|---|---|
| 1904 | 40,000 | 45.00 | 95.00 | 145 | 265 | — |
| 1904 Proof | 700 | Value: 550 | | | | |

**Note:** Obverse matte, reverse polished.

**20 MARK** **KM# 371** **Weight:** 7.9650 g. **Composition:** 0.9000 Gold .2304 oz. AGW **Ruler:** Ernst Ludwig

| Date | Mintage | F | VF | XF | Unc | BU |
|---|---|---|---|---|---|---|
| 1901A | 80,000 | 125 | 175 | 325 | 500 | — |
| 1901A Proof | 600 | Value: 1,300 | | | | |
| 1903A | 40,000 | 125 | 175 | 350 | 750 | — |
| 1903A Proof | 100 | Value: 1,500 | | | | |

**20 MARK** **KM# 374** **Weight:** 7.9650 g. **Composition:** 0.9000 Gold .2304 oz. AGW **Ruler:** Ernst Ludwig

| Date | Mintage | F | VF | XF | Unc | BU |
|---|---|---|---|---|---|---|
| 1905A | 45,000 | 125 | 200 | 300 | 500 | — |
| 1905A Proof | 200 | Value: 1,500 | | | | |
| 1906A | 85,000 | 125 | 175 | 250 | 425 | — |
| 1906A Proof | 199 | Value: 1,500 | | | | |
| 1908A | 40,000 | 125 | 175 | 265 | 450 | — |
| 1911A | 150,000 | 125 | 175 | 250 | 425 | — |

## PATTERNS

Including off metal strikes

| KM# | Date | Mintage | Identification | Mkt Val |
|---|---|---|---|---|
| Pn31 | 1910 | — | 3 Mark. Silver. | — |
| Pn32 | 1917 | — | 3 Mark. Silver. | — |
| Pn33 | 1917 | — | 3 Mark. Silver. Plain edge. Y82. | — |

# LIPPE-DETMOLD

After the division of 1613, the Counts of Lippe-Detmold, as the senior branch of the family, ruled over the largest portion of Lippe (see), a small patrimony in northwestern Germany. In 1620, Lippe-Sternberg became extinct and its lands and titles reverted to Lippe-Detmold. The younger brother of Hermann Adolf founded the line of Lippe-Sternberg-Schwalenberg (Biesterfeld) in 1652, which lasted into the 20th century. In 1720, the count was raised to the rank of prince, but did not use the title until 1789. Lippe joined the North German Confederation in 1866 and became part of the German Empire in 1871. Prince Alexander was declared insane and placed under a regency during his entire reign. There ensued a ten-year testamentary dispute between the Lippe-Biesterfeld and the Schaumburg-Lippe lines over the succession to the childless Alexander - a Wilhelmine cause célèbre. Leopold (V) of the Biesterfeld line gained the principality in 1905, but was forced to abdicate in 1918, at the end of World War I. In 1947, Lippe was absorbed by the German state of North Rhine-Westphalia.

**RULERS**

Alexander, 1895-1905

Leopold IV, 1905-1918

**MINT MARKS**

A= Berlin mint, 1843-1918

## PRINCIPALITY

**2 MARK** **KM# 270** **Weight:** 11.1110 g. **Composition:** 0.9000 Silver .3215 oz. ASW **Ruler:** Leopold IV

| Date | Mintage | F | VF | XF | Unc | BU |
|---|---|---|---|---|---|---|
| 1906A | 20,000 | 100 | 200 | 300 | 475 | — |
| 1906A Proof | 1,100 | Value: 525 | | | | |

**3 MARK** **KM# 275** **Weight:** 16.6670 g. **Composition:** 0.9000 Silver .4823 oz. ASW **Ruler:** Leopold IV

| Date | Mintage | F | VF | XF | Unc | BU |
|---|---|---|---|---|---|---|
| 1913A | 15,000 | 125 | 250 | 335 | 500 | — |
| 1913A Proof | 100 | Value: 675 | | | | |

# LUBECK

The original settlement was called Liubice, the capital of a Slavic principality. It was located at the confluence of the Schwartau with the Trave Rivers and contained a castle with a merchant town on a harbor. The town was burned down in 1138 and Count Adolf II of Holstein (1128-64) refounded the city four miles (6.5 kilometers) up the Trave in 1143. Duke Heinirich III the Lion of Saxony (1153-80) forced Adolf II to relinquish Lübeck to him as his feudal overlord. Heinrich III no sooner had the city in his possession when a fire destroyed it. Heinrich III began rebuilding it in 1159 and this is now considered the traditional date of it founding. As the city and its trade on the Baltic grew in importance, special rights and privileges were granted to it in 1188 by Emperor Friedrich I Barbarossa. In 1226, Friedrich II raised Lübeck to the status of a free imperial city and a long period of self-government began. From about 1190 and into the 13th century, an imperial mint operated in the town. Although Lübeck was granted the mint right in 1188, reiterated in 1226 and 1340, its earliest civic coinage only began about 1350. The commercial importance of the city became even greater when it joined with Hamburg in 1241 to form the nucleus of what was to become the Hanseatic League. In 1358, the member cities of the League, which had grown very powerful during the preceding century, elected Lübeck as the administrative capital. By the beginning of the 15th century, the city was second only to Cologne as the largest in northern Germany.

The Protestant Reformation swept through Lübeck in 1529-30 (see Bishopric) and changes came rapidly as the governing city council was removed from office, only to be replaced by a revolutionary *burgomeister*, Jürgen Wullenwever. An unsuccessful war ensued against Denmark, Sweden and the Netherlands and caused the city to lose its powerful position in northern Europe. This began the dismemberment of the Hanseatic League and even a victorious war against Sweden during 1563-1570 was not enough to prevent the decline of Lübeck's fortunes. The demise of the League in 1630, during the Thirty Years' War, may have actually been beneficial to the city as it was able to remain neutral during the long years of struggle throughout Germany. The city was able to regain much of its lost economic power during the 18th century, partly due to increased trade with Russia through its new Baltic port of St. Petersburg. Lübeck's economy was completely ruined, however, during the Napoleonic Wars (1792-1815). Occupied by the French from 1811 to 1813, it was restored as a free city in the latter year. After 1815, the city was a member of the German Confederation and joined the North German Confederation in 1866. It remained a free city as part of the German Empire from 1871 until the end of World War I in 1918. However, its status as a self-governing entity, which had begun in 1226, did not end until 1937, when it was made a part of the province of Schleswig-Holstein.

## FREE CITY

**2 MARK** **KM# 210** **Weight:** 11.1110 g. **Composition:** 0.9000 Silver .3215 oz. ASW

| Date | Mintage | F | VF | XF | Unc | BU |
|---|---|---|---|---|---|---|
| 1901A | 25,000 | 100 | 175 | 225 | 400 | — |
| 1901A Proof | — | Value: 450 | | | | |

**2 MARK** **KM# 212** **Weight:** 11.1110 g. **Composition:** 0.9000 Silver .3215 oz. ASW

| Date | Mintage | F | VF | XF | Unc | BU |
|---|---|---|---|---|---|---|
| 1904A | 25,000 | 45.00 | 75.00 | 130 | 220 | — |
| 1904A Proof | 200 | Value: 300 | | | | |
| 1905A | 25,000 | 45.00 | 75.00 | 130 | 225 | — |
| 1905A Proof | 178 | Value: 300 | | | | |
| 1906A | 25,000 | 45.00 | 75.00 | 130 | 225 | — |
| 1906A Proof | 200 | Value: 300 | | | | |
| 1907A | 25,000 | 45.00 | 75.00 | 130 | 225 | — |
| 1911A | 25,000 | 45.00 | 75.00 | 130 | 225 | — |
| 1911A Proof | — | Value: 350 | | | | |
| 1912A | 25,000 | 45.00 | 75.00 | 130 | 225 | — |
| 1912A Proof | — | Value: 350 | | | | |

**3 MARK** **KM# 215** **Weight:** 16.6670 g. **Composition:** 0.9000 Silver .4823 oz. ASW

| Date | Mintage | F | VF | XF | Unc | BU |
|---|---|---|---|---|---|---|
| 1908 | 33,000 | 25.00 | 65.00 | 110 | 185 | — |
| 1909A | 33,000 | 25.00 | 65.00 | 110 | 185 | — |
| 1910A | 33,000 | 25.00 | 65.00 | 110 | 185 | — |
| 1911A | 33,000 | 25.00 | 65.00 | 110 | 185 | — |
| 1912A | 34,000 | 25.00 | 65.00 | 110 | 185 | — |
| 1913A | 30,000 | 25.00 | 65.00 | 110 | 185 | — |
| 1914A | 10,000 | 35.00 | 85.00 | 150 | 250 | — |
| Common dateA Proof | — | Value: 275 | | | | |

**5 MARK** KM# 213 **Weight:** 27.7770 g. **Composition:** 0.9000 Silver .8038 oz. ASW

| Date | Mintage | F | VF | XF | Unc | BU |
|---|---|---|---|---|---|---|
| 1904A | 10,000 | 100 | 250 | 375 | 500 | — |
| 1904A Proof | 200 | Value: 850 | | | | |
| 1907A | 10,000 | 100 | 250 | 375 | 550 | — |
| 1908A | 10,000 | 100 | 275 | 400 | 600 | — |
| 1913A | 6,000 | 100 | 275 | 425 | 650 | — |

**10 MARK** KM# 211 **Weight:** 3.9820 g. **Composition:** 0.9000 Gold .1152 oz. AGW

| Date | Mintage | F | VF | XF | Unc | BU |
|---|---|---|---|---|---|---|
| 1901A | 10,000 | 300 | 500 | 1,000 | 1,300 | — |
| 1901A Proof | 200 | Value: 2,250 | | | | |
| 1904A | 10,000 | 300 | 500 | 1,000 | 1,300 | — |
| 1904A Proof | 130 | Value: 2,250 | | | | |

**10 MARK** KM# 214 **Weight:** 3.9820 g. **Composition:** 0.9000 Gold .1152 oz. AGW

| Date | Mintage | F | VF | XF | Unc | BU |
|---|---|---|---|---|---|---|
| 1905A | 10,000 | 300 | 500 | 1,000 | 1,300 | — |
| 1905A Proof | 247 | Value: 2,750 | | | | |
| 1906A | 10,000 | 300 | 500 | 1,000 | 1,300 | — |
| 1906A Proof | 216 | Value: 2,750 | | | | |
| 1909A | 10,000 | 300 | 500 | 1,000 | 1,300 | — |
| 1910A | 10,000 | 300 | 500 | 1,000 | 1,300 | — |

## PATTERNS

Including off metal strikes

| KM# | Date | Mintage | Identification | Mkt Val |
|---|---|---|---|---|
| Pn38 | 1915 | — | 3 Mark. Copper. Aluminum-plated. | — |
| Pn39 | 1915 | — | 3 Mark. Zinc. Aluminum-plated. | — |
| Pn40 | 1915 | — | 3 Mark. Silver. | — |

# MECKLENBURG-SCHWERIN

The Duchy of Mecklenburg was divided in 1592 to form the branches of Mecklenburg-Schwerin and Mecklenburg-Güstrow. During the Thirty Years' War, the several dukes of the Mecklenburg states sided with the Protestant forces against the emperor. Albrecht von Wallenstein, Duke of Friedland and imperial general, ousted the Mecklenburg dukes from their territories in 1628. The rightful rulers were each restored to their lands in 1632. In 1658, Mecklenburg-Schwerin was divided by the four sons of Adolf Friedrich into the lines of Mecklenburg-Schwerin, Mecklenburg-Grabow, Mecklenburg-Mirow (extinct in 1675) and Mecklenburg-Strelitz (see). Mecklenburg-Schwerin and Mecklenburg-Güstrow fell extinct in the male line in 1692 and 1695 respectively, becoming a source of dispute between Mecklenburg-Grabow and Mecklenburg-Strelitz. Both parties finally agreed to a settlement in 1701 which awarded about eighty percent of all Mecklenburg territory to Grabow, which became the main Schwerin line, and the rest to Strelitz. No coinage was produced for Mecklenburg-Schwerin from 1708 until 1750. In 1815, the Congress of Vienna elevated the ruler to the rank of Grand Duke. Mecklenburg-Schwerin became a part of the German Empire in 1871. The last grand duke abdicated at the end of World War I in 1918.

**RULERS**

Friedrich Franz IV, 1897-1918

**MINT MARKS**

A= Berlin mint, 1852-1915

## GRAND DUCHY

**2 MARK** KM# 330 **Weight:** 11.1110 g. **Composition:** 0.9000 Silver .3215 oz. ASW **Ruler:** Friedrich Franz IV **Subject:** Grand duke coming of age

| Date | Mintage | F | VF | XF | Unc | BU |
|---|---|---|---|---|---|---|
| 1901A | 50,000 | 125 | 300 | 465 | 1,100 | — |
| 1901A Proof | 1,000 | Value: 1,200 | | | | |

**2 MARK** KM# 333 **Weight:** 11.1110 g. **Composition:** 0.9000 Silver .3215 oz. ASW **Ruler:** Friedrich Franz IV **Subject:** Friedrich Franz IV wedding

| Date | Mintage | F | VF | XF | Unc | BU |
|---|---|---|---|---|---|---|
| 1904A | 100,000 | 15.00 | 35.00 | 65.00 | 100 | — |
| 1904A Proof | 6,000 | Value: 175 | | | | |

**3 MARK** KM# 340 **Weight:** 16.6670 g. **Composition:** 0.9000 Silver .4823 oz. ASW **Ruler:** Friedrich Franz IV **Subject:** 100 years as grand duchy

| Date | Mintage | F | VF | XF | Unc | BU |
|---|---|---|---|---|---|---|
| 1915A | 33,000 | 40.00 | 85.00 | 150 | 235 | — |
| 1915A Proof | — | Value: 450 | | | | |

**5 MARK** KM# 334 **Weight:** 27.7770 g. **Composition:** 0.9000 Silver .8038 oz. ASW **Ruler:** Friedrich Franz IV **Subject:** Friedrich Franz IV wedding

| Date | Mintage | F | VF | XF | Unc | BU |
|---|---|---|---|---|---|---|
| 1904A | 40,000 | 40.00 | 100 | 175 | 250 | — |
| 1904A Proof | 2,500 | Value: 500 | | | | |

**5 MARK** KM# 341 **Weight:** 27.7770 g. **Composition:** 0.9000 Silver .8038 oz. ASW **Ruler:** Friedrich Franz IV **Subject:** 100 years as grand duchy

| Date | Mintage | F | VF | XF | Unc | BU |
|---|---|---|---|---|---|---|
| 1915A | 10,000 | 125 | 265 | 500 | 850 | — |
| 1915A Proof | — | Value: 1,000 | | | | |

**10 MARK** KM# 331 **Weight:** 3.9820 g. **Composition:** 0.9000 Gold .1152 oz. AGW **Ruler:** Friedrich Franz IV **Subject:** Grand duke coming of age **Reverse:** Type III

| Date | Mintage | F | VF | XF | Unc | BU |
|---|---|---|---|---|---|---|
| 1901A | 10,000 | 450 | 1,000 | 1,500 | 2,500 | — |
| 1901A Proof | 200 | Value: 3,250 | | | | |

**20 MARK** KM# 332 **Weight:** 7.9650 g. **Composition:** 0.9000 Gold .2304 oz. AGW **Ruler:** Friedrich Franz IV **Subject:** Grand duke coming of age **Reverse:** Type III

| Date | Mintage | F | VF | XF | Unc | BU |
|---|---|---|---|---|---|---|
| 1901A | 5,000 | 900 | 1,750 | 2,750 | 3,750 | — |
| 1901A Proof | 200 | Value: 4,000 | | | | |

## PATTERNS

Including off metal strikes

| KM# | Date | Mintage | Identification | Mkt Val |
|---|---|---|---|---|
| Pn26 | 1915 | — | 3 Mark. Silver. Plain edge. KM340. | — |
| Pn27 | 1915 | — | 3 Mark. Silver. | — |
| Pn28 | 1915 | — | 5 Mark. Silver. KM341. | — |

# MECKLENBURG-STRELITZ

The Duchy of Mecklenburg-Strelitz was the youngest branch of the dynasty established when Mecklenburg-Schwerin was divided in 1658. Like its parent senior line, Mecklenburg-Strelitz became a grand duchy in 1815 as enacted by the Congress of Vienna. It became a constituent part of the German Empire in 1871, but all sovereignty ended with the conclusion of World War I in 1918.

**RULERS**

Friedrich Wilhelm, 1860-1904
Adolf Friedrich V, 1904-1914
Adolf Friedrich VI, 1914-1918

## GRAND DUCHY

**2 MARK** KM# 115 **Weight:** 11.1110 g. **Composition:** 0.9000 Silver .3215 oz. ASW **Ruler:** Adolph Friedrich V

| Date | Mintage | F | VF | XF | Unc | BU |
|---|---|---|---|---|---|---|
| 1905A | 10,000 | 135 | 300 | 575 | 775 | — |
| 1905A Proof | 2,500 | Value: 800 | | | | |

**3 MARK** KM# 120 **Weight:** 16.6670 g. **Composition:** 0.9000 Silver .4823 oz. ASW **Ruler:** Adolph Friedrich V

| Date | Mintage | F | VF | XF | Unc | BU |
|---|---|---|---|---|---|---|
| 1913A | 7,000 | 250 | 450 | 900 | 1,650 | — |
| 1913A Proof | — | Value: 1,850 | | | | |

**10 MARK** **KM# 116** **Weight:** 3.9820 g. **Composition:** 0.9000 Gold .1152 oz. AGW **Ruler:** Adolph Friedrich V

| Date | Mintage | F | VF | XF | Unc | BU |
|---|---|---|---|---|---|---|
| 1905A | 1,000 | 1,500 | 2,250 | 3,000 | 4,800 | — |
| 1905A Proof | 150 | Value: 5,000 | | | | |

**20 MARK** **KM# 117** **Weight:** 7.9650 g. **Composition:** 0.9000 Gold .2304 oz. AGW **Ruler:** Adolph Friedrich V **Reverse:** Type III

| Date | Mintage | F | VF | XF | Unc | BU |
|---|---|---|---|---|---|---|
| 1905A | 1,000 | 1,750 | 3,000 | 4,750 | 6,500 | — |
| 1905A Proof | 160 | Value: 7,000 | | | | |

### PATTERNS

Including off metal strikes

| KM# | Date | Mintage | Identification | Mkt Val |
|---|---|---|---|---|
| Pn41 | 1913 | — | 3 Mark. Silver. KM120. | — |

## OLDENBURG

The county of Oldenburg was situated on the North Seacoast, to the east of the principality of East Friesland. It was originally part of the old duchy of Saxony and the first recorded lord ruled from the beginning of the 11th century. The first count was named in 1091 and had already acquired the county of Delmenhorst prior to that time. The first identifiable Oldenburg coinage was struck in the first half of the 13th century. Oldenburg was divided into Oldenburg and Delmenhorst in 1270, but the two lines were reunited by marriage five generations later. Through another marriage to the heiress of the duchy of Schleswig and county of Holstein, the royal house of Denmark descended through the Oldenburg line beginning in 1448, while a junior branch continued as counts of Oldenburg. The lordship of Jever was added to the county's domains in 1575. In 1667, the last count died without a direct heir and Oldenburg reverted to Denmark until 1773. In the following year, Oldenburg was given to the bishop of Lübeck, of the Holstein-Gottorp line, and raised to the status of a duchy. Oldenburg was occupied several times during the Napoleonic Wars and became a grand duchy in 1829. In 1817, Oldenburg acquired the principality of Birkenfeld from Prussia and struck coins in denominations used there. World War I spelled the end of temporal power for the Grand Duke in 1918, but the title has continued up to the present time. Grand Duke Anton Günther was born in 1923.

**RULERS**

Friedrich August, 1900-1918

**MINT MARKS**

A - Berlin mint, 1891-1901

## GRAND DUCHY

**2 MARK** **KM# 202** **Weight:** 11.1110 g. **Composition:** 0.9000 Silver .3215 oz. ASW **Ruler:** Friedrich August

| Date | Mintage | F | VF | XF | Unc | BU |
|---|---|---|---|---|---|---|
| 1901A | 75,000 | 85.00 | 200 | 450 | 900 | — |
| 1901A Proof | 260 | Value: 1,000 | | | | |

**5 MARK** **KM# 203** **Weight:** 27.7770 g. **Composition:** 0.9000 Silver .8038 oz. ASW **Ruler:** Friedrich August

| Date | Mintage | F | VF | XF | Unc | BU |
|---|---|---|---|---|---|---|
| 1901A | 10,000 | 350 | 800 | 1,600 | 3,250 | — |
| 1901A | 10,000 | 350 | 800 | 1,600 | 3,750 | — |
| 1901A Proof | 170 | Value: 4,500 | | | | |
| 1901A Proof | 170 | Value: 4,000 | | | | |

## PRUSSIA

**(Preussen)**

Elector Friedrich III of Brandenburg-Prussia (1688-1713) was accorded the title of "King in Prussia" in 1701 as a reward for his support of Austria during the War of the Spanish Succession. Under successive strong leaders, Prussia gained increasing importance and added to its territories to become one of the leading countries of Europe in the course of the 18th century. As part of the reforms instituted by Friedrich II, the system of single letter mintmarks representing specific mints replaced the traditional incorporation of mint officials' symbols and/or initials as part of coin designs. Some of these very same mintmarks are still in use on modern German coins up to the present day. During the Napoleonic Wars (1792-1815), Prussia was allied with Saxony and they were soundly defeated at Jena in 1806. Prussia was forced to cede large portions of its territory at the time, but played a large part in the final defeat of Napoleon. The Congress of Vienna awarded Prussia part of Pomerania, the northern half of Saxony, much of Westphalia and the Rhineland, thus making it the largest state in Germany and a major power in European affairs. After defeating Denmark in 1864 and Austria in 1866, Prussia acquired Schleswig-Holstein, Hannover, Hesse-Cassel, Nassau and Frankfurt am Main. By this time, Prussia encompassed a large part of German territory and its population included two-thirds of all the German people. By winning the Franco-Prussian War (1870-71), Prussia became the pivotal state in the unification of Germany in 1871. King Wilhelm I was proclaimed Kaiser (Emperor) of all Germany, but World War I brought an end to both the Empire and the Kingdom of Prussia in 1918.

**NOTE:**

For coins of Neuchatel previously listed here, see Switzerland.

**RULERS**

Wilhelm II, 1888-1918

**MINT MARKS**

A - Berlin = Prussia, East Friesland, East Prussia, Posen

## KINGDOM

**2 MARK** **KM# 522** **Weight:** 11.1110 g. **Composition:** 0.9000 Silver .2215 oz. ASW **Ruler:** Wilhelm II

| Date | Mintage | F | VF | XF | Unc | BU |
|---|---|---|---|---|---|---|
| 1901 | 398,000 | 25.00 | 50.00 | 125 | 800 | — |
| 1901 Proof | — | Value: 2,500 | | | | |
| 1902 | 3,948,000 | 7.00 | 13.50 | 40.00 | 125 | — |
| 1903 | 4,079,000 | 7.00 | 13.50 | 40.00 | 125 | — |
| 1904A | 9,981,000 | 7.00 | 13.50 | 40.00 | 125 | — |
| 1905A | 6,493,000 | 7.00 | 13.50 | 35.00 | 95.00 | — |
| 1905A Proof | 620 | Value: 300 | | | | |
| 1906A | 4,019,000 | 7.00 | 13.50 | 30.00 | 85.00 | — |
| 1906A Proof | 85 | Value: 300 | | | | |
| 1907A | 8,110,000 | 7.00 | 13.50 | 25.00 | 75.00 | — |
| 1908A | 2,389,000 | 7.00 | 13.50 | 30.00 | 100 | — |
| 1911A | 1,181,000 | 8.00 | 16.50 | 30.00 | 110 | — |
| 1912A | 733,000 | 8.00 | 16.50 | 30.00 | 110 | — |

**2 MARK** **KM# 525** **Weight:** 11.1110 g. **Composition:** 0.9000 Silver .3215 oz. ASW **Ruler:** Wilhelm II **Subject:** 200 Years - Kingdom of Prussia

| Date | Mintage | F | VF | XF | Unc | BU |
|---|---|---|---|---|---|---|
| 1901A | 2,600,000 | 4.50 | 8.50 | 13.50 | 27.50 | — |
| 1901A Proof | — | Value: 70.00 | | | | |

**2 MARK** **KM# 532** **Weight:** 11.1110 g. **Composition:** 0.9000 Silver .3215 oz. ASW **Ruler:** Wilhelm II **Subject:** 100 Years - defeat of Napoleon

| Date | Mintage | F | VF | XF | Unc | BU |
|---|---|---|---|---|---|---|
| 1913A | 1,500,000 | 8.00 | 12.00 | 18.50 | 32.00 | — |
| 1913A Proof | — | Value: 70.00 | | | | |

**2 MARK** **KM# 533** **Weight:** 11.1110 g. **Composition:** 0.9000 Silver .3215 oz. ASW **Ruler:** Wilhelm II **Subject:** 25th year of reign

| Date | Mintage | F | VF | XF | Unc | BU |
|---|---|---|---|---|---|---|
| 1913A | 1,500,000 | 8.00 | 12.00 | 17.50 | 30.00 | — |
| 1913A Proof | 5,000 | Value: 75.00 | | | | |

**3 MARK** **KM# 527** **Weight:** 16.6670 g. **Composition:** 0.9000 Silver .4823 oz. ASW **Ruler:** Wilhelm II

| Date | Mintage | F | VF | XF | Unc | BU |
|---|---|---|---|---|---|---|
| 1908A | 2,859,000 | 6.50 | 12.00 | 18.50 | 45.00 | — |
| 1909A | 6,344,000 | 6.50 | 12.00 | 18.50 | 45.00 | — |
| 1910A | 5,591,000 | 6.50 | 12.00 | 18.50 | 45.00 | — |
| 1911A | 3,242,000 | 6.50 | 12.00 | 18.50 | 45.00 | — |
| 1912A | 4,626,000 | 6.50 | 12.00 | 18.50 | 45.00 | — |
| (1908-1912)A Proof | — | Value: 175 | | | | |

**3 MARK** **KM# 530** **Weight:** 16.6670 g. **Composition:** 0.9000 Silver .4823 oz. ASW **Ruler:** Wilhelm II **Subject:** Berlin University

| Date | Mintage | F | VF | XF | Unc | BU |
|---|---|---|---|---|---|---|
| 1910A | 200,000 | 15.00 | 30.00 | 55.00 | 85.00 | — |
| 1910A Proof | 2,000 | Value: 300 | | | | |

**3 MARK** **KM# 531** **Weight:** 16.6670 g. **Composition:** 0.9000 Silver .4823 oz. ASW **Ruler:** Wilhelm II **Subject:** Breslau University

| Date | Mintage | F | VF | XF | Unc | BU |
|---|---|---|---|---|---|---|
| 1911A | 400,000 | 12.50 | 25.00 | 45.00 | 70.00 | — |
| 1911A Proof | — | Value: 235 | | | | |

**3 MARK** **KM# 534** **Weight:** 16.6670 g. **Composition:** 0.9000 Silver .4823 oz. ASW **Ruler:** Wilhelm II **Subject:** 100 years - defeat of Napoleon

| Date | Mintage | F | VF | XF | Unc | BU |
|---|---|---|---|---|---|---|
| 1913A | 2,000,000 | 8.00 | 13.00 | 20.00 | 35.00 | — |
| 1913A Proof | — | Value: 100 | | | | |

**3 MARK** **KM# 535** **Weight:** 16.6670 g. **Composition:** 0.9000 Silver .4823 oz. ASW **Ruler:** Wilhelm II **Subject:** 25th year of reign

| Date | Mintage | F | VF | XF | Unc | BU |
|---|---|---|---|---|---|---|
| 1913A | 2,000,000 | 8.00 | 13.00 | 20.00 | 35.00 | — |
| 1913A Proof | 6,000 | Value: 90.00 | | | | |

**3 MARK** **KM# 538** **Weight:** 16.6670 g. **Composition:** 0.9000 Silver .4823 oz. ASW **Ruler:** Wilhelm II

| Date | Mintage | F | VF | XF | Unc | BU |
|---|---|---|---|---|---|---|
| 1914A | 2,564,000 | 8.00 | 13.00 | 20.00 | 32.50 | — |
| 1914A Proof | — | Value: 75.00 | | | | |

**3 MARK** **KM# 539** **Weight:** 16.6670 g. **Composition:** 0.9000 Silver .4823 oz. ASW **Ruler:** Wilhelm II **Subject:** Centenary - absorption of Mansfeld

| Date | Mintage | F | VF | XF | Unc | BU |
|---|---|---|---|---|---|---|
| 1915A | 30,000 | 100 | 400 | 600 | 750 | — |
| 1915A Proof | — | Value: 800 | | | | |

**5 MARK** **KM# 523** **Weight:** 27.7770 g. **Composition:** 0.9000 Silver .8038 oz. ASW **Ruler:** Wilhelm II **Reverse:** Type III

| Date | Mintage | F | VF | XF | Unc | BU |
|---|---|---|---|---|---|---|
| 1898A | 1,134,000 | 15.00 | 30.00 | 100 | 450 | — |
| 1901A | 668,000 | 15.00 | 30.00 | 80.00 | 325 | — |
| 1902A | 1,951,000 | 15.00 | 25.00 | 70.00 | 275 | — |
| 1903A | 3,856,000 | 15.00 | 22.50 | 65.00 | 275 | — |
| 1904A | 2,060,000 | 15.00 | 22.50 | 65.00 | 275 | — |
| 1906A | 231,000 | 20.00 | 35.00 | 90.00 | 400 | — |
| 1907A | 2,902,000 | 15.00 | 22.50 | 50.00 | 250 | — |
| 1908A | 2,231,000 | 15.00 | 22.50 | 50.00 | 250 | — |
| (1891-1908)A | — | Value: 900 | | | | |

**5 MARK** **KM# 526** **Weight:** 27.7770 g. **Composition:** 0.9000 Silver .8038 oz. ASW **Ruler:** Wilhelm II **Subject:** 200 years - Kingdom of Prussia

| Date | Mintage | F | VF | XF | Unc | BU |
|---|---|---|---|---|---|---|
| 1901A | 460,000 | 22.50 | 37.50 | 65.00 | 100 | — |
| 1901A Proof | — | Value: 175 | | | | |

**5 MARK** **KM# 536** **Weight:** 27.7770 g. **Composition:** 0.9000 Silver .8038 oz. ASW **Ruler:** Wilhelm II

| Date | Mintage | F | VF | XF | Unc | BU |
|---|---|---|---|---|---|---|
| 1913A | 1,962,000 | 14.00 | 22.00 | 32.00 | 70.00 | — |
| 1914A | 1,587,000 | 16.00 | 24.00 | 35.00 | 85.00 | — |
| (1913-1914)A Proof | — | Value: 600 | | | | |

**10 MARK** **KM# 520** **Weight:** 3.9820 g. **Composition:** 0.9000 Gold .1152 oz. AGW **Ruler:** Wilhelm II **Reverse:** Type III

| Date | Mintage | F | VF | XF | Unc | BU |
|---|---|---|---|---|---|---|
| 1901A | 702,000 | 55.00 | 95.00 | 120 | 275 | — |
| 1901A Proof | — | Value: 750 | | | | |
| 1902A | 271,000 | 55.00 | 95.00 | 120 | 275 | — |
| 1902A Proof | — | Value: 750 | | | | |
| 1903A | 1,685,000 | 55.00 | 95.00 | 120 | 275 | — |
| 1903A Proof | — | Value: 750 | | | | |
| 1904A | 1,178,000 | 55.00 | 95.00 | 120 | 275 | — |
| 1905A | 1,063,000 | 55.00 | 95.00 | 120 | 275 | — |
| 1905A Proof | 117 | Value: 750 | | | | |
| 1906A | 542,000 | 55.00 | 95.00 | 120 | 275 | — |
| 1906A Proof | 150 | Value: 750 | | | | |
| 1907A | 813,000 | 55.00 | 95.00 | 120 | 275 | — |
| 1907A Proof | — | Value: 750 | | | | |
| 1909A | 532,000 | 55.00 | 95.00 | 120 | 275 | — |
| 1909A Proof | — | Value: 750 | | | | |
| 1910A | 803,000 | 55.00 | 95.00 | 120 | 275 | — |
| 1911A | 271,000 | 55.00 | 95.00 | 120 | 275 | — |
| 1911A Proof | — | Value: 750 | | | | |
| 1912A | 542,000 | 55.00 | 95.00 | 120 | 275 | — |
| 1912A Proof | — | Value: 750 | | | | |

**20 MARK** **KM# 521** **Weight:** 7.9650 g. **Composition:** 0.9000 Gold .2304 oz. AGW **Ruler:** Wilhelm II **Reverse:** Type III

| Date | Mintage | F | VF | XF | Unc | BU |
|---|---|---|---|---|---|---|
| 1901A | 5,188,000 | BV | 100 | 110 | 130 | — |
| 1901A Proof | — | Value: 600 | | | | |
| 1902A | 4,138,000 | BV | 100 | 110 | 130 | — |
| 1903A | 2,870,000 | BV | 100 | 110 | 130 | — |
| 1904A | 3,453,000 | BV | 100 | 110 | 130 | — |
| 1905A | 4,176,000 | BV | 100 | 110 | 130 | — |
| 1905A Proof | 287 | Value: 600 | | | | |
| 1905J | 921,000 | BV | 100 | 150 | 200 | — |
| 1906A | 7,788,000 | BV | 100 | 110 | 130 | — |
| 1906A Proof | 124 | Value: 600 | | | | |
| 1906J | 82,000 | 125 | 200 | 300 | 450 | — |
| 1907A | 2,576,000 | BV | 100 | 110 | 130 | — |
| 1908A | 3,274,000 | BV | 100 | 110 | 130 | — |
| 1909A | 5,213,000 | BV | 100 | 110 | 130 | — |
| 1909J | 350,000 | 115 | 150 | 175 | 200 | — |
| 1909J Proof | — | Value: 800 | | | | |
| 1910A | 8,646,000 | BV | 100 | 110 | 130 | — |
| 1910J | 753,000 | BV | 100 | 150 | 200 | — |
| 1911A | 4,746,000 | BV | 100 | 110 | 130 | — |
| 1912A | 5,569,000 | BV | 100 | 110 | 130 | — |
| 1912J | 503,000 | BV | 100 | 150 | 200 | — |
| 1913A | 6,102,000 | BV | 100 | 110 | 130 | — |
| 1913A Proof | — | Value: 600 | | | | |

**20 MARK** **KM# 537** **Weight:** 7.9650 g. **Composition:** 0.9000 Gold .2304 oz. AGW **Ruler:** Wilhelm II

| Date | Mintage | F | VF | XF | Unc | BU |
|---|---|---|---|---|---|---|
| 1913A | — | BV | 115 | 135 | 175 | — |
| 1913A Proof | — | Value: 1,200 | | | | |
| 1914A | 2,137,000 | BV | 115 | 135 | 175 | — |
| 1914A Proof | — | Value: 1,200 | | | | |
| 1915A | 1,271,000 | 550 | 1,000 | 1,650 | 3,000 | — |

## PATTERNS

Including off metal strikes

| KM# | Date | Mintage | Identification | Mkt Val |
|---|---|---|---|---|
| PnA30 | 1901 | — | 20 Mark. Silver. Plain edge. | — |
| Pn28 | 1901 | — | 5 Mark. Silver. Larger design. KM526. | — |
| Pn29 | 1901 | — | 5 Mark. Silver. Larger design. KM526. | — |
| Pn30 | 1904 | — | 2 Mark. Silver. Plain edge. Broader rim. KM522. | — |
| Pn31 | 1904 | — | 5 Mark. Silver. | — |

| KM# | Date | Mintage | Identification | Mkt Val |
|---|---|---|---|---|
| Pn32 | 1904 | — | 5 Mark. Copper. "N.A." countermarked. | — |
| Pn33 | 1904 | — | 5 Mark. Silver. Reeded edge. Without beaded rims. KM523. | — |
| Pn34 | 1904 | — | 5 Mark. Silver. Smaller lettering. KM523. | — |
| Pn35 | 1904 | — | 5 Mark. Silver. Eagle in ornamental in inner border. | — |
| Pn36 | 1905 | — | 3 Mark. Silver. | — |
| Pn37 | 1905 | — | 3 Mark. Silver. Legend in different position. | — |
| Pn39 | 1905 | — | 3 Mark. Silver. KM527. | — |
| Pn38 | 1905 | — | 3 Mark. Copper. | — |
| PnA40 | 1907 | — | 20 Mark. Copper. 4.1100 g. | — |
| Pn40 | 1908 | — | 5 Mark. Silver. | — |
| Pn42 | 1908 | — | 20 Mark. Gold. KM521.2 | — |
| Pn41 | 1908 | — | 5 Mark. Brass. | — |
| Pn43 | 1909 | — | 2 Mark. Nickel. KM522. | — |
| Pn44 | 1910 | — | 3 Mark. Silver. | — |
| Pn45 | 1910 | — | 3 Mark. Copper. | — |
| Pn46 | 1911 | — | 3 Mark. Silver. KM531. | — |
| Pn47 | 1911 | — | 3 Mark. Silver. | — |
| Pn48 | 1911 | — | 3 Mark. Silver. KM531. | 400 |
| Pn49 | 1912 | — | 2 Mark. Silver. KM533. | — |
| Pn50 | 1912 | — | 3 Mark. Silver. | — |
| Pn52 | 1912 | — | 3 Mark. Silver. | — |
| Pn53 | 1912 | — | 3 Mark. Bronze. | — |
| Pn51 | 1912 | — | 3 Mark. Bronze. | — |
| Pn54 | 1913 | — | 2 Mark. Silver. Dots above "O" in KONIG. KM533. | — |
| Pn55 | 1913 | — | 3 Mark. Silver. | — |
| Pn61 | 1913 | — | 5 Mark. Silver. Extra sharp design. KM536. | — |
| Pn56 | 1913 | — | 3 Mark. Bronze. | — |
| Pn57 | 1913 | — | 3 Mark. Silver. | — |
| Pn58 | 1913 | — | 3 Mark. Bronze. | — |
| Pn59 | 1913 | — | 3 Mark. Silver. Dots above O in KONIG. KM535. | — |
| Pn60 | 1913 | — | 3 Mark. Copper. | — |
| Pn62 | 1914 | — | 3 Mark. Silver. Extra sharp design. KM538. | — |
| Pn63 | 1915 | — | 3 Mark. Silver. Gothic script. KM539. | — |
| Pn64 | 1915 | — | 3 Mark. White Metal. | — |
| Pn65 | 1915 | — | 3 Mark. Tin-iron. | — |

## REUSS-OBERGREIZ

The other branch of the division of 1635, Obergreiz went through a number of consolidations and further divisions. Upon the extinction of the Ruess-Untergreiz linein 1768, the latter passed to Reuss-Obergreiz and this line continued on into the 20th century, obtaining the rank of count back in 1673 and that of prince in 1778.

**RULERS**

Heinrich XXII, 1859-1902
Heinrich XXIV, 1902-1918

### PRINCIPALITY

**2 MARK** **KM# 128** **Weight:** 11.1110 g. **Composition:** 0.9000 Silver .3215 oz. ASW **Ruler:** Heinrich XXII

| Date | Mintage | F | VF | XF | Unc | BU |
|---|---|---|---|---|---|---|
| 1899A | 10,000 | 100 | 200 | 400 | 650 | — |
| 1899A Proof | 120 | Value: 800 | | | | |
| 1901A | 10,000 | 100 | 200 | 400 | 650 | — |
| 1901A Proof | — | Value: 800 | | | | |

**3 MARK** **KM# 130** **Weight:** 16.6670 g. **Composition:** 0.9000 Silver .4823 oz. ASW **Ruler:** Heinrich XXIV

| Date | Mintage | F | VF | XF | Unc | BU |
|---|---|---|---|---|---|---|
| 1909A | 10,000 | 120 | 275 | 450 | 800 | — |
| 1909A Proof | 400 | Value: 1,250 | | | | |

## PATTERNS

Including off metal strikes

| KM# | Date | Mintage | Identification | Mkt Val |
|---|---|---|---|---|
| Pn4 | 1909 | — | 3 Mark. Silver. Head faces left. KM130 | — |

## SAXE-ALTENBURG

**(Sachsen-Neu-Altenburg)**

A new line was established at Altenburg when the Duke of Saxe-Hildburghausen exchanged Hildburghausen for Altenburg in 1826. This line lasted until the end of World War I, when the last duke was forced to abdicate.

**RULERS**

Ernst I, 1853-1908
Ernst II, 1908-1918

**MINT MARKS**

A – Berlin Mint, 1886-1918

### DUCHY

**2 MARK** **KM# 144** **Weight:** 11.1110 g. **Composition:** 0.9000 Silver .3215 oz. ASW **Ruler:** Ernst I **Subject:** Ernst 75th birthday

| Date | Mintage | F | VF | XF | Unc | BU |
|---|---|---|---|---|---|---|
| 1901A | 50,000 | 100 | 200 | 400 | 650 | — |
| 1901A Proof | 500 | Value: 800 | | | | |

**5 MARK** **KM# 145** **Weight:** 27.7770 g. **Composition:** 0.9000 Silver .8038 oz. ASW **Ruler:** Ernst I **Subject:** Ernst 75th birthday

| Date | Mintage | F | VF | XF | Unc | BU |
|---|---|---|---|---|---|---|
| 1901A | 20,000 | 200 | 425 | 800 | 1,400 | — |
| 1901A Proof | 500 | Value: 1,750 | | | | |

**5 MARK** **KM# 147** **Weight:** 27.7770 g. **Composition:** 0.9000 Silver .8038 oz. ASW **Ruler:** Ernst I **Subject:** Ernst 50th year of reign

| Date | Mintage | F | VF | XF | Unc | BU |
|---|---|---|---|---|---|---|
| 1903 | 20,000 | 100 | 200 | 300 | 425 | — |
| 1903A Proof | 300 | Value: 500 | | | | |

## SAXE-COBURG-GOTHA

**(Sachsen-Coburg-Gotha)**

Upon the extinction of the ducal line in Saxe-Gotha-Altenburg in 1826, Gotha was assigned to Saxe-Coburg-Saalfeld and Saxe-Meiningen received Saalfeld. The resulting duchy became called Saxe-Coburg-Gotha. Albert, the son of Ernst I and younger brother of Ernst II, married Queen Victoria of Great Britain and the British royal dynastic name was that of Saxe-Coburg-Gotha. Their son, Alfred was made the Duke of Edinburgh and succeeded his uncle, Ernst II, as Duke of Saxe-Coburg-Gotha. Alfred's oldler brother, Eduard Albert, followed their mother as King Edward VII (1901-1910). The last duke of Saxe-Coburg-Gotha was Alfred's son, Karl Eduard, forced to abdicate in 1918 as a result of World War I, which was fought in part against his cousin, King George V.

**RULERS**

Karl Eduard, 1900-1918

**MINT MARKS**

A – Berlin Mint, 1886-1911

### DUCHY

**2 MARK** **KM# 152** **Weight:** 11.1110 g. **Composition:** 0.9000 Silver .3215 oz. ASW **Ruler:** Karl Eduard

| Date | Mintage | F | VF | XF | Unc | BU |
|---|---|---|---|---|---|---|
| 1905A | 10,000 | 125 | 275 | 600 | 1,100 | — |
| 1905A Proof | 2,000 | Value: 1,100 | | | | |
| 1911A Proof | 100 | Value: 12,500 | | | | |

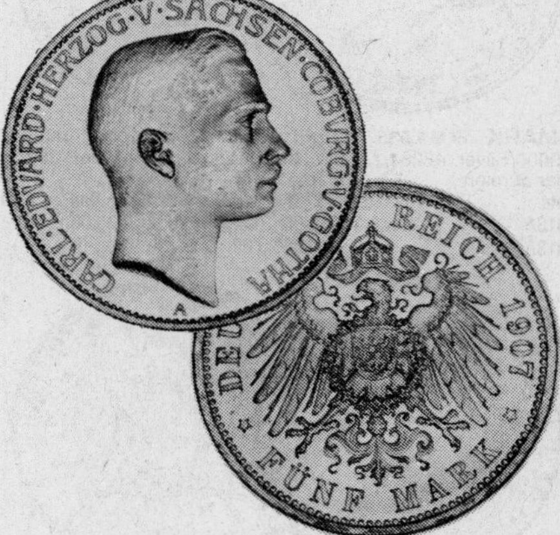

**5 MARK** **KM# 153** **Weight:** 27.7770 g. **Composition:** 0.9000 Silver .8038 oz. ASW **Ruler:** Karl Eduard

| Date | Mintage | F | VF | XF | Unc | BU |
|---|---|---|---|---|---|---|
| 1907A | 10,000 | 300 | 600 | 1,000 | 1,500 | — |
| 1907A Proof | — | Value: 2,250 | | | | |

**10 MARK** **KM# 154** **Weight:** 3.9820 g. **Composition:** 0.9000 Gold .1152 oz. AGW **Ruler:** Karl Eduard

| Date | Mintage | F | VF | XF | Unc | BU |
|---|---|---|---|---|---|---|
| 1905A | 9,511 | 400 | 600 | 1,200 | 1,800 | — |
| 1905A Proof | 489 | Value: 3,500 | | | | |

**20 MARK** **KM# 155** **Weight:** 7.9650 g. **Composition:** 0.9000 Gold .2304 oz. AGW **Ruler:** Karl Eduard **Reverse:** Type I

| Date | Mintage | F | VF | XF | Unc | BU |
|---|---|---|---|---|---|---|
| 1905A | 10,000 | 400 | 750 | 1,400 | 2,000 | — |
| 1905A Proof | 484 | Value: 3,750 | | | | |

# SAXE-MEININGEN

**(Sachsen-Meiningen)**

The duchy of Saxe-Meiningen was located in Thuringia (Thüringen), sandwiched between Saxe-Weimar-Eisenach on the west and north and the enclave of Schmalkalden belonging to Hesse-Cassel on the east. It was founded upon the division of the Ernestine line in Saxe-Gotha in 1680. In 1735, due to an exchange of some territory, the duchy became known as Saxe-Coburg-Meiningen. In 1826, Saxe-Coburg-Gotha assigned Saalfeld to Saxe-Meiningen. The duchy came under the strong influence of Prussia from 1866, when Bernhard II was forced to abdicate because of his support of Austria. The last duke was forced to give up his sovereign power at the end of World War I in 1918.

**RULERS**

Georg II, 1866-1914
Bernhard III, 1914-1918

## DUCHY

**2 MARK** **KM# 196** **Weight:** 11.1110 g. **Composition:** 0.9000 Silver .3215 oz. ASW **Ruler:** Georg II **Subject:** Duke's 75th birthday

| Date | Mintage | F | VF | XF | Unc | BU |
|---|---|---|---|---|---|---|
| 1901D | 20,000 | 100 | 250 | 400 | 750 | — |
| 1901D Proof | — | Value: 1,000 | | | | |

**2 MARK** **KM# 198** **Weight:** 11.1110 g. **Composition:** 0.9000 Silver .3215 oz. ASW **Ruler:** Georg II **Obverse:** Long beard

| Date | Mintage | F | VF | XF | Unc | BU |
|---|---|---|---|---|---|---|
| 1902D | 20,000 | 225 | 750 | 1,200 | 2,000 | — |

**2 MARK** **KM# 199** **Weight:** 11.1110 g. **Composition:** 0.9000 Silver .3215 oz. ASW **Ruler:** Georg II **Obverse:** Short beard

| Date | Mintage | F | VF | XF | Unc | BU |
|---|---|---|---|---|---|---|
| 1902D | Inc. above | 100 | 200 | 350 | 750 | — |
| 1913D | 5,000 | 150 | 250 | 450 | 1,250 | — |

**2 MARK** **KM# 206** **Weight:** 11.1110 g. **Composition:** 0.9000 Silver .3215 oz. ASW **Ruler:** Bernhard III **Subject:** Death of Georg II

| Date | Mintage | F | VF | XF | Unc | BU |
|---|---|---|---|---|---|---|
| 1915 | 30,000 | 35.00 | 60.00 | 140 | 200 | — |

**3 MARK** **KM# 203** **Weight:** 16.6670 g. **Composition:** 0.9000 Silver .4823 oz. ASW **Ruler:** Georg II

| Date | Mintage | F | VF | XF | Unc | BU |
|---|---|---|---|---|---|---|
| 1908D | 35,000 | 35.00 | 100 | 140 | 200 | — |
| 1908D Proof | — | Value: 430 | | | | |
| 1913D | 20,000 | 35.00 | 100 | 140 | 200 | — |

**3 MARK** **KM# 207** **Weight:** 16.6670 g. **Composition:** 0.9000 Silver .4823 oz. ASW **Ruler:** Bernhard III **Subject:** Death of Georg II

| Date | Mintage | F | VF | XF | Unc | BU |
|---|---|---|---|---|---|---|
| 1915 | 30,000 | 30.00 | 65.00 | 135 | 200 | — |
| 1915 Proof | — | Value: 225 | | | | |

**5 MARK** **KM# 197** **Weight:** 27.7770 g. **Composition:** 0.9000 Silver .8038 oz. ASW **Ruler:** Georg II **Subject:** Duke's 75th birthday

| Date | Mintage | F | VF | XF | Unc | BU |
|---|---|---|---|---|---|---|
| 1901D | 20,000 | 85.00 | 225 | 425 | 1,000 | — |
| 1901D Proof | — | Value: 1,500 | | | | |

**5 MARK** **KM# 200** **Weight:** 27.7770 g. **Composition:** 0.9000 Silver .8038 oz. ASW **Ruler:** Georg II **Obverse:** Long beard

| Date | Mintage | F | VF | XF | Unc | BU |
|---|---|---|---|---|---|---|
| 1902D | 20,000 | 60.00 | 175 | 325 | 1,000 | — |

**5 MARK** **KM# 201** **Weight:** 27.7770 g. **Composition:** 0.9000 Silver .8038 oz. ASW **Ruler:** Georg II **Obverse:** Short beard

| Date | Mintage | F | VF | XF | Unc | BU |
|---|---|---|---|---|---|---|
| 1902D | Inc. above | 60.00 | 150 | 325 | 1,000 | — |
| 1908D | 60,000 | 50.00 | 150 | 275 | 850 | — |

**10 MARK** **KM# 202** **Weight:** 3.9820 g. **Composition:** 0.9000 Gold .1152 oz. AGW **Ruler:** Georg II

| Date | Mintage | F | VF | XF | Unc | BU |
|---|---|---|---|---|---|---|
| 1902D | 2,000 | 600 | 1,400 | 2,500 | 3,500 | — |
| 1902D Proof | — | Value: 4,250 | | | | |
| 1909D | 2,000 | 600 | 1,400 | 2,500 | 3,500 | — |
| 1909D Proof | — | Value: 4,250 | | | | |
| 1914D | 1,002 | 800 | 1,600 | 2,500 | 3,500 | — |
| 1914D Proof | — | Value: 4,250 | | | | |

**20 MARK** **KM# 195** **Weight:** 7.9650 g. **Composition:** 0.9000 Gold .2304 oz. AGW **Ruler:** Georg II **Reverse:** Type III

| Date | Mintage | F | VF | XF | Unc | BU |
|---|---|---|---|---|---|---|
| 1900D | 1,005 | 1,500 | 3,000 | 3,500 | 7,000 | — |
| 1900D Proof | — | Value: 11,000 | | | | |
| 1905D | 1,000 | 1,500 | 3,000 | 3,500 | 7,000 | — |
| 1905D Proof | — | Value: 11,000 | | | | |

**20 MARK** **KM# 205** **Weight:** 7.9650 g. **Composition:** 0.9000 Gold .2304 oz. AGW **Ruler:** Georg II

| Date | Mintage | F | VF | XF | Unc | BU |
|---|---|---|---|---|---|---|
| 1910D | 1,004 | 1,500 | 3,000 | 4,000 | 5,500 | — |
| 1910D Proof | — | Value: 7,000 | | | | |
| 1914D | 1,000 | 1,500 | 3,000 | 4,000 | 5,500 | — |
| 1914D Proof | — | Value: 7,000 | | | | |

## PATTERNS

Including off metal strikes

| KM# | Date | Mintage | Identification | Mkt Val |
|---|---|---|---|---|
| Pn16 | 1901 | — | 10 Mark. Gold. With neck and beard variety. KM202. | — |
| Pn17 | 1901 | — | 10 Mark. Gold. KM202. | — |
| Pn18 | 1915 | — | 2 Mark. KM206. | — |
| Pn19 | 1915 | — | 3 Mark. KM207. | — |

# SAXE-WEIMAR-EISENACH

**(Sachsen-Weimar-Eisenach)**

When the death of the duke of Saxe-Eisenach in 1741 heralded the extinction of that line, its possessions reverted to Saxe-Weimar, which henceforth was known as Saxe-Weimar-Eisenach. Because of the strong role played by the duke during the Napoleonic Wars, Saxe-Weimar-Eisenach was raised to the rank of a grand duchy in 1814 and granted the territory of Neustadt, taken from Saxony. The last grand duke abdicated at the end of World War I.

**RULERS**
Karl Alexander, 1853-1901
Wilhelm Ernst, 1901-1918

**MINT MARKS**
A – Berlin Mint, 1840-1915

## GRAND DUCHY

**2 MARK** **Y# 170** **Weight:** 11.1110 g. **Composition:** 0.9000 Silver .3215 oz. ASW **Ruler:** Wilhelm Ernst

| Date | Mintage | F | VF | XF | Unc | BU |
|---|---|---|---|---|---|---|
| 1901A | 100,000 | 100 | 300 | 425 | 850 | — |
| 1901A Proof | — | Value: 1,200 | | | | |

**2 MARK** **Y# 172** **Weight:** 11.1110 g. **Composition:** 0.9000 Silver .3215 oz. ASW **Ruler:** Wilhelm Ernst **Subject:** Grand Duke's First Marriage

| Date | Mintage | F | VF | XF | Unc | BU |
|---|---|---|---|---|---|---|
| 1903A | 40,000 | 35.00 | 60.00 | 100 | 140 | — |
| 1903A Proof | Est. 1,000 | Value: 180 | | | | |

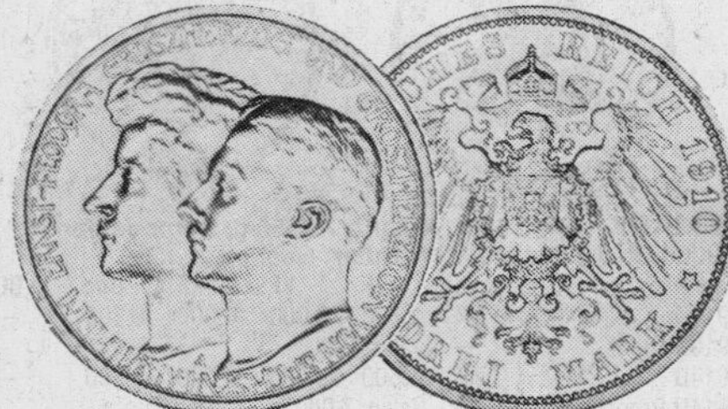

**2 MARK** **Y# 174** **Weight:** 11.1110 g. **Composition:** 0.9000 Silver .3215 oz. ASW **Ruler:** Wilhelm Ernst **Subject:** Jena University 350th Anniversary

| Date | Mintage | F | VF | XF | Unc | BU |
|---|---|---|---|---|---|---|
| 1908 | 50,000 | 25.00 | 50.00 | 100 | 125 | — |

**3 MARK** **Y# 176** **Weight:** 16.6670 g. **Composition:** 0.9000 Silver .4823 oz. ASW **Ruler:** Wilhelm Ernst **Subject:** Grand Duke's Second Marriage

| Date | Mintage | F | VF | XF | Unc | BU |
|---|---|---|---|---|---|---|
| 1910 | 133,000 | 15.00 | 35.00 | 70.00 | 85.00 | — |
| 1910A Proof | — | Value: 125 | | | | |

**3 MARK** **Y# 177** **Weight:** 16.6670 g. **Composition:** 0.9000 Silver .4823 oz. ASW **Ruler:** Wilhelm Ernst **Subject:** Centenary of Grand Duchy

| Date | Mintage | F | VF | XF | Unc | BU |
|---|---|---|---|---|---|---|
| 1915A | 50,000 | 25.00 | 75.00 | 125 | 175 | — |
| 1915A Proof | 200 | Value: 400 | | | | |

**5 MARK** **Y# 173** **Weight:** 27.7770 g. **Composition:** 0.9000 Silver .8038 oz. ASW **Ruler:** Wilhelm Ernst **Subject:** Grand Dule's First Marriage

| Date | Mintage | F | VF | XF | Unc | BU |
|---|---|---|---|---|---|---|
| 1903A | 24,000 | 50.00 | 100 | 225 | 300 | — |
| 1903A Proof | Est. 1,000 | Value: 425 | | | | |

**5 MARK** **Y# 175** **Weight:** 27.7770 g. **Composition:** 0.9000 Silver .8038 oz. ASW **Ruler:** Wilhelm Ernst **Subject:** Jena University 350th Anniversary

| Date | Mintage | F | VF | XF | Unc | BU |
|---|---|---|---|---|---|---|
| 1908A | 40,000 | 60.00 | 100 | 180 | 220 | — |
| 1908A Proof | — | Value: 625 | | | | |

**20 MARK** **Y# 171** **Weight:** 7.9650 g. **Composition:** 0.9000 Gold .2304 oz. AGW **Ruler:** Wilhelm Ernst **Subject:** Golden Wedding of Carl Alexander

| Date | Mintage | F | VF | XF | Unc | BU |
|---|---|---|---|---|---|---|
| 1901A | 5,000 | 750 | 1,500 | 2,000 | 3,000 | — |
| 1901A Proof | — | Value: 5,000 | | | | |

### PATTERNS

Including off metal strikes

| KM# | Date | Mintage | Identification | Mkt Val |
|---|---|---|---|---|
| Pn1 | 1908 | — | 5 Mark. Silver. Figure smaller. Y#175. | — |

| KM# | Date | Mintage | Identification | Mkt Val |
|---|---|---|---|---|
| Pn2 | 1910 | — | 3 Mark. Silver. | — |
| Pn3 | 1910 | — | 3 Mark. Brass. | — |

## SAXONY

Saxony, located in southeast Germany was founded in 850. The first coinage was struck c. 990. It was divided into two lines in 1464. The electoral right was obtained by the elder line in 1547. During the time of the Reformation, Saxony was one of the more powerful states in central Europe. It became a kingdom in 1806. At the Congress of Vienna in 1815, they were forced to cede half its territories to Prussia.

**RULERS**
Albert, 1873-1902
Georg, 1902-1904
Friedrich August III, 1904-1918

**MINT MARKS**
L - Leipzig

## KINGDOM

**2 MARK** **KM# 1245** **Weight:** 11.1110 g. **Composition:** 0.9000 Silver .3215 oz. ASW **Ruler:** Albert **Note:** Similar to KM#185.

| Date | Mintage | F | VF | XF | Unc | BU |
|---|---|---|---|---|---|---|
| 1901E | 440,000 | 12.50 | 55.00 | 100 | 275 | — |
| 1902E | 543,000 | 10.00 | 55.00 | 100 | 200 | — |

**2 MARK** **KM# 1255** **Weight:** 11.1110 g. **Composition:** 0.9000 Silver .3215 oz. ASW **Ruler:** Georg **Subject:** Death of Albert

| Date | Mintage | F | VF | XF | Unc | BU |
|---|---|---|---|---|---|---|
| 1902E | 168,000 | 15.00 | 40.00 | 65.00 | 100 | — |
| 1902E Proof | 250 | Value: 200 | | | | |

**2 MARK** **KM# 1257** **Weight:** 11.1110 g. **Composition:** 0.9000 Silver .3215 oz. ASW **Ruler:** Georg

| Date | Mintage | F | VF | XF | Unc | BU |
|---|---|---|---|---|---|---|
| 1903E | 746,000 | 30.00 | 60.00 | 140 | 350 | — |
| 1903E Proof | 50 | Value: 600 | | | | |
| 1904E | 1,266,000 | 17.50 | 50.00 | 100 | 250 | — |

**2 MARK** **KM# 1261** **Weight:** 11.1110 g. **Composition:** 0.9000 Silver .3215 oz. ASW **Ruler:** Friedrich August III **Subject:** Death of Georg

| Date | Mintage | F | VF | XF | Unc | BU |
|---|---|---|---|---|---|---|
| 1904E | 150,000 | 15.00 | 35.00 | 60.00 | 95.00 | — |
| 1904E Proof | 55 | Value: 225 | | | | |

**2 MARK** **KM# 1263** **Weight:** 11.1110 g. **Composition:** 0.9000 Silver .3215 oz. ASW **Ruler:** Friedrich August III

| Date | Mintage | F | VF | XF | Unc | BU |
|---|---|---|---|---|---|---|
| 1905E | 559,000 | 20.00 | 35.00 | 60.00 | 155 | — |
| 1905E Proof | 100 | Value: 300 | | | | |
| 1906E | 559,000 | 20.00 | 35.00 | 60.00 | 155 | — |
| 1907E | 1,118,000 | 20.00 | 35.00 | 60.00 | 155 | — |
| 1908E | 336,000 | 20.00 | 35.00 | 55.00 | 150 | — |
| 1911E | 186,000 | 20.00 | 35.00 | 55.00 | 150 | — |
| 1912E | 168,000 | 20.00 | 35.00 | 55.00 | 150 | — |
| 1914E | 298,000 | 20.00 | 35.00 | 55.00 | 150 | — |
| (1905-1914)E Proof | — | Value: 300 | | | | |

**2 MARK** **KM# 1268** **Weight:** 11.1110 g. **Composition:** 0.9000 Silver .3215 oz. ASW **Ruler:** Friedrich August III **Subject:** 500th anniversary - Leipzig University

| Date | Mintage | F | VF | XF | Unc | BU |
|---|---|---|---|---|---|---|
| 1909 | 125,000 | 15.00 | 30.00 | 65.00 | 90.00 | — |
| 1909 Proof | 300 | Value: 200 | | | | |

**3 MARK** **KM# 1267** **Weight:** 16.6670 g. **Composition:** 0.9000 Silver .4823 oz. ASW **Ruler:** Friedrich August III

| Date | Mintage | F | VF | XF | Unc | BU |
|---|---|---|---|---|---|---|
| 1908E | 276,000 | 10.00 | 20.00 | 40.00 | 65.00 | — |
| 1909E | 1,197,000 | 10.00 | 18.00 | 28.00 | 60.00 | — |
| 1910E | 745,000 | 10.00 | 18.00 | 28.00 | 60.00 | — |
| 1911E | 581,000 | 10.00 | 18.00 | 28.00 | 60.00 | — |
| 1912E | 379,000 | 10.00 | 18.00 | 28.00 | 60.00 | — |
| 1913E | 307,000 | 10.00 | 18.00 | 28.00 | 60.00 | — |
| (1908-1913)E Proof | — | Value: 225 | | | | |

**3 MARK** **KM# 1275** **Weight:** 16.6670 g. **Composition:** 0.9000 Silver .4823 oz. ASW **Ruler:** Friedrich August III **Subject:** Battle of Leipzig centennial

| Date | Mintage | F | VF | XF | Unc | BU |
|---|---|---|---|---|---|---|
| 1913E | 1,000,000 | 12.00 | 18.00 | 28.00 | 45.00 | — |
| 1913E Proof | 17,000 | Value: 100 | | | | |

**3 MARK** **KM# 1276** **Weight:** 16.6670 g. **Composition:** 0.9000 Silver .4823 oz. ASW **Ruler:** Friedrich August III **Subject:** Jubilee of Reformation

| Date | Mintage | F | VF | XF | Unc | BU |
|---|---|---|---|---|---|---|
| 1917E Proof | 100 | Value: 60,000 | | | | |

**5 MARK** **KM# 1246** **Weight:** 27.7770 g. **Composition:** 0.9000 Silver .8038 oz. ASW **Ruler:** Albert **Note:** Similar to KM#1256.

| Date | Mintage | F | VF | XF | Unc | BU |
|---|---|---|---|---|---|---|
| 1901E | 156,000 | 25.00 | 55.00 | 300 | 700 | — |
| 1902E | 168,000 | 20.00 | 40.00 | 250 | 500 | — |
| 1902E Proof | — | Value: 2,400 | | | | |

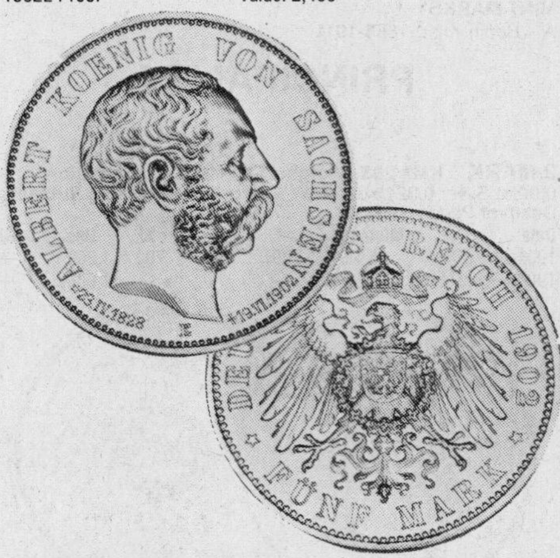


**5 MARK** **KM# 1256** **Weight:** 27.7770 g. **Composition:** 0.9000 Silver .8038 oz. ASW **Ruler:** Georg **Subject:** Death of Albert

| Date | Mintage | F | VF | XF | Unc | BU |
|---|---|---|---|---|---|---|
| 1902E | 100,000 | 30.00 | 60.00 | 125 | 175 | — |
| 1902E Proof | 250 | Value: 425 | | | | |

**5 MARK** **KM# 1258** **Weight:** 27.7770 g. **Composition:** 0.9000 Silver .8038 oz. ASW **Ruler:** Georg

| Date | Mintage | F | VF | XF | Unc | BU |
|---|---|---|---|---|---|---|
| 1903E | 536,000 | 20.00 | 40.00 | 125 | 650 | — |
| 1903E Proof | 50 | Value: 1,000 | | | | |
| 1904E | 291,000 | 25.00 | 50.00 | 160 | 750 | — |
| 1904E Proof | — | Value: 1,100 | | | | |

**5 MARK** **KM# 1262** **Weight:** 27.7770 g. **Composition:** 0.9000 Silver .8038 oz. ASW **Ruler:** Friedrich August III **Subject:** Death of Georg

| Date | Mintage | F | VF | XF | Unc | BU |
|---|---|---|---|---|---|---|
| 1904E | 37,000 | 40.00 | 125 | 225 | 300 | — |
| 1904E Proof | 70 | Value: 500 | | | | |

**5 MARK** **KM# 1266** **Weight:** 27.7770 g. **Composition:** 0.9000 Silver .8038 oz. ASW **Ruler:** Friedrich August III

| Date | Mintage | F | VF | XF | Unc | BU |
|---|---|---|---|---|---|---|
| 1907E | 398,000 | 20.00 | 40.00 | 85.00 | 300 | — |
| 1908E | 317,000 | 20.00 | 40.00 | 85.00 | 250 | — |
| 1914E | 298,000 | 17.50 | 35.00 | 80.00 | 200 | — |
| 1914E Proof | — | Value: 1,100 | | | | |

**5 MARK** **KM# 1269** **Weight:** 27.7770 g. **Composition:** 0.9000 Silver .8038 oz. ASW **Ruler:** Friedrich August III **Subject:** 500th anniversary - Leipzig University

| Date | Mintage | F | VF | XF | Unc | BU |
|---|---|---|---|---|---|---|
| 1909 | 50,000 | 40.00 | 90.00 | 165 | 235 | — |
| 1909 Proof | 300 | Value: 525 | | | | |

**10 MARK** **KM# 1247** **Weight:** 3.9820 g. **Composition:** 0.9000 Gold .1152 oz. AGW **Ruler:** Albert **Reverse:** Type III

| Date | Mintage | F | VF | XF | Unc | BU |
|---|---|---|---|---|---|---|
| 1901E | 75,000 | 80.00 | 125 | 175 | 450 | — |
| 1902E | 37,000 | 80.00 | 125 | 175 | 475 | — |

**10 MARK** **KM# 1259** **Weight:** 3.9820 g. **Composition:** 0.9000 Gold .1152 oz. AGW **Ruler:** Georg

| Date | Mintage | F | VF | XF | Unc | BU |
|---|---|---|---|---|---|---|
| 1903E | 284,000 | 80.00 | 200 | 300 | 500 | — |
| 1903E Proof | 100 | Value: 1,450 | | | | |
| 1904E | 149,000 | 80.00 | 200 | 300 | 500 | — |

**10 MARK** **KM# 1264** **Weight:** 3.9820 g. **Composition:** 0.9000 Gold .1152 oz. AGW **Ruler:** Friedrich August III

| Date | Mintage | F | VF | XF | Unc | BU |
|---|---|---|---|---|---|---|
| 1905E | 112,000 | 70.00 | 200 | 250 | 400 | — |
| 1905E Proof | 100 | Value: 1,400 | | | | |
| 1906E | 75,000 | 70.00 | 200 | 250 | 400 | — |
| 1907E | 112,000 | 70.00 | 200 | 250 | 400 | — |
| 1909E | 112,000 | 70.00 | 200 | 250 | 400 | — |
| 1910E | 75,000 | 70.00 | 200 | 250 | 400 | — |
| 1910E Proof | — | Value: 1,400 | | | | |
| 1911E | 38,000 | 70.00 | 200 | 250 | 425 | — |
| 1912E | 75,000 | 70.00 | 200 | 250 | 400 | — |

**20 MARK** **KM# 1260** **Weight:** 7.9650 g. **Composition:** 0.9000 Gold .2304 oz. AGW **Ruler:** Georg **Reverse:** Type III

| Date | Mintage | F | VF | XF | Unc | BU |
|---|---|---|---|---|---|---|
| 1903E | 250,000 | 120 | 150 | 250 | 400 | — |
| 1903E Proof | — | Value: 1,800 | | | | |

## MEDALLIC COINAGE

**2 MARK** **KM# M13** **Composition:** Silver **Ruler:** Georg **Subject:** Visit of King George

| Date | Mintage | F | VF | XF | Unc | BU |
|---|---|---|---|---|---|---|
| 1903 Proof | — | Value: 1,250 | | | | |

**2 MARK** **KM# M14** **Composition:** Silver **Ruler:** Friedrich August III **Subject:** Visit of King Friedrich August

| Date | Mintage | F | VF | XF | Unc | BU |
|---|---|---|---|---|---|---|
| 1905 Proof | — | Value: 1,200 | | | | |

## PATTERNS

Including off metal strikes

| KM# | Date | Mintage | Identification | Mkt Val |
|---|---|---|---|---|
| Pn78 | 1902 | — | 5 Mark. Silver. KM1258. | — |
| PnA78 | 1905 | — | 20 Mark. Copper. 4.0600 g. | — |
| PnB78 | 1905 | — | 20 Mark. Copper. 4.8900 g. Bust in uniform. | — |
| Pn79 | 1913 | — | 3 Mark. Silver. | — |
| Pn80 | 1917 | — | 3 Mark. Aluminum. KM1267. | — |

# SCHAUMBURG-LIPPE

The tiny countship of Schaumburg-Lippe, with an area of only 131 square miles (218 square kilometers) in northwest Germany, was surrounded by the larger states of Brunswick-Lüneburg-Calenberg, an enclave of Hesse-Cassel, and the bishopric of Minden (part of Brandenburg-Prussia from 1648). It was founded in 1640 when Schaumburg-Gehmen was divided between Hesse-Cassel and Lippe-Alverdissen. The two became known as Schaumburg-Hessen and Schaumburg-Lippe. Philipp II, the youngest son of Count Simon VI of Lippe came into the possession of Alverdissen and Lipperode upon his father's death in 1613. In 1640, he also inherited half of Schaumburg-Bückeburg, becoming the first Count of Schaumburg-Lippe. A separate line of Schaumburg-Alverdissen was established in 1681 and, upon the extinction of the elder line in 1777, the lands and titles devolved onto Alverdissen, becoming the ruling line in the countship. In 1806, the count was raised to the rank of prince and Schaumburg-Lippe was incorporated into the Rhine Confederation. It became a part of the German Confederation in 1815 and joined the North German Confederation in 1866. The principality became a member state in the German Empire in 1871. The last sovereign prince resigned as a result of World War I.

**RULERS**

Albrecht Georg, 1893-1911
Adolf II Bernhard, 1911-1918

**MINT MARKS**

A - Berlin mint, 1858-1911

## PRINCIPALITY

**2 MARK** **KM# 203** **Weight:** 11.1110 g. **Composition:** 0.9000 Silver 0.3215 oz. ASW **Ruler:** Albrecht Georg **Subject:** Death of Prince George

| Date | Mintage | F | VF | XF | Unc | BU |
|---|---|---|---|---|---|---|
| 1904A | 5,000 | 200 | 400 | 700 | 1,250 | — |
| 1904A Proof | 200 | — | — | — | 1,600 | — |

**3 MARK** **KM# 206** **Weight:** 16.6670 g. **Composition:** 0.9000 Silver 0.4823 oz. ASW **Ruler:** Albrecht Georg **Subject:** Death of Prince George

| Date | Mintage | F | VF | XF | Unc | BU |
|---|---|---|---|---|---|---|
| 1911A | 50,000 | 30.00 | 60.00 | 90.00 | 175 | — |
| 1911A Proof | — | — | — | — | 300 | — |

**5 MARK** **KM# 204** **Weight:** 27.7770 g. **Composition:** 0.9000 Silver 0.8038 oz. ASW **Ruler:** Albrecht Georg **Subject:** Death of Prince George

| Date | Mintage | F | VF | XF | Unc | BU |
|---|---|---|---|---|---|---|
| 1904A | 3,000 | 350 | 775 | 1,200 | 2,450 | — |
| 1904A Proof | 200 | — | — | — | 3,500 | — |

**20 MARK** **KM# 205** **Weight:** 7.9650 g. **Composition:** 0.9000 Gold 0.2304 oz. AGW **Ruler:** Albrecht Georg **Subject:** Death of Prince George

| Date | Mintage | F | VF | XF | Unc | BU |
|---|---|---|---|---|---|---|
| 1904A | 5,500 | 600 | 1,000 | 2,000 | 3,000 | — |
| 1904A Proof | 132 | — | — | — | 4,500 | — |

# SCHLESWIG-HOLSTEIN

Schleswig-Holstein is located along the border area between Denmark and Germany. The Duchy of Schleswig was predominantly Danish while the Duchy of Holstein was mostly German. Holstein-Gottorp was the ruling line in most of the territory from 1533 and lost Schleswig to Denmark permanently in 1721. Holstein-Gottorp was transferred by the 1773 Treaty of Zarskoje Selo to Denmark in exchange for Oldenburg. There was a great deal of trouble in the area during the 19th century and as a result of a war with Denmark, Prussia annexed the territory in 1864. After World War I, a plebiscite was held and the area was divided in 1920. North Slesvig went to Denmark while South Schleswig and Holstein became a permanent part of Germany.

## STATE

### GUTSCHRIFTSMARKE

**5/100 GUTSCHRIFTSMARKE** **KM# Tn1** **Composition:** Aluminum **Obverse:** Provincial arms **Reverse:** Denomination **Size:** 23 mm.

| Date | Mintage | F | VF | XF | Unc | BU |
|---|---|---|---|---|---|---|
| 1923 | 3,330,000 | 3.00 | 7.00 | 14.00 | 22.50 | — |

**10/100 GUTSCHRIFTSMARKE** **KM# Tn2** **Composition:** Aluminum **Obverse:** Provincial arms **Reverse:** Denomination **Size:** 27 mm.

| Date | Mintage | F | VF | XF | Unc | BU |
|---|---|---|---|---|---|---|
| 1923 | 4,500,000 | 4.00 | 8.00 | 16.00 | 25.00 | — |

# SCHWARZBURG-RUDOLSTADT

The Countship of Schwarzburg-Rudolstadt came into being as the younger line upon the division of Schwarzburg-Blankenburg in 1552. Its territory of about 360 square miles (600 square kilometers) is located in the center of Thuringia (Thüringen), surrounded by several of the Saxon duchies and Reuss-Obergreiz. The count attained the rank of prince in 1711 and the small state was able to weather the political perils of the Napoleonic Wars (1792-1815). Schwarzburg-Rudolstadt joined the German Confederation at the end of hostilities and subsequently became a member of the North German Confederation in 1867, then the German Empire in 1871. The last prince obtained Schwarzburg-Sondershausen upon the latter's extinction in 1909, then was forced to abdicate in 1918.

**RULERS**

Günther Viktor, 1890-1918

**MINT MARKS**

A - Berlin mint, 1841-1901

## PATTERNS

Including off metal strikes

| KM# | Date | Mintage | Identification | Mkt Val |
|---|---|---|---|---|
| Pn3 | 1901 | — | 2 Mark. Y207. | — |

# SCHWARZBURG-SONDERSHAUSEN

The Countship of Schwarzburg-Sondershausen was established as the elder line of the family upon the division of Schwarzburg-Blankenburg in 1552. It contains territory of about 330 square miles (550 square kilometers) and is located just north of Thuringia (Thüringen), surrounded by the Prussian province of Saxony, between the ducal enclaves of Gotha and Weimar. The count was raised to the rank of prince in 1697 and underwent several minor divisions during the 18th century. Schwarzburg-

Sondershausen joined the German Confederation in 1815 and became a member of the North German Confederation in 1867, as well as the German Empire in 1871. When Karl Günther died without an heir in 1909, his lands and titles went to Schwarzburg-Rudolstadt (see).

**RULERS**
Karl Günther, 1880-1909

**MINT MARKS**
A - Berlin mint, 1846-1909

## PRINCIPALITY

**2 MARK** Y# 211 **Weight:** 11.1110 g. **Composition:** 0.9000 Silver .3215 oz. ASW **Ruler:** Karl Gunther **Subject:** 25th anniversary of reign **Note:** Thick rim.

| Date | Mintage | F | VF | XF | Unc | BU |
|---|---|---|---|---|---|---|
| 1905 | 13,000 | 40.00 | 75.00 | 145 | 220 | — |
| 1905 Proof | 5,000 | Value: 250 | | | | |

**2 MARK** Y# 211a **Weight:** 11.1110 g. **Composition:** 0.9000 Silver .3215 oz. ASW **Ruler:** Karl Gunther **Subject:** 25th anniversary of reign **Note:** Thin rim.

| Date | Mintage | F | VF | XF | Unc | BU |
|---|---|---|---|---|---|---|
| 1905 Proof | 5,000 | Value: 150 | | | | |
| 1905 | 62,000 | 25.00 | 40.00 | 90.00 | 125 | — |

**3 MARK** Y# 212 **Weight:** 16.6670 g. **Composition:** 0.9000 Silver .4823 oz. ASW **Ruler:** Karl Gunther **Subject:** Death of Karl Gunther

| Date | Mintage | F | VF | XF | Unc | BU |
|---|---|---|---|---|---|---|
| 1909A | 70,000 | 30.00 | 60.00 | 100 | 185 | — |
| 1909A Proof | 100 | Value: 350 | | | | |

### PATTERNS
Including off metal strikes

| KM# | Date | Mintage | Identification | Mkt Val |
|---|---|---|---|---|
| Pn1 | 1901 | — | 2 Mark. Y209. | — |
| Pn2 | 1901 | — | 2 Mark. Y211. | — |
| Pn3 | 1909 | — | 3 Mark. Silver. | — |

## WALDECK-PYRMONT

The Count of Waldeck-Eisenberg inherited the Countship of Pyrmont, located between Lippe and Hannover, in 1625, thus creating an entity which encompassed about 672 square miles (1120 square kilometers). Waldeck and Pyrmont were permanently united in 1668, thus continuing the Eisenberg line as Waldeck-Pyrmont from that date. The count was raised to the rank of prince in 1712 and the unification of the two territories was confirmed in 1812. Waldeck-Pyrmont joined the German Confederation in 1815 and the North German Confederation in 1867. The prince renounced his sovereignty on 1 October of that year and Waldeck-Pyrmont was incorporated into Prussia. However, coinage was struck into the early 20th century for Waldeck-Pyrmont as a member of the German Empire. The hereditary territorial titles were lost along with the war in 1918. Some coins were struck for issue in Pyrmont only in the 18th through 20th centuries and those are listed separately under that name.

**RULERS**
Friedrich, 1893-1918 (d.1946)

**MINT OFFICIALS**
AW - Albert Welle, mintmaster in Arolsen 1827-1840
FW, F*w, W, .W. – Friedrich Welle

**MINT MARKS**
A - Berlin mint, 1842-1903
B - Hannover mint, 1867

## PRINCIPALITY

**5 MARK** Y# 213 **Weight:** 27.7770 g. **Composition:** 0.9000 Silver .8038 oz. ASW **Ruler:** Friedrich

| Date | Mintage | F | VF | XF | Unc | BU |
|---|---|---|---|---|---|---|
| 1903A | 2,000 | 700 | 1,500 | 3,000 | 5,000 | — |
| 1903A Proof | 300 | Value: 5,500 | | | | |

**20 MARK** Y# 214 **Weight:** 7.9650 g. **Composition:** 0.9000 Gold .2304 oz. AGW **Ruler:** Friedrich

| Date | Mintage | F | VF | XF | Unc | BU |
|---|---|---|---|---|---|---|
| 1903A | 2,000 | 1,000 | 2,500 | 3,500 | 5,500 | — |
| 1903A Proof | 150 | Value: 7,500 | | | | |

## WURTTEMBERG

## KINGDOM

**2 MARK** KM# 631 **Weight:** 11.1110 g. **Composition:** 0.9000 Silver .3215 oz. ASW **Ruler:** Wilhelm II

| Date | Mintage | F | VF | XF | Unc | BU |
|---|---|---|---|---|---|---|
| 1892F | 177,000 | 16.00 | 30.00 | 95.00 | 250 | — |
| 1893F | 174,000 | 16.00 | 30.00 | 75.00 | 225 | — |
| 1896F | 351,000 | 12.00 | 25.00 | 50.00 | 200 | — |
| 1898F | 144,000 | 20.00 | 30.00 | 90.00 | 250 | — |
| 1899F | 538,000 | 9.00 | 19.00 | 40.00 | 175 | — |
| 1900F | 516,000 | 8.00 | 16.00 | 40.00 | 125 | — |
| (1892-1900)F Proof | — | Value: 175 | | | | |
| 1901F | 592,000 | 9.00 | 19.00 | 40.00 | 125 | — |
| 1902F | 816,000 | 8.00 | 17.00 | 45.00 | 125 | — |
| 1903F | 811,000 | 9.00 | 19.00 | 40.00 | 125 | — |
| 1904F | 1,988,000 | 8.00 | 15.00 | 30.00 | 100 | — |
| 1905F | 250,000 | 9.00 | 20.00 | 35.00 | 100 | — |
| 1906F | 1,505,000 | 9.00 | 20.00 | 35.00 | 100 | — |
| 1907F | 1,504,000 | 8.00 | 15.00 | 30.00 | 100 | — |
| 1908F | 451,000 | 8.00 | 22.00 | 40.00 | 125 | — |
| 1912F | 251,000 | 8.00 | 15.00 | 30.00 | 100 | — |
| 1913F | 226,000 | 8.00 | 17.00 | 40.00 | 125 | — |
| 1914F | 318,000 | 8.00 | 17.00 | 45.00 | 125 | — |
| (1901-1914) Proof | — | Value: 175 | | | | |

**3 MARK** KM# 635 **Weight:** 16.6670 g. **Composition:** 0.9000 Silver .4823 oz. ASW **Ruler:** Wilhelm II

| Date | Mintage | F | VF | XF | Unc | BU |
|---|---|---|---|---|---|---|
| 1908F | 300,000 | 10.00 | 20.00 | 30.00 | 65.00 | — |
| 1909F | 1,907,000 | 10.00 | 20.00 | 30.00 | 60.00 | — |
| 1910F | 837,000 | 10.00 | 20.00 | 30.00 | 60.00 | — |
| 1911F | 425,000 | 10.00 | 20.00 | 30.00 | 60.00 | — |
| 1912F | 849,000 | 10.00 | 17.50 | 25.00 | 50.00 | — |
| 1913F | 267,000 | 10.00 | 20.00 | 30.00 | 70.00 | — |
| 1914F | 733,000 | 10.00 | 17.50 | 25.00 | 50.00 | — |
| (1908-1914)F Proof | — | Value: 250 | | | | |

**3 MARK** KM# 636 **Weight:** 16.6670 g. **Composition:** 0.9000 Silver .4823 oz. ASW **Ruler:** Wilhelm II **Subject:** Silver wedding anniversary **Obverse:** Normal bar in H of CHARLOTTE

| Date | Mintage | F | VF | XF | Unc | BU |
|---|---|---|---|---|---|---|
| 1911F | 493,000 | 11.50 | 17.50 | 35.00 | 60.00 | — |
| 1911F Proof | — | Value: 125 | | | | |

**3 MARK** KM# 637 **Weight:** 16.6670 g. **Composition:** 0.9000 Silver .4823 oz. ASW **Ruler:** Wilhelm II **Subject:** Silver wedding anniversary **Obverse:** High bar in H of CHARLOTTE

| Date | Mintage | F | VF | XF | Unc | BU |
|---|---|---|---|---|---|---|
| 1911F | 7,000 | 100 | 250 | 450 | 600 | — |
| 1911F Proof | — | Value: 1,100 | | | | |

**3 MARK** KM# 638 **Weight:** 16.6670 g. **Composition:** 0.9000 Silver .4823 oz. ASW **Ruler:** Wilhelm II **Subject:** 25th year of reign **Note:** 5,650 were melted.

| Date | Mintage | F | VF | XF | Unc | BU |
|---|---|---|---|---|---|---|
| 1916F Proof | 1,000 | Value: 6,500 | | | | |

**5 MARK** KM# 632 **Weight:** 27.7770 g. **Composition:** 0.9000 Silver .8038 oz. ASW **Ruler:** Wilhelm II

| Date | Mintage | F | VF | XF | Unc | BU |
|---|---|---|---|---|---|---|
| 1892F | 69,000 | 20.00 | 50.00 | 150 | 600 | — |
| 1893F | 71,000 | 20.00 | 50.00 | 150 | 600 | — |
| 1894F | 20,000 | 150 | 300 | 900 | 3,000 | — |

| Date | Mintage | F | VF | XF | Unc | BU |
|---|---|---|---|---|---|---|
| 1895F | 201,000 | 20.00 | 40.00 | 125 | 500 | — |
| 1898F | 216,000 | 15.00 | 30.00 | 125 | 500 | — |
| 1899F | 112,000 | 15.00 | 30.00 | 125 | 500 | — |
| 1900F | 211,000 | 15.00 | 30.00 | 85.00 | 350 | — |
| (1892-1900)F Proof | — | Value: 600 | | | | |
| 1901F | 211,000 | 15.00 | 30.00 | 80.00 | 400 | — |
| 1902F | 361,000 | 15.00 | 30.00 | 80.00 | 400 | — |
| 1903F | 722,000 | 15.00 | 30.00 | 65.00 | 375 | — |
| 1904F | 391,000 | 15.00 | 30.00 | 65.00 | 375 | — |
| 1906F | 64,000 | 25.00 | 60.00 | 185 | 600 | — |
| 1906F Proof | 50 | Value: 1,500 | | | | |
| 1907F | 417,000 | 15.00 | 30.00 | 65.00 | 250 | — |
| 1908F | 532,000 | 15.00 | 30.00 | 55.00 | 250 | — |
| 1913F | 401,000 | 15.00 | 30.00 | 50.00 | 250 | — |
| (1901-1913)F Proof | — | Value: 700 | | | | |

**10 MARK** KM# 633 **Weight:** 3.9820 g. **Composition:** 0.9000 Gold .1152 oz. AGW **Ruler:** Wilhelm II

| Date | Mintage | F | VF | XF | Unc | BU |
|---|---|---|---|---|---|---|
| 1893F | 300,000 | 80.00 | 120 | 160 | 300 | — |
| 1896F | 200,000 | 80.00 | 120 | 160 | 300 | — |
| 1898F | 420,000 | 80.00 | 120 | 160 | 300 | — |
| 1900F | 90,000 | 80.00 | 120 | 160 | 300 | — |
| 1901F | 110,000 | 65.00 | 120 | 160 | 300 | — |
| 1902F | 50,000 | 125 | 150 | 200 | 375 | — |
| 1903F | 180,000 | 65.00 | 100 | 160 | 300 | — |
| 1904F | 350,000 | 65.00 | 100 | 150 | 300 | — |
| 1904F Proof | — | Value: 1,200 | | | | |
| 1905F | 200,000 | 65.00 | 100 | 150 | 300 | — |
| 1905F Proof | — | Value: 1,200 | | | | |
| 1906F | 100,000 | 65.00 | 100 | 160 | 300 | — |
| 1906F Proof | 50 | Value: 1,200 | | | | |
| 1907F | 150,000 | 65.00 | 100 | 150 | 300 | — |
| 1907F Proof | — | Value: 1,200 | | | | |
| 1909F | 100,000 | 65.00 | 120 | 160 | 300 | — |
| 1909F Proof | — | Value: 1,200 | | | | |
| 1910F | 150,000 | 65.00 | 120 | 160 | 300 | — |
| 1910F Proof | — | Value: 1,200 | | | | |
| 1911F | 50,000 | 140 | 275 | 425 | 650 | — |
| 1911F Proof | — | Value: 1,200 | | | | |
| 1912F | 49,000 | 140 | 275 | 425 | 750 | — |
| 1912F Proof | — | Value: 1,200 | | | | |
| 1913F | 50,000 | 140 | 275 | 425 | 650 | — |
| 1913F Proof | — | Value: 1,200 | | | | |

**20 MARK** KM# 634 **Weight:** 7.9650 g. **Composition:** 0.9000 Gold .2304 oz. AGW **Ruler:** Wilhelm II

| Date | Mintage | F | VF | XF | Unc | BU |
|---|---|---|---|---|---|---|
| 1894F | 501,000 | 100 | 120 | 145 | 250 | — |
| 1897F | 400,000 | 100 | 120 | 145 | 250 | — |
| 1897F Proof | — | Value: 1,000 | | | | |
| 1898F | 106,000 | 100 | 120 | 145 | 275 | — |
| 1900F | 500,000 | 100 | 120 | 145 | 250 | — |
| 1900F Proof | — | Value: 1,000 | | | | |
| 1905F | 506,000 | 100 | 120 | 145 | 250 | — |
| 1905F Proof | — | Value: 500 | | | | |
| 1913F | 43,000 | 4,000 | 8,000 | 25,000 | 35,000 | — |
| 1913F Proof | — | Value: 40,000 | | | | |
| 1914F | 558,000 | 2,800 | 4,000 | 6,000 | 8,500 | — |
| 1914F Proof | — | Value: 15,000 | | | | |

## GERMANY

### 1871-1918

Germany, a nation of north-central Europe which from1871 to 1945 was, successively, an empire, a republic and a totalitarian state, attained its territorial peak as an empire when it comprised a 208,780 sq. mi. (540,740 sq. km.) homeland and an overseas colonial empire.

As the power of the Roman Empire waned, several war-like tribes residing in northern Germany moved south and west, invading France, Belgium, England, Italy and Spain. In 800 A.D. the Frankish king Charlemagne, who ruled most of France and Germany, was crowned Emperor of the Holy Roman Empire, a loose federation of an estimated 1,800 German States that lasted until 1806. Modern Germany was formed from the eastern part of Charlemagne's empire.

After 1812, the German States were reduced to a federation of 32, of which Prussia was the strongest. In 1871, Prussian chancellor Otto von Bismarck united the German States into an empire ruled by William I, the Prussian king. The empire initiated a colonial endeavor and became one of the world's greatest powers. Germany disintegrated as a result of World War I.

It was reestablished as the Weimar Republic. The humiliation of defeat, economic depression, poverty and discontent gave rise to Adolf Hitler, 1933, who reconstituted Germany as the Third Reich and after initial diplomatic and military triumphs, expanded his goals beyond Europe into Africa and USSR which led it into final disaster in World War II, ending on VE Day, May 7, 1945.

**RULERS**

Wilhelm II, 1888-1918

**MINT MARKS**

A - Berlin
D - Munich
E - Muldenhutten (1887-1953)
F - Stuttgart
G - Karlsruhe
J - Hamburg

**MONETARY SYSTEM**

(Until 1923)
100 Pfennig = 1 Mark

(Commencing 1945)
100 Pfennig = 1 Mark

# EMPIRE

## STANDARD COINAGE

**PFENNIG** KM# 10 **Composition:** Copper

| Date | Mintage | F | VF | XF | Unc | BU |
|---|---|---|---|---|---|---|
| 1890-1900 Common date proof | — | Value: 70.00 | | | | |
| 1890A | 17,295,000 | 0.50 | 1.50 | 3.50 | 10.00 | — |
| 1890D | 7,030,000 | 1.00 | 2.50 | 5.00 | 12.50 | — |
| 1890E | 3,730,000 | 0.50 | 2.00 | 6.50 | 12.50 | — |
| 1890F | 4,189,000 | 0.50 | 2.00 | 6.50 | 15.00 | — |
| 1890G | 3,050,000 | 1.50 | 3.00 | 6.50 | 15.00 | — |
| 1890J | 2,247,000 | 1.50 | 3.00 | 6.50 | 15.00 | — |
| 1891A | 12,040,000 | 1.50 | 3.00 | 5.00 | 10.00 | — |
| 1891D | 876,000 | 10.00 | 25.00 | 75.00 | 135 | — |
| 1891E | 528,000 | 20.00 | 40.00 | 85.00 | 140 | — |
| 1891F | 1,263,000 | 5.00 | 10.00 | 25.00 | 65.00 | — |
| 1891G | 360,000 | 40.00 | 75.00 | 145 | 300 | — |
| 1891J | 1,837,000 | 7.50 | 25.00 | 75.00 | 135 | — |
| 1892A | 22,341,000 | 0.25 | 0.50 | 1.50 | 20.00 | — |
| 1892D | 6,139,000 | 2.00 | 4.00 | 9.00 | 40.00 | — |
| 1892E | 3,195,000 | 2.00 | 4.00 | 9.00 | 35.00 | — |
| 1892F | 5,013,000 | 1.00 | 2.00 | 5.00 | 30.00 | — |
| 1892G | 2,689,000 | 5.00 | 10.00 | 25.00 | 65.00 | — |
| 1892J | 3,980,000 | 0.50 | 1.50 | 4.00 | 20.00 | — |
| 1893A | 18,966,000 | 0.25 | 0.50 | 2.00 | 12.00 | — |
| 1893D | 7,027,000 | 0.25 | 1.00 | 4.00 | 20.00 | — |
| 1893E | 1,218,000 | 10.00 | 20.00 | 30.00 | 60.00 | — |
| 1893F | 1,460,000 | 5.00 | 10.00 | 20.00 | 40.00 | — |
| 1893G | 700,000 | 12.50 | 25.00 | 40.00 | 120 | — |
| 1893J | 1,825,000 | 2.00 | 7.00 | 25.00 | 80.00 | — |
| 1894A | 17,592,000 | 0.25 | 0.50 | 2.00 | 7.50 | — |
| 1894D | 5,530,000 | 0.25 | 1.00 | 4.00 | 12.50 | — |
| 1894E | 5,040,000 | 0.50 | 1.50 | 5.00 | 15.00 | — |
| 1894F | 4,206,000 | 0.20 | 1.00 | 4.00 | 15.00 | — |
| 1894G | 2,351,000 | 3.00 | 9.00 | 20.00 | 40.00 | — |
| 1894J | 2,619,000 | 0.50 | 2.00 | 6.00 | 12.50 | — |
| 1895A | 20,152,000 | 0.25 | 1.00 | 2.50 | 8.50 | — |
| 1895D | 1,496,000 | 10.00 | 25.00 | 35.00 | 100 | — |
| 1895E | 1,191,000 | 5.00 | 10.00 | 25.00 | 35.00 | — |
| 1895F | 4,366,000 | 0.25 | 2.50 | 6.50 | 12.50 | — |
| 1895G | 3,051,000 | 1.00 | 3.00 | 7.50 | 25.00 | — |
| 1895J | 3,839,000 | 2.00 | 4.00 | 10.00 | 20.00 | — |
| 1896A | 27,094,000 | 0.10 | 0.25 | 1.50 | 6.50 | — |
| 1896D | 7,025,000 | 0.10 | 0.25 | 1.50 | 6.50 | — |
| 1896E | 3,725,000 | 0.25 | 2.50 | 5.00 | 10.00 | — |
| 1896F | 3,450,000 | 0.10 | 0.20 | 1.50 | 6.50 | — |
| 1896G | 3,028,000 | 0.25 | 4.00 | 7.50 | 15.00 | — |
| 1897A | 8,534,000 | 0.25 | 1.00 | 3.50 | 8.50 | — |
| 1897D | 2,600,000 | 1.00 | 2.50 | 6.00 | 15.00 | — |
| 1897E | 1,294,000 | 3.50 | 7.50 | 15.00 | 45.00 | — |
| 1897F | 2,390,000 | 5.00 | 10.00 | 30.00 | 70.00 | — |
| 1897G | 1,122,000 | 10.00 | 20.00 | 50.00 | 100 | — |
| 1897J | 4,941,000 | 1.00 | 2.00 | 5.00 | 10.00 | — |
| 1898A | 18,564,000 | 0.10 | 0.25 | 1.50 | 6.50 | — |
| 1898D | 4,430,000 | 0.25 | 2.00 | 5.00 | 15.00 | — |
| 1898E | 2,432,000 | 0.50 | 5.00 | 10.00 | 20.00 | — |
| 1898F | 4,193,000 | 0.20 | 1.00 | 2.50 | 7.50 | — |
| 1898G | 1,951,000 | 0.25 | 5.00 | 15.00 | 30.00 | — |
| 1898J | 3,231,000 | 0.25 | 2.50 | 5.00 | 10.00 | — |
| 1899A | 22,009,000 | 0.10 | 0.25 | 2.00 | 6.00 | — |
| 1899D | 4,590,000 | 0.10 | 0.25 | 2.00 | 6.00 | — |
| 1899E | 3,725,000 | 0.25 | 2.50 | 5.00 | 12.50 | — |
| 1899F | 4,300,000 | 0.10 | 0.20 | 1.50 | 5.50 | — |
| 1899G | 2,550,000 | 0.20 | 1.50 | 5.00 | 15.00 | — |
| 1899J | 2,416,000 | 0.20 | 1.00 | 4.00 | 10.00 | — |
| 1900A | 51,804,000 | 0.10 | 0.25 | 1.50 | 5.50 | — |
| 1900D | 14,635,000 | 0.10 | 0.25 | 1.50 | 5.50 | — |
| 1900E | 7,887,000 | 0.20 | 1.00 | 3.50 | 8.50 | — |
| 1900F | 10,312,000 | 0.10 | 0.50 | 1.50 | 6.00 | — |
| 1900G | 6,138,000 | 0.20 | 1.00 | 3.50 | 8.50 | — |
| 1900J | 9,917,000 | 0.20 | 1.00 | 3.50 | 8.50 | — |
| 1901-16 Common date proof | — | Value: 75.00 | | | | |
| 1901A | 21,045,000 | 0.10 | 0.25 | 1.50 | 9.00 | — |
| 1901D | 5,337,000 | 0.25 | 1.00 | 3.50 | 9.00 | — |
| 1901E | 1,397,000 | 1.00 | 6.00 | 14.00 | 35.00 | — |
| 1901F | 2,925,000 | 0.25 | 2.50 | 5.00 | 12.00 | — |
| 1901G | 1,977,000 | 2.50 | 6.50 | 20.00 | 75.00 | — |
| 1901J | 2,011,000 | 3.00 | 12.50 | 75.00 | 125 | — |
| 1902A | 7,474,000 | 0.50 | 1.00 | 5.00 | 10.00 | — |
| 1902D | 2,811,000 | 1.00 | 5.00 | 20.00 | 50.00 | — |
| 1902E | 1,183,000 | 2.50 | 5.00 | 20.00 | 35.00 | — |
| 1902F | 1,250,000 | 2.50 | 5.00 | 20.00 | 35.00 | — |
| 1902G | 881,000 | 5.00 | 20.00 | 45.00 | 100 | — |
| 1902J | 150 | 375 | 1,000 | 1,500 | 4,000 | — |
| 1903A | 12,690,000 | 0.10 | 0.50 | 1.50 | 10.00 | — |
| 1903D | 3,140,000 | 1.00 | 2.00 | 5.00 | 20.00 | — |
| 1903E | 1,956,000 | 2.00 | 4.00 | 10.00 | 30.00 | — |
| 1903F | 2,945,000 | 1.00 | 5.00 | 30.00 | 45.00 | — |
| 1903G | 1,377,000 | 5.00 | 10.00 | 50.00 | 125 | — |
| 1903J | 2,832,000 | 2.50 | 10.00 | 25.00 | 60.00 | — |
| 1904A | 28,625,000 | 0.10 | 0.25 | 1.50 | 10.00 | — |
| 1904D | 4,118,000 | 1.00 | 2.00 | 9.00 | 25.00 | — |
| 1904E | 2,778,000 | 1.00 | 2.00 | 9.00 | 20.00 | — |
| 1904F | 4,520,000 | 2.00 | 4.00 | 9.00 | 20.00 | — |
| 1904G | 3,232,000 | 2.00 | 9.00 | 20.00 | 45.00 | — |
| 1904J | 4,467,000 | 1.00 | 2.00 | 9.00 | 15.00 | — |
| 1905A | 19,631,000 | 0.10 | 0.25 | 1.50 | 5.00 | — |
| 1905D | 6,084,000 | 0.10 | 0.25 | 4.00 | 20.00 | — |
| 1905E | 3,564,000 | 0.10 | 0.50 | 4.00 | 15.00 | — |
| 1905E Cross under denomination | Inc. above | — | — | 2,500 | — | — |
| 1905F | 4,153,000 | 0.10 | 0.20 | 1.50 | 20.00 | — |
| 1905G | 3,051,000 | 0.20 | 1.00 | 3.00 | 15.00 | — |
| 1905J | 4,085,000 | 0.10 | 0.20 | 1.50 | 30.00 | — |
| 1906A | 46,921,000 | 0.10 | 0.50 | 1.50 | 6.00 | — |
| 1906D | 5,633,000 | 0.10 | 0.50 | 1.50 | 20.00 | — |
| 1906E | 7,278,000 | 0.10 | 0.50 | 1.50 | 10.00 | — |
| 1906F | 7,173,000 | 0.10 | 0.50 | 1.50 | 12.50 | — |
| 1906G | 5,194,000 | 0.10 | 0.50 | 1.50 | 25.00 | — |
| 1906J | 3,622,000 | 0.10 | 0.50 | 1.50 | 25.00 | — |
| 1907A | 33,711,000 | 0.10 | 0.50 | 1.50 | 6.00 | — |
| 1907D | 14,691,000 | 0.10 | 0.50 | 1.50 | 12.50 | — |
| 1907E | 3,719,000 | 0.10 | 0.50 | 1.50 | 17.50 | — |
| 1907F | 7,026,000 | 0.10 | 0.20 | 1.50 | 12.50 | — |
| 1907G | 3,052,000 | 0.10 | 0.50 | 1.50 | 22.50 | — |
| 1907J | 6,722,000 | 0.10 | 0.50 | 1.50 | 17.50 | — |
| 1908A | 21,922,000 | 0.10 | 0.50 | 1.50 | 9.00 | — |
| 1908D | 10,629,000 | 0.10 | 0.50 | 1.50 | 12.50 | — |
| 1908E | 3,400,000 | 0.10 | 0.50 | 1.50 | 17.50 | — |
| 1908F | 6,112,000 | 0.10 | 0.20 | 1.50 | 17.50 | — |

| Date | Mintage | F | VF | XF | Unc | BU |
|---|---|---|---|---|---|---|
| 1908G | 3,663,000 | 0.10 | 0.50 | 1.50 | 12.50 | — |
| 1908J | 5,581,000 | 0.10 | 0.50 | 1.50 | 12.50 | — |
| 1909A | 21,430,000 | 0.10 | 0.25 | 1.00 | 3.50 | — |
| 1909D | 2,814,000 | 0.20 | 1.00 | 2.50 | 8.50 | — |
| 1909E | 2,562,000 | 1.50 | 4.00 | 6.00 | 12.00 | — |
| 1909F | 2,425,000 | 1.50 | 4.00 | 6.00 | 12.00 | — |
| 1909G | 1,220,000 | 1.50 | 4.00 | 7.50 | 17.50 | — |
| 1909J | 1,634,000 | 1.50 | 4.00 | 6.50 | 15.00 | — |
| 1910A | 10,761,000 | 0.10 | 0.50 | 1.50 | 6.00 | — |
| 1910D | 4,221,000 | 0.10 | 0.25 | 1.00 | 4.00 | — |
| 1910E | 1,600,000 | 0.25 | 1.50 | 5.00 | 12.00 | — |
| 1910F | 3,009,000 | 0.20 | 1.50 | 5.00 | 8.50 | — |
| 1910G | 1,834,000 | 0.25 | 4.00 | 6.00 | 12.00 | — |
| 1910J | 2,450,000 | 0.25 | 5.00 | 7.50 | 17.50 | — |
| 1911A | 38,172,000 | 0.10 | 0.50 | 1.50 | 5.00 | — |
| 1911D | 8,657,000 | 0.10 | 0.50 | 1.50 | 5.50 | — |
| 1911E | 5,236,000 | 0.10 | 0.50 | 1.50 | 6.00 | — |
| 1911F | 5,780,000 | 0.10 | 0.50 | 1.50 | 6.00 | — |
| 1911G | 2,075,000 | 0.10 | 0.50 | 1.50 | 6.00 | — |
| 1911J | 5,594,000 | 0.10 | 0.50 | 1.50 | 6.00 | — |
| 1912A | 42,693,000 | 0.10 | 0.50 | 1.50 | 5.00 | — |
| 1912D | 10,173,000 | 0.10 | 0.50 | 1.50 | 5.50 | — |
| 1912E | 5,689,000 | 0.10 | 0.50 | 1.50 | 6.00 | — |
| 1912F | 7,441,000 | 0.10 | 0.50 | 1.50 | 6.00 | — |
| 1912G | 5,526,000 | 0.10 | 0.50 | 1.50 | 6.00 | — |
| 1912J | 5,615,000 | 0.10 | 0.50 | 1.50 | 6.00 | — |
| 1913A | 32,671,000 | 0.10 | 0.50 | 1.50 | 5.00 | — |
| 1913D | 8,161,000 | 0.10 | 0.50 | 1.50 | 5.50 | — |
| 1913E | 2,258,000 | 1.50 | 4.00 | 7.50 | 17.50 | — |
| 1913F | 6,620,000 | 0.10 | 0.20 | 1.00 | 4.00 | — |
| 1913G | 3,209,000 | 0.10 | 0.50 | 1.50 | 6.00 | — |
| 1913J | 1,456,000 | 0.50 | 5.00 | 10.00 | 25.00 | — |
| 1914A | 9,976,000 | 0.10 | 0.50 | 1.50 | 5.50 | — |
| 1914D | 1,842,000 | 0.10 | 0.50 | 1.50 | 6.00 | — |
| 1914E | 2,926,000 | 0.20 | 1.00 | 2.00 | 7.00 | — |
| 1914F | 3,316,000 | 0.10 | 0.50 | 1.50 | 6.00 | — |
| 1914G | 2,100,000 | 0.20 | 1.00 | 2.00 | 7.00 | — |
| 1914J | 4,368,000 | 0.10 | 0.50 | 1.50 | 5.50 | — |
| 1915A | 14,738,000 | 0.10 | 0.50 | 1.50 | 5.50 | — |
| 1915D | 1,771,000 | 0.10 | 0.25 | 2.50 | 7.00 | — |
| 1915E | 2,779,000 | 0.20 | 1.50 | 3.50 | 8.50 | — |
| 1915F | 1,411,000 | 0.20 | 1.50 | 3.50 | 11.50 | — |
| 1915G | 2,041,000 | 0.20 | 1.50 | 4.00 | 10.00 | — |
| 1915J | 2,981,000 | 0.20 | 1.50 | 3.50 | 8.50 | — |
| 1916A | 5,960,000 | 0.10 | 0.50 | 1.50 | 5.50 | — |
| 1916D | 5,401,000 | 0.20 | 1.00 | 3.00 | 8.00 | — |
| 1916E | 818,000 | 1.00 | 5.00 | 7.50 | 12.00 | — |
| 1916F | 1,104,000 | 0.50 | 2.00 | 5.00 | 10.00 | — |
| 1916G | 671,000 | 1.50 | 7.50 | 10.00 | 18.50 | — |
| 1916J | 898,000 | 1.50 | 6.00 | 9.00 | 15.00 | — |

**PFENNIG** **KM# 24** **Composition:** Aluminum

| Date | Mintage | F | VF | XF | Unc | BU |
|---|---|---|---|---|---|---|
| 1916-18 Common date proof | — | Value: 90.00 | | | | |
| 1916G | — | 125 | 225 | 350 | 600 | — |
| 1917A | 27,159,000 | 0.15 | 0.50 | 2.00 | 5.00 | — |
| 1917A Proof | — | Value: 40.00 | | | | |
| 1917D | 6,940,000 | 0.15 | 0.50 | 2.00 | 6.00 | — |
| 1917E | 3,862,000 | 0.50 | 2.00 | 4.50 | 8.00 | — |
| 1917E Proof | — | Value: 40.00 | | | | |
| 1917F | 5,125,000 | 0.25 | 2.00 | 4.00 | 7.00 | — |
| 1917G | 3,139,000 | 0.25 | 2.00 | 4.50 | 8.00 | — |
| 1917G Proof | — | Value: 40.00 | | | | |
| 1917J | 4,182,000 | 0.25 | 2.00 | 4.00 | 8.00 | — |
| 1917J Proof | — | Value: 40.00 | | | | |
| 1918A | — | 300 | 500 | 3,500 | 6,000 | — |
| 1918D | 318,000 | 10.00 | 20.00 | 27.50 | 40.00 | — |
| 1918F | — | 500 | 1,000 | 1,500 | 2,500 | — |

**Note:** The 1918F 1 Pfennigs are from the burned out ruins of the Stuttgart Mint destroyed in World War II

**2 PFENNIG** **KM# 16** **Composition:** Copper

| Date | Mintage | F | VF | XF | Unc | BU |
|---|---|---|---|---|---|---|
| 1904-16 Common date proof | — | Value: 150 | | | | |
| 1904A | 5,414,000 | 0.10 | 0.25 | 2.00 | 10.00 | — |
| 1904D | 1,404,000 | 0.10 | 0.50 | 2.50 | 30.00 | — |
| 1904E | 744,000 | 2.50 | 7.00 | 14.50 | 40.00 | — |
| 1904F | 1,002,000 | 0.10 | 1.00 | 4.50 | 75.00 | — |
| 1904G | 495,000 | 3.50 | 8.00 | 16.50 | 100 | — |
| 1904J | 44,000 | 4.00 | 10.00 | 35.00 | 110 | — |
| 1905A | 5,172,000 | 0.10 | 0.25 | 2.00 | 20.00 | — |
| 1905D | 1,570,000 | 0.10 | 0.50 | 2.50 | 40.00 | — |
| 1905E | 924,000 | 0.10 | 1.00 | 4.00 | 75.00 | — |
| 1905F | 1,115,000 | 0.10 | 1.00 | 3.00 | 60.00 | — |
| 1905G | 1,030,000 | 0.10 | 1.00 | 3.50 | 90.00 | — |
| 1905J | 1,609,000 | 0.10 | 1.00 | 3.50 | 125 | — |
| 1906A | 8,459,000 | 0.10 | 0.25 | 2.00 | 20.00 | — |
| 1906D | 3,539,000 | 0.10 | 0.25 | 2.00 | 25.00 | — |
| 1906E | 2,055,000 | 0.10 | 0.25 | 2.00 | 60.00 | — |
| 1906F | 2,840,000 | 0.10 | 0.25 | 2.00 | 30.00 | — |
| 1906G | 1,527,000 | 0.10 | 0.25 | 2.00 | 50.00 | — |
| 1906J | 1,908,000 | 0.10 | 0.25 | 2.00 | 100 | — |
| 1907A | 13,468,000 | 0.10 | 0.25 | 2.00 | 30.00 | — |
| 1907D | 1,921,000 | 0.10 | 0.25 | 2.00 | 30.00 | — |
| 1907E | 744,000 | 0.25 | 2.00 | 6.00 | 50.00 | — |
| 1907F | 1,059,000 | 0.10 | 0.50 | 2.00 | 75.00 | — |
| 1907G | 610,000 | 0.25 | 1.00 | 3.50 | 100 | — |
| 1907J | 952,000 | 0.10 | 0.50 | 2.00 | 60.00 | — |
| 1908A | 5,421,000 | 0.10 | 0.25 | 2.00 | 22.50 | — |
| 1908D | 1,407,000 | 0.10 | 0.50 | 2.00 | 30.00 | — |
| 1908E | 745,000 | 1.00 | 5.00 | 8.00 | 40.00 | — |
| 1908F | 1,003,000 | 0.10 | 0.50 | 2.50 | 40.00 | — |
| 1908G | 610,000 | 0.25 | 1.00 | 4.50 | 70.00 | — |
| 1908J | 817,000 | 0.10 | 0.50 | 3.00 | 70.00 | — |
| 1910A | 5,421,000 | 0.10 | 0.25 | 2.00 | 20.00 | — |
| 1910D | 1,407,000 | 0.10 | 0.50 | 2.00 | 35.00 | — |
| 1910E | 745,000 | 0.25 | 4.00 | 7.00 | 35.00 | — |
| 1910F | 1,003,000 | 0.25 | 1.50 | 4.50 | 35.00 | — |
| 1910G | 517,000 | 0.25 | 1.50 | 5.50 | 75.00 | — |
| 1910J | 568,000 | 0.25 | 1.00 | 4.00 | 75.00 | — |
| 1911A | 8,187,000 | 0.10 | 1.00 | 3.00 | 8.00 | — |
| 1911D | 2,100,000 | 0.10 | 0.50 | 3.00 | 8.00 | — |
| 1911E | 1,133,000 | 0.10 | 0.50 | 3.50 | 8.00 | — |
| 1911F | 1,490,000 | 0.10 | 0.50 | 3.50 | 8.00 | — |
| 1911G | 1,313,000 | 0.10 | 0.50 | 3.50 | 8.00 | — |
| 1911J | 1,883,000 | 0.10 | 0.50 | 3.00 | 8.00 | — |
| 1912A | 13,580,000 | 0.10 | 0.25 | 2.00 | 8.00 | — |
| 1912D | 3,109,000 | 0.10 | 0.50 | 2.50 | 8.00 | — |
| 1912E | 1,808,000 | 0.10 | 1.00 | 3.50 | 8.00 | — |
| 1912F | 2,366,000 | 0.10 | 0.50 | 2.50 | 8.00 | — |
| 1912G | 1,395,000 | 0.10 | 0.50 | 3.00 | 8.00 | — |
| 1912J | 1,605,000 | 0.10 | 0.50 | 3.00 | 8.00 | — |
| 1913A | 4,212,000 | 0.10 | 0.25 | 2.00 | 8.00 | — |
| 1913D | 2,525,000 | 0.10 | 0.50 | 2.00 | 8.00 | — |
| 1913E | 413,000 | 3.00 | 15.00 | 22.00 | 40.00 | — |
| 1913F | 1,602,000 | 0.10 | 0.50 | 2.50 | 8.00 | — |
| 1913G | 741,000 | 0.25 | 1.00 | 3.50 | 8.00 | — |
| 1913J | 1,254,000 | 0.10 | 0.50 | 2.00 | 8.00 | — |
| 1914A | 5,350,000 | 0.10 | 0.25 | 2.00 | 8.00 | — |
| 1914E | 1,201,000 | 1.00 | 3.50 | 9.00 | 22.00 | — |
| 1914F | 158,000 | 12.00 | 45.00 | 85.00 | 150 | — |
| 1914G | 610,000 | 2.00 | 6.00 | 17.50 | 125 | — |
| 1914J | 817,000 | 0.10 | 1.00 | 3.50 | 9.00 | — |
| 1915A | 3,897,000 | 0.10 | 1.00 | 3.50 | 8.00 | — |
| 1915D | 1,407,000 | 0.10 | 1.00 | 2.50 | 8.00 | — |
| 1915E | 288,000 | 5.00 | 15.00 | 28.00 | 55.00 | — |
| 1915F | 904,000 | 0.10 | 0.25 | 2.00 | 40.00 | — |
| 1916A | 3,524,000 | 0.10 | 1.00 | 3.50 | 8.00 | — |
| 1916D | 915,000 | 0.25 | 1.00 | 2.50 | 8.00 | — |
| 1916E | 484,000 | 0.25 | 1.00 | 4.50 | 9.00 | — |
| 1916F | 651,000 | 0.25 | 1.00 | 4.50 | 20.00 | — |
| 1916G | 397,000 | 0.50 | 2.50 | 6.50 | 50.00 | — |
| 1916J | 531,000 | 0.50 | 2.50 | 6.50 | 30.00 | — |

**5 PFENNIG** **KM# 11** **Composition:** Copper-Nickel

| Date | Mintage | F | VF | XF | Unc | BU |
|---|---|---|---|---|---|---|
| 1908/10G | 3,357,000 | — | — | — | — | — |
| 1890-1900 Common date proof | — | Value: 80.00 | | | | |
| 1890A | 4,548,000 | 0.10 | 0.50 | 4.00 | 12.50 | — |
| 1890D | 2,813,000 | 0.25 | 1.00 | 5.00 | 15.00 | — |
| 1890E | 1,318,000 | 0.25 | 1.00 | 6.00 | 17.50 | — |
| 1890F | 1,068,000 | 0.25 | 1.00 | 5.00 | 15.00 | — |
| 1890G | 948,000 | 0.25 | 1.00 | 6.00 | 17.50 | — |
| 1890J | 1,629,000 | 0.20 | 1.00 | 5.00 | 15.00 | — |
| 1891A | 6,313,000 | 0.10 | 0.50 | 4.00 | 12.50 | — |
| 1891E | 173,000 | 12.50 | 35.00 | 50.00 | 80.00 | — |
| 1891F | 942,000 | 0.25 | 1.00 | 5.00 | 15.00 | — |
| 1891G | 271,000 | 5.00 | 17.50 | 30.00 | 55.00 | — |
| 1892A | 2,279,000 | 0.10 | 1.00 | 4.00 | 12.50 | — |
| 1892D | 920,000 | 0.25 | 1.00 | 5.00 | 15.00 | — |
| 1892E | 346,000 | 2.50 | 12.50 | 20.00 | 35.00 | — |
| 1892F | 464,000 | 4.00 | 15.00 | 25.00 | 45.00 | — |
| 1892G | 800,000 | 3.00 | 15.00 | 22.50 | 35.00 | — |
| 1892J | 93,000 | 50.00 | 90.00 | 150 | 225 | — |
| 1893A | 8,572,000 | 0.10 | 0.50 | 4.00 | 15.00 | — |
| 1893D | 1,892,000 | 0.25 | 1.00 | 5.00 | 16.50 | — |
| 1893E | 1,149,000 | 0.25 | 1.00 | 6.00 | 17.50 | — |
| 1893F | 1,546,000 | 0.15 | 1.00 | 5.00 | 15.00 | — |
| 1893G | 422,000 | 4.00 | 15.00 | 20.00 | 40.00 | — |
| 1893J | 1,544,000 | 0.20 | 1.00 | 5.00 | 15.00 | — |
| 1894A | 10,830,000 | 0.10 | 0.50 | 4.00 | 12.50 | — |
| 1894D | 2,812,000 | 0.25 | 1.00 | 5.00 | 15.00 | — |
| 1894E | 802,000 | 0.25 | 1.50 | 6.00 | 17.50 | — |
| 1894F | 300,000 | 1.00 | 4.00 | 10.00 | 30.00 | — |
| 1894G | 280,000 | 1.00 | 5.00 | 12.50 | 35.00 | — |
| 1894J | 1,634,000 | 0.20 | 1.00 | 5.00 | 15.00 | — |
| 1895E | 686,000 | 0.25 | 2.50 | 7.50 | 22.50 | — |
| 1895F | 1,705,000 | 0.15 | 1.50 | 5.00 | 15.00 | — |
| 1895G | 940,000 | 0.25 | 2.00 | 6.00 | 17.50 | — |
| 1896A | 1,459,000 | 0.25 | 1.00 | 5.00 | 15.00 | — |
| 1896E | 658,000 | 0.25 | 2.50 | 7.50 | 17.50 | — |
| 1896F | 2,009,000 | 0.10 | 1.00 | 5.00 | 15.00 | — |
| 1896G | 1,221,000 | 1,500 | 2,500 | — | — | — |
| 1896J | 1,634,000 | 0.20 | 1.00 | 5.00 | 15.00 | — |
| 1897A | 9,390,000 | 0.10 | 0.50 | 3.00 | 11.50 | — |
| 1897D | 2,812,000 | 0.25 | 1.00 | 3.00 | 11.50 | — |
| 1897E | 833,000 | 0.25 | 2.00 | 5.00 | 15.00 | — |
| 1897/797G | Inc. above | 1.00 | 4.00 | 10.00 | 30.00 | — |
| 1897G | Inc. above | 0.10 | 1.00 | 4.50 | 15.00 | — |
| 1898A | 10,836,000 | 0.10 | 0.30 | 2.25 | 10.00 | — |
| 1898D | 2,812,000 | 0.10 | 0.50 | 2.25 | 11.50 | — |
| 1898E | 1,492,000 | 0.10 | 0.50 | 2.75 | 14.00 | — |
| 1898F | 2,007,000 | 0.10 | 0.50 | 2.75 | 14.00 | — |
| 1898G | 1,220,000 | 0.10 | 0.50 | 2.25 | 17.50 | — |
| 1898J | 1,635,000 | 0.20 | 1.00 | 2.25 | 12.00 | — |
| 1899A | 10,884,000 | 0.10 | 0.30 | 2.00 | 11.50 | — |
| 1899D | 2,812,000 | 0.10 | 0.50 | 2.75 | 14.00 | — |
| 1899E | 1,488,000 | 0.10 | 0.50 | 3.00 | 17.50 | — |
| 1899F | 2,006,000 | 0.10 | 0.50 | 2.75 | 14.00 | — |
| 1899G | 1,222,000 | 0.10 | 0.50 | 2.25 | 12.00 | — |
| 1899J | 1,634,000 | 0.10 | 0.50 | 2.25 | 12.00 | — |
| 1900A | 18,941,000 | 0.10 | 0.30 | 2.00 | 10.00 | — |
| 1900D | 4,254,000 | 0.10 | 0.50 | 2.25 | 12.00 | — |
| 1900E | 2,236,000 | 0.10 | 0.50 | 2.75 | 14.00 | — |
| 1900F | 3,209,000 | 0.10 | 0.25 | 2.25 | 12.00 | — |
| 1900G | 2,136,000 | 0.10 | 0.50 | 2.25 | 12.00 | — |
| 1900J | 2,859,000 | 0.10 | 0.50 | 2.25 | 12.00 | — |
| 1901-15 Common date proof | — | Value: 100 | | | | |
| 1901A | 8,155,000 | 0.10 | 0.30 | 2.00 | 9.00 | — |
| 1901D | 2,779,000 | 0.10 | 0.30 | 2.25 | 11.50 | — |
| 1901E | 1,492,000 | 0.10 | 0.50 | 2.25 | 12.50 | — |
| 1901F | 1,810,000 | 0.10 | 0.30 | 2.00 | 11.50 | — |
| 1901G | 915,000 | 0.10 | 0.50 | 15.00 | 50.00 | — |
| 1901J | 1,226,000 | 0.10 | 0.30 | 20.00 | 100 | — |
| 1902A | 8,949,000 | 0.10 | 0.30 | 2.00 | 9.00 | — |
| 1902D | 2,812,000 | 0.10 | 0.30 | 2.00 | 12.50 | — |
| 1902E | 1,120,000 | 0.10 | 0.50 | 2.75 | 14.50 | — |
| 1902F | 1,800,000 | 0.10 | 0.50 | 2.75 | 14.50 | — |
| 1902G | 1,220,000 | 0.10 | 0.50 | 3.50 | 17.50 | — |
| 1902J | 1,636,000 | 0.10 | 0.25 | 2.25 | 12.50 | — |
| 1903A | 5,932,000 | 0.10 | 0.30 | 2.00 | 9.00 | — |
| 1903D | 1,406,000 | 0.10 | 0.50 | 2.75 | 10.00 | — |
| 1903E | 1,114,000 | 0.10 | 1.00 | 4.00 | 12.50 | — |
| 1903F | 1,209,000 | 0.10 | 0.50 | 4.00 | 12.50 | — |
| 1903G | 610,000 | 0.10 | 1.50 | 5.00 | 15.00 | — |
| 1903J | 817,000 | 0.10 | 1.00 | 4.00 | 12.50 | — |
| 1904A | 6,791,000 | 0.10 | 0.30 | 2.00 | 9.00 | — |
| 1904D | 1,408,000 | 0.10 | 0.50 | 2.25 | 12.50 | — |
| 1904E | 746,000 | 0.10 | 1.50 | 4.00 | 12.50 | — |
| 1904F | 1,006,000 | 0.10 | 0.50 | 2.75 | 12.50 | — |
| 1904G | 610,000 | 0.10 | 1.00 | 3.00 | 14.00 | — |
| 1904J | 818,000 | 0.10 | 0.50 | 2.75 | 14.00 | — |
| 1905A | 8,129,000 | 0.10 | 0.20 | 0.75 | 8.50 | — |
| 1905D | 2,109,000 | 0.10 | 0.20 | 0.75 | 8.50 | — |
| 1905E | 1,117,000 | 0.10 | 0.20 | 0.75 | 8.50 | — |
| 1905F | 1,505,000 | 0.10 | 0.20 | 0.75 | 8.50 | — |
| 1905G | 915,000 | 0.10 | 0.50 | 2.50 | 10.00 | — |
| 1905J | 1,226,000 | 0.10 | 0.20 | 0.75 | 8.50 | — |
| 1906A | 18,970,000 | 0.10 | 0.20 | 0.50 | 7.00 | — |
| 1906D | 4,922,000 | 0.10 | 0.20 | 0.50 | 7.50 | — |
| 1906E | 2,605,000 | 0.10 | 0.20 | 0.50 | 7.50 | — |
| 1906F | 3,512,000 | 0.10 | 0.20 | 0.50 | 7.50 | — |
| 1906G | 2,136,000 | 0.10 | 0.25 | 1.00 | 9.00 | — |
| 1906J | 2,859,000 | 0.10 | 0.20 | 0.50 | 7.50 | — |
| 1907A | 11,930,000 | 0.10 | 0.20 | 0.50 | 7.00 | — |
| 1907D | 2,113,000 | 0.10 | 0.20 | 0.50 | 7.50 | — |
| 1907E | 1,517,000 | 0.10 | 0.25 | 1.00 | 9.00 | — |
| 1907F | 1,845,000 | 0.10 | 0.20 | 0.50 | 7.50 | — |
| 1907G | 915,000 | 0.10 | 0.50 | 1.00 | 9.00 | — |
| 1907J | 1,636,000 | 0.10 | 0.20 | 0.50 | 7.50 | — |
| 1908A | 22,114,000 | 0.10 | 0.20 | 0.50 | 6.50 | — |
| 1908D | 4,991,000 | 0.10 | 0.20 | 0.50 | 7.00 | — |
| 1908E | 2,919,000 | 0.10 | 0.20 | 0.50 | 8.00 | — |
| 1908/7F | 5,124,000 | 30.00 | 60.00 | 80.00 | 150 | — |
| 1908F | Inc. above | 0.10 | 0.20 | 0.50 | 7.50 | — |
| 1908G | Inc. above | 0.10 | 0.15 | 0.50 | 7.00 | — |
| 1908J | 3,264,000 | 0.10 | 0.20 | 0.50 | 6.00 | — |
| 1909A | 5,797,000 | 0.10 | 0.30 | 2.00 | 8.00 | — |
| 1909D | 2,753,000 | 0.10 | 0.50 | 2.50 | 9.00 | — |
| 1909E | 984,000 | 0.25 | 2.50 | 5.00 | 15.00 | — |
| 1909F | 252,000 | 2.00 | 5.00 | 7.50 | 20.00 | — |
| 1909/8J | 1,632,000 | 1.00 | 5.00 | 15.00 | 45.00 | — |
| 1909J | Inc. above | 0.10 | 2.50 | 5.00 | 15.00 | — |
| 1910A | 7,344,000 | 0.10 | 0.20 | 1.00 | 6.50 | — |
| 1910D | 2,814,000 | 0.10 | 0.20 | 0.50 | 8.50 | — |
| 1910E | 1,290,000 | 0.10 | 0.50 | 2.00 | 12.00 | — |
| 1910F | 1,721,000 | 0.10 | 0.20 | 0.50 | 8.50 | — |
| 1910G | 1,222,000 | 0.10 | 0.20 | 0.50 | 8.50 | — |
| 1910J | 152,000 | 30.00 | 42.50 | 70.00 | 125 | — |
| 1911A | 15,660,000 | 0.10 | 0.15 | 0.50 | 6.50 | — |
| 1911D | 2,221,000 | 0.10 | 0.20 | 0.50 | 7.00 | — |
| 1911E | 1,770,000 | 0.10 | 0.20 | 0.50 | 7.00 | — |

| Date | Mintage | F | VF | XF | Unc | BU |
|---|---|---|---|---|---|---|
| 1911F | 2,714,000 | 0.10 | 0.20 | 0.50 | 7.00 | — |
| 1911G | 1,833,000 | 0.10 | 0.20 | 1.00 | 7.00 | — |
| 1911J | 3,116,000 | 0.10 | 0.15 | 0.50 | 7.00 | — |
| 1912A | 19,320,000 | 0.10 | 0.15 | 0.50 | 6.50 | — |
| 1912D | 4,015,000 | 0.10 | 0.20 | 0.50 | 7.00 | — |
| 1912E | 2,568,000 | 0.10 | 0.20 | 0.50 | 7.00 | — |
| 1912F | 3,679,000 | 0.10 | 0.15 | 0.50 | 7.00 | — |
| 1912G | 2,440,000 | 0.10 | 0.20 | 0.50 | 7.00 | — |
| 1912J | 3,020,000 | 0.10 | 0.15 | 0.50 | 7.00 | — |
| 1913A | 15,506,000 | 0.10 | 0.15 | 0.50 | 6.50 | — |
| 1913D | 5,519,000 | 0.10 | 0.20 | 0.50 | 7.00 | — |
| 1913E | 2,373,000 | 0.10 | 0.20 | 0.50 | 9.00 | — |
| 1913F | 2,054,000 | 0.10 | 0.20 | 0.50 | 6.00 | — |
| 1913G | 1,221,000 | 0.10 | 0.20 | 0.50 | 6.00 | — |
| 1913J | 253,000 | 15.00 | 25.00 | 40.00 | 60.00 | — |
| 1914A | 23,605,000 | 0.10 | 0.15 | 0.50 | 6.00 | — |
| 1914D | 3,014,000 | 0.10 | 0.20 | 0.50 | 6.00 | — |
| 1914E | 1,710,000 | 0.10 | 0.20 | 0.50 | 6.00 | — |
| 1914F | 2,206,000 | 0.10 | 0.20 | 0.50 | 6.00 | — |
| 1914G | 1,218,000 | 0.10 | 0.20 | 0.50 | 6.00 | — |
| 1914J | 3,235,000 | 0.10 | 0.15 | 0.50 | 6.00 | — |
| 1915D | 3,516,000 | 0.10 | 0.50 | 2.00 | 7.00 | — |
| 1915E | 834,000 | 1.00 | 6.00 | 8.00 | 15.00 | — |
| 1915F | 1,894,000 | 0.10 | 0.50 | 2.00 | 6.00 | — |
| 1915G | 894,000 | 0.50 | 5.00 | 6.50 | 10.00 | — |
| 1915J | 1,669,000 | 0.10 | 0.50 | 3.50 | 10.00 | — |

## 5 PFENNIG KM# 19 Composition: Iron

| Date | Mintage | F | VF | XF | Unc | BU |
|---|---|---|---|---|---|---|
| 1915-22 Common date proof | — | Value: 90.00 | | | | |
| 1915A | 34,631,000 | 0.10 | 0.25 | 2.00 | 9.00 | — |
| 1915D | 2,021,000 | 0.50 | 6.50 | 10.00 | 17.50 | — |
| 1915E | 4,670,000 | 0.50 | 4.00 | 7.50 | 15.00 | — |
| 1915F | 3,500,000 | 0.25 | 2.50 | 5.00 | 7.50 | — |
| 1915G | 3,676,000 | 0.25 | 2.00 | 5.00 | 7.50 | — |
| 1915J | 2,100,000 | 0.25 | 2.00 | 5.00 | 7.50 | — |
| 1916A | 51,003,000 | 0.10 | 0.25 | 1.50 | 6.00 | — |
| 1916D | 19,590,000 | 0.10 | 0.50 | 1.50 | 6.00 | — |
| 1916E | 2,271,000 | 1.00 | 10.00 | 30.00 | 40.00 | — |
| 1916F | 10,479,000 | 0.15 | 1.00 | 2.00 | 6.00 | — |
| 1916G | 5,599,000 | 0.25 | 1.50 | 3.50 | 20.00 | — |
| 1916J | 10,253,000 | 0.25 | 3.00 | 7.50 | 15.00 | — |
| 1917A | 87,315,000 | 0.10 | 0.50 | 1.00 | 9.00 | — |
| 1917D | 19,581,000 | 0.10 | 0.50 | 1.00 | 9.00 | — |
| 1917E | 11,092,000 | 0.50 | 5.00 | 7.50 | 12.00 | — |
| 1917F | 10,930,000 | 0.10 | 0.50 | 2.00 | 10.00 | — |
| 1917F | — | — | — | — | — | — |
| **Note:** Mule with Polish reverse of Y#5, see Poland | | | | | | |
| 1917G | 6,720,000 | 0.25 | 3.00 | 6.00 | 12.00 | — |
| 1917J | 11,686,000 | 0.25 | 2.00 | 5.00 | 12.00 | — |
| 1918A | 223,516,000 | 0.10 | 0.50 | 1.00 | 8.00 | — |
| 1918D | 29,130,000 | 0.10 | 0.50 | 1.00 | 8.00 | — |
| 1918E | 23,600,000 | 0.25 | 1.00 | 6.00 | 15.00 | — |
| 1918F | 24,598,000 | 0.10 | 0.25 | 1.00 | 8.00 | — |
| 1918G | 12,697,000 | 0.10 | 0.50 | 1.00 | 8.00 | — |
| 1918J | 20,240,000 | 0.10 | 0.50 | 1.00 | 8.00 | — |
| 1919A | 112,102,000 | 0.10 | 0.20 | 0.50 | 7.00 | — |
| 1919D | 41,163,000 | 0.10 | 0.25 | 1.00 | 8.00 | — |
| 1919E | 20,608,000 | 0.25 | 3.00 | 6.00 | 15.00 | — |
| 1919F | 32,700,000 | 0.10 | 0.25 | 1.00 | 8.00 | — |
| 1919G | 13,925,000 | 0.10 | 0.50 | 2.50 | 12.00 | — |
| 1919J | 16,249,000 | 0.15 | 1.00 | 2.00 | 9.00 | — |
| 1920A | 80,300,000 | 0.10 | 0.20 | 0.50 | 7.00 | — |
| 1920D | 25,502,000 | 0.10 | 0.50 | 1.00 | 8.00 | — |
| 1920E | 11,646,000 | 0.25 | 2.50 | 8.00 | 25.00 | — |
| 1920F | 24,300,000 | 0.10 | 0.25 | 1.00 | 8.00 | — |
| 1920G | 10,244,000 | 0.20 | 2.00 | 3.50 | 15.00 | — |
| 1920J | 16,857,000 | 0.10 | 0.20 | 1.00 | 8.00 | — |
| 1921A | 143,418,000 | 0.10 | 0.20 | 0.50 | 7.00 | — |
| 1921D | 38,133,000 | 0.10 | 0.25 | 1.00 | 8.00 | — |
| 1921E | 21,104,000 | 2.50 | 5.00 | 10.00 | 20.00 | — |
| 1921F | 24,800,000 | 0.10 | 0.25 | 1.00 | 8.00 | — |
| 1921G | 21,289,000 | 0.10 | 0.25 | 1.00 | 8.00 | — |
| 1921J | 28,928,000 | 0.15 | 1.00 | 3.00 | 12.00 | — |
| 1922A Rare | 89,062,000 | — | — | — | — | — |
| 1922G | 31,240,000 | 0.10 | 0.25 | 1.00 | 8.00 | — |
| 1922E | 19,156,000 | 2.50 | 5.00 | 10.00 | 20.00 | — |
| 1922F | 16,436,000 | 0.10 | 0.25 | 1.00 | 8.00 | — |
| 1922G | 19,708,000 | 0.10 | 0.25 | 1.00 | 8.00 | — |
| 1922J | 16,820,000 | 0.25 | 2.50 | 6.00 | 15.00 | — |

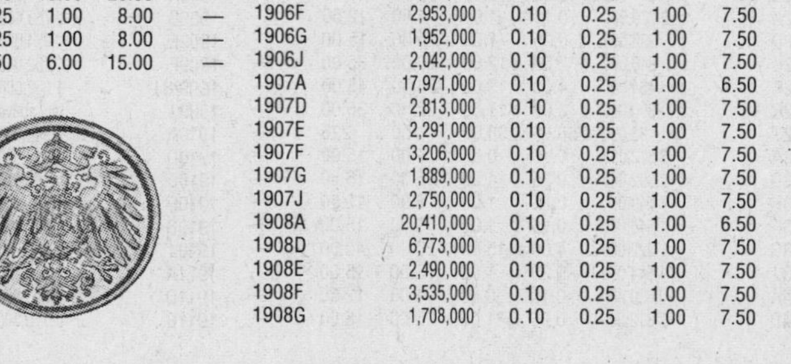

## 10 PFENNIG KM# 12 Composition: Copper-Nickel

| Date | Mintage | F | VF | XF | Unc | BU |
|---|---|---|---|---|---|---|
| 1901-16 Common date proof | — | Value: 80.00 | | | | |
| 1890-1900 Common date proof | — | Value: 95.00 | | | | |
| 1890A | 6,878,000 | 0.10 | 0.25 | 6.00 | 18.00 | — |
| 1890F | 784,000 | 0.25 | 1.50 | 8.00 | 25.00 | — |
| 1890G | 976,000 | 0.25 | 2.00 | 8.00 | 25.00 | — |
| 1890J | 1,637,000 | 0.25 | 1.00 | 8.00 | 25.00 | — |
| 1891A | 4,239,000 | 0.10 | 0.25 | 3.00 | 15.00 | — |
| 1891D | 2,812,000 | 0.10 | 0.30 | 4.00 | 16.00 | — |
| 1891E | 1,489,000 | 0.20 | 1.00 | 4.00 | 16.00 | — |
| 1891F | 1,226,000 | 0.25 | 2.50 | 5.00 | 20.00 | — |
| 1891G | 247,000 | 7.00 | 20.00 | 40.00 | 70.00 | — |
| 1892A | 2,413,000 | 0.15 | 0.50 | 4.00 | 18.00 | — |
| 1892D | 2,812,000 | 0.15 | 0.50 | 4.00 | 18.00 | — |
| 1892E | 870,000 | 0.25 | 2.50 | 5.00 | 20.00 | — |
| 1892F | 663,000 | 0.25 | 2.50 | 5.00 | 20.00 | — |
| 1892G | 300,000 | 6.00 | 15.00 | 30.00 | 65.00 | — |
| 1892J | — | 2,150 | 3,600 | — | — | — |
| 1893A | 8,435,000 | 0.10 | 0.25 | 2.25 | 10.00 | — |
| 1893E | 362,000 | 0.50 | 6.00 | 12.50 | 35.00 | — |
| 1893F | 1,345,000 | 0.15 | 0.50 | 3.00 | 16.00 | — |
| 1893G | 921,000 | 0.25 | 1.50 | 5.00 | 16.00 | — |
| 1893J | 1,636,000 | 0.20 | 1.00 | 5.00 | 16.00 | — |
| 1894E | 260,000 | 7.50 | 25.00 | 40.00 | 65.00 | — |
| 1896A | 4,996,000 | 0.10 | 1.00 | 2.25 | 10.00 | — |
| 1896D | 2,812,000 | 0.20 | 1.00 | 4.00 | 12.00 | — |
| 1896E | 1,495,000 | 0.20 | 1.00 | 4.00 | 15.00 | — |
| 1896F | 2,009,000 | 0.15 | 1.00 | 4.00 | 15.00 | — |
| 1896G | 200,000 | 6.00 | 15.00 | 25.00 | 40.00 | — |
| 1896J | 1,632,000 | 0.10 | 0.30 | 4.00 | 15.00 | — |
| 1897A | 5,842,000 | 0.10 | 0.25 | 2.25 | 10.00 | — |
| 1897G | 1,020,000 | 0.25 | 1.50 | 4.00 | 15.00 | — |
| 1898A | 10,833,000 | 0.10 | 0.25 | 2.00 | 9.00 | — |
| 1898D | 2,814,000 | 0.10 | 0.25 | 3.00 | 12.00 | — |
| 1898E | 805,000 | 0.20 | 0.50 | 3.00 | 14.00 | — |
| 1898F | 2,007,000 | 0.15 | 0.50 | 2.25 | 14.00 | — |
| 1898G | 480,000 | 0.50 | 3.00 | 6.00 | 22.50 | — |
| 1898J | 1,635,000 | 0.10 | 0.30 | 2.25 | 14.00 | — |
| 1899A | 10,838,000 | 0.10 | 0.25 | 2.00 | 9.00 | — |
| 1899D | 3,813,000 | 0.10 | 0.25 | 3.00 | 12.00 | — |
| 1899E | 2,175,000 | 0.10 | 0.30 | 3.00 | 14.00 | — |
| 1899F | 2,008,000 | 0.10 | 0.25 | 3.00 | 12.00 | — |
| 1899G | 1,382,000 | 0.10 | 0.25 | 3.00 | 12.00 | — |
| 1899J | 1,635,000 | 0.10 | 0.25 | 3.00 | 12.00 | — |
| 1900A | 34,559,000 | 0.10 | 0.25 | 1.75 | 8.00 | — |
| 1900D | 8,694,000 | 0.10 | 0.25 | 1.75 | 12.00 | — |
| 1900E | 4,490,000 | 0.10 | 0.30 | 2.00 | 12.00 | — |
| 1900F | 5,933,000 | 0.10 | 0.25 | 1.75 | 12.00 | — |
| 1900G | 4,239,000 | 0.10 | 0.25 | 2.00 | 14.00 | — |
| 1900J | 5,720,000 | 0.10 | 0.25 | 1.75 | 14.00 | — |
| 1901A | 10,200,000 | 0.10 | 0.25 | 1.00 | 7.00 | — |
| 1901D | 3,259,000 | 0.10 | 0.25 | 1.00 | 12.00 | — |
| 1901E | 1,863,000 | 0.10 | 0.30 | 1.00 | 12.00 | — |
| 1901F | 2,594,000 | 0.10 | 0.25 | 1.00 | 12.00 | — |
| 1901G | 1,527,000 | 0.10 | 0.25 | 1.00 | 12.00 | — |
| 1901J | 1,225,000 | 0.10 | 0.25 | 1.00 | 12.00 | — |
| 1902A | 5,878,000 | 0.10 | 0.25 | 1.00 | 6.00 | — |
| 1902D | 1,406,000 | 0.10 | 0.25 | 1.00 | 12.00 | — |
| 1902E | 502,000 | 0.25 | 3.00 | 6.00 | 15.00 | — |
| 1902F | 1,003,000 | 0.10 | 0.25 | 1.00 | 14.00 | — |
| 1902G | 610,000 | 0.25 | 1.50 | 3.50 | 14.00 | — |
| 1902J | 815,000 | 0.25 | 1.50 | 3.00 | 14.00 | — |
| 1903A | 5,131,000 | 0.10 | 0.25 | 1.00 | 7.00 | — |
| 1903D | 1,406,000 | 0.10 | 0.30 | 1.50 | 12.00 | — |
| 1903E | 988,000 | 0.15 | 0.30 | 1.00 | 12.00 | — |
| 1903F | 1,003,000 | 0.10 | 0.25 | 1.00 | 12.00 | — |
| 1903G | 610,000 | 0.25 | 0.50 | 1.50 | 14.00 | — |
| 1903J | 816,000 | 0.20 | 0.40 | 1.50 | 14.00 | — |
| 1904A | 5,189,000 | 0.10 | 0.25 | 1.00 | 6.00 | — |
| 1904D | 1,056,000 | 0.10 | 0.30 | 1.00 | 12.00 | — |
| 1904E | 559,000 | 0.25 | 1.00 | 2.50 | 12.00 | — |
| 1904F | 753,000 | 0.10 | 0.25 | 1.00 | 12.00 | — |
| 1904G | 457,000 | 1.00 | 5.00 | 7.50 | 16.00 | — |
| 1904J | 612,000 | 0.25 | 1.50 | 3.50 | 16.00 | — |
| 1905A | 8,650,000 | 0.10 | 0.25 | 1.00 | 6.00 | — |
| 1905A Proof | 250 | Value: 100 | | | | |
| 1905D | 1,846,000 | 0.10 | 0.25 | 1.00 | 7.50 | — |
| 1905E | 980,000 | 0.15 | 0.30 | 1.00 | 7.50 | — |
| 1905F | 1,310,000 | 0.10 | 0.25 | 1.00 | 7.50 | — |
| 1905G | 642,000 | 0.25 | 1.00 | 2.00 | 10.00 | — |
| 1905J | 1,430,000 | 0.10 | 0.25 | 1.00 | 7.50 | — |
| 1906A | 14,470,000 | 0.10 | 0.25 | 1.00 | 7.50 | — |
| 1906D | 4,132,000 | 0.10 | 0.25 | 1.00 | 7.50 | — |
| 1906E | 2,189,000 | 0.10 | 0.25 | 1.00 | 7.50 | — |
| 1906F | 2,953,000 | 0.10 | 0.25 | 1.00 | 7.50 | — |
| 1906G | 1,952,000 | 0.10 | 0.25 | 1.00 | 7.50 | — |
| 1906J | 2,042,000 | 0.10 | 0.25 | 1.00 | 7.50 | — |
| 1907A | 17,971,000 | 0.10 | 0.25 | 1.00 | 6.50 | — |
| 1907D | 2,813,000 | 0.10 | 0.25 | 1.00 | 7.50 | — |
| 1907E | 2,291,000 | 0.10 | 0.25 | 1.00 | 7.50 | — |
| 1907F | 3,206,000 | 0.10 | 0.25 | 1.00 | 7.50 | — |
| 1907G | 1,889,000 | 0.10 | 0.25 | 1.00 | 7.50 | — |
| 1907J | 2,750,000 | 0.10 | 0.25 | 1.00 | 7.50 | — |
| 1908A | 20,410,000 | 0.10 | 0.25 | 1.00 | 6.50 | — |
| 1908D | 6,773,000 | 0.10 | 0.25 | 1.00 | 7.50 | — |
| 1908E | 2,490,000 | 0.10 | 0.25 | 1.00 | 7.50 | — |
| 1908F | 3,535,000 | 0.10 | 0.25 | 1.00 | 7.50 | — |
| 1908G | 1,708,000 | 0.10 | 0.25 | 1.00 | 7.50 | — |
| 1908J | 2,649,000 | 0.10 | 0.25 | 1.00 | 7.50 | — |
| 1909A | 2,270,000 | 0.25 | 1.00 | 7.50 | 20.00 | — |
| 1909D | 966,000 | 0.25 | 1.50 | 9.00 | 40.00 | — |
| 1909E | 806,000 | 2.00 | 10.00 | 22.50 | 40.00 | — |
| 1909F | 780,000 | 2.00 | 10.00 | 22.50 | 60.00 | — |
| 1909G | 980,000 | 2.00 | 10.00 | 30.00 | 75.00 | — |
| 1909J | 725,000 | 2.00 | 10.00 | 30.00 | 75.00 | — |
| 1910A | 3,734,000 | 0.10 | 0.20 | 0.50 | 6.00 | — |
| 1910D | 1,406,000 | 0.25 | 0.50 | 1.00 | 7.50 | — |
| 1910E | 300,000 | 3.50 | 8.50 | 17.50 | 60.00 | — |
| 1910F | 1,003,000 | 0.25 | 0.50 | 1.00 | 7.50 | — |
| 1910G | 610,000 | 4.00 | 8.50 | 17.50 | 70.00 | — |
| 1911A | 13,554,000 | 0.10 | 0.15 | 0.50 | 6.00 | — |
| 1911D | 2,508,000 | 0.10 | 0.15 | 0.50 | 7.00 | — |
| 1911E | 2,246,000 | 0.10 | 0.15 | 0.50 | 7.00 | — |
| 1911F | 2,235,000 | 0.10 | 0.15 | 0.50 | 7.00 | — |
| 1911G | 1,678,000 | 0.10 | 0.15 | 0.50 | 7.00 | — |
| 1911J | 3,062,000 | 0.10 | 0.15 | 0.50 | 7.00 | — |
| 1912A | 21,312,000 | 0.10 | 0.15 | 0.50 | 6.00 | — |
| 1912D | 6,988,000 | 0.10 | 0.15 | 0.50 | 7.00 | — |
| 1912E | 2,649,000 | 0.10 | 0.15 | 0.50 | 7.00 | — |
| 1912F | 3,787,000 | 0.10 | 0.15 | 0.50 | 7.00 | — |
| 1912G | 2,441,000 | 0.10 | 0.15 | 0.50 | 7.00 | — |
| 1912J | 2,730,000 | 0.10 | 0.15 | 0.50 | 7.00 | — |
| 1913A | 13,466,000 | 0.10 | 0.15 | 0.50 | 6.00 | — |
| 1913D | 3,164,000 | 0.10 | 0.15 | 0.50 | 7.00 | — |
| 1913E | 1,478,000 | 0.10 | 0.15 | 0.50 | 7.00 | — |
| 1913F | 1,991,000 | 0.10 | 0.15 | 0.50 | 7.00 | — |
| 1913G | 1,373,000 | 0.10 | 0.15 | 0.50 | 7.00 | — |
| 1913J | 1,550,000 | 0.10 | 0.15 | 0.50 | 7.00 | — |
| 1914A | 18,570,000 | 0.10 | 0.15 | 0.50 | 6.00 | — |
| 1914D | 2,301,000 | 0.10 | 0.15 | 0.50 | 7.00 | — |
| 1914E | 3,478,000 | 0.10 | 0.15 | 0.50 | 7.00 | — |
| 1914F | 4,515,000 | 0.10 | 0.15 | 0.50 | 7.00 | — |
| 1914G | 2,689,000 | 0.10 | 0.15 | 0.50 | 7.00 | — |
| 1914J | 1,589,000 | 0.10 | 0.15 | 0.50 | 7.00 | — |
| 1915A | 10,639,000 | 0.10 | 0.15 | 0.50 | 7.00 | — |
| 1915D | 2,277,000 | 0.10 | 0.15 | 0.50 | 7.00 | — |
| 1915E | 1,027,000 | 0.25 | 2.50 | 5.00 | 15.00 | — |
| 1915F | 1,508,000 | 0.10 | 0.15 | 0.50 | 7.00 | — |
| 1915G | 363,000 | 35.00 | 100 | 140 | 200 | — |
| 1915J | 2,677,000 | 0.20 | 1.00 | 2.50 | 7.50 | — |
| 1916D | 1,128,000 | 0.15 | 1.00 | 2.50 | 10.00 | — |

## 10 PFENNIG KM# 20 Composition: Iron

| Date | Mintage | F | VF | XF | Unc | BU |
|---|---|---|---|---|---|---|
| 1916-22 Common date proof | — | Value: 95.00 | | | | |
| 1916A | 69,143,000 | 0.10 | 0.35 | 2.00 | 8.00 | — |
| 1916D | 11,609,000 | 0.10 | 0.30 | 2.00 | 9.00 | — |
| 1916E | 8,280,000 | 0.15 | 0.50 | 5.00 | 10.00 | — |
| 1916F | 7,473,000 | 0.15 | 0.50 | 5.00 | 10.00 | — |
| 1916G | 5,878,000 | 0.15 | 0.50 | 5.00 | 10.00 | — |
| 1916J | 11,683,000 | 0.15 | 0.50 | 4.00 | 9.00 | — |
| 1916 Rare | — | — | — | — | — | — |
| 1917A | 53,198,000 | 0.10 | 0.20 | 1.50 | 4.00 | — |
| 1917D | 16,370,000 | 0.10 | 0.30 | 2.00 | 5.00 | — |
| 1917E | 9,182,000 | 0.15 | 0.50 | 3.00 | 7.00 | — |
| 1917F | 11,341,000 | 0.15 | 0.50 | 3.00 | 7.00 | — |
| 1917F | — | — | — | — | — | — |
| **Note:** Mule with Polish reverse of Y#6, see Poland | | | | | | |
| 1917G | 7,088,000 | 0.15 | 0.50 | 4.00 | 10.00 | — |
| 1917J | 9,205,000 | 0.15 | 0.50 | 4.00 | 10.00 | — |
| 1918D | 42,000 | 600 | 1,000 | 2,000 | 3,000 | — |
| 1921A | 16,265,000 | 1.00 | 4.00 | 7.00 | 15.00 | — |
| 1922D | — | 2.00 | 7.50 | 14.00 | 25.00 | — |
| 1922E | 2,235,000 | 12.50 | 25.00 | 45.00 | 100 | — |
| 1922F | 1,928,000 | 0.50 | 3.00 | 6.00 | 12.00 | — |
| 1922G | 1,358,000 | 15.00 | 30.00 | 50.00 | 110 | — |
| 1922J | 2,420,000 | 1.00 | 4.00 | 7.00 | 15.00 | — |
| 1922 | — | 100 | 175 | 250 | 450 | — |

**Note:** There are several 1915A patterns for this type

## 10 PFENNIG KM# 26 Composition: Zinc Note: 3.10-3.60 grams. Without mint mark.

| Date | Mintage | F | VF | XF | Unc | BU |
|---|---|---|---|---|---|---|
| 1917 | 75,073,000 | 0.10 | 0.20 | 1.00 | 4.50 | — |
| 1918 | 202,008,000 | 0.10 | 0.20 | 1.00 | 4.50 | — |
| 1918 Proof | 28 | Value: 300 | | | | |
| 1919 | 147,800,000 | 0.10 | 0.20 | 1.00 | 4.50 | — |
| 1919 Proof | 50 | Value: 100 | | | | |
| 1920 | 223,019,000 | 0.10 | 0.20 | 1.00 | 4.50 | — |
| 1920 Proof | 40 | Value: 100 | | | | |

| Date | Mintage | F | VF | XF | Unc | BU |
|---|---|---|---|---|---|---|
| 1921 | 319,334,000 | 0.10 | 0.20 | 1.00 | 4.50 | — |
| 1921 Proof | 24 | Value: 300 | | | | |
| 1922 | 274,499,000 | 0.10 | 0.20 | 1.00 | 4.50 | — |
| 1922 Proof | 12 | Value: 400 | | | | |

**10 PFENNIG** KM# 25 **Composition:** Zinc **Note:** Eagle and beaded border similar to KM#20.

| Date | Mintage | F | VF | XF | Unc | BU |
|---|---|---|---|---|---|---|
| 1917 | — | 100 | 200 | 250 | 350 | — |

**PFENNIG** KM# 18 **Composition:** Nickel

| te | Mintage | F | VF | XF | Unc | BU |
|---|---|---|---|---|---|---|
| 09-12 Common date roof | — | Value: 150 | | | | |
| 09A | 962,000 | 2.50 | 7.00 | 11.50 | 25.00 | — |
| 09D | 1,406,000 | 2.50 | 7.00 | 11.50 | 25.00 | — |
| 09E | 250,000 | 15.00 | 27.50 | 40.00 | 90.00 | — |
| 09F | 400,000 | 4.00 | 10.00 | 20.00 | 40.00 | — |
| 09G | 610,000 | 4.00 | 10.00 | 20.00 | 40.00 | — |
| 09J | 10,000 | 500 | 750 | 1,200 | 1,500 | — |
| 10A | 9,522,000 | 2.50 | 7.00 | 11.50 | 22.50 | — |
| 10D | 1,408,000 | 2.50 | 7.00 | 11.50 | 22.50 | — |
| 10E | 1,242,000 | 2.50 | 7.00 | 11.50 | 22.50 | — |
| 10F | 1,605,000 | 2.50 | 7.00 | 15.00 | 25.00 | — |
| 10G | 330,000 | 3.00 | 8.00 | 18.50 | 35.00 | — |
| 10J | 1,561,000 | 2.50 | 7.00 | 15.00 | 25.00 | — |
| 11A | 3,179,000 | 2.50 | 7.00 | 11.50 | 20.00 | — |
| 11D | 506,000 | 3.00 | 8.00 | 18.50 | 40.00 | — |
| 11E | 747,000 | 3.00 | 8.00 | 18.50 | 40.00 | — |
| 11G | 892,000 | 3.00 | 8.00 | 18.50 | 40.00 | — |
| 11J | 516,000 | 3.00 | 8.00 | 18.50 | 40.00 | — |
| 12A | 2,590,000 | 2.50 | 7.00 | 11.50 | — | — |
| 12D | 900,000 | 3.00 | 8.00 | 17.50 | 32.50 | — |
| 12F | 1,003,000 | 3.00 | 8.00 | 18.50 | 35.00 | — |
| 12J | 362,000 | 12.50 | 25.00 | 35.00 | 80.00 | — |

**0 PFENNIG** KM# 15 **Weight:** 2.7770 g. **Composition:** .9000 Silver .0803 oz. ASW

| ate | Mintage | F | VF | XF | Unc | BU |
|---|---|---|---|---|---|---|
| 896-1900 Common date proof | — | Value: 525 | | | | |
| 896A | 389,000 | 100 | 220 | 325 | 475 | — |
| 898A | 387,000 | 100 | 220 | 325 | 475 | — |
| 900J | 192,000 | 100 | 235 | 375 | 550 | — |
| 900J Proof | — | Value: 650 | | | | |
| 901-03 Common date proof | — | Value: 500 | | | | |
| 901A | 194,000 | 150 | 250 | 300 | 400 | — |
| 902F | 95,000 | 250 | 300 | 475 | 1,150 | — |
| 902F Proof | — | Value: 800 | | | | |
| 903A | 384,000 | 125 | 200 | 250 | 325 | — |

**1/2 MARK** KM# 17 **Weight:** 2.7770 g. **Composition:** 0.9000 Silver .0803 oz. ASW

| Date | Mintage | F | VF | XF | Unc | BU |
|---|---|---|---|---|---|---|
| 1905-19 Common date proof | — | Value: 115 | | | | |
| 1905A | 37,766,000 | 0.75 | 1.00 | 4.50 | 12.00 | — |
| 1905D | 7,636,000 | 0.75 | 1.50 | 4.50 | 12.00 | — |
| 1905E | 4,908,000 | 0.75 | 1.50 | 4.50 | 12.00 | — |
| 1905F | 6,310,000 | 0.75 | 1.50 | 4.50 | 12.00 | — |
| 1905G | 3,886,000 | 0.75 | 1.50 | 4.50 | 15.00 | — |
| 1905J | 6,316,000 | 0.75 | 1.50 | 4.50 | 12.00 | — |
| 1906A | 29,754,000 | 0.75 | 1.50 | 4.50 | 12.00 | — |
| 1906D | 11,977,000 | 0.75 | 1.50 | 4.50 | 12.00 | — |
| 1906E | 5,821,000 | 0.75 | 1.50 | 4.50 | 15.00 | — |
| 1906F | 8,036,000 | 0.75 | 1.50 | 4.50 | 12.00 | — |
| 1906G | 4,273,000 | 0.75 | 1.50 | 4.50 | 18.00 | — |
| 1906J | 2,179,000 | 0.75 | 2.50 | 7.50 | 60.00 | — |
| 1907A | 14,168,000 | 0.75 | 1.50 | 4.50 | 12.00 | — |
| 1907D | 2,884,000 | 0.75 | 1.50 | 4.50 | 12.00 | — |
| 1907E | 600,000 | 2.50 | 9.00 | 20.00 | 60.00 | — |

| Date | Mintage | F | VF | XF | Unc | BU |
|---|---|---|---|---|---|---|
| 1907F | 1,202,000 | 0.75 | 1.50 | 4.50 | 12.00 | — |
| 1907G | 927,000 | 3.00 | 10.00 | 20.00 | 60.00 | — |
| 1907J | 3,268,000 | 0.75 | 1.50 | 20.00 | 45.00 | — |
| 1908A | 5,018,000 | 0.75 | 1.50 | 4.50 | 12.00 | — |
| 1908D | 400,000 | 7.50 | 17.50 | 32.50 | 70.00 | — |
| 1908E | 591,000 | 2.50 | 10.00 | 25.00 | 60.00 | — |
| 1908F | 1,000 | 2,000 | 5,000 | 7,000 | 9,000 | — |
| 1908G | 675,000 | 1.25 | 30.00 | 60.00 | 200 | — |
| 1808/7J | 1,309,000 | 1.25 | 30.00 | 60.00 | 200 | — |
| 1908J | Inc. above | 1.25 | 10.00 | 80.00 | 200 | — |
| 1909A | 5,404,000 | 0.75 | 1.50 | 4.50 | 12.00 | — |
| 1909/5D | 1,001,000 | 0.75 | 1.50 | 4.50 | 12.00 | — |
| 1909D | Inc. above | 0.75 | 1.50 | 4.50 | 12.00 | — |
| 1909E | 745,000 | 1.25 | 5.00 | 10.00 | 28.00 | — |
| 1909F | 999,000 | 0.75 | 2.50 | 7.50 | 15.00 | — |
| 1909G | 607,000 | 1.25 | 5.00 | 10.00 | 75.00 | — |
| 1909J | 816,000 | 1.25 | 5.00 | 10.00 | 20.00 | — |
| 1911A | 2,710,000 | 1.25 | 5.00 | 7.50 | 22.00 | — |
| 1911/05D | 703,000 | 1.25 | 5.00 | 7.50 | 22.00 | — |
| 1911D | Inc. above | 1.25 | 5.00 | 7.50 | 22.00 | — |
| 1911E | 376,000 | 5.00 | 17.50 | 25.00 | 70.00 | — |
| 1911F | 502,000 | 2.50 | 7.50 | 17.50 | 50.00 | — |
| 1911G | 610,000 | 2.50 | 7.50 | 17.50 | 50.00 | — |
| 1911J | 418,000 | 5.00 | 17.50 | 27.50 | 85.00 | — |
| 1912A | 2,709,000 | 1.25 | 5.00 | 7.50 | 25.00 | — |
| 1912/5D | 703,000 | 1.50 | 10.00 | 15.00 | 30.00 | — |
| 1912D | Inc. above | 1.50 | 10.00 | 15.00 | 30.00 | — |
| 1912E | 369,000 | 5.00 | 17.50 | 25.00 | 65.00 | — |
| 1912F | 501,000 | 2.50 | 7.50 | 12.50 | 65.00 | — |
| 1912J | 399,000 | 6.00 | 20.00 | 50.00 | 120 | — |
| 1913A | 5,419,000 | 0.75 | 1.50 | 4.50 | 12.00 | — |
| 1913/05D | 1,406,000 | 0.75 | 1.50 | 4.50 | 12.00 | — |
| 1913D | Inc. above | 0.75 | 1.50 | 4.50 | 12.00 | — |
| 1913E | 745,000 | 2.50 | 5.00 | 10.00 | 22.00 | — |
| 1913F | 1,003,000 | 0.75 | 1.50 | 5.00 | 12.00 | — |
| 1913G | 610,000 | 1.25 | 5.00 | 10.00 | 22.00 | — |
| 1913J | 817,000 | 1.25 | 5.00 | 10.00 | 28.00 | — |
| 1914A | 13,525,000 | 0.75 | 1.50 | 3.50 | 10.00 | — |
| 1914/05D | 328,000 | 2.50 | 10.00 | 15.00 | 35.00 | — |
| 1914D | Inc. above | 2.50 | 10.00 | 15.00 | 35.00 | — |
| 1914J | 2,292,000 | 0.75 | 3.00 | 5.00 | 12.00 | — |
| 1915A | 13,015,000 | 0.75 | 1.50 | 3.50 | 10.00 | — |
| 1915/05D | 5,117,000 | 0.75 | 1.50 | 3.00 | 10.00 | — |
| 1915D | Inc. above | 0.75 | 1.50 | 3.00 | 10.00 | — |
| 1915E | 3,308,000 | 0.75 | 1.50 | 3.00 | 10.00 | — |
| 1915F | 5,309,000 | 0.75 | 1.50 | 3.00 | 10.00 | — |
| 1915G | 2,730,000 | 0.75 | 1.50 | 3.00 | 10.00 | — |
| 1915E | 2,285,000 | 0.75 | 1.50 | 3.00 | 10.00 | — |
| 1916A | 9,750,000 | 0.75 | 1.50 | 3.00 | 10.00 | — |
| 1916/616D | 4,397,000 | 0.75 | 1.50 | 3.00 | 10.00 | — |
| 1916/05D | Inc. above | 0.75 | 1.50 | 3.00 | 10.00 | — |
| 1916/5D | Inc. above | 0.75 | 1.50 | 3.00 | 10.00 | — |
| 1916D | Inc. above | 0.75 | 1.50 | 3.00 | 10.00 | — |
| 1916E | 1,640,000 | 0.75 | 1.50 | 3.00 | 10.00 | — |
| 1916F | 2,410,000 | 0.75 | 1.50 | 3.00 | 10.00 | — |
| 1916G | 1,779,000 | 0.75 | 1.50 | 3.00 | 10.00 | — |
| 1916J | 1,464,000 | 0.75 | 1.50 | 3.00 | 10.00 | — |
| 1917A | 14,692,000 | 0.75 | 1.50 | 3.00 | 10.00 | — |
| 1917/05D | 979,000 | 0.75 | 1.50 | 3.00 | 10.00 | — |
| 1917D | Inc. above | 0.75 | 1.50 | 3.00 | 10.00 | — |
| 1917E | 1,561,000 | 0.75 | 1.50 | 3.00 | 10.00 | — |
| 1917F | 450,000 | 2.50 | 10.00 | 15.00 | 50.00 | — |
| 1917G | 619,000 | 2.50 | 10.00 | 15.00 | 50.00 | — |
| 1917J | 1,039,000 | 1.50 | 4.00 | 6.00 | 15.00 | — |
| 1918A | 14,622,000 | 0.75 | 1.50 | 3.00 | 10.00 | — |
| **Note:** Some were issued with a black finish to prevent hoarding | | | | | | |
| 1918/05D | 3,670,000 | 0.75 | 1.50 | 3.00 | 10.00 | — |
| 1918D | Inc. above | 0.75 | 1.50 | 3.00 | 10.00 | — |
| **Note:** Some were issued with a black finish to prevent hoarding | | | | | | |
| 1918E | 2,807,000 | 1.50 | 6.00 | 10.00 | 20.00 | — |
| **Note:** Some were issued with a black finish to prevent hoarding | | | | | | |
| 1918E Proof | 19 | — | — | — | — | — |
| 1918F | 4,010,000 | 0.75 | 1.50 | 3.50 | 10.00 | — |
| **Note:** Some were issued with a black finish to prevent hoarding | | | | | | |
| 1918G | 1,032,000 | 1.50 | 6.00 | 10.00 | 15.00 | — |
| **Note:** Some were issued with a black finish to prevent hoarding | | | | | | |
| 1918J | 3,452,000 | 0.75 | 1.50 | 4.00 | 12.00 | — |
| **Note:** Some were issued with a black finish to prevent hoarding | | | | | | |
| 1919A | 9,124,000 | 0.75 | 1.50 | 4.00 | 12.00 | — |
| **Note:** Some were issued with a black finish to prevent hoarding | | | | | | |
| 1919/1619D | 2,195,000 | 0.75 | 1.50 | 5.00 | 15.00 | — |
| 1919/05D | Inc. above | 0.75 | 1.50 | 5.00 | 15.00 | — |
| 1919D | Inc. above | 0.75 | 1.50 | 5.00 | 15.00 | — |
| **Note:** Some were issued with a black finish to prevent hoarding | | | | | | |
| 1919E | 1,767,000 | 2.50 | 7.50 | 12.50 | 20.00 | — |
| **Note:** Some were issued with a black finish to prevent hoarding | | | | | | |
| 1919F | 1,559,000 | 2.00 | 6.00 | 12.00 | 25.00 | — |
| **Note:** Some were issued with a black finish to prevent hoarding | | | | | | |
| 1919J | 1,875,000 | 1.00 | 3.00 | 5.00 | 15.00 | — |
| **Note:** Some were issued with a black finish to prevent hoarding | | | | | | |

**MARK** KM# 14 **Weight:** 5.5500 g. **Composition:** 0.9000 Silver .1606 oz. ASW

| Date | Mintage | F | VF | XF | Unc | BU |
|---|---|---|---|---|---|---|
| 1891-1900 Proof | — | Value: 150 | | | | |
| 1891A | 711,000 | 7.50 | 12.50 | 22.00 | 90.00 | — |
| 1891D | 450 | 900 | 1,350 | 2,750 | | — |
| 1892A | 909,000 | 5.00 | 12.50 | 22.00 | 90.00 | — |
| 1892D | 418,000 | 5.00 | 15.00 | 32.00 | 120 | — |
| 1892E | 223,000 | 10.00 | 17.50 | 45.00 | 185 | — |
| 1892F | 302,000 | 5.00 | 15.00 | 32.00 | 145 | — |
| 1892G | 183,000 | 20.00 | 40.00 | 100 | 300 | — |
| 1892J | 237,000 | 14.00 | 25.00 | 70.00 | 150 | — |
| 1893A | 1,633,000 | 2.50 | 5.00 | 12.00 | 80.00 | — |
| 1893D | 425,000 | 2.50 | 5.00 | 32.00 | 145 | — |
| 1893E | 224,000 | 7.50 | 17.50 | 45.00 | 140 | — |
| 1893F | 300,000 | 7.50 | 15.00 | 32.00 | 120 | — |
| 1893J | 254,000 | 8.00 | 20.00 | 50.00 | 150 | — |
| 1894G | 184,000 | 20.00 | 45.00 | 150 | 350 | — |
| 1896A | 2,160,000 | 2.50 | 5.00 | 15.00 | 60.00 | — |
| 1896D | 562,000 | 2.50 | 6.00 | 18.00 | 90.00 | — |
| 1896E | 297,000 | 5.00 | 15.00 | 45.00 | 120 | — |
| 1896F | 401,000 | 2.50 | 6.00 | 32.00 | 95.00 | — |
| 1896G | 243,000 | 7.50 | 20.00 | 70.00 | 185 | — |
| 1896J | 326,000 | 5.00 | 15.00 | 45.00 | 145 | — |
| 1898A | 1,000,000 | 5.00 | 12.50 | 22.00 | 95.00 | — |
| 1899A | 1,439,000 | 2.50 | 5.00 | 15.00 | 70.00 | — |
| 1899D | 633,000 | 2.50 | 5.00 | 18.00 | 75.00 | — |
| 1899E | 335,000 | 5.00 | 15.00 | 28.00 | 100 | — |
| 1899F | 393,000 | 4.00 | 10.00 | 22.00 | 85.00 | — |
| 1899G | 274,000 | 4.00 | 10.00 | 28.00 | 160 | — |
| 1899J | 368,000 | 4.00 | 10.00 | 28.00 | 135 | — |
| 1900A | 1,625,000 | 2.50 | 5.00 | 12.00 | 40.00 | — |
| 1900/800D | 421,000 | 2.50 | 5.00 | 12.00 | 70.00 | — |
| 1900/801D | 915,000 | 2.50 | 5.00 | 12.00 | 70.00 | — |
| 1900D | Inc. above | 2.50 | 5.00 | 12.00 | 70.00 | — |
| 1900E | 223,000 | 10.00 | 25.00 | 50.00 | 150 | — |
| 1900F | 301,000 | 7.50 | 17.50 | 35.00 | 100 | — |
| 1900G | 183,000 | 12.00 | 27.00 | 65.00 | 185 | — |
| 1900J | 246,000 | 10.00 | 25.00 | 50.00 | 150 | — |
| 1901-16 Common date proof | — | Value: 150 | | | | |
| 1901A | 3,821,000 | 2.50 | 5.00 | 12.00 | 35.00 | — |
| 1901/800D | Inc. above | 2.50 | 5.00 | 12.00 | 35.00 | — |
| 1901/801D | Inc. above | 2.50 | 5.00 | 12.00 | 35.00 | — |
| 1901D | Inc. above | 2.50 | 5.00 | 15.00 | 40.00 | — |
| 1901E | 484,000 | 2.50 | 6.00 | 20.00 | 70.00 | — |
| 1901F | 802,000 | 2.50 | 5.00 | 12.00 | 60.00 | — |
| 1901G | 579,000 | 3.00 | 7.50 | 35.00 | 150 | — |
| 1901J | 531,000 | 2.50 | 5.00 | 30.00 | 100 | — |
| 1902A | 5,222,000 | 1.50 | 4.00 | 10.00 | 30.00 | — |
| 1902D | 1,546,000 | 1.50 | 4.00 | 10.00 | 30.00 | — |
| 1902E | 819,000 | 1.50 | 4.00 | 12.00 | 80.00 | — |
| 1902F | 953,000 | 1.50 | 4.00 | 10.00 | 75.00 | — |
| 1902G | 270,000 | 6.00 | 25.00 | 45.00 | 135 | — |
| 1902J | 898,000 | 3.50 | 7.50 | 25.00 | 145 | — |
| 1903A | 3,965,000 | 1.25 | 2.00 | 5.50 | 28.00 | — |
| 1903/803D | 914,000 | 1.25 | 2.50 | 6.50 | 30.00 | — |
| 1903D | Inc. above | 1.25 | 2.50 | 6.50 | 30.00 | — |
| 1903E | 485,000 | 5.00 | 12.00 | 22.00 | 75.00 | — |
| 1903F | 652,000 | 5.00 | 7.50 | 20.00 | 110 | — |
| 1903G | 614,000 | 2.50 | 5.00 | 15.00 | 70.00 | — |
| 1903J | 531,000 | 5.00 | 12.00 | 28.00 | 200 | — |
| 1904A | 3,243,000 | 1.25 | 2.00 | 5.50 | 28.00 | — |
| 1904D | 1,761,000 | 1.25 | 2.00 | 6.50 | 35.00 | — |
| 1904E | 931,000 | 2.50 | 4.00 | 10.00 | 40.00 | — |
| 1904F | 1,255,000 | 2.00 | 3.50 | 9.00 | 35.00 | — |
| 1904G | 664,000 | 2.50 | 5.00 | 20.00 | 50.00 | — |
| 1904J | 1,021,000 | 2.50 | 5.00 | 25.00 | 200 | — |
| 1905A | 10,303,000 | 1.25 | 2.00 | 5.00 | 20.00 | — |
| 1905D | 1,759,000 | 1.25 | 2.00 | 6.50 | 28.00 | — |
| 1905E | 931,000 | 2.50 | 4.00 | 10.00 | 40.00 | — |
| 1905F | Inc. above | 2,000 | 2,800 | 4,500 | 6,000 | — |
| 1905G | 860,000 | 2.50 | 4.00 | 12.50 | 50.00 | — |
| 1905J | 1,021,000 | 1.50 | 5.00 | 25.00 | 125 | — |
| 1906A | 5,414,000 | 1.25 | 2.50 | 5.50 | 28.00 | — |
| 1906D | 1,412,000 | 1.25 | 2.50 | 7.50 | 28.00 | — |
| 1906E | 745,000 | 1.50 | 5.00 | 12.00 | 40.00 | — |
| 1906F | 2,257,000 | 1.25 | 2.50 | 5.50 | 35.00 | — |
| 1906G | 609,000 | 2.50 | 10.00 | 40.00 | 100 | — |
| 1906G Proof | — | — | — | — | — | — |
| 1906J | 372,000 | 5.00 | 12.00 | 35.00 | 200 | — |
| 1907A | 9,201,000 | 1.25 | 2.50 | 5.00 | 20.00 | — |
| 1907D | 2,387,000 | 1.25 | 2.50 | 5.00 | 20.00 | — |
| 1907E | 1,265,000 | 1.25 | 2.50 | 6.50 | 25.00 | — |
| 1907F | 1,704,000 | 1.25 | 2.50 | 6.50 | 20.00 | — |
| 1907G | 1,035,000 | 1.25 | 2.50 | 12.00 | 30.00 | — |
| 1907J | 1,833,000 | 1.25 | 2.50 | 12.00 | 90.00 | — |
| 1908A | 4,338,000 | 1.25 | 2.50 | 5.00 | 15.00 | — |
| 1908D | 1,126,000 | 1.25 | 2.50 | 5.50 | 20.00 | — |

| Date | Mintage | F | VF | XF | Unc | BU |
|---|---|---|---|---|---|---|
| 1908E | 596,000 | 2.50 | 5.00 | 12.50 | 45.00 | — |
| 1908F | 802,000 | 1.25 | 2.50 | 6.50 | 40.00 | — |
| 1908G | 488,000 | 2.50 | 5.00 | 12.00 | 45.00 | — |
| 1908J | 653,000 | 2.50 | 5.00 | 12.00 | 75.00 | — |
| 1909A | 4,151,000 | 1.25 | 2.50 | 5.00 | 25.00 | — |
| 1909D | 1,968,000 | 1.25 | 2.50 | 5.50 | 15.00 | — |
| 1909E | — | 35.00 | 90.00 | 150 | 245 | — |
| 1909G | 854,000 | 4.00 | 12.00 | 22.00 | 35.00 | — |
| 1909J | 53,000 | 85.00 | 175 | 285 | 650 | — |
| 1910A | 5,870,000 | 1.25 | 1.50 | 5.00 | 17.50 | — |
| 1910D | 1,406,000 | 1.25 | 2.50 | 5.50 | 20.00 | — |
| 1910E | 1,050,000 | 2.50 | 4.50 | 7.00 | 25.00 | — |
| 1910F | 1,631,000 | 2.50 | 4.50 | 7.00 | 20.00 | — |
| 1910G | 610,000 | 2.50 | 5.00 | 12.00 | 55.00 | — |
| 1910J | 1,094,000 | 2.50 | 5.00 | 12.00 | 75.00 | — |
| 1911A | 5,693,000 | 1.25 | 2.50 | 5.50 | 15.00 | — |
| 1911D | 126,000 | 10.00 | 20.00 | 40.00 | 100 | — |
| 1911E | 738,000 | 4.00 | 6.00 | 15.00 | 50.00 | — |
| 1911F | 773,000 | 2.50 | 6.00 | 45.00 | 200 | — |
| 1911G | 305,000 | 4.00 | 6.00 | 15.00 | 50.00 | — |
| 1911J | 812,000 | 4.00 | 6.00 | 40.00 | 175 | — |
| 1912A | 2,439,000 | 1.25 | 2.50 | 5.50 | 15.00 | — |
| 1912D | 632,000 | 1.25 | 2.50 | 5.50 | 20.00 | — |
| 1912E | 708,000 | 2.50 | 5.00 | 10.00 | 20.00 | — |
| 1912F | 502,000 | 2.50 | 5.00 | 12.00 | 40.00 | — |
| 1912J | 409,000 | 5.00 | 10.00 | 20.00 | 125 | — |
| 1913F | 450,000 | 15.00 | 25.00 | 40.00 | 60.00 | — |
| 1913G | 275,000 | 20.00 | 30.00 | 45.00 | 65.00 | — |
| 1913J | 368,000 | 20.00 | 30.00 | 45.00 | 70.00 | — |
| 1914A | 11,304,000 | 1.25 | 1.50 | 3.50 | 15.00 | — |
| 1914/9D | 3,515,000 | 1.25 | 1.50 | 3.00 | 14.00 | — |
| 1914D | Inc. above | 1.25 | 1.50 | 3.50 | 15.00 | — |
| 1914E | 2,235,000 | 1.25 | 1.50 | 3.50 | 15.00 | — |
| 1914F | 2,300,000 | 1.25 | 1.50 | 3.50 | 15.00 | — |
| 1914G | 1,911,000 | 1.25 | 1.50 | 3.50 | 15.00 | — |
| 1914J | 2,978,000 | 1.25 | 1.50 | 3.50 | 15.00 | — |
| 1915A | 13,817,000 | 1.25 | 1.50 | 3.50 | 15.00 | — |
| 1915D | 4,218,000 | 1.25 | 1.50 | 3.50 | 15.00 | — |
| 1915E | 2,235,000 | 1.25 | 1.50 | 3.50 | 15.00 | — |
| 1915F | 2,911,000 | 1.25 | 1.50 | 3.50 | 15.00 | — |
| 1915G | 1,749,000 | 1.25 | 1.50 | 3.50 | 15.00 | — |
| 1915J | 1,634,000 | 1.25 | 1.50 | 3.50 | 15.00 | — |
| 1916F | 306,000 | 12.00 | 22.00 | 35.00 | 75.00 | — |

## MILITARY COINAGE - WWI

Issued under the authority of the German Military Commander of the East for use in Estonia, Latvia, Lithuania, Poland, and Northwest Russia.

**KOPEK** KM# 21 **Composition:** Iron

| Date | Mintage | F | VF | XF | Unc | BU |
|---|---|---|---|---|---|---|
| 1916A | 11,942,000 | 2.50 | 5.00 | 10.00 | 25.00 | — |
| 1916A Proof | — | Value: 125 | | | | |
| 1916J | 8,000,000 | 2.50 | 5.00 | 10.00 | 25.00 | — |
| 1916J Proof | — | Value: 125 | | | | |

**2 KOPEKS** KM# 22 **Composition:** Iron

| Date | Mintage | F | VF | XF | Unc | BU |
|---|---|---|---|---|---|---|
| 1916A | 6,973,000 | 2.50 | 5.00 | 12.50 | 30.00 | — |
| 1916A Proof | — | Value: 125 | | | | |
| 1916J | 8,000,000 | 2.50 | 5.00 | 12.50 | 30.00 | — |
| 1916J Proof | — | Value: 125 | | | | |

**3 KOPEKS** KM# 23 **Composition:** Iron

| Date | Mintage | F | VF | XF | Unc | BU |
|---|---|---|---|---|---|---|
| 1916A | 8,670,000 | 2.50 | 5.00 | 12.50 | 35.00 | — |
| 1916A Proof | — | Value: 125 | | | | |
| 1916J | 8,000,000 | 2.50 | 5.00 | 12.50 | 35.00 | — |
| 1916J Proof | — | Value: 125 | | | | |

## PATTERNS

### Including off metal strikes

| KM# | Date | Mintage | Identification | Mkt Val |
|---|---|---|---|---|
| Pn66 | 1901 | — | 50 Pfennig. Plain 2mm edge. KM#15. | 200 |
| Pn67 | 1901 | — | 50 Pfennig. Plain 3.5mm edge. KM#15. | 200 |
| Pn68 | 1901 | — | 50 Pfennig. Coarse reeding. KM#15. | 200 |
| Pn69 | 1901 | — | 50 Pfennig. Coarse wavy reeding. KM#15. | 200 |

| KM# | Date | Mintage | Identification | Mkt Val |
|---|---|---|---|---|
| Pn70 | 1901 | — | 1/2 Mark. Silver. | 400 |
| Pn71 | 1901 | — | 1/2 Mark. Silver. Date. | 400 |
| Pn72 | 1901 | — | 1/2 Mark. Silver. Incuse diamond. | 400 |
| Pn73 | 1901 | — | 1/2 Mark. Brass. Incuse diamond. | 200 |
| Pn74 | 1901 | — | 1/2 Mark. Brass. Incuse diamond, beaded circle. | 200 |
| Pn75 | 1901 | — | 1/2 Mark. Silver. Diamond within beads. | 375 |
| Pn76 | 1901 | — | 1/2 Mark. Brass. Beaded diamond. | 200 |
| Pn77 | 1901 | — | 1/2 Mark. Silver. Beaded diamond. | 375 |

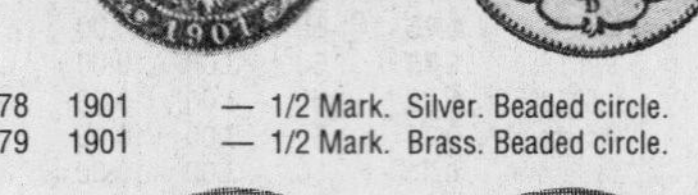

| KM# | Date | Mintage | Identification | Mkt Val |
|---|---|---|---|---|
| Pn78 | 1901 | — | 1/2 Mark. Silver. Beaded circle. | 375 |
| Pn79 | 1901 | — | 1/2 Mark. Brass. Beaded circle. | 200 |

| KM# | Date | Mintage | Identification | Mkt Val |
|---|---|---|---|---|
| Pn80 | 1901 | — | 1/2 Mark. Silver. Diamnd within beads. | 375 |
| Pn81 | 1901 | — | 1/2 Mark. Silver. Incuse diamond. | 375 |
| Pn82 | 1901 | — | 1/2 Mark. Brass. Incuse diamond. | 200 |
| Pn83 | 1901 | — | 1/2 Mark. Silver. Date. | 375 |
| Pn84 | 1901 | — | 1/2 Mark. Silver. Beaded circle. | 375 |
| Pn85 | 1901 | — | 1/2 Mark. Brass. Beaded circle. | 200 |
| Pn86 | 1902 | — | 50 Pfennig. Without beaded rims, coarse reeding; KM#15. | 375 |
| Pn87 | 1902 | — | 50 Pfennig. Without beaded rims, reeded edge; KM#15. | 375 |

| KM# | Date | Mintage | Identification | Mkt Val |
|---|---|---|---|---|
| Pn88 | 1902 | — | 50 Pfennig. 0.7100 Silver. Incuse circle. | 500 |
| Pn89 | 1902 | — | 1/2 Mark. Silver. Incuse circle. | 400 |
| Pn90 | 1903 | — | 50 Pfennig. Without beaded rim, coarse reeding; KM#15. | 375 |
| Pn91 | 1903 | — | 50 Pfennig. Coarse reeding; KM#15. | 375 |

| KM# | Date | Mintage | Identification | Mkt Val |
|---|---|---|---|---|
| Pn92 | 1903 | — | 50 Pfennig. Silver. Crown. | 400 |
| Pn93 | 1903 | — | 50 Pfennig. Eagle. | 400 |
| Pn94 | 1903 | — | 50 Pfennig. Brass. Otto of Bavaria. | 375 |
| Pn95 | 1903 | — | 50 Pfennig. Copper. Otto of Bavaria. | 375 |
| Pn96 | 1903 | — | 50 Pfennig. Brass. Crown. Otto of Bavaria. | 375 |
| Pn97 | 1903 | — | 50 Pfennig. Brass. Germania. | 350 |
| Pn98 | 1904 | — | 1/2 Mark. KM#17. | 400 |
| Pn99 | | — | 25 Pfennig. Nickel-Silver. Value within beaded circle. | 200 |
| Pn100 | | — | 25 Pfennig. Copper-Nickel. Beaded circle. | 200 |
| Pn101 | | — | 25 Pfennig. Tin Alloy. Beaded circle. | 200 |
| Pn102 | 1907 | — | 25 Pfennig. Nickel. Germania. | 150 |
| Pn103 | 1907 | — | 25 Pfennig. Copper. Crown. | 150 |
| Pn104 | 1907 | — | 25 Pfennig. Nickel. Crown. | 150 |
| Pn105 | 1907 | — | 1/2 Mark. Coarse reeding; KM#17. | 200 |

| KM# | Date | Mintage | Identification | Mkt Val |
|---|---|---|---|---|
| Pn106 | 1908 | — | 25 Pfennig. Nickel. | 300 |

| KM# | Date | Mintage | Identification | Mkt Val |
|---|---|---|---|---|
| Pn107 | 1908 | — | 25 Pfennig. Nickel-Silver. Eagle plain. | 200 |
| Pn108 | 1908 | — | 25 Pfennig. Silver. Eagle plain. | 30 |
| Pn109 | 1908 | — | 25 Pfennig. Nickel-Silver. Eagle within beads. | 20 |
| Pn110 | 1908 | — | 25 Pfennig. Nickel-Silver. Eagle within beads. | 20 |
| Pn111 | 1908 | — | 25 Pfennig. Eagle plain. | 20 |

| KM# | Date | Mintage | Identification | Mkt Val |
|---|---|---|---|---|
| Pn112 | 1908 | — | 25 Pfennig. Copper-Nickel. | 200 |

| KM# | Date | Mintage | Identification | Mkt Val |
|---|---|---|---|---|
| Pn113 | 1908 | — | 25 Pfennig. Nickel-Silver. | 20 |
| Pn114 | 1908 | — | 25 Pfennig. Nickel. | 20 |

| KM# | Date | Mintage | Identification | Mkt Val |
|---|---|---|---|---|
| Pn115 | 1908 | — | 25 Pfennig. Nickel-Silver. | 200 |
| Pn116 | 1908 | — | 25 Pfennig. Aluminum. | 200 |
| Pn117 | 1908 | — | 25 Pfennig. Copper-Nickel. | 150 |
| Pn118 | 1908 | — | 25 Pfennig. Silver. | 250 |
| Pn119 | 1908 | — | 25 Pfennig. Bronze. | 150 |
| Pn120 | 1908 | — | 25 Pfennig. Copper. | 150 |

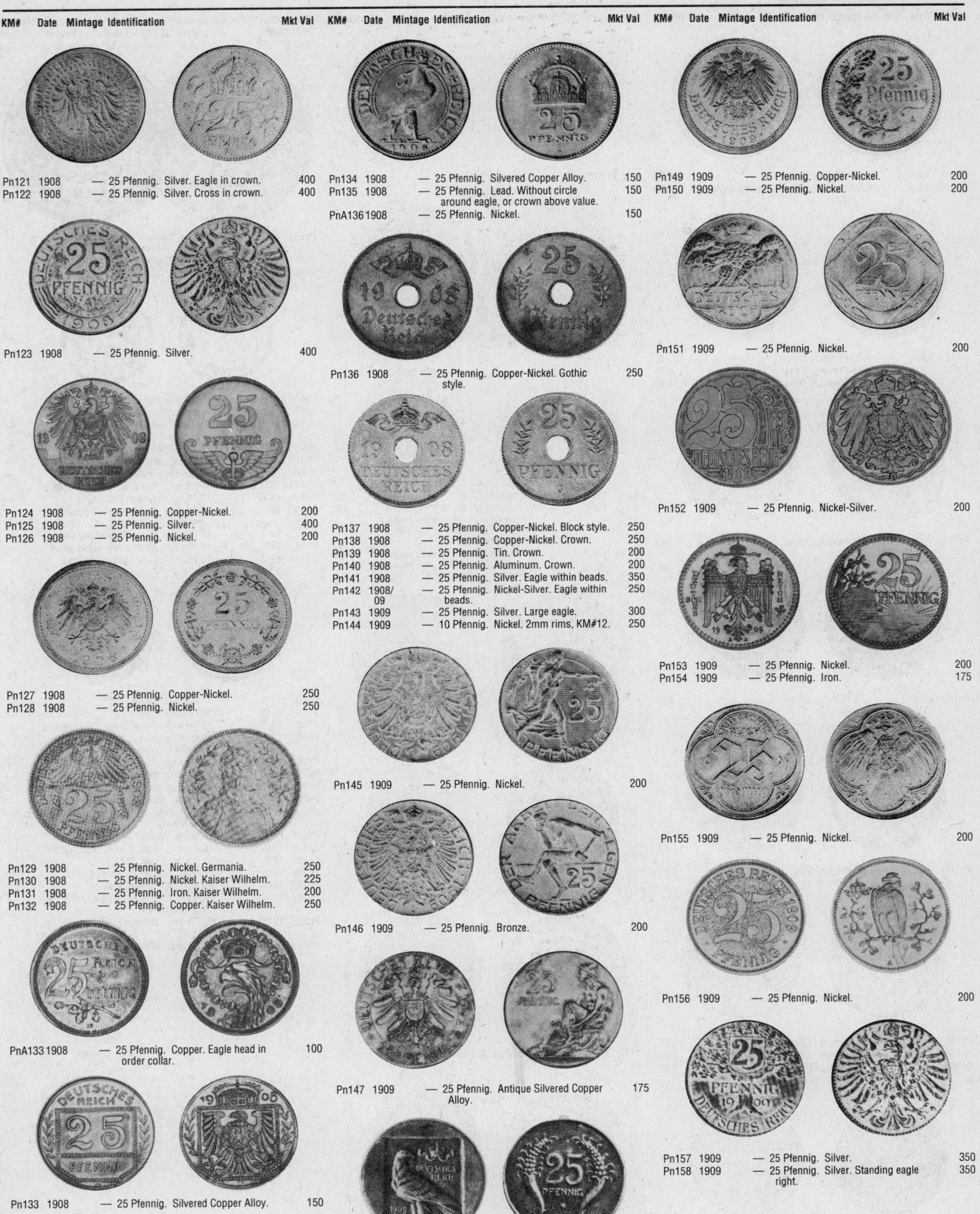

| KM# | Date | Mintage | Identification | Mkt Val |
|---|---|---|---|---|
| Pn121 | 1908 | — | 25 Pfennig. Silver. Eagle in crown. | 400 |
| Pn122 | 1908 | — | 25 Pfennig. Silver. Cross in crown. | 400 |
| Pn123 | 1908 | — | 25 Pfennig. Silver. | 400 |
| Pn124 | 1908 | — | 25 Pfennig. Copper-Nickel. | 200 |
| Pn125 | 1908 | — | 25 Pfennig. Silver. | 400 |
| Pn126 | 1908 | — | 25 Pfennig. Nickel. | 200 |
| Pn127 | 1908 | — | 25 Pfennig. Copper-Nickel. | 250 |
| Pn128 | 1908 | — | 25 Pfennig. Nickel. | 250 |
| Pn129 | 1908 | — | 25 Pfennig. Nickel. Germania. | 250 |
| Pn130 | 1908 | — | 25 Pfennig. Nickel. Kaiser Wilhelm. | 225 |
| Pn131 | 1908 | — | 25 Pfennig. Iron. Kaiser Wilhelm. | 200 |
| Pn132 | 1908 | — | 25 Pfennig. Copper. Kaiser Wilhelm. | 250 |
| PnA133 | 1908 | — | 25 Pfennig. Copper. Eagle head in order collar. | 100 |
| Pn133 | 1908 | — | 25 Pfennig. Silvered Copper Alloy. | 150 |
| Pn134 | 1908 | — | 25 Pfennig. Silvered Copper Alloy. | 150 |
| Pn135 | 1908 | — | 25 Pfennig. Lead. Without circle around eagle, or crown above value. | 150 |
| PnA136 | 1908 | — | 25 Pfennig. Nickel. | 150 |
| Pn136 | 1908 | — | 25 Pfennig. Copper-Nickel. Gothic style. | 250 |
| Pn137 | 1908 | — | 25 Pfennig. Copper-Nickel. Block style. | 250 |
| Pn138 | 1908 | — | 25 Pfennig. Copper-Nickel. Crown. | 250 |
| Pn139 | 1908 | — | 25 Pfennig. Tin. Crown. | 200 |
| Pn140 | 1908 | — | 25 Pfennig. Aluminum. Crown. | 200 |
| Pn141 | 1908 | — | 25 Pfennig. Silver. Eagle within beads. | 350 |
| Pn142 | 1908/09 | — | 25 Pfennig. Nickel-Silver. Eagle within beads. | 250 |
| Pn143 | 1909 | — | 25 Pfennig. Silver. Large eagle. | 300 |
| Pn144 | 1909 | — | 10 Pfennig. Nickel. 2mm rims, KM#12. | 250 |
| Pn145 | 1909 | — | 25 Pfennig. Nickel. | 200 |
| Pn146 | 1909 | — | 25 Pfennig. Bronze. | 200 |
| Pn147 | 1909 | — | 25 Pfennig. Antique Silvered Copper Alloy. | 175 |
| Pn148 | 1909 | — | 25 Pfennig. Cast | 200 |
| Pn149 | 1909 | — | 25 Pfennig. Copper-Nickel. | 200 |
| Pn150 | 1909 | — | 25 Pfennig. Nickel. | 200 |
| Pn151 | 1909 | — | 25 Pfennig. Nickel. | 200 |
| Pn152 | 1909 | — | 25 Pfennig. Nickel-Silver. | 200 |
| Pn153 | 1909 | — | 25 Pfennig. Nickel. | 200 |
| Pn154 | 1909 | — | 25 Pfennig. Iron. | 175 |
| Pn155 | 1909 | — | 25 Pfennig. Nickel. | 200 |
| Pn156 | 1909 | — | 25 Pfennig. Nickel. | 200 |
| Pn157 | 1909 | — | 25 Pfennig. Silver. | 350 |
| Pn158 | 1909 | — | 25 Pfennig. Silver. Standing eagle right. | 350 |

| KM# | Date | Mintage | Identification | Mkt Val |
|---|---|---|---|---|
| Pn159 | 1909 | — | 25 Pfennig. Silver. | 350 |
| Pn160 | 1909 | — | 25 Pfennig. Silver. Standing eagle right. | 350 |
| Pn161 | 1909 | — | 25 Pfennig. Silver. | 300 |
| Pn162 | 1909 | — | 25 Pfennig. Nickel. | 200 |
| Pn163 | 1909 | — | 25 Pfennig. Copper-Nickel. | 200 |
| Pn164 | 1909 | — | 25 Pfennig. Silver. Legend over value. | 300 |
| Pn165 | 1909 | — | 25 Pfennig. Silver. Standing eagle right. | 350 |
| Pn166 | 1909 | — | 25 Pfennig. Antique Silvered Copper Alloy. | 200 |
| Pn167 | 1909 | — | 25 Pfennig. Silver. | 300 |
| Pn168 | 1909 | — | 25 Pfennig. Silver. Eagle within legend. | 300 |
| Pn169 | 1909 | — | 25 Pfennig. Silver. Large eagle, legend above crowned value. | 300 |
| Pn170 | 1909 | — | 25 Pfennig. Silver. | 350 |

| KM# | Date | Mintage | Identification | Mkt Val |
|---|---|---|---|---|
| PnA171 | 1909 | — | 25 Pfennig. | 250 |
| Pn171 | 1909 | — | 25 Pfennig. Silver. | 300 |
| Pn172 | 1909 | — | 25 Pfennig. Silver. | 300 |
| Pn173 | 1909 | — | 25 Pfennig. Nickel. GOTT MITUNS above crowned eagle with spread wings. DEUTSCHES REICH above large numerals. | 250 |
| Pn174 | 1909 | — | 25 Pfennig. Nickel. Stockier eagle, countermarked mm. Large munerals and countermarked date. | 250 |
| Pn175 | 1909 | — | 25 Pfennig. | 250 |
| Pn176 | 1909 | — | 25 Pfennig. Silver Or Copper-Nickel. | 300 |
| Pn177 | 1909 | — | 25 Pfennig. Antique Silvered Copper Alloy. | 250 |
| Pn178 | | — | 25 Pfennig. Silver. Large eagle. | 350 |
| Pn179 | 1910 | — | 25 Pfennig. Silver. Eagle within legend. | 250 |
| Pn180 | 1910 | — | 1/2 Mark. Silver. KM#17. | 350 |
| Pn181 | 1910 | — | Mark. Silver. Without mint mark, KM#7. | — |
| PnD182 | 1910 | — | 3 Mark. Ernst Ludwig | — |
| PnA182 | 1911 | — | Mark. Aluminum Clad Zinc. | — |

| KM# | Date | Mintage | Identification | Mkt Val |
|---|---|---|---|---|
| PnB182 | 1911 | — | 2 Mark. Aluminum Clad Zinc. Bavaria | — |
| PnC182 | 1912 | — | 3 Mark. Aluminum Clad Zinc. Bavaria | — |
| PnE182 | 1913 | — | 3 Mark. Silver. Without mint mark, Kaiser on horseback. | — |
| PnF182 | 1913 | — | 3 Mark. Copper. | — |
| Pn182 | 1914 | — | 5 Pfennig. Reeded edge. KM#11 | — |
| PnA183 | 1915 | — | (No Denomination). Gilt Bronze. | — |
| Pn183 | 1915 | — | Pfennig. Zinc. Reeded edge. KM#10 | — |
| Pn184 | 1915 | — | Pfennig. Iron. Date below value, KM#24. | — |
| Pn185 | 1915 | — | Pfennig. Aluminum. | — |
| Pn186 | 1915 | — | 5 Pfennig. Without mint mark, KM#11. | — |
| Pn187 | 1915 | — | 10 Pfennig. Brass. KM#17. KM#12. | — |
| Pn188 | 1915 | — | 10 Pfennig. Brass. Broad rims, KM#12. | — |
| Pn189 | 1915 | — | 10 Pfennig. Nickel. Broad rims. | — |
| Pn190 | 1915 | — | 10 Pfennig. Copper-Nickel. Broad rims. | — |
| Pn192 | 1915 | — | 10 Pfennig. Brass. Date above value. | — |
| Pn193 | 1915 | — | 10 Pfennig. Nickel. Date above value. | — |
| Pn194 | 1915 | — | 10 Pfennig. Iron. Date above value. | — |
| Pn195 | 1915 | — | 10 Pfennig. Small "10". | — |
| Pn196 | 1915 | — | 10 Pfennig. Large "10". | — |
| Pn197 | 1915 | — | 10 Pfennig. Brass. Small "10", KM#20. | — |
| Pn198 | 1915 | — | 10 Pfennig. Nickel. Small "10", KM#20. | — |
| Pn199 | 1915 | — | 10 Pfennig. Iron. 67 beads on rim. | — |
| Pn200 | 1915 | — | 10 Pfennig. Nickel. 67 beads on rim. | — |
| Pn201 | 1915 | — | 10 Pfennig. Copper-Nickel. KM#20. | — |
| Pn203 | 1915 | — | 1/2 Mark. Silver. Large eagle. | — |
| Pn204 | 1915 | — | Mark. Aluminum. GOTT MIT UNS on rim, KM#14. | — |
| PnA205 | | — | Pfenning. Copper. KM#24. | — |
| Pn191 | 1915 | — | 10 Pfennig. Rusted Iron. Broad rims. | 100 |
| Pn202 | 1915 | — | 10 Pfennig. Iron. KM#20. | 500 |
| Pn205 | 1916 | — | Pfennig. Aluminum. KM#24. | — |
| Pn206 | 1916 | — | Pfennig. Aluminum. KM#24. | — |
| Pn207 | 1917 | — | Pfennig. Aluminum. Without mint mark, KM#24. | — |
| Pn208 | 1917 | — | 10 Pfennig. Without mint mark, KM#20. | — |
| Pn209 | 1917 | — | 10 Pfennig. Mint mark, KM#26. | — |

| Date | Mintage | F | VF | XF | Unc | BU |
|---|---|---|---|---|---|---|
| 1924E | 6,595,000 | 0.15 | 0.50 | 3.00 | 12.00 | — |
| 1924F | 14,969,000 | 0.15 | 0.50 | 3.00 | 10.00 | — |
| 1924G | 10,349,000 | 0.15 | 0.50 | 3.00 | 10.00 | — |
| 1924J | 21,196,000 | 0.25 | 1.00 | 5.00 | 10.00 | — |

# WEIMAR REPUBLIC

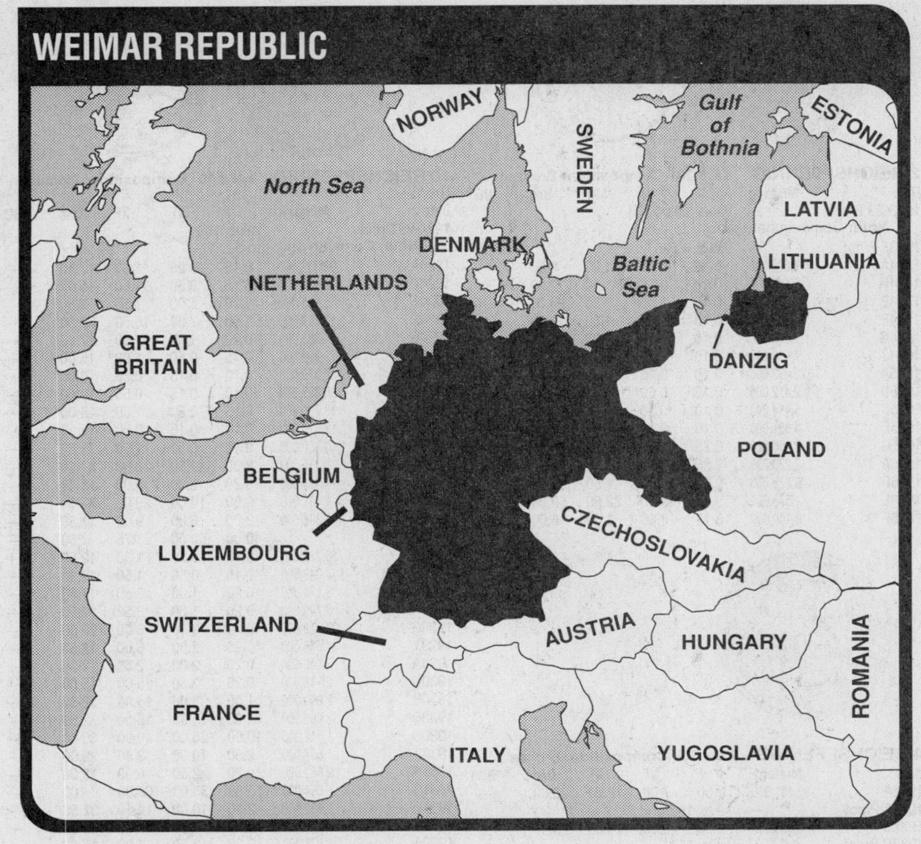


**1919-1933**

The Imperial German government disintegrated in a flurry of royal abdications as World War I ended. Desperate German parliamentarians, fearful of impending anarchy and civil war, hastily declared a German Republic. The new National Assembly, which was convened Feb. 6, 1919 in Weimar had to establish a legal government, draft a constitution, and then conclude a peace treaty with the Allies. Friedrich Ebert was elected as Reichs President. The harsh terms of the peace treaty imposed on Germany were economically and psychologically unacceptable to the German population regardless of political persuasion and the problem of German treaty compliance was to plague the Republic until the worldwide Great Depression of 1929. The new constitution paid less attention to fundamental individual rights and concentrated more power in the President and Central Government to insure a more stable social and economic order. The German bureaucracy survived the transition intact and had a stifling effect on the democratic process. The army started training large numbers of reservists in conjunction with the U.S.S.R. thereby circumventing treaty limitations on the size of the German military.

New anti-democratic ideologies were forming. Communism and Fascism were spreading. The National Socialist German Workers Party, under Hitler's leadership, incorporated the ever-present anti-Semitism into a new virulent Nazi Catechism.

In spite of the historic German inflation, the French occupation of the Rhineland, and the loss of vast territories and resources, the republic survived. By 1929 the German economy had been restored to its pre-war level. Much of the economic gains however were dependent on the extensive assistance provided by the U.S.A. and collapsed along with the world economy in 1929. Even during the good times, the Republic was never able to muster any loyal public support or patriotism. By 1930, Nationalists, Nazis, and Communists held nearly half of the Reichstag seats and the government was forced to rely more and more on presidential decrees as the only means to effectuate policy. In 1932, the Nazis won 230 Reichstag seats. As head of the largest party, Hitler claimed the right to form the next government. President Hindenburg's opposition forced a second election in which the Nazis lost 34 seats. Von Papen, however, convinced Hindenburg to name Hitler Chancellor by arguing that Hitler could be controlled! Hitler formed his cabinet and immediately began consolidating his power and laying the groundwork for the Third Reich.

**MONETARY SYSTEM**

(During 1923-1924)
100 Rentenpfennig = 1 Rentenmark

(Commencing 1924)
100 Reichspfennig = 1 Reichsmark

# WEIMAR REPUBLIC

## STANDARD COINAGE

**RENTENPFENNIG** **KM# 30** **Composition:** Bronze

| Date | Mintage | F | VF | XF | Unc | BU |
|---|---|---|---|---|---|---|
| 1923-29 Proof | — | Value: 120 | | | | |
| **Note:** Common date proof | | | | | | |
| 1923A | 12,629,000 | 0.15 | 0.50 | 1.50 | 5.00 | — |
| 1923D | Est. 2,314,000 | 0.25 | 2.00 | 5.00 | 22.00 | — |
| 1923E | 2,200,000 | 1.50 | 4.00 | 12.00 | 35.00 | — |
| 1923F | 160,000 | 1.50 | 4.00 | 12.00 | 35.00 | — |
| 1923G | 1,004,000 | 0.25 | 1.50 | 8.00 | 30.00 | — |
| 1923J | 1,470,000 | 0.25 | 1.50 | 6.00 | 20.00 | — |
| 1924A | 55,273,000 | 0.15 | 0.50 | 2.50 | 7.50 | — |
| 1924D | 17,540,000 | 0.20 | 1.50 | 5.00 | 10.00 | — |
| 1924E | 6,838,000 | 0.20 | 1.50 | 6.00 | 12.50 | — |
| 1924F | 10,347,000 | 0.20 | 1.50 | 5.00 | 10.00 | — |
| 1924G | 7,366,000 | 0.25 | 1.50 | 6.00 | 12.50 | — |
| 1924J | 11,024,000 | 0.20 | 1.50 | 5.00 | 10.00 | — |
| 1925A | — | 300 | 500 | 1,000 | 2,000 | — |
| 1929F | — | 125 | 225 | 350 | 500 | — |

**2 RENTENPFENNIG** **KM# 31** **Composition:** Bronze

| Date | Mintage | F | VF | XF | Unc | BU |
|---|---|---|---|---|---|---|
| 1923-29 Proof | — | Value: 140 | | | | |
| **Note:** Common date proof | | | | | | |
| 1923A | 8,587,000 | 0.15 | 0.50 | 2.50 | 12.50 | — |
| 1923D | 1,490,000 | 0.15 | 0.50 | 3.00 | 10.00 | — |
| 1923F | Inc. above | 0.50 | 5.00 | 15.00 | 35.00 | — |
| 1923G | Inc. above | 0.25 | 1.00 | 6.50 | 15.00 | — |
| 1923J | Inc. above | 0.50 | 5.00 | 12.50 | 25.00 | — |
| 1924A | 80,864,000 | 0.10 | 0.25 | 2.50 | 10.00 | — |
| 1924D | 19,899,000 | 0.10 | 0.25 | 2.50 | 10.00 | — |

**5 RENTENPFENNIG** **KM# 32** **Composition:** Aluminum-Bronze

| Date | Mintage | F | VF | XF | Unc | BU |
|---|---|---|---|---|---|---|
| 1923-29 Proof | — | Value: 150 | | | | |
| **Note:** Common date proof | | | | | | |
| 1923A | 3,083,000 | 0.20 | 1.00 | 2.50 | 10.00 | — |
| 1923D | | 0.30 | 1.50 | 3.00 | 17.50 | — |
| 1923F | | 35.00 | 75.00 | 125 | 175 | — |
| 1923G | | 30.00 | 60.00 | 90.00 | 125 | — |
| 1924A | 171,966,000 | 0.10 | 0.50 | 2.00 | 7.50 | — |
| 1924D | 31,163,000 | 0.20 | 0.50 | 1.00 | 6.00 | — |
| 1924E | 12,206,000 | 0.20 | 0.50 | 1.00 | 7.50 | — |
| 1924F | 29,032,000 | 0.20 | 0.50 | 1.00 | 7.50 | — |
| 1924G | 19,217,000 | 0.20 | 0.50 | 1.00 | 7.50 | — |
| 1924J | 32,332,000 | 0.20 | 0.50 | 1.00 | 7.50 | — |
| 1925F 1 known | — | — | 4,800 | — | — | — |

**10 RENTENPFENNIG** **KM# 33** **Composition:** Aluminum-Bronze

| Date | Mintage | F | VF | XF | Unc | BU |
|---|---|---|---|---|---|---|
| 1923-1925 Proof | — | Value: 150 | | | | |
| **Note:** Common date proof | | | | | | |
| 1923A | | 0.25 | 2.50 | 6.00 | 17.50 | — |
| 1923D | | 0.50 | 5.00 | 10.00 | 25.00 | — |
| 1923F | | 70.00 | 110 | 160 | 225 | — |
| 1923G | | 2.50 | 12.50 | 25.00 | 50.00 | — |
| 1924A | 169,956,000 | 0.20 | 0.40 | 2.50 | 7.50 | — |
| 1924D | 33,894,000 | 0.15 | 0.50 | 1.00 | 10.00 | — |
| 1924E | 18,679,000 | 0.20 | 1.00 | 1.50 | 15.00 | — |
| 1924F | 42,237,000 | 0.15 | 0.50 | 1.00 | 10.00 | — |
| 1924F Proof | — | Value: 95.00 | | | | |
| 1924G | 18,758,000 | 0.20 | 0.50 | 1.00 | 15.00 | — |
| 1924J | 33,928,000 | 0.15 | 0.50 | 1.00 | 15.00 | — |
| 1925F | 13,000 | 500 | 1,000 | 1,500 | 2,000 | — |

**50 PFENNIG** **KM# 27** **Composition:** Aluminum

| Date | Mintage | F | VF | XF | Unc | BU |
|---|---|---|---|---|---|---|
| 1919A | 7,173,000 | 0.25 | 1.50 | 4.00 | 6.00 | — |
| 1919D | 791,000 | 0.50 | 1.50 | 3.50 | 10.00 | — |
| 1919E | 930,000 | 2.00 | 7.00 | 15.00 | 30.00 | — |
| 1919E Proof | 35 | — | — | — | — | — |
| 1919F | 160,000 | 5.00 | 10.00 | 20.00 | 50.00 | — |
| 1919G | 660,000 | 0.75 | 5.00 | 7.50 | 12.50 | — |
| 1919J | 800,000 | 3.00 | 8.00 | 17.00 | 40.00 | — |
| 1920A | 119,793,000 | 0.10 | 0.15 | 0.25 | 1.50 | — |
| 1920D | 28,306,000 | 0.10 | 0.15 | 0.25 | 1.50 | — |
| 1920E | 14,400,000 | 0.25 | 1.50 | 4.00 | 10.00 | — |
| 1920E Proof | 226 | Value: 65.00 | | | | |
| 1920F | 10,932,000 | 0.10 | 0.15 | 0.25 | 1.50 | — |
| 1920G | 5,040,000 | 0.20 | 1.50 | 2.50 | 5.00 | — |
| 1920J | 15,423,000 | 0.10 | 0.25 | 1.00 | 4.00 | — |
| 1921A | 184,468,000 | 0.10 | 0.15 | 0.25 | 1.50 | — |
| 1921D | 48,729,000 | 0.10 | 0.15 | 0.25 | 1.50 | — |
| 1921E | 31,210,000 | 0.15 | 1.50 | 2.50 | 5.00 | — |
| 1921E Proof | 332 | Value: 65.00 | | | | |
| 1921F | 46,950,000 | 0.10 | 0.15 | 0.25 | 1.50 | — |
| 1921G | 19,107,000 | 0.10 | 0.20 | 0.50 | 1.50 | — |
| 1921J | 28,013,000 | 0.10 | 0.25 | 1.00 | 4.00 | — |
| 1922A | 145,215,000 | 0.10 | 0.15 | 0.25 | 1.50 | — |
| 1922D | 58,019,000 | 0.10 | 0.15 | 0.25 | 1.50 | — |
| 1922E | 33,930,000 | 0.15 | 1.50 | 2.50 | 5.00 | — |
| 1922E Proof | 333 | Value: 65.00 | | | | |
| 1922F | 33,000,000 | 0.10 | 0.15 | 0.25 | 1.50 | — |
| 1922G | 36,745,000 | 0.10 | 0.20 | 0.50 | 1.50 | — |
| 1922J | 36,202,000 | 0.25 | 2.50 | 4.50 | 9.00 | — |

**50 RENTENPFENNIG** **KM# 34** **Composition:** Aluminum-Bronze

| Date | Mintage | F | VF | XF | Unc | BU |
|---|---|---|---|---|---|---|
| 1923-29 Proof | — | Value: 200 | | | | |
| **Note:** Common date proof | | | | | | |
| 1923A | 451,000 | 5.00 | 15.00 | 27.50 | 55.00 | — |
| 1923D | 192,000 | 12.50 | 17.50 | 32.50 | 60.00 | — |
| 1923F | 120,000 | 45.00 | 90.00 | 120 | 220 | — |
| 1923G | 120,000 | 15.00 | 25.00 | 55.00 | 90.00 | — |
| 1923J | 4,000 | 600 | 1,200 | 1,600 | 2,200 | — |
| 1924A | 117,365,000 | 5.00 | 10.00 | 17.50 | 35.00 | — |
| 1924D | 30,971,000 | 5.00 | 10.00 | 17.50 | 45.00 | — |
| 1924E | 14,668,000 | 5.00 | 10.00 | 22.50 | 50.00 | — |
| 1924F | 21,968,000 | 5.00 | 10.00 | 17.50 | 45.00 | — |
| 1924G | 13,349,000 | 7.50 | 15.00 | 27.50 | 55.00 | — |
| 1924J | 17,252,000 | 5.00 | 10.00 | 17.50 | 45.00 | — |

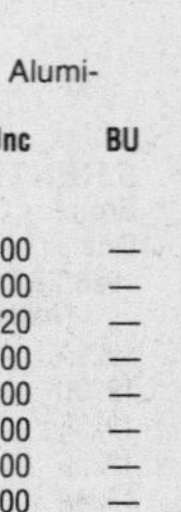
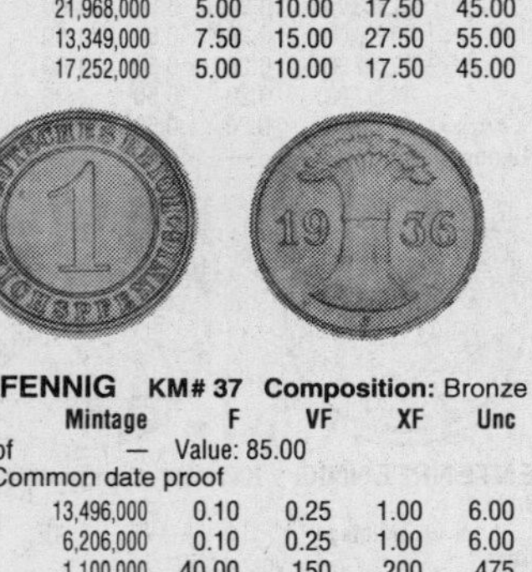

**REICHSPFENNIG** **KM# 37** **Composition:** Bronze

| Date | Mintage | F | VF | XF | Unc | BU |
|---|---|---|---|---|---|---|
| 1924-29 Proof | — | Value: 85.00 | | | | |
| **Note:** Common date proof | | | | | | |
| 1924A | 13,496,000 | 0.10 | 0.25 | 1.00 | 6.00 | — |
| 1924D | 6,206,000 | 0.10 | 0.25 | 1.00 | 6.00 | — |
| 1924E | 1,100,000 | 40.00 | 150 | 200 | 475 | — |
| 1924F | 2,650,000 | 0.15 | 0.30 | 1.00 | 6.00 | — |
| 1924G | 5,100,000 | 0.15 | 0.50 | 2.00 | 8.50 | — |
| 1924J | 24,400,000 | 0.10 | 0.25 | 1.00 | 6.00 | — |
| 1925A | 40,925,000 | 0.10 | 0.25 | 1.00 | 5.00 | — |
| 1925D | 1,558,000 | 5.00 | 12.50 | 22.50 | 40.00 | — |
| 1925E | 10,460,000 | 0.10 | 0.25 | 1.00 | 6.00 | — |
| 1925F | 5,673,000 | 0.10 | 0.25 | 1.00 | 6.00 | — |
| 1925G | 13,502,000 | 0.10 | 0.25 | 1.00 | 6.00 | — |
| 1925J | 30,300,000 | 0.10 | 0.25 | 1.00 | 6.00 | — |
| 1927A | 4,671,000 | 0.10 | 0.25 | 1.00 | 6.00 | — |
| 1927D | 4,203,000 | 0.15 | 0.50 | 2.00 | 8.50 | — |
| 1927E | 8,000,000 | 0.15 | 0.50 | 3.50 | 12.00 | — |
| 1927F | 2,350,000 | 0.25 | 1.00 | 2.00 | 8.50 | — |
| 1927G | 3,236,000 | 0.15 | 0.50 | 3.50 | 12.00 | — |
| 1928A | 19,300,000 | 0.10 | 0.25 | 1.00 | 3.50 | — |
| 1928D | 10,200,000 | 0.10 | 0.25 | 1.00 | 3.50 | — |
| 1928F | 8,672,000 | 0.10 | 0.25 | 1.00 | 3.50 | — |
| 1928G | 3,764,000 | 0.15 | 0.50 | 2.00 | 6.00 | — |
| 1929A | 37,170,000 | 0.10 | 0.25 | 1.00 | 3.50 | — |
| 1929D | 9,337,000 | 0.10 | 0.25 | 1.00 | 3.50 | — |
| 1929E | 6,600,000 | 0.15 | 0.30 | 1.00 | 5.00 | — |
| 1929F | 3,150,000 | 0.10 | 0.25 | 1.50 | 6.00 | — |
| 1929G | 1,986,000 | 0.15 | 0.50 | 2.00 | 6.00 | — |
| 1930A | 40,997,000 | 0.10 | 0.25 | 1.00 | 3.50 | — |
| 1930D | 6,441,000 | 0.10 | 0.25 | 1.00 | 3.50 | — |
| 1930E | 1,412,000 | 6.00 | 12.00 | 25.00 | 60.00 | — |
| 1930F | 6,415,000 | 0.10 | 0.50 | 1.50 | 6.00 | — |
| 1930G | 5,017,000 | 0.10 | 0.25 | 1.00 | 3.50 | — |
| 1931A | 38,481,000 | 0.10 | 0.25 | 1.00 | 3.50 | — |
| 1931D | 5,998,000 | 0.10 | 0.25 | 1.00 | 3.50 | — |
| 1931E | 12,800,000 | 0.15 | 0.50 | 2.00 | 6.00 | — |
| 1931F | 12,591,000 | 0.10 | 0.25 | 1.00 | 3.50 | — |
| 1931G | 2,622,000 | 0.15 | 0.50 | 2.50 | 7.50 | — |
| 1932A | 17,096,000 | 0.10 | 0.25 | 1.00 | 3.50 | — |
| 1933A | 37,846,000 | 0.10 | 0.25 | 1.00 | 3.50 | — |
| 1933E | 2,945,000 | 0.35 | 2.00 | 4.50 | 9.00 | — |
| 1933F | 5,023,000 | 0.10 | 0.50 | 1.00 | 5.00 | — |
| 1934A | 51,214,000 | 0.10 | 0.25 | 1.00 | 5.00 | — |
| 1934D | 7,408,000 | 0.10 | 0.25 | 1.00 | 5.00 | — |
| 1934E | 4,628,000 | 0.50 | 3.50 | 7.50 | 15.00 | — |
| 1934F | 5,667,000 | 0.10 | 0.25 | 1.00 | 5.00 | — |
| 1934G | 2,450,000 | 0.15 | 0.30 | 1.00 | 5.00 | — |
| 1934J | 4,271,000 | 0.15 | 0.50 | 3.00 | 8.50 | — |
| 1935A | 35,894,000 | 0.10 | 0.25 | 1.00 | 5.00 | — |
| 1935D | 15,489,000 | 0.10 | 0.25 | 1.00 | 5.00 | — |
| 1935E | 8,351,000 | 0.15 | 0.50 | 2.50 | 7.50 | — |
| 1935F | 12,094,000 | 0.10 | 0.25 | 1.00 | 5.00 | — |
| 1935G | 7,454,000 | 0.10 | 0.25 | 1.00 | 5.00 | — |
| 1935J | 8,505,000 | 0.10 | 0.25 | 1.00 | 5.00 | — |
| 1936A | Est. 50,949,000 | 0.10 | 0.25 | 1.00 | 5.00 | — |
| 1936D | 12,262,000 | 0.10 | 0.25 | 1.00 | 5.00 | — |
| 1936E | 2,576,000 | 0.50 | 3.00 | 10.00 | 15.00 | — |
| 1936F | 6,915,000 | 0.10 | 0.25 | 1.00 | 5.00 | — |
| 1936G | Est. 2,940,000 | 0.15 | 0.30 | 1.00 | 5.00 | — |
| 1936J | Est. 5,421,000 | 0.15 | 0.50 | 2.00 | 7.50 | — |

**2 REICHSPFENNIG** **KM# 38** **Composition:** Bronze

| Date | Mintage | F | VF | XF | Unc | BU |
|---|---|---|---|---|---|---|
| 1923-29 Proof | — | Value: 90.00 | | | | |
| **Note:** Common date proof | | | | | | |
| 1923F Proof | — | Value: 4,500 | | | | |
| 1924A | 19,620,000 | 0.10 | 0.25 | 1.00 | 6.00 | — |
| 1924D | 3,482,000 | 0.10 | 0.30 | 1.50 | 12.00 | — |
| 1924E | 4,253,000 | 0.15 | 1.50 | 7.50 | 20.00 | — |
| 1924F | 4,567,000 | 0.10 | 0.20 | 1.00 | 10.00 | — |
| 1924G | 7,560,000 | 0.10 | 0.20 | 1.00 | 10.00 | — |
| 1924J | 7,489,000 | 0.10 | 0.25 | 1.00 | 10.00 | — |
| 1925A | 22,433,000 | 0.10 | 0.25 | 1.00 | 6.00 | — |
| 1925D | 2,412,000 | 0.15 | 0.60 | 2.50 | 15.00 | — |
| 1925E | 5,414,000 | 0.10 | 0.30 | 1.50 | 10.00 | — |
| 1925F | 4,851,000 | 0.10 | 0.30 | 1.50 | 10.00 | — |
| 1925G | 2,456,000 | 0.25 | 1.50 | 7.50 | 20.00 | — |
| 1936A | 3,220,000 | 0.25 | 2.00 | 7.50 | 17.50 | — |
| 1936D | 6,525,000 | 0.10 | 0.30 | 1.50 | 10.00 | — |
| 1936E | 573,000 | 5.00 | 15.00 | 22.50 | 50.00 | — |
| 1936F | 3,100,000 | 0.15 | 0.50 | 1.00 | 6.00 | — |

**4 REICHSPFENNIG** **KM# 75** **Composition:** Bronze

| Date | Mintage | F | VF | XF | Unc | BU |
|---|---|---|---|---|---|---|
| 1932A | 27,101,000 | 2.50 | 7.00 | 12.00 | 22.00 | — |
| 1932A Proof | — | Value: 150 | | | | |
| 1932D | 7,055,000 | 2.50 | 6.00 | 14.00 | 25.00 | — |
| 1932D Proof | — | Value: 150 | | | | |
| 1932E | 3,729,000 | 2.50 | 9.00 | 16.50 | 45.00 | — |
| 1932E Proof | — | Value: 150 | | | | |
| 1932F | 5,022,000 | 2.50 | 9.00 | 16.50 | 45.00 | — |
| 1932F Proof | — | Value: 150 | | | | |
| 1932G | 3,050,000 | 3.00 | 12.00 | 20.00 | 55.00 | — |
| 1932G Proof | — | Value: 150 | | | | |
| 1932J | 4,094,000 | 2.50 | 9.00 | 16.50 | 45.00 | — |
| 1932J Proof | — | Value: 150 | | | | |

**5 REICHSPFENNIG** **KM# 39** **Composition:** Aluminum-Bronze

| Date | Mintage | F | VF | XF | Unc | BU |
|---|---|---|---|---|---|---|
| 1924-29 Proof | — | Value: 100 | | | | |
| **Note:** Common date proof | | | | | | |
| 1924A | 14,469,000 | 0.20 | 0.50 | 2.50 | 15.00 | — |
| 1924D | 8,139,000 | 0.20 | 0.50 | 2.50 | 8.00 | — |
| 1924E | 5,976,000 | 0.20 | 1.00 | 5.00 | 15.00 | — |
| 1924F | 3,134,000 | 0.20 | 1.00 | 5.00 | 15.00 | — |
| 1924G | 4,790,000 | 0.20 | 1.00 | 7.50 | 17.50 | — |
| 1924J | 2,200,000 | 0.25 | 1.00 | 3.50 | 12.00 | — |
| 1925A | 85,239,000 | 0.15 | 0.40 | 2.00 | 7.00 | — |
| 1925D | 39,750,000 | 0.15 | 0.35 | 2.00 | 7.00 | — |
| 1925E | 17,554,000 | 0.20 | 1.00 | 5.00 | 12.00 | — |
| 1925F Large 5 | 20,990,000 | 0.15 | 0.35 | 2.50 | 6.00 | — |
| 1925F Small 5 | Inc. above | 0.15 | 0.35 | 2.50 | 6.00 | — |
| 1925G | 10,232,000 | 0.20 | 1.00 | 5.00 | 17.50 | — |
| 1925J | 10,950,000 | 0.20 | 1.00 | 5.00 | 17.50 | — |
| 1926A | 22,377,000 | 0.15 | 0.40 | 2.00 | 12.00 | — |
| 1926E | 5,990,000 | 10.00 | 20.00 | 35.00 | 50.00 | — |
| 1926F | 2,871,000 | 5.00 | 12.50 | 25.00 | 35.00 | — |
| 1930A | 7,418,000 | 0.20 | 0.50 | 3.00 | 15.00 | — |
| 1935A | 19,178,000 | 0.15 | 0.25 | 0.50 | 6.00 | — |
| 1935D | 5,480,000 | 0.15 | 0.35 | 1.00 | 8.00 | — |
| 1935E | 2,384,000 | 0.20 | 0.50 | 3.00 | 12.00 | — |
| 1935F | 4,585,000 | 0.15 | 0.40 | 1.50 | 8.00 | — |
| 1935G | 2,652,000 | 0.20 | 0.50 | 3.00 | 12.00 | — |
| 1935J | 2,614,000 | 0.20 | 0.50 | 3.00 | 12.00 | — |
| 1936A | 36,992,000 | 0.15 | 0.25 | 0.50 | 6.00 | — |
| 1936D | 8,108,000 | 0.15 | 0.35 | 1.00 | 8.00 | — |
| 1936E | 2,981,000 | 0.20 | 0.50 | 3.00 | 12.00 | — |
| 1936F | 6,643,000 | 0.15 | 0.30 | 1.00 | 7.00 | — |
| 1936G | 2,274,000 | 0.20 | 0.35 | 1.00 | 8.00 | — |
| 1936J | 4,470,000 | 0.20 | 0.50 | 3.00 | 12.00 | — |

**10 REICHSPFENNIG** **KM# 40** **Composition:** Aluminum-Bronze

| Date | Mintage | F | VF | XF | Unc | BU |
|---|---|---|---|---|---|---|
| 1924-29 Proof | — | Value: 100 | | | | |
| **Note:** Common date proof | | | | | | |
| 1924A | 20,883,000 | 0.15 | 0.25 | 1.00 | 12.50 | — |
| 1924D | 9,639,000 | 0.15 | 0.50 | 1.50 | 15.00 | — |
| 1924E | 5,185,000 | 0.20 | 1.00 | 1.50 | 17.50 | — |
| 1924F | 2,758,000 | 1.00 | 7.50 | 15.00 | 37.50 | — |
| 1924G | 4,363,000 | 0.20 | 1.00 | 1.50 | 17.50 | — |
| 1924J | 3,993,000 | 0.15 | 0.50 | 1.00 | 15.00 | — |
| 1925A | 102,319,000 | 0.10 | 0.15 | 0.50 | 10.00 | — |
| 1925D | 36,853,000 | 0.10 | 0.15 | 0.50 | 10.00 | — |
| 1925E | 18,700,000 | 0.15 | 0.50 | 1.00 | 15.00 | — |
| 1925F | 12,516,000 | 0.10 | 0.15 | 0.50 | 12.50 | — |
| 1925G | 10,360,000 | 0.10 | 0.50 | 1.00 | 12.50 | — |
| 1925J | 8,755,000 | 8.00 | 12.50 | 20.00 | 37.50 | — |
| 1926A | 14,390,000 | 0.20 | 2.00 | 4.00 | 15.00 | — |
| 1926G | 1,481,000 | 2.50 | 10.00 | 20.00 | 37.50 | — |
| 1928A | 2,308,000 | 2.00 | 6.00 | 9.00 | 17.50 | — |
| 1928G | | 40.00 | 60.00 | 175 | 250 | — |
| 1929A | 25,712,000 | 0.15 | 0.50 | 1.50 | 12.50 | — |
| 1929D | 7,049,000 | 0.15 | 0.50 | 1.50 | 12.50 | — |
| 1929E | 3,138,000 | 0.20 | 1.00 | 2.50 | 17.50 | — |
| 1929F | 3,740,000 | 0.20 | 1.00 | 2.50 | 17.50 | — |
| 1929G | 2,729,000 | 0.30 | 3.50 | 6.00 | 22.00 | — |
| 1929J | 4,086,000 | 0.20 | 2.50 | 5.00 | 18.50 | — |
| 1930A | 7,540,000 | 0.20 | 2.00 | 2.50 | 12.50 | — |
| 1930D | 2,148,000 | 0.25 | 3.50 | 5.00 | 15.00 | — |
| 1930E | 2,090,000 | 1.00 | 5.00 | 15.00 | 32.50 | — |
| 1930F | 2,006,000 | 1.00 | 5.00 | 15.00 | 32.50 | — |
| 1930G | 1,542,000 | 10.00 | 25.00 | 40.00 | 60.00 | — |
| 1930J | 1,637,000 | 2.50 | 10.00 | 12.50 | 22.00 | — |
| 1931A | 9,661,000 | 0.20 | 2.50 | 5.00 | 15.00 | — |
| 1931D | 664,000 | 15.00 | 35.00 | 65.00 | 100 | — |
| 1931F | 1,482,000 | 2.50 | 10.00 | 12.50 | 32.50 | — |
| 1931G | 38,000 | 200 | 350 | 550 | 700 | — |
| 1932A | 4,528,000 | 0.25 | 3.50 | 6.00 | 17.50 | — |
| 1932D | 2,812,000 | 0.50 | 5.00 | 7.50 | 17.50 | — |
| 1932E | 1,491,000 | 6.00 | 12.50 | 17.50 | 40.00 | — |
| 1932F | 1,806,000 | 6.00 | 12.50 | 17.50 | 40.00 | — |
| 1932G | 137,000 | 350 | 750 | 1,150 | 1,500 | — |
| 1933A | 1,349,000 | 15.00 | 25.00 | 50.00 | 100 | — |
| 1933/2G | 1,046,000 | 6.00 | 12.50 | 17.50 | 40.00 | — |
| 1933G | Inc. above | 5.00 | 10.00 | 16.50 | 40.00 | — |
| 1933J | 1,634,000 | 1.00 | 8.50 | 15.00 | 35.00 | — |
| 1934A | 3,200,000 | 0.20 | 1.00 | 6.00 | 17.50 | — |
| 1934D | 1,252,000 | 1.00 | 7.50 | 10.00 | 25.00 | — |
| 1934E | | 20.00 | 35.00 | 50.00 | 100 | — |
| 1934F | 100,000 | 15.00 | 30.00 | 50.00 | 100 | — |
| 1934G | 150,000 | 15.00 | 30.00 | 50.00 | 125 | — |
| 1935A | 35,890,000 | 0.10 | 0.15 | 1.00 | 8.50 | — |
| 1935D | 8,960,000 | 0.10 | 0.25 | 1.50 | 12.50 | — |
| 1935E | 5,966,000 | 0.15 | 0.35 | 2.00 | 15.00 | — |
| 1935F | 7,944,000 | 0.10 | 0.30 | 1.50 | 12.50 | — |
| 1935G | 4,847,000 | 0.10 | 0.50 | 3.00 | 15.00 | — |
| 1935J | 8,995,000 | 0.10 | 0.30 | 1.50 | 12.50 | — |
| 1936A | 24,527,000 | 0.10 | 0.15 | 0.50 | 7.50 | — |
| 1936D | 8,092,000 | 0.10 | 0.20 | 1.00 | 12.50 | — |
| 1936E | 2,441,000 | 0.20 | 0.50 | 2.50 | 15.00 | — |
| 1936F | 4,889,000 | 0.10 | 0.30 | 1.50 | 12.50 | — |
| 1936G | 1,715,000 | 0.15 | 0.60 | 2.50 | 15.00 | — |
| 1936J | 1,632,000 | 0.25 | 3.00 | 8.00 | 17.50 | — |

**50 REICHSPFENNIG** **KM# 41** **Composition:** Aluminum-Bronze

| Date | Mintage | F | VF | XF | Unc | BU |
|---|---|---|---|---|---|---|
| 1924A | 801,000 | 500 | 900 | 1,200 | 1,500 | — |
| 1924A | — | Value: 1,750 | | | | |
| 1924E | | 1,200 | 2,000 | 3,000 | 3,500 | — |
| 1924F | 55,000 | 2,000 | 4,000 | 5,000 | 7,500 | — |
| 1924F Proof | — | Value: 10,500 | | | | |
| **Note:** Peus Auction #324 4-89 proof realized $10,360 | | | | | | |
| 1924G | 11,000 | 3,500 | 5,000 | 6,750 | 10,000 | — |
| 1924G Proof | — | — | — | — | — | — |
| 1925E | 1,805,000 | 500 | 750 | 1,000 | 1,250 | — |
| 1925E | 196 | Value: 2,000 | | | | |
| 1925F | — | 5,000 | 9,000 | 12,500 | 20,000 | — |
| 1925F Proof | — | Value: 30,000 | | | | |

**Note:** Peus Auction #324 4-89 proof realized $23,830. Kurpfalische Munzhandlung Mannheim 6-91 proof realized $37,600

**50 REICHSPFENNIG** KM# 49 **Composition:** Nickel

| Date | Mintage | F | VF | XF | Unc | BU |
|---|---|---|---|---|---|---|
| 1927-29 Proof | — | Value: 150 | | | | |
| **Note:** Common date proof | | | | | | |
| 1927A | 16,309,000 | 2.00 | 3.50 | 5.00 | 10.00 | — |
| 1927D | 2,228,000 | 2.50 | 5.00 | 7.50 | 12.50 | — |
| 1927E | 1,070,000 | 5.00 | 10.00 | 15.00 | 20.00 | — |
| 1927F | 1,940,000 | 2.50 | 5.00 | 7.50 | 12.50 | — |
| 1927G | 1,756,000 | 4.00 | 7.50 | 10.00 | 17.50 | — |
| 1927J | 4,056,000 | 2.50 | 5.00 | 7.50 | 12.50 | — |
| 1928A | 43,864,000 | 0.25 | 1.50 | 3.50 | 7.50 | — |
| 1928D | 14,088,000 | 0.50 | 2.50 | 5.00 | 10.00 | — |
| 1928E | 8,618,000 | 0.50 | 3.50 | 6.00 | 12.50 | — |
| 1928F | 9,954,000 | 0.50 | 2.50 | 5.00 | 10.00 | — |
| 1928G | 6,177,000 | 0.50 | 4.50 | 7.50 | 15.00 | — |
| 1928J | 6,565,000 | 0.50 | 2.50 | 5.00 | 10.00 | — |
| 1929A | 10,298,000 | 0.50 | 2.00 | 4.00 | 7.50 | — |
| 1929D | 1,965,000 | 0.50 | 3.50 | 6.00 | 12.50 | — |
| 1929F | 1,162,000 | 5.00 | 12.50 | 20.00 | 32.50 | — |
| 1930A | 4,128,000 | 0.50 | 4.50 | 7.50 | 12.50 | — |
| 1930D | 1,406,000 | 2.00 | 12.00 | 17.50 | 30.00 | — |
| 1930E | 745,000 | 15.00 | 40.00 | 50.00 | 100 | — |
| 1930F | 320,000 | 40.00 | 100 | 130 | 200 | — |
| 1930G | 610,000 | 15.00 | 40.00 | 80.00 | 125 | — |
| 1930J | 526,000 | 15.00 | 25.00 | 40.00 | 75.00 | — |
| 1931A | 5,624,000 | 0.50 | 4.00 | 7.50 | 10.00 | — |
| 1931D | 1,125,000 | 1.50 | 12.50 | 17.50 | 30.00 | — |
| 1931F | 1,484,000 | 1.50 | 12.00 | 16.00 | 25.00 | — |
| 1931G | 60,000 | 175 | 300 | 450 | 675 | — |
| 1931J | 291,000 | 30.00 | 90.00 | 150 | 200 | — |
| 1932E | 598,000 | 30.00 | 80.00 | 150 | 225 | — |
| 1932G | 96,000 | 800 | 1,200 | 1,500 | 2,250 | — |
| 1933G | 333,000 | 40.00 | 85.00 | 135 | 200 | — |
| 1933J | 654,000 | 35.00 | 75.00 | 120 | 175 | — |
| 1935A | 6,390,000 | 0.50 | 4.00 | 6.00 | 8.50 | — |
| 1935D | 2,812,000 | 2.50 | 7.50 | 15.00 | 20.00 | — |
| 1935E | 745,000 | 7.50 | 30.00 | 40.00 | 50.00 | — |
| 1935F | 2,006,000 | 2.50 | 7.50 | 10.00 | 15.00 | — |
| 1935G | 650,000 | 12.50 | 37.50 | 50.00 | 70.00 | — |
| 1935J | 1,635,000 | 2.00 | 15.00 | 20.00 | 27.50 | — |
| 1935 | — | 1.00 | 6.00 | 12.50 | 25.00 | — |
| 1936A | 7,696,000 | 2.50 | 5.00 | 7.50 | 12.50 | — |
| 1936D | 844,000 | 4.00 | 20.00 | 35.00 | 70.00 | — |
| 1936E | 1,190,000 | 5.00 | 15.00 | 30.00 | 60.00 | — |
| 1936F | 602,000 | 7.50 | 17.50 | 35.00 | 75.00 | — |
| 1936G | 936,000 | 5.00 | 15.00 | 30.00 | 40.00 | — |
| 1936J | 490,000 | 25.00 | 75.00 | 110 | 150 | — |
| 1937A | 10,842,000 | 0.25 | 2.50 | 5.00 | 7.50 | — |
| 1937D | 2,814,000 | 0.50 | 4.00 | 7.50 | 10.00 | — |
| 1937F | 1,700,000 | 0.50 | 2.50 | 10.00 | 12.50 | — |
| 1937J | 300,000 | 60.00 | 120 | 200 | 275 | — |
| 1938E | 1,200,000 | 7.50 | 12.50 | 22.50 | 30.00 | — |
| 1938G | 1,299,000 | 7.50 | 12.50 | 25.00 | 35.00 | — |
| 1938J | 1,333,000 | 7.50 | 15.00 | 25.00 | 35.00 | — |

**MARK** KM# 42 **Weight:** 5.0000 g. **Composition:** 0.5000 Silver .0803 oz. ASW

| Date | Mintage | F | VF | XF | Unc | BU |
|---|---|---|---|---|---|---|
| 1924-29 Proof | — | Value: 250 | | | | |
| **Note:** Common date proof | | | | | | |
| 1924A | 75,536,000 | 4.00 | 9.00 | 16.50 | 38.00 | — |
| 1924D | 17,099,000 | 5.00 | 10.00 | 22.50 | 45.00 | — |
| 1924E | 12,293,000 | 5.00 | 10.00 | 22.50 | 45.00 | — |
| 1924E Proof | 115 | Value: 275 | | | | |
| 1924F | 16,550,000 | 5.00 | 10.00 | 18.00 | 40.00 | — |
| 1924G | 10,065,000 | 6.00 | 12.00 | 25.00 | 65.00 | — |
| 1924J | 13,481,000 | 5.00 | 10.00 | 20.00 | 45.00 | — |
| 1925A | 13,878,000 | 6.00 | 12.00 | 35.00 | 100 | — |
| 1925D | 6,100,000 | 8.00 | 15.00 | 35.00 | 80.00 | — |

**3 MARK** KM# 28 **Composition:** Aluminum **Edge:** Reeded

| Date | Mintage | F | VF | XF | Unc | BU |
|---|---|---|---|---|---|---|
| 1922A | 15,497,000 | 0.25 | 2.50 | 5.00 | 10.00 | — |
| 1922A Proof | — | Value: 75.00 | | | | |
| 1922E | 2,000 | 125 | 200 | 300 | 500 | — |
| 1922E Proof | 1,000 | Value: 325 | | | | |
| 1922F | — | 200 | 300 | 400 | 1,000 | — |

**3 MARK** KM# 29 **Composition:** Aluminum **Subject:** 3rd Anniversary Weimar Constitution

| Date | Mintage | F | VF | XF | Unc | BU |
|---|---|---|---|---|---|---|
| 1922A | 32,514,000 | 0.25 | 1.00 | 1.50 | 2.50 | — |
| 1922D | 8,441,000 | 175 | 250 | 400 | 550 | — |
| 1922D Proof | — | Value: 600 | | | | |
| 1922E | 2,440,000 | 0.50 | 5.00 | 7.50 | 15.00 | — |
| 1922E Proof | 22,000 | Value: 30.00 | | | | |
| 1922F | 6,023,000 | 2.50 | 12.50 | 17.50 | 30.00 | — |
| 1922G | 3,655,000 | 0.25 | 2.50 | 5.00 | 12.50 | — |
| 1922J | 4,896,000 | 0.25 | 1.50 | 4.00 | 7.50 | — |
| 1923E | 2,060,000 | 17.50 | 40.00 | 60.00 | 85.00 | — |
| 1923E Proof | 2,291 | Value: 75.00 | | | | |
| 1923F | — | 175 | 400 | 700 | 1,500 | — |

**3 MARK** KM# 43 **Weight:** 15.0000 g. **Composition:** 0.5000 Silver .2411 oz. ASW

| Date | Mintage | F | VF | XF | Unc | BU |
|---|---|---|---|---|---|---|
| 1924A | 24,386,000 | 11.50 | 30.00 | 45.00 | 90.00 | — |
| 1924D | 3,769,000 | 12.50 | 35.00 | 55.00 | 120 | — |
| 1924E | 3,353,000 | 20.00 | 35.00 | 55.00 | 120 | — |
| 1924E Proof | 115 | Value: 350 | | | | |
| 1924F | 4,518,000 | 20.00 | 32.00 | 50.00 | 110 | — |
| 1924G | 2,745,000 | 20.00 | 35.00 | 60.00 | 130 | — |
| 1924J | 3,677,000 | 20.00 | 35.00 | 55.00 | 120 | — |
| 1925D | 2,558,000 | 35.00 | 75.00 | 110 | 175 | — |
| 1925-29 Proof | — | Value: 280 | | | | |
| **Note:** Common date proof | | | | | | |

**REICHSMARK** KM# 44 **Weight:** 5.0000 g. **Composition:** 0.5000 Silver .0803 oz. ASW

| Date | Mintage | F | VF | XF | Unc | BU |
|---|---|---|---|---|---|---|
| 1925A | 34,527,000 | 3.00 | 10.00 | 20.00 | 40.00 | — |
| 1925A Proof | 600 | Value: 200 | | | | |
| 1925D | 13,854,000 | 3.00 | 12.50 | 22.50 | 50.00 | — |
| 1925E | 6,460,000 | 7.50 | 20.00 | 32.00 | 60.00 | — |
| 1925F | 8,035,000 | 7.50 | 15.00 | 27.50 | 55.00 | — |
| 1925G | 4,520,000 | 7.50 | 15.00 | 30.00 | 55.00 | — |
| 1925J | 6,800,000 | 7.50 | 15.00 | 25.00 | 55.00 | — |
| 1926A | 35,555,000 | 6.50 | 10.00 | 22.50 | 45.00 | — |
| 1926D | 4,424,000 | 7.50 | 15.00 | 27.50 | 60.00 | — |
| 1926E | 3,225,000 | 7.50 | 15.00 | 45.00 | 90.00 | — |
| 1926E Proof | 31 | Value: 200 | | | | |
| 1926F | 3,045,000 | 7.50 | 27.50 | 40.00 | 75.00 | — |
| 1926G | 3,410,000 | 7.50 | 27.50 | 40.00 | 75.00 | — |
| 1926J | 1,290,000 | 25.00 | 75.00 | 120 | 225 | — |
| 1927A | 364,000 | 200 | 300 | 425 | 600 | — |
| 1927F | 1,959,000 | 40.00 | 60.00 | 90.00 | 125 | — |
| 1927J | 2,451,000 | 35.00 | 55.00 | 75.00 | 120 | — |

**2 REICHSMARK** KM# 45 **Weight:** 10.0000 g. **Composition:** 0.5000 Silver .1608 oz. ASW

| Date | Mintage | F | VF | XF | Unc | BU |
|---|---|---|---|---|---|---|
| 1925-29 Proof | — | Value: 160 | | | | |
| **Note:** Common date proof | | | | | | |
| 1925A | 16,145,000 | 7.50 | 12.50 | 22.00 | 55.00 | — |
| 1925D | 2,272,000 | 10.00 | 15.00 | 35.00 | 65.00 | — |
| 1925E | 1,971,000 | 10.00 | 17.50 | 40.00 | 75.00 | — |
| 1925E Proof | 101 | Value: 200 | | | | |
| 1925F | 2,414,000 | 10.00 | 17.50 | 35.00 | 65.00 | — |
| 1925G | 929,000 | 10.00 | 20.00 | 45.00 | 80.00 | — |
| 1925J | 2,326,000 | 10.00 | 17.50 | 35.00 | 65.00 | — |
| 1926A | 31,645,000 | 5.00 | 10.00 | 20.00 | 45.00 | — |
| 1926D | 11,322,000 | 5.00 | 10.00 | 22.00 | 55.00 | — |
| 1926E | 5,107,000 | 7.50 | 12.50 | 30.00 | 60.00 | — |
| 1926E Proof | 30 | — | — | — | — | — |
| 1926F | 7,115,000 | 7.50 | 12.50 | 30.00 | 55.00 | — |
| 1926G | 5,171,000 | 7.50 | 12.50 | 30.00 | 65.00 | — |
| 1926J | 5,305,000 | 7.50 | 12.50 | 30.00 | 65.00 | — |
| 1927A | 6,399,000 | 7.50 | 12.50 | 30.00 | 60.00 | — |
| 1927D | 466,000 | 750 | 1,100 | 1,500 | 2,000 | — |
| 1927E | 373,000 | 200 | 325 | 650 | 1,200 | — |
| 1927E Proof | 53 | Value: 2,150 | | | | |
| 1927F | 502,000 | 35.00 | 125 | 160 | 300 | — |
| 1927J | 540,000 | 35.00 | 75.00 | 125 | 200 | — |
| 1931D | 2,109,000 | 20.00 | 35.00 | 60.00 | 115 | — |
| 1931E | 1,118,000 | 22.50 | 45.00 | 85.00 | 140 | — |
| 1931F | 1,505,000 | 22.50 | 45.00 | 75.00 | 125 | — |
| 1931G | 915,000 | 40.00 | 75.00 | 120 | 200 | — |
| 1931J | 1,226,000 | 22.50 | 40.00 | 70.00 | 140 | — |

**3 REICHSMARK** KM# 46 **Weight:** 15.0000 g. **Composition:** 0.5000 Silver .2411 oz. ASW **Subject:** 1000th Year of the Rhineland

| Date | Mintage | F | VF | XF | Unc | BU |
|---|---|---|---|---|---|---|
| 1925A | 3,052,000 | 17.50 | 30.00 | 40.00 | 50.00 | — |
| 1925A Proof | — | Value: 150 | | | | |
| 1925D | 1,123,000 | 22.50 | 35.00 | 45.00 | 70.00 | — |
| 1925D Proof | — | Value: 165 | | | | |
| 1925E | 441,000 | 22.50 | 40.00 | 60.00 | 75.00 | — |
| 1925E Proof | 229 | Value: 175 | | | | |
| 1925F | 173,000 | 30.00 | 45.00 | 60.00 | 100 | — |
| 1925F Proof | — | Value: 250 | | | | |
| 1925G | 300,000 | 22.50 | 40.00 | 55.00 | 75.00 | — |
| 1925G Proof | — | Value: 150 | | | | |
| 1925J | 492,000 | 22.50 | 40.00 | 55.00 | 75.00 | — |
| 1925J Proof | — | Value: 185 | | | | |

**3 REICHSMARK** KM# 48 **Weight:** 15.0000 g. **Composition:** 0.5000 Silver .2411 oz. ASW **Subject:** 700 Years of Freedom for Lubeck

| Date | Mintage | F | VF | XF | Unc | BU |
|---|---|---|---|---|---|---|
| 1926A | 200,000 | 50.00 | 80.00 | 110 | 175 | — |
| 1926A Proof | — | Value: 265 | | | | |

**3 REICHSMARK** KM# 50 **Weight:** 15.0000 g. **Composition:** 0.5000 Silver .2411 oz. ASW **Subject:** 100th Anniversary of Bremerhaven

| Date | Mintage | F | VF | XF | Unc | BU |
|---|---|---|---|---|---|---|
| 1927A | 150,000 | 60.00 | 100 | 130 | 200 | — |
| 1927A Proof | — | Value: 330 | | | | |

**3 REICHSMARK** **KM# 52** **Weight:** 15.0000 g. **Composition:** 0.5000 Silver .2411 oz. ASW **Subject:** 1000th Anniversary - Founding of Nordhausen

| Date | Mintage | F | VF | XF | Unc | BU |
|---|---|---|---|---|---|---|
| 1927A | 100,000 | 50.00 | 80.00 | 130 | 200 | — |
| 1927A Proof | — | Value: 350 | | | | |

**3 REICHSMARK** **KM# 53** **Weight:** 15.0000 g. **Composition:** 0.5000 Silver .2411 oz. ASW **Subject:** 400th Anniversary - Philipps University in Marburg

| Date | Mintage | F | VF | XF | Unc | BU |
|---|---|---|---|---|---|---|
| 1927A | 130,000 | 50.00 | 80.00 | 115 | 175 | — |
| 1927A Proof | — | Value: 250 | | | | |

**3 REICHSMARK** **KM# 54** **Weight:** 15.0000 g. **Composition:** 0.5000 Silver .2411 oz. ASW **Subject:** 450th Anniversary - Tubingen University

| Date | Mintage | F | VF | XF | Unc | BU |
|---|---|---|---|---|---|---|
| 1927F | 50,000 | 150 | 225 | 325 | 450 | — |
| 1927F Proof | — | Value: 625 | | | | |

**3 REICHSMARK** **KM# 57** **Weight:** 15.0000 g. **Composition:** 0.5000 Silver .2411 oz. ASW **Subject:** 900th Anniversary - Founding of Naumburg

| Date | Mintage | F | VF | XF | Unc | BU |
|---|---|---|---|---|---|---|
| 1928A | 100,000 | 60.00 | 100 | 145 | 200 | — |
| 1928A Matte proof | — | Value: 500 | | | | |

**3 REICHSMARK** **KM# 58** **Weight:** 15.0000 g. **Composition:** 0.5000 Silver .2411 oz. ASW **Subject:** 400th Anniversary - Death of Albrecht Durer

| Date | Mintage | F | VF | XF | Unc | BU |
|---|---|---|---|---|---|---|
| 1928D | 50,000 | 125 | 225 | 325 | 450 | — |
| 1928D Matte proof | — | Value: 1,600 | | | | |

**3 REICHSMARK** **KM# 59** **Weight:** 15.0000 g. **Composition:** 0.5000 Silver .2411 oz. ASW **Subject:** 1000th Anniversary - Founding of Dinkelsbuhl

| Date | Mintage | F | VF | XF | Unc | BU |
|---|---|---|---|---|---|---|
| 1928D | 40,000 | 225 | 400 | 600 | 800 | — |
| 1928D Proof | — | Value: 2,000 | | | | |

**3 REICHSMARK** **KM# 65** **Weight:** 15.0000 g. **Composition:** 0.5000 Silver .2411 oz. ASW **Subject:** 1000th Anniversary - Meissen

| Date | Mintage | F | VF | XF | Unc | BU |
|---|---|---|---|---|---|---|
| 1929E | 200,000 | 25.00 | 45.00 | 65.00 | 100 | — |
| 1929E Proof | — | Value: 320 | | | | |

**3 REICHSMARK** **KM# 62** **Weight:** 15.0000 g. **Composition:** 0.5000 Silver .2411 oz. ASW **Subject:** Waldeck-Prussia Union

| Date | Mintage | F | VF | XF | Unc | BU |
|---|---|---|---|---|---|---|
| 1929A | 170,000 | 50.00 | 95.00 | 125 | 200 | — |
| 1929A Proof | — | Value: 250 | | | | |

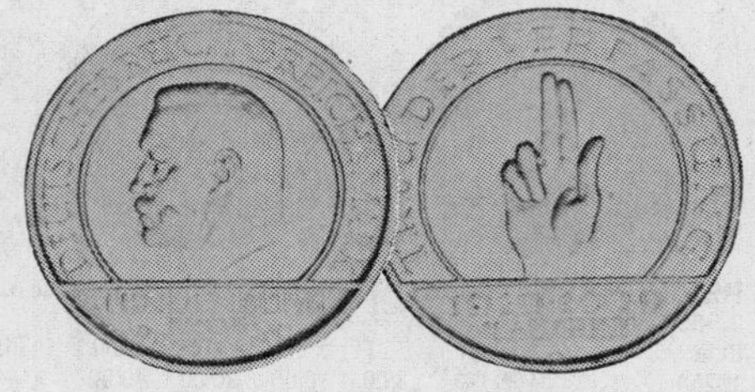

**3 REICHSMARK** **KM# 63** **Weight:** 15.0000 g. **Composition:** 0.5000 Silver .2411 oz. ASW **Subject:** 10th Anniversary - Weimar Constitution

| Date | Mintage | F | VF | XF | Unc | BU |
|---|---|---|---|---|---|---|
| 1929A | 1,421,000 | 17.50 | 35.00 | 50.00 | 65.00 | — |
| 1929A Proof | — | Value: 225 | | | | |
| 1929A Matte proof | — | — | — | — | — | — |
| 1929D | 499,000 | 17.50 | 35.00 | 55.00 | 70.00 | — |
| 1929D Proof | — | Value: 225 | | | | |
| 1929E | 122,000 | 22.50 | 45.00 | 55.00 | 80.00 | — |
| 1929E Proof | — | Value: 300 | | | | |
| 1929F | 370,000 | 17.50 | 35.00 | 55.00 | 70.00 | — |
| 1929F Proof | — | Value: 250 | | | | |
| 1929G | 256,000 | 22.50 | 45.00 | 60.00 | 80.00 | — |
| 1929G Proof | — | Value: 250 | | | | |
| 1929J | 342,000 | 17.50 | 35.00 | 55.00 | 70.00 | — |
| 1929J Proof | — | Value: 250 | | | | |

**3 REICHSMARK** **KM# 60** **Weight:** 15.0000 g. **Composition:** 0.5000 Silver .2411 oz. ASW **Subject:** 200th Anniversary - Birth of Gotthold Lessing

| Date | Mintage | F | VF | XF | Unc | BU |
|---|---|---|---|---|---|---|
| 1929A | 217,000 | 17.50 | 30.00 | 60.00 | 90.00 | — |
| 1929A Proof | — | Value: 175 | | | | |
| 1929D | 56,000 | 20.00 | 35.00 | 65.00 | 100 | — |
| 1929D Proof | — | Value: 250 | | | | |
| 1929E | 30,000 | 20.00 | 35.00 | 70.00 | 110 | — |
| 1929E Proof | — | Value: 275 | | | | |
| 1929F | 40,000 | 20.00 | 35.00 | 65.00 | 100 | — |
| 1929F Proof | — | Value: 250 | | | | |
| 1929G | 24,000 | 20.00 | 35.00 | 80.00 | 110 | — |
| 1929G Proof | — | Value: 300 | | | | |
| 1929J | 33,000 | 20.00 | 35.00 | 80.00 | 100 | — |
| 1929J Proof | — | Value: 300 | | | | |

**3 REICHSMARK** **KM# 67** **Weight:** 15.0000 g. **Composition:** 0.5000 Silver .2411 oz. ASW **Subject:** Graf Zeppelin Flight

| Date | Mintage | F | VF | XF | Unc | BU |
|---|---|---|---|---|---|---|
| 1930A | 542,000 | 40.00 | 60.00 | 85.00 | 110 | — |
| 1930A Proof | — | Value: 350 | | | | |
| 1930D | 141,000 | 35.00 | 60.00 | 90.00 | 125 | — |
| 1930D Proof | — | Value: 250 | | | | |
| 1930E | 75,000 | 35.00 | 60.00 | 90.00 | 140 | — |
| 1930E Proof | — | Value: 335 | | | | |
| 1930F | 100,000 | 35.00 | 60.00 | 90.00 | 125 | — |
| 1930F Proof | — | Value: 275 | | | | |
| 1930G | 61,000 | 40.00 | 65.00 | 95.00 | 150 | — |
| 1930G Proof | — | Value: 335 | | | | |
| 1930J | 82,000 | 40.00 | 65.00 | 95.00 | 130 | — |
| 1930J Proof | — | Value: 325 | | | | |

**3 REICHSMARK** **KM# 69** **Weight:** 15.0000 g. **Composition:** 0.5000 Silver .2411 oz. ASW **Subject:** 700th Anniversary - Death of Von Der Vogelweide

| Date | Mintage | F | VF | XF | Unc | BU |
|---|---|---|---|---|---|---|
| 1930A | 163,000 | 35.00 | 55.00 | 85.00 | 125 | — |
| 1930A Proof | — | Value: 200 | | | | |
| 1930A Matte proof | — | — | — | — | — | — |
| 1930D | 42,000 | 35.00 | 55.00 | 85.00 | 125 | — |
| 1930D Proof | — | Value: 225 | | | | |
| 1930E | 22,000 | 37.50 | 75.00 | 100 | 150 | — |
| 1930E Proof | — | Value: 225 | | | | |
| 1930F | 30,000 | 37.50 | 75.00 | 100 | 125 | — |
| 1930F Proof | — | Value: 325 | | | | |
| 1930G | 18,000 | 45.00 | 85.00 | 120 | 150 | — |
| 1930G Proof | — | Value: 225 | | | | |
| 1930J | 25,000 | 35.00 | 55.00 | 85.00 | 130 | — |
| 1930J Proof | — | Value: 225 | | | | |

**3 REICHSMARK** **KM# 70** **Weight:** 15.0000 g. **Composition:** 0.5000 Silver .2411 oz. ASW **Subject:** Liberation of Rhineland

| Date | Mintage | F | VF | XF | Unc | BU |
|---|---|---|---|---|---|---|
| 1930A | 1,734,000 | 22.50 | 35.00 | 60.00 | 85.00 | — |
| 1930A Proof | — | Value: 150 | | | | |
| 1930A Matte proof | — | — | — | — | — | — |
| 1930D | 450,000 | 22.50 | 35.00 | 60.00 | 85.00 | — |
| 1930D Proof | — | Value: 200 | | | | |
| 1930E | 38,000 | 65.00 | 125 | 175 | 250 | — |
| 1930E Proof | — | Value: 200 | | | | |
| 1930F | 321,000 | 22.50 | 35.00 | 60.00 | 85.00 | — |
| 1930F Proof | — | Value: 160 | | | | |
| 1930G | 195,000 | 22.50 | 35.00 | 65.00 | 85.00 | — |
| 1930G Proof | — | Value: 200 | | | | |
| 1930J | 261,000 | 22.50 | 35.00 | 65.00 | 85.00 | — |
| 1930J Proof | — | Value: 200 | | | | |

**3 REICHSMARK** **KM# 72** **Weight:** 15.0000 g. **Composition:** 0.5000 Silver .2411 oz. ASW **Subject:** 300th Anniversary - Magdeburg Rebuilding

| Date | Mintage | F | VF | XF | Unc | BU |
|---|---|---|---|---|---|---|
| 1931A | 100,000 | 80.00 | 150 | 200 | 275 | — |
| 1931A Proof | — | Value: 450 | | | | |

**3 REICHSMARK** **KM# 73** **Weight:** 15.0000 g. **Composition:** 0.5000 Silver .2411 oz. ASW **Subject:** Centenary - Death of vom Stein

| Date | Mintage | F | VF | XF | Unc | BU |
|---|---|---|---|---|---|---|
| 1931A | 150,000 | 40.00 | 90.00 | 150 | 200 | — |
| 1931A Proof | — | Value: 300 | | | | |

**3 REICHSMARK** **KM# 74** **Weight:** 15.0000 g. **Composition:** 0.5000 Silver .2411 oz. ASW

| Date | Mintage | F | VF | XF | Unc | BU |
|---|---|---|---|---|---|---|
| 1931-33 Proof | — | Value: 1,250 | | | | |
| **Note:** Common date proof | | | | | | |
| 1931A | 13,324,000 | 100 | 200 | 275 | 400 | — |
| 1931D | 2,232,000 | 125 | 225 | 350 | 450 | — |
| 1931E | 2,235,000 | 140 | 275 | 350 | 550 | — |
| 1931F | 2,357,000 | 125 | 225 | 350 | 450 | — |
| 1931G | 1,468,000 | 145 | 275 | 375 | 600 | — |
| 1931J | 1,115,000 | 145 | 275 | 375 | 600 | — |
| 1932A | 2,933,000 | 125 | 200 | 275 | 400 | — |
| 1932D | 1,986,000 | 145 | 250 | 375 | 500 | — |
| 1932F | 653,000 | 300 | 500 | 800 | 1,150 | — |
| 1932G | 210,000 | 550 | 800 | 1,400 | 3,000 | — |
| 1932J | 1,336,000 | 145 | 225 | 375 | 500 | — |
| 1933G | 152,000 | 800 | 1,300 | 2,200 | 4,000 | — |

**Note:** Less than 10 percent of issue was released

**3 REICHSMARK** **KM# 76** **Weight:** 15.0000 g. **Composition:** 0.5000 Silver .2411 oz. ASW **Subject:** Centenary - Death of Goethe

| Date | Mintage | F | VF | XF | Unc | BU |
|---|---|---|---|---|---|---|
| 1932A | 217,000 | 30.00 | 60.00 | 100 | 130 | — |
| 1932A Proof | — | Value: 250 | | | | |
| 1932D | 56,000 | 30.00 | 60.00 | 100 | 130 | — |
| 1932D Proof | — | Value: 250 | | | | |
| 1932E | 30,000 | 40.00 | 70.00 | 100 | 160 | — |
| 1932E Proof | — | Value: 300 | | | | |
| 1932F | 40,000 | 25.00 | 50.00 | 85.00 | 145 | — |
| 1932F Proof | — | Value: 250 | | | | |
| 1932F Matte proof | — | — | — | — | — | — |
| 1932G | 24,000 | 45.00 | 80.00 | 110 | 160 | — |
| 1932G | — | Value: 300 | | | | |
| 1932J | 33,000 | 45.00 | 80.00 | 110 | 160 | — |
| 1932J | — | Value: 265 | | | | |
| 1933J | 423,000 | 600 | 1,100 | 2,200 | 3,250 | — |
| 1933J Proof | — | Value: 4,250 | | | | |

**5 REICHSMARK** **KM# 56** **Weight:** 25.0000 g. **Composition:** 0.5000 Silver .4019 oz. ASW

| Date | Mintage | F | VF | XF | Unc | BU |
|---|---|---|---|---|---|---|
| 1927-33 Proof | — | Value: 700 | | | | |
| **Note:** Common date proof | | | | | | |
| 1927A | 7,926,000 | 27.00 | 70.00 | 110 | 180 | — |
| 1927D | 1,471,000 | 32.00 | 80.00 | 120 | 200 | — |
| 1927E | 1,100,000 | 35.00 | 110 | 160 | 250 | — |
| 1927F | 700,000 | 27.00 | 100 | 150 | 225 | — |
| 1927G | 759,000 | 50.00 | 130 | 220 | 400 | — |
| 1927J | 1,006,000 | 32.00 | 80.00 | 110 | 225 | — |
| 1928A | 15,466,000 | 27.00 | 70.00 | 125 | 175 | — |
| 1928D | 4,613,000 | 27.00 | 75.00 | 135 | 200 | — |
| 1928E | 2,310,000 | 35.00 | 100 | 150 | 225 | — |
| 1928F | 3,771,000 | 30.00 | 70.00 | 130 | 200 | — |
| 1928G | 1,923,000 | 35.00 | 110 | 150 | 250 | — |
| 1928J | 2,450,000 | 35.00 | 100 | 150 | 225 | — |
| 1929A | 6,730,000 | 30.00 | 70.00 | 125 | 175 | — |
| 1929D | 2,020,000 | 35.00 | 100 | 145 | 250 | — |
| 1929E | 860,000 | 150 | 400 | 600 | 900 | — |
| 1929F | 814,000 | 60.00 | 165 | 255 | 400 | — |
| 1929G | 950,000 | 80.00 | 175 | 300 | 450 | — |
| 1929J | 779,000 | 80.00 | 175 | 300 | 425 | — |
| 1930A | 3,790,000 | 50.00 | 120 | 180 | 300 | — |
| 1930D | 606,000 | 125 | 325 | 575 | 800 | — |
| 1930E | 354,000 | 400 | 1,100 | 1,750 | 2,250 | — |
| 1930F | 630,000 | 125 | 325 | 575 | 800 | — |
| 1930G | 367,000 | 400 | 700 | 1,400 | 2,000 | — |
| 1930J | 740,000 | 125 | 325 | 600 | 1,000 | — |
| 1931A | 14,651,000 | 27.00 | 70.00 | 120 | 175 | — |
| 1931D | 3,254,000 | 32.00 | 80.00 | 130 | 200 | — |
| 1931E | 2,245,000 | 35.00 | 100 | 150 | 225 | — |
| 1931F | 4,152,000 | 32.00 | 80.00 | 130 | 180 | — |
| 1931G | 1,620,000 | 35.00 | 110 | 200 | 400 | — |
| 1931J | 3,092,000 | 40.00 | 110 | 150 | 225 | — |
| 1932A | 32,303,000 | 32.00 | 70.00 | 125 | 175 | — |
| 1932D | 8,556,000 | 32.00 | 70.00 | 135 | 180 | — |
| 1932E | 4,013,000 | 45.00 | 100 | 150 | 225 | — |
| 1932F | 5,019,000 | 32.00 | 80.00 | 130 | 175 | — |
| 1932G | 3,504,000 | 32.00 | 100 | 150 | 225 | — |
| 1932J | 3,752,000 | 40.00 | 100 | 160 | 260 | — |

**5 REICHSMARK** **KM# 47** **Weight:** 25.0000 g. **Composition:** 0.5000 Silver .4019 oz. ASW **Subject:** 1000th Year of the Rhineland

| Date | Mintage | F | VF | XF | Unc | BU |
|---|---|---|---|---|---|---|
| 1925A | 684,000 | 35.00 | 60.00 | 100 | 130 | — |
| 1925A Proof | — | Value: 325 | | | | |
| 1925D | 452,000 | 35.00 | 60.00 | 100 | 140 | — |
| 1925D Proof | — | Value: 400 | | | | |
| 1925E | 204,000 | 50.00 | 75.00 | 110 | 150 | — |
| 1925E Proof | 226 | Value: 400 | | | | |
| 1925F | 212,000 | 40.00 | 65.00 | 100 | 140 | — |
| 1925F Proof | — | Value: 425 | | | | |
| 1925G | 89,000 | 45.00 | 70.00 | 110 | 150 | — |
| 1925G Proof | — | Value: 475 | | | | |
| 1925J | 43,000 | 70.00 | 140 | 200 | 275 | — |
| 1925J Proof | — | Value: 550 | | | | |

**5 REICHSMARK** **KM# 51** **Weight:** 25.0000 g. **Composition:** 0.5000 Silver .4019 oz. ASW **Subject:** 100th Anniversary - Bremerhaven

| Date | Mintage | F | VF | XF | Unc | BU |
|---|---|---|---|---|---|---|
| 1927A | 50,000 | 175 | 300 | 500 | 700 | — |
| 1927A Proof | — | Value: 1,000 | | | | |

**5 REICHSMARK** **KM# 55** **Weight:** 25.0000 g. **Composition:** 0.5000 Silver .4019 oz. ASW **Subject:** 450th Anniversary - University of Tubingen

| Date | Mintage | F | VF | XF | Unc | BU |
|---|---|---|---|---|---|---|
| 1927F | 40,000 | 175 | 250 | 375 | 500 | — |
| 1927F Proof | — | Value: 800 | | | | |

**5 REICHSMARK** **KM# 66** **Weight:** 25.0000 g. **Composition:** 0.5000 Silver .4019 oz. ASW **Subject:** 1000th Anniversary - Meissen

| Date | Mintage | F | VF | XF | Unc | BU |
|---|---|---|---|---|---|---|
| 1929E | 120,000 | 140 | 225 | 375 | 550 | — |
| 1929E Proof | — | Value: 1,000 | | | | |

**5 REICHSMARK** **KM# 61** **Weight:** 25.0000 g. **Composition:** 0.5000 Silver .4019 oz. ASW **Subject:** 200th Anniversasry - Birth of Gotthold Lessing

| Date | Mintage | F | VF | XF | Unc | BU |
|---|---|---|---|---|---|---|
| 1929A | 87,000 | 50.00 | 100 | 135 | 200 | — |
| 1929A Proof | — | Value: 350 | | | | |
| 1929D | 22,000 | 50.00 | 100 | 150 | 225 | — |
| 1929D Proof | — | Value: 350 | | | | |
| 1929E | 12,000 | 60.00 | 120 | 165 | 250 | — |
| 1929E Proof | — | Value: 425 | | | | |
| 1929F | 16,000 | 50.00 | 100 | 150 | 225 | — |
| 1929F Proof | — | Value: 375 | | | | |
| 1929G | 9,760 | 60.00 | 120 | 165 | 250 | — |
| 1929G Proof | — | Value: 425 | | | | |
| 1929J | 13,000 | 55.00 | 110 | 150 | 225 | — |
| 1929J Proof | — | Value: 400 | | | | |

**5 REICHSMARK** **KM# 64** **Weight:** 25.0000 g. **Composition:** 0.5000 Silver .4019 oz. ASW **Subject:** 10th Anniversary - Weimar Constitution

| Date | Mintage | F | VF | XF | Unc | BU |
|---|---|---|---|---|---|---|
| 1929A | 325,000 | 45.00 | 65.00 | 125 | 200 | — |
| 1929A Proof | — | Value: 450 | | | | |
| 1929D | 84,000 | 50.00 | 90.00 | 135 | 200 | — |
| 1929D Proof | — | Value: 400 | | | | |
| 1929E | 45,000 | 50.00 | 90.00 | 135 | 225 | — |
| 1929E Proof | — | Value: 625 | | | | |
| 1929F | 60,000 | 60.00 | 100 | 150 | 200 | — |
| 1929F Proof | — | Value: 400 | | | | |
| 1929G | 37,000 | 60.00 | 100 | 160 | 225 | — |
| 1929G Proof | — | Value: 500 | | | | |
| 1929J | 49,000 | 50.00 | 90.00 | 160 | 225 | — |
| 1929J Proof | — | Value: 650 | | | | |

**5 REICHSMARK** **KM# 68** **Weight:** 25.0000 g. **Composition:** 0.5000 Silver .4019 oz. ASW **Subject:** Graf Zeppelin Flight

| Date | Mintage | F | VF | XF | Unc | BU |
|---|---|---|---|---|---|---|
| 1930A | 217,000 | 60.00 | 100 | 165 | 250 | — |
| 1930A Proof | — | Value: 450 | | | | |
| 1930A Matte proof | — | — | — | — | — | — |
| 1930D | 56,000 | 70.00 | 110 | 170 | 250 | — |
| 1930D Proof | — | Value: 650 | | | | |
| 1930E | 30,000 | 70.00 | 110 | 200 | 300 | — |
| 1930E Proof | — | Value: 700 | | | | |
| 1930F | 40,000 | 70.00 | 110 | 170 | 250 | — |
| 1930F Proof | — | Value: 600 | | | | |
| 1930G | 24,000 | 75.00 | 115 | 175 | 300 | — |
| 1930G Proof | — | Value: 700 | | | | |
| 1930J | 33,000 | 70.00 | 110 | 175 | 300 | — |
| 1930J Proof | — | Value: 700 | | | | |

**5 REICHSMARK** **KM# 71** **Weight:** 25.0000 g. **Composition:** 0.5000 Silver .4019 oz. ASW **Subject:** Liberation of Rhineland

| Date | Mintage | F | VF | XF | Unc | BU |
|---|---|---|---|---|---|---|
| 1930A | 325,000 | 60.00 | 100 | 160 | 225 | — |
| 1930A Proof | — | Value: 425 | | | | |
| 1930D | 84,000 | 60.00 | 100 | 170 | 225 | — |
| 1930D Proof | — | Value: 575 | | | | |
| 1930E | 45,000 | 70.00 | 125 | 180 | 250 | — |
| 1930E Proof | — | Value: 500 | | | | |
| 1930F | 60,000 | 60.00 | 100 | 165 | 225 | — |
| 1930F Proof | — | Value: 475 | | | | |
| 1930G | 37,000 | 85.00 | 165 | 190 | 250 | — |
| 1930G Proof | — | Value: 575 | | | | |
| 1930J | 49,000 | 75.00 | 135 | 190 | 250 | — |
| 1930J Proof | — | Value: 550 | | | | |

**5 REICHSMARK** **KM# 77** **Weight:** 25.0000 g. **Composition:** 0.5000 Silver .4019 oz. ASW **Subject:** Centenary - Death of Goethe

| Date | Mintage | F | VF | XF | Unc | BU |
|---|---|---|---|---|---|---|
| 1932A | 11,000 | 500 | 1,500 | 2,100 | 2,800 | — |
| 1932A Proof | — | Value: 4,500 | | | | |
| 1932D | 2,812 | 600 | 1,600 | 2,200 | 2,900 | — |
| 1932D Proof | — | Value: 4,000 | | | | |
| 1932E | 1,490 | 700 | 1,600 | 2,400 | 3,000 | — |
| 1932E Proof | — | Value: 4,500 | | | | |
| 1932F | 2,006 | 600 | 1,600 | 2,200 | 2,900 | — |
| 1932F Proof | — | Value: 5,500 | | | | |
| 1932G | 1,220 | 700 | 1,600 | 2,400 | 3,000 | — |
| 1932G Proof | — | Value: 5,000 | | | | |
| 1932J | 1,634 | 700 | 1,600 | 2,400 | 3,000 | — |
| 1932J Proof | — | Value: 5,000 | | | | |

**200 MARK** **KM# 35** **Composition:** Aluminum

| Date | Mintage | F | VF | XF | Unc | BU |
|---|---|---|---|---|---|---|
| 1923A | 174,900,000 | 0.15 | 0.50 | 1.00 | 1.75 | — |
| 1923A Proof | — | Value: 50.00 | | | | |
| 1923D | 35,189,000 | 0.20 | 0.60 | 1.00 | 1.75 | — |
| 1923D Proof | — | Value: 50.00 | | | | |
| 1923E | 11,250,000 | 0.20 | 1.00 | 2.50 | 5.00 | — |
| 1923E Proof | 4,095 | Value: 50.00 | | | | |
| 1923F | 20,090,000 | 0.25 | 1.00 | 2.00 | 4.00 | — |
| 1923F Proof | — | Value: 50.00 | | | | |
| 1923G | 24,923,000 | 0.25 | 1.00 | 2.00 | 4.00 | — |
| 1923G Proof | — | Value: 50.00 | | | | |
| 1923J | 16,258,000 | 0.20 | 1.00 | 2.50 | 5.00 | — |
| 1923J Proof | — | Value: 50.00 | | | | |

**500 MARK** **KM# 36** **Composition:** Aluminum

| Date | Mintage | F | VF | XF | Unc | BU |
|---|---|---|---|---|---|---|
| 1923A | 59,278,000 | 0.20 | 1.00 | 1.50 | 2.50 | — |
| 1923A Proof | — | Value: 75.00 | | | | |
| 1923D | 13,683,000 | 0.25 | 1.00 | 1.50 | 3.00 | — |
| 1923D Proof | — | Value: 75.00 | | | | |
| 1923E | 2,128,000 | 1.00 | 7.50 | 12.50 | 15.00 | — |
| 1923E Proof | 2,053 | Value: 75.00 | | | | |
| 1923F | 7,963,000 | 0.25 | 1.50 | 2.00 | 5.00 | — |
| 1923F Proof | — | Value: 75.00 | | | | |
| 1923G | 4,404,000 | 0.25 | 2.50 | 5.00 | 7.50 | — |
| 1923G Proof | — | Value: 75.00 | | | | |
| 1923J | 1,008,000 | 10.00 | 18.00 | 35.00 | 65.00 | — |
| 1923J Proof | — | Value: 250 | | | | |

## MEDALLIC COINAGE

**5 MARK** **KM# M1** **Composition:** Silver **Subject:** Von Hindenburg by Goetz

| Date | Mintage | F | VF | XF | Unc | BU |
|---|---|---|---|---|---|---|
| 1927D | — | — | — | — | 30.00 | — |

**5 MARK** **KM# M1a** **Weight:** 22.4700 g. **Composition:** Gold **Subject:** Von Hindenburg by Goetz

| Date | Mintage | F | VF | XF | Unc | BU |
|---|---|---|---|---|---|---|
| 1927D | — | — | — | — | 475 | — |

**5 MARK** **KM# M1b** **Weight:** 43.2600 g. **Composition:** Platinum APW

| Date | Mintage | F | VF | XF | Unc | BU |
|---|---|---|---|---|---|---|
| 1927D | — | — | — | — | 1,500 | — |

**5 MARK** **KM# M2** **Composition:** Silver **Subject:** Von Hindenburg by Bernhart

| Date | Mintage | F | VF | XF | Unc | BU |
|---|---|---|---|---|---|---|
| 1928 Proof | — | Value: 30.00 | | | | |

**5 MARK** **KM# M2a** **Weight:** 23.0000 g. **Composition:** Gold **Subject:** Von Hindenburg by Bernhart

| Date | Mintage | F | VF | XF | Unc | BU |
|---|---|---|---|---|---|---|
| 1928 Proof | — | Value: 450 | | | | |

**10 MARK** **KM# M3** **Weight:** 3.4200 g. **Composition:** 0.7500 Gold .0824 oz. AGW **Subject:** Von Hindenburg by Bernhart

| Date | Mintage | F | VF | XF | Unc | BU |
|---|---|---|---|---|---|---|
| 1928 Proof | — | Value: 150 | | | | |

**10 MARK** **KM# M3a** **Composition:** Silver

| Date | Mintage | F | VF | XF | Unc | BU |
|---|---|---|---|---|---|---|
| 1928 Proof | — | Value: 25.00 | | | | |

**10 MARK** **KM# M5** **Composition:** Gold **Subject:** Von Hindenburg by Goetz

| Date | Mintage | F | VF | XF | Unc | BU |
|---|---|---|---|---|---|---|
| 1928 Proof | — | Value: 175 | | | | |

**10 MARK** **KM# M5a** **Composition:** Silver

| Date | Mintage | F | VF | XF | Unc | BU |
|---|---|---|---|---|---|---|
| 1928 | — | — | — | — | 35.00 | — |

**20 MARK** **KM# M4** **Weight:** 6.3900 g. **Composition:** 0.7500 Gold .1541 oz. AGW **Subject:** Von Hindenburg by Bernhart

| Date | Mintage | F | VF | XF | Unc | BU |
|---|---|---|---|---|---|---|
| 1928 Proof | — | Value: 200 | | | | |

**20 MARK** **KM# M4a** **Composition:** Silver

| Date | Mintage | F | VF | XF | Unc | BU |
|---|---|---|---|---|---|---|
| 1928 Proof | — | Value: 35.00 | | | | |

**20 MARK** **KM# M6** **Weight:** 6.4900 g. **Composition:** Gold **Subject:** Von Hindenburg by Goetz

| Date | Mintage | F | VF | XF | Unc | BU |
|---|---|---|---|---|---|---|
| 1928 Proof | — | Value: 225 | | | | |

**20 MARK** **KM# M6a** **Composition:** Silver

| Date | Mintage | F | VF | XF | Unc | BU |
|---|---|---|---|---|---|---|
| 1928 | — | — | — | — | 45.00 | — |

**25 MARK** **KM# M7** **Weight:** 6.9400 g. **Composition:** Gold

| Date | Mintage | F | VF | XF | Unc | BU |
|---|---|---|---|---|---|---|
| 1932 | — | — | — | — | 285 | — |

**25 MARK** **KM# M7a** **Weight:** 10.1500 g. **Composition:** Platinum APW

| Date | Mintage | F | VF | XF | Unc | BU |
|---|---|---|---|---|---|---|
| 1932 | 5 | — | — | — | 1,000 | — |

## PATTERNS

Including off metal strikes

| KM# | Date | Mintage | Identification | Mkt Val |
|---|---|---|---|---|
| PnA331 | 1927 | — | 3 Mark. Silver. Justus Von Liebig; never issued. | — |

**Note:** An XF-AU example brought $15,957 at the Emporium Hamburg 1987 sale.

| KM# | Date | Mintage | Identification | Mkt Val |
|---|---|---|---|---|
| Pn212 | 1919 | — | 50 Pfennig. Brass. | 200 |
| Pn213 | 1919 | — | 50 Pfennig. Silver. | 300 |
| Pn214 | 1919 | — | 50 Pfennig. Nickel. | 150 |
| Pn215 | 1919 | — | 50 Pfennig. Aluminum. | 150 |
| Pn216 | 1919 | — | 50 Pfennig. Zinc. | 150 |
| Pn218 | 1919 | — | 50 Pfennig. Aluminum. Reeded edge. | 110 |
| Pn217 | 1919 | — | 50 Pfennig. Zinc. Reeded edge. | — |
| Pn219 | 1919 | — | 50 Pfennig. Aluminum. Plain edge. | — |
| Pn220 | 1919 | — | 50 Pfennig. Aluminum. Ornamental edge. | — |
| Pn221 | 1919 | — | 50 Pfennig. Zinc. Ornamental edge. | — |
| Pn222 | 1919 | — | 1/2 Mark. KM#17. | — |
| Pn223 | 1919 | — | Mark. Copper. KM#14. | — |
| Pn224 | 19xx | — | Mark. Aluminum. | — |
| Pn225 | 1921 | — | Mark. Brass Plated Aluminum. | — |
| Pn226 | 1921 | — | Mark. Zinc. | — |
| Pn227 | 1921 | — | Mark. | — |
| Pn228 | 1921 | — | Mark. Aluminum Plated Steel. | — |
| Pn230 | 1921 | — | Mark. Silver. | — |
| Pn231 | 1921 | — | Mark. Iron. | — |
| Pn232 | 1921 | — | Mark. Copper Strips Inlaid On Silver Or Copper-Nickel. | — |
| Pn233 | 1921 | — | Mark. Copper Strips Inlaid On Aluminum. | — |
| Pn229 | 1921 | — | Mark. Nickel. | 125 |
| PnA234 | 1922 | — | 10 Pfennig. Iron. | 200 |
| Pn235 | 1922 | — | 3 Mark. KM#28; GOTT MIT UNS. | 750 |

**Note:** Most 1922F lettered-edge 3 Marks were recovered from the burned-out ruins of the Stuttgart Mint destroyed in World War II; the above value is for the one known perfect example, blackened VF examples are valued between $175 and $350

| KM# | Date | Mintage | Identification | Mkt Val |
|---|---|---|---|---|
| Pn239 | 1922 | — | 5 Mark. Aluminum. | 100 |
| Pn239a | 1922 | — | 5 Mark. Aluminum Plated Copper. | 700 |
| Pn234 | 1922 | — | 50 Pfennig. Iron. Plain with 6 ridges edge. KM#27. | — |
| Pn236 | 1922 | — | 3 Mark. Reeded edge. KM#28. | — |
| Pn237 | 1922 | — | 3 Mark. Plain edge. KM#28. | — |
| Pn238 | 1922 | — | 3 Mark. Reeded edge. KM#28. | — |
| Pn240 | 1922 | — | 5 Mark. Roman lettering. | — |
| Pn241 | 1923 | — | 2 Pfennig. Without mintmark; KM#31. | — |
| Pn242 | 1923 | — | 50 Pfennig. Without mintmark; KM#34. | — |
| Pn244 | 1923 | — | 20 Mark. Aluminum. | — |
| Pn245 | 1923 | — | 100 Mark. Aluminum. | — |
| Pn246 | 1923 | — | 200 Mark. Doubled reeding; KM#35. | — |
| Pn248 | 1923 | — | 1000 Mark. Silver. Reeded edge. | — |
| Pn249 | 1923 | — | 1000 Mark. Aluminum. Plain edge. | — |
| Pn243 | 1923 | — | 3 Mark. KM#29.4. | 225 |

**Note:** All pattern 1923F 3 Marks were recovered from the burned out ruins of the Stuttgart Mint destroyed in World War II; blackened VF examples range in value from $225 to $400

| KM# | Date | Mintage | Identification | Mkt Val |
|---|---|---|---|---|
| Pn247 | 1923 | — | 1000 Mark. Aluminum. Reeded edge. | 300 |
| PnA250 | 1924 | — | 2 Pfennig. Brass. KM#31. | 125 |
| Pn250 | 1924 | — | 2 Pfennig. Copper. Eagle head left. | — |
| Pn251 | 1924 | — | 10 Pfennig. Copper. | — |
| Pn252 | 1924 | — | 10 Pfennig. Aluminum. | — |
| Pn253 | 1924 | — | 10 Pfennig. Copper. Full eagle | — |
| Pn254 | 1924 | — | 10 Pfennig. Aluminum. Full eagle | — |
| Pn255 | 1924 | — | 10 Pfennig. Nickel. Full eagle. | — |
| Pn256 | 1924 | — | 50 Pfennig. Lead. KM#41. | — |

**Note:** 1

| KM# | Date | Mintage | Identification | Mkt Val |
|---|---|---|---|---|
| Pn257 | 1924 | — | Mark. Silver. Reeded, lettered edge. | — |
| Pn258 | 1924 | — | 3 Mark. 0.5000 Silver. Ornamental edge. | — |
| Pn259 | 1924 | — | 5 Mark. Silver. | — |
| Pn260 | 1925 | — | Pfennig. Copper. | — |
| Pn261 | 1925 | — | 2 Pfennig. Copper. | — |
| Pn262 | 1925 | — | 5 Pfennig. Copper-Nickel. | — |
| Pn263 | 1925 | — | 5 Pfennig. Copper-Nickel. Larger eagle head. | — |
| Pn264 | 1925 | — | 10 Pfennig. Copper-Nickel. | — |
| Pn272 | 1925 | — | 50 Pfennig. Brass. Mercury | — |
| Pn273 | 1925 | — | Mark. Silver. Thick wreath. | — |
| Pn274 | 1925 | — | Mark. Nickel. Thick wreath. | — |
| Pn275 | 1925 | — | Mark. 0.4500 Silver. Thin wreath. | — |
| PnA276 | 1925 | — | 3 Mark. Brass. | — |
| PnA277 | 1925 | — | 3 Mark. Brass. Woman's head. | — |
| Pn277 | 1925 | — | 3 Mark. Iron. KM#46. | — |
| Pn283 | 1925 | — | 20 Mark. Gold. | — |
| Pn284 | 1925 | — | 20 Mark. Brass. | — |
| Pn265 | 1925 | 6 | 50 Pfennig. KM#41. | 16,500 |

**Note:** An XF-AU example brought $15,957, Emporium Hamburg 1987 sale

| KM# | Date | Mintage | Identification | Mkt Val |
|---|---|---|---|---|
| Pn266 | 1925 | — | 50 Pfennig. Brass. Bundle. | 100 |
| Pn267 | 1925 | — | 50 Pfennig. Bronze. Bundle. | 100 |
| Pn268 | 1925 | — | 50 Pfennig. Copper-Nickel. Bundle. | 100 |
| Pn269 | 1925 | — | 50 Pfennig. Nickel. Bundle. | 100 |
| Pn270 | 1925 | — | 50 Pfennig. Nickel-Silver. Mercury | 125 |
| Pn271 | 1925 | — | 50 Pfennig. Nickel. Mercury | 125 |
| Pn276 | 1925 | — | 2 Mark. 0.5000 Silver. Thick wreath. | 150 |
| Pn278 | 1925 | — | 3 Mark. Silver. | 400 |
| Pn279 | 1925 | — | 5 Mark. Silver. | 750 |
| Pn280 | 1925 | — | 5 Mark. Silver. | 750 |
| Pn281 | 1925 | — | 5 Mark. Silver. | 1,750 |
| Pn281a | 1925 | — | 5 Mark. Silvered-Bronze. | 150 |
| Pn282 | 1925 | — | 5 Mark. Silver. | 1,400 |
| Pn287 | 1926 | — | 50 Pfennig. Copper-Nickel. Leaves through value | 125 |
| Pn291 | 1926 | — | 50 Pfennig. Copper-Nickel. Cornucopia. | 125 |
| Pn305 | 1926 | — | 50 Pfennig. Nickel. | 100 |
| Pn307 | 1926 | — | Mark. Brass. | 100 |
| Pn310 | 1926 | — | 5 Mark. Silver. | 750 |
| Pn311 | 1926 | — | 5 Mark. Silver. | 750 |
| Pn312 | 1926 | — | 5 Mark. Silver. | 1,000 |
| Pn312a | 1926 | — | 5 Mark. Silver. Ship sailing right. | 500 |
| Pn313 | 1926 | — | 5 Mark. Silver. Large eagle, small mint mark. | 500 |
| Pn314 | 1926 | — | 5 Mark. Silver. Small eagle, large mint mark. | 500 |
| Pn315 | 1926 | — | 5 Mark. Silver. | 800 |
| Pn316 | 1926 | — | 5 Mark. Silver. | 800 |
| Pn318 | 1926 | — | 5 Mark. Silver. With motto. | 650 |
| Pn320 | 1926 | — | 5 Mark. Silver. Without motto.. | 800 |
| Pn285 | 1926 | — | 50 Pfennig. Copper-Nickel. | — |
| Pn286 | 1926 | — | 50 Pfennig. | — |
| Pn288 | 1926 | — | 50 Pfennig. Leaves below value | — |
| Pn289 | 1926 | — | 50 Pfennig. Copper-Nickel. Leaves below value | — |
| Pn290 | 1926 | — | 50 Pfennig. Leaves below value. | — |
| Pn292 | 1926 | — | 50 Pfennig. Copper-Nickel. Two leaves. | — |
| Pn293 | 1926 | — | 50 Pfennig. Copper-Nickel. Wreath. | — |
| Pn294 | 1926 | — | 50 Pfennig. Copper-Nickel. Wheat. | — |
| Pn295 | 1926 | — | 50 Pfennig. Copper-Nickel. Eagle. | — |
| Pn296 | 1926 | — | 50 Pfennig. Copper-Nickel. Two leaves. | — |
| Pn297 | 1926 | — | 50 Pfennig. Copper-Nickel. Eagle. | — |
| Pn298 | 1926 | — | 50 Pfennig. Copper-Nickel. Wheat. | — |
| Pn299 | 1926 | — | 50 Pfennig. Copper-Nickel. Two leaves. | — |
| Pn300 | 1926 | — | 50 Pfennig. Copper-Nickel. Eagle. | — |
| Pn301 | 1926 | — | 50 Pfennig. Copper-Nickel. "Reichspfennig" | — |
| Pn302 | 1926 | — | 50 Pfennig. Copper-Nickel. | — |
| Pn303 | 1926 | — | 50 Pfennig. Nickel. | — |

| KM# | Date | Mintage | Identification | Mkt Val |
|---|---|---|---|---|
| Pn304 | 1926 | — | 50 Pfennig. Copper-Nickel. | — |
| Pn306 | 1926 | — | 50 Pfennig. Nickel. Smaller eagle. | — |
| Pn307a | 1926 | — | Mark. Silver. | — |
| PnA308 | 1926 | — | 3 Mark. | — |
| Pn308 | 1926 | — | 5 Mark. Silver. | — |
| Pn309 | 1926 | — | 5 Mark. Silver. Wreath aaround eagle. | — |
| Pn317 | 1926 | — | 5 Mark. Silver. "PROBE"; with motto. | — |
| Pn319 | 1926 | — | 5 Mark. Silver. "PROBE" without motto. | — |
| Pn321 | 1927 | — | 50 Pfennig. Deeper relief, KM#49. | — |
| Pn322 | 1927 | — | 50 Pfennig. Silver. | — |
| Pn324 | 1927 | — | Mark. Pn307. | — |
| Pn327 | 1927 | — | 3 Mark. 0.9930 Silver. | — |
| Pn328 | 1927 | — | 3 Mark. Silver. Lettered edge. "PROBE" | — |
| Pn329 | 1927 | — | 3 Mark. Silver. Lettered edge. | — |
| PnA331 | 1927 | — | 3 Mark. Silver. Justus Von Liebig; never issued. | — |
| Pn323 | 1927 | — | 50 Pfennig. Copper-Nickel. | 150 |
| Pn325 | 1927 | — | Mark. 0.5000 Silver. Ornamental edge. | 175 |
| Pn326 | 1927 | — | Mark. 0.9930 Silver. Plain edge. | 225 |
| Pn327a | 1927 | — | 3 Mark. Copper-Nickel. | 1,000 |
| Pn330 | 1927 | — | 3 Mark. Plain edge. | 825 |
| Pn331 | 1927 | — | 5 Mark. Silver. Large eagle. | — |
| Pn332 | | — | 5 Mark. Silvered Tin. Small eagle. | — |
| Pn334 | 1927 | — | 5 Mark. 50 stars; KM#56. | — |
| Pn335 | 1927 | — | 5 Mark. 47 stars; KM#56. | — |
| Pn336 | 1927 | — | 5 Mark. 73 stars; KM#56. | — |
| Pn338 | 1929 | — | 3 Mark. Silver. "PROBE"; KM#62. | — |
| Pn339 | 1929 | — | 5 Mark. Silver. Plain rims; "PROBE". | — |
| Pn340 | 1929 | — | 5 Mark. Silver. Star rims; "PROBE". | — |
| Pn342 | 1929 | — | 5 Mark. Pn346. | — |
| PnA343 | 1929 | — | 3 Mark. PROBE | — |
| Pn337 | 1929 | — | 3 Mark. Script on edge; KM#60. | 825 |
| Pn341 | 1929 | — | 5 Mark. Silver. "PROBE". | 1,850 |
| Pn344 | 1930 | — | 3 Mark. Silver. "PROBE" | 850 |
| Pn345 | 1930 | — | 3 Mark. Silver. "PROBE"; KM#69. | 850 |
| Pn343 | 1930 | — | 3 Mark. Silver. "PROBE"; KM#70. | — |
| Pn346 | 1930 | — | 5 Mark. Silver. "PROBE"; KM#68. | — |
| Pn347 | 1930 | — | 5 Mark. Silver. | — |
| Pn348 | 1931 | — | 3 Mark. | — |
| Pn349 | 1931 | — | 5 Mark. | — |
| PnA347 | 1931 | — | Pfennig. Brass. | 75.00 |
| Pn351 | 1932 | — | 3 Mark. 0.7500 Silver. KM#74. | 700 |
| Pn353a | 1932 | — | 5 Mark. Nickel. "PROBE". KM#76. | 350 |
| Pn350 | 1932 | — | 4 Pfennig. Silvered Copper. "PROBE" | — |
| PnA351 | 1932 | — | 3 Mark. Silver. | — |
| Pn352 | 1932 | — | 3 Mark. Silver. Reeded edge. "PROBE"; KM#74. | — |
| Pn353 | 1932 | — | 3 Mark. Silver. Reeded edge. Without "PROBE"; KM#74. | — |

**1933-1945**

A wide range of factors, such as humiliation of defeat, economic depression, poverty, and a pervasive feeling of discontent aided Hitler in his climb to power. After the unsuccessful Putsch (uprising against the Bavarian Government) in 1923, Hitler was imprisoned in Landsberg Fortress. While imprisoned Hitler dictated his book *"Mein Kampf"* which became the cornerstone of Nazism espousing Hitler's irrational ideology and the manipulation of power without moral constraint as the basis of strategy.

Master propagandist Josef Goebbels tried to attract the sympathetic attention of the German public. The usual tactic was to have Hitler promise all things to all people provided that they in turn would pledge to him their complete faith and obedience.

Once in power, coercion was used to elicit the appearance of unanimous endorsement. Public works and military rearmament helped overcome the depression. It took the Nazis only about two years to consolidate their system politically. The combined terrorism of the storm troops and the police forces, including the Gestapo, stifled potential opposition. By 1935, Nazi affiliated organizations controlled all German cultural, professional, and economic fields, assuring strict compliance with the party line.

With the passage of the Nurnberg Laws in 1935, the more ominous aspects of Nazi anti-Semitism came to light. Jews were deprived of their citizenship and forbidden to marry non-Jews. This was followed by confiscation of property and the required wearing of the Star of David for identification purposes, eventually culminating in the mass deportation to concentration and death camps.

By 1936, unemployment was virtually eliminated and economic production was up to 1929 levels. All sources of information were under the control of Josef Goebbels, while all police power was in the hands of Heinrich Himmler. Germans who were not convinced by Goebbel's propaganda machine would be silenced by Himmler's Gestapo. Usually the implied threat was enough. The majority of Germans did not suffer any ill effects at first and national pride stirred once again.

Hitler's audacity in foreign affairs met with success due to the trend of appeasement by the western powers. First, Germany withdrew from the League of Nations and the World Disarmament Council. In 1935, the Saar voted to return to Germany and Hitler renounced the reviled 1921 peace treaty and related pacts. In 1936, German forces reoccupied the Rhineland. In 1938, Austria was annexed and at the Munich Conference, which excluded Czechoslovakia, Great Britain and France agreed that the Sudatenland was to become German territory. In 1939, Slovakia became an independent Nazi Puppet State and the "Protectorate" of Bohemia and Moravia was established. Next came the German-Soviet non-aggression pact which secretly divided up Poland between the two totalitarian powers. Great Britain and France finally declared war when Poland was invaded. The years of 1939-1942 were a period of impressive victories for Germany's well-trained and equipped forces. However, when Hitler expanded his war beyond Western Europe by invading Africa and Russia and declaring war on the U.S.A., it started the chain of events which would culminate in the total and final German defeat on May 7, 1945, VE Day, ending the European theater of the Second World War and The Third Reich.

**MINT MARKS**

A - Berlin
B - Vienna, 1938-1944
D - Munich
E - Muldenhutten
F - Stuttgart
G - Karlsruhe
J - Hamburg

**MONETARY SYSTEMS**

(During 1923-1924)
100 Rentenpfennig = 1 Rentenmark

(Commencing 1924)
100 Reichspfennig = 1 Reichsmark

# THIRD REICH

## STANDARD COINAGE

**REICHSPFENNIG** **KM# 89** **Composition:** Bronze

| Date | Mintage | F | VF | XF | Unc | BU |
|---|---|---|---|---|---|---|
| 1936A | — | 1.50 | 4.00 | 7.50 | 20.00 | — |
| **Note:** Mintage included with KM#37. | | | | | | |
| 1936E | 150,000 | 25.00 | 50.00 | 100 | 150 | — |
| 1936F | 4,600,000 | 22.50 | 50.00 | 95.00 | 145 | — |
| 1936G | — | 15.00 | 30.00 | 50.00 | 75.00 | — |
| **Note:** Mintage included with KM#37. | | | | | | |
| 1936J | — | 10.00 | 30.00 | 50.00 | 85.00 | — |
| **Note:** Mintage included with KM#37. | | | | | | |
| 1937A | 67,180,000 | 0.10 | 0.25 | 0.50 | 2.50 | — |
| 1937D | 14,060,000 | 0.10 | 0.25 | 0.50 | 2.50 | — |
| 1937E | 10,700,000 | 0.15 | 0.35 | 1.00 | 5.00 | — |
| 1937F | 11,058,000 | 0.15 | 0.35 | 1.00 | 5.00 | — |
| 1937G | 4,250,000 | 0.15 | 0.35 | 1.00 | 5.00 | — |
| 1937J | 6,714,000 | 0.15 | 0.35 | 1.00 | 5.00 | — |
| 1938A | 75,707,000 | 0.10 | 0.25 | 0.50 | 5.00 | — |
| 1938B | 2,378,000 | 0.50 | 6.00 | 9.00 | 12.50 | — |
| 1938D | 13,930,000 | 0.10 | 0.25 | 0.50 | 5.00 | — |
| 1938E | 14,503,000 | 0.10 | 0.25 | 0.50 | 5.00 | — |
| 1938F | 11,714,000 | 0.10 | 0.25 | 0.50 | 5.00 | — |
| 1938G | 8,390,000 | 0.10 | 0.25 | 0.50 | 5.00 | — |
| 1938J | 15,458,000 | 0.10 | 0.25 | 0.50 | 6.00 | — |
| 1939A | 97,541,000 | 0.10 | 0.25 | 0.50 | 5.00 | — |
| 1939B | 22,732,000 | 0.15 | 0.35 | 1.00 | 7.50 | — |
| 1939D | 20,760,000 | 0.10 | 0.25 | 0.50 | 5.00 | — |

| Date | Mintage | F | VF | XF | Unc | BU |
|---|---|---|---|---|---|---|
| 1939E | 12,478,000 | 0.10 | 0.25 | 0.50 | 7.50 | — |
| 1939F | 12,482,000 | 0.10 | 0.25 | 0.50 | 5.00 | — |
| 1939G | 12,250,000 | 0.10 | 0.25 | 0.50 | 5.00 | — |
| 1939J | 8,368,000 | 0.10 | 0.25 | 0.50 | 7.50 | — |
| 1940A | 27,094,000 | 0.10 | 0.25 | 0.50 | 6.00 | — |
| 1940F | 7,850,000 | 0.15 | 0.35 | 1.00 | 6.00 | — |
| 1940G | 3,875,000 | 1.00 | 5.00 | 7.50 | 15.00 | — |
| 1940J | 7,450,000 | 0.50 | 4.00 | 5.00 | 8.00 | — |
| 1936-1940 Proof | — | Value: 75.00 | | | | |

## REICHSPFENNIG KM# 97 Composition: Zinc

| Date | Mintage | F | VF | XF | Unc | BU |
|---|---|---|---|---|---|---|
| 1940A | 223,948,000 | 0.10 | 0.20 | 1.00 | 5.00 | — |
| 1940B | 62,198,000 | 0.10 | 0.20 | 1.00 | 2.50 | — |
| 1940D | 43,951,000 | 0.10 | 0.20 | 1.00 | 5.00 | — |
| 1940E | 20,749,000 | 0.20 | 1.00 | 5.00 | 7.50 | — |
| 1940F | 33,854,000 | 0.10 | 0.20 | 1.00 | 5.00 | — |
| 1940G | 20,165,000 | 0.10 | 0.20 | 1.00 | 5.00 | — |
| 1940J | 24,459,000 | 0.10 | 0.20 | 1.00 | 5.00 | — |
| 1941A | 281,618,000 | 0.10 | 0.15 | 0.50 | 4.00 | — |
| 1941B | 62,285,000 | 0.20 | 1.00 | 1.50 | 7.50 | — |
| 1941D | 73,745,000 | 0.10 | 0.15 | 0.50 | 5.00 | — |
| 1941E | 49,041,000 | 0.10 | 0.50 | 1.50 | 7.50 | — |
| 1941F | 51,017,000 | 0.10 | 0.15 | 0.50 | 5.00 | — |
| 1941G | 44,810,000 | 0.10 | 0.50 | 1.00 | 7.50 | — |
| 1941J | 57,625,000 | 0.10 | 0.15 | 0.50 | 5.00 | — |
| 1942A | 558,877,000 | 0.10 | 0.15 | 0.50 | 5.00 | — |
| 1942B | 124,740,000 | 0.10 | 0.20 | 1.00 | 6.00 | — |
| 1942D | 134,145,000 | 0.10 | 0.15 | 0.50 | 6.00 | — |
| 1942E | 84,674,000 | 0.15 | 1.50 | 2.50 | 8.50 | — |
| 1942F | 90,788,000 | 0.10 | 0.15 | 0.50 | 6.00 | — |
| 1942G | 59,858,000 | 0.10 | 0.15 | 0.50 | 6.00 | — |
| 1942J | 122,934,000 | 0.10 | 0.50 | 1.00 | 6.00 | — |
| 1943A | 372,401,000 | 0.10 | 0.15 | 0.50 | 6.00 | — |
| 1943B | 79,315,000 | 0.10 | 0.50 | 1.00 | 6.00 | — |
| 1943D | 91,629,000 | 0.10 | 0.15 | 0.50 | 6.00 | — |
| 1943E | 34,191,000 | 0.50 | 2.50 | 7.50 | 10.00 | — |
| 1943F | 70,269,000 | 0.10 | 0.50 | 1.00 | 6.00 | — |
| 1943G | 24,688,000 | 0.15 | 1.50 | 2.50 | 7.50 | — |
| 1943J | 37,695,000 | 0.15 | 1.50 | 2.50 | 7.50 | — |
| 1944A | 124,421,000 | 0.10 | 0.50 | 2.00 | 5.00 | — |
| 1944B | 87,850,000 | 0.20 | 1.00 | 2.00 | 5.00 | — |
| 1944D | 56,755,000 | 0.20 | 1.00 | 2.50 | 7.00 | — |
| 1944E | 41,729,000 | 0.20 | 2.00 | 5.00 | 10.00 | — |
| 1944F | 15,580,000 | 0.50 | 4.00 | 6.00 | 12.00 | — |
| 1944G | 34,967,000 | 0.10 | 0.50 | 1.00 | 4.00 | — |
| 1945A | 17,145,000 | 0.25 | 2.50 | 7.50 | 20.00 | — |
| 1945E | 6,800,000 | 45.00 | 65.00 | 90.00 | 150 | — |
| 1940-1945 Proof | — | Value: 100 | | | | |

## 2 REICHSPFENNIG KM# 90 Composition: Bronze

| Date | Mintage | F | VF | XF | Unc | BU |
|---|---|---|---|---|---|---|
| 1936A | | 0.50 | 3.00 | 8.00 | 25.00 | — |
| 1936D | | 0.50 | 3.00 | 8.00 | 25.00 | — |
| 1936F | 3,100,000 | 5.00 | 15.00 | 40.00 | 60.00 | — |
| 1937A | 34,404,000 | 0.10 | 0.50 | 1.50 | 7.00 | — |
| 1937D | 9,016,000 | 0.10 | 0.50 | 1.50 | 7.00 | — |
| 1937E | | 15.00 | 20.00 | 35.00 | 60.00 | — |
| 1937F | 7,487,000 | 0.10 | 0.50 | 1.50 | 7.00 | — |
| 1937G | 490,000 | 2.00 | 8.50 | 15.00 | 27.50 | — |
| 1937J | 450,000 | 2.00 | 8.50 | 15.00 | 25.00 | — |
| 1938A | 27,264,000 | 0.10 | 0.15 | 0.50 | 6.00 | — |
| 1938B | 2,714,000 | 1.50 | 4.00 | 8.00 | 22.00 | — |
| 1938D | 8,770,000 | 0.10 | 0.25 | 1.00 | 6.00 | — |
| 1938E | 5,450,000 | 0.25 | 1.00 | 2.00 | 6.00 | — |
| 1938F | 10,090,000 | 0.10 | 0.25 | 1.00 | 6.00 | — |
| 1938G | 3,685,000 | 0.10 | 0.25 | 1.00 | 6.00 | — |
| 1938J | 7,243,000 | 0.10 | 0.25 | 1.00 | 6.00 | — |
| 1939A | 37,348,000 | 0.10 | 0.25 | 1.00 | 6.00 | — |
| 1939B | 9,361,000 | 0.10 | 0.25 | 1.00 | 6.00 | — |
| 1939D | 7,555,000 | 0.10 | 0.25 | 1.00 | 6.00 | — |
| 1939E | 6,650,000 | 0.25 | 1.00 | 4.50 | 10.00 | — |
| 1939F | 7,019,000 | 0.10 | 0.25 | 1.00 | 6.00 | — |
| 1939G | 4,885,000 | 0.10 | 0.25 | 1.00 | 6.00 | — |
| 1939J | 6,996,000 | 0.10 | 0.25 | 1.00 | 6.00 | — |
| 1940A | 22,681,000 | 0.10 | 0.25 | 1.00 | 6.00 | — |
| 1940D | 3,855,000 | 0.50 | 3.00 | 6.50 | 12.50 | — |
| 1940E | 3,412,000 | 2.50 | 10.00 | 15.00 | 30.00 | — |
| 1940G | 1,161,000 | 40.00 | 70.00 | 110 | 150 | — |
| 1940J | 2,357,000 | 1.50 | 7.50 | 12.50 | 25.00 | — |
| 1936-1940 Proof | — | Value: 100 | | | | |

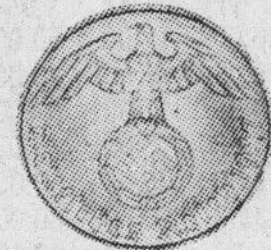

## 5 REICHSPFENNIG KM# 91 Composition: Aluminum-Bronze

| Date | Mintage | F | VF | XF | Unc | BU |
|---|---|---|---|---|---|---|
| 1936A | | 25.00 | 60.00 | 80.00 | 120 | — |
| 1936D | | 25.00 | 60.00 | 80.00 | 120 | — |
| 1936G | | 45.00 | 80.00 | 120 | 175 | — |
| 1937A | 29,700,000 | 0.10 | 0.20 | 1.00 | 6.00 | — |
| 1937D | 4,992,000 | 0.10 | 0.20 | 1.00 | 7.50 | — |
| 1937E | 4,474,000 | 0.20 | 1.00 | 3.00 | 10.00 | — |
| 1937F | 2,092,000 | 0.10 | 0.20 | 1.00 | 8.00 | — |
| 1937G | 2,749,000 | 2.50 | 7.50 | 15.00 | 20.00 | — |
| 1937J | 6,991,000 | 0.25 | 2.50 | 5.00 | 12.50 | — |
| 1938A | 54,012,000 | 0.25 | 2.50 | 5.00 | 7.50 | — |
| 1938B | 3,447,000 | 0.25 | 1.50 | 5.00 | 10.00 | — |
| 1938D | 17,708,000 | 0.10 | 0.25 | 1.50 | 6.00 | — |
| 1938E | 8,602,000 | 0.10 | 0.40 | 4.00 | 8.00 | — |
| 1938F | 8,147,000 | 0.10 | 0.25 | 1.50 | 7.00 | — |
| 1938G | 7,323,000 | 0.10 | 0.25 | 1.50 | 7.00 | — |
| 1938J | 7,646,000 | 0.10 | 0.25 | 1.50 | 7.00 | — |
| 1939A | 35,337,000 | 0.10 | 0.25 | 1.50 | 7.00 | — |
| 1939B | 8,313,000 | 0.10 | 0.20 | 1.00 | 7.50 | — |
| 1939D | 8,304,000 | 0.20 | 1.00 | 2.00 | 7.50 | — |
| 1939E | 5,138,000 | 0.20 | 1.00 | 2.00 | 7.50 | — |
| 1939F | 10,339,000 | 0.10 | 0.20 | 1.00 | 6.00 | — |
| 1939G | 4,266,000 | 0.25 | 2.50 | 7.50 | 12.50 | — |
| 1939J | 4,177,000 | 0.20 | 2.00 | 7.50 | 10.00 | — |
| 1936-1939 Proof | — | Value: 100 | | | | |

## 5 REICHSPFENNIG KM# 100 Composition: Zinc

| Date | Mintage | F | VF | XF | Unc | BU |
|---|---|---|---|---|---|---|
| 1940A | 174,684,000 | 0.10 | 0.20 | 1.00 | 5.00 | — |
| 1940B | 63,469,000 | 0.20 | 1.00 | 1.50 | 6.00 | — |
| 1940D | 44,364,000 | 0.20 | 1.00 | 1.50 | 6.00 | — |
| 1940E | 25,800,000 | 0.30 | 2.00 | 4.00 | 6.00 | — |
| 1940F | 31,381,000 | 0.20 | 1.00 | 2.00 | 6.00 | — |
| 1940G | 24,148,000 | 0.20 | 1.00 | 2.50 | 6.00 | — |
| 1940J | 30,518,000 | 0.20 | 1.00 | 2.00 | 6.00 | — |
| 1941A | 246,216,000 | 0.10 | 0.20 | 1.00 | 5.00 | — |
| 1941B | 60,297,000 | 0.10 | 0.30 | 2.00 | 7.50 | — |
| 1941D | 51,100,000 | 0.10 | 0.30 | 2.00 | 7.50 | — |
| 1941E | 26,354,000 | 0.10 | 0.30 | 2.00 | 7.50 | — |
| 1941F | 36,725,000 | 0.10 | 0.30 | 2.00 | 7.50 | — |
| 1941G | 21,276,000 | 0.10 | 0.30 | 2.00 | 7.50 | — |
| 1941J | 52,872,000 | 0.10 | 0.30 | 2.00 | 7.50 | — |
| 1942A | 161,042,000 | 0.10 | 0.20 | 1.00 | 5.00 | — |
| 1942B | 12,405,000 | 0.25 | 1.50 | 5.00 | 7.50 | — |
| 1942D | 15,486,000 | 0.10 | 0.35 | 2.50 | 5.00 | — |
| 1942E | 8,800,000 | 7.50 | 17.50 | 22.50 | 35.00 | — |
| 1942F | 24,662,000 | 0.10 | 0.25 | 1.50 | 5.00 | — |
| 1942G | 12,749,000 | 0.10 | 0.35 | 2.50 | 7.50 | — |
| 1943A | 46,830,000 | 0.15 | 0.50 | 2.00 | 12.50 | — |
| 1943B | 833,000 | 30.00 | 50.00 | 75.00 | 125 | — |
| 1943D | 13,650,000 | 0.15 | 0.50 | 4.00 | 10.00 | — |
| 1943E | 16,581,000 | 2.50 | 7.50 | 12.50 | 17.50 | — |
| 1943F | 9,891,000 | 0.20 | 1.00 | 2.50 | 6.00 | — |
| 1943G | 7,237,000 | 0.15 | 0.50 | 2.00 | 6.00 | — |
| 1944A | 23,699,000 | 3.50 | 15.00 | 27.50 | 37.50 | — |
| 1944D | 26,340,000 | 0.25 | 1.50 | 3.00 | 5.00 | — |
| 1944E | 19,720,000 | 0.50 | 4.00 | 9.00 | 15.00 | — |
| 1944F | 6,853,000 | 0.25 | 1.50 | 3.00 | 7.50 | — |
| 1944G | 3,540,000 | 90.00 | 175 | 210 | 300 | — |
| 1940-1944 Proof | — | Value: 200 | | | | |

## 10 REICHSPFENNIG KM# 92 Composition: Aluminum-Bronze

| Date | Mintage | F | VF | XF | Unc | BU |
|---|---|---|---|---|---|---|
| 1936A | | 17.50 | 35.00 | 50.00 | 90.00 | — |
| 1936E | 245,000 | 80.00 | 135 | 175 | 275 | — |
| 1936G | 129,000 | 175 | 225 | 300 | 400 | — |
| 1937A | 36,830,000 | 0.10 | 0.50 | 2.00 | 7.50 | — |
| 1937D | 6,882,000 | 0.25 | 1.50 | 3.00 | 10.00 | — |
| 1937E | 3,786,000 | 2.00 | 10.00 | 18.00 | 40.00 | — |
| 1937F | 5,934,000 | 0.50 | 2.50 | 5.00 | 12.50 | — |
| 1937G | 2,131,000 | 1.00 | 5.00 | 7.50 | 17.50 | — |
| 1937J | 4,439,000 | 0.50 | 2.50 | 5.00 | 15.00 | — |

| Date | Mintage | F | VF | XF | Unc | BU |
|---|---|---|---|---|---|---|
| 1938A | 70,068,000 | 0.10 | 0.20 | 1.00 | 6.00 | — |
| 1938B | 7,852,000 | 0.50 | 2.50 | 5.00 | 12.50 | — |
| 1938D | 16,990,000 | 0.10 | 0.50 | 2.00 | 8.00 | — |
| 1938E | 10,739,000 | 0.20 | 1.00 | 2.50 | 9.00 | — |
| 1938F | 12,307,000 | 0.20 | 1.00 | 2.50 | 9.00 | — |
| 1938G | 8,584,000 | 0.20 | 1.00 | 2.50 | 9.00 | — |
| 1938J | 10,389,000 | 0.20 | 1.00 | 2.50 | 9.00 | — |
| 1939A | 40,171,000 | 0.20 | 1.00 | 2.00 | 8.00 | — |
| 1939B | 7,814,000 | 0.20 | 1.00 | 2.00 | 9.00 | — |
| 1939D | 11,307,000 | 0.20 | 1.00 | 2.00 | 9.00 | — |
| 1939E | 5,079,000 | 0.50 | 2.50 | 7.50 | 15.00 | — |
| 1939F | 6,993,000 | 0.25 | 1.50 | 3.00 | 10.00 | — |
| 1939G | 5,532,000 | 0.50 | 5.00 | 10.00 | 20.00 | — |
| 1939J | 5,557,000 | 0.20 | 1.00 | 2.00 | 6.00 | — |
| 1936-1939 Proof | — | Value: 95.00 | | | | |

## 10 REICHSPFENNIG KM# 101 Composition: Zinc

| Date | Mintage | F | VF | XF | Unc | BU |
|---|---|---|---|---|---|---|
| 1940A | 212,948,000 | 0.10 | 0.35 | 1.50 | 6.00 | — |
| 1940B | 76,274,000 | 0.15 | 0.50 | 2.50 | 7.50 | — |
| 1940D | 45,434,000 | 0.15 | 0.50 | 2.00 | 6.50 | — |
| 1940E | 34,350,000 | 0.15 | 0.50 | 2.00 | 6.50 | — |
| 1940F | 27,603,000 | 0.15 | 0.50 | 2.00 | 6.50 | — |
| 1940G | 27,308,000 | 0.15 | 0.50 | 2.00 | 6.50 | — |
| 1940J | 41,678,000 | 0.15 | 0.50 | 2.00 | 6.50 | — |
| 1941A | 240,284,000 | 0.10 | 0.35 | 1.50 | 6.00 | — |
| 1941B | 70,747,000 | 0.15 | 0.50 | 2.50 | 7.50 | — |
| 1941D | 77,560,000 | 0.15 | 0.50 | 2.00 | 6.50 | — |
| 1941E | 36,548,000 | 0.15 | 0.50 | 2.00 | 6.50 | — |
| 1941F | 42,834,000 | 0.15 | 0.50 | 2.00 | 6.50 | — |
| 1941G | 28,765,000 | 0.15 | 0.50 | 2.00 | 6.50 | — |
| 1941J | 30,525,000 | 0.15 | 0.50 | 2.00 | 6.50 | — |
| 1942A | 184,545,000 | 0.10 | 0.20 | 0.50 | 2.00 | — |
| 1942B | 16,329,000 | 0.25 | 2.50 | 3.50 | 10.00 | — |
| 1942D | 40,852,000 | 0.20 | 1.00 | 2.50 | 7.50 | — |
| 1942E | 18,334,000 | 0.25 | 1.50 | 3.00 | 7.50 | — |
| 1942F | 32,690,000 | 0.10 | 0.35 | 1.50 | 6.00 | — |
| 1942G | 20,295,000 | 0.25 | 1.50 | 2.50 | 6.00 | — |
| 1942J | 29,957,000 | 0.25 | 1.50 | 2.50 | 10.00 | — |
| 1943A | 157,357,000 | 0.15 | 1.50 | 2.50 | 6.00 | — |
| 1943B | 11,940,000 | 2.50 | 7.50 | 15.00 | 25.00 | — |
| 1943D | 17,304,000 | 0.25 | 2.00 | 3.00 | 15.00 | — |
| 1943E | 10,445,000 | 2.50 | 7.50 | 15.00 | 25.00 | — |
| 1943F | 24,804,000 | 0.25 | 2.50 | 5.00 | 25.00 | — |
| 1943G | 3,618,000 | 0.25 | 2.50 | 6.00 | 50.00 | — |
| 1943J | 1,821,000 | 20.00 | 40.00 | 70.00 | 125 | — |
| 1944A | 84,164,000 | 0.15 | 1.00 | 2.50 | 7.50 | — |
| 1944B | 40,781,000 | 0.50 | 1.50 | 3.00 | 8.00 | — |
| 1944D | 30,369,000 | 0.35 | 1.50 | 3.00 | 8.00 | — |
| 1944E | 29,963,000 | 0.50 | 2.00 | 4.00 | 8.00 | — |
| 1944F | 19,639,000 | 0.50 | 2.00 | 4.00 | 8.00 | — |
| 1944G | 13,023,000 | 0.50 | 2.00 | 4.00 | 8.00 | — |
| 1945A | 7,112,000 | 5.00 | 12.50 | 25.00 | 50.00 | — |
| 1945E | 4,897,000 | 12.50 | 27.50 | 50.00 | 90.00 | — |
| 1940-1945 Proof | — | Value: 200 | | | | |

## 50 REICHSPFENNIG KM# 87 Composition: Aluminum

| Date | Mintage | F | VF | XF | Unc | BU |
|---|---|---|---|---|---|---|
| 1935A | 75,912,000 | 0.25 | 2.50 | 6.00 | 20.00 | — |
| 1935A Proof | — | Value: 200 | | | | |
| 1935D | 19,688,000 | 0.25 | 1.00 | 2.50 | 17.50 | — |
| 1935D Proof | — | Value: 75.00 | | | | |
| 1935E | 10,418,000 | 0.50 | 5.00 | 7.50 | 22.50 | — |
| 1935E Proof | — | Value: 200 | | | | |
| 1935F | 14,061,000 | 0.25 | 1.00 | 3.00 | 22.50 | — |
| 1935F Proof | — | Value: 200 | | | | |
| 1935G | 8,540,000 | 0.50 | 4.00 | 9.00 | 32.50 | — |
| 1935G Proof | — | Value: 200 | | | | |
| 1935J | 11,438,000 | 0.35 | 3.50 | 7.50 | 27.50 | — |
| 1935J Proof | — | Value: 200 | | | | |

## 50 REICHSPFENNIG KM# 95 Composition: Nickel

| Date | Mintage | F | VF | XF | Unc | BU |
|---|---|---|---|---|---|---|
| 1938A | 5,051,000 | 15.00 | 30.00 | 40.00 | 60.00 | — |
| 1938B | 1,124,000 | 20.00 | 40.00 | 50.00 | 80.00 | — |
| 1938D | 1,260,000 | 20.00 | 40.00 | 60.00 | 75.00 | — |
| 1938E | 949,000 | 20.00 | 40.00 | 60.00 | 85.00 | — |
| 1938F | 1,210,000 | 12.50 | 28.00 | 50.00 | 60.00 | — |
| 1938G | 460,000 | 25.00 | 70.00 | 90.00 | 150 | — |
| 1938J | 730,000 | 20.00 | 90.00 | 110 | 175 | — |
| 1939A | 15,037,000 | 17.50 | 30.00 | 50.00 | 70.00 | — |
| 1939B | 2,826,000 | 17.50 | 30.00 | 55.00 | 75.00 | — |
| 1939D | 3,648,000 | 15.00 | 30.00 | 55.00 | 75.00 | — |
| 1939E | 1,924,000 | 15.00 | 32.00 | 60.00 | 85.00 | — |
| 1939F | 2,602,000 | 15.00 | 32.00 | 60.00 | 85.00 | — |
| 1939G | 1,565,000 | 15.00 | 32.00 | 65.00 | 125 | — |
| 1939J | 2,114,000 | 15.00 | 32.00 | 60.00 | 90.00 | — |
| 1938-1939 Proof | — | Value: 245 | | | | |

**50 REICHSPFENNIG** **KM# 96** **Composition:** Aluminum

| Date | Mintage | F | VF | XF | Unc | BU |
|---|---|---|---|---|---|---|
| 1939A | 5,000,000 | 0.35 | 2.50 | 5.00 | 25.00 | — |
| 1939B | 5,482,000 | 0.35 | 2.50 | 5.00 | 35.00 | — |
| 1939D | 600,000 | 2.50 | 12.50 | 25.00 | 100 | — |
| 1939E | 2,000,000 | 0.50 | 5.00 | 7.50 | 50.00 | — |
| 1939F | 3,600,000 | 0.35 | 3.00 | 6.00 | 35.00 | — |
| 1939G | 560,000 | 10.00 | 20.00 | 75.00 | 140 | — |
| 1939J | 1,000,000 | 2.50 | 10.00 | 15.00 | 60.00 | — |
| 1940A | 56,128,000 | 0.15 | 0.50 | 2.50 | 25.00 | — |
| 1940B | 10,016,000 | 0.35 | 3.00 | 5.00 | 35.00 | — |
| 1940D | 13,800,000 | 0.25 | 1.50 | 3.00 | 75.00 | — |
| 1940E | 5,618,000 | 1.50 | 10.00 | 15.00 | 90.00 | — |
| 1940F | 6,663,000 | 0.25 | 1.50 | 3.00 | 35.00 | — |
| 1940G | 5,616,000 | 1.50 | 9.00 | 12.50 | 90.00 | — |
| 1940J | 7,335,000 | 2.00 | 12.50 | 17.50 | 90.00 | — |
| 1941A | 31,263,000 | 0.25 | 1.50 | 3.00 | 60.00 | — |
| 1941B | 4,291,000 | 2.00 | 5.00 | 7.00 | 75.00 | — |
| 1941D | 7,200,000 | 0.35 | 3.00 | 5.00 | 50.00 | — |
| 1941E | 3,806,000 | 0.50 | 4.00 | 7.50 | 50.00 | — |
| 1941F | 5,128,000 | 0.30 | 2.00 | 5.00 | 60.00 | — |
| 1941G | 3,091,000 | 2.50 | 4.00 | 7.50 | 110 | — |
| 1941J | 4,165,000 | 1.00 | 6.00 | 8.00 | 60.00 | — |
| 1942A | 11,580,000 | 0.15 | 0.50 | 2.50 | 25.00 | — |
| 1942B | 2,876,000 | 3.50 | 15.00 | 25.00 | 45.00 | — |
| 1942D | 2,247,000 | 0.35 | 3.00 | 6.00 | 20.00 | — |
| 1942E | 3,810,000 | 2.50 | 5.00 | 7.50 | 40.00 | — |
| 1942F | 5,133,000 | 1.00 | 3.50 | 5.00 | 35.00 | — |
| 1942G | 1,400,000 | 2.50 | 5.00 | 10.00 | 110 | — |
| 1943A | 29,325,000 | 0.15 | 0.50 | 2.50 | 25.00 | — |
| 1943B | 8,229,000 | 0.50 | 4.50 | 7.50 | 20.00 | — |
| 1943D | 5,315,000 | 0.20 | 1.00 | 3.50 | 20.00 | — |
| 1943G | 2,892,000 | 1.25 | 7.50 | 12.50 | 60.00 | — |
| 1943J | 4,166,000 | 5.00 | 10.00 | 15.00 | 45.00 | — |
| 1944B | 5,622,000 | 1.00 | 7.50 | 10.00 | 35.00 | — |
| 1944D | 4,886,000 | 7.50 | 15.00 | 25.00 | 110 | — |
| 1944F | 3,739,000 | 1.25 | 7.50 | 10.00 | 90.00 | — |
| 1944G | 1,190,000 | 55.00 | 90.00 | 150 | 250 | — |
| 1940-1944 Proof | — | Value: 250 | | | | |

**REICHSMARK** **KM# 78** **Composition:** Nickel

| Date | Mintage | F | VF | XF | Unc | BU |
|---|---|---|---|---|---|---|
| 1933A | 6,030,000 | 0.75 | 2.50 | 7.50 | 20.00 | — |
| 1933D | 4,562,000 | 1.00 | 3.00 | 9.00 | 20.00 | — |
| 1933E | 3,500,000 | 2.50 | 7.50 | 12.50 | 20.00 | — |
| 1933F | 1,400,000 | 4.00 | 8.50 | 15.00 | 20.00 | — |
| 1933G | 2,000,000 | 2.50 | 7.50 | 15.00 | 20.00 | — |
| 1934A | 52,345,000 | 0.50 | 1.50 | 2.50 | 10.00 | — |
| 1934D | 30,597,000 | 0.50 | 1.50 | 2.50 | 10.00 | — |
| 1934E | 15,135,000 | 1.00 | 3.00 | 7.00 | 15.00 | — |
| 1934F | 23,672,000 | 0.75 | 2.50 | 5.00 | 12.50 | — |
| 1934G | 13,252,000 | 1.50 | 5.00 | 10.00 | 18.00 | — |
| 1934J | 16,820,000 | 1.00 | 3.50 | 7.50 | 15.00 | — |
| 1935A | 57,896,000 | 0.75 | 2.50 | 5.00 | 12.50 | — |
| 1935J | 3,621,000 | 2.50 | 7.50 | 20.00 | 40.00 | — |
| 1936A | 20,287,000 | 1.25 | 4.00 | 7.00 | 12.50 | — |
| 1936D | 4,940,000 | 2.50 | 7.50 | 15.00 | 27.50 | — |
| 1936E | 3,200,000 | 2.50 | 10.00 | 25.00 | 35.00 | — |
| 1936F | 2,075,000 | 25.00 | 40.00 | 70.00 | 100 | — |
| 1936G | 620,000 | 50.00 | 120 | 150 | 225 | — |
| 1936J | 2,975,000 | 2.50 | 7.50 | 12.50 | 60.00 | — |
| 1937A | 49,976,000 | 0.50 | 1.50 | 2.50 | 8.00 | — |
| 1937D | 10,529,000 | 1.00 | 3.00 | 6.00 | 12.00 | — |
| 1937E | 2,926,000 | 3.00 | 15.00 | 30.00 | 50.00 | — |
| 1937F | 6,221,000 | 2.50 | 6.00 | 12.00 | 50.00 | — |
| 1937G | 2,143,000 | 2.50 | 10.00 | 17.50 | 40.00 | — |
| 1937J | 4,721,000 | 2.50 | 10.00 | 17.50 | 60.00 | — |
| 1938A | 9,829,000 | 1.25 | 4.00 | 10.00 | 30.00 | — |
| 1938E | 2,073,000 | 4.00 | 17.50 | 25.00 | 80.00 | — |
| 1938F | 2,739,000 | 5.00 | 17.50 | 22.50 | 80.00 | — |
| 1938G | 4,381,000 | 10.00 | 20.00 | 35.00 | 90.00 | — |
| 1938J | 1,269,000 | 27.50 | 70.00 | 90.00 | 150 | — |
| 1939A | 52,150,000 | 5.00 | 12.50 | 15.00 | 35.00 | — |
| 1939B | 9,836,000 | 50.00 | 125 | 160 | 250 | — |
| 1939D | 12,522,000 | 9.00 | 22.50 | 37.50 | 75.00 | — |
| 1939E | 6,570,000 | 20.00 | 35.00 | 80.00 | 120 | — |
| 1939F | 10,033,000 | 10.00 | 20.00 | 40.00 | 100 | — |
| 1939G | 5,475,000 | 60.00 | 130 | 200 | 350 | — |
| 1939J | 8,478,000 | 15.00 | 35.00 | 60.00 | 100 | — |
| 1933-1939 Proof | — | Value: 225 | | | | |

**2 REICHSMARK** **KM# 79** **Weight:** 8.0000 g. **Composition:** 0.6250 Silver .1607 oz. ASW **Subject:** 450th anniversary - birth of Martin Luther

| Date | Mintage | F | VF | XF | Unc | BU |
|---|---|---|---|---|---|---|
| 1933A | 542,000 | 9.00 | 22.50 | 30.00 | 50.00 | — |
| 1933A Proof | — | Value: 200 | | | | |
| 1933D | 141,000 | 10.00 | 25.00 | 32.00 | 60.00 | — |
| 1933D Proof | — | Value: 200 | | | | |
| 1933E | 75,000 | 12.50 | 30.00 | 40.00 | 60.00 | — |
| 1933E Proof | — | Value: 250 | | | | |
| 1933F | 100,000 | 10.00 | 25.00 | 35.00 | 60.00 | — |
| 1933F Proof | — | Value: 250 | | | | |
| 1933G | 61,000 | 14.00 | 30.00 | 42.00 | 75.00 | — |
| 1933G Proof | — | Value: 250 | | | | |
| 1933J | 82,000 | 10.00 | 25.00 | 40.00 | 70.00 | — |
| 1933J Proof | — | Value: 235 | | | | |

**2 REICHSMARK** **KM# 81** **Weight:** 8.0000 g. **Composition:** 0.6250 Silver .1607 oz. ASW **Subject:** 1st anniversary - Nazi rule **Reverse:** Potsdam Garrison Church

| Date | Mintage | F | VF | XF | Unc | BU |
|---|---|---|---|---|---|---|
| 1934A | 2,710,000 | 4.50 | 10.00 | 22.00 | 50.00 | — |
| 1934A Proof | — | Value: 200 | | | | |
| 1934D | 703,000 | 5.50 | 12.00 | 30.00 | 70.00 | — |
| 1934D Proof | — | Value: 200 | | | | |
| 1934E | 373,000 | 7.50 | 16.50 | 40.00 | 90.00 | — |
| 1934E Proof | — | Value: 200 | | | | |
| 1934F | 502,000 | 6.00 | 12.00 | 32.50 | 75.00 | — |
| 1934F Proof | — | Value: 200 | | | | |
| 1934G | 305,000 | 7.00 | 15.00 | 50.00 | 115 | — |
| 1934G Proof | — | Value: 200 | | | | |
| 1934J | 409,000 | 7.00 | 15.00 | 40.00 | 100 | — |
| 1934J Proof | — | Value: 200 | | | | |

**2 REICHSMARK** **KM# 84** **Weight:** 8.0000 g. **Composition:** 0.6250 Silver .1607 oz. ASW **Subject:** 175th anniversary - birth of Schiller

| Date | Mintage | F | VF | XF | Unc | BU |
|---|---|---|---|---|---|---|
| 1934F | 300,000 | 25.00 | 60.00 | 80.00 | 120 | — |
| 1934F Proof | — | Value: 225 | | | | |

**2 REICHSMARK** **KM# 93** **Weight:** 8.0000 g. **Composition:** 0.6250 Silver .1607 oz. ASW **Subject:** Swastika-Hindenburg issue

| Date | Mintage | F | VF | XF | Unc | BU |
|---|---|---|---|---|---|---|
| 1936D | 840,000 | 3.00 | 6.00 | 20.00 | 35.00 | — |
| 1936E | | 8.00 | 30.00 | 50.00 | 100 | — |
| 1936G | | 6.00 | 20.00 | 30.00 | 50.00 | — |
| 1936J | | 20.00 | 60.00 | 120 | 275 | — |
| 1937A | 23,425,000 | 2.50 | 3.50 | 5.00 | 10.00 | — |
| 1937D | 6,190,000 | 2.50 | 3.50 | 5.00 | 10.00 | — |
| 1937E | 3,725,000 | 2.50 | 3.50 | 5.00 | 10.00 | — |
| 1937F | 5,015,000 | 2.50 | 3.50 | 5.00 | 10.00 | — |
| 1937G | 1,913,000 | 2.50 | 3.50 | 5.00 | 10.00 | — |
| 1937J | 2,756,000 | 2.50 | 3.50 | 5.00 | 12.00 | — |
| 1938A | 13,201,000 | 2.50 | 3.50 | 5.00 | 10.00 | — |
| 1938B | 13,163,000 | 2.50 | 3.50 | 5.00 | 10.00 | — |
| 1938D | 3,711,000 | 2.50 | 3.50 | 5.00 | 10.00 | — |
| 1938E | 4,731,000 | 2.50 | 3.50 | 5.00 | 10.00 | — |
| 1938F | 1,882,000 | 3.00 | 4.00 | 6.00 | 12.50 | — |
| 1938G | 2,313,000 | 2.50 | 3.50 | 5.00 | 10.00 | — |
| 1938J | 2,306,000 | 3.00 | 4.00 | 5.00 | 10.00 | — |
| 1939A | 26,855,000 | 2.50 | 3.50 | 5.00 | 10.00 | — |
| 1939B | 3,522,000 | 2.50 | 3.50 | 5.00 | 10.00 | — |
| 1939D | 5,357,000 | 2.50 | 3.50 | 5.00 | 10.00 | — |
| 1939E | 251,000 | 12.50 | 30.00 | 40.00 | 75.00 | — |
| 1939F | 3,180,000 | 2.50 | 3.50 | 5.00 | 10.00 | — |
| 1939G | 2,305,000 | 2.50 | 3.50 | 7.50 | 10.00 | — |
| 1939J | 3,414,000 | 2.50 | 3.50 | 7.50 | 10.00 | — |
| 1936-1939 Proof | — | Value: 185 | | | | |

**5 REICHSMARK** **KM# 80** **Weight:** 13.8800 g. **Composition:** 0.9000 Silver .4016 oz. ASW **Subject:** 450th anniversary - birth of Martin Luther

| Date | Mintage | F | VF | XF | Unc | BU |
|---|---|---|---|---|---|---|
| 1933A | 108,000 | 50.00 | 100 | 150 | 250 | — |
| 1933A Proof | — | Value: 350 | | | | |
| 1933D | 28,000 | 60.00 | 125 | 185 | 300 | — |
| 1933D Proof | — | Value: 400 | | | | |
| 1933E | 12,000 | 70.00 | 145 | 200 | 300 | — |
| 1933F Proof | — | Value: 485 | | | | |
| 1933F | 20,000 | 60.00 | 125 | 150 | 250 | — |
| 1933F Proof | — | Value: 400 | | | | |
| 1933G | 12,000 | 100 | 175 | 250 | 350 | — |
| 1933G Proof | — | Value: 485 | | | | |
| 1933J | 16,000 | 75.00 | 145 | 200 | 300 | — |
| 1933J Proof | — | Value: 400 | | | | |

**5 REICHSMARK** **KM# 82** **Weight:** 13.8800 g. **Composition:** 0.9000 Silver .4016 oz. ASW **Subject:** 1st anniversary - Nazi rule **Reverse:** Potsdam Garrison Church

| Date | Mintage | F | VF | XF | Unc | BU |
|---|---|---|---|---|---|---|
| 1934A | 2,168,000 | 7.50 | 11.50 | 32.00 | 100 | — |
| 1934D | 562,000 | 7.50 | 11.50 | 32.00 | 120 | — |
| 1934E | 298,000 | 10.00 | 18.00 | 50.00 | 165 | — |
| 1934F | 401,000 | 8.00 | 14.00 | 45.00 | 125 | — |
| 1934G | 244,000 | 10.00 | 18.00 | 50.00 | 165 | — |
| 1934J | 327,000 | 9.00 | 18.00 | 45.00 | 140 | — |
| 1934 Proof | — | Value: 300 | | | | |

**Note:** Impaired proofs are common and valued around $200.

**5 REICHSMARK** **KM# 83** **Weight:** 13.8800 g. **Composition:** 0.9000 Silver .4016 oz. ASW **Subject:** 1st anniversary - Nazi rule **Reverse:** Potsdam Garrison Church, date 21 MARZ 1933 dropped

| Date | Mintage | F | VF | XF | Unc | BU |
|---|---|---|---|---|---|---|
| 1934A | 14,526,000 | 4.00 | 6.00 | 12.00 | 35.00 | — |
| 1934D | 6,303,000 | 4.00 | 6.00 | 15.00 | 50.00 | — |
| 1934E | 2,739,000 | 5.00 | 7.50 | 17.50 | 65.00 | — |
| 1934F | 4,844,000 | 4.00 | 6.00 | 15.00 | 50.00 | — |
| 1934G | 2,304,000 | 5.00 | 7.50 | 17.50 | 65.00 | — |
| 1934J | 4,294,000 | 4.00 | 6.00 | 15.00 | 50.00 | — |
| 1935A | 23,407,000 | 3.00 | 5.00 | 10.00 | 30.00 | — |
| 1935D | 3,539,000 | 4.00 | 6.00 | 15.00 | 50.00 | — |
| 1935E | 2,476,000 | 5.00 | 7.50 | 17.50 | 65.00 | — |
| 1935F | 2,177,000 | 5.00 | 7.50 | 17.50 | 75.00 | — |
| 1935G | 1,966,000 | 5.00 | 7.50 | 17.50 | 75.00 | — |
| 1935J | 1,425,000 | 6.00 | 10.00 | 25.00 | 110 | — |
| 1934-1935 Proof | — | Value: 250 | | | | |

**5 REICHSMARK** **KM# 85** **Weight:** 13.8800 g. **Composition:** 0.9000 Silver .4016 oz. ASW **Subject:** 175th anniversary - birth of Schiller

| Date | Mintage | F | VF | XF | Unc | BU |
|---|---|---|---|---|---|---|
| 1934F | 100,000 | 110 | 225 | 300 | 450 | — |
| 1934F Proof | — | Value: 700 | | | | |

**5 REICHSMARK** **KM# 86** **Weight:** 13.8800 g. **Composition:** 0.9000 Silver .4016 oz. ASW **Subject:** Hindenburg issue

| Date | Mintage | F | VF | XF | Unc | BU |
|---|---|---|---|---|---|---|
| 1935A | 19,325,000 | 3.00 | 6.00 | 10.00 | 25.00 | — |
| 1935D | 6,596,000 | 3.00 | 6.00 | 10.00 | 25.00 | — |
| 1935E | 3,260,000 | 4.00 | 6.50 | 12.50 | 30.00 | — |
| 1935F | 4,372,000 | 3.00 | 6.00 | 10.00 | 27.50 | — |
| 1935G | 2,371,000 | 3.00 | 6.00 | 12.50 | 32.50 | — |
| 1935J | 2,830,000 | 3.00 | 6.00 | 12.50 | 32.50 | — |
| 1936A | 30,611,000 | 3.00 | 6.00 | 10.00 | 16.00 | — |
| 1936D | 7,032,000 | 3.00 | 6.00 | 10.00 | 18.00 | — |
| 1936E | 3,320,000 | 3.00 | 6.00 | 12.50 | 27.50 | — |
| 1936F | 4,926,000 | 3.00 | 6.00 | 12.50 | 27.50 | — |
| 1936G | 2,734,000 | 3.00 | 6.00 | 12.50 | 30.00 | — |
| 1936J | 3,706,000 | 3.00 | 6.00 | 12.50 | 30.00 | — |
| 1935-1936 Proof | — | Value: 200 | | | | |

**5 REICHSMARK** **KM# 94** **Weight:** 13.8800 g. **Composition:** 0.9000 Silver .4016 oz. ASW **Subject:** Swastika-Hindenburg issue

| Date | Mintage | F | VF | XF | Unc | BU |
|---|---|---|---|---|---|---|
| 1936A | 8,430,000 | 3.00 | 6.00 | 10.00 | 17.50 | — |
| 1936D | 1,872,000 | 3.00 | 7.00 | 15.00 | 27.50 | — |
| 1936E | 870,000 | 5.00 | 8.00 | 17.50 | 30.00 | — |
| 1936F | 1,732,000 | 3.00 | 7.00 | 15.00 | 27.50 | — |
| 1936G | 743,000 | 5.00 | 8.50 | 20.00 | 35.00 | — |
| 1936J | 640,000 | 8.00 | 20.00 | 30.00 | 75.00 | — |
| 1937A | 6,662,000 | 3.00 | 6.00 | 10.00 | 20.00 | — |
| 1937D | 2,173,000 | 3.00 | 6.00 | 10.00 | 15.00 | — |
| 1937E | 1,490,000 | 5.00 | 8.00 | 15.00 | 27.50 | — |
| 1937F | 1,578,000 | 4.00 | 7.50 | 15.00 | 27.50 | — |
| 1937G | 1,472,000 | 5.00 | 8.00 | 15.00 | 27.50 | — |
| 1937J | 2,191,000 | 3.00 | 6.00 | 12.50 | 25.00 | — |
| 1938A | 6,789,000 | 3.00 | 6.00 | 10.00 | 15.00 | — |
| 1938D | 1,304,000 | 3.00 | 6.00 | 12.50 | 17.50 | — |
| 1938E | 425,000 | 5.00 | 8.00 | 15.00 | 27.50 | — |
| 1938F | 740,000 | 3.50 | 6.50 | 12.50 | 22.50 | — |
| 1938G | 861,000 | 4.00 | 7.50 | 15.00 | 25.00 | — |
| 1938J | 1,302,000 | 3.50 | 6.50 | 12.50 | 20.00 | — |
| 1939A | 3,428,000 | 4.00 | 7.50 | 12.50 | 20.00 | — |
| 1939B | 1,942,000 | 5.00 | 8.00 | 15.00 | 25.00 | — |
| 1939D | 1,216,000 | 7.50 | 12.50 | 20.00 | 30.00 | — |
| 1939E | 1,320,000 | 15.00 | 20.00 | 40.00 | 80.00 | — |
| 1939F | 1,060,000 | 7.50 | 12.50 | 25.00 | 45.00 | — |
| 1939G | 567,000 | 12.50 | 18.00 | 35.00 | 75.00 | — |
| 1939J | 1,710,000 | 5.00 | 8.00 | 15.00 | 25.00 | — |
| 1936-1939 Proof | — | Value: 200 | | | | |

## MILITARY COINAGE

WWII

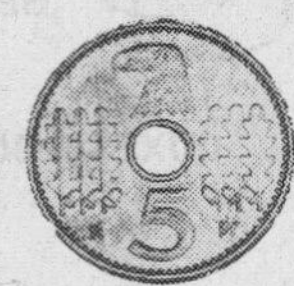

**5 REICHSPFENNIG** **KM# 98** **Composition:** Zinc **Note:** Circulated only in occupied territories.

| Date | Mintage | F | VF | XF | Unc | BU |
|---|---|---|---|---|---|---|
| 1940A | — | 10.00 | 15.00 | 22.50 | 35.00 | — |
| 1940B | 3,020,000 | 50.00 | 125 | 200 | 300 | — |
| 1940D | — | 17.50 | 45.00 | 60.00 | 100 | — |
| 1940E | 2,445,000 | 90.00 | 175 | 275 | 400 | — |
| 1940F | — | 125 | 250 | 350 | 500 | — |
| 1940G | — | — | 12,000 | — | — | — |
| 1940J | — | 90.00 | 200 | 300 | 450 | — |
| 1941A | — | 175 | 300 | 600 | 900 | — |
| 1941F | — | — | 11,000 | — | — | — |
| 1940-1941 Proof | — | Value: 750 | | | | |

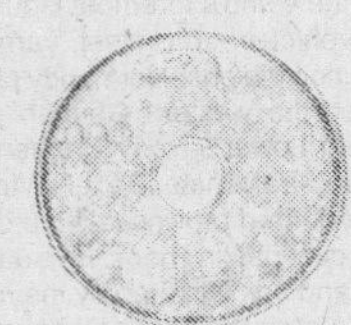

**10 REICHSPFENNIG** **KM# 99** **Composition:** Zinc **Note:** Circulated only in occupied territories.

| Date | Mintage | F | VF | XF | Unc | BU |
|---|---|---|---|---|---|---|
| 1940A | — | 8.00 | 14.00 | 22.50 | 35.00 | — |
| 1940B | 840,000 | 90.00 | 250 | 600 | 900 | — |
| 1940D | — | — | — | 10,000 | — | — |
| 1940E | 5,100,000 | — | — | 6,000 | — | — |
| 1940F | — | 200 | 400 | 1,500 | 2,250 | — |
| 1940G | 150,000 | 40.00 | 75.00 | 225 | 300 | — |
| 1940J | — | 350 | 1,000 | 1,300 | 2,000 | — |
| 1941A | — | 500 | 900 | 2,250 | 3,000 | — |
| 1941F 2 known | — | — | — | — | 14,500 | — |

# ALLIED OCCUPATION

## POST WW II COINAGE

**REICHSPFENNIG** **KM# A102** **Composition:** Zinc **Obverse:** Modified design, swastika and wreath removed **Reverse:** Eagle missing tail feathers

| Date | Mintage | F | VF | XF | Unc | BU |
|---|---|---|---|---|---|---|
| 1944D | — | — | — | 10,000 | — | — |

**Note:** Possibly a pattern

**REICHSPFENNIG** **KM# A103** **Composition:** Zinc

| Date | Mintage | F | VF | XF | Unc | BU |
|---|---|---|---|---|---|---|
| 1945F | 2,984,000 | 5.00 | 10.00 | 18.00 | 35.00 | — |
| 1946F | 1,633,000 | 15.00 | 35.00 | 80.00 | 130 | — |
| 1946G | 1,500,000 | 35.00 | 75.00 | 125 | 165 | — |
| 1945-1946 Proof | — | Value: 185 | | | | |

**5 REICHSPFENNIG** **KM# A105** **Composition:** Zinc

| Date | Mintage | F | VF | XF | Unc | BU |
|---|---|---|---|---|---|---|
| 1947A | — | 2.50 | 7.50 | 15.00 | 25.00 | — |
| 1947D | 16,528,000 | 2.50 | 4.50 | 6.50 | 20.00 | — |
| 1948A | — | 5.00 | 15.00 | 25.00 | 35.00 | — |
| 1948E | 7,666,000 | 150 | 300 | 425 | 750 | — |

**10 REICHSPFENNIG** **KM# A104** **Composition:** Zinc

| Date | Mintage | F | VF | XF | Unc | BU |
|---|---|---|---|---|---|---|
| 1945F | 5,942,000 | 4.50 | 7.50 | 15.00 | 25.00 | — |
| 1946F | 3,738,000 | 10.00 | 20.00 | 30.00 | 100 | — |
| 1946G | 1,600,000 | 35.00 | 65.00 | 100 | 175 | — |
| 1947A | — | 4.50 | 10.00 | 20.00 | 30.00 | — |
| 1947E | 2,612,000 | 200 | 400 | 650 | 950 | — |
| 1947F | 1,269,000 | 1.50 | 3.50 | 8.00 | 17.50 | — |
| 1948A | — | 5.00 | 20.00 | 25.00 | 35.00 | — |
| 1948F | 19,579,000 | 1.50 | 3.50 | 8.00 | 15.00 | — |
| 1946-1948 Proof | — | Value: 180 | | | | |

## PATTERNS

Including off metal strikes

| KM# | Date | Mintage | Identification | Mkt Val |
|---|---|---|---|---|
| Pn354 | 1933 | — | Mark. Nickel. Legend above eagle. PROBE. | 250 |
| Pn355 | 1933 | — | Mark. Nickel. "PROBE." | 250 |
| Pn356 | 1933 | — | Mark. Nickel. Rays above eagle. | 250 |
| Pn357 | 1933 | — | Mark. Nickel. Plain above eagle. | 250 |
| Pn358 | 1933 | — | Mark. Nickel. Large 1 with rays. "PROBE." | 250 |
| Pn359 | 1933 | — | Mark. Nickel. "PROBE." | 250 |
| Pn360 | 1933 | — | Mark. Nickel. KM78. | 250 |
| PnA361 | 1933/6 | — | 5 Mark. Copper-Nickel. Martin Luther. Eagle. KM94. | — |
| Pn361 | 1934 | — | 2 Mark. KM79. KM81. | — |
| Pn362 | 1934 | — | 2 Mark. Silver. KM84. | — |
| Pn363 | | — | 5 Mark. Similar to Pn351 edge. KM80. | — |
| Pn364 | 1934 | — | 5 Mark. Silver. KM85. "PROBE". | — |
| Pn365 | 1934 | — | 5 Pfennig. Brass. KM91. | — |
| Pn366 | 1934 | — | 5 Pfennig. Aluminum-Bronze. KM91.1. "PROBE." | — |
| Pn367 | 1935 | — | 50 Pfennig. Aluminum. | — |
| Pn370 | 1935 | — | 5 Mark. Silver. "PROBE." | — |
| Pn371 | 1935 | — | 5 Mark. Silver. "PROBE." | — |
| Pn368 | 1935 | — | 50 Pfennig. Oak leaves next to date. "PROBE". Wavy edge. | — |
| Pn369 | 1935 | — | Mark. KM78. | — |
| Pn372 | 1935 | — | 5 Mark. Silver. Masses entering. "PROBE." | — |
| Pn373 | 1935 | — | 5 Mark. 0.9000 Silver. Family entering. "PROBE." | — |
| Pn374 | 1935 | — | 5 Mark. Electrotype. | — |
| Pn375 | 1936 | — | Pfennig. Copper Plated Iron. KM89. | — |
| PnA375 | 1936 | — | Reichspfennig. Copper Plated Iron. KM30. | — |
| Pn376 | 1937 | — | 5 Pfennig. Iron. KM91. Hindenburg. | — |
| Pn377 | 1937 | — | 50 Pfennig. Nickel. KM95. "PROBE." | — |
| Pn378 | 1939 | — | 5 Pfennig. KM100. | — |
| Pn379 | 1939 | — | Mark. Nickel. "PROBE" on rim. | — |
| Pn380 | 1939 | — | Mark. Pn379. Pn381. | — |
| Pn381 | 1939 | — | Mark. | 225 |
| Pn382 | 1939 | — | Mark. Aluminum. KM78. Pn381. | — |
| Pn383 | 1939/1940 | — | Mark. Iron. "PROBE." Copper-nickel plated. | 200 |
| Pn384 | 1940 | — | Mark. Silver. | 400 |
| Pn385 | 1942 | — | 5 Mark. Silvered Copper. Eagle. | — |
| Pn386 | 1942 | — | 5 Reichspfennig. Copper. Klippe. | — |
| Pn388 | 1942 | — | 5 Mark. Silvered Copper. Steel helmet in laurel wreath. | — |
| Pn387 | 1942 | — | 5 Reichsmark. Silver. Klippe. | 6,500 |
| PnB390 | 1946 | — | 10 Pfennig. Brass. | 900 |
| PnA389 | 1946 | — | Pfennig. Aluminum. | — |
| Pn390 | 1947 | — | 50 Pfennig. Aluminum. | — |
| Pn391 | 1947 | — | 5 Pfennig. Aluminum. | — |
| Pn394 | 1947 | — | 10 Pfennig. Aluminum. | — |
| pnc389 | 1947 | — | 5 Pfennig. Aluminum. reeded edge. | — |
| pnc390 | 1947 | — | 10 Pfennig. Dur-Aluminum. | — |

| KM# | Date | Mintage | Identification | Mkt Val |
|---|---|---|---|---|
| pnb389 | 1947 | — | 5 Pfennig. Zinc. without swastika. KM100. | 3,350 |
| pnd389 | 1947 | — | 10 Pfennig. Zinc. with slavic 7. KM104 | 6,000 |
| Pn389 | 1947 | — | 10 Pfennig. Zinc. Without swastika. KM101. | 3,350 |
| Pn395 | 1947 | — | 10 Pfennig. Iron. Copper-nickel plated. | — |
| Pn392 | 1947 | — | 5 Pfennig. Brass Plated Aluminum. | — |
| Pn393 | 1947 | — | 5 Pfennig. Copper-Nickel Plated Iron. Copper-nickel plated. | — |
| PnA390 | 1947 | — | 10 Pfennig. Aluminum. Plain edge. | — |
| Pn396 | 1948 | — | 10 Pfennig. Zinc. | — |

# GERMANY-FEDERAL REPUBLIC

The Federal Republic of Germany, located in north-central Europe, has an area of 137,744 sq. mi. (356,910sq. km.) and a population of 81.1 million. Capital: Berlin. The economy centers about one of the world's foremost industrial establishments. Machinery, motor vehicles, iron, steel, yarns and fabrics are exported.

During the post-Normandy phase of World War II, Allied troops occupied the western German provinces of Schleswig-Holstein, Hamburg, Lower Saxony, Bremen, North Rhine-Westphalia, Hesse, Rhineland-Palatinate, Baden-Wurttemberg, Bavaria and Saarland. The conquered provinces were divided into American, British and French occupation zones. Five eastern German provinces were occupied and administered by the forces of the Soviet Union.

The post-World War II division of Germany was ended Oct. 3, 1990, when the German Democratic Republic (East Germany) ceased to exist and its five constituent provinces were formally admitted to the Federal Republic of Germany. An election Dec. 2, 1990, chose representatives to the united federal parliament (Bundestag), which then conducted its opening session in Berlin in the old Reichstag building. Though Berlin technically is the capital of a united Germany, the actual seat of government remains for the time being in Bonn.

**MINT MARKS**

A - Berlin
D - Munich
F - Stuttgart
G - Karlsruhe
J - Hamburg

**MONETARY SYSTEM**

100 Pfennig = 1 Deutsche Mark (DM)

## FEDERAL REPUBLIC
### STANDARD COINAGE

**PFENNIG** **KM# A101** **Composition:** Bronze-Clad Steel
**Note:** Currency reform.

| Date | Mintage | F | VF | XF | Unc | BU |
|---|---|---|---|---|---|---|
| 1948D | 46,325,000 | — | 0.50 | 15.00 | 40.00 | — |
| 1948F | 68,203,000 | — | 0.50 | 8.00 | 32.50 | — |
| 1948F Prof | 250 | Value: 150 | | | | |
| 1948G | 45,604,000 | — | 0.50 | 15.00 | 60.00 | — |
| 1948J | 79,304,000 | — | 0.50 | 15.00 | 50.00 | — |
| 1949D | 99,863,000 | — | 0.50 | 6.00 | 27.50 | — |
| 1949D Proof | — | Value: 100 | | | | |
| 1949F | 70,900,000 | — | 0.50 | 6.00 | 22.50 | — |
| 1949F Proof | 250 | Value: 60.00 | | | | |
| 1949G | 50,500,000 | — | 0.50 | 10.00 | 40.00 | — |
| 1949J | 101,932,000 | — | 0.50 | 6.00 | 27.50 | — |
| 1949J Proof | — | Value: 85.00 | | | | |

**PFENNIG** **KM# 105** **Composition:** Copper Plated Steel
**Note:** Federal Republic.

| Date | Mintage | F | VF | XF | Unc | BU |
|---|---|---|---|---|---|---|
| 1950D | 772,592,000 | — | — | 0.10 | 1.00 | — |
| 1950F | 898,277,000 | — | — | 0.10 | 1.00 | — |
| 1950F Proof | 620 | Value: 27.50 | | | | |
| 1950G | 515,673,000 | — | — | 0.10 | 1.00 | — |
| 1950G Proof | 1,800 | Value: 5.00 | | | | |
| 1950J | 784,424,000 | — | — | 0.10 | 1.00 | — |
| 1950J Proof | — | Value: 12.00 | | | | |
| 1966D | 65,063,000 | — | — | 0.10 | 2.00 | — |
| 1966F | 75,031,000 | — | — | 0.10 | 2.00 | — |
| 1966F Proof | 100 | Value: 35.00 | | | | |
| 1966G | 48,261,000 | — | — | 0.10 | 2.00 | — |
| 1966G Proof | 3,070 | Value: 4.00 | | | | |
| 1966J | 66,842,000 | — | — | 0.10 | 3.00 | — |
| 1966J Proof | 1,000 | Value: 8.00 | | | | |
| 1967D | 39,082,000 | — | — | 0.10 | 3.00 | — |
| 1967F | 45,003,000 | — | — | 0.10 | 3.00 | — |
| 1967F Proof | 1,500 | Value: 6.00 | | | | |
| 1967G | 20,787,000 | — | — | 0.10 | 3.00 | — |
| 1967G Proof | 4,500 | Value: 3.50 | | | | |
| 1967J | 42,583,000 | — | — | 0.10 | 4.00 | — |
| 1967J Proof | 1,500 | Value: 8.00 | | | | |
| 1968D | 32,796,999 | — | — | 0.10 | 1.00 | — |
| 1968F | 26,338,000 | — | — | 0.10 | 1.00 | — |
| 1968F Proof | 3,000 | Value: 5.00 | | | | |
| 1968G | 20,382,000 | — | — | 0.10 | 1.00 | — |
| 1968G Proof | 6,023 | Value: 4.00 | | | | |
| 1968J | 23,414,000 | — | — | 0.25 | 1.00 | — |
| 1968J Proof | 2,000 | Value: 6.50 | | | | |
| 1969D | 78,177,000 | — | — | 0.10 | 0.50 | — |
| 1969F | 90,172,000 | — | — | 0.10 | 0.50 | — |
| 1969F Proof | 5,100 | Value: 1.50 | | | | |
| 1969G | 61,836,000 | — | — | 0.10 | 0.50 | — |
| 1969G Proof | 8,700 | Value: 1.25 | | | | |
| 1969J | 80,221,000 | — | — | 0.10 | 0.50 | — |
| 1969J Proof | 5,000 | Value: 1.50 | | | | |
| 1970D | 91,151,000 | — | — | 0.10 | 0.25 | — |
| 1970F | 105,236,000 | — | — | 0.10 | 0.25 | — |
| 1970F Proof | 5,240 | Value: 1.50 | | | | |
| 1970G | 82,421,000 | — | — | 0.10 | 0.25 | — |
| 1970G Proof | 10,200 | Value: 1.00 | | | | |
| 1970 Small J | 93,455,000 | — | — | 0.10 | 0.25 | — |
| 1970 Large J | Inc. above | — | — | 0.10 | 0.25 | — |
| 1970J Proof | 5,000 | Value: 1.50 | | | | |
| 1971D | 116,612,000 | — | — | 0.10 | 0.25 | — |
| 1971D Proof | 8,000 | Value: 1.00 | | | | |
| 1971F | 157,393,000 | — | — | 0.10 | 0.25 | — |

| Date | Mintage | F | VF | XF | Unc | BU |
|---|---|---|---|---|---|---|
| 1971F Proof | 8,000 | Value: 1.00 | | | | |
| 1971G | 77,674,000 | — | — | 0.10 | 0.25 | — |
| 1971G Proof | 10,200 | Value: 1.00 | | | | |
| 1971J | 120,218,000 | — | — | 0.10 | 0.25 | — |
| 1971J Proof | 8,000 | Value: 1.00 | | | | |
| 1972D | 90,696,000 | — | — | 0.10 | 0.25 | — |
| 1972D Proof | 8,000 | Value: 1.00 | | | | |
| 1972F | 105,006,000 | — | — | 0.10 | 0.25 | — |
| 1972F Proof | 8,000 | Value: 1.00 | | | | |
| 1972G | 60,660,000 | — | — | 0.10 | 0.25 | — |
| 1972G Proof | 10,000 | Value: 1.00 | | | | |
| 1972J | 93,492,000 | — | — | 0.10 | 0.25 | — |
| 1972J Proof | 8,000 | Value: 1.00 | | | | |
| 1973D | 38,976,000 | — | — | 0.10 | 0.25 | — |
| 1973D Proof | 9,000 | Value: 1.00 | | | | |
| 1973F | 45,006,000 | — | — | 0.10 | 0.25 | — |
| 1973F Proof | 9,000 | Value: 1.00 | | | | |
| 1973G | 25,811,000 | — | — | 0.10 | 0.25 | — |
| 1973G Proof | 9,000 | Value: 1.00 | | | | |
| 1973J | 40,057,000 | — | — | 0.10 | 0.25 | — |
| 1973J Proof | 9,000 | Value: 1.00 | | | | |
| 1974D | 90,951,000 | — | — | 0.10 | 0.25 | — |
| 1974D Proof | 35,000 | Value: 0.40 | | | | |
| 1974F | 105,091,000 | — | — | 0.10 | 0.25 | — |
| 1974F Proof | 35,000 | Value: 0.40 | | | | |
| 1974G | 60,548,000 | — | — | 0.10 | 0.25 | — |
| 1974G Proof | 35,000 | Value: 0.40 | | | | |
| 1974J | 93,527,000 | — | — | 0.10 | 0.25 | — |
| 1974J Proof | 35,000 | Value: 0.40 | | | | |
| 1975D | 91,053,000 | — | — | 0.10 | 0.25 | — |
| 1975D Proof | 43,000 | Value: 0.40 | | | | |
| 1975F | 105,007,000 | — | — | 0.10 | 0.25 | — |
| 1975F Proof | 43,000 | Value: 0.40 | | | | |
| 1975G | 60,704,000 | — | — | 0.10 | 0.25 | — |
| 1975G Proof | 43,000 | Value: 0.40 | | | | |
| 1975J | 93,495,000 | — | — | 0.10 | 0.25 | — |
| 1975J Proof | 43,000 | Value: 0.40 | | | | |
| 1976D | 130,227,000 | — | — | 0.10 | 0.25 | — |
| 1976D Proof | 43,000 | Value: 0.40 | | | | |
| 1976F | 150,037,000 | — | — | 0.10 | 0.25 | — |
| 1976F Proof | 43,000 | Value: 0.40 | | | | |
| 1976G | 86,586,000 | — | — | 0.10 | 0.25 | — |
| 1976G Proof | 43,000 | Value: 0.40 | | | | |
| 1976J | 133,500,000 | — | — | 0.10 | 0.25 | — |
| 1976J Proof | 43,000 | Value: 0.40 | | | | |
| 1977D | 143,000,000 | — | — | 0.10 | 0.25 | — |
| 1977D Proof | 52,000 | Value: 0.40 | | | | |
| 1977F | 165,000,000 | — | — | 0.10 | 0.25 | — |
| 1977F Proof | 51,000 | Value: 0.40 | | | | |
| 1977G | 95,201,000 | — | — | 0.10 | 0.25 | — |
| 1977G Proof | 51,000 | Value: 0.40 | | | | |
| 1977J | 146,788,000 | — | — | 0.10 | 0.25 | — |
| 1977J Proof | 51,000 | Value: 0.40 | | | | |
| 1978D | 156,000,000 | — | — | 0.10 | 0.25 | — |
| 1978D Proof | 54,000 | Value: 0.40 | | | | |
| 1978F | 180,000,000 | — | — | 0.10 | 0.25 | — |
| 1978F Proof | 54,000 | Value: 0.40 | | | | |
| 1978G | 103,800,000 | — | — | 0.10 | 0.25 | — |
| 1978G Proof | 54,000 | Value: 0.40 | | | | |
| 1978J | 160,200,000 | — | — | 0.10 | 0.25 | — |
| 1978J Proof | 54,000 | Value: 0.40 | | | | |
| 1979D | 156,000,000 | — | — | 0.10 | 0.25 | — |
| 1979D Proof | 89,000 | Value: 0.40 | | | | |
| 1979F | 180,000,000 | — | — | 0.10 | 0.25 | — |
| 1979F Proof | 89,000 | Value: 0.40 | | | | |
| 1979G | 103,800,000 | — | — | 0.10 | 0.25 | — |
| 1979G Proof | 89,000 | Value: 0.40 | | | | |
| 1979J | 160,200,000 | — | — | 0.10 | 0.25 | — |
| 1979J Proof | 89,000 | Value: 0.40 | | | | |
| 1980D | 200,080,000 | — | — | 0.10 | 0.25 | — |
| 1980D Proof | 110,000 | Value: 0.40 | | | | |
| 1980F | 200,620,000 | — | — | 0.10 | 0.25 | — |
| 1980F Proof | 110,000 | Value: 0.40 | | | | |
| 1980G | 71,940,000 | — | — | 0.10 | 0.25 | — |
| 1980G Proof | 110,000 | Value: 0.40 | | | | |
| 1980J | 143,110,000 | — | — | 0.10 | 0.25 | — |
| 1980J Proof | 110,000 | Value: 0.40 | | | | |
| 1981D | 169,550,000 | — | — | 0.10 | 0.25 | — |
| 1981D Proof | 91,000 | Value: 0.40 | | | | |
| 1981F | 274,010,000 | — | — | 0.10 | 0.25 | — |
| 1981F Proof | 91,000 | Value: 0.40 | | | | |
| 1981G | 178,010,000 | — | — | 0.10 | 0.25 | — |
| 1981G Proof | 91,000 | Value: 0.40 | | | | |
| 1981J | 189,090,000 | — | — | 0.10 | 0.25 | — |
| 1981J Proof | 91,000 | Value: 0.40 | | | | |
| 1982D | 130,090,000 | — | — | 0.10 | 0.20 | — |
| 1982D Proof | 78,000 | Value: 0.40 | | | | |
| 1982F | 108,390,000 | — | — | 0.10 | 0.20 | — |
| 1982F Proof | 78,000 | Value: 0.40 | | | | |
| 1982G | 77,740,000 | — | — | 0.10 | 0.20 | — |
| 1982G Proof | 78,000 | Value: 0.40 | | | | |
| 1982J | 124,720,000 | — | — | 0.10 | 0.20 | — |
| 1982J Proof | 78,000 | Value: 0.40 | | | | |
| 1983D | 46,800,000 | — | — | 0.10 | 0.20 | — |
| 1983D Proof | 75,000 | Value: 0.40 | | | | |
| 1983F | 54,000,000 | — | — | 0.10 | 0.20 | — |
| 1983F Proof | 75,000 | Value: 0.40 | | | | |
| 1983G | 31,140,000 | — | — | 0.10 | 0.20 | — |
| 1983G Proof | 75,000 | Value: 0.40 | | | | |
| 1983J | 48,060,000 | — | — | 0.10 | 0.20 | — |
| 1983J Proof | 75,000 | Value: 0.40 | | | | |
| 1984D | 58,500,000 | — | — | 0.10 | 0.20 | — |
| 1984D Proof | 64,000 | Value: 0.40 | | | | |
| 1984F | 67,500,000 | — | — | 0.10 | 0.20 | — |
| 1984F Proof | 64,000 | Value: 0.40 | | | | |
| 1984G | 38,900,000 | — | — | 0.10 | 0.20 | — |
| 1984G Proof | 64,000 | Value: 0.40 | | | | |
| 1984J | 60,100,000 | — | — | 0.10 | 0.20 | — |
| 1984J Proof | 64,000 | Value: 0.40 | | | | |
| 1985D | 19,500,000 | — | — | 0.10 | 0.20 | — |
| 1985D Proof | 56,000 | Value: 0.40 | | | | |
| 1985F | 22,500,000 | — | — | 0.10 | 0.20 | — |
| 1985F Proof | 54,000 | Value: 0.40 | | | | |
| 1985G | 13,000,000 | — | — | — | 0.10 | — |
| 1985G Proof | 55,000 | Value: 0.40 | | | | |
| 1985J | 20,000,000 | — | — | — | 0.10 | — |
| 1985J Proof | 54,000 | Value: 0.40 | | | | |
| 1986D | 39,000,000 | — | — | — | 0.10 | — |
| 1986D Proof | 44,000 | Value: 0.40 | | | | |
| 1986F | 45,000,000 | — | — | — | 0.10 | — |
| 1986F Proof | 44,000 | Value: 0.40 | | | | |
| 1986G | 25,900,000 | — | — | — | 0.10 | — |
| 1986G Proof | 44,000 | Value: 0.40 | | | | |
| 1986J | 40,100,000 | — | — | — | 0.10 | — |
| 1986J Proof | 44,000 | Value: 0.40 | | | | |
| 1987D | 6,500,000 | — | — | — | 0.10 | — |
| 1987D Proof | 45,000 | Value: 0.40 | | | | |
| 1987F | 7,500,000 | — | — | — | 0.10 | — |
| 1987F Proof | 45,000 | Value: 0.40 | | | | |
| 1987G | 4,330,000 | — | — | — | 0.10 | — |
| 1987G Proof | 45,000 | Value: 0.40 | | | | |
| 1987J | 6,680,000 | — | — | — | 0.10 | — |
| 1987J Proof | 45,000 | Value: 0.40 | | | | |
| 1988D | 52,000,000 | — | — | — | 0.10 | — |
| 1988D Proof | 45,000 | Value: 0.40 | | | | |
| 1988F | 60,000,000 | — | — | — | 0.10 | — |
| 1988F Proof | 45,000 | Value: 0.40 | | | | |
| 1988G | 34,600,000 | — | — | — | 0.10 | — |
| 1988G Proof | 45,000 | Value: 0.40 | | | | |
| 1988J | 53,400,000 | — | — | — | 0.10 | — |
| 1988J Proof | 45,000 | Value: 0.40 | | | | |
| 1989D | 104,000,000 | — | — | — | 0.10 | — |
| 1989D Proof | 45,000 | Value: 0.40 | | | | |
| 1989F | 120,000,000 | — | — | — | 0.10 | — |
| 1989F Proof | 45,000 | Value: 0.40 | | | | |
| 1989G | 69,200,000 | — | — | — | 0.10 | — |
| 1989G Proof | 45,000 | Value: 0.40 | | | | |
| 1989J | 106,800,000 | — | — | — | 0.10 | — |
| 1989J Proof | 45,000 | Value: 0.40 | | | | |
| 1990D | 169,000,000 | — | — | — | 0.10 | — |
| 1990D Proof | 45,000 | Value: 0.40 | | | | |
| 1990F | 195,000,000 | — | — | — | 0.10 | — |
| 1990F Proof | 45,000 | Value: 0.40 | | | | |
| 1990G | 112,450,000 | — | — | — | 0.10 | — |
| 1990G Proof | 45,000 | Value: 0.40 | | | | |
| 1990J | 173,550,000 | — | — | — | 0.10 | — |
| 1990J Proof | 45,000 | Value: 0.40 | | | | |
| 1991A | 260,000,000 | — | — | — | 0.10 | — |
| 1991A Proof | 45,000 | Value: 0.40 | | | | |
| 1991D | 273,000,000 | — | — | — | 0.10 | — |
| 1991D Proof | 45,000 | Value: 0.40 | | | | |
| 1991F | 312,000,000 | — | — | — | 0.10 | — |
| 1991F Proof | 45,000 | Value: 0.40 | | | | |
| 1991G | 182,000,000 | — | — | — | 0.10 | — |
| 1991G Proof | 45,000 | Value: 0.40 | | | | |
| 1991J | 273,000,000 | — | — | — | 0.10 | — |
| 1991J Proof | 45,000 | Value: 0.40 | | | | |
| 1992A | 40,000,000 | — | — | — | 0.10 | — |
| 1992A Proof | 45,000 | Value: 0.40 | | | | |
| 1992D | 42,000,000 | — | — | — | 0.10 | — |
| 1992D Proof | 45,000 | Value: 0.40 | | | | |
| 1992F | 48,000,000 | — | — | — | 0.10 | — |
| 1992F Proof | 45,000 | Value: 0.40 | | | | |
| 1992G | 28,000,000 | — | — | — | 0.10 | — |
| 1992G Proof | 45,000 | Value: 0.40 | | | | |
| 1992J | 42,000,000 | — | — | — | 0.10 | — |
| 1992J Proof | 45,000 | Value: 0.40 | | | | |
| 1993A | 40,000,000 | — | — | — | 0.10 | — |
| 1993A Proof | 45,000 | Value: 0.40 | | | | |
| 1993D | 42,000,000 | — | — | — | 0.10 | — |
| 1993D Proof | 45,000 | Value: 0.40 | | | | |
| 1993F | 48,000,000 | — | — | — | 0.10 | — |
| 1993F Proof | 45,000 | Value: 0.40 | | | | |
| 1993G | 28,000,000 | — | — | — | 0.10 | — |
| 1993G Prof | 45,000 | Value: 0.40 | | | | |
| 1993J | 42,000,000 | — | — | — | 0.10 | — |
| 1993J Proof | 45,000 | Value: 0.40 | | | | |
| 1994A | 100,000,000 | — | — | — | 0.10 | — |
| 1994A Proof | 45,000 | Value: 0.40 | | | | |
| 1994D | 105,000,000 | — | — | — | 0.10 | — |
| 1994D Proof | 45,000 | Value: 0.40 | | | | |
| 1994F | 120,000,000 | — | — | — | 0.10 | — |
| 1994F Proof | 45,000 | Value: 0.40 | | | | |
| 1994G | 70,000,000 | — | — | — | 0.10 | — |
| 1994G Proof | 45,000 | Value: 0.40 | | | | |
| 1994J | 105,000,000 | — | — | — | 0.10 | — |
| 1994J Proof | 45,000 | Value: 0.40 | | | | |
| 1995A | 100,000,000 | — | — | — | 0.15 | — |
| 1995A Proof | 45,000 | Value: 0.45 | | | | |
| 1995D | 105,000,000 | — | — | — | 0.15 | — |
| 1995D Proof | 45,000 | Value: 0.45 | | | | |
| 1995F | 120,000,000 | — | — | — | 0.15 | — |
| 1995F Proof | 45,000 | Value: 0.45 | | | | |
| 1995G | 70,000,000 | — | — | — | 0.15 | — |
| 1995G Proof | 45,000 | Value: 0.45 | | | | |
| 1995J | 105,000,000 | — | — | — | 0.15 | — |
| 1995J Proof | 45,000 | Value: 0.45 | | | | |
| 1996A | 80,000,000 | — | — | — | 0.20 | — |
| 1996A Proof | 45,000 | Value: 0.50 | | | | |
| 1996D | 84,000,000 | — | — | — | 0.20 | — |
| 1996D Proof | 45,000 | Value: 0.50 | | | | |
| 1996F | 96,000,000 | — | — | — | 0.20 | — |
| 1996F Proof | 45,000 | Value: 0.50 | | | | |
| 1996G | 56,000,000 | — | — | — | 0.20 | — |
| 1996G Proof | 45,000 | Value: 0.50 | | | | |
| 1996J | 84,000,000 | — | — | — | 0.20 | — |
| 1996J Proof | 45,000 | Value: 0.50 | | | | |
| 1997A In sets only | 70,000 | — | — | — | 1.75 | — |
| 1997A Proof | 45,000 | Value: 2.00 | | | | |
| 1997D In sets only | 70,000 | — | — | — | 1.75 | — |
| 1997D Proof | 45,000 | Value: 2.00 | | | | |
| 1997F In sets only | 70,000 | — | — | — | 1.75 | — |
| 1997F Proof | 45,000 | Value: 2.00 | | | | |
| 1997G In sets only | 70,000 | — | — | — | 1.75 | — |
| 1997G Proof | 45,000 | Value: 2.00 | | | | |
| 1997J In sets only | 70,000 | — | — | — | 1.75 | — |
| 1997J Proof | 45,000 | Value: 2.00 | | | | |
| 1998A In sets only | 70,000 | — | — | — | 1.75 | — |
| 1998A Proof | 45,000 | Value: 2.00 | | | | |
| 1998D In sets only | 70,000 | — | — | — | 1.75 | — |
| 1998D Proof | 45,000 | Value: 2.00 | | | | |
| 1998F In sets only | 70,000 | — | — | — | 1.75 | — |
| 1998F Proof | 45,000 | Value: 2.00 | | | | |
| 1998G In sets only | 70,000 | — | — | — | 1.75 | — |
| 1998G Proof | 45,000 | Value: 2.00 | | | | |
| 1998J In sets only | 70,000 | — | — | — | 1.75 | — |
| 1998J Proof | 45,000 | Value: 2.00 | | | | |
| 1999A In sets only | 70,000 | — | — | — | 1.75 | — |
| 1999A Proof | 45,000 | Value: 2.00 | | | | |
| 1999D In sets only | 70,000 | — | — | — | 1.75 | — |
| 1999D Proof | 45,000 | Value: 2.00 | | | | |
| 1999F In sets only | 70,000 | — | — | — | 1.75 | — |
| 1999F Proof | 45,000 | Value: 2.00 | | | | |
| 1999G In sets only | 70,000 | — | — | — | 1.75 | — |
| 1999G Proof | 45,000 | Value: 2.00 | | | | |
| 1999J In sets only | 70,000 | — | — | — | 1.75 | — |
| 1999J Proof | 45,000 | Value: 2.00 | | | | |
| 2000A In sets only | 20,000 | — | — | — | 1.75 | — |
| 2000A Proof | 45,000 | — | — | — | 2.00 | — |
| 2000D In sets only | 20,000 | — | — | — | 1.75 | — |
| 2000D Proof | 45,000 | Value: 2.00 | | | | |
| 2000F In sets only | 20,000 | — | — | — | 1.75 | — |
| 2000F Proof | 45,000 | Value: 2.00 | | | | |
| 2000G In sets only | 20,000 | — | — | — | 1.75 | — |
| 2000G Proof | 45,000 | Value: 2.00 | | | | |
| 2000J In sets only | 20,000 | — | — | — | 1.75 | — |
| 2000J Proof | 45,000 | Value: 2.00 | | | | |
| 2001A In sets only | 130,000 | — | — | — | 5.00 | — |
| 2001A Proof | 78,000 | Value: 5.00 | | | | |
| 2001D In sets only | 130,000 | — | — | — | 5.00 | — |
| 2001D Proof | 78,000 | Value: 5.00 | | | | |
| 2001F In sets only | 130,000 | — | — | — | 5.00 | — |
| 2001F Proof | 78,000 | Value: 5.00 | | | | |
| 2001G In sets only | 130,000 | — | — | — | 5.00 | — |
| 2001G Proof | 78,000 | Value: 5.00 | | | | |
| 2001J In sets only | 130,000 | — | — | — | 5.00 | — |
| 2001J Proof | 78,000 | Value: 5.00 | | | | |

**2 PFENNIG** **KM# 106** **Composition:** Bronze **Note:** Federal Republic.

| Date | Mintage | F | VF | XF | Unc | BU |
|---|---|---|---|---|---|---|
| 1950D | 26,263,000 | — | 0.10 | 1.00 | 10.00 | — |
| 1950D Proof | — | Value: 50.00 | | | | |
| 1950F | 30,278,000 | — | 0.10 | 1.00 | 10.00 | — |
| 1950F Proof | 200 | — | — | — | — | — |
| 1950G | 17,151,000 | — | 0.10 | 50.00 | 75.00 | — |
| 1950G Proof | — | Value: 90.00 | | | | |
| 1950J | 27,216,000 | — | 0.10 | 1.00 | 10.00 | — |
| 1950J Proof | — | Value: 40.00 | | | | |
| 1958D | 19,440,000 | — | 0.10 | 1.00 | 10.00 | — |
| 1958F | 24,122,000 | — | 0.10 | 1.00 | 10.00 | — |
| 1958F Proof | 100 | — | — | — | — | — |
| 1958G | 15,255,000 | — | 0.10 | 1.00 | 10.00 | — |
| 1958J | 21,250,000 | — | 0.10 | 1.00 | 10.00 | — |
| 1959D | 19,690,000 | — | — | 0.25 | 10.00 | — |
| 1959F | 25,017,000 | — | — | 0.25 | 10.00 | — |
| 1959F Proof | 75 | — | — | — | — | — |
| 1959G | 12,899,000 | — | — | 0.25 | 10.00 | — |
| 1959J | 25,482,000 | — | — | 0.25 | 10.00 | — |
| 1960D | 21,979,000 | — | — | 0.25 | 6.00 | — |
| 1960F | 13,060,000 | — | — | 0.25 | 6.00 | — |
| 1960F Proof | 75 | — | — | — | — | — |
| 1960G | 5,657,000 | — | 0.10 | 0.25 | 6.00 | — |
| 1960J | 17,799,000 | — | — | 0.25 | 6.00 | — |
| 1961D | 26,662,000 | — | — | 0.25 | 6.00 | — |
| 1961F | 24,990,000 | — | — | 0.25 | 6.00 | — |
| 1961G | 18,060,000 | — | — | 0.25 | 6.00 | — |

| Date | Mintage | F | VF | XF | Unc | BU |
|---|---|---|---|---|---|---|
| 1961J | 22,147,000 | — | — | 0.25 | 6.00 | — |
| 1962D | 21,297,000 | — | — | 0.25 | 6.00 | — |
| 1962F | 42,189,000 | — | — | 0.25 | 4.00 | — |
| 1962G | 17,297,000 | — | — | 0.25 | 4.00 | — |
| 1962J | 30,706,000 | — | — | 0.25 | 4.00 | — |
| 1963D | 7,648,000 | — | — | 0.25 | 7.00 | — |
| 1963F | 18,299,000 | — | — | 0.25 | 2.00 | — |
| 1963G | 35,838,000 | — | — | 0.25 | 2.00 | — |
| 1963G Proof | — | — | — | — | — | — |
| 1963J | 42,884,000 | — | — | 0.25 | 2.00 | — |
| 1964D | 20,336,000 | — | — | 0.25 | 3.00 | — |
| 1964F | 31,400,000 | — | — | 0.10 | 1.00 | — |
| 1964G | 18,431,000 | — | — | 0.10 | 1.00 | — |
| 1964G Proof | Est. 600 | Value: 12.00 | | | | |
| 1964J | 13,370,000 | — | — | 0.10 | 1.00 | — |
| 1965D | 48,541,000 | — | — | 0.10 | 1.00 | — |
| 1965F | 27,000,000 | — | — | 0.10 | 1.00 | — |
| 1965F Proof | Est. 80 | Value: 70.00 | | | | |
| 1965G | 13,584,000 | — | — | 0.10 | 1.00 | — |
| 1965G Proof | 1,200 | Value: 5.00 | | | | |
| 1965J | 33,397,000 | — | — | 0.10 | 1.00 | — |
| 1966D | 65,077,000 | — | — | 0.10 | 0.25 | — |
| 1966F | 52,543,000 | — | — | 0.10 | 0.25 | — |
| 1966F Proof | 100 | Value: 80.00 | | | | |
| 1966G | 40,804,000 | — | — | 0.10 | 0.25 | — |
| 1966G Proof | 3,070 | Value: 5.50 | | | | |
| 1966J | 46,754,000 | — | — | 0.10 | 0.25 | — |
| 1966J Proof | 1,000 | Value: 40.00 | | | | |
| 1967D | 25,997,000 | — | — | 0.10 | 2.00 | — |
| 1967F | 30,004,000 | — | — | 0.10 | 1.00 | — |
| 1967F Proof | 1,500 | Value: 7.00 | | | | |
| 1967G | 6,280,000 | — | — | 1.00 | 3.00 | — |
| 1967G Proof | 4,500 | Value: 4.50 | | | | |
| 1967J | 26,725,000 | — | — | 0.10 | 1.00 | — |
| 1967J Proof | 1,500 | Value: 10.00 | | | | |
| 1968D | 19,523,000 | — | — | 1.00 | 3.00 | — |
| 1968G | 15,357,000 | — | — | 0.10 | 1.00 | — |
| 1968G Proof | 3,651 | Value: 4.00 | | | | |
| 1968J | — | — | 150 | 225 | 350 | — |
| 1969J | — | — | 150 | 225 | 350 | — |

## 2 PFENNIG KM# 106a Composition: Bronze Clad Steel

| Date | Mintage | F | VF | XF | Unc | BU |
|---|---|---|---|---|---|---|
| 1967G Proof | 520 | Value: 720 | | | | |
| 1968D | 19,523,000 | — | — | 0.10 | 0.25 | — |
| 1968F | 30,000,000 | — | — | 0.10 | 0.25 | — |
| 1968F Proof | 3,000 | Value: 6.00 | | | | |
| 1968G | 13,004,000 | — | — | 0.10 | 0.25 | — |
| 1968G Proof | 2,372 | Value: 4.00 | | | | |
| 1968J | 20,026,000 | — | — | 0.10 | 0.25 | — |
| 1968J Proof | 2,000 | Value: 7.50 | | | | |
| 1969D | 39,012,000 | — | — | 0.10 | 0.25 | — |
| 1969D Proof | — | Value: 1.25 | | | | |
| 1969F | 45,029,000 | — | — | 0.10 | 0.25 | — |
| 1969F Proof | 5,100 | Value: 1.25 | | | | |
| 1969G | 32,156,999 | — | — | 0.10 | 0.25 | — |
| 1969G Proof | 8,700 | Value: 1.25 | | | | |
| 1969J | 40,102,000 | — | — | 0.10 | 0.25 | — |
| 1969J Proof | 5,000 | Value: 2.50 | | | | |
| 1970D | 45,525,000 | — | — | 0.10 | 0.25 | — |
| 1970F | 73,851,000 | — | — | 0.10 | 0.25 | — |
| 1970F Proof | 5,140 | Value: 1.25 | | | | |
| 1970G | 30,330,000 | — | — | 0.10 | 0.25 | — |
| 1970G Proof | 10,200 | Value: 1.25 | | | | |
| 1970 Small J | 46,730,000 | — | — | 0.10 | 0.25 | — |
| 1970 Large J | Inc. above | — | — | 0.10 | 0.25 | — |
| 1970J Proof | 5,000 | Value: 1.75 | | | | |
| 1971D | 71,755,000 | — | — | 0.10 | 0.25 | — |
| 1971D Proof | 8,000 | Value: 1.25 | | | | |
| 1971F | 82,765,000 | — | — | 0.10 | 0.25 | — |
| 1971F Proof | 8,000 | Value: 1.25 | | | | |
| 1971G | 47,850,000 | — | — | 0.10 | 0.25 | — |
| 1971G Proof | 10,000 | Value: 1.25 | | | | |
| 1971J | 73,641,000 | — | — | 0.10 | 0.25 | — |
| 1971J Proof | 8,000 | Value: 1.25 | | | | |
| 1972D | 52,403,000 | — | — | 0.10 | 0.25 | — |
| 1972D Proof | 8,000 | Value: 1.00 | | | | |
| 1972F | 60,272,000 | — | — | 0.10 | 0.25 | — |
| 1972F Proof | 8,000 | Value: 1.00 | | | | |
| 1972G | 34,864,000 | — | — | 0.10 | 0.25 | — |
| 1972G Proof | 10,000 | Value: 1.00 | | | | |
| 1972J | 53,673,000 | — | — | 0.10 | 0.25 | — |
| 1972J Proof | 8,000 | Value: 1.00 | | | | |
| 1973D | 26,190,000 | — | — | 0.10 | 0.25 | — |
| 1973D Proof | 9,000 | Value: 1.00 | | | | |
| 1973F | 30,160,000 | — | — | 0.10 | 0.25 | — |
| 1973F Proof | 9,000 | Value: 1.00 | | | | |
| 1973G | 17,379,000 | — | — | 0.10 | 0.25 | — |
| 1973G Proof | 9,000 | Value: 1.00 | | | | |
| 1973J | 26,830,000 | — | — | 0.10 | 0.25 | — |
| 1973J Proof | 9,000 | Value: 1.00 | | | | |
| 1974D | 58,667,000 | — | — | 0.10 | 0.25 | — |
| 1974D Proof | 35,000 | Value: 0.50 | | | | |
| 1974F | 67,596,000 | — | — | 0.10 | 0.25 | — |
| 1974F Proof | 35,000 | Value: 0.50 | | | | |
| 1974G | 39,007,000 | — | — | 0.10 | 0.25 | — |
| 1974G Proof | 35,000 | Value: 0.50 | | | | |
| 1974J | 60,195,000 | — | — | 0.10 | 0.25 | — |
| 1974J Proof | 35,000 | Value: 0.50 | | | | |
| 1975D | 58,634,000 | — | — | 0.10 | 0.25 | — |
| 1975D Proof | 43,000 | Value: 0.50 | | | | |
| 1975F | 67,685,000 | — | — | 0.10 | 0.25 | — |
| 1975F Proof | 43,000 | Value: 0.50 | | | | |
| 1975G | 39,391,000 | — | — | 0.10 | 0.25 | — |
| 1975G Proof | 43,000 | Value: 0.50 | | | | |
| 1975J | 60,207,000 | — | — | 0.10 | 0.25 | — |
| 1975J Proof | 43,000 | Value: 0.50 | | | | |
| 1976D | 78,074,000 | — | — | 0.10 | 0.25 | — |
| 1976D Proof | 43,000 | Value: 0.50 | | | | |
| 1976F | 90,130,000 | — | — | 0.10 | 0.25 | — |
| 1976F Proof | 43,000 | Value: 0.50 | | | | |
| 1976G | 51,988,000 | — | — | 0.10 | 0.25 | — |
| 1976G Proof | 43,000 | Value: 0.50 | | | | |
| 1976J | 80,145,000 | — | — | 0.10 | 0.25 | — |
| 1976J Proof | 43,000 | Value: 0.50 | | | | |
| 1977D | 84,516,000 | — | — | 0.10 | 0.20 | — |
| 1977D Proof | 51,000 | Value: 0.40 | | | | |
| 1977F | 97,504,000 | — | — | 0.10 | 0.20 | — |
| 1977F Proof | 51,000 | Value: 0.40 | | | | |
| 1977G | 56,276,000 | — | — | 0.10 | 0.20 | — |
| 1977G Proof | 51,000 | Value: 0.40 | | | | |
| 1977J | 86,888,000 | — | — | 0.10 | 0.20 | — |
| 1977J Proof | 51,000 | Value: 0.40 | | | | |
| 1978D | 84,500,000 | — | — | 0.10 | 0.20 | — |
| 1978D Proof | 54,000 | Value: 0.40 | | | | |
| 1978F | 97,500,000 | — | — | 0.10 | 0.20 | — |
| 1978F Proof | 54,000 | Value: 0.40 | | | | |
| 1978G | 56,225,000 | — | — | 0.10 | 0.20 | — |
| 1978G Proof | 54,000 | Value: 0.40 | | | | |
| 1978J | 86,775,000 | — | — | 0.10 | 0.20 | — |
| 1978J Proof | 54,000 | Value: 0.40 | | | | |
| 1979D | 91,000,000 | — | — | 0.10 | 0.20 | — |
| 1979D Proof | 89,000 | Value: 0.40 | | | | |
| 1979F | 105,000,000 | — | — | 0.10 | 0.20 | — |
| 1979F Proof | 89,000 | Value: 0.40 | | | | |
| 1979G | 60,550,000 | — | — | 0.10 | 0.20 | — |
| 1979G Proof | 89,000 | Value: 0.40 | | | | |
| 1979J | 93,480,000 | — | — | 0.10 | 0.20 | — |
| 1979J Proof | 89,000 | Value: 0.40 | | | | |
| 1980D | 93,360,000 | — | — | 0.10 | 0.20 | — |
| 1980D Proof | 110,000 | Value: 0.40 | | | | |
| 1980F | 120,360,000 | — | — | 0.10 | 0.20 | — |
| 1980F Proof | 110,000 | Value: 0.40 | | | | |
| 1980G | 50,830,000 | — | — | 0.10 | 0.20 | — |
| 1980G Proof | 110,000 | Value: 0.40 | | | | |
| 1980J | 102,260,000 | — | — | 0.10 | 0.20 | — |
| 1980J Proof | 110,000 | Value: 0.40 | | | | |
| 1981D | 93,910,000 | — | — | 0.10 | 0.20 | — |
| 1981D Proof | 91,000 | Value: 0.40 | | | | |
| 1981F | 83,710,000 | — | — | 0.10 | 0.20 | — |
| 1981F Proof | 91,000 | Value: 0.40 | | | | |
| 1981G | 89,850,000 | — | — | 0.10 | 0.20 | — |
| 1981G Proof | 91,000 | Value: 0.40 | | | | |
| 1981J | 87,250,000 | — | — | 0.10 | 0.20 | — |
| 1981J Proof | 91,000 | Value: 0.40 | | | | |
| 1982D | 64,390,000 | — | — | 0.10 | 0.20 | — |
| 1982D Proof | 78,000 | Value: 0.40 | | | | |
| 1982F | 36,870,000 | — | — | 0.10 | 0.20 | — |
| 1982F Proof | 78,000 | Value: 0.40 | | | | |
| 1982G | 58,590,000 | — | — | 0.10 | 0.20 | — |
| 1982G Proof | 78,000 | Value: 0.40 | | | | |
| 1982J | 57,690,000 | — | — | 0.10 | 0.20 | — |
| 1982J Proof | 78,000 | Value: 0.40 | | | | |
| 1983D | 71,500,000 | — | — | 0.10 | 0.20 | — |
| 1983D Proof | 75,000 | Value: 0.40 | | | | |
| 1983F | 82,500,000 | — | — | 0.10 | 0.20 | — |
| 1983F Proof | 75,000 | Value: 0.40 | | | | |
| 1983G | 47,575,000 | — | — | 0.10 | 0.20 | — |
| 1983G Proof | 75,000 | Value: 0.40 | | | | |
| 1983J | 73,425,000 | — | — | 0.10 | 0.20 | — |
| 1983J Proof | 75,000 | Value: 0.40 | | | | |
| 1984D | 58,500,000 | — | — | 0.10 | 0.20 | — |
| 1984D Proof | 64,000 | Value: 0.40 | | | | |
| 1984F | 67,500,000 | — | — | 0.10 | 0.20 | — |
| 1984F Proof | 64,000 | Value: 0.40 | | | | |
| 1984G | 38,900,000 | — | — | 0.10 | 0.20 | — |
| 1984G Proof | 64,000 | Value: 0.40 | | | | |
| 1984J | 60,100,000 | — | — | 0.10 | 0.20 | — |
| 1984J Proof | 64,000 | Value: 0.40 | | | | |
| 1985D | 19,500,000 | — | — | — | 0.10 | — |
| 1985D Proof | 56,000 | Value: 0.40 | | | | |
| 1985F | 22,500,000 | — | — | — | 0.10 | — |
| 1985F Proof | 54,000 | Value: 0.40 | | | | |
| 1985G | 13,000,000 | — | — | — | 0.10 | — |
| 1985G Proof | 55,000 | Value: 0.40 | | | | |
| 1985J | 20,000,000 | — | — | — | 0.10 | — |
| 1985J Proof | 54,000 | Value: 0.40 | | | | |
| 1986D | 39,000,000 | — | — | — | 0.10 | — |
| 1986D Proof | 44,000 | Value: 0.40 | | | | |
| 1986F | 45,000,000 | — | — | — | 0.10 | — |
| 1986F Proof | 44,000 | Value: 0.40 | | | | |
| 1986G | 25,900,000 | — | — | — | 0.10 | — |
| 1986G Proof | 44,000 | Value: 0.40 | | | | |
| 1986J | 40,100,000 | — | — | — | 0.10 | — |
| 1986J Proof | 44,000 | Value: 0.40 | | | | |
| 1987D | 6,500,000 | — | 1.00 | 2.50 | 5.00 | — |
| 1987D Proof | 45,000 | Value: 0.40 | | | | |
| 1987F | 7,500,000 | — | 1.00 | 2.50 | 5.00 | — |
| 1987F Proof | 45,000 | Value: 0.40 | | | | |
| 1987G | 4,330,000 | — | 1.00 | 2.50 | 5.00 | — |
| 1987G Proof | 45,000 | Value: 0.40 | | | | |
| 1987J | 6,680,000 | — | 1.00 | 2.50 | 5.00 | — |
| 1987J Proof | 45,000 | Value: 0.40 | | | | |
| 1988D | 52,000,000 | — | — | — | 0.10 | — |
| 1988D Proof | 45,000 | Value: 0.40 | | | | |
| 1988F | 60,000,000 | — | — | — | 0.10 | — |
| 1988F Proof | 45,000 | Value: 0.40 | | | | |
| 1988G | 34,600,000 | — | — | — | 0.10 | — |
| 1988G Proof | 45,000 | Value: 0.40 | | | | |
| 1988J | 53,400,000 | — | — | — | 0.10 | — |
| 1988J Proof | 45,000 | Value: 0.40 | | | | |
| 1989D | 52,000,000 | — | — | — | 0.10 | — |
| 1989D Proof | 45,000 | Value: 0.40 | | | | |
| 1989F | 60,000,000 | — | — | — | 0.10 | — |
| 1989F Proof | 45,000 | Value: 0.40 | | | | |
| 1989G | 34,600,000 | — | — | — | 0.10 | — |
| 1989G Proof | 45,000 | Value: 0.40 | | | | |
| 1989J | 53,400,000 | — | — | — | 0.10 | — |
| 1989J Proof | 45,000 | Value: 0.40 | | | | |
| 1990D | 71,500,000 | — | — | — | 0.10 | — |
| 1990D Proof | 45,000 | Value: 0.40 | | | | |
| 1990F | 82,500,000 | — | — | — | 0.10 | — |
| 1990F Proof | 45,000 | Value: 0.40 | | | | |
| 1990G | 47,570,000 | — | — | — | 0.10 | — |
| 1990G Proof | 45,000 | Value: 0.40 | | | | |
| 1990J | 73,420,000 | — | — | — | 0.10 | — |
| 1990J Proof | 45,000 | Value: 0.40 | | | | |
| 1991A | 115,000,000 | — | — | — | 0.10 | — |
| 1991A Proof | 45,000 | Value: 0.40 | | | | |
| 1991D | 120,750,000 | — | — | — | 0.10 | — |
| 1991D Proof | 45,000 | Value: 0.40 | | | | |
| 1991F | 138,000,000 | — | — | — | 0.10 | — |
| 1991F Proof | 45,000 | Value: 0.40 | | | | |
| 1991G | 80,500,000 | — | — | — | 0.10 | — |
| 1991G Proof | 45,000 | Value: 0.40 | | | | |
| 1991J | 120,750,000 | — | — | — | 0.10 | — |
| 1991J Proof | 45,000 | Value: 0.40 | | | | |
| 1992A | 60,000,000 | — | — | — | 0.10 | — |
| 1992A Proof | 45,000 | Value: 0.40 | | | | |
| 1992D | 63,000,000 | — | — | — | 0.10 | — |
| 1992D Proof | 45,000 | Value: 0.40 | | | | |
| 1992F | 72,000,000 | — | — | — | 0.10 | — |
| 1992F Proof | 45,000 | Value: 0.40 | | | | |
| 1992G | 42,000,000 | — | — | — | 0.10 | — |
| 1992G Proof | 45,000 | Value: 0.40 | | | | |
| 1992J | 63,000,000 | — | — | — | 0.10 | — |
| 1992J Proof | 45,000 | Value: 0.40 | | | | |
| 1993A | 10,000,000 | — | — | — | 0.10 | — |
| 1993A Proof | 45,000 | Value: 0.40 | | | | |
| 1993D | 10,500,000 | — | — | — | 0.10 | — |
| 1993D Proof | 45,000 | Value: 0.40 | | | | |
| 1993F | 12,000,000 | — | — | — | 0.10 | — |
| 1993F Proof | 45,000 | Value: 0.40 | | | | |
| 1993G | 7,000,000 | — | — | — | 0.10 | — |
| 1993G Proof | 45,000 | Value: 0.40 | | | | |
| 1993J | 10,000,000 | — | — | — | 0.10 | — |
| 1993J Proof | 45,000 | Value: 0.40 | | | | |
| 1994A | 55,000,000 | — | — | — | 0.10 | — |
| 1994A Proof | 45,000 | Value: 0.40 | | | | |
| 1994D | 57,750,000 | — | — | — | 0.10 | — |
| 1994D Proof | 45,000 | Value: 0.40 | | | | |
| 1994F | 66,000,000 | — | — | — | 0.10 | — |
| 1994F Proof | 45,000 | Value: 0.40 | | | | |
| 1994G | 38,500,000 | — | — | — | 0.10 | — |
| 1994G Proof | 45,000 | Value: 0.40 | | | | |
| 1994J | 57,750,000 | — | — | — | 0.10 | — |
| 1994J Proof | 45,000 | Value: 0.40 | | | | |
| 1995A | 1,000,000,000 | — | — | — | 0.15 | — |
| 1995A Proof | 45,000 | Value: 0.45 | | | | |
| 1995D | 105,000,000 | — | — | — | 0.15 | — |
| 1995D Proof | 45,000 | Value: 0.45 | | | | |
| 1995F | 120,000,000 | — | — | — | 0.15 | — |
| 1995F Proof | 45,000 | Value: 0.45 | | | | |
| 1995G | 70,000,000 | — | — | — | 0.15 | — |
| 1995G Proof | 45,000 | Value: 0.45 | | | | |
| 1995J | 105,000,000 | — | — | — | 0.15 | — |
| 1995J Proof | 45,000 | Value: 0.45 | | | | |
| 1996A | 40,000,000 | — | — | — | 0.20 | — |
| 1996A Proof | 45,000 | Value: 0.50 | | | | |
| 1996D | 42,000,000 | — | — | — | 0.20 | — |
| 1996D Proof | 45,000 | Value: 0.50 | | | | |
| 1996F | 48,000,000 | — | — | — | 0.20 | — |
| 1996F Proof | 45,000 | Value: 0.50 | | | | |
| 1996G | 28,000,000 | — | — | — | 0.20 | — |
| 1996G Proof | 45,000 | Value: 0.50 | | | | |
| 1996J | 42,000,000 | — | — | — | 0.20 | — |
| 1996J Proof | 45,000 | Value: 0.50 | | | | |
| 1997A In sets only | 70,000 | — | — | — | 1.75 | — |
| 1997A Proof | 45,000 | Value: 2.00 | | | | |
| 1997D In sets only | 70,000 | — | — | — | 1.75 | — |
| 1997D Proof | 45,000 | Value: 2.00 | | | | |
| 1997F In sets only | 70,000 | — | — | — | 1.75 | — |
| 1997F Proof | 45,000 | Value: 2.00 | | | | |
| 1997G In sets only | 70,000 | — | — | — | 1.75 | — |
| 1997G Proof | 45,000 | Value: 2.00 | | | | |
| 1997J In sets only | 70,000 | — | — | — | 1.75 | — |
| 1997J Proof | 45,000 | Value: 2.00 | | | | |
| 1998A In sets only | 70,000 | — | — | — | 1.75 | — |
| 1998A Proof | 45,000 | Value: 2.00 | | | | |
| 1998D In sets only | 70,000 | — | — | — | 1.75 | — |
| 1998D Proof | 45,000 | Value: 2.00 | | | | |
| 1998F In sets only | 70,000 | — | — | — | 1.75 | — |
| 1998F Proof | 45,000 | Value: 2.00 | | | | |
| 1998G In sets only | 70,000 | — | — | — | 1.75 | — |
| 1998G Proof | 45,000 | Value: 2.00 | | | | |
| 1998J In sets only | 70,000 | — | — | — | 1.75 | — |

| Date | Mintage | F | VF | XF | Unc | BU |
|---|---|---|---|---|---|---|
| 1998J Proof | 45,000 | Value: 2.00 | | | | |
| 1999A In sets only | 70,000 | — | — | — | 1.75 | — |
| 1999A Proof | 45,000 | Value: 2.00 | | | | |
| 1999D In sets only | 70,000 | — | — | — | 1.75 | — |
| 1999D Proof | 45,000 | Value: 2.00 | | | | |
| 1999F In sets only | 70,000 | — | — | — | 1.75 | — |
| 1999F Proof | 45,000 | Value: 2.00 | | | | |
| 1999G In sets only | 70,000 | — | — | — | 1.75 | — |
| 1999G Proof | 45,000 | Value: 2.00 | | | | |
| 1999J In sets only | 70,000 | — | — | — | 1.75 | — |
| 1999J Proof | 45,000 | Value: 2.00 | | | | |
| 2000A In sets only | 70,000 | — | — | — | 1.75 | — |
| 2000A Proof | 45,000 | Value: 2.00 | | | | |
| 2000D In sets only | 70,000 | — | — | — | 1.75 | — |
| 2000D Proof | 45,000 | Value: 2.00 | | | | |
| 2000F In sets only | 70,000 | — | — | — | 1.75 | — |
| 2000F Proof | 45,000 | Value: 2.00 | | | | |
| 2000G In sets only | 70,000 | — | — | — | 1.75 | — |
| 2000G Proof | 45,000 | Value: 2.00 | | | | |
| 2000J In sets only | 70,000 | — | — | — | 1.75 | — |
| 2000J Proof | 45,000 | Value: 2.00 | | | | |
| 2001A In sets only | 130,000 | — | — | — | 5.00 | — |
| 2001A Proof | 78,000 | Value: 5.00 | | | | |
| 2001D In sets only | 130,000 | — | — | — | 5.00 | — |
| 2001D Proof | 78,000 | Value: 5.00 | | | | |
| 2001F In sets only | 130,000 | — | — | — | 5.00 | — |
| 2001F Proof | 78,000 | Value: 5.00 | | | | |
| 2001G In sets only | 130,000 | — | — | — | 5.00 | — |
| 2001G Proof | 78,000 | Value: 5.00 | | | | |
| 2001J In sets only | 130,000 | — | — | — | 5.00 | — |
| 2001J Proof | 78,000 | Value: 5.00 | | | | |

**5 PFENNIG** KM# 102 **Composition:** Bronze-Clad Steel
**Note:** Currency Reform.

| Date | Mintage | F | VF | XF | Unc | BU |
|---|---|---|---|---|---|---|
| 1949D | 60,026,000 | — | 0.20 | 7.50 | 45.00 | — |
| 1949D Proof | — | Value: 150 | | | | |
| 1949F | 66,081,999 | — | 0.20 | 7.50 | 35.00 | — |
| 1949F Proof | 250 | Value: 80.00 | | | | |
| 1949G | 57,356,000 | — | 0.20 | 7.50 | 50.00 | — |
| 1949J | 68,977,000 | — | 0.20 | 7.50 | 40.00 | — |
| 1949J Proof | — | Value: 80.00 | | | | |

**5 PFENNIG** KM# 107 **Composition:** Brass Plated Steel

| Date | Mintage | F | VF | XF | Unc | BU |
|---|---|---|---|---|---|---|
| 1950D | 271,962,000 | — | — | 1.50 | 5.00 | — |
| 1950F | 362,880,000 | — | — | 1.50 | 5.00 | — |
| 1950F Proof | 500 | Value: 65.00 | | | | |
| 1950G | 180,492,000 | — | — | 1.50 | 5.00 | — |
| 1950G | 1,800 | — | — | 1.50 | 4.00 | — |
| 1950J Large J | 285,283,000 | — | — | 1.50 | 5.00 | — |
| 1950J Small J | Inc. above | — | — | 1.50 | 5.00 | — |
| 1966D | 26,036,000 | — | — | 1.50 | 8.50 | — |
| 1966F | 30,047,000 | — | — | 1.50 | 8.50 | — |
| 1966F Proof | 100 | — | — | — | 60.00 | — |
| 1966G | 17,333,000 | — | — | 1.50 | 8.50 | — |
| 1966G Proof | 3,070 | — | — | — | 7.50 | — |
| 1966J | 26,741,000 | — | — | 1.50 | 8.50 | — |
| 1966J Proof | 1,000 | — | — | 1.50 | 17.50 | — |
| 1967D | 10,418,000 | — | — | 1.50 | 8.50 | — |
| 1967F | 12,012,000 | — | — | 1.50 | 8.50 | — |
| 1967F Proof | 1,500 | Value: 15.00 | | | | |
| 1967G | 1,736,000 | — | 2.00 | 4.00 | 25.00 | — |
| 1967G Proof | 4,500 | Value: 7.50 | | | | |
| 1967J | 10,706,000 | — | — | 1.50 | 8.50 | — |
| 1967J Proof | 1,500 | Value: 15.00 | | | | |
| 1968D | 13,047,000 | — | — | 0.25 | 5.00 | — |
| 1968F | 15,026,000 | — | — | 0.25 | 5.00 | — |
| 1968F Proof | 3,000 | Value: 9.00 | | | | |
| 1968G | 13,855,000 | — | — | 0.25 | 5.00 | — |
| 1968G Proof | 6,023 | Value: 6.00 | | | | |
| 1968J | 13,362,000 | — | — | 0.25 | 5.00 | — |
| 1968J Proof | 2,000 | Value: 15.00 | | | | |
| 1969D | 23,488,000 | — | — | 0.10 | 1.50 | — |
| 1969F | 27,046,000 | — | — | 0.10 | 1.50 | — |
| 1969F Proof | 5,000 | Value: 3.00 | | | | |
| 1969G | 15,631,000 | — | — | 0.10 | 1.50 | — |
| 1969G Proof | 8,700 | Value: 2.50 | | | | |
| 1969J | 24,120,000 | — | — | 0.10 | 1.50 | — |
| 1969J Proof | 5,000 | Value: 2.00 | | | | |
| 1970D | 39,940,000 | — | — | 0.10 | 0.25 | — |
| 1970F | 45,517,000 | — | — | 0.10 | 0.25 | — |
| 1970F Proof | 5,140 | Value: 2.50 | | | | |
| 1970G | 27,638,000 | — | — | 0.10 | 0.25 | — |
| 1970G Proof | 10,200 | Value: 1.50 | | | | |
| 1970J | 40,873,000 | — | — | 0.10 | 0.25 | — |
| 1970J Proof | 5,000 | Value: 2.50 | | | | |
| 1971D | 57,345,000 | — | — | 0.10 | 0.25 | — |
| 1971D Proof | 8,000 | Value: 1.50 | | | | |
| 1971F | 66,426,000 | — | — | 0.10 | 0.25 | — |
| 1971F Proof | 8,000 | Value: 1.50 | | | | |
| 1971G | 38,284,000 | — | — | 0.10 | 0.25 | — |
| 1971G Proof | 10,000 | Value: 1.50 | | | | |
| 1971J | 58,566,000 | — | — | 0.10 | 0.25 | — |
| 1971J Proof | 8,000 | Value: 1.50 | | | | |
| 1972D | 52,325,000 | — | — | 0.10 | 0.25 | — |
| 1972D Proof | 8,000 | Value: 1.50 | | | | |
| 1972F | 60,292,000 | — | — | 0.10 | 0.25 | — |
| 1972F Proof | 8,000 | Value: 1.50 | | | | |
| 1972G | 34,719,000 | — | — | 0.10 | 0.25 | — |
| 1972G Proof | 10,000 | Value: 1.50 | | | | |
| 1972J | 54,218,000 | — | — | 0.10 | 0.25 | — |
| 1972J Proof | 8,000 | Value: 1.50 | | | | |
| 1973D | 15,596,000 | — | — | 0.10 | 0.25 | — |
| 1973D Proof | 9,000 | Value: 1.50 | | | | |
| 1973F | 18,039,000 | — | — | 0.10 | 0.25 | — |
| 1973F Proof | 9,000 | Value: 1.50 | | | | |
| 1973G | 10,391,000 | — | — | 0.10 | 0.25 | — |
| 1973G Proof | 9,000 | Value: 1.50 | | | | |
| 1973J | 16,035,000 | — | — | 0.10 | 0.25 | — |
| 1973J Proof | 9,000 | Value: 1.50 | | | | |
| 1974D | 15,769,000 | — | — | 0.10 | 0.25 | — |
| 1974D Proof | 35,000 | Value: 0.50 | | | | |
| 1974F | 18,143,000 | — | — | 0.10 | 0.25 | — |
| 1974F Proof | 35,000 | Value: 0.50 | | | | |
| 1974G | 10,508,000 | — | — | 0.10 | 0.25 | — |
| 1974G Proof | 35,000 | Value: 0.50 | | | | |
| 1974J | 16,055,000 | — | — | 0.10 | 0.25 | — |
| 1974J Proof | 35,000 | Value: 0.50 | | | | |
| 1975D | 15,715,000 | — | — | 0.10 | 0.25 | — |
| 1975D Proof | 43,000 | Value: 0.50 | | | | |
| 1975F | 18,013,000 | — | — | 0.10 | 0.25 | — |
| 1975F Proof | 43,000 | Value: 0.50 | | | | |
| 1975G | 10,466,000 | — | — | 0.10 | 0.25 | — |
| 1975G Proof | 43,000 | Value: 0.50 | | | | |
| 1975J | 16,201,000 | — | — | 0.10 | 0.25 | — |
| 1975J Proof | 43,000 | Value: 0.50 | | | | |
| 1976D | 47,091,000 | — | — | 0.10 | 0.25 | — |
| 1976D Proof | 43,000 | Value: 0.50 | | | | |
| 1976F | 54,370,000 | — | — | 0.10 | 0.25 | — |
| 1976F Proof | 43,000 | Value: 0.50 | | | | |
| 1976G | 31,367,000 | — | — | 0.10 | 0.25 | — |
| 1976G Proof | 43,000 | Value: 0.50 | | | | |
| 1976J | 48,321,000 | — | — | 0.10 | 0.25 | — |
| 1976J Proof | 43,000 | Value: 0.50 | | | | |
| 1977D | 52,159,000 | — | — | 0.10 | 0.20 | — |
| 1977D Proof | 51,000 | Value: 0.40 | | | | |
| 1977F | 60,124,000 | — | — | 0.10 | 0.20 | — |
| 1977F Proof | 51,000 | Value: 0.40 | | | | |
| 1977G | 34,600,000 | — | — | 0.10 | 0.20 | — |
| 1977G Proof | 51,000 | Value: 0.40 | | | | |
| 1977J | 53,481,000 | — | — | 0.10 | 0.20 | — |
| 1977J Proof | 51,000 | Value: 0.40 | | | | |
| 1978D | 41,600,000 | — | — | 0.10 | 0.20 | — |
| 1978D Proof | 54,000 | Value: 0.40 | | | | |
| 1978F | 48,000,000 | — | — | 0.10 | 0.20 | — |
| 1978F Proof | 54,000 | Value: 0.40 | | | | |
| 1978G | 27,680,000 | — | — | 0.10 | 0.20 | — |
| 1978G Proof | 54,000 | Value: 0.40 | | | | |
| 1978J | 42,720,000 | — | — | 0.10 | 0.20 | — |
| 1978J Proof | 54,000 | Value: 0.40 | | | | |
| 1979D | 41,600,000 | — | — | 0.10 | 0.20 | — |
| 1979D Proof | 89,000 | Value: 0.40 | | | | |
| 1979F | 48,000,000 | — | — | 0.10 | 0.20 | — |
| 1979F Proof | 89,000 | Value: 0.40 | | | | |
| 1979G | 27,680,000 | — | — | 0.10 | 0.20 | — |
| 1979G Proof | 89,000 | Value: 0.40 | | | | |
| 1979J | 42,711,000 | — | — | 0.10 | 0.20 | — |
| 1979J Proof | 89,000 | Value: 0.40 | | | | |
| 1980D | 39,880,000 | — | — | 0.10 | 0.20 | — |
| 1980D Proof | 110,000 | Value: 0.40 | | | | |
| 1980F | 53,270,000 | — | — | 0.10 | 0.20 | — |
| 1980F Proof | 110,000 | Value: 0.40 | | | | |
| 1980G | 43,070,000 | — | — | 0.10 | 0.20 | — |
| 1980G Proof | 110,000 | Value: 0.40 | | | | |
| 1980J | 59,130,000 | — | — | 0.10 | 0.20 | — |
| 1980J Proof | 110,000 | Value: 0.40 | | | | |
| 1981D | 82,250,000 | — | — | 0.10 | 0.20 | — |
| 1981D Proof | 91,000 | Value: 0.40 | | | | |
| 1981F | 84,910,000 | — | — | 0.10 | 0.20 | — |
| 1981F Proof | 91,000 | Value: 0.40 | | | | |
| 1981G | 41,910,000 | — | — | 0.10 | 0.20 | — |
| 1981G Proof | 91,000 | Value: 0.40 | | | | |
| 1981J | 49,290,000 | — | — | 0.10 | 0.20 | — |
| 1981J Proof | 91,000 | Value: 0.40 | | | | |
| 1982D | 57,500,000 | — | — | 0.10 | 0.20 | — |
| 1982D Proof | 78,000 | Value: 0.40 | | | | |
| 1982F | 53,290,000 | — | — | 0.10 | 0.20 | — |
| 1982F Proof | 78,000 | Value: 0.40 | | | | |
| 1982G | 23,750,000 | — | — | 0.10 | 0.20 | — |
| 1982G Proof | 78,000 | Value: 0.40 | | | | |
| 1982J | 62,000,000 | — | — | 0.10 | 0.20 | — |
| 1982J Proof | 78,000 | Value: 0.40 | | | | |
| 1983D | 46,800,000 | — | — | 0.10 | 0.20 | — |
| 1983D Proof | 75,000 | Value: 0.40 | | | | |
| 1983F | 54,000,000 | — | — | 0.10 | 0.20 | — |
| 1983F Proof | 75,000 | Value: 0.40 | | | | |
| 1983G | 31,140,000 | — | — | 0.10 | 0.20 | — |
| 1983G Proof | 75,000 | Value: 0.40 | | | | |
| 1983J | 48,060,000 | — | — | 0.10 | 0.20 | — |
| 1983J Proof | 75,000 | Value: 0.40 | | | | |
| 1984D | 36,400,000 | — | — | 0.10 | 0.20 | — |
| 1984D Proof | 64,000 | Value: 0.40 | | | | |
| 1984F | 42,000,000 | — | — | 0.10 | 0.20 | — |
| 1984F Proof | 64,000 | Value: 0.40 | | | | |
| 1984G | 24,200,000 | — | — | 0.10 | 0.20 | — |
| 1984G Proof | 64,000 | Value: 0.40 | | | | |
| 1984J | 37,400,000 | — | — | 0.10 | 0.20 | — |
| 1984J Proof | 64,000 | Value: 0.40 | | | | |
| 1985D | 15,600,000 | — | — | — | 0.10 | — |
| 1985D Proof | 56,000 | Value: 0.40 | | | | |
| 1985F | 18,000,000 | — | — | — | 0.10 | — |
| 1985F Proof | 54,000 | Value: 0.40 | | | | |
| 1985G | 10,400,000 | — | — | — | 0.10 | — |
| 1985G Proof | 55,000 | Value: 0.40 | | | | |
| 1985J | 16,000,000 | — | — | — | 0.10 | — |
| 1985J Proof | 54,000 | Value: 0.40 | | | | |
| 1986D | 36,400,000 | — | — | — | 0.10 | — |
| 1986D Proof | 44,000 | Value: 0.40 | | | | |
| 1986F | 42,000,000 | — | — | — | 0.10 | — |
| 1986F Proof | 44,000 | Value: 0.40 | | | | |
| 1986G | 24,200,000 | — | — | — | 0.10 | — |
| 1986G Proof | 44,000 | Value: 0.40 | | | | |
| 1986J | 37,400,000 | — | — | — | 0.10 | — |
| 1986J Proof | 44,000 | Value: 0.40 | | | | |
| 1987D | 52,000,000 | — | — | — | 0.10 | — |
| 1987D Proof | 45,000 | Value: 0.40 | | | | |
| 1987F | 60,000,000 | — | — | — | 0.10 | — |
| 1987F Proof | 45,000 | Value: 0.40 | | | | |
| 1987G | 34,600,000 | — | — | — | 0.10 | — |
| 1987G Proof | 45,000 | Value: 0.40 | | | | |
| 1987J | 53,400,000 | — | — | — | 0.10 | — |
| 1987J Proof | 45,000 | Value: 0.40 | | | | |
| 1988D | 52,400,000 | — | — | — | 0.10 | — |
| 1988D Proof | 45,000 | Value: 0.40 | | | | |
| 1988F | 72,000,000 | — | — | — | 0.10 | — |
| 1988F Proof | 45,000 | Value: 0.40 | | | | |
| 1988G | 41,500,000 | — | — | — | 0.10 | — |
| 1988G Proof | 45,000 | Value: 0.40 | | | | |
| 1988J | 64,099,999 | — | — | — | 0.10 | — |
| 1988J Proof | 45,000 | Value: 0.40 | | | | |
| 1989D | 93,600,000 | — | — | — | 0.10 | — |
| 1989D Proof | 45,000 | Value: 0.40 | | | | |
| 1989F | 108,000,000 | — | — | — | 0.10 | — |
| 1989F Proof | 45,000 | Value: 0.40 | | | | |
| 1989G | 62,280,000 | — | — | — | 0.10 | — |
| 1989G Proof | 45,000 | Value: 0.40 | | | | |
| 1989J | 96,120,000 | — | — | — | 0.10 | — |
| 1989J Proof | 45,000 | Value: 0.40 | | | | |
| 1990A | 70,000,000 | — | — | — | 0.10 | — |
| 1990D | 93,600,000 | — | — | — | 0.10 | — |
| 1990D Proof | 45,000 | Value: 0.40 | | | | |
| 1990F | 108,000,000 | — | — | — | 0.10 | — |
| 1990F Proof | 45,000 | Value: 0.40 | | | | |
| 1990G | 62,280,000 | — | — | — | 0.10 | — |
| 1990G Proof | 45,000 | Value: 0.40 | | | | |
| 1990J | 96,120,000 | — | — | — | 0.10 | — |
| 1990J Proof | 45,000 | Value: 0.40 | | | | |
| 1991A | 128,000,000 | — | — | — | 0.10 | — |
| 1991A Proof | 45,000 | Value: 0.40 | | | | |
| 1991D | 134,400,000 | — | — | — | 0.10 | — |
| 1991D Proof | 45,000 | Value: 0.40 | | | | |
| 1991F | 153,600,000 | — | — | — | 0.10 | — |
| 1991F Proof | 45,000 | Value: 0.40 | | | | |
| 1991G | 89,600,000 | — | — | — | 0.10 | — |
| 1991G Proof | 45,000 | Value: 0.40 | | | | |
| 1991J | 134,400,000 | — | — | — | 0.10 | — |
| 1991J Proof | 45,000 | Value: 0.40 | | | | |
| 1992A | 28,000,000 | — | — | — | 0.10 | — |
| 1992A Proof | 45,000 | Value: 0.40 | | | | |
| 1992D | 29,400,000 | — | — | — | 0.10 | — |
| 1992D Proof | 45,000 | Value: 0.40 | | | | |
| 1992F | 33,600,000 | — | — | — | 0.10 | — |
| 1992F Proof | 45,000 | Value: 0.40 | | | | |
| 1992G | 19,600,000 | — | — | — | 0.10 | — |
| 1992G Proof | 45,000 | Value: 0.40 | | | | |
| 1992J | 29,400,000 | — | — | — | 0.10 | — |
| 1992J Proof | 45,000 | Value: 0.40 | | | | |
| 1993A | 36,000,000 | — | — | — | 0.10 | — |
| 1993A Proof | 45,000 | Value: 0.40 | | | | |
| 1993D | 37,800,000 | — | — | — | 0.10 | — |
| 1993D Proof | 45,000 | Value: 0.40 | | | | |
| 1993F | 43,200,000 | — | — | — | 0.10 | — |
| 1993F Proof | 45,000 | Value: 0.40 | | | | |
| 1993G | 25,200,000 | — | — | — | 0.10 | — |
| 1993G Proof | 45,000 | Value: 0.40 | | | | |
| 1993J | 37,800,000 | — | — | — | 0.10 | — |
| 1993J Proof | 45,000 | Value: 0.40 | | | | |
| 1994A | 38,000,000 | — | — | — | 0.10 | — |
| 1994A Proof | 45,000 | Value: 0.40 | | | | |
| 1994D | 39,900,000 | — | — | — | 0.10 | — |
| 1994D Proof | 45,000 | Value: 0.40 | | | | |
| 1994F | 45,600,000 | — | — | — | 0.10 | — |
| 1994F Proof | 45,000 | Value: 0.40 | | | | |
| 1994G | 26,600,000 | — | — | — | 0.10 | — |
| 1994G Proof | 45,000 | Value: 0.40 | | | | |
| 1994J | 39,900,000 | — | — | — | 0.10 | — |
| 1994J Proof | 45,000 | Value: 0.40 | | | | |
| 1995A | 48,000,000 | — | — | — | 0.15 | — |

| Date | Mintage | F | VF | XF | Unc | BU |
|---|---|---|---|---|---|---|
| 1995A Proof | 45,000 | Value: 0.45 | | | | |
| 1995D | 50,400,000 | — | — | — | 0.15 | — |
| 1995D Proof | 45,000 | Value: 0.45 | | | | |
| 1995F | 57,600,000 | — | — | — | 0.15 | — |
| 1995F Proof | 45,000 | Value: 0.45 | | | | |
| 1995G | 33,600,000 | — | — | — | 0.15 | — |
| 1995G Proof | 45,000 | Value: 0.45 | | | | |
| 1995J | 50,400,000 | — | — | — | 0.15 | — |
| 1995J Proof | 45,000 | Value: 0.45 | | | | |
| 1996A | 48,000,000 | — | — | — | 0.20 | — |
| 1996A Proof | 45,000 | Value: 0.50 | | | | |
| 1996D | 50,400,000 | — | — | — | 0.20 | — |
| 1996D Proof | 45,000 | Value: 0.50 | | | | |
| 1996F | 57,600,000 | — | — | — | 0.20 | — |
| 1996F Proof | 45,000 | Value: 0.50 | | | | |
| 1996G | 33,600,000 | — | — | — | 0.20 | — |
| 1996G Proof | 45,000 | Value: 0.50 | | | | |
| 1996J | 50,400,000 | — | — | — | 0.20 | — |
| 1996J Proof | 45,000 | Value: 0.50 | | | | |
| 1996A In sets only | 70,000 | — | — | — | 1.75 | — |
| 1997A Proof | 45,000 | Value: 2.00 | | | | |
| 1997D In sets only | 70,000 | — | — | — | 1.75 | — |
| 1997D Proof | 45,000 | Value: 2.00 | | | | |
| 1997F In sets only | 70,000 | — | — | — | 1.75 | — |
| 1997F Proof | 45,000 | Value: 2.00 | | | | |
| 1997G In sets only | 70,000 | — | — | — | 1.75 | — |
| 1997G Proof | 45,000 | Value: 2.00 | | | | |
| 1997J In sets only | 70,000 | — | — | — | 1.75 | — |
| 1997J Proof | 45,000 | Value: 2.00 | | | | |
| 1998A In sets only | 70,000 | — | — | — | 1.75 | — |
| 1998A Proof | 45,000 | Value: 2.00 | | | | |
| 1998D In sets only | 70,000 | — | — | — | 1.75 | — |
| 1998D Proof | 45,000 | Value: 2.00 | | | | |
| 1998F In sets only | 70,000 | — | — | — | 1.75 | — |
| 1998F Proof | 45,000 | Value: 2.00 | | | | |
| 1998G In sets only | 70,000 | — | — | — | 1.75 | — |
| 1998G Proof | 45,000 | Value: 2.00 | | | | |
| 1998J In sets only | 70,000 | — | — | — | 1.75 | — |
| 1998J Proof | 45,000 | Value: 2.00 | | | | |
| 1999A In sets only | 70,000 | — | — | — | 1.75 | — |
| 1999A Proof | 45,000 | Value: 2.00 | | | | |
| 1999D In sets only | 70,000 | — | — | — | 1.75 | — |
| 1999D Proof | 45,000 | Value: 2.00 | | | | |
| 1999F In sets only | 70,000 | — | — | — | 1.75 | — |
| 1999F Proof | 45,000 | Value: 2.00 | | | | |
| 1999G In sets only | 70,000 | — | — | — | 1.75 | — |
| 1999G Proof | 45,000 | Value: 2.00 | | | | |
| 1999J In sets only | 70,000 | — | — | — | 1.75 | — |
| 1999J Proof | 45,000 | Value: 2.00 | | | | |
| 2000A In sets only | 45,000 | — | — | — | 1.75 | — |
| 2000A Proof | 70,000 | Value: 2.00 | | | | |
| 2000D In sets only | 45,000 | — | — | — | 1.75 | — |
| 2000D Proof | 70,000 | Value: 2.00 | | | | |
| 2000F In sets only | 45,000 | — | — | — | 1.75 | — |
| 2000F Proof | 70,000 | Value: 2.00 | | | | |
| 2000G In sets only | 45,000 | — | — | — | 1.75 | — |
| 2000G Proof | 70,000 | Value: 2.00 | | | | |
| 2000J In sets only | 45,000 | — | — | — | 1.75 | — |
| 2000J Proof | 70,000 | Value: 2.00 | | | | |
| 2001A In sets only | 130,000 | — | — | — | 5.00 | — |
| 2001A Proof | 78,000 | Value: 5.00 | | | | |
| 2001D In sets only | 130,000 | — | — | — | 5.00 | — |
| 2001D Proof | 78,000 | Value: 5.00 | | | | |
| 2001F In sets only | 130,000 | — | — | — | 5.00 | — |
| 2001F Proof | 78,000 | Value: 5.00 | | | | |
| 2001G In sets only | 130,000 | — | — | — | 5.00 | — |
| 2001G Proof | 78,000 | Value: 5.00 | | | | |
| 2001J In sets only | 130,000 | — | — | — | 5.00 | — |
| 2001J Proof | 78,000 | Value: 5.00 | | | | |

## 10 PFENNIG KM# 103 Composition: Brass Clad Steel

**Note:** Currency Reform.

| Date | Mintage | F | VF | XF | Unc | BU |
|---|---|---|---|---|---|---|
| 1949D | 140,558,000 | — | 0.50 | 7.50 | 30.00 | — |
| 1949D Proof | — | Value: 150 | | | | |
| 1949F | 120,932,000 | — | 0.50 | 7.50 | 30.00 | — |
| 1949F Proof | 250 | Value: 140 | | | | |
| 1949G | 82,933,000 | — | 1.00 | 7.50 | 40.00 | — |
| 1949 Large J | 154,095,000 | — | 0.50 | 7.50 | 30.00 | — |
| 1949J Proof | — | Value: 60.00 | | | | |
| 1949 Small J | Inc. above | — | 0.50 | 7.50 | 30.00 | — |
| 1949J Proof | — | Value: 60.00 | | | | |

## 10 PFENNIG KM# 108 Composition: Brass Plated Steel

**Note:** Federal Republic.

| Date | Mintage | F | VF | XF | Unc | BU |
|---|---|---|---|---|---|---|
| 1950D | 393,209,000 | — | — | 0.20 | 4.00 | — |
| 1950F | 584,340,000 | — | — | 0.20 | 4.00 | — |
| 1950F Proof | 500 | Value: 45.00 | | | | |
| 1950G | 309,045,000 | — | — | 0.20 | 4.00 | — |
| 1950G Proof | 1,800 | Value: 5.00 | | | | |
| 1950J | 402,452,000 | — | — | 0.20 | 4.00 | — |
| 1950J Proof | — | Value: 20.00 | | | | |
| 1966D | 31,220,000 | — | — | 0.20 | 4.00 | — |
| 1966F | 36,097,000 | — | — | 0.20 | 4.00 | — |
| 1966F Proof | 100 | Value: 75.00 | | | | |
| 1966G | 25,338,000 | — | — | 0.20 | 4.00 | — |
| 1966G Proof | 3,070 | Value: 7.50 | | | | |
| 1966J | 32,116,000 | — | — | 0.20 | 4.00 | — |
| 1966J Proof | 1,000 | Value: 12.50 | | | | |
| 1967D | 15,632,000 | — | — | 0.20 | 5.00 | — |
| 1967F | 18,049,000 | — | — | 0.20 | 5.00 | — |
| 1967F Proof | 1,500 | Value: 15.00 | | | | |
| 1967G | 1,518,000 | — | 2.00 | 6.00 | 20.00 | — |
| 1967G Proof | 4,500 | Value: 7.50 | | | | |
| 1967J | 16,050,999 | — | — | 0.20 | 5.00 | — |
| 1967J Proof | 1,500 | Value: 12.50 | | | | |
| 1968D | 5,207,000 | — | — | 0.20 | 3.50 | — |
| 1968F | 6,010,000 | — | — | 0.20 | 3.50 | — |
| 1968F Proof | 3,000 | Value: 10.00 | | | | |
| 1968G | 12,384,000 | — | 0.15 | 0.50 | 3.50 | — |
| 1968G Proof | 6,023 | Value: 5.00 | | | | |
| 1968J | 5,422,000 | — | — | 0.20 | 4.00 | — |
| 1968J Proof | 2,000 | Value: 10.00 | | | | |
| 1969D | 41,693,000 | — | — | 0.15 | 2.50 | — |
| 1969F | 48,084,000 | — | — | 0.15 | 0.25 | — |
| 1969F Proof | 5,000 | Value: 3.00 | | | | |
| 1969G | 48,760,000 | — | — | 0.15 | 0.25 | — |
| 1969G Proof | 8,700 | Value: 2.50 | | | | |
| 1969J | 42,756,000 | — | — | 0.15 | 0.25 | — |
| 1969J Proof | 5,000 | Value: 2.50 | | | | |
| 1970D | 54,085,000 | — | — | 0.15 | 0.25 | — |
| 1970F | 60,086,000 | — | — | 0.15 | 0.25 | — |
| 1970F Proof | 5,140 | Value: 3.00 | | | | |
| 1970G | 35,900,000 | — | — | 0.15 | 0.25 | — |
| 1970G Proof | 10,200 | Value: 2.00 | | | | |
| 1970J | 40,115,000 | — | — | 0.15 | 0.25 | — |
| 1970J Proof | 5,000 | Value: 2.50 | | | | |
| 1971D | 54,022,000 | — | — | 0.15 | 0.25 | — |
| 1971D Proof | 8,000 | Value: 2.50 | | | | |
| 1971F | 92,534,000 | — | — | 0.15 | 0.25 | — |
| 1971F Proof | 8,000 | Value: 2.50 | | | | |
| 1971G | 88,614,000 | — | — | 0.15 | 0.25 | — |
| 1971G Proof | 10,000 | Value: 2.00 | | | | |
| 1971 Small J | 65,622,000 | — | — | 0.15 | 0.25 | — |
| 1971 Large J | Inc. above | — | — | 0.15 | 0.25 | — |
| 1971J Proof | 8,000 | Value: 1.50 | | | | |
| 1972D | 104,345,000 | — | — | 0.15 | 0.25 | — |
| 1972D Proof | 8,000 | Value: 1.50 | | | | |
| 1972F | 110,177,000 | — | — | 0.15 | 0.25 | — |
| 1972F Proof | 8,000 | Value: 1.50 | | | | |
| 1972G | 71,766,000 | — | — | 0.15 | 0.25 | — |
| 1972G Proof | 10,000 | Value: 1.50 | | | | |
| 1972J | 96,991,000 | — | — | 0.15 | 0.25 | — |
| 1972J Proof | 8,000 | Value: 1.50 | | | | |
| 1973D | 26,052,000 | — | — | 0.15 | 0.25 | — |
| 1973D Proof | 9,000 | Value: 1.50 | | | | |
| 1973F | 30,070,000 | — | — | 0.15 | 0.25 | — |
| 1973F Proof | 9,000 | Value: 1.50 | | | | |
| 1973G | 17,294,000 | — | — | 0.15 | 0.25 | — |
| 1973G Proof | 9,000 | Value: 1.50 | | | | |
| 1973J | 26,774,000 | — | — | 0.15 | 0.25 | — |
| 1973J Proof | 9,000 | Value: 1.50 | | | | |
| 1974D | 15,707,000 | — | — | 0.15 | 0.25 | — |
| 1974D Proof | 35,000 | Value: 0.75 | | | | |
| 1974F | 18,135,000 | — | — | 0.15 | 0.25 | — |
| 1974F Proof | 35,000 | Value: 0.75 | | | | |
| 1974G | 10,450,000 | — | — | 0.15 | 0.25 | — |
| 1974G Proof | 35,000 | Value: 0.75 | | | | |
| 1974J | 16,056,000 | — | — | 0.15 | 0.25 | — |
| 1974J Proof | 35,000 | Value: 0.75 | | | | |
| 1975D | 15,654,000 | — | — | 0.15 | 0.25 | — |
| 1975D Proof | 43,000 | Value: 0.75 | | | | |
| 1975F | 18,043,000 | — | — | 0.15 | 0.25 | — |
| 1975F Proof | 43,000 | Value: 0.75 | | | | |
| 1975G | 10,403,000 | — | — | 0.15 | 0.25 | — |
| 1975G Proof | 43,000 | Value: 0.75 | | | | |
| 1975J | 16,111,000 | — | — | 0.15 | 0.25 | — |
| 1975J Proof | 43,000 | Value: 0.75 | | | | |
| 1976D | 65,200,000 | — | — | 0.15 | 0.25 | — |
| 1976D Proof | 43,000 | Value: 0.75 | | | | |
| 1976F | 75,282,000 | — | — | 0.15 | 0.25 | — |
| 1976F Proof | 43,000 | Value: 0.75 | | | | |
| 1976G | 43,372,000 | — | — | 0.15 | 0.25 | — |
| 1976G Proof | 43,000 | Value: 0.75 | | | | |
| 1976J | 66,930,000 | — | — | 0.15 | 0.25 | — |
| 1976J Proof | 43,000 | Value: 0.75 | | | | |
| 1977D | 64,989,000 | — | — | 0.10 | 0.20 | — |
| 1977D Proof | 51,000 | Value: 0.50 | | | | |
| 1977F | 75,052,000 | — | — | 0.10 | 0.20 | — |
| 1977F Proof | 51,000 | Value: 0.50 | | | | |
| 1977G | 43,300,000 | — | — | 0.10 | 0.20 | — |
| 1977G Proof | 51,000 | Value: 0.50 | | | | |
| 1977J | 66,800,000 | — | — | 0.10 | 0.20 | — |
| 1977J Proof | 51,000 | Value: 0.50 | | | | |
| 1978D | 91,000,000 | — | — | 0.10 | 0.20 | — |
| 1978D Proof | 54,000 | Value: 0.50 | | | | |
| 1978F | 105,000,000 | — | — | 0.10 | 0.20 | — |
| 1978F Proof | 54,000 | Value: 0.50 | | | | |
| 1978G | 60,590,000 | — | — | 0.10 | 0.20 | — |
| 1978G Proof | 54,000 | Value: 0.50 | | | | |
| 1978J | 93,490,000 | — | — | 0.10 | 0.20 | — |
| 1978J Proof | 54,000 | Value: 0.50 | | | | |
| 1979D | 104,000,000 | — | — | 0.10 | 0.20 | — |
| 1979D Proof | 89,000 | Value: 0.50 | | | | |
| 1979F | 120,000,000 | — | — | 0.10 | 0.20 | — |
| 1979F Proof | 89,000 | Value: 0.50 | | | | |
| 1979G | 69,200,000 | — | — | 0.10 | 0.20 | — |
| 1979G Proof | 89,000 | Value: 0.50 | | | | |
| 1979J | 106,800,000 | — | — | 0.10 | 0.20 | — |
| 1979J Proof | 89,000 | Value: 0.50 | | | | |
| 1980D | 65,450,000 | — | — | 0.10 | 0.20 | — |
| 1980D Proof | 110,000 | Value: 0.50 | | | | |
| 1980F | 122,780,000 | — | — | 0.10 | 0.20 | — |
| 1980F Proof | 110,000 | Value: 0.50 | | | | |
| 1980G | 75,410,000 | — | — | 0.10 | 0.20 | — |
| 1980G Proof | 110,000 | Value: 0.50 | | | | |
| 1980J | 70,960,000 | — | — | 0.10 | 0.20 | — |
| 1980J Proof | 110,000 | Value: 0.50 | | | | |
| 1981D | 135,200,000 | — | — | 0.10 | 0.20 | — |
| 1981D Proof | 91,000 | Value: 0.50 | | | | |
| 1981F | 117,410,000 | — | — | 0.10 | 0.20 | — |
| 1981F Proof | 91,000 | Value: 0.50 | | | | |
| 1981G | 69,440,000 | — | — | 0.10 | 0.20 | — |
| 1981G Proof | 91,000 | Value: 0.50 | | | | |
| 1981J | 138,360,000 | — | — | 0.10 | 0.20 | — |
| 1981J Proof | 91,000 | Value: 0.50 | | | | |
| 1982D | 74,690,000 | — | — | 0.10 | 0.20 | — |
| 1982D Proof | 78,000 | Value: 0.50 | | | | |
| 1982F | 85,140,000 | — | — | 0.10 | 0.20 | — |
| 1982F Proof | 78,000 | Value: 0.50 | | | | |
| 1982G | 50,840,000 | — | — | 0.10 | 0.20 | — |
| 1982G Proof | 78,000 | Value: 0.50 | | | | |
| 1982J | 80,620,000 | — | — | 0.10 | 0.20 | — |
| 1982J Proof | 78,000 | Value: 0.50 | | | | |
| 1983D | 33,800,000 | — | — | 0.10 | 0.20 | — |
| 1983D Proof | 75,000 | Value: 0.50 | | | | |
| 1983F | 39,000,000 | — | — | 0.10 | 0.20 | — |
| 1983F Proof | 75,000 | Value: 0.50 | | | | |
| 1983G | 22,490,000 | — | — | 0.10 | 0.20 | — |
| 1983G Proof | 75,000 | Value: 0.50 | | | | |
| 1983J | 34,710,000 | — | — | 0.10 | 0.20 | — |
| 1983J Proof | 75,000 | Value: 0.50 | | | | |
| 1984D | 52,000,000 | — | — | 0.10 | 0.20 | — |
| 1984D Proof | 64,000 | Value: 0.50 | | | | |
| 1984F | 60,000,000 | — | — | 0.10 | 0.20 | — |
| 1984G Proof | 64,000 | Value: 0.50 | | | | |
| 1984G | 34,600,000 | — | — | 0.10 | 0.20 | — |
| 1984G Proof | 64,000 | Value: 0.50 | | | | |
| 1984J | 53,400,000 | — | — | 0.10 | 0.20 | — |
| 1984J Proof | 64,000 | Value: 0.50 | | | | |
| 1985D | 78,000,000 | — | — | — | 0.15 | — |
| 1985D Proof | 56,000 | Value: 0.50 | | | | |
| 1985F | 90,000,000 | — | — | — | 0.15 | — |
| 1985F Proof | 54,000 | Value: 0.50 | | | | |
| 1985G | 51,900,000 | — | — | — | 0.15 | — |
| 1985G Proof | 55,000 | Value: 0.50 | | | | |
| 1985J | 80,100,000 | — | — | — | 0.15 | — |
| 1985J Proof | 54,000 | Value: 0.50 | | | | |
| 1986D | 41,600,000 | — | — | — | 0.15 | — |
| 1986D Proof | 44,000 | Value: 0.50 | | | | |
| 1986F | 48,000,000 | — | — | — | 0.15 | — |
| 1986F Proof | 44,000 | Value: 0.50 | | | | |
| 1986G | 27,700,000 | — | — | — | 0.15 | — |
| 1986G Proof | 44,000 | Value: 0.50 | | | | |
| 1986J | 42,700,000 | — | — | — | 0.15 | — |
| 1986J Proof | 44,000 | Value: 0.15 | | | | |
| 1987D | 58,500,000 | — | — | — | 0.10 | — |
| 1987D Proof | 45,000 | Value: 0.15 | | | | |
| 1987F | 67,500,000 | — | — | — | 0.10 | — |
| 1987F Proof | 45,000 | Value: 0.15 | | | | |
| 1987G | 38,900,000 | — | — | — | 0.10 | — |
| 1987G Proof | 45,000 | Value: 0.50 | | | | |
| 1987J | 60,100,000 | — | — | — | 0.15 | — |
| 1987J Proof | 45,000 | Value: 0.50 | | | | |
| 1988D | 109,200,000 | — | — | — | 0.15 | — |
| 1988D Proof | 45,000 | Value: 0.50 | | | | |
| 1988F | 126,000,000 | — | — | — | 0.15 | — |
| 1988F Proof | 45,000 | Value: 0.50 | | | | |
| 1988G | 72,700,000 | — | — | — | 0.15 | — |
| 1988G Proof | 45,000 | Value: 0.50 | | | | |
| 1988J | 112,100,000 | — | — | — | 0.15 | — |
| 1988J Proof | 45,000 | Value: 0.50 | | | | |
| 1989D | 119,600,000 | — | — | — | 0.15 | — |
| 1989D Proof | 45,000 | Value: 0.50 | | | | |
| 1989F | 138,000,000 | — | — | — | 0.15 | — |
| 1989F Proof | 45,000 | Value: 0.50 | | | | |

| Date | Mintage | F | VF | XF | Unc | BU |
|---|---|---|---|---|---|---|
| 1989G | 79,580,000 | — | — | — | 0.15 | — |
| 1989G Proof | 45,000 | Value: 0.50 | | | | |
| 1989J | 122,820,000 | — | — | — | 0.15 | — |
| 1989J Proof | 45,000 | Value: 0.50 | | | | |
| 1990A | 100,000,000 | — | — | — | 0.15 | — |
| 1990D | 156,000,000 | — | — | — | 0.15 | — |
| 1990D Proof | 45,000 | Value: 0.50 | | | | |
| 1990F | 180,000,000 | — | — | — | 0.15 | — |
| 1990F Proof | 45,000 | Value: 0.50 | | | | |
| 1990G | 103,800,000 | — | — | — | 0.15 | — |
| 1990G Proof | 45,000 | Value: 0.50 | | | | |
| 1990J | 160,200,000 | — | — | — | 0.15 | — |
| 1990J Proof | 45,000 | Value: 0.50 | | | | |
| 1991A | 170,000,000 | — | — | — | 0.15 | — |
| 1991A Proof | 45,000 | Value: 0.40 | | | | |
| 1991D | 178,550,000 | — | — | — | 0.15 | — |
| 1991D Proof | 45,000 | Value: 0.40 | | | | |
| 1991F | 204,000,000 | — | — | — | 0.15 | — |
| 1991F Proof | 45,000 | Value: 0.40 | | | | |
| 1991G | 119,000,000 | — | — | — | 0.15 | — |
| 1991G Proof | 45,000 | Value: 0.40 | | | | |
| 1991J | 178,500,000 | — | — | — | 0.15 | — |
| 1991J Proof | 45,000 | Value: 0.40 | | | | |
| 1992A | 80,000,000 | — | — | — | 0.10 | — |
| 1992A Proof | 45,000 | Value: 0.40 | | | | |
| 1992D | 84,000,000 | — | — | — | 0.10 | — |
| 1992D Proof | 45,000 | Value: 0.40 | | | | |
| 1992F | 96,000,000 | — | — | — | 0.10 | — |
| 1992F Proof | 45,000 | Value: 0.40 | | | | |
| 1992G | 56,000,000 | — | — | — | 0.10 | — |
| 1992G Proof | 45,000 | Value: 0.40 | | | | |
| 1992J | 84,000,000 | — | — | — | 0.10 | — |
| 1992J Proof | 45,000 | Value: 0.40 | | | | |
| 1993A | 80,000,000 | — | — | — | 0.10 | — |
| 1993A Proof | 45,000 | Value: 0.40 | | | | |
| 1993D | 84,000,000 | — | — | — | 0.10 | — |
| 1993D Proof | 45,000 | Value: 0.40 | | | | |
| 1993F | 96,000,000 | — | — | — | 0.10 | — |
| 1993F Proof | 45,000 | Value: 0.40 | | | | |
| 1993G | 56,000,000 | — | — | — | 0.10 | — |
| 1993G Proof | 45,000 | Value: 0.40 | | | | |
| 1993J | 84,000,000 | — | — | — | 0.10 | — |
| 1993J Proof | 45,000 | Value: 0.40 | | | | |
| 1994A | 100,000,000 | — | — | — | 0.10 | — |
| 1994A Proof | 45,000 | Value: 0.40 | | | | |
| 1994D | 105,000,000 | — | — | — | 0.10 | — |
| 1994D Proof | 45,000 | Value: 0.40 | | | | |
| 1994F | 120,000,000 | — | — | — | 0.10 | — |
| 1994F Proof | 45,000 | Value: 0.40 | | | | |
| 1994G | 70,000,000 | — | — | — | 0.10 | — |
| 1994G Proof | 45,000 | Value: 0.40 | | | | |
| 1994J | 105,000,000 | — | — | — | 0.10 | — |
| 1994J Proof | 45,000 | Value: 0.40 | | | | |
| 1995A | 110,000,000 | — | — | — | 0.15 | — |
| 1995A Proof | 45,000 | Value: 0.45 | | | | |
| 1995D | 115,000,000 | — | — | — | 0.15 | — |
| 1995D Proof | 45,000 | Value: 0.45 | | | | |
| 1995F | 132,000,000 | — | — | — | 0.15 | — |
| 1995F Proof | 45,000 | Value: 0.45 | | | | |
| 1995G | 77,000,000 | — | — | — | 0.15 | — |
| 1995G Proof | 45,000 | Value: 0.45 | | | | |
| 1995J | 115,500,000 | — | — | — | 0.15 | — |
| 1995J Proof | 45,000 | Value: 0.45 | | | | |
| 1996A | 90,000,000 | — | — | — | 0.20 | — |
| 1996A Proof | 45,000 | Value: 0.50 | | | | |
| 1996D | 94,500,000 | — | — | — | 0.20 | — |
| 1996D Proof | 45,000 | Value: 0.50 | | | | |
| 1996F | 108,000,000 | — | — | — | 0.20 | — |
| 1996F Proof | 45,000 | Value: 0.50 | | | | |
| 1996G | 63,000,000 | — | — | — | 0.20 | — |
| 1996G Proof | 45,000 | Value: 0.50 | | | | |
| 1996J | 94,500,000 | — | — | — | 0.20 | — |
| 1996J Proof | 45,000 | Value: 0.50 | | | | |
| 1997A In sets only | 70,000 | — | — | — | 1.75 | — |
| 1997A Proof | 45,000 | Value: 2.00 | | | | |
| 1997D In sets only | 70,000 | — | — | — | 1.75 | — |
| 1997D Proof | 45,000 | Value: 2.00 | | | | |
| 1997F In sets only | 70,000 | — | — | — | 1.75 | — |
| 1997F Proof | 45,000 | Value: 2.00 | | | | |
| 1997G In sets only | 70,000 | — | — | — | 1.75 | — |
| 1997G Proof | 45,000 | Value: 2.00 | | | | |
| 1997J In sets only | 70,000 | — | — | — | 1.75 | — |
| 1997J Proof | 45,000 | Value: 2.00 | | | | |
| 1998A | — | — | — | — | 1.75 | — |
| 1998A Proof | — | Value: 2.00 | | | | |
| 1998D | — | — | — | — | 1.75 | — |
| 1998D Proof | — | Value: 2.00 | | | | |
| 1998F In sets only | 70,000 | — | — | — | 1.75 | — |
| 1998F Proof | 45,000 | Value: 2.00 | | | | |
| 1998G | — | — | — | — | 1.75 | — |
| 1998G Proof | — | Value: 2.00 | | | | |
| 1998J | — | — | — | — | 1.75 | — |
| 1998J Proof | — | Value: 2.00 | | | | |
| 1999A | — | — | — | — | 1.75 | — |
| 1999A Proof | — | Value: 2.00 | | | | |
| 1999D | — | — | — | — | 1.75 | — |
| 1999D Proof | — | Value: 2.00 | | | | |
| 1999F In sets only | 70,000 | — | — | — | 1.75 | — |
| 1999F Proof | 45,000 | Value: 2.00 | | | | |
| 1999G | — | — | — | — | 1.75 | — |
| 1999G Proof | — | Value: 2.00 | | | | |
| 1999J | — | — | — | — | 1.75 | — |
| 1999J Proof | — | Value: 2.00 | | | | |
| 2000A In sets only | 70,000 | — | — | — | 1.75 | — |
| 2000A Proof | 45,000 | Value: 2.00 | | | | |
| 2000D In sets only | 70,000 | — | — | — | 1.75 | — |
| 2000D Proof | 45,000 | Value: 2.00 | | | | |
| 2000F In sets only | 70,000 | — | — | — | 1.75 | — |
| 2000F Proof | 45,000 | Value: 2.00 | | | | |
| 2000G In sets only | 70,000 | — | — | — | 1.75 | — |
| 2000G Proof | 45,000 | Value: 2.00 | | | | |
| 2000J In sets only | 70,000 | — | — | — | 1.75 | — |
| 2000J Proof | 45,000 | Value: 2.00 | | | | |
| 2001A In sets only | 130,000 | — | — | — | 5.00 | — |
| 2001A Proof | 78,000 | Value: 5.00 | | | | |
| 2001D In sets only | 130,000 | — | — | — | 5.00 | — |
| 2001D Proof | 78,000 | Value: 5.00 | | | | |
| 2001F In sets only | 130,000 | — | — | — | 5.00 | — |
| 2001F Proof | 78,000 | Value: 5.00 | | | | |
| 2001G In sets only | 130,000 | — | — | — | 5.00 | — |
| 2001G Proof | 78,000 | Value: 5.00 | | | | |
| 2001J In sets only | 130,000 | — | — | — | 5.00 | — |
| 2001J Proof | 78,000 | Value: 5.00 | | | | |

### 50 PFENNIG KM# 104 Composition: Copper-Nickel

**Note:** Currency Reform.

| Date | Mintage | F | VF | XF | Unc | BU |
|---|---|---|---|---|---|---|
| 1949D | 39,108,000 | — | 0.75 | 4.50 | 45.00 | — |
| 1949F | 45,118,000 | — | 0.75 | 4.50 | 45.00 | — |
| 1949F Proof | 200 | Value: 125 | | | | |
| 1949G | 25,924,000 | — | 0.75 | 5.00 | 55.00 | — |
| 1949J | 42,303,000 | — | 0.75 | 4.50 | 55.00 | — |
| 1949J Proof | — | Value: 135 | | | | |
| 1950G | 30,000 | — | 250 | 400 | 700 | — |

**Note:** The 1950G dated coin was restruck without authorization by a mint official using genuine dies - quantity unknow.

### 50 PFENNIG KM# 109.1 Composition: Copper-Nickel

**Edge:** Reeded **Note:** Federal Republic

| Date | Mintage | F | VF | XF | Unc | BU |
|---|---|---|---|---|---|---|
| 1950D | 100,735,000 | — | 0.50 | 0.75 | 9.00 | — |
| 1950F | 143,510,000 | — | 0.50 | 0.75 | 9.00 | — |
| 1950F Proof | 450 | Value: 85.00 | | | | |
| 1950G | 66,421,000 | — | 0.50 | 0.75 | 10.00 | — |
| 1950G Proof | 1,800 | Value: 5.00 | | | | |
| 1950J | 102,736,000 | — | 0.50 | 0.75 | 9.00 | — |
| 1950J Proof | — | Value: 25.00 | | | | |
| 1966D | 8,327,999 | — | 0.50 | 0.75 | 15.00 | — |
| 1966F | 9,605,000 | — | 0.50 | 0.75 | 15.00 | — |
| 1966F Proof | 100 | Value: 125 | | | | |
| 1966G | 5,543,000 | — | 0.50 | 0.65 | 15.00 | — |
| 1966G Proof | 3,070 | Value: 10.00 | | | | |
| 1966J | 8,569,000 | — | 0.50 | 0.65 | 15.00 | — |
| 1966J Proof | 1,000 | Value: 20.00 | | | | |
| 1967D | 5,207,000 | — | 0.50 | 0.65 | 15.00 | — |
| 1967F | 6,005,000 | — | 0.50 | 0.65 | 15.00 | — |
| 1967F Proof | 1,500 | Value: 18.00 | | | | |
| 1967G | 1,843,000 | — | 0.50 | 1.00 | 18.00 | — |
| 1967G Proof | 4,500 | Value: 15.00 | | | | |
| 1967J | 10,684,000 | — | 0.50 | 0.65 | 15.00 | — |
| 1967J Proof | 1,500 | Value: 18.00 | | | | |
| 1968D | 7,809,000 | — | 0.50 | 0.60 | 12.00 | — |
| 1968F | 3,000,000 | — | 0.50 | 0.60 | 12.00 | — |
| 1968F Proof | 3,000 | Value: 15.00 | | | | |
| 1968G | 6,818,000 | — | 0.50 | 0.60 | 12.00 | — |
| 1968G Proof | 6,023 | Value: 8.00 | | | | |
| 1968J | 2,672,000 | — | 0.50 | 0.65 | 17.50 | — |
| 1968J Proof | 2,000 | Value: 15.00 | | | | |
| 1969D | 14,561,000 | — | 0.45 | 0.55 | 2.50 | — |
| 1969F | 16,804,000 | — | 0.45 | 0.55 | 2.50 | — |
| 1969F Proof | 5,000 | Value: 4.00 | | | | |
| 1969G | 9,704,000 | — | 0.45 | 0.55 | 2.50 | — |
| 1969G Proof | 8,700 | Value: 3.50 | | | | |
| 1969J | 14,969,000 | — | 0.45 | 0.55 | 2.50 | — |
| 1969J Proof | 5,000 | Value: 10.00 | | | | |
| 1970D | 25,294,000 | — | 0.45 | 0.55 | 1.00 | — |
| 1970F | 26,455,000 | — | 0.45 | 0.55 | 1.00 | — |
| 1970F Proof | 5,140 | Value: 3.50 | | | | |
| 1970G | 11,955,000 | — | 0.45 | 0.55 | 1.00 | — |
| 1970G Proof | 10,200 | Value: 3.00 | | | | |
| 1970J | 10,683,000 | — | 0.45 | 0.55 | 1.00 | — |
| 1970J Proof | 5,000 | Value: 3.50 | | | | |
| 1971D | 23,393,000 | — | 0.45 | 0.55 | 0.75 | — |
| 1971D Proof | 8,000 | Value: 3.00 | | | | |
| 1971F | 29,746,000 | — | 0.45 | 0.55 | 0.75 | — |
| 1971F Proof | 8,000 | Value: 3.00 | | | | |
| 1971G | 15,556,000 | — | 0.45 | 0.55 | 0.75 | — |
| 1971G Proof | 10,000 | Value: 3.00 | | | | |
| 1971 Large J | 24,044,000 | — | 0.45 | 0.55 | 0.75 | — |
| 1971 Small J | Inc. above | — | 0.45 | 0.55 | 0.75 | — |
| 1971J Proof | 8,000 | Value: 3.00 | | | | |

### MARK KM# 110 Composition: Copper-Nickel Note: Federal Republic.

| Date | Mintage | F | VF | XF | Unc | BU |
|---|---|---|---|---|---|---|
| 1950D | 60,467,000 | — | 0.75 | 4.00 | 55.00 | — |
| 1950D Proof | — | Value: 200 | | | | |
| 1950F | 69,183,000 | — | 0.75 | 5.00 | 65.00 | — |
| 1950F Proof | 150 | Value: 450 | | | | |
| 1950G | 39,826,000 | — | 0.75 | 5.00 | 100 | — |
| 1950G Proof | Est. 200 | Value: 375 | | | | |
| 1950J | 61,483,000 | — | 0.75 | 4.00 | 60.00 | — |
| 1950J Proof | — | Value: 200 | | | | |
| 1954D | 5,202,000 | — | 1.00 | 15.00 | 385 | — |
| 1954D Proof | — | Value: 925 | | | | |
| 1954F | 6,000,000 | — | 1.00 | 15.00 | 450 | — |
| 1954F Proof | 175 | Value: 800 | | | | |
| 1954G | 3,459,000 | — | 20.00 | 450 | 1,750 | — |
| 1954G Proof | 15 | Value: 2,250 | | | | |
| 1954J | 5,341,000 | — | 1.00 | 15.00 | 385 | — |
| 1954J Proof | — | Value: 1,000 | | | | |
| 1955D | 3,093,000 | — | 1.00 | 15.00 | 325 | — |
| 1955D Proof | — | Value: 1,000 | | | | |
| 1955F | 4,909,000 | — | 1.00 | 15.00 | 300 | — |
| 1955F Proof | Est. 20 | Value: 900 | | | | |
| 1955G | 2,500,000 | — | 8.00 | 100 | 1,500 | — |
| 1955G Proof | — | Value: 2,750 | | | | |
| 1955J | 5,294,000 | — | 1.00 | 10.00 | 200 | — |
| 1955J Proof | — | Value: 450 | | | | |
| 1956D | 13,231,000 | — | 1.00 | 8.50 | 215 | — |
| 1956D Proof | — | Value: 525 | | | | |
| 1956F | 14,700,000 | — | 1.00 | 12.50 | 325 | — |
| 1956F Proof | 100 | Value: 475 | | | | |
| 1956G | 8,362,000 | — | 1.00 | 6.50 | 165 | — |
| 1956G Proof | — | Value: 325 | | | | |
| 1956J | 11,478,000 | — | 1.00 | 9.00 | 185 | — |
| 1956J Proof | — | Value: 1,000 | | | | |
| 1957D | 6,820,000 | — | 1.00 | 9.00 | 175 | — |
| 1957D Proof | 100 | Value: 450 | | | | |
| 1957F | 6,390,000 | — | 1.00 | 9.00 | 180 | — |
| 1957F Proof | 100 | Value: 475 | | | | |
| 1957G | 3,841,000 | — | 1.00 | 15.00 | 600 | — |
| 1957G Proof | 27 | Value: 1,650 | | | | |
| 1957J | 6,632,000 | — | 1.00 | 9.00 | 170 | — |
| 1957J Proof | 200 | Value: 325 | | | | |
| 1958D | 4,150,000 | — | 1.00 | 6.50 | 160 | — |
| 1958D Proof | 200 | Value: 350 | | | | |
| 1958F | 4,109,000 | — | 1.00 | 7.50 | 210 | — |
| 1958F Proof | 100 | Value: 575 | | | | |
| 1958G | 3,460,000 | — | 1.00 | 8.50 | 300 | — |
| 1958G Proof | 20 | Value: 2,100 | | | | |
| 1958J | 4,656,000 | — | 1.00 | 7.00 | 185 | — |
| 1958J Proof | 37 | Value: 1,150 | | | | |
| 1959D | 10,409,000 | — | 0.85 | 6.00 | 140 | — |
| 1959D Proof | 40 | Value: 850 | | | | |
| 1959F | 11,972,000 | — | 0.85 | 5.00 | 125 | — |
| 1959F Proof | 100 | Value: 525 | | | | |
| 1959G | 6,921,000 | — | 0.85 | 5.00 | 225 | — |
| 1959G Proof | 20 | Value: 2,100 | | | | |
| 1959J | 10,691,000 | — | 0.85 | 5.00 | 250 | — |
| 1959J Proof | 25 | Value: 1,800 | | | | |
| 1960D | 5,453,000 | — | 0.85 | 5.00 | 150 | — |
| 1960D Proof | 100 | Value: 475 | | | | |
| 1960F | 5,709,000 | — | 0.85 | 5.00 | 125 | — |
| 1960F Proof | 100 | Value: 475 | | | | |
| 1960G | 3,632,000 | — | 0.85 | 6.00 | 250 | — |
| 1960G Proof | 100 | Value: 500 | | | | |
| 1960J | 5,612,000 | — | 0.85 | 5.00 | 175 | — |
| 1960J Proof | 36 | Value: 1,150 | | | | |
| 1961D | 7,536,000 | — | 0.85 | 5.00 | 100 | — |
| 1961D Proof | 60 | Value: 650 | | | | |
| 1961F | 6,029,000 | — | 0.85 | 5.00 | 100 | — |
| 1961F Proof | 50 | Value: 700 | | | | |
| 1961G | 4,843,000 | — | 0.85 | 6.50 | 400 | — |
| 1961G Proof | 70 | Value: 600 | | | | |
| 1961J | 7,483,000 | — | 0.85 | 6.00 | 325 | — |
| 1961J Proof | 28 | Value: 1,200 | | | | |
| 1962D | 10,327,000 | — | 0.85 | 4.00 | 65.00 | — |
| 1962D Proof | 40 | Value: 600 | | | | |
| 1962F | 11,122,000 | — | 0.85 | 4.00 | 75.00 | — |
| 1962F Proof | 45 | Value: 550 | | | | |
| 1962G | 6,054,000 | — | 0.85 | 5.50 | 200 | — |
| 1962G Proof | 100 | Value: 450 | | | | |
| 1962J | 10,822,000 | — | 0.85 | 4.00 | 125 | — |
| 1962J Proof | 28 | Value: 1,200 | | | | |
| 1963D | 12,624,000 | — | 0.85 | 4.00 | 80.00 | — |
| 1963D Proof | 40 | Value: 600 | | | | |

| Date | Mintage | F | VF | XF | Unc | BU |
|---|---|---|---|---|---|---|
| 1963F | 18,292,000 | — | 0.85 | 4.00 | 90.00 | — |
| 1963F Proof | 45 | Value: 550 | | | | |
| 1963G | 11,253,000 | — | 0.85 | 4.00 | 80.00 | — |
| 1963G Proof | 200 | Value: 300 | | | | |
| 1963J | 15,906,000 | — | 0.85 | 4.00 | 80.00 | — |
| 1963J Proof | 28 | Value: 1,200 | | | | |
| 1964D | 8,048,000 | — | 0.85 | 4.00 | 100 | — |
| 1964D Proof | 30 | Value: 1,000 | | | | |
| 1964F | 12,796,000 | — | 0.85 | 4.00 | 90.00 | — |
| 1964F Proof | 25 | Value: 1,900 | | | | |
| 1964G | 3,465,000 | — | 0.85 | 4.00 | 120 | — |
| 1964G Proof | 368 | Value: 145 | | | | |
| 1964J | 6,958,000 | — | 0.85 | 4.00 | 75.00 | — |
| 1964J Proof | 33 | Value: 900 | | | | |
| 1965D | 9,388,000 | — | 0.75 | 3.00 | 37.50 | — |
| 1965F | 9,013,000 | — | 0.75 | 3.00 | 40.00 | — |
| 1965F Proof | Est. 80 | Value: 175 | | | | |
| 1965G | 6,232,000 | — | 0.75 | 3.00 | 47.50 | — |
| 1965G Proof | 1,200 | Value: 65.00 | | | | |
| 1965J | 8,023,999 | — | 0.75 | 3.00 | 55.00 | — |
| 1966D | 11,717,000 | — | 0.75 | 3.00 | 42.50 | — |
| 1966F | 11,368,000 | — | 0.75 | 3.00 | 42.50 | — |
| 1966F Proof | 100 | Value: 150 | | | | |
| 1966G | 7,799,000 | — | 0.75 | 3.00 | 55.00 | — |
| 1966G Proof | 3,070 | Value: 35.00 | | | | |
| 1966J | 12,030,000 | — | 0.75 | 3.00 | 42.50 | — |
| 1966J Proof | 1,000 | Value: 65.00 | | | | |
| 1967D | 13,017,000 | — | 0.75 | 3.00 | 32.50 | — |
| 1967F | 7,500,000 | — | 0.75 | 5.00 | 100 | — |
| 1967F Proof | 1,500 | Value: 65.00 | | | | |
| 1967G | 4,324,000 | — | 0.75 | 3.00 | 55.00 | — |
| 1967G Proof | 4,500 | Value: 50.00 | | | | |
| 1967J | 13,357,000 | — | 0.75 | 3.00 | 40.00 | — |
| 1967J Proof | 1,500 | Value: 65.00 | | | | |
| 1968D | 1,303,000 | — | 0.75 | 4.00 | 55.00 | — |
| 1968F | 1,500,000 | — | 0.75 | 4.00 | 40.00 | — |
| 1968F Proof | 3,000 | Value: 35.00 | | | | |
| 1968G | 5,198,000 | — | 0.75 | 4.00 | 55.00 | — |
| 1968G Proof | 6,023 | Value: 15.00 | | | | |
| 1968J | 1,338,000 | — | 0.75 | 5.50 | 165 | — |
| 1968J Proof | 2,000 | Value: 75.00 | | | | |
| 1969D | 13,025,000 | — | 0.75 | 1.50 | 20.00 | — |
| 1969F | 15,021,000 | — | 0.75 | 1.50 | 20.00 | — |
| 1969F Proof | 5,000 | Value: 15.00 | | | | |
| 1969G | 8,665,000 | — | 0.75 | 1.50 | 32.50 | — |
| 1969G Proof | 8,700 | Value: 12.50 | | | | |
| 1969J | 13,370,000 | — | 0.75 | 1.50 | 25.00 | — |
| 1969J Proof | 5,000 | Value: 15.00 | | | | |
| 1970D | 17,928,000 | — | 0.75 | 1.00 | 20.00 | — |
| 1970F | 19,408,000 | — | 0.75 | 1.00 | 25.00 | — |
| 1970F Proof | 5,140 | Value: 15.00 | | | | |
| 1970G | 20,386,000 | — | 0.75 | 1.00 | 32.50 | — |
| 1970G Proof | 10,200 | Value: 9.00 | | | | |
| 1970J | 10,707,000 | — | 0.75 | 1.00 | 20.00 | — |
| 1970J Proof | 5,000 | Value: 15.00 | | | | |
| 1971D | 24,513,000 | — | 0.75 | 1.00 | 10.00 | — |
| 1971D Proof | 8,000 | Value: 8.00 | | | | |
| 1971F | 28,275,000 | — | 0.75 | 1.00 | 10.00 | — |
| 1971F Proof | 8,000 | Value: 8.00 | | | | |
| 1971G | 16,375,000 | — | 0.75 | 1.00 | 12.50 | — |
| 1971G Proof | 10,000 | Value: 8.00 | | | | |
| 1971J | 25,214,000 | — | 0.75 | 1.00 | 10.00 | — |
| 1971J Proof | 8,000 | Value: 8.00 | | | | |
| 1972D | 20,904,000 | — | 0.75 | 1.00 | 10.00 | — |
| 1972D Proof | 8,000 | Value: 7.00 | | | | |
| 1972F | 24,086,000 | — | 0.75 | 1.00 | 10.00 | — |
| 1972F Proof | 8,000 | Value: 7.00 | | | | |
| 1972G | 13,868,000 | — | 0.75 | 1.00 | 10.00 | — |
| 1972G Proof | 10,000 | Value: 7.00 | | | | |
| 1972J | 21,360,000 | — | 0.75 | 1.00 | 10.00 | — |
| 1972J Proof | 8,000 | Value: 7.00 | | | | |
| 1973D | 14,327,000 | — | 0.75 | 1.00 | 6.00 | — |
| 1973D Proof | 9,000 | Value: 5.00 | | | | |
| 1973F | 16,591,999 | — | 0.75 | 1.00 | 6.00 | — |
| 1973F Proof | 9,000 | Value: 5.00 | | | | |
| 1973G | 10,409,000 | — | 0.75 | 1.00 | 6.00 | — |
| 1973G Proof | 9,000 | Value: 5.00 | | | | |
| 1973J | 14,704,000 | — | 0.75 | 1.00 | 6.00 | — |
| 1973J Proof | 9,000 | Value: 5.00 | | | | |
| 1974D | 20,876,000 | — | 0.75 | 1.00 | 6.00 | — |
| 1974D Proof | 35,000 | Value: 4.00 | | | | |
| 1974F | 24,057,000 | — | 0.75 | 1.00 | 6.00 | — |
| 1974F Proof | 35,000 | Value: 4.00 | | | | |
| 1974G | 13,931,000 | — | 0.75 | 1.00 | 6.00 | — |
| 1974G Proof | 35,000 | Value: 4.00 | | | | |
| 1974J | 21,440,000 | — | 0.75 | 1.00 | 6.00 | — |
| 1974J Proof | 35,000 | Value: 4.00 | | | | |
| 1975D | 18,241,000 | — | 0.75 | 1.00 | 6.00 | — |
| 1975D Proof | 43,000 | Value: 4.00 | | | | |
| 1975F | 21,059,000 | — | 0.75 | 1.00 | 6.00 | — |
| 1975F Proof | 43,000 | Value: 4.00 | | | | |
| 1975G | 12,142,000 | — | 0.75 | 1.00 | 6.50 | — |
| 1975G Proof | 43,000 | Value: 4.00 | | | | |
| 1975J | 18,770,000 | — | 0.75 | 1.00 | 6.00 | — |
| 1975J Proof | 43,000 | Value: 4.00 | | | | |
| 1976D | 15,670,000 | — | 0.75 | 1.00 | 6.00 | — |
| 1976D Proof | 43,000 | Value: 4.00 | | | | |
| 1976F | 18,105,000 | — | 0.75 | 1.00 | 6.00 | — |
| 1976F Proof | 43,000 | Value: 4.00 | | | | |
| 1976G | 10,382,000 | — | 0.75 | 1.00 | 6.00 | — |
| 1976G Proof | 43,000 | Value: 4.00 | | | | |
| 1976J | 16,046,000 | — | 0.75 | 1.00 | 6.00 | — |
| 1976J Proof | 43,000 | Value: 4.00 | | | | |
| 1977D | 20,801,000 | — | 0.75 | 0.85 | 3.00 | — |
| 1977D Proof | 51,000 | Value: 2.00 | | | | |
| 1977F | 24,026,000 | — | 0.75 | 0.85 | 3.00 | — |
| 1977F Proof | 51,000 | Value: 2.00 | | | | |
| 1977G | 13,849,000 | — | 0.75 | 0.85 | 3.00 | — |
| 1977G Proof | 51,000 | Value: 2.00 | | | | |
| 1977J | 21,416,000 | — | 0.75 | 0.85 | 3.00 | — |
| 1977J Proof | 51,000 | Value: 2.00 | | | | |
| 1978D | 15,600,000 | — | 0.75 | 0.85 | 2.00 | — |
| 1978D Proof | 54,000 | Value: 1.25 | | | | |
| 1978F | 18,000,000 | — | 0.75 | 0.85 | 2.00 | — |
| 1978F Proof | 54,000 | Value: 1.25 | | | | |
| 1978G | 10,380,000 | — | 0.75 | 0.85 | 2.00 | — |
| 1978G Proof | 54,000 | Value: 1.25 | | | | |
| 1978J | 16,020,000 | — | 0.75 | 0.85 | 2.00 | — |
| 1978J Proof | 54,000 | Value: 1.25 | | | | |
| 1979D | 18,200,000 | — | 0.75 | 0.85 | 2.00 | — |
| 1979D Proof | 89,000 | Value: 1.25 | | | | |
| 1979F | 21,000,000 | — | 0.75 | 0.85 | 2.00 | — |
| 1979F Proof | 89,000 | Value: 1.25 | | | | |
| 1979G | 12,110,000 | — | 0.75 | 0.85 | 2.00 | — |
| 1979G Proof | 89,000 | Value: 1.25 | | | | |
| 1979J | 18,690,000 | — | 0.75 | 0.85 | 2.00 | — |
| 1979J Proof | 89,000 | Value: 1.25 | | | | |
| 1980D | 24,330,000 | — | — | 0.75 | 0.90 | — |
| 1980D Proof | 110,000 | Value: 1.00 | | | | |
| 1980F | 9,670,000 | — | — | 0.75 | 0.90 | — |
| 1980F Proof | 110,000 | Value: 1.00 | | | | |
| 1980G | 8,540,000 | — | — | 0.75 | 0.90 | — |
| 1980G Proof | 110,000 | Value: 1.00 | | | | |
| 1980J | 16,010,000 | — | — | 0.75 | 0.90 | — |
| 1980J Proof | 110,000 | Value: 1.00 | | | | |
| 1981D | 21,150,000 | — | — | 0.75 | 0.90 | — |
| 1981D Proof | 91,000 | Value: 1.00 | | | | |
| 1981F | 25,910,000 | — | — | 0.75 | 0.90 | — |
| 1981F Proof | 91,000 | Value: 1.00 | | | | |
| 1981G | 14,090,000 | — | — | 0.75 | 0.90 | — |
| 1981G Proof | 91,000 | Value: 1.00 | | | | |
| 1981J | 18,800,000 | — | — | 0.75 | 0.90 | — |
| 1981J Proof | 91,000 | Value: 1.00 | | | | |
| 1982D | 20,590,000 | — | — | 0.75 | 0.90 | — |
| 1982D Proof | 78,000 | Value: 1.00 | | | | |
| 1982F | 22,990,000 | — | — | 0.75 | 0.90 | — |
| 1982F Proof | 78,000 | Value: 1.00 | | | | |
| 1982G | 14,900,000 | — | — | 0.75 | 0.90 | — |
| 1982G Proof | 78,000 | Value: 1.00 | | | | |
| 1982J | 11,520,000 | — | — | 0.75 | 0.90 | — |
| 1982J Proof | 78,000 | Value: 1.00 | | | | |
| 1983D | 18,200,000 | — | — | 0.75 | 0.90 | — |
| 1983D Proof | 75,000 | Value: 1.00 | | | | |
| 1983F | 21,000,000 | — | — | 0.75 | 0.90 | — |
| 1983F Proof | 75,000 | Value: 1.00 | | | | |
| 1983G | 12,100,000 | — | — | 0.75 | 0.90 | — |
| 1983G Proof | 75,000 | Value: 1.00 | | | | |
| 1983J | 18,690,000 | — | — | 0.75 | 0.90 | — |
| 1983J Proof | 75,000 | Value: 1.00 | | | | |
| 1984D | 8,400,000 | — | — | 0.75 | 0.90 | — |
| 1984D Proof | 64,000 | Value: 1.50 | | | | |
| 1984F | 9,700,000 | — | — | 0.75 | 0.90 | — |
| 1984F Proof | 64,000 | Value: 1.50 | | | | |
| 1984G | 5,600,000 | — | — | 0.75 | 0.90 | — |
| 1984G Proof | 64,000 | Value: 1.50 | | | | |
| 1984J | 8,700,000 | — | — | 0.75 | 0.90 | — |
| 1984J Proof | 64,000 | Value: 1.50 | | | | |
| 1985D | 11,700,000 | — | — | — | 0.85 | — |
| 1985D Proof | 56,000 | Value: 1.50 | | | | |
| 1985F | 13,500,000 | — | — | — | 0.85 | — |
| 1985F Proof | 54,000 | Value: 1.50 | | | | |
| 1985G | 7,800,000 | — | — | — | 0.85 | — |
| 1985G Proof | 55,000 | Value: 1.50 | | | | |
| 1985J | 12,000,000 | — | — | — | 0.85 | — |
| 1985J Proof | 54,000 | Value: 1.50 | | | | |
| 1986D | 10,400,000 | — | — | — | 0.85 | — |
| 1986D Proof | 44,000 | Value: 1.50 | | | | |
| 1986F | 12,000,000 | — | — | — | 0.85 | — |
| 1986F Proof | 44,000 | Value: 1.50 | | | | |
| 1986G | 6,900,000 | — | — | — | 0.85 | — |
| 1986G Proof | 44,000 | Value: 1.50 | | | | |
| 1986J | 10,700,000 | — | — | — | 0.85 | — |
| 1986J Proof | 44,000 | Value: 1.50 | | | | |
| 1987D | 3,120,000 | — | 3.50 | 7.50 | 15.00 | — |
| 1987D Proof | 45,000 | Value: 1.50 | | | | |
| 1987F | 3,600,000 | — | 3.50 | 7.50 | 15.00 | — |
| 1987F Proof | 45,000 | Value: 1.50 | | | | |
| 1987G | 2,080,000 | — | 3.50 | 7.50 | 15.00 | — |
| 1987G Proof | 45,000 | Value: 1.50 | | | | |
| 1987J | 3,200,000 | — | 3.50 | 7.50 | 15.00 | — |
| 1987J Proof | 45,000 | Value: 1.50 | | | | |
| 1988D | 20,800,000 | — | — | — | 0.85 | — |
| 1988D Proof | 45,000 | Value: 1.50 | | | | |
| 1988F | 24,000,000 | — | — | — | 0.85 | — |
| 1988F Proof | 45,000 | Value: 1.50 | | | | |
| 1988G | 13,800,000 | — | — | — | 0.85 | — |
| 1988G Proof | 45,000 | Value: 1.50 | | | | |
| 1988J | 21,400,000 | — | — | — | 0.85 | — |
| 1988J Proof | 45,000 | Value: 1.50 | | | | |
| 1989D | 39,000,000 | — | — | — | 0.85 | — |
| 1989D Proof | 45,000 | Value: 1.50 | | | | |
| 1989F | 45,000,000 | — | — | — | 0.85 | — |
| 1989F Proof | 45,000 | Value: 1.50 | | | | |
| 1989G | 25,950,000 | — | — | — | 0.85 | — |
| 1989G Proof | 45,000 | Value: 1.50 | | | | |
| 1989J | 40,050,000 | — | — | — | 0.85 | — |
| 1989J Proof | 45,000 | Value: 1.50 | | | | |
| 1990A | 55,000,000 | — | — | — | 2.00 | — |
| 1990D | 77,740,000 | — | — | — | 0.85 | — |
| 1990D Proof | 45,000 | Value: 1.50 | | | | |
| 1990F | 89,700,000 | — | — | — | 0.85 | — |
| 1990F Proof | 45,000 | Value: 1.50 | | | | |
| 1990G | 51,720,000 | — | — | — | 0.85 | — |
| 1990G Proof | 45,000 | Value: 1.50 | | | | |
| 1990J | 79,830,000 | — | — | — | 0.85 | — |
| 1990J Proof | 45,000 | Value: 1.50 | | | | |
| 1991A | 30,000,000 | — | — | — | 0.85 | — |
| 1991A Proof | 45,000 | Value: 1.50 | | | | |
| 1991D | 31,500,000 | — | — | — | 0.85 | — |
| 1991D Proof | 45,000 | Value: 1.50 | | | | |
| 1991F | 36,000,000 | — | — | — | 0.85 | — |
| 1991F Proof | 45,000 | Value: 1.50 | | | | |
| 1991G | 21,000,000 | — | — | — | 0.85 | — |
| 1991G Proof | 45,000 | Value: 1.50 | | | | |
| 1991J | 31,500,000 | — | — | — | 0.85 | — |
| 1991J Proof | 45,000 | Value: 1.50 | | | | |
| 1992A | 30,000,000 | — | — | — | 0.85 | — |
| 1992A Proof | 45,000 | Value: 1.50 | | | | |
| 1992D | 31,500,000 | — | — | — | 0.85 | — |
| 1992D Proof | 45,000 | Value: 1.50 | | | | |
| 1992F | 36,000,000 | — | — | — | 0.85 | — |
| 1992F Proof | 45,000 | Value: 1.50 | | | | |
| 1992G | 21,000,000 | — | — | — | 0.85 | — |
| 1992G Proof | 45,000 | Value: 1.50 | | | | |
| 1992J | 31,500,000 | — | — | — | 0.85 | — |
| 1992J Proof | 45,000 | Value: 1.50 | | | | |
| 1993A | 8,000,000 | — | — | — | 0.85 | — |
| 1993A Proof | 45,000 | Value: 1.50 | | | | |
| 1993D | 8,400,000 | — | — | — | 0.85 | — |
| 1993D Proof | 45,000 | Value: 1.50 | | | | |
| 1993F | 9,600,000 | — | — | — | 0.85 | — |
| 1993F Proof | 45,000 | Value: 1.50 | | | | |
| 1993G | 5,600,000 | — | — | — | 0.85 | — |
| 1993G Proof | 45,000 | Value: 1.50 | | | | |
| 1993J | 8,400,000 | — | — | — | 0.85 | — |
| 1993J Proof | 45,000 | Value: 1.50 | | | | |
| 1994A | 18,000,000 | — | — | — | 0.85 | — |
| 1994A Proof | 45,000 | Value: 1.50 | | | | |
| 1994D | 18,900,000 | — | — | — | 0.85 | — |
| 1994D Proof | 45,000 | Value: 1.50 | | | | |
| 1994F | 21,800,000 | — | — | — | 0.85 | — |
| 1994F Proof | 45,000 | Value: 1.50 | | | | |
| 1994G | 12,800,000 | — | — | — | 0.85 | — |
| 1994G Proof | 45,000 | Value: 1.50 | | | | |
| 1994J | 18,900,000 | — | — | — | 0.85 | — |
| 1994J Proof | 45,000 | Value: 1.50 | | | | |
| 1995A In sets only | 20,000 | — | — | — | 70.00 | — |
| 1995A Proof | 45,000 | Value: 20.00 | | | | |
| 1995D In sets only | 20,000 | — | — | — | 70.00 | — |
| 1995D Proof | 45,000 | Value: 20.00 | | | | |
| 1995F In sets only | 20,000 | — | — | — | 70.00 | — |
| 1995F Proof | 45,000 | Value: 20.00 | | | | |
| 1995G In sets only | 20,000 | — | — | — | 70.00 | — |
| 1995G Proof | 45,000 | Value: 20.00 | | | | |
| 1995J | 100,000 | — | — | — | 18.00 | — |
| 1995J Proof | 45,000 | Value: 20.00 | | | | |
| 1996A In sets only | 50,000 | — | — | — | 12.50 | — |
| 1996A Proof | 45,000 | Value: 14.00 | | | | |
| 1996D In sets only | 50,000 | — | — | — | 12.50 | — |
| 1996D Proof | 45,000 | Value: 14.00 | | | | |
| 1996F In sets only | 50,000 | — | — | — | 12.50 | — |
| 1996F Proof | 45,000 | Value: 14.00 | | | | |
| 1996G In sets only | 50,000 | — | — | — | 12.50 | — |
| 1996G Proof | 45,000 | Value: 14.00 | | | | |
| 1996J In sets only | 50,000 | — | — | — | 12.50 | — |
| 1996J Proof | 45,000 | Value: 14.00 | | | | |
| 1997A In sets only | 70,000 | — | — | — | 4.75 | — |
| 1997A Proof | 45,000 | Value: 5.00 | | | | |
| 1997D In sets only | 70,000 | — | — | — | 4.75 | — |
| 1997D Proof | 45,000 | Value: 5.00 | | | | |
| 1997F In sets only | 70,000 | — | — | — | 4.75 | — |
| 1997F Proof | 45,000 | Value: 5.00 | | | | |
| 1997G In sets only | 70,000 | — | — | — | 4.75 | — |
| 1997G Proof | 45,000 | Value: 5.00 | | | | |
| 1997J In sets only | 70,000 | — | — | — | 4.75 | — |
| 1997J Proof | 45,000 | Value: 5.00 | | | | |
| 1998A In sets only | 70,000 | — | — | — | 4.75 | — |
| 1998A Proof | 45,000 | Value: 5.00 | | | | |
| 1998D In sets only | 70,000 | — | — | — | 4.75 | — |
| 1998D Proof | 45,000 | Value: 5.00 | | | | |
| 1998F In sets only | 70,000 | — | — | — | 4.75 | — |
| 1998F Proof | 45,000 | Value: 5.00 | | | | |
| 1998G In sets only | 70,000 | — | — | — | 4.75 | — |
| 1998G Proof | 45,000 | Value: 5.00 | | | | |
| 1998J In sets only | 70,000 | — | — | — | 4.75 | — |
| 1998J Proof | 45,000 | Value: 5.00 | | | | |
| 1999A In sets only | 70,000 | — | — | — | 4.75 | — |
| 1999A Proof | 45,000 | Value: 5.00 | | | | |
| 1999D In sets only | 70,000 | — | — | — | 4.75 | — |
| 1999D Proof | 45,000 | Value: 5.00 | | | | |
| 1999F In sets only | 70,000 | — | — | — | 4.75 | — |
| 1999F Proof | 45,000 | Value: 5.00 | | | | |
| 1999G In sets only | 70,000 | — | — | — | 4.75 | — |
| 1999G Proof | 45,000 | Value: 5.00 | | | | |
| 1999J In sets only | 70,000 | — | — | — | 4.75 | — |
| 1999J Proof | 45,000 | Value: 5.00 | | | | |

| Date | Mintage | F | VF | XF | Unc | BU |
|---|---|---|---|---|---|---|
| 2000A In sets only | 70,000 | — | — | — | 5.00 | — |
| 2000A Proof | 45,000 | Value: 5.00 | | | | |
| 2000D In sets only | 70,000 | — | — | — | 5.00 | — |
| 2000D Proof | 45,000 | Value: 5.00 | | | | |
| 2000F In sets only | 70,000 | — | — | — | 5.00 | — |
| 2000F Proof | 45,000 | Value: 5.00 | | | | |
| 2000G In sets only | 70,000 | — | — | — | 5.00 | — |
| 2000G Proof | 45,000 | Value: 5.00 | | | | |
| 2000J In sets only | 70,000 | — | — | — | 5.00 | — |
| 2000J Proof | 45,000 | Value: 5.00 | | | | |
| 2001A In sets only | 130,000 | — | — | — | 15.00 | — |
| 2001A Proof | 78,000 | Value: 15.00 | | | | |
| 2001D In sets only | 130,000 | — | — | — | 15.00 | — |
| 2001D Proof | 78,000 | Value: 15.00 | | | | |
| 2001F In sets only | 130,000 | — | — | — | 15.00 | — |
| 2001F Proof | 78,000 | Value: 15.00 | | | | |
| 2001G In sets only | 130,000 | — | — | — | 15.00 | — |
| 2001G Proof | 78,000 | Value: 15.00 | | | | |
| 2001J In sets only | 130,000 | — | — | — | 15.00 | — |
| 2001J Proof | 78,000 | Value: 15.00 | | | | |

**MARK KM# 203 Weight:** 11.8500 g. **Composition:** 0.9990 Gold .3806 oz. AGW **Subject:** Retirement of the mark currency **Obverse:** Denomination **Reverse:** Eagle **Edge:** Lettered **Size:** 23.5 mm.

| Date | Mintage | F | VF | XF | Unc | BU |
|---|---|---|---|---|---|---|
| 2001A Proof | 200,000 | Value: 230 | | | | |
| 2001D Proof | 200,000 | Value: 230 | | | | |
| 2001G Proof | 200,000 | Value: 230 | | | | |
| 2001J Proof | 200,000 | Value: 230 | | | | |
| 2001F Proof | 200,000 | Value: 230 | | | | |

**2 MARK KM# 111 Composition:** Copper-Nickel **Note:** Federal Republic.

| Date | Mintage | F | VF | XF | Unc | BU |
|---|---|---|---|---|---|---|
| 1951D | 19,564,000 | — | 30.00 | 55.00 | 150 | — |
| 1951D Proof | 200 | Value: 450 | | | | |
| 1951F | 22,609,000 | — | 20.00 | 45.00 | 110 | — |
| 1951F Proof | 150 | Value: 500 | | | | |
| 1951G | Est. 13,012,000 | — | 40.00 | 100 | 210 | — |

**Note:** The 1951G dated coin was restruck without authorization by a mint official using genuine dies - quantity unknown

| Date | Mintage | F | VF | XF | Unc | BU |
|---|---|---|---|---|---|---|
| 1951G Proof | 33 | Value: 1,200 | | | | |

**Note:** The 1951G dated coin was restruck without authorization by a mint official using genuine dies - quantity unknown

| Date | Mintage | F | VF | XF | Unc | BU |
|---|---|---|---|---|---|---|
| 1951J | 20,104,000 | — | 28.00 | 45.00 | 110 | — |
| 1951J Proof | 180 | Value: 450 | | | | |

**2 MARK KM# 116 Composition:** Copper-Nickel **Reverse:** Head of Max Planck facing left

| Date | Mintage | F | VF | XF | Unc | BU |
|---|---|---|---|---|---|---|
| 1957D | 7,452,000 | — | 2.00 | 6.00 | 65.00 | — |
| 1957D Proof | 350 | Value: 235 | | | | |
| 1957F | 6,337,000 | — | 2.00 | 6.00 | 65.00 | — |
| 1957F Proof | 100 | Value: 325 | | | | |
| 1957G | 2,598,000 | — | 3.00 | 7.50 | 135 | — |
| 1957G Proof | 56 | Value: 600 | | | | |
| 1957J | 11,210,000 | — | 2.00 | 6.00 | 60.00 | — |
| 1957J Proof | 370 | Value: 175 | | | | |
| 1958D | 12,623,000 | — | 1.50 | 5.00 | 50.00 | — |
| 1958D Proof | 1,240 | Value: 85.00 | | | | |
| 1958F | 16,825,000 | — | 1.50 | 4.00 | 45.00 | — |
| 1958F Proof | 300 | Value: 200 | | | | |
| 1958G | 10,744,000 | — | 1.50 | 4.00 | 45.00 | — |
| 1958G Proof | 45 | Value: 700 | | | | |
| 1958J | 9,408,000 | — | 1.50 | 4.00 | 45.00 | — |
| 1958J Proof | 100 | Value: 400 | | | | |
| 1959D | 1,020,000 | — | 4.00 | 10.00 | 220 | — |
| 1959D Proof | 38 | Value: 800 | | | | |
| 1959F | 203,000 | — | 15.00 | 60.00 | 365 | — |
| 1959F Proof | 24 | Value: 900 | | | | |
| 1960D | 3,535,000 | — | 1.50 | 4.00 | 35.00 | — |
| 1960D Proof | 100 | Value: 325 | | | | |
| 1960F | 3,692,000 | — | 1.50 | 4.00 | 35.00 | — |
| 1960F Proof | 50 | Value: 600 | | | | |
| 1960G | 2,695,000 | — | 2.00 | 4.00 | 35.00 | — |
| 1960G Proof | 130 | Value: 300 | | | | |
| 1960J | 4,676,000 | — | 1.50 | 4.00 | 35.00 | — |
| 1960J Proof | 36 | Value: 800 | | | | |
| 1961D | 3,918,000 | — | 1.50 | 4.00 | 35.00 | — |
| 1961D Proof | 50 | Value: 600 | | | | |
| 1961F | 3,872,000 | — | 1.50 | 4.00 | 35.00 | — |
| 1961F Proof | 46 | Value: 650 | | | | |
| 1961G | 2,776,000 | — | 2.00 | 4.00 | 35.00 | — |
| 1961G Proof | 100 | Value: 325 | | | | |
| 1961J | 2,940,000 | — | 1.50 | 4.00 | 35.00 | — |
| 1961J Proof | 28 | Value: 750 | | | | |
| 1962D | 4,105,000 | — | 2.00 | 6.00 | 35.00 | — |
| 1962D Proof | 50 | Value: 600 | | | | |
| 1962F | 3,344,000 | — | 2.00 | 6.00 | 35.00 | — |
| 1962F Proof | 42 | Value: 625 | | | | |
| 1962G | 1,800,000 | — | 2.00 | 6.00 | 35.00 | — |
| 1962G Proof | 130 | Value: 300 | | | | |
| 1962J | 3,609,000 | — | 2.00 | 6.00 | 25.00 | — |
| 1962J Proof | 28 | Value: 750 | | | | |
| 1963D | 4,411,000 | — | 1.50 | 4.00 | 25.00 | — |
| 1963D Proof | 40 | Value: 650 | | | | |
| 1963F | 3,752,000 | — | 1.50 | 4.00 | 25.00 | — |
| 1963F Proof | 47 | Value: 600 | | | | |
| 1963G | 3,448,000 | — | 1.50 | 4.00 | 25.00 | — |
| 1963G Proof | 200 | Value: 250 | | | | |
| 1963J | 7,348,000 | — | 1.50 | 4.00 | 25.00 | — |
| 1963J Proof | 32 | Value: 700 | | | | |
| 1964D | 5,205,000 | — | 1.50 | 4.00 | 20.00 | — |
| 1964D Proof | 40 | Value: 650 | | | | |
| 1964F | 4,834,000 | — | 1.50 | 4.00 | 20.00 | — |
| 1964F Proof | 36 | Value: 800 | | | | |
| 1964G | 3,044,000 | — | 1.50 | 4.00 | 20.00 | — |
| 1964G Proof | 368 | Value: 150 | | | | |
| 1964J | 2,681,000 | — | 1.50 | 4.00 | 20.00 | — |
| 1964J Proof | 43 | Value: 600 | | | | |
| 1965D | 3,903,000 | — | 1.50 | 2.50 | 15.00 | — |
| 1965D Proof | 35 | Value: 800 | | | | |
| 1965F | 4,045,000 | — | 1.50 | 2.50 | 15.00 | — |
| 1965F Proof | 300 | Value: 250 | | | | |
| 1965G | 2,599,000 | — | 1.50 | 2.50 | 15.00 | — |
| 1965G Proof | 8,233 | Value: 5.00 | | | | |
| 1965J | 4,006,999 | — | 1.50 | 2.50 | 15.00 | — |
| 1965J Proof | 36 | Value: 750 | | | | |
| 1966D | 5,855,000 | — | 1.50 | 2.50 | 12.00 | — |
| 1966D Proof | 20 | Value: 900 | | | | |
| 1966F | 3,750,000 | — | 1.50 | 2.50 | 12.00 | — |
| 1966F Proof | 450 | Value: 250 | | | | |
| 1966G | 3,895,000 | — | 1.50 | 2.50 | 12.00 | — |
| 1966G Proof | 3,070 | Value: 20.00 | | | | |
| 1966J | 6,014,000 | — | 1.50 | 2.50 | 12.00 | — |
| 1966J Proof | 1,000 | Value: 35.00 | | | | |
| 1967D | 3,254,000 | — | 1.50 | 2.50 | 12.00 | — |
| 1967D Proof | 20 | Value: 900 | | | | |
| 1967F | 3,758,000 | — | 1.50 | 2.50 | 12.00 | — |
| 1967F Proof | 1,600 | Value: 32.00 | | | | |
| 1967G | 1,878,000 | — | 1.50 | 4.00 | 16.50 | — |
| 1967G Proof | 5,363 | Value: 28.00 | | | | |
| 1967J | 6,684,000 | — | 1.25 | 2.50 | 12.00 | — |
| 1967J Proof | 1,500 | Value: 32.00 | | | | |
| 1968D | 4,166,000 | — | 1.50 | 2.50 | 15.00 | — |
| 1968D Proof | 30 | Value: 850 | | | | |
| 1968F | 1,050,000 | — | 2.00 | 5.00 | 20.00 | — |
| 1968F Proof | 3,100 | Value: 22.00 | | | | |
| 1968G | 3,060,000 | — | 2.00 | 2.50 | 12.00 | — |
| 1968G Proof | 6,023 | Value: 15.00 | | | | |
| 1968J | 939,000 | — | 2.00 | 4.00 | 20.00 | — |
| 1968J Proof | 2,000 | Value: 28.00 | | | | |
| 1969D | 2,602,000 | — | 2.00 | 2.50 | 15.00 | — |
| 1969F | 3,005,000 | — | 2.00 | 2.50 | 15.00 | — |
| 1969F Proof | 5,100 | Value: 6.00 | | | | |
| 1969G | 1,754,000 | — | 2.00 | 2.50 | 16.50 | — |
| 1969G Proof | 8,700 | Value: 6.00 | | | | |
| 1969J | 2,680,000 | — | 2.00 | 2.50 | 10.00 | — |
| 1969J Proof | 5,000 | Value: 6.00 | | | | |
| 1970D | 5,203,000 | — | 1.50 | 2.00 | 4.00 | — |
| 1970F | 6,018,000 | — | 1.50 | 2.00 | 4.00 | — |
| 1970F Proof | 5,140 | Value: 7.50 | | | | |
| 1970G | 3,461,000 | — | 1.50 | 2.00 | 4.00 | — |
| 1970G Proof | 10,000 | Value: 5.00 | | | | |
| 1970J | 5,691,000 | — | 1.50 | 2.00 | 4.00 | — |
| 1970J Proof | 5,000 | Value: 6.00 | | | | |
| 1971D | 8,451,000 | — | 1.00 | 1.25 | 3.00 | — |
| 1971D Proof | 8,000 | Value: 5.00 | | | | |
| 1971F | 10,017,000 | — | 1.00 | 1.25 | 3.00 | — |
| 1971F Proof | 8,000 | Value: 5.00 | | | | |
| 1971G | 5,631,000 | — | 1.00 | 1.25 | 3.00 | — |
| 1971G Proof | 10,000 | Value: 5.00 | | | | |
| 1971J | 8,786,000 | — | 1.00 | 1.25 | 3.00 | — |
| 1971J Proof | 8,000 | Value: 6.00 | | | | |

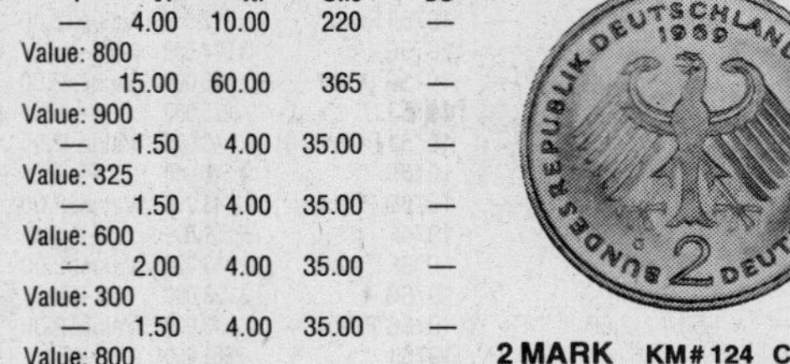

**2 MARK KM# 124 Composition:** Copper-Nickel Clad Nickel **Reverse:** Head of Konrad Adenauer facing left

| Date | Mintage | F | VF | XF | Unc | BU |
|---|---|---|---|---|---|---|
| 1969D | 7,001,000 | — | — | 1.50 | 3.00 | — |
| 1969F | 7,006,000 | — | — | 1.50 | 3.00 | — |
| 1969G | 7,010,000 | — | — | 1.50 | 3.00 | — |
| 1969J | 7,000,000 | — | — | 1.50 | 3.00 | — |
| 1970D | 7,318,000 | — | — | 1.50 | 3.00 | — |
| 1970F | 8,422,000 | — | — | 1.50 | 3.00 | — |
| 1970G | 4,844,000 | — | — | 1.50 | 3.00 | — |
| 1970J | 7,476,000 | — | — | 1.50 | 3.00 | — |
| 1971D | 7,287,000 | — | — | 1.50 | 3.00 | — |
| 1971F | 8,400,000 | — | — | 1.50 | 3.00 | — |
| 1971G | 4,848,000 | — | — | 1.50 | 3.00 | — |
| 1971J | 7,476,000 | — | — | 1.50 | 3.00 | — |
| 1972D | 7,286,000 | — | — | 1.50 | 3.00 | — |
| 1972D Proof | 8,000 | Value: 4.50 | | | | |
| 1972F | 8,392,000 | — | — | 1.50 | 3.00 | — |
| 1972F Proof | 8,000 | Value: 4.50 | | | | |
| 1972G | 4,848,000 | — | — | 1.50 | 3.00 | — |
| 1972G Proof | 10,000 | Value: 4.50 | | | | |
| 1972J | 7,476,000 | — | — | 1.50 | 3.00 | — |
| 1972J Proof | 8,000 | Value: 4.50 | | | | |
| 1973D | 10,393,000 | — | — | 1.50 | 3.00 | — |
| 1973D Proof | 9,000 | Value: 4.50 | | | | |
| 1973F | 11,015,000 | — | — | 1.50 | 3.00 | — |
| 1973F Proof | 9,000 | Value: 4.50 | | | | |
| 1973G | 9,022,000 | — | — | 1.50 | 3.00 | — |
| 1973G Proof | 9,000 | Value: 4.50 | | | | |
| 1973J | 12,272,000 | — | — | 1.50 | 3.00 | — |
| 1973J Proof | 9,000 | Value: 4.50 | | | | |
| 1974D | 5,151,000 | — | — | 1.50 | 3.00 | — |
| 1974D Proof | 35,000 | Value: 2.25 | | | | |
| 1974F | 5,894,000 | — | — | 1.50 | 3.00 | — |
| 1974F Proof | 35,000 | Value: 2.25 | | | | |
| 1974G | 3,790,000 | — | — | 1.50 | 3.00 | — |
| 1974G Proof | 35,000 | Value: 2.25 | | | | |
| 1974J | 5,282,000 | — | — | 1.50 | 3.00 | — |
| 1974J Proof | 35,000 | Value: 2.25 | | | | |
| 1975D | 4,553,000 | — | — | 1.50 | 2.50 | — |
| 1975D Proof | 43,000 | Value: 2.25 | | | | |
| 1975F | 5,270,000 | — | — | 1.50 | 2.50 | — |
| 1975F Proof | 43,000 | Value: 2.25 | | | | |
| 1975G | 3,035,000 | — | — | 1.50 | 2.50 | — |
| 1975G Proof | 43,000 | Value: 2.25 | | | | |
| 1975J | 4,673,000 | — | — | 1.50 | 2.50 | — |
| 1975J Proof | 43,000 | Value: 2.25 | | | | |
| 1976D | 4,576,000 | — | — | 1.50 | 2.50 | — |
| 1976D Proof | 43,000 | Value: 2.25 | | | | |
| 1976F | 5,257,000 | — | — | 1.50 | 2.50 | — |
| 1976F Proof | 43,000 | Value: 2.25 | | | | |
| 1976G | 3,028,000 | — | — | 1.50 | 2.50 | — |
| 1976G Proof | 43,000 | Value: 2.25 | | | | |
| 1976J | 4,673,000 | — | — | 1.50 | 2.50 | — |
| 1976J Proof | 43,000 | Value: 2.25 | | | | |
| 1977D | 5,906,000 | — | — | 1.50 | 2.50 | — |
| 1977D Proof | 51,000 | Value: 2.00 | | | | |
| 1977F | 6,765,000 | — | — | 1.50 | 2.50 | — |
| 1977F Proof | 51,000 | Value: 2.00 | | | | |
| 1977G | 3,892,000 | — | — | 1.50 | 2.50 | — |
| 1977G Proof | 51,000 | Value: 2.00 | | | | |
| 1977J | 6,007,000 | — | — | 1.50 | 2.50 | — |
| 1977J Proof | 51,000 | Value: 2.00 | | | | |
| 1978D | 3,304,000 | — | — | 1.50 | 2.50 | — |
| 1978D Proof | 54,000 | Value: 2.00 | | | | |
| 1978F | 3,804 | — | — | 1.50 | 2.50 | — |
| 1978F Proof | 54,000 | Value: 2.00 | | | | |
| 1978G | 2,217,000 | — | — | 1.50 | 2.50 | — |
| 1978G Proof | 54,000 | Value: 2.00 | | | | |
| 1978J | 3,392,000 | — | — | 1.50 | 2.50 | — |
| 1978J Proof | 54,000 | Value: 2.00 | | | | |
| 1979D | 3,209,000 | — | — | 1.50 | 2.50 | — |
| 1979D Proof | 89,000 | Value: 2.00 | | | | |
| 1979F | 3,689,000 | — | — | 1.50 | 2.50 | — |
| 1979F Proof | 89,000 | Value: 2.00 | | | | |
| 1979G | 2,165,000 | — | — | 1.50 | 2.50 | — |
| 1979G Proof | 89,000 | Value: 2.00 | | | | |
| 1979J | 3,293,000 | — | — | 1.50 | 2.50 | — |
| 1979J Proof | 89,000 | Value: 2.00 | | | | |
| 1980D | 10,810,000 | — | — | 1.50 | 2.00 | — |
| 1980D Proof | 110,000 | Value: 2.00 | | | | |
| 1980F | 8,910,000 | — | — | 1.50 | 2.00 | — |
| 1980F Proof | 110,000 | Value: 2.00 | | | | |
| 1980G | 1,170,000 | — | — | 1.50 | 2.00 | — |
| 1980G Proof | 110,000 | Value: 2.00 | | | | |
| 1980J | 4,670,000 | — | — | 1.50 | 2.00 | — |
| 1980J Proof | 110,000 | Value: 2.00 | | | | |
| 1981D | 8,180,000 | — | — | 1.50 | 2.00 | — |
| 1981D Proof | 91,000 | Value: 2.00 | | | | |
| 1981F | 7,690,000 | — | — | 1.50 | 2.00 | — |
| 1981F Proof | 91,000 | Value: 2.00 | | | | |

| Date | Mintage | F | VF | XF | Unc | BU |
|---|---|---|---|---|---|---|
| 1981G | 7,070,000 | — | — | 1.50 | 2.00 | — |
| 1981G Proof | 91,000 | Value: 2.00 | | | | |
| 1981J | 8,289,999 | — | — | 1.50 | 2.00 | — |
| 1981J Proof | 91,000 | Value: 2.00 | | | | |
| 1982D | 9,220,000 | — | — | 1.50 | 2.00 | — |
| 1982D Proof | 78,000 | Value: 2.00 | | | | |
| 1982F | 11,260,000 | — | — | 1.50 | 2.00 | — |
| 1982F Proof | 78,000 | Value: 2.00 | | | | |
| 1982G | 6,640,000 | — | — | 1.50 | 2.00 | — |
| 1982G Proof | 78,000 | Value: 2.00 | | | | |
| 1982J | 9,790,000 | — | — | 1.50 | 2.00 | — |
| 1982J Proof | 78,000 | Value: 2.00 | | | | |
| 1983D | 1,560,000 | — | — | 1.50 | 2.00 | — |
| 1983D Proof | 75,000 | Value: 2.00 | | | | |
| 1983F | 1,800,000 | — | — | 1.50 | 2.00 | — |
| 1983F Proof | 75,000 | Value: 2.00 | | | | |
| 1983G | 1,030,000 | — | — | 1.50 | 2.00 | — |
| 1983G Proof | 75,000 | Value: 2.00 | | | | |
| 1983J | 1,600,000 | — | — | 1.50 | 2.00 | — |
| 1983J Proof | 75,000 | Value: 2.00 | | | | |
| 1984D | 52,000 | — | 2.00 | 4.50 | 8.50 | — |
| 1984D Proof | 64,000 | Value: 2.00 | | | | |
| 1984F | 60,000 | — | 2.00 | 4.50 | 8.50 | — |
| 1984F Proof | 64,000 | Value: 2.00 | | | | |
| 1984G | 35,000 | — | 3.00 | 6.00 | 11.50 | — |
| 1984G Proof | 64,000 | Value: 2.00 | | | | |
| 1984J | 53,000 | — | 2.00 | 4.50 | 8.50 | — |
| 1984J Proof | 64,000 | Value: 2.00 | | | | |
| 1985D | 2,600,000 | — | — | — | 2.00 | — |
| 1985D Proof | 56,000 | Value: 2.25 | | | | |
| 1985F | 3,000,000 | — | — | — | 1.75 | — |
| 1985F Proof | 54,000 | Value: 2.25 | | | | |
| 1985G | 1,730,000 | — | — | — | 1.75 | — |
| 1985G Proof | 55,000 | Value: 2.25 | | | | |
| 1985J | 2,670,000 | — | — | — | 1.75 | — |
| 1985J Proof | 54,000 | Value: 2.25 | | | | |
| 1986D | 2,600,000 | — | — | — | 1.75 | — |
| 1986D Proof | 44,000 | Value: 2.25 | | | | |
| 1986F | 3,000,000 | — | — | — | 1.75 | — |
| 1986F Proof | 44,000 | Value: 2.25 | | | | |
| 1986G | 1,730,000 | — | — | — | 1.75 | — |
| 1986G Proof | 44,000 | Value: 2.25 | | | | |
| 1986J | 2,670,000 | — | — | — | 1.75 | — |
| 1986J Proof | 44,000 | Value: 2.25 | | | | |
| 1987D | 4,420,000 | — | — | — | 1.75 | — |
| 1987D Proof | 45,000 | Value: 2.25 | | | | |
| 1987F | 5,100,000 | — | — | — | 1.75 | — |
| 1987F Proof | 45,000 | Value: 2.25 | | | | |
| 1987G | 2,940,000 | — | — | — | 1.75 | — |
| 1987G Proof | 45,000 | Value: 2.25 | | | | |
| 1987J | 4,540,000 | — | — | — | 1.75 | — |
| 1987J Proof | 45,000 | Value: 2.25 | | | | |

**2 MARK KM# A127 Composition:** Copper-Nickel Clad Nickel **Reverse:** Head of Theodor Heuss facing left

| Date | Mintage | F | VF | XF | Unc | BU |
|---|---|---|---|---|---|---|
| 1970D | 7,317,000 | — | — | 1.50 | 3.00 | — |
| 1970F | 8,426,000 | — | — | 1.50 | 3.00 | — |
| 1970G | 4,844,000 | — | — | 1.50 | 3.00 | — |
| 1970J | 7,476,000 | — | — | 1.50 | 3.00 | — |
| 1971D | 7,280,000 | — | — | 1.50 | 3.00 | — |
| 1971F | 8,403,000 | — | — | 1.50 | 3.00 | — |
| 1971G | 4,841,000 | — | — | 1.50 | 3.00 | — |
| 1971J | 7,476,000 | — | — | 1.50 | 3.00 | — |
| 1972D | 7,288,000 | — | — | 1.50 | 3.00 | — |
| 1972D Proof | 8,000 | Value: 4.50 | | | | |
| 1972F | 8,401,000 | — | — | 1.50 | 3.00 | — |
| 1972F Proof | 8,000 | Value: 4.50 | | | | |
| 1972G | 4,859,000 | — | — | 1.50 | 3.00 | — |
| 1972G Proof | 10,000 | Value: 4.50 | | | | |
| 1972J | 7,476,000 | — | — | 1.50 | 3.00 | — |
| 1972J Proof | 8,000 | Value: 4.50 | | | | |
| 1973D | 10,379,000 | — | — | 1.50 | 3.00 | — |
| 1973D Proof | 9,000 | Value: 4.50 | | | | |
| 1973F | 11,018,000 | — | — | 1.50 | 3.00 | — |
| 1973F Proof | 9,000 | Value: 4.50 | | | | |
| 1973G | 8,975,000 | — | — | 1.50 | 3.00 | — |
| 1973G Proof | 9,000 | Value: 4.50 | | | | |
| 1973J | 12,360,000 | — | — | 1.50 | 3.00 | — |
| 1973J Proof | 9,000 | Value: 4.50 | | | | |
| 1974D | 5,147,000 | — | — | 1.50 | 3.00 | — |
| 1974D Proof | 35,000 | Value: 2.00 | | | | |
| 1974F | 5,899,000 | — | — | 1.50 | 3.00 | — |
| 1974F Proof | 35,000 | Value: 2.00 | | | | |
| 1974G | 3,820,000 | — | — | 1.50 | 3.00 | — |
| 1974G Proof | 35,000 | Value: 2.00 | | | | |
| 1974J | 5,280,000 | — | — | 1.50 | 3.00 | — |
| 1974J Proof | 35,000 | Value: 2.00 | | | | |
| 1975D | 4,623,000 | — | — | 1.50 | 2.00 | — |
| 1975D Proof | 43,000 | Value: 2.00 | | | | |
| 1975F | 5,251,000 | — | — | 1.50 | 2.00 | — |
| 1975F Proof | 43,000 | Value: 2.00 | | | | |
| 1975G | 3,034,000 | — | — | 1.50 | 2.00 | — |
| 1975G Proof | 43,000 | Value: 2.00 | | | | |
| 1975J | 4,675,000 | — | — | 1.50 | 2.00 | — |
| 1975J Proof | 43,000 | Value: 2.00 | | | | |
| 1976D | 4,546,000 | — | — | 1.50 | 2.00 | — |
| 1976D Proof | 43,000 | Value: 2.00 | | | | |
| 1976F | 5,259,000 | — | — | 1.50 | 2.00 | — |
| 1976F Proof | 43,000 | Value: 2.00 | | | | |
| 1976G | 3,028,000 | — | — | 1.50 | 2.00 | — |
| 1976G Proof | 43,000 | Value: 2.00 | | | | |
| 1976J | 4,681,000 | — | — | 1.50 | 2.00 | — |
| 1976J Proof | 43,000 | Value: 2.00 | | | | |
| 1977D | 5,857,000 | — | — | 1.50 | 2.00 | — |
| 1977D Proof | 51,000 | Value: 1.75 | | | | |
| 1977F | 6,752,000 | — | — | 1.50 | 2.00 | — |
| 1977F Proof | 51,000 | Value: 1.75 | | | | |
| 1977G | 3,892,000 | — | — | 1.50 | 2.00 | — |
| 1977G Proof | 51,000 | Value: 1.75 | | | | |
| 1977J | 6,009,000 | — | — | 1.50 | 2.00 | — |
| 1977J Proof | 51,000 | Value: 1.75 | | | | |
| 1978D | 3,804,000 | — | — | 1.50 | 2.00 | — |
| 1978D Proof | 54,000 | Value: 1.75 | | | | |
| 1978F | 3,804,000 | — | — | 1.50 | 2.00 | — |
| 1978F Proof | 54,000 | Value: 1.75 | | | | |
| 1978G | 2,217,000 | — | — | 1.50 | 2.00 | — |
| 1978G Proof | 54,000 | Value: 1.75 | | | | |
| 1978J | 3,392,000 | — | — | 1.50 | 2.00 | — |
| 1978J Proof | 54,000 | Value: 1.75 | | | | |
| 1979D | 3,209,000 | — | — | 1.50 | 2.00 | — |
| 1979D Proof | 89,000 | Value: 1.75 | | | | |
| 1979F | 3,689,000 | — | — | 1.50 | 2.00 | — |
| 1979F Proof | 89,000 | Value: 1.75 | | | | |
| 1979G | 2,165,000 | — | — | 1.50 | 2.00 | — |
| 1979G Proof | 89,000 | Value: 1.75 | | | | |
| 1979J | 3,293,000 | — | — | 1.50 | 2.00 | — |
| 1979J Proof | 89,000 | Value: 1.75 | | | | |
| 1980D | 2,000,000 | — | — | 1.50 | 1.75 | — |
| 1980D Proof | 110,000 | Value: 1.75 | | | | |
| 1980F | 2,300,000 | — | — | 1.50 | 1.75 | — |
| 1980F Proof | 110,000 | Value: 1.75 | | | | |
| 1980G | 1,300,000 | — | — | 1.50 | 1.75 | — |
| 1980G Proof | 110,000 | Value: 1.75 | | | | |
| 1980J | 2,000,000 | — | — | 1.50 | 1.75 | — |
| 1980J Proof | 110,000 | Value: 1.75 | | | | |
| 1981D | 2,000,000 | — | — | 1.50 | 1.75 | — |
| 1981D Proof | 91,000 | Value: 1.75 | | | | |
| 1981F | 2,300,000 | — | — | 1.50 | 1.75 | — |
| 1981F Proof | 91,000 | Value: 1.75 | | | | |
| 1981G | 1,300,000 | — | — | 1.50 | 1.75 | — |
| 1981G Proof | 91,000 | Value: 1.75 | | | | |
| 1981J | 2,000,000 | — | — | 1.50 | 1.75 | — |
| 1981J Proof | 91,000 | Value: 1.75 | | | | |
| 1982D | 3,100,000 | — | — | 1.50 | 1.75 | — |
| 1982D Proof | 78,000 | Value: 1.75 | | | | |
| 1982F | 3,600,000 | — | — | 1.50 | 1.75 | — |
| 1982F Proof | 78,000 | Value: 1.75 | | | | |
| 1982G | 2,100,000 | — | — | 1.50 | 1.75 | — |
| 1982G Proof | 78,000 | Value: 1.75 | | | | |
| 1982J | 3,200,000 | — | — | 1.50 | 1.75 | — |
| 1982J Proof | 78,000 | Value: 1.75 | | | | |
| 1983D | 1,560,000 | — | — | 1.50 | 1.75 | — |
| 1983D Proof | 75,000 | Value: 1.75 | | | | |
| 1983F | 1,800,000 | — | — | 1.50 | 1.75 | — |
| 1983F Proof | 75,000 | Value: 1.75 | | | | |
| 1983G | 1,030,000 | — | — | 1.50 | 1.75 | — |
| 1983G Proof | 75,000 | Value: 1.75 | | | | |
| 1983J | 1,600,000 | — | — | 1.50 | 1.75 | — |
| 1983J Proof | 75,000 | Value: 1.75 | | | | |
| 1984D | 52,000 | — | 2.00 | 4.50 | 8.50 | — |
| 1984D Proof | 64,000 | Value: 2.00 | | | | |
| 1984F | 60,000 | — | 2.00 | 4.50 | 8.50 | — |
| 1984F Proof | 64,000 | Value: 2.00 | | | | |
| 1984G | 35,000 | — | 3.00 | 6.00 | 11.50 | — |
| 1984G Proof | 64,000 | Value: 2.00 | | | | |
| 1984J | 53,000 | — | 2.00 | 4.50 | 8.50 | — |
| 1984J Proof | 64,000 | Value: 2.00 | | | | |
| 1985D | 2,600,000 | — | — | — | 1.75 | — |
| 1985D Proof | 56,000 | Value: 2.25 | | | | |
| 1985F | 3,000,000 | — | — | — | 1.75 | — |
| 1985F Proof | 54,000 | Value: 2.25 | | | | |
| 1985G | 1,730,000 | — | — | — | 1.75 | — |
| 1985G Proof | 55,000 | Value: 2.25 | | | | |
| 1985J | 2,670,000 | — | — | — | 1.75 | — |
| 1985J Proof | 54,000 | Value: 2.25 | | | | |
| 1986D | 2,600,000 | — | — | — | 1.75 | — |
| 1986D Proof | 44,000 | Value: 2.25 | | | | |
| 1986F | 3,000,000 | — | — | — | 1.75 | — |
| 1986F Proof | 44,000 | Value: 2.25 | | | | |
| 1986G | 1,730,000 | — | — | — | 1.75 | — |
| 1986G Proof | 44,000 | Value: 2.25 | | | | |
| 1986J | 2,670,000 | — | — | — | 1.75 | — |
| 1986J Proof | 44,000 | Value: 2.25 | | | | |
| 1987D | 4,420,000 | — | — | — | 1.75 | — |
| 1987D Proof | 45,000 | Value: 2.25 | | | | |
| 1987F | 5,100,000 | — | — | — | 1.75 | — |
| 1987F Proof | 45,000 | Value: 2.25 | | | | |
| 1987G | 2,940,000 | — | — | — | 1.75 | — |
| 1987G Proof | 45,000 | Value: 2.25 | | | | |
| 1987J | 4,540,000 | — | — | — | 1.75 | — |
| 1987J Proof | 45,000 | Value: 2.25 | | | | |

**2 MARK KM# 149 Composition:** Copper-Nickel Clad Nickel **Reverse:** Head of Dr. Kurt Schumacher facing forward

| Date | Mintage | F | VF | XF | Unc | BU |
|---|---|---|---|---|---|---|
| 1979D | 3,209,000 | — | — | 1.50 | 2.00 | — |
| 1979D Proof | 89,000 | Value: 1.75 | | | | |
| 1979F | 3,689,000 | — | — | 1.50 | 2.00 | — |
| 1979F Proof | 89,000 | Value: 1.75 | | | | |
| 1979G | 2,165,000 | — | — | 1.50 | 2.00 | — |
| 1979G Proof | 89,000 | Value: 1.75 | | | | |
| 1979J | 3,293,000 | — | — | 1.50 | 2.00 | — |
| 1979J Proof | 89,000 | Value: 1.75 | | | | |
| 1980D | 2,000,000 | — | — | 1.50 | 2.00 | — |
| 1980D Proof | 110,000 | Value: 1.75 | | | | |
| 1980F | 2,300,000 | — | — | 1.50 | 2.00 | — |
| 1980F Proof | 110,000 | Value: 1.75 | | | | |
| 1980G | 1,300,000 | — | — | 1.50 | 2.00 | — |
| 1980G Proof | 110,000 | Value: 1.75 | | | | |
| 1980J | 2,000,000 | — | — | 1.50 | 2.00 | — |
| 1980J Proof | 110,000 | Value: 1.75 | | | | |
| 1981D | 2,000,000 | — | — | 1.50 | 2.00 | — |
| 1981D Proof | 91,000 | Value: 1.75 | | | | |
| 1981F | 2,000,000 | — | — | 1.50 | 2.00 | — |
| 1981F Proof | 91,000 | Value: 1.75 | | | | |
| 1981G | 1,300,000 | — | — | 1.50 | 2.00 | — |
| 1981G Proof | 91,000 | Value: 1.75 | | | | |
| 1981J | 2,000,000 | — | — | 1.50 | 2.00 | — |
| 1981J Proof | 91,000 | Value: 1.75 | | | | |
| 1982D | 3,100,000 | — | — | 1.50 | 2.00 | — |
| 1982D Proof | 78,000 | Value: 1.75 | | | | |
| 1982F | 3,600,000 | — | — | 1.50 | 2.00 | — |
| 1982F Proof | 78,000 | Value: 1.75 | | | | |
| 1982G | 2,100,000 | — | — | 1.50 | 2.00 | — |
| 1982G Proof | 78,000 | Value: 1.75 | | | | |
| 1982J | 3,200,000 | — | — | 1.50 | 2.00 | — |
| 1982J Proof | 78,000 | Value: 1.75 | | | | |
| 1983D | 1,560,000 | — | — | 1.50 | 2.00 | — |
| 1983D Proof | 75,000 | Value: 1.75 | | | | |
| 1983F | 1,800,000 | — | — | 1.50 | 2.00 | — |
| 1983F Proof | 75,000 | Value: 1.75 | | | | |
| 1983G | 1,030,000 | — | — | 1.50 | 2.00 | — |
| 1983G Proof | 75,000 | Value: 1.75 | | | | |
| 1983J | 1,600,000 | — | — | 1.50 | 2.00 | — |
| 1983J Proof | 75,000 | Value: 1.75 | | | | |
| 1984D | 52,000 | — | 2.00 | 4.50 | 8.50 | — |
| 1984D Proof | 64,000 | Value: 1.75 | | | | |
| 1984F | 60,000 | — | 2.00 | 4.50 | 8.50 | — |
| 1984F Proof | 64,000 | Value: 1.75 | | | | |
| 1984G | 35,000 | — | 3.00 | 6.00 | 11.50 | — |
| 1984G Proof | 64,000 | Value: 1.75 | | | | |
| 1984J | 53,000 | — | 2.00 | 4.50 | 8.50 | — |
| 1984J Proof | 64,000 | Value: 1.75 | | | | |
| 1985D | 2,600,000 | — | — | — | 1.75 | — |
| 1985D Proof | 56,000 | Value: 2.25 | | | | |
| 1985F | 3,000,000 | — | — | — | 1.75 | — |
| 1985F Proof | 54,000 | Value: 2.25 | | | | |
| 1985G | 1,730,000 | — | — | — | 1.75 | — |
| 1985G Proof | 55,000 | Value: 2.25 | | | | |
| 1985J | 2,670,000 | — | — | — | 1.75 | — |
| 1985J Proof | 54,000 | Value: 2.25 | | | | |
| 1986D | 2,600,000 | — | — | — | 1.75 | — |
| 1986D Proof | 44,000 | Value: 2.25 | | | | |
| 1986F | 3,000,000 | — | — | — | 1.75 | — |
| 1986F Proof | 44,000 | Value: 2.25 | | | | |
| 1986G | 1,730,000 | — | — | — | 1.75 | — |
| 1986G Proof | 44,000 | Value: 2.25 | | | | |
| 1986J | 2,670,000 | — | — | — | 1.75 | — |
| 1986J Proof | 44,000 | Value: 2.25 | | | | |
| 1987D | 4,420,000 | — | — | — | 1.75 | — |
| 1987D Proof | 45,000 | Value: 2.25 | | | | |
| 1987F | 5,100,000 | — | — | — | 1.75 | — |
| 1987F Proof | 45,000 | Value: 2.25 | | | | |
| 1987G | 2,940,000 | — | — | — | 1.75 | — |
| 1987G Proof | 45,000 | Value: 2.25 | | | | |
| 1987J | 4,540,000 | — | — | — | 1.75 | — |
| 1987J Proof | 45,000 | Value: 2.25 | | | | |
| 1988D | 5,850,000 | — | — | — | 1.75 | — |
| 1988D Proof | 45,000 | Value: 2.25 | | | | |
| 1988F | 6,750,000 | — | — | — | 1.75 | — |
| 1988F Proof | 45,000 | Value: 2.25 | | | | |
| 1988G | 3,890,000 | — | — | — | 1.75 | — |
| 1988G Proof | 45,000 | Value: 2.25 | | | | |
| 1988J | 6,010,000 | — | — | — | 1.75 | — |
| 1988J Proof | 45,000 | Value: 2.25 | | | | |
| 1989D | 10,400,000 | — | — | — | 1.75 | — |
| 1989D Proof | 45,000 | Value: 2.25 | | | | |
| 1989F | 12,000,000 | — | — | — | 1.75 | — |
| 1989F Proof | 45,000 | Value: 2.25 | | | | |
| 1989G | 6,920,000 | — | — | — | 1.75 | — |
| 1989G Proof | 45,000 | Value: 2.25 | | | | |
| 1989J | 10,680,000 | — | — | — | 1.75 | — |

| Date | Mintage | F | VF | XF | Unc | BU |
|---|---|---|---|---|---|---|
| 1989J Proof | 45,000 | Value: 2.25 | | | | |
| 1990D | 18,370,000 | — | — | — | 1.75 | — |
| 1990D Proof | 45,000 | Value: 2.25 | | | | |
| 1990F | 21,200,000 | — | — | — | 1.75 | — |
| 1990F Proof | 45,000 | Value: 2.25 | | | | |
| 1990G | 12,220,000 | — | — | — | 1.75 | — |
| 1990G Proof | 45,000 | Value: 2.25 | | | | |
| 1990J | 18,870,000 | — | — | — | 1.75 | — |
| 1990J Proof | 45,000 | Value: 2.25 | | | | |
| 1991A | 4,000,000 | — | — | — | 1.75 | — |
| 1991A Proof | 45,000 | Value: 2.25 | | | | |
| 1991D | 4,200,000 | — | — | — | 1.75 | — |
| 1991D Proof | 45,000 | Value: 2.25 | | | | |
| 1991F | 4,800,000 | — | — | — | 1.75 | — |
| 1991F Proof | 45,000 | Value: 2.25 | | | | |
| 1991G | 2,800,000 | — | — | — | 1.75 | — |
| 1991G Proof | 45,000 | Value: 2.25 | | | | |
| 1991J | 4,200,000 | — | — | — | 1.75 | — |
| 1991J Proof | 45,000 | Value: 2.25 | | | | |
| 1992A | 7,330,000 | — | — | — | 1.75 | — |
| 1992A Proof | 45,000 | Value: 2.25 | | | | |
| 1992D | 7,700,000 | — | — | — | 1.75 | — |
| 1992D Proof | 45,000 | Value: 2.25 | | | | |
| 1992F | 8,800,000 | — | — | — | 1.75 | — |
| 1992F Proof | 45,000 | Value: 2.25 | | | | |
| 1992G | 5,130,000 | — | — | — | 1.75 | — |
| 1992G Proof | 45,000 | Value: 2.25 | | | | |
| 1992J | 7,700,000 | — | — | — | 1.75 | — |
| 1992J Proof | 45,000 | Value: 2.25 | | | | |
| 1993A | 600,000 | — | — | 3.00 | 7.00 | — |
| 1993A Proof | 45,000 | Value: 2.25 | | | | |
| 1993D | 630,000 | — | — | 3.00 | 7.00 | — |
| 1993D Proof | 45,000 | Value: 2.25 | | | | |
| 1993F | 720,000 | — | — | 3.00 | 7.00 | — |
| 1993F Proof | 45,000 | Value: 2.25 | | | | |
| 1993G | 420,000 | — | — | 4.00 | 10.00 | — |
| 1993G Proof | 45,000 | Value: 2.25 | | | | |
| 1993J | 630,000 | — | — | 3.00 | 7.00 | — |
| 1993J Proof | 45,000 | Value: 2.25 | | | | |

**2 MARK** **KM# 170** **Composition:** Copper-Nickel Clad Nickel **Reverse:** Head of Ludwig Erhard facing forward

| Date | Mintage | F | VF | XF | Unc | BU |
|---|---|---|---|---|---|---|
| 1988D | 5,850,000 | — | — | — | 1.65 | — |
| 1988D Proof | 45,000 | Value: 2.00 | | | | |
| 1988F | 6,750,000 | — | — | — | 1.65 | — |
| 1988F Proof | 45,000 | Value: 2.00 | | | | |
| 1988G | 3,890,000 | — | — | — | 1.65 | — |
| 1988G Proof | 45,000 | Value: 2.00 | | | | |
| 1988J | 6,010,000 | — | — | — | 1.65 | — |
| 1988J Proof | 45,000 | Value: 2.00 | | | | |
| 1989D | 10,400,000 | — | — | — | 1.65 | — |
| 1989D Proof | 45,000 | Value: 2.00 | | | | |
| 1989F | 12,000,000 | — | — | — | 1.65 | — |
| 1989F Proof | 45,000 | Value: 2.00 | | | | |
| 1989G | 6,920,000 | — | — | — | 1.65 | — |
| 1989G Proof | 45,000 | Value: 2.00 | | | | |
| 1989J | 10,680,000 | — | — | — | 1.65 | — |
| 1989J Proof | 45,000 | Value: 2.00 | | | | |
| 1990D | 18,370,000 | — | — | — | 1.65 | — |
| 1990D Proof | 45,000 | Value: 2.00 | | | | |
| 1990F | 21,200,000 | — | — | — | 1.65 | — |
| 1990F Proof | 45,000 | Value: 2.00 | | | | |
| 1990G | 12,220,000 | — | — | — | 1.65 | — |
| 1990G Proof | 45,000 | Value: 2.00 | | | | |
| 1990J | 18,870,000 | — | — | — | 1.65 | — |
| 1990J Proof | 45,000 | Value: 2.00 | | | | |
| 1991A | 4,000,000 | — | — | — | 1.65 | — |
| 1991A Proof | 45,000 | Value: 2.00 | | | | |
| 1991D | 4,200,000 | — | — | — | 1.65 | — |
| 1991D Proof | 45,000 | Value: 2.00 | | | | |
| 1991F | 4,800,000 | — | — | — | 1.65 | — |
| 1991F Proof | 45,000 | Value: 2.00 | | | | |
| 1991G | 2,800,000 | — | — | — | 1.65 | — |
| 1991G Proof | 45,000 | Value: 2.00 | | | | |
| 1991J | 4,200,000 | — | — | — | 1.65 | — |
| 1991J Proof | 45,000 | Value: 2.00 | | | | |
| 1992A | 7,330,000 | — | — | — | 1.75 | — |
| 1992A Proof | 45,000 | Value: 2.25 | | | | |
| 1992D | 7,700,000 | — | — | — | 1.75 | — |
| 1992D Proof | 45,000 | Value: 2.25 | | | | |
| 1992F | 8,800,000 | — | — | — | 1.75 | — |
| 1992F Proof | 45,000 | Value: 2.25 | | | | |
| 1992G | 5,130,000 | — | — | — | 1.75 | — |
| 1992G Proof | 45,000 | Value: 2.25 | | | | |
| 1992J | 7,700,000 | — | — | — | 1.75 | — |
| 1992J Proof | 45,000 | Value: 2.25 | | | | |
| 1993A | 600,000 | — | — | 3.00 | 7.00 | — |
| 1993A Proof | 45,000 | Value: 2.25 | | | | |
| 1993D | 630,000 | — | — | 3.00 | 7.00 | — |
| 1993D Proof | 45,000 | Value: 2.25 | | | | |

| Date | Mintage | F | VF | XF | Unc | BU |
|---|---|---|---|---|---|---|
| 1993F | 720,000 | — | — | 3.00 | 7.00 | — |
| 1993F Proof | 45,000 | Value: 2.25 | | | | |
| 1993G | 420,000 | — | — | 4.00 | 10.00 | — |
| 1993G Proof | 45,000 | Value: 2.25 | | | | |
| 1993J | 630,000 | — | — | 3.00 | 7.00 | — |
| 1993J Proof | 45,000 | Value: 2.25 | | | | |
| 1994A | 5,000,000 | — | — | — | 1.75 | — |
| 1994A Proof | 45,000 | Value: 2.25 | | | | |
| 1994D | 5,250,000 | — | — | — | 1.75 | — |
| 1994D Proof | 45,000 | Value: 2.25 | | | | |
| 1994F | 6,000,000 | — | — | — | 1.75 | — |
| 1994F Proof | 45,000 | Value: 2.25 | | | | |
| 1994G | 3,500,000 | — | — | — | 1.75 | — |
| 1994G Proof | 45,000 | Value: 2.25 | | | | |
| 1994J | 5,250,000 | — | — | — | 1.75 | — |
| 1994J Proof | 45,000 | Value: 2.25 | | | | |
| 1995A | 1,595,000 | — | — | — | 3.50 | — |
| 1995A Proof | 45,000 | Value: 17.50 | | | | |
| 1995D In sets only | 20,000 | — | — | — | 60.00 | — |
| 1995D Proof | 45,000 | Value: 17.50 | | | | |
| 1995F In sets only | 20,000 | — | — | — | 60.00 | — |
| 1995F Proof | 45,000 | Value: 17.50 | | | | |
| 1995G | 920,000 | — | — | — | 6.00 | — |
| 1995G Proof | 45,000 | Value: 17.50 | | | | |
| 1995J In sets only | 20,000 | — | — | — | 60.00 | — |
| 1995J Proof | 45,000 | Value: 17.50 | | | | |
| 1996A | — | — | — | — | 5.00 | — |
| 1996A Proof | 45,000 | Value: 6.00 | | | | |
| 1996D | — | — | — | — | 5.00 | — |
| 1996D Proof | 45,000 | Value: 6.00 | | | | |
| 1996F | — | — | — | — | 5.00 | — |
| 1996F Proof | 45,000 | Value: 6.00 | | | | |
| 1996G | — | — | — | — | 5.00 | — |
| 1996G Proof | 45,000 | Value: 6.00 | | | | |
| 1996J | — | — | — | — | 5.00 | — |
| 1996J Proof | 45,000 | Value: 6.00 | | | | |
| 1997A In sets only | 70,000 | — | — | — | 4.25 | — |
| 1997A Proof | 45,000 | Value: 5.00 | | | | |
| 1997D In sets only | 70,000 | — | — | — | 4.25 | — |
| 1997D Proof | 45,000 | Value: 5.00 | | | | |
| 1997F In sets only | 70,000 | — | — | — | 4.25 | — |
| 1997F Proof | 45,000 | Value: 5.00 | | | | |
| 1997G In sets only | 70,000 | — | — | — | 4.25 | — |
| 1997G Proof | 45,000 | Value: 5.00 | | | | |
| 1997J In sets only | 70,000 | — | — | — | 4.25 | — |
| 1997J Proof | 45,000 | Value: 5.00 | | | | |
| 1998A In sets only | 70,000 | — | — | — | 4.25 | — |
| 1998A Proof | 45,000 | Value: 5.00 | | | | |
| 1998D In sets only | 70,000 | — | — | — | 4.25 | — |
| 1998D Proof | 45,000 | Value: 5.00 | | | | |
| 1998F In sets only | 70,000 | — | — | — | 4.25 | — |
| 1998F Proof | 45,000 | Value: 5.00 | | | | |
| 1998G In sets only | 70,000 | — | — | — | 4.25 | — |
| 1998G Proof | 45,000 | Value: 5.00 | | | | |
| 1998J In sets only | 70,000 | — | — | — | 4.25 | — |
| 1998J Proof | 45,000 | Value: 5.00 | | | | |
| 1999A In sets only | 70,000 | — | — | — | 4.25 | — |
| 1999A Proof | 45,000 | Value: 5.00 | | | | |
| 1999D In sets only | 70,000 | — | — | — | 4.25 | — |
| 1999D Proof | 45,000 | Value: 5.00 | | | | |
| 1999F In sets only | 70,000 | — | — | — | 4.25 | — |
| 1999F Proof | 45,000 | Value: 5.00 | | | | |
| 1999G In sets only | 70,000 | — | — | — | 4.75 | — |
| 1999G Proof | 45,000 | Value: 5.00 | | | | |
| 1999J In sets only | 70,000 | — | — | — | 4.75 | — |
| 1999J Proof | 45,000 | Value: 5.00 | | | | |
| 2000A In sets only | 70,000 | — | — | — | 5.00 | — |
| 2000A Proof | 45,000 | Value: 5.00 | | | | |
| 2000D In sets only | 70,000 | — | — | — | 5.00 | — |
| 2000D Proof | 45,000 | Value: 5.00 | | | | |
| 2000F In sets only | 70,000 | — | — | — | 5.00 | — |
| 2000F Proof | 45,000 | Value: 5.00 | | | | |
| 2000G In sets only | 70,000 | — | — | — | 5.00 | — |
| 2000G Proof | 45,000 | Value: 5.00 | | | | |
| 2000J In sets only | 70,000 | — | — | — | 5.00 | — |
| 2000J Proof | 45,000 | Value: 5.00 | | | | |
| 2001A In sets only | 130,000 | — | — | — | 10.00 | — |
| 2001A Proof | 78,000 | Value: 10.00 | | | | |
| 2001D In sets only | 130,000 | — | — | — | 10.00 | — |
| 2001D Proof | 78,000 | Value: 10.00 | | | | |
| 2001F In sets only | 130,000 | — | — | — | 10.00 | — |
| 2001F Proof | 78,000 | Value: 10.00 | | | | |
| 2001G In sets only | 130,000 | — | — | — | 10.00 | — |
| 2001G Proof | 78,000 | Value: 10.00 | | | | |
| 2001J In sets only | 130,000 | — | — | — | 10.00 | — |
| 2001J Proof | 78,000 | Value: 10.00 | | | | |

**2 MARK** **KM# 175** **Composition:** Copper-Nickel Clad Nickel **Reverse:** Head of Franz Joseph Strauss facing left

| Date | Mintage | F | VF | XF | Unc | BU |
|---|---|---|---|---|---|---|
| 1990D | 18,370,000 | — | — | — | 1.75 | — |
| 1990D Proof | 45,000 | Value: 2.25 | | | | |
| 1990F | 21,200,000 | — | — | — | 1.75 | — |
| 1990F Proof | 45,000 | Value: 2.25 | | | | |
| 1990G | 12,220,000 | — | — | — | 1.75 | — |
| 1990G Proof | 45,000 | Value: 2.25 | | | | |
| 1990J | 18,870,000 | — | — | — | 1.75 | — |
| 1990J Proof | 45,000 | Value: 2.25 | | | | |
| 1991A | 4,000,000 | — | — | — | 1.75 | — |
| 1991A Proof | 45,000 | Value: 2.25 | | | | |
| 1991D | 4,200,000 | — | — | — | 1.75 | — |
| 1991D Proof | 45,000 | Value: 2.25 | | | | |
| 1991F | 4,800,000 | — | — | — | 1.75 | — |
| 1991F Proof | 45,000 | Value: 2.25 | | | | |
| 1991G | 2,800,000 | — | — | — | 1.75 | — |
| 1991G Proof | 45,000 | Value: 2.25 | | | | |
| 1991J | 4,200,000 | — | — | — | 1.75 | — |
| 1991J Proof | 45,000 | Value: 2.25 | | | | |
| 1992A | 7,330,000 | — | — | — | 1.75 | — |
| 1992A Proof | 45,000 | Value: 2.25 | | | | |
| 1992D | 7,700,000 | — | — | — | 1.75 | — |
| 1992D Proof | 45,000 | Value: 2.25 | | | | |
| 1992F | 8,800,000 | — | — | — | 1.75 | — |
| 1992F Proof | 45,000 | Value: 2.25 | | | | |
| 1992G | 5,130,000 | — | — | — | 1.75 | — |
| 1992G Proof | 45,000 | Value: 2.25 | | | | |
| 1992J | 7,700,000 | — | — | — | 1.75 | — |
| 1992J Proof | 45,000 | Value: 2.25 | | | | |
| 1993A | 600,000 | — | — | 3.00 | 7.00 | — |
| 1993A Proof | 45,000 | Value: 2.25 | | | | |
| 1993D | 630,000 | — | — | 3.00 | 7.00 | — |
| 1993D Proof | 45,000 | Value: 2.25 | | | | |
| 1993F | 720,000 | — | — | 3.00 | 7.00 | — |
| 1993F Proof | 45,000 | Value: 2.25 | | | | |
| 1993G | 420,000 | — | — | 4.00 | 10.00 | — |
| 1993G Proof | 45,000 | Value: 2.25 | | | | |
| 1993J | 630,000 | — | — | 3.00 | 7.00 | — |
| 1993J Proof | 45,000 | Value: 2.25 | | | | |
| 1994A | 5,000,000 | — | — | — | 1.75 | — |
| 1994A Proof | 45,000 | Value: 2.25 | | | | |
| 1994D | 5,250,000 | — | — | — | 1.75 | — |
| 1994D Proof | 45,000 | Value: 2.25 | | | | |
| 1994F | 6,000,000 | — | — | — | 1.75 | — |
| 1994F Proof | 45,000 | Value: 2.25 | | | | |
| 1994G | 3,500,000 | — | — | — | 1.75 | — |
| 1994G Proof | 45,000 | Value: 2.25 | | | | |
| 1994J | 5,250,000 | — | — | — | 1.75 | — |
| 1994J Proof | 45,000 | Value: 2.25 | | | | |
| 1995A | 1,595,000 | — | — | — | 3.50 | — |
| 1995A Proof | 45,000 | Value: 17.50 | | | | |
| 1995D In sets only | 20,000 | — | — | — | 60.00 | — |
| 1995D Proof | 45,000 | Value: 17.50 | | | | |
| 1995F In sets only | 20,000 | — | — | — | 60.00 | — |
| 1995F Proof | 45,000 | Value: 17.50 | | | | |
| 1995G | 620,000 | — | — | — | 7.00 | — |
| 1995G Proof | 45,000 | Value: 17.50 | | | | |
| 1995J In sets only | 20,000 | — | — | — | 60.00 | — |
| 1995J Proof | 45,000 | Value: 17.50 | | | | |
| 1996A | — | — | — | — | 5.00 | — |
| 1996A Proof | 45,000 | Value: 6.00 | | | | |
| 1996D | — | — | — | — | 5.00 | — |
| 1996D Proof | 45,000 | Value: 6.00 | | | | |
| 1996F | — | — | — | — | 5.00 | — |
| 1996F Proof | 45,000 | Value: 6.00 | | | | |
| 1996G | — | — | — | — | 5.00 | — |
| 1996G Proof | 45,000 | Value: 6.00 | | | | |
| 1996J | — | — | — | — | 5.00 | — |
| 1996J Proof | 45,000 | Value: 6.00 | | | | |
| 1997A In sets only | 70,000 | — | — | — | 4.25 | — |
| 1997A Proof | 45,000 | Value: 5.00 | | | | |
| 1997D In sets only | 70,000 | — | — | — | 4.25 | — |
| 1997D Proof | 45,000 | Value: 5.00 | | | | |
| 1997F In sets only | 70,000 | — | — | — | 4.25 | — |
| 1997F Proof | 45,000 | Value: 5.00 | | | | |
| 1997G In sets only | 70,000 | — | — | — | 4.25 | — |
| 1997G Proof | 45,000 | Value: 5.00 | | | | |
| 1997J In sets only | 70,000 | — | — | — | 4.25 | — |
| 1997J Proof | 45,000 | Value: 5.00 | | | | |
| 1998A In sets only | 70,000 | — | — | — | 4.25 | — |
| 1998A Proof | 45,000 | Value: 5.00 | | | | |
| 1998D In sets only | 70,000 | — | — | — | 4.25 | — |
| 1998D Proof | 45,000 | Value: 5.00 | | | | |
| 1998F In sets only | 70,000 | — | — | — | 4.25 | — |
| 1998F Proof | 45,000 | Value: 5.00 | | | | |
| 1998G In sets only | 70,000 | — | — | — | 4.25 | — |
| 1998G Proof | 45,000 | Value: 5.00 | | | | |
| 1998J In sets only | 70,000 | — | — | — | 4.25 | — |
| 1998J Proof | 45,000 | Value: 5.00 | | | | |
| 1999A In sets only | 70,000 | — | — | — | 4.25 | — |
| 1999A Proof | 45,000 | Value: 5.00 | | | | |
| 1999D In sets only | 70,000 | — | — | — | 4.25 | — |
| 1999D Proof | 45,000 | Value: 5.00 | | | | |
| 1999F In sets only | 70,000 | — | — | — | 4.25 | — |
| 1999F Proof | 45,000 | Value: 5.00 | | | | |
| 1999G In sets only | 70,000 | — | — | — | 4.25 | — |
| 1999G Proof | 45,000 | Value: 5.00 | | | | |
| 1999J In sets only | 70,000 | — | — | — | 4.25 | — |
| 1999J Proof | 45,000 | Value: 5.00 | | | | |
| 2000A In sets only | 70,000 | — | — | — | 5.00 | — |
| 2000A Proof | 45,000 | Value: 5.00 | | | | |
| 2000D In sets only | 70,000 | — | — | — | 5.00 | — |
| 2000D Proof | 45,000 | Value: 5.00 | | | | |

| Date | Mintage | F | VF | XF | Unc | BU |
|---|---|---|---|---|---|---|
| 2000F In sets only | 70,000 | — | — | — | 5.00 | — |
| 2000F Proof | 45,000 | Value: 5.00 | | | | |
| 2000G In sets only | 70,000 | — | — | — | 5.00 | — |
| 2000G Proof | 45,000 | Value: 5.00 | | | | |
| 2000J In sets only | 70,000 | — | — | — | 5.00 | — |
| 2000J Proof | 45,000 | Value: 5.00 | | | | |
| 2001A In sets only | 130,000 | — | — | — | 10.00 | — |
| 2001A Proof | 78,000 | Value: 10.00 | | | | |
| 2001D In sets only | 130,000 | — | — | — | 10.00 | — |
| 2001D Proof | 78,000 | Value: 10.00 | | | | |
| 2001F In sets only | 130,000 | — | — | — | 10.00 | — |
| 2001F Proof | 78,000 | Value: 10.00 | | | | |
| 2001G In sets only | 130,000 | — | — | — | 10.00 | — |
| 2001G Proof | 78,000 | Value: 10.00 | | | | |
| 2001J In sets only | 130,000 | — | — | — | 10.00 | — |
| 2001J Proof | 78,000 | Value: 10.00 | | | | |

**2 MARK** **KM# 183** **Composition:** Copper-Nickel Clad Nickel **Reverse:** Head of Willy Brandt facing forward

| Date | Mintage | F | VF | XF | Unc | BU |
|---|---|---|---|---|---|---|
| 1994A | 5,000,000 | — | — | — | 2.00 | — |
| 1994A Proof | 45,000 | Value: 2.50 | | | | |
| 1994D | 5,250,000 | — | — | — | 2.00 | — |
| 1994D Proof | 45,000 | Value: 2.50 | | | | |
| 1994F | 6,000,000 | — | — | — | 2.00 | — |
| 1994F Proof | 45,000 | Value: 2.50 | | | | |
| 1994G | 3,600,000 | — | — | — | 2.00 | — |
| 1994G Proof | 45,000 | Value: 2.50 | | | | |
| 1994J | 5,250,000 | — | — | — | 2.00 | — |
| 1994J Proof | 45,000 | Value: 2.50 | | | | |
| 1995A | 1,595,000 | — | — | — | 3.50 | — |
| 1995A Proof | 45,000 | Value: 17.50 | | | | |
| 1995D In sets only | 20,000 | — | — | — | 65.00 | — |
| 1995D Proof | 45,000 | Value: 17.50 | | | | |
| 1995F In sets only | 20,000 | — | — | — | 65.00 | — |
| 1995F Proof | 45,000 | Value: 17.50 | | | | |
| 1995G | 1,220,000 | — | — | — | 4.50 | — |
| 1995G Proof | 45,000 | Value: 17.50 | | | | |
| 1995J | 75,000 | — | — | — | 30.00 | — |
| 1995J Proof | 45,000 | Value: 17.50 | | | | |
| 1996A | — | — | — | — | 5.50 | — |
| 1996A Proof | 45,000 | Value: 6.50 | | | | |
| 1996D | — | — | — | — | 5.50 | — |
| 1996D Proof | 45,000 | Value: 6.50 | | | | |
| 1996F | — | — | — | — | 5.50 | — |
| 1996F Proof | 45,000 | Value: 6.50 | | | | |
| 1996G | — | — | — | — | 5.50 | — |
| 1996G Proof | 45,000 | Value: 6.50 | | | | |
| 1996J | — | — | — | — | 5.50 | — |
| 1996J Proof | 45,000 | Value: 6.50 | | | | |
| 1997A In sets only | 70,000 | — | — | — | 4.25 | — |
| 1997A Proof | 45,000 | Value: 5.00 | | | | |
| 1997D In sets only | 70,000 | — | — | — | 4.25 | — |
| 1997D Proof | 45,000 | Value: 5.00 | | | | |
| 1997F In sets only | 70,000 | — | — | — | 4.25 | — |
| 1997F Proof | 45,000 | Value: 5.00 | | | | |
| 1997G In sets only | 70,000 | — | — | — | 4.25 | — |
| 1997G Proof | 45,000 | Value: 5.00 | | | | |
| 1997J In sets only | 70,000 | — | — | — | 4.25 | — |
| 1997J Proof | 45,000 | Value: 5.00 | | | | |
| 1998A In sets only | 70,000 | — | — | — | 4.25 | — |
| 1998A Proof | 45,000 | Value: 5.00 | | | | |
| 1998D In sets only | 70,000 | — | — | — | 4.25 | — |
| 1998D Proof | 45,000 | Value: 5.00 | | | | |
| 1998F In sets only | 70,000 | — | — | — | 4.25 | — |
| 1998F Proof | 45,000 | Value: 5.00 | | | | |
| 1998G In sets only | 70,000 | — | — | — | 4.25 | — |
| 1998G Proof | 45,000 | Value: 5.00 | | | | |
| 1998J In sets only | 70,000 | — | — | — | 4.25 | — |
| 1998J Proof | 45,000 | Value: 5.00 | | | | |
| 1999A In sets only | 70,000 | — | — | — | 4.25 | — |
| 1999A Proof | 45,000 | Value: 5.00 | | | | |
| 1999D In sets only | 70,000 | — | — | — | 4.25 | — |
| 1999D Proof | 45,000 | Value: 5.00 | | | | |
| 1999F In sets only | 70,000 | — | — | — | 4.25 | — |
| 1999F Proof | 45,000 | Value: 5.00 | | | | |
| 1999G In sets only | 70,000 | — | — | — | 4.25 | — |
| 1999G Proof | 45,000 | Value: 5.00 | | | | |
| 1999J In sets only | 70,000 | — | — | — | 4.25 | — |
| 1999J Proof | 45,000 | Value: 5.00 | | | | |
| 2000A In sets only | 70,000 | — | — | — | 5.00 | — |
| 2000A Proof | 45,000 | Value: 5.00 | | | | |
| 2000D In sets only | 70,000 | — | — | — | 5.00 | — |
| 2000D Proof | 45,000 | Value: 5.00 | | | | |
| 2000F In sets only | 70,000 | — | — | — | 5.00 | — |
| 2000F Proof | 45,000 | Value: 5.00 | | | | |
| 2000G In sets only | 70,000 | — | — | — | 5.00 | — |
| 2000G Proof | 45,000 | Value: 5.00 | | | | |
| 2000J In sets only | 70,000 | — | — | — | 5.00 | — |
| 2000J Proof | 45,000 | Value: 5.00 | | | | |
| 2001A In sets only | 130,000 | — | — | — | 10.00 | — |
| 2001A Proof | 78,000 | Value: 10.00 | | | | |
| 2001D In sets only | 130,000 | — | — | — | 10.00 | — |
| 2001D Proof | 78,000 | Value: 10.00 | | | | |
| 2001F In sets only | 130,000 | — | — | — | 10.00 | — |
| 2001F Proof | 78,000 | Value: 10.00 | | | | |
| 2001G In sets only | 130,000 | — | — | — | 10.00 | — |
| 2001G Proof | 78,000 | Value: 10.00 | | | | |
| 2001J In sets only | 130,000 | — | — | — | 10.00 | — |
| 2001J Proof | 78,000 | Value: 10.00 | | | | |

**5 MARK** **KM# 112.1** **Weight:** 11.2000 g. **Composition:** 0.6250 Silver .2250 oz. ASW **Note:** Federal Republic.

| Date | Mintage | F | VF | XF | Unc | BU |
|---|---|---|---|---|---|---|
| 1951D | 20,600,000 | — | 4.00 | 15.00 | 65.00 | — |
| 1951D Proof | — | Value: 250 | | | | |
| 1951F | 24,000,000 | — | 4.00 | 15.00 | 75.00 | — |
| 1951F Proof | 280 | Value: 250 | | | | |
| 1951G | 13,840,000 | — | 4.00 | 15.00 | 75.00 | — |
| 1951G Proof | — | Value: 450 | | | | |
| 1951J | 21,360,000 | — | 4.00 | 15.00 | 60.00 | — |
| 1951J Proof | — | Value: 225 | | | | |
| 1956D | 1,092,000 | — | 15.00 | 60.00 | 225 | — |
| 1956D Proof | — | Value: 450 | | | | |
| 1956F | 1,200,000 | — | 10.00 | 75.00 | 375 | — |
| 1956F Proof | 23 | Value: 1,000 | | | | |
| 1956J | 1,068,000 | — | 10.00 | 60.00 | 225 | — |
| 1956J Proof | — | Value: 450 | | | | |
| 1957D | 566,000 | — | 10.00 | 85.00 | 400 | — |
| 1957D Proof | — | Value: 475 | | | | |
| 1957F | 2,100,000 | — | 7.50 | 50.00 | 300 | — |
| 1957F Proof | — | Value: 500 | | | | |
| 1957G | 692,000 | — | 10.00 | 65.00 | 350 | — |
| 1957G Proof | — | Value: 400 | | | | |
| 1957J | 1,630,000 | — | 7.50 | 30.00 | 150 | — |
| 1957J Proof | — | Value: 250 | | | | |
| 1958D | 1,226,000 | — | 7.50 | 30.00 | 150 | — |
| 1958D Proof | — | Value: 300 | | | | |
| 1958F | 600,000 | — | 20.00 | 125 | 600 | — |
| 1958F Proof | 100 | Value: 800 | | | | |
| 1958G | 1,557,000 | — | 7.50 | 28.00 | 130 | — |
| 1958G Proof | — | Value: 400 | | | | |
| 1958J | 60,000 | — | 1,100 | 2,500 | 3,750 | — |
| 1958J Proof | — | Value: 4,000 | | | | |
| 1959D | 496,000 | — | 10.00 | 45.00 | 245 | — |
| 1959D Proof | — | Value: 400 | | | | |
| 1959G | 692,000 | — | 15.00 | 55.00 | 235 | — |
| 1959G Proof | — | Value: 500 | | | | |
| 1959J | 713,000 | — | 8.00 | 40.00 | 225 | — |
| 1959J Proof | — | Value: 375 | | | | |
| 1960D | 1,040,000 | — | 7.00 | 20.00 | 110 | — |
| 1960D Proof | — | Value: 300 | | | | |
| 1960F | 1,576,000 | — | 7.00 | 20.00 | 110 | — |
| 1960F Proof | 50 | Value: 700 | | | | |
| 1960G | 692,000 | — | 7.00 | 22.00 | 125 | — |
| 1960G Proof | — | Value: 250 | | | | |
| 1960J | 1,618,000 | — | 7.00 | 18.00 | 90.00 | — |
| 1960J Proof | — | Value: 400 | | | | |
| 1961D | 1,040,000 | — | 4.50 | 15.00 | 80.00 | — |
| 1961D Proof | — | Value: 225 | | | | |
| 1961F | 824,000 | — | 4.50 | 22.00 | 125 | — |
| 1961F Proof | — | Value: 450 | | | | |
| 1961J | 518,000 | — | 6.00 | 28.00 | 135 | — |
| 1961J Proof | — | Value: 550 | | | | |
| 1963D | 2,080,000 | — | 4.50 | 15.00 | 60.00 | — |
| 1963D Proof | — | Value: 350 | | | | |
| 1963F | 1,254,000 | — | 4.50 | 18.00 | 70.00 | — |
| 1963F Proof | — | Value: 350 | | | | |
| 1963G | 600,000 | — | 7.50 | 20.00 | 100 | — |
| 1963G Proof | Est. 100 | Value: 400 | | | | |
| 1963J | 2,136,000 | — | 4.50 | 15.00 | 60.00 | — |
| 1963J Proof | — | Value: 350 | | | | |
| 1964D | 456,000 | — | 15.00 | 50.00 | 175 | — |
| 1964D Proof | — | Value: 375 | | | | |
| 1964F | 2,646,000 | — | 4.50 | 15.00 | 60.00 | — |
| 1964F Proof | — | Value: 350 | | | | |
| 1964G | 1,649,000 | — | 4.50 | 15.00 | 45.00 | — |
| 1964G Proof | Est. 600 | Value: 80.00 | | | | |
| 1964J | 1,335,000 | — | 4.00 | 15.00 | 45.00 | — |
| 1964J Proof | — | Value: 200 | | | | |
| 1965D | 4,354,000 | — | 4.00 | 12.50 | 30.00 | — |
| 1965D Proof | — | Value: 175 | | | | |
| 1965F | 4,050,000 | — | 4.00 | 8.00 | 30.00 | — |
| 1965F Proof | Est. 80 | Value: 385 | | | | |
| 1965G | 2,335,000 | — | 4.00 | 7.00 | 25.00 | — |
| 1965G Proof | 8,233 | Value: 42.00 | | | | |
| 1965J | 3,605,000 | — | 4.00 | 7.00 | 25.00 | — |
| 1965J Proof | — | Value: 250 | | | | |
| 1966D | 5,200,000 | — | 4.00 | 7.00 | 22.50 | — |
| 1966D Proof | — | Value: 250 | | | | |
| 1966F | 6,000,000 | — | 4.00 | 7.00 | 22.50 | — |
| 1966F Proof | 100 | Value: 385 | | | | |
| 1966G | 3,460,000 | — | 4.00 | 7.00 | 22.50 | — |
| 1966G Proof | 3,070 | Value: 45.00 | | | | |
| 1966J | 5,340,000 | — | 4.00 | 7.00 | 22.50 | — |
| 1966J Proof | 1,000 | Value: 110 | | | | |
| 1967D | 3,120,000 | — | 4.00 | 7.00 | 22.50 | — |
| 1967D Proof | — | Value: 200 | | | | |
| 1967F | 3,598,000 | — | 4.00 | 7.00 | 22.50 | — |
| 1967F Proof | 1,500 | Value: 75.00 | | | | |
| 1967G | 1,406,000 | — | 4.00 | 7.00 | 25.00 | — |
| 1967G Proof | 4,500 | Value: 35.00 | | | | |
| 1967J | 3,204,000 | — | 4.00 | 7.00 | 22.50 | — |
| 1967J Proof | 1,500 | Value: 90.00 | | | | |
| 1968D | 1,300,000 | — | 4.00 | 10.00 | 35.00 | — |
| 1968D Proof | — | Value: 60.00 | | | | |
| 1968F | 1,497,000 | — | 4.00 | 10.00 | 35.00 | — |
| 1968F Proof | 3,000 | Value: 75.00 | | | | |
| 1968G | 1,535,000 | — | 4.00 | 10.00 | 35.00 | — |
| 1968G Proof | 6,023 | Value: 35.00 | | | | |
| 1968J | 1,335,000 | — | 4.00 | 10.00 | 35.00 | — |
| 1968J Proof | 2,000 | Value: 65.00 | | | | |
| 1969D | 2,080,000 | — | 4.00 | 7.00 | 20.00 | — |
| 1969D Proof | — | Value: 25.00 | | | | |
| 1969F | 2,395,000 | — | 4.00 | 7.00 | 20.00 | — |
| 1969F Proof | 5,000 | Value: 25.00 | | | | |
| 1969G | 3,484,000 | — | 4.00 | 7.00 | 20.00 | — |
| 1969G Proof | 8,700 | Value: 20.00 | | | | |
| 1969J | 2,136,000 | — | 4.00 | 7.00 | 20.00 | — |
| 1969J Proof | 5,000 | Value: 25.00 | | | | |
| 1970D | 2,000,000 | — | 4.00 | 7.00 | 20.00 | — |
| 1970D Proof | — | Value: 20.00 | | | | |
| 1970F | 1,995,000 | — | 4.00 | 7.00 | 20.00 | — |
| 1970F Proof | 5,140 | Value: 25.00 | | | | |
| 1970G | 6,000,000 | — | 3.50 | 4.50 | 8.50 | — |
| 1970G Proof | 10,200 | Value: 18.00 | | | | |
| 1970J | 4,000,000 | — | 3.50 | 4.50 | 8.50 | — |
| 1970J Proof | 5,000 | Value: 25.00 | | | | |
| 1971D | 4,000,000 | — | 3.50 | 4.50 | 8.50 | — |
| 1971D Proof | 8,000 | Value: 20.00 | | | | |
| 1971F | 3,993,000 | — | 3.50 | 4.50 | 8.50 | — |
| 1971F Proof | 8,000 | Value: 20.00 | | | | |
| 1971G | 6,010,000 | — | 3.50 | 4.50 | 8.50 | — |
| 1971G Proof | 10,000 | Value: 18.00 | | | | |
| 1971J | 6,000,000 | — | 3.50 | 4.50 | 8.50 | — |
| 1971J Proof | 8,000 | Value: 20.00 | | | | |
| 1972D | 3,000,000 | — | 3.50 | 4.50 | 8.50 | — |
| 1972D Proof | 8,000 | Value: 20.00 | | | | |
| 1972F | 8,992,000 | — | 3.50 | 4.50 | 8.50 | — |
| 1972F Proof | 8,100 | Value: 20.00 | | | | |
| 1972G | 4,999,000 | — | 3.50 | 4.50 | 8.50 | — |
| 1972G Proof | 10,000 | Value: 18.00 | | | | |
| 1972J | 6,000,000 | — | 3.50 | 4.50 | 7.50 | — |
| 1972J Proof | 8,000 | Value: 20.00 | | | | |
| 1973D | 3,380,000 | — | 3.50 | 4.50 | 7.50 | — |
| 1973D Proof | 9,000 | Value: 18.00 | | | | |
| 1973F | 3,891,000 | — | 3.50 | 4.50 | 7.50 | — |
| 1973F Proof | 9,100 | Value: 18.00 | | | | |
| 1973G | 2,240,000 | — | 3.50 | 4.50 | 7.50 | — |
| 1973G Proof | 9,000 | Value: 18.00 | | | | |
| 1973J | 5,571,000 | — | 3.50 | 4.50 | 7.50 | — |
| 1973J Proof | 9,000 | Value: 18.00 | | | | |
| 1974D | 4,594,000 | — | 3.50 | 4.50 | 7.50 | — |
| 1974D Proof | 35,000 | Value: 15.00 | | | | |
| 1974F | 6,514,000 | — | 3.50 | 4.50 | 7.50 | — |
| 1974F Proof | 35,000 | Value: 15.00 | | | | |
| 1974G | 3,708,000 | — | 3.50 | 4.50 | 7.50 | — |
| 1974G Proof | 35,000 | Value: 15.00 | | | | |
| 1974J | 2,968,000 | — | 3.50 | 4.50 | 7.50 | — |
| 1974J Proof | 35,000 | Value: 15.00 | | | | |

**5 MARK** **KM# 112.3** **Weight:** 11.2000 g. **Composition:** 0.6250 Silver .2250 oz. ASW **Note:** Error. With edge lettering. GRUSS DICH DEUTSCHLAND AUS HERZENSGRUND.

| Date | Mintage | F | VF | XF | Unc | BU |
|---|---|---|---|---|---|---|
| 1957J | Inc. above | — | 1,250 | 1,650 | 2,400 | — |

**5 MARK** **KM# 112.2** **Weight:** 11.2000 g. **Composition:** 0.6250 Silver .2250 oz. ASW **Note:** Uninscribed plain edge errors.

| Date | Mintage | F | VF | XF | Unc | BU |
|---|---|---|---|---|---|---|
| 1959D | Inc. above | — | 60.00 | 120 | 175 | — |
| 1959J | Inc. above | — | 60.00 | 120 | 175 | — |
| 1963J | Inc. above | — | 60.00 | 120 | 175 | — |
| 1964F | Inc. above | — | 60.00 | 120 | 175 | — |
| 1965F | Inc. above | — | 60.00 | 120 | 175 | — |
| 1965G | Inc. above | — | 60.00 | 120 | 175 | — |
| 1966F | Inc. above | — | 125 | 250 | 345 | — |
| 1966G | Inc. above | — | 60.00 | 120 | 175 | — |
| 1967D | Inc. above | — | 125 | 250 | 345 | — |
| 1967G | Inc. above | — | 60.00 | 120 | 175 | — |

**5 MARK** **KM# 112.4** **Weight:** 11.2000 g. **Composition:** 0.6250 Silver .2250 oz. ASW **Note:** Error. With edge lettering. ALLE MENSCHEN WERDEN BRUDER.

| Date | Mintage | F | VF | XF | Unc | BU |
|---|---|---|---|---|---|---|
| 1970F | — | — | 1,250 | 1,650 | 2,400 | — |

**5 MARK** KM# 140.1 **Weight:** 10.0000 g. **Composition:** Copper-Nickel Clad Nickel

| Date | Mintage | F | VF | XF | Unc | BU |
|---|---|---|---|---|---|---|
| 1975D | 65,663,000 | — | — | 3.50 | 4.50 | — |
| 1975D Proof | 43,000 | Value: 7.00 | | | | |
| 1975F | 75,002,000 | — | — | 3.50 | 4.50 | — |
| 1975F Proof | 43,000 | Value: 7.00 | | | | |
| 1975G | 43,297,000 | — | — | 3.50 | 4.50 | — |
| 1975G Proof | 43,000 | Value: 7.00 | | | | |
| 1975J | 67,372,000 | — | — | 3.50 | 4.50 | — |
| 1975J Proof | 43,000 | Value: 7.00 | | | | |
| 1976D | 7,821,000 | — | — | 3.50 | 5.00 | — |
| 1976D Proof | 43,000 | Value: 7.00 | | | | |
| 1976F | 9,072,000 | — | — | 3.50 | 5.00 | — |
| 1976F Proof | 43,000 | Value: 7.00 | | | | |
| 1976G | 5,784,000 | — | — | 3.50 | 5.00 | — |
| 1976G Proof | 43,000 | Value: 7.00 | | | | |
| 1976J | 8,068,000 | — | — | 3.50 | 5.00 | — |
| 1976J Proof | 43,000 | Value: 7.00 | | | | |
| 1977D | 8,321,000 | — | — | 3.50 | 5.00 | — |
| 1977D Proof | 51,000 | Value: 6.00 | | | | |
| 1977F | 9,612,000 | — | — | 3.50 | 5.00 | — |
| 1977F Proof | 51,000 | Value: 6.00 | | | | |
| 1977G | 5,746,000 | — | — | 3.50 | 5.00 | — |
| 1977G Proof | 51,000 | Value: 6.00 | | | | |
| 1977J | 8,577,000 | — | — | 3.50 | 5.00 | — |
| 1977J Proof | 51,000 | Value: 6.00 | | | | |
| 1978D | 7,854,000 | — | — | 3.50 | 5.00 | — |
| 1978D Proof | 54,000 | Value: 6.00 | | | | |
| 1978F | 9,054,000 | — | — | 3.50 | 5.00 | — |
| 1978F Proof | 54,000 | Value: 6.00 | | | | |
| 1978G | 5,244,000 | — | — | 3.50 | 5.00 | — |
| 1978G Proof | 54,000 | Value: 6.00 | | | | |
| 1978J | 8,064,000 | — | — | 3.50 | 5.00 | — |
| 1978J Proof | 54,000 | Value: 6.00 | | | | |
| 1979D | 7,889,000 | — | — | 3.50 | 5.00 | — |
| 1979D Proof | 89,000 | Value: 6.00 | | | | |
| 1979F | 9,089,000 | — | — | 3.50 | 5.00 | — |
| 1979F Proof | 89,000 | Value: 6.00 | | | | |
| 1979G | 5,279,000 | — | — | 3.50 | 5.00 | — |
| 1979G Proof | 89,000 | Value: 6.00 | | | | |
| 1979J | 8,099,000 | — | — | 3.50 | 5.00 | — |
| 1979J Proof | 89,000 | Value: 6.00 | | | | |
| 1980D | 8,300,000 | — | — | 3.50 | 5.00 | — |
| 1980D Proof | 110,000 | Value: 6.00 | | | | |
| 1980F | 9,640,000 | — | — | 3.50 | 5.00 | — |
| 1980F Proof | 110,000 | Value: 6.00 | | | | |
| 1980G | 5,500,000 | — | — | 3.50 | 5.00 | — |
| 1980G Proof | 110,000 | Value: 6.00 | | | | |
| 1980J | 8,500,000 | — | — | 3.50 | 5.00 | — |
| 1980J Proof | 110,000 | Value: 6.00 | | | | |
| 1981D | 8,300,000 | — | — | 3.50 | 5.00 | — |
| 1981D Proof | 91,000 | Value: 6.00 | | | | |
| 1981F | 9,600,000 | — | — | 3.50 | 5.00 | — |
| 1981F Proof | 91,000 | Value: 6.00 | | | | |
| 1981G | 5,500,000 | — | — | 3.50 | 5.00 | — |
| 1981G Proof | 91,000 | Value: 6.00 | | | | |
| 1981J | 8,500,000 | — | — | 3.50 | 5.00 | — |
| 1981J Proof | 91,000 | Value: 6.00 | | | | |
| 1982D | 8,900,000 | — | — | 3.50 | 5.00 | — |
| 1982D Proof | 78,000 | Value: 6.00 | | | | |
| 1982F | 10,300,000 | — | — | 3.50 | 5.00 | — |
| 1982F Proof | 78,000 | Value: 6.00 | | | | |
| 1982G | 5,990,000 | — | — | 3.50 | 5.00 | — |
| 1982G Proof | 78,000 | Value: 6.00 | | | | |
| 1982J | 9,100,000 | — | — | 3.50 | 5.00 | — |
| 1982J Proof | 78,000 | Value: 6.00 | | | | |
| 1983D | 6,240,000 | — | — | 3.50 | 5.00 | — |
| 1983D Proof | 75,000 | Value: 6.00 | | | | |
| 1983F | 7,200,000 | — | — | 3.50 | 5.00 | — |
| 1983F Proof | 75,000 | Value: 6.00 | | | | |
| 1983G | 4,152,000 | — | — | 3.50 | 5.00 | — |
| 1983G Proof | 75,000 | Value: 6.00 | | | | |
| 1983J | 6,408,000 | — | — | 3.50 | 5.00 | — |
| 1983J Proof | 75,000 | Value: 6.00 | | | | |
| 1984D | 6,000,000 | — | — | 3.50 | 5.00 | — |
| 1984D Proof | 64,000 | Value: 6.00 | | | | |
| 1984F | 6,900,000 | — | — | 3.50 | 5.00 | — |
| 1984F Proof | 64,000 | Value: 6.00 | | | | |
| 1984G | 4,000,000 | — | — | 3.50 | 5.00 | — |
| 1984G Proof | 64,000 | Value: 6.00 | | | | |
| 1984J | 6,100,000 | — | — | 3.50 | 5.00 | — |
| 1984J Proof | 64,000 | Value: 6.00 | | | | |
| 1985D | 4,900,000 | — | — | 3.50 | 5.00 | — |
| 1985D Proof | 56,000 | Value: 6.00 | | | | |
| 1985F | 5,700,000 | — | — | 3.50 | 5.00 | — |
| 1985F Proof | 54,000 | Value: 6.00 | | | | |
| 1985G | 3,300,000 | — | — | 3.50 | 5.00 | — |
| 1985G Proof | 55,000 | Value: 6.00 | | | | |
| 1985J | 5,100,000 | — | — | 3.50 | 5.00 | — |
| 1985J Proof | 54,000 | Value: 6.00 | | | | |
| 1986D | 4,900,000 | — | — | 3.50 | 5.00 | — |
| 1986D Proof | 44,000 | Value: 6.00 | | | | |
| 1986F | 5,700,000 | — | — | 3.50 | 5.00 | — |
| 1986F Proof | 44,000 | Value: 6.00 | | | | |
| 1986G | 3,300,000 | — | — | 3.50 | 5.00 | — |
| 1986G Proof | 44,000 | Value: 6.00 | | | | |
| 1986J | 5,100,000 | — | — | 3.50 | 5.00 | — |
| 1986J Proof | 44,000 | Value: 6.00 | | | | |
| 1987D | 6,760,000 | — | — | 3.50 | 5.00 | — |
| 1987D Proof | 45,000 | Value: 6.00 | | | | |
| 1987F | 7,800,000 | — | — | 3.50 | 5.00 | — |
| 1987F Proof | 45,000 | Value: 6.00 | | | | |
| 1987G | 4,500,000 | — | — | 3.50 | 5.00 | — |
| 1987G Proof | 45,000 | Value: 6.00 | | | | |
| 1987J | 6,940,000 | — | — | 3.50 | 5.00 | — |
| 1987J Proof | 45,000 | Value: 6.00 | | | | |
| 1988D | 11,960,000 | — | — | — | 4.00 | — |
| 1988D Proof | 45,000 | Value: 5.00 | | | | |
| 1988F | 13,800,000 | — | — | — | 4.00 | — |
| 1988F Proof | 45,000 | Value: 5.00 | | | | |
| 1988G | 7,960,000 | — | — | — | 4.00 | — |
| 1988G Proof | 45,000 | Value: 5.00 | | | | |
| 1988J | 12,280,000 | — | — | — | 4.00 | — |
| 1988J Proof | 45,000 | Value: 5.00 | | | | |
| 1989D | 17,160,000 | — | — | — | 4.00 | — |
| 1989D Proof | 45,000 | Value: 5.00 | | | | |
| 1989F | 19,800,000 | — | — | — | 4.00 | — |
| 1989F Proof | 45,000 | Value: 5.00 | | | | |
| 1989G | 11,420,000 | — | — | — | 4.00 | — |
| 1989G Proof | 45,000 | Value: 5.00 | | | | |
| 1989J | 17,620,000 | — | — | — | 4.00 | — |
| 1989J Proof | 45,000 | Value: 5.00 | | | | |
| 1990D | 20,900,000 | — | — | — | 4.00 | — |
| 1990D Proof | 45,000 | Value: 5.00 | | | | |
| 1990F | 24,120,000 | — | — | — | 4.00 | — |
| 1990F Proof | 45,000 | Value: 5.00 | | | | |
| 1990G | 13,910,000 | — | — | — | 4.00 | — |
| 1990G Proof | 45,000 | Value: 5.00 | | | | |
| 1990J | 21,470,000 | — | — | — | 4.00 | — |
| 1990J Proof | 45,000 | Value: 5.00 | | | | |
| 1991A | 18,000,000 | — | — | — | 4.00 | — |
| 1991A Proof | 45,000 | Value: 5.00 | | | | |
| 1991D | 18,900,000 | — | — | — | 4.00 | — |
| 1991D Proof | 45,000 | Value: 5.00 | | | | |
| 1991F | 21,600,000 | — | — | — | 4.00 | — |
| 1991F Proof | 45,000 | Value: 5.00 | | | | |
| 1991G | 12,600,000 | — | — | — | 4.00 | — |
| 1991G Proof | 45,000 | Value: 5.00 | | | | |
| 1991J | 18,900,000 | — | — | — | 4.00 | — |
| 1991J Proof | 45,000 | Value: 5.00 | | | | |
| 1992A | 16,000,000 | — | — | — | 4.00 | — |
| 1992A Proof | 45,000 | Value: 5.00 | | | | |
| 1992D | 16,800,000 | — | — | — | 4.00 | — |
| 1992D Proof | 45,000 | Value: 5.00 | | | | |
| 1992F | 19,200,000 | — | — | — | 4.00 | — |
| 1992F Proof | 45,000 | Value: 5.00 | | | | |
| 1992G | 11,200,000 | — | — | — | 4.00 | — |
| 1992G Proof | 45,000 | Value: 5.00 | | | | |
| 1992J | 16,800,000 | — | — | — | 4.00 | — |
| 1992J Proof | 45,000 | Value: 5.00 | | | | |
| 1993A | 3,200,000 | — | — | — | 4.00 | — |
| 1993A Proof | 45,000 | Value: 5.00 | | | | |
| 1993D | 3,380,000 | — | — | — | 4.00 | — |
| 1993D Proof | 45,000 | Value: 5.00 | | | | |
| 1993F | 3,840,000 | — | — | — | 4.00 | — |
| 1993F Proof | 45,000 | Value: 5.00 | | | | |
| 1993G | 2,240,000 | — | — | — | 4.00 | — |
| 1993G Proof | 45,000 | Value: 5.00 | | | | |
| 1993J | 3,360,000 | — | — | — | 4.00 | — |
| 1993J Proof | 45,000 | Value: 5.00 | | | | |
| 1994A | 4,000,000 | — | — | — | 4.00 | — |
| 1994A Proof | 45,000 | Value: 5.00 | | | | |
| 1994D | 4,200,000 | — | — | — | 4.00 | — |
| 1994D Proof | 45,000 | Value: 5.00 | | | | |
| 1994F | 4,800,000 | — | — | — | 4.00 | — |
| 1994F Proof | 45,000 | Value: 5.00 | | | | |
| 1994G | 2,800,000 | — | — | — | 4.00 | — |
| 1994G Proof | 45,000 | Value: 5.00 | | | | |
| 1994J | 4,200,000 | — | — | — | 4.00 | — |
| 1994J Proof | 45,000 | Value: 5.00 | | | | |
| 1995A In sets only | 20,000 | — | — | — | 80.00 | — |
| 1995A Proof | 45,000 | Value: 30.00 | | | | |
| 1995D In sets only | 20,000 | — | — | — | 80.00 | — |
| 1995D Proof | 45,000 | Value: 30.00 | | | | |
| 1995F In sets only | 20,000 | — | — | — | 80.00 | — |
| 1995F Proof | 45,000 | Value: 30.00 | | | | |
| 1995G In sets only | 20,000 | — | — | — | 80.00 | — |
| 1995G Proof | 45,000 | Value: 30.00 | | | | |
| 1995J In sets only | 20,000 | — | — | — | 80.00 | — |
| 1995J Proof | 45,000 | Value: 30.00 | | | | |
| 1996A In sets only | 50,000 | — | — | — | 15.00 | — |
| 1996A Proof | 45,000 | Value: 17.50 | | | | |
| 1996D In sets only | 50,000 | — | — | — | 15.00 | — |
| 1996D Proof | 45,000 | Value: 17.50 | | | | |
| 1996F In sets only | 50,000 | — | — | — | 15.00 | — |
| 1996F Proof | 45,000 | Value: 17.50 | | | | |
| 1996G In sets only | 50,000 | — | — | — | 15.00 | — |
| 1996G Proof | 45,000 | Value: 17.50 | | | | |
| 1996J In sets only | 50,000 | — | — | — | 15.00 | — |
| 1996J Proof | 45,000 | Value: 17.50 | | | | |
| 1997A In sets only | 70,000 | — | — | — | 6.00 | — |
| 1997A Proof | 45,000 | Value: 7.00 | | | | |
| 1997D In sets only | 70,000 | — | — | — | 6.00 | — |
| 1997D Proof | 45,000 | Value: 7.00 | | | | |
| 1997F In sets only | 70,000 | — | — | — | 6.00 | — |
| 1997F Proof | 45,000 | Value: 7.00 | | | | |
| 1997G In sets only | 70,000 | — | — | — | 6.00 | — |
| 1997G Proof | 45,000 | Value: 7.00 | | | | |
| 1997J In sets only | 70,000 | — | — | — | 6.00 | — |
| 1997J Proof | 45,000 | Value: 7.00 | | | | |
| 1998A In sets only | 70,000 | — | — | — | 6.00 | — |
| 1998A Proof | 45,000 | Value: 7.00 | | | | |
| 1998D In sets only | 70,000 | — | — | — | 6.00 | — |
| 1998D Proof | 45,000 | Value: 7.00 | | | | |
| 1998F In sets only | 70,000 | — | — | — | 6.00 | — |
| 1998F Proof | 45,000 | Value: 7.00 | | | | |
| 1998G In sets only | 70,000 | — | — | — | 6.00 | — |
| 1998G Proof | 45,000 | Value: 7.00 | | | | |
| 1998J In sets only | 70,000 | — | — | — | 6.00 | — |
| 1998J Proof | 45,000 | Value: 7.00 | | | | |
| 1999A In sets only | 70,000 | — | — | — | 6.00 | — |
| 1999A Proof | 45,000 | Value: 7.00 | | | | |
| 1999D In sets only | 70,000 | — | — | — | 6.00 | — |
| 1999D Proof | 45,000 | Value: 7.00 | | | | |
| 1999F In sets only | 70,000 | — | — | — | 6.00 | — |
| 1999F Proof | 45,000 | Value: 7.00 | | | | |
| 1999G In sets only | 70,000 | — | — | — | 6.00 | — |
| 1999G Proof | 45,000 | Value: 7.00 | | | | |
| 1999J In sets only | 70,000 | — | — | — | 6.00 | — |
| 1999J Proof | 45,000 | Value: 7.00 | | | | |
| 2000A In sets only | 70,000 | — | — | — | 15.00 | — |
| 2000A Proof | 45,000 | Value: 15.00 | | | | |
| 2000D In sets only | 70,000 | — | — | — | 15.00 | — |
| 2000D Proof | 45,000 | Value: 15.00 | | | | |
| 2000F In sets only | 70,000 | — | — | — | 15.00 | — |
| 2000F Proof | 45,000 | Value: 15.00 | | | | |
| 2000G In sets only | 70,000 | — | — | — | 15.00 | — |
| 2000G Proof | 45,000 | Value: 15.00 | | | | |
| 2000J In sets only | 70,000 | — | — | — | 15.00 | — |
| 2000J Proof | 45,000 | Value: 15.00 | | | | |
| 2001A In sets only | 130,000 | — | — | — | 30.00 | — |
| 2001A Proof | 78,000 | Value: 30.00 | | | | |
| 2001D In sets only | 130,000 | — | — | — | 30.00 | — |
| 2001D Proof | 78,000 | Value: 30.00 | | | | |
| 2001F In sets only | 130,000 | — | — | — | 30.00 | — |
| 2001F Proof | 78,000 | Value: 30.00 | | | | |
| 2001G In sets only | 130,000 | — | — | — | 30.00 | — |
| 2001G Proof | 78,000 | Value: 30.00 | | | | |
| 2001J In sets only | 130,000 | — | — | — | 30.00 | — |
| 2001J Proof | 78,000 | Value: 30.00 | | | | |

**5 MARK** KM# 140.2 **Weight:** 5.4400 g. **Composition:** Copper-Nickel Clad Nickel **Note:** Thin variety.

| Date | Mintage | F | VF | XF | Unc | BU |
|---|---|---|---|---|---|---|
| 1975 | — | — | — | 90.00 | 150 | — |

**Note:** Illegally produced by a German Mint official

**10 MARK** KM# 201 **Weight:** 15.5000 g. **Composition:** 0.9250 Silver .4610 oz. ASW **Subject:** 10th Anniversary of Reunification **Obverse:** Eagle and denomination **Reverse:** Parliament building **Edge Lettering:** "WIR SIND DAS VOLK WIR SIND EIN VOLK" **Size:** 32.5 mm.

| Date | Mintage | F | VF | XF | Unc | BU |
|---|---|---|---|---|---|---|
| 2000A Proof | — | Value: 22.50 | | | | |
| 2000J Proof | — | Value: 22.50 | | | | |
| 2000D | — | — | — | — | 10.00 | — |
| 2000D Proof | — | Value: 22.50 | | | | |
| 2000F Proof | — | Value: 22.50 | | | | |
| 2000G Proof | — | Value: 22.50 | | | | |

**10 MARK** KM# 202 **Weight:** 15.5000 g. **Composition:** 0.9250 Silver .4610 oz. ASW **Obverse:** Eagle and denomination **Reverse:** Portrait **Edge Lettering:** "JOHANN SEBASTIAN BACH 250 TODESTAG" **Size:** 32.5 mm.

| Date | Mintage | F | VF | XF | Unc | BU |
|---|---|---|---|---|---|---|
| 2000A Proof | — | Value: 22.50 | | | | |
| 2000D Proof | — | Value: 22.50 | | | | |

| Date | Mintage | F | VF | XF | Unc | BU |
|---|---|---|---|---|---|---|
| 2000F Proof | — | Value: 10.00 | | | | |
| 2000F Proof | — | Value: 22.50 | | | | |
| 2000G Proof | — | Value: 22.50 | | | | |
| 2000J Proof | — | Value: 22.50 | | | | |

## COMMEMORATIVE COINAGE

**5 MARK** **KM# 113** **Weight:** 11.2000 g. **Composition:** 0.6250 Silver .2250 oz. ASW **Subject:** Centenary - Nurnberg Museum

| Date | Mintage | F | VF | XF | Unc | BU |
|---|---|---|---|---|---|---|
| 1952D | 199,000 | — | 450 | 750 | 1,150 | — |
| 1952D Proof | 1,345 | Value: 3,250 | | | | |

**5 MARK** **KM# 114** **Weight:** 11.2000 g. **Composition:** 0.6250 Silver .2250 oz. ASW **Subject:** 150th Anniversary - Death of Friedrich von Schiller

| Date | Mintage | F | VF | XF | Unc | BU |
|---|---|---|---|---|---|---|
| 1955F | 199,000 | — | 200 | 450 | 650 | — |
| 1955F Proof | 1,217 | Value: 1,650 | | | | |

**5 MARK** **KM# 115** **Weight:** 11.2000 g. **Composition:** 0.6250 Silver .2250 oz. ASW **Subject:** 300th Anniversary - Birth of Ludwig von Baden

| Date | Mintage | F | VF | XF | Unc | BU |
|---|---|---|---|---|---|---|
| 1955G | 198,000 | — | 200 | 325 | 550 | — |
| 1955G Proof | Est. 2,000 | Value: 1,550 | | | | |

**Note:** This coin was restruck without authorization by a mint official using genuine dies - quantity unknown

**5 MARK** **KM# 117** **Weight:** 11.2000 g. **Composition:** 0.6250 Silver .2250 oz. ASW **Subject:** Centenary - Death of Joseph Freiherr von Eichendorff

| Date | Mintage | F | VF | XF | Unc | BU |
|---|---|---|---|---|---|---|
| 1957J | 198,000 | — | 200 | 325 | 575 | — |
| 1957J Proof | 2,000 | Value: 1,600 | | | | |

**5 MARK** **KM# 118.1** **Weight:** 11.2000 g. **Composition:** 0.6250 Silver .2250 oz. ASW **Subject:** 150th Anniversary - Death of Johann Gottlieb Fichte

| Date | Mintage | F | VF | XF | Unc | BU |
|---|---|---|---|---|---|---|
| 1964J | 495,000 | — | 50.00 | 95.00 | 185 | — |
| 1964J Proof | 5,000 | Value: 700 | | | | |

**5 MARK** **KM# 118.2** **Weight:** 11.2000 g. **Composition:** 0.6250 Silver .2250 oz. ASW **Note:** Error. Plain edge.

| Date | Mintage | F | VF | XF | Unc | BU |
|---|---|---|---|---|---|---|
| 1964J | — | — | 250 | 500 | 900 | — |

**5 MARK** **KM# 119.2** **Weight:** 11.2000 g. **Composition:** 0.6250 Silver .2250 oz. ASW **Note:** Error. Plain edge.

| Date | Mintage | F | VF | XF | Unc | BU |
|---|---|---|---|---|---|---|
| 1966D | — | — | 225 | 425 | 700 | — |

**5 MARK** **KM# 119.1** **Weight:** 11.2000 g. **Composition:** 0.6250 Silver .2250 oz. ASW **Subject:** 250th Anniversary - Death of Gottfried Wilhelm Leibniz

| Date | Mintage | F | VF | XF | Unc | BU |
|---|---|---|---|---|---|---|
| 1966D | 1,940,000 | — | 10.00 | 20.00 | 35.00 | — |
| 1966D Proof | 60,000 | Value: 95.00 | | | | |

**5 MARK** **KM# 120.1** **Weight:** 11.2000 g. **Composition:** 0.6250 Silver .2250 oz. ASW **Subject:** Wilhelm & Alexander von Humboldt

| Date | Mintage | F | VF | XF | Unc | BU |
|---|---|---|---|---|---|---|
| 1967F | 2,000,000 | — | 12.00 | 20.00 | 40.00 | — |
| 1967F Proof | 60,000 | Value: 110 | | | | |

**5 MARK** **KM# 120.2** **Weight:** 11.2000 g. **Composition:** 0.6250 Silver .2250 oz. ASW **Note:** Error. Plain edge.

| Date | Mintage | F | VF | XF | Unc | BU |
|---|---|---|---|---|---|---|
| 1967F | — | — | 225 | 425 | 700 | — |

**5 MARK** **KM# 123.2** **Weight:** 11.2000 g. **Composition:** 0.6250 Silver .2250 oz. ASW **Note:** Polished devices.

| Date | Mintage | F | VF | XF | Unc | BU |
|---|---|---|---|---|---|---|
| 1968D Proof | — | Value: 300 | | | | |

**5 MARK** **KM# 121** **Weight:** 11.2000 g. **Composition:** 0.6250 Silver .2250 oz. ASW **Subject:** 150th Anniversary - Birth of Friedrich Raiffeisen

| Date | Mintage | F | VF | XF | Unc | BU |
|---|---|---|---|---|---|---|
| 1968J | 3,860,000 | — | 3.50 | 5.00 | 9.00 | — |
| 1968J Proof | 140,000 | Value: 32.00 | | | | |

**5 MARK** **KM# 122** **Weight:** 11.2000 g. **Composition:** 0.6250 Silver .2250 oz. ASW **Subject:** 500th Anniversary - Death of Johannes Gutenberg

| Date | Mintage | F | VF | XF | Unc | BU |
|---|---|---|---|---|---|---|
| 1968G | 2,900,000 | — | 4.00 | 9.00 | 15.00 | — |
| 1968G Proof | 100,000 | Value: 45.00 | | | | |

**5 MARK** **KM# 123.1** **Weight:** 11.2000 g. **Composition:** 0.6250 Silver .2250 oz. ASW **Subject:** 150th Anniversary - Birth of Max von Pettenkofer

| Date | Mintage | F | VF | XF | Unc | BU |
|---|---|---|---|---|---|---|
| 1968D | 2,900,000 | — | 4.00 | 8.50 | 13.50 | — |
| 1968D Proof | 100,000 | Value: 37.50 | | | | |

**5 MARK** **KM# 125.1** **Weight:** 11.2000 g. **Composition:** 0.6250 Silver .2250 oz. ASW **Subject:** 150th Anniversary - Birth of Theodor Fontane

| Date | Mintage | F | VF | XF | Unc | BU |
|---|---|---|---|---|---|---|
| 1969G | 2,830,000 | — | 4.00 | 8.50 | 14.50 | — |
| 1969G Proof | 170,000 | Value: 27.50 | | | | |

**5 MARK** **KM# 126.1** **Weight:** 11.2000 g. **Composition:** 0.6250 Silver .2250 oz. ASW **Subject:** 375th Anniversary - Death of Gerhard Mercator

| Date | Mintage | F | VF | XF | Unc | BU |
|---|---|---|---|---|---|---|
| 1969F | 5,004,000 | — | — | — | 5.50 | — |
| 1969F Proof | 200,000 | Value: 15.00 | | | | |

**5 MARK** **KM# 125.2** **Weight:** 11.2000 g. **Composition:** 0.6250 Silver .2250 oz. ASW **Note:** Error. Incomplete nose and hair.

| Date | Mintage | F | VF | XF | Unc | BU |
|---|---|---|---|---|---|---|
| 1969G Proof | — | Value: 140 | | | | |

**5 MARK** **KM# 126.2** **Weight:** 11.2000 g. **Composition:** 0.6250 Silver .2250 oz. ASW **Note:** Error. Plain edge.

| Date | Mintage | F | VF | XF | Unc | BU |
|---|---|---|---|---|---|---|
| 1969F | — | — | 250 | 450 | 750 | — |

**5 MARK** **KM# 126.3** **Weight:** 11.2000 g. **Composition:** 0.6250 Silver .2250 oz. ASW **Note:** Error. With edge lettering; Einigkeit und Recht und Freiheit.

| Date | Mintage | F | VF | XF | Unc | BU |
|---|---|---|---|---|---|---|
| 1969F | — | — | 600 | 1,000 | 1,600 | — |

**5 MARK** **KM# 126.4** **Weight:** 11.2000 g. **Composition:** 0.6250 Silver .2250 oz. ASW **Note:** Error. With long R.

| Date | Mintage | F | VF | XF | Unc | BU |
|---|---|---|---|---|---|---|
| 1969F | — | — | 25.00 | 55.00 | 100 | — |

**5 MARK** **KM# 127** **Weight:** 11.2000 g. **Composition:** 0.6250 Silver .2250 oz. ASW **Subject:** 200th Anniversary - Birth of Ludwig van Beethoven

| Date | Mintage | F | VF | XF | Unc | BU |
|---|---|---|---|---|---|---|
| 1970F | 5,000,000 | — | — | 4.00 | 7.50 | — |
| 1970F Proof | 200,000 | Value: 15.00 | | | | |

**5 MARK** **KM# 128.1** **Weight:** 11.2000 g. **Composition:** 0.6250 Silver .2250 oz. ASW **Subject:** German Unification

| Date | Mintage | F | VF | XF | Unc | BU |
|---|---|---|---|---|---|---|
| 1971G | 5,000,000 | — | 4.00 | 5.50 | 10.00 | — |
| 1971G Proof | 200,000 | Value: 20.00 | | | | |

**5 MARK** **KM# 129** **Weight:** 11.2000 g. **Composition:** 0.6250 Silver .2250 oz. ASW **Subject:** 500th Anniversary - Birth of Albrecht Durer

| Date | Mintage | F | VF | XF | Unc | BU |
|---|---|---|---|---|---|---|
| 1971D | 8,000,000 | — | — | — | 5.00 | — |
| 1971D Proof | 200,000 | Value: 20.00 | | | | |

**5 MARK** **KM# 128.2** **Weight:** 11.2000 g. **Composition:** 0.6250 Silver .2250 oz. ASW **Note:** Error. With weak window details.

| Date | Mintage | F | VF | XF | Unc |
|---|---|---|---|---|---|
| 1971F Proof | — | Value: 100 | | | |

**5 MARK** **KM# 136** **Weight:** 11.2000 g. **Composition:** 0.6250 Silver .2250 oz. ASW **Subject:** 500th Anniversary - Birth of Nicholas Copernicus

| Date | Mintage | F | VF | XF | Unc | BU |
|---|---|---|---|---|---|---|
| 1973J | 8,000,000 | — | — | — | 5.00 | — |
| 1973J Proof | 250,000 | Value: 12.00 | | | | |

**5 MARK** **KM# 137** **Weight:** 11.2000 g. **Composition:** 0.6250 Silver .2250 oz. ASW **Subject:** 125th Anniversary - Frankfurt Parliament

| Date | Mintage | F | VF | XF | Unc | BU |
|---|---|---|---|---|---|---|
| 1973G | 8,000,000 | — | — | — | 5.00 | — |
| 1973G Proof | 250,000 | Value: 12.00 | | | | |

**5 MARK** **KM# 138** **Weight:** 11.2000 g. **Composition:** 0.6250 Silver .2250 oz. ASW **Subject:** 25th Anniversary - Constitutional Law

| Date | Mintage | F | VF | XF | Unc | BU |
|---|---|---|---|---|---|---|
| 1974F | 8,000,000 | — | — | — | 5.00 | — |
| 1974F Proof | 250,000 | Value: 12.00 | | | | |

**5 MARK** **KM# 139** **Weight:** 11.2000 g. **Composition:** 0.6250 Silver .2250 oz. ASW **Subject:** 250th Anniversary - Birth of Immanuel Kant

| Date | Mintage | F | VF | XF | Unc | BU |
|---|---|---|---|---|---|---|
| 1974D | 8,000,000 | — | — | — | 5.00 | — |
| 1974D Proof | 250,000 | Value: 14.00 | | | | |

**5 MARK** **KM# 141** **Weight:** 11.2000 g. **Composition:** 0.6250 Silver .2250 oz. ASW **Subject:** 50th Anniversary - Death of Friedrich Ebert

| Date | Mintage | F | VF | XF | Unc | BU |
|---|---|---|---|---|---|---|
| 1975J | 8,000,000 | — | — | — | 5.00 | — |
| 1975J Proof | 250,000 | Value: 14.00 | | | | |

**5 MARK** **KM# 143** **Weight:** 5.3000 g. **Composition:** 0.6250 Silver .2250 oz. ASW **Subject:** Centenary - Birth of Albert Schweitzer

| Date | Mintage | F | VF | XF | Unc | BU |
|---|---|---|---|---|---|---|
| 1975G | 8,000,000 | — | — | — | 5.00 | — |
| 1975G Proof | 250,000 | Value: 14.00 | | | | |

**5 MARK** **KM# 142.2** **Weight:** 5.3000 g. **Composition:** 0.6250 Silver .2250 oz. ASW **Note:** 1.4mm thick.

| Date | Mintage | F | VF | XF | Unc | BU |
|---|---|---|---|---|---|---|
| 1975F | Inc. above | — | — | — | 5.00 | — |

**5 MARK** **KM# 142.1** **Weight:** 11.2000 g. **Composition:** 0.6250 Silver .2250 oz. ASW **Subject:** European Monument Proctection Year **Note:** 2.1mm thick.

| Date | Mintage | F | VF | XF | Unc | BU |
|---|---|---|---|---|---|---|
| 1975F | 8,000,000 | — | — | — | 5.00 | — |
| 1975F Proof | 250,000 | Value: 12.00 | | | | |

**5 MARK** **KM# 144** **Weight:** 5.3000 g. **Composition:** 0.6250 Silver .2250 oz. ASW **Subject:** 300th Anniversary - Death of von Grimmelshausen

| Date | Mintage | F | VF | XF | Unc | BU |
|---|---|---|---|---|---|---|
| 1976D | 8,000,000 | — | — | — | 5.00 | — |
| 1976D Proof | 250,000 | Value: 18.00 | | | | |

**5 MARK** **KM# 145** **Weight:** 5.3000 g. **Composition:** 0.6250 Silver .2250 oz. ASW **Subject:** 200th Anniversary - Birth of Carl Friedrich Gauss

| Date | Mintage | F | VF | XF | Unc | BU |
|---|---|---|---|---|---|---|
| 1977J | 8,000,000 | — | — | — | 5.00 | — |
| 1977J Proof | 250,000 | Value: 18.00 | | | | |

**5 MARK** **KM# 146** **Weight:** 5.3000 g. **Composition:** 0.6250 Silver .2250 oz. ASW **Subject:** 200th Anniversary - Birth of Heinrich von Kleist

| Date | Mintage | F | VF | XF | Unc | BU |
|---|---|---|---|---|---|---|
| 1977G | 8,000,000 | — | — | — | 5.00 | — |
| 1977G Proof | 250,000 | Value: 14.00 | | | | |

**5 MARK** **KM# 147** **Weight:** 5.3000 g. **Composition:** 0.6250 Silver .2250 oz. ASW **Subject:** 100th Anniversary - Birth of Gustav Stresemann

| Date | Mintage | F | VF | XF | Unc | BU |
|---|---|---|---|---|---|---|
| 1978D | 8,000,000 | — | — | — | 5.00 | — |
| 1978D Proof | 250,000 | Value: 14.00 | | | | |

**5 MARK** **KM# 148** **Weight:** 5.3000 g. **Composition:** 0.6250 Silver .2250 oz. ASW **Subject:** 225th Anniversary - Death of Balthasar Neumann

| Date | Mintage | F | VF | XF | Unc | BU |
|---|---|---|---|---|---|---|
| 1978F | 8,000,000 | — | — | — | 5.00 | — |
| 1978F Proof | 259,000 | Value: 12.00 | | | | |

**5 MARK** **KM# 150** **Weight:** 5.3000 g. **Composition:** 0.6250 Silver .2250 oz. ASW **Subject:** 150th Anniversary - German Archeological Institute

| Date | Mintage | F | VF | XF | Unc | BU |
|---|---|---|---|---|---|---|
| 1979J | 8,000,000 | — | — | — | 5.00 | — |
| 1979J Proof | 250,000 | Value: 14.00 | | | | |

**5 MARK** **KM# 151** **Weight:** 10.0000 g. **Composition:** Copper-Nickel Clad Nickel **Subject:** 100th Anniversary - Birth of Otto Hahn

| Date | Mintage | F | VF | XF | Unc | BU |
|---|---|---|---|---|---|---|
| 1979G | 5,000,000 | — | — | 4.00 | 7.00 | — |
| 1979G Proof | 350,000 | Value: 10.00 | | | | |

**5 MARK** **KM# 151a** **Weight:** 11.2000 g. **Composition:** 0.6250 Silver .2250 oz. ASW

| Date | Mintage | F | VF | XF | Unc | BU |
|---|---|---|---|---|---|---|
| 1979G | 18 | — | — | — | 22,500 | — |

**5 MARK** **KM# 152** **Composition:** Copper-Nickel Clad Nickel **Subject:** 750th Anniversary - Death of von der Vogelweide

| Date | Mintage | F | VF | XF | Unc | BU |
|---|---|---|---|---|---|---|
| 1980D | 5,000,000 | — | — | 4.00 | 7.00 | — |
| 1980D Proof | 350,000 | Value: 11.50 | | | | |

**5 MARK** **KM# 153** **Composition:** Copper-Nickel Clad Nickel **Subject:** 100th Anniversary - Cologne Cathedral

| Date | Mintage | F | VF | XF | Unc | BU |
|---|---|---|---|---|---|---|
| 1980F | 5,000,000 | — | — | 4.50 | 8.50 | — |
| 1980F Proof | 350,000 | Value: 13.50 | | | | |

**5 MARK** **KM# 154** **Composition:** Copper-Nickel Clad Nickel **Subject:** 200th Anniversary - Death of Gotthold Ephraim Lessing

| Date | Mintage | F | VF | XF | Unc | BU |
|---|---|---|---|---|---|---|
| 1981J | 6,500,000 | — | — | — | 4.50 | — |
| 1981J Proof | 350,000 | Value: 10.00 | | | | |

**5 MARK** **KM# 155** **Composition:** Copper-Nickel Clad Nickel **Subject:** 150th Anniversary - Death of Carl vom Stein

| Date | Mintage | F | VF | XF | Unc | BU |
|---|---|---|---|---|---|---|
| 1981G | 6,500,000 | — | — | — | 4.50 | — |
| 1981G Proof | 350,000 | Value: 10.00 | | | | |

**5 MARK** **KM# 156** **Composition:** Copper-Nickel Clad Nickel **Subject:** 150th Anniversary - Death of Johann Wolfgang von Goethe

| Date | Mintage | F | VF | XF | Unc | BU |
|---|---|---|---|---|---|---|
| 1982D | 8,000,000 | — | — | — | 4.50 | — |
| 1982D Proof | 350,000 | Value: 11.50 | | | | |

**5 MARK** **KM# 157** **Composition:** Copper-Nickel Clad Nickel **Subject:** 10th Anniversary - U.N. Environmental Conference

| Date | Mintage | F | VF | XF | Unc | BU |
|---|---|---|---|---|---|---|
| 1982F | 8,000,000 | — | — | — | 4.50 | — |
| 1982F Proof | 350,000 | Value: 10.00 | | | | |

**5 MARK** **KM# 158** **Composition:** Copper-Nickel Clad Nickel **Subject:** 100th Anniversary - Death of Karl Marx

| Date | Mintage | F | VF | XF | Unc | BU |
|---|---|---|---|---|---|---|
| 1983J | 8,000,000 | — | — | — | 4.50 | — |
| 1983J Proof | 350,000 | Value: 10.00 | | | | |

**5 MARK** **KM# 159** **Composition:** Copper-Nickel Clad Nickel **Subject:** 500th Anniversary - Birth of Martin Luther

| Date | Mintage | F | VF | XF | Unc | BU |
|---|---|---|---|---|---|---|
| 1983G | 8,000,000 | — | — | — | 4.50 | — |
| 1983G Proof | 350,000 | Value: 13.50 | | | | |

**5 MARK** **KM# 160** **Composition:** Copper-Nickel Clad Nickel **Subject:** 150th Anniversary - German Customs Union

| Date | Mintage | F | VF | XF | Unc | BU |
|---|---|---|---|---|---|---|
| 1984D | 8,000,000 | — | — | — | 4.50 | — |
| 1984D Proof | 350,000 | Value: 11.50 | | | | |

**5 MARK** **KM# 161** **Composition:** Copper-Nickel Clad Nickel **Subject:** 175th Anniversary - Birth of Felix Bartholdy

| Date | Mintage | F | VF | XF | Unc | BU |
|---|---|---|---|---|---|---|
| 1984J | 8,000,000 | — | — | — | 4.50 | — |
| 1984J Proof | 350,000 | Value: 12.50 | | | | |

**5 MARK** **KM# 162** **Composition:** Copper-Nickel Clad Nickel **Subject:** European Year of Music

| Date | Mintage | F | VF | XF | Unc | BU |
|---|---|---|---|---|---|---|
| 1985F | 8,000,000 | — | — | — | 4.50 | — |
| 1985F Proof | 350,000 | Value: 11.50 | | | | |

**5 MARK** **KM# 163** **Composition:** Copper-Nickel Clad Nickel **Subject:** 150th Anniversary - German Railroad

| Date | Mintage | F | VF | XF | Unc | BU |
|---|---|---|---|---|---|---|
| 1985G | 8,000,000 | — | — | — | 4.50 | — |
| 1985G Proof | 350,000 | Value: 10.00 | | | | |

**5 MARK** **KM# 164** **Composition:** Copper-Nickel Clad Nickel **Subject:** 600th Anniversary - Heidelberg University

| Date | Mintage | F | VF | XF | Unc | BU |
|---|---|---|---|---|---|---|
| 1986D | 8,000,000 | — | — | — | 4.50 | — |
| 1986D Proof | 350,000 | Value: 10.00 | | | | |

**5 MARK** **KM# 165** **Composition:** Copper-Nickel Clad Nickel **Subject:** 200th Anniversary - Death of Frederick the Great

| Date | Mintage | F | VF | XF | Unc | BU |
|---|---|---|---|---|---|---|
| 1986F | 8,000,000 | — | — | — | 4.50 | — |
| 1986F Proof | 350,000 | Value: 12.50 | | | | |

**10 MARK** **KM# 130** **Weight:** 15.5000 g. **Composition:** 0.6250 Silver .3115 oz. ASW **Series:** Munich Olympics **Reverse:** "In Deutschland" with spiraling symbol

| Date | Mintage | F | VF | XF | Unc | BU |
|---|---|---|---|---|---|---|
| 1972D | 2,500,000 | — | — | — | 9.50 | — |
| 1972D Proof | 125,000 | Value: 32.00 | | | | |
| 1972F | 2,375,000 | — | — | — | 9.50 | — |
| 1972F Proof | 125,000 | Value: 32.00 | | | | |
| 1972G | 2,500,000 | — | — | — | 9.50 | — |
| 1972G Proof | 125,000 | Value: 32.00 | | | | |
| 1972J | 2,500,000 | — | — | — | 9.50 | — |
| 1972J Proof | 125,000 | Value: 32.00 | | | | |

**10 MARK** **KM# 131** **Weight:** 15.5000 g. **Composition:** 0.6250 Silver .3115 oz. ASW **Series:** Munich Olympics **Reverse:** Schleife (knot)

| Date | Mintage | F | VF | XF | Unc | BU |
|---|---|---|---|---|---|---|
| 1972D | 5,000,000 | — | — | — | 9.50 | — |
| 1972D Proof | 125,000 | Value: 25.00 | | | | |
| 1972F | 4,875,000 | — | — | — | 9.50 | — |
| 1972F Proof | 125,000 | Value: 25.00 | | | | |
| 1972G | 5,000,000 | — | — | — | 9.50 | — |
| 1972G Proof | 125,000 | Value: 25.00 | | | | |
| 1972J | 5,000,000 | — | — | — | 9.50 | — |
| 1972J Proof | 125,000 | Value: 25.00 | | | | |

**10 MARK** **KM# 132** **Weight:** 15.5000 g. **Composition:** 0.6250 Silver .3115 oz. ASW **Series:** Munich Olympics **Reverse:** Athletes kneeling

| Date | Mintage | F | VF | XF | Unc | BU |
|---|---|---|---|---|---|---|
| 1972D | 5,000,000 | — | — | — | 8.50 | — |
| 1972D Proof | 150,000 | Value: 20.00 | | | | |
| 1972F | 4,850,000 | — | — | — | 8.50 | — |
| 1972F Proof | 150,000 | Value: 20.00 | | | | |
| 1972G | 5,000,000 | — | — | — | 8.50 | — |
| 1972G Proof | 150,000 | Value: 20.00 | | | | |
| 1972J | 5,000,000 | — | — | — | 8.50 | — |
| 1972J Proof | 150,000 | Value: 20.00 | | | | |

**10 MARK** **KM# 133** **Weight:** 15.5000 g. **Composition:** 0.6250 Silver .3115 oz. ASW **Series:** Munich Olympics **Reverse:** Stadium - ariel view

| Date | Mintage | F | VF | XF | Unc | BU |
|---|---|---|---|---|---|---|
| 1972D | 5,000,000 | — | — | — | 8.50 | — |
| 1972D Proof | 150,000 | Value: 20.00 | | | | |
| 1972F | 4,850,000 | — | — | — | 8.50 | — |
| 1972F Proof | 150,000 | Value: 20.00 | | | | |
| 1972G | 5,000,000 | — | — | — | 8.50 | — |
| 1972G Proof | 150,000 | Value: 20.00 | | | | |
| 1972J | 5,000,000 | — | — | — | 8.50 | — |
| 1972J Proof | 150,000 | Value: 20.00 | | | | |

**10 MARK** **KM# 135** **Weight:** 15.5000 g. **Composition:** 0.6250 Silver .3115 oz. ASW **Series:** Munich Olympics **Reverse:** Olympic Flame - Rings and spiral symbol

| Date | Mintage | F | VF | XF | Unc | BU |
|---|---|---|---|---|---|---|
| 1972D | 5,000,000 | — | — | — | 8.50 | — |
| 1972D Proof | 150,000 | Value: 20.00 | | | | |
| 1972F | 4,850,000 | — | — | — | 8.50 | — |
| 1972F Proof | 150,000 | Value: 20.00 | | | | |
| 1972G | 5,000,000 | — | — | — | 8.50 | — |
| 1972G Proof | 150,000 | Value: 20.00 | | | | |
| 1972J | 5,000,000 | — | — | — | 8.50 | — |
| 1972J Proof | 150,000 | Value: 20.00 | | | | |

**10 MARK** **KM# 134.1** **Weight:** 15.5000 g. **Composition:** 0.6250 Silver .3115 oz. ASW **Series:** Munich Olympics **Reverse:** "In Munchen" - with spiral symbol **Note:** Edge lettering separated by periods.

| Date | Mintage | F | VF | XF | Unc | BU |
|---|---|---|---|---|---|---|
| 1972D | 2,500,000 | — | — | — | 9.50 | — |
| 1972D Proof | 150,000 | Value: 25.00 | | | | |
| 1972F | 2,350,000 | — | — | — | 9.50 | — |
| 1972F Proof | 150,000 | Value: 25.00 | | | | |
| 1972G | 2,500,000 | — | — | — | 9.50 | — |
| 1972G Proof | 150,000 | Value: 25.00 | | | | |
| 1972J | 2,500,000 | — | — | — | 9.50 | — |
| 1972J Proof | 150,000 | Value: 25.00 | | | | |

**10 MARK** **KM# 134.2** **Weight:** 15.5000 g. **Composition:** 0.6250 Silver .3115 oz. ASW **Note:** Error. With edge lettering separated by arabesques.

| Date | Mintage | F | VF | XF | Unc | BU |
|---|---|---|---|---|---|---|
| 1972D | — | — | — | — | 2,760 | — |
| 1972F | — | — | — | — | 2,760 | — |
| 1972G | — | — | — | — | 2,760 | — |
| 1972J | 600 | — | 200 | 300 | 550 | — |

**10 MARK** **KM# 166** **Weight:** 15.5000 g. **Composition:** 0.6250 Silver .3115 oz. ASW **Subject:** 750th Anniversary - Berlin

| Date | Mintage | F | VF | XF | Unc | BU |
|---|---|---|---|---|---|---|
| 1987J | 8,000,000 | — | — | — | 10.00 | — |
| 1987J Proof | 350,000 | Value: 85.00 | | | | |

**10 MARK** **KM# 167** **Weight:** 15.5000 g. **Composition:** 0.6250 Silver .3115 oz. ASW **Subject:** European Unity

| Date | Mintage | F | VF | XF | Unc | BU |
|---|---|---|---|---|---|---|
| 1987G | 8,000,000 | — | — | — | 8.00 | — |
| 1987G Prof | 350,000 | Value: 65.00 | | | | |

**10 MARK** **KM# 168** **Weight:** 15.5000 g. **Composition:** 0.6250 Silver .3115 oz. ASW **Subject:** 200th Anniversary - Birth of Arthur Schopenhauer

| Date | Mintage | F | VF | XF | Unc | BU |
|---|---|---|---|---|---|---|
| 1988D | 8,000,000 | — | — | — | 8.00 | — |
| 1988D Proof | 350,000 | Value: 30.00 | | | | |

**10 MARK** **KM# 169** **Weight:** 15.5000 g. **Composition:** 0.6250 Silver .3115 oz. ASW **Subject:** 100th Anniversary - Death of Carl Zeiss

| Date | Mintage | F | VF | XF | Unc | BU |
|---|---|---|---|---|---|---|
| 1988F | 8,000,000 | — | — | — | 8.00 | — |
| 1988F Proof | 350,000 | Value: 22.00 | | | | |

**10 MARK** **KM# 171** **Weight:** 15.5000 g. **Composition:** 0.6250 Silver .3115 oz. ASW **Subject:** 800th Year - Port of Hamburg

| Date | Mintage | F | VF | XF | Unc | BU |
|---|---|---|---|---|---|---|
| 1989J | 8,000,000 | — | — | — | 8.00 | — |
| 1989J Proof | 350,000 | Value: 25.00 | | | | |

**10 MARK** **KM# 172** **Weight:** 15.5000 g. **Composition:** 0.6250 Silver .3115 oz. ASW **Subject:** 2000th Anniversary - City of Bonn

| Date | Mintage | F | VF | XF | Unc | BU |
|---|---|---|---|---|---|---|
| 1989D | 8,000,000 | — | — | — | 8.00 | — |
| 1989D Proof | 350,000 | Value: 25.00 | | | | |

**10 MARK** **KM# 173** **Weight:** 15.5000 g. **Composition:** 0.6250 Silver .3115 oz. ASW **Subject:** 40th Anniversary - Republic

| Date | Mintage | F | VF | XF | Unc | BU |
|---|---|---|---|---|---|---|
| 1989G | 8,000,000 | — | — | — | 8.00 | — |
| 1989G Proof | 350,000 | Value: 25.00 | | | | |

**10 MARK** **KM# 174** **Weight:** 15.5000 g. **Composition:** 0.6250 Silver .3115 oz. ASW **Subject:** Death of Kaiser Friedrich Barbarossa

| Date | Mintage | F | VF | XF | Unc | BU |
|---|---|---|---|---|---|---|
| 1990F | 7,850,000 | — | — | — | 8.00 | — |
| 1990F Proof | 400,000 | Value: 20.00 | | | | |

**10 MARK** **KM# 176** **Weight:** 15.5000 g. **Composition:** 0.6250 Silver .3115 oz. ASW **Subject:** 800th Anniversary - The Teutonic Order

| Date | Mintage | F | VF | XF | Unc | BU |
|---|---|---|---|---|---|---|
| 1990J | 8,850,000 | — | — | — | 8.00 | — |
| 1990J Proof | 450,000 | Value: 12.50 | | | | |

**10 MARK** **KM# 177** **Weight:** 15.5000 g. **Composition:** 0.6250 Silver .3115 oz. ASW **Subject:** German Unity - Brandenburg Gate

| Date | Mintage | F | VF | XF | Unc | BU |
|---|---|---|---|---|---|---|
| 1991A | 8,850,000 | — | — | — | 8.00 | — |
| 1991A Proof | 450,000 | Value: 13.50 | | | | |

**10 MARK** **KM# 178** **Weight:** 15.5000 g. **Composition:** 0.6250 Silver .3115 oz. ASW **Subject:** Kathe Kollwitz - Artist

| Date | Mintage | F | VF | XF | Unc | BU |
|---|---|---|---|---|---|---|
| 1992G | 8,450,000 | — | — | — | 8.00 | — |
| 1992G Proof | 450,000 | Value: 11.50 | | | | |

**10 MARK** **KM# 179** **Weight:** 15.5000 g. **Composition:** 0.6250 Silver .3115 oz. ASW **Subject:** Civil Pour-le-Merite Order

| Date | Mintage | F | VF | XF | Unc | BU |
|---|---|---|---|---|---|---|
| 1992D | 8,450,000 | — | — | — | 8.00 | — |
| 1992D Proof | 450,000 | Value: 11.50 | | | | |

**10 MARK** **KM# 180** **Weight:** 15.5000 g. **Composition:** 0.6250 Silver .3115 oz. ASW **Subject:** 1000 Anniversary - Potsdam

| Date | Mintage | F | VF | XF | Unc | BU |
|---|---|---|---|---|---|---|
| 1993F | 7,950,000 | — | — | — | 8.00 | — |
| 1993F Proof | 450,000 | Value: 11.50 | | | | |

**10 MARK** **KM# 181** **Weight:** 15.5000 g. **Composition:** 0.6250 Silver .3115 oz. ASW **Reverse:** Head of Robert Koch facing forward

| Date | Mintage | F | VF | XF | Unc | BU |
|---|---|---|---|---|---|---|
| 1993J | 7,450,000 | — | — | — | 8.00 | — |
| 1993J Proof | 450,000 | Value: 11.50 | | | | |

**10 MARK** **KM# 182** **Weight:** 15.5000 g. **Composition:** 0.6250 Silver .3115 oz. ASW **Subject:** Attempt on Hitler's Life, July 20, 1944

| Date | Mintage | F | VF | XF | Unc | BU |
|---|---|---|---|---|---|---|
| 1994A | 7,450,000 | — | — | — | 8.00 | — |
| 1994A Proof | 450,000 | Value: 11.50 | | | | |

**10 MARK** **KM# 184** **Weight:** 15.5000 g. **Composition:** 0.6250 Silver .3115 oz. ASW **Reverse:** Head of Johann Gottfried Herder facing right

| Date | Mintage | F | VF | XF | Unc | BU |
|---|---|---|---|---|---|---|
| 1994G | 7,450,000 | — | — | — | 8.00 | — |
| 1994G Proof | 450,000 | Value: 11.50 | | | | |

**10 MARK** **KM# 185** **Weight:** 15.5000 g. **Composition:** 0.6250 Silver .3115 oz. ASW **Subject:** 50th Anniversary of Peace and Reconciliation **Edge Lettering:** STEINERNE GLOCKE SYMBOL FUER TOLERANZ

| Date | Mintage | F | VF | XF | Unc | BU |
|---|---|---|---|---|---|---|
| 1995J | 7,450,000 | — | — | — | 8.00 | — |
| 1995J Proof | 450,000 | Value: 11.50 | | | | |

**10 MARK** **KM# 186** **Weight:** 15.5000 g. **Composition:** 0.6250 Silver .3115 oz. ASW **Subject:** Henry the Lion **Edge Lettering:** HEINRICH DER LOEWE AUS KAISERLICHEM STAMM

| Date | Mintage | F | VF | XF | Unc | BU |
|---|---|---|---|---|---|---|
| 1995F | 7,450,000 | — | — | — | 8.00 | — |
| 1995F Proof | 450,000 | Value: 11.50 | | | | |

**10 MARK** **KM# 187** **Weight:** 15.5000 g. **Composition:** 0.6250 Silver .3115 oz. ASW **Subject:** Wilhelm Conrad Rontgen **Reverse:** Hand and X-rayed hand **Edge Lettering:** ERSTER NOBEL PREIS FUER PHYSIK

| Date | Mintage | F | VF | XF | Unc | BU |
|---|---|---|---|---|---|---|
| 1995D | 6,900,000 | — | — | — | 8.00 | — |
| 1995D Proof | 450,000 | Value: 11.50 | | | | |

**10 MARK** **KM# 188** **Weight:** 15.5000 g. **Composition:** 0.6250 Silver .3115 oz. ASW **Subject:** Kolpingwerk **Edge Lettering:** TAETIGE LIEBE HEILT ALLE WUNDEN

| Date | Mintage | F | VF | XF | Unc | BU |
|---|---|---|---|---|---|---|
| 1996A | 5,600,000 | — | — | — | 8.00 | — |
| 1996A Proof | 400,000 | Value: 11.50 | | | | |

**10 MARK** **KM# 189.1** **Weight:** 15.5000 g. **Composition:** 0.6250 Silver .3115 oz. ASW **Subject:** Philipp Melanchthon **Obverse:** Stylized eagle **Reverse:** Portrait, dates

| Date | Mintage | F | VF | XF | Unc | BU |
|---|---|---|---|---|---|---|
| 1997A Proof | 150,000 | Value: 22.50 | | | | |
| 1997D Proof | 150,000 | Value: 22.50 | | | | |
| 1997F Proof | 150,000 | Value: 22.50 | | | | |
| 1997G Proof | 150,000 | Value: 22.50 | | | | |
| 1997J | 3,000,000 | — | — | — | 10.00 | — |
| 1997J Proof | 150,000 | Value: 22.50 | | | | |

**10 MARK** **KM# 189.2** **Weight:** 15.5000 g. **Composition:** 0.6250 Silver .3115 oz. ASW **Reverse:** Different forelock on portrait

| Date | Mintage | F | VF | XF | Unc | BU |
|---|---|---|---|---|---|---|
| 1997J | — | — | — | — | 10.00 | — |
| 1997J Proof | — | Value: 28.00 | | | | |

**10 MARK KM# 190 Weight:** 15.5000 g. **Composition:** 0.6250 Silver .3115 oz. ASW **Subject:** Heinrich Heine **Obverse:** Stylized eagle **Reverse:** Portrait with handwritten text in background

| Date | Mintage | F | VF | XF | Unc | BU |
|---|---|---|---|---|---|---|
| 1997A Proof | 150,000 | Value: 22.50 | | | | |
| 1997D | 3,000,000 | — | — | — | 10.00 | — |
| 1997D Proof | 750,000 | Value: 22.50 | | | | |
| 1997F Proof | 150,000 | Value: 22.50 | | | | |
| 1997G Proof | 150,000 | Value: 22.50 | | | | |
| 1997J Proof | 150,000 | Value: 22.50 | | | | |

**10 MARK KM# 192 Weight:** 15.5000 g. **Composition:** 0.6250 Silver .3115 oz. ASW **Subject:** Diesel Engine Centennial **Obverse:** Stylized eagle **Reverse:** First diesel engine

| Date | Mintage | F | VF | XF | Unc | BU |
|---|---|---|---|---|---|---|
| 1997A Proof | 150,000 | Value: 22.50 | | | | |
| 1997D Proof | 150,000 | Value: 22.50 | | | | |
| 1997F | 3,000,000 | — | — | — | 10.00 | — |
| 1997F Proof | 150,000 | Value: 22.50 | | | | |
| 1997G Proof | 150,000 | Value: 22.50 | | | | |
| 1997J Proof | 150,000 | Value: 22.50 | | | | |

**10 MARK KM# 191 Weight:** 15.5000 g. **Composition:** 0.9250 Silver .4610 oz. ASW **Subject:** 300th Anniversary - Peace of Westphalia **Obverse:** Stylized eagle **Reverse:** Clasped hands, dove and quill

| Date | Mintage | F | VF | XF | Unc | BU |
|---|---|---|---|---|---|---|
| 1998A Proof | 200,000 | Value: 22.50 | | | | |
| 1998D Proof | 200,000 | Value: 22.50 | | | | |
| 1998F Proof | 200,000 | Value: 22.50 | | | | |
| 1998G Proof | 200,000 | Value: 22.50 | | | | |
| 1998J | 3,500,000 | — | — | — | 10.00 | — |
| 1998J Proof | 200,000 | Value: 22.50 | | | | |

**Note:** A 1997 strike of this coin does not exist

**10 MARK KM# 193 Weight:** 15.5000 g. **Composition:** 0.9000 Silver .5345 oz. ASW **Subject:** 900th Birthday of Hildegard von Bingen **Obverse:** Stylized eagle **Reverse:** Seated nun writing **Edge Lettering:** WISSE DIE WEGE DES HERRN

| Date | Mintage | F | VF | XF | Unc | BU |
|---|---|---|---|---|---|---|
| 1998A Proof | 200,000 | Value: 22.50 | | | | |
| 1998D Proof | 200,000 | Value: 22.50 | | | | |
| 1998F Proof | 200,000 | Value: 22.50 | | | | |
| 1998G | 3,500,000 | — | — | — | 10.00 | — |
| 1998G Proof | 200,000 | Value: 22.50 | | | | |
| 1998J Proof | 200,000 | Value: 22.50 | | | | |

**10 MARK KM# 194 Weight:** 15.5000 g. **Composition:** 0.9000 Silver .5345 oz. ASW **Subject:** 300th Anniversary Franckesche Charitable Endowment

| Date | Mintage | F | VF | XF | Unc | BU |
|---|---|---|---|---|---|---|
| 1998A | — | — | — | — | 10.00 | — |
| 1998A Proof | — | Value: 22.50 | | | | |
| 1998D Proof | — | Value: 22.50 | | | | |
| 1998F Proof | — | Value: 22.50 | | | | |
| 1998G Proof | — | Value: 22.50 | | | | |
| 1998J Proof | — | Value: 22.50 | | | | |

**10 MARK KM# 195 Weight:** 15.5000 g. **Composition:** 0.9250 Silver .4610 oz. ASW **Subject:** 50 Years of German Deutsch Mark **Obverse:** Denomination above eagle **Reverse:** Seven coin designs **Edge Lettering:** EINIGKEIT UND RECHT UND FREIHEIT

| Date | Mintage | F | VF | XF | Unc | BU |
|---|---|---|---|---|---|---|
| 1998A Proof | — | Value: 21.50 | | | | |
| 1998D Proof | — | Value: 21.50 | | | | |
| 1998F | — | — | — | — | 10.00 | — |
| 1998F Proof | — | Value: 21.50 | | | | |
| 1998G Proof | — | Value: 21.50 | | | | |
| 1998J Proof | — | Value: 21.50 | | | | |

**10 MARK KM# 196 Weight:** 15.5000 g. **Composition:** 0.9250 Silver .4610 oz. ASW **Subject:** 50th Anniversary - German Constitution **Obverse:** Denomination below eagle **Reverse:** German constitution **Edge Lettering:** FUR DAS GESAMTE DEUTSCH VOLK

| Date | Mintage | F | VF | XF | Unc | BU |
|---|---|---|---|---|---|---|
| 1999A Proof | — | Value: 20.00 | | | | |
| 1999D | — | — | — | — | 10.00 | — |
| 1999D Proof | — | Value: 20.00 | | | | |
| 1999F Proof | — | Value: 20.00 | | | | |
| 1999G Proof | — | Value: 20.00 | | | | |
| 1999J Proof | — | Value: 20.00 | | | | |

**10 MARK KM# 197 Weight:** 15.5000 g. **Composition:** 0.9250 Silver .4610 oz. ASW **Subject:** 250th Anniversary - Birth of J.W. von Goethe **Obverse:** Denomination below eagle **Reverse:** Portrait of von Goethe facing inscribed field **Edge Lettering:** WIRKE GUT SO WIRKST DU LANGER

| Date | Mintage | F | VF | XF | Unc | BU |
|---|---|---|---|---|---|---|
| 1999A Proof | — | Value: 20.00 | | | | |
| 1999D Proof | — | Value: 20.00 | | | | |
| 1999F | — | — | — | — | 10.00 | — |
| 1999F Proof | — | Value: 20.00 | | | | |
| 1999G Proof | — | Value: 20.00 | | | | |
| 1999J Proof | — | Value: 20.00 | | | | |

**10 MARK KM# 198 Weight:** 15.5000 g. **Composition:** 0.9250 Silver .4610 oz. ASW **Subject:** SOS Kinderdorfs **Obverse:** Denomination below eagle **Reverse:** Stylized globe, children playing **Edge Lettering:** SOS - KINDERDORFS - EINE IDEE FUR DIE WELT

| Date | Mintage | F | VF | XF | Unc | BU |
|---|---|---|---|---|---|---|
| 1999A Proof | — | Value: 20.00 | | | | |
| 1999D Proof | — | Value: 20.00 | | | | |
| 1999F Proof | — | Value: 20.00 | | | | |
| 1999G Proof | — | Value: 20.00 | | | | |
| 1999J | — | — | — | — | 10.00 | — |
| 1999J Proof | — | Value: 20.00 | | | | |

**Note:** A 1997 strike of this coin does not exist.

**10 MARK KM# 199 Weight:** 15.5000 g. **Composition:** 0.9250 Silver .4610 oz. ASW **Subject:** Expo 2000 **Obverse:** Stylized eagle **Reverse:** Childlike drawing of human balance scale **Edge Lettering:** WELTAUSSTELLUNG EXPO 2000 HANNOVER

| Date | Mintage | F | VF | XF | Unc | BU |
|---|---|---|---|---|---|---|
| 2000A | 3,000,000 | — | — | — | 10.00 | — |
| 2000A Proof | 160,000 | Value: 20.00 | | | | |
| 2000D Proof | 160,000 | Value: 20.00 | | | | |
| 2000F Proof | 160,000 | Value: 20.00 | | | | |
| 2000G Proof | 160,000 | Value: 20.00 | | | | |
| 2000J Proof | 160,000 | Value: 20.00 | | | | |

**10 MARK KM# 200 Weight:** 15.5000 g. **Composition:** 0.9250 Silver .4610 oz. ASW **Subject:** Charlemagne **Obverse:** Stylized eagle **Reverse:** Charlemagne handing church model to Madonna and child **Edge Lettering:** URBS AQUENSIS - URBS REGALIS

| Date | Mintage | F | VF | XF | Unc | BU |
|---|---|---|---|---|---|---|
| 2000A Proof | 160,000 | Value: 20.00 | | | | |
| 2000D Proof | 160,000 | Value: 20.00 | | | | |
| 2000F Proof | 160,000 | Value: 20.00 | | | | |
| 2000G | 3,000,000 | — | — | — | 10.00 | — |
| 2000G Proof | 160,000 | Value: 20.00 | | | | |
| 2000J Proof | 160,000 | Value: 20.00 | | | | |

**10 MARK KM# 204 Weight:** 15.5000 g. **Composition:** 0.9250 Silver .4610 oz. ASW **Edge Lettering:** "OHNE WASSER KEIN LEBEN" **Size:** 32.5 mm.

| Date | Mintage | F | VF | XF | Unc | BU |
|---|---|---|---|---|---|---|
| 2001A | 2,500,000 | — | — | — | 10.00 | — |
| 2001A Proof | 160,000 | Value: 22.50 | | | | |
| 2001D Proof | 160,000 | Value: 22.50 | | | | |
| 2001F Proof | 160,000 | Value: 22.50 | | | | |
| 2001G Proof | 160,000 | Value: 22.50 | | | | |
| 2001J Proof | 160,000 | Value: 22.50 | | | | |

**10 MARK KM# 205 Weight:** 15.5000 g. **Composition:** 0.9250 Silver .4610 oz. ASW **Subject:** Albert Gustav Lortzing **Obverse:** Stylized eagle **Reverse:** Portrait and music **Edge Lettering:** "WILDSCHUETZ*UNDINE"ZAR UND ZIMMER MANN" **Size:** 32.5 mm.

| Date | Mintage | F | VF | XF | Unc | BU |
|---|---|---|---|---|---|---|
| 2001A Proof | 160,000 | Value: 22.50 | | | | |
| 2001D Proof | 160,000 | Value: 22.50 | | | | |
| 2001F Proof | 160,000 | Value: 22.50 | | | | |
| 2001G Proof | 160,000 | Value: 22.50 | | | | |
| 2001J | 2,500,000 | — | — | — | 10.00 | — |
| 2001J Proof | 160,000 | Value: 22.50 | | | | |

**10 MARK** KM# 206 **Weight:** 15.5000 g. **Composition:** 0.9250 Silver .4610 oz. ASW **Subject:** Federal Constitution: 50th Anniversary **Obverse:** Stylized eagle **Reverse:** Justice holding books and scale **Edge:** Lettered **Size:** 32.5 mm.

| Date | Mintage | F | VF | XF | Unc | BU |
|---|---|---|---|---|---|---|
| 2001A Proof | 160,000 | Value: 22.50 | | | | |
| 2001D Proof | 160,000 | Value: 22.50 | | | | |
| 2001F Proof | 160,000 | Value: 22.50 | | | | |
| 2001G | 2,500,000 | — | — | — | 10.00 | — |
| 2001G Proof | 160,000 | Value: 22.50 | | | | |
| 2001J Proof | 160,000 | Value: 22.50 | | | | |

## EURO COINAGE

European Economic Community Issues

**EURO CENT** KM# 207 **Weight:** 2.2700 g. **Composition:** Copper Plated Steel **Obverse:** Oak leaves. **Reverse:** Denomination and globe. **Edge:** Plain. **Size:** 16.3 mm.

| Date | Mintage | F | VF | XF | Unc | BU |
|---|---|---|---|---|---|---|
| 2002A | 2,400,000,000 | — | — | — | 0.15 | — |
| 2002A Proof | Inc. above | Value: 0.25 | | | | |
| 2002D | Inc. above | — | — | — | 0.15 | — |
| 2002D Proof | Inc. above | Value: 0.25 | | | | |
| 2002F | Inc. above | — | — | — | 0.15 | — |
| 2002F Proof | Inc. above | Value: 0.25 | | | | |
| 2002G | Inc. above | — | — | — | 0.15 | — |
| 2002G Proof | Inc. above | Value: 0.25 | | | | |
| 2002J | Inc. above | — | — | — | 0.15 | — |
| 2002J Proof | Inc. above | Value: 0.25 | | | | |

**2 EURO CENTS** KM# 208 **Weight:** 3.0000 g. **Composition:** Copper Plated Steel **Obverse:** Oak leaves. **Reverse:** Denomination and globe. **Edge:** Grooved. **Size:** 18.7 mm.

| Date | Mintage | F | VF | XF | Unc | BU |
|---|---|---|---|---|---|---|
| 2002A | 1,100,000,000 | — | — | — | 0.25 | — |
| 2002A Proof | Inc. above | Value: 0.35 | | | | |
| 2002D | Inc. above | — | — | — | 0.25 | — |
| 2002D Proof | Inc. above | Value: 0.35 | | | | |
| 2002F | Inc. above | — | — | — | 0.25 | — |
| 2002F Proof | Inc. above | Value: 0.35 | | | | |
| 2002G | Inc. above | — | — | — | 0.25 | — |
| 2002G Proof | Inc. above | Value: 0.35 | | | | |
| 2002J | Inc. above | — | — | — | 0.25 | — |
| 2002J Proof | Inc. above | Value: 0.35 | | | | |

**5 EURO CENTS** KM# 209 **Weight:** 3.8600 g. **Composition:** Copper Plated Steel **Obverse:** Oak leaves. **Reverse:** Denomination and globe. **Edge:** Plain. **Size:** 21.2 mm.

| Date | Mintage | F | VF | XF | Unc | BU |
|---|---|---|---|---|---|---|
| 2002A | 2,200,000,000 | — | — | — | 0.35 | — |
| 2002A Proof | Inc. above | Value: 0.50 | | | | |
| 2002D | Inc. above | — | — | — | 0.35 | — |
| 2002D Proof | Inc. above | Value: 0.50 | | | | |
| 2002F | Inc. above | — | — | — | 0.35 | — |
| 2002F Proof | Inc. above | Value: 0.50 | | | | |
| 2002G | Inc. above | — | — | — | 0.35 | — |
| 2002G Proof | Inc. above | Value: 0.50 | | | | |
| 2002J | Inc. above | — | — | — | 0.35 | — |
| 2002J Proof | Inc. above | Value: 0.50 | | | | |

**10 EURO CENTS** KM# 210 **Weight:** 4.0000 g. **Composition:** Brass **Obverse:** Brandenburg Gate. **Reverse:** Denomination and map. **Edge:** Reeded. **Size:** 19.7 mm.

| Date | Mintage | F | VF | XF | Unc | BU |
|---|---|---|---|---|---|---|
| 2002A | 2,400,000,000 | — | — | — | 0.50 | — |
| 2002A Proof | Inc. above | Value: 0.75 | | | | |
| 2002D | Inc. above | — | — | — | 0.50 | — |
| 2002D Proof | Inc. above | Value: 0.75 | | | | |
| 2002F | Inc. above | — | — | — | 0.50 | — |
| 2002F Proof | Inc. above | Value: 0.75 | | | | |
| 2002G | Inc. above | — | — | — | 0.50 | — |
| 2002G Proof | Inc. above | Value: 0.75 | | | | |
| 2002J | Inc. above | — | — | — | 0.50 | — |
| 2002J Proof | Inc. above | Value: 0.75 | | | | |

**20 EURO CENTS** KM# 211 **Weight:** 5.7300 g. **Composition:** Brass **Obverse:** Brandenburg Gate. **Reverse:** Denomination and map. **Edge:** Notched. **Size:** 22.2 mm.

| Date | Mintage | F | VF | XF | Unc | BU |
|---|---|---|---|---|---|---|
| 2002A | 1,100,000,000 | — | — | — | 0.75 | — |
| 2002A Proof | Inc. above | Value: 1.25 | | | | |
| 2002D | Inc. above | — | — | — | 0.75 | — |
| 2002D Proof | Inc. above | Value: 1.25 | | | | |
| 2002F | Inc. above | — | — | — | 0.75 | — |
| 2002F Proof | Inc. above | Value: 1.25 | | | | |
| 2002G | Inc. above | — | — | — | 0.75 | — |
| 2002G Proof | Inc. above | Value: 1.25 | | | | |
| 2002J | Inc. above | — | — | — | 0.75 | — |
| 2002J Proof | Inc. above | Value: 1.25 | | | | |

**50 EURO CENTS** KM# 212 **Weight:** 7.8100 g. **Composition:** Brass **Obverse:** Brandenburg Gate. **Reverse:** Denomination and map. **Edge:** Reeded. **Size:** 24.2 mm.

| Date | Mintage | F | VF | XF | Unc | BU |
|---|---|---|---|---|---|---|
| 2002A | 900,000,000 | — | — | — | 1.75 | — |
| 2002A Proof | Inc. above | Value: 3.25 | | | | |
| 2002D | Inc. above | — | — | — | 1.75 | — |
| 2002D Proof | Inc. above | Value: 3.25 | | | | |
| 2002F | Inc. above | — | — | — | 1.75 | — |
| 2002F Proof | Inc. above | Value: 3.25 | | | | |
| 2002G | Inc. above | — | — | — | 1.75 | — |
| 2002G Proof | Inc. above | Value: 3.25 | | | | |
| 2002J | Inc. above | — | — | — | 1.75 | — |
| 2002J Proof | Inc. above | Value: 3.25 | | | | |

**EURO** KM# 213 **Ring Composition:** Brass **Center Weight:** 7.5000 g. **Center Composition:** Copper Nickel **Subject:** Currency Reform **Obverse:** Stylized eagle. **Reverse:** Denomination over map. **Edge:** Three normally reeded and three very finely reeded sections. **Size:** 23.3 mm.

| Date | Mintage | F | VF | XF | Unc | BU |
|---|---|---|---|---|---|---|
| 2002A | 1,200,000,000 | — | — | — | 2.50 | — |
| 2002A Proof | Inc. above | Value: 6.50 | | | | |
| 2002D | Inc. above | — | — | — | 2.50 | — |
| 2002D Proof | Inc. above | Value: 6.50 | | | | |
| 2002F | Inc. above | — | — | — | 2.50 | — |
| 2002F Proof | Inc. above | Value: 6.50 | | | | |
| 2002G | Inc. above | — | — | — | 2.50 | — |
| 2002G Proof | Inc. above | Value: 6.50 | | | | |
| 2002J | Inc. above | — | — | — | 2.50 | — |
| 2002J Proof | Inc. above | Value: 6.50 | | | | |

**2 EUROS** KM# 214 **Ring Composition:** Copper Nickel **Center Weight:** 8.5200 g. **Center Composition:** Brass **Obverse:** Stylized eagle. **Reverse:** Denomination and map. **Edge:** Reeded and "EINIGKEIT UND RECHT UND FREIHEIT." **Size:** 25.6 mm.

| Date | Mintage | F | VF | XF | Unc | BU |
|---|---|---|---|---|---|---|
| 2002A | 800,000,000 | — | — | — | 5.50 | — |
| 2002A Proof | Inc. above | Value: 12.50 | | | | |
| 2002D | Inc. above | — | — | — | 5.50 | — |
| 2002D Proof | Inc. above | Value: 12.50 | | | | |
| 2002F | Inc. above | — | — | — | 5.50 | — |
| 2002F Proof | Inc. above | Value: 12.50 | | | | |
| 2002G | Inc. above | — | — | — | 5.50 | — |
| 2002G Proof | Inc. above | Value: 12.50 | | | | |
| 2002J | Inc. above | — | — | — | 5.50 | — |
| 2002J Proof | Inc. above | Value: 12.50 | | | | |

## PATTERNS

Including off metal strikes

| KM# | Date | Mintage | Identification | Mkt Val |
|---|---|---|---|---|
| Pn397 | 1950 | — | 2 Mark. Copper-Nickel. With Hole, PN#400. | — |
| Pn398 | 1951 | — | 2 Mark. Copper-Nickel. Max Planck. | — |
| Pn399 | 1951 | — | 2 Mark. Copper-Nickel. Max Planck. | — |
| Pn400 | 1955 | — | 2 Mark. | — |
| Pn401 | 1959 | — | 2 Pfennig. Brass. | — |
| Pn402 | 1960 | — | 2 Pfennig. Zinc. | — |

## TRIAL STRIKES

| KM# | Date | Mintage | Identification | Mkt Val |
|---|---|---|---|---|
| TS1 | | — | 10 Pfennig. KM#4. Uniface. | — |
| TS2 | | — | 2 Mark. Silver. Pn400. Uniface. | — |
| TS4 | | — | 2 Mark. Lead. Pn400. Uniface. | — |
| TS7 | | — | 2 Mark. Lead. Max Planck. Uniface. | — |
| TS9 | | — | 2 Mark. Iron. Max Planck. Uniface. | — |
| TS11 | | — | 2 Mark. Lead. Max Planck. Uniface. | — |
| TS5 | 1950 | — | 2 Mark. Lead. Pn400. Uniface. | — |
| TS3 | 1950 | — | 2 Mark. Silver. Pn400. Uniface. | — |
| TS6 | 1951 | — | 2 Mark. Lead. Max Planck. Uniface. | — |
| TS10 | 1951 | — | 2 Mark. Lead. Max Planck. Uniface. | — |
| TS8 | 1951 | — | 2 Mark. Iron. Max Planck. Uniface. | — |

## MINT SETS

| KM# | Date | Mintage | Identification | Issue Price | Mkt Val |
|---|---|---|---|---|---|
| MS106 | 1998F (10) | 70,000 | KM105, 106a, 107-108, 109.2, 110, 140.1, 170, 175, 183 | — | 35.00 |
| MS1 | 1974D (9) | 20,000 | KM#105, 106a, 107-108, 109.2, 110, 112.1, 124, A127 | — | 45.00 |
| MS2 | 1974F (9) | 20,000 | KM#105, 106a, 107-108, 109.2, 110, 112.1, 124, A127 | — | 45.00 |
| MS3 | 1974G (9) | 20,000 | KM#105, 106a, 107-108, 109.2, 110, 112.1, 124, A127 | — | 45.00 |
| MS4 | 1974J (9) | 20,000 | KM#105, 106a, 107-108, 109.2, 110, 112.1, 124, A127 | — | 45.00 |
| MS5 | 1975D (9) | 26,000 | KM#105, 106a, 107-108, 109.2, 110, 124, A127, 140.1 | — | 28.00 |
| MS6 | 1975F (9) | 26,000 | KM#105, 106a, 107-108, 109.2, 110, 124, A127, 140.1 | — | 28.00 |
| MS7 | 1975G (9) | 26,000 | KM#105, 106a, 107-108, 109.2, 110, 124, A127, 140.1 | — | 28.00 |
| MS8 | 1975J (9) | 26,000 | KM#105, 106a, 107-108, 109.2, 110, 124, A127, 140.1 | — | 28.00 |
| MS9 | 1976D (9) | 26,000 | KM#105, 106a, 107-108, 109.2, 110, 124, A127, 140.1 | — | 28.00 |
| MS10 | 1976F (9) | 26,000 | KM#105, 106a, 107-108, 1092., 110, 124, A127, 140.1 | — | 28.00 |
| MS11 | 1976G (9) | 26,000 | KM#105, 106a, 107-108, 109.2, 110, 124, A127, 140.1 | — | 28.00 |
| MS12 | 1976J (9) | 26,000 | KM#105, 106a, 107-108, 109.2, 110, 124, A127, 140.1 | — | 28.00 |
| MS13 | 1977D (9) | 29,000 | KM#105, 106a, 107-108, 109.2, 110, 124, A127, 140.1 | — | 20.00 |
| MS14 | 1977F (9) | 29,000 | KM#105, 106a, 107-108, 109.2, 110, 124, A127, 140.1 | — | 20.00 |
| MS15 | 1977G (9) | 29,000 | KM#105, 106a, 107-108, 109.2, 110, 124, A127, 140.1 | — | 20.00 |
| MS16 | 1977J (9) | 29,000 | KM#105, 106a, 107-108, 109.2, 110, 124, A127, 140.1 | — | 20.00 |
| MS17 | 1978D (9) | 30,000 | KM#105, 106a, 107-108, 109.2, 110, 124, A127, 140.1 | — | 17.50 |
| MS18 | 1978F (9) | 30,000 | KM#105, 106a, 107-108, 109.2, 110, 124, A127, 140.1 | — | 17.50 |
| MS19 | 1978g (9) | 30,000 | KM#105, 106a, 107-108, 109.2, 110, 124, A127, 140.1 | — | 17.50 |
| MS20 | 1978J (9) | 30,000 | KM#105, 106a, 107-108, 109.2, 110, 124, A127, 140.1 | — | 17.50 |
| MS21 | 1979D (10) | 34,000 | KM105, 106a, 107-108, 109.2, 110, 124, A127, 140.1, 149 | 11.00 | 17.50 |
| MS22 | 1979F (10) | 34,000 | KM105, 106a, 107-108, 109.2, 110, 124, A127, 140.1, 149 | 11.00 | 17.50 |
| MS23 | 1979G (10) | 34,000 | KM105, 106a, 107-108, 109.2, 110, 124, A127, 140.1, 149 | 11.00 | 17.50 |
| MS24 | 1979J (10) | 34,000 | KM105, 106a, 107-108, 109.2, 110, 124, A127, 140.1, 149 | 11.00 | 17.50 |
| MS25 | 1980D (10) | 36,000 | KM105, 106a, 107-108, 109.2, 110, 124, A127, 140.1, 149 | 11.00 | 17.50 |
| MS26 | 1980F (10) | 36,000 | KM105, 106a, 107-108, 109.2, 110, 124, A127, 140.1, 149 | 11.00 | 17.50 |
| MS27 | 1980G (10) | 36,000 | KM105, 106a, 107-108, 109.2, 110, 124, A127, 140.1, 149 | 11.00 | 17.50 |
| MS28 | 1980J (10) | 36,000 | KM105, 106a, 107-108, 109.2, 110, 124, A127, 140.1, 149 | 11.00 | 17.50 |
| MS29 | 1981D (10) | 38,000 | KM105, 106a, 107-108, 109.2, 110, 124, A127, 140.1, 149 | 11.00 | 17.50 |
| MS30 | 1981F (10) | 38,000 | KM105, 106a, 107-108, 109.2, 110, 124, A127, 140.1, 149 | 11.00 | 17.50 |
| MS31 | 1981G (10) | 38,000 | KM105, 106a, 107-108, 109.2, 110, 124, A127, 140.1, 149 | 11.00 | 17.50 |
| MS32 | 1981J (10) | 38,000 | KM105, 106a, 107-108, 109.2, 110, 124, A127, 140.1, 149 | 11.00 | 17.50 |

| KM# | Date | Mintage | Identification | Issue Price | Mkt Val |
|---|---|---|---|---|---|
| MS33 | 1982D (10) | 33,000 | KM105, 106a, 107-108, 109.2, 110, 124, A127, 140.1, 149 | 11.00 | 17.50 |
| MS34 | 1982F (10) | 33,000 | KM105, 106a, 107-108, 109.2, 110, 124, A127, 140.1, 149 | 11.00 | 17.50 |
| MS35 | 1982G (10) | 33,000 | KM105, 106a, 107-108, 109.2, 110, 124, A127, 140.1, 149 | 11.00 | 17.50 |
| MS36 | 1982J (10) | 33,000 | KM105, 106a, 107-108, 109.2, 110, 124, A127, 140.1, 149 | 11.00 | 17.50 |
| MS37 | 1983D (10) | 31,000 | KM105, 106a, 107-108, 109.2, 110, 124, A127, 140.1, 149 | 11.00 | 17.50 |
| MS38 | 1983F (10) | 31,000 | KM105, 106a, 107-108, 109.2, 110, 124, A127, 140.1, 149 | 11.00 | 17.50 |
| MS39 | 1983G (10) | 31,000 | KM105, 106a, 107-108, 109.2, 110, 124, A127, 140.1, 149 | 11.00 | 17.50 |
| MS40 | 1983J (10) | 31,000 | KM105, 106a, 107-108, 109.2, 110, 124, A127, 140.1, 149 | 11.00 | 17.50 |
| MS41 | 1984D (10) | 25,000 | KM105, 106a, 107-108, 109.2, 110, 124, A127, 140.1, 149 | 11.00 | 35.00 |
| MS42 | 1984F (10) | 25,000 | KM105, 106a, 107-108, 109.2, 110, 124, A127, 140.1, 149 | 11.00 | 35.00 |
| MS43 | 1984G (10) | 25,000 | KM105, 106a, 107-108, 109.2, 110, 124, A127, 140.1, 149 | 11.00 | 40.00 |
| MS44 | 1984J (10) | 25,000 | KM105, 106a, 107-108, 109.2, 110, 124, A127, 140.1, 149 | 11.00 | 35.00 |
| MS45 | 1985D (10) | 23,000 | KM105, 106a, 107-108, 109.2, 110, 124, A127, 140.1, 149 | 11.00 | 27.50 |
| MS46 | 1985F (10) | 23,000 | KM105, 106a, 107-108, 109.2, 110, 124, A127, 140.1, 149 | 11.00 | 27.50 |
| MS47 | 1985G (10) | 23,000 | KM105, 106a, 107-108, 109.2, 110, 124, A127, 140.1, 149 | 11.00 | 27.50 |
| MS48 | 1985J (10) | 23,000 | KM105, 106a, 107-108, 109.2, 110, 124, A127, 140.1, 149 | 11.00 | 27.50 |
| MS49 | 1986D (10) | 15,000 | KM105, 106a, 107-108, 109.2, 110, 124, A127, 140.1, 149 | 11.00 | 50.00 |
| MS50 | 1986F (10) | 15,000 | KM105, 106a, 107-108, 109.2, 110, 124, A127, 140.1, 149 | 11.00 | 50.00 |
| MS51 | 1986G (10) | 15,000 | KM105, 106a, 107-108, 109.2, 110, 124, A127, 140.1, 149 | 11.00 | 50.00 |
| MS52 | 1986J (10) | 15,000 | KM105, 106a, 107-108, 109.2, 110, 124, A127, 140.1, 149 | 11.00 | 50.00 |
| MS53 | 1987D (10) | 18,000 | KM105, 106a, 107-108, 109.2, 110, 124, A127, 140.1, 149 | 11.00 | 35.00 |
| MS54 | 1987F (10) | 18,000 | KM105, 106a, 107-108, 109.2, 110, 124, A127, 140.1, 149 | 11.00 | 35.00 |
| MS55 | 1987G (10) | 18,000 | KM105, 106a, 107-108, 109.2, 110, 124, A127, 140.1, 149 | 11.00 | 45.00 |
| MS56 | 1987J (10) | 18,000 | KM105, 106a, 107-108, 109.2, 110, 124, A127, 140.1, 149 | 11.00 | 35.00 |
| MS57 | 1988D (9) | 18,000 | KM105, 106a, 107-108, 109.2, 110, 140.1, 149, 170 | — | 27.50 |
| MS58 | 1988F (9) | 18,000 | KM105, 106a, 107-108, 109.2, 110, 140.1, 149, 170 | — | 27.50 |
| MS59 | 1988G (9) | 18,000 | KM105, 106a, 107-108, 109.2, 110, 140.1, 149, 170 | — | 27.50 |
| MS60 | 1988J (9) | 18,000 | KM105, 106a, 107-108, 109.2, 110, 140.1, 149, 170 | — | 27.50 |
| MS61 | 1989D (9) | 18,000 | KM105, 106a, 107-108, 109.2, 110, 140.1, 149, 170 | — | 27.50 |
| MS62 | 1989F (9) | 18,000 | KM105, 106a, 107-108, 109.2, 110, 140.1, 149, 170 | — | 27.50 |
| MS63 | 1989G (9) | 18,000 | KM105, 106a, 107-108, 109.2, 110, 140.1, 149, 170 | — | 27.50 |
| MS64 | 1989J (9) | 18,000 | KM105, 106a, 107-108, 109.2, 110, 140.1, 149, 170 | — | 27.50 |
| MS65 | 1990D (10) | 20,000 | KM105, 106a, 107-108, 109.2, 110, 140.1, 149, 170, 175 | — | 25.00 |
| MS66 | 1990F (10) | 20,000 | KM105, 106a, 107-108, 109.2, 110, 140.1, 149, 170, 175 | — | 25.00 |
| MS67 | 1990G (10) | 20,000 | KM105, 106a, 107-108, 109.2, 110, 140.1, 149, 170, 175 | — | 25.00 |
| MS68 | 1990J (10) | 20,000 | KM105, 106a, 107-108, 109.2, 110, 140.1, 149, 170, 175 | — | 25.00 |
| MS69 | 1991A (10) | 20,000 | KM105, 106a, 107-108, 109.2, 110, 140.1, 149, 170, 175 | — | 22.50 |
| MS70 | 1991D (10) | 20,000 | KM105, 106a, 107-108, 109.2, 110, 140.1, 149, 170, 175 | — | 22.50 |
| MS71 | 1991F (10) | 20,000 | KM105, 106a, 107-108, 109.2, 110, 140.1, 149, 170, 175 | — | 22.50 |
| MS72 | 1991G (10) | 20,000 | KM105, 106a, 107-108, 109.2, 110, 140.1, 149, 170, 175 | — | 22.50 |
| MS73 | 1991J (10) | 20,000 | KM105, 106a, 107-108, 109.2, 110, 140.1, 149, 170, 175 | — | 22.50 |
| MS74 | 1992A (10) | 20,000 | KM105, 106a, 107-108, 109.2, 110, 140.1, 149, 170, 175 | — | 22.50 |
| MS75 | 1992D (10) | 20,000 | KM105, 106a, 107-108, 109.2, 110, 140.1, 149, 170, 175 | — | 22.50 |
| MS76 | 1992F (10) | 20,000 | KM105, 106a, 107-108, 109.2, 110, 140.1, 149, 170, 175 | — | 22.50 |
| MS77 | 1992G (10) | 20,000 | KM105, 106a, 107-108, 109.2, 110, 140.1, 149, 170, 175 | — | 22.50 |
| MS78 | 1992J (10) | 20,000 | KM105, 106a, 107-108, 109.2, 110, 140.1, 149, 170, 175 | — | 22.50 |
| MS79 | 1993A (10) | 20,000 | KM105, 106a, 107-108, 109.2, 110, 140.1, 149, 170, 175 | — | 40.00 |
| MS80 | 1993D (10) | 20,000 | KM105, 106a, 107-108, 109.2, 110, 140.1, 149, 170, 175 | — | 40.00 |
| MS81 | 1993F (10) | 20,000 | KM105, 106a, 107-108, 109.2, 110, 140.1, 149, 170, 175 | — | 40.00 |
| MS82 | 1993G (10) | 20,000 | KM105, 106a, 107-108, 109.2, 110, 140.1, 149, 170, 175 | — | 40.00 |
| MS83 | 1993J (10) | 20,000 | KM105, 106a, 107-108, 109.2, 110, 140.1, 149, 170, 175 | — | 40.00 |
| MS84 | 1994A (10) | 10,000 | KM105, 106A, 107-108, 109.2, 110, 140.1, 170, 175, 183 | — | 37.50 |
| MS85 | 1994D (10) | 20,000 | KM105, 106a, 107-108, 109.2, 110, 140.1, 170, 175, 183 | — | 37.50 |
| MS86 | 1994F (10) | 20,000 | KM105, 106a, 107-108, 109.2, 110, 140.1, 170, 175, 183 | — | 37.50 |
| MS87 | 1994G (10) | 20,000 | KM105, 106a, 107-108, 109.2, 110, 140.1, 170, 175, 183 | — | 37.50 |
| MS88 | 1994J (10) | 20,000 | KM105, 106a, 107-108, 109.2, 110, 140.1, 170, 175, 183 | — | 37.50 |
| MS89 | 1995A (10) | 20,000 | KM105, 106a, 107-108, 109.2, 110, 140.1, 170, 175, 183 | — | 175 |
| MS90 | 1995D (10) | 20,000 | KM105, 106a, 107-108, 109.2, 110, 140.1, 170, 175, 183 | — | 335 |
| MS91 | 1995F (10) | 20,000 | KM105, 106a, 107-108, 109.2, 110, 140.1, 170, 175, 183 | — | 425 |
| MS92 | 1995G (10) | 20,000 | KM105, 106a, 107-108, 109.2, 110, 140.1, 170, 175, 183 | — | 265 |
| MS93 | 1995J (10) | 20,000 | KM105, 106A, 107-108, 109.2, 110, 140.1, 170, 175, 183 | — | 260 |
| MS94 | 1996A (10) | 50,000 | KM105, 106a, 107-108, 109.2, 110, 140.1, 170, 175, 183 | — | 55.00 |
| MS95 | 1996D (10) | 50,000 | KM105, 106a, 107-108, 109.2, 110, 140.1, 170, 175, 183 | — | 55.00 |
| MS96 | 1996F (10) | 50,000 | KM105, 106a, 107-108, 109.2, 110, 140.1, 170, 175, 183 | — | 55.00 |
| MS97 | 1996G (10) | 50,000 | KM105, 106a, 107-108, 109.2, 110, 140.1, 170, 175, 183 | — | 55.00 |
| MS98 | 1996J (10) | 50,000 | KM105, 106a, 107-108, 109.2, 110, 140.1, 170, 175, 183 | — | 55.00 |
| MS99 | 1997A (9) | 70,000 | KM105, 106a, 108, 109.2, 110, 140.1, 170, 175, 183 | — | 35.00 |
| MS100 | 1997D (10) | 70,000 | KM105, 106a, 107-108, 109.2, 110, 140.1, 170, 175, 183 | — | 35.00 |
| MS101 | 1997F (10) | 70,000 | KM105, 106a, 107-108, 109.2, 110, 140.1, 170, 175, 183 | — | 35.00 |
| MS102 | 1997G (10) | 70,000 | KM105, 106a, 107-108, 109.2, 110, 140.1, 170, 175, 183 | — | 35.00 |
| MS103 | 1997J (10) | 70,000 | KM105, 106a, 107-108, 109.2, 110, 140.1, 170, 175, 183 | — | 35.00 |
| MS104 | 1998A (10) | 70,000 | KM105, 106a, 107-108, 109.2, 110, 140.1, 170, 175, 183 | — | 35.00 |
| MS105 | 1998D (10) | 70,000 | KM105, 106a, 107-108, 109.2, 110, 140.1, 170, 175, 183 | — | 35.00 |
| MS107 | 1998G (10) | 70,000 | KM105, 106a, 107-108, 109.2, 110, 140.1, 170, 175, 183 | — | 35.00 |
| MS108 | 1998J (10) | 70,000 | KM105, 106a, 107-108, 109.2, 110, 140.1, 170, 175, 183 | — | 35.00 |
| MS109 | 1999A (10) | 70,000 | KM105, 106a, 107-108, 109.2, 110, 140.1, 170, 175, 183 | — | 35.00 |
| MS110 | 1999D (10) | 70,000 | km105, 106A, 107-108, 109.2, 110, 140.1, 170, 175, 183 | — | 35.00 |
| MS112 | 1999G (10) | 70,000 | KM105, 106a, 107-108, 109.2, 110, 140.1, 170, 175, 183 | — | 35.00 |
| MS114 | 1999J (10) | 70,000 | KM105, 106a, 107-108, 109.2, 110, 140.1, 170, 175, 183 | — | 35.00 |
| MS115 | 2000D (10) | 20,000 | KM105, 106a, 107-108, 109.2, 110, 140.1, 170, 175, 183 | — | 40.00 |
| MS116 | 2000F (10) | 20,000 | KM105, 160a, 107-108, 109.2, 110, 140.1, 170, 175, 183 | — | 40.00 |
| MS117 | 2000G (10) | 20,000 | KM105, 106a, 107-108, 109.2, 110, 140.1, 170, 175, 183 | — | 40.00 |
| MS118 | 2000J (10) | 20,000 | KM105, 106a, 107-108, 109.2, 110, 140.1, 170, 175, 183 | — | 40.00 |
| MS119 | 2001A (10) | 130,000 | KM105,106a,107-108,109.2,110,140.1,170,175,183 | — | 30.00 |
| MS120 | 2001D (10) | 130,000 | KM105,106a,107-108,109.2,110,140.1,170,175,183 | — | 30.00 |
| MS121 | 2001F (10) | 130,000 | KM105,106a,107-108,109.2,110,140.1,170,175,183 | — | 30.00 |
| MS122 | 2001G (10) | 130,000 | KM105,106a,107-108,109.2,110,140.1,170,175,183 | — | 30.00 |
| MS123 | 2001J (10) | 130,000 | KM105,106a,107-108,109.2,110,140.1,170,175,183 | — | 30.00 |
| MS124 | 2002A (8) | — | KM#207-214 | — | 20.00 |
| MS125 | 2002D (8) | — | KM#207-214 | — | 20.00 |
| MS126 | 2002F (8) | — | KM#207-214 | — | 20.00 |
| MS127 | 2002G (8) | — | KM#207-214 | — | 20.00 |
| MS128 | 2002J (8) | — | KM#207-214 | — | 20.00 |

## PROOF SETS

| KM# | Date | Mintage | Identification | Issue Price | Mkt Val |
|---|---|---|---|---|---|
| PS1 | 1950-64G (8) | 600 | KM105-108, 109.1, 110, 112.1, 116 | — | 500 |
| PS2 | 1950-65F (8) | 300 | KM105-108, 109.1, 110, 112.1, 116 | — | 1,500 |
| PS3 | 1950-65G (8) | 8,233 | KM105-108, 109.1, 110, 112.1, 116 | — | 85.00 |
| PS76 | 1985D | 56,000 | MK#105, 106a, 107-108, 109.2, 110, 124, A127, 140.1, 149 | 15.00 | 25.00 |
| PS4 | 1966F (8) | 450 | KM105-108, 109.1, 110, 112.1, 116 | — | 2,000 |
| PS5 | 1966G (8) | 3,070 | KM105-108, 109.1, 110, 112.1, 116 | — | 175 |
| PS6 | 1966J (8) | 1,000 | KM105-108, 109.1, 110, 112.1, 116 | — | 450 |
| PS9 | 1967G (8) | 520 | KM105, 106a*, 107-108, 109.1, 110, 112.1, 116 | — | 1,600 |
| PS7 | 1967F (8) | 1,600 | KM105-108, 109.1, 110, 112.1, 116 | — | 350 |
| PS8 | 1967G (8) | 3,630 | KM105-108, 109.1, 110, 112.1, 116 | — | 175 |
| PS10 | 1967J (8) | 1,500 | KM105, 106a, 107-108, 109.1, 110, 112.1, 116 | — | 450 |
| PS11 | 1968F (8) | 3,000 | KM105, 106a, 107-108, 109.1, 110, 112.1, 116 | — | 350 |
| PS12 | 1968G (8) | 3,651 | KM105, 106, 107-108, 109.1, 110, 112.1, 116 | — | 175 |
| PS12a | 1968G (8) | 2,372 | KM105, 106a, 107-108, 109.1, 110, 112.1, 116 | — | 225 |
| PS13 | 1968J (8) | 2,000 | KM105, 106a, 107-108, 109.1, 110, 112.1, 116 | — | 375 |
| PS14 | 1969F (8) | 5,000 | KM105, 106a, 107-108, 109.1, 110, 112.1, 116 | — | 100 |
| PS15 | 1969G (8) | 8,700 | KM105, 106a, 107-108, 109.1, 110, 112.1, 116 | — | 85.00 |
| PS16 | 1969J (8) | 5,000 | KM105, 106a, 107-108, 109.1, 110, 112.1, 116 | — | 100 |
| PS17 | 1970F (8) | 5,140 | KM105, 106a, 107-108, 109.1, 110, 112.1, 116 | — | 100 |
| PS18 | 1970G (8) | 10,200 | KM105, 106a, 107-108, 109.1, 110, 112.1, 116 | — | 80.00 |
| PS19 | 1970J (8) | 5,000 | KM105, 106a, 107-108, 109.1, 110, 112.1, 116 | — | 90.00 |
| PS20 | 1971D (8) | 8,000 | KM105, 106a, 107-108, 109.1, 110, 112.1, 116 | — | 95.00 |
| PS21 | 1971F (8) | 8,000 | KM105, 106a, 107-108, 109.1, 110, 112.1, 116 | — | 90.00 |
| PS22 | 1971G (8) | 10,200 | KM105, 106a, 107-108, 109.1, 110, 112.1, 116 | — | 90.00 |
| PS23 | 1971J (8) | 8,000 | KM105, 106a, 107-108, 109.1, 110, 112.1, 116 | — | 95.00 |
| PS24 | 1972D (9) | 8,000 | KM105, 106a, 107-108, 109.2, 110, 112.1, 124, A127 | — | 95.00 |
| PS25 | 1972F (9) | 8,000 | KM105, 106a, 107-108, 109.2, 110, 112.1, 124, A127 | — | 95.00 |
| PS26 | 1972G (9) | 10,000 | KM105, 106a, 107-108, 109.2, 110, 112.1, 124, A127 | — | 85.00 |
| PS27 | 1972J (9) | 8,000 | KM105, 106a, 107-108, 109.2, 110, 112.1, 124, A127 | — | 85.00 |
| PS28 | 1973D (9) | 9,000 | KM105, 106a, 107-108, 109.2, 110, 112.1, 124, A127 | — | 85.00 |
| PS29 | 1973F (9) | 9,000 | KM105, 106a, 107-108, 109.2, 110, 112.1, 124, A127 | — | 85.00 |
| PS30 | 1973G (9) | 9,000 | KM105, 106a, 107-108, 109.2, 110, 112.1, 124, A127 | — | 85.00 |
| PS31 | 1973J (9) | 9,000 | KM105, 106a, 107-108, 109.2, 110, 112.1, 124, A127 | — | 85.00 |
| PS32 | 1974D (9) | 35,000 | KM105, 106a, 107-108, 109.2, 110,112.1, 124, A127 | 10.00 | 30.00 |
| PS33 | 1974F (9) | 35,000 | KM105, 106a, 107-108, 109.2, 110, 112.1, 124, A127 | 10.00 | 30.00 |
| PS34 | 1974G (9) | 35,000 | KM105, 106a, 107-108, 109.2, 110, 112.1, 124, A127 | 10.00 | 30.00 |
| PS35 | 1974J (9) | 35,000 | KM105, 106a, 107-108, 109.2, 110, 112.1, 124, A127 | 10.00 | 30.00 |
| PS36 | 1975D (9) | 43,120 | KM105, 106a, 107-108, 109.2, 110, 124, A127, 140.1 | 10.00 | 20.00 |
| PS37 | 1975F (9) | 43,100 | KM105, 106a, 107-108, 109.2, 110, 124, A127, 140.1 | 10.00 | 20.00 |
| PS38 | 1975G (9) | 43,100 | KM105, 106a, 107-108, 109.2, 110, 124, A127, 140.1 | 10.00 | 20.00 |
| PS39 | 1975J (9) | 43,120 | KM105, 106a, 107-108, 109.2, 110, 124, A127, 140.1 | 10.00 | 20.00 |
| PS40 | 1976D (9) | 43,120 | KM105, 106a, 107-108, 109.2, 110, 124, A127,140.1 | 10.00 | 20.00 |
| PS41 | 1976F (9) | 43,100 | KM105, 106a, 107-108, 109.2, 110, 124, A127, 140.1 | 10.00 | 20.00 |
| PS42 | 1976G (9) | 43,100 | KM105, 106a, 107-108, 109.2, 110, 124, A127, 140.1 | 10.00 | 20.00 |
| PS43 | 1976J (9) | 43,120 | KM105, 106a, 107-108, 109.2, 110, 124, A127, 140.1 | 10.00 | 20.00 |
| PS44 | 1977D (9) | 50,620 | KM105, 106a, 107-108, 109.2, 110, 124, A127, 140.1 | 12.50 | 17.50 |
| PS45 | 1977F (9) | 50,600 | KM105, 106a, 107-108, 109.2, 110, 124, A127, 140.1 | 12.50 | 17.50 |
| PS46 | 1977G (9) | 50,600 | KM105, 106a, 107-108, 109.2, 110, 124, A127, 140.1 | 12.50 | 17.50 |
| PS47 | 1977J (9) | 50,620 | KM105, 106a, 107-108, 109.2, 110, 124, A127, 140.1 | 12.50 | 17.50 |
| PS48 | 1978D (9) | 54,000 | KM105, 106A, 107-108, 109.2, 110, 124, A127, 140.1 | 13.00 | 17.50 |
| PS49 | 1978F (9) | 54,000 | KM105, 106a, 107-108, 109.2, 110, 124, A127, 140.1 | 13.00 | 17.50 |
| PS50 | 1978G (9) | 54,000 | KM105, 106a, 107-108, 109.2, 110, 124, A127, 140.1 | 13.00 | 17.50 |

| KM# | Date | Mintage | Identification | Issue Price | Mkt Val |
|---|---|---|---|---|---|
| PS51 | 1978J (9) | 54,000 | KM105, 106a, 107-108, 109.2, 110, 124, A127, 140.1 | 13.00 | 17.50 |
| PS52 | 1979D (10) | 89,000 | KM105, 106a, 107-108, 109.2, 110, 124, A127, 140.1, 149 | 15.00 | 17.50 |
| PS53 | 1979F (10) | 89,000 | KM105, 106a, 107-108, 109.2, 110, 124, A127, 140.1, 149 | 15.00 | 17.50 |
| PS54 | 1979G (10) | 89,000 | KM105, 106a, 107-108, 109.2, 110, 124, A127, 140.1, 149 | 15.00 | 17.50 |
| PS55 | 1979J (10) | 89,000 | KM105, 106a, 107-108, 109.2, 110, 124, A127, 140.1, 149 | 15.00 | 17.50 |
| PS56 | 1980D (10) | 60,000 | KM105, 106a, 107-108, 109.2, 110, 124, A127, 140.1, 149 | 15.00 | 17.50 |
| PS57 | 1980F (10) | 60,000 | KM105, 106a, 107-108, 109.2, 110, 124, A127, 140.1, 149 | 15.00 | 17.50 |
| PS58 | 1980G (10) | 60,000 | KM105, 106a, 107-108, 109.2, 110, 124, A127, 140.1, 149 | 15.00 | 17.50 |
| PS59 | 1980J (10) | 60,000 | KM105, 106a, 107-108, 109.2, 110, 124, A127, 140.1, 149 | 15.00 | 17.50 |
| PS60 | 1981D (10) | 60,000 | KM105, 106a, 107-108, 109.2, 110, 124, A127, 140.1, 149 | 15.00 | 17.50 |
| PS61 | 1981F (10) | 91,000 | KM105, 106a, 107-108, 109.2, 110, 124, A127, 140.1, 149 | 15.00 | 17.50 |
| PS62 | 1981G (10) | 91,000 | KM105, 106a, 107-108, 109.2, 110, 124, A127, 140.1, 149 | 15.00 | 17.50 |
| PS63 | 1981J (10) | 78,000 | KM105, 106a, 107-108, 109.2, 110, 124, A127, 140.1, 149 | 15.00 | 17.50 |
| PS64 | 1982D (10) | 78,000 | KM105, 106a, 107-108, 109.2, 110, 124, A127, 140.1, 149 | 15.00 | 17.50 |
| PS65 | 1982F (10) | 78,000 | KM105, 106a,107-108, 109.2, 110, 124, A127, 140.1, 149 | 15.00 | 17.50 |
| PS66 | 1982G (10) | 78,000 | KM105, 106a, 107-108, 109.2, 110, 124, A127, 140.1, 149 | 15.00 | 17.50 |
| PS67 | 1982J (10) | 78,000 | KM105, 106a, 107-108, 109.2, 110, 124, A127, 140.1, 149 | 15.00 | 17.50 |
| PS68 | 1983D (10) | 75,000 | KM105, 106a, 107-108, 109.2, 110, 124, A127, 140.1, 149 | 15.00 | 17.50 |
| PS69 | 1983F (10) | 75,000 | KM105, 106a, 107-108, 109.2, 110, 124, A127, 140.1, 149 | 15.00 | 17.50 |
| PS70 | 1983G (10) | 75,000 | KM105, 106a, 107-108, 109.2, 110, 124, A127, 140.1, 149 | 15.00 | 17.50 |
| PS71 | 1983J (10) | 75,000 | KM105, 106a, 107-108, 109.2, 110, 124, A127, 140.1, 149 | 15.00 | 17.50 |
| PS72 | 1984D (10) | 64,000 | KM105, 106a, 107-108, 109.2, 110, 124, A127, 140.1, 149 | 15.00 | 26.50 |
| PS73 | 1984F (10) | 64,000 | KM105, 106a, 107-108, 109.2, 110, 124, A127, 140.1, 149 | 15.00 | 26.50 |
| PS74 | 1984G (10) | 64,000 | KM105, 106a, 107-108, 109.2, 110, 124, A127, 140.1, 149 | 15.00 | 26.50 |
| PS75 | 1985D (10) | 56,000 | KM105, 106a, 107-108, 109.2, 110, 124, A127, 140.1, 149 | 15.00 | 26.50 |
| PS77 | 1985F (10) | 54,000 | KM105, 106a, 107-108, 109.2, 110, 124, A127, 140.1, 149 | 15.00 | 25.00 |
| PS78 | 1985G (10) | 55,000 | KM105, 106a, 107-108, 109.2, 110, 124, A127, 140.1, 149 | 15.00 | 25.00 |
| PS79 | 1985J (10) | 54,000 | KM105, 106a, 107-108, 109.2, 110, 124, A127, 140.1, 149 | 15.00 | 25.00 |
| PS80 | 1986D (10) | 44,000 | KM105, 106a, 107-108, 109.2, 110, 124, A127, 140.1, 149 | 15.00 | 27.50 |
| PS81 | 1986F (10) | 44,000 | KM105, 106a, 107-108, 109.2, 110, 124, A127, 140.1, 149 | 15.00 | 27.50 |
| PS82 | 1986G (10) | 44,000 | KM105, 106a, 107-108, 109.2, 110, 124, A127, 140.1, 149 | 15.00 | 27.50 |
| PS83 | 1986J (10) | 44,000 | KM105, 106a, 107-108, 109.2, 110, 124, A127, 140.1, 149 | 15.00 | 27.50 |
| PS84 | 1987D (10) | 45,000 | KM105, 106a, 107-108, 109.2, 110, 124, A127, 140.1, 149 | 15.00 | 25.00 |
| PS85 | 1987F (10) | 45,000 | KM105, 106a, 107-108, 109.2, 110, 124, A127, 140.1, 149 | 15.00 | 25.00 |
| PS86 | 1987G (10) | 45,000 | KM105, 106a, 107-108, 109.2, 110, 124, A127, 140.1, 149 | 15.00 | 25.00 |
| PS87 | 1987J (10) | 45,000 | KM105, 106a, 107-108, 109.2, 110, 124, A127, 140.1, 149 | 15.00 | 25.00 |
| PS88 | 1988D (9) | 45,000 | KM105, 106a, 107-108, 109.2, 110, 140.1, 149, 170 | — | 25.00 |
| PS89 | 1988F (9) | 45,000 | KM105, 106a, 107-108, 109.2, 110, 140.1, 149, 170 | — | 25.00 |
| PS90 | 1988G (9) | 45,000 | KM105, 106a, 107-108, 109.2, 110, 140.1, 149, 170 | — | 25.00 |
| PS91 | 1988J (9) | 45,000 | KM105, 106a, 107-108, 109.2, 110, 140.1, 149, 170 | — | 25.00 |
| PS92 | 1989D (9) | 45,000 | KM105, 106a, 107-108, 109.2, 110, 140.1, 149, 170 | — | 25.00 |
| PS93 | 1989F (9) | 45,000 | KM105, 106a, 107-108, 109.2, 110, 140.1, 149, 170 | — | 25.00 |
| PS94 | 1989G (9) | 45,000 | KM105-106a, 107-108, 109.2, 110, 140.1, 149, 170 | — | 25.00 |
| PS95 | 1989J (9) | 45,000 | KM105-106a, 107-108, 109.2, 110, 140.1, 149, 170 | — | 25.00 |
| PS96 | 1990D (10) | 45,000 | KM105, 106a, 107-108, 109.2, 110, 140.1, 149, 170, 175 | — | 25.00 |
| PS97 | 1990F (10) | 45,000 | KM105, 106a, 107-108, 109.2, 110, 140.1, 149, 170, 175 | — | 25.00 |
| PS98 | 1990G (10) | 45,000 | KM105,106a,107-180,109.2,110,140.1,149, 170,175 | — | 25.00 |
| PS99 | 1990J (10) | 45,000 | KM105,106a,107-108,109.2,110,140.1,149, 170,175 | — | 25.00 |
| PS100 | 1991A (10) | 45,000 | KM105,106a,107-108,109.2,110,140.1,149, 170,175 | — | 27.50 |
| PS101 | 1991D (10) | 45,000 | KM105,106a,107-108,109.2,110,140.1,149, 170,175 | — | 27.50 |
| PS102 | 1991F (10) | 45,000 | KM105,106a,107-108,109.2,110,140.1,149, 170,175 | — | 27.50 |
| PS103 | 1991G (10) | 45,000 | KM105,106a,107-108,109.2,110,140.1,149, 170,175 | — | 27.50 |
| PS104 | 1991J (10) | 45,000 | KM105,106a,107-108,109.2,110,140.1,149, 170,175 | — | 27.50 |
| PS105 | 1992A (10) | 45,000 | KM105,106a,107-108,109.2,110,140.1,149, 170,175 | — | 27.50 |
| PS106 | 1992D (10) | 45,000 | KM105,106a,107-108,109.2,110,140.1,149, 170,175 | — | 27.50 |
| PS107 | 1992F (10) | 45,000 | KM105,106a,107-108,109.2,110,140.1,149, 170,175 | — | 27.50 |
| PS108 | 1992G (10) | 45,000 | KM105,106a,107,108,109. 2,110,140.1,149,170,175 | — | 27.50 |
| PS109 | 1992J (10) | 45,000 | KM105,106a,107-108,109.2,110,140.1,149, 170,175 | — | 27.50 |
| PS110 | 1993A (10) | 45,000 | KM105,106a,107-108,109.2,110,140.1,149, 170,175 | — | 35.00 |
| PS111 | 1993D (10) | 45,000 | KM105,106a,107-108,109.2,110,140.1,149, 170,175 | — | 35.00 |
| PS112 | 1993F (10) | 45,000 | KM105,106a,107-108,109.2,110,140.1,149, 170,175 | — | 35.00 |
| PS113 | 1993J (10) | 45,000 | KM105,106a,107-108,109.2,110,140.1,149, 170,175 | — | 35.00 |
| PS114 | 1993J | 45,000 | KM105,106a,107-108,109.2,110,140.1,149, 170,175 | — | 35.00 |
| PS115 | 1994A (10) | 45,000 | KM105,106a,107-108,109.2,110,140.1,170, 175,183 | — | 35.00 |
| PS116 | 1994D (10) | 45,000 | KM105,106a,107-108,109.2,110,140.1,170, 175,183 | — | 35.00 |
| PS117 | 1994F (10) | 45,000 | KM105,106a,107-108,109.2,110,140,1,170, 175,183 | — | 35.00 |
| PS118 | 1994G (10) | 45,000 | KM105,106a,107-108,109.2,110,140.1,170, 175,183 | — | 35.00 |
| PS119 | 1994J (10) | 45,000 | KM105,106a,107-108,109.2,110,140.1,170, 175,183 | — | 35.00 |
| PS120 | 1995A (10) | 45,000 | KM105,106a,107-108,109.2,110,140.1,170, 175,183 | — | 115 |
| PS121 | 1995D (10) | 45,000 | KM105,106a,107-108,109.2,110,140.1,170, 175,183 | — | 115 |
| PS123 | 1995G (10) | 45,000 | KM105,106a,107-108,109.2,110,140.1,170, 175,183 | — | 115 |
| PS122 | 1995F (10) | 45,000 | KM105,106a,107-108,109.2,110,140.1,170, 175,183 | — | 115 |
| PS124 | 1995J (10) | 45,000 | KM105,106a,107-108,109.2,110,140.1,170, 175,183 | — | 115 |
| PS125 | 1996A (10) | 45,000 | KM105,106a,107-108,109.2,110,140.1,170, 175,183 | — | 60.00 |
| PS126 | 1996D (10) | 45,000 | KM105,106a,107-108,109.2,110,140.1,170, 175,183 | — | 60.00 |
| PS127 | 1996F (10) | 45,000 | KM105,106a,107-108,109.2,110,140.1,170, 175,183 | — | 60.00 |
| PS128 | 1996G (10) | 45,000 | KM105,106a,107-108,109.2,110,140.1,170, 175,183 | — | 60.00 |
| PS129 | 1996J (10) | 45,000 | KM105,106a,107-108,109.2,110,140.1,170, 175,183 | — | 60.00 |
| PS130 | 1997A (10) | 45,000 | KM105,106a,107-108,109.2,110,140.1,170, 175,183 | — | 37.50 |
| PS131 | 1997D (10) | 45,000 | KM105,106a,107-108,109.2,110,140.1,170, 175,183 | — | 37.50 |
| PS132 | 1997F (10) | 45,000 | KM105,106a,107-108,109.2,11o,140.1,170, 175,183 | — | 37.50 |
| PS133 | 1997G (10) | 45,000 | KM105,106a,107-108,109.2,110,140.1,170, 175,183 | — | 37.50 |
| PS134 | 1997J (10) | 45,000 | KM105,106a,107-108,109.2,110,140.1,170, 175,183 | — | 37.50 |
| PS135 | 1998A (10) | 45,000 | KM105,106a,107-108,109.2,110,140.1,170, 175,183 | — | 37.50 |
| PS136 | 1998D (10) | 45,000 | KM105,106a,107-108,109.2,110,140.1,170, 175,183 | — | 37.50 |
| PS137 | 1998F (10) | 45,000 | KM105,106a,107-108,109.2,110,140.1,170, 175,183 | — | 37.50 |
| PS142 | 1999F (10) | 45,000 | KM105,106a,107-108,109.2,110,140.1,170, 175,183 | — | 37.50 |
| PS138 | 1998G (10) | 45,000 | KM105,106a,107-108,109.2,110,140.1,170, 175,183 | — | 37.50 |
| PS139 | 1998J (10) | 45,000 | KM105,106a,107-108,109.2,110,140.1,170, 175,183 | — | 37.50 |
| PS144 | 1999J (10) | 45,000 | KM105,106a,107-108,109.2,110,140.1,170, 175,183 | — | 50.00 |
| PS140 | 1999A (10) | 45,000 | KM105,106a,107-108,109.2,110,140.1,170, 175,183 | — | 37.50 |
| PS141 | 1999D (10) | 45,000 | KM105,106a,107-108,109.2,110,140.1,170, 175,183 | — | 37.50 |
| PS143 | 1999G (10) | 45,000 | KM105,106a,107-108,109.2,110,140.1,170, 175,183 | — | 37.50 |
| PS145 | 2000A (10) | 45,000 | KM105,106a,107-108,109.2,110,140.1,170, 175,183 | — | 50.00 |
| PS146 | 2000D (10) | 45,000 | KM105,106a,107-108,109.2,110,140.1,170, 175,183 | — | 50.00 |
| PS147 | 2000F (10) | 45,000 | KM105,106a,107,108,109. 2,110,140.1,170,175,183 | — | 50.00 |
| PS148 | 2000G (10) | 45,000 | KM105,106a,107-108,109.2,110,140.1,170, 175,183 | — | 50.00 |
| PS149 | 2000J (10) | 45,000 | KM105,106a,107-108,109.2,110,140.1,170, 175,183 | — | 50.00 |
| PS150 | 2001A (10) | 78,000 | KM105,106a,107-108,109.2,110,140.1,170, 175,183 | — | 65.00 |
| PS151 | 2001D (10) | 78,000 | KM105,106a,107-108,109.2,110,140.1,170, 175,183 | — | 65.00 |
| PS152 | 2001F (10) | 78,000 | KM105,106a,107-108,110,140.1,170,175,1 83 | — | 65.00 |
| PS153 | 2001G (10) | 78,000 | KM105,106a,107-108,109.2,110,140.1,170, 175,183 | — | 65.00 |
| PS154 | 2001J (10) | 78,000 | KM105,106a,107-108,109.2,110,140.1,170, 175,183 | — | 65.00 |
| PS155 | 2002A (8) | — | KM#207-214 | — | 25.00 |
| PS156 | 2002D (8) | — | KM#207-214 | — | 25.00 |
| PS157 | 2002F (8) | — | KM#207-214 | — | 25.00 |
| PS158 | 2002G (8) | — | KM#207-214 | — | 25.00 |
| PS159 | 2002J (8) | — | KM#207-214 | — | 25.00 |

**1949-1990**

The German Democratic Republic, formerly East Germany, was located on the great north European plain, had an area of 41,768 sq. mi. (108,330 sq. km.) and a population of 16.6 million. The figures included East Berlin, which had been incorporated into the G.D.R. Capital: East Berlin. The economy was highly industrialized. Machinery, transport equipment chemicals, and lignite were exported.

During the closing days of World War II in Europe, Soviet troops advancing into Germany from the east occupied the German provinces of Mecklenburg, Brandenburg, Lusatia, Saxony and Thuringia. These five provinces comprised the occupation zone administered by the Soviet Union after the cessation of hostilities. The other three zones were administered by the U.S., Great Britain and France. Under the Potsdam agreement, questions affecting Germany as a whole were to be settled by the commanders of the occupation zones acting jointly and by unanimous decision. When Soviet intransigence rendered the quadripartite commission inoperable, the three western zones were united to form the Federal Republic of Germany, May 23, 1949. Thereupon the Soviet Union dissolved its occupation zone and established it as the Democratic Republic of Germany, Oct. 7, 1949.

The post-WW II division of Germany was ended Oct. 3,1990, when the German Democratic Republic (East Germany) ceased to exist and its five constituent provinces were formally admitted to the Federal Republic of Germany. An election Dec. 2, 1990, chose representatives to the united federal parliament (Bundestag), which then conducted its opening session in Berlin in the old Reichstag building. Although Berlin technically is the capital of the reunited Germany, the actual seat of government remains for the time being in Bonn.

**MINT MARKS**

A - Berlin
E - Muldenhutten

**MONETARY SYSTEM**

100 Pfennig = 1 Mark

# DEMOCRATIC REPUBLIC

## STANDARD COINAGE

**PFENNIG** **KM# 1** **Composition:** Aluminum

| Date | Mintage | F | VF | XF | Unc | BU |
|---|---|---|---|---|---|---|
| 1948A | 243,000,000 | — | 1.00 | 8.00 | 35.00 | — |
| 1949A | Inc. above | — | 1.00 | 8.00 | 35.00 | — |
| 1949E | 55,200,000 | — | 11.50 | 45.00 | 300 | — |
| 1950A | — | — | 1.00 | 8.00 | 35.00 | — |
| 1950E | — | — | 7.50 | 20.00 | 100 | — |

**PFENNIG** **KM# 5** **Composition:** Aluminum

| Date | Mintage | F | VF | XF | Unc | BU |
|---|---|---|---|---|---|---|
| 1952A | 297,213,000 | — | 0.50 | 1.75 | 6.00 | — |
| 1952E | 49,296,000 | — | 5.00 | 12.00 | 55.00 | — |
| 1953A | 114,002,000 | — | 0.50 | 1.75 | 6.00 | — |
| 1953E | 50,876,000 | — | 5.00 | 15.00 | 60.00 | — |

**PFENNIG** **KM# 8.1** **Composition:** Aluminum

| Date | Mintage | F | VF | XF | Unc | BU |
|---|---|---|---|---|---|---|
| 1960A | 101,808,000 | — | 0.25 | 0.75 | 3.50 | — |
| 1961A | 101,776,000 | — | 0.25 | 0.75 | 3.50 | — |
| 1962A | 81,459,000 | — | 0.25 | 0.75 | 3.50 | — |
| 1963A | 101,402,000 | — | 0.25 | 0.75 | 3.50 | — |
| 1964A | 98,967,000 | — | 0.25 | 0.75 | 3.50 | — |
| 1965A | 38,585,000 | — | 3.00 | 15.00 | 35.00 | — |
| 1968A | 813,680,000 | — | 0.25 | 0.75 | 2.50 | — |
| 1972A | 4,801,000 | — | 2.00 | 10.00 | 25.00 | — |
| 1973A | 5,518,000 | — | 1.50 | 8.00 | 22.50 | — |
| 1975A | 202,752,000 | — | 0.25 | 0.75 | 2.50 | — |

**PFENNIG** **KM# 8.2** **Composition:** Aluminum **Obverse:** Smaller design features **Reverse:** Small design features

| Date | Mintage | F | VF | XF | Unc | BU |
|---|---|---|---|---|---|---|
| 1977A | 61,560,000 | — | 0.10 | 0.25 | 2.00 | — |
| 1978A | 200,050,000 | — | 0.10 | 0.20 | 0.50 | — |
| 1979A | 100,640,000 | — | 0.10 | 0.20 | 0.50 | — |
| 1979A Proof | — | Value: 45.00 | | | | |
| 1980A | 153,000,000 | — | 0.10 | 0.20 | 0.50 | — |
| 1980A Proof | — | Value: 45.00 | | | | |
| 1981A | 200,436,000 | — | 0.10 | 0.20 | 0.50 | — |
| 1981A Proof | 40 | — | — | — | — | — |
| 1982A | 99,200,000 | — | 0.10 | 0.20 | 0.50 | — |
| 1982A Proof | 2,500 | Value: 10.00 | | | | |
| 1983A | 150,000,000 | — | 0.10 | 0.20 | 0.50 | — |
| 1983A Proof | 2,550 | Value: 18.00 | | | | |
| 1984A | 137,600,000 | — | 0.10 | 0.20 | 0.50 | — |
| 1984A Proof | 3,015 | Value: 4.50 | | | | |
| 1985A | 125,060,000 | — | 0.10 | 0.20 | 0.50 | — |
| 1985A Proof | 2,816 | Value: 4.50 | | | | |
| 1986A | 73,900,000 | — | 0.10 | 0.20 | 0.50 | — |
| 1986A Proof | 2,800 | Value: 4.50 | | | | |
| 1987A | 50,015,000 | — | 0.10 | 0.20 | 0.50 | — |
| 1987A Proof | 2,345 | Value: 4.50 | | | | |
| 1988A | 75,450,000 | — | 0.10 | 0.20 | 0.50 | — |
| 1988A Proof | 2,300 | Value: 4.50 | | | | |
| 1989A | 84,410,000 | — | 0.10 | 0.20 | 0.50 | — |
| 1989A Proof | 2,300 | Value: 4.50 | | | | |
| 1990A | 15,670,000 | — | 0.10 | 0.20 | 2.00 | — |

**5 PFENNIG** **KM# 2** **Composition:** Aluminum

| Date | Mintage | F | VF | XF | Unc | BU |
|---|---|---|---|---|---|---|
| 1948A | 205,072,000 | — | 2.50 | 5.50 | 50.00 | — |
| 1949A | Inc. above | — | 2.50 | 5.50 | 45.00 | — |
| 1950A | Inc. above | — | 2.50 | 5.50 | 35.00 | — |

**5 PFENNIG** **KM# 6** **Composition:** Aluminum

| Date | Mintage | F | VF | XF | Unc | BU |
|---|---|---|---|---|---|---|
| 1952A | 113,397,000 | — | 2.00 | 5.00 | 12.50 | — |
| 1952E | 24,024,000 | — | 3.50 | 8.00 | 35.00 | — |
| 1953A | 40,994,000 | — | 2.00 | 5.00 | 17.50 | — |
| 1953E | 28,665,000 | — | 5.00 | 17.50 | 90.00 | — |

**5 PFENNIG** **KM# 9.1** **Composition:** Aluminum

| Date | Mintage | F | VF | XF | Unc | BU |
|---|---|---|---|---|---|---|
| 1968A | 282,303,000 | — | 0.50 | 1.00 | 2.00 | — |
| 1972A | 51,462,000 | — | 0.50 | 1.00 | 3.50 | — |
| 1975A | 84,710,000 | — | 0.50 | 1.00 | 2.00 | — |

**5 PFENNIG** **KM# 9.2** **Composition:** Aluminum **Obverse:** Smaller design features **Reverse:** Smaller design features **Note:** Varieties exist.

| Date | Mintage | F | VF | XF | Unc | BU |
|---|---|---|---|---|---|---|
| 1978A | 43,257,000 | — | 0.15 | 0.25 | 0.60 | — |
| 1979A | 46,194,000 | — | 0.15 | 0.25 | 0.60 | — |
| 1979A Proof | — | Value: 45.00 | | | | |
| 1980A | 31,977,000 | — | 0.15 | 0.25 | 0.60 | — |
| 1980A Proof | — | Value: 45.00 | | | | |
| 1981A | 33,101,999 | — | 0.15 | 0.25 | 0.60 | — |
| 1981A Proof | 40 | — | — | — | — | — |
| 1982A | 916,000 | — | 1.75 | 7.50 | 22.50 | — |
| 1982A Proof | 2,500 | Value: 10.00 | | | | |
| 1983A | 100,890,000 | — | 0.15 | 0.25 | 0.60 | — |
| 1983A Proof | 2,550 | Value: 18.00 | | | | |
| 1984A | Est. 6,000 | — | — | — | 30.00 | — |
| 1984A Proof | 3,015 | Value: 4.50 | | | | |
| 1985A | 1,000,000 | — | 1.50 | 6.50 | 18.50 | — |
| 1985A Proof | 2,816 | Value: 4.50 | | | | |
| 1986A | 1,000,000 | — | 1.50 | 6.50 | 18.50 | — |
| 1986A Proof | 2,800 | Value: 4.50 | | | | |
| 1987A | Est. 20,000 | — | — | — | 12.50 | — |
| 1987A Proof | 2,345 | Value: 4.50 | | | | |
| 1988A | 35,930,000 | — | 0.15 | 0.25 | 0.60 | — |
| 1988A Proof | 2,300 | Value: 4.50 | | | | |
| 1989A | 21,550,000 | — | 0.15 | 0.25 | 0.60 | — |
| 1989A Proof | 2,300 | Value: 4.50 | | | | |
| 1990A | 50,640,000 | — | 0.15 | 0.25 | 0.60 | — |

**10 PFENNIG** **KM# 3** **Composition:** Aluminum **Note:** Also exists with medallic die rotation (1950E).

| Date | Mintage | F | VF | XF | Unc | BU |
|---|---|---|---|---|---|---|
| 1948A | 216,537,000 | — | 2.50 | 17.50 | 75.00 | — |
| 1949A | Inc. above | — | 2.50 | 17.50 | 70.00 | — |
| 1950A | Inc. above | — | 2.50 | 8.50 | 70.00 | — |
| 1950E | 16,000,000 | — | 17.50 | 175 | 1,000 | — |

**10 PFENNIG** **KM# 7** **Composition:** Aluminum

| Date | Mintage | F | VF | XF | Unc | BU |
|---|---|---|---|---|---|---|
| 1952A | 70,427,000 | — | 1.50 | 11.50 | 55.00 | — |
| 1952E | 21,498,000 | — | 15.00 | 40.00 | 280 | — |
| 1953A | 18,611,000 | — | 3.50 | 17.50 | 75.00 | — |
| 1953E | 11,500,000 | — | 15.00 | 70.00 | 650 | — |

**10 PFENNIG** **KM# 10** **Composition:** Aluminum

| Date | Mintage | F | VF | XF | Unc | BU |
|---|---|---|---|---|---|---|
| 1963A | 21,063,000 | — | 6.00 | 30.00 | 85.00 | — |
| 1965A | 55,313,000 | — | 0.15 | 0.25 | 2.50 | — |
| 1967A | 96,955,000 | — | 0.15 | 0.25 | 2.50 | — |
| 1968A | 207,461,000 | — | 0.15 | 0.25 | 0.75 | — |
| 1970A | 13,387,000 | — | 0.15 | 0.25 | 1.00 | — |
| 1971A | 66,617,999 | — | 0.15 | 0.25 | 0.75 | — |
| 1972A | 5,702,000 | — | 0.50 | 3.00 | 12.00 | — |
| 1973A | 11,257,000 | — | 0.15 | 0.25 | 1.50 | — |
| 1978A | 40,000,000 | — | 0.15 | 0.25 | 1.50 | — |
| 1979A | 54,665,000 | — | 0.15 | 0.25 | 0.60 | — |
| 1979A Proof | — | Value: 45.00 | | | | |
| 1980A | 20,664,000 | — | 0.15 | 0.25 | 0.60 | — |
| 1980A Proof | — | Value: 45.00 | | | | |
| 1981A | 40,704,000 | — | 0.15 | 0.25 | 0.60 | — |
| 1981A Proof | 40 | — | — | — | — | — |
| 1982A | 40,212,000 | — | 0.15 | 0.25 | 1.50 | — |
| 1982A Proof | 2,500 | Value: 10.00 | | | | |
| 1983A | 40,699,000 | — | 0.15 | 0.25 | 0.60 | — |
| 1983A Proof | 2,550 | Value: 20.00 | | | | |
| 1984A | Est. 12,000 | — | — | — | 25.00 | — |
| **Note:** Issued in sets only, remainder unaccountable | | | | | | |
| 1984A Proof | 3,015 | Value: 4.50 | | | | |
| 1985A | 1,010,000 | — | 0.35 | 4.50 | 17.50 | — |
| 1985A Proof | 2,816 | Value: 4.50 | | | | |
| 1986A | 1,000,000 | — | 0.35 | 4.50 | 17.50 | — |
| 1986A Proof | 2,800 | Value: 4.50 | | | | |
| 1987A | Est. 20,000 | — | — | — | 12.00 | — |
| **Note:** Issued in sets only, remainder unaccountable | | | | | | |
| 1987A Proof | 2,345 | Value: 4.50 | | | | |
| 1988A | 10,705,000 | — | 0.15 | 0.25 | 0.75 | — |

| Date | Mintage | F | VF | XF | Unc | BU |
|---|---|---|---|---|---|---|
| 1988A Proof | 2,300 | Value: 4.50 | | | | |
| 1989A | 37,640,000 | — | 0.15 | 0.25 | 0.60 | — |
| 1989A Proof | 2,300 | Value: 4.50 | | | | |
| 1990A | Est. 14,000 | — | — | — | 15.00 | — |

**Note:** Issued in sets only, remainder unaccountable

**20 PFENNIG** KM# 11 **Composition:** Brass **Note:** Ribbon width varieties exist.

| Date | Mintage | F | VF | XF | Unc | BU |
|---|---|---|---|---|---|---|
| 1969 | 167,168,000 | — | 0.25 | 1.50 | 4.00 | — |
| 1971 | 24,563,000 | — | 0.25 | 2.50 | 6.00 | — |
| 1972A | 5,007,000 | — | 0.25 | 2.50 | 10.00 | — |
| 1973A | 2,524,000 | — | 0.25 | 4.50 | 20.00 | — |
| 1974A | 7,458,000 | — | 0.25 | 2.50 | 10.00 | — |
| 1979A | 293,000 | — | 0.25 | 1.50 | 7.50 | — |
| 1979A Proof | — | Value: 50.00 | | | | |
| 1980A | 2,190,000 | — | 0.20 | 0.50 | 5.00 | — |
| 1980A Proof | — | Value: 50.00 | | | | |
| 1981A | 983,000 | — | 0.20 | 0.75 | 7.50 | — |
| 1981A Proof | 40 | — | — | — | — | — |
| 1982A | 10,458,000 | — | 0.20 | 2.50 | 8.50 | — |
| 1982A Proof | 2,500 | Value: 12.50 | | | | |
| 1983A | 25,809,000 | — | 0.20 | 0.50 | 3.00 | — |
| 1983A Proof | 2,550 | Value: 25.00 | | | | |
| 1984A | 25,009,000 | — | 0.20 | 0.50 | 3.00 | — |
| 1984A Proof | 3,015 | Value: 5.50 | | | | |
| 1985A | 1,559,000 | — | 0.20 | 0.50 | 4.00 | — |
| 1985A Proof | 2,816 | Value: 5.50 | | | | |
| 1986A | 1,147,000 | — | 0.20 | 0.50 | 4.00 | — |
| 1986A Proof | 2,800 | Value: 5.50 | | | | |
| 1987A | Est. 20,000 | — | — | — | 8.00 | — |

**Note:** Issued in sets only, remainder unaccountable

| Date | Mintage | F | VF | XF | Unc | BU |
|---|---|---|---|---|---|---|
| 1987A Proof | 2,345 | Value: 5.50 | | | | |
| 1988A | Est. 15,000 | — | — | — | 10.00 | — |

**Note:** Issued in sets only, remainder unaccountable

| Date | Mintage | F | VF | XF | Unc | BU |
|---|---|---|---|---|---|---|
| 1988A Proof | 2,300 | Value: 5.50 | | | | |
| 1989A | 14,690,000 | — | 0.20 | 0.50 | 2.00 | — |
| 1989A Proof | 2,300 | Value: 5.50 | | | | |
| 1990A | Est. 14,000 | — | — | — | 15.00 | — |

**Note:** Issued in sets only, remainder unaccountable

**50 PFENNIG** KM# 4 **Composition:** Aluminum-Bronze

| Date | Mintage | F | VF | XF | Unc | BU |
|---|---|---|---|---|---|---|
| 1949A | | — | — | 7,500 | — | — |
| 1950A | 67,703,000 | — | 3.50 | 8.50 | 32.50 | — |

**Note:** Some authorities believe the 1949 dated piece is a pattern

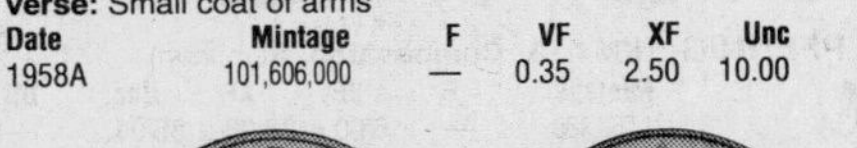

**50 PFENNIG** KM# 12.1 **Composition:** Aluminum **Obverse:** Small coat of arms

| Date | Mintage | F | VF | XF | Unc | BU |
|---|---|---|---|---|---|---|
| 1958A | 101,606,000 | — | 0.35 | 2.50 | 10.00 | — |

**50 PFENNIG** KM# 12.2 **Composition:** Aluminum **Obverse:** Larger coat of arms **Note:** Inscription varieties exist.

| Date | Mintage | F | VF | XF | Unc | BU |
|---|---|---|---|---|---|---|
| 1968A | 19,860,000 | — | 0.35 | 0.75 | 5.00 | — |
| 1971A | 35,829,000 | — | 0.35 | 0.75 | 3.00 | — |
| 1972A | 8,117,000 | — | 0.35 | 0.75 | 4.50 | — |
| 1973A | 6,530,000 | — | 0.35 | 0.75 | 7.50 | — |
| 1979A | 1,026,999 | — | 0.35 | 0.75 | 7.50 | — |
| 1979A Proof | — | — | — | — | — | — |
| 1980A | 1,118,000 | — | 0.35 | 0.75 | 8.00 | — |
| 1980A Proof | — | — | — | — | — | — |
| 1981A | 10,546,000 | — | 0.35 | 0.75 | 2.50 | — |
| 1981A Proof | 40 | — | — | — | — | — |
| 1982A | 79,832,000 | — | 0.35 | 0.75 | 2.50 | — |
| 1982A Proof | 2,500 | Value: 12.50 | | | | |
| 1983A | 1,309,000 | — | 0.35 | 0.75 | 7.50 | — |
| 1983A Proof | 2,550 | Value: 25.00 | | | | |
| 1984A | Est. 5,000 | — | — | — | 30.00 | — |
| 1984A Proof | 3,015 | Value: 5.50 | | | | |
| 1985A | 1,565,000 | — | 0.35 | 0.75 | 7.50 | — |
| 1985A Proof | 2,816 | Value: 5.50 | | | | |
| 1986A | 776,000 | — | 0.35 | 0.75 | 7.50 | — |
| 1986A Proof | 2,800 | Value: 5.50 | | | | |
| 1987A | Est. 21,000 | — | — | — | 12.00 | — |

**Note:** Issued in sets only, remainder unaccountable

| Date | Mintage | F | VF | XF | Unc | BU |
|---|---|---|---|---|---|---|
| 1987A Proof | 2,345 | Value: 5.50 | | | | |
| 1988A | Est. 15,000 | — | — | — | 14.00 | — |

**Note:** Issued in sets only, remainder unaccountable

| Date | Mintage | F | VF | XF | Unc | BU |
|---|---|---|---|---|---|---|
| 1988A Proof | 2,300 | Value: 5.50 | | | | |
| 1989A | 31,000 | — | 0.35 | 0.75 | 7.50 | — |
| 1989A Proof | 2,300 | Value: 5.50 | | | | |
| 1990A | Est. 14,000 | — | — | — | 15.00 | — |

**Note:** Issued in sets only, remainder unaccountable

**MARK** KM# 13 **Composition:** Aluminum

| Date | Mintage | F | VF | XF | Unc | BU |
|---|---|---|---|---|---|---|
| 1956A | 112,108,000 | — | 0.50 | 1.00 | 9.00 | — |
| 1962A | 45,920,000 | — | 0.50 | 2.00 | 10.00 | — |
| 1963A | 31,910,000 | — | 0.50 | 2.50 | 12.00 | — |

**MARK** KM# 35.1 **Composition:** Aluminum **Reverse:** Large 1

| Date | Mintage | F | VF | XF | Unc | BU |
|---|---|---|---|---|---|---|
| 1972A | 30,288,000 | — | 0.50 | 2.50 | 5.00 | — |

**MARK** KM# 35.2 **Composition:** Aluminum **Reverse:** Small 1

| Date | Mintage | F | VF | XF | Unc | BU |
|---|---|---|---|---|---|---|
| 1973A | 6,972,000 | — | 0.50 | 2.00 | 10.00 | — |
| 1975A | 32,094,000 | — | 0.50 | 1.00 | 6.50 | — |
| 1977A | 119,813,000 | — | 0.50 | 1.00 | 2.00 | — |
| 1978A | 18,824,000 | — | 0.50 | 1.00 | 2.50 | — |
| 1979A | 1,002,999 | — | 0.50 | 1.25 | 7.50 | — |
| 1979A Proof | — | — | — | — | — | — |
| 1980A | 1,069,000 | — | 0.50 | 1.25 | 7.50 | — |
| 1980A Proof | — | — | — | — | — | — |
| 1981A | 1,006,000 | — | 0.50 | 1.25 | 7.50 | — |
| 1981A Proof | 40 | — | — | — | — | — |
| 1982A | 51,619,000 | — | 0.50 | 1.00 | 2.00 | — |
| 1982A Proof | 2,500 | Value: 25.00 | | | | |
| 1983A | 1,065,000 | — | 0.50 | 1.25 | 7.50 | — |
| 1983A Proof | 2,550 | Value: 30.00 | | | | |
| 1984A | Est. 5,000 | — | — | — | 65.00 | — |
| 1984A Proof | 3,015 | Value: 7.50 | | | | |
| 1985A | 1,128,000 | — | — | 1.25 | 7.50 | — |
| 1985A Proof | 2,816 | Value: 7.50 | | | | |
| 1986A | 1,000,000 | — | 0.50 | 1.25 | 7.50 | — |
| 1986A Proof | 2,800 | Value: 7.50 | | | | |
| 1987A | Est. 21,000 | — | — | — | 5.50 | — |

**Note:** Issued in sets only, reminader unaccountable

| Date | Mintage | F | VF | XF | Unc | BU |
|---|---|---|---|---|---|---|
| 1987A Proof | 2,345 | Value: 7.50 | | | | |
| 1988A | Est. 15,000 | — | — | — | 7.50 | — |

**Note:** Issued in sets only, remainder unaccountable

| Date | Mintage | F | VF | XF | Unc | BU |
|---|---|---|---|---|---|---|
| 1988A Proof | 2,300 | Value: 7.50 | | | | |
| 1989A | 33,000 | — | 0.50 | 1.00 | 5.00 | — |
| 1989A Proof | 2,300 | Value: 7.50 | | | | |
| 1990A | Est. 14,000 | — | — | — | 20.00 | — |

**Note:** Issued in sets only, remainder unaccountable

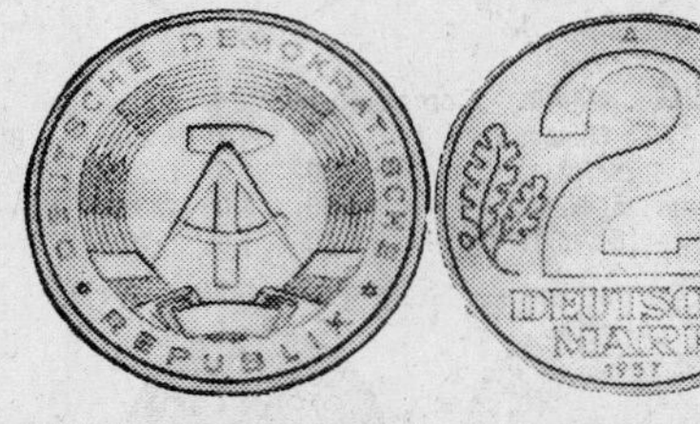


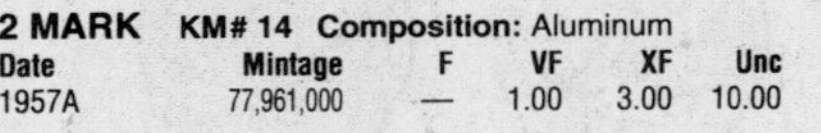

**2 MARK** KM# 14 **Composition:** Aluminum

| Date | Mintage | F | VF | XF | Unc | BU |
|---|---|---|---|---|---|---|
| 1957A | 77,961,000 | — | 1.00 | 3.00 | 10.00 | — |

**2 MARK** KM# 48 **Composition:** Aluminum

| Date | Mintage | F | VF | XF | Unc | BU |
|---|---|---|---|---|---|---|
| 1974A | 5,790,000 | — | 1.00 | 3.50 | 12.00 | — |
| 1975A | 32,464,000 | — | 0.90 | 2.00 | 10.00 | — |
| 1977A | 27,859,000 | — | 0.90 | 2.00 | 10.00 | — |
| 1978A | 23,415,000 | — | 0.90 | 2.00 | 10.00 | — |
| 1979A | 985,000 | — | 0.90 | 1.75 | 7.50 | — |
| 1979A Proof | — | — | — | — | — | — |
| 1980A | 1,018,999 | — | 0.90 | 1.75 | 7.50 | — |
| 1980A Proof | — | — | — | — | — | — |
| 1981A | 939,000 | — | 0.90 | 1.75 | 7.50 | — |
| 1981A Proof | 40 | — | — | — | — | — |
| 1982A | 60,488,000 | — | 0.80 | 1.00 | 2.00 | — |
| 1982A Proof | 2,500 | Value: 55.00 | | | | |
| 1983A | 1,030,000 | — | 0.90 | 1.25 | 5.00 | — |
| 1983A Proof | 2,550 | Value: 75.00 | | | | |
| 1984A | Est. 6,000 | — | — | — | 30.00 | — |
| 1984A Proof | 3,015 | Value: 20.00 | | | | |
| 1985A | 1,310,000 | — | 0.90 | 1.25 | 5.00 | — |
| 1985A Proof | 2,816 | Value: 20.00 | | | | |
| 1986A | 1,000,000 | — | 0.90 | 1.25 | 6.00 | — |
| 1986A Proof | 2,800 | Value: 20.00 | | | | |
| 1987A | Est. 30,000 | — | — | — | 6.00 | — |

**Note:** Issued in sets only, remainder unaccountable

| Date | Mintage | F | VF | XF | Unc | BU |
|---|---|---|---|---|---|---|
| 1987A Proof | 2,345 | Value: 20.00 | | | | |
| 1988A | Est. 15,000 | — | — | — | 6.50 | — |

**Note:** Issued in sets only, remainder unaccountable

| Date | Mintage | F | VF | XF | Unc | BU |
|---|---|---|---|---|---|---|
| 1988A Proof | 2,300 | Value: 20.00 | | | | |
| 1989A | 46,000 | — | 0.90 | 1.25 | 6.50 | — |
| 1989A Proof | 2,300 | Value: 20.00 | | | | |
| 1990A | Est. 14,000 | — | — | — | 20.00 | — |

**Note:** Issued in sets only, remainder unaccountable

**5 MARK** KM# 19.1 **Composition:** Copper-Nickel **Subject:** 125th Anniversary of Birth of Robert Koch

| Date | Mintage | F | VF | XF | Unc | BU |
|---|---|---|---|---|---|---|
| 1968 | 100,000 | — | — | — | — | 30.00 |

**5 MARK** KM# 19.2 **Composition:** Copper-Nickel **Note:** Error: plain edge.

| Date | Mintage | F | VF | XF | Unc | BU |
|---|---|---|---|---|---|---|
| 1968 | — | — | — | — | — | 450 |

**5 MARK** KM# 22.2 **Composition:** Nickel-Bronze **Note:** Error: plain edge.

| Date | Mintage | F | VF | XF | Unc | BU |
|---|---|---|---|---|---|---|
| 1969 | — | — | — | — | — | 150 |

**5 MARK** KM# 22.3 **Composition:** Nickel-Bronze **Note:** Error: Mongolian inscription and dates on edge.

| Date | Mintage | F | VF | XF | Unc | BU |
|---|---|---|---|---|---|---|
| 1969 | — | — | — | — | — | — |

**5 MARK** KM# 22.1 **Composition:** Nickel-Bronze **Subject:** 20th Anniversary D.D.R

| Date | Mintage | F | VF | XF | Unc | BU |
|---|---|---|---|---|---|---|
| 1969 | 50,222,000 | — | — | 3.00 | 4.50 | 7.50 |

**Note:** 10% nickel and 90% copper

**5 MARK** KM# 22.1a **Composition:** Copper-Nickel

| Date | Mintage | F | VF | XF | Unc | BU |
|---|---|---|---|---|---|---|
| 1969 | 12,741 | — | 50.00 | 75.00 | — | — |

**Note:** 25% nickel and 75% copper

**5 MARK** **KM# 23** **Composition:** Copper-Nickel **Subject:** Heinrich Hertz

| Date | Mintage | F | VF | XF | Unc | BU |
|---|---|---|---|---|---|---|
| 1969 | 100,000 | — | — | — | — | 24.50 |

**5 MARK** **KM# 26** **Composition:** Copper-Nickel **Subject:** Wilhelm Conrad Rontgen

| Date | Mintage | F | VF | XF | Unc | BU |
|---|---|---|---|---|---|---|
| 1970 | 100,000 | — | — | — | — | 24.50 |

**5 MARK** **KM# 29** **Composition:** Copper-Nickel **Subject:** Brandenburg Gate

| Date | Mintage | F | VF | XF | Unc | BU |
|---|---|---|---|---|---|---|
| 1971A | 4,000,000 | — | — | — | — | 10.00 |
| 1979A | 32,000 | — | — | — | — | 35.00 |
| 1979A Proof | 2,500 | — | — | — | — | — |
| 1980A | 30,000 | — | — | — | — | 32.00 |
| 1980A Proof | 2,500 | — | — | — | — | — |
| 1981A | 30,000 | — | — | — | — | 28.00 |
| 1981A Proof | 2,500 | — | — | — | — | — |
| 1982A | 28,000 | — | — | — | — | 26.50 |
| 1982A Proof | 2,500 | Value: 195 | | | | |
| 1983A | 3,000 | — | — | — | — | 1,100 |
| 1984A | 28,000 | — | — | — | — | 95.00 |
| 1984A Proof | 3,015 | Value: 135 | | | | |
| 1985A | 3,000 | — | — | — | — | 1,100 |
| 1986A | 28,000 | — | — | — | — | 125 |
| 1986A Proof | 2,800 | Value: 140 | | | | |
| 1987A | 220,000 | — | — | — | — | 20.00 |
| 1987A Proof | 6,424 | Value: 75.00 | | | | |
| 1988A | 28,000 | — | — | — | — | 40.00 |
| 1988A Proof | 2,300 | Value: 115 | | | | |
| 1989A | 28,000 | — | — | — | — | 40.00 |
| 1989A Proof | 2,405 | Value: 115 | | | | |
| 1990A | 50,000 | — | — | — | — | 50.00 |

**5 MARK** **KM# 30** **Composition:** Copper-Nickel **Subject:** Johannes Kepler

| Date | Mintage | F | VF | XF | Unc | BU |
|---|---|---|---|---|---|---|
| 1971 | 100,000 | — | — | — | — | 24.50 |

**5 MARK** **KM# 36.1** **Composition:** Copper-Nickel **Subject:** 75th Anniversary - Death of Johannes Brahms

| Date | Mintage | F | VF | XF | Unc | BU |
|---|---|---|---|---|---|---|
| 1972 | 55,000 | — | — | — | — | 26.50 |

**5 MARK** **KM# 37** **Composition:** Copper-Nickel **Subject:** City of Meissen

| Date | Mintage | F | VF | XF | Unc | BU |
|---|---|---|---|---|---|---|
| 1972A | 3,500,000 | — | — | — | 4.00 | 8.50 |
| 1981A Proof | 40 | Value: 2,750 | | | | |
| 1983A | 28,000 | — | — | — | — | 180 |
| 1983A Proof | 2,550 | Value: 300 | | | | |

**5 MARK** **KM# 36.2** **Composition:** Copper-Nickel **Note:** Error: Double edge inscription.

| Date | Mintage | F | VF | XF | Unc | BU |
|---|---|---|---|---|---|---|
| 1972 | — | — | — | — | — | 575 |

**5 MARK** **KM# 43** **Composition:** Copper-Nickel **Subject:** 125th Anniversary - Birth of Otto Lilienthal

| Date | Mintage | F | VF | XF | Unc | BU |
|---|---|---|---|---|---|---|
| 1973 | 100,000 | — | — | — | — | 38.00 |

**5 MARK** **KM# 49** **Composition:** Copper-Nickel **Subject:** Centenary - Death of Philipp Reis

| Date | Mintage | F | VF | XF | Unc | BU |
|---|---|---|---|---|---|---|
| 1974 | 100,000 | — | — | — | — | 24.50 |

**5 MARK** **KM# 54** **Composition:** Copper-Nickel **Subject:** 100th Anniversary - Birth of Thomas Mann

| Date | Mintage | F | VF | XF | Unc | BU |
|---|---|---|---|---|---|---|
| 1975 | 100,000 | — | — | — | — | 18.50 |

**5 MARK** **KM# 55** **Composition:** Copper-Nickel **Subject:** International Women's Year

| Date | Mintage | F | VF | XF | Unc | BU |
|---|---|---|---|---|---|---|
| 1975 | 250,000 | — | — | — | — | 20.00 |

**5 MARK** **KM# 60** **Composition:** Copper-Nickel **Subject:** 200th Anniversary - Birth of Ferdinand von Schill

| Date | Mintage | F | VF | XF | Unc | BU |
|---|---|---|---|---|---|---|
| 1976 | 100,000 | — | — | — | — | 30.00 |

**5 MARK** **KM# 64** **Composition:** Copper-Nickel **Subject:** 125th Anniversary - Death of Friedrich Ludwig Jahn

| Date | Mintage | F | VF | XF | Unc | BU |
|---|---|---|---|---|---|---|
| 1977 | 90,000 | — | — | — | — | 42.00 |
| 1977 Proof | 10,000 | Value: 48.00 | | | | |

**5 MARK** **KM# 67** **Composition:** Copper-Nickel **Subject:** 175th Anniversary - Death of Friedrich Klopstock

| Date | Mintage | F | VF | XF | Unc | BU |
|---|---|---|---|---|---|---|
| 1978 | 96,000 | — | — | — | — | 38.00 |
| 1978 Proof | 4,500 | Value: 65.00 | | | | |

**5 MARK** **KM# 68** **Composition:** Copper-Nickel **Subject:** Anti-Apartheid Year

| Date | Mintage | F | VF | XF | Unc | BU |
|---|---|---|---|---|---|---|
| 1978A | 196,000 | — | — | — | — | 24.50 |
| 1978A Proof | 4,000 | Value: 70.00 | | | | |

**5 MARK** **KM# 72** **Composition:** Copper-Nickel **Subject:** 100th Anniversary - Birth of Albert Einstein

| Date | Mintage | F | VF | XF | Unc | BU |
|---|---|---|---|---|---|---|
| 1979 | 56,000 | — | — | — | — | 65.00 |
| 1979 Proof | 4,500 | Value: 85.00 | | | | |

**5 MARK** **KM# 76** **Composition:** Copper-Nickel **Subject:** 75th Anniversary - Death of Adolph von Menzel

| Date | Mintage | F | VF | XF | Unc | BU |
|---|---|---|---|---|---|---|
| 1980 | 55,000 | — | — | — | — | 37.50 |
| 1980 Proof | 5,500 | Value: 60.00 | | | | |

**5 MARK** **KM# 79** **Composition:** Copper-Nickel **Subject:** 450th Anniversary - Death of Tilman Riemenschneider

| Date | Mintage | F | VF | XF | Unc | BU |
|---|---|---|---|---|---|---|
| 1981 | 55,000 | — | — | — | — | 65.00 |
| 1981 Proof | 5,500 | Value: 85.00 | | | | |

**5 MARK** **KM# 84** **Composition:** Copper-Nickel **Subject:** 200th Anniversary - Birth of Friedrich Frobel

| Date | Mintage | F | VF | XF | Unc | BU |
|---|---|---|---|---|---|---|
| 1982 | 55,000 | — | — | — | — | 60.00 |
| 1982 Proof | 5,500 | Value: 75.00 | | | | |

**5 MARK** **KM# 85** **Composition:** Copper-Nickel-Zinc **Subject:** Goethe's Weimar Cottage

| Date | Mintage | F | VF | XF | Unc | BU |
|---|---|---|---|---|---|---|
| 1982A | 245,000 | — | — | — | — | 35.00 |
| 1982A Proof | 5,500 | Value: 75.00 | | | | |
| 1982A Matte | 210 | Value: 3,000 | | | | |

**5 MARK** **KM# 86** **Composition:** Copper-Nickel-Zinc **Subject:** Wartburg Castle

| Date | Mintage | F | VF | XF | Unc | BU |
|---|---|---|---|---|---|---|
| 1982A | 245,000 | — | — | — | — | 32.50 |
| 1982A Proof | 5,500 | Value: 70.00 | | | | |
| 1983A | 10,000 | — | — | — | — | 375 |

**5 MARK** **KM# 89** **Composition:** Copper-Nickel **Subject:** Wittenberg Church

| Date | Mintage | F | VF | XF | Unc | BU |
|---|---|---|---|---|---|---|
| 1983A | 245,000 | — | — | — | — | 30.00 |
| 1983A Proof | 5,500 | Value: 70.00 | | | | |

**5 MARK** **KM# 90** **Composition:** Copper-Nickel **Subject:** Martin Luther's Birth Place

| Date | Mintage | F | VF | XF | Unc | BU |
|---|---|---|---|---|---|---|
| 1983A | 245,000 | — | — | — | — | 35.00 |
| 1983A Proof | 5,500 | Value: 65.00 | | | | |

**5 MARK** **KM# 91** **Composition:** Copper-Nickel-Zinc **Subject:** 125th Anniversary - Birth of Max Planck

| Date | Mintage | F | VF | XF | Unc | BU |
|---|---|---|---|---|---|---|
| 1983 | 56,000 | — | — | — | — | 38.00 |
| 1983 Proof | 4,200 | Value: 70.00 | | | | |

**5 MARK** **KM# 96** **Composition:** Copper-Nickel **Subject:** Leipzig Old City Hall

| Date | Mintage | F | VF | XF | Unc | BU |
|---|---|---|---|---|---|---|
| 1984A | 245,000 | — | — | — | — | 30.00 |
| 1984A Proof | 5,500 | Value: 60.00 | | | | |

**5 MARK** **KM# 97** **Composition:** Copper-Nickel **Subject:** Thomas Church of Leipzig

| Date | Mintage | F | VF | XF | Unc | BU |
|---|---|---|---|---|---|---|
| 1984A | 245,000 | — | — | — | — | 30.00 |
| 1984A Proof | 5,500 | Value: 60.00 | | | | |

**5 MARK** **KM# 98** **Composition:** Copper-Nickel **Subject:** 150th Anniversary - Death of Adolf Freiherr von Lutzow

| Date | Mintage | F | VF | XF | Unc | BU |
|---|---|---|---|---|---|---|
| 1984A | 55,000 | — | — | — | — | 58.00 |
| 1984A Proof | 5,000 | Value: 90.00 | | | | |

**5 MARK** **KM# 102** **Composition:** Copper-Nickel **Subject:** Restoration of Dresden Women's Church

| Date | Mintage | F | VF | XF | Unc | BU |
|---|---|---|---|---|---|---|
| 1985A | 245,000 | — | — | — | — | 32.00 |
| 1985A Proof | 8,476 | Value: 60.00 | | | | |

**5 MARK** **KM# 103** **Composition:** Copper-Nickel **Subject:** Restoration of Dresden Zwinger

| Date | Mintage | F | VF | XF | Unc | BU |
|---|---|---|---|---|---|---|
| 1985A | 245,000 | — | — | — | — | 32.00 |
| 1985A Proof | 5,500 | Value: 60.00 | | | | |

**5 MARK** **KM# 104** **Composition:** Copper-Nickel **Subject:** 225th Anniversary - Death of Caroline Neuber

| Date | Mintage | F | VF | XF | Unc | BU |
|---|---|---|---|---|---|---|
| 1985A | 56,000 | — | — | — | — | 70.00 |
| 1985A Proof | 4,000 | Value: 90.00 | | | | |

**5 MARK** **KM# 110** **Composition:** Copper-Nickel **Subject:** Potsdam - Sanssouci Palace

| Date | Mintage | F | VF | XF | Unc | BU |
|---|---|---|---|---|---|---|
| 1986A | 296,000 | — | — | — | — | 12.50 |
| 1986A Proof | 4,200 | Value: 65.00 | | | | |

**5 MARK** **KM# 111** **Composition:** Copper-Nickel **Subject:** Potsdam - New Palace

| Date | Mintage | F | VF | XF | Unc | BU |
|---|---|---|---|---|---|---|
| 1986A | 296,000 | — | — | — | — | 12.50 |
| 1986A Proof | 4,200 | Value: 65.00 | | | | |

**5 MARK** **KM# 112** **Composition:** Copper-Nickel **Subject:** 175th Anniversary - Death of Heinrich von Kleist

| Date | Mintage | F | VF | XF | Unc | BU |
|---|---|---|---|---|---|---|
| 1986A | 56,000 | — | — | — | — | 125 |
| 1986A Proof | 4,000 | Value: 135 | | | | |

**5 MARK** **KM# 114** **Composition:** Copper-Zinc-Nickel **Subject:** Berlin - Nikolai Quarter

| Date | Mintage | F | VF | XF | Unc | BU |
|---|---|---|---|---|---|---|
| 1987A | 496,000 | — | — | — | — | 11.50 |
| 1987A Proof | 4,200 | Value: 52.50 | | | | |

**5 MARK** **KM# 115** **Composition:** Copper-Zinc-Nickel **Subject:** Berlin - Red City Hall

| Date | Mintage | F | VF | XF | Unc | BU |
|---|---|---|---|---|---|---|
| 1987A | 496,000 | — | — | — | — | 11.50 |
| 1987A Proof | 4,200 | Value: 52.50 | | | | |

**5 MARK** **KM# 116** **Composition:** Copper-Zinc-Nickel **Subject:** Berlin - Universal Time Clock

| Date | Mintage | F | VF | XF | Unc | BU |
|---|---|---|---|---|---|---|
| 1987A | 496,000 | — | — | — | — | 11.50 |
| 1987A Proof | 4,200 | Value: 52.50 | | | | |

**5 MARK** **KM# 120** **Composition:** Copper-Nickel **Subject:** Germany's First Railroad

| Date | Mintage | F | VF | XF | Unc | BU |
|---|---|---|---|---|---|---|
| 1988A | 496,000 | — | — | — | — | 12.50 |
| 1988A Proof | 4,200 | Value: 100 | | | | |

**5 MARK** **KM# 121** **Composition:** Copper-Nickel **Subject:** Port City of Rostock

| Date | Mintage | F | VF | XF | Unc | BU |
|---|---|---|---|---|---|---|
| 1988A | 496,000 | — | — | — | — | 12.50 |
| 1988A Proof | 4,200 | Value: 72.50 | | | | |

**5 MARK** **KM# 122** **Composition:** Copper-Nickel **Subject:** 50th Anniversary - Death of Ernst Barlach

| Date | Mintage | F | VF | XF | Unc | BU |
|---|---|---|---|---|---|---|
| 1988A | 56,000 | — | — | — | — | 55.00 |
| 1988A Proof | 4,000 | Value: 100 | | | | |

**5 MARK** **KM# 129** **Composition:** Copper-Zinc-Nickel **Subject:** Katharinen Kirche in Zwickau

| Date | Mintage | F | VF | XF | Unc | BU |
|---|---|---|---|---|---|---|
| 1989A | 496,000 | — | — | — | — | 9.50 |
| 1989A Proof | 4,200 | Value: 67.50 | | | | |

**5 MARK** **KM# 130** **Composition:** Copper-Zinc-Nickel **Subject:** Marien Kirche in Muhlhausen

| Date | Mintage | F | VF | XF | Unc | BU |
|---|---|---|---|---|---|---|
| 1989A | 496,000 | — | — | — | — | 9.50 |
| 1989A Proof | 4,200 | Value: 67.50 | | | | |

**5 MARK** **KM# 131** **Composition:** Copper-Zinc-Nickel **Subject:** 100th Anniversary - Birth of Carl von Ossietzky

| Date | Mintage | F | VF | XF | Unc | BU |
|---|---|---|---|---|---|---|
| 1989A | 56,000 | — | — | — | — | 72.50 |
| 1989A Proof | 4,000 | Value: 90.00 | | | | |

**5 MARK** **KM# 133** **Composition:** Copper-Zinc-Nickel **Subject:** 100th Anniversary - Birth of Kurt Tucholsky

| Date | Mintage | F | VF | XF | Unc | BU |
|---|---|---|---|---|---|---|
| 1990A | 51,000 | — | — | — | — | 42.50 |
| 1990A Proof | 4,000 | Value: 72.50 | | | | |

**5 MARK** **KM# 134** **Composition:** Copper-Zinc-Nickel **Subject:** 500 Years of Postal Service

| Date | Mintage | F | VF | XF | Unc | BU |
|---|---|---|---|---|---|---|
| 1990A | 496,000 | — | — | — | — | 9.50 |
| 1990A Proof | 4,200 | Value: 55.00 | | | | |

**5 MARK** **KM# 135** **Composition:** Copper-Zinc-Nickel **Subject:** Zeughaus Museum

| Date | Mintage | F | VF | XF | Unc | BU |
|---|---|---|---|---|---|---|
| 1990A | 496,000 | — | — | — | — | 7.50 |
| 1990A Proof | 4,200 | Value: 50.00 | | | | |

**10 MARK** **KM# 15.1** **Weight:** 17.0000 g. **Composition:** 0.8000 Silver .4373 oz. ASW **Subject:** 125th Anniversary - Death of Karl Friedrich Schinkel **Edge Lettering:** 10 MARK DER DEUTSCHEN NOTEN BANK

| Date | Mintage | F | VF | XF | Unc | BU |
|---|---|---|---|---|---|---|
| 1966 | 50,000 | — | — | — | — | 345 |

**10 MARK** **KM# 15.2** **Weight:** 17.0000 g. **Composition:** 0.8000 Silver .4373 oz. ASW **Note:** Error: Plain edge.

| Date | Mintage | F | VF | XF | Unc | BU |
|---|---|---|---|---|---|---|
| 1966 | — | — | — | — | — | — |

**10 MARK** **KM# 17.2** **Weight:** 17.0000 g. **Composition:** 0.8000 Silver .4373 oz. ASW **Note:** Error, edge: 10 MARK*10 MARK*10 MARK*

| Date | Mintage | F | VF | XF | Unc | BU |
|---|---|---|---|---|---|---|
| 1967 | 3,000 | — | — | — | — | 225 |

**10 MARK** **KM# 17.1** **Weight:** 17.0000 g. **Composition:** 0.8000 Silver .4373 oz. ASW **Subject:** 100th Anniversary - Birth of Kathe Kollwitz

| Date | Mintage | F | VF | XF | Unc | BU |
|---|---|---|---|---|---|---|
| 1967 | 97,000 | — | — | — | — | 70.00 |

**10 MARK** **KM# 20.1** **Weight:** 17.0000 g. **Composition:** 0.6250 Silver .3416 oz. ASW **Subject:** 500th Anniversary - Death of Johann Gutenberg

| Date | Mintage | F | VF | XF | Unc | BU |
|---|---|---|---|---|---|---|
| 1968 | 100,000 | — | — | — | — | 55.00 |

**10 MARK** **KM# 20.2** **Weight:** 17.0000 g. **Composition:** 0.6250 Silver .3416 oz. ASW **Note:** Error: Plain edge.

| Date | Mintage | F | VF | XF | Unc | BU |
|---|---|---|---|---|---|---|
| 1968 | — | — | — | — | — | 700 |

**10 MARK** **KM# 24** **Weight:** 17.0000 g. **Composition:** 0.6250 Silver .3416 oz. ASW **Subject:** 250th Anniversary - Death of Johann Friedrich Bottger

| Date | Mintage | F | VF | XF | Unc | BU |
|---|---|---|---|---|---|---|
| 1969 | 100,000 | — | — | — | — | 55.00 |

**10 MARK** **KM# 27.1** **Weight:** 17.0000 g. **Composition:** 0.6250 Silver .3416 oz. ASW **Subject:** Ludwig van Beethoven

| Date | Mintage | F | VF | XF | Unc | BU |
|---|---|---|---|---|---|---|
| 1970 | 100,000 | — | — | — | — | 55.00 |

**10 MARK** **KM# 27.2** **Weight:** 17.0000 g. **Composition:** 0.6250 Silver .3416 oz. ASW **Note:** Error: Plain edge.

| Date | Mintage | F | VF | XF | Unc | BU |
|---|---|---|---|---|---|---|
| 1970 | — | — | — | — | — | 575 |

**10 MARK** **KM# 31** **Weight:** 17.0000 g. **Composition:** 0.6250 Silver .3416 oz. ASW **Subject:** Albrecht Durer

| Date | Mintage | F | VF | XF | Unc | BU |
|---|---|---|---|---|---|---|
| 1971 | 100,000 | — | — | — | — | 57.50 |

**10 MARK** **KM# 38** **Composition:** Copper-Nickel **Subject:** Buchenwald Memorial

| Date | Mintage | F | VF | XF | Unc | BU |
|---|---|---|---|---|---|---|
| 1972A | 2,500,000 | — | — | — | 5.00 | 7.50 |

**10 MARK** **KM# 39** **Weight:** 17.0000 g. **Composition:** 0.6250 Silver .3416 oz. ASW **Subject:** 175th Anniversary - Birth of Heinrich Heine

| Date | Mintage | F | VF | XF | Unc | BU |
|---|---|---|---|---|---|---|
| 1972 | 100,000 | — | — | — | — | 60.00 |

**10 MARK** **KM# 44** **Composition:** Copper-Nickel **Subject:** 10th Youth Festival Games

| Date | Mintage | F | VF | XF | Unc | BU |
|---|---|---|---|---|---|---|
| 1973A | 1,500,000 | — | — | — | 5.50 | 8.00 |

**10 MARK** **KM# 45** **Weight:** 17.0000 g. **Composition:** 0.6250 Silver .3416 oz. ASW **Subject:** 75th Anniversary - Birth of Bertolt Brecht

| Date | Mintage | F | VF | XF | Unc | BU |
|---|---|---|---|---|---|---|
| 1973 | 100,000 | — | — | — | — | 58.00 |

**10 MARK** **KM# 50** **Composition:** Copper-Nickel **Subject:** 25th Anniversary, with state motto

| Date | Mintage | F | VF | XF | Unc | BU |
|---|---|---|---|---|---|---|
| 1974A | 3,000,000 | — | — | — | 5.50 | 8.50 |

**10 MARK** **KM# 51** **Weight:** 17.0000 g. **Composition:** 0.6250 Silver .3416 oz. ASW **Subject:** 25th Anniversary D.D.R

| Date | Mintage | F | VF | XF | Unc | BU |
|---|---|---|---|---|---|---|
| 1974 | 70,000 | — | — | — | — | 58.00 |
| 1974 Proof | 200 | Value: 2,500 | | | | |

**10 MARK** **KM# 52** **Weight:** 17.0000 g. **Composition:** 0.6250 Silver .3416 oz. ASW **Subject:** 200th Anniversary - Birth of Caspar David Friedrich

| Date | Mintage | F | VF | XF | Unc | BU |
|---|---|---|---|---|---|---|
| 1974 | 75,000 | — | — | — | — | 57.50 |

**10 MARK** **KM# 56** **Weight:** 17.0000 g. **Composition:** 0.6250 Silver .3416 oz. ASW **Subject:** Centenary - Birth of Albert Schweitzer

| Date | Mintage | F | VF | XF | Unc | BU |
|---|---|---|---|---|---|---|
| 1975 | 99,000 | — | — | — | — | 57.50 |
| 1975 Proof | 1,040 | Value: 1,450 | | | | |

**10 MARK** **KM# 57** **Weight:** 17.0000 g. **Composition:** 0.5000 Silver .2733 oz. ASW **Subject:** Mule **Obverse:** KM#58 **Reverse:** KM#56 **Edge:** Plain

| Date | Mintage | F | VF | XF | Unc | BU |
|---|---|---|---|---|---|---|
| 1975A | 6,700 | — | — | — | — | 150 |

**10 MARK** **KM# 58** **Composition:** Copper-Nickel **Subject:** 20th Anniversary - Warsaw Pact

| Date | Mintage | F | VF | XF | Unc | BU |
|---|---|---|---|---|---|---|
| 1975A | 2,500,000 | — | — | — | 5.50 | 8.50 |

**10 MARK** **KM# 61** **Composition:** Copper-Nickel **Subject:** 20th Anniversary - National People's Army

| Date | Mintage | F | VF | XF | Unc | BU |
|---|---|---|---|---|---|---|
| 1976A | 750,000 | — | — | — | — | 9.00 |

**10 MARK** **KM# 62** **Weight:** 17.0000 g. **Composition:** 0.5000 Silver .2733 oz. ASW **Subject:** 150th Anniversary - Death of Carl Maria von Weber

| Date | Mintage | F | VF | XF | Unc | BU |
|---|---|---|---|---|---|---|
| 1976 | 94,000 | — | — | — | — | 70.00 |
| 1976 Proof | 6,037 | Value: 90.00 | | | | |

**10 MARK** **KM# 65** **Weight:** 17.0000 g. **Composition:** 0.5000 Silver .2733 oz. ASW **Subject:** 375th Anniversary - Birth of Otto von Guericke

| Date | Mintage | F | VF | XF | Unc | BU |
|---|---|---|---|---|---|---|
| 1977 | 69,000 | — | — | — | — | 82.50 |
| 1977 Proof | 6,000 | Value: 97.50 | | | | |

**10 MARK** **KM# 69** **Weight:** 17.0000 g. **Composition:** 0.5000 Silver .2733 oz. ASW **Subject:** 175th Anniversary - Birth of Justus von Liebig

| Date | Mintage | F | VF | XF | Unc | BU |
|---|---|---|---|---|---|---|
| 1978 | 71,000 | — | — | — | — | 77.50 |
| 1978 Proof | 4,500 | Value: 92.50 | | | | |

**10 MARK** **KM# 70** **Composition:** Copper-Nickel **Subject:** Joint USSR-DDR Orbital Flight

| Date | Mintage | F | VF | XF | Unc | BU |
|---|---|---|---|---|---|---|
| 1978A | 748,000 | — | — | — | — | 25.00 |
| 1978A Proof | 2,200 | Value: 520 | | | | |

**10 MARK** **KM# 73** **Weight:** 17.0000 g. **Composition:** 0.5000 Silver .2733 oz. ASW **Subject:** 175th Anniversary - Birth of Ludwig Feuerbach

| Date | Mintage | F | VF | XF | Unc | BU |
|---|---|---|---|---|---|---|
| 1979 | 51,000 | — | — | — | — | 85.00 |
| 1979 Proof | 4,500 | Value: 100 | | | | |

**10 MARK** **KM# 77** **Weight:** 17.0000 g. **Composition:** 0.5000 Silver .2733 oz. ASW **Subject:** 225th Anniversary - Birth of Gerhard von Scharnhorst

| Date | Mintage | F | VF | XF | Unc | BU |
|---|---|---|---|---|---|---|
| 1980 | 55,000 | — | — | — | — | 52.50 |
| 1980 Proof | 5,500 | Value: 75.00 | | | | |

**10 MARK** **KM# 80** **Composition:** Copper-Nickel **Subject:** 25th Anniversary - National People's Army

| Date | Mintage | F | VF | XF | Unc | BU |
|---|---|---|---|---|---|---|
| 1981A | 745,000 | — | — | — | — | 15.00 |
| 1981A Proof | 5,500 | Value: 60.00 | | | | |

**10 MARK** **KM# 81** **Weight:** 17.0000 g. **Composition:** 0.5000 Silver .2733 oz. ASW **Subject:** 150th Anniversary - Death of Georg Hegel

| Date | Mintage | F | VF | XF | Unc | BU |
|---|---|---|---|---|---|---|
| 1981 | 50,000 | — | — | — | — | 52.50 |
| 1981 Proof | 5,500 | Value: 80.00 | | | | |

**10 MARK** **KM# 82** **Composition:** Copper-Nickel **Subject:** 700th Anniversary - Berlin Mint

| Date | Mintage | F | VF | XF | Unc | BU |
|---|---|---|---|---|---|---|
| 1981 | 55,000 | — | — | — | — | 48.00 |
| 1981 Proof | 5,500 | Value: 82.00 | | | | |

**10 MARK** **KM# 87** **Weight:** 17.0000 g. **Composition:** 0.5000 Silver .2733 oz. ASW **Subject:** Leipzig Gewandhaus

| Date | Mintage | F | VF | XF | Unc | BU |
|---|---|---|---|---|---|---|
| 1982 | 50,000 | — | — | — | — | 52.50 |
| 1982 Proof | 5,500 | Value: 85.00 | | | | |

**10 MARK** **KM# 92** **Weight:** 17.1100 g. **Composition:** 0.5000 Silver .2751 oz. ASW **Subject:** 100th Anniversary - Death of Richard Wagner

| Date | Mintage | F | VF | XF | Unc | BU |
|---|---|---|---|---|---|---|
| 1983 | 44,000 | — | — | — | — | 52.50 |
| 1983 Proof | 5,500 | Value: 85.00 | | | | |

**10 MARK** **KM# 93** **Composition:** Copper-Nickel-Zinc **Subject:** 30th Anniversary - Worker's Militia

| Date | Mintage | F | VF | XF | Unc | BU |
|---|---|---|---|---|---|---|
| 1983A | 495,000 | — | — | — | — | 17.50 |
| 1983A Proof | 5,000 | Value: 55.00 | | | | |

**10 MARK** **KM# 99** **Weight:** 17.0000 g. **Composition:** 0.5000 Silver .2733 oz. ASW **Subject:** 100th Anniversary - Death of Alfred Brehm

| Date | Mintage | F | VF | XF | Unc | BU |
|---|---|---|---|---|---|---|
| 1984A | 50,000 | — | — | — | — | 80.00 |
| 1984A Proof | 5,000 | Value: 95.00 | | | | |

**10 MARK** **KM# 101** **Weight:** 17.0000 g. **Composition:** 0.5000 Silver .2733 oz. ASW **Subject:** Restoration of Semper Opera in Dresden

| Date | Mintage | F | VF | XF | Unc | BU |
|---|---|---|---|---|---|---|
| 1985A | 50,000 | — | — | — | — | 62.50 |
| 1985A Proof | 5,000 | Value: 97.50 | | | | |

**10 MARK** **KM# 106** **Composition:** Copper-Nickel-Zinc **Subject:** 40th Anniversary - Liberation from Fascism

| Date | Mintage | F | VF | XF | Unc | BU |
|---|---|---|---|---|---|---|
| 1985A | 745,000 | — | — | — | — | 14.50 |
| 1985A Proof | 5,500 | Value: 65.00 | | | | |

**10 MARK** **KM# 107** **Composition:** Copper-Nickel-Zinc **Subject:** 175th Anniversary - Humboldt University

| Date | Mintage | F | VF | XF | Unc | BU |
|---|---|---|---|---|---|---|
| 1985A | 51,000 | — | — | — | — | 77.50 |
| 1985A Proof | 4,000 | Value: 97.50 | | | | |

**10 MARK** **KM# 109** **Composition:** Copper-Nickel **Subject:** 100th Anniversary - Birth of Ernst Thalmann

| Date | Mintage | F | VF | XF | Unc | BU |
|---|---|---|---|---|---|---|
| 1986A | 746,000 | — | — | — | — | 12.50 |
| 1986A Proof | 4,000 | Value: 65.00 | | | | |

**10 MARK** **KM# 113** **Weight:** 17.0000 g. **Composition:** 0.5000 Silver .2733 oz. ASW **Subject:** Charite - Berlin

| Date | Mintage | F | VF | XF | Unc | BU |
|---|---|---|---|---|---|---|
| 1986A | 51,000 | — | — | — | — | 60.00 |
| 1986A Proof | 4,000 | Value: 90.00 | | | | |

**10 MARK** **KM# 118** **Weight:** 17.0000 g. **Composition:** 0.5000 Silver .2733 oz. ASW **Subject:** Berlin - Theater

| Date | Mintage | F | VF | XF | Unc | BU |
|---|---|---|---|---|---|---|
| 1987A | 51,000 | — | — | — | — | 60.00 |
| 1987A Proof | 4,000 | Value: 92.50 | | | | |

**10 MARK** **KM# 123** **Weight:** 17.0000 g. **Composition:** 0.5000 Silver .2733 oz. ASW **Subject:** 500th Anniversary - Birth of Ulrich von Hutten

| Date | Mintage | F | VF | XF | Unc | BU |
|---|---|---|---|---|---|---|
| 1988A | 52,000 | — | — | — | — | 85.00 |
| 1988A Proof | 3,500 | Value: 200 | | | | |

**10 MARK** **KM# 125** **Composition:** Copper-Nickel **Subject:** East German Sports

| Date | Mintage | F | VF | XF | Unc | BU |
|---|---|---|---|---|---|---|
| 1988A | 747,000 | — | — | — | — | 12.50 |
| 1988A Proof | 3,200 | Value: 120 | | | | |

**10 MARK** **KM# 126** **Composition:** Copper-Nickel **Subject:** Council of Mutual Economic Aid

| Date | Mintage | F | VF | XF | Unc | BU |
|---|---|---|---|---|---|---|
| 1989A | — | — | — | — | — | 40.00 |
| 1989A Proof | 3,000 | Value: 185 | | | | |

**10 MARK** **KM# 128** **Weight:** 17.0000 g. **Composition:** 0.5000 Silver .2733 oz. ASW **Subject:** 225th Anniversary - Birth of Johann Gottfried Schadow

| Date | Mintage | F | VF | XF | Unc | BU |
|---|---|---|---|---|---|---|
| 1989A | 51,000 | — | — | — | — | 115 |
| 1989A Proof | 4,000 | Value: 245 | | | | |

**10 MARK** **KM# 132** **Composition:** Copper-Nickel-Zinc **Subject:** 40th Anniversary - East German Government

| Date | Mintage | F | VF | XF | Unc | BU |
|---|---|---|---|---|---|---|
| 1989A | 746,000 | — | — | — | — | 14.50 |
| 1989A Proof | 3,080 | Value: 175 | | | | |

**10 MARK** **KM# 136** **Composition:** Copper-Nickel-Zinc **Subject:** International Labor Day

| Date | Mintage | F | VF | XF | Unc | BU |
|---|---|---|---|---|---|---|
| 1990A | 747,000 | — | — | — | — | 9.00 |
| 1990A Proof | 4,367 | Value: 60.00 | | | | |

**10 MARK** **KM# 137** **Weight:** 17.0000 g. **Composition:** 0.5000 Silver .2733 oz. ASW **Subject:** Johann Gottlieb Fichte

| Date | Mintage | F | VF | XF | Unc | BU |
|---|---|---|---|---|---|---|
| 1990A | 37,000 | — | — | — | — | 85.00 |
| 1990A Proof | 4,900 | Value: 135 | | | | |

**20 MARK** **KM# 16.1** **Weight:** 20.9000 g. **Composition:** 0.8000 Silver .5376 oz. ASW **Subject:** 250th Anniversary - Death of Gottfried Wilhelm Leibniz **Edge Lettering:** 20 MARK DER DEUTSCHEN NOTEN BANK

| Date | Mintage | F | VF | XF | Unc | BU |
|---|---|---|---|---|---|---|
| 1966 | 50,000 | — | — | — | — | 210 |

**20 MARK** **KM# 16.2** **Weight:** 20.9000 g. **Composition:** 0.8000 Silver .5376 oz. ASW **Edge:** Error: In inscription **Edge Lettering:** 10 MARK DER DEUTSCHEN NOTEN BANK

| Date | Mintage | F | VF | XF | Unc | BU |
|---|---|---|---|---|---|---|
| 1966 | — | — | — | — | — | — |

**20 MARK** **KM# 18.1** **Weight:** 20.9000 g. **Composition:** 0.8000 Silver .5376 oz. ASW **Subject:** 200th Anniversary - Birth of Wilhelm von Humboldt

| Date | Mintage | F | VF | XF | Unc | BU |
|---|---|---|---|---|---|---|
| 1967 | 97,000 | — | — | — | — | 160 |

**20 MARK** **KM# 18.2** **Weight:** 20.9000 g. **Composition:** 0.8000 Silver .5376 oz. ASW **Edge:** Error: In inscription **Edge Lettering:** 20 MARK*20 MARK*20 MARK*20 MARK

| Date | Mintage | F | VF | XF | Unc | BU |
|---|---|---|---|---|---|---|
| 1967 | 3,000 | — | — | — | — | 220 |

**20 MARK** **KM# 21** **Weight:** 20.9000 g. **Composition:** 0.8000 Silver .5376 oz. ASW **Subject:** 150th Anniversary - Birth of Karl Marx

| Date | Mintage | F | VF | XF | Unc | BU |
|---|---|---|---|---|---|---|
| 1968 | 100,000 | — | — | — | — | 90.00 |

**20 MARK** **KM# 25** **Weight:** 20.9000 g. **Composition:** 0.6250 Silver .4200 oz. ASW **Subject:** Johann Wolfgang von Goethe

| Date | Mintage | F | VF | XF | Unc | BU |
|---|---|---|---|---|---|---|
| 1969 | 100,000 | — | — | — | — | 135 |
| 1969 Proof; Rare | — | — | — | — | — | — |

**20 MARK** **KM# 28** **Weight:** 20.9000 g. **Composition:** 0.6250 Silver .4200 oz. ASW **Subject:** 150th Anniversary - Birth of Friedrich Engels

| Date | Mintage | F | VF | XF | Unc | BU |
|---|---|---|---|---|---|---|
| 1970 | 100,000 | — | — | — | — | 100 |
| 1970 Proof; Rare | — | — | — | — | — | — |

**20 MARK** **KM# 32** **Weight:** 20.9000 g. **Composition:** 0.6250 Silver .4200 oz. ASW **Subject:** Karl Kiebknecht - Rosa Luxemburg

| Date | Mintage | F | VF | XF | Unc | BU |
|---|---|---|---|---|---|---|
| 1971 | 100,000 | — | — | — | — | 75.00 |

**20 MARK** **KM# 33** **Composition:** Copper-Nickel **Subject:** 100th Anniversary - Birth of Heinrich Mann

| Date | Mintage | F | VF | XF | Unc | BU |
|---|---|---|---|---|---|---|
| 1971 | 2,000,000 | — | — | 4.00 | 5.00 | 9.00 |

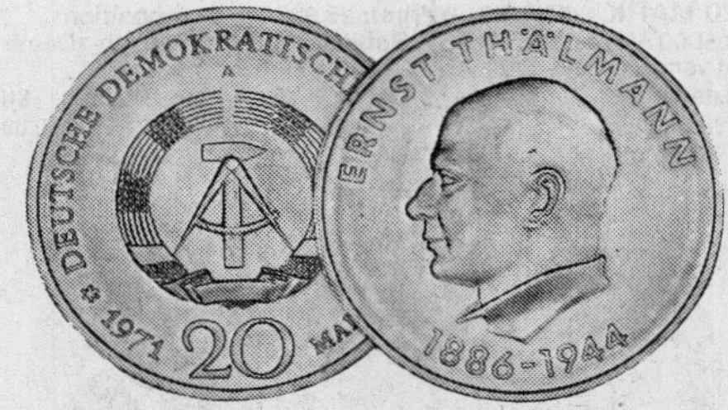


**20 MARK** **KM# 34** **Composition:** Copper-Nickel **Subject:** 85th Birthday of Ernst Thalmann **Note:** Edge varieties exist.

| Date | Mintage | F | VF | XF | Unc | BU |
|---|---|---|---|---|---|---|
| 1971A | 2,500,000 | — | — | 4.00 | 5.00 | 9.00 |

**20 MARK** **KM# 40** **Composition:** Copper-Nickel **Subject:** Friedrich von Schiller

| Date | Mintage | F | VF | XF | Unc | BU |
|---|---|---|---|---|---|---|
| 1972A | 3,000,000 | — | — | 4.00 | 5.00 | 9.00 |

**20 MARK** **KM# 41** **Weight:** 20.9000 g. **Composition:** 0.6250 Silver .4200 oz. ASW **Subject:** 500th Anniversary - Birth of Lucas Cranach

| Date | Mintage | F | VF | XF | Unc | BU |
|---|---|---|---|---|---|---|
| 1972 | 100,000 | — | — | — | — | 82.00 |

**20 MARK** **KM# 42** **Composition:** Copper-Nickel **Subject:** Wilhelm Pieck

| Date | Mintage | F | VF | XF | Unc | BU |
|---|---|---|---|---|---|---|
| 1972A | 2,500,000 | — | — | 4.00 | 5.00 | 9.00 |

**20 MARK** **KM# 46** **Weight:** 20.9000 g. **Composition:** 0.6250 Silver .4200 oz. ASW **Subject:** 60th Anniversary - Death of August Bebel

| Date | Mintage | F | VF | XF | Unc | BU |
|---|---|---|---|---|---|---|
| 1973 | 100,000 | — | — | — | — | 70.00 |

**20 MARK** **KM# 47** **Composition:** Copper-Nickel **Subject:** Otto Grotewohl

| Date | Mintage | F | VF | XF | Unc | BU |
|---|---|---|---|---|---|---|
| 1973A | 2,500,000 | — | — | 5.00 | 6.00 | 10.00 |

**20 MARK** **KM# 53** **Weight:** 20.9000 g. **Composition:** 0.6250 Silver .4200 oz. ASW **Subject:** 250th Anniversary - Death of Immanuel Kant

| Date | Mintage | F | VF | XF | Unc | BU |
|---|---|---|---|---|---|---|
| 1974 | 96,000 | — | — | — | — | 72.00 |
| 1974 Proof | 4,221 | Value: 140 | | | | |

**20 MARK** **KM# 59** **Weight:** 20.9000 g. **Composition:** 0.6250 Silver .4200 oz. ASW **Subject:** 225th Anniversary - Death of Johann Sebastian Bach

| Date | Mintage | F | VF | XF | Unc | BU |
|---|---|---|---|---|---|---|
| 1975 | 100,000 | — | — | — | — | 100 |
| 1975 Proof | Inc. above | Value: 3,500 | | | | |

**20 MARK** **KM# 63** **Weight:** 20.9000 g. **Composition:** 0.6250 Silver .4200 oz. ASW **Subject:** 150th Anniversary - Birth of Wilhelm Liebknecht

| Date | Mintage | F | VF | XF | Unc | BU |
|---|---|---|---|---|---|---|
| 1976 | 96,000 | — | — | — | — | 75.00 |
| 1976 Proof | 4,000 | Value: 150 | | | | |

**20 MARK** **KM# 66** **Weight:** 20.9000 g. **Composition:** 0.5000 Silver .3360 oz. ASW **Subject:** 200th Anniversary - Birth of Carl Friedrich Gauss

| Date | Mintage | F | VF | XF | Unc | BU |
|---|---|---|---|---|---|---|
| 1977 | 55,000 | — | — | — | — | 90.00 |

**20 MARK** **KM# 71** **Weight:** 20.9000 g. **Composition:** 0.5000 Silver .3360 oz. ASW **Subject:** 175th Anniversary - Death of Johann von Herder

| Date | Mintage | F | VF | XF | Unc | BU |
|---|---|---|---|---|---|---|
| 1978 | 51,000 | — | — | — | — | 87.50 |
| 1978 Proof | 4,500 | Value: 120 | | | | |

**20 MARK** **KM# 74** **Weight:** 20.9000 g. **Composition:** 0.5000 Silver .3360 oz. ASW **Subject:** 250th Anniversary - Birth of Gotthold Ephraim Lessing

| Date | Mintage | F | VF | XF | Unc | BU |
|---|---|---|---|---|---|---|
| 1979 | 41,000 | — | — | — | — | 100 |
| 1979 Proof | 4,500 | Value: 150 | | | | |

**20 MARK** **KM# 75** **Composition:** Copper-Nickel **Subject:** 30th Anniversary - Eath German Regime

| Date | Mintage | F | VF | XF | Unc | BU |
|---|---|---|---|---|---|---|
| 1979A | 1,000,000 | — | — | — | — | 14.50 |

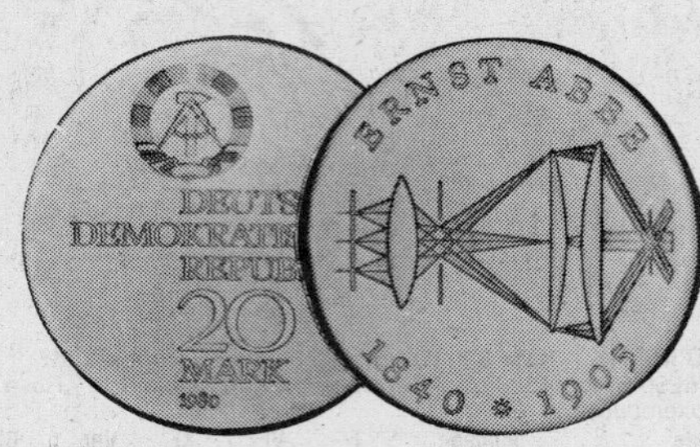


**20 MARK** **KM# 78** **Weight:** 20.9200 g. **Composition:** 0.5000 Silver .3360 oz. ASW **Subject:** 75th Anniversary - Death of Ernst Abbe

| Date | Mintage | F | VF | XF | Unc | BU |
|---|---|---|---|---|---|---|
| 1980 | 40,000 | — | — | — | — | 70.00 |
| 1980 Proof | 5,500 | Value: 120 | | | | |

**20 MARK** **KM# 83** **Weight:** 20.9200 g. **Composition:** 0.5000 Silver .3360 oz. ASW **Subject:** 150th Anniversary - Death of vom Stein

| Date | Mintage | F | VF | XF | Unc | BU |
|---|---|---|---|---|---|---|
| 1981 | 40,000 | — | — | — | — | 60.00 |
| 1981 Proof | 5,500 | Value: 100 | | | | |

**20 MARK** **KM# 88** **Weight:** 20.9200 g. **Composition:** 0.5000 Silver .3360 oz. ASW **Subject:** 125th Anniversary - Birth of Clara Zetkin

| Date | Mintage | F | VF | XF | Unc | BU |
|---|---|---|---|---|---|---|
| 1982 | 40,000 | — | — | — | — | 60.00 |
| 1982 Proof | 5,500 | Value: 90.00 | | | | |

**20 MARK** **KM# 94** **Weight:** 20.9200 g. **Composition:** 0.5000 Silver .3360 oz. ASW **Subject:** 500th Anniversary - Birth of Martin Luther

| Date | Mintage | F | VF | XF | Unc | BU |
|---|---|---|---|---|---|---|
| 1983 | 45,000 | — | — | — | — | 540 |
| 1983 Proof | 5,000 | Value: 550 | | | | |

**20 MARK** **KM# 95** **Composition:** Copper-Nickel **Subject:** 100th Anniversary - Death of Karl Marx

| Date | Mintage | F | VF | XF | Unc | BU |
|---|---|---|---|---|---|---|
| 1983A | 995,000 | — | — | — | — | 14.50 |
| 1983A Proof | 5,000 | Value: 65.00 | | | | |

**20 MARK** **KM# 100** **Weight:** 20.9200 g. **Composition:** 0.5000 Silver .3360 oz. ASW **Subject:** 225th Anniversary - Death of Georg Friedrich Handel

| Date | Mintage | F | VF | XF | Unc | BU |
|---|---|---|---|---|---|---|
| 1984A | 41,000 | — | — | — | — | 165 |
| 1984A Proof | 4,500 | Value: 195 | | | | |

**20 MARK** **KM# 105** **Weight:** 20.9200 g. **Composition:** 0.5000 Silver .3360 oz. ASW **Subject:** 125th Anniversary - Death of Ernst Moritz Arndt

| Date | Mintage | F | VF | XF | Unc | BU |
|---|---|---|---|---|---|---|
| 1985A | 41,000 | — | — | — | — | 95.00 |
| 1985A Proof | 4,000 | Value: 115 | | | | |

**20 MARK** **KM# 108** **Weight:** 20.9000 g. **Composition:** 0.6250 Silver .4200 oz. ASW **Subject:** 200th Anniversary - Birth of Jacob and Wilhelm Grimm

| Date | Mintage | F | VF | XF | Unc | BU |
|---|---|---|---|---|---|---|
| 1986A | 37,000 | — | — | — | — | 220 |
| 1986A Proof | 3,500 | Value: 285 | | | | |

**20 MARK** **KM# 119.1** **Weight:** 20.9000 g. **Composition:** 0.6250 Silver .4200 oz. ASW **Subject:** Berlin - City Seal

| Date | Mintage | F | VF | XF | Unc | BU |
|---|---|---|---|---|---|---|
| 1987A | 42,000 | — | — | — | — | 450 |
| 1987A Proof | 2,100 | Value: 1,650 | | | | |

**Note:** Seal on reverse totally frosted on proof coins

**20 MARK** **KM# 119.2** **Weight:** 20.9000 g. **Composition:** 0.6250 Silver .4200 oz. ASW **Reverse:** Fields in seal polished

| Date | Mintage | F | VF | XF | Unc | BU |
|---|---|---|---|---|---|---|
| 1987A Proof | 2,100 | Value: 1,650 | | | | |

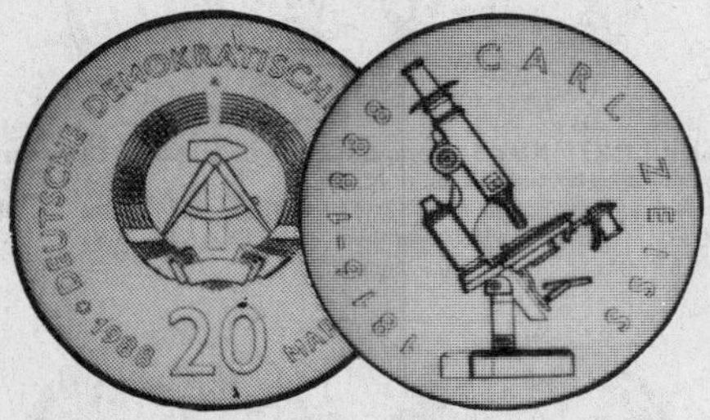

**20 MARK** **KM# 124** **Weight:** 20.9000 g. **Composition:** 0.6250 Silver .4200 oz. ASW **Subject:** 100th Anniversary - Death of Carl Zeiss

| Date | Mintage | F | VF | XF | Unc | BU |
|---|---|---|---|---|---|---|
| 1988A | 37,000 | — | — | — | — | 195 |
| 1988A Proof | 3,500 | Value: 245 | | | | |

**20 MARK** **KM# 127** **Weight:** 20.9000 g. **Composition:** 0.6250 Silver .4200 oz. ASW **Subject:** 500th Anniversary - Birth of Thomas Muntzer

| Date | Mintage | F | VF | XF | Unc | BU |
|---|---|---|---|---|---|---|
| 1989A | 37,000 | — | — | — | — | 90.00 |
| 1989A Proof | 3,500 | Value: 185 | | | | |

**20 MARK** **KM# 138** **Weight:** 20.9000 g. **Composition:** 0.6250 Silver .4200 oz. ASW **Subject:** Andreas Schluter

| Date | Mintage | F | VF | XF | Unc | BU |
|---|---|---|---|---|---|---|
| 1990A | 37,000 | — | — | — | — | 110 |
| 1990A Proof | 3,500 | Value: 180 | | | | |

**20 MARK** **KM# 139** **Composition:** Copper-Nickel **Subject:** Opening of Brandenburg Gate **Obverse:** State emblem, value and legend

| Date | Mintage | F | VF | XF | Unc | BU |
|---|---|---|---|---|---|---|
| 1990A | 300,000 | — | — | — | — | 12.50 |

**20 MARK** **KM# 139a** **Weight:** 18.2000 g. **Composition:** 0.9990 Silver .5852 oz. ASW

| Date | Mintage | F | VF | XF | Unc | BU |
|---|---|---|---|---|---|---|
| 1990A | 145,000 | — | — | — | — | 25.00 |
| 1990A Proof | 5,000 | Value: 75.00 | | | | |

## PIEFORTS

| KM# | Date | Mintage | Identification | Mkt Val |
|---|---|---|---|---|
| P1 | (1985) | — | 5 Mark. Copper-Zinc-Nickel. KM#110, Unc. | — |

## PROBAS

| KM# | Date | Mintage | Identification | Mkt Val |
|---|---|---|---|---|
| PR2 | | — | Pfennig. Aluminum. Mule - obv: obv. of KM#8.1, rev: obverse of KM#5. | — |
| PR1 | 1948 | — | Pfennig. Zinc. | 1,750 |
| PR3 | (1967) | — | 10 Mark. Silver. Neubauer. | 3,750 |
| PR5 | 1968 | — | 10 Pfennig. Brass Plated Steel. KM#10.1 | 375 |
| PR6 | 1968 | — | 50 Pfennig. Brass. KM#12. | 450 |
| PR4 | 1968 | — | 5 Pfennig. Brass. KM#9.1. | — |
| PR7 | 1968 | — | 20 Mark. 0.9990 Gold. KM#21. | — |
| PR8 | (1969) | — | 20 Pfennig. Brass. Mule - 2 obverses of KM#11. | — |
| PR9 | 1969 | — | 20 Pfennig. Nickel. KM#11. | — |
| PR10 | 1969 | 12,741 | 5 Mark. Copper-Nickel-Zinc. PROBE. | 500 |
| PR11 | 1972 | — | 10 Pfennig. Steel. KM#10.1. | — |
| PRA12 | 1972 | — | 2 Mark. Aluminum. KM#48. | — |
| PR12 | 1973 | — | 10 Mark. Copper-Nickel. Edge: 10 MARK* 10 MARK * 10 MARK * | — |
| PR13 | 1974 | 1,500 | 10 Mark. 0.5000 Silver. KM#50. | 1,500 |
| PR14 | 1974 | 100 | 10 Mark. 0.6250 Silver. Mintage numbered on lead seal, PROBE, KM#52. | 5,750 |
| PR16 | 1975 | 10,261 | 20 Mark. Silver. Incuse notes, Unc, KM#59. | 135 |
| PR17 | 1975 | I.A. | 20 Mark. Silver. Incuse notes, matte fields, proof, KM#59. | 4,500 |
| PR18 | 1975 | 8,810 | 10 Mark. Silver. PROBE, KM#57. | 145 |
| PR15 | 1975 | — | 5 Pfennig. Nickel. KM#9.1, | — |
| PRA19 | 1976 | — | 5 Pfennig. Aluminum. KM#9.2. | — |
| PR19 | (1977) | 6,000 | 10 Mark. Silver. Guericke. | 425 |
| PR20 | 1978 | 100 | 10 Mark. Silver. KM#70. | — |
| PR21 | 1979 | — | 20 Mark. Copper-Nickel-Zinc. Obverse: PROBA instead of date, KM#75. | — |
| PR22 | 1979 | 10,000 | 20 Mark. Copper-Nickel-Zinc. | 135 |
| PR23 | 1981 | | 10 Mark. 0.5000 Silver. PROBE on obverse, Unc. | 1,250 |
| PR24 | 1981 | 2,250 | 10 Mark. 0.5000 Silver. PROBE on obverse, Proof. | 1,200 |
| PR25 | 1982 | — | 5 Pfennig. Aluminum. Reeded edge, PROBA, KM#9.2. | 325 |
| PR26 | 1982 | — | 20 Pfennig. Brass Plated Steel. KM#11. | 500 |
| PR27 | 1982 | 210 | 5 Mark. Copper-Zinc-Nickel. House frosted on reverse, K#85, Proof. | 5,000 |
| PR28 | 1982 | 90 | 20 Mark. Silver. Countermark number of issue right of date, KM#88, Unc. | 8,500 |
| PR29 | 1983 | 100 | 10 Mark. Copper-Zinc-Nickel. Countermark PROBE and number on obverse, KM#93, Unc. | 1,500 |
| PR30 | 1983 | 100 | 20 Mark. Copper-Zinc-Nickel. PROBE and number beow date, KM#94, Unc. | 3,000 |
| PRA29 | 1983 | — | 5 Pfennig. Nickel. KM#9.2. | — |
| PR31 | 1983 | 100 | 20 Mark. Copper-Zinc-Nickel. PROBE and issue number left and right of denomination, KM#95, Unc. | — |
| PR32 | (1985) | 300 | 5 Mark. Copper-Zinc-Nickel. Incusely numbered, PROBA, Unc. | — |
| PR35 | 1985 | — | 10 Mark. 0.5000 Silver. KM#106, Unc. | — |
| PR37 | 1985 | 266 | 10 Mark. 0.3330 Gold. Alloyed with silver, KM#16, Proof. | — |
| PR33 | 1985 | 112 | 10 Mark. Silver. KM#107. | 6,500 |
| PR34 | 1985 | 50 | 10 Mark. Copper-Zinc-Nickel. Reverse large design size, KM#106, Unc. | 4,200 |
| PR36 | 1985 | — | 10 Mark. 0.5000 Silver. KM#106, Proof. | 12,500 |
| PR41 | 1986 | 107 | 10 Mark. 0.5000 Silver. P next to state emblem, KM#109, Unc. | 2,000 |
| PR38 | 1986 | — | Mark. Copper-Zinc-Nickel. PROBE, KM#35. | — |
| PR39 | 1986 | — | 2 Mark. Copper-Zinc-Nickel. PROBE, KM#48. | — |
| PR40 | 1986 | 110 | 5 Mark. Copper-Zinc-Nickel. P below tower, Unc. | — |
| PR42 | 1988 | 1,000 | 10 Mark. 0.5000 Silver. P below value, KM#125, Proof. | 1,200 |
| PR43 | 1988 | 15 | 20 Mark. Silver. PROBE, large inscription, KM#124, Unc. | 9,500 |
| PR44 | 1989 | — | 10 Mark. 0.5000 Silver. KM#132, Proof. | 11,500 |

## TRIAL STRIKES

| KM# | Date | Mintage | Identification | Mkt Val |
|---|---|---|---|---|
| TS1 | (1966) | 300 | 10 Mark. Aluminum. Uniface, Reverse of KM#15. | 230 |
| TS2 | (1966) | 300 | 20 Mark. Aluminum. Uniface, Reverse of KM#16. | 270 |

| KM# | Date | Mintage | Identification | Mkt Val |
|---|---|---|---|---|
| TS3 | (1967) | 400 | 10 Mark. Aluminum. Uniface, Reverse of KM#17. | 230 |
| TS4 | (1967) | 400 | 20 Mark. Aluminum. Uniface, Reverse of KM#18. | 270 |
| TS5 | 1968 | 350 | 5 Mark. Aluminum. Uniface, Reverse of KM#19. | 235 |
| TS6 | (1968) | 300 | 10 Mark. Aluminum. Uniface, Reverse of KM#20. | 250 |
| TS7 | (1968) | 300 | 20 Mark. Aluminum. Uniface, Reverse of KM#21. | 270 |
| TS9 | (1969) | 350 | 5 Mark. Aluminum. Uniface, reverse of KM#23. | 235 |
| TS10 | (1969) | 300 | 10 Mark. Aluminum. Uniface, reverse of KM#24. | 250 |
| TS11 | (1969) | 300 | 20 Mark. Aluminum. Uniface, reverse of KM#25. | 260 |
| TS8 | (1969) | — | 5 Mark. Nickel-Bronze. Uniface, obverse of KM#14, edge 5 MARK * 5 MARK * 5 MARK * | — |
| TS12 | (1970) | 350 | 5 Mark. Aluminum. Uniface, reverse of KM#26. | 235 |
| TS13 | (1970) | 300 | 10 Mark. Aluminum. Uniface, reverse of KM#27. | 250 |
| TS14 | (1970) | 330 | 20 Mark. Aluminum. Uniface, reverse of KM#28. | 260 |
| TS15 | (1971) | 450 | 5 Mark. Aluminum. Uniface, reverse of KM#30. | 235 |
| TS16 | (1971) | 300 | 10 Mark. Aluminum. Uniface, reverse of KM#31. | 250 |
| TS17 | (1971) | 410 | 20 Mark. Aluminum. Uniface, reverse of KM#32. | 250 |
| TS18 | (1972) | 300 | 5 Mark. Aluminum. Uniface, reverse of KM#36. | 235 |
| TS19 | (1972) | 300 | 10 Mark. Aluminum. Uniface, reverse of KM#39. | 250 |
| TS20 | (1972) | 300 | 20 Mark. Aluminum. Uniface, reverse of KM#41. | 260 |
| TS21 | (1973) | 300 | 5 Mark. Aluminum. Uniface, reverse of KM#43. | 235 |
| TS22 | (1973) | — | 20 Mark. Copper-Zinc-Nickel. Uniface, reverse of KM#47. | — |
| TS23 | (1973) | — | 20 Mark. Copper-Zinc-Nickel. Uniface, reverse with portrait within circular legend, KM#47. | — |
| TS24 | (1975) | 306 | 10 Mark. Aluminum. Uniface, reverse of KM#56. | 220 |
| TS25 | 1979 | — | 20 Mark. Copper-Zinc-Nickel. Uniface, reverse of PR22. | — |

## MINT SETS

| KM# | Date | Mintage | Identification | Mkt Val |
|---|---|---|---|---|
| MS1 | 1979A (8) | 26,000 | KM#8.2-10, 11-12.2, 29, 35.2, 48 | 50.00 |
| MS2 | 1980A (8) | 25,000 | KM#8.2-10, 11-12.2, 35.2, 48 | 65.00 |
| MS3 | 1981 (8) | 25,000 | KM#8.2-10, 11-12.2, 29, 35.2, 48 | 55.00 |
| MS4 | 1982 (8) | 21,000 | KM#8.2-10, 11-12.2, 29, 35.2, 48 | 80.00 |
| MS5 | 1982 (7) | 4,500 | KM#8.2-10, 11-12.2, 35.2, 48 | 90.00 |
| MS6 | 1983 (8) | 19,000 | KM#8.2-10, 11-12.2, 35.2, 37, 48 | 200 |
| MS7 | 1983 (7) | 4,500 | KM#8.2-10, 11-12.2, 35.2, 48 | 150 |
| MS8 | 1984 (8) | 19,000 | KM#8.2-10, 11-12.2, 29, 35.2, 48 | 125 |
| MS9 | 1984 (7) | 4,500 | KM#8.2-10, 11-12.2, 35.2, 48 | 100 |
| MS10 | 1985 (8) | 6,000 | KM#8.2-10, 11-12.2, 35.2, 48, 102 | 60.00 |
| MS11 | 1985 (7) | 4,500 | KM#8.2-10, 11-12.2, 35.2, 48 | 55.00 |
| MS12 | 1986 (8) | 7,000 | KM#8.2-10, 11-12, 29, 35.2, 48 | 110 |
| MS13 | 1986 (7) | 4,500 | KM#8.2-10, 11-12.2, 35.2, 48 | 65.00 |
| MS14 | 1987 (8) | 8,000 | KM#8.2-10, 11-12.2, 29, 35.2, 48 | 50.00 |
| MS15 | 1987 (7) | 4,500 | KM#8.2-10, 11-12.2, 35.2, 48 | 60.00 |
| MS16 | 1988 (8) | 11,000 | KM#8.2-10, 11-12.2, 29, 35.2, 48 | 55.00 |
| MS17 | 1988 (7) | 4,500 | KM#8.2-10, 11-12.2, 35.2, 48 | 60.00 |
| MS18 | 1989 (8) | 11,000 | KM8.2-10, 11-12.2, 29, 35.2, 48 | 55.00 |
| MS19 | 1989 (7) | 4,500 | KM#8.2-10, 11-12.2, 35.2,48 | 60.00 |
| MS20 | 1990 (8) | 11,000 | KM#8.2-10, 11-12.2, 29, 35.2, 48 | 125 |
| MS21 | 1990 (7) | 4,500 | KM#8.2-10, 11-12.2, 35.2, 48 | 100 |

## PROOF SETS

| KM# | Date | Mintage | Identification | Mkt Val |
|---|---|---|---|---|
| PS1 | 1981 (8) | 20 | KM#8.2-10, 11-12.2, 35.2, 48, 79 | — |
| PS2 | 1981 (8) | 20 | KM#8.2-10, 11-12.2, 35.2, 37, 48 | — |
| PS3 | 1982 (8) | 2,500 | KM#8.2-10, 11-12.2, 29, 35.2, 48 | 410 |
| PS4 | 1983 (8) | 2,550 | KM#8.2-10, 11-12.2, 35.2, 37, 48 | 300 |
| PS5 | 1984 (8) | 3,015 | KM#8.2-10, 11-12.2, 29, 35.2, 48 | 120 |
| PS6 | 1985 (8) | 2,816 | KM#8.2-10, 11-12.2, 35.2, 48, 102 | 95.00 |
| PS7 | 1986 (8) | 2,800 | KM#8.2-10, 11-12.2, 29, 35.2, 48 | 120 |
| PS8 | 1987 (8) | 2,345 | KM#8.2-10, 11-12.2, 29, 35.2, 48 | 115 |
| PS9 | 1988 (8) | 2,300 | KM#8.2-10, 11-12.2, 28, 35.2, 48 | 120 |
| PS10 | 1989 (8) | 2,300 | KM#8.2-10, 11-12.2, 28, 35.2, 48 | 130 |

# GHANA

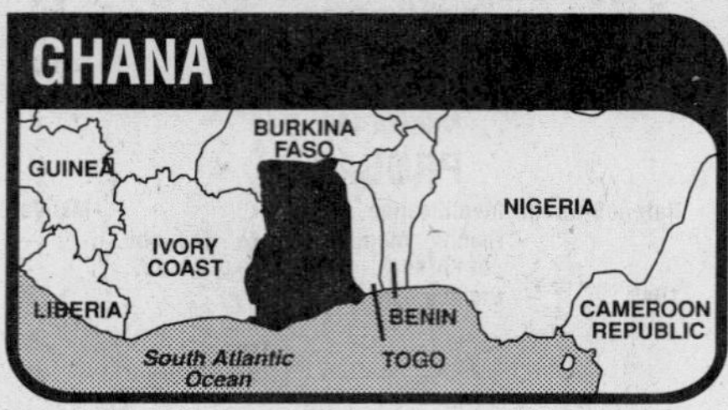


The Republic of Ghana, a member of the British Commonwealth situated on the West Coast of Africa between Ivory Coast and Togo, has an area of 92,100 sq. mi. (238,540 sq. km.) and a population of 14 million, almost entirely African. Capital: Accra. Cocoa (the major crop), coconuts, palm kernels and coffee are exported. Mining, second in importance to agriculture, is concentrated on gold, manganese and industrial diamonds.

The state of Ghana, comprising the Gold Coast and British Togoland, obtained independence on March 6, 1957, becoming the first Negro African colony to do so. On July l, 1960, Ghana adopted a republican constitution, changing from a ministerial to a presidential form of government. The government was overthrown, the constitution suspended and the National Assembly dissolved by the Ghanaian army and police on Feb. 24, 1966. The government was returned to civilian authority in Oct. 1969, but was again seized by military officers in a bloodless coup on Jan. 13, 1972, but 3 further coups occurred in 1978, 1979 and 1981. The latter 2 coups were followed by suspension of the constitution and banning of political parties. A new constitution, which allowed multiparty politics, was approved in April 1992.

Ghana's monetary denomination of Cedi' is derived from the word 'sedie' meaning cowrie, a shell money commonly employed by coastal tribes.

**MONETARY SYSTEM**

12 Pence = 1 Shilling

# REPUBLIC

## STANDARD COINAGE

**1/2 PENNY** **KM# 1** **Composition:** Bronze **Obverse:** Dr. Kwame Nkrumah bust right

| Date | Mintage | F | VF | XF | Unc | BU |
|---|---|---|---|---|---|---|
| 1958 | 32,200,000 | — | 0.10 | 0.25 | 0.50 | — |
| 1958 Proof | 20,000 | Value: 0.75 | | | | |

**PENNY** **KM#2** **Composition:** Bronze **Obverse:** Dr. Kwame Nkrumah bust right

| Date | Mintage | F | VF | XF | Unc | BU |
|---|---|---|---|---|---|---|
| 1958 | 60,000,000 | — | 0.15 | 0.35 | 0.75 | — |
| 1958 Proof | 20,000 | Value: 1.00 | | | | |

**3 PENCE** **KM# 3** **Composition:** Copper Nickel **Obverse:** Dr. Kwame Nkrumah bust right

| Date | Mintage | F | VF | XF | Unc | BU |
|---|---|---|---|---|---|---|
| 1958 | 25,200,000 | — | 0.20 | 0.45 | 1.00 | — |
| 1958 Proof | 20,000 | Value: 1.50 | | | | |

**6 PENCE** **KM# 4** **Composition:** Copper Nickel **Obverse:** Dr. Kwame Nkrumah bust right

| Date | Mintage | F | VF | XF | Unc | BU |
|---|---|---|---|---|---|---|
| 1958 | 15,200,000 | — | 0.20 | 0.45 | 1.00 | — |
| 1958 Proof | — | Value: 1.50 | | | | |

**SHILLING** **KM# 5** **Composition:** Copper Nickel **Obverse:** Dr. Kwame Nkrumah bust right

| Date | Mintage | F | VF | XF | Unc | BU |
|---|---|---|---|---|---|---|
| 1958 | 34,400,000 | — | 0.25 | 0.50 | 1.75 | — |
| 1958 Proof | 20,000 | Value: 2.50 | | | | |

**2 SHILLING** **KM# 6** **Composition:** Copper Nickel **Obverse:** Dr. Kwame Nkrumah bust right

| Date | Mintage | F | VF | XF | Unc | BU |
|---|---|---|---|---|---|---|
| 1958 | 72,700,000 | — | 0.35 | 0.75 | 2.25 | — |
| 1958 Proof | 20,000 | Value: 3.50 | | | | |

**10 SHILLING** **KM# 7** **Weight:** 28.2800 g. **Composition:** 0.9250 Silver .8411 oz. ASW **Obverse:** Dr. Kwame Nkrumah bust right

| Date | Mintage | F | VF | XF | Unc | BU |
|---|---|---|---|---|---|---|
| 1958 Proof | 11,000 | Value: 12.50 | | | | |

## DECIMAL COINAGE

**1/2 PESEWA** **KM# 12** **Composition:** Bronze **Obverse:** Brush drums

| Date | Mintage | F | VF | XF | Unc | BU |
|---|---|---|---|---|---|---|
| 1967 | 30,000,000 | — | 0.10 | 0.20 | 0.50 | — |
| 1967 Proof | 2,000 | Value: 1.00 | | | | |

**PESEWA** **KM# 13** **Composition:** Bronze **Obverse:** Brush drums

| Date | Mintage | F | VF | XF | Unc | BU |
|---|---|---|---|---|---|---|
| 1967 | 30,000,000 | — | 0.15 | 0.25 | 0.60 | — |
| 1967 Proof | 2,000 | Value: 1.25 | | | | |

| ate | Mintage | F | VF | XF | Unc | BU |
|---|---|---|---|---|---|---|
| 975 | 50,250,000 | — | 0.10 | 0.20 | 0.50 | — |
| 979 | 50,000,000 | — | 0.10 | 0.20 | 0.50 | — |

**2-1/2 PESEWAS** **KM# 14** **Composition:** Copper-Nickel **Obverse:** Cocoa beans

| Date | Mintage | F | VF | XF | Unc | BU |
|---|---|---|---|---|---|---|
| 1967 | 6,000,000 | — | 0.10 | 0.20 | 0.75 | — |
| 1967 Proof | 2,000 | Value: 1.50 | | | | |

**5 PESEWAS** **KM# 8** **Composition:** Copper-Nickel **Obverse:** Dr. Kwame Nkrumah bust right

| Date | Mintage | F | VF | XF | Unc | BU |
|---|---|---|---|---|---|---|
| 1965 | 30,000,000 | — | 0.20 | 0.35 | 1.25 | — |

**5 PESEWAS** **KM# 15** **Composition:** Copper-Nickel **Obverse:** Cocoa beans

| Date | Mintage | F | VF | XF | Unc | BU |
|---|---|---|---|---|---|---|
| 1967 | 30,000,000 | — | 0.15 | 0.25 | 0.75 | — |
| 1967 | 2,000 | — | 0.15 | 0.25 | 2.00 | — |
| 1973 | 8,000,000 | — | 0.15 | 0.25 | 0.75 | — |
| 1975 | 20,000,000 | — | 0.15 | 0.25 | 0.75 | — |

**10 PESEWAS** **KM# 9** **Composition:** Copper-Nickel **Obverse:** Dr. Kwame Nkrumah bust right

| Date | Mintage | F | VF | XF | Unc | BU |
|---|---|---|---|---|---|---|
| 1965 | 50,000,000 | — | 0.25 | 0.50 | 1.25 | — |

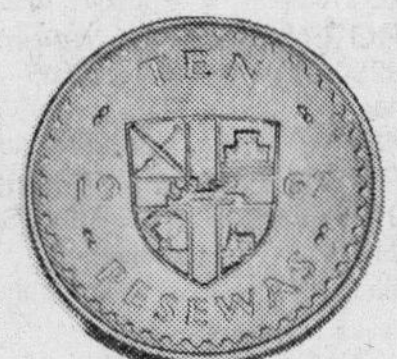


**10 PESEWAS** **KM# 16** **Composition:** Copper-Nickel **Obverse:** Cocoa beans

| Date | Mintage | F | VF | XF | Unc | BU |
|---|---|---|---|---|---|---|
| 1967 | 13,200,000 | — | 0.20 | 0.40 | 1.50 | — |
| 1967 Proof | 2,000 | Value: 2.50 | | | | |
| 1975 | 20,000,000 | — | 0.20 | 0.40 | 1.25 | — |
| 1979 | 5,500,000 | — | 0.20 | 0.40 | 1.25 | — |

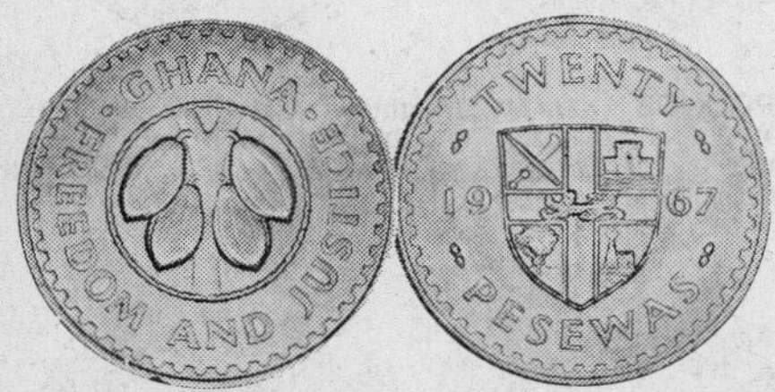


**20 PESEWAS** **KM# 17** **Composition:** Copper-Nickel **Obverse:** Cocoa beans

| Date | Mintage | F | VF | XF | Unc | BU |
|---|---|---|---|---|---|---|
| 1967 | 25,800,000 | — | 0.25 | 0.50 | 1.75 | — |
| 1967 Proof | 2,000 | Value: 3.00 | | | | |
| 1975 | — | — | 0.25 | 0.50 | 1.75 | — |
| 1979 | 5,000,000 | — | 0.25 | 0.50 | 1.75 | — |

**25 PESEWAS** **KM# 10** **Composition:** Copper-Nickel **Obverse:** Dr. Kwame Nkrumah bust right

| Date | Mintage | F | VF | XF | Unc | BU |
|---|---|---|---|---|---|---|
| 1965 | 60,100,000 | — | 0.35 | 0.75 | 2.00 | — |

**50 PESEWAS** **KM# 11** **Composition:** Copper-Nickel **Obverse:** Dr. Kwame Nkrumah bust right

| Date | Mintage | F | VF | XF | Unc | BU |
|---|---|---|---|---|---|---|
| 1965 | 18,200,000 | — | 0.75 | 1.50 | 3.50 | — |

**50 PESEWAS** **KM# 18** **Composition:** Brass **Series:** F.A.O. **Obverse:** Cocoa beans

| Date | Mintage | F | VF | XF | Unc | BU |
|---|---|---|---|---|---|---|
| 1979 | 60,000,000 | — | 0.45 | 0.75 | 2.25 | — |

**50 PESEWAS** **KM# 24** **Composition:** Brass **Obverse:** Cocoa beans

| Date | Mintage | F | VF | XF | Unc | BU |
|---|---|---|---|---|---|---|
| 1984 | 10,000,000 | — | 0.10 | 0.25 | 0.60 | — |

**CEDI** **KM# 19** **Composition:** Brass **Series:** F.A.O. **Obverse:** Cauri

| Date | Mintage | F | VF | XF | Unc | BU |
|---|---|---|---|---|---|---|
| 1979 | 160,000,000 | — | 0.35 | 0.85 | 3.00 | — |

**CEDI** **KM# 25** **Composition:** Brass **Obverse:** Cauri

| Date | Mintage | F | VF | XF | Unc | BU |
|---|---|---|---|---|---|---|
| 1984 | 40,000,000 | — | 0.10 | 0.25 | 0.75 | — |

**5 CEDIS** **KM# 26** **Composition:** Brass **Obverse:** Bush drums

| Date | Mintage | F | VF | XF | Unc | BU |
|---|---|---|---|---|---|---|
| 1984 | 88,920,000 | — | 0.10 | 0.20 | 0.50 | — |

**5 CEDIS** **KM# 33** **Composition:** Brass Plated Steel **Obverse:** Bush drums

| Date | Mintage | F | VF | XF | Unc | BU |
|---|---|---|---|---|---|---|
| 1991 | — | — | 0.10 | 0.20 | 0.50 | — |

**10 CEDIS** **KM# 29** **Composition:** Nickel Clad Steel

| Date | Mintage | F | VF | XF | Unc | BU |
|---|---|---|---|---|---|---|
| 1991 | — | — | — | 0.25 | 0.75 | — |

**20 CEDIS** **KM# 30** **Composition:** Nickel Clad Steel

| Date | Mintage | F | VF | XF | Unc | BU |
|---|---|---|---|---|---|---|
| 1991 | — | — | — | 0.35 | 1.00 | — |
| 1995 | — | — | — | 0.35 | 1.00 | — |

**50 CEDIS** **KM# 20** **Weight:** 28.2800 g. **Composition:** 0.9250 Silver .8411 oz. ASW **Subject:** International Year of Disabled Persons

| Date | Mintage | F | VF | XF | Unc | BU |
|---|---|---|---|---|---|---|
| 1981 | 10,000 | — | — | — | 25.00 | — |
| 1981 Proof | 10,000 | Value: 35.00 | | | | |

**50 CEDIS** KM# 21 **Composition:** Copper Nickel **Series:** F.A.O. **Subject:** World Fisheries Conference

| Date | Mintage | F | VF | XF | Unc | BU |
|---|---|---|---|---|---|---|
| ND(1984) | 100,000 | — | — | — | 6.50 | — |

**50 CEDIS** KM# 21a **Weight:** 28.2800 g. **Composition:** 0.9250 Silver .8411 oz. ASW **Series:** F.A.O. **Subject:** World Fisheries Conference

| Date | Mintage | F | VF | XF | Unc | BU |
|---|---|---|---|---|---|---|
| ND(1984) Proof | 21,000 | Value: 55.00 | | | | |

**50 CEDIS** KM# 21b **Weight:** 47.5400 g. **Composition:** 0.9170 Gold 1.4017 oz. AGW **Series:** F.A.O. **Subject:** World Fisheries Conference

| Date | Mintage | F | VF | XF | Unc | BU |
|---|---|---|---|---|---|---|
| ND(1984) Proof | 105 | Value: 2,000 | | | | |

**50 CEDIS** KM# 22 **Weight:** 28.2800 g. **Composition:** 0.9250 Silver .8411 oz. ASW **Subject:** Year of the Scout

| Date | Mintage | F | VF | XF | Unc | BU |
|---|---|---|---|---|---|---|
| ND(1984) | 10,000 | — | — | — | 40.00 | — |
| ND(1984) Proof | Inc. above | Value: 50.00 | | | | |

**50 CEDIS** KM# 31 **Composition:** Nickel Clad Steel

| Date | Mintage | F | VF | XF | Unc | BU |
|---|---|---|---|---|---|---|
| 1991 | — | — | — | 1.00 | 2.25 | — |
| 1997 | — | — | — | 1.00 | 2.25 | — |

**100 CEDIS** KM# 27 **Weight:** 28.2800 g. **Composition:** 0.5000 Silver .4546 oz. ASW **Subject:** Commonwealth Games

| Date | Mintage | F | VF | XF | Unc | BU |
|---|---|---|---|---|---|---|
| 1986 | 50,000 | — | — | — | 17.50 | — |

**100 CEDIS** KM# 27a **Weight:** 28.2800 g. **Composition:** 0.9250 Silver .8411 oz. ASW **Subject:** Commonwealth Games

| Date | Mintage | F | VF | XF | Unc | BU |
|---|---|---|---|---|---|---|
| 1986 Proof | 20,000 | Value: 27.50 | | | | |

**100 CEDIS** KM# 32 **Ring Composition:** Copper-Nickel **Center Composition:** Brass **Obverse:** Cocoa beans

| Date | Mintage | F | VF | XF | Unc | BU |
|---|---|---|---|---|---|---|
| 1991 | — | — | — | 1.75 | 3.75 | — |
| 1997 | — | — | — | 1.50 | 3.00 | — |

**200 CEDIS** KM# 35 **Composition:** Nickel Plated Steel **Obverse:** Cowrie shell **Reverse:** National arms, denomination

| Date | Mintage | F | VF | XF | Unc | BU |
|---|---|---|---|---|---|---|
| 1996 | — | — | — | — | 3.75 | — |
| 1998 | — | — | — | — | 3.00 | — |

**500 CEDIS** KM# 28 **Weight:** 15.9800 g. **Composition:** 0.9170 Gold .4711 oz. AGW **Subject:** International Year of Disabled Persons

| Date | Mintage | F | VF | XF | Unc | BU |
|---|---|---|---|---|---|---|
| 1981 | — | — | — | — | 325 | — |
| 1981 Proof | — | Value: 400 | | | | |

**500 CEDIS** KM# 23 **Weight:** 15.9800 g. **Composition:** 0.9170 Gold .4711 oz. AGW **Subject:** Year of the Scout

| Date | Mintage | F | VF | XF | Unc | BU |
|---|---|---|---|---|---|---|
| ND(1984) | 2,000 | — | — | — | 300 | — |
| ND(1984) Proof | 2,000 | Value: 375 | | | | |

**500 CEDIS** KM# 34 **Composition:** Nickel-Brass **Obverse:** Drums **Reverse:** National arms, denomination

| Date | Mintage | F | VF | XF | Unc | BU |
|---|---|---|---|---|---|---|
| 1996 | — | — | — | — | 4.75 | — |

## MEDALLIC COINAGE

**CROWN** KM# M1 **Composition:** Copper-Nickel **Subject:** OAU summit meeting

| Date | Mintage | F | VF | XF | Unc | BU |
|---|---|---|---|---|---|---|
| 1965 Proof | 10,000 | Value: 16.50 | | | | |

**CROWN** KM# M2 **Weight:** 28.2800 g. **Composition:** 0.9250 Silver .8411 oz. ASW

| Date | Mintage | F | VF | XF | Unc | BU |
|---|---|---|---|---|---|---|
| 1965 Proof | 1,000 | Value: 40.00 | | | | |

**CROWN** KM# M3 **Weight:** 28.2800 g. **Composition:** 0.9170 Gold .8338 oz. AGW **Subject:** OAU summit meeting

| Date | Mintage | F | VF | XF | Unc | BU |
|---|---|---|---|---|---|---|
| 1965 Proof | 50 | Value: 700 | | | | |

**2 POUNDS** KM# M5 **Weight:** 15.9800 g. **Composition:** 0.9170 Gold .4711 oz. AGW **Subject:** Republic day

| Date | Mintage | F | VF | XF | Unc | BU |
|---|---|---|---|---|---|---|
| ND(1960) Proof | 15,000 | Value: 225 | | | | |

**2 POUNDS** KM# M4 **Weight:** 15.9800 g. **Composition:** 0.9170 Gold .4711 oz. AGW **Subject:** OAU summit meeting

| Date | Mintage | F | VF | XF | Unc | BU |
|---|---|---|---|---|---|---|
| 1965 Proof | 2,020 | Value: 250 | | | | |

**2 POUNDS** KM# M6 **Weight:** 15.9800 g. **Composition:** 0.9170 Gold .4711 oz. AGW **Obverse:** Arms with date below **Reverse:** Bust of Kotoka 1/2 left

| Date | Mintage | F | VF | XF | Unc | BU |
|---|---|---|---|---|---|---|
| 1968 Proof | 2,000 | Value: 250 | | | | |

**2 POUNDS** KM# M7 **Weight:** 15.9800 g. **Composition:** 0.9170 Gold .4711 oz. AGW **Subject:** Freedom in Unity

| Date | Mintage | F | VF | XF | Unc | BU |
|---|---|---|---|---|---|---|
| 1973 Proof | 2,000 | Value: 250 | | | | |

**2 POUNDS** KM# M8 **Weight:** 15.9800 g. **Composition:** 0.9170 Gold .4711 oz. AGW **Subject:** Operation Feed Yourself **Obverse:** Native planting crops **Reverse:** Arms and date

| Date | Mintage | F | VF | XF | Unc | BU |
|---|---|---|---|---|---|---|
| 1975 Proof | — | Value: 175 | | | | |

**2 POUNDS** KM# M9 **Weight:** 19.6700 g. **Composition:** 0.9170 Gold .5799 oz. AGW **Subject:** 20th anniversary of independence

| Date | Mintage | F | VF | XF | Unc | BU |
|---|---|---|---|---|---|---|
| ND(1977) Proof | 4,397 | Value: 325 | | | | |

**2 POUNDS** KM# M9a **Weight:** 11.8800 g. **Composition:** Silver **Subject:** 20th anniversary of independence

| Date | Mintage | F | VF | XF | Unc | BU |
|---|---|---|---|---|---|---|
| ND(1977) Proof | — | Value: 20.00 | | | | |

**4 POUNDS** KM# M10 **Weight:** 39.5400 g. **Composition:** 0.9170 Gold 1.1658 oz. AGW **Subject:** 20th anniversary of independence

| Date | Mintage | F | VF | XF | Unc | BU |
|---|---|---|---|---|---|---|
| ND(1977) Proof | 300 | Value: 800 | | | | |

## PIEFORTS

| KM# | Date | Mintage | Identification | Issue Price | Mkt Val |
|---|---|---|---|---|---|
| P1 | 1981 | 1,050 | 50 Cedis. Silver. KM20. | — | 65.00 |
| P2 | 1981 | — | 500 Cedis. Gold. KM28. | — | 1,200 |
| P3 | (1984) | 520 | 50 Cedis. Silver. KM21a. | — | 80.00 |

## PROOF SETS

| KM# | Date | Mintage | Identification | Issue Price | Mkt Val |
|---|---|---|---|---|---|
| PS1 | 1958 (7) | 6,431 | KM1-7 | — | 23.50 |
| PS2 | 1967 (6) | 100 | KM12-17 | 8.53 | 11.50 |

# GIBRALTAR

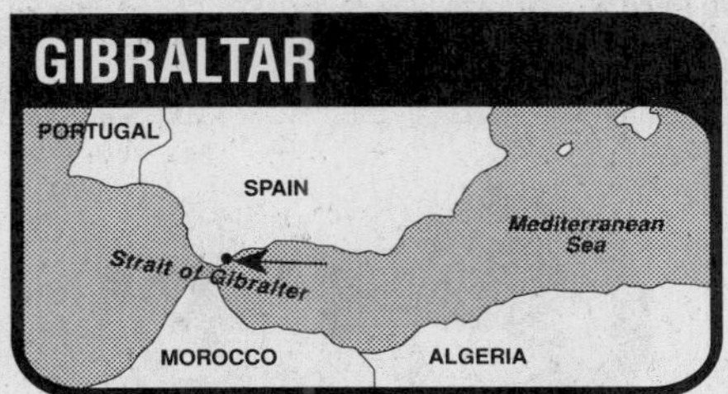


The British Colony of Gibraltar, located at the southernmost point of the Iberian Peninsula, has an area of 2.25sq. mi. (6.5 sq. km.) and a population of 29,651. Capital (and only town): Gibraltar. Aside from its strategic importance as guardian of the western entrance to the Mediterranean Sea, Gibraltar is also a free port and a British naval base.

Gibraltar, rooted in Greek mythology as one of the Pillars of Hercules, has long been a coveted stronghold. Moslems took it from Spain and fortified it in 711. Spain retook it in 1309, lost it again to the Moors in 1333 and retook it in 1462. After 1540 Spain strengthened its defenses and held it until the War of the Spanish Succession when it was captured by a combined British and Dutch force in 1704. Britain held it against the Franco-Spanish attacks of 1704-05 and through the historic Great Siege of 1779-83.Recently Spain has attempted to discourage British occupancy by harassment and economic devices. In 1967, Gibraltar's inhabitants voted 12,138 to 44 to remain under British rule.

Gibraltar's celebrated Barbary Ape, the last monkey to be found in a wild state in Europe, is featured on the colony's first decimal crown, released in 1972.

**RULERS**
British

**MINT MARKS**
PM - Pobjoy Mint

**MINT PRIVY MARKS**
U - Unc finish

**DIE MARKS**
1988: AA-AE
1989: AA-AF
1990: AA-AB
1991: AA
1992: AA-BB
1993: AA-BB
1994-1999: AA

**MONETARY SYSTEM**
4 Farthings = 1 Penny
12 Pence = 1 Shilling
2 Shillings = 1 Crown
5 Shillings = 1 Crown
20 Shillings = 1 Pound

## BRITISH COLONY

### CROWN COINAGE

**CROWN** KM# 4 **Composition:** Copper-Nickel

| Date | Mintage | F | VF | XF | Unc | BU |
|---|---|---|---|---|---|---|
| 1967 | 125,000 | — | 0.50 | 1.00 | 2.50 | — |
| 1968 | 40,000 | — | 0.65 | 1.25 | 3.00 | — |
| 1969 | 40,000 | — | 0.65 | 1.25 | 3.00 | — |
| 1970 | 45,000 | — | 0.65 | 1.25 | 3.00 | — |

**CROWN** KM# 4a **Weight:** 28.2800 g. **Composition:** 0.5000 Silver .4546 oz. ASW

| Date | Mintage | F | VF | XF | Unc | BU |
|---|---|---|---|---|---|---|
| 1967 Proof | 10,000 | Value: 12.50 | | | | |
| 1967 Frosted Proof | 50 | Value: 200 | | | | |

### DECIMAL COINAGE

**PENNY** KM# 20 **Composition:** Bronze **Reverse:** Barbary partridge

| Date | Mintage | F | VF | XF | Unc | BU |
|---|---|---|---|---|---|---|
| 1988 AA | — | — | — | — | 0.25 | — |
| 1988 AB | — | — | — | — | 0.25 | — |
| 1988 AC | — | — | — | — | 0.25 | — |
| 1988 AD | — | — | — | — | 0.25 | — |
| 1988 AE | — | — | — | — | 0.25 | — |
| 1989 AA | — | — | — | — | 0.25 | — |
| 1989 AB | — | — | — | — | 0.25 | — |
| 1989 AC | — | — | — | — | 0.25 | — |
| 1989 AD | — | — | — | — | 0.25 | — |
| 1989 AE | — | — | — | — | 0.25 | — |
| 1989 AF | — | — | — | — | 0.25 | — |
| 1990 AA | — | — | — | — | 0.25 | — |
| 1990 AB | — | — | — | — | 0.25 | — |
| 1991 AA | — | — | — | — | 0.25 | — |
| 1992 AA | — | — | — | — | 0.25 | — |
| 1992 BB | — | — | — | — | 0.25 | — |
| 1993 AA | — | — | — | — | 0.25 | — |
| 1993 BB | — | — | — | — | 0.25 | — |
| 1994 AA | — | — | — | — | 0.25 | — |

**PENNY** KM# 20a **Composition:** Bronze Plated Steel

| Date | Mintage | F | VF | XF | Unc | BU |
|---|---|---|---|---|---|---|
| 1995 AA | — | — | — | — | 0.25 | — |
| 1996 AA | — | — | — | — | 0.25 | — |
| 1997 AA | — | — | — | — | 0.25 | — |

**PENNY** KM# 773 **Composition:** Bronze Plated Steel **Obverse:** Rank-Broadley portrait of Queen Elizabeth II **Reverse:** Barbary partridge

| Date | Mintage | F | VF | XF | Unc | BU |
|---|---|---|---|---|---|---|
| 1998 AA | — | — | — | — | 0.25 | — |
| 1999 AA | — | — | — | — | 0.25 | — |

**2 PENCE** KM# 21 **Composition:** Bronze **Reverse:** Lighthouse on Europa Point

| Date | Mintage | F | VF | XF | Unc | BU |
|---|---|---|---|---|---|---|
| 1988 AA | — | — | — | — | 0.50 | — |
| 1988 AB | — | — | — | — | 0.50 | — |
| 1988 AC | — | — | — | — | 0.50 | — |
| 1988 AD | — | — | — | — | 0.50 | — |
| 1988 AE | — | — | — | — | 0.50 | — |
| 1989 AA | — | — | — | — | 0.50 | — |
| 1989 AB | — | — | — | — | 0.50 | — |
| 1989 AC | — | — | — | — | 0.50 | — |
| 1989 AD | — | — | — | — | 0.50 | — |
| 1989 AE | — | — | — | — | 0.50 | — |
| 1989 AF | — | — | — | — | 0.50 | — |
| 1990 AA | — | — | — | — | 0.50 | — |
| 1990 AB | — | — | — | — | 0.50 | — |
| 1991 AA | — | — | — | — | 0.50 | — |
| 1992 AA | — | — | — | — | 0.50 | — |
| 1992 BB | — | — | — | — | 0.50 | — |
| 1993 AA | — | — | — | — | 0.50 | — |
| 1993 BB | — | — | — | — | 0.50 | — |
| 1994 AA | — | — | — | — | 0.50 | — |

**2 PENCE** KM# 21a **Composition:** Bronze Plated Steel

| Date | Mintage | F | VF | XF | Unc | BU |
|---|---|---|---|---|---|---|
| 1995 AA | — | — | — | — | 0.50 | — |
| 1996 AA | — | — | — | — | 0.50 | — |
| 1997 AA | — | — | — | — | 0.50 | — |

**2 PENCE** KM# 774 **Composition:** Bronze Plated Steel **Obverse:** Rank-Broadley portrait of Queen Elizabeth II

| Date | Mintage | F | VF | XF | Unc | BU |
|---|---|---|---|---|---|---|
| 1998 AA | — | — | — | — | 0.50 | — |
| 1999 AA | — | — | — | — | 0.50 | — |

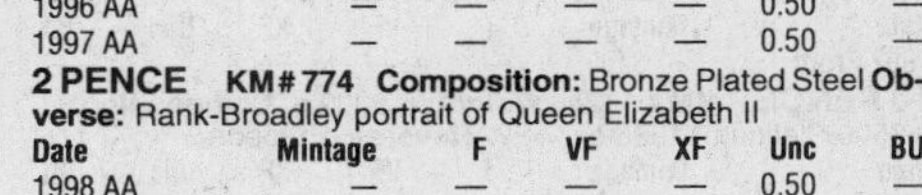
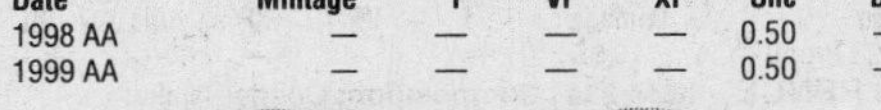

**5 PENCE** KM# 22 **Composition:** Copper-Nickel **Reverse:** Barbary Ape

| Date | Mintage | F | VF | XF | Unc | BU |
|---|---|---|---|---|---|---|
| 1988 AA | — | — | — | — | 0.75 | — |
| 1989 AA | — | — | — | — | 0.75 | — |

**5 PENCE** **KM# 22b** **Weight:** 3.2500 g. **Composition:** 0.9250 Silver .0966 oz. ASW

| Date | Mintage | F | VF | XF | Unc | BU |
|---|---|---|---|---|---|---|
| 1990 Proof | 5,000 | Value: 25.00 | | | | |

**5 PENCE** **KM# 22c** **Weight:** 3.2500 g. **Composition:** 0.9170 Gold .0958 oz. AGW **Obverse:** Queen's portrait **Reverse:** Barbary Ape

| Date | Mintage | F | VF | XF | Unc | BU |
|---|---|---|---|---|---|---|
| 1990 Proof | 1,000 | Value: 125 | | | | |

**5 PENCE** **KM# 22a** **Composition:** Copper-Nickel **Note:** Reduced size, 18 millimeters.

| Date | Mintage | F | VF | XF | Unc | BU |
|---|---|---|---|---|---|---|
| 1990 AA | — | — | — | — | 0.50 | — |
| 1991 AA | — | — | — | — | 0.50 | — |
| 1992 AA | — | — | — | — | 0.50 | — |
| 1992 AB | — | — | — | — | 0.50 | — |
| 1993 AA | — | — | — | — | 0.50 | — |
| 1994 AA | — | — | — | — | 0.50 | — |
| 1995 AA | — | — | — | — | 0.50 | — |
| 1996 AA | — | — | — | — | 0.50 | — |
| 1997 AA | — | — | — | — | 0.50 | — |

**5 PENCE** **KM# 775** **Composition:** Copper-Nickel **Obverse:** Rank-Broadley portrait of Queen Elizabeth II

| Date | Mintage | F | VF | XF | Unc | BU |
|---|---|---|---|---|---|---|
| 1998 AA | — | — | — | — | 0.50 | — |
| 1999 AA | — | — | — | — | 0.50 | — |

**10 PENCE** **KM# 23** **Composition:** Copper-Nickel **Reverse:** Moorish castle

| Date | Mintage | F | VF | XF | Unc | BU |
|---|---|---|---|---|---|---|
| 1988 AA | — | — | — | — | 1.00 | — |
| 1988 AB | — | — | — | — | 1.00 | — |
| 1989 AA | — | — | — | — | 1.00 | — |
| 1990 AA | — | — | — | — | 1.00 | — |
| 1991 AA | — | — | — | — | 1.00 | — |
| 1991 AB | — | — | — | — | 1.00 | — |

**10 PENCE** **KM# 112** **Composition:** Copper-Nickel **Reverse:** Europort

| Date | Mintage | F | VF | XF | Unc | BU |
|---|---|---|---|---|---|---|
| 1992 AA | — | — | — | — | 0.75 | — |
| 1993 AA | — | — | — | — | 0.75 | — |
| 1995 AA | — | — | — | — | 0.75 | — |
| 1996 AA | — | — | — | — | 0.75 | — |
| 1997 AA | — | — | — | — | 0.75 | — |

**10 PENCE** **KM# 112a** **Weight:** 6.5000 g. **Composition:** 0.9250 Silver .1933 oz. ASW **Reverse:** Europort

| Date | Mintage | F | VF | XF | Unc | BU |
|---|---|---|---|---|---|---|
| 1992 Proof | 25,000 | Value: 25.00 | | | | |

**10 PENCE** **KM# 112b** **Weight:** 6.5000 g. **Composition:** 0.9170 Gold .1916 oz. AGW **Reverse:** Europort

| Date | Mintage | F | VF | XF | Unc | BU |
|---|---|---|---|---|---|---|
| 1992 Proof | 3,500 | — | — | — | — | — |

**10 PENCE** **KM# 112c** **Weight:** 6.5000 g. **Composition:** 0.9500 Platinum .1985 oz. APW **Reverse:** Europort

| Date | Mintage | F | VF | XF | Unc | BU |
|---|---|---|---|---|---|---|
| 1992 Proof | 3,500 | — | — | — | — | — |

**10 PENCE** **KM# 23a** **Composition:** Copper-Nickel

| Date | Mintage | F | VF | XF | Unc | BU |
|---|---|---|---|---|---|---|
| 1994 | — | — | — | — | 1.00 | — |

**10 PENCE** **KM# 776** **Weight:** 6.5000 g. **Composition:** 0.9500 Platinum .1985 oz. APW **Obverse:** Rank-Broadley portrait of Queen Elizabeth II

| Date | Mintage | F | VF | XF | Unc | BU |
|---|---|---|---|---|---|---|
| 1998 AA | — | — | — | — | 1.00 | — |
| 1999 AA | — | — | — | — | 1.00 | — |

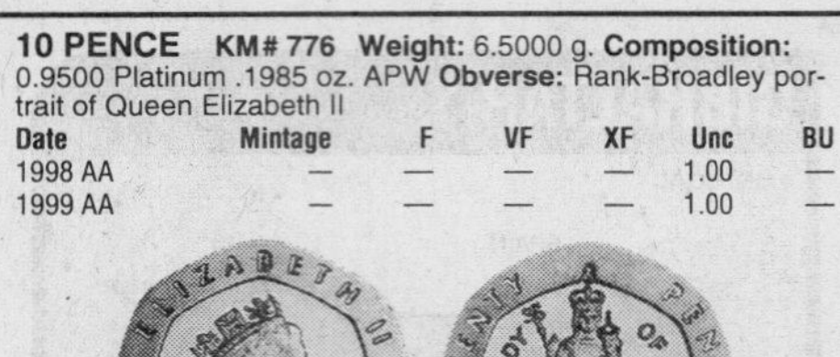

**20 PENCE** **KM# 16** **Composition:** Copper-Nickel **Reverse:** Our Lady of Europe

| Date | Mintage | F | VF | XF | Unc | BU |
|---|---|---|---|---|---|---|
| 1988 AA | — | — | — | — | 1.50 | — |
| 1988 AA Proof | — | — | — | — | — | — |
| 1989 AA | — | — | — | — | 1.50 | — |
| 1990 AA | — | — | — | — | 1.50 | — |
| 1991 AA | — | — | — | — | 1.50 | — |
| 1992 AA | — | — | — | — | 1.50 | — |
| 1993 AA | — | — | — | — | 1.50 | — |
| 1994 AA | — | — | — | — | 1.50 | — |
| 1995 AA | — | — | — | — | 1.50 | — |
| 1995 AA Proof | — | — | — | — | — | — |
| 1996 AA | — | — | — | — | 1.50 | — |
| 1997 AA | — | — | — | — | 1.50 | — |

**20 PENCE** **KM# 777** **Composition:** Copper-Nickel **Obverse:** Rank-Broadley portrait of Queen Elizabeth II

| Date | Mintage | F | VF | XF | Unc | BU |
|---|---|---|---|---|---|---|
| 1998 AA | — | — | — | — | 1.50 | — |
| 1999 AA | — | — | — | — | 1.50 | — |

**25 NEW PENCE** **KM# 5** **Composition:** Copper-Nickel **Reverse:** Barbary Ape

| Date | Mintage | F | VF | XF | Unc | BU |
|---|---|---|---|---|---|---|
| 1971 | 75,000 | — | — | 2.00 | 5.00 | — |

**25 NEW PENCE** **KM# 5a** **Weight:** 28.2800 g. **Composition:** 0.5000 Silver .4546 oz. ASW

| Date | Mintage | F | VF | XF | Unc | BU |
|---|---|---|---|---|---|---|
| 1971 Proof | 20,000 | Value: 10.00 | | | | |
| 1971 Frosted Proof | 50 | Value: 200 | | | | |

**25 NEW PENCE** **KM# 6** **Composition:** Copper-Nickel **Subject:** 25th Wedding Anniversary **Reverse:** Arms of Queen Elizabeth II and Prince Philip

| Date | Mintage | F | VF | XF | Unc | BU |
|---|---|---|---|---|---|---|
| 1972 | 70,000 | — | — | 1.50 | 3.50 | — |

**25 NEW PENCE** **KM# 6a** **Weight:** 28.2800 g. **Composition:** 0.9250 Silver .8411 oz. ASW

| Date | Mintage | F | VF | XF | Unc | BU |
|---|---|---|---|---|---|---|
| 1972 Proof | 15,000 | Value: 12.50 | | | | |

**25 NEW PENCE** **KM# 10** **Composition:** Silver **Subject:** Queen's Silver Jubilee **Reverse:** Shield within wreath of apes and laurel

| Date | Mintage | F | VF | XF | Unc | BU |
|---|---|---|---|---|---|---|
| 1977 | 65,000 | — | — | 1.50 | 3.50 | — |

**25 NEW PENCE** **KM# 10a** **Weight:** 28.2800 g. **Composition:** 0.9250 Silver .8411 oz. ASW

| Date | Mintage | F | VF | XF | Unc | BU |
|---|---|---|---|---|---|---|
| 1977 Proof | 24,000 | Value: 12.50 | | | | |

**50 PENCE** **KM# 17** **Composition:** Copper-Nickel **Reverse:** Denomination in wreath of Candytuft flowers

| Date | Mintage | F | VF | XF | Unc | BU |
|---|---|---|---|---|---|---|
| 1988 AA | 30,000 | — | — | — | 2.00 | — |
| 1988 AB | — | — | — | — | 2.00 | — |
| 1989 AA | — | — | — | — | 2.00 | — |
| 1989 AB | — | — | — | — | 2.00 | — |

**50 PENCE** **KM# 19** **Composition:** Copper-Nickel **Subject:** Christmas **Reverse:** The Three Wise Men

| Date | Mintage | F | VF | XF | Unc | BU |
|---|---|---|---|---|---|---|
| 1988 | — | — | — | — | 4.00 | — |
| 1988 Proof | Est. 30,000 | Value: 15.00 | | | | |

**50 PENCE** **KM# 19a** **Weight:** 15.5000 g. **Composition:** 0.9250 Silver .4610 oz. ASW **Subject:** Christmas **Reverse:** The Three Wise Men

| Date | Mintage | F | VF | XF | Unc | BU |
|---|---|---|---|---|---|---|
| 1988 Proof | Est. 5,000 | Value: 15.00 | | | | |

**50 PENCE** **KM# 19b** **Weight:** 26.0000 g. **Composition:** 0.9170 Gold .7665 oz. AGW **Subject:** Christmas **Reverse:** The Three Wise Men

| Date | Mintage | F | VF | XF | Unc | BU |
|---|---|---|---|---|---|---|
| 1988 Proof | 250 | Value: 450 | | | | |

**50 PENCE** **KM# 19c** **Weight:** 30.4000 g. **Composition:** 0.9950 Platinum .9725 oz. APW **Subject:** Christmas **Reverse:** The Three Wise Men

| Date | Mintage | F | VF | XF | Unc | BU |
|---|---|---|---|---|---|---|
| 1988 Proof | 50 | Value: 700 | | | | |

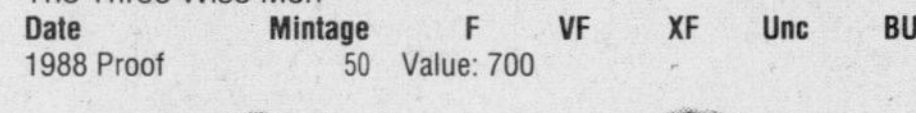

**50 PENCE** **KM#31** **Composition:** Copper-Nickel **Reverse:** Christmas - Choir Boy

| Date | Mintage | F | VF | XF | Unc | BU |
|---|---|---|---|---|---|---|
| 1989 AA | — | — | — | — | 4.00 | — |
| 1989 AA Proof | Est. 30,000 | Value: 6.50 | | | | |

**50 PENCE** **KM# 31a** **Weight:** 15.5000 g. **Composition:** 0.9250 Silver .4610 oz. ASW **Reverse:** Christmas - Choir Boy

| Date | Mintage | F | VF | XF | Unc | BU |
|---|---|---|---|---|---|---|
| 1989 Proof | Est. 5,000 | Value: 45.00 | | | | |

**50 PENCE** **KM# 31b** **Weight:** 26.0000 g. **Composition:** 0.9170 Gold .7665 oz. AGW **Reverse:** Christmas - Choir Boy

| Date | Mintage | F | VF | XF | Unc | BU |
|---|---|---|---|---|---|---|
| 1989 Proof | Est. 250 | Value: 750 | | | | |

**50 PENCE** **KM# 31c** **Weight:** 30.4000 g. **Composition:** 0.9950 Platinum .9628 oz. APW **Reverse:** Christmas - Choir Boy

| Date | Mintage | F | VF | XF | Unc | BU |
|---|---|---|---|---|---|---|
| 1989 Proof | Est. 50 | Value: 1,000 | | | | |

**50 PENCE** **KM#39** **Composition:** Copper-Nickel **Reverse:** Dolphins

| Date | Mintage | F | VF | XF | Unc | BU |
|---|---|---|---|---|---|---|
| 1990 AA | — | — | — | — | 4.00 | — |
| 1991 AA | — | — | — | — | 4.00 | — |
| 1992 AA | — | — | — | — | 4.00 | — |
| 1993 AA | — | — | — | — | 4.00 | — |
| 1994 AA | — | — | — | — | 4.00 | — |
| 1995 AA | — | — | — | — | 4.00 | — |
| 1996 AA | — | — | — | — | 4.00 | — |

**50 PENCE** **KM# 39a** **Weight:** 15.5000 g. **Composition:** 0.9250 Silver .4610 oz. ASW

| Date | Mintage | F | VF | XF | Unc | BU |
|---|---|---|---|---|---|---|
| 1990 Proof | 2,500 | Value: 47.50 | | | | |
| 1993 Proof | — | Value: 50.00 | | | | |

**50 PENCE** **KM# 39b** **Weight:** 26.0000 g. **Composition:** 0.9170 Gold .7665 oz. AGW **Reverse:** Dolphins

| Date | Mintage | F | VF | XF | Unc | BU |
|---|---|---|---|---|---|---|
| 1990 Proof | 250 | Value: 800 | | | | |

**50 PENCE** **KM#47** **Composition:** Copper-Nickel **Reverse:** Christmas - Two women with child

| Date | Mintage | F | VF | XF | Unc | BU |
|---|---|---|---|---|---|---|
| 1990 Proof | Est. 30,000 | Value: 8.00 | | | | |

**50 PENCE** **KM# 47a** **Weight:** 15.5000 g. **Composition:** 0.9250 Silver .4610 oz. ASW **Reverse:** Christmas - Two women with child

| Date | Mintage | F | VF | XF | Unc | BU |
|---|---|---|---|---|---|---|
| 1990 Proof | 5,000 | Value: 45.00 | | | | |

**50 PENCE** **KM# 47b** **Weight:** 26.0000 g. **Composition:** 0.9170 Gold .7665 oz. AGW **Reverse:** Christmas - Two women with child

| Date | Mintage | F | VF | XF | Unc | BU |
|---|---|---|---|---|---|---|
| 1990 Proof | 250 | Value: 700 | | | | |

**50 PENCE** **KM# 47c** **Weight:** 30.4000 g. **Composition:** 0.9950 Platinum .9723 oz. APW **Reverse:** Christmas - Two women with child

| Date | Mintage | F | VF | XF | Unc | BU |
|---|---|---|---|---|---|---|
| 1990 Proof | 50 | Value: 1,000 | | | | |

**50 PENCE** **KM#83** **Composition:** Copper-Nickel **Reverse:** Christmas - Family caroling

| Date | Mintage | F | VF | XF | Unc | BU |
|---|---|---|---|---|---|---|
| 1991 AA | — | — | — | — | 4.00 | — |
| 1991 AA Proof | Est. 30,000 | Value: 6.50 | | | | |

**50 PENCE** **KM# 83a** **Weight:** 15.5000 g. **Composition:** 0.9250 Silver .4610 oz. ASW **Reverse:** Christmas - Family caroling

| Date | Mintage | F | VF | XF | Unc | BU |
|---|---|---|---|---|---|---|
| 1991 Proof | Est. 5,000 | Value: 40.00 | | | | |

**50 PENCE** **KM# 83b** **Weight:** 26.0000 g. **Composition:** 0.9170 Gold .7665 oz. AGW **Reverse:** Christmas - Family caroling

| Date | Mintage | F | VF | XF | Unc | BU |
|---|---|---|---|---|---|---|
| 1991 Proof | 250 | Value: 685 | | | | |

**50 PENCE** **KM# 83c** **Weight:** 30.4000 g. **Composition:** 0.9500 Platinum .9286 oz. APW **Reverse:** Christmas - Family caroling

| Date | Mintage | F | VF | XF | Unc | BU |
|---|---|---|---|---|---|---|
| 1991 Proof | 50 | Value: 860 | | | | |

**50 PENCE** **KM# 108** **Composition:** Copper-Nickel **Reverse:** Christmas - Bust of Santa

| Date | Mintage | F | VF | XF | Unc | BU |
|---|---|---|---|---|---|---|
| 1992 AA | Est. 30,000 | — | — | — | 3.50 | — |
| 1992 AA Proof | — | Value: 6.50 | | | | |

**50 PENCE** **KM# 108a** **Weight:** 15.5000 g. **Composition:** 0.9250 Silver .4610 oz. ASW **Reverse:** Christmas - Bust of Santa

| Date | Mintage | F | VF | XF | Unc | BU |
|---|---|---|---|---|---|---|
| 1992 Proof | Est. 5,000 | Value: 40.00 | | | | |

**50 PENCE** **KM# 108b** **Weight:** 26.0000 g. **Composition:** 0.9170 Gold .7665 oz. AGW **Reverse:** Christmas - Bust of Santa

| Date | Mintage | F | VF | XF | Unc | BU |
|---|---|---|---|---|---|---|
| 1992 Proof | 250 | Value: 685 | | | | |

**50 PENCE** **KM# 108c** **Weight:** 30.4000 g. **Composition:** 0.9950 Platinum .9725 oz. APW **Reverse:** Christmas - Bust of Santa

| Date | Mintage | F | VF | XF | Unc | BU |
|---|---|---|---|---|---|---|
| 1992 Proof | 50 | Value: 860 | | | | |

**50 PENCE** **KM# 190** **Composition:** Copper-Nickel **Reverse:** Christmas - Santa in automobile

| Date | Mintage | F | VF | XF | Unc | BU |
|---|---|---|---|---|---|---|
| 1993 AA | 30,000 | — | — | — | 3.50 | — |

**50 PENCE** **KM# 190a** **Weight:** 15.5000 g. **Composition:** 0.9250 Silver .4610 oz. ASW **Reverse:** Christmas - Santa in automobile

| Date | Mintage | F | VF | XF | Unc | BU |
|---|---|---|---|---|---|---|
| 1993 Proof | Est. 5,000 | Value: 40.00 | | | | |

**50 PENCE** **KM# 190b** **Weight:** 26.0000 g. **Composition:** 0.9170 Gold .7665 oz. AGW **Reverse:** Christmas - Santa in automobile

| Date | Mintage | F | VF | XF | Unc | BU |
|---|---|---|---|---|---|---|
| 1993 Proof | Est. 250 | Value: 685 | | | | |

**50 PENCE** **KM# 190c** **Weight:** 30.4000 g. **Composition:** 0.9500 Platinum .9286 oz. APW **Reverse:** Christmas - Santa in automobile

| Date | Mintage | F | VF | XF | Unc | BU |
|---|---|---|---|---|---|---|
| 1993 Proof | Est. 50 | Value: 860 | | | | |

**50 PENCE** **KM# 294** **Composition:** Copper-Nickel **Reverse:** Christmas - Santa, balloon and sack

| Date | Mintage | F | VF | XF | Unc | BU |
|---|---|---|---|---|---|---|
| 1994 AA | 30,000 | — | — | — | 3.50 | — |

**50 PENCE** **KM# 294a** **Weight:** 15.5000 g. **Composition:** 0.9250 Silver .4610 oz. ASW **Reverse:** Christmas - Santa, baloon and sack

| Date | Mintage | F | VF | XF | Unc | BU |
|---|---|---|---|---|---|---|
| 1994 Proof | Est. 5,000 | Value: 40.00 | | | | |

**50 PENCE** **KM# 294b** **Weight:** 26.0000 g. **Composition:** 0.9170 Gold .7665 oz. AGW **Reverse:** Christmas - Santa, balloon and sack

| Date | Mintage | F | VF | XF | Unc | BU |
|---|---|---|---|---|---|---|
| 1994 Proof | Est. 250 | Value: 700 | | | | |

**50 PENCE** **KM# 294c** **Weight:** 30.4000 g. **Composition:** 0.9500 Platinum .9286 oz. APW **Reverse:** Christmas - Santa, baloon and sack

| Date | Mintage | F | VF | XF | Unc | BU |
|---|---|---|---|---|---|---|
| 1994 Proof | Est. 50 | Value: 875 | | | | |

**50 PENCE** **KM# 336** **Composition:** Copper-Nickel **Reverse:** Christmas - Penguins parading

| Date | Mintage | F | VF | XF | Unc | BU |
|---|---|---|---|---|---|---|
| 1995 AA | Est. 30,000 | — | — | — | 4.00 | — |

**50 PENCE** **KM# 336a** **Weight:** 15.5000 g. **Composition:** 0.9250 Silver .4610 oz. ASW **Reverse:** Christmas - Penguins parading

| Date | Mintage | F | VF | XF | Unc | BU |
|---|---|---|---|---|---|---|
| 1995 Proof | Est. 5,000 | Value: 40.00 | | | | |

**50 PENCE** **KM# 336b** **Weight:** 26.0000 g. **Composition:** 0.9170 Gold .7665 oz. AGW **Reverse:** Christmas - Penguins parading

| Date | Mintage | F | VF | XF | Unc | BU |
|---|---|---|---|---|---|---|
| 1995 Proof | Est. 250 | Value: 700 | | | | |

**50 PENCE** **KM# 336c** **Weight:** 30.4000 g. **Composition:** 0.9950 Platinum .9769 oz. APW **Reverse:** Christmas - Penguins parading

| Date | Mintage | F | VF | XF | Unc | BU |
|---|---|---|---|---|---|---|
| 1995 Proof | 50 | Value: 875 | | | | |

**50 PENCE** **KM# 453** **Composition:** Copper-Nickel **Reverse:** Christmas - Santa Claus and biplane

| Date | Mintage | F | VF | XF | Unc | BU |
|---|---|---|---|---|---|---|
| 1996 | Est. 30,000 | — | — | — | 4.00 | — |

**50 PENCE** **KM# 453a** **Weight:** 15.0000 g. **Composition:** 0.9250 Silver .4610 oz. ASW **Reverse:** Christmas - Santa Claus and biplane

| Date | Mintage | F | VF | XF | Unc | BU |
|---|---|---|---|---|---|---|
| 1996 Proof | Est. 5,000 | Value: 35.00 | | | | |

**50 PENCE** **KM# 453b** **Weight:** 26.0000 g. **Composition:** 0.9170 Gold .7665 oz. AGW **Reverse:** Christmas - Santa Claus and biplane

| Date | Mintage | F | VF | XF | Unc | BU |
|---|---|---|---|---|---|---|
| 1996 Proof | Est. 250 | Value: 645 | | | | |

**50 PENCE** **KM# 606** **Composition:** Copper-Nickel **Obverse:** Queen's portrait **Reverse:** Christmas - Santa Claus in sleigh

| Date | Mintage | F | VF | XF | Unc | BU |
|---|---|---|---|---|---|---|
| 1997 | Est. 30,000 | — | — | — | 4.00 | — |

**50 PENCE** **KM# 606a** **Weight:** 8.0000 g. **Composition:** 0.9250 Silver .2379 oz. ASW **Reverse:** Christmas - Santa Claus in sleigh

| Date | Mintage | F | VF | XF | Unc | BU |
|---|---|---|---|---|---|---|
| 1997 Proof | Est. 5,000 | Value: 35.00 | | | | |

**50 PENCE** **KM# 606b** **Weight:** 8.0000 g. **Composition:** 0.9170 Gold .2359 oz. AGW **Obverse:** Queen's portrait **Reverse:** Christmas - Santa in sleigh

| Date | Mintage | F | VF | XF | Unc | BU |
|---|---|---|---|---|---|---|
| 1997 Proof | Est. 250 | Value: 645 | | | | |

**50 PENCE** **KM# 39.1** **Weight:** 8.0000 g. **Composition:** Copper-Nickel 27.30 oz. **Obverse:** Queen's portrait **Reverse:** Configuration of five dolphins and denomination

| Date | Mintage | F | VF | XF | Unc | BU |
|---|---|---|---|---|---|---|
| 1997 AA | — | — | — | — | 4.00 | — |
| 1998 AA | — | — | — | — | 4.00 | — |
| 1999 AA | — | — | — | — | 4.00 | — |

**50 PENCE** **KM# 39.1a** **Weight:** 8.0000 g. **Composition:** 0.9250 Silver .2379 oz. ASW

| Date | Mintage | F | VF | XF | Unc | BU |
|---|---|---|---|---|---|---|
| 1997 Proof | Est. 5,000 | Value: 35.00 | | | | |

**50 PENCE** **KM# 39.1b** **Weight:** 8.0000 g. **Composition:** 0.9999 Gold .2569 oz. AGW

| Date | Mintage | F | VF | XF | Unc | BU |
|---|---|---|---|---|---|---|
| 1997 Proof | Est. 250 | Value: 400 | | | | |

**50 PENCE** **KM# 769** **Composition:** Copper-Nickel **Obverse:** Queen's portrait **Reverse:** Santa Claus in chimney

| Date | Mintage | F | VF | XF | Unc | BU |
|---|---|---|---|---|---|---|
| 1998 | Est. 30,000 | — | — | — | 4.00 | — |

**50 PENCE** **KM# 769a** **Weight:** 8.0000 g. **Composition:** 0.9250 Silver .2379 oz. ASW **Reverse:** Santa Claus in Chimney

| Date | Mintage | F | VF | XF | Unc | BU |
|---|---|---|---|---|---|---|
| 1998 Proof | Est. 5,000 | Value: 35.00 | | | | |

**50 PENCE** **KM# 769b** **Weight:** 8.0000 g. **Composition:** 0.9170 Gold .2359 oz. AGW **Obverse:** Queen's portrait **Reverse:** Santa Claus in chimney

| Date | Mintage | F | VF | XF | Unc | BU |
|---|---|---|---|---|---|---|
| 1998 Proof | Est. 250 | Value: 645 | | | | |

**50 PENCE** **KM# 866** **Composition:** Copper-Nickel **Obverse:** Rank-Broadley portrait of Queen Elizabeth II **Reverse:** Santa with pair of monkeys

| Date | Mintage | F | VF | XF | Unc | BU |
|---|---|---|---|---|---|---|
| 1999 BB | Est. 30,000 | — | — | — | 4.00 | — |
| 1999 BB | Est. 30,000 | — | — | — | 4.00 | — |

**50 PENCE** **KM# 866a** **Weight:** 8.0000 g. **Composition:** 0.9250 Silver .2379 oz. ASW **Reverse:** Santa with pair of monkeys

| Date | Mintage | F | VF | XF | Unc | BU |
|---|---|---|---|---|---|---|
| 1999 Proof | Est. 5,000 | Value: 35.00 | | | | |

**50 PENCE** **KM# 866b** **Weight:** 8.0000 g. **Composition:** 0.9170 Gold .2359 oz. AGW **Reverse:** Santa with pair of monkeys

| Date | Mintage | F | VF | XF | Unc | BU |
|---|---|---|---|---|---|---|
| 1999 Proof | Est. 250 | Value: 645 | | | | |

**50 PENCE** **KM# 887** **Weight:** 8.0000 g. **Composition:** Copper-Nickel **Obverse:** Bust Queen right **Reverse:** Christmas - Madonna and child with angels **Edge:** Plain **Shape:** 7-sided

| Date | Mintage | F | VF | XF | Unc | BU |
|---|---|---|---|---|---|---|
| 2000 | 30,000 | — | — | — | 4.00 | — |

**50 PENCE** **KM# 887a** **Weight:** 8.0000 g. **Composition:** 0.9250 Silver .2379 oz. ASW **Reverse:** Christmas - Madonna and child with angels

| Date | Mintage | F | VF | XF | Unc | BU |
|---|---|---|---|---|---|---|
| 2000 Proof | 5,000 | Value: 35.00 | | | | |

**50 PENCE** **KM# 887b** **Weight:** 8.0000 g. **Composition:** 0.9160 Gold .2356 oz. AGW **Reverse:** Christmas - Madonna and child with angels **Note:** KM#310-317 previously listed here do not exist and have been removed.

| Date | Mintage | F | VF | XF | Unc | BU |
|---|---|---|---|---|---|---|
| 2000 Proof | 250 | Value: 645 | | | | |

**50 PENCE** **KM# 971** **Weight:** 8.0000 g. **Composition:** Copper-Nickel **Subject:** Christmas **Obverse:** Queen's portrait **Reverse:** Three wise men **Edge:** Plain, seven sided **Size:** 27.3 mm.

| Date | Mintage | F | VF | XF | Unc | BU |
|---|---|---|---|---|---|---|
| 2001 | 30,000 | — | — | — | 10.00 | — |

**50 PENCE** **KM# 971a** **Weight:** 8.0000 g. **Composition:** 0.9250 Silver .2379 oz. ASW **Edge:** Plain, seven sided **Size:** 27.3 mm.

| Date | Mintage | F | VF | XF | Unc | BU |
|---|---|---|---|---|---|---|
| 2001 Proof | 5,000 | Value: 34.00 | | | | |

**50 PENCE** **KM# 971b** **Weight:** 8.0000 g. **Composition:** 0.9167 Gold .2358 oz. AGW **Edge:** Plain, seven sided **Size:** 27.3 mm.

| Date | Mintage | F | VF | XF | Unc | BU |
|---|---|---|---|---|---|---|
| 2001 Proof | 250 | Value: 645 | | | | |

**1/25 CROWN** **KM# 124** **Weight:** 1.2440 g. **Composition:** 0.9999 Gold .0400 oz. AGW **Reverse:** Japanese Royal Wedding

| Date | Mintage | F | VF | XF | Unc | BU |
|---|---|---|---|---|---|---|
| 1993 Proof | Est. 25,000 | Value: 50.00 | | | | |

**1/25 CROWN** **KM# 202a** **Weight:** 1.2440 g. **Composition:** 0.9950 Platinum .0400 oz. APW

| Date | Mintage | F | VF | XF | Unc | BU |
|---|---|---|---|---|---|---|
| 1993 Proof | 7,500 | Value: 55.00 | | | | |

**1/25 CROWN** **KM# 202** **Weight:** 1.2440 g. **Composition:** 0.9999 Gold .0400 oz. AGW **Series:** Peter Rabbit Centennial **Subject:** Peter Rabbit **Obverse:** Portrait of Queen Elizabeth II **Reverse:** Peter Rabbit eating carrots **Note:** Similar to 1 Crown, KM#201.

| Date | Mintage | F | VF | XF | Unc | BU |
|---|---|---|---|---|---|---|
| 1993 Proof | Est. 25,000 | Value: 40.00 | | | | |

**1/25 CROWN** **KM# 206** **Weight:** 1.2440 g. **Composition:** 0.9999 Gold .0400 oz. AGW **Series:** Peter Rabbit Centennial **Subject:** Tiggy-Winkel **Reverse:** Mrs. Tiggy-Winkel ironing **Note:** Similar to 1 Crown, KM#205.

| Date | Mintage | F | VF | XF | Unc | BU |
|---|---|---|---|---|---|---|
| 1993 Proof | Est. 25,000 | Value: 40.00 | | | | |

**1/25 CROWN** **KM# 210** **Weight:** 1.2440 g. **Composition:** 0.9999 Gold .0400 oz. AGW **Series:** Peter Rabbit Centennial **Subject:** Jeremy Fisher **Reverse:** Jeremy Fisher fishing **Note:** Similar to 1 Crown, KM#209.

| Date | Mintage | F | VF | XF | Unc | BU |
|---|---|---|---|---|---|---|
| 1993 Proof | Est. 25,000 | Value: 40.00 | | | | |

**1/25 CROWN** **KM# 214** **Weight:** 1.2440 g. **Composition:** 0.9999 Gold .0400 oz. AGW **Series:** Peter Rabbit Centennial **Subject:** Tom Kitten **Reverse:** Tom Kitten with mother cat **Note:** Similar to 1 Crown, KM#213.

| Date | Mintage | F | VF | XF | Unc | BU |
|---|---|---|---|---|---|---|
| 1993 Proof | Est. 25,000 | Value: 40.00 | | | | |

**1/25 CROWN** **KM# 218** **Weight:** 1.2440 g. **Composition:** 0.9999 Gold .0400 oz. AGW **Series:** Peter Rabbit Centennial **Subject:** Benjamin Bunny **Reverse:** Benjamin Bunny wearing hat and holding coat **Note:** Similar to 1 Crown, KM#217.

| Date | Mintage | F | VF | XF | Unc | BU |
|---|---|---|---|---|---|---|
| 1993 Proof | Est. 25,000 | Value: 40.00 | | | | |

**1/25 CROWN** **KM# 222** **Weight:** 1.2440 g. **Composition:** 0.9999 Gold .0400 oz. AGW **Series:** Peter Rabbit Centennial **Subject:** Jemima Puddle-Duck **Reverse:** Jemima Puddle Duck talking with fox **Note:** Similar to 1 Crown, KM#221.

| Date | Mintage | F | VF | XF | Unc | BU |
|---|---|---|---|---|---|---|
| 1993 Proof | Est. 25,000 | Value: 40.00 | | | | |

**1/25 CROWN** **KM# 437** **Weight:** 1.2440 g. **Composition:** 0.9999 Gold .0400 oz. AGW **Series:** Peter Rabbit Centennial **Subject:** Mother and Bunnies **Note:** Similar to 1 Crown, KM#444.

| Date | Mintage | F | VF | XF | Unc | BU |
|---|---|---|---|---|---|---|
| 1994 Proof | 25,000 | Value: 45.00 | | | | |

**1/25 CROWN** **KM# 437a** **Weight:** 1.2440 g. **Composition:** 0.9950 Platinum .0400 oz. APW **Series:** Peter Rabbit Centennial **Subject:** Mother and Bunnies **Note:** Similar to 1 Crown, KM#444.

| Date | Mintage | F | VF | XF | Unc | BU |
|---|---|---|---|---|---|---|
| 1994 Proof | Est. 7,500 | Value: 55.00 | | | | |

**1/25 CROWN** **KM# 454** **Weight:** 1.2441 g. **Composition:** 0.9999 Gold .0400 oz. AGW **Series:** Centenary of the Cinema **Subject:** Wizard of Oz **Note:** Similar to 1 Crown, KM#457.

| Date | Mintage | F | VF | XF | Unc | BU |
|---|---|---|---|---|---|---|
| 1996 Proof | Est. 25,000 | Value: 45.00 | | | | |

**1/25 CROWN** **KM# 458** **Weight:** 1.2441 g. **Composition:** 0.9999 Gold .0400 oz. AGW **Series:** Centenary of the Cinema **Subject:** Marx Brothers **Note:** Similar to 1 Crown, KM#461.

| Date | Mintage | F | VF | XF | Unc | BU |
|---|---|---|---|---|---|---|
| 1996 Proof | Est. 25,000 | Value: 45.00 | | | | |

**1/25 CROWN** **KM# 462** **Weight:** 1.2441 g. **Composition:** 0.9999 Gold .0400 oz. AGW **Series:** Centenary of the Cinema **Subject:** Elvis Presley **Note:** Similar to 1 Crown, KM#465.

| Date | Mintage | F | VF | XF | Unc | BU |
|---|---|---|---|---|---|---|
| 1996 Proof | Est. 25,000 | Value: 45.00 | | | | |

**1/25 CROWN** **KM# 466** **Weight:** 1.2441 g. **Composition:** 0.9999 Gold .0400 oz. AGW **Series:** Centenary of the Cinema **Subject:** Casablanca **Note:** Similar to 1 Crown, KM#469.

| Date | Mintage | F | VF | XF | Unc | BU |
|---|---|---|---|---|---|---|
| 1996 Proof | Est. 25,000 | Value: 45.00 | | | | |

**1/25 CROWN** **KM# 470** **Weight:** 1.2441 g. **Composition:** 0.9999 Gold .0400 oz. AGW **Series:** Centenary of the Cinema **Subject:** E.T. **Note:** Similar to 1 Crown, KM#473.

| Date | Mintage | F | VF | XF | Unc | BU |
|---|---|---|---|---|---|---|
| 1996 Proof | Est. 25,000 | Value: 45.00 | | | | |

**1/25 CROWN** **KM# 474** **Weight:** 1.2441 g. **Composition:** 0.9999 Gold .0400 oz. AGW **Series:** Centenary of the Cinema **Subject:** Alfred Hitchcock **Note:** Similar to 1 Crown, KM#477.

| Date | Mintage | F | VF | XF | Unc | BU |
|---|---|---|---|---|---|---|
| 1996 Proof | Est. 25,000 | Value: 45.00 | | | | |

**1/25 CROWN** **KM# 368** **Weight:** 1.2441 g. **Composition:** 0.9999 Gold .0400 oz. AGW **Reverse:** Roses **Note:** Similar to 1 Crown, KM#373.

| Date | Mintage | F | VF | XF | Unc | BU |
|---|---|---|---|---|---|---|
| 1996 Proof | Est. 25,000 | Value: 45.00 | | | | |

**1/25 CROWN** **KM# 390** **Weight:** 1.2441 g. **Composition:** 0.9999 Gold .0400 oz. AGW **Series:** Centenary of the Cinema **Subject:** Grace Kelly **Note:** Similar to 1 Crown, KM#393.

| Date | Mintage | F | VF | XF | Unc | BU |
|---|---|---|---|---|---|---|
| 1996 Proof | Est. 25,000 | Value: 45.00 | | | | |

**1/25 CROWN** **KM# 395** **Weight:** 1.2441 g. **Composition:** 0.9999 Gold .0400 oz. AGW **Series:** Centenary of the Cinema **Subject:** James Dean **Note:** Similar to 1 Crown, KM#398.

| Date | Mintage | F | VF | XF | Unc | BU |
|---|---|---|---|---|---|---|
| 1996 Proof | Est. 25,000 | Value: 45.00 | | | | |

**1/25 CROWN** **KM# 400** **Weight:** 1.2441 g. **Composition:** 0.9999 Gold .0400 oz. AGW **Series:** Centenary of the Cinema **Subject:** Marilyn Monroe **Note:** Similar to 1 Crown, KM#403.

| Date | Mintage | F | VF | XF | Unc | BU |
|---|---|---|---|---|---|---|
| 1996 Proof | Est. 25,000 | Value: 45.00 | | | | |

**1/25 CROWN** **KM# 405** **Weight:** 1.2441 g. **Composition:** 0.9999 Gold .0400 oz. AGW **Series:** Centenary of the Cinema **Subject:** Audrey Hepburn **Note:** Similar to 1 Crown, KM#408.

| Date | Mintage | F | VF | XF | Unc | BU |
|---|---|---|---|---|---|---|
| 1996 Proof | 25,000 | Value: 45.00 | | | | |

**1/25 CROWN** **KM# 410** **Weight:** 1.2441 g. **Composition:** 0.9999 Gold .0400 oz. AGW **Series:** Centenary of the Cinema **Subject:** Bruce Lee **Note:** Similar to 1 Crown, KM#413.

| Date | Mintage | F | VF | XF | Unc | BU |
|---|---|---|---|---|---|---|
| 1996 Proof | Est. 25,000 | Value: 55.00 | | | | |

**1/25 CROWN** **KM# 415** **Weight:** 1.2441 g. **Composition:** 0.9999 Gold .0400 oz. AGW **Series:** Centenary of the Cinema **Subject:** Charlie Chaplin **Note:** Similar to 1 Crown, KM#418.

| Date | Mintage | F | VF | XF | Unc | BU |
|---|---|---|---|---|---|---|
| 1996 Proof | Est. 25,000 | Value: 55.00 | | | | |

**1/25 CROWN** **KM# 420** **Weight:** 1.2441 g. **Composition:** 0.9999 Gold .0400 oz. AGW **Series:** Centenary of the Cinema **Subject:** Gone With The Wind **Note:** Similar to 1 Crown, KM#423.

| Date | Mintage | F | VF | XF | Unc | BU |
|---|---|---|---|---|---|---|
| 1996 Proof | Est. 25,000 | Value: 55.00 | | | | |

**1/25 CROWN** **KM# 425** **Weight:** 1.2441 g. **Composition:** 0.9999 Gold .0400 oz. AGW **Series:** Centenary of the Cinema **Subject:** The Flintstones **Note:** Similar to 1 Crown, KM#428.

| Date | Mintage | F | VF | XF | Unc | BU |
|---|---|---|---|---|---|---|
| 1996 Proof | Est. 25,000 | Value: 55.00 | | | | |

**1/25 CROWN** **KM# 375** **Weight:** 1.2441 g. **Composition:** 0.9999 Gold .0400 oz. AGW **Series:** Peter Rabbit Centennial **Subject:** Rabbit Escaping

| Date | Mintage | F | VF | XF | Unc | BU |
|---|---|---|---|---|---|---|
| 1996 Proof | Est. 25,000 | Value: 45.00 | | | | |

**1/25 CROWN** **KM# 375a** **Weight:** 1.2500 g. **Composition:** 0.9950 Platinum .0400 oz. APW **Series:** Peter Rabbit Centennial **Subject:** Rabbit Escaping

| Date | Mintage | F | VF | XF | Unc | BU |
|---|---|---|---|---|---|---|
| 1996 Proof | Est. 7,500 | Value: 55.00 | | | | |

**1/25 CROWN** **KM# 405a** **Weight:** 1.2500 g. **Composition:** 0.9950 Platinum .0400 oz. APW

| Date | Mintage | F | VF | XF | Unc | BU |
|---|---|---|---|---|---|---|
| 1996 Proof | Est. 1,000 | Value: 65.00 | | | | |

**1/25 CROWN** **KM# 452** **Weight:** 1.2441 g. **Composition:** 0.9999 Gold .0400 oz. AGW **Series:** Centenary of the Cinema **Subject:** James Dean **Note:** Similar to 1/10 Crown, KM#453.

| Date | Mintage | F | VF | XF | Unc | BU |
|---|---|---|---|---|---|---|
| 1996 Proof | Est. 25,000 | Value: 60.00 | | | | |

**1/25 CROWN** **KM# 518a** **Weight:** 1.2504 g. **Composition:** 0.9950 Platinum .0400 oz. APW

| Date | Mintage | F | VF | XF | Unc | BU |
|---|---|---|---|---|---|---|
| 1997 Proof | Est. 7,500 | Value: 55.00 | | | | |

**1/25 CROWN** **KM# 518** **Weight:** 1.2441 g. **Composition:** 0.9999 Gold .0400 oz. AGW **Subject:** The Tale of Peter Rabbit **Note:** Similar to 1 Crown, KM#525.

| Date | Mintage | F | VF | XF | Unc | BU |
|---|---|---|---|---|---|---|
| 1997 Proof | Est. 25,000 | Value: 45.00 | | | | |

**1/25 CROWN** **KM# 537** **Weight:** 1.2440 g. **Composition:** 0.9999 Gold .0400 oz. AGW **Subject:** Peonies **Note:** Similar to 1 Crown, KM#540.

| Date | Mintage | F | VF | XF | Unc | BU |
|---|---|---|---|---|---|---|
| 1997 Proof | Est. 25,000 | Value: 45.00 | | | | |

**1/25 CROWN** **KM# 541** **Weight:** 1.2440 g. **Composition:** 0.9999 Gold .0400 oz. AGW **Subject:** Nefertiti **Note:** Similar to 1 Crown, KM#544.

| Date | Mintage | F | VF | XF | Unc | BU |
|---|---|---|---|---|---|---|
| 1997 Proof | Est. 10,000 | Value: 45.00 | | | | |

**1/25 CROWN** **KM# 545** **Weight:** 1.2440 g. **Composition:** 0.9999 Gold .0400 oz. AGW **Subject:** Cleopatra **Note:** Similar to 1 Crown, KM#548.

| Date | Mintage | F | VF | XF | Unc | BU |
|---|---|---|---|---|---|---|
| 1997 Proof | Est. 10,000 | Value: 45.00 | | | | |

**1/25 CROWN** **KM# 549** **Weight:** 1.2440 g. **Composition:** 0.9999 Gold .0400 oz. AGW **Subject:** Europa **Note:** Similar to 1 Crown, KM#552.

| Date | Mintage | F | VF | XF | Unc | BU |
|---|---|---|---|---|---|---|
| 1997 Proof | Est. 10,000 | Value: 45.00 | | | | |

**1/25 CROWN** **KM# 553** **Weight:** 1.2440 g. **Composition:** 0.9999 Gold .0400 oz. AGW **Subject:** Liberty **Note:** Similar to 1 Crown, KM#556.

| Date | Mintage | F | VF | XF | Unc | BU |
|---|---|---|---|---|---|---|
| 1997 Proof | Est. 10,000 | Value: 45.00 | | | | |

**1/25 CROWN** **KM# 581** **Weight:** 1.2440 g. **Composition:** 0.9999 Gold .0400 oz. AGW **Series:** Evolution of Mankind **Subject:** Egypt **Note:** Similar to 1 Crown, KM#582.

| Date | Mintage | F | VF | XF | Unc | BU |
|---|---|---|---|---|---|---|
| 1997 Proof | Est. 15,000 | Value: 40.00 | | | | |

**1/25 CROWN** **KM# 583** **Weight:** 1.2440 g. **Composition:** 0.9999 Gold .0400 oz. AGW **Series:** Evolution of Mankind **Subject:** Israel **Note:** Similar to 1 Crown, KM#584.

| Date | Mintage | F | VF | XF | Unc | BU |
|---|---|---|---|---|---|---|
| 1997 Proof | Est. 15,000 | Value: 40.00 | | | | |

**1/25 CROWN** **KM# 585** **Weight:** 1.2440 g. **Composition:** 0.9999 Gold .0400 oz. AGW **Series:** Evolution of Mankind **Subject:** China **Note:** Similar to 1 Crown, KM#586.

| Date | Mintage | F | VF | XF | Unc | BU |
|---|---|---|---|---|---|---|
| 1997 Proof | Est. 15,000 | Value: 40.00 | | | | |

**1/25 CROWN** **KM# 587** **Weight:** 1.2440 g. **Composition:** 0.9999 Gold .0400 oz. AGW **Series:** Evolution of Mankind **Subject:** Greece **Note:** Similar to 1 Crown, KM#588.

| Date | Mintage | F | VF | XF | Unc | BU |
|---|---|---|---|---|---|---|
| 1997 Proof | Est. 15,000 | Value: 40.00 | | | | |

**1/25 CROWN** **KM# 589** **Weight:** 1.2440 g. **Composition:** 0.9999 Gold .0400 oz. AGW **Series:** Evolution of Mankind **Subject:** Rome **Note:** Similar to 1 Crown, KM#590.

| Date | Mintage | F | VF | XF | Unc | BU |
|---|---|---|---|---|---|---|
| 1997 Proof | Est. 15,000 | Value: 40.00 | | | | |

**1/25 CROWN** **KM# 591** **Weight:** 1.2440 g. **Composition:** 0.9999 Gold .0400 oz. AGW **Series:** Evolution of Mankind **Subject:** India **Note:** Similar to 1 Crown, KM#592.

| Date | Mintage | F | VF | XF | Unc | BU |
|---|---|---|---|---|---|---|
| 1997 Proof | Est. 15,000 | Value: 40.00 | | | | |

**1/25 CROWN** **KM# 593** **Weight:** 1.2440 g. **Composition:** 0.9999 Gold .0400 oz. AGW **Series:** Evolution of Mankind **Subject:** Holy Roman Empire **Note:** Similar to 1 Crown, KM#594.

| Date | Mintage | F | VF | XF | Unc | BU |
|---|---|---|---|---|---|---|
| 1997 Proof | Est. 15,000 | Value: 40.00 | | | | |

**1/25 CROWN** **KM# 595** **Weight:** 1.2440 g. **Composition:** 0.9999 Gold .0400 oz. AGW **Series:** Evolution of Mankind **Subject:** Macedonia **Note:** Similar to 1 Crown, KM#596.

| Date | Mintage | F | VF | XF | Unc | BU |
|---|---|---|---|---|---|---|
| 1997 Proof | Est. 15,000 | Value: 40.00 | | | | |

**1/25 CROWN** **KM# 597** **Weight:** 1.2440 g. **Composition:** 0.9999 Gold .0400 oz. AGW **Series:** Evolution of Mankind **Subject:** Native America **Note:** Similar to 1 Crown, KM#598.

| Date | Mintage | F | VF | XF | Unc | BU |
|---|---|---|---|---|---|---|
| 1997 Proof | Est. 15,000 | Value: 40.00 | | | | |

**1/25 CROWN** **KM# 599** **Weight:** 1.2440 g. **Composition:** 0.9999 Gold .0400 oz. AGW **Series:** Evolution of Mankind **Subject:** Asia **Note:** Similar to 1 Crown, KM#600.

| Date | Mintage | F | VF | XF | Unc | BU |
|---|---|---|---|---|---|---|
| 1997 Proof | Est. 15,000 | Value: 40.00 | | | | |

**1/25 CROWN** **KM# 601** **Weight:** 1.2440 g. **Composition:** 0.9999 Gold .0400 oz. AGW **Series:** Evolution of Mankind **Subject:** Inca Empire **Note:** Similar to 1 Crown, KM#602.

| Date | Mintage | F | VF | XF | Unc | BU |
|---|---|---|---|---|---|---|
| 1997 Proof | Est. 15,000 | Value: 40.00 | | | | |

**1/25 CROWN** **KM# 603** **Weight:** 1.2440 g. **Composition:** 0.9999 Gold .0400 oz. AGW **Series:** Evolution of Mankind **Subject:** Islamic Civilization **Note:** Similar to 1 Crown, KM#604.

| Date | Mintage | F | VF | XF | Unc | BU |
|---|---|---|---|---|---|---|
| 1997 Proof | Est. 15,000 | Value: 40.00 | | | | |

**1/25 CROWN** **KM# 608** **Weight:** 1.2440 g. **Composition:** 0.9999 Gold .0400 oz. AGW **Series:** Traders of the World **Subject:** Sir Francis Drake **Obverse:** Queen's portrait **Reverse:** Sir Francis Drake, ship and beach **Note:** Similar to 1 Crown, KM#609.

| Date | Mintage | F | VF | XF | Unc | BU |
|---|---|---|---|---|---|---|
| 1997 Proof | Est. 15,000 | Value: 45.00 | | | | |

**1/25 CROWN** **KM# 610** **Weight:** 1.2440 g. **Composition:** 0.9999 Gold .0400 oz. AGW **Series:** Traders of the World **Subject:** Romans **Obverse:** Queen's portrait **Reverse:** Lion, lioness, ship, map **Note:** Similar to 1 Crown, KM#611.

| Date | Mintage | F | VF | XF | Unc | BU |
|---|---|---|---|---|---|---|
| 1997 Proof | Est. 15,000 | Value: 45.00 | | | | |

**1/25 CROWN** **KM# 612** **Weight:** 1.2440 g. **Composition:** 0.9999 Gold .0400 oz. AGW **Series:** Traders of the World **Subject:** Venetians **Obverse:** Queen's portrait **Reverse:** Pair of oysters with pearls, Venetian canal scene **Note:** Similar to 1 Crown, KM#613.

| Date | Mintage | F | VF | XF | Unc | BU |
|---|---|---|---|---|---|---|
| 1997 Proof | Est. 15,000 | Value: 45.00 | | | | |

**1/25 CROWN** **KM# 614** **Weight:** 1.2440 g. **Composition:** 0.9999 Gold .0400 oz. AGW **Series:** Traders of the World **Subject:** Portuguese **Obverse:** Queen's portrait **Reverse:** Gold ingots and Portuguese ship **Note:** Similar to 1 Crown, KM#615.

| Date | Mintage | F | VF | XF | Unc | BU |
|---|---|---|---|---|---|---|
| 1997 Proof | Est. 15,000 | Value: 45.00 | | | | |

**1/25 CROWN** **KM# 616** **Weight:** 1.2440 g. **Composition:** 0.9999 Gold .0400 oz. AGW **Series:** Traders of the World **Subject:** Spanish **Obverse:** Queen's portrait **Reverse:** Tobacco leaves, ship, map and gems **Note:** Similar to 1 Crown, KM#617.

| Date | Mintage | F | VF | XF | Unc | BU |
|---|---|---|---|---|---|---|
| 1997 Proof | Est. 15,000 | Value: 45.00 | | | | |

**1/25 CROWN** **KM# 618** **Weight:** 1.2440 g. **Composition:** 0.9999 Gold .0400 oz. AGW **Series:** Traders of the World **Subject:** English **Obverse:** Queen's portrait **Reverse:** Profile of Queen above fighting ships **Note:** Similar to 1 Crown, KM#619.

| Date | Mintage | F | VF | XF | Unc | BU |
|---|---|---|---|---|---|---|
| 1997 Proof | Est. 15,000 | Value: 45.00 | | | | |

**1/25 CROWN** **KM# 620** **Weight:** 1.2440 g. **Composition:** 0.9999 Gold .0400 oz. AGW **Series:** Traders of the World **Subject:** Captain Bligh **Obverse:** Queen's portrait **Reverse:** Captain Bligh on beach, ship **Note:** Similar to 1 Crown, KM#621.

| Date | Mintage | F | VF | XF | Unc | BU |
|---|---|---|---|---|---|---|
| 1997 Proof | Est. 15,000 | Value: 45.00 | | | | |

**1/25 CROWN** **KM# 622** **Weight:** 1.2440 g. **Composition:** 0.9999 Gold .0400 oz. AGW **Series:** Traders of the World **Subject:** Captain Cook **Obverse:** Queen's portrait **Reverse:** Beaver on rock, ship, Captain Cook **Note:** Similar to 1 Crown, KM#623.

| Date | Mintage | F | VF | XF | Unc | BU |
|---|---|---|---|---|---|---|
| 1997 Proof | Est. 15,000 | Value: 45.00 | | | | |

**1/25 CROWN** **KM# 649** **Weight:** 1.2440 g. **Composition:** 0.9999 Gold .0400 oz. AGW **Subject:** The Tale of Peter Rabbit **Obverse:** Queen's portrait **Reverse:** Peter Rabbit **Note:** Similar to 1 Crown, KM#656.

| Date | Mintage | F | VF | XF | Unc | BU |
|---|---|---|---|---|---|---|
| 1998 Proof | Est. 25,000 | Value: 45.00 | | | | |

**1/25 CROWN** **KM# 657** **Weight:** 1.2441 g. **Composition:** 0.9999 Gold .0400 oz. AGW **Subject:** Chrysanthemum **Obverse:** Queen's portrait **Reverse:** Three blossoms **Note:** Similar to 1 Crown, KM#661.

| Date | Mintage | F | VF | XF | Unc | BU |
|---|---|---|---|---|---|---|
| 1998 Proof | Est. 25,000 | Value: 45.00 | | | | |

**1/25 CROWN** **KM# 662** **Weight:** 1.2441 g. **Composition:** 0.9999 Gold .0400 oz. AGW **Subject:** Brittania **Obverse:** Queen's portrait **Reverse:** Profile of helmeted Brittania **Note:** Similar to 1 Crown, KM#674.

| Date | Mintage | F | VF | XF | Unc | BU |
|---|---|---|---|---|---|---|
| 1998 Proof | Est. 10,000 | Value: 45.00 | | | | |

**1/25 CROWN** **KM# 663** **Weight:** 1.2441 g. **Composition:** 0.9999 Gold .0400 oz. AGW **Subject:** Juno **Obverse:** Queen's portrait **Reverse:** Facing portrait **Note:** Similar to 1 Crown, KM#675.

| Date | Mintage | F | VF | XF | Unc | BU |
|---|---|---|---|---|---|---|
| 1998 Proof | Est. 10,000 | Value: 45.00 | | | | |

**1/25 CROWN** **KM# 664** **Weight:** 1.2441 g. **Composition:** 0.9999 Gold .0400 oz. AGW **Subject:** Athena **Obverse:** Queen's portrait **Reverse:** Profile of helmeted Athena **Note:** Similar to 1 Crown, KM#676.

| Date | Mintage | F | VF | XF | Unc | BU |
|---|---|---|---|---|---|---|
| 1998 Proof | Est. 10,000 | Value: 45.00 | | | | |

**1/25 CROWN** **KM# 665** **Weight:** 1.2441 g. **Composition:** 0.9999 Gold .0400 oz. AGW **Subject:** Arethusa **Obverse:** Queen's portrait **Reverse:** Profile with dolphins **Note:** Similar to 1 Crown, KM#677.

| Date | Mintage | F | VF | XF | Unc | BU |
|---|---|---|---|---|---|---|
| 1998 Proof | Est. 10,000 | Value: 45.00 | | | | |

**1/25 CROWN** **KM# 678** **Weight:** 1.2441 g. **Composition:** 0.9999 Gold .0400 oz. AGW **Subject:** Paddington Bear **Obverse:** Queen's portrait **Reverse:** Paddington with suitcase **Note:** Similar to 1 Crown, KM#682.

| Date | Mintage | F | VF | XF | Unc | BU |
|---|---|---|---|---|---|---|
| 1998 Proof | Est. 7,500 | Value: 45.00 | | | | |

**1/25 CROWN** **KM# 691** **Weight:** 1.2440 g. **Composition:** 0.9999 Gold .0400 oz. AGW **Subject:** Traders of the World **Obverse:** Queen's portrait **Reverse:** Phoenician Galley (200 BC-600AD), shells below **Note:** Similar to 1 Crown, KM#692.

| Date | Mintage | F | VF | XF | Unc | BU |
|---|---|---|---|---|---|---|
| 1998 Proof | Est. 10,000 | Value: 45.00 | | | | |

**1/25 CROWN** **KM# 693** **Weight:** 1.2440 g. **Composition:** 0.9999 Gold .0400 oz. AGW **Subject:** Traders of the World **Obverse:** Queen's portrait **Reverse:** Viking ship (900 AD), pair of fish **Note:** Similar to 1 Crown, KM#694.

| Date | Mintage | F | VF | XF | Unc | BU |
|---|---|---|---|---|---|---|
| 1998 Proof | Est. 10,000 | Value: 45.00 | | | | |

**1/25 CROWN** **KM# 695** **Weight:** 1.2440 g. **Composition:** 0.9999 Gold .0400 oz. AGW **Subject:** Traders of the World **Obverse:** Queen's portrait **Reverse:** Marco Polo with ship (1254-1324) **Note:** Similar to 1 Crown, KM#696.

| Date | Mintage | F | VF | XF | Unc | BU |
|---|---|---|---|---|---|---|
| 1998 Proof | Est. 10,000 | Value: 45.00 | | | | |

**1/25 CROWN** **KM# 697** **Weight:** 1.2440 g. **Composition:** 0.9999 Gold .0400 oz. AGW **Subject:** Traders of the World **Obverse:** Queen's portrait **Reverse:** Hanseatic Kogge (circa 1350), coins **Note:** Similar to 1 Crown, KM#698.

| Date | Mintage | F | VF | XF | Unc | BU |
|---|---|---|---|---|---|---|
| 1998 Proof | Est. 10,000 | Value: 45.00 | | | | |

**1/25 CROWN** **KM# 699** **Weight:** 1.2440 g. **Composition:** 0.9999 Gold .0400 oz. AGW **Subject:** Traders of the World **Obverse:** Queen's portrait **Reverse:** Chinese Junk (1400s) **Note:** Similar to 1 Crown, KM#700.

| Date | Mintage | F | VF | XF | Unc | BU |
|---|---|---|---|---|---|---|
| 1998 Proof | Est. 10,000 | Value: 45.00 | | | | |

**1/25 CROWN** **KM# 701** **Weight:** 1.2440 g. **Composition:** 0.9999 Gold .0400 oz. AGW **Subject:** Traders of the World **Obverse:** Queen's portrait **Reverse:** Christopher Columbus (1451-1506) and ship **Note:** Similar to 1 Crown, KM#702.

| Date | Mintage | F | VF | XF | Unc | BU |
|---|---|---|---|---|---|---|
| 1998 Proof | Est. 10,000 | Value: 45.00 | | | | |

**1/25 CROWN** **KM# 703** **Weight:** 1.2440 g. **Composition:** 0.9999 Gold .0400 oz. AGW **Subject:** Traders of the World **Obverse:** Queen's portrait **Reverse:** Sir Walter Raleigh (1552-1618) **Note:** Similar to 1 Crown, KM#704.

| Date | Mintage | F | VF | XF | Unc | BU |
|---|---|---|---|---|---|---|
| 1998 Proof | Est. 10,000 | Value: 45.00 | | | | |

**1/25 CROWN** **KM# 705** **Weight:** 1.2440 g. **Composition:** 0.9999 Gold .0400 oz. AGW **Subject:** Traders of the World **Obverse:** Queen's portrait **Reverse:** Sinking ships at the Boston Tea Party (1773), tea leaf **Note:** Similar to 1 Crown, KM#706.

| Date | Mintage | F | VF | XF | Unc | BU |
|---|---|---|---|---|---|---|
| 1998 Proof | Est. 10,000 | Value: 45.00 | | | | |

**1/25 CROWN** **KM# 709** **Weight:** 1.2440 g. **Composition:** 0.9999 Gold .0400 oz. AGW **Subject:** Evolution of Mankind **Obverse:** Queen's portrait **Reverse:** Homo-Habilis, using tools **Note:** Similar to 1 Crown, KM#710.

| Date | Mintage | F | VF | XF | Unc | BU |
|---|---|---|---|---|---|---|
| 1998 Proof | Est. 15,000 | Value: 45.00 | | | | |

**1/25 CROWN** **KM# 711** **Weight:** 1.2440 g. **Composition:** 0.9999 Gold .0400 oz. AGW **Subject:** Evolution of Mankind **Obverse:** Queen's portrait **Reverse:** Homo Erectus - using fire **Note:** Similar to 1 Crown, KM#712.

| Date | Mintage | F | VF | XF | Unc | BU |
|---|---|---|---|---|---|---|
| 1998 Proof | Est. 15,000 | Value: 45.00 | | | | |

**1/25 CROWN** **KM# 713** **Weight:** 1.2440 g. **Composition:** 0.9999 Gold .0400 oz. AGW **Subject:** Evolution of Mankind **Obverse:** Queen's portrait **Reverse:** Gibraltar skull, man and "The Rock" **Note:** Similar to 1 Crown, KM#714.

| Date | Mintage | F | VF | XF | Unc | BU |
|---|---|---|---|---|---|---|
| 1998 Proof | Est. 15,000 | Value: 45.00 | | | | |

**1/25 CROWN** **KM# 715** **Weight:** 1.2440 g. **Composition:** 0.9999 Gold .0400 oz. AGW **Subject:** Evolution of Mankind **Obverse:** Queen's portrait **Reverse:** Neanderthal Man, burial scene **Note:** Similar to 1 Crown, KM#716.

| Date | Mintage | F | VF | XF | Unc | BU |
|---|---|---|---|---|---|---|
| 1998 Proof | Est. 15,000 | Value: 45.00 | | | | |

**1/25 CROWN** **KM# 717** **Weight:** 1.2440 g. **Composition:** 0.9999 Gold .0400 oz. AGW **Subject:** Evolution of Mankind **Obverse:** Queen's portrait **Reverse:** Homo Sapiens and cave painting **Note:** Similar to 1 Crown, KM#718.

| Date | Mintage | F | VF | XF | Unc | BU |
|---|---|---|---|---|---|---|
| 1998 Proof | Est. 15,000 | Value: 45.00 | | | | |

**1/25 CROWN** **KM# 719** **Weight:** 1.2440 g. **Composition:** 0.9999 Gold .0400 oz. AGW **Subject:** Evolution of Mankind **Obverse:** Queen's portrait **Reverse:** Homo Sapiens killing mammoth **Note:** Similar to 1 Crown, KM#720.

| Date | Mintage | F | VF | XF | Unc | BU |
|---|---|---|---|---|---|---|
| 1998 Proof | Est. 15,000 | Value: 45.00 | | | | |

**1/25 CROWN** **KM# 722** **Weight:** 1.2440 g. **Composition:** 0.9999 Gold .0400 oz. AGW **Subject:** Evolution of Mankind **Obverse:** Queen's portrait **Reverse:** Illustrated theory of evolution **Note:** Similar to 1 Crown, KM#722.

| Date | Mintage | F | VF | XF | Unc | BU |
|---|---|---|---|---|---|---|
| 1998 Proof | Est. 15,000 | Value: 45.00 | | | | |

**1/25 CROWN** **KM# 723** **Weight:** 1.2440 g. **Composition:** 0.9999 Gold .0400 oz. AGW **Subject:** Evolution of Mankind **Obverse:** Queen's portrait **Reverse:** Human and primate mothers with young **Note:** Similar to 1 Crown, KM#724.

| Date | Mintage | F | VF | XF | Unc | BU |
|---|---|---|---|---|---|---|
| 1998 Proof | Est. 15,000 | Value: 45.00 | | | | |

**1/25 CROWN** **KM# 725** **Weight:** 1.2440 g. **Composition:** 0.9999 Gold .0400 oz. AGW **Subject:** Evolution of Mankind **Obverse:** Queen's portrait **Reverse:** Charles Darwin **Note:** Similar to 1 Crown, KM#726.

| Date | Mintage | F | VF | XF | Unc | BU |
|---|---|---|---|---|---|---|
| 1998 Proof | Est. 15,000 | Value: 45.00 | | | | |

**1/25 CROWN** **KM# 727** **Weight:** 1.2440 g. **Composition:** 0.9999 Gold .0400 oz. AGW **Subject:** Evolution of Mankind **Obverse:** Queen's portrait **Reverse:** Raymond Dart with skull **Note:** Similar to 1 Crown, KM#728.

| Date | Mintage | F | VF | XF | Unc | BU |
|---|---|---|---|---|---|---|
| 1998 Proof | Est. 15,000 | Value: 45.00 | | | | |

**1/25 CROWN** **KM# 729** **Weight:** 1.2440 g. **Composition:** 0.9999 Gold .0400 oz. AGW **Subject:** Evolution of Mankind **Obverse:** Queen's portrait **Reverse:** 20th century Homo Sapiens **Note:** Similar to 1 Crown, KM#730.

| Date | Mintage | F | VF | XF | Unc | BU |
|---|---|---|---|---|---|---|
| 1998 Proof | Est. 15,000 | Value: 45.00 | | | | |

**1/25 CROWN** **KM# 649a** **Weight:** 1.2441 g. **Composition:** 0.9950 Platinum .0398 oz. APW

| Date | Mintage | F | VF | XF | Unc | BU |
|---|---|---|---|---|---|---|
| 1998 Proof | Est. 7,500 | Value: 55.00 | | | | |

**1/25 CROWN** **KM# 678a** **Weight:** 1.2440 g. **Composition:** 0.9950 Platinum .0400 oz. APW

| Date | Mintage | F | VF | XF | Unc | BU |
|---|---|---|---|---|---|---|
| 1998 Proof | Est. 5,000 | Value: 55.00 | | | | |

**1/25 CROWN** **KM# 707** **Weight:** 1.2440 g. **Composition:** 0.9999 Gold .0400 oz. AGW **Subject:** Evolution of Mankind **Obverse:** Queen's portrait **Reverse:** Australopithecus - Lucy **Note:** Similar to 1 Crwn, KM#708.

| Date | Mintage | F | VF | XF | Unc | BU |
|---|---|---|---|---|---|---|
| 1998 Proof | Est. 15,000 | Value: 45.00 | | | | |

**1/25 CROWN** **KM# 779.2** **Weight:** 1.2440 g. **Composition:** 0.9999 Gold .0400 oz. AGW **Reverse:** Rabbit reading, sparrow. Without Chinese characters

| Date | Mintage | F | VF | XF | Unc | BU |
|---|---|---|---|---|---|---|
| 1999 Proof | Inc. above | Value: 45.00 | | | | |

**1/25 CROWN** **KM# 779.1a** **Weight:** 1.2400 g. **Composition:** 0.9950 Platinum .0400 oz. APW

| Date | Mintage | F | VF | XF | Unc | BU |
|---|---|---|---|---|---|---|
| 1999 Proof | Est. 3,000 | Value: 55.00 | | | | |

**1/25 CROWN** **KM# 779.2a** **Weight:** 1.2400 g. **Composition:** 0.9950 Platinum .0400 oz. APW **Reverse:** Rabbit reading, sparrow. Without Chinese characters

| Date | Mintage | F | VF | XF | Unc | BU |
|---|---|---|---|---|---|---|
| 1999 Proof | Inc. above | Value: 55.00 | | | | |

**1/25 CROWN** **KM# 779.1** **Weight:** 1.2440 g. **Composition:** 0.9999 Gold .0400 oz. AGW **Subject:** 1999 The Year of the Rabbit **Obverse:** Queen's portrait **Reverse:** Sparrow, Peter Rabbit reading, Chinese characters **Note:** Similar to 1 Crown, KM#783.1.

| Date | Mintage | F | VF | XF | Unc | BU |
|---|---|---|---|---|---|---|
| 1999 Proof | Est. 5,000 | Value: 45.00 | | | | |

**1/10 CROWN** **KM# 51** **Weight:** 3.1100 g. **Composition:** 0.9999 Gold .1000 oz. AGW **Series:** Barcelona Olympics **Subject:** Chariot Racing **Note:** Similar to 1 Crown, KM#67.

| Date | Mintage | F | VF | XF | Unc | BU |
|---|---|---|---|---|---|---|
| 1991 Proof | Est. 20,000 | Value: 75.00 | | | | |
| 1992 Proof | Est. 20,000 | Value: 90.00 | | | | |

**1/10 CROWN** **KM# 50** **Weight:** 3.1100 g. **Composition:** 0.9999 Gold .1000 oz. AGW **Series:** Barcelona Olympics **Subject:** Discus Thrower **Note:** Similar to 1 Crown, KM#66.

| Date | Mintage | F | VF | XF | Unc | BU |
|---|---|---|---|---|---|---|
| 1991 Proof | Est. 20,000 | Value: 75.00 | | | | |
| 1992 Proof | Est. 20,000 | Value: 90.00 | | | | |

**1/10 CROWN** **KM# 52** **Weight:** 3.1100 g. **Composition:** 0.9999 Gold .1000 oz. AGW **Series:** Barcelona Olympics **Subject:** Runners **Note:** Similar to 1 Crown, KM#68.

| Date | Mintage | F | VF | XF | Unc | BU |
|---|---|---|---|---|---|---|
| 1991 Proof | Est. 20,000 | Value: 75.00 | | | | |
| 1992 Proof | Est. 20,000 | Value: 90.00 | | | | |

**1/10 CROWN** **KM# 53** **Weight:** 3.1100 g. **Composition:** 0.9999 Gold .1000 oz. AGW **Series:** Barcelona Olympics **Subject:** Javelin Thrower **Note:** Similar to 1 Crown, KM#69.

| Date | Mintage | F | VF | XF | Unc | BU |
|---|---|---|---|---|---|---|
| 1991 Proof | Est. 20,000 | Value: 75.00 | | | | |
| 1992 Proof | Est. 20,000 | Value: 90.00 | | | | |

**1/10 CROWN** **KM# 54** **Weight:** 3.1100 g. **Composition:** 0.9999 Gold .1000 oz. AGW **Series:** Barcelona Olympics **Subject:** Wrestlers **Note:** Similar to 1 Crown, KM#70.

| Date | Mintage | F | VF | XF | Unc | BU |
|---|---|---|---|---|---|---|
| 1991 Proof | Est. 20,000 | Value: 75.00 | | | | |
| 1992 Proof | Est. 20,000 | Value: 90.00 | | | | |

**1/10 CROWN** **KM# 55** **Weight:** 3.1100 g. **Composition:** 0.9999 Gold .1000 oz. AGW **Series:** Barcelona Olympics **Subject:** Boxers **Note:** Similar to 1 Crown, KM#71.

| Date | Mintage | F | VF | XF | Unc | BU |
|---|---|---|---|---|---|---|
| 1991 Proof | Est. 20,000 | Value: 75.00 | | | | |
| 1992 Proof | Est. 20,000 | Value: 90.00 | | | | |

**1/10 CROWN KM# 56 Weight:** 3.1100 g. **Composition:** 0.9999 Gold .1000 oz. AGW **Series:** Barcelona Olympics **Subject:** Long Jumper **Note:** Similar to 1 Crown, KM#72.

| Date | Mintage | F | VF | XF | Unc | BU |
|---|---|---|---|---|---|---|
| 1991 Proof | Est. 20,000 | Value: 75.00 | | | | |
| 1992 Proof | Est. 20,000 | Value: 90.00 | | | | |

**1/10 CROWN KM# 57 Weight:** 3.1100 g. **Composition:** 0.9999 Gold .1000 oz. AGW **Series:** Barcelona Olympics **Subject:** Olympic Victor **Note:** Similar to 1 Crown, KM#73.

| Date | Mintage | F | VF | XF | Unc | BU |
|---|---|---|---|---|---|---|
| 1991 Proof | Est. 20,000 | Value: 75.00 | | | | |
| 1992 Proof | Est. 20,000 | Value: 90.00 | | | | |

**1/10 CROWN KM# 125 Weight:** 3.1100 g. **Composition:** 0.9999 Gold .1000 oz. AGW **Subject:** Japanese Royal Wedding

| Date | Mintage | F | VF | XF | Unc | BU |
|---|---|---|---|---|---|---|
| 1993 Proof | Est. 10,000 | Value: 95.00 | | | | |

**1/10 CROWN KM# 203a Weight:** 3.1100 g. **Composition:** 0.9990 Platinum .1000 oz. APW

| Date | Mintage | F | VF | XF | Unc | BU |
|---|---|---|---|---|---|---|
| 1993 Proof | Est. 5,000 | Value: 120 | | | | |

**1/10 CROWN KM# 203 Weight:** 3.1100 g. **Composition:** 0.9999 Gold .1000 oz. AGW **Series:** Peter Rabbit Centennial **Subject:** Peter Rabbit **Obverse:** Queen's portrait **Reverse:** Peter Rabbit eating carrots **Note:** Similar to 1 Crown, KM#201.

| Date | Mintage | F | VF | XF | Unc | BU |
|---|---|---|---|---|---|---|
| 1993 Proof | Est. 20,000 | Value: 80.00 | | | | |

**1/10 CROWN KM# 207 Weight:** 3.1100 g. **Composition:** 0.9990 Platinum .1000 oz. APW **Series:** Peter Rabbit Centennial **Subject:** Tiggy-Winkel **Reverse:** Mrs. Tiggy-Winkel ironing **Note:** Similar to 1 Crown, KM#205.

| Date | Mintage | F | VF | XF | Unc | BU |
|---|---|---|---|---|---|---|
| 1993 Proof | Est. 20,000 | Value: 80.00 | | | | |

**1/10 CROWN KM# 211 Weight:** 3.1100 g. **Composition:** 0.9990 Platinum .1000 oz. APW **Series:** Peter Rabbit Centennial **Subject:** Jeremy Fisher **Reverse:** Jeremy Fisher fishing **Note:** Similar to 1 Crown, KM#209.

| Date | Mintage | F | VF | XF | Unc | BU |
|---|---|---|---|---|---|---|
| 1993 Proof | Est. 20,000 | Value: 80.00 | | | | |

**1/10 CROWN KM# 215 Weight:** 3.1100 g. **Composition:** 0.9990 Platinum .1000 oz. APW **Series:** Peter Rabbit Centennial **Subject:** Tom Kitten **Reverse:** Tom Kitten with mother cat **Note:** Similar to 1 Crown, KM#213.

| Date | Mintage | F | VF | XF | Unc | BU |
|---|---|---|---|---|---|---|
| 1993 Proof | Est. 20,000 | Value: 80.00 | | | | |

**1/10 CROWN KM# 219 Weight:** 3.1100 g. **Composition:** 0.9990 Platinum .1000 oz. APW **Series:** Peter Rabbit Centennial **Subject:** Benjamin Bunny **Reverse:** Benjamin Bunny wearing hat and holding coat **Note:** Similar to 1 Crown, KM#217.

| Date | Mintage | F | VF | XF | Unc | BU |
|---|---|---|---|---|---|---|
| 1993 Proof | Est. 20,000 | Value: 80.00 | | | | |

**1/10 CROWN KM# 223 Weight:** 3.1100 g. **Composition:** 0.9990 Platinum .1000 oz. APW **Series:** Peter Rabbit Centennial **Subject:** Jemima Puddle-Duck **Reverse:** Jemima Puddle Duck talking with fox **Note:** Similar to 1 Crown, KM#221.

| Date | Mintage | F | VF | XF | Unc | BU |
|---|---|---|---|---|---|---|
| 1993 Proof | Est. 20,000 | Value: 80.00 | | | | |

**1/10 CROWN KM# 439 Weight:** 3.1100 g. **Composition:** 0.9990 Platinum .1000 oz. APW **Series:** Peter Rabbit Centennial **Subject:** Mother and Bunnies **Note:** Similar to 1 Crown, KM#444.

| Date | Mintage | F | VF | XF | Unc | BU |
|---|---|---|---|---|---|---|
| 1994 Proof | Est. 20,000 | Value: 95.00 | | | | |

**1/10 CROWN KM# 439a Weight:** 3.1103 g. **Composition:** 0.9950 Platinum .1000 oz. APW **Note:** Similar to 1 Crown, KM#444.

| Date | Mintage | F | VF | XF | Unc | BU |
|---|---|---|---|---|---|---|
| 1994 Proof | Est. 5,000 | Value: 120 | | | | |

**1/10 CROWN KM# 446 Weight:** 3.1103 g. **Composition:** 0.9999 Gold .1000 oz. AGW **Subject:** Lord Buddha **Note:** Similar to 1 Crown, KM#449.

| Date | Mintage | F | VF | XF | Unc | BU |
|---|---|---|---|---|---|---|
| 1996 Proof | Est. 10,000 | Value: 95.00 | | | | |

**1/10 CROWN KM# 455 Weight:** 3.1103 g. **Composition:** 0.9999 Gold .1000 oz. AGW **Series:** Centenary of the Cinema **Subject:** Wizard of Oz **Note:** Similar to 1 Crown, KM#457.

| Date | Mintage | F | VF | XF | Unc | BU |
|---|---|---|---|---|---|---|
| 1996 Proof | Est. 20,000 | Value: 80.00 | | | | |

**1/10 CROWN KM# 459 Weight:** 3.1103 g. **Composition:** 0.9999 Gold .1000 oz. AGW **Series:** Centenary of the Cinema **Subject:** Marx Brothers **Note:** Similar to 1 Crown, KM#461.

| Date | Mintage | F | VF | XF | Unc | BU |
|---|---|---|---|---|---|---|
| 1996 Proof | Est. 20,000 | Value: 80.00 | | | | |

**1/10 CROWN KM# 463 Weight:** 3.1103 g. **Composition:** 0.9999 Gold .1000 oz. AGW **Series:** Centenary of the Cinema **Subject:** Elvis Presley **Note:** Similar to 1 Crown, KM#465.

| Date | Mintage | F | VF | XF | Unc | BU |
|---|---|---|---|---|---|---|
| 1996 Proof | Est. 20,000 | Value: 80.00 | | | | |

**1/10 CROWN KM# 467 Weight:** 3.1103 g. **Composition:** 0.9999 Gold .1000 oz. AGW **Series:** Centenary of the Cinema **Subject:** Casablanca **Note:** Similar to 1 Crown, KM#469.

| Date | Mintage | F | VF | XF | Unc | BU |
|---|---|---|---|---|---|---|
| 1996 Proof | Est. 20,000 | Value: 80.00 | | | | |

**1/10 CROWN KM# 471 Weight:** 3.1103 g. **Composition:** 0.9999 Gold .1000 oz. AGW **Series:** Centenary of the Cinema **Subject:** E.T. **Note:** Similar to 1 Crown, KM#473.

| Date | Mintage | F | VF | XF | Unc | BU |
|---|---|---|---|---|---|---|
| 1996 Proof | Est. 20,000 | Value: 80.00 | | | | |

**1/10 CROWN KM# 475 Weight:** 3.1103 g. **Composition:** 0.9999 Gold .1000 oz. AGW **Series:** Centenary of the Cinema **Subject:** Alfred Hitchcock **Note:** Similar to 1 Crown, KM#477.

| Date | Mintage | F | VF | XF | Unc | BU |
|---|---|---|---|---|---|---|
| 1996 Proof | Est. 20,000 | Value: 80.00 | | | | |

**1/10 CROWN KM# 369 Weight:** 3.1103 g. **Composition:** 0.9999 Gold .1000 oz. AGW **Subject:** Roses **Note:** Similar to 1 Crown, KM#373.

| Date | Mintage | F | VF | XF | Unc | BU |
|---|---|---|---|---|---|---|
| 1996 Proof | Est. 20,000 | Value: 80.00 | | | | |

**1/10 CROWN KM# 377a Weight:** 3.1259 g. **Composition:** 0.9950 Platinum .1000 oz. APW **Note:** Similar to 1 Crown, KM#382.

| Date | Mintage | F | VF | XF | Unc | BU |
|---|---|---|---|---|---|---|
| 1996 Proof | Est. 10,000 | Value: 95.00 | | | | |

**1/10 CROWN KM# 391 Weight:** 3.1103 g. **Composition:** 0.9999 Gold .1000 oz. AGW **Series:** Centenary of the Cinema **Subject:** Grace Kelly **Note:** Similar to 1 Crown, KM#393.

| Date | Mintage | F | VF | XF | Unc | BU |
|---|---|---|---|---|---|---|
| 1996 Proof | Est. 20,000 | Value: 80.00 | | | | |

**1/10 CROWN KM# 396 Weight:** 3.1103 g. **Composition:** 0.9999 Gold .1000 oz. AGW **Series:** Centenary of the Cinema **Subject:** James Dean **Note:** Similar to 1 Crown, KM#398.

| Date | Mintage | F | VF | XF | Unc | BU |
|---|---|---|---|---|---|---|
| 1996 Proof | Est. 20,000 | Value: 80.00 | | | | |

**1/10 CROWN KM# 401 Weight:** 3.1103 g. **Composition:** 0.9999 Gold .1000 oz. AGW **Series:** Centenary of the Cinema **Subject:** Marilyn Monroe **Note:** Similar to 1 Crown, KM#403.

| Date | Mintage | F | VF | XF | Unc | BU |
|---|---|---|---|---|---|---|
| 1996 Proof | Est. 20,000 | Value: 80.00 | | | | |

**1/10 CROWN KM# 406 Weight:** 3.1103 g. **Composition:** 0.9999 Gold .1000 oz. AGW **Series:** Centenary of the Cinema **Subject:** Audrey Hepburn **Note:** Similar to 1 Crown, KM#408.

| Date | Mintage | F | VF | XF | Unc | BU |
|---|---|---|---|---|---|---|
| 1996 Proof | Est. 20,000 | Value: 80.00 | | | | |

**1/10 CROWN KM# 411 Weight:** 3.1103 g. **Composition:** 0.9999 Gold .1000 oz. AGW **Series:** Centenary of the Cinema **Subject:** Bruce Lee **Note:** Similar to 1 Crown, KM#413.

| Date | Mintage | F | VF | XF | Unc | BU |
|---|---|---|---|---|---|---|
| 1996 Proof | Est. 20,000 | Value: 80.00 | | | | |

**1/10 CROWN KM# 416 Weight:** 3.1103 g. **Composition:** 0.9999 Gold .1000 oz. AGW **Series:** Centenary of the Cinema **Subject:** Charlie Chaplin **Note:** Similar to 1 Crown, KM#418.

| Date | Mintage | F | VF | XF | Unc | BU |
|---|---|---|---|---|---|---|
| 1996 Proof | Est. 20,000 | Value: 80.00 | | | | |

**1/10 CROWN KM# 421 Weight:** 3.1103 g. **Composition:** 0.9999 Gold .1000 oz. AGW **Series:** Centenary of the Cinema **Subject:** Gone With The Wind **Note:** Similar to 1 Crown, KM#423.

| Date | Mintage | F | VF | XF | Unc | BU |
|---|---|---|---|---|---|---|
| 1996 Proof | Est. 20,000 | Value: 80.00 | | | | |

**1/10 CROWN KM# 426 Weight:** 3.1103 g. **Composition:** 0.9999 Gold .1000 oz. AGW **Series:** Centenary of the Cinema **Subject:** The Flintstones **Note:** Similar to 1 Crown, KM#428.

| Date | Mintage | F | VF | XF | Unc | BU |
|---|---|---|---|---|---|---|
| 1996 Proof | Est. 20,000 | Value: 80.00 | | | | |

**1/10 CROWN KM# 377 Weight:** 3.1103 g. **Composition:** 0.9999 Gold .1000 oz. AGW **Series:** Peter Rabbit Centennial **Subject:** Rabbit Escaping

| Date | Mintage | F | VF | XF | Unc | BU |
|---|---|---|---|---|---|---|
| 1996 Proof | Est. 20,000 | Value: 80.00 | | | | |

**1/10 CROWN KM# 406a Weight:** 3.1103 g. **Composition:** 0.9950 Platinum .1000 oz. APW

| Date | Mintage | F | VF | XF | Unc | BU |
|---|---|---|---|---|---|---|
| 1996 Proof | Est. 1,000 | Value: 135 | | | | |

**1/10 CROWN KM# A453 Weight:** 3.1103 g. **Composition:** 0.9999 Gold .1000 oz. AGW **Series:** Centenary of the Cinema **Subject:** James Dean

| Date | Mintage | F | VF | XF | Unc | BU |
|---|---|---|---|---|---|---|
| 1996 Proof | 20,000 | Value: 95.00 | | | | |

**1/10 CROWN KM# 520a Weight:** 3.1259 g. **Composition:** 0.9950 Platinum .1000 oz. APW

| Date | Mintage | F | VF | XF | Unc | BU |
|---|---|---|---|---|---|---|
| 1997 Proof | Est. 5,000 | Value: 120 | | | | |

**1/10 CROWN KM# 520 Weight:** 3.1103 g. **Composition:** 0.9999 Gold .1000 oz. AGW **Subject:** Tale of Peter Rabbit **Note:** Similar to 1 Crown, KM#525.

| Date | Mintage | F | VF | XF | Unc | BU |
|---|---|---|---|---|---|---|
| 1997 Proof | Est. 20,000 | Value: 80.00 | | | | |

**1/10 CROWN KM# 538 Weight:** 3.1100 g. **Composition:** 0.9999 Gold .1000 oz. AGW **Subject:** Peonies **Note:** Similar to 1 Crown, KM#540.

| Date | Mintage | F | VF | XF | Unc | BU |
|---|---|---|---|---|---|---|
| 1997 Proof | Est. 20,000 | Value: 75.00 | | | | |

**1/10 CROWN KM# 542 Weight:** 3.1100 g. **Composition:** 0.9999 Gold .1000 oz. AGW **Subject:** Nefertiti **Note:** Similar to 1 Crown, KM#544.

| Date | Mintage | F | VF | XF | Unc | BU |
|---|---|---|---|---|---|---|
| 1997 Proof | Est. 7,500 | Value: 75.00 | | | | |

**1/10 CROWN KM# 546 Weight:** 3.1100 g. **Composition:** 0.9999 Gold .1000 oz. AGW **Subject:** Cleopatra **Note:** Similar to 1 Crown, KM#548.

| Date | Mintage | F | VF | XF | Unc | BU |
|---|---|---|---|---|---|---|
| 1997 Proof | Est. 7,500 | Value: 75.00 | | | | |

**1/10 CROWN KM# 550 Weight:** 3.1100 g. **Composition:** 0.9999 Gold .1000 oz. AGW **Subject:** Europa **Note:** Similar to 1 Crown, KM#552.

| Date | Mintage | F | VF | XF | Unc | BU |
|---|---|---|---|---|---|---|
| 1997 Proof | Est. 7,500 | Value: 75.00 | | | | |

**1/10 CROWN KM# 554 Weight:** 3.1100 g. **Composition:** 0.9999 Gold .1000 oz. AGW **Subject:** Liberty **Note:** Similar to 1 Crown, KM#556.

| Date | Mintage | F | VF | XF | Unc | BU |
|---|---|---|---|---|---|---|
| 1997 Proof | Est. 7,500 | Value: 75.00 | | | | |

**1/10 CROWN KM# 651 Weight:** 3.1100 g. **Composition:** 0.9999 Gold .1000 oz. AGW **Subject:** Tale of Peter Rabbit **Obverse:** Queen's portrait **Reverse:** Peter Rabbit **Note:** Similar to 1 Crown, KM#656.

| Date | Mintage | F | VF | XF | Unc | BU |
|---|---|---|---|---|---|---|
| 1998 Proof | Est. 20,000 | Value: 90.00 | | | | |

**1/10 CROWN KM# 651a Weight:** 3.1103 g. **Composition:** 0.9950 Platinum .1000 oz. APW

| Date | Mintage | F | VF | XF | Unc | BU |
|---|---|---|---|---|---|---|
| 1998 Proof | Est. 5,000 | Value: 120 | | | | |

**1/10 CROWN KM# 679a Weight:** 3.1103 g. **Composition:** 0.9950 Platinum .1000 oz. APW

| Date | Mintage | F | VF | XF | Unc | BU |
|---|---|---|---|---|---|---|
| 1998 Proof | Est. 5,000 | Value: 120 | | | | |

**1/10 CROWN KM# 679 Weight:** 3.1100 g. **Composition:** 0.9999 Gold .1000 oz. AGW **Subject:** Paddington Bear **Obverse:** Queen's portrait **Reverse:** Bear with suitcase **Note:** Similar to 1 Crown, KM#682.

| Date | Mintage | F | VF | XF | Unc | BU |
|---|---|---|---|---|---|---|
| 1998 Proof | Est. 7,500 | Value: 90.00 | | | | |

**1/10 CROWN KM# 658 Weight:** 3.1100 g. **Composition:** 0.9999 Gold .1000 oz. AGW **Subject:** Chrysanthemum **Obverse:** Queen's portrait **Reverse:** Three blossoms **Note:** Similar to 1 Crown, KM#661.

| Date | Mintage | F | VF | XF | Unc | BU |
|---|---|---|---|---|---|---|
| 1998 Proof | Est. 20,000 | Value: 90.00 | | | | |

**1/10 CROWN KM# 666 Weight:** 3.1100 g. **Composition:** 0.9999 Gold .1000 oz. AGW **Subject:** Brittania **Obverse:** Queen's portrait **Reverse:** Helmeted Brittania **Note:** Similar to 1 Crown, KM#674.

| Date | Mintage | F | VF | XF | Unc | BU |
|---|---|---|---|---|---|---|
| 1998 Proof | Est. 7,500 | Value: 90.00 | | | | |

**1/10 CROWN KM# 667 Weight:** 3.1100 g. **Composition:** 0.9999 Gold .1000 oz. AGW **Subject:** Juno **Obverse:** Queen's portrait **Reverse:** Facing portrait of Juno **Note:** Similar to 1 Crown KM#675.

| Date | Mintage | F | VF | XF | Unc | BU |
|---|---|---|---|---|---|---|
| 1998 Proof | Est. 7,500 | Value: 90.00 | | | | |

**1/10 CROWN KM# 668 Weight:** 3.1100 g. **Composition:** 0.9999 Gold .1000 oz. AGW **Subject:** Athena **Obverse:** Queen's portrait **Reverse:** Helmeted Athena **Note:** Similar to 1 Crown, KM#676.

| Date | Mintage | F | VF | XF | Unc | BU |
|---|---|---|---|---|---|---|
| 1998 Proof | Est. 7,500 | Value: 90.00 | | | | |

**1/10 CROWN KM# 669 Weight:** 3.1100 g. **Composition:** 0.9999 Gold .1000 oz. AGW **Subject:** Arethusa **Obverse:** Queen's portrait **Reverse:** Portrait with dolphins **Note:** Similar to 1 Crown, KM#677.

| Date | Mintage | F | VF | XF | Unc | BU |
|---|---|---|---|---|---|---|
| 1998 Proof | Est. 7,500 | Value: 90.00 | | | | |

**1/5 CROWN KM# 76a Weight:** 6.2200 g. **Composition:** 0.9950 Platinum .2000 oz. APW

| Date | Mintage | F | VF | XF | Unc | BU |
|---|---|---|---|---|---|---|
| 1990 Proof | Est. 1,000 | Value: 325 | | | | |

**1/5 CROWN KM# 77a Weight:** 6.2200 g. **Composition:** 0.9950 Platinum .2000 oz. APW

| Date | Mintage | F | VF | XF | Unc | BU |
|---|---|---|---|---|---|---|
| 1990 Proof | Est. 1,000 | Value: 325 | | | | |

**1/5 CROWN KM# 78a Weight:** 6.2200 g. **Composition:** 0.9950 Platinum .2000 oz. APW

| Date | Mintage | F | VF | XF | Unc | BU |
|---|---|---|---|---|---|---|
| 1990 Proof | Est. 1,000 | Value: 325 | | | | |

**1/5 CROWN KM# 79a Weight:** 6.2200 g. **Composition:** 0.9950 Platinum .2000 oz. APW

| Date | Mintage | F | VF | XF | Unc | BU |
|---|---|---|---|---|---|---|
| 1990 Proof | Est. 1,000 | Value: 325 | | | | |

**1/5 CROWN KM# 80a Weight:** 6.2200 g. **Composition:** 0.9950 Platinum .2000 oz. APW

| Date | Mintage | F | VF | XF | Unc | BU |
|---|---|---|---|---|---|---|
| 1990 Proof | Est. 1,000 | Value: 325 | | | | |

**1/5 CROWN KM# 81a Weight:** 6.2200 g. **Composition:** 0.9950 Platinum .2000 oz. APW

| Date | Mintage | F | VF | XF | Unc | BU |
|---|---|---|---|---|---|---|
| 1990 Proof | Est. 1,000 | Value: 325 | | | | |

**1/5 CROWN KM# 76 Weight:** 6.2200 g. **Composition:** 0.9990 Gold .2000 oz. AGW **Series:** World Cup Soccer **Subject:** Italian Flag **Note:** Similar to 1 Crown, KM#33.

| Date | Mintage | F | VF | XF | Unc | BU |
|---|---|---|---|---|---|---|
| 1990 Proof | Est. 5,000 | Value: 215 | | | | |

**1/5 CROWN KM# 77 Weight:** 6.2200 g. **Composition:** 0.9999 Gold .2000 oz. AGW **Series:** World Cup Soccer **Subject:** Map of Italy **Note:** Similar to 1 Crown, KM#34.

| Date | Mintage | F | VF | XF | Unc | BU |
|---|---|---|---|---|---|---|
| 1990 Proof | Est. 5,000 | Value: 215 | | | | |

**1/5 CROWN KM# 78 Weight:** 6.2200 g. **Composition:** 0.9999 Gold .2000 oz. AGW **Series:** World Cup Soccer **Subject:** Goalie Catching Ball **Note:** Similar to 1 Crown, KM#35.

| Date | Mintage | F | VF | XF | Unc | BU |
|---|---|---|---|---|---|---|
| 1990 Proof | Est. 5,000 | Value: 215 | | | | |

**1/5 CROWN KM# 81 Weight:** 6.2200 g. **Composition:** 0.9999 Gold .2000 oz. AGW **Series:** World Cup Soccer **Subject:** 3 Players **Note:** Similar to 1 Crown, KM#38.

| Date | Mintage | F | VF | XF | Unc | BU |
|---|---|---|---|---|---|---|
| 1990 Proof | Est. 5,000 | Value: 215 | | | | |

**1/5 CROWN** **KM# 48** **Weight:** 6.2200 g. **Composition:** 0.9990 Gold .2000 oz. AGW **Subject:** Penny Black Stamp **Note:** Similar to 1 Crown, KM#49.

| Date | Mintage | F | VF | XF | Unc | BU |
|---|---|---|---|---|---|---|
| 1990 Proof | Est. 5,000 | Value: 215 | | | | |

**1/5 CROWN** **KM# 79** **Weight:** 6.2200 g. **Composition:** 0.9999 Gold .2000 oz. AGW **Series:** World Cup Soccer **Subject:** 1 Player **Note:** Similar to 1 Crown, KM#36.

| Date | Mintage | F | VF | XF | Unc | BU |
|---|---|---|---|---|---|---|
| 1990 Proof | Est. 5,000 | Value: 215 | | | | |

**1/5 CROWN** **KM# 80** **Weight:** 6.2200 g. **Composition:** 0.9999 Gold .2000 oz. AGW **Series:** World Cup Soccer **Subject:** 2 Players **Note:** Similar to 1 Crown, KM#37.

| Date | Mintage | F | VF | XF | Unc | BU |
|---|---|---|---|---|---|---|
| 1990 Proof | Est. 5,000 | Value: 215 | | | | |

**1/5 CROWN** **KM# 58** **Weight:** 6.2200 g. **Composition:** 0.9999 Gold .2000 oz. AGW **Series:** Barcelona Olympics **Subject:** Discus Thrower **Note:** Similar to 1 Crown, KM#66.

| Date | Mintage | F | VF | XF | Unc | BU |
|---|---|---|---|---|---|---|
| 1991 Proof | Est. 5,000 | Value: 150 | | | | |
| 1992 Proof | Est. 5,000 | Value: 150 | | | | |

**1/5 CROWN** **KM# 59** **Weight:** 6.2200 g. **Composition:** 0.9999 Gold .2000 oz. AGW **Series:** Barcelona Olympics **Subject:** Chariot Racing **Note:** Similar to 1 Crown, KM#67.

| Date | Mintage | F | VF | XF | Unc | BU |
|---|---|---|---|---|---|---|
| 1991 Proof | Est. 5,000 | Value: 150 | | | | |
| 1992 Proof | Est. 5,000 | Value: 150 | | | | |

**1/5 CROWN** **KM# 62** **Weight:** 6.2200 g. **Composition:** 0.9999 Gold .2000 oz. AGW **Series:** Barcelona Olympics **Subject:** Wrestlers **Note:** Similar to 1 Crown, KM#70.

| Date | Mintage | F | VF | XF | Unc | BU |
|---|---|---|---|---|---|---|
| 1991 Proof | Est. 5,000 | Value: 150 | | | | |
| 1992 Proof | Est. 5,000 | Value: 150 | | | | |

**1/5 CROWN** **KM# 63** **Weight:** 6.2200 g. **Composition:** 0.9999 Gold .2000 oz. AGW **Series:** Barcelona Olympics **Subject:** Boxers **Note:** Similar to 1 Crown, KM#71.

| Date | Mintage | F | VF | XF | Unc | BU |
|---|---|---|---|---|---|---|
| 1991 Proof | Est. 5,000 | Value: 150 | | | | |
| 1992 Proof | Est. 5,000 | Value: 150 | | | | |

**1/5 CROWN** **KM# 64** **Weight:** 6.2200 g. **Composition:** 0.9999 Gold .2000 oz. AGW **Series:** Barcelona Olympics **Subject:** Long Jumper **Note:** Similar to 1 Crown, KM#72.

| Date | Mintage | F | VF | XF | Unc | BU |
|---|---|---|---|---|---|---|
| 1991 Proof | Est. 5,000 | Value: 150 | | | | |
| 1992 Proof | Est. 5,000 | Value: 150 | | | | |

**1/5 CROWN** **KM# 65** **Weight:** 6.2200 g. **Composition:** 0.9999 Gold .2000 oz. AGW **Series:** Barcelona Olympics **Subject:** Olympic Victor **Note:** Similar to 1 Crown, KM#73.

| Date | Mintage | F | VF | XF | Unc | BU |
|---|---|---|---|---|---|---|
| 1991 Proof | Est. 5,000 | Value: 150 | | | | |
| 1992 Proof | — | Value: 150 | | | | |

**1/5 CROWN** **KM# 60** **Weight:** 6.2200 g. **Composition:** 0.9999 Gold .2000 oz. AGW **Series:** Barcelona Olympics **Subject:** Runners **Note:** Similar to 1 Crown, KM#68.

| Date | Mintage | F | VF | XF | Unc | BU |
|---|---|---|---|---|---|---|
| 1991 Proof | Est. 5,000 | Value: 150 | | | | |
| 1992 Proof | Est. 5,000 | Value: 150 | | | | |

**1/5 CROWN** **KM# 61** **Weight:** 6.2200 g. **Composition:** 0.9999 Gold .2000 oz. AGW **Series:** Barcelona Olympics **Subject:** Javelin Thrower **Note:** Similar to 1 Crown, KM#69.

| Date | Mintage | F | VF | XF | Unc | BU |
|---|---|---|---|---|---|---|
| 1991 Proof | Est. 5,000 | Value: 150 | | | | |
| 1992 Proof | Est. 5,000 | Value: 150 | | | | |

**1/5 CROWN** **KM# 58a** **Weight:** 6.2200 g. **Composition:** 0.9950 Platinum .2000 oz. APW

| Date | Mintage | F | VF | XF | Unc | BU |
|---|---|---|---|---|---|---|
| 1991 Proof | Est. 1,000 | Value: 275 | | | | |

**1/5 CROWN** **KM# 59a** **Weight:** 6.2200 g. **Composition:** 0.9950 Platinum .2000 oz. APW

| Date | Mintage | F | VF | XF | Unc | BU |
|---|---|---|---|---|---|---|
| 1991 Proof | Est. 1,000 | Value: 275 | | | | |

**1/5 CROWN** **KM# 60a** **Weight:** 6.2200 g. **Composition:** 0.9950 Platinum .2000 oz. APW

| Date | Mintage | F | VF | XF | Unc | BU |
|---|---|---|---|---|---|---|
| 1991 Proof | Est. 1,000 | Value: 275 | | | | |

**1/5 CROWN** **KM# 61a** **Weight:** 6.2200 g. **Composition:** 0.9950 Platinum .2000 oz. APW

| Date | Mintage | F | VF | XF | Unc | BU |
|---|---|---|---|---|---|---|
| 1991 Proof | Est. 1,000 | Value: 275 | | | | |

**1/5 CROWN** **KM# 62a** **Weight:** 6.2200 g. **Composition:** 0.9950 Platinum .2000 oz. APW

| Date | Mintage | F | VF | XF | Unc | BU |
|---|---|---|---|---|---|---|
| 1991 Proof | Est. 1,000 | Value: 275 | | | | |

**1/5 CROWN** **KM# 63a** **Weight:** 6.2200 g. **Composition:** 0.9950 Platinum .2000 oz. APW

| Date | Mintage | F | VF | XF | Unc | BU |
|---|---|---|---|---|---|---|
| 1991 Proof | Est. 1,000 | Value: 275 | | | | |

**1/5 CROWN** **KM# 64a** **Weight:** 6.2200 g. **Composition:** 0.9950 Platinum .2000 oz. APW

| Date | Mintage | F | VF | XF | Unc | BU |
|---|---|---|---|---|---|---|
| 1991 Proof | Est. 1,000 | Value: 275 | | | | |

**1/5 CROWN** **KM# 65a** **Weight:** 6.2200 g. **Composition:** 0.9950 Platinum .2000 oz. APW

| Date | Mintage | F | VF | XF | Unc | BU |
|---|---|---|---|---|---|---|
| 1991 Proof | Est. 1,000 | Value: 275 | | | | |

**1/5 CROWN** **KM# 150** **Weight:** 6.2200 g. **Composition:** 0.9999 Gold .2000 oz. AGW **Series:** Preserve Planet Earth **Subject:** Cetiosaurus **Obverse:** Queen's portrait **Reverse:** Long-necked dinosaur

| Date | Mintage | F | VF | XF | Unc | BU |
|---|---|---|---|---|---|---|
| 1993 Proof | Est. 5,000 | Value: 125 | | | | |

**1/5 CROWN** **KM# 152** **Weight:** 6.2200 g. **Composition:** 0.9999 Gold .2000 oz. AGW **Series:** Preserve Planet Earth **Subject:** Stegosaurus **Obverse:** Queen's portrait **Reverse:** Dinosaur with pointed plates along spine

| Date | Mintage | F | VF | XF | Unc | BU |
|---|---|---|---|---|---|---|
| 1993 Proof | Est. 5,000 | Value: 135 | | | | |

**1/5 CROWN** **KM# 153** **Weight:** 6.2200 g. **Composition:** 0.9999 Gold .2000 oz. AGW **Series:** WWII Warships **Subject:** USS Philadelphia

| Date | Mintage | F | VF | XF | Unc | BU |
|---|---|---|---|---|---|---|
| 1993 Proof | Est. 5,000 | Value: 165 | | | | |

**1/5 CROWN** **KM# 154** **Weight:** 6.2200 g. **Composition:** 0.9999 Gold .2000 oz. AGW **Series:** WWII Warships **Subject:** USS McLanahan

| Date | Mintage | F | VF | XF | Unc | BU |
|---|---|---|---|---|---|---|
| 1993 Proof | Est. 5,000 | Value: 165 | | | | |

**1/5 CROWN** **KM# 155** **Weight:** 6.2200 g. **Composition:** 0.9999 Gold .2000 oz. AGW **Series:** WWII Warships **Subject:** HNLMS Isaac Sweers

| Date | Mintage | F | VF | XF | Unc | BU |
|---|---|---|---|---|---|---|
| 1993 Proof | Est. 5,000 | Value: 165 | | | | |

**1/5 CROWN** **KM# 156** **Weight:** 6.2200 g. **Composition:** 0.9999 Gold .2000 oz. AGW **Series:** WWII Warships **Subject:** USS Weehawken

| Date | Mintage | F | VF | XF | Unc | BU |
|---|---|---|---|---|---|---|
| 1993 Proof | Est. 5,000 | Value: 165 | | | | |

**1/5 CROWN** **KM# 157** **Weight:** 6.2200 g. **Composition:** 0.9999 Gold .2000 oz. AGW **Series:** WWII Warships **Subject:** HMS Warspite

| Date | Mintage | F | VF | XF | Unc | BU |
|---|---|---|---|---|---|---|
| 1993 Proof | Est. 5,000 | Value: 165 | | | | |

**1/5 CROWN** **KM# 158** **Weight:** 6.2200 g. **Composition:** 0.9999 Gold .2000 oz. AGW **Series:** WWII Warships **Subject:** HMS Hood

| Date | Mintage | F | VF | XF | Unc | BU |
|---|---|---|---|---|---|---|
| 1993 Proof | Est. 5,000 | Value: 165 | | | | |

**1/5 CROWN** **KM# 159** **Weight:** 6.2200 g. **Composition:** 0.9999 Gold .2000 oz. AGW **Series:** WWII Warships **Subject:** HMS Penelope

| Date | Mintage | F | VF | XF | Unc | BU |
|---|---|---|---|---|---|---|
| 1993 Proof | Est. 5,000 | Value: 165 | | | | |

**1/5 CROWN** **KM# 160** **Weight:** 6.2200 g. **Composition:** 0.9999 Gold .2000 oz. AGW **Series:** WWII Warships **Subject:** HMCS Prescott

| Date | Mintage | F | VF | XF | Unc | BU |
|---|---|---|---|---|---|---|
| 1993 Proof | Est. 5,000 | Value: 165 | | | | |

**1/5 CROWN** **KM# 161** **Weight:** 6.2200 g. **Composition:** 0.9999 Gold .2000 oz. AGW **Series:** WWII Warships **Subject:** HMS Ark Royal

| Date | Mintage | F | VF | XF | Unc | BU |
|---|---|---|---|---|---|---|
| 1993 Proof | Est. 5,000 | Value: 165 | | | | |

**1/5 CROWN** **KM# 162** **Weight:** 6.2200 g. **Composition:** 0.9999 Gold .2000 oz. AGW **Series:** WWII Warships **Subject:** USS Gleaves

| Date | Mintage | F | VF | XF | Unc | BU |
|---|---|---|---|---|---|---|
| 1993 Proof | Est. 5,000 | Value: 165 | | | | |

**1/5 CROWN** **KM# 163** **Weight:** 6.2200 g. **Composition:** 0.9999 Gold .2000 oz. AGW **Series:** WWII Warships **Subject:** HMAS Waterhen

| Date | Mintage | F | VF | XF | Unc | BU |
|---|---|---|---|---|---|---|
| 1993 Proof | Est. 5,000 | Value: 165 | | | | |

**1/5 CROWN** **KM# 164** **Weight:** 6.2200 g. **Composition:** 0.9999 Gold .2000 oz. AGW **Series:** WWII Warships **Subject:** FSS Savorgnan de Brazza

| Date | Mintage | F | VF | XF | Unc | BU |
|---|---|---|---|---|---|---|
| 1993 Proof | Est. 5,000 | Value: 165 | | | | |

**1/5 CROWN** **KM# 165** **Weight:** 6.2200 g. **Composition:** 0.9999 Gold .2000 oz. AGW **Subject:** Queen Anne

| Date | Mintage | F | VF | XF | Unc | BU |
|---|---|---|---|---|---|---|
| 1993 Proof | Est. 5,000 | Value: 150 | | | | |

**1/5 CROWN** **KM# 166** **Weight:** 6.2200 g. **Composition:** 0.9999 Gold .2000 oz. AGW **Subject:** King George I

| Date | Mintage | F | VF | XF | Unc | BU |
|---|---|---|---|---|---|---|
| 1993 Proof | Est. 5,000 | Value: 150 | | | | |

**1/5 CROWN** **KM# 167** **Weight:** 6.2200 g. **Composition:** 0.9999 Gold .2000 oz. AGW **Subject:** King George II

| Date | Mintage | F | VF | XF | Unc | BU |
|---|---|---|---|---|---|---|
| 1993 Proof | Est. 5,000 | Value: 150 | | | | |

**1/5 CROWN** **KM# 168** **Weight:** 6.2200 g. **Composition:** 0.9999 Gold .2000 oz. AGW **Subject:** King George III

| Date | Mintage | F | VF | XF | Unc | BU |
|---|---|---|---|---|---|---|
| 1993 Proof | Est. 5,000 | Value: 150 | | | | |

**1/5 CROWN** **KM# 169** **Weight:** 6.2200 g. **Composition:** 0.9999 Gold .2000 oz. AGW **Subject:** King George IV

| Date | Mintage | F | VF | XF | Unc | BU |
|---|---|---|---|---|---|---|
| 1993 Proof | Est. 5,000 | Value: 150 | | | | |

**1/5 CROWN** **KM# 170** **Weight:** 6.2200 g. **Composition:** 0.9999 Gold .2000 oz. AGW **Subject:** King William IV

| Date | Mintage | F | VF | XF | Unc | BU |
|---|---|---|---|---|---|---|
| 1993 Proof | Est. 5,000 | Value: 150 | | | | |

**1/5 CROWN** **KM# 171** **Weight:** 6.2200 g. **Composition:** 0.9999 Gold .2000 oz. AGW **Subject:** Queen Victoria

| Date | Mintage | F | VF | XF | Unc | BU |
|---|---|---|---|---|---|---|
| 1993 Proof | Est. 5,000 | Value: 150 | | | | |

**1/5 CROWN** **KM# 172** **Weight:** 6.2200 g. **Composition:** 0.9999 Gold .2000 oz. AGW **Subject:** King Edward VII

| Date | Mintage | F | VF | XF | Unc | BU |
|---|---|---|---|---|---|---|
| 1993 Proof | Est. 5,000 | Value: 150 | | | | |

**1/5 CROWN** **KM# 173** **Weight:** 6.2200 g. **Composition:** 0.9999 Gold .2000 oz. AGW **Subject:** King George V

| Date | Mintage | F | VF | XF | Unc | BU |
|---|---|---|---|---|---|---|
| 1993 Proof | Est. 5,000 | Value: 150 | | | | |

**1/5 CROWN** **KM# 174** **Weight:** 6.2200 g. **Composition:** 0.9999 Gold .2000 oz. AGW **Subject:** King Edward VIII

| Date | Mintage | F | VF | XF | Unc | BU |
|---|---|---|---|---|---|---|
| 1993 Proof | Est. 5,000 | Value: 150 | | | | |

**1/5 CROWN** **KM# 175** **Weight:** 6.2200 g. **Composition:** 0.9999 Gold .2000 oz. AGW **Subject:** King George VI

| Date | Mintage | F | VF | XF | Unc | BU |
|---|---|---|---|---|---|---|
| 1993 Proof | Est. 5,000 | Value: 150 | | | | |

**1/5 CROWN** **KM# 176** **Weight:** 6.2200 g. **Composition:** 0.9999 Gold .2000 oz. AGW **Subject:** Queen Elizabeth II

| Date | Mintage | F | VF | XF | Unc | BU |
|---|---|---|---|---|---|---|
| 1993 Proof | Est. 5,000 | Value: 150 | | | | |

**1/5 CROWN** **KM# 204a** **Weight:** 6.2200 g. **Composition:** 0.9950 Platinum .2000 oz. APW

| Date | Mintage | F | VF | XF | Unc | BU |
|---|---|---|---|---|---|---|
| 1993 Proof | Est. 5,000 | Value: 200 | | | | |

**1/5 CROWN** **KM# 643** **Weight:** 6.2200 g. **Composition:** 0.9999 Gold .2000 oz. AGW **Series:** XVII Winter Olympics **Subject:** Figure Skaters **Note:** Similar to 1 Crown, KM#145.

| Date | Mintage | F | VF | XF | Unc | BU |
|---|---|---|---|---|---|---|
| 1993 Proof | Est. 5,000 | Value: 185 | | | | |

**1/5 CROWN** **KM# 644** **Weight:** 6.2200 g. **Composition:** 0.9999 Gold .2000 oz. AGW **Series:** XVII Winter Olympics **Subject:** Ice Hockey **Note:** Similar to 1 Crown, KM#146.

| Date | Mintage | F | VF | XF | Unc | BU |
|---|---|---|---|---|---|---|
| 1993 Proof | Est. 5,000 | Value: 185 | | | | |

**1/5 CROWN** **KM# 645** **Weight:** 6.2200 g. **Composition:** 0.9999 Gold .2000 oz. AGW **Series:** XVII Winter Olympics **Subject:** Bobsledding **Note:** Similar to 1 Crown, KM#147.

| Date | Mintage | F | VF | XF | Unc | BU |
|---|---|---|---|---|---|---|
| 1993 Proof | Est. 5,000 | Value: 185 | | | | |

**1/5 CROWN** **KM# 646** **Weight:** 6.2200 g. **Composition:** 0.9999 Gold .2000 oz. AGW **Series:** XVII Winter Olympics **Subject:** Skiers **Note:** Similar to 1 Crown, KM#148.

| Date | Mintage | F | VF | XF | Unc | BU |
|---|---|---|---|---|---|---|
| 1993 Proof | Est. 5,000 | Value: 185 | | | | |

**1/5 CROWN** **KM# 181** **Weight:** 6.2200 g. **Composition:** 0.9999 Gold .2000 oz. AGW **Series:** International Friendship **Obverse:** Queen's portrait right **Reverse:** Stylized panda **Note:** Similar to 1 Crown, KM#180.

| Date | Mintage | F | VF | XF | Unc | BU |
|---|---|---|---|---|---|---|
| 1993 Proof | Est. 5,000 | Value: 165 | | | | |

**1/5 CROWN** **KM# 185** **Weight:** 6.2200 g. **Composition:** 0.9999 Gold .2000 oz. AGW **Series:** International Friendship **Obverse:** Queen's portrait right **Reverse:** Natural panda **Note:** Similar to 1 Crown, KM#184.

| Date | Mintage | F | VF | XF | Unc | BU |
|---|---|---|---|---|---|---|
| 1993 Proof | Est. 5,000 | Value: 165 | | | | |

**1/5 CROWN** **KM# 189** **Weight:** 6.2200 g. **Composition:** 0.9999 Gold .2000 oz. AGW **Series:** International Friendship **Obverse:** Queen's portrait right **Reverse:** General Sikarski portrait above B-24 bomber with Rock of Gibraltar in background **Note:** Similar to 1 Crown, KM#188.

| Date | Mintage | F | VF | XF | Unc | BU |
|---|---|---|---|---|---|---|
| 1993 Proof | Est. 5,000 | Value: 165 | | | | |

**1/5 CROWN** **KM# 199** **Weight:** 6.2143 g. **Composition:** 0.9999 Gold .1998 oz. AGW **Subject:** Dependent Territories Conference **Obverse:** Queen's portrait right **Reverse:** 7 shields, 2 in center, 5 around with rope loops **Note:** Similar to 1 Crown, KM#200.

| Date | Mintage | F | VF | XF | Unc | BU |
|---|---|---|---|---|---|---|
| 1993 Proof | Est. 5,000 | Value: 150 | | | | |

**1/5 CROWN** **KM# 204** **Weight:** 6.2200 g. **Composition:** 0.9999 Gold .2000 oz. AGW **Series:** Peter Rabbit Centennial **Subject:** Peter Rabbit **Obverse:** Queen's portrait **Reverse:** Peter Rabbit eating carrots **Note:** Similar to 1 Crown, KM#201.

| Date | Mintage | F | VF | XF | Unc | BU |
|---|---|---|---|---|---|---|
| 1993 Proof | Est. 5,000 | Value: 150 | | | | |

**1/5 CROWN** **KM# 208** **Weight:** 6.2200 g. **Composition:** 0.9999 Gold .2000 oz. AGW **Series:** Peter Rabbit Centennial **Subject:** Tiggy-Winkel **Reverse:** Mrs. Tiggy-Winkel ironing **Note:** Similar to 1 Crown, KM#205.

| Date | Mintage | F | VF | XF | Unc | BU |
|---|---|---|---|---|---|---|
| 1993 Proof | Est. 5,000 | Value: 150 | | | | |

**1/5 CROWN** **KM# 212** **Weight:** 6.2200 g. **Composition:** 0.9999 Gold .2000 oz. AGW **Series:** Peter Rabbit Centennial **Subject:** Jeremy Fisher **Reverse:** Jeremy Fisher fishing **Note:** Similar to 1 Crown, KM#209.

| Date | Mintage | F | VF | XF | Unc | BU |
|---|---|---|---|---|---|---|
| 1993 Proof | Est. 5,000 | Value: 150 | | | | |

**1/5 CROWN** **KM# 216** **Weight:** 6.2200 g. **Composition:** 0.9999 Gold .2000 oz. AGW **Series:** Peter Rabbit Centennial **Subject:** Tom Kitten **Reverse:** Tom Kitten with mother cat **Note:** Similar to 1 Crown, KM#213.

| Date | Mintage | F | VF | XF | Unc | BU |
|---|---|---|---|---|---|---|
| 1993 Proof | Est. 5,000 | Value: 150 | | | | |

**1/5 CROWN** **KM# 220** **Weight:** 6.2200 g. **Composition:** 0.9999 Gold .2000 oz. AGW **Series:** Peter Rabbit Centennial **Subject:** Benjamin Bunny **Reverse:** Benjamin Bunny wearing hat and holding coat **Note:** Similar to 1 Crown, KM#217.

| Date | Mintage | F | VF | XF | Unc | BU |
|---|---|---|---|---|---|---|
| 1993 Proof | Est. 5,000 | Value: 150 | | | | |

**1/5 CROWN** **KM# 224** **Weight:** 6.2200 g. **Composition:** 0.9999 Gold .2000 oz. AGW **Series:** Peter Rabbit Centennial **Subject:** Jemima Puddle-Duck **Reverse:** Jemima Puddle Duck talking with fox **Note:** Similar to 1 Crown, KM#221.

| Date | Mintage | F | VF | XF | Unc | BU |
|---|---|---|---|---|---|---|
| 1993 Proof | Est. 5,000 | Value: 150 | | | | |

**1/5 CROWN** **KM# 126** **Weight:** 6.2200 g. **Composition:** 0.9999 Gold .2000 oz. AGW **Subject:** Japanese Royal Wedding **Note:** Similar to 1/2 Crown, KM#127.

| Date | Mintage | F | VF | XF | Unc | BU |
|---|---|---|---|---|---|---|
| 1993 Proof | Est. 10,000 | Value: 125 | | | | |

**1/5 CROWN** **KM# 441** **Weight:** 6.2200 g. **Composition:** 0.9999 Gold .2000 oz. AGW **Subject:** The Tale of Peter Rabbit **Note:** Similar to 1 Crown, KM#444.

| Date | Mintage | F | VF | XF | Unc | BU |
|---|---|---|---|---|---|---|
| 1994 Proof | Est. 10,000 | Value: 185 | | | | |

**1/5 CROWN** **KM# 226** **Weight:** 6.2200 g. **Composition:** 0.9999 Gold .2000 oz. AGW **Series:** World Cup Soccer **Obverse:** Queen's portrait **Reverse:** 3 players kicking ball up field **Note:** Similar to 1 Crown, KM#225.

| Date | Mintage | F | VF | XF | Unc | BU |
|---|---|---|---|---|---|---|
| 1994 Proof | Est. 5,000 | Value: 150 | | | | |

**1/5 CROWN** **KM# 228** **Weight:** 6.2200 g. **Composition:** 0.9999 Gold .2000 oz. AGW **Series:** World Cup Soccer **Reverse:** 2 players facing; 1 kicking and 1 defending **Note:** Similar to 1 Crown, KM#227.

| Date | Mintage | F | VF | XF | Unc | BU |
|---|---|---|---|---|---|---|
| 1994 Proof | Est. 5,000 | Value: 150 | | | | |

**1/5 CROWN** **KM# 230** **Weight:** 6.2200 g. **Composition:** 0.9999 Gold .2000 oz. AGW **Series:** World Cup Soccer **Reverse:** 2 players; 1 goalie and 1 trying to score **Note:** Similar to 1 Crown, KM#229.

| Date | Mintage | F | VF | XF | Unc | BU |
|---|---|---|---|---|---|---|
| 1994 Proof | Est. 5,000 | Value: 150 | | | | |

**1/5 CROWN** **KM# 232** **Weight:** 6.2200 g. **Composition:** 0.9999 Gold .2000 oz. AGW **Series:** World Cup Soccer **Reverse:** 1 player looking up **Note:** Similar to 1 Crown, KM#231.

| Date | Mintage | F | VF | XF | Unc | BU |
|---|---|---|---|---|---|---|
| 1994 Proof | Est. 5,000 | Value: 150 | | | | |

**1/5 CROWN** **KM# 234** **Weight:** 6.2200 g. **Composition:** 0.9999 Gold .2000 oz. AGW **Series:** World Cup Soccer **Reverse:** 1 player kicking, 1 player running forward **Note:** Similar to 1 Crown, KM#233.

| Date | Mintage | F | VF | XF | Unc | BU |
|---|---|---|---|---|---|---|
| 1994 Proof | Est. 5,000 | Value: 150 | | | | |

**1/5 CROWN** **KM# 236** **Weight:** 6.2200 g. **Composition:** 0.9999 Gold .2000 oz. AGW **Series:** World Cup Soccer **Reverse:** Player in foreground heading ball to player **Note:** Similar to 1 Crown, KM#235.

| Date | Mintage | F | VF | XF | Unc | BU |
|---|---|---|---|---|---|---|
| 1994 Proof | Est. 5,000 | Value: 150 | | | | |

**1/5 CROWN** **KM# 240** **Weight:** 6.2200 g. **Composition:** 0.9999 Gold .2000 oz. AGW **Series:** Preserve Planet Earth **Subject:** Spanish Imperial Eagle **Reverse:** Eagle flying above island **Note:** Similar to 1 Crown, KM#241.

| Date | Mintage | F | VF | XF | Unc | BU |
|---|---|---|---|---|---|---|
| 1994 Proof | Est. 5,000 | Value: 150 | | | | |

**1/5 CROWN** **KM# 242** **Weight:** 6.2200 g. **Composition:** 0.9999 Gold .2000 oz. AGW **Series:** Preserve Planet Earth **Subject:** Striped Dolphins **Reverse:** 3 dolphins **Note:** Similar to 1 Crown, KM#243.

| Date | Mintage | F | VF | XF | Unc | BU |
|---|---|---|---|---|---|---|
| 1994 Proof | Est. 5,000 | Value: 150 | | | | |

**1/5 CROWN** **KM# 244** **Weight:** 6.2200 g. **Composition:** 0.9999 Gold .2000 oz. AGW **Series:** Preserve Planet Earth **Subject:** African Elephants **Reverse:** Mother and baby elephants **Note:** Similar to 1 Crown, KM#245.

| Date | Mintage | F | VF | XF | Unc | BU |
|---|---|---|---|---|---|---|
| 1994 Proof | Est. 5,000 | Value: 150 | | | | |

**1/5 CROWN** **KM# 254** **Weight:** 6.2200 g. **Composition:** 0.9999 Gold .2000 oz. AGW **Series:** World War II **Subject:** Squadron 202 in Gibraltar **Reverse:** Planes flying, Gibraltar in background **Note:** Similar to 1 Crown, KM#250.

| Date | Mintage | F | VF | XF | Unc | BU |
|---|---|---|---|---|---|---|
| 1994 Proof | Est. 5,000 | Value: 165 | | | | |

**1/5 CROWN** **KM# 253** **Weight:** 6.2200 g. **Composition:** 0.9999 Gold .2000 oz. AGW **Series:** World War II **Subject:** Maltese Convoy **Reverse:** Convoy of ships **Note:** Similar to 1 Crown, KM#259.

| Date | Mintage | F | VF | XF | Unc | BU |
|---|---|---|---|---|---|---|
| 1994 Proof | Est. 5,000 | Value: 165 | | | | |

**1/5 CROWN** **KM# 255** **Weight:** 6.2200 g. **Composition:** 0.9999 Gold .2000 oz. AGW **Series:** World War II **Reverse:** Admiral Somerville, ship in background **Note:** Similar to 1 Crown, KM#261.

| Date | Mintage | F | VF | XF | Unc | BU |
|---|---|---|---|---|---|---|
| 1994 Proof | Est. 5,000 | Value: 165 | | | | |

**1/5 CROWN** **KM# 256** **Weight:** 6.2200 g. **Composition:** 0.9999 Gold .2000 oz. AGW **Series:** World War II **Reverse:** Glen Miller and band **Note:** Similar to 1 Crown, KM#262.

| Date | Mintage | F | VF | XF | Unc | BU |
|---|---|---|---|---|---|---|
| 1994 Proof | Est. 5,000 | Value: 165 | | | | |

**1/5 CROWN** **KM# 257** **Weight:** 6.2200 g. **Composition:** 0.9999 Gold .2000 oz. AGW **Series:** World War II **Reverse:** King George VI congratulating pilots **Note:** Similar to 1 Crown, KM#263.

| Date | Mintage | F | VF | XF | Unc | BU |
|---|---|---|---|---|---|---|
| 1994 Proof | Est. 5,000 | Value: 165 | | | | |

**1/5 CROWN** **KM# 258** **Weight:** 6.2200 g. **Composition:** 0.9999 Gold .2000 oz. AGW **Series:** World War II **Reverse:** General Eisenhower, planes and ships in background **Note:** Similar to 1 Crown, KM#264.

| Date | Mintage | F | VF | XF | Unc | BU |
|---|---|---|---|---|---|---|
| 1994 Proof | Est. 5,000 | Value: 165 | | | | |

**1/5 CROWN** **KM# 265** **Weight:** 6.2200 g. **Composition:** 0.9999 Gold .2000 oz. AGW **Series:** First Man on Moon **Reverse:** Dr. Wernher von Braun with replica of rocket **Note:** Similar to 1 Crown, KM#271.

| Date | Mintage | F | VF | XF | Unc | BU |
|---|---|---|---|---|---|---|
| 1994 Proof | Est. 5,000 | Value: 165 | | | | |

**1/5 CROWN** **KM# 266** **Weight:** 6.2200 g. **Composition:** 0.9999 Gold .2000 oz. AGW **Series:** First Man on Moon **Reverse:** Rocket on pad before lift-off **Note:** Similar to 1 Crown, KM#272.

| Date | Mintage | F | VF | XF | Unc | BU |
|---|---|---|---|---|---|---|
| 1994 Proof | Est. 5,000 | Value: 165 | | | | |

**1/5 CROWN** **KM# 267** **Weight:** 6.2200 g. **Composition:** 0.9999 Gold .2000 oz. AGW **Series:** First Man on Moon **Reverse:** Recovering space capsule after splashdown **Note:** Similar to 1 Crown, KM#273.

| Date | Mintage | F | VF | XF | Unc | BU |
|---|---|---|---|---|---|---|
| 1994 Proof | Est. 5,000 | Value: 165 | | | | |

**1/5 CROWN** **KM# 268** **Weight:** 6.2200 g. **Composition:** 0.9999 Gold .2000 oz. AGW **Series:** First Man on Moon **Reverse:** Lunar Module landing on the moon **Note:** Similar to 1 Crown, KM#274.

| Date | Mintage | F | VF | XF | Unc | BU |
|---|---|---|---|---|---|---|
| 1994 Proof | Est. 5,000 | Value: 165 | | | | |

**1/5 CROWN** **KM# 269** **Weight:** 6.2200 g. **Composition:** 0.9999 Gold .2000 oz. AGW **Series:** First Man on Moon **Reverse:** Astronaut stepping on the moon **Note:** Similar to 1 Crown, KM#275.

| Date | Mintage | F | VF | XF | Unc | BU |
|---|---|---|---|---|---|---|
| 1994 Proof | Est. 5,000 | Value: 165 | | | | |

**1/5 CROWN** **KM# 270** **Weight:** 6.2200 g. **Composition:** 0.9999 Gold .2000 oz. AGW **Series:** First Man on Moon **Reverse:** Astronaut setting up flag on the moon **Note:** Similar to 1 Crown, KM#276.

| Date | Mintage | F | VF | XF | Unc | BU |
|---|---|---|---|---|---|---|
| 1994 Proof | Est. 5,000 | Value: 165 | | | | |

**1/5 CROWN** **KM# 277** **Weight:** 6.2200 g. **Composition:** 0.9999 Gold .2000 oz. AGW **Series:** Sherlock Holmes **Reverse:** Holmes sitting with pipe in hand **Note:** Similar to 1 Crown, KM#285.

| Date | Mintage | F | VF | XF | Unc | BU |
|---|---|---|---|---|---|---|
| 1994 Proof | Est. 5,000 | Value: 165 | | | | |

**1/5 CROWN** **KM# 278** **Weight:** 6.2200 g. **Composition:** 0.9999 Gold .2000 oz. AGW **Series:** Sherlock Holmes **Reverse:** Holmes playing violin, Dr. Watson watching **Note:** Similar to 1 Crown, KM#286.

| Date | Mintage | F | VF | XF | Unc | BU |
|---|---|---|---|---|---|---|
| 1994 Proof | Est. 5,000 | Value: 165 | | | | |

**1/5 CROWN** **KM# 279** **Weight:** 6.2200 g. **Composition:** 0.9999 Gold .2000 oz. AGW **Series:** Sherlock Holmes **Reverse:** People talking before 221 B Baker St. **Note:** Similar to 1 Crown, KM#287.

| Date | Mintage | F | VF | XF | Unc | BU |
|---|---|---|---|---|---|---|
| 1994 Proof | Est. 5,000 | Value: 165 | | | | |

**1/5 CROWN** **KM# 280** **Weight:** 6.2200 g. **Composition:** 0.9999 Gold .2000 oz. AGW **Series:** Sherlock Holmes **Reverse:** Scene from book "The Empty House" **Note:** Similar to 1 Crown, KM#288.

| Date | Mintage | F | VF | XF | Unc | BU |
|---|---|---|---|---|---|---|
| 1994 Proof | Est. 5,000 | Value: 165 | | | | |

**1/5 CROWN** **KM# 281** **Weight:** 6.2200 g. **Composition:** 0.9999 Gold .2000 oz. AGW **Series:** Sherlock Holmes **Reverse:** Sailing ship "Mary Celeste" **Note:** Similar to 1 Crown, KM#289.

| Date | Mintage | F | VF | XF | Unc | BU |
|---|---|---|---|---|---|---|
| 1994 Proof | Est. 5,000 | Value: 175 | | | | |

**1/5 CROWN** **KM# 282** **Weight:** 6.2200 g. **Composition:** 0.9999 Gold .2000 oz. AGW **Series:** Sherlock Holmes **Reverse:** Scene from the "Hound of the Baskervilles" **Note:** Similar to 1 Crown, KM#290.

| Date | Mintage | F | VF | XF | Unc | BU |
|---|---|---|---|---|---|---|
| 1994 Proof | Est. 5,000 | Value: 170 | | | | |

**1/5 CROWN** **KM# 283** **Weight:** 6.2200 g. **Composition:** 0.9999 Gold .2000 oz. AGW **Series:** Sherlock Holmes **Reverse:** Scene from the "Three Garriders" **Note:** Similar to 1 Crown, KM#291.

| Date | Mintage | F | VF | XF | Unc | BU |
|---|---|---|---|---|---|---|
| 1994 Proof | Est. 5,000 | Value: 165 | | | | |

**1/5 CROWN** **KM# 284** **Weight:** 6.2200 g. **Composition:** 0.9999 Gold .2000 oz. AGW **Series:** Sherlock Holmes **Reverse:** Scene from the "Final Problem" **Note:** Similar to 1 Crown, KM#292.

| Date | Mintage | F | VF | XF | Unc | BU |
|---|---|---|---|---|---|---|
| 1994 Proof | Est. 5,000 | Value: 165 | | | | |

**1/5 CROWN** **KM# 238** **Weight:** 6.2200 g. **Composition:** 0.9999 Gold .2000 oz. AGW **Series:** Preserve Planet Earth **Subject:** Sabre Tooth Tiger

| Date | Mintage | F | VF | XF | Unc | BU |
|---|---|---|---|---|---|---|
| 1994 Proof | Est. 5,000 | Value: 150 | | | | |

**1/5 CROWN** **KM# 442** **Weight:** 6.2200 g. **Composition:** 0.9950 Platinum .2000 oz. APW

| Date | Mintage | F | VF | XF | Unc | BU |
|---|---|---|---|---|---|---|
| 1994 Proof | Est. 2,500 | Value: 185 | | | | |

**1/5 CROWN** **KM# 295** **Weight:** 6.2200 g. **Composition:** 0.9999 Gold .2000 oz. AGW **Series:** Atlanta Olympics **Subject:** Long Jumpers

| Date | Mintage | F | VF | XF | Unc | BU |
|---|---|---|---|---|---|---|
| 1995 Proof | Est. 5,000 | Value: 160 | | | | |

**1/5 CROWN** **KM# 296** **Weight:** 6.2200 g. **Composition:** 0.9999 Gold .2000 oz. AGW **Series:** Atlanta Olympics **Subject:** Discus Throwers

| Date | Mintage | F | VF | XF | Unc | BU |
|---|---|---|---|---|---|---|
| 1995 Proof | Est. 5,000 | Value: 160 | | | | |

**1/5 CROWN** **KM# 297** **Weight:** 6.2200 g. **Composition:** 0.9999 Gold .2000 oz. AGW **Series:** Atlanta Olympics **Subject:** Relay Racers

| Date | Mintage | F | VF | XF | Unc | BU |
|---|---|---|---|---|---|---|
| 1995 Proof | Est. 5,000 | Value: 160 | | | | |

**1/5 CROWN** **KM# 298** **Weight:** 6.2200 g. **Composition:** 0.9999 Gold .2000 oz. AGW **Series:** Atlanta Olympics **Subject:** Javelin Throwers

| Date | Mintage | F | VF | XF | Unc | BU |
|---|---|---|---|---|---|---|
| 1995 Proof | Est. 5,000 | Value: 160 | | | | |

**1/5 CROWN** **KM# 326** **Weight:** 6.2200 g. **Composition:** 0.9999 Gold .2000 oz. AGW **Subject:** Peter Rabbit

| Date | Mintage | F | VF | XF | Unc | BU |
|---|---|---|---|---|---|---|
| 1995 Proof | Est. 5,000 | Value: 165 | | | | |

**1/5 CROWN** **KM# 326a** **Weight:** 6.2200 g. **Composition:** 0.9950 Platinum .2000 oz. APW

| Date | Mintage | F | VF | XF | Unc | BU |
|---|---|---|---|---|---|---|
| 1995 Proof | Est. 2,500 | Value: 210 | | | | |

**1/5 CROWN** **KM# 303** **Weight:** 6.2200 g. **Composition:** 0.9999 Gold .2000 oz. AGW **Obverse:** Queen's portrait **Reverse:** Rock of Gibraltar and rising sun **Note:** Similar to 1 Crown, KM#304.

| Date | Mintage | F | VF | XF | Unc | BU |
|---|---|---|---|---|---|---|
| 1995 Proof | Est. 5,000 | Value: 165 | | | | |

**1/5 CROWN** **KM# 328** **Weight:** 6.2200 g. **Composition:** 0.9999 Gold .2000 oz. AGW **Series:** Island Games **Subject:** Female Discus Thrower **Reverse:** Circle of athletes with female discus thrower **Note:** Similar to 1 Crown, KM#329.

| Date | Mintage | F | VF | XF | Unc | BU |
|---|---|---|---|---|---|---|
| 1995 Proof | Est. 5,000 | Value: 160 | | | | |

**1/5 CROWN** **KM# 330** **Weight:** 6.2200 g. **Composition:** 0.9999 Gold .2000 oz. AGW **Series:** Island Games **Subject:** High Jumper **Reverse:** Circle of athletes with high jumper **Note:** Similar to 1 Crown, KM#331.

| Date | Mintage | F | VF | XF | Unc | BU |
|---|---|---|---|---|---|---|
| 1995 Proof | Est. 5,000 | Value: 160 | | | | |

**1/5 CROWN** **KM# 342** **Weight:** 6.2200 g. **Composition:** 0.9999 Gold .2000 oz. AGW **Series:** Olympics **Subject:** Tennis **Obverse:** Queen's portrait **Reverse:** Tennis player **Note:** Similar to 1 Crown, KM#348.

| Date | Mintage | F | VF | XF | Unc | BU |
|---|---|---|---|---|---|---|
| 1996 Proof | Est. 5,000 | Value: 165 | | | | |

**1/5 CROWN** **KM# 343** **Weight:** 6.2200 g. **Composition:** 0.9999 Gold .2000 oz. AGW **Series:** Olympics **Subject:** Wrestlers **Note:** Similar to 1 Crown, KM#349.

| Date | Mintage | F | VF | XF | Unc | BU |
|---|---|---|---|---|---|---|
| 1996 Proof | Est. 5,000 | Value: 165 | | | | |

**1/5 CROWN** **KM# 344** **Weight:** 6.2200 g. **Composition:** 0.9999 Gold .2000 oz. AGW **Series:** Olympics **Subject:** Baseball **Note:** Similar to 1 Crown, KM#350.

| Date | Mintage | F | VF | XF | Unc | BU |
|---|---|---|---|---|---|---|
| 1996 Proof | Est. 5,000 | Value: 165 | | | | |

**1/5 CROWN** **KM# 345** **Weight:** 6.2200 g. **Composition:** 0.9999 Gold .2000 oz. AGW **Series:** Olympics **Subject:** Flame **Note:** Similar to 1 Crown, KM#351.

| Date | Mintage | F | VF | XF | Unc | BU |
|---|---|---|---|---|---|---|
| 1996 Proof | Est. 5,000 | Value: 165 | | | | |

**1/5 CROWN** **KM# 346** **Weight:** 6.2200 g. **Composition:** 0.9999 Gold .2000 oz. AGW **Series:** Olympics **Subject:** Volleyball **Note:** Similar to 1 Crown, KM#352.

| Date | Mintage | F | VF | XF | Unc | BU |
|---|---|---|---|---|---|---|
| 1996 Proof | Est. 5,000 | Value: 165 | | | | |

**1/5 CROWN** **KM# 347** **Weight:** 6.2200 g. **Composition:** 0.9999 Gold .2000 oz. AGW **Series:** Olympics **Subject:** Basketball **Note:** Similar to 1 Crown, KM#353.

| Date | Mintage | F | VF | XF | Unc | BU |
|---|---|---|---|---|---|---|
| 1996 Proof | Est. 5,000 | Value: 165 | | | | |

**1/5 CROWN** **KM# 357** **Weight:** 6.2200 g. **Composition:** 0.9999 Gold .2000 oz. AGW **Subject:** Nefusat Yehuda Synagogue Renovation **Obverse:** Queen's portrait **Reverse:** Hebrew symbol, rock, arms and building **Note:** Similar to 1 Crown, KM#358.

| Date | Mintage | F | VF | XF | Unc | BU |
|---|---|---|---|---|---|---|
| 1996 Proof | Est. 5,000 | Value: 165 | | | | |

**1/5 CROWN** **KM# 379** **Weight:** 6.2207 g. **Composition:** 0.9999 Gold .2000 oz. AGW **Series:** Peter Rabbit Centennial **Subject:** Rabbit Escaping **Note:** Similar to 1 Crown, KM#382.

| Date | Mintage | F | VF | XF | Unc | BU |
|---|---|---|---|---|---|---|
| 1996 Proof | Est. 7,500 | Value: 165 | | | | |

**1/5 CROWN** **KM# 384** **Weight:** 6.2207 g. **Composition:** 0.9999 Gold .2000 oz. AGW **Series:** Preserve Planet Earth **Subject:** Shag Birds **Note:** Similar to 1 Crown, KM#386.

| Date | Mintage | F | VF | XF | Unc | BU |
|---|---|---|---|---|---|---|
| 1996 Proof | Est. 5,000 | Value: 165 | | | | |

**1/5 CROWN** **KM# 385** **Weight:** 6.2207 g. **Composition:** 0.9999 Gold .2000 oz. AGW **Series:** Preserve Planet Earth **Subject:** Puffins **Note:** Similar to 1 Crown, KM#387.

| Date | Mintage | F | VF | XF | Unc | BU |
|---|---|---|---|---|---|---|
| 1996 Proof | Est. 5,000 | Value: 165 | | | | |

**1/5 CROWN** **KM# 392** **Weight:** 6.2207 g. **Composition:** 0.9999 Gold .2000 oz. AGW **Series:** Cinema Centennial **Subject:** Grace Kelly **Note:** Similar to 1 Crown, KM#393.

| Date | Mintage | F | VF | XF | Unc | BU |
|---|---|---|---|---|---|---|
| 1996 Proof | Est. 5,000 | Value: 165 | | | | |

**1/5 CROWN** **KM# 397** **Weight:** 6.2207 g. **Composition:** 0.9999 Gold .2000 oz. AGW **Series:** Centenary of the Cinema **Subject:** James Dean **Note:** Similar to 1 Crown, KM#398.

| Date | Mintage | F | VF | XF | Unc | BU |
|---|---|---|---|---|---|---|
| 1996 Proof | Est. 5,000 | Value: 165 | | | | |

**1/5 CROWN** **KM# 402** **Weight:** 6.2207 g. **Composition:** 0.9999 Gold .2000 oz. AGW **Series:** Centenary of the Cinema **Subject:** Marilyn Monroe **Note:** Similar to 1 Crown, KM#403.

| Date | Mintage | F | VF | XF | Unc | BU |
|---|---|---|---|---|---|---|
| 1996 Proof | Est. 5,000 | Value: 165 | | | | |

**1/5 CROWN** **KM# 407** **Weight:** 6.2207 g. **Composition:** 0.9999 Gold .2000 oz. AGW **Series:** Centenary of the Cinema **Subject:** Audrey Hepburn **Note:** Similar to 1 Crown, KM#408.

| Date | Mintage | F | VF | XF | Unc | BU |
|---|---|---|---|---|---|---|
| 1996 Proof | Est. 5,000 | Value: 165 | | | | |

**1/5 CROWN** **KM# 412** **Weight:** 6.2207 g. **Composition:** 0.9999 Gold .2000 oz. AGW **Series:** Centenary of the Cinema **Subject:** Bruce Lee **Note:** Similar to 1 Crown, KM#413.

| Date | Mintage | F | VF | XF | Unc | BU |
|---|---|---|---|---|---|---|
| 1996 Proof | Est. 5,000 | Value: 165 | | | | |

**1/5 CROWN** **KM# 417** **Weight:** 6.2207 g. **Composition:** 0.9999 Gold .2000 oz. AGW **Series:** Centenary of the Cinema **Subject:** Charlie Chaplin **Note:** Similar to 1 Crown, KM#418.

| Date | Mintage | F | VF | XF | Unc | BU |
|---|---|---|---|---|---|---|
| 1996 Proof | Est. 5,000 | Value: 165 | | | | |

**1/5 CROWN** **KM# 422** **Weight:** 6.2207 g. **Composition:** 0.9999 Gold .2000 oz. AGW **Series:** Centenary of the Cinema **Subject:** Gone With The Wind **Note:** Similar to 1 Crown, KM#423.

| Date | Mintage | F | VF | XF | Unc | BU |
|---|---|---|---|---|---|---|
| 1996 Proof | Est. 5,000 | Value: 165 | | | | |

**1/5 CROWN** **KM# 427** **Weight:** 6.2207 g. **Composition:** 0.9999 Gold .2000 oz. AGW **Series:** Centenary of the Cinema **Subject:** The Flintstones **Note:** Similar to 1 Crown, KM#428.

| Date | Mintage | F | VF | XF | Unc | BU |
|---|---|---|---|---|---|---|
| 1996 Proof | Est. 5,000 | Value: 165 | | | | |

**1/5 CROWN** **KM# 431** **Weight:** 6.2207 g. **Composition:** 0.9999 Gold .2000 oz. AGW **Series:** Duke of Edinburgh Awards Scheme **Subject:** 7 Events **Note:** Similar to 1 Crown, KM#432.

| Date | Mintage | F | VF | XF | Unc | BU |
|---|---|---|---|---|---|---|
| 1996 Proof | Est. 5,000 | Value: 165 | | | | |

**1/5 CROWN** **KM# 434** **Weight:** 6.2207 g. **Composition:** 0.9999 Gold .2000 oz. AGW **Series:** Duke of Edinburgh Awards Scheme **Subject:** Cameo/Horses **Note:** Similar to 1 Crown, KM#435.

| Date | Mintage | F | VF | XF | Unc | BU |
|---|---|---|---|---|---|---|
| 1996 Proof | Est. 5,000 | Value: 165 | | | | |

**1/5 CROWN** **KM# 360** **Weight:** 6.2200 g. **Composition:** 0.9999 Gold .2000 oz. AGW **Series:** Euro 96 **Subject:** England

| Date | Mintage | F | VF | XF | Unc | BU |
|---|---|---|---|---|---|---|
| 1996 Proof | Est. 5,000 | Value: 175 | | | | |

**1/5 CROWN** **KM# 370a** **Weight:** 6.2518 g. **Composition:** 0.9950 Platinum .2000 oz. APW **Subject:** Roses

| Date | Mintage | F | VF | XF | Unc | BU |
|---|---|---|---|---|---|---|
| 1996 Proof | Est. 1,000 | Value: 220 | | | | |

**1/5 CROWN** **KM# 379a** **Weight:** 6.2200 g. **Composition:** 0.9950 Platinum .2000 oz. APW

| Date | Mintage | F | VF | XF | Unc | BU |
|---|---|---|---|---|---|---|
| 1996 Proof | Est. 5,000 | Value: 210 | | | | |

**1/5 CROWN** **KM# 392a** **Weight:** 6.2200 g. **Composition:** 0.9950 Platinum .2000 oz. APW

| Date | Mintage | F | VF | XF | Unc | BU |
|---|---|---|---|---|---|---|
| 1996 Proof | Est. 1,000 | Value: 220 | | | | |

**1/5 CROWN** **KM# 397a** **Weight:** 6.2200 g. **Composition:** 0.9950 Platinum .2000 oz. APW

| Date | Mintage | F | VF | XF | Unc | BU |
|---|---|---|---|---|---|---|
| 1996 Proof | Est. 1,000 | Value: 220 | | | | |

**1/5 CROWN** **KM# 402a** **Weight:** 6.2200 g. **Composition:** 0.9950 Platinum .2000 oz. APW

| Date | Mintage | F | VF | XF | Unc | BU |
|---|---|---|---|---|---|---|
| 1996 Proof | Est. 1,000 | Value: 220 | | | | |

**1/5 CROWN** **KM# 407a** **Weight:** 6.2200 g. **Composition:** 0.9950 Platinum .2000 oz. APW

| Date | Mintage | F | VF | XF | Unc | BU |
|---|---|---|---|---|---|---|
| 1996 Proof | Est. 1,000 | Value: 220 | | | | |

**1/5 CROWN** **KM# 447** **Weight:** 6.2207 g. **Composition:** 0.9999 Gold .2000 oz. AGW **Subject:** Lord Buddah **Note:** Similar to 1 Crown, KM#449.

| Date | Mintage | F | VF | XF | Unc | BU |
|---|---|---|---|---|---|---|
| 1996 Proof | Est. 8,000 | Value: 185 | | | | |

**1/5 CROWN** **KM# 456** **Weight:** 6.2207 g. **Composition:** 0.9999 Gold .2000 oz. AGW **Series:** Centenary of the Cinema **Subject:** Wizard of Oz **Note:** Similar to 1 Crown, KM#457.

| Date | Mintage | F | VF | XF | Unc | BU |
|---|---|---|---|---|---|---|
| 1996 Proof | Est. 5,000 | Value: 165 | | | | |

**1/5 CROWN** **KM# 460** **Weight:** 6.2207 g. **Composition:** 0.9999 Gold .2000 oz. AGW **Series:** Centenary of the Cinema **Subject:** Marx Brothers **Note:** Similar to 1 Crown, KM#461.

| Date | Mintage | F | VF | XF | Unc | BU |
|---|---|---|---|---|---|---|
| 1996 Proof | Est. 5,000 | Value: 165 | | | | |

**1/5 CROWN** **KM# 464** **Weight:** 6.2207 g. **Composition:** 0.9999 Gold .2000 oz. AGW **Series:** Centenary of the Cinema **Subject:** Elvis Presley **Note:** Similar to 1 Crown, KM#465.

| Date | Mintage | F | VF | XF | Unc | BU |
|---|---|---|---|---|---|---|
| 1996 Proof | Est. 5,000 | Value: 165 | | | | |

**1/5 CROWN** **KM# 468** **Weight:** 6.2207 g. **Composition:** 0.9999 Gold .2000 oz. AGW **Series:** Centenary of the Cinema **Subject:** Casablanca **Note:** Similar to 1 Crown, KM#469.

| Date | Mintage | F | VF | XF | Unc | BU |
|---|---|---|---|---|---|---|
| 1996 Proof | Est. 5,000 | Value: 165 | | | | |

**1/5 CROWN** **KM# 472** **Weight:** 6.2207 g. **Composition:** 0.9999 Gold .2000 oz. AGW **Series:** Centenary of the Cinema **Subject:** E.T. **Note:** Similar to 1 Crown, KM#473.

| Date | Mintage | F | VF | XF | Unc | BU |
|---|---|---|---|---|---|---|
| 1996 Proof | Est. 5,000 | Value: 165 | | | | |

**1/5 CROWN** **KM# 476** **Weight:** 6.2207 g. **Composition:** 0.9999 Gold .2000 oz. AGW **Series:** Centenary of the Cinema **Subject:** Alfred Hitchcock **Note:** Similar to 1 Crown, KM#477.

| Date | Mintage | F | VF | XF | Unc | BU |
|---|---|---|---|---|---|---|
| 1996 Proof | Est. 5,000 | Value: 165 | | | | |

**1/5 CROWN** **KM# 370** **Weight:** 6.2200 g. **Composition:** 0.9999 Gold .2000 oz. AGW **Subject:** Roses **Note:** Similar to 1 Crown, KM#373.

| Date | Mintage | F | VF | XF | Unc | BU |
|---|---|---|---|---|---|---|
| 1996 Proof | Est. 5,000 | Value: 165 | | | | |

**1/5 CROWN** **KM# 522a** **Weight:** 6.2518 g. **Composition:** 0.9950 Platinum .2000 oz. APW

| Date | Mintage | F | VF | XF | Unc | BU |
|---|---|---|---|---|---|---|
| 1997 Proof | Est. 2,500 | Value: 210 | | | | |

**1/5 CROWN** **KM# 539a** **Weight:** 6.2200 g. **Composition:** 0.9950 Platinum .1990 oz. APW

| Date | Mintage | F | VF | XF | Unc | BU |
|---|---|---|---|---|---|---|
| 1997 Proof | Est. 1,000 | Value: 200 | | | | |

**1/5 CROWN** **KM# 543a** **Weight:** 6.2200 g. **Composition:** 0.9950 Platinum .1990 oz. APW

| Date | Mintage | F | VF | XF | Unc | BU |
|---|---|---|---|---|---|---|
| 1997 Proof | Est. 1,000 | Value: 200 | | | | |

**1/5 CROWN** **KM# 547a** **Weight:** 6.2200 g. **Composition:** 0.9950 Platinum .1990 oz. APW

| Date | Mintage | F | VF | XF | Unc | BU |
|---|---|---|---|---|---|---|
| 1997 Proof | Est. 1,000 | Value: 200 | | | | |

**1/5 CROWN** **KM# 551a** **Weight:** 6.2200 g. **Composition:** 0.9950 Platinum .1990 oz. APW

| Date | Mintage | F | VF | XF | Unc | BU |
|---|---|---|---|---|---|---|
| 1997 Proof | Est. 1,000 | Value: 200 | | | | |

**1/5 CROWN** **KM# 555a** **Weight:** 6.2200 g. **Composition:** 0.9950 Platinum .1990 oz. APW

| Date | Mintage | F | VF | XF | Unc | BU |
|---|---|---|---|---|---|---|
| 1997 Proof | Est. 1,000 | Value: 200 | | | | |

**1/5 CROWN** **KM# 513** **Weight:** 6.2207 g. **Composition:** 0.9999 Gold .2000 oz. AGW **Subject:** Peacock **Note:** Similar to 1 Crown, KM#514.

| Date | Mintage | F | VF | XF | Unc | BU |
|---|---|---|---|---|---|---|
| 1997 Proof | Est. 5,000 | Value: 185 | | | | |

**1/5 CROWN** **KM# 522** **Weight:** 6.2207 g. **Composition:** 0.9999 Gold .2000 oz. AGW **Subject:** Tale of Peter Rabbit **Note:** Similar to 1 Crown, KM#525.

| Date | Mintage | F | VF | XF | Unc | BU |
|---|---|---|---|---|---|---|
| 1997 Proof | Est. 10,000 | Value: 165 | | | | |

**1/5 CROWN** **KM# 529** **Weight:** 6.2207 g. **Composition:** 0.9999 Gold .2000 oz. AGW **Series:** Golden Wedding Anniversary **Subject:** Queen Elizabeth and Prince Philip **Note:** Similar to 1 Crown, KM#530.

| Date | Mintage | F | VF | XF | Unc | BU |
|---|---|---|---|---|---|---|
| 1997 Proof | Est. 3,500 | Value: 150 | | | | |

**1/5 CROWN** **KM# 531** **Weight:** 6.2207 g. **Composition:** 0.9999 Gold .2000 oz. AGW **Series:** Golden Wedding Anniversary **Subject:** Queen Elizabeth and Prince Philip **Note:** Similar to 1 Crown, KM#532.

| Date | Mintage | F | VF | XF | Unc | BU |
|---|---|---|---|---|---|---|
| 1997 Proof | Est. 3,500 | Value: 150 | | | | |

**1/5 CROWN** **KM# 533** **Weight:** 6.2207 g. **Composition:** 0.9999 Gold .2000 oz. AGW **Series:** Golden Wedding Anniversary **Subject:** Queen Elizabeth and Prince Philip **Note:** Similar to 1 Crown, KM#534.

| Date | Mintage | F | VF | XF | Unc | BU |
|---|---|---|---|---|---|---|
| 1997 Proof | Est. 3,500 | Value: 150 | | | | |

**1/5 CROWN** **KM# 535** **Weight:** 6.2207 g. **Composition:** 0.9999 Gold .2000 oz. AGW **Series:** Golden Wedding Anniversary **Subject:** Queen Elizabeth and Prince Philip **Note:** Similar to 1 Crown, KM#536.

| Date | Mintage | F | VF | XF | Unc | BU |
|---|---|---|---|---|---|---|
| 1997 Proof | Est. 3,500 | Value: 150 | | | | |

**1/5 CROWN** **KM# 539** **Weight:** 6.2207 g. **Composition:** 0.9999 Gold .2000 oz. AGW **Subject:** Peonies **Note:** Similar to 1 Crown, KM#540.

| Date | Mintage | F | VF | XF | Unc | BU |
|---|---|---|---|---|---|---|
| 1997 Proof | Est. 5,000 | Value: 150 | | | | |

**1/5 CROWN** **KM# 543** **Weight:** 6.2200 g. **Composition:** 0.9999 Gold .2000 oz. AGW **Subject:** Nefertiti **Note:** Similar to 1 Crown, KM#544.

| Date | Mintage | F | VF | XF | Unc | BU |
|---|---|---|---|---|---|---|
| 1997 Proof | Est. 5,000 | Value: 150 | | | | |

**1/5 CROWN** **KM# 547** **Weight:** 6.2200 g. **Composition:** 0.9999 Gold .2000 oz. AGW **Subject:** Cleopatra **Note:** Similar to 1 Crown, KM#548.

| Date | Mintage | F | VF | XF | Unc | BU |
|---|---|---|---|---|---|---|
| 1997 Proof | Est. 5,000 | Value: 150 | | | | |

**1/5 CROWN** **KM# 551** **Weight:** 6.2200 g. **Composition:** 0.9999 Gold .2000 oz. AGW **Subject:** Europa **Note:** Similar to 1 Crown, KM#552.

| Date | Mintage | F | VF | XF | Unc | BU |
|---|---|---|---|---|---|---|
| 1997 Proof | Est. 5,000 | Value: 150 | | | | |

**1/5 CROWN** **KM# 555** **Weight:** 6.2200 g. **Composition:** 0.9999 Gold .2000 oz. AGW **Subject:** Liberty **Note:** Similar to 1 Crown, KM#556.

| Date | Mintage | F | VF | XF | Unc | BU |
|---|---|---|---|---|---|---|
| 1997 Proof | Est. 5,000 | Value: 150 | | | | |

**1/5 CROWN** **KM# 562** **Weight:** 6.2200 g. **Composition:** 0.9999 Gold .2000 oz. AGW **Series:** Queen's Birthday Series **Note:** Similar to 1 Crown, KM#566.

| Date | Mintage | F | VF | XF | Unc | BU |
|---|---|---|---|---|---|---|
| 1997 Proof | Est. 5,000 | Value: 165 | | | | |

**1/5 CROWN** **KM# 563** **Weight:** 6.2200 g. **Composition:** 0.9999 Gold .2000 oz. AGW **Series:** Queen's Birthday Series **Note:** Similar to 1 Crown, KM#567.

| Date | Mintage | F | VF | XF | Unc | BU |
|---|---|---|---|---|---|---|
| 1997 Proof | Est. 5,000 | Value: 165 | | | | |

**1/5 CROWN** **KM# 564** **Weight:** 6.2200 g. **Composition:** 0.9999 Gold .2000 oz. AGW **Series:** Queen's Birthday Series **Note:** Similar to 1 Crown, KM#568.

| Date | Mintage | F | VF | XF | Unc | BU |
|---|---|---|---|---|---|---|
| 1997 Proof | Est. 5,000 | Value: 165 | | | | |

**1/5 CROWN** **KM# 565** **Weight:** 6.2200 g. **Composition:** 0.9999 Gold .2000 oz. AGW **Series:** Queen's Birthday Series **Note:** Similar to 1 Crown, KM#569.

| Date | Mintage | F | VF | XF | Unc | BU |
|---|---|---|---|---|---|---|
| 1997 Proof | Est. 5,000 | Value: 165 | | | | |

**1/5 CROWN** **KM# 570** **Weight:** 6.2200 g. **Composition:** 0.9999 Gold .2000 oz. AGW **Subject:** The New Mosque **Note:** Similar to 1 Crown, KM#571.

| Date | Mintage | F | VF | XF | Unc | BU |
|---|---|---|---|---|---|---|
| 1997 Proof | Est. 5,000 | Value: 165 | | | | |

**1/5 CROWN** **KM# 635** **Weight:** 6.2200 g. **Composition:** 0.9999 Gold .2000 oz. AGW **Subject:** Winter Olympics Japan **Obverse:** Queen's portrait **Reverse:** Speed skater and "Bullet Train" **Note:** Similar to 1 Crown, KM#636.

| Date | Mintage | F | VF | XF | Unc | BU |
|---|---|---|---|---|---|---|
| 1998 Proof | Est. 5,000 | Value: 165 | | | | |

**1/5 CROWN** **KM# 637** **Weight:** 6.2200 g. **Composition:** 0.9999 Gold .2000 oz. AGW **Subject:** Winter Olympics Japan **Obverse:** Queen's portrait **Reverse:** Ski jumper and Buddha **Note:** Similar to 1 Crown, KM#638.

| Date | Mintage | F | VF | XF | Unc | BU |
|---|---|---|---|---|---|---|
| 1998 Proof | Est. 5,000 | Value: 165 | | | | |

**1/5 CROWN** **KM# 639** **Weight:** 6.2200 g. **Composition:** 0.9999 Gold .2000 oz. AGW **Subject:** Winter Olympics Japan **Obverse:** Queen's portrait **Reverse:** Cross country skiers **Note:** Similar to 1 Crown, KM#640.

| Date | Mintage | F | VF | XF | Unc | BU |
|---|---|---|---|---|---|---|
| 1998 Proof | Est. 5,000 | Value: 165 | | | | |

**1/5 CROWN** **KM# 641** **Weight:** 6.2200 g. **Composition:** 0.9999 Gold .2000 oz. AGW **Subject:** Winter Olympics Japan **Obverse:** Queen's portrait **Reverse:** Slalom skier and Zenkoji temple **Note:** Similar to 1 Crown, KM#642.

| Date | Mintage | F | VF | XF | Unc | BU |
|---|---|---|---|---|---|---|
| 1998 Proof | Est. 5,000 | Value: 165 | | | | |

**1/5 CROWN** **KM# 653** **Weight:** 6.2200 g. **Composition:** 0.9999 Gold .2000 oz. AGW **Subject:** Peter Rabbit **Obverse:** Queen's portrait **Reverse:** Peter Rabbit **Note:** Similar to 1 Crown, KM#656.

| Date | Mintage | F | VF | XF | Unc | BU |
|---|---|---|---|---|---|---|
| 1998 Proof | Est. 10,000 | Value: 165 | | | | |

**1/5 CROWN** **KM# 653a** **Weight:** 6.2200 g. **Composition:** 0.9950 Platinum .2000 oz. APW

| Date | Mintage | F | VF | XF | Unc | BU |
|---|---|---|---|---|---|---|
| 1998 Proof | Est. 2,500 | Value: 200 | | | | |

**1/5 CROWN** **KM# 659a** **Weight:** 6.2200 g. **Composition:** 0.9950 Platinum .2000 oz. APW

| Date | Mintage | F | VF | XF | Unc | BU |
|---|---|---|---|---|---|---|
| 1998 Proof | Est. 1,000 | Value: 200 | | | | |

**1/5 CROWN** **KM# 671a** **Weight:** 6.2200 g. **Composition:** 0.9950 Platinum .2000 oz. APW

| Date | Mintage | F | VF | XF | Unc | BU |
|---|---|---|---|---|---|---|
| 1998 Proof | Est. 1,000 | Value: 200 | | | | |

**1/5 CROWN** **KM# 672a** **Weight:** 6.2200 g. **Composition:** 0.9950 Platinum .2000 oz. APW

| Date | Mintage | F | VF | XF | Unc | BU |
|---|---|---|---|---|---|---|
| 1998 Proof | Est. 1,000 | Value: 200 | | | | |

**1/5 CROWN** **KM# 673a** **Weight:** 6.2200 g. **Composition:** 0.9950 Platinum .2000 oz. APW

| Date | Mintage | F | VF | XF | Unc | BU |
|---|---|---|---|---|---|---|
| 1998 Proof | Est. 1,000 | Value: 200 | | | | |

**1/5 CROWN** **KM# 680a** **Weight:** 6.2200 g. **Composition:** 0.9950 Platinum .2000 oz. APW

| Date | Mintage | F | VF | XF | Unc | BU |
|---|---|---|---|---|---|---|
| 1998 Proof | Est. 2,000 | Value: 200 | | | | |

**1/5 CROWN** **KM# 741** **Weight:** 6.2200 g. **Composition:** 0.9999 Gold .2000 oz. AGW **Subject:** Year of the Ocean **Obverse:** Queen's portrait **Reverse:** Polar bear and walrus

| Date | Mintage | F | VF | XF | Unc | BU |
|---|---|---|---|---|---|---|
| 1998 Proof | Est. 5,000 | Value: 165 | | | | |

**1/5 CROWN** **KM# 742** **Weight:** 6.2200 g. **Composition:** 0.9999 Gold .2000 oz. AGW **Subject:** Year of the Ocean **Obverse:** Queen's portrait **Reverse:** Seals and penguins

| Date | Mintage | F | VF | XF | Unc | BU |
|---|---|---|---|---|---|---|
| 1998 Proof | Est. 5,000 | Value: 165 | | | | |

**1/5 CROWN** **KM# 743** **Weight:** 6.2200 g. **Composition:** 0.9999 Gold .2000 oz. AGW **Subject:** Year of the Ocean **Obverse:** Queen's portrait **Reverse:** Sea cow with calf

| Date | Mintage | F | VF | XF | Unc | BU |
|---|---|---|---|---|---|---|
| 1998 Proof | Est. 5,000 | Value: 165 | | | | |

**1/5 CROWN** **KM# 744** **Weight:** 6.2200 g. **Composition:** 0.9999 Gold .2000 oz. AGW **Subject:** Year of the Ocean **Obverse:** Queen's portrait **Reverse:** Surfer

| Date | Mintage | F | VF | XF | Unc | BU |
|---|---|---|---|---|---|---|
| 1998 Proof | Est. 5,000 | Value: 165 | | | | |

**1/5 CROWN** **KM# 659** **Weight:** 6.2200 g. **Composition:** 0.9999 Gold .2000 oz. AGW **Subject:** Chrysanthemum **Note:** Similar to 1 Crown, KM#661.

| Date | Mintage | F | VF | XF | Unc | BU |
|---|---|---|---|---|---|---|
| 1998 Proof | Est. 5,000 | Value: 165 | | | | |

**1/5 CROWN** **KM# 671** **Weight:** 6.2200 g. **Composition:** 0.9999 Gold .2000 oz. AGW **Subject:** Juno **Obverse:** Queen's portrait **Reverse:** Facing portrait of Juno **Note:** Similar to 1 Crown, KM#675.

| Date | Mintage | F | VF | XF | Unc | BU |
|---|---|---|---|---|---|---|
| 1998 Proof | Est. 5,000 | Value: 165 | | | | |

**1/5 CROWN** **KM# 672** **Weight:** 6.2200 g. **Composition:** 0.9999 Gold .2000 oz. AGW **Subject:** Athena **Obverse:** Queen's portrait **Reverse:** Helmeted portrait of Athena **Note:** Similar to 1 Crown, KM#676.

| Date | Mintage | F | VF | XF | Unc | BU |
|---|---|---|---|---|---|---|
| 1998 Proof | Est. 5,000 | Value: 165 | | | | |

**1/5 CROWN** **KM# 673** **Weight:** 6.2200 g. **Composition:** 0.9999 Gold .2000 oz. AGW **Subject:** Arethusa **Obverse:** Queen's portrait **Reverse:** Portrait of Arethusa with dolphins **Note:** Similar to 1 Crown, KM#677.

| Date | Mintage | F | VF | XF | Unc | BU |
|---|---|---|---|---|---|---|
| 1998 Proof | Est. 5,000 | Value: 165 | | | | |

**1/5 CROWN** **KM# 798** **Weight:** 6.2200 g. **Composition:** 0.9999 Gold .2000 oz. AGW **Obverse:** Queen's portrait **Reverse:**

Portrait of Dwight D. Eisenhower, North African invasion scene **Note:** Similar to 1 Crown, KM#799.

| Date | Mintage | F | VF | XF | Unc | BU |
|---|---|---|---|---|---|---|
| 1998 Proof | Est. 5,000 | Value: 165 | | | | |

**1/5 CROWN** **KM# 731** **Weight:** 6.2200 g. **Composition:** 0.9999 Gold .2000 oz. AGW **Obverse:** Queen's portrait **Reverse:** Cupid with hologram heart **Note:** Similar to 1/2 Crown, KM#647.

| Date | Mintage | F | VF | XF | Unc | BU |
|---|---|---|---|---|---|---|
| 1998 Proof | Est. 5,000 | Value: 165 | | | | |

**1/5 CROWN** **KM# 686** **Weight:** 6.2200 g. **Composition:** 0.9999 Gold .2000 oz. AGW **Subject:** World Cup France 1998 **Obverse:** Queen's portrait **Reverse:** Two players, map of Europe **Note:** Similar to 1 Crown, KM#690.

| Date | Mintage | F | VF | XF | Unc | BU |
|---|---|---|---|---|---|---|
| 1998 Proof | Est. 5,000 | Value: 165 | | | | |

**1/5 CROWN** **KM# 680** **Weight:** 6.2200 g. **Composition:** 0.9999 Gold .2000 oz. AGW **Subject:** Paddington Bear **Obverse:** Queen's portrait **Reverse:** Bear with suitcase **Note:** Similar to 1 Crown, KM#682.

| Date | Mintage | F | VF | XF | Unc | BU |
|---|---|---|---|---|---|---|
| 1998 Proof | Est. 5,000 | Value: 165 | | | | |

**1/5 CROWN** **KM# 683** **Weight:** 6.2200 g. **Composition:** 0.9999 Gold .2000 oz. AGW **Subject:** World Cup France 1998 **Obverse:** Queen's portrait **Reverse:** Goalie, map of Europe **Note:** Similar to 1 Crown, KM#687.

| Date | Mintage | F | VF | XF | Unc | BU |
|---|---|---|---|---|---|---|
| 1998 Proof | Est. 5,000 | Value: 165 | | | | |

**1/5 CROWN** **KM# 684** **Weight:** 6.2200 g. **Composition:** 0.9999 Gold .2000 oz. AGW **Subject:** World Cup France 1998 **Obverse:** Queen's portrait **Reverse:** Player kicking to left **Note:** Similar to 1 Crown, KM#688.

| Date | Mintage | F | VF | XF | Unc | BU |
|---|---|---|---|---|---|---|
| 1998 Proof | Est. 5,000 | Value: 165 | | | | |

**1/5 CROWN** **KM# 685** **Weight:** 6.2200 g. **Composition:** 0.9999 Gold .2000 oz. AGW **Subject:** World Cup France 1998 **Obverse:** Queen's portrait **Reverse:** Player dribbling **Note:** Similar to 1 Crown, KM#689.

| Date | Mintage | F | VF | XF | Unc | BU |
|---|---|---|---|---|---|---|
| 1998 Proof | Est. 5,000 | Value: 165 | | | | |

**1/5 CROWN** **KM# 767** **Weight:** 6.2200 g. **Composition:** 0.9999 Gold .2000 oz. AGW **Subject:** Gibraltar Regiment New Colours **Obverse:** Queen's portrait **Reverse:** Soldiers presenting keys **Note:** Similar to 1 Crown, KM#758.

| Date | Mintage | F | VF | XF | Unc | BU |
|---|---|---|---|---|---|---|
| 1998 Proof | Est. 5,000 | Value: 165 | | | | |

**1/5 CROWN** **KM# 786** **Weight:** 6.2200 g. **Composition:** 0.9999 Gold .2000 oz. AGW **Series:** Summer Olympics **Subject:** Sydney **Obverse:** Queen's portrait **Reverse:** Sailboats and platypus **Note:** Similar to 1 Crown, KM#787.

| Date | Mintage | F | VF | XF | Unc | BU |
|---|---|---|---|---|---|---|
| 1999 Proof | Est. 5,000 | Value: 165 | | | | |

**1/5 CROWN** **KM# 788** **Weight:** 6.2200 g. **Composition:** 0.9999 Gold .2000 oz. AGW **Series:** Summer Olympics **Subject:** Sydney **Obverse:** Queen's portrait **Reverse:** Swimmer and koala bear **Note:** Similar to 1 Crown, KM#789.

| Date | Mintage | F | VF | XF | Unc | BU |
|---|---|---|---|---|---|---|
| 1999 Proof | Est. 5,000 | Value: 165 | | | | |

**1/5 CROWN** **KM# 792** **Weight:** 6.2200 g. **Composition:** 0.9999 Gold .2000 oz. AGW **Series:** Summer Olympics **Subject:** Sydney **Obverse:** Queen's portrait **Reverse:** Man with torch and dog **Note:** Similar to 1 Crown, KM#793.

| Date | Mintage | F | VF | XF | Unc | BU |
|---|---|---|---|---|---|---|
| 1999 Proof | Est. 5,000 | Value: 165 | | | | |

**1/5 CROWN** **KM# 796** **Weight:** 6.2200 g. **Composition:** 0.9999 Gold .2000 oz. AGW **Subject:** Millennium 2000 **Obverse:** Queen's portrait **Reverse:** Sundial, digital clock face, candle and traditional clock face **Note:** Similar to 5 Pounds, KM#797.

| Date | Mintage | F | VF | XF | Unc | BU |
|---|---|---|---|---|---|---|
| 1999 Proof | Est. 5,000 | Value: 165 | | | | |

**1/5 CROWN** **KM# 800** **Weight:** 6.2200 g. **Composition:** 0.9999 Gold .2000 oz. AGW **Subject:** King Alfred the Great **Obverse:** Queen's portrait **Reverse:** Alfred the Great, dates **Note:** Similar to 1 Crown, KM#801.

| Date | Mintage | F | VF | XF | Unc | BU |
|---|---|---|---|---|---|---|
| 1999 Proof | Est. 5,000 | Value: 165 | | | | |

**1/5 CROWN** **KM# 802** **Weight:** 6.2200 g. **Composition:** 0.9999 Gold .2000 oz. AGW **Subject:** King Canute **Obverse:** Queen's portrait **Reverse:** King Canute, dates **Note:** Similar to 1 Crown, KM#803.

| Date | Mintage | F | VF | XF | Unc | BU |
|---|---|---|---|---|---|---|
| 1999 Proof | Est. 5,000 | Value: 165 | | | | |

**1/5 CROWN** **KM# 804** **Weight:** 6.2200 g. **Composition:** 0.9999 Gold .2000 oz. AGW **Subject:** King Edward the Confessor **Obverse:** Queen's portrait **Reverse:** Edward the Confessor, dates **Note:** Similar to 1 Crown, KM#805.

| Date | Mintage | F | VF | XF | Unc | BU |
|---|---|---|---|---|---|---|
| 1999 Proof | Est. 5,000 | Value: 165 | | | | |

**1/5 CROWN** **KM# 806** **Weight:** 6.2200 g. **Composition:** 0.9999 Gold .2000 oz. AGW **Series:** House of Normandy **Subject:** King William I **Obverse:** Queen's portrait **Reverse:** William I, dates **Note:** Similar to 1 Crown, KM#807.

| Date | Mintage | F | VF | XF | Unc | BU |
|---|---|---|---|---|---|---|
| 1999 Proof | Est. 5,000 | Value: 165 | | | | |

**1/5 CROWN** **KM# 808** **Weight:** 6.2200 g. **Composition:** 0.9999 Gold .2000 oz. AGW **Series:** House of Plantagenet **Subject:** King Richard I **Obverse:** Queen's portrait **Reverse:** Richard I, dates **Note:** Similar to 1 Crown, KM#809.

| Date | Mintage | F | VF | XF | Unc | BU |
|---|---|---|---|---|---|---|
| 1999 Proof | Est. 5,000 | Value: 165 | | | | |

**1/5 CROWN** **KM# 810** **Weight:** 6.2200 g. **Composition:** 0.9999 Gold .2000 oz. AGW **Series:** House of Plantagenet **Subject:** King John **Obverse:** Queen's portrait **Reverse:** King John, dates **Note:** Similar to 1 Crown, KM#811.

| Date | Mintage | F | VF | XF | Unc | BU |
|---|---|---|---|---|---|---|
| 1999 Proof | Est. 5,000 | Value: 165 | | | | |

**1/5 CROWN** **KM# 812** **Weight:** 6.2200 g. **Composition:** 0.9999 Gold .2000 oz. AGW **Series:** House of Lancaster **Subject:** King Henry V **Obverse:** Queen's portrait **Reverse:** King Henry V, dates **Note:** Similar to 1 Crown, KM#813.

| Date | Mintage | F | VF | XF | Unc | BU |
|---|---|---|---|---|---|---|
| 1999 Proof | Est. 5,000 | Value: 165 | | | | |

**1/5 CROWN** **KM# 814** **Weight:** 6.2200 g. **Composition:** 0.9999 Gold .2000 oz. AGW **Series:** House of York **Subject:** King Richard III **Obverse:** Queen's portrait **Reverse:** King Richard III, dates **Note:** Similar to 1 Crown, KM#815.

| Date | Mintage | F | VF | XF | Unc | BU |
|---|---|---|---|---|---|---|
| 1999 Proof | Est. 5,000 | Value: 165 | | | | |

**1/5 CROWN** **KM# 816** **Weight:** 6.2200 g. **Composition:** 0.9999 Gold .2000 oz. AGW **Series:** House of Tudor **Subject:** King Henry VIII **Obverse:** Queen's portrait **Reverse:** King Henry VIII, dates **Note:** Similar to 1 Crown, KM#817.

| Date | Mintage | F | VF | XF | Unc | BU |
|---|---|---|---|---|---|---|
| 1999 Proof | Est. 5,000 | Value: 165 | | | | |

**1/5 CROWN** **KM# 818** **Weight:** 6.2200 g. **Composition:** 0.9999 Gold .2000 oz. AGW **Series:** House of Tudor **Subject:** Queen Elizabeth I **Obverse:** Queen's portrait **Reverse:** Queen Elizabeth I, dates **Note:** Similar to 1 Crown, KM#819.

| Date | Mintage | F | VF | XF | Unc | BU |
|---|---|---|---|---|---|---|
| 1999 Proof | Est. 5,000 | Value: 165 | | | | |

**1/5 CROWN** **KM# 820** **Weight:** 6.2200 g. **Composition:** 0.9999 Gold .2000 oz. AGW **Series:** House of Stuart **Subject:** King Charles I **Obverse:** Queen's portrait **Reverse:** King Charles I, dates **Note:** Similar to 1 Crown, KM#821.

| Date | Mintage | F | VF | XF | Unc | BU |
|---|---|---|---|---|---|---|
| 1999 Proof | Est. 5,000 | Value: 165 | | | | |

**1/5 CROWN** **KM# 822** **Weight:** 6.2200 g. **Composition:** 0.9999 Gold .2000 oz. AGW **Series:** House of Stuart **Subject:** King Charles II **Obverse:** Queen's portrait **Reverse:** Charles II, dates **Note:** Similar to 1 Crown, KM#823.

| Date | Mintage | F | VF | XF | Unc | BU |
|---|---|---|---|---|---|---|
| 1999 Proof | Est. 5,000 | Value: 165 | | | | |

**1/5 CROWN** **KM# 824** **Weight:** 6.2200 g. **Composition:** 0.9999 Gold .2000 oz. AGW **Subject:** The Wedding of Prince Edward **Obverse:** Queen's portrait **Reverse:** Prince and bride **Note:** Similar to 1 Crown, KM#826.

| Date | Mintage | F | VF | XF | Unc | BU |
|---|---|---|---|---|---|---|
| 1999 Proof | Est. 5,000 | Value: 165 | | | | |

**1/5 CROWN** **KM# 826** **Weight:** 6.2200 g. **Composition:** 0.9999 Gold .2000 oz. AGW **Subject:** The Wedding of Prince Edward **Obverse:** Queen's portrait **Reverse:** St. George's Chapel **Note:** Similar to 1 Crown, KM#827.

| Date | Mintage | F | VF | XF | Unc | BU |
|---|---|---|---|---|---|---|
| 1999 Proof | Est. 5,000 | Value: 165 | | | | |

**1/5 CROWN** **KM# 834** **Weight:** 6.2200 g. **Composition:** 0.9999 Gold .2000 oz. AGW **Subject:** The Life of Queen Elizabeth **Obverse:** Queen's portrait **Reverse:** 1905 portrait of Queen Mother as a girl **Note:** Similar to 1 Crown, KM#835.

| Date | Mintage | F | VF | XF | Unc | BU |
|---|---|---|---|---|---|---|
| 1999 Proof | Est. 5,000 | Value: 165 | | | | |

**1/5 CROWN** **KM# 836** **Weight:** 6.2200 g. **Composition:** 0.9999 Gold .2000 oz. AGW **Subject:** The Life of Queen Elizabeth **Obverse:** Queen's portrait **Reverse:** 1918 portrait of Queen Mother with wounded veteran **Note:** Similar to 1 Crown, KM#837.

| Date | Mintage | F | VF | XF | Unc | BU |
|---|---|---|---|---|---|---|
| 1999 Proof | Est. 5,000 | Value: 165 | | | | |

**1/5 CROWN** **KM# 838** **Weight:** 6.2200 g. **Composition:** 0.9999 Gold .2000 oz. AGW **Subject:** The Life of Queen Elizabeth **Obverse:** Queen's portrait **Reverse:** 1923 wedding portrait **Note:** Similar to 1 Crown, KM#839.

| Date | Mintage | F | VF | XF | Unc | BU |
|---|---|---|---|---|---|---|
| 1999 Proof | Est. 5,000 | Value: 165 | | | | |

**1/5 CROWN** **KM# 840** **Weight:** 6.2200 g. **Composition:** 0.9999 Gold .2000 oz. AGW **Subject:** The Life of Queen Elizabeth **Obverse:** Queen's portrait **Reverse:** 1936 family portrait **Note:** Similar to 1 Crown, KM#841.

| Date | Mintage | F | VF | XF | Unc | BU |
|---|---|---|---|---|---|---|
| 1999 Proof | Est. 5,000 | Value: 165 | | | | |

**1/5 CROWN** **KM# 843** **Weight:** 6.2200 g. **Composition:** 0.9999 Gold .2000 oz. AGW **Subject:** The World of War **Obverse:** Queen's portrait **Reverse:** Franklin D. Roosevelt and Zero fighter **Note:** Similar to 1 Crown, KM#843.1.

| Date | Mintage | F | VF | XF | Unc | BU |
|---|---|---|---|---|---|---|
| 1999 Proof | — | Value: 165 | | | | |

**1/5 CROWN** **KM# 844** **Weight:** 6.2200 g. **Composition:** 0.9999 Gold .2000 oz. AGW **Subject:** The World At War **Obverse:** Queen's portrait **Reverse:** Operation Manna, bomber dropping food packets **Note:** Similar to 1 Crown, KM#845.

| Date | Mintage | F | VF | XF | Unc | BU |
|---|---|---|---|---|---|---|
| 1999 Proof | Est. 5,000 | Value: 165 | | | | |

**1/5 CROWN** **KM# 847** **Weight:** 6.2200 g. **Composition:** 0.9999 Gold .2000 oz. AGW **Subject:** The World At War **Obverse:** Queen's portrait **Reverse:** Robert Oppenheimer, B-29 and mushroom cloud **Note:** Similar to 1 Crown, KM#847.

| Date | Mintage | F | VF | XF | Unc | BU |
|---|---|---|---|---|---|---|
| 1999 Proof | Est. 5,000 | Value: 165 | | | | |

**1/5 CROWN** **KM# 848** **Weight:** 6.2200 g. **Composition:** 0.9999 Gold .2000 oz. AGW **Subject:** The World At War **Obverse:** Queen's portrait **Reverse:** Barnes Wallis portrait, bomber above dam **Note:** Similar to 1 Crown, KM#849.

| Date | Mintage | F | VF | XF | Unc | BU |
|---|---|---|---|---|---|---|
| 1999 Proof | Est. 5,000 | Value: 165 | | | | |

**1/5 CROWN** **KM# 850** **Weight:** 6.2200 g. **Composition:** 0.9999 Gold .2000 oz. AGW **Subject:** The World At War **Obverse:** Queen's portrait **Reverse:** Douglas Bader portrait, planes in combat **Note:** Similar to 1 Crown, KM#851.

| Date | Mintage | F | VF | XF | Unc | BU |
|---|---|---|---|---|---|---|
| 1999 Proof | Est. 5,000 | Value: 165 | | | | |

**1/5 CROWN** **KM# 852** **Weight:** 6.2200 g. **Composition:** 0.9999 Gold .2000 oz. AGW **Subject:** The World At War **Obverse:** Queen's portrait **Reverse:** Winston Churchill, crowd **Note:** Similar to 1 Crown, KM#853.

| Date | Mintage | F | VF | XF | Unc | BU |
|---|---|---|---|---|---|---|
| 1999 Proof | Est. 5,000 | Value: 165 | | | | |

**1/5 CROWN** **KM# 854** **Weight:** 6.2200 g. **Composition:** 0.9999 Gold .2000 oz. AGW **Subject:** The World At War **Obverse:** Queen's portrait **Reverse:** Tirpitz, battleship and sailor **Note:** Similar to 1 Crown, KM#855.

| Date | Mintage | F | VF | XF | Unc | BU |
|---|---|---|---|---|---|---|
| 1999 Proof | Est. 5,000 | Value: 165 | | | | |

**1/5 CROWN** **KM# 856** **Weight:** 6.2200 g. **Composition:** 0.9999 Gold .2000 oz. AGW **Subject:** The World At War **Obverse:** Queen's portrait **Reverse:** Soldier kissing child goodbye **Note:** Similar to 1 Crown, KM#857.

| Date | Mintage | F | VF | XF | Unc | BU |
|---|---|---|---|---|---|---|
| 1999 Proof | Est. 5,000 | Value: 165 | | | | |

**1/5 CROWN** **KM# 858** **Weight:** 6.2200 g. **Composition:** 0.9999 Gold .2000 oz. AGW **Subject:** The World At War **Obverse:** Queen's portrait **Reverse:** 2 firemen in action after air raid **Note:** Similar to 1 Crown, KM#859.

| Date | Mintage | F | VF | XF | Unc | BU |
|---|---|---|---|---|---|---|
| 1999 Proof | Est. 5,000 | Value: 165 | | | | |

**1/5 CROWN** **KM# 860** **Weight:** 6.2200 g. **Composition:** 0.9999 Gold .2000 oz. AGW **Subject:** The World At War **Obverse:** Queen's portrait **Reverse:** D-Day landing scene **Note:** Similar to 1 Crown, KM#861.

| Date | Mintage | F | VF | XF | Unc | BU |
|---|---|---|---|---|---|---|
| 1999 Proof | Est. 5,000 | Value: 165 | | | | |

**1/5 CROWN** **KM# 862** **Weight:** 6.2200 g. **Composition:** 0.9999 Gold .2000 oz. AGW **Subject:** The World At War **Obverse:** Queen's portrait **Reverse:** Operation Heavywater military skier **Note:** Similar to 1 Crown, KM#863.

| Date | Mintage | F | VF | XF | Unc | BU |
|---|---|---|---|---|---|---|
| 1999 Proof | Est. 5,000 | Value: 165 | | | | |

**1/5 CROWN** **KM# 864** **Weight:** 6.2200 g. **Composition:** 0.9999 Gold .2000 oz. AGW **Subject:** The World At War **Obverse:** Queen's portrait **Reverse:** German tanks in Russia **Note:** Similar to 1 Crown, KM#865.

| Date | Mintage | F | VF | XF | Unc | BU |
|---|---|---|---|---|---|---|
| 1999 Proof | Est. 5,000 | Value: 165 | | | | |

**1/5 CROWN** **KM# 781.1** **Weight:** 6.2200 g. **Composition:** 0.9999 Gold .2000 oz. AGW **Subject:** 1999 Year of the Rabbit **Obverse:** Queen's portrait **Reverse:** Rabbit reading, sparrow, Chinese characters

| Date | Mintage | F | VF | XF | Unc | BU |
|---|---|---|---|---|---|---|
| 1999 Proof | Est. 3,500 | Value: 165 | | | | |

**1/5 CROWN** **KM# 781.2** **Weight:** 6.2200 g. **Composition:** 0.9999 Gold .2000 oz. AGW **Reverse:** Rabbit reading, sparrow. Without Chinese characters

| Date | Mintage | F | VF | XF | Unc | BU |
|---|---|---|---|---|---|---|
| 1999 Proof | Inc. above | Value: 165 | | | | |

**1/5 CROWN** **KM# 781.1a** **Weight:** 6.2200 g. **Composition:** 0.9950 Platinum .2000 oz. APW

| Date | Mintage | F | VF | XF | Unc | BU |
|---|---|---|---|---|---|---|
| 1999 Proof | Est. 1,500 | Value: 200 | | | | |

**1/5 CROWN** **KM# 781.2a** **Weight:** 6.2200 g. **Composition:** 0.9950 Platinum .2000 oz. APW

| Date | Mintage | F | VF | XF | Unc | BU |
|---|---|---|---|---|---|---|
| 1999 Proof | Inc. above | Value: 200 | | | | |

**1/5 CROWN** **KM# 784** **Weight:** 6.2200 g. **Composition:** 0.9999 Gold .2000 oz. AGW **Series:** Summer Olympics **Subject:** Sydney **Obverse:** Queen's portrait **Reverse:** Broad Jumper with kangaroo

| Date | Mintage | F | VF | XF | Unc | BU |
|---|---|---|---|---|---|---|
| 1999 Proof | Est. 5,000 | Value: 165 | | | | |

**1/5 CROWN** **KM# 791** **Weight:** 6.2200 g. **Composition:** 0.9999 Gold .2000 oz. AGW **Series:** Summer Olympics **Subject:** Sydney **Obverse:** Queen's portrait **Reverse:** Two oarsmen and cockatoos

| Date | Mintage | F | VF | XF | Unc | BU |
|---|---|---|---|---|---|---|
| 1999 Proof | Est. 5,000 | Value: 165 | | | | |

**1/5 CROWN** **KM# 794** **Weight:** 6.2200 g. **Composition:** 0.9999 Gold .2000 oz. AGW **Series:** Summer Olympics **Subject:** Sydney **Obverse:** Queen's portrait **Reverse:** Torch runner, portrait of Aboriginal and Ayers Rock

| Date | Mintage | F | VF | XF | Unc | BU |
|---|---|---|---|---|---|---|
| 1999 Proof | Est. 5,000 | Value: 165 | | | | |

**1/5 CROWN** **KM# 870** **Weight:** 6.2200 g. **Composition:** 0.9999 Gold .2000 oz. AGW **Series:** Queen Mother Series **Obverse:** Bust Queen right **Reverse:** 1937 Coronation scene

| Date | Mintage | F | VF | XF | Unc | BU |
|---|---|---|---|---|---|---|
| 2000 Proof | 5,000 | Value: 175 | | | | |

**1/5 CROWN** **KM# 872** **Weight:** 6.2200 g. **Composition:** 0.9999 Gold .2000 oz. AGW **Series:** Queen Mother Series **Obverse:** Bust Queen right **Reverse:** 1938 Visit to France

| Date | Mintage | F | VF | XF | Unc | BU |
|---|---|---|---|---|---|---|
| 2000 Proof | 5,000 | Value: 175 | | | | |

**1/5 CROWN** **KM# 874** **Weight:** 6.2200 g. **Composition:** 0.9999 Gold .2000 oz. AGW **Series:** Queen Mother Series **Obverse:** Bust Queen right **Reverse:** 1940 Bomb damage

| Date | Mintage | F | VF | XF | Unc | BU |
|---|---|---|---|---|---|---|
| 2000 Proof | 5,000 | Value: 175 | | | | |

**1/5 CROWN** **KM# 876** **Weight:** 6.2200 g. **Composition:** 0.9999 Gold .2000 oz. AGW **Series:** Queen Mother Series **Obverse:** Bust Queen right

| Date | Mintage | F | VF | XF | Unc | BU |
|---|---|---|---|---|---|---|
| 2000 Proof | 5,000 | Value: 175 | | | | |

**1/5 CROWN** **KM# 879** **Weight:** 6.2200 g. **Composition:** 0.9999 Gold .2000 oz. AGW **Series:** 18th Birthday **Subject:** Prince William **Obverse:** Bust Queen right **Reverse:** Bust Prince William facing **Edge:** Reeded

| Date | Mintage | F | VF | XF | Unc | BU |
|---|---|---|---|---|---|---|
| 2000 Proof | 5,000 | Value: 175 | | | | |

**1/5 CROWN** **KM# 881** **Weight:** 6.2200 g. **Composition:** 0.9999 Gold .2000 oz. AGW **Series:** 100 Birthday **Subject:** Queen Elizabeth, The Queen Mother **Obverse:** Bust Queen right **Reverse:** Queen Mother's portrait facing **Note:** Queen Mother's portrait has a real diamond chip (.015) set in her crown.

| Date | Mintage | F | VF | XF | Unc | BU |
|---|---|---|---|---|---|---|
| 2000 Proof | 2,000 | Value: 175 | | | | |

**1/5 CROWN** **KM# 902** **Weight:** 6.2200 g. **Composition:** 0.9999 Gold .2000 oz. AGW **Subject:** Queen Mother **Obverse:** Queen's portrait **Reverse:** 1953 Coronation scene **Edge:** Reeded **Size:** 22 mm.

| Date | Mintage | F | VF | XF | Unc | BU |
|---|---|---|---|---|---|---|
| 2001 Proof | 5,000 | Value: 175 | | | | |

**1/5 CROWN** **KM# 903** **Weight:** 6.2200 g. **Composition:** 0.9999 Gold .2000 oz. AGW **Obverse:** Queen's portrait **Reverse:** Queen Mother and Prince Charles in 1954

| Date | Mintage | F | VF | XF | Unc | BU |
|---|---|---|---|---|---|---|
| 2001 Proof | 5,000 | Value: 175 | | | | |

**1/5 CROWN** **KM# 909** **Weight:** 6.2200 g. **Composition:** 0.9999 Gold .2000 oz. AGW **Series:** Victorian Era **Subject:** Victoria's Coronation 1838 **Obverse:** Queen's portrait **Reverse:** 1838 Coronation scene **Edge:** Reeded **Size:** 22 mm.

| Date | Mintage | F | VF | XF | Unc | BU |
|---|---|---|---|---|---|---|
| 2001 Proof | 5,000 | Value: 175 | | | | |

**1/5 CROWN** **KM# 909.1** **Weight:** 6.2200 g. **Composition:** 0.9999 Gold Clad Silver .2000 oz. **Series:** Victorian Era **Reverse:** 1838 Coronation scene with a tiny emerald set in the field below the 1838 date **Edge:** Reeded **Size:** 22 mm.

| Date | Mintage | F | VF | XF | Unc | BU |
|---|---|---|---|---|---|---|
| 2001 Proof | 2,001 | Value: 200 | | | | |

**1/5 CROWN** **KM# 911** **Weight:** 6.2200 g. **Composition:** 0.9999 Gold .2000 oz. AGW **Series:** Victorian Era **Subject:** Empress of India 1876 **Obverse:** Queen's portrait **Reverse:** Crowned portrait of Victoria and two elephants **Edge:** Reeded **Size:** 22 mm.

| Date | Mintage | F | VF | XF | Unc | BU |
|---|---|---|---|---|---|---|
| 2001 Proof | 5,000 | Value: 175 | | | | |

**1/5 CROWN** **KM# 911.1** **Weight:** 6.2200 g. **Composition:** 0.9999 Gold .2000 oz. AGW **Series:** Victorian Era **Reverse:** Same but with a tiny ruby set in the field behind Victoria's head **Edge:** Reeded **Size:** 22 mm.

| Date | Mintage | F | VF | XF | Unc | BU |
|---|---|---|---|---|---|---|
| 2001 Proof | 2,001 | Value: 200 | | | | |

**1/5 CROWN** **KM# 913** **Weight:** 6.2200 g. **Composition:** 0.9999 Gold .2000 oz. AGW **Series:** Victorian Era **Subject:** Diamond Jubilee 1897 **Obverse:** Queen's portrait **Reverse:** Victoria's cameo portrait above naval ships **Edge:** Reeded **Size:** 22 mm.

| Date | Mintage | F | VF | XF | Unc | BU |
|---|---|---|---|---|---|---|
| 2001 Proof | 5,000 | Value: 175 | | | | |

**1/5 CROWN** **KM# 913.1** **Weight:** 6.2200 g. **Composition:** 0.9999 Gold .2000 oz. AGW **Series:** Victorian Era **Reverse:** Same but with a tiny diamond set at the top of the fourth mast **Edge:** Reeded **Size:** 22 mm.

| Date | Mintage | F | VF | XF | Unc | BU |
|---|---|---|---|---|---|---|
| 2001 Proof | 2,001 | Value: 200 | | | | |

**1/5 CROWN** **KM# 915** **Weight:** 6.2200 g. **Composition:** 0.9999 Gold .2000 oz. AGW **Series:** Victorian Era **Subject:** Victoria's Death 1901 **Obverse:** Queen's portrait **Reverse:** Victoria's cameo portrait and Osborne Manor **Edge:** Reeded **Size:** 22 mm.

| Date | Mintage | F | VF | XF | Unc | BU |
|---|---|---|---|---|---|---|
| 2001 Proof | 5,000 | Value: 175 | | | | |

**1/5 CROWN** **KM# 915.1** **Weight:** 6.2200 g. **Composition:** 0.9999 Gold .2000 oz. AGW **Series:** Victorian Era **Reverse:** Same but with a tiny sapphire set in the field between the towers **Edge:** Reeded **Size:** 22 mm.

| Date | Mintage | F | VF | XF | Unc | BU |
|---|---|---|---|---|---|---|
| 2001 Proof | 2,001 | Value: 200 | | | | |

**1/5 CROWN** **KM# 921** **Weight:** 6.2200 g. **Composition:** 0.9999 Gold .2000 oz. AGW **Series:** Victorian Era **Subject:** Charles Dickens **Obverse:** Queen's portrait **Reverse:** Portrait and scene from "Oliver Twist" **Edge:** Reeded **Size:** 22 mm.

| Date | Mintage | F | VF | XF | Unc | BU |
|---|---|---|---|---|---|---|
| 2001 Proof | 5,000 | Value: 175 | | | | |

**1/5 CROWN** **KM# 917** **Weight:** 6.2200 g. **Composition:** 0.9999 Gold .2000 oz. AGW **Series:** Victorian Era **Subject:** Prince Albert and the Great Exhibition 1851 **Obverse:** Queen's portrait **Reverse:** Albert's cameo portrait and the exhibit hall **Edge:** Reeded **Size:** 22 mm.

| Date | Mintage | F | VF | XF | Unc | BU |
|---|---|---|---|---|---|---|
| 2001 Proof | 5,000 | Value: 175 | | | | |

**1/5 CROWN** **KM# 919** **Weight:** 6.2200 g. **Composition:** 0.9999 Gold .2000 oz. AGW **Series:** Victorian Era **Subject:** Isambard K. Brunel **Obverse:** Queen's portrait **Reverse:** Portrait in top hat and railroad bridge **Edge:** Reeded **Size:** 22 mm.

| Date | Mintage | F | VF | XF | Unc | BU |
|---|---|---|---|---|---|---|
| 2001 Proof | 5,000 | Value: 175 | | | | |

**1/5 CROWN** **KM# 923** **Weight:** 6.2200 g. **Composition:** 0.9999 Gold .2000 oz. AGW **Series:** Victorian Era **Subject:** Charles Darwin **Obverse:** Queen's portrait **Reverse:** Portrait, ship and a squatting aboriginal figure **Edge:** Reeded **Size:** 22 mm.

| Date | Mintage | F | VF | XF | Unc | BU |
|---|---|---|---|---|---|---|
| 2001 Proof | 5,000 | Value: 175 | | | | |

**1/5 CROWN** **KM# 925** **Weight:** 6.2200 g. **Composition:** 0.9999 Gold .2000 oz. AGW **Series:** Mythology of the Solar System **Obverse:** Queen's portrait **Reverse:** Standing goddess with snake basket **Edge:** Reeded **Size:** 22 mm.

| Date | Mintage | F | VF | XF | Unc | BU |
|---|---|---|---|---|---|---|
| 2001 Proof | 5,000 | Value: 175 | | | | |

**1/5 CROWN** **KM# 926** **Ring Weight:** 12.1100 g. **Ring Composition:** 0.9999 Gold .3893 oz. AGW **Center Weight:** 5.7900 g. **Center Composition:** 0.9250 Silver .1722 oz. ASW **Series:** Mythology of the Solar System **Subject:** Solar System **Obverse:** Queen's portrait **Reverse:** Standing goddess with snake basket **Edge:** Reeded **Size:** 32.25 mm.

| Date | Mintage | F | VF | XF | Unc | BU |
|---|---|---|---|---|---|---|
| 2001 In Proof sets only | 999 | Value: 350 | | | | |

**1/5 CROWN** **KM# 929** **Weight:** 6.2200 g. **Composition:** 0.9999 Gold .2000 oz. AGW **Series:** Mythology of the Solar System **Subject:** Sun **Obverse:** Queen's portrait **Reverse:** Helios in chariot and the sun **Edge:** Reeded **Size:** 22 mm.

| Date | Mintage | F | VF | XF | Unc | BU |
|---|---|---|---|---|---|---|
| 2001 Proof | 5,000 | Value: 175 | | | | |

**1/5 CROWN** **KM# 929.1** **Weight:** 6.2200 g. **Composition:** 0.9999 Gold .2000 oz. AGW **Series:** Mythology of the Solar System **Reverse:** Similar but with a fiery hologram in the sun **Edge:** Reeded **Size:** 22 mm.

| Date | Mintage | F | VF | XF | Unc | BU |
|---|---|---|---|---|---|---|
| 2001 In Proof sets only | 999 | Value: 350 | | | | |

**1/5 CROWN** **KM# 931** **Weight:** 6.2200 g. **Composition:** 0.9999 Gold .2000 oz. AGW **Series:** Mythology of the Solar System **Subject:** Moon **Obverse:** Queen's portrait **Reverse:** Goddess Diana and the moon **Edge:** Reeded **Size:** 22 mm.

| Date | Mintage | F | VF | XF | Unc | BU |
|---|---|---|---|---|---|---|
| 2001 Proof | 5,000 | Value: 175 | | | | |

**1/5 CROWN** **KM# 931.1** **Weight:** 6.2200 g. **Composition:** 0.9999 Gold .2000 oz. AGW **Series:** Mythology of the Solar System **Reverse:** Similar but with a small pearl set in the moon **Edge:** Reeded **Size:** 22 mm.

| Date | Mintage | F | VF | XF | Unc | BU |
|---|---|---|---|---|---|---|
| 2001 In Proof sets only | 999 | Value: 350 | | | | |

**1/5 CROWN** **KM# 933** **Weight:** 6.2200 g. **Composition:** 0.9999 Gold .2000 oz. AGW **Series:** Mythology of the Solar System **Subject:** Earth **Obverse:** Queen's portrait **Reverse:** Atlas carrying the earth **Edge:** Reeded **Size:** 22 mm.

| Date | Mintage | F | VF | XF | Unc | BU |
|---|---|---|---|---|---|---|
| 2001 Proof | 5,000 | Value: 175 | | | | |

**1/5 CROWN** **KM# 933.1** **Weight:** 6.2200 g. **Composition:** 0.9999 Gold .2000 oz. AGW **Series:** Mythology of the Solar System **Reverse:** Similar but with a tiny diamond set in the earth **Edge:** Reeded **Size:** 22 mm.

| Date | Mintage | F | VF | XF | Unc | BU |
|---|---|---|---|---|---|---|
| 2001 In Proof sets only | 999 | Value: 350 | | | | |

**1/5 CROWN** **KM# 935** **Weight:** 6.2200 g. **Composition:** 0.9999 Gold .2000 oz. AGW **Series:** Mythology of the Solar System **Subject:** Neptune **Obverse:** Queen's portrait **Reverse:** Seated god with trident and ringed planet **Edge:** Reeded **Size:** 22 mm.

| Date | Mintage | F | VF | XF | Unc | BU |
|---|---|---|---|---|---|---|
| 2001 Proof | 5,000 | Value: 175 | | | | |

**1/5 CROWN** **KM# 937** **Weight:** 6.2200 g. **Composition:** 0.9999 Gold .2000 oz. AGW **Series:** Mythology of the Solar System **Subject:** Jupiter **Obverse:** Queen's portrait **Reverse:** Seated god with lightening bolts and a planet **Edge:** Reeded **Size:** 22 mm.

| Date | Mintage | F | VF | XF | Unc | BU |
|---|---|---|---|---|---|---|
| 2001 Proof | 5,000 | Value: 175 | | | | |

**1/5 CROWN** **KM# 939** **Weight:** 6.2200 g. **Composition:** 0.9999 Gold .2000 oz. AGW **Series:** Mythology of the Solar System **Subject:** Mars **Obverse:** Queen's portrait **Reverse:** Standing Roman solider and a planet **Edge:** Reeded **Size:** 22 mm.

| Date | Mintage | F | VF | XF | Unc | BU |
|---|---|---|---|---|---|---|
| 2001 Proof | 5,000 | Value: 175 | | | | |

**1/5 CROWN** **KM# 941** **Weight:** 6.2200 g. **Composition:** 0.9999 Gold .2000 oz. AGW **Series:** Mythology of the Solar System **Subject:** Mercury **Obverse:** Queen's portrait **Reverse:** Seated god with cadceus and a planet **Edge:** Reeded **Size:** 22 mm.

| Date | Mintage | F | VF | XF | Unc | BU |
|---|---|---|---|---|---|---|
| 2001 Proof | 5,000 | Value: 175 | | | | |

**1/5 CROWN** **KM# 943** **Weight:** 6.2200 g. **Composition:** 0.9999 Gold .2000 oz. AGW **Series:** Mythology of the Solar System **Subject:** Uranus **Obverse:** Queen's portrait **Reverse:** Seated god with scepter **Edge:** Reeded **Size:** 22 mm.

| Date | Mintage | F | VF | XF | Unc | BU |
|---|---|---|---|---|---|---|
| 2001 Proof | 5,000 | Value: 175 | | | | |

**1/5 CROWN** **KM# 945** **Weight:** 6.2200 g. **Composition:** 0.9999 Gold .2000 oz. AGW **Series:** Mythology of the Solar System **Subject:** Saturn **Obverse:** Queen's portrait **Reverse:** Seated god with long handled sickle and a ringed planet **Edge:** Reeded **Size:** 22 mm.

| Date | Mintage | F | VF | XF | Unc | BU |
|---|---|---|---|---|---|---|
| 2001 Proof | 5,000 | Value: 175 | | | | |

**1/5 CROWN** **KM# 947** **Weight:** 6.2200 g. **Composition:** 0.9999 Gold .2000 oz. AGW **Series:** Mythology of the Solar System **Subject:** Pluto **Obverse:** Queen's portrait **Reverse:** Seated god with dogs and a planet **Edge:** Reeded **Size:** 22 mm.

| Date | Mintage | F | VF | XF | Unc | BU |
|---|---|---|---|---|---|---|
| 2001 Proof | 5,000 | Value: 175 | | | | |

**1/5 CROWN** **KM# 949** **Weight:** 6.2200 g. **Composition:** 0.9999 Gold .2000 oz. AGW **Series:** Mythology of the Solar System **Subject:** Venus **Obverse:** Queen's portrait **Reverse:** Goddess seated on a half shell **Edge:** Reeded **Size:** 22 mm.

| Date | Mintage | F | VF | XF | Unc | BU |
|---|---|---|---|---|---|---|
| 2001 Proof | 5,000 | Value: 175 | | | | |

**1/5 CROWN** **KM# 951** **Weight:** 6.2200 g. **Composition:** 0.9999 Gold .2000 oz. AGW **Subject:** Queen's 76th Birthday **Obverse:** Queen's portrait **Reverse:** Queen in Order of the Garter robes with a tiny in set diamond **Edge:** Reeded **Size:** 22 mm.

| Date | Mintage | F | VF | XF | Unc | BU |
|---|---|---|---|---|---|---|
| 2001 Proof | 2,001 | Value: 200 | | | | |

**1/5 CROWN** **KM# 954** **Weight:** 6.2200 g. **Composition:** 0.9999 Gold .2000 oz. AGW **Series:** Victorian Age Part II **Subject:** Victoria's Accession to the Throne **Obverse:** Queen's portrait **Reverse:** Victoria learning of her accession **Edge:** Reeded **Size:** 22 mm.

| Date | Mintage | F | VF | XF | Unc | BU |
|---|---|---|---|---|---|---|
| 2001 Proof | 5,000 | Value: 175 | | | | |

**1/5 CROWN** **KM# 956** **Weight:** 6.2200 g. **Composition:** 0.9999 Gold .2000 oz. AGW **Series:** Victorian Age Part II **Subject:** Royal Family **Reverse:** Victoria and Albert seated with children **Edge:** Reeded **Size:** 22 mm.

| Date | Mintage | F | VF | XF | Unc | BU |
|---|---|---|---|---|---|---|
| 2001 Proof | 5,000 | Value: 175 | | | | |

**1/5 CROWN** **KM# 958** **Weight:** 6.2200 g. **Composition:** 0.9999 Gold .2000 oz. AGW **Series:** Victorian Age Part II **Subject:** Victoria in Scotland **Reverse:** Victoria on horse and servant **Edge:** Reeded **Size:** 22 mm.

| Date | Mintage | F | VF | XF | Unc | BU |
|---|---|---|---|---|---|---|
| 2001 Proof | 5,000 | Value: 175 | | | | |

**1/5 CROWN** **KM# 960** **Weight:** 6.2200 g. **Composition:** 0.9999 Gold .2000 oz. AGW **Series:** Victorian Age Part II **Subject:** Gladstone and Disaraeli **Reverse:** Portraits of both politicians **Edge:** Reeded **Size:** 22 mm.

| Date | Mintage | F | VF | XF | Unc | BU |
|---|---|---|---|---|---|---|
| 2001 Proof | 5,000 | Value: 175 | | | | |

**1/5 CROWN** **KM# 962** **Weight:** 6.2200 g. **Composition:** 0.9999 Gold .2000 oz. AGW **Series:** Victorian Age Part II **Subject:** Florence Nightingale **Reverse:** Woman holding lantern **Edge:** Reeded **Size:** 22 mm.

| Date | Mintage | F | VF | XF | Unc | BU |
|---|---|---|---|---|---|---|
| 2001 Proof | 5,000 | Value: 175 | | | | |

**1/5 CROWN** **KM# 964** **Weight:** 6.2200 g. **Composition:** 0.9999 Gold .2000 oz. AGW **Series:** Victorian Age Part II **Subject:** Lord Tennyson **Reverse:** Portrait with the Light Brigade in background **Edge:** Reeded **Size:** 22 mm.

| Date | Mintage | F | VF | XF | Unc | BU |
|---|---|---|---|---|---|---|
| 2001 Proof | 5,000 | Value: 175 | | | | |

**1/5 CROWN** **KM# 966** **Weight:** 6.2200 g. **Composition:** 0.9999 Gold .2000 oz. AGW **Series:** Victorian Age Part II **Subject:** Stanley and Livingstone **Reverse:** Stanly meeting Dr. Livingstone **Edge:** Reeded **Size:** 22 mm.

| Date | Mintage | F | VF | XF | Unc | BU |
|---|---|---|---|---|---|---|
| 2001 Proof | 5,000 | Value: 175 | | | | |

**1/5 CROWN** **KM# 968** **Weight:** 6.2200 g. **Composition:** 0.9999 Gold .2000 oz. AGW **Series:** Victorian Age Part II **Subject:** Bronte Sisters **Reverse:** Portraits of three women **Edge:** Reeded **Size:** 22 mm.

| Date | Mintage | F | VF | XF | Unc | BU |
|---|---|---|---|---|---|---|
| 2001 Proof | 5,000 | Value: 175 | | | | |

**1/4 CROWN** **KM# 868.2** **Weight:** 7.7800 g. **Composition:** 0.9250 Silver .2314 oz. ASW **Reverse:** Rabbit reading, sparrow. Without Chinese characters

| Date | Mintage | F | VF | XF | Unc | BU |
|---|---|---|---|---|---|---|
| 1999 Proof | Inc. above | Value: 35.00 | | | | |

**1/4 CROWN** **KM# 868.1** **Weight:** 7.7800 g. **Composition:** 0.9250 Silver .2314 oz. ASW **Subject:** 1999 The Year of the Rabbit **Obverse:** Queen's portrait **Reverse:** Peter Rabbit reading, sparrow, Chinese characters **Note:** Similar to 1 Crown, KM#783.1.

| Date | Mintage | F | VF | XF | Unc | BU |
|---|---|---|---|---|---|---|
| 1999 Proof | Est. 25,000 | Value: 35.00 | | | | |

**1/2 CROWN** **KM# 886** **Weight:** 15.5500 g. **Composition:** 0.9999 Gold .5000 oz. AGW **Subject:** Rotary Club of Gibraltar

| Date | Mintage | F | VF | XF | Unc | BU |
|---|---|---|---|---|---|---|
| 1991 Proof | 5,000 | Value: 500 | | | | |

**1/2 CROWN** **KM# 127** **Weight:** 15.5500 g. **Composition:** 0.9999 Gold .5000 oz. AGW **Subject:** Japanese Royal Wedding

| Date | Mintage | F | VF | XF | Unc | BU |
|---|---|---|---|---|---|---|
| 1993 Proof | 5,000 | Value: 260 | | | | |

**1/2 CROWN** **KM# 177** **Weight:** 15.5500 g. **Composition:** 0.9990 Silver .5000 oz. ASW **Series:** WWII Warships **Subject:** HMS Hood

| Date | Mintage | F | VF | XF | Unc | BU |
|---|---|---|---|---|---|---|
| 1993 | Est. 30,000 | — | — | — | 35.00 | — |

**1/2 CROWN** **KM# 198** **Weight:** 15.5500 g. **Composition:** 0.9990 Silver .5000 oz. ASW **Subject:** Edward VIII

| Date | Mintage | F | VF | XF | Unc | BU |
|---|---|---|---|---|---|---|
| 1993 Proof | Est. 30,000 | Value: 30.00 | | | | |

**1/2 CROWN** **KM# 572** **Weight:** 15.5500 g. **Composition:** 0.9990 Silver .5000 oz. ASW **Subject:** Sherlock Holmes **Obverse:** Queen's portrait **Reverse:** Holmes smoking pipe

| Date | Mintage | F | VF | XF | Unc | BU |
|---|---|---|---|---|---|---|
| 1994 Proof | Est. 30,000 | Value: 20.00 | | | | |

**1/2 CROWN** **KM# 443** **Weight:** 15.5500 g. **Composition:** 0.9999 Gold .5000 oz. AGW **Series:** Peter Rabbit Centennial **Subject:** Mother and Bunnies **Note:** Similar to 1 Crown, KM#444.

| Date | Mintage | F | VF | XF | Unc | BU |
|---|---|---|---|---|---|---|
| 1994 Proof | Est. 5,000 | Value: 350 | | | | |

**1/2 CROWN** **KM# 448** **Weight:** 15.5500 g. **Composition:** 0.9999 Gold .5000 oz. AGW **Subject:** Lord Buddha **Note:** Similar to 1 Crown, KM#449.

| Date | Mintage | F | VF | XF | Unc | BU |
|---|---|---|---|---|---|---|
| 1996 Proof | Est. 5,000 | Value: 350 | | | | |

**1/2 CROWN** **KM# 372** **Weight:** 15.5500 g. **Composition:** 0.9999 Gold .5000 oz. AGW **Subject:** Roses **Note:** Similar to 1 Crown, KM#373.

| Date | Mintage | F | VF | XF | Unc | BU |
|---|---|---|---|---|---|---|
| 1996 Proof | Est. 3,000 | Value: 350 | | | | |

**1/2 CROWN** **KM# 381** **Weight:** 15.5500 g. **Composition:** 0.9999 Gold .5000 oz. AGW **Series:** Peter Rabbit Centennial **Subject:** Rabbit Escaping

| Date | Mintage | F | VF | XF | Unc | BU |
|---|---|---|---|---|---|---|
| 1996 Proof | Est. 5,000 | Value: 350 | | | | |

**1/2 CROWN** **KM# 524** **Weight:** 15.5500 g. **Composition:** 0.9999 Gold .5000 oz. AGW **Subject:** Tale of Peter Rabbit **Note:** Similar to 1 Crown, KM#525.

| Date | Mintage | F | VF | XF | Unc | BU |
|---|---|---|---|---|---|---|
| 1997 Proof | Est. 2,500 | Value: 350 | | | | |

**1/2 CROWN** **KM# 655** **Weight:** 15.5500 g. **Composition:** 0.9999 Gold .5000 oz. AGW **Subject:** Peter Rabbit **Obverse:** Queen's portrait **Reverse:** Peter Rabbit **Note:** Similar to 1 Crown, KM#656.

| Date | Mintage | F | VF | XF | Unc | BU |
|---|---|---|---|---|---|---|
| 1998 Proof | Est. 2,500 | Value: 325 | | | | |

**1/2 CROWN** **KM# 681** **Weight:** 15.5500 g. **Composition:** 0.9999 Gold .5000 oz. AGW **Subject:** Paddington Bear **Obverse:** Queen's portrait **Reverse:** Bear with suitcase **Note:** Similar to 1 Crown, KM#682.

| Date | Mintage | F | VF | XF | Unc | BU |
|---|---|---|---|---|---|---|
| 1998 Proof | Est. 2,500 | Value: 325 | | | | |

**1/2 CROWN** **KM# 895** **Weight:** 15.7800 g. **Composition:** 0.9990 Silver .5068 oz. ASW **Subject:** Cupid **Obverse:** Queen's portrait **Reverse:** Cupid with multicolor holographic heat similar to 1/2 crown KM#-647 but without the metal content statement **Edge:** Reeded **Size:** 32.25 mm.

| Date | Mintage | F | VF | XF | Unc | BU |
|---|---|---|---|---|---|---|
| 1998 Proof | 10,000 | Value: 50.00 | | | | |

**1/2 CROWN** **KM# 647** **Weight:** 15.5500 g. **Composition:** 0.9999 Gold .5000 oz. AGW **Subject:** Cupid **Obverse:** Queen's portrait **Reverse:** Cupid with hologram heart

| Date | Mintage | F | VF | XF | Unc | BU |
|---|---|---|---|---|---|---|
| 1998 Proof | Est. 10,000 | Value: 325 | | | | |

**1/2 CROWN** **KM# 732** **Weight:** 15.5500 g. **Composition:** 0.9999 Gold .5000 oz. AGW **Subject:** Peacocks **Obverse:** Queen's portrait **Reverse:** Pair of peacocks, one with full display in hologram

| Date | Mintage | F | VF | XF | Unc | BU |
|---|---|---|---|---|---|---|
| 1998 Proof | Est. 3,500 | Value: 325 | | | | |

**1/2 CROWN** **KM# 782.2** **Weight:** 15.5500 g. **Composition:** 0.9999 Gold .5000 oz. AGW **Reverse:** Rabbit reading, sparrow. Without Chinese characters

| Date | Mintage | F | VF | XF | Unc | BU |
|---|---|---|---|---|---|---|
| 1999 | Inc. above | — | — | — | 325 | — |

**1/2 CROWN** **KM# 782.1** **Weight:** 15.5500 g. **Composition:** 0.9999 Gold .5000 oz. AGW **Subject:** 1999 The Year of the Rabbit **Obverse:** Queen's portrait **Reverse:** Rabbit reading, sparrow, Chinese characters **Note:** Similar to 1 Crown, KM#783.1.

| Date | Mintage | F | VF | XF | Unc | BU |
|---|---|---|---|---|---|---|
| 1999 Proof | Est. 1,000 | Value: 325 | | | | |

**1/2 CROWN** **KM# 894** **Weight:** 15.5517 g. **Composition:** 0.9990 Gold .5000 oz. AGW **Edge:** Reeded **Note:** Similar to 1/2 Crown, KM#883.

| Date | Mintage | F | VF | XF | Unc | BU |
|---|---|---|---|---|---|---|
| 2000 Proof | 999 | Value: 325 | | | | |

**1/2 CROWN** **KM# 883** **Ring Weight:** 9.0000 g. **Ring Composition:** 0.9990 Gold .2893 oz. AGW **Center Composition:** Titanium **Series:** 160th Anniversary **Subject:** Uniform Penny Post **Obverse:** Bust Queen right **Reverse:** Postage stamp design **Edge:** Reeded

| Date | Mintage | F | VF | XF | Unc | BU |
|---|---|---|---|---|---|---|
| 2000 Proof | 5,000 | Value: 175 | | | | |

**CROWN** **KM# 11** **Composition:** Copper-Nickel **Reverse:** 80th Birthday of Queen Mother

| Date | Mintage | F | VF | XF | Unc | BU |
|---|---|---|---|---|---|---|
| 1980 | — | — | — | 1.50 | 3.00 | — |

**CROWN** **KM# 11a** **Weight:** 28.2800 g. **Composition:** 0.9250 Silver .8411 oz. ASW

| Date | Mintage | F | VF | XF | Unc | BU |
|---|---|---|---|---|---|---|
| 1980 Proof | Est. 25,000 | Value: 15.00 | | | | |

**CROWN** **KM# 12** **Composition:** Copper-Nickel **Reverse:** 175th Anniversary - Death of Nelson

| Date | Mintage | F | VF | XF | Unc | BU |
|---|---|---|---|---|---|---|
| 1980 | Est. 100,000 | — | — | 1.00 | 2.00 | — |

**CROWN** **KM# 12a** **Weight:** 28.2800 g. **Composition:** 0.9250 Silver .8411 oz. ASW

| Date | Mintage | F | VF | XF | Unc | BU |
|---|---|---|---|---|---|---|
| 1980 Proof | Est. 15,000 | Value: 20.00 | | | | |

**CROWN** **KM# 14** **Composition:** Copper-Nickel **Reverse:** Wedding fo Prince Charles and Lady Diana

| Date | Mintage | F | VF | XF | Unc | BU |
|---|---|---|---|---|---|---|
| 1981 | — | — | — | 1.00 | 2.50 | — |

**CROWN** **KM# 14a** **Weight:** 28.2800 g. **Composition:** 0.9250 Silver .8411 oz. ASW

| Date | Mintage | F | VF | XF | Unc | BU |
|---|---|---|---|---|---|---|
| 1981 Proof | Est. 30,000 | Value: 13.50 | | | | |

**CROWN** **KM# 33** **Composition:** Copper-Nickel **Reverse:** World Cup Soccer - Italian Flag

| Date | Mintage | F | VF | XF | Unc | BU |
|---|---|---|---|---|---|---|
| 1990 | — | — | — | — | 3.50 | — |

**CROWN** **KM# 33a** **Weight:** 28.2800 g. **Composition:** 0.9250 Silver .8411 oz. ASW

| Date | Mintage | F | VF | XF | Unc | BU |
|---|---|---|---|---|---|---|
| 1990 Proof | Est. 30,000 | Value: 32.50 | | | | |

**CROWN** **KM# 34** **Composition:** Copper-Nickel **Obverse:** Similar to KM#33 **Reverse:** World Cup Soccer - Map of Italy

| Date | Mintage | F | VF | XF | Unc | BU |
|---|---|---|---|---|---|---|
| 1990 | — | — | — | — | 3.50 | — |

**CROWN** **KM# 34a** **Weight:** 28.2800 g. **Composition:** 0.9250 Silver .8411 oz. ASW

| Date | Mintage | F | VF | XF | Unc | BU |
|---|---|---|---|---|---|---|
| 1990 Proof | Est. 30,000 | Value: 32.50 | | | | |

**CROWN** **KM# 35** **Composition:** Copper-Nickel **Obverse:** Similar to KM#33. **Reverse:** World Cup Soccer - Goalie Catching Ball

| Date | Mintage | F | VF | XF | Unc | BU |
|---|---|---|---|---|---|---|
| 1990 | — | — | — | — | 3.50 | — |

**CROWN** **KM# 35a** **Weight:** 28.2800 g. **Composition:** 0.9250 Silver .8411 oz. ASW

| Date | Mintage | F | VF | XF | Unc | BU |
|---|---|---|---|---|---|---|
| 1990 Proof | Est. 30,000 | Value: 32.50 | | | | |

**CROWN** **KM# 36** **Composition:** Copper-Nickel **Obverse:** Similar to KM#33. **Reverse:** World Cup Soccer - Ball at Head

| Date | Mintage | F | VF | XF | Unc | BU |
|---|---|---|---|---|---|---|
| 1990 | — | — | — | — | 3.50 | — |

**CROWN** **KM# 36a** **Weight:** 28.2800 g. **Composition:** 0.9250 Silver .8411 oz. ASW

| Date | Mintage | F | VF | XF | Unc | BU |
|---|---|---|---|---|---|---|
| 1990 Proof | Est. 30,000 | Value: 32.50 | | | | |

**CROWN** **KM# 37** **Composition:** Copper-Nickel **Obverse:** Similar to KM#33. **Reverse:** World Cup Soccer - Ball at Feet

| Date | Mintage | F | VF | XF | Unc | BU |
|---|---|---|---|---|---|---|
| 1990 | — | — | — | — | 3.50 | — |

**CROWN** **KM# 37a** **Weight:** 28.2800 g. **Composition:** 0.9250 Silver .8411 oz. ASW

| Date | Mintage | F | VF | XF | Unc | BU |
|---|---|---|---|---|---|---|
| 1990 Proof | Est. 30,000 | Value: 32.50 | | | | |

**CROWN** **KM# 38** **Composition:** Copper-Nickel **Obverse:** Similar to KM#33. **Reverse:** World Cup Soccer - 3 Players

| Date | Mintage | F | VF | XF | Unc | BU |
|---|---|---|---|---|---|---|
| 1990 | — | — | — | — | 3.50 | — |

**CROWN** **KM# 38a** **Weight:** 28.2800 g. **Composition:** 0.9250 Silver .8411 oz. ASW

| Date | Mintage | F | VF | XF | Unc | BU |
|---|---|---|---|---|---|---|
| 1990 Proof | Est. 30,000 | Value: 32.50 | | | | |

**CROWN** **KM# 40** **Composition:** Copper-Nickel **Obverse:** Similar to KM#33. **Reverse:** 21st Anniversary - Constitution

| Date | Mintage | F | VF | XF | Unc | BU |
|---|---|---|---|---|---|---|
| 1990 | — | — | — | — | 6.50 | — |

**CROWN** **KM# 40a** **Weight:** 28.2800 g. **Composition:** 0.9250 Silver .8411 oz. ASW

| Date | Mintage | F | VF | XF | Unc | BU |
|---|---|---|---|---|---|---|
| 1990 Proof | Est. 30,000 | Value: 50.00 | | | | |

**CROWN** **KM# 46** **Composition:** Copper-Nickel **Obverse:** Similar to KM#33. **Reverse:** Queen Mother

| Date | Mintage | F | VF | XF | Unc | BU |
|---|---|---|---|---|---|---|
| 1990 | — | — | — | — | 4.50 | — |

**CROWN** **KM# 46a** **Weight:** 28.2800 g. **Composition:** 0.9250 Silver .8411 oz. ASW **Reverse:** Queen Mother

| Date | Mintage | F | VF | XF | Unc | BU |
|---|---|---|---|---|---|---|
| 1990 Proof | Est. 30,000 | Value: 16.50 | | | | |

**CROWN** **KM# 46b** **Weight:** 6.2200 g. **Composition:** 0.9999 Gold .2000 oz. AGW **Subject:** Queen Mother

| Date | Mintage | F | VF | XF | Unc | BU |
|---|---|---|---|---|---|---|
| 1990 Proof | Est. 5,000 | Value: 175 | | | | |

**CROWN** **KM# 46c** **Weight:** 6.2200 g. **Composition:** 0.9950 Platinum .2000 oz. APW **Reverse:** Queen Mother

| Date | Mintage | F | VF | XF | Unc | BU |
|---|---|---|---|---|---|---|
| 1990 Proof | Est. 1,000 | Value: 200 | | | | |

**CROWN** **KM# 49** **Composition:** Copper-Nickel **Reverse:** Penny Black Stamp

| Date | Mintage | F | VF | XF | Unc | BU |
|---|---|---|---|---|---|---|
| 1990 | — | — | — | — | 7.50 | — |
| 1990 Proof | Est. 50,000 | Value: 18.00 | | | | |

**CROWN** **KM# 49a** **Weight:** 28.2800 g. **Composition:** 0.9250 Silver .8411 oz. ASW

| Date | Mintage | F | VF | XF | Unc | BU |
|---|---|---|---|---|---|---|
| 1990 Proof | Est. 30,000 | Value: 45.00 | | | | |

**CROWN** **KM# 49b** **Weight:** 31.1000 g. **Composition:** 0.9999 Gold .9999 oz. AGW **Reverse:** Penny Black Stamp

| Date | Mintage | F | VF | XF | Unc | BU |
|---|---|---|---|---|---|---|
| 1990 Proof | Est. 1,000 | Value: 1,100 | | | | |

**CROWN** **KM# 49c** **Weight:** 15.5500 g. **Composition:** 0.9999 Gold .4999 oz. AGW

| Date | Mintage | F | VF | XF | Unc | BU |
|---|---|---|---|---|---|---|
| 1990 Proof | Est. 2,500 | Value: 500 | | | | |

**CROWN** **KM# 66** **Composition:** Copper-Nickel **Reverse:** Barcelona Olympics - Discus Thrower

| Date | Mintage | F | VF | XF | Unc | BU |
|---|---|---|---|---|---|---|
| 1991 | — | — | — | — | 4.50 | — |
| 1991 Proof | Est. 8,000 | Value: 25.00 | | | | |
| 1992 | — | — | — | — | 5.00 | — |

**CROWN** **KM# 66a** **Weight:** 28.2800 g. **Composition:** 0.9250 Silver .8411 oz. ASW

| Date | Mintage | F | VF | XF | Unc | BU |
|---|---|---|---|---|---|---|
| 1991 Proof | Est. 30,000 | Value: 30.00 | | | | |
| 1992 Proof | — | Value: 100 | | | | |

**CROWN KM# 67 Composition:** Copper-Nickel **Obverse:** Similar to KM#66 **Reverse:** Barcelona Olympics - Chariot Racing

| Date | Mintage | F | VF | XF | Unc | BU |
|---|---|---|---|---|---|---|
| 1991 | — | — | — | — | 4.50 | — |
| 1991 Proof | Est. 8,000 | Value: 25.00 | | | | |
| 1992 | — | — | — | — | 5.00 | — |

**CROWN KM# 67a Weight:** 28.2800 g. **Composition:** 0.9250 Silver .8411 oz. ASW

| Date | Mintage | F | VF | XF | Unc | BU |
|---|---|---|---|---|---|---|
| 1991 Proof | Est. 30,000 | Value: 30.00 | | | | |

**CROWN KM# 68 Composition:** Copper-Nickel **Obverse:** Similar to KM#66 **Reverse:** Barcelona Olympics - Runners

| Date | Mintage | F | VF | XF | Unc | BU |
|---|---|---|---|---|---|---|
| 1991 | — | — | — | — | 4.50 | — |
| 1991 Proof | Est. 8,000 | Value: 25.00 | | | | |
| 1992 | — | — | — | — | 5.00 | — |

**CROWN KM# 68a Weight:** 28.2800 g. **Composition:** 0.9250 Silver .8411 oz. ASW

| Date | Mintage | F | VF | XF | Unc | BU |
|---|---|---|---|---|---|---|
| 1991 Proof | Est. 30,000 | Value: 30.00 | | | | |

**CROWN KM# 69 Composition:** Copper-Nickel **Obverse:** Similar to KM#66. **Reverse:** Barcelona Olympics - Javelin Thrower

| Date | Mintage | F | VF | XF | Unc | BU |
|---|---|---|---|---|---|---|
| 1991 | — | — | — | — | 4.50 | — |
| 1991 Proof | Est. 8,000 | Value: 25.00 | | | | |
| 1992 | — | — | — | — | 5.00 | — |

**CROWN KM# 69a Weight:** 28.2800 g. **Composition:** 0.9250 Silver .8411 oz. ASW

| Date | Mintage | F | VF | XF | Unc | BU |
|---|---|---|---|---|---|---|
| 1991 Proof | Est. 30,000 | Value: 40.00 | | | | |

**CROWN KM# 70 Composition:** Copper-Nickel **Obverse:** Similar to KM#66 **Reverse:** Barcelona Olympics - Wrestlers

| Date | Mintage | F | VF | XF | Unc | BU |
|---|---|---|---|---|---|---|
| 1991 | — | — | — | — | 4.50 | — |
| 1991 Proof | Est. 8,000 | Value: 25.00 | | | | |
| 1992 | — | — | — | — | 5.00 | — |

**CROWN KM# 70a Weight:** 28.2800 g. **Composition:** 0.9250 Silver .8411 oz. ASW

| Date | Mintage | F | VF | XF | Unc | BU |
|---|---|---|---|---|---|---|
| 1991 Proof | Est. 30,000 | Value: 30.00 | | | | |

**CROWN KM# 71 Composition:** Copper-Nickel **Obverse:** Similar to KM#66 **Reverse:** Barcelona Olympics - Boxers

| Date | Mintage | F | VF | XF | Unc | BU |
|---|---|---|---|---|---|---|
| 1991 | — | — | — | — | 4.50 | — |
| 1991 Proof | Est. 8,000 | Value: 25.00 | | | | |
| 1992 | — | — | — | — | 5.00 | — |

**CROWN KM# 71a Weight:** 28.2800 g. **Composition:** 0.9250 Silver .8411 oz. ASW

| Date | Mintage | F | VF | XF | Unc | BU |
|---|---|---|---|---|---|---|
| 1991 Proof | Est. 30,000 | Value: 30.00 | | | | |

**CROWN KM# 72 Composition:** Copper-Nickel **Obverse:** Similar to KM#66 **Reverse:** Barcelona Olympics - Long Jumper

| Date | Mintage | F | VF | XF | Unc | BU |
|---|---|---|---|---|---|---|
| 1991 | — | — | — | — | 4.50 | — |
| 1991 Proof | Est. 8,000 | Value: 25.00 | | | | |
| 1992 | — | — | — | — | 5.00 | — |

**CROWN KM# 72a Weight:** 28.2800 g. **Composition:** 0.9250 Silver .8411 oz. ASW

| Date | Mintage | F | VF | XF | Unc | BU |
|---|---|---|---|---|---|---|
| 1991 Proof | Est. 30,000 | Value: 30.00 | | | | |

**CROWN KM# 73 Composition:** Copper-Nickel **Obverse:** Similar to KM#66 **Reverse:** Barcelona Olympics - Olympic Victor

| Date | Mintage | F | VF | XF | Unc | BU |
|---|---|---|---|---|---|---|
| 1991 | — | — | — | — | 4.50 | — |
| 1991 Proof | Est. 8,000 | Value: 25.00 | | | | |
| 1992 | — | — | — | — | 5.00 | — |

**CROWN KM# 73a Weight:** 28.2800 g. **Composition:** 0.9250 Silver .8411 oz. ASW

| Date | Mintage | F | VF | XF | Unc | BU |
|---|---|---|---|---|---|---|
| 1991 Proof | Est. 30,000 | Value: 30.00 | | | | |

**CROWN KM# 74 Composition:** Copper-Nickel **Reverse:** Rotary Club of Gibraltar

| Date | Mintage | F | VF | XF | Unc | BU |
|---|---|---|---|---|---|---|
| 1991 | — | — | — | — | 4.50 | — |

**CROWN KM# 74a Weight:** 28.2800 g. **Composition:** 0.9250 Silver .8411 oz. ASW **Reverse:** Rotary Club of Gibraltar

| Date | Mintage | F | VF | XF | Unc | BU |
|---|---|---|---|---|---|---|
| 1991 Proof | Est. 30,000 | Value: 27.50 | | | | |

**CROWN KM# 84 Composition:** Copper-Nickel **Subject:** 10th Wedding Anniversary **Reverse:** Prince Charles

| Date | Mintage | F | VF | XF | Unc | BU |
|---|---|---|---|---|---|---|
| 1991 | — | — | — | — | 4.00 | — |

**CROWN KM# 84a Weight:** 28.2800 g. **Composition:** 0.9250 Silver .8411 oz. ASW **Subject:** 10th Wedding Anniversary **Reverse:** Prince Charles

| Date | Mintage | F | VF | XF | Unc | BU |
|---|---|---|---|---|---|---|
| 1991 Proof | Est. 30,000 | Value: 35.00 | | | | |

**CROWN KM# 84b Weight:** 6.2200 g. **Composition:** 0.9999 Gold .2000 oz. AGW **Reverse:** Prince Charles

| Date | Mintage | F | VF | XF | Unc | BU |
|---|---|---|---|---|---|---|
| 1991 Proof | Est. 5,000 | Value: 185 | | | | |

**CROWN KM# 85 Composition:** Copper-Nickel **Subject:** 10th Wedding Anniversary **Reverse:** Princess Diana

| Date | Mintage | F | VF | XF | Unc | BU |
|---|---|---|---|---|---|---|
| 1991 | — | — | — | — | 4.00 | — |

**CROWN KM# 85a Weight:** 28.2800 g. **Composition:** 0.9250 Silver .8411 oz. ASW **Subject:** 10th Wedding Anniversary **Reverse:** Princess Diana

| Date | Mintage | F | VF | XF | Unc | BU |
|---|---|---|---|---|---|---|
| 1991 Proof | — | Value: 37.50 | | | | |

**CROWN KM# 85b Weight:** 6.2200 g. **Composition:** 0.9999 Gold .2000 oz. AGW **Reverse:** Princess Diana

| Date | Mintage | F | VF | XF | Unc | BU |
|---|---|---|---|---|---|---|
| 1991 Proof | — | Value: 185 | | | | |

**CROWN** **KM# 86** **Composition:** Copper-Nickel **Reverse:** Royal Yacht "Britannia"

| Date | Mintage | F | VF | XF | Unc | BU |
|---|---|---|---|---|---|---|
| 1991 | — | — | — | — | 4.00 | — |

**CROWN** **KM# 86a** **Weight:** 28.2800 g. **Composition:** 0.9250 Silver .8411 oz. ASW **Subject:** 10th Wedding Anniversary **Reverse:** Royal Yacht "Britannia"

| Date | Mintage | F | VF | XF | Unc | BU |
|---|---|---|---|---|---|---|
| 1991 Proof | Est. 30,000 | Value: 35.00 | | | | |

**CROWN** **KM# 86b** **Weight:** 6.2200 g. **Composition:** 0.9999 Gold .2000 oz. AGW **Subject:** 10th Wedding Anniversary **Reverse:** Royal Yacht "Britannia"

| Date | Mintage | F | VF | XF | Unc | BU |
|---|---|---|---|---|---|---|
| 1991 Proof | Est. 5,000 | Value: 185 | | | | |

**CROWN** **KM# 95** **Composition:** Copper-Nickel **Reverse:** Corgi Dog

| Date | Mintage | F | VF | XF | Unc | BU |
|---|---|---|---|---|---|---|
| 1991 | — | — | — | — | 9.00 | — |

**CROWN** **KM# 95a** **Weight:** 31.1030 g. **Composition:** 0.9990 Silver 1.0000 oz. ASW

| Date | Mintage | F | VF | XF | Unc | BU |
|---|---|---|---|---|---|---|
| 1991 Proof | Est. 50,000 | Value: 28.50 | | | | |

**CROWN** **KM# 103** **Composition:** Copper-Nickel **Obverse:** Similar to KM#95 **Reverse:** Cocker Spaniel

| Date | Mintage | F | VF | XF | Unc | BU |
|---|---|---|---|---|---|---|
| 1992 | — | — | — | — | 9.00 | — |

**CROWN** **KM# 103a** **Weight:** 28.2800 g. **Composition:** 0.9250 Silver .8411 oz. ASW

| Date | Mintage | F | VF | XF | Unc | BU |
|---|---|---|---|---|---|---|
| 1992 | — | — | — | — | 26.50 | — |

**CROWN** **KM# 178** **Composition:** Copper-Nickel **Reverse:** Gibraltar City Charter

| Date | Mintage | F | VF | XF | Unc | BU |
|---|---|---|---|---|---|---|
| 1992 | — | — | — | — | 5.00 | — |

**CROWN** **KM# 178a** **Weight:** 28.2800 g. **Composition:** 0.9250 Silver .8411 oz. ASW

| Date | Mintage | F | VF | XF | Unc | BU |
|---|---|---|---|---|---|---|
| 1992 Proof | Est. 30,000 | Value: 35.00 | | | | |

**CROWN** **KM# 113** **Composition:** Copper-Nickel **Reverse:** WWII Warships - USS Philadelphia

| Date | Mintage | F | VF | XF | Unc | BU |
|---|---|---|---|---|---|---|
| 1993 | — | — | — | — | 4.00 | — |

**CROWN** **KM# 113a** **Weight:** 28.2800 g. **Composition:** 0.9250 Silver .8411 oz. ASW

| Date | Mintage | F | VF | XF | Unc | BU |
|---|---|---|---|---|---|---|
| 1993 Proof | Est. 30,000 | Value: 26.50 | | | | |

**CROWN** **KM# 114** **Composition:** Copper-Nickel **Reverse:** WWII Warships - USS McLanahan

| Date | Mintage | F | VF | XF | Unc | BU |
|---|---|---|---|---|---|---|
| 1993 | — | — | — | — | 4.00 | — |

**CROWN** **KM# 114a** **Weight:** 28.2800 g. **Composition:** 0.9250 Silver .8411 oz. ASW

| Date | Mintage | F | VF | XF | Unc | BU |
|---|---|---|---|---|---|---|
| 1993 Proof | Est. 30,000 | Value: 26.50 | | | | |

**CROWN** **KM# 115** **Composition:** Copper-Nickel **Reverse:** WWII Warships - HNLMS Isaac Sweers

| Date | Mintage | F | VF | XF | Unc | BU |
|---|---|---|---|---|---|---|
| 1993 | — | — | — | — | 4.00 | — |

**CROWN** **KM# 115a** **Weight:** 28.2800 g. **Composition:** 0.9250 Silver .8411 oz. ASW

| Date | Mintage | F | VF | XF | Unc | BU |
|---|---|---|---|---|---|---|
| 1993 Proof | Est. 30,000 | Value: 26.50 | | | | |

**CROWN** **KM# 116** **Composition:** Copper-Nickel **Reverse:** WWII Warships - USS Weehawken

| Date | Mintage | F | VF | XF | Unc | BU |
|---|---|---|---|---|---|---|
| 1993 | — | — | — | — | 4.00 | — |

**CROWN** **KM# 116a** **Weight:** 28.2800 g. **Composition:** 0.9250 Silver .8411 oz. ASW

| Date | Mintage | F | VF | XF | Unc | BU |
|---|---|---|---|---|---|---|
| 1993 Proof | Est. 30,000 | Value: 26.50 | | | | |

**CROWN** **KM# 117** **Composition:** Copper-Nickel **Reverse:** WWII Warships - HMS Warspite

| Date | Mintage | F | VF | XF | Unc | BU |
|---|---|---|---|---|---|---|
| 1993 | — | — | — | — | 4.00 | — |

**CROWN** **KM# 117a** **Weight:** 28.2800 g. **Composition:** 0.9250 Silver .8411 oz. ASW

| Date | Mintage | F | VF | XF | Unc | BU |
|---|---|---|---|---|---|---|
| 1993 Proof | Est. 30,000 | Value: 26.50 | | | | |

**CROWN** **KM# 118** **Composition:** Copper-Nickel **Reverse:** WWII Warships - HMS Hood

| Date | Mintage | F | VF | XF | Unc | BU |
|---|---|---|---|---|---|---|
| 1993 | — | — | — | — | 4.00 | — |

**CROWN** **KM# 118a** **Weight:** 28.2800 g. **Composition:** 0.9250 Silver .8411 oz. ASW

| Date | Mintage | F | VF | XF | Unc | BU |
|---|---|---|---|---|---|---|
| 1993 Proof | Est. 30,000 | Value: 26.50 | | | | |

**CROWN** **KM# 119** **Composition:** Copper-Nickel **Reverse:** WWII Warships - HMS Penelope

| Date | Mintage | F | VF | XF | Unc | BU |
|---|---|---|---|---|---|---|
| 1993 | — | — | — | — | 4.00 | — |

**CROWN** **KM# 119a** **Weight:** 28.2800 g. **Composition:** 0.9250 Silver .8411 oz. ASW

| Date | Mintage | F | VF | XF | Unc | BU |
|---|---|---|---|---|---|---|
| 1993 Proof | Est. 30,000 | Value: 26.50 | | | | |

**CROWN** **KM# 120** **Composition:** Copper-Nickel **Reverse:** WWII Warships - HMCS Prescott

| Date | Mintage | F | VF | XF | Unc | BU |
|---|---|---|---|---|---|---|
| 1993 | — | — | — | — | 4.00 | — |

**CROWN** **KM# 120a** **Weight:** 28.2800 g. **Composition:** 0.9250 Silver .8411 oz. ASW

| Date | Mintage | F | VF | XF | Unc | BU |
|---|---|---|---|---|---|---|
| 1993 Proof | Est. 30,000 | Value: 26.50 | | | | |

**CROWN** **KM# 121** **Composition:** Copper-Nickel **Reverse:** WWII Warships - HMS Ark Royal

| Date | Mintage | F | VF | XF | Unc | BU |
|---|---|---|---|---|---|---|
| 1993 | — | — | — | — | 4.00 | — |

**CROWN** **KM# 121a** **Weight:** 28.2800 g. **Composition:** 0.9250 Silver .8411 oz. ASW

| Date | Mintage | F | VF | XF | Unc | BU |
|---|---|---|---|---|---|---|
| 1993 Proof | Est. 30,000 | Value: 26.50 | | | | |

**CROWN** **KM# 122** **Composition:** Copper-Nickel **Reverse:** WWII Warships - USS Gleaves

| Date | Mintage | F | VF | XF | Unc | BU |
|---|---|---|---|---|---|---|
| 1993 | — | — | — | — | 4.00 | — |

**CROWN** **KM# 122a** **Weight:** 28.2800 g. **Composition:** 0.9250 Silver .8411 oz. ASW

| Date | Mintage | F | VF | XF | Unc | BU |
|---|---|---|---|---|---|---|
| 1993 Proof | Est. 30,000 | Value: 26.50 | | | | |

**CROWN** **KM# 123** **Composition:** Copper-Nickel **Reverse:** WWII Warships - HMAS Waterhen

| Date | Mintage | F | VF | XF | Unc | BU |
|---|---|---|---|---|---|---|
| 1993 | — | — | — | — | 4.00 | — |

**CROWN** **KM# 123a** **Weight:** 28.2800 g. **Composition:** 0.9250 Silver .8411 oz. ASW

| Date | Mintage | F | VF | XF | Unc | BU |
|---|---|---|---|---|---|---|
| 1993 Proof | Est. 30,000 | Value: 26.50 | | | | |

**CROWN** **KM# 132** **Composition:** Copper-Nickel **Reverse:** Queen Anne - 1702-1714

| Date | Mintage | F | VF | XF | Unc | BU |
|---|---|---|---|---|---|---|
| 1993 Prooflike | — | — | — | — | 4.00 | — |

**CROWN** **KM# 132a** **Weight:** 28.2800 g. **Composition:** 0.9250 Silver .8411 oz. ASW

| Date | Mintage | F | VF | XF | Unc | BU |
|---|---|---|---|---|---|---|
| 1993 Proof | Est. 30,000 | Value: 35.00 | | | | |

**CROWN** **KM# 133** **Composition:** Copper-Nickel **Reverse:** King George I - 1714-1727

| Date | Mintage | F | VF | XF | Unc | BU |
|---|---|---|---|---|---|---|
| 1993 Prooflike | — | — | — | — | 4.00 | — |

**CROWN** **KM# 133a** **Weight:** 28.2800 g. **Composition:** 0.9250 Silver .8411 oz. ASW

| Date | Mintage | F | VF | XF | Unc | BU |
|---|---|---|---|---|---|---|
| 1993 Proof | Est. 30,000 | Value: 35.00 | | | | |

**CROWN** **KM# 134** **Composition:** Copper-Nickel **Reverse:** King George II - 1727-1760

| Date | Mintage | F | VF | XF | Unc | BU |
|---|---|---|---|---|---|---|
| 1993 Prooflike | — | — | — | — | 4.00 | — |

**CROWN** **KM# 134a** **Weight:** 28.2800 g. **Composition:** 0.9250 Silver .8411 oz. ASW

| Date | Mintage | F | VF | XF | Unc | BU |
|---|---|---|---|---|---|---|
| 1993 Proof | Est. 30,000 | Value: 35.00 | | | | |

**CROWN** **KM# 135** **Composition:** Copper-Nickel **Reverse:** King George III - 1760-1820

| Date | Mintage | F | VF | XF | Unc | BU |
|---|---|---|---|---|---|---|
| 1993 Prooflike | — | — | — | — | 4.00 | — |

**CROWN** **KM# 135a** **Weight:** 28.2800 g. **Composition:** 0.9250 Silver .8411 oz. ASW

| Date | Mintage | F | VF | XF | Unc | BU |
|---|---|---|---|---|---|---|
| 1993 Proof | Est. 30,000 | Value: 35.00 | | | | |

**CROWN** **KM# 136** **Composition:** Copper-Nickel **Reverse:** King George IV - 1820-1830

| Date | Mintage | F | VF | XF | Unc | BU |
|---|---|---|---|---|---|---|
| 1993 Prooflike | — | — | — | — | 4.00 | — |

**CROWN** **KM# 136a** **Weight:** 28.2800 g. **Composition:** 0.9250 Silver .8411 oz. ASW

| Date | Mintage | F | VF | XF | Unc | BU |
|---|---|---|---|---|---|---|
| 1993 Proof | Est. 30,000 | Value: 35.00 | | | | |

**CROWN** **KM# 137** **Composition:** Copper-Nickel **Reverse:** King William IV - 1830-1837

| Date | Mintage | F | VF | XF | Unc | BU |
|---|---|---|---|---|---|---|
| 1993 Prooflike | — | — | — | — | 4.00 | — |

**CROWN** **KM# 137a** **Weight:** 28.2800 g. **Composition:** 0.9250 Silver .8411 oz. ASW

| Date | Mintage | F | VF | XF | Unc | BU |
|---|---|---|---|---|---|---|
| 1993 Proof | Est. 30,000 | Value: 35.00 | | | | |

**CROWN** **KM# 138** **Composition:** Copper-Nickel **Reverse:** Queen Victoria - 1837-1901

| Date | Mintage | F | VF | XF | Unc | BU |
|---|---|---|---|---|---|---|
| 1993 Prooflike | — | — | — | — | 4.00 | — |

**CROWN** **KM# 138a** **Weight:** 28.2800 g. **Composition:** 0.9250 Silver .8411 oz. ASW

| Date | Mintage | F | VF | XF | Unc | BU |
|---|---|---|---|---|---|---|
| 1993 Proof | Est. 30,000 | Value: 35.00 | | | | |

**CROWN** **KM# 139** **Composition:** Copper-Nickel **Reverse:** King Edward VII - 1901-1910

| Date | Mintage | F | VF | XF | Unc | BU |
|---|---|---|---|---|---|---|
| 1993 Prooflike | — | — | — | — | 4.00 | — |

**CROWN** **KM# 139a** **Weight:** 28.2800 g. **Composition:** 0.9250 Silver .8411 oz. ASW

| Date | Mintage | F | VF | XF | Unc | BU |
|---|---|---|---|---|---|---|
| 1993 Proof | Est. 30,000 | Value: 35.00 | | | | |

**CROWN** **KM# 140** **Composition:** Copper-Nickel **Reverse:** King George V - 1910-1936

| Date | Mintage | F | VF | XF | Unc | BU |
|---|---|---|---|---|---|---|
| 1993 Prooflike | — | — | — | — | 4.00 | — |

**CROWN** **KM# 140a** **Weight:** 28.2800 g. **Composition:** 0.9250 Silver .8411 oz. ASW

| Date | Mintage | F | VF | XF | Unc | BU |
|---|---|---|---|---|---|---|
| 1993 Proof | Est. 30,000 | Value: 35.00 | | | | |

**CROWN** **KM# 141** **Composition:** Copper-Nickel **Reverse:** King Edward VIII - 1936

| Date | Mintage | F | VF | XF | Unc | BU |
|---|---|---|---|---|---|---|
| 1993 Prooflike | — | — | — | — | 4.00 | — |

**CROWN** **KM# 141a** **Weight:** 28.2800 g. **Composition:** 0.9250 Silver .8411 oz. ASW

| Date | Mintage | F | VF | XF | Unc | BU |
|---|---|---|---|---|---|---|
| 1993 Proof | Est. 30,000 | Value: 35.00 | | | | |

**CROWN** **KM# 142** **Composition:** Copper-Nickel **Reverse:** King George VI - 1936-1952

| Date | Mintage | F | VF | XF | Unc | BU |
|---|---|---|---|---|---|---|
| 1993 Prooflike | — | — | — | — | 4.00 | — |

**CROWN** **KM# 142a** **Weight:** 28.2800 g. **Composition:** 0.9250 Silver .8411 oz. ASW

| Date | Mintage | F | VF | XF | Unc | BU |
|---|---|---|---|---|---|---|
| 1993 Proof | Est. 30,000 | Value: 35.00 | | | | |

**CROWN** **KM# 143** **Composition:** Copper-Nickel **Reverse:** Coronation of Queen Elizabeth II

| Date | Mintage | F | VF | XF | Unc | BU |
|---|---|---|---|---|---|---|
| 1993 | — | — | — | — | 4.00 | — |

**CROWN** **KM# 143a** **Weight:** 28.2800 g. **Composition:** 0.9250 Silver .8411 oz. ASW

| Date | Mintage | F | VF | XF | Unc | BU |
|---|---|---|---|---|---|---|
| 1993 Proof | Est. 30,000 | Value: 35.00 | | | | |

**CROWN** **KM# 144** **Composition:** Copper-Nickel **Reverse:** WWII Warships - FSS Savorgnan de Brazza

| Date | Mintage | F | VF | XF | Unc | BU |
|---|---|---|---|---|---|---|
| 1993 | — | — | — | — | 4.00 | — |

**CROWN** **KM# 144a** **Weight:** 28.2800 g. **Composition:** 0.9250 Silver .8411 oz. ASW

| Date | Mintage | F | VF | XF | Unc | BU |
|---|---|---|---|---|---|---|
| 1993 Proof | Est. 30,000 | Value: 26.50 | | | | |

**CROWN** **KM# 145** **Composition:** Copper-Nickel **Reverse:** XVII Winter Olympics - Skaters

| Date | Mintage | F | VF | XF | Unc | BU |
|---|---|---|---|---|---|---|
| 1993 Proof | — | Value: 4.00 | | | | |

**CROWN** **KM# 145a** **Weight:** 28.2800 g. **Composition:** 0.9250 Silver .8411 oz. ASW

| Date | Mintage | F | VF | XF | Unc | BU |
|---|---|---|---|---|---|---|
| 1993 Proof | Est. 30,000 | Value: 35.00 | | | | |

**CROWN** **KM# 145b** **Weight:** 6.2200 g. **Composition:** 0.9999 Gold .2000 oz. AGW **Reverse:** XVII Winter Olympics - Skaters

| Date | Mintage | F | VF | XF | Unc | BU |
|---|---|---|---|---|---|---|
| 1993 Proof | Est. 5,000 | Value: 200 | | | | |

**CROWN** **KM# 146** **Composition:** Copper-Nickel **Reverse:** XVII Winter Olympics - Ice Hockey

| Date | Mintage | F | VF | XF | Unc | BU |
|---|---|---|---|---|---|---|
| 1993 Proof | — | Value: 4.00 | | | | |

**CROWN** **KM# 146a** **Weight:** 28.2800 g. **Composition:** 0.9250 Silver .8411 oz. ASW

| Date | Mintage | F | VF | XF | Unc | BU |
|---|---|---|---|---|---|---|
| 1993 Proof | Est. 30,000 | Value: 35.00 | | | | |

**CROWN** **KM# 146b** **Weight:** 6.2200 g. **Composition:** 0.9999 Gold .2000 oz. AGW **Reverse:** XVII Winter Olympics - Ice Hockey

| Date | Mintage | F | VF | XF | Unc | BU |
|---|---|---|---|---|---|---|
| 1993 Proof | Est. 5,000 | Value: 200 | | | | |

**CROWN** **KM# 147** **Composition:** Copper-Nickel **Reverse:** XVII Winter Olympics - Bobsledding

| Date | Mintage | F | VF | XF | Unc | BU |
|---|---|---|---|---|---|---|
| 1993 Proof | — | Value: 4.00 | | | | |

**CROWN** **KM# 147a** **Weight:** 28.2800 g. **Composition:** 0.9250 Silver .8411 oz. ASW

| Date | Mintage | F | VF | XF | Unc | BU |
|---|---|---|---|---|---|---|
| 1993 Proof | Est. 30,000 | Value: 35.00 | | | | |

**CROWN** **KM# 147b** **Weight:** 6.2200 g. **Composition:** 0.9999 Gold .2000 oz. AGW **Reverse:** XVII Winter Olympics - Bobsledding

| Date | Mintage | F | VF | XF | Unc | BU |
|---|---|---|---|---|---|---|
| 1993 Proof | Est. 5,000 | Value: 200 | | | | |

**CROWN** **KM# 148** **Composition:** Copper-Nickel **Reverse:** XVII Winter Olympics - Skiers

| Date | Mintage | F | VF | XF | Unc | BU |
|---|---|---|---|---|---|---|
| 1993 Proof | — | Value: 4.00 | | | | |

**CROWN** **KM# 148a** **Weight:** 28.2800 g. **Composition:** 0.9250 Silver .8411 oz. ASW

| Date | Mintage | F | VF | XF | Unc | BU |
|---|---|---|---|---|---|---|
| 1993 Proof | Est. 30,000 | Value: 35.00 | | | | |

**CROWN** **KM# 148b** **Weight:** 6.2200 g. **Composition:** 0.9999 Gold .2000 oz. AGW **Reverse:** XVII Winter Olympics

| Date | Mintage | F | VF | XF | Unc | BU |
|---|---|---|---|---|---|---|
| 1993 Proof | Est. 5,000 | Value: 200 | | | | |

**CROWN** **KM# 149** **Composition:** Copper-Nickel **Reverse:** Preserve Planet Earth - Cetiosaurus

| Date | Mintage | F | VF | XF | Unc | BU |
|---|---|---|---|---|---|---|
| 1993 | — | — | — | — | 8.00 | — |

**CROWN** **KM# 149a** **Weight:** 28.2800 g. **Composition:** 0.9250 Silver .8411 oz. ASW

| Date | Mintage | F | VF | XF | Unc | BU |
|---|---|---|---|---|---|---|
| 1993 Proof | Est. 30,000 | Value: 32.50 | | | | |

**CROWN** **KM# 151** **Composition:** Copper-Nickel **Reverse:** Preserve Planet Earth - Stegosaurus

| Date | Mintage | F | VF | XF | Unc | BU |
|---|---|---|---|---|---|---|
| 1993 | — | — | — | — | 8.50 | — |

**CROWN** **KM# 151a** **Weight:** 28.2800 g. **Composition:** 0.9250 Silver .8411 oz. ASW

| Date | Mintage | F | VF | XF | Unc | BU |
|---|---|---|---|---|---|---|
| 1993 Proof | Est. 30,000 | Value: 32.50 | | | | |

**CROWN** **KM# 180** **Composition:** Copper-Nickel **Obverse:** Similar to KM#178 **Reverse:** International Friendship - Stylized Panda

| Date | Mintage | F | VF | XF | Unc | BU |
|---|---|---|---|---|---|---|
| 1993 | — | — | — | — | 6.50 | — |

**CROWN** **KM# 180a** **Weight:** 28.2800 g. **Composition:** 0.9250 Silver .8411 oz. ASW

| Date | Mintage | F | VF | XF | Unc | BU |
|---|---|---|---|---|---|---|
| 1993 Proof | Est. 30,000 | Value: 35.00 | | | | |

**CROWN** **KM# 184** **Composition:** Copper-Nickel **Reverse:** International Friendship - Natural Panda

| Date | Mintage | F | VF | XF | Unc | BU |
|---|---|---|---|---|---|---|
| 1993 | — | — | — | — | 6.50 | — |

**CROWN** **KM# 184a** **Weight:** 28.2800 g. **Composition:** 0.9250 Silver .8411 oz. ASW

| Date | Mintage | F | VF | XF | Unc | BU |
|---|---|---|---|---|---|---|
| 1993 Proof | Est. 30,000 | Value: 35.00 | | | | |

**CROWN** **KM# 188** **Composition:** Copper-Nickel **Reverse:** International Friendship - General Sikorski

| Date | Mintage | F | VF | XF | Unc | BU |
|---|---|---|---|---|---|---|
| 1993 | — | — | — | — | 5.00 | — |

**CROWN** **KM# 188a** **Weight:** 28.2800 g. **Composition:** 0.9250 Silver .8411 oz. ASW

| Date | Mintage | F | VF | XF | Unc | BU |
|---|---|---|---|---|---|---|
| 1993 Proof | Est. 30,000 | Value: 35.00 | | | | |

**CROWN** **KM# 192.1** **Composition:** Copper-Nickel **Reverse:** Long-Haried Dachshund

| Date | Mintage | F | VF | XF | Unc | BU |
|---|---|---|---|---|---|---|
| 1993 | — | — | — | — | 8.50 | — |

**CROWN** **KM# 192.1a** **Weight:** 31.1030 g. **Composition:** 0.9250 Silver 1.0000 oz. ASW

| Date | Mintage | F | VF | XF | Unc | BU |
|---|---|---|---|---|---|---|
| 1993 Proof | Est. 50,000 | Value: 30.00 | | | | |

**CROWN** **KM# 192.2** **Composition:** Copper-Nickel **Reverse:** Mint mark left of dog

| Date | Mintage | F | VF | XF | Unc | BU |
|---|---|---|---|---|---|---|
| 1993(c) | — | — | — | — | 8.00 | — |

**CROWN** **KM# 192.2a** **Weight:** 28.2800 g. **Composition:** 0.9250 Silver .8411 oz. ASW

| Date | Mintage | F | VF | XF | Unc | BU |
|---|---|---|---|---|---|---|
| 1993 | — | — | — | — | 27.50 | — |

**CROWN** **KM# 200** **Composition:** Copper-Nickel **Reverse:** Dependent Territories Conference

| Date | Mintage | F | VF | XF | Unc | BU |
|---|---|---|---|---|---|---|
| 1993 | — | — | — | — | 5.50 | — |

**CROWN** **KM# 200a** **Weight:** 28.2800 g. **Composition:** 0.9250 Silver .8411 oz. ASW

| Date | Mintage | F | VF | XF | Unc | BU |
|---|---|---|---|---|---|---|
| 1993 Proof | Est. 30,000 | Value: 35.00 | | | | |

**CROWN** **KM# 201** **Composition:** Copper-Nickel **Reverse:** Peter Rabbit Centennial - Peter Rabbit

| Date | Mintage | F | VF | XF | Unc | BU |
|---|---|---|---|---|---|---|
| 1993 | — | — | — | — | 7.50 | — |

**CROWN** **KM# 201a** **Weight:** 28.2800 g. **Composition:** 0.9250 Silver .8411 oz. ASW

| Date | Mintage | F | VF | XF | Unc | BU |
|---|---|---|---|---|---|---|
| 1993 Proof | Est. 30,000 | Value: 37.50 | | | | |

**CROWN** **KM# 205** **Composition:** Copper-Nickel **Reverse:** Peter Rabbit Centennial - Tiggy-Winkel

| Date | Mintage | F | VF | XF | Unc | BU |
|---|---|---|---|---|---|---|
| 1993 | — | — | — | — | 7.50 | — |

**CROWN** **KM# 205a** **Weight:** 28.2800 g. **Composition:** 0.9250 Silver .8411 oz. ASW

| Date | Mintage | F | VF | XF | Unc | BU |
|---|---|---|---|---|---|---|
| 1993 Proof | Est. 30,000 | Value: 25.00 | | | | |

**CROWN** **KM# 209** **Composition:** Copper-Nickel **Reverse:** Peter Rabbit Centennial - Jeremy Fisher

| Date | Mintage | F | VF | XF | Unc | BU |
|---|---|---|---|---|---|---|
| 1993 | — | — | — | — | 7.50 | — |

**CROWN** **KM# 209a** **Weight:** 28.2800 g. **Composition:** 0.9250 Silver .8411 oz. ASW

| Date | Mintage | F | VF | XF | Unc | BU |
|---|---|---|---|---|---|---|
| 1993 Proof | Est. 30,000 | Value: 25.00 | | | | |

**CROWN** **KM# 213** **Composition:** Copper-Nickel **Reverse:** Peter Rabbit Centennial - Tom Kitten

| Date | Mintage | F | VF | XF | Unc | BU |
|---|---|---|---|---|---|---|
| 1993 | — | — | — | — | 7.50 | — |

**CROWN** **KM# 213a** **Weight:** 28.2800 g. **Composition:** 0.9250 Silver .8411 oz. ASW

| Date | Mintage | F | VF | XF | Unc | BU |
|---|---|---|---|---|---|---|
| 1993 Proof | Est. 30,000 | Value: 25.00 | | | | |

**CROWN** **KM# 217** **Composition:** Copper-Nickel **Reverse:** Peter Rabbit Centennial - Benjamin Bunny

| Date | Mintage | F | VF | XF | Unc | BU |
|---|---|---|---|---|---|---|
| 1993 | — | — | — | — | 7.50 | — |

**CROWN** **KM# 217a** **Weight:** 28.2800 g. **Composition:** 0.9250 Silver .8411 oz. ASW

| Date | Mintage | F | VF | XF | Unc | BU |
|---|---|---|---|---|---|---|
| 1993 Proof | Est. 30,000 | Value: 25.00 | | | | |

**CROWN** **KM# 221** **Composition:** Copper-Nickel **Reverse:** Peter Rabbit Centennial - Jemima Puddle-Duck

| Date | Mintage | F | VF | XF | Unc | BU |
|---|---|---|---|---|---|---|
| 1993 | — | — | — | — | 7.50 | — |

**CROWN** **KM# 221a** **Weight:** 28.2800 g. **Composition:** 0.9250 Silver .8411 oz. ASW

| Date | Mintage | F | VF | XF | Unc | BU |
|---|---|---|---|---|---|---|
| 1993 Proof | Est. 30,000 | Value: 25.00 | | | | |

**CROWN** KM# 342C **Composition:** Copper-Nickel **Subject:** Year of the Cockerel **Obverse:** Queen's portrait **Reverse:** Cockerel (rooster)

| Date | Mintage | F | VF | XF | Unc | BU |
|---|---|---|---|---|---|---|
| 1993 | — | — | — | — | 6.00 | — |

**CROWN** KM# 225 **Composition:** Copper-Nickel **Subject:** World Cup Soccer **Reverse:** 3 Players

| Date | Mintage | F | VF | XF | Unc | BU |
|---|---|---|---|---|---|---|
| 1994 | — | — | — | — | 4.75 | — |

**CROWN** KM# 225a **Weight:** 28.2800 g. **Composition:** 0.9250 Silver .8411 oz. ASW

| Date | Mintage | F | VF | XF | Unc | BU |
|---|---|---|---|---|---|---|
| 1994 Proof | Est. 30,000 | Value: 30.00 | | | | |

**CROWN** KM# 227 **Composition:** Copper-Nickel **Subject:** World Cup Soccer **Reverse:** 2 Players Facing

| Date | Mintage | F | VF | XF | Unc | BU |
|---|---|---|---|---|---|---|
| 1994 | — | — | — | — | 4.75 | |

**CROWN** KM# 227a **Weight:** 28.2800 g. **Composition:** 0.9250 Silver .8411 oz. ASW

| Date | Mintage | F | VF | XF | Unc | BU |
|---|---|---|---|---|---|---|
| 1994 Proof | Est. 30,000 | Value: 30.00 | | | | |

**CROWN** KM# 229 **Composition:** Copper-Nickel **Subject:** World Cup Soccer **Reverse:** Goalie and Scorer

| Date | Mintage | F | VF | XF | Unc | BU |
|---|---|---|---|---|---|---|
| 1994 | — | — | — | — | 4.75 | — |

**CROWN** KM# 229a **Weight:** 28.2800 g. **Composition:** 0.9250 Silver .8411 oz. ASW

| Date | Mintage | F | VF | XF | Unc | BU |
|---|---|---|---|---|---|---|
| 1994 Proof | Est. 30,000 | Value: 30.00 | | | | |

**CROWN** KM# 231 **Composition:** Copper-Nickel **Subject:** World Cup Soccer **Reverse:** 1 Player

| Date | Mintage | F | VF | XF | Unc | BU |
|---|---|---|---|---|---|---|
| 1994 | — | — | — | — | 4.75 | — |

**CROWN** KM# 231a **Weight:** 28.2800 g. **Composition:** 0.9250 Silver .8411 oz. ASW

| Date | Mintage | F | VF | XF | Unc | BU |
|---|---|---|---|---|---|---|
| 1994 | Est. 30,000 | Value: 30.00 | | | | |

**CROWN** KM# 233 **Composition:** Copper-Nickel **Reverse:** World Cup Soccer - 2 Players, 1 Kicking

| Date | Mintage | F | VF | XF | Unc | BU |
|---|---|---|---|---|---|---|
| 1994 | — | — | — | — | 4.75 | — |

**CROWN** KM# 233a **Weight:** 28.2800 g. **Composition:** 0.9250 Silver .8411 oz. ASW

| Date | Mintage | F | VF | XF | Unc | BU |
|---|---|---|---|---|---|---|
| 1994 Proof | Est. 30,000 | Value: 30.00 | | | | |

**CROWN** KM# 235 **Composition:** Copper-Nickel **Subject:** World Cup Soccer **Reverse:** 2 Players Sideways

| Date | Mintage | F | VF | XF | Unc | BU |
|---|---|---|---|---|---|---|
| 1994 | — | — | — | — | 4.75 | — |

**CROWN** KM# 235a **Weight:** 28.2800 g. **Composition:** 0.9250 Silver .8411 oz. ASW

| Date | Mintage | F | VF | XF | Unc | BU |
|---|---|---|---|---|---|---|
| 1994 Proof | Est. 30,000 | Value: 30.00 | | | | |

**CROWN** KM# 239a **Weight:** 28.2800 g. **Composition:** 0.9250 Silver .8411 oz. ASW

| Date | Mintage | F | VF | XF | Unc | BU |
|---|---|---|---|---|---|---|
| 1994 Proof | Est. 30,000 | Value: 35.00 | | | | |

**CROWN** KM# 241 **Composition:** Copper-Nickel **Reverse:** Preserve Planet Earth - Spanish Imperial Eagle

| Date | Mintage | F | VF | XF | Unc | BU |
|---|---|---|---|---|---|---|
| 1994 | — | — | — | — | 7.00 | — |

**CROWN** KM# 241a **Weight:** 28.2800 g. **Composition:** 0.9250 Silver .8411 oz. ASW

| Date | Mintage | F | VF | XF | Unc | BU |
|---|---|---|---|---|---|---|
| 1994 Proof | Est. 30,000 | Value: 37.50 | | | | |

**CROWN** KM# 243 **Composition:** Copper-Nickel **Reverse:** Preserve Planet Earth - Striped Dolphins

| Date | Mintage | F | VF | XF | Unc | BU |
|---|---|---|---|---|---|---|
| 1994 | — | — | — | — | 7.00 | — |

**CROWN** KM# 243a **Weight:** 28.2800 g. **Composition:** 0.9250 Silver .8411 oz. ASW

| Date | Mintage | F | VF | XF | Unc | BU |
|---|---|---|---|---|---|---|
| 1994 Proof | Est. 30,000 | Value: 37.50 | | | | |

**CROWN** KM# 245 **Composition:** Copper-Nickel **Reverse:** Preserve Planet Earth - African Elephants

| Date | Mintage | F | VF | XF | Unc | BU |
|---|---|---|---|---|---|---|
| 1994 | — | — | — | — | 8.50 | — |

**CROWN** KM# 245a **Weight:** 28.2800 g. **Composition:** 0.9250 Silver .8411 oz. ASW

| Date | Mintage | F | VF | XF | Unc | BU |
|---|---|---|---|---|---|---|
| 1994 Proof | Est. 30,000 | Value: 37.50 | | | | |

**CROWN** KM# 246 **Composition:** Copper-Nickel **Reverse:** Pekingese Dog

| Date | Mintage | F | VF | XF | Unc | BU |
|---|---|---|---|---|---|---|
| 1994 | — | — | — | — | 7.00 | — |

**CROWN** KM# 259 **Composition:** Copper-Nickel **Reverse:** World War II - Maltese Convoy

| Date | Mintage | F | VF | XF | Unc | BU |
|---|---|---|---|---|---|---|
| 1994 | — | — | — | — | 6.00 | — |

**CROWN** KM# 259a **Weight:** 28.2800 g. **Composition:** 0.9250 Silver .8411 oz. ASW

| Date | Mintage | F | VF | XF | Unc | BU |
|---|---|---|---|---|---|---|
| 1994 Proof | Est. 30,000 | Value: 35.00 | | | | |

**CROWN** KM# 260 **Composition:** Copper-Nickel **Reverse:** World War II - Squadron 202 in Gibraltar

| Date | Mintage | F | VF | XF | Unc | BU |
|---|---|---|---|---|---|---|
| 1994 | — | — | — | — | 6.00 | — |

**CROWN** **KM# 260a** **Weight:** 28.2800 g. **Composition:** 0.9250 Silver .8411 oz. ASW

| Date | Mintage | F | VF | XF | Unc | BU |
|---|---|---|---|---|---|---|
| 1994 Proof | Est. 30,000 | Value: 35.00 | | | | |

**CROWN** **KM# 261** **Composition:** Copper-Nickel **Reverse:** World War II - Admiral Somerville

| Date | Mintage | F | VF | XF | Unc | BU |
|---|---|---|---|---|---|---|
| 1994 | — | — | — | — | 6.00 | — |

**CROWN** **KM# 261a** **Weight:** 28.2800 g. **Composition:** 0.9250 Silver .8411 oz. ASW

| Date | Mintage | F | VF | XF | Unc | BU |
|---|---|---|---|---|---|---|
| 1994 Proof | Est. 30,000 | Value: 35.00 | | | | |

**CROWN** **KM# 262** **Composition:** Copper-Nickel **Reverse:** World War II - Glen Miller

| Date | Mintage | F | VF | XF | Unc | BU |
|---|---|---|---|---|---|---|
| 1994 | — | — | — | — | 6.00 | — |

**CROWN** **KM# 262a** **Weight:** 28.2800 g. **Composition:** 0.9250 Silver .8411 oz. ASW

| Date | Mintage | F | VF | XF | Unc | BU |
|---|---|---|---|---|---|---|
| 1994 Proof | Est. 30,000 | Value: 32.50 | | | | |

**CROWN** **KM# 263** **Composition:** Copper-Nickel **Reverse:** World War II - King George VI and Pilots

| Date | Mintage | F | VF | XF | Unc | BU |
|---|---|---|---|---|---|---|
| 1994 | — | — | — | — | 6.00 | — |

**CROWN** **KM# 263a** **Weight:** 28.2800 g. **Composition:** 0.9250 Silver .8411 oz. ASW

| Date | Mintage | F | VF | XF | Unc | BU |
|---|---|---|---|---|---|---|
| 1994 Proof | Est. 30,000 | Value: 35.00 | | | | |

**CROWN** **KM# 264** **Composition:** Copper-Nickel **Reverse:** World War II - General Eisenhower

| Date | Mintage | F | VF | XF | Unc | BU |
|---|---|---|---|---|---|---|
| 1994 | — | — | — | — | 6.00 | — |

**CROWN** **KM# 264a** **Weight:** 28.2800 g. **Composition:** 0.9250 Silver .8411 oz. ASW

| Date | Mintage | F | VF | XF | Unc | BU |
|---|---|---|---|---|---|---|
| 1994 Proof | — | Value: 35.00 | | | | |

**CROWN** **KM# 271** **Composition:** Copper-Nickel **Reverse:** First Man on Moon - Dr. Wernher von Braun

| Date | Mintage | F | VF | XF | Unc | BU |
|---|---|---|---|---|---|---|
| 1994 | — | — | — | — | 5.75 | — |

**CROWN** **KM# 271a** **Weight:** 28.2800 g. **Composition:** 0.9250 Silver .8411 oz. ASW

| Date | Mintage | F | VF | XF | Unc | BU |
|---|---|---|---|---|---|---|
| 1994 Proof | Est. 30,000 | Value: 30.00 | | | | |

**CROWN** **KM# 272** **Composition:** Copper-Nickel **Reverse:** First Man on Moon - Rocket Launching

| Date | Mintage | F | VF | XF | Unc | BU |
|---|---|---|---|---|---|---|
| 1994 | — | — | — | — | 5.75 | — |

**CROWN** **KM# 272a** **Weight:** 28.2800 g. **Composition:** 0.9250 Silver .8411 oz. ASW

| Date | Mintage | F | VF | XF | Unc | BU |
|---|---|---|---|---|---|---|
| 1994 Proof | Est. 30,000 | Value: 30.00 | | | | |

**CROWN** **KM# 273** **Composition:** Copper-Nickel **Reverse:** First Man on Moon - Space Capsule Recovery

| Date | Mintage | F | VF | XF | Unc | BU |
|---|---|---|---|---|---|---|
| 1994 | — | — | — | — | 5.75 | — |

**CROWN** **KM# 273a** **Weight:** 28.2800 g. **Composition:** 0.9250 Silver .8411 oz. ASW

| Date | Mintage | F | VF | XF | Unc | BU |
|---|---|---|---|---|---|---|
| 1994 Proof | Est. 30,000 | Value: 30.00 | | | | |

**CROWN** **KM# 274** **Composition:** Copper-Nickel **Reverse:** First Man on Moon - First Manned Lunar Landing

| Date | Mintage | F | VF | XF | Unc | BU |
|---|---|---|---|---|---|---|
| 1994 | — | — | — | — | 5.75 | — |

**CROWN** **KM# 274a** **Weight:** 28.2800 g. **Composition:** 0.9250 Silver .8411 oz. ASW

| Date | Mintage | F | VF | XF | Unc | BU |
|---|---|---|---|---|---|---|
| 1994 Proof | Est. 30,000 | Value: 30.00 | | | | |

**CROWN** **KM# 275** **Composition:** Copper-Nickel **Reverse:** First Man on Moon - First Step on Moon

| Date | Mintage | F | VF | XF | Unc | BU |
|---|---|---|---|---|---|---|
| 1994 | — | — | — | — | 5.75 | — |

**CROWN** **KM# 275a** **Weight:** 28.2800 g. **Composition:** 0.9250 Silver .8411 oz. ASW

| Date | Mintage | F | VF | XF | Unc | BU |
|---|---|---|---|---|---|---|
| 1994 Proof | Est. 30,000 | Value: 30.00 | | | | |

**CROWN** **KM# 276** **Composition:** Copper-Nickel **Reverse:** First Man on Moon - First Flag Planted on Moon

| Date | Mintage | F | VF | XF | Unc | BU |
|---|---|---|---|---|---|---|
| 1994 | — | — | — | — | 5.75 | — |

**CROWN** **KM# 276a** **Weight:** 28.2800 g. **Composition:** 0.9250 Silver .8411 oz. ASW

| Date | Mintage | F | VF | XF | Unc | BU |
|---|---|---|---|---|---|---|
| 1994 Proof | Est. 30,000 | Value: 30.00 | | | | |

**CROWN** **KM# 285** **Composition:** Copper-Nickel **Reverse:** Sherlock Holmes - Holmes Holding Pipe

| Date | Mintage | F | VF | XF | Unc | BU |
|---|---|---|---|---|---|---|
| 1994 | — | — | — | — | 6.00 | — |

**CROWN** **KM# 285a** **Weight:** 28.2800 g. **Composition:** 0.9250 Silver .8411 oz. ASW

| Date | Mintage | F | VF | XF | Unc | BU |
|---|---|---|---|---|---|---|
| 1994 Proof | Est. 30,000 | Value: 27.50 | | | | |

**CROWN** **KM# 286** **Composition:** Copper-Nickel **Reverse:** Sherlock Holmes - Holmes Playing Violin for Dr. Watson

| Date | Mintage | F | VF | XF | Unc | BU |
|---|---|---|---|---|---|---|
| 1994 | — | — | — | — | 6.00 | — |

**CROWN** **KM# 286a** **Weight:** 28.2800 g. **Composition:** 0.9250 Silver .8411 oz. ASW

| Date | Mintage | F | VF | XF | Unc | BU |
|---|---|---|---|---|---|---|
| 1994 Proof | Est. 30,000 | Value: 27.50 | | | | |

**CROWN** **KM# 287** **Composition:** Copper-Nickel **Reverse:** Sherlock Holmes - 221 B Baker Street

| Date | Mintage | F | VF | XF | Unc | BU |
|---|---|---|---|---|---|---|
| 1994 | — | — | — | — | 6.00 | — |

**CROWN** **KM# 287a** **Weight:** 28.2800 g. **Composition:** 0.9250 Silver .8411 oz. ASW

| Date | Mintage | F | VF | XF | Unc | BU |
|---|---|---|---|---|---|---|
| 1994 Proof | Est. 30,000 | Value: 22.50 | | | | |

**CROWN** **KM# 288** **Composition:** Copper-Nickel **Reverse:** Sherlock Holmes - The Empty House

| Date | Mintage | F | VF | XF | Unc | BU |
|---|---|---|---|---|---|---|
| 1994 | — | — | — | — | 6.00 | — |

**CROWN** **KM# 288a** **Weight:** 28.2800 g. **Composition:** 0.9250 Silver .8411 oz. ASW

| Date | Mintage | F | VF | XF | Unc | BU |
|---|---|---|---|---|---|---|
| 1994 Proof | Est. 30,000 | Value: 22.50 | | | | |

**CROWN** **KM# 289** **Composition:** Copper-Nickel **Reverse:** Sherlock Holmes - The Mary Celeste

| Date | Mintage | F | VF | XF | Unc | BU |
|---|---|---|---|---|---|---|
| 1994 | — | — | — | — | 6.00 | — |

**CROWN** **KM# 289a** **Weight:** 28.2800 g. **Composition:** 0.9250 Silver .8411 oz. ASW

| Date | Mintage | F | VF | XF | Unc | BU |
|---|---|---|---|---|---|---|
| 1994 Proof | Est. 30,000 | Value: 37.50 | | | | |

**CROWN** **KM# 290** **Composition:** Copper-Nickel **Reverse:** Sherlock Holmes - The Hound of the Baskervilles

| Date | Mintage | F | VF | XF | Unc | BU |
|---|---|---|---|---|---|---|
| 1994 | — | — | — | — | 6.00 | — |

**CROWN** **KM# 290a** **Weight:** 28.2800 g. **Composition:** 0.9250 Silver .8411 oz. ASW

| Date | Mintage | F | VF | XF | Unc | BU |
|---|---|---|---|---|---|---|
| 1994 Proof | Est. 30,000 | Value: 35.00 | | | | |

**CROWN** **KM# 291** **Composition:** Copper-Nickel **Reverse:** Sherlock Holmes - The Three Garriders

| Date | Mintage | F | VF | XF | Unc | BU |
|---|---|---|---|---|---|---|
| 1994 | — | — | — | — | 6.00 | — |

**CROWN** **KM# 291a** **Weight:** 28.2800 g. **Composition:** 0.9250 Silver .8411 oz. ASW

| Date | Mintage | F | VF | XF | Unc | BU |
|---|---|---|---|---|---|---|
| 1994 Proof | Est. 30,000 | Value: 20.00 | | | | |

**CROWN** **KM# 292** **Composition:** Copper-Nickel **Reverse:** Sherlock Holmes - The Final Problem

| Date | Mintage | F | VF | XF | Unc | BU |
|---|---|---|---|---|---|---|
| 1994 | — | — | — | — | 6.00 | — |

**CROWN** **KM# 292a** **Weight:** 28.2800 g. **Composition:** 0.9250 Silver .8411 oz. ASW

| Date | Mintage | F | VF | XF | Unc | BU |
|---|---|---|---|---|---|---|
| 1994 Proof | Est. 30,000 | Value: 20.00 | | | | |

**CROWN** **KM# 444** **Composition:** Copper-Nickel **Reverse:** The Tale of Peter Rabbit

| Date | Mintage | F | VF | XF | Unc | BU |
|---|---|---|---|---|---|---|
| 1994 | — | — | — | — | 7.50 | — |

**CROWN** **KM# 444a** **Weight:** 28.2800 g. **Composition:** 0.9250 Silver .8411 oz. ASW

| Date | Mintage | F | VF | XF | Unc | BU |
|---|---|---|---|---|---|---|
| 1994 Proof | Est. 30,000 | Value: 40.00 | | | | |

**CROWN** **KM# 239** **Composition:** Copper-Nickel **Series:** Preserve Planet Earth **Subject:** Sabre Tooth Tiger **Obverse:** Similar to KM#241 **Reverse:** Sabre Tooth Tiger **Note:** Similar to 1/5 Crown, KM#238.

| Date | Mintage | F | VF | XF | Unc | BU |
|---|---|---|---|---|---|---|
| 1994 | — | — | — | — | 7.00 | — |

**CROWN** **KM# 327** **Composition:** Copper-Nickel **Reverse:** Peter Rabbit **Note:** Similar to 1/5 Crown, KM#326.

| Date | Mintage | F | VF | XF | Unc | BU |
|---|---|---|---|---|---|---|
| 1995 | — | — | — | — | 6.50 | — |

**CROWN** **KM# 299** **Composition:** Copper-Nickel **Reverse:** Atlanta Olympics - Long Jumper

| Date | Mintage | F | VF | XF | Unc | BU |
|---|---|---|---|---|---|---|
| 1995 Proof | — | Value: 5.50 | | | | |

**CROWN** **KM# 299a** **Weight:** 28.2800 g. **Composition:** 0.9250 Silver .8411 oz. ASW

| Date | Mintage | F | VF | XF | Unc | BU |
|---|---|---|---|---|---|---|
| 1995 Proof | Est. 30,000 | Value: 30.00 | | | | |

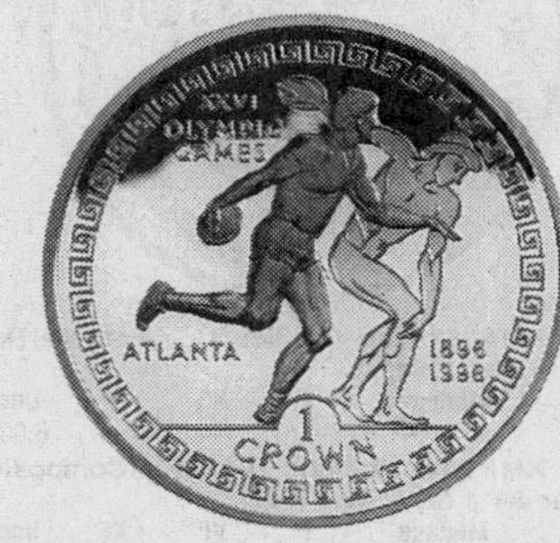


**CROWN** **KM# 300** **Composition:** Copper-Nickel **Reverse:** Atlanta Olympics - Discus Thrower

| Date | Mintage | F | VF | XF | Unc | BU |
|---|---|---|---|---|---|---|
| 1995 | — | — | — | — | 5.50 | — |

**CROWN** **KM# 300a** **Weight:** 28.2800 g. **Composition:** 0.9250 Silver .8411 oz. ASW

| Date | Mintage | F | VF | XF | Unc | BU |
|---|---|---|---|---|---|---|
| 1995 Proof | Est. 30,000 | Value: 30.00 | | | | |

**CROWN** **KM# 301** **Composition:** Copper-Nickel **Reverse:** Atlanta Olympics - Relay Runners

| Date | Mintage | F | VF | XF | Unc | BU |
|---|---|---|---|---|---|---|
| 1995 | — | — | — | — | 5.50 | — |

**CROWN** **KM# 301a** **Weight:** 28.2800 g. **Composition:** 0.9250 Silver .8411 oz. ASW

| Date | Mintage | F | VF | XF | Unc | BU |
|---|---|---|---|---|---|---|
| 1995 Proof | Est. 30,000 | Value: 30.00 | | | | |

**CROWN** **KM# 302** **Composition:** Copper-Nickel **Reverse:** Atlanta Olympics - Javelin Throwers

| Date | Mintage | F | VF | XF | Unc | BU |
|---|---|---|---|---|---|---|
| 1995 | — | — | — | — | 5.50 | — |

**CROWN** **KM# 302a** **Weight:** 28.2800 g. **Composition:** 0.9250 Silver .8411 oz. ASW

| Date | Mintage | F | VF | XF | Unc | BU |
|---|---|---|---|---|---|---|
| 1995 Proof | Est. 30,000 | Value: 30.00 | | | | |

**CROWN** **KM# 304** **Composition:** Copper-Nickel **Reverse:** Sun rising over Rock of Gibraltar

| Date | Mintage | F | VF | XF | Unc | BU |
|---|---|---|---|---|---|---|
| 1995 | — | — | — | — | 6.50 | — |

**CROWN** **KM# 304a** **Weight:** 28.2800 g. **Composition:** 0.9250 Silver .8411 oz. ASW

| Date | Mintage | F | VF | XF | Unc | BU |
|---|---|---|---|---|---|---|
| 1995 Proof | Est. 30,000 | Value: 40.00 | | | | |

**CROWN** **KM# 306** **Composition:** Copper-Nickel **Reverse:** Preserve Planet Earth - Monkeys

| Date | Mintage | F | VF | XF | Unc | BU |
|---|---|---|---|---|---|---|
| 1995 | — | — | — | — | 7.00 | — |

**CROWN** **KM# 306a** **Weight:** 28.2800 g. **Composition:** 0.9250 Silver .8411 oz. ASW

| Date | Mintage | F | VF | XF | Unc | BU |
|---|---|---|---|---|---|---|
| 1995 Proof | Est. 30,000 | Value: 42.50 | | | | |

**CROWN** **KM# 308** **Composition:** Copper-Nickel **Reverse:** Preserve Planet Earth - Sperm Whale

| Date | Mintage | F | VF | XF | Unc | BU |
|---|---|---|---|---|---|---|
| 1995 | — | — | — | — | 8.50 | — |

**CROWN** **KM# 308a** **Weight:** 28.2800 g. **Composition:** 0.9250 Silver .8411 oz. ASW

| Date | Mintage | F | VF | XF | Unc | BU |
|---|---|---|---|---|---|---|
| 1995 Proof | Est. 30,000 | Value: 42.50 | | | | |

**CROWN** **KM# 327a** **Weight:** 28.2800 g. **Composition:** 0.9250 Silver .8411 oz. ASW

| Date | Mintage | F | VF | XF | Unc | BU |
|---|---|---|---|---|---|---|
| 1995 Proof | Est. 30,000 | Value: 37.50 | | | | |

**CROWN** **KM# 329** **Composition:** Copper-Nickel **Reverse:** Island Games - Numerous Athletes

| Date | Mintage | F | VF | XF | Unc | BU |
|---|---|---|---|---|---|---|
| 1995 | — | — | — | — | 6.00 | — |

**CROWN** **KM# 329a** **Weight:** 28.2800 g. **Composition:** 0.9250 Silver .8411 oz. ASW

| Date | Mintage | F | VF | XF | Unc | BU |
|---|---|---|---|---|---|---|
| 1995 Proof | Est. 30,000 | Value: 35.00 | | | | |

**CROWN** **KM# 331** **Composition:** Copper-Nickel **Reverse:** Island Games - High Jumpers

| Date | Mintage | F | VF | XF | Unc | BU |
|---|---|---|---|---|---|---|
| 1995 | — | — | — | — | 6.00 | — |

**CROWN** **KM# 331a** **Weight:** 28.2800 g. **Composition:** 0.9250 Silver .8411 oz. ASW

| Date | Mintage | F | VF | XF | Unc | BU |
|---|---|---|---|---|---|---|
| 1995 Proof | Est. 30,000 | Value: 35.00 | | | | |

**CROWN** **KM# 348** **Composition:** Copper-Nickel **Reverse:** Olympics - Tennis

| Date | Mintage | F | VF | XF | Unc | BU |
|---|---|---|---|---|---|---|
| 1996 | — | — | — | — | 6.00 | — |

**CROWN** **KM# 348a** **Weight:** 28.2800 g. **Composition:** 0.9250 Silver .8411 oz. ASW

| Date | Mintage | F | VF | XF | Unc | BU |
|---|---|---|---|---|---|---|
| 1996 Proof | Est. 30,000 | Value: 42.50 | | | | |

**CROWN** **KM# 349** **Weight:** 28.2800 g. **Composition:** 0.9250 Silver .8411 oz. ASW **Reverse:** Olympics - Wrestlers

| Date | Mintage | F | VF | XF | Unc | BU |
|---|---|---|---|---|---|---|
| 1996 | — | — | — | — | 6.00 | — |

**CROWN** **KM# 349a** **Weight:** 28.2800 g. **Composition:** 0.9250 Silver .8411 oz. ASW

| Date | Mintage | F | VF | XF | Unc | BU |
|---|---|---|---|---|---|---|
| 1996 Proof | Est. 30,000 | Value: 42.50 | | | | |

**CROWN** **KM# 350** **Composition:** Copper-Nickel **Reverse:** Olympics - Baseball

| Date | Mintage | F | VF | XF | Unc | BU |
|---|---|---|---|---|---|---|
| 1996 | — | — | — | — | 6.00 | — |

**CROWN** **KM# 350a** **Weight:** 28.2800 g. **Composition:** 0.9250 Silver .8411 oz. ASW

| Date | Mintage | F | VF | XF | Unc | BU |
|---|---|---|---|---|---|---|
| 1996 Proof | Est. 30,000 | Value: 42.50 | | | | |

**CROWN** **KM# 351** **Composition:** Copper-Nickel **Reverse:** Olympics - Flame

| Date | Mintage | F | VF | XF | Unc | BU |
|---|---|---|---|---|---|---|
| 1996 | — | — | — | — | 6.00 | — |

**CROWN** **KM# 351a** **Weight:** 28.2800 g. **Composition:** 0.9250 Silver .8411 oz. ASW

| Date | Mintage | F | VF | XF | Unc | BU |
|---|---|---|---|---|---|---|
| 1996 Proof | Est. 30,000 | Value: 42.50 | | | | |

**CROWN** **KM# 352** **Composition:** Copper-Nickel **Reverse:** Olympics - Volleyball

| Date | Mintage | F | VF | XF | Unc | BU |
|---|---|---|---|---|---|---|
| 1996 | — | — | — | — | 6.00 | — |

**CROWN** **KM# 352a** **Weight:** 28.2800 g. **Composition:** 0.9250 Silver .8411 oz. ASW

| Date | Mintage | F | VF | XF | Unc | BU |
|---|---|---|---|---|---|---|
| 1996 Proof | Est. 30,000 | Value: 42.50 | | | | |

**CROWN** **KM# 353** **Composition:** Copper-Nickel **Reverse:** Olympics - Basketball

| Date | Mintage | F | VF | XF | Unc | BU |
|---|---|---|---|---|---|---|
| 1996 | — | — | — | — | 6.00 | — |

**CROWN** **KM# 353a** **Weight:** 28.2800 g. **Composition:** 0.9250 Silver .8411 oz. ASW

| Date | Mintage | F | VF | XF | Unc | BU |
|---|---|---|---|---|---|---|
| 1996 Proof | Est. 30,000 | Value: 42.50 | | | | |

**CROWN** **KM# 358** **Composition:** Copper-Nickel **Reverse:** Mefusot Yehuda Synagogue Renovation

| Date | Mintage | F | VF | XF | Unc | BU |
|---|---|---|---|---|---|---|
| 1996 | — | — | — | — | 7.00 | — |

**CROWN** **KM# 358a** **Weight:** 28.2800 g. **Composition:** 0.9250 Silver .8411 oz. ASW

| Date | Mintage | F | VF | XF | Unc | BU |
|---|---|---|---|---|---|---|
| 1996 Proof | Est. 30,000 | Value: 40.00 | | | | |

**CROWN** **KM# 359** **Composition:** Copper-Nickel **Reverse:** Euro Soccer

| Date | Mintage | F | VF | XF | Unc | BU |
|---|---|---|---|---|---|---|
| 1996 | — | — | — | — | 8.00 | — |

**CROWN** **KM# 373** **Composition:** Copper-Nickel **Reverse:** Roses

| Date | Mintage | F | VF | XF | Unc | BU |
|---|---|---|---|---|---|---|
| 1996 | — | — | — | — | 8.00 | — |

**CROWN** **KM# 373a** **Weight:** 28.2800 g. **Composition:** 0.9250 Silver .8411 oz. ASW

| Date | Mintage | F | VF | XF | Unc | BU |
|---|---|---|---|---|---|---|
| 1996 Proof | Est. 30,000 | Value: 40.00 | | | | |

**CROWN** **KM# 382** **Composition:** Copper-Nickel **Reverse:** Peter Rabbit Centennial - Rabbit Escaping

| Date | Mintage | F | VF | XF | Unc | BU |
|---|---|---|---|---|---|---|
| 1996 | — | — | — | — | 6.50 | — |

**CROWN** **KM# 382a** **Weight:** 28.2800 g. **Composition:** 0.9250 Silver .8411 oz. ASW

| Date | Mintage | F | VF | XF | Unc | BU |
|---|---|---|---|---|---|---|
| 1996 Proof | Est. 30,000 | Value: 40.00 | | | | |

**CROWN** **KM# 386** **Composition:** Copper-Nickel **Reverse:** Preserve Planet Earth - Shag Birds

| Date | Mintage | F | VF | XF | Unc | BU |
|---|---|---|---|---|---|---|
| 1996 | — | — | — | — | 8.50 | — |

**CROWN** **KM# 386a** **Weight:** 28.2800 g. **Composition:** 0.9250 Silver .8411 oz. ASW

| Date | Mintage | F | VF | XF | Unc | BU |
|---|---|---|---|---|---|---|
| 1996 Proof | Est. 30,000 | Value: 40.00 | | | | |

**CROWN** **KM# 387** **Composition:** Copper-Nickel **Reverse:** Preserve Planet Earth - Atlantic Puffins

| Date | Mintage | F | VF | XF | Unc | BU |
|---|---|---|---|---|---|---|
| 1996 | — | — | — | — | 8.50 | — |

**CROWN** **KM# 387a** **Weight:** 28.2800 g. **Composition:** 0.9250 Silver .8411 oz. ASW

| Date | Mintage | F | VF | XF | Unc | BU |
|---|---|---|---|---|---|---|
| 1996 Proof | Est. 30,000 | Value: 40.00 | | | | |

**CROWN** **KM# 393** **Composition:** Copper-Nickel **Reverse:** Cinema Centennial - Grace Kelly

| Date | Mintage | F | VF | XF | Unc | BU |
|---|---|---|---|---|---|---|
| 1996 | — | — | — | — | 8.00 | — |

**CROWN** **KM# 393a** **Weight:** 28.2800 g. **Composition:** 0.9250 Silver .8411 oz. ASW

| Date | Mintage | F | VF | XF | Unc | BU |
|---|---|---|---|---|---|---|
| 1996 Proof | Est. 30,000 | Value: 40.00 | | | | |

**CROWN** **KM# 398** **Composition:** Copper-Nickel **Reverse:** Centenary of the Cinema - James Dean

| Date | Mintage | F | VF | XF | Unc | BU |
|---|---|---|---|---|---|---|
| 1996 | — | — | — | — | 8.00 | — |

**CROWN** **KM# 398a** **Weight:** 28.2800 g. **Composition:** 0.9250 Silver .8411 oz. ASW

| Date | Mintage | F | VF | XF | Unc | BU |
|---|---|---|---|---|---|---|
| 1996 Proof | Est. 30,000 | Value: 40.00 | | | | |

**CROWN** **KM# 403** **Composition:** Copper-Nickel **Reverse:** Centenary of the Cinema - Marilyn Monroe

| Date | Mintage | F | VF | XF | Unc | BU |
|---|---|---|---|---|---|---|
| 1996 | — | — | — | — | 8.00 | — |

**CROWN** **KM# 403a** **Weight:** 28.2800 g. **Composition:** 0.9250 Silver .8411 oz. ASW

| Date | Mintage | F | VF | XF | Unc | BU |
|---|---|---|---|---|---|---|
| 1996 | — | — | — | — | 40.00 | — |

**CROWN** **KM# 408** **Composition:** Copper-Nickel **Reverse:** Centenary of the Cinema - Audrey Hepburn

| Date | Mintage | F | VF | XF | Unc | BU |
|---|---|---|---|---|---|---|
| 1996 | — | — | — | — | 8.00 | — |

**CROWN** **KM# 408a** **Weight:** 28.2800 g. **Composition:** 0.9250 Silver .8411 oz. ASW

| Date | Mintage | F | VF | XF | Unc | BU |
|---|---|---|---|---|---|---|
| 1996 Proof | Est. 30,000 | Value: 40.00 | | | | |

**CROWN** **KM# 413** **Composition:** Copper-Nickel **Reverse:** Centenary of the Cinema - Bruce Lee

| Date | Mintage | F | VF | XF | Unc | BU |
|---|---|---|---|---|---|---|
| 1996 | — | — | — | — | 8.00 | — |

**CROWN** **KM# 413a** **Weight:** 28.2800 g. **Composition:** 0.9250 Silver .8411 oz. ASW

| Date | Mintage | F | VF | XF | Unc | BU |
|---|---|---|---|---|---|---|
| 1996 Proof | Est. 30,000 | Value: 40.00 | | | | |

**CROWN** **KM# 418** **Composition:** Copper-Nickel **Reverse:** Centenary of the Cinema - Charlie Chaplin

| Date | Mintage | F | VF | XF | Unc | BU |
|---|---|---|---|---|---|---|
| 1996 | — | — | — | — | 8.00 | — |

**CROWN** **KM# 418a** **Weight:** 28.2800 g. **Composition:** 0.9250 Silver .8411 oz. ASW

| Date | Mintage | F | VF | XF | Unc | BU |
|---|---|---|---|---|---|---|
| 1996 Proof | Est. 30,000 | Value: 40.00 | | | | |

**CROWN** **KM# 423** **Composition:** Copper-Nickel **Reverse:** Centenary of the Cinema - Gone WIth The Wind

| Date | Mintage | F | VF | XF | Unc | BU |
|---|---|---|---|---|---|---|
| 1996 | — | — | — | — | 8.00 | — |

**CROWN** **KM# 423a** **Weight:** 28.2800 g. **Composition:** 0.9250 Silver .8411 oz. ASW

| Date | Mintage | F | VF | XF | Unc | BU |
|---|---|---|---|---|---|---|
| 1996 Proof | Est. 30,000 | Value: 40.00 | | | | |

**CROWN** **KM# 428** **Composition:** Copper-Nickel **Reverse:** Centenary of the Cinema - The Flintstones

| Date | Mintage | F | VF | XF | Unc | BU |
|---|---|---|---|---|---|---|
| 1996 | — | — | — | — | 8.00 | — |

**CROWN** **KM# 428a** **Weight:** 28.2800 g. **Composition:** 0.9250 Silver .8411 oz. ASW

| Date | Mintage | F | VF | XF | Unc | BU |
|---|---|---|---|---|---|---|
| 1996 Proof | Est. 30,000 | Value: 40.00 | | | | |

**CROWN** **KM# 430** **Weight:** 28.2800 g. **Composition:** 0.9250 Silver .8411 oz. ASW **Reverse:** European Football Championship - Goliath

| Date | Mintage | F | VF | XF | Unc | BU |
|---|---|---|---|---|---|---|
| 1996 Proof | Est. 10,000 | Value: 32.50 | | | | |

**CROWN** **KM# 432** **Composition:** Copper-Nickel **Reverse:** Duke of Edinburgh Awards Scheme - 7 Scenes

| Date | Mintage | F | VF | XF | Unc | BU |
|---|---|---|---|---|---|---|
| 1996 | — | — | — | — | 8.00 | — |

**CROWN** **KM# 432a** **Weight:** 28.2800 g. **Composition:** 0.9250 Silver .8411 oz. ASW

| Date | Mintage | F | VF | XF | Unc | BU |
|---|---|---|---|---|---|---|
| 1996 Proof | Est. 30,000 | Value: 40.00 | | | | |

**CROWN** **KM# 435** **Composition:** Copper-Nickel **Reverse:** Duke of Edinburgh Awards Scheme - Cameo/Horses

| Date | Mintage | F | VF | XF | Unc | BU |
|---|---|---|---|---|---|---|
| 1996 | — | — | — | — | 8.00 | — |

**CROWN** **KM# 435a** **Weight:** 28.2800 g. **Composition:** 0.9250 Silver .8411 oz. ASW

| Date | Mintage | F | VF | XF | Unc | BU |
|---|---|---|---|---|---|---|
| 1996 Proof | Est. 30,000 | Value: 40.00 | | | | |

**CROWN** **KM# 449** **Composition:** Copper-Nickel **Reverse:** Lord Buddha

| Date | Mintage | F | VF | XF | Unc | BU |
|---|---|---|---|---|---|---|
| 1996 | — | — | — | — | 7.50 | — |

**CROWN** **KM# 449a** **Weight:** 28.2800 g. **Composition:** 0.9250 Silver .8411 oz. ASW

| Date | Mintage | F | VF | XF | Unc | BU |
|---|---|---|---|---|---|---|
| 1996 Proof | Est. 15,000 | Value: 27.50 | | | | |

**CROWN** **KM# 457** **Composition:** Copper-Nickel **Reverse:** Centenary of the Cinema - Wizard of Oz

| Date | Mintage | F | VF | XF | Unc | BU |
|---|---|---|---|---|---|---|
| 1996 | — | — | — | — | 7.75 | — |

**CROWN** **KM# 457a** **Weight:** 28.2800 g. **Composition:** 0.9250 Silver .8411 oz. ASW

| Date | Mintage | F | VF | XF | Unc | BU |
|---|---|---|---|---|---|---|
| 1996 Proof | Est. 30,000 | Value: 40.00 | | | | |

**CROWN** **KM# 461** **Composition:** Copper-Nickel **Reverse:** Centenary of the Cinema - Marx Brothers

| Date | Mintage | F | VF | XF | Unc | BU |
|---|---|---|---|---|---|---|
| 1996 | — | — | — | — | 7.75 | — |

**CROWN** **KM# 461a** **Weight:** 28.2800 g. **Composition:** 0.9250 Silver .8411 oz. ASW

| Date | Mintage | F | VF | XF | Unc | BU |
|---|---|---|---|---|---|---|
| 1996 Proof | Est. 30,000 | Value: 40.00 | | | | |

**CROWN** **KM# 465** **Composition:** Copper-Nickel **Reverse:** Centenary of the Cinema - Elvis Presley

| Date | Mintage | F | VF | XF | Unc | BU |
|---|---|---|---|---|---|---|
| 1996 | — | — | — | — | 7.75 | — |

**CROWN** **KM# 465a** **Weight:** 28.0000 g. **Composition:** 0.9250 Silver .8411 oz. ASW

| Date | Mintage | F | VF | XF | Unc | BU |
|---|---|---|---|---|---|---|
| 1996 Proof | Est. 30,000 | Value: 40.00 | | | | |

**CROWN** **KM# 469** **Composition:** Copper-Nickel **Reverse:** Centenary of the Cinema - Casablanca

| Date | Mintage | F | VF | XF | Unc | BU |
|---|---|---|---|---|---|---|
| 1996 | — | — | — | — | 7.75 | — |

**CROWN** **KM# 469a** **Weight:** 28.0000 g. **Composition:** 0.9250 Silver .8411 oz. ASW

| Date | Mintage | F | VF | XF | Unc | BU |
|---|---|---|---|---|---|---|
| 1996 Proof | Est. 30,000 | Value: 40.00 | | | | |

**CROWN** **KM# 473** **Composition:** Copper-Nickel **Reverse:** Centenary of the Cinema - E.T.

| Date | Mintage | F | VF | XF | Unc | BU |
|---|---|---|---|---|---|---|
| 1996 | — | — | — | — | 7.75 | — |

**CROWN** **KM# 473a** **Weight:** 28.0000 g. **Composition:** 0.9250 Silver .8411 oz. ASW

| Date | Mintage | F | VF | XF | Unc | BU |
|---|---|---|---|---|---|---|
| 1996 Proof | Est. 30,000 | Value: 40.00 | | | | |

**CROWN** **KM# 477** **Composition:** Copper-Nickel **Reverse:** Centenary of the Cinema - Alfred Hitchcock

| Date | Mintage | F | VF | XF | Unc | BU |
|---|---|---|---|---|---|---|
| 1996 | — | — | — | — | 7.75 | — |

**CROWN** **KM# 477a** **Weight:** 28.0000 g. **Composition:** 0.9250 Silver .8411 oz. ASW

| Date | Mintage | F | VF | XF | Unc | BU |
|---|---|---|---|---|---|---|
| 1996 Proof | Est. 30,000 | Value: 40.00 | | | | |

**CROWN** **KM# 359a** **Weight:** 28.2800 g. **Composition:** 0.9250 Silver .8411 oz. ASW **Note:** For KM#365-365b previously listed here, see Royal Series, KM#365-365b.

| Date | Mintage | F | VF | XF | Unc | BU |
|---|---|---|---|---|---|---|
| 1996 Proof | Est. 30,000 | Value: 45.00 | | | | |

**CROWN** **KM# 561** **Composition:** Copper-Nickel **Subject:** Yorkshire Terrier **Note:** Similar to 1 Royal, KM#561a.

| Date | Mintage | F | VF | XF | Unc | BU |
|---|---|---|---|---|---|---|
| 1997 | — | — | — | — | 9.00 | — |

**CROWN** **KM# 514** **Composition:** Copper-Nickel **Reverse:** Peacock

| Date | Mintage | F | VF | XF | Unc | BU |
|---|---|---|---|---|---|---|
| 1997 | — | — | — | — | 8.00 | — |

**CROWN** **KM# 514a** **Weight:** 28.2800 g. **Composition:** 0.9250 Silver .8411 oz. ASW

| Date | Mintage | F | VF | XF | Unc | BU |
|---|---|---|---|---|---|---|
| 1997 | Est. 30,000 | Value: 40.00 | | | | |

**CROWN** **KM# 525** **Composition:** Copper-Nickel **Reverse:** Tale of Peter Rabbit - Peter Rabbit standing

| Date | Mintage | F | VF | XF | Unc | BU |
|---|---|---|---|---|---|---|
| 1997 | — | — | — | — | 8.50 | — |

**CROWN** **KM# 526** **Weight:** 28.2800 g. **Composition:** 0.9250 Silver .8411 oz. ASW

| Date | Mintage | F | VF | XF | Unc | BU |
|---|---|---|---|---|---|---|
| 1997 Proof | Est. 30,000 | Value: 40.00 | | | | |

**CROWN** **KM# 530** **Composition:** Copper-Nickel **Subject:** Queen Elizabeth and Prince Phillip **Obverse:** Queen's portrait **Reverse:** Engagement portrait of Queen and Prince

| Date | Mintage | F | VF | XF | Unc | BU |
|---|---|---|---|---|---|---|
| 1997 | — | — | — | — | 7.50 | — |

**CROWN** **KM# 530a** **Weight:** 28.2800 g. **Composition:** 0.9250 Gold Clad Silver .8411 oz.

| Date | Mintage | F | VF | XF | Unc | BU |
|---|---|---|---|---|---|---|
| 1997 Proof | Est. 10,000 | Value: 45.00 | | | | |

**CROWN** **KM# 532** **Composition:** Copper-Nickel **Subject:** Golden Wedding Anniversary - Queen Elizabeth and Prince Philip **Obverse:** Queen's portrait **Reverse:** The Queen with her first born, Prince Charles

| Date | Mintage | F | VF | XF | Unc | BU |
|---|---|---|---|---|---|---|
| 1997 | — | — | — | — | 7.50 | — |

**CROWN** **KM# 532a** **Weight:** 28.2800 g. **Composition:** 0.9250 Gold Clad Silver .8411 oz.

| Date | Mintage | F | VF | XF | Unc | BU |
|---|---|---|---|---|---|---|
| 1997 Proof | Est. 10,000 | Value: 45.00 | | | | |

**CROWN** **KM# 534** **Composition:** Copper-Nickel **Subject:** Golden Wedding Anniversary - Queen Elizabeth and Prince Philip **Obverse:** Queen's portrait **Reverse:** The Queen, two children and a monkey

| Date | Mintage | F | VF | XF | Unc | BU |
|---|---|---|---|---|---|---|
| 1997 | — | — | — | — | 7.50 | — |

**CROWN** **KM# 534a** **Weight:** 28.2800 g. **Composition:** 0.9250 Gold Clad Silver .8411 oz.

| Date | Mintage | F | VF | XF | Unc | BU |
|---|---|---|---|---|---|---|
| 1997 Proof | Est. 10,000 | Value: 45.00 | | | | |

**CROWN** **KM# 536** **Composition:** Copper-Nickel **Subject:** Golden Wedding Anniversary - Queen Elizabeth and Prince Philip **Obverse:** Queen's portrait **Reverse:** The Queen and adoring crowd

| Date | Mintage | F | VF | XF | Unc | BU |
|---|---|---|---|---|---|---|
| 1997 | — | — | — | — | 7.50 | — |

**CROWN** **KM# 536a** **Weight:** 28.2800 g. **Composition:** 0.9250 Gold Clad Silver .8411 oz.

| Date | Mintage | F | VF | XF | Unc | BU |
|---|---|---|---|---|---|---|
| 1997 Proof | Est. 10,000 | Value: 45.00 | | | | |

**CROWN** **KM# 540** **Composition:** Copper-Nickel **Subject:** Peonies **Obverse:** Queen's portrait **Reverse:** Peony flowers

| Date | Mintage | F | VF | XF | Unc | BU |
|---|---|---|---|---|---|---|
| 1997 | — | — | — | — | 8.00 | — |

**CROWN** **KM# 540a** **Weight:** 28.2800 g. **Composition:** 0.9250 Silver .8411 oz. ASW

| Date | Mintage | F | VF | XF | Unc | BU |
|---|---|---|---|---|---|---|
| 1997 Proof | Est. 30,000 | Value: 40.00 | | | | |

**CROWN** **KM# 544** **Weight:** 28.2800 g. **Composition:** 0.9250 Silver .8411 oz. ASW **Subject:** Nefertiti **Obverse:** Queen's portrait **Reverse:** Head of Nefertiti right

| Date | Mintage | F | VF | XF | Unc | BU |
|---|---|---|---|---|---|---|
| 1997 Proof | Est. 10,000 | Value: 40.00 | | | | |

**CROWN** **KM# 548** **Weight:** 28.2800 g. **Composition:** 0.9250 Silver .8411 oz. ASW **Subject:** Cleopatra **Obverse:** Queen's portrait **Reverse:** Facing head of Cleopatra

| Date | Mintage | F | VF | XF | Unc | BU |
|---|---|---|---|---|---|---|
| 1997 Proof | Est. 10,000 | Value: 40.00 | | | | |

**CROWN** **KM# 552** **Weight:** 28.2800 g. **Composition:** 0.9250 Silver .8411 oz. ASW **Subject:** Europa **Obverse:** Queen's portrait **Reverse:** Europa portrait

| Date | Mintage | F | VF | XF | Unc | BU |
|---|---|---|---|---|---|---|
| 1997 Proof | Est. 10,000 | Value: 40.00 | | | | |

**CROWN** **KM# 556** **Weight:** 28.2800 g. **Composition:** 0.9250 Silver .8411 oz. ASW **Subject:** Liberty U.S.A. **Obverse:** Queen's portrait **Reverse:** Head of Liberty, right

| Date | Mintage | F | VF | XF | Unc | BU |
|---|---|---|---|---|---|---|
| 1997 Proof | Est. 10,000 | Value: 40.00 | | | | |

**CROWN** **KM# 566** **Composition:** Copper-Nickel **Series:** Queen's Birthday **Obverse:** Queen's portrait **Reverse:** Queen on horse, Gibraltar in background

| Date | Mintage | F | VF | XF | Unc | BU |
|---|---|---|---|---|---|---|
| 1997 | — | — | — | — | 8.50 | — |

**CROWN** **KM# 566a** **Weight:** 28.2800 g. **Composition:** 0.9250 Silver .8411 oz. ASW

| Date | Mintage | F | VF | XF | Unc | BU |
|---|---|---|---|---|---|---|
| 1997 Proof | Est. 30,000 | Value: 40.00 | | | | |

**CROWN** **KM# 567** **Composition:** Copper-Nickel **Series:** Queen's Birthday **Obverse:** Queen's portrait **Reverse:** Queen on horseback returning salute

| Date | Mintage | F | VF | XF | Unc | BU |
|---|---|---|---|---|---|---|
| 1997 | — | — | — | — | 8.50 | — |

**CROWN** **KM# 567a** **Weight:** 28.2800 g. **Composition:** 0.9250 Silver .8411 oz. ASW

| Date | Mintage | F | VF | XF | Unc | BU |
|---|---|---|---|---|---|---|
| 1997 Proof | Est. 30,000 | Value: 40.00 | | | | |

**CROWN** **KM# 568** **Composition:** Copper-Nickel **Series:** Queen's Birthday **Obverse:** Queen's portrait **Reverse:** Trooping the Clors scene, portrait of Queen

| Date | Mintage | F | VF | XF | Unc | BU |
|---|---|---|---|---|---|---|
| 1997 | — | — | — | — | 8.50 | — |

**CROWN** **KM# 568a** **Weight:** 28.2800 g. **Composition:** 0.9250 Silver .8411 oz. ASW

| Date | Mintage | F | VF | XF | Unc | BU |
|---|---|---|---|---|---|---|
| 1997 Proof | Est. 30,000 | Value: 40.00 | | | | |

**CROWN** **KM# 569** **Composition:** Copper-Nickel **Series:** Queen's Birthday **Obverse:** Queen's portrait **Reverse:** Gurkha troops with dragons

| Date | Mintage | F | VF | XF | Unc | BU |
|---|---|---|---|---|---|---|
| 1997 | — | — | — | — | 8.50 | — |

**CROWN** **KM# 569a** **Weight:** 28.2800 g. **Composition:** 0.9250 Silver .8411 oz. ASW

| Date | Mintage | F | VF | XF | Unc | BU |
|---|---|---|---|---|---|---|
| 1997 | — | — | — | — | 40.00 | — |

**CROWN** **KM# 571** **Composition:** Copper-Nickel **Subject:** The New Mosque **Obverse:** Queen's portrait **Reverse:** Two Moorish calvary riders with mosque in background

| Date | Mintage | F | VF | XF | Unc | BU |
|---|---|---|---|---|---|---|
| 1997 | — | — | — | — | 8.00 | — |

**CROWN** **KM# 571a** **Weight:** 28.2800 g. **Composition:** 0.9250 Silver .8411 oz. ASW

| Date | Mintage | F | VF | XF | Unc | BU |
|---|---|---|---|---|---|---|
| 1997 Proof | Est. 30,000 | Value: 40.00 | | | | |

**CROWN** **KM# 573** **Weight:** 28.2800 g. **Composition:** 0.9250 Silver .8411 oz. ASW **Series:** Wonders of the World **Subject:** Mausoleum at Halicarnassus **Obverse:** Queen's portrait **Reverse:** Gold coin design inset on mausoleum

| Date | Mintage | F | VF | XF | Unc | BU |
|---|---|---|---|---|---|---|
| 1997 Proof | Est. 7,500 | Value: 50.00 | | | | |

**CROWN** **KM# 574** **Weight:** 28.2800 g. **Composition:** 0.9250 Silver .8411 oz. ASW **Series:** Wonders of the World **Subject:** Statue of Zeus at Olympia **Obverse:** Queen's portrait **Reverse:** Gold coin design inset on statue of Zeus

| Date | Mintage | F | VF | XF | Unc | BU |
|---|---|---|---|---|---|---|
| 1997 Proof | Est. 7,500 | Value: 50.00 | | | | |

**CROWN** **KM# 575** **Weight:** 28.2800 g. **Composition:** 0.9250 Silver .8411 oz. ASW **Series:** Wonders of the World **Subject:** The Pharos of Alexandria **Obverse:** Queen's portrait **Reverse:** Gold coin design inset on lighthouse

| Date | Mintage | F | VF | XF | Unc | BU |
|---|---|---|---|---|---|---|
| 1997 Proof | Est. 7,500 | Value: 50.00 | | | | |

**CROWN** **KM# 576** **Weight:** 28.2800 g. **Composition:** 0.9250 Silver .8411 oz. ASW **Series:** Wonders of the World **Subject:** The Pillars of Hercules **Obverse:** Queen's portrait **Reverse:** Gold coin design inset on the Rock of Gibraltar

| Date | Mintage | F | VF | XF | Unc | BU |
|---|---|---|---|---|---|---|
| 1997 Proof | Est. 7,500 | Value: 50.00 | | | | |

**CROWN** **KM# 577** **Weight:** 28.2800 g. **Composition:** 0.9250 Silver .8411 oz. ASW **Series:** Wonders of the World **Subject:** The Colossus of Rhodes **Obverse:** Queen's portrait **Reverse:** Gold coin design inset on large statue

| Date | Mintage | F | VF | XF | Unc | BU |
|---|---|---|---|---|---|---|
| 1997 Proof | Est. 7,500 | Value: 50.00 | | | | |

**CROWN** **KM# 578** **Weight:** 28.2800 g. **Composition:** 0.9250 Silver .8411 oz. ASW **Series:** Wonders of the World **Subject:** The Pyramids of Egypt **Obverse:** Queen's portrait **Reverse:** Gold coin design inset on pyramids

| Date | Mintage | F | VF | XF | Unc | BU |
|---|---|---|---|---|---|---|
| 1997 Proof | Est. 7,500 | Value: 50.00 | | | | |

**CROWN** **KM# 579** **Weight:** 28.2800 g. **Composition:** 0.9250 Silver .8411 oz. ASW **Series:** Wonders of the World **Subject:** The Hanging Gardens of Babylon **Obverse:** Queen's portrait **Reverse:** Gold coin design inset on an overgrown building

| Date | Mintage | F | VF | XF | Unc | BU |
|---|---|---|---|---|---|---|
| 1997 Proof | Est. 7,500 | Value: 50.00 | | | | |

**CROWN** **KM# 580** **Weight:** 28.2800 g. **Composition:** 0.9250 Silver .8411 oz. ASW **Series:** Wonders of the World **Subject:** The Temple of Artemis at Ephesus **Obverse:** Queen's portrait **Reverse:** Gold coin design inset on classic Greek building

| Date | Mintage | F | VF | XF | Unc | BU |
|---|---|---|---|---|---|---|
| 1997 | Est. 7,500 | Value: 50.00 | | | | |

**CROWN** **KM# 582** **Weight:** 28.2800 g. **Composition:** 0.9250 Silver .8411 oz. ASW **Series:** Evolution of Mankind **Subject:** Egypt **Obverse:** Queen's portrait **Reverse:** Three ancient Egyptians, pyramids, hieroglyphics

| Date | Mintage | F | VF | XF | Unc | BU |
|---|---|---|---|---|---|---|
| 1997 Proof | Est. 10,000 | Value: 40.00 | | | | |

**CROWN KM# 584 Weight:** 28.2800 g. **Composition:** 0.9250 Silver .8411 oz. ASW **Series:** Evolution of Mankind **Subject:** Israel **Obverse:** Queen's portrait **Reverse:** Star of David, Moses and Temple of Solomon

| Date | Mintage | F | VF | XF | Unc | BU |
|---|---|---|---|---|---|---|
| 1997 Proof | Est. 10,000 | Value: 40.00 | | | | |

**CROWN KM# 586 Weight:** 28.2800 g. **Composition:** 0.9250 Silver .8411 oz. ASW **Series:** Evolution of Mankind **Subject:** China **Obverse:** Queen's portrait **Reverse:** Emporer and the Great Wall

| Date | Mintage | F | VF | XF | Unc | BU |
|---|---|---|---|---|---|---|
| 1997 Proof | Est. 10,000 | Value: 40.00 | | | | |

**CROWN KM# 588 Weight:** 28.2800 g. **Composition:** 0.9250 Silver .8411 oz. ASW **Series:** Evolution of Mankind **Subject:** Greece **Obverse:** Queen's portrait **Reverse:** Aristotle, classic Greek building

| Date | Mintage | F | VF | XF | Unc | BU |
|---|---|---|---|---|---|---|
| 1997 Proof | Est. 10,000 | Value: 40.00 | | | | |

**CROWN KM# 590 Weight:** 28.2800 g. **Composition:** 0.9250 Silver .8411 oz. ASW **Series:** Evolution of Mankind **Subject:** Rome **Obverse:** Queen's portrait **Reverse:** Julius Caesar and Stonehenge

| Date | Mintage | F | VF | XF | Unc | BU |
|---|---|---|---|---|---|---|
| 1997 Proof | Est. 10,000 | Value: 40.00 | | | | |

**CROWN KM# 592 Weight:** 28.2800 g. **Composition:** 0.9250 Silver .8411 oz. ASW **Series:** Evolution of Mankind **Subject:** India **Obverse:** Queen's portrait **Reverse:** Krishna playing flute by a temple

| Date | Mintage | F | VF | XF | Unc | BU |
|---|---|---|---|---|---|---|
| 1997 Proof | Est. 10,000 | Value: 40.00 | | | | |

**CROWN KM# 594 Weight:** 28.2800 g. **Composition:** 0.9250 Silver .8411 oz. ASW **Series:** Evolution of Mankind **Subject:** Holy Roman Empire **Obverse:** Queen's portrait **Reverse:** Charlemagne and soldiers on horseback

| Date | Mintage | F | VF | XF | Unc | BU |
|---|---|---|---|---|---|---|
| 1997 Proof | Est. 10,000 | Value: 40.00 | | | | |

**CROWN KM# 596 Weight:** 28.2800 g. **Composition:** 0.9250 Silver .8411 oz. ASW **Series:** Evolution of Mankind **Subject:** Macedonia **Obverse:** Queen's portrait **Reverse:** Alexander the Great on horseback

| Date | Mintage | F | VF | XF | Unc | BU |
|---|---|---|---|---|---|---|
| 1997 Proof | Est. 10,000 | Value: 40.00 | | | | |

**CROWN KM# 598 Weight:** 28.2800 g. **Composition:** 0.9250 Silver .8411 oz. ASW **Series:** Evolution of Mankind **Subject:** Native America **Obverse:** Queen's portrait **Reverse:** North American native on horseback and totem pole

| Date | Mintage | F | VF | XF | Unc | BU |
|---|---|---|---|---|---|---|
| 1997 Proof | Est. 10,000 | Value: 40.00 | | | | |

**CROWN KM# 600 Weight:** 28.2800 g. **Composition:** 0.9250 Silver .8411 oz. ASW **Series:** Evolution of Mankind **Subject:** Asia **Obverse:** Queen's portrait **Reverse:** Buddha and temple

| Date | Mintage | F | VF | XF | Unc | BU |
|---|---|---|---|---|---|---|
| 1997 Proof | Est. 10,000 | Value: 40.00 | | | | |

**CROWN KM# 602 Weight:** 28.2800 g. **Composition:** 0.9250 Silver .8411 oz. ASW **Series:** Evolution of Mankind **Subject:** Inca Empire **Obverse:** Queen's portrait **Reverse:** Incan Emporer and Machu Picchu

| Date | Mintage | F | VF | XF | Unc | BU |
|---|---|---|---|---|---|---|
| 1997 Proof | Est. 10,000 | Value: 40.00 | | | | |

**CROWN KM# 604 Weight:** 28.2800 g. **Composition:** 0.9250 Silver .8411 oz. ASW **Series:** Evolution of Mankind **Subject:** Islamic Civilization **Obverse:** Queen's portrait **Reverse:** General Tariq Ibn Ziyad and building

| Date | Mintage | F | VF | XF | Unc | BU |
|---|---|---|---|---|---|---|
| 1997 Proof | Est. 10,000 | Value: 40.00 | | | | |

**CROWN KM# 609 Weight:** 28.2800 g. **Composition:** 0.9250 Silver .8410 oz. ASW **Series:** Traders of the World **Subject:** Sir Francis Drake **Obverse:** Queen's portrait **Reverse:** Sir Francis Drake, ship and beach

| Date | Mintage | F | VF | XF | Unc | BU |
|---|---|---|---|---|---|---|
| 1997 Proof | Est. 10,000 | Value: 45.00 | | | | |

**CROWN** **KM# 611** **Weight:** 28.2800 g. **Composition:** 0.9250 Silver .8410 oz. ASW **Series:** Traders of the World **Subject:** Romans **Obverse:** Queen's portrait **Reverse:** Lion, lioness, ship, map

| Date | Mintage | F | VF | XF | Unc | BU |
|---|---|---|---|---|---|---|
| 1997 Proof | Est. 10,000 | Value: 45.00 | | | | |

**CROWN** **KM# 613** **Weight:** 28.2800 g. **Composition:** 0.9250 Silver .8410 oz. ASW **Series:** Traders of the World **Subject:** Venetians **Obverse:** Queen's portrait **Reverse:** Pair of oysters with pearls, Venetian canal scene

| Date | Mintage | F | VF | XF | Unc | BU |
|---|---|---|---|---|---|---|
| 1997 Proof | Est. 10,000 | Value: 45.00 | | | | |

**CROWN** **KM# 615** **Weight:** 28.2800 g. **Composition:** 0.9250 Silver .8410 oz. ASW **Series:** Traders of the World **Subject:** Portuguese **Obverse:** Queen's portrait **Reverse:** Gold ingots and Portuguese ship

| Date | Mintage | F | VF | XF | Unc | BU |
|---|---|---|---|---|---|---|
| 1997 Proof | Est. 10,000 | Value: 45.00 | | | | |

**CROWN** **KM# 617** **Weight:** 28.2800 g. **Composition:** 0.9250 Silver .8410 oz. ASW **Series:** Traders of the World **Subject:** Spanish **Obverse:** Queen's portrait **Reverse:** Tobacco leaves, ship, map, gems

| Date | Mintage | F | VF | XF | Unc | BU |
|---|---|---|---|---|---|---|
| 1997 Proof | Est. 10,000 | Value: 45.00 | | | | |

**CROWN** **KM# 619** **Weight:** 28.2800 g. **Composition:** 0.9250 Silver .8410 oz. ASW **Series:** Traders of the World **Subject:** English **Obverse:** Queen's portrait **Reverse:** Profile of Queen Elizabeth I above fighting ships

| Date | Mintage | F | VF | XF | Unc | BU |
|---|---|---|---|---|---|---|
| 1997 Proof | Est. 10,000 | Value: 45.00 | | | | |

**CROWN** **KM# 621** **Weight:** 28.2800 g. **Composition:** 0.9250 Silver .8410 oz. ASW **Series:** Traders of the World **Subject:** Captain Bligh **Obverse:** Queen's portrait **Reverse:** Captain Bligh on beach, ship

| Date | Mintage | F | VF | XF | Unc | BU |
|---|---|---|---|---|---|---|
| 1997 Proof | Est. 10,000 | Value: 45.00 | | | | |

**CROWN** **KM# 623** **Weight:** 28.2800 g. **Composition:** 0.9250 Silver .8410 oz. ASW **Series:** Traders of the World **Subject:** Captain Cook **Obverse:** Queen's portrait **Reverse:** Beaver on rock, ship, Captain Cook

| Date | Mintage | F | VF | XF | Unc | BU |
|---|---|---|---|---|---|---|
| 1997 Proof | Est. 10,000 | Value: 45.00 | | | | |

**CROWN** **KM# 636** **Composition:** Copper-Nickel **Subject:** Winter Olympics Japan **Obverse:** Queen's portrait **Reverse:** Speed skater and Bullet Train

| Date | Mintage | F | VF | XF | Unc | BU |
|---|---|---|---|---|---|---|
| 1998 | — | — | — | — | 8.00 | — |

**CROWN** **KM# 636a** **Weight:** 28.2800 g. **Composition:** 0.9250 Silver .8410 oz. ASW

| Date | Mintage | F | VF | XF | Unc | BU |
|---|---|---|---|---|---|---|
| 1998 Proof | Est. 30,000 | Value: 45.00 | | | | |

**CROWN** **KM# 638** **Composition:** Copper-Nickel **Subject:** Winter Olympics Japan **Obverse:** Queen's portrait **Reverse:** Ski jumper and Buddha

| Date | Mintage | F | VF | XF | Unc | BU |
|---|---|---|---|---|---|---|
| 1998 | — | — | — | — | 8.00 | — |

**CROWN** **KM# 638a** **Weight:** 28.2800 g. **Composition:** 0.9250 Silver .8410 oz. ASW

| Date | Mintage | F | VF | XF | Unc | BU |
|---|---|---|---|---|---|---|
| 1998 Proof | Est. 30,000 | Value: 45.00 | | | | |

**CROWN** **KM# 640** **Composition:** Copper-Nickel **Subject:** Winter Olympics Japan **Obverse:** Queen's portrait **Reverse:** Cross country skiers

| Date | Mintage | F | VF | XF | Unc | BU |
|---|---|---|---|---|---|---|
| 1998 | — | — | — | — | 8.00 | — |

**CROWN** **KM# 640a** **Weight:** 28.2800 g. **Composition:** 0.9250 Silver .8410 oz. ASW

| Date | Mintage | F | VF | XF | Unc | BU |
|---|---|---|---|---|---|---|
| 1998 Proof | Est. 30,000 | Value: 45.00 | | | | |

**CROWN** **KM# 642** **Composition:** Copper-Nickel **Subject:** Winter Olympics Japan **Obverse:** Queen's portrait **Reverse:** Slalom skier, Zenkoji temple

| Date | Mintage | F | VF | XF | Unc | BU |
|---|---|---|---|---|---|---|
| 1998 | — | — | — | — | 8.00 | — |

**CROWN** **KM# 642a** **Weight:** 28.2800 g. **Composition:** 0.9250 Silver .8410 oz. ASW

| Date | Mintage | F | VF | XF | Unc | BU |
|---|---|---|---|---|---|---|
| 1998 Proof | Est. 30,000 | Value: 45.00 | | | | |

**CROWN** **KM# 656** **Composition:** Copper-Nickel **Subject:** The Tale of Peter Rabbit **Obverse:** Queen's portrait **Reverse:** Peter Rabbit

| Date | Mintage | F | VF | XF | Unc | BU |
|---|---|---|---|---|---|---|
| 1998 | — | — | — | — | 8.00 | — |

**CROWN** **KM# 656a** **Weight:** 28.2800 g. **Composition:** 0.9250 Silver .8411 oz. ASW

| Date | Mintage | F | VF | XF | Unc | BU |
|---|---|---|---|---|---|---|
| 1998 Proof | Est. 30,000 | Value: 50.00 | | | | |

**CROWN** KM# 661 **Composition:** Copper-Nickel **Subject:** Chrysanthemum **Obverse:** Queen's portrait **Reverse:** Three blossoms

| Date | Mintage | F | VF | XF | Unc | BU |
|---|---|---|---|---|---|---|
| 1998 | — | — | — | — | 10.00 | — |

**CROWN** KM# 661a **Weight:** 28.2800 g. **Composition:** 0.9250 Silver .8411 oz. ASW

| Date | Mintage | F | VF | XF | Unc | BU |
|---|---|---|---|---|---|---|
| 1998 Proof | Est. 30,000 | Value: 50.00 | | | | |

**CROWN** KM# 674 **Weight:** 28.2800 g. **Composition:** 0.9250 Silver .8411 oz. ASW **Subject:** Brittania **Obverse:** Queen's portrait **Reverse:** Helmeted portrait of Brittania

| Date | Mintage | F | VF | XF | Unc | BU |
|---|---|---|---|---|---|---|
| 1998 Proof | Est. 10,000 | Value: 50.00 | | | | |

**CROWN** KM# 675 **Weight:** 28.2800 g. **Composition:** 0.9250 Silver .8411 oz. ASW **Subject:** Juno **Obverse:** Queen's portrait **Reverse:** Frontal portrait of Juno

| Date | Mintage | F | VF | XF | Unc | BU |
|---|---|---|---|---|---|---|
| 1998 Proof | Est. 10,000 | Value: 50.00 | | | | |

**CROWN** KM# 676 **Weight:** 28.2800 g. **Composition:** 0.9250 Silver .8411 oz. ASW **Subject:** Athena **Obverse:** Queen's portrait **Reverse:** Helmeted portrait of Athena

| Date | Mintage | F | VF | XF | Unc | BU |
|---|---|---|---|---|---|---|
| 1998 Proof | Est. 10,000 | Value: 50.00 | | | | |

**CROWN** KM# 677 **Weight:** 28.2800 g. **Composition:** 0.9250 Silver .8411 oz. ASW **Subject:** Arethusa **Obverse:** Queen's portrait **Reverse:** Portrait of Arethusa with dolphins

| Date | Mintage | F | VF | XF | Unc | BU |
|---|---|---|---|---|---|---|
| 1998 Proof | Est. 10,000 | Value: 50.00 | | | | |

**CROWN** KM# 682 **Composition:** Copper-Nickel **Subject:** Paddington Bear **Obverse:** Queen's portrait **Reverse:** Bear with suitcase

| Date | Mintage | F | VF | XF | Unc | BU |
|---|---|---|---|---|---|---|
| 1998 | — | — | — | — | 10.00 | — |

**CROWN** KM# 682a **Weight:** 28.2800 g. **Composition:** 0.9250 Silver .8410 oz. ASW

| Date | Mintage | F | VF | XF | Unc | BU |
|---|---|---|---|---|---|---|
| 1998 Proof | Est. 30,000 | Value: 50.00 | | | | |

**CROWN** KM# 687 **Composition:** Copper-Nickel **Series:** World Cup France 1998 **Obverse:** Queen's portrait **Reverse:** Goalie

| Date | Mintage | F | VF | XF | Unc | BU |
|---|---|---|---|---|---|---|
| 1998 | — | — | — | — | 8.00 | — |

**CROWN** KM# 687a **Weight:** 28.2800 g. **Composition:** 0.9250 Silver .8410 oz. ASW

| Date | Mintage | F | VF | XF | Unc | BU |
|---|---|---|---|---|---|---|
| 1998 Proof | Est. 30,000 | Value: 50.00 | | | | |

**CROWN** KM# 688 **Composition:** Copper-Nickel **Series:** World Cup France 1998 **Obverse:** Queen's portrait **Reverse:** Player kicking to the left

| Date | Mintage | F | VF | XF | Unc | BU |
|---|---|---|---|---|---|---|
| 1998 | — | — | — | — | 8.00 | — |

**CROWN** KM# 688a **Weight:** 28.2800 g. **Composition:** 0.9250 Silver .8410 oz. ASW

| Date | Mintage | F | VF | XF | Unc | BU |
|---|---|---|---|---|---|---|
| 1998 | Est. 30,000 | — | — | — | 50.00 | — |

**CROWN** KM# 689 **Composition:** Copper-Nickel **Series:** World Cup France 1998 **Obverse:** Queen's portrait **Reverse:** Player advancing ball

| Date | Mintage | F | VF | XF | Unc | BU |
|---|---|---|---|---|---|---|
| 1998 | — | — | — | — | 8.00 | — |

**CROWN** KM# 689a **Weight:** 28.2800 g. **Composition:** 0.9250 Silver .8410 oz. ASW

| Date | Mintage | F | VF | XF | Unc | BU |
|---|---|---|---|---|---|---|
| 1998 Proof | Est. 30,000 | Value: 50.00 | | | | |

**CROWN** KM# 690 **Composition:** Copper-Nickel **Series:** World Cup France 1998 **Obverse:** Queen's portrait **Reverse:** Two players

| Date | Mintage | F | VF | XF | Unc | BU |
|---|---|---|---|---|---|---|
| 1998 | — | — | — | — | 8.00 | — |

**CROWN** KM# 690a **Weight:** 28.2800 g. **Composition:** 0.9250 Silver .8410 oz. ASW

| Date | Mintage | F | VF | XF | Unc | BU |
|---|---|---|---|---|---|---|
| 1998 Proof | Est. 30,000 | Value: 50.00 | | | | |

**CROWN** KM# 692 **Weight:** 28.2800 g. **Composition:** 0.9250 Silver .8410 oz. ASW **Series:** Traders of the World **Obverse:** Queen's portrait **Reverse:** Phoenecian Galley (200BC-600AD), shells below

| Date | Mintage | F | VF | XF | Unc | BU |
|---|---|---|---|---|---|---|
| 1998 Proof | Est. 10,000 | Value: 50.00 | | | | |

**CROWN** KM# 694 **Weight:** 28.2800 g. **Composition:** 0.9250 Silver .8410 oz. ASW **Series:** Traders of the World **Obverse:** Queen's portrait **Reverse:** Viking ship (900AD), pair of fish and elephant tusks

| Date | Mintage | F | VF | XF | Unc | BU |
|---|---|---|---|---|---|---|
| 1998 Proof | Est. 10,000 | Value: 50.00 | | | | |

**CROWN** **KM# 696** **Weight:** 28.2800 g. **Composition:** 0.9250 Silver .8410 oz. ASW **Series:** Traders of the World **Obverse:** Queen's portrait **Reverse:** Marco Polo (1254-1324), ship, chop sticks with noodles below

| Date | Mintage | F | VF | XF | Unc | BU |
|---|---|---|---|---|---|---|
| 1998 Proof | Est. 10,000 | Value: 50.00 | | | | |

**CROWN** **KM# 698** **Weight:** 28.2800 g. **Composition:** 0.9250 Silver .8410 oz. ASW **Series:** Traders of the World **Obverse:** Queen's portrait **Reverse:** Hanseatic Kogge (circa 1350) coins of the Hanseatic League nations above, map

| Date | Mintage | F | VF | XF | Unc | BU |
|---|---|---|---|---|---|---|
| 1998 Proof | Est. 10,000 | Value: 50.00 | | | | |

**CROWN** **KM# 700** **Weight:** 28.2800 g. **Composition:** 0.9250 Silver .8410 oz. ASW **Series:** Traders of the World **Obverse:** Queen's portrait **Reverse:** Chinese Junk (1400s), silk worm, pottery

| Date | Mintage | F | VF | XF | Unc | BU |
|---|---|---|---|---|---|---|
| 1998 Proof | Est. 10,000 | Value: 50.00 | | | | |

**CROWN** **KM# 702** **Weight:** 28.2800 g. **Composition:** 0.9250 Silver .8410 oz. ASW **Series:** Traders of the World **Obverse:** Queen's portrait **Reverse:** Christopher Columbus (1451-1506) and ship

| Date | Mintage | F | VF | XF | Unc | BU |
|---|---|---|---|---|---|---|
| 1998 Proof | Est. 10,000 | Value: 50.00 | | | | |

**CROWN** **KM# 704** **Composition:** Copper-Nickel **Series:** Traders of the World **Obverse:** Queen's portrait **Reverse:** Sir Walter Raleigh (1552-1618)

| Date | Mintage | F | VF | XF | Unc | BU |
|---|---|---|---|---|---|---|
| 1998 | — | — | — | — | 10.00 | — |

**CROWN** **KM# 704a** **Weight:** 28.2800 g. **Composition:** 0.9250 Silver .8410 oz. ASW

| Date | Mintage | F | VF | XF | Unc | BU |
|---|---|---|---|---|---|---|
| 1998 Proof | Est. 10,000 | Value: 50.00 | | | | |

**CROWN** **KM# 706** **Weight:** 28.2800 g. **Composition:** 0.9250 Silver .8410 oz. ASW **Series:** Traders of the World **Obverse:** Queen's portrait **Reverse:** Boston Tea Party (1773) scene, tea leaf above

| Date | Mintage | F | VF | XF | Unc | BU |
|---|---|---|---|---|---|---|
| 1998 Proof | Est. 10,000 | Value: 50.00 | | | | |

**CROWN** **KM# 708** **Composition:** Copper-Nickel **Series:** Evolution of Mankind **Obverse:** Queen's portrait **Reverse:** Australopithecus, Lucy

| Date | Mintage | F | VF | XF | Unc | BU |
|---|---|---|---|---|---|---|
| 1998 | — | — | — | — | 10.00 | — |

**CROWN** **KM# 708a** **Weight:** 28.2800 g. **Composition:** 0.9250 Silver .8410 oz. ASW

| Date | Mintage | F | VF | XF | Unc | BU |
|---|---|---|---|---|---|---|
| 1998 Proof | Est. 10,000 | Value: 50.00 | | | | |

**CROWN** **KM# 710** **Composition:** Copper-Nickel **Series:** Evolution of Mankind **Obverse:** Queen's portrait **Reverse:** Homo Habilis, use of tools

| Date | Mintage | F | VF | XF | Unc | BU |
|---|---|---|---|---|---|---|
| 1998 | — | — | — | — | 10.00 | — |

**CROWN** **KM# 710a** **Weight:** 28.2800 g. **Composition:** 0.9250 Silver .8410 oz. ASW

| Date | Mintage | F | VF | XF | Unc | BU |
|---|---|---|---|---|---|---|
| 1998 Proof | Est. 10,000 | Value: 50.00 | | | | |

**CROWN** **KM# 712** **Composition:** Copper-Nickel **Series:** Evolution of Mankind **Obverse:** Queen's portrait **Reverse:** Homo Erectus, use of fire

| Date | Mintage | F | VF | XF | Unc | BU |
|---|---|---|---|---|---|---|
| 1998 | — | — | — | — | 10.00 | — |

**CROWN** **KM# 712a** **Weight:** 28.2800 g. **Composition:** 0.9250 Silver .8410 oz. ASW

| Date | Mintage | F | VF | XF | Unc | BU |
|---|---|---|---|---|---|---|
| 1998 Proof | Est. 10,000 | Value: 50.00 | | | | |

**CROWN** **KM# 714** **Composition:** Copper-Nickel **Series:** Evolution of Mankind **Obverse:** Queen's portrait **Reverse:** Skull, 1848, Rock of Gibraltar

| Date | Mintage | F | VF | XF | Unc | BU |
|---|---|---|---|---|---|---|
| 1998 | — | — | — | — | 10.00 | — |

**CROWN** **KM# 714a** **Weight:** 28.2800 g. **Composition:** 0.9250 Silver .8410 oz. ASW

| Date | Mintage | F | VF | XF | Unc | BU |
|---|---|---|---|---|---|---|
| 1998 Proof | Est. 10,000 | Value: 50.00 | | | | |

**CROWN** **KM# 716** **Composition:** Copper-Nickel **Series:** Evolution of Mankind **Obverse:** Queen's portrait **Reverse:** Neanderthal Man, burial scene

| Date | Mintage | F | VF | XF | Unc | BU |
|---|---|---|---|---|---|---|
| 1998 | — | — | — | — | 10.00 | — |

**CROWN** **KM# 716a** **Weight:** 28.2800 g. **Composition:** 0.9250 Silver .8410 oz. ASW

| Date | Mintage | F | VF | XF | Unc | BU |
|---|---|---|---|---|---|---|
| 1998 Proof | Est. 10,000 | Value: 50.00 | | | | |

**CROWN** **KM# 718** **Composition:** Copper-Nickel **Series:** Evolution of Mankind **Obverse:** Queen's portrait **Reverse:** Homo Sapiens, cave painting

| Date | Mintage | F | VF | XF | Unc | BU |
|---|---|---|---|---|---|---|
| 1998 | — | — | — | — | 10.00 | — |

**CROWN** **KM# 718a** **Weight:** 28.2800 g. **Composition:** 0.9250 Silver .8410 oz. ASW

| Date | Mintage | F | VF | XF | Unc | BU |
|---|---|---|---|---|---|---|
| 1998 Proof | Est. 10,000 | Value: 50.00 | | | | |

**CROWN** **KM# 720** **Composition:** Copper-Nickel **Series:** Evolution of Mankind **Obverse:** Queen's portrait **Reverse:** Homo Sapiens hunting mammoth

| Date | Mintage | F | VF | XF | Unc | BU |
|---|---|---|---|---|---|---|
| 1998 | — | — | — | — | 10.00 | — |

**CROWN** **KM# 720a** **Weight:** 28.2800 g. **Composition:** 0.9250 Silver .8410 oz. ASW

| Date | Mintage | F | VF | XF | Unc | BU |
|---|---|---|---|---|---|---|
| 1998 Proof | Est. 10,000 | Value: 50.00 | | | | |

**CROWN** **KM# 722a** **Weight:** 28.2800 g. **Composition:** 0.9250 Silver .8410 oz. ASW

| Date | Mintage | F | VF | XF | Unc | BU |
|---|---|---|---|---|---|---|
| 1998 Proof | Est. 10,000 | Value: 50.00 | | | | |

**CROWN** **KM# 724** **Composition:** Copper-Nickel **Series:** Evolution of Mankind **Obverse:** Queen's portrait **Reverse:** Human and primate mothers with young, "The Common Ancentry of Ape and Man"

| Date | Mintage | F | VF | XF | Unc | BU |
|---|---|---|---|---|---|---|
| 1998 | — | — | — | — | 10.00 | — |

**CROWN** **KM# 724a** **Weight:** 28.2800 g. **Composition:** 0.9250 Silver .8410 oz. ASW

| Date | Mintage | F | VF | XF | Unc | BU |
|---|---|---|---|---|---|---|
| 1998 Proof | Est. 10,000 | Value: 50.00 | | | | |

**CROWN** **KM# 726** **Composition:** Copper-Nickel **Series:** Evolution of Mankind **Obverse:** Queen's portrait **Reverse:** Charles Darwin, dates

| Date | Mintage | F | VF | XF | Unc | BU |
|---|---|---|---|---|---|---|
| 1998 | — | — | — | — | 10.00 | — |

**CROWN** **KM# 726a** **Weight:** 28.2800 g. **Composition:** 0.9250 Silver .8410 oz. ASW

| Date | Mintage | F | VF | XF | Unc | BU |
|---|---|---|---|---|---|---|
| 1998 Proof | Est. 10,000 | Value: 50.00 | | | | |

**CROWN** **KM# 728** **Composition:** Copper-Nickel **Series:** Evolution fo Mankind **Obverse:** Queen's portrait **Reverse:** Raymond Dart, dates, the Tuang Skull

| Date | Mintage | F | VF | XF | Unc | BU |
|---|---|---|---|---|---|---|
| 1998 | — | — | — | — | 10.00 | — |

**CROWN** **KM# 722.1** **Composition:** Copper-Nickel **Series:** Evolution of Mankind **Obverse:** Queen's portrait **Reverse:** Pictorial representation of theory of evolution

| Date | Mintage | F | VF | XF | Unc | BU |
|---|---|---|---|---|---|---|
| 1998 | — | — | — | — | 10.00 | — |

**CROWN** **KM# 728a** **Weight:** 28.2800 g. **Composition:** 0.9250 Silver .8410 oz. ASW

| Date | Mintage | F | VF | XF | Unc | BU |
|---|---|---|---|---|---|---|
| 1998 Proof | Est. 10,000 | Value: 50.00 | | | | |

**CROWN** **KM# 730** **Composition:** Copper-Nickel **Series:** Evolution of Mankind **Obverse:** Queen's portrait **Reverse:** Four people of different races

| Date | Mintage | F | VF | XF | Unc | BU |
|---|---|---|---|---|---|---|
| 1998 | — | — | — | — | 10.00 | — |

**CROWN** **KM# 730a** **Weight:** 28.2800 g. **Composition:** 0.9250 Silver .8410 oz. ASW

| Date | Mintage | F | VF | XF | Unc | BU |
|---|---|---|---|---|---|---|
| 1998 Proof | Est. 10,000 | Value: 50.00 | | | | |

**CROWN** **KM# 733** **Weight:** 28.2800 g. **Composition:** 0.9250 Silver .8410 oz. ASW **Series:** Wonders of the World **Obverse:** Queen's portrait **Reverse:** Guilin Hills, China with Chinese coin design inlay

| Date | Mintage | F | VF | XF | Unc | BU |
|---|---|---|---|---|---|---|
| 1998 Proof | Est. 7,500 | Value: 60.00 | | | | |

**CROWN** **KM# 734** **Weight:** 28.2800 g. **Composition:** 0.9250 Silver .8410 oz. ASW **Series:** Wonders of the World **Obverse:** Queen's portrait **Reverse:** Victorial Falls, Africa, with African coin design inlay

| Date | Mintage | F | VF | XF | Unc | BU |
|---|---|---|---|---|---|---|
| 1998 Proof | Est. 7,500 | Value: 60.00 | | | | |

**CROWN** **KM# 735** **Weight:** 28.2800 g. **Composition:** 0.9250 Silver .8410 oz. ASW **Series:** Wonders of the World **Obverse:** Queen's portrait **Reverse:** The Matterhorn, Switzerland, Italy with Swiss coin design inlay

| Date | Mintage | F | VF | XF | Unc | BU |
|---|---|---|---|---|---|---|
| 1998 Proof | Est. 7,500 | Value: 60.00 | | | | |

**CROWN** **KM# 736** **Weight:** 28.2800 g. **Composition:** 0.9250 Silver .8410 oz. ASW **Series:** Wonders of the World **Obverse:** Queen's portrait **Reverse:** Taroko Gorge, Taiwan, with Taiwanese coin design inlay

| Date | Mintage | F | VF | XF | Unc | BU |
|---|---|---|---|---|---|---|
| 1998 Proof | Est. 7,500 | Value: 60.00 | | | | |

**CROWN** **KM# 737** **Weight:** 28.2800 g. **Composition:** 0.9250 Silver .8410 oz. ASW **Series:** Wonders of the World **Obverse:** Queen's portrait **Reverse:** Niagara Falls, Canada, USA, with American coin design inlay

| Date | Mintage | F | VF | XF | Unc | BU |
|---|---|---|---|---|---|---|
| 1998 Proof | Est. 7,500 | Value: 60.00 | | | | |

**CROWN** **KM# 738** **Weight:** 28.2800 g. **Composition:** 0.9250 Silver .8410 oz. ASW **Series:** Wonders of the World **Obverse:** Queen's portrait **Reverse:** Mount Fuji, Japan, with Japanese coin design inlay

| Date | Mintage | F | VF | XF | Unc | BU |
|---|---|---|---|---|---|---|
| 1998 Proof | Est. 7,500 | Value: 60.00 | | | | |

**CROWN** **KM# 739** **Weight:** 28.2800 g. **Composition:** 0.9250 Silver .8410 oz. ASW **Series:** Wonders of the World **Obverse:** Queen's portrait **Reverse:** Ulura, Australia with Australian coin design inlay

| Date | Mintage | F | VF | XF | Unc | BU |
|---|---|---|---|---|---|---|
| 1998 Proof | Est. 7,500 | Value: 60.00 | | | | |

**CROWN** **KM# 745** **Composition:** Copper-Nickel **Series:** Year of the Ocean **Obverse:** Queen's portrait **Reverse:** Mermaid and dolphin

| Date | Mintage | F | VF | XF | Unc | BU |
|---|---|---|---|---|---|---|
| 1998 | — | — | — | — | 9.00 | — |

**CROWN** **KM# 745a** **Weight:** 28.2800 g. **Composition:** 0.9250 Silver .8410 oz. ASW

| Date | Mintage | F | VF | XF | Unc | BU |
|---|---|---|---|---|---|---|
| 1998 Proof | Est. 30,000 | Value: 50.00 | | | | |

**CROWN** **KM# 746** **Composition:** Copper-Nickel **Series:** Year of the Ocean **Obverse:** Queen's portrait **Reverse:** Octopus, fish and coral

| Date | Mintage | F | VF | XF | Unc | BU |
|---|---|---|---|---|---|---|
| 1998 | — | — | — | — | 9.00 | — |

**CROWN** **KM# 746a** **Weight:** 28.2800 g. **Composition:** 0.9250 Silver .8410 oz. ASW

| Date | Mintage | F | VF | XF | Unc | BU |
|---|---|---|---|---|---|---|
| 1998 Proof | Est. 30,000 | Value: 50.00 | | | | |

**CROWN** **KM# 747** **Composition:** Copper-Nickel **Series:** Year of the Ocean **Obverse:** Queen's portrait **Reverse:** Jelly fish, stingray, fish

| Date | Mintage | F | VF | XF | Unc | BU |
|---|---|---|---|---|---|---|
| 1998 | — | — | — | — | 9.00 | — |

**CROWN** **KM# 747a** **Weight:** 28.2800 g. **Composition:** 0.9250 Silver .8410 oz. ASW

| Date | Mintage | F | VF | XF | Unc | BU |
|---|---|---|---|---|---|---|
| 1998 Proof | Est. 30,000 | Value: 60.00 | | | | |

**CROWN** **KM# 748** **Composition:** Copper-Nickel **Series:** Year of the Ocean **Obverse:** Queen's portrait **Reverse:** Two wind surfers

| Date | Mintage | F | VF | XF | Unc | BU |
|---|---|---|---|---|---|---|
| 1998 | — | — | — | — | 9.00 | — |

**CROWN** **KM# 748a** **Weight:** 28.2800 g. **Composition:** 0.9250 Silver .8410 oz. ASW

| Date | Mintage | F | VF | XF | Unc | BU |
|---|---|---|---|---|---|---|
| 1998 Proof | Est. 30,000 | Value: 60.00 | | | | |

**CROWN** **KM# 768** **Composition:** Copper-Nickel **Subject:** The Gibraltar Regiment New Colors **Obverse:** Queen's portrait **Reverse:** Soldier presenting keys

| Date | Mintage | F | VF | XF | Unc | BU |
|---|---|---|---|---|---|---|
| 1998 | — | — | — | — | 10.00 | — |

**CROWN** **KM# 768a** **Weight:** 28.2800 g. **Composition:** 0.9250 Silver .8410 oz. ASW

| Date | Mintage | F | VF | XF | Unc | BU |
|---|---|---|---|---|---|---|
| 1998 Proof | Est. 30,000 | Value: 50.00 | | | | |

**CROWN** **KM# 799** **Composition:** Copper-Nickel **Subject:** General Dwight D. Eisenhower **Obverse:** Queen's portrait **Reverse:** Portrait of Eisenhower and North African invasion scene

| Date | Mintage | F | VF | XF | Unc | BU |
|---|---|---|---|---|---|---|
| 1998 | — | — | — | — | 8.00 | — |

**CROWN** **KM# 799a** **Weight:** 28.2800 g. **Composition:** 0.9250 Silver .8410 oz. ASW

| Date | Mintage | F | VF | XF | Unc | BU |
|---|---|---|---|---|---|---|
| 1998 Proof | Est. 10,000 | Value: 50.00 | | | | |

**CROWN** **KM# 783.1** **Composition:** Copper-Nickel **Subject:** 1999 The Year of the Rabbit **Obverse:** Queen's portrait **Reverse:** Rabbit reading, sparrow, Chinese characters

| Date | Mintage | F | VF | XF | Unc | BU |
|---|---|---|---|---|---|---|
| 1999 | — | — | — | — | 10.00 | — |

**CROWN** **KM# 783.2** **Composition:** Copper-Nickel **Reverse:** Rabbit reading, sparrow. Without Chinese characters

| Date | Mintage | F | VF | XF | Unc | BU |
|---|---|---|---|---|---|---|
| 1999 | Inc. above | — | — | — | 10.00 | — |

**CROWN** **KM# 783.1a** **Weight:** 28.2800 g. **Composition:** 0.9250 Silver .8410 oz. ASW

| Date | Mintage | F | VF | XF | Unc | BU |
|---|---|---|---|---|---|---|
| 1999 Proof | Est. 10,000 | Value: 50.00 | | | | |

**CROWN** **KM# 783.2a** **Weight:** 28.2800 g. **Composition:** 0.9250 Silver .8410 oz. ASW **Reverse:** Rabbit reading, sparrow. Without Chinese characters

| Date | Mintage | F | VF | XF | Unc | BU |
|---|---|---|---|---|---|---|
| 1999 Proof | Inc. above | Value: 50.00 | | | | |

**CROWN** **KM# 785** **Composition:** Copper-Nickel **Series:** Summer Olympics **Subject:** Sydney **Obverse:** Queen's portrait **Reverse:** Broad jumper and kangaroo

| Date | Mintage | F | VF | XF | Unc | BU |
|---|---|---|---|---|---|---|
| 1999 | — | — | — | — | 8.00 | — |

**CROWN** **KM# 785a** **Weight:** 28.2800 g. **Composition:** 0.9250 Silver .8410 oz. ASW

| Date | Mintage | F | VF | XF | Unc | BU |
|---|---|---|---|---|---|---|
| 1999 Proof | Est. 30,000 | Value: 50.00 | | | | |

**CROWN** **KM# 787** **Composition:** Copper-Nickel **Series:** Summer Olympics **Subject:** Sydney **Obverse:** Queen's portrait **Reverse:** Sailboats and platypus

| Date | Mintage | F | VF | XF | Unc | BU |
|---|---|---|---|---|---|---|
| 1999 | — | — | — | — | 8.00 | — |

**CROWN** **KM# 787a** **Weight:** 28.2800 g. **Composition:** 0.9250 Silver .8410 oz. ASW

| Date | Mintage | F | VF | XF | Unc | BU |
|---|---|---|---|---|---|---|
| 1999 Proof | Est. 30,000 | Value: 50.00 | | | | |

**CROWN** **KM# 789** **Composition:** Copper-Nickel **Series:** Summer Olympics **Subject:** Sydney **Obverse:** Queen's portrait **Reverse:** Swimmer and koala bear

| Date | Mintage | F | VF | XF | Unc | BU |
|---|---|---|---|---|---|---|
| 1999 | — | — | — | — | 8.00 | — |

**CROWN** **KM# 789a** **Weight:** 28.2800 g. **Composition:** 0.9250 Silver .8410 oz. ASW

| Date | Mintage | F | VF | XF | Unc | BU |
|---|---|---|---|---|---|---|
| 1999 Proof | Est. 30,000 | Value: 50.00 | | | | |

**CROWN** **KM# 791a** **Weight:** 28.2800 g. **Composition:** 0.9250 Silver .8410 oz. ASW

| Date | Mintage | F | VF | XF | Unc | BU |
|---|---|---|---|---|---|---|
| 1999 Proof | Est. 30,000 | Value: 50.00 | | | | |

**CROWN** **KM# 793** **Composition:** Copper-Nickel **Obverse:** Queen's portrait **Reverse:** Man with torch and dog

| Date | Mintage | F | VF | XF | Unc | BU |
|---|---|---|---|---|---|---|
| 1999 | — | — | — | — | 8.00 | — |

**CROWN** **KM# 793a** **Weight:** 28.2800 g. **Composition:** 0.9250 Silver .8410 oz. ASW

| Date | Mintage | F | VF | XF | Unc | BU |
|---|---|---|---|---|---|---|
| 1999 Proof | Est. 30,000 | Value: 50.00 | | | | |

**CROWN** **KM# 795** **Composition:** Copper-Nickel **Obverse:** Queen's portrait **Reverse:** Runner with torch, Aboriginal portrait and Ayer's Rock

| Date | Mintage | F | VF | XF | Unc | BU |
|---|---|---|---|---|---|---|
| 1999 | — | — | — | — | 8.00 | — |

**CROWN** **KM# 795a** **Weight:** 28.2800 g. **Composition:** 0.9250 Silver .8410 oz. ASW

| Date | Mintage | F | VF | XF | Unc | BU |
|---|---|---|---|---|---|---|
| 1999 Proof | Est. 30,000 | Value: 50.00 | | | | |

**CROWN** **KM# 801** **Composition:** Copper-Nickel **Subject:** King Alfred the Great **Obverse:** Queen's portrait **Reverse:** Alfred the Great, date

| Date | Mintage | F | VF | XF | Unc | BU |
|---|---|---|---|---|---|---|
| 1999 | — | — | — | — | 7.50 | — |

**Note:**

**CROWN** **KM# 801a** **Weight:** 28.2800 g. **Composition:** 0.9250 Silver .8410 oz. ASW

| Date | Mintage | F | VF | XF | Unc | BU |
|---|---|---|---|---|---|---|
| 1999 Proof | Est. 10,000 | Value: 50.00 | | | | |

**CROWN** **KM# 791.1** **Composition:** Copper-Nickel **Series:** Summer Olympics **Subject:** Sydney **Obverse:** Queen's portrait **Reverse:** Two oarsmen below cockatoos

| Date | Mintage | F | VF | XF | Unc | BU |
|---|---|---|---|---|---|---|
| 1999 | — | — | — | — | 8.00 | — |

**CROWN** **KM# 803** **Composition:** Copper-Nickel **Subject:** King Canute **Obverse:** Queen's portrait **Reverse:** King Canute, dates

| Date | Mintage | F | VF | XF | Unc | BU |
|---|---|---|---|---|---|---|
| 1999 | — | — | — | — | 7.50 | — |

**CROWN** **KM# 803a** **Weight:** 28.2800 g. **Composition:** 0.9250 Silver .8410 oz. ASW

| Date | Mintage | F | VF | XF | Unc | BU |
|---|---|---|---|---|---|---|
| 1999 Proof | Est. 10,000 | Value: 50.00 | | | | |

**CROWN** **KM# 805** **Composition:** Copper-Nickel **Subject:** King Edward the Confessor **Obverse:** Queen's portrait **Reverse:** King Edward, dates

| Date | Mintage | F | VF | XF | Unc | BU |
|---|---|---|---|---|---|---|
| 1999 | — | — | — | — | 7.50 | — |

**CROWN** **KM# 805a** **Weight:** 28.2800 g. **Composition:** 0.9250 Silver .8410 oz. ASW

| Date | Mintage | F | VF | XF | Unc | BU |
|---|---|---|---|---|---|---|
| 1999 Proof | Est. 10,000 | Value: 50.00 | | | | |

**CROWN** **KM# 807** **Composition:** Copper-Nickel **Subject:** King William I **Obverse:** Queen's portrait **Reverse:** King William, dates

| Date | Mintage | F | VF | XF | Unc | BU |
|---|---|---|---|---|---|---|
| 1999 | — | — | — | — | 7.50 | — |

**CROWN** **KM# 807a** **Weight:** 28.2800 g. **Composition:** 0.9250 Silver .8410 oz. ASW

| Date | Mintage | F | VF | XF | Unc | BU |
|---|---|---|---|---|---|---|
| 1999 Proof | Est. 10,000 | Value: 50.00 | | | | |

**CROWN** **KM# 809** **Composition:** Copper-Nickel **Subject:** King Richard I **Obverse:** Queen's portrait **Reverse:** King Richard, dates

| Date | Mintage | F | VF | XF | Unc | BU |
|---|---|---|---|---|---|---|
| 1999 | — | — | — | — | 7.50 | — |

**CROWN** **KM# 809a** **Weight:** 28.2800 g. **Composition:** 0.9250 Silver .8410 oz. ASW

| Date | Mintage | F | VF | XF | Unc | BU |
|---|---|---|---|---|---|---|
| 1999 Proof | Est. 10,000 | Value: 50.00 | | | | |

**CROWN** **KM# 811** **Composition:** Copper-Nickel **Subject:** King John **Obverse:** Queen's portrait **Reverse:** King John, dates

| Date | Mintage | F | VF | XF | Unc | BU |
|---|---|---|---|---|---|---|
| 1999 | — | — | — | — | 7.50 | — |

**CROWN** **KM# 811a** **Weight:** 28.2800 g. **Composition:** 0.9250 Silver .8410 oz. ASW

| Date | Mintage | F | VF | XF | Unc | BU |
|---|---|---|---|---|---|---|
| 1999 Proof | Est. 10,000 | Value: 50.00 | | | | |

**CROWN** **KM# 813** **Composition:** Copper-Nickel **Subject:** King Henry V **Obverse:** Queen's portrait **Reverse:** King Henry, dates

| Date | Mintage | F | VF | XF | Unc | BU |
|---|---|---|---|---|---|---|
| 1999 | — | — | — | — | 7.50 | — |

**CROWN** **KM# 813a** **Weight:** 28.2800 g. **Composition:** 0.9250 Silver .8410 oz. ASW

| Date | Mintage | F | VF | XF | Unc | BU |
|---|---|---|---|---|---|---|
| 1999 Proof | Est. 10,000 | Value: 50.00 | | | | |

**CROWN** **KM# 815** **Composition:** Copper-Nickel **Subject:** King Richard III **Obverse:** Queen's portrait **Reverse:** King Richard, dates

| Date | Mintage | F | VF | XF | Unc | BU |
|---|---|---|---|---|---|---|
| 1999 | — | — | — | — | 7.50 | — |

**CROWN** **KM# 815a** **Weight:** 28.2800 g. **Composition:** 0.9250 Silver .8410 oz. ASW

| Date | Mintage | F | VF | XF | Unc | BU |
|---|---|---|---|---|---|---|
| 1999 Proof | Est. 10,000 | Value: 50.00 | | | | |

**CROWN** **KM# 817** **Composition:** Copper-Nickel **Subject:** King Henry VIII **Obverse:** Queen's portrait **Reverse:** King Henry, dates

| Date | Mintage | F | VF | XF | Unc | BU |
|---|---|---|---|---|---|---|
| 1999 | — | — | — | — | 7.50 | — |

**CROWN** **KM# 817a** **Weight:** 28.2800 g. **Composition:** 0.9250 Silver .8410 oz. ASW

| Date | Mintage | F | VF | XF | Unc | BU |
|---|---|---|---|---|---|---|
| 1999 Proof | Est. 10,000 | Value: 50.00 | | | | |

**CROWN** **KM# 819** **Composition:** Copper-Nickel **Subject:** Queen Elizabeth I **Obverse:** Queen's portrait **Reverse:** Queen Elizabeth, dates

| Date | Mintage | F | VF | XF | Unc | BU |
|---|---|---|---|---|---|---|
| 1999 | — | — | — | — | 7.50 | — |

**CROWN** **KM# 819a** **Weight:** 28.2800 g. **Composition:** 0.9250 Silver .8410 oz. ASW

| Date | Mintage | F | VF | XF | Unc | BU |
|---|---|---|---|---|---|---|
| 1999 Proof | Est. 10,000 | Value: 50.00 | | | | |

**CROWN** **KM# 821** **Composition:** Copper-Nickel **Subject:** King Charles I **Obverse:** Queen's portrait **Reverse:** King Charles, dates

| Date | Mintage | F | VF | XF | Unc | BU |
|---|---|---|---|---|---|---|
| 1999 | — | — | — | — | 7.50 | — |

**CROWN** **KM# 821a** **Weight:** 28.2800 g. **Composition:** 0.9250 Silver .8410 oz. ASW

| Date | Mintage | F | VF | XF | Unc | BU |
|---|---|---|---|---|---|---|
| 1999 Proof | Est. 10,000 | Value: 50.00 | | | | |

**CROWN** **KM# 823** **Composition:** Copper-Nickel **Subject:** King Charles II **Obverse:** Queen's portrait **Reverse:** King Charles, dates

| Date | Mintage | F | VF | XF | Unc | BU |
|---|---|---|---|---|---|---|
| 1999 | — | — | — | — | 7.50 | — |

**CROWN** **KM# 823a** **Weight:** 28.2800 g. **Composition:** 0.9250 Silver .8410 oz. ASW

| Date | Mintage | F | VF | XF | Unc | BU |
|---|---|---|---|---|---|---|
| 1999 Proof | Est. 10,000 | Value: 50.00 | | | | |

**CROWN** **KM# 826a** **Weight:** 28.2800 g. **Composition:** 0.9250 Silver .8410 oz. ASW

| Date | Mintage | F | VF | XF | Unc | BU |
|---|---|---|---|---|---|---|
| 1999 Proof | 10,000 | Value: 50.00 | | | | |

**CROWN** **KM# 827** **Weight:** 28.2800 g. **Composition:** 0.9250 Silver .8410 oz. ASW **Subject:** The Wedding of Prince Edward and Miss Sophie Rhys-Jones **Obverse:** Queen's portrait **Reverse:** St. George's Chapel

| Date | Mintage | F | VF | XF | Unc | BU |
|---|---|---|---|---|---|---|
| 1999 | — | — | — | — | 8.00 | — |

**CROWN** **KM# 827a** **Weight:** 28.2800 g. **Composition:** 0.9250 Silver .8410 oz. ASW

| Date | Mintage | F | VF | XF | Unc | BU |
|---|---|---|---|---|---|---|
| 1999 Proof | Est. 10,000 | Value: 50.00 | | | | |

**CROWN** **KM# 835** **Composition:** Copper-Nickel **Subject:** The Life of Queen Elizabeth **Obverse:** Queen's portrait **Reverse:** 1903 portrait of Queen Mother as a girl

| Date | Mintage | F | VF | XF | Unc | BU |
|---|---|---|---|---|---|---|
| 1999 | — | — | — | — | 8.00 | — |

**CROWN** **KM# 835a** **Weight:** 28.2800 g. **Composition:** 0.9250 Silver .8410 oz. ASW

| Date | Mintage | F | VF | XF | Unc | BU |
|---|---|---|---|---|---|---|
| 1999 Proof | Est. 10,000 | Value: 50.00 | | | | |

**CROWN** **KM# 837** **Composition:** Copper-Nickel **Subject:** The Life of Queen Elizabeth **Obverse:** Queen's portrait **Reverse:** 1918 portrait with wounded soldier

| Date | Mintage | F | VF | XF | Unc | BU |
|---|---|---|---|---|---|---|
| 1999 | — | — | — | — | 8.00 | — |

**CROWN** **KM# 826.1** **Composition:** Copper-Nickel **Subject:** The Wedding of Prince Edward and Miss Sophie Rhys-Jones **Obverse:** Queen's portrait **Reverse:** Prince and bride

| Date | Mintage | F | VF | XF | Unc | BU |
|---|---|---|---|---|---|---|
| 1999 | — | — | — | — | 8.00 | — |

**CROWN** **KM# 837a** **Weight:** 28.2800 g. **Composition:** 0.9250 Silver .8410 oz. ASW

| Date | Mintage | F | VF | XF | Unc | BU |
|---|---|---|---|---|---|---|
| 1999 Proof | Est. 10,000 | Value: 50.00 | | | | |

**CROWN** **KM# 839** **Composition:** Copper-Nickel **Subject:** The Life of Queen Elizabeth **Obverse:** Queen's portrait **Reverse:** 1923 wedding portrait

| Date | Mintage | F | VF | XF | Unc | BU |
|---|---|---|---|---|---|---|
| 1999 | — | — | — | — | 8.00 | — |

**CROWN** **KM# 839a** **Weight:** 28.2800 g. **Composition:** 0.9250 Silver .8410 oz. ASW

| Date | Mintage | F | VF | XF | Unc | BU |
|---|---|---|---|---|---|---|
| 1999 Proof | Est. 10,000 | Value: 50.00 | | | | |

**CROWN** **KM# 841** **Composition:** Copper-Nickel **Subject:** The Life of Queen Elizabeth **Obverse:** Queen's portrait **Reverse:** 1936 family protrait

| Date | Mintage | F | VF | XF | Unc | BU |
|---|---|---|---|---|---|---|
| 1999 | — | — | — | — | 8.00 | — |

**CROWN** **KM# 841a** **Weight:** 28.2800 g. **Composition:** 0.9250 Silver .8410 oz. ASW

| Date | Mintage | F | VF | XF | Unc | BU |
|---|---|---|---|---|---|---|
| 1999 Proof | Est. 10,000 | Value: 50.00 | | | | |

**CROWN** **KM# 843a** **Weight:** 28.2800 g. **Composition:** 0.9250 Silver .8410 oz. ASW

| Date | Mintage | F | VF | XF | Unc | BU |
|---|---|---|---|---|---|---|
| 1999 Proof | Est. 10,000 | Value: 50.00 | | | | |

**CROWN KM# 845 Composition:** Copper-Nickel **Subject:** The World at War **Obverse:** Queen's portrait **Reverse:** Operation Manna, bomber dropping food packets

| Date | Mintage | F | VF | XF | Unc | BU |
|---|---|---|---|---|---|---|
| 1999 | — | — | — | — | 10.00 | — |

**CROWN KM# 845a Weight:** 28.2800 g. **Composition:** 0.9250 Silver .8410 oz. ASW

| Date | Mintage | F | VF | XF | Unc | BU |
|---|---|---|---|---|---|---|
| 1999 Proof | Est. 10,000 | Value: 50.00 | | | | |

**CROWN KM# 843.1 Weight:** 28.2800 g. **Composition:** 0.9250 Silver .8410 oz. ASW **Obverse:** Queen's portrait **Reverse:** Franklin Roosevelt and Zero fighter

| Date | Mintage | F | VF | XF | Unc | BU |
|---|---|---|---|---|---|---|
| 1999 | — | — | — | — | 10.00 | — |

**CROWN KM# 847.1 Composition:** Copper-Nickel **Subject:** The World at War **Obverse:** Queen's portrait **Reverse:** Robert Oppenheimer, B-29 and mushroom cloud

| Date | Mintage | F | VF | XF | Unc | BU |
|---|---|---|---|---|---|---|
| 1999 | — | — | — | — | 10.00 | — |

**CROWN KM# 847a Weight:** 28.2800 g. **Composition:** 0.9250 Silver .8410 oz. ASW

| Date | Mintage | F | VF | XF | Unc | BU |
|---|---|---|---|---|---|---|
| 1999 Proof | Est. 10,000 | Value: 50.00 | | | | |

**CROWN KM# 849 Composition:** Copper-Nickel **Subject:** The World at War **Obverse:** Queen's portrait **Reverse:** Barnes Wallis portrait, bomber above dam

| Date | Mintage | F | VF | XF | Unc | BU |
|---|---|---|---|---|---|---|
| 1999 | — | — | — | — | 10.00 | — |

**CROWN KM# 849a Weight:** 28.2800 g. **Composition:** 0.9250 Silver .8410 oz. ASW

| Date | Mintage | F | VF | XF | Unc | BU |
|---|---|---|---|---|---|---|
| 1999 Proof | Est. 10,000 | Value: 50.00 | | | | |

**CROWN KM# 851 Composition:** Copper-Nickel **Subject:** The World at War **Obverse:** Queen's portrait **Reverse:** Douglas Bader portrait, planes in combat

| Date | Mintage | F | VF | XF | Unc | BU |
|---|---|---|---|---|---|---|
| 1999 | — | — | — | — | 10.00 | — |

**CROWN KM# 851a Weight:** 28.2800 g. **Composition:** 0.9250 Silver .8410 oz. ASW

| Date | Mintage | F | VF | XF | Unc | BU |
|---|---|---|---|---|---|---|
| 1999 Proof | Est. 10,000 | Value: 50.00 | | | | |

**CROWN KM# 853 Composition:** Copper-Nickel **Subject:** The World at War **Obverse:** Queen's portrait **Reverse:** Winston Churchill and crowd

| Date | Mintage | F | VF | XF | Unc | BU |
|---|---|---|---|---|---|---|
| 1999 | — | — | — | — | 10.00 | — |

**CROWN KM# 853a Weight:** 28.2800 g. **Composition:** 0.9250 Silver .8410 oz. ASW

| Date | Mintage | F | VF | XF | Unc | BU |
|---|---|---|---|---|---|---|
| 1999 Proof | Est. 10,000 | Value: 50.00 | | | | |

**CROWN KM# 855 Composition:** Copper-Nickel **Subject:** The World at War **Obverse:** Queen's portrait **Reverse:** Tirpitz, battleship and sailor

| Date | Mintage | F | VF | XF | Unc | BU |
|---|---|---|---|---|---|---|
| 1999 | — | — | — | — | 10.00 | — |

**CROWN KM# 855a Weight:** 28.2800 g. **Composition:** 0.9250 Silver .8410 oz. ASW

| Date | Mintage | F | VF | XF | Unc | BU |
|---|---|---|---|---|---|---|
| 1999 Proof | Est. 10,000 | Value: 50.00 | | | | |

**CROWN KM# 857 Composition:** Copper-Nickel **Subject:** The World at War **Obverse:** Queen's portrait **Reverse:** Soldier kissing child goodbye

| Date | Mintage | F | VF | XF | Unc | BU |
|---|---|---|---|---|---|---|
| 1999 | — | — | — | — | 10.00 | — |

**CROWN KM# 857a Weight:** 28.2800 g. **Composition:** 0.9250 Silver .8410 oz. ASW

| Date | Mintage | F | VF | XF | Unc | BU |
|---|---|---|---|---|---|---|
| 1999 Proof | Est. 10,000 | Value: 50.00 | | | | |

**CROWN KM# 859 Composition:** Copper-Nickel **Subject:** The World at War **Obverse:** Queen's portrait **Reverse:** Fire fighters in action after air raid

| Date | Mintage | F | VF | XF | Unc | BU |
|---|---|---|---|---|---|---|
| 1999 | — | — | — | — | 10.00 | — |

**CROWN KM# 859a Weight:** 28.2800 g. **Composition:** 0.9250 Silver .8410 oz. ASW

| Date | Mintage | F | VF | XF | Unc | BU |
|---|---|---|---|---|---|---|
| 1999 Proof | Est. 10,000 | Value: 50.00 | | | | |

**CROWN KM# 861 Composition:** Copper-Nickel **Subject:** The World at War **Obverse:** Queen's portrait **Reverse:** D-Day landing scene

| Date | Mintage | F | VF | XF | Unc | BU |
|---|---|---|---|---|---|---|
| 1999 | — | — | — | — | 10.00 | — |

**CROWN KM# 861a Weight:** 28.2800 g. **Composition:** 0.9250 Silver .8410 oz. ASW

| Date | Mintage | F | VF | XF | Unc | BU |
|---|---|---|---|---|---|---|
| 1999 Proof | Est. 10,000 | Value: 50.00 | | | | |

**CROWN KM# 863 Composition:** Copper-Nickel **Subject:** The World at War **Obverse:** Queen's portrait **Reverse:** Operation Heavywater military skier

| Date | Mintage | F | VF | XF | Unc | BU |
|---|---|---|---|---|---|---|
| 1999 | — | — | — | — | 10.00 | — |

**CROWN KM# 863a Weight:** 28.2800 g. **Composition:** 0.9250 Silver .8410 oz. ASW

| Date | Mintage | F | VF | XF | Unc | BU |
|---|---|---|---|---|---|---|
| 1999 Proof | Est. 10,000 | Value: 50.00 | | | | |

**CROWN KM# 865 Composition:** Copper-Nickel **Subject:** The World at War **Obverse:** Queen's portrait **Reverse:** German tanks in Russia

| Date | Mintage | F | VF | XF | Unc | BU |
|---|---|---|---|---|---|---|
| 1999 | — | — | — | — | 10.00 | — |

**CROWN KM# 865a Weight:** 28.2800 g. **Composition:** 0.9250 Silver .8410 oz. ASW

| Date | Mintage | F | VF | XF | Unc | BU |
|---|---|---|---|---|---|---|
| 1999 Proof | Est. 10,000 | Value: 50.00 | | | | |

**CROWN KM# 796.1 Weight:** 6.2200 g. **Composition:** 0.9999 Gold .2000 oz. AGW **Subject:** Millenium 2000 **Obverse:** Rank-Broadley portrait of Queen Elizabeth II **Reverse:** Sundial, digital clock face, candle and traditional clock face **Note:** Similar to 5 Pounds, KM#796.

| Date | Mintage | F | VF | XF | Unc | BU |
|---|---|---|---|---|---|---|
| 1999 Proof | 5,000 | Value: 175 | | | | |

**CROWN KM# 871 Weight:** 28.2800 g. **Composition:** Copper-Nickel **Subject:** The Life of Queen Elizabeth - The Queen Mother **Obverse:** Queen's head right **Reverse:** 1937 coronation scene

| Date | Mintage | F | VF | XF | Unc | BU |
|---|---|---|---|---|---|---|
| 2000 | — | — | — | — | 10.00 | — |

**CROWN KM# 871a Weight:** 28.2800 g. **Composition:** 0.9250 Silver .8410 oz. ASW

| Date | Mintage | F | VF | XF | Unc | BU |
|---|---|---|---|---|---|---|
| 2000 Proof | 10,000 | Value: 50.00 | | | | |

**CROWN KM# 873 Composition:** Copper-Nickel **Subject:** The Life of Queen Elizabeth - The Queen Mother **Reverse:** 1938 visit to France

| Date | Mintage | F | VF | XF | Unc | BU |
|---|---|---|---|---|---|---|
| 2000 | — | — | — | — | 10.00 | — |

**CROWN KM# 873a Weight:** 28.2800 g. **Composition:** 0.9250 Silver .8410 oz. ASW

| Date | Mintage | F | VF | XF | Unc | BU |
|---|---|---|---|---|---|---|
| 2000 Proof | 10,000 | Value: 50.00 | | | | |

**CROWN KM# 875 Composition:** Copper-Nickel **Subject:** The Life of Queen Elizabeth - The Queen Mother **Reverse:** 1940 bomb damage

| Date | Mintage | F | VF | XF | Unc | BU |
|---|---|---|---|---|---|---|
| 2000 | — | — | — | — | 10.00 | — |

**CROWN KM# 875a Weight:** 28.2800 g. **Composition:** 0.9250 Silver .8410 oz. ASW

| Date | Mintage | F | VF | XF | Unc | BU |
|---|---|---|---|---|---|---|
| 2000 Proof | 10,000 | Value: 50.00 | | | | |

**CROWN KM# 877 Composition:** Copper-Nickel **Subject:** The Life of Queen Elizabeth - The Queen Mother **Reverse:** 1945 victory

| Date | Mintage | F | VF | XF | Unc | BU |
|---|---|---|---|---|---|---|
| 2000 | — | — | — | — | 10.00 | — |

**CROWN KM# 877a Weight:** 28.2800 g. **Composition:** 0.9250 Silver .8410 oz. ASW

| Date | Mintage | F | VF | XF | Unc | BU |
|---|---|---|---|---|---|---|
| 2000 Proof | 10,000 | Value: 50.00 | | | | |

**CROWN KM# 880 Weight:** 28.2800 g. **Composition:** Copper-Nickel **Subject:** 18th Birthday - H.R.H. The Prince William **Obverse:** Queen's head right **Reverse:** Prince William's head right

| Date | Mintage | F | VF | XF | Unc | BU |
|---|---|---|---|---|---|---|
| 2000 | — | — | — | — | 10.00 | — |

**CROWN KM# 880a Weight:** 28.2800 g. **Composition:** 0.9250 Silver .8410 oz. ASW

| Date | Mintage | F | VF | XF | Unc | BU |
|---|---|---|---|---|---|---|
| 2000 Proof | 10,000 | Value: 50.00 | | | | |

**CROWN KM# 882 Composition:** Copper-Nickel **Subject:** Queen Mother **Obverse:** Queen's portrait **Reverse:** Queen Mother's portrait

| Date | Mintage | F | VF | XF | Unc | BU |
|---|---|---|---|---|---|---|
| 2000 | — | — | — | — | 10.00 | — |

**CROWN KM# 884 Ring Weight:** 26.3000 g. **Ring Composition:** 0.9990 Gold .8455 oz. AGW **Center Composition:** Titanium **Subject:** 160th Anniversary - Uniform Penny Post **Reverse:** Postage stamp design **Edge:** Reeded

| Date | Mintage | F | VF | XF | Unc | BU |
|---|---|---|---|---|---|---|
| 2000 Proof | 999 | Value: 600 | | | | |

**CROWN KM# 904 Weight:** 28.2800 g. **Composition:** Copper-Nickel **Subject:** Queen Mother **Obverse:** Queen's portrait **Reverse:** 1953 Coronation scene **Edge:** Reeded **Size:** 38.6 mm.

| Date | Mintage | F | VF | XF | Unc | BU |
|---|---|---|---|---|---|---|
| 2001 | — | — | — | — | 10.00 | — |

**CROWN KM# 904a Weight:** 28.2800 g. **Composition:** 0.9250 Silver .8410 oz. ASW

| Date | Mintage | F | VF | XF | Unc | BU |
|---|---|---|---|---|---|---|
| 2001 Proof | 10,000 | Value: 47.50 | | | | |

**CROWN KM# 905 Weight:** 28.2800 g. **Composition:** Copper-Nickel **Subject:** Queen Mother **Obverse:** Queen's portrait **Reverse:** Queen Mother with Prince Charles in 1954 **Edge:** Reeded **Size:** 38.6 mm.

| Date | Mintage | F | VF | XF | Unc | BU |
|---|---|---|---|---|---|---|
| 2001 | — | — | — | — | 10.00 | — |

**CROWN KM# 905a Weight:** 28.2800 g. **Composition:** 0.9250 Silver .8410 oz. ASW

| Date | Mintage | F | VF | XF | Unc | BU |
|---|---|---|---|---|---|---|
| 2001 Proof | 10,000 | Value: 47.50 | | | | |

**CROWN KM# 906 Weight:** 28.2800 g. **Composition:** Copper-Nickel **Subject:** 21st Century **Obverse:** Queen's portrait **Reverse:** Celtic cross, Viking ship and modern technological items **Edge:** Reeded **Size:** 38.6 mm.

| Date | Mintage | F | VF | XF | Unc | BU |
|---|---|---|---|---|---|---|
| 2001 | — | — | — | — | 10.00 | — |

**CROWN KM# 906b Ring Weight:** 14.2000 g. **Ring Composition:** 0.9999 Silver .4565 oz. ASW **Center Weight:** 5.2000 g. **Center Composition:** 0.9995 Platinum .1671 oz. APW

| Date | Mintage | F | VF | XF | Unc | BU |
|---|---|---|---|---|---|---|
| 2001 Proof | 999 | Value: 400 | | | | |

**CROWN KM# 910 Weight:** 28.2800 g. **Composition:** Copper-Nickel **Series:** Victorian Era **Obverse:** Queen's portrait **Reverse:** 1838 Coronation scene **Edge:** Reeded **Size:** 38.6 mm.

| Date | Mintage | F | VF | XF | Unc | BU |
|---|---|---|---|---|---|---|
| 2001 | — | — | — | — | 10.00 | — |

**CROWN KM# 910a Weight:** 28.2800 g. **Composition:** 0.9250 Silver .8410 oz. ASW **Series:** Victorian Era

| Date | Mintage | F | VF | XF | Unc | BU |
|---|---|---|---|---|---|---|
| 2001 Proof | 10,000 | Value: 47.50 | | | | |

**CROWN KM# 912 Composition:** Copper-Nickel **Series:** Victorian Era **Subject:** Empress of India 1876 **Obverse:** Queen's portrait **Reverse:** Crowned portrait of Victoria and two elephants

| Date | Mintage | F | VF | XF | Unc | BU |
|---|---|---|---|---|---|---|
| 2001 | — | — | — | — | 10.00 | — |

**CROWN KM# 912a Weight:** 28.2800 g. **Composition:** 0.9250 Silver .8410 oz. ASW **Series:** Victorian Era

| Date | Mintage | F | VF | XF | Unc | BU |
|---|---|---|---|---|---|---|
| 2001 Proof | 10,000 | Value: 47.50 | | | | |

**CROWN KM# 914 Composition:** Copper-Nickel **Series:** Victorian Era **Subject:** Diamond Jubilee 1897 **Obverse:** Queen's portrait **Reverse:** Victoria's cameo portrait above naval ships

| Date | Mintage | F | VF | XF | Unc | BU |
|---|---|---|---|---|---|---|
| 2001 | — | — | — | — | 10.00 | — |

**CROWN KM# 914a Weight:** 28.2800 g. **Composition:** 0.9250 Silver .8410 oz. ASW **Series:** Victorian Era

| Date | Mintage | F | VF | XF | Unc | BU |
|---|---|---|---|---|---|---|
| 2001 Proof | 10,000 | Value: 47.50 | | | | |

**CROWN KM# 916 Composition:** Copper-Nickel **Series:** Victorian Era **Subject:** Victoria's Death 1901 **Obverse:** Queen's portrait **Reverse:** Victoria's cameo portrait and Osborne Manor

| Date | Mintage | F | VF | XF | Unc | BU |
|---|---|---|---|---|---|---|
| 2001 | — | — | — | — | 10.00 | — |

**CROWN KM# 916a Weight:** 28.2800 g. **Composition:** 0.9250 Silver .8410 oz. ASW **Series:** Victorian Era

| Date | Mintage | F | VF | XF | Unc | BU |
|---|---|---|---|---|---|---|
| 2001 Proof | 10,000 | Value: 47.50 | | | | |

**CROWN KM# 918 Composition:** Copper-Nickel **Series:** Victorian Era **Subject:** Prince Albert and the Great Exhibition 1851 **Obverse:** Queen's portrait **Reverse:** Albert's cameo portrait and the exhibit hall

| Date | Mintage | F | VF | XF | Unc | BU |
|---|---|---|---|---|---|---|
| 2001 Proof | 5,000 | Value: 175 | | | | |

**CROWN KM# 918a Weight:** 28.2800 g. **Composition:** 0.9250 Silver .8410 oz. ASW **Series:** Victorian Era

| Date | Mintage | F | VF | XF | Unc | BU |
|---|---|---|---|---|---|---|
| 2001 Proof | 10,000 | Value: 47.50 | | | | |

**CROWN KM# 920 Composition:** Copper-Nickel **Series:** Victorian Era **Subject:** Isambard K. Brunel **Obverse:** Queen's portrait **Reverse:** Portrait in top hat and railroad bridge

| Date | Mintage | F | VF | XF | Unc | BU |
|---|---|---|---|---|---|---|
| 2001 | — | — | — | — | 10.00 | — |

**CROWN KM# 920a Weight:** 28.2800 g. **Composition:** 0.9250 Silver .8410 oz. ASW **Series:** Victorian Era

| Date | Mintage | F | VF | XF | Unc | BU |
|---|---|---|---|---|---|---|
| 2001 Proof | 10,000 | Value: 47.50 | | | | |

**CROWN KM# 922 Composition:** Copper-Nickel **Series:** Victorian Era **Subject:** Charles Dickens **Obverse:** Queen's portrait **Reverse:** Portrait and scene from "Oliver Twist"

| Date | Mintage | F | VF | XF | Unc | BU |
|---|---|---|---|---|---|---|
| 2001 | — | — | — | — | 10.00 | — |

**CROWN KM# 922a Weight:** 28.2800 g. **Composition:** 0.9250 Silver .8410 oz. ASW **Series:** Victorian Era

| Date | Mintage | F | VF | XF | Unc | BU |
|---|---|---|---|---|---|---|
| 2001 Proof | 10,000 | Value: 47.50 | | | | |

**CROWN KM# 924 Composition:** Copper-Nickel **Series:** Victorian Era **Subject:** Charles Darwin **Obverse:** Queen's portrait **Reverse:** Portrait, ship and a squatting aboriginal figure

| Date | Mintage | F | VF | XF | Unc | BU |
|---|---|---|---|---|---|---|
| 2001 | — | — | — | — | 10.00 | — |

**CROWN KM# 924a Weight:** 28.2800 g. **Composition:** 0.9250 Silver .8410 oz. ASW **Series:** Victorian Era

| Date | Mintage | F | VF | XF | Unc | BU |
|---|---|---|---|---|---|---|
| 2001 Proof | 10,000 | Value: 47.50 | | | | |

**CROWN KM# 927 Weight:** 28.2800 g. **Composition:** Copper-Nickel **Series:** Mythology of the Solar System **Obverse:** Queen's portrait **Reverse:** Standing goddess with snake basket **Edge:** Reeded **Size:** 38.6 mm.

| Date | Mintage | F | VF | XF | Unc | BU |
|---|---|---|---|---|---|---|
| 2001 | — | — | — | — | 10.00 | — |

**CROWN KM# 927a Weight:** 28.2800 g. **Composition:** 0.9250 Silver .8410 oz. ASW **Series:** Mythology of the Solar System **Edge:** Reeded **Size:** 38.6 mm.

| Date | Mintage | F | VF | XF | Unc | BU |
|---|---|---|---|---|---|---|
| 2001 Proof | 10,000 | Value: 47.50 | | | | |

**CROWN KM# 928 Ring Weight:** 12.9900 g. **Ring Composition:** 0.9250 Silver .3863 oz. ASW **Center Weight:** 5.0000 g. **Center Composition:** Titanium **Series:** Mythology of the Solar System **Subject:** Solar System **Obverse:** Queen's portrait **Reverse:** Standing goddess with snake basket **Edge:** Reeded **Size:** 32.25 mm.

| Date | Mintage | F | VF | XF | Unc | BU |
|---|---|---|---|---|---|---|
| 2001 In Proof sets only | 2,001 | Value: 87.50 | | | | |

**CROWN KM# 930 Composition:** Copper-Nickel **Series:** Mythology of the Solar System **Subject:** Sun **Obverse:** Queen's portrait **Reverse:** Helios in chariot and the sun

| Date | Mintage | F | VF | XF | Unc | BU |
|---|---|---|---|---|---|---|
| 2001 | — | — | — | — | 10.00 | — |

**CROWN KM# 930a Weight:** 28.2800 g. **Composition:** 0.9250 Silver .8410 oz. ASW **Series:** Mythology of the Solar System

| Date | Mintage | F | VF | XF | Unc | BU |
|---|---|---|---|---|---|---|
| 2001 Proof | 10,000 | Value: 47.50 | | | | |

**CROWN KM# 930a.1 Weight:** 28.2800 g. **Composition:** 0.9250 Silver .8410 oz. ASW **Series:** Mythology of the Solar System **Reverse:** Similar but with a fiery hologram in the sun

| Date | Mintage | F | VF | XF | Unc | BU |
|---|---|---|---|---|---|---|
| 2001 In Proof sets only | 2,001 | Value: 87.50 | | | | |

**CROWN** **KM# 932** **Composition:** Copper-Nickel **Series:** Mythology of the Solar System **Subject:** Moon **Obverse:** Queen's portrait **Reverse:** Goddess Diana and the moon

| Date | Mintage | F | VF | XF | Unc | BU |
|---|---|---|---|---|---|---|
| 2001 Proof | 5,000 | Value: 175 | | | | |

**CROWN** **KM# 932a** **Weight:** 28.2800 g. **Composition:** 0.9250 Silver .8410 oz. ASW **Series:** Mythology of the Solar System

| Date | Mintage | F | VF | XF | Unc | BU |
|---|---|---|---|---|---|---|
| 2001 Proof | 10,000 | Value: 47.50 | | | | |

**CROWN** **KM# 932a.1** **Weight:** 28.2800 g. **Composition:** 0.9250 Silver .8410 oz. ASW **Series:** Mythology of the Solar System **Reverse:** Similar but with a small pearl set in the moon

| Date | Mintage | F | VF | XF | Unc | BU |
|---|---|---|---|---|---|---|
| 2001 In Proof sets only | 2,001 | Value: 87.50 | | | | |

**CROWN** **KM# 934** **Composition:** Copper-Nickel **Series:** Mythology of the Solar System **Subject:** Earth **Obverse:** Queen's portrait **Reverse:** Atlas carrying the earth

| Date | Mintage | F | VF | XF | Unc | BU |
|---|---|---|---|---|---|---|
| 2001 | — | — | — | — | 10.00 | — |

**CROWN** **KM# 934a** **Weight:** 28.2800 g. **Composition:** 0.9250 Silver .8410 oz. ASW **Series:** Mythology of the Solar System

| Date | Mintage | F | VF | XF | Unc | BU |
|---|---|---|---|---|---|---|
| 2001 Proof | 10,000 | Value: 47.50 | | | | |

**CROWN** **KM# 934a.1** **Weight:** 28.2800 g. **Composition:** 0.9250 Silver .8410 oz. ASW **Series:** Mythology of the Solar System **Reverse:** Similar but with a fancy diamond set in the earth

| Date | Mintage | F | VF | XF | Unc | BU |
|---|---|---|---|---|---|---|
| 2001 In Proof sets only | 2,001 | Value: 87.50 | | | | |

**CROWN** **KM# 936** **Composition:** Copper-Nickel **Series:** Mythology of the Solar System **Subject:** Neptune **Obverse:** Queen's portrait **Reverse:** Seated god with trident and ringed planet

| Date | Mintage | F | VF | XF | Unc | BU |
|---|---|---|---|---|---|---|
| 2001 | — | — | — | — | 10.00 | — |

**CROWN** **KM# 936a** **Weight:** 28.2800 g. **Composition:** 0.9250 Silver .8410 oz. ASW **Series:** Mythology of the Solar System

| Date | Mintage | F | VF | XF | Unc | BU |
|---|---|---|---|---|---|---|
| 2001 Proof | 10,000 | Value: 47.50 | | | | |

**CROWN** **KM# 938** **Composition:** Copper-Nickel **Series:** Mythology of the Solar System **Subject:** Jupiter **Obverse:** Queen's portrait **Reverse:** Seated god with lightening bolts and a planet

| Date | Mintage | F | VF | XF | Unc | BU |
|---|---|---|---|---|---|---|
| 2001 | — | — | — | — | 10.00 | — |

**CROWN** **KM# 938a** **Weight:** 28.2800 g. **Composition:** 0.9250 Silver .8410 oz. ASW **Series:** Mythology of the Solar System

| Date | Mintage | F | VF | XF | Unc | BU |
|---|---|---|---|---|---|---|
| 2001 Proof | 10,000 | Value: 47.50 | | | | |

**CROWN** **KM# 940** **Composition:** Copper-Nickel **Series:** Mythology of the Solar System **Subject:** Mars **Obverse:** Queen's portrait **Reverse:** Standing Roman soldier and a planet

| Date | Mintage | F | VF | XF | Unc | BU |
|---|---|---|---|---|---|---|
| 2001 | — | Value: 10.00 | | | | |

**CROWN** **KM# 940a** **Weight:** 28.2800 g. **Composition:** 0.9250 Silver .8410 oz. ASW **Series:** Mythology of the Solar System

| Date | Mintage | F | VF | XF | Unc | BU |
|---|---|---|---|---|---|---|
| 2001 Proof | 10,000 | Value: 47.50 | | | | |

**CROWN** **KM# 942** **Composition:** Copper-Nickel **Series:** Mythology of the Solar System **Subject:** Mercury **Obverse:** Queen's portrait **Reverse:** Seated god with cadceus and a planet

| Date | Mintage | F | VF | XF | Unc | BU |
|---|---|---|---|---|---|---|
| 2001 | — | — | — | — | 10.00 | — |

**CROWN** **KM# 942a** **Weight:** 28.2800 g. **Composition:** 0.9250 Silver .8410 oz. ASW **Series:** Mythology of the Solar System

| Date | Mintage | F | VF | XF | Unc | BU |
|---|---|---|---|---|---|---|
| 2001 Proof | 10,000 | Value: 47.50 | | | | |

**CROWN** **KM# 944** **Composition:** Copper-Nickel **Series:** Mythology of the Solar System **Subject:** Uranus **Obverse:** Queen's portrait **Reverse:** Seated god with scepter

| Date | Mintage | F | VF | XF | Unc | BU |
|---|---|---|---|---|---|---|
| 2001 | — | — | — | — | 10.00 | — |

**CROWN** **KM# 944a** **Weight:** 28.2800 g. **Composition:** 0.9250 Silver .8410 oz. ASW **Series:** Mythology of the Solar System

| Date | Mintage | F | VF | XF | Unc | BU |
|---|---|---|---|---|---|---|
| 2001 Proof | 10,000 | Value: 47.50 | | | | |

**CROWN** **KM# 946** **Composition:** Copper-Nickel **Series:** Mythology of the Solar System **Subject:** Saturn **Obverse:** Queen's portrait **Reverse:** Seated god with long handled sickle and a ringed planet

| Date | Mintage | F | VF | XF | Unc | BU |
|---|---|---|---|---|---|---|
| 2001 | — | — | — | — | 10.00 | — |

**CROWN** **KM# 946a** **Weight:** 28.2800 g. **Composition:** 0.9250 Silver .8410 oz. ASW **Series:** Mythology of the Solar System

| Date | Mintage | F | VF | XF | Unc | BU |
|---|---|---|---|---|---|---|
| 2001 Proof | 10,000 | Value: 47.50 | | | | |

**CROWN** **KM# 948** **Composition:** Copper-Nickel **Series:** Mythology of the Solar System **Subject:** Pluto **Obverse:** Queen's portrait **Reverse:** Seated god with dogs and planet

| Date | Mintage | F | VF | XF | Unc | BU |
|---|---|---|---|---|---|---|
| 2001 | — | — | — | — | 10.00 | — |

**CROWN** **KM# 948a** **Weight:** 28.2800 g. **Composition:** 0.9250 Silver .8410 oz. ASW **Series:** Mythology of the Solar System

| Date | Mintage | F | VF | XF | Unc | BU |
|---|---|---|---|---|---|---|
| 2001 Proof | 10,000 | Value: 47.50 | | | | |

**CROWN** **KM# 950** **Composition:** Copper-Nickel **Series:** Mythology of the Solar System **Subject:** Venus **Obverse:** Queen's portrait **Reverse:** Goddess seated on a half shell

| Date | Mintage | F | VF | XF | Unc | BU |
|---|---|---|---|---|---|---|
| 2001 | — | — | — | — | 10.00 | — |

**CROWN** **KM# 950a** **Weight:** 28.2800 g. **Composition:** 0.9250 Silver .8410 oz. ASW **Series:** Mythology of the Solar System

| Date | Mintage | F | VF | XF | Unc | BU |
|---|---|---|---|---|---|---|
| 2001 Proof | 10,000 | Value: 47.50 | | | | |

**CROWN** **KM# 952** **Weight:** 28.2800 g. **Composition:** Copper-Nickel **Subject:** Queen's 75th Birthday **Obverse:** Queen's portrait **Reverse:** Queen in Order of Garter robes **Edge:** Reeded **Size:** 38.6 mm.

| Date | Mintage | F | VF | XF | Unc | BU |
|---|---|---|---|---|---|---|
| 2001 | — | — | — | — | 10.00 | — |

**CROWN** **KM# 952a** **Weight:** 28.2800 g. **Composition:** 0.9250 Silver .8410 oz. ASW

| Date | Mintage | F | VF | XF | Unc | BU |
|---|---|---|---|---|---|---|
| 2001 Proof | 10,000 | Value: 47.50 | | | | |

**CROWN** **KM# 955** **Weight:** 28.2800 g. **Composition:** Copper-Nickel **Series:** Victorian Age Part II **Obverse:** Queen's portrait **Reverse:** Victoria learning of her accession **Edge:** Reeded **Size:** 38.6 mm.

| Date | Mintage | F | VF | XF | Unc | BU |
|---|---|---|---|---|---|---|
| 2001 | — | — | — | — | 10.00 | — |

**CROWN** **KM# 955a** **Weight:** 28.2800 g. **Composition:** 0.9250 Silver .8410 oz. ASW **Series:** Victorian Age Part II **Edge:** Reeded **Size:** 38.6 mm.

| Date | Mintage | F | VF | XF | Unc | BU |
|---|---|---|---|---|---|---|
| 2001 Proof | 10,000 | Value: 47.50 | | | | |

**CROWN** **KM# 957** **Composition:** Copper-Nickel **Series:** Victorian Age Part II **Subject:** Royal Family **Reverse:** Victoria and Albert seated with children **Edge:** Reeded **Size:** 38.6 mm.

| Date | Mintage | F | VF | XF | Unc | BU |
|---|---|---|---|---|---|---|
| 2001 | — | — | — | — | 10.00 | — |

**CROWN** **KM# 957a** **Weight:** 28.2800 g. **Composition:** 0.9250 Silver .8410 oz. ASW **Series:** Victorian Age Part II **Edge:** Reeded **Size:** 38.6 mm.

| Date | Mintage | F | VF | XF | Unc | BU |
|---|---|---|---|---|---|---|
| 2001 Proof | 10,000 | Value: 47.50 | | | | |

**CROWN** **KM# 959** **Composition:** Copper-Nickel **Series:** Victorian Age Part II **Subject:** Victoria in Scotland **Reverse:** Victoria on horse with servant **Edge:** Reeded **Size:** 38.6 mm.

| Date | Mintage | F | VF | XF | Unc | BU |
|---|---|---|---|---|---|---|
| 2001 | 2,001 | — | — | — | 10.00 | — |

**CROWN** **KM# 959a** **Weight:** 28.2800 g. **Composition:** 0.9250 Silver .8410 oz. ASW **Series:** Victorian Age Part II **Edge:** Reeded **Size:** 38.6 mm.

| Date | Mintage | F | VF | XF | Unc | BU |
|---|---|---|---|---|---|---|
| 2001 Proof | 10,000 | Value: 47.50 | | | | |

**CROWN** **KM# 961** **Composition:** Copper-Nickel **Series:** Victorian Age Part II **Subject:** Gladstone and Disraeli **Reverse:** Portraits of both politicians **Edge:** Reeded **Size:** 38.6 mm.

| Date | Mintage | F | VF | XF | Unc | BU |
|---|---|---|---|---|---|---|
| 2001 | — | — | — | — | 10.00 | — |

**CROWN** **KM# 961a** **Weight:** 28.2800 g. **Composition:** 0.9250 Silver .8410 oz. ASW **Series:** Victorian Age Part II **Edge:** Reeded **Size:** 38.6 mm.

| Date | Mintage | F | VF | XF | Unc | BU |
|---|---|---|---|---|---|---|
| 2001 Proof | 10,000 | Value: 47.50 | | | | |

**CROWN** **KM# 963** **Composition:** Copper-Nickel **Series:** Victorian Age Part II **Subject:** Florence Nightingale **Reverse:** Woman holding lantern **Edge:** Reeded **Size:** 38.6 mm.

| Date | Mintage | F | VF | XF | Unc | BU |
|---|---|---|---|---|---|---|
| 2001 | — | — | — | — | 10.00 | — |

**CROWN** **KM# 963a** **Weight:** 28.2800 g. **Composition:** 0.9250 Silver .8410 oz. ASW **Series:** Victorian Age Part II **Edge:** Reeded **Size:** 38.6 mm.

| Date | Mintage | F | VF | XF | Unc | BU |
|---|---|---|---|---|---|---|
| 2001 Proof | 10,000 | Value: 47.50 | | | | |

**CROWN** **KM# 965** **Composition:** Copper-Nickel **Series:** Victorian Age Part II **Subject:** Lord Tennyson **Reverse:** Portrait with the Light Brigade in background **Edge:** Reeded **Size:** 38.6 mm.

| Date | Mintage | F | VF | XF | Unc | BU |
|---|---|---|---|---|---|---|
| 2001 | — | — | — | — | 10.00 | — |

**CROWN** **KM# 965a** **Weight:** 28.2800 g. **Composition:** 0.9250 Silver .8410 oz. ASW **Series:** Victorian Age Part II **Edge:** Reeded **Size:** 38.6 mm.

| Date | Mintage | F | VF | XF | Unc | BU |
|---|---|---|---|---|---|---|
| 2001 Proof | 10,000 | Value: 47.50 | | | | |

**CROWN** **KM# 967** **Composition:** Copper-Nickel **Series:** Victorian Age Part II **Subject:** Stanley and Livingstone **Reverse:** Stanley meeting Dr. Livingstone **Edge:** Reeded **Size:** 38.6 mm.

| Date | Mintage | F | VF | XF | Unc | BU |
|---|---|---|---|---|---|---|
| 2001 | — | — | — | — | 10.00 | — |

**CROWN** **KM# 967a** **Weight:** 28.2800 g. **Composition:** 0.9250 Silver .8410 oz. ASW **Series:** Victorian Age Part II **Edge:** Reeded **Size:** 38.6 mm.

| Date | Mintage | F | VF | XF | Unc | BU |
|---|---|---|---|---|---|---|
| 2001 Proof | 10,000 | Value: 47.50 | | | | |

**CROWN** **KM# 969** **Composition:** Copper-Nickel **Series:** Victorian Age Part II **Subject:** Bronte Sisters **Reverse:** Portraits of three women **Edge:** Reeded **Size:** 38.6 mm.

| Date | Mintage | F | VF | XF | Unc | BU |
|---|---|---|---|---|---|---|
| 2001 | — | — | — | — | 10.00 | — |

**CROWN** **KM# 969a** **Weight:** 28.2800 g. **Composition:** 0.9250 Silver .8410 oz. ASW **Edge:** Reeded **Size:** 38.6 mm.

| Date | Mintage | F | VF | XF | Unc | BU |
|---|---|---|---|---|---|---|
| 2001 Proof | 10,000 | Value: 47.50 | | | | |

**CROWN** **KM# 906a** **Weight:** 31.1035 g. **Composition:** 0.9990 Silver 1.0000 oz. ASW **Note:** 31.1035 .999 Silver, 1.0000 ASW with a gold plated inner ring and a blackened outer ring.

| Date | Mintage | F | VF | XF | Unc | BU |
|---|---|---|---|---|---|---|
| 2001 Proof | 2,001 | Value: 47.50 | | | | |

**2 CROWN** **KM# 128** **Weight:** 62.2070 g. **Composition:** 0.9990 Silver 2.0000 oz. ASW **Subject:** Japanese Royal Wedding **Obverse:** Queen's portrait **Reverse:** Pair of peacocks at ease

| Date | Mintage | F | VF | XF | Unc | BU |
|---|---|---|---|---|---|---|
| 1993 Proof | Est. 20,000 | Value: 65.00 | | | | |

**2 CROWN** **KM# 128a** **Weight:** 62.2070 g. **Composition:** 0.9999 Gold 2.0000 oz. AGW **Subject:** Japanese Royal Wedding **Obverse:** Queen's portrait **Reverse:** Pair of peacocks at ease

| Date | Mintage | F | VF | XF | Unc | BU |
|---|---|---|---|---|---|---|
| 1993 Proof | Est. 2,500 | Value: 1,000 | | | | |

**2 CROWN** **KM# 129** **Weight:** 62.2070 g. **Composition:** 0.9990 Silver 2.0000 oz. ASW **Subject:** Japanese Royal Wedding **Obverse:** Queen's portrait **Reverse:** Two peacocks, one in full display

| Date | Mintage | F | VF | XF | Unc | BU |
|---|---|---|---|---|---|---|
| 1993 Proof | Est. 20,000 | Value: 37.50 | | | | |

**2 CROWN** **KM# 129a** **Weight:** 62.2070 g. **Composition:** 0.9999 Gold 2.0000 oz. AGW **Subject:** Japanese Royal Wedding **Obverse:** Queen's portrait **Reverse:** Two peacocks, one in full display

| Date | Mintage | F | VF | XF | Unc | BU |
|---|---|---|---|---|---|---|
| 1993 Proof | Est. 2,500 | Value: 900 | | | | |

**5 CROWN** **KM# 106** **Weight:** 155.9230 g. **Composition:** 0.9990 Silver 5.0000 oz. ASW **Subject:** Olympics - Discus Thrower **Obverse:** Queen's portrait **Note:** Illustration reduced. Actual size 65 millimeters.

| Date | Mintage | F | VF | XF | Unc | BU |
|---|---|---|---|---|---|---|
| 1991 Proof | Est. 1,000 | Value: 225 | | | | |

**5 CROWN** **KM# 451** **Weight:** 155.5175 g. **Composition:** 0.9999 Gold 5.0000 oz. AGW **Subject:** Lord Buddha **Note:** Similar to 1 Crown, KM#449.

| Date | Mintage | F | VF | XF | Unc | BU |
|---|---|---|---|---|---|---|
| 1996 Proof | Est. 250 | — | — | — | — | — |

**5 CROWN** **KM# 907** **Ring Weight:** 73.4100 g. **Ring Composition:** 0.9999 Silver 2.3599 oz. ASW **Center Weight:** 26.9000 g. **Center Composition:** 0.9995 Platinum .8644 oz. APW **Subject:** 21st Century **Obverse:** Like crown KM#906 **Reverse:** Like Crown KM#906 **Edge:** Reeded **Size:** 50 mm.

| Date | Mintage | F | VF | XF | Unc | BU |
|---|---|---|---|---|---|---|
| 2001 Proof | 199 | Value: 1,740 | | | | |

**10 CROWN** KM# 107 **Weight:** 311.8460 g. **Composition:** 0.9990 Silver 10.0000 oz. ASW **Subject:** Olympics - Ancient Runners **Obverse:** Queen's portrait **Size:** 73 mm. **Note:** Illustration reudced.

| Date | Mintage | F | VF | XF | Unc | BU |
|---|---|---|---|---|---|---|
| 1991 Proof | Est. 1,000 | Value: 300 | | | | |

**10 CROWN** KM# 130 **Weight:** 311.8460 g. **Composition:** 0.9990 Silver 10.0000 oz. ASW **Subject:** Japanese Royal Wedding **Note:** Similar to 2 Crown, KM#128.

| Date | Mintage | F | VF | XF | Unc | BU |
|---|---|---|---|---|---|---|
| 1993 Proof | Est. 5,000 | Value: 285 | | | | |

**10 CROWN** KM# 131 **Weight:** 311.8460 g. **Composition:** 0.9990 Silver 10.0000 oz. ASW **Subject:** Japanese Royal Wedding **Note:** Similar to 2 Crown, KM#129.

| Date | Mintage | F | VF | XF | Unc | BU |
|---|---|---|---|---|---|---|
| 1993 Proof | Est. 5,000 | Value: 285 | | | | |

**40 CROWN** KM# 333 **Weight:** 1244.1400 g. **Composition:** 0.9990 Silver 40.0000 oz. ASW **Subject:** Rock of Gibraltar and The Rising Sun **Size:** 100 mm. **Note:** Illustration reduced.

| Date | Mintage | F | VF | XF | Unc | BU |
|---|---|---|---|---|---|---|
| 1994 Proof | Est. 1,500 | Value: 550 | | | | |

**POUND** KM# 18 **Composition:** Nickel-Brass **Reverse:** Gibraltar Castle and Key

| Date | Mintage | F | VF | XF | Unc | BU |
|---|---|---|---|---|---|---|
| 1988 AA | — | — | — | — | 3.50 | — |
| 1990 AA | — | — | — | — | 3.50 | — |
| 1991 AA | — | — | — | — | 3.50 | — |
| 1992 AA | — | — | — | — | 3.50 | — |
| 1993 AA | — | — | — | — | 3.50 | — |
| 1996 AA | — | — | — | — | 3.50 | — |
| 1997 AA | — | — | — | — | 3.50 | — |

**POUND** KM# 18a **Weight:** 9.5000 g. **Composition:** 0.9250 Silver .2825 oz. ASW

| Date | Mintage | F | VF | XF | Unc | BU |
|---|---|---|---|---|---|---|
| 1988 Proof | — | Value: 15.00 | | | | |

**POUND** KM# 18b **Weight:** 9.5000 g. **Composition:** 0.9170 Gold .2801 oz. AGW

| Date | Mintage | F | VF | XF | Unc | BU |
|---|---|---|---|---|---|---|
| 1988 Proof | — | Value: 350 | | | | |

**POUND** KM# 32 **Composition:** Nickel-Brass **Reverse:** 150th Anniversary of Gibraltar Coinage

| Date | Mintage | F | VF | XF | Unc | BU |
|---|---|---|---|---|---|---|
| 1989 | — | — | — | — | 4.00 | — |

**POUND** KM# 32a **Weight:** 9.5000 g. **Composition:** 0.9250 Silver .2826 oz. ASW

| Date | Mintage | F | VF | XF | Unc | BU |
|---|---|---|---|---|---|---|
| 1989 Proof | Est. 2,500 | Value: 35.00 | | | | |

**POUND** KM# 32b **Weight:** 9.5000 g. **Composition:** 0.9170 Gold .2801 oz. AGW **Reverse:** 150th Anniversary of Gibraltar Coinage

| Date | Mintage | F | VF | XF | Unc | BU |
|---|---|---|---|---|---|---|
| 1989 Proof | 150 | Value: 350 | | | | |

**POUND** KM# 32c **Weight:** 9.0000 g. **Composition:** 0.9500 Platinum .2749 oz. APW

| Date | Mintage | F | VF | XF | Unc | BU |
|---|---|---|---|---|---|---|
| 1989 Proof | 100 | Value: 375 | | | | |

**POUND** KM# 191 **Composition:** Nickel-Brass **Reverse:** Referendum of 1967

| Date | Mintage | F | VF | XF | Unc | BU |
|---|---|---|---|---|---|---|
| 1993 | — | — | — | — | 4.50 | — |

**POUND** KM# 191a **Weight:** 9.5000 g. **Composition:** 0.9250 Silver .2825 oz. ASW

| Date | Mintage | F | VF | XF | Unc | BU |
|---|---|---|---|---|---|---|
| 1993 Proof | Est. 5,000 | Value: 35.00 | | | | |

**POUND** KM# 191b **Weight:** 9.5000 g. **Composition:** 0.9170 Gold .2801 oz. AGW **Subject:** Referendum of 1967 **Obverse:** Queen's portrait right **Reverse:** Gibraltar arms above Rock of Gibraltar with Union Jack background

| Date | Mintage | F | VF | XF | Unc | BU |
|---|---|---|---|---|---|---|
| 1993 Proof | Est. 3,500 | Value: 350 | | | | |

**POUND** KM# 324 **Composition:** Virenium **Reverse:** 40th Anniversary - Queen Elizabeth II's 1st Royal Visit to Gibraltar

| Date | Mintage | F | VF | XF | Unc | BU |
|---|---|---|---|---|---|---|
| 1994 AA | Est. 3,500 | — | — | — | 7.50 | — |

**POUND** KM# 340 **Composition:** Nickel-Brass **Reverse:** National Day - Rock of Gibraltar

| Date | Mintage | F | VF | XF | Unc | BU |
|---|---|---|---|---|---|---|
| 1995 AA | — | — | — | — | 3.50 | — |

**POUND** KM# 340a **Weight:** 9.5000 g. **Composition:** 0.9250 Silver .2825 oz. ASW

| Date | Mintage | F | VF | XF | Unc | BU |
|---|---|---|---|---|---|---|
| 1995 Proof | 3,500 | Value: 35.00 | | | | |

**POUND** KM# 869 **Composition:** Nickel-Brass **Obverse:** Rank-Broadley portrait of Queen Elizabeth II **Reverse:** Gibraltar castle and key

| Date | Mintage | F | VF | XF | Unc | BU |
|---|---|---|---|---|---|---|
| 1998 AA | — | — | — | — | 3.50 | — |
| 1999 AA | — | — | — | — | 3.50 | — |

**2 POUNDS** KM# 24 **Composition:** Virenium **Reverse:** Cannon in tunnel of fortress

| Date | Mintage | F | VF | XF | Unc | BU |
|---|---|---|---|---|---|---|
| 1988 AA | — | — | — | — | 7.50 | — |
| 1989 AA | — | — | — | — | 7.50 | — |
| 1990 AA | — | — | — | — | 7.50 | — |
| 1991 AA | — | — | — | — | 7.50 | — |
| 1993 AA | — | — | — | — | 7.50 | — |
| 1995 AA | — | — | — | — | 7.50 | — |
| 1995 AB | — | — | — | — | 7.50 | — |
| 1995 AC | — | — | — | — | 7.50 | — |
| 1996 AA | — | — | — | — | 7.50 | — |

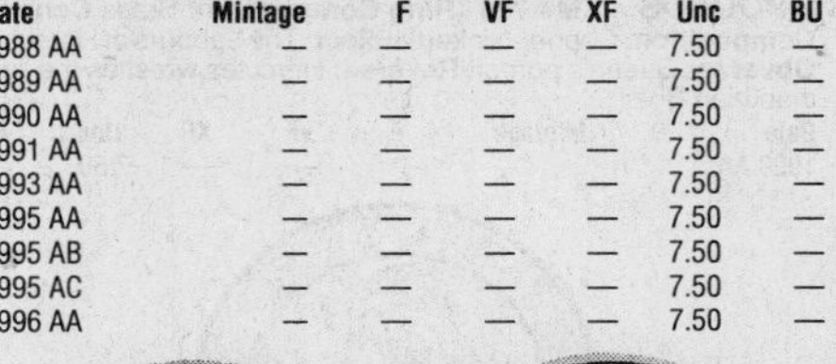

**2 POUNDS** KM# 98 **Composition:** Virenium **Reverse:** Columbus and Ship

| Date | Mintage | F | VF | XF | Unc | BU |
|---|---|---|---|---|---|---|
| 1992 AA | — | — | — | — | 6.50 | — |

**2 POUNDS** KM# 98a **Weight:** 9.3000 g. **Composition:** 0.9250 Silver .2766 oz. ASW

| Date | Mintage | F | VF | XF | Unc | BU |
|---|---|---|---|---|---|---|
| 1992 Proof | Est. 5,000 | Value: 40.00 | | | | |

**2 POUNDS** KM# 98b **Weight:** 15.9400 g. **Composition:** 0.9170 Gold .4700 oz. AGW **Reverse:** Columbus and Ship

| Date | Mintage | F | VF | XF | Unc | BU |
|---|---|---|---|---|---|---|
| 1992 Proof | Est. 5,000 | — | — | — | — | — |

**2 POUNDS** KM# 98c **Weight:** 18.0000 g. **Composition:** 0.9500 Platinum .5498 oz. APW

| Date | Mintage | F | VF | XF | Unc | BU |
|---|---|---|---|---|---|---|
| 1992 Proof | Est. 1,000 | — | — | — | — | — |

**2 POUNDS** KM# 325 **Composition:** Virenium **Reverse:** 40th Anniversary - Queen Elizabeth II's 1st Royal Visit to Gibraltar

| Date | Mintage | F | VF | XF | Unc | BU |
|---|---|---|---|---|---|---|
| 1994 AA | Est. 5,000 | — | — | — | 6.50 | — |

**2 POUNDS** KM# 755 **Ring Composition:** Brass **Center Composition:** Copper-Nickel **Subject:** The Labours of Hercules **Obverse:** Queen's portrait by Maklouf **Reverse:** Hercules wrestling the Nimean Lion

| Date | Mintage | F | VF | XF | Unc | BU |
|---|---|---|---|---|---|---|
| 1997 | — | — | — | — | 7.50 | — |

**2 POUNDS** KM# 755a **Weight:** 12.0000 g. **Composition:** 0.9990 Gold Plated Silver .999 oz. ASW AGW

| Date | Mintage | F | VF | XF | Unc | BU |
|---|---|---|---|---|---|---|
| 1997 Proof | Est. 7,500 | Value: 60.00 | | | | |

**2 POUNDS** KM# 758a **Composition:** 0.9990 Gold Plated Silver .999 oz. ASW AGW

| Date | Mintage | F | VF | XF | Unc | BU |
|---|---|---|---|---|---|---|
| 1997 Proof | 7,500 | Value: 60.00 | | | | |

**2 POUNDS** KM# 756a **Weight:** 12.0000 g. **Composition:** 0.9990 Gold Plated Silver .999 oz. ASW AGW

| Date | Mintage | F | VF | XF | Unc | BU |
|---|---|---|---|---|---|---|
| 1997 Proof | Est. 7,500 | Value: 60.00 | | | | |

**2 POUNDS** KM# 757a **Weight:** 12.0000 g. **Composition:** 0.9990 Gold Plated Silver .999 oz. ASW AGW

| Date | Mintage | F | VF | XF | Unc | BU |
|---|---|---|---|---|---|---|
| 1997 Proof | Est. 7,500 | Value: 60.00 | | | | |

**2 POUNDS** **KM# 758** **Ring Composition:** Brass **Center Composition:** Copper-Nickel **Subject:** The Labours of Hercules **Obverse:** Queen's portrait **Reverse:** Hercules wrestles the Erymanthian Boar

| Date | Mintage | F | VF | XF | Unc | BU |
|---|---|---|---|---|---|---|
| 1998 AA | — | — | — | — | 7.50 | — |

**2 POUNDS** **KM# 757** **Ring Composition:** Brass **Center Composition:** Copper-Nickel **Subject:** The Labours of Hercules **Obverse:** Queen's portrait **Reverse:** Hercules and the Ceryneian Hind

| Date | Mintage | F | VF | XF | Unc | BU |
|---|---|---|---|---|---|---|
| 1998 AA | — | — | — | — | 7.50 | — |

**2 POUNDS** **KM# 756** **Ring Composition:** Brass **Center Composition:** Copper-Nickel **Subject:** The Labours of Hercules **Obverse:** Rank-Broadley portrait of Queen Elizabeth II **Reverse:** Hercules fighting the Hydra

| Date | Mintage | F | VF | XF | Unc | BU |
|---|---|---|---|---|---|---|
| 1998 AA | — | — | — | — | 7.50 | — |

**2 POUNDS** **KM# 759** **Composition:** 0.9990 Gold Plated Silver .999 oz. ASW AGW **Subject:** The Labours of Hercules **Obverse:** Queen's portrait **Reverse:** Hercules and teh Augean Stables

| Date | Mintage | F | VF | XF | Unc | BU |
|---|---|---|---|---|---|---|
| 1999 AA | — | — | — | — | 7.50 | — |

**2 POUNDS** **KM# 759a** **Weight:** 10.0000 g. **Composition:** 0.9990 Gold Plated Silver .999 oz. ASW AGW

| Date | Mintage | F | VF | XF | Unc | BU |
|---|---|---|---|---|---|---|
| 1999 Proof | Est. 25,000 | Value: 60.00 | | | | |

**2 POUNDS** **KM# 760** **Center Composition:** Copper-Nickel **Subject:** The Labours of Hercules **Obverse:** Queen's portrait **Reverse:** Hercules and the Cretan Bull

| Date | Mintage | F | VF | XF | Unc | BU |
|---|---|---|---|---|---|---|
| 1999 AA | — | — | — | — | 7.50 | — |

**2 POUNDS** **KM# 760a** **Weight:** 10.0000 g. **Composition:** 0.9990 Gold Plated Silver .999 oz. ASW AGW

| Date | Mintage | F | VF | XF | Unc | BU |
|---|---|---|---|---|---|---|
| 1999 Proof | Est. 25,000 | Value: 60.00 | | | | |

**2 POUNDS** **KM# 761** **Ring Composition:** Brass **Center Composition:** Copper-Nickel **Subject:** The Labours of Hercules **Obverse:** Queen's portrait **Reverse:** Hercules and the Stymphalian Birds

| Date | Mintage | F | VF | XF | Unc | BU |
|---|---|---|---|---|---|---|
| 1999 AA | — | — | — | — | 7.50 | — |

**2 POUNDS** **KM# 761a** **Weight:** 10.0000 g. **Composition:** 0.9990 Gold Plated Silver .999 oz. ASW AGW

| Date | Mintage | F | VF | XF | Unc | BU |
|---|---|---|---|---|---|---|
| 1999 Proof | Est. 25,000 | Value: 60.00 | | | | |

**2 POUNDS** **KM# 762** **Ring Composition:** Brass **Center Composition:** Copper-Nickel **Subject:** The Labours of Hercules **Obverse:** Queen's portrait **Reverse:** Hercules and the Mares of Diomedes

| Date | Mintage | F | VF | XF | Unc | BU |
|---|---|---|---|---|---|---|
| 1999 AA | — | — | — | — | 7.50 | — |

**2 POUNDS** **KM# 762a** **Weight:** 10.0000 g. **Composition:** 0.9990 Gold Plated Silver .999 oz. ASW AGW

| Date | Mintage | F | VF | XF | Unc | BU |
|---|---|---|---|---|---|---|
| 1999 Proof | Est. 25,000 | Value: 60.00 | | | | |

**2 POUNDS** **KM# 763** **Ring Composition:** Brass **Center Composition:** Copper-Nickel **Subject:** The Labours of Hercules **Obverse:** Queen's portrait **Reverse:** Hercules and Hippolyta's Girdle **Edge:** Reeded

| Date | Mintage | F | VF | XF | Unc | BU |
|---|---|---|---|---|---|---|
| 2000 AA | Est. 2,000 | — | — | — | 7.50 | — |

**2 POUNDS** **KM# 764** **Ring Composition:** Brass **Center Weight:** 12.0000 g. **Center Composition:** Copper-Nickel **Subject:** The Labours of Hercules - Geryon's Cattle **Obverse:** Queen's portrait **Reverse:** Hercules with cow and three devils shot by one arrow **Edge:** Reeded

| Date | Mintage | F | VF | XF | Unc | BU |
|---|---|---|---|---|---|---|
| 2000 AA | — | — | — | — | 7.50 | — |

**2 POUNDS** **KM# 765** **Ring Composition:** Brass **Center Composition:** Copper-Nickel **Subject:** The Labours of Hercules **Obverse:** Queen's portrait **Reverse:** Hercules carrying the world while facing a man with a bushel of apples **Edge:** Reeded

| Date | Mintage | F | VF | XF | Unc | BU |
|---|---|---|---|---|---|---|
| 2000 AA | — | — | — | — | 7.50 | — |
| 2000 AA | — | — | — | — | 7.50 | — |

**2 POUNDS** **KM# 766** **Ring Composition:** Brass **Center Composition:** Copper-Nickel **Subject:** The Labours of Hercules **Obverse:** Queen's portrait **Reverse:** Hercules chaining Cerberus

| Date | Mintage | F | VF | XF | Unc | BU |
|---|---|---|---|---|---|---|
| 2000 AA | — | — | — | — | 7.50 | — |
| 2000 AA | — | — | — | — | 7.50 | — |

**2 POUNDS** **KM# 763a** **Weight:** 12.0000 g. **Composition:** 0.9990 Silver .3854 oz. ASW **Subject:** The Labours of Hercules **Note:** Partially gold plated.

| Date | Mintage | F | VF | XF | Unc | BU |
|---|---|---|---|---|---|---|
| 2000 Proof | 7,500 | Value: 60.00 | | | | |

**2 POUNDS** **KM# 764a** **Weight:** 12.0000 g. **Composition:** 0.9990 Silver .3854 oz. ASW **Subject:** The Labours of Hercules **Note:** Partially gold plated.

| Date | Mintage | F | VF | XF | Unc | BU |
|---|---|---|---|---|---|---|
| 2000 Proof | 7,500 | Value: 60.00 | | | | |

**2 POUNDS** **KM# 765a** **Weight:** 12.0000 g. **Composition:** 0.9990 Silver .3854 oz. ASW **Subject:** The Labours of Hercules **Note:** Partially gold plated.

| Date | Mintage | F | VF | XF | Unc | BU |
|---|---|---|---|---|---|---|
| 2000 Proof | 7,500 | Value: 60.00 | | | | |

**2 POUNDS** **KM# 766a** **Weight:** 12.0000 g. **Composition:** 0.9990 Silver .3854 oz. ASW **Subject:** The Labours of Hercules **Note:** Partially gold plated.

| Date | Mintage | F | VF | XF | Unc | BU |
|---|---|---|---|---|---|---|
| 2000 Proof | 7,500 | Value: 60.00 | | | | |

**2 POUNDS** **KM# 970a** **Ring Composition:** 0.9990 Gold Plated Silver .3854 oz. ASW AGW **Center Weight:** 12.0000 g. **Center Composition:** 0.9990 Silver **Edge:** Reeded **Size:** 28.4 mm.

| Date | Mintage | F | VF | XF | Unc | BU |
|---|---|---|---|---|---|---|
| 2001 | 7,500 | — | — | — | 30.00 | — |

**2 POUNDS** **KM# 970** **Ring Weight:** 12.0000 g. **Ring Composition:** Brass **Center Composition:** Steel Copper-Nickel **Subject:** Bicentennial of the Union Jack **Obverse:** Queen's portrait **Reverse:** Standing Britannia wearing flag as a cape **Edge:** Reeded **Size:** 28.4 mm.

| Date | Mintage | F | VF | XF | Unc | BU |
|---|---|---|---|---|---|---|
| 2001 | — | — | — | — | 10.00 | — |

**5 POUNDS** **KM# 25** **Composition:** Virenium **Reverse:** Hercules

| Date | Mintage | F | VF | XF | Unc | BU |
|---|---|---|---|---|---|---|
| 1988 AA | — | — | — | — | 15.00 | — |
| 1989 AA | — | — | — | — | 15.00 | — |
| 1990 AA | — | — | — | — | 15.00 | — |
| 1991 AA | — | — | — | — | 15.00 | — |
| 1992 AA | — | — | — | — | 15.00 | — |
| 1993 AA | — | — | — | — | 15.00 | — |

**5 POUNDS** **KM# 309** **Composition:** Virenium **Reverse:** D-Day - Solider, sailor and pilot

| Date | Mintage | F | VF | XF | Unc | BU |
|---|---|---|---|---|---|---|
| 1994 | — | — | — | — | 16.50 | — |
| 1994 Proof | Est. 5,000 | Value: 20.00 | | | | |

**5 POUNDS** **KM# 309a** **Weight:** 23.5000 g. **Composition:** 0.9250 Silver .6989 oz. ASW

| Date | Mintage | F | VF | XF | Unc | BU |
|---|---|---|---|---|---|---|
| 1994 Proof | Est. 5,000 | Value: 40.00 | | | | |

**5 POUNDS** **KM# 309b** **Weight:** 39.8300 g. **Composition:** 0.9170 Gold 1.1743 oz. AGW **Reverse:** D-Day - Soldier, sailor and pilot

| Date | Mintage | F | VF | XF | Unc | BU |
|---|---|---|---|---|---|---|
| 1994 Proof | Est. 850 | — | — | — | — | — |

**5 POUNDS** **KM# 332** **Composition:** Virenium **Reverse:** 50th Anniversary - VE Day

| Date | Mintage | F | VF | XF | Unc | BU |
|---|---|---|---|---|---|---|
| 1995 | — | — | — | — | 16.50 | — |
| 1995 Proof | Est. 5,000 | Value: 20.00 | | | | |

**5 POUNDS** **KM# 332a** **Weight:** 23.5000 g. **Composition:** 0.9250 Silver .6989 oz. ASW

| Date | Mintage | F | VF | XF | Unc | BU |
|---|---|---|---|---|---|---|
| 1995 Proof | Est. 5,000 | Value: 40.00 | | | | |

**5 POUNDS** **KM# 332b** **Weight:** 39.8300 g. **Composition:** 0.9170 Gold 1.1743 oz. AGW **Reverse:** 50th Anniversary - VE Day

| Date | Mintage | F | VF | XF | Unc | BU |
|---|---|---|---|---|---|---|
| 1995 Proof | Est. 850 | Value: 850 | | | | |

**5 POUNDS** **KM# 334** **Composition:** Virenium **Reverse:** Queen Mother viewing bomb damaged Buckingham Palace

| Date | Mintage | F | VF | XF | Unc | BU |
|---|---|---|---|---|---|---|
| 1995 | — | — | — | — | 15.00 | — |

**5 POUNDS** **KM# 334a** **Weight:** 25.5000 g. **Composition:** 0.9250 Silver .6980 oz. ASW

| Date | Mintage | F | VF | XF | Unc | BU |
|---|---|---|---|---|---|---|
| 1995 Proof | Est. 5,000 | Value: 40.00 | | | | |

**5 POUNDS** **KM# 334b** **Weight:** 39.8300 g. **Composition:** 0.9170 Gold 1.1743 oz. AGW **Reverse:** Queen Mother viewing bomb damaged Buckingham Palace

| Date | Mintage | F | VF | XF | Unc | BU |
|---|---|---|---|---|---|---|
| 1995 Proof | Est. 850 | Value: 750 | | | | |

**5 POUNDS** **KM# 335** **Composition:** Virenium **Reverse:** VJ Day - Flag Raising

| Date | Mintage | F | VF | XF | Unc | BU |
|---|---|---|---|---|---|---|
| 1995 | — | — | — | — | 16.50 | — |
| 1995 Proof | Est. 5,000 | Value: 20.00 | | | | |

**5 POUNDS** **KM# 335a** **Weight:** 23.5000 g. **Composition:** 0.9250 Silver .6989 oz. ASW

| Date | Mintage | F | VF | XF | Unc | BU |
|---|---|---|---|---|---|---|
| 1995 Proof | Est. 5,000 | Value: 40.00 | | | | |

**5 POUNDS** **KM# 335b** **Weight:** 39.8300 g. **Composition:** 0.9170 Gold 1.1743 oz. AGW **Reverse:** VJ Day - Flag Raising

| Date | Mintage | F | VF | XF | Unc | BU |
|---|---|---|---|---|---|---|
| 1995 Proof | Est. 850 | Value: 850 | | | | |

**5 POUNDS** **KM# 341** **Composition:** Virenium **Reverse:** 190th Anniversary - Death of Admiral Nelson

| Date | Mintage | F | VF | XF | Unc | BU |
|---|---|---|---|---|---|---|
| 1995 | — | — | — | — | 15.00 | — |

**5 POUNDS** **KM# 341a** **Weight:** 23.5000 g. **Composition:** 0.9250 Silver .6989 oz. ASW

| Date | Mintage | F | VF | XF | Unc | BU |
|---|---|---|---|---|---|---|
| 1995 Proof | Est. 5,000 | Value: 40.00 | | | | |

**5 POUNDS** **KM# 341b** **Weight:** 39.0830 g. **Composition:** 0.9170 Gold 1.1743 oz. AGW **Reverse:** 190th Anniversary - Death of Admiral Nelson

| Date | Mintage | F | VF | XF | Unc | BU |
|---|---|---|---|---|---|---|
| 1995 Proof | Est. 850 | Value: 900 | | | | |

**5 POUNDS** **KM# 354** **Composition:** Virenium **Reverse:** 70th Birthday of Queen Elizabeth II

| Date | Mintage | F | VF | XF | Unc | BU |
|---|---|---|---|---|---|---|
| 1996 | — | — | — | — | 16.50 | — |

**5 POUNDS** **KM# 354a** **Weight:** 23.5000 g. **Composition:** 0.9250 Silver .6989 oz. ASW

| Date | Mintage | F | VF | XF | Unc | BU |
|---|---|---|---|---|---|---|
| 1996 Proof | Est. 5,000 | Value: 40.00 | | | | |

**5 POUNDS** **KM# 354b** **Weight:** 39.8300 g. **Composition:** 0.9170 Gold 1.1743 oz. AGW **Reverse:** 70th Birthday of Queen Elizabeth II

| Date | Mintage | F | VF | XF | Unc | BU |
|---|---|---|---|---|---|---|
| 1996 Proof | Est. 850 | Value: 650 | | | | |

**5 POUNDS** **KM# 355** **Composition:** Virenium **Reverse:** Olympics- Zeus on Throne

| Date | Mintage | F | VF | XF | Unc | BU |
|---|---|---|---|---|---|---|
| 1996 | — | — | — | — | 16.50 | — |

**5 POUNDS** **KM# 355a** **Weight:** 23.5000 g. **Composition:** 0.9250 Silver .3989 oz. ASW

| Date | Mintage | F | VF | XF | Unc | BU |
|---|---|---|---|---|---|---|
| 1996 Proof | Est. 5,000 | Value: 40.00 | | | | |

**5 POUNDS** **KM# 355b** **Weight:** 39.8300 g. **Composition:** 0.9170 Gold 1.1743 oz. AGW **Reverse:** Olympics - Zeus on Throne

| Date | Mintage | F | VF | XF | Unc | BU |
|---|---|---|---|---|---|---|
| 1996 Proof | 850 | Value: 750 | | | | |

**5 POUNDS** **KM# 527** **Composition:** Virenium **Subject:** Queen Elizabeth II's Golden Wedding Anniversary **Obverse:** Queen's portrait **Reverse:** Two hands

| Date | Mintage | F | VF | XF | Unc | BU |
|---|---|---|---|---|---|---|
| 1997 | — | — | — | — | 17.50 | — |

**5 POUNDS** **KM# 527a** **Weight:** 25.5000 g. **Composition:** 0.9250 Silver .6989 oz. ASW

| Date | Mintage | F | VF | XF | Unc | BU |
|---|---|---|---|---|---|---|
| 1997 Proof | Est. 10,000 | Value: 40.00 | | | | |

**5 POUNDS** **KM# 527b** **Weight:** 39.8300 g. **Composition:** 0.9170 Gold 1.1743 oz. AGW **Subject:** Queen Elizabeth II's Golden Wedding Anniversary **Obverse:** Queen's portrait **Reverse:** Two hands

| Date | Mintage | F | VF | XF | Unc | BU |
|---|---|---|---|---|---|---|
| 1997 Proof | Est. 850 | Value: 750 | | | | |

**5 POUNDS** **KM# 605** **Composition:** Virenium **Subject:** Bicentennial - Arrival of Commodore Nelson **Obverse:** Queen's portrait **Reverse:** Cameo portrait of Nelson above left of his ship

| Date | Mintage | F | VF | XF | Unc | BU |
|---|---|---|---|---|---|---|
| 1997 AA | — | — | — | — | 16.50 | — |

**5 POUNDS** **KM# 605a** **Weight:** 23.5000 g. **Composition:** 0.9250 Silver .6989 oz. ASW

| Date | Mintage | F | VF | XF | Unc | BU |
|---|---|---|---|---|---|---|
| 1997 Proof | Est. 10,000 | Value: 40.00 | | | | |

**5 POUNDS** **KM# 605b** **Weight:** 39.8300 g. **Composition:** 0.9170 Gold 1.1743 oz. AGW **Subject:** Bicentennial - Arrival of Commodore Nelson **Obverse:** Queen's portrait **Reverse:** Cameo portrait of Nelson above left of his ship

| Date | Mintage | F | VF | XF | Unc | BU |
|---|---|---|---|---|---|---|
| 1997 Proof | Est. 850 | Value: 850 | | | | |

**5 POUNDS** **KM# 607** **Composition:** Virenium **Subject:** Last Voyage of Britannia **Obverse:** Queen's portrait **Reverse:** Ship sailing past Gibraltar

| Date | Mintage | F | VF | XF | Unc | BU |
|---|---|---|---|---|---|---|
| 1997 AA | — | — | — | — | 16.50 | — |

**5 POUNDS** **KM# 607a** **Weight:** 23.5000 g. **Composition:** 0.9250 Silver .6989 oz. ASW

| Date | Mintage | F | VF | XF | Unc | BU |
|---|---|---|---|---|---|---|
| 1997 Proof | Est. 5,000 | Value: 50.00 | | | | |

**5 POUNDS** **KM# 607b** **Weight:** 39.8300 g. **Composition:** 0.9170 Gold 1.1743 oz. AGW **Subject:** Last Voyage of Britannia **Obverse:** Queen's portrait **Reverse:** Ship sailing past Gibraltar

| Date | Mintage | F | VF | XF | Unc | BU |
|---|---|---|---|---|---|---|
| 1997 Proof | Est. 850 | Value: 850 | | | | |

**5 POUNDS** **KM# 740** **Composition:** Virenium **Subject:** 40th Anniversary of Radio Gibraltar **Obverse:** Queen's portrait **Reverse:** Radio broadcaster on the job

| Date | Mintage | F | VF | XF | Unc | BU |
|---|---|---|---|---|---|---|
| 1998 | — | — | — | — | 16.00 | — |

**5 POUNDS** **KM# 740a** **Weight:** 23.5000 g. **Composition:** 0.9250 Silver .6989 oz. ASW

| Date | Mintage | F | VF | XF | Unc | BU |
|---|---|---|---|---|---|---|
| 1998 Proof | Est. 5,000 | Value: 40.00 | | | | |

**5 POUNDS** **KM# 740b** **Weight:** 39.8300 g. **Composition:** 0.9170 Gold 1.1743 oz. AGW **Subject:** 40th Anniversary of Radio Gibraltar **Obverse:** Queen's portrait **Reverse:** Radio broadcaster on the job

| Date | Mintage | F | VF | XF | Unc | BU |
|---|---|---|---|---|---|---|
| 1998 Proof | Est. 850 | Value: 850 | | | | |

**5 POUNDS** **KM# 770** **Composition:** Virenium **Subject:** 80th Anniversary of the RAF **Obverse:** Queen's portrait **Reverse:** Eurofighter over map

| Date | Mintage | F | VF | XF | Unc | BU |
|---|---|---|---|---|---|---|
| 1998 | — | — | — | — | 16.00 | — |

**5 POUNDS** **KM# 770a** **Weight:** 23.5000 g. **Composition:** 0.9250 Silver .6989 oz. ASW

| Date | Mintage | F | VF | XF | Unc | BU |
|---|---|---|---|---|---|---|
| 1998 Proof | Est. 5,000 | Value: 50.00 | | | | |

**5 POUNDS** **KM# 770b** **Weight:** 39.8300 g. **Composition:** 0.9170 Gold 1.1743 oz. AGW **Subject:** 80th Anniversary of the RAF **Obverse:** Queen's portrait

| Date | Mintage | F | VF | XF | Unc | BU |
|---|---|---|---|---|---|---|
| 1998 Proof | Est. 850 | Value: 850 | | | | |

**5 POUNDS** **KM# 771** **Composition:** Virenium **Subject:** Millennium 2000 **Obverse:** Queen's portrait **Reverse:** Landmarks of London

| Date | Mintage | F | VF | XF | Unc | BU |
|---|---|---|---|---|---|---|
| 1998 | — | — | — | — | 16.00 | — |

**5 POUNDS** **KM# 771a** **Weight:** 23.5000 g. **Composition:** 0.9250 Silver .6989 oz. ASW

| Date | Mintage | F | VF | XF | Unc | BU |
|---|---|---|---|---|---|---|
| 1998 Proof | Est. 5,000 | Value: 50.00 | | | | |

**5 POUNDS** **KM# 771b** **Weight:** 39.8300 g. **Composition:** 0.9170 Gold 1.1743 oz. AGW **Reverse:** Millenium 2000

| Date | Mintage | F | VF | XF | Unc | BU |
|---|---|---|---|---|---|---|
| 1998 Proof | 850 | Value: 875 | | | | |

**5 POUNDS** **KM# 772** **Composition:** Virenium **Subject:** 50th Birthday of Prince Charles **Obverse:** Queen's portrait **Reverse:** Portraits of Prince Charles and sons William and Harry

| Date | Mintage | F | VF | XF | Unc | BU |
|---|---|---|---|---|---|---|
| 1998 AA | — | — | — | — | 16.00 | — |

**5 POUNDS** **KM# 772a** **Weight:** 23.5000 g. **Composition:** 0.9250 Silver .6989 oz. ASW

| Date | Mintage | F | VF | XF | Unc | BU |
|---|---|---|---|---|---|---|
| 1998 Proof | 5,000 | Value: 50.00 | | | | |

**5 POUNDS** **KM# 772b** **Weight:** 39.8300 g. **Composition:** 0.9170 Gold 1.1743 oz. AGW

| Date | Mintage | F | VF | XF | Unc | BU |
|---|---|---|---|---|---|---|
| 1998 Proof | 850 | Value: 875 | | | | |

**5 POUNDS** **KM# 797** **Composition:** Virenium **Subject:** Millennium 2000 **Obverse:** Rank-Broadley portrait of Queen Elizabeth II **Reverse:** Sundial, digital clock face, candle and traditional clock face

| Date | Mintage | F | VF | XF | Unc | BU |
|---|---|---|---|---|---|---|
| 1999 | — | — | — | — | 16.00 | — |

**5 POUNDS** **KM# 797a** **Composition:** Titanium

| Date | Mintage | F | VF | XF | Unc | BU |
|---|---|---|---|---|---|---|
| 1999 | Est. 25,000 | — | — | — | 35.00 | — |

**5 POUNDS** **KM# 797b** **Weight:** 28.2800 g. **Composition:** 0.9250 Silver .8410 oz. ASW

| Date | Mintage | F | VF | XF | Unc | BU |
|---|---|---|---|---|---|---|
| 1999 Proof | Est. 5,000 | Value: 65.00 | | | | |

**5 POUNDS** **KM# 867** **Composition:** Virenium **Subject:** Mediterranean Rowing Club **Obverse:** Rank-Broadley portrait of Queen Elizabeth II **Reverse:** A one-man and a four-man row boat

| Date | Mintage | F | VF | XF | Unc | BU |
|---|---|---|---|---|---|---|
| 1999 | — | — | — | — | 16.00 | — |

**5 POUNDS** **KM# 867a** **Weight:** 23.5000 g. **Composition:** 0.8250 Silver .6989 oz. ASW

| Date | Mintage | F | VF | XF | Unc | BU |
|---|---|---|---|---|---|---|
| 1999 Proof | Est. 5,000 | Value: 65.00 | | | | |

**5 POUNDS** **KM# 867b** **Weight:** 39.8300 g. **Composition:** 0.9170 Gold 1.1743 oz. AGW

| Date | Mintage | F | VF | XF | Unc | BU |
|---|---|---|---|---|---|---|
| 1999 Proof | Est. 850 | Value: 885 | | | | |

**5 POUNDS** **KM# 878** **Composition:** Virenium **Subject:** Battle of Britain **Obverse:** Queen's portrait **Reverse:** Spitfire in flight

| Date | Mintage | F | VF | XF | Unc | BU |
|---|---|---|---|---|---|---|
| 2000 | — | — | — | — | 15.00 | — |

**5 POUNDS** **KM# 878a** **Weight:** 23.5000 g. **Composition:** 0.9250 Silver 69.89 oz. ASW

| Date | Mintage | F | VF | XF | Unc | BU |
|---|---|---|---|---|---|---|
| 2000 Proof | Est. 10,000 | Value: 50.00 | | | | |

**5 POUNDS** **KM# 878b** **Weight:** 39.8300 g. **Composition:** 0.9160 Gold 1.1738 oz. AGW **Subject:** Battle of Britain **Obverse:** Queen's portrait **Reverse:** Spitfire in flight

| Date | Mintage | F | VF | XF | Unc | BU |
|---|---|---|---|---|---|---|
| 2000 Proof | Est. 850 | Value: 885 | | | | |

**5 POUNDS** **KM# 885** **Weight:** 10.0000 g. **Composition:** Titanium **Subject:** 160th Anniversary - Uniform Penny Post **Ob-**

**verse:** Bust Queen right **Reverse:** Postage stamp design **Edge:** Reeded

| Date | Mintage | F | VF | XF | Unc | BU |
|---|---|---|---|---|---|---|
| 2000 Proof | 15,000 | Value: 35.00 | | | | |

**5 POUNDS** **KM# 953** **Weight:** 20.0000 g. **Composition:** Virenium **Subject:** Gibraltar Chronicle 200 Years **Obverse:** Queen's portrait **Reverse:** Naval battle scene with newspaper in background **Edge:** Reeded **Size:** 36.1 mm.

| Date | Mintage | F | VF | XF | Unc | BU |
|---|---|---|---|---|---|---|
| 2001 | — | — | — | — | 15.00 | — |

**5 POUNDS** **KM# 953a** **Weight:** 23.5000 g. **Composition:** 0.9250 Silver .6989 oz. ASW **Edge:** Reeded **Size:** 36.1 mm.

| Date | Mintage | F | VF | XF | Unc | BU |
|---|---|---|---|---|---|---|
| 2001 Proof | 10,000 | Value: 50.00 | | | | |

**5 POUNDS** **KM# 953b** **Weight:** 39.8300 g. **Composition:** 0.9167 Gold 1.1739 oz. AGW **Edge:** Reeded **Size:** 36.1 mm.

| Date | Mintage | F | VF | XF | Unc | BU |
|---|---|---|---|---|---|---|
| 2001 Proof | 850 | Value: 885 | | | | |

**25 POUNDS** **KM# 7** **Weight:** 7.7700 g. **Composition:** 0.9170 Gold .2291 oz. AGW **Subject:** 250th Anniversary - Introduction of British Sterling

| Date | Mintage | F | VF | XF | Unc | BU |
|---|---|---|---|---|---|---|
| 1975 | 2,395 | — | — | — | 120 | — |
| 1975 Proof | 750 | Value: 180 | | | | |

**50 POUNDS** **KM# 8** **Weight:** 15.5500 g. **Composition:** 0.9170 Gold .4585 oz. AGW **Subject:** 250th Anniversary - Introduction of British Sterling **Obverse:** Similar to 25 Pounds, KM#7

| Date | Mintage | F | VF | XF | Unc | BU |
|---|---|---|---|---|---|---|
| 1975 | 1,625 | — | — | — | 220 | — |
| 1975 Proof | 750 | Value: 320 | | | | |

**50 POUNDS** **KM# 13** **Weight:** 15.9760 g. **Composition:** 0.9170 Gold .4711 oz. AGW **Reverse:** 175th Anniversary of Death of Nelson

| Date | Mintage | F | VF | XF | Unc | BU |
|---|---|---|---|---|---|---|
| 1980 | Est. 7,500 | — | — | — | 200 | — |
| 1980 Proof | Est. 5,000 | Value: 225 | | | | |

**50 POUNDS** **KM# 15** **Weight:** 15.9760 g. **Composition:** 0.9170 Gold .4711 oz. AGW **Reverse:** Wedding of Prince Charles and Lady Diana

| Date | Mintage | F | VF | XF | Unc | BU |
|---|---|---|---|---|---|---|
| 1981 | — | — | — | — | 210 | — |
| 1981 Proof | Est. 2,500 | Value: 235 | | | | |

**100 POUNDS** **KM# 9** **Weight:** 31.1000 g. **Composition:** 0.9170 Gold .9170 oz. AGW **Subject:** 250th Anniversary - Introduction of British Sterling **Obverse:** Similar to 25 Pounds, KM#7

| Date | Mintage | F | VF | XF | Unc | BU |
|---|---|---|---|---|---|---|
| 1975 | 1,625 | — | — | — | 420 | — |
| 1975 Proof | 750 | Value: 500 | | | | |

**1/25 ROYAL** **KM# 896** **Weight:** 1.2441 g. **Composition:** 0.9999 Gold .0400 oz. AGW **Subject:** Bullion **Obverse:** Queen's portrait **Reverse:** Two cherubs **Edge:** Reeded **Size:** 13.92 mm.

| Date | Mintage | F | VF | XF | Unc | BU |
|---|---|---|---|---|---|---|
| 2001 | — | — | — | — | 32.00 | — |
| 2001 In Proof sets only | 1,000 | Value: 50.00 | | | | |

**1/10 ROYAL** **KM# 897** **Weight:** 3.1100 g. **Composition:** 0.9999 Gold .1000 oz. AGW **Subject:** Bullion **Obverse:** Queen's portrait **Reverse:** Two cherubs **Edge:** Reeded **Size:** 18 mm.

| Date | Mintage | F | VF | XF | Unc | BU |
|---|---|---|---|---|---|---|
| 2001 | — | — | — | — | 70.00 | — |
| 2001 In Proof sets only | 1,000 | Value: 100 | | | | |

**1/5 ROYAL** **KM# 898** **Weight:** 6.2200 g. **Composition:** 0.9990 Gold .2000 oz. AGW **Subject:** Bullion **Obverse:** Queen's portrait **Reverse:** Two cherubs **Edge:** Reeded **Size:** 22 mm.

| Date | Mintage | F | VF | XF | Unc | BU |
|---|---|---|---|---|---|---|
| 2001 | — | — | — | — | 109 | — |
| 2001 In Proof sets only | 1,000 | Value: 185 | | | | |

**1/2 ROYAL** **KM# 899** **Weight:** 15.5517 g. **Composition:** 0.9999 Gold .5000 oz. AGW **Subject:** Bullion **Obverse:** Queen's portrait **Reverse:** Two cherubs **Edge:** Reeded **Size:** 30 mm.

| Date | Mintage | F | VF | XF | Unc | BU |
|---|---|---|---|---|---|---|
| 2001 | — | — | — | — | 250 | — |
| 2001 In Proof sets only | 1,000 | Value: 365 | | | | |

**ROYAL** **KM# 318** **Weight:** 28.6200 g. **Composition:** Copper-Nickel **Obverse:** Queen's portrait **Reverse:** Seated dog above denomination **Edge:** Reeded **Size:** 38.8 mm.

| Date | Mintage | F | VF | XF | Unc | BU |
|---|---|---|---|---|---|---|
| 1995 | — | — | — | — | 10.00 | — |

**ROYAL** **KM# 900** **Weight:** 28.2800 g. **Composition:** Copper-Nickel **Obverse:** Queen's portrait **Reverse:** Two cherubs **Edge:** Reeded **Size:** 38.6 mm.

| Date | Mintage | F | VF | XF | Unc | BU |
|---|---|---|---|---|---|---|
| 2001 | — | — | — | — | 10.00 | — |

**ROYAL** **KM# 900a** **Weight:** 31.1035 g. **Composition:** 0.9990 Silver 1.0000 oz. ASW

| Date | Mintage | F | VF | XF | Unc | BU |
|---|---|---|---|---|---|---|
| 2001 Proof | 10,000 | Value: 47.50 | | | | |

**ROYAL** **KM# 901** **Weight:** 31.1035 g. **Composition:** 0.9999 Gold 1.0000 oz. AGW **Subject:** Bullion **Obverse:** Queen's portrait **Reverse:** Two cherubs **Edge:** Reeded **Size:** 32.7 mm.

| Date | Mintage | F | VF | XF | Unc | BU |
|---|---|---|---|---|---|---|
| 2001 | — | — | — | — | 470 | — |
| 2001 In Proof sets only | 1,000 | Value: 650 | | | | |

## SOVEREIGN COINAGE

**1/4 SOVEREIGN** **KM# 26** **Weight:** 1.9900 g. **Composition:** 0.9170 Gold .0587 oz. AGW **Subject:** 150th Anniversary of Regal Coinage Una and the Lion **Note:** Similar to 5 Sovereigns, KM#30.

| Date | Mintage | F | VF | XF | Unc | BU |
|---|---|---|---|---|---|---|
| 1989 U | — | — | — | — | — | — |
| 1989 Proof | Est. 1,989 | Value: 70.00 | | | | |

**1/4 SOVEREIGN** **KM# 41** **Weight:** 1.9900 g. **Composition:** 0.9170 Gold .0587 oz. AGW **Subject:** 21st Anniversary - Constitution **Obverse:** Similar to 5 Sovereigns, KM#30.1 **Reverse:** Similar to 5 Sovereigns, KM#45

| Date | Mintage | F | VF | XF | Unc | BU |
|---|---|---|---|---|---|---|
| 1990 Proof | Est. 1,000 | Value: 65.00 | | | | |

**1/4 SOVEREIGN** **KM# 515** **Weight:** 1.2241 g. **Composition:** 0.9999 Gold .0400 oz. AGW **Subject:** Una and the Lion **Note:** Similar to 1 Sovereign, KM#517.

| Date | Mintage | F | VF | XF | Unc | BU |
|---|---|---|---|---|---|---|
| 1997 Proof | — | Value: 50.00 | | | | |

**1/2 SOVEREIGN** **KM# 27** **Weight:** 3.9800 g. **Composition:** 0.9170 Gold .1173 oz. AGW **Subject:** 150th Anniversary of Regal Coinage Una and the Lion **Note:** Similar to 5 Sovereigns, KM#30.2.

| Date | Mintage | F | VF | XF | Unc | BU |
|---|---|---|---|---|---|---|
| 1989 U | — | — | — | — | — | — |
| 1989 Proof | Est. 1,989 | Value: 135 | | | | |

**1/2 SOVEREIGN** **KM# 42** **Weight:** 3.9800 g. **Composition:** 0.9170 Gold .1173 oz. AGW **Subject:** 21st Anniversary - Constitution **Obverse:** Similar to 5 Sovereigns, KM#30.1 **Reverse:** Similar to 5 Sovereigns, KM#45

| Date | Mintage | F | VF | XF | Unc | BU |
|---|---|---|---|---|---|---|
| 1990 Proof | 1,000 | Value: 125 | | | | |

**1/2 SOVEREIGN** **KM# 516** **Weight:** 3.1103 g. **Composition:** 0.9999 Gold .10000 oz. AGW **Subject:** Una and the Lion **Note:** Similar to 1 Sovereign, KM#517.

| Date | Mintage | F | VF | XF | Unc | BU |
|---|---|---|---|---|---|---|
| 1997 Proof | — | Value: 85.00 | | | | |

**SOVEREIGN** **KM# 28** **Weight:** 7.9600 g. **Composition:** 0.9170 Gold .2347 oz. AGW **Subject:** 150th Anniversary of Regal Coinage **Note:** Similar to 5 Sovereigns, KM#30.2.

| Date | Mintage | F | VF | XF | Unc | BU |
|---|---|---|---|---|---|---|
| 1989 U | — | — | — | — | — | — |
| 1989 Proof | Est. 1,989 | Value: 265 | | | | |

**SOVEREIGN** **KM# 43** **Weight:** 7.9600 g. **Composition:** 0.9170 Gold .2347 oz. AGW **Subject:** 21st Anniversary - Constitution **Obverse:** Similar to 5 Sovereigns, KM#30.1 **Reverse:** Similar to 5 Sovereigns, KM#45

| Date | Mintage | F | VF | XF | Unc | BU |
|---|---|---|---|---|---|---|
| 1990 Proof | Est. 1,000 | Value: 250 | | | | |

**SOVEREIGN** **KM# 517** **Weight:** 6.2207 g. **Composition:** 0.9999 Gold .2000 oz. AGW **Subject:** Una and the Lion **Obverse:** Queen's portrait **Reverse:** Woman in toga with scepter and lion

| Date | Mintage | F | VF | XF | Unc | BU |
|---|---|---|---|---|---|---|
| 1997 Proof | — | Value: 175 | | | | |

**2 SOVEREIGNS** **KM# 29** **Weight:** 15.9400 g. **Composition:** 0.9170 Gold .4700 oz. AGW **Subject:** 150th Anniversary of Regal Coinage **Reverse:** Una and the Lion **Note:** Similar to 5 Sovereigns, KM#30.

| Date | Mintage | F | VF | XF | Unc | BU |
|---|---|---|---|---|---|---|
| 1989 Proof | 1,989 | Value: 550 | | | | |

**2 SOVEREIGNS** **KM# 44** **Weight:** 15.9400 g. **Composition:** 0.9170 Gold .4700 oz. AGW **Subject:** 21st Anniversary - Constitution **Obverse:** Similar to 5 Sovereigns, KM#30.1 **Reverse:** Similar to 5 Sovereigns, KM#45

| Date | Mintage | F | VF | XF | Unc | BU |
|---|---|---|---|---|---|---|
| 1990 Proof | 1,000 | Value: 500 | | | | |

**5 SOVEREIGNS** **KM# 30** **Weight:** 39.8300 g. **Composition:** 0.9170 Gold 1.1743 oz. AGW **Subject:** 150th Anniversary of Regal Coinage **Reverse:** Una and the Lion

| Date | Mintage | F | VF | XF | Unc | BU |
|---|---|---|---|---|---|---|
| 1989 Proof | 1,989 | Value: 1,100 | | | | |

**5 SOVEREIGNS** **KM# 45** **Weight:** 39.8300 g. **Composition:** 0.9170 Gold 1.1743 oz. AGW **Subject:** 21st Anniversary - Constitution **Obverse:** Similar to KM#30

| Date | Mintage | F | VF | XF | Unc | BU |
|---|---|---|---|---|---|---|
| 1990 Proof | Est. 1,000 | Value: 950 | | | | |

## ROYAL COINAGE

**1/25 ROYAL** **KM# 91** **Weight:** 1.2400 g. **Composition:** 0.9999 Gold .0400 oz. AGW **Reverse:** Corgi Dog **Note:** Similar to 1 Royal, KM#97.

| Date | Mintage | F | VF | XF | Unc | BU |
|---|---|---|---|---|---|---|
| 1991 | — | — | — | — | 75.00 | — |
| 1991 Proof | Est. 1,000 | Value: 76.50 | | | | |

**1/25 ROYAL** **KM# 99** **Weight:** 1.2400 g. **Composition:** 0.9999 Gold .0400 oz. AGW **Reverse:** Cocker Spaniel **Note:** Similar to 1 Royal, KM#105.

| Date | Mintage | F | VF | XF | Unc | BU |
|---|---|---|---|---|---|---|
| 1992 | — | — | — | — | 35.00 | — |
| 1992 Proof | Est. 1,000 | Value: 36.50 | | | | |

**1/25 ROYAL** **KM# 193** **Weight:** 1.2400 g. **Composition:** 0.9999 Gold .0400 oz. AGW **Reverse:** Long-haired Dahshund **Note:** Similar to 1 Royal, KM#197.

| Date | Mintage | F | VF | XF | Unc | BU |
|---|---|---|---|---|---|---|
| 1993 | — | — | — | — | 35.00 | — |
| 1993 Proof | Est. 1,000 | Value: 36.50 | | | | |

**1/25 ROYAL** **KM# 248** **Weight:** 1.2400 g. **Composition:** 0.9999 Gold .0400 oz. AGW **Reverse:** Pekingese **Note:** Similar to 1/5 Royal, KM#250.

| Date | Mintage | F | VF | XF | Unc | BU |
|---|---|---|---|---|---|---|
| 1994 | — | — | — | — | 35.00 | — |
| 1994 Proof | Est. 1,000 | Value: 36.50 | | | | |

**1/25 ROYAL** **KM# 319** **Weight:** 1.2400 g. **Composition:** 0.9999 Gold .0400 oz. AGW **Reverse:** Collie **Note:** Similar to 1 Royal, KM#323.

| Date | Mintage | F | VF | XF | Unc | BU |
|---|---|---|---|---|---|---|
| 1995 | — | — | — | — | 35.00 | — |
| 1995 Proof | Est. 1,000 | Value: 36.50 | | | | |

**1/25 ROYAL** **KM# 361** **Weight:** 1.2400 g. **Composition:** 0.9999 Gold .0400 oz. AGW **Reverse:** Bull Dog **Note:** Similar to 1 Royal, KM#365b.

| Date | Mintage | F | VF | XF | Unc | BU |
|---|---|---|---|---|---|---|
| 1996 | — | — | — | — | 35.00 | — |
| 1996 Proof | Est. 1,000 | Value: 36.50 | | | | |

**1/25 ROYAL** **KM# 557** **Weight:** 1.2400 g. **Composition:** 0.9999 Gold .0400 oz. AGW **Reverse:** Yorkshire Terrier **Note:** Similar to 1 Royal, KM#561b.

| Date | Mintage | F | VF | XF | Unc | BU |
|---|---|---|---|---|---|---|
| 1997 | — | — | — | — | 50.00 | — |
| 1997 Proof | Est. 1,000 | Value: 52.00 | | | | |

**1/25 ROYAL** **KM# 749** **Weight:** 1.2400 g. **Composition:** 0.9999 Gold .0400 oz. AGW **Obverse:** Queen's portrait **Reverse:** Kissing cherubs **Note:** Similar to 1 Royal, KM#754.

| Date | Mintage | F | VF | XF | Unc | BU |
|---|---|---|---|---|---|---|
| 1998 | — | — | — | — | 50.00 | — |
| 1998 Proof | Est. 1,000 | Value: 52.00 | | | | |

**1/25 ROYAL** **KM# 749a** **Weight:** 1.2400 g. **Composition:** 0.9950 Platinum .0400 oz. APW **Reverse:** Kissing cherubs

| Date | Mintage | F | VF | XF | Unc | BU |
|---|---|---|---|---|---|---|
| 1998 Proof | — | Value: 75.00 | | | | |

**1/25 ROYAL** **KM# 828** **Weight:** 1.2400 g. **Composition:** 0.9990 Gold .0400 oz. AGW **Obverse:** Queen's portrait **Reverse:** Cherub

| Date | Mintage | F | VF | XF | Unc | BU |
|---|---|---|---|---|---|---|
| 1999 U | — | — | — | — | 35.00 | — |
| 1999 U Y2K | Est. 20,000 | — | — | — | 35.00 | — |
| 1999 Proof | Est. 1,000 | Value: 36.50 | | | | |

**1/25 ROYAL** **KM# 828a** **Weight:** 1.2400 g. **Composition:** 0.9950 Platinum .0400 oz. APW **Obverse:** Queen's portrait **Reverse:** One cherubim

| Date | Mintage | F | VF | XF | Unc | BU |
|---|---|---|---|---|---|---|
| 1999 Proof | Est. 1,000 | Value: 75.00 | | | | |

**1/10 ROYAL** **KM# 92** **Weight:** 3.1100 g. **Composition:** 0.9999 Gold .1000 oz. AGW **Reverse:** Corgi Dog **Note:** Similar to 1 Royal, KM#97.

| Date | Mintage | F | VF | XF | Unc | BU |
|---|---|---|---|---|---|---|
| 1991 | — | — | — | — | 75.00 | — |
| 1991 Proof | Est. 1,000 | Value: 76.50 | | | | |

**1/10 ROYAL** **KM# 100** **Weight:** 3.1100 g. **Composition:** 0.9999 Gold .1000 oz. AGW **Reverse:** Cocker Spaniel **Note:** Similar to 1 Royal, KM#105.

| Date | Mintage | F | VF | XF | Unc | BU |
|---|---|---|---|---|---|---|
| 1992 | — | — | — | — | 75.00 | — |
| 1992 Proof | Est. 1,000 | Value: 76.50 | | | | |

**1/10 ROYAL** **KM# 194** **Weight:** 3.1100 g. **Composition:** 0.9999 Gold .1000 oz. AGW **Reverse:** Long-haired Dashshund

| Date | Mintage | F | VF | XF | Unc | BU |
|---|---|---|---|---|---|---|
| 1993 | — | — | — | — | 60.00 | — |
| 1993 Proof | Est. 1,000 | Value: 62.00 | | | | |

**1/10 ROYAL** **KM# 249** **Weight:** 3.1100 g. **Composition:** 0.9999 Gold .1000 oz. AGW **Reverse:** Pekingese **Note:** Similar to 1/5 Royal, KM#250.

| Date | Mintage | F | VF | XF | Unc | BU |
|---|---|---|---|---|---|---|
| 1994 | — | — | — | — | 60.00 | — |
| 1994 Proof | Est. 1,000 | Value: 62.00 | | | | |

**1/10 ROYAL** **KM# 320** **Weight:** 3.1100 g. **Composition:** 0.9999 Gold .1000 oz. AGW **Reverse:** Collie **Note:** Similar to 1 Royal, KM#323.

| Date | Mintage | F | VF | XF | Unc | BU |
|---|---|---|---|---|---|---|
| 1995 | — | — | — | — | 60.00 | — |
| 1995 Proof | Est. 1,000 | Value: 62.00 | | | | |

**1/10 ROYAL** **KM# 362** **Weight:** 3.1100 g. **Composition:** 0.9999 Gold .1000 oz. AGW **Reverse:** Bull Dog **Note:** Similar to 1 Royal, KM#365b.

| Date | Mintage | F | VF | XF | Unc | BU |
|---|---|---|---|---|---|---|
| 1996 | — | — | — | — | 60.00 | — |
| 1996 Proof | Est. 1,000 | Value: 62.00 | | | | |

**1/10 ROYAL** **KM# 558** **Weight:** 3.1100 g. **Composition:** 0.9999 Gold .1000 oz. AGW **Reverse:** Yorkshire Terrier **Note:** Similar to 1 Royal, KM#561b.

| Date | Mintage | F | VF | XF | Unc | BU |
|---|---|---|---|---|---|---|
| 1997 | — | — | — | — | 75.00 | — |
| 1997 Proof | Est. 1,000 | Value: 76.50 | | | | |

**1/10 ROYAL** **KM# 750** **Weight:** 3.1100 g. **Composition:** 0.9999 Gold .1000 oz. AGW **Subject:** Kissing Cherubs **Obverse:** Queen's portrait **Reverse:** Kissing cherubs **Note:** Similar to 1 Royal, KM#754.

| Date | Mintage | F | VF | XF | Unc | BU |
|---|---|---|---|---|---|---|
| 1998 | — | — | — | — | 75.00 | — |
| 1998 Proof | Est. 1,000 | Value: 76.50 | | | | |

**1/10 ROYAL** **KM# 829** **Weight:** 3.1100 g. **Composition:** 0.9999 Gold .1000 oz. AGW **Obverse:** Queen's portrait **Reverse:** Cherubim

| Date | Mintage | F | VF | XF | Unc | BU |
|---|---|---|---|---|---|---|
| 1999 U | — | — | — | — | 50.00 | — |
| 1999 U Y2K | Est. 10,000 | — | — | — | 50.00 | — |
| 1999 Proof | — | Value: 52.00 | | | | |

**1/10 ROYAL** **KM# 829a** **Weight:** 3.1100 g. **Composition:** 0.9950 Platinum .0999 oz. APW **Reverse:** Cherubim

| Date | Mintage | F | VF | XF | Unc | BU |
|---|---|---|---|---|---|---|
| 1999 Proof | Est. 1,000 | — | — | — | — | — |

**1/10 ROYAL** **KM# 889** **Weight:** 3.1100 g. **Composition:** 0.9990 Gold .1000 oz. AGW **Subject:** Bullion **Obverse:** Bust Queen right **Reverse:** 2 cherubs **Edge:** Reeded

| Date | Mintage | F | VF | XF | Unc | BU |
|---|---|---|---|---|---|---|
| 2000 | — | — | — | — | 75.00 | — |
| 2000 In mint sets only | 1,000 | Value: 76.50 | | | | |

**1/5 ROYAL** **KM# 93** **Weight:** 6.2200 g. **Composition:** 0.9999 Gold .20000 oz. AGW **Reverse:** Corgi Dog **Note:** Similar to 1 Royal, KM#97.

| Date | Mintage | F | VF | XF | Unc | BU |
|---|---|---|---|---|---|---|
| 1991 | — | — | — | — | 175 | — |
| 1991 Proof | Est. 1,000 | Value: 177 | | | | |

**1/5 ROYAL** **KM# 101** **Weight:** 6.2200 g. **Composition:** 0.9999 Gold .20000 oz. AGW **Reverse:** Cocker Spaniel **Note:** Similar to 1 Royal, KM#105.

| Date | Mintage | F | VF | XF | Unc | BU |
|---|---|---|---|---|---|---|
| 1992 | — | — | — | — | 125 | — |
| 1992 Proof | Est. 1,000 | Value: 127 | | | | |

**1/5 ROYAL** **KM# 195** **Weight:** 6.2200 g. **Composition:** 0.9999 Gold .20000 oz. AGW **Reverse:** Long-haired Dashshund

| Date | Mintage | F | VF | XF | Unc | BU |
|---|---|---|---|---|---|---|
| 1993 | — | — | — | — | 125 | — |
| 1993 Proof | Est. 1,000 | Value: 127 | | | | |

**1/5 ROYAL** **KM# 250** **Weight:** 6.2200 g. **Composition:** 0.9999 Gold .20000 oz. AGW **Reverse:** Pekingese

| Date | Mintage | F | VF | XF | Unc | BU |
|---|---|---|---|---|---|---|
| 1994 | — | — | — | — | 125 | — |
| 1994 Proof | Est. 1,000 | Value: 127 | | | | |

**1/5 ROYAL** **KM# 321** **Weight:** 6.2200 g. **Composition:** 0.9999 Gold .20000 oz. AGW **Reverse:** Collie **Note:** Similar to 1 Royal, KM#323.

| Date | Mintage | F | VF | XF | Unc | BU |
|---|---|---|---|---|---|---|
| 1995 | — | — | — | — | 125 | — |
| 1995 Proof | Est. 1,000 | Value: 127 | | | | |

**1/5 ROYAL** **KM# 363** **Weight:** 6.2200 g. **Composition:** 0.9999 Gold .20000 oz. AGW **Reverse:** Bull Dog **Note:** Similar to 1 Royal, KM#365b.

| Date | Mintage | F | VF | XF | Unc | BU |
|---|---|---|---|---|---|---|
| 1996 | — | — | — | — | 125 | — |
| 1996 Proof | Est. 1,000 | Value: 127 | | | | |

**1/5 ROYAL** **KM# 559** **Weight:** 6.2200 g. **Composition:** 0.9999 Gold .20000 oz. AGW **Reverse:** Yorkshire Terrier **Note:** Similar to 1 Royal, KM#561b.

| Date | Mintage | F | VF | XF | Unc | BU |
|---|---|---|---|---|---|---|
| 1997 | — | — | — | — | 150 | — |
| 1997 Proof | Est. 1,000 | Value: 152 | | | | |

**1/5 ROYAL** **KM# 751** **Weight:** 6.2200 g. **Composition:** 0.9999 Gold .20000 oz. AGW **Obverse:** Queen's portrait **Reverse:** Kissing cherubs **Note:** Similar to 1 Royal, KM#754.

| Date | Mintage | F | VF | XF | Unc | BU |
|---|---|---|---|---|---|---|
| 1998 | — | — | — | — | 125 | — |
| 1998 Proof | Est. 1,000 | Value: 127 | | | | |

**1/5 ROYAL** **KM# 830** **Weight:** 6.2200 g. **Composition:** 0.9999 Gold .2000 oz. AGW **Obverse:** Queen's portrait **Reverse:** 4 cherubim

| Date | Mintage | F | VF | XF | Unc | BU |
|---|---|---|---|---|---|---|
| 1999 U | — | — | — | — | 100 | — |
| 1999 U Y2K | Est. 5,000 | — | — | — | 100 | — |
| 1999 Proof | — | Value: 102 | | | | |

**1/5 ROYAL** **KM# 830a** **Weight:** 6.2200 g. **Composition:** 0.9950 Platinum .2000 oz. APW **Reverse:** 4 cherubim

| Date | Mintage | F | VF | XF | Unc | BU |
|---|---|---|---|---|---|---|
| 1999 Proof | Est. 1,000 | — | — | — | — | — |

**1/5 ROYAL** **KM# 890** **Weight:** 6.2200 g. **Composition:** 0.9990 Gold .2000 oz. AGW **Subject:** Bullion **Obverse:** Bust Queen right **Reverse:** 2 cherubs **Edge:** Reeded

| Date | Mintage | F | VF | XF | Unc | BU |
|---|---|---|---|---|---|---|
| 2000 | — | — | — | — | 125 | — |
| 2000 In proof sets only | 1,000 | — | — | — | — | — |

**1/2 ROYAL** **KM# 94** **Weight:** 15.5500 g. **Composition:** 0.9999 Gold .5000 oz. AGW **Reverse:** Corgi Dog **Note:** Similar to 1 Royal, KM#97.

| Date | Mintage | F | VF | XF | Unc | BU |
|---|---|---|---|---|---|---|
| 1991 | — | — | — | — | 375 | — |
| 1991 Proof | Est. 1,000 | Value: 377 | | | | |

**1/2 ROYAL** **KM# 102** **Weight:** 15.5500 g. **Composition:** 0.9999 Gold .5000 oz. AGW **Reverse:** Cocker Spaniel **Note:** Simuler to 1 Royal, KM#105.

| Date | Mintage | F | VF | XF | Unc | BU |
|---|---|---|---|---|---|---|
| 1992 | — | — | — | — | 300 | — |
| 1992 Proof | Est. 1,000 | Value: 302 | | | | |

**1/2 ROYAL** **KM# 196** **Weight:** 15.5500 g. **Composition:** 0.9999 Gold .5000 oz. AGW **Reverse:** Long-haired Dashshund

| Date | Mintage | F | VF | XF | Unc | BU |
|---|---|---|---|---|---|---|
| 1993 | — | — | — | — | 225 | — |
| 1993 Proof | Est. 1,000 | Value: 227 | | | | |

**1/2 ROYAL** **KM# 251** **Weight:** 15.5500 g. **Composition:** 0.9999 Gold .5000 oz. AGW **Reverse:** Pekingese **Note:** Similar to 1/5 Royal, KM#250.

| Date | Mintage | F | VF | XF | Unc | BU |
|---|---|---|---|---|---|---|
| 1994 | — | — | — | — | 225 | — |
| 1994 Proof | Est. 1,000 | Value: 227 | | | | |

**1/2 ROYAL** **KM# 322** **Weight:** 15.5500 g. **Composition:** 0.9999 Gold .5000 oz. AGW **Reverse:** Collie **Note:** Similar to 1 Royal, KM#323.

| Date | Mintage | F | VF | XF | Unc | BU |
|---|---|---|---|---|---|---|
| 1995 | — | — | — | — | 225 | — |
| 1995 Proof | Est. 1,000 | Value: 227 | | | | |

**1/2 ROYAL** **KM# 364** **Weight:** 15.5500 g. **Composition:** 0.9999 Gold .5000 oz. AGW **Reverse:** Bull Dog **Note:** Similar to 1 Royal, KM#365b.

| Date | Mintage | F | VF | XF | Unc | BU |
|---|---|---|---|---|---|---|
| 1996 | — | — | — | — | 225 | — |
| 1996 Proof | Est. 1,000 | Value: 227 | | | | |

**1/2 ROYAL** **KM# 560** **Weight:** 15.5500 g. **Composition:** 0.9999 Gold .5000 oz. AGW **Reverse:** Yorkshire Terrier **Note:** Similar to 1 Royal, KM#561.

| Date | Mintage | F | VF | XF | Unc | BU |
|---|---|---|---|---|---|---|
| 1997 | — | — | — | — | 300 | — |
| 1997 Proof | Est. 1,000 | Value: 302 | | | | |

**1/2 ROYAL** **KM# 752** **Weight:** 15.5500 g. **Composition:** 0.9999 Gold .5000 oz. AGW **Obverse:** Queen's portrait **Reverse:** Kissing cherubs **Note:** Similar to 1 Royal, KM#754.

| Date | Mintage | F | VF | XF | Unc | BU |
|---|---|---|---|---|---|---|
| 1998 | — | — | — | — | 225 | — |
| 1998 Proof | Est. 1,000 | Value: 227 | | | | |

**1/2 ROYAL** **KM# 831** **Weight:** 15.5500 g. **Composition:** 0.9999 Gold .5000 oz. AGW **Obverse:** Queen's portrait **Reverse:** 4 cherubim

| Date | Mintage | F | VF | XF | Unc | BU |
|---|---|---|---|---|---|---|
| 1999 | — | — | — | — | 200 | — |
| 1999 Proof | — | Value: 202 | | | | |

**1/2 ROYAL** **KM# 891** **Weight:** 15.5500 g. **Composition:** 0.9999 Gold .5000 oz. AGW **Subject:** Bullion **Obverse:** Bust Queen right **Reverse:** 2 cherubs **Edge:** Reeded

| Date | Mintage | F | VF | XF | Unc | BU |
|---|---|---|---|---|---|---|
| 2000 | — | — | — | — | 225 | — |
| 2000 In proof sets only | 1,000 | Value: 227 | | | | |

**ROYAL** **KM# 97** **Weight:** 31.1030 g. **Composition:** 0.9999 Gold 1.0000 oz. AGW **Reverse:** Corgi Dog

| Date | Mintage | F | VF | XF | Unc | BU |
|---|---|---|---|---|---|---|
| 1991 | — | — | — | — | 600 | — |
| 1991 | Est. 1,000 | Value: 602 | | | | |

**ROYAL** **KM# 105** **Weight:** 31.1030 g. **Composition:** 0.9999 Gold 1.0000 oz. AGW **Reverse:** Cocker Spaniel

| Date | Mintage | F | VF | XF | Unc | BU |
|---|---|---|---|---|---|---|
| 1992 | — | — | — | — | 600 | — |
| 1992 Proof | Est. 1,000 | Value: 602 | | | | |

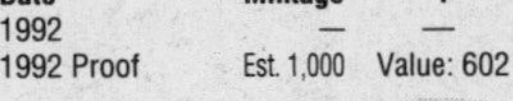

**ROYAL** **KM# 197** **Weight:** 31.1030 g. **Composition:** 0.9999 Gold 1.0000 oz. AGW **Reverse:** Long-haired Bachshund

| Date | Mintage | F | VF | XF | Unc | BU |
|---|---|---|---|---|---|---|
| 1993 | — | — | — | — | 450 | — |
| 1993 Proof | Est. 1,000 | Value: 452 | | | | |

**ROYAL** **KM# 252a** **Weight:** 31.1030 g. **Composition:** 0.9999 Gold 1.0000 oz. AGW **Reverse:** Pekingese

| Date | Mintage | F | VF | XF | Unc | BU |
|---|---|---|---|---|---|---|
| 1994 | — | — | — | — | 450 | — |
| 1994 Proof | Est. 1,000 | Value: 452 | | | | |

**ROYAL** **KM# 252** **Weight:** 31.1000 g. **Composition:** 0.9990 Silver .9989 oz. ASW **Reverse:** Pekingese **Note:** Similar to 1/5 Royal, KM#250.

| Date | Mintage | F | VF | XF | Unc | BU |
|---|---|---|---|---|---|---|
| 1994 Proof | Est. 50,000 | Value: 30.00 | | | | |

**ROYAL** **KM# 323** **Weight:** 31.1030 g. **Composition:** 0.9999 Gold 1.0000 oz. AGW **Reverse:** Collie

| Date | Mintage | F | VF | XF | Unc | BU |
|---|---|---|---|---|---|---|
| 1995 | — | — | — | — | 450 | — |
| 1995 Proof | Est. 1,000 | Value: 452 | | | | |

**ROYAL** **KM# 356** **Weight:** 31.1030 g. **Composition:** 0.9990 Silver 1.0000 oz. ASW **Reverse:** Collie

| Date | Mintage | F | VF | XF | Unc | BU |
|---|---|---|---|---|---|---|
| 1995 Proof | Est. 50,000 | Value: 30.00 | | | | |

**ROYAL** **KM# 365** **Weight:** 31.1030 g. **Composition:** 0.9990 Silver 1.0000 oz. ASW **Obverse:** Queen's portrait **Reverse:** Bull dog

| Date | Mintage | F | VF | XF | Unc | BU |
|---|---|---|---|---|---|---|
| 1996 Proof | Est. 50,000 | Value: 30.00 | | | | |

**ROYAL** **KM# 365b** **Weight:** 31.1030 g. **Composition:** 0.9999 Gold 1.0000 oz. AGW **Reverse:** Bull Dog

| Date | Mintage | F | VF | XF | Unc | BU |
|---|---|---|---|---|---|---|
| 1996 | — | — | — | — | 500 | — |
| 1996 Proof | Est. 1,000 | Value: 502 | | | | |

**ROYAL** **KM# 561a** **Weight:** 31.1035 g. **Composition:** 0.9999 Silver 1.0000 oz. ASW **Obverse:** Queen's portrait **Reverse:** Yorkshire terrier

| Date | Mintage | F | VF | XF | Unc | BU |
|---|---|---|---|---|---|---|
| 1997 Proof | Est. 50,000 | Value: 30.00 | | | | |

**ROYAL** **KM# 561b** **Weight:** 31.1035 g. **Composition:** 0.9999 Gold 1.0000 oz. AGW **Obverse:** Queen's portrait **Reverse:** Yorkshire terrier

| Date | Mintage | F | VF | XF | Unc | BU |
|---|---|---|---|---|---|---|
| 1997 | — | — | — | — | 500 | — |
| 1997 Proof | Est. 1,000 | Value: 502 | | | | |

**ROYAL** **KM# 753** **Composition:** Copper-Nickel **Subject:** Kissing Cherubs **Obverse:** Queen's portrait **Reverse:** Kissing cherubs

| Date | Mintage | F | VF | XF | Unc | BU |
|---|---|---|---|---|---|---|
| 1998 | — | — | — | — | 10.00 | — |

**ROYAL** **KM# 753a** **Weight:** 28.2800 g. **Composition:** 0.9990 Silver 1.0000 oz. ASW

| Date | Mintage | F | VF | XF | Unc | BU |
|---|---|---|---|---|---|---|
| 1998 Proof | Est. 20,000 | Value: 45.00 | | | | |

**ROYAL** **KM# 754** **Weight:** 31.1030 g. **Composition:** 0.9999 Gold 1.0000 oz. AGW **Obverse:** Queen's portrait **Reverse:** Kissing cherubs

| Date | Mintage | F | VF | XF | Unc | BU |
|---|---|---|---|---|---|---|
| 1998 | — | — | — | — | 400 | — |
| 1998 Proof | Est. 1,000 | Value: 402 | | | | |

**ROYAL** **KM# 832** **Composition:** Copper-Nickel **Obverse:** Queen's portrait **Reverse:** 4 cherubim

| Date | Mintage | F | VF | XF | Unc | BU |
|---|---|---|---|---|---|---|
| 1999 | — | — | — | — | 10.00 | — |

**ROYAL** **KM# 832a** **Weight:** 31.1035 g. **Composition:** 0.9990 Silver 1.0000 oz. ASW

| Date | Mintage | F | VF | XF | Unc | BU |
|---|---|---|---|---|---|---|
| 1999 Proof | Est. 50,000 | Value: 50.00 | | | | |

**ROYAL** **KM# 833** **Weight:** 31.1030 g. **Composition:** 0.9999 Gold 1.0000 oz. AGW **Obverse:** Queen's portrait **Reverse:** Four cherubim

| Date | Mintage | F | VF | XF | Unc | BU |
|---|---|---|---|---|---|---|
| 1999 U | — | — | — | — | 350 | — |
| 1999 Proof | — | Value: 352 | | | | |

**ROYAL** **KM# 892** **Weight:** 28.2800 g. **Composition:** Copper-Nickel **Obverse:** Bust Queen right **Reverse:** 2 cherubs **Edge:** Reeded

| Date | Mintage | F | VF | XF | Unc | BU |
|---|---|---|---|---|---|---|
| 2000 | — | — | — | — | 10.00 | — |

**ROYAL KM# 892a Weight:** 31.1035 g. **Composition:** 0.9990 Silver 1.0000 oz. ASW

| Date | Mintage | F | VF | XF | Unc | BU |
|---|---|---|---|---|---|---|
| 2000 Proof | 10,000 | Value: 50.00 | | | | |

**ROYAL KM# 893 Weight:** 31.1035 g. **Composition:** 0.9990 Gold 1.0000 oz. AGW **Obverse:** Bust Queen right **Reverse:** 2 cherubs **Edge:** Reeded

| Date | Mintage | F | VF | XF | Unc | BU |
|---|---|---|---|---|---|---|
| 2000 | — | — | — | — | 400 | — |
| 2000 In proof sets only | 1,000 | Value: 402 | | | | |

## EUROPEAN CURRENCY UNITS

**2 POUNDS (2.8 ECUS) KM# 293 Composition:** Copper-Nickel

| Date | Mintage | F | VF | XF | Unc | BU |
|---|---|---|---|---|---|---|
| 1992 | — | — | — | — | 12.50 | — |

**10 POUNDS (14 ECUS) KM# 87 Weight:** 10.0000 g. **Composition:** 0.9250 Silver .2974 oz. ASW **Subject:** European Currency Unit **Obverse:** Uncouped portrait **Reverse:** Mounted rider left

| Date | Mintage | F | VF | XF | Unc | BU |
|---|---|---|---|---|---|---|
| 1991 Proof | Est. 10,000 | Value: 20.00 | | | | |
| 1992 Proof | Est. 5,000 | Value: 30.00 | | | | |
| 1993 | — | — | — | — | 75.00 | — |
| 1994 | — | — | — | — | 75.00 | — |

**10 POUNDS (14 ECUS) KM# 109 Weight:** 10.0000 g. **Composition:** 0.9250 Silver .2974 oz. ASW **Obverse:** Couped portrait **Reverse:** Mounted rider right

| Date | Mintage | F | VF | XF | Unc | BU |
|---|---|---|---|---|---|---|
| 1992 | — | — | — | — | 15.00 | — |
| 1992 Proof | — | — | — | — | — | — |
| 1993 Proof | — | Value: 35.00 | | | | |

**10 POUNDS (14 ECUS) KM# 624 Weight:** 10.0000 g. **Composition:** 0.9250 Silver .2974 oz. ASW **Obverse:** Queen's portrait **Reverse:** Knight on horseback jumping left, shield

| Date | Mintage | F | VF | XF | Unc | BU |
|---|---|---|---|---|---|---|
| 1992 Proof | Est. 2,500 | Value: 25.00 | | | | |

**10 POUNDS (14 ECUS) KM# 89 Weight:** 10.0000 g. **Composition:** 0.9250 Silver .2974 oz. ASW **Obverse:** Couped portrait **Reverse:** Knight on horse jumping right

| Date | Mintage | F | VF | XF | Unc | BU |
|---|---|---|---|---|---|---|
| 1992A Matte | — | — | — | — | 20.00 | — |

**10 POUNDS (14 ECUS) KM# 337 Weight:** 10.0000 g. **Composition:** 0.9250 Silver .2974 oz. ASW **Reverse:** Olympics - Torch Shield

| Date | Mintage | F | VF | XF | Unc | BU |
|---|---|---|---|---|---|---|
| 1992 Proof | 2,500 | Value: 25.00 | | | | |

**10 POUNDS (14 ECUS) KM# 627 Weight:** 10.0000 g. **Composition:** 0.9250 Silver .2974 oz. ASW **Obverse:** Queen's portrait **Reverse:** Knight on horseback jumping right, 3 lions on shield

| Date | Mintage | F | VF | XF | Unc | BU |
|---|---|---|---|---|---|---|
| 1993 Proof | Est. 2,500 | Value: 25.00 | | | | |

**25 POUNDS (35 ECUS) KM# 88 Weight:** 28.2800 g. **Composition:** 0.9250 Silver .8411 oz. ASW **Obverse:** Uncouped portrait **Reverse:** Knight left **Note:** Similar to 10 Pounds - 14 Ecus, KM#87.

| Date | Mintage | F | VF | XF | Unc | BU |
|---|---|---|---|---|---|---|
| 1991 Proof | Est. 10,000 | Value: 60.00 | | | | |
| 1992 | — | — | — | — | 40.00 | — |
| 1992 Proof | Est. 15,000 | Value: 60.00 | | | | |

**25 POUNDS (35 ECUS) KM# 110 Weight:** 28.2800 g. **Composition:** 0.9250 Silver .8411 oz. ASW **Obverse:** Uncouped portrait **Reverse:** Knight right

| Date | Mintage | F | VF | XF | Unc | BU |
|---|---|---|---|---|---|---|
| 1992 Proof | Est. 15,000 | Value: 50.00 | | | | |
| 1993 Proof | — | Value: 70.00 | | | | |

**25 POUNDS (35 ECUS) KM# 338 Weight:** 28.2800 g. **Composition:** 0.9250 Silver .8411 oz. ASW **Reverse:** Olympics - Torch Shield

| Date | Mintage | F | VF | XF | Unc | BU |
|---|---|---|---|---|---|---|
| 1992 Proof | Est. 2,000 | Value: 100 | | | | |

**25 POUNDS (35 ECUS) KM# 625 Weight:** 28.2800 g. **Composition:** 0.9250 Silver .8411 oz. ASW **Obverse:** Queen's portrait **Reverse:** Knight on horseback jumping left, small horse on shield

| Date | Mintage | F | VF | XF | Unc | BU |
|---|---|---|---|---|---|---|
| 1992 Proof | Est. 2,000 | Value: 100 | | | | |

**25 POUNDS (35 ECUS) KM# 628 Weight:** 28.2800 g. **Composition:** 0.9250 Silver .8411 oz. ASW **Obverse:** Queen's portrait **Reverse:** Knight on horseback jumping right, 3 lions on shield

| Date | Mintage | F | VF | XF | Unc | BU |
|---|---|---|---|---|---|---|
| 1993 Proof | Est. 2,000 | Value: 75.00 | | | | |

**50 POUNDS (70 ECUS) KM# 75 Weight:** 6.1200 g. **Composition:** 0.5000 Gold .1000 oz. AGW **Obverse:** Couped portrait

| Date | Mintage | F | VF | XF | Unc | BU |
|---|---|---|---|---|---|---|
| 1991 | — | — | — | — | 85.00 | — |
| 1991 Proof | Est. 5,000 | Value: 200 | | | | |
| 1992 | — | — | — | — | 85.00 | — |
| 1992 Proof | Est. 2,000 | Value: 225 | | | | |
| 1994 | — | — | — | — | 250 | — |

**50 POUNDS (70 ECUS) KM# 111 Weight:** 6.1200 g. **Composition:** 0.5000 Gold .1000 oz. AGW **Reverse:** Knight charging right

| Date | Mintage | F | VF | XF | Unc | BU |
|---|---|---|---|---|---|---|
| 1992 Proof | Est. 2,000 | Value: 175 | | | | |
| 1993 Proof | Est. 1,000 | Value: 200 | | | | |

**50 POUNDS (70 ECUS) KM# 339 Weight:** 6.1200 g. **Composition:** 0.5000 Gold .1000 oz. AGW **Reverse:** Olympics - Torch Shield

| Date | Mintage | F | VF | XF | Unc | BU |
|---|---|---|---|---|---|---|
| 1992 Proof | Est. 1,000 | Value: 200 | | | | |

**50 POUNDS (70 ECUS)** **KM# 626** **Weight:** 6.1200 g. **Composition:** 0.5000 Gold .1000 oz. AGW **Obverse:** Queen's portrait **Reverse:** Knight on horseback jumping left, small horse on shield

| Date | Mintage | F | VF | XF | Unc | BU |
|---|---|---|---|---|---|---|
| 1992 Proof | Est. 1,000 | Value: 200 | | | | |

**50 POUNDS (70 ECUS)** **KM# 629** **Weight:** 6.1200 g. **Composition:** 0.5000 Gold .1000 oz. AGW **Obverse:** Queen's portrait **Reverse:** Knight on horseback jumping right, 3 lions on shield

| Date | Mintage | F | VF | XF | Unc | BU |
|---|---|---|---|---|---|---|
| 1993 Proof | Est. 1,000 | Value: 150 | | | | |

## STERLING ECU

**2.8 ECUS** **KM# 478** **Composition:** Copper-Nickel **Reverse:** Euro Tunnel - Train Exiting Tunnel

| Date | Mintage | F | VF | XF | Unc | BU |
|---|---|---|---|---|---|---|
| 1993 | — | — | — | — | 9.50 | — |

**2.8 ECUS** **KM# 630** **Composition:** Copper-Nickel **Subject:** A'riane - European Space Programme **Obverse:** Queen's portrait **Reverse:** Rocket orbitting Earth **Note:** Similar to 70 Ecus, KM#634.

| Date | Mintage | F | VF | XF | Unc | BU |
|---|---|---|---|---|---|---|
| 1993 | — | — | — | — | 7.50 | — |

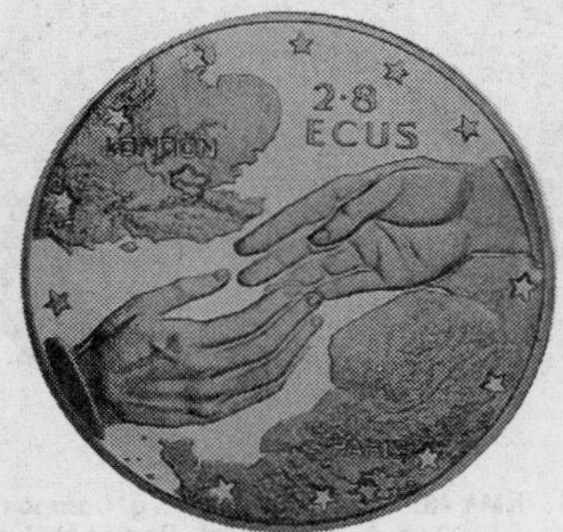


**2.8 ECUS** **KM# 484** **Composition:** Copper-Nickel **Reverse:** Euro Tunnel - Clasping Hands

| Date | Mintage | F | VF | XF | Unc | BU |
|---|---|---|---|---|---|---|
| 1994 | — | — | — | — | 9.00 | — |

**2.8 ECUS** **KM# 489** **Composition:** Copper-Nickel **Reverse:** Mythology - WInged Victory Above Chariot

| Date | Mintage | F | VF | XF | Unc | BU |
|---|---|---|---|---|---|---|
| 1994 | — | — | — | — | 8.50 | — |

**2.8 ECUS** **KM# 494** **Composition:** Copper-Nickel **Reverse:** Admiral Nelson and Ship

| Date | Mintage | F | VF | XF | Unc | BU |
|---|---|---|---|---|---|---|
| 1995 | — | — | — | — | 8.50 | — |

**2.8 ECUS** **KM# 508** **Composition:** Copper-Nickel **Reverse:** Austrian Knight **Note:** Similar to 70 Ecus, KM#512.

| Date | Mintage | F | VF | XF | Unc | BU |
|---|---|---|---|---|---|---|
| 1996 | — | — | — | — | 8.50 | — |

**14 ECUS** **KM# 479** **Weight:** 10.0000 g. **Composition:** 0.9250 Silver .2974 oz. ASW **Reverse:** Euro Tunnel - Train Exiting Tunnel

| Date | Mintage | F | VF | XF | Unc | BU |
|---|---|---|---|---|---|---|
| 1993 Proof | 30,000 | Value: 15.00 | | | | |

**14 ECUS** **KM# 631** **Weight:** 10.0000 g. **Composition:** 0.9250 Silver .2974 oz. ASW **Subject:** Sir Winston Churchill **Obverse:** Queen's portrait **Reverse:** Churchill in uniform

| Date | Mintage | F | VF | XF | Unc | BU |
|---|---|---|---|---|---|---|
| 1993 Proof | Est. 20,000 | Value: 15.00 | | | | |

**14 ECUS** **KM# 483** **Weight:** 10.0000 g. **Composition:** 0.9250 Silver .2974 oz. ASW **Reverse:** International Aid for Europe

| Date | Mintage | F | VF | XF | Unc | BU |
|---|---|---|---|---|---|---|
| 1994 Proof | Est. 30,000 | Value: 18.50 | | | | |

**14 ECUS** **KM# 485** **Weight:** 10.0000 g. **Composition:** 0.9250 Silver .2974 oz. ASW **Reverse:** Euro Tunnel - Train Exiting Tunnel

| Date | Mintage | F | VF | XF | Unc | BU |
|---|---|---|---|---|---|---|
| 1994 Proof | Est. 30,000 | Value: 22.50 | | | | |

**14 ECUS** **KM# 490** **Weight:** 10.0000 g. **Composition:** 0.9250 Silver .2974 oz. ASW **Reverse:** Parthenon and Brandenburg Gate

| Date | Mintage | F | VF | XF | Unc | BU |
|---|---|---|---|---|---|---|
| 1994 Proof | Est. 30,000 | Value: 16.50 | | | | |

**14 ECUS** **KM# 495** **Weight:** 10.0000 g. **Composition:** 0.9250 Silver .2974 oz. ASW **Reverse:** L'Arc de Triumph - Ceres

| Date | Mintage | F | VF | XF | Unc | BU |
|---|---|---|---|---|---|---|
| 1995 Proof | Est. 30,000 | Value: 18.50 | | | | |

**14 ECUS** **KM# 496** **Weight:** 10.0000 g. **Composition:** 0.9250 Silver .2974 oz. ASW **Reverse:** Richard the Lionheart

| Date | Mintage | F | VF | XF | Unc | BU |
|---|---|---|---|---|---|---|
| 1995 Proof | Est. 30,000 | Value: 18.50 | | | | |

**14 ECUS** **KM# 509** **Weight:** 10.0000 g. **Composition:** 0.9250 Silver .2974 oz. ASW **Reverse:** Napoleon Above European Battle Site

| Date | Mintage | F | VF | XF | Unc | BU |
|---|---|---|---|---|---|---|
| 1996 Proof | Est. 30,000 | Value: 18.50 | | | | |

**14 ECUS** **KM# 510** **Weight:** 10.0000 g. **Composition:** 0.9250 Silver .2974 oz. ASW **Reverse:** Leaning Tower of Pisa, Irish Harp

| Date | Mintage | F | VF | XF | Unc | BU |
|---|---|---|---|---|---|---|
| 1996 Proof | Est. 30,000 | Value: 18.50 | | | | |

**15 ECUS** **KM# 497** **Weight:** 1.2400 g. **Composition:** 0.9999 Gold .0399 oz. AGW **Reverse:** Knight with shield and banner

| Date | Mintage | F | VF | XF | Unc | BU |
|---|---|---|---|---|---|---|
| 1995 Proof | 15,000 | Value: 30.00 | | | | |

**15 ECUS** **KM# 504** **Weight:** 1.2400 g. **Composition:** 0.9999 Gold .0399 oz. AGW **Reverse:** Sir Francis Drake's ship "Golden Hind"

| Date | Mintage | F | VF | XF | Unc | BU |
|---|---|---|---|---|---|---|
| 1996 Proof | Est. 1,500 | Value: 40.00 | | | | |

**21 ECUS** **KM# 480** **Weight:** 19.2000 g. **Composition:** 0.9250 Silver .5710 oz. ASW **Reverse:** Euro Tunnel - Trains Exiting Tunnel

| Date | Mintage | F | VF | XF | Unc | BU |
|---|---|---|---|---|---|---|
| 1993 Proof | Est. 15,000 | Value: 32.50 | | | | |

**21 ECUS** **KM# 482** **Weight:** 19.2000 g. **Composition:** 0.9250 Silver .5710 oz. ASW **Reverse:** Euro Tunnel - Tunnel View and Napoleon

| Date | Mintage | F | VF | XF | Unc | BU |
|---|---|---|---|---|---|---|
| 1993 Proof | Est. 15,000 | Value: 22.50 | | | | |

**21 ECUS** **KM# 632** **Weight:** 19.2000 g. **Composition:** 0.9250 Silver .5710 oz. ASW **Subject:** European Economic Community **Obverse:** Queen's portrait **Reverse:** European coins

| Date | Mintage | F | VF | XF | Unc | BU |
|---|---|---|---|---|---|---|
| 1993 Proof | Est. 15,000 | Value: 30.00 | | | | |

**21 ECUS** **KM# 486** **Weight:** 19.2000 g. **Composition:** 0.9250 Silver .5710 oz. ASW **Reverse:** Euro Tunnel - 2 Trains and Motor Vehicle

| Date | Mintage | F | VF | XF | Unc | BU |
|---|---|---|---|---|---|---|
| 1994 Proof | Est. 15,000 | Value: 30.00 | | | | |

**21 ECUS** **KM# 491** **Weight:** 19.2000 g. **Composition:** 0.9250 Silver .5710 oz. ASW **Reverse:** 21 Years - European Community Membership

| Date | Mintage | F | VF | XF | Unc | BU |
|---|---|---|---|---|---|---|
| 1994 Proof | Est. 15,000 | Value: 30.00 | | | | |

**21 ECUS** **KM# 498** **Weight:** 19.2000 g. **Composition:** 0.9250 Silver .5710 oz. ASW **Reverse:** Europa with Shields of Austria, Sweden and Finland

| Date | Mintage | F | VF | XF | Unc | BU |
|---|---|---|---|---|---|---|
| 1995 Proof | Est. 15,000 | Value: 35.00 | | | | |

**21 ECUS** **KM# 499** **Weight:** 19.2000 g. **Composition:** 0.9250 Silver .5710 oz. ASW **Subject:** Agreement of Cooperation between Russia and the European Union

| Date | Mintage | F | VF | XF | Unc | BU |
|---|---|---|---|---|---|---|
| 1995 Proof | Est. 15,000 | Value: 35.00 | | | | |

**35 ECUS** **KM# 505** **Weight:** 3.1100 g. **Composition:** 0.9999 Gold .1000 oz. AGW **Reverse:** Ship "Hanseatic Kogge"

| Date | Mintage | F | VF | XF | Unc | BU |
|---|---|---|---|---|---|---|
| 1996 Proof | Est. 1,500 | Value: 75.00 | | | | |

**70 ECUS** **KM# 634** **Weight:** 6.2200 g. **Composition:** 0.9999 Gold .2000 oz. AGW **Subject:** Ariane - European Space Programme **Obverse:** Queen's portrait **Reverse:** Rocket orbitting Earth

| Date | Mintage | F | VF | XF | Unc | BU |
|---|---|---|---|---|---|---|
| 1993 Proof | Est. 2,000 | Value: 165 | | | | |
| 1993 Proof | Est. 1,000 | Value: 170 | | | | |

**70 ECUS** **KM# 633** **Weight:** 155.5175 g. **Composition:** 0.9990 Silver 5.0000 oz. ASW **Subject:** Ariane - European Space Programme **Obverse:** Queen's portrait **Reverse:** Rocket orbitting Earth **Note:** Similar to 70 Ecus, KM#634.

| Date | Mintage | F | VF | XF | Unc | BU |
|---|---|---|---|---|---|---|
| 1993 Proof | Est. 2,000 | Value: 165 | | | | |

**70 ECUS** **KM# 487** **Weight:** 155.5175 g. **Composition:** 0.9990 Silver 5.0000 oz. ASW **Obverse:** Portrait of Queen **Reverse:** Euro Tunnel - Tunnel View and Napoleon **Shape:** 65 **Note:** Illustration reduced.

| Date | Mintage | F | VF | XF | Unc | BU |
|---|---|---|---|---|---|---|
| 1994 Proof | Est. 2,000 | Value: 135 | | | | |

**70 ECUS** **KM# 492** **Weight:** 155.5175 g. **Composition:** 0.9990 Silver 5.0000 oz. ASW **Subject:** European Unity **Reverse:** Goddesses with quadrigia **Size:** 65 mm. **Note:** Illustration reduced.

| Date | Mintage | F | VF | XF | Unc | BU |
|---|---|---|---|---|---|---|
| 1994 Proof | Est. 2,000 | Value: 135 | | | | |

**70 ECUS** **KM# 488** **Weight:** 6.2200 g. **Composition:** 0.9999 Gold .2000 oz. AGW **Reverse:** Euro Tunnel - Outreached Hands Above English Channel

| Date | Mintage | F | VF | XF | Unc | BU |
|---|---|---|---|---|---|---|
| 1994 Proof | Est. 2,000 | Value: 125 | | | | |

**70 ECUS** **KM# 493** **Weight:** 6.2200 g. **Composition:** 0.9999 Gold .2000 oz. AGW **Reverse:** Mythology - Europa Sowing Seeds

| Date | Mintage | F | VF | XF | Unc | BU |
|---|---|---|---|---|---|---|
| 1994 Proof | Est. 2,000 | Value: 125 | | | | |

**70 ECUS** **KM# 501** **Weight:** 155.9200 g. **Composition:** 0.9990 Silver 5.0079 oz. ASW **Reverse:** Liberty and Brittania seated above Euro Tunnel

| Date | Mintage | F | VF | XF | Unc | BU |
|---|---|---|---|---|---|---|
| 1995 Proof | Est. 2,000 | Value: 165 | | | | |

**70 ECUS** **KM# 502** **Weight:** 6.2200 g. **Composition:** 0.9999 Gold .2000 oz. AGW **Reverse:** Mercury above Ship

| Date | Mintage | F | VF | XF | Unc | BU |
|---|---|---|---|---|---|---|
| 1995 Proof | Est. 2,000 | Value: 160 | | | | |

**70 ECUS** **KM# 503** **Weight:** 6.2200 g. **Composition:** 0.9999 Gold .2000 oz. AGW **Reverse:** Richard the Lionheart

| Date | Mintage | F | VF | XF | Unc | BU |
|---|---|---|---|---|---|---|
| 1995 Proof | Est. 2,000 | Value: 160 | | | | |

**70 ECUS** **KM# 500** **Weight:** 155.9200 g. **Composition:** 0.9990 Silver 5.0079 oz. ASW **Reverse:** Admiral Nelson and HMS Victory **Size:** 65 mm. **Note:** Illustration reduced.

| Date | Mintage | F | VF | XF | Unc | BU |
|---|---|---|---|---|---|---|
| 1995 Proof | 2,000 | Value: 165 | | | | |

**70 ECUS** **KM# 512** **Weight:** 6.2200 g. **Composition:** 0.9999 Gold .2000 oz. AGW **Note:** Similar to 2.8 Ecus, KM#508.

| Date | Mintage | F | VF | XF | Unc | BU |
|---|---|---|---|---|---|---|
| 1996 Proof | 2,000 | Value: 160 | | | | |

**70 ECUS** **KM# 506** **Weight:** 6.2200 g. **Composition:** 0.9999 Gold .2000 oz. AGW **Reverse:** HMS Victory

| Date | Mintage | F | VF | XF | Unc | BU |
|---|---|---|---|---|---|---|
| 1996 Proof | Est. 1,500 | Value: 165 | | | | |

**70 ECUS** **KM# 511** **Weight:** 155.5175 g. **Composition:** 0.9990 Silver 5.000 oz. ASW **Reverse:** Sir Francis Drake and "Golden Hind"

| Date | Mintage | F | VF | XF | Unc | BU |
|---|---|---|---|---|---|---|
| 1996 Proof | Est. 2,000 | Value: 165 | | | | |

**75 ECUS** **KM# 528** **Ring Weight:** 3.8880 g. **Ring Composition:** 0.9999 Gold .1250 oz. AGW **Center Weight:** 3.8880 g. **Center Composition:** 0.9995 Platinum .1250 oz. APW **Subject:** Austrian Centennial **Obverse:** Queen's portrait **Reverse:** Standing allegorical figure with shield and trident

| Date | Mintage | F | VF | XF | Unc | BU |
|---|---|---|---|---|---|---|
| 1996 Proof | 1,500 | Value: 250 | | | | |

**140 ECUS** **KM# 507** **Center Weight:** 15.5500 g. **Center Composition:** 0.9999 Gold .4999 oz. AGW **Reverse:** Viking Longship

| Date | Mintage | F | VF | XF | Unc | BU |
|---|---|---|---|---|---|---|
| 1996 In Proof sets only | Est. 1,500 | — | — | — | 350 | — |

## PATTERNS

Including off metal strikes

| KM# | Date | Mintage | Identification | Mkt Val |
|---|---|---|---|---|
| Pn4 | 1989 | — | 1/4 Sovereign. Gold. Similar to Pn8. | — |
| Pn5 | 1989 | — | 1/2 Sovereign. Gold. Similar to Pn8. | — |
| Pn6 | 1989 | — | Sovereign. Gold. Similar to Pn8. | — |
| Pn7 | 1989 | — | 2 Sovereigns. Gold. Similar to Pn8. | — |
| Pn8 | 1989 | — | 5 Sovereigns. Gold. Una and the lion with the Rock of Gibraltar in background. | — |

## PIEFORTS

| KM# | Date | Mintage | Identification | Mkt Val |
|---|---|---|---|---|
| P2 | 1990 | 1,000 | 5 Pence. 0.9160 Gold. 6.0000 g. KM#22c. | — |
| P1 | 1990 | 5,000 | 5 Pence. 0.9250 Silver. 6.0000 g. KM#22b. | 65.00 |
| P3 | 1993 | 5,000 | 14 Ecus. 0.9250 Silver. KM#631. | 50.00 |

## MINT SETS

| KM# | Date | Mintage | Identification | Issue Price | Mkt Val |
|---|---|---|---|---|---|
| MS10 | 1998 (9) | — | KM#16, 18, 20-21, 22a, 24, 39, 112, 355 | — | 35.00 |
| MS11 | 1999 (9) | — | KM#16, 18, 20-21, 22a, 24, 39, 112, 355 | — | 35.00 |
| MS1 | 1975 (3) | 1,625 | KM#7-9 | — | 750 |
| MS2 | 1988 (9) | — | KM#16-18, 20-25 | 21.00 | 32.00 |
| MS3 | 1989 (9) | — | KM#16-17, 20-25, 32 | — | 35.00 |
| MS4 | 1990 (9) | — | km#16, 18, 20-21, 22A, 23-25, 39 | 25.00 | 35.00 |
| ms5 | 1991 (9) | — | KM#16, 18, 20-21, 22a, 23-25, 39 | 25.00 | 35.00 |
| MS7 | 1995 (9) | — | KM#16, 20-21, 22A, 24, 39, 112, 334, 340 | — | 35.00 |
| MS6 | 1996-1998 (6) | 5,000 | KM#201, 327, 382,444, 525, 656 | — | 45.00 |
| MS8 | 1996 (9) | — | KM#16, 18, 20-21, 22, 24, 39, 112, 355 | — | 35.00 |
| MS9 | 1997 (9) | — | KM#16, 18, 20-21, 22a, 24, 39, 113, 355 | — | 35.00 |

## PROOF SETS

| KM# | Date | Mintage | Identification | Issue Price | Mkt Val |
|---|---|---|---|---|---|
| PS27 | 2001 (4) | 999 | KM#665, 668.1, 670.1, 672.1 | 1,400 | — |
| PS28 | 2001 (4) | 2,001 | KM#667, 669a.1, 671a.1, 673a.1 | 350 | — |
| PS1 | 1975 (3) | 750 | KM#7-9 | 875 | 1,000 |
| PS2 | 1989 (5) | — | KM#26-30 | — | 2,130 |
| PS3 | 1989 (2) | — | KM#29-30 | — | 1,650 |
| PS4 | 1990 (6) | 500 | KM#76-81 | — | 1,500 |
| PS5 | 1990 (6) | 250 | KM#76a-81a | — | 2,100 |
| PS6 | 1990 (5) | 1,000 | KM#41-45 | 1,800 | 1,900 |
| PS11 | 1991 (5) | 1,000 | KM#91-94, 97 | — | 1,310 |
| PS7 | 1991 (8) | 20,000 | KM#50-57 | — | 640 |
| PS8 | 1991 (8) | 5,000 | KM#58-65 | — | 1,280 |
| PS9 | 1991 (8) | 1,000 | KM#58a-65a | — | 2,200 |

| KM# | Date | Mintage | Identification | Issue Price | Mkt Val |
|---|---|---|---|---|---|
| PS10 | 1991 (8) | 50 | KM#66-73 | 120 | 120 |
| PS12 | 1992 (5) | 1,000 | KM#99-102, 105 | — | 1,150 |
| PS14 | 1993 (5) | 300 | KM#124-128 | — | 625 |
| PS13 | 1993 (5) | 1,000 | KM#193-197 | — | 910 |
| PS16 | 1994-95 (3) | 5,000 | KM#309, 332, 335 | — | 60.00 |
| PS17 | 1994-95 (3) | 3,000 | KM#309a, 332a, 335a | — | 120 |
| PS18 | 1994-95 (3) | 3,000 | KM#309, 332, 335 | — | 120 |
| PS15 | 1994 (5) | 1,000 | KM#248-251, 252a | — | 910 |
| PS19 | 1995 (5) | 1,000 | KM#319-323 | — | 910 |
| PS22 | 1996 (4) | 1,500 | KM#504-507 | — | 650 |
| PS21 | 1996 (5) | 1,000 | KM#361-364, 365b | — | 960 |
| PS23 | 1997 (5) | 1,000 | KM#557-560, 561b | — | 1,100 |
| PS24 | 1998 (5) | 1,000 | KM#749-752, 754 | 1,309 | 890 |
| PS25 | 1999 (5) | 1,000 | KM#828-831, 833 | 1,310 | 750 |
| PS26 | 2000 (5) | 1,000 | KM#888-891, 893 | — | 875 |

## PROOF-LIKE SETS (PL)

| KM# | Date | Mintage | Identification | Issue Price | Mkt Val |
|---|---|---|---|---|---|
| PL1 | 1992 (8) | — | KM#66-73 | — | 100 |

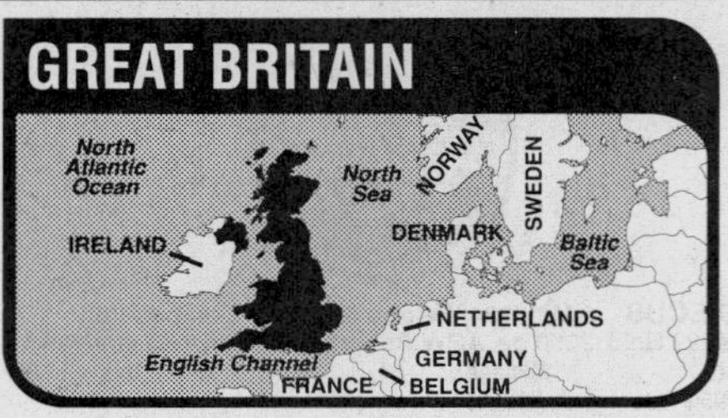


The United Kingdom of Great Britain and Northern Ireland, located off the northwest coast of the European continent, has an area of 94,227sq. mi. (244,820 sq. km.) and a population of 54 million. Capital: London. The economy is based on industrial activity and trading. Machinery, motor vehicles, chemicals, and textile yarns and fabrics are exported.

After the departure of the Romans, who brought Britain into a more active relationship with Europe, it fell prey to invaders from Scandinavia and the Low Countries who drove the original Britons into Scotland and Wales, and established a profusion of kingdoms that finally united in the 11th century under the Danish King Canute. Norman rule, following the conquest of 1066, stimulated the development of those institutions, which have since distinguished British life. Henry VIII (1509-47) turned Britain from continental adventuring and faced it to the sea - a decision that made Britain a world power during the reign of Elizabeth I (1558-1603). Strengthened by the Industrial Revolution and the defeat of Napoleon, 19thcentury Britain turned to the remote parts of the world and established a colonial empire of such extent and prosperity that the world has never seen its like. World Wars I and II sealed the fate of the Empire and relegated Britain to a lesser role in world affairs by draining her resources and inaugurating a worldwide movement toward national self-determination in her former colonies.

By the mid-20th century, most of the territories formerly comprising the British Empire had gained independence, and the empire had evolved into the Commonwealth of Nations, an association of equal and autonomous states, which enjoy special trade interests. The Commonwealth is presently composed of 50 member nations, including the United Kingdom. All recognize the British monarch as head of the Commonwealth. Sixteen continue to recognize the British monarch as Head of State. They are: United Kingdom, Antigua and Barbuda, Australia, Bahamas, Barbados, Belize, Canada, Grenada, Jamaica, New Zealand, Papua New Guinea, St. Christopher & Nevis, Saint Lucia, Saint Vincent and the Grenadines, Solomon Islands, and Tuvalu. Elizabeth II is personally, and separately, the Queen of the sovereign, independent countries just mentioned. There is no other British connection between the several individual, national sovereignties, except that they are each represented by High Commissioners instead of ambassadors in each others countries.

**RULERS**

Victoria, 1837-1901
Edward VII, 1901-1910
George V, 1910-1936
Edward VIII, 1936
George VI, 1936-1952
Elizabeth II, 1952--

**Mint Marks**

H - Heaton
KN - King's Norton

**MONETARY SYSTEM**

**(Until 1970)**

4 Farthings = 1 Penny
12 Pence = 1 Shilling
2 Shillings = 1 Florin
5 Shillings = 1 Crown
20 Shillings = 1 Pound (Sovereign)
21 Shillings = 1 Guinea

NOTE: Proofs exist for many dates of British coins in the 19th and early 20th centuries and for virtually all coins between 1926 and 1964. Those not specifically listed here are extremely rare.

# KINGDOM

## POUND COINAGE

**1/3 FARTHING** **KM# 791** **Composition:** Bronze **Ruler:** Edward VII **Obverse:** Bust of Edward VII right **Note:** Homeland style stuck for Malta.

| Date | Mintage | F | VF | XF | Unc | BU |
|---|---|---|---|---|---|---|
| 1902 | 288,000 | 2.50 | 5.00 | 8.00 | 18.00 | — |

**1/3 FARTHING** **KM# 823** **Composition:** Bronze **Ruler:** George V **Obverse:** Bust of George V left **Note:** Homeland style struck for Malta.

| Date | Mintage | F | VF | XF | Unc | BU |
|---|---|---|---|---|---|---|
| 1913 | 288,000 | 2.50 | 5.00 | 8.00 | 16.00 | — |

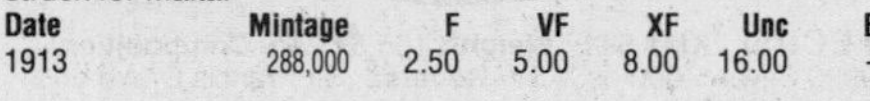

**FARTHING** **KM# 788.2** **Composition:** Bronze **Ruler:** Victoria **Note:** Blackened finish.

| Date | Mintage | F | VF | XF | Unc | BU |
|---|---|---|---|---|---|---|
| 1901 | 8,016,000 | 0.30 | 0.50 | 2.00 | 8.00 | — |

**FARTHING** **KM# 792** **Composition:** Bronze **Ruler:** Edward VII

| Date | Mintage | F | VF | XF | Unc | BU |
|---|---|---|---|---|---|---|
| 1902 | 5,125,000 | 0.50 | 1.50 | 3.00 | 10.00 | — |
| 1903 | 5,331,000 | 0.75 | 1.75 | 6.00 | 22.50 | — |
| 1903 Shield heraldically colored; Proof | — | Value: 800 | | | | |
| 1904 | 3,629,000 | 1.50 | 3.00 | 6.00 | 22.50 | — |
| 1905 | 4,077,000 | 0.50 | 1.50 | 6.00 | 22.50 | — |
| 1906 | 5,340,000 | 0.50 | 1.50 | 6.00 | 22.50 | — |
| 1907 | 4,399,000 | 0.50 | 1.50 | 6.00 | 22.50 | — |
| 1908 | 4,265,000 | 0.75 | 1.50 | 6.00 | 22.50 | — |
| 1909 | 8,852,000 | 0.75 | 1.50 | 6.00 | 22.50 | — |
| 1910 | 2,598,000 | 1.00 | 4.00 | 8.00 | 30.00 | — |

**FARTHING** **KM# 808.1** **Composition:** Bronze **Ruler:** George V

| Date | Mintage | F | VF | XF | Unc | BU |
|---|---|---|---|---|---|---|
| 1911 | 5,197,000 | 0.60 | 1.00 | 3.00 | 8.00 | — |
| 1912 | 7,670,000 | 0.35 | 0.75 | 2.50 | 8.00 | — |
| 1913 | 4,184,000 | 0.50 | 0.75 | 2.50 | 8.00 | — |
| 1914 | 6,127,000 | 0.35 | 0.75 | 2.50 | 8.00 | — |
| 1915 | 7,129,000 | 0.50 | 0.75 | 5.00 | 9.00 | — |
| 1916 | 10,993,000 | 0.35 | 0.75 | 1.75 | 7.00 | — |
| 1917 | 21,435,000 | 0.15 | 0.35 | 1.50 | 5.00 | — |
| 1918 | 19,363,000 | 0.75 | 1.50 | 10.00 | 16.50 | — |

**FARTHING** **KM# 808.2** **Composition:** Bronze **Ruler:** George V **Note:** Bright finish.

| Date | Mintage | F | VF | XF | Unc | BU |
|---|---|---|---|---|---|---|
| 1918 | Inc. above | 0.20 | 0.40 | 1.00 | 5.00 | — |
| 1919 | 15,089,000 | 0.20 | 0.40 | 1.00 | 5.00 | — |
| 1920 | 11,481,000 | 0.20 | 0.40 | 1.00 | 5.00 | — |
| 1921 | 9,469,000 | 0.20 | 0.40 | 1.00 | 6.00 | — |
| 1922 | 9,957,000 | 0.20 | 0.40 | 1.00 | 6.00 | — |
| 1923 | 8,034,000 | 0.20 | 0.40 | 1.00 | 7.00 | — |
| 1924 | 8,733,000 | 0.20 | 0.40 | 1.00 | 7.00 | — |
| 1925 | 12,635,000 | 0.20 | 0.40 | 1.00 | 5.00 | — |

**FARTHING** **KM# 825** **Composition:** Bronze **Ruler:** George V **Obverse:** Modified effigy

| Date | Mintage | F | VF | XF | Unc | BU |
|---|---|---|---|---|---|---|
| 1926 | 9,792,000 | 0.15 | 0.40 | 1.00 | 6.50 | — |
| 1926 Proof | — | Value: 275 | | | | |
| 1927 | 7,868,000 | 0.15 | 0.40 | 1.00 | 6.00 | — |
| 1927 Proof | — | Value: 250 | | | | |
| 1928 | 11,626,000 | 0.15 | 0.35 | 0.85 | 4.00 | — |
| 1928 Proof | — | Value: 200 | | | | |
| 1929 | 8,419,000 | 0.15 | 0.35 | 0.85 | 4.00 | — |
| 1929 Proof | — | Value: 200 | | | | |
| 1930 | 4,195,000 | 0.25 | 0.50 | 1.00 | 6.00 | — |
| 1930 Proof | — | Value: 200 | | | | |
| 1931 | 6,595,000 | 0.15 | 0.35 | 0.85 | 4.00 | — |
| 1931 Proof | — | Value: 200 | | | | |
| 1932 | 9,293,000 | 0.15 | 0.35 | 0.75 | 2.50 | — |
| 1932 Proof | — | Value: 200 | | | | |
| 1933 | 4,560,000 | 0.15 | 0.35 | 1.00 | 4.00 | — |
| 1933 Proof | — | Value: 200 | | | | |
| 1934 | 3,053,000 | 0.35 | 0.75 | 1.75 | 7.00 | — |
| 1934 Proof | — | Value: 200 | | | | |
| 1935 | 2,227,000 | 1.00 | 2.00 | 3.50 | 10.00 | — |
| 1935 Proof | — | Value: 200 | | | | |
| 1936 | 9,734,000 | 0.15 | 0.35 | 0.75 | 3.50 | — |
| 1936 Proof | — | Value: 200 | | | | |

**FARTHING** **KM# 843** **Composition:** Bronze **Ruler:** George VI

| Date | Mintage | F | VF | XF | Unc | BU |
|---|---|---|---|---|---|---|
| 1937 | 8,131,000 | 0.15 | 0.25 | 0.50 | 1.50 | — |
| 1937 Matte Proof; Rare | — | — | — | — | — | — |

**Note:** There are reportedly 3-4 pieces known of this variety struck specifically for use in photographs.

| Date | Mintage | F | VF | XF | Unc | BU |
|---|---|---|---|---|---|---|
| 1937 Proof | 26,000 | Value: 4.00 | | | | |
| 1938 | 7,450,000 | 0.15 | 0.30 | 0.60 | 3.50 | — |
| 1938 Proof | — | Value: 175 | | | | |
| 1939 | 31,440,000 | 0.10 | 0.25 | 0.40 | 1.75 | — |
| 1939 Proof | — | Value: 175 | | | | |
| 1940 | 18,360,000 | 0.10 | 0.25 | 0.50 | 2.50 | — |
| 1940 Proof | — | Value: 175 | | | | |
| 1941 | 27,312,000 | 0.10 | 0.25 | 0.40 | 1.75 | — |
| 1941 Proof | — | Value: 175 | | | | |
| 1942 | 28,858,000 | 0.10 | 0.20 | 0.35 | 1.75 | — |
| 1942 Proof | — | Value: 175 | | | | |
| 1943 | 33,345,999 | 0.10 | 0.15 | 0.30 | 1.75 | — |
| 1943 Proof | — | Value: 175 | | | | |
| 1944 | 25,138,000 | 0.10 | 0.15 | 0.30 | 1.75 | — |
| 1944 Proof | — | Value: 175 | | | | |
| 1945 | 23,736,000 | 0.10 | 0.20 | 0.35 | 1.75 | — |
| 1945 Proof | — | Value: 175 | | | | |
| 1946 | 24,365,000 | 0.10 | 0.20 | 0.35 | 1.75 | — |
| 1946 Proof | — | Value: 175 | | | | |
| 1947 | 14,746,000 | 0.10 | 0.20 | 0.35 | 1.75 | — |
| 1947 Proof | — | Value: 175 | | | | |
| 1948 | 16,622,000 | 0.10 | 0.20 | 0.35 | 1.75 | — |
| 1948 Proof | — | Value: 175 | | | | |

**FARTHING** **KM# 867** **Composition:** Bronze **Ruler:** George VI **Obv. Legend:** Without IND IMP

| Date | Mintage | F | VF | XF | Unc | BU |
|---|---|---|---|---|---|---|
| 1949 | 8,424,000 | 0.10 | 0.20 | 0.35 | 1.75 | — |
| 1949 Proof | — | Value: 175 | | | | |
| 1950 | 10,325,000 | 0.10 | 0.20 | 0.35 | 1.75 | — |
| 1950 Matte Proof; Rare | — | Value: 3.50 | | | | |

**Note:** There are reportedly 3-4 known of this variety, struck specifically for use in photographs

| Date | Mintage | F | VF | XF | Unc | BU |
|---|---|---|---|---|---|---|
| 1950 Proof | 18,000 | Value: 5.00 | | | | |
| 1951 | 14,016,000 | 0.10 | 0.20 | 0.35 | 2.00 | — |
| 1951 Matte Proof; Rare | — | — | — | — | — | — |

**Note:** There are reportedly 3-4 known of this variety, struck specifically for use in photographs

| Date | Mintage | F | VF | XF | Unc | BU |
|---|---|---|---|---|---|---|
| 1951 Proof | 20,000 | Value: 3.50 | | | | |
| 1952 | 5,251,000 | 0.10 | 0.20 | 0.35 | 2.00 | — |
| 1952 Proof | — | Value: 175 | | | | |

**FARTHING** **KM# 881** **Composition:** Bronze **Ruler:** Elizabeth II

| Date | Mintage | F | VF | XF | Unc | BU |
|---|---|---|---|---|---|---|
| 1953 | 6,131,000 | 0.15 | 0.25 | 0.35 | 2.00 | — |
| 1953 Proof | 40,000 | Value: 5.00 | | | | |
| 1953 Matte Proof; Rare | — | — | — | — | — | — |

**Note:** There are reportedly 1-2 known of this variety, struck specifically for use in photographs

**FARTHING** **KM# 895** **Composition:** Bronze **Ruler:** Elizabeth II **Obv. Legend:** Without BRITT OMN

| Date | Mintage | F | VF | XF | Unc | BU |
|---|---|---|---|---|---|---|
| 1954 | 6,566,000 | 0.10 | 0.15 | 0.30 | 2.00 | — |
| 1954 Proof | — | Value: 175 | | | | |
| 1955 | 5,779,000 | 0.10 | 0.15 | 0.30 | 2.00 | — |
| 1955 Proof | — | Value: 175 | | | | |
| 1956 | 1,997,000 | 0.25 | 0.50 | 0.75 | 4.00 | — |
| 1956 Proof | — | Value: 175 | | | | |

**1/2 PENNY** **KM# 789** **Composition:** Bronze **Ruler:** Victoria

| Date | Mintage | F | VF | XF | Unc | BU |
|---|---|---|---|---|---|---|
| 1901 | 11,127,000 | 0.40 | 0.75 | 5.00 | 12.50 | — |
| 1901 Proof | — | Value: 500 | | | | |

**1/2 PENNY** **KM# 793.1** **Composition:** Bronze **Ruler:** Edward VII **Reverse:** Low horizon

| Date | Mintage | F | VF | XF | Unc | BU |
|---|---|---|---|---|---|---|
| 1902 | 13,673,000 | 8.00 | 15.00 | 50.00 | 140 | — |

**1/2 PENNY** **KM# 793.2** **Composition:** Bronze **Ruler:** Edward VII **Reverse:** High horizon

| Date | Mintage | F | VF | XF | Unc | BU |
|---|---|---|---|---|---|---|
| 1902 | Inc. above | 0.50 | 1.50 | 5.00 | 18.00 | — |
| 1903 | 11,451,000 | 0.75 | 2.50 | 8.00 | 37.50 | — |
| 1904 | 8,131,000 | 1.50 | 3.50 | 12.00 | 45.00 | — |
| 1905 | 10,125,000 | 1.00 | 3.00 | 8.00 | 30.00 | — |
| 1906 | 11,101,000 | 0.75 | 2.00 | 6.00 | 30.00 | — |
| 1907 | 16,849,000 | 0.75 | 2.00 | 6.00 | 30.00 | — |
| 1908 | 16,620,999 | 0.75 | 2.00 | 6.00 | 30.00 | — |
| 1909 | 8,279,000 | 1.00 | 3.00 | 8.00 | 30.00 | — |
| 1910 | 10,770,000 | 1.00 | 3.00 | 8.00 | 30.00 | — |

**1/2 PENNY** **KM# 809** **Composition:** Bronze **Ruler:** George V

| Date | Mintage | F | VF | XF | Unc | BU |
|---|---|---|---|---|---|---|
| 1911 | 12,571,000 | 0.75 | 1.50 | 4.50 | 22.50 | — |
| 1912 | 21,186,000 | 0.50 | 1.25 | 4.00 | 22.50 | — |
| 1913 | 17,476,000 | 0.75 | 2.25 | 8.00 | 30.00 | — |
| 1914 | 20,289,000 | 0.75 | 1.50 | 5.00 | 22.50 | — |
| 1915 | 21,563,000 | 0.75 | 1.50 | 5.00 | 22.50 | — |
| 1916 | 39,386,000 | 0.75 | 1.50 | 5.00 | 22.50 | — |
| 1917 | 38,245,000 | 0.75 | 1.50 | 5.00 | 22.50 | — |
| 1918 | 22,321,000 | 0.75 | 1.50 | 5.00 | 22.50 | — |
| 1919 | 28,104,000 | 0.50 | 1.50 | 5.00 | 22.50 | — |
| 1920 | 35,147,000 | 0.50 | 1.50 | 5.00 | 22.50 | — |
| 1921 | 28,027,000 | 0.75 | 1.50 | 3.00 | 18.00 | — |
| 1922 | 10,735,000 | 1.00 | 2.00 | 6.00 | 20.00 | — |
| 1923 | 12,266,000 | 0.50 | 1.50 | 5.00 | 15.00 | — |
| 1924 | 13,971,000 | 0.75 | 2.00 | 5.00 | 15.00 | — |
| 1925 | 12,216,000 | 1.00 | 2.00 | 5.00 | 15.00 | — |

**1/2 PENNY** **KM# 824** **Composition:** Bronze **Ruler:** George V **Obverse:** Modified effigy

| Date | Mintage | F | VF | XF | Unc | BU |
|---|---|---|---|---|---|---|
| 1925 | Inc. above | 1.50 | 4.00 | 8.00 | 35.00 | — |
| 1926 | 6,712,000 | 1.50 | 3.00 | 6.00 | 17.00 | — |
| 1926 Proof | — | Value: 325 | | | | |
| 1927 | 15,590,000 | 0.75 | 1.50 | 3.00 | 12.00 | — |
| 1927 Proof | — | Value: 325 | | | | |

**1/2 PENNY** **KM# 837** **Composition:** Bronze **Ruler:** George V **Obverse:** Smaller head

| Date | Mintage | F | VF | XF | Unc | BU |
|---|---|---|---|---|---|---|
| 1928 | 20,935,000 | 0.25 | 0.50 | 2.50 | 10.00 | — |
| 1928 Proof | — | Value: 325 | | | | |
| 1929 | 25,680,000 | 0.25 | 0.50 | 2.50 | 10.00 | — |
| 1929 Proof | — | Value: 325 | | | | |
| 1930 | 12,533,000 | 0.25 | 0.50 | 2.50 | 10.00 | — |
| 1930 Proof | — | Value: 325 | | | | |
| 1931 | 16,138,000 | 0.25 | 0.50 | 2.50 | 10.00 | — |
| 1931 Proof | — | Value: 325 | | | | |
| 1932 | 14,448,000 | 0.25 | 0.50 | 2.50 | 12.00 | — |
| 1932 Proof | — | Value: 325 | | | | |
| 1933 | 10,560,000 | 0.25 | 0.50 | 2.50 | 10.00 | — |
| 1933 Proof | — | Value: 325 | | | | |
| 1934 | 7,704,000 | 0.50 | 0.50 | 3.50 | 14.00 | — |
| 1934 Proof | — | Value: 350 | | | | |
| 1935 | 12,180,000 | 0.25 | 0.50 | 2.00 | 8.00 | — |
| 1935 Proof | — | Value: 300 | | | | |
| 1936 | 23,009,000 | 0.25 | 0.50 | 1.50 | 6.00 | — |
| 1936 Proof | — | Value: 300 | | | | |

**1/2 PENNY** **KM# 844** **Composition:** Bronze **Ruler:** George VI

| Date | Mintage | F | VF | XF | Unc | BU |
|---|---|---|---|---|---|---|
| 1937 | 24,504,000 | 0.25 | 0.35 | 0.50 | 1.75 | — |
| 1937 Proof | 26,000 | Value: 5.00 | | | | |
| 1937 Matte Proof; Rare | — | — | — | — | — | — |
| 1938 | 40,320,000 | 0.25 | 0.50 | 1.25 | 3.75 | — |
| 1938 Proof | — | Value: 300 | | | | |
| 1939 | 28,925,000 | 0.25 | 0.50 | 1.25 | 3.50 | — |
| 1939 Proof | — | Value: 300 | | | | |
| 1940 | 32,162,000 | 0.25 | 0.50 | 2.00 | 5.50 | — |
| 1940 Proof | — | Value: 300 | | | | |
| 1941 | 45,120,000 | 0.20 | 0.50 | 1.50 | 5.00 | — |
| 1941 Proof | — | Value: 300 | | | | |
| 1942 | 71,909,000 | 0.10 | 0.20 | 0.60 | 2.25 | — |
| 1942 Proof | — | Value: 300 | | | | |
| 1943 | 76,200,000 | 0.10 | 0.25 | 1.00 | 2.25 | — |
| 1943 Proof | — | Value: 300 | | | | |
| 1944 | 81,840,000 | 0.10 | 0.25 | 1.00 | 3.00 | — |
| 1944 Proof | — | Value: 300 | | | | |
| 1945 | 57,000,000 | 0.10 | 0.25 | 0.90 | 2.75 | — |
| 1945 Proof | — | Value: 300 | | | | |
| 1946 | 22,726,000 | 0.20 | 0.50 | 2.75 | 7.00 | — |
| 1946 Proof | — | Value: 300 | | | | |
| 1947 | 21,266,000 | 0.10 | 0.25 | 2.00 | 5.00 | — |
| 1947 Proof | — | Value: 300 | | | | |
| 1948 | 26,947,000 | 0.10 | 0.25 | 0.90 | 2.25 | — |
| 1948 Proof | — | Value: 300 | | | | |

**1/2 PENNY** **KM# 868** **Composition:** Bronze **Ruler:** George VI **Obv. Legend:** Without IND IMP

| Date | Mintage | F | VF | XF | Unc | BU |
|---|---|---|---|---|---|---|
| 1949 | 24,744,000 | 0.10 | 0.25 | 1.00 | 5.00 | — |
| 1949 Proof | — | Value: 250 | | | | |
| 1950 | 24,154,000 | 0.10 | 0.25 | 0.75 | 4.00 | — |
| 1950 Proof | 18,000 | Value: 5.00 | | | | |
| 1950 Matte Proof; Rare | — | — | — | — | — | — |

**Note:** There are reportedly 1-2 known of this variety, struck specifically for use in photographs

| Date | Mintage | F | VF | XF | Unc | BU |
|---|---|---|---|---|---|---|
| 1951 | 14,868,000 | 0.25 | 0.50 | 1.50 | 6.00 | — |
| 1951 Proof | 20,000 | Value: 6.00 | | | | |
| 1951 Matte Proof; Rare | — | — | — | — | — | — |

| Date | Mintage | F | VF | XF | Unc | BU |
|---|---|---|---|---|---|---|

**Note:** There are reportedly 1-2 known of this variety, struck specifically for use in photographs

| Date | Mintage | F | VF | XF | Unc | BU |
|---|---|---|---|---|---|---|
| 1952 | 33,278,000 | 0.10 | 0.25 | 0.50 | 3.00 | — |
| 1952 Proof | — | Value: 275 | | | | |

**1/2 PENNY KM# 882 Composition:** Bronze **Ruler:** Elizabeth II

| Date | Mintage | F | VF | XF | Unc | BU |
|---|---|---|---|---|---|---|
| 1953 | 8,926,000 | 0.20 | 0.40 | 1.00 | 2.25 | — |
| 1953 Proof | 40,000 | Value: 4.00 | | | | |
| 1953 Matte Proof; Rare | — | — | — | — | — | — |

**Note:** There are reportedly 1-2 known of this variety, struck specifically for use in photographs.

**1/2 PENNY KM# 896 Composition:** Bronze **Ruler:** Elizabeth II **Obv. Legend:** Without BRITT OMN

| Date | Mintage | F | VF | XF | Unc | BU |
|---|---|---|---|---|---|---|
| 1954 | 19,375,000 | 0.10 | 0.25 | 1.50 | 4.50 | — |
| 1954 Proof | — | Value: 250 | | | | |
| 1955 | 18,799,000 | 0.10 | 0.25 | 1.50 | 3.25 | — |
| 1955 Proof | — | Value: 250 | | | | |
| 1956 | 21,799,000 | 0.15 | 0.50 | 1.50 | 3.25 | — |
| 1956 Proof | — | Value: 250 | | | | |
| 1957 | 43,684,000 | 0.10 | 0.25 | 0.50 | 1.50 | — |
| 1957 Proof | — | Value: 250 | | | | |
| 1958 | 62,318,000 | — | 0.10 | 0.20 | 0.75 | — |
| 1958 Proof | — | Value: 250 | | | | |
| 1959 | 79,176,000 | — | 0.10 | 0.15 | 0.40 | — |
| 1959 Proof | — | Value: 250 | | | | |
| 1960 | 41,340,000 | — | 0.10 | 0.15 | 0.30 | — |
| 1960 Proof | — | Value: 250 | | | | |
| 1962 | 41,779,000 | — | — | 0.10 | 0.20 | — |
| 1962 Proof | — | Value: 250 | | | | |
| 1963 | 45,036,000 | — | — | 0.10 | 0.20 | — |
| 1963 Proof | — | Value: 250 | | | | |
| 1964 | 78,583,000 | — | — | 0.10 | 0.15 | — |
| 1964 Proof | — | Value: 250 | | | | |
| 1965 | 98,083,000 | — | — | — | 0.10 | — |
| 1965 Proof | — | — | — | — | — | — |
| 1966 | 95,289,000 | — | — | — | 0.10 | — |
| 1966 Proof | — | — | — | — | — | — |
| 1967 | 146,491,000 | — | — | — | 0.10 | — |
| 1967 Proof | — | — | — | — | — | — |
| 1970 Proof | 750,000 | Value: 1.50 | | | | |

**PENNY KM# 775 Weight:** 0.4713 g. **Composition:** 0.9250 Silver .0140 oz. ASW **Ruler:** Victoria

| Date | Mintage | F | VF | XF | Unc | BU |
|---|---|---|---|---|---|---|
| 1901 Prooflike | 18,000 | — | — | — | 12.50 | — |

**PENNY KM# 790 Composition:** Bronze **Ruler:** Victoria

| Date | Mintage | F | VF | XF | Unc | BU |
|---|---|---|---|---|---|---|
| 1901 | 22,206,000 | 0.30 | 0.75 | 3.00 | 12.50 | — |
| 1901 Proof | — | — | — | — | — | — |

**PENNY KM# 794.1 Composition:** Bronze **Ruler:** Edward VII **Reverse:** Low sea level

| Date | Mintage | F | VF | XF | Unc | BU |
|---|---|---|---|---|---|---|
| 1902 | 26,977,000 | 4.00 | 9.00 | 22.50 | 90.00 | — |

**PENNY KM# 794.2 Composition:** Bronze **Ruler:** Edward VII **Reverse:** High sea level

| Date | Mintage | F | VF | XF | Unc | BU |
|---|---|---|---|---|---|---|
| 1902 | Inc. above | 0.50 | 2.00 | 4.00 | 30.00 | — |
| 1903 | 21,415,000 | 0.50 | 2.50 | 6.00 | 35.00 | — |
| 1904 | 12,913,000 | 1.00 | 3.00 | 15.00 | 60.00 | — |
| 1905 | 17,784,000 | 0.50 | 2.50 | 8.00 | 45.00 | — |
| 1906 | 37,990,000 | 0.50 | 2.00 | 7.00 | 45.00 | — |
| 1907 | 47,322,000 | 0.50 | 2.00 | 7.00 | 45.00 | — |
| 1908 | 31,506,000 | 0.50 | 2.00 | 7.00 | 45.00 | — |
| 1908 Matte Proof; Rare | — | — | — | — | — | — |
| 1909 | 19,617,000 | 0.50 | 2.00 | 7.00 | 45.00 | — |
| 1910 | 29,549,000 | 0.35 | 1.50 | 6.00 | 35.00 | — |

**PENNY KM# 795 Weight:** 0.4713 g. **Composition:** 0.9250 Silver .0140 oz. ASW **Ruler:** Edward VII

| Date | Mintage | F | VF | XF | Unc | BU |
|---|---|---|---|---|---|---|
| 1902 Prooflike | 21,000 | — | — | — | 12.50 | — |
| 1903 Prooflike | 17,000 | — | — | — | 12.50 | — |
| 1904 Prooflike | 19,000 | — | — | — | 12.50 | — |
| 1905 Prooflike | 18,000 | — | — | — | 12.50 | — |
| 1906 Prooflike | 19,000 | — | — | — | 12.50 | — |
| 1907 Prooflike | 18,000 | — | — | — | 12.50 | — |
| 1908 Prooflike | 18,000 | — | — | — | 12.50 | — |
| 1909 Prooflike | 2,948 | — | — | — | 15.00 | — |
| 1910 Prooflike | 3,392 | — | — | — | 20.00 | — |

**PENNY KM# 810 Composition:** Bronze **Ruler:** George V

| Date | Mintage | F | VF | XF | Unc | BU |
|---|---|---|---|---|---|---|
| 1911 | 23,079,000 | 0.40 | 1.25 | 5.00 | 25.00 | — |
| 1912 | 48,306,000 | 0.35 | 1.00 | 5.00 | 22.50 | — |
| 1912H | 16,800,000 | 1.00 | 3.00 | 18.00 | 75.00 | — |
| 1913 | 65,497,000 | 0.40 | 1.25 | 6.00 | 22.50 | — |
| 1914 | 50,821,000 | 0.35 | 1.00 | 5.00 | 22.50 | — |
| 1915 | 47,311,000 | 0.50 | 1.25 | 6.00 | 27.50 | — |
| 1916 | 86,411,000 | 0.35 | 1.00 | 4.50 | 22.50 | — |
| 1917 | 107,905,000 | 0.35 | 1.00 | 4.50 | 22.50 | — |
| 1918 | 84,227,000 | 0.35 | 1.00 | 4.50 | 22.50 | — |
| 1918H | 2,573,000 | 2.00 | 15.00 | 70.00 | 350 | — |
| 1918KN | Inc. above | 3.50 | 17.50 | 120 | 550 | — |
| 1919 | 113,761,000 | 0.50 | 1.00 | 4.00 | 22.50 | — |
| 1919H | 4,526,000 | 1.25 | 6.00 | 70.00 | 375 | — |
| 1919KN | Inc. above | 5.00 | 25.00 | 120 | 600 | — |
| 1920 | 124,693,000 | 0.50 | 1.50 | 4.00 | 18.00 | — |
| 1921 | 129,717,999 | 0.30 | 0.60 | 3.00 | 16.00 | — |
| 1922 | 16,347,000 | 0.75 | 2.50 | 10.00 | 50.00 | — |
| 1926 | 4,499,000 | 2.50 | 8.00 | 20.00 | 75.00 | — |
| 1926 Proof | — | Value: 850 | | | | |

**PENNY KM# 811 Weight:** 0.4713 g. **Composition:** 0.9250 Silver .0140 oz. ASW **Ruler:** George V

| Date | Mintage | F | VF | XF | Unc | BU |
|---|---|---|---|---|---|---|
| 1911 Prooflike | 1,913 | — | — | — | 15.00 | — |
| 1912 Prooflike | 1,616 | — | — | — | 15.00 | — |
| 1913 Prooflike | 1,590 | — | — | — | 15.00 | — |
| 1914 Prooflike | 1,818 | — | — | — | 15.00 | — |
| 1915 Prooflike | 2,072 | — | — | — | 15.00 | — |
| 1916 Prooflike | 1,647 | — | — | — | 15.00 | — |
| 1917 Prooflike | 1,820 | — | — | — | 15.00 | — |
| 1918 Prooflike | 1,911 | — | — | — | 15.00 | — |
| 1919 Prooflike | 1,699 | — | — | — | 15.00 | — |
| 1920 Prooflike | 1,715 | — | — | — | 15.00 | — |

**PENNY KM# 811a Weight:** 0.4713 g. **Composition:** 0.5000 Silver .0076 oz. ASW **Ruler:** George V

| Date | Mintage | F | VF | XF | Unc | BU |
|---|---|---|---|---|---|---|
| 1921 Prooflike | 1,847 | — | — | — | 15.00 | — |
| 1922 Prooflike | 1,758 | — | — | — | 15.00 | — |
| 1923 Prooflike | 1,840 | — | — | — | 15.00 | — |
| 1924 Prooflike | 1,619 | — | — | — | 15.00 | — |
| 1925 Prooflike | 1,890 | — | — | — | 15.00 | — |
| 1926 Prooflike | 2,180 | — | — | — | 15.00 | — |
| 1927 Prooflike | 1,647 | — | — | — | 15.00 | — |

**PENNY KM# 826 Composition:** Bronze **Ruler:** George V **Obverse:** Modified head

| Date | Mintage | F | VF | XF | Unc | BU |
|---|---|---|---|---|---|---|
| 1926 | — | 8.00 | 40.00 | 450 | 2,000 | — |
| 1926 Proof | — | — | — | — | — | — |
| 1927 | 60,990,000 | 0.35 | 0.75 | 4.00 | 12.50 | — |
| 1927 Proof | — | Value: 750 | | | | |

**PENNY KM# 838 Composition:** Bronze **Ruler:** George V **Obverse:** Smaller head

| Date | Mintage | F | VF | XF | Unc | BU |
|---|---|---|---|---|---|---|
| 1928 | 50,178,000 | 0.25 | 0.50 | 2.00 | 10.00 | — |
| 1928 Proof | — | Value: 500 | | | | |
| 1929 | 49,133,000 | 0.25 | 0.50 | 2.00 | 10.00 | — |
| 1929 Proof | — | Value: 400 | | | | |
| 1930 | 29,098,000 | 0.25 | 1.00 | 4.00 | 20.00 | — |
| 1930 Proof | — | Value: 400 | | | | |
| 1931 | 19,843,000 | 0.25 | 1.00 | 4.00 | 22.50 | — |
| 1931 Proof | — | Value: 400 | | | | |
| 1932 | 8,278,000 | 1.00 | 3.50 | 12.50 | 50.00 | — |
| 1932 Proof | — | Value: 500 | | | | |
| 1933 Rare | — | — | — | — | — | — |
| 1933 Proof | — | — | — | — | — | — |
| 1934 | 13,966,000 | 0.50 | 3.00 | 8.50 | 40.00 | — |
| 1934 Proof | — | Value: 500 | | | | |
| 1935 | 56,070,000 | 0.25 | 0.50 | 1.50 | 8.00 | — |
| 1935 Proof | — | Value: 375 | | | | |
| 1936 | 154,296,000 | 0.25 | 0.40 | 1.00 | 8.00 | — |
| 1936 Proof | — | Value: 375 | | | | |

**PENNY KM# 839 Weight:** 0.4713 g. **Composition:** 0.5000 Silver .0076 oz. ASW **Ruler:** George V **Obverse:** Modified effigy

| Date | Mintage | F | VF | XF | Unc | BU |
|---|---|---|---|---|---|---|
| 1928 Prooflike | 1,846 | — | — | — | 15.00 | — |
| 1929 Prooflike | 1,837 | — | — | — | 15.00 | — |
| 1930 Prooflike | 1,724 | — | — | — | 15.00 | — |
| 1931 Prooflike | 1,759 | — | — | — | 15.00 | — |
| 1932 Prooflike | 1,835 | — | — | — | 15.00 | — |
| 1933 Prooflike | 1,872 | — | — | — | 15.00 | — |
| 1934 Prooflike | 1,919 | — | — | — | 15.00 | — |
| 1935 Prooflike | 1,975 | — | — | — | 15.00 | — |
| 1936 Prooflike | 1,329 | — | — | — | 15.00 | — |

**PENNY** KM# 845 **Composition:** Bronze **Ruler:** George VI

| Date | Mintage | F | VF | XF | Unc | BU |
|---|---|---|---|---|---|---|
| 1937 | 88,896,000 | 0.20 | 0.35 | 1.25 | 3.50 | — |
| 1937 Proof | 26,000 | Value: 10.00 | | | | |
| 1937 Matte Proof; Rare | — | — | — | — | — | — |
| 1938 | 121,560,000 | 0.20 | 0.35 | 1.25 | 3.50 | — |
| 1938 Proof | — | Value: 350 | | | | |
| 1939 | 55,560,000 | 0.25 | 0.50 | 1.50 | 6.50 | — |
| 1939 Proof | — | Value: 350 | | | | |
| 1940 | 42,284,000 | 0.25 | 0.50 | 2.00 | 10.00 | — |
| 1940 Proof | — | Value: 350 | | | | |
| 1944 | 42,600,000 | 0.25 | 0.50 | 2.25 | 8.00 | — |
| 1944 Proof | — | — | — | — | — | — |
| 1945 | 79,531,000 | 0.20 | 0.35 | 1.50 | 7.75 | — |
| 1945 Proof | — | — | — | — | — | — |
| 1946 | 66,855,999 | 0.20 | 0.35 | 1.00 | 7.75 | — |
| 1946 Proof | — | — | — | — | — | — |
| 1947 | 52,220,000 | 0.15 | 0.25 | 0.75 | 3.50 | — |
| 1947 Proof | — | — | — | — | — | — |
| 1948 | 63,961,000 | 0.15 | 0.25 | 0.75 | 3.50 | — |
| 1948 Proof | — | — | — | — | — | — |

**PENNY** KM# 846 **Weight:** 0.4713 g. **Composition:** 0.5000 Silver .0076 oz. ASW **Ruler:** George VI

| Date | Mintage | F | VF | XF | Unc | BU |
|---|---|---|---|---|---|---|
| 1937 Prooflike | 1,329 | — | — | — | 15.00 | — |
| 1938 Prooflike | 1,275 | — | — | — | 15.00 | — |
| 1939 Prooflike | 1,253 | — | — | — | 15.00 | — |
| 1940 Prooflike | 1,375 | — | — | — | 15.00 | — |
| 1941 Prooflike | 1,255 | — | — | — | 15.00 | — |
| 1942 Prooflike | 1,243 | — | — | — | 15.00 | — |
| 1943 Prooflike | 1,347 | — | — | — | 15.00 | — |
| 1944 Prooflike | 1,259 | — | — | — | 15.00 | — |
| 1945 Prooflike | 1,367 | — | — | — | 15.00 | — |
| 1946 Prooflike | 1,479 | — | — | — | 15.00 | — |

**PENNY** KM# 846a **Weight:** 0.4713 g. **Composition:** 0.9250 Silver .0140 oz. ASW **Ruler:** George VI

| Date | Mintage | F | VF | XF | Unc | BU |
|---|---|---|---|---|---|---|
| 1947 Prooflike | 1,387 | — | — | — | 15.00 | — |
| 1948 Prooflike | 1,397 | — | — | — | 15.00 | — |

**PENNY** KM# 869 **Composition:** Bronze **Ruler:** George VI **Obv. Legend:** Without IND IMP

| Date | Mintage | F | VF | XF | Unc | BU |
|---|---|---|---|---|---|---|
| 1949 | 14,324,000 | 0.20 | 0.35 | 1.00 | 4.00 | — |
| 1949 Proof | — | — | — | — | — | — |
| 1950 | 240,000 | 2.00 | 6.00 | 21.00 | 37.00 | — |
| 1950 Matte Proof; Rare | — | — | — | — | — | — |

**Note:** There are reportedly 1-2 known of this variety, struck specifically for use in photography

| Date | Mintage | F | VF | XF | Unc | BU |
|---|---|---|---|---|---|---|
| 1950 Proof | 18,000 | Value: 30.00 | | | | |
| 1951 | 120,000 | 3.00 | 7.00 | 15.00 | 25.00 | — |
| 1951 Matte Proof; Rare | — | — | — | — | — | — |

**Note:** There are reportedly 1-2 known of this variety, struck specifically for use in photography

| Date | Mintage | F | VF | XF | Unc | BU |
|---|---|---|---|---|---|---|
| 1951 Proof | 20,000 | Value: 50.00 | | | | |
| 1952 Unique | — | — | — | — | — | — |

**PENNY** KM# 870 **Weight:** 0.4713 g. **Composition:** 0.9250 Silver .0140 oz. ASW **Ruler:** George VI **Obv. Legend:** Without IND IMP

| Date | Mintage | F | VF | XF | Unc | BU |
|---|---|---|---|---|---|---|
| 1949 Prooflike | 1,407 | — | — | — | 15.00 | — |
| 1950 Prooflike | 1,527 | — | — | — | 15.00 | — |
| 1951 Prooflike | 1,480 | — | — | — | 15.00 | — |
| 1952 Prooflike | 1,024 | — | — | — | 15.00 | — |

**PENNY** KM# 883 **Composition:** Bronze **Ruler:** Elizabeth II

| Date | Mintage | F | VF | XF | Unc | BU |
|---|---|---|---|---|---|---|
| 1953 | 1,308,000 | 0.75 | 1.50 | 2.50 | 4.50 | — |
| 1953 Proof | 40,000 | Value: 9.00 | | | | |
| 1953 Matte Proof; Rare | — | — | — | — | — | — |

**Note:** There are reportedly 1-2 known of this variety, struck specifically for use in photography

**PENNY** KM# 884 **Weight:** 0.4713 g. **Composition:** 0.9250 Silver .0140 oz. ASW **Ruler:** Elizabeth II

| Date | Mintage | F | VF | XF | Unc | BU |
|---|---|---|---|---|---|---|
| 1953 Prooflike | 1,050 | — | — | — | 95.00 | — |

**PENNY** KM# 897 **Composition:** Bronze **Ruler:** Elizabeth II **Obv. Legend:** Without BRITT OMN

| Date | Mintage | F | VF | XF | Unc | BU |
|---|---|---|---|---|---|---|
| 1954 1 Known | — | — | — | — | — | — |
| 1961 | 48,313,000 | — | 0.10 | 0.15 | 0.80 | — |
| 1961 Proof | — | — | — | — | — | — |
| 1962 | 143,309,000 | — | — | 0.10 | 0.15 | — |
| 1962 Proof | — | — | — | — | — | — |
| 1963 | 125,236,000 | — | — | 0.10 | 0.15 | — |
| 1963 Proof | — | — | — | — | — | — |
| 1964 | 153,294,000 | — | — | — | 0.10 | — |
| 1964 Proof | — | — | — | — | — | — |
| 1965 | 121,310,000 | — | — | — | 0.10 | — |
| 1966 | 165,739,000 | — | — | — | 0.10 | — |
| 1967 | 654,564,000 | — | — | — | 0.10 | — |
| 1970 Proof | 750,000 | Value: 5.00 | | | | |

**PENNY** KM# 898 **Weight:** 0.4713 g. **Composition:** 0.9250 Silver .0140 oz. ASW **Ruler:** Elizabeth II

| Date | Mintage | F | VF | XF | Unc | BU |
|---|---|---|---|---|---|---|
| 1954 Prooflike | 1,088 | — | — | — | 15.00 | — |
| 1955 Prooflike | 1,036 | — | — | — | 15.00 | — |
| 1956 Prooflike | 1,100 | — | — | — | 15.00 | — |
| 1957 Prooflike | 1,168 | — | — | — | 15.00 | — |
| 1958 Prooflike | 1,112 | — | — | — | 15.00 | — |
| 1959 Prooflike | 1,118 | — | — | — | 15.00 | — |
| 1960 Prooflike | 1,124 | — | — | — | 15.00 | — |
| 1961 Prooflike | 1,200 | — | — | — | 15.00 | — |
| 1962 Prooflike | 1,127 | — | — | — | 15.00 | — |
| 1963 Prooflike | 1,133 | — | — | — | 15.00 | — |
| 1964 Prooflike | 1,215 | — | — | — | 15.00 | — |
| 1965 Prooflike | 1,143 | — | — | — | 15.00 | — |
| 1966 Prooflike | 1,206 | — | — | — | 15.00 | — |
| 1967 Prooflike | 1,068 | — | — | — | 15.00 | — |
| 1968 Prooflike | 964 | — | — | — | 15.00 | — |
| 1969 Prooflike | 1,002 | — | — | — | 15.00 | — |
| 1970 Prooflike | 980 | — | — | — | 15.00 | — |
| 1971 Prooflike | 1,108 | — | — | — | 15.00 | — |
| 1972 Prooflike | 1,026 | — | — | — | 15.00 | — |
| 1973 Prooflike | 1,004 | — | — | — | 15.00 | — |
| 1974 Prooflike | 1,138 | — | — | — | 15.00 | — |
| 1975 Prooflike | 1,050 | — | — | — | 15.00 | — |
| 1976 Prooflike | 1,158 | — | — | — | 15.00 | — |
| 1977 Prooflike | 1,240 | — | — | — | 17.50 | — |
| 1978 Prooflike | 1,178 | — | — | — | 17.50 | — |
| 1979 Prooflike | 1,188 | — | — | — | 17.50 | — |
| 1980 Prooflike | 1,198 | — | — | — | 17.50 | — |
| 1981 Prooflike | 1,288 | — | — | — | 17.50 | — |
| 1982 Prooflike | 1,218 | — | — | — | 17.50 | — |
| 1983 Prooflike | 1,228 | — | — | — | 17.50 | — |
| 1984 Prooflike | 1,354 | — | — | — | 17.50 | — |
| 1985 Prooflike | 1,248 | — | — | — | 17.50 | — |
| 1986 Prooflike | 1,378 | — | — | — | 17.50 | — |
| 1987 Prooflike | 1,512 | — | — | — | 17.50 | — |
| 1988 Prooflike | 1,402 | — | — | — | 17.50 | — |
| 1989 Prooflike | 1,353 | — | — | — | 17.50 | — |
| 1990 Prooflike | 1,523 | — | — | — | 17.50 | — |
| 1991 Prooflike | 1,514 | — | — | — | 17.50 | — |
| 1992 Prooflike | 1,556 | — | — | — | 17.50 | — |
| 1993 Prooflike | 1,440 | — | — | — | 17.50 | — |
| 1994 Prooflike | 1,443 | — | — | — | 17.50 | — |
| 1995 Prooflike | 1,466 | — | — | — | 17.50 | — |
| 1996 Prooflike | 1,629 | — | — | — | 17.50 | — |
| 1997 Prooflike | 1,786 | — | — | — | 17.50 | — |
| 1998 Prooflike | — | — | — | — | 17.50 | — |
| 1999 Prooflike | — | — | — | — | 17.50 | — |

**2 PENCE** KM# 776 **Weight:** 0.9426 g. **Composition:** 0.9250 Silver .0280 oz. ASW **Ruler:** Victoria

| Date | Mintage | F | VF | XF | Unc | BU |
|---|---|---|---|---|---|---|
| 1901 Prooflike | 14,000 | — | — | — | 12.50 | — |

**2 PENCE** KM# 796 **Weight:** 0.9426 g. **Composition:** 0.9250 Silver .0280 oz. ASW **Ruler:** Edward VII

| Date | Mintage | F | VF | XF | Unc | BU |
|---|---|---|---|---|---|---|
| 1902 Prooflike | 14,000 | — | — | — | 12.50 | — |
| 1903 Prooflike | 13,000 | — | — | — | 12.50 | — |
| 1904 Prooflike | 14,000 | — | — | — | 12.50 | — |
| 1905 Prooflike | 11,000 | — | — | — | 12.50 | — |
| 1906 Prooflike | 11,000 | — | — | — | 12.50 | — |
| 1907 Prooflike | 8,760 | — | — | — | 12.50 | — |
| 1908 Prooflike | 15,000 | — | — | — | 12.50 | — |
| 1909 Prooflike | 2,695 | — | — | — | 15.00 | — |
| 1910 Prooflike | 2,998 | — | — | — | 20.00 | — |

**2 PENCE** KM# 812 **Weight:** 0.9426 g. **Composition:** 0.9250 Silver .0280 oz. ASW **Ruler:** George V

| Date | Mintage | F | VF | XF | Unc | BU |
|---|---|---|---|---|---|---|
| 1911 Prooflike | 1,635 | — | — | — | 17.50 | — |
| 1912 Prooflike | 1,678 | — | — | — | 17.50 | — |
| 1913 Prooflike | 1,880 | — | — | — | 17.50 | — |
| 1914 Prooflike | 1,659 | — | — | — | 17.50 | — |
| 1915 Prooflike | 1,465 | — | — | — | 17.50 | — |
| 1916 Prooflike | 1,509 | — | — | — | 17.50 | — |
| 1917 Prooflike | 1,506 | — | — | — | 17.50 | — |
| 1918 Prooflike | 1,547 | — | — | — | 17.50 | — |
| 1919 Prooflike | 1,567 | — | — | — | 17.50 | — |
| 1920 Prooflike | 1,630 | — | — | — | 17.50 | — |

**2 PENCE** KM# 812a **Weight:** 0.9426 g. **Composition:** 0.5000 Silver .0152 oz. ASW **Ruler:** George V

| Date | Mintage | F | VF | XF | Unc | BU |
|---|---|---|---|---|---|---|
| 1921 Prooflike | 1,794 | — | — | — | 20.00 | — |
| 1922 Prooflike | 3,074 | — | — | — | 20.00 | — |
| 1923 Prooflike | 1,527 | — | — | — | 20.00 | — |
| 1924 Prooflike | 1,602 | — | — | — | 20.00 | — |
| 1925 Prooflike | 1,670 | — | — | — | 20.00 | — |
| 1926 Prooflike | 1,902 | — | — | — | 20.00 | — |
| 1927 Prooflike | 1,766 | — | — | — | 20.00 | — |

**2 PENCE** KM# 840 **Weight:** 0.9426 g. **Composition:** 0.5000 Silver .0152 oz. ASW **Ruler:** George V **Obverse:** Modified effigy

| Date | Mintage | F | VF | XF | Unc | BU |
|---|---|---|---|---|---|---|
| 1928 Prooflike | 1,706 | — | — | — | 17.50 | — |
| 1929 Prooflike | 1,862 | — | — | — | 17.50 | — |
| 1930 Prooflike | 1,901 | — | — | — | 17.50 | — |
| 1931 Prooflike | 1,897 | — | — | — | 17.50 | — |
| 1932 Prooflike | 1,960 | — | — | — | 17.50 | — |
| 1933 Prooflike | 2,066 | — | — | — | 17.50 | — |
| 1934 Prooflike | 1,927 | — | — | — | 17.50 | — |
| 1935 Prooflike | 1,928 | — | — | — | 17.50 | — |
| 1936 Prooflike | 1,365 | — | — | — | 20.00 | — |

**2 PENCE** KM# 847 **Weight:** 0.9426 g. **Composition:** 0.5000 Silver .0152 oz. ASW **Ruler:** George VI

| Date | Mintage | F | VF | XF | Unc | BU |
|---|---|---|---|---|---|---|
| 1937 Prooflike | 1,472 | — | — | — | 17.50 | — |
| 1938 Prooflike | 1,374 | — | — | — | 17.50 | — |
| 1939 Prooflike | 1,436 | — | — | — | 17.50 | — |
| 1940 Prooflike | 1,277 | — | — | — | 17.50 | — |
| 1941 Prooflike | 1,345 | — | — | — | 17.50 | — |
| 1942 Prooflike | 1,231 | — | — | — | 17.50 | — |
| 1943 Prooflike | 1,239 | — | — | — | 17.50 | — |

| Date | Mintage | F | VF | XF | Unc | BU |
|---|---|---|---|---|---|---|
| 1944 Prooflike | 1,345 | — | — | — | 17.50 | — |
| 1945 Prooflike | 1,355 | — | — | — | 17.50 | — |
| 1946 Prooflike | 1,365 | — | — | — | 17.50 | — |

**2 PENCE** **KM# 847a** **Weight:** 0.9426 g. **Composition:** 0.9250 Silver .0280 oz. ASW **Ruler:** George VI

| Date | Mintage | F | VF | XF | Unc | BU |
|---|---|---|---|---|---|---|
| 1947 Prooflike | 1,479 | — | — | — | 17.50 | — |
| 1948 Prooflike | 1,385 | — | — | — | 17.50 | — |

**2 PENCE** **KM# 871** **Weight:** 0.9426 g. **Composition:** 0.9250 Silver .0280 oz. ASW **Ruler:** George VI **Obv. Legend:** Without IND IMP

| Date | Mintage | F | VF | XF | Unc | BU |
|---|---|---|---|---|---|---|
| 1949 Prooflike | 1,395 | — | — | — | 17.50 | — |
| 1950 Prooflike | 1,405 | — | — | — | 17.50 | — |
| 1951 Prooflike | 1,580 | — | — | — | 17.50 | — |
| 1952 Prooflike | 1,064 | — | — | — | 17.50 | — |

**2 PENCE** **KM# 885** **Weight:** 0.9426 g. **Composition:** 0.9250 Silver .0280 oz. ASW **Ruler:** Elizabeth II

| Date | Mintage | F | VF | XF | Unc | BU |
|---|---|---|---|---|---|---|
| 1953 Prooflike | 1,025 | — | — | — | 85.00 | — |

**2 PENCE** **KM# 899** **Weight:** 0.9426 g. **Composition:** 0.9250 Silver .0280 oz. ASW **Ruler:** Elizabeth II **Obv. Legend:** Without BRITT OMN

| Date | Mintage | F | VF | XF | Unc | BU |
|---|---|---|---|---|---|---|
| 1954 Prooflike | 1,020 | — | — | — | 20.00 | — |
| 1955 Prooflike | 1,082 | — | — | — | 20.00 | — |
| 1956 Prooflike | 1,088 | — | — | — | 20.00 | — |
| 1957 Prooflike | 1,094 | — | — | — | 20.00 | — |
| 1958 Prooflike | 1,164 | — | — | — | 20.00 | — |
| 1959 Prooflike | 1,106 | — | — | — | 20.00 | — |
| 1960 Prooflike | 1,112 | — | — | — | 20.00 | — |
| 1961 Prooflike | 1,118 | — | — | — | 20.00 | — |
| 1962 Prooflike | 1,197 | — | — | — | 20.00 | — |
| 1963 Prooflike | 1,131 | — | — | — | 20.00 | — |
| 1964 Prooflike | 1,137 | — | — | — | 20.00 | — |
| 1965 Prooflike | 1,221 | — | — | — | 20.00 | — |
| 1966 Prooflike | 1,206 | — | — | — | 20.00 | — |
| 1967 Prooflike | 986 | — | — | — | 20.00 | — |
| 1968 Prooflike | 1,048 | — | — | — | 20.00 | — |
| 1969 Prooflike | 1,002 | — | — | — | 20.00 | — |
| 1970 Prooflike | 980 | — | — | — | 20.00 | — |
| 1971 Prooflike | 1,018 | — | — | — | 20.00 | — |
| 1972 Prooflike | 1,026 | — | — | — | 20.00 | — |
| 1973 Prooflike | 1,004 | — | — | — | 20.00 | — |
| 1974 Prooflike | 1,042 | — | — | — | 20.00 | — |
| 1975 Prooflike | 1,148 | — | — | — | 20.00 | — |
| 1976 Prooflike | 1,158 | — | — | — | 20.00 | — |
| 1977 Prooflike | 1,138 | — | — | — | 22.00 | — |
| 1978 Prooflike | 1,282 | — | — | — | 22.00 | — |
| 1979 Prooflike | 1,188 | — | — | — | 22.00 | — |
| 1980 Prooflike | 1,198 | — | — | — | 22.00 | — |
| 1981 Prooflike | 1,178 | — | — | — | 22.00 | — |
| 1982 Prooflike | 1,330 | — | — | — | 22.00 | — |
| 1983 Prooflike | 1,228 | — | — | — | 22.00 | — |
| 1984 Prooflike | 1,238 | — | — | — | 22.00 | — |
| 1985 Prooflike | 1,366 | — | — | — | 22.00 | — |
| 1986 Prooflike | 1,378 | — | — | — | 22.00 | — |
| 1987 Prooflike | 1,390 | — | — | — | 22.00 | — |
| 1988 Prooflike | 1,526 | — | — | — | 22.00 | — |
| 1989 Prooflike | 1,353 | — | — | — | 22.00 | — |
| 1990 Prooflike | 1,523 | — | — | — | 22.00 | — |
| 1991 Prooflike | 1,384 | — | — | — | 22.00 | — |
| 1992 Prooflike | 1,424 | — | — | — | 22.00 | — |
| 1993 Prooflike | 1,440 | — | — | — | 22.00 | — |
| 1994 Prooflike | 1,443 | — | — | — | 22.00 | — |
| 1995 Prooflike | 1,466 | — | — | — | 22.00 | — |
| 1996 Prooflike | 1,629 | — | — | — | 22.00 | — |
| 1997 Prooflike | 1,786 | — | — | — | 22.00 | — |
| 1998 Prooflike | — | — | — | — | 22.00 | — |
| 1999 Prooflike | — | — | — | — | 22.00 | — |

**3 PENCE** **KM# 777** **Weight:** 1.4138 g. **Composition:** 0.9250 Silver .0420 oz. ASW **Ruler:** Victoria

| Date | Mintage | F | VF | XF | Unc | BU |
|---|---|---|---|---|---|---|
| 1901 | 6,100,000 | 1.00 | 2.00 | 4.00 | 20.00 | — |
| 1901 Prooflike | 8,976 | — | — | — | 30.00 | |

**3 PENCE** **KM# 797.1** **Weight:** 1.4138 g. **Composition:** 0.9250 Silver .0420 oz. ASW **Ruler:** Edward VII

| Date | Mintage | F | VF | XF | Unc | BU |
|---|---|---|---|---|---|---|
| 1902 | 8,287,000 | 0.50 | 1.25 | 4.00 | 15.00 | — |
| 1902 Prooflike | 8,976 | — | — | — | 18.00 | — |
| 1902 Matte Proof | 15,000 | Value: 22.50 | | | | |
| 1903 | 5,235,000 | 2.50 | 4.50 | 12.00 | 40.00 | — |
| 1903 Prooflike | 8,976 | — | — | — | 18.00 | — |
| 1904 | 3,630,000 | 5.00 | 12.00 | 32.00 | 75.00 | — |
| 1904 Prooflike | 8,876 | — | — | — | 25.00 | — |

**3 PENCE** **KM# 797.2** **Weight:** 1.4138 g. **Composition:** 0.9250 Silver .0420 oz. ASW **Ruler:** Edward VII **Note:** The below Prooflike listings can be of mirror or satin-line finish, which are more difficult to separate from the currency strikes, especially for the years 1903-1906.

| Date | Mintage | F | VF | XF | Unc | BU |
|---|---|---|---|---|---|---|
| 1904 | Inc. above | 4.50 | 10.00 | 30.00 | 70.00 | — |
| 1905 | 3,563,000 | 3.00 | 8.00 | 22.50 | 50.00 | — |
| 1905 Prooflike | 8,976 | — | — | — | 22.50 | — |
| 1906 | 3,174,000 | 4.00 | 10.00 | 30.00 | 100 | — |
| 1906 Prooflike | 8,800 | — | — | — | 22.50 | — |
| 1907 | 4,841,000 | 2.00 | 4.00 | 15.00 | 40.00 | — |
| 1907 Prooflike | 11,000 | — | — | — | 22.50 | — |
| 1908 | 8,176,000 | 2.00 | 4.00 | 15.00 | 35.00 | — |
| 1908 Prooflike | 8,760 | — | — | — | 22.50 | — |
| 1909 | 4,054,999 | 2.00 | 3.50 | 12.00 | 35.00 | — |
| 1909 Prooflike | 1,983 | — | — | — | 30.00 | — |
| 1910 | 4,565,000 | 1.00 | 2.00 | 7.00 | 25.00 | — |
| 1910 Prooflike | 1,140 | — | — | — | 30.00 | — |

**3 PENCE** **KM# 813** **Weight:** 1.4138 g. **Composition:** 0.9250 Silver .0420 oz. ASW **Ruler:** George V

| Date | Mintage | F | VF | XF | Unc | BU |
|---|---|---|---|---|---|---|
| 1911 | 5,843,000 | 0.50 | 1.00 | 3.00 | 12.50 | — |
| 1911 Prooflike | 1,991 | — | — | — | 22.50 | — |
| 1911 Proof | 6,007 | Value: 35.00 | | | | |
| 1912 | 8,934,000 | 0.50 | 1.00 | 3.00 | 12.50 | — |
| 1912 Prooflike | 1,246 | — | — | — | 22.50 | — |
| 1913 | 7,144,000 | 0.50 | 1.00 | 4.00 | 15.00 | — |
| 1913 Prooflike | 1,228 | — | — | — | 30.00 | — |
| 1914 | 6,735,000 | 0.50 | 1.00 | 3.00 | 15.00 | — |
| 1914 Prooflike | 982 | — | — | — | 32.50 | — |
| 1915 | 5,452,000 | 0.50 | 1.00 | 2.00 | 12.50 | — |
| 1915 Prooflike | 1,293 | — | — | — | 25.00 | — |
| 1916 | 18,556,000 | 0.40 | 0.75 | 3.00 | 12.50 | — |
| 1916 Prooflike | 1,128 | — | — | — | 22.50 | — |
| 1917 | 21,664,000 | 0.40 | 0.75 | 3.00 | 12.50 | — |
| 1917 Prooflike | 1,237 | — | — | — | 22.50 | — |
| 1918 | 20,632,000 | 0.40 | 0.75 | 3.00 | 12.50 | — |
| 1918 Prooflike | 1,375 | — | — | — | 22.50 | — |
| 1919 | 16,846,000 | 0.40 | 0.75 | 3.00 | 12.50 | — |
| 1919 Prooflike | 1,258 | — | — | — | 22.50 | — |
| 1920 | 16,704,999 | 0.40 | 0.75 | 3.00 | 15.00 | — |
| 1920 Prooflike | 1,399 | — | — | — | 25.00 | — |

**3 PENCE** **KM# 813a** **Weight:** 1.4138 g. **Composition:** 0.5000 Silver .0227 oz. ASW **Ruler:** George V

| Date | Mintage | F | VF | XF | Unc | BU |
|---|---|---|---|---|---|---|
| 1920 | Inc. above | — | BV | 2.50 | 10.00 | — |
| 1921 | 8,751,000 | — | BV | 3.00 | 15.00 | — |
| 1921 Prooflike | 1,386 | — | — | — | 20.00 | — |
| 1922 | 7,981,000 | — | BV | 2.00 | 16.00 | — |
| 1922 Prooflike | 1,373 | — | — | — | 20.00 | — |
| 1923 Prooflike | 1,430 | — | — | — | 25.00 | — |
| 1924 Prooflike | 1,515 | — | — | — | 25.00 | — |
| 1925 | 3,733,000 | 0.50 | 2.00 | 8.00 | 25.00 | — |
| 1925 Prooflike | 1,438 | — | — | — | 25.00 | — |
| 1926 | 4,109,000 | 1.50 | 5.00 | 17.50 | 60.00 | — |
| 1926 Prooflike | 1,504 | — | — | — | 25.00 | — |
| 1927 Prooflike | 1,690 | — | — | — | 25.00 | — |

**3 PENCE** **KM# 827** **Weight:** 1.4138 g. **Composition:** 0.5000 Silver .0227 oz. ASW **Ruler:** George V **Obverse:** Modified effigy

| Date | Mintage | F | VF | XF | Unc | BU |
|---|---|---|---|---|---|---|
| 1926 | Inc. above | 1.00 | 2.50 | 8.00 | 40.00 | — |
| 1928 Prooflike | 1,835 | — | — | — | 22.50 | — |
| 1929 Prooflike | 1,761 | — | — | — | 22.50 | — |
| 1930 Prooflike | 1,948 | — | — | — | 22.50 | — |
| 1931 Prooflike | 1,818 | — | — | — | 22.50 | — |
| 1932 Prooflike | 2,042 | — | — | — | 22.50 | — |
| 1933 Prooflike | 1,920 | — | — | — | 22.50 | — |
| 1934 Prooflike | 1,887 | — | — | — | 22.50 | — |
| 1935 Prooflike | 2,007 | — | — | — | 22.50 | — |
| 1936 Prooflike | 1,307 | — | — | — | 25.00 | — |

**3 PENCE** **KM# 830** **Weight:** 1.4138 g. **Composition:** 0.5000 Silver .0227 oz. ASW **Ruler:** George V **Reverse:** Oak sprigs with acorns

| Date | Mintage | F | VF | XF | Unc | BU |
|---|---|---|---|---|---|---|
| 1927 Proof | 15,000 | Value: 45.00 | | | | |

**3 PENCE** **KM# 831** **Weight:** 1.4138 g. **Composition:** 0.5000 Silver .0227 oz. ASW **Ruler:** George V

| Date | Mintage | F | VF | XF | Unc | BU |
|---|---|---|---|---|---|---|
| 1927 Proof | 15,000 | Value: 45.00 | | | | |
| 1928 | 1,302,000 | 2.50 | 4.00 | 10.00 | 30.00 | — |
| 1928 Proof | — | Value: 275 | | | | |
| 1930 | 1,319,000 | 2.00 | 3.50 | 7.50 | 27.50 | — |
| 1930 Proof | — | Value: 250 | | | | |
| 1931 | 6,252,000 | BV | 0.50 | 1.50 | 5.00 | — |
| 1931 Proof | — | Value: 225 | | | | |
| 1932 | 5,887,000 | BV | 0.50 | 1.50 | 5.00 | — |
| 1932 Proof | — | Value: 225 | | | | |
| 1933 | 5,579,000 | BV | 0.50 | 1.50 | 5.00 | — |
| 1933 Proof | — | Value: 225 | | | | |
| 1934 | 7,406,000 | BV | 0.50 | 1.50 | 5.00 | — |
| 1934 Proof | — | Value: 225 | | | | |
| 1935 | 7,028,000 | BV | 0.50 | 1.50 | 5.00 | — |
| 1935 Proof | — | Value: 225 | | | | |
| 1936 | 3,239,000 | BV | 0.50 | 1.50 | 5.00 | — |
| 1936 Proof | — | Value: 225 | | | | |

**3 PENCE** **KM# 848** **Weight:** 1.4138 g. **Composition:** 0.5000 Silver .0227 oz. ASW **Ruler:** George VI

| Date | Mintage | F | VF | XF | Unc | BU |
|---|---|---|---|---|---|---|
| 1937 | 8,148,000 | BV | 0.50 | 1.50 | 5.00 | — |
| 1937 Proof | 26,000 | Value: 8.00 | | | | |
| 1937 Matte Proof; Rare | — | — | — | — | — | — |

**Note:** There are reportedly 2-4 known of this variety, struck specifically for use in photography

| Date | Mintage | F | VF | XF | Unc | BU |
|---|---|---|---|---|---|---|
| 1938 | 6,402,000 | BV | 0.50 | 1.50 | 5.00 | — |
| 1938 Proof | — | Value: 200 | | | | |
| 1939 | 1,356,000 | BV | 0.75 | 2.50 | 12.00 | — |
| 1939 Proof | — | Value: 225 | | | | |
| 1940 | 7,914,000 | BV | 0.50 | 1.00 | 5.00 | — |
| 1940 Proof | — | Value: 200 | | | | |
| 1941 | 7,979,000 | BV | 0.50 | 1.00 | 5.00 | — |
| 1941 Proof | — | Value: 200 | | | | |
| 1942 | 4,144,000 | BV | 1.50 | 3.50 | 20.00 | — |
| 1942 Proof | — | Value: 200 | | | | |
| 1943 | 1,379,000 | BV | 2.00 | 3.50 | 22.50 | — |
| 1943 Proof | — | Value: 225 | | | | |
| 1944 | 2,005,999 | 1.00 | 5.00 | 12.00 | 35.00 | — |
| 1944 Proof | — | Value: 300 | | | | |
| 1945 Rare | 320,000 | — | — | — | — | — |

**Note:** Issue melted, only one known

**3 PENCE** **KM# 849** **Composition:** Nickel-Brass **Ruler:** George VI

| Date | Mintage | F | VF | XF | Unc | BU |
|---|---|---|---|---|---|---|
| 1937 | 45,708,000 | 0.25 | 0.40 | 1.00 | 6.50 | — |
| 1937 Proof | 26,000 | Value: 8.50 | | | | |
| 1937 Matte Proof ; Rare | — | — | — | — | — | — |

**Note:** There are reportedly 2-4 known of this variety, struck specifically for use in photography

| Date | Mintage | F | VF | XF | Unc | BU |
|---|---|---|---|---|---|---|
| 1938 | 14,532,000 | 0.40 | 0.80 | 3.50 | 17.50 | — |
| 1938 Proof | — | Value: 250 | | | | |
| 1939 | 5,603,000 | 0.40 | 0.80 | 4.00 | 22.50 | — |
| 1939 Proof | — | Value: 250 | | | | |
| 1940 | 12,636,000 | 0.25 | 0.50 | 2.50 | 12.00 | — |
| 1940 Proof | — | Value: 250 | | | | |
| 1941 | 60,239,000 | 0.25 | 0.40 | 1.00 | 7.50 | — |
| 1941 Proof | — | Value: 250 | | | | |
| 1942 | 103,214,000 | 0.25 | 0.40 | 1.00 | 5.00 | — |
| 1942 Proof | — | — | — | — | — | — |
| 1943 | 101,702,000 | 0.25 | 0.40 | 1.00 | 5.00 | — |
| 1943 Proof | — | — | — | — | — | — |
| 1944 | 69,760,000 | 0.25 | 0.40 | 1.00 | 6.00 | — |
| 1944 Proof | — | — | — | — | — | — |

| Date | Mintage | F | VF | XF | Unc | BU |
|---|---|---|---|---|---|---|
| 1945 | 33,942,000 | 0.25 | 0.50 | 1.50 | 10.00 | — |
| 1945 Proof | — | — | — | — | — | — |
| 1946 | 621,000 | 2.50 | 8.00 | 35.00 | 225 | — |
| 1946 Proof | — | Value: 375 | | | | |
| 1948 | 4,230,000 | 0.60 | 1.50 | 5.50 | 30.00 | — |
| 1948 Proof | — | — | — | — | — | — |

**3 PENCE KM# 850 Weight:** 1.4138 g. **Composition:** 0.5000 Silver .0227 oz. ASW **Ruler:** George VI

| Date | Mintage | F | VF | XF | Unc | BU |
|---|---|---|---|---|---|---|
| 1937 Prooflike | 1,351 | — | — | — | 20.00 | — |
| 1938 Prooflike | 1,350 | — | — | — | 20.00 | — |
| 1939 Prooflike | 1,234 | — | — | — | 20.00 | — |
| 1940 Prooflike | 1,290 | — | — | — | 20.00 | — |
| 1941 Prooflike | 1,253 | — | — | — | 20.00 | — |
| 1942 Prooflike | 1,325 | — | — | — | 20.00 | — |
| 1943 Prooflike | 1,335 | — | — | — | 20.00 | — |
| 1944 Prooflike | 1,345 | — | — | — | 20.00 | — |
| 1945 Prooflike | 1,355 | — | — | — | 20.00 | — |
| 1946 Prooflike | 1,365 | — | — | — | 20.00 | — |

**3 PENCE KM# 850a Weight:** 1.4138 g. **Composition:** 0.9250 Silver .0420 oz. ASW **Ruler:** George VI

| Date | Mintage | F | VF | XF | Unc | BU |
|---|---|---|---|---|---|---|
| 1947 Prooflike | 1,375 | — | — | — | 20.00 | — |
| 1948 Prooflike | 1,491 | — | — | — | 20.00 | — |

**3 PENCE KM# 872 Weight:** 1.4138 g. **Composition:** 0.9250 Silver .0420 oz. ASW **Ruler:** George VI **Obv. Legend:** Without IND IMP

| Date | Mintage | F | VF | XF | Unc | BU |
|---|---|---|---|---|---|---|
| 1949 Prooflike | 1,395 | — | — | — | 20.00 | — |
| 1950 Prooflike | 1,405 | — | — | — | 20.00 | — |
| 1951 Prooflike | 1,468 | — | — | — | 20.00 | — |
| 1952 Prooflike | 1,012 | — | — | — | 22.50 | — |

**3 PENCE KM# 873 Composition:** Nickel-Brass **Ruler:** George VI **Obv. Legend:** Without IND IMP

| Date | Mintage | F | VF | XF | Unc | BU |
|---|---|---|---|---|---|---|
| 1949 | 464,000 | 5.00 | 10.00 | 50.00 | 225 | — |
| 1949 Proof | — | Value: 350 | | | | |
| 1950 | 1,600,000 | 1.00 | 3.00 | 12.00 | 50.00 | — |
| 1950 Proof | 18,000 | Value: 22.50 | | | | |
| 1950 Matte Proof; Rare | — | — | — | — | — | — |

**Note:** There are reportedly 2-4 known of this variety, struck specifically for use in photography

| Date | Mintage | F | VF | XF | Unc | BU |
|---|---|---|---|---|---|---|
| 1951 | 1,184,000 | 1.00 | 3.00 | 12.00 | 30.00 | — |
| 1951 Proof | 20,000 | Value: 22.50 | | | | |
| 1951 Matte Proof; Rare | — | — | — | — | — | — |

**Note:** There are reportedly 2-4 known of this variety, struck specifically for use in photography

| Date | Mintage | F | VF | XF | Unc | BU |
|---|---|---|---|---|---|---|
| 1952 | 25,494,000 | 0.25 | 0.50 | 1.00 | 6.00 | — |
| 1952 Proof | — | Value: 250 | | | | |

**3 PENCE KM# 886 Composition:** Nickel-Brass **Ruler:** Elizabeth II

| Date | Mintage | F | VF | XF | Unc | BU |
|---|---|---|---|---|---|---|
| 1953 | 30,618,000 | 0.25 | 0.50 | 1.00 | 3.00 | — |
| 1953 Proof | 40,000 | Value: 4.50 | | | | |
| 1953 Matte Proof; Rare | — | — | — | — | — | — |

**Note:** There are reportedly 2-4 known of this variety, struck specifically for use in photography

**3 PENCE KM# 887 Weight:** 1.4138 g. **Composition:** 0.9250 Silver .0420 oz. ASW **Ruler:** Elizabeth II

| Date | Mintage | F | VF | XF | Unc | BU |
|---|---|---|---|---|---|---|
| 1953 Prooflike | 1,078 | — | — | — | 85.00 | — |

**3 PENCE KM# 900 Composition:** Nickel-Brass **Ruler:** Elizabeth II **Obv. Legend:** Without BRITT OMN

| Date | Mintage | F | VF | XF | Unc | BU |
|---|---|---|---|---|---|---|
| 1954 | 41,720,000 | — | 0.25 | 0.50 | 3.00 | — |
| 1954 Proof | — | Value: 200 | | | | |
| 1955 | 41,075,000 | — | — | 0.75 | 4.00 | — |
| 1955 Proof | — | Value: 200 | | | | |
| 1956 | 36,902,000 | — | — | 1.00 | 5.00 | — |
| 1956 Proof | — | Value: 200 | | | | |
| 1957 | 24,294,000 | — | — | 0.50 | 4.00 | — |
| 1957 Proof | — | Value: 200 | | | | |
| 1958 | 20,504,000 | — | 0.25 | 0.50 | 5.00 | — |
| 1958 Proof | — | Value: 250 | | | | |
| 1959 | 28,499,000 | — | — | 0.50 | 3.50 | — |
| 1959 Proof | — | Value: 200 | | | | |
| 1960 | 83,078,000 | — | — | 0.40 | 2.75 | — |
| 1960 Proof | — | Value: 200 | | | | |
| 1961 | 41,102,000 | — | — | 0.25 | 1.00 | — |
| 1961 Proof | — | Value: 200 | | | | |
| 1962 | 47,242,000 | — | — | 0.25 | 1.00 | — |
| 1962 Proof | — | Value: 200 | | | | |
| 1963 | 35,280,000 | — | — | 0.25 | 0.50 | — |
| 1963 Proof | — | Value: 200 | | | | |
| 1964 | 47,440,000 | — | — | 0.25 | 0.50 | — |
| 1964 Proof | — | Value: 200 | | | | |
| 1965 | 23,907,000 | — | — | 0.25 | 0.50 | — |
| 1965 Proof | — | Value: 250 | | | | |
| 1966 | 55,320,000 | — | — | 0.25 | 0.50 | — |
| 1966 Proof | — | Value: 250 | | | | |
| 1967 | 49,000,000 | — | 0.15 | 0.25 | 0.50 | — |
| 1967 Proof | — | — | — | — | — | — |
| 1970 Proof | 750,000 | Value: 2.50 | | | | |

**3 PENCE KM# 901 Weight:** 1.4138 g. **Composition:** 0.9250 Silver .0420 oz. ASW **Ruler:** Elizabeth II **Obv. Legend:** Without BRITT OMN

| Date | Mintage | F | VF | XF | Unc | BU |
|---|---|---|---|---|---|---|
| 1954 Prooflike | 1,076 | — | — | — | 20.00 | — |
| 1955 Prooflike | 1,082 | — | — | — | 20.00 | — |
| 1956 Prooflike | 1,088 | — | — | — | 20.00 | — |
| 1957 Prooflike | 1,094 | — | — | — | 20.00 | — |
| 1958 Prooflike | 1,100 | — | — | — | 20.00 | — |
| 1959 Prooflike | 1,172 | — | — | — | 20.00 | — |
| 1960 Prooflike | 1,112 | — | — | — | 20.00 | — |
| 1961 Prooflike | 1,118 | — | — | — | 20.00 | — |
| 1962 Prooflike | 1,125 | — | — | — | 20.00 | — |
| 1963 Prooflike | 1,205 | — | — | — | 20.00 | — |
| 1964 Prooflike | 1,213 | — | — | — | 20.00 | — |
| 1965 Prooflike | 1,221 | — | — | — | 20.00 | — |
| 1966 Prooflike | 1,206 | — | — | — | 20.00 | — |
| 1967 Prooflike | 986 | — | — | — | 20.00 | — |
| 1968 Prooflike | 964 | — | — | — | 20.00 | — |
| 1969 Prooflike | 1,088 | — | — | — | 20.00 | — |
| 1970 Prooflike | 980 | — | — | — | 20.00 | — |
| 1971 Prooflike | 1,018 | — | — | — | 20.00 | — |
| 1972 Prooflike | 1,026 | — | — | — | 20.00 | — |
| 1973 Prooflike | 1,098 | — | — | — | 20.00 | — |
| 1974 Prooflike | 1,138 | — | — | — | 20.00 | — |
| 1975 Prooflike | 1,148 | — | — | — | 20.00 | — |
| 1976 Prooflike | 1,158 | — | — | — | 20.00 | — |
| 1977 Prooflike | 1,138 | — | — | — | 22.00 | — |
| 1978 Prooflike | 1,178 | — | — | — | 22.00 | — |
| 1979 Prooflike | 1,294 | — | — | — | 22.00 | — |
| 1980 Prooflike | 1,198 | — | — | — | 22.00 | — |
| 1981 Prooflike | 1,178 | — | — | — | 22.00 | — |
| 1982 Prooflike | 1,218 | — | — | — | 22.00 | — |
| 1983 Prooflike | 1,342 | — | — | — | 22.00 | — |
| 1984 Prooflike | 1,354 | — | — | — | 22.00 | — |
| 1985 Prooflike | 1,366 | — | — | — | 22.00 | — |
| 1986 Prooflike | 1,378 | — | — | — | 22.00 | — |
| 1987 Prooflike | 1,390 | — | — | — | 22.00 | — |
| 1988 Prooflike | 1,528 | — | — | — | 22.00 | — |
| 1989 Prooflike | 1,353 | — | — | — | 22.00 | — |
| 1990 Prooflike | 1,523 | — | — | — | 22.00 | — |
| 1991 Prooflike | 1,384 | — | — | — | 22.00 | — |
| 1992 Prooflike | 1,424 | — | — | — | 22.00 | — |
| 1993 Prooflike | 1,440 | — | — | — | 22.00 | — |
| 1994 Prooflike | 1,433 | — | — | — | 22.00 | — |
| 1995 Prooflike | 1,466 | — | — | — | 22.00 | — |
| 1996 Prooflike | 1,629 | — | — | — | 22.00 | — |
| 1997 Prooflike | 1,786 | — | — | — | 22.00 | — |
| 1998 Prooflike | — | — | — | — | 22.00 | — |
| 1999 Prooflike | — | — | — | — | 22.00 | — |

**4 PENCE (Groat) KM# 778 Weight:** 1.8851 g. **Composition:** 0.9250 Silver .0561 oz. ASW **Ruler:** Victoria

| Date | Mintage | F | VF | XF | Unc | BU |
|---|---|---|---|---|---|---|
| 1901 Prooflike | 12,000 | — | — | — | 15.00 | — |

**4 PENCE (Groat) KM# 798 Weight:** 1.8851 g. **Composition:** 0.9250 Silver .0561 oz. ASW **Ruler:** Edward VII

| Date | Mintage | F | VF | XF | Unc | BU |
|---|---|---|---|---|---|---|
| 1902 Prooflike | 10,000 | — | — | — | 15.00 | — |
| 1903 Prooflike | 9,729 | — | — | — | 15.00 | — |
| 1904 Prooflike | 12,000 | — | — | — | 15.00 | — |
| 1905 Prooflike | 11,000 | — | — | — | 15.00 | — |
| 1906 Prooflike | 11,000 | — | — | — | 15.00 | — |
| 1907 Prooflike | 11,000 | — | — | — | 15.00 | — |
| 1908 Prooflike | 9,929 | — | — | — | 15.00 | — |
| 1909 Prooflike | 2,428 | — | — | — | 20.00 | — |
| 1910 Prooflike | 2,755 | — | — | — | 22.50 | — |

**4 PENCE (Groat) KM# 814 Weight:** 1.8851 g. **Composition:** 0.9250 Silver .0561 oz. ASW **Ruler:** George V

| Date | Mintage | F | VF | XF | Unc | BU |
|---|---|---|---|---|---|---|
| 1911 Prooflike | 1,768 | — | — | — | 17.50 | — |
| 1912 Prooflike | 1,700 | — | — | — | 17.50 | — |
| 1913 Prooflike | 1,798 | — | — | — | 17.50 | — |
| 1914 Prooflike | 1,651 | — | — | — | 17.50 | — |
| 1915 Prooflike | 1,441 | — | — | — | 17.50 | — |
| 1916 Prooflike | 1,499 | — | — | — | 17.50 | — |
| 1917 Prooflike | 1,478 | — | — | — | 17.50 | — |
| 1918 Prooflike | 1,479 | — | — | — | 17.50 | — |
| 1919 Prooflike | 1,524 | — | — | — | 17.50 | — |
| 1920 Prooflike | 1,460 | — | — | — | 17.50 | — |

**4 PENCE (Groat) KM# 814a Weight:** 1.8851 g. **Composition:** 0.5000 Silver .0303 oz. ASW **Ruler:** George V

| Date | Mintage | F | VF | XF | Unc | BU |
|---|---|---|---|---|---|---|
| 1921 Prooflike | 1,542 | — | — | — | 17.50 | — |
| 1922 Prooflike | 1,609 | — | — | — | 17.50 | — |
| 1923 Prooflike | 1,635 | — | — | — | 17.50 | — |
| 1924 Prooflike | 1,665 | — | — | — | 17.50 | — |
| 1925 Prooflike | 1,786 | — | — | — | 17.50 | — |
| 1926 Prooflike | 1,762 | — | — | — | 17.50 | — |
| 1927 Prooflike | 1,681 | — | — | — | 17.50 | — |

**4 PENCE (Groat) KM# 841 Weight:** 1.8851 g. **Composition:** 0.5000 Silver .0303 oz. ASW **Ruler:** George V **Obverse:** Modified effigy

| Date | Mintage | F | VF | XF | Unc | BU |
|---|---|---|---|---|---|---|
| 1928 Prooflike | 1,642 | — | — | — | 20.00 | — |
| 1929 Prooflike | 1,969 | — | — | — | 20.00 | — |
| 1930 Prooflike | 1,744 | — | — | — | 20.00 | — |
| 1931 Prooflike | 1,915 | — | — | — | 20.00 | — |
| 1932 Prooflike | 1,937 | — | — | — | 20.00 | — |
| 1933 Prooflike | 1,931 | — | — | — | 20.00 | — |
| 1934 Prooflike | 1,893 | — | — | — | 20.00 | — |
| 1935 Prooflike | 1,995 | — | — | — | 20.00 | — |
| 1936 Prooflike | 1,323 | — | — | — | 22.50 | — |

**4 PENCE (Groat) KM# 851 Weight:** 1.8851 g. **Composition:** 0.5000 Silver .0303 oz. ASW **Ruler:** George VI

| Date | Mintage | F | VF | XF | Unc | BU |
|---|---|---|---|---|---|---|
| 1937 Prooflike | 1,325 | — | — | — | 20.00 | — |
| 1938 Prooflike | 1,424 | — | — | — | 20.00 | — |
| 1939 Prooflike | 1,332 | — | — | — | 20.00 | — |
| 1940 Prooflike | 1,367 | — | — | — | 20.00 | — |
| 1941 Prooflike | 1,345 | — | — | — | 20.00 | — |
| 1942 Prooflike | 1,325 | — | — | — | 20.00 | — |
| 1943 Prooflike | 1,335 | — | — | — | 20.00 | — |
| 1944 Prooflike | 1,345 | — | — | — | 20.00 | — |
| 1945 Prooflike | 1,355 | — | — | — | 20.00 | — |
| 1946 Prooflike | 1,365 | — | — | — | 20.00 | — |

**4 PENCE (Groat)** **KM# 851a** **Weight:** 1.8851 g. **Composition:** 0.9250 Silver .0561 oz. ASW **Ruler:** George VI

| Date | Mintage | F | VF | XF | Unc | BU |
|---|---|---|---|---|---|---|
| 1947 Prooflike | 1,375 | — | — | — | 20.00 | — |
| 1948 Prooflike | 1,385 | — | — | — | 20.00 | — |

**4 PENCE (Groat)** **KM# 874** **Weight:** 1.8851 g. **Composition:** 0.9250 Silver .0561 oz. ASW **Ruler:** George VI
**Obv. Legend:** Without IND IMP

| Date | Mintage | F | VF | XF | Unc | BU |
|---|---|---|---|---|---|---|
| 1949 Prooflike | 1,503 | — | — | — | 20.00 | — |
| 1950 Prooflike | 1,515 | — | — | — | 20.00 | — |
| 1951 Prooflike | 1,580 | — | — | — | 20.00 | — |
| 1952 Prooflike | 1,064 | — | — | — | 22.50 | — |

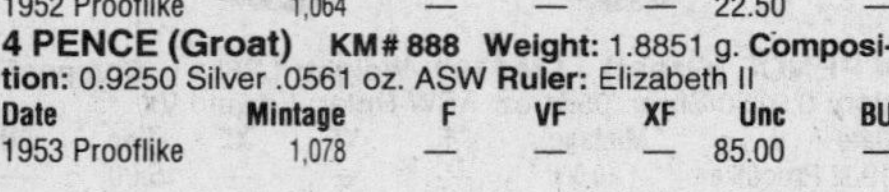

**4 PENCE (Groat)** **KM# 888** **Weight:** 1.8851 g. **Composition:** 0.9250 Silver .0561 oz. ASW **Ruler:** Elizabeth II

| Date | Mintage | F | VF | XF | Unc | BU |
|---|---|---|---|---|---|---|
| 1953 Prooflike | 1,078 | — | — | — | 85.00 | — |

**4 PENCE (Groat)** **KM# 902** **Weight:** 1.8851 g. **Composition:** 0.9250 Silver .0561 oz. ASW **Ruler:** Elizabeth II
**Obv. Legend:** Without BRITT OMN

| Date | Mintage | F | VF | XF | Unc | BU |
|---|---|---|---|---|---|---|
| 1954 Prooflike | 1,076 | — | — | — | 20.00 | — |
| 1955 Prooflike | 1,082 | — | — | — | 20.00 | — |
| 1956 Prooflike | 1,088 | — | — | — | 20.00 | — |
| 1957 Prooflike | 1,094 | — | — | — | 20.00 | — |
| 1958 Prooflike | 1,100 | — | — | — | 20.00 | — |
| 1959 Prooflike | 1,106 | — | — | — | 20.00 | — |
| 1960 Prooflike | 1,180 | — | — | — | 20.00 | — |
| 1961 Prooflike | 1,118 | — | — | — | 20.00 | — |
| 1962 Prooflike | 1,197 | — | — | — | 20.00 | — |
| 1963 Prooflike | 1,205 | — | — | — | 20.00 | — |
| 1964 Prooflike | 1,213 | — | — | — | 20.00 | — |
| 1965 Prooflike | 1,221 | — | — | — | 20.00 | — |
| 1966 Prooflike | 1,206 | — | — | — | 20.00 | — |
| 1967 Prooflike | 986 | — | — | — | 20.00 | — |
| 1968 Prooflike | 964 | — | — | — | 20.00 | — |
| 1969 Prooflike | 1,002 | — | — | — | 20.00 | — |
| 1970 Prooflike | 1,068 | — | — | — | 20.00 | — |
| 1971 Prooflike | 1,108 | — | — | — | 20.00 | — |
| 1972 Prooflike | 1,118 | — | — | — | 20.00 | — |
| 1973 Prooflike | 1,098 | — | — | — | 20.00 | — |
| 1974 Prooflike | 1,138 | — | — | — | 20.00 | — |
| 1975 Prooflike | 1,148 | — | — | — | 20.00 | — |
| 1976 Prooflike | 1,158 | — | — | — | 20.00 | — |
| 1977 Prooflike | 1,138 | — | — | — | 22.00 | — |
| 1978 Prooflike | 1,178 | — | — | — | 22.00 | — |
| 1979 Prooflike | 1,188 | — | — | — | 22.00 | — |
| 1980 Prooflike | 1,306 | — | — | — | 22.00 | — |
| 1981 Prooflike | 1,288 | — | — | — | 22.00 | — |
| 1982 Prooflike | 1,330 | — | — | — | 22.00 | — |
| 1983 Prooflike | 1,342 | — | — | — | 22.00 | — |
| 1984 Prooflike | 1,354 | — | — | — | 22.00 | — |
| 1985 Prooflike | 1,366 | — | — | — | 22.00 | — |
| 1986 Prooflike | 1,378 | — | — | — | 22.00 | — |
| 1987 Prooflike | 1,390 | — | — | — | 22.00 | — |
| 1988 Prooflike | 1,402 | — | — | — | 22.00 | — |
| 1989 Prooflike | 1,353 | — | — | — | 22.00 | — |
| 1990 Prooflike | 1,523 | — | — | — | 22.00 | — |
| 1991 Prooflike | 1,514 | — | — | — | 22.00 | — |
| 1992 Prooflike | 1,556 | — | — | — | 22.00 | — |
| 1993 Prooflike | 1,440 | — | — | — | 22.00 | — |
| 1994 Prooflike | 1,433 | — | — | — | 22.00 | — |
| 1995 Prooflike | 1,466 | — | — | — | 22.00 | — |
| 1996 Prooflike | 1,629 | — | — | — | 22.00 | — |
| 1997 Prooflike | 1,786 | — | — | — | 22.00 | — |
| 1998 Prooflike | — | — | — | — | 22.00 | — |
| 1999 Prooflike | — | — | — | — | 22.00 | — |

**6 PENCE** **KM# 779** **Weight:** 3.0100 g. **Composition:** 0.9250 Silver .0895 oz. ASW **Ruler:** Victoria

| Date | Mintage | F | VF | XF | Unc | BU |
|---|---|---|---|---|---|---|
| 1901 | 5,109,000 | 1.50 | 2.50 | 8.00 | 22.50 | — |

**6 PENCE** **KM# 799** **Weight:** 3.0100 g. **Composition:** 0.9250 Silver .0895 oz. ASW **Ruler:** Edward VII

| Date | Mintage | F | VF | XF | Unc | BU |
|---|---|---|---|---|---|---|
| 1902 | 6,356,000 | 1.50 | 2.50 | 15.00 | 35.00 | — |
| 1902 Matte Proof | 15,000 | Value: 32.50 | | | | |
| 1903 | 5,411,000 | 2.50 | 8.00 | 25.00 | 65.00 | — |
| 1904 | 4,487,000 | 3.50 | 10.00 | 35.00 | 120 | — |
| 1905 | 4,236,000 | 3.00 | 8.00 | 25.00 | 80.00 | — |
| 1906 | 7,641,000 | 1.50 | 3.00 | 15.00 | 40.00 | — |
| 1907 | 8,734,000 | 1.75 | 3.25 | 17.50 | 60.00 | — |
| 1908 | 6,739,000 | 3.00 | 8.00 | 27.50 | 90.00 | — |
| 1909 | 6,584,000 | 2.50 | 7.50 | 25.00 | 80.00 | — |
| 1910 | 12,491,000 | 1.50 | 3.00 | 15.00 | 40.00 | — |

**6 PENCE** **KM# 815** **Weight:** 3.0100 g. **Composition:** 0.9250 Silver .0895 oz. ASW **Ruler:** George V

| Date | Mintage | F | VF | XF | Unc | BU |
|---|---|---|---|---|---|---|
| 1911 | 9,165,000 | 1.00 | 2.00 | 8.00 | 30.00 | — |
| 1911 Proof | 6,007 | Value: 40.00 | | | | |
| 1912 | 10,984,000 | 1.00 | 3.00 | 12.00 | 42.50 | — |
| 1913 | 7,500,000 | 1.50 | 4.00 | 15.00 | 55.00 | — |
| 1914 | 22,715,000 | 1.00 | 1.50 | 6.00 | 24.00 | — |
| 1915 | 15,695,000 | 1.00 | 1.50 | 6.00 | 24.00 | — |
| 1916 | 22,207,000 | 1.00 | 1.50 | 6.00 | 22.00 | — |
| 1917 | 7,725,000 | 1.50 | 2.00 | 9.00 | 45.00 | — |
| 1918 | 27,559,000 | 1.00 | 1.50 | 6.00 | 22.00 | — |
| 1919 | 13,375,000 | 1.00 | 2.00 | 8.00 | 32.50 | — |
| 1920 | 14,136,000 | 1.00 | 2.00 | 8.00 | 35.00 | — |

**6 PENCE** **KM# 815a.1** **Weight:** 2.8276 g. **Composition:** 0.5000 Silver .0455 oz. ASW **Ruler:** George V **Note:** Narrow rim.

| Date | Mintage | F | VF | XF | Unc | BU |
|---|---|---|---|---|---|---|
| 1920 | Inc. above | 0.75 | 1.50 | 7.00 | 32.00 | — |
| 1921 | 30,340,000 | 0.75 | 1.50 | 6.00 | 32.00 | — |
| 1922 | 16,879,000 | 0.75 | 2.00 | 8.00 | 35.00 | — |
| 1923 | 6,383,000 | 1.00 | 3.00 | 18.00 | 40.00 | — |
| 1924 | 17,444,000 | 0.75 | 1.50 | 8.00 | 30.00 | — |
| 1925 | 12,721,000 | 1.00 | 2.50 | 9.00 | 35.00 | — |

**6 PENCE** **KM# 815a.2** **Weight:** 2.8276 g. **Composition:** 0.5000 Silver .0455 oz. ASW **Ruler:** George V **Note:** Wide rim.

| Date | Mintage | F | VF | XF | Unc | BU |
|---|---|---|---|---|---|---|
| 1925 | Inc. above | 0.75 | 2.00 | 8.00 | 35.00 | — |
| 1926 | 21,810,000 | 1.00 | 2.50 | 10.00 | 35.00 | — |

**6 PENCE** **KM# 828** **Weight:** 2.8276 g. **Composition:** 0.5000 Silver .0455 oz. ASW **Ruler:** George V **Obverse:** Modified effigy, slightly smaller bust

| Date | Mintage | F | VF | XF | Unc | BU |
|---|---|---|---|---|---|---|
| 1926 | Inc. above | BV | 1.00 | 5.00 | 22.50 | — |
| 1927 | 8,925,000 | BV | 1.50 | 8.00 | 25.00 | — |
| 1927 Proof | — | Value: 500 | | | | |

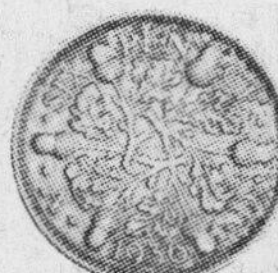

**6 PENCE** **KM# 832** **Weight:** 2.8276 g. **Composition:** 0.5000 Silver .0455 oz. ASW **Ruler:** George V **Reverse:** Oak sprigs with acorns **Note:** Varieties in edge milling exist.

| Date | Mintage | F | VF | XF | Unc | BU |
|---|---|---|---|---|---|---|
| 1927 Proof | 15,000 | Value: 25.00 | | | | |
| 1927 Matte Proof; Rare | — | — | — | — | — | — |

**Note:** There are reportedly 3-4 known of this variety, struck specifically for use in photographs

| Date | Mintage | F | VF | XF | Unc | BU |
|---|---|---|---|---|---|---|
| 1928 | 23,123,000 | BV | 1.00 | 3.00 | 20.00 | — |
| 1928 Proof | — | Value: 325 | | | | |
| 1929 | 28,319,000 | BV | 1.00 | 3.50 | 22.00 | — |
| 1929 Proof | — | Value: 350 | | | | |
| 1930 | 16,990,000 | BV | 1.00 | 3.00 | 18.00 | — |
| 1930 Proof | — | Value: 325 | | | | |
| 1931 | 16,873,000 | BV | 1.00 | 5.00 | 18.00 | — |
| 1931 Proof | — | Value: 325 | | | | |
| 1932 | 9,406,000 | 0.75 | 1.75 | 12.00 | 28.00 | — |
| 1932 Proof | — | Value: 350 | | | | |
| 1933 | 22,185,000 | BV | 1.00 | 5.00 | 15.00 | — |
| 1933 Proof | — | Value: 325 | | | | |
| 1934 | 9,304,000 | BV | 1.00 | 7.00 | 17.00 | — |
| 1934 Proof | — | Value: 325 | | | | |
| 1935 | 13,996,000 | — | BV | 2.25 | 12.50 | — |
| 1935 Proof | — | Value: 325 | | | | |
| 1936 | 24,380,000 | BV | 0.75 | 2.25 | 12.50 | — |
| 1936 Proof | — | Value: 325 | | | | |

**6 PENCE** **KM# 852** **Weight:** 2.8276 g. **Composition:** 0.5000 Silver .0455 oz. ASW **Ruler:** George VI

| Date | Mintage | F | VF | XF | Unc | BU |
|---|---|---|---|---|---|---|
| 1937 | 22,303,000 | — | BV | 1.00 | 4.00 | — |
| 1937 Proof | 26,000 | Value: 9.00 | | | | |
| 1937 Matte Proof; Rare | — | — | — | — | — | — |

**Note:** There are reportedly 3-4 known of this variety, struck specifically for use in photographs

| Date | Mintage | F | VF | XF | Unc | BU |
|---|---|---|---|---|---|---|
| 1938 | 13,403,000 | BV | 1.50 | 3.00 | 12.00 | — |
| 1938 Proof | — | Value: 250 | | | | |
| 1939 | 28,670,000 | — | BV | 1.00 | 5.00 | — |
| 1939 Proof | — | Value: 235 | | | | |
| 1940 | 20,875,000 | — | BV | 1.00 | 5.00 | — |
| 1940 Proof | — | Value: 250 | | | | |
| 1941 | 23,087,000 | — | BV | 1.00 | 5.00 | — |
| 1941 Proof | — | Value: 235 | | | | |
| 1942 | 44,943,000 | — | BV | 1.00 | 5.00 | — |
| 1942 Proof | — | Value: 235 | | | | |
| 1943 | 46,927,000 | — | BV | 1.00 | 5.00 | — |
| 1943 Proof | — | Value: 235 | | | | |
| 1944 | 36,953,000 | — | BV | 1.00 | 5.00 | — |
| 1944 Proof | — | Value: 250 | | | | |
| 1945 | 39,939,000 | — | BV | 1.00 | 5.00 | — |
| 1945 Proof | — | Value: 250 | | | | |
| 1946 | 43,466,000 | — | BV | 1.00 | 5.00 | — |
| 1946 Proof | — | Value: 250 | | | | |

**6 PENCE** **KM# 862** **Composition:** Copper-Nickel **Ruler:** George VI

| Date | Mintage | F | VF | XF | Unc | BU |
|---|---|---|---|---|---|---|
| 1947 | 29,993,000 | — | 0.20 | 0.50 | 5.00 | — |
| 1947 Proof | — | Value: 250 | | | | |
| 1948 | 88,324,000 | — | 0.20 | 0.50 | 5.00 | — |
| 1948 Proof | — | Value: 275 | | | | |

**6 PENCE** **KM# 875** **Composition:** Copper-Nickel **Ruler:** George VI **Rev. Legend:** Without IND IMP

| Date | Mintage | F | VF | XF | Unc | BU |
|---|---|---|---|---|---|---|
| 1949 | 41,336,000 | — | 0.20 | 0.50 | 6.00 | — |
| 1949 Proof | — | Value: 275 | | | | |
| 1950 | 32,741,999 | — | 0.20 | 0.50 | 6.00 | — |
| 1950 Proof | 18,000 | Value: 7.00 | | | | |
| 1950 Matte Proof; Rare | — | — | — | — | — | — |

**Note:** There are reportedly 3-4 known of this variety, struck specifically for use in photographs

| Date | Mintage | F | VF | XF | Unc | BU |
|---|---|---|---|---|---|---|
| 1951 | 40,399,000 | — | 0.20 | 0.50 | 6.00 | — |
| 1951 Proof | 20,000 | Value: 7.00 | | | | |
| 1951 Matte Proof; Rare | — | — | — | — | — | — |

**Note:** There are reportedly 3-4 known of this variety, struck specifically for use in photographs

| Date | Mintage | F | VF | XF | Unc | BU |
|---|---|---|---|---|---|---|
| 1952 | 1,012,999 | 1.25 | 2.50 | 12.50 | 28.00 | — |
| 1952 Proof | — | Value: 800 | | | | |

**6 PENCE** **KM# 889** **Composition:** Copper-Nickel **Ruler:** Elizabeth II

| Date | Mintage | F | VF | XF | Unc | BU |
|---|---|---|---|---|---|---|
| 1953 | 70,324,000 | — | 0.15 | 0.50 | 1.00 | — |
| 1953 Proof | 40,000 | Value: 3.50 | | | | |
| 1953 Matte Proof; Rare | — | — | — | — | — | — |

**Note:** There are reportedly 3-4 known of this variety, struck specifically for use in photographs

**6 PENCE** KM# 903 **Composition:** Copper-Nickel **Ruler:** Elizabeth II **Obv. Legend:** Without BRITT OMN

| Date | Mintage | F | VF | XF | Unc | BU |
|---|---|---|---|---|---|---|
| 1954 | 105,241,000 | — | 0.15 | 0.50 | 4.00 | — |
| 1954 Proof | — | Value: 200 | | | | |
| 1955 | 109,930,000 | — | 0.15 | 0.35 | 2.00 | — |
| 1955 Proof | — | Value: 200 | | | | |
| 1956 | 109,842,000 | — | 0.15 | 0.35 | 2.00 | — |
| 1956 Proof | — | Value: 200 | | | | |
| 1957 | 105,654,000 | — | 0.15 | 0.35 | 1.50 | — |
| 1957 Proof | — | Value: 200 | | | | |
| 1958 | 123,519,000 | — | 0.15 | 0.50 | 4.00 | — |
| 1958 Proof | — | Value: 200 | | | | |
| 1959 | 93,089,000 | — | 0.15 | 0.35 | 1.00 | — |
| 1959 Proof | — | Value: 200 | | | | |
| 1960 | 103,283,000 | — | 0.15 | 0.35 | 3.50 | — |
| 1960 Proof | — | Value: 200 | | | | |
| 1961 | 115,052,000 | — | 0.15 | 0.35 | 2.50 | — |
| 1961 Proof | — | Value: 200 | | | | |
| 1962 | 166,484,000 | — | 0.15 | 0.35 | 1.00 | — |
| 1962 Proof | — | Value: 200 | | | | |
| 1963 | 120,056,000 | — | 0.15 | 0.30 | 0.60 | — |
| 1963 Proof | — | Value: 200 | | | | |
| 1964 | 152,336,000 | — | 0.15 | 0.25 | 0.50 | — |
| 1964 Proof | — | Value: 200 | | | | |
| 1965 | 129,644,000 | — | 0.10 | 0.20 | 0.40 | — |
| 1965 Proof | — | Value: 250 | | | | |
| 1966 | 175,676,000 | — | 0.10 | 0.20 | 0.40 | — |
| 1966 Proof | — | Value: 250 | | | | |
| 1967 Proof | — | Value: 250 | | | | |
| 1967 | 240,788,000 | — | 0.10 | 0.20 | 0.40 | — |
| 1970 Proof | 750,000 | Value: 2.00 | | | | |

**SHILLING** KM# 780 **Weight:** 5.6552 g. **Composition:** 0.9250 Silver .1682 oz. ASW **Ruler:** Victoria

| Date | Mintage | F | VF | XF | Unc | BU |
|---|---|---|---|---|---|---|
| 1901 | 3,426,000 | 3.00 | 6.00 | 15.00 | 50.00 | — |

**SHILLING** KM# 800 **Weight:** 5.6552 g. **Composition:** 0.9250 Silver .1682 oz. ASW **Ruler:** Edward VII

| Date | Mintage | F | VF | XF | Unc | BU |
|---|---|---|---|---|---|---|
| 1902 | 7,890,000 | 2.50 | 7.00 | 16.00 | 60.00 | — |
| 1902 Matte Proof | 15,000 | Value: 60.00 | | | | |
| 1903 | 2,061,999 | 5.00 | 15.00 | 65.00 | 225 | — |
| 1904 | 2,040,000 | 5.00 | 15.00 | 70.00 | 210 | — |
| 1905 | 488,000 | 30.00 | 55.00 | 275 | 1,200 | — |
| 1906 | 10,791,000 | 3.00 | 8.00 | 28.00 | 70.00 | — |
| 1907 | 14,083,000 | 3.50 | 10.00 | 32.50 | 100 | — |
| 1908 | 3,807,000 | 5.00 | 15.00 | 75.00 | 280 | — |
| 1909 | 5,665,000 | 5.00 | 15.00 | 70.00 | 280 | — |
| 1910 | 26,547,000 | 3.00 | 8.00 | 26.00 | 60.00 | — |

**SHILLING** KM# 816 **Weight:** 5.6552 g. **Composition:** 0.9250 Silver .1682 oz. ASW **Ruler:** George V

| Date | Mintage | F | VF | XF | Unc | BU |
|---|---|---|---|---|---|---|
| 1911 | 20,066,000 | 2.00 | 3.25 | 17.50 | 40.00 | — |
| 1911 Proof | 6,007 | Value: 60.00 | | | | |
| 1912 | 15,594,000 | 2.00 | 3.25 | 17.50 | 60.00 | — |
| 1913 | 9,002,000 | 3.00 | 6.00 | 28.50 | 75.00 | — |
| 1914 | 23,416,000 | 2.00 | 3.25 | 8.00 | 40.00 | — |
| 1915 | 39,279,000 | 2.00 | 3.25 | 8.00 | 40.00 | — |
| 1916 | 35,862,000 | 2.00 | 3.00 | 6.50 | 30.00 | — |
| 1917 | 22,203,000 | 2.00 | 3.25 | 8.00 | 40.00 | — |
| 1918 | 34,916,000 | 2.00 | 3.00 | 6.50 | 30.00 | — |
| 1919 | 10,824,000 | 2.00 | 3.00 | 10.00 | 55.00 | — |

**SHILLING** KM# 816a **Weight:** 5.6552 g. **Composition:** 0.5000 Silver .0909 oz. ASW **Ruler:** George V

| Date | Mintage | F | VF | XF | Unc | BU |
|---|---|---|---|---|---|---|
| 1920 | 22,825,000 | BV | 2.50 | 10.00 | 40.00 | — |
| 1921 | 22,649,000 | BV | 2.50 | 18.00 | 60.00 | — |
| 1922 | 27,216,000 | BV | 3.00 | 16.00 | 55.00 | — |
| 1923 | 14,575,000 | BV | 2.50 | 12.00 | 40.00 | — |
| 1924 | 9,250,000 | BV | 3.00 | 22.50 | 55.00 | — |
| 1925 | 5,419,000 | 3.00 | 5.00 | 45.00 | 90.00 | — |
| 1926 | 22,516,000 | BV | 4.00 | 15.00 | 50.00 | — |

**SHILLING** KM# 829 **Weight:** 5.6552 g. **Composition:** 0.5000 Silver .0909 oz. ASW **Ruler:** George V **Obverse:** Modified effigy, slightly smaller bust

| Date | Mintage | F | VF | XF | Unc | BU |
|---|---|---|---|---|---|---|
| 1926 | Inc. above | BV | 3.00 | 15.00 | 42.50 | — |
| 1927 | 9,262,000 | BV | 3.00 | 16.00 | 40.00 | — |

**SHILLING** KM# 833 **Weight:** 5.6552 g. **Composition:** 0.5000 Silver .0909 oz. ASW **Ruler:** George V

| Date | Mintage | F | VF | XF | Unc | BU |
|---|---|---|---|---|---|---|
| 1927 | Inc. above | BV | 2.50 | 15.00 | 40.00 | — |
| 1927 Proof | 15,000 | Value: 45.00 | | | | |
| 1927 Matte Proof; Rare | — | — | — | — | — | — |

**Note:** There are reportedly 1-2 of this variety, struck specifically for use in photographs

| Date | Mintage | F | VF | XF | Unc | BU |
|---|---|---|---|---|---|---|
| 1928 | 18,137,000 | — | BV | 8.00 | 22.50 | — |
| 1928 Proof | — | Value: 425 | | | | |
| 1929 | 19,343,000 | — | BV | 7.00 | 20.00 | — |
| 1929 Proof | — | Value: 500 | | | | |
| 1930 | 3,137,000 | 2.00 | 4.00 | 22.50 | 50.00 | — |
| 1930 Proof | — | Value: 500 | | | | |
| 1931 | 6,994,000 | 1.50 | 3.50 | 8.00 | 22.50 | — |
| 1931 Proof | — | Value: 425 | | | | |
| 1932 | 12,168,000 | 1.50 | 3.50 | 8.00 | 20.00 | — |
| 1932 Proof | — | Value: 425 | | | | |
| 1933 | 11,512,000 | 1.50 | 3.00 | 7.00 | 20.00 | — |
| 1933 Proof | — | Value: 425 | | | | |
| 1934 | 6,138,000 | 1.50 | 3.25 | 10.00 | 40.00 | — |
| 1934 Proof | — | Value: 450 | | | | |
| 1935 | 9,183,000 | 1.50 | 3.00 | 7.50 | 20.00 | — |
| 1935 Proof | — | Value: 425 | | | | |
| 1936 | 11,911,000 | 1.50 | 2.50 | 6.00 | 20.00 | — |
| 1936 Proof | — | Value: 425 | | | | |

**SHILLING** KM# 853 **Weight:** 5.6552 g. **Composition:** 0.5000 Silver .0909 oz. ASW **Ruler:** George VI **Reverse:** English crest

| Date | Mintage | F | VF | XF | Unc | BU |
|---|---|---|---|---|---|---|
| 1937 | 8,359,000 | BV | 1.00 | 3.00 | 8.00 | — |
| 1937 Proof | 26,000 | Value: 12.50 | | | | |
| 1937 Matte Proof; Rare | — | — | — | — | — | — |

**Note:** There are reportedly 1-2 known of this variety, struck specifically for use in photographs

| Date | Mintage | F | VF | XF | Unc | BU |
|---|---|---|---|---|---|---|
| 1938 | 4,833,000 | BV | 1.00 | 4.00 | 20.00 | — |
| 1938 Proof | — | Value: 450 | | | | |
| 1939 | 11,053,000 | BV | 1.00 | 3.00 | 17.50 | — |
| 1939 Proof | — | Value: 400 | | | | |
| 1940 | 11,099,000 | — | BV | 2.50 | 8.00 | — |
| 1940 Proof | — | Value: 400 | | | | |
| 1941 | 11,392,000 | — | BV | 2.00 | 8.00 | — |
| 1941 Proof | — | Value: 400 | | | | |
| 1942 | 17,454,000 | — | BV | 2.00 | 7.50 | — |
| 1942 Proof | — | Value: 400 | | | | |
| 1943 | 11,404,000 | — | BV | 2.00 | 7.50 | — |
| 1943 Proof | — | Value: 350 | | | | |
| 1944 | 11,587,000 | — | BV | 2.00 | 7.50 | — |
| 1944 Proof | — | Value: 350 | | | | |
| 1945 | 15,143,000 | — | BV | 2.00 | 7.50 | — |
| 1945 Proof | — | Value: 400 | | | | |
| 1946 | 18,664,000 | — | BV | 1.50 | 7.00 | — |
| 1946 Proof | — | Value: 400 | | | | |

**SHILLING** KM# 854 **Weight:** 5.6552 g. **Composition:** 0.5000 Silver .0909 oz. ASW **Ruler:** George VI **Reverse:** Scottish crest

| Date | Mintage | F | VF | XF | Unc | BU |
|---|---|---|---|---|---|---|
| 1937 | 6,749,000 | — | BV | 2.50 | 8.00 | — |
| 1937 Proof | 26,000 | Value: 12.50 | | | | |
| 1937 Matte Proof; Rare | — | — | — | — | — | — |

**Note:** There are reportedly 1-2 known of this variety, struck specifically for use in photographs

| Date | Mintage | F | VF | XF | Unc | BU |
|---|---|---|---|---|---|---|
| 1938 | 4,798,000 | — | BV | 4.00 | 18.00 | — |
| 1938 Proof | — | Value: 400 | | | | |
| 1939 | 10,264,000 | — | BV | 3.00 | 8.00 | — |
| 1939 Proof | — | Value: 400 | | | | |
| 1940 | 9,913,000 | — | BV | 2.50 | 7.50 | — |
| 1940 Proof | — | Value: 400 | | | | |
| 1941 | 8,086,000 | — | BV | 2.00 | 7.00 | — |
| 1941 Proof | — | Value: 400 | | | | |
| 1942 | 13,677,000 | — | BV | 2.00 | 7.00 | — |
| 1942 Proof | — | Value: 375 | | | | |
| 1943 Proof | — | Value: 350 | | | | |
| 1943 | 9,824,000 | — | BV | 2.00 | 7.00 | — |
| 1944 | 10,990,000 | — | BV | 2.00 | 7.00 | — |
| 1944 Proof | — | Value: 350 | | | | |
| 1945 | 15,106,000 | — | BV | 2.00 | 7.00 | — |
| 1945 Proof | — | Value: 400 | | | | |
| 1946 | 16,382,000 | — | BV | 2.00 | 7.00 | — |
| 1946 Proof | — | — | — | — | — | — |

**SHILLING** KM# 863 **Composition:** Copper-Nickel **Ruler:** George VI **Reverse:** English crest

| Date | Mintage | F | VF | XF | Unc | BU |
|---|---|---|---|---|---|---|
| 1947 | 12,121,000 | 0.10 | 0.25 | 1.00 | 5.00 | — |
| 1947 Proof | — | Value: 325 | | | | |
| 1948 | 45,577,000 | 0.10 | 0.20 | 1.00 | 5.00 | — |
| 1948 Proof | — | Value: 350 | | | | |

**SHILLING** KM# 864 **Composition:** Copper-Nickel **Ruler:** George VI **Reverse:** Scottish crest

| Date | Mintage | F | VF | XF | Unc | BU |
|---|---|---|---|---|---|---|
| 1947 | 12,283,000 | 0.10 | 0.25 | 1.00 | 5.50 | — |
| 1947 Proof | — | Value: 325 | | | | |
| 1948 | 45,352,000 | 0.10 | 0.20 | 1.00 | 5.00 | — |
| 1948 Proof | — | Value: 350 | | | | |

**SHILLING** **KM# 876** **Composition:** Copper-Nickel **Ruler:** George VI **Reverse:** English crest **Rev. Legend:** Without IND IMP

| Date | Mintage | F | VF | XF | Unc | BU |
|---|---|---|---|---|---|---|
| 1949 | 19,328,000 | 0.10 | 0.25 | 1.50 | 7.50 | — |
| 1949 Proof | — | Value: 400 | | | | |
| 1950 | 19,244,000 | 0.10 | 0.25 | 1.50 | 7.50 | — |
| 1950 Proof | 18,000 | Value: 11.00 | | | | |
| 1950 Matte Proof; Rare | — | — | — | — | — | — |

**Note:** There are reportedly 1-2 known of this variety, struck specifically for use in photographs

| Date | Mintage | F | VF | XF | Unc | BU |
|---|---|---|---|---|---|---|
| 1951 | 9,957,000 | 0.10 | 0.25 | 1.50 | 7.50 | — |
| 1951 Proof | 20,000 | Value: 11.00 | | | | |
| 1951 Matte Proof; Rare | — | — | — | — | — | — |

**Note:** There are reportedly 1-2 known of this variety, struck specifically for use in photographs

| Date | Mintage | F | VF | XF | Unc | BU |
|---|---|---|---|---|---|---|
| 1952 Matte Proof; Rare | — | — | — | — | — | — |

**Note:** There are reportedly 1-2 known of this variety, struck specifically for use in photographs

**SHILLING** **KM# 877** **Composition:** Copper-Nickel **Ruler:** George VI **Reverse:** Scottish crest

| Date | Mintage | F | VF | XF | Unc | BU |
|---|---|---|---|---|---|---|
| 1949 | 21,243,000 | 0.10 | 0.25 | 1.50 | 7.50 | — |
| 1949 Proof | — | Value: 400 | | | | |
| 1950 | 14,300,000 | 0.10 | 0.25 | 1.50 | 7.50 | — |
| 1950 Proof | 18,000 | Value: 11.00 | | | | |
| 1950 Matte Proof; Rare | — | — | — | — | — | — |

**Note:** There are reportedly 1-2 known of this variety, struck specifically for use in photographs

| Date | Mintage | F | VF | XF | Unc | BU |
|---|---|---|---|---|---|---|
| 1951 | 10,961,000 | 0.10 | 0.25 | 1.50 | 7.50 | — |
| 1951 Proof | 20,000 | Value: 11.00 | | | | |
| 1951 Matte Proof; Rare | — | — | — | — | — | — |

**Note:** There are reportedly 1-2 known of this variety, struck specifically for use in photographs

**SHILLING** **KM# 890** **Composition:** Copper-Nickel **Ruler:** Elizabeth II **Reverse:** English arms

| Date | Mintage | F | VF | XF | Unc | BU |
|---|---|---|---|---|---|---|
| 1953 | 41,943,000 | — | 0.15 | 0.50 | 2.50 | — |
| 1953 Proof | 40,000 | Value: 8.00 | | | | |
| 1953 Matte Proof; Rare | — | — | — | — | — | — |

**Note:** There are reportedly 1-2 known of this variety, struck specifically for use in photographs

**SHILLING** **KM# 891** **Composition:** Copper-Nickel **Ruler:** Elizabeth II **Reverse:** Scottish arms

| Date | Mintage | F | VF | XF | Unc | BU |
|---|---|---|---|---|---|---|
| 1953 | 20,664,000 | — | 0.15 | 0.50 | 2.50 | — |
| 1953 Proof | 40,000 | Value: 8.00 | | | | |
| 1953 Matte Proof; Rare | — | — | — | — | — | — |

**Note:** There are reportedly 1-2 known of this variety, struck specifically for use in photographs

**SHILLING** **KM# 904** **Composition:** Copper-Nickel **Ruler:** Elizabeth II **Obv. Legend:** Without BRITT OMN **Reverse:** English arms

| Date | Mintage | F | VF | XF | Unc | BU |
|---|---|---|---|---|---|---|
| 1954 | 30,162,000 | — | 0.15 | 0.50 | 2.00 | — |
| 1954 Proof | — | Value: 300 | | | | |
| 1955 | 45,260,000 | — | 0.15 | 0.50 | 2.00 | — |
| 1955 Proof | — | Value: 300 | | | | |
| 1956 | 44,970,000 | — | 0.15 | 0.50 | 6.00 | — |
| 1956 Proof | — | Value: 300 | | | | |
| 1957 | 42,774,000 | — | 0.15 | 0.50 | 2.00 | — |
| 1957 Proof | — | Value: 300 | | | | |
| 1958 | 14,392,000 | 0.25 | 0.50 | 2.50 | 18.50 | — |
| 1958 Proof | — | Value: 325 | | | | |
| 1959 | 19,443,000 | — | 0.15 | 0.40 | 2.00 | — |
| 1959 Proof | — | Value: 300 | | | | |
| 1960 | 27,028,000 | — | 0.15 | 0.35 | 2.00 | — |
| 1960 Proof | — | Value: 300 | | | | |
| 1961 | 39,817,000 | — | 0.15 | 0.35 | 2.00 | — |
| 1961 Proof | — | Value: 275 | | | | |
| 1962 | 36,704,000 | — | 0.15 | 0.25 | 1.75 | — |
| 1962 Proof | — | Value: 275 | | | | |
| 1963 | 49,434,000 | — | — | 0.25 | 0.50 | — |
| 1963 Proof | — | Value: 275 | | | | |
| 1964 | 8,591,000 | — | — | 0.25 | 0.50 | — |
| 1964 Proof | — | Value: 300 | | | | |
| 1965 | 9,216,000 | — | — | 0.25 | 0.50 | — |
| 1965 Proof | — | Value: 300 | | | | |
| 1966 | 15,002,000 | — | — | 0.25 | 0.50 | — |
| 1966 Proof | — | Value: 300 | | | | |
| 1970 Proof | 750,000 | Value: 4.00 | | | | |

**SHILLING** **KM# 905** **Composition:** Copper-Nickel **Ruler:** Elizabeth II **Reverse:** Scottish arms

| Date | Mintage | F | VF | XF | Unc | BU |
|---|---|---|---|---|---|---|
| 1954 | 26,772,000 | — | 0.15 | 0.25 | 2.25 | — |
| 1954 Proof | — | Value: 300 | | | | |
| 1954 Matte Proof; Rare | — | — | — | — | — | — |
| 1955 | 27,951,000 | — | 0.15 | 0.35 | 2.50 | — |
| 1955 Proof | — | Value: 300 | | | | |
| 1956 | 42,854,000 | — | 0.15 | 1.00 | 12.00 | — |
| 1956 Proof | — | Value: 300 | | | | |
| 1957 | 17,960,000 | — | 0.25 | 1.50 | 18.50 | — |
| 1957 Proof | — | Value: 325 | | | | |
| 1958 | 40,823,000 | — | 0.15 | 0.50 | 2.25 | — |
| 1958 Proof | — | Value: 300 | | | | |
| 1959 | 1,012,999 | 1.00 | 2.00 | 5.00 | 22.50 | — |
| 1959 Proof | — | Value: 325 | | | | |
| 1960 | 14,376,000 | — | 0.15 | 0.50 | 2.25 | — |
| 1960 Proof | — | Value: 300 | | | | |
| 1961 | 2,763,000 | 0.25 | 0.20 | 1.25 | 7.00 | — |
| 1961 Proof | — | Value: 300 | | | | |
| 1962 | 17,475,000 | — | 0.15 | 0.25 | 1.50 | — |
| 1962 Proof | — | Value: 275 | | | | |
| 1963 | 32,299,999 | — | 0.15 | 0.25 | 0.75 | — |
| 1963 Proof | — | Value: 275 | | | | |
| 1964 | 5,239,000 | — | 0.15 | 0.25 | 1.50 | — |
| 1964 Proof | — | Value: 300 | | | | |
| 1965 | 2,774,000 | — | 0.15 | 0.25 | 1.50 | — |
| 1965 Proof | — | Value: 325 | | | | |
| 1966 | 15,604,000 | — | 0.15 | 0.25 | 0.85 | — |
| 1966 Proof | — | Value: 325 | | | | |
| 1970 Proof | 750,000 | Value: 4.00 | | | | |

**FLORIN (Two Shillings)** **KM# 781** **Weight:** 11.3104 g. **Composition:** 0.9250 Silver .3364 oz. ASW **Ruler:** Victoria

| Date | Mintage | F | VF | XF | Unc | BU |
|---|---|---|---|---|---|---|
| 1901 | 2,649,000 | 6.00 | 12.50 | 20.00 | 70.00 | — |

**FLORIN (Two Shillings)** **KM# 801** **Weight:** 11.3104 g. **Composition:** 0.9250 Silver .3364 oz. ASW **Ruler:** Edward VII

| Date | Mintage | F | VF | XF | Unc | BU |
|---|---|---|---|---|---|---|
| 1902 | 2,190,000 | 7.50 | 15.00 | 30.00 | 80.00 | — |
| 1902 Matte Proof | 15,000 | Value: 85.00 | | | | |
| 1903 | 995,000 | 10.00 | 20.00 | 60.00 | 225 | — |
| 1904 | 2,770,000 | 10.00 | 40.00 | 85.00 | 270 | — |
| 1905 | 1,188,000 | 25.00 | 50.00 | 125 | 900 | — |
| 1906 | 6,910,000 | 8.00 | 20.00 | 50.00 | 200 | — |
| 1907 | 5,948,000 | 8.00 | 20.00 | 50.00 | 225 | — |
| 1908 | 3,280,000 | 10.00 | 25.00 | 100 | 375 | — |
| 1909 | 3,483,000 | 10.00 | 25.00 | 85.00 | 250 | — |
| 1910 | 5,651,000 | 8.00 | 20.00 | 45.00 | 100 | — |

**FLORIN (Two Shillings)** **KM# 817** **Weight:** 11.3104 g. **Composition:** 0.9250 Silver .3364 oz. ASW **Ruler:** George V

| Date | Mintage | F | VF | XF | Unc | BU |
|---|---|---|---|---|---|---|
| 1911 | 5,951,000 | 4.00 | 8.00 | 30.00 | 85.00 | — |
| 1911 Proof | 6,007 | Value: 110 | | | | |
| 1912 | 8,572,000 | 5.00 | 10.00 | 40.00 | 90.00 | — |
| 1913 | 4,545,000 | 5.50 | 12.00 | 40.00 | 140 | — |
| 1914 | 21,253,000 | 2.50 | 4.00 | 20.00 | 50.00 | — |
| 1915 | 12,358,000 | 2.50 | 4.00 | 20.00 | 75.00 | — |
| 1916 | 21,064,000 | 2.50 | 4.00 | 15.00 | 80.00 | — |
| 1917 | 11,182,000 | 2.50 | 4.00 | 15.00 | 40.00 | — |
| 1918 | 29,212,000 | 2.50 | 4.00 | 14.00 | 65.00 | — |
| 1919 | 9,469,000 | 3.50 | 6.00 | 20.00 | 55.00 | — |

**FLORIN (Two Shillings)** **KM# 817a** **Weight:** 11.3104 g. **Composition:** 0.5000 Silver .1818 oz. ASW **Ruler:** George V

| Date | Mintage | F | VF | XF | Unc | BU |
|---|---|---|---|---|---|---|
| 1920 | 15,388,000 | 2.00 | 4.00 | 20.00 | 50.00 | — |
| 1921 | 34,864,000 | 2.00 | 3.50 | 18.00 | 45.00 | — |
| 1922 | 23,861,000 | 2.00 | 3.50 | 18.00 | 45.00 | — |
| 1923 | 21,547,000 | 2.00 | 3.00 | 15.00 | 40.00 | — |
| 1924 | 4,582,000 | 2.50 | 4.00 | 22.50 | 60.00 | — |
| 1925 | 1,404,000 | 10.00 | 20.00 | 80.00 | 200 | — |
| 1926 | 5,125,000 | 3.50 | 7.50 | 40.00 | 90.00 | — |

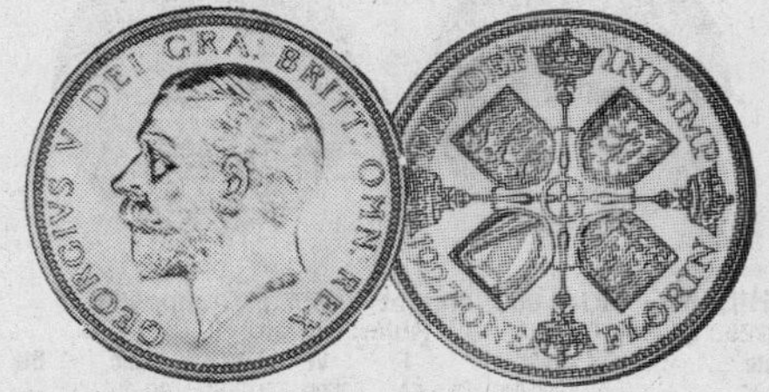

**FLORIN (Two Shillings)** **KM# 834** **Weight:** 11.3104 g. **Composition:** 0.5000 Silver .1818 oz. ASW **Ruler:** George V

| Date | Mintage | F | VF | XF | Unc | BU |
|---|---|---|---|---|---|---|
| 1927 Proof | 15,000 | Value: 75.00 | | | | |
| 1928 | 11,088,000 | 1.50 | 2.50 | 7.00 | 25.00 | — |
| 1928 Proof | — | Value: 500 | | | | |
| 1929 | 16,397,000 | 1.50 | 2.50 | 7.00 | 25.00 | — |
| 1929 Proof | — | Value: 600 | | | | |
| 1930 | 5,734,000 | 2.00 | 4.00 | 15.00 | 37.50 | — |
| 1930 Proof | — | Value: 500 | | | | |
| 1931 | 6,556,000 | 2.00 | 4.00 | 12.00 | 35.00 | — |
| 1931 Proof | — | Value: 500 | | | | |
| 1932 | 717,000 | 12.50 | 25.00 | 85.00 | 240 | — |
| 1932 Proof | — | Value: 1,200 | | | | |
| 1933 | 8,685,000 | 1.50 | 2.50 | 8.00 | 25.00 | — |
| 1933 Proof | — | Value: 500 | | | | |
| 1935 | 7,541,000 | 1.50 | 2.50 | 6.00 | 22.50 | — |
| 1935 Proof | — | Value: 500 | | | | |
| 1936 | 9,897,000 | 1.50 | 2.50 | 7.00 | 22.50 | — |
| 1936 Proof | — | Value: 500 | | | | |

**FLORIN (Two Shillings)** **KM# 855** **Weight:** 11.3104 g. **Composition:** 0.5000 Silver .1818 oz. ASW **Ruler:** George VI

| Date | Mintage | F | VF | XF | Unc | BU |
|---|---|---|---|---|---|---|
| 1937 | 13,007,000 | — | BV | 3.00 | 8.00 | — |
| 1937 Proof | 26,000 | Value: 18.00 | | | | |
| 1937 Matte Proof; Rare | — | — | — | — | — | — |

**Note:** There are reportedly 1-2 known of this variety, struck specifically for use in photographs

| Date | Mintage | F | VF | XF | Unc | BU |
|---|---|---|---|---|---|---|
| 1938 | 7,909,000 | BV | 2.50 | 7.50 | 24.00 | — |
| 1938 Proof | — | Value: 450 | | | | |
| 1939 | 20,851,000 | — | BV | 3.50 | 9.00 | — |
| 1939 Proof | — | Value: 400 | | | | |
| 1940 | 18,700,000 | — | BV | 3.00 | 8.00 | — |
| 1940 Proof | — | Value: 400 | | | | |
| 1941 | 24,451,000 | — | BV | 3.00 | 7.00 | — |
| 1941 Proof | — | Value: 400 | | | | |
| 1942 | 39,895,000 | — | BV | 3.00 | 7.00 | — |
| 1942 Proof | — | Value: 400 | | | | |
| 1943 | 26,712,000 | — | BV | 3.00 | 7.00 | — |
| 1943 Proof | — | Value: 400 | | | | |
| 1944 | 27,560,000 | — | BV | 3.00 | 7.00 | — |
| 1944 Proof | — | Value: 400 | | | | |
| 1945 | 25,858,000 | — | BV | 3.00 | 7.00 | — |
| 1945 Proof | — | Value: 600 | | | | |
| 1946 | 22,300,000 | — | BV | 3.00 | 7.00 | — |
| 1946 Proof | — | Value: 600 | | | | |

**FLORIN (Two Shillings)** **KM# 865** **Composition:** Copper-Nickel **Ruler:** George VI

| Date | Mintage | F | VF | XF | Unc | BU |
|---|---|---|---|---|---|---|
| 1947 | 22,910,000 | 0.20 | 0.35 | 1.00 | 4.00 | — |
| 1947 Proof | — | Value: 325 | | | | |
| 1948 | 67,554,000 | 0.20 | 0.35 | 1.00 | 3.50 | — |
| 1948 Proof | — | Value: 325 | | | | |

**FLORIN (Two Shillings)** **KM# 878** **Composition:** Copper-Nickel **Ruler:** George VI **Rev. Legend:** Without IND IMP

| Date | Mintage | F | VF | XF | Unc | BU |
|---|---|---|---|---|---|---|
| 1949 | 28,615,000 | 0.20 | 0.35 | 1.00 | 6.00 | — |
| 1949 Proof | — | Value: 325 | | | | |
| 1950 | 24,357,000 | 0.20 | 0.35 | 1.00 | 7.00 | — |
| 1950 Proof | 18,000 | Value: 15.00 | | | | |
| 1950 Matte Proof; Rare | — | — | — | — | — | — |

**Note:** There are reportedly 1-2 known of this variety, struck specifically for use in photographs

| Date | Mintage | F | VF | XF | Unc | BU |
|---|---|---|---|---|---|---|
| 1951 | 27,412,000 | 0.20 | 0.35 | 1.00 | 6.00 | — |
| 1951 Proof | 20,000 | Value: 12.00 | | | | |
| 1951 Matte Proof; Rare | — | — | — | — | — | — |

**Note:** There are reportedly 1-2 known of this variety, struck specifically for use in photographs

**FLORIN (Two Shillings)** **KM# 892** **Composition:** Copper-Nickel **Ruler:** Elizabeth II

| Date | Mintage | F | VF | XF | Unc | BU |
|---|---|---|---|---|---|---|
| 1953 | 11,959,000 | 0.25 | 0.50 | 1.00 | 5.00 | — |
| 1953 Proof | 40,000 | Value: 10.00 | | | | |
| 1953 Matte Proof; Rare | — | — | — | — | — | — |

**Note:** There are reportedly 1-2 known of this variety, struck specifically for use in photographs

**FLORIN (Two Shillings)** **KM# 906** **Composition:** Copper-Nickel **Ruler:** Elizabeth II **Obv. Legend:** Without BRITT OMN

| Date | Mintage | F | VF | XF | Unc | BU |
|---|---|---|---|---|---|---|
| 1954 | 13,085,000 | 0.20 | 0.50 | 3.00 | 30.00 | — |
| 1954 Proof | — | Value: 325 | | | | |
| 1955 | 25,887,000 | 0.20 | 0.30 | 1.00 | 4.00 | — |
| 1955 Proof | — | Value: 300 | | | | |
| 1956 | 47,824,000 | 0.20 | 0.30 | 1.00 | 4.00 | — |
| 1956 Proof | — | Value: 300 | | | | |
| 1957 | 33,070,999 | 0.20 | 0.40 | 2.00 | 27.50 | — |
| 1957 Proof | — | Value: 300 | | | | |
| 1958 | 9,565,000 | 0.25 | 0.50 | 1.75 | 10.00 | — |
| 1958 Proof | — | Value: 350 | | | | |
| 1959 | 14,080,000 | 0.25 | 0.50 | 3.00 | 27.50 | — |
| 1959 Proof | — | Value: 300 | | | | |
| 1960 | 13,832,000 | — | 0.20 | 1.50 | 4.00 | — |
| 1960 Proof | — | Value: 300 | | | | |
| 1961 | 37,735,000 | — | 0.20 | 1.00 | 4.00 | — |
| 1961 Proof | — | Value: 300 | | | | |
| 1962 | 35,148,000 | — | 0.20 | 0.75 | 2.50 | — |
| 1962 Proof | — | Value: 300 | | | | |
| 1963 | 26,471,000 | — | 0.20 | 0.75 | 2.00 | — |
| 1963 Proof | — | Value: 300 | | | | |
| 1964 | 16,539,000 | — | 0.20 | 0.50 | 2.00 | — |
| 1965 | 48,163,000 | — | 0.20 | 0.50 | 1.50 | — |
| 1966 | 83,999,000 | — | 0.20 | 0.30 | 1.50 | — |
| 1967 | 39,718,000 | — | 0.20 | 0.30 | 1.50 | — |
| 1970 Proof | 750,000 | Value: 4.00 | | | | |

**1/2 CROWN** **KM# 782** **Weight:** 14.1380 g. **Composition:** 0.9250 Silver .4205 oz. ASW **Ruler:** Victoria

| Date | Mintage | F | VF | XF | Unc | BU |
|---|---|---|---|---|---|---|
| 1901 | 1,577,000 | 5.00 | 12.50 | 35.00 | 85.00 | — |

**1/2 CROWN** **KM# 802** **Weight:** 14.1380 g. **Composition:** 0.9250 Silver .4205 oz. ASW **Ruler:** Edward VII

| Date | Mintage | F | VF | XF | Unc | BU |
|---|---|---|---|---|---|---|
| 1902 | 1,316,000 | 10.00 | 20.00 | 40.00 | 90.00 | — |
| 1902 Matte Proof | 15,000 | Value: 100 | | | | |
| 1903 | 275,000 | 30.00 | 80.00 | 800 | 1,800 | — |
| 1904 | 710,000 | 25.00 | 60.00 | 350 | 1,250 | — |
| 1905 | 166,000 | 75.00 | 250 | 1,200 | 2,500 | — |
| 1906 | 2,886,000 | 20.00 | 40.00 | 120 | 350 | — |
| 1907 | 3,694,000 | 20.00 | 40.00 | 120 | 400 | — |
| 1908 | 1,759,000 | 20.00 | 40.00 | 150 | 500 | — |
| 1909 | 3,052,000 | 20.00 | 40.00 | 120 | 400 | — |
| 1910 | 2,558,000 | 10.00 | 20.00 | 70.00 | 200 | — |

**1/2 CROWN** **KM# 818.1** **Weight:** 14.1380 g. **Composition:** 0.9250 Silver .4205 oz. ASW **Ruler:** George V

| Date | Mintage | F | VF | XF | Unc | BU |
|---|---|---|---|---|---|---|
| 1911 | 2,915,000 | 5.00 | 10.00 | 30.00 | 125 | — |
| 1911 Proof | 6,007 | Value: 125 | | | | |
| 1912 | 4,701,000 | 5.00 | 10.00 | 40.00 | 150 | — |
| 1913 | 4,090,000 | 5.00 | 12.00 | 45.00 | 150 | — |
| 1914 | 18,333,000 | 4.00 | 6.00 | 15.00 | 50.00 | — |
| 1915 | 32,433,000 | 4.00 | 6.00 | 15.00 | 45.00 | — |
| 1916 | 29,530,000 | 4.00 | 6.00 | 15.00 | 40.00 | — |
| 1917 | 11,172,000 | 4.50 | 7.00 | 20.00 | 60.00 | — |
| 1918 | 29,080,000 | 4.00 | 6.00 | 15.00 | 40.00 | — |
| 1919 | 10,267,000 | 4.00 | 6.00 | 18.00 | 60.00 | — |

**1/2 CROWN** **KM# 818.1a** **Weight:** 14.1380 g. **Composition:** 0.5000 Silver .2273 oz. ASW **Ruler:** George V **Reverse:** Crown touches shield

| Date | Mintage | F | VF | XF | Unc | BU |
|---|---|---|---|---|---|---|
| 1920 | 17,983,000 | 3.00 | 5.00 | 18.00 | 75.00 | — |
| 1921 | 23,678,000 | 3.00 | 5.00 | 20.00 | 85.00 | — |
| 1922 | 16,396,999 | 3.00 | 5.00 | 25.00 | 85.00 | — |

**1/2 CROWN** **KM# 818.2** **Weight:** 14.1380 g. **Composition:** 0.5000 Silver .2273 oz. ASW **Ruler:** George V **Reverse:** Groove between crown and shield

| Date | Mintage | F | VF | XF | Unc | BU |
|---|---|---|---|---|---|---|
| 1922 | Inc. above | 3.00 | 5.00 | 25.00 | 85.00 | — |
| 1923 | 26,309,000 | 2.50 | 4.00 | 15.00 | 40.00 | — |
| 1924 | 5,866,000 | 3.00 | 7.00 | 28.00 | 70.00 | — |
| 1925 | 1,413,000 | 12.50 | 30.00 | 125 | 350 | — |
| 1926 | 4,474,000 | 4.00 | 10.00 | 40.00 | 125 | — |

**1/2 CROWN** **KM# 830** **Weight:** 14.1380 g. **Composition:** 0.5000 Silver .2273 oz. ASW **Ruler:** George V **Obverse:** Modified effigy, larger beads

| Date | Mintage | F | VF | XF | Unc | BU |
|---|---|---|---|---|---|---|
| 1926 | Inc. above | 4.00 | 10.00 | 50.00 | 135 | — |
| 1927 | 6,838,000 | 2.00 | 7.00 | 15.00 | 60.00 | — |

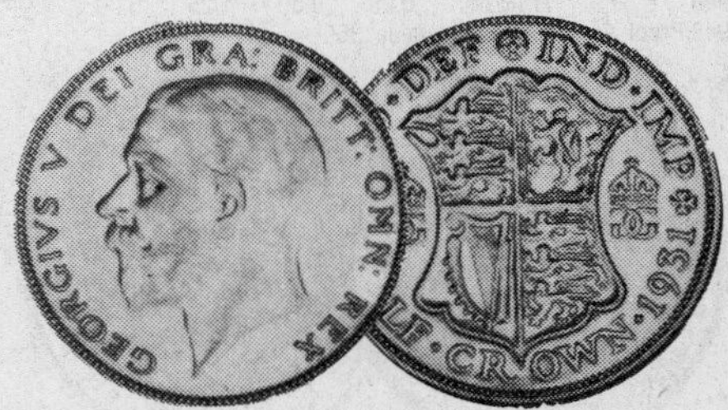

**1/2 CROWN** **KM# 835** **Weight:** 14.1380 g. **Composition:** 0.5000 Silver .2273 oz. ASW **Ruler:** George V

| Date | Mintage | F | VF | XF | Unc | BU |
|---|---|---|---|---|---|---|
| 1927 Proof | 15,000 | Value: 50.00 | | | | |
| 1927 Matte Proof; Rare | — | — | — | — | — | — |

**Note:** There are reportedly 1-2 known of this variety, struck specifically for use in photographs

| Date | Mintage | F | VF | XF | Unc | BU |
|---|---|---|---|---|---|---|
| 1928 | 18,763,000 | 2.00 | 3.00 | 8.00 | 30.00 | — |
| 1928 Proof | — | Value: 600 | | | | |
| 1929 | 17,633,000 | 2.00 | 3.00 | 8.00 | 30.00 | — |
| 1929 Proof | — | Value: 600 | | | | |
| 1930 | 810,000 | 10.00 | 25.00 | 80.00 | 285 | — |
| 1930 Proof | — | Value: 1,000 | | | | |
| 1931 | 11,264,000 | 2.00 | 3.00 | 8.00 | 30.00 | — |
| 1931 Proof | — | Value: 600 | | | | |
| 1932 | 4,794,000 | 4.00 | 8.00 | 18.00 | 60.00 | — |
| 1932 Proof | — | Value: 700 | | | | |
| 1933 | 10,311,000 | 2.00 | 3.00 | 8.00 | 30.00 | — |
| 1933 Proof | — | Value: 600 | | | | |
| 1934 | 2,422,000 | 3.50 | 8.00 | 25.00 | 85.00 | — |
| 1934 Proof | — | Value: 750 | | | | |
| 1935 | 7,022,000 | 2.00 | 3.00 | 8.00 | 28.00 | — |
| 1935 Proof | — | Value: 600 | | | | |
| 1936 | 7,039,000 | 2.00 | 3.00 | 7.00 | 25.00 | — |
| 1936 Proof | — | Value: 600 | | | | |

**1/2 CROWN** **KM# 856** **Weight:** 14.1380 g. **Composition:** 0.5000 Silver .2273 oz. ASW **Ruler:** George VI

| Date | Mintage | F | VF | XF | Unc | BU |
|---|---|---|---|---|---|---|
| 1937 | 9,106,000 | — | BV | 3.50 | 12.00 | — |
| 1937 Proof | 26,000 | Value: 20.00 | | | | |
| 1937 Matte Proof; Rare | — | — | — | — | — | — |

**Note:** There are reportedly 1-2 known of this variety, struck specifically for use in photographs

| Date | Mintage | F | VF | XF | Unc | BU |
|---|---|---|---|---|---|---|
| 1938 | 6,426,000 | BV | 2.50 | 7.50 | 30.00 | — |
| 1938 Proof | — | Value: 750 | | | | |
| 1939 | 15,479,000 | BV | 2.00 | 3.50 | 12.00 | — |
| 1939 Proof | — | Value: 500 | | | | |
| 1940 | 17,948,000 | BV | 2.00 | 3.00 | 10.00 | — |
| 1940 Proof | — | Value: 500 | | | | |
| 1941 | 15,774,000 | BV | 1.75 | 3.00 | 10.00 | — |
| 1941 Proof | — | Value: 500 | | | | |

| Date | Mintage | F | VF | XF | Unc | BU |
|---|---|---|---|---|---|---|
| 1942 | 31,220,000 | BV | 1.75 | 3.00 | 10.00 | — |
| 1942 Proof | — | Value: 400 | | | | |
| 1943 | 15,463,000 | BV | 1.75 | 3.00 | 10.00 | — |
| 1943 Proof | — | Value: 400 | | | | |
| 1944 | 15,255,000 | BV | 1.75 | 3.00 | 10.00 | — |
| 1944 Proof | — | Value: 400 | | | | |
| 1945 | 19,849,000 | BV | 1.75 | 3.00 | 10.00 | — |
| 1945 Proof | — | Value: 500 | | | | |
| 1946 | 22,725,000 | BV | 1.50 | 3.00 | 8.00 | — |
| 1946 Proof | — | Value: 500 | | | | |

**1/2 CROWN** **KM# 866** **Composition:** Copper-Nickel **Ruler:** George VI

| Date | Mintage | F | VF | XF | Unc | BU |
|---|---|---|---|---|---|---|
| 1947 | 21,910,000 | 0.25 | 0.50 | 1.25 | 5.00 | — |
| 1947 Proof | — | Value: 400 | | | | |
| 1948 | 71,165,000 | 0.25 | 0.50 | 1.25 | 5.00 | — |
| 1948 Proof | — | Value: 350 | | | | |

**1/2 CROWN** **KM# 879** **Composition:** Copper-Nickel **Ruler:** George VI **Rev. Legend:** Without IND IMP

| Date | Mintage | F | VF | XF | Unc | BU |
|---|---|---|---|---|---|---|
| 1949 | 28,273,000 | 0.25 | 0.50 | 1.25 | 8.00 | — |
| 1949 Proof | — | Value: 400 | | | | |
| 1950 | 28,336,000 | 0.25 | 0.50 | 1.25 | 8.00 | — |
| 1950 Proof | 18,000 | Value: 12.00 | | | | |
| 1950 Matte Proof; Rare | — | — | — | — | — | — |

**Note:** There are reportedly 1-2 known of this variety, struck specifically for use in photographs

| Date | Mintage | F | VF | XF | Unc | BU |
|---|---|---|---|---|---|---|
| 1951 | 9,004,000 | 0.50 | 0.75 | 1.50 | 8.00 | — |
| 1951 Proof | 20,000 | Value: 12.00 | | | | |
| 1951 Matte Proof; Rare | — | — | — | — | — | — |

**Note:** There are reportedly 1-2 known of this variety, struck specifically for use in photographs

| Date | Mintage | F | VF | XF | Unc | BU |
|---|---|---|---|---|---|---|
| 1952 | — | — | 12,000 | — | — | — |
| 1952 Proof | — | Value: 40,000 | | | | |

**1/2 CROWN** **KM# 893** **Composition:** Copper-Nickel **Ruler:** Elizabeth II

| Date | Mintage | F | VF | XF | Unc | BU |
|---|---|---|---|---|---|---|
| 1953 | 4,333,000 | 0.50 | 0.75 | 1.75 | 4.00 | — |
| 1953 Proof | 40,000 | Value: 12.00 | | | | |
| 1953 Matte Proof; Rare | — | — | — | — | — | — |

**Note:** There are reportedly 1-2 known of this variety, struck specifically for use in photographs

**1/2 CROWN** **KM# 907** **Composition:** Copper-Nickel **Ruler:** Elizabeth II **Obv. Legend:** Without BRITT OMN

| Date | Mintage | F | VF | XF | Unc | BU |
|---|---|---|---|---|---|---|
| 1954 | 11,615,000 | 0.50 | 1.00 | 5.00 | 25.00 | — |
| 1954 Proof | — | Value: 400 | | | | |
| 1955 | 23,629,000 | 0.25 | 0.50 | 1.00 | 6.00 | — |
| 1955 Proof | — | — | — | — | — | — |
| 1956 | 33,935,000 | 0.25 | 0.50 | 1.00 | 6.00 | — |
| 1956 Proof | — | — | — | — | — | — |
| 1957 | 34,201,000 | 0.25 | 0.50 | 0.75 | 4.50 | — |
| 1957 Proof | — | — | — | — | — | — |
| 1958 | 15,746,000 | 0.25 | 0.75 | 4.00 | 15.00 | — |
| 1958 Proof | — | — | — | — | — | — |
| 1959 | 9,029,000 | 1.00 | 1.50 | 6.50 | 30.00 | — |
| 1959 Proof | — | — | — | — | — | — |
| 1960 | 19,929,000 | 0.25 | 0.50 | 0.75 | 6.00 | — |
| 1960 Proof | — | — | — | — | — | — |
| 1961 | 25,888,000 | 0.25 | 0.50 | 0.75 | 2.50 | — |
| 1961 Prooflike | — | — | — | — | 10.00 | — |
| 1961 Proof | — | — | — | — | — | — |
| 1962 | 24,013,000 | 0.25 | 0.50 | 0.75 | 2.50 | — |
| 1962 Proof | — | — | — | — | — | — |
| 1963 | 17,625,000 | 0.25 | 0.50 | 0.75 | 2.50 | — |
| 1963 Proof | — | — | — | — | — | — |
| 1964 | 5,974,000 | 0.25 | 0.50 | 0.75 | 3.50 | — |
| 1965 | 9,778,000 | 0.20 | 0.30 | 0.50 | 2.00 | — |
| 1966 | 13,375,000 | 0.20 | 0.30 | 0.50 | 1.50 | — |
| 1967 | 33,058,000 | 0.20 | 0.30 | 0.50 | 1.50 | — |
| 1970 Proof | 750,000 | Value: 4.00 | | | | |

**CROWN** **KM# 803** **Weight:** 28.2759 g. **Composition:** 0.9250 Silver .8409 oz. ASW **Ruler:** Edward VII

| Date | Mintage | F | VF | XF | Unc | BU |
|---|---|---|---|---|---|---|
| 1902 | 256,000 | 25.00 | 40.00 | 80.00 | 175 | — |
| 1902 Matte Proof | 15,000 | Value: 175 | | | | |

**CROWN** **KM# 836** **Weight:** 28.2759 g. **Composition:** 0.5000 Silver .4546 oz. ASW **Ruler:** George V

| Date | Mintage | F | VF | XF | Unc | BU |
|---|---|---|---|---|---|---|
| 1927 Proof | 15,000 | Value: 200 | | | | |
| 1928 | 9,034 | 50.00 | 80.00 | 125 | 225 | — |
| 1928 Proof | — | Value: 1,800 | | | | |
| 1929 | 4,994 | 60.00 | 80.00 | 125 | 285 | — |
| 1929 Proof | — | Value: 2,000 | | | | |
| 1930 | 4,847 | 70.00 | 100 | 150 | 300 | — |
| 1930 Proof | — | Value: 2,000 | | | | |
| 1931 | 4,056 | 70.00 | 100 | 150 | 350 | — |
| 1931 Proof | — | Value: 2,000 | | | | |
| 1932 | 2,395 | 100 | 200 | 325 | 500 | — |
| 1932 Proof | — | Value: 2,500 | | | | |
| 1933 | 7,132 | 60.00 | 80.00 | 125 | 285 | — |
| 1933 Proof | — | Value: 2,000 | | | | |
| 1934 | 932 | 450 | 750 | 1,200 | 1,800 | — |
| 1934 Proof | — | Value: 3,500 | | | | |
| 1936 | 2,473 | 100 | 200 | 325 | 500 | — |
| 1936 Proof | — | Value: 2,500 | | | | |

**CROWN** **KM# 842** **Weight:** 28.2759 g. **Composition:** 0.5000 Silver .4546 oz. ASW **Ruler:** George V **Subject:** Silver Jubilee **Obverse:** Bust of George V left **Reverse:** St. George slaying the dragon

| Date | Mintage | F | VF | XF | Unc | BU |
|---|---|---|---|---|---|---|
| 1935 Incused edge lettering | 715,000 | 10.00 | 15.00 | 18.00 | 35.00 | — |
| 1935 Proof | — | Value: 2,000 | | | | |
| 1935 Specimen in box of issue | — | — | — | — | 75.00 | — |
| 1935 | Inc. above | — | 250 | 500 | 1,000 | — |

**Note:** (Error) Edge lettering: MEN.ANNO-REGNIXXV

**CROWN** **KM# 842a** **Composition:** 0.9250 Silver **Ruler:** George V **Subject:** Silver Jubilee

| Date | Mintage | F | VF | XF | Unc | BU |
|---|---|---|---|---|---|---|
| 1935 Raised edge lettering | 2,500 | Value: 400 | | | | |
| 1935 Proof | — | Value: 1,250 | | | | |

**Note:** (Error) Edge lettering: DECUS ANNO REGNI TUTAMEN•XXV•

**CROWN** **KM# 842b** **Weight:** 47.8300 g. **Composition:** 0.9170 Gold 1.4096 oz. AGW **Ruler:** George V **Subject:** Silver Jubilee

| Date | Mintage | F | VF | XF | Unc | BU |
|---|---|---|---|---|---|---|
| 1935 Proof | 28 | Value: 14,500 | | | | |

**CROWN** **KM# 857** **Composition:** 0.5000 Silver **Ruler:** George VI

| Date | Mintage | F | VF | XF | Unc | BU |
|---|---|---|---|---|---|---|
| 1937 | 419,000 | 8.00 | 12.00 | 18.00 | 35.00 | — |
| 1937 Proof | 26,000 | Value: 60.00 | | | | |
| 1937 Frosted cameo relief; V.I.P. Proof | — | Value: 500 | | | | |
| 1937 Matte Proof; Rare; 1-2 pieces | — | — | — | — | — | — |

**CROWN** **KM# 880** **Composition:** Copper-Nickel **Ruler:** George VI **Subject:** Festival of Britain

| Date | Mintage | F | VF | XF | Unc | BU |
|---|---|---|---|---|---|---|
| 1951 Prooflike | 2,004,000 | — | — | — | 12.00 | — |
| 1951 Proof | — | Value: 25.00 | | | | |
| 1951 30-50 pieces; Frosted cameo relief; V.I.P. Proof | — | Value: 450 | | | | |
| 1951 Matte Proof; Rare; 1-2 pieces | — | — | — | — | — | — |

**CROWN** **KM# 894** **Composition:** Copper-Nickel **Ruler:** Elizabeth II **Subject:** Coronation of Queen Elizabeth II

| Date | Mintage | F | VF | XF | Unc | BU |
|---|---|---|---|---|---|---|
| 1953 | 5,963,000 | — | — | 5.00 | 10.00 | — |
| 1953 Proof | 40,000 | Value: 25.00 | | | | |
| 1953 20-30 pieces; V.I.P. Proof | — | Value: 450 | | | | |
| 1953 Matte Proof; Rare; 1-2 pieces | — | — | — | — | — | — |

**CROWN** **KM# 909** **Composition:** Copper-Nickel **Ruler:** Elizabeth II **Subject:** British Exhibition in New York

| Date | Mintage | F | VF | XF | Unc | BU |
|---|---|---|---|---|---|---|
| 1960 | 1,024,000 | — | — | 6.50 | 9.50 | — |
| 1960 Prooflike | 70,000 | — | — | — | 22.00 | — |
| 1960 V.I.P. Proof; 30-50 pieces | — | Value: 450 | | | | |

**CROWN** **KM# 910** **Composition:** Copper-Nickel **Ruler:** Elizabeth II **Reverse:** Head of Winston Churchill right **Note:** The Specimen is struck with satin-finish.

| Date | Mintage | F | VF | XF | Unc | BU |
|---|---|---|---|---|---|---|
| 1965 | 9,640,000 | — | — | 0.65 | 1.00 | — |
| 1965 Specimen | — | — | — | — | 600 | — |

## SOVEREIGN COINAGE

**1/2 SOVEREIGN** **KM# 784** **Weight:** 3.9940 g. **Composition:** 0.9170 Gold .1177 oz. AGW **Ruler:** Victoria

| Date | Mintage | F | VF | XF | Unc | BU |
|---|---|---|---|---|---|---|
| 1901 | 2,037,999 | BV | 50.00 | 75.00 | 125 | — |

**1/2 SOVEREIGN** **KM# 804** **Weight:** 3.9940 g. **Composition:** 0.9170 Gold .1177 oz. AGW **Ruler:** Edward VII

| Date | Mintage | F | VF | XF | Unc | BU |
|---|---|---|---|---|---|---|
| 1902 | 4,244,000 | BV | 65.00 | 75.00 | 100 | — |
| 1902 Proof | 15,000 | Value: 175 | | | | |
| 1903 | 2,522,000 | BV | 65.00 | 75.00 | 100 | — |
| 1904 | 1,717,000 | BV | 65.00 | 75.00 | 100 | — |
| 1905 | 3,024,000 | BV | 65.00 | 75.00 | 100 | — |
| 1906 | 4,245,000 | BV | 65.00 | 75.00 | 100 | — |
| 1907 | 4,233,000 | BV | 65.00 | 75.00 | 100 | — |
| 1908 | 3,997,000 | BV | 65.00 | 75.00 | 100 | — |
| 1909 | 4,011,000 | BV | 65.00 | 75.00 | 100 | — |
| 1910 | 5,024,000 | BV | 65.00 | 75.00 | 100 | — |

**1/2 SOVEREIGN** **KM# 819** **Weight:** 3.9940 g. **Composition:** 0.9170 Gold .1177 oz. AGW **Ruler:** George V

| Date | Mintage | F | VF | XF | Unc | BU |
|---|---|---|---|---|---|---|
| 1911 | 6,104,000 | BV | 65.00 | 75.00 | 100 | — |
| 1911 Proof | 3,764 | Value: 325 | | | | |
| 1912 | 6,224,000 | BV | 65.00 | 75.00 | 100 | — |
| 1913 | 6,094,000 | BV | 65.00 | 75.00 | 100 | — |
| 1914 | 7,251,000 | BV | 65.00 | 75.00 | 100 | — |
| 1915 | 2,043,000 | BV | 65.00 | 75.00 | 100 | — |

**1/2 SOVEREIGN** **KM# 858** **Weight:** 3.9940 g. **Composition:** 0.9170 Gold .1177 oz. AGW **Ruler:** George VI

| Date | Mintage | F | VF | XF | Unc | BU |
|---|---|---|---|---|---|---|
| 1937 Proof | 5,500 | Value: 275 | | | | |
| 1937 Matte Proof; Unique | — | — | — | — | — | — |

**1/2 SOVEREIGN** **KM# 922** **Weight:** 3.9900 g. **Composition:** 0.9170 Gold .1176 oz. AGW **Ruler:** Elizabeth II

| Date | Mintage | F | VF | XF | Unc | BU |
|---|---|---|---|---|---|---|
| 1980 Proof | 10,000 | Value: 60.00 | | | | |
| 1982 | 2,500,000 | — | — | — | 50.00 | — |
| 1982 Proof | 23,000 | Value: 60.00 | | | | |
| 1983 Proof | 22,000 | Value: 60.00 | | | | |
| 1984 Proof | 22,000 | Value: 60.00 | | | | |

**1/2 SOVEREIGN** **KM# 942** **Weight:** 3.9900 g. **Composition:** 0.9170 Gold .1176 oz. AGW **Ruler:** Elizabeth II **Obverse:** New portrait of Elizabeth II

| Date | Mintage | F | VF | XF | Unc | BU |
|---|---|---|---|---|---|---|
| 1985 Proof | 25,000 | Value: 60.00 | | | | |
| 1986 Proof | 25,000 | Value: 60.00 | | | | |
| 1987 Proof | 23,000 | Value: 60.00 | | | | |
| 1988 Proof | Est. 23,000 | Value: 60.00 | | | | |
| 1990 Proof | Est. 20,000 | Value: 85.00 | | | | |
| 1991 Proof | Est. 9,000 | Value: 100 | | | | |
| 1992 Proof | 7,500 | Value: 100 | | | | |
| 1993 Proof | 7,500 | Value: 100 | | | | |
| 1994 Proof | Est. 7,500 | Value: 100 | | | | |
| 1995 Proof | 4,900 | Value: 100 | | | | |
| 1996 Proof | 5,730 | Value: 125 | | | | |
| 1997 Proof | 7,500 | Value: 125 | | | | |

**1/2 SOVEREIGN** **KM# 955** **Weight:** 3.9900 g. **Composition:** 0.9170 Gold .1176 oz. AGW **Ruler:** Elizabeth II **Subject:** 500th Anniversary of the Gold Sovereign

| Date | Mintage | F | VF | XF | Unc | BU |
|---|---|---|---|---|---|---|
| ND(1989) Proof | Est. 25,000 | Value: 85.00 | | | | |

**1/2 SOVEREIGN** **KM# 1001** **Weight:** 3.9900 g. **Composition:** 0.9170 Gold .1176 oz. AGW **Ruler:** Elizabeth II **Obverse:** Rank-Broadley portrait of Queen Elizabeth II **Reverse:** St. George slaying the dragon

| Date | Mintage | F | VF | XF | Unc | BU |
|---|---|---|---|---|---|---|
| 1998 Proof | 6,144 | Value: 125 | | | | |
| 1999 Proof | 7,500 | Value: 125 | | | | |
| 2000 Proof | 7,500 | Value: 125 | | | | |

**SOVEREIGN** **KM# 785** **Weight:** 7.9881 g. **Composition:** 0.9170 Gold .2354 oz. AGW **Ruler:** Victoria

| Date | Mintage | F | VF | XF | Unc | BU |
|---|---|---|---|---|---|---|
| 1901 | 1,579,000 | — | — | BV | 115 | — |

**SOVEREIGN** **KM# 805** **Weight:** 7.9881 g. **Composition:** 0.9170 Gold .2354 oz. AGW **Ruler:** Edward VII

| Date | Mintage | F | VF | XF | Unc | BU |
|---|---|---|---|---|---|---|
| 1902 | 4,738,000 | — | — | BV | 110 | — |
| 1902 Proof | 15,000 | Value: 275 | | | | |
| 1903 | 8,889,000 | — | — | BV | 110 | — |
| 1904 | 10,041,000 | — | — | BV | 110 | — |
| 1905 | 5,910,000 | — | — | BV | 110 | — |
| 1906 | 10,467,000 | — | — | BV | 110 | — |
| 1907 | 18,459,000 | — | — | BV | 110 | — |
| 1908 | 11,729,000 | — | — | BV | 110 | — |
| 1909 | 12,157,000 | — | — | BV | 110 | — |
| 1910 | 22,380,000 | — | — | BV | 110 | — |

**SOVEREIGN** **KM# 820** **Weight:** 7.9881 g. **Composition:** 0.9170 Gold .2354 oz. AGW **Ruler:** George V

| Date | Mintage | F | VF | XF | Unc | BU |
|---|---|---|---|---|---|---|
| 1911 | 30,044,000 | — | — | BV | 110 | — |
| 1911 Proof | 3,764 | Value: 500 | | | | |
| 1912 | 30,318,000 | — | — | BV | 110 | — |
| 1913 | 24,540,000 | — | — | BV | 110 | — |
| 1914 | 11,501,000 | — | — | BV | 110 | — |
| 1915 | 20,295,000 | — | — | BV | 110 | — |
| 1916 | 1,554,000 | — | — | BV | 115 | — |
| 1917 | 1,014,999 | 2,850 | 3,175 | 5,500 | 10,000 | — |
| 1925 | 4,406,000 | — | — | BV | 110 | — |

**SOVEREIGN** **KM# 859** **Weight:** 7.9881 g. **Composition:** 0.9170 Gold .2354 oz. AGW **Ruler:** George VI

| Date | Mintage | F | VF | XF | Unc | BU |
|---|---|---|---|---|---|---|
| 1937 Proof | 5,500 | Value: 550 | | | | |
| 1937 Matte Proof; Unique | — | — | — | — | — | — |

**SOVEREIGN** **KM# 908** **Weight:** 7.9881 g. **Composition:** 0.9170 Gold .2354 oz. AGW **Ruler:** Elizabeth II

| Date | Mintage | F | VF | XF | Unc | BU |
|---|---|---|---|---|---|---|
| 1957 | 2,072,000 | — | — | BV | 95.00 | — |
| 1957 Proof | — | — | — | — | — | — |
| 1958 | 8,700,000 | — | — | BV | 90.00 | — |
| 1958 Proof | — | — | — | — | — | — |
| 1959 | 1,358,000 | — | — | BV | 115 | — |
| 1959 Proof | — | — | — | — | — | — |
| 1962 | 3,000,000 | — | — | BV | 90.00 | — |
| 1962 Proof | — | — | — | — | — | — |
| 1963 | 7,400,000 | — | — | BV | 90.00 | — |
| 1963 Proof | — | — | — | — | — | — |
| 1964 | 3,000,000 | — | — | BV | 90.00 | — |
| 1965 | 3,800,000 | — | — | BV | 90.00 | — |
| 1966 | 7,050,000 | — | — | BV | 90.00 | — |
| 1967 | 5,000,000 | — | — | BV | 90.00 | — |
| 1968 | 4,203,000 | — | — | BV | 90.00 | — |

**SOVEREIGN** **KM# 919** **Weight:** 7.9881 g. **Composition:** 0.9170 Gold .2354 oz. AGW **Ruler:** Elizabeth II

| Date | Mintage | F | VF | XF | Unc | BU |
|---|---|---|---|---|---|---|
| 1974 | 5,003,000 | — | — | BV | 90.00 | — |
| 1976 | 4,150,000 | — | — | BV | 90.00 | — |
| 1978 | 6,350,000 | — | — | BV | 90.00 | — |
| 1979 | 9,100,000 | — | — | BV | 90.00 | — |
| 1979 Proof | 50,000 | Value: 110 | | | | |
| 1980 | 5,100,000 | — | — | BV | 90.00 | — |
| 1980 Proof | 91,000 | Value: 110 | | | | |
| 1981 | 5,000,000 | — | — | BV | 90.00 | — |
| 1981 Proof | 33,000 | Value: 110 | | | | |
| 1982 | 2,950,000 | — | — | BV | 90.00 | — |
| 1982 Proof | 23,000 | Value: 110 | | | | |
| 1983 Proof | 21,000 | Value: 110 | | | | |
| 1984 Proof | 20,000 | Value: 110 | | | | |

**SOVEREIGN** **KM# 943** **Weight:** 7.9881 g. **Composition:** 0.9170 Gold .2354 oz. AGW **Ruler:** Elizabeth II **Obverse:** New portrait of Elizabeth II

| Date | Mintage | F | VF | XF | Unc | BU |
|---|---|---|---|---|---|---|
| 1985 Proof | 17,000 | Value: 135 | | | | |
| 1986 Proof | 25,000 | Value: 135 | | | | |
| 1987 Proof | 22,000 | Value: 135 | | | | |
| 1988 Proof | Est. 25,000 | Value: 135 | | | | |
| 1990 Proof | Est. 20,000 | Value: 150 | | | | |
| 1991 Proof | Est. 9,000 | Value: 150 | | | | |
| 1992 Proof | 7,500 | Value: 175 | | | | |
| 1993 Proof | 7,500 | Value: 175 | | | | |
| 1994 Proof | Est. 7,500 | Value: 175 | | | | |
| 1995 Proof | 7,500 | Value: 175 | | | | |
| 1996 Proof | 7,500 | Value: 175 | | | | |
| 1997 Proof | 7,500 | Value: 175 | | | | |

**SOVEREIGN** **KM# 956** **Weight:** 7.9881 g. **Composition:** 0.9170 Gold .2354 oz. AGW **Ruler:** Elizabeth II **Subject:** 500th Anniversary of the Gold Sovereign

| Date | Mintage | F | VF | XF | Unc | BU |
|---|---|---|---|---|---|---|
| ND(1989) Proof | Est. 28,000 | Value: 175 | | | | |

**SOVEREIGN** **KM# 1002** **Weight:** 7.9881 g. **Composition:** 0.9170 Gold .2354 oz. AGW **Ruler:** Elizabeth II **Obverse:** Rank-Broadley portrait of Queen Elizabeth II **Reverse:** St. George slaying the dragon

| Date | Mintage | F | VF | XF | Unc | BU |
|---|---|---|---|---|---|---|
| 1998 Proof | 10,000 | Value: 175 | | | | |
| 1999 Proof | 10,000 | Value: 175 | | | | |
| 2000 Proof | 10,000 | Value: 175 | | | | |

**2 POUNDS** **KM# 806** **Weight:** 15.9761 g. **Composition:** 0.9170 Gold .4708 oz. AGW **Ruler:** Edward VII

| Date | Mintage | F | VF | XF | Unc | BU |
|---|---|---|---|---|---|---|
| 1902 | 46,000 | 250 | 300 | 450 | 550 | — |
| 1902 Proof | 8,066 | Value: 650 | | | | |

**Note:** Proof issues with mint mark S below right rear hoof of horse were struck at Sydney, refer to Australia listings

**2 POUNDS** **KM# 821** **Weight:** 15.9761 g. **Composition:** 0.9170 Gold .4708 oz. AGW **Ruler:** George V

| Date | Mintage | F | VF | XF | Unc | BU |
|---|---|---|---|---|---|---|
| 1911 Proof | 2,812 | Value: 1,200 | | | | |

**2 POUNDS** **KM# 860** **Weight:** 15.9761 g. **Composition:** 0.9170 Gold .4708 oz. AGW **Ruler:** George VI

| Date | Mintage | F | VF | XF | Unc | BU |
|---|---|---|---|---|---|---|
| 1937 Proof | 5,500 | Value: 600 | | | | |
| 1937 Matte Proof; Unique | — | — | — | — | — | — |

**2 POUNDS** **KM# 923** **Weight:** 15.9200 g. **Composition:** 0.9170 Gold .4694 oz. AGW **Ruler:** Elizabeth II

| Date | Mintage | F | VF | XF | Unc | BU |
|---|---|---|---|---|---|---|
| 1980 Proof | 10,000 | Value: 225 | | | | |
| 1982 Proof | 2,500 | Value: 250 | | | | |
| 1983 Proof | 13,000 | Value: 225 | | | | |

**2 POUNDS** **KM# 944** **Weight:** 15.9200 g. **Composition:** 0.9170 Gold .4694 oz. AGW **Ruler:** Elizabeth II **Obverse:** New portrait of Elizabeth II

| Date | Mintage | F | VF | XF | Unc | BU |
|---|---|---|---|---|---|---|
| 1985 Proof | 5,849 | Value: 275 | | | | |
| 1987 Proof | 14,000 | Value: 275 | | | | |
| 1988 Proof | 15,000 | Value: 275 | | | | |
| 1990 Proof | Est. 12,000 | Value: 275 | | | | |
| 1991 Proof | Est. 5,000 | Value: 300 | | | | |
| 1992 Proof | 3,000 | Value: 300 | | | | |
| 1993 Proof | 3,000 | Value: 300 | | | | |
| 1999 Proof | — | Value: 400 | | | | |

**2 POUNDS** **KM# 957** **Weight:** 15.9800 g. **Composition:** 0.9170 Gold .4708 oz. AGW **Ruler:** Elizabeth II **Subject:** 500th Anniversary of the Gold Sovereign

| Date | Mintage | F | VF | XF | Unc | BU |
|---|---|---|---|---|---|---|
| ND(1989) Proof | Est. 17,000 | Value: 350 | | | | |

**5 POUNDS** **KM# 807** **Weight:** 39.9403 g. **Composition:** 0.9170 Gold 1.1773 oz. AGW **Ruler:** Edward VII

| Date | Mintage | F | VF | XF | Unc | BU |
|---|---|---|---|---|---|---|
| 1902 | Est. 35,000 | 600 | 650 | 750 | 1,000 | — |

**Note:** 27,000 pieces were remelted

| Date | Mintage | F | VF | XF | Unc | BU |
|---|---|---|---|---|---|---|
| 1902 Proof | 8,066 | Value: 1,250 | | | | |

**Note:** Proof issues with mint mark S below right rear hoof of horse were struck at Sydney, refer to Australia listings

**5 POUNDS** **KM# 822** **Weight:** 39.9403 g. **Composition:** 0.9170 Gold 1.1773 oz. AGW **Ruler:** George V

| Date | Mintage | F | VF | XF | Unc | BU |
|---|---|---|---|---|---|---|
| 1911 Proof | 2,812 | Value: 2,000 | | | | |

**5 POUNDS** **KM# 861** **Weight:** 39.9403 g. **Composition:** 0.9170 Gold 1.1773 oz. AGW **Ruler:** George V

| Date | Mintage | F | VF | XF | Unc | BU |
|---|---|---|---|---|---|---|
| 1937 Proof | 5,500 | Value: 1,000 | | | | |

**Note:** Impaired and blemished proofs of the 1937 issue are common and trade at much lower values. The value listed here is for blemish free examples

| Date | Mintage | F | VF | XF | Unc | BU |
|---|---|---|---|---|---|---|
| 1937 Matte Proof; Unique | — | — | — | — | — | — |

**5 POUNDS** **KM# 924** **Weight:** 39.9400 g. **Composition:** 0.9170 Gold 1.1775 oz. AGW **Ruler:** Elizabeth II

| Date | Mintage | F | VF | XF | Unc | BU |
|---|---|---|---|---|---|---|
| 1980 Proof | 10,000 | Value: 550 | | | | |
| 1981 Proof | 5,400 | Value: 650 | | | | |
| 1982 Proof | 2,500 | Value: 650 | | | | |
| 1984 | 25,000 | — | — | — | 550 | — |
| 1984 Proof | 8,000 | Value: 650 | | | | |

**5 POUNDS** **KM# 945** **Weight:** 39.9400 g. **Composition:** 0.9170 Gold 1.1775 oz. AGW **Ruler:** Elizabeth II **Obverse:** New portrait of Elizabeth II

| Date | Mintage | F | VF | XF | Unc | BU |
|---|---|---|---|---|---|---|
| 1985 | 14,000 | — | — | — | 550 | — |
| 1985 Proof | 13,000 | Value: 650 | | | | |
| 1986 | 7,723 | — | — | — | 550 | — |
| 1990 | 1,226 | — | — | — | 550 | — |
| 1990 Proof | Est. 2,500 | Value: 650 | | | | |
| 1991 | 976 | — | — | — | 575 | — |
| 1991 Proof | Est. 1,500 | Value: 675 | | | | |
| 1992 Proof | 1,250 | Value: 675 | | | | |
| 1992 | 797 | — | — | — | 575 | — |
| 1993 | 906 | — | — | — | 575 | — |
| 1994 Proof | Est. 1,250 | Value: 675 | | | | |
| 1995 Proof | Est. 1,000 | Value: 675 | | | | |
| 1995 Proof | Est. 1,250 | Value: 675 | | | | |
| 1996 | 901 | — | — | — | 575 | — |
| 1997 | 802 | — | — | — | 575 | — |

**5 POUNDS** **KM# 949** **Weight:** 39.9400 g. **Composition:** 0.9170 Gold 1.1775 oz. AGW **Ruler:** Elizabeth II **Obverse:** Draped bust

| Date | Mintage | F | VF | XF | Unc | BU |
|---|---|---|---|---|---|---|
| 1987 | 10,000 | — | — | — | 550 | — |
| 1988 | Est. 10,000 | — | — | — | 550 | — |

**5 POUNDS** **KM# 958** **Weight:** 39.9400 g. **Composition:** 0.9170 Gold 1.1775 oz. AGW **Ruler:** Elizabeth II **Subject:** 500th Anniversary of the Gold Sovereign

| Date | Mintage | F | VF | XF | Unc | BU |
|---|---|---|---|---|---|---|
| 1989 | 10,000 | — | — | — | 600 | — |
| 1989 Proof | Est. 5,000 | Value: 650 | | | | |



**5 POUNDS** **KM# 1003** **Weight:** 39.9400 g. **Composition:** 0.9170 Gold 1.1775 oz. AGW **Ruler:** Elizabeth II **Obverse:** Rank-Broadley portrait of Queen Elizabeth II **Reverse:** St. George slaying dragon **Edge:** Reeded **Size:** 36 mm.

| Date | Mintage | F | VF | XF | Unc | BU |
|---|---|---|---|---|---|---|
| 1999 Proof | — | Value: 925 | | | | |
| 2000 | 10,000 | — | — | — | 525 | — |

## DECIMAL COINAGE

1971-1981, 100 New Pence = 1 Pound; 1982, 100 Pence = 1 Pound

**1/2 NEW PENNY** **KM# 914** **Composition:** Bronze **Ruler:** Elizabeth II

| Date | Mintage | F | VF | XF | Unc | BU |
|---|---|---|---|---|---|---|
| 1971 | 1,394,188,000 | — | — | 0.10 | 0.20 | — |
| 1971 Proof | 350,000 | Value: 1.00 | | | | |
| 1972 Proof | 150,000 | Value: 3.00 | | | | |
| 1973 | 365,680,000 | — | — | 0.15 | 0.40 | — |
| 1973 Proof | 100,000 | Value: 1.00 | | | | |
| 1974 | 365,448,000 | — | — | 0.15 | 0.35 | — |
| 1974 Proof | 100,000 | Value: 1.00 | | | | |
| 1975 | 197,600,000 | — | — | 0.15 | 0.45 | — |
| 1975 Proof | 100,000 | Value: 1.00 | | | | |
| 1976 | 412,172,000 | — | — | 0.15 | 0.35 | — |
| 1976 Proof | 100,000 | Value: 1.00 | | | | |
| 1977 | 66,367,999 | — | — | 0.15 | 0.25 | — |
| 1977 Proof | 194,000 | Value: 1.00 | | | | |
| 1978 | 59,532,000 | — | — | 0.15 | 0.25 | — |
| 1978 Proof | 88,000 | Value: 1.00 | | | | |
| 1979 | 219,132,000 | — | — | 0.15 | 0.25 | — |
| 1979 Proof | 81,000 | Value: 1.00 | | | | |
| 1980 | 202,788,000 | — | — | 0.15 | 0.25 | — |
| 1980 Proof | 143,000 | Value: 1.00 | | | | |
| 1981 | 32,484,000 | — | — | 0.15 | 0.45 | — |
| 1981 Proof | 100,000 | Value: 1.00 | | | | |

**1/2 PENNY** **KM# 926** **Composition:** Bronze **Ruler:** Elizabeth II **Reverse:** HALF PENNY above crown and fraction **Note:** Denomination now demonitized.

| Date | Mintage | F | VF | XF | Unc | BU |
|---|---|---|---|---|---|---|
| 1982 | 190,752,000 | — | — | 0.15 | 0.25 | — |
| 1982 Proof | 107,000 | Value: 1.00 | | | | |
| 1983 | 7,600,000 | — | — | 0.25 | 0.60 | — |
| 1983 Proof | 108,000 | Value: 1.50 | | | | |
| 1984 In sets only | Est. 159,000 | — | — | — | 2.00 | — |
| 1984 Proof | 107,000 | Value: 2.50 | | | | |

**NEW PENNY** **KM# 915** **Composition:** Bronze **Ruler:** Elizabeth II

| Date | Mintage | F | VF | XF | Unc | BU |
|---|---|---|---|---|---|---|
| 1971 | 1,521,666,000 | — | — | 0.15 | 0.25 | — |
| 1971 Proof | 350,000 | Value: 1.25 | | | | |
| 1972 Proof | 150,000 | Value: 3.00 | | | | |
| 1973 | 280,196,000 | — | — | 0.15 | 0.45 | — |
| 1973 Proof | 100,000 | Value: 1.25 | | | | |
| 1974 | 330,892,000 | — | — | 0.15 | 0.45 | — |
| 1974 Proof | 100,000 | Value: 1.25 | | | | |
| 1975 | 221,604,000 | — | — | 0.15 | 0.60 | — |
| 1975 Proof | 100,000 | Value: 1.25 | | | | |
| 1976 | 241,800,000 | — | — | 0.15 | 0.30 | — |
| 1976 Proof | 100,000 | Value: 1.25 | | | | |
| 1977 | 285,430,000 | — | — | 0.15 | 0.25 | — |
| 1977 Proof | 194,000 | Value: 1.25 | | | | |
| 1978 | 292,770,000 | — | — | 0.15 | 0.50 | — |
| 1978 Proof | 88,000 | Value: 1.25 | | | | |
| 1979 | 459,000,000 | — | — | 0.15 | 0.25 | — |
| 1979 Proof | 81,000 | Value: 1.25 | | | | |
| 1980 | 416,304,000 | — | — | 0.15 | 0.25 | — |
| 1980 Proof | 143,000 | Value: 1.25 | | | | |
| 1981 | 301,800,000 | — | — | 0.15 | 0.25 | — |
| 1981 Proof | 100,000 | Value: 1.25 | | | | |

**PENNY** **KM# 927** **Composition:** Bronze **Ruler:** Elizabeth II

| Date | Mintage | F | VF | XF | Unc | BU |
|---|---|---|---|---|---|---|
| 1982 | 121,429,000 | — | — | 0.15 | 0.25 | — |
| 1982 Proof | 107,000 | Value: 1.25 | | | | |
| 1983 | 243,002,000 | — | — | 0.15 | 0.40 | — |
| 1983 Proof | 108,000 | Value: 1.25 | | | | |
| 1984 | 154,760,000 | — | — | 0.20 | 1.25 | — |
| 1984 Proof | 107,000 | Value: 1.25 | | | | |

**PENNY** **KM# 935** **Composition:** Bronze **Ruler:** Elizabeth II **Note:** Reduced size.

| Date | Mintage | F | VF | XF | Unc | BU |
|---|---|---|---|---|---|---|
| 1985 | 200,605,000 | — | — | 0.15 | 0.35 | — |
| 1985 Proof | 102,000 | Value: 1.25 | | | | |
| 1986 | 369,989,000 | — | — | 0.15 | 0.35 | — |

| Date | Mintage | F | VF | XF | Unc | BU |
|---|---|---|---|---|---|---|
| 1986 Proof | 125,000 | Value: 1.25 | | | | |
| 1987 | 499,946,000 | — | — | 0.15 | 0.25 | — |
| 1987 Proof | 89,000 | Value: 1.25 | | | | |
| 1988 | 793,492,000 | — | — | 0.15 | 0.25 | — |
| 1988 Proof | 125,000 | Value: 1.25 | | | | |
| 1989 | 658,142,000 | — | — | 0.15 | 0.25 | — |
| 1989 Proof | 100,000 | Value: 1.25 | | | | |
| 1990 | 529,048,000 | — | — | 0.15 | 0.25 | — |
| 1990 Proof | 100,000 | Value: 1.25 | | | | |
| 1991 | 206,458,000 | — | — | 0.15 | 0.25 | — |
| 1991 Proof | — | Value: 1.25 | | | | |
| 1992 | — | — | — | — | 0.50 | — |
| 1992 Proof | — | Value: 1.75 | | | | |

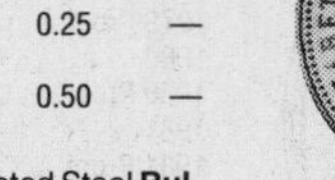

**PENNY** **KM# 935a** **Composition:** Copper Plated Steel **Ruler:** Elizabeth II

| Date | Mintage | F | VF | XF | Unc | BU |
|---|---|---|---|---|---|---|
| 1992 | 253,867,000 | — | — | 0.15 | 0.25 | — |
| 1993 | 602,590,000 | — | — | 0.15 | 0.25 | — |
| 1993 Proof | — | Value: 1.25 | | | | |
| 1994 | 843,834,000 | — | — | 0.15 | 0.25 | — |
| 1994 Proof | — | Value: 1.25 | | | | |
| 1995 | 303,314,000 | — | — | 0.15 | 0.25 | — |
| 1995 Proof | — | Value: 1.25 | | | | |
| 1996 | 723,840,000 | — | — | — | 0.25 | — |
| 1996 Proof | — | Value: 1.25 | | | | |
| 1997 | 396,874,000 | — | — | — | 0.25 | — |
| 1997 Proof | — | Value: 1.25 | | | | |

**PENNY** **KM# 935b** **Composition:** 0.9250 Silver **Ruler:** Elizabeth II

| Date | Mintage | F | VF | XF | Unc | BU |
|---|---|---|---|---|---|---|
| 1996 Proof | — | Value: 16.50 | | | | |

**PENNY** **KM# 986** **Composition:** Copper Plated Steel **Ruler:** Elizabeth II **Obverse:** Rank-Broadley effigy of Queen Elizabeth II **Reverse:** Crowned portcullis

| Date | Mintage | F | VF | XF | Unc | BU |
|---|---|---|---|---|---|---|
| 1998 | 680,054,000 | — | — | — | 0.20 | — |
| 1998 Proof | Est. 100,000 | Value: 3.25 | | | | |

**PENNY** **KM# 986a** **Composition:** Bronze **Ruler:** Elizabeth II

| Date | Mintage | F | VF | XF | Unc | BU |
|---|---|---|---|---|---|---|
| 1999 | 916,000,000 | — | — | — | 0.20 | — |
| 1999 Proof | 79,401 | Value: 1.25 | | | | |
| 2000 | — | — | — | — | 0.20 | — |
| 2000 Proof | 100,000 | Value: 1.25 | | | | |
| 2001 | — | — | — | — | 0.20 | — |
| 2001 Proof | 100,000 | Value: 1.25 | | | | |

**2 NEW PENCE** **KM# 916** **Composition:** Bronze **Ruler:** Elizabeth II

| Date | Mintage | F | VF | XF | Unc | BU |
|---|---|---|---|---|---|---|
| 1971 | 1,454,856,000 | — | — | 0.10 | 0.20 | — |
| 1971 Proof | 350,000 | Value: 1.50 | | | | |
| 1972 Proof | 150,000 | Value: 3.50 | | | | |
| 1973 Proof | 100,000 | Value: 3.50 | | | | |
| 1974 Proof | 100,000 | Value: 3.50 | | | | |
| 1975 | 145,545,000 | — | — | 0.15 | 0.40 | — |
| 1975 Proof | 100,000 | Value: 1.50 | | | | |
| 1976 | 181,379,000 | — | — | 0.15 | 0.30 | — |
| 1976 Proof | 100,000 | Value: 1.50 | | | | |
| 1977 | 109,281,000 | — | — | 0.15 | 0.25 | — |
| 1977 Proof | 194,000 | Value: 1.50 | | | | |
| 1978 | 189,658,000 | — | — | 0.15 | 0.40 | — |
| 1978 Proof | 88,000 | Value: 1.50 | | | | |
| 1979 | 268,300,000 | — | — | 0.15 | 0.25 | — |
| 1979 Proof | 81,000 | Value: 1.50 | | | | |
| 1980 | 408,527,000 | — | — | 0.15 | 0.25 | — |
| 1980 Proof | 143,000 | Value: 1.50 | | | | |
| 1981 | 353,191,000 | — | — | 0.15 | 0.25 | — |
| 1981 Proof | 100,000 | Value: 1.50 | | | | |

**2 PENCE** **KM# 928** **Composition:** Bronze **Ruler:** Elizabeth II

| Date | Mintage | F | VF | XF | Unc | BU |
|---|---|---|---|---|---|---|
| 1982 In sets only | 205,000 | — | — | — | 1.00 | — |
| 1982 Proof | 107,000 | Value: 1.50 | | | | |
| 1983 In sets only | 631,000 | — | — | — | 1.00 | — |
| 1983 Proof | 108,000 | Value: 1.50 | | | | |
| 1984 In sets only | 159,000 | — | — | — | 1.50 | — |
| 1984 Proof | 107,000 | Value: 1.50 | | | | |

**2 PENCE** **KM# 936** **Composition:** Bronze **Ruler:** Elizabeth II

| Date | Mintage | F | VF | XF | Unc | BU |
|---|---|---|---|---|---|---|
| 1985 | 107,113,000 | — | — | 0.15 | 0.25 | — |
| 1985 Proof | 102,000 | Value: 1.50 | | | | |
| 1986 | 168,968,000 | — | — | 0.15 | 0.50 | — |
| 1986 Proof | 125,000 | Value: 1.50 | | | | |
| 1987 | 218,101,000 | — | — | 0.15 | 0.25 | — |
| 1987 Proof | 89,000 | Value: 1.50 | | | | |
| 1988 | 419,889,000 | — | — | 0.15 | 0.25 | — |
| 1988 Proof | 125,000 | Value: 1.50 | | | | |
| 1989 | 359,226,000 | — | — | 0.15 | 0.25 | — |
| 1989 Proof | 100,000 | Value: 1.50 | | | | |
| 1990 | 204,500,000 | — | — | 0.15 | 0.25 | — |
| 1990 Proof | 100,000 | Value: 1.50 | | | | |
| 1991 | 86,625,000 | — | — | 0.15 | 0.25 | — |
| 1991 Proof | — | Value: 1.50 | | | | |
| 1992 | 96,000,000 | — | — | — | 0.50 | — |

**2 PENCE** **KM# 936a** **Composition:** Copper Plated Steel **Ruler:** Elizabeth II

| Date | Mintage | F | VF | XF | Unc | BU |
|---|---|---|---|---|---|---|
| 1992 | 102,247,000 | — | — | 0.15 | 0.25 | — |
| 1993 | 235,674,000 | — | — | 0.15 | 0.25 | — |
| 1993 Proof | — | Value: 1.50 | | | | |
| 1994 | 531,628,000 | — | — | 0.10 | 0.25 | — |
| 1994 Proof | — | Value: 1.50 | | | | |
| 1995 | 124,482,000 | — | — | 0.10 | 0.25 | — |
| 1995 Proof | — | Value: 1.50 | | | | |
| 1996 | 296,278,000 | — | — | 0.10 | 0.25 | — |
| 1996 Proof | — | Value: 1.50 | | | | |
| 1997 | 439,975,000 | — | — | 0.10 | 0.25 | — |
| 1997 Proof | — | Value: 1.50 | | | | |

**2 PENCE** **KM# 936b** **Composition:** 0.9250 Silver **Ruler:** Elizabeth II

| Date | Mintage | F | VF | XF | Unc | BU |
|---|---|---|---|---|---|---|
| 1996 Proof | — | Value: 17.50 | | | | |

**2 PENCE** **KM# 987** **Composition:** Copper Plated Steel **Ruler:** Elizabeth II **Obverse:** Rank-Broadley effigy of Queen Elizabeth II **Reverse:** Prince of Wales badge

| Date | Mintage | F | VF | XF | Unc | BU |
|---|---|---|---|---|---|---|
| 1998 | 96,084,000 | — | — | — | 0.25 | — |
| 1998 Proof | Est. 100,000 | Value: 3.25 | | | | |

**2 PENCE** **KM# 987a** **Composition:** Bronze **Ruler:** Elizabeth II

| Date | Mintage | F | VF | XF | Unc | BU |
|---|---|---|---|---|---|---|
| 1999 | 460,000,000 | — | — | — | 0.25 | — |
| 1999 Proof | 79,401 | Value: 1.50 | | | | |
| 2000 | — | — | — | — | 0.25 | — |
| 2000 Proof | Est. 100,000 | Value: 1.50 | | | | |
| 2001 | — | — | — | — | 0.25 | — |
| 2001 Proof | Est. 100,000 | Value: 1.50 | | | | |

**5 NEW PENCE** **KM# 911** **Composition:** Copper-Nickel **Ruler:** Elizabeth II

| Date | Mintage | F | VF | XF | Unc | BU |
|---|---|---|---|---|---|---|
| 1968 | 98,868,000 | — | — | 0.15 | 0.30 | — |
| 1969 | 119,270,000 | — | — | 0.15 | 0.40 | — |
| 1970 | 225,948,000 | — | — | 0.15 | 0.40 | — |
| 1971 | 81,783,000 | — | — | 0.15 | 0.50 | — |
| 1971 Proof | 350,000 | Value: 1.75 | | | | |
| 1972 Proof | 150,000 | Value: 3.50 | | | | |
| 1973 Proof | 100,000 | Value: 3.50 | | | | |
| 1974 Proof | 100,000 | Value: 3.50 | | | | |
| 1975 | 116,906,000 | — | — | 0.15 | 0.30 | — |
| 1975 Proof | 100,000 | Value: 1.50 | | | | |
| 1976 Proof | 100,000 | Value: 3.50 | | | | |
| 1977 | 24,308,000 | — | — | 0.15 | 0.35 | — |
| 1977 Proof | 194,000 | Value: 1.50 | | | | |
| 1978 | 61,094,000 | — | — | 0.15 | 0.55 | — |
| 1978 Proof | 88,000 | Value: 1.50 | | | | |
| 1979 | 155,456,000 | — | — | 0.15 | 0.30 | — |
| 1979 Proof | 81,000 | Value: 1.50 | | | | |
| 1980 | 203,020,000 | — | — | 0.15 | 0.30 | — |
| 1980 Proof | 143,000 | Value: 1.50 | | | | |
| 1981 Proof | 100,000 | Value: 1.75 | | | | |

**5 PENCE** **KM# 929** **Composition:** Copper-Nickel **Ruler:** Elizabeth II

| Date | Mintage | F | VF | XF | Unc | BU |
|---|---|---|---|---|---|---|
| 1982 In sets only | 205,000 | — | — | — | 2.25 | — |
| 1982 Proof | 107,000 | Value: 1.75 | | | | |
| 1983 In sets only | 637,000 | — | — | — | 1.75 | — |
| 1983 Proof | 108,000 | Value: 1.75 | | | | |
| 1984 In sets only | 159,000 | — | — | — | 1.75 | — |
| 1984 Proof | 107,000 | Value: 1.50 | | | | |

**5 PENCE** **KM# 937** **Composition:** Copper-Nickel **Ruler:** Elizabeth II

| Date | Mintage | F | VF | XF | Unc | BU |
|---|---|---|---|---|---|---|
| 1985 In sets only | 178,000 | — | — | — | 2.00 | — |
| 1985 Proof | 102,000 | Value: 1.50 | | | | |
| 1986 In sets only | 167,000 | — | — | — | 1.00 | — |
| 1986 Proof | 125,000 | Value: 1.50 | | | | |
| 1987 | 48,220,000 | — | — | 0.15 | 0.30 | — |
| 1987 Proof | 89,000 | Value: 1.75 | | | | |
| 1988 | 120,775,000 | — | — | 0.15 | 0.30 | — |
| 1988 Proof | 125,000 | Value: 1.75 | | | | |
| 1989 | 101,406,000 | — | — | 0.15 | 0.30 | — |
| 1989 Proof | 100,000 | Value: 1.75 | | | | |
| 1990 In sets only | — | — | — | — | 2.50 | — |
| 1990 Proof | — | Value: 2.75 | | | | |

**5 PENCE** **KM# 937a** **Weight:** 5.6000 g. **Composition:** 0.9250 Silver .1683 oz. ASW **Ruler:** Elizabeth II

| Date | Mintage | F | VF | XF | Unc | BU |
|---|---|---|---|---|---|---|
| 1990 Proof | 35,000 | Value: 22.00 | | | | |

**5 PENCE** **KM# 937c** **Weight:** 3.2500 g. **Composition:** 0.9250 Silver .0999 oz. ASW **Ruler:** Elizabeth II

| Date | Mintage | F | VF | XF | Unc | BU |
|---|---|---|---|---|---|---|
| 1990 Proof | 35,000 | Value: 20.00 | | | | |
| 1996 Proof | — | Value: 20.00 | | | | |

**5 PENCE** **KM# 937d** **Weight:** 6.5000 g. **Composition:** 0.9250 Silver .1933 oz. ASW **Ruler:** Elizabeth II

| Date | Mintage | F | VF | XF | Unc | BU |
|---|---|---|---|---|---|---|
| 1990 Proof | 20,000 | Value: 25.00 | | | | |

**5 PENCE** **KM# 937b** **Composition:** Copper-Nickel **Ruler:** Elizabeth II **Note:** Reduced size. Varieties in thickness and edge milling exist.

| Date | Mintage | F | VF | XF | Unc | BU |
|---|---|---|---|---|---|---|
| 1990 | 1,634,840,000 | — | — | — | 0.35 | — |
| 1990 Proof | — | Value: 1.75 | | | | |
| 1991 | 724,979,000 | — | — | — | 0.35 | — |
| 1991 Proof | — | Value: 1.75 | | | | |
| 1992 | 453,174,000 | — | — | — | 0.35 | — |
| 1992 Proof | — | Value: 1.75 | | | | |
| 1993 In sets only | 56,945 | — | — | — | 1.25 | — |
| 1993 Proof | — | Value: 1.75 | | | | |
| 1994 | 93,602,000 | — | — | — | 0.35 | — |
| 1994 Proof | — | Value: 1.75 | | | | |
| 1995 | 183,384,000 | — | — | — | 0.35 | — |
| 1995 Proof | — | Value: 1.75 | | | | |
| 1996 | 302,902,000 | — | — | — | 0.35 | — |
| 1996 Proof | — | Value: 1.75 | | | | |
| 1997 | 736,596,000 | — | — | — | 0.35 | — |
| 1997 Proof | — | Value: 1.50 | | | | |

**5 PENCE** **KM# 988** **Composition:** Copper-Nickel **Ruler:** Elizabeth II **Obverse:** Rank-Broadley effigy of Queen Elizabeth II **Reverse:** Crowned Scottish thistle

| Date | Mintage | F | VF | XF | Unc | BU |
|---|---|---|---|---|---|---|
| 1998 | 88,396,000 | — | — | — | 0.30 | — |
| 1998 Proof | Est. 100,000 | Value: 3.25 | | | | |
| 1999 | — | — | — | — | 0.30 | — |
| 1999 Proof | 79,401 | Value: 3.00 | | | | |

| Date | Mintage | F | VF | XF | Unc | BU |
|---|---|---|---|---|---|---|
| 2000 | — | — | — | — | 0.30 | — |
| 2000 Proof | Est. 100,000 | Value: 3.00 | | | | |
| 2001 | — | — | — | — | 0.30 | — |
| 2001 Proof | Est. 100,000 | Value: 3.00 | | | | |

**10 NEW PENCE** **KM# 912** **Composition:** Copper-Nickel **Ruler:** Elizabeth II

| Date | Mintage | F | VF | XF | Unc | BU |
|---|---|---|---|---|---|---|
| 1968 | 336,143,000 | — | — | 0.25 | 0.50 | — |
| 1969 | 314,008,000 | — | — | 0.25 | 0.60 | — |
| 1970 | 133,571,000 | — | — | 0.25 | 0.75 | — |
| 1971 | 63,205,000 | — | — | 0.25 | 1.00 | — |
| 1971 Proof | 350,000 | Value: 1.75 | | | | |
| 1972 Proof | 150,000 | Value: 3.75 | | | | |
| 1973 | 152,174,000 | — | — | 0.25 | 0.50 | — |
| 1973 Proof | 100,000 | Value: 1.75 | | | | |
| 1974 | 92,741,000 | — | — | 0.25 | 0.50 | — |
| 1974 Proof | 100,000 | Value: 1.75 | | | | |
| 1975 | 181,559,000 | — | — | 0.25 | 0.50 | — |
| 1975 Proof | 100,000 | Value: 1.75 | | | | |
| 1976 | 228,220,000 | — | — | 0.25 | 0.50 | — |
| 1976 Proof | 100,000 | Value: 1.75 | | | | |
| 1977 | 59,323,000 | — | — | 0.25 | 0.60 | — |
| 1977 Proof | 194,000 | Value: 1.75 | | | | |
| 1978 Proof | 88,000 | Value: 5.25 | | | | |
| 1979 | 115,457,000 | — | — | 0.25 | 0.60 | — |
| 1979 Proof | 81,000 | Value: 1.75 | | | | |
| 1980 | 88,650,000 | — | — | 0.25 | 0.65 | — |
| 1980 Proof | 143,000 | Value: 1.75 | | | | |
| 1981 | 3,433,000 | — | 0.25 | 0.50 | 2.00 | — |
| 1981 Proof | 100,000 | Value: 1.75 | | | | |

**10 PENCE** **KM# 930** **Composition:** Copper-Nickel **Ruler:** Elizabeth II

| Date | Mintage | F | VF | XF | Unc | BU |
|---|---|---|---|---|---|---|
| 1982 In sets only | 205,000 | — | — | — | 2.75 | — |
| 1982 Proof | 107,000 | Value: 1.75 | | | | |
| 1983 In sets only | 637,000 | — | — | — | 2.75 | — |
| 1983 Proof | 108,000 | Value: 1.75 | | | | |
| 1984 In sets only | 159,000 | — | — | — | 2.00 | — |
| 1984 Proof | 107,000 | Value: 1.75 | | | | |

**10 PENCE** **KM# 938** **Composition:** Copper-Nickel **Ruler:** Elizabeth II

| Date | Mintage | F | VF | XF | Unc | BU |
|---|---|---|---|---|---|---|
| 1985 In sets only | 178,000 | — | — | — | 2.75 | — |
| 1985 Proof | 102,000 | Value: 1.75 | | | | |
| 1986 In sets only | 167,000 | — | — | — | 1.75 | — |
| 1986 Proof | 125,000 | Value: 1.75 | | | | |
| 1987 In sets only | 172,000 | — | — | — | 2.75 | — |
| 1987 Proof | 89,000 | Value: 2.75 | | | | |
| 1988 In sets only | 134,000 | — | — | — | 2.75 | — |
| 1988 Proof | 125,000 | Value: 2.75 | | | | |
| 1989 In sets only | 78,000 | — | — | — | 3.50 | — |
| 1989 Proof | 100,000 | Value: 2.75 | | | | |
| 1990 | — | — | — | — | 3.50 | — |
| 1990 Proof | 100,000 | Value: 2.75 | | | | |
| 1991 In sets only | — | — | — | — | 3.50 | — |
| 1991 Proof | — | Value: 2.75 | | | | |
| 1992 In sets only | — | — | — | — | 2.75 | — |
| 1992 Proof | — | Value: 3.50 | | | | |

**10 PENCE** **KM# 938c** **Weight:** 6.5000 g. **Composition:** 0.9250 Silver .1933 oz. ASW **Ruler:** Elizabeth II

| Date | Mintage | F | VF | XF | Unc | BU |
|---|---|---|---|---|---|---|
| 1992 Proof | 35,000 | Value: 17.50 | | | | |
| 1996 Proof | — | Value: 17.50 | | | | |

**10 PENCE** **KM# 938a** **Weight:** 11.3100 g. **Composition:** 0.9250 Silver .3363 oz. ASW **Ruler:** Elizabeth II **Note:** Date varieties exist.

| Date | Mintage | F | VF | XF | Unc | BU |
|---|---|---|---|---|---|---|
| 1992 Proof | 35,000 | Value: 25.00 | | | | |

**10 PENCE** **KM# 938b** **Composition:** Copper-Nickel **Ruler:** Elizabeth II **Note:** Reduced size. Varieties in thickness and edge milling exist.

| Date | Mintage | F | VF | XF | Unc | BU |
|---|---|---|---|---|---|---|
| 1992 | 1,395,497,000 | — | — | 0.25 | 0.50 | — |
| 1992 Proof | — | Value: 2.75 | | | | |
| 1993 In sets only | — | — | — | — | 1.00 | — |
| 1993 Proof | — | Value: 1.75 | | | | |
| 1994 In sets only | — | — | — | — | 1.00 | — |
| 1994 Proof | — | Value: 1.75 | | | | |
| 1995 | 43,259,000 | — | — | — | 1.00 | — |
| 1995 Proof | — | Value: 1.75 | | | | |
| 1996 | 118,738,000 | — | — | — | 1.00 | — |
| 1996 Proof | — | Value: 1.75 | | | | |
| 1997 | 8,786,000 | — | — | — | 1.00 | — |
| 1997 Proof | — | Value: 1.75 | | | | |

**10 PENCE** **KM# 989** **Composition:** Copper-Nickel **Ruler:** Elizabeth II **Obverse:** Rank-Broadley effigy of Queen Elizabeth II **Reverse:** Crowned lion

| Date | Mintage | F | VF | XF | Unc | BU |
|---|---|---|---|---|---|---|
| 1998 Proof | — | Value: 4.50 | | | | |
| 1999 In sets only | 136,492 | — | — | — | 1.25 | — |
| 1999 Proof | 79,401 | Value: 3.25 | | | | |
| 2000 | — | — | — | — | 0.40 | — |
| 2000 Proof | Est. 100,000 | Value: 3.25 | | | | |
| 2001 | — | — | — | — | 0.40 | — |
| 2001 Proof | Est. 100,000 | Value: 3.25 | | | | |

**20 PENCE** **KM# 931** **Composition:** Copper-Nickel **Ruler:** Elizabeth II

| Date | Mintage | F | VF | XF | Unc | BU |
|---|---|---|---|---|---|---|
| 1982 | 740,815,000 | — | — | 0.45 | 0.65 | — |
| 1982 Proof | 107,000 | Value: 5.00 | | | | |
| 1983 | 158,463,000 | — | — | 0.45 | 0.65 | — |
| 1983 Proof | 108,000 | Value: 2.50 | | | | |
| 1984 | 65,351,000 | — | — | 0.45 | 0.65 | — |
| 1984 Proof | 107,000 | Value: 2.50 | | | | |

**20 PENCE** **KM# 939** **Composition:** Copper-Nickel **Ruler:** Elizabeth II

| Date | Mintage | F | VF | XF | Unc | BU |
|---|---|---|---|---|---|---|
| 1985 | 74,274,000 | — | — | 0.45 | 0.75 | — |
| 1985 Proof | 102,000 | Value: 5.00 | | | | |
| 1986 In sets only | 167,000 | — | — | — | 1.00 | — |
| 1986 Proof | 125,000 | Value: 5.00 | | | | |
| 1987 | 137,450,000 | — | — | 0.45 | 0.75 | — |
| 1987 Proof | 89,000 | Value: 5.00 | | | | |
| 1988 | 38,038,000 | — | — | 0.45 | 0.75 | — |
| 1988 Proof | 125,000 | Value: 5.00 | | | | |
| 1989 | 132,014,000 | — | — | 0.45 | 0.75 | — |
| 1989 Proof | 100,000 | Value: 5.00 | | | | |
| 1990 | 88,098,000 | — | — | 0.45 | 0.75 | — |
| 1990 Proof | 100,000 | Value: 5.00 | | | | |
| 1991 | 35,901,000 | — | — | 0.45 | 1.00 | — |
| 1991 Proof | — | Value: 5.00 | | | | |
| 1992 | 31,205,000 | — | — | 0.45 | 1.00 | — |
| 1992 Proof | — | Value: 5.00 | | | | |
| 1993 | 123,124,000 | — | — | 0.45 | 0.75 | — |
| 1993 Proof | — | Value: 5.00 | | | | |
| 1994 | 67,131,000 | — | — | 0.45 | 1.00 | — |
| 1994 Proof | — | Value: 5.00 | | | | |
| 1995 | 102,005,000 | — | — | 0.45 | 0.75 | — |
| 1995 Proof | — | Value: 5.00 | | | | |
| 1996 | 83,164,000 | — | — | 0.45 | 0.75 | — |
| 1996 Proof | — | Value: 5.00 | | | | |
| 1997 | 89,519,000 | — | — | 0.45 | 0.75 | — |
| 1997 Proof | — | Value: 5.00 | | | | |

**20 PENCE** **KM# 939a** **Composition:** 0.9250 Silver **Ruler:** Elizabeth II

| Date | Mintage | F | VF | XF | Unc | BU |
|---|---|---|---|---|---|---|
| 1996 Proof | — | Value: 18.50 | | | | |

**20 PENCE** **KM# 978** **Weight:** 3.2400 g. **Composition:** 0.9580 Silver .0998 oz. ASW **Ruler:** Elizabeth II **Obverse:** Queen's portrait **Reverse:** Britannia in chariot **Note:** Similar to 2 Pounds, KM#981.

| Date | Mintage | F | VF | XF | Unc | BU |
|---|---|---|---|---|---|---|
| 1997 Proof | 8,686 | Value: 25.00 | | | | |

**20 PENCE** **KM# 990** **Composition:** Copper-Nickel **Ruler:** Elizabeth II **Obverse:** Rank-Broadley effigy of Queen Elizabeth II **Reverse:** Tudor rose

| Date | Mintage | F | VF | XF | Unc | BU |
|---|---|---|---|---|---|---|
| 1998 | 35,709,000 | — | — | — | 0.60 | — |
| 1998 Proof | Est. 100,000 | Value: 3.50 | | | | |
| 1999 | 106,000,000 | — | — | — | 0.60 | — |
| 1999 Proof | 79,401 | Value: 2.00 | | | | |
| 2000 | — | — | — | — | 0.60 | — |
| 2000 Proof | Est. 100,000 | Value: 3.25 | | | | |
| 2001 | — | — | — | — | 0.60 | — |
| 2001 Proof | Est. 100,000 | Value: 3.25 | | | | |

**20 PENCE** **KM# 1016** **Weight:** 3.2400 g. **Composition:** 0.9584 Silver .0998 oz. ASW **Ruler:** Elizabeth II **Subject:** Britannia Bullion **Obverse:** Queen's portrait **Reverse:** Stylized "Una and the Lion" **Edge:** Reeded **Size:** 16.5 mm.

| Date | Mintage | F | VF | XF | Unc | BU |
|---|---|---|---|---|---|---|
| 2001 Proof | 15,000 | Value: 25.00 | | | | |

**25 NEW PENCE** **KM# 917** **Composition:** Copper-Nickel **Ruler:** Elizabeth II **Subject:** Royal Silver Wedding Anniversary

| Date | Mintage | F | VF | XF | Unc | BU |
|---|---|---|---|---|---|---|
| ND(1972) | 7,452,000 | — | — | 0.65 | 1.75 | — |
| ND(1972) Proof | 150,000 | Value: 7.50 | | | | |

**25 NEW PENCE** **KM# 917a** **Weight:** 28.2759 g. **Composition:** 0.9250 Silver .8409 oz. ASW **Ruler:** Elizabeth II

| Date | Mintage | F | VF | XF | Unc | BU |
|---|---|---|---|---|---|---|
| ND(1972) Proof | 100,000 | Value: 25.00 | | | | |

**25 NEW PENCE** **KM# 920** **Composition:** Copper-Nickel **Ruler:** Elizabeth II **Subject:** Silver Jubilee of Reign

| Date | Mintage | F | VF | XF | Unc | BU |
|---|---|---|---|---|---|---|
| 1977 | 36,989,000 | — | — | 0.65 | 1.50 | — |
| 1977 Proof | 194,000 | Value: 6.00 | | | | |
| 1977 (RMF) | — | — | — | — | 4.00 | — |
| **Note:** Seated in Royal Mint Folder and First Day Covers | | | | | | |
| 1981 (RMF) Reported, not confirmed | — | — | — | — | — | — |

**25 NEW PENCE** **KM# 920a** **Weight:** 28.2759 g. **Composition:** 0.9250 Silver .8409 oz. ASW **Ruler:** Elizabeth II

| Date | Mintage | F | VF | XF | Unc | BU |
|---|---|---|---|---|---|---|
| 1977 Proof | 377,000 | Value: 20.00 | | | | |

**25 NEW PENCE** **KM# 921** **Composition:** Copper-Nickel **Ruler:** Elizabeth II **Subject:** 80th Birthday of Queen Mother

| Date | Mintage | F | VF | XF | Unc | BU |
|---|---|---|---|---|---|---|
| ND(1980) | 9,478,000 | — | — | 0.65 | 1.75 | — |

**25 NEW PENCE** **KM# 921a** **Weight:** 28.2759 g. **Composition:** 0.9250 Silver .8409 oz. ASW **Ruler:** Elizabeth II

| Date | Mintage | F | VF | XF | Unc | BU |
|---|---|---|---|---|---|---|
| ND(1980) Proof | 84,000 | Value: 30.00 | | | | |

**25 NEW PENCE** **KM# 925** **Composition:** Copper-Nickel **Ruler:** Elizabeth II **Subject:** Wedding of Prince Charles and Lady Diana

| Date | Mintage | F | VF | XF | Unc | BU |
|---|---|---|---|---|---|---|
| 1981 | 27,360,000 | — | — | 0.65 | 1.75 | — |

**25 NEW PENCE** **KM# 925a** **Weight:** 28.2759 g. **Composition:** 0.9250 Silver .8409 oz. ASW **Ruler:** Elizabeth II

| Date | Mintage | F | VF | XF | Unc | BU |
|---|---|---|---|---|---|---|
| 1981 Proof | 218,000 | Value: 27.50 | | | | |

**50 NEW PENCE** **KM# 913** **Composition:** Copper-Nickel **Ruler:** Elizabeth II

| Date | Mintage | F | VF | XF | Unc | BU |
|---|---|---|---|---|---|---|
| 1969 | 188,400,000 | — | — | 1.25 | 2.50 | — |
| 1970 | 19,461,000 | — | — | 1.25 | 3.50 | — |
| 1971 Proof | 350,000 | Value: 3.50 | | | | |
| 1972 Proof | 150,000 | Value: 6.50 | | | | |
| 1974 Proof | 100,000 | Value: 3.00 | | | | |
| 1975 Proof | 100,000 | Value: 3.00 | | | | |
| 1976 | 43,747,000 | — | — | 1.75 | 3.50 | — |
| 1976 Proof | 100,000 | Value: 2.50 | | | | |
| 1977 | 49,536,000 | — | — | 1.75 | 3.50 | — |
| 1977 Proof | 194,000 | Value: 2.50 | | | | |
| 1978 | 72,005,000 | — | — | 1.75 | 3.50 | — |
| 1978 Proof | 88,000 | Value: 2.75 | | | | |
| 1979 | 58,680,000 | — | — | 1.75 | 2.25 | — |
| 1979 Proof | 81,000 | Value: 2.75 | | | | |
| 1980 | 89,086,000 | — | — | 1.75 | 2.25 | — |
| 1980 Proof | 143,000 | Value: 2.50 | | | | |
| 1981 | 74,003,000 | — | — | 1.75 | 2.25 | — |
| 1981 Proof | 100,000 | Value: 2.50 | | | | |

**50 PENCE** **KM# 918** **Composition:** Copper-Nickel **Ruler:** Elizabeth II **Subject:** Entry Into E.E.C

| Date | Mintage | F | VF | XF | Unc | BU |
|---|---|---|---|---|---|---|
| 1973 | 89,775,000 | — | — | 1.25 | 2.00 | — |
| 1973 Proof | 357,000 | Value: 6.00 | | | | |

**50 PENCE** **KM# 932** **Composition:** Copper-Nickel **Ruler:** Elizabeth II

| Date | Mintage | F | VF | XF | Unc | BU |
|---|---|---|---|---|---|---|
| 1982 | 51,312,000 | — | — | 1.25 | 1.75 | — |
| 1982 Proof | 107,000 | Value: 2.50 | | | | |
| 1983 | 23,436,000 | — | — | 1.25 | 2.00 | — |
| 1983 Proof | 125,000 | Value: 2.50 | | | | |
| 1984 In sets only | Est. 107,000 | — | — | — | 2.75 | — |
| 1984 Proof | 125,000 | Value: 2.50 | | | | |

**50 PENCE** **KM# 940.1** **Composition:** Copper-Nickel **Ruler:** Elizabeth II

| Date | Mintage | F | VF | XF | Unc | BU |
|---|---|---|---|---|---|---|
| 1985 | 680,000 | — | — | 1.25 | 3.50 | — |
| 1985 Proof | 102,000 | Value: 2.75 | | | | |
| 1986 In sets only | 167,000 | — | — | — | 2.75 | — |
| 1986 Proof | 125,000 | Value: 2.75 | | | | |
| 1987 In sets only | 172,000 | — | — | — | 2.75 | — |
| 1987 Proof | 89,000 | Value: 2.75 | | | | |
| 1988 In sets only | 134,000 | — | — | — | 2.75 | — |
| 1988 Proof | 125,000 | Value: 3.50 | | | | |
| 1989 In sets only | 78,000 | — | — | — | 3.50 | — |
| 1989 Proof | 100,000 | Value: 2.75 | | | | |
| 1990 In sets only | — | — | — | — | 3.50 | — |
| 1990 Proof | 100,000 | Value: 6.00 | | | | |
| 1991 In sets only | — | — | — | — | 3.50 | — |
| 1991 Proof | — | Value: 6.50 | | | | |
| 1992 In sets only | — | — | — | — | 3.50 | — |
| 1992 Proof | — | Value: 6.50 | | | | |
| 1993 In sets only | — | — | — | — | 3.50 | — |
| 1993 Proof | — | Value: 3.50 | | | | |
| 1995 | — | — | — | — | 2.75 | — |
| 1995 Proof | — | Value: 3.50 | | | | |
| 1996 | — | — | — | — | 2.75 | — |
| 1996 Proof | — | Value: 3.50 | | | | |
| 1997 In sets only | — | — | — | — | 2.75 | — |
| 1997 Proof | — | Value: 3.50 | | | | |

**50 PENCE** **KM# 963** **Composition:** Copper-Nickel **Ruler:** Elizabeth II **Subject:** British Presidency of European Council of Ministers

| Date | Mintage | F | VF | XF | Unc | BU |
|---|---|---|---|---|---|---|
| ND(1992) | 109,000 | — | — | — | 5.75 | — |
| ND(1992) Proof | Est. 100,000 | Value: 13.50 | | | | |

**50 PENCE** **KM# 963a** **Weight:** 13.5000 g. **Composition:** 0.9250 Silver .4014 oz. ASW **Ruler:** Elizabeth II

| Date | Mintage | F | VF | XF | Unc | BU |
|---|---|---|---|---|---|---|
| ND(1992) Proof | Est. 35,000 | Value: 30.00 | | | | |

**50 PENCE** **KM# 963b** **Weight:** 26.3200 g. **Composition:** 0.9170 Gold .7757 oz. AGW **Ruler:** Elizabeth II **Subject:** British Presidency of European Council of Ministers

| Date | Mintage | F | VF | XF | Unc | BU |
|---|---|---|---|---|---|---|
| ND(1992) Proof | Est. 2,500 | Value: 350 | | | | |

**50 PENCE** **KM# 966** **Composition:** Copper-Nickel **Ruler:** Elizabeth II **Subject:** 50th Anniversary of Normandy Invasion

| Date | Mintage | F | VF | XF | Unc | BU |
|---|---|---|---|---|---|---|
| 1994 | 6,673,000 | — | — | — | 2.50 | — |
| 1994 Proof | — | Value: 13.50 | | | | |

**50 PENCE** **KM# 966a** **Weight:** 13.5000 g. **Composition:** 0.9250 Silver .4014 oz. ASW **Ruler:** Elizabeth II

| Date | Mintage | F | VF | XF | Unc | BU |
|---|---|---|---|---|---|---|
| 1994 Proof | — | Value: 45.00 | | | | |

**50 PENCE** **KM# 966b** **Weight:** 27.0000 g. **Composition:** 0.9250 Silver .8028 oz. ASW **Ruler:** Elizabeth II

| Date | Mintage | F | VF | XF | Unc | BU |
|---|---|---|---|---|---|---|
| 1994 Proof | 10,000 | Value: 85.00 | | | | |

**50 PENCE** **KM# 966c** **Weight:** 26.3200 g. **Composition:** 0.9170 Gold .7757 oz. AGW **Ruler:** Elizabeth II

| Date | Mintage | F | VF | XF | Unc | BU |
|---|---|---|---|---|---|---|
| 1994 Proof | — | Value: 500 | | | | |

**50 PENCE** **KM# 940.1a** **Composition:** Silver **Ruler:** Elizabeth II

| Date | Mintage | F | VF | XF | Unc | BU |
|---|---|---|---|---|---|---|
| 1996 In Proof sets only | — | Value: 30.00 | | | | |

**50 PENCE** **KM# 940.2** **Composition:** Copper-Nickel **Ruler:** Elizabeth II **Note:** Reduced size.

| Date | Mintage | F | VF | XF | Unc | BU |
|---|---|---|---|---|---|---|
| 1997 | 456,364,000 | — | — | — | 2.75 | — |
| 1997 Proof | — | Value: 3.50 | | | | |

**50 PENCE** **KM# 979** **Weight:** 8.1100 g. **Composition:** 0.9580 Silver .2498 oz. ASW **Ruler:** Elizabeth II **Obverse:** Queen's portrait **Reverse:** Britannia in chariot **Note:** Similar to 2 Pounds, KM#981.

| Date | Mintage | F | VF | XF | Unc | BU |
|---|---|---|---|---|---|---|
| 1997 In proof sets only | Est. 15,000 | Value: 25.00 | | | | |

**50 PENCE** **KM# 991** **Composition:** Copper-Nickel **Ruler:** Elizabeth II **Obverse:** Rank-Broadley portrait of Queen Elizabeth II **Reverse:** Seated Brittania

| Date | Mintage | F | VF | XF | Unc | BU |
|---|---|---|---|---|---|---|
| 1998 | 42,705,000 | — | — | — | 1.75 | — |
| 1998 Proof | Est. 100,000 | Value: 2.50 | | | | |
| 1999 | 44,000,000 | — | — | — | 1.75 | — |
| 1999 Proof | 79,401 | Value: 2.50 | | | | |
| 2000 | — | — | — | — | 1.75 | — |
| 2000 Proof | Est. 100,000 | Value: 2.50 | | | | |
| 2001 | — | — | — | — | 1.75 | — |
| 2001 Proof | Est. 100,000 | Value: 2.50 | | | | |

**50 PENCE** **KM# 992** **Composition:** Copper-Nickel **Ruler:** Elizabeth II **Subject:** 25th Anniversary - Britain in the Common Market **Obverse:** Rank-Broadley portrait of Queen Elizabeth II **Reverse:** Bouquet of stars

| Date | Mintage | F | VF | XF | Unc | BU |
|---|---|---|---|---|---|---|
| 1998 | 4,967,000 | — | — | — | 2.75 | — |
| 1998 Proof | Est. 100,000 | Value: 10.00 | | | | |

**50 PENCE** **KM# 992a** **Weight:** 8.0000 g. **Composition:** 0.9250 Silver .2379 oz. ASW **Ruler:** Elizabeth II

| Date | Mintage | F | VF | XF | Unc | BU |
|---|---|---|---|---|---|---|
| 1998 Proof | — | Value: 45.00 | | | | |

**50 PENCE** **KM# 996** **Composition:** Copper-Nickel **Ruler:** Elizabeth II **Subject:** National Health Service **Obverse:** Rank-Broadley portrait of Queen Elizabeth II **Reverse:** Radiant hands

| Date | Mintage | F | VF | XF | Unc | BU |
|---|---|---|---|---|---|---|
| 1998 | 5,001,000 | — | — | — | 2.75 | — |
| 1998 BU with folder | — | — | — | — | 8.50 | — |
| 1998 Proof | — | Value: 14.00 | | | | |

**50 PENCE** **KM# 996a** **Weight:** 8.0000 g. **Composition:** 0.9250 Silver .2379 oz. ASW **Ruler:** Elizabeth II

| Date | Mintage | F | VF | XF | Unc | BU |
|---|---|---|---|---|---|---|
| 1998 Proof | Est. 25,000 | Value: 45.00 | | | | |

**50 PENCE** **KM# 996b** **Weight:** 15.5000 g. **Composition:** 0.9167 Gold .4568 oz. AGW **Ruler:** Elizabeth II **Subject:** National Health Service **Obverse:** Rank-Broadley portrait of Queen Elizabeth II **Reverse:** Radiant hands

| Date | Mintage | F | VF | XF | Unc | BU |
|---|---|---|---|---|---|---|
| 1998 Proof | Est. 1,500 | Value: 475 | | | | |

**50 PENCE** **KM# 1004** **Composition:** Copper-Nickel **Ruler:** Elizabeth II **Subject:** Public Library **Obverse:** Bust Queen right **Reverse:** Open book above building and CD's **Edge:** Plain edge

| Date | Mintage | F | VF | XF | Unc | BU |
|---|---|---|---|---|---|---|
| 2000 | Est. 5,000,000 | — | — | — | 2.75 | — |
| 2000 Proof | 100,000 | Value: 15.00 | | | | |

**50 PENCE** **KM# 1017** **Weight:** 8.1100 g. **Composition:** 0.9584 Silver .2499 oz. ASW **Ruler:** Elizabeth II **Subject:** Britannia Bullion **Obverse:** Queen's portrait **Reverse:** Stylized "Una and the Lion" **Edge:** Reeded **Size:** 22 mm.

| Date | Mintage | F | VF | XF | Unc | BU |
|---|---|---|---|---|---|---|
| 2001 Proof | 5,000 | Value: 25.00 | | | | |

**POUND** **KM# 933** **Composition:** Nickel-Brass **Ruler:** Elizabeth II **Edge Lettering:** DECUS ET TUTAMEN

| Date | Mintage | F | VF | XF | Unc | BU |
|---|---|---|---|---|---|---|
| 1983 | 443,054,000 | — | — | 2.25 | 3.50 | — |
| 1983 Proof | 108,000 | Value: 6.00 | | | | |

**POUND** **KM# 933a** **Weight:** 9.5000 g. **Composition:** 0.9250 Silver .2825 oz. ASW **Ruler:** Elizabeth II

| Date | Mintage | F | VF | XF | Unc | BU |
|---|---|---|---|---|---|---|
| 1983 Proof | 50,000 | Value: 27.50 | | | | |

**POUND** **KM# 934** **Composition:** Nickel-Brass **Ruler:** Elizabeth II **Reverse:** Scottish thistle **Edge Lettering:** NEMO ME IMPUNE LACESSIT

| Date | Mintage | F | VF | XF | Unc | BU |
|---|---|---|---|---|---|---|
| 1984 | 146,257,000 | — | — | 2.25 | 3.50 | — |
| 1984 Proof | 107,000 | Value: 6.00 | | | | |

**POUND** **KM# 934a** **Weight:** 9.5000 g. **Composition:** 0.9250 Silver .2825 oz. ASW **Ruler:** Elizabeth II

| Date | Mintage | F | VF | XF | Unc | BU |
|---|---|---|---|---|---|---|
| 1984 Proof | 45,000 | Value: 27.50 | | | | |

**POUND** **KM# 941** **Composition:** Nickel-Brass **Ruler:** Elizabeth II **Reverse:** Welsh leek **Edge Lettering:** PLEIDIOL WYF I'M GWLAD

| Date | Mintage | F | VF | XF | Unc | BU |
|---|---|---|---|---|---|---|
| 1985 | 228,431,000 | — | — | 2.00 | 3.50 | — |
| 1985 Proof | 102,000 | Value: 6.00 | | | | |
| 1990 | 97,269,000 | — | — | 2.00 | 3.50 | — |
| 1990 Proof | 100,000 | Value: 6.00 | | | | |

**POUND** **KM# 941a** **Weight:** 9.5000 g. **Composition:** 0.9250 Silver .2825 oz. ASW **Ruler:** Elizabeth II

| Date | Mintage | F | VF | XF | Unc | BU |
|---|---|---|---|---|---|---|
| 1985 Proof | 50,000 | Value: 27.50 | | | | |
| 1990 Proof | Est. 25,000 | Value: 36.50 | | | | |

**POUND** **KM# 946** **Composition:** Nickel-Brass **Ruler:** Elizabeth II **Reverse:** Northern Ireland - Blooming Flax

| Date | Mintage | F | VF | XF | Unc | BU |
|---|---|---|---|---|---|---|
| 1986 | 10,410,000 | — | — | 2.00 | 3.50 | — |
| 1986 Proof | 125,000 | Value: 6.00 | | | | |
| 1991 | 38,444,000 | — | — | 2.00 | 3.50 | — |
| 1991 Proof | — | Value: 6.00 | | | | |

**POUND** **KM# 946a** **Weight:** 9.5000 g. **Composition:** 0.9250 Silver .2825 oz. ASW **Ruler:** Elizabeth II

| Date | Mintage | F | VF | XF | Unc | BU |
|---|---|---|---|---|---|---|
| 1986 Proof | 50,000 | Value: 27.50 | | | | |
| 1991 Proof | Est. 25,000 | Value: 35.00 | | | | |

**POUND** **KM# 948** **Composition:** Nickel-Brass **Ruler:** Elizabeth II **Reverse:** Oak tree **Edge Lettering:** DECUS ET TUTAMEN

| Date | Mintage | F | VF | XF | Unc | BU |
|---|---|---|---|---|---|---|
| 1987 | 39,299,000 | — | — | — | 3.50 | — |
| 1987 Proof | 125,000 | Value: 6.00 | | | | |
| 1992 | 36,320,000 | — | — | — | 3.50 | — |
| 1992 Proof | — | Value: 6.00 | | | | |

**POUND** **KM# 948a** **Weight:** 9.5000 g. **Composition:** 0.9250 Silver .2825 oz. ASW **Ruler:** Elizabeth II

| Date | Mintage | F | VF | XF | Unc | BU |
|---|---|---|---|---|---|---|
| 1987 Proof | 50,000 | Value: 27.50 | | | | |
| 1992 Proof | Est. 25,000 | Value: 36.50 | | | | |

**POUND** **KM# 954** **Composition:** Copper-Zinc-Nickel **Ruler:** Elizabeth II **Edge Lettering:** DECUS ET TUTAMEN

| Date | Mintage | F | VF | XF | Unc | BU |
|---|---|---|---|---|---|---|
| 1988 | 7,119,000 | — | — | — | 3.50 | — |
| 1988 Proof | Est. 125,000 | Value: 7.00 | | | | |

**POUND** **KM# 954a** **Weight:** 9.5000 g. **Composition:** 0.9250 Silver .2825 oz. ASW **Ruler:** Elizabeth II

| Date | Mintage | F | VF | XF | Unc | BU |
|---|---|---|---|---|---|---|
| 1988 Proof | Est. 50,000 | Value: 27.50 | | | | |

**POUND** **KM# 959** **Composition:** Nickel-Brass **Ruler:** Elizabeth II **Obverse:** Queen's portrait **Reverse:** Scottish thistle **Edge Lettering:** NEMO ME IMPUNE LACESSIT

| Date | Mintage | F | VF | XF | Unc | BU |
|---|---|---|---|---|---|---|
| 1989 | 70,581,000 | — | — | — | 3.50 | — |
| 1989 Proof | 100,000 | Value: 6.00 | | | | |

**POUND** **KM# 959a** **Weight:** 9.5000 g. **Composition:** 0.9250 Silver .2825 oz. ASW **Ruler:** Elizabeth II

| Date | Mintage | F | VF | XF | Unc | BU |
|---|---|---|---|---|---|---|
| 1989 Proof | Est. 25,000 | Value: 32.50 | | | | |

**POUND** **KM# 964** **Composition:** Nickel-Brass **Ruler:** Elizabeth II **Reverse:** Royal coat of arms **Edge Lettering:** DECUS ET TUTAMEN

| Date | Mintage | F | VF | XF | Unc | BU |
|---|---|---|---|---|---|---|
| 1993 | 114,745,000 | — | — | — | 3.50 | — |
| 1993 Proof | — | Value: 6.00 | | | | |

**POUND** **KM# 964a** **Weight:** 9.5000 g. **Composition:** 0.9250 Silver .2825 oz. ASW **Ruler:** Elizabeth II

| Date | Mintage | F | VF | XF | Unc | BU |
|---|---|---|---|---|---|---|
| 1993 Proof | Est. 25,000 | Value: 40.00 | | | | |

**POUND** **KM# 967** **Composition:** Nickel-Brass **Ruler:** Elizabeth II **Reverse:** Scotland arms **Edge Lettering:** NEMO ME IMPUNE LACESSIT

| Date | Mintage | F | VF | XF | Unc | BU |
|---|---|---|---|---|---|---|
| 1994 | 29,753,000 | — | — | — | 3.50 | — |
| 1994 Proof | — | Value: 6.00 | | | | |

**POUND** **KM# 967a** **Weight:** 9.5000 g. **Composition:** 0.9250 Silver .2825 oz. ASW **Ruler:** Elizabeth II

| Date | Mintage | F | VF | XF | Unc | BU |
|---|---|---|---|---|---|---|
| 1994 Proof | Est. 25,000 | Value: 40.00 | | | | |

**POUND** **KM# 969** **Composition:** Nickel-Brass **Ruler:** Elizabeth II **Reverse:** Wales - Welsh Dragon **Edge Lettering:** PLEIDIOL WYF I'M GWLAD

| Date | Mintage | F | VF | XF | Unc | BU |
|---|---|---|---|---|---|---|
| 1995 | 34,504,000 | — | — | — | 3.50 | — |
| 1995 Proof | 100,000 | Value: 6.00 | | | | |

**POUND** **KM# 969a** **Weight:** 9.5000 g. **Composition:** 0.9250 Silver .2825 oz. ASW **Ruler:** Elizabeth II

| Date | Mintage | F | VF | XF | Unc | BU |
|---|---|---|---|---|---|---|
| 1995 Proof | 27,000 | Value: 37.50 | | | | |

**POUND** **KM# 972** **Composition:** Nickel-Brass **Ruler:** Elizabeth II **Reverse:** Northern Ireland - Celtic Collar on Cross **Edge Lettering:** DECUS ET TUTAMEN

| Date | Mintage | F | VF | XF | Unc | BU |
|---|---|---|---|---|---|---|
| 1996 | 89,886,000 | — | — | — | 3.50 | — |
| 1996 Proof | Est. 100,000 | Value: 6.00 | | | | |

**POUND** **KM# 972a** **Weight:** 9.5000 g. **Composition:** 0.9250 Silver .2825 oz. ASW **Ruler:** Elizabeth II

| Date | Mintage | F | VF | XF | Unc | BU |
|---|---|---|---|---|---|---|
| 1996 Proof | 40,000 | Value: 37.50 | | | | |

**POUND** **KM# 975** **Composition:** Nickel-Brass **Ruler:** Elizabeth II **Obverse:** Queen's portrait **Reverse:** Plantagenet lions **Edge Lettering:** DECUS ET TUTAMEN

| Date | Mintage | F | VF | XF | Unc | BU |
|---|---|---|---|---|---|---|
| 1997 | 47,707,000 | — | — | — | 3.50 | — |
| 1997 Proof | Est. 100,000 | Value: 6.00 | | | | |

**POUND** **KM# 975a** **Weight:** 9.5000 g. **Composition:** 0.9250 Silver .2825 oz. ASW **Ruler:** Elizabeth II **Edge Lettering:** DECUS ET TUTAMEN

| Date | Mintage | F | VF | XF | Unc | BU |
|---|---|---|---|---|---|---|
| 1997 Proof | 30,000 | Value: 40.00 | | | | |

**POUND** **KM# 980** **Weight:** 16.2200 g. **Composition:** 0.9580 Silver .4996 oz. ASW **Ruler:** Elizabeth II **Obverse:** Queen's portrait **Reverse:** Britannia in chariot **Note:** Similar to 2 Pounds, KM#981.

| Date | Mintage | F | VF | XF | Unc | BU |
|---|---|---|---|---|---|---|
| 1997 Proof | Est. 15,000 | Value: 40.00 | | | | |

**POUND** **KM# 993** **Composition:** Nickel-Brass **Ruler:** Elizabeth II **Obverse:** Rank-Broadley portrait of Queen Elizabeth II **Reverse:** British Royal Arms **Edge Lettering:** DECUS ET TUTAMEN

| Date | Mintage | F | VF | XF | Unc | BU |
|---|---|---|---|---|---|---|
| 1998 | Est. 100,000 | — | — | — | 7.00 | — |

**POUND** **KM# 993a** **Weight:** 9.5000 g. **Composition:** 0.9250 Silver .2825 oz. ASW **Ruler:** Elizabeth II

| Date | Mintage | F | VF | XF | Unc | BU |
|---|---|---|---|---|---|---|
| 1998 | 13,863 | — | — | — | 40.00 | — |

**POUND** **KM# 998** **Composition:** Nickel-Brass **Ruler:** Elizabeth II **Obverse:** Rank-Broadley portrait of Queen Elizabeth II **Reverse:** Scottish lion

| Date | Mintage | F | VF | XF | Unc | BU |
|---|---|---|---|---|---|---|
| 1999 In mint sets only | — | — | — | — | 3.50 | — |
| 1999 Proof | Est. 100,000 | Value: 6.00 | | | | |

**POUND** **KM# 998a** **Weight:** 9.5000 g. **Composition:** 0.9250 Silver .2825 oz. ASW **Ruler:** Elizabeth II

| Date | Mintage | F | VF | XF | Unc | BU |
|---|---|---|---|---|---|---|
| 1999 frosted reverse | Est. 2,000 | — | — | — | — | — |
| 1999 Proof | 23,000 | Value: 40.00 | | | | |

**POUND** **KM# 1005** **Composition:** Nickel-Brass **Ruler:** Elizabeth II **Obverse:** Bust Queen right **Reverse:** Welsh dragon **Edge:** Reeded and lettered **Edge Lettering:** PLEIDOL WYF I'M GWLAD

| Date | Mintage | F | VF | XF | Unc | BU |
|---|---|---|---|---|---|---|
| 2000 | — | — | — | — | 3.50 | — |
| 2000 Proof | Est. 100,000 | Value: 6.00 | | | | |

**POUND** **KM# 1013** **Weight:** 9.5000 g. **Composition:** Nickel-Brass **Ruler:** Elizabeth II **Subject:** Northern Ireland **Obverse:** Queen's new portrait **Reverse:** Celtic style cross **Edge:** Reeding **Edge Lettering:** "DEBUS ET TUTAMEN" **Size:** 22.5 mm.

| Date | Mintage | F | VF | XF | Unc | BU |
|---|---|---|---|---|---|---|
| 2001 | — | — | — | — | 3.50 | — |
| 2001 Proof | — | Value: 6.00 | | | | |

**POUND** **KM# 1018** **Weight:** 16.2200 g. **Composition:** 0.9584 Silver .4998 oz. ASW **Ruler:** Elizabeth II **Subject:** Britannia Bullion **Obverse:** Queen's portrait **Reverse:** Stylized "Una and the Lion" **Edge:** Reeded **Size:** 27 mm.

| Date | Mintage | F | VF | XF | Unc | BU |
|---|---|---|---|---|---|---|
| 2001 Proof | 5,000 | Value: 40.00 | | | | |

**2 POUNDS** **KM# 947** **Composition:** Nickel-Brass **Ruler:** Elizabeth II **Subject:** Commonwealth Games **Edge Lettering:** XIII COMMONWEALTH GAMES SCOTLAND 1986

| Date | Mintage | F | VF | XF | Unc | BU |
|---|---|---|---|---|---|---|
| 1986 | 8,212,000 | — | — | 4.50 | 6.50 | — |
| 1986 Proof | 125,000 | Value: 12.00 | | | | |

**2 POUNDS** **KM# 947a** **Weight:** 15.9800 g. **Composition:** 0.5000 Silver .2569 oz. ASW **Ruler:** Elizabeth II

| Date | Mintage | F | VF | XF | Unc | BU |
|---|---|---|---|---|---|---|
| 1986 | 125,000 | — | — | — | 15.00 | — |

**2 POUNDS** **KM# 947b** **Weight:** 15.9800 g. **Composition:** 0.9250 Silver .4752 oz. ASW **Ruler:** Elizabeth II

| Date | Mintage | F | VF | XF | Unc | BU |
|---|---|---|---|---|---|---|
| 1986 Proof | 75,000 | Value: 25.00 | | | | |

**2 POUNDS** **KM# 947c** **Weight:** 15.9800 g. **Composition:** 0.9170 Gold .4710 oz. AGW **Ruler:** Elizabeth II **Subject:** Commonwealth Games

| Date | Mintage | F | VF | XF | Unc | BU |
|---|---|---|---|---|---|---|
| 1986 Proof | 18,000 | Value: 200 | | | | |

**2 POUNDS** **KM# 960** **Composition:** Nickel-Brass **Ruler:** Elizabeth II **Subject:** Tercentenary - Bill of Rights

| Date | Mintage | F | VF | XF | Unc | BU |
|---|---|---|---|---|---|---|
| ND(1989) | 4,397,000 | — | — | — | 6.50 | — |
| ND(1989) Proof | 100,000 | Value: 12.00 | | | | |

**2 POUNDS** **KM# 960a** **Weight:** 15.9800 g. **Composition:** 0.9250 Silver .4752 oz. ASW **Ruler:** Elizabeth II

| Date | Mintage | F | VF | XF | Unc | BU |
|---|---|---|---|---|---|---|
| ND(1989) Proof | 25,000 | Value: 25.00 | | | | |

**2 POUNDS** **KM# 961** **Composition:** Nickel-Brass **Ruler:** Elizabeth II **Subject:** Tercentenary - Claim of Right

| Date | Mintage | F | VF | XF | Unc | BU |
|---|---|---|---|---|---|---|
| ND(1989) | 346,000 | — | — | — | 9.00 | — |
| ND(1989) Proof | 100,000 | Value: 12.00 | | | | |

**2 POUNDS** **KM# 961a** **Weight:** 15.9800 g. **Composition:** 0.9250 Silver .4752 oz. ASW **Ruler:** Elizabeth II

| Date | Mintage | F | VF | XF | Unc | BU |
|---|---|---|---|---|---|---|
| ND(1989) Proof | 25,000 | Value: 25.00 | | | | |

**2 POUNDS** **KM# 968** **Composition:** Nickel-Brass **Ruler:** Elizabeth II **Subject:** 300th Anniversary - Bank of England **Edge Lettering:** SIC VOS NON VOBIS

| Date | Mintage | F | VF | XF | Unc | BU |
|---|---|---|---|---|---|---|
| ND(1994) | 1,441,000 | — | — | — | 5.50 | — |
| ND(1994) Proof | — | Value: 9.00 | | | | |

**2 POUNDS** **KM# 968a** **Weight:** 15.9800 g. **Composition:** 0.9250 Silver .4752 oz. ASW **Ruler:** Elizabeth II

| Date | Mintage | F | VF | XF | Unc | BU |
|---|---|---|---|---|---|---|
| ND(1994) Proof | Est. 40,000 | Value: 40.00 | | | | |

**2 POUNDS** **KM# 968c** **Weight:** 15.9800 g. **Composition:** 0.9170 Gold .4710 oz. AGW **Ruler:** Elizabeth II **Subject:** 300th Anniversary - Bank of England

| Date | Mintage | F | VF | XF | Unc | BU |
|---|---|---|---|---|---|---|
| ND(1994) Proof | Est. 3,500 | Value: 470 | | | | |

**2 POUNDS** **KM# 1012** **Weight:** 15.9800 g. **Composition:** 0.9170 Gold .4710 oz. AGW **Ruler:** Elizabeth II **Obverse:** 2 Pounds, KM#944 **Reverse:** 2 Pounds, KM#968c **Note:** Muled die error.

| Date | Mintage | F | VF | XF | Unc | BU |
|---|---|---|---|---|---|---|
| ND(1994) Rare | — | — | — | — | — | — |

**2 POUNDS** **KM# 971** **Composition:** Nickel-Brass **Ruler:** Elizabeth II **Subject:** 50th Anniversary - United Nations **Note:** Mintage included with KM#970.

| Date | Mintage | F | VF | XF | Unc | BU |
|---|---|---|---|---|---|---|
| ND(1995) | — | — | — | — | 6.00 | — |

**2 POUNDS** **KM# 970** **Composition:** Nickel-Brass **Ruler:** Elizabeth II **Subject:** End of World War II - Dove **Edge Lettering:** 1945 IN PEACE GOODWILL 1995

| Date | Mintage | F | VF | XF | Unc | BU |
|---|---|---|---|---|---|---|
| ND(1995) | 6,033,000 | — | — | — | 6.00 | — |
| ND(1995) Proof | 100,000 | Value: 9.00 | | | | |

**2 POUNDS** **KM# 970a** **Weight:** 15.9800 g. **Composition:** 0.9250 Silver .4752 oz. ASW **Ruler:** Elizabeth II

| Date | Mintage | F | VF | XF | Unc | BU |
|---|---|---|---|---|---|---|
| ND(1995) Proof | 50,000 | Value: 40.00 | | | | |

**2 POUNDS** **KM# 970c** **Weight:** 15.9800 g. **Composition:** 0.9170 Gold .4710 oz. AGW **Ruler:** Elizabeth II **Subject:** End of World War II - Dove

| Date | Mintage | F | VF | XF | Unc | BU |
|---|---|---|---|---|---|---|
| ND(1995) Proof | 2,500 | Value: 470 | | | | |

**2 POUNDS** **KM# 971a** **Weight:** 15.9760 g. **Composition:** 0.9250 Silver .4751 oz. ASW **Ruler:** Elizabeth II

| Date | Mintage | F | VF | XF | Unc | BU |
|---|---|---|---|---|---|---|
| ND(1995) Proof | Est. 175,000 | Value: 40.00 | | | | |

**2 POUNDS** **KM# 971c** **Weight:** 15.9760 g. **Composition:** 0.9170 Gold .4708 oz. AGW **Ruler:** Elizabeth II **Subject:** 50th Anniversary - United Nations

| Date | Mintage | F | VF | XF | Unc | BU |
|---|---|---|---|---|---|---|
| ND(1995) Proof | Est. 5,000 | Value: 475 | | | | |

**2 POUNDS** **KM# 973** **Composition:** Nickel-Brass **Ruler:** Elizabeth II **Reverse:** Soccer ball **Edge Lettering:** TENTH EUROPEAN CHAMPIONSHIP

| Date | Mintage | F | VF | XF | Unc | BU |
|---|---|---|---|---|---|---|
| 1996 | 5,141,000 | — | — | — | 6.50 | — |
| 1996 Proof | Est. 100,000 | Value: 10.00 | | | | |

**2 POUNDS** **KM# 973a** **Weight:** 15.9760 g. **Composition:** 0.9250 Silver .4751 oz. ASW **Ruler:** Elizabeth II

| Date | Mintage | F | VF | XF | Unc | BU |
|---|---|---|---|---|---|---|
| 1996 Proof | — | Value: 40.00 | | | | |

**2 POUNDS** **KM# 976** **Ring Composition:** Brass **Center Composition:** Copper-Nickel **Ruler:** Elizabeth II **Obverse:** Queen's new portrait **Reverse:** Celtic designs **Edge Lettering:** STANDING ON THE SHOULDERS OF GIANTS

| Date | Mintage | F | VF | XF | Unc | BU |
|---|---|---|---|---|---|---|
| 1997 | 13,735,000 | — | — | — | 7.50 | — |
| 1997 Proof | Est. 100,000 | Value: 10.00 | | | | |

**2 POUNDS** **KM# 981** **Weight:** 32.5400 g. **Composition:** 0.9580 Silver .9995 oz. ASW **Ruler:** Elizabeth II **Obverse:** Queen's portrait **Reverse:** Britannia in chariot

| Date | Mintage | F | VF | XF | Unc | BU |
|---|---|---|---|---|---|---|
| 1997 Proof | Est. 35,000 | Value: 50.00 | | | | |

**2 POUNDS** **KM# 976a** **Weight:** 12.0000 g. **Composition:** 0.9250 Silver .3568 oz. ASW **Ruler:** Elizabeth II **Note:** Gold plated silver ring, silver center.

| Date | Mintage | F | VF | XF | Unc | BU |
|---|---|---|---|---|---|---|
| 1997 Proof | Est. 40,000 | Value: 45.00 | | | | |

**2 POUNDS** **KM# 976b** **Weight:** 15.9800 g. **Composition:** 0.9170 Gold .4710 oz. AGW **Ruler:** Elizabeth II **Note:** Red gols ring, yellow gold center.

| Date | Mintage | F | VF | XF | Unc | BU |
|---|---|---|---|---|---|---|
| 1997 Proof | Est. 2,500 | Value: 675 | | | | |

**2 POUNDS** **KM# 994b** **Weight:** 12.0000 g. **Composition:** 0.9250 Silver .3568 oz. ASW **Ruler:** Elizabeth II **Note:** without gold plating

| Date | Mintage | | | | | |
|---|---|---|---|---|---|---|
| | 19,978 | Value: 40.00 | | | | |

**2 POUNDS** **KM# 994a** **Weight:** 12.0000 g. **Composition:** 0.9250 Silver .3568 oz. ASW **Ruler:** Elizabeth II **Note:** Gold plated silver ring, silver center.

| Date | Mintage | F | VF | XF | Unc | BU |
|---|---|---|---|---|---|---|
| 1998 Proof | 7,646 | Value: 50.00 | | | | |

**2 POUNDS** **KM# 1029** **Weight:** 32.5400 g. **Composition:** 0.9580 Silver .9995 oz. ASW **Ruler:** (no Ruler Name) **Subject:** Britannia Bullion **Obverse:** Queen's new portrait **Reverse:** Standing Britannia **Edge:** Reeded **Size:** 40 mm.

| Date | Mintage | F | VF | XF | Unc | BU |
|---|---|---|---|---|---|---|
| 1998 | — | — | — | — | 20.00 | — |

**2 POUNDS** **KM# 994** **Ring Composition:** Nickel-Brass **Center Composition:** Copper-Nickel **Ruler:** Elizabeth II **Obverse:** Rank-Broadley portrait of Queen Elizabeth II **Reverse:** Celtic design **Edge Lettering:** STANDING ON THE SHOULDERS OF GIANTS

| Date | Mintage | F | VF | XF | Unc | BU |
|---|---|---|---|---|---|---|
| 1998 | 67,268,000 | — | — | — | 5.00 | — |
| 1998 Proof | Est. 100,000 | Value: 7.50 | | | | |

**2 POUNDS** **KM# 999** **Ring Composition:** Nickel-Brass **Center Composition:** Copper-Nickel **Ruler:** Elizabeth II **Subject:** Rugby World Cup **Obverse:** Rank-Broadley portrait of Queen Elizabeth II **Reverse:** 2-tone rugby design

| Date | Mintage | F | VF | XF | Unc | BU |
|---|---|---|---|---|---|---|
| 1999 | 5,000,000 | — | — | — | 7.50 | — |
| 1999 Proof | Est. 100,000 | Value: 10.00 | | | | |

**2 POUNDS** **KM# 999b** **Weight:** 15.9800 g. **Composition:** 0.9170 Gold .4710 oz. AGW **Ruler:** Elizabeth II

| Date | Mintage | F | VF | XF | Unc | BU |
|---|---|---|---|---|---|---|
| 1999 Proof | 4,250 | Value: 525 | | | | |

**2 POUNDS** **KM# 999c** **Weight:** 24.0000 g. **Composition:** 0.9250 Silver .7137 oz. ASW **Ruler:** Elizabeth II **Obverse:** Queen's portrait within gold plated legend **Reverse:** Multicolor hologram center within gold plated legend **Edge:** Reeded, lettered edge

| Date | Mintage | F | VF | XF | Unc | BU |
|---|---|---|---|---|---|---|
| 1999 Proof | 10,000 | Value: 80.00 | | | | |

**2 POUNDS** **KM# 1000** **Weight:** 32.5400 g. **Composition:** 0.9580 Silver .9995 oz. ASW **Ruler:** Elizabeth II **Obverse:** Rank-Broadley portrait of Queen Elizabeth II **Reverse:** Britannia in chariot

| Date | Mintage | F | VF | XF | Unc | BU |
|---|---|---|---|---|---|---|
| 1999 Proof | Est. 100,000 | Value: 45.00 | | | | |

**2 POUNDS** **KM# 999a** **Weight:** 12.0000 g. **Composition:** 0.9250 Silver .3569 oz. ASW **Ruler:** Elizabeth II **Edge:** Reeded, lettered edge **Note:** Gold plated legends.

| Date | Mintage | F | VF | XF | Unc | BU |
|---|---|---|---|---|---|---|
| 1999 Proof | Est. 25,000 | Value: 47.50 | | | | |

**2 POUNDS** **KM# 1019** **Weight:** 32.4500 g. **Composition:** 0.9584 Silver .9999 oz. ASW **Ruler:** Elizabeth II **Subject:** Britannia Bullion **Obverse:** Queen's portrait **Reverse:** Stylized "Una and the Lion" **Edge:** Reeded **Size:** 40 mm.

| Date | Mintage | F | VF | XF | Unc | BU |
|---|---|---|---|---|---|---|
| 2001 | 100,000 | — | — | — | 15.75 | — |
| 2001 Proof | 15,000 | Value: 55.00 | | | | |

**2 POUNDS** **KM# 1014a** **Weight:** 12.0000 g. **Composition:** 0.9250 Silver .3569 oz. ASW **Ring Composition:** Gold Plated **Ruler:** Elizabeth II **Edge:** Reeded and inscribed **Edge Lettering:** "WIRELESS BRIDGES THE ATLANTIC...MARCONI 1901..." **Size:** 28.4 mm.

| Date | Mintage | F | VF | XF | Unc | BU |
|---|---|---|---|---|---|---|
| 2001 Proof | 25,000 | Value: 45.00 | | | | |

**2 POUNDS** **KM# 1014b** **Weight:** 15.9700 g. **Composition:** 0.9166 Gold .4706 oz. AGW **Ring Composition:** Red Gold **Center Composition:** Yellow Gold Plated Red Gold **Ruler:** Elizabeth II

| Date | Mintage | F | VF | XF | Unc | BU |
|---|---|---|---|---|---|---|
| 2001 Proof | 2,500 | Value: 445 | | | | |

**2 POUNDS** **KM# 1014** **Ring Weight:** 11.9700 g. **Ring Composition:** Nickel-Brass **Center Composition:** Copper-Nickel **Ruler:** Elizabeth II **Subject:** First Transatlantic Radio Transmission **Obverse:** Queen's new portrait **Reverse:** Symbolic design **Edge:** Reeded and inscribed **Size:** 28.4 mm.

| Date | Mintage | F | VF | XF | Unc | BU |
|---|---|---|---|---|---|---|
| 2001 | — | — | — | — | 5.00 | — |
| 2001 Proof | — | Value: 10.00 | | | | |

**5 POUNDS** **KM# 962** **Composition:** Copper-Nickel **Ruler:** Elizabeth II **Subject:** 90th Birthday of Queen Mother

| Date | Mintage | F | VF | XF | Unc | BU |
|---|---|---|---|---|---|---|
| ND(1990) | 2,755,000 | — | — | — | 15.00 | — |

**5 POUNDS** **KM# 962a** **Weight:** 28.2800 g. **Composition:** 0.9250 Silver .8411 oz. ASW **Ruler:** Elizabeth II

| Date | Mintage | F | VF | XF | Unc | BU |
|---|---|---|---|---|---|---|
| ND(1990) Proof | Est. 150,000 | Value: 40.00 | | | | |

**5 POUNDS** **KM# 962b** **Weight:** 39.9400 g. **Composition:** 0.9170 Gold 1.1775 oz. AGW **Ruler:** Elizabeth II **Subject:** 90th Birthday of Queen Mother

| Date | Mintage | F | VF | XF | Unc | BU |
|---|---|---|---|---|---|---|
| ND(1990) Proof | Est. 2,500 | Value: 650 | | | | |

**5 POUNDS** **KM# 965** **Composition:** Copper-Nickel **Ruler:** Elizabeth II **Subject:** 40th Anniversary of Reign

| Date | Mintage | F | VF | XF | Unc | BU |
|---|---|---|---|---|---|---|
| ND(1993) | 1,822,000 | — | — | — | 14.00 | — |
| ND(1993) Proof | Est. 100,000 | Value: 20.00 | | | | |

**5 POUNDS** **KM# 965a** **Weight:** 28.2800 g. **Composition:** 0.9250 Silver .8411 oz. ASW **Ruler:** Elizabeth II

| Date | Mintage | F | VF | XF | Unc | BU |
|---|---|---|---|---|---|---|
| ND(1993) Proof | Est. 100,000 | Value: 45.00 | | | | |

**5 POUNDS** **KM# 965b** **Weight:** 39.9400 g. **Composition:** 0.9170 Gold 1.1775 oz. AGW **Ruler:** Elizabeth II **Subject:** 40th Anniversary of Reign

| Date | Mintage | F | VF | XF | Unc | BU |
|---|---|---|---|---|---|---|
| ND(1993) Proof | Est. 2,500 | Value: 950 | | | | |

**5 POUNDS** **KM# 974** **Composition:** Copper-Nickel **Ruler:** Elizabeth II **Subject:** 70th Birthday of Queen Elizabeth II

| Date | Mintage | F | VF | XF | Unc | BU |
|---|---|---|---|---|---|---|
| ND(1996) | 2,936,000 | — | — | — | 15.00 | — |
| ND(1996) Proof | — | Value: 22.00 | | | | |

**5 POUNDS** **KM# 974a** **Weight:** 28.2800 g. **Composition:** 0.9250 Silver .8411 oz. ASW **Ruler:** Elizabeth II

| Date | Mintage | F | VF | XF | Unc | BU |
|---|---|---|---|---|---|---|
| ND(1996) Proof | Est. 70,000 | Value: 45.00 | | | | |

**5 POUNDS** **KM# 974b** **Weight:** 39.9400 g. **Composition:** 0.9170 Gold 1.1775 oz. AGW **Ruler:** Elizabeth II **Subject:** 70th Birthday of Queen Elizabeth II

| Date | Mintage | F | VF | XF | Unc | BU |
|---|---|---|---|---|---|---|
| ND(1996) Proof | Est. 2,750 | Value: 1,000 | | | | |

**5 POUNDS** **KM# 977** **Composition:** Copper-Nickel **Ruler:** Elizabeth II **Subject:** Queen Elizabeth II's Golden Wedding Anniversary **Obverse:** Portrait of the Queen Elizabeth II and Prince Philip **Reverse:** Two coats of arms

| Date | Mintage | F | VF | XF | Unc | BU |
|---|---|---|---|---|---|---|
| ND(1997) | 1,733,000 | — | — | — | 16.50 | — |
| ND(1997) Proof | — | Value: 22.00 | | | | |

**5 POUNDS** **KM# 977a** **Weight:** 28.2800 g. **Composition:** 0.9250 Silver .8411 oz. ASW **Ruler:** Elizabeth II

| Date | Mintage | F | VF | XF | Unc | BU |
|---|---|---|---|---|---|---|
| ND(1997) Proof | Est. 70,000 | Value: 50.00 | | | | |

**5 POUNDS** **KM# 977b** **Weight:** 39.9400 g. **Composition:** 0.9170 Gold 1.1775 oz. AGW **Ruler:** Elizabeth II

| Date | Mintage | F | VF | XF | Unc | BU |
|---|---|---|---|---|---|---|
| ND(1997) Proof | Est. 2,750 | Value: 995 | | | | |

**5 POUNDS** **KM# 995** **Composition:** Copper-Nickel **Ruler:** Elizabeth II **Subject:** 50th Birthday - Prince Charles **Obverse:** Rank-Broadley portrait of Queen Elizabeth II **Reverse:** Portrait of Prince Charles

| Date | Mintage | F | VF | XF | Unc | BU |
|---|---|---|---|---|---|---|
| 1998 | 1,407,000 | — | — | — | 16.50 | — |
| 1998 Proof | Est. 100,000 | Value: 20.00 | | | | |

**5 POUNDS** **KM# 995a** **Weight:** 28.2800 g. **Composition:** 0.9250 Silver .8411 oz. ASW **Ruler:** Elizabeth II

| Date | Mintage | F | VF | XF | Unc | BU |
|---|---|---|---|---|---|---|
| 1998 Proof | — | Value: 50.00 | | | | |

**5 POUNDS** **KM# 995b** **Weight:** 39.9400 g. **Composition:** 0.9167 Gold 1.1771 oz. AGW **Ruler:** Elizabeth II

| Date | Mintage | F | VF | XF | Unc | BU |
|---|---|---|---|---|---|---|
| 1998 Proof | — | Value: 900 | | | | |

**5 POUNDS** **KM# 997** **Weight:** 28.2800 g. **Composition:** 0.9250 Silver .8411 oz. ASW **Ruler:** Elizabeth II **Obverse:** Rank-Broadley portrait of Queen Elizabeth II **Reverse:** Portrait of Princess Diana, dates

| Date | Mintage | F | VF | XF | Unc | BU |
|---|---|---|---|---|---|---|
| 1999 | 5,000,000 | — | — | — | 16.50 | — |
| 1999 Proof | Est. 100,000 | Value: 22.00 | | | | |

**5 POUNDS** **KM# 997a** **Weight:** 28.2800 g. **Composition:** 0.9250 Silver .8410 oz. ASW **Ruler:** Elizabeth II

| Date | Mintage | F | VF | XF | Unc | BU |
|---|---|---|---|---|---|---|
| 1999 Proof | Est. 350,000 | Value: 50.00 | | | | |

**5 POUNDS** **KM# 997b** **Weight:** 39.9400 g. **Composition:** 0.9170 Gold 1.1775 oz. AGW **Ruler:** Elizabeth II

| Date | Mintage | F | VF | XF | Unc | BU |
|---|---|---|---|---|---|---|
| 1999 Proof | Est. 7,500 | Value: 925 | | | | |

**5 POUNDS** **KM# 1006** **Composition:** Copper-Nickel **Ruler:** Elizabeth II **Obverse:** Bust Queen right **Reverse:** Map with Greenwich Meridian **Edge Lettering:** WHAT'S PAST IS PROLOGUE

| Date | Mintage | F | VF | XF | Unc | BU |
|---|---|---|---|---|---|---|
| 1999 | — | — | — | — | 15.00 | — |
| 1999 Proof | — | Value: 20.00 | | | | |
| 2000 | — | — | — | — | 15.00 | — |
| 2000 Proof | Est. 100,000 | Value: 20.00 | | | | |

**5 POUNDS** **KM# 1006a** **Weight:** 28.2800 g. **Composition:** 0.9250 Silver .8410 oz. ASW **Ruler:** Elizabeth II

| Date | Mintage | F | VF | XF | Unc | BU |
|---|---|---|---|---|---|---|
| 1999 Proof | 75,000 | Value: 55.00 | | | | |
| 2000 Proof | 50,000 | Value: 55.00 | | | | |

**5 POUNDS** **KM# 1006b** **Weight:** 39.9400 g. **Composition:** 0.9170 Gold 1.1771 oz. AGW **Ruler:** Elizabeth II

| Date | Mintage | F | VF | XF | Unc | BU |
|---|---|---|---|---|---|---|
| 1999 Proof | 2,500 | Value: 995 | | | | |
| 2000 Proof | 2,500 | Value: 995 | | | | |

**5 POUNDS** **KM# 1007** **Composition:** Copper-Nickel **Ruler:** Elizabeth II **Subject:** 100th Birthday - Queen Elizabeth, The Queen Mother **Reverse:** Bust Queen Mother left with signature **Edge:** Reeded

| Date | Mintage | F | VF | XF | Unc | BU |
|---|---|---|---|---|---|---|
| 2000 | — | — | — | — | 16.50 | — |

**5 POUNDS** **KM# 1007a** **Weight:** 28.2800 g. **Composition:** 0.9250 Silver .8410 oz. ASW **Ruler:** Elizabeth II **Subject:** Queen Mother's Centennial **Obverse:** Queen's portrait **Reverse:** Queen Mother's portrait and signature **Edge:** Reeded

| Date | Mintage | F | VF | XF | Unc | BU |
|---|---|---|---|---|---|---|
| 2000 Proof | 100,000 | Value: 55.00 | | | | |

**5 POUNDS** **KM# 1007b** **Weight:** 39.9400 g. **Composition:** 0.9167 Gold 1.0003 oz. AGW **Ruler:** Elizabeth II

| Date | Mintage | F | VF | XF | Unc | BU |
|---|---|---|---|---|---|---|
| 2000 Proof | 3,000 | Value: 950 | | | | |

**5 POUNDS** **KM# 1006.1** **Composition:** Copper-Nickel **Ruler:** Elizabeth II **Reverse:** Same as KM#1006 but with the addition of a world globe at 3 o'clock in inner circle

| Date | Mintage | F | VF | XF | Unc | BU |
|---|---|---|---|---|---|---|
| 2000 | — | — | — | — | 20.00 | — |

**5 POUNDS** **KM# 1015** **Weight:** 28.2800 g. **Composition:** Copper-Nickel **Ruler:** Elizabeth II **Subject:** Centennial of Queen Victoria **Obverse:** Queen Elizabeth's portrait **Reverse:** Queen Victoria's portrait **Edge:** Reeded **Size:** 38.6 mm.

| Date | Mintage | F | VF | XF | Unc | BU |
|---|---|---|---|---|---|---|
| 2001 | — | — | — | — | 15.00 | — |
| 2001 Proof | — | Value: 20.00 | | | | |

**5 POUNDS** **KM# 1024** **Weight:** 28.2800 g. **Composition:** Copper-Nickel **Ruler:** Elizabeth II **Subject:** Queen's Golden Jubilee of Reign **Obverse:** Queen's portrait **Reverse:** Queen on horse **Edge:** Reeded **Size:** 38.6 mm.

| Date | Mintage | F | VF | XF | Unc | BU |
|---|---|---|---|---|---|---|
| 2002 | — | — | — | — | 15.00 | — |
| 2002 Proof | — | Value: 20.00 | | | | |

**5 POUNDS** **KM# 1024a** **Weight:** 28.2800 g. **Composition:** 0.9250 Silver .8410 oz. ASW **Ruler:** Elizabeth II **Edge:** Reeded **Size:** 38.6 mm.

| Date | Mintage | F | VF | XF | Unc | BU |
|---|---|---|---|---|---|---|
| 2002 Proof | — | Value: 50.00 | | | | |

**5 POUNDS** **KM# 1024b** **Weight:** 39.9400 g. **Composition:** 0.9167 Gold 1.0003 oz. AGW **Ruler:** Elizabeth II **Edge:** Reeded **Size:** 38.6 mm.

| Date | Mintage | F | VF | XF | Unc | BU |
|---|---|---|---|---|---|---|
| 2002 Proof | — | Value: 950 | | | | |

## BULLION COINAGE

Until 1990, .917 Gold was commonly alloyed with copper by the British Royal Mint.

All proof issues have designers name as P. Nathan. The uncirculated issues use only Nathan.

**10 POUNDS (1/10 Ounce - Britannia)** **KM# 950** **Weight:** 3.4120 g. **Composition:** 0.9170 Gold .1000 oz. AGW **Ruler:** Elizabeth II **Note:** Copper alloy.

| Date | Mintage | F | VF | XF | Unc | BU |
|---|---|---|---|---|---|---|
| 1987 | — | — | — | — | BV+16% | — |
| 1987 Proof | 26,000 | Value: 60.00 | | | | |
| 1988 | — | — | — | — | BV+16% | — |
| 1988 Proof | Est. 19,000 | Value: 60.00 | | | | |
| 1989 | — | — | — | — | BV+16% | — |
| 1989 Proof | Est. 6,500 | Value: 60.00 | | | | |

**10 POUNDS (1/10 Ounce - Britannia)** **KM# 950a** **Weight:** 3.4120 g. **Composition:** 0.9170 Gold .1000 oz. AGW **Ruler:** Elizabeth II **Note:** Silver alloy.

| Date | Mintage | F | VF | XF | Unc | BU |
|---|---|---|---|---|---|---|
| 1990 Proof | Est. 5,000 | Value: 60.00 | | | | |
| 1991 Proof | 2,750 | Value: 100 | | | | |
| 1992 Proof | 1,500 | Value: 100 | | | | |
| 1993 Proof | Est. 1,000 | Value: 100 | | | | |
| 1994 Proof | 1,500 | Value: 95.00 | | | | |
| 1995 Proof | 1,500 | Value: 95.00 | | | | |
| 1996 Proof | Est. 3,000 | Value: 90.00 | | | | |
| 1999 Proof | Est. 5,750 | Value: 80.00 | | | | |

**10 POUNDS (1/10 Ounce - Britannia)** **KM# 982** **Weight:** 3.4100 g. **Composition:** 0.9167 Gold .1005 oz. AGW **Ruler:** Elizabeth II **Obverse:** Queen's portrait **Reverse:** Britannia in chariot **Note:** Similar to 2 Pounds, KM#981.

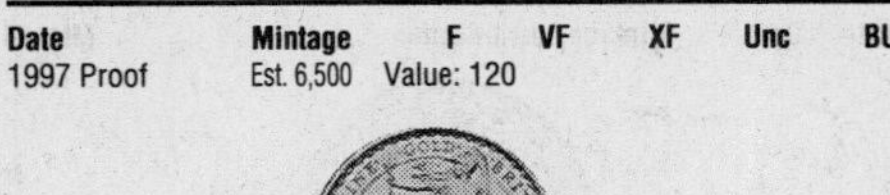

| Date | Mintage | F | VF | XF | Unc | BU |
|---|---|---|---|---|---|---|
| 1997 Proof | Est. 6,500 | Value: 120 | | | | |

**10 POUNDS (1/10 Ounce - Britannia)** **KM# 1008**
**Weight:** 3.4100 g. **Composition:** 0.9167 Gold .1005 oz. AGW **Ruler:** Elizabeth II **Reverse:** Britannia standing **Edge:** Reeded

| Date | Mintage | F | VF | XF | Unc | BU |
|---|---|---|---|---|---|---|
| 1999 Proof | — | Value: 115 | | | | |
| 2000 Proof | 3,250 | Value: 100 | | | | |

**10 POUNDS (1/10 Ounce - Britannia)** **KM# 1020**
**Weight:** 3.4100 g. **Composition:** 0.9167 Gold .1005 oz. AGW **Ruler:** Elizabeth II **Subject:** Britannia Bullion **Obverse:** Queen's portrait **Reverse:** Stylized "Una and the Lion" **Edge:** Reeded **Size:** 16.5 mm.

| Date | Mintage | F | VF | XF | Unc | BU |
|---|---|---|---|---|---|---|
| 2001 | 25,000 | — | — | — | BV+16% | — |
| 2001 Proof | 3,500 | Value: 115 | | | | |

**25 POUNDS (1/4 Ounce - Britannia)** **KM# 951**
**Weight:** 8.5130 g. **Composition:** 0.9170 Gold .2500 oz. AGW **Ruler:** Elizabeth II **Note:** Copper alloy.

| Date | Mintage | F | VF | XF | Unc | BU |
|---|---|---|---|---|---|---|
| 1987 | — | — | — | — | BV+8% | — |
| 1987 Proof | 26,000 | Value: 125 | | | | |
| 1988 | — | — | — | — | BV+8% | — |
| 1988 Proof | Est. 14,000 | Value: 125 | | | | |
| 1989 | — | — | — | — | BV+8% | — |
| 1989 Proof | Est. 4,000 | Value: 125 | | | | |

**25 POUNDS (1/4 Ounce - Britannia)** **KM# 951a**
**Weight:** 8.5130 g. **Composition:** 0.9170 Gold .2500 oz. AGW **Ruler:** Elizabeth II **Note:** Silver alloy.

| Date | Mintage | F | VF | XF | Unc | BU |
|---|---|---|---|---|---|---|
| 1990 Proof | Est. 2,500 | Value: 125 | | | | |
| 1991 Proof | 750 | Value: 225 | | | | |
| 1992 Proof | 500 | Value: 225 | | | | |
| 1993 Proof | Est. 500 | Value: 225 | | | | |
| 1994 Proof | 500 | Value: 210 | | | | |
| 1995 Proof | 500 | Value: 210 | | | | |
| 1996 Proof | 2,500 | Value: 210 | | | | |
| 1999 Proof | 1,750 | Value: 210 | | | | |

**25 POUNDS (1/4 Ounce - Britannia)** **KM# 983**
**Weight:** 8.5100 g. **Composition:** 0.9167 Gold .2508 oz. AGW **Ruler:** Elizabeth II **Obverse:** Queen's portrait **Reverse:** Britannia in chariot **Note:** Similar to 2 Pounds, KM#981.

| Date | Mintage | F | VF | XF | Unc | BU |
|---|---|---|---|---|---|---|
| 1997 Proof | Est. 4,000 | Value: 215 | | | | |

**25 POUNDS (1/4 Ounce - Britannia)** **KM# 1009**
**Weight:** 8.5100 g. **Composition:** 0.9167 Gold .2508 oz. AGW **Ruler:** Elizabeth II **Reverse:** Britannia standing **Edge:** Reeded

| Date | Mintage | F | VF | XF | Unc | BU |
|---|---|---|---|---|---|---|
| 1999 Proof | — | Value: 220 | | | | |
| 2000 Proof | Est. 1,250 | Value: 200 | | | | |

**25 POUNDS (1/4 Ounce - Britannia)** **KM# 1021**
**Weight:** 8.5100 g. **Composition:** 0.9167 Gold .2508 oz. AGW **Ruler:** Elizabeth II **Subject:** Britannia Bullion **Obverse:** Queen's portrait **Reverse:** Stylized "Una and the Lion" **Edge:** Reeded **Size:** 22 mm.

| Date | Mintage | F | VF | XF | Unc | BU |
|---|---|---|---|---|---|---|
| 2001 | 25,000 | — | — | — | BV+8% | — |
| 2001 Proof | 1,500 | Value: 225 | | | | |

**50 POUNDS (1/2 Ounce - Britannia)** **KM# 952**
**Weight:** 17.0250 g. **Composition:** 0.9170 Gold .5000 oz. AGW **Ruler:** Elizabeth II **Note:** Copper alloy.

| Date | Mintage | F | VF | XF | Unc | BU |
|---|---|---|---|---|---|---|
| 1987 | — | — | — | — | BV+6% | — |
| 1987 Proof | 13,000 | Value: 245 | | | | |
| 1988 | — | — | — | — | BV+6% | — |
| 1988 Proof | Est. 6,500 | Value: 245 | | | | |
| 1989 | — | — | — | — | BV+6% | — |
| 1989 Proof | Est. 2,500 | Value: 250 | | | | |

**50 POUNDS (1/2 Ounce - Britannia)** **KM# 952a**
**Weight:** 17.0250 g. **Composition:** 0.9170 Gold .5000 oz. AGW **Ruler:** Elizabeth II **Note:** Silver alloy.

| Date | Mintage | F | VF | XF | Unc | BU |
|---|---|---|---|---|---|---|
| 1990 Proof | Est. 2,500 | Value: 250 | | | | |
| 1991 Proof | 750 | Value: 380 | | | | |
| 1992 Proof | 500 | Value: 420 | | | | |
| 1993 Proof | Est. 500 | — | — | — | — | — |
| 1994 Proof | 500 | Value: 420 | | | | |
| 1995 Proof | 500 | Value: 420 | | | | |
| 1996 Proof | Est. 2,500 | Value: 395 | | | | |
| 1999 Proof | Est. 750 | Value: 440 | | | | |

**50 POUNDS (1/2 Ounce - Britannia)** **KM# 984**
**Weight:** 17.0300 g. **Composition:** 0.9167 Gold .5019 oz. AGW **Ruler:** Elizabeth II **Obverse:** Queen's portrait **Reverse:** Britannia in chariot **Note:** Similar to 2 Pounds, KM#281.

| Date | Mintage | F | VF | XF | Unc | BU |
|---|---|---|---|---|---|---|
| 1997 Proof | Est. 1,500 | Value: 400 | | | | |

**50 POUNDS (1/2 Ounce - Britannia)** **KM# 1010**
**Weight:** 17.0300 g. **Composition:** 0.9167 Gold .5019 oz. AGW **Ruler:** Elizabeth II **Reverse:** Britannia standing **Edge:** Reeded

| Date | Mintage | F | VF | XF | Unc | BU |
|---|---|---|---|---|---|---|
| 1999 Proof | — | Value: 425 | | | | |
| 2000 Proof | 750 | Value: 425 | | | | |

**50 POUNDS (1/2 Ounce - Britannia)** **KM# 1022**
**Weight:** 17.0200 g. **Composition:** 0.9167 Gold .5016 oz. AGW **Ruler:** Elizabeth II **Subject:** Britannia Bullion **Obverse:** Queen's portrait **Reverse:** Stylized "Una and the Lion" **Edge:** Reeded **Size:** 27 mm.

| Date | Mintage | F | VF | XF | Unc | BU |
|---|---|---|---|---|---|---|
| 2001 | 25,000 | — | — | — | BV+6% | — |
| 2001 Proof | 1,000 | Value: 432 | | | | |

**100 POUNDS (1 Ounce - Britannia)** **KM# 953** **Weight:** 34.0500 g. **Composition:** 0.9170 Gold 1.0000 oz. AGW **Ruler:** Elizabeth II **Note:** Copper alloy.

| Date | Mintage | F | VF | XF | Unc | BU |
|---|---|---|---|---|---|---|
| 1987 | — | — | — | — | BV+4% | — |
| 1987 Proof | 13,000 | Value: 500 | | | | |
| 1988 | — | — | — | — | BV+4% | — |
| 1988 Proof | Est. 8,500 | Value: 500 | | | | |
| 1989 | — | — | — | — | BV+4% | — |
| 1989 Proof | Est. 2,600 | Value: 500 | | | | |

**100 POUNDS (1 Ounce - Britannia)** **KM# 953a**
**Weight:** 34.0500 g. **Composition:** 0.9170 Gold 1.0000 oz. AGW **Ruler:** Elizabeth II **Note:** Silver alloy.

| Date | Mintage | F | VF | XF | Unc | BU |
|---|---|---|---|---|---|---|
| 1990 Proof | 3,500 | Value: 500 | | | | |
| 1991 Proof | 1,250 | Value: 750 | | | | |
| 1992 Proof | 500 | Value: 785 | | | | |
| 1993 Proof | Est. 500 | Value: 785 | | | | |
| 1994 Proof | Est. 500 | Value: 760 | | | | |
| 1995 Proof | Est. 500 | Value: 800 | | | | |
| 1996 Proof | 2,500 | Value: 395 | | | | |
| 1999 Proof | Est. 750 | Value: 835 | | | | |

**100 POUNDS (1 Ounce - Britannia)** **KM# 985** **Weight:** 34.0500 g. **Composition:** 0.9167 Gold 1.0035 oz. AGW **Ruler:** Elizabeth II **Obverse:** Queen's portrait **Reverse:** Britannia in chariot

| Date | Mintage | F | VF | XF | Unc | BU |
|---|---|---|---|---|---|---|
| 1997 Proof | Est. 2,500 | Value: 845 | | | | |

**100 POUNDS (1 Ounce - Britannia)** **KM# 1011**
**Weight:** 34.0500 g. **Composition:** 0.9167 Gold 1.0035 oz. AGW **Ruler:** Elizabeth II **Reverse:** Britannia standing **Edge:** Reeded

| Date | Mintage | F | VF | XF | Unc | BU |
|---|---|---|---|---|---|---|
| 1999 Proof | — | Value: 850 | | | | |
| 2000 Proof | 750 | Value: 850 | | | | |

**100 POUNDS (1 Ounce - Britannia)** **KM# 1023**
**Weight:** 34.0500 g. **Composition:** 0.9167 Gold 1.0035 oz. AGW **Ruler:** Elizabeth II **Subject:** Britannia Bullion **Obverse:** Queen's portrait **Reverse:** Stylized "Una and the Lion" **Edge:** Reeded **Size:** 32.7 mm.

| Date | Mintage | F | VF | XF | Unc | BU |
|---|---|---|---|---|---|---|
| 2001 | 25,000 | — | — | — | BV+4% | — |
| 2001 Proof | 1,000 | Value: 865 | | | | |

## TRADE COINAGE

### Britannia Series

Issued to facilitate British trade in the Orient, the reverse design incorporated the denomination in Chinese characters and Malay script.

This issue was struck at the Bombay (B) and Calcutta (C) Mints in India, except for 1925 and 1930 issues which were struck at London. Through error the mint marks did not appear on some early (1895-1900) issues as ndicated.

**DOLLAR** **KM# T5** **Weight:** 26.9568 g. **Composition:** 0.9000 Silver .7800 oz. ASW **Ruler:** (no Ruler Name)

| Date | Mintage | F | VF | XF | Unc | BU |
|---|---|---|---|---|---|---|
| 1901/0B | 25,680,000 | 40.00 | 60.00 | 100 | 200 | — |
| 1901B | Inc. above | 15.00 | 20.00 | 25.00 | 60.00 | — |
| 1901B Proof | Inc. above | Value: 800 | | | | |
| 1901C | 1,514,000 | 25.00 | 45.00 | 100 | 200 | — |
| 1902B | 30,404,000 | 15.00 | 20.00 | 25.00 | 60.00 | — |
| 1902B Proof | Inc. above | Value: 800 | | | | |
| 1902C | 1,267,000 | 25.00 | 45.00 | 80.00 | 175 | — |
| 1902C Proof | Inc. above | Value: 800 | | | | |
| 1903/2B | 3,956,000 | 12.00 | 25.00 | 40.00 | 75.00 | — |
| 1903B | Inc. above | 12.00 | 20.00 | — | 60.00 | — |
| 1903B Proof | Inc. above | Value: 800 | | | | |

| Date | Mintage | F | VF | XF | Unc | BU |
|---|---|---|---|---|---|---|
| 1904/898B | 649,000 | 50.00 | 80.00 | 125 | 200 | — |
| 1904/3B | Inc. above | 30.00 | 50.00 | 100 | 225 | — |
| 1904/0B | Inc. above | 80.00 | 125 | 175 | 300 | — |
| 1904B | Inc. above | 40.00 | 60.00 | 100 | 250 | — |
| 1904B Proof | Inc. above | Value: 700 | | | | |
| 1907B | 1,946,000 | 12.00 | 20.00 | 25.00 | 60.00 | — |
| 1908/3B | 6,871,000 | 40.00 | 60.00 | 100 | 175 | — |
| 1908/7B | Inc. above | 35.00 | 50.00 | 90.00 | 125 | — |
| 1908B | Inc. above | 12.00 | 20.00 | 25.00 | 60.00 | — |
| 1908B Proof | Inc. above | Value: 700 | | | | |
| 1909/8B | 5,954,000 | 30.00 | 45.00 | 80.00 | 125 | — |
| 1909B | Inc. above | 12.00 | 20.00 | 25.00 | 60.00 | — |
| 1910/00B | 553,000 | 40.00 | 60.00 | 100 | 175 | — |
| 1910B | Inc. above | 12.00 | 20.00 | 25.00 | 60.00 | — |
| 1911/00B | — | 30.00 | 50.00 | 100 | 150 | — |
| 1911B | 37,471,000 | 12.00 | 20.00 | 25.00 | 60.00 | — |
| 1912B | 5,672,000 | 12.00 | 20.00 | 25.00 | 60.00 | — |
| 1912B Proof | Inc. above | Value: 800 | | | | |
| 1913/2B | — | 100 | 150 | 250 | 700 | — |
| 1913B | 1,567,000 | 30.00 | 60.00 | 125 | 300 | — |
| 1913B Proof | Inc. above | Value: 800 | | | | |
| 1921B | 5 | — | — | — | 15,000 | — |
| **Note:** Original mintage 50,211 | | | | | | |
| 1921B Restrike; Proof | — | Value: 4,500 | | | | |
| 1925 | 6,870,000 | 15.00 | 20.00 | 25.00 | 70.00 | — |
| 1929/1B | 5,100,000 | 30.00 | 50.00 | 80.00 | 200 | — |
| 1929B | Inc. above | 12.00 | 20.00 | 25.00 | 60.00 | — |
| 1929B Proof | Inc. above | Value: 800 | | | | |
| 1930B | 10,400,000 | 12.00 | 20.00 | 25.00 | 60.00 | — |
| 1930B Proof | Inc. above | Value: 800 | | | | |
| 1930 | 666,000 | 12.00 | 20.00 | 25.00 | 60.00 | — |
| 1934B | 17,335,000 | 75.00 | 150 | 200 | 500 | — |
| 1934B Proof | Inc. above | Value: 3,500 | | | | |
| 1934B Restrike; Proof | 20 | Value: 3,000 | | | | |
| 1935B | 5 | 1,000 | 1,500 | 2,500 | 5,000 | — |
| **Note:** Original mintage 6,811,995 | | | | | | |
| 1935B Proof | 20 | Value: 7,500 | | | | |
| 1935B Restrike; Proof | 20 | Value: 4,000 | | | | |

**DOLLAR** KM# T5a **Composition:** Gold **Ruler:** (no Ruler Name)

| Date | Mintage | F | VF | XF | Unc | BU |
|---|---|---|---|---|---|---|
| 1901B Restrike; Proof | — | Value: 7,500 | | | | |
| 1902B Restrike; Proof | — | Value: 7,500 | | | | |

## PATTERNS

Including off metal strikes

| KM# | Date | Mintage | Identification | Mkt Val |
|---|---|---|---|---|
| PnA121 | 1922 | — | Florin. Gold. KM817a | 15,000 |
| PnC121 | 1923 | — | Shilling. Nickel. KM816a | 1,000 |
| PnB121 | 1923 | — | 3 Pence. Nickel. KM#813a. | — |
| PnF121 | 1924 | — | Shilling. Nickel. 5.0000 g. KM816a | 1,000 |
| PnD121 | 1924 | — | 3 Pence. Gold. KM813a | 10,000 |
| | 1924 | — | 6 Pence. Gold. KM815.a1 | 10,000 |
| Pn121 | 1924 | — | Shilling. Nickel. KM816a | 1,000 |
| PnE122 | 1925 | — | Shilling. Nickel. Modified effigy. KM#833. | 2,000 |
| PnF122 | 1925 | — | Shilling. Silver. MODEL. Matte proof; KM#833. | 2,000 |
| PnA122 | 1925 | — | 3 Pence. Nickel. Modified effigy. KM#831. | — |
| PnB122 | 1925 | — | 3 Pence. Silver. MODEL. Matte proof; KM#831. | — |
| PnC122 | 1925 | — | 6 Pence. Nickel. Modified effigy. KM#832. | — |
| PnD122 | 1925 | — | 6 Pence. Silver. MODEL. Matte proof; KM#832. | — |
| PnG122 | 1926 | — | 1/2 Crown. Silver. MODEL. Matte proof; KM#835. | — |
| PnJ122 | 1927 | — | Florin. Silver. MODEL. Matte proof, KM#834. | — |
| PnI122 | 1927 | — | 6 Pence. Nickel. KM#828 | — |
| PnK122 | 1927 | — | 1/2 Crown. Nickel. Modified Effigy. KM830 | — |
| PnL122 | 1927 | — | 1/2 Crown. Gold. Modified Effigy. KM830 | — |
| PnM122 | 1935 | — | Crown. Silver. similar to KM842. | — |
| Pn122 | 1937 | 18,000 | Farthing. Bronze. Edward VIII. | — |
| Pn126 | 1937 | — | 3 Pence. Nickel-Brass. Inner circle. Edward VIII. | 45,000 |
| Pn128 | 1937 | 25,000 | Shilling. 0.5000 Silver. Edward VIII. | 37,000 |
| Pn132 | 1937 | 6 | Sovereign. 0.9160 Gold. Edward VIII. | 120,000 |
| Pn123 | 1937 | 18,000 | 1/2 Penny. Bronze. Edward VIII. | — |
| Pn124 | 1937 | 25,000 | Penny. Bronze. Edward VIII. | — |
| Pn125 | 1937 | — | 3 Pence. Nickel-Brass. Edward VIII. | — |
| Pn127 | 1937 | 18,000 | 6 Pence. 0.5000 Silver. Edward VIII. | — |
| Pn129 | 1937 | 35,000 | Florin. 0.5000 Silver. Edward VIII. | — |
| Pn130 | 1937 | 60,000 | 1/2 Crown. 0.5000 Silver. Edward VIII. | — |
| Pn131 | 1937 | 120,000 | Crown. 0.5000 Silver. Edward VIII. | — |
| Pn133 | 1946 | — | 6 Pence. Copper-Nickel. | — |
| PnA134 | 1950 | — | 4 Shilling. Copper-Nickel. | — |
| PnB134 | 1952 | — | Shilling. KM#876. | — |
| Pn134 | 1953 | — | Penny. Bronze. Dentilated border. | — |
| PnA135 | 1953 | — | Crown. Matte, KM#894. | — |
| Pn135 | 1953 | — | 1/2 Sovereign. 0.9160 Gold. | — |
| Pn137 | 1953 | — | 2 Pounds. 0.9160 Gold. | — |
| Pn138 | 1953 | — | 5 Pounds. 0.9160 Gold. | — |
| Pn136 | 1953 | — | Sovereign. 0.9160 Gold. Y#137. | 40,000 |
| Pn139 | 1961 | — | Cent. | — |
| Pn140 | 1961 | — | 2 Cents. | — |
| Pn141 | 1961 | — | 5 Cents. | — |
| Pn142 | 1961 | — | 10 Cents. | — |
| Pn143 | 1961 | — | 20 Cents. | — |
| Pn144 | 1961 | — | 50 Cents. | — |
| Pn145 | 1963 | — | 1/2 Penny. Decimal. | — |
| Pn146 | 1963 | — | Penny. Decimal. | — |

## PRIVATE PATTERNS

| KM# | Date | Mintage | Identification | Mkt Val |
|---|---|---|---|---|
| PPn119 | 1902 | — | Crown. Silver. | 1,700 |
| PPn120 | 1902 | — | Crown. Gold. | 5,000 |
| PPn121 | 1902 | — | 1/2 Pound. Silver. | 4,000 |
| PPn122 | 1902 | — | Pound. Silver. | 3,250 |
| PPn-C123 | MDCDX | — | Crown. Silver. Plain edge. | 3,500 |
| PPn-D123 | MDCDX | — | Crown. Silver. Milled edge. | 3,500 |
| PPn-E123 | MDCDX | 2 | Crown. Silver Plated Copper. Matte. | 8,000 |
| PPn-I123 | 1910 | 10 | Crown. Silver. Plain edge. | 3,500 |
| PPn-J123 | 1910 | 10 | Crown. Silver. 32.6300 g. Milled edge. | 3,500 |
| PPn-A123 | MDCDX | — | Crown. Gold. Plain edge. | — |
| PPn-B123 | MDCDX | — | Crown. Gold. Milled edge. | — |
| PPn-F123 | MDCDX | — | Crown. Copper. Matte. | — |
| PPn-G123 | 1910 | — | Crown. Gold. Plain edge. | — |
| PPn-H123 | 1910 | — | Crown. Gold. Milled edge. | — |
| PPn-K123 | 1910 | — | Crown. Silver. Milled edge. Weight varies 27.54-28.38 grams; Matte. | — |
| PPn-L123 | 1910 | — | Crown. Copper. | — |
| PPn123 | 1911 | — | 2 Florins. Silver. Plain edge. | 900 |
| PPn124 | 1911 | — | 2 Florins. Silver. Reeded edge. | 900 |
| PPn125 | 1911 | — | 2 Florins. Silver. REX 19 11 BRI. Plain edge. | 1,000 |
| PPn126 | 1913 | — | Octorino. Silver. Reeded edge. | 800 |
| PPn127 | 1913 | — | Octorino. Gold. Reeded edge. | 3,000 |
| PPn128 | 1913 | — | Octorino. Platinum. Reeded edge. | 2,850 |
| PPn129 | 1913 | — | Octorino. Copper. Reeded edge. | 500 |
| PPn130 | 1913 | — | Octorino. Lead. Plain edge. | 450 |
| PPn-A130 | 1913 | — | Octorino. Iron. | 2,000 |
| PPn131 | 1913 | — | 8 Pence. Silver. Reeded edge. | 500 |
| PPn132 | 1913 | — | 8 Pence. Gold. Reeded edge. | 2,000 |
| PPn133 | 1913 | — | 8 Pence. Platinum. Reeded edge. | 2,000 |
| PPn134 | 1913 | — | 8 Pence. Copper. Reeded edge. | 350 |
| PPn135 | 1913 | — | 8 Pence. Nickel. Reeded edge. | 350 |
| PPn136 | 1914 | — | 12 Groats. Silver. Plain edge. | 750 |
| PPn-A136 | 1914 | — | 12 Groats. Silver. Reeded edge. | 750 |
| PPn137 | 1914 | — | 12 Groats. Platinum. Plain edge. | 3,000 |
| PPn138 | 1914 | — | 12 Groats. Platinum. Reeded edge. | 3,000 |
| PPn139 | 1914 | — | 12 Groats. Gold. Reeded edge. | 2,400 |
| PPn140 | 1933 | 4 | Penny. Bronze. Plain edge. | — |

## PIEFORTS

| KM# | Date | Mintage | Identification | Mkt Val |
|---|---|---|---|---|
| P1 | 1973 | — | 50 Pence. 0.9250 Silver. | 1,250 |
| P2 | 1982 | — | 20 Pence. 0.9250 Silver. | 50.00 |
| P3 | 1983 | 10,000 | Pound. 0.9250 Silver. KM#933. | 125 |
| P4 | 1984 | 15,000 | Pound. 0.9250 Silver. KM#934. | 50.00 |
| P5 | 1985 | 15,000 | Pound. 0.9250 Silver. KM#941. | 40.00 |
| P6 | 1986 | 15,000 | Pound. 0.9250 Silver. KM#946. | 40.00 |
| P7 | 1987 | 15,000 | Pound. 0.9250 Silver. KM#948. | 40.00 |
| P8 | 1988 | 15,000 | Pound. 0.9250 Silver. KM#954. | 40.00 |
| P9 | 1989 | 15,000 | Pound. 0.9250 Silver. KM#959. | 40.00 |
| P10 | 1989 | 25,000 | 2 Pounds. 0.9250 Silver. KM#960a. | 45.00 |
| P11 | 1989 | 10,000 | 2 Pounds. 0.9250 Silver. KM#961a. | 45.00 |
| P12 | 1990 | 20,000 | 5 Pence. 0.9250 Silver. KM#937c. | 25.00 |
| P13 | 1992 | 15,000 | 10 Pence. 0.9250 Silver. KM#938b. | 50.00 |
| P15 | 1992 | — | 50 Pence. 0.9250 Silver. KM#963a. | 70.00 |
| P16 | 1993 | — | Pound. 0.9250 Silver. KM#964. | 45.00 |
| P17 | 1994 | — | 50 Pence. 0.9250 Silver. KM#966b. | 65.00 |
| P18 | 1994 | — | Pound. 0.9250 Silver. KM#967. | 70.00 |
| P19 | 1994 | — | 2 Pounds. 0.9250 Silver. KM#968a. | 80.00 |
| P20 | 1995 | 8,458 | Pound. 0.9250 Silver. KM#969. | 65.00 |
| P21 | 1995 | — | 2 Pounds. 0.9250 Silver. KM#970a. | 70.00 |
| P22 | 1995 | — | 2 Pounds. 0.9250 Silver. KM#971a. | 70.00 |
| P23 | 1996 | 10,000 | Pound. 0.9250 Silver. KM#972. | 60.00 |
| P24 | 1997 | — | 50 Pence. 0.9250 Silver. KM#963. | 70.00 |
| P25 | 1997 | — | Pound. 0.9250 Silver. KM#975. | 70.00 |
| P26 | 1998 | — | Pound. 0.9250 Silver. KM#993a. | — |
| P27 | 1997 | — | 2 Pounds. 0.9250 Silver. KM#976a. | 75.00 |
| P28 | 1998 | — | 50 Pence. 0.9250 Silver. KM#992a. | 70.00 |
| P29 | 1998 | — | 50 Pence. 0.9250 Silver. KM#996a. | 70.00 |
| P30 | 1998 | — | 2 Pounds. 0.9250 Silver. KM#994a. | 75.00 |
| P31 | 1999 | — | Pound. 0.9250 Silver. KM998a | — |

## TRIAL STRIKES

| KM# | Date | Mintage | Identification | Mkt Val |
|---|---|---|---|---|
| TS1 | 1926 | — | 3 Pence. Silver. MODEL. | 1,000 |
| TS2 | 1926 | — | 6 Pence. Silver. MODEL. | 1,000 |
| TS3 | 1926 | — | Shilling. Silver. MODEL. | 1,250 |
| TS4 | 1926 | — | 2 Shilling. Silver. MODEL. | 1,350 |
| TS5 | 1926 | — | 1/2 Crown. Silver. MODEL. | 1,500 |
| TSA6 | 1926 | — | Crown. Silver. MODEL. | — |

**Note:** A complete set of silver plated copper electro types officially prepared for the designer has been recorded. Market value $2,000

| KM# | Date | Mintage | Identification | Mkt Val |
|---|---|---|---|---|
| TS6 | 1926 | — | Crown. Silver. Blank. | — |
| TS7 | 1963 | — | 1/4 New Penny. Aluminum. Uniface. | — |
| TS8 | 1963 | — | 1/2 New Penny. Bronze. Uniface. | — |
| TS9 | 1963 | — | New Penny. Bronze. Uniface. | — |
| TS10 | 1963 | — | 2 New Pence. Bronze. Uniface. | — |
| TS11 | 1963 | — | 5 New Pence. Silver. Uniface. | — |
| TS12 | 1963 | — | 10 New Pence. Silver. Uniface. | — |
| TS13 | 1963 | — | 20 New Pence. Silver. Uniface. | — |
| TS14 | 1963 | — | 20 New Pence. Silver. Uniface. | — |

## MAUNDY SETS

| KM# | Date | Mintage | Identification | Issue Price | Mkt Val |
|---|---|---|---|---|---|
| MDS157 | 1901 | 8,976 | KM#775-778 | — | 80.00 |
| MDS158 | 1902 | 8,976 | KM#795-796, 797.1-798 | — | 80.00 |
| MDS159 | 1902 | — | KM#795-796, 797.1-798 Proof | — | 80.00 |
| MDS160 | 1903 | 8,976 | KM#795-796, 797.1-798 | — | 75.00 |
| MDS161 | 1904 | 8,976 | KM#795-796, 797.1-798 | — | 75.00 |
| MDS162 | 1905 | 8,976 | KM#795-796, 797.2-798 | — | 75.00 |
| MDS163 | 1906 | 8,800 | KM#795-796, 797.2-798 | — | 75.00 |
| MDS164 | 1907 | 8,760 | KM#795-796, 797.2-798 | — | 75.00 |
| MDS165 | 1908 | 8,760 | KM#795-796, 797.2-798 | — | 75.00 |
| MDS166 | 1909 | 1,983 | KM#795-796, 797.2-798 | — | 110 |
| MDS167 | 1910 | 1,440 | KM#795-796, 797.2-798 | — | 110 |
| MDS168 | 1911 | 1,768 | KM#811-814 | — | 95.00 |
| MDS169 | 1911 | 6,007 | KM#811-814 Proof | — | 110 |
| MDS170 | 1912 | 1,246 | KM#811-814 | — | 95.00 |
| MDS171 | 1913 | 1,228 | KM#811-814 | — | 95.00 |
| MDS172 | 1914 | 982 | KM#811-814 | — | 95.00 |
| MDS173 | 1915 | 1,293 | KM#811-814 | — | 95.00 |
| MDS174 | 1916 | 1,128 | KM#811-814 | — | 95.00 |
| MDS175 | 1917 | 1,237 | KM#811-814 | — | 95.00 |
| MDS176 | 1918 | 1,375 | KM#811-814 | — | 95.00 |
| MDS177 | 1919 | 1,258 | KM#811-814 | — | 95.00 |
| MDS178 | 1920 | 1,399 | KM#811-814 | — | 110 |
| MDS179 | 1921 | 1,386 | KM#811a-814a | — | 95.00 |
| MDS180 | 1922 | 1,373 | KM#811a-814a | — | 95.00 |
| MDS181 | 1923 | 1,430 | KM#811a-814a | — | 95.00 |
| MDS182 | 1924 | 1,515 | KM#811a-814a | — | 95.00 |
| MDS183 | 1925 | 1,438 | KM#811a-814a | — | 95.00 |
| MDS184 | 1926 | 1,504 | KM#811a-814a | — | 95.00 |
| MDS185 | 1927 | 1,647 | KM#811a-814a | — | 95.00 |
| MDS186 | 1928 | 1,642 | KM#827, 839-841 | — | 95.00 |
| MDS187 | 1929 | 1,761 | KM#827, 839-841 | — | 110 |
| MDS188 | 1930 | 1,724 | KM#827, 839-841 | — | 95.00 |
| MDS189 | 1931 | 1,759 | KM#827, 839-841 | — | 95.00 |
| MDS190 | 1932 | 1,835 | KM#827, 839-841 | — | 95.00 |
| MDS191 | 1933 | 1,872 | KM#827, 839-841 | — | 95.00 |
| MDS192 | 1934 | 1,887 | KM#827, 839-841 | — | 95.00 |
| MDS193 | 1935 | 1,926 | KM#827, 839-841 | — | 110 |
| MDS194 | 1936 | 1,323 | KM#827, 839-841 | — | 180 |
| MDS195 | 1937 | 1,325 | KM#846-847, 850-851 | — | 90.00 |
| MDS196 | 1937 | 26,000 | KM#846-847, 850-851 Proof | — | 95.00 |
| MDS197 | 1938 | 1,275 | KM#846-847, 850-851 | — | 95.00 |
| MDS198 | 1939 | 1,234 | KM#846-847, 850-851 | — | 95.00 |
| MDS199 | 1940 | 1,277 | KM#846-847, 850-851 | — | 110 |
| MDS200 | 1941 | 1,253 | KM#846-847, 850-851 | — | 95.00 |
| MDS201 | 1942 | 1,231 | KM#846-847, 850-851 | — | 95.00 |
| MDS202 | 1943 | 1,239 | KM#846-847, 850-851 | — | 95.00 |
| MDS203 | 1944 | 1,259 | KM#846-847, 850-851 | — | 95.00 |
| MDS204 | 1945 | 1,355 | KM#846-847, 850-851 | — | 95.00 |
| MDS205 | 1946 | 1,365 | KM#846-847, 850-851 | — | 95.00 |
| MDS206 | 1947 | 1,375 | KM#846a-847a, 850a-851a | — | 95.00 |
| MDS207 | 1948 | 1,385 | KM#846a-847a, 850a-851a | — | 95.00 |
| MDS208 | 1949 | 1,395 | KM#870-872, 874 | — | 95.00 |
| MDS209 | 1950 | 1,405 | KM#870-872, 874 | — | 120 |
| MDS210 | 1951 | 1,468 | KM#870-872, 874 | — | 95.00 |
| MDS211 | 1952 | 1,012 | KM#870-872, 874 | — | 95.00 |
| MDS212 | 1953 | 1,025 | KM#884-885, 887-888 | — | 450 |
| MDS213 | 1954 | 1,020 | KM#898-899, 901-902 | — | 95.00 |
| MDS214 | 1955 | 1,036 | KM#898-899, 901-902 | — | 95.00 |
| MDS215 | 1956 | 1,088 | KM#898-899, 901-902 | — | 95.00 |
| MDS216 | 1957 | 1,094 | KM#898-899, 901-902 | — | 95.00 |
| MDS217 | 1958 | 1,100 | KM#898-899, 901-902 | — | 95.00 |
| MDS218 | 1959 | 1,106 | KM#898-899, 901-902 | — | 95.00 |
| MDS219 | 1960 | 1,112 | KM#898-899, 901-902 | — | 110 |
| MDS220 | 1961 | — | KM#898-899, 901-902 | — | 95.00 |
| MDS221 | 1962 | 1,125 | KM#898-899, 901-902 | — | 95.00 |
| MDS222 | 1963 | 1,131 | KM#898-899, 901-902 | — | 95.00 |
| MDS223 | 1964 | 1,137 | KM#898-899, 901-902 | — | 95.00 |
| MDS224 | 1965 | 1,143 | KM#898-899, 901-902 | — | 95.00 |
| MDS225 | 1966 | 1,206 | KM#898-899, 901-902 | — | 95.00 |
| MDS226 | 1967 | 986 | KM#898-899, 901-902 | — | 95.00 |
| MDS227 | 1968 | 964 | KM#898-899, 901-902 | — | 95.00 |
| MDS228 | 1969 | 1,002 | KM#898-899, 901-902 | — | 110 |
| MDS229 | 1970 | 980 | KM#898-899, 901-902 | — | 110 |
| MDS230 | 1971 | 1,018 | KM#898-899, 901-902 | — | 80.00 |
| MDS231 | 1972 | 1,026 | KM#898-899, 901-902 | — | 80.00 |
| MDS232 | 1973 | 1,004 | KM#898-899, 901-902 | — | 80.00 |
| MDS233 | 1974 | 1,042 | KM#898-899, 901-902 | — | 80.00 |
| MDS234 | 1975 | 1,050 | KM#898-899, 901-902 | — | 80.00 |
| MDS235 | 1976 | 1,257 | KM#898-899, 901-902 | — | 80.00 |
| MDS236 | 1977 | 1,248 | KM#898-899, 901-902 | — | 85.00 |
| MDS237 | 1978 | 1,179 | KM#898-899, 901-902 | — | 85.00 |
| MDS238 | 1979 | 1,180 | KM#898-899, 901-902 | — | 85.00 |
| MDS239 | 1980 | 1,148 | KM#898-899, 901-902 | — | 85.00 |
| MDS240 | 1981 | 1,398 | KM#898-899, 901-902 | — | 85.00 |
| MDS241 | 1982 | 1,220 | KM#898-899, 901-902 | — | 85.00 |
| MDS242 | 1983 | 1,228 | KM#898-899, 901-902 | — | 85.00 |
| MDS243 | 1984 | 1,238 | KM#898-899, 901-902 | — | 85.00 |
| MDS244 | 1985 | 1,248 | KM#898-899, 901-902 | — | 85.00 |
| MDS245 | 1986 | 1,378 | KM#898-899, 901-902 | — | 85.00 |
| MDS246 | 1987 | 1,390 | KM#898-899, 901-902 | — | 110 |
| MDS247 | 1988 | 1,402 | KM#898-899, 901-902 | — | 110 |
| MDS248 | 1989 | 1,353 | KM#898-899, 901-902 | — | 110 |
| MDS249 | 1990 | 1,523 | KM#898-899, 901-902 | — | 110 |
| MDS250 | 1991 | 1,384 | KM#898-899, 901-902 | — | 110 |
| MDS251 | 1992 | 1,424 | KM#898-899, 901-902 | — | 110 |
| MDS252 | 1993 | 1,440 | KM#898-899, 901-902 | — | 110 |
| MDS253 | 1994 | 1,433 | KM#898-899, 901-902 | — | 110 |
| MDS254 | 1995 | 1,466 | KM#898-899, 901-902 | — | 120 |
| MDS255 | 1996 | 1,629 | KM#898-899, 901-902 | — | 125 |
| MDS256 | 1997 | 1,786 | KM#898-899, 901-902 | — | 135 |
| MDS257 | 1998 | 1,619 | KM#898-899, 901-902 | — | 140 |
| MDS258 | 1999 | — | KM#898-899, 901-902 | — | 145 |

## MINT SETS

| KM# | Date | Mintage | Identification | Issue Price | Mkt Val |
|---|---|---|---|---|---|
| MS101 | 1953 (9) | — | KM#881-883, 886, 889-893 | 1.25 | 12.00 |
| MS102 | 1968/71 (5) | — | KM#911-912 (1968), 914-916 (1971), blue wallet | 0.50 | 2.00 |
| MS103 | 1982 (7) | 205,000 | KM#926-932 | 6.00 | 12.50 |
| MS104 | 1983 (8) | 637,100 | KM#926-933 | 8.75 | 22.00 |
| MS105 | 1984 (8) | 158,820 | KM#926-932, 934 | 8.75 | 19.00 |
| MS106 | 1985 (7) | 178,375 | KM#935-940.1, 941 | 8.75 | 15.00 |
| MS107 | 1986 (8) | 167,224 | KM#935-940.1, 946-947 | 9.75 | 20.00 |
| MS108 | 1987 (7) | 172,425 | KM#935-940.1, 948 | 9.00 | 21.50 |
| MS109 | 1988 (7) | 134,067 | KM#935-940.1, 954 | 9.00 | 17.50 |
| MS110 | 1989 (7) | 77,569 | KM#935-940.1, 959 | 10.00 | 26.00 |
| MS111 | 1989 (2) | — | KM#960-961 | 11.00 | 11.00 |
| MS112 | 1990 (8) | 102,606 | KM#935-936, 937, 936b, 938-940.1, 941 | 15.00 | 23.50 |
| MS113 | 1991 (7) | 74,975 | KM#935-936, 937b, 938-940.1, 946 | 15.00 | 20.00 |
| MS114 | 1991 (7) | — | KM#935-936, 937b, 938-940.1, 946 Baby Pack | 18.50 | 22.50 |
| MS115 | 1992 (9) | 78,421 | KM#935-936, 937b, 938, 938b, 939-940.1, 948, 963 Baby Pack | 17.50 | 20.00 |
| MS116 | 1992 (9) | — | KM#935-936, 937b, 938, 938b, 939-940.1, 948, 963 Baby Pack | 22.50 | 20.00 |
| MS117 | 1993 (8) | 56,945 | KM#935a-936a, 937b, 938b, 939-940.1, 963-964 | 22.50 | 22.50 |
| MS118 | 1994 (8) | 177,971 | KM#935a-936a, 937b, 938b, 939, 966-968 | 22.50 | 20.00 |
| MS119 | 1995 (8) | 105,647 | KM#935a-936a, 937b-938b, 939-940.1, 969-970 | — | 20.00 |
| MS120 | 1996 (8) | 86,501 | KM#935a-936a, 937b-938b, 939-940.1, 972-973 | 18.50 | 20.00 |
| MS121 | 1997 (9) | 109,557 | KM#935a, 936a, 937b, 938b, 939-940.1, 940.2, 975-976 | — | 20.00 |
| MS122 | 1998 (9) | — | KM#986-994 | 25.00 | 15.00 |
| MS124 | 1998 (2) | 96,149 | KM#991-992 | 15.00 | 9.50 |
| MS125 | 1999 (8) | 136,492 | KM#986a-991, 998-999 | 20.00 | 18.00 |
| MS126 | 2000 (9) | — | KM#986a-991, 994, 1004-1005 Wedding Collection | 20.00 | 20.00 |
| MS127 | 2000 (9) | — | KM#986a-991, 994, 1004-1005 | 25.00 | 25.00 |
| MS128 | 2000 (9) | — | M#986a-991, 994, 1004-1005 Baby Gift Set | 25.00 | 25.00 |

## PROOF SETS

| KM# | Date | Mintage | Identification | Issue Price | Mkt Val |
|---|---|---|---|---|---|
| PS115 | 2001 (4) | 5,000 | KM#1016-1019 | — | 140 |
| PS116 | 2001 (4) | 1,000 | KM#1020-1023 | 1,595 | — |
| PS65 | 1989 (2) | — | KM#960b-961b | — | 95.00 |
| PS15 | 1902 (13) | 8,066 | KM#795-797.1, 798-807 | — | 2,000 |
| PS16 | 1902 (11) | 7,057 | KM#795-797.1, 798-805 | — | 550 |
| PS17 | 1911 (12) | 2,812 | KM#811-818.1, 819-822 | — | 3,500 |
| PS18 | 1911 (10) | 952 | KM#811-818.1, 819-820 | — | 900 |
| PS19 | 1911 (8) | 2,241 | KM#811-818.1 | — | 400 |
| PS20 | 1927 (6) | 15,030 | KM#831-836 | — | 375 |
| PSA20 | 1927 (6) | — | KM#831-836 Matte Proof; Rare | — | — |
| PS21 | 1937 (15) | 26,402 | KM#843-857 | — | 225 |
| PSA21 | 1937 (15) | — | KM#843-857 Matte Proof; Rare | — | — |
| PS-A221 | 1937 (4) | 1 | KM#858-861 Matte Proof; Unique | — | — |
| PS22 | 1937 (4) | 5,500 | KM#858-861 | — | 2,250 |
| PS23 | 1950 (9) | 17,513 | KM#867-869, 873, 875-879 | 2.50 | 75.00 |
| PSA23 | 1950 (9) | — | KM#867-869, 873, 875-879; Rare | — | — |
| PS24 | 1951 (10) | 20,000 | KM#867-869, 873, 875-880 | 2.80 | 80.00 |
| PSA24 | 1951 (10) | — | KM#867-869, 873, 875-880; Rare | — | — |
| PS25 | 1953 (10) | 40,000 | KM#881-883, 886, 889-894 | 3.50 | 60.00 |
| PSA25 | 1953 (10) | — | KM#881-883, 886, 889-894; Rare | — | — |
| PS26 | 1970 (8) | 750,000 | KM#896-897, 900, 903-907 (Issued 1971) | 8.75 | 20.00 |
| PS27 | 1971 (6) | 350,000 | KM#911-916 (Issued 1973) | 8.85 | 14.50 |
| PS28 | 1972 (7) | 150,000 | KM#911-917 (Issued 1976) | 13.00 | 19.00 |
| PS29 | 1973 (6) | 100,000 | KM#911-912, 914-916, 918 (Issued 1976) | 13.00 | 17.50 |
| PS30 | 1974 (6) | 100,000 | KM#911-916 (Issued 1976) | 13.00 | 13.50 |
| PS31 | 1975 (6) | 100,000 | KM#911-916 (Issued 1976) | 13.00 | 13.50 |
| PS32 | 1976 (6) | 100,000 | KM#911-916 | 13.00 | 14.00 |
| PS33 | 1977 (7) | 193,800 | KM#911-916, 920 | 17.00 | 17.50 |
| PS34 | 1978 (6) | 88,100 | KM#911-916 | 15.00 | 19.50 |
| PS35 | 1979 (6) | 81,000 | KM#911-916 | 15.00 | 16.00 |
| PS37 | 1980 (4) | 10,000 | KM#919, 922-924 | 2,650 | 1,150 |
| PS36 | 1980 (6) | 143,400 | KM#911-916 | 23.00 | 15.50 |
| PS38 | 1981 (2) | 2,500 | KM#919, 925a | — | 160 |
| PS39 | 1981 (6) | — | KM#911-916 | 26.00 | 15.50 |
| PS40 | 1981 (9) | 5,000 | KM#911-916, 919, 924, 925a | — | 935 |
| PS42 | 1982 (4) | 2,500 | KM#919, 922-924 | — | 1,350 |
| PS41 | 1982 (7) | — | KM#926-932 | 21.60 | 16.00 |
| PS44 | 1983 (3) | — | KM#919, 922-923 | 775 | 535 |
| PS43 | 1983 (8) | 125,000 | KM#926-933 | 29.95 | 25.00 |
| PS46 | 1984 (3) | — | KM#919, 922, 924 | 1,275 | 910 |
| PS45 | 1984 (8) | 125,000 | KM#926-932, 934 | 29.95 | 23.50 |
| PS48 | 1985 (4) | 12,500 | KM#942-945 | 1,395 | 1,175 |
| PS47 | 1985 (7) | 125,000 | KM#935-940.1, 941 | 29.75 | 23.50 |
| PS50 | 1986 (3) | 12,500 | KM#942-943, 947c | 675 | 535 |
| PS49 | 1986 (8) | 125,000 | KM#935-940.1, 946-947 | 29.75 | 28.50 |
| PS53 | 1987 (3) | 12,500 | KM#942-944 | 675 | 535 |
| PS51 | 1987 (7) | 125,000 | KM#935-940.1, 948 | 29.75 | 25.00 |
| PS52 | 1987 (4) | 10,000 | KM#950-953 | 1,595 | 1,000 |
| PS54 | 1987 (2) | 12,500 | KM#950-951 | 325 | 190 |
| PS57 | 1988 (3) | — | KM#942-944 | 775 | 510 |
| PS55 | 1988 (7) | 125,000 | KM#935-940.1, 954 | 29.75 | 27.50 |
| PS56 | 1988 (4) | 6,500 | KM#950-953 | 1,595 | 1,000 |
| PS58 | 1988 (2) | 7,500 | KM#950-951 | 340 | 190 |
| PS61 | 1989 (4) | 5,000 | KM#955-958 | 1,595 | 1,600 |
| PS62 | 1989 (3) | 15,000 | KM#955-957 | 775 | 675 |
| PS64 | 1989 (2) | — | KM#960a-961a | — | 55.00 |
| PS59 | 1989 (9) | 100,000 | KM#935-940.1, 959-961 | 34.95 | 46.00 |
| PS60 | 1989 (4) | 2,500 | KM#950-953 | 1,595 | 1,000 |
| PS63 | 1989 (2) | 1,500 | KM#950-951 | 340 | 200 |
| PS68 | 1990 (4) | 2,500 | KM#942-944, 949 | 1,595 | 1,400 |
| PS69 | 1990 (4) | 2,500 | KM#950a-953a | 1,595 | 1,000 |
| PS70 | 1990 (3) | 7,500 | KM#942-944 | 775 | 570 |
| PS71 | 1990 (2) | 35,000 | KM#937a-937c | 47.50 | 39.00 |
| PS66 | 1990 (8) | 100,000 | KM#935-937, 937b, 938-940.1, 941 Leatherette Case | 35.00 | 36.00 |
| PS67 | 1990 (8) | I.A. | KM#935-937, 937b, 938-940.1, 941 Leather Case | 45.00 | 35.00 |
| PS74 | 1991 (4) | 1,500 | KM#942-944, 949 | 1,750 | 1,500 |
| PS75 | 1991 (4) | 750 | KM#950a-953a | 1,750 | 1,500 |
| PS76 | 1991 (3) | 2,500 | KM#942-944 | 895 | 665 |
| PS72 | 1991 (7) | 10,000 | KM#935-936, 937b, 938-940.1, 946 Leatherette Case | 38.50 | 22.50 |
| PS73 | 1991 (7) | 10,000 | KM#935-936, 937b, 938-940.1, 946 Leather Case | 48.50 | 27.50 |
| PS79 | 1992 (4) | 1,250 | KM#942-945 | 1,750 | 1,450 |
| PS80 | 1992 (4) | 1,000 | KM#938b, 938c, 948a, 963a | 122 | 125 |
| PS81 | 1992 (3) | 1,250 | KM#942-944 | 895 | 710 |
| PS82 | 1992 (2) | — | KM#938a-938c | 59.45 | 46.00 |
| PS77 | 1992 (9) | 100,000 | KM#935-936, 937b, 938, 938b, 939-94.1, 948, 963 Leatherette Case | 44.50 | 46.00 |
| PS78 | 1992 (9) | 100,000 | KM#935-936, 937b, 938, 938b, 939-940.1, 948, 963 Leather Case | 44.50 | 40.00 |
| PS85 | 1993 (4) | 500 | KM#950a-953a | 1,755 | 1,600 |
| PS86 | 1993 (4) | 1,250 | KM#942-945 | 1,560 | 1,530 |
| PS87 | 1993 (3) | 1,250 | KM#942-944 | 800 | 670 |
| PS83 | 1993 (8) | 100,000 | KM#935a-936a, 937b, 938b, 939-940.1, 964-965 Standard Case | 50.00 | 47.00 |
| PS84 | 1993 (8) | I.A. | KM#935a-936a, 937b, 938b, 939-940.1, 964-965 Deluxe Case | 60.00 | 55.00 |
| PS90 | 1994 (4) | 500 | KM#950a-953a | 1,499 | 1,500 |
| PS91 | 1994 (4) | 1,250 | KM#942-943, 945, 968c | — | 1,550 |
| PS92 | 1994 (3) | 1,250 | KM#942-943, 968c | — | 760 |
| PS88 | 1994 (8) | 100,000 | KM#935a-936a, 937b, 938b, 939, 966-968 Standard Case | 45.00 | 34.00 |
| PS89 | 1994 (8) | I.A. | KM#935a-936a, 937b, 938b, 939, 966-968 Deluxe Case | 55.00 | 50.00 |
| PS93 | 1995 (8) | 42,842 | KM#935a-936a, 937b-938b, 939-940.1, 969-970 | — | 41.50 |
| PS94 | 1995 (8) | 17,797 | KM#935a-936a, 937b-938b, 939-940.1, 969-970 Deluxe Case | — | 60.00 |
| PS95 | 1995 (4) | 1,250 | KM#942-943, 945, 971c | — | 1,675 |
| PS96 | 1995 (4) | 500 | KM#950a-953a | 1,500 | 1,500 |
| PS97 | 1995 (3) | 1,250 | KM#942-943, 945 | — | 860 |
| PS100 | 1996 (4) | 2,500,000 | KM#950a-953a | 1,600 | 1,500 |
| PS101 | 1996 (7) | — | KM#935b, 936b, 937c, 938c, 939a, 940.1a, 972a | — | 155 |
| PS98 | 1996 (9) | 100,000 | KM#935a-936a, 937b-938b, 939-940.1, 972-973 | 44.75 | 42.50 |
| PS99 | 1996 (9) | — | KM#935a-936a, 937b-938b, 939-940.1, 972-973 Deluxe Case | 56.00 | 55.00 |
| PS102 | 1997 (10) | 70,000 | KM#935a, 936a, 937b, 938b, 939, 940.1, 940.2, 975-976, 977a | — | 50.00 |
| PS103 | 1997 (4) | 15,000 | KM#978-981 | 145 | 135 |
| PS104 | 1997 (4) | 1,500 | KM#982-985 | 1,600 | 1,650 |
| PS105 | 1998 (10) | 100,000 | KM#986-995 | 55.00 | 50.00 |
| PS107 | 1999 (4) | 1,000 | KM#999a, 1001-1003 | 1,725 | 1,725 |
| PS108 | 1999 (3) | 1,250 | KM#1001-1003 | — | 955 |
| PS109 | 1999 (4) | 750 | KM#950a-953a | 1,495 | 1,500 |
| PS110 | 1999 (4) | — | KM#1008-1011 | 1,595 | — |
| PS106 | 1999 (9) | 100,000 | KM#986a-987a, 988-991, 997-999 | 50.00 | 50.00 |
| PS114 | 2000 (4) | 750 | KM#1008-1011 | 1,495 | 1,498 |
| PS111 | 2000 (10) | 90,000 | KM#986a-991, 994, 1004-1006 Standard Set | 50.00 | 50.00 |
| PS112 | 2000 (10) | 10,000 | KM#986a-991, 994, 1004-1006 Deluxe Set | 65.00 | 65.00 |
| PS113 | 2000 (10) | 15,000 | KM#986-991, 994, 1004-1006 Executive Set | 115 | 115 |

# GREECE

The Hellenic (Greek) Republic is situated in southeastern Europe on the southern tip of the Balkan Peninsula. The republic includes many islands, the most important of which are Crete and the Ionian Islands. Greece (including islands) has an area of 50,944 sq. mi. (131,940 sq. km.) and a population of 10.3 million. Capital: Athens. Greece is still largely agricultural. Tobacco, cotton, fruit and wool are exported.

Greece, the Mother of Western civilization, attained the peak of its culture in the 5th century B.C., when it contributed more to government, drama, art and architecture than any other people to this time. Greece fell under Roman domination in the 2nd and 1st centuries B.C., becoming part of the Byzantine Empire until Constantinople fell to the Crusaders in 1202. With the fall of Constantinople to the Turks in 1453, Greece became part of the Ottoman Empire. Independence from Turkey was won with the revolution of 1821-27. In 1833, Greece was established as a monarchy, with sovereignty guaranteed by Britain, France and Russia. After a lengthy power struggle between the monarchist forces and democratic factions, Greece was proclaimed a republic in 1925. The monarchy was restored in 1935 and reconfirmed by a plebiscite in 1946. The Italians invaded Greece via Albania on Oct. 28, 1940 but were driven back well within the Albanian border. Germany began their invasion in April 1941 and quickly overran the entire country and drove off a British Expeditionary force by the end of April. King George II and his new government went into exile. The German--Italian occupation of Greece lasted until Oct. 1944 after which only German troops remained until the end of the occupation. On April 21, 1967, a military junta took control of the government and suspended the constitution. King Constantine II made an unsuccessful attempt against the junta in the fall of 1968 and consequently fled to Italy. The monarchy was formally abolished by plebiscite, Dec. 8, 1974, and Greece was established as the Hellenic Republic, the third republic in Greek history.

**RULERS**

George I, 1863-1913
Constantine I, 1913-1917, 1920-1922
Alexander I, 1917-1920
George II, 1922-1923, 1935-1947
Paul I, 1947-1964
Constantine II, 1964-1973

**MINT MARKS**

(a) - Paris, privy marks only
A - Paris
B - Vienna
BB - Strassburg
H - Heaton, Birmingham
K - Bordeaux
KN - King's Norton
(p) - Poissy - Thunderbolt

**MONETARY SYSTEM**

Commencing 1831
100 Lepta = 1 Drachma

## KINGDOM

### DECIMAL COINAGE

**5 LEPTA** **KM# 62** **Composition:** Nickel **Reverse:** Owl on amphora

| Date | Mintage | F | VF | XF | Unc | BU |
|---|---|---|---|---|---|---|
| 1912(a) | 25,053,000 | 0.75 | 1.50 | 4.50 | 25.00 | — |

**10 LEPTA** **KM# 63** **Composition:** Nickel **Reverse:** Owl on amphora

| Date | Mintage | F | VF | XF | Unc | BU |
|---|---|---|---|---|---|---|
| 1912(a) | 28,973,000 | 0.75 | 1.50 | 3.50 | 25.00 | — |

**10 LEPTA** **KM# 66.1** **Weight:** 1.5200 g. **Composition:** Aluminum **Note:** 1.77mm thick.

| Date | Mintage | F | VF | XF | Unc | BU |
|---|---|---|---|---|---|---|
| 1922(p) | 120,000,000 | 1.00 | 2.00 | 5.50 | 25.00 | — |

**10 LEPTA** **KM# 66.2** **Weight:** 1.6500 g. **Composition:** Aluminum **Note:** 2.2mm thick.

| Date | Mintage | F | VF | XF | Unc | BU |
|---|---|---|---|---|---|---|
| 1922(p) | — | — | — | — | — | — |

**20 LEPTA** **KM# 64** **Composition:** Nickel **Rev. Legend:** Goddess Athena

| Date | Mintage | F | VF | XF | Unc | BU |
|---|---|---|---|---|---|---|
| 1912(a) | 10,145,000 | 0.75 | 1.50 | 5.00 | 38.00 | — |

**50 LEPTA** **KM# 65** **Composition:** Copper-Nickel

| Date | Mintage | F | VF | XF | Unc | BU |
|---|---|---|---|---|---|---|
| 1921H | 1,000,000 | 300 | 600 | 1,200 | 2,500 | — |
| 1921KN | 1,524,000 | 500 | 1,000 | 2,000 | 3,750 | — |

**DRACHMA** **KM# 60** **Weight:** 5.0000 g. **Composition:** 0.8350 Silver .1342 oz. ASW **Obverse:** George I **Reverse:** Mythological figure Thetis with shield of Achilles, seated on sea-horse

| Date | Mintage | F | VF | XF | Unc | BU |
|---|---|---|---|---|---|---|
| 1910(a) | 4,570,000 | 6.00 | 12.50 | 25.00 | 80.00 | — |
| 1911(a) | 1,881,000 | 7.00 | 15.00 | 30.00 | 100 | — |

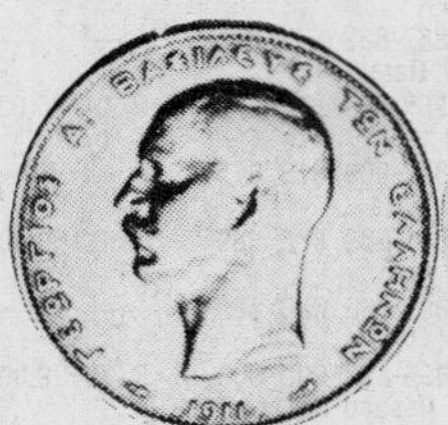

**2 DRACHMAI** **KM# 61** **Weight:** 10.0000 g. **Composition:** 0.8350 Silver .2684 oz. ASW **Obverse:** George I **Reverse:** Mythological figure Thetis with shield of Achilles seated on sea-horse

| Date | Mintage | F | VF | XF | Unc | BU |
|---|---|---|---|---|---|---|
| 1911(a) | 1,500,000 | 8.00 | 25.00 | 55.00 | 150 | — |

## REPUBLIC

### DECIMAL COINAGE

**20 LEPTA** **KM# 67** **Composition:** Copper-Nickel **Reverse:** Helmeted goddess Athena

| Date | Mintage | F | VF | XF | Unc | BU |
|---|---|---|---|---|---|---|
| 1926 | 20,000,000 | 0.75 | 1.50 | 4.50 | 12.50 | — |

**50 LEPTA** **KM# 68** **Composition:** Copper-Nickel

| Date | Mintage | F | VF | XF | Unc | BU |
|---|---|---|---|---|---|---|
| 1926 | 20,000,000 | 0.45 | 1.00 | 3.50 | 12.50 | — |
| 1926B (1930) | 20,000,000 | 0.45 | 1.00 | 3.50 | 12.50 | — |

**DRACHMA** **KM# 69** **Composition:** Copper-Nickel

| Date | Mintage | F | VF | XF | Unc | BU |
|---|---|---|---|---|---|---|
| 1926 | 15,000,000 | 0.45 | 1.00 | 3.50 | 20.00 | — |
| 1926B (193 | 20,000,000 | 0.45 | 1.00 | 3.50 | 20.00 | — |

**2 DRACHMAI** **KM# 70** **Composition:** Copper-Nickel

| Date | Mintage | F | VF | XF | Unc | BU |
|---|---|---|---|---|---|---|
| 1926 | 22,000,000 | 1.00 | 2.00 | 5.00 | 25.00 | — |

**5 DRACHMAI** **KM# 71.2** **Composition:** Nickel **Note:** BRUSSELLS MINT: 2 berries will have dots.

| Date | Mintage | F | VF | XF | Unc | BU |
|---|---|---|---|---|---|---|
| 1930 | 1,500,000 | 1.50 | 3.50 | 10.00 | 50.00 | — |

**5 DRACHMAI** **KM# 71.1** **Composition:** Nickel **Obverse:** Phoenix **Note:** LONDON MINT: In second set of berries on left only 1 berry will have a dot on it.

| Date | Mintage | F | VF | XF | Unc | BU |
|---|---|---|---|---|---|---|
| 1930 | 23,500,000 | 0.75 | 1.50 | 5.00 | 28.00 | — |
| 1930 Proof | — | Value: 400 | | | | |

**10 DRACHMAI** **KM# 72** **Weight:** 7.0000 g. **Composition:** 0.5000 Silver .1125 oz. ASW

| Date | Mintage | F | VF | XF | Unc | BU |
|---|---|---|---|---|---|---|
| 1930 | 7,500,000 | 4.50 | 9.00 | 18.50 | 85.00 | — |
| 1930 Proof | — | Value: 500 | | | | |

**20 DRACHMAI** KM# 73 **Weight:** 11.3100 g. **Composition:** 0.5000 Silver .1818 oz. ASW **Obverse:** Prow of ancinet ship **Reverse:** Neptune

| Date | Mintage | F | VF | XF | Unc | BU |
|---|---|---|---|---|---|---|
| 1930 | 11,500,000 | 5.00 | 10.00 | 20.00 | 125 | — |
| 1930 Proof | — | Value: 600 | | | | |

# KINGDOM

## DECIMAL COINAGE

**5 LEPTA** KM# 77 **Composition:** Aluminum

| Date | Mintage | F | VF | XF | Unc | BU |
|---|---|---|---|---|---|---|
| 1954 | 15,000,000 | — | 0.10 | 0.50 | 2.00 | — |
| 1971 | 1,002,000 | 0.20 | 0.50 | 1.00 | 5.00 | — |

**Note:** 1971 dated coins have smaller hole at center

**10 LEPTA** KM# 78 **Composition:** Aluminum

| Date | Mintage | F | VF | XF | Unc | BU |
|---|---|---|---|---|---|---|
| 1954 | 48,000,000 | — | 0.10 | 0.35 | 2.00 | — |
| 1959 | 20,000,000 | — | 0.10 | 0.35 | 2.00 | — |
| 1964 | 12,000,000 | — | 0.10 | 0.35 | 2.00 | — |
| 1965 In sets only | — | — | — | — | 3.00 | — |
| 1965 In proof sets only | 4,987 | Value: 5.00 | | | | |
| 1966 | 20,000,000 | — | 0.10 | 0.35 | 2.00 | — |
| 1969 | 20,000,000 | — | 0.10 | 0.35 | 2.00 | — |
| 1971 Small center hole | 5,922,000 | — | 0.25 | 1.00 | 5.00 | — |

**10 LEPTA** KM# 102 **Composition:** Aluminum **Obverse:** Soldier and Phoenix

| Date | Mintage | F | VF | XF | Unc | BU |
|---|---|---|---|---|---|---|
| 1973 | 2,742,000 | — | 0.10 | 1.00 | 4.00 | — |

**20 LEPTA** KM# 79 **Composition:** Aluminum

| Date | Mintage | F | VF | XF | Unc | BU |
|---|---|---|---|---|---|---|
| 1954 | 24,000,000 | — | 0.10 | 0.50 | 2.00 | — |
| 1959 | 20,000,000 | — | 0.10 | 0.50 | 2.00 | — |
| 1964 | 8,000,000 | — | 0.10 | 0.50 | 2.00 | — |
| 1966 | 15,000,000 | — | 0.10 | 0.50 | 2.00 | — |
| 1969 | 20,000,000 | — | 0.10 | 0.50 | 2.00 | — |
| 1971 Small center hole | 4,108,000 | — | 0.20 | 1.00 | 2.50 | — |

**20 LEPTA** KM# 104 **Composition:** Aluminum **Obverse:** Soldier in front of phoenix, anniverary date below **Reverse:** Olive branch, denomination

| Date | Mintage | F | VF | XF | Unc | BU |
|---|---|---|---|---|---|---|
| 1973 | 2,718,000 | — | 0.20 | 0.60 | 4.00 | — |

**50 LEPTA** KM# 80 **Composition:** Copper-Nickel

| Date | Mintage | F | VF | XF | Unc | BU |
|---|---|---|---|---|---|---|
| ERR | — | — | — | — | — | — |
| 1954 | 37,228,000 | 0.15 | 0.25 | 1.00 | 5.50 | — |
| 1957 | 5,108,000 | 0.25 | 1.00 | 10.00 | 30.00 | — |
| 1957 Proof | — | Value: 150 | | | | |
| 1959 | 10,160,000 | 0.15 | 0.25 | 1.00 | 5.50 | — |
| 1962 Plain edge | 20,500,000 | 0.15 | 0.25 | 0.75 | 4.50 | — |
| 1962 Serrated edge | Inc. above | 0.15 | 0.25 | 0.75 | 4.50 | — |
| 1962 | — | — | — | — | — | — |
| 1964 | 20,000,000 | 0.15 | 0.25 | 0.75 | 4.50 | — |
| 1965 In sets only | — | — | — | — | 6.00 | — |
| 1965 In proof sets only | 4,987 | Value: 6.50 | | | | |

**50 LEPTA** KM# 88 **Composition:** Copper-Nickel

| Date | Mintage | F | VF | XF | Unc | BU |
|---|---|---|---|---|---|---|
| 1966 | 30,000,000 | 0.20 | 0.50 | 1.00 | 4.50 | — |
| 1970 | 10,160,000 | 0.30 | 0.60 | 1.50 | 5.00 | — |

**50 LEPTA** KM# 97.1 **Composition:** Copper-Nickel **Obverse:** Small head

| Date | Mintage | F | VF | XF | Unc | BU |
|---|---|---|---|---|---|---|
| 1971 | 10,999,000 | — | 0.10 | 0.15 | 3.00 | — |
| 1973 | 9,342,000 | — | 0.20 | 0.50 | 4.00 | — |

**50 LEPTA** KM# 97.2 **Composition:** Copper-Nickel **Obverse:** Large head

| Date | Mintage | F | VF | XF | Unc | BU |
|---|---|---|---|---|---|---|
| 1973 | Inc. above | — | 0.20 | 0.50 | 4.00 | — |

**DRACHMA** KM# 81 **Composition:** Copper-Nickel

| Date | Mintage | F | VF | XF | Unc | BU |
|---|---|---|---|---|---|---|
| 1954 | 24,091,000 | 0.15 | 0.25 | 0.75 | 5.50 | — |
| 1957 | 8,151,000 | 0.15 | 0.25 | 2.00 | 18.00 | — |
| 1957 Proof | — | Value: 200 | | | | |
| 1959 | 10,180,000 | 0.15 | 0.25 | 2.00 | 10.00 | — |
| 1962 | 20,060,000 | 0.15 | 0.25 | 0.75 | 5.50 | — |
| 1965 In sets only | — | — | — | — | 6.00 | — |
| 1965 In proof sets only | 4,987 | Value: 6.50 | | | | |

**DRACHMA** KM# 89 **Composition:** Copper-Nickel

| Date | Mintage | F | VF | XF | Unc | BU |
|---|---|---|---|---|---|---|
| 1966 | 20,000,000 | — | 0.15 | 0.45 | 3.50 | — |

| Date | Mintage | F | VF | XF | Unc | BU |
|---|---|---|---|---|---|---|
| 1967 | 20,000,000 | — | 0.15 | 0.45 | 3.50 | — |
| 1970 | 7,001,000 | — | 0.50 | 1.00 | 6.00 | — |

**DRACHMA** KM# 98 **Composition:** Copper-Nickel

| Date | Mintage | F | VF | XF | Unc | BU |
|---|---|---|---|---|---|---|
| 1971 | 11,985,000 | — | 0.20 | 0.75 | 3.50 | — |
| 1973 | 8,196,000 | — | 0.25 | 1.00 | 4.50 | — |

**2 DRACHMAI** KM# 82 **Composition:** Copper-Nickel

| Date | Mintage | F | VF | XF | Unc | BU |
|---|---|---|---|---|---|---|
| 1954 | 12,609,000 | 0.50 | 0.75 | 1.50 | 6.00 | — |
| 1957 | 10,171,000 | 0.50 | 0.75 | 2.50 | 15.00 | — |
| 1957 Proof | — | Value: 300 | | | | |
| 1959 | 5,000,000 | 0.50 | 0.75 | 2.50 | 10.00 | — |
| 1962 | 10,096,000 | 0.50 | 0.75 | 1.50 | 6.00 | — |
| 1965 In sets only | — | — | — | — | 5.00 | — |
| 1965 In proof sets only | 4,987 | Value: 6.50 | | | | |

**2 DRACHMAI** KM# 90 **Composition:** Copper-Nickel

| Date | Mintage | F | VF | XF | Unc | BU |
|---|---|---|---|---|---|---|
| 1966 | 10,000,000 | 0.15 | 0.25 | 0.50 | 3.50 | — |
| 1967 | 10,000,000 | 0.15 | 0.25 | 0.50 | 3.50 | — |
| 1970 | 7,000,000 | 0.50 | 1.00 | 2.00 | 7.00 | — |

**2 DRACHMAI** KM# 99 **Composition:** Copper-Nickel

| Date | Mintage | F | VF | XF | Unc | BU |
|---|---|---|---|---|---|---|
| 1971 | 9,998,000 | 0.15 | 0.25 | 0.75 | 3.50 | — |
| 1973 | 7,972,000 | 0.20 | 0.50 | 1.50 | 4.50 | — |

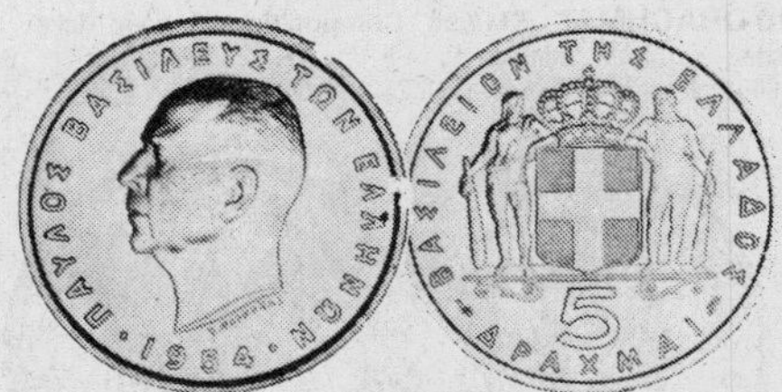

**5 DRACHMAI** KM# 83 **Composition:** Copper-Nickel

| Date | Mintage | F | VF | XF | Unc | BU |
|---|---|---|---|---|---|---|
| 1954 | 21,000,000 | 0.25 | 0.50 | 1.00 | 6.00 | — |
| 1965 In sets only | — | — | — | — | 5.50 | — |
| 1965 In proof sets only | 4,987 | Value: 7.50 | | | | |

**5 DRACHMAI** KM# 91 **Composition:** Copper-Nickel

| Date | Mintage | F | VF | XF | Unc | BU |
|---|---|---|---|---|---|---|
| 1966 | 12,000,000 | 0.15 | 0.25 | 1.00 | 5.00 | — |
| 1970 | 5,000,000 | 0.50 | 1.00 | 3.00 | 9.00 | — |

**5 DRACHMAI** KM# 100 **Composition:** Copper-Nickel

| Date | Mintage | F | VF | XF | Unc | BU |
|---|---|---|---|---|---|---|
| 1971 | 4,014,000 | 0.25 | 0.50 | 2.00 | 5.00 | — |
| 1973 | 3,166,000 | 0.25 | 0.50 | 1.50 | 4.50 | — |

**10 DRACHMAI** KM# 84 **Composition:** Nickel

| Date | Mintage | F | VF | XF | Unc | BU |
|---|---|---|---|---|---|---|
| 1959 | 20,000,000 | 0.30 | 0.50 | 1.50 | 6.00 | — |
| 1959 Proof | — | Value: 200 | | | | |
| 1965 In sets only | — | — | — | — | 5.50 | — |
| 1965 In proof sets only | 4,987 | Value: 7.50 | | | | |

**10 DRACHMAI** KM# 84a **Composition:** Silver

| Date | Mintage | F | VF | XF | Unc | BU |
|---|---|---|---|---|---|---|
| 1959 Proof | — | Value: 600 | | | | |

**10 DRACHMAI** KM# 96 **Composition:** Copper-Nickel

| Date | Mintage | F | VF | XF | Unc | BU |
|---|---|---|---|---|---|---|
| 1968 | 40,000,000 | 0.25 | 0.50 | 0.75 | 4.50 | — |

**10 DRACHMAI** KM# 101 **Composition:** Copper-Nickel
**Reverse:** Phoenix

| Date | Mintage | F | VF | XF | Unc | BU |
|---|---|---|---|---|---|---|
| 1971 | 502,000 | 0.25 | 0.50 | 1.00 | 6.50 | — |
| 1973 | 541,000 | 0.50 | 1.00 | 2.50 | 7.00 | — |

**20 DRACHMAI** KM# 74 **Weight:** 6.4516 g. **Composition:** 0.9000 Gold .1867 oz. AGW **Subject:** 5th Anniversary - Restoration of Monarchy

| Date | Mintage | F | VF | XF | Unc | BU |
|---|---|---|---|---|---|---|
| ND Proof | 200 | Value: 5,000 | | | | |

**20 DRACHMAI** KM# 85 **Weight:** 7.5000 g. **Composition:** 0.8350 Silver .2013 oz. ASW

| Date | Mintage | F | VF | XF | Unc | BU |
|---|---|---|---|---|---|---|
| 1960 | 20,000,000 | — | BV | 2.50 | 6.00 | — |
| 1960 Proof | — | Value: 350 | | | | |
| 1965 | — | — | — | — | 7.00 | — |
| 1965 In proof sets only | 4,987 | Value: 9.00 | | | | |

**20 DRACHMAI** KM# 92 **Weight:** 6.4516 g. **Composition:** 0.9000 Gold .1867 oz. AGW

| Date | Mintage | F | VF | XF | Unc | BU |
|---|---|---|---|---|---|---|
| ND (1970) | 20,000 | — | — | — | 225 | — |

**20 DRACHMAI** KM# 111.1 **Composition:** Copper-Nickel
**Reverse:** Narrow rim with faint veil or no veil

| Date | Mintage | F | VF | XF | Unc | BU |
|---|---|---|---|---|---|---|
| 1973 | 3,092,000 | 0.25 | 0.50 | 1.50 | 6.00 | — |

**20 DRACHMAI** KM# 111.2 **Composition:** Copper-Nickel
**Reverse:** Wide rim with heavy veil and broken wave design at rear hoof

| Date | Mintage | F | VF | XF | Unc | BU |
|---|---|---|---|---|---|---|
| 1973 | Inc. above | 1.00 | 2.00 | 4.00 | 12.00 | — |

**20 DRACHMAI** KM# 111.3 **Composition:** Copper-Nickel
**Reverse:** Wide rim with continuous wave design at rear hoof

| Date | Mintage | F | VF | XF | Unc | BU |
|---|---|---|---|---|---|---|
| 1973 | Inc. above | 0.25 | 0.50 | 1.00 | 6.00 | — |

**30 DRACHMAI** KM# 93 **Weight:** 12.5000 g. **Composition:** 0.8350 Silver .3355 oz. ASW **Subject:** 1967 Revolution

| Date | Mintage | F | VF | XF | Unc | BU |
|---|---|---|---|---|---|---|
| 1967(1970) | 100,000 | — | — | 25.00 | 30.00 | — |

**30 DRACHMAI** KM# 86 **Weight:** 18.0000 g. **Composition:** 0.8350 Silver .4832 oz. ASW **Subject:** Centennial - Royal Greek Dynasty

| Date | Mintage | F | VF | XF | Unc | BU |
|---|---|---|---|---|---|---|
| ND (1963) | 3,000,000 | BV | 3.00 | 5.00 | 9.00 | — |

**30 DRACHMAI** KM# 87 **Weight:** 12.0000 g. **Composition:** 0.8350 Silver .3221 oz. ASW **Subject:** Constantine and Anne-Marie Wedding

| Date | Mintage | F | VF | XF | Unc | BU |
|---|---|---|---|---|---|---|
| 1964 Berne: small edge lettering | 1,000 | BV | 2.00 | 4.00 | 7.50 | — |
| 1964 Kongsberg: large edge lettering | 1,000 | BV | 2.00 | 4.00 | 6.50 | — |

**100 DRACHMAI** KM# 75 **Weight:** 25.0000 g. **Composition:** 0.9000 Silver .7235 oz. ASW **Subject:** 5th Anniversary - Restoration of Monarchy **Obverse:** George I **Reverse:** Crowned and mantled arms

| Date | Mintage | F | VF | XF | Unc | BU |
|---|---|---|---|---|---|---|
| ND (1940) Proof | 500 | Value: 1,200 | | | | |

**100 DRACHMAI** KM# 76 **Weight:** 32.2580 g. **Composition:** 0.9000 Gold .9335 oz. AGW

| Date | Mintage | F | VF | XF | Unc | BU |
|---|---|---|---|---|---|---|
| ND (1940) Proof | 140 | Value: 11,000 | | | | |

**100 DRACHMAI** KM# 94 **Weight:** 25.0000 g. **Composition:** 0.8350 Silver .6712 oz. ASW **Subject:** 1967 Revolution

| Date | Mintage | F | VF | XF | Unc | BU |
|---|---|---|---|---|---|---|
| ND (1970) | 30,000 | — | — | 35.00 | 60.00 | — |

**100 DRACHMAI** KM# 95 **Weight:** 32.2580 g. **Composition:** 0.9000 Gold .9335 oz. AGW **Subject:** 1967 Revolution

| Date | Mintage | F | VF | XF | Unc | BU |
|---|---|---|---|---|---|---|
| ND (1970) | 10,000 | — | — | — | 700 | — |
| ND (1970) | 10,000 | — | — | — | 700 | — |

## REPUBLIC

### DECIMAL COINAGE

**10 LEPTA** KM# 103 **Composition:** Aluminum **Obverse:** Modified design; soldier replaced with phoenix **Reverse:** Pair of dolphins flank trident

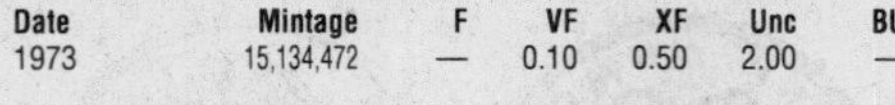

| Date | Mintage | F | VF | XF | Unc | BU |
|---|---|---|---|---|---|---|
| 1973 | 15,134,472 | — | 0.10 | 0.50 | 2.00 | — |

**10 LEPTA** KM# 113 **Composition:** Aluminum **Obverse:** Shield in wereath **Reverse:** Charging bull, right

| Date | Mintage | F | VF | XF | Unc | BU |
|---|---|---|---|---|---|---|
| 1976 | 2,043,000 | — | 0.10 | 0.30 | 2.00 | — |
| 1978 | 791,000 | 0.50 | 1.00 | 2.50 | 5.00 | — |
| 1978 Proof | 20,000 | Value: 5.00 | | | | |

**20 LEPTA** KM# 105 **Composition:** Aluminum **Obverse:** Modified design; soldier replaced with phoenix

| Date | Mintage | F | VF | XF | Unc | BU |
|---|---|---|---|---|---|---|
| 1973 | 15,265,797 | — | 0.20 | 0.50 | 2.50 | — |

**20 LEPTA** KM# 114 **Composition:** Aluminum **Obverse:** Shield in wreath **Reverse:** Bust of stallion, left

| Date | Mintage | F | VF | XF | Unc | BU |
|---|---|---|---|---|---|---|
| 1976 | 2,506,000 | — | 0.20 | 0.40 | 2.50 | — |
| 1978 | 803,000 | 0.50 | 1.00 | 2.50 | 5.00 | — |
| 1978 Proof | 20,000 | Value: 5.00 | | | | |

**50 LEPTA** KM# 106 **Composition:** Nickel-Brass

| Date | Mintage | F | VF | XF | Unc | BU |
|---|---|---|---|---|---|---|
| 1973 | 55,231,898 | — | 0.10 | 0.15 | 1.00 | — |

**50 LEPTA** KM# 115 **Composition:** Nickel-Brass **Reverse:** Markos Botsaris

| Date | Mintage | F | VF | XF | Unc | BU |
|---|---|---|---|---|---|---|
| 1976 | 51,016,000 | — | 0.10 | 0.15 | 1.00 | — |
| 1978 | 12,010,000 | — | 0.10 | 0.15 | 1.00 | — |
| 1978 Proof | 20,000 | Value: 3.00 | | | | |
| 1980 | 6,682,000 | — | 0.10 | 0.15 | 1.25 | — |
| 1982 | 3,365,000 | — | 0.10 | 0.15 | 1.25 | — |
| 1984 | 1,208,000 | — | 0.10 | 0.15 | 1.25 | — |
| 1986 | — | — | 0.10 | 0.15 | 1.25 | — |

**DRACHMA** KM# 107 **Composition:** Nickel-Brass

| Date | Mintage | F | VF | XF | Unc | BU |
|---|---|---|---|---|---|---|
| 1973 | 45,218,431 | 0.15 | 0.20 | 0.50 | 1.50 | — |

**DRACHMA** KM# 116 **Composition:** Nickel-Brass **Reverse:** Konstantinos Kanaris

| Date | Mintage | F | VF | XF | Unc | BU |
|---|---|---|---|---|---|---|
| 1976 | 102,060,000 | — | 0.10 | 0.15 | 1.00 | — |
| **Note:** Varieties exist | | | | | | |
| 1978 | 21,200,000 | — | 0.10 | 0.15 | 1.00 | — |
| 1978 Proof | 20,000 | Value: 2.50 | | | | |
| 1980 | 52,503,000 | — | 0.10 | 0.15 | 1.00 | — |
| 1982 | 54,186,000 | — | 0.10 | 0.15 | 1.00 | — |
| 1984 | 33,665,000 | — | 0.10 | 0.15 | 1.00 | — |
| 1986 | 17,901,000 | — | 0.10 | 0.15 | 1.00 | — |

**DRACHMA** KM# 150 **Composition:** Copper **Obverse:** Sailing ship **Reverse:** Bouboulina - Heroine

| Date | Mintage | F | VF | XF | Unc | BU |
|---|---|---|---|---|---|---|
| 1988 | 36,707,000 | — | — | — | 0.20 | — |
| 1990 | — | — | — | — | 0.20 | — |
| 1992 | — | — | — | — | 0.20 | — |
| 1993 | — | — | — | — | 0.20 | — |
| 1993 Proof | — | Value: 3.50 | | | | |
| 1998 | — | — | — | — | — | — |
| 2000 | — | — | — | — | 0.20 | — |

**2 DRACHMAI** KM# 108 **Composition:** Nickel-Brass

| Date | Mintage | F | VF | XF | Unc | BU |
|---|---|---|---|---|---|---|
| 1973 | 51,163,812 | 0.20 | 0.40 | 1.00 | 2.50 | — |

**2 DRACHMAI** KM# 117 **Composition:** Nickel-Brass **Reverse:** Georgios Karaiskakis

| Date | Mintage | F | VF | XF | Unc | BU |
|---|---|---|---|---|---|---|
| 1976 | 92,401,000 | — | 0.15 | 0.25 | 1.00 | — |
| 1978 | 16,772,000 | — | 0.15 | 0.25 | 1.00 | — |
| 1978 Proof | 20,000 | Value: 2.50 | | | | |
| 1980 | 45,955,000 | — | 0.15 | 0.25 | 1.00 | — |

**2 DRACHMES** KM# 130 **Composition:** Nickel-Brass **Reverse:** Georgios Karaiskakis

| Date | Mintage | F | VF | XF | Unc | BU |
|---|---|---|---|---|---|---|
| 1982 | 64,414,000 | — | 0.10 | 0.20 | 1.00 | — |
| 1984 | 37,861,000 | — | 0.10 | 0.20 | 1.00 | — |
| 1986 | 21,019,000 | — | 0.10 | 0.20 | 1.00 | — |

**2 DRACHMES** KM# 151 **Composition:** Copper **Reverse:** Manto Mavrogenous

| Date | Mintage | F | VF | XF | Unc | BU |
|---|---|---|---|---|---|---|
| 1988 | 36,707,000 | — | — | — | 0.30 | — |
| 1990 | — | — | — | — | 0.30 | — |
| 1992 | — | — | — | — | 0.30 | — |
| 1993 | — | — | — | — | 0.30 | — |
| 1993 Proof | — | Value: 4.50 | | | | |
| 1994 | — | — | — | — | 0.30 | — |
| 1998 | — | — | — | — | 0.30 | — |
| 2000 | — | — | — | — | 0.30 | — |

**5 DRACHMAI** KM# 109.2 **Composition:** Copper-Nickel **Note:** Denomination spelling ends with A.

| Date | Mintage | F | VF | XF | Unc | BU |
|---|---|---|---|---|---|---|
| 1973 | Inc. above | 1.00 | 2.00 | 4.00 | 10.00 | — |

**5 DRACHMAI** KM# 109.1 **Composition:** Copper-Nickel **Note:** Denomination spelling ends with I.

| Date | Mintage | F | VF | XF | Unc | BU |
|---|---|---|---|---|---|---|
| 1973 | 33,957,473 | 0.50 | 1.00 | 1.50 | 2.50 | — |

**5 DRACHMAI** KM# 118 **Composition:** Copper-Nickel **Reverse:** Aristotle

| Date | Mintage | F | VF | XF | Unc | BU |
|---|---|---|---|---|---|---|
| 1976 | 85,187,000 | 0.10 | 0.20 | 0.35 | 1.00 | — |
| 1978 | 17,404,000 | 0.10 | 0.20 | 0.35 | 1.00 | — |
| 1978 Proof | 20,000 | Value: 2.00 | | | | |
| 1980 | 33,701,000 | 0.10 | 0.20 | 0.35 | 1.00 | — |

**5 DRACHMES** KM# 131 **Composition:** Copper-Nickel

| Date | Mintage | F | VF | XF | Unc | BU |
|---|---|---|---|---|---|---|
| 1982 | 42,647,000 | 0.10 | 0.20 | 0.35 | 1.00 | — |
| 1984 | 29,778,000 | 0.10 | 0.20 | 0.35 | 1.00 | — |
| 1986 | 16,730,000 | 0.10 | 0.20 | 0.35 | 1.00 | — |
| 1988 | 30,273,000 | — | — | 0.30 | 0.65 | — |
| 1990 | — | — | — | 0.30 | 0.65 | — |
| 1992 | — | — | — | 0.30 | 0.65 | — |
| 1993 | — | — | — | 0.30 | 0.65 | — |
| 1993 Proof | — | Value: 4.50 | | | | |
| 1994 | — | — | — | — | 0.65 | — |
| 1998 | — | — | — | 0.30 | 0.65 | — |
| 1999 | — | — | — | — | 0.65 | — |
| 2000 | — | — | — | — | 0.65 | — |

**10 DRACHMAI** KM# 110 **Composition:** Copper-Nickel

| Date | Mintage | F | VF | XF | Unc | BU |
|---|---|---|---|---|---|---|
| 1973 | 22,599,848 | 0.50 | 1.00 | 1.75 | 3.50 | — |

**10 DRACHMAI** KM# 119 **Composition:** Copper-Nickel **Reverse:** Democritus

| Date | Mintage | F | VF | XF | Unc | BU |
|---|---|---|---|---|---|---|
| 1976 | 76,816,000 | 0.15 | 0.25 | 0.50 | 1.00 | — |
| 1978 | 14,637,000 | 0.15 | 0.25 | 0.50 | 1.00 | — |
| 1978 Proof | 20,000 | Value: 2.50 | | | | |
| 1980 | 28,733,000 | 0.15 | 0.25 | 0.50 | 1.00 | — |

**10 DRACHMES** KM# 132 **Composition:** Copper-Nickel

| Date | Mintage | F | VF | XF | Unc | BU |
|---|---|---|---|---|---|---|
| 1982 | 35,539,000 | 0.15 | 0.25 | 0.50 | 1.00 | — |
| 1984 | 23,802,000 | 0.15 | 0.25 | 0.50 | 1.00 | — |
| 1986 | 24,441,000 | 0.15 | 0.25 | 0.50 | 1.00 | — |
| 1988 | 16,869,000 | — | 0.20 | 0.40 | 0.85 | — |
| 1990 | — | — | 0.20 | 0.40 | 0.85 | — |
| 1992 | — | — | 0.20 | 0.40 | 0.85 | — |
| 1993 | — | — | 0.20 | 0.40 | 0.85 | — |
| 1993 Proof | — | Value: 5.00 | | | | |
| 1998 | — | — | 0.20 | 0.40 | 0.85 | — |
| 2000 | — | — | — | — | 0.85 | — |

**20 DRACHMAI** KM# 112 **Composition:** Copper-Nickel

| Date | Mintage | F | VF | XF | Unc | BU |
|---|---|---|---|---|---|---|
| 1973 | 20,650,087 | 0.20 | 0.30 | 0.50 | 1.50 | — |

**20 DRACHMAI** KM# 120 **Composition:** Copper-Nickel **Reverse:** Pericles

| Date | Mintage | F | VF | XF | Unc | BU |
|---|---|---|---|---|---|---|
| 1976 | 53,167,500 | 0.20 | 0.30 | 0.50 | 1.25 | — |
| 1978 | 65,353,000 | 0.20 | 0.30 | 0.50 | 1.50 | — |
| 1978 Proof | 20,000 | Value: 3.00 | | | | |
| 1980 | 17,562,000 | 0.20 | 0.30 | 0.50 | 1.25 | — |

**20 DRACHMES** KM# 133 **Composition:** Copper-Nickel

| Date | Mintage | F | VF | XF | Unc | BU |
|---|---|---|---|---|---|---|
| 1982 | 24,299,000 | 0.20 | 0.30 | 0.50 | 1.00 | — |
| 1984 | 13,412,000 | 0.20 | 0.30 | 0.50 | 1.25 | — |
| 1986 | 10,553,000 | 0.20 | 0.30 | 0.50 | 1.00 | — |
| 1988 | 16,196,000 | — | — | 0.50 | 1.00 | — |

**20 DRACHMES** KM# 154 **Composition:** Nickel-Bronze **Reverse:** Dionysus Solomos, composer of National Anthem

| Date | Mintage | F | VF | XF | Unc | BU |
|---|---|---|---|---|---|---|
| 1990 | — | — | — | — | 1.25 | — |
| 1992 | — | — | — | — | 1.25 | — |
| 1993 | — | — | — | — | 1.25 | — |
| 1993 Proof | — | Value: 6.50 | | | | |
| 1994 | — | — | — | — | 1.25 | — |
| 1998 | — | — | — | — | 1.25 | — |
| 2000 | — | — | — | — | 1.25 | — |

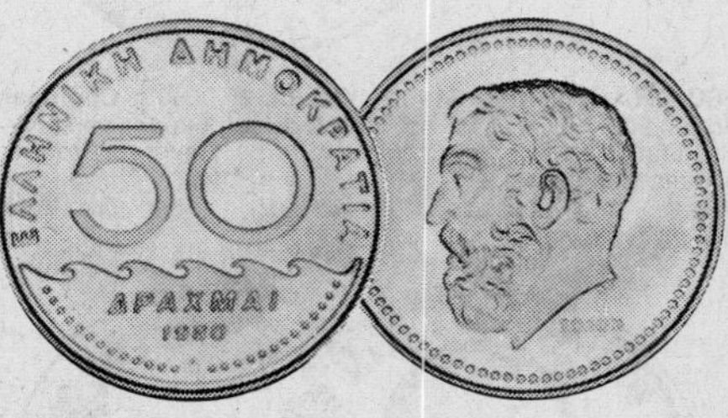

**50 DRACHMAI** KM# 124 **Composition:** Copper-Nickel **Reverse:** Solon teh Archon of Athens

| Date | Mintage | F | VF | XF | Unc | BU |
|---|---|---|---|---|---|---|
| 1980 | 32,250,999 | 0.50 | 0.75 | 1.50 | 3.50 | — |

**50 DRACHMES** KM# 134 **Composition:** Copper-Nickel **Obverse:** Denomination in modern Greek

| Date | Mintage | F | VF | XF | Unc | BU |
|---|---|---|---|---|---|---|
| 1982 | 18,899,000 | 0.40 | 0.60 | 1.00 | 1.50 | — |
| 1984 | 11,411,000 | 0.40 | 0.60 | 1.00 | 1.50 | — |

**50 DRACHMES** KM# 147 **Composition:** Nickel-Brass **Obverse:** Ancient sailing boat

| Date | Mintage | F | VF | XF | Unc | BU |
|---|---|---|---|---|---|---|
| 1986 | 12,078,000 | — | 0.50 | 1.00 | 2.50 | — |
| 1988 | 23,589,000 | — | — | 0.75 | 1.50 | — |
| 1990 | — | — | — | 0.75 | 1.75 | — |
| 1992 | — | — | — | 0.75 | 1.75 | — |
| 1993 | — | — | — | 0.75 | 1.75 | — |
| 1993 Proof | — | Value: 7.50 | | | | |
| 1994 | — | — | — | 0.75 | 1.75 | — |
| 1998 | — | — | — | — | 1.75 | — |
| 2000 | — | — | — | — | 1.75 | — |

**50 DRACHMES** KM# 164 **Composition:** Brass **Subject:** 150th Anniversary of the Constitution **Obverse:** Portrait of Dimitrois Kallergis

| Date | Mintage | F | VF | XF | Unc | BU |
|---|---|---|---|---|---|---|
| ND (1994) | 7,500,000 | — | — | — | 3.00 | — |

**50 DRACHMES** **KM# 168** **Composition:** Brass **Subject:** 150th Anniversary of the Constitution **Obverse:** Portrait of Makrygiannis **Reverse:** Center of Parliament Building

| Date | Mintage | F | VF | XF | Unc | BU |
|---|---|---|---|---|---|---|
| ND (1994) | 7,500,000 | — | — | — | 3.00 | — |

**50 DRACHMES** **KM# 171** **Composition:** Brass **Obverse:** National arms **Reverse:** Portrait of Rhgas Feriaou, dates flanking

| Date | Mintage | F | VF | XF | Unc | BU |
|---|---|---|---|---|---|---|
| ND (1998) | 2,500 | — | — | — | 3.50 | — |

**50 DRACHMES** **KM# 172** **Composition:** Brass **Obverse:** National arms **Reverse:** Portrait of Dionysious Solomou, date flanking

| Date | Mintage | F | VF | XF | Unc | BU |
|---|---|---|---|---|---|---|
| ND (1998) | 2,500 | — | — | — | 3.50 | — |

**100 DRACHMAI** **KM# 121** **Weight:** 13.0000 g. **Composition:** 0.6500 Silver .2717 oz. ASW **Subject:** 50th Anniversary - Bank of Greece

| Date | Mintage | F | VF | XF | Unc | BU |
|---|---|---|---|---|---|---|
| 1978 Proof | 25,000 | Value: 45.00 | | | | |

**100 DRACHMAI** **KM# 125** **Weight:** 5.7800 g. **Composition:** 0.9000 Silver .1672 oz. ASW **Subject:** Pan-European Games **Reverse:** Ancient olympic broad jump

| Date | Mintage | F | VF | XF | Unc | BU |
|---|---|---|---|---|---|---|
| 1981 | 150,000 | — | — | — | 7.00 | — |
| 1981 Proof | 150,000 | Value: 12.50 | | | | |

**100 DRACHMAI** **KM# 135** **Weight:** 5.7800 g. **Composition:** 0.9000 Silver .1672 oz. ASW **Subject:** Pan-European Games **Reverse:** Olympic high jump

| Date | Mintage | F | VF | XF | Unc | BU |
|---|---|---|---|---|---|---|
| 1982 | 150,000 | — | — | — | 7.00 | — |
| 1982 Proof | Inc. above | Value: 12.50 | | | | |

**100 DRACHMAI** **KM# 136** **Weight:** 5.7800 g. **Composition:** 0.9000 Silver .1672 oz. ASW **Subject:** Pan-European Games **Reverse:** Pole vault

| Date | Mintage | F | VF | XF | Unc | BU |
|---|---|---|---|---|---|---|
| 1982 | 150,000 | — | — | — | 7.00 | — |
| 1982 Proof | Inc. above | Value: 12.50 | | | | |

**100 DRACHMES** **KM# 152** **Composition:** Copper-Nickel **Subject:** 28th Chess Olympics

| Date | Mintage | F | VF | XF | Unc | BU |
|---|---|---|---|---|---|---|
| 1988 | 30,000 | — | — | — | 12.00 | — |

**100 DRACHMES** **KM# 159** **Composition:** Brass **Subject:** Macedonia - Alexander the Great

| Date | Mintage | F | VF | XF | Unc | BU |
|---|---|---|---|---|---|---|
| 1990 | — | — | — | — | 2.35 | — |
| 1992 | — | — | — | — | 2.35 | — |
| 1993 | — | — | — | — | 2.35 | — |
| 1993 Proof | — | Value: 8.50 | | | | |
| 1994 | — | — | — | — | 2.35 | — |
| 1998 | — | — | — | — | 2.35 | — |
| 2000 | — | — | — | — | 2.35 | — |

**100 DRACHMES** **KM# 169** **Composition:** Brass **Subject:** VI Universal Track Championship Games **Obverse:** Ancient city view and track above denomination **Reverse:** Runner

| Date | Mintage | F | VF | XF | Unc | BU |
|---|---|---|---|---|---|---|
| 1997 | 5,000,000 | — | — | — | 2.75 | — |

**100 DRACHMES** **KM# 170** **Composition:** Brass **Subject:** 13th World Basketball Championships **Obverse:** Cup in ball design above denomination **Reverse:** Four basketball players in action

| Date | Mintage | F | VF | XF | Unc | BU |
|---|---|---|---|---|---|---|
| 1998 | — | — | — | — | 3.50 | — |

**100 DRACHMES** **KM# 173** **Weight:** 10.0000 g. **Composition:** Brass **Obverse:** Ancient wrestlers **Reverse:** Modern wrestlers **Edge:** Reeded and plain sectioned edge

| Date | Mintage | F | VF | XF | Unc | BU |
|---|---|---|---|---|---|---|
| 1999 | — | — | — | — | 3.50 | — |

**100 DRACHMES** **KM# 174** **Weight:** 10.0000 g. **Composition:** Brass **Obverse:** Statue of Atlas **Reverse:** Weight lifter **Edge:** Reeded and plain sectioned edge

| Date | Mintage | F | VF | XF | Unc | BU |
|---|---|---|---|---|---|---|
| 1999 | — | — | — | — | 3.50 | — |

**250 DRACHMAI** **KM# 126** **Weight:** 14.4400 g. **Composition:** 0.9000 Silver .4178 oz. ASW **Subject:** Pan-European Games **Reverse:** Ancient olympic javelin throwing

| Date | Mintage | F | VF | XF | Unc | BU |
|---|---|---|---|---|---|---|
| 1981 | 150,000 | — | — | — | 10.00 | — |
| 1981 Proof | 150,000 | Value: 17.50 | | | | |

**250 DRACHMAI** **KM# 137** **Weight:** 14.4400 g. **Composition:** 0.9000 Silver .4178 oz. ASW **Subject:** Pan-European Games **Reverse:** 1896 olympic discus throwing

| Date | Mintage | F | VF | XF | Unc | BU |
|---|---|---|---|---|---|---|
| 1982 | 150,000 | — | — | — | 10.00 | — |
| 1982 Proof | Inc. above | Value: 17.50 | | | | |

**250 DRACHMAI** **KM# 138** **Weight:** 14.4400 g. **Composition:** 0.9000 Silver .4178 oz. ASW **Subject:** Pan-European Games **Reverse:** Shot put

| Date | Mintage | F | VF | XF | Unc | BU |
|---|---|---|---|---|---|---|
| 1982 | 150,000 | — | — | — | 10.00 | — |
| 1982 Proof | Inc. above | Value: 17.50 | | | | |

**500 DRACHMAI** **KM# 127** **Weight:** 28.8800 g. **Composition:** 0.9000 Silver .8357 oz. ASW **Subject:** Pan-European Games **Reverse:** Ancient olympic relay race

| Date | Mintage | F | VF | XF | Unc | BU |
|---|---|---|---|---|---|---|
| 1981 | 150,000 | — | — | — | 17.50 | — |
| 1981 Proof | 150,000 | Value: 24.00 | | | | |

**500 DRACHMAI** **KM# 139** **Weight:** 28.8800 g. **Composition:** 0.9000 Silver .8357 oz. ASW **Subject:** Pan-European Games **Reverse:** 1896 olympic racers at starting blocks

| Date | Mintage | F | VF | XF | Unc | BU |
|---|---|---|---|---|---|---|
| 1982 | 150,000 | — | — | — | 17.50 | — |
| 1982 Proof | Inc. above | Value: 24.00 | | | | |

**500 DRACHMAI** **KM# 140** **Weight:** 28.8800 g. **Composition:** 0.9000 Silver .8357 oz. ASW **Subject:** Pan-European Games **Reverse:** Racers

| Date | Mintage | F | VF | XF | Unc | BU |
|---|---|---|---|---|---|---|
| 1982 | 150,000 | — | — | — | 17.50 | — |
| 1982 Proof | Inc. above | Value: 24.00 | | | | |

**500 DRACHMES** **KM# 122** **Weight:** 13.0000 g. **Composition:** 0.9000 Silver .3762 oz. ASW **Subject:** Common Market Membership

| Date | Mintage | F | VF | XF | Unc | BU |
|---|---|---|---|---|---|---|
| ND (1979) | — | — | — | — | — | — |
| ND (1979) Proof | 18,000 | Value: 200 | | | | |

**500 DRACHMES** **KM# 145** **Weight:** 18.0000 g. **Composition:** 0.9000 Silver .5209 oz. ASW **Subject:** Olympics **Obverse:** Torch

| Date | Mintage | F | VF | XF | Unc | BU |
|---|---|---|---|---|---|---|
| 1984 | 25,000 | — | — | — | 75.00 | — |
| 1984 Proof | 25,000 | Value: 100 | | | | |

**500 DRACHMES** **KM# 153** **Weight:** 18.1100 g. **Composition:** 0.9000 Silver .5240 oz. ASW **Subject:** 28rh Chess Olympics

| Date | Mintage | F | VF | XF | Unc | BU |
|---|---|---|---|---|---|---|
| 1988 Proof | 3,000 | Value: 125 | | | | |

**500 DRACHMES** **KM# 157** **Weight:** 18.0000 g. **Composition:** 0.9000 Silver .5208 oz. ASW **Subject:** XI Mediterranean Games

| Date | Mintage | F | VF | XF | Unc | BU |
|---|---|---|---|---|---|---|
| 1991 Proof | 10,000 | Value: 45.00 | | | | |

**500 DRACHMES** **KM# 160** **Weight:** 17.0000 g. **Composition:** 0.9250 Silver .5056 oz. ASW **Subject:** 2500th Anniversary of Democracy

| Date | Mintage | F | VF | XF | Unc | BU |
|---|---|---|---|---|---|---|
| 1993 Proof | Est. 30,000 | Value: 45.00 | | | | |

**500 DRACHMES** **KM# 162** **Weight:** 17.0000 g. **Composition:** 0.9250 Silver .5056 oz. ASW **Subject:** Volleyball Centennial

| Date | Mintage | F | VF | XF | Unc | BU |
|---|---|---|---|---|---|---|
| 1994 Proof | 1,750 | Value: 75.00 | | | | |

**500 DRACHMES** **KM# 175** **Weight:** 9.5400 g. **Composition:** Copper-Nickel **Subject:** 2004 Olympics **Obverse:** Laurel wreath, games logo **Reverse:** Arched entry to ancient Olympic stadium **Edge:** Plain

| Date | Mintage | F | VF | XF | Unc | BU |
|---|---|---|---|---|---|---|
| 2000 | — | — | — | — | 4.50 | — |

**500 DRACHMES** **KM# 176** **Weight:** 9.5400 g. **Composition:** Copper-Nickel **Reverse:** Runner receiving Olympic torch **Edge:** Plain

| Date | Mintage | F | VF | XF | Unc | BU |
|---|---|---|---|---|---|---|
| 2000 | — | — | — | — | 4.50 | — |

**500 DRACHMES** KM# 177 **Weight:** 9.5400 g. **Composition:** Copper-Nickel **Reverse:** Ancient winner Diagoras being carried **Edge:** Plain

| Date | Mintage | F | VF | XF | Unc | BU |
|---|---|---|---|---|---|---|
| 2000 | — | — | — | — | 4.50 | — |

**500 DRACHMES** KM# 178 **Weight:** 9.5400 g. **Composition:** Copper-Nickel **Reverse:** Conjoined busts of President Vikelas and Baron Couberten **Edge:** Plain

| Date | Mintage | F | VF | XF | Unc | BU |
|---|---|---|---|---|---|---|
| 2000 | — | — | — | — | 4.50 | — |

**500 DRACHMES** KM# 179 **Weight:** 9.5400 g. **Composition:** Copper-Nickel **Reverse:** Standing Spyros Louis, 1896 marathon winner **Edge:** Plain

| Date | Mintage | F | VF | XF | Unc | BU |
|---|---|---|---|---|---|---|
| 2000 | — | — | — | — | 4.50 | — |

**500 DRACHMES** KM# 180 **Weight:** 9.5400 g. **Composition:** Copper-Nickel **Reverse:** 1896 Olympicgold medal design **Edge:** Plain

| Date | Mintage | F | VF | XF | Unc | BU |
|---|---|---|---|---|---|---|
| 2000 | — | — | — | — | 4.50 | — |

**1000 DRACHMES** KM# 148 **Weight:** 23.3300 g. **Composition:** 0.9250 Silver .6939 oz. ASW **Subject:** Decade For Women

| Date | Mintage | F | VF | XF | Unc | BU |
|---|---|---|---|---|---|---|
| 1985 Proof | 3,660 | Value: 65.00 | | | | |

**1000 DRACHMES** KM# 155 **Weight:** 18.0000 g. **Composition:** 0.9000 Silver .5208 oz. ASW **Subject:** 50th Anniversary - Italian Invasion of Greece

| Date | Mintage | F | VF | XF | Unc | BU |
|---|---|---|---|---|---|---|
| 1990 Proof | 7,000 | Value: 75.00 | | | | |

**1000 DRACHMES** KM# 165 **Weight:** 33.6300 g. **Composition:** 0.9250 Silver 1.001 oz. ASW **Subject:** Olympics **Reverse:** 4 ancient runners

| Date | Mintage | F | VF | XF | Unc | BU |
|---|---|---|---|---|---|---|
| 1996 Proof | 100,000 | Value: 45.00 | | | | |

**1000 DRACHMES** KM# 166 **Weight:** 33.6300 g. **Composition:** 0.9250 Silver 1.001 oz. ASW **Subject:** Olympics **Reverse:** 2 ancient wrestlers

| Date | Mintage | F | VF | XF | Unc | BU |
|---|---|---|---|---|---|---|
| 1996 Proof | 100,000 | Value: 45.00 | | | | |

**2500 DRACHMAI** KM# 128 **Weight:** 6.4500 g. **Composition:** 0.9000 Gold .1866 oz. AGW **Subject:** Pan-European Games - Ancient Olympics

| Date | Mintage | F | VF | XF | Unc | BU |
|---|---|---|---|---|---|---|
| 1981 Proof | 75,000 | Value: 100 | | | | |

**2500 DRACHMAI** KM# 141 **Weight:** 6.4500 g. **Composition:** 0.9000 Gold .1866 oz. AGW **Subject:** Pan-European Games - 1896 Olympics

| Date | Mintage | F | VF | XF | Unc | BU |
|---|---|---|---|---|---|---|
| 1982 Proof | 50,000 | Value: 100 | | | | |

**2500 DRACHMAI** KM# 142 **Weight:** 6.4500 g. **Composition:** 0.9000 Gold .1866 oz. AGW **Subject:** Pan-European Games

| Date | Mintage | F | VF | XF | Unc | BU |
|---|---|---|---|---|---|---|
| 1982 Proof | 50,000 | Value: 100 | | | | |

**5000 DRACHMAI** KM# 129 **Weight:** 12.5000 g. **Composition:** 0.9000 Gold .3617 oz. AGW **Subject:** Pan-European Games - Ancient Olympics

| Date | Mintage | F | VF | XF | Unc | BU |
|---|---|---|---|---|---|---|
| 1981 Proof | 75,000 | Value: 220 | | | | |

**5000 DRACHMAI** KM# 143 **Weight:** 12.5000 g. **Composition:** 0.9000 Gold .3617 oz. AGW **Subject:** Pan-European Games - 1896 Olympics

| Date | Mintage | F | VF | XF | Unc | BU |
|---|---|---|---|---|---|---|
| 1982 Proof | 50,000 | Value: 185 | | | | |

**5000 DRACHMAI** KM# 144 **Weight:** 12.5000 g. **Composition:** 0.9000 Gold .3617 oz. AGW **Subject:** Pan-European Games

| Date | Mintage | F | VF | XF | Unc | BU |
|---|---|---|---|---|---|---|
| 1982 Proof | 50,000 | Value: 185 | | | | |

**5000 DRACHMAI** KM# 146 **Weight:** 8.0000 g. **Composition:** 0.9000 Gold .2315 oz. AGW **Subject:** Olympics **Obverse:** Arms at left, torch at right, similar to 500 Drachmai, KM#145 **Reverse:** Apollo

| Date | Mintage | F | VF | XF | Unc | BU |
|---|---|---|---|---|---|---|
| 1984 Proof | 15,000 | Value: 400 | | | | |

**10000 DRACHMES** KM# 123 **Weight:** 20.0000 g. **Composition:** 0.9000 Gold .5787 oz. AGW **Subject:** Common Market Membership

| Date | Mintage | F | VF | XF | Unc | BU |
|---|---|---|---|---|---|---|
| ND (1979) | — | — | — | — | 400 | — |

**10000 DRACHMES** KM# 149 **Weight:** 7.1300 g. **Composition:** 0.9000 Gold .2063 oz. AGW **Subject:** Decade For Women

| Date | Mintage | F | VF | XF | Unc | BU |
|---|---|---|---|---|---|---|
| 1985 Proof | 2,835 | Value: 285 | | | | |

**10000 DRACHMES** **KM# 158** **Weight:** 8.0000 g. **Composition:** 0.9000 Gold .2315 oz. AGW **Subject:** XI Mediterranean Games

| Date | Mintage | F | VF | XF | Unc | BU |
|---|---|---|---|---|---|---|
| 1991 Proof | 2,000 | Value: 300 | | | | |

**10000 DRACHMES** **KM# 161** **Weight:** 8.5000 g. **Composition:** 0.9170 Gold .2506 oz. AGW **Subject:** 2500th Anniversary of Democracy

| Date | Mintage | F | VF | XF | Unc | BU |
|---|---|---|---|---|---|---|
| 1993 Proof | Est. 10,000 | Value: 250 | | | | |

**10000 DRACHMES** **KM# 163** **Weight:** 8.5000 g. **Composition:** 0.9170 Gold .2506 oz. AGW **Subject:** Volleyball Centennial

| Date | Mintage | F | VF | XF | Unc | BU |
|---|---|---|---|---|---|---|
| 1994 Proof | 500 | Value: 400 | | | | |

**20000 DRACHMES** **KM# 156** **Weight:** 8.0000 g. **Composition:** 0.9000 Gold .2315 oz. AGW **Subject:** 50th Anniversary - Italian Invasion of Greece

| Date | Mintage | F | VF | XF | Unc | BU |
|---|---|---|---|---|---|---|
| 1990 Proof | 1,000 | Value: 1,000 | | | | |

**20000 DRACHMES** **KM# 167** **Weight:** 16.9700 g. **Composition:** 0.9170 Gold .5001 oz. AGW **Subject:** Olympics **Reverse:** Ancient javelin throwers

| Date | Mintage | F | VF | XF | Unc | BU |
|---|---|---|---|---|---|---|
| 1996 Proof | 60,000 | Value: 350 | | | | |

## ESSAIS

| KM# | Date | Mintage | Identification | Mkt Val |
|---|---|---|---|---|
| E23 | 1911 | 4 | 2 Drachmai. Silver. 1868 2 Drachmai. ESSAI to right of denomination. | 8,250 |
| EA23 | 1911 | 2 | 2 Drachmai. Silver. Without mintmark, ESSAI to right of sea-horse. | 8,500 |
| E24 | 1912 | — | 5 Lepta. Nickel. ESSAI, plain edge, without mintmark | 550 |
| E25 | 1912 | — | 5 Lepta. Zinc. ESSAI | 650 |
| E26 | 1912 | — | 10 Lepta. Nickel. ESSAI, plain edge, without mintmark. | 575 |
| E27 | 1912 | — | 10 Lepta. Zinc. ESSAI. | 700 |
| E28 | 1912 | — | 10 Lepta. Nickel. ESSAI, with mintmark | 600 |
| E29 | 1912 | — | 20 Lepta. Nickel. ESSAI. | 600 |
| E30 | 1912 | — | 20 Lepta. Zinc. ESSAI. | 800 |
| E31 | 1913 | — | Drachma. Silver. ESSAI. | 5,000 |
| E32 | 1915 | — | Drachma. Copper-Nickel. ESSAI. | 3,650 |
| E33 | 1915 | — | Drachma. Silver. ESSAI. | 4,000 |
| E34 | 1915 | — | Drachma. Gold. 9.2000 g. ESSAI. | 9,000 |
| E35 | 1915 | — | 2 Drachmai. Silver. ESSAI. | 5,000 |
| E36 | 1915 | — | 2 Drachmai. Gold. 15.9000 g. ESSAI. | 12,500 |
| E37 | 1922 | — | 10 Lepta. Aluminum. ESSAI. | 825 |

## PATTERNS

Including off metal strikes

| KM# | Date | Mintage | Identification | Mkt Val |
|---|---|---|---|---|
| Pn40 | 1910 | — | Drachma. Silver. Value in lower case letters. | 3,500 |
| Pn41 | 1910 | — | Drachma. Without mintmark. | 3,500 |
| Pn42 | 1911 | — | 2 Drachmai. Silver. Sea-horse. Without mintmark. | 8,500 |
| Pn44 | 1926 | — | Drachma. Nickel. Large letters. | 500 |
| Pn54 | 1926 | — | 2 Drachmai. Nickel. Large letters. | 800 |
| Pn55 | 1930 | — | 5 Drachmai. Nickel. With "MODEL" edge. | 750 |
| Pn59 | | — | 20 Drachmai. Copper. 21mm, KM74. | 2,800 |
| PnA59 | | — | 20 Drachmai. Copper. 22mm, KM74. | 3,500 |
| Pn60 | | — | 20 Drachmai. Gold. Without "20", KM74. | 22,750 |
| Pn61 | | — | 100 Drachmai. Copper. KM75. | 2,650 |
| Pn62 | | — | 100 Drachmai. Copper. KM76. | 3,000 |
| Pn63 | 1954 | 50 | 50 Lepta. Copper-Nickel. "ANAMN-KETIKON" above date. | 500 |
| Pn64 | 1954 | 10 | 50 Lepta. Gold. | 5,000 |
| Pn65 | 1954 | — | 50 Lepta. "hollow cheek". | 50.00 |
| Pn66 | 1954 | 50 | Drachma. Copper Nickel. "ANAMN-KETIKON" above date. | 500 |
| Pn67 | 1954 | 10 | Drachma. Gold. | 5,000 |
| Pn70 | 1954 | 10 | 2 Drachmai. Gold. | 5,000 |
| Pn73 | 1954 | 10 | 5 Drachmai. Gold. | 5,000 |
| Pn68 | 1954 | — | Drachma. "hollow cheek". | 50.00 |
| Pn71 | 1954 | — | 2 Drachmai. "hollow cheek". | 200 |
| Pn69 | 1954 | 50 | 2 Drachmai. Copper-Nickel. "ANAMN-KETIKON" above date. | 500 |
| Pn72 | 1954 | 50 | 5 Drachmai. Copper-Nickel. "ANAMN-KETIKON" above date. | 500 |
| Pn74 | 1954 | — | 5 Drachmai. Copper-Nickel. "hollow cheek". | — |
| Pn75 | 1959 | 10 | 10 Drachmai. Gold. | 5,000 |
| Pn77 | 1960 | 57 | 20 Drachmai. Gold. | 5,000 |

| KM# | Date | Mintage | Identification | Mkt Val |
|---|---|---|---|---|
| Pn78 | 1963 | — | 30 Drachmai. Silver. With "ANAMN-KETIKON." | 1,500 |
| Pn79 | 1964 | — | 30 Drachmai. Gold. | 5,000 |
| Pn82 | 1966 | — | Drachma. Gold. | — |
| Pn84 | 1966 | — | 2 Drachmai. Gold. | — |
| Pn86 | 1966 | — | 5 Drachmai. Gold. | — |
| Pn81 | 1966 | — | 50 Lepta. Platinum. | 5,000 |
| Pn83 | 1966 | — | Drachma. Platinum. | 5,000 |
| Pn85 | 1966 | — | 2 Drachmai. Platinum. | 5,000 |
| Pn87 | 1966 | — | 5 Drachmai. Platinum. | 5,000 |
| Pn88 | 1973 | — | 20 Drachmai. Bronze-Nickel. Low relief and date, without veil. | 50.00 |
| Pn89 | 1976 | — | Drachma. Nickel. 4 sails and 2 waves. | 300 |
| Pn90 | 1986 | 4 | Drachma. Aluminum. | 1,500 |
| Pn91 | 1986 | 4 | 2 Drachmai. Aluminum. | 1,500 |
| pn92 | 1987 | — | Drachma. Copper. | — |
| pn93 | 1987 | — | 2 Drachmes. Nickel-Brass. | — |
| Pn80 | 1996 | — | 50 Lepta. Gold. | — |

## PIEFORTS

| KM# | Date | Mintage | Identification | Mkt Val |
|---|---|---|---|---|
| P1 | 1922 | — | 10 Lepta. Copper. With ESSAI. | 500 |
| P3 | | 2 | 20 Drachmai. Lead. KM74. | 2,200 |

## TRIAL STRIKES

| KM# | Date | Mintage | Identification | Mkt Val |
|---|---|---|---|---|
| TS19 | 1921 | — | 5 Lepta. Aluminum. Uniface. | — |
| TS20 | 1921 | — | 5 Lepta. Aluminum. Uniface. | — |
| TS21 | 1921 | — | 50 Lepta. Aluminum. Uniface. | 500 |
| TS22 | 1926 | — | 2 Drachmai. Copper. With E. | 50.00 |
| TS23 | 1930 | — | 5 Drachmai. Copper. Uniface. With E. | 50.00 |
| TS24 | 1930 | — | 20 Drachmai. Brass. Test marks. | 50.00 |
| TS25 | 1960 | — | 20 Drachmai. Copper. | 100 |

## MINT SETS

| KM# | Date | Mintage | Identification | Issue Price | Mkt Val |
|---|---|---|---|---|---|
| MS1 | 1965 (7) | — | KM78, 80-85 | — | 15.00 |
| MS2 | 1978 | 50,000 | | — | 15.00 |
| MS3 | 1982 (7) | — | KM115-116, 130-134 | — | 5.00 |
| MS4 | 1993 (7) | — | KM#131-132, 147, 150-151, 154, 159 | — | 8.50 |
| MS5 | 2000 | — | KM#131-132, 147, 150-151, 154, 159 | — | 8.50 |

## PROOF SETS

| KM# | Date | Mintage | Identification | Issue Price | Mkt Val |
|---|---|---|---|---|---|
| PS1 | 1965 (7) | 4,987 | KM78, 80-85 | 10.25 | 25.00 |
| PS2 | 1978 (8) | 20,000 | KM113-120 | — | 25.00 |
| PS3 | 1993 (8) | — | KM131-132, 147, 150-151, 154, 159-160 | — | 85.00 |
| PS4 | 1994 (2) | — | KM162-163 | — | 475 |

# GREENLAND

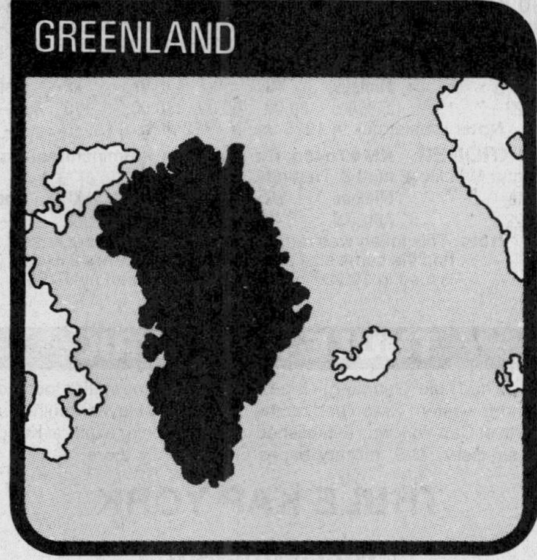

Greenland, an integral part of the Danish realm is situated between the North Atlantic Ocean and the Polar Sea, almost entirely within the Arctic Circle. An island nation, it has an area of 840,000 sq. mi. (2,175,600 sq. km.) and a population of 57,000 Capital: Nuuk (formerly Godthaab). Greenland is the world's only source of natural cryolite, a fluoride of sodium and aluminum important in making aluminum. Fish products and minerals are exported.

Eric the Red discovered Greenland in 982 and established the first settlement in 986. Greenland was a republic until 1261, when the sovereignty of Norway was extended to the island. The original colony was abandoned about 1400 when increasing cold interfered with the breeding of cattle. Successful recolonization was undertaken by Denmark in 1721. In 1921 Denmark extended its claim to include the entire island, and made it a colony of the crown in 1924. The island's colonial status was abolished by amendment to the Danish constitution on June 5, 1953, and Greenland became an integral part of the Kingdom of Denmark. It has been an autonomous state since May 1, 1979.

**RULERS**

Danish

**MINT MARKS**

Heart (h) Copenhagen (Kobenhavn)

**MINTMASTERS INITIALS**

HCN - Hans Christian Nielsen, 1919-1927
C - Alfred Kristian Frederik Christiansen, 1956-1971
GJ - Knud Gunnar Jensen, 1901-1933
S - Harald Salomon, 1933-1968

**MONETARY SYSTEM**

100 Øre = 1 Krone

# DANISH COLONY

## MILLED COINAGE

**25 ORE KM# 5 Composition:** Copper-Nickel **Obverse:** Crowned arms of Denmark **Obv. Legend:** GRONLANDS STYRELSE **Reverse:** Value over polar bear walking left, date below

| Date | Mintage | F | VF | XF | Unc | BU |
|---|---|---|---|---|---|---|
| 1926(h) HCN, GJ | 310,000 | 4.00 | 7.00 | 12.50 | 25.00 | — |

**Note:** Was withdrawn from circulation during 1940-42 and sent to the United States for alteration.

**25 ORE KM# 6 Composition:** Copper-Nickel **Note:** Center hole added to KM#5.

| Date | Mintage | F | VF | XF | Unc | BU |
|---|---|---|---|---|---|---|
| 1926(h) HCN, GJ | 60,000 | 20.00 | 40.00 | — | — | — |

**Note:** The hole was added to avoid confusion with the 1 Krone coins of Denmark.

**50 ORE KM# 7 Composition:** Aluminum-Bronze **Obverse:** Crowned arms of Denmark **Obv. Legend:** GRONLANDS STYRELSE **Reverse:** Value over polar bear walking left, date below.

| Date | Mintage | F | VF | XF | Unc | BU |
|---|---|---|---|---|---|---|
| 1926(h) HCN, CJ | 196,000 | 5.50 | 9.00 | 15.00 | 30.00 | — |

**KRONE KM# 8 Composition:** Aluminum-Bronze **Obverse:** Crowned arms of Denmark **Obv. Legend:** GRONLANDS STYRELSE **Reverse:** Value over polar bear walking left, date below.

| Date | Mintage | F | VF | XF | Unc | BU |
|---|---|---|---|---|---|---|
| 1926(h) HCN, CJ | 287,000 | 4.50 | 8.50 | 18.00 | 45.00 | — |

**KRONE KM# 10 Composition:** Aluminum-Bronze **Issuer:** Royal Greenland Trade Company **Obverse:** Crowned arms of Denmark and Greenland **Obv. Legend:** DEN KONGELIGE GRONLANDSKE HANDEL **Reverse:** Value in sprays

| Date | Mintage | F | VF | XF | Unc | BU |
|---|---|---|---|---|---|---|
| 1957(h) C, S | 100,000 | 6.00 | 10.00 | 20.00 | 45.00 | — |

**KRONE KM# 10a Composition:** Copper-Nickel **Issuer:** Royal Greenland Trade Company

| Date | Mintage | F | VF | XF | Unc | BU |
|---|---|---|---|---|---|---|
| 1960(h) C, S | 109,000 | 3.00 | 6.00 | 10.00 | 18.50 | — |
| 1964(h) C, S | 110,000 | 4.00 | 8.00 | 12.50 | 20.00 | — |

**5 KRONER KM# 9 Composition:** Brass **Obverse:** Crowned arms of Denmark **Obv. Legend:** GRONLANDS STYRELSE **Reverse:** Value over polar bear walking left, date below.

| Date | Mintage | F | VF | XF | Unc | BU |
|---|---|---|---|---|---|---|
| 1944 | 100,000 | 30.00 | 45.00 | 65.00 | 100 | — |

## TOKEN COINAGE

**10 ORE KM# Tn1 Composition:** Nickel Plated Zinc **Issuer:** Greenland Mining Ltd; Josvas Copper Mines **Obv. Legend:** GRONLANDSK MINEDRIFTS-ARTIESELSKAB **Reverse:** Crossed hammers over "10"

| Date | Mintage | VG | F | VF | XF | Unc |
|---|---|---|---|---|---|---|
| 1911 | 5,000 | 3.00 | 8.00 | 12.00 | 25.00 | — |

**25 ORE** **KM# Tn2** **Composition:** Nickel Plated Zinc **Issuer:** Greenland Mining Ltd; Josvas Copper Mines **Obv. Legend:** GRONLANDSK MINEDRIFTS-ARTIESELSKAB **Reverse:** Crossed hammers over "25"

| Date | Mintage | VG | F | VF | XF | Unc |
|---|---|---|---|---|---|---|
| 1911 | 5,000 | 3.00 | 8.00 | 12.00 | 25.00 | — |

**100 ORE** **KM# Tn3** **Composition:** Nickel Plated Zinc **Issuer:** Greenland Mining Ltd; Josvas Copper Mines **Obv. Legend:** GRONLANDSK MINEDRIFTS-ARTIESELSKAB **Reverse:** Crossed hammers over "100"

| Date | Mintage | VG | F | VF | XF | Unc |
|---|---|---|---|---|---|---|
| 1911 | 5,000 | 3.00 | 8.00 | 12.00 | 25.00 | — |

**Note:** Struck at L. Chr. Lauer, Nurnberg, Germany

## TOKEN COINAGE

Series IV, 1922

**50 ORE** **KM# Tn47** **Composition:** Copper-Nickel **Issuer:** Ivigtut Cryolite Mining & Trading Co. **Obverse:** Seated polar bear on frame **Obv. Legend:** IVIGTUT KRYOLITHBRUD **Rev. Legend:** KRYOLITH MINE HANDELS SELSKABET

| Date | Mintage | VG | F | VF | XF | Unc |
|---|---|---|---|---|---|---|
| 1922 | 4,018,000 | 16.00 | 40.00 | 65.00 | 90.00 | — |

**10 ORE** **KM# Tn46** **Composition:** Copper-Nickel **Issuer:** Ivigtut Cryolite Mining & Trading Co. **Obverse:** Seated polar bear on frame **Obv. Legend:** IVIGTUT KRYOLITHBRUD **Rev. Legend:** KRYOLITH MINE HANDELS SELSKABET

| Date | Mintage | F | VF | XF | Unc | BU |
|---|---|---|---|---|---|---|
| 1922 | 10,018,000 | 10.00 | 15.00 | 30.00 | — | — |

**2 KRONER** **KM# Tn48** **Composition:** Copper-Nickel **Issuer:** Ivigtut Cryolite Mining & Trading Co. **Obverse:** Seated polar bear on frame **Obv. Legend:** IVIGTUT KRYOLITHBRUD **Rev. Legend:** KRYOLITH MINE HANDELS SELSKABET

| Date | Mintage | VG | F | VF | XF | Unc |
|---|---|---|---|---|---|---|
| 1922 | 4,018,000 | 15.00 | 35.00 | 60.00 | 85.00 | — |

**10 KRONER** **KM# Tn49** **Composition:** Copper-Nickel **Issuer:** Ivigtut Cryolite Mining & Trading Co. **Obverse:** Seated polar bear on frame **Obv. Legend:** IVIGTUT KRYOLITHBRUD **Rev. Legend:** KRYOLITH MINE HANDELS SELSKABET

| Date | Mintage | VG | F | VF | XF | Unc |
|---|---|---|---|---|---|---|
| 1922 | 10,706,000 | 20.00 | 50.00 | 80.00 | 110 | — |

**Note:** Was struck in 1926 using 1922 dies

**10 KRONER** **KM# Tn49a** **Composition:** Aluminum **Issuer:** Ivigtut Cryolite Mining & Trading Co.

| Date | Mintage | VG | F | VF | XF | Unc |
|---|---|---|---|---|---|---|
| 1922 | 7,018,000 | — | — | 750 | 900 | — |

**Note:** This token was removed from circulation because it had the same size and weight of Denmark's 2 Kroner, issued in 1924. These tokens were used until 1957

# THULE-KAP YORK

The Thule (Gaanaaq)-Cape York Artic trading station located in northwestern Greenland on the coast of the Hayes Peninsula north of Cap York was established in 1910 by polar explorer Knud Rasmussen. U.S. military bases are currently there.

## THULE KAP YORK

## TOKEN COINAGE

**5 ORE** **KM# Tn5.1** **Composition:** Aluminum **Obv. Legend:** THULE *KAP YORK* **Reverse:** "5" above date, with hole in center

| Date | Mintage | F | VF | XF | Unc | BU |
|---|---|---|---|---|---|---|
| 1910 | 5,000 | 2.00 | 4.50 | 8.00 | 15.00 | — |

**Note:** Struck in 1913

**5 ORE** **KM# Tn5.2** **Composition:** Aluminum **Note:** Without center hole

| Date | Mintage | F | VF | XF | Unc | BU |
|---|---|---|---|---|---|---|
| 1910 Rare | — | — | — | — | — | — |

**Note:** Struck in 1913

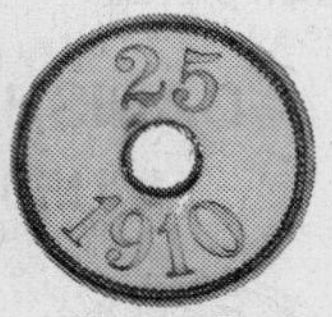

**25 ORE** **KM# Tn6** **Composition:** Aluminum **Obv. Legend:** THULE *KAP YORK* **Reverse:** "25" above date, with hole in center

| Date | Mintage | F | VF | XF | Unc | BU |
|---|---|---|---|---|---|---|
| 1910 | 5,000 | 2.00 | 3.50 | 6.00 | 12.00 | — |

**100 ORE** **KM# Tn7** **Composition:** Aluminum **Obv. Legend:** THULE *KAP YORK* **Reverse:** "100" above date, with hole in center

| Date | Mintage | F | VF | XF | Unc | BU |
|---|---|---|---|---|---|---|
| 1910 | 2,000 | 4.00 | 10.00 | 16.00 | 30.00 | — |

**500 ORE** **KM# Tn8** **Composition:** Aluminum **Obv. Legend:** THULE *KAP YORK* **Reverse:** "500" above date, with hole in center

| Date | Mintage | F | VF | XF | Unc | BU |
|---|---|---|---|---|---|---|
| 1910 | 2,000 | 6.00 | 15.00 | 22.00 | 40.00 | — |

**Note:** Tn5-8 were struck at L. Chr. Lauer, Nurnberg, Germany

**5 KRONER** **KM# Tn9** **Composition:** Aluminum **Obv. Legend:** THULE *KAP YORK* **Reverse:** "5" above date, with hole in center

| Date | Mintage | F | VF | XF | Unc | BU |
|---|---|---|---|---|---|---|
| 1932 | 500 | 15.00 | 30.00 | 50.00 | 90.00 | — |

**10 KRONER** **KM# Tn10** **Composition:** Aluminum **Obv. Legend:** THULE *KAP YORK* **Reverse:** "10" above date, with hole in center

| Date | Mintage | F | VF | XF | Unc | BU |
|---|---|---|---|---|---|---|
| 1932 | 500 | 40.00 | 85.00 | 140 | 200 | — |

**Note:** Tn9-10 were struck at a private mint in Copenhagen

# GRENADA

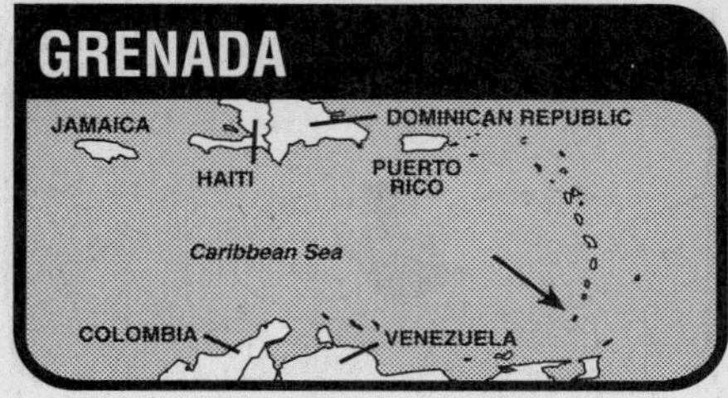


The State of Grenada, located in the Windward Islands of the Caribbean Sea 90 miles (145 km.) north of Trinidad, has(with Carriacou and Petit Martinique) an area of 133 sq. mi. (344 sq. km.) and a population of 94,000. Capital: St.George's. Grenada is the smallest independent nation in the Western Hemisphere. The economy is based on agriculture and tourism. Sugar, coconuts, nutmeg, cocoa and bananas are exported.

Columbus discovered Grenada in 1498 during his third voyage to the Americas. Spain failed to colonize the island, and in 1627 granted it to the British who sold it to the French who colonized it in 1650. Grenada was captured by the British in 1763, retaken by the French in 1779, and finally ceded to the British in 1783. In 1958 Grenada joined the Federation of the West Indies, which was dissolved in 1962. In 1967 it became an internally self-governing British associated state. Full independence was attained on Feb. 4, 1974. Grenada is a member of the Commonwealth of Nations. The prime minister is the Head of Government. Elizabeth II is Head of State as Queen of Grenada.

The early coinage of Grenada consists of cut and countermarked pieces of Spanish or Spanish Colonial Reales, which were valued at 11 Bits. In 1787 8 Reales coins were cut into 11 triangular pieces and countermarked with an incuse G. Later in 1814 large denomination cut pieces were issued being 1/2, 1/3 or 1/6 cuts and countermarked with a TR, incuse G and a number 6, 4,2, or 1 indicating the value in bitts.

**RULERS**

British

**MONETARY SYSTEM**

1789-1798

1 Bit = 9 Pence

11 Bits = 8 Shillings 3 Pence = 1 Dollar

1798-1840

12 Bits = 9 Shillings = 1 Dollar

## STATE

### MODERN COINAGE

**4 DOLLARS** **KM# 15** **Composition:** Copper-Nickel **Series:** F.A.O.

| Date | Mintage | F | VF | XF | Unc | BU |
|---|---|---|---|---|---|---|
| 1970 | 13,000 | — | 4.50 | 7.50 | 13.50 | — |
| 1970 Proof | 2,000 | Value: 32.50 | | | | |

**10 DOLLARS** **KM# 16** **Composition:** Copper-Nickel **Subject:** Royal Visit

| Date | Mintage | F | VF | XF | Unc | BU |
|---|---|---|---|---|---|---|
| 1985 | Est. 100,000 | — | — | 4.50 | 9.00 | — |

**10 DOLLARS** **KM# 16a** **Weight:** 28.2800 g. **Composition:** 0.9250 Silver .8411 oz. ASW **Subject:** Royal Visit

| Date | Mintage | F | VF | XF | Unc | BU |
|---|---|---|---|---|---|---|
| 1985 Proof | Est. 5,000 | Value: 55.00 | | | | |

**10 DOLLARS** **KM# 16b** **Weight:** 47.5400 g. **Composition:** 0.9170 Gold 1.4013 oz. AGW **Subject:** Royal Visit

| Date | Mintage | F | VF | XF | Unc | BU |
|---|---|---|---|---|---|---|
| 1985 Proof | Est. 250 | Value: 1,200 | | | | |

**100 DOLLARS** **KM# 17** **Weight:** 129.5900 g. **Composition:** 0.9250 Silver 3.8543 oz. ASW **Subject:** Tropical Birds - Grenada Dove **Obverse:** Arms in circle, country name above, date below **Size:** 63 mm. **Note:** Illustration reduced.

| Date | Mintage | F | VF | XF | Unc | BU |
|---|---|---|---|---|---|---|
| 1988 Proof | Est. 10,000 | Value: 125 | | | | |

### MEDALLIC COINAGE

**25 DOLLARS** **KM# M1** **Weight:** 29.9700 g. **Composition:** 0.9990 Silver .9627 oz. ASW **Subject:** Carifta Exposition

| Date | Mintage | F | VF | XF | Unc | BU |
|---|---|---|---|---|---|---|
| 1969 Proof | — | Value: 65.00 | | | | |

**200 DOLLARS** **KM# M2** **Weight:** 37.9400 g. **Composition:** 0.9160 Gold 1.1174 oz. AGW **Subject:** Carifta Exposition

| Date | Mintage | F | VF | XF | Unc | BU |
|---|---|---|---|---|---|---|
| 1969 Proof | — | Value: 850 | | | | |

# GUADELOUPE

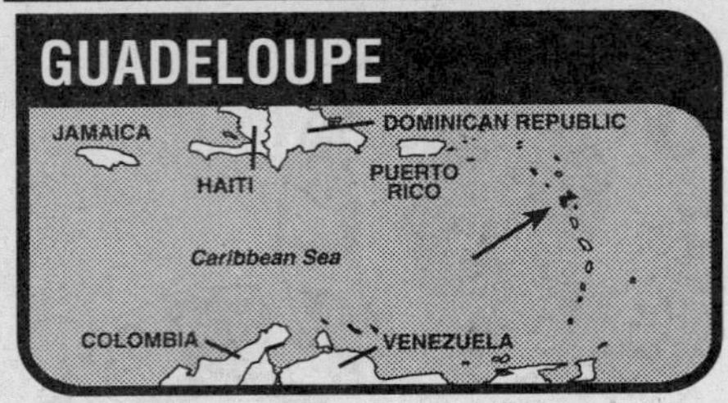


The French Overseas Department of Guadeloupe, located in the Leeward Islands of the West Indies about300 miles (493 km.) southeast of Puerto Rico, has an area of 687 sq. mi. (1,780 sq. km.) and a population of 306,000. Actually it is two islands separated by a narrow saltwater stream: volcanic Basse-Terre to the west and the flatter limestone formation of Grande-Terre to the east. Capital: Basse-Terre, on the island of that name. The principal industries are agriculture, the distillation of liquors, and tourism. Sugar, bananas, and rum are exported.

Guadeloupe was discovered by Columbus in 1493 and settled in 1635 by two Frenchmen, L'Olive and Duplessis, who took possession in the name of the French Company of the Islands of America. When repeated efforts by private companies to colonize the island failed, it was relinquished to the French crown in 1674, and established as a dependency of Martinique. The British occupied the island on two occasions, 1759-63 and 1810-16, before it passed permanently to France. A colony until 1946 Guadeloupe was then made an overseas territory of the FrenchUnion. In 1958 it voted to become an Overseas Department within the new French Community.

The well-known R.F. in garland oval countermark of the French Government is only legitimate if on a French Colonies 12 deniers 1767 C#4. Two other similar but incuse RF countermarks are on cut pieces in the values of 1 and 4 escalins. Contemporary and modern counterfeits are known of both these types.

**RULERS**

French 1816-

**MONETARY SYSTEM**

100 Centimes = 1 Franc

## FRENCH COLONY

### MODERN COINAGE

**50 CENTIMES** **KM# 45** **Composition:** Copper-Nickel

| Date | Mintage | F | VF | XF | Unc | BU |
|---|---|---|---|---|---|---|
| 1903 | 600,000 | 16.00 | 35.00 | 75.00 | 235 | — |
| 1921 | 600,000 | 12.00 | 30.00 | 65.00 | 185 | — |

**FRANC** **KM# 46** **Composition:** Copper-Nickel

| Date | Mintage | F | VF | XF | Unc | BU |
|---|---|---|---|---|---|---|
| 1903 | 700,000 | 20.00 | 40.00 | 80.00 | 240 | — |
| 1921 | 700,000 | 15.00 | 30.00 | 70.00 | 200 | — |

### ESSAIS

| KM# | Date | Mintage | Identification | Mkt Val |
|---|---|---|---|---|
| E1 | 1903 | — | 50 Centimes. Copper-Nickel. | 175 |
| E2 | 1903 | — | 50 Centimes. Silver. | 300 |
| E3 | 1903 | — | Franc. Copper-Nickel. | 265 |
| E4 | 1903 | — | Franc. Silver. | 525 |
| E5 | 19(21) | — | Franc. Bronze. | 160 |

### PIEFORTS

| KM# | Date | Mintage | Identification | Mkt Val |
|---|---|---|---|---|
| P1 | 1903 | — | 50 Centimes. Copper-Nickel. | 400 |
| P2 | 1903 | — | Franc. Copper-Nickel. | 500 |

# GUATEMALA

The Republic of Guatemala, the northernmost of the five Central American republics, has an area of 42,042 sq. mi. (108,890 sq. km.) and a population of 10.7 million. Capital: Guatemala City. The economy of Guatemala is heavily dependent on agriculture, however, the country is rich in nickel resources which are being developed. Coffee, cotton and bananas are exported.

Guatemala, once the site of an ancient Mayan civilization, was conquered by Pedro de Alvarado, the resourceful lieutenant of Cortes who undertook the conquest from Mexico. Cruel but strategically skillful, he progressed rapidly along the Pacific coastal lowlands to the highland plain of Quetzaltenango where the decisive battle for Guatemala was fought. After routing the Indian forces, he established the city of Guatemala in 1524. The Spanish Captaincy-General of Guatemala included all Central America but Panama. Guatemala declared its independence of Spain in 1821 and was absorbed into the Mexican empire of Augustin Iturbide (1822-23). From1823 to 1839 Guatemala was a constituent state of the Central American Republic. Upon dissolution of that confederation, Guatemala proclaimed itself an independent republic. Like El Salvador, Guatemala suffered from internal strife between right-wing, US-backed military government and leftist indigenous peoples from ca. 1954 to ca. 1997.

**MINT MARKS**

Antigua, the old capital city of Santiago de los Caballeros, including the mint, was destroyed by a volcanic eruption and earthquake in 1773. A new mint and capital city was established in Nueva Guatemala City. Coin production recommenced in late 1776 using the NG mint mark.

G or G-G - Guatemala until 1776, 1878-1889
H - Heaton, Birmingham
(KN) – Birmingham, King's Norton Mint
(L) – London, Royal Mint
(P) – Philadelphia, USA
NG - Nueva Guatemala, 1777-1829, 1992
(S) – San Francisco, USA

## REPUBLIC

### REAL COINAGE

8 Reales = 1 Peso;
100 Centavos = 1 Peso; 1859-1924;
100 Centavos = 1 Quetzal, 1925-

**1/4 REAL** **KM# 175** **Composition:** Copper-Nickel

| Date | Mintage | F | VF | XF | Unc | BU |
|---|---|---|---|---|---|---|
| 1901 H | 5,056,000 | 0.15 | 0.35 | 0.75 | 2.00 | — |

**1/2 REAL (Medio)** **KM# 176** **Composition:** Copper-Nickel

| Date | Mintage | F | VF | XF | Unc | BU |
|---|---|---|---|---|---|---|
| 1901 | 6,652,000 | 0.35 | 0.65 | 1.00 | 2.50 | — |

**REAL** **KM# 177** **Composition:** Copper-Nickel

| Date | Mintage | F | VF | XF | Unc | BU |
|---|---|---|---|---|---|---|
| 1901 | 7,388,000 | — | 0.30 | 0.85 | 1.50 | — |
| 1910 | 4,000,000 | — | 0.35 | 0.85 | 1.75 | — |

| Date | Mintage | F | VF | XF | Unc | BU |
|---|---|---|---|---|---|---|
| 1911 | 2,000,000 | — | 0.40 | 1.25 | 2.50 | — |
| 1912 | 8,000,000 | — | 0.30 | 0.85 | 1.50 | — |

## PROVISIONAL COINAGE

1915-1923

### 12-1/2 CENTAVOS KM# 230 Composition: Copper

| Date | Mintage | F | VF | XF | Unc | BU |
|---|---|---|---|---|---|---|
| 1915 | 6,000,000 | 0.75 | 1.25 | 3.00 | 8.00 | — |

### 25 CENTAVOS KM# 231 Composition: Copper

| Date | Mintage | F | VF | XF | Unc | BU |
|---|---|---|---|---|---|---|
| 1915 | 4,000,000 | 0.75 | 1.25 | 2.50 | 7.00 | — |

### 50 CENTAVOS KM# 232.2 Composition: Aluminum-Bronze Note: Thick numerals in denomination.

| Date | Mintage | F | VF | XF | Unc | BU |
|---|---|---|---|---|---|---|
| 1922 | Inc. above | 0.65 | 1.00 | 3.00 | 12.00 | — |

### 50 CENTAVOS KM# 232.1 Composition: Aluminum-Bronze Note: Thin numerals in denomination.

| Date | Mintage | F | VF | XF | Unc | BU |
|---|---|---|---|---|---|---|
| 1922 | 3,803,000 | 0.65 | 1.00 | 3.00 | 12.00 | — |

### PESO KM# 233 Composition: Aluminum-Bronze

| Date | Mintage | F | VF | XF | Unc | BU |
|---|---|---|---|---|---|---|
| 1923 | 1,477,000 | 1.00 | 1.50 | 4.00 | 18.00 | — |

### 5 PESOS KM# 234 Composition: Aluminum-Bronze

| Date | Mintage | F | VF | XF | Unc | BU |
|---|---|---|---|---|---|---|
| 1923 | 440,000 | 1.50 | 2.75 | 7.00 | 28.00 | — |

### 5 PESOS KM# 234a Composition: Copper

| Date | Mintage | F | VF | XF | Unc | BU |
|---|---|---|---|---|---|---|
| 1923 | Inc. above | 1.50 | 2.75 | 7.00 | 28.00 | — |

## REFORM COINAGE

100 Centavos = 1 Quetzol

### 1/2 CENTAVO (Medio) KM# 248 Composition: Brass

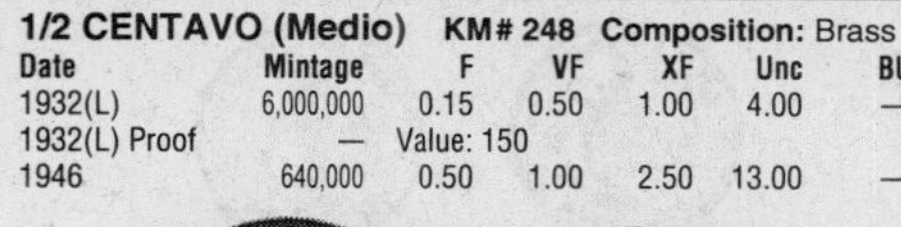

| Date | Mintage | F | VF | XF | Unc | BU |
|---|---|---|---|---|---|---|
| 1932(L) | 6,000,000 | 0.15 | 0.50 | 1.00 | 4.00 | — |
| 1932(L) Proof | — | Value: 150 | | | | |
| 1946 | 640,000 | 0.50 | 1.00 | 2.50 | 13.00 | — |

### CENTAVO (Un) KM# 237 Composition: Copper Obverse: Incuse legend on scroll

| Date | Mintage | F | VF | XF | Unc | BU |
|---|---|---|---|---|---|---|
| 1925 | 357,000 | 3.50 | 6.50 | 13.50 | 30.00 | — |

### CENTAVO (Un) KM# 237a Composition: Bronze

| Date | Mintage | F | VF | XF | Unc | BU |
|---|---|---|---|---|---|---|
| 1925 | Inc. above | 5.00 | 8.00 | 15.00 | 40.00 | — |

### CENTAVO (Un) KM# 247 Composition: Copper

| Date | Mintage | F | VF | XF | Unc | BU |
|---|---|---|---|---|---|---|
| 1929(L) | 500,000 | 2.00 | 3.00 | 6.00 | 22.50 | |
| 1929(L) Proof | — | — | — | — | — | — |

### CENTAVO (Un) KM# 249 Composition: Brass

| Date | Mintage | F | VF | XF | Unc | BU |
|---|---|---|---|---|---|---|
| 1932(L) | 3,000,000 | 0.40 | 1.00 | 3.00 | 10.00 | — |
| 1932(L) Proof | — | — | — | — | — | — |
| 1933(L) | 1,500,000 | 0.60 | 1.50 | 4.50 | 12.00 | — |
| 1933(L) Proof | — | — | — | — | — | — |
| 1934(L) | 1,000,000 | 0.50 | 1.25 | 4.50 | 12.00 | — |
| 1934(L) Proof | — | — | — | — | — | — |
| 1936(L) | 1,500,000 | 0.40 | 1.00 | 4.50 | 12.00 | — |
| 1936(L) Proof | — | — | — | — | — | — |
| 1938/7(L) | 1,000,000 | 0.40 | 1.00 | 5.00 | 12.50 | — |
| 1938(L) | Inc. above | 0.40 | 1.00 | 4.50 | 12.00 | — |
| 1938(L) Proof | — | — | — | — | — | — |
| 1939(L) | 1,500,000 | 0.50 | 1.25 | 4.50 | 9.50 | — |
| 1939(L) Proof | — | — | — | — | — | — |
| 1946 | 539,000 | — | 0.15 | 0.65 | 4.50 | — |
| 1947 | 1,121,000 | — | 0.15 | 0.35 | 2.50 | — |
| 1948 | 1,651,000 | — | 0.15 | 0.35 | 3.50 | — |
| 1949 | 1,022,000 | — | 0.15 | 0.45 | 3.50 | — |

### CENTAVO (Un) KM# 251 Composition: Brass

| Date | Mintage | F | VF | XF | Unc | BU |
|---|---|---|---|---|---|---|
| 1943 (P) | 450,000 | 3.00 | 6.00 | 10.00 | 30.00 | — |
| 1944 (S) | 2,049,999 | 0.50 | 1.25 | 2.50 | 8.00 | — |

### CENTAVO (Un) KM# 254 Composition: Brass Reverse: Fray Bartolome de las Casas

| Date | Mintage | F | VF | XF | Unc | BU |
|---|---|---|---|---|---|---|
| 1949 | 1,091,000 | — | 0.15 | 0.35 | 5.00 | — |
| 1950 | 3,663,000 | — | 0.15 | 0.25 | 1.75 | — |
| 1951 | 3,586,000 | — | 0.15 | 0.50 | 15.00 | — |
| 1952 | 1,445,000 | — | 0.15 | 0.30 | 5.00 | — |
| 1953 | 2,214,000 | — | 0.15 | 0.25 | 1.00 | — |
| 1954 | 1,455,000 | — | 0.15 | 0.30 | 2.25 | — |

### CENTAVO (Un) KM# 259 Composition: Nickel-Brass Reverse: Larger bust

| Date | Mintage | F | VF | XF | Unc | BU |
|---|---|---|---|---|---|---|
| 1954(KN) | 10,000,000 | — | — | 0.15 | 1.50 | — |
| 1957(KN) | 1,600,000 | — | 0.15 | 0.25 | 0.75 | — |
| 1958(KN) | 2,000,000 | — | 0.15 | 0.25 | 1.00 | — |

### CENTAVO (Un) KM# 260 Composition: Brass Obverse: Larger legend

| Date | Mintage | F | VF | XF | Unc | BU |
|---|---|---|---|---|---|---|
| 1958 | 10,001,000 | — | — | 0.15 | 0.50 | — |
| 1961 | 1,826,000 | — | — | 0.15 | 0.30 | — |
| 1963 | 4,926,000 | — | — | 0.15 | 0.30 | — |
| 1964 | 4,280,000 | — | — | 0.15 | 0.30 | — |

### CENTAVO (Un) KM# 265 Composition: Brass Size: 19 mm. Note: Size reduced. Varieties in size and style of date exist.

| Date | Mintage | F | VF | XF | Unc | BU |
|---|---|---|---|---|---|---|
| 1965 | 3,845,000 | — | — | 0.15 | 0.75 | — |
| 1966 | 6,100,000 | — | — | 0.15 | 0.25 | — |
| 1967 | 6,400,000 | — | — | 0.15 | 0.25 | — |
| 1968 | 2,590,000 | — | — | 0.15 | 0.25 | — |
| 969 | 13,780,000 | — | — | 0.15 | 0.25 | — |
| 970 | 10,511,000 | — | — | 0.15 | 0.25 | — |

### CENTAVO (Un) KM# 273 Composition: Brass Obverse: Smaller legend and date

| Date | Mintage | F | VF | XF | Unc | BU |
|---|---|---|---|---|---|---|
| 1972 | 11,500,000 | — | — | 0.15 | 0.25 | — |
| 1973 | 12,000,000 | — | — | 0.15 | 0.25 | — |

### CENTAVO (Un) KM# 275.1 Composition: Brass Obverse: Larger legend and date Reverse: Large head

| Date | Mintage | F | VF | XF | Unc | BU |
|---|---|---|---|---|---|---|
| 1974 | 10,000,000 | — | — | 0.15 | 0.25 | — |
| 1975 | 15,000,000 | — | — | 0.15 | 0.25 | — |
| 1976 | 15,230,000 | — | — | 0.15 | 0.25 | — |
| 1977 | 30,000,000 | — | — | 0.15 | 0.25 | — |
| 1978 | 30,000,000 | — | — | 0.15 | 0.25 | — |
| 1979 | 30,000,000 | — | — | 0.15 | 0.25 | — |

### CENTAVO (Un) KM# 275.2 Composition: Brass Reverse: Smaller head, legend and date Note: Varieties exist.

| Date | Mintage | F | VF | XF | Unc | BU |
|---|---|---|---|---|---|---|
| 1979 | Inc. above | — | — | 0.15 | 0.25 | — |
| 1980 | 20,000,000 | — | — | 0.15 | 0.25 | — |
| 1984 | 20,000,000 | — | — | 0.15 | 0.25 | — |
| 1985 | — | — | — | 0.15 | 0.25 | — |

| Date | Mintage | F | VF | XF | Unc | BU |
|---|---|---|---|---|---|---|
| 1986 | — | — | — | 0.15 | 0.25 | — |
| 1987 | 50,000,000 | — | — | 0.15 | 0.25 | — |
| 1988 | 51,400,000 | — | — | 0.15 | 0.25 | — |
| 1989 | — | — | — | 0.15 | 0.25 | — |
| 1990 | — | — | — | 0.15 | 0.25 | — |
| 1991 | — | — | — | 0.15 | 0.25 | — |
| 1992 | — | — | — | 0.15 | 0.25 | — |

**CENTAVO (Un)** **KM# 275.4** **Composition:** Brass **Obverse:** Legend on scroll in relief **Note:** Varieties exist.

| Date | Mintage | F | VF | XF | Unc | BU |
|---|---|---|---|---|---|---|
| 1981 | 30,000,000 | — | — | 0.15 | 0.25 | — |
| 1982 | 30,000,000 | — | — | 0.15 | 0.25 | — |

**CENTAVO (Un)** **KM# 275.5** **Composition:** Brass **Reverse:** New portrait of Fray de las Casas

| Date | Mintage | F | VF | XF | Unc | BU |
|---|---|---|---|---|---|---|
| 1993 | — | — | — | 0.15 | 0.25 | — |
| 1994 | — | — | — | 0.15 | 0.25 | — |
| 1995 | — | — | — | 0.15 | 0.25 | — |

**CENTAVO (Un)** **KM# 282** **Weight:** 0.8000 g. **Composition:** Aluminum **Obverse:** National arms **Reverse:** Bust of Las Casas left **Edge:** Plain

| Date | Mintage | F | VF | XF | Unc | BU |
|---|---|---|---|---|---|---|
| 1999 | — | — | — | 0.15 | 0.25 | — |

**2 CENTAVOS (Dos)** **KM# 250** **Composition:** Brass

| Date | Mintage | F | VF | XF | Unc | BU |
|---|---|---|---|---|---|---|
| 1932(L) | 3,000,000 | 0.50 | 1.25 | 3.50 | 17.50 | — |
| 1932(L) Proof | — | — | — | — | — | — |

**2 CENTAVOS (Dos)** **KM# 252** **Composition:** Brass

| Date | Mintage | F | VF | XF | Unc | BU |
|---|---|---|---|---|---|---|
| 1943 (P) | 150,000 | 3.00 | 7.50 | 12.00 | 32.00 | — |
| 1944 (S) | 1,100,000 | 0.60 | 2.00 | 3.75 | 10.00 | — |

**5 CENTAVOS** **KM# 238.1** **Weight:** 1.6667 g. **Composition:** 0.7200 Silver .0386 oz. ASW **Obverse:** Long-tailed quetzal **Reverse:** Engraver's initials below "Centavos"

| Date | Mintage | F | VF | XF | Unc | BU |
|---|---|---|---|---|---|---|
| 1925 | 573,000 | 3.00 | 5.75 | 11.50 | 25.00 | — |
| 1944 | 1,026,000 | BV | 1.25 | 2.50 | 12.00 | — |
| 1945 | 4,026,000 | BV | 0.75 | 2.00 | 9.00 | — |
| 1947 | 1,834,000 | BV | 1.00 | 2.00 | 7.50 | — |
| 1948 | 1,103,000 | BV | 1.00 | 2.00 | 10.00 | — |
| 1949 | 551,000 | 0.50 | 1.50 | 3.00 | 20.00 | — |

**5 CENTAVOS** **KM# 238.1a** **Weight:** 2.5000 g. **Composition:** 0.9000 Gold .0723 oz. AGW

| Date | Mintage | F | VF | XF | Unc | BU |
|---|---|---|---|---|---|---|
| 1925 | 8 | — | — | 750 | 950 | — |

**5 CENTAVOS** **KM# 238.2** **Weight:** 1.6667 g. **Composition:** 0.7200 Silver .0386 oz. ASW **Obverse:** Short-tailed quetzal **Reverse:** Without engraver's initials

| Date | Mintage | F | VF | XF | Unc | BU |
|---|---|---|---|---|---|---|
| 1928(L) | 1,000,000 | BV | 1.00 | 2.00 | 28.00 | — |
| 1928(L) Proof | — | Value: 400 | | | | |
| 1929(L) | 1,000,000 | BV | 1.00 | 2.00 | 7.50 | — |
| 1929(L) Proof | — | — | — | — | — | — |
| 1932(L) | 2,000,000 | BV | 1.00 | 1.50 | 6.50 | — |
| 1932(L) Proof | — | — | — | — | — | — |
| 1933(L) | 600,000 | BV | 1.00 | 2.50 | 9.00 | — |
| 1933(L) Proof | — | — | — | — | — | — |
| 1934(L) | 1,200,000 | BV | 1.00 | 2.00 | 7.50 | — |
| 1934(L) Proof | — | — | — | — | — | — |
| 1937(L) | 400,000 | BV | 1.00 | 1.50 | 7.50 | — |
| 1937(L) Proof | — | — | — | — | — | — |
| 1938(L) | 300,000 | 0.50 | 1.50 | 2.50 | 14.00 | — |
| 1938(L) Proof | — | — | — | — | — | — |
| 1943(P) | 900,000 | BV | 0.75 | 1.50 | 7.00 | — |

**5 CENTAVOS** **KM# 255** **Weight:** 1.6667 g. **Composition:** 0.7200 Silver .0386 oz. ASW **Note:** Varieties exist with and without dashes.

| Date | Mintage | F | VF | XF | Unc | BU |
|---|---|---|---|---|---|---|
| 1949 | 305,000 | 0.50 | 1.50 | 3.50 | 22.00 | — |

**5 CENTAVOS** **KM# 257.1** **Weight:** 1.6667 g. **Composition:** 0.7200 Silver .0386 oz. ASW

| Date | Mintage | F | VF | XF | Unc | BU |
|---|---|---|---|---|---|---|
| 1950 | 453,000 | BV | 1.00 | 2.00 | 9.00 | — |
| 1951 | 1,032,000 | BV | 1.00 | 1.50 | 5.00 | — |
| 1952 | 913,000 | BV | 1.00 | 1.50 | 4.00 | — |
| 1953 | 447,000 | BV | 1.00 | 2.50 | 4.00 | — |
| 1954 | 520,000 | BV | 1.00 | 1.50 | 8.00 | — |
| 1955 | 2,061,999 | BV | 1.00 | 1.50 | 3.00 | — |
| 1956 | 1,301,000 | BV | 1.00 | 1.50 | 3.00 | — |
| 1957 | 2,941,000 | BV | 1.00 | 1.50 | 2.50 | — |

**5 CENTAVOS** **KM# 257.1a** **Weight:** 2.7300 g. **Composition:** 0.6200 Gold .0544 oz. AGW **Note:** Distributed among delegates.

| Date | Mintage | F | VF | XF | Unc | BU |
|---|---|---|---|---|---|---|
| 1953 | 25 | — | — | — | 550 | — |

**5 CENTAVOS** **KM# 257.2** **Weight:** 1.6670 g. **Composition:** 0.7200 Silver .0386 oz. ASW **Obverse:** Long-tailed quetzal **Note:** Small crude date and large crude dates.

| Date | Mintage | F | VF | XF | Unc | BU |
|---|---|---|---|---|---|---|
| 1958 Small date | 3,025,000 | BV | 0.75 | 1.00 | 2.50 | — |
| 1958 Large date | Inc. above | BV | 1.00 | 1.75 | 3.50 | — |
| 1959 | 232,000 | BV | 1.00 | 1.50 | 2.00 | — |

**5 CENTAVOS** **KM# 257.3** **Weight:** 1.6670 g. **Composition:** 0.7200 Silver .0386 oz. ASW **Obverse:** Short-tailed quetzal

| Date | Mintage | F | VF | XF | Unc | BU |
|---|---|---|---|---|---|---|
| 1958 Small date | Inc. above | BV | 1.00 | 1.75 | 3.50 | — |

**5 CENTAVOS** **KM# 261** **Weight:** 1.6670 g. **Composition:** 0.7200 Silver .0386 oz. ASW **Reverse:** Level ground at tree

| Date | Mintage | F | VF | XF | Unc | BU |
|---|---|---|---|---|---|---|
| 1960 | 4,770,000 | — | BV | 0.50 | 1.00 | — |
| 1961 | 6,756,000 | — | BV | 0.50 | 1.00 | — |
| 1964 | 1,529,000 | — | BV | 0.50 | 1.00 | — |

**5 CENTAVOS** **KM# 266** **Composition:** Copper-Nickel **Note:** Date size varieties exist.

| Date | Mintage | F | VF | XF | Unc | BU |
|---|---|---|---|---|---|---|
| 1965 | 1,642,000 | — | 0.15 | 0.50 | 4.00 | — |
| 1966 | 3,600,000 | — | — | 0.15 | 0.35 | — |
| 1967 | 2,800,000 | — | — | 0.15 | 0.35 | — |
| 1968 | 4,030,000 | — | — | 0.15 | 0.35 | — |
| 1969 | 7,210,000 | — | — | 0.15 | 0.35 | — |
| 1970 | 8,121,000 | — | — | 0.15 | 0.35 | — |

**5 CENTAVOS** **KM# 270** **Composition:** Copper-Nickel **Obverse:** Legend on scroll incuse. Small shield and quetzal

| Date | Mintage | F | VF | XF | Unc | BU |
|---|---|---|---|---|---|---|
| 1971 | 8,270,000 | — | — | 0.15 | 0.35 | — |
| 1974 | 10,575,000 | — | — | 0.15 | 0.35 | — |
| 1975 | 10,000,000 | — | — | 0.15 | 0.35 | — |
| 1976 | 6,000,000 | — | — | 0.15 | 0.35 | — |
| 1977 | 20,000,000 | — | — | 0.15 | 0.35 | — |

**5 CENTAVOS** **KM# 276.1** **Composition:** Copper-Nickel **Obverse:** Large shield and quetzal

| Date | Mintage | F | VF | XF | Unc | BU |
|---|---|---|---|---|---|---|
| 1977 | Inc. above | — | — | 0.15 | 0.35 | — |
| 1978 | 15,000,000 | — | — | 0.15 | 0.30 | — |
| 1979 | 12,000,000 | — | — | 0.15 | 0.30 | — |

**5 CENTAVOS** **KM# 276.2** **Composition:** Copper-Nickel **Obverse:** Legend on scroll in relief

| Date | Mintage | F | VF | XF | Unc | BU |
|---|---|---|---|---|---|---|
| 1980 | 8,000,000 | — | — | 0.15 | 0.30 | — |

**5 CENTAVOS** **KM# 276.3** **Composition:** Copper-Nickel **Reverse:** Different tree

| Date | Mintage | F | VF | XF | Unc | BU |
|---|---|---|---|---|---|---|
| 1981 | 8,000,000 | — | — | 0.15 | 0.30 | — |
| 1985 | — | — | — | 0.15 | 0.30 | — |

**5 CENTAVOS** **KM# 276.4** **Composition:** Copper-Nickel **Obverse:** Legend on scroll incuse **Reverse:** Smaller tree, less ground below **Note:** Varieties exist.

| Date | Mintage | F | VF | XF | Unc | BU |
|---|---|---|---|---|---|---|
| 1985 | — | — | — | 0.15 | 0.30 | — |
| 1986 Large date | — | — | — | 0.15 | 0.30 | — |
| 1986 Small date | — | — | — | — | — | — |
| 1987 | 25,000,000 | — | — | 0.15 | 0.30 | — |
| 1988 | 21,800,000 | — | — | 0.15 | 0.30 | — |
| 1989 | — | — | — | 0.15 | 0.30 | — |
| 1990 | — | — | — | 0.15 | 0.30 | — |
| 1991 | — | — | — | 0.15 | 0.30 | — |
| 1992 | — | — | — | 0.15 | 0.30 | — |
| 1993 | — | — | — | 0.15 | 0.30 | — |
| 1994 | — | — | — | 0.15 | 0.30 | — |
| 1995 | — | — | — | 0.15 | 0.30 | — |
| 1996 | — | — | — | 0.15 | 0.30 | — |
| 1998 | — | — | — | 0.15 | 0.30 | — |

**5 CENTAVOS** **KM# 276.5** **Composition:** Copper-Nickel **Obverse:** Smaller letters, REPUBLICA DE GUATEMALA

| Date | Mintage | F | VF | XF | Unc | BU |
|---|---|---|---|---|---|---|
| 1995 | — | — | — | 0.15 | 0.30 | — |

**5 CENTAVOS** **KM# 276.6** **Composition:** Copper-Nickel **Obverse:** Smaller sized emblem

| Date | Mintage | F | VF | XF | Unc | BU |
|---|---|---|---|---|---|---|
| 1997 | — | — | — | 0.15 | 0.30 | — |

**10 CENTAVOS** **KM# 239.1a** **Weight:** 5.0000 g. **Composition:** 0.9000 Gold .1446 oz. AGW

| Date | Mintage | F | VF | XF | Unc | BU |
|---|---|---|---|---|---|---|
| 1925 Rare | 8 | — | — | — | — | — |

**10 CENTAVOS** **KM# 239.1** **Weight:** 3.3333 g. **Composition:** 0.7200 Silver .0772 oz. ASW **Obverse:** Long-tailed quetzal **Reverse:** Engraver's initials below "CENTAVOS" **Note:** Varieties exist.

| Date | Mintage | F | VF | XF | Unc | BU |
|---|---|---|---|---|---|---|
| 1925 | 573,000 | 3.50 | 6.50 | 15.00 | 32.50 | — |
| 1944 | 155,000 | 1.25 | 3.50 | 7.00 | 16.50 | — |
| 1945 | 1,499,000 | BV | 1.25 | 2.00 | 4.00 | — |
| 1947 | 471,000 | BV | 1.50 | 2.50 | 8.00 | — |
| 1948 | 324,000 | BV | 1.50 | 2.50 | 5.50 | — |
| 1949 | 145,000 | BV | 2.00 | 4.50 | 10.00 | — |

**10 CENTAVOS** **KM# 239.2** **Weight:** 3.3333 g. **Composition:** 0.7200 Silver .0772 oz. ASW **Obverse:** Short-tailed quetzal **Reverse:** Without engraver's initials

| Date | Mintage | F | VF | XF | Unc | BU |
|---|---|---|---|---|---|---|
| 1928(L) | 500,000 | BV | 2.50 | 5.00 | 25.00 | — |
| 1928(L) Proof | — | Value: 250 | | | | |
| 1929(L) | 500,000 | BV | 2.00 | 3.50 | 22.50 | — |
| 1929(L) Proof | — | — | — | — | — | — |
| 1932(L) | 500,000 | BV | 2.00 | 3.50 | 12.00 | — |
| 1932(L) Proof | — | — | — | — | — | — |
| 1933(L) | 650,000 | BV | 1.75 | 3.00 | 15.00 | — |
| 1933(L) Proof | — | — | — | — | — | — |
| 1934(L) | 300,000 | BV | 1.75 | 3.00 | 15.00 | — |
| 1934(L) Proof | — | — | — | — | — | — |
| 1936(L) | 200,000 | BV | 2.50 | 4.50 | 17.50 | — |
| 1936(L) Proof | — | — | — | — | — | — |
| 1938(L) | 150,000 | 1.00 | 3.00 | 5.00 | 12.50 | — |
| 1938(L) Proof | — | — | — | — | — | — |
| 1943(P) | 600,000 | BV | 1.25 | 2.50 | 7.50 | — |

**10 CENTAVOS** **KM# 239.3** **Weight:** 3.3333 g. **Composition:** 0.7200 Silver .0772 oz. ASW **Reverse:** With engraver's initials **Note:** Mintage included above, in KM#239.1. Varieties exist.

| Date | Mintage | F | VF | XF | Unc | BU |
|---|---|---|---|---|---|---|
| 1947 | — | BV | 3.00 | 4.00 | 8.50 | — |

**10 CENTAVOS** **KM# 256.1** **Weight:** 3.3333 g. **Composition:** 0.7200 Silver .0772 oz. ASW **Reverse:** Small monolith

| Date | Mintage | F | VF | XF | Unc | BU |
|---|---|---|---|---|---|---|
| 1949 | 281,000 | BV | 2.50 | 3.50 | 10.00 | — |
| 1950 | 550,000 | BV | 1.50 | 2.50 | 5.00 | — |
| 1951 | 263,000 | BV | 2.50 | 4.50 | 12.50 | — |
| 1952 | 307,000 | BV | 1.50 | 2.50 | 5.00 | — |
| 1953 | 388,000 | BV | 1.50 | 2.50 | 5.00 | — |
| 1955 | 896,000 | BV | 1.50 | 2.50 | 5.00 | — |
| 1956 | 501,000 | BV | 1.50 | 2.50 | 12.50 | — |
| 1958 | 1,528,000 | BV | 1.50 | 2.50 | 6.00 | — |

**10 CENTAVOS** **KM# 256.2** **Weight:** 3.3333 g. **Composition:** 0.7200 Silver .0772 oz. ASW **Reverse:** Larger monolith

| Date | Mintage | F | VF | XF | Unc | BU |
|---|---|---|---|---|---|---|
| 1957 | 1,123,000 | BV | 1.25 | 2.00 | 3.00 | — |
| 1958 | Inc. above | BV | 1.50 | 2.50 | 5.00 | — |
| 1958 Medallic die alignment | Inc. above | 6.00 | 12.00 | 22.50 | 40.00 | — |

**10 CENTAVOS** **KM# 256.3** **Weight:** 3.3333 g. **Composition:** 0.7200 Silver .0772 oz. ASW **Obverse:** Long-tailed quetzal **Reverse:** Small monolith

| Date | Mintage | F | VF | XF | Unc | BU |
|---|---|---|---|---|---|---|
| 1958 | Inc. above | BV | 1.25 | 2.00 | 3.00 | — |
| 1959 | 461,000 | BV | 1.25 | 2.00 | 3.00 | — |
| 1959 Medallic die alignment | Inc. above | 6.00 | 12.00 | 22.50 | 37.50 | — |

**10 CENTAVOS** **KM# 262** **Weight:** 3.3333 g. **Composition:** 0.7200 Silver .0772 oz. ASW

| Date | Mintage | F | VF | XF | Unc | BU |
|---|---|---|---|---|---|---|
| 1960 | 1,743,000 | BV | 1.50 | 2.00 | 2.50 | — |
| 1961 | 2,647,000 | BV | 1.50 | 2.00 | 2.50 | — |
| 1964 | 965,000 | BV | 1.50 | 2.00 | 2.50 | — |

**10 CENTAVOS** **KM# 267** **Composition:** Copper-Nickel **Note:** Varieties of 9 in date exist.

| Date | Mintage | F | VF | XF | Unc | BU |
|---|---|---|---|---|---|---|
| 1965 | 2,227,000 | — | 0.15 | 0.25 | 0.75 | — |
| 1966 | 1,550,000 | — | 0.15 | 0.35 | 0.85 | — |
| 1967 | 3,120,000 | — | 0.15 | 0.25 | 0.75 | — |
| 1968 | 3,220,000 | — | 0.15 | 0.25 | 0.75 | — |
| 1969 | 3,530,000 | — | 0.15 | 0.25 | 0.75 | — |
| 1970 | 4,153,000 | — | 0.15 | 0.25 | 0.75 | — |

**10 CENTAVOS** **KM# 271.1** **Composition:** Copper-Nickel **Obverse:** Small wreath

| Date | Mintage | F | VF | XF | Unc | BU |
|---|---|---|---|---|---|---|
| 1971 | 4,580,000 | — | 0.15 | 0.25 | 0.75 | — |

**10 CENTAVOS** **KM# 271.2** **Composition:** Copper-Nickel **Obverse:** Large wreath

| Date | Mintage | F | VF | XF | Unc | BU |
|---|---|---|---|---|---|---|
| 1971 | Inc. above | — | 0.15 | 0.25 | 0.75 | — |
| 1973 | — | — | 0.15 | 0.25 | 0.75 | — |

**10 CENTAVOS** **KM# 274** **Composition:** Copper-Nickel

| Date | Mintage | F | VF | XF | Unc | BU |
|---|---|---|---|---|---|---|
| 1974 | 3,500,000 | — | 0.15 | 0.25 | 0.75 | — |
| 1975 Dots flank date | 6,000,000 | — | 0.15 | 0.25 | 0.75 | — |

**10 CENTAVOS** **KM# 277.1** **Composition:** Copper-Nickel **Note:** Wide rim toothed border.

| Date | Mintage | F | VF | XF | Unc | BU |
|---|---|---|---|---|---|---|
| 1976 | 2,000,000 | — | 0.15 | 0.25 | 0.75 | — |
| 1977 | 5,000,000 | — | 0.15 | 0.25 | 0.75 | — |

**10 CENTAVOS** **KM# 277.2** **Composition:** Copper-Nickel **Note:** Round beads instead of toothed border.

| Date | Mintage | F | VF | XF | Unc | BU |
|---|---|---|---|---|---|---|
| 1978 | 8,500,000 | — | 0.15 | 0.25 | 0.75 | — |
| 1979 | 11,000,000 | — | 0.15 | 0.25 | 0.75 | — |

**10 CENTAVOS** **KM# 277.3** **Composition:** Copper-Nickel **Obverse:** Legend on scroll in relief, quetzal in silhouette **Reverse:** Different design

| Date | Mintage | F | VF | XF | Unc | BU |
|---|---|---|---|---|---|---|
| 1980 | 5,000,000 | — | 0.15 | 0.25 | 0.75 | — |
| 1981 | 4,000,000 | — | 0.15 | 0.25 | 0.75 | — |

**10 CENTAVOS** **KM# 277.4** **Composition:** Copper-Nickel **Obverse:** Quetzal is solid, larger monolith

| Date | Mintage | F | VF | XF | Unc | BU |
|---|---|---|---|---|---|---|
| 1983 | 20,000,000 | — | 0.15 | 0.25 | 0.75 | — |
| 1986 | — | — | 0.15 | 0.25 | 0.75 | — |

**10 CENTAVOS** **KM# 277.5** **Composition:** Copper-Nickel **Reverse:** Larger 10 **Note:** Varieties exist.

| Date | Mintage | F | VF | XF | Unc | BU |
|---|---|---|---|---|---|---|
| 1986 | — | — | 0.15 | 0.25 | 0.75 | — |
| 1987 | 17,000,000 | — | 0.15 | 0.25 | 0.75 | — |
| 1988 | 13,250,000 | — | 0.15 | 0.25 | 0.75 | — |
| 1989 | — | — | 0.15 | 0.25 | 0.75 | — |
| 1990 | — | — | 0.15 | 0.25 | 0.75 | — |
| 1991 | — | — | 0.15 | 0.25 | 0.75 | — |
| 1992 | — | — | 0.15 | 0.25 | 0.75 | — |
| 1993 | — | — | 0.15 | 0.25 | 0.75 | — |
| 1994 | — | — | 0.15 | 0.25 | 0.75 | — |

**10 CENTAVOS** **KM# 277.6** **Composition:** Copper-Nickel **Obverse:** Smaller letters in REPUBLICA DE GUATEMALA

| Date | Mintage | F | VF | XF | Unc | BU |
|---|---|---|---|---|---|---|
| 1995 | — | — | 0.15 | 0.25 | 0.75 | — |
| 1996 | — | — | 0.15 | 0.25 | 0.75 | — |
| 1997 | — | — | 0.15 | 0.25 | 0.75 | — |
| 1998 | — | — | 0.15 | 0.25 | 0.75 | — |

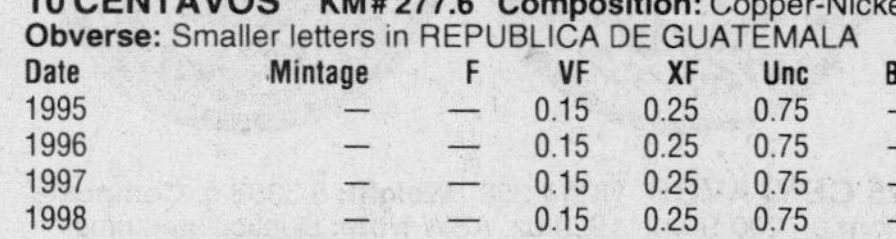

**1/4 QUETZAL** **KM# 240.1** **Weight:** 8.3333 g. **Composition:** 0.7200 Silver .1929 oz. ASW **Edge:** Lettered

| Date | Mintage | F | VF | XF | Unc | BU |
|---|---|---|---|---|---|---|
| 1925 (P) | 1,160,000 | 3.75 | 8.00 | 25.00 | 50.00 | — |

**1/4 QUETZAL** **KM# 240.2** **Weight:** 8.3333 g. **Composition:** 0.7200 Silver .1929 oz. ASW **Obverse:** Without NOBLES below scroll

| Date | Mintage | F | VF | XF | Unc | BU |
|---|---|---|---|---|---|---|
| 1925 (P) | Inc. above | 37.50 | 75.00 | 175 | 400 | — |

**1/4 QUETZAL** **KM# 240a** **Composition:** 0.9000 Gold

| Date | Mintage | F | VF | XF | Unc | BU |
|---|---|---|---|---|---|---|
| 1925 (P) Rare | 8 | — | — | — | — | — |

**1/4 QUETZAL** **KM# 243.1** **Weight:** 8.3333 g. **Composition:** 0.7200 Silver .1929 oz. ASW **Reverse:** Larger design

| Date | Mintage | F | VF | XF | Unc | BU |
|---|---|---|---|---|---|---|
| 1926(L) | 2,000,000 | 2.00 | 3.50 | 10.00 | 55.00 | — |
| 1926(L) Proof | — | — | — | — | — | — |
| 1928(L) | 400,000 | 2.50 | 4.00 | 10.00 | 55.00 | — |
| 1928(L) Proof | — | — | — | — | — | — |
| 1929(L) | 400,000 | 2.50 | 4.50 | 12.50 | 45.00 | — |
| 1929(L) Proof | — | — | — | — | — | — |

**1/4 QUETZAL** **KM# 243.2** **Weight:** 8.3333 g. **Composition:** 0.7200 Silver .1929 oz. ASW **Edge:** Reeded

| Date | Mintage | F | VF | XF | Unc | BU |
|---|---|---|---|---|---|---|
| 1946 | 203,000 | 3.00 | 6.50 | 13.50 | 22.00 | — |
| 1947 | 134,000 | 3.75 | 8.00 | 12.50 | 20.00 | — |
| 1948 | 129,000 | 3.75 | 7.50 | 12.00 | 20.00 | — |
| 1949/8 | 25,000 | 5.25 | 10.00 | 16.50 | 30.00 | — |
| 1949 | Inc. above | 12.50 | 27.50 | 55.00 | 100 | — |

**25 CENTAVOS** **KM# 253** **Weight:** 8.3333 g. **Composition:** 0.7200 Silver .1929 oz. ASW

| Date | Mintage | F | VF | XF | Unc | BU |
|---|---|---|---|---|---|---|
| 1943 (P) | 900,000 | 2.50 | 5.50 | 10.00 | 40.00 | — |

**25 CENTAVOS** **KM# 258** **Weight:** 8.3333 g. **Composition:** 0.7200 Silver .1929 oz. ASW **Note:** Denticulated rims.

| Date | Mintage | F | VF | XF | Unc | BU |
|---|---|---|---|---|---|---|
| 1950 | 81,000 | 2.25 | 4.00 | 8.00 | 30.00 | — |
| 1951 | 11,000 | 8.50 | 17.50 | 27.50 | 70.00 | — |
| 1952 | 112,000 | BV | 2.75 | 6.00 | 15.00 | — |
| 1954 | 246,000 | BV | 2.75 | 5.00 | 10.00 | — |
| 1955 | 409,000 | BV | 2.75 | 5.00 | 10.00 | — |
| 1956 | 342,000 | BV | 2.75 | 5.00 | 10.00 | — |
| 1957 | 257,000 | BV | 2.75 | 5.00 | 9.00 | — |
| 1958 | 394,000 | BV | 2.75 | 5.00 | 9.00 | — |
| 1959/8 | 277,000 | BV | 2.75 | 5.00 | 9.00 | — |
| 1959 | Inc. above | BV | 2.75 | 6.00 | 12.50 | — |

**25 CENTAVOS** **KM# 263** **Weight:** 8.3333 g. **Composition:** 0.7200 Silver .1929 oz. ASW **Note:** Scalloped rims.

| Date | Mintage | F | VF | XF | Unc | BU |
|---|---|---|---|---|---|---|
| 1960 | 560,000 | BV | 2.25 | 3.25 | 6.00 | — |
| 1960 Medallic die alignment | Inc. above | 20.00 | 50.00 | 100 | 175 | — |

**Note:** Planchet size and weight vary in 1960 type as well as density of reeding

| Date | Mintage | F | VF | XF | Unc | BU |
|---|---|---|---|---|---|---|
| 1961 | 750,000 | BV | 2.25 | 3.25 | 6.00 | — |
| 1963 | 1,100,000 | BV | 2.00 | 3.00 | 5.50 | — |
| 1964 | 299,000 | BV | 2.25 | 3.25 | 6.00 | — |

**25 CENTAVOS** **KM# 268** **Composition:** Copper-Nickel

| Date | Mintage | F | VF | XF | Unc | BU |
|---|---|---|---|---|---|---|
| 1965 | 1,178,000 | 0.15 | 0.25 | 0.60 | 1.75 | — |
| 1966 | 910,000 | 0.15 | 0.25 | 0.60 | 1.75 | — |

**25 CENTAVOS** **KM# 269** **Composition:** Copper-Nickel **Reverse:** Modified design

| Date | Mintage | F | VF | XF | Unc | BU |
|---|---|---|---|---|---|---|
| 1967 | 1,140,000 | 0.15 | 0.25 | 0.60 | 1.75 | — |
| 1968 | 1,540,000 | 0.15 | 0.25 | 0.60 | 1.50 | — |
| 1969 Large date | 2,069,000 | 0.15 | 0.25 | 0.60 | 1.50 | — |
| 1970 | 2,501,000 | 0.15 | 0.25 | 0.60 | 1.50 | — |

**25 CENTAVOS** **KM# 272** **Composition:** Copper-Nickel **Obverse:** Smaller arms, legend on scroll incuse

| Date | Mintage | F | VF | XF | Unc | BU |
|---|---|---|---|---|---|---|
| 1971 | 2,850,000 | 0.15 | 0.25 | 0.50 | 1.00 | — |
| 1975 | 1,592,000 | 0.15 | 0.25 | 0.50 | 1.00 | — |
| 1976 | 2,000,000 | 0.15 | 0.25 | 0.50 | 1.00 | — |

**25 CENTAVOS** **KM# 278.1** **Composition:** Copper-Nickel **Reverse:** Large head

| Date | Mintage | F | VF | XF | Unc | BU |
|---|---|---|---|---|---|---|
| 1977 | 2,000,000 | 0.15 | 0.25 | 0.50 | 1.00 | — |
| 1978 | 4,400,000 | 0.15 | 0.25 | 0.35 | 0.85 | — |
| 1979 | 5,400,000 | 0.15 | 0.25 | 0.35 | 0.85 | — |

**25 CENTAVOS** **KM# 278.2** **Composition:** Copper-Nickel **Obverse:** Legend on scroll in relief **Reverse:** Small head **Note:** Wide rim

| Date | Mintage | F | VF | XF | Unc | BU |
|---|---|---|---|---|---|---|
| 1981 | 1,600,000 | 0.15 | 0.25 | 0.50 | 1.00 | — |

**25 CENTAVOS** **KM# 278.4** **Composition:** Copper-Nickel **Obverse:** Quetzal is solid **Note:** Narrow rim.

| Date | Mintage | F | VF | XF | Unc | BU |
|---|---|---|---|---|---|---|
| 1982 | 2,000,000 | 0.15 | 0.25 | 0.50 | 1.00 | — |

**25 CENTAVOS** **KM# 278.3** **Composition:** Copper-Nickel **Obverse:** Legend on scroll incuse **Reverse:** Small head and denomination

| Date | Mintage | F | VF | XF | Unc | BU |
|---|---|---|---|---|---|---|
| 1984 | 2,000,000 | 0.15 | 0.25 | 0.50 | 1.00 | — |

**25 CENTAVOS** **KM# 278.5** **Composition:** Copper-Nickel **Reverse:** Large head and denomination **Note:** Varieties exist in number of wing feathers and details on head.

| Date | Mintage | F | VF | XF | Unc | BU |
|---|---|---|---|---|---|---|
| 1985 | — | 0.15 | 0.25 | 0.35 | 0.85 | — |
| 1986 | — | 0.15 | 0.25 | 0.35 | 0.85 | — |
| 1987 | 13,316,000 | 0.15 | 0.25 | 0.35 | 0.85 | — |
| 1988 | 6,600,000 | 0.15 | 0.25 | 0.35 | 0.85 | — |
| 1989 | — | 0.15 | 0.25 | 0.35 | 0.85 | — |
| 1990 | — | 0.15 | 0.25 | 0.35 | 0.85 | — |
| 1991 | — | 0.15 | 0.25 | 0.35 | 0.85 | — |
| 1992 | — | 0.15 | 0.25 | 0.35 | 0.85 | — |
| 1993 | — | 0.15 | 0.25 | 0.35 | 0.85 | — |
| 1994 | — | 0.15 | 0.25 | 0.35 | 0.85 | — |
| 1995 | — | 0.15 | 0.25 | 0.35 | 0.85 | — |

**25 CENTAVOS** **KM# 278.6** **Composition:** Copper-Nickel **Obverse:** Smaller design with wider rims **Reverse:** Smaller design with wider rims **Edge Lettering:** REPUBLICA DE GUATEMALA CA

| Date | Mintage | F | VF | XF | Unc | BU |
|---|---|---|---|---|---|---|
| 1996 | — | 0.15 | 0.25 | 0.35 | 0.85 | — |
| 1997 | — | 0.15 | 0.25 | 0.35 | 0.85 | — |

**1/2 QUETZAL** **KM# 241.1** **Weight:** 16.6667 g. **Composition:** 0.7200 Silver .3858 oz. ASW

| Date | Mintage | F | VF | XF | Unc | BU |
|---|---|---|---|---|---|---|
| 1925 (P) | 400,000 | 16.50 | 27.50 | 58.00 | 220 | — |

**1/2 QUETZAL** **KM# 241.2** **Weight:** 16.6667 g. **Composition:** 0.7200 Silver .3858 oz. ASW **Obverse:** Without NOBLES below scroll

| Date | Mintage | F | VF | XF | Unc | BU |
|---|---|---|---|---|---|---|
| 1925 (P) | Inc. above | 70.00 | 100 | 200 | 550 | — |

**50 CENTAVOS** KM# 264 **Weight:** 12.0000 g. **Composition:** 0.7200 Silver .2777 oz. ASW

| Date | Mintage | F | VF | XF | Unc | BU |
|---|---|---|---|---|---|---|
| 1962 | 1,983,000 | — | BV | 2.50 | 5.00 | — |
| 1963/2 | 350,000 | 3.50 | 7.50 | 12.50 | 20.00 | — |
| 1963 | Inc. above | — | — | 2.50 | 5.00 | — |

**50 CENTAVOS** KM# 283 **Weight:** 5.5400 g. **Composition:** Brass **Obverse:** National arms **Reverse:** National flower "MONJA BLANCA" **Edge:** Reeded **Size:** 24.2 mm.

| Date | Mintage | F | VF | XF | Unc | BU |
|---|---|---|---|---|---|---|
| 1998 | — | — | — | 0.50 | 1.25 | — |

**QUETZAL** KM# 242 **Weight:** 33.3333 g. **Composition:** 0.7200 Silver .7716 oz. ASW

| Date | Mintage | F | VF | XF | Unc | BU |
|---|---|---|---|---|---|---|
| 1925 (P) | Est. 10,000 | 475 | 650 | 950 | 2,000 | — |

**Note:** 7,000 pieces were withdrawn and remelted soon after issue and more met with the same fate in 1932

**QUETZAL** KM# 279 **Weight:** 27.0000 g. **Composition:** 0.9250 Silver .8030 oz. ASW **Note:** Carlos Merida

| Date | Mintage | F | VF | XF | Unc | BU |
|---|---|---|---|---|---|---|
| 1992NG Proof | — | Value: 50.00 | | | | |

**QUETZAL** KM# 280 **Weight:** 27.0000 g. **Composition:** 0.9250 Silver .8030 oz. ASW **Subject:** Environmental Protection **Reverse:** Horned Guan

| Date | Mintage | F | VF | XF | Unc | BU |
|---|---|---|---|---|---|---|
| 1994 Proof | 20,000 | Value: 50.00 | | | | |

**QUETZAL** KM# 281 **Weight:** 27.0000 g. **Composition:** 0.9250 Silver .8030 oz. ASW **Subject:** 50th Anniversary - National Bank of Guatemala **Obverse:** Coin designs around national emblem **Reverse:** Pre-Columbian artisans

| Date | Mintage | F | VF | XF | Unc | BU |
|---|---|---|---|---|---|---|
| 1996 Proof | — | Value: 45.00 | | | | |

**QUETZAL** KM# 284 **Weight:** 11.1000 g. **Composition:** Brass **Obverse:** National arms **Reverse:** Signature **Edge:** Reeded

| Date | Mintage | F | VF | XF | Unc | BU |
|---|---|---|---|---|---|---|
| 1999 | — | — | — | 1.00 | 2.50 | — |

**5 QUETZALES** KM# 244 **Weight:** 8.3592 g. **Composition:** 0.9000 Gold .2419 oz. AGW

| Date | Mintage | F | VF | XF | Unc | BU |
|---|---|---|---|---|---|---|
| 1926 | 48,000 | 125 | 185 | 250 | 325 | — |

**10 QUETZALES** KM# 245 **Weight:** 16.7185 g. **Composition:** 0.9000 Gold .4838 oz. AGW

| Date | Mintage | F | VF | XF | Unc | BU |
|---|---|---|---|---|---|---|
| 1926 | 18,000 | 250 | 325 | 425 | 700 | — |

**20 QUETZALES** KM# 246 **Weight:** 33.4370 g. **Composition:** 0.9000 Gold .9676 oz. AGW

| Date | Mintage | F | VF | XF | Unc | BU |
|---|---|---|---|---|---|---|
| 1926 | 49,000 | 350 | 450 | 600 | 900 | — |

## PATTERNS

Including off metal strikes

| KM# | Date | Mintage | Identification | Mkt Val |
|---|---|---|---|---|
| Pn18 | 1921 | — | Peso. Copper-Nickel. MONEDA NACIONAL NIQUEL. | — |
| Pn19 | 1922 | — | 5 Pesos. Silver. 3/4 facing bust of Barrios. | — |
| Pn20 | 1922 | — | 5 Pesos. Aluminum-Brass. 3/4 facing bust of Barrios. | — |
| Pn21 | 1923 | — | 5 Pesos. Gold. KM234 | — |
| Pn22 | 1949 | 20 | Centavo. Brass. large bust. | 450 |
| Pn23 | 1949 | 20 | 5 Centavos. 0.7200 Silver. | 475 |
| Pn24 | 1949 | 20 | 10 Centavos. 0.7200 Silver. | 525 |
| Pn25 | 1949 | 20 | 25 Centavos. 0.7200 Silver. | 575 |
| Pn26 | 1960 | — | 25 Centavos. Aluminum. Plain edge. KM#263. | — |
| Pn27 | 1995 | 100 | Quetzal. Brass center. Silver ring. 22.4300 g. 38 mm. National arms. Humming bird flying above lake. Reeded edge. Brass center in Silver ring within Brass ring. | 100 |
| Pn28 | 1995 | 100 | Quetzal. Brass center. Silver ring. 22.2400 g. 38 mm. National arms. Parrot on branch, buildings in back. Reeded edge. Brass center in Silver ring within Brass ring. | 100 |

## PROOF SETS

| KM# | Date | Mintage | Identification | Issue Price | Mkt Val |
|---|---|---|---|---|---|
| PS1 | 1894 (6) | — | KM#162, 165-167, 168.1, 210 | — | 1,800 |
| PS2 | 1895/1896 (6) | — | Rare. KM#162, 165-167, 210, 4 Reales 1895 Pn9 | — | — |

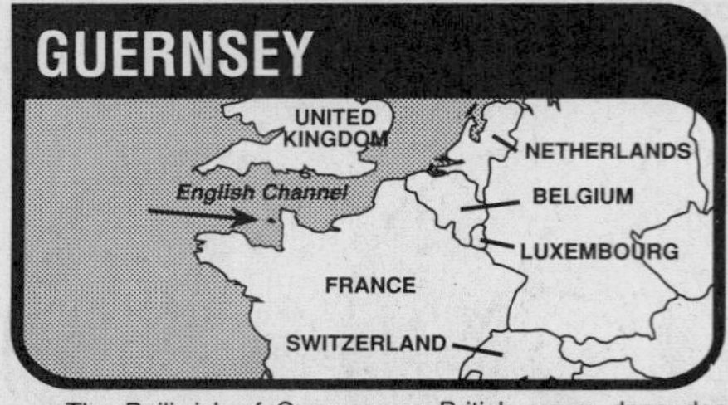


The Bailiwick of Guernsey, a British crown dependency located in the English Channel 30 miles (48 km.) west of Normandy, France, has an area of 30 sq. mi. (194 sq. km.)(including the isles of Alderney, Jethou, Herm, Brechou, and Sark), and a population of 54,000. Capital: St. Peter Port. Agriculture and cattle breeding are the main occupations.

Militant monks from the duchy of Normandy established the first permanent settlements on Guernsey prior to the Norman invasion of England, but the prevalence of prehistoric monuments suggests an earlier occupancy. The island, the only part of the duchy of Normandy belonging to the British crown, has been a possession of Britain since the Norman Conquest of 1066. During the Anglo-French wars, the harbors of Guernsey were employed in the building and out-fitting of ships for the English privateers preying on French shipping. Guernsey is administered by its own laws and customs. Unless the island is mentioned specifically, acts passed by the British Parliament are not applicable to Guernsey. During World War II, German troops occupied the island from June 30, 1940 till May 9,1945.

**RULERS**
British

**MINT MARKS**
H - Heaton, Birmingham

**MONETARY SYSTEM**
8 Doubles = 1 Penny
12 Pence = 1 Shilling
5 Shillings = 1 Crown
20 Shillings = 1 Pound

1 Stem + 3 Stems

## BRITISH DEPENDENCY

### STANDARD COINAGE

**DOUBLE** KM# 10 **Composition:** Bronze

| Date | Mintage | F | VF | XF | Unc | BU |
|---|---|---|---|---|---|---|
| 1902H | 84,000 | 0.20 | 0.60 | 2.25 | 4.00 | — |
| 1902H Proof | — | Value: 250 | | | | |
| 1903H | 112,000 | 0.15 | 0.30 | 1.25 | 2.50 | — |
| 1911H | 45,000 | 0.50 | 1.50 | 4.00 | 12.00 | — |

**DOUBLE** KM# 11 **Composition:** Bronze

| Date | Mintage | F | VF | XF | Unc | BU |
|---|---|---|---|---|---|---|
| 1911H | 90,000 | 0.30 | 1.20 | 3.00 | 6.00 | — |
| 1914H | 45,000 | 1.50 | 3.00 | 6.00 | 12.00 | — |
| 1929H | 79,000 | 0.30 | 0.85 | 2.50 | 5.50 | — |
| 1933H | 96,000 | 0.30 | 0.85 | 2.50 | 5.50 | — |
| 1938H | 96,000 | 0.30 | 0.85 | 2.50 | 5.50 | — |

**2 DOUBLES** KM# 9 **Composition:** Bronze **Obverse:** Leaves with 3 stems above shield

| Date | Mintage | F | VF | XF | Unc | BU |
|---|---|---|---|---|---|---|
| 1902H | 18,000 | 4.50 | 9.00 | 18.00 | 30.00 | — |
| 1902H Proof | — | Value: 250 | | | | |
| 1903H | 18,000 | 6.00 | 12.50 | 22.00 | 35.00 | — |
| 1906H | 18,000 | 6.00 | 12.50 | 22.00 | 35.00 | — |
| 1908H | 18,000 | 6.00 | 12.50 | 22.00 | 35.00 | — |
| 1911H | 29,000 | 4.50 | 9.00 | 15.00 | 27.50 | — |

**2 DOUBLES** KM# 12 **Composition:** Bronzed Copper

| Date | Mintage | F | VF | XF | Unc | BU |
|---|---|---|---|---|---|---|
| 1914H | 29,000 | 4.50 | 9.00 | 18.50 | 27.50 | — |
| 1914H Proof | — | Value: 125 | | | | |
| 1917H | 15,000 | 20.00 | 35.00 | 70.00 | 155 | — |
| 1918H | 57,000 | 1.25 | 2.50 | 9.00 | 15.00 | — |
| 1920H | 57,000 | 1.25 | 2.50 | 9.00 | 15.00 | — |
| 1929H | 79,000 | 0.35 | 1.25 | 6.00 | 10.00 | — |

**4 DOUBLES** KM# 5 **Composition:** Bronze **Obverse:** Leaves with 3 stems above shield **Note:** Varieties exist.

| Date | Mintage | F | VF | XF | Unc | BU |
|---|---|---|---|---|---|---|
| 1874 | 69,000 | 1.50 | 3.00 | 11.50 | 22.50 | — |
| 1902H | 105,000 | 0.85 | 1.75 | 3.00 | 7.50 | — |
| 1902H Proof | — | Value: 250 | | | | |
| 1903H | 52,000 | 1.50 | 3.00 | 9.00 | 25.00 | — |
| 1906H | 52,000 | 1.50 | 3.00 | 9.00 | 25.00 | — |
| 1908H | 26,000 | 3.00 | 7.50 | 15.00 | 30.00 | — |
| 1910H | 52,000 | 1.50 | 3.00 | 9.00 | 25.00 | — |
| 1910H Proof | — | Value: 250 | | | | |
| 1911H | 52,000 | 2.25 | 4.50 | 13.50 | 27.50 | — |

**4 DOUBLES** KM# 13 **Composition:** Bronze

| Date | Mintage | F | VF | XF | Unc | BU |
|---|---|---|---|---|---|---|
| 1914H | 209,000 | 0.75 | 1.50 | 4.50 | 12.50 | — |
| 1918H | 157,000 | 0.75 | 1.50 | 6.00 | 17.50 | — |
| 1920H | 157,000 | 0.45 | 1.25 | 4.50 | 10.00 | — |
| 1945H | 96,000 | 0.45 | 1.25 | 4.50 | 10.00 | — |
| 1949H | 19,000 | 1.50 | 3.00 | 12.00 | 20.00 | — |

**4 DOUBLES** KM# 15 **Composition:** Bronze **Note:** Guernsey Lily

| Date | Mintage | F | VF | XF | Unc | BU |
|---|---|---|---|---|---|---|
| 1956 | 240,000 | 0.25 | 0.45 | 0.75 | 2.00 | — |
| 1956 Proof | 2,100 | Value: 4.00 | | | | |
| 1966 Proof | 10,000 | Value: 1.75 | | | | |

**8 DOUBLES** KM# 7 **Composition:** Bronze

| Date | Mintage | F | VF | XF | Unc | BU |
|---|---|---|---|---|---|---|
| 1902H | 235,000 | 1.25 | 2.25 | 6.00 | 12.50 | — |
| 1902H Proof | — | Value: 250 | | | | |
| 1903H | 118,000 | 0.50 | 1.75 | 4.50 | 10.00 | — |
| 1910H | 91,000 | 1.25 | 2.50 | 12.50 | 25.00 | — |
| 1910H Proof | — | Value: 250 | | | | |
| 1911H | 78,000 | 3.00 | 8.50 | 15.00 | 30.00 | — |

**8 DOUBLES** KM# 14 **Composition:** Bronze

| Date | Mintage | F | VF | XF | Unc | BU |
|---|---|---|---|---|---|---|
| 1914H | 157,000 | 0.65 | 1.75 | 4.50 | 10.00 | — |
| 1914H Proof | — | Value: 150 | | | | |
| 1918H | 157,000 | 0.65 | 1.75 | 4.50 | 10.00 | — |
| 1920H | 157,000 | 0.50 | 1.50 | 4.00 | 9.00 | — |
| 1920H Proof | — | Value: 150 | | | | |
| 1934H | 124,000 | 0.50 | 1.50 | 4.00 | 9.00 | — |
| 1934H Proof | 500 | Value: 175 | | | | |
| 1938H | 120,000 | 0.50 | 1.50 | 4.00 | 9.00 | — |
| 1938H Proof | — | Value: 250 | | | | |
| 1945H | 192,000 | 0.40 | 0.85 | 2.00 | 5.50 | — |
| 1947H | 240,000 | 0.30 | 0.60 | 2.25 | 5.00 | — |
| 1949H | 230,000 | 0.30 | 0.60 | 2.25 | 5.00 | — |

**8 DOUBLES** KM# 16 **Composition:** Bronze **Obverse:** Three-flowered lily

| Date | Mintage | F | VF | XF | Unc | BU |
|---|---|---|---|---|---|---|
| 1956 | 500,000 | 0.10 | 0.20 | 0.50 | 1.25 | — |
| 1956 Proof | 2,100 | Value: 4.00 | | | | |
| 1959 | 500,000 | 0.10 | 0.20 | 0.50 | 1.25 | — |
| 1959 Proof | — | — | — | — | — | — |
| 1966 Proof | 10,000 | Value: 1.75 | | | | |

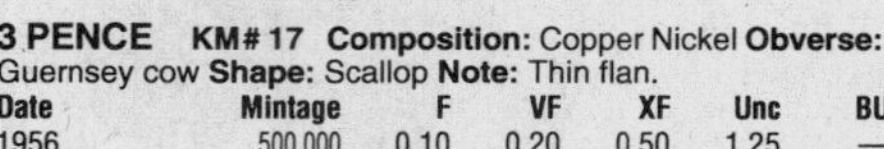

**3 PENCE** KM# 17 **Composition:** Copper Nickel **Obverse:** Guernsey cow **Shape:** Scallop **Note:** Thin flan.

| Date | Mintage | F | VF | XF | Unc | BU |
|---|---|---|---|---|---|---|
| 1956 | 500,000 | 0.10 | 0.20 | 0.50 | 1.25 | — |
| 1956 Proof | 2,100 | Value: 4.00 | | | | |

**3 PENCE** KM# 18 **Composition:** Copper Nickel **Obverse:** Guernsey cow **Shape:** Scallop **Note:** Thick flan.

| Date | Mintage | F | VF | XF | Unc | BU |
|---|---|---|---|---|---|---|
| 1959 | 500,000 | 0.10 | 0.20 | 0.50 | 1.00 | — |
| 1959 Proof | — | Value: 150 | | | | |
| 1966 Proof | 10,000 | Value: 1.75 | | | | |

**10 SHILLING** KM# 19 **Composition:** Copper Nickel **Subject:** 900th Anniversary - Norman Conquest **Reverse:** William I portrait left

| Date | Mintage | F | VF | XF | Unc | BU |
|---|---|---|---|---|---|---|
| 1966 | 300,000 | — | 1.00 | 1.25 | 1.75 | — |
| 1966 Proof | 10,000 | Value: 3.00 | | | | |

## DECIMAL COINAGE

100 Pence = 1 Pound

**1/2 NEW PENNY** KM# 20 **Composition:** Bronze

| Date | Mintage | F | VF | XF | Unc | BU |
|---|---|---|---|---|---|---|
| 1971 | 2,066,000 | — | — | 0.15 | 0.30 | — |
| 1971 Proof | 10,000 | Value: 1.00 | | | | |

**1/2 PENNY** KM# 33 **Composition:** Bronze

| Date | Mintage | F | VF | XF | Unc | BU |
|---|---|---|---|---|---|---|
| 1979 Proof | 20,000 | Value: 1.00 | | | | |

**NEW PENNY** KM# 21 **Composition:** Bronze **Reverse:** Gannet

| Date | Mintage | F | VF | XF | Unc | BU |
|---|---|---|---|---|---|---|
| 1971 | 1,922,000 | — | — | 0.15 | 0.25 | — |
| 1971 Proof | 10,000 | Value: 1.00 | | | | |

**PENNY** KM# 27 **Composition:** Bronze **Reverse:** Gannet

| Date | Mintage | F | VF | XF | Unc | BU |
|---|---|---|---|---|---|---|
| 1977 | 640,000 | — | — | 0.15 | 0.25 | — |
| 1979 | 2,400,000 | — | — | 0.15 | 0.25 | — |
| 1979 Proof | 20,000 | Value: 1.00 | | | | |
| 1981 Proof | 10,000 | Value: 2.00 | | | | |

**PENNY** KM# 40 **Composition:** Bronze **Reverse:** Chancre crab

| Date | Mintage | F | VF | XF | Unc | BU |
|---|---|---|---|---|---|---|
| 1985 | 60,000 | — | — | 0.15 | 0.30 | — |
| 1985 Proof | 2,500 | Value: 2.00 | | | | |
| 1986 | 1,010,000 | — | — | 0.15 | 0.30 | — |
| 1986 Proof | 2,500 | Value: 2.00 | | | | |
| 1987 | 5,000 | — | — | 0.15 | 0.30 | — |
| 1987 In proof sets only | 2,500 | Value: 2.00 | | | | |
| 1988 | 500,000 | — | — | 0.15 | 0.30 | — |
| 1988 Proof | 2,500 | Value: 2.00 | | | | |
| 1989 | 1,000,000 | — | — | 0.15 | 0.30 | — |
| 1989 In proof sets only | 2,500 | Value: 2.00 | | | | |
| 1990 | 5,000 | — | — | 0.15 | 0.30 | — |
| 1990 Proof | 700 | Value: 4.00 | | | | |

**PENNY** KM# 40a **Composition:** Copper Plated Steel **Reverse:** Chancre crab

| Date | Mintage | F | VF | XF | Unc | BU |
|---|---|---|---|---|---|---|
| 1992 In sets only | — | — | — | — | 0.30 | — |
| 1992 In proof sets only | — | Value: 5.00 | | | | |
| 1994 | 750,000 | — | — | — | 0.30 | — |
| 1997 | 2,000,000 | — | — | — | 0.30 | — |

**PENNY** KM# 89 **Composition:** Copper Plated Steel **Obverse:** Rank-Broadley portrait of Queen Elizabeth II **Reverse:** Chancre crab

| Date | Mintage | F | VF | XF | Unc | BU |
|---|---|---|---|---|---|---|
| 1998 | — | — | — | — | 0.30 | — |

**2 NEW PENCE** KM# 22 **Composition:** Bronze **Reverse:** Windmill from Sark

| Date | Mintage | F | VF | XF | Unc | BU |
|---|---|---|---|---|---|---|
| 1971 | 1,680,000 | — | — | 0.15 | 0.35 | — |
| 1971 Proof | 10,000 | Value: 1.00 | | | | |

**2 PENCE** KM# 28 **Composition:** Bronze **Reverse:** Windmill from Sark

| Date | Mintage | F | VF | XF | Unc | BU |
|---|---|---|---|---|---|---|
| 1977 | 700,000 | — | — | 0.15 | 0.25 | — |
| 1979 | 2,400,000 | — | — | 0.15 | 0.25 | — |
| 1979 Proof | 20,000 | Value: 1.00 | | | | |
| 1981 Proof | 10,000 | Value: 2.00 | | | | |

**2 PENCE** KM# 41 **Composition:** Bronze **Reverse:** Guernsey cow

| Date | Mintage | F | VF | XF | Unc | BU |
|---|---|---|---|---|---|---|
| 1985 | 60,000 | — | — | 0.15 | 0.30 | — |
| 1985 Proof | 2,500 | Value: 2.00 | | | | |
| 1986 | 510,000 | — | — | 0.15 | 0.30 | — |
| 1986 Proof | 2,500 | Value: 2.00 | | | | |
| 1987 | 5,000 | — | — | 0.15 | 0.30 | — |
| 1987 In proof sets only | 2,500 | Value: 2.00 | | | | |
| 1988 | 500,000 | — | — | 0.15 | 0.30 | — |
| 1988 Proof | 2,500 | Value: 2.00 | | | | |
| 1989 | 500,000 | — | — | 0.15 | 0.30 | — |
| 1989 In proof sets only | 2,500 | Value: 2.00 | | | | |
| 1990 | 380,000 | — | — | 0.15 | 0.30 | — |
| 1990 Proof | 700 | Value: 4.00 | | | | |

**2 PENCE** KM# 41a **Weight:** 7.2000 g. **Composition:** Copper Plated Steel **Reverse:** Guernsey cow **Edge:** Plain **Size:** 25.9 mm. **Note:** British Royal Mint.

| Date | Mintage | F | VF | XF | Unc | BU |
|---|---|---|---|---|---|---|
| 1992 In sets only | — | — | — | — | 0.30 | — |
| 1992 In proof sets only | — | Value: 5.00 | | | | |
| 1996 | 500,000 | — | — | — | 0.30 | — |
| 1997 | — | — | — | — | 0.30 | — |
| 1999 | 600,000 | — | — | — | 0.25 | — |

**2 PENCE** KM# 96 **Weight:** 7.2000 g. **Composition:** Copper Plated Steel **Obverse:** Queen's new portrait **Reverse:** Guernsey cow **Edge:** Plain

| Date | Mintage | F | VF | XF | Unc | BU |
|---|---|---|---|---|---|---|
| 1999 | — | — | — | — | 0.25 | — |

**5 NEW PENCE** KM# 23 **Composition:** Copper-Nickel **Reverse:** Guernsey lilly

| Date | Mintage | F | VF | XF | Unc | BU |
|---|---|---|---|---|---|---|
| 1968 | 800,000 | — | 0.15 | 0.25 | 0.40 | — |
| 1971 Proof | 10,000 | Value: 1.50 | | | | |

**5 PENCE** KM# 29 **Composition:** Copper-Nickel **Reverse:** Guernsey lilly

| Date | Mintage | F | VF | XF | Unc | BU |
|---|---|---|---|---|---|---|
| 1977 | 250,000 | — | — | 0.20 | 0.45 | — |
| 1979 | 200,000 | — | — | 0.20 | 0.45 | — |
| 1979 Proof | 20,000 | Value: 2.00 | | | | |
| 1981 Proof | 10,000 | Value: 3.00 | | | | |
| 1982 | 200,000 | — | — | 0.20 | 0.45 | — |

**5 PENCE** KM# 42.1 **Composition:** Copper-Nickel

| Date | Mintage | F | VF | XF | Unc | BU |
|---|---|---|---|---|---|---|
| 1985 | 35,000 | — | — | 0.20 | 0.45 | — |
| 1985 Proof | 2,500 | Value: 2.50 | | | | |
| 1986 | 100,000 | — | — | 0.20 | 0.45 | — |
| 1986 Proof | 2,500 | Value: 2.50 | | | | |
| 1987 | 300,000 | — | — | 0.20 | 0.45 | — |
| 1987 In proof sets only | Est. 2,5002,500 | Value: 2.50 | | | | |
| 1988 | 405,000 | — | — | 0.20 | 0.45 | — |
| 1988 Proof | 2,500 | Value: 2.50 | | | | |
| 1989 | 5,000 | — | — | 0.20 | 0.50 | — |
| 1989 In proof sets only | 2,500 | Value: 2.50 | | | | |
| 1990 In sets only | Est. 2,520 | — | — | — | 0.60 | — |
| 1990 Proof | 700 | Value: 5.00 | | | | |

**5 PENCE** KM# 42.2 **Weight:** 3.2600 g. **Composition:** Copper-Nickel **Size:** 18 mm. **Note:** Reduced size. British Royal Mint.

| Date | Mintage | F | VF | XF | Unc | BU |
|---|---|---|---|---|---|---|
| 1990 | 2,400,000 | — | — | 0.20 | 0.45 | — |
| 1990 Proof | 700 | Value: 5.00 | | | | |
| 1992 | 1,300,000 | — | — | — | 0.50 | — |
| 1997 | — | — | — | — | 0.50 | — |
| 1999 | 1,700,000 | — | — | — | 0.50 | — |

**5 PENCE** KM# 97 **Weight:** 3.2600 g. **Composition:** Copper-Nickel **Obverse:** Queen's new portrait **Reverse:** Sail boats **Edge:** Reeded

| Date | Mintage | F | VF | XF | Unc | BU |
|---|---|---|---|---|---|---|
| 1999 | — | — | — | — | 0.45 | — |

**10 NEW PENCE** **KM# 24** **Composition:** Copper-Nickel **Reverse:** Guernsey cow

| Date | Mintage | F | VF | XF | Unc | BU |
|---|---|---|---|---|---|---|
| 1968 | 600,000 | — | 0.20 | 0.40 | 1.00 | — |
| 1970 | 300,000 | — | 0.20 | 0.40 | 1.00 | — |
| 1971 Proof | 10,000 | Value: 2.00 | | | | |

**10 PENCE** **KM# 30** **Composition:** Copper-Nickel **Reverse:** Guernsey cow

| Date | Mintage | F | VF | XF | Unc | BU |
|---|---|---|---|---|---|---|
| 1977 | 480,000 | — | — | 0.25 | 0.85 | — |
| 1979 | 659,000 | — | — | 0.25 | 0.85 | — |
| 1979 Proof | 20,000 | Value: 2.00 | | | | |
| 1981 Proof | 10,000 | Value: 3.00 | | | | |
| 1982 | 200,000 | — | — | 0.25 | 1.00 | — |
| 1984 | 400,000 | — | — | 0.25 | 0.85 | — |

**10 PENCE** **KM# 43.1** **Composition:** Copper-Nickel **Reverse:** Tomato plant

| Date | Mintage | F | VF | XF | Unc | BU |
|---|---|---|---|---|---|---|
| 1985 | 110,000 | — | — | 0.25 | 0.60 | — |
| 1985 Proof | 2,500 | Value: 2.50 | | | | |
| 1986 | 300,000 | — | — | 0.25 | 0.60 | — |
| 1986 Proof | 2,500 | Value: 6.00 | | | | |
| 1987 | 250,000 | — | — | 0.25 | 0.60 | — |
| 1987 In proof sets only | 2,500 | Value: 2.50 | | | | |
| 1988 | 300,000 | — | — | 0.25 | 0.60 | — |
| 1988 Proof | 2,500 | Value: 2.50 | | | | |
| 1989 | 200,000 | — | — | 0.25 | 0.60 | — |
| 1989 In proof sets only | 2,500 | Value: 2.50 | | | | |
| 1990 | 3,500 | — | — | 0.25 | 0.60 | — |
| 1990 Proof | 700 | Value: 5.00 | | | | |

**10 PENCE** **KM# 43.2** **Composition:** Copper-Nickel **Reverse:** Tomato plant **Note:** Reduced size.

| Date | Mintage | F | VF | XF | Unc | BU |
|---|---|---|---|---|---|---|
| 1992 | 3,500,000 | — | — | — | 0.60 | — |
| 1992 In proof sets only | — | Value: 6.00 | | | | |
| 1997 | — | — | — | — | 0.60 | — |

**20 PENCE** **KM# 38** **Composition:** Copper-Nickel **Reverse:** Guernsey milk can

| Date | Mintage | F | VF | XF | Unc | BU |
|---|---|---|---|---|---|---|
| 1982 | 500,000 | — | — | 0.45 | 0.90 | — |
| 1983 | 500,000 | — | — | 0.45 | 0.90 | — |

**20 PENCE** **KM# 44** **Composition:** Copper-Nickel

| Date | Mintage | F | VF | XF | Unc | BU |
|---|---|---|---|---|---|---|
| 1985 | 35,000 | — | — | 0.45 | 0.85 | — |
| 1985 Proof | 2,500 | Value: 3.00 | | | | |
| 1986 | 10,000 | — | — | 0.45 | 0.85 | — |
| 1986 Proof | 2,500 | Value: 3.00 | | | | |
| 1987 | 5,000 | — | — | 0.45 | 0.85 | — |
| 1987 Proof | 2,500 | Value: 3.00 | | | | |
| 1988 | 5,000 | — | — | 0.45 | 0.85 | — |
| 1988 Proof | 2,500 | Value: 3.00 | | | | |
| 1989 | 93,000 | — | — | 0.45 | 0.85 | — |
| 1989 Proof | Est. 2,5002,500 | Value: 3.00 | | | | |
| 1990 | 113,000 | — | — | 0.45 | 0.85 | — |
| 1990 Proof | 700 | Value: 6.00 | | | | |
| 1992 | 800,000 | — | — | — | 1.00 | — |
| 1992 Proof | — | Value: 7.00 | | | | |
| 1997 | — | — | — | — | 1.00 | — |

**20 PENCE** **KM# 90** **Composition:** Copper-Nickel **Obverse:** Rank-Broadley portrait of Queen Elizabeth II

| Date | Mintage | F | VF | XF | Unc | BU |
|---|---|---|---|---|---|---|
| 1999 | — | — | — | — | 0.90 | — |
| 1999 Proof | — | Value: 3.00 | | | | |

**25 PENCE** **KM# 26** **Composition:** Copper-Nickel **Subject:** 25th Wedding Anniversary - Elizabeth and Philip

| Date | Mintage | F | VF | XF | Unc | BU |
|---|---|---|---|---|---|---|
| 1972 | 56,000 | — | — | 2.50 | 5.50 | — |

**25 PENCE** **KM# 26a** **Weight:** 28.2759 g. **Composition:** 0.9250 Silver .8410 oz. ASW **Subject:** 25th Wedding Anniversary - Elizabeth and Philip

| Date | Mintage | F | VF | XF | Unc | BU |
|---|---|---|---|---|---|---|
| 1972 Proof | 15,000 | Value: 12.50 | | | | |

**25 PENCE** **KM# 31** **Composition:** Copper-Nickel **Subject:** Queen's Silver Jubilee

| Date | Mintage | F | VF | XF | Unc | BU |
|---|---|---|---|---|---|---|
| ND(1977) | 207,000 | — | — | 1.25 | 2.25 | — |

**25 PENCE** **KM# 31a** **Weight:** 28.2759 g. **Composition:** 0.9250 Silver .8410 oz. ASW **Subject:** Queen's Silver Jubilee

| Date | Mintage | F | VF | XF | Unc | BU |
|---|---|---|---|---|---|---|
| ND(1977) Proof | 25,000 | Value: 11.50 | | | | |

**25 PENCE** **KM# 32** **Composition:** Copper-Nickel **Subject:** Royal Visit

| Date | Mintage | F | VF | XF | Unc | BU |
|---|---|---|---|---|---|---|
| 1978 | 105,000 | — | — | 1.25 | 2.50 | — |

**25 PENCE** **KM# 32a** **Weight:** 28.2759 g. **Composition:** 0.9250 Silver .8410 oz. ASW **Subject:** Royal Visit

| Date | Mintage | F | VF | XF | Unc | BU |
|---|---|---|---|---|---|---|
| 1978 Proof | 25,000 | Value: 12.50 | | | | |

**25 PENCE** **KM# 35** **Composition:** Copper-Nickel **Subject:** Queen Mother's 80th Birthday

| Date | Mintage | F | VF | XF | Unc | BU |
|---|---|---|---|---|---|---|
| ND(1980) | 150,000 | — | — | 1.25 | 2.50 | — |

**25 PENCE** **KM# 35a** **Weight:** 28.2759 g. **Composition:** 0.9250 Silver .8410 oz. ASW **Subject:** Queen Mother's 80th Birthday

| Date | Mintage | F | VF | XF | Unc | BU |
|---|---|---|---|---|---|---|
| ND(1980) Proof | 25,000 | Value: 13.50 | | | | |

**25 PENCE** **KM# 36** **Composition:** Copper-Nickel **Subject:** Wedding of Prince Charles and Lady Diana **Obverse:** Similar to 25 New Pence, KM#35

| Date | Mintage | F | VF | XF | Unc | BU |
|---|---|---|---|---|---|---|
| 1981 | 114,000 | — | — | 1.50 | 3.00 | — |

**25 PENCE** **KM# 36a** **Weight:** 28.2759 g. **Composition:** 0.9250 Silver .8410 oz. ASW **Subject:** Wedding of Prince Charles and Lady Diana **Obverse:** Similar to 25 New Pence, KM#35

| Date | Mintage | F | VF | XF | Unc | BU |
|---|---|---|---|---|---|---|
| 1981 Proof | 12,000 | Value: 16.50 | | | | |

**50 NEW PENCE** **KM# 25** **Composition:** Copper-Nickel **Reverse:** Ducal cap of the Duke of Normandy

| Date | Mintage | F | VF | XF | Unc | BU |
|---|---|---|---|---|---|---|
| 1969 | 200,000 | — | 1.00 | 1.50 | 2.50 | — |
| 1970 | 200,000 | — | 1.00 | 1.50 | 2.50 | — |
| 1971 Proof | 10,000 | Value: 3.00 | | | | |

**50 PENCE** **KM#34** **Composition:** Copper-Nickel **Reverse:** Ducal cap of the Duke of Normandy

| Date | Mintage | F | VF | XF | Unc | BU |
|---|---|---|---|---|---|---|
| 1979 Proof | 20,000 | Value: 4.50 | | | | |
| 1981 | 200,000 | — | — | 0.90 | 1.45 | — |
| 1981 Proof | 10,000 | Value: 5.50 | | | | |
| 1982 | 150,000 | — | — | 0.90 | 1.45 | — |
| 1983 | 200,000 | — | — | 0.90 | 1.45 | — |
| 1984 | 200,000 | — | — | 0.90 | 1.45 | — |

**50 PENCE** **KM# 45.1** **Composition:** Copper-Nickel

| Date | Mintage | F | VF | XF | Unc | BU |
|---|---|---|---|---|---|---|
| 1985 | 35,000 | — | — | 0.90 | 1.45 | — |
| 1985 Proof | 2,500 | Value: 4.00 | | | | |
| 1986 | 10,000 | — | — | 0.90 | 1.45 | — |
| 1986 Proof | 2,500 | Value: 4.00 | | | | |
| 1987 | 5,000 | — | — | 0.90 | 1.45 | — |
| 1987 In proof sets only | 2,500 | Value: 4.50 | | | | |
| 1988 | 6,000 | — | — | 0.90 | 1.45 | — |
| 1988 Proof | 2,500 | Value: 4.50 | | | | |
| 1989 | 55,000 | — | — | 0.90 | 1.45 | — |
| 1989 In proof sets only | 2,500 | Value: 4.50 | | | | |
| 1990 | 80,000 | — | — | 0.90 | 1.45 | — |
| 1990 Proof | 700 | Value: 7.50 | | | | |
| 1992 | 65,000 | — | — | — | 2.00 | — |
| 1997 In proof sets only | — | Value: 7.50 | | | | |

**50 PENCE** **KM# 45.2** **Composition:** Copper-Nickel **Obverse:** Queen's portrait **Reverse:** Crossed flowers **Size:** 27.3 mm.

| Date | Mintage | F | VF | XF | Unc | BU |
|---|---|---|---|---|---|---|
| 1997 | 1,000,000 | — | — | — | 1.75 | — |

**50 PENCE** **KM# 105** **Weight:** 7.9700 g. **Composition:** Copper-Nickel **Subject:** Battle of Britain **Obverse:** Queen's portrait **Reverse:** Pilot and figher plane **Edge:** Plain, seven sided **Size:** 27.3 mm.

| Date | Mintage | F | VF | XF | Unc | BU |
|---|---|---|---|---|---|---|
| 2000 | 10,000 | — | — | — | 1.50 | — |

**50 PENCE** **KM# 105a** **Weight:** 8.1000 g. **Composition:** 0.9250 Silver .2409 oz. ASW

| Date | Mintage | F | VF | XF | Unc | BU |
|---|---|---|---|---|---|---|
| 2000 Proof | 15,000 | Value: 25.00 | | | | |

**50 PENCE** **KM# 105b** **Weight:** 15.5000 g. **Composition:** 0.9170 Gold .4570 oz. AGW **Edge:** Plain, seven-sided **Size:** 27.3 mm.

| Date | Mintage | F | VF | XF | Unc | BU |
|---|---|---|---|---|---|---|
| 2000 Proof | 1,500 | Value: 300 | | | | |

**POUND** **KM# 37** **Composition:** Copper-Nickel-Zinc **Reverse:** Guernsey lily

| Date | Mintage | F | VF | XF | Unc | BU |
|---|---|---|---|---|---|---|
| 1981 | 200,000 | — | 1.80 | 2.00 | 3.50 | — |
| 1981 Proof | 10,000 | Value: 4.50 | | | | |

**POUND** **KM# 37a** **Weight:** 8.0000 g. **Composition:** 0.9170 Gold .2358 oz. AGW **Reverse:** Guernsey lily

| Date | Mintage | F | VF | XF | Unc | BU |
|---|---|---|---|---|---|---|
| 1981 Proof | 4,500 | Value: 125 | | | | |

**POUND** **KM# 39** **Composition:** Aluminum-Bronze **Reverse:** H.M.S. Crescent

| Date | Mintage | F | VF | XF | Unc | BU |
|---|---|---|---|---|---|---|
| 1983 | 269,000 | — | 1.80 | 2.00 | 3.50 | — |

**POUND** **KM# 46** **Composition:** Copper-Nickel-Zinc

| Date | Mintage | F | VF | XF | Unc | BU |
|---|---|---|---|---|---|---|
| 1985 | 35,000 | — | — | 1.75 | 2.50 | — |
| 1985 Proof | 2,500 | Value: 6.50 | | | | |
| 1986 | 10,000 | — | — | 1.75 | 2.50 | — |
| 1986 Proof | 2,500 | Value: 6.50 | | | | |
| 1987 | 5,000 | — | — | 1.75 | 2.50 | — |
| 1987 In proof sets only | 2,500 | Value: 6.50 | | | | |
| 1988 | 5,000 | — | — | 1.75 | 2.50 | — |
| 1988 Proof | 2,500 | Value: 6.50 | | | | |
| 1989 | 5,000 | — | — | 1.75 | 2.50 | — |
| 1989 In proof sets only | 2,500 | Value: 6.50 | | | | |
| 1990 | 3,500 | — | — | 1.75 | 2.50 | — |
| 1990 Proof | 700 | Value: 10.00 | | | | |
| 1992 Proof | — | — | — | — | 12.50 | — |
| 1997 Proof | — | — | — | — | 3.50 | — |

**POUND** **KM# 77** **Weight:** 9.5000 g. **Composition:** 0.9250 Silver .2825 oz. ASW **Subject:** Queen Elizabeth the Queen Mother **Note:** Similar to 5 Pounds, KM#66

| Date | Mintage | F | VF | XF | Unc | BU |
|---|---|---|---|---|---|---|
| 1995 Proof | — | Value: 30.00 | | | | |

**POUND** **KM# 78** **Weight:** 9.5000 g. **Composition:** 0.9250 Silver .2825 oz. ASW **Subject:** 70th Birthday of Queen Elizabeth II

| Date | Mintage | F | VF | XF | Unc | BU |
|---|---|---|---|---|---|---|
| 1996 Proof | — | Value: 20.00 | | | | |

**POUND** **KM# 70** **Weight:** 9.5000 g. **Composition:** 0.9250 Silver .2825 oz. ASW **Subject:** Golden Wedding Anniversary **Obverse:** Queen's portrait **Reverse:** Queen Elizabeth II and Prince Philip, monogrammed shield, Westminster Abbey.

| Date | Mintage | F | VF | XF | Unc | BU |
|---|---|---|---|---|---|---|
| 1997 Proof | Est. 50,000 | Value: 20.00 | | | | |

**POUND** **KM# 73** **Weight:** 9.5000 g. **Composition:** 0.9250 Silver .2825 oz. ASW **Series:** Castle **Subject:** Tower of London

| Date | Mintage | F | VF | XF | Unc | BU |
|---|---|---|---|---|---|---|
| 1997 Proof | 15,000 | Value: 32.50 | | | | |

**POUND** **KM# 84** **Weight:** 9.5000 g. **Composition:** 0.9250 Silver .2825 oz. ASW **Subject:** 80th Anniversary - Royal Air Force **Obverse:** Rank-Broadley portrait of Queen Elizabeth II **Reverse:** Three Spitfires and RAF Benevolent Fund Crest

| Date | Mintage | F | VF | XF | Unc | BU |
|---|---|---|---|---|---|---|
| 1998 Proof | Est. 30,000 | Value: 45.00 | | | | |

**POUND** **KM# 109** **Weight:** 9.5000 g. **Composition:** 0.9250 Silver .2825 oz. ASW **Subject:** Winston Churchill **Obverse:** Queen's portrait **Reverse:** Churchill's portrait **Edge:** Reeded **Size:** 22.5 mm.

| Date | Mintage | F | VF | XF | Unc | BU |
|---|---|---|---|---|---|---|
| 1999 Proof | — | Value: 25.00 | | | | |

**POUND** **KM# 95** **Weight:** 9.5000 g. **Composition:** 0.9250 Silver .2825 oz. ASW **Subject:** Prince Edward's Wedding **Obverse:** Queen's portrait **Reverse:** Portraits of Edward and Sophie **Edge:** Reeded **Size:** 22.5 mm. **Note:** British Royal Mint.

| Date | Mintage | F | VF | XF | Unc | BU |
|---|---|---|---|---|---|---|
| 1999 Proof | 50,000 | Value: 35.00 | | | | |

**POUND** **KM# 87** **Weight:** 9.5000 g. **Composition:** 0.9250 Gold Plated Silver .2825 oz. ASW AGW **Subject:** Year 2000 **Obverse:** Queen's portrait **Reverse:** Handheld planet Earth **Note:** Millennium insert for 5 pounds, KM#86.

| Date | Mintage | F | VF | XF | Unc | BU |
|---|---|---|---|---|---|---|
| 2000 | Est. 50,000 | — | — | — | — | — |

**POUND** **KM# 99** **Weight:** 9.5000 g. **Composition:** 0.9250 Silver .2825 oz. ASW **Subject:** Queen Mother's 100th Birthday **Obverse:** Queen's portrait **Reverse:** Queen Mother's portrait **Edge:** Reeded **Size:** 22.5 mm.

| Date | Mintage | F | VF | XF | Unc | BU |
|---|---|---|---|---|---|---|
| 2000 Proof | 30,000 | Value: 25.00 | | | | |

**POUND** **KM# 110** **Weight:** 9.5000 g. **Composition:** Copper-Nickel-Zinc **Subject:** Circulation Type **Obverse:** Queen's new portrait **Reverse:** Denomination **Edge:** Reeded **Size:** 22.5 mm.

| Date | Mintage | F | VF | XF | Unc | BU |
|---|---|---|---|---|---|---|
| 2001 | — | — | — | — | 2.50 | — |

**POUND** **KM# 111** **Weight:** 9.5000 g. **Composition:** 0.9250 Silver .2825 oz. ASW **Subject:** Queen's 75th Birthday **Obverse:** Queen's portrait **Reverse:** Queen's portrait in wreath **Edge:** Reeded **Size:** 22.5 mm.

| Date | Mintage | F | VF | XF | Unc | BU |
|---|---|---|---|---|---|---|
| 2001 Proof | — | Value: 25.00 | | | | |

**2 POUNDS** **KM# 47** **Composition:** Copper-Nickel **Subject:** 40th Anniversary - Liberation from Germany

| Date | Mintage | F | VF | XF | Unc | BU |
|---|---|---|---|---|---|---|
| ND(1985) | 75,000 | — | — | 3.50 | 6.00 | — |
| ND(1985) Proof | 2,500 | Value: 8.00 | | | | |

**2 POUNDS** **KM# 47a** **Weight:** 28.2800 g. **Composition:** 0.9250 Silver .8411 oz. ASW **Subject:** 40th Anniversary - Liberation from Germany

| Date | Mintage | F | VF | XF | Unc | BU |
|---|---|---|---|---|---|---|
| ND (1985) Proof | 2,500 | Value: 30.00 | | | | |

**2 POUNDS** **KM# 48** **Composition:** Copper-Nickel **Subject:** Commonwealth Games

| Date | Mintage | F | VF | XF | Unc | BU |
|---|---|---|---|---|---|---|
| 1986 | 18,000 | — | — | — | 6.00 | — |
| 1986 In proof sets only | Est. 2,500 | Value: 10.00 | | | | |

**2 POUNDS** **KM# 48a** **Weight:** 28.2800 g. **Composition:** 0.5000 Silver .4547 oz. ASW **Subject:** Commonwealth Games

| Date | Mintage | F | VF | XF | Unc | BU |
|---|---|---|---|---|---|---|
| 1986 | Est. 50,000 | — | — | — | 13.50 | — |

**2 POUNDS** **KM# 48b** **Weight:** 28.2800 g. **Composition:** 0.9250 Silver .8411 oz. ASW **Subject:** Commonwealth Games

| Date | Mintage | F | VF | XF | Unc | BU |
|---|---|---|---|---|---|---|
| 1986 Proof | Est. 20,000 | Value: 22.50 | | | | |

**2 POUNDS** **KM# 49** **Composition:** Copper-Nickel **Subject:** 900th Anniversary - Death of William the Conqueror

| Date | Mintage | F | VF | XF | Unc | BU |
|---|---|---|---|---|---|---|
| ND(1987) | 18,000 | — | — | — | 6.50 | — |
| ND(1987) Proof | Est. 2,500 | Value: 10.00 | | | | |

**2 POUNDS** **KM# 49a** **Weight:** 28.2800 g. **Composition:** 0.9250 Silver .8411 oz. ASW **Subject:** 900th Anniversary - Death of William the Conqueror

| Date | Mintage | F | VF | XF | Unc | BU |
|---|---|---|---|---|---|---|
| ND(1987) Proof | 2,500 | Value: 30.00 | | | | |

**2 POUNDS** **KM# 49b** **Weight:** 47.5400 g. **Composition:** 0.9170 Gold 1.4012 oz. AGW **Subject:** 900th Anniversary - Death of William the Conqueror

| Date | Mintage | F | VF | XF | Unc | BU |
|---|---|---|---|---|---|---|
| ND(1987) Proof | 90 | Value: 1,550 | | | | |

**2 POUNDS** **KM# 50** **Composition:** Copper-Nickel **Reverse:** William II

| Date | Mintage | F | VF | XF | Unc | BU |
|---|---|---|---|---|---|---|
| 1988 | 7,500 | — | — | — | 6.50 | — |
| 1988 Proof | 2,500 | Value: 10.00 | | | | |

**2 POUNDS** **KM# 50a** **Weight:** 28.2800 g. **Composition:** 0.9250 Silver .8411 oz. ASW **Reverse:** William II

| Date | Mintage | F | VF | XF | Unc | BU |
|---|---|---|---|---|---|---|
| 1988 Proof | 2,500 | Value: 30.00 | | | | |

**2 POUNDS** **KM# 51** **Composition:** Copper-Nickel **Reverse:** Henry I

| Date | Mintage | F | VF | XF | Unc | BU |
|---|---|---|---|---|---|---|
| 1989 | 10,000 | — | — | — | 7.00 | — |
| 1989 Proof | Est. 2,500 | Value: 10.00 | | | | |

**2 POUNDS** **KM# 52** **Composition:** Copper-Nickel **Subject:** Royal Visit

| Date | Mintage | F | VF | XF | Unc | BU |
|---|---|---|---|---|---|---|
| 1989 | 5,000 | — | — | — | 8.00 | — |

**2 POUNDS** **KM# 51a** **Weight:** 28.2800 g. **Composition:** 0.9250 Silver .8411 oz. ASW **Reverse:** Henry I

| Date | Mintage | F | VF | XF | Unc | BU |
|---|---|---|---|---|---|---|
| 1989 Proof | Est. 2,500 | Value: 30.00 | | | | |

**2 POUNDS** **KM# 52a** **Weight:** 28.2800 g. **Composition:** 0.9250 Silver .8411 oz. ASW **Subject:** Royal Visit

| Date | Mintage | F | VF | XF | Unc | BU |
|---|---|---|---|---|---|---|
| 1989 Proof | 5,000 | Value: 40.00 | | | | |

**2 POUNDS** **KM# 53** **Composition:** Copper-Nickel **Subject:** 90th Birthday of Queen Mother

| Date | Mintage | F | VF | XF | Unc | BU |
|---|---|---|---|---|---|---|
| ND(1990) | 9,000 | — | — | — | 7.00 | — |

**2 POUNDS** **KM# 53a** **Weight:** 28.2800 g. **Composition:** 0.9250 Silver .8411 oz. ASW **Subject:** 90th Birthday of Queen Mother

| Date | Mintage | F | VF | XF | Unc | BU |
|---|---|---|---|---|---|---|
| ND(1990) Proof | 1,302 | Value: 50.00 | | | | |

**2 POUNDS** **KM# 54** **Composition:** Copper-Nickel **Reverse:** Henry II

| Date | Mintage | F | VF | XF | Unc | BU |
|---|---|---|---|---|---|---|
| 1991 | 1,200 | — | — | — | 7.00 | — |

**2 POUNDS** **KM# 54a** **Weight:** 28.2800 g. **Composition:** 0.9250 Silver .8411 oz. ASW **Reverse:** Henry II

| Date | Mintage | F | VF | XF | Unc | BU |
|---|---|---|---|---|---|---|
| 1991 Proof | Est. 2,500 | Value: 50.00 | | | | |

**2 POUNDS** **KM# 55** **Composition:** Copper-Nickel **Subject:** 40th Anniversary of Coronation

| Date | Mintage | F | VF | XF | Unc | BU |
|---|---|---|---|---|---|---|
| ND(1993) | 13,000 | — | — | — | 6.50 | — |

**2 POUNDS** **KM# 55a** **Weight:** 28.2800 g. **Composition:** 0.9250 Silver .8411 oz. ASW **Subject:** 40th Anniversary of Coronation

| Date | Mintage | F | VF | XF | Unc | BU |
|---|---|---|---|---|---|---|
| ND(1993) Proof | Est. 10,000 | Value: 45.00 | | | | |

**2 POUNDS** **KM# 56** **Composition:** Copper-Nickel **Subject:** 50th Anniversary - Normandy Landing

| Date | Mintage | F | VF | XF | Unc | BU |
|---|---|---|---|---|---|---|
| ND(1994) | 49,000 | — | — | — | 7.50 | — |

**2 POUNDS** **KM# 56a** **Weight:** 28.2800 g. **Composition:** 0.9250 Silver .8411 oz. ASW **Subject:** 50th Anniversary - Normandy Landing

| Date | Mintage | F | VF | XF | Unc | BU |
|---|---|---|---|---|---|---|
| ND(1994) Proof | Est. 10,000 | Value: 37.50 | | | | |

**2 POUNDS** **KM# 61** **Composition:** Copper-Nickel **Subject:** 50th Anniversary of Liberation

| Date | Mintage | F | VF | XF | Unc | BU |
|---|---|---|---|---|---|---|
| ND(1995) | 42,000 | — | — | — | 7.50 | — |

**2 POUNDS** **KM# 66** **Composition:** Copper-Nickel **Reverse:** Queen Mother

| Date | Mintage | F | VF | XF | Unc | BU |
|---|---|---|---|---|---|---|
| 1995 | 56,000 | — | — | — | 15.00 | — |

**2 POUNDS** **KM# 61a** **Weight:** 28.2800 g. **Composition:** 0.9250 Silver .8411 oz. ASW **Subject:** 50th Anniversary of Liberation

| Date | Mintage | F | VF | XF | Unc | BU |
|---|---|---|---|---|---|---|
| ND(1995) Proof | 7,000 | Value: 37.50 | | | | |

**2 POUNDS** **KM# 61b** **Weight:** 56.5600 g. **Composition:** 0.9250 Silver .16822 oz. ASW **Subject:** 50th Anniversary of Liberation

| Date | Mintage | F | VF | XF | Unc | BU |
|---|---|---|---|---|---|---|
| ND(1995) Proof | 800 | Value: 70.00 | | | | |

**2 POUNDS** **KM# 80** **Composition:** Copper-Nickel **Subject:** WWF Conserving Nature **Obverse:** Queen's portrait **Reverse:** Emperor moth

| Date | Mintage | F | VF | XF | Unc | BU |
|---|---|---|---|---|---|---|
| 1997 | — | — | — | — | 8.50 | — |

**2 POUNDS** **KM# 80a** **Weight:** 28.2800 g. **Composition:** 0.9250 Silver .841 oz. ASW **Subject:** WWF Conserving Nature **Obverse:** Queen's portrait **Reverse:** Emperor moth

| Date | Mintage | F | VF | XF | Unc | BU |
|---|---|---|---|---|---|---|
| 1997 Proof | Est. 15,000 | Value: 50.00 | | | | |

**2 POUNDS** **KM# 88** **Ring Composition:** Brass **Center Composition:** Copper Nickel **Obverse:** Queen's portrait by Maklouf **Reverse:** Arms on cross design

| Date | Mintage | F | VF | XF | Unc | BU |
|---|---|---|---|---|---|---|
| 1997 | — | — | — | — | 8.50 | — |

**Note:** In mint sets only

| Date | Mintage | F | VF | XF | Unc | BU |
|---|---|---|---|---|---|---|
| 1997 Proof | — | Value: 12.00 | | | | |

**Note:** In proof sets only

**2 POUNDS** **KM# 83** **Ring Composition:** Brass **Center Composition:** Copper Nickel **Obverse:** Rank-Broadley portrait of Queen Elizabeth II **Reverse:** Latent image arms on cross **Edge:** Bailiwick of Guernsey

| Date | Mintage | F | VF | XF | Unc | BU |
|---|---|---|---|---|---|---|
| 1998 | Est. 150,000 | — | — | — | 8.50 | — |

**2 POUNDS** **KM# 81** **Composition:** Copper-Nickel **Subject:** WWF Conserving Nature **Obverse:** Queen's portrait **Reverse:** Brimstone butterfly

| Date | Mintage | F | VF | XF | Unc | BU |
|---|---|---|---|---|---|---|
| 1998 | — | — | — | — | 8.50 | — |

**5 POUNDS** **KM# 66a** **Weight:** 28.2800 g. **Composition:** 0.9250 Silver .8411 oz. ASW **Reverse:** Queen Mother

| Date | Mintage | F | VF | XF | Unc | BU |
|---|---|---|---|---|---|---|
| 1995 Proof | Est. 40,000 | Value: 50.00 | | | | |

**5 POUNDS** **KM# 67** **Weight:** 7.8100 g. **Composition:** 0.9990 Gold .2508 oz. AGW **Reverse:** Queen Mother

| Date | Mintage | F | VF | XF | Unc | BU |
|---|---|---|---|---|---|---|
| 1995 Proof | Est. 2,500 | Value: 210 | | | | |

**5 POUNDS** **KM# 68** **Composition:** Copper-Nickel **Subject:** European Football **Reverse:** Soccer ball and European map

| Date | Mintage | F | VF | XF | Unc | BU |
|---|---|---|---|---|---|---|
| 1996 | — | — | — | — | 15.00 | — |

**5 POUNDS** **KM# 68a** **Weight:** 28.2800 g. **Composition:** 0.9250 Silver .8411 oz. ASW **Subject:** European Football **Reverse:** Soccer ball and European map

| Date | Mintage | F | VF | XF | Unc | BU |
|---|---|---|---|---|---|---|
| 1996 Proof | Est. 20,000 | Value: 65.00 | | | | |

**5 POUNDS** **KM# 79** **Composition:** Copper-Nickel **Subject:** 70th Birthday of Queen Elizabeth II

| Date | Mintage | F | VF | XF | Unc | BU |
|---|---|---|---|---|---|---|
| 1996 | — | — | — | — | 15.00 | — |

**5 POUNDS** **KM# 79a** **Weight:** 28.2800 g. **Composition:** 0.9250 Silver .8411 oz. ASW **Subject:** 70th Birthday of Queen Elizabeth II

| Date | Mintage | F | VF | XF | Unc | BU |
|---|---|---|---|---|---|---|
| 1996 Proof | — | Value: 45.00 | | | | |

**5 POUNDS** **KM# 71** **Composition:** Copper-Nickel **Subject:** Queen Elizabeth II's Golden Wedding Anniversary **Note:** Similar to Pound, KM#70.

| Date | Mintage | F | VF | XF | Unc | BU |
|---|---|---|---|---|---|---|
| 1997 | 22,000 | — | — | — | 12.50 | — |

**5 POUNDS** **KM# 71a** **Weight:** 28.2800 g. **Composition:** 0.9250 Silver .8411 oz. ASW **Subject:** Queen Elizabeth II's Golden Wedding Anniversary **Note:** Similar to Pound, KM#70.

| Date | Mintage | F | VF | XF | Unc | BU |
|---|---|---|---|---|---|---|
| 1997 Proof | Est. 20,000 | Value: 65.00 | | | | |

**5 POUNDS** **KM# 74** **Composition:** Copper-Nickel **Subject:** Castle Cornet **Obverse:** Queen's portrait **Reverse:** Castle

| Date | Mintage | F | VF | XF | Unc | BU |
|---|---|---|---|---|---|---|
| 1997 | — | — | — | — | 10.00 | — |

**5 POUNDS** **KM# 74a** **Weight:** 28.2800 g. **Composition:** 0.9250 Silver .8411 oz. ASW **Subject:** Castle Cornet **Obverse:** Queen's portrait **Reverse:** Castle

| Date | Mintage | F | VF | XF | Unc | BU |
|---|---|---|---|---|---|---|
| 1997 Proof | Est. 10,000 | Value: 60.00 | | | | |

**5 POUNDS** **KM# 75** **Weight:** 28.2800 g. **Composition:** 0.9250 Silver .8411 oz. ASW **Subject:** Castle Caernarfon **Obverse:** Queen's portrait **Reverse:** Caernarfon castle

| Date | Mintage | F | VF | XF | Unc | BU |
|---|---|---|---|---|---|---|
| 1997 Proof | Est. 10,000 | Value: 60.00 | | | | |

**5 POUNDS** **KM# 76** **Weight:** 28.2800 g. **Composition:** 0.9250 Silver .8411 oz. ASW **Subject:** Castle Leeds **Obverse:** Queen's portrait **Reverse:** Leeds castle

| Date | Mintage | F | VF | XF | Unc | BU |
|---|---|---|---|---|---|---|
| 1997 Proof | Est. 10,000 | Value: 60.00 | | | | |

**5 POUNDS** **KM# 98** **Weight:** 1.2000 g. **Composition:** 0.9167 Gold .0354 oz. AGW **Subject:** Queen's 50th Wedding Anniversary **Reverse:** Royal couple, shield and church **Edge:** Reeded **Size:** 9 mm. **Note:** Struck at the British Royal Mint.

| Date | Mintage | F | VF | XF | Unc | BU |
|---|---|---|---|---|---|---|
| 1997 Proof | — | Value: 35.00 | | | | |

**5 POUNDS** **KM# 82** **Composition:** Copper-Nickel **Subject:** 80th Anniversary of the Royal Air Force **Obverse:** Rank-Broadley portrait of Queen Elizabeth II **Reverse:** Three Spitfires and an oval crest

| Date | Mintage | F | VF | XF | Unc | BU |
|---|---|---|---|---|---|---|
| 1998 | — | — | — | — | 12.50 | — |

**5 POUNDS** **KM# 82a** **Weight:** 28.2800 g. **Composition:** 0.9250 Silver .8410 oz. ASW **Subject:** 80th Anniversary of the Royal Air Force **Obverse:** Rank-Broadley portrait of Queen Elizabeth II **Reverse:** Three Spitfires and an oval crest

| Date | Mintage | F | VF | XF | Unc | BU |
|---|---|---|---|---|---|---|
| 1998 Proof | 15,000 | Value: 55.00 | | | | |

**5 POUNDS** **KM# 86** **Weight:** 28.2800 g. **Composition:** 0.9250 Silver .8410 oz. ASW **Subject:** Millennium 2000 **Obverse:** Queen's portrait and legend **Reverse:** Rising sun design, denomination, date

| Date | Mintage | F | VF | XF | Unc | BU |
|---|---|---|---|---|---|---|
| 1999 Proof | Est. 50,000 | Value: 40.00 | | | | |

**5 POUNDS** **KM# 91** **Ring Composition:** Copper-Nickel **Center Composition:** Brass **Subject:** Millennium 2000 **Obverse:** Queen's portrait in center and below **Reverse:** Hands holding planet earth in center, rising sun design around

| Date | Mintage | F | VF | XF | Unc | BU |
|---|---|---|---|---|---|---|
| 1999 | 22,000 | — | — | — | 18.00 | — |

**5 POUNDS** **KM# 92** **Weight:** 27.7100 g. **Composition:** Copper Nickel **Subject:** Prince Edward's Marriage **Obverse:** Queen's portrait **Reverse:** Portraits of Edward and Sophie **Edge:** Reeded **Size:** 38.6 mm.

| Date | Mintage | F | VF | XF | Unc | BU |
|---|---|---|---|---|---|---|
| 1999 | 19,000 | — | — | — | 15.00 | — |

**5 POUNDS** **KM# 92a** **Weight:** 28.2800 g. **Composition:** 0.9250 Silver .8410 oz. ASW **Subject:** Prince Edward's Marriage **Obverse:** Queen's portrait **Reverse:** Portrait's of Edward and Sophie

| Date | Mintage | F | VF | XF | Unc | BU |
|---|---|---|---|---|---|---|
| 1999 Proof | — | Value: 37.50 | | | | |

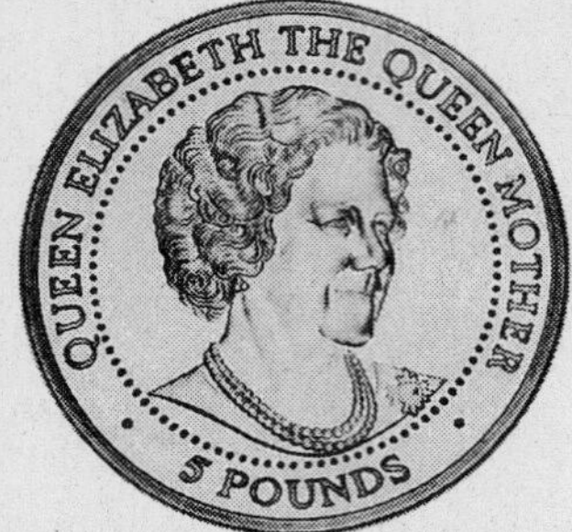


**5 POUNDS** **KM# 93** **Weight:** 27.7100 g. **Composition:** Copper-Nickel **Subject:** Queen Mother **Obverse:** Queen's portrait **Reverse:** Queen Mother's portrait

| Date | Mintage | F | VF | XF | Unc | BU |
|---|---|---|---|---|---|---|
| 1999 | 5,000 | — | — | — | 16.50 | — |

**5 POUNDS** **KM# 94a** **Weight:** 47.5400 g. **Composition:** 0.9166 Gold 1.4011 oz. AGW **Subject:** Winston Churchill **Obverse:** Queen's portrait **Reverse:** Churchill's portrait **Edge:** Reeded **Note:** British Royal Mint

| Date | Mintage | F | VF | XF | Unc | BU |
|---|---|---|---|---|---|---|
| 1999 Proof | 125,000 | Value: 865 | | | | |

**5 POUNDS** **KM# 113** **Weight:** 1.1300 g. **Composition:** 0.9170 Gold .0333 oz. AGW **Subject:** 20th Century Monarchy **Obverse:** Queen's portrait **Reverse:** Five portraits **Edge:** Reeded **Size:** 13.9 mm.

| Date | Mintage | F | VF | XF | Unc | BU |
|---|---|---|---|---|---|---|
| 2000 Proof | — | Value: 57.50 | | | | |

**5 POUNDS** **KM# 102** **Weight:** 27.9500 g. **Composition:** Copper-Nickel **Subject:** Century of Monarchy **Obverse:** Queen's portrait **Reverse:** Portraits of past five sovereigns **Edge:** Reeded **Size:** 38.4 mm.

| Date | Mintage | F | VF | XF | Unc | BU |
|---|---|---|---|---|---|---|
| 2000 | — | — | — | — | 11.00 | — |

**5 POUNDS** **KM# 100** **Weight:** 28.2800 g. **Composition:** Copper-Nickel **Obverse:** Queen's portrait **Reverse:** Queen Mother's portrait **Edge:** Reeded **Size:** 38.6 mm.

| Date | Mintage | F | VF | XF | Unc | BU |
|---|---|---|---|---|---|---|
| 2000 | — | — | — | — | 7.50 | — |

**5 POUNDS** **KM# 100a** **Weight:** 28.2800 g. **Composition:** 0.9250 Silver .8410 oz. ASW **Subject:** Queen Mother's 100th Birthday **Obverse:** Queen Mother's portrait with gld plated "100" **Edge:** Reeded **Size:** 38.6 mm.

| Date | Mintage | F | VF | XF | Unc | BU |
|---|---|---|---|---|---|---|
| 2000 Proof | 20,000 | Value: 47.50 | | | | |

**5 POUNDS** **KM# 101** **Weight:** 1.1300 g. **Composition:** 0.9170 Gold .0333 oz. AGW **Subject:** Queen Mother's 100th Birthday **Obverse:** Queen's portrait **Reverse:** Queen Mother's portrait **Edge:** Reeded **Size:** 13.9 mm.

| Date | Mintage | F | VF | XF | Unc | BU |
|---|---|---|---|---|---|---|
| 2000 Proof | 20,000 | Value: 57.50 | | | | |

**5 POUNDS** **KM# 102a** **Weight:** 28.2800 g. **Composition:** 0.9250 Silver .8410 oz. ASW **Subject:** Century of Monarchy **Obverse:** Queen's portrait **Reverse:** Five royal portraits **Edge:** Reeded **Size:** 38.6 mm.

| Date | Mintage | F | VF | XF | Unc | BU |
|---|---|---|---|---|---|---|
| 2000 Proof | 20,000 | Value: 47.50 | | | | |

**5 POUNDS** **KM# 106** **Weight:** 28.2600 g. **Composition:** Copper-Nickel **Subject:** Queen Victoria Centennial **Obverse:** Queen Elizabeth's portrait **Reverse:** Queen Victoria's portrait **Edge:** Reeded **Size:** 38.6 mm.

| Date | Mintage | F | VF | XF | Unc | BU |
|---|---|---|---|---|---|---|
| 2001 | — | — | — | — | 7.50 | — |
| 2001 Proof | 30,000 | Value: 20.00 | | | | |

**5 POUNDS** **KM# 106a** **Weight:** 28.2800 g. **Composition:** 0.9250 Silver .8410 oz. ASW **Subject:** Queen Victoria 1837-1901 **Obverse:** Queen's portrait **Reverse:** Queen Victoria's portrait **Edge:** Reeded **Size:** 38.6 mm.

| Date | Mintage | F | VF | XF | Unc | BU |
|---|---|---|---|---|---|---|
| 2001 Proof | 10,000 | Value: 47.50 | | | | |

**5 POUNDS** **KM# 108** **Weight:** 28.0000 g. **Composition:** Copper-Nickel **Subject:** Queen Elizabeth's 75th Birthday **Obverse:** Queen Elizabeth's portrait **Reverse:** Queen's portrait in wreath **Edge:** Reeded **Size:** 38.6 mm.

| Date | Mintage | F | VF | XF | Unc | BU |
|---|---|---|---|---|---|---|
| 2001 | — | — | — | — | 6.00 | — |

**5 POUNDS** **KM# 108a** **Weight:** 28.2800 g. **Composition:** 0.9250 Silver .8410 oz. ASW **Subject:** Queen's 75th Birthday **Obverse:** Queen's portrait **Reverse:** Queen's portrait in wreath **Edge:** Reeded **Size:** 38.6 mm.

| Date | Mintage | F | VF | XF | Unc | BU |
|---|---|---|---|---|---|---|
| 2001 Proof | — | Value: 55.00 | | | | |

**5 POUNDS** **KM# 118** **Weight:** 1.1300 g. **Composition:** 0.9170 Gold .0333 oz. AGW **Subject:** Queen's 75th Birthday **Obverse:** Queen's portrait **Reverse:** Queen's portrait in wreath **Edge:** Reeded **Size:** 13.9 mm.

| Date | Mintage | F | VF | XF | Unc | BU |
|---|---|---|---|---|---|---|
| 2001 Proof | — | Value: 57.50 | | | | |

**5 POUNDS** **KM# 117** **Weight:** 1.1300 g. **Composition:** 0.9170 Gold .0333 oz. AGW **Subject:** Queen Victoria 1837-1901 **Obverse:** Queen's portrait **Reverse:** Queen Victoria's portrait **Edge:** Reeded **Size:** 13.9 mm.

| Date | Mintage | F | VF | XF | Unc | BU |
|---|---|---|---|---|---|---|
| 2001 Proof | — | Value: 55.00 | | | | |

**5 POUNDS** **KM# 114** **Weight:** 28.2800 g. **Composition:** Copper-Nickel **Subject:** 19th Century Monarchy **Obverse:** Queen's portrait **Reverse:** Four portraits **Edge:** Reeded **Size:** 38.6 mm.

| Date | Mintage | F | VF | XF | Unc | BU |
|---|---|---|---|---|---|---|
| 2001 | — | — | — | — | 11.50 | — |

**5 POUNDS** **KM# 114a** **Weight:** 28.2800 g. **Composition:** 0.9250 Silver .8410 oz. ASW **Edge:** Reeded **Size:** 38.6 mm.

| Date | Mintage | F | VF | XF | Unc | BU |
|---|---|---|---|---|---|---|
| 2001 Proof | — | Value: 55.00 | | | | |

**5 POUNDS** KM# 115 **Weight:** 1.1300 g. **Composition:** 0.9170 Gold .0333 oz. AGW **Subject:** 19th Century Monarchy **Obverse:** Queen's portrait **Reverse:** Four portraits **Edge:** Reeded **Size:** 13.9 mm.

| Date | Mintage | F | VF | XF | Unc | BU |
|---|---|---|---|---|---|---|
| 2001 Proof | — | Value: 57.50 | | | | |

**10 POUNDS** KM# 57 **Weight:** 3.1300 g. **Composition:** 0.9990 Gold .1005 oz. AGW **Subject:** 50th Anniversary - Normandy Invasion

| Date | Mintage | F | VF | XF | Unc | BU |
|---|---|---|---|---|---|---|
| ND(1994) | Est. 500 | Value: 75.00 | | | | |

**Note:** Sold only in sets

**10 POUNDS** KM# 62 **Weight:** 3.1300 g. **Composition:** 0.9990 Gold .1005 oz. AGW **Subject:** 50th Anniversary of Liberation

| Date | Mintage | F | VF | XF | Unc | BU |
|---|---|---|---|---|---|---|
| ND(1995) Proof | Est. 500 | Value: 75.00 | | | | |

**Note:** Sold only in sets

**10 POUNDS** KM# 104 **Weight:** 141.7500 g. **Composition:** 0.9990 Silver 4.5528 oz. ASW **Subject:** Century of Monarchy **Obverse:** Queen's portrait **Reverse:** Five royal portraits **Edge:** Reeded **Size:** 65 mm.

| Date | Mintage | F | VF | XF | Unc | BU |
|---|---|---|---|---|---|---|
| 2000 Proof | 950 | Value: 200 | | | | |

**10 POUNDS** KM# 116 **Weight:** 141.7500 g. **Composition:** 0.9990 Silver 4.5528 oz. ASW **Subject:** 19th Century Monarchy **Obverse:** Queen's portrait **Reverse:** Four portraits **Edge:** Reeded **Size:** 65 mm.

| Date | Mintage | F | VF | XF | Unc | BU |
|---|---|---|---|---|---|---|
| 2001 Proof | — | Value: 200 | | | | |

**25 POUNDS** KM# 58 **Weight:** 7.8100 g. **Composition:** 0.9990 Gold .2509 oz. AGW **Subject:** 50th Anniversary - Normandy Invasion

| Date | Mintage | F | VF | XF | Unc | BU |
|---|---|---|---|---|---|---|
| ND(1994) | Est. 500 | — | — | — | 200 | — |
| ND(1994) Proof | Est. 500 | Value: 185 | | | | |

**Note:** Sold only in sets

**25 POUNDS** KM# 63 **Weight:** 7.8100 g. **Composition:** 0.9990 Gold .2509 oz. AGW **Subject:** 50th Anniversary of Liberation

| Date | Mintage | F | VF | XF | Unc | BU |
|---|---|---|---|---|---|---|
| ND(1995) In proof sets only | Est. 500 | Value: 185 | | | | |

**25 POUNDS** KM# 69 **Weight:** 7.8100 g. **Composition:** 0.9990 Gold .2509 oz. AGW **Subject:** European Football **Reverse:** Soccer ball and European map **Note:** Similar to 5 Pounds, KM#68.

| Date | Mintage | F | VF | XF | Unc | BU |
|---|---|---|---|---|---|---|
| 1996 Proof | 1,500 | Value: 175 | | | | |

**25 POUNDS** KM# 72 **Weight:** 7.8100 g. **Composition:** 0.9990 Gold .2509 oz. AGW **Subject:** Queen Elizabeth II's Golden Wedding Anniversary **Note:** Similar to Pound, KM#70.

| Date | Mintage | F | VF | XF | Unc | BU |
|---|---|---|---|---|---|---|
| 1997 Proof | Est. 5,000 | Value: 275 | | | | |

**25 POUNDS** KM# 85 **Weight:** 7.8100 g. **Composition:** 0.9990 Gold .2509 oz. AGW **Subject:** 80th Anniversary - Royal Air Force **Obverse:** Rank-Broadley portrait of Queen Elizabeth II **Reverse:** Three Spitfires and RAF Benevolent Fund Crest

| Date | Mintage | F | VF | XF | Unc | BU |
|---|---|---|---|---|---|---|
| 1998 Proof | Est. 2,500 | Value: 175 | | | | |

**25 POUNDS** KM# 103 **Weight:** 7.8100 g. **Composition:** 0.9170 Gold .2303 oz. AGW **Subject:** Queen Mother's 100th Birthday **Obverse:** Queen's portrait **Reverse:** Queen Mother's portrait **Edge:** Reeded **Size:** 22 mm.

| Date | Mintage | F | VF | XF | Unc | BU |
|---|---|---|---|---|---|---|
| 2000 Proof | 5,000 | Value: 230 | | | | |

**25 POUNDS** KM# 107 **Weight:** 7.8100 g. **Composition:** 0.9170 Gold .2303 oz. AGW **Subject:** Queen Victoria Centennial **Obverse:** Queen Elizabeth's portrait **Reverse:** Queen Victoria's portrait **Edge:** Reeded **Size:** 22 mm.

| Date | Mintage | F | VF | XF | Unc | BU |
|---|---|---|---|---|---|---|
| 2001 Proof | 2,500 | Value: 267 | | | | |

**25 POUNDS** KM# 112 **Weight:** 7.8100 g. **Composition:** 0.9170 Gold .2303 oz. AGW **Subject:** Queen's 75th Birthday **Obverse:** Queen's portrait **Reverse:** Queen's portrait in wreath **Edge:** Reeded **Size:** 22 mm.

| Date | Mintage | F | VF | XF | Unc | BU |
|---|---|---|---|---|---|---|
| 2001 Proof | — | Value: 230 | | | | |

**50 POUNDS** KM# 59 **Weight:** 15.6100 g. **Composition:** 0.9990 Gold .5014 oz. AGW **Subject:** 50th Anniversary - Normandy Invasion

| Date | Mintage | F | VF | XF | Unc | BU |
|---|---|---|---|---|---|---|
| ND(1994) In proof sets only | Est. 500 | Value: 365 | | | | |

**50 POUNDS** KM# 64 **Weight:** 15.6100 g. **Composition:** 0.9990 Gold .5014 oz. AGW **Subject:** 50th Anniversary of Liberation

| Date | Mintage | F | VF | XF | Unc | BU |
|---|---|---|---|---|---|---|
| ND(1995) In proof sets only | Est. 500 | Value: 365 | | | | |

**100 POUNDS** KM# 60 **Weight:** 31.2100 g. **Composition:** 0.9990 Gold 1.0025 oz. AGW **Subject:** 50th Anniversary - Normandy Invasion

| Date | Mintage | F | VF | XF | Unc | BU |
|---|---|---|---|---|---|---|
| ND(1994) In proof sets only | Est. 500 | Value: 725 | | | | |

**100 POUNDS** KM# 65 **Weight:** 31.2100 g. **Composition:** 0.9990 Gold 1.0025 oz. AGW **Subject:** 50th Anniversary of Liberation

| Date | Mintage | F | VF | XF | Unc | BU |
|---|---|---|---|---|---|---|
| ND(1995) In proof sets only | Est. 500 | Value: 725 | | | | |

## PIEFORTS

| KM# | Date | Mintage | Identification | Mkt Val |
|---|---|---|---|---|
| P1 | 1981 | 500 | Pound. 16.0000 g. KM#37a. | 265 |
| P2 | 2000 | 10,000 | 50 Pence. 0.9250 Silver. 16.2000 g. KM#105a. | 55.00 |

## MINT SETS

| KM# | Date | Mintage | Identification | Issue Price | Mkt Val |
|---|---|---|---|---|---|
| MS1 | 1985 (8) | 10,000 | KM40-41, 42.1, 43-47 | 8.75 | 12.50 |
| MS2 | 1985 (7) | — | KM40-41, 42.1, 43-46 | — | — |
| MS3 | 1986 (7) | 5,000 | KM40-46 | 8.75 | 6.50 |
| MS4 | 1987 (7) | 7,500 | KM40-46 | 11.00 | 6.50 |
| MS5 | 1988 (7) | 5,000 | KM40-46 | 13.00 | 15.00 |
| MS6 | 1989 (7) | 5,000 | KM40-46 | 17.00 | 16.50 |
| MS7 | 1990 (8) | 2,520 | KM40-41, 42.1-42.2, 43-46 | 16.00 | 20.00 |
| MS8 | 1992 (7) | 1,500 | KM40-41, 42.2, 43-46 | 22.50 | 25.00 |
| MS9 | 1997 (7) | — | KM40-41, 42.2, 43-46 | — | 25.00 |

## PROOF SETS

| KM# | Date | Mintage | Identification | Issue Price | Mkt Val |
|---|---|---|---|---|---|
| PS2 | 1885H (4) | — | KM5a, 7a, 8a, 10a | — | 1,150 |
| PS1 | 1885H (4) | — | KM5, 7, 8, 10 | — | 725 |
| PS3 | 1902H (4) | — | KM5, 7-8, 10 | — | 1,000 |
| PS4 | 1910H (2) | — | KM5, 7 | — | 500 |
| PS5 | 1956 (6) | 1,050 | KM15-17 double set | — | 22.50 |
| PS6 | 1966 (4) | 10,000 | KM15-16, 18, 19 | — | 8.50 |
| PS7 | 1971 (6) | 10,000 | KM20-25 | 16.00 | 9.50 |
| PS8 | 1979 (6) | 4,963 | KM27-30, 33-34 | 25.00 | 11.50 |
| PS9 | 1981 (6) | 10,000 | KM27-30, 34, 37 | 29.00 | 20.00 |
| PS10 | 1985 (8) | 2,500 | KM40-47 | 29.75 | 30.00 |
| PS11 | 1986 (8) | 2,500 | KM40-46, 48 | 35.00 | 32.00 |
| PS12 | 1987 (8) | 2,500 | KM40-46, 49 | 33.00 | 32.00 |
| PS13 | 1988 (8) | 2,500 | KM40-46, 50 | 45.00 | 32.00 |
| PS14 | 1989 (8) | 2,500 | KM40-46, 51 | 45.00 | 32.00 |
| PS15 | 1990 (9) | 700 | KM40-41, 42.1-42.2, 43-46 | 46.00 | 46.00 |
| PS16 | 1992 (7) | 500 | KM40-41, 42.2, 43.2, 44-46 | 52.50 | 55.00 |
| PS17 | 1994 (4) | 500 | KM57-60 | 1,595 | 1,350 |
| PS18 | ND (1995) (4) | 500 | KM62-65 | 1,600 | 1,350 |
| PS19 | 1996 (2) | 1,500 | KM68a, 69 | — | 275 |
| PS20 | 1997 (3) | — | KM70, 71a, 72 | — | 420 |
| PS21 | 1997 (4) | — | KM73, 74a, 75-76 | 181 | 215 |

The Republic of Guinea, situated on the Atlantic Coast of Africa between Sierra Leone and Guinea-Bissau, has an area of 94,964 sq. mi. (245,860 sq. km.) and a population of 6.4 million. Capital: Conakry. Although Guinea contains one-third of the world's reserves of bauxite and significant deposits of iron ore, gold and diamonds, the economy is still dependent on agriculture, aluminum, bananas, copra and coffee are exported.

The coast of Guinea was known to Portuguese navigators of the 15th century but was seldom visited by European traders of the 16th-18th centuries because of its dangerous coastal waters. French penetration of the area began in the mid-19th century with the entering into of protectorate treaties with several of the coastal chiefs. After a long struggle with Guinea's native leader Samory Toure, France secured the area and until 1890 administered it as a part of Senegal. In 1895 the colony (Guinee Francais) became an autonomous part of the federation of French West Africa. The inhabitants were extended French citizenship in 1946 when the colony became an overseas territory of the French Union. Guinea became an independent republic on Oct. 2, 1958, when it declined to enter the new French Community.

**MONETARY SYSTEM**
100 Centimes = 1 Franc

# REPUBLIC

## DECIMAL COINAGE

**FRANC KM# 4 Composition:** Copper-Nickel **Obverse:** Ahmed Sekou Toure

| Date | Mintage | F | VF | XF | Unc | BU |
|---|---|---|---|---|---|---|
| 1962 | — | 1.25 | 2.00 | 3.50 | 7.00 | — |
| 1962 Proof | — | Value: 50.00 | | | | |

**5 FRANCS KM# 1 Composition:** Aluminum-Bronze **Obverse:** Ahmed Sekou Toure

| Date | Mintage | F | VF | XF | Unc | BU |
|---|---|---|---|---|---|---|
| 1959 | — | 2.75 | 4.75 | 9.00 | 22.50 | — |

**5 FRANCS KM# 5 Composition:** Copper-Nickel **Note:** Mule with two obverses exists.

| Date | Mintage | F | VF | XF | Unc | BU |
|---|---|---|---|---|---|---|
| 1962 | — | 1.25 | 2.00 | 3.00 | 6.50 | — |
| 1962 Proof | — | Value: 70.00 | | | | |

**10 FRANCS KM# 2 Composition:** Aluminum-Bronze **Obverse:** Ahmed Sekou Toure

| Date | Mintage | F | VF | XF | Unc | BU |
|---|---|---|---|---|---|---|
| 1959 | — | 5.00 | 10.00 | 20.00 | 45.00 | — |

**10 FRANCS KM# 6 Composition:** Copper-Nickel **Obverse:** Ahmed Sekou Toure

| Date | Mintage | F | VF | XF | Unc | BU |
|---|---|---|---|---|---|---|
| 1962 | — | 1.75 | 2.75 | 6.00 | 12.00 | — |
| 1962 Proof | — | Value: 85.00 | | | | |

**25 FRANCS KM# 3 Composition:** Aluminum-Bronze **Obverse:** Ahmed Sekou Toure

| Date | Mintage | F | VF | XF | Unc | BU |
|---|---|---|---|---|---|---|
| 1959 | — | 9.00 | 16.00 | 30.00 | 90.00 | — |

**25 FRANCS KM# 7 Composition:** Copper-Nickel **Obverse:** Ahmed Sekou Toure

| Date | Mintage | F | VF | XF | Unc | BU |
|---|---|---|---|---|---|---|
| 1962 | — | 2.50 | 4.00 | 7.50 | 15.00 | — |
| 1962 Proof | — | Value: 120 | | | | |

**50 FRANCS KM# 8 Composition:** Copper-Nickel **Obverse:** Ahmed Sekou Toure **Note:** Not released into circulation.

| Date | Mintage | F | VF | XF | Unc | BU |
|---|---|---|---|---|---|---|
| 1969 | 4,000,000 | — | — | 35.00 | 55.00 | — |

**100 FRANCS KM# 9 Weight:** 5.6500 g. **Composition:** 0.9990 Silver .1816 oz. ASW **Subject:** 10th Anniversary of Independence **Obverse:** Dr. Martin Luther King

| Date | Mintage | F | VF | XF | Unc | BU |
|---|---|---|---|---|---|---|
| 1969 Proof | 9,700 | Value: 7.00 | | | | |
| 1970 Proof | Inc. above | Value: 7.00 | | | | |

**100 FRANCS KM# 41 Composition:** Copper-Nickel **Obverse:** Ahmed Sekou Toure **Note:** Not released into circulation.

| Date | Mintage | F | VF | XF | Unc | BU |
|---|---|---|---|---|---|---|
| 1971 | 2,585,000 | — | — | 22.50 | 45.00 | — |

**200 FRANCS KM# 10 Weight:** 11.7000 g. **Composition:** 0.9990 Silver .3761 oz. ASW **Subject:** 10th Anniversary of Independence **Obverse:** John and Robert Kennedy

| Date | Mintage | F | VF | XF | Unc | BU |
|---|---|---|---|---|---|---|
| 1969 Proof | 10,000 | Value: 10.00 | | | | |
| 1970 Proof | Inc. above | Value: 10.00 | | | | |

**200 FRANCS KM# 11 Weight:** 11.7000 g. **Composition:** 0.9990 Silver .3761 oz. ASW **Subject:** 10th Anniversary of Independence **Obverse:** Almamy Toure

| Date | Mintage | F | VF | XF | Unc | BU |
|---|---|---|---|---|---|---|
| 1969 Proof | 6,100 | Value: 10.00 | | | | |
| 1970 Proof | Inc. above | Value: 10.00 | | | | |

**250 FRANCS KM# 12 Weight:** 14.5300 g. **Composition:** 0.9990 Silver .4671 oz. ASW **Subject:** 10th Anniversary of Independence **Obverse:** Lunar landing

| Date | Mintage | F | VF | XF | Unc | BU |
|---|---|---|---|---|---|---|
| 1969 Proof | 26,000 | Value: 11.50 | | | | |
| 1970 Proof | Inc. above | Value: 11.50 | | | | |

**250 FRANCS KM# 13 Weight:** 14.5300 g. **Composition:** 0.9990 Silver .4671 oz. ASW **Subject:** 10th Anniversary of Independence **Obverse:** Alpha Yaya Diallo

| Date | Mintage | F | VF | XF | Unc | BU |
|---|---|---|---|---|---|---|
| 1969 Proof | 6,100 | Value: 11.50 | | | | |
| 1970 Proof | Inc. above | Value: 11.50 | | | | |

**250 FRANCS** **KM# 14** **Weight:** 14.5300 g. **Composition:** 0.9990 Silver .4671 oz. ASW **Subject:** 10th Anniversary of Independence **Obverse:** Apollo XIII

| Date | Mintage | F | VF | XF | Unc | BU |
|---|---|---|---|---|---|---|
| 1969 Proof | 4,450 | Value: 17.50 | | | | |
| 1970 Proof | Inc. above | Value: 17.50 | | | | |

**250 FRANCS** **KM# 21** **Weight:** 14.5300 g. **Composition:** 0.9990 Silver .4671 oz. ASW **Subject:** 10th Anniversary of Independence **Obverse:** Spacecraft Soyuz

| Date | Mintage | F | VF | XF | Unc | BU |
|---|---|---|---|---|---|---|
| 1970 Proof | 3,500 | Value: 20.00 | | | | |

**500 FRANCS** **KM# 15** **Weight:** 29.0800 g. **Composition:** 0.9990 Silver .9349 oz. ASW **Subject:** 10th Anniversary of Independence **Obverse:** Munich Olympics

| Date | Mintage | F | VF | XF | Unc | BU |
|---|---|---|---|---|---|---|
| 1969 Proof | 7,200 | Value: 32.50 | | | | |
| 1970 Proof | 1,900 | Value: 42.50 | | | | |

**500 FRANCS** **KM# 16** **Weight:** 29.0800 g. **Composition:** 0.9990 Silver .9349 oz. ASW **Subject:** 10th Anniversary of Independence **Obverse:** Oiseaux Dancers **Reverse:** Similar to KM#15

| Date | Mintage | F | VF | XF | Unc | BU |
|---|---|---|---|---|---|---|
| 1969 Proof | 7,150 | Value: 35.00 | | | | |
| 1970 Proof | — | Value: 45.00 | | | | |

**500 FRANCS** **KM# 22** **Weight:** 29.0800 g. **Composition:** 0.9990 Silver .9349 oz. ASW **Subject:** 10th Anniversary of Independence **Obverse:** Ikhnaton **Reverse:** Similar to KM#15

| Date | Mintage | F | VF | XF | Unc | BU |
|---|---|---|---|---|---|---|
| 1970 Proof | 4,180 | Value: 30.00 | | | | |

**500 FRANCS** **KM# 23** **Weight:** 29.0800 g. **Composition:** 0.9990 Silver .9349 oz. ASW **Subject:** 10th Anniversary of Independence **Obverse:** Chephren **Reverse:** Similar to KM#15

| Date | Mintage | F | VF | XF | Unc | BU |
|---|---|---|---|---|---|---|
| 1970 Proof | 4,150 | Value: 30.00 | | | | |

**500 FRANCS** **KM# 24** **Weight:** 29.0800 g. **Composition:** 0.9990 Silver .9349 oz. ASW **Subject:** 10th Anniversary of Independence **Obverse:** Cleopatra **Reverse:** Similar to KM#15

| Date | Mintage | F | VF | XF | Unc | BU |
|---|---|---|---|---|---|---|
| 1970 Proof | 5,250 | Value: 35.00 | | | | |

**500 FRANCS** **KM# 25** **Weight:** 29.0800 g. **Composition:** 0.9990 Silver .9349 oz. ASW **Subject:** 10th Anniversary of Independence **Obverse:** Queen Nefertiti **Reverse:** Similar to KM#15

| Date | Mintage | F | VF | XF | Unc | BU |
|---|---|---|---|---|---|---|
| 1970 Proof | 4,610 | Value: 35.00 | | | | |

**500 FRANCS** **KM# 26** **Weight:** 29.0800 g. **Composition:** 0.9990 Silver .9349 oz. ASW **Subject:** 10th Anniversary of Independence **Obverse:** Ramses III **Reverse:** Similar to KM#15

| Date | Mintage | F | VF | XF | Unc | BU |
|---|---|---|---|---|---|---|
| 1970 Proof | 4,330 | Value: 30.00 | | | | |

**500 FRANCS** **KM# 27** **Weight:** 29.0800 g. **Composition:** 0.9990 Silver .9349 oz. ASW **Subject:** 10th Anniversary of Independence **Obverse:** Tutankhamen **Reverse:** Similar to KM#15

| Date | Mintage | F | VF | XF | Unc | BU |
|---|---|---|---|---|---|---|
| 1970 Proof | 4,280 | Value: 37.50 | | | | |

**500 FRANCS** **KM# 28** **Weight:** 29.0800 g. **Composition:** 0.9990 Silver .9349 oz. ASW **Subject:** 10th Anniversary of Independence **Obverse:** Queen Teyi **Reverse:** Similar to KM#15

| Date | Mintage | F | VF | XF | Unc | BU |
|---|---|---|---|---|---|---|
| 1970 Proof | 4,120 | Value: 30.00 | | | | |

**500 FRANCS** KM# 29 **Weight:** 29.0800 g. **Composition:** 0.9990 Silver .9349 oz. ASW **Subject:** 10th Anniversary of Independence **Obverse:** Gamal Abdel Nasser **Reverse:** Similar to KM#15

| Date | Mintage | F | VF | XF | Unc | BU |
|---|---|---|---|---|---|---|
| 1970 Proof | 950 | Value: 55.00 | | | | |

**1000 FRANCS** KM# 17 **Weight:** 4.0000 g. **Composition:** 0.9000 Gold .1157 oz. AGW **Subject:** 10th Anniversary of Independence **Obverse:** John and Robert Kennedy

| Date | Mintage | F | VF | XF | Unc | BU |
|---|---|---|---|---|---|---|
| 1969 Proof | 6,600 | Value: 75.00 | | | | |
| 1970 Proof | Inc. above | Value: 75.00 | | | | |

**2000 FRANCS** KM# 18 **Weight:** 8.0000 g. **Composition:** 0.9000 Gold .2315 oz. AGW **Subject:** 10th Anniversary of Independence **Obverse:** Lunar landing

| Date | Mintage | F | VF | XF | Unc | BU |
|---|---|---|---|---|---|---|
| 1969 Proof | 15,000 | Value: 125 | | | | |

**2000 FRANCS** KM# 30 **Weight:** 8.0000 g. **Composition:** 0.9000 Gold .2315 oz. AGW **Subject:** 10th Anniversary of Independence **Obverse:** Apollo XIII

| Date | Mintage | F | VF | XF | Unc | BU |
|---|---|---|---|---|---|---|
| 1970 Proof | 1,775 | Value: 165 | | | | |

**2000 FRANCS** KM# 31 **Weight:** 8.0000 g. **Composition:** 0.9000 Gold .2315 oz. AGW **Subject:** 10th Anniversary of Independence **Obverse:** Spacecraft Soyuz, similar to 250 Francs, KM#21

| Date | Mintage | F | VF | XF | Unc | BU |
|---|---|---|---|---|---|---|
| 1970 Proof | 2,840 | Value: 150 | | | | |

**5000 FRANCS** KM# 32 **Weight:** 20.0000 g. **Composition:** 0.9000 Gold .5787 oz. AGW **Subject:** 10th Anniversary of Independence **Obverse:** Munich Olympics

| Date | Mintage | F | VF | XF | Unc | BU |
|---|---|---|---|---|---|---|
| 1969 Proof | 2,740 | Value: 250 | | | | |
| 1970 Proof | 500 | Value: 350 | | | | |

**5000 FRANCS** KM# 19 **Weight:** 20.0000 g. **Composition:** 0.9000 Gold .5787 oz. AGW **Subject:** 10th Anniversary of Independence **Obverse:** Gamal Abedel Nasser

| Date | Mintage | F | VF | XF | Unc | BU |
|---|---|---|---|---|---|---|
| 1970 Proof | 4,000 | Value: 325 | | | | |

**5000 FRANCS** KM# 33 **Weight:** 20.0000 g. **Composition:** 0.9000 Gold .5787 oz. AGW **Subject:** 10th Anniversary of Independence **Obverse:** Ikhnaton, similar to 500 Francs, KM#22

| Date | Mintage | F | VF | XF | Unc | BU |
|---|---|---|---|---|---|---|
| 1970 Proof | 685 | Value: 475 | | | | |

**5000 FRANCS** KM# 34 **Weight:** 20.0000 g. **Composition:** 0.9000 Gold .5787 oz. AGW **Subject:** 10th Anniversary of Independence **Obverse:** Chephren, similar to 500 Francs, KM#23

| Date | Mintage | F | VF | XF | Unc | BU |
|---|---|---|---|---|---|---|
| 1970 Proof | 675 | Value: 475 | | | | |

**5000 FRANCS** KM# 35 **Weight:** 20.0000 g. **Composition:** 0.9000 Gold .5787 oz. AGW **Subject:** 10th Anniversary of Independence **Obverse:** Cleopatra, similar to 500 Francs, KM#24

| Date | Mintage | F | VF | XF | Unc | BU |
|---|---|---|---|---|---|---|
| 1970 Proof | 789 | Value: 475 | | | | |

**5000 FRANCS** KM# 36 **Weight:** 20.0000 g. **Composition:** 0.9000 Gold .5787 oz. AGW **Subject:** 10th Anniversary of Independence **Obverse:** Queen Nefertiti, similar to 500 Francs, KM#25

| Date | Mintage | F | VF | XF | Unc | BU |
|---|---|---|---|---|---|---|
| 1970 Proof | 774 | Value: 475 | | | | |

**5000 FRANCS** KM# 37 **Weight:** 20.0000 g. **Composition:** 0.9000 Gold .5787 oz. AGW **Subject:** 10th Anniversary of Independence **Obverse:** Ramses III, similar to 500 Francs, KM#26

| Date | Mintage | F | VF | XF | Unc | BU |
|---|---|---|---|---|---|---|
| 1970 Proof | 695 | Value: 475 | | | | |

**5000 FRANCS** KM# 39 **Weight:** 20.0000 g. **Composition:** 0.9000 Gold .5787 oz. AGW **Subject:** 10th Anniversary of Independence **Obverse:** Queen Teyi, similar to 500 Francs, KM#28

| Date | Mintage | F | VF | XF | Unc | BU |
|---|---|---|---|---|---|---|
| 1970 Proof | 685 | Value: 475 | | | | |

**5000 FRANCS** KM# 40 **Weight:** 20.0000 g. **Composition:** 0.9000 Gold .5787 oz. AGW **Subject:** 10th Anniversary of Independence **Obverse:** Gamal Abdel Nasser, similar to 500 Francs, KM#29

| Date | Mintage | F | VF | XF | Unc | BU |
|---|---|---|---|---|---|---|
| 1970 Proof | 185 | Value: 600 | | | | |

**10000 FRANCS** KM# 20 **Weight:** 40.0000 g. **Composition:** 0.9000 Gold 1.1575 oz. AGW **Subject:** 10th Anniversary of Independence **Obverse:** Ahmed Sekou Toure **Reverse:** Similar to 5000 Francs, KM#19

| Date | Mintage | F | VF | XF | Unc | BU |
|---|---|---|---|---|---|---|
| 1969 Proof | 2,300 | Value: 750 | | | | |
| 1970 Proof | — | Value: 950 | | | | |

**20000 FRANCS** KM# 64 **Weight:** 31.4700 g. **Composition:** 0.9250 Silver .9359 oz. ASW **Subject:** 35th Anniversary of Guinea Franc **Reverse:** Woman planting palm tree

| Date | Mintage | F | VF | XF | Unc | BU |
|---|---|---|---|---|---|---|
| ND(1995) | Est. 5,000 | — | — | — | 40.00 | — |

## DECIMAL COINAGE

100 Cauris = 1 Syli

**50 CAURIS** KM# 42 **Composition:** Aluminum **Note:** Nkrumah

| Date | Mintage | F | VF | XF | Unc | BU |
|---|---|---|---|---|---|---|
| 1971 | — | 1.00 | 2.00 | 3.50 | 6.00 | — |

**SYLI** KM# 43 **Composition:** Aluminum

| Date | Mintage | F | VF | XF | Unc | BU |
|---|---|---|---|---|---|---|
| 1971 | — | 2.00 | 3.00 | 5.50 | 12.50 | — |

**2 SYLIS** KM# 44 **Composition:** Aluminum

| Date | Mintage | F | VF | XF | Unc | BU |
|---|---|---|---|---|---|---|
| 1971 | — | 1.00 | 2.00 | 4.00 | 8.00 | — |

**5 SYLI** KM# 45 **Composition:** Aluminum

| Date | Mintage | F | VF | XF | Unc | BU |
|---|---|---|---|---|---|---|
| 1971 | — | 1.25 | 2.25 | 4.50 | 9.00 | — |

**500 SYLI** KM# 46 **Weight:** 40.0000 g. **Composition:** 0.9250 Silver 1.1897 oz. ASW **Obverse:** Miriam Makeba

| Date | Mintage | F | VF | XF | Unc | BU |
|---|---|---|---|---|---|---|
| 1977 | 500 | — | — | — | 100 | — |
| 1977 Proof | 500 | Value: 125 | | | | |

**500 SYLI** KM# 47 **Weight:** 40.0000 g. **Composition:** 0.9250 Silver 1.1897 oz. ASW **Obverse:** Patrice Lumumba **Reverse:** Similar to KM#46

| Date | Mintage | F | VF | XF | Unc | BU |
|---|---|---|---|---|---|---|
| 1977 | 250 | — | — | — | 150 | — |
| 1977 Proof | 150 | Value: 200 | | | | |

**1000 SYLI** KM# 48 **Weight:** 2.9300 g. **Composition:** 0.9000 Gold .0847 oz. AGW **Obverse:** Miriam Makeba **Reverse:** Similar to 2000 Sylis, KM#50

| Date | Mintage | F | VF | XF | Unc | BU |
|---|---|---|---|---|---|---|
| 1977 | 300 | — | — | — | 80.00 | — |
| 1977 Proof | 250 | Value: 90.00 | | | | |

**1000 SYLI** KM# 49 **Weight:** 2.9300 g. **Composition:** 0.9000 Gold .0847 oz. AGW **Obverse:** Nkrumah **Reverse:** Similar to 2000 Sylis, KM#50

| Date | Mintage | F | VF | XF | Unc | BU |
|---|---|---|---|---|---|---|
| 1977 | 150 | — | — | — | 100 | — |
| 1977 Proof | 150 | Value: 115 | | | | |

**2000 SYLI** KM# 50 **Weight:** 5.8700 g. **Composition:** 0.9000 Gold .1698 oz. AGW **Obverse:** Mao Tse Tung

| Date | Mintage | F | VF | XF | Unc | BU |
|---|---|---|---|---|---|---|
| 1977 | 200 | — | — | — | 200 | — |
| 1977 Proof | 200 | Value: 250 | | | | |

**2000 SYLI** KM# 51 **Weight:** 5.8700 g. **Composition:** 0.9000 Gold .1698 oz. AGW **Obverse:** Sekou Toure

| Date | Mintage | F | VF | XF | Unc | BU |
|---|---|---|---|---|---|---|
| 1977 | 100 | — | — | — | 200 | — |
| 1977 Proof | 50 | Value: 275 | | | | |

## REFORM COINAGE

**FRANC** KM# 56 **Composition:** Brass Clad Steel

| Date | Mintage | F | VF | XF | Unc | BU |
|---|---|---|---|---|---|---|
| 1985 | — | 0.10 | 0.20 | 0.40 | 1.00 | — |

**5 FRANCS** KM# 53 **Composition:** Brass Clad Steel

| Date | Mintage | F | VF | XF | Unc | BU |
|---|---|---|---|---|---|---|
| 1985 | — | 0.10 | 0.20 | 0.40 | 1.00 | — |

**10 FRANCS** KM# 52 **Composition:** Brass Clad Steel

| Date | Mintage | F | VF | XF | Unc | BU |
|---|---|---|---|---|---|---|
| 1985 | — | 0.20 | 0.40 | 0.80 | 1.25 | — |

**25 FRANCS** KM# 60 **Composition:** Brass

| Date | Mintage | F | VF | XF | Unc | BU |
|---|---|---|---|---|---|---|
| 1987 | — | 0.20 | 0.40 | 0.85 | 1.75 | — |

**50 FRANCS** KM# 63 **Composition:** Copper-Nickel

| Date | Mintage | F | VF | XF | Unc | BU |
|---|---|---|---|---|---|---|
| 1994 | — | 0.30 | 0.60 | 1.25 | 2.75 | — |

**100 FRANCS** KM# 57 **Weight:** 16.0000 g. **Composition:** 0.9990 Silver .5144 oz. ASW **Subject:** 1992 Olympics **Reverse:** Discus thrower

| Date | Mintage | F | VF | XF | Unc | BU |
|---|---|---|---|---|---|---|
| 1988 Matte | Est. 5,000 | — | — | — | 50.00 | — |

**200 FRANCS** KM# 58 **Weight:** 16.0000 g. **Composition:** 0.9990 Silver .5144 oz. ASW **Subject:** 1992 Olympics **Reverse:** Basketball players

| Date | Mintage | F | VF | XF | Unc | BU |
|---|---|---|---|---|---|---|
| 1988 Matte | Est. 5,000 | — | — | — | 55.00 | — |

**300 FRANCS** KM# 59 **Weight:** 16.0000 g. **Composition:** 0.9990 Silver .5144 oz. ASW **Subject:** 1992 Olympics **Reverse:** Stadium

| Date | Mintage | F | VF | XF | Unc | BU |
|---|---|---|---|---|---|---|
| 1988 | Est. 5,000 | — | — | — | 65.00 | — |

**10000 FRANCS** KM# 61 **Weight:** 25.0000 g. **Composition:** 0.9990 Silver .8038 oz. ASW **Subject:** 30th Anniversary of Currency **Reverse:** Palm branches and denomination

| Date | Mintage | F | VF | XF | Unc | BU |
|---|---|---|---|---|---|---|
| ND(1990) Proof | 1,000 | Value: 75.00 | | | | |

**10000 FRANCS** KM# 62 **Weight:** 15.9760 g. **Composition:** 0.9170 Gold .4708 oz. AGW **Subject:** 30th Anniversary of Currency **Obverse:** Arms with dates on each side **Reverse:** Palm branches and denomination

| Date | Mintage | F | VF | XF | Unc | BU |
|---|---|---|---|---|---|---|
| 1990 Proof | Est. 200 | — | — | — | — | — |

## MEDALLIC COINAGE

**5000 FRANCS** KM# 38 **Weight:** 20.0000 g. **Composition:** 0.9000 Gold .5787 oz. AGW **Subject:** 10th Anniversary of Independence **Obverse:** Tutankhamen, similar to 500 Francs, KM#27

| Date | Mintage | F | VF | XF | Unc | BU |
|---|---|---|---|---|---|---|
| 1970 Proof | 675 | Value: 475 | | | | |

**200 SYLI** KM# M1 **Composition:** Copper Nickel **Subject:** International Games **Reverse:** Race walking

| Date | Mintage | F | VF | XF | Unc | BU |
|---|---|---|---|---|---|---|
| 1984 Plain proof | — | Value: 13.50 | | | | |
| 1984 Frosted pr | — | Value: 18.50 | | | | |

**500 SYLI** KM# M2 **Weight:** 31.0600 g. **Composition:** 0.9990 Silver .9976 oz. ASW **Subject:** International Games **Reverse:** Race walking

| Date | Mintage | F | VF | XF | Unc | BU |
|---|---|---|---|---|---|---|
| 1984 Proof | — | Value: 45.00 | | | | |

## TRIAL STRIKES

| KM# | Date | Mintage | Identification | Mkt Val |
|---|---|---|---|---|
| TS1 | (1969) | — | 100 Francs. KM#9. | 30.00 |
| TS2 | (1969) | — | 200 Francs. KM#11. | 30.00 |
| TS3 | (1969) | — | 250 Francs. KM#13. | 35.00 |
| TS4 | (1969) | — | 500 Francs. KM#16. | 55.00 |

| KM# | Date | Mintage | Identification | Mkt Val |
|---|---|---|---|---|
| TS5 | (1969) | — | 1000 Francs. Goldine. KM#17. | 65.00 |

| KM# | Date | Mintage | Identification | Mkt Val |
|---|---|---|---|---|
| TS6 | (1984) | — | 200 Syli. Lead. M1. | 35.00 |

## MINT SETS

| KM# | Date | Mintage | Identification | Issue Price | Mkt Val |
|---|---|---|---|---|---|
| MS1 | 1977 (6) | — | KM46-51 | — | 830 |
| MS2 | 1988 (3) | 5,000 | KM57-59 | 150 | 170 |

## PROOF SETS

| KM# | Date | Mintage | Identification | Issue Price | Mkt Val |
|---|---|---|---|---|---|
| PS1 | 1962 (4) | — | KM4-7 | — | 325 |
| PS2 | 1969 (7) | — | KM9-13,15-16 | 62.50 | 120 |
| PS3 | 1969 (4) | — | KM17-20 | 236 | 1,275 |
| PS4 | 1970 (7) | — | | 62.50 | 140 |
| PS5 | 1970 (7) | — | KM22-28 | 85.00 | 265 |
| PS7 | 1970 (3) | — | KM12, 14, 21 | 29.95 | 50.00 |
| PS6 | 1970 (7) | — | KM33-39 | 440 | 3,325 |
| PS8 | 1977 (6) | — | KM46-51. Coins were issued in sets made per order containing from 1 to 11 different coins | — | 1,050 |

# GUINEA-BISSAU

The Republic of Guinea-Bissau, formerly Portuguese Guinea, an overseas province on the west coast of Africa between Senegal and Guinea, has an area of 13,948 sq. mi. (36,120sq. km.) and a population of 1.1 million. Capital: Bissau. The country has undeveloped deposits of oil and bauxite. Peanuts, oil-palm kernels and hides are exported.

Portuguese Guinea was discovered by Portuguese navigator, Nuno Tristao, in 1446. Trading rights in the area were granted to Cape Verde islanders but few prominent posts were established before 1851, and they were principally coastal installations. The chief export of this colony's early period was slaves for South America, a practice that adversely affected trade with the native people and retarded subjection of the interior. Territorial disputes with France delayed final demarcation of the colony's frontiers until 1905.

The African Party for the Independence of Guinea-Bissau was founded in 1956, and several years later began a guerrilla warfare that grew in effectiveness until 1974,when the rebels controlled most of the colony. Portugal's costly overseas wars in her African territories resulted in a military coup in Portugal in April 1974, which appreciably brightened the prospects for freedom for Guinea-Bissau. In August 1974, the Lisbon government signed an agreement granting independence to Portuguese Guinea effective Sept. 10, 1974. The new republic took the name of Guinea-Bissau.

**RULERS**

Portuguese until 1974

# PORTUGUESE GUINEA

## DECIMAL COINAGE

**5 CENTAVOS** KM# 1 **Composition:** Bronze

| Date | Mintage | F | VF | XF | Unc | BU |
|---|---|---|---|---|---|---|
| 1933 | 100,000 | 30.00 | 60.00 | 90.00 | 160 | — |

**10 CENTAVOS** KM# 2 **Composition:** Bronze

| Date | Mintage | F | VF | XF | Unc | BU |
|---|---|---|---|---|---|---|
| 1933 | 250,000 | 28.00 | 85.00 | 500 | 1,000 | — |

**10 CENTAVOS** KM# 12 **Composition:** Aluminum

| Date | Mintage | F | VF | XF | Unc | BU |
|---|---|---|---|---|---|---|
| 1973 | 100,000 | 4.00 | 8.00 | 15.00 | 30.00 | — |

**20 CENTAVOS** KM# 3 **Composition:** Bronze

| Date | Mintage | F | VF | XF | Unc | BU |
|---|---|---|---|---|---|---|
| 1933 | 350,000 | 3.50 | 7.50 | 35.00 | 60.00 | — |

**20 CENTAVOS** KM# 13 **Composition:** Bronze

| Date | Mintage | F | VF | XF | Unc | BU |
|---|---|---|---|---|---|---|
| 1973 | 100,000 | 3.00 | 6.00 | 15.00 | 30.00 | — |

**50 CENTAVOS** KM# 4 **Composition:** Nickel-Bronze

| Date | Mintage | F | VF | XF | Unc | BU |
|---|---|---|---|---|---|---|
| 1933 | 600,000 | 12.00 | 50.00 | 200 | 450 | — |

**50 CENTAVOS** KM# 6 **Composition:** Bronze **Subject:** 500th Anniversary of Discovery

| Date | Mintage | F | VF | XF | Unc | BU |
|---|---|---|---|---|---|---|
| ND(1946) | 2,000,000 | 1.00 | 3.00 | 15.00 | 30.00 | — |

**50 CENTAVOS** KM# 8 **Composition:** Bronze

| Date | Mintage | F | VF | XF | Unc | BU |
|---|---|---|---|---|---|---|
| 1952 | 10,000,000 | 0.35 | 0.75 | 2.00 | 5.00 | — |

**ESCUDO** KM# 5 **Composition:** Nickel-Bronze

| Date | Mintage | F | VF | XF | Unc | BU |
|---|---|---|---|---|---|---|
| 1933 | 800,000 | 6.00 | 18.00 | 200 | 450 | — |

**ESCUDO** KM# 7 **Composition:** Bronze **Subject:** 500th Anniversary of Discovery

| Date | Mintage | F | VF | XF | Unc | BU |
|---|---|---|---|---|---|---|
| ND(1946) | 2,000,000 | 0.75 | 2.00 | 6.00 | 18.00 | — |

**ESCUDO** **KM# 14** **Composition:** Bronze

| Date | Mintage | F | VF | XF | Unc | BU |
|---|---|---|---|---|---|---|
| 1973 | 250,000 | 6.50 | 12.50 | 22.50 | 40.00 | — |

**2-1/2 ESCUDOS** **KM# 9** **Composition:** Copper-Nickel

| Date | Mintage | F | VF | XF | Unc | BU |
|---|---|---|---|---|---|---|
| 1952 | 3,010,000 | 0.50 | 1.50 | 3.00 | 7.00 | — |

**5 ESCUDOS** **KM# 15** **Composition:** Copper-Nickel

| Date | Mintage | F | VF | XF | Unc | BU |
|---|---|---|---|---|---|---|
| 1973 | 800,000 | 2.50 | 5.00 | 10.00 | 20.00 | — |

**10 ESCUDOS** **KM# 10** **Weight:** 5.0000 g. **Composition:** 0.7200 Silver .1157 oz. ASW

| Date | Mintage | F | VF | XF | Unc | BU |
|---|---|---|---|---|---|---|
| 1952 | 1,200,000 | 3.50 | 18.00 | 70.00 | 140 | — |

**10 ESCUDOS** **KM# 16** **Composition:** Copper-Nickel

| Date | Mintage | F | VF | XF | Unc | BU |
|---|---|---|---|---|---|---|
| 1973 | 1,700,000 | 2.50 | 10.00 | 20.00 | 40.00 | — |

**20 ESCUDOS** **KM# 11** **Weight:** 10.0000 g. **Composition:** 0.7200 Silver .2315 oz. ASW

| Date | Mintage | F | VF | XF | Unc | BU |
|---|---|---|---|---|---|---|
| 1952 | 750,000 | 5.00 | 15.00 | 45.00 | 90.00 | — |

# GUINEA-BISSAU

## DECIMAL COINAGE

**50 CENTAVOS** **KM# 17** **Composition:** Aluminum **Series:** F.A.O.

| Date | Mintage | F | VF | XF | Unc | BU |
|---|---|---|---|---|---|---|
| 1977 | 6,000,000 | 2.00 | 3.00 | 4.50 | 8.00 | — |

**PESO** **KM# 18** **Composition:** Aluminum-Bronze **Series:** F.A.O.

| Date | Mintage | F | VF | XF | Unc | BU |
|---|---|---|---|---|---|---|
| 1977 | 7,000,000 | 2.25 | 3.50 | 5.50 | 9.00 | — |

**2-1/2 PESOS** **KM# 19** **Composition:** Aluminum-Bronze **Series:** F.A.O.

| Date | Mintage | F | VF | XF | Unc | BU |
|---|---|---|---|---|---|---|
| 1977 | 4,000,000 | 2.25 | 4.50 | 6.50 | 10.00 | — |

**5 PESOS** **KM# 20** **Composition:** Copper-Nickel **Series:** F.A.O.

| Date | Mintage | F | VF | XF | Unc | BU |
|---|---|---|---|---|---|---|
| 1977 | 6,000,000 | 2.50 | 5.00 | 7.00 | 11.50 | — |

**20 PESOS** **KM# 21** **Composition:** Copper-Nickel **Series:** F.A.O.

| Date | Mintage | F | VF | XF | Unc | BU |
|---|---|---|---|---|---|---|
| 1977 | 2,500,000 | 4.00 | 6.50 | 11.50 | 18.00 | — |

**2000 PESOS** **KM# 28** **Composition:** Nickel Plated Steel **Reverse:** Olympics - Handball Player

| Date | Mintage | F | VF | XF | Unc | BU |
|---|---|---|---|---|---|---|
| 1991 | 5,000 | — | — | — | 17.50 | — |

**2000 PESOS** **KM# 38** **Composition:** Nickel Plated Steel **Subject:** 50th Anniversary - FAO **Obverse:** National emblem **Reverse:** Pineapple harvest

| Date | Mintage | F | VF | XF | Unc | BU |
|---|---|---|---|---|---|---|
| ND(1995) | — | — | — | — | 17.50 | — |

**10000 PESOS** **KM# 27** **Weight:** 16.0000 g. **Composition:** 0.9990 Silver .5144 oz. ASW **Reverse:** Nuno Tristad - Discovery of Guinea-Bissau

| Date | Mintage | F | VF | XF | Unc | BU |
|---|---|---|---|---|---|---|
| 1991 Proof | — | Value: 32.50 | | | | |

**10000 PESOS** **KM# 29** **Weight:** 11.9700 g. **Composition:** 0.9990 Silver .3848 oz. ASW **Reverse:** Soccer Player

| Date | Mintage | F | VF | XF | Unc | BU |
|---|---|---|---|---|---|---|
| 1991 | — | — | — | — | 32.00 | — |

**10000 PESOS** **KM# 30** **Weight:** 19.6700 g. **Composition:** 0.9990 Silver .6324 oz. ASW **Reverse:** XXV Olympics - Floor Exercise

| Date | Mintage | F | VF | XF | Unc | BU |
|---|---|---|---|---|---|---|
| 1992 Proof | Est. 10,000 | Value: 25.00 | | | | |

**10000 PESOS** KM# 31 **Weight:** 15.0000 g. **Composition:** 0.9990 Silver .4823 oz. ASW **Reverse:** Elephant Standing on Africa

| Date | Mintage | F | VF | XF | Unc | BU |
|---|---|---|---|---|---|---|
| 1993 Proof | — | Value: 28.00 | | | | |

**10000 PESOS** KM# 32 **Weight:** 15.0000 g. **Composition:** 0.9990 Silver .4823 oz. ASW **Reverse:** Prehistoric Life - Stegosaurus

| Date | Mintage | F | VF | XF | Unc | BU |
|---|---|---|---|---|---|---|
| 1993 Proof | — | Value: 27.50 | | | | |

**10000 PESOS** KM# 35 **Weight:** 16.1000 g. **Composition:** 0.9990 Silver .5177 oz. ASW **Reverse:** Prehistoric Life - Vulcanodon

| Date | Mintage | F | VF | XF | Unc | BU |
|---|---|---|---|---|---|---|
| 1994 Proof | — | Value: 45.00 | | | | |

**20000 NUEVO PESOS** KM# 25 **Weight:** 25.0000 g. **Composition:** 0.9990 Silver .8039 oz. ASW **Reverse:** II Extraordinary Congress

| Date | Mintage | F | VF | XF | Unc | BU |
|---|---|---|---|---|---|---|
| ND(1990) | 2,000 | — | — | — | 42.50 | — |

**20000 NUEVO PESOS** KM# 26 **Weight:** 25.0000 g. **Composition:** 0.9990 Silver .8039 oz. ASW **Reverse:** 10th Anniversary - L. Cabral Deposed

| Date | Mintage | F | VF | XF | Unc | BU |
|---|---|---|---|---|---|---|
| 1990 Proof | Est. 2,500 | Value: 47.50 | | | | |

**20000 NUEVO PESOS** KM# 33 **Weight:** 20.0000 g. **Composition:** 0.9990 Silver .6430 oz. ASW **Reverse:** Defense of Nature - Elephant

| Date | Mintage | F | VF | XF | Unc | BU |
|---|---|---|---|---|---|---|
| 1993 Proof | — | Value: 37.50 | | | | |

**20000 NUEVO PESOS** KM# 34 **Weight:** 20.1000 g. **Composition:** 0.9990 Silver .6456 oz. ASW **Reverse:** Sailing Ship - Passat

| Date | Mintage | F | VF | XF | Unc | BU |
|---|---|---|---|---|---|---|
| 1993 | 100 | — | — | — | 275 | — |
| 1993 Proof | — | Value: 37.50 | | | | |

**50000 PESOS** KM# 36 **Weight:** 31.4700 g. **Composition:** 0.9250 Silver .9359 oz. ASW **Reverse:** Hippopotamus Female and Calf

| Date | Mintage | F | VF | XF | Unc | BU |
|---|---|---|---|---|---|---|
| 1996 Proof | Est. 15,000 | Value: 55.00 | | | | |

**50000 PESOS** KM# 37 **Weight:** 31.4700 g. **Composition:** 0.9250 Silver .9359 oz. ASW **Reverse:** Alvise Da Cadamosto - Sailing Ship

| Date | Mintage | F | VF | XF | Unc | BU |
|---|---|---|---|---|---|---|
| 1996 Proof | Est. 10,000 | Value: 50.00 | | | | |

## MEDALLIC COINAGE

**250 PESOS** KM# M1.1 **Composition:** Copper-Nickel **Reverse:** International Games - Balance Beam; engraver's initials on balance beam

| Date | Mintage | F | VF | XF | Unc | BU |
|---|---|---|---|---|---|---|
| 1984 Proof | — | Value: 11.50 | | | | |

**250 PESOS** KM# M1.2 **Composition:** Copper-Nickel **Reverse:** Without initials on balance beam

| Date | Mintage | F | VF | XF | Unc | BU |
|---|---|---|---|---|---|---|
| 1984 Proof | — | Value: 11.50 | | | | |

**250 PESOS** KM# M2 **Composition:** Copper-Nickel **Reverse:** International Games - Horizontal Bar

| Date | Mintage | F | VF | XF | Unc | BU |
|---|---|---|---|---|---|---|
| 1984 Proof | — | Value: 11.50 | | | | |

**1000 PESOS** KM# M3 **Weight:** 31.2400 g. **Composition:** Silver **Reverse:** International Games - Balance Beam **Note:** According to official information released by the Bank National of Guinea-Bissau, KM#M1-M3 are not legal tender and were issued without the authorization of their government.

| Date | Mintage | F | VF | XF | Unc | BU |
|---|---|---|---|---|---|---|
| 1984 Proof | — | Value: 50.00 | | | | |

## PROVAS

Standard metals; stamped "PROVA" in field

| KM# | Date | Mintage | Identification | Issue Price | Mkt Val |
|---|---|---|---|---|---|
| Pr1 | 1933 | — | 5 Centavos. KM#1. | — | 30.00 |
| Pr2 | 1933 | — | 10 Centavos. KM#2. | — | 30.00 |
| Pr3 | 1933 | — | 20 Centavos. KM#3. | — | 30.00 |
| Pr4 | 1933 | — | 50 Centavos. KM#4. | — | 40.00 |
| Pr5 | 1933 | — | Escudo. KM#5. | — | 45.00 |
| Pr6 | 1946 | — | 50 Centavos. KM#6. | — | 15.00 |
| Pr7 | 1946 | — | Escudo. KM#7. | — | 15.00 |
| Pr8 | 1952 | — | 50 Centavos. KM#8. | — | 15.00 |
| Pr9 | 1952 | — | 2-1/2 Escudos. KM#9. | — | 20.00 |
| Pr10 | 1952 | — | 10 Escudos. KM#10. | — | 45.00 |
| Pr11 | 1952 | — | 20 Escudos. KM#11. | — | 50.00 |
| Pr12 | 1973 | — | Escudo. KM#14. | — | 20.00 |
| Pr13 | 1973 | — | 10 Escudos. KM#16. | — | 25.00 |

## TRIAL STRIKES

| KM# | Date | Mintage | Identification | Mkt Val |
|---|---|---|---|---|
| TS1 | 1984 | — | 250 Pesos. Lead. KM-M1. | 35.00 |

# GUYANA (British Guiana)

The Cooperative Republic of Guyana, an independent member of the British Commonwealth situated on the northeast coast of South America, has an area of 83,000sq. mi. (214,970 sq. km.) and a population of 729,000. Capital: Georgetown. The economy is basically agrarian. Sugar, rice and bauxite are exported.

The original area of Essequibo and Demerary, which included present-day Suriname, French Guiana, and parts of Brazil and Venezuela was sighted by Columbus in 1498.The first European settlement was made late in the 16th century by the Dutch, however, the region was claimed for the British by Sir Walter Raleigh during the reign of Elizabeth I. For the next 150 years, possession alternated between the Dutch and the British, with a short interval of French control. The British exercised de facto control after 1796, although the area, which included the Dutch colonies of Essequibo, Demerary and Berbice, was not ceded to them by the Dutch until 1814. From 1803 to1831, Essequibo and Demerary were administered separately from Berbice. The three colonies were united in the British Crown Colony of British Guiana in 1831. British Guiana won internal self-government in 1952 and full independence, under the traditional name of Guyana, on May 26,1966. Guyana became a republic on Feb. 23, 1970. It is a member of the Commonwealth of Nations. The president is the Chief of State. The prime minister is the Head of Government.

**RULERS**

British, until 1966

## BRITISH GUIANA AND WEST INDIES

### STERLING COINAGE

**4 PENCE** KM#26 **Weight:** 1.8851 g. **Composition:** 0.9250 Silver .0560 oz. ASW

| Date | Mintage | F | VF | XF | Unc | BU |
|---|---|---|---|---|---|---|
| 1901 | 60,000 | 3.00 | 7.50 | 17.50 | 55.00 | — |

**4 PENCE** KM#27 **Weight:** 1.8851 g. **Composition:** 0.9250 Silver .0560 oz. ASW

| Date | Mintage | F | VF | XF | Unc | BU |
|---|---|---|---|---|---|---|
| 1903 | 60,000 | 3.00 | 7.50 | 17.50 | 55.00 | — |
| 1903 Matte proof | — | Value: 450 | | | | |
| 1908 | 30,000 | 5.00 | 12.50 | 25.00 | 90.00 | — |
| 1909 | 36,000 | 5.00 | 12.50 | 25.00 | 90.00 | — |
| 1910 | 66,000 | 3.00 | 10.00 | 22.50 | 85.00 | — |

**4 PENCE** KM#28 **Weight:** 1.8851 g. **Composition:** 0.9250 Silver .0560 oz. ASW

| Date | Mintage | F | VF | XF | Unc | BU |
|---|---|---|---|---|---|---|
| 1911 | 30,000 | 6.00 | 14.50 | 35.00 | 115 | — |
| 1913 | 30,000 | 6.00 | 14.50 | 35.00 | 115 | — |
| 1916 | 30,000 | 6.00 | 14.50 | 35.00 | 115 | — |

## BRITISH GUIANA

### STERLING COINAGE

**4 PENCE** KM#29 **Weight:** 1.8851 g. **Composition:** 0.9250 Silver .0560 oz. ASW

| Date | Mintage | F | VF | XF | Unc | BU |
|---|---|---|---|---|---|---|
| 1917 | 72,000 | 3.00 | 7.50 | 22.50 | 90.00 | — |
| 1917 Matte proof | — | Value: 450 | | | | |
| 1918 | 210,000 | 1.25 | 3.50 | 15.00 | 55.00 | — |
| 1921 | 90,000 | 3.00 | 7.50 | 17.50 | 70.00 | — |
| 1923 | 12,000 | 20.00 | 45.00 | 85.00 | 160 | — |
| 1925 | 30,000 | 3.50 | 8.50 | 32.50 | 100 | — |
| 1926 | 30,000 | 3.50 | 8.50 | 25.00 | 65.00 | — |
| 1931 | 15,000 | 10.00 | 25.00 | 60.00 | 120 | — |
| 1931 Proof | — | Value: 175 | | | | |
| 1935 | 36,000 | 3.00 | 7.50 | 20.00 | 175 | — |
| 1935 Proof | — | Value: 175 | | | | |
| 1936 | 63,000 | 1.75 | 2.50 | 10.00 | 30.00 | — |
| 1936 Proof | — | Value: 225 | | | | |

**4 PENCE** KM#30 **Weight:** 1.8851 g. **Composition:** 0.9250 Silver .0560 oz. ASW

| Date | Mintage | F | VF | XF | Unc | BU |
|---|---|---|---|---|---|---|
| 1938 | 30,000 | 1.75 | 2.50 | 10.00 | 25.00 | — |
| 1938 Proof | — | Value: 175 | | | | |
| 1939 | 48,000 | 1.75 | 2.50 | 7.50 | 20.00 | — |
| 1939 Proof | — | Value: 175 | | | | |
| 1940 | 90,000 | 1.25 | 2.00 | 3.50 | 18.50 | — |
| 1940 Proof | — | Value: 175 | | | | |
| 1941 | 120,000 | 1.25 | 1.75 | 3.00 | 12.50 | — |
| 1941 Proof | — | Value: 175 | | | | |
| 1942 | 180,000 | 1.25 | 1.75 | 3.00 | 12.50 | — |
| 1942 Proof | — | Value: 175 | | | | |
| 1943 | — | 1.25 | 1.75 | 2.50 | 8.00 | — |
| 1943 Proof | — | Value: 400 | | | | |

**4 PENCE** KM# 30a **Weight:** 1.8851 g. **Composition:** 0.5000 Silver .0303 oz. ASW

| Date | Mintage | F | VF | XF | Unc | BU |
|---|---|---|---|---|---|---|
| 1944 | 90,000 | 0.75 | 1.25 | 2.50 | 8.00 | — |
| 1945 | 120,000 | 0.50 | 1.00 | 2.00 | 7.00 | — |
| 1945 Proof | — | Value: 200 | | | | |

## REPUBLIC OF GUYANA

### DECIMAL COINAGE

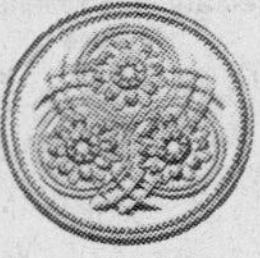

**CENT** KM# 31 **Composition:** Nickel-Brass **Reverse:** Stylized lotus flower

| Date | Mintage | F | VF | XF | Unc | BU |
|---|---|---|---|---|---|---|
| 1967 | 6,000,000 | — | — | 0.10 | 0.25 | — |
| 1967 Proof | 5,100 | Value: 2.00 | | | | |
| 1969 | 4,000,000 | — | — | 0.10 | 0.25 | — |
| 1970 | 6,000,000 | — | — | 0.10 | 0.25 | — |
| 1971 | 4,000,000 | — | — | 0.10 | 0.25 | — |
| 1972 | 4,000,000 | — | — | 0.10 | 0.25 | — |
| 1973 | 4,000,000 | — | — | 0.10 | 0.25 | — |
| 1974 | 11,000,000 | — | — | 0.10 | 0.20 | — |
| 1975 | — | — | — | 0.10 | 0.25 | — |
| 1976 | — | — | — | 0.10 | 0.25 | — |
| 1977 | 16,000,000 | — | — | 0.10 | 0.20 | — |
| 1978 | 10,450,000 | — | — | 0.10 | 0.20 | — |
| 1979 | — | — | — | 0.10 | 0.20 | — |
| 1980 | 12,000,000 | — | — | 0.10 | 0.20 | — |
| 1981 | 10,000,000 | — | — | 0.10 | 0.20 | — |
| 1982 | 8,000,000 | — | — | 0.10 | 0.20 | — |
| 1983 | 12,000,000 | — | — | 0.10 | 0.20 | — |
| 1985 | 8,000,000 | — | — | 0.10 | 0.20 | — |
| 1987 | 6,000,000 | — | — | 0.10 | 0.20 | — |
| 1988 | 80,000 | — | — | 0.10 | 0.20 | — |
| 1989 | — | — | — | 0.10 | 0.20 | — |
| 1991 | — | — | — | 0.10 | 0.20 | — |
| 1992 | — | — | — | 0.10 | 0.20 | — |

**CENT** KM# 37 **Composition:** Nickel-Brass **Subject:** 10th Anniversary of Independence **Reverse:** Manatee

| Date | Mintage | F | VF | XF | Unc | BU |
|---|---|---|---|---|---|---|
| 1976FM (M) | 15,000 | — | — | 0.15 | 1.00 | — |
| 1976FM (U) | 50 | — | — | — | — | — |
| 1976FM (P) | 28,000 | Value: 1.25 | | | | |
| 1977FM (M) | — | — | — | — | 3.00 | — |
| 1977FM (U) | 15,000 | — | — | 0.20 | 1.00 | — |
| 1977FM (P) | 7,215 | Value: 1.25 | | | | |
| 1978FM (M) | — | — | — | — | 3.00 | — |

| Date | Mintage | F | VF | XF | Unc | BU |
|---|---|---|---|---|---|---|
| 1978FM (U) | 15,000 | — | — | 0.20 | 1.00 | — |
| 1978FM (P) | 5,044 | Value: 1.25 | | | | |
| 1979FM (U) | 15,000 | — | — | 0.20 | 1.00 | — |
| 1979FM (P) | 3,547 | Value: 1.25 | | | | |
| 1980FM (U) | 30,000 | — | — | 0.20 | 1.00 | — |
| 1980FM (P) | 2,763 | Value: 1.50 | | | | |

**5 CENTS** **KM# 32** **Composition:** Nickel-Brass **Reverse:** Stylized lotus flower **Note:** Varieties exist.

| Date | Mintage | F | VF | XF | Unc | BU |
|---|---|---|---|---|---|---|
| 1967 | 4,600,000 | — | — | 0.10 | 0.25 | — |
| 1967 Proof | 5,100 | Value: 2.00 | | | | |
| 1972 | 1,200,000 | — | — | 0.10 | 0.30 | — |
| 1974 | 3,000,000 | — | — | 0.10 | 0.30 | — |
| 1975 | — | — | — | 0.10 | 0.30 | — |
| 1976 | — | — | — | 0.10 | 0.30 | — |
| 1977 | 1,500,000 | — | — | 0.10 | 0.30 | — |
| 1978 | 2,000 | — | — | 0.50 | 4.00 | — |
| 1979 | — | — | — | — | — | — |
| 1980 | 1,000,000 | — | — | 0.10 | 0.30 | — |
| 1981 | 1,000,000 | — | — | 0.10 | 0.30 | — |
| 1982 | 2,000,000 | — | — | 0.10 | 0.30 | — |
| 1985 | 3,000,000 | — | — | 0.10 | 0.30 | — |
| 1986 | 4,000,000 | — | — | 0.10 | 0.30 | — |
| 1987 | 3,000,000 | — | — | 0.10 | 0.30 | — |
| 1988 | 2,000,000 | — | — | 0.10 | 0.30 | — |
| 1989 | — | — | — | 0.10 | 0.30 | — |
| 1990 | — | — | — | 0.10 | 0.30 | — |
| 1991 | — | — | — | 0.10 | 0.30 | — |
| 1992 | — | — | — | 0.10 | 0.30 | — |

**5 CENTS** **KM# 38** **Composition:** Nickel-Brass **Subject:** 10th Anniversary of Independence **Reverse:** Jaguar

| Date | Mintage | F | VF | XF | Unc | BU |
|---|---|---|---|---|---|---|
| 1976FM (M) | 15,000 | — | — | 0.20 | 1.50 | — |
| 1976FM (U) | 50 | — | — | — | — | — |
| 1976FM (P) | 28,000 | Value: 1.50 | | | | |
| 1977FM (M) | — | — | — | — | 5.00 | — |
| 1977FM (U) | 15,000 | — | — | 0.20 | 1.50 | — |
| 1977FM (P) | 7,215 | Value: 1.75 | | | | |
| 1978FM (M) | — | — | — | — | 5.00 | — |
| 1978FM (U) | 15,000 | — | — | 0.20 | 1.50 | — |
| 1978FM (P) | 5,044 | Value: 1.75 | | | | |
| 1979FM (U) | 15,000 | — | — | 0.20 | 1.50 | — |
| 1979FM (P) | 3,547 | Value: 1.75 | | | | |
| 1980FM (U) | 30,000 | — | — | 0.20 | 1.50 | — |
| 1980FM (P) | 2,763 | Value: 2.00 | | | | |

**10 CENTS** **KM# 33** **Composition:** Copper-Nickel

| Date | Mintage | F | VF | XF | Unc | BU |
|---|---|---|---|---|---|---|
| 1967 | 4,000,000 | — | 0.10 | 0.20 | 0.35 | — |
| 1967 Proof | 5,100 | Value: 2.50 | | | | |
| 1973 | 1,500,000 | — | 0.10 | 0.20 | 0.35 | — |
| 1974 | 1,700,000 | — | 0.10 | 0.20 | 0.35 | — |
| 1976 | — | — | 0.10 | 0.20 | 0.35 | — |
| 1977 | 4,000,000 | — | 0.10 | 0.20 | 0.35 | — |
| 1978 | 2,010,000 | — | 0.10 | 0.20 | 0.35 | — |
| 1979 | — | — | 0.10 | 0.20 | 0.35 | — |
| 1980 | 1,000,000 | — | 0.10 | 0.20 | 0.35 | — |
| 1981 | 1,000,000 | — | 0.10 | 0.20 | 0.35 | — |
| 1982 | 2,000,000 | — | 0.10 | 0.20 | 0.35 | — |
| 1985 | 3,000,000 | — | 0.10 | 0.20 | 0.35 | — |
| 1986 | 4,000,000 | — | 0.10 | 0.20 | 0.35 | — |
| 1987 | 3,000,000 | — | 0.10 | 0.20 | 0.35 | — |
| 1988 | 2,000,000 | — | 0.10 | 0.20 | 0.35 | — |
| 1989 | — | — | 0.10 | 0.20 | 0.35 | — |
| 1990 | — | — | 0.10 | 0.20 | 0.35 | — |
| 1991 | — | — | 0.10 | 0.20 | 0.35 | — |
| 1992 | — | — | 0.10 | 0.20 | 0.35 | — |

**10 CENTS** **KM# 39** **Composition:** Copper-Nickel **Subject:** 10th Anniversary of Independence **Reverse:** Squirrel Monkey

| Date | Mintage | F | VF | XF | Unc | BU |
|---|---|---|---|---|---|---|
| 1976 | 2,006,000 | — | — | 0.20 | 1.00 | — |
| 1976FM (M) | 10,000 | — | — | 0.20 | 1.00 | — |
| 1976FM (U) | 50 | — | — | — | — | — |
| 1976FM (P) | 28,000 | Value: 3.00 | | | | |
| 1977 | 1,500,000 | — | — | 0.20 | 1.00 | — |
| 1977FM (M) | — | — | — | — | 8.00 | — |
| 1977FM (U) | 10,000 | — | — | 0.20 | 1.00 | — |
| 1977FM (P) | 7,215 | Value: 3.00 | | | | |
| 1978FM (M) | — | — | — | — | 8.00 | — |
| 1978FM (U) | 10,000 | — | — | 0.20 | 1.00 | — |
| 1978FM (P) | 5,044 | Value: 3.00 | | | | |
| 1979FM (U) | 10,000 | — | — | 0.20 | 1.00 | — |
| 1979FM (P) | 3,547 | Value: 3.00 | | | | |
| 1980FM (U) | 20,000 | — | — | 0.20 | 1.00 | — |
| 1980FM (P) | 2,763 | Value: 4.00 | | | | |

**25 CENTS** **KM# 34** **Composition:** Copper-Nickel

| Date | Mintage | F | VF | XF | Unc | BU |
|---|---|---|---|---|---|---|
| 1967 | 3,500,000 | — | 0.15 | 0.25 | 0.65 | — |
| 1967 Proof | 5,100 | Value: 2.50 | | | | |
| 1972 | 1,000,000 | — | 0.15 | 0.25 | 0.65 | — |
| 1974 | 4,000,000 | — | 0.15 | 0.25 | 0.65 | — |
| 1975 | — | — | 0.15 | 0.25 | 0.65 | — |
| 1976 | — | — | 0.15 | 0.25 | 0.65 | — |
| 1977 | 4,000,000 | — | 0.15 | 0.25 | 0.65 | — |
| 1978 | 2,006,000 | — | 0.15 | 0.25 | 0.65 | — |
| 1981 | 1,000,000 | — | 0.15 | 0.25 | 0.65 | — |
| 1982 | 1,500,000 | — | 0.15 | 0.25 | 0.65 | — |
| 1984 | 1,000,000 | — | 0.15 | 0.25 | 0.65 | — |
| 1985 | 2,000,000 | — | 0.15 | 0.25 | 0.65 | — |
| 1986 | 4,000,000 | — | 0.15 | 0.25 | 0.65 | — |
| 1987 | 3,000,000 | — | 0.15 | 0.25 | 0.65 | — |
| 1988 | 4,000,000 | — | 0.15 | 0.25 | 0.65 | — |
| 1989 | — | — | 0.15 | 0.25 | 0.65 | — |
| 1990 | — | — | 0.15 | 0.25 | 0.65 | — |
| 1991 | — | — | 0.15 | 0.25 | 0.65 | — |
| 1992 | — | — | 0.15 | 0.25 | 0.65 | — |

**25 CENTS** **KM# 40** **Composition:** Copper-Nickel **Subject:** 10th Anniversary of Independence **Reverse:** Harpy Eagle

| Date | Mintage | F | VF | XF | Unc | BU |
|---|---|---|---|---|---|---|
| 1976FM (M) | 4,000 | — | — | 0.30 | 2.00 | — |
| 1976FM (U) | 50 | — | — | — | — | — |
| 1976FM (P) | 28,000 | Value: 3.00 | | | | |
| 1977 | 2,000,000 | — | 0.15 | 0.25 | 1.00 | — |
| 1977FM (M) | — | — | — | — | 10.00 | — |
| 1977FM (U) | 4,000 | — | — | 0.30 | 4.00 | — |
| 1977FM (P) | 7,215 | Value: 3.00 | | | | |
| 1978FM (M) | — | — | — | — | 10.00 | — |
| 1978FM (U) | 4,000 | — | — | 0.30 | 4.00 | — |
| 1978FM (P) | 5,044 | Value: 3.00 | | | | |
| 1979FM (U) | 4,000 | — | — | 0.30 | 4.00 | — |
| 1979FM (P) | 3,547 | Value: 3.00 | | | | |
| 1980FM (U) | 8,437 | — | — | 0.30 | 4.00 | — |
| 1980FM (P) | 2,763 | Value: 4.00 | | | | |

**50 CENTS** **KM# 35** **Composition:** Copper-Nickel

| Date | Mintage | F | VF | XF | Unc | BU |
|---|---|---|---|---|---|---|
| 1967 | 1,000,000 | — | 0.25 | 0.35 | 0.75 | — |
| 1967 Proof | 5,100 | Value: 3.50 | | | | |

**50 CENTS** **KM# 41** **Composition:** Copper-Nickel **Subject:** 10th Anniversary of Independence **Reverse:** Hoatzin

| Date | Mintage | F | VF | XF | Unc | BU |
|---|---|---|---|---|---|---|
| 1976FM (M) | 2,000 | — | — | 0.40 | 5.00 | — |
| 1976FM (U) | 50 | — | — | — | — | — |
| 1976FM (P) | 28,000 | Value: 4.00 | | | | |
| 1977FM (M) | — | — | — | — | 20.00 | — |
| 1977FM (U) | 2,000 | — | — | 0.40 | 5.00 | — |
| 1977FM (P) | 7,215 | Value: 4.00 | | | | |
| 1978FM (M) | — | — | — | — | 20.00 | — |
| 1978FM (U) | 2,000 | — | — | 0.40 | 5.00 | — |
| 1978FM (P) | 5,044 | Value: 4.00 | | | | |
| 1979FM (U) | 2,000 | — | — | 0.40 | 5.00 | — |
| 1979FM (P) | 3,547 | Value: 4.00 | | | | |
| 1980FM (U) | 4,437 | — | — | 0.40 | 3.50 | — |
| 1980FM (P) | 2,763 | Value: 5.00 | | | | |

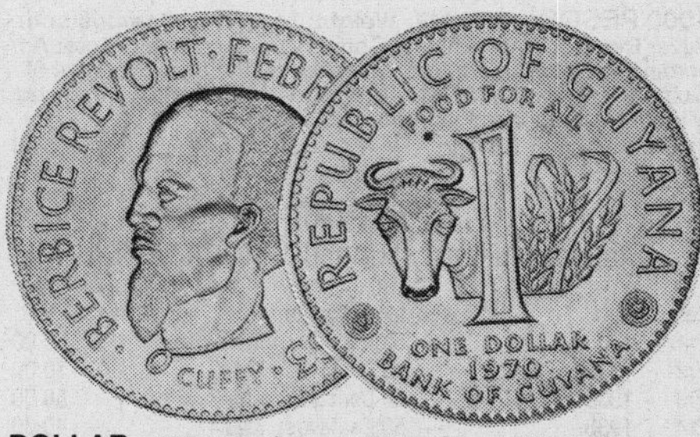


**DOLLAR** **KM# 36** **Composition:** Copper-Nickel **Series:** F.A.O.

| Date | Mintage | F | VF | XF | Unc | BU |
|---|---|---|---|---|---|---|
| 1970 | 500,000 | — | 0.50 | 1.50 | 3.50 | — |
| 1970 Proof | 5,000 | Value: 5.00 | | | | |

**DOLLAR** **KM# 42** **Composition:** Copper-Nickel **Series:** F.A.O. **Subject:** 10th Anniversary of Independence **Reverse:** Common Caiman

| Date | Mintage | F | VF | XF | Unc | BU |
|---|---|---|---|---|---|---|
| 1976FM (M) | 600 | — | — | 0.50 | 5.00 | — |
| 1976FM (U) | 50 | — | — | — | — | — |
| 1976FM (P) | 28,000 | Value: 5.00 | | | | |
| 1977FM (M) | — | — | — | — | 30.00 | — |
| 1977FM (U) | 500 | — | — | 0.50 | 5.00 | — |
| 1977FM (P) | 7,215 | Value: 7.00 | | | | |
| 1978FM (M) | — | — | — | — | 30.00 | — |
| 1978FM (U) | 500 | — | — | 0.50 | 5.00 | — |
| 1978FM (P) | 5,044 | Value: 7.00 | | | | |
| 1979FM (U) | 500 | — | — | 0.50 | 5.00 | — |
| 1979FM (P) | 3,547 | Value: 7.00 | | | | |
| 1980FM (U) | 1,437 | — | — | 0.50 | 5.00 | — |
| 1980FM (P) | 2,763 | Value: 8.00 | | | | |

**DOLLAR** **KM# 50** **Composition:** Copper Plated Steel **Reverse:** Hand gathering rice

| Date | Mintage | F | VF | XF | Unc | BU |
|---|---|---|---|---|---|---|
| 1996 | — | — | — | — | 0.50 | — |

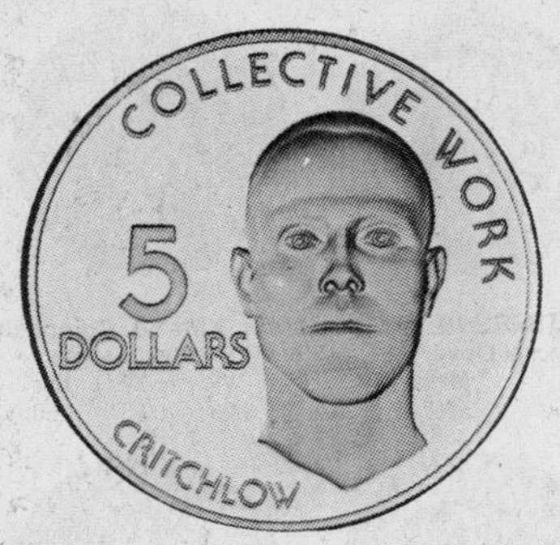


**5 DOLLARS** **KM# 43** **Composition:** Copper-Nickel **Subject:** 10th Anniversary of Independence **Obverse:** Similar to 1 Dollar, KM#42.

| Date | Mintage | F | VF | XF | Unc | BU |
|---|---|---|---|---|---|---|
| 1976FM (M) | 400 | — | — | — | 15.00 | — |
| 1976FM (U) | 150 | — | — | — | 17.50 | — |
| 1977FM (M) | — | — | — | — | 45.00 | — |
| 1977FM (U) | 100 | — | — | — | 25.00 | — |
| 1978FM (M) | — | — | — | — | 45.00 | — |
| 1978FM (U) | 100 | — | — | — | 25.00 | — |
| 1979FM (U) | 100 | — | — | — | 25.00 | — |
| 1980FM (U) | 200 | — | — | — | 15.00 | — |

**5 DOLLARS** **KM# 43a** **Weight:** 37.3000 g. **Composition:** 0.5000 Silver .5996 oz. ASW

| Date | Mintage | F | VF | XF | Unc | BU |
|---|---|---|---|---|---|---|
| 1976FM (P) | 18,000 | Value: 8.50 | | | | |
| 1977FM (P) | 5,685 | Value: 10.00 | | | | |
| 1978FM (P) | 3,825 | Value: 12.00 | | | | |
| 1979FM (P) | 2,665 | Value: 15.00 | | | | |
| 1980FM (P) | 2,763 | Value: 15.00 | | | | |

**5 DOLLARS** **KM# 51** **Composition:** Copper Plated Steel **Reverse:** Sugar cane

| Date | Mintage | F | VF | XF | Unc | BU |
|---|---|---|---|---|---|---|
| 1996 | — | — | — | — | 0.75 | — |

**10 DOLLARS** **KM# 44** **Composition:** Copper-Nickel **Subject:** 10th Anniversary of Independence **Obverse:** Similar to 1 Dollar, KM#42

| Date | Mintage | F | VF | XF | Unc | BU |
|---|---|---|---|---|---|---|
| 1976FM (M) | 300 | — | — | — | 30.00 | — |
| 1976FM (U) | 300 | — | — | — | 30.00 | — |
| 1977FM (M) | — | — | — | — | 80.00 | — |
| 1977FM (U) | 100 | — | — | — | 50.00 | — |
| 1978FM (M) | — | — | — | — | 80.00 | — |
| 1978FM (U) | 100 | — | — | — | 50.00 | — |
| 1979FM (U) | 100 | — | — | — | 50.00 | — |
| 1980FM (U) | 200 | — | — | — | 40.00 | — |

**10 DOLLARS** **KM# 44a** **Weight:** 43.2300 g. **Composition:** 0.9250 Silver 1.2856 oz. ASW

| Date | Mintage | F | VF | XF | Unc | BU |
|---|---|---|---|---|---|---|
| 1976FM (P) | 18,000 | Value: 12.50 | | | | |
| 1977FM (P) | 5,685 | Value: 15.00 | | | | |
| 1978FM (P) | 3,825 | Value: 18.00 | | | | |
| 1979FM (P) | 2,665 | Value: 20.00 | | | | |
| 1980FM (P) | 2,763 | Value: 20.00 | | | | |

**10 DOLLARS** **KM# 52** **Composition:** Nickel Plated Steel **Reverse:** Gold mining scene **Edge:** Plain **Shape:** 7-sided

| Date | Mintage | F | VF | XF | Unc | BU |
|---|---|---|---|---|---|---|
| 1996 | — | — | — | — | 1.25 | — |

**50 DOLLARS** **KM# 45** **Weight:** 48.3000 g. **Composition:** 0.9250 Silver 1.4365 oz. ASW **Subject:** 10th Anniversary of Independence **Note:** Enmore Martyrs

| Date | Mintage | F | VF | XF | Unc | BU |
|---|---|---|---|---|---|---|
| 1976FM (U) | 100 | — | — | — | 110 | — |
| 1976FM (P) | 1,001 | Value: 75.00 | | | | |

**50 DOLLARS** **KM# 48** **Weight:** 28.2800 g. **Composition:** 0.9250 Silver .8411 oz. ASW **Subject:** Royal Visit **Note:** Similar to 500 Dollars, KM#49.

| Date | Mintage | F | VF | XF | Unc | BU |
|---|---|---|---|---|---|---|
| 1994 Proof | — | Value: 50.00 | | | | |

**100 DOLLARS** **KM# 46** **Weight:** 5.7400 g. **Composition:** 0.5000 Gold .0923 oz. AGW **Subject:** 10th Anniversary of Independence **Reverse:** Arawak Indian

| Date | Mintage | F | VF | XF | Unc | BU |
|---|---|---|---|---|---|---|
| 1976FM (U) | 100 | — | — | — | 80.00 | — |
| 1976FM (P) | 21,000 | Value: 60.00 | | | | |

**100 DOLLARS** **KM# 47** **Weight:** 5.5800 g. **Composition:** 0.5000 Gold .0897 oz. AGW **Note:** Legendary Golden Man

| Date | Mintage | F | VF | XF | Unc | BU |
|---|---|---|---|---|---|---|
| 1977FM (U) | 100 | — | — | — | 85.00 | — |
| 1977FM (P) | 7,635 | Value: 65.00 | | | | |

**500 DOLLARS** **KM# 49** **Weight:** 47.5400 g. **Composition:** 0.9170 Gold 1.4017 oz. AGW **Subject:** Royal Visit

| Date | Mintage | F | VF | XF | Unc | BU |
|---|---|---|---|---|---|---|
| 1994 Proof | 100 | Value: 1,000 | | | | |

**2000 DOLLARS** **KM# 53** **Composition:** 0.9250 Silver **Subject:** Millennium **Obverse:** National arms **Reverse:** World globe and radiant sun **Edge:** Plain **Shape:** 12-sided

| Date | Mintage | F | VF | XF | Unc | BU |
|---|---|---|---|---|---|---|
| ND(1999) Proof | Est. 30,000 | Value: 40.00 | | | | |

## PATTERNS

Including off metal strikes

| KM# | Date | Mintage | Identification | Mkt Val |
|---|---|---|---|---|
| Pn1 | 1967 | — | 5 Cents. Silver. KM#32. | — |

## MINT SETS

| KM# | Date | Mintage | Identification | Issue Price | Mkt Val |
|---|---|---|---|---|---|
| MS1 | 1977 (8) | — | KM#37-44 | — | 150 |
| MS2 | 1978 (8) | — | KM#37-44 | — | 150 |

## PROOF SETS

| KM# | Date | Mintage | Identification | Issue Price | Mkt Val |
|---|---|---|---|---|---|
| PS1 | 1967 (5) | 5,100 | KM#31-35 | 10.50 | 9.00 |
| PS2 | 1976 (8) | 17,536 | KM#37-42, 43a, 44a | 45.00 | 37.50 |
| PS3 | 1976 (6) | 10,302 | KM#37-42 | 15.00 | 17.00 |
| PS4 | 1977 (8) | 5,685 | KM#37-42, 43a, 44a | 45.00 | 42.00 |
| PS5 | 1977 (6) | 1,530 | KM#37-42 | 15.00 | 20.00 |
| PS6 | 1978 (8) | 3,825 | KM#37-42, 43a, 44a | 47.50 | 47.50 |
| PS7 | 1978 (6) | 1,219 | KM#37-42 | 16.00 | 20.00 |
| PS8 | 1979 (8) | 2,665 | KM#37-42, 43a, 44a | 47.50 | 52.00 |
| PS9 | 1979 (6) | 882 | KM#37-42 | 16.00 | 20.00 |
| PS10 | 1980 (8) | 1,900 | KM#37-42, 43a, 44a | 100 | 58.00 |
| PS11 | 1980 (6) | 863 | KM#37-42 | 19.00 | 22.50 |

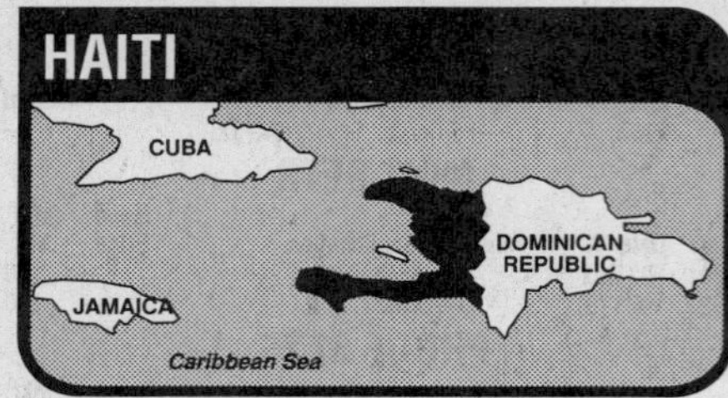


The Republic of Haiti, which occupies the western one-third of the island of Hispaniola in the Caribbean Sea between Puerto Rico and Cuba, has an area of 10,714 sq. mi. (27,750 sq. km.) and a population of 6.5 million. Capital: Port-au-Prince. The economy is based on agriculture; but light manufacturing and tourism are increasingly important. Coffee, bauxite, sugar, essential oils and handicrafts are exported.

Columbus discovered Hispaniola in 1492. Spain colonized the island, making Santo Domingo the base for exploration of the Western Hemisphere. The area that is now Haiti was ceded to France by Spain in 1697. Slaves brought from Africa to work the coffee and sugar cane plantations made it one of the richest colonies of the French Empire. A slave revolt in the 1790's led to the establishment of the Republic of Haiti in1804, making it the oldest Black republic in the world and the second oldest republic (after the United States) in the Western Hemisphere.

The French language is used on Haitian coins although it is spoken by only about 10% of the populace. A form of Creole is the language of the Haitians.

Two dating systems are used on Haiti's 19th century coins. One is Christian, the other Revolutionary – beginning in 1803 when the French were permanently ousted by a native revolt. Thus, a date of AN30, (i.e., year 30) is equivalent to 1833 A.D. Some coins carry both date forms. In the listings which follow, coins dated only in the Revolutionary system are listed by AN years in the date column.

**MINT MARKS**

A - Paris
(a) - Paris, privy marks only
HEATON - Birmingham
R - Rome
(w) = Waterbury (Connecticut, USA) (Scoville Mfg. Co.)
(p) – Philadelphia (U.S.A. mint)

**MONETARY SYSTEM**

100 Centimes = 1 Gourde

# THIRD REPUBLIC

## DECIMAL COINAGE

100 Centimes = 1 Gourde

**5 CENTIMES** **KM# 53** **Composition:** Copper-Nickel **Obverse:** President Nord Alexis

| Date | Mintage | F | VF | XF | Unc | BU |
|---|---|---|---|---|---|---|
| 1904(w) | 2,000,000 | 0.50 | 2.00 | 4.00 | 15.00 | — |
| 1904(w) Proof | — | Value: 90.00 | | | | |
| 1905(w) | 20,000,000 | 0.30 | 1.00 | 2.50 | 10.00 | — |
| 1905(w) Proof | — | Value: 100 | | | | |
| 1906(w) | 10,000,000 | — | — | — | — | — |

Reported, not confirmed.

**5 CENTIMES** **KM# 52** **Composition:** Copper-Nickel **Note:** Struck at the Scovill Mfg. Co., Waterbury, Connecticut; design incorporates Paris privy and mint director's marks.

| Date | Mintage | F | VF | XF | Unc | BU |
|---|---|---|---|---|---|---|
| 1904(w) | — | 2.50 | 5.50 | 12.50 | 35.00 | — |
| 1904(w) Proof | — | Value: 120 | | | | |

**5 CENTIMES** **KM# 57** **Composition:** Copper-Nickel **Obverse:** President Dumarsais Estime

| Date | Mintage | F | VF | XF | Unc | BU |
|---|---|---|---|---|---|---|
| 1949(p) | 10,000,000 | 0.10 | 0.20 | 0.40 | 1.25 | — |

**5 CENTIMES** **KM# 59** **Composition:** Nickel-Silver **Obverse:** President Paul E. Magloire

| Date | Mintage | F | VF | XF | Unc | BU |
|---|---|---|---|---|---|---|
| 1953(p) | 3,000,000 | 0.15 | 0.25 | 0.50 | 1.50 | — |

**5 CENTIMES** **KM# 62** **Composition:** Copper-Nickel **Obverse:** President Francois Duvalier

| Date | Mintage | F | VF | XF | Unc | BU |
|---|---|---|---|---|---|---|
| 1958(p) | 15,000,000 | — | — | 0.10 | 0.25 | — |
| 1970 | 5,000,000 | — | — | 0.10 | 0.20 | — |

**5 CENTIMES** **KM# 119** **Composition:** Copper-Nickel **Series:** F.A.O **Obverse:** President Jean-Claude Duvalier

| Date | Mintage | F | VF | XF | Unc | BU |
|---|---|---|---|---|---|---|
| 1975 | 16,000,000 | — | — | 0.10 | 0.20 | — |

**5 CENTIMES** **KM# 145** **Composition:** Copper-Nickel **Series:** F.A.O.

| Date | Mintage | F | VF | XF | Unc | BU |
|---|---|---|---|---|---|---|
| 1981 | 15,000 | — | 0.10 | 0.25 | 0.65 | — |

**5 CENTIMES** **KM# 154** **Composition:** Steel **Obverse:** Portrait of national hero, Charlemagne Peralte **Reverse:** National emblem

| Date | Mintage | F | VF | XF | Unc | BU |
|---|---|---|---|---|---|---|
| 1995 | — | — | — | — | 0.25 | — |

**5 CENTIMES** **KM# 154a** **Composition:** Nickel Plated Steel

| Date | Mintage | F | VF | XF | Unc | BU |
|---|---|---|---|---|---|---|
| 1995 | — | — | — | — | 0.35 | — |
| 1997 | — | — | — | — | 0.35 | — |

**10 CENTIMES (0.10 Gourdes)** **KM# 54** **Composition:** Copper-Nickel **Obverse:** President Nord Alexis

| Date | Mintage | F | VF | XF | Unc | BU |
|---|---|---|---|---|---|---|
| 1906(w) | 10,000,000 | 0.50 | 1.50 | 5.00 | 15.00 | — |
| 1906(w) Proof | — | Value: 100 | | | | |

**10 CENTIMES (0.10 Gourdes)** **KM# 58** **Composition:** Copper-Nickel **Obverse:** President Dumarsais Estime

| Date | Mintage | F | VF | XF | Unc | BU |
|---|---|---|---|---|---|---|
| 1949(p) | 5,000,000 | 0.15 | 0.25 | 0.50 | 1.50 | — |

**10 CENTIMES (0.10 Gourdes)** **KM# 60** **Composition:** Nickel-Silver **Obverse:** President Paul E. Magloire

| Date | Mintage | F | VF | XF | Unc | BU |
|---|---|---|---|---|---|---|
| 1953(p) | 1,500,000 | — | 0.10 | 0.25 | 1.25 | — |

**10 CENTIMES (0.10 Gourdes)** **KM# 63** **Composition:** Copper-Nickel **Obverse:** President Francois Duvalier

| Date | Mintage | F | VF | XF | Unc | BU |
|---|---|---|---|---|---|---|
| 1958(p) | 7,500,000 | — | 0.10 | 0.15 | 0.35 | — |
| 1970 | 2,500,000 | — | — | 0.10 | 0.20 | — |

**10 CENTIMES (0.10 Gourdes)** **KM# 120** **Composition:** Copper-Nickel **Series:** F.A.O. **Obverse:** President Jean-Claude Duvalier

| Date | Mintage | F | VF | XF | Unc | BU |
|---|---|---|---|---|---|---|
| 1975 | 12,000,000 | — | — | 0.10 | 0.20 | — |
| 1983 | 2,000,000 | — | — | 0.10 | 0.30 | — |

**10 CENTIMES (0.10 Gourdes)** **KM# 146** **Composition:** Copper-Nickel **Series:** F.A.O.

| Date | Mintage | F | VF | XF | Unc | BU |
|---|---|---|---|---|---|---|
| 1981R | 15,000 | — | 0.10 | 0.25 | 0.85 | — |

**10 CENTIMES (0.10 Gourdes)** **KM# 157** **Composition:** Copper-Nickel **Series:** F.A.O. **Obverse:** Portrait **Reverse:** National emblem

| Date | Mintage | F | VF | XF | Unc | BU |
|---|---|---|---|---|---|---|
| 1995 | — | — | — | — | 0.45 | — |

**20 CENTIMES** **KM# 55** **Composition:** Copper-Nickel **Obverse:** President Nord Alexis

| Date | Mintage | F | VF | XF | Unc | BU |
|---|---|---|---|---|---|---|
| 1907(w) | 5,000,000 | 1.00 | 2.00 | 4.50 | 15.00 | — |
| 1907(w) Proof | — | Value: 125 | | | | |
| 1908(w) | — | — | — | — | — | — |

Reported, not confirmed

**20 CENTIMES** **KM# 61** **Composition:** Nickel-Silver **Obverse:** President Paul E. Magliore

| Date | Mintage | F | VF | XF | Unc | BU |
|---|---|---|---|---|---|---|
| 1956(p) | 2,500,000 | 0.20 | 0.35 | 0.75 | 2.50 | — |

**20 CENTIMES** **KM# 77** **Composition:** Nickel-Silver **Obverse:** President Francios Duvalier

| Date | Mintage | F | VF | XF | Unc | BU |
|---|---|---|---|---|---|---|
| 1970 | 1,000,000 | — | 0.10 | 0.20 | 0.80 | — |

**20 CENTIMES** **KM# 100** **Composition:** Copper-Nickel **Series:** F.A.O. **Obverse:** President Jean-Claude Duvalier

| Date | Mintage | F | VF | XF | Unc | BU |
|---|---|---|---|---|---|---|
| 1972 | 1,500,000 | — | 0.10 | 0.25 | 1.00 | — |
| 1975 | 4,000,000 | — | 0.10 | 0.20 | 0.80 | — |
| 1983 | 1,500,000 | — | 0.10 | 0.20 | 0.80 | — |

**20 CENTIMES** **KM# 147** **Composition:** Copper-Nickel **Series:** F.A.O.

| Date | Mintage | F | VF | XF | Unc | BU |
|---|---|---|---|---|---|---|
| 1981R | 15,000 | — | 0.10 | 0.25 | 1.00 | — |

**20 CENTIMES** **KM# 152** **Composition:** Copper-Nickel **Obverse:** Portrait of national hero, Charlemagne Perlalte **Reverse:** National emblem

| Date | Mintage | F | VF | XF | Unc | BU |
|---|---|---|---|---|---|---|
| 1986 | 2,500,000 | — | 0.10 | 0.20 | 0.60 | — |
| 1989 | — | — | 0.10 | 0.20 | 0.60 | — |
| 1991 | — | — | 0.10 | 0.20 | 0.60 | — |

**20 CENTIMES** **KM# 152a** **Composition:** Nickel Plated Steel

| Date | Mintage | F | VF | XF | Unc | BU |
|---|---|---|---|---|---|---|
| 1995 | — | — | — | — | 0.75 | — |

**50 CENTIMES (0.50 Gourdes)** **KM# 56** **Composition:** Copper-Nickel **Obverse:** President Nord Alexis

| Date | Mintage | F | VF | XF | Unc | BU |
|---|---|---|---|---|---|---|
| 1907(w) | 2,000,000 | 0.90 | 1.75 | 5.50 | 15.00 | — |
| 1907(w) Proof | — | Value: 175 | | | | |
| 1908(w) | 800,000 | 1.00 | 2.50 | 8.50 | 20.00 | — |
| 1908(w) Proof | — | Value: 200 | | | | |

**50 CENTIMES (0.50 Gourdes)** **KM# 101** **Composition:** Copper-Nickel **Series:** F.A.O. **Obverse:** President Jean-Claude Duvalier

| Date | Mintage | F | VF | XF | Unc | BU |
|---|---|---|---|---|---|---|
| 1972 | 600,000 | — | 0.10 | 0.25 | 1.50 | — |

**50 CENTIMES (0.50 Gourdes)** **KM# 101a** **Composition:** Copper-Nickel-Zinc **Note:** Varieties exist.

| Date | Mintage | F | VF | XF | Unc | BU |
|---|---|---|---|---|---|---|
| 1975 | 1,200,000 | — | 0.10 | 0.20 | 1.00 | — |
| 1979 | 2,000,000 | — | 0.10 | 0.20 | 1.00 | — |
| 1983 | 1,000,000 | — | 0.10 | 0.20 | 1.00 | — |
| 1985 | — | — | — | — | 0.75 | — |

**50 CENTIMES (0.50 Gourdes)** **KM# 148** **Composition:** Copper-Nickel **Series:** F.A.O.

| Date | Mintage | F | VF | XF | Unc | BU |
|---|---|---|---|---|---|---|
| 1981R | 15,000 | — | 0.10 | 0.50 | 1.50 | — |

**50 CENTIMES (0.50 Gourdes)** **KM# 153** **Composition:** Copper-Nickel **Obverse:** Portrait of national hero, Charlemagne Peralte **Reverse:** National emblem

| Date | Mintage | F | VF | XF | Unc | BU |
|---|---|---|---|---|---|---|
| 1986 | 2,000,000 | — | 0.10 | 0.25 | 1.00 | — |
| 1989 | — | — | 0.10 | 0.25 | 1.00 | — |
| 1991 | — | — | 0.10 | 0.25 | 1.00 | — |

**50 CENTIMES (0.50 Gourdes)** **KM# 153a** **Composition:** Nickel Plated Steel

| Date | Mintage | F | VF | XF | Unc | BU |
|---|---|---|---|---|---|---|
| 1995 | — | — | 0.10 | 0.25 | 1.25 | — |

**GOURDE** **KM# 155** **Composition:** Aluminum-Bronze **Obverse:** Hilltop ediface **Reverse:** National emblem **Shape:** 7-sided

| Date | Mintage | F | VF | XF | Unc | BU |
|---|---|---|---|---|---|---|
| 1995 | — | — | — | — | 1.75 | — |

**GOURDE** **KM# 155a** **Composition:** Brass Plated Steel

| Date | Mintage | F | VF | XF | Unc | BU |
|---|---|---|---|---|---|---|
| 1995 | — | — | — | — | 2.00 | — |

**5 GOURDES** **KM# 64.1** **Weight:** 23.5200 g. **Composition:** 0.9990 Silver .7555 oz. ASW **Series:** 10th Anniversary of Revolution **Subject:** Columbus Discovers America

| Date | Mintage | F | VF | XF | Unc | BU |
|---|---|---|---|---|---|---|
| 1967 IC Proof | 4,650 | Value: 11.50 | | | | |
| 1968 IC Proof | 5,750 | Value: 11.50 | | | | |
| 1969 IC Proof | 1,175 | Value: 20.00 | | | | |
| 1970 IC Proof | 2,060 | Value: 18.00 | | | | |

**5 GOURDES** **KM# 64.2** **Weight:** 23.5200 g. **Composition:** 0.9990 Silver .7555 oz. ASW **Reverse:** Additional "1 AR" countermark at 8 o'clock

| Date | Mintage | F | VF | XF | Unc | BU |
|---|---|---|---|---|---|---|
| 1970 Proof | — | Value: 25.00 | | | | |

**5 GOURDES** **KM# 78** **Weight:** 23.5200 g. **Composition:** 0.9990 Silver .7555 oz. ASW **Reverse:** Similar to KM#64 **Note:** Haitienne Paradise

| Date | Mintage | F | VF | XF | Unc | BU |
|---|---|---|---|---|---|---|
| 1971 IC Proof | 1,585 | Value: 60.00 | | | | |

**5 GOURDES** **KM# 156** **Composition:** Brass **Obverse:** Four portraits **Reverse:** National emblem

| Date | Mintage | F | VF | XF | Unc | BU |
|---|---|---|---|---|---|---|
| 1995 | — | — | — | — | 2.75 | — |

**5 GOURDES** **KM# 156a** **Composition:** Bronze Plated Steel

| Date | Mintage | F | VF | XF | Unc | BU |
|---|---|---|---|---|---|---|
| 1995 | — | — | — | — | 3.00 | — |

**10 GOURDES** **KM# 65.1** **Weight:** 47.0500 g. **Composition:** 0.9990 Silver 1.5113 oz. ASW **Series:** 10th Anniversary of Revolution **Obverse:** General Louverture

| Date | Mintage | F | VF | XF | Unc | BU |
|---|---|---|---|---|---|---|
| 1967 IC Proof | 6,750 | Value: 22.00 | | | | |
| 1968 IC Proof | 5,725 | Value: 22.00 | | | | |
| 1969 IC Proof | 1,100 | Value: 30.00 | | | | |
| 1970 IC Proof | 1,500 | Value: 30.00 | | | | |

**10 GOURDES** **KM# 65.2** **Weight:** 47.0500 g. **Composition:** 0.9990 Silver 1.5113 oz. ASW **Reverse:** Additional "1 AR" countermark left of the initials "IC"

| Date | Mintage | F | VF | XF | Unc | BU |
|---|---|---|---|---|---|---|
| 1970 IC Proof | — | Value: 65.50 | | | | |

**10 GOURDES** **KM# 79** **Weight:** 47.0500 g. **Composition:** 0.9990 Silver 1.5113 oz. ASW **Obverse:** Seminole Chief - Osceola **Reverse:** Similar to KM#65

| Date | Mintage | F | VF | XF | Unc | BU |
|---|---|---|---|---|---|---|
| 1971 IC Proof | 3,535 | Value: 35.00 | | | | |

**10 GOURDES** **KM# 80** **Weight:** 47.0500 g. **Composition:** 0.9990 Silver 1.5113 oz. ASW **Obverse:** Sioux Chief - Sitting Bull **Reverse:** Similar to KM#65

| Date | Mintage | F | VF | XF | Unc | BU |
|---|---|---|---|---|---|---|
| 1971 IC Proof | 3,185 | Value: 35.00 | | | | |

**10 GOURDES** **KM# 81** **Weight:** 47.0500 g. **Composition:** 0.9990 Silver 1.5113 oz. ASW **Obverse:** Fox Chief - Playing Fox **Reverse:** Similar to KM#65

| Date | Mintage | F | VF | XF | Unc | BU |
|---|---|---|---|---|---|---|
| 1971 IC Proof | 3,035 | Value: 35.00 | | | | |

**10 GOURDES** **KM# 82** **Weight:** 47.0500 g. **Composition:** 0.9990 Silver 1.5113 oz. ASW **Obverse:** Chiricahua Chief - Geronimo **Reverse:** Similar to KM#65

| Date | Mintage | F | VF | XF | Unc | BU |
|---|---|---|---|---|---|---|
| 1971 IC Proof | 3,285 | Value: 35.00 | | | | |

**10 GOURDES** **KM# 83** **Weight:** 47.0500 g. **Composition:** 0.9990 Silver 1.5113 oz. ASW **Obverse:** Seminole Chief - Billy Bowlegs **Reverse:** Similar to KM#65

| Date | Mintage | F | VF | XF | Unc | BU |
|---|---|---|---|---|---|---|
| 1971 IC Proof | 3,735 | Value: 35.00 | | | | |

**10 GOURDES** **KM# 84** **Weight:** 47.0500 g. **Composition:** 0.9990 Silver 1.5113 oz. ASW **Obverse:** Nez Perce Chief - Joseph **Reverse:** Similar to KM#65

| Date | Mintage | F | VF | XF | Unc | BU |
|---|---|---|---|---|---|---|
| 1971 IC Proof | 3,235 | Value: 35.00 | | | | |

**10 GOURDES** **KM# 85** **Weight:** 47.0500 g. **Composition:** 0.9990 Silver 1.5113 oz. ASW **Obverse:** Yankton Sioux Chief - War Eagle **Reverse:** Similar to KM#65

| Date | Mintage | F | VF | XF | Unc | BU |
|---|---|---|---|---|---|---|
| 1971 IC Proof | 3,135 | Value: 35.00 | | | | |

**10 GOURDES** **KM# 86** **Weight:** 47.0500 g. **Composition:** 0.9990 Silver 1.5113 oz. ASW **Obverse:** Oglala Sioux Chief - Red Cloud **Reverse:** Similar to KM#65

| Date | Mintage | F | VF | XF | Unc | BU |
|---|---|---|---|---|---|---|
| 1971 IC Proof | 3,235 | Value: 35.00 | | | | |

**10 GOURDES** **KM# 87** **Weight:** 47.0500 g. **Composition:** 0.9990 Silver 1.5113 oz. ASW **Obverse:** Cherokee Chief - Stalking Turkey **Reverse:** Similar to KM#65

| Date | Mintage | F | VF | XF | Unc | BU |
|---|---|---|---|---|---|---|
| 1971 IC Proof | 3,185 | Value: 35.00 | | | | |

**20 GOURDES** **KM# 66** **Weight:** 3.9500 g. **Composition:** 0.9000 Gold .1143 oz. AGW **Series:** 10th Anniversary of Revolution **Note:** Mackandal

| Date | Mintage | F | VF | XF | Unc | BU |
|---|---|---|---|---|---|---|
| 1967 IC Proof | 10,351 | Value: 50.00 | | | | |
| 1968 IC Proof | — | Value: 50.00 | | | | |
| 1969 IC Proof | — | Value: 60.00 | | | | |
| 1970 IC Proof | — | Value: 65.00 | | | | |

**25 GOURDES** **KM# 67.1** **Weight:** 117.6000 g. **Composition:** 0.9990 Silver 3.7809 oz. ASW **Subject:** 10th Anniversary of Revolution **Obverse:** Art objects **Reverse:** Similar to 5 Gourdes, KM#64 **Size:** 60 mm. **Note:** Illustration reduced.

| Date | Mintage | F | VF | XF | Unc | BU |
|---|---|---|---|---|---|---|
| 1967 IC Proof | 4,650 | Value: 45.00 | | | | |
| 1968 IC Proof | 5,810 | Value: 45.00 | | | | |
| 1969 IC Proof | 1,115 | Value: 65.00 | | | | |
| 1970 IC Proof | 1,000 | Value: 65.00 | | | | |

**25 GOURDES** **KM# 67** **Weight:** 117.6000 g. **Composition:** 0.9990 Silver 3. oz. ASW **Subject:** 10th Anniversary of Revolution - Art Objects **Reverse:** Similar to 5 Gourdes, KM#64 **Size:** 60 mm. **Note:** Illustration reduced.

| Date | Mintage | F | VF | XF | Unc | BU |
|---|---|---|---|---|---|---|
| 1967 IC Proof | 4,650 | Value: 45.00 | | | | |
| 1968 IC Proof | 5,810 | Value: 45.00 | | | | |
| 1969 IC Proof | 1,115 | Value: 70.00 | | | | |
| 1970 IC Proof | 1,000 | Value: 70.00 | | | | |

**25 GOURDES** **KM# 67.2** **Weight:** 117.6000 g. **Composition:** 0.9990 Silver 3.7809 oz. ASW **Reverse:** Additional "1 AR" countermark at 8 o'clock **Size:** 60 mm.

| Date | Mintage | F | VF | XF | Unc | BU |
|---|---|---|---|---|---|---|
| 1970 Proof | — | Value: 160 | | | | |

**25 GOURDES** **KM# 88** **Weight:** 117.6000 g. **Composition:** 0.9990 Silver 3.7809 oz. ASW **Obverse:** International airport **Reverse:** Similar to KM#67; similar to 5 Gourdes KM#64 **Note:** Illustration reduced.

| Date | Mintage | F | VF | XF | Unc | BU |
|---|---|---|---|---|---|---|
| 1971 IC Proof | 1,935 | Value: 75.00 | | | | |

**25 GOURDES** **KM# 102** **Weight:** 10.0000 g. **Composition:** 0.9250 Silver .2973 oz. ASW

| Date | Mintage | F | VF | XF | Unc | BU |
|---|---|---|---|---|---|---|
| 1973 | 6,100 | — | — | — | 6.00 | — |
| 1973 Proof | 5,470 | Value: 7.00 | | | | |
| 1974 Proof | — | Value: 30.00 | | | | |

**25 GOURDES** **KM# 103** **Weight:** 10.0000 g. **Composition:** 0.9250 Silver .2973 oz. ASW **Subject:** World Soccer Championship Games

| Date | Mintage | F | VF | XF | Unc | BU |
|---|---|---|---|---|---|---|
| 1973 | 57,000 | — | — | — | 5.50 | — |
| 1973 Proof | 6,430 | Value: 7.00 | | | | |

**25 GOURDES** **KM# 112.1** **Weight:** 8.3750 g. **Composition:** 0.9250 Silver .2491 oz. ASW **Series:** United States Bicentennial

| Date | Mintage | F | VF | XF | Unc | BU |
|---|---|---|---|---|---|---|
| 1974 | 25,000 | — | — | — | 6.00 | — |
| 1974 Proof | 600 | Value: 20.00 | | | | |
| 1975 Proof | — | Value: 35.00 | | | | |
| 1976 Proof | 10,000 | Value: 12.50 | | | | |

**25 GOURDES** **KM# 112.2** **Weight:** 8.3750 g. **Composition:** 0.9250 Silver .2491 oz. ASW **Obverse:** Error; without country name at top

| Date | Mintage | F | VF | XF | Unc | BU |
|---|---|---|---|---|---|---|
| 1974 | 25,000 | — | — | — | 40.00 | — |

**25 GOURDES** **KM# 121** **Weight:** 8.3750 g. **Composition:** 0.9250 Silver .2491 oz. ASW **Series:** International Women's Year **Reverse:** Similar to KM#67

| Date | Mintage | F | VF | XF | Unc | BU |
|---|---|---|---|---|---|---|
| 1975 | 7,180 | — | — | — | 16.50 | — |
| 1975 Proof | 1,440 | Value: 35.00 | | | | |

**30 GOURDES** **KM# 72** **Weight:** 9.1100 g. **Composition:** 0.8580 Gold .1713 oz. AGW **Series:** 10th Anniversary of Revolution **Obverse:** Citadel of Saint Christopher

| Date | Mintage | F | VF | XF | Unc | BU |
|---|---|---|---|---|---|---|
| 1969 IC Proof | 1,185 | Value: 125 | | | | |
| 1970 IC Proof | Inc. above | Value: 150 | | | | |

**40 GOURDES** **KM# 73** **Weight:** 12.1500 g. **Composition:** 0.5850 Gold .2285 oz. AGW **Series:** 10th Anniversary of Revolution **Obverse:** J. J. Dessalines

| Date | Mintage | F | VF | XF | Unc | BU |
|---|---|---|---|---|---|---|
| 1969 Proof | 1,005 | Value: 200 | | | | |
| 1970 Proof | Inc. above | Value: 220 | | | | |

**50 GOURDES** **KM# 68** **Weight:** 9.8700 g. **Composition:** 0.9000 Gold .2856 oz. AGW **Series:** 10th Anniversary of Revolution **Obverse:** Dancer

| Date | Mintage | F | VF | XF | Unc | BU |
|---|---|---|---|---|---|---|
| 1967 IC Proof | 8,681 | Value: 130 | | | | |
| 1968 IC Proof | — | Value: 180 | | | | |
| 1969 IC Proof | — | Value: 210 | | | | |
| 1970 IC Proof | — | Value: 235 | | | | |

**50 GOURDES** **KM# 89** **Weight:** 9.8700 g. **Composition:** 0.9000 Gold .2856 oz. AGW **Series:** 10th Anniversary of Revolution **Reverse:** Similar to KM#68 **Note:** Heros de Vertieres

| Date | Mintage | F | VF | XF | Unc | BU |
|---|---|---|---|---|---|---|
| 1971 IC Proof | 485 | Value: 300 | | | | |

**50 GOURDES** **KM# 104** **Weight:** 20.0000 g. **Composition:** 0.9250 Silver .5949 oz. ASW **Obverse:** Woman on the beach

| Date | Mintage | F | VF | XF | Unc | BU |
|---|---|---|---|---|---|---|
| 1973 | 8,685 | — | — | — | 16.50 | — |
| 1973 Proof | 5,973 | Value: 20.00 | | | | |
| 1974 Proof | — | Value: 45.00 | | | | |

**50 GOURDES KM# 105 Weight:** 20.0000 g. **Composition:** 0.9250 Silver .5949 oz. ASW **Obverse:** Woman and child

| Date | Mintage | F | VF | XF | Unc | BU |
|---|---|---|---|---|---|---|
| 1973 | 7,300 | — | — | — | 13.50 | — |
| 1973 Proof | 5,853 | Value: 16.50 | | | | |
| 1974 | — | — | — | — | 37.50 | — |
| 1974 Proof | — | Value: 45.00 | | | | |

**50 GOURDES KM# 106 Weight:** 16.7500 g. **Composition:** 0.9250 Silver .4982 oz. ASW **Series:** World Soccer Championship Games

| Date | Mintage | F | VF | XF | Unc | BU |
|---|---|---|---|---|---|---|
| 1973 Proof | 12,000 | Value: 15.00 | | | | |

**50 GOURDES KM# 113 Weight:** 16.7500 g. **Composition:** 0.9250 Silver .4982 oz. ASW **Series:** 1976 Montreal Olympiad

| Date | Mintage | F | VF | XF | Unc | BU |
|---|---|---|---|---|---|---|
| 1974 | 21,000 | — | — | — | 15.00 | — |
| 1974 Proof | 2,358 | Value: 22.00 | | | | |
| 1975 Proof | — | Value: 27.50 | | | | |
| 1976 | — | — | — | — | — | — |
| 1976 Thin 6; Proof | 8,000 | Value: 25.00 | | | | |
| 1976 Thick 6; Proof | Inc. above | Value: 30.00 | | | | |

**50 GOURDES KM# 114 Weight:** 16.7500 g. **Composition:** 0.9250 Silver .4982 oz. ASW **Reverse:** Smaller 4 in date

| Date | Mintage | F | VF | XF | Unc | BU |
|---|---|---|---|---|---|---|
| 1974 | — | — | — | — | 20.00 | — |
| 1974 Proof | — | Value: 30.00 | | | | |

**50 GOURDES KM# 123 Weight:** 16.7500 g. **Composition:** 0.9250 Silver .4982 oz. ASW **Note:** Holy Year

| Date | Mintage | F | VF | XF | Unc | BU |
|---|---|---|---|---|---|---|
| 1974 | — | — | — | — | 12.50 | — |
| 1974 Proof | 960 | Value: 25.00 | | | | |
| 1975 | — | — | — | — | 35.00 | — |
| 1976 Proof | 6,000 | Value: 25.00 | | | | |

**50 GOURDES KM# 131 Weight:** 21.3000 g. **Composition:** 0.9250 Silver .6334 oz. ASW **Obverse:** Queen of the sugar **Reverse:** Similar to KM#104

| Date | Mintage | F | VF | XF | Unc | BU |
|---|---|---|---|---|---|---|
| 1977 | 321 | — | — | — | 30.00 | — |
| 1977 Proof | 602 | Value: 37.50 | | | | |

**50 GOURDES KM# 127 Weight:** 21.3000 g. **Composition:** 0.9250 Silver .6334 oz. ASW **Series:** World Soccer Championsip Games **Reverse:** Similar to KM#104

| Date | Mintage | F | VF | XF | Unc | BU |
|---|---|---|---|---|---|---|
| 1977 | 11,000 | — | — | — | 20.00 | — |
| 1977 Proof | 9,000 | Value: 25.00 | | | | |

**50 GOURDES KM# 128 Weight:** 21.3000 g. **Composition:** 0.9250 Silver .6334 oz. ASW **Subject:** Human Rights **Reverse:** Similar to KM#104

| Date | Mintage | F | VF | XF | Unc | BU |
|---|---|---|---|---|---|---|
| 1977 | 800 | — | — | — | 27.50 | — |
| 1977 Proof | 545 | Value: 35.00 | | | | |

**50 GOURDES KM# 129 Weight:** 21.3000 g. **Composition:** 0.9250 Silver .6334 oz. ASW **Series:** 1980 Moscow Olympics

| Date | Mintage | F | VF | XF | Unc | BU |
|---|---|---|---|---|---|---|
| 1977 | 3,969 | — | — | — | 22.50 | — |
| 1977 Proof | 3,720 | Value: 27.50 | | | | |
| 1978 Proof | Est. 350 | Value: 225 | | | | |

**50 GOURDES KM# 130.1 Weight:** 21.3000 g. **Composition:** 0.9250 Silver .6334 oz. ASW **Series:** 20th Anniversary of European Market

| Date | Mintage | F | VF | XF | Unc | BU |
|---|---|---|---|---|---|---|
| 1977 | 421 | — | — | — | 65.00 | — |
| 1977 Proof | 364 | Value: 80.00 | | | | |

**50 GOURDES KM# 130.2 Weight:** 21.3000 g. **Composition:** 0.9250 Silver .6334 oz. ASW **Obverse:** Entire area within circle frosted **Reverse:** Date added below arms

| Date | Mintage | F | VF | XF | Unc | BU |
|---|---|---|---|---|---|---|
| 1978 | — | — | — | — | 75.00 | — |
| 1978 Proof | — | Value: 90.00 | | | | |

**50 GOURDES KM# 149 Weight:** 20.0000 g. **Composition:** 0.9250 Silver .5948 oz. ASW **Series:** F.A.O.

| Date | Mintage | F | VF | XF | Unc | BU |
|---|---|---|---|---|---|---|
| 1981R | Est. 14,000 | — | — | — | 30.00 | — |
| 1981R Proof | — | Value: 55.00 | | | | |

**50 GOURDES** **KM# 150** **Weight:** 20.0000 g. **Composition:** 0.9250 Silver .5948 oz. ASW **Subject:** Holy Year

| Date | Mintage | F | VF | XF | Unc | BU |
|---|---|---|---|---|---|---|
| 1983R Proof | 1,000 | Value: 85.00 | | | | |

**60 GOURDES** **KM# 74** **Weight:** 18.2200 g. **Composition:** 0.5850 Gold .3427 oz. AGW **Series:** 10th Anniversary of the Revolution **Obverse:** Alexandre Petion

| Date | Mintage | F | VF | XF | Unc | BU |
|---|---|---|---|---|---|---|
| 1969 IC Proof | 935 | Value: 225 | | | | |
| 1970 IC Proof | Inc. above | Value: 375 | | | | |

**100 GOURDES** **KM# 69** **Weight:** 19.7500 g. **Composition:** 0.9000 Gold .5715 oz. AGW **Series:** 10th Anniversary of the Revolution **Obverse:** Marie Jeanne

| Date | Mintage | F | VF | XF | Unc | BU |
|---|---|---|---|---|---|---|
| 1967 IC Proof | Est. 8,682 | Value: 285 | | | | |
| 1968 IC Proof | — | Value: 325 | | | | |
| 1969 IC Proof | — | Value: 325 | | | | |
| 1970 IC Proof | — | Value: 350 | | | | |

**100 GOURDES** **KM# 90** **Weight:** 19.7500 g. **Composition:** 0.9000 Gold .5715 oz. AGW **Obverse:** Seminole Tribal Chief - Osceola **Reverse:** Similar to KM#69

| Date | Mintage | F | VF | XF | Unc | BU |
|---|---|---|---|---|---|---|
| 1971 IC Proof | 435 | Value: 375 | | | | |

**100 GOURDES** **KM# 91** **Weight:** 19.7500 g. **Composition:** 0.9000 Gold .5715 oz. AGW **Obverse:** Sioux Chief - Sitting Bull **Reverse:** Similar to KM#69

| Date | Mintage | F | VF | XF | Unc | BU |
|---|---|---|---|---|---|---|
| 1971 IC Proof | 475 | Value: 375 | | | | |

**100 GOURDES** **KM# 92** **Weight:** 19.7500 g. **Composition:** 0.9000 Gold .5715 oz. AGW **Obverse:** Fox Chief - Playing Fox **Reverse:** Similar to KM#69

| Date | Mintage | F | VF | XF | Unc | BU |
|---|---|---|---|---|---|---|
| 1971 IC Proof | 425 | Value: 375 | | | | |

**100 GOURDES** **KM# 93** **Weight:** 19.7500 g. **Composition:** 0.9000 Gold .5715 oz. AGW **Obverse:** Chiricahua Chief - Geronimo **Reverse:** Similar to KM#69

| Date | Mintage | F | VF | XF | Unc | BU |
|---|---|---|---|---|---|---|
| 1971 IC Proof | 520 | Value: 375 | | | | |

**100 GOURDES** **KM# 94** **Weight:** 19.7500 g. **Composition:** 0.9000 Gold .5715 oz. AGW **Obverse:** Seminole Chiel - Billy Bowlegs **Reverse:** Similar to KM#69

| Date | Mintage | F | VF | XF | Unc | BU |
|---|---|---|---|---|---|---|
| 1971 IC Proof | 425 | Value: 375 | | | | |

**100 GOURDES** **KM# 95** **Weight:** 19.7500 g. **Composition:** 0.9000 Gold .5715 oz. AGW **Obverse:** Nez Perce Chief - Joseph **Reverse:** Similar to KM#69

| Date | Mintage | F | VF | XF | Unc | BU |
|---|---|---|---|---|---|---|
| 1971 IC Proof | 455 | Value: 375 | | | | |

**100 GOURDES** **KM# 96** **Weight:** 19.7500 g. **Composition:** 0.9000 Gold .5715 oz. AGW **Obverse:** Yankton Sioux Chief - War Eagle **Reverse:** Similar to KM#69

| Date | Mintage | F | VF | XF | Unc | BU |
|---|---|---|---|---|---|---|
| 1971 IC Proof | 455 | Value: 375 | | | | |

**100 GOURDES** **KM# 97** **Weight:** 19.7500 g. **Composition:** 0.9000 Gold .5715 oz. AGW **Obverse:** Oglala Sioux Chief - War Eagle **Reverse:** Similar to KM#69

| Date | Mintage | F | VF | XF | Unc | BU |
|---|---|---|---|---|---|---|
| 1971 IC Proof | 455 | Value: 375 | | | | |

**100 GOURDES** **KM# 98** **Weight:** 19.7500 g. **Composition:** 0.9000 Gold .5715 oz. AGW **Obverse:** Cherokee Chief - Stalking Turkey **Reverse:** Similar to KM#69

| Date | Mintage | F | VF | XF | Unc | BU |
|---|---|---|---|---|---|---|
| 1971 IC Proof | 425 | Value: 375 | | | | |

**100 GOURDES** **KM# 107** **Weight:** 1.4500 g. **Composition:** 0.9000 Gold .0419 oz. AGW **Obverse:** Christopher Columbus

| Date | Mintage | F | VF | XF | Unc | BU |
|---|---|---|---|---|---|---|
| 1973 | 3,233 | — | — | — | 32.00 | — |
| 1973 Proof | 915 | Value: 55.00 | | | | |

**100 GOURDES** **KM# 132** **Weight:** 43.0000 g. **Composition:** 0.9250 Silver 1.2789 oz. ASW **Obverse:** Presidents Sadat and Begin **Reverse:** Similar to KM#69

| Date | Mintage | F | VF | XF | Unc | BU |
|---|---|---|---|---|---|---|
| 1977 | 550 | — | — | — | 55.00 | — |
| 1977 Proof | 500 | Value: 80.00 | | | | |

**100 GOURDES** **KM# 133** **Weight:** 43.0000 g. **Composition:** 0.9250 Silver 1.2789 oz. ASW **Subject:** 20th Anniversary of European Market **Reverse:** Similar to KM#69; similar to KM#132

| Date | Mintage | F | VF | XF | Unc | BU |
|---|---|---|---|---|---|---|
| 1977 | 321 | — | — | — | 85.00 | — |
| 1977 Proof | 214 | Value: 100 | | | | |

**100 GOURDES** **KM# 134** **Weight:** 43.0000 g. **Composition:** 0.9250 Silver 1.2789 oz. ASW **Subject:** 50th Anniversary of Lindbergh's New York to Paris Flight **Reverse:** Similar to KM#69; similar to KM#132

| Date | Mintage | F | VF | XF | Unc | BU |
|---|---|---|---|---|---|---|
| 1977 | 321 | — | — | — | 80.00 | — |
| 1977 Proof | 214 | Value: 125 | | | | |

**100 GOURDES** **KM# 135** **Weight:** 43.0000 g. **Composition:** 0.9250 Silver 1.2789 oz. ASW **Obverse:** Statue of Liberty **Reverse:** Similar to KM#69; similar to KM#132

| Date | Mintage | F | VF | XF | Unc | BU |
|---|---|---|---|---|---|---|
| 1977 | 321 | — | — | — | 80.00 | — |
| 1977 Proof | 214 | Value: 125 | | | | |

**100 GOURDES** **KM# 158** **Weight:** 40.0000 g. **Composition:** 0.9250 Silver 1.1896 oz. ASW **Subject:** 10th Anniversary of the Presidency of Jean Claude Duvalier **Obverse:** Similar to 50 Centimes KM#148 but without FAO **Reverse:** Nurse and child

| Date | Mintage | F | VF | XF | Unc | BU |
|---|---|---|---|---|---|---|
| 1981R Proof | — | Value: 150 | | | | |

**100 GOURDES** **KM# 159** **Weight:** 40.0000 g. **Composition:** 0.9250 Silver 1.1896 oz. ASW **Subject:** 10th Anniversary of the Presidency of Jean Claude Duvalier **Obverse:** Similar to 50 Centimes KM#148 but without FAO **Reverse:** Infants on open book

| Date | Mintage | F | VF | XF | Unc | BU |
|---|---|---|---|---|---|---|
| 1981R Proof | — | Value: 150 | | | | |

**100 GOURDES** **KM# 160** **Weight:** 40.0000 g. **Composition:** 0.9250 Silver 1.1896 oz. ASW **Subject:** 10th Anniversary of the Presidency of Jean Claude Duvalier **Obverse:** Similar to 50 Centimes KM#148 but without FAO **Reverse:** Nude woman and man

| Date | Mintage | F | VF | XF | Unc | BU |
|---|---|---|---|---|---|---|
| 1981R Proof | — | Value: 175 | | | | |

**200 GOURDES** **KM# 70** **Weight:** 39.4900 g. **Composition:** 0.9000 Gold 1.1427 oz. AGW **Series:** 10th Anniversary of Revolution **Subject:** Revolt of Santo Domingo

| Date | Mintage | F | VF | XF | Unc | BU |
|---|---|---|---|---|---|---|
| 1967 IC Proof | Est. 4,199 | Value: 485 | | | | |
| 1968 IC Proof | — | Value: 500 | | | | |
| 1969 IC Proof | — | Value: 500 | | | | |
| 1970 IC Proof | — | Value: 550 | | | | |

**200 GOURDES** **KM# 99** **Weight:** 39.4900 g. **Composition:** 0.9000 Gold 1.1427 oz. AGW **Reverse:** Similar to 100 Gourdes, KM#69 **Note:** Revolutionist from Saint Dominique

| Date | Mintage | F | VF | XF | Unc | BU |
|---|---|---|---|---|---|---|
| 1971 IC Proof | 235 | Value: 800 | | | | |

**200 GOURDES** **KM# 108** **Weight:** 2.9100 g. **Composition:** 0.9000 Gold .0842 oz. AGW **Series:** World Soccer Championship Games

| Date | Mintage | F | VF | XF | Unc | BU |
|---|---|---|---|---|---|---|
| 1973 | 5,167 | — | — | — | 55.00 | — |
| 1973 Proof | 915 | Value: 80.00 | | | | |

**200 GOURDES** **KM# 115** **Weight:** 2.9100 g. **Composition:** 0.9000 Gold .0842 oz. AGW **Subject:** Holy Year **Reverse:** Finess stamped on hexagonal mound, spears with spearheads

| Date | Mintage | F | VF | XF | Unc | BU |
|---|---|---|---|---|---|---|
| 1974 | 4,965 | — | — | — | 55.00 | — |
| 1974 Proof | 660 | Value: 75.00 | | | | |

**200 GOURDES** **KM# 124** **Weight:** 2.9100 g. **Composition:** 0.9000 Gold .0842 oz. AGW **Subject:** Holy Year **Reverse:** Finess stamped on oval mound, spears with arrowheads

| Date | Mintage | F | VF | XF | Unc | BU |
|---|---|---|---|---|---|---|
| 1975 Proof | — | Value: 85.00 | | | | |

**200 GOURDES** **KM# 125** **Weight:** 2.9100 g. **Composition:** 0.9000 Gold .0842 oz. AGW **Series:** International Women's Year **Reverse:** Similar to KM#124

| Date | Mintage | F | VF | XF | Unc | BU |
|---|---|---|---|---|---|---|
| 1975 | 2,260 | — | — | — | 65.00 | — |
| 1975 Proof | 840 | Value: 125 | | | | |

**250 GOURDES** **KM# 75** **Weight:** 75.9500 g. **Composition:** 0.5850 Gold 1.4286 oz. AGW **Series:** 10th Anniversary of Revolution **Obverse:** King H. Christophe **Reverse:** Similar to KM#136

| Date | Mintage | F | VF | XF | Unc | BU |
|---|---|---|---|---|---|---|
| 1969 IC Proof | 470 | Value: 700 | | | | |
| 1970 IC Proof | — | Value: 1,000 | | | | |

**250 GOURDES** **KM# 136** **Weight:** 4.2500 g. **Composition:** 0.9000 Gold .1229 oz. AGW **Subject:** Human Rights

| Date | Mintage | F | VF | XF | Unc | BU |
|---|---|---|---|---|---|---|
| 1977 | 282 | — | — | — | 100 | — |
| 1977 Proof | 288 | Value: 115 | | | | |

**250 GOURDES** **KM# 137** **Weight:** 4.2500 g. **Composition:** 0.9000 Gold .1229 oz. AGW **Obverse:** Presidents Sadat and Begin

| Date | Mintage | F | VF | XF | Unc | BU |
|---|---|---|---|---|---|---|
| 1977 | 270 | — | — | — | 100 | — |
| 1977 Proof | 520 | Value: 95.00 | | | | |

**250 GOURDES** **KM# 138** **Weight:** 4.2500 g. **Composition:** 0.9000 Gold .1229 oz. AGW **Subject:** 20th Anniversary of European Market

| Date | Mintage | F | VF | XF | Unc | BU |
|---|---|---|---|---|---|---|
| 1977 | 107 | — | — | — | 165 | — |
| 1977 Proof | 107 | Value: 185 | | | | |

**250 GOURDES** **KM# 139** **Weight:** 4.2500 g. **Composition:** 0.9000 Gold .1229 oz. AGW **Subject:** 50th Anniversary of Lindbergh's New York to Paris Flight **Obverse:** Portrait of Lindbergh in flier's cap above "Spirit of St. Louis" **Reverse:** Similar to KM#137

| Date | Mintage | F | VF | XF | Unc | BU |
|---|---|---|---|---|---|---|
| 1977 | 107 | — | — | — | 215 | — |
| 1977 Proof | 107 | Value: 225 | | | | |

**500 GOURDES** **KM# 76** **Weight:** 151.9000 g. **Composition:** 0.5850 Gold 2.8572 oz. AGW **Series:** 10th Anniversary of Revolution **Obverse:** Haitian native art **Reverse:** Similar to KM#141 **Size:** 68 mm. **Note:** Illustration reduced.

| Date | Mintage | F | VF | XF | Unc | BU |
|---|---|---|---|---|---|---|
| 1969 IC Proof | 435 | Value: 2,000 | | | | |
| 1970 IC Proof | — | Value: 2,500 | | | | |

**500 GOURDES** **KM# 109** **Weight:** 7.2800 g. **Composition:** 0.9000 Gold .2106 oz. AGW

| Date | Mintage | F | VF | XF | Unc | BU |
|---|---|---|---|---|---|---|
| 1973 | 2,380 | — | — | — | 135 | — |
| 1973 Proof | 915 | Value: 160 | | | | |

**500 GOURDES** **KM# 110** **Weight:** 7.2800 g. **Composition:** 0.9000 Gold .2106 oz. AGW

| Date | Mintage | F | VF | XF | Unc | BU |
|---|---|---|---|---|---|---|
| 1973 | 2,265 | — | — | — | 115 | — |
| 1973 Proof | 915 | Value: 130 | | | | |

**500 GOURDES** **KM# 116** **Weight:** 6.5000 g. **Composition:** 0.9000 Gold .1881 oz. AGW **Obverse:** Same as 1000 Gourdes, KM#118 **Reverse:** Similar to KM#141

| Date | Mintage | F | VF | XF | Unc | BU |
|---|---|---|---|---|---|---|
| 1974 Proof | — | Value: 135 | | | | |

**500 GOURDES** **KM# 117** **Weight:** 6.5000 g. **Composition:** 0.9000 Gold .1881 oz. AGW **Series:** 1976 Montreal Olympics **Reverse:** Fineness stamped on hexagonal mound, spears with spearheads

| Date | Mintage | F | VF | XF | Unc | BU |
|---|---|---|---|---|---|---|
| 1974 | 3,489 | — | — | — | 100 | — |
| 1974 Proof | 1,140 | Value: 125 | | | | |

**500 GOURDES** **KM# 126** **Weight:** 6.5000 g. **Composition:** 0.9000 Gold .1881 oz. AGW **Series:** 1976 Montreal Olympics **Reverse:** Fineness stamped on hexagonal mound, spears with arrowheads

| Date | Mintage | F | VF | XF | Unc | BU |
|---|---|---|---|---|---|---|
| 1975 | 120 | — | — | — | 450 | — |

**500 GOURDES** **KM# 140** **Weight:** 8.5000 g. **Composition:** 0.9000 Gold .2459 oz. AGW **Series:** World Soccer Championship Games

| Date | Mintage | F | VF | XF | Unc | BU |
|---|---|---|---|---|---|---|
| 1977 | 450 | — | — | — | 175 | — |
| 1977 Proof | 200 | Value: 250 | | | | |

**500 GOURDES** **KM# 141** **Weight:** 8.5000 g. **Composition:** 0.9000 Gold .2459 oz. AGW **Series:** 1980 Moscow Olympics

| Date | Mintage | F | VF | XF | Unc | BU |
|---|---|---|---|---|---|---|
| 1977 | 695 | — | — | — | 165 | — |
| 1977 Proof | 504 | Value: 195 | | | | |
| 1978 Proof | Est. 350 | Value: 350 | | | | |

**500 GOURDES** **KM# 142** **Weight:** 8.5000 g. **Composition:** 0.9000 Gold .2459 oz. AGW **Subject:** 20th Anniversary of European Common Market **Obverse:** Map of Europe **Reverse:** Similar to KM#141

| Date | Mintage | F | VF | XF | Unc | BU |
|---|---|---|---|---|---|---|
| 1977 | 207 | — | — | — | 225 | — |
| 1977 Proof | 257 | Value: 265 | | | | |
| 1978 | — | — | — | — | 300 | — |
| 1978 Proof | 150 | Value: 400 | | | | |

**500 GOURDES** **KM# 143** **Weight:** 8.5000 g. **Composition:** 0.9000 Gold .2459 oz. AGW **Subject:** Economic Connections

| Date | Mintage | F | VF | XF | Unc | BU |
|---|---|---|---|---|---|---|
| 1977 | 107 | — | — | — | 225 | — |
| 1977 Proof | 107 | Value: 300 | | | | |

**500 GOURDES** **KM# 144** **Weight:** 8.5000 g. **Composition:** 0.9000 Gold .2459 oz. AGW **Obverse:** Jean-Claude Duvalier

| Date | Mintage | F | VF | XF | Unc | BU |
|---|---|---|---|---|---|---|
| 1977 | 107 | — | — | — | 225 | — |
| 1977 Proof | 328 | Value: 200 | | | | |

**500 GOURDES** **KM# 161** **Weight:** 7.0000 g. **Composition:** 0.9000 Gold .2025 oz. AGW **Subject:** 10th Anniversary of the Presidency of Jean Claud Duvalier **Obverse:** Similar to 10 Centimes KM#146 without FAO **Reverse:** Similar to 10 Centimes, KM#146

| Date | Mintage | F | VF | XF | Unc | BU |
|---|---|---|---|---|---|---|
| 1981R Proof | — | Value: 650 | | | | |

**500 GOURDES** **KM# 162** **Weight:** 7.0000 g. **Composition:** 0.9000 Gold .2025 oz. AGW **Subject:** 10th Anniversary of the Presidency of Jean Claud Duvalier **Obverse:** Similar to 20 Centimes KM#147 but without FAO **Reverse:** Similar to 20 Centimes, KM#147

| Date | Mintage | F | VF | XF | Unc | BU |
|---|---|---|---|---|---|---|
| 1981R Proof | — | Value: 650 | | | | |

**500 GOURDES** **KM# 163** **Weight:** 7.0000 g. **Composition:** 0.9000 Gold .2025 oz. AGW **Subject:** 10th Anniversary of the Presidency of Jean Claud Duvalier **Obverse:** Similar to 50 Centimes KM#148 but without FAO **Reverse:** Similar to 50 Centimes, KM#148

| Date | Mintage | F | VF | XF | Unc | BU |
|---|---|---|---|---|---|---|
| 1981R Proof | — | Value: 650 | | | | |

**500 GOURDES** **KM# 151** **Weight:** 10.5000 g. **Composition:** 0.9000 Gold .3038 oz. AGW **Subject:** Papal Visit

| Date | Mintage | F | VF | XF | Unc | BU |
|---|---|---|---|---|---|---|
| 1983R Proof | 1,000 | Value: 185 | | | | |

**1000 GOURDES** KM# 71 **Weight:** 197.4800 g. **Composition:** 0.9000 Gold 5.7148 oz. AGW **Series:** 10th Anniversary of Revolution **Obverse:** Dr. Francios Duvalier **Reverse:** Similar to KM#118

| Date | Mintage | F | VF | XF | Unc | BU |
|---|---|---|---|---|---|---|
| 1967 IC Proof | Est. 2,950 | Value: 2,400 | | | | |
| 1968 IC Proof | — | Value: 2,600 | | | | |
| 1969 IC Proof | — | Value: 2,850 | | | | |
| 1970 IC Proof | — | Value: 3,100 | | | | |

**1000 GOURDES** KM# 111 **Weight:** 14.5600 g. **Composition:** 0.9000 Gold .4213 oz. AGW **Obverse:** President Jean Claude Duvalier

| Date | Mintage | F | VF | XF | Unc | BU |
|---|---|---|---|---|---|---|
| 1973 | — | — | — | — | 200 | — |
| 1973 Proof | 915 | Value: 250 | | | | |

**1000 GOURDES** KM# 118.1 **Weight:** 13.0000 g. **Composition:** 0.9000 Gold .3762 oz. AGW **Series:** United States Bicentennial

| Date | Mintage | F | VF | XF | Unc | BU |
|---|---|---|---|---|---|---|
| 1974 | 3,040 | — | — | — | 190 | — |
| 1974 Proof | 480 | Value: 275 | | | | |
| 1975 Proof | — | Value: 600 | | | | |

**1000 GOURDES** KM# 118.2 **Weight:** 13.0000 g. **Composition:** 0.9000 Gold .3762 oz. AGW **Obverse:** Error; without country name at top

| Date | Mintage | F | VF | XF | Unc | BU |
|---|---|---|---|---|---|---|
| 1974 | — | — | — | — | 750 | — |

**1000 GOURDES** KM# 164 **Weight:** 14.0000 g. **Composition:** 0.9000 Gold .4051 oz. AGW **Subject:** 10th Anniversary of the Presidency of Jean Claude Duvalier **Obverse:** Similar to 50 Centimes KM#148 but without FAO **Reverse:** Three nudes and flag

| Date | Mintage | F | VF | XF | Unc | BU |
|---|---|---|---|---|---|---|
| 1981R Proof | — | Value: 1,150 | | | | |

## PATTERNS

Including off metal strikes

| KM# | Date | Mintage | Identification | Mkt Val |
|---|---|---|---|---|
| Pn87 | 1974 | — | 25 Gourdes. 0.9250 Silver. KM#112 | — |

## TRIAL STRIKES

| KM# | Date | Mintage | Identification | Mkt Val |
|---|---|---|---|---|
| TS1 | (1971) | — | 100 Gourdes. Gilt Bronze. KM#93 | 85.00 |

## MINT SETS

| KM# | Date | Mintage | Identification | Issue Price | Mkt Val |
|---|---|---|---|---|---|
| MS1 | 1973 (8) | 8,000 | KM#102, 104-105, 107-111, | 490 | 580 |
| MS2 | 1973 (4) | — | KM#102-105 | 60.00 | 37.50 |
| MS3 | 1974 (2) | — | KM#115, 123 | — | 70.00 |
| MS4 | 1975 (2) | — | KM#121, 125 | 50.25 | 65.00 |
| MS5 | 1976 (2) | — | KM#113, 117 | — | — |
| MS6 | 1995 (5) | — | KM#152a-156a | — | 10.00 |

## PROOF SETS

| KM# | Date | Mintage | Identification | Issue Price | Mkt Val |
|---|---|---|---|---|---|
| PS1 | 1967 (5) | 2,525 | KM#66, 68-71 | 722 | 3,250 |
| PSA1 | 1967 (8) | — | KM#64.1, 65-71 | — | 3,350 |
| PS2 | 1967 (3) | 4,650 | KM#64, 65, 67 | 47.00 | 85.00 |
| PS3 | 1968 (5) | 475 | KM#66, 68-71 | 823 | 3,875 |
| PS4 | 1968 (3) | 5,725 | KM#64, 65, 67 | 53.50 | 95.00 |
| PS5 | 1969 (5) | 435 | KM#72-76 | 475 | 3,250 |
| PS6 | 1969 (5) | 140 | KM#66, 68-71 | 823 | 4,150 |
| PS7 | 1969 (3) | 1,100 | KM#64, 65, 67 | 53.50 | 140 |
| PS8 | 1970 (5) | — | KM#66, 68-71 | 823 | 4,500 |
| PS9 | 1970 (3) | — | KM#64.2, 65.2, 67.2 | — | 260 |
| PSA9 | 1970 (3) | 1,000 | KM#64, 65, 67 | 53.50 | 140 |
| PS10 | 1971 (9) | — | KM#79-87 | 135 | 320 |
| PS11 | 1971 (9) | — | KM#90-98 | — | 3,375 |
| PSA11 | 1971 (18) | — | KM#79-87, 90-98 | — | 3,700 |
| PS12 | 1973 (8) | 1,250 | KM#102-105, 107-109, 111 | 830 | 575 |
| PS13 | 1973 (4) | 3,500 | KM#102-105 | 60.00 | 50.00 |
| PS14 | 1975 (2) | — | KM#121, 125 | 67.25 | 150 |
| PS17 | 1976 (3) | — | KM#112, 113, 123 | — | 60.00 |
| PS18 | 1978 (2) | 350 | KM#129, 141 | — | 475 |
| PS19 | 1978 (2) | — | KM#130.2, 142 | — | 450 |
| PS20 | 1981R (7) | 10 | KM#158-164 | — | 3,450 |

# HEJAZ

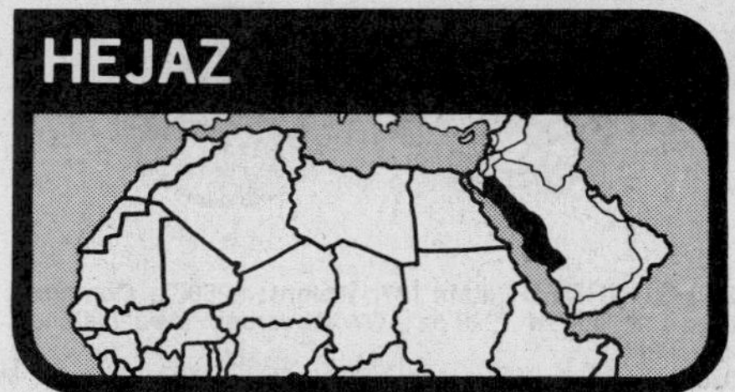

Hejaz, a province of Saudi Arabia and a former vilayet of the Ottoman Empire, occupies an 800-mile long (1,287km.) coastal strip between Nejd and the Red Sea. The province was a Turkish dependency until freed in World War I. Husain Ibn Ali, Amir of Mecca, opposed the Turkish control and, with the aid of Lawrence of Arabia, wrested much of Hejaz from the Turks and in 1916 assumed the title of King of Hejaz. Abd Al-Aziz Bin Sa'ud, of Nejd conquered Hejaz in 1925, and in 1926 combined it and Nejd into a single kingdom.

**TITLES**

**al-Hejaz** الحجاز

**RULERS**

al Husain Ibn Ali, AH1334-42/1916-24AD
Abd Al-Aziz Bin Sa'ud, AH1343-1373/1925-1953AD

**MONETARY SYSTEM**

40 Para = 1 Piastre (Ghirsh)
20 Piastres = 1 Riyal
100 Piastres = 1 Dinar

## KINGDOM

### COUNTERMARKED COINAGE

Minor Coins

Following the defeat of the Ottomans in 1916, Turkish 20 and 40 Para coins of Muhammed V and Muhammed VI were countermarked "al-Hejaz" in Arabic. The countermark was applied to the obverse side effacing the Ottoman Sultan's toughra, and thus refuting Turkish rule in Hejaz.

Countermarks on the reverse are rare errors. The 10 Para of Muhammed V and 10 and 20 Para (billon) of Abdul Mejid exist with a smaller, 6-milimeter countermark. These are probably unofficial and not contemporary. Other host coins are considered spurious.

**10 PARA** KM# 2 **Composition:** Nickel **Countermark:** "Hejaz"(Reshat) **Note:** Large countermark on Turkey 10 Para, KM#760. Accession date: AH1327.

| CM Date | Host Date | Good | VG | F | VF | XF |
|---|---|---|---|---|---|---|
| ND(1916-21) | AH1327//2-7 Rare | — | — | — | — | — |

**20 PARA** KM# 3 **Composition:** Nickel **Countermark:** "Hejaz" **Note:** Countermark on Turkey 20 Para, KM#761. Accession date: AH1327.

| CM Date | Host Date | Good | VG | F | VF | XF |
|---|---|---|---|---|---|---|
| ND(1916-21) | AH1327//2 | 5.00 | 9.00 | 18.00 | 35.00 | — |
| ND(1916-21) | AH1327//3 | 4.00 | 7.00 | 15.00 | 30.00 | — |
| ND(1916-21) | AH1327//4 | 3.00 | 6.00 | 12.00 | 25.00 | — |
| ND(1916-21) | AH1327//5 | 3.00 | 6.00 | 12.00 | 25.00 | — |
| ND(1916-21) | AH1327//6 | 3.00 | 6.00 | 12.00 | 25.00 | — |
| ND(1916-21) | AH1327//x r.y. obliterated | 2.00 | 5.00 | 10.00 | 20.00 | — |

**40 PARA** KM# 4 **Composition:** Nickel **Countermark:** "Hejaz" **Note:** Countermark on Turkey 40 Para, KM#766. Accession date: AH1327.

| CM Date | Host Date | Good | VG | F | VF | XF |
|---|---|---|---|---|---|---|
| ND(1916-21) | AH1327//3 | 6.00 | 10.00 | 20.00 | 40.00 | — |
| ND(1916-21) | AH1327//4 | 3.00 | 6.00 | 12.00 | 25.00 | — |
| ND(1916-21) | AH1327//5 | 3.00 | 6.00 | 12.00 | 25.00 | — |
| ND(1916-21) | AH1327//x r.y. obliterated | 2.00 | 5.00 | 10.00 | 20.00 | — |

**40 PARA** KM# 5 **Composition:** Copper-Nickel
**Countermark:** "Hejaz" **Note:** Countermark on Turkey 40 Para, KM#779. Accession date: AH1327.

| CM Date | Host Date | Good | VG | F | VF | XF |
|---|---|---|---|---|---|---|
| ND(1916-21) | AH1327//8 | 4.00 | 6.00 | 12.00 | 25.00 | — |
| ND(1916-21) | AH1327//9 | 9.00 | 18.00 | 35.00 | 75.00 | — |
| ND(1916-21) | AH1327//x p.y. obliterated | 3.00 | 6.00 | 10.00 | 20.00 | — |

**40 PARA** KM# 6 **Composition:** Copper-Nickel
**Countermark:** "Hejaz" **Note:** Countermark on Turkey 40 Para, KM#828. Accession date: AH1336.

| CM Date | Host Date | Good | VG | F | VF | XF |
|---|---|---|---|---|---|---|
| ND(1916-21) | AH1336//4 | 15.00 | 30.00 | 60.00 | 100 | — |
| ND(1916-21) | AH1336//x | 10.00 | 20.00 | 40.00 | 75.00 | — |

## COUNTERMARKED COINAGE

### Silver Coins

Silver coins of various sizes were also countermarked "al-Hejaz". The most common host coins include the Maria Theresa Thaler of Austria, and 5, 10, and 20 Kurush or Qirsh of Turkey and Egypt. The countermark occurs in various sizes and styles of script. These countermarks may have been applied by local silversmiths to discourage re-exportation of the badly needed hard currency and silver of known fineness.

Some crown-sized examples exist with both the "al-Hejaz" and "Nejd" countermarks. The authenticity of the silver countermarked coins has long been discussed, and it is likely that most were privatley produced. Other host coins are considered spurious.

**5 PIASTRES** KM# 12 **Composition:** Silver
**Countermark:** "Hejaz" **Note:** Countermark on Egypt 5 Qirsh, KM#308. Accession date: 1327.

| CM Date | Host Date | Good | VG | F | VF | XF |
|---|---|---|---|---|---|---|
| ND(1916-20) | ND(AH1327//2H-4H, 6H) | 20.00 | 40.00 | 75.00 | 150 | — |

**5 PIASTRES** KM# 10 **Composition:** Silver
**Countermark:** "Hejaz" **Note:** Countermark on Turkey 5 Kurush, KM#750. Accession date: AH1327.

| CM Date | Host Date | Good | VG | F | VF | XF |
|---|---|---|---|---|---|---|
| ND(1916-21) | ND(AH1327//1-7) | 20.00 | 40.00 | 75.00 | 150 | — |

**5 PIASTRES** KM# 11 **Composition:** Silver
**Countermark:** "Hejaz" **Note:** Countermark on Turkey 5 Kurush, KM#771. Accession date: AH1327.

| CM Date | Host Date | Good | VG | F | VF | XF |
|---|---|---|---|---|---|---|
| ND(1916-21) | ND(AH1327//7-9) | 20.00 | 40.00 | 75.00 | 150 | — |

**10 PIASTRES** KM# 15 **Composition:** Silver
**Countermark:** "Hejaz" **Note:** Countermark on Egypt 10 Qirsh, KM#309. Accession date: AH1327.

| CM Date | Host Date | Good | VG | F | VF | XF |
|---|---|---|---|---|---|---|
| ND(1916-21) | ND(AH1327//2H-4H, 6H) | 25.00 | 45.00 | 80.00 | 160 | — |

**10 PIASTRES** KM# 13 **Composition:** Silver
**Countermark:** "Hejaz" **Note:** Countermark on Turkey 10 Kurush, KM#751. Accession date: AH1327.

| CM Date | Host Date | Good | VG | F | VF | XF |
|---|---|---|---|---|---|---|
| ND(1916-21) | ND(AH1327//1-7) | 25.00 | 45.00 | 80.00 | 160 | — |

**10 PIASTRES** KM# 14 **Composition:** Silver
**Countermark:** "Hejaz" **Note:** Countermark on Turkey 10 Kurush, KM#772. Accession date: AH1327.

| CM Date | Host Date | Good | VG | F | VF | XF |
|---|---|---|---|---|---|---|
| ND(1916-21) | ND(AH1327//7-10) | 25.00 | 45.00 | 80.00 | 160 | — |

**20 PIASTRES** KM# 18 **Composition:** Silver
**Countermark:** "Hejaz" **Note:** Countermark on Austria Maria Theresa Thaler, KM#T1. Accession date: 1327.

| CM Date | Host Date | Good | VG | F | VF | XF |
|---|---|---|---|---|---|---|
| (1916-21) | 1780 restrike | 15.00 | 30.00 | 60.00 | 125 | — |

**20 PIASTRES** KM# 16 **Composition:** Silver
**Countermark:** "Hejaz" **Note:** Countermark on Egypt 20 Qirsh, KM#310. Accession date: 1327.

| CM Date | Host Date | Good | VG | F | VF | XF |
|---|---|---|---|---|---|---|
| ND(1916-21) | ND(AH1327//2H-4H, 6H) | 35.00 | 60.00 | 100 | 150 | — |

**20 PIASTRES** KM# 17 **Composition:** Silver
**Countermark:** "Hejaz" **Note:** Countermark on Turkey 20 Kurush, KM#780. Accession date: 1327.

| CM Date | Host Date | Good | VG | F | VF | XF |
|---|---|---|---|---|---|---|
| ND(1916-21) | ND(AH1327//8-10) | 35.00 | 60.00 | 100 | 150 | — |

## REGULAR COINAGE

All the regular coins of Hejaz bear the accessional date AH1334 of Al-Husain Ibn Ali, plus the regnal year. Many of the bronze coins occur with a light silver wash mostly on thicker specimens. A variety of planchet thicknesses exist.

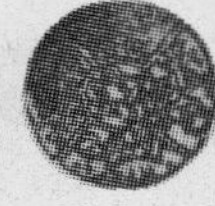

**1/8 PIASTRE** KM# 21 **Composition:** Bronze **Note:** Reeded and plain edge varieties exist.

| Date | Mintage | Good | VG | F | VF | XF |
|---|---|---|---|---|---|---|
| AH1334//5 | — | — | 25.00 | 50.00 | 100 | 200 |

**1/4 PIASTRE** KM# 22 **Weight:** 1.1400 g. **Composition:** Bronze **Note:** Reeded and plain edge varieties exist.

| Date | Mintage | Good | VG | F | VF | XF |
|---|---|---|---|---|---|---|
| AH1334//5 | — | — | 4.00 | 10.00 | 20.00 | 35.00 |
| AH1334//6/5 | — | — | 75.00 | 300 | 600 | 1,200 |
| AH1334//6 | — | — | 150 | 400 | 800 | 1,500 |

**1/4 PIASTRE** KM# 25 **Composition:** Bronze **Edge:** Plain

| Date | Mintage | Good | VG | F | VF | XF |
|---|---|---|---|---|---|---|
| AH1334//8 | — | — | 5.00 | 10.00 | 20.00 | 35.00 |

**1/2 PIASTRE** KM# 23 **Composition:** Bronze **Note:** Reeded and plain edge varieties exist.

| Date | Mintage | Good | VG | F | VF | XF |
|---|---|---|---|---|---|---|
| AH1334//5 | — | — | 3.00 | 10.00 | 20.00 | 35.00 |

**1/2 PIASTRE** KM# 26 **Composition:** Bronze **Note:** Similar to 1/4 Piatre, KM#25. All known specimens were overstruck as "Nejd" KM#1.

| Date | Mintage | Good | VG | F | VF | XF |
|---|---|---|---|---|---|---|
| AH1334//8 Rare | — | — | — | — | — | — |

**PIASTRE** KM# 24 **Composition:** Bronze **Edge:** Reeded

| Date | Mintage | Good | VG | F | VF | XF |
|---|---|---|---|---|---|---|
| AH1334//5 | — | — | 6.00 | 10.00 | 20.00 | 35.00 |
| AH1334//6/5 | — | — | 100 | 200 | 400 | 600 |

**PIASTRE** KM# 27 **Composition:** Bronze **Edge:** Plain

| Date | Mintage | Good | VG | F | VF | XF |
|---|---|---|---|---|---|---|
| AH1334//8 | — | — | 10.00 | 20.00 | 35.00 | 60.00 |

**5 PIASTRES** KM# 28 **Weight:** 6.1000 g. **Composition:** 0.9170 Silver .1798 oz. ASW

| Date | Mintage | Good | VG | F | VF | XF |
|---|---|---|---|---|---|---|
| AH1334//8 | — | — | 15.00 | 40.00 | 75.00 | 150 |

**10 PIASTRES** KM# 29 **Weight:** 12.0500 g. **Composition:** 0.9170 Silver .3552 oz. ASW

| Date | Mintage | Good | VG | F | VF | XF |
|---|---|---|---|---|---|---|
| AH1334//8 | — | — | 100 | 200 | 400 | 800 |

**20 PIASTRES (1 Riyal)** **KM# 30** **Weight:** 24.1000 g. **Composition:** 0.9170 Silver .7105 oz. ASW

| Date | Mintage | Good | VG | F | VF | XF |
|---|---|---|---|---|---|---|
| AH1334//8 | — | — | 20.00 | 45.00 | 90.00 | 120 |
| AH1334//9 | — | — | 30.00 | 62.50 | 125 | 200 |

**DINAR HASHIMI** **KM# 31** **Composition:** Gold

| Date | Mintage | Good | VG | F | VF | XF |
|---|---|---|---|---|---|---|
| AH1334//8 | — | — | — | 125 | 250 | 350 |

# MECCA

## KINGDOM

### TRANSITIONAL COINAGE

Struck at Hejaz Mint during occupied Mecca by Abd Al-Aziz Bin Sa'ud while establishing his kingdom.

**1/4 GHIRSH** **KM# 1** **Composition:** Copper Or Bronze
**Note:** Several varieties exist, including reeded and plain edges. Some specimens struck over bronze Hejaz 1/4 and 1/2 Piastres (KM#23 and KM#26), and some occur with a light silver wash.

| Date | Mintage | Good | VG | F | VF | XF |
|---|---|---|---|---|---|---|
| AH1343 | — | — | 15.00 | 25.00 | 50.00 | 75.00 |

**1/2 GHIRSH** **KM# 2.1** **Composition:** Copper Or Bronze
**Obverse:** Legend right of toughra **Obv. Legend:** "Al-Faisal al Saud"

| Date | Mintage | Good | VG | F | VF | XF |
|---|---|---|---|---|---|---|
| AH1343 | — | — | 10.00 | 20.00 | 40.00 | 75.00 |

**1/2 GHIRSH** **KM# 2.2** **Composition:** Copper Or Bronze
**Obverse:** Legend right of toughra **Obv. Legend:** "al-Faisal"

| Date | Mintage | Good | VG | F | VF | XF |
|---|---|---|---|---|---|---|
| AH1343 | — | — | 18.00 | 35.00 | 75.00 | 150 |

### REGULAR COINAGE

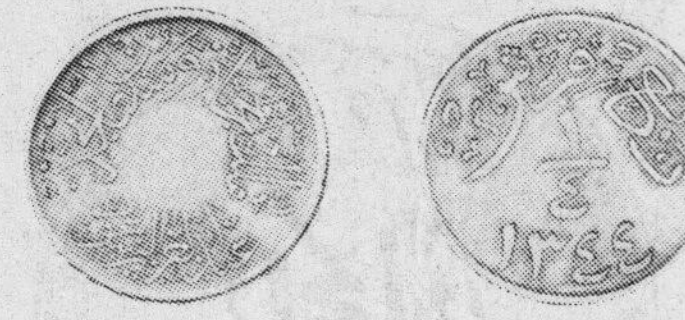

**1/4 GHIRSH** **KM# 4** **Composition:** Copper-Nickel

| Date | Mintage | Good | VG | F | VF | XF |
|---|---|---|---|---|---|---|
| AH1344 | — | — | 1.25 | 2.00 | 6.00 | 15.00 |
| AH1344 Proof | — | — | — | — | — | — |

**1/2 GHIRSH** **KM# 5** **Composition:** Copper-Nickel

| Date | Mintage | Good | VG | F | VF | XF |
|---|---|---|---|---|---|---|
| AH1344 | — | — | 2.50 | 4.00 | 12.00 | 18.00 |
| AH1344 Proof | — | — | — | — | — | — |

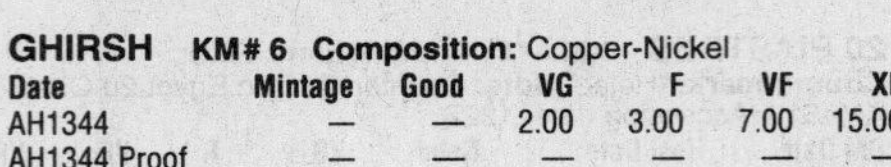

**GHIRSH** **KM# 6** **Composition:** Copper-Nickel

| Date | Mintage | Good | VG | F | VF | XF |
|---|---|---|---|---|---|---|
| AH1344 | — | — | 2.00 | 3.00 | 7.00 | 15.00 |
| AH1344 Proof | — | — | — | — | — | — |

# HEJAZ & NEJD

## KINGDOM

### REGULAR COINAGE

**1/4 GHIRSH** **KM# 7** **Composition:** Copper-Nickel

| Date | Mintage | VG | F | VF | XF | Unc |
|---|---|---|---|---|---|---|
| AH1346 | 3,000,000 | 3.00 | 5.00 | 8.00 | 20.00 | — |

**1/4 GHIRSH** **KM# 13** **Composition:** Copper-Nickel

| Date | Mintage | VG | F | VF | XF | Unc |
|---|---|---|---|---|---|---|
| AH1348 | — | 3.00 | 5.00 | 8.00 | 20.00 | — |
| AH1348 Proof | — | — | — | — | — | — |

**1/2 GHIRSH** **KM# 8** **Composition:** Copper-Nickel

| Date | Mintage | VG | F | VF | XF | Unc |
|---|---|---|---|---|---|---|
| AH1346 | 3,000,000 | 3.00 | 5.00 | 8.00 | 20.00 | — |

**1/2 GHIRSH** **KM# 14** **Composition:** Copper-Nickel

| Date | Mintage | VG | F | VF | XF | Unc |
|---|---|---|---|---|---|---|
| AH1348 | — | 3.00 | 5.00 | 8.00 | 25.00 | — |
| AH1348 Proof | — | — | — | — | — | — |

**GHIRSH** **KM# 9** **Composition:** Copper-Nickel

| Date | Mintage | VG | F | VF | XF | Unc |
|---|---|---|---|---|---|---|
| AH1346 | 3,000,000 | 3.00 | 5.00 | 10.00 | 35.00 | — |

**GHIRSH** **KM# 15** **Composition:** Copper-Nickel

| Date | Mintage | VG | F | VF | XF | Unc |
|---|---|---|---|---|---|---|
| AH1348 | — | 3.00 | 5.00 | 8.50 | 25.00 | — |
| AH1348 Proof | — | — | — | — | — | — |

**1/4 RIYAL** **KM# 10** **Weight:** 6.0500 g. **Composition:** 0.9170 Silver .1783 oz. ASW

| Date | Mintage | VG | F | VF | XF | Unc |
|---|---|---|---|---|---|---|
| AH1346 | 400,000 | 12.50 | 20.00 | 45.00 | 75.00 | — |
| AH1346 Proof | — | — | — | — | — | — |
| AH1348 | 200,000 | 17.50 | 30.00 | 60.00 | 100 | — |
| AH1348 Proof | — | — | — | — | — | — |

**1/2 RIYAL** **KM# 11** **Weight:** 12.1000 g. **Composition:** 0.9170 Silver .3567 oz. ASW

| Date | Mintage | VG | F | VF | XF | Unc |
|---|---|---|---|---|---|---|
| AH1346 | 200,000 | 55.00 | 100 | 165 | 300 | — |
| AH1346 Proof | — | Value: 200 | | | | |
| AH1348 | 100,000 | 55.00 | 100 | 165 | 300 | — |
| AH1348 Proof | — | — | — | — | — | — |

**RIYAL** **KM# 12** **Weight:** 24.1000 g. **Composition:** 0.9170 Silver .7105 oz. ASW

| Date | Mintage | VG | F | VF | XF | Unc |
|---|---|---|---|---|---|---|
| AH1346 | 800,000 | 15.00 | 25.00 | 50.00 | 80.00 | — |
| AH1346 Proof | — | Value: 350 | | | | |
| AH1348 | 400,000 | 20.00 | 30.00 | 85.00 | 120 | — |
| AH1348 Proof | — | — | — | — | — | — |

# HONDURAS

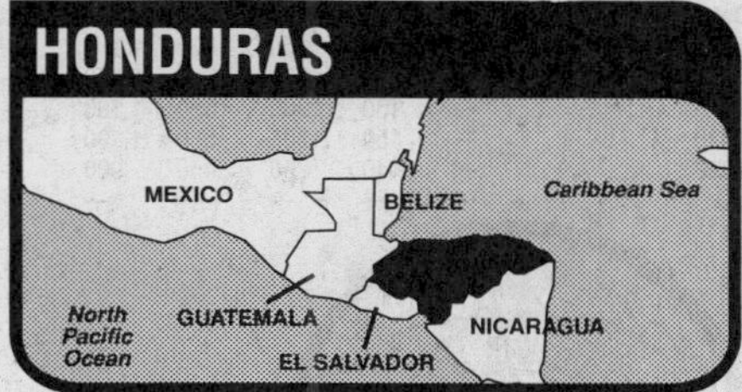


The Republic of Honduras, situated in Central America alongside El Salvador, between Nicaragua and Guatemala, has an area of 43,277sq. mi. (112,090 sq. km.) and a population of 5.6 million. Capital: Tegucigalpa. Agriculture, mining (gold and silver), and logging are the major economic activities, with increasing tourism and emerging petroleum resource discoveries. Precious metals, bananas, timber and coffee are exported.

The eastern part of Honduras was part of the ancient Mayan Empire; however, the largest Indian community in Honduras was the not too well known Lencas. Honduras was claimed for Spain by Columbus in 1502, during his last voyage to the Americas. The first settlement was made by Cristobal de Olid under orders from Hernando Cortes, then in Mexico. The area, regarded as one of the most promising sources of gold and silver in the New World, was a part of the Captaincy General of Guatemala throughout the colonial period. After declaring its independence from Spain on September 15, 1821, Honduras fell under the Mexican empire of Augustin de Iturbide, and then joined the Central American Republic (1823-39). Upon the effective dissolution of that federation (ca. 1840), Honduras reclaimed its independence as a self-standing republic. Honduras forces played a major part in permanently ending the threat of William Walker to establish a slave holding empire in Central America based on his self engineered elections to the Presidency of Nicaragua. Thrice expelled from Central America, Walker was shot by a Honduran firing squad in 1860. 1876 to 1933 saw a period of instability and for some months U.S. Marine Corp military occupation. From 1933 to 1940 General Tiburcio Carias Andino was dictator president of the Republic. Since 1990 democratic practices have become more consistent.

**MONETARY SYSTEM**
100 Centavos = 1 Peso

## REPUBLIC

### DECIMAL COINAGE

100 Centavos = 1 Peso

**CENTAVO** **KM# 46** **Composition:** Bronze **Edge:** Plain, reeded, and plain and reeded **Note:** Varieties exist.

| Date | Mintage | VG | F | VF | XF | Unc |
|---|---|---|---|---|---|---|
| 1901/0 | 98,000 | 5.00 | 12.50 | 22.00 | 37.50 | — |
| 1901 | Inc. above | 5.00 | 12.50 | 22.00 | 37.50 | — |
| 1902 large 0 | — | 3.50 | 8.00 | 15.00 | 32.50 | — |
| 1902 small 0 | — | 3.50 | 8.00 | 15.00 | 32.50 | — |
| 1903/2/0 | — | 5.50 | 15.00 | 25.00 | 45.00 | — |
| 1903/2/1 5 known | — | — | — | — | — | — |
| 1904 | — | 4.50 | 15.00 | 25.00 | 45.00 | — |
| 1907/4 | 234,000 | 6.50 | 16.50 | 25.00 | 45.00 | — |
| 1907 | Inc. above | 6.50 | 16.50 | 25.00 | 45.00 | — |

**CENTAVO** **KM# 59** **Composition:** Bronze **Obverse:** KM#46 **Reverse:** Altered KM#49 **Note:** Varieties exist.

| Date | Mintage | VG | F | VF | XF | Unc |
|---|---|---|---|---|---|---|
| 1907 large UN | — | 0.50 | 1.50 | 3.25 | 6.00 | — |
| **Note:** Mintage included in KM#46 | | | | | | |
| 1907 small UN | — | 0.50 | 1.50 | 3.25 | 6.00 | — |
| **Note:** Mintage included in KM#46 | | | | | | |
| 1908/7 | 263,000 | 8.00 | 15.00 | 32.00 | 50.00 | — |
| 1908 | — | 8.00 | 15.00 | 32.50 | 50.00 | — |

**CENTAVO** **KM# 61** **Composition:** Bronze **Obverse:** KM#49 **Reverse:** Altered KM#49 **Note:** The 1890, 1891 and 1908 dates are found with a die-cutting error or broken die that reads REPLBLICA. Other varieties exist.

| Date | Mintage | VG | F | VF | XF | Unc |
|---|---|---|---|---|---|---|
| 1908 | — | 6.00 | 13.50 | 25.00 | 40.00 | — |

**CENTAVO** **KM# 65** **Composition:** Bronze **Obverse:** KM#45 **Reverse:** Altered KM#45 **Note:** Varieties exist.

| Date | Mintage | VG | F | VF | XF | Unc |
|---|---|---|---|---|---|---|
| 1910/5 | 410,000 | 10.00 | 22.00 | 35.00 | 60.00 | — |
| 1910 large 0 | 410,000 | 8.50 | 20.00 | 32.50 | 50.00 | — |
| 1911/811 | 62,000 | 10.00 | 22.00 | 35.00 | 60.00 | — |
| 1911/885 | Inc. above | 10.00 | 22.00 | 35.00 | 60.00 | — |
| 1911/886 | Inc. above | 10.00 | 22.00 | 35.00 | 60.00 | — |
| 1911 CENTAVO | Inc. above | 6.00 | 15.00 | 25.00 | 40.00 | — |
| 1911 CENTAVOS; rare | Inc. above | — | — | — | — | — |

**CENTAVO** **KM# 66** **Composition:** Bronze **Obverse:** KM#48 **Reverse:** Altered KM#45

| Date | Mintage | VG | F | VF | XF | Unc |
|---|---|---|---|---|---|---|
| 1910 | Inc. above | 8.00 | 22.50 | 37.50 | 75.00 | — |
| 1610 error, inverted 9 | Inc. above | 50.00 | 100 | 175 | 350 | — |
| 1910 error, second 1 inverted | Inc. above | 15.00 | 30.00 | 55.00 | 100 | — |

**CENTAVO** **KM# 67** **Composition:** Bronze **Obverse:** KM#48 **Reverse:** Altered KM#48

| Date | Mintage | VG | F | VF | XF | Unc |
|---|---|---|---|---|---|---|
| 1910 | Inc. above | 4.00 | 8.50 | 15.00 | 35.00 | — |

**CENTAVO** **KM# 68** **Composition:** Bronze **Obverse:** KM#45 **Reverse:** Altered KM#48

| Date | Mintage | VG | F | VF | XF | Unc |
|---|---|---|---|---|---|---|
| 1910 | Inc. above | 20.00 | 45.00 | 85.00 | 170 | — |

**CENTAVO** **KM# 70** **Composition:** Bronze **Note:** Similar to KM#65, CENTAVO omitted.

| Date | Mintage | VG | F | VF | XF | Unc |
|---|---|---|---|---|---|---|
| 1919 | 168,000 | 1.75 | 3.50 | 6.00 | 25.00 | — |
| 1920 | 30,000 | 3.00 | 6.00 | 12.50 | 35.00 | — |

**2 CENTAVOS** **KM# 64** **Composition:** Bronze **Obverse:** KM#46 **Reverse:** Altered KM#49

| Date | Mintage | VG | F | VF | XF | Unc |
|---|---|---|---|---|---|---|
| 1907 Rare | — | — | — | — | — | — |
| 1908 | — | 40.00 | 80.00 | 150 | 300 | — |

**2 CENTAVOS** **KM# 69** **Composition:** Bronze **Obverse:** KM#46 **Reverse:** Altered KM#46 **Note:** Reverse dies often very crudely recut, especially 1910 and 1911. Some coins of 1910 appear to be struck over earlier 1 or 2 Centavos, probably 1907 or 1908.

| Date | Mintage | VG | F | VF | XF | Unc |
|---|---|---|---|---|---|---|
| 1910 | 435,000 | 1.50 | 3.50 | 6.00 | 16.00 | — |
| 1911 | 68,000 | 4.00 | 9.00 | 25.00 | 50.00 | — |
| 1912 CENTAVOS | 88,000 | 1.00 | 2.50 | 4.50 | 14.00 | — |
| 1912 CENTAVO | Inc. above | 3.00 | 6.00 | 12.00 | 25.00 | — |
| 1913 | 258,000 | 1.00 | 2.50 | 5.00 | 15.00 | — |

**2 CENTAVOS** **KM# 71** **Composition:** Bronze **Reverse:** CENTAVOS omitted **Note:** Varieties exist.

| Date | Mintage | VG | F | VF | XF | Unc |
|---|---|---|---|---|---|---|
| 1919 | 117,000 | 1.50 | 3.25 | 7.50 | 20.00 | — |
| 1920 | 283,000 | 0.65 | 1.25 | 2.75 | 12.50 | — |
| 1920 Dot | Inc. above | 0.85 | 1.50 | 3.00 | 12.50 | — |

**5 CENTAVOS** **KM# 48** **Weight:** 1.2500 g. **Composition:** 0.8350 Silver .0336 oz. ASW

| Date | Mintage | VG | F | VF | XF | Unc |
|---|---|---|---|---|---|---|
| 1902 | — | 27.50 | 55.00 | 135 | 300 | — |

**25 CENTAVOS** **KM# 50a** **Weight:** 6.2500 g. **Composition:** 0.8350 Silver .1678 oz. ASW **Note:** Varieties exist.

| Date | Mintage | VG | F | VF | XF | Unc |
|---|---|---|---|---|---|---|
| 1901/801 | — | 4.00 | 6.50 | 13.50 | 30.00 | — |
| 1901/11 | — | 4.00 | 6.50 | 15.00 | 40.00 | — |
| 1901 large first 1 | 54,000 | 3.00 | 5.00 | 10.00 | 20.00 | — |
| 1902/801 | — | 12.00 | 20.00 | 30.00 | 50.00 | — |
| 1902/802 | — | 12.00 | 20.00 | 30.00 | 50.00 | — |
| 1902/812 | — | 12.00 | 20.00 | 30.00 | 50.00 | — |
| 1902/891 | — | 12.00 | 20.00 | 30.00 | 50.00 | — |
| 1902/1 F | — | 4.00 | 6.00 | 10.00 | 20.00 | — |
| 1902 F | — | 4.00 | 7.50 | 13.50 | 25.00 | — |
| 1904 | — | 13.50 | 27.50 | 47.50 | 80.00 | — |
| 1907/4 | 14,000 | 6.00 | 10.00 | 17.50 | 30.00 | — |
| 1907 | Inc. above | 6.50 | 11.50 | 20.00 | 32.00 | — |
| 1913/0 | 52,000 | — | — | — | — | — |
| 1913/2 | Inc. above | — | — | — | — | — |
| 1913 | Inc. above | 10.00 | 18.50 | 30.00 | 55.00 | — |

**50 CENTAVOS** **KM# 51a** **Weight:** 12.5000 g. **Composition:** Silver .3355 oz. ASW **Note:** Fineness can be .8350 or .9000.

| Date | Mintage | VG | F | VF | XF | Unc |
|---|---|---|---|---|---|---|
| 1908/897 | 447 | 32.50 | 75.00 | 140 | 220 | — |
| 1908 | Inc. above | 25.00 | 55.00 | 85.00 | 190 | — |

**50 CENTAVOS** **KM# 51** **Weight:** 12.5000 g. **Composition:** 0.9000 Silver .3617 oz. ASW

| Date | Mintage | VG | F | VF | XF | Unc |
|---|---|---|---|---|---|---|
| 1910 | 602 | 500 | 900 | — | — | — |

**PESO** **KM# 56** **Weight:** 1.6120 g. **Composition:** 0.9000 Gold .0467 oz. AGW

| Date | Mintage | F | VF | XF | Unc | BU |
|---|---|---|---|---|---|---|
| 1901 | — | 150 | 300 | 600 | 1,150 | — |
| 1902 | — | 140 | 300 | 500 | 1,000 | — |
| 1907 | — | 140 | 250 | 450 | 900 | — |
| 1914/882 | — | 275 | 450 | 600 | 1,150 | — |
| 1914/03 | — | 275 | 450 | 600 | 1,150 | — |
| 1919 | — | 150 | 300 | 550 | 1,100 | — |
| 1920 | — | 150 | 300 | 550 | 1,100 | — |
| 1922 | — | 140 | 250 | 450 | 900 | — |
| ND | — | — | — | — | — | — |

**PESO** **KM# 52** **Weight:** 25.0000 g. **Composition:** 0.9000 Silver .7234 oz. ASW **Reverse:** Large CENTRO-AMERICA **Note:** Overdates and recut dies are prevalent.

| Date | Mintage | VG | F | VF | XF | Unc |
|---|---|---|---|---|---|---|
| 1902 | — | 27.50 | 50.00 | 80.00 | 130 | — |
| 1903 flat-top 3 | — | 27.50 | 45.00 | 70.00 | 120 | — |
| 1903 round-top 3 | — | 30.00 | 55.00 | 90.00 | 160 | — |
| 1904 | 20,000 | 30.00 | 55.00 | 90.00 | 160 | — |
| 1914 | — | 200 | 500 | 900 | 1,500 | — |

**5 PESOS** **KM# 53** **Weight:** 8.0645 g. **Composition:** 0.9000 Gold .2333 oz. AGW

| Date | Mintage | F | VF | XF | Unc | BU |
|---|---|---|---|---|---|---|
| 1902 | — | 450 | 650 | 1,000 | 2,500 | — |
| 1908/888 | — | 450 | 650 | 1,000 | 2,500 | — |
| 1913 | 1,200 | 450 | 650 | 1,000 | 2,500 | — |

**20 PESOS** **KM# 57** **Weight:** 32.2580 g. **Composition:** 0.9000 Gold .9335 oz. AGW

| Date | Mintage | F | VF | XF | Unc | BU |
|---|---|---|---|---|---|---|
| 1908/888 | — | 9,000 | 12,000 | 17,500 | — | — |
| 1908/897 Rare | — | — | — | — | — | — |

**Note:** Stack's Hammel sale 9-82 VF 1908/897 realized $12,000. Ponterio & Associates NYINC. sale 12-86 choice XF realized $30,800. Superior Casterline sale 5-89 choice XF realized $28,600.

| Date | Mintage | F | VF | XF | Unc | BU |
|---|---|---|---|---|---|---|
| 1908 | — | 9,000 | 12,000 | 17,500 | — | — |

## REFORM COINAGE

100 Centavos = 1 Lempira

**CENTAVO** **KM# 77.1** **Weight:** 2.0000 g. **Composition:** Bronze **Size:** 15 mm. **Note:** Thick planchet.

| Date | Mintage | F | VF | XF | Unc | BU |
|---|---|---|---|---|---|---|
| 1935 | 2,000,000 | 0.25 | 0.75 | 2.00 | 7.50 | — |
| 1939 | 2,000,000 | 0.25 | 0.50 | 1.50 | 6.00 | — |
| 1949 | 4,000,000 | 0.10 | 0.30 | 0.75 | 2.50 | — |

**CENTAVO** **KM# 77.2** **Weight:** 1.5000 g. **Composition:** Bronze **Size:** 15 mm. **Note:** Thin planchet.

| Date | Mintage | F | VF | XF | Unc | BU |
|---|---|---|---|---|---|---|
| 1954 | 3,500,000 | 0.10 | 0.15 | 0.25 | 1.00 | — |
| 1956 | 2,000,000 | 0.10 | 0.15 | 0.25 | 0.50 | — |
| 1957/6 | 28,000,000 | — | — | — | — | — |
| 1957 | Inc. above | — | 0.10 | 0.15 | 0.30 | — |

**CENTAVO** **KM# 77a** **Composition:** Copper Clad Steel **Obverse:** Without clouds behind pyramids

| Date | Mintage | F | VF | XF | Unc | BU |
|---|---|---|---|---|---|---|
| 1974 | — | — | 0.10 | 0.15 | 0.25 | — |
| 1985 | — | — | 0.10 | 0.15 | 0.25 | — |
| 1992 | — | — | 0.10 | 0.15 | 0.25 | — |
| 1998 | — | — | 0.10 | 0.15 | 0.25 | — |

**CENTAVO** **KM# 77b** **Composition:** Copper Plated Steel **Obverse:** Clouds behind pyramids

| Date | Mintage | F | VF | XF | Unc | BU |
|---|---|---|---|---|---|---|
| 1988 | 50,000,000 | — | 0.10 | 0.15 | 0.25 | — |

**2 CENTAVOS** **KM# 78** **Composition:** Bronze

| Date | Mintage | F | VF | XF | Unc | BU |
|---|---|---|---|---|---|---|
| 1939 | 2,000,000 | 0.25 | 0.50 | 1.50 | 6.00 | — |
| 1949 | 3,000,000 | 0.10 | 0.25 | 1.00 | 4.00 | — |
| 1954 | 2,000,000 | 0.10 | 0.25 | 1.00 | 3.00 | — |
| 1956 | 20,000,000 | — | 0.10 | 0.15 | 0.40 | — |

**2 CENTAVOS** **KM# 78a** **Composition:** Bronze Clad Steel

| Date | Mintage | F | VF | XF | Unc | BU |
|---|---|---|---|---|---|---|
| 1974 | — | — | 0.10 | 0.15 | 0.25 | — |

**5 CENTAVOS** **KM# 72.1** **Composition:** Copper-Nickel **Note:** Dentilated border.

| Date | Mintage | F | VF | XF | Unc | BU |
|---|---|---|---|---|---|---|
| 1931 | 2,000,000 | 0.50 | 1.50 | 2.50 | 15.00 | — |
| 1932 | 1,000,000 | 0.35 | 0.75 | 1.50 | 10.00 | — |
| 1949 | 2,000,000 | 0.20 | 0.50 | 1.00 | 6.00 | — |
| 1956 | 10,070,000 | — | 0.15 | 0.25 | 0.60 | — |
| 1972 | 5,000,000 | — | 0.10 | 0.15 | 0.35 | — |

**5 CENTAVOS** **KM# 72.2** **Composition:** Copper-Nickel **Note:** Beaded border.

| Date | Mintage | F | VF | XF | Unc | BU |
|---|---|---|---|---|---|---|
| 1954 | 1,400,000 | 0.15 | 0.25 | 0.60 | 2.50 | — |
| 1980 | 20,000,000 | — | 0.10 | 0.15 | 0.35 | — |

**5 CENTAVOS** **KM# 72.2a** **Composition:** Brass **Obverse:** Large letters and coat of arms, without clouds behind pyramids

| Date | Mintage | F | VF | XF | Unc | BU |
|---|---|---|---|---|---|---|
| 1975 | 20,000,000 | — | 0.10 | 0.15 | 0.35 | — |
| 1989 | — | — | 0.10 | 0.15 | 0.35 | — |

**5 CENTAVOS** **KM# 72.3** **Composition:** Brass **Obverse:** Small letters and coat of arms, with clouds behind pyramids

| Date | Mintage | F | VF | XF | Unc | BU |
|---|---|---|---|---|---|---|
| 1993 | — | — | 0.10 | 0.15 | 0.35 | — |
| 1994 | — | — | 0.10 | 0.15 | 0.35 | — |

**5 CENTAVOS** **KM# 72.4** **Composition:** Brass **Obverse:** Without clouds behind pyramids

| Date | Mintage | F | VF | XF | Unc | BU |
|---|---|---|---|---|---|---|
| 1995 | — | — | 0.10 | 0.15 | 0.35 | — |
| 1999 | — | — | 0.10 | 0.15 | 0.35 | — |

**10 CENTAVOS** **KM# 76.1** **Composition:** Copper-Nickel **Note:** Dentilated border.

| Date | Mintage | F | VF | XF | Unc | BU |
|---|---|---|---|---|---|---|
| 1932 | 1,500,000 | 0.75 | 1.50 | 4.00 | 25.00 | — |
| 1951 | 1,000,000 | 0.25 | 0.75 | 1.50 | 4.00 | — |
| 1956 | 7,560,000 | 0.10 | 0.15 | 0.25 | 0.75 | — |

**10 CENTAVOS** **KM# 76.2** **Composition:** Copper-Nickel **Note:** Beaded border.

| Date | Mintage | F | VF | XF | Unc | BU |
|---|---|---|---|---|---|---|
| 1954 | 1,200,000 | 0.10 | 0.25 | 0.75 | 5.00 | — |
| 1967 | — | 0.10 | 0.25 | 0.50 | 2.00 | — |
| 1980 | 15,000,000 | 0.10 | 0.25 | 0.50 | 2.00 | — |
| 1993 | — | 0.10 | 0.25 | 0.50 | 2.00 | — |

**10 CENTAVOS** **KM# 76.1a** **Composition:** Brass **Obverse:** Large letters and coat of arms **Note:** Dentilated border.

| Date | Mintage | F | VF | XF | Unc | BU |
|---|---|---|---|---|---|---|
| 1976 | — | 0.10 | 0.15 | 0.25 | 0.60 | — |
| 1989 | — | 0.10 | 0.15 | 0.25 | 0.60 | — |

**10 CENTAVOS** **KM# 76.2a** **Composition:** Brass **Obverse:** Small letters and coat of arms, clouds behind pyramids **Note:** Beaded border.

| Date | Mintage | F | VF | XF | Unc | BU |
|---|---|---|---|---|---|---|
| 1993 | — | — | 0.10 | 0.20 | 0.45 | — |
| 1994 | — | — | 0.10 | 0.20 | 0.45 | — |

**10 CENTAVOS** **KM# 76.3** **Composition:** Brass **Obverse:** Small letters and coat of arms, no clouds

| Date | Mintage | F | VF | XF | Unc | BU |
|---|---|---|---|---|---|---|
| 1995 | — | — | 0.10 | 0.20 | 0.45 | — |
| 1999 | — | — | 0.10 | 0.20 | 0.45 | — |

**20 CENTAVOS** **KM# 73** **Weight:** 2.5000 g. **Composition:** 0.9000 Silver .0723 oz. ASW **Note:** Chief of the Lempira.

| Date | Mintage | F | VF | XF | Unc | BU |
|---|---|---|---|---|---|---|
| 1931 | 1,000,000 | 1.25 | 3.25 | 7.00 | 25.00 | — |
| 1932 | 750,000 | 1.25 | 3.25 | 7.00 | 20.00 | — |
| 1951 | 1,500,000 | BV | 1.25 | 2.50 | 7.00 | — |
| 1952 | 2,500,000 | BV | 1.25 | 2.00 | 6.00 | — |
| 1958 | 2,000,000 | BV | 1.25 | 2.00 | 5.00 | — |

**20 CENTAVOS** **KM# 79** **Composition:** Copper-Nickel

| Date | Mintage | F | VF | XF | Unc | BU |
|---|---|---|---|---|---|---|
| 1967 | 12,000,000 | — | 0.10 | 0.20 | 0.40 | — |

**20 CENTAVOS** **KM# 81** **Composition:** Copper-Nickel **Note:** Different style lettering.

| Date | Mintage | F | VF | XF | Unc | BU |
|---|---|---|---|---|---|---|
| 1973 | 15,000,000 | — | 0.10 | 0.20 | 0.60 | — |

**20 CENTAVOS** **KM# 83.1** **Composition:** Copper-Nickel **Obverse:** National arms **Reverse:** Lempira brave

| Date | Mintage | F | VF | XF | Unc | BU |
|---|---|---|---|---|---|---|
| 1978 | 30,000,000 | — | 0.10 | 0.20 | 0.60 | — |
| 1990 | — | — | 0.10 | 0.20 | 0.60 | — |

**20 CENTAVOS** **KM# 83.1a** **Composition:** Nickel Plated Steel **Obverse:** Small arms and legend, with clouds

| Date | Mintage | F | VF | XF | Unc | BU |
|---|---|---|---|---|---|---|
| 1991 | — | — | 0.10 | 0.20 | 0.60 | — |
| 1993 | — | — | 0.10 | 0.20 | 0.60 | — |
| 1994 | — | — | 0.10 | 0.20 | 0.60 | — |

**20 CENTAVOS** **KM# 83.2a** **Composition:** Nickel Plated Steel **Obverse:** Without clouds

| Date | Mintage | F | VF | XF | Unc | BU |
|---|---|---|---|---|---|---|
| 1995 | — | — | 0.10 | 0.20 | 0.60 | — |
| 1996 | — | — | 0.10 | 0.20 | 0.60 | — |
| 1999 | — | — | 0.10 | 0.20 | 0.60 | — |

**50 CENTAVOS** **KM# 74** **Weight:** 6.2500 g. **Composition:** 0.9000 Silver .1808 oz. ASW **Note:** Chief of the Lempira.

| Date | Mintage | F | VF | XF | Unc | BU |
|---|---|---|---|---|---|---|
| 1931 | 500,000 | 1.00 | 3.00 | 6.00 | 30.00 | — |
| 1932 | 1,100,000 | 1.00 | 2.00 | 5.00 | 25.00 | — |
| 1937 | 1,000,000 | 1.00 | 2.00 | 5.00 | 25.00 | — |
| 1951 | 500,000 | 1.00 | 2.00 | 4.00 | 20.00 | — |

**50 CENTAVOS** **KM# 80** **Composition:** Copper-Nickel

| Date | Mintage | F | VF | XF | Unc | BU |
|---|---|---|---|---|---|---|
| 1967 | 4,800,000 | — | 0.25 | 0.35 | 1.25 | — |

**50 CENTAVOS** **KM# 82** **Composition:** Copper-Nickel **Obverse:** National arms **Reverse:** Lempira brave **Note:** F.A.O. issue.

| Date | Mintage | F | VF | XF | Unc | BU |
|---|---|---|---|---|---|---|
| 1973 | 4,400,000 | — | 0.25 | 0.35 | 1.25 | — |

**50 CENTAVOS** **KM# 84** **Composition:** Copper-Nickel

| Date | Mintage | F | VF | XF | Unc | BU |
|---|---|---|---|---|---|---|
| 1978 | 12,000,000 | — | 0.25 | 0.35 | 1.00 | — |
| 1990 | — | — | 0.25 | 0.35 | 1.00 | — |

**50 CENTAVOS** **KM# 84.a1** **Composition:** Nickel Plated Steel

| Date | Mintage | F | VF | XF | Unc | BU |
|---|---|---|---|---|---|---|
| 1991 | — | — | 0.25 | 0.35 | 1.00 | — |
| 1994 | — | — | 0.25 | 0.35 | 1.00 | — |

**50 CENTAVOS** **KM# 88** **Composition:** Nickel-Steel **Subject:** 50th Anniversary F.A.O. **Obverse:** National arms **Reverse:** Lempira brave

| Date | Mintage | F | VF | XF | Unc | BU |
|---|---|---|---|---|---|---|
| 1994 | 2,000,000 | — | — | — | 1.50 | — |

**50 CENTAVOS** **KM# 84.a2** **Composition:** Nickel Plated Steel **Obverse:** No clouds behind pyramid in arms

| Date | Mintage | F | VF | XF | Unc | BU |
|---|---|---|---|---|---|---|
| 1995 | — | — | 0.25 | 0.35 | 1.00 | — |
| 1996 | — | — | 0.25 | 0.35 | 1.00 | — |

**LEMPIRA** **KM# 75** **Weight:** 12.5000 g. **Composition:** 0.9000 Silver .3617 oz. ASW **Note:** Chief of the Lempira.

| Date | Mintage | F | VF | XF | Unc | BU |
|---|---|---|---|---|---|---|
| 1931 | 550,000 | BV | 3.50 | 7.00 | 50.00 | — |
| 1932 | 1,000,000 | BV | 3.50 | 7.00 | 40.00 | — |
| 1933 | 400,000 | BV | 3.50 | 7.00 | 30.00 | — |
| 1934 | 600,000 | BV | 3.50 | 7.00 | 25.00 | — |
| 1935 | 1,000,000 | — | BV | 6.00 | 25.00 | — |
| 1937 | 4,000,000 | — | BV | 5.00 | 20.00 | — |

**LEMPIRA** **KM# 89** **Weight:** 33.6250 g. **Composition:** 0.9250 Silver 1.0000 oz. ASW **Subject:** Central Bank's 50th Anniversary **Obverse:** National arms **Reverse:** Building **Edge:** Plain **Size:** 38 mm.

| Date | Mintage | F | VF | XF | Unc | BU |
|---|---|---|---|---|---|---|
| ND(2001) Proof | 3,000 | Value: 25.00 | | | | |

**LEMPIRA** **KM# 90** **Weight:** 7.7750 g. **Composition:** 0.9990 Gold .2497 oz. AGW **Subject:** Central Bank's 50th Anniversary **Obverse:** National arms **Reverse:** Building **Edge:** Reeded **Size:** 24 mm.

| Date | Mintage | F | VF | XF | Unc | BU |
|---|---|---|---|---|---|---|
| ND(2001) Proof | 1,200 | Value: 150 | | | | |

**100 LEMPIRAS** KM# 85 **Weight:** 27.0000 g. **Composition:** 0.9250 Silver .8030 oz. ASW **Subject:** 500th Anniversary - Discovery of America **Reverse:** Ship approaching curved wall

| Date | Mintage | F | VF | XF | Unc | BU |
|---|---|---|---|---|---|---|
| 1992 Proof | 5,000,000 | Value: 60.00 | | | | |

**200 LEMPIRAS** KM# 86 **Weight:** 6.5000 g. **Composition:** 0.9000 Gold .1881 oz. AGW **Subject:** Bicentenary of Birth - Gen. Francisco Morazan

| Date | Mintage | F | VF | XF | Unc | BU |
|---|---|---|---|---|---|---|
| 1992 Proof | 1,500,000 | Value: 150 | | | | |

**500 LEMPIRAS** KM# 87 **Weight:** 12.5000 g. **Composition:** 0.9000 Gold .3617 oz. AGW **Subject:** Bicentenary of Birth - Gen. Francisco Morazan

| Date | Mintage | F | VF | XF | Unc | BU |
|---|---|---|---|---|---|---|
| 1992 | 1,500,000 | Value: 240 | | | | |

## PATTERNS

Including off-metal strikes

Rosettes separate legends on Pn1-Pn5a.

| KM# | Date | Mintage | Identification | Mkt Val |
|---|---|---|---|---|
| Pn22 | 1909 | — | Centavo. Copper. | 150 |
| Pn23 | 1919 | — | Peso. Copper. KM#56. | 100 |

# HONG KONG

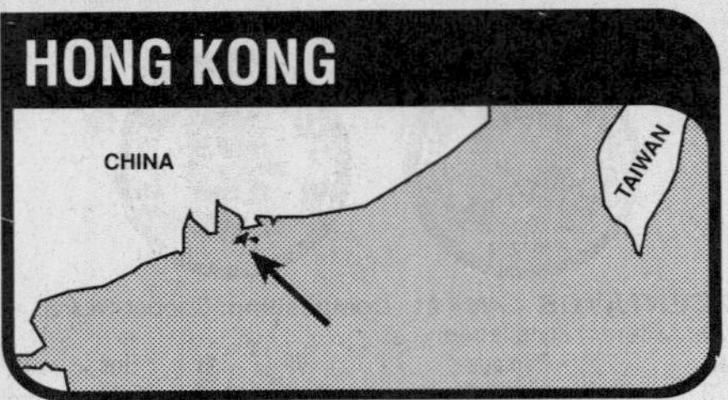


Hong Kong, a former British colony, reverted to control of the People's Republic of China on July 1, 1997 as a Special Administrative Region. It is situated at the mouth of the Canton or Pearl River 90miles (145 km.) southeast of Canton, has an area of 403 sq. mi. (1,040 sq. km.) and an estimated population of 6.3 million. Capital: Victoria. The free port of Hong Kong, the commercial center of the Far East, is a trans-shipment point for goods destined for China and the countries of the Pacific Rim. Light manufacturing and tourism are important components of the economy.

Long a haven for fishermen-pirates and opium smugglers, the island of Hong Kong was ceded to Britain at the conclusion of the first Opium War, 1839-1842. At the time, the acquisition of a 'barren rock' was ridiculed by both London and English merchants operating in the Far East. The Kowloon Peninsula and Stonecutter's Island were ceded in 1860, and the so-called New Territories, comprising most of the mainland of the colony, were leased to Britain for99 years in 1898.

The legends on Hong Kong coinage are bilingual: English and Chinese. The rare 1941 cent was dispatched to Hong Kong in several shipments. One fell into Japanese hands, while another was melted down by the British and a third was sunk during enemy action.

**RULERS**

British 1842-1997

**MINT MARKS**

H - Heaton

KN - King's Norton

**MONETARY SYSTEM**

10 Mils (Wen, Ch'ien) = 1 Cent (Hsien)

10 Cents = 1 Chiao

100 Cents = 10 Chiao = 1 Dollar (Yuan)

## BRITISH COLONY

### DECIMAL COINAGE

**CENT** KM# 4.3 **Composition:** Bronze **Obverse:** 5 pearls in center of crown

| Date | Mintage | F | VF | XF | Unc | BU |
|---|---|---|---|---|---|---|
| 1901 | 5,000,000 | 2.50 | 5.50 | 16.00 | 70.00 | — |
| 1901H | 10,000,000 | 2.50 | 5.50 | 16.00 | 60.00 | — |

**CENT** KM# 11 **Composition:** Bronze

| Date | Mintage | F | VF | XF | Unc | BU |
|---|---|---|---|---|---|---|
| 1902 | 5,000,000 | 2.50 | 4.50 | 15.00 | 40.00 | — |
| 1903 | 5,000,000 | 2.50 | 4.50 | 15.00 | 40.00 | — |
| 1904H | 10,000,000 | 1.75 | 3.50 | 12.00 | 32.00 | — |
| 1905 | 2,500,000 | 3.75 | 7.50 | 20.00 | 55.00 | — |
| 1905H | 12,500,000 | 2.50 | 4.50 | 15.00 | 40.00 | — |

**CENT** KM# 16 **Composition:** Bronze

| Date | Mintage | F | VF | XF | Unc | BU |
|---|---|---|---|---|---|---|
| 1919 | 2,500,000 | 2.00 | 4.00 | 14.00 | 40.00 | — |
| 1923 | 2,500,000 | 1.50 | 3.00 | 10.00 | 28.00 | — |
| 1924 | 5,000,000 | 1.25 | 2.50 | 5.50 | 20.00 | — |
| 1925 | 2,500,000 | 1.25 | 2.50 | 5.50 | 20.00 | — |
| 1926 | 2,500,000 | 1.25 | 2.50 | 5.50 | 20.00 | — |
| 1926 Proof | — | Value: 350 | | | | |

**CENT** KM# 17 **Composition:** Bronze

| Date | Mintage | F | VF | XF | Unc | BU |
|---|---|---|---|---|---|---|
| 1931 | 5,000,000 | 0.75 | 1.00 | 2.00 | 5.50 | — |
| 1931 Proof | — | Value: 250 | | | | |
| 1933 | 6,500,000 | 0.75 | 1.00 | 2.00 | 5.50 | — |
| 1933 Proof | — | Value: 250 | | | | |
| 1934 | 5,000,000 | 0.75 | 1.00 | 2.00 | 5.50 | — |
| 1934 Proof | — | Value: 250 | | | | |

**CENT** KM# 24 **Composition:** Bronze

| Date | Mintage | F | VF | XF | Unc | BU |
|---|---|---|---|---|---|---|
| 1941 | 5,000,000 | 750 | 1,500 | 3,250 | 5,750 | — |
| 1941 Proof | — | Value: 8,500 | | | | |

**5 CENTS** KM# 5 **Weight:** 1.3577 g. **Composition:** 0.8000 Silver .0349 oz. ASW **Note:** Coins dated 1866-1868 struck at the Hong Kong Mint; coins dated 1872-1901 struck at the British Royal Mint.

| Date | Mintage | F | VF | XF | Unc | BU |
|---|---|---|---|---|---|---|
| 1901 | 10,000,000 | 1.00 | 2.50 | 5.00 | 15.00 | — |

**5 CENTS** KM# 12 **Weight:** 1.3577 g. **Composition:** 0.8000 Silver .0349 oz. ASW

| Date | Mintage | F | VF | XF | Unc | BU |
|---|---|---|---|---|---|---|
| 1903 | 6,000,000 | 1.00 | 2.00 | 4.00 | 12.50 | — |
| 1903 Proof | — | Value: 225 | | | | |
| 1904 | 8,000,000 | 1.00 | 2.00 | 4.00 | 12.50 | — |
| 1904 Proof | — | Value: 200 | | | | |
| 1905 | 1,000,000 | 1.25 | 3.00 | 6.50 | 17.50 | — |
| 1905H | 7,000,000 | 1.00 | 2.00 | 4.00 | 12.50 | — |

**5 CENTS** KM# 18 **Weight:** 1.3577 g. **Composition:** 0.8000 Silver .0349 oz. ASW

| Date | Mintage | F | VF | XF | Unc | BU |
|---|---|---|---|---|---|---|
| 1932 | 3,000,000 | 1.00 | 1.50 | 2.50 | 6.50 | — |
| 1932 Proof | — | Value: 165 | | | | |
| 1933 | 2,000,000 | 1.00 | 1.50 | 2.75 | 7.50 | — |
| 1933 Proof | — | Value: 165 | | | | |

**5 CENTS** **KM# 18a** **Composition:** Copper-Nickel

| Date | Mintage | F | VF | XF | Unc | BU |
|---|---|---|---|---|---|---|
| 1935 | 1,000,000 | 1.00 | 2.00 | 4.50 | 16.50 | — |
| 1935 Proof | — | Value: 115 | | | | |

**5 CENTS** **KM# 20** **Composition:** Nickel

| Date | Mintage | F | VF | XF | Unc | BU |
|---|---|---|---|---|---|---|
| 1937 | 3,000,000 | 0.75 | 1.25 | 2.25 | 7.50 | — |
| 1937 Proof | — | Value: 85.00 | | | | |

**5 CENTS** **KM# 22** **Composition:** Nickel

| Date | Mintage | F | VF | XF | Unc | BU |
|---|---|---|---|---|---|---|
| 1938 | 3,000,000 | 0.50 | 1.00 | 2.00 | 6.50 | — |
| 1938 Proof | — | Value: 125 | | | | |
| 1939H | 3,090,000 | 0.50 | 1.00 | 2.00 | 6.50 | — |
| 1939H Proof | — | Value: 125 | | | | |
| 1939KN | 4,710,000 | 0.50 | 1.00 | 2.00 | 6.50 | — |
| 1941H | 777,000 | 350 | 750 | 1,400 | 2,850 | — |
| 1941KN | 1,075,000 | 100 | 175 | 350 | 700 | — |

**5 CENTS** **KM# 26** **Composition:** Nickel-Brass

| Date | Mintage | F | VF | XF | Unc | BU |
|---|---|---|---|---|---|---|
| 1949 | 15,000,000 | 0.25 | 0.50 | 1.25 | 7.50 | — |
| 1949 Proof | — | Value: 125 | | | | |
| 1950 | 20,400,000 | 0.25 | 0.50 | 1.25 | 7.50 | — |
| 1950 Proof | — | Value: 125 | | | | |

**5 CENTS** **KM# 29.1** **Composition:** Nickel-Brass **Edge:** Reeded and security

| Date | Mintage | F | VF | XF | Unc | BU |
|---|---|---|---|---|---|---|
| 1958H | 5,000,000 | — | 0.25 | 0.75 | 4.50 | — |
| 1960 | 5,000,000 | — | 0.15 | 0.50 | 3.50 | — |
| 1960 Proof | — | Value: 65.00 | | | | |
| 1963 | 7,000,000 | — | 0.15 | 0.50 | 3.50 | — |
| 1963 Proof | — | Value: 65.00 | | | | |
| 1964 | — | 16.00 | 35.00 | 90.00 | 225 | — |
| 1965 | 18,000,000 | — | 0.10 | 0.40 | 2.00 | — |
| 1965H | 6,000,000 | — | 0.10 | 0.40 | 2.00 | — |
| 1967 | 10,000,000 | — | 0.10 | 0.40 | 2.00 | — |

**5 CENTS** **KM# 29.2** **Composition:** Nickel-Brass **Edge:** Reeded without security **Note:** Error.

| Date | Mintage | F | VF | XF | Unc | BU |
|---|---|---|---|---|---|---|
| 1958H | Inc. above | 2.50 | 5.00 | 9.00 | 20.00 | — |
| 1960 | Inc. above | 2.50 | 5.00 | 9.00 | 20.00 | — |

**5 CENTS** **KM# 29.3** **Composition:** Nickel-Brass **Edge:** Reeded

| Date | Mintage | F | VF | XF | Unc | BU |
|---|---|---|---|---|---|---|
| 1971KN | 14,000,000 | — | — | 0.25 | 0.50 | — |
| 1971H | 6,000,000 | — | — | 0.25 | 0.50 | — |
| 1972H | 14,000,000 | — | — | 0.25 | 0.50 | — |
| 1977 | 6,000,000 | — | — | 0.25 | 0.50 | — |
| 1978 | 10,000,000 | — | — | 0.25 | 0.50 | — |
| 1979 | 4,000,000 | — | — | 0.25 | 0.50 | — |

**5 CENTS** **KM# 61** **Composition:** Nickel-Brass **Subject:** Queen's portrait **Reverse:** Legend around inscription

| Date | Mintage | F | VF | XF | Unc | BU |
|---|---|---|---|---|---|---|
| 1988 | 50,000 | — | — | — | 4.00 | — |
| 1988 Proof | 25,000 | Value: 5.00 | | | | |

**10 CENTS** **KM# 6.3** **Weight:** 2.7154 g. **Composition:** 0.8000 Silver .0698 oz. ASW **Obverse:** 11 pearls on right arch of crown **Note:** Coins dated 1866-1868 struck at the Hong Kong Mint; coins dated 1869-1901 struck at the British Royal Mint.

| Date | Mintage | F | VF | XF | Unc | BU |
|---|---|---|---|---|---|---|
| 1901 | 25,000,000 | 1.00 | 2.00 | 4.00 | 18.50 | — |

**10 CENTS** **KM# 13** **Weight:** 2.7154 g. **Composition:** 0.8000 Silver .0698 oz. ASW

| Date | Mintage | F | VF | XF | Unc | BU |
|---|---|---|---|---|---|---|
| 1902 | 18,000,000 | 1.00 | 2.00 | 4.00 | 16.50 | — |
| 1902 Proof | — | Value: 200 | | | | |
| 1903 | 25,000,000 | 1.00 | 2.00 | 4.00 | 16.50 | — |
| 1903 Proof | — | Value: 200 | | | | |
| 1904 | 30,000,000 | 1.00 | 2.00 | 4.00 | 16.50 | — |
| 1904 Proof | — | Value: 165 | | | | |
| 1905 | 33,487,000 | 225 | 400 | 650 | 1,500 | — |
| 1905 Proof | — | Value: 1,750 | | | | |

**10 CENTS** **KM# 19** **Composition:** Copper-Nickel

| Date | Mintage | F | VF | XF | Unc | BU |
|---|---|---|---|---|---|---|
| 1935 | 10,000,000 | 0.50 | 1.00 | 3.50 | 15.00 | — |
| 1935 Proof | — | Value: 75.00 | | | | |
| 1936 | 5,000,000 | 0.50 | 1.00 | 3.50 | 15.00 | — |
| 1936 Proof | — | Value: 75.00 | | | | |

**10 CENTS** **KM# 21** **Composition:** Nickel

| Date | Mintage | F | VF | XF | Unc | BU |
|---|---|---|---|---|---|---|
| 1937 | 17,500,000 | 0.50 | 0.80 | 1.50 | 6.50 | — |
| 1937 Proof | — | Value: 85.00 | | | | |

**10 CENTS** **KM# 23** **Composition:** Nickel

| Date | Mintage | F | VF | XF | Unc | BU |
|---|---|---|---|---|---|---|
| 1938 | 7,500,000 | 0.65 | 1.00 | 2.25 | 7.50 | — |
| 1938 Proof | — | Value: 85.00 | | | | |
| 1939H | 5,000,000 | 0.65 | 1.00 | 2.25 | 7.50 | — |
| 1939KN | 5,000,000 | 0.65 | 1.00 | 2.25 | 7.50 | — |
| 1939KN Proof | — | Value: 85.00 | | | | |

**10 CENTS** **KM# 25** **Composition:** Nickel-Brass **Edge:** Reeded and security

| Date | Mintage | F | VF | XF | Unc | BU |
|---|---|---|---|---|---|---|
| 1948 | 30,000,000 | 0.25 | 0.50 | 1.25 | 6.50 | — |
| 1948 Proof | — | Value: 65.00 | | | | |
| 1949 | 35,000,000 | 0.25 | 0.50 | 1.25 | 6.50 | — |
| 1949 Proof | — | Value: 65.00 | | | | |
| 1950 | 20,000,000 | 0.25 | 0.50 | 1.25 | 6.50 | — |
| 1950 Proof | — | Value: 65.00 | | | | |
| 1951 | 5,000,000 | 0.50 | 1.00 | 3.00 | 22.50 | — |
| 1951 Proof | — | Value: 85.00 | | | | |

**10 CENTS** **KM# 25a** **Composition:** Nickel-Brass **Edge:** Reeded without security **Note:** Error.

| Date | Mintage | F | VF | XF | Unc | BU |
|---|---|---|---|---|---|---|
| 1950 | Inc. above | 3.50 | 6.50 | 12.50 | 25.00 | — |

**10 CENTS** **KM# 28.1** **Composition:** Nickel-Brass **Edge:** Reeded with security

| Date | Mintage | F | VF | XF | Unc | BU |
|---|---|---|---|---|---|---|
| 1955 | 10,000,000 | 0.15 | 0.25 | 0.50 | 5.50 | — |
| 1955 Proof | — | Value: 50.00 | | | | |
| 1956 | 3,110,000 | 0.25 | 0.50 | 1.25 | 15.00 | — |
| 1956 Proof | — | Value: 50.00 | | | | |
| 1956H | 4,488,000 | 0.15 | 0.25 | 1.00 | 10.00 | — |
| 1956KN | 2,500,000 | 0.25 | 0.50 | 2.00 | 16.50 | — |
| 1957H | 5,250,000 | 0.15 | 0.25 | 0.50 | 10.00 | — |
| 1957KN | 2,800,000 | 0.15 | 0.25 | 1.00 | 15.00 | — |
| 1958KN | 10,000,000 | 0.15 | 0.25 | 0.50 | 10.00 | — |
| 1959H | 20,000,000 | 0.10 | 0.15 | 0.25 | 6.00 | — |
| 1960 | 12,500,000 | 0.10 | 0.15 | 0.25 | 6.00 | — |
| 1960 Proof | — | Value: 50.00 | | | | |
| 1960H | 10,000,000 | 0.10 | 0.15 | 0.25 | 6.00 | — |
| 1961 | 20,000,000 | 0.10 | 0.15 | 0.25 | 4.00 | — |
| 1961 Proof | — | Value: 50.00 | | | | |
| 1961H | 5,000,000 | 0.15 | 0.25 | 0.50 | 5.00 | — |
| 1961KN | 5,000,000 | 0.15 | 0.25 | 0.50 | 5.00 | — |
| 1963 | 27,000,000 | 0.10 | 0.15 | 0.25 | 4.00 | — |
| 1963 Proof | — | Value: 50.00 | | | | |
| 1963H | 3,000,000 | 0.20 | 0.30 | 0.50 | 4.00 | — |
| 1963KN | Inc. above | 0.10 | 0.15 | 0.25 | 3.50 | — |
| 1964 | 9,000,000 | 0.10 | 0.15 | 0.25 | 2.00 | — |
| 1964H | 21,000,000 | 0.10 | 0.15 | 0.25 | 2.00 | — |
| 1965 | 40,000,000 | 0.10 | 0.15 | 0.25 | 2.00 | — |
| 1965H | 8,000,000 | 0.10 | 0.15 | 0.25 | 2.50 | — |
| 1965KN | Inc. above | 0.10 | 0.15 | 0.25 | 2.50 | — |
| 1967 | 10,000,000 | 0.10 | 0.15 | 0.25 | 2.00 | — |
| 1968H | 15,000,000 | 0.10 | 0.15 | 0.25 | 2.00 | — |

**10 CENTS** **KM# 28.2** **Composition:** Nickel-Brass **Edge:** Reeded without security **Note:** Error.

| Date | Mintage | F | VF | XF | Unc | BU |
|---|---|---|---|---|---|---|
| 1956 | Inc. above | 2.25 | 4.50 | 8.50 | 25.00 | — |
| 1963 | — | 2.25 | 4.50 | 8.50 | 25.00 | — |

**10 CENTS** **KM# 28.3** **Composition:** Nickel-Brass **Edge:** Reeded

| Date | Mintage | F | VF | XF | Unc | BU |
|---|---|---|---|---|---|---|
| 1971H | 22,000,000 | — | 0.10 | 0.15 | 0.65 | — |
| 1972KN | 20,000,000 | — | 0.10 | 0.15 | 0.65 | — |
| 1973 | 2,250,000 | 0.15 | 0.25 | 0.65 | 3.50 | — |
| 1974 | 4,600,000 | — | 0.10 | 0.15 | 0.65 | — |
| 1975 | 44,840,000 | — | 0.10 | 0.15 | 0.65 | — |
| 1978 | 57,500,000 | — | 0.10 | 0.15 | 0.65 | — |
| 1979 | 101,500,000 | — | 0.10 | 0.15 | 0.65 | — |
| 1980 | 24,000,000 | — | 7.00 | 15.00 | 35.00 | — |

**Note:** Few pieces were released for circulation in 1980, but large numbers have found their way onto the market in subsequent years. About 3,500 are known to exist.

**10 CENTS** **KM# 49** **Composition:** Nickel-Brass

| Date | Mintage | F | VF | XF | Unc | BU |
|---|---|---|---|---|---|---|
| 1982 | — | — | 0.10 | 0.15 | 0.25 | — |
| 1983 | 110,016,000 | — | 0.10 | 0.15 | 0.25 | — |
| 1984 | 30,016,000 | — | 0.10 | 0.15 | 0.25 | — |

**10 CENTS** **KM# 55** **Composition:** Nickel-Brass

| Date | Mintage | F | VF | XF | Unc | BU |
|---|---|---|---|---|---|---|
| 1985 | 34,016,000 | — | 0.10 | 0.15 | 0.25 | — |
| 1986 | 40,000,000 | — | 0.10 | 0.15 | 0.25 | — |
| 1987 | — | — | 0.10 | 0.15 | 0.25 | — |
| 1988 | 30,000,000 | — | 0.10 | 0.15 | 0.25 | — |
| 1988 Proof | 20,000 | Value: 5.00 | | | | |
| 1989 | 40,000,000 | — | 0.10 | 0.15 | 0.25 | — |

| Date | Mintage | F | VF | XF | Unc | BU |
|---|---|---|---|---|---|---|
| 1990 | — | — | 0.10 | 0.15 | 0.25 | — |
| 1991 | — | — | 0.10 | 0.15 | 0.25 | — |
| 1992 | 24,000,000 | — | 0.10 | 0.15 | 0.25 | — |

**10 CENTS** KM# 66 **Composition:** Brass Plated Steel **Obverse:** Bauhinia flower

| Date | Mintage | F | VF | XF | Unc | BU |
|---|---|---|---|---|---|---|
| 1993 | — | — | 0.10 | 0.15 | 0.30 | — |
| 1993 Proof | — | Value: 2.50 | | | | |
| 1994 | — | — | 0.10 | 0.15 | 0.30 | — |
| 1995 | — | — | 0.10 | 0.15 | 0.30 | — |
| 1996 | — | — | 0.10 | 0.15 | 0.30 | — |
| 1997 | — | — | 0.10 | 0.15 | 0.30 | — |
| 1998 | — | — | 0.10 | 0.15 | 0.30 | — |

**20 CENTS** KM# 14 **Weight:** 5.4308 g. **Composition:** 0.8000 Silver .1397 oz. ASW

| Date | Mintage | F | VF | XF | Unc | BU |
|---|---|---|---|---|---|---|
| 1902 | 250,000 | 20.00 | 40.00 | 90.00 | 250 | — |
| 1902 Proof | — | Value: 1,200 | | | | |
| 1904 | 250,000 | 20.00 | 40.00 | 90.00 | 250 | — |
| 1905 | 750,000 | 300 | 600 | 1,200 | 1,850 | — |
| 1905 Proof | — | Value: 3,000 | | | | |

**20 CENTS** KM# 36 **Composition:** Nickel-Brass

| Date | Mintage | F | VF | XF | Unc | BU |
|---|---|---|---|---|---|---|
| 1975 | 71,000,000 | — | 0.10 | 0.20 | 0.35 | — |
| 1976 | 42,000,000 | — | 0.10 | 0.20 | 0.35 | — |
| 1977 | Inc. above | — | 0.10 | 0.20 | 0.35 | — |
| 1978 | 86,000,000 | — | 0.10 | 0.20 | 0.35 | — |
| 1979 | 94,500,000 | — | 0.10 | 0.20 | 0.35 | — |
| 1980 | 65,000,000 | — | 0.10 | 0.20 | 0.35 | — |
| 1982 | 30,000,000 | — | 0.10 | 0.20 | 0.35 | — |
| 1983 | 15,000,000 | — | 0.10 | 0.20 | 0.35 | — |

**20 CENTS** KM# 59 **Composition:** Brass **Obverse:** Mature queen's portrait

| Date | Mintage | F | VF | XF | Unc | BU |
|---|---|---|---|---|---|---|
| 1985 | 10,000,000 | — | 0.10 | 0.20 | 0.35 | — |
| 1988 | Est. 40,000 | — | 0.10 | 0.20 | 0.35 | — |
| 1988 Proof | Est. 20,000 | Value: 5.00 | | | | |
| 1989 | 17,000,000 | — | 0.10 | 0.20 | 0.35 | — |
| 1990 | — | — | 0.10 | 0.20 | 0.35 | — |
| 1991 | — | — | 0.10 | 0.20 | 0.35 | — |
| 1992 | 131,000,000 | — | 0.10 | 0.20 | 0.35 | — |

**20 CENTS** KM# 67 **Composition:** Nickel-Brass **Obverse:** Bauhinia flower

| Date | Mintage | F | VF | XF | Unc | BU |
|---|---|---|---|---|---|---|
| 1993 | — | — | 0.10 | 0.20 | 0.40 | — |
| 1993 Proof | — | Value: 2.50 | | | | |
| 1994 | — | — | 0.10 | 0.20 | 0.40 | — |
| 1995 | — | — | 0.10 | 0.20 | 0.40 | — |
| 1997 | — | — | 0.10 | 0.20 | 0.40 | — |

**50 CENTS** KM# 15 **Weight:** 13.5769 g. **Composition:** 0.8000 Silver .3492 oz. ASW

| Date | Mintage | F | VF | XF | Unc | BU |
|---|---|---|---|---|---|---|
| 1902 | 100,000 | 25.00 | 35.00 | 50.00 | 135 | — |
| 1902 Proof | — | Value: 650 | | | | |
| 1904 | 100,000 | 25.00 | 35.00 | 60.00 | 125 | — |
| 1904 Proof | — | Value: 650 | | | | |
| 1905 | 300,000 | 20.00 | 25.00 | 50.00 | 110 | — |
| 1905 Proof | — | Value: 650 | | | | |

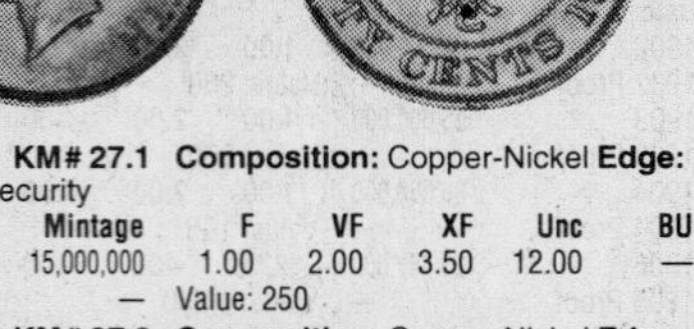

**50 CENTS** KM# 27.1 **Composition:** Copper-Nickel **Edge:** Reeded and security

| Date | Mintage | F | VF | XF | Unc | BU |
|---|---|---|---|---|---|---|
| 1951 | 15,000,000 | 1.00 | 2.00 | 3.50 | 12.00 | — |
| 1951 Proof | — | Value: 250 | | | | |

**50 CENTS** KM# 27.2 **Composition:** Copper-Nickel **Edge:** Reeded without security **Note:** Error.

| Date | Mintage | F | VF | XF | Unc | BU |
|---|---|---|---|---|---|---|
| 1951 | Inc. above | 3.00 | 5.00 | 10.00 | 22.00 | — |

**50 CENTS** KM# 30.1 **Composition:** Copper-Nickel **Edge:** Reeded and security

| Date | Mintage | F | VF | XF | Unc | BU |
|---|---|---|---|---|---|---|
| 1958H | 4,000,000 | — | 0.50 | 1.25 | 4.50 | — |
| 1960 | 4,000,000 | — | 0.40 | 1.00 | 4.00 | — |
| 1960 Proof | — | Value: 100 | | | | |
| 1961 | 6,000,000 | — | 0.40 | 1.00 | 3.50 | — |
| 1961 Proof | — | Value: 100 | | | | |
| 1963H | 10,000,000 | — | 0.40 | 1.00 | 3.50 | — |
| 1964 | 5,000,000 | — | 0.40 | 1.00 | 3.50 | — |
| 1965KN | 8,000,000 | — | 0.40 | 1.00 | 3.00 | — |
| 1966 | 5,000,000 | — | 0.40 | 1.00 | 3.50 | — |
| 1967 | 12,000,000 | — | 0.40 | 1.00 | 3.00 | — |
| 1968H | 12,000,000 | — | 0.40 | 1.00 | 3.00 | — |
| 1970H | 4,600,000 | — | 0.40 | 1.00 | 3.00 | — |

**50 CENTS** KM# 30.2 **Composition:** Copper-Nickel **Edge:** Reeded without security **Note:** Error.

| Date | Mintage | F | VF | XF | Unc | BU |
|---|---|---|---|---|---|---|
| 1958H | Inc. above | 2.00 | 4.00 | 8.00 | 20.00 | — |

**50 CENTS** KM# 34 **Composition:** Copper-Nickel **Edge:** Reeded

| Date | Mintage | F | VF | XF | Unc | BU |
|---|---|---|---|---|---|---|
| 1971KN | — | — | 0.20 | 0.40 | 1.50 | — |
| 1972 | 30,000,000 | — | 0.20 | 0.40 | 1.50 | — |
| 1973 | 36,800,000 | — | 0.20 | 0.40 | 1.50 | — |
| 1974 | 6,000,000 | — | 0.20 | 0.40 | 1.50 | — |
| 1975 | 8,000,000 | — | 0.20 | 0.40 | 1.50 | — |

**50 CENTS** KM# 41 **Composition:** Nickel-Brass

| Date | Mintage | F | VF | XF | Unc | BU |
|---|---|---|---|---|---|---|
| 1977 | 60,001,000 | — | 0.20 | 0.30 | 0.80 | — |
| 1978 | 70,000,000 | — | 0.20 | 0.30 | 0.80 | — |
| 1979 | 60,640,000 | — | 0.20 | 0.30 | 0.80 | — |
| 1980 | 120,000,000 | — | 0.20 | 0.30 | 0.80 | — |

**50 CENTS** KM# 62 **Composition:** Nickel-Brass **Obverse:** Mature queen's portrait

| Date | Mintage | F | VF | XF | Unc | BU |
|---|---|---|---|---|---|---|
| 1988 | 50,000 | — | — | — | 8.00 | — |
| 1988 Proof | 25,000 | Value: 10.00 | | | | |
| 1990 | 27,000 | — | 0.20 | 0.30 | 0.80 | — |

**50 CENTS** KM# 68 **Composition:** Brass Plated Steel **Obverse:** Bauhinia flower

| Date | Mintage | F | VF | XF | Unc | BU |
|---|---|---|---|---|---|---|
| 1993 | — | — | 0.20 | 0.30 | 0.80 | — |
| 1993 Proof | — | Value: 5.50 | | | | |
| 1994 | — | — | 0.20 | 0.30 | 0.80 | — |
| 1995 | — | — | 0.20 | 0.30 | 0.80 | — |
| 1997 | — | — | 0.20 | 0.30 | 0.80 | — |

**DOLLAR** KM# 31.1 **Composition:** Copper-Nickel **Reverse:** Mint mark is below "LL" of "DOLLAR"

| Date | Mintage | F | VF | XF | Unc | BU |
|---|---|---|---|---|---|---|
| 1960H | 40,000,000 | — | 0.60 | 1.75 | 5.50 | — |
| 1960H Proof | — | Value: 3,350 | | | | |
| 1960KN | 40,000,000 | — | 0.60 | 1.75 | 5.50 | — |
| 1970H | 15,000,000 | — | 0.60 | 1.25 | 4.50 | — |

**DOLLAR** KM# 31.2 **Composition:** Copper-Nickel **Reverse:** Mint mark is below "LL" of "DOLLAR" **Edge:** Reeded without security **Note:** Error.

| Date | Mintage | F | VF | XF | Unc | BU |
|---|---|---|---|---|---|---|
| 1960H | Inc. above | 4.00 | 7.00 | 15.00 | 30.00 | — |

**DOLLAR** KM# 35 **Composition:** Copper-Nickel **Edge:** Reeded

| Date | Mintage | F | VF | XF | Unc | BU |
|---|---|---|---|---|---|---|
| 1971H | 8,000,000 | — | 0.60 | 1.25 | 4.50 | — |
| 1972 | 20,000,000 | — | 0.60 | 1.25 | 3.50 | — |
| 1973 | 8,125,000 | — | 0.60 | 1.25 | 4.50 | — |

| Date | Mintage | F | VF | XF | Unc | BU |
|---|---|---|---|---|---|---|
| 1974 | 26,000,000 | — | 0.60 | 1.25 | 3.50 | — |
| 1975 | 22,500,000 | — | 0.60 | 1.25 | 3.50 | — |

**DOLLAR** KM# 43 **Composition:** Copper-Nickel

| Date | Mintage | F | VF | XF | Unc | BU |
|---|---|---|---|---|---|---|
| 1978 | 120,000,000 | — | 0.40 | 0.70 | 1.50 | — |
| 1979 | 104,908,000 | — | 0.40 | 0.70 | 1.50 | — |
| 1980 | 100,000,000 | — | 0.40 | 0.70 | 1.50 | — |

**DOLLAR** KM# 63 **Composition:** Copper-Nickel **Obverse:** Mature queen's portrait **Reverse:** Lion within legend

| Date | Mintage | F | VF | XF | Unc | BU |
|---|---|---|---|---|---|---|
| 1987 | — | — | 0.30 | 0.50 | 1.00 | — |
| 1988 | 20,000,000 | — | 0.30 | 0.50 | 1.00 | — |
| 1988 Proof | 20,000 | Value: 20.00 | | | | |
| 1989 | 20,000,000 | — | 0.30 | 0.50 | 1.00 | — |
| 1990 | — | — | 0.30 | 0.50 | 1.00 | — |
| 1991 | — | — | 0.30 | 0.50 | 1.00 | — |
| 1992 | 25,000,000 | — | 0.30 | 0.50 | 1.00 | — |

**DOLLAR** KM# 69 **Composition:** Nickel Plated Steel **Obverse:** Bauhinia flower

| Date | Mintage | F | VF | XF | Unc | BU |
|---|---|---|---|---|---|---|
| 1993 | — | — | 0.30 | 0.50 | 1.00 | — |
| 1993 Proof | — | Value: 10.00 | | | | |

**DOLLAR** KM# 69a **Composition:** Copper-Nickel **Obverse:** Bauhinia flower

| Date | Mintage | F | VF | XF | Unc | BU |
|---|---|---|---|---|---|---|
| 1994 | — | — | 0.30 | 0.50 | 1.00 | — |
| 1995 | — | — | 0.30 | 0.50 | 1.00 | — |
| 1996 | — | — | 0.30 | 0.50 | 1.00 | — |
| 1997 | — | — | 0.30 | 0.50 | 1.00 | — |

**2 DOLLARS** KM# 37 **Composition:** Copper-Nickel

| Date | Mintage | F | VF | XF | Unc | BU |
|---|---|---|---|---|---|---|
| 1975 | 60,000,000 | — | 0.45 | 0.85 | 1.75 | — |
| 1978 | 504,000 | — | 0.45 | 1.00 | 10.00 | — |
| 1979 | 9,032,000 | — | 0.45 | 0.85 | 1.75 | — |
| 1980 | 30,000,000 | — | 0.45 | 0.85 | 1.75 | — |
| 1981 | 30,000,000 | — | 0.45 | 0.85 | 1.75 | — |
| 1982 | 30,000,000 | — | 0.45 | 0.85 | 1.75 | — |
| 1983 | 7,002,000 | — | 0.45 | 0.85 | 1.75 | — |
| 1984 | 22,002,000 | — | 0.45 | 0.85 | 1.75 | — |

**2 DOLLARS** KM# 60 **Composition:** Copper-Nickel **Obverse:** Mature queen's portrait

| Date | Mintage | F | VF | XF | Unc | BU |
|---|---|---|---|---|---|---|
| 1985 | 10,002,000 | — | 0.45 | 0.65 | 1.25 | — |
| 1986 | 15,000,000 | — | 0.45 | 0.65 | 1.25 | — |
| 1987 | — | — | 0.45 | 0.65 | 1.25 | — |
| 1988 | 5,000,000 | — | 0.45 | 0.65 | 1.25 | — |
| 1988 Proof | 20,000 | Value: 35.00 | | | | |
| 1989 | 33,000,000 | — | 0.45 | 0.65 | 1.25 | — |
| 1990 | — | — | 0.45 | 0.65 | 1.25 | — |
| 1991 | — | — | 0.45 | 0.65 | 1.25 | — |
| 1992 | 4,370,000 | — | 0.45 | 0.65 | 1.25 | — |

**2 DOLLARS** KM# 64 **Composition:** Copper-Nickel **Obverse:** Bauhinia flower

| Date | Mintage | F | VF | XF | Unc | BU |
|---|---|---|---|---|---|---|
| 1993 | — | — | 0.45 | 0.65 | 1.25 | — |
| 1993 Proof | — | Value: 12.50 | | | | |
| 1994 | — | — | 0.45 | 0.65 | 1.25 | — |
| 1995 | — | — | 0.45 | 0.65 | 1.25 | — |
| 1997 | — | — | 0.45 | 0.65 | 1.25 | — |

**5 DOLLARS** KM# 39 **Composition:** Copper-Nickel

| Date | Mintage | F | VF | XF | Unc | BU |
|---|---|---|---|---|---|---|
| 1976 | 30,000,000 | — | 1.00 | 1.50 | 2.50 | — |
| 1978 | 10,000,000 | — | 1.00 | 1.50 | 3.00 | — |
| 1979 | 12,000,000 | — | 1.00 | 1.50 | 2.50 | — |

**5 DOLLARS** KM# 46 **Composition:** Copper-Nickel

| Date | Mintage | F | VF | XF | Unc | BU |
|---|---|---|---|---|---|---|
| 1980 | 40,000,000 | — | 1.00 | 1.50 | 2.50 | — |
| 1981 | 20,000,000 | — | 1.00 | 1.50 | 2.50 | — |
| 1982 | 10,000,000 | — | 1.00 | 1.50 | 2.50 | — |
| 1983 | 4,000,000 | — | 1.00 | 1.50 | 2.50 | — |
| 1984 | 4,500,000 | — | 1.00 | 1.50 | 2.50 | — |

**5 DOLLARS** KM# 56 **Composition:** Copper-Nickel

| Date | Mintage | F | VF | XF | Unc | BU |
|---|---|---|---|---|---|---|
| 1985 | 6,000,000 | — | 0.75 | 1.25 | 2.25 | — |
| 1986 | 8,000,000 | — | 0.75 | 1.25 | 2.25 | — |
| 1987 | — | — | 0.75 | 1.25 | 2.25 | — |
| 1988 | 16,000,000 | — | 0.75 | 1.25 | 2.25 | — |
| 1988 Proof | 25,000 | Value: 45.00 | | | | |
| 1989 | 37,000,000 | — | 0.75 | 1.25 | 2.25 | — |
| 1991 | — | — | 0.75 | 1.25 | 2.25 | — |

**5 DOLLARS** KM# 65 **Composition:** Copper-Nickel **Obverse:** Bauhinia flower

| Date | Mintage | F | VF | XF | Unc | BU |
|---|---|---|---|---|---|---|
| 1993 | — | — | 0.75 | 1.25 | 2.25 | — |
| 1993 Proof | — | Value: 20.00 | | | | |
| 1994 | — | — | 0.75 | 1.25 | 2.25 | — |
| 1995 | — | — | 0.75 | 1.25 | 2.25 | — |
| 1997 | — | — | 0.75 | 1.25 | 2.25 | — |

**10 DOLLARS** KM# 70 **Ring Composition:** Copper Nickel **Center Composition:** Nickel-Brass **Obverse:** Bauhinia flower **Reverse:** Shou character

| Date | Mintage | F | VF | XF | Unc | BU |
|---|---|---|---|---|---|---|
| 1993 | — | — | 2.50 | 4.50 | 10.00 | — |
| 1993 Proof | Est. 30,000 | Value: 20.00 | | | | |
| 1994 | — | — | 1.50 | 2.50 | 5.00 | — |
| 1995 | — | — | 1.50 | 2.50 | 5.00 | — |

**10 DOLLARS** KM# 70a **Ring Composition:** 0.3750 Gold **Center Weight:** 18.3000 g. **Center Composition:** 0.9170 Gold .3826 oz. AGW **Obverse:** Bauhinia flower **Reverse:** Shou character

| Date | Mintage | F | VF | XF | Unc | BU |
|---|---|---|---|---|---|---|
| 1994 Proof | 20,000 | Value: 200 | | | | |

**1000 DOLLARS** KM# 38 **Weight:** 15.9700 g. **Composition:** 0.9170 Gold .4708 oz. AGW **Subject:** Visit of Queen Elizabeth

| Date | Mintage | F | VF | XF | Unc | BU |
|---|---|---|---|---|---|---|
| 1975 | 15,000 | — | — | — | 275 | — |
| 1975 Proof | 5,005 | Value: 1,250 | | | | |

**1000 DOLLARS** KM# 40 **Weight:** 15.9700 g. **Composition:** 0.9170 Gold .4708 oz. AGW **Subject:** Year of the Dragon

| Date | Mintage | F | VF | XF | Unc | BU |
|---|---|---|---|---|---|---|
| 1976 | 20,000 | — | — | — | 465 | — |
| 1976 Proof | 6,911 | Value: 1,150 | | | | |

**1000 DOLLARS** **KM# 42** **Weight:** 15.9700 g. **Composition:** 0.9170 Gold .4708 oz. AGW **Subject:** Year of the Snake

| Date | Mintage | F | VF | XF | Unc | BU |
|---|---|---|---|---|---|---|
| 1977 | 20,000 | — | — | — | 300 | — |
| 1977 Proof | 10,000 | Value: 525 | | | | |

**1000 DOLLARS** **KM# 44** **Weight:** 15.9700 g. **Composition:** 0.9170 Gold .4708 oz. AGW **Subject:** Year of the Horse

| Date | Mintage | F | VF | XF | Unc | BU |
|---|---|---|---|---|---|---|
| 1978 | 20,000 | — | — | — | 250 | — |
| 1978 Proof | 10,000 | Value: 450 | | | | |

**1000 DOLLARS** **KM# 45** **Weight:** 15.9700 g. **Composition:** 0.9170 Gold .4708 oz. AGW **Subject:** Year of the Goat

| Date | Mintage | F | VF | XF | Unc | BU |
|---|---|---|---|---|---|---|
| 1979 | 30,000 | — | — | — | 225 | — |
| 1979 Proof | 15,000 | Value: 325 | | | | |

**1000 DOLLARS** **KM# 47** **Weight:** 15.9700 g. **Composition:** 0.9170 Gold .4708 oz. AGW **Subject:** Year of the Monkey

| Date | Mintage | F | VF | XF | Unc | BU |
|---|---|---|---|---|---|---|
| 1980 | 31,000 | — | — | — | 220 | — |
| 1980 Proof | 18,000 | Value: 300 | | | | |

**1000 DOLLARS** **KM# 48** **Weight:** 15.9700 g. **Composition:** 0.9170 Gold .4708 oz. AGW **Subject:** Year of the Cockerel

| Date | Mintage | F | VF | XF | Unc | BU |
|---|---|---|---|---|---|---|
| 1981 | 33,000 | — | — | — | 220 | — |
| 1981 Proof | 22,000 | Value: 300 | | | | |

**1000 DOLLARS** **KM# 50** **Weight:** 15.9700 g. **Composition:** 0.9170 Gold .4708 oz. AGW **Subject:** Year of the Dog

| Date | Mintage | F | VF | XF | Unc | BU |
|---|---|---|---|---|---|---|
| 1982 | 33,000 | — | — | — | 225 | — |
| 1982 Proof | 22,000 | Value: 320 | | | | |

**1000 DOLLARS** **KM# 51** **Weight:** 15.9700 g. **Composition:** 0.9170 Gold .4708 oz. AGW **Subject:** Year of the Pig

| Date | Mintage | F | VF | XF | Unc | BU |
|---|---|---|---|---|---|---|
| 1983 | 33,000 | — | — | — | 550 | — |
| 1983 Proof | 22,000 | Value: 700 | | | | |

**1000 DOLLARS** **KM# 52** **Weight:** 15.9700 g. **Composition:** 0.9170 Gold .4708 oz. AGW **Subject:** Year of the Rat

| Date | Mintage | F | VF | XF | Unc | BU |
|---|---|---|---|---|---|---|
| 1984 | 20,000 | — | — | — | 325 | — |
| 1984 Proof | 10,000 | Value: 550 | | | | |

**1000 DOLLARS** **KM# 53** **Weight:** 15.9700 g. **Composition:** 0.9170 Gold .4708 oz. AGW **Subject:** Year of the Ox

| Date | Mintage | F | VF | XF | Unc | BU |
|---|---|---|---|---|---|---|
| 1985 | 30,000 | — | — | — | 345 | — |
| 1985 Proof | 10,000 | Value: 575 | | | | |

**1000 DOLLARS** **KM# 54** **Weight:** 15.9700 g. **Composition:** 0.9170 Gold .4708 oz. AGW **Subject:** Year of the Tiger

| Date | Mintage | F | VF | XF | Unc | BU |
|---|---|---|---|---|---|---|
| 1986 | 20,000 | — | — | — | 325 | — |
| 1986 Proof | 10,000 | Value: 500 | | | | |

**1000 DOLLARS** **KM# 57** **Weight:** 15.9700 g. **Composition:** 0.9170 Gold .4708 oz. AGW **Subject:** Royal visit of Queen Elizabeth II

| Date | Mintage | F | VF | XF | Unc | BU |
|---|---|---|---|---|---|---|
| 1986 | 20,000 | — | — | — | 235 | — |
| 1986 Proof | 12,000 | Value: 350 | | | | |

**1000 DOLLARS** **KM# 58** **Weight:** 15.9700 g. **Composition:** 0.9170 Gold .4708 oz. AGW **Subject:** Year of the Rabbitt

| Date | Mintage | F | VF | XF | Unc | BU |
|---|---|---|---|---|---|---|
| 1987 | 20,000 | — | — | — | 235 | — |
| 1987 Proof | 12,000 | Value: 350 | | | | |

# HONG KONG S.A.R.

## DECIMAL COINAGE

**10 CENTS** **KM# 72** **Composition:** Brass Plated Steel **Obverse:** Bauhinia flower **Reverse:** Sailing junk

| Date | Mintage | F | VF | XF | Unc | BU |
|---|---|---|---|---|---|---|
| 1997 | — | — | 0.15 | 0.15 | 0.30 | — |
| 1997 Proof | Est. 97,000 | Value: 1.50 | | | | |

**20 CENTS** **KM# 73** **Composition:** Nickel-Brass **Obverse:** Bauhinia flower **Reverse:** Butterfly kites

| Date | Mintage | F | VF | XF | Unc | BU |
|---|---|---|---|---|---|---|
| 1997 | — | — | 0.10 | 0.20 | 0.40 | — |
| 1997 Proof | — | Value: 1.50 | | | | |

**50 CENTS** **KM# 74** **Composition:** Brass Plated Steel **Obverse:** Bauhinia flower **Reverse:** Ox

| Date | Mintage | F | VF | XF | Unc | BU |
|---|---|---|---|---|---|---|
| 1997 | — | — | 0.20 | 0.30 | 0.80 | — |
| 1997 Proof | Est. 97,000 | Value: 2.50 | | | | |

**DOLLAR** **KM# 75** **Composition:** Copper-Nickel **Obverse:** Bauhinia flower **Reverse:** Chinese unicorn

| Date | Mintage | F | VF | XF | Unc | BU |
|---|---|---|---|---|---|---|
| 1997 | — | — | 0.30 | 0.50 | 1.00 | — |
| 1997 Proof | — | Value: 5.50 | | | | |

**2 DOLLARS** KM# 76 **Composition:** Copper-Nickel **Obverse:** Bauhinia flower **Reverse:** Ho Ho brothers

| Date | Mintage | F | VF | XF | Unc | BU |
|---|---|---|---|---|---|---|
| 1997 | — | — | 0.45 | 0.65 | 1.25 | — |
| 1997 Proof | Est. 97,000 | Value: 8.00 | | | | |

**5 DOLLARS** KM# 77 **Composition:** Copper-Nickel **Obverse:** Bauhinia flower **Reverse:** Shou character

| Date | Mintage | F | VF | XF | Unc | BU |
|---|---|---|---|---|---|---|
| 1997 | — | — | 0.75 | 1.25 | 2.25 | — |
| 1997 Proof | Est. 97,000 | Value: 12.50 | | | | |

**10 DOLLARS** KM# 78 **Ring Composition:** Copper Nickel **Center Composition:** Nickel-Brass **Obverse:** Bauhinia flower **Reverse:** Suspension bridge

| Date | Mintage | F | VF | XF | Unc | BU |
|---|---|---|---|---|---|---|
| 1997 | — | — | 1.75 | 3.50 | 6.50 | — |
| 1997 Proof | Est. 97,000 | Value: 13.50 | | | | |

**1000 DOLLARS** KM# 71 **Weight:** 15.9700 g. **Composition:** 0.9170 Gold .4708 oz. AGW **Subject:** Return of Hong Kong to China

| Date | Mintage | F | VF | XF | Unc | BU |
|---|---|---|---|---|---|---|
| 1997 Proof | 97,000 | Value: 300 | | | | |

**1000 DOLLARS** KM# 79 **Weight:** 15.9700 g. **Composition:** 0.9170 Gold .4708 oz. AGW **Subject:** Hong Kong International Airport

| Date | Mintage | F | VF | XF | Unc | BU |
|---|---|---|---|---|---|---|
| 1998 Proof | 15,000 | Value: 450 | | | | |

## MINT SETS

| KM# | Date | Mintage | Identification | Issue Price | Mkt Val |
|---|---|---|---|---|---|
| MS1 | 1988 (7) | 50,000 | KM55-56, 59-63 | 13.00 | 65.00 |
| MS2 | 1993 (7) | — | KM64-70 | 20.00 | 32.50 |
| MS3 | 1997 (7) | — | KM72-78 | 30.00 | 12.50 |

## PROOF SETS

| KM# | Date | Mintage | Identification | Issue Price | Mkt Val |
|---|---|---|---|---|---|
| PS4 | 1988 (7) | 25,000 | KM55-56, 59-63 | 39.75 | 125 |
| PS5 | 1993 (7) | 30,000 | KM64-70 | 50.00 | 72.50 |
| PS6 | 1997 (7) | 97,000 | KM72-78 | — | 45.00 |

The Republic of Hungary, located in central Europe, has an area of 35,929 sq. mi. (93,030 sq. km.) and a population of 10.7 million. Capital: Budapest. The economy is based on agriculture, bauxite and a rapidly expanding industrial sector. Machinery, chemicals, iron and steel, and fruits and vegetables are exported.

The ancient kingdom of Hungary, founded by the Magyars in the 9th century, achieved its greatest extension in the mid-14th century when its dominions touched the Baltic, Black and Mediterranean Seas. After suffering repeated Turkish invasions, Hungary accepted Habsburg rule to escape Turkish occupation, regaining independence in 1867 with the Emperor of Austria as king of a dual Austro-Hungarian monarchy.

After World War I, Hungary lost 2/3 of its territory and 1/2 of its population and underwent a period of drastic political revision. The short-lived republic of 1918 was followed by a chaotic interval of communist rule, 1919, and the restoration of the monarchy in 1920 with Admiral Horthy as regent of the kingdom. Although a German ally in World War II, Hungary was occupied by German troops who imposed a pro-Nazi dictatorship, 1944. Soviet armies drove out the Germans in 1945 and assisted the communist minority in seizing power. A revised constitution published on Aug. 20, 1949, established Hungary as a People's Republic of the Soviet type. On October 23, 1989, Hungary was pro-claimed the Republic of Hungary.

**RULERS**

Franz Joseph I, 1848-1916
Karl I, 1916-1918

**MINT MARKS**

B, K, KB - Kremnitz (Kormoczbanya)
BP - Budapest

**MONETARY SYSTEM**

**1892-1925**

100 Filler = 1 Korona

**1926-1945**

100 Filler = 1 Pengo

**Commencing 1946**

100 Filler = 1 Forint

NOTE: Many coins of Hungary through 1948, especially1925-1945, have been restruck in recent times. These may be identified by a rosette in the vicinity of the mintmark. Restrike mintages for KM#440-449, 451-458, 468-469,475-477, 480-483, 494, 496-498 are usually about1000 pieces, later date mintages are not known.

# KINGDOM

## REFORM COINAGE

100 Filler = 1 Korona

**FILLER** KM# 480 **Composition:** Bronze

| Date | Mintage | F | VF | XF | Unc | BU |
|---|---|---|---|---|---|---|
| 1901KB | 5,994,000 | 4.00 | 8.00 | 17.00 | 32.50 | — |
| 1902KB | 16,299,000 | 0.20 | 0.50 | 1.25 | 4.00 | — |
| 1903KB | 2,291,000 | 12.00 | 25.00 | 65.00 | 110 | — |
| 1906KB | 61,000 | 65.00 | 120 | 180 | 275 | — |
| 1914KB | — | 65.00 | 90.00 | 135 | 210 | — |
| 1914KB Proof | — | Value: 350 | | | | |

**2 FILLER** KM# 481 **Composition:** Bronze

| Date | Mintage | F | VF | XF | Unc | BU |
|---|---|---|---|---|---|---|
| 1901KB | 25,805,000 | 0.50 | 1.00 | 2.50 | 5.00 | — |
| 1902KB | 6,937,000 | 5.50 | 8.50 | 13.50 | 20.00 | — |
| 1903KB | 4,052,000 | 12.00 | 20.00 | 35.00 | 50.00 | — |
| 1904KB | 4,203,000 | 6.00 | 12.00 | 25.00 | 40.00 | — |
| 1905KB | 9,335,000 | 0.70 | 1.75 | 3.00 | 6.00 | — |
| 1906KB | 3,140,000 | 1.75 | 2.50 | 5.00 | 7.50 | — |
| 1907KB | 9,943,000 | 5.50 | 9.00 | 12.00 | 17.50 | — |
| 1908KB | 16,486,000 | 0.50 | 1.00 | 2.50 | 5.00 | — |
| 1909KB | 19,075,000 | 0.50 | 1.00 | 2.50 | 5.00 | — |
| 1910KB | 5,338,000 | 4.50 | 7.50 | 10.00 | 15.00 | — |
| 1910KB Restrike with rosette; proof | — | Value: 10.00 | | | | |
| 1914KB | 4,106,000 | 0.50 | 1.00 | 2.50 | 5.00 | — |
| 1915KB | 1,294,000 | 1.50 | 2.00 | 4.00 | 7.00 | — |

**2 FILLER** KM# 497 **Composition:** Iron **Note:** Varieties in planchet thickness exist for 1917.

| Date | Mintage | F | VF | XF | Unc | BU |
|---|---|---|---|---|---|---|
| 1916 | — | 6.00 | 10.00 | 15.00 | 25.00 | — |
| 1917 | — | 1.00 | 2.50 | 6.00 | 12.00 | — |
| 1918 | — | 2.00 | 4.50 | 9.00 | 15.00 | — |

**10 FILLER** KM# 482 **Composition:** Nickel **Note:** Edge varieties exist.

| Date | Mintage | F | VF | XF | Unc | BU |
|---|---|---|---|---|---|---|
| 1906KB | 56,000 | 75.00 | 175 | 250 | 325 | — |
| 1908KB | 6,819,000 | 0.25 | 0.50 | 1.50 | 4.00 | — |
| 1909KB | 17,204,000 | 0.30 | 0.60 | 2.00 | 4.00 | — |
| 1914KB | — | 175 | 275 | 550 | 900 | — |

**10 FILLER** KM# 494 **Composition:** Copper-Nickel-Zinc **Note:** Varieties exist.

| Date | Mintage | F | VF | XF | Unc | BU |
|---|---|---|---|---|---|---|
| 1914 | 4,400,000 | 200 | 300 | 500 | 900 | — |
| 1915 | Inc. above | 0.30 | 0.60 | 1.50 | 4.00 | — |
| 1915 Restrike with rosette; proof | Inc. above | Value: 4.00 | | | | |
| 1916 | Inc. above | 0.50 | 1.25 | 2.50 | 5.00 | — |

**10 FILLER** KM# 496 **Composition:** Iron **Note:** Varieties exist.

| Date | Mintage | F | VF | XF | Unc | BU |
|---|---|---|---|---|---|---|
| 1915 | 11,500,000 | 9.00 | 20.00 | 32.50 | 55.00 | — |
| 1916 Rare | Inc. above | — | — | — | — | — |
| 1918 | Inc. above | 15.00 | 30.00 | 55.00 | 85.00 | — |
| 1918 Restrike; proof | — | Value: 18.00 | | | | |
| 1920 | 3,275,000 | 4.50 | 9.00 | 15.00 | 25.00 | — |
| 1920 Restrike; proof | — | Value: 18.00 | | | | |

**20 FILLER** KM# 483 **Composition:** Nickel **Note:** Edge varieties exist.

| Date | Mintage | F | VF | XF | Unc | BU |
|---|---|---|---|---|---|---|
| 1906KB | 67,000 | 275 | 400 | 600 | 1,250 | — |
| 1907KB | 1,248,000 | 3.00 | 6.00 | 12.00 | 24.00 | — |
| 1908KB | 10,770,000 | 0.75 | 1.75 | 3.75 | 7.50 | — |
| 1914KB | 5,387,000 | 3.75 | 6.50 | 10.00 | 15.00 | — |
| 1914KB Restrike; proof | — | Value: 12.50 | | | | |

**20 FILLER** KM# 498 **Composition:** Iron **Note:** Edge varieties exist.

| Date | Mintage | F | VF | XF | Unc | BU |
|---|---|---|---|---|---|---|
| 1914 | 18,826,000 | 18.00 | 32.50 | 45.00 | 70.00 | — |
| 1916 | Inc. above | 0.50 | 1.25 | 2.50 | 7.00 | — |
| 1917 | Inc. above | 0.75 | 1.75 | 3.50 | 8.00 | — |
| 1918 | Inc. above | 0.75 | 1.75 | 3.50 | 8.00 | — |
| 1918 Restrike; proof | — | Value: 6.00 | | | | |
| 1920 | 12,000,000 | 2.50 | 5.00 | 9.00 | 18.00 | — |
| 1921 | Inc. above | 18.00 | 32.50 | 45.00 | 70.00 | — |
| 1921 Restrike; proof | — | Value: 12.00 | | | | |
| 1922 Rare | — | — | — | — | — | — |
| 1922 Restrike; proof | — | Value: 12.00 | | | | |

**20 FILLER** KM# 498a **Composition:** Brass

| Date | Mintage | F | VF | XF | Unc | BU |
|---|---|---|---|---|---|---|
| 1922 | 400 | — | — | — | — | — |
| 1922 Restrike | — | Value: 30.00 | | | | |

**KORONA** KM# 484 **Weight:** 5.0000 g. **Composition:** 0.8350 Silver .1342 oz. ASW **Note:** Obverse varieties exist.

| Date | Mintage | F | VF | XF | Unc | BU |
|---|---|---|---|---|---|---|
| 1906KB | 24,000 | 150 | 200 | 300 | 425 | — |

**KORONA** KM# 492 **Weight:** 5.0000 g. **Composition:** 0.8350 Silver .1342 oz. ASW

| Date | Mintage | F | VF | XF | Unc | BU |
|---|---|---|---|---|---|---|
| 1912 | 4,004,000 | 2.50 | 5.00 | 10.00 | 15.00 | — |
| 1913 | 5,214 | 50.00 | 80.00 | 140 | 200 | — |
| 1914 | 5,886,000 | BV | 3.75 | 6.50 | 10.00 | — |
| 1915 | 3,934,000 | BV | 3.00 | 4.50 | 6.00 | — |
| 1916 | — | BV | 3.50 | 6.00 | 8.00 | — |

**2 KORONA** KM# 493 **Weight:** 10.0000 g. **Composition:** 0.8350 Silver .2685 oz. ASW

| Date | Mintage | F | VF | XF | Unc | BU |
|---|---|---|---|---|---|---|
| 1912KB | 4,000,000 | BV | 4.50 | 6.50 | 13.50 | — |
| 1913KB | 3,000,000 | BV | 4.50 | 6.50 | 13.50 | — |
| 1914KB | 500,000 | 20.00 | 30.00 | 50.00 | 80.00 | — |

**5 KORONA** KM# 488 **Weight:** 24.0000 g. **Composition:** 0.9000 Silver .6944 oz. ASW

| Date | Mintage | F | VF | XF | Unc | BU |
|---|---|---|---|---|---|---|
| 1906KB | 1,263 | 1,000 | 1,500 | 2,000 | 2,500 | — |
| 1907KB | 500,000 | 12.00 | 20.00 | 40.00 | 85.00 | — |
| 1908KB | 1,742,000 | 10.00 | 18.00 | 40.00 | 75.00 | — |
| 1909KB | 1,299,000 | 10.00 | 18.00 | 40.00 | 90.00 | — |
| 1909KB U.P. Restrike; proof | — | Value: 35.00 | | | | |

**5 KORONA** KM# 489 **Weight:** 24.0000 g. **Composition:** 0.9000 Silver .6944 oz. ASW **Subject:** 40th Anniversary - Coronation of Franz Josef

| Date | Mintage | F | VF | XF | Unc | BU |
|---|---|---|---|---|---|---|
| 1907 | 300,000 | 15.00 | 22.00 | 35.00 | 55.00 | — |
| 1907 Restrike; proof | — | Value: 30.00 | | | | |
| 1907 Restrike; proof | — | Value: 30.00 | | | | |

**10 KORONA** KM# 485 **Weight:** 3.3875 g. **Composition:** 0.9000 Gold .0980 oz. AGW

| Date | Mintage | F | VF | XF | Unc | BU |
|---|---|---|---|---|---|---|
| 1901KB | 230,000 | BV | 45.00 | 55.00 | 85.00 | — |
| 1902KB | 243,000 | BV | 45.00 | 55.00 | 85.00 | — |
| 1903KB | 228,000 | BV | 45.00 | 55.00 | 85.00 | — |
| 1904KB | 1,531,000 | BV | 45.00 | 55.00 | 85.00 | — |
| 1905KB | 869,000 | BV | 45.00 | 55.00 | 85.00 | — |
| 1906KB | 748,000 | BV | 45.00 | 55.00 | 85.00 | — |
| 1907KB | 752,000 | BV | 45.00 | 55.00 | 85.00 | — |
| 1908KB | 509,000 | BV | 45.00 | 55.00 | 85.00 | — |
| 1909KB | 574,000 | BV | 45.00 | 55.00 | 85.00 | — |
| 1910KB | 1,362,000 | BV | 45.00 | 55.00 | 85.00 | — |
| 1911KB | 1,828,000 | BV | 45.00 | 55.00 | 85.00 | — |
| 1912KB | 739,000 | 50.00 | 60.00 | 70.00 | 100 | — |
| 1913KB | 137,000 | 50.00 | 75.00 | 100 | 130 | — |
| 1914KB | 115,000 | 50.00 | 80.00 | 135 | 165 | — |
| 1915KB | 54,000 | 1,000 | 2,000 | 3,000 | 4,000 | — |

**20 KORONA** KM# 486 **Weight:** 6.7750 g. **Composition:** 0.9000 Gold .1960 oz. AGW

| Date | Mintage | F | VF | XF | Unc | BU |
|---|---|---|---|---|---|---|
| 1901KB | 510,000 | BV | 80.00 | 90.00 | 135 | — |
| 1901KB | 510,000 | BV | 80.00 | 90.00 | 135 | — |
| 1902KB | 523,000 | BV | 80.00 | 90.00 | 135 | — |
| 1903KB | 505,000 | BV | 80.00 | 90.00 | 135 | — |
| 1904KB | 572,000 | BV | 80.00 | 90.00 | 135 | — |
| 1905KB | 526,000 | BV | 80.00 | 90.00 | 135 | — |
| 1906KB | 353,000 | BV | 80.00 | 90.00 | 135 | — |
| 1907KB | 194,000 | 100 | 150 | 175 | 200 | — |
| 1908KB | 138,000 | BV | 80.00 | 90.00 | 135 | — |
| 1909KB | 459,000 | BV | 80.00 | 90.00 | 135 | — |
| 1910KB | 85,000 | 125 | 175 | 250 | 300 | — |
| 1911KB | 63,000 | BV | 80.00 | 90.00 | 135 | — |
| 1912KB | 211,000 | BV | 80.00 | 90.00 | 135 | — |
| 1913KB | 320,000 | 110 | 140 | 165 | 200 | — |
| 1914KB | 176,000 | BV | 80.00 | 90.00 | 135 | — |
| 1915KB | 690,000 | 110 | 140 | 165 | 200 | — |

**20 KORONA** KM# 495 **Weight:** 6.7750 g. **Composition:** 0.9000 Gold .1960 oz. AGW **Reverse:** Bosnian arms added

| Date | Mintage | F | VF | XF | Unc | BU |
|---|---|---|---|---|---|---|
| 1914 | — | BV | 90.00 | 100 | 145 | — |
| 1915 | — | — | — | — | — | — |
| 1916 | — | 125 | 175 | 275 | 400 | — |

**20 KORONA** KM# 500 **Weight:** 6.7750 g. **Composition:** 0.9000 Gold .1960 oz. AGW **Obv. Legend:** KAROLY...

| Date | Mintage | F | VF | XF | Unc | BU |
|---|---|---|---|---|---|---|
| 1918 Rare | — | — | — | — | — | — |

**100 KORONA** KM# 490 **Weight:** 33.8753 g. **Composition:** 0.9000 Gold .9802 oz. AGW **Subject:** 40th Anniversary - Coronation of Franz Josef

| Date | Mintage | F | VF | XF | Unc | BU |
|---|---|---|---|---|---|---|
| 1907KB | 11,000 | 500 | 650 | 900 | 1,350 | — |
| 1907KB U.P. Restrike | — | — | — | — | 800 | — |

**100 KORONA** KM# 491 **Weight:** 33.8753 g. **Composition:** 0.9000 Gold .9802 oz. AGW

| Date | Mintage | F | VF | XF | Unc | BU |
|---|---|---|---|---|---|---|
| 1907 | 1,088 | 600 | 1,100 | 1,450 | 1,900 | — |
| 1907 U.P. Restrike | — | — | — | — | 350 | — |
| 1908 | 4,038 | 550 | 850 | 1,250 | 1,800 | — |
| 1908 U.P Restrike | — | — | — | — | 350 | — |

## REGENCY COINAGE

1926 - 1945

**FILLER** KM# 505 **Composition:** Bronze

| Date | Mintage | F | VF | XF | Unc | BU |
|---|---|---|---|---|---|---|
| 1926BP | 6,471,000 | 0.50 | 1.00 | 2.00 | 4.00 | — |
| 1927BP | 16,529,000 | 0.10 | 0.20 | 0.50 | 3.00 | — |
| 1928BP | 7,000,000 | 0.25 | 0.50 | 1.00 | 3.75 | — |
| 1929BP | 418,000 | 5.00 | 10.00 | 20.00 | 35.00 | — |
| 1930BP | 3,734,000 | 0.30 | 0.60 | 1.50 | 5.00 | — |
| 1931BP | 10,849,000 | 0.10 | 0.20 | 0.60 | 3.00 | — |
| 1932BP | 5,000,000 | 0.25 | 0.50 | 1.00 | 4.00 | — |
| 1932BP Restrike; proof | — | Value: 3.75 | | | | |
| 1933BP | 5,000,000 | 0.25 | 0.50 | 1.00 | 4.00 | — |
| 1934BP | 3,111,000 | 0.30 | 0.60 | 1.20 | 4.50 | — |
| 1935BP | 6,889,000 | 0.25 | 0.50 | 1.00 | 4.00 | — |
| 1936BP | 10,000,000 | 0.10 | 0.20 | 0.60 | 2.50 | — |
| 1938BP | 10,575,000 | 0.10 | 0.20 | 0.60 | 2.50 | — |
| 1939BP | 10,425,000 | 0.10 | 0.20 | 0.60 | 2.50 | — |

**2 FILLER** **KM# 506** **Composition:** Bronze

| Date | Mintage | F | VF | XF | Unc | BU |
|---|---|---|---|---|---|---|
| 1926BP | 17,777,000 | 0.10 | 0.20 | 0.40 | 2.00 | — |
| 1927BP | 44,836,000 | 0.10 | 0.20 | 0.40 | 2.00 | — |
| 1928BP | 11,448,000 | 0.10 | 0.20 | 0.40 | 2.00 | — |
| 1929BP | 8,995,000 | 0.10 | 0.25 | 0.50 | 2.50 | — |
| 1930BP | 6,943,000 | 0.10 | 0.25 | 0.50 | 2.50 | — |
| 1931BP | 826,000 | 0.40 | 0.90 | 2.50 | 6.50 | — |
| 1932BP | 4,174,000 | 4.00 | 8.00 | 15.00 | 25.00 | — |
| 1933BP | 501,000 | 3.00 | 6.00 | 10.00 | 18.00 | — |
| 1934BP | 9,499,000 | 0.10 | 0.20 | 0.40 | 2.00 | — |
| 1935BP | 10,000,000 | 0.10 | 0.20 | 0.40 | 2.00 | — |
| 1936BP | 2,049,000 | 0.15 | 0.30 | 0.75 | 4.00 | — |
| 1937BP | 7,951,000 | 0.10 | 0.25 | 0.50 | 2.00 | — |
| 1938BP | 14,125,000 | 0.10 | 0.20 | 0.40 | 1.50 | — |
| 1939BP | 16,875,000 | 0.10 | 0.20 | 0.40 | 1.50 | — |
| 1940BP | 7,000,000 | 0.10 | 0.25 | 0.50 | 1.50 | — |

**2 FILLER** **KM# 518.1** **Composition:** Steel

| Date | Mintage | F | VF | XF | Unc | BU |
|---|---|---|---|---|---|---|
| 1940 | 64,500,000 | 1.00 | 2.00 | 5.00 | 10.00 | — |

**2 FILLER** **KM# 518.2** **Composition:** Steel

| Date | Mintage | F | VF | XF | Unc | BU |
|---|---|---|---|---|---|---|
| 1940 | 78,000,000 | 0.50 | 1.00 | 2.00 | 4.50 | — |
| 1941 | 12,000,000 | 30.00 | 65.00 | 125 | 200 | — |
| 1942 | 13,000,000 | 0.50 | 1.00 | 2.00 | 4.50 | — |
| 1942 Restrike; proof | — | Value: 6.50 | | | | |

**2 FILLER** **KM# 519** **Composition:** Zinc **Note:** Variations in planchets exist.

| Date | Mintage | F | VF | XF | Unc | BU |
|---|---|---|---|---|---|---|
| 1943 | 37,000,000 | 0.10 | 0.20 | 0.70 | 3.00 | — |
| 1943 Restrike; proof | — | Value: 6.50 | | | | |
| 1944 | 55,159,000 | 0.10 | 0.20 | 0.70 | 2.50 | — |

**10 FILLER** **KM# 507** **Composition:** Copper-Nickel

| Date | Mintage | F | VF | XF | Unc | BU |
|---|---|---|---|---|---|---|
| 1926BP | 20,001,000 | 0.50 | 1.50 | 3.00 | 10.00 | — |
| 1927BP | 12,255,000 | 0.50 | 1.50 | 3.00 | 7.00 | — |
| 1935BP | 4,740,000 | 0.50 | 1.50 | 3.00 | 4.50 | — |
| 1936BP | 3,005,000 | 0.50 | 1.50 | 3.00 | 4.50 | — |
| 1938BP | 6,700,000 | 0.50 | 1.50 | 3.00 | 4.50 | — |
| 1939BP | 4,460,000 | 3.00 | 5.00 | 10.00 | 20.00 | — |
| 1940BP | 960,000 | 15.00 | 30.00 | 50.00 | 75.00 | — |

**10 FILLER** **KM# 507a** **Composition:** Steel

| Date | Mintage | F | VF | XF | Unc | BU |
|---|---|---|---|---|---|---|
| 1940 | 45,927,000 | 0.10 | 0.20 | 0.80 | 3.50 | — |
| 1941 | 24,963,000 | 0.10 | 0.20 | 0.80 | 3.50 | — |
| 1942 | 44,110,000 | 0.10 | 0.20 | 0.80 | 3.50 | — |

**20 FILLER** **KM# 508** **Composition:** Copper-Nickel

| Date | Mintage | F | VF | XF | Unc | BU |
|---|---|---|---|---|---|---|
| 1926BP | 25,000,000 | 1.50 | 3.50 | 10.00 | 15.00 | — |
| 1927BP | 830,000 | 10.00 | 30.00 | 60.00 | 100 | — |
| 1938BP | 20,150,000 | 0.10 | 0.25 | 1.00 | 2.50 | — |
| 1939BP | 2,020,000 | 6.50 | 10.00 | 20.00 | 35.00 | — |
| 1940BP | 2,470,000 | 4.00 | 7.50 | 18.00 | 30.00 | — |

**20 FILLER** **KM# 520** **Composition:** Steel

| Date | Mintage | F | VF | XF | Unc | BU |
|---|---|---|---|---|---|---|
| 1941 | 75,007,000 | 0.10 | 0.20 | 0.90 | 4.00 | — |
| 1943 | 7,500,000 | 0.10 | 0.20 | 0.90 | 4.00 | — |
| 1944 | 25,000,000 | 0.10 | 0.20 | 0.90 | 4.00 | — |
| 1944 Restrike; proof | — | Value: 7.00 | | | | |

**50 FILLER** **KM# 509** **Composition:** Copper-Nickel

| Date | Mintage | F | VF | XF | Unc | BU |
|---|---|---|---|---|---|---|
| 1926BP | 14,921,000 | 0.75 | 2.00 | 3.50 | 6.00 | — |
| 1938BP | 20,079,000 | 0.20 | 0.40 | 1.00 | 3.00 | — |
| 1939BP | 2,770,000 | 6.50 | 15.00 | 30.00 | 50.00 | — |
| 1939BP Restrike; proof | — | Value: 20.00 | | | | |
| 1940BP | 6,230,000 | 4.00 | 7.50 | 18.00 | 30.00 | — |

**PENGO** **KM# 510** **Weight:** 5.0000 g. **Composition:** 0.6400 Silver .1029 oz. ASW

| Date | Mintage | F | VF | XF | Unc | BU |
|---|---|---|---|---|---|---|
| 1926BP | 15,000,000 | BV | 2.50 | 6.50 | 20.00 | — |
| 1927BP | 18,000,000 | BV | 1.50 | 4.50 | 12.00 | — |
| 1937BP | 4,000,000 | BV | 1.50 | 2.50 | 6.00 | — |
| 1938BP | 5,000,000 | BV | 1.50 | 2.50 | 6.00 | — |
| 1939BP | 13,000,000 | BV | 1.00 | 2.00 | 5.00 | — |

**PENGO** **KM# 521** **Composition:** Aluminum

| Date | Mintage | F | VF | XF | Unc | BU |
|---|---|---|---|---|---|---|
| 1941 | 80,000,000 | 0.10 | 0.20 | 0.50 | 1.00 | — |
| 1942 | 19,000,000 | 0.10 | 0.20 | 0.50 | 1.00 | — |
| 1943 | 2,000,000 | 1.00 | 4.00 | 8.00 | 15.00 | — |
| 1944 | 16,000,000 | 0.10 | 0.20 | 0.50 | 1.00 | — |

**2 PENGO** **KM# 511** **Weight:** 10.0000 g. **Composition:** 0.6400 Silver .2058 oz. ASW

| Date | Mintage | F | VF | XF | Unc | BU |
|---|---|---|---|---|---|---|
| 1929BP | 5,000,000 | 1.25 | 3.00 | 6.50 | 12.50 | — |
| 1931BP | 110,000 | 10.00 | 25.00 | 45.00 | 90.00 | — |
| 1932BP | 602,000 | 1.50 | 4.00 | 8.00 | 15.00 | — |
| 1933BP | 1,051,000 | 1.25 | 3.00 | 6.00 | 12.50 | — |
| 1935BP | 50,000 | 25.00 | 65.00 | 120 | 250 | — |
| 1936BP | 711,000 | 2.00 | 5.00 | 10.00 | 20.00 | — |
| 1937BP | 1,500,000 | 1.25 | 3.00 | 4.75 | 8.50 | — |
| 1938BP | 6,417,000 | 1.25 | 3.00 | 4.75 | 8.50 | — |
| 1939BP | 2,103,000 | 1.25 | 3.00 | 4.75 | 8.50 | — |

**2 PENGO** **KM# 513** **Weight:** 10.0000 g. **Composition:** 0.6400 Silver .2058 oz. ASW **Subject:** Tercentenerary - Founding of Pazmany University

| Date | Mintage | F | VF | XF | Unc | BU |
|---|---|---|---|---|---|---|
| 1935 | 50,000 | 3.00 | 6.00 | 10.00 | 20.00 | — |
| 1935 Restrike not marked; proof | — | Value: 22.50 | | | | |

**2 PENGO** **KM# 514** **Weight:** 10.0000 g. **Composition:** 0.6400 Silver .2058 oz. ASW **Subject:** Death of Rakoczi Bicentennial

| Date | Mintage | F | VF | XF | Unc | BU |
|---|---|---|---|---|---|---|
| 1935 | 100,000 | 2.00 | 4.00 | 6.00 | 10.00 | — |
| 1935 Restrike not marked; proof | — | Value: 22.50 | | | | |

**2 PENGO** **KM# 515** **Weight:** 10.0000 g. **Composition:** 0.6400 Silver .2058 oz. ASW **Subject:** 50th Anniversary - Death of Liszt

| Date | Mintage | F | VF | XF | Unc | BU |
|---|---|---|---|---|---|---|
| 1936 | 200,000 | 1.50 | 2.50 | 4.50 | 8.00 | — |
| 1936 Restrike not marked; proof | — | Value: 18.00 | | | | |

**2 PENGO** **KM# 522.1** **Composition:** Aluminum

| Date | Mintage | F | VF | XF | Unc | BU |
|---|---|---|---|---|---|---|
| 1941 | 24,000,000 | 0.15 | 0.30 | 0.50 | 0.80 | — |
| 1942 | 8,000,000 | 0.15 | 0.30 | 0.50 | 0.80 | — |
| 1943 | 10,000,000 | 0.15 | 0.30 | 0.50 | 0.80 | — |

**2 PENGO** **KM# 522.2** **Composition:** Aluminum **Reverse:** Base of 2 is wavy

| Date | Mintage | F | VF | XF | Unc | BU |
|---|---|---|---|---|---|---|
| 1941 | 40,000 | 10.00 | 20.00 | 35.00 | 65.00 | — |
| 1941 Restrike, rose | — | — | — | — | — | — |

**5 PENGO** **KM# 512.2** **Weight:** 25.3300 g. **Composition:** 0.6400 Silver .5213 oz. ASW

| Date | Mintage | F | VF | XF | Unc | BU |
|---|---|---|---|---|---|---|
| 1930 Restrike; proof | — | Value: 18.50 | | | | |

**5 PENGO** **KM# 512.1** **Weight:** 25.0000 g. **Composition:** 0.6400 Silver .5145 oz. ASW **Subject:** 10th Anniversary - Regency of Admiral Horthy **Note:** Raised, sharp edge reeding.

| Date | Mintage | F | VF | XF | Unc | BU |
|---|---|---|---|---|---|---|
| 1930BP | 3,650,000 | 4.50 | 7.00 | 12.00 | 17.50 | — |

**5 PENGO** **KM# 517** **Weight:** 25.0000 g. **Composition:** 0.6400 Silver .5145 oz. ASW **Subject:** Admiral Miklos Horthy **Note:** Smooth, ornamented edge

| Date | Mintage | F | VF | XF | Unc | BU |
|---|---|---|---|---|---|---|
| 1938 | 60 | — | — | — | 800 | — |
| 1939 | 408,000 | 4.50 | 7.50 | 12.50 | 25.00 | — |

**5 PENGO** **KM# 516** **Weight:** 25.0000 g. **Composition:** 0.6400 Silver .5145 oz. ASW **Subject:** 900th Anniversary - Death of St. Stephan

| Date | Mintage | F | VF | XF | Unc | BU |
|---|---|---|---|---|---|---|
| 1938 | 600,000 | 4.50 | 7.50 | 12.50 | 25.00 | — |
| 1938 Restrike not marked; proof | — | Value: 28.50 | | | | |

**5 PENGO** **KM# 523** **Composition:** Aluminum **Subject:** 75th Birthday of Admiral Horthy

| Date | Mintage | F | VF | XF | Unc | BU |
|---|---|---|---|---|---|---|
| 1943 | 2,000,000 | 0.50 | 1.00 | 2.00 | 4.00 | — |
| 1943 Restrike; proof | — | Value: 6.00 | | | | |

# PROVISIONAL GOVERNMENT
## 1944-1946
## STANDARD COINAGE

**5 PENGO** **KM# 525** **Composition:** Aluminum

| Date | Mintage | F | VF | XF | Unc | BU |
|---|---|---|---|---|---|---|
| 1945BP | 5,002,000 | 0.50 | 1.00 | 3.00 | 6.50 | — |
| 1945BP PROBAVERET Restrike; proof | — | Value: 17.50 | | | | |

# 1ST REPUBLIC
## 1946-1949
## DECIMAL COINAGE

**2 FILLER** **KM# 529** **Composition:** Bronze

| Date | Mintage | F | VF | XF | Unc | BU |
|---|---|---|---|---|---|---|
| 1946BP | 13,665,000 | 0.15 | 0.25 | 0.50 | 1.00 | — |
| 1947BP | 23,865,000 | 0.15 | 0.25 | 0.50 | 1.00 | — |
| 1947BP Restrike; proof | — | Value: 5.00 | | | | |

**5 FILLER** **KM# 535** **Composition:** Aluminum

| Date | Mintage | F | VF | XF | Unc | BU |
|---|---|---|---|---|---|---|
| 1948BP | 24,000,000 | 0.25 | 0.50 | 1.00 | 3.00 | — |
| 1951BP | 15,000,000 | 0.20 | 0.40 | 0.80 | 2.00 | — |

**10 FILLER** **KM# 530** **Composition:** Aluminum-Bronze

| Date | Mintage | F | VF | XF | Unc | BU |
|---|---|---|---|---|---|---|
| 1946BP | 23,565,000 | 0.15 | 0.30 | 0.70 | 2.00 | — |
| 1947BP | 29,580,000 | 0.15 | 0.30 | 0.70 | 2.00 | — |
| 1947BP Restrike; proof | — | Value: 4.50 | | | | |
| 1948BP | 4,885,000 | 1.00 | 2.00 | 3.00 | 6.50 | — |
| 1950BP | 8,000,000 | 0.50 | 1.00 | 2.50 | 5.00 | — |

**10 FILLER** **KM# 530a** **Composition:** Aluminum

| Date | Mintage | F | VF | XF | Unc | BU |
|---|---|---|---|---|---|---|
| 1950 | — | — | — | 55.00 | 85.00 | — |

**20 FILLER** **KM# 531** **Composition:** Aluminum-Bronze

| Date | Mintage | F | VF | XF | Unc | BU |
|---|---|---|---|---|---|---|
| 1946BP | 16,560,000 | 0.25 | 0.50 | 1.00 | 2.00 | — |
| 1946BP Restrike; proof | — | Value: 4.50 | | | | |
| 1947BP | 18,260,000 | 0.25 | 0.50 | 1.25 | 2.50 | — |
| 1948BP | 5,180,000 | 1.00 | 2.00 | 3.00 | 8.00 | — |
| 1950BP | 6,000,000 | 0.75 | 1.50 | 2.50 | 7.00 | — |

**50 FILLER** **KM# 536** **Composition:** Aluminum

| Date | Mintage | F | VF | XF | Unc | BU |
|---|---|---|---|---|---|---|
| 1948BP | 15,000,000 | 50.00 | 70.00 | 120 | — | — |
| 1948BP Restrike; proof | — | — | — | — | — | — |

**FORINT** **KM# 532** **Composition:** Aluminum

| Date | Mintage | F | VF | XF | Unc | BU |
|---|---|---|---|---|---|---|
| 1946BP | 38,900,000 | 1.00 | 2.00 | 3.00 | 8.00 | — |
| 1947BP | 2,600,000 | 3.00 | 6.00 | 10.00 | 20.00 | — |
| 1949BP | 17,000,000 | 1.50 | 2.50 | 5.00 | 10.00 | — |

**2 FORINT** **KM# 533** **Composition:** Aluminum

| Date | Mintage | F | VF | XF | Unc | BU |
|---|---|---|---|---|---|---|
| 1946BP | 10,000,000 | 1.50 | 2.50 | 5.00 | 12.00 | — |
| 1947BP | 3,500,000 | 3.00 | 5.00 | 10.00 | 20.00 | — |

**5 FORINT** **KM# 534** **Weight:** 20.0000 g. **Composition:** 0.8350 Silver .5369 oz. ASW **Reverse:** Lajos Kossuth **Note:** Thick planchet.

| Date | Mintage | F | VF | XF | Unc | BU |
|---|---|---|---|---|---|---|
| 1946BP | 40,000 | 5.00 | 10.00 | 15.00 | 30.00 | — |

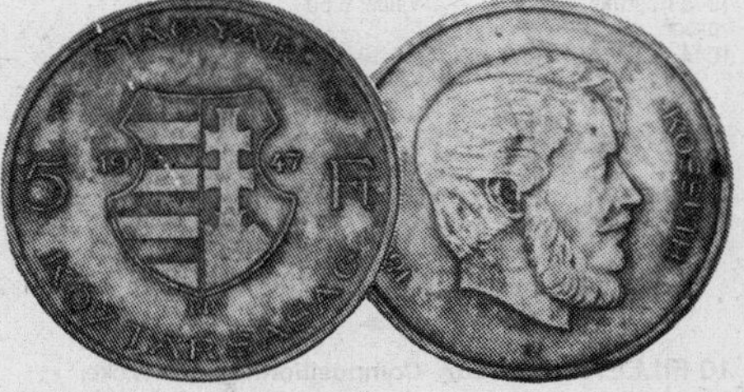

**5 FORINT** **KM# 534a** **Weight:** 12.0000 g. **Composition:** 0.5000 Silver .1929 oz. ASW **Reverse:** Lajos Kossuth **Note:** 1.7 millimeter thin planchet.

| Date | Mintage | F | VF | XF | Unc | BU |
|---|---|---|---|---|---|---|
| 1947 | 10,000,000 | BV | 1.75 | 3.00 | 5.00 | — |
| 1947 Restrike; proof | — | Value: 8.00 | | | | |

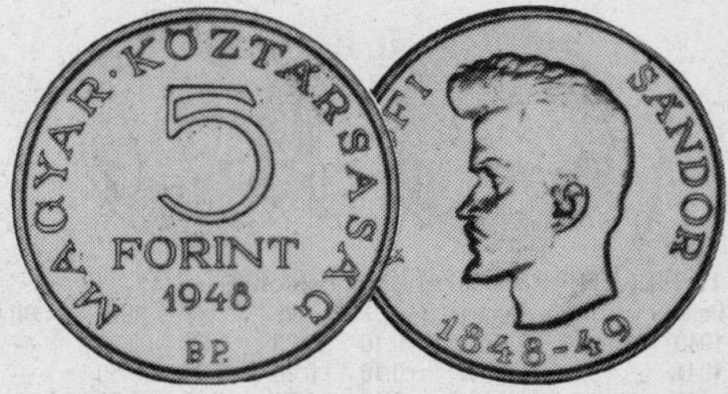

**5 FORINT** **KM# 537** **Weight:** 12.0000 g. **Composition:** 0.5000 Silver .1929 oz. ASW **Subject:** Centenerary of 1848 Revolution **Reverse:** Sandor Petofi

| Date | Mintage | F | VF | XF | Unc | BU |
|---|---|---|---|---|---|---|
| 1948 | 100,000 | BV | 2.00 | 4.00 | 8.00 | — |
| 1948 Restrike; proof | — | Value: 15.00 | | | | |

**5 FORINT** KM# 534b **Weight:** 13.0000 g. **Composition:** 0.8350 Silver .3490 oz. ASW

| Date | Mintage | F | VF | XF | Unc | BU |
|---|---|---|---|---|---|---|
| 1966 Restrike; proof | 5,000 | Value: 15.00 | | | | |
| 1967 Restrike; proof | 5,000 | Value: 15.00 | | | | |

**10 FORINT** KM# 538 **Weight:** 20.0000 g. **Composition:** 0.5000 Silver .3215 oz. ASW **Subject:** Centenerary of 1848 Revolution **Reverse:** Istvan Szechenyi

| Date | Mintage | F | VF | XF | Unc | BU |
|---|---|---|---|---|---|---|
| 1948BP | 100,000 | 2.50 | 3.50 | 6.50 | 12.00 | — |
| 1948BP Restrike; proof | — | Value: 20.00 | | | | |

**20 FORINT** KM# 539 **Weight:** 28.0000 g. **Composition:** 0.5000 Silver .4501 oz. ASW **Subject:** Centenerary of 1848 Revolution **Reverse:** Mihaly Tancsics

| Date | Mintage | F | VF | XF | Unc | BU |
|---|---|---|---|---|---|---|
| 1948BP | 50,000 | 5.00 | 9.00 | 15.00 | 20.00 | — |
| 1948BP Restrike; proof | — | Value: 35.00 | | | | |

# PEOPLES REPUBLIC

## 1949-1989

## DECIMAL COINAGE

**2 FILLER** KM# 546 **Composition:** Aluminum

| Date | Mintage | F | VF | XF | Unc | BU |
|---|---|---|---|---|---|---|
| 1950BP | 24,990,000 | — | 0.10 | 0.20 | 0.50 | — |
| 1952BP | 5,600,000 | — | 0.10 | 0.30 | 1.00 | — |
| 1953BP | 9,400,000 | — | 0.10 | 0.20 | 0.50 | — |
| 1954BP | 10,000,000 | — | 0.10 | 0.20 | 0.50 | — |
| 1955BP | 6,029,000 | — | 0.10 | 0.25 | 0.75 | — |
| 1956BP | 4,000,000 | — | 0.15 | 0.30 | 1.00 | — |
| 1957BP | 5,000,000 | — | 0.10 | 0.25 | 0.50 | — |
| 1960BP | 3,000,000 | 0.10 | 0.15 | 0.30 | 0.60 | — |
| 1961BP | 2,000,000 | 0.20 | 0.40 | 0.60 | 1.00 | — |
| 1962BP | 3,000,000 | 0.10 | 0.15 | 0.30 | 0.60 | — |
| 1963BP | 2,082,000 | 0.10 | 0.20 | 0.35 | 0.70 | — |
| 1965BP | 540,000 | — | 4.00 | 8.00 | 16.00 | — |
| 1971BP | 1,041,000 | 0.10 | 0.15 | 0.30 | 0.60 | — |
| 1972BP | 1,000,000 | 0.10 | 0.15 | 0.30 | 0.60 | — |
| 1973BP | 2,820,000 | 0.10 | 0.15 | 0.30 | 0.60 | — |
| 1974BP | 50,000 | — | 0.40 | 0.80 | 1.50 | — |
| 1975BP | 50,000 | — | 0.40 | 0.80 | 1.50 | — |
| 1976BP | 50,000 | — | 0.40 | 0.80 | 1.50 | — |
| 1977BP | 60,000 | — | 0.40 | 0.80 | 1.50 | — |
| 1978BP | 50,000 | — | 0.40 | 0.80 | 1.50 | — |
| 1979BP | 30,000 | — | 0.75 | 1.25 | 2.50 | — |
| 1980BP | 30,000 | — | 0.75 | 1.25 | 2.50 | — |
| 1981BP | 30,000 | — | 0.75 | 1.25 | 2.50 | — |
| 1982BP | 30,000 | — | 0.75 | 1.25 | 2.50 | — |
| 1983BP | 30,000 | — | 0.75 | 1.25 | 2.50 | — |
| 1984BP | 30,000 | — | 0.75 | 1.25 | 2.50 | — |
| 1985BP | 30,000 | — | 0.75 | 1.25 | 2.50 | — |
| 1986BP | 30,000 | — | 0.75 | 1.25 | 2.50 | — |
| 1987BP | 30,000 | — | 0.75 | 1.25 | 2.50 | — |
| 1988BP | 30,000 | — | 0.75 | 1.25 | 2.50 | — |
| 1989BP | 30,000 | — | 0.75 | 1.25 | 2.50 | — |

**2 FILLER** KM# 546a **Composition:** Copper-Nickel

| Date | Mintage | F | VF | XF | Unc | BU |
|---|---|---|---|---|---|---|
| 1966 Proof | 5,000 | Value: 4.00 | | | | |
| 1967 Proof | 5,000 | Value: 4.00 | | | | |

**5 FILLER** KM# 549 **Composition:** Aluminum

| Date | Mintage | F | VF | XF | Unc | BU |
|---|---|---|---|---|---|---|
| 1953BP | 10,000,000 | 0.10 | 0.15 | 0.30 | 0.50 | — |
| 1955BP | 6,005,000 | 0.15 | 0.20 | 0.50 | 1.00 | — |
| 1956BP | 6,012,000 | 0.15 | 0.20 | 0.50 | 1.00 | — |
| 1957BP | 5,000,000 | 0.20 | 0.30 | 0.60 | 1.20 | — |
| 1959BP | 8,000,000 | 0.15 | 0.20 | 0.50 | 1.00 | — |
| 1960BP | 7,000,000 | 0.15 | 0.20 | 0.50 | 1.00 | — |
| 1961BP | 4,410,000 | 0.20 | 0.30 | 0.60 | 1.20 | — |
| 1962BP | 5,590,000 | 0.20 | 0.30 | 0.60 | 1.20 | — |
| 1963BP | 4,020,000 | 0.20 | 0.30 | 0.60 | 1.20 | — |
| 1964BP | 3,600,000 | 0.20 | 0.30 | 0.60 | 1.20 | — |
| 1965BP | 6,000,000 | 0.20 | 0.30 | 0.60 | 1.20 | — |
| 1970BP | 3,900,000 | — | 2.50 | 5.00 | 10.00 | — |
| 1971BP | 100,000 | — | 0.25 | 0.50 | 1.00 | — |
| 1972BP | 50,000 | — | 0.25 | 0.50 | 1.00 | — |
| 1973BP | 105,000 | — | 0.25 | 0.50 | 1.00 | — |
| 1974BP | 60,000 | — | 0.25 | 0.50 | 1.00 | — |
| 1975BP | 60,000 | — | 0.25 | 0.50 | 1.00 | — |
| 1976BP | 50,000 | — | 0.25 | 0.50 | 1.00 | — |
| 1977BP | 60,000 | — | 0.25 | 0.50 | 1.00 | — |
| 1978BP | 50,000 | — | 0.25 | 0.50 | 1.00 | — |
| 1979BP | 30,000 | — | 0.50 | 1.00 | 2.00 | — |
| 1980BP | 30,000 | — | 0.50 | 1.00 | 2.00 | — |
| 1981BP | 30,000 | — | 0.50 | 1.00 | 2.00 | — |
| 1982BP | 30,000 | — | 0.50 | 1.00 | 2.00 | — |
| 1983BP | 30,000 | — | 0.50 | 1.00 | 2.00 | — |
| 1984BP | 30,000 | — | 0.50 | 1.00 | 2.00 | — |
| 1985BP | 30,000 | — | 0.50 | 1.00 | 2.00 | — |
| 1986BP | 30,000 | — | 0.50 | 1.00 | 2.00 | — |
| 1987BP | 30,000 | — | 0.50 | 1.00 | 2.00 | — |
| 1988BP | 30,000 | — | 0.50 | 1.00 | 2.00 | — |
| 1989BP | 30,000 | — | 0.50 | 1.00 | 2.00 | — |

**5 FILLER** KM# 549a **Composition:** Copper-Nickel

| Date | Mintage | F | VF | XF | Unc | BU |
|---|---|---|---|---|---|---|
| 1966 Proof | 5,000 | Value: 5.00 | | | | |
| 1967 Proof | 5,000 | Value: 5.00 | | | | |

**10 FILLER** KM# 547 **Composition:** Aluminum

| Date | Mintage | F | VF | XF | Unc | BU |
|---|---|---|---|---|---|---|
| 1950BP | 5,040,000 | 10.00 | 20.00 | 30.00 | 50.00 | — |
| 1951BP | 80,950,000 | 1.50 | 3.00 | 5.00 | 10.00 | — |
| 1955BP | 10,019,000 | 2.00 | 4.00 | 7.00 | 15.00 | — |
| 1957BP | 13,000,000 | 2.00 | 4.00 | 7.00 | 15.00 | — |
| 1958BP | 12,015,000 | 2.00 | 4.00 | 7.00 | 15.00 | — |
| 1959BP | 15,000,000 | 2.00 | 4.00 | 7.00 | 15.00 | — |
| 1960BP | 5,000,000 | 2.50 | 5.00 | 8.00 | 17.00 | — |
| 1961BP | 13,000,000 | 2.00 | 4.00 | 7.00 | 15.00 | — |
| 1962BP | 4,000,000 | 2.50 | 5.00 | 9.00 | 18.00 | — |
| 1963BP | 8,000,000 | 2.50 | 5.00 | 8.00 | 17.00 | — |
| 1964BP | 17,008,000 | 2.00 | 4.00 | 7.00 | 15.00 | — |
| 1965BP | 21,880,000 | 2.00 | 4.00 | 7.00 | 15.00 | — |
| 1966BP | 8,120,000 | 2.50 | 5.00 | 8.00 | 17.00 | — |

**10 FILLER** KM# 547a **Composition:** Copper-Nickel

| Date | Mintage | F | VF | XF | Unc | BU |
|---|---|---|---|---|---|---|
| 1966 Proof | 5,000 | Value: 6.00 | | | | |
| 1967 Proof | 5,000 | Value: 6.00 | | | | |

**10 FILLER** KM# 572 **Composition:** Aluminum **Note:** Reduced size.

| Date | Mintage | F | VF | XF | Unc | BU |
|---|---|---|---|---|---|---|
| 1967 | 5,000 | 5.00 | 10.00 | 20.00 | 45.00 | — |
| 1968 | 16,000,000 | 0.50 | 1.00 | 2.50 | 5.00 | — |
| 1969 | 50,760,000 | 0.50 | 1.00 | 2.50 | 5.00 | — |
| 1970 | 28,470,000 | 0.50 | 1.00 | 2.50 | 5.00 | — |
| 1971 | 28,800,000 | — | 0.50 | 1.25 | 2.50 | — |
| 1972 | 17,220,000 | — | 0.50 | 1.25 | 2.50 | — |
| 1973 | 33,720,000 | — | 0.50 | 1.25 | 2.50 | — |
| 1974 | 24,930,000 | — | 0.50 | 1.25 | 2.50 | — |
| 1975 | 30,000,000 | — | 0.50 | 1.25 | 2.50 | — |
| 1976 | 20,025,000 | — | 0.50 | 1.25 | 2.50 | — |
| 1977 | 30,075,000 | — | 0.50 | 1.25 | 2.50 | — |
| 1978 | 36,005,000 | — | 0.40 | 1.00 | 2.00 | — |
| 1979 | 36,060,000 | — | 0.40 | 1.00 | 2.00 | — |
| 1980 | 36,010,000 | — | 0.40 | 1.00 | 2.00 | — |
| 1981 | 36,000,000 | — | 0.40 | 1.00 | 2.00 | — |
| 1982 | 45,015,000 | — | 0.30 | 0.75 | 1.50 | — |
| 1983 | 45,030,000 | — | 0.30 | 0.75 | 1.50 | — |
| 1984 | 42,075,000 | — | 0.30 | 0.75 | 1.50 | — |
| 1985 | 40,035,000 | — | 0.30 | 0.75 | 1.50 | — |
| 1986 | 48,075,000 | — | 0.30 | 0.75 | 1.50 | — |
| 1987 | 45,000,000 | — | 0.30 | 0.75 | 1.50 | — |
| 1988 | 48,015,000 | — | 0.30 | 0.75 | 1.50 | — |
| 1989 | 55,515,000 | — | — | 0.10 | 0.50 | — |

**20 FILLER** KM# 550 **Composition:** Aluminum

| Date | Mintage | F | VF | XF | Unc | BU |
|---|---|---|---|---|---|---|
| 1953BP | 45,000,000 | 1.00 | 2.00 | 4.00 | 8.00 | — |
| 1955BP | 10,023,000 | 1.25 | 2.50 | 5.00 | 10.00 | — |
| 1957BP | 5,000,000 | 1.75 | 3.50 | 7.00 | 15.00 | — |
| 1958BP | 10,000,000 | 1.25 | 2.50 | 5.00 | 10.00 | — |
| 1959BP | 13,000,000 | 1.25 | 2.50 | 5.00 | 10.00 | — |
| 1961BP | 9,000,000 | 1.25 | 2.50 | 5.00 | 10.00 | — |
| 1963BP | 7,000,000 | 1.50 | 3.00 | 6.00 | 12.00 | — |
| 1964BP | 10,400,000 | 1.25 | 2.50 | 5.00 | 10.00 | — |
| 1965BP | 15,000,000 | 1.25 | 2.50 | 5.00 | 10.00 | — |
| 1966BP | 5,000,000 | 1.50 | 3.00 | 6.50 | 12.50 | — |

**20 FILLER** KM# 550a **Composition:** Copper-Nickel

| Date | Mintage | F | VF | XF | Unc | BU |
|---|---|---|---|---|---|---|
| 1966 Proof | 5,000 | Value: 8.00 | | | | |
| 1967 Proof | 5,000 | Value: 8.00 | | | | |

**20 FILLER** KM# 573 **Composition:** Aluminum **Note:** Reduced size.

| Date | Mintage | F | VF | XF | Unc | BU |
|---|---|---|---|---|---|---|
| 1967 | 10,000,000 | 0.25 | 0.75 | 2.50 | 6.00 | — |
| 1968 | 56,500,000 | 0.10 | 0.40 | 1.25 | 3.00 | — |
| 1969 | 28,550,000 | 0.15 | 0.45 | 1.50 | 4.00 | — |
| 1970 | 19,960,000 | 0.20 | 0.60 | 2.00 | 5.00 | — |
| 1971 | 31,090,000 | 0.10 | 0.20 | 0.75 | 2.00 | — |
| 7971 Error | 11,000 | 3.50 | 7.50 | 15.00 | 30.00 | — |
| 1972 | 21,070,000 | 0.15 | 0.30 | 0.75 | 1.50 | — |
| 1973 | 22,970,000 | 0.15 | 0.30 | 0.75 | 1.50 | — |
| 1974 | 35,010,000 | 0.15 | 0.30 | 0.75 | 1.50 | — |
| 1975 | 30,010,000 | 0.15 | 0.30 | 0.75 | 1.50 | — |
| 1976 | 30,010,000 | 0.15 | 0.30 | 0.75 | 1.50 | — |
| 1977 | 30,050,000 | 0.15 | 0.30 | 0.75 | 1.50 | — |
| 1978 | 30,140,000 | 0.15 | 0.30 | 0.75 | 1.50 | — |
| 1979 | 32,010,000 | 0.15 | 0.30 | 0.75 | 1.50 | — |
| 1980 | 45,010,000 | 0.10 | 0.20 | 0.50 | 1.00 | — |
| 1981 | 34,030,000 | 0.10 | 0.20 | 0.50 | 1.00 | — |
| 1982 | 35,010,000 | 0.10 | 0.20 | 0.50 | 1.00 | — |
| 1983 | 43,210,000 | 0.10 | 0.20 | 0.50 | 1.00 | — |
| 1984 | 42,270,000 | 0.10 | 0.20 | 0.50 | 1.00 | — |
| 1985 | 40,440,000 | 0.10 | 0.20 | 0.50 | 1.00 | — |
| 1986 | 48,000,000 | 0.10 | 0.20 | 0.50 | 1.00 | — |
| 1987 | 55,000,000 | 0.10 | 0.20 | 0.50 | 1.00 | — |
| 1988 | 48,010,000 | 0.10 | 0.20 | 0.50 | 1.00 | — |
| 1989 | 64,660,000 | — | — | 0.10 | 0.50 | — |

**20 FILLER** KM# 627 **Composition:** Aluminum **Series:** F.A.O.

| Date | Mintage | F | VF | XF | Unc | BU |
|---|---|---|---|---|---|---|
| 1983 | 50,000 | — | 0.50 | 1.00 | 2.50 | — |

**50 FILLER** KM# 551 **Composition:** Aluminum

| Date | Mintage | F | VF | XF | Unc | BU |
|---|---|---|---|---|---|---|
| 1953BP | 10,017,000 | 1.50 | 3.00 | 6.00 | 12.00 | — |
| 1965BP | 3,005,000 | 1.25 | 2.50 | 5.00 | 10.00 | — |
| 1966BP | 1,500,000 | 1.75 | 3.50 | 7.00 | 15.00 | — |

**50 FILLER** KM# 551a **Composition:** Copper-Nickel

| Date | Mintage | F | VF | XF | Unc | BU |
|---|---|---|---|---|---|---|
| 1966 Proof | 5,000 | Value: 10.00 | | | | |
| 1967 Proof | 5,000 | Value: 10.00 | | | | |

**50 FILLER** KM# 574 **Composition:** Aluminum

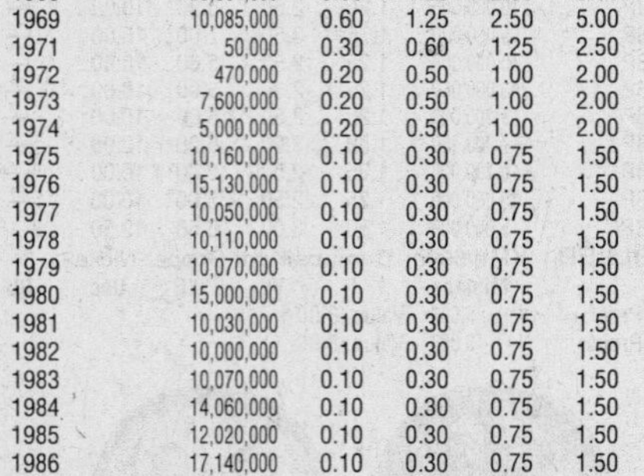

| Date | Mintage | F | VF | XF | Unc | BU |
|---|---|---|---|---|---|---|
| 1967 | 20,000,000 | 0.50 | 1.00 | 2.00 | 4.00 | — |
| 1968 | 13,861,000 | 0.60 | 1.25 | 2.50 | 5.00 | — |
| 1969 | 10,085,000 | 0.60 | 1.25 | 2.50 | 5.00 | — |
| 1971 | 50,000 | 0.30 | 0.60 | 1.25 | 2.50 | — |
| 1972 | 470,000 | 0.20 | 0.50 | 1.00 | 2.00 | — |
| 1973 | 7,600,000 | 0.20 | 0.50 | 1.00 | 2.00 | — |
| 1974 | 5,000,000 | 0.20 | 0.50 | 1.00 | 2.00 | — |
| 1975 | 10,160,000 | 0.10 | 0.30 | 0.75 | 1.50 | — |
| 1976 | 15,130,000 | 0.10 | 0.30 | 0.75 | 1.50 | — |
| 1977 | 10,050,000 | 0.10 | 0.30 | 0.75 | 1.50 | — |
| 1978 | 10,110,000 | 0.10 | 0.30 | 0.75 | 1.50 | — |
| 1979 | 10,070,000 | 0.10 | 0.30 | 0.75 | 1.50 | — |
| 1980 | 15,000,000 | 0.10 | 0.30 | 0.75 | 1.50 | — |
| 1981 | 10,030,000 | 0.10 | 0.30 | 0.75 | 1.50 | — |
| 1982 | 10,000,000 | 0.10 | 0.30 | 0.75 | 1.50 | — |
| 1983 | 10,070,000 | 0.10 | 0.30 | 0.75 | 1.50 | — |
| 1984 | 14,060,000 | 0.10 | 0.30 | 0.75 | 1.50 | — |
| 1985 | 12,020,000 | 0.10 | 0.30 | 0.75 | 1.50 | — |
| 1986 | 17,140,000 | 0.10 | 0.30 | 0.75 | 1.50 | — |
| 1987 | 23,000,000 | — | 0.10 | 0.50 | 1.00 | — |
| 1988 | 18,050,000 | — | 0.10 | 0.50 | 1.00 | — |
| 1989 | 18,200,000 | — | 0.10 | 0.50 | 1.00 | — |

**FORINT** KM# 545 **Composition:** Aluminum

| Date | Mintage | F | VF | XF | Unc | BU |
|---|---|---|---|---|---|---|
| 1949BP | 19,440,000 | 1.50 | 3.00 | 6.00 | 12.00 | — |
| 1950BP | 39,060,000 | 2.25 | 4.50 | 9.00 | 18.00 | — |
| 1952BP | 63,018,000 | 2.00 | 4.00 | 8.00 | 16.00 | — |

**FORINT** KM# 555 **Composition:** Aluminum

| Date | Mintage | F | VF | XF | Unc | BU |
|---|---|---|---|---|---|---|
| 1957 | 7,500,000 | 2.00 | 4.00 | 8.00 | 16.00 | — |
| 1958 | 5,070,000 | 1.50 | 3.00 | 6.00 | 12.00 | — |
| 1960 | 5,000,000 | 1.25 | 2.50 | 5.00 | 10.00 | — |
| 1961 | 5,000,000 | 1.25 | 2.50 | 5.00 | 10.00 | — |
| 1963 | 3,000,000 | 1.50 | 3.00 | 6.50 | 12.50 | — |
| 1964 | 6,080,000 | 1.00 | 2.00 | 4.00 | 8.00 | — |
| 1965 | 9,810,000 | 1.00 | 2.00 | 4.00 | 8.00 | — |
| 1966 | 5,680,000 | 1.75 | 3.50 | 7.50 | 15.00 | — |

**FORINT** KM# 555a **Weight:** 5.8500 g. **Composition:** 0.8350 Silver .0570 oz. ASW

| Date | Mintage | F | VF | XF | Unc | BU |
|---|---|---|---|---|---|---|
| 1966 Proof | 5,000 | Value: 12.00 | | | | |
| 1967 Proof | 5,000 | Value: 12.00 | | | | |

**FORINT** KM# 575 **Composition:** Aluminum

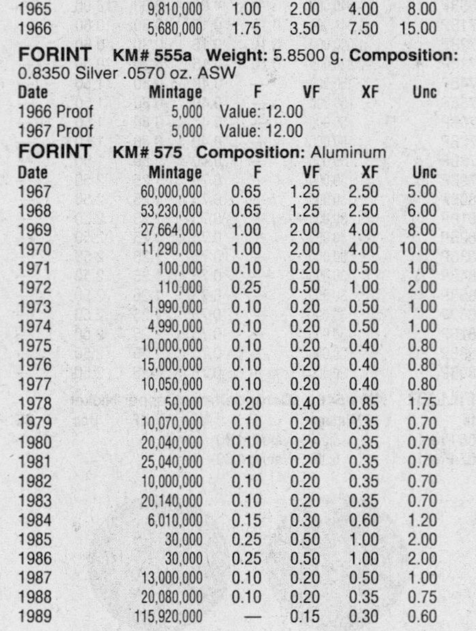

| Date | Mintage | F | VF | XF | Unc | BU |
|---|---|---|---|---|---|---|
| 1967 | 60,000,000 | 0.65 | 1.25 | 2.50 | 5.00 | — |
| 1968 | 53,230,000 | 0.65 | 1.25 | 2.50 | 6.00 | — |
| 1969 | 27,664,000 | 1.00 | 2.00 | 4.00 | 8.00 | — |
| 1970 | 11,290,000 | 1.00 | 2.00 | 4.00 | 10.00 | — |
| 1971 | 100,000 | 0.10 | 0.20 | 0.50 | 1.00 | — |
| 1972 | 110,000 | 0.25 | 0.50 | 1.00 | 2.00 | — |
| 1973 | 1,990,000 | 0.10 | 0.20 | 0.50 | 1.00 | — |
| 1974 | 4,990,000 | 0.10 | 0.20 | 0.50 | 1.00 | — |
| 1975 | 10,000,000 | 0.10 | 0.20 | 0.40 | 0.80 | — |
| 1976 | 15,000,000 | 0.10 | 0.20 | 0.40 | 0.80 | — |
| 1977 | 10,050,000 | 0.10 | 0.20 | 0.40 | 0.80 | — |
| 1978 | 50,000 | 0.20 | 0.40 | 0.85 | 1.75 | — |
| 1979 | 10,070,000 | 0.10 | 0.20 | 0.35 | 0.70 | — |
| 1980 | 20,040,000 | 0.10 | 0.20 | 0.35 | 0.70 | — |
| 1981 | 25,040,000 | 0.10 | 0.20 | 0.35 | 0.70 | — |
| 1982 | 10,000,000 | 0.10 | 0.20 | 0.35 | 0.70 | — |
| 1983 | 20,140,000 | 0.10 | 0.20 | 0.35 | 0.70 | — |
| 1984 | 6,010,000 | 0.15 | 0.30 | 0.60 | 1.20 | — |
| 1985 | 30,000 | 0.25 | 0.50 | 1.00 | 2.00 | — |
| 1986 | 30,000 | 0.25 | 0.50 | 1.00 | 2.00 | — |
| 1987 | 13,000,000 | 0.10 | 0.20 | 0.50 | 1.00 | — |
| 1988 | 20,080,000 | 0.10 | 0.20 | 0.35 | 0.75 | — |
| 1989 | 115,920,000 | — | 0.15 | 0.30 | 0.60 | — |

**2 FORINT** KM# 548 **Composition:** Copper-Nickel

| Date | Mintage | F | VF | XF | Unc | BU |
|---|---|---|---|---|---|---|
| 1950BP | 18,500,000 | 1.75 | 3.50 | 7.00 | 15.00 | — |
| 1951BP | 4,000,000 | 2.00 | 4.00 | 8.00 | 16.00 | — |
| 1952BP | 4,530,000 | 2.00 | 4.00 | 8.00 | 16.00 | — |

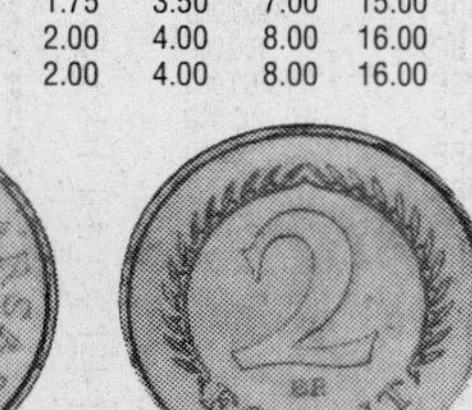

**2 FORINT** KM# 556 **Composition:** Copper-Nickel

| Date | Mintage | F | VF | XF | Unc | BU |
|---|---|---|---|---|---|---|
| 1957 | 5,000,000 | 1.50 | 3.00 | 6.00 | 12.50 | — |
| 1958 | 1,033,000 | 1.75 | 3.50 | 7.00 | 15.00 | — |
| 1960 | 4,000,000 | 1.50 | 3.00 | 6.00 | 12.50 | — |
| 1961 | 690,000 | 2.00 | 4.00 | 8.00 | 16.00 | — |
| 1962 | 1,190,000 | 1.50 | 3.00 | 6.00 | 12.50 | — |

**2 FORINT** KM# 556a **Composition:** Copper-Nickel-Zinc

| Date | Mintage | F | VF | XF | Unc | BU |
|---|---|---|---|---|---|---|
| 1962 | 1,210,000 | 1.25 | 2.50 | 5.00 | 10.00 | — |
| 1963 | 3,100,000 | 1.25 | 2.50 | 5.00 | 10.00 | — |
| 1964 | 3,250,000 | 1.25 | 2.50 | 5.00 | 10.00 | — |
| 1965 | 4,395,000 | 1.25 | 2.50 | 5.00 | 10.00 | — |
| 1966 | 6,630,000 | 1.25 | 2.50 | 5.00 | 10.00 | — |

**2 FORINT** KM# 556b **Weight:** 6.1200 g. **Composition:** 0.8350 Silver .1643 oz. ASW

| Date | Mintage | F | VF | XF | Unc | BU |
|---|---|---|---|---|---|---|
| 1966 Proof | 5,000 | Value: 14.00 | | | | |
| 1967 Proof | 5,000 | Value: 14.00 | | | | |

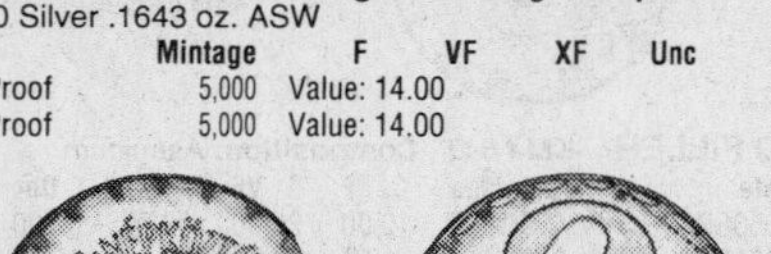

**2 FORINT** KM# 591 **Composition:** Brass

| Date | Mintage | F | VF | XF | Unc | BU |
|---|---|---|---|---|---|---|
| 1970 | 49,195,000 | 0.50 | 1.00 | 2.00 | 4.00 | — |
| 1971 | 10,830,000 | 0.10 | 0.50 | 1.00 | 2.00 | — |
| 1972 | 10,015,000 | 0.10 | 0.50 | 1.00 | 2.00 | — |
| 1973 | 820,000 | 1.00 | 2.00 | 4.00 | 8.00 | — |
| 1974 | 10,000,000 | 0.25 | 0.75 | 1.50 | 3.00 | — |
| 1975 | 20,030,000 | 0.25 | 0.75 | 1.50 | 3.00 | — |
| 1976 | 15,000,000 | 0.25 | 0.75 | 1.50 | 3.00 | — |
| 1977 | 10,115,000 | 0.25 | 0.75 | 1.50 | 3.00 | — |
| 1978 | 12,000,000 | 0.25 | 0.75 | 1.50 | 3.00 | — |
| 1979 | 10,127,000 | 0.25 | 0.75 | 1.50 | 3.00 | — |
| 1980 | 12,005,000 | 0.25 | 0.75 | 1.50 | 3.00 | — |
| 1981 | 10,010,000 | 0.25 | 0.75 | 1.50 | 3.00 | — |
| 1982 | 10,005,000 | 0.25 | 0.75 | 1.50 | 3.00 | — |
| 1983 | 20,160,000 | 0.25 | 0.75 | 1.50 | 3.00 | — |
| 1984 | 5,000,000 | 0.75 | 1.50 | 3.00 | 6.00 | — |
| 1985 | 10,675,000 | 0.25 | 0.75 | 1.50 | 3.00 | — |
| 1986 | 30,000 | 1.50 | 3.00 | 6.00 | 12.00 | — |
| 1987 | 5,030,000 | 0.50 | 1.00 | 2.00 | 4.00 | — |
| 1988 | 5,035,000 | 0.50 | 1.00 | 2.00 | 4.00 | — |
| 1989 | 79,223,000 | 0.10 | 0.25 | 0.50 | 1.00 | — |

**5 FORINT** KM# 576 **Composition:** Copper-Nickel **Note:** Lajos Kossuth.

| Date | Mintage | F | VF | XF | Unc | BU |
|---|---|---|---|---|---|---|
| 1967BP | 20,000,000 | 0.50 | 1.00 | 2.50 | 5.00 | — |
| 1968BP | 29,000 | 5.00 | 10.00 | 20.00 | 35.00 | — |

**5 FORINT** KM# 594 **Composition:** Nickel

| Date | Mintage | F | VF | XF | Unc | BU |
|---|---|---|---|---|---|---|
| 1971 | 20,004,000 | 0.20 | 0.35 | 0.75 | 1.50 | — |
| 1972 | 5,000,000 | 0.25 | 0.50 | 1.00 | 2.00 | — |
| 1973 | 100,000 | 0.35 | 0.75 | 1.50 | 3.00 | — |
| 1974 | 50,000 | 0.35 | 0.75 | 1.50 | 3.00 | — |
| 1975 | 50,000 | 0.35 | 0.75 | 1.50 | 3.00 | — |
| 1976 | 5,090,000 | 0.25 | 0.50 | 1.00 | 2.00 | — |
| 1977 | 50,000 | 0.35 | 0.75 | 1.50 | 3.00 | — |
| 1978 | 6,000,000 | 0.25 | 0.50 | 1.00 | 2.00 | — |
| 1979 | 10,000,000 | 0.25 | 0.50 | 1.00 | 2.00 | — |
| 1980 | 6,002,000 | 0.25 | 0.50 | 1.00 | 2.00 | — |
| 1981 | 5,002,000 | 0.25 | 0.50 | 1.00 | 2.00 | — |
| 1982 | 936,000 | 0.30 | 0.60 | 1.25 | 2.50 | — |

**5 FORINT** KM# 628 **Composition:** Nickel **Series:** F.A.O.

| Date | Mintage | F | VF | XF | Unc | BU |
|---|---|---|---|---|---|---|
| 1983 | 50,000 | — | 1.00 | 2.00 | 3.50 | — |

**5 FORINT** KM# 635 **Composition:** Copper-Nickel **Note:** Lajos Kossuth.

| Date | Mintage | F | VF | XF | Unc | BU |
|---|---|---|---|---|---|---|
| 1983 | 15,240,000 | 0.15 | 0.25 | 0.50 | 1.00 | — |
| 1984 | 25,018,000 | 0.15 | 0.25 | 0.50 | 1.00 | — |
| 1985 | 25,286,000 | 0.15 | 0.25 | 0.50 | 1.00 | — |
| 1986 | 1,030,000 | 0.20 | 0.35 | 0.75 | 1.50 | — |
| 1987 | 30,000 | 0.30 | 0.60 | 1.25 | 2.50 | — |
| 1988 | 4,050,000 | 0.20 | 0.35 | 0.75 | 1.50 | — |
| 1989 | 39,014,000 | 0.15 | 0.25 | 0.50 | 1.00 | — |

**10 FORINT** **KM# 552** **Weight:** 12.5000 g. **Composition:** 0.8000 Silver .3215 oz. ASW **Subject:** 10th Anniversary of Forint

| Date | Mintage | F | VF | XF | Unc | BU |
|---|---|---|---|---|---|---|
| 1956BP | 22,000 | 3.00 | 5.00 | 8.00 | 16.00 | — |

**10 FORINT** **KM# 595** **Composition:** Nickel

| Date | Mintage | F | VF | XF | Unc | BU |
|---|---|---|---|---|---|---|
| 1971 | 24,998,000 | 0.35 | 0.75 | 1.50 | 3.00 | — |
| 1972 | 25,078,000 | 0.35 | 0.75 | 1.50 | 3.00 | — |
| 1973 | 78,000 | 0.60 | 1.25 | 2.50 | 5.00 | — |
| 1974 | 50,000 | 0.60 | 1.25 | 2.50 | 5.00 | — |
| 1975 | 50,000 | 0.60 | 1.25 | 2.50 | 5.00 | — |
| 1976 | 3,568,000 | 0.50 | 1.00 | 2.00 | 4.00 | — |
| 1977 | 4,618,000 | 0.50 | 1.00 | 2.00 | 4.00 | — |
| 1978 | 50,000 | 0.60 | 1.25 | 2.50 | 5.00 | — |
| 1979 | 5,000,000 | 0.50 | 1.00 | 2.00 | 4.00 | — |
| 1980 | 2,550,000 | 0.50 | 1.00 | 2.00 | 4.00 | — |
| 1982 | 30,000 | 0.60 | 1.25 | 2.50 | 5.00 | — |

**10 FORINT** **KM# 620** **Composition:** Nickel **Series:** F.A.O.

| Date | Mintage | F | VF | XF | Unc | BU |
|---|---|---|---|---|---|---|
| 1981 | 60,000 | — | — | 2.50 | 5.00 | — |

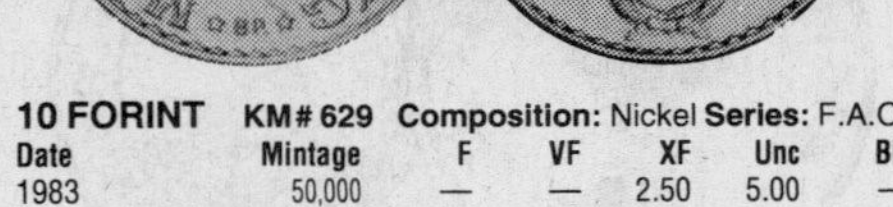

**10 FORINT** **KM# 629** **Composition:** Nickel **Series:** F.A.O.

| Date | Mintage | F | VF | XF | Unc | BU |
|---|---|---|---|---|---|---|
| 1983 | 50,000 | — | — | 2.50 | 5.00 | — |

**10 FORINT** **KM# 636** **Composition:** Aluminum-Bronze **Note:** Circulation coinage.

| Date | Mintage | F | VF | XF | Unc | BU |
|---|---|---|---|---|---|---|
| 1983 | 11,004,000 | 0.25 | 0.50 | 1.00 | 2.00 | — |
| 1984 | 7,578,000 | 0.25 | 0.50 | 1.00 | 2.00 | — |
| 1985 | 27,648,000 | 0.25 | 0.50 | 1.00 | 2.00 | — |
| 1986 | 15,006,000 | 0.25 | 0.50 | 1.00 | 2.00 | — |
| 1987 | 10,000,000 | 0.25 | 0.50 | 1.00 | 2.00 | — |
| 1988 | 5,000,000 | 0.25 | 0.50 | 1.00 | 2.00 | — |
| 1989 | 37,094,000 | 0.25 | 0.50 | 1.00 | 2.00 | — |

**20 FORINT** **KM# 553** **Weight:** 17.5000 g. **Composition:** 0.8000 Silver .4501 oz. ASW **Subject:** 10th Anniversary of Forint

| Date | Mintage | F | VF | XF | Unc | BU |
|---|---|---|---|---|---|---|
| 1956BP | 22,000 | 4.50 | 8.00 | 12.00 | 20.00 | — |

**20 FORINT** **KM# 630** **Composition:** Copper-Nickel **Obverse:** Dozsa

| Date | Mintage | F | VF | XF | Unc | BU |
|---|---|---|---|---|---|---|
| 1982 | 13,404,000 | 0.25 | 0.50 | 0.80 | 1.60 | — |
| 1983 | 18,006,000 | 0.25 | 0.50 | 0.80 | 1.60 | — |
| 1984 | 31,016,000 | 0.25 | 0.50 | 0.80 | 1.60 | — |
| 1985 | 20,122,000 | 0.25 | 0.50 | 0.80 | 1.60 | — |
| 1986 | 6,000,000 | 0.35 | 0.65 | 1.25 | 2.25 | — |
| 1987 | 30,000 | 0.40 | 0.75 | 1.50 | 3.00 | — |
| 1988 | 30,000 | 0.40 | 0.75 | 1.50 | 3.00 | — |
| 1989 | 31,890,000 | 0.25 | 0.50 | 0.80 | 1.60 | — |

**20 FORINT** **KM# 637** **Composition:** Copper-Nickel **Subject:** Forestry for Development

| Date | Mintage | F | VF | XF | Unc | BU |
|---|---|---|---|---|---|---|
| 1984 | 15,000 | — | — | — | 3.00 | — |
| 1984 Proof | 5,000 | Value: 7.00 | | | | |

**20 FORINT** **KM# 653** **Composition:** Copper-Nickel **Series:** F.A.O.

| Date | Mintage | F | VF | XF | Unc | BU |
|---|---|---|---|---|---|---|
| 1985 | 25,000 | — | — | — | 3.00 | — |
| 1985 Proof | — | Value: 6.50 | | | | |

**25 FORINT (Huszonot)** **KM# 554** **Weight:** 20.0000 g. **Composition:** 0.8000 Silver .5144 oz. ASW **Subject:** 10th Anniversary Forint

| Date | Mintage | F | VF | XF | Unc | BU |
|---|---|---|---|---|---|---|
| 1956BP | 22,000 | 5.00 | 10.00 | 15.00 | 20.00 | — |

**25 FORINT (Huszonot)** **KM# 557** **Weight:** 17.5000 g. **Composition:** 0.7500 Silver .4220 oz. ASW **Subject:** 150th Anniversary - Birth of Liszt

| Date | Mintage | F | VF | XF | Unc | BU |
|---|---|---|---|---|---|---|
| 1961 Proof | 15,000 | Value: 15.50 | | | | |

**25 FORINT (Huszonot)** **KM# 558** **Weight:** 17.5000 g. **Composition:** 0.7500 Silver .4220 oz. ASW **Subject:** 80th Anniversary - Birth of Bartok

| Date | Mintage | F | VF | XF | Unc | BU |
|---|---|---|---|---|---|---|
| 1961 Proof | 15,000 | Value: 16.50 | | | | |

**25 FORINT (Huszonot)** **KM# 567** **Weight:** 12.0000 g. **Composition:** 0.6400 Silver .2469 oz. ASW **Subject:** 40th Anniversary - Death of Zrinyi

| Date | Mintage | F | VF | XF | Unc | BU |
|---|---|---|---|---|---|---|
| 1966 Proof | 11,000 | Value: 20.00 | | | | |

**25 FORINT (Huszonot)** **KM# 577** **Weight:** 12.0000 g. **Composition:** 0.7500 Silver .2893 oz. ASW **Subject:** 85th Birthday of Kodaly

| Date | Mintage | F | VF | XF | Unc | BU |
|---|---|---|---|---|---|---|
| 1967 | 15,000 | — | — | — | 10.00 | — |
| 1967 Proof | — | Value: 12.50 | | | | |

**50 FORINT (Otven)** **KM# 559** **Weight:** 20.0000 g. **Composition:** 0.7500 Silver .4922 oz. ASW **Subject:** 150th Anniversary - Birth of Liszt

| Date | Mintage | F | VF | XF | Unc | BU |
|---|---|---|---|---|---|---|
| 1961BP Proof | 15,000 | Value: 20.00 | | | | |

**50 FORINT (Otven)** **KM# 560** **Weight:** 3.8380 g. **Composition:** 0.9860 Gold .1217 oz. AGW **Subject:** 150th Anniversary - Birth of Liszt

| Date | Mintage | F | VF | XF | Unc | BU |
|---|---|---|---|---|---|---|
| 1961 Proof | 2,503 | Value: 90.00 | | | | |

**50 FORINT (Otven)** **KM# 561** **Weight:** 20.0000 g. **Composition:** 0.7500 Silver .4822 oz. ASW **Subject:** 80th Anniversary - Birth of Bartok

| Date | Mintage | F | VF | XF | Unc | BU |
|---|---|---|---|---|---|---|
| 1961 Proof | 15,000 | Value: 20.00 | | | | |

**50 FORINT (Otven)** **KM# 562** **Weight:** 3.8380 g. **Composition:** 0.9860 Gold .1217 oz. AGW **Subject:** 80th Anniversary - Birth of Bartok

| Date | Mintage | F | VF | XF | Unc | BU |
|---|---|---|---|---|---|---|
| 1961 Proof | 2,503 | Value: 90.00 | | | | |

**50 FORINT (Otven)** **KM# 568** **Weight:** 20.0000 g. **Composition:** 0.6400 Silver .4115 oz. ASW **Subject:** 400th Anniversary - Death of Zrinyi

| Date | Mintage | F | VF | XF | Unc | BU |
|---|---|---|---|---|---|---|
| 1966BP Proof | 11,000 | Value: 25.00 | | | | |

**50 FORINT (Otven)** **KM# 578** **Weight:** 20.0000 g. **Composition:** 0.7500 Silver .4822 oz. ASW **Subject:** 85th Birthday of Kodaly

| Date | Mintage | F | VF | XF | Unc | BU |
|---|---|---|---|---|---|---|
| 1967 | 15,000 | — | — | — | 10.00 | — |
| 1967 Proof | — | Value: 12.50 | | | | |

**50 FORINT (Otven)** **KM# 582** **Weight:** 20.0000 g. **Composition:** 0.6400 Silver .4115 oz. ASW **Subject:** 150th Anniversary - Birth of Semmelweis

| Date | Mintage | F | VF | XF | Unc | BU |
|---|---|---|---|---|---|---|
| 1968 | 20,000 | — | — | — | 10.00 | — |
| 1968 Proof | 4,750 | Value: 12.50 | | | | |

**50 FORINT (Otven)** **KM# 583** **Weight:** 4.2050 g. **Composition:** 0.9000 Gold .1217 oz. AGW **Subject:** 150th Anniversary - Birth of Semmelweis

| Date | Mintage | F | VF | XF | Unc | BU |
|---|---|---|---|---|---|---|
| 1968 Proof | 25,000 | Value: 75.00 | | | | |

**50 FORINT (Otven)** **KM# 589** **Weight:** 16.0000 g. **Composition:** 0.6400 Silver .3292 oz. ASW **Subject:** 50th Anniversary - Republic of Councils

| Date | Mintage | F | VF | XF | Unc | BU |
|---|---|---|---|---|---|---|
| 1969 | 12,000 | — | — | — | 10.00 | — |
| 1969 Proof | 3,000 | Value: 15.00 | | | | |

**50 FORINT (Otven)** **KM# 592** **Weight:** 16.0000 g. **Composition:** 0.6400 Silver .3292 oz. ASW **Subject:** 25th Anniversary of Liberation

| Date | Mintage | F | VF | XF | Unc | BU |
|---|---|---|---|---|---|---|
| 1970 | 20,000 | — | — | — | 9.00 | — |
| 1970 Proof | 5,000 | Value: 12.50 | | | | |

**50 FORINT (Otven)** **KM# 596** **Weight:** 16.0000 g. **Composition:** 0.6400 Silver .3292 oz. ASW **Subject:** 1000th Anniversary - Birth of St. Stephen

| Date | Mintage | F | VF | XF | Unc | BU |
|---|---|---|---|---|---|---|
| 1972 | 24,000 | — | — | — | 12.00 | — |
| 1972 Proof | 6,000 | Value: 15.00 | | | | |

**50 FORINT (Otven)** **KM# 599** **Weight:** 16.0000 g. **Composition:** 0.6400 Silver .3292 oz. ASW **Subject:** 150th Anniversary - Birth of Sandor Petofi

| Date | Mintage | F | VF | XF | Unc | BU |
|---|---|---|---|---|---|---|
| 1973 | 24,000 | — | — | — | 8.00 | — |
| 1973 Proof | 6,000 | Value: 12.00 | | | | |

**50 FORINT (Otven)** **KM# 601** **Weight:** 16.0000 g. **Composition:** 0.6400 Silver .3292 oz. ASW **Subject:** 50th Anniversary of National Bank

| Date | Mintage | F | VF | XF | Unc | BU |
|---|---|---|---|---|---|---|
| 1974 | 24,000 | — | — | — | 8.00 | — |
| 1974 Proof | 6,000 | Value: 10.00 | | | | |

**50 FORINT (Otven)** **KM# 663** **Composition:** Copper-Nickel **Subject:** 25th Anniversary of World Wildlife Foundation **Reverse:** Red-footed Falcon

| Date | Mintage | F | VF | XF | Unc | BU |
|---|---|---|---|---|---|---|
| 1988 | 45,000 | — | — | — | 6.50 | — |

**100 FORINT (Szaz)** **KM# 563** **Weight:** 7.6760 g. **Composition:** 0.9860 Gold .2431 oz. AGW **Subject:** 150th Anniversary - Birth of Liszt

| Date | Mintage | F | VF | XF | Unc | BU |
|---|---|---|---|---|---|---|
| 1961BP Proof | 2,500 | Value: 155 | | | | |

**100 FORINT (Szaz)** **KM# 564** **Weight:** 7.6760 g. **Composition:** 0.9860 Gold .2431 oz. AGW **Subject:** 80th Anniversary - Birth of Bartok

| Date | Mintage | F | VF | XF | Unc | BU |
|---|---|---|---|---|---|---|
| 1961 Proof | 2,500 | Value: 155 | | | | |

**100 FORINT (Szaz)** **KM# 569** **Weight:** 8.4100 g. **Composition:** 0.9000 Gold .2433 oz. AGW **Subject:** 400th Anniversary - Death of Zrinyi

| Date | Mintage | F | VF | XF | Unc | BU |
|---|---|---|---|---|---|---|
| 1966 Proof | 3,300 | Value: 155 | | | | |

**100 FORINT (Szaz)** **KM# 579** **Weight:** 28.0000 g. **Composition:** 0.7500 Silver .6752 oz. ASW **Subject:** 85th Birthday of Kodaly

| Date | Mintage | F | VF | XF | Unc | BU |
|---|---|---|---|---|---|---|
| 1967BP | 10,000 | — | — | — | 25.00 | — |
| 1967BP Proof | — | Value: 40.00 | | | | |

**100 FORINT (Szaz)** **KM# 584** **Weight:** 28.0000 g. **Composition:** 0.6400 Silver .5762 oz. ASW **Subject:** 150th Anniversary - Birth of Semmelweis

| Date | Mintage | F | VF | XF | Unc | BU |
|---|---|---|---|---|---|---|
| 1968 | 20,000 | — | — | — | 9.00 | — |
| 1968 Proof | 4,750 | Value: 17.50 | | | | |

**100 FORINT (Szaz)** **KM# 585** **Weight:** 8.4100 g. **Composition:** 0.9000 Gold .2433 oz. AGW **Subject:** 150th Anniversary - Birth of Semmelweis

| Date | Mintage | F | VF | XF | Unc | BU |
|---|---|---|---|---|---|---|
| 1968 Proof | 23,000 | Value: 135 | | | | |

**100 FORINT (Szaz)** **KM# 590** **Weight:** 22.0000 g. **Composition:** 0.6400 Silver .4527 oz. ASW **Subject:** 50th Anniversary - Republic of Councils

| Date | Mintage | F | VF | XF | Unc | BU |
|---|---|---|---|---|---|---|
| 1969 | 12,000 | — | — | — | 12.00 | — |
| 1969 Proof | 3,000 | Value: 15.00 | | | | |

**100 FORINT (Szaz)** **KM# 593** **Weight:** 22.0000 g. **Composition:** 0.6400 Silver .4527 oz. ASW **Subject:** 25th Anniversary of Liberation

| Date | Mintage | F | VF | XF | Unc | BU |
|---|---|---|---|---|---|---|
| 1970 | 20,000 | — | — | — | 10.00 | — |
| 1970 Proof | 5,000 | Value: 12.00 | | | | |

**100 FORINT (Szaz)** **KM# 597** **Weight:** 22.0000 g. **Composition:** 0.6400 Silver .4527 oz. ASW **Subject:** 1000th Anniversary - Birth of St. Stephen

| Date | Mintage | F | VF | XF | Unc | BU |
|---|---|---|---|---|---|---|
| 1972 | 24,000 | — | — | — | 12.00 | — |
| 1972 Proof | 6,000 | Value: 15.00 | | | | |

**100 FORINT (Szaz)** **KM# 598** **Weight:** 22.0000 g. **Composition:** 0.6400 Silver .4527 oz. ASW **Subject:** Buda and Pest Union Centennial

| Date | Mintage | F | VF | XF | Unc | BU |
|---|---|---|---|---|---|---|
| 1972 | 25,000 | — | — | — | 12.00 | — |
| 1972 Proof | 6,000 | Value: 15.00 | | | | |

**100 FORINT (Szaz)** **KM# 600** **Weight:** 22.0000 g. **Composition:** 0.6400 Silver .4527 oz. ASW **Subject:** 150th Anniversary - Birth of Sandor Petofi

| Date | Mintage | F | VF | XF | Unc | BU |
|---|---|---|---|---|---|---|
| 1973 | 24,000 | — | — | — | 8.50 | — |
| 1973 Proof | 6,000 | Value: 12.50 | | | | |

**100 FORINT (Szaz)** **KM# 602** **Weight:** 22.0000 g. **Composition:** 0.6400 Silver .4527 oz. ASW **Subject:** 25th Anniversary of KGST

| Date | Mintage | F | VF | XF | Unc | BU |
|---|---|---|---|---|---|---|
| 1974 | 20,000 | — | — | — | 8.50 | — |
| 1974 Proof | 5,000 | Value: 12.50 | | | | |

**100 FORINT (Szaz)** **KM# 603** **Weight:** 22.0000 g. **Composition:** 0.6400 Silver .4527 oz. ASW **Subject:** 50th Anniversary of National Bank

| Date | Mintage | F | VF | XF | Unc | BU |
|---|---|---|---|---|---|---|
| 1974 | 24,000 | — | — | — | 8.50 | — |
| 1974 Proof | 6,000 | Value: 12.50 | | | | |

**100 FORINT (Szaz)** **KM# 617** **Composition:** Nickel **Subject:** 1st Soviet-Hungarian Space Flight

| Date | Mintage | F | VF | XF | Unc | BU |
|---|---|---|---|---|---|---|
| 1980 | 180,000 | — | — | — | 4.00 | — |
| 1980 Proof | 20,000 | Value: 8.00 | | | | |

**100 FORINT (Szaz)** **KM# 621** **Composition:** Nickel **Subject:** World Food Day

| Date | Mintage | F | VF | XF | Unc | BU |
|---|---|---|---|---|---|---|
| 1981 | 80,000 | — | — | — | 5.00 | — |
| 1981 | 20,000 | Value: 10.00 | | | | |

**100 FORINT (Szaz)** **KM# 622** **Composition:** Copper-Nickel-Zinc **Subject:** 1300th Anniversary of Bulgarian Statehood

| Date | Mintage | F | VF | XF | Unc | BU |
|---|---|---|---|---|---|---|
| 1981 Proof | 50,000 | Value: 8.00 | | | | |

**100 FORINT (Szaz)** **KM# 626** **Composition:** Copper-Nickel **Subject:** World Football Championship

| Date | Mintage | F | VF | XF | Unc | BU |
|---|---|---|---|---|---|---|
| 1982 | 150,000 | — | — | — | 2.50 | — |

**100 FORINT (Szaz)** **KM# 631** **Composition:** Copper-Nickel **Series:** F.A.O.

| Date | Mintage | F | VF | XF | Unc | BU |
|---|---|---|---|---|---|---|
| 1983 | 50,000 | — | — | — | 3.50 | — |
| 1983 Proof | 10,000 | Value: 5.50 | | | | |

**100 FORINT (Szaz)** **KM# 632** **Composition:** Copper-Nickel-Zinc **Subject:** 200th Anniversary - Birth of Simon Bolivar **Reverse:** Andean Condor

| Date | Mintage | F | VF | XF | Unc | BU |
|---|---|---|---|---|---|---|
| 1983 | 20,000 | — | — | — | 6.50 | — |
| 1983 Proof | 10,000 | Value: 7.50 | | | | |

**100 FORINT (Szaz)** **KM# 633** **Composition:** Copper-Nickel-Zinc **Reverse:** Count Istvan Szechenyi

| Date | Mintage | F | VF | XF | Unc | BU |
|---|---|---|---|---|---|---|
| 1983 | 30,000 | — | — | — | 6.00 | — |
| 1983 Proof | 20,000 | Value: 9.00 | | | | |

**100 FORINT (Szaz)** **KM# 634** **Composition:** Copper-Nickel-Zinc **Subject:** 100th Anniversary - Birth of Bela Czobel - Painter

| Date | Mintage | F | VF | XF | Unc | BU |
|---|---|---|---|---|---|---|
| 1983 | 20,000 | — | — | — | 6.00 | — |
| 1983 Proof | 10,000 | Value: 10.00 | | | | |

**100 FORINT (Szaz)** **KM# 638** **Composition:** Copper-Nickel-Zinc **Subject:** 200th Anniversary - Birth of Sandor Korosi Csoma

| Date | Mintage | F | VF | XF | Unc | BU |
|---|---|---|---|---|---|---|
| 1984 | 20,000 | — | — | — | 6.00 | — |
| 1984 Proof | 10,000 | Value: 10.00 | | | | |

**100 FORINT (Szaz)** **KM# 639** **Composition:** Copper-Nickel-Zinc **Subject:** Forestry for Development

| Date | Mintage | F | VF | XF | Unc | BU |
|---|---|---|---|---|---|---|
| 1984 | 15,000 | — | — | — | 6.00 | — |
| 1984 Proof | 5,000 | Value: 10.00 | | | | |

**100 FORINT (Szaz)** **KM# 644** **Composition:** Copper-Nickel-Zinc **Subject:** Wildlife Preservation **Reverse:** Pond Turtle

| Date | Mintage | F | VF | XF | Unc | BU |
|---|---|---|---|---|---|---|
| 1985 | 20,000 | — | — | — | 9.00 | — |

**100 FORINT (Szaz)** **KM# 645** **Composition:** Copper-Nickel-Zinc **Subject:** Wildlife Preservation **Reverse:** European Otter

| Date | Mintage | F | VF | XF | Unc | BU |
|---|---|---|---|---|---|---|
| 1985 | 20,000 | — | — | — | 9.00 | — |

**100 FORINT (Szaz)** **KM# 646** **Composition:** Copper-Nickel-Zinc **Subject:** Wildlife Preservation **Reverse:** Wildcat

| Date | Mintage | F | VF | XF | Unc | BU |
|---|---|---|---|---|---|---|
| 1985 | 20,000 | — | — | — | 9.00 | — |

**100 FORINT (Szaz)** **KM# 647** **Composition:** Copper-Nickel-Zinc **Subject:** World Football - Map of Mexico

| Date | Mintage | F | VF | XF | Unc | BU |
|---|---|---|---|---|---|---|
| 1985 | 30,000 | — | — | — | 7.50 | — |

**100 FORINT (Szaz)** **KM# 648** **Composition:** Copper-Nickel-Zinc **Subject:** World Football - Native Mexican Artifacts

| Date | Mintage | F | VF | XF | Unc | BU |
|---|---|---|---|---|---|---|
| 1985 | 30,000 | — | — | — | 7.50 | — |

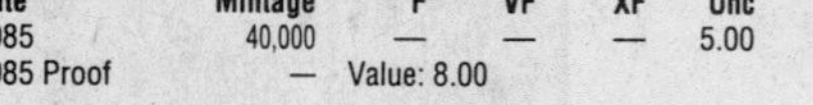

**100 FORINT (Szaz)** **KM# 651** **Composition:** Copper-Nickel-Zinc **Subject:** Budapest Cultural Forum

| Date | Mintage | F | VF | XF | Unc | BU |
|---|---|---|---|---|---|---|
| 1985 | 40,000 | — | — | — | 5.00 | — |
| 1985 Proof | — | Value: 8.00 | | | | |

**100 FORINT (Szaz)** **KM# 654** **Composition:** Copper-Nickel-Zinc **Series:** F.A.O.

| Date | Mintage | F | VF | XF | Unc | BU |
|---|---|---|---|---|---|---|
| 1985 | 20,000 | — | — | — | 5.00 | — |
| 1985 Proof | 5,000 | Value: 8.00 | | | | |

**100 FORINT (Szaz)** **KM# 655** **Composition:** Copper-Nickel-Zinc **Subject:** 200th Anniversary - Birth of Andras Fay

| Date | Mintage | F | VF | XF | Unc | BU |
|---|---|---|---|---|---|---|
| 1986 | 42,000 | — | — | — | 5.00 | — |
| 1986 Proof | 8,000 | Value: 8.00 | | | | |

**100 FORINT (Szaz)** **KM# 664** **Composition:** Copper-Nickel **Subject:** 1990 World Cup Soccer

| Date | Mintage | F | VF | XF | Unc | BU |
|---|---|---|---|---|---|---|
| 1988 | 23,000 | — | — | — | 9.00 | — |

**100 FORINT (Szaz)** **KM# 665** **Composition:** Copper-Nickel-Zinc **Subject:** Europe Football Championship

| Date | Mintage | F | VF | XF | Unc | BU |
|---|---|---|---|---|---|---|
| 1988 | 20,000 | — | — | — | 9.00 | — |

**100 FORINT (Szaz)** **KM# 668** **Composition:** Copper-Nickel **Subject:** 1990 World Cup Soccer

| Date | Mintage | F | VF | XF | Unc | BU |
|---|---|---|---|---|---|---|
| 1989 | 23,000 | — | — | — | 9.00 | — |

**200 FORINT (Ketszaz)** **KM# 586** **Weight:** 16.8210 g. **Composition:** 0.9000 Gold .4867 oz. AGW **Subject:** 150th Anniversary - Birth of Ignac Semmelweis

| Date | Mintage | F | VF | XF | Unc | BU |
|---|---|---|---|---|---|---|
| 1968BP Proof | 14,000 | Value: 240 | | | | |

**200 FORINT (Ketszaz)** **KM# 604** **Weight:** 28.0000 g. **Composition:** 0.6400 Silver .5762 oz. ASW **Subject:** 30th Anniversary of Liberation

| Date | Mintage | F | VF | XF | Unc | BU |
|---|---|---|---|---|---|---|
| 1975BP | 20,000 | — | — | — | 11.50 | — |
| 1975BP Proof | 10,000 | Value: 13.50 | | | | |

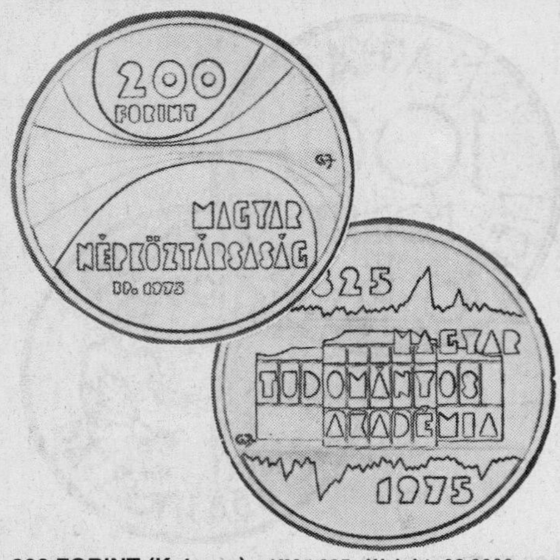


**200 FORINT (Ketszaz)** **KM# 605** **Weight:** 28.0000 g. **Composition:** 0.6400 Silver .5762 oz. ASW **Subject:** 150th Anniversary - Academy of Science

| Date | Mintage | F | VF | XF | Unc | BU |
|---|---|---|---|---|---|---|
| 1975 | 20,000 | — | — | — | 11.50 | — |
| 1975 Proof | 10,000 | Value: 13.50 | | | | |

**200 FORINT (Ketszaz)** **KM# 608** **Weight:** 28.0000 g. **Composition:** 0.6400 Silver .5762 oz. ASW **Reverse:** Pal Szinyei Merse

| Date | Mintage | F | VF | XF | Unc | BU |
|---|---|---|---|---|---|---|
| 1976 | 25,000 | — | — | — | 11.50 | — |
| 1976 Proof | 5,000 | Value: 13.50 | | | | |

**200 FORINT (Ketszaz)** **KM# 611** **Weight:** 28.0000 g. **Composition:** 0.6400 Silver .5762 oz. ASW **Reverse:** Tivadar CS. Kosztka

| Date | Mintage | F | VF | XF | Unc | BU |
|---|---|---|---|---|---|---|
| 1977 | 25,000 | — | — | — | 11.50 | — |
| 1977 Proof | 5,000 | Value: 13.50 | | | | |

**200 FORINT (Ketszaz)** **KM# 606** **Weight:** 28.0000 g. **Composition:** 0.6400 Silver .5762 oz. ASW **Subject:** 300th Anniversary - Birth of Ferencz Rakoczi II

| Date | Mintage | F | VF | XF | Unc | BU |
|---|---|---|---|---|---|---|
| 1976 | 25,000 | — | — | — | 11.50 | — |
| 1976 Proof | 5,000 | Value: 15.00 | | | | |

**200 FORINT (Ketszaz)** **KM# 609** **Weight:** 28.0000 g. **Composition:** 0.6400 Silver .5762 oz. ASW **Reverse:** Gyula Derkovits

| Date | Mintage | F | VF | XF | Unc | BU |
|---|---|---|---|---|---|---|
| 1976 | 25,000 | — | — | — | 11.50 | — |
| 1976 Proof | 5,000 | Value: 13.50 | | | | |

**200 FORINT (Ketszaz)** **KM# 612** **Weight:** 28.0000 g. **Composition:** 0.6400 Silver .5762 oz. ASW **Reverse:** Jozsef Rippl-Ronai

| Date | Mintage | F | VF | XF | Unc | BU |
|---|---|---|---|---|---|---|
| 1977 | 25,000 | — | — | — | 11.50 | — |
| 1977 Proof | 5,000 | Value: 13.50 | | | | |

**200 FORINT (Ketszaz)** **KM# 607** **Weight:** 28.0000 g. **Composition:** 0.6400 Silver .5762 oz. ASW **Reverse:** Mihaly Munkacsy

| Date | Mintage | F | VF | XF | Unc | BU |
|---|---|---|---|---|---|---|
| 1976 | 25,000 | — | — | — | 11.50 | — |
| 1976 Proof | 5,000 | Value: 13.50 | | | | |

**200 FORINT (Ketszaz)** **KM# 610** **Weight:** 28.0000 g. **Composition:** 0.6400 Silver .5762 oz. ASW **Reverse:** Adam Manyoki

| Date | Mintage | F | VF | XF | Unc | BU |
|---|---|---|---|---|---|---|
| 1977 | 25,000 | — | — | — | 11.50 | — |
| 1977 Proof | 5,000 | Value: 13.50 | | | | |

**200 FORINT (Ketszaz)** **KM# 613** **Weight:** 28.0000 g. **Composition:** 0.6400 Silver .5762 oz. ASW **Subject:** 175th Anniversary of National Museum

| Date | Mintage | F | VF | XF | Unc | BU |
|---|---|---|---|---|---|---|
| 1977 | 25,000 | — | — | — | 12.00 | — |
| 1977 Proof | 5,000 | Value: 16.50 | | | | |

**200 FORINT (Ketszaz)** **KM# 614** **Weight:** 28.0000 g. **Composition:** 0.6400 Silver .5762 oz. ASW **Subject:** First Hungarian Gold Forint

| Date | Mintage | F | VF | XF | Unc | BU |
|---|---|---|---|---|---|---|
| 1978 | 25,000 | — | — | — | 12.00 | — |
| 1978 Proof | 5,000 | Value: 16.50 | | | | |

**200 FORINT (Ketszaz)** **KM# 615** **Weight:** 28.0000 g. **Composition:** 0.6400 Silver .5762 oz. ASW **Subject:** International Year of the Child

| Date | Mintage | F | VF | XF | Unc | BU |
|---|---|---|---|---|---|---|
| 1979 | 9,000 | — | — | — | 9.00 | — |
| 1979 Proof | 21,000 | Value: 12.50 | | | | |

**200 FORINT (Ketszaz)** **KM# 616** **Weight:** 22.0000 g. **Composition:** 0.6400 Silver .4527 oz. ASW **Subject:** 350th Anniversary - Death of Gabor Bethlen

| Date | Mintage | F | VF | XF | Unc | BU |
|---|---|---|---|---|---|---|
| 1979 | 15,000 | — | — | — | 12.50 | — |
| 1979 Proof | 5,000 | Value: 17.50 | | | | |

**200 FORINT (Ketszaz)** **KM# 618** **Weight:** 16.0000 g. **Composition:** 0.6400 Silver .3292 oz. ASW **Subject:** XIII Winter Olympics - Lake Placid

| Date | Mintage | F | VF | XF | Unc | BU |
|---|---|---|---|---|---|---|
| 1980 Proof | 15,000 | Value: 11.50 | | | | |

**200 FORINT (Ketszaz)** **KM# 643** **Weight:** 16.0000 g. **Composition:** 0.6400 Silver .3292 oz. ASW **Subject:** Wildlife Preservation **Reverse:** Otter

| Date | Mintage | F | VF | XF | Unc | BU |
|---|---|---|---|---|---|---|
| 1985 | 13,000 | — | — | — | 10.00 | — |
| 1985 Proof | 2,000 | Value: 13.50 | | | | |

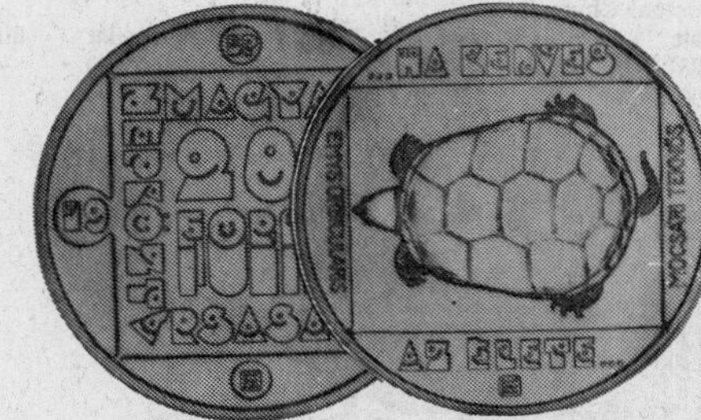

**200 FORINT (Ketszaz)** **KM# 649** **Weight:** 16.0000 g. **Composition:** 0.6400 Silver .3292 oz. ASW **Subject:** Wildlife Preservation **Reverse:** Pond Turtle

| Date | Mintage | F | VF | XF | Unc | BU |
|---|---|---|---|---|---|---|
| 1985 | 13,000 | — | — | — | 10.00 | — |
| 1985 Proof | 2,000 | Value: 13.50 | | | | |

**200 FORINT (Ketszaz)** **KM# 650** **Weight:** 16.0000 g. **Composition:** 0.6400 Silver .3292 oz. ASW **Subject:** Wildlife Preservation **Reverse:** Wildcat

| Date | Mintage | F | VF | XF | Unc | BU |
|---|---|---|---|---|---|---|
| 1985 | 13,000 | — | — | — | 10.00 | — |
| 1985 Proof | 2,000 | Value: 13.50 | | | | |

**500 FORINT (Otszaz)** **KM# 565** **Weight:** 38.3800 g. **Composition:** 0.9860 Gold 1.2168 oz. AGW **Subject:** 150th Anniversary - Birth of Ferenc Liszt

| Date | Mintage | F | VF | XF | Unc | BU |
|---|---|---|---|---|---|---|
| 1961BP | 2,503 | — | — | — | — | — |

**500 FORINT (Otszaz)** **KM# 566** **Weight:** 38.3800 g. **Composition:** 0.9860 Gold 1.2168 oz. AGW **Subject:** 80th Aniversry - Birth of Bela Bartok

| Date | Mintage | F | VF | XF | Unc | BU |
|---|---|---|---|---|---|---|
| 1961 | 2,503 | — | — | — | — | — |

**500 FORINT (Otszaz)** **KM# 570** **Weight:** 42.0522 g. **Composition:** 0.9000 Gold 1.2169 oz. AGW **Subject:** 400th Anniversary - Death of Miklos Zrinyl

| Date | Mintage | F | VF | XF | Unc | BU |
|---|---|---|---|---|---|---|
| 1966 Proof | 1,100 | Value: 750 | | | | |

**500 FORINT (Otszaz)** **KM# 580** **Weight:** 42.0522 g. **Composition:** 0.9000 Gold 1.2169 oz. AGW **Subject:** 85th Birthday of Zoltan Kodaly

| Date | Mintage | F | VF | XF | Unc | BU |
|---|---|---|---|---|---|---|
| 1967 | — | — | — | — | 600 | — |
| 1967 Proof | 1,000 | Value: 750 | | | | |

**500 FORINT (Otszaz)** **KM# 587** **Weight:** 42.0522 g. **Composition:** 0.9000 Gold 1.2169 oz. AGW **Subject:** 150th Anniversary - Birth of Ignacz Semmelweis **Reverse:** Similar to 50 Forint, KM#583

| Date | Mintage | F | VF | XF | Unc | BU |
|---|---|---|---|---|---|---|
| 1968 Proof | 9,000 | Value: 550 | | | | |

**Note:**

**500 FORINT (Otszaz)** **KM# 619** **Weight:** 39.0000 g. **Composition:** 0.6400 Silver .8025 oz. ASW **Subject:** XIII Winter Olympics - Lake Placid **Reverse:** Similar to 200 Forint, KM#618

| Date | Mintage | F | VF | XF | Unc | BU |
|---|---|---|---|---|---|---|
| 1980BP Proof | 13,000 | Value: 55.00 | | | | |

**500 FORINT (Otszaz)** **KM# 623** **Weight:** 25.0000 g. **Composition:** 0.6400 Silver .5144 oz. ASW **Subject:** Centennial - Birth of Bela Bartok

| Date | Mintage | F | VF | XF | Unc | BU |
|---|---|---|---|---|---|---|
| 1981 | 13,000 | — | — | — | 18.50 | — |
| 1981 Proof | 13,000 | Value: 22.50 | | | | |

**500 FORINT (Otszaz)** **KM# 624** **Weight:** 28.0000 g. **Composition:** 0.6400 Silver .5762 oz. ASW **Subject:** World Football Championship

| Date | Mintage | F | VF | XF | Unc | BU |
|---|---|---|---|---|---|---|
| 1981 | 6,000 | — | — | — | 22.00 | — |
| 1981 Proof | 40,000 | Value: 18.00 | | | | |

**500 FORINT (Otszaz)** **KM# 625** **Weight:** 28.0000 g. **Composition:** 0.6400 Silver .5762 oz. ASW **Subject:** World Football Championship

| Date | Mintage | F | VF | XF | Unc | BU |
|---|---|---|---|---|---|---|
| 1981 | 6,000 | — | — | — | 22.00 | — |
| 1981 Proof | 40,000 | Value: 18.00 | | | | |

**500 FORINT (Otszaz)** **KM# 640** **Weight:** 28.0000 g. **Composition:** 0.6400 Silver .5762 oz. ASW **Subject:** Decade for Women

| Date | Mintage | F | VF | XF | Unc | BU |
|---|---|---|---|---|---|---|
| 1984 | 8,000 | — | — | — | 20.00 | — |
| 1984 Proof | 20,000 | Value: 25.00 | | | | |

**500 FORINT (Otszaz)** **KM# 641** **Weight:** 28.0000 g. **Composition:** 0.6400 Silver .5762 oz. ASW **Subject:** Winter Olympics **Reverse:** Cross country skiers

| Date | Mintage | F | VF | XF | Unc | BU |
|---|---|---|---|---|---|---|
| 1984 | 8,000 | — | — | — | 12.50 | — |
| 1984 Proof | 12,000 | Value: 18.00 | | | | |

**500 FORINT (Otszaz)** **KM# 642** **Weight:** 28.0000 g. **Composition:** 0.6400 Silver .5762 oz. ASW **Subject:** Los Angeles Olympics **Reverse:** Gymnast

| Date | Mintage | F | VF | XF | Unc | BU |
|---|---|---|---|---|---|---|
| 1984 | 8,000 | — | — | — | 13.50 | — |
| 1984 Proof | 12,000 | Value: 18.00 | | | | |

**500 FORINT (Otszaz)** **KM# 652** **Weight:** 28.0000 g. **Composition:** 0.6400 Silver .5762 oz. ASW **Subject:** Budapest Cultural Forum

| Date | Mintage | F | VF | XF | Unc | BU |
|---|---|---|---|---|---|---|
| 1985 | 15,000 | — | — | — | 12.50 | — |
| 1985 Proof | 10,000 | Value: 18.50 | | | | |

**500 FORINT (Otszaz)** **KM# 656** **Weight:** 28.0000 g. **Composition:** 0.6400 Silver .5762 oz. ASW **Subject:** World Football Championship **Reverse:** Football players

| Date | Mintage | F | VF | XF | Unc | BU |
|---|---|---|---|---|---|---|
| 1986 | 8,000 | — | — | — | 15.00 | — |
| 1986 Proof | 17,000 | Value: 13.50 | | | | |

**500 FORINT (Otszaz)** **KM# 659** **Weight:** 28.0000 g. **Composition:** 0.9000 Silver .8102 oz. ASW **Subject:** Winter Olympics - Speed Skating

| Date | Mintage | F | VF | XF | Unc | BU |
|---|---|---|---|---|---|---|
| 1986 | 15,000 | — | — | — | 15.00 | — |
| 1986 Proof | 15,000 | Value: 22.50 | | | | |

**500 FORINT (Otszaz)** **KM# 662** **Weight:** 28.0000 g. **Composition:** 0.9000 Silver .8102 oz. ASW **Subject:** 950th Anniversary - Death of St. Stephan

| Date | Mintage | F | VF | XF | Unc | BU |
|---|---|---|---|---|---|---|
| 1988 | 5,000 | — | — | — | 38.00 | — |
| 1988 Proof | 15,000 | Value: 30.00 | | | | |



**500 FORINT (Otszaz)** **KM# 657** **Weight:** 28.0000 g. **Composition:** 0.6400 Silver .5762 oz. ASW **Subject:** World Football Championship **Reverse:** Stadium

| Date | Mintage | F | VF | XF | Unc | BU |
|---|---|---|---|---|---|---|
| 1986 | 8,000 | — | — | — | 15.00 | — |
| 1986 Proof | 17,000 | Value: 13.50 | | | | |

**500 FORINT (Otszaz)** **KM# 660** **Weight:** 28.0000 g. **Composition:** 0.9000 Silver .8102 oz. ASW **Subject:** Seoul Olympics **Reverse:** Wrestlers

| Date | Mintage | F | VF | XF | Unc | BU |
|---|---|---|---|---|---|---|
| 1987 | 15,000 | — | — | — | 16.50 | — |
| 1987 Proof | 15,000 | Value: 22.50 | | | | |

**500 FORINT (Otszaz)** **KM# 666** **Weight:** 28.0000 g. **Composition:** 0.9000 Silver .8102 oz. ASW **Subject:** Europe Football Championship

| Date | Mintage | F | VF | XF | Unc | BU |
|---|---|---|---|---|---|---|
| 1988 | 8,000 | — | — | — | 20.00 | — |
| 1988 Proof | 12,000 | Value: 18.00 | | | | |

**500 FORINT (Otszaz)** **KM# 658** **Weight:** 28.0000 g. **Composition:** 0.9000 Silver .8102 oz. ASW **Subject:** 300th Anniversary - Repossession of Buda from the Turks

| Date | Mintage | F | VF | XF | Unc | BU |
|---|---|---|---|---|---|---|
| 1986 | 20,000 | — | — | — | 22.50 | — |
| 1986 Proof | 10,000 | Value: 28.00 | | | | |

**500 FORINT (Otszaz)** **KM# 661** **Weight:** 28.0000 g. **Composition:** 0.9000 Silver .8102 oz. ASW **Subject:** World Wildlife Fund **Reverse:** Montagu's Harrier

| Date | Mintage | F | VF | XF | Unc | BU |
|---|---|---|---|---|---|---|
| 1988 | 10,000 | — | — | — | 22.50 | — |
| 1988 Proof | 25,000 | Value: 25.00 | | | | |

**500 FORINT (Otszaz)** **KM# 667** **Weight:** 28.0000 g. **Composition:** 0.9000 Silver .8102 oz. ASW **Subject:** World Football Championship

| Date | Mintage | F | VF | XF | Unc | BU |
|---|---|---|---|---|---|---|
| 1988 | 7,000 | — | — | — | 20.00 | — |
| 1988 Proof | 15,000 | Value: 18.00 | | | | |

**500 FORINT (Otszaz)** **KM# 669** **Weight:** 28.0000 g. **Composition:** 0.9000 Silver .8102 oz. ASW **Subject:** World Football Championship **Reverse:** Two players

| Date | Mintage | F | VF | XF | Unc | BU |
|---|---|---|---|---|---|---|
| 1989 | 7,000 | — | — | — | 16.50 | — |
| 1989 Proof | 15,000 | Value: 20.00 | | | | |

**500 FORINT (Otszaz)** **KM# 670** **Weight:** 28.0000 g. **Composition:** 0.9000 Silver .8102 oz. ASW **Subject:** Save the Children Fund

| Date | Mintage | F | VF | XF | Unc | BU |
|---|---|---|---|---|---|---|
| 1989 | 10,000 | — | — | — | 20.00 | — |
| 1989 Proof | 20,000 | Value: 22.50 | | | | |

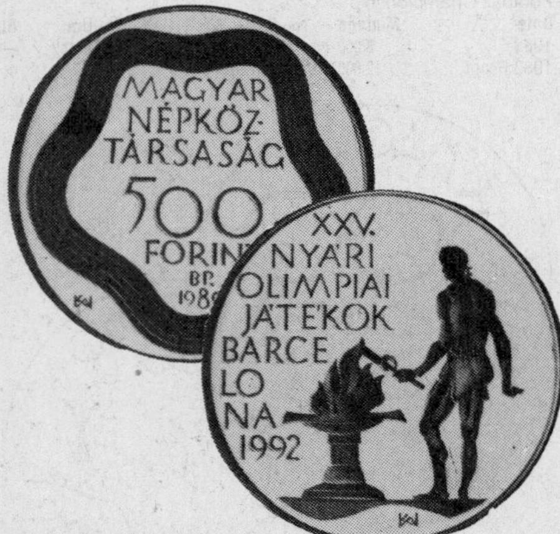


**500 FORINT (Otszaz)** **KM# 671** **Weight:** 28.0000 g. **Composition:** 0.9000 Silver .8102 oz. ASW **Subject:** 1992 Barcelona Olympics - Flame

| Date | Mintage | F | VF | XF | Unc | BU |
|---|---|---|---|---|---|---|
| 1989 | 15,000 | — | — | — | 25.00 | — |
| 1989 Proof | 15,000 | Value: 30.00 | | | | |

**1000 FORINT (Ezer)** **KM# 571** **Weight:** 84.1040 g. **Composition:** 0.9000 Gold 2.4339 oz. AGW **Subject:** 400th Anniversary - Death of Miklos Zrinyi **Obverse:** Similar to 500 Forint, KM#570

| Date | Mintage | F | VF | XF | Unc | BU |
|---|---|---|---|---|---|---|
| 1966 Proof | 330 | Value: 1,750 | | | | |

**1000 FORINT (Ezer)** **KM# 581** **Weight:** 84.1040 g. **Composition:** 0.9000 Gold 2.4339 oz. AGW **Subject:** 85th Birthday of Zoltan Kodaly **Obverse:** Similar to 500 Forint, KM#580

| Date | Mintage | F | VF | XF | Unc | BU |
|---|---|---|---|---|---|---|
| 1967 Proof | 500 | Value: 1,500 | | | | |

**1000 FORINT (Ezer)** **KM# 588** **Weight:** 84.1040 g. **Composition:** 0.9000 Gold 2.4339 oz. AGW **Subject:** 150th Anniversary - Birth of Ignacz Semmelweis **Reverse:** Similar to 500 forint, KM#587

| Date | Mintage | F | VF | XF | Unc | BU |
|---|---|---|---|---|---|---|
| 1968 | 7,000 | Value: 1,250 | | | | |

## TRANSITIONAL COINAGE

**2 FORINT** **KM# 737** **Composition:** Brass **Note:** Similar to 2 Forint, KM#591. Communist design type with New Republic legends.

| Date | Mintage | F | VF | XF | Unc | BU |
|---|---|---|---|---|---|---|
| 1990 | 10,000 | — | — | — | 15.00 | — |

**5 FORINT** **KM# 738** **Composition:** Copper-Nickel **Note:** Similar to 5 Forint, KM#635. Communist design with New Republic legends.

| Date | Mintage | F | VF | XF | Unc | BU |
|---|---|---|---|---|---|---|
| 1990 | 10,000 | — | — | — | 20.00 | — |

**10 FORINT** **KM# 739** **Composition:** Aluminum-Bronze **Note:** Similar to 10 Forint, KM#636.

| Date | Mintage | F | VF | XF | Unc | BU |
|---|---|---|---|---|---|---|
| 1990 | 10,000 | — | — | — | 25.00 | — |

**20 FORINT** **KM# 740** **Composition:** Copper-Nickel **Note:** Similar to 20 Forint, KM#630.

| Date | Mintage | F | VF | XF | Unc | BU |
|---|---|---|---|---|---|---|
| 1990 | 10,000 | — | — | — | 30.00 | — |

# 2ND REPUBLIC

## 1989-present

## DECIMAL COINAGE

**2 FILLER** **KM# 673** **Composition:** Aluminum

| Date | Mintage | F | VF | XF | Unc | BU |
|---|---|---|---|---|---|---|
| 1990BP | 10,000 | — | — | — | 2.00 | — |
| 1991BP | 10,000 | — | — | — | 3.00 | — |
| 1992BP | 30,000 | — | — | — | 3.50 | — |

**5 FILLER** **KM# 674** **Composition:** Aluminum

| Date | Mintage | F | VF | XF | Unc | BU |
|---|---|---|---|---|---|---|
| 1990BP | 10,000 | — | — | — | 2.00 | — |
| 1991BP | 10,000 | — | — | — | 3.00 | — |
| 1992BP | 30,000 | — | — | — | 3.50 | — |

**10 FILLER** **KM# 675** **Composition:** Aluminum

| Date | Mintage | F | VF | XF | Unc | BU |
|---|---|---|---|---|---|---|
| 1990BP | 46,515,000 | 0.10 | 0.15 | 0.20 | 0.35 | — |
| 1991BP | 2,370,000 | 0.25 | 0.35 | 0.50 | 0.70 | — |
| 1992BP | 15,828,000 | 0.15 | 0.25 | 0.35 | 0.50 | — |
| 1993BP | 30,000 | — | — | — | 0.75 | — |
| 1994BP | 30,000 | — | — | — | 0.75 | — |
| 1995BP | 30,000 | — | — | — | 0.75 | — |
| 1996BP | 20,000 | — | — | — | 1.00 | — |

**20 FILLER** **KM# 676** **Composition:** Aluminum

| Date | Mintage | F | VF | XF | Unc | BU |
|---|---|---|---|---|---|---|
| 1990BP | 59,360,000 | 0.10 | 0.15 | 0.20 | 0.35 | — |
| 1991BP | 20,210,000 | 0.20 | 0.35 | 0.50 | 0.75 | — |
| 1992BP | 30,000 | — | — | — | 1.00 | — |
| 1993BP | 30,000 | — | — | — | 1.00 | — |
| 1994BP | 30,000 | — | — | — | 1.00 | — |
| 1995BP | 30,000 | — | — | — | 1.00 | — |
| 1996BP | 20,000 | — | — | — | 1.25 | — |

**50 FILLER** **KM# 677** **Composition:** Aluminum

| Date | Mintage | F | VF | XF | Unc | BU |
|---|---|---|---|---|---|---|
| 1990BP | 20,550,000 | — | 0.10 | 0.20 | 0.30 | — |
| 1991BP | 31,250,000 | — | — | 0.10 | 0.25 | — |
| 1992BP | 440,000 | — | — | — | 0.75 | — |
| 1993BP | 30,000 | — | — | — | 1.00 | — |
| 1994BP | 30,000 | — | — | — | 1.00 | — |
| 1995BP | 30,000 | — | — | — | 1.00 | — |
| 1996BP | 20,000 | — | — | — | 1.00 | — |
| 1997BP | 10,000 | — | — | — | 1.25 | — |
| 1998BP | 10,000 | — | — | — | 1.25 | — |
| 1999BP | 10,000 | — | — | — | 1.25 | — |

**FORINT** KM# 692 **Composition:** Brass

| Date | Mintage | F | VF | XF | Unc | BU |
|---|---|---|---|---|---|---|
| 1992 | 23,890,000 | — | 0.10 | 0.25 | 0.35 | — |
| 1992 Proof | 1,000 | Value: 5.00 | | | | |
| 1993 | 75,100,000 | — | — | 0.10 | 0.25 | — |
| 1993 Proof | 30,000 | Value: 1.00 | | | | |
| 1994 | 66,605,000 | — | — | 0.10 | 0.25 | — |
| 1994 Proof | 15,000 | Value: 1.00 | | | | |
| 1995 | 50,535,000 | — | — | 0.10 | 0.25 | — |
| 1995 Proof | 15,000 | Value: 1.00 | | | | |
| 1996 | 67,000,000 | — | — | 0.10 | 0.25 | — |
| 1996 Proof | 10,000 | Value: 1.25 | | | | |
| 1997 | — | — | — | — | 0.25 | — |
| 1997 Proof | 3,000 | Value: 2.50 | | | | |
| 1998 | — | — | — | — | 0.25 | — |
| 1998 Proof | 3,000 | Value: 2.50 | | | | |
| 1999 | — | — | — | — | 0.25 | — |
| 1999 Proof | 3,000 | Value: 2.50 | | | | |
| 2000 | — | — | — | — | 0.25 | — |
| 2000 Proof | 3,000 | Value: 2.50 | | | | |
| 2001 | — | — | — | — | 0.25 | — |
| 2001 | 3,000 | Value: 2.50 | | | | |

**2 FORINT** KM# 693 **Composition:** Copper-Nickel

| Date | Mintage | F | VF | XF | Unc | BU |
|---|---|---|---|---|---|---|
| 1992 | 10,380,000 | 0.10 | 0.25 | 0.35 | 0.50 | — |
| 1992 Proof | 1,000 | Value: 6.00 | | | | |
| 1993 | 82,915,000 | — | 0.10 | 0.25 | 0.35 | — |
| 1993 Proof | 30,000 | Value: 1.50 | | | | |
| 1994 | 68,370,000 | — | 0.10 | 0.25 | 0.35 | — |
| 1994 Proof | 15,000 | Value: 1.50 | | | | |
| 1995 | 60,945,000 | — | 0.10 | 0.25 | 0.35 | — |
| 1995 Proof | 15,000 | Value: 1.50 | | | | |
| 1996 | 50,010,000 | — | 0.10 | 0.25 | 0.35 | — |
| 1996 Proof | 10,000 | Value: 1.75 | | | | |
| 1997 | — | — | — | — | 0.35 | — |
| 1997 Proof | 3,000 | Value: 3.50 | | | | |
| 1998 | — | — | — | — | 0.35 | — |
| 1998 P[roof | 3,000 | Value: 3.50 | | | | |
| 1999 | — | — | — | — | 0.35 | — |
| 1999 Proof | 3,000 | Value: 3.50 | | | | |
| 2000 | — | — | — | — | 0.35 | — |
| 2000 Proof | 3,000 | Value: 3.50 | | | | |
| 2001 | — | — | — | — | 0.35 | — |
| 2001 Proof | 3,000 | Value: 3.50 | | | | |

**5 FORINT** KM# 694 **Composition:** Brass **Obverse:** Great White Egret

| Date | Mintage | F | VF | XF | Unc | BU |
|---|---|---|---|---|---|---|
| 1992 | 1,145,000 | 0.15 | 0.30 | 0.60 | 1.00 | — |
| 1992 Proof | 1,000 | Value: 6.50 | | | | |
| 1993 | 37,180,000 | 0.10 | 0.25 | 0.45 | 0.75 | — |
| 1993 Proof | 30,000 | Value: 2.00 | | | | |
| 1994 | 53,615,000 | 0.10 | 0.20 | 0.30 | 0.65 | — |
| 1994 Proof | 15,000 | Value: 2.00 | | | | |
| 1995 | 24,670,000 | 0.10 | 0.20 | 0.30 | 0.75 | — |
| 1995 Proof | 15,000 | Value: 2.00 | | | | |
| 1996 | — | — | — | — | 0.75 | — |
| 1996 Proof | 10,000 | Value: 2.00 | | | | |
| 1997 | 3,000 | — | — | — | 0.75 | — |
| 1997 Proof | 3,000 | Value: 4.50 | | | | |
| 1998 | — | — | — | — | 0.75 | — |
| 1998 Proof | 3,000 | Value: 4.50 | | | | |
| 1999 | — | — | — | — | 0.75 | — |
| 1999 Proof | 3,000 | Value: 4.50 | | | | |
| 2000 | — | — | — | — | 0.75 | — |
| 2000 Proof | 3,000 | Value: 4.50 | | | | |
| 2001 | — | — | — | — | 0.75 | — |
| 2001 Proof | 3,000 | Value: 4.50 | | | | |

**10 FORINT** KM# 695 **Composition:** Copper-Nickel Clad Brass

| Date | Mintage | F | VF | XF | Unc | BU |
|---|---|---|---|---|---|---|
| 1992 | 2,000 | — | — | — | 6.00 | — |
| 1992 Proof | 1,000 | Value: 8.00 | | | | |
| 1993 | 35,565,000 | 0.10 | 0.25 | 0.45 | 1.00 | — |
| 1993 Proof | 30,000 | Value: 3.00 | | | | |
| 1994 | 69,078,000 | — | 0.15 | 0.35 | 0.85 | — |
| 1994 Proof | 15,000 | Value: 3.00 | | | | |
| 1995 | 40,910,000 | 0.10 | 0.25 | 0.45 | 1.00 | — |
| 1995 Proof | 15,000 | Value: 3.00 | | | | |
| 1996 | 13,010,000 | 0.15 | 0.30 | 0.50 | 1.00 | — |
| 1996 Proof | 10,000 | Value: 3.50 | | | | |
| 1997 | — | — | — | — | 1.00 | — |
| 1997 Proof | 3,000 | Value: 5.00 | | | | |
| 1998 | — | — | — | — | 1.00 | — |
| 1998 Proof | 3,000 | Value: 5.00 | | | | |
| 1999 | — | — | — | — | 1.00 | — |
| 1999 Proof | 3,000 | Value: 5.00 | | | | |
| 2000 | — | — | — | — | 1.00 | — |
| 2000 Proof | 3,000 | Value: 5.00 | | | | |
| 2001 | — | — | — | — | 1.00 | — |
| 2001 Proof | 3,000 | Value: 5.00 | | | | |

**20 FORINT** KM# 696 **Composition:** Nickel-Brass

| Date | Mintage | F | VF | XF | Unc | BU |
|---|---|---|---|---|---|---|
| 1992 | 2,000 | — | — | — | 8.00 | — |
| 1992 Proof | 1,000 | Value: 10.00 | | | | |
| 1993 | 42,965,000 | 0.20 | 0.30 | 0.60 | 1.50 | — |
| 1993 Proof | 30,000 | Value: 4.00 | | | | |
| 1994 | 68,965,000 | 0.15 | 0.25 | 0.50 | 1.25 | — |
| 1994 Proof | 15,000 | Value: 4.00 | | | | |
| 1995 | 53,395,000 | 0.15 | 0.25 | 0.50 | 1.25 | — |
| 1995 Proof | 15,000 | Value: 4.00 | | | | |
| 1996 | 6,010,000 | 0.20 | 0.30 | 0.65 | 1.50 | — |
| 1996 Proof | 10,000 | Value: 4.00 | | | | |
| 1997 | 7,000 | — | — | — | 3.50 | — |
| 1997 Proof | 3,000 | Value: 6.00 | | | | |
| 1998 | — | — | — | — | 1.50 | — |
| 1998 Proof | 3,000 | Value: 6.00 | | | | |
| 1999 | — | — | — | — | 1.50 | — |
| 1999 Proof | 3,000 | Value: 6.00 | | | | |
| 2000 | — | — | — | — | 1.50 | — |
| 2000 Proof | 3,000 | Value: 6.00 | | | | |
| 2001 | — | — | — | — | 1.50 | — |
| 2001 Proof | 3,000 | Value: 6.00 | | | | |

**50 FORINT** KM# 697 **Composition:** Copper-Nickel Clad Brass **Obverse:** Saker falcon

| Date | Mintage | F | VF | XF | Unc | BU |
|---|---|---|---|---|---|---|
| 1992 | 2,000 | — | — | — | 10.00 | — |
| 1992 Proof | 1,000 | Value: 12.00 | | | | |
| 1993 | 861,000 | 0.50 | 0.65 | 1.25 | 3.00 | — |
| 1993 Proof | 30,000 | Value: 5.00 | | | | |
| 1994 | 8,397,000 | 0.25 | 0.45 | 0.85 | 3.00 | — |
| 1994 Proof | 15,000 | Value: 5.00 | | | | |
| 1995 | 36,985,000 | — | 0.25 | 0.50 | 2.50 | — |
| 1995 Proof | 15,000 | Value: 5.00 | | | | |
| 1996 | — | 0.30 | 0.50 | 1.00 | 3.00 | — |
| 1996 Proof | 10,000 | Value: 5.00 | | | | |
| 1997 | — | — | — | — | 3.00 | — |
| 1997 Proof | 3,000 | Value: 6.50 | | | | |
| 1998 | — | — | — | — | 3.00 | — |
| 1998 Proof | 3,000 | Value: 6.50 | | | | |
| 1999 | — | — | — | — | 3.00 | — |
| 1999 Proof | 3,000 | Value: 6.50 | | | | |

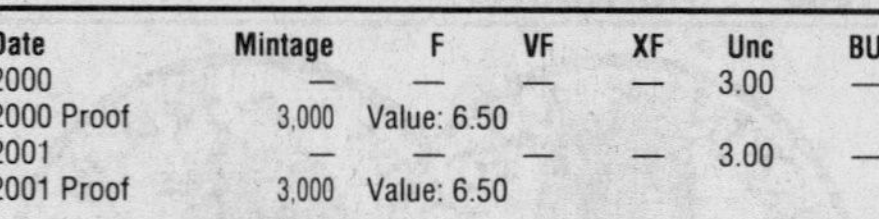

| Date | Mintage | F | VF | XF | Unc | BU |
|---|---|---|---|---|---|---|
| 2000 | — | — | — | — | 3.00 | — |
| 2000 Proof | 3,000 | Value: 6.50 | | | | |
| 2001 | — | — | — | — | 3.00 | — |
| 2001 Proof | 3,000 | Value: 6.50 | | | | |

**75 FORINT** KM# 734 **Weight:** 31.4600 g. **Composition:** 0.9250 Silver .9356 oz. ASW **Subject:** 75th Anniversary - Hungarian National Bank **Obverse:** National arms above denomination **Reverse:** Goddess Juno

| Date | Mintage | F | VF | XF | Unc | BU |
|---|---|---|---|---|---|---|
| 1999 | Est. 3,000 | — | — | — | 35.00 | — |
| 1999 Proof | Est. 4,500 | Value: 45.00 | | | | |

**100 FORINT (Szaz)** KM# 678 **Composition:** Copper-Nickel-Zinc **Reverse:** Adreas Fay

| Date | Mintage | F | VF | XF | Unc | BU |
|---|---|---|---|---|---|---|
| 1990BP | 20,000 | — | — | — | 5.00 | — |
| 1990BP Proof | 10,000 | Value: 7.00 | | | | |

**100 FORINT (Szaz)** KM# 700 **Composition:** Copper-Nickel **Subject:** S.O.S. Gyermekfalu, Children's Village

| Date | Mintage | F | VF | XF | Unc | BU |
|---|---|---|---|---|---|---|
| 1990 Proof | 50,000 | Value: 12.00 | | | | |

**100 FORINT (Szaz)** KM# 701 **Composition:** Copper-Nickel **Subject:** Hungarian Theatre

| Date | Mintage | F | VF | XF | Unc | BU |
|---|---|---|---|---|---|---|
| 1990 | 5,000 | — | — | — | 12.00 | — |
| 1990 Proof | 5,000 | Value: 12.00 | | | | |

**100 FORINT (Szaz)** KM# 682 **Composition:** Copper-Nickel-Zinc **Subject:** Papal Visit

| Date | Mintage | F | VF | XF | Unc | BU |
|---|---|---|---|---|---|---|
| 1991 | 30,000 | — | — | — | 3.00 | — |
| 1991 Proof | 30,000 | Value: 6.00 | | | | |

**100 FORINT (Szaz)** KM# 698 **Composition:** Brass

| Date | Mintage | F | VF | XF | Unc | BU |
|---|---|---|---|---|---|---|
| 1992 | 2,000 | — | — | — | 12.00 | — |
| 1992 Proof | 1,000 | Value: 15.00 | | | | |
| 1993 | 925,000 | — | — | — | 3.00 | — |
| 1993 Proof | 30,000 | Value: 6.00 | | | | |
| 1994 | 7,861,000 | — | — | — | 2.50 | — |
| 1994 Proof | 15,000 | Value: 6.00 | | | | |
| 1995 | 27,485,000 | — | — | — | 2.50 | — |
| 1995 Proof | 15,000 | Value: 6.00 | | | | |
| 1996 | 6,210,000 | — | — | — | 2.50 | — |
| 1996 Proof | 10,000 | Value: 6.00 | | | | |
| 1997 | 7,000 | — | — | — | 5.00 | — |
| 1997 Proof | 3,000 | Value: 7.50 | | | | |
| 1998 | 7,000 | — | — | — | 5.00 | — |
| 1998 Proof | 3,000 | Value: 7.50 | | | | |

**100 FORINT (Szaz)** KM# 721 **Ring Composition:** Stainless Steel **Center Composition:** Brass Plated Steel **Obverse:** Crowned arms **Reverse:** Denomination in inner circle

| Date | Mintage | F | VF | XF | Unc | BU |
|---|---|---|---|---|---|---|
| 1996 | — | — | — | — | 4.50 | — |
| 1996 Proof | — | Value: 12.00 | | | | |
| 1997 | — | — | — | — | 4.50 | — |
| 1997 Proof | 3,000 | Value: 9.00 | | | | |
| 1998 | — | — | — | — | 4.50 | — |
| 1998 Proof | 3,000 | Value: 9.00 | | | | |
| 1999 | — | — | — | — | 4.50 | — |
| 1999 Proof | 3,000 | Value: 9.00 | | | | |
| 2000 | — | — | — | — | 4.50 | — |
| 2000 Proof | 3,000 | Value: 9.00 | | | | |
| 2001 | — | — | — | — | 4.50 | — |
| 2001 Proof | 3,000 | Value: 9.00 | | | | |

**100 FORINT (Szaz)** KM# 726 **Composition:** Bronze **Subject:** Revolution of 1848 **Obverse:** Hungarian Order of Military Merit (1848-1849) II Class **Reverse:** Revolutionary ribbon badge above poetry verse

| Date | Mintage | F | VF | XF | Unc | BU |
|---|---|---|---|---|---|---|
| 1998 | 15,000 | — | — | — | 7.00 | — |
| 1998 Proof | 15,000 | Value: 9.00 | | | | |

**200 FORINT** KM# 688 **Weight:** 10.0000 g. **Composition:** 0.5000 Silver .1608 oz. ASW **Reverse:** White storks

| Date | Mintage | F | VF | XF | Unc | BU |
|---|---|---|---|---|---|---|
| 1992BP | 20,000 | — | — | — | 7.00 | — |
| 1992BP Proof | 80,000 | Value: 10.00 | | | | |

**200 FORINT** KM# 689 **Weight:** 12.0000 g. **Composition:** 0.5000 Silver .1929 oz. ASW **Reverse:** National Bank

| Date | Mintage | F | VF | XF | Unc | BU |
|---|---|---|---|---|---|---|
| 1992 | 3,514,000 | — | — | — | 6.50 | — |
| 1992 Proof | 30,000 | Value: 9.00 | | | | |
| 1993 | 2,541,000 | — | — | — | 6.50 | — |
| 1993 Proof | 30,000 | Value: 9.00 | | | | |

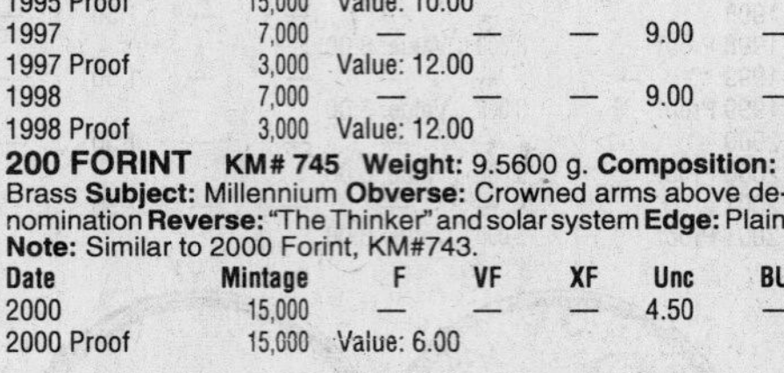


**200 FORINT** KM# 707 **Weight:** 12.0000 g. **Composition:** 0.5000 Silver .1929 oz. ASW **Reverse:** Ferenc Deak

| Date | Mintage | F | VF | XF | Unc | BU |
|---|---|---|---|---|---|---|
| 1994 | 5,000,000 | — | — | — | 7.00 | — |
| 1994 Proof | 15,000 | Value: 10.00 | | | | |
| 1995 | 85,000 | — | — | — | 8.00 | — |
| 1995 Proof | 15,000 | Value: 10.00 | | | | |
| 1997 | 7,000 | — | — | — | 9.00 | — |
| 1997 Proof | 3,000 | Value: 12.00 | | | | |
| 1998 | 7,000 | — | — | — | 9.00 | — |
| 1998 Proof | 3,000 | Value: 12.00 | | | | |

**200 FORINT** KM# 745 **Weight:** 9.5600 g. **Composition:** Brass **Subject:** Millennium **Obverse:** Crowned arms above denomination **Reverse:** "The Thinker" and solar system **Edge:** Plain **Note:** Similar to 2000 Forint, KM#743.

| Date | Mintage | F | VF | XF | Unc | BU |
|---|---|---|---|---|---|---|
| 2000 | 15,000 | — | — | — | 4.50 | — |
| 2000 Proof | 15,000 | Value: 6.00 | | | | |

**200 FORINT** KM# 754 **Weight:** 9.4000 g. **Composition:** Brass **Subject:** Childrens Literature: Ludas Matyi **Obverse:** Denomination **Reverse:** Man holding a goose **Edge:** Plain **Size:** 29.2 mm.

| Date | Mintage | F | VF | XF | Unc | BU |
|---|---|---|---|---|---|---|
| 2001 | 12,000 | — | — | — | 7.50 | — |
| 2001 Proof | 5,000 | Value: 15.00 | | | | |

**200 FORINT** KM# 755 **Composition:** Brass **Subject:** Childrens Literature: Janos Vitez **Obverse:** Denomination **Reverse:** Soldier riding a flying bird **Edge:** Plain **Size:** 29.2 mm.

| Date | Mintage | F | VF | XF | Unc | BU |
|---|---|---|---|---|---|---|
| 2001 | 12,000 | — | — | — | 7.50 | — |
| 2001 Proof | 5,000 | Value: 15.00 | | | | |

**200 FORINT** KM# 756 **Composition:** Brass **Subject:** Childrens Literature: Toldi **Obverse:** Denomination **Reverse:** Knight kicking a boat off the shore **Edge:** Plain **Size:** 29.2 mm.

| Date | Mintage | F | VF | XF | Unc | BU |
|---|---|---|---|---|---|---|
| 2001 | 12,000 | — | — | — | 7.50 | — |
| 2001 Proof | 5,000 | Value: 15.00 | | | | |

**200 FORINT** KM# 757 **Composition:** Brass **Subject:** Childrens Literature: A Pal Utcai Fiuk **Obverse:** Denomination **Reverse:** Two men and cord wood **Edge:** Plain **Size:** 29.2 mm.

| Date | Mintage | F | VF | XF | Unc | BU |
|---|---|---|---|---|---|---|
| 2001 | 12,000 | — | — | — | 7.50 | — |
| 2001 Proof | 5,000 | Value: 15.00 | | | | |

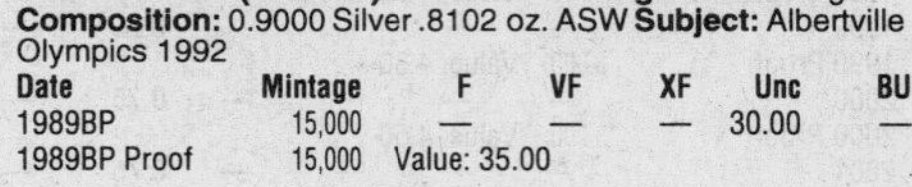

**500 FORINT (Otszaz)** KM# 672 **Weight:** 28.0000 g. **Composition:** 0.9000 Silver .8102 oz. ASW **Subject:** Albertville Olympics 1992

| Date | Mintage | F | VF | XF | Unc | BU |
|---|---|---|---|---|---|---|
| 1989BP | 15,000 | — | — | — | 30.00 | — |
| 1989BP Proof | 15,000 | Value: 35.00 | | | | |

**500 FORINT (Otszaz)** **KM# 680** **Weight:** 28.0000 g. **Composition:** 0.9000 Silver .8102 oz. ASW **Reverse:** 2 capital cities of King Mathias

| Date | Mintage | F | VF | XF | Unc | BU |
|---|---|---|---|---|---|---|
| 1990 | 15,000 | — | — | — | 35.00 | — |
| 1990 Proof | 15,000 | Value: 40.00 | | | | |

**500 FORINT (Otszaz)** **KM# 683** **Weight:** 28.0000 g. **Composition:** 0.9000 Silver .8102 oz. ASW **Subject:** Papal Visit

| Date | Mintage | F | VF | XF | Unc | BU |
|---|---|---|---|---|---|---|
| 1991 | 10,000 | — | — | — | 25.00 | — |
| 1991 Proof | 20,000 | Value: 30.00 | | | | |

**500 FORINT (Otszaz)** **KM# 690** **Weight:** 31.4600 g. **Composition:** 0.9250 Silver .9357 oz. ASW **Subject:** Telstar I satelite

| Date | Mintage | F | VF | XF | Unc | BU |
|---|---|---|---|---|---|---|
| 1992 | Est. 5,000 | — | — | — | 21.50 | — |
| 1992 Proof | Est. 15,000 | Value: 25.00 | | | | |

**500 FORINT (Otszaz)** **KM# 699** **Weight:** 28.0000 g. **Composition:** 0.9000 Silver .8102 oz. ASW **Subject:** 200th Anniversary - Birth of Kolcsey Ferenc

| Date | Mintage | F | VF | XF | Unc | BU |
|---|---|---|---|---|---|---|
| 1990 | 10,000 | — | — | — | 40.00 | — |
| 1990 Proof | 5,000 | Value: 50.00 | | | | |

**500 FORINT (Otszaz)** **KM# 685** **Weight:** 28.0000 g. **Composition:** 0.9000 Silver .8102 oz. ASW **Subject:** 200th Anniversary - Birth of Count Szechenyi

| Date | Mintage | F | VF | XF | Unc | BU |
|---|---|---|---|---|---|---|
| 1991 | 15,000 | — | — | — | 28.00 | — |
| 1991 Proof | 15,000 | Value: 35.00 | | | | |

**500 FORINT (Otszaz)** **KM# 686** **Weight:** 28.0000 g. **Composition:** 0.9000 Silver .8102 oz. ASW **Note:** Karoly Robert Emlekere

| Date | Mintage | F | VF | XF | Unc | BU |
|---|---|---|---|---|---|---|
| 1992 | 10,000 | — | — | — | 30.00 | — |
| 1992 Proof | 20,000 | Value: 27.50 | | | | |

**500 FORINT (Otszaz)** **KM# 679** **Weight:** 28.0000 g. **Composition:** 0.9000 Silver .8102 oz. ASW **Note:** King Mathias and Queen Beatrix

| Date | Mintage | F | VF | XF | Unc | BU |
|---|---|---|---|---|---|---|
| 1990 | 15,000 | — | — | — | 35.00 | — |
| 1990 Proof | 15,000 | Value: 40.00 | | | | |

**500 FORINT (Otszaz)** **KM# 687** **Weight:** 28.0000 g. **Composition:** 0.9000 Silver .8102 oz. ASW **Subject:** Canonization of King Ladislaus

| Date | Mintage | F | VF | XF | Unc | BU |
|---|---|---|---|---|---|---|
| 1992 | 10,000 | — | — | — | 22.50 | — |
| 1992 Proof | 20,000 | Value: 25.00 | | | | |

**500 FORINT (Otszaz)** **KM# 704** **Weight:** 31.4600 g. **Composition:** 0.9250 Silver .9357 oz. ASW **Note:** European Currency Union.

| Date | Mintage | F | VF | XF | Unc | BU |
|---|---|---|---|---|---|---|
| 1993 | 10,000 | — | — | — | 20.00 | — |
| 1993 Proof | 30,000 | Value: 22.50 | | | | |

**500 FORINT (Otszaz)** **KM# 702** **Weight:** 31.4600 g. **Composition:** 0.9250 Silver .9357 oz. ASW **Reverse:** Old Danube Ship "Arpad"

| Date | Mintage | F | VF | XF | Unc | BU |
|---|---|---|---|---|---|---|
| 1993 | 10,000 | — | — | — | 16.50 | — |
| 1993 Proof | 15,000 | Value: 18.00 | | | | |

**500 FORINT (Otszaz)** **KM# 705** **Weight:** 31.4600 g. **Composition:** 0.9250 Silver .9357 oz. ASW **Subject:** Expo '96

| Date | Mintage | F | VF | XF | Unc | BU |
|---|---|---|---|---|---|---|
| 1993 | 20,000 | — | — | — | 22.50 | — |
| 1993 Proof | 80,000 | Value: 28.50 | | | | |

**500 FORINT (Otszaz)** **KM# 709** **Weight:** 31.4600 g. **Composition:** 0.9250 Silver .9357 oz. ASW **Subject:** Death of Lajos Kossuth

| Date | Mintage | F | VF | XF | Unc | BU |
|---|---|---|---|---|---|---|
| 1994 | 10,000 | — | — | — | 22.50 | — |
| 1994 Proof | 10,000 | Value: 27.50 | | | | |

**500 FORINT (Otszaz)** **KM# 710** **Weight:** 31.4600 g. **Composition:** 0.9250 Silver .9357 oz. ASW **Subject:** International European Union

| Date | Mintage | F | VF | XF | Unc | BU |
|---|---|---|---|---|---|---|
| 1994 | 10,000 | — | — | — | 22.50 | — |
| 1994 Proof | 30,000 | Value: 27.50 | | | | |

**500 FORINT (Otszaz)** **KM# 708** **Weight:** 31.4600 g. **Composition:** 0.9250 Silver .9357 oz. ASW **Reverse:** Old Danube Ship "Carolina" **Note:** Old Danube Ships - Carolina

| Date | Mintage | F | VF | XF | Unc | BU |
|---|---|---|---|---|---|---|
| 1994 | 10,000 | — | — | — | 18.00 | — |
| 1994 Proof | 15,000 | Value: 20.00 | | | | |

**750 FORINT** **KM# 723** **Weight:** 10.0000 g. **Composition:** 0.5000 Silver .1607 oz. ASW **Subject:** Soccer **Obverse:** Denomination in goal **Reverse:** Ball in net above the Eiffel Tower

| Date | Mintage | F | VF | XF | Unc | BU |
|---|---|---|---|---|---|---|
| 1997 | 3,000 | — | — | — | 30.00 | — |
| 1997 Proof | 12,000 | Value: 22.50 | | | | |

**750 FORINT** **KM# 725** **Weight:** 10.0000 g. **Composition:** 0.5000 Silver .1607 oz. ASW **Subject:** 125th Anniversary - Budapest **Obverse:** Bridge **Reverse:** City map and arms

| Date | Mintage | F | VF | XF | Unc | BU |
|---|---|---|---|---|---|---|
| 1998 | 3,000 | — | — | — | 35.00 | — |
| 1998 Proof | 12,000 | Value: 25.00 | | | | |

**1000 FORINT** **KM# 706** **Weight:** 31.4600 g. **Composition:** 0.9250 Silver .9357 oz. ASW **Subject:** World Cup Soccer **Reverse:** Goalie

| Date | Mintage | F | VF | XF | Unc | BU |
|---|---|---|---|---|---|---|
| 1993BP | 10,000 | — | — | — | 22.50 | — |
| 1993BP Proof | 15,000 | Value: 27.50 | | | | |

**1000 FORINT** **KM# 712** **Weight:** 31.4600 g. **Composition:** 0.9250 Silver .9357 oz. ASW **Subject:** Atlanta Olympics **Reverse:** Swimmers

| Date | Mintage | F | VF | XF | Unc | BU |
|---|---|---|---|---|---|---|
| 1994 | 10,000 | — | — | — | 20.00 | — |
| 1994 Proof | 40,000 | Value: 23.50 | | | | |

**1000 FORINT** KM# 713 **Weight:** 31.4600 g. **Composition:** 0.9250 Silver .9357 oz. ASW **Subject:** Protect Our World **Reverse:** Globe in trunk

| Date | Mintage | F | VF | XF | Unc | BU |
|---|---|---|---|---|---|---|
| 1994 | 10,000 | — | — | — | 30.00 | — |
| 1994 Proof | 10,000 | Value: 30.00 | | | | |

**1000 FORINT** KM# 714 **Weight:** 31.4600 g. **Composition:** 0.9250 Silver .9357 oz. ASW **Reverse:** Old Danube Ship "Hableany" **Note:** Old Danube Ships - Hableany

| Date | Mintage | F | VF | XF | Unc | BU |
|---|---|---|---|---|---|---|
| 1995 | 10,000 | — | — | — | 30.00 | — |
| 1995 Proof | 20,000 | Value: 27.50 | | | | |

**2000 FORINT** KM# 717 **Weight:** 31.4600 g. **Composition:** 0.9250 Silver .9357 oz. ASW **Subject:** 50th Anniversary Forint Rebirth **Reverse:** 13-coin designs **Note:**

| Date | Mintage | F | VF | XF | Unc | BU |
|---|---|---|---|---|---|---|
| 1996 | 5,000 | — | — | — | 37.50 | — |
| 1996 Proof | 5,000 | Value: 47.50 | | | | |

**1000 FORINT** KM# 716 **Weight:** 31.4600 g. **Composition:** 0.9250 Silver .9357 oz. ASW **Subject:** Olympics **Reverse:** Fencing match

| Date | Mintage | F | VF | XF | Unc | BU |
|---|---|---|---|---|---|---|
| 1995 | 5,000 | — | — | — | 32.50 | — |
| 1995 Proof | 25,000 | Value: 30.00 | | | | |

**1000 FORINT** KM# 715 **Weight:** 31.4600 g. **Composition:** 0.9250 Silver .9357 oz. ASW **Note:** Pannonhalma Ruins

| Date | Mintage | F | VF | XF | Unc | BU |
|---|---|---|---|---|---|---|
| 1995 | 10,000 | — | — | — | 30.00 | — |
| 1995 Proof | 10,000 | Value: 37.50 | | | | |

**2000 FORINT** KM# 722 **Weight:** 31.4600 g. **Composition:** 0.9250 Silver .9357 oz. ASW **Obverse:** Lake Balaton view above denomination **Reverse:** Steam ships "Helka" and "Kelen"

| Date | Mintage | F | VF | XF | Unc | BU |
|---|---|---|---|---|---|---|
| 1997 | 5,000 | — | — | — | 38.00 | — |
| 1997 Proof | 15,000 | Value: 35.00 | | | | |

**1000 FORINT** KM# 720 **Weight:** 31.4600 g. **Composition:** 0.9250 Silver .9357 oz. ASW **Subject:** European Union **Obverse:** Crowned arms divide date **Reverse:** Hungarian Parliament building, "ecu" **Note:**

| Date | Mintage | F | VF | XF | Unc | BU |
|---|---|---|---|---|---|---|
| 1995 | 5,000 | — | — | — | 35.00 | — |
| 1995 Proof | 18,000 | Value: 40.00 | | | | |

**2000 FORINT** KM# 718 **Weight:** 31.4600 g. **Composition:** 0.9250 Silver .9357 oz. ASW **Subject:** 1100th Anniversary of Hungarian Nartionhood **Reverse:** Three equestrian archers above old shield

| Date | Mintage | F | VF | XF | Unc | BU |
|---|---|---|---|---|---|---|
| 1996 | 10,000 | — | — | — | 35.00 | — |
| 1996 Proof | 10,000 | Value: 45.00 | | | | |

**2000 FORINT** KM# 724 **Weight:** 31.1035 g. **Composition:** 0.9250 Silver .9250 oz. ASW **Subject:** European Union **Obverse:** Crowned arms divide date above denomination **Reverse:** Royal Palace of Budapest

| Date | Mintage | F | VF | XF | Unc | BU |
|---|---|---|---|---|---|---|
| 1997 | 3,000 | — | — | — | 40.00 | — |
| 1997 Proof | 27,000 | Value: 50.00 | | | | |

**2000 FORINT** **KM# 727** **Weight:** 31.4600 g. **Composition:** 0.9250 Silver .9356 oz. ASW **Subject:** Revolution of 1848 **Obverse:** Hungarian Order of Military Merit (1848-1849) I Class **Reverse:** Hungarian military flag over European map

| Date | Mintage | F | VF | XF | Unc | BU |
|---|---|---|---|---|---|---|
| 1998 | 5,000 | — | — | — | 40.00 | — |
| 1998 Proof | 10,000 | Value: 55.00 | | | | |

**2000 FORINT** **KM# 729** **Weight:** 31.4600 g. **Composition:** 0.9250 Silver .9356 oz. ASW **Subject:** UNICEF - For the Children of the World **Obverse:** UNICEF logo above denomination **Reverse:** Child's drawing of a princess

| Date | Mintage | F | VF | XF | Unc | BU |
|---|---|---|---|---|---|---|
| 1998 Proof | Est. 28,000 | Value: 45.00 | | | | |

**2000 FORINT** **KM# 730** **Weight:** 31.4600 g. **Composition:** 0.9250 Silver .9356 oz. ASW **Subject:** World Wildlife Fund **Obverse:** World Wildlife Fund logo above Hungarian arms and denomination **Reverse:** Barn swallows feeding

| Date | Mintage | F | VF | XF | Unc | BU |
|---|---|---|---|---|---|---|
| 1998 Proof | Est. 18,000 | Value: 50.00 | | | | |

**2000 FORINT** **KM# 731** **Weight:** 31.4600 g. **Composition:** 0.9250 Silver .9356 oz. ASW **Obverse:** Sailboats on Lake Balaton above denomination **Reverse:** The "Phoenix" under full sail

| Date | Mintage | F | VF | XF | Unc | BU |
|---|---|---|---|---|---|---|
| 1998 | Est. 5,000 | — | — | — | 37.50 | — |
| 1998 Proof | Est. 10,000 | Value: 32.50 | | | | |

**2000 FORINT** **KM# 732** **Weight:** 31.4600 g. **Composition:** 0.9250 Silver .9356 oz. ASW **Subject:** 150th Birthday - Lorand Eotvos **Obverse:** Denomination **Reverse:** Framed portrait and scientific instrument

| Date | Mintage | F | VF | XF | Unc | BU |
|---|---|---|---|---|---|---|
| 1998 | 3,000 | — | — | — | 35.00 | — |
| 1998 Proof | 3,000 | Value: 45.00 | | | | |

**2000 FORINT** **KM# 733** **Weight:** 31.4600 g. **Composition:** 0.9250 Silver .9356 oz. ASW **Subject:** European Union **Obverse:** National arms **Reverse:** Monuments, Euro logo

| Date | Mintage | F | VF | XF | Unc | BU |
|---|---|---|---|---|---|---|
| 1998 | 3,000 | — | — | — | 40.00 | — |
| 1998 Proof | 12,000 | Value: 50.00 | | | | |

**2000 FORINT** **KM# 743** **Weight:** 20.0000 g. **Composition:** 0.9250 Silver .5948 oz. ASW **Subject:** Millennium **Obverse:** National arms **Reverse:** "The Thinker" and solar system **Edge:** 7-sided plain

| Date | Mintage | F | VF | XF | Unc | BU |
|---|---|---|---|---|---|---|
| 1999 | — | — | — | — | 30.00 | — |
| 1999 Proof | — | Value: 35.00 | | | | |

**2000 FORINT** **KM# 744** **Weight:** 20.0000 g. **Composition:** 0.9250 Silver .5948 oz. ASW **Subject:** Olympics **Obverse:** National arms **Reverse:** Hammer throw

| Date | Mintage | F | VF | XF | Unc | BU |
|---|---|---|---|---|---|---|
| 1999 | — | — | — | — | 30.00 | — |
| 1999 Proof | — | Value: 35.00 | | | | |

**2000 FORINT** **KM# 747** **Weight:** 15.7240 g. **Composition:** 0.9250 Silver .4676 oz. ASW **Obverse:** Country name, denomination and date **Reverse:** Angel in wreath **Edge:** Reeded and plain sectioned **Note:** 19.3 x 38.4 millimeters. Koll. Saraspatak 1531.

| Date | Mintage | F | VF | XF | Unc | BU |
|---|---|---|---|---|---|---|
| 2000 | — | — | — | — | 20.00 | — |
| 2000 Proof | — | Value: 22.50 | | | | |

**2000 FORINT** **KM# 748** **Weight:** 15.7240 g. **Composition:** 0.9250 Silver .4676 oz. ASW **Obverse:** Country name, denomination and date **Reverse:** Seal and inscription **Note:** Lorantffy Zsuzsanna 1600-1660.

| Date | Mintage | F | VF | XF | Unc | BU |
|---|---|---|---|---|---|---|
| 2000 | Est. 3,000 | — | — | — | 20.00 | — |
| 2000 Proof | 3,000 | Value: 22.50 | | | | |

**3000 FORINT** **KM# 735** **Weight:** 31.4600 g. **Composition:** 0.9250 Silver .9356 oz. ASW **Subject:** European Union **Obverse:** Crowned arms above denomination **Reverse:** Statue and Euro logo

| Date | Mintage | F | VF | XF | Unc | BU |
|---|---|---|---|---|---|---|
| 1999 | 3,000 | — | — | — | 40.00 | — |
| 1999 Proof | 17,000 | Value: 50.00 | | | | |

**3000 FORINT** **KM# 741** **Weight:** 31.4600 g. **Composition:** 0.9250 Silver .9356 oz. ASW **Subject:** Hungarian Millennium **Obverse:** Crown above denomination **Reverse:** Round window design **Edge:** Plain **Note:** Gold-plated center.

| Date | Mintage | F | VF | XF | Unc | BU |
|---|---|---|---|---|---|---|
| 1999 | Est. 5,000 | — | — | — | 37.50 | — |
| 1999 Proof | 5,000 | Value: 45.00 | | | | |

**3000 FORINT** **KM# 746** **Weight:** 31.4600 g. **Composition:** 0.9250 Silver .9356 oz. ASW **Obverse:** Denomination **Reverse:** Beaver **Edge:** Reeded

| Date | Mintage | F | VF | XF | Unc | BU |
|---|---|---|---|---|---|---|
| 2000 | 3,000 | — | — | — | 40.00 | — |
| 2000 Proof | 7,000 | Value: 50.00 | | | | |

**3000 FORINT** **KM# 749** **Weight:** 31.4600 g. **Composition:** 0.9250 Silver .9356 oz. ASW **Subject:** Hologram inventor - Dennis Gabor **Obverse:** Hologram initials in center **Reverse:** Bust of Dennis Gabor right **Edge:** Reeded

| Date | Mintage | F | VF | XF | Unc | BU |
|---|---|---|---|---|---|---|
| 2000 | Est. 3,000 | — | — | — | 45.00 | — |
| 2000 Proof | 3,000 | Value: 55.00 | | | | |

**3000 FORINT** **KM# 750** **Weight:** 31.4600 g. **Composition:** 0.9250 Silver .9356 oz. ASW **Subject:** 125th Anniversary - Franz Liszt Music Academy **Obverse:** 1/2-length Franz Liszt right **Reverse:** Academy entrance **Edge:** Reeded

| Date | Mintage | F | VF | XF | Unc | BU |
|---|---|---|---|---|---|---|
| 2000 | Est. 3,000 | — | — | — | 45.00 | — |
| 2000 Proof | 3,000 | Value: 55.00 | | | | |

**3000 FORINT** **KM# 752** **Weight:** 31.4600 g. **Composition:** 0.9250 Silver .9356 oz. ASW **Subject:** Hungarian Silver Coinage Millennium **Obverse:** Denomination in ornamental frame **Reverse:** Thaler design circa 1500 portaying Ladislaus I (1077-95) with the title of saint **Edge:** Reeding over "1001-2001" **Edge Lettering:** "BP.NX.KB.HX.GY.F.AF.MM.C+" **Size:** 238.5 mm.

| Date | Mintage | F | VF | XF | Unc | BU |
|---|---|---|---|---|---|---|
| 2001 | 5,000 | — | — | — | 32.50 | — |
| 2001 Proof | 5,000 | Value: 37.50 | | | | |

**3000 FORINT** **KM# 759** **Weight:** 31.8000 g. **Composition:** 0.9250 Silver .9457 oz. ASW **Subject:** Centennial of First Hungarian Film "The Dance" **Obverse:** Denomination in ornamental frame **Reverse:** Two dancers on film **Edge:** Reeded **Size:** 38.7 mm.

| Date | Mintage | F | VF | XF | Unc | BU |
|---|---|---|---|---|---|---|
| 2001 | 3,500 | — | — | — | 40.00 | — |
| 2001 Proof | 3,500 | Value: 50.00 | | | | |

**4000 FORINT** **KM# 751** **Weight:** 31.4600 g. **Composition:** 0.9250 Silver .9356 oz. ASW **Subject:** Godollo Artist Colony Centennial **Obverse:** Denomination **Reverse:** "Sisters" stained glass window design **Edge:** Plain **Size:** 26.4x39.6 mm.

| Date | Mintage | F | VF | XF | Unc | BU |
|---|---|---|---|---|---|---|
| 2001 | 4,000 | — | — | — | 35.00 | — |
| 2001 Proof | 4,000 | Value: 45.00 | | | | |

**5000 FORINT** **KM# 681** **Weight:** 6.9820 g. **Composition:** 0.9860 Gold .2213 oz. AGW **Subject:** 500th Anniversary - Death of Mathias I

| Date | Mintage | F | VF | XF | Unc | BU |
|---|---|---|---|---|---|---|
| 1990BP Proof | 10,000 | Value: 145 | | | | |

**5000 FORINT** **KM# 711** **Weight:** 7.7700 g. **Composition:** 0.5840 Gold .1459 oz. AGW **Reverse:** Great Bustard Bird

| Date | Mintage | F | VF | XF | Unc | BU |
|---|---|---|---|---|---|---|
| 1994 Proof | 5,000 | Value: 115 | | | | |

**10000 FORINT (Tizezer)** **KM# 684** **Weight:** 6.9820 g. **Composition:** 0.9860 Gold .2213 oz. AGW **Subject:** Papal visit

| Date | Mintage | F | VF | XF | Unc | BU |
|---|---|---|---|---|---|---|
| 1991BP Proof | 10,000 | Value: 165 | | | | |

**10000 FORINT (Tizezer)** **KM# 691** **Weight:** 6.9820 g. **Composition:** 0.9860 Gold .2213 oz. AGW **Subject:** 650th Anniversary - Death of Charles Robert

| Date | Mintage | F | VF | XF | Unc | BU |
|---|---|---|---|---|---|---|
| 1992 Proof | 10,000 | Value: 145 | | | | |

**10000 FORINT (Tizezer)** **KM# 703** **Weight:** 6.9820 g. **Composition:** 0.9860 Gold .2213 oz. AGW **Subject:** Centennial - Death of Ferenc Erkel

| Date | Mintage | F | VF | XF | Unc | BU |
|---|---|---|---|---|---|---|
| 1993 Proof | 5,000 | Value: 150 | | | | |

**20000 FORINT** **KM# 719** **Weight:** 6.9820 g. **Composition:** 0.9860 Gold .2213 oz. AGW **Subject:** 1100th Anniversary of Hungarian Nationhood **Reverse:** Two equestrian archers

| Date | Mintage | F | VF | XF | Unc | BU |
|---|---|---|---|---|---|---|
| 1996 Proof | 5,000 | Value: 225 | | | | |

**20000 FORINT** KM# 728 **Weight:** 6.9820 g. **Composition:** 0.9860 Gold .2213 oz. AGW **Subject:** Revolution of 1848 **Obverse:** Hungarian Order of Military Merit III Class **Reverse:** Portrait of Lajos Batthyany

| Date | Mintage | F | VF | XF | Unc | BU |
|---|---|---|---|---|---|---|
| 1998 Proof | Est. 5,000 | Value: 245 | | | | |

**20000 FORINT** KM# 742 **Weight:** 6.9820 g. **Composition:** 0.9860 Gold .2213 oz. AGW **Subject:** Hungarian State Millennium **Obverse:** Portrait of St. Michael the Archangel **Reverse:** Crown **Edge:** Plain

| Date | Mintage | F | VF | XF | Unc | BU |
|---|---|---|---|---|---|---|
| 1999 Proof | Est. 3,000 | — | — | — | 230 | — |

**20000 FORINT** KM# 753 **Weight:** 6.9820 g. **Composition:** 0.9860 Gold .2213 oz. AGW **Subject:** Hungarian Coinage Millennium **Obverse:** Denomination **Reverse:** Hammered coinage minting scene above old coin design **Edge:** Plain **Size:** 22 mm.

| Date | Mintage | F | VF | XF | Unc | BU |
|---|---|---|---|---|---|---|
| 2001 Proof | 3,000 | Value: 200 | | | | |

**100000 FORINT** KM# 758 **Weight:** 31.1040 g. **Composition:** 0.9860 Gold .9860 oz. AGW **Subject:** Saint Stephen **Obverse:** Angels crowning coat of arms **Reverse:** King seated on throne **Edge:** Reeded **Size:** 37 mm.

| Date | Mintage | F | VF | XF | Unc | BU |
|---|---|---|---|---|---|---|
| 2001 | — | — | — | — | 400 | — |
| 2001 Proof | 3,000 | Value: 550 | | | | |

## TRANSITIONAL COINAGE

**FORINT** KM# 736 **Composition:** Aluminum **Note:** Similar to Forint, KM#575. Communist design type with New Republic legends.

| Date | Mintage | F | VF | XF | Unc | BU |
|---|---|---|---|---|---|---|
| 1990 | 10,000 | — | — | — | 10.00 | — |

## PATTERNS

Including off metal strikes

| KM# | Date | Mintage | Identification | Mkt Val |
|---|---|---|---|---|
| Pn126 | 1910 | — | 2 Korona. Lead. KM#493. | — |
| Pn127 | 1913 | — | 2 Korona. Aluminum. KM#493. | — |
| Pn128 | 1914 | — | Filler. Steel. KM#480. | — |

| KM# | Date | Mintage | Identification | Mkt Val |
|---|---|---|---|---|
| Pn129 | 1914 | — | 10 Filler. Silver. KM#482. | 800 |
| Pn130 | 1914 | — | 2 Korona. Aluminum. KM#493. | — |
| Pn131 | 1915 | — | 2 Filler. New Silver. KM#481 | 130 |
| Pn134 | 1915 | — | 20 Filler. Iron. KM#498. | 250 |
| Pn136 | 1915 | — | 20 Filler. Silver. KM#483. | 1,000 |
| Pn137 | 1915 | — | 1/2 Korona. Silver. Franz Joseph I bust right. Value in wreath. | 1,000 |
| Pn132 | 1915 | — | 10 Filler. Nickel. KM#494. | — |
| Pn133 | 1915 | — | 10 Filler. Nickel. KM#496. | — |
| Pn135 | 1915 | — | 20 Filler. Iron. Circle around crown. | — |
| Pn138 | 1916 | — | 2 Heller. Lead. One side. | — |
| Pn140 | 1916 | — | 2 Filler. Iron. 2 in square. | — |
| Pn141 | 1916 | — | 2 Filler. Iron. Circle around crown. | — |
| Pn142 | ND(1916) | — | 2 Filler. Lead. Ornaments around 2, without legend. | — |
| Pn143 | 1916 | — | 10 Filler. Iron. KM#496 | — |
| Pn144 | 1916 | — | 20 Filler. Lead. KM#498. | — |
| Pn139 | 1916 | — | 2 Filler. Iron. KM#481 | 350 |
| Pn145 | 1917 | — | 20 Filler. Zinc. | — |
| Pn146 | 1917 | — | 2 Filler. Steel. With rosette. | — |
| Pn147 | 1917 | — | 10 Filler. Iron. Crown above sceptor and wsord. Value between wheat. | — |
| Pn148 | 1917 | — | 10 Filler. Zinc. | — |
| Pn149 | 1917 | — | 10 Filler. New Silver. | — |
| Pn150 | 1918 | — | 2 Filler. Aluminum. KM#497 | — |
| Pn151 | 1918 | — | 50 Filler. Iron. Large crown. | — |
| Pn152 | 1918 | — | 50 Filler. Lead. | — |
| Pn153 | ND | — | 10 Korona. Silver. | — |
| Pn154 | ND | 3 | 10 Korona. Bronze. | — |
| Pn155 | 1922 | — | 20 Filler. Bronze. | — |
| Pn156 | 1922 | — | 20 Filler. New Silver. | — |
| Pn157 | 1922 | — | 20 Filler. Nickel. | — |
| Pn158 | 1922 | — | 5 Korona. Aluminum. | — |

| KM# | Date | Mintage | Identification | Mkt Val |
|---|---|---|---|---|
| Pn159 | 1922 | — | 5 Korona. Brass. | — |
| Pn160 | 1926 | — | 10 Filler. Lead. KM#507 | — |
| Pn161 | 1927 | — | 10 Pengo. Brass. Fr#100 | — |
| Pn162 | 1927 | — | 10 Pengo. Gold. | — |
| Pn163 | 1927 | — | 20 Pengo. Brass. Denomination in grape-wheat ear wreath. Fr#99. | — |
| Pn164 | 1927 | — | 20 Pengo. Brass. Denomination in wreath. Fr#99. | — |
| Pn165 | 1927 | — | 20 Pengo. Gold. Denomination in grape-wheat ear wreath. | — |
| Pn166 | 1927 | — | 20 Pengo. Gold. Denomination in laurel wreath. | 2,500 |

| KM# | Date | Mintage | Identification | Mkt Val |
|---|---|---|---|---|
| Pn167 | 1928 | — | 10 Pengo. Gold. Fr#100 | 2,500 |

| KM# | Date | Mintage | Identification | Mkt Val |
|---|---|---|---|---|
| Pn169 | 1928 | — | 20 Pengo. Gold. Fr#99. | 2,500 |
| Pn168 | 1928 | — | 20 Pengo. Brass. Smaller arms. Fr#99a. | — |
| Pn170 | 1929 | — | 5 Pengo. Lead. | — |
| Pn171 | 1929 | — | 5 Pengo. Silver. | — |
| Pn172 | 1929 | — | 20 Pengo. Gold. Fr#99a. | 2,500 |
| Pn173 | 1930 | — | 5 Pengo. Y#44 | — |
| Pn174 | 1935 | — | 2 Filler. Nickel. KM#506. | — |
| Pn175 | 1935 | — | 2 Pengo. | — |
| Pn176 | 1938 | — | 50 Filler. Aluminum. KM#509. | — |
| Pn177 | 1939 | — | Filler. Aluminum. KM#505. | — |
| Pn178 | 1940 | — | Filler. Iron. KM#505. | — |
| Pn179 | 1940 | — | 10 Filler. Lead. KM#507. | — |
| Pn180 | 1941 | — | 50 Filler. Iron. KM#509. | — |
| Pn181 | 1943 | — | 2 Filler. Aluminum. KM#519. | — |

## PIEFORTS

| KM# | Date | Mintage | Identification | Mkt Val |
|---|---|---|---|---|
| P22 | 1979 | 2,500 | 200 Forint. Silver. 0.6400 g. KM#615 | 65.00 |
| P23 | 1979 | 2,500 | 200 Forint. Silver. 0.6400 g. KM#616 | 35.00 |
| P24 | 1980 | 3,000 | 100 Forint. KM#617 | 30.00 |
| P25 | 1980 | 3,000 | 200 Forint. Silver. 0.6400 g. KM#618 | 30.00 |
| P26 | 1980 | 1,500 | 500 Forint. Silver. 0.6400 g. KM#619 | 125 |

## PROBA

| KM# | Date | Mintage | Identification | Mkt Val |
|---|---|---|---|---|
| Pr1 | 1986 | — | 500 Forint. Silver. KM#656. Soccer players. | 325 |

| KM# | Date | Mintage | Identification | Mkt Val |
|---|---|---|---|---|
| Pr2 | 1986 | — | 500 Forint. Silver. KM#657. Stadium. | 325 |
| Pr3 | 1988 | — | 100 Forint. Copper-Nickel. KM#664. Soccer players. | — |

| KM# | Date | Mintage | Identification | Mkt Val |
|---|---|---|---|---|
| Pr4 | 1988 | — | 100 Forint. Copper-Nickel. KM#665. Soccer goalie in net. | — |
| Pr5 | 1989 | — | 100 Forint. Copper-Nickel. KM#668. Soccer players shaking hands. | — |

## TRIAL STRIKES

| KM# | Date | Mintage | Identification | Mkt Val |
|---|---|---|---|---|
| TS39 | 1907 | — | 100 Korona. Bronze. KM#491. | — |
| TS40 | 1907 | — | 100 Korona. Bronze. KM#490. Without legend. | — |
| TS41 | 1910 | — | 2 Korona. Lead. KM#493. | — |
| TS42 | 1913 | — | 2 Korona. Aluminum. KM#493. | — |
| TS43 | 1914 | — | Filler. Iron. KM#480. | — |
| TS44 | 1914 | — | 2 Filler. Nickel. KM#481. | — |
| TS45 | 1914 | — | 10 Filler. Copper-Zinc. KM#482. | — |
| TS46 | 1914 | — | 10 Filler. Silver Plated Copper-Nickel-Zinc. | — |
| TS47 | 1914 | — | 10 Filler. Silver. KM#482. | — |
| TS48 | 1914 | — | 20 Filler. Iron. KM#483. | — |
| TS49 | 1914 | — | 2 Korona. Aluminum. KM#493. | — |
| TS50 | 1914 | — | 2 Korona. Bronze. KM#486. | — |
| TS51 | 1915 | — | 2 Filler. Iron. KM#481. | — |
| TS52 | 1915 | — | 10 Filler. Nickel. KM#496. | — |
| TS53 | 1915 | — | 20 Filler. Silver. KM#483. | 1,200 |
| TS55 | 1916 | — | 1/2 Korona. Silver. | 1,200 |
| TS54 | 1916 | — | 20 Filler. Lead. KM#498. | — |
| TS56 | 1917 | — | 10 Filler. Lead. | — |
| TS57 | 1917 | — | 10 Filler. Zinc. | — |
| TS58 | 1917 | — | 10 Filler. Copper-Nickel-Zinc. | — |
| TS59 | 1918 | — | 50 Filler. Lead. | — |
| TS60 | 1918 | — | 20 Korona. Lead. KM#486. | — |
| TS61 | 1920 | — | 10 Filler. Copper-Nickel-Zinc. KM#496. | — |
| TS62 | 1922 | — | 20 Filler. Nickel. KM#498. | — |
| TS63 | 1922 | — | 20 Filler. Bronze. KM#498. | — |
| TS64 | 1922 | — | 20 Filler. Brass. KM#498. | — |
| TS65 | 1922 | — | 20 Filler. Copper-Nickel-Zinc. KM#498. | — |
| TS66 | 1930 | — | 5 Pengo. Lead. Obverse only, KM#512. | — |
| TS67 | 1930 | — | 5 Pengo. Lead. Reverse only, KM#512. | — |
| TS68 | 1935 | — | 2 Filler. Nickel. KM#506 | — |
| TS69 | 1935 | — | 2 Pengo. Lead. Reverse only, KM#514. | — |
| TS70 | 1936 | — | 2 Pengo. Lead. Obverse only, KM#515. | — |
| TS71 | 1938 | — | 5 Pengo. Copper-Zinc. KM#517. | — |
| TS72 | 1938 | — | 5 Pengo. Copper-Zinc. KM#516. | — |
| TS73 | 1938 | — | 5 Pengo. Lead. Obverse only, KM#516. | — |
| TS74 | 1938 | — | 5 Pengo. Lead. Reverse only, KM#516. | — |
| TS75 | 1939 | — | Filler. Aluminum. KM#505. | — |
| TS76 | 1939 | — | 50 Filler. Aluminum. KM#509. | — |
| TS77 | 1941 | — | 50 Filler. Iron. KM#509. | — |
| TS78 | 1943 | — | 2 Filler. Aluminum. KM#519. | — |
| TS79 | 1943 | — | 5 Pengo. Copper-Zinc. KM#523. | — |

## MINT SETS

| KM# | Date | Mintage | Identification | Issue Price | Mkt Val |
|---|---|---|---|---|---|
| MS-A1 | 1956 (3) | — | KM#552, 553, 554 | — | 55.00 |
| MS1 | 1971 (9) | — | KM#546, 549, 572-575, 591, 594, 595 | — | 5.00 |
| MS2 | 1972 (9) | — | KM#546, 549, 572-575, 591, 594, 595 | — | 5.00 |
| MS3 | 1973 (9) | — | KM#546, 549, 572-575, 591, 594, 595 | — | 5.00 |
| MS4 | 1974 (9) | — | KM#546, 549, 572-575, 591, 594, 595 | — | 5.00 |
| MS5 | 1975 (9) | — | KM#546, 549, 572-575, 591, 594, 595 | — | 5.00 |
| MS6 | 1976 (9) | — | KM#546, 549, 572-575, 591, 594, 595 | — | 5.00 |
| MS7 | 1977 (9) | — | KM#546, 549, 572-575, 591, 594, 595 | — | 5.00 |
| MSA7 | 1977 (3) | — | KM#610-612 | — | 35.00 |
| MS8 | 1978 (9) | — | KM#546, 549, 572-575, 591, 594, 595 | — | 5.00 |
| MS9 | 1979 (9) | — | KM#546, 549, 572-575, 591, 594, 595 | — | 5.00 |
| MS10 | 1980 (9) | — | KM#546, 549, 572-575, 591, 594, 595 | — | 5.00 |
| MS11 | 1981 (9) | — | KM#546, 549, 572-575, 591, 594, 620 | — | 5.00 |
| MS12 | 1982 (9) | — | KM#546, 549, 572-575, 591, 594, 595 | — | 5.00 |
| MS13 | 1983 (10) | — | KM#546, 549, 572-575, 591, 630, 635, 636 | — | 5.50 |
| MSA13 | 1983 (3) | — | KM#627, 628, 629 | — | 10.00 |
| MS14 | 1984 (10) | — | KM#546, 549, 572-575, 591, 630, 635, 636 | — | 5.50 |
| MS15 | 1985 (10) | — | KM#546, 549, 572-575, 591, 630, 635, 636 | — | 5.50 |
| MS16 | 1986 (10) | — | KM#546, 549, 572-575, 591, 630, 635, 636 | — | 5.50 |
| MS17 | 1987 (10) | — | KM#546, 549, 572-575, 591, 630, 635, 636 | — | 5.50 |
| MS18 | 1988 (10) | — | KM#546, 549, 572-575, 591, 630, 635, 636 | — | 5.50 |
| MS19 | 1989 (10) | — | KM#546, 549, 572-575, 591, 630, 635, 636 | — | 5.50 |
| MS20 | 1990 (5) | — | KM673-677 | — | 5.00 |
| MS21 | 1991 (5) | — | KM673-677 | — | 7.00 |
| MS22 | 1992 (8) | — | KM689, 692-698 | — | 30.00 |
| MSA22 | 1992 (5) | — | KM673-677 | — | 9.00 |
| MS23 | 1993 (11) | — | KM675-677, 689, 692-698 | — | 20.00 |
| MS24 | 1994 (11) | — | KM675-677, 692-698, 707 | — | 18.00 |
| MS25 | 1995 (10) | — | KM675-677, 692-698 | — | 10.00 |
| MS26 | 1995 (11) | — | KM675-677, 692-698, 707 | 17.50 | 20.00 |
| MS27 | 1996 (10) | — | KM675-677, 692-698 | — | 10.00 |
| MS28 | 1997 (10) | 7,000 | KM677, 692-698, 707, 721 | 18.50 | 20.00 |
| MS29 | 1998 (11) | — | KM677, 692-698, 707, 721, 726 | 22.50 | 30.00 |
| MS30 | 1999 (8) | — | KM677, 692-697, 721 | — | 17.50 |
| MS31 | 2000 (8) | — | KM692-697, 721, 745 | — | 17.50 |

## PROOF SETS

| KM# | Date | Mintage | Identification | Issue Price | Mkt Val |
|---|---|---|---|---|---|
| PSA1 | 1948 (3) | — | KM537-539 | 70.00 | 70.00 |
| PS1 | 1961 (6) | 2,500 | KM560, 562-566 | — | 2,100 |
| PS2 | 1961 (4) | — | KM557-559, 561 | — | 80.00 |
| PS3 | 1966 (8) | 2,000 | KM534b, 546a, 547a, 549a-551a, 555a, 556b | 15.00 | 48.00 |
| PS4 | 1966 (3) | 330 | KM569-571 | 430 | 2,675 |
| PS5 | 1966 (2) | 11,000 | KM567-568 | 7.50 | 45.00 |
| PS6 | 1967 (8) | 5,000 | KM534b, 546a, 547a, 549a-551a, 555a, 556b | 15.00 | 55.00 |
| PS7 | 1967 (2) | 500 | KM580, 581 | — | 2,250 |
| PS8 | 1968 (5) | 7,000 | KM583, 585-588 | — | 2,850 |
| PS9 | 1968 (2) | 4,750 | KM582, 584 | 35.00 | 30.00 |
| PS10 | 1969 (2) | 3,000 | KM589, 590 | 35.00 | 30.00 |
| PS11 | 1970 (2) | 4,000 | KM592, 593 | 25.00 | 25.00 |
| PS12 | 1972 (2) | 6,000 | KM596, 597 | 25.00 | 32.50 |
| PS13 | 1973 (2) | 6,000 | KM599, 600 | — | 27.50 |
| PS14 | 1974 (2) | — | KM601, 603 | — | 25.00 |
| PS15 | 1976 (3) | 5,000 | KM607-609 | — | 50.00 |
| PS16 | 1977 (3) | — | KM610-612 | — | 50.00 |
| PS17 | 1992 (8) | 1,000 | KM689, 692-698 | — | 80.00 |
| PS18 | 1993 (8) | — | KM 689, 692-698 | — | 47.50 |
| PSA19 | 1993/4 (2) | — | KM704, 710 | — | 52.50 |
| PS19 | 1994 (8) | — | KM692-698, 707 | — | 47.50 |
| PS20 | 1995 (8) | — | KM692-698, 707 | 24.50 | 47.50 |
| PS21 | 1997 (8) | 3,000 | KM692-698, 707, 721 | 29.50 | 55.00 |
| PS22 | 1998 (3) | 5,000 | KM726-728 | 267 | 270 |
| PS24 | 1999 (2) | — | KM741, 742 | 239 | 265 |
| PS23 | 1999 (7) | — | KM692-697, 721 | — | 37.50 |
| PS25 | 2000 (8) | — | KM692-697, 721, 745 | — | 42.50 |

## SPECIMEN SETS (SS)

| KM# | Date | Mintage | Identification | Issue Price | Mkt Val |
|---|---|---|---|---|---|
| SS1 | 1977 (9) | — | KM546, 549, 572-575, 591, 594-595 | — | 10.00 |
| SS2 | 1978 (9) | — | KM546, 549, 572-575, 591, 594-595 | — | 10.00 |
| SS3 | 1979 (9) | — | KM546, 549, 572-575, 591, 594-595 | — | 10.00 |
| SS4 | 1981 (9) | — | KM546, 549, 572-575, 591, 594, 620 | — | 10.00 |
| SS5 | 1989 (10) | — | KM546, 549, 572-575, 591, 630, 635, 636 | — | 9.00 |

# ICELAND

The Republic of Iceland, an island of recent volcanic origin in the North Atlantic east of Greenland and immediately south of the Arctic Circle, has an area of 39,768sq. mi. (103,000 sq. km.) and a population of 275,264. Capital: Reykjavik. Fishing is the chief industry and accounts for more than 70 percent of the exports.

Iceland was settled by Norwegians in the 9th century and established as an independent republic in 930. The Icelandic assembly called the Althingi', also established in 930, is the oldest parliament in the world. Iceland came under Norwegian sovereignty in 1262, and passed to Denmark when Norway and Denmark were united under the Danish crown in 1380. In 1918 it was established as a virtually independent kingdom in union with Denmark. On June 17, 1944, while Denmark was still under occupation by troops of the Third Reich, Iceland was established by plebiscite as an independent republic.

**RULERS**
Christian X, 1912-1944

**MINT MARKS**
Heart (h) - Copenhagen

**MINTMASTERS INITIALS**
HCN - Hans Christian Nielsen, 1919-1927
(for Iceland, 1922-1926)
N - Niels Peter Nielsen, 1927-1955
(for Iceland, 1929-1940)

**MONEYERS INITIALS**
GJ - Knud Gunnar Jensen, 1901-1933

**MONETARY SYSTEM**
100 Aurar = 1 Krona

## KINGDOM

### DECIMAL COINAGE

**EYRIR KM# 5.1 Composition:** Bronze

| Date | Mintage | F | VF | XF | Unc | BU |
|---|---|---|---|---|---|---|
| 1926(h) HCN-GJ | 405,000 | 1.50 | 3.00 | 7.50 | 28.50 | — |
| 1931(h) N-GJ | 462,000 | 1.00 | 2.50 | 6.00 | 26.00 | — |
| 1937(h) N-GJ Wide date | 211,000 | 2.00 | 4.00 | 8.00 | 32.00 | — |
| 1938(h) N-GJ | 279,000 | 1.00 | 2.00 | 4.00 | 13.50 | — |
| 1938(h) N-GJ Large 3 over small 3 | — | 1.00 | 2.00 | 3.50 | 12.50 | — |
| 1939(h) N-GJ Large 3 | 305,000 | 1.00 | 2.00 | 3.50 | 12.50 | — |
| 1939(h) N-GJ Small 3 | Inc. above | 1.00 | 2.00 | 3.50 | 12.50 | — |

**EYRIR KM# 5.2 Composition:** Bronze

| Date | Mintage | F | VF | XF | Unc | BU |
|---|---|---|---|---|---|---|
| 1940 | 1,000,000 | 0.25 | 0.50 | 1.00 | 2.50 | — |
| 1940 Proof | — | Value: 225 | | | | |
| 1942 | 2,000,000 | 0.25 | 0.40 | 0.75 | 2.00 | — |

**2 AURAR KM# 6.1 Composition:** Bronze **Note:** Varieties exist in the appearance of the numeral 8 in 1938 dated coins. As the die slowly deteriorated, "globs" were added to the upper loop and later to the lower loop.

| Date | Mintage | F | VF | XF | Unc | BU |
|---|---|---|---|---|---|---|
| 1926(h) HCN-GJ | 498,000 | 1.50 | 3.00 | 8.00 | 32.00 | — |
| 1931(h) N-GJ | 446,000 | 1.00 | 2.50 | 7.00 | 26.50 | — |
| 1938(h) N-GJ | 206,000 | 6.00 | 12.00 | 17.50 | 42.50 | — |
| 1940(h) N-GJ | 257,000 | 5.00 | 10.00 | 15.00 | 33.50 | — |

**2 AURAR KM# 6.2 Composition:** Bronze

| Date | Mintage | F | VF | XF | Unc | BU |
|---|---|---|---|---|---|---|
| 1940 | 1,000,000 | 0.40 | 0.75 | 1.50 | 3.00 | — |
| 1940 Proof | — | Value: 265 | | | | |
| 1942 | 2,000,000 | 0.20 | 0.50 | 1.00 | 2.00 | — |

**5 AURAR KM# 7.1 Composition:** Bronze

| Date | Mintage | F | VF | XF | Unc | BU |
|---|---|---|---|---|---|---|
| 1926(h) HCN-GJ | 355,000 | 5.00 | 10.00 | 25.00 | 72.50 | — |
| 1931(h) N-GJ | 311,000 | 5.00 | 10.00 | 25.00 | 72.50 | — |

**5 AURAR KM# 7.2 Composition:** Bronze

| Date | Mintage | F | VF | XF | Unc | BU |
|---|---|---|---|---|---|---|
| 1940 | 1,000,000 | 0.60 | 1.25 | 2.50 | 5.00 | — |
| 1940 Proof | — | Value: 285 | | | | |
| 1942 | 2,000,000 | 0.35 | 0.85 | 1.50 | 3.00 | — |

**10 AURAR KM# 1.1 Composition:** Copper-Nickel

| Date | Mintage | F | VF | XF | Unc | BU |
|---|---|---|---|---|---|---|
| 1922(h) HCN GJ | 300,000 | 2.00 | 3.50 | 7.00 | 36.50 | — |
| 1923(h) HCN GJ | 302,000 | 3.00 | 4.50 | 9.00 | 40.00 | — |
| 1925(h) HCN GJ | 321,000 | 15.00 | 25.00 | 40.00 | 90.00 | — |
| 1929(h) N-GJ | 176,000 | 15.00 | 25.00 | 45.00 | 95.00 | — |
| 1933(h) N-GJ | 157,000 | 10.00 | 20.00 | 30.00 | 75.00 | — |
| 1936(h) | 213,000 | 3.00 | 6.00 | 10.00 | 35.00 | — |
| 1939/6(h) N-GJ | 208,000 | 5.00 | 10.00 | 15.00 | 42.50 | — |
| 1939(h) N-GJ | Inc. above | 4.00 | 8.00 | 12.00 | 32.50 | — |

**10 AURAR KM# 1.2 Composition:** Copper-Nickel

| Date | Mintage | F | VF | XF | Unc | BU |
|---|---|---|---|---|---|---|
| 1940 | 1,500,000 | 0.35 | 0.75 | 1.50 | 4.50 | — |
| 1940 Proof | — | Value: 225 | | | | |

**10 AURAR KM# 1a Composition:** Zinc

| Date | Mintage | F | VF | XF | Unc | BU |
|---|---|---|---|---|---|---|
| 1942 | 2,000,000 | 1.50 | 3.00 | 6.00 | 28.50 | — |
| 1942 Prooflike | — | — | — | — | — | — |

**25 AURAR KM# 2.1 Composition:** Copper-Nickel

| Date | Mintage | F | VF | XF | Unc | BU |
|---|---|---|---|---|---|---|
| 1922(h) HCN GJ | 300,000 | 1.00 | 2.50 | 4.00 | 32.50 | — |
| 1923(h) HCN GJ | 304,000 | 1.00 | 2.50 | 4.00 | 32.50 | — |
| 1925(h) HCN GJ | 207,000 | 2.50 | 4.50 | 10.00 | 42.50 | — |
| 1933(h) N-GJ | 104,000 | 10.00 | 15.00 | 25.00 | 85.00 | — |
| 1937(h) N-GJ Near 7 | 201,000 | 3.00 | 5.00 | 9.00 | 40.00 | — |
| 1937(h) N-GJ Far 7 | Inc. above | 3.00 | 5.00 | 9.00 | 40.00 | — |

**25 AURAR KM# 2.2 Composition:** Copper-Nickel

| Date | Mintage | F | VF | XF | Unc | BU |
|---|---|---|---|---|---|---|
| 1940 | 1,500,000 | 0.25 | 0.50 | 1.00 | 2.50 | — |
| 1940 Proof | — | Value: 245 | | | | |

**25 AURAR KM# 2a Composition:** Zinc

| Date | Mintage | F | VF | XF | Unc | BU |
|---|---|---|---|---|---|---|
| 1942 | 2,000,000 | 1.00 | 2.50 | 5.00 | 26.50 | — |
| 1942 Prooflike | — | — | — | — | — | — |

**KRONA KM# 3.1 Composition:** Aluminum-Bronze

| Date | Mintage | F | VF | XF | Unc | BU |
|---|---|---|---|---|---|---|
| 1925(h) HCN GJ | 252,000 | 3.00 | 6.00 | 25.00 | 155 | — |
| 1929(h) N-GJ | 154,000 | 5.00 | 10.00 | 32.00 | 180 | — |
| 1940(h) N-GJ | 209,000 | 1.50 | 2.50 | 5.00 | 15.00 | — |

**KRONA KM# 3.2 Composition:** Aluminum-Bronze

| Date | Mintage | F | VF | XF | Unc | BU |
|---|---|---|---|---|---|---|
| 1940 | 715,000 | 1.00 | 2.00 | 4.00 | 10.00 | — |
| 1940 Proof; rare | — | — | — | — | — | — |

**2 KRONUR KM# 4.1 Composition:** Aluminum-Bronze

| Date | Mintage | F | VF | XF | Unc | BU |
|---|---|---|---|---|---|---|
| 1925(h) HCN GJ | 126,000 | 7.50 | 12.50 | 40.00 | 185 | — |
| 1929(h) N-GJ | 77,000 | 10.00 | 20.00 | 65.00 | 285 | — |

**2 KRONUR KM# 4.2 Composition:** Aluminum-Bronze

| Date | Mintage | F | VF | XF | Unc | BU |
|---|---|---|---|---|---|---|
| 1940 | 546,000 | 0.75 | 1.50 | 3.50 | 10.00 | — |
| 1940 Proof; rare | — | — | — | — | — | — |

### MEDALLIC COINAGE

**2 KRONUR KM# M1 Composition:** Bronze **Subject:** 1000 Years Althing **Obv. Designer:** BB - Baldvin Bjornsson **Rev. Designer:** TM - Tryggvi Magnusson **Note:** Struck privately by the Saxon State Mint, Muldenhutten, Germany, at the instigation of a Parliamentary committee.

| Date | Mintage | F | VF | XF | Unc | BU |
|---|---|---|---|---|---|---|
| 1930 | 20,000 | — | 20.00 | 30.00 | 50.00 | — |

**5 KRONUR** **KM# M2** **Composition:** Silver **Subject:** 1000 Years Althing **Obv. Designer:** BB - Baldvin Bjornsson **Rev. Designer:** GE - Gudmundur Einarsson **Note:** Struck privately by the Saxon State Mint, Muldenhutten, Germany, at the instigation of a Parliamentary committee.

| Date | Mintage | F | VF | XF | Unc | BU |
|---|---|---|---|---|---|---|
| 1930 | 10,000 | — | 45.00 | 60.00 | 100 | — |

**10 KRONUR** **KM# M3** **Composition:** Silver **Subject:** 1000 Years Althing **Obv. Designer:** EJ - Einar Jonsson **Rev. Designer:** BB - Baldvin Bjornsson **Note:** FH stands for Friedrich Hornlein, the engraver. Struck privately by the Saxon State Mint, Muldenhutten, Germany, at the instigation of a Parliamentary committee.

| Date | Mintage | F | VF | XF | Unc | BU |
|---|---|---|---|---|---|---|
| 1930 FH | 10,000 | — | 60.00 | 100 | 175 | — |

## TOKEN COINAGE

Under the Scandinavian Monetary Convention of 1873, the coinage of Denmark, Norway, and Sweden could circulate with validity in Iceland. Despite the various options for exchange, very few coins appear to have made their way to Iceland. As a result, Icelandic merchants resorted to manufacturing their own tokens. While some bare the crudeness of a homemade token, others had been elaborately struck by such well known manufacturers as L. Chr. Lauer of Nurnberg, who most likely had N. Chr. Hansen and Co., Copenhagen as an agent.

Merchants posting inflated token prices alongside legal coinage prices on goods for sale led to the 1901 law which prohibited the manufacture and usage of private coinage, ending the token era which started in the mid 1800s.

NOTE: There are at least four different types of tokens for this time period. Only Type I tokens are cataloged here.

TYPE I: Tokens with stated values; first in shillings, later in kronur and aurar.

TYPE II: Bread Tokens, used to barter for prearranged quantities of goods or labor.

TYPE III: Advertising or Address Tokens.

TYPE IV: Miscellaneous Tokens.

**10 AURAR** **KM# Tn12** **Weight:** 1.7000 g. **Composition:** Brass **Issuer:** P.J. Thorsteinsson, Bildudal **Note:** Similar to 100 Aurar, KM#Tn21. Struck by L. Chr. Lauer of Nurnberg.

| Date | Mintage | VG | F | VF | XF | Unc |
|---|---|---|---|---|---|---|
| ND(1901) | — | 12.00 | 25.00 | 50.00 | 110 | — |

**25 AURAR** **KM# Tn15** **Weight:** 1.7000 g. **Composition:** Brass **Issuer:** P.J. Thorsteinsson, Bildudal **Note:** Similar to 100 Aurar, KM#Tn21. Struck by L. Chr. Lauer of Nurnberg.

| Date | Mintage | VG | F | VF | XF | Unc |
|---|---|---|---|---|---|---|
| ND(1901) | — | 6.00 | 12.00 | 25.00 | 55.00 | — |

**50 AURAR** **KM# Tn18** **Weight:** 2.2000 g. **Composition:** Brass **Issuer:** P.J. Thorsteinsson, Bildudal **Note:** Similar to 100 Aurar, KM#Tn21. Struck by L. Chr. Lauer of Nurnberg.

| Date | Mintage | VG | F | VF | XF | Unc |
|---|---|---|---|---|---|---|
| ND(1901) | — | 6.00 | 12.00 | 25.00 | 55.00 | — |

**100 AURAR** **KM# Tn21** **Weight:** 1.1000 g. **Composition:** Aluminum **Issuer:** P.J. Thorsteinsson, Bildudal **Note:** Struck by L. Chr. Lauer of Nurnberg.

| Date | Mintage | VG | F | VF | XF | Unc |
|---|---|---|---|---|---|---|
| ND(1901) Rare | — | — | — | — | — | — |

**500 AURAR** **KM# Tn22** **Weight:** 1.1000 g. **Composition:** Aluminum **Issuer:** P.J. Thorsteinsson, Bildudal **Note:** Similar to 100 Aurar, KM#Tn21. Struck by L. Chr. Lauer of Nurnberg.

| Date | Mintage | VG | F | VF | XF | Unc |
|---|---|---|---|---|---|---|
| ND(1901) | — | 7.00 | 15.00 | 30.00 | 65.00 | — |

**10 ORE** **KM# Tn3** **Composition:** Bronze **Issuer:** N. Chr. Gram., Thingeyri **Note:** Similar to 25 Ore, KM#Tn4.

| Date | Mintage | VG | F | VF | XF | Unc |
|---|---|---|---|---|---|---|
| ND(1902) Rare | — | — | — | — | — | — |

**25 ORE** **KM# Tn4** **Composition:** Bronze **Issuer:** N. Chr. Gram., Thingeyri

| Date | Mintage | VG | F | VF | XF | Unc |
|---|---|---|---|---|---|---|
| ND(1902) Rare | — | — | — | — | — | — |

**50 ORE** **KM# Tn23** **Composition:** Bronze **Issuer:** N. Chr. Gram., Thingeyri **Note:** Similar to 25 Ore, KM#Tn4.

| Date | Mintage | VG | F | VF | XF | Unc |
|---|---|---|---|---|---|---|
| ND(1902) Rare | — | — | — | — | — | — |

## REPUBLIC
### DECIMAL COINAGE

**EYRIR** **KM# 8** **Composition:** Bronze **Note:** Values for the 1953-59 proof issues are for impaired proofs. Brilliant proofs may bring 3 to 4 times these figures.

| Date | Mintage | F | VF | XF | Unc | BU |
|---|---|---|---|---|---|---|
| 1946 | 4,000,000 | 0.10 | 0.15 | 0.50 | 1.00 | — |
| 1946 Proof | — | Value: 250 | | | | |
| 1953 | 4,000,000 | 0.10 | 0.15 | 0.40 | 0.75 | — |
| 1953 Proof | — | Value: 65.00 | | | | |
| 1956 | 2,000,000 | 0.10 | 0.15 | 0.40 | 0.75 | — |
| 1956 Proof | — | Value: 65.00 | | | | |
| 1957 | 2,000,000 | 0.10 | 0.15 | 0.40 | 0.75 | — |
| 1957 Proof | — | Value: 65.00 | | | | |
| 1958 | 2,000,000 | 0.10 | 0.15 | 0.40 | 0.75 | — |
| 1958 Proof | — | Value: 65.00 | | | | |
| 1959 | 1,600,000 | 0.10 | 0.15 | 0.40 | 0.75 | — |
| 1959 Proof | — | Value: 65.00 | | | | |
| 1966 | 1,000,000 | 0.10 | 0.15 | 0.40 | 0.75 | — |
| 1966 Proof | 15,000 | Value: 3.25 | | | | |

**5 AURAR** **KM# 9** **Composition:** Bronze **Note:** Values for the 1958-63 proof issues are for impaired proofs. Brilliant proofs may bring 3 to 4 times these figures.

| Date | Mintage | F | VF | XF | Unc | BU |
|---|---|---|---|---|---|---|
| 1946 | 4,000,000 | 0.10 | 0.25 | 0.50 | 1.25 | — |
| 1946 Proof | — | Value: 400 | | | | |
| 1958 | 400,000 | 0.50 | 2.00 | 3.50 | 5.00 | — |
| 1958 Proof | — | Value: 100 | | | | |
| 1959 | 600,000 | 0.50 | 2.00 | 3.00 | 4.50 | — |
| 1959 Proof | — | Value: 100 | | | | |
| 1960 | 1,200,000 | 0.15 | 0.40 | 1.00 | 1.75 | — |
| 1960 Proof | — | Value: 100 | | | | |
| 1961 | 1,200,000 | 0.15 | 0.40 | 1.00 | 1.75 | — |
| 1961 Proof | — | Value: 100 | | | | |
| 1963 | 1,200,000 | 0.10 | 0.30 | 0.75 | 1.50 | — |
| 1963 Proof | — | Value: 100 | | | | |
| 1965 | 800,000 | 0.10 | 0.20 | 0.50 | 1.00 | — |
| 1966 | 1,000,000 | 0.10 | 0.20 | 0.50 | 1.00 | — |
| 1966 Proof | 15,000 | Value: 3.25 | | | | |

**10 AURAR** **KM# 10** **Composition:** Copper-Nickel **Note:** Values for the 1953-63 proof issues are for impaired proofs. Brilliant proofs may bring 3 to 4 times these figures.

| Date | Mintage | F | VF | XF | Unc | BU |
|---|---|---|---|---|---|---|
| 1946 | 4,000,000 | — | 0.10 | 0.20 | 0.60 | — |
| 1946 Proof | — | Value: 400 | | | | |
| 1953 | 4,000,000 | — | 0.10 | 0.20 | 0.50 | — |
| 1953 Proof | — | Value: 65.00 | | | | |
| 1957 | 1,200,000 | 0.25 | 0.75 | 2.00 | 5.00 | — |
| 1957 Proof | — | Value: 65.00 | | | | |
| 1958 | 500,000 | 0.20 | 0.50 | 1.00 | 2.00 | — |
| 1958 Proof | — | Value: 65.00 | | | | |
| 1959 | 3,000,000 | 0.20 | 0.50 | 1.50 | 4.00 | — |
| 1959 Proof | — | Value: 65.00 | | | | |
| 1960 | 1,000,000 | 0.10 | 0.20 | 0.40 | 1.00 | — |
| 1960 Proof | — | Value: 65.00 | | | | |
| 1961 | 2,000,000 | — | — | 0.10 | 0.30 | — |
| 1961 Proof | — | Value: 65.00 | | | | |
| 1962 | 3,000,000 | — | — | 0.10 | 0.20 | — |
| 1962 Proof | — | Value: 65.00 | | | | |
| 1963 | 4,000,000 | — | — | 0.10 | 0.20 | — |
| 1963 Proof | — | Value: 65.00 | | | | |
| 1965 | 2,000,000 | — | — | 0.10 | 0.20 | — |
| 1966 | 4,000,000 | — | — | 0.10 | 0.20 | — |
| 1967 | 2,000,000 | — | — | 0.10 | 0.20 | — |
| 1969 Coarse edge reeding | 3,200,000 | — | — | 0.10 | 0.20 | — |
| 1969 Fine edge reeding | Inc. above | — | — | 0.10 | 0.20 | — |

**10 AURAR** **KM# 10a** **Composition:** Aluminum

| Date | Mintage | F | VF | XF | Unc | BU |
|---|---|---|---|---|---|---|
| 1970 | 4,800,000 | — | — | 0.10 | 0.20 | — |
| 1971 | 11,200,000 | — | — | 0.10 | 0.20 | — |
| 1973 | 4,800,000 | — | — | 0.10 | 0.20 | — |
| 1974 | 4,800,000 | — | — | 0.10 | 0.20 | — |
| 1974 Proof | 15,000 | Value: 3.25 | | | | |

**25 AURAR** **KM# 11** **Composition:** Copper-Nickel **Note:** Values for the 1951-63 proof issues are for impaired proofs. Brilliant proofs may bring 3 to 4 times these figures.

| Date | Mintage | F | VF | XF | Unc | BU |
|---|---|---|---|---|---|---|
| 1946 | 2,000,000 | 0.10 | 0.15 | 0.35 | 1.25 | — |
| 1946 Proof | — | Value: 400 | | | | |
| 1951 | 2,000,000 | 0.10 | 0.15 | 0.35 | 0.75 | — |
| 1951 Proof | — | Value: 75.00 | | | | |
| 1954 | 2,000,000 | 0.10 | 0.15 | 0.35 | 0.75 | — |
| 1954 Proof | — | Value: 75.00 | | | | |
| 1957 | 1,000,000 | 0.20 | 0.50 | 1.50 | 3.50 | — |
| 1957 Proof | — | Value: 75.00 | | | | |
| 1958 | 500,000 | 0.20 | 0.40 | 0.60 | 1.00 | — |
| 1958 Proof | — | Value: 75.00 | | | | |
| 1959 | 2,000,000 | 0.20 | 0.50 | 1.50 | 3.00 | — |
| 1959 Proof | — | Value: 75.00 | | | | |
| 1960 | 1,000,000 | — | — | 0.10 | 0.30 | — |
| 1960 Proof | — | Value: 75.00 | | | | |
| 1961 | 1,200,000 | — | — | 0.10 | 0.30 | — |
| 1961 Proof | — | Value: 75.00 | | | | |
| 1962 | 2,000,000 | — | — | 0.10 | 0.25 | — |
| 1962 Proof | — | Value: 75.00 | | | | |
| 1963 | 3,000,000 | — | — | 0.10 | 0.25 | — |
| 1963 Proof | — | Value: 75.00 | | | | |
| 1965 | 4,000,000 | — | — | 0.10 | 0.25 | — |
| 1966 | 2,000,000 | — | — | 0.10 | 0.25 | — |
| 1967 | 3,000,000 | — | — | 0.10 | 0.25 | — |
| 1967 Proof | 15,000 | Value: 3.25 | | | | |

**50 AURAR** **KM# 17** **Composition:** Nickel-Brass

| Date | Mintage | F | VF | XF | Unc | BU |
|---|---|---|---|---|---|---|
| 1969 | 1,000,000 | — | — | 0.10 | 0.30 | — |
| 1970 | 2,000,000 | — | — | 0.10 | 0.30 | — |
| 1971 | 2,000,000 | — | — | 0.10 | 0.30 | — |
| 1973 | 1,000,000 | — | — | 0.10 | 0.30 | — |
| 1974 | 2,000,000 | — | — | 0.10 | 0.30 | — |
| 1974 Proof | 15,000 | Value: 3.25 | | | | |

**KRONA** KM# 12 **Composition:** Aluminum-Bronze

| Date | Mintage | F | VF | XF | Unc | BU |
|---|---|---|---|---|---|---|
| 1946 | 2,175,000 | — | 0.10 | 0.40 | 1.50 | — |
| 1946 Proof | — | Value: 400 | | | | |

**KRONA** KM# 12a **Composition:** Nickel-Brass **Note:** Values for the 1957-63 proof issues are for impaired proofs. Brilliant proofs may bring 3 to 4 times these figures.

| Date | Mintage | F | VF | XF | Unc | BU |
|---|---|---|---|---|---|---|
| 1957 | 1,000,000 | 0.10 | 0.15 | 0.40 | 1.50 | — |
| 1957 Proof | — | Value: 85.00 | | | | |
| 1959 | 500,000 | 0.10 | 0.20 | 0.75 | 2.00 | — |
| 1959 Proof | — | Value: 85.00 | | | | |
| 1961 | 500,000 | 0.10 | 0.20 | 0.75 | 2.00 | — |
| 1961 Proof | — | Value: 85.00 | | | | |
| 1962 | 1,000,000 | 0.10 | 0.15 | 0.20 | 0.60 | — |
| 1962 Proof | — | Value: 85.00 | | | | |
| 1963 | 1,500,000 | — | 0.10 | 0.15 | 0.50 | — |
| 1963 Proof | — | Value: 85.00 | | | | |
| 1965 | 2,000,000 | — | — | 0.10 | 0.50 | — |
| 1966 | 2,000,000 | — | — | 0.10 | 0.50 | — |
| 1969 | 2,000,000 | — | — | 0.10 | 0.25 | — |
| 1970 | 3,000,000 | — | — | 0.10 | 0.25 | — |
| 1971 | 2,500,000 | — | — | 0.10 | 0.25 | — |

| Date | Mintage | F | VF | XF | Unc | BU |
|---|---|---|---|---|---|---|
| 1973 Large round knob 3 | 2,500,000 | — | — | 0.10 | 0.50 | — |
| 1973 Thin, sharp end 3 | 3,500,000 | — | — | 0.10 | 0.25 | — |
| 1974 | 5,000,000 | — | — | 0.10 | 0.25 | — |
| 1975 | 10,500,000 | — | — | 0.10 | 0.25 | — |
| 1975 Proof | 15,000 | Value: 3.25 | | | | |

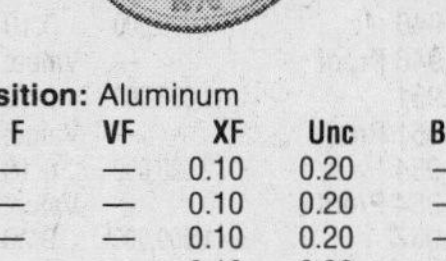

**KRONA** KM# 23 **Composition:** Aluminum

| Date | Mintage | F | VF | XF | Unc | BU |
|---|---|---|---|---|---|---|
| 1976 | 10,000,000 | — | — | 0.10 | 0.20 | — |
| 1977 | 10,000,000 | — | — | 0.10 | 0.20 | — |
| 1978 | 13,000,000 | — | — | 0.10 | 0.20 | — |
| 1980 | 7,225,000 | — | — | 0.10 | 0.20 | — |
| 1980 Proof | 15,000 | Value: 3.25 | | | | |

**2 KRONUR** KM# 13 **Composition:** Aluminum-Bronze **Note:** Republic

| Date | Mintage | F | VF | XF | Unc | BU |
|---|---|---|---|---|---|---|
| 1946 | 1,086,000 | 0.20 | 0.40 | 0.80 | 3.50 | — |
| 1946 Proof | — | Value: 450 | | | | |

**2 KRONUR** KM# 13a.1 **Composition:** Nickel-Brass **Note:** Values for the 1958-63 proof issues are for impaired proofs. Brilliant proofs may bring 3 to 4 times these figures.

| Date | Mintage | F | VF | XF | Unc | BU |
|---|---|---|---|---|---|---|
| 1958 | 500,000 | 0.20 | 0.50 | 1.00 | 3.00 | — |
| 1958 Proof | — | Value: 115 | | | | |
| 1962 | 500,000 | 0.20 | 0.50 | 1.00 | 3.00 | — |
| 1962 Proof | — | Value: 115 | | | | |
| 1963 | 750,000 | 0.15 | 0.30 | 0.60 | 2.00 | — |
| 1963 Proof | — | Value: 115 | | | | |
| 1966 | 1,000,000 | 0.10 | 0.20 | 0.40 | 1.50 | — |
| 1966 Proof | 15,000 | Value: 3.25 | | | | |

**2 KRONUR** KM# 13a.2 **Weight:** 11.5000 g. **Composition:** Nickel-Brass **Note:** Thick planchet.

| Date | Mintage | F | VF | XF | Unc | BU |
|---|---|---|---|---|---|---|
| 1966 | 300 | — | — | 325 | 400 | — |

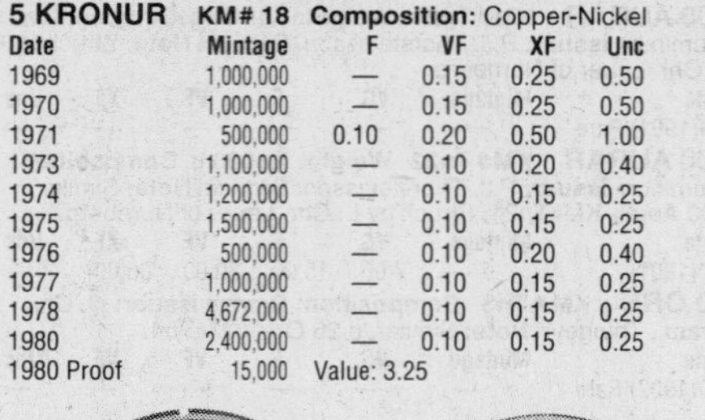

**5 KRONUR** KM# 18 **Composition:** Copper-Nickel

| Date | Mintage | F | VF | XF | Unc | BU |
|---|---|---|---|---|---|---|
| 1969 | 1,000,000 | — | 0.15 | 0.25 | 0.50 | — |
| 1970 | 1,000,000 | — | 0.15 | 0.25 | 0.50 | — |
| 1971 | 500,000 | 0.10 | 0.20 | 0.50 | 1.00 | — |
| 1973 | 1,100,000 | — | 0.10 | 0.20 | 0.40 | — |
| 1974 | 1,200,000 | — | 0.10 | 0.15 | 0.25 | — |
| 1975 | 1,500,000 | — | 0.10 | 0.15 | 0.25 | — |
| 1976 | 500,000 | — | 0.10 | 0.20 | 0.40 | — |
| 1977 | 1,000,000 | — | 0.10 | 0.15 | 0.25 | — |
| 1978 | 4,672,000 | — | 0.10 | 0.15 | 0.25 | — |
| 1980 | 2,400,000 | — | 0.10 | 0.15 | 0.25 | — |
| 1980 Proof | 15,000 | Value: 3.25 | | | | |

**10 KRONUR** KM# 15 **Composition:** Copper-Nickel

| Date | Mintage | F | VF | XF | Unc | BU |
|---|---|---|---|---|---|---|
| 1967 | 1,000,000 | 0.15 | 0.25 | 0.50 | 1.50 | — |
| 1969 | 500,000 | 0.15 | 0.30 | 0.75 | 2.00 | — |
| 1970 | 1,000,000 | — | 0.15 | 0.30 | 0.75 | — |
| 1971 | 1,500,000 | — | 0.15 | 0.30 | 0.75 | — |
| 1973 | 1,500,000 | — | 0.15 | 0.30 | 0.75 | — |
| 1974 | 2,000,000 | — | 0.10 | 0.25 | 0.60 | — |
| 1975 | 2,500,000 | — | 0.10 | 0.25 | 0.60 | — |
| 1976 | 2,500,000 | — | 0.10 | 0.25 | 0.60 | — |
| 1977 | 2,000,000 | — | 0.10 | 0.25 | 0.60 | — |
| 1978 | 10,500,000 | — | 0.10 | 0.25 | 0.60 | — |
| 1980 | 4,600,000 | — | 0.10 | 0.25 | 0.60 | — |
| 1980 Proof | 15,000 | Value: 3.25 | | | | |

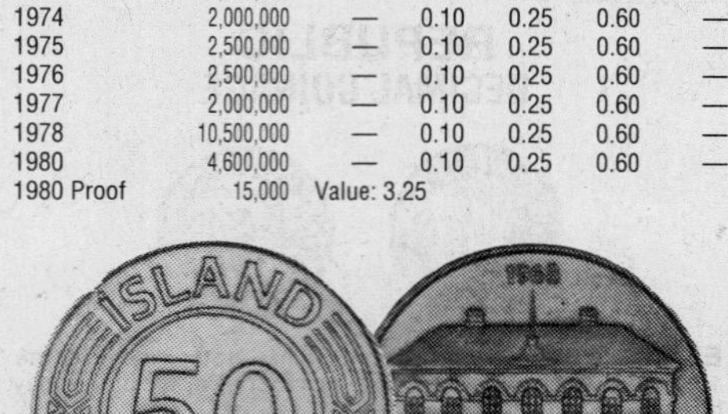

**50 KRONUR** KM# 16 **Composition:** Nickel **Subject:** 50th Anniversary of Sovereignty

| Date | Mintage | F | VF | XF | Unc | BU |
|---|---|---|---|---|---|---|
| 1968 | 100,000 | 1.50 | 2.50 | 4.00 | 7.00 | — |

**50 KRONUR** KM# 19 **Composition:** Copper-Nickel **Reverse:** Parliament building

| Date | Mintage | F | VF | XF | Unc | BU |
|---|---|---|---|---|---|---|
| 1970 | 800,000 | 0.25 | 0.50 | 1.00 | 2.00 | — |
| 1971 | 500,000 | 0.25 | 0.50 | 1.00 | 2.50 | — |
| 1973 | 50,000 | 1.00 | 1.50 | 2.50 | 4.00 | — |
| 1974 | 200,000 | 0.25 | 0.50 | 1.00 | 2.00 | — |
| 1975 | 500,000 | 0.20 | 0.35 | 0.75 | 1.50 | — |
| 1976 | 500,000 | 0.20 | 0.35 | 0.75 | 1.50 | — |
| 1977 | 200,000 | 0.20 | 0.35 | 0.75 | 1.50 | — |
| 1978 | 2,040,000 | 0.20 | 0.35 | 0.50 | 1.00 | — |
| 1980 | 1,500,000 | 0.20 | 0.35 | 0.50 | 1.00 | — |
| 1980 Proof | 15,000 | Value: 3.25 | | | | |

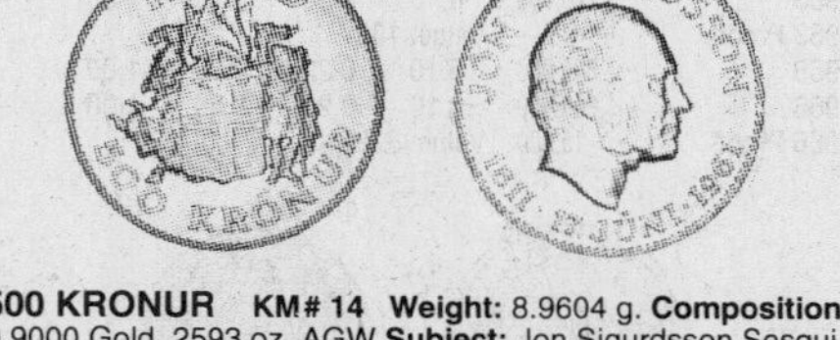

**500 KRONUR** KM# 14 **Weight:** 8.9604 g. **Composition:** 0.9000 Gold .2593 oz. AGW **Subject:** Jon Sigurdsson Sesquicentennial

| Date | Mintage | F | VF | XF | Unc | BU |
|---|---|---|---|---|---|---|
| ND(1961) | 10,000 | — | — | — | 150 | — |
| ND(1961) Proof | — | Value: 775 | | | | |

**500 KRONUR** KM# 20 **Weight:** 20.0000 g. **Composition:** 0.9250 Silver .5968 oz. ASW **Subject:** 1100th Anniversary - 1st Settlement

| Date | Mintage | F | VF | XF | Unc | BU |
|---|---|---|---|---|---|---|
| ND(1974) | 70,000 | — | — | — | 8.50 | — |
| ND(1974) Proof | Est. 58,000 | Value: 12.50 | | | | |

**Note:** 17,000 proof coins were remelted

**1000 KRONUR** KM# 21 **Weight:** 30.0000 g. **Composition:** 0.9250 Silver .8923 oz. ASW **Subject:** 1100th Anniversary - 1st Settlement

| Date | Mintage | F | VF | XF | Unc | BU |
|---|---|---|---|---|---|---|
| ND(1974) | 70,000 | — | — | — | 12.50 | — |
| ND(1974) Proof | Est. 58,000 | Value: 17.50 | | | | |

**Note:** 17,000 proof coins were remelted

**10000 KRONUR** KM# 22 **Weight:** 15.5000 g. **Composition:** 0.9000 Gold .4485 oz. AGW **Subject:** 1100th Anniversary - 1st Settlement

| Date | Mintage | F | VF | XF | Unc | BU |
|---|---|---|---|---|---|---|
| ND(1974) | 12,000 | — | — | — | 200 | — |
| ND(1974) Proof | 8,000 | Value: 260 | | | | |

## REFORM COINAGE

100 Old Kronur = 1 New Krona

**5 AURAR** KM# 24 **Composition:** Bronze **Note:** Skate

| Date | Mintage | F | VF | XF | Unc | BU |
|---|---|---|---|---|---|---|
| 1981 | 15,000,000 | — | — | — | 0.25 | — |
| 1981 Proof | 15,000 | Value: 3.50 | | | | |

**10 AURAR** KM# 25 **Composition:** Bronze **Note:** Cuttle-fish

| Date | Mintage | F | VF | XF | Unc | BU |
|---|---|---|---|---|---|---|
| 1981 | 50,000,000 | — | — | — | 0.25 | — |
| 1981 Proof | 15,000 | Value: 5.00 | | | | |

**50 AURAR** KM# 26 **Composition:** Bronze **Note:** Shrimp

| Date | Mintage | F | VF | XF | Unc | BU |
|---|---|---|---|---|---|---|
| 1981 | 10,000,000 | — | — | 0.10 | 0.35 | — |
| 1981 Proof | 15,000 | Value: 6.00 | | | | |

**50 AURAR** KM# 26a **Composition:** Bronze Coated Steel

| Date | Mintage | F | VF | XF | Unc | BU |
|---|---|---|---|---|---|---|
| 1986 | 2,000,000 | — | — | — | 0.30 | — |

**KRONA** KM# 27 **Composition:** Copper-Nickel **Note:** Cod

| Date | Mintage | F | VF | XF | Unc | BU |
|---|---|---|---|---|---|---|
| 1981 | 18,000,000 | — | — | 0.15 | 0.50 | — |
| 1981 Proof | 15,000 | Value: 8.00 | | | | |
| 1984 | 7,000,000 | — | — | 0.15 | 0.50 | — |
| 1987 | 7,500,000 | — | — | 0.15 | 0.50 | — |

**KRONA** KM# 27a **Composition:** Nickel Coated Steel

| Date | Mintage | F | VF | XF | Unc | BU |
|---|---|---|---|---|---|---|
| 1989 | 5,000,000 | — | — | — | 0.50 | — |
| 1991 | 5,180,000 | — | — | — | 0.50 | — |
| 1992 | 5,000,000 | — | — | — | 0.50 | — |
| 1994 | 5,000,000 | — | — | — | 0.50 | — |
| 1996 | 6,000,000 | — | — | — | 0.50 | — |
| 1999 | 5,000,000 | — | — | — | 0.50 | — |
| 2000 | 10,000 | — | — | — | 1.00 | — |

**5 KRONUR** KM# 28 **Composition:** Copper-Nickel **Obverse:** Four national icons **Reverse:** Two dolphins, denomination

| Date | Mintage | F | VF | XF | Unc | BU |
|---|---|---|---|---|---|---|
| 1981 | 4,350,000 | — | — | 0.25 | 1.25 | — |
| 1981 Proof | 15,000 | Value: 10.00 | | | | |
| 1984 | 1,000,000 | — | — | 0.25 | 1.25 | — |
| 1987 | 3,000,000 | — | — | 0.25 | 1.25 | — |
| 1992 | 2,000,000 | — | — | 0.25 | 1.25 | — |

**5 KRONUR** KM# 28a **Composition:** Nickel Clad Steel

| Date | Mintage | F | VF | XF | Unc | BU |
|---|---|---|---|---|---|---|
| 1996 | 1,500,000 | — | — | — | 1.25 | — |
| 1999 | 2,000,000 | — | — | — | 1.25 | — |
| 2000 | 10,000 | — | — | — | 1.50 | — |

**10 KRONUR** KM# 29.1 **Composition:** Copper-Nickel **Obverse:** Four national icons **Reverse:** Four capelins, denomination **Edge:** Reeded

| Date | Mintage | F | VF | XF | Unc | BU |
|---|---|---|---|---|---|---|
| 1984 | 10,000,000 | — | — | 0.35 | 1.50 | — |
| 1987 | 7,500,000 | — | — | 0.35 | 1.50 | — |
| 1994 | 2,500,000 | — | — | 0.35 | 1.50 | — |

**10 KRONUR** KM# 29.2 **Composition:** Nickel Clad Steel **Note:** Security edge. (Struck on flan of Indian Rupee in error.)

| Date | Mintage | F | VF | XF | Unc | BU |
|---|---|---|---|---|---|---|
| 1984 | Inc. above | — | — | — | 85.00 | — |

**10 KRONUR** KM# 29.1a **Composition:** Nickel Clad Steel

| Date | Mintage | F | VF | XF | Unc | BU |
|---|---|---|---|---|---|---|
| 1996 | 4,000,000 | — | — | — | 1.50 | — |
| 2000 | 10,000 | — | — | — | 2.00 | — |

**50 KRONUR** KM# 31 **Composition:** Copper-Zinc-Nickel **Note:** Crab

| Date | Mintage | F | VF | XF | Unc | BU |
|---|---|---|---|---|---|---|
| 1987 | 4,000,000 | — | — | — | 3.25 | — |
| 1992 | 2,000,000 | — | — | — | 3.25 | — |
| 2000 | 10,000 | — | — | — | 4.00 | — |
| 2001 | 2,000,000 | — | — | — | 3.25 | — |

**100 KRONUR** KM# 35 **Composition:** Nickel-Brass **Note:** Lumpfish

| Date | Mintage | F | VF | XF | Unc | BU |
|---|---|---|---|---|---|---|
| 1995 | 6,000,000 | — | — | — | 5.00 | — |
| 2000 | 10,000 | — | — | — | 6.00 | — |
| 2001 | 2,140,000 | — | — | — | 5.00 | — |

**500 KRONUR** KM# 30 **Weight:** 20.0000 g. **Composition:** 0.5000 Silver .3215 oz. ASW **Subject:** 100th Anniversary of Icelandic Banknotes

| Date | Mintage | F | VF | XF | Unc | BU |
|---|---|---|---|---|---|---|
| ND(1986) | 15,000 | — | — | — | 45.00 | — |

**500 KRONUR** KM# 30a **Weight:** 20.0000 g. **Composition:** 0.9250 Silver .5968 oz. ASW

| Date | Mintage | F | VF | XF | Unc | BU |
|---|---|---|---|---|---|---|
| ND(1986) Proof | 5,000 | Value: 65.00 | | | | |

**1000 KRONUR** KM# 32 **Weight:** 30.0000 g. **Composition:** 0.9250 Silver .8922 oz. ASW **Subject:** 50th Anniversary of Icelandic Republic **Obverse:** Arms **Reverse:** Head of Sveinn Bjornsson left **Note:** In sets only.

| Date | Mintage | F | VF | XF | Unc | BU |
|---|---|---|---|---|---|---|
| ND(1994) | 6,000 | — | — | — | 55.00 | — |
| ND(1994) Proof | 3,000 | Value: 82.50 | | | | |

**1000 KRONUR** KM# 33 **Weight:** 30.0000 g. **Composition:** 0.9250 Silver .8922 oz. ASW **Obverse:** Arms **Reverse:** Head of Asgeir Asgeirsson left **Note:** In sets only.

| Date | Mintage | F | VF | XF | Unc | BU |
|---|---|---|---|---|---|---|
| ND(1994) | 6,000 | — | — | — | 55.00 | — |
| ND(1994) Proof | 3,000 | Value: 82.50 | | | | |

**1000 KRONUR** KM# 34 **Weight:** 30.0000 g. **Composition:** 0.9250 Silver .8922 oz. ASW **Obverse:** Arms **Reverse:** Head of Kristjan Eldjarn left **Note:** In sets only.

| Date | Mintage | F | VF | XF | Unc | BU |
|---|---|---|---|---|---|---|
| ND(1994) | 6,000 | — | — | — | 55.00 | — |
| ND(1994) Proof | 3,000 | Value: 82.50 | | | | |

**10000 KRONUR** KM# 36 **Weight:** 8.6500 g. **Composition:** 0.9000 Gold .2503 oz. AGW **Subject:** 1000 Years of Christianity **Obverse:** National arms **Reverse:** Old crosier top

| Date | Mintage | F | VF | XF | Unc | BU |
|---|---|---|---|---|---|---|
| ND(2000) Proof | 3,000 | Value: 225 | | | | |

**10000 KRONUR** KM# 37 **Weight:** 27.7300 g. **Composition:** 0.9000 Silver .7720 oz. ASW **Subject:** Lief Ericson Millennium

| Date | Mintage | F | VF | XF | Unc | BU |
|---|---|---|---|---|---|---|
| 2000 Proof | 150,000 | — | — | — | 55.00 | — |

## MINT SETS

| KM# | Date | Mintage | Identification | Issue Price | Mkt Val |
|---|---|---|---|---|---|
| MS1 | 1930 (3) | 10,000 | KM#M1-M3 | — | 350 |
| MS2 | 1970 (6) | — | KM#10a, 12a, 15, 17-19 | — | 11.50 |
| MS3 | 1971 (6) | — | KM#10a, 12a, 15, 17-19 | — | 10.00 |
| MS4 | 1973 (6) | — | KM#10a, 12a (knob 3), 15, 17-19 | 3.25 | 9.00 |
| MS5 | 1974 (6) | — | KM#10a, 12a, 15, 17-19 | 3.25 | 7.50 |
| MS6 | 1974 (2) | 70,000 | KM#20-21 | 30.00 | 20.00 |
| MS7 | 1975 (4) | — | KM#12a, 15, 18-19 | — | 5.50 |
| MS8 | 1976 (4) | — | KM#15, 18-19, 23 | — | 5.50 |
| MS9 | 1977 (4) | — | KM#15, 18-19, 23 | — | 5.50 |
| MS10 | 1978 (4) | — | KM#15, 18-19, 23 | — | 5.50 |
| MS11 | 1980 (4) | — | KM#15, 18-19, 23 | — | 5.50 |
| MS12 | 1981 (5) | — | KM#24-28 | — | 5.50 |
| MS13 | 1981-1996 (8) | — | 1981: KM#24-25; 1986: KM#26a; 1992: KM#31; 1995: KM#35; 1996: KM#27a, 28a, 29.1a | — | 12.50 |
| MS14 | 1994 (3) | 6,000 | KM#32-34 | 110 | 165 |
| MS15 | 2000 (5) | 10,000 | KM#27a, 28a, 29.1a, 31, 35 | — | 14.50 |

## PROOF SETS

| KM# | Date | Mintage | Identification | Issue Price | Mkt Val |
|---|---|---|---|---|---|
| PS1 | 1974 (3) | 8,000 | KM#20-22 | 272 | 300 |
| PS2 | 1974 (2) | 58,000 | KM#20-21 | 38.00 | 32.00 |
| PS3 | 1966-1980 (11) | 15,000 | 1966: KM#8-9, 13a.1; 1967: KM#11; 1974: KM#10a, 17; 1975: KM#12a; 1980: KM#15, 18-19, 23 | 40.00 | 37.50 |
| PS4 | 1981 (5) | 15,000 | KM#24-28 | 32.00 | 37.50 |
| PS5 | 1994 (3) | 3,000 | KM#32-34 | 155 | 265 |
| PS6 | 2000 (2) | 150,000 | KM#37 and US Ericson Dollar | 68.00 | 82.50 |

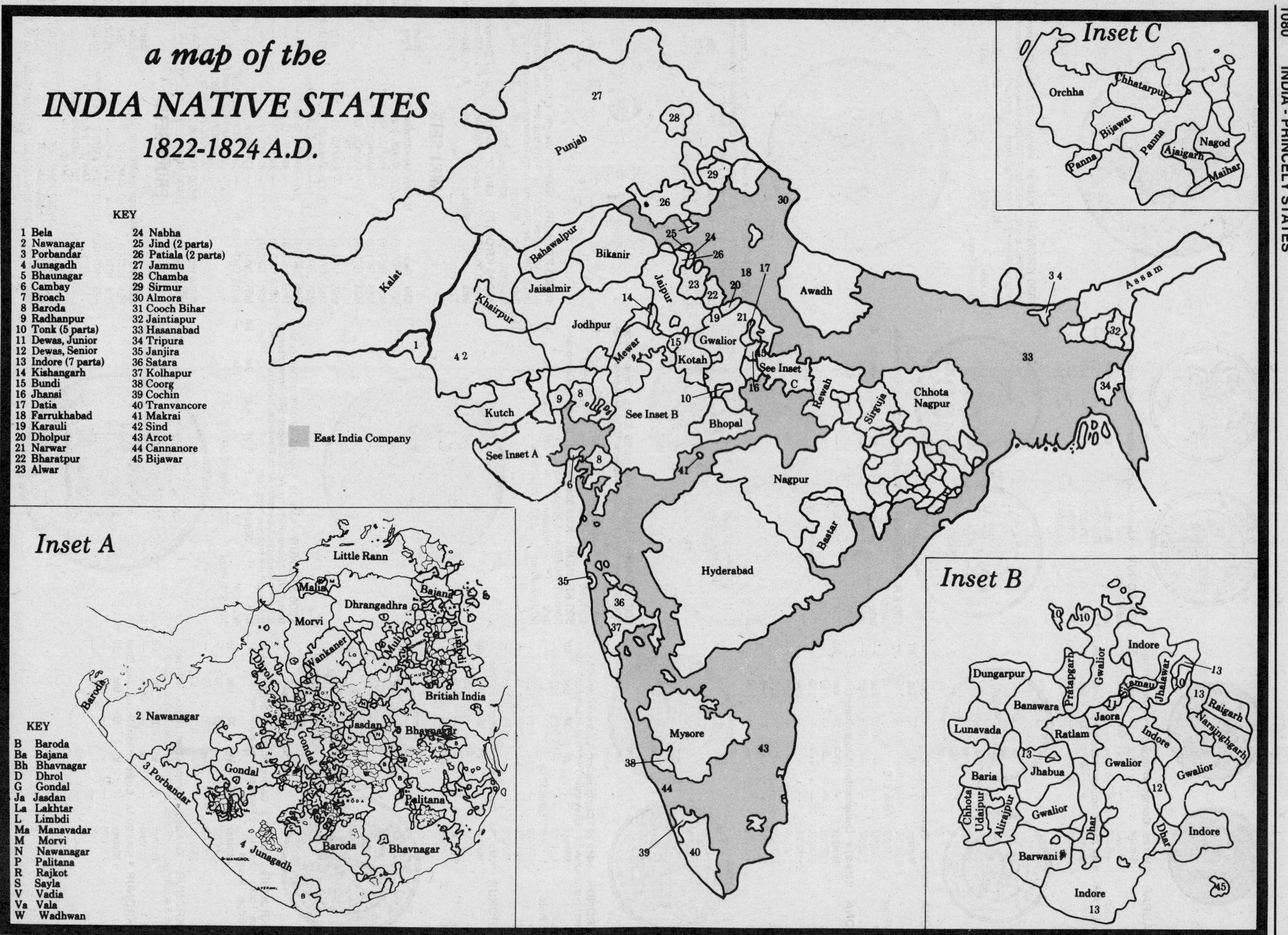
a map of the
INDIA NATIVE STATES
1822-1824 A.D.
KEY
1 Bela
2 Nawanagar
3 Porbandar
4 Junagadh
5 Bhaunagar
6 Cambay
7 Broach
8 Baroda
9 Radhanpur
10 Tonk (5 parts)
11 Dewas, Junior
12 Dewas, Senior
13 Indore (7 parts)
14 Kishangarh
15 Bundi
16 Jhansi
17 Datia
18 Farrukhabad
19 Karauli
20 Dholpur
21 Narwar
22 Bharatpur
23 Alwar
24 Nabha
25 Jind (2 parts)
26 Patiala (2 parts)
27 Jammu
28 Chamba
29 Sirmur
30 Almora
31 Cooch Bihar
32 Jaintiapur
33 Hasanabad
34 Tripura
35 Janjira
36 Satara
37 Kolhapur
38 Coorg
39 Cochin
40 Tranvancore
41 Makrai
42 Sind
43 Arcot
44 Cannanore
45 Bijawar
East India Company
Punjab
Kalat
Bahawalpur
Bikanir
Jaisalmir
Khairpur
Jodhpur
Jaipur
Mewar
Gwalior
Kotah
Kutch
See Inset A
See Inset B
Bhopal
See Inset C
Awadh
Rewah
Sirguja
Chhota Nagpur
Assam
Nagpur
Bastar
Hyderabad
Mysore
Inset A
Little Rann
Malia
Dhrangadhra
Morvi
Bajana
Wankaner
Muli
Limbdi
Dhrol
British India
Baroda
2 Nawanagar
Jasdan
Gondal
Bhavnagar
3 Porbandar
Palitana
4 Junagadh
KEY
B Baroda
Ba Bajana
Bh Bhavnagar
D Dhrol
G Gondal
Ja Jasdan
La Lakhtar
L Limbdi
Ma Manavadar
M Morvi
N Nawanagar
P Palitana
R Rajkot
S Sayla
V Vadia
Va Vala
W Wadhwan
Inset B
Indore
Dungarpur
Pratapgarh
Gwalior
Jhalawar
Banswara
Jaora
Raigarh
Narsinghgarh
Lunavada
Ratlam
Jhabua
Baria
Chhota Udaipur
Alirajpur
Dhar
Barwani
Inset C
Orchha
Chhatarpur
Bijawar
Panna
Ajaigarh
Nagod
Maihar

# INDIA - PRINCELY STATES

**MONETARY SYSTEMS**

In each state, local rates of exchange prevailed. There was no fixed rate between copper, silver or gold coin, but the rates varied in accordance with the values of the metal and by the edict of the local authority.

Within the subcontinent, different regions used distinctive coinage standards. In North India and the Deccan, the silver rupee (11.6 g) and gold mohur (11.0 g) predominated. In Gujarat, the silver kori (4.7 g) and gold kori (6.4 g) were the main currency. In South India the silver fanam (0.7-1.0 g) and gold hun or Pagoda (3.4 g) were current. Copper coins in all parts of India were produced to a myriad of local metrologies with seemingly endless varieties.

**NAZARANA ISSUES**

Throughout the Indian Princely States listings are Nazarana designations for special full flan strikings of copper, silver and some gold coinage. The purpose of these issues was for presentation to the local monarch to gain favor. For example if one had an audience with one's ruler he would exchange goods, currency notes or the cruder struck circulating coinage for Nazarana pieces which he would present to the ruler as a gift. The borderline between true Nazarana pieces and well struck regular issues is often indistinct. The Nazaranas sometimes circulated alongside the cruder "dump" issues.

**PRICING**

As the demand for Indian Princely coinage develops, and more dealers handle the material, sale records and price lists enable a firmer basis for pricing most series. For scarcer types adequate sale records are often not available, and prices must be regarded as tentative. Inasmuch as date collectors of Princely States series are few, dates known to be scarce are usually worth little more than common ones. Coins of a dated type, which do not show the full date on their flans should be valued at about 70 per cent of the prices indicated.

**DATING**

Coins are dated in several eras. Arabic and Devanagari numerals are used in conjunction with the Hejira era (AH), the Vikrama Samvat (VS), Saka Samvat (Saka), Fasli era(FE) Mauludi era (AM), and Malabar era (ME), as well as the Christian era (AD).

**GRADING**

Copper coins are rarely found in high grade, as they were the workhorse of coinage circulation, and were everywhere used for day-to-day transactions. Moreover, they were carelessly struck and even when 'new', can often only be distinguished from VF coins with difficulty, if at all.

Silver coins were often hoarded and not infrequently, turn up in nearly as-struck condition. The silver coins of Hyderabad (dump coins) are common in high grades, and the rupees of some states are scarcer 'used' than 'new'. Great caution must be exercised in determining the value or scarcity of high grade dump coins.

Dump gold was rarely circulated, and usually occurs in high grades, or is found made into jewelry.

## BAHAWALPUR

The Amirs of Bahawalpur established their independence from Afghan control towards the close of the 18th century. In the 1830's the state's independence under British suzerainty became guaranteed by treaty. With the creation of Pakistan in 1947 Bahawalpur, with an area of almost 17,500 square miles, became its premier Princely State. Bahawalpur State, named after its capital, stretched for almost three hundred miles along the left bank of the Sutlej, Panjnad and Indus rivers.

For earlier issues in the names of the Durrani rulers, see Afghanistan.

**RULERS**

Amirs

Alhaj Muhammad Bahawal Khan V, AH1317-1325/1899-1907AD

Sir Sadiq Muhammad Khan V, AH1325-1365/1907-1947AD

## PRINCELY STATE

### ANONYMOUS HAMMERED 'DUMP' COINAGE

**PAISA** **Y# 2.1** **Composition:** Copper **Ruler:** Anonymous (Alhaj Muhammad Bahawal Khan V) **Note:** Struck at Bahawalpur Mint.

| Date | Mintage | Good | VG | F | VF | XF |
|---|---|---|---|---|---|---|
| AH1321(1903-1904) | — | 3.50 | 6.00 | 8.50 | 12.50 | 20.00 |
| AH1325(1907-1908) | — | 3.50 | 6.00 | 8.50 | 12.50 | 20.00 |

**PAISA** **Y# 2.2** **Composition:** Copper **Ruler:** Anonymous (Alhaj Muhammad Bahawal Khan V) **Note:** Struck at Bahawalpur Mint.

| Date | Mintage | Good | VG | F | VF | XF |
|---|---|---|---|---|---|---|
| ND(c. 1909) | — | 4.00 | 7.50 | 12.00 | 20.00 | 32.50 |

### HAMMERED 'DUMP' COINAGE

**PAISA** **Y# 6** **Composition:** Copper **Ruler:** Alhaj Muhammad Bahawal Khan V AH1317-1325 / 1899-1907AD **Obverse:** Legend in Persian **Obv. Legend:** Muhammad Bahawal ... **Note:** Struck at Bahawalpur Mint. For anonymous Paisas struck during the years of his reign, see Y#2.1, 2.2.

| Date | Mintage | Good | VG | F | VF | XF |
|---|---|---|---|---|---|---|
| AH1324(1906-1907) | — | 3.50 | 6.00 | 8.00 | 12.50 | 20.00 |
| AH1325(1907-1908) | — | 3.50 | 6.00 | 8.00 | 12.50 | 20.00 |

**PAISA** **Y# 7.1** **Composition:** Copper **Ruler:** Sir Sadiq Muhammad Khan V AH1325-1365 / 1907-1947 **Obverse:** Legend in Persian **Obv. Legend:** Sadiq Muhammad ... **Note:** Struck at Bahawalpur Mint.

| Date | Mintage | Good | VG | F | VF | XF |
|---|---|---|---|---|---|---|
| AH1326(1908-1909) | — | 3.50 | 6.00 | 9.00 | 12.50 | 20.00 |
| AH1327(1909-1910) | — | 3.50 | 6.00 | 9.00 | 12.50 | 20.00 |

**PAISA** **Y# 7.2** **Composition:** Copper **Ruler:** Sir Sadiq Muhammad Khan V AH1325-1365 / 1907-1947 **Obverse:** Legend in Persian **Obv. Legend:** Sadiq Muhammad ... **Reverse:** Without date **Note:** Struck at Bahawalpur Mint.

| Date | Mintage | Good | VG | F | VF | XF |
|---|---|---|---|---|---|---|
| ND(c. 1910) | — | 4.00 | 7.50 | 12.50 | 20.00 | 32.50 |

**PAISA** **Y# 7.3** **Composition:** Copper **Ruler:** Sir Sadiq Muhammad Khan V AH1325-1365 / 1907-1947 **Obverse:** Legend in Persian **Obv. Legend:** Sadiq Muhammad ... **Reverse:** Without date or star **Note:** Struck at Bahawalpur Mint.

| Date | Mintage | Good | VG | F | VF | XF |
|---|---|---|---|---|---|---|
| ND(c. 1910) | — | 5.50 | 9.00 | 13.50 | 20.00 | 32.50 |

**PAISA** **Y# 8** **Composition:** Copper **Ruler:** Sir Sadiq Muhammad Khan V AH1325-1365 / 1907-1947 **Obverse:** Toughra **Note:** Struck at Bahawalpur Mint.

| Date | Mintage | Good | VG | F | VF | XF |
|---|---|---|---|---|---|---|
| AH1342(1923-1924) | — | 7.50 | 11.00 | 15.00 | 20.00 | 32.50 |
| AH1343(1924-1925) | — | 7.50 | 11.00 | 15.00 | 20.00 | 32.50 |

### MILLED COINAGE

**PAISA** **Y# 9** **Composition:** Copper Or Bronze **Ruler:** Sir Sadiq Muhammad Khan V AH1325-1365 / 1907-1947 **Obverse:** Toughra **Reverse:** Three branches in square **Note:** Struck at Bahawalpur Mint.

| Date | Mintage | VG | F | VF | XF | Unc |
|---|---|---|---|---|---|---|
| AH1343(1924-25) | — | 4.50 | 11.50 | 17.50 | 25.00 | 40.00 |

**PAISA** **Y# 9a** **Composition:** Brass **Ruler:** Sir Sadiq Muhammad Khan V AH1325-1365 / 1907-1947 **Obverse:** Toughra **Reverse:** Three branches in square **Note:** Struck at Bahawalpur Mint.

| Date | Mintage | VG | F | VF | XF | Unc |
|---|---|---|---|---|---|---|
| AH1343(1924-25) | — | — | 11.50 | 17.50 | 25.00 | 40.00 |

**PAISA** **Y# 13** **Composition:** Brass **Ruler:** Sir Sadiq Muhammad Khan V AH1325-1365 / 1907-1947 **Obverse:** Bust of Muhammad Bahawal Khan V left **Reverse:** Toughra **Note:** Struck at Bahawalpur Mint.

| Date | Mintage | VG | F | VF | XF | Unc |
|---|---|---|---|---|---|---|
| AH1359(1940-41) | — | 0.30 | 0.75 | 1.25 | 2.00 | 3.00 |
| AH1359(1940-41) Proof | — | — | — | — | — | — |

**RUPEE** **Y# 14** **Weight:** 6.5000 g. **Composition:** Silver **Ruler:** Sir Sadiq Muhammad Khan V AH1325-1365 / 1907-1947 **Obverse:** Toughra **Note:** Struck at Bahawalpur Mint. Possible pattern.

| Date | Mintage | VG | F | VF | XF | Unc |
|---|---|---|---|---|---|---|
| AH1343(1924-25) | — | 16.50 | 40.00 | 55.00 | 75.00 | 100 |

**1/2 PICE** **Y# 12** **Composition:** Copper **Ruler:** Sir Sadiq Muhammad Khan V AH1325-1365 / 1907-1947 **Obverse:** Bust of Muhammad Bahawal Khan V left **Reverse:** Toughra **Note:** Struck at Bahawalpur Mint.

| Date | Mintage | VG | F | VF | XF | Unc |
|---|---|---|---|---|---|---|
| AH1359(1940-41) | — | 0.15 | 0.35 | 0.75 | 1.25 | 2.00 |
| AH1359(1940-41) Proof | — | — | — | — | — | — |

**NAZARANA RUPEE** **Y# 10** **Weight:** 12.3000 g. **Composition:** Silver **Ruler:** Sir Sadiq Muhammad Khan V AH1325-1365 / 1907-1947 **Obverse:** Bust of Muhammad Bahawal Khan V left **Reverse:** Ornate helmeted arms **Note:** Struck at Bahawalpur Mint. Design prepared for the nawab by Spink & Son Ltd., London.

| Date | Mintage | VG | F | VF | XF | Unc |
|---|---|---|---|---|---|---|
| AH1343(1924-25) | — | — | — | 250 | 325 | 400 |

**ASHRAFI** **Y# 11** **Weight:** 7.0000 g. **Composition:** Gold **Ruler:** Sir Sadiq Muhammad Khan V AH1325-1365 / 1907-1947 **Obverse:** Bust of Muhammad Bahawal Khan V left **Reverse:** Ornate helmeted arms **Size:** 22.5 mm. **Note:** Struck at Bahawalpur Mint. Design prepared for the nawab by Spink & Son Ltd., London.

| Date | Mintage | VG | F | VF | XF | Unc |
|---|---|---|---|---|---|---|
| AH1343(1924-25) | — | — | — | 400 | 500 | 650 |

**ASHRAFI** **Y# 11a** **Weight:** 10.0000 g. **Composition:** Gold **Ruler:** Sir Sadiq Muhammad Khan V AH1325-1365 / 1907-1947 **Obverse:** Bust of Muhammad Bahawal Khan V left **Reverse:** Ornate helmeted arms **Note:** Struck at Bahawalpur Mint. Design prepared for the nawab by Spink & Son Ltd., London.

| Date | Mintage | VG | F | VF | XF | Unc |
|---|---|---|---|---|---|---|
| AH1343(1924-25) Proof | — | Value: 2,000 | | | | |

## BARODA

Maratha state located in western India. The ruling line was descended from Damaji, a Maratha soldier, who received the title of "Distinguished Swordsman" in 1721 (hence the scimitar on most Baroda coins). The Baroda title "Gaikwara" comes from "gaikwar" or cow herd, Damaji's father's occupation.

The Maratha rulers of Baroda, the Gaekwar family rose to prominence in the mid-18th century by carving out for themselves a dominion from territories, which were previously under the control of the Poona Marathas, and to a lesser extent, of the Raja of Jodhpur. Chronic internal disputes regarding the succession to the masnad culminated in the intervention of British troops in support of one candidate, Anand Rao Gaekwar, in 1800. Then, in 1802, an agreement with the East India Company released the Baroda princes from their fear of domination by the Maratha Peshwa of Poona but subordinated them to Company interests. Nevertheless, for almost the next century and a half Baroda maintained a good relationship with the British and continued as a major Princely State right up to 1947, when it acceded to the Indian Union.

**RULERS**

Gaekwars

Sayaji Rao III, AH1292-1357/VS1932-1995/1875-1938AD

Pratap Singh, VS1995-2008/1938-1951AD

## PRINCELY STATE

### MILLED COINAGE

**1/6 MOHUR** **Y# 37** **Composition:** Gold **Ruler:** Sayaji Rao II AH1292-1357 / VS1932-1995 / 1875-1938AD **Obverse:** Bust of Sayaji Rao III right **Size:** 14.5 mm. **Note:** 1.04-1.18 grams.

| Date | Mintage | VG | F | VF | XF | Unc |
|---|---|---|---|---|---|---|
| VS1951(1894) | — | — | 165 | 225 | 275 | 350 |
| VS1953(1896) | — | — | 165 | 225 | 275 | 350 |
| VS1959(1902) | — | — | 165 | 225 | 275 | 350 |

**1/3 MOHUR** **Y# 38** **Composition:** Gold **Ruler:** Sayaji Rao II AH1292-1357 / VS1932-1995 / 1875-1938AD **Obverse:** Bust of Sayaji Rao III right **Size:** 16 mm. **Note:** 2.07-2.39 grams.

| Date | Mintage | VG | F | VF | XF | Unc |
|---|---|---|---|---|---|---|
| VS1959(1902) | — | — | 185 | 250 | 325 | 400 |

**1/3 MOHUR** **Y# 40** **Composition:** Gold **Ruler:** Pratap Singh VS1995-2008 / 1938-1951AD **Obverse:** Bust of Pratap Singh right **Size:** 18 mm. **Note:** 2.07-2.13 grams.

| Date | Mintage | VG | F | VF | XF | Unc |
|---|---|---|---|---|---|---|
| VS1995(1938) | — | — | — | 400 | 600 | 900 |

**MOHUR** **Y# 39** **Composition:** Gold **Ruler:** Sayaji Rao II AH1292-1357 / VS1932-1995 / 1875-1938AD **Obverse:** Bust of Sayaji Rao III right **Size:** 21 mm. **Note:** 6.20-6.40 grams.

| Date | Mintage | VG | F | VF | XF | Unc |
|---|---|---|---|---|---|---|
| VS1959(1902) | — | — | 250 | 325 | 450 | 650 |

**MOHUR** **Y# 41** **Composition:** Gold **Ruler:** Pratap Singh VS1995-2008 / 1938-1951AD **Obverse:** Bust of Pratap Singh right **Size:** 21 mm. **Note:** 6.20-6.40 grams.

| Date | Mintage | VG | F | VF | XF | Unc |
|---|---|---|---|---|---|---|
| VS1995(1938) | — | — | — | 400 | 600 | 900 |

## BHAUNAGAR

State located in northwest India on the west shore of the Gulf of Cambay.

The Thakurs of Bhaunagar, as the rulers were titled, were Gohel Rajputs. They traced their control of the area back to the 13th century. Under the umbrella of British paramountcy, the Thakurs of Bhaunagar were regarded as relatively enlightened rulers. The State was absorbed into Saurashtra in February 1948.

Anonymous Types: Bearing the distinguishing Nagari legend *Bahadur* in addition to the Mughal legends.

**MONETARY SYSTEM**

2 Trambiyo = 1 Dokda

1-1/2 Dokda = 1 Dhingla

## PRINCELY STATE

### ANONYMOUS HAMMERED 'DUMP' COINAGE

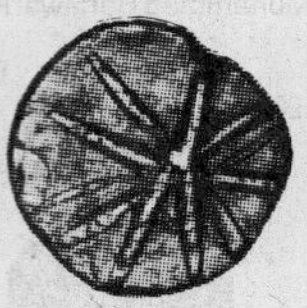

**DOKDA** **KM# 1** **Composition:** Copper **Ruler:** Thakurs of Bhaunagar Gohel Rajputs

| Date | Mintage | Good | VG | F | VF | XF |
|---|---|---|---|---|---|---|
| VS2004(1947) | — | 4.00 | 6.00 | 10.00 | 15.00 | — |

## BIKANIR

Bikanir, located in Rajputana was established as a state sometime between 1465 and 1504 by Jodhpur Rathor Rajput named Rao Bikaji. During the period of the Great Mughals Bikanir was intimately linked to Delhi by ties of both loyalty and marriage. Both Akbar and Jahangir contracted marriages with princesses of the Bikanir Rajputs,and the Bikanir nobility rendered outstanding service in the Mughal armies. Bikanir came under British influence in 1817 and after 1947 was incorporated into Rajasthan.

**RULERS**

Ganga Singhji, VS1944-1999/1887-1942AD

Sadul Singh, VS1999-2004/1942-1947AD

**MINT**

Bikanir

## PRINCELY STATE

### MEDALLIC COINAGE

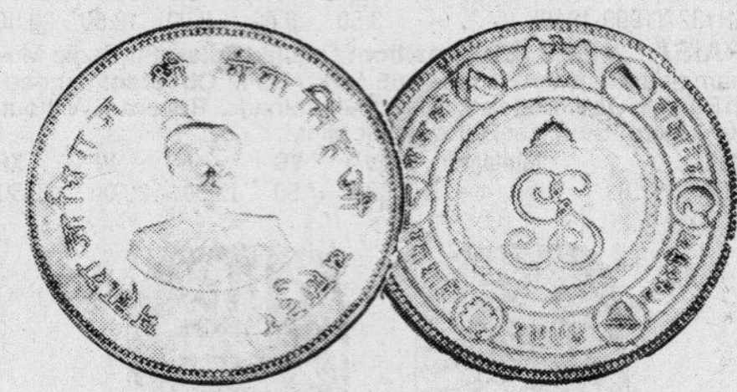

**NAZARANA RUPEE** **KM# M1** **Composition:** Silver **Ruler:** Ganga Singhji VS1994-1999 / 1887-1942AD **Subject:** 50th anniversary of reign **Obverse:** Bust of Ganga Singh facing **Reverse:** Crowned monogram

| Date | Mintage | VG | F | VF | XF | Unc |
|---|---|---|---|---|---|---|
| VS1994(1937) | — | 5.00 | 12.50 | 16.50 | 22.50 | 35.00 |
| VS1994(1937) Prooflike, restrike | — | — | — | — | — | 16.50 |

**NAZARANA RUPEE** **KM# M1a** **Composition:** Gold **Ruler:** Ganga Singhji VS1994-1999 / 1887-1942AD **Subject:** 50th anniversary of reign **Obverse:** Bust of Ganga Singh facing **Reverse:** Crowned monogram

| Date | Mintage | VG | F | VF | XF | Unc |
|---|---|---|---|---|---|---|
| VS1994(1937) Prooflike, restrike, rare | — | — | — | — | — | — |

**NAZARANA 1/2 MOHUR** **KM# M2** **Weight:** 4.4000 g. **Composition:** Gold **Ruler:** Ganga Singhji VS1994-1999 / 1887-1942AD **Subject:** 50th anniversary of reign **Obverse:** Bust of Ganga Singh facing **Size:** 19 mm.

| Date | Mintage | VG | F | VF | XF | Unc |
|---|---|---|---|---|---|---|
| VS1994(1937) | — | — | 100 | 125 | 150 | 275 |
| VS1994(1937) Prooflike, restrike | — | — | — | — | — | 150 |

**NAZARANA 1/2 MOHUR** **KM# M2a** **Composition:** Silver **Ruler:** Ganga Singhji VS1994-1999 / 1887-1942AD **Subject:** 50th anniversary of reign **Obverse:** Bust of Ganga Singh facing

| Date | Mintage | VG | F | VF | XF | Unc |
|---|---|---|---|---|---|---|
| VS1994(1937) Prooflike, restrike | — | — | — | — | — | 50.00 |

**NAZARANA MOHUR** **KM# M3** **Weight:** 8.5000 g. **Composition:** Gold **Ruler:** Ganga Singhji VS1994-1999 / 1887-1942AD **Subject:** 50th anniversary of reign **Obverse:** Bust of Ganga Singh facing **Size:** 21 mm.

| Date | Mintage | VG | F | VF | XF | Unc |
|---|---|---|---|---|---|---|
| VS1994(1937) | — | — | 175 | 225 | 275 | 400 |
| VS1994(1937) Prooflike, restrike | — | — | — | — | — | 250 |

**NAZARANA MOHUR** **KM# M3a** **Composition:** Silver **Ruler:** Ganga Singhji VS1994-1999 / 1887-1942AD **Subject:** 50th anniversary of reign **Obverse:** Bust of Ganga Singh facing

| Date | Mintage | VG | F | VF | XF | Unc |
|---|---|---|---|---|---|---|
| VS1994(1937) | — | — | — | — | 12.50 | 20.00 |
| VS1994(1937) Prooflike, restrike | — | — | — | — | — | 50.00 |

**NAZARANA MOHUR** **KM# M4** **Weight:** 8.6800 g. **Composition:** Gold **Ruler:** Sadul Singh VS1999-2004 / 1942-1947AD

| Date | Mintage | VG | F | VF | XF | Unc |
|---|---|---|---|---|---|---|
| VS1999(1942) | — | — | — | — | 800 | 1,300 |

## BUNDI

State in Rajputana in northwest India.

Bundi was founded in 1342 by a Chauhan Rajput, Rao Dewa (Deoraj). Until the Maratha defeat early in the 19th century, Bundi was greatly harassed by the forces of Holkar and Sindhia. In 1818 it came under British protection and control and remained so until 1947.In 1948 the State was absorbed into Rajasthan.

**RULERS**

Raghubir Singh VS1946-1984/1889-1927AD

Ishwari Singh VS1984-2004/1927-1947AD

**MINT**

| | PERSO-ARABIC | DEVANAGARI |
|---|---|---|
| Bundi | بندي | बूंदी |
| Mintname: Bundi | بوندي | |

## PRINCELY STATE

### REGAL COINAGE

(Hammered "Dump" Coinage)

**1/2 PAISA** **Y# A12** **Composition:** Copper **Ruler:** Edward VII **Obverse:** Katar **Obv. Legend:** EDWARD VII EMPEROR **Note:** 4.70-5.10 grams.

| Date | Mintage | Good | VG | F | VF | XF |
|---|---|---|---|---|---|---|
| ND(VS1963-1976) Date off flan | — | 3.00 | 4.50 | 6.50 | 8.50 | — |
| VS1965(1908) | — | 6.00 | 9.00 | 12.50 | 16.50 | — |
| VS1973(1916) | — | 6.00 | 9.00 | 12.50 | 16.50 | — |
| VS1974(1917) | — | 6.00 | 9.00 | 12.50 | 16.50 | — |
| VS1976(1919) | — | 6.00 | 9.00 | 12.50 | 16.50 | — |

**1/2 PAISA** **Y# YA2** **Composition:** Copper **Ruler:** Victoria **Obverse:** Katar, inscription: VIC/TORIA/QUEEN **Obv. Legend:** EMPEROR EDWARD **Note:** 5.00-5.20 grams.

| Date | Mintage | Good | VG | F | VF | XF |
|---|---|---|---|---|---|---|
| VS1963(1906) | — | 0.75 | 1.25 | 2.25 | 3.50 | — |
| VS1965(1908) | — | 0.75 | 1.25 | 2.25 | 3.50 | — |
| VS1966(1909) | — | 0.75 | 1.25 | 2.25 | 3.50 | — |
| VS1967(1910) | — | 0.75 | 1.25 | 2.25 | 3.50 | — |

**1/2 PAISA** **Y# 15.1** **Composition:** Copper **Ruler:** George V **Obverse:** Katar **Obv. Legend:** EMPEROR-GEORGE V **Note:** 5.00-5.35 grams.

| Date | Mintage | Good | VG | F | VF | XF |
|---|---|---|---|---|---|---|
| VS1973(1916) | — | 1.50 | 2.25 | 3.00 | 4.00 | — |
| VS1974(1917) | — | 1.50 | 2.25 | 3.00 | 4.00 | — |
| VS1976(1919) | — | 1.50 | 2.25 | 3.00 | 4.00 | — |
| VS1977(1920) | — | 1.50 | 2.25 | 3.00 | 4.00 | — |

**1/2 PAISA** **Y# 15.2** **Composition:** Copper **Ruler:** George V **Obverse:** Katar **Obv. Legend:** GEORGE V EMPEROR **Note:** 5.00-5.35 grams. Size and weight vary.

| Date | Mintage | Good | VG | F | VF | XF |
|---|---|---|---|---|---|---|
| VS1980(1923) | — | 1.50 | 2.25 | 3.00 | 4.00 | — |
| VS1981(1924) | — | 1.50 | 2.25 | 3.00 | 4.00 | — |
| VS1982(1925) | — | 1.50 | 2.25 | 3.00 | 4.00 | — |
| VS1983(1926) | — | 1.50 | 2.25 | 3.00 | 4.00 | — |
| VS1984(1927) | — | 1.50 | 2.25 | 3.00 | 4.00 | — |
| VS1986(1929) | — | 2.00 | 3.00 | 4.00 | 5.00 | — |
| VS1987(1930) | — | 2.00 | 3.00 | 4.00 | 5.00 | — |
| VS1988(1931) | — | 3.00 | 4.00 | 5.50 | 7.50 | — |
| VS1990(1933) | — | 3.00 | 4.00 | 5.50 | 7.50 | — |
| VS1991(1934) | — | 3.00 | 4.00 | 5.50 | 7.50 | — |
| VS1992(1935) | — | 3.00 | 4.00 | 5.50 | 7.50 | — |

**1/4 RUPEE** **Y# B11** **Composition:** Silver **Ruler:** Edward VII **Obverse:** Seated figure holding katar **Obv. Legend:** EMPER-OR-EDWARD VII **Note:** 2.65-2.70 grams.

| Date | Mintage | Good | VG | F | VF | XF |
|---|---|---|---|---|---|---|
| VS1958(1901) | — | 5.50 | 13.50 | 21.50 | 30.00 | 40.00 |
| VS1959(1902) | — | 5.50 | 13.50 | 21.50 | 30.00 | 40.00 |
| VS1961(1904) | — | 5.50 | 13.50 | 21.50 | 30.00 | 40.00 |
| VS1962(1905) | — | 5.50 | 13.50 | 21.50 | 30.00 | 40.00 |

**1/4 RUPEE** **Y# 12** **Composition:** Silver **Ruler:** Edward VII **Obverse:** Katar **Obv. Legend:** EDWARD VII EMPEROR **Note:** 2.65-2.70 grams.

| Date | Mintage | Good | VG | F | VF | XF |
|---|---|---|---|---|---|---|
| VS1963(1906) | — | 1.50 | 4.00 | 6.00 | 9.00 | 13.50 |
| VS1964(1907) | — | 1.50 | 4.00 | 6.00 | 9.00 | 13.50 |
| VS1965(1908) | — | 1.50 | 4.00 | 6.00 | 9.00 | 13.50 |
| VS1966(1909) | — | 1.50 | 4.00 | 6.00 | 9.00 | 13.50 |

**1/4 RUPEE** **Y# 16.1** **Composition:** Silver **Ruler:** George V **Obverse:** Katar **Obv. Legend:** EMPEROR-GEORGE V **Note:** 2.60-2.70 grams.

| Date | Mintage | Good | VG | F | VF | XF |
|---|---|---|---|---|---|---|
| VS1972(1915) | — | 1.25 | 3.00 | 4.50 | 6.50 | 10.00 |
| VS1973(1916) | — | 1.25 | 3.00 | 4.50 | 6.50 | 10.00 |
| VS1974(1917) | — | 1.25 | 3.00 | 4.50 | 6.50 | 10.00 |

**1/4 RUPEE** **Y# 16.2** **Composition:** Silver **Ruler:** George V **Obverse:** Katar **Obv. Legend:** GEORGE V EMPEROR **Note:** 2.60-2.70 grams.

| Date | Mintage | Good | VG | F | VF | XF |
|---|---|---|---|---|---|---|
| VS1980(1923) | — | 1.25 | 3.00 | 4.50 | 6.50 | 10.00 |
| VS1981(1924) | — | 1.25 | 3.00 | 4.50 | 6.50 | 10.00 |
| VS1982(1925) | — | 1.25 | 3.00 | 4.50 | 6.50 | 10.00 |

**1/4 RUPEE** **Y# A19** **Composition:** Silver **Ruler:** George V **Obverse:** Date 1925 at center **Obv. Legend:** EMPEROR GEORGE V **Size:** 13 mm. **Note:** 2.60-2.70 grams.

| Date | Mintage | Good | VG | F | VF | XF |
|---|---|---|---|---|---|---|
| VS1915(1925) | — | 10.00 | 20.00 | 31.50 | 42.50 | 60.00 |

**1/2 RUPEE** **Y# A11** **Composition:** Silver **Ruler:** Edward VII **Obverse:** Seated figure holding katar **Obv. Legend:** EMPER-OR-EDWARD VII **Size:** 16-18 mm. **Note:** 5.30-5.40 grams.

| Date | Mintage | Good | VG | F | VF | XF |
|---|---|---|---|---|---|---|
| VS1958(1901) | — | 6.00 | 15.00 | 21.50 | 30.00 | 40.00 |

**1/2 RUPEE** **Y# 13** **Composition:** Silver **Ruler:** Edward VII **Obverse:** Katar **Obv. Legend:** EDWARD VII EMPEROR **Size:** 16-18 mm. **Note:** 5.30-5.40 grams.

| Date | Mintage | Good | VG | F | VF | XF |
|---|---|---|---|---|---|---|
| VS1963(1906) | — | 2.25 | 5.50 | 8.00 | 12.50 | 18.50 |
| VS1964(1907) | — | 2.00 | 5.00 | 7.00 | 10.00 | 15.00 |
| VS1965(1908) | — | 2.00 | 5.00 | 7.00 | 10.00 | 15.00 |
| VS1966(1909) | — | 2.00 | 5.00 | 7.00 | 10.00 | 15.00 |

**1/2 RUPEE** **Y# 17.1** **Composition:** Silver **Ruler:** George V **Note:** 5.30-5.40 grams.

| Date | Mintage | Good | VG | F | VF | XF |
|---|---|---|---|---|---|---|
| VS1972(1915) | — | 2.00 | 5.00 | 7.00 | 10.00 | 15.00 |
| VS1973(1916) | — | 2.00 | 5.00 | 7.00 | 10.00 | 15.00 |
| VS1974(1917) | — | 1.50 | 4.00 | 6.00 | 9.00 | 13.50 |
| VS1979(1922) | — | 1.50 | 4.00 | 6.00 | 9.00 | 13.50 |

**1/2 RUPEE** **Y# 17.2** **Composition:** Silver **Ruler:** George V **Obverse:** Legend arranged differently **Note:** 5.30-5.40 grams.

| Date | Mintage | Good | VG | F | VF | XF |
|---|---|---|---|---|---|---|
| VS1979(1922) | — | 1.50 | 4.00 | 6.00 | 9.00 | 13.50 |
| VS1980(1923) | — | 1.50 | 4.00 | 6.00 | 9.00 | 13.50 |
| VS1981(1924) | — | 1.50 | 4.00 | 6.00 | 9.00 | 13.50 |
| VS1982(1925) | — | 1.50 | 4.00 | 6.00 | 9.00 | 13.50 |
| VS1983(1926) | — | 1.50 | 4.00 | 6.00 | 9.00 | 13.50 |
| VS1984(1927) | — | 1.50 | 4.00 | 6.00 | 9.00 | 13.50 |

**1/2 RUPEE** **Y# 19** **Composition:** Silver **Ruler:** George V **Obverse:** Date 1925 at center **Obv. Legend:** EMPEROR GEORGE V **Note:** 5.30-5.40 grams.

| Date | Mintage | Good | VG | F | VF | XF |
|---|---|---|---|---|---|---|
| VS1915(1925) | — | 11.50 | 23.50 | 38.50 | 55.00 | 80.00 |

**RUPEE** **Y# 11** **Composition:** Silver **Ruler:** Edward VII **Obverse:** Seated figure holding katar **Obv. Legend:** EMPEROR-EDWARD VII **Note:** 10.60-10.70 grams.

| Date | Mintage | Good | VG | F | VF | XF |
|---|---|---|---|---|---|---|
| VS1958(1901) | — | 2.75 | 6.50 | 10.00 | 15.00 | 22.50 |
| VS1959(1902) | — | 2.75 | 6.50 | 10.00 | 15.00 | 22.50 |
| VS1960(1903) | — | 2.75 | 6.50 | 10.00 | 15.00 | 22.50 |
| VS1961(1904) | — | 2.75 | 6.50 | 10.00 | 15.00 | 22.50 |
| VS1962(1905) | — | 2.75 | 6.50 | 10.00 | 15.00 | 22.50 |
| VS1963(1906) | — | 2.75 | 6.50 | 10.00 | 15.00 | 22.50 |

**RUPEE** **Y# 14** **Composition:** Silver **Ruler:** Edward VII **Obverse:** Katar **Obv. Legend:** EDWARD VII EMPEROR **Note:** 10.60-10.70 grams.

| Date | Mintage | Good | VG | F | VF | XF |
|---|---|---|---|---|---|---|
| VS1963(1906) | — | 2.75 | 6.50 | 10.00 | 15.00 | 22.50 |
| VS1964(1907) | — | 2.75 | 6.50 | 10.00 | 15.00 | 22.50 |
| VS1965(1908) | — | 2.75 | 6.50 | 10.00 | 15.00 | 22.50 |
| VS1966(1909) | — | 2.75 | 6.50 | 10.00 | 15.00 | 22.50 |
| VS1967(1910) | — | 2.75 | 6.50 | 10.00 | 15.00 | 22.50 |
| VS1968(1911) | — | 2.75 | 6.50 | 10.00 | 15.00 | 22.50 |
| VS1969(1912) | — | 2.75 | 6.50 | 10.00 | 15.00 | 22.50 |

**RUPEE** **Y# 18.1** **Composition:** Silver **Ruler:** George V **Obverse:** Katar **Obv. Legend:** EMPEROR GEORGE V **Note:** 10.60-10.70 grams.

| Date | Mintage | Good | VG | F | VF | XF |
|---|---|---|---|---|---|---|
| VS1972(1915) | — | 2.50 | 6.00 | 9.00 | 13.50 | 20.00 |
| VS1973(1916) | — | 2.50 | 6.00 | 9.00 | 13.50 | 20.00 |
| VS1974(1917) | — | 2.50 | 6.00 | 9.00 | 13.50 | 20.00 |
| VS1975(1918) | — | 2.50 | 6.00 | 9.00 | 13.50 | 20.00 |
| VS1979(1922) | — | 2.50 | 6.00 | 9.00 | 13.50 | 20.00 |

**RUPEE** **Y# 18.2** **Composition:** Silver **Ruler:** George V **Obverse:** Katar **Obv. Legend:** GEORGE V EMPEROR **Note:** 10.60-10.70 grams.

| Date | Mintage | Good | VG | F | VF | XF |
|---|---|---|---|---|---|---|
| VS1979(1922) | — | 2.50 | 6.00 | 9.00 | 13.50 | 20.00 |
| VS1980(1923) | — | 2.50 | 6.00 | 9.00 | 13.50 | 20.00 |
| VS1981(1924) | — | 2.50 | 6.00 | 9.00 | 13.50 | 20.00 |
| VS1982(1925) | — | 2.50 | 6.00 | 9.00 | 13.50 | 20.00 |
| VS1983(1926) | — | 2.50 | 6.00 | 9.00 | 13.50 | 20.00 |
| VS1984(1927) | — | 2.50 | 6.00 | 9.00 | 13.50 | 20.00 |
| VS1985(1928) | — | 2.50 | 6.00 | 9.00 | 13.50 | 20.00 |
| VS1987(1930) | — | 2.50 | 6.00 | 9.00 | 13.50 | 20.00 |
| VS1989(1932) | — | 2.50 | 6.00 | 9.00 | 13.50 | 20.00 |
| VS1979-1989 Date off flan | — | 1.50 | 4.00 | 6.00 | 9.00 | 13.50 |

**RUPEE** **Y# 20** **Composition:** Silver **Ruler:** George V **Obverse:** Date 1925 at center **Obv. Legend:** EMPEROR GEORGE V **Note:** 10.60-10.70 grams.

| Date | Mintage | Good | VG | F | VF | XF |
|---|---|---|---|---|---|---|
| VS1915(1925) | — | — | 45.00 | 70.00 | 100 | 140 |

**NAZARANA RUPEE** **Y# 10** **Composition:** Silver **Ruler:** Victoria **Obverse:** Seated figure holding katar **Obv. Legend:** VICTORIA QUEEN

| Date | Mintage | Good | VG | F | VF | XF |
|---|---|---|---|---|---|---|
| VS1958(1901) | — | 18.50 | 37.50 | 55.00 | 90.00 | 140 |

**NAZARANA RUPEE** **Y# 11a** **Composition:** Silver **Ruler:** Edward VII **Obverse:** Seated figure holding katar **Obv. Legend:** EMPEROR-EDWARD VII **Note:** 10.60-10.70 grams. Broad, square flan.

| Date | Mintage | Good | VG | F | VF | XF |
|---|---|---|---|---|---|---|
| VS1962(1905) | — | 18.50 | 37.50 | 60.00 | 100 | 175 |

**NAZARANA RUPEE** **Y# 14a** **Composition:** Silver **Ruler:** Edward VII **Obverse:** Katar **Obv. Legend:** EDWARD VII EMPEROR **Note:** 10.60-10.70 grams.

| Date | Mintage | Good | VG | F | VF | XF |
|---|---|---|---|---|---|---|
| VS1965(1908) | — | 17.50 | 35.00 | 55.00 | 90.00 | 150 |
| VS1966(1909) | — | 17.50 | 35.00 | 55.00 | 90.00 | 150 |
| VS1967(1910) | — | 17.50 | 35.00 | 55.00 | 90.00 | 150 |
| VS1968(1911) | — | 17.50 | 35.00 | 55.00 | 90.00 | 150 |
| VS1969(1912) | — | 17.50 | 35.00 | 55.00 | 90.00 | 150 |
| VS1970(1913) | — | 17.50 | 35.00 | 55.00 | 90.00 | 150 |

**NAZARANA RUPEE** **Y# 18a.1** **Composition:** Silver **Ruler:** George V **Obverse:** Katar **Obv. Legend:** EMPEROR GEORGE V **Note:** 10.55-10.80 grams. Square.

| Date | Mintage | Good | VG | F | VF | XF |
|---|---|---|---|---|---|---|
| VS1965(1908) | — | 13.50 | 27.50 | 45.00 | 75.00 | 125 |
| VS1971(1914) | — | 13.50 | 27.50 | 45.00 | 75.00 | 125 |
| VS1974(1917) | — | 13.50 | 27.50 | 45.00 | 75.00 | 125 |
| VS1975(1918) | — | 13.50 | 27.50 | 45.00 | 75.00 | 125 |
| VS1977(1920) | — | 13.50 | 27.50 | 45.00 | 75.00 | 125 |

**NAZARANA RUPEE** **Y# 14b** **Composition:** Silver **Ruler:** Edward VII **Obverse:** Katar **Obv. Legend:** EDWARD VII EMPEROR **Note:** 10.60-10.70 grams. Round flan.

| Date | Mintage | Good | VG | F | VF | XF |
|---|---|---|---|---|---|---|
| VS1966(1909) | — | 5.00 | 12.50 | 20.00 | 35.00 | 60.00 |
| VS1967(1910) | — | 5.00 | 12.50 | 20.00 | 35.00 | 60.00 |
| VS1968(1911) | — | 5.00 | 12.50 | 20.00 | 35.00 | 60.00 |
| VS1969(1912) | — | 6.00 | 15.00 | 21.50 | 30.00 | 40.00 |
| VS1970(1913) | — | 6.00 | 15.00 | 21.50 | 30.00 | 40.00 |

**NAZARANA RUPEE** **Y# 18a.2** **Composition:** Silver **Ruler:** George V **Obverse:** Katar **Obv. Legend:** GEORGE V **Note:** 10.55-10.80 grams. Square.

| Date | Mintage | Good | VG | F | VF | XF |
|---|---|---|---|---|---|---|
| VS1979(1922) | — | 13.50 | 27.50 | 45.00 | 75.00 | 125 |
| VS1980(1923) | — | 13.50 | 27.50 | 45.00 | 75.00 | 125 |
| VS1981(1924) | — | 13.50 | 27.50 | 45.00 | 75.00 | 125 |
| VS1983(1926) | — | 13.50 | 27.50 | 45.00 | 75.00 | 125 |
| VS1984(1927) | — | 13.50 | 27.50 | 45.00 | 75.00 | 125 |
| VS1987(1930) | — | 13.50 | 27.50 | 45.00 | 75.00 | 125 |

**NAZARANA RUPEE** **Y# 20a** **Composition:** Silver **Ruler:** George V **Obverse:** Date 1925 at center **Obv. Legend:** EMPEROR GEORGE V **Note:** 10.55-10.80 grams.

| Date | Mintage | Good | VG | F | VF | XF |
|---|---|---|---|---|---|---|
| VS1915(1925) | — | 22.50 | 45.00 | 75.00 | 110 | 150 |

## CAMBAY

**Khanbayat**

Although of very ancient origins as a port, located at the head of the Gulf of Cambay in West India, Cambay did not come into existence as a separate state until about 1730 after the breakdown of Mughal authority in Delhi. The nawabs of Cambay traced their ancestry to Momin Khan II, the last of the Muslim governors of Gujerat. The State came under British control after two decades of Maratha rule.

**RULERS**

Ja'far Ali Khan, AH1297-1333/VS1937-1972/1880-1915AD

Mint: Khanbayat

## PRINCELY STATE

### ANONYMOUS HAMMERED 'DUMP' COINAGE

**1/2 PAISA** **Y# 5** **Composition:** Copper **Ruler:** Jafar Ali Khan VS1937-1972 **Obverse:** Persian legend **Obv. Legend:** Cambay **Reverse:** Denomination in words

| Date | Mintage | Good | VG | F | VF | XF |
|---|---|---|---|---|---|---|
| VS1963(1906) | — | 3.50 | 6.50 | 9.00 | 12.50 | — |
| VS1964(1907) | — | 3.50 | 6.50 | 9.00 | 12.50 | — |

**1/2 PAISA** **Y# 5a** **Composition:** Copper **Ruler:** Jafar Ali Khan VS1937-1972 **Obverse:** Persian legend **Obv. Legend:** Cambay **Reverse:** Denomination in numerals

| Date | Mintage | Good | VG | F | VF | XF |
|---|---|---|---|---|---|---|
| VS1964(1907) | — | 3.00 | 5.00 | 7.50 | 10.00 | — |
| VS1965(1908) | — | 3.00 | 5.00 | 7.50 | 10.00 | — |
| VS1966(1909) | — | 3.00 | 5.00 | 7.50 | 10.00 | — |

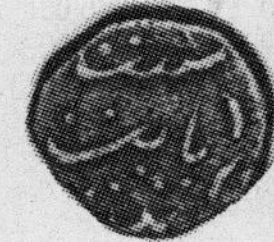

**PAISA** **Y# 6** **Composition:** Copper **Ruler:** Jafar Ali Khan VS1937-1972 **Obverse:** Persian legend **Obv. Legend:** Cambay **Note:** Varieties exist.

| Date | Mintage | Good | VG | F | VF | XF |
|---|---|---|---|---|---|---|
| VS1962(1905) | — | 1.00 | 1.50 | 2.00 | 3.50 | — |
| VS1963(1906) | — | 1.00 | 1.50 | 2.00 | 3.50 | — |
| VS1964(1907) | — | 1.25 | 1.75 | 2.50 | 4.25 | — |
| VS1965(1908) | — | 1.00 | 1.50 | 2.00 | 3.50 | — |
| VS1966(1909) | — | 1.00 | 1.50 | 2.00 | 3.50 | — |
| VS1968(1911) | — | 1.00 | 1.50 | 2.00 | 3.50 | — |
| VS1970(1913) | — | 1.65 | 2.50 | 4.00 | 5.00 | — |

**RUPEE** **Y# 10** **Composition:** Silver **Ruler:** Jafar Ali Khan VS1937-1972 **Obverse:** Persian legend **Obv. Legend:** Ja'afar Ali Khan **Reverse:** Mint name **Note:** Struck at Cambay. 10.70-11.60 grams.

| Date | Mintage | Good | VG | F | VF | XF |
|---|---|---|---|---|---|---|
| AH1319(1901-1902) | — | 15.00 | 30.00 | 50.00 | 80.00 | 120 |

### COUNTERMARKED 'DUMP' COINAGE

**1/4 PAISA** **Y# 2** **Composition:** Copper **Ruler:** Jafar Ali Khan VS1937-1972 **Countermark:** Persian "Shah"

| Date | Mintage | Good | VG | F | VF | XF |
|---|---|---|---|---|---|---|
| ND(c. 1905-1909) | — | 3.00 | 5.50 | 7.50 | 10.00 | — |

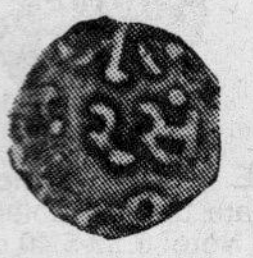

**1/2 PAISA** **Y# 3** **Composition:** Copper **Ruler:** Jafar Ali Khan VS1937-1972 **Countermark:** Persian "Shah" **Note:** Round flan.

| Date | Mintage | Good | VG | F | VF | XF |
|---|---|---|---|---|---|---|
| VS(19)62(1905) | — | 3.00 | 5.50 | 7.50 | 10.00 | — |

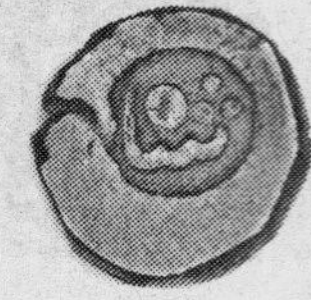

**PAISA** **Y# 4** **Composition:** Copper **Ruler:** Jafar Ali Khan VS1937-1972 **Countermark:** Persian "Shah" **Note:** Round flan.

| Date | Mintage | Good | VG | F | VF | XF |
|---|---|---|---|---|---|---|
| VS194x | — | 1.25 | 2.00 | 3.00 | 4.25 | — |

**PAISA** **Y# 4a** **Composition:** Copper **Ruler:** Jafar Ali Khan VS1937-1972 **Countermark:** Persian "Shah" **Note:** Square flan.

| Date | Mintage | Good | VG | F | VF | XF |
|---|---|---|---|---|---|---|
| ND | — | 1.50 | 2.25 | 3.25 | 4.50 | — |

## CIS-SUTLEJ STATES - FARIDKOT

State located in the Punjab.

**RULERS**

Harindar Singh, 1918-1949AD

## PRINCELY STATE

### MEDALLIC COINAGE

**NAZARANA 1/2 RUPEE** **KM# M1** **Composition:** Silver **Ruler:** Harindar Singh 1918 - 1949AD **Obverse:** Bust of Harindar Singh left **Reverse:** Arms **Note:** Prev. Y#B1.

| Date | Mintage | VG | F | VF | XF | Unc |
|---|---|---|---|---|---|---|
| 1941 | — | — | — | — | — | — |

**NAZARANA RUPEE** **KM# M2** **Composition:** Silver **Ruler:** Harindar Singh 1918 - 1949AD **Obverse:** Bust of Harindar Singh left **Reverse:** Arms **Note:** Prev. Y#A1.

| Date | Mintage | VG | F | VF | XF | Unc |
|---|---|---|---|---|---|---|
| 1941 Rare | — | — | — | — | — | — |

**NAZARANA 1/3 MOHUR** **KM# M3** **Composition:** Gold **Ruler:** Harindar Singh 1918 - 1949AD **Obverse:** Bust of Harindar Singh left **Reverse:** Arms **Note:** 3.57-3.80 grams, Prev. Y#1.

| Date | Mintage | VG | F | VF | XF | Unc |
|---|---|---|---|---|---|---|
| 1941 | — | — | — | 700 | 1,500 | 2,000 |

## CIS-SUTLEJ STATES - JIND

State located in the southern Punjab and north Haryana states.

The ruling princes belonged to the same Jat family as the maharajas of Patiala. Like them, they traced their ancestry back to Baryam, a revenue collector under Babur (1526). The State was founded by Gajpat Singh after he took part in the Sikh uprising against the Afghan governor of Sirhind in 1763. One of Gajpat Singh's daughters became the mother of Ranjit Singh.

## PRINCELY STATE

### MEDALLIC COINAGE

**NAZARANA RUPEE** **KM# M1** **Composition:** Silver **Ruler:** Ranbir Singh VS1943 - / 1886 - AD **Subject:** 50th anniversary of reign **Obverse:** Persian inscription **Reverse:** Persian inscription **Note:** 10.70-11.60 grams; Prev. Y#2.

| Date | Mintage | VG | F | VF | XF | Unc |
|---|---|---|---|---|---|---|
| VS1993(1936) | — | 100 | 175 | 250 | 350 | — |

## CIS-SUTLEJ STATES - MALER KOLTA

State located in the Punjab in northwest India, founded by the Maler Kotla family who were Sherwani Afghans who had travelled to India from Kabul in 1467 as officials of the Delhi emperors.

Coins are rupees of Ahmad Shah Durrani, and except for the last ruler, contain the chief's initial on the reverse. The chiefs were called Ra'is until 1821, Nawabs thereafter.

For similar issues see Jind, Nabha and Patiala.

**RULERS**

Ibrahim Ali Khan, AH1288-1326/1871-1908AD

Ahmad Ali Khan, AH1326-/1908-AD

## PRINCELY STATE

### HAMMERED 'DUMP' COINAGE

**1/2 PAISA** **Y# 7** **Composition:** Copper **Ruler:** Ahmad Ali Khan AH1326-/1908-AD **Obverse:** Persian inscription: Ahmad Ali Khan ...

| Date | Mintage | Good | VG | F | VF | XF |
|---|---|---|---|---|---|---|
| ND(1908) | — | 7.00 | 11.00 | 16.50 | 25.00 | — |

**PAISA** **Y# 8** **Composition:** Copper **Ruler:** Ahmad Ali Khan AH1326-/1908-AD **Obverse:** Persian inscription: Ahmad Ali Khan ...

| Date | Mintage | Good | VG | F | VF | XF |
|---|---|---|---|---|---|---|
| AH1326(1908-09) | — | 17.50 | 25.00 | — | 35.00 | 50.00 |

**Note:** Error for 1326

**RUPEE** Y# 9 **Composition:** Silver **Ruler:** Ahmad Ali Khan AH1326-/1908-AD **Obverse:** Persian inscription: Ahmad Ali Khan ... **Note:** 10.70-11.60 grams.

| Date | Mintage | Good | VG | F | VF | XF |
|---|---|---|---|---|---|---|
| ND(1908) | — | — | 6.00 | 9.00 | 13.50 | 20.00 |

**NAZARANA 2 RUPEE** Y# 10 **Weight:** 22.0000 g. **Composition:** Silver **Ruler:** Ahmad Ali Khan AH1326-/1908-AD **Obverse:** Persian inscription: Ahmad Ali Khan ...

| Date | Mintage | Good | VG | F | VF | XF |
|---|---|---|---|---|---|---|
| AH1326(1908-09) Rare | — | — | — | — | — | — |

## CIS-SUTLEJ STATES - PATIALA

State located in the Punjab in northwest India In the mid-18th century the Raja was given his title and mint right by Ahmad Shah Durrani of Afghanistan, whose coin he copied.

The rulers became Maharajas in 1810AD. The maharaja of Patiala was also recognized as the leader of the Phulkean tribe. Unlike others, Patiala's Sikh rulers had never hesitated to seek British assistance at those times when they felt threatened by their co-religionist neighbors. In 1857 Patiala's forces were immediately made available on the side of the British.

**RULERS**

Bhupindar Singh, VS1958-1994/1900-1937AD
Yadvindar Singh, VS1994-2005/1937-1948AD

## PRINCELY STATE

### UNCERTAIN COINAGE

**RUPEE** KM# 1 **Composition:** Silver **Note:** 10.70-11.60 grams, unknown date (ca.1900's).

| Date | Mintage | Good | VG | F | VF | XF |
|---|---|---|---|---|---|---|
| AHxxxx // 4(1938) | — | — | 12.50 | 18.50 | 25.00 | 35.00 |

### HAMMERED 'DUMP' COINAGE

**RUPEE** Y# A3 **Composition:** Silver **Ruler:** Bhupindar Singh VS1958-94/1900-37AD **Obverse:** Persian inscription: Guru Govind Singh **Note:** 11.10-11.20 grams.

| Date | Mintage | VG | F | VF | XF | Unc |
|---|---|---|---|---|---|---|
| VS1958(1901) | — | — | — | — | — | — |

**RUPEE** Y# A1 **Composition:** Silver **Ruler:** Yadvindar Singh VS1994-2005/1934-48AD **Obverse:** Persian inscription: Guru Govind Singh **Note:** 11.10-11.20 grams.

| Date | Mintage | VG | F | VF | XF | Unc |
|---|---|---|---|---|---|---|
| VS1994(1937) | — | — | — | — | — | — |

**1/6 MOHUR** Y# 14 **Weight:** 1.7500 g. **Composition:** Gold **Ruler:** Bhupindar Singh VS1958-94/1900-37AD **Obverse:** Persian inscription: Ahmad Shah Durrani **Reverse:** Dagger at left

| Date | Mintage | VG | F | VF | XF | Unc |
|---|---|---|---|---|---|---|
| VS(19)58(1901) | — | — | 85.00 | 100 | 125 | 175 |

**1/6 MOHUR** Y# 19 **Weight:** 1.7500 g. **Composition:** Gold **Ruler:** Yadvindar Singh VS1994-2005/1934-48AD **Obverse:** Persian inscription: Ahmad Shah Durrani **Reverse:** Bayoneted rifle at left

| Date | Mintage | VG | F | VF | XF | Unc |
|---|---|---|---|---|---|---|
| VS(19)94(1937) | — | — | 75.00 | 100 | 125 | 175 |

**1/3 MOHUR** KM# 15 **Weight:** 3.5000 g. **Composition:** Gold **Ruler:** Bhupindar Singh VS1958-94/1900-37AD **Obverse:** Persian inscription: Ahmad Shah Durrani

| Date | Mintage | VG | F | VF | XF | Unc |
|---|---|---|---|---|---|---|
| VS(19)58(1901) | — | — | 85.00 | 100 | 125 | 175 |

**1/3 MOHUR** KM# 20 **Weight:** 3.5000 g. **Composition:** Gold **Ruler:** Yadvindar Singh VS1994-2005/1934-48AD **Obverse:** Persian inscription: Ahmad Shah Durrani

| Date | Mintage | VG | F | VF | XF | Unc |
|---|---|---|---|---|---|---|
| VS(19)94(1937) | — | — | 75.00 | 100 | 125 | 175 |

**2/3 MOHUR** Y# 16 **Weight:** 7.0000 g. **Composition:** Gold **Ruler:** Bhupindar Singh VS1958-94/1900-37AD **Obverse:** Persian inscription: Ahmad Shah Durrani **Size:** 18 mm.

| Date | Mintage | VG | F | VF | XF | Unc |
|---|---|---|---|---|---|---|
| VS(19)58(1901) | — | — | 125 | 140 | 200 | 300 |

**2/3 MOHUR** Y# 21 **Weight:** 7.0000 g. **Composition:** Gold **Ruler:** Yadvindar Singh VS1994-2005/1934-48AD **Obverse:** Persian inscription: Ahmad Shah Durrani

| Date | Mintage | VG | F | VF | XF | Unc |
|---|---|---|---|---|---|---|
| VS(19)94(1937) | — | — | 150 | 185 | 225 | 275 |

**MOHUR** Y# 17 **Weight:** 10.5000 g. **Composition:** Gold **Ruler:** Bhupindar Singh VS1958-94/1900-37AD **Obverse:** Persian inscription: Ahmad Shah Durrani

| Date | Mintage | VG | F | VF | XF | Unc |
|---|---|---|---|---|---|---|
| VS(19)58(1901) | — | — | 150 | 200 | 275 | 400 |

## COOCH BEHAR

Cooch Behar was relatively peaceful until there was a dispute over the succession in 1772. After a confusing period during which the Bhutanese installed their own nominated ruler and captured Dhairyendra Narandra, the Chief Minister appealed to the British for assistance. With an eye on the potentially lucrative Tibetan trade, which had increased somewhat in volume since Prithvi Narayan's rise to power in Nepal, the British agreed to support Darendra Narayan, so long as British suzeraintv was acknowledged.

Over the following decades the British gradually increased their control over the state. After large numbers of debased silver half, or "Narainy" rupees had been struck, the British decided to close the mint, and after that a few coins only were struck at the coronation of each ruler, although it was only in 1866 that the local coins ceased to be legal tender.

**RULERS**

Nripendra Narayan, CB353-401/SE1785-1833/1863-1911AD
Raja Rajendra Narayan, CB401-403/SE1833-1835/1911-1913AD
Jitendra Narayan, CB403-412/SE1835-1844/1913-1922AD
Jagaddipendra Narayan, CB412-439/SE1844-1871/1922-1949AD

## PRINCELY STATE

### MILLED COINAGE

**NAZARANA 1/2 RUPEE** KM# 195 **Weight:** 4.7000 g. **Composition:** Silver **Ruler:** Raja Rajendra Narayan CB401-403; SE1833-1835; 1911-1913AD **Obverse:** Arms

| Date | Mintage | VG | F | VF | XF | Unc |
|---|---|---|---|---|---|---|
| CB402(1912) | 1,001 | — | — | 50.00 | 70.00 | 100 |

**NAZARANA 1/2 RUPEE** KM# 210 **Weight:** 4.7000 g. **Composition:** Silver **Ruler:** Jitendra Narayan CB403-412; SE1835-1844; 1913-1922AD **Obverse:** Arms

| Date | Mintage | VG | F | VF | XF | Unc |
|---|---|---|---|---|---|---|
| CB404(1914) | 1,004 | — | — | 50.00 | 70.00 | 100 |

**NAZARANA 1/2 RUPEE** KM# 225 **Weight:** 5.4000 g. **Composition:** Silver **Ruler:** Jagaddipendra Narayan CB412-439; SE1844-1871; 1922-1949AD **Obverse:** Arms

| Date | Mintage | VG | F | VF | XF | Unc |
|---|---|---|---|---|---|---|
| CB413(1923) | — | — | — | 35.00 | 50.00 | 70.00 |

**NAZARANA MOHUR** KM# 200 **Weight:** 8.5000 g. **Composition:** Gold **Ruler:** Raja Rajendra Narayan CB401-403; SE1833-1835; 1911-1913AD **Obverse:** Arms

| Date | Mintage | VG | F | VF | XF | Unc |
|---|---|---|---|---|---|---|
| CB402(1912) | 100 | — | — | — | 1,200 | 1,800 |

**NAZARANA MOHUR** KM# 215 **Weight:** 8.0000 g. **Composition:** Gold **Ruler:** Jitendra Narayan CB403-412; SE1835-1844; 1913-1922AD **Obverse:** Arms

| Date | Mintage | VG | F | VF | XF | Unc |
|---|---|---|---|---|---|---|
| CB404(1914) | 100 | — | — | — | 1,200 | 1,800 |

## DATIA

State located in north-central India, governed by Maharajas.

Datia was founded in 1735 by Bhagwan Das, son of Narsingh Dev of the Orchha royal house. In 1804 the State concluded its first treaty with the East India Company and thereafter came under British protection and control.

**RULERS**

Bhawani Singh, AH1274-1325/1857-1907AD
Govind Singh, AH1325-1368/1907-1948AD

**MINT**

Dalipnagar

**Gaja Shahi Series**

Struck for more than 100 years, with the AH date on the obverse and the regnal year on the reverse bearing little relationship to each other. These are close copies of Orchha C#24-32 and can only be distinguished by the symbols, which are always different from those of Orchha, except for the Gaja (mace):

Gaja always on reverse

On obverse (Datia Mint Symbol)

On reverse

# PRINCELY STATE

## MEDALLIC COINAGE

**1/2 MOHUR (Nazarana 1/2 Mohur)** KM# M1 **Composition:** Gold **Ruler:** Govind Singh AH1325-1368/1907-1948AD **Obverse:** Bust of Govind Singh 3/4 right **Reverse:** Arms **Note:** Weight varies 5.35 - 5.78 grams.

| Date | Mintage | F | VF | XF | Unc | BU |
|---|---|---|---|---|---|---|
| ND(1940) | — | — | 750 | 1,500 | 2,000 | — |

## HAMMERED 'DUMP' COINAGE

Gaja Shahi Series

Struck for more than 100 years, with the AH date on the obverse and the regnal year on the reverse bearing little relationship to each other. These are close copies of Orchha C#24-32 and can only be distinguished by the symbols, which are different from those of Orchha, accept for the Gaja (mace).

**1/2 PAISA** C# 22 **Weight:** 6.0000 g. **Composition:** Copper **Ruler:** Bhawani Singh AH1274-1325/1857-1907AD

| Date | Mintage | Good | VG | F | VF | XF |
|---|---|---|---|---|---|---|
| AH1320(1902) | — | 3.00 | 4.50 | 6.50 | 10.00 | — |

**PAISA** C# 23 **Composition:** Copper **Ruler:** Bhawani Singh AH1274-1325/1857-1907AD **Note:** Round or somewhat square shape, weight varies 12 - 13 grams.

| Date | Mintage | Good | VG | F | VF | XF |
|---|---|---|---|---|---|---|
| AH1320 / yr.46(1902-03) | — | 2.50 | 3.25 | 4.00 | 5.50 | — |

# DEWAS

A Maratha state located in west-central India. The raja, the brother of the raja of Dewas Senior Branch had a palace in Dewas City. They descended from two brothers, Tukoji and Jiwaji who were given Dewas City in 1726 by Peshwa Baji Rao as a reward for army services.

Largely due to its geographical location Dewas suffered much at the hands of the armies of Holkar and Sindhia,and from Pindari incursions. In 1818 the State came under British protection.

**LOCAL RULERS**

Vikrama Simha Rao, 1937-1948AD

# PRINCELY STATE

### Senior Branch

## MILLED COINAGE

**PAISA** KM# 13 **Composition:** Copper **Ruler:** Vikrama Simha Rao VS1994-2005/1937-1948AD **Obverse:** Bust of Vikrama Simha Rao right **Reverse:** Arms

| Date | Mintage | VG | F | VF | XF | Unc |
|---|---|---|---|---|---|---|
| 2000/1944 | — | 11.50 | 27.50 | 55.00 | 90.00 | 150 |
| 2001/1944 | — | 11.50 | 22.50 | 45.00 | 75.00 | 125 |

# DHAR

The territory in central India in which Dhar was located had been controlled by the Paramara clan of Rajputs from the 9th century to the 13th century, after which it passed into Muslim hands. The modern Princely State of Dhar originated in the first half of the 18th century when the Maratha Peshwa, Baji Rao, handed over the region as a fiefdom to Anand Rao Ponwar. Anand Rao Ponwar was of the same stock as the rulers of Dewas and a descendant of the original Paramara Rajputs. Sometimes in conflict with Holkar, sometimes with Sindhia, in 1819 Dhar came under British protection. No silver or gold coinage was ever struck at Dhar. In 1895 the British silver rupee was adopted.

**LOCAL RULERS**

Anand Rao IV, AH1363-1368/1943-1948AD

# PRINCELY STATE

## MEDALLIC COINAGE

**NAZARANA MOHUR** KM# M1 **Composition:** Gold **Ruler:** Anand Rao IV AH1363-1368/1943-1948AD

| Date | Mintage | VG | F | VF | XF | Unc |
|---|---|---|---|---|---|---|
| 1943 | — | — | — | 600 | 900 | 1,200 |

# DUNGARPUR

A district in northwest India which became part of Rajasthan in 1948.

The maharawals of Dungarpur were descended from the Mewar chieftains of the 12th century. In 1527 the upper Mahi basin was bifurcated to form the Princely States of Dungarpur and Banswara. Thereafter Dungarpur came successively under Mughal and Maratha control until in 1818 it came under British protection.

**RULERS**

Bijey Singh, VS1955-1975/1898-1918AD
Lakshman Singh, VS1975-2005/1918-1948AD

# PRINCELY STATE

## HAMMERED 'DUMP' COINAGE

**NAZARANA MOHUR** KM# 9 **Weight:** 11.0000 g. **Composition:** Gold **Ruler:** Lakshman Singh VS1975-2005/1918-1948AD

| Date | Mintage | Good | VG | F | VF | XF |
|---|---|---|---|---|---|---|
| VS1996(1939) Rare | — | — | — | — | — | — |
| VS2001(1944) Rare | — | — | — | — | — | — |

## WW II EMERGENCY COINAGE

**PAISA** KM# 7 **Composition:** Copper **Ruler:** Lakshman Singh VS1975-2005/1918-1948AD **Reverse:** 2 bars above 'P' in "Paisa"

| Date | Mintage | VG | F | VF | XF | Unc |
|---|---|---|---|---|---|---|
| VS2001(1944) | — | 18.50 | 30.00 | 50.00 | 75.00 | — |

**PAISA** KM# 8 **Composition:** Copper **Ruler:** Lakshman Singh VS1975-2005/1918-1948AD **Reverse:** One bar above 'P' in "Paisa"

| Date | Mintage | VG | F | VF | XF | Unc |
|---|---|---|---|---|---|---|
| VS2001(1944) | — | 9.00 | 15.00 | 25.00 | 37.50 | — |

# GWALIOR

### Sindhia

State located in central India. Capital originally was Ujjain (= Daru-l-fath), but was later transferred to Gwalior in 1810. The Gwalior ruling family, the Sindhias, were descendants of the Maratha chief Ranoji Sindhia (d.1750). His youngest son, Mahadji Sindhia (d.1794) was anxious to establish his independence from the overlordship of the Peshwas of Poona. Unable to achieve this alone, it was the Peshwa's crushing defeat by Ahmad Shah Durrani at Panipat in 1761, which helped realize his ambitions. Largely in the interests of sustaining this autonomy, but partly as a result of a defeat at East India Company hands in 1781, Mahadji concluded an alliance with the British in 1782. In 1785, he reinstalled the fallen Mughal Emperor, Shah Alam, on the throne at Dehli. Very early in the 19th century, Gwalior's relationship with the British began to deteriorate, a situation which culminated in the Anglo-Maratha War of 1803. Gwalior's forces under Daulat Rao were defeated. In consequence, and by the terms of the peace treaty which followed, his territory was truncated. In 1818, Gwalior suffered a further loss of land at British hands. In the years that ensued, as the East India Company's possessions became transformed into empire and as the Pax Britannica swept across the subcontinent, the Sindhia family's relationship with their British overlords steadily improved.

**RULERS**

Madho Rao, VS1943-1982/1886-1925AD
Jivaji Rao, VS1982-2005/1925-1948AD

**MINTS**

گواليار

Gwalior Fort

# PRINCELY STATE

## MILLED COINAGE

**1/2 PICE** KM# 164 **Composition:** Copper **Ruler:** Madho Rao VS1943-82/1886-1925AD **Obverse:** Plumes above crossed spear and trident **Size:** 20 mm.

| Date | Mintage | F | VF | XF | Unc | BU |
|---|---|---|---|---|---|---|
| VS1958(1901) | — | 0.65 | 2.00 | 4.00 | 10.00 | — |

**1/4 ANNA** KM# 169 **Composition:** Copper **Ruler:** Madho Rao VS1943-82/1886-1925AD **Obverse:** Plumes above crossed spear and trident

| Date | Mintage | F | VF | XF | Unc | BU |
|---|---|---|---|---|---|---|
| VS1958(1901) | — | 0.75 | 2.25 | 4.50 | 11.00 | — |

**1/4 ANNA** KM# 170 **Weight:** 6.6000 g. **Composition:** Copper **Ruler:** Madho Rao VS1943-82/1886-1925AD **Obverse:** Bust of Madho Rao right **Reverse:** Arms **Note:** Thick planchet (2.2 millimeters).

| Date | Mintage | F | VF | XF | Unc | BU |
|---|---|---|---|---|---|---|
| VS1970(1913) | — | 0.25 | 0.75 | 1.50 | 3.00 | — |

**1/4 ANNA** KM# 171 **Weight:** 5.1000 g. **Composition:** Copper **Ruler:** Madho Rao VS1943-82/1886-1925AD **Obverse:** Bust of Madho Rao right **Reverse:** Arms **Note:** Thin planchet (1.6 millimeters).

| Date | Mintage | F | VF | XF | Unc | BU |
|---|---|---|---|---|---|---|
| VS1970(1913) | — | 1.25 | 3.50 | 5.00 | 7.00 | — |
| VS1974(1917) | — | 0.25 | 0.75 | 1.50 | 3.00 | — |

**1/4 ANNA** KM# 172 **Composition:** Copper **Ruler:** Madho Rao VS1943-82/1886-1925AD **Obverse:** Bust of Madho Rao right, continuous legend around portrait **Reverse:** Arms

| Date | Mintage | F | VF | XF | Unc | BU |
|---|---|---|---|---|---|---|
| VS1974(1917) | — | 4.00 | 6.00 | 9.00 | 12.50 | — |

**1/4 ANNA** KM# 177 **Composition:** Copper **Ruler:** Jivaji Rao VS1985-2005/1925-48AD **Obverse:** Crude style bust of Jivaji Rao left **Reverse:** Arms **Note:** Thin planchet. 3.00-3.15 grams.

| Date | Mintage | F | VF | XF | Unc | BU |
|---|---|---|---|---|---|---|
| VS1986(1929) | — | 0.75 | 2.50 | 3.50 | 6.00 | — |
| VS1999(1942) | — | 1.00 | 3.50 | 5.00 | 7.50 | — |

**1/4 ANNA** KM# 176.1 **Composition:** Copper **Ruler:** Jivaji Rao VS1985-2005/1925-48AD **Obverse:** Fine style bust of Jivaji Rao left **Reverse:** Arms **Note:** Thick planchet. 4.65-5.15 grams.

| Date | Mintage | F | VF | XF | Unc | BU |
|---|---|---|---|---|---|---|
| VS1986(1929) | — | 0.25 | 0.75 | 1.50 | 3.00 | — |

**1/4 ANNA** KM# 176.2 **Composition:** Copper **Ruler:** Jivaji Rao VS1985-2005/1925-48AD **Obverse:** Crude style "pug-nose" bust of Jivaji Rao left **Reverse:** Arms

| Date | Mintage | F | VF | XF | Unc | BU |
|---|---|---|---|---|---|---|
| VS1986(1929) | — | 0.25 | 0.75 | 1.50 | 3.00 | — |

**1/4 ANNA** KM# 178.1 **Composition:** Copper **Ruler:** Jivaji Rao VS1985-2005/1925-48AD **Obverse:** Facing coiled cobras below bust of Jivaji Rao left **Reverse:** Arms, without inscription on side

| Date | Mintage | F | VF | XF | Unc | BU |
|---|---|---|---|---|---|---|
| VS1999(1942) | — | 0.20 | 0.60 | 1.00 | 2.00 | — |

**1/4 ANNA** KM# 178.2 **Composition:** Copper **Ruler:** Jivaji Rao VS1985-2005/1925-48AD **Obverse:** Without facing coiled cobras below bust of Jivaji Rao left **Reverse:** Arms

| Date | Mintage | F | VF | XF | Unc | BU |
|---|---|---|---|---|---|---|
| VS1999(1942) | — | 0.20 | 0.60 | 1.00 | 2.00 | — |

**1/2 ANNA** KM# 179 **Composition:** Brass **Ruler:** Jivaji Rao VS1985-2005/1925-48AD **Obverse:** Bust of Jivaji Rao left **Reverse:** Arms

| Date | Mintage | F | VF | XF | Unc | BU |
|---|---|---|---|---|---|---|
| VS1999(1942) | — | 0.20 | 0.60 | 1.00 | 2.00 | — |
| VS1999(1942) Proof | — | Value: 50.00 | | | | |

**1/3 MOHUR** KM# 175 **Weight:** 3.4500 g. **Composition:** Gold **Ruler:** Madho Rao VS1943-82/1886-1925AD **Obverse:** Bust of Madho Rao right **Reverse:** Arms

| Date | Mintage | F | VF | XF | Unc | BU |
|---|---|---|---|---|---|---|
| VS1959(1902) | — | 265 | 550 | 900 | 1,300 | — |

## PATTERNS

Including off metal strikes

| KM# | Date | Mintage | Identification | Mkt Val |
|---|---|---|---|---|
| Pn1 | 1977(1920) | — | 4 Anna. Silver. | — |

# HYDERABAD

**Haidarabad**

Hyderabad State, the largest Indian State and the last remnant of Mughal suzerainty in South or Central India, traced its foundation to Nizam-ul Mulk, the Mughal viceroy in the Deccan. From about 1724 the first nizam, as the rulers of Hyderabad came to be called, took advantage of Mughal decline in the North to assert an all but ceremonial independence of the emperor. The East India Company defeated Hyderabad's natural enemies, the Muslim rulers of Mysore and the Marathas, with the help of troops furnished under alliances between them and the Nizam. This formed the beginning of a relationship, which persisted for a century and a half until India's Independence. Hyderabad was the premier Princely State, with a population (in 1935) of fourteen and a half million. It was not absorbed into the Indian Union until 1948. Hyderabad City is located beside Golkonda, the citadel of the Qutb Shahi sultans until they were overthrown by Aurangzeb in 1687. A beautifully located city on the bank of the Musi river, the mint epithet was appropriately Farkhanda Bunyad, "of happy foundation".

Hyderabad exercised authority over a number of feudatories or samasthans. Some of these, such as Gadwal and Shorapur, paid tribute to both the Nizam and the Marathas. These feudatories were generally in the hands of local rajas whose ancestry predated the establishment of Hyderabad State. There were also many mints in the State, both private and government. There was little or no standardization of the purity of silver coinage until the 20th century. At least one banker, Pestonji Meherji by name, was distinguished by minting his own coins.

**RULERS**

Mir Mahbub Ali Khan II, AH1285-1329/1869-1911AD
Mir Usman Ali Khan, AH1329-1367/1911-1948AD

**MINTS**

فرخنده بنیاد حیدراباد

Haidarabad
Mintname: Farkhanda Bunyad Haidarabad

## PRINCELY STATE

### HAMMERED 'DUMP' COINAGE

**1/16 RUPEE** Y# 13 **Weight:** 0.6980 g. **Composition:** 0.8180 Silver .0183 oz. ASW **Ruler:** Mir Mahbub Ali Khan II AH1285-1329/1869-1911AD **Obverse:** Inscription: Asaf Jah, Nizam al-Mulk, Founder of the Nizami line; Persian letter "M' for Mahbub above "k" of "Mulk"

| Date | Mintage | VG | F | VF | XF | Unc |
|---|---|---|---|---|---|---|
| AH1321/37(1903-04) | — | 1.00 | 1.75 | 2.50 | 4.00 | — |

**1/8 RUPEE** Y# 14 **Weight:** 1.3970 g. **Composition:** 0.8180 Silver .0367 oz. ASW **Ruler:** Mir Mahbub Ali Khan II AH1285-1329/1869-1911AD **Obverse:** Inscription: Asaf Jah, Nizam al-Mulk, Founder of the Nizami line; Persian letter "M' for Mahbub above "k" of "Mulk"

| Date | Mintage | VG | F | VF | XF | Unc |
|---|---|---|---|---|---|---|
| AH1321/37(1903-04) | — | 1.75 | 2.25 | 3.00 | 4.50 | — |

**1/4 RUPEE** Y# 15 **Weight:** 2.7940 g. **Composition:** 0.8180 Silver .0735 oz. ASW **Ruler:** Mir Mahbub Ali Khan II AH1285-1329/1869-1911AD **Obverse:** Inscription: Asaf Jah, Nizam al-Mulk, Founder of the Nizami line; Persian letter "M' for Mahbub above "k" of "Mulk"

| Date | Mintage | VG | F | VF | XF | Unc |
|---|---|---|---|---|---|---|
| AH1321/37(1903-04) | — | 2.00 | 2.75 | 4.50 | 7.00 | — |

**RUPEE** Y# 17 **Weight:** 11.1780 g. **Composition:** 0.8180 Silver .2940 oz. ASW **Ruler:** Mir Mahbub Ali Khan II AH1285-1329/1869-1911AD **Obverse:** Inscription: Asaf Jah, Nizam al-Mulk, Founder of the Nizami line; Persian letter "M' for Mahbub above "k" of "Mulk"

| Date | Mintage | VG | F | VF | XF | Unc |
|---|---|---|---|---|---|---|
| AH1318/34(1900-01) | — | 4.50 | 5.50 | 7.00 | 14.00 | — |

**1/16 ASHRAFI** Y# 18 **Weight:** 0.6980 g. **Composition:** 0.9100 Gold **Ruler:** Mir Mahbub Ali Khan II AH1285-1329/1869-1911AD **Obverse:** Inscription: Asaf Jah, Nizam al-Mulk, Founder of the Nizami line; Persian letter "M" for Mahbub above "k" of "Mulk"

| Date | Mintage | VG | F | VF | XF | Unc |
|---|---|---|---|---|---|---|
| AH1321/37(1903-04) | — | 20.00 | 30.00 | 40.00 | 60.00 | — |

**1/8 ASHRAFI** Y# 19 **Weight:** 1.3970 g. **Composition:** 0.9100 Gold **Ruler:** Mir Mahbub Ali Khan II AH1285-1329/1869-1911AD **Obverse:** Inscription: Asaf Jah, Nizam al-Mulk, Founder of the Nizami line; Persian letter "M" for Mahbub above "k" of "Mulk"

| Date | Mintage | VG | F | VF | XF | Unc |
|---|---|---|---|---|---|---|
| AH1293 | — | 25.00 | 40.00 | 60.00 | 75.00 | — |
| AH1302 | — | 25.00 | 40.00 | 60.00 | 75.00 | — |
| AH1306 | — | 25.00 | 40.00 | 60.00 | 75.00 | — |
| AH1309 | — | 25.00 | 40.00 | 60.00 | 75.00 | — |
| AH1313 | — | 25.00 | 40.00 | 60.00 | 75.00 | — |
| AH1316 | — | 25.00 | 40.00 | 60.00 | 75.00 | — |
| AH1317/33 | — | 25.00 | 40.00 | 60.00 | 75.00 | — |
| AH1318 | — | 25.00 | 40.00 | 60.00 | 75.00 | — |
| AH1320(1902-03) | — | 25.00 | 40.00 | 60.00 | 75.00 | — |
| AH1321(1903-04) | — | 25.00 | 40.00 | 60.00 | 75.00 | — |

**1/4 ASHRAFI** Y# 20 **Weight:** 2.7940 g. **Composition:** 0.9100 Gold **Ruler:** Mir Mahbub Ali Khan II AH1285-1329/1869-1911AD **Obverse:** Inscription: Asaf Jah, Nizam al-Mulk, Founder of the Nizami line; Persian letter "M" for Mahbub above "k" of "Mulk"

| Date | Mintage | VG | F | VF | XF | Unc |
|---|---|---|---|---|---|---|
| AH1301 | — | 45.00 | 60.00 | 80.00 | 100 | — |
| AH1304 | — | 45.00 | 60.00 | 80.00 | 100 | — |
| AH1306 | — | 45.00 | 60.00 | 80.00 | 100 | — |
| AH1309 | — | 45.00 | 60.00 | 80.00 | 100 | — |
| AH1314/30 | — | 45.00 | 60.00 | 80.00 | 100 | — |
| AH1315 | — | 45.00 | 60.00 | 80.00 | 100 | — |
| AH1316 | — | 45.00 | 60.00 | 80.00 | 100 | — |
| AH1318/35(1901) | — | 45.00 | 60.00 | 80.00 | 100 | — |
| AH1319/35(1901-02) | — | 45.00 | 60.00 | 80.00 | 100 | — |

**1/2 ASHRAFI** Y# 21 **Weight:** 5.5890 g. **Composition:** 0.9100 Gold **Ruler:** Mir Mahbub Ali Khan II AH1285-1329/1869-1911AD **Obverse:** Inscription: Asaf Jah, Nizam al-Mulk, Founder of the Nizami line; Persian letter "M" for Mahbub above "k" of "Mulk"

| Date | Mintage | VG | F | VF | XF | Unc |
|---|---|---|---|---|---|---|
| AH1320(1902-03) | — | 75.00 | 90.00 | 110 | 140 | — |
| AH1321(1903-04)(1903) | — | 75.00 | 90.00 | 110 | 140 | — |

**1/2 ASHRAFI** Y# 21 **Weight:** 5.5890 g. **Composition:** 0.9100 Gold **Ruler:** Mir Mahbub Ali Khan II AH1285-1329/1869-1911AD **Obverse:** Inscription: Asaf Jah, Nizam al-Mulk, Founder of the Nizami line; Persian letter "M" for Mahbub above "k" of "Mulk"

| Date | Mintage | VG | F | VF | XF | Unc |
|---|---|---|---|---|---|---|
| AH1320(1902-03) | — | 75.00 | 90.00 | 110 | 140 | — |
| AH1321(1903-04)(1903) | — | 75.00 | 90.00 | 110 | 140 | — |

**ASHRAFI** Y# 22 **Weight:** 11.1780 g. **Composition:** 0.9100 Gold **Ruler:** Mir Mahbub Ali Khan II AH1285-1329/1869-1911AD **Obverse:** Inscription: Asaf Jah, Nizam al-Mulk, Founder of the Nizami line; Persian letter "M" for Mahbub above "k" of "Mulk"

| Date | Mintage | VG | F | VF | XF | Unc |
|---|---|---|---|---|---|---|
| AH1319(1901) | — | 150 | 170 | 200 | 250 | — |
| AH1320 | — | 150 | 170 | 200 | 250 | — |
| AH1321 | — | 150 | 170 | 200 | 250 | — |

**ASHRAFI** Y# 22 **Weight:** 11.1780 g. **Composition:** 0.9100 Gold **Ruler:** Mir Mahbub Ali Khan II AH1285-1329/1869-1911AD **Obverse:** Inscription: Asaf Jah, Nizam al-Mulk, Founder of the Nizami line; Persian letter "M" for Mahbub above "k" of "Mulk"

| Date | Mintage | VG | F | VF | XF | Unc |
|---|---|---|---|---|---|---|
| AH1319(1901) | — | 150 | 170 | 200 | 250 | — |
| AH1320 | — | 150 | 170 | 200 | 250 | — |
| AH1321 | — | 150 | 170 | 200 | 250 | — |

## MILLED COINAGE

### Provisional Series

**2 ANNAS Y# 29 Weight:** 1.3970 g. **Composition:** 0.8180 Silver **Ruler:** Mir Mahbub Ali Khan II AH1285-1329/1869-1911AD **Obverse:** Inscription: Asaf Jah, Nizam al-Mulk, Founder of the Nizami line; Persian letter "M" for Mahbub above "k" of "Mulk"

| Date | Mintage | VG | F | VF | XF | Unc |
|---|---|---|---|---|---|---|
| AH1318/35(1901) | — | 10.00 | 17.50 | 27.50 | 37.50 | — |

**4 ANNAS Y# 30 Weight:** 2.7940 g. **Composition:** 0.8180 Silver **Ruler:** Mir Mahbub Ali Khan II AH1285-1329/1869-1911AD **Obverse:** Inscription: Asaf Jah, Nizam al-Mulk, Founder of the Nizami line; Persian letter "M" for Mahbub above "k" of "Mulk"

| Date | Mintage | VG | F | VF | XF | Unc |
|---|---|---|---|---|---|---|
| AH1318/34(1900-01) | — | 8.50 | 16.50 | 25.00 | 33.50 | — |
| AH1318/35(1901) | — | 8.50 | 16.50 | 25.00 | 33.50 | — |

**8 ANNAS Y# 31 Weight:** 5.5890 g. **Composition:** 0.8180 Silver **Ruler:** Mir Mahbub Ali Khan II AH1285-1329/1869-1911AD **Obverse:** Inscription: Asaf Jah, Nizam al-Mulk, Founder of the Nizami line; Persian letter "M" for Mahbub above "k" of "Mulk"

| Date | Mintage | VG | F | VF | XF | Unc |
|---|---|---|---|---|---|---|
| AH1318/34 (1900-01) | — | 10.00 | 20.00 | 30.00 | 40.00 | — |
| AH1318/35(1901) | — | 10.00 | 20.00 | 30.00 | 40.00 | — |

## MILLED COINAGE

### Standard Series

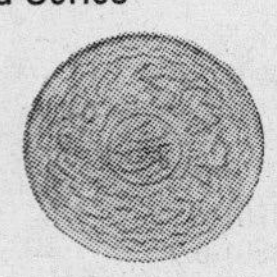

**PAI Y# 34 Composition:** Copper **Ruler:** Mir Mahbub Ali Khan II AH1285-1329/1869-1911AD **Obverse:** Toughra

| Date | Mintage | F | VF | XF | Unc | BU |
|---|---|---|---|---|---|---|
| AH1326/42(1908) | — | 4.00 | 6.00 | 9.00 | 15.00 | — |
| AH1327/42(1909) | — | 4.00 | 6.00 | 9.00 | 15.00 | — |

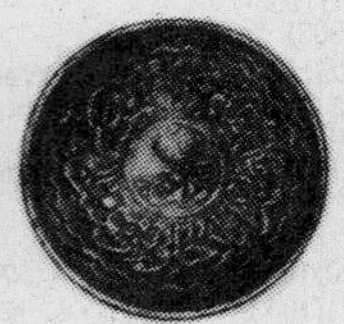

**2 PAI Y# 35 Composition:** Copper **Ruler:** Mir Mahbub Ali Khan II AH1285-1329/1869-1911AD **Obverse:** Toughra

| Date | Mintage | F | VF | XF | Unc | BU |
|---|---|---|---|---|---|---|
| AH1322/37(1904) | — | 1.00 | 1.25 | 1.75 | 2.75 | — |
| AH1322/38(1904) | — | 0.75 | 1.00 | 1.50 | 2.50 | — |
| AH1322/39(1905) | — | 1.00 | 1.25 | 1.75 | 2.75 | — |
| AH1323/38(1905) | — | 1.00 | 1.25 | 1.75 | 2.75 | — |
| AH1323/39(1905) | — | 0.60 | 0.75 | 1.00 | 1.50 | — |
| AH1323/40(1906) | — | 0.75 | 1.00 | 1.50 | 2.50 | — |
| AH1323/41(1906) | — | 0.75 | 1.00 | 1.50 | 2.50 | — |
| AH1324/39(1906) | — | 1.00 | 1.25 | 1.75 | 2.75 | — |
| AH1324/40(1906) | — | 0.60 | 0.85 | 1.25 | 1.75 | — |
| AH1324/41(1907) | — | 0.75 | 1.00 | 1.50 | 2.50 | — |
| AH1325/40(1907) | — | 1.00 | 1.25 | 1.75 | 2.75 | — |
| AH1325/41(1907) | — | 0.75 | 1.00 | 1.50 | 2.50 | — |
| AH1329/43(1911) | — | 0.50 | 0.65 | 1.00 | 1.75 | — |
| AH1329/44(1911) | — | 0.50 | 0.65 | 1.00 | 1.75 | — |
| AH1329/45(1911) | — | 0.50 | 0.65 | 1.00 | 1.75 | — |

**1/2 ANNA Y# 36 Composition:** Copper **Ruler:** Mir Mahbub Ali Khan II AH1285-1329/1869-1911AD **Obverse:** Toughra

| Date | Mintage | VG | F | VF | XF | Unc |
|---|---|---|---|---|---|---|
| AH1324/38(1906) | — | 1.00 | 2.50 | 4.00 | 6.00 | 10.00 |
| AH1324/40(1906-07) | — | 0.60 | 1.50 | 2.25 | 3.00 | 4.00 |
| AH1325/40(1907) | — | 0.80 | 2.00 | 3.25 | 3.75 | 5.50 |
| AH1325/41(1907) | — | 0.80 | 2.00 | 3.25 | 3.75 | 5.50 |
| AH1324/41(1907-08) | — | 0.90 | 2.25 | 3.00 | 3.50 | 4.50 |
| AH1326/41(1908) | — | 1.00 | 2.50 | 3.75 | 4.50 | 7.00 |
| AH1329/44(1911) | — | 0.60 | 1.50 | 2.50 | 3.00 | 4.00 |

**2 ANNAS Y# 37 Weight:** 1.3900 g. **Composition:** 0.8180 Silver .0367 oz. ASW **Ruler:** Mir Mahbub Ali Khan II AH1285-1329/1869-1911AD **Obverse:** Chahar Minar gateway

| Date | Mintage | VG | F | VF | XF | Unc |
|---|---|---|---|---|---|---|
| AH1323/34(1905) | — | 0.60 | 1.50 | 2.50 | 5.00 | 8.00 |
| **Note:** R.Y. '34' error for '39' | | | | | | |
| AH1323/39(1905-06) | — | 0.30 | 0.75 | 1.25 | 3.00 | 5.00 |

**4 ANNAS Y# 38.1 Weight:** 2.7940 g. **Composition:** 0.8180 Silver .0735 oz. ASW **Ruler:** Mir Mahbub Ali Khan II AH1285-1329/1869-1911AD **Obverse:** Chahar Minar gateway, signature variety Type I between minarets

| Date | Mintage | VG | F | VF | XF | Unc |
|---|---|---|---|---|---|---|
| AH1323/39(1905-06) | — | 1.50 | 4.00 | 4.75 | 5.50 | 9.00 |
| AH1326/43(1909) | — | 3.50 | 8.50 | 16.50 | 25.00 | 32.50 |

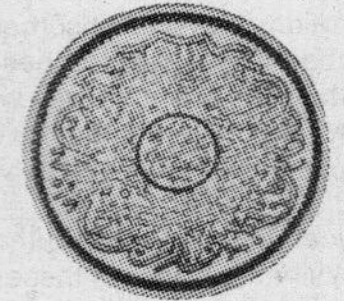

**4 ANNAS Y# 38.2 Weight:** 2.7940 g. **Composition:** 0.8180 Silver .0735 oz. ASW **Ruler:** Mir Mahbub Ali Khan II AH1285-1329/1869-1911AD **Obverse:** Chahar Minar gateway, signature variety Type I between minarets **Note:** Struck with dies of 1/2 Ashrafi.

| Date | Mintage | VG | F | VF | XF | Unc |
|---|---|---|---|---|---|---|
| AH1324/40(1906-07) | — | — | — | — | — | — |

**4 ANNAS Y# 38.3 Weight:** 2.7940 g. **Composition:** 0.8180 Silver .0735 oz. ASW **Ruler:** Mir Mahbub Ali Khan II AH1285-1329/1869-1911AD **Obverse:** Chahar Minar gateway, signature variety Type II between minarets

| Date | Mintage | VG | F | VF | XF | Unc |
|---|---|---|---|---|---|---|
| AH1328/43(1910) | — | 1.50 | 4.00 | 4.75 | 6.00 | 10.00 |
| AH1329/44(1911) | — | 1.50 | 4.00 | 4.75 | 5.50 | 9.00 |

**8 ANNAS Y# 39.1 Weight:** 5.5890 g. **Composition:** 0.8180 Silver .1470 oz. ASW **Ruler:** Mir Mahbub Ali Khan II AH1285-1329/1869-1911AD **Obverse:** Chahar Minar gateway, signature variety Type I

| Date | Mintage | VG | F | VF | XF | Unc |
|---|---|---|---|---|---|---|
| AH1322/38(1904-05) | — | — | — | — | — | — |

**8 ANNAS Y# 39.2 Weight:** 5.5890 g. **Composition:** 0.8180 Silver .1470 oz. ASW **Ruler:** Mir Mahbub Ali Khan II AH1285-1329/1869-1911AD **Obverse:** Chahar Minar gateway, signature variety Type II between minarets

| Date | Mintage | VG | F | VF | XF | Unc |
|---|---|---|---|---|---|---|
| AH1328/43(1910) | — | 2.75 | 6.50 | 7.50 | 9.00 | 15.00 |
| AH1329/44(1911) | — | 2.75 | 6.50 | 7.50 | 9.00 | 15.00 |

**RUPEE Y# 40.1 Weight:** 11.1780 g. **Composition:** 0.8180 Silver .2940 oz. ASW **Ruler:** Mir Mahbub Ali Khan II AH1285-1329/1869-1911AD **Obverse:** Chahar Minar gateway, signature variety Type I between minarets

| Date | Mintage | VG | F | VF | XF | Unc |
|---|---|---|---|---|---|---|
| AH1319/35(1901-02) | — | 4.75 | 11.50 | 13.50 | 16.50 | 27.50 |
| AH1321/37(1903-04) | — | 4.75 | 11.50 | 13.50 | 16.50 | 27.50 |
| AH1322/38(1904) | — | 4.75 | 11.50 | 13.50 | 15.00 | 25.00 |
| AH1321/38(1904-05) | — | 4.75 | 11.50 | 13.50 | 15.00 | 25.00 |
| AH1323/39(1905-06) | — | 4.75 | 11.50 | 13.50 | 15.00 | 25.00 |
| AH1322/39(1905) | — | 4.75 | 11.50 | 13.50 | 15.00 | 25.00 |
| AH1324/40(1906-07) | — | 4.75 | 11.50 | 13.50 | 15.00 | 25.00 |
| AH1325/41(1907) | — | 4.75 | 11.50 | 13.50 | 15.00 | 25.00 |
| AH1326/41(1908) | — | 4.75 | 11.50 | 13.50 | 15.00 | 25.00 |

**RUPEE Y# 40.2 Weight:** 11.1780 g. **Composition:** 0.8180 Silver .2940 oz. ASW **Ruler:** Mir Mahbub Ali Khan II AH1285-1329/1869-1911AD **Obverse:** Chahar Minar gateway, signature variety Type II between minarets

| Date | Mintage | VG | F | VF | XF | Unc |
|---|---|---|---|---|---|---|
| AH1328/43(1910) | — | 4.75 | 11.50 | 13.50 | 15.00 | 25.00 |
| AH1329/44(1911) | — | 4.75 | 11.50 | 13.50 | 15.00 | 25.00 |

**1/8 ASHRAFI Y# 41.1 Weight:** 1.3940 g. **Composition:** 0.9100 Gold **Ruler:** Mir Mahbub Ali Khan II AH1285-1329/1869-1911AD **Obverse:** Chahar Minar gateway, signature variety Type I between minarets

| Date | Mintage | VG | F | VF | XF | Unc |
|---|---|---|---|---|---|---|
| AH1325/41 (1907-08) | — | — | 35.00 | 50.00 | 65.00 | 85.00 |

**1/8 ASHRAFI Y# 41.2 Weight:** 1.3940 g. **Composition:** 0.9100 Gold **Ruler:** Mir Mahbub Ali Khan II AH1285-1329/1869-1911AD **Obverse:** Chahar Minar gateway, signature variety Type II between minarets

| Date | Mintage | VG | F | VF | XF | Unc |
|---|---|---|---|---|---|---|
| AH1329/44 | — | — | 35.00 | 50.00 | 65.00 | 85.00 |

**1/4 ASHRAFI Y# 42.1 Weight:** 2.7940 g. **Composition:** 0.9100 Gold **Ruler:** Mir Mahbub Ali Khan II AH1285-1329/1869-1911AD **Obverse:** Chahar Minar gateway, signature variety Type I between minarets

| Date | Mintage | VG | F | VF | XF | Unc |
|---|---|---|---|---|---|---|
| AH1325/41(1907-08) | — | — | 50.00 | 65.00 | 85.00 | 125 |

**1/4 ASHRAFI Y# 42.2 Weight:** 2.7940 g. **Composition:** 0.9100 Gold **Ruler:** Mir Mahbub Ali Khan II AH1285-1329/1869-1911AD **Obverse:** Chahar Minar gateway, signature variety Type II between minarets

| Date | Mintage | VG | F | VF | XF | Unc |
|---|---|---|---|---|---|---|
| AH1328/43 | — | — | 50.00 | 65.00 | 85.00 | 125 |
| AH1329/44 | — | — | 50.00 | 65.00 | 85.00 | 125 |

**1/2 ASHRAFI Y# 43.1 Weight:** 5.5890 g. **Composition:** 0.9100 Gold **Ruler:** Mir Mahbub Ali Khan II AH1285-1329/1869-1911AD **Obverse:** Chahar Minar gateway, signature variety Type I between minarets

| Date | Mintage | VG | F | VF | XF | Unc |
|---|---|---|---|---|---|---|
| AH1325/41 | — | — | 80.00 | 110 | 150 | 250 |
| AH1326/41 | — | — | 80.00 | 110 | 150 | 250 |

**1/2 ASHRAFI Y# 43.2 Weight:** 5.5890 g. **Composition:** 0.9100 Gold **Ruler:** Mir Mahbub Ali Khan II AH1285-1329/1869-1911AD **Obverse:** Chahar Minar gateway, signature variety Type II between minarets

| Date | Mintage | VG | F | VF | XF | Unc |
|---|---|---|---|---|---|---|
| AH1328/43 | — | — | 80.00 | 110 | 150 | 250 |
| AH1329/44 | — | — | 80.00 | 110 | 150 | 250 |

**ASHRAFI** **Y# 44.1** **Weight:** 11.1780 g. **Composition:** 0.9100 Gold **Ruler:** Mir Mahbub Ali Khan II AH1285-1329/1869-1911AD **Obverse:** Chahar Minar gateway, signature variety Type I between minarets

| Date | Mintage | F | VF | XF | Unc | BU |
|---|---|---|---|---|---|---|
| AH1325/41(1907) | — | 165 | 225 | 300 | 400 | — |

**ASHRAFI** **Y# 44.2** **Weight:** 11.1780 g. **Composition:** 0.9100 Gold **Ruler:** Mir Mahbub Ali Khan II AH1285-1329/1869-1911AD **Obverse:** Chahar Minar gateway, signature variety Type II between minarets

| Date | Mintage | F | VF | XF | Unc | BU |
|---|---|---|---|---|---|---|
| AH1328/43(1910) | — | 165 | 225 | 300 | 400 | — |
| AH1329/44(1911) | — | 165 | 225 | 300 | 400 | — |

## MILLED COINAGE

First Series

**PAI** **Y# 45** **Composition:** Bronze **Ruler:** Mir Usman Ali Khan AH1329-67/1911-48AD **Obverse:** Toughra

| Date | Mintage | F | VF | XF | Unc | BU |
|---|---|---|---|---|---|---|
| AH1338(1919) | — | 1.50 | 2.00 | 2.50 | 4.00 | — |
| AH1344/15(1925) | — | 0.60 | 0.75 | 1.00 | 1.50 | — |
| AH1349/20(1930) | — | 0.60 | 0.75 | 1.00 | 1.50 | — |
| AH1352/23(1933) | — | 1.00 | 1.25 | 1.50 | 2.50 | — |
| AH1352/24(1934) | — | 1.00 | 1.25 | 1.50 | 2.50 | — |
| AH1353/23(1934) | — | 1.00 | 1.25 | 1.50 | 2.50 | — |
| AH1353/24(1934) | — | 0.70 | 0.85 | 1.10 | 1.75 | — |

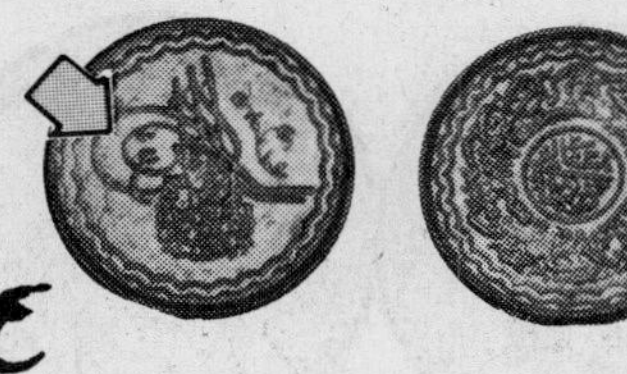

**2 PAI** **Y# 46a** **Composition:** Bronze **Ruler:** Mir Usman Ali Khan AH1329-67/1911-48AD **Obverse:** Full "Ain" in toughra

| Date | Mintage | F | VF | XF | Unc | BU |
|---|---|---|---|---|---|---|
| AH1330/1(1911) | — | 1.50 | 2.00 | 2.50 | 3.50 | — |
| AH1331/2(1912) | — | 0.35 | 0.50 | 0.65 | 1.00 | — |
| AH1330/2(1912) | — | 0.35 | 0.50 | 0.65 | 1.00 | — |
| AH1332/3(1913) | — | 0.35 | 0.50 | 0.65 | 1.00 | — |
| AH1331/3(1913) | — | 0.50 | 0.65 | 0.75 | 1.00 | — |
| AH1333/3(1914) | — | 0.60 | 0.75 | 1.00 | 1.50 | — |
| AH1333/4(1914) | — | 0.35 | 0.50 | 0.65 | 1.00 | — |
| AH1332/4(1914) | — | 0.60 | 0.75 | 1.00 | 1.50 | — |
| AH1334/3(1915) | — | 0.60 | 0.75 | 1.00 | 1.50 | — |
| AH1333/5(1915) | — | 0.75 | 1.00 | 1.25 | 2.00 | — |
| AH1335/6(1916) | — | 0.35 | 0.50 | 0.65 | 1.00 | — |
| AH1336/7(1917) | — | 0.35 | 0.50 | 0.65 | 1.00 | — |
| AH1335/7(1917) | — | 0.35 | 0.50 | 0.65 | 1.00 | — |
| AH1337/7(1918) | — | 0.75 | 1.00 | 1.25 | 2.00 | — |
| AH1337/8(1918) | — | 0.60 | 0.75 | 1.00 | 1.50 | — |
| AH1336/8(1918) | — | 0.50 | 0.65 | 0.80 | 1.25 | — |
| AH1338/8(1919) | — | 0.75 | 1.00 | 1.25 | 2.00 | — |
| AH1338/9(1919) | — | 0.35 | 0.50 | 0.65 | 1.00 | — |
| AH1339/10(1920) | — | 0.75 | 1.00 | 1.25 | 2.00 | — |
| AH1338/11(1920) | — | 0.50 | 0.75 | 1.00 | 1.50 | — |
| AH1339/11(1921) | — | 0.75 | 1.00 | 1.25 | 2.00 | — |
| AH1342/13(1923) | — | 0.60 | 0.75 | 1.00 | 1.50 | — |
| AH1343/14(1924) | — | 0.35 | 0.50 | 0.65 | 1.00 | — |
| AH1342/14(1924) | — | 0.35 | 0.50 | 0.65 | 1.00 | — |
| AH1344/15(1925) | — | 0.50 | 0.65 | 0.80 | 1.25 | — |
| AH1343/15(1925) | — | 0.40 | 0.60 | 0.75 | 1.25 | — |
| AH1345/16(1926) | — | 0.35 | 0.50 | 0.65 | 1.00 | — |
| AH1347/18(1928) | — | 0.75 | 1.00 | 1.25 | 2.00 | — |
| AH1348/19(1929) | — | 0.35 | 0.50 | 0.65 | 1.00 | — |
| AH1347/19(1929) | — | 0.75 | 1.00 | 1.25 | 2.00 | — |
| AH1349/20(1930) | — | 0.35 | 0.50 | 0.65 | 1.00 | — |

**2 PAI** **Y# 46** **Composition:** Bronze **Ruler:** Mir Usman Ali Khan AH1329-67/1911-48AD **Obverse:** Short "Ain" in toughra **Note:** See also 1 Rupee, Y#53 and Y#53a.

| Date | Mintage | F | VF | XF | Unc | BU |
|---|---|---|---|---|---|---|
| AH1329/1(1911) | — | 10.00 | 15.00 | 22.50 | 35.00 | — |
| AH1330/1(1911) | — | 8.00 | 12.50 | 20.00 | 32.50 | — |

**1/2 ANNA** **Y# 47** **Composition:** Bronze **Ruler:** Mir Usman Ali Khan AH1329-67/1911-48AD **Obverse:** Toughra

| Date | Mintage | F | VF | XF | Unc | BU |
|---|---|---|---|---|---|---|
| AH1332/2(1913) | — | 0.75 | 1.00 | 1.25 | 2.00 | — |
| AH1332/3(1913) | — | 0.75 | 1.00 | 1.25 | 2.00 | — |
| AH1334/4(1915) | — | 1.25 | 1.50 | 2.00 | 3.25 | — |
| AH1344/15(1925) | — | 1.25 | 1.50 | 2.00 | 3.25 | — |
| AH1348/20(1930) | — | 1.00 | 1.35 | 1.75 | 2.75 | — |

**ANNA** **Y# 48** **Composition:** Copper-Nickel **Ruler:** Mir Usman Ali Khan AH1329-67/1911-48AD **Obverse:** Toughra **Note:** Round flan.

| Date | Mintage | F | VF | XF | Unc | BU |
|---|---|---|---|---|---|---|
| AH1338(1919) | — | 0.50 | 0.75 | 1.00 | 1.50 | — |
| AH1339(1920) | — | 1.00 | 1.35 | 1.75 | 2.75 | — |
| AH1340(1921) | — | 0.60 | 0.85 | 1.25 | 1.75 | — |
| AH1341(1922) | — | 0.75 | 1.00 | 1.35 | 2.00 | — |
| AH1344(1925) | — | 0.50 | 0.75 | 1.00 | 1.50 | — |
| AH1347(1928) | — | 0.50 | 0.75 | 1.00 | 1.50 | — |
| AH1348(1929) | — | 0.60 | 0.85 | 1.25 | 1.75 | — |
| AH1349(1930) | — | 0.50 | 0.75 | 1.00 | 1.50 | — |
| AH1351(1932) | — | 0.50 | 0.75 | 1.00 | 1.50 | — |
| AH1352(1933) | — | 1.00 | 1.35 | 1.75 | 2.75 | — |
| AH1353(1934) | — | 0.50 | 0.75 | 1.00 | 1.50 | — |
| AH1354(1935) | — | 0.50 | 0.75 | 1.00 | 1.50 | — |

**ANNA** **Y# 49** **Composition:** Copper-Nickel **Ruler:** Mir Usman Ali Khan AH1329-67/1911-48AD **Obverse:** Toughra **Note:** Square flan.

| Date | Mintage | F | VF | XF | Unc | BU |
|---|---|---|---|---|---|---|
| AH1356(1937) | — | 0.35 | 0.50 | 0.65 | 1.00 | — |
| AH1357(1938) | — | 0.50 | 0.65 | 0.85 | 1.35 | — |
| AH1358(1939) | — | 0.35 | 0.50 | 0.65 | 1.00 | — |
| AH1359(1940) | — | 0.75 | 1.00 | 1.25 | 2.00 | — |
| AH1360(1941) | — | 0.75 | 1.00 | 1.25 | 2.00 | — |
| AH1361(1942) | — | 0.75 | 1.00 | 1.25 | 2.00 | — |

**2 ANNAS** **Y# 50** **Weight:** 1.3970 g. **Composition:** 0.8180 Silver .0367 oz. ASW **Ruler:** Mir Usman Ali Khan AH1329-67/1911-48AD **Obverse:** Chahar Minar gateway

| Date | Mintage | F | VF | XF | Unc | BU |
|---|---|---|---|---|---|---|
| AH1335/6(1916) | — | 1.25 | 1.75 | 2.50 | 4.00 | — |
| AH1337/9(1919) | — | 1.00 | 1.50 | 2.50 | 4.00 | — |
| AH1338/10(1920) | — | 1.00 | 1.50 | 2.50 | 4.00 | — |
| AH1340/11(1921) | — | 1.00 | 1.50 | 2.50 | 4.00 | — |
| AH1341/13(1923) | — | 1.00 | 1.50 | 2.50 | 4.00 | — |
| AH1342/13(1923) | — | 1.00 | 1.50 | 2.50 | 4.00 | — |
| AH1341/14(1923) | — | 1.25 | 2.00 | 3.00 | 5.00 | — |
| AH1343/14(1924) | — | 1.00 | 1.50 | 2.25 | 3.50 | — |
| AH1343/15(1925) | — | 1.00 | 1.50 | 2.25 | 3.50 | — |
| AH1347(1928) | — | 1.25 | 2.00 | 3.00 | 5.00 | — |
| AH1348/19(1929) | — | 1.00 | 1.50 | 2.25 | 3.50 | — |
| AH1351/22(1932) | — | 1.00 | 1.50 | 2.50 | 4.00 | — |
| AH1355/26(1936) | — | 1.00 | 1.50 | 2.50 | 4.00 | — |

**4 ANNAS** **Y# 51** **Weight:** 2.7940 g. **Composition:** 0.8180 Silver .0735 oz. ASW **Ruler:** Mir Usman Ali Khan AH1329-67/1911-48AD **Obverse:** Chahar Minar gateway

| Date | Mintage | F | VF | XF | Unc | BU |
|---|---|---|---|---|---|---|
| AH1337/9(1919) | — | 1.75 | 3.00 | 4.50 | 7.00 | — |
| AH1340/11(1921) | — | 1.75 | 3.00 | 4.50 | 7.00 | — |
| AH1342/13(1923) | — | 1.75 | 3.00 | 4.50 | 7.00 | — |
| AH1342/14(1924) | — | 1.75 | 3.00 | 4.50 | 7.00 | — |
| AH1348/19(1929) | — | 1.75 | 3.00 | 4.50 | 7.00 | — |
| AH1351/22(1932) | — | 1.75 | 3.00 | 4.50 | 7.00 | — |
| AH1354/25(1935) | — | 1.75 | 3.00 | 4.50 | 7.00 | — |
| AH1358/30(1940) | — | 1.75 | 3.00 | 4.50 | 7.00 | — |

**8 ANNAS** **Y# 52** **Weight:** 5.5890 g. **Composition:** 0.8180 Silver .1470 oz. ASW **Ruler:** Mir Usman Ali Khan AH1329-67/1911-48AD **Obverse:** Chahar Minar gateway

| Date | Mintage | F | VF | XF | Unc | BU |
|---|---|---|---|---|---|---|
| AH1337/9(1919) | — | 3.50 | 5.00 | 8.00 | 12.00 | — |
| AH1342/13(1923) | — | 3.50 | 5.00 | 8.00 | 12.00 | — |
| AH1343/13(1924) | — | 3.50 | 5.00 | 8.00 | 12.00 | — |
| AH1354/25(1935) | — | 3.50 | 5.00 | 8.00 | 12.00 | — |

**RUPEE** **Y# 53** **Weight:** 11.1780 g. **Composition:** 0.8180 Silver .2940 oz. ASW **Ruler:** Mir Usman Ali Khan AH1329-67/1911-48AD **Obverse:** Chahar Minar gateway with partial initials "Ain" in doorway

| Date | Mintage | F | VF | XF | Unc | BU |
|---|---|---|---|---|---|---|
| AH1330/1(1911) | — | 5.50 | 9.00 | 15.00 | 25.00 | — |

**RUPEE** **Y# 53a** **Weight:** 11.1780 g. **Composition:** 0.8180 Silver .2940 oz. ASW **Ruler:** Mir Usman Ali Khan AH1329-67/1911-48AD **Obverse:** Chahar Minar gateway with full "Ain" in doorway

| Date | Mintage | F | VF | XF | Unc | BU |
|---|---|---|---|---|---|---|
| AH1330/1(1911) | — | 5.50 | 9.00 | 15.00 | 25.00 | — |
| AH1331/2(1912) | — | 4.50 | 7.50 | 12.50 | 20.00 | — |
| AH1330/2(1912) | — | 5.50 | 9.00 | 15.00 | 25.00 | — |
| AH1332/3(1913) | — | 4.50 | 7.50 | 12.50 | 20.00 | — |
| AH1331/3(1913) | — | 4.50 | 7.50 | 12.50 | 20.00 | — |
| AH1334/6(1916) | — | 4.50 | 7.50 | 12.50 | 20.00 | — |
| AH1335/6(1916) | — | 4.50 | 7.50 | 12.50 | 20.00 | — |
| AH1335/7(1917) | — | 4.50 | 7.50 | 12.50 | 20.00 | — |
| AH1336/7(1917) | — | 4.50 | 7.50 | 12.50 | 20.00 | — |
| AH1337/8(1918) | — | 4.50 | 7.50 | 12.50 | 20.00 | — |
| AH1338/9(1919) | — | 4.50 | 7.50 | 12.50 | 20.00 | — |
| AH1337/9(1919) | — | 7.50 | 12.50 | 20.00 | 35.00 | — |
| AH1339/9(1920) | — | 4.50 | 7.50 | 12.50 | 20.00 | — |
| AH1340/11(1921) | — | 4.50 | 7.50 | 12.50 | 20.00 | — |
| AH1341/12(1922) | — | 4.50 | 7.50 | 12.50 | 20.00 | — |
| AH1342/13(1923) | — | 4.50 | 7.50 | 12.50 | 20.00 | — |
| AH1343/14(1924) | — | 4.50 | 7.50 | 12.50 | 20.00 | — |

**1/8 ASHRAFI** **Y# 54.1** **Weight:** 1.3940 g. **Composition:** 0.9100 Gold **Ruler:** Mir Usman Ali Khan AH1329-67/1911-48AD **Obverse:** Chahar Minar gateway with partial "Ain" in doorway

| Date | Mintage | F | VF | XF | Unc | BU |
|---|---|---|---|---|---|---|
| AH1329/1(1911) Rare | — | — | — | — | — | — |

**1/8 ASHRAFI** **Y# 54.2** **Weight:** 1.3940 g. **Composition:** 0.9100 Gold **Ruler:** Mir Usman Ali Khan AH1329-67/1911-48AD **Obverse:** Chahar Minar gateway with full "Ain" in doorway

| Date | Mintage | F | VF | XF | Unc | BU |
|---|---|---|---|---|---|---|
| AH1337/8(1918) | — | 30.00 | 37.50 | 50.00 | 70.00 | — |
| AH1340/11(1921) | — | 30.00 | 37.50 | 50.00 | 70.00 | — |
| AH1343(1924) | — | 30.00 | 37.50 | 50.00 | 70.00 | — |
| AH1344/15(1925) | — | 30.00 | 37.50 | 50.00 | 70.00 | — |
| AH1353(1934) | — | 30.00 | 37.50 | 50.00 | 70.00 | — |
| AH1354/25(1935) | — | 30.00 | 37.50 | 50.00 | 70.00 | — |
| AH1356/27(1937) | — | 30.00 | 37.50 | 50.00 | 70.00 | — |
| AH1360(1941) | — | 30.00 | 37.50 | 50.00 | 70.00 | — |
| AH1366/37(1947) | — | 30.00 | 37.50 | 50.00 | 70.00 | — |
| AH1368/39(1950) | — | 30.00 | 37.50 | 50.00 | 70.00 | — |

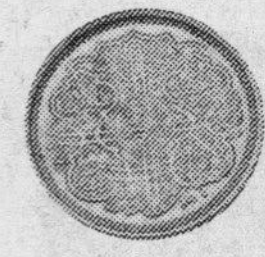

**1/4 ASHRAFI** **Y# 55** **Weight:** 2.7940 g. **Composition:** 0.9100 Gold **Ruler:** Mir Usman Ali Khan AH1329-67/1911-48AD **Obverse:** Chahar Minar gateway

| Date | Mintage | F | VF | XF | Unc | BU |
|---|---|---|---|---|---|---|
| AH1337/8(1918) | — | 40.00 | 60.00 | 85.00 | 125 | — |
| AH1342/13(1923) | — | 40.00 | 60.00 | 85.00 | 125 | — |
| AH1342/14(1924) | — | 40.00 | 60.00 | 85.00 | 125 | — |
| AH1349/20(1930) | — | 40.00 | 60.00 | 85.00 | 125 | — |
| AH1353/23(1934) | — | 40.00 | 60.00 | 85.00 | 125 | — |
| AH1354/25(1935) | — | 40.00 | 60.00 | 85.00 | 125 | — |
| AH1357(1938) | — | 40.00 | 60.00 | 85.00 | 125 | — |
| AH1360/31(1941) | — | 40.00 | 60.00 | 85.00 | 125 | — |
| AH1367/38(1948) | — | 40.00 | 60.00 | 85.00 | 125 | — |

**1/2 ASHRAFI** **Y# 56.1** **Weight:** 5.5890 g. **Composition:** 0.9100 Gold **Ruler:** Mir Usman Ali Khan AH1329-67/1911-48AD **Obverse:** Chahar Minar gateway with partial "Ain" in doorway

| Date | Mintage | F | VF | XF | Unc | BU |
|---|---|---|---|---|---|---|
| AH1329/1(1911) | — | 85.00 | 125 | 175 | 250 | — |

**1/2 ASHRAFI** **Y# 56.2** **Weight:** 5.5890 g. **Composition:** 0.9100 Gold **Ruler:** Mir Usman Ali Khan AH1329-67/1911-48AD **Obverse:** Chahar Minar gateway with full "Ain" in doorway

| Date | Mintage | F | VF | XF | Unc | BU |
|---|---|---|---|---|---|---|
| AH1337/8(1918) | — | 75.00 | 100 | 140 | 200 | — |
| AH1342/14(1924) | — | 75.00 | 100 | 140 | 200 | — |
| AH1343/14(1924) | — | 75.00 | 100 | 140 | 200 | — |
| AH1344/14(1925) | — | 75.00 | 100 | 140 | 200 | — |
| AH1345/16(1926) | — | 75.00 | 100 | 140 | 200 | — |
| AH1349/20(1930) | — | 75.00 | 100 | 140 | 200 | — |
| AH1354/25(1935) | — | 75.00 | 100 | 140 | 200 | — |
| AH1357/29(1939) | — | 75.00 | 100 | 140 | 200 | — |
| AH1366/37(1947) | — | 75.00 | 100 | 140 | 200 | — |
| AH1367/38(1948) | — | 75.00 | 100 | 140 | 200 | — |

**ASHRAFI** **Y# 57** **Weight:** 11.1780 g. **Composition:** 0.9100 Gold **Ruler:** Mir Usman Ali Khan AH1329-67/1911-48AD **Obverse:** Chahar Minar gateway with partial initial "Ain" in doorway

| Date | Mintage | F | VF | XF | Unc | BU |
|---|---|---|---|---|---|---|
| AH1329/1(1911) | — | 165 | 220 | 325 | 450 | — |
| AH1330/1(1911) | — | 165 | 220 | 325 | 450 | — |

**ASHRAFI** **Y# 57a** **Weight:** 11.1780 g. **Composition:** 0.9100 Gold **Ruler:** Mir Usman Ali Khan AH1329-67/1911-48AD **Obverse:** Chahar Minar gateway with full initial "Ain" in doorway

| Date | Mintage | F | VF | XF | Unc | BU |
|---|---|---|---|---|---|---|
| AH1331/3(1913) | — | 140 | 160 | 240 | 350 | — |
| AH1333/4(1914) | — | 140 | 160 | 240 | 350 | — |
| AH1337/8(1918) | — | 140 | 160 | 240 | 350 | — |
| AH1337/9(1919) | — | 140 | 160 | 240 | 350 | — |
| AH1338/9(1919) | — | 140 | 160 | 240 | 350 | — |
| AH1340/11(1921) | — | 140 | 160 | 240 | 350 | — |
| AH1342/14(1924) | — | 140 | 165 | 240 | 350 | — |
| AH1343/14(1924) | — | 140 | 160 | 240 | 350 | — |
| AH1344/15(1925) | — | 140 | 160 | 240 | 350 | — |
| AH1348/19(1929) | — | 140 | 160 | 240 | 350 | — |
| AH1349/20(1930) | — | 140 | 160 | 240 | 350 | — |
| AH1354/25(1935) | — | 140 | 160 | 240 | 350 | — |
| AH1358/30(1940) | — | 140 | 160 | 240 | 350 | — |
| AH1360/31(1941) | — | 140 | 160 | 240 | 350 | — |
| AH1362/34(1943) | — | 140 | 160 | 240 | 350 | — |

## MILLED COINAGE

### Second Series

**2 PAI** **Y# 58** **Composition:** Bronze **Ruler:** Mir Usman Ali Khan AH1329-67/1911-48AD

| Date | Mintage | F | VF | XF | Unc | BU |
|---|---|---|---|---|---|---|
| AH1362/33(1943) | — | 0.25 | 0.35 | 0.50 | 0.75 | — |
| AH1363/34(1944) | — | 0.25 | 0.35 | 0.50 | 0.75 | — |
| AH1363/35(1945) | — | 0.20 | 0.25 | 0.50 | 0.75 | — |
| AH1364/35(1945) | — | 0.20 | 0.25 | 0.50 | 0.75 | — |
| AH1365/36(1946) | — | 0.20 | 0.25 | 0.50 | 0.75 | — |
| AH1366/37(1947) | — | 0.20 | 0.25 | 0.50 | 0.75 | — |
| AH1368/39(1950) | — | 0.20 | 0.25 | 0.50 | 0.75 | — |

**ANNA** **Y# 59** **Composition:** Bronze **Ruler:** Mir Usman Ali Khan AH1329-67/1911-48AD **Obverse:** Toughra **Note:** Square flan.

| Date | Mintage | F | VF | XF | Unc | BU |
|---|---|---|---|---|---|---|
| AH1361(1942) | — | 0.40 | 0.50 | 0.75 | 1.50 | — |
| AH1362(1943) | — | 0.40 | 0.50 | 0.75 | 1.50 | — |
| AH1364(1945) | — | 0.40 | 0.50 | 0.75 | 1.50 | — |
| AH1365(1946) | — | 0.40 | 0.50 | 0.75 | 1.50 | — |
| AH1366(1946) | — | 0.40 | 0.50 | 0.75 | 1.50 | — |
| AH1368(1948) | — | 0.40 | 0.50 | 0.75 | 1.50 | — |

**2 ANNAS** **Y# 60** **Weight:** 1.3970 g. **Composition:** Silver .0367 oz. ASW **Ruler:** Mir Usman Ali Khan AH1329-67/1911-48AD

| Date | Mintage | F | VF | XF | Unc | BU |
|---|---|---|---|---|---|---|
| AH1362/33(1943) | — | 0.40 | 0.60 | 1.00 | 2.00 | — |

**2 ANNAS** **Y# 64** **Composition:** Nickel **Ruler:** Mir Usman Ali Khan AH1329-67/1911-48AD

| Date | Mintage | F | VF | XF | Unc | BU |
|---|---|---|---|---|---|---|
| AH1366/37(1947) | — | 0.15 | 0.25 | 0.35 | 1.00 | — |
| AH1368/39(1950) | — | 0.25 | 0.35 | 0.45 | 1.50 | — |

**4 ANNAS** **Y# 61** **Weight:** 2.7940 g. **Composition:** Silver .0735 oz. ASW **Ruler:** Mir Usman Ali Khan AH1329-67/1911-48AD

| Date | Mintage | F | VF | XF | Unc | BU |
|---|---|---|---|---|---|---|
| AH1362/33(1943) | — | 0.60 | 0.80 | 1.00 | 2.00 | — |
| AH1362/34(1944) | — | 0.75 | 0.90 | 1.10 | 2.25 | — |
| AH1364/33(1945) | — | 0.80 | 1.00 | 1.25 | 2.50 | — |
| AH1364/35(1945) | — | 0.80 | 1.00 | 1.25 | 2.50 | — |
| AH1364/36(1946) | — | 0.80 | 1.00 | 1.25 | 2.50 | — |
| AH1365/36(1946) | — | 0.80 | 1.00 | 1.25 | 2.50 | — |

**4 ANNAS** **Y# 65** **Composition:** Nickel **Ruler:** Mir Usman Ali Khan AH1329-67/1911-48AD

| Date | Mintage | F | VF | XF | Unc | BU |
|---|---|---|---|---|---|---|
| AH1366/37(1947) | — | 0.40 | 0.50 | 0.75 | 1.50 | — |
| AH1368/39(1950) | — | 0.40 | 0.50 | 0.75 | 1.50 | — |

**8 ANNAS** **Y# 62** **Weight:** 5.5890 g. **Composition:** Silver .1470 oz. ASW **Ruler:** Mir Usman Ali Khan AH1329-67/1911-48AD

| Date | Mintage | F | VF | XF | Unc | BU |
|---|---|---|---|---|---|---|
| AH1363/34(1944) | — | 3.50 | 6.00 | 10.00 | 17.50 | — |

**8 ANNAS** **Y# 66** **Composition:** Nickel **Ruler:** Mir Usman Ali Khan AH1329-67/1911-48AD

| Date | Mintage | F | VF | XF | Unc | BU |
|---|---|---|---|---|---|---|
| AH1366/37(1947) | — | 0.60 | 0.80 | 1.00 | 2.00 | — |

**RUPEE** **Y# 63** **Weight:** 11.1780 g. **Composition:** Silver .2940 oz. ASW **Ruler:** Mir Usman Ali Khan AH1329-67/1911-48AD

| Date | Mintage | F | VF | XF | Unc | BU |
|---|---|---|---|---|---|---|
| AH1361/31(1942) | — | 4.50 | 7.50 | 12.50 | 20.00 | — |
| AH1361/32(1942) | — | 4.50 | 7.50 | 12.50 | 20.00 | — |
| AH1362/34(1944) | — | 4.50 | 7.50 | 12.50 | 20.00 | — |
| AH1364/35(1945) | — | 4.50 | 7.50 | 12.50 | 20.00 | — |
| AH1364/36(1946) | — | 4.50 | 7.50 | 12.50 | 20.00 | — |
| AH1365/36(1946) | — | 4.50 | 7.50 | 12.50 | 20.00 | — |

**ASHRAFI** **Y# 67** **Weight:** 11.1780 g. **Composition:** Gold **Ruler:** Mir Usman Ali Khan AH1329-67/1911-48AD

| Date | Mintage | F | VF | XF | Unc | BU |
|---|---|---|---|---|---|---|
| AH1368/39(1950) | — | — | — | — | — | — |

## PATTERNS

### Including off metal strikes

| KM# | Date | Mintage | Identification | Mkt Val |
|---|---|---|---|---|
| Pn10 | 1319/35 | — | Rupee. Silver. Y#53a. | — |
| Pn11 | 1324/40 | — | 1/2 Ashrafi. Silver. Y#43. | — |
| Pn12 | 1324/40 | — | Ashrafi. Silver. Y#44. | — |

## INDORE

The Holkars were one of the three dominant Maratha powers (with the Peshwas and Sindhias), with major landholdings in Central India.

Indore State originated in 1728 with a grant of land north of the Narbada river by the Maratha Peshwa of Poona to Malhar Rao Holkar, a cavalry commander in his service. After Holkar's death (ca.1765) his daughter-in-law, Ahalya Bai, assumed the position of Queen Regent.Together with Tukoji Rao she effectively ruled the State until her death thirty years later. But it was left to Tukoji's son, Jaswant Rao, to challenge the dominance of the Poona Marathas in the Maratha Confederacy, eventually defeating the Peshwa's army in 1802. But at this point the fortunes of the Holkars suffered a serious reverse. Although Jaswant Rao had initially defeated a small British force under Col. William Monson, he was badly beaten by a contingent under Lord Lake. As a result Holkar was forced to cede a considerable portion of his territory and from this time until India's independence in 1947, the residual State of Indore was obliged to accept British protection.

For more detailed data on the Indore series, see *A Study of Holkar State Coinage*, by P.K.Sethi, S.K. Bhatt and R. Holkar (1976).

**HOLKAR RULERS**

Shivaji Rao, VS1943-1960/FE1296-1313/1886-1903AD
Tukoji Rao III, VS1960-1983/1903-1926AD
Yashwant Rao, VS1983-2005/1926-1948AD

**HONORIFIC TITLE**

Bahadur

**MINTS**

Indore  or इंदौर

**INDORE MINT**

Coins issued intermittently from 1772-1935AD.

# PRINCELY STATE

## MILLED COINAGE

**1/4 ANNA** **KM# 33.3** **Composition:** Copper **Ruler:** Shivaji Rao VS1743-1960/FE1296-1313/1886-1903AD **Obverse:** Continuous legend around reclining bull **Obv. Legend:** Shivaji Rao...Bahadur **Reverse:** "Indore" above denomination and date **Note:** Floral border varieties exist. Struck at the Indore Mint.

| Date | Mintage | VG | F | VF | XF | Unc |
|---|---|---|---|---|---|---|
| VS1958 | — | 1.25 | 1.75 | 3.50 | 7.00 | — |
| VS1959 | — | 1.25 | 1.75 | 3.50 | 7.00 | — |

**1/2 ANNA** **KM# 35.3** **Composition:** Copper **Ruler:** Shivaji Rao VS1743-1960/FE1296-1313/1886-1903AD **Obverse:** Continuous legend around reclining bull **Obv. Legend:** Shivaji Rao **Reverse:** "Indore" above denomination and date **Note:** Struck at the Indore Mint.

| Date | Mintage | VG | F | VF | XF | Unc |
|---|---|---|---|---|---|---|
| VS1958 | — | 1.50 | 2.00 | 4.00 | 8.00 | — |
| VS1959 | — | 1.50 | 2.00 | 4.00 | 8.00 | — |

## MILLED COINAGE

Third Series

This series was introduced in 1898 to counteract counterfeiting of the second series which had begun to proliferate as a result of a sharp fall in the price of silver. Idle minting machines were reactivated for this purpose, but the series was short-lived.

**RUPEE** **KM# 47.2** **Weight:** 11.2000 g. **Composition:** Silver **Ruler:** Shivaji Rao VS1743-1960/FE1296-1313/1886-1903AD **Obverse:** Bust of Shivaji Rao facing; continuous legend **Reverse:** Arms **Note:** Struck at the Indore Mint.

| Date | Mintage | VG | F | VF | XF | Unc |
|---|---|---|---|---|---|---|
| VS1958 | — | 70.00 | 140 | 200 | 275 | 400 |

## MILLED COINAGE

Fourth Series

**1/4 ANNA** **KM# 49** **Composition:** Copper **Ruler:** Yashwant Rao VS1983-2005/1926-1948AD **Obverse:** Bust of Yeshwant Rao facing 3/4 right **Note:** Struck at the Indore Mint.

| Date | Mintage | VG | F | VF | XF | Unc |
|---|---|---|---|---|---|---|
| VS1992 | — | 0.40 | 1.00 | 2.00 | 3.50 | 6.00 |

**1/4 ANNA** **KM# 50** **Composition:** Copper **Ruler:** Yashwant Rao VS1983-2005/1926-1948AD **Obverse:** Bust of Yeshwant Rao facing **Note:** Struck at the Indore Mint.

| Date | Mintage | VG | F | VF | XF | Unc |
|---|---|---|---|---|---|---|
| VS1992 | — | 0.50 | 1.25 | 2.50 | 4.00 | 7.00 |

# JAIPUR

Tradition has it that the region of Jaipur, located in northwest India, once belonged to an ancient Kachwaha Rajput dynasty which claimed descent from Kush, one of the sons of Rama, King of Ayodhya. But the Princely State of Jaipur originated in the 12th century. Comparatively small in size, the State remained largely unnoticed until after the 16th century when the Jaipur royal house became famous for its military skills and thereafter supplied the Mughals with some of their more distinguished generals. The city of Jaipur was founded about 1728 by Maharaja Jai Singh II who was well known for his knowledge of mathematics and astronomy. The late 18th and early 19th centuries were difficult times for Jaipur. They were marked by internal rivalry, exacerbated by Maratha or Pindari incursions. In 1818 this culminated with a treaty whereby Jaipur came under British protection and oversight.

**RULERS**

Madho Singh II, 1880-1922AD
Man Singh II, 1922-1949AD

**MINTNAMES**

Coins were struck at two mints, which bear the following characteristic marks on the reverse:

Sawai Jaipur

Sawai Madhopur

**JAIPUR MINT**

In the names of Queen Victoria

کوین وکٹوریا

And Madho Singh II

**Years 1-43/1880-1922AD**

NOTE: Queen Victoria's name was retained on Madho Singh II's coinage until 1922AD. No coins were struck with Edward VII's name by Madho Singh II.

# PRINCELY STATE

## HAMMERED 'DUMP' COINAGE

**1/2 PAISA** **KM# 175** **Composition:** Copper **Ruler:** Man Singh II 1922-49AD **Obverse:** Inscription: Edward VIII.... **Reverse:** Jhar; inscription: Singh II....

| Date | Mintage | VG | F | VF | XF | Unc |
|---|---|---|---|---|---|---|
| ND(1942)/21 | — | 1.00 | 1.75 | 2.50 | 4.50 | — |

**PAISA** **KM# 130** **Composition:** Copper **Ruler:** Madho Singh 1880-1922AD **Obverse:** Inscription: Queen Victoria... **Reverse:** Jhar; inscription: Madho Singh II.... **Note:** Weight varies 6.15-6.30g .

| Date | Mintage | VG | F | VF | XF | Unc |
|---|---|---|---|---|---|---|
| ND(1901)/22 | — | 0.65 | 1.35 | 2.00 | — | — |
| ND(1902)/23 | — | 0.65 | 1.35 | 2.00 | — | — |
| ND(1903)/24 | — | 0.65 | 1.35 | 2.00 | — | — |
| ND(1904)/25 | — | 0.65 | 1.35 | 2.00 | — | — |
| ND(1906)/27 | — | 0.65 | 1.35 | 2.00 | — | — |
| ND(1907)/28 | — | 0.65 | 1.35 | 2.00 | — | — |
| ND(1908)/29 | — | 0.65 | 1.35 | 2.00 | — | — |
| ND(1916)/37 | — | 0.65 | 1.35 | 2.00 | — | — |
| ND(1917)/38 | — | 0.65 | 1.35 | 2.00 | — | — |
| ND(1918)/39 | — | 0.65 | 1.35 | 2.00 | — | — |
| ND(1920)/41 | — | 0.65 | 1.35 | 2.00 | — | — |

**1/16 RUPEE** **KM# 135** **Composition:** Silver **Ruler:** Madho Singh 1880-1922AD **Obverse:** Inscription: Queen Victoria... **Reverse:** Jhar; inscription: Madho Singh II.... **Note:** Weight varies 0.67-0.72g.

| Date | Mintage | VG | F | VF | XF | Unc |
|---|---|---|---|---|---|---|
| ND(1912)/33 | — | 5.00 | 7.00 | 10.00 | 15.00 | — |

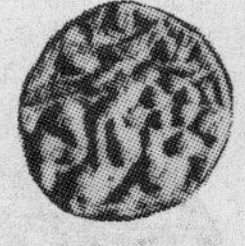 

**1/8 RUPEE** **KM# 137** **Composition:** Silver **Ruler:** Madho Singh 1880-1922AD **Obverse:** Inscription: Queen Victoria... **Reverse:** Jhar; inscription: Madho Singh II.... **Note:** Weight varies 1.34-1.45g.

| Date | Mintage | VG | F | VF | XF | Unc |
|---|---|---|---|---|---|---|
| ND(1901)/22 | — | 2.50 | 3.50 | 5.00 | 8.00 | — |
| ND(1902)/23 | — | 2.50 | 3.50 | 5.00 | 8.00 | — |
| ND(1905)/26 | — | 2.50 | 3.50 | 5.00 | 8.00 | — |
| ND(1906)/27 | — | 2.50 | 3.50 | 5.00 | 8.00 | — |
| ND(1907)/28 | — | 2.50 | 3.50 | 5.00 | 8.00 | — |
| ND(1908)/29 | — | 2.50 | 3.50 | 5.00 | 8.00 | — |
| ND(1920)/41 | — | 2.50 | 3.50 | 5.00 | 8.00 | — |
| ND(1921)/42 | — | 2.50 | 3.50 | 5.00 | 8.00 | — |
| ND(1933)/4 | — | 2.50 | 3.50 | 5.00 | 8.00 | — |

**1/4 RUPEE** **KM# 139** **Composition:** Silver **Ruler:** Madho Singh 1880-1922AD **Obverse:** Inscription: Queen Victoria... **Reverse:** Jhar; inscription: Madho Singh II.... **Note:** Weight varies 2.68-2.90g.

| Date | Mintage | VG | F | VF | XF | Unc |
|---|---|---|---|---|---|---|
| ND(1901)/22 | — | 3.00 | 4.50 | 6.50 | 10.00 | — |
| ND(1902)/23 | — | 3.00 | 4.50 | 6.50 | 10.00 | — |
| ND(1903)/24 | — | 3.00 | 4.50 | 6.50 | 10.00 | — |
| ND(1905)/26 | — | 3.00 | 4.50 | 6.50 | 10.00 | — |
| ND(1906)/27 | — | 3.00 | 4.50 | 6.50 | 10.00 | — |
| ND(1907)/28 | — | 3.00 | 4.50 | 6.50 | 10.00 | — |
| ND(1908)/29 | — | 3.00 | 4.50 | 6.50 | 10.00 | — |
| ND(1909)/30 | — | 3.00 | 4.50 | 6.50 | 10.00 | — |
| ND(1913)/34 | — | 3.00 | 4.50 | 6.50 | 10.00 | — |
| ND(1916)/37 | — | 3.00 | 4.50 | 6.50 | 10.00 | — |
| ND(1917)/38 | — | 3.00 | 4.50 | 6.50 | 10.00 | — |
| ND(1921)/42 | — | 3.00 | 4.50 | 6.50 | 10.00 | — |

**1/2 RUPEE** **KM# 142** **Composition:** Silver **Ruler:** Madho Singh 1880-1922AD **Obverse:** Inscription: Queen Victoria... **Reverse:** Jhar; inscription: Madho Singh II.... **Note:** Weight varies 5.35-5.80g.

| Date | Mintage | VG | F | VF | XF | Unc |
|---|---|---|---|---|---|---|
| ND(1901)/22 | — | 3.50 | 5.00 | 7.50 | 12.50 | — |
| ND(1902)/23 | — | 3.50 | 5.00 | 7.50 | 12.50 | — |
| ND(1904)/25 | — | 3.50 | 5.00 | 7.50 | 12.50 | — |
| ND(1905)/26 | — | 3.50 | 5.00 | 7.50 | 12.50 | — |
| ND(1906)/27 | — | 3.50 | 5.00 | 7.50 | 12.50 | — |
| ND(1907)/28 | — | 3.50 | 5.00 | 7.50 | 12.50 | — |
| ND(1908)/29 | — | 3.50 | 5.00 | 7.50 | 12.50 | — |
| ND(1909)/30 | — | 3.50 | 5.00 | 7.50 | 12.50 | — |
| ND(1913)/34 | — | 3.50 | 5.00 | 7.50 | 12.50 | — |
| ND(1916)/37 | — | 3.50 | 5.00 | 7.50 | 12.50 | — |

**RUPEE** **KM# 145** **Composition:** Silver **Ruler:** Madho Singh 1880-1922AD **Obverse:** Inscription: Queen Victoria... **Reverse:** Jhar; inscription: Madho Singh II.... **Note:** Weight varies 10.70-11.60g.

| Date | Mintage | VG | F | VF | XF | Unc |
|---|---|---|---|---|---|---|
| ND(1902)/23 | — | 4.00 | 6.00 | 9.00 | 14.00 | — |
| ND(1903)/24 | — | 4.00 | 6.00 | 9.00 | 14.00 | — |
| ND(1904)/25 | — | 4.00 | 6.00 | 9.00 | 14.00 | — |
| ND(1905)/26 | — | 4.00 | 6.00 | 9.00 | 14.00 | — |
| ND(1906)/27 | — | 4.00 | 6.00 | 9.00 | 14.00 | — |
| ND(1908)/29 | — | 4.00 | 6.00 | 9.00 | 14.00 | — |
| ND(1909)/30 | — | 4.00 | 6.00 | 9.00 | 14.00 | — |
| ND(1910)/31 | — | 4.00 | 6.00 | 9.00 | 14.00 | — |
| ND(1912)/33 | — | 4.00 | 6.00 | 9.00 | 14.00 | — |
| ND(1916)/37 | — | 4.00 | 6.00 | 9.00 | 14.00 | — |
| 191(8)/39 | — | 4.00 | 6.00 | 9.00 | 14.00 | — |
| ND(1919)/40 | — | 4.00 | 6.00 | 9.00 | 14.00 | — |
| ND(1921)/42 | — | 4.00 | 6.00 | 9.00 | 14.00 | — |
| 1922/43 | — | 4.00 | 6.00 | 9.00 | 14.00 | — |

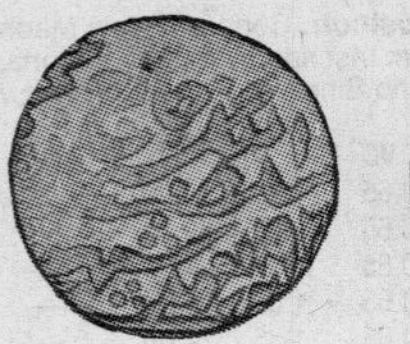

**RUPEE** **KM# 158** **Weight:** 10.7000 g. **Composition:** Silver **Ruler:** Man Singh II 1922-49AD **Obverse:** Inscription: George V.... **Reverse:** Jhar; inscription: Man Singh II....

| Date | Mintage | VG | F | VF | XF | Unc |
|---|---|---|---|---|---|---|
| 1922/1 | — | 25.00 | 40.00 | 65.00 | 90.00 | — |

**MOHUR** **KM# 150** **Composition:** Gold **Ruler:** Madho Singh 1880-1922AD **Obverse:** Inscription: Queen Victoria.... **Reverse:** Jhar; inscription: Madho Singh II.... **Note:** Weight varies 10.70-11.40 g.

| Date | Mintage | VG | F | VF | XF | Unc |
|---|---|---|---|---|---|---|
| ND(1904)/25 | — | 135 | 155 | 185 | 225 | — |
| ND(1916)/37 | — | 135 | 155 | 185 | 225 | — |
| ND(1916)/37 | — | 135 | 155 | 185 | 225 | — |
| ND(1919)/40 | — | 135 | 155 | 185 | 225 | — |
| ND(1920)/41 | — | 135 | 155 | 185 | 225 | — |

**MOHUR** **KM# 163** **Composition:** Gold **Ruler:** Man Singh II 1922-49AD **Obverse:** Inscription: George V.... **Reverse:** Jhar; inscription: Man Singh II.... **Note:** Weight varies 10.70-11.40 g.

| Date | Mintage | VG | F | VF | XF | Unc |
|---|---|---|---|---|---|---|
| ND(1923)/2 | — | 150 | 200 | 300 | 425 | — |
| 1(924)/3 | — | 150 | 200 | 300 | 425 | — |
| 1925/4 | — | 150 | 200 | 300 | 425 | — |
| 19(28)/7 | — | 150 | 200 | 300 | 425 | — |

**MOHUR** **KM# 200** **Composition:** Gold **Ruler:** Man Singh II 1922-49AD **Obverse:** Inscription: George VI.... **Reverse:** Madho Singh II.... **Note:** Weight varies 10.70-11.40 g.

| Date | Mintage | VG | F | VF | XF | Unc |
|---|---|---|---|---|---|---|
| ND(1941)/20 | — | 135 | 155 | 185 | 250 | — |
| ND(1943)/22 | — | 135 | 155 | 185 | 250 | — |
| ND(1947)/26 | — | 135 | 155 | 185 | 250 | — |
| ND(1948)/27 | — | 135 | 155 | 185 | 250 | — |
| 1949/28 | — | 135 | 155 | 185 | 250 | — |

## MILLED COINAGE

**ANNA** **KM# 185** **Composition:** Brass **Ruler:** Man Singh II 1922-49AD **Obverse:** Jhar

| Date | Mintage | Good | VG | F | VF | XF |
|---|---|---|---|---|---|---|
| 1943 | — | — | 0.20 | 0.40 | 0.60 | 1.00 |
| 1944/3 | — | 0.15 | 0.40 | 0.80 | 1.20 | 2.00 |
| 1944 | — | — | 0.20 | 0.40 | 0.60 | 1.00 |

**ANNA** **KM# 186** **Weight:** 5.1700 g. **Composition:** Brass **Ruler:** Man Singh II 1922-49AD **Obverse:** Jhar **Note:** Brass, thick planchet.

| Date | Mintage | Good | VG | F | VF | XF |
|---|---|---|---|---|---|---|
| 1943 | — | 0.10 | 0.25 | 0.50 | 0.80 | 1.50 |

**ANNA** **KM# 187** **Weight:** 2.7800 g. **Composition:** Brass **Ruler:** Man Singh II 1922-49AD **Obverse:** Jhar **Note:** Brass, thin planchet.

| Date | Mintage | Good | VG | F | VF | XF |
|---|---|---|---|---|---|---|
| 1943 | — | — | 0.20 | 0.40 | 0.60 | 1.00 |

**ANNA** **KM# 188** **Composition:** Brass **Ruler:** Man Singh II 1922-49AD **Obverse:** Bust of Man Singh II right **Reverse:** Jhar

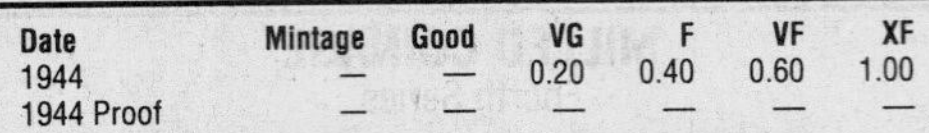

| Date | Mintage | Good | VG | F | VF | XF |
|---|---|---|---|---|---|---|
| 1944 | — | — | 0.20 | 0.40 | 0.60 | 1.00 |
| 1944 Proof | — | — | — | — | — | — |

**2 ANNA** **KM# 190** **Composition:** Brass **Ruler:** Man Singh II 1922-49AD **Reverse:** Jhar **Note:** Square flan.

| Date | Mintage | Good | VG | F | VF | XF |
|---|---|---|---|---|---|---|
| 1942/21 | — | 1.25 | 3.00 | 4.50 | 6.00 | 10.00 |

**1/2 PAISA** **KM# 176** **Composition:** Copper **Ruler:** Man Singh II 1922-49AD **Obverse:** Inscription: Edward VIII.... **Reverse:** Jhar; inscription: Man Singh II.... **Note:** Crude struck in collar.

| Date | Mintage | Good | VG | F | VF | XF |
|---|---|---|---|---|---|---|
| ND(1943)/22 | — | 0.40 | 1.00 | 1.75 | 2.50 | 4.50 |
| ND(1944)/23 | — | 0.40 | 1.00 | 1.75 | 2.50 | 4.50 |

**NAZARANA PAISA** **KM# 155** **Composition:** Copper **Ruler:** Man Singh II 1922-49AD **Obverse:** Inscription: George V.... **Reverse:** Jhar; inscription: Man Singh II....

| Date | Mintage | Good | VG | F | VF | XF |
|---|---|---|---|---|---|---|
| 1922/1 | — | 6.00 | 15.00 | 25.00 | 40.00 | 60.00 |
| 1923/2 | — | 6.00 | 15.00 | 25.00 | 40.00 | 60.00 |
| 1924/3 | — | 6.00 | 15.00 | 25.00 | 40.00 | 60.00 |
| 1924/4 | — | 6.00 | 15.00 | 25.00 | 40.00 | 60.00 |
| 1925/4 | — | 6.00 | 15.00 | 25.00 | 40.00 | 60.00 |
| 1926/5 | — | 6.00 | 15.00 | 25.00 | 40.00 | 60.00 |
| 1927/5 | — | 6.00 | 15.00 | 25.00 | 40.00 | 60.00 |
| 1927/6 | — | 6.00 | 15.00 | 25.00 | 40.00 | 60.00 |
| 1928/7 | — | 6.00 | 15.00 | 25.00 | 40.00 | 60.00 |
| 1929/8 | — | 6.00 | 15.00 | 25.00 | 40.00 | 60.00 |
| 1930/9 | — | 6.00 | 15.00 | 25.00 | 40.00 | 60.00 |
| 19(30)/10 | — | 6.00 | 15.00 | 25.00 | 40.00 | 60.00 |
| 1931/10 | — | 6.00 | 15.00 | 25.00 | 40.00 | 60.00 |
| 1932/11 | — | 6.00 | 15.00 | 25.00 | 40.00 | 60.00 |
| 1933/12 | — | 6.00 | 15.00 | 25.00 | 40.00 | 60.00 |
| 1934/13 | — | 6.00 | 15.00 | 25.00 | 40.00 | 60.00 |
| 1935/14 | — | 6.00 | 15.00 | 25.00 | 40.00 | 60.00 |

**NAZARANA PAISA** **KM# 157** **Composition:** Copper **Ruler:** Man Singh II 1922-49AD **Obverse:** Inscription: George V.... **Reverse:** Jhar; inscription: Man Singh II....

| Date | Mintage | Good | VG | F | VF | XF |
|---|---|---|---|---|---|---|
| 1929/8 | — | 6.00 | 15.00 | 25.00 | 40.00 | 60.00 |

**NAZARANA PAISA** **KM# 167** **Weight:** 6.4400 g. **Composition:** Copper **Ruler:** Man Singh II 1922-49AD **Obverse:** Inscription: Edward VIII.... **Reverse:** Jhar; inscription: Man Singh II....

| Date | Mintage | Good | VG | F | VF | XF |
|---|---|---|---|---|---|---|
| 1936/15 | — | 125 | 250 | 275 | 325 | 400 |

**NAZARANA PAISA** **KM# 180** **Composition:** Copper **Ruler:** Man Singh II 1922-49AD **Obverse:** Inscription: Edward VIII.... **Reverse:** Jhar; inscription: Man Singh II....

| Date | Mintage | Good | VG | F | VF | XF |
|---|---|---|---|---|---|---|
| 1937/16 | — | 4.00 | 10.00 | 17.50 | 25.00 | 40.00 |
| 1938/17 | — | 4.00 | 10.00 | 17.50 | 25.00 | 40.00 |
| 1939/18 | — | 4.00 | 10.00 | 17.50 | 25.00 | 40.00 |
| 1940/19 | — | 4.00 | 10.00 | 17.50 | 25.00 | 40.00 |
| 1941/19 | — | 4.00 | 10.00 | 17.50 | 25.00 | 40.00 |
| 1941/20 | — | 4.00 | 10.00 | 17.50 | 25.00 | 40.00 |
| 1942/21 | — | 4.00 | 10.00 | 17.50 | 25.00 | 40.00 |
| 1943/22 | — | 4.00 | 10.00 | 17.50 | 25.00 | 40.00 |
| 19(44)/23 | — | 4.00 | 10.00 | 17.50 | 25.00 | 40.00 |
| 1945/24 | — | 4.00 | 10.00 | 17.50 | 25.00 | 40.00 |
| 1946/25 | — | 4.00 | 10.00 | 17.50 | 25.00 | 40.00 |
| 1947/26 | — | 4.00 | 10.00 | 17.50 | 25.00 | 40.00 |
| 1947/27 | — | 4.00 | 10.00 | 17.50 | 25.00 | 40.00 |
| 1948/27 | — | 4.00 | 10.00 | 17.50 | 25.00 | 40.00 |
| 1949/28 | — | 4.00 | 10.00 | 17.50 | 25.00 | 40.00 |

**NAZARANA NEW PAISA** **KM# 132** **Composition:** Copper **Ruler:** Madho Singh 1880-1922AD **Obverse:** Inscription: Queen Victoria... **Reverse:** Jhar; inscription: Madho Singh II.... **Note:** Well-centered issues on thin planchets may be restrikes.

| Date | Mintage | VG | F | VF | XF | Unc |
|---|---|---|---|---|---|---|
| 1880/1 | — | 12.50 | 17.50 | 25.00 | 40.00 | — |
| 1901/22 | — | 12.50 | 17.50 | 25.00 | 40.00 | — |
| 1902/23 | — | 12.50 | 17.50 | 25.00 | 40.00 | — |
| 1903/24 | — | 12.50 | 17.50 | 25.00 | 40.00 | — |
| 1904/25 | — | 12.50 | 17.50 | 25.00 | 40.00 | — |
| 1905/26 | — | 12.50 | 17.50 | 25.00 | 40.00 | — |
| 1906/27 | — | 12.50 | 17.50 | 25.00 | 40.00 | — |
| 1907/28 | — | 12.50 | 17.50 | 25.00 | 40.00 | — |
| 1908/29 | — | 12.50 | 17.50 | 25.00 | 40.00 | — |
| 1909/30 | — | 12.50 | 17.50 | 25.00 | 40.00 | — |
| 1910/31 | — | 12.50 | 17.50 | 25.00 | 40.00 | — |
| 1911/32 | — | 12.50 | 17.50 | 25.00 | 40.00 | — |
| 1912/33 | — | 12.50 | 17.50 | 25.00 | 40.00 | — |
| 1913/34 | — | 12.50 | 17.50 | 25.00 | 40.00 | — |
| 1914/35 | — | 12.50 | 17.50 | 25.00 | 40.00 | — |
| 1915/36 | — | 12.50 | 17.50 | 25.00 | 40.00 | — |
| 1916/37 | — | 12.50 | 17.50 | 25.00 | 40.00 | — |
| 1917/38 | — | 12.50 | 17.50 | 25.00 | 40.00 | — |

**NAZARANA RUPEE** **KM# 147** **Composition:** Silver **Ruler:** Madho Singh 1880-1922AD **Obverse:** Inscription: Queen Victoria.... **Reverse:** Jhar; inscription: Madho Singh II.... **Note:** Size varies 36-37mm.

| Date | Mintage | VG | F | VF | XF | Unc |
|---|---|---|---|---|---|---|
| 1901/22 | — | 27.50 | 40.00 | 52.50 | 75.00 | — |
| 1903/24 | — | 27.50 | 40.00 | 52.50 | 75.00 | — |
| 1904/25 | — | 27.50 | 40.00 | 52.50 | 75.00 | — |
| 1906/27 | — | 27.50 | 40.00 | 52.50 | 75.00 | — |
| 1908/29 | — | 27.50 | 40.00 | 52.50 | 75.00 | — |
| 1909/30 | — | 27.50 | 40.00 | 52.50 | 75.00 | — |
| 1910/31 | — | 27.50 | 40.00 | 52.50 | 75.00 | — |
| 1911/32 | — | 27.50 | 40.00 | 52.50 | 75.00 | — |
| 1912/33 | — | 27.50 | 40.00 | 52.50 | 75.00 | — |
| 1913/34 | — | 27.50 | 40.00 | 52.50 | 75.00 | — |
| 1916/37 | — | 27.50 | 40.00 | 52.50 | 75.00 | — |
| 1920/41 | — | 27.50 | 40.00 | 52.50 | 75.00 | — |
| 1921/42 | — | 27.50 | 40.00 | 52.50 | 75.00 | — |

**NAZARANA RUPEE KM# 159 Weight:** 10.7000 g. **Composition:** Silver **Ruler:** Man Singh II 1922-49AD **Obverse:** Inscription: George V.... **Reverse:** Jhar; inscription: Man Singh II....

| Date | Mintage | VG | F | VF | XF | Unc |
|---|---|---|---|---|---|---|
| 1924/3 | — | 40.00 | 62.50 | 85.00 | 120 | — |
| 1928/7 | — | 40.00 | 62.50 | 85.00 | 120 | — |
| 1932/11 | — | 40.00 | 62.50 | 85.00 | 120 | — |

**NAZARANA RUPEE KM# 170 Weight:** 10.7000 g. **Composition:** Silver **Ruler:** Man Singh II 1922-49AD **Obverse:** Inscription: Edward VIII.... **Reverse:** Jhar; inscription: Man Singh II....

| Date | Mintage | VG | F | VF | XF | Unc |
|---|---|---|---|---|---|---|
| 1936/15 Rare | — | — | — | — | — | — |

**NAZARANA RUPEE KM# 196 Composition:** Silver **Ruler:** Man Singh II 1922-49AD **Obverse:** Inscription: George VI.... **Reverse:** Madho Singh II.... **Note:** Similar rupees approximately 30mm in diameter are modern forgeries.

| Date | Mintage | VG | F | VF | XF | Unc |
|---|---|---|---|---|---|---|
| 1938/20 | — | — | — | 70.00 | 100 | — |
| 1939/18 | — | 10.00 | 16.00 | 28.50 | 40.00 | — |
| 1941/20 | — | 10.00 | 16.00 | 28.50 | 40.00 | — |
| 1943/22 | — | 10.00 | 16.00 | 28.50 | 40.00 | — |
| 1945/24 | — | 10.00 | 16.00 | 28.50 | 40.00 | — |
| 1948/27 | — | 10.00 | 16.00 | 28.50 | 40.00 | — |
| 1949/28 | — | 10.00 | 16.00 | 28.50 | 40.00 | — |

**NAZARANA RUPEE KM# 195 Composition:** Silver **Ruler:** Man Singh II 1922-49AD **Obverse:** Mule; inscription: George VI.... **Reverse:** Madho Singh II.... **Note:** Weight varies 10.70-11.60 g.

| Date | Mintage | Good | VG | F | VF | XF |
|---|---|---|---|---|---|---|
| 1949/3 | — | 12.50 | 25.00 | 32.50 | 55.00 | 80.00 |

**NAZARANA MOHUR KM# 201 Composition:** Gold **Ruler:** Man Singh II 1922-49AD **Obverse:** Inscription: George VI.... **Reverse:** Man Singh II....

| Date | Mintage | Good | VG | F | VF | XF |
|---|---|---|---|---|---|---|
| ND(1949)/28 | — | — | — | — | — | — |

## JODHPUR

Jodhpur, also known as Marwar, located in northwest India, was the largest Princely State in the Rajputana Agency. Its population in 1941 exceeded two and a half million. The "Maharajadhirajas" ("Great Kings of Kings") of Jodhpur were Rathor Rajputs who claimed an extremely ancient ancestry from Rama, king of Ayodhya. With the collapse of the Rathor rulers of Kanauj in 1194 the family entered Marwar where they laid the foundation of the new state. The city of Jodhpur was built by Rao Jodha in 1459, and the city and the state were named after him. In 1561 the Mughal Emperor Akbar invaded Jodhpur, forcing its submission. In 1679 Emperor Aurangzeb sacked the city, an experience which stimulated the Rajput royal house to forge a new unity among themselves in order to extricate themselves from Mughal hegemony. Internal dissension once again asserted itself and Rajput unity, which had both benefited from and accelerated Mughal decline, fell apart before the Marathas. In 1818 Jodhpur came under British protection and control and after Indian independence in 1947 the State was merged into Rajasthan. Jodhpur is best known for its particular style of riding breeches (jodpurs) which became very popular in the West in the late 19th century.

**RULERS**

Sardar Singh, VS1952-1968/1895-1911AD
Sumer Singh, VS1968-1975/1911-1918AD
Umaid Singh, VS1975-2004/1918-1947AD
Hanwant Singh, as Titular Ruler, VS2004-2009/1947-1949AD

**MINTS**

Jodhpur جودہ پور

Jodpur جود پور

Dar-al-Mansur دار المنصور

**MINT MARKS**

**Before 1858AD**

Sojat, always on reverse. (KM#226)

Sojat, sometimes on obverse. (KM#226)

Pali, (KM#227)

Pali, Sojat
Nagor, (on reverse of KM#177.2)
Usually on obverse.

Jodhpur, on obverse. (KM#47)

**Issues of 1858-1873AD**

After 1858AD, the mint marks vary, and are given for each listing, wherever there is a difference.

All gold coins struck at Jodhpur Mint. All mints except Jodhpur closed by or before 1893AD. All copper coins were probably struck at the Jodhpur Mint, but if struck elsewhere, they bear no distinguishing marks.

In addition to the mint marks indicating the mint cities, there are also the marks of the Darogas (mint overseers), which are very useful in identifying the mints, especially when the city marks are missing or off the flan. These are given by cat.# and mint: (Only one of the marks appears on any one coin, always on the obverse.)

**Issues of Edward VII and George V and Sardar Singh and Sumer Singh**

Jodhpur (KM#91-95, 98-100, 109, 113-115) 

Jodhpur (KM#120)

**Issues of George V and Sumer Singh**

Jodhpur (KM#111-112) 

**Issues of George V and Umaid Singh**

Jodhpur (KM#128 & 129) 

Jodhpur (KM#129)

**Issues of Edward VIII and Umaid Singh**

Jodhpur all 

**Issues of George VI and Umaid Singh**

Jodhpur (KM#141-143) 

Jodhpur (KM#144-147, 150-151) 

**Issues of George VI and Hanwant Singh**

Jodhpur all 

The Daroga's marks generally consist of a symbol or a single Nagari letter, sometimes inverted, and even lying on its side. Some letters are found on more than one series, so that the mark is not a positive identification, but taken together with the city mark and the style of the coin, will provide a correct attribution.

**JODHPUR MINT**

Operative between 1761AD (AH1175) and 1945AD (VS2002). There are a number of mules of late Jodhpur types struck in 1945 and later for collectors.

# PRINCELY STATE

## HAMMERED 'DUMP' COINAGE

**1/4 ANNA** KM# 91.1 **Weight:** 10.5000 g. **Composition:** Copper **Ruler:** Sardar Singh VS1952-68/1895-1911AD **Obverse:** Inscription: Edward (VII)... **Reverse:** Inscription: Sardar Singh...; date at top **Note:** Other blundered dates may exist. Cross reference Y#20. Struck at the Jodhpur Mint.

| Date | Mintage | Good | VG | F | VF | XF |
|---|---|---|---|---|---|---|
| 1901 | — | 1.50 | 2.50 | 3.75 | 5.50 | — |
| 1902 | — | 1.50 | 2.50 | 3.75 | 5.50 | — |
| 1903 | — | 1.50 | 2.50 | 3.75 | 5.50 | — |
| 1904 | — | 1.50 | 2.50 | 3.75 | 5.50 | — |
| 1905 | — | 1.50 | 2.50 | 3.75 | 5.50 | — |
| 1906 | — | 0.50 | 1.00 | 1.75 | 2.50 | — |
| 1609 | — | 1.50 | 2.50 | 3.75 | 5.50 | — |
| 1907 | — | 1.00 | 2.00 | 3.25 | 4.50 | — |
| 1908 | — | 1.00 | 2.00 | 3.25 | 4.50 | — |
| 1909 | — | 1.00 | 2.00 | 3.25 | 4.50 | — |
| 1910 | — | 1.00 | 2.00 | 3.25 | 4.50 | — |
| 1290(1910) Error | — | 1.25 | 2.25 | 3.00 | 4.00 | — |
| 1291(1910) Error | — | 0.75 | 1.50 | 2.25 | 3.25 | — |
| 1292(1910) Error | — | — | — | — | — | — |
| 1967(1910) Error | — | 1.25 | 2.25 | 3.00 | 4.00 | — |
| 2091(1910) Error | — | 1.25 | 2.25 | 3.00 | 4.00 | — |
| 5201(1910) Error | — | 1.25 | 2.25 | 3.00 | 4.00 | — |
| 5291(1910) Error | — | — | — | — | — | — |

**1/4 ANNA** KM# 91.2 **Weight:** 10.5000 g. **Composition:** Copper **Ruler:** Sardar Singh VS1952-68/1895-1911AD **Obverse:** Inscription: Edward (VII)... **Reverse:** Inscription: Sardar Singh...; date at bottom **Note:** Cross reference Y#20. Struck at the Jodhpur Mint.

| Date | Mintage | Good | VG | F | VF | XF |
|---|---|---|---|---|---|---|
| 1906 | — | — | — | — | — | — |

**1/4 ANNA** KM# 110 **Weight:** 10.5000 g. **Composition:** Copper **Ruler:** Sumar Singh VS1968-75/1911-18AD **Obverse:** Inscription: George V, "Emperor"... **Reverse:** Inscription: Sumar Singh... **Note:** Cross reference Y#27. Struck at the Jodhpur Mint.

| Date | Mintage | Good | VG | F | VF | XF |
|---|---|---|---|---|---|---|
| 1914 | — | 6.50 | 9.00 | 12.50 | 17.50 | — |

**1/4 ANNA** KM# 111 **Weight:** 10.5000 g. **Composition:** Copper **Ruler:** Sumar Singh VS1968-75/1911-18AD **Obverse:** Inscription: George V, "Shah"... **Reverse:** Inscription: Sumar Singh... **Note:** Cross reference Y#27. Struck at the Jodhpur Mint.

| Date | Mintage | Good | VG | F | VF | XF |
|---|---|---|---|---|---|---|
| 1914 | — | — | — | — | — | — |

**1/4 ANNA** KM# 131 **Weight:** 10.5000 g. **Composition:** Copper **Ruler:** Umaid Singh VS1975-2004/1918-47AD **Obverse:** Inscription: Edward (VIII)...; without Persian "8" left of Daroga's mark **Reverse:** Inscription: Umaid Singh... **Note:** Cross reference Y#39. Struck at the Jodhpur Mint.

| Date | Mintage | Good | VG | F | VF | XF |
|---|---|---|---|---|---|---|
| 1936 | — | 1.75 | 2.75 | 4.00 | 6.50 | — |

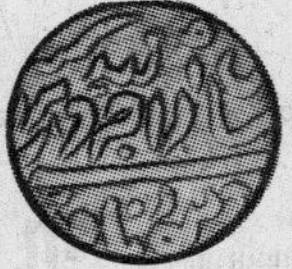

**1/4 ANNA** KM# 132 **Weight:** 10.5000 g. **Composition:** Copper **Ruler:** Umaid Singh VS1975-2004/1918-47AD **Obverse:** Inscription: Edward (VIII)...; large Persian "8" left of Daroga's mark **Reverse:** Inscription: Umaid Singh... **Note:** Struck at the Jodhpur Mint.

| Date | Mintage | Good | VG | F | VF | XF |
|---|---|---|---|---|---|---|
| 1936 | — | 1.75 | 2.75 | 4.00 | 6.50 | — |

**Note:** Blundered legend varieties also exist

**1/4 ANNA** KM# 133 **Weight:** 10.5000 g. **Composition:** Copper **Ruler:** Umaid Singh VS1975-2004/1918-47AD **Obverse:** Inscription: Edward (VIII)...; small Persian "8" left of Daroga's mark **Reverse:** Inscription: Umaid Singh... **Note:** Struck at the Jodhpur Mint.

| Date | Mintage | Good | VG | F | VF | XF |
|---|---|---|---|---|---|---|
| 1936 | — | 1.75 | 2.75 | 4.00 | 6.50 | — |

**1/4 ANNA** KM# 141 **Composition:** Copper **Ruler:** Umaid Singh VS1975-2004/1918-47AD **Obverse:** Inscription: George (VI)... **Reverse:** Inscription: Umaid Singh...; date at top **Note:** Thick, 10.50-10.70 grams. Cross reference Y#40. Struck at the Jodhpur Mint.

| Date | Mintage | Good | VG | F | VF | XF |
|---|---|---|---|---|---|---|
| 1937 | — | 1.25 | 1.75 | 2.50 | 3.50 | — |
| 1938 | — | 1.25 | 1.75 | 2.50 | 3.50 | — |
| 1939 | — | 1.25 | 1.75 | 2.50 | 3.50 | — |

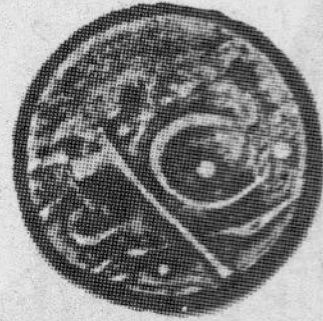

**1/4 ANNA** KM# 142 **Composition:** Copper **Ruler:** Umaid Singh VS1975-2004/1918-47AD **Obverse:** Inscription: George (VI)... **Reverse:** Inscription: Umaid Singh... **Note:** Struck at the Jodhpur Mint.

| Date | Mintage | Good | VG | F | VF | XF |
|---|---|---|---|---|---|---|
| VS1996 | — | 2.00 | 3.00 | 4.00 | 6.00 | — |

**1/4 ANNA** KM# 143 **Composition:** Copper **Ruler:** Umaid Singh VS1975-2004/1918-47AD **Obverse:** Inscription: George (VI)... **Reverse:** Inscription: Umaid Singh... **Note:** Struck at the Jodhpur Mint.

| Date | Mintage | Good | VG | F | VF | XF |
|---|---|---|---|---|---|---|
| ND | — | 3.00 | 4.50 | 6.50 | 10.00 | — |

**1/4 ANNA** KM# 152 **Weight:** 4.2000 g. **Composition:** Copper **Ruler:** Hanwant Singh, as Titular Ruler VS2004-09/1947-49AD **Obverse:** Inscription: George (VI)... **Reverse:** Inscription: Hanwant Singh... **Note:** Cross reference Y#43. Struck at the Jodhpur Mint.

| Date | Mintage | Good | VG | F | VF | XF |
|---|---|---|---|---|---|---|
| VS(2004) | — | 12.50 | 20.00 | 32.50 | 50.00 | — |

**1/2 ANNA** KM# 92.1 **Composition:** Copper **Ruler:** Sardar Singh VS1952-68/1895-1911AD **Obverse:** Inscription: Edward (VII)... **Reverse:** Inscription: Sardar Singh... **Note:** 20.00-21.00 grams. Cross reference Y#21. Struck at the Jodhpur Mint.

| Date | Mintage | Good | VG | F | VF | XF |
|---|---|---|---|---|---|---|
| 1906 | — | 3.50 | 5.00 | 7.50 | 11.50 | — |

**1/2 ANNA** KM# 92.2 **Composition:** Copper **Ruler:** Sardar Singh VS1952-68/1895-1911AD **Obverse:** Inscription: Edward (VII)... **Reverse:** Inscription: Sardar Singh...; legend differs **Note:** Cross reference Y#21. Struck at the Jodhpur Mint.

| Date | Mintage | Good | VG | F | VF | XF |
|---|---|---|---|---|---|---|
| 1906 | — | 3.50 | 5.00 | 7.50 | 11.50 | — |
| 1908 | — | 3.50 | 5.00 | 7.50 | 11.50 | — |

**1/2 ANNA** KM# 112.1 **Weight:** 21.0000 g. **Composition:** Copper **Ruler:** Sumar Singh VS1968-75/1911-18AD **Obverse:** Inscription: George V, "Emperor"... **Reverse:** Inscription: Sumar Singh... **Note:** Cross reference Y#28. Struck at the Jodhpur Mint.

| Date | Mintage | Good | VG | F | VF | XF |
|---|---|---|---|---|---|---|
| 1914 | — | 5.00 | 8.50 | 12.50 | 20.00 | — |

**1/2 ANNA** KM# 112.2 **Weight:** 21.0000 g. **Composition:** Copper **Ruler:** Sumar Singh VS1968-75/1911-18AD **Obverse:** Inscription: George V, "Shah"... **Reverse:** Inscription: Sumar Singh... **Note:** Cross reference Y#28. Struck at the Jodhpur Mint.

| Date | Mintage | Good | VG | F | VF | XF |
|---|---|---|---|---|---|---|
| 1914 | — | 5.00 | 8.50 | 12.50 | 20.00 | — |

**1/8 RUPEE** KM# 93 **Weight:** 1.4000 g. **Composition:** Silver **Ruler:** Sardar Singh VS1952-68/1895-1911AD **Obverse:** Inscription: Edward (VII)... **Reverse:** Inscription: Sardar Singh...

| Date | Mintage | VG | F | VF | XF | Unc |
|---|---|---|---|---|---|---|
| ND(1908) | — | 17.50 | 25.00 | 35.00 | 50.00 | — |

**1/8 RUPEE** KM# 113 **Weight:** 1.4000 g. **Composition:** Silver **Ruler:** Sumar Singh VS1968-75/1911-18AD **Obverse:** Inscription: George V, "Shah"... **Reverse:** Inscription: Sumar Singh... **Note:** Cross reference Y#29. Struck at the Jodhpur Mint.

| Date | Mintage | VG | F | VF | XF | Unc |
|---|---|---|---|---|---|---|
| ND(1911-18) | — | 15.00 | 21.50 | 30.00 | 40.00 | — |

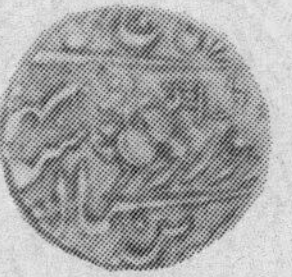

**1/4 RUPEE** KM# 94 **Weight:** 2.8000 g. **Composition:** Silver **Ruler:** Sardar Singh VS1952-68/1895-1911AD **Obverse:** Inscription: Edward (VII)... **Reverse:** Inscription: Sardar Singh... **Note:** Cross reference Y#22.

| Date | Mintage | VG | F | VF | XF | Unc |
|---|---|---|---|---|---|---|
| VS1965 | — | 18.50 | 26.50 | 37.50 | 55.00 | — |

**1/4 RUPEE** KM# 114 **Weight:** 2.8000 g. **Composition:** Silver **Ruler:** Sumar Singh VS1968-75/1911-18AD **Note:** Cross reference Y#30. Struck at the Jodhpur Mint.

| Date | Mintage | Good | VG | F | VF | XF |
|---|---|---|---|---|---|---|
| ND(1911-18) | — | 15.00 | 21.50 | 30.00 | 40.00 | — |

**1/4 RUPEE** KM# 124 **Weight:** 3.1000 g. **Composition:** Silver **Ruler:** Umaid Singh VS1975-2004/1918-47AD **Obverse:** Inscription: George (V)... **Reverse:** Inscription: Umaid Singh... **Note:** Cross reference Y#35. Struck at the Jodhpur Mint.

| Date | Mintage | VG | F | VF | XF | Unc |
|---|---|---|---|---|---|---|
| ND(1918-35) | — | 18.50 | 26.50 | 37.50 | 55.00 | — |

**1/2 RUPEE** KM# 95 **Weight:** 5.6000 g. **Composition:** Silver **Ruler:** Sardar Singh VS1952-68/1895-1911AD **Obverse:** Inscription: Edward (VII)... **Reverse:** Inscription: Sardar Singh... **Note:** Struck at the Jodhpur Mint.

| Date | Mintage | VG | F | VF | XF | Unc |
|---|---|---|---|---|---|---|
| ND | — | 20.00 | 31.50 | 42.50 | 60.00 | — |

**1/2 RUPEE** KM# 115 **Weight:** 5.6000 g. **Composition:** Silver **Ruler:** Sumar Singh VS1968-75/1911-18AD **Note:** Cross reference Y#31. Struck at the Jodhpur Mint.

| Date | Mintage | Good | VG | F | VF | XF |
|---|---|---|---|---|---|---|
| ND(1911-18) | — | 15.00 | 21.50 | 30.00 | 40.00 | — |

**1/2 RUPEE** KM# 125 **Composition:** Silver **Ruler:** Umaid Singh VS1975-2004/1918-47AD **Obverse:** Inscription: George (V)... **Reverse:** Inscription: Umaid Singh... **Note:** Round. Struck at the Jodhpur Mint.

| Date | Mintage | VG | F | VF | XF | Unc |
|---|---|---|---|---|---|---|
| ND(1918-35) | — | — | — | — | — | — |

**1/2 RUPEE** KM# 125a **Composition:** Silver **Ruler:** Umaid Singh VS1975-2004/1918-47AD **Obverse:** Inscription: George

(V)... **Reverse:** Inscription: Umaid Singh... **Note:** Square flan. Struck at the Jodhpur Mint.

| Date | Mintage | VG | F | VF | XF | Unc |
|---|---|---|---|---|---|---|
| ND(1918-35) | — | — | — | — | — | — |

**RUPEE KM# 116 Weight:** 11.2000 g. **Composition:** Silver **Ruler:** Sumar Singh VS1968-75/1911-18AD **Note:** Cross reference Y#32. Struck at the Jodhpur Mint.

| Date | Mintage | Good | VG | F | VF | XF |
|---|---|---|---|---|---|---|
| ND(1911-18) | — | 18.50 | 26.50 | 37.50 | 55.00 | — |

**RUPEE KM# 126 Composition:** Silver **Ruler:** Umaid Singh VS1975-2004/1918-47AD **Obverse:** Inscription: George (V)... **Reverse:** Inscription: Umaid Singh... **Note:** Struck at the Jodhpur Mint.

| Date | Mintage | VG | F | VF | XF | Unc |
|---|---|---|---|---|---|---|
| ND(1918-35) | — | — | — | — | — | — |

**1/4 MOHUR KM# 98 Weight:** 2.8000 g. **Composition:** Gold **Ruler:** Sardar Singh VS1952-68/1895-1911AD **Obverse:** Inscription: Edward (VII)... **Reverse:** Inscription: Sardar Singh... **Note:** Cross reference Y#23. Struck at the Jodhpur Mint.

| Date | Mintage | VG | F | VF | XF | Unc |
|---|---|---|---|---|---|---|
| ND(1906) | — | 60.00 | 85.00 | 110 | 165 | — |

**1/4 MOHUR KM# 127.1 Weight:** 2.7000 g. **Composition:** Gold **Ruler:** Umaid Singh VS1975-2004/1918-47AD **Obverse:** Inscription: George (V)...; "OM" or "AVM" **Reverse:** Inscription: Umaid Singh... **Note:** Cross reference Y#36. Struck at the Jodhpur Mint.

| Date | Mintage | VG | F | VF | XF | Unc |
|---|---|---|---|---|---|---|
| ND(1918-35) | — | 60.00 | 90.00 | 120 | 175 | — |

**1/4 MOHUR KM# 127.2 Weight:** 2.7000 g. **Composition:** Gold **Ruler:** Umaid Singh VS1975-2004/1918-47AD **Obverse:** Inscription: George (V)...; "Shri." **Reverse:** Inscription: Umaid Singh... **Note:** Cross reference Y#36. Struck at the Jodhpur Mint.

| Date | Mintage | VG | F | VF | XF | Unc |
|---|---|---|---|---|---|---|
| ND(1918-35) | — | 60.00 | 90.00 | 120 | 175 | — |

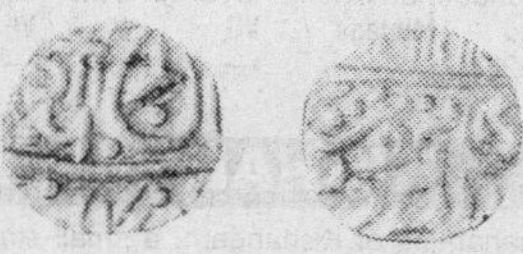

**1/4 MOHUR KM# 158 Weight:** 2.7000 g. **Composition:** Gold **Ruler:** Hanwant Singh, as Titular Ruler VS2004-09/1947-49AD **Obverse:** Inscription: George (VI)... **Reverse:** Inscription: Hanwant Singh... **Note:** Struck at the Jodhpur Mint.

| Date | Mintage | VG | F | VF | XF | Unc |
|---|---|---|---|---|---|---|
| VS(2004) Rare | — | — | — | — | — | — |

**1/2 MOHUR KM# 99 Weight:** 5.5000 g. **Composition:** Gold **Ruler:** Sardar Singh VS1952-68/1895-1911AD **Obverse:** Inscription: Edward (VII)... **Reverse:** Inscription: Sardar Singh... **Note:** Cross reference Y#24. Struck at the Jodhpur Mint.

| Date | Mintage | VG | F | VF | XF | Unc |
|---|---|---|---|---|---|---|
| ND(1906) | — | 100 | 150 | 210 | 300 | — |

**1/2 MOHUR KM# 119 Weight:** 5.5000 g. **Composition:** Gold **Ruler:** Sumar Singh VS1968-75/1911-18AD **Note:** Cross reference Y#26. Struck at the Jodhpur Mint.

| Date | Mintage | VG | F | VF | XF | Unc |
|---|---|---|---|---|---|---|
| ND(1911-18) | — | 87.50 | 125 | 175 | 250 | — |

**1/2 MOHUR KM# 128 Weight:** 5.5000 g. **Composition:** Gold **Ruler:** Umaid Singh VS1975-2004/1918-47AD **Obverse:** Inscription: George (V)... **Reverse:** Inscription: Umaid Singh... **Note:** Cross reference Y#37. Struck at the Jodhpur Mint.

| Date | Mintage | VG | F | VF | XF | Unc |
|---|---|---|---|---|---|---|
| ND(1918-35) | — | 100 | 150 | 210 | 300 | — |

**MOHUR KM# 100.1 Weight:** 11.0000 g. **Composition:** Gold **Ruler:** Sardar Singh VS1952-68/1895-1911AD **Obverse:** Inscription: Edward (VII)...; "Ma." **Reverse:** Inscription: Sardar Singh... **Note:** Cross reference Y#25. Struck at the Jodhpur Mint.

| Date | Mintage | VG | F | VF | XF | Unc |
|---|---|---|---|---|---|---|
| 1906 | — | 175 | 250 | 350 | 550 | — |

**MOHUR KM# 100.2 Weight:** 11.0000 g. **Composition:** Gold **Ruler:** Sardar Singh VS1952-68/1895-1911AD **Obverse:** Inscription: Edward (VII)...; "Sa." **Reverse:** Inscription: Sardar Singh... **Note:** Cross reference Y#25. Struck at the Jodhpur Mint.

| Date | Mintage | VG | F | VF | XF | Unc |
|---|---|---|---|---|---|---|
| 1906 | — | 175 | 250 | 350 | 550 | — |

**MOHUR KM# 120.1 Weight:** 11.0000 g. **Composition:** Gold **Ruler:** Sumar Singh VS1968-75/1911-18AD **Obverse:** "Ma." **Note:** Cross reference Y#33. Struck at the Jodhpur Mint.

| Date | Mintage | VG | F | VF | XF | Unc |
|---|---|---|---|---|---|---|
| ND(1911-18) | — | 175 | 250 | 350 | 550 | — |

**MOHUR KM# 120.2 Weight:** 11.0000 g. **Composition:** Gold **Ruler:** Sumar Singh VS1968-75/1911-18AD **Obverse:** "Ha." **Note:** Cross reference Y#33. Struck at the Jodhpur Mint.

| Date | Mintage | VG | F | VF | XF | Unc |
|---|---|---|---|---|---|---|
| ND(1911-18) | — | 200 | 300 | 400 | 600 | — |

**MOHUR KM# 129 Weight:** 11.0000 g. **Composition:** Gold **Ruler:** Umaid Singh VS1975-2004/1918-47AD **Obverse:** Inscription: George (V)...; "170m" **Reverse:** Inscription: Umaid Singh... **Note:** Cross reference Y#38. Struck at the Jodhpur Mint.

| Date | Mintage | VG | F | VF | XF | Unc |
|---|---|---|---|---|---|---|
| 19x8 | — | 175 | 250 | 350 | 550 | — |

**MOHUR KM# 130 Weight:** 11.0000 g. **Composition:** Gold **Ruler:** Umaid Singh VS1975-2004/1918-47AD **Obverse:** Inscription: George (V)...; "Shri. " **Reverse:** Inscription: Umaid Singh... **Note:** Cross reference Y#38. Struck at the Jodhpur Mint.

| Date | Mintage | VG | F | VF | XF | Unc |
|---|---|---|---|---|---|---|
| ND(1918-35) | — | 165 | 210 | 300 | 450 | — |

**MOHUR KM# 140 Weight:** 11.0100 g. **Composition:** Gold **Ruler:** Umaid Singh VS1975-2004/1918-47AD **Note:** Struck at the Jodhpur Mint.

| Date | Mintage | VG | F | VF | XF | Unc |
|---|---|---|---|---|---|---|
| 1936 | — | — | — | — | — | — |

**MOHUR KM# 151 Weight:** 11.0200 g. **Composition:** Gold **Ruler:** Umaid Singh VS1975-2004/1918-47AD **Obverse:** Inscription: George (VI)...; small legend, without Persian "6" **Reverse:** Inscription: Umaid Singh...; small legend, without Persian "6" **Note:** Struck at the Jodhpur Mint.

| Date | Mintage | VG | F | VF | XF | Unc |
|---|---|---|---|---|---|---|
| ND | — | 165 | 225 | 350 | 650 | — |
| VS2000 | — | 165 | 225 | 350 | 650 | — |

**MOHUR Weight:** 11.0200 g. **Composition:** Gold **Ruler:** Umaid Singh VS1975-2004/1918-47AD **Obverse:** Inscription: George (VI)...; Daroga's mark similar to KM#144-146 **Reverse:** Inscription: Umaid Singh... **Note:** Struck at the Jodhpur Mint.

| Date | Mintage | VG | F | VF | XF | Unc |
|---|---|---|---|---|---|---|
| ND | — | 165 | 225 | 350 | 650 | — |

**MOHUR KM# 150 Weight:** 11.0000 g. **Composition:** Gold **Ruler:** Umaid Singh VS1975-2004/1918-47AD **Obverse:** Inscription: George (VI)...; large legend, Persian "6" after "George" **Reverse:** Inscription: Umaid Singh...; large legend, Persian "6" after "George" **Note:** Cross reference Y#42. Struck at the Jodhpur Mint.

| Date | Mintage | VG | F | VF | XF | Unc |
|---|---|---|---|---|---|---|
| ND | — | 165 | 225 | 350 | 650 | — |

**MOHUR KM# 160 Weight:** 11.0000 g. **Composition:** Gold **Ruler:** Hanwant Singh, as Titular Ruler VS2004-09/1947-49AD **Obverse:** Inscription: George (VI)... **Reverse:** Inscription: Hanwant Singh... **Note:** Struck at the Jodhpur Mint.

| Date | Mintage | VG | F | VF | XF | Unc |
|---|---|---|---|---|---|---|
| VS(2004) | — | 250 | 350 | 500 | 650 | — |

## MILLED COINAGE

**1/4 ANNA KM# 147 Weight:** 2.6000 g. **Composition:** Copper **Ruler:** Umaid Singh VS1975-2004/1918-47AD **Obverse:** Inscription: George (VI)...; cock with wings raised facing left, legend around **Reverse:** Inscription: Umaid Singh...; date and "Rajya Marwar" **Note:** Struck at the Jodhpur Mint.

| Date | Mintage | Good | VG | F | VF | XF |
|---|---|---|---|---|---|---|
| VS2000 Rare | — | — | — | — | — | — |

**1/4 ANNA KM# 144 Weight:** 3.0000 g. **Composition:** Copper **Ruler:** Umaid Singh VS1975-2004/1918-47AD **Obverse:** Inscription: George (VI)...; without Persian "6" below Daroga's mark **Reverse:** Inscription: Umaid Singh... **Note:** Thin flan. Cross reference Y#41. Struck at the Jodhpur Mint.

| Date | Mintage | Good | VG | F | VF | XF |
|---|---|---|---|---|---|---|
| VS2000 | — | 1.75 | 2.75 | 4.00 | 5.50 | — |
| ND Date off flan | — | 0.20 | 0.30 | 0.50 | 1.00 | — |

**1/4 ANNA KM# 145 Weight:** 2.6000 g. **Composition:** Copper **Ruler:** Umaid Singh VS1975-2004/1918-47AD **Obverse:** Inscription: George (VI)...; Persian "6" below Daroga's mark **Reverse:** Inscription: Umaid Singh... **Note:** Varieties exist. Struck at the Jodhpur Mint.

| Date | Mintage | Good | VG | F | VF | XF |
|---|---|---|---|---|---|---|
| VS2001 | — | 1.75 | 2.75 | 4.00 | 5.50 | — |
| VS2002 | — | 1.75 | 2.75 | 4.00 | 5.50 | — |

**1/4 ANNA KM# 146 Weight:** 2.6000 g. **Composition:** Copper **Ruler:** Umaid Singh VS1975-2004/1918-47AD **Obverse:** Inscription: George (VI)...; Persian 2 (error for 6) below Daroga's mark **Reverse:** Inscription: Umaid Singh... **Note:** Struck at the Jodhpur Mint.

| Date | Mintage | Good | VG | F | VF | XF |
|---|---|---|---|---|---|---|
| VS | — | — | — | — | — | — |

# JUBBAL

## PRINCELY STATE

### MEDALLIC COINAGE

**1/2 MOHUR KM# M1 Weight:** 5.5800 g. **Composition:** Gold **Ruler:** Raja Bhayay Chandra Bahadur VS1967-2004/1910-1947AD **Obverse:** Supported arms **Reverse:** "Shri" in hexagram

| Date | Mintage | VG | F | VF | XF | Unc |
|---|---|---|---|---|---|---|
| VS1988(1931) | — | — | — | — | 900 | 1,200 |

**MOHUR KM# M2 Weight:** 11.5900 g. **Composition:** Gold **Ruler:** Raja Bhayay Chandra Bahadur VS1967-2004/1910-1947AD **Obverse:** Supported Arms **Rev. Designer:** "Shri" in hexagram

| Date | Mintage | VG | F | VF | XF | Unc |
|---|---|---|---|---|---|---|
| VS1988(1931) | — | — | — | — | 1,200 | 1,500 |

# JUNAGADH

A state located in the Kathiawar peninsula of Western India was originally a petty Rajput kingdom until conquered by the Sultan of Ahmadabad in 1472. It became a Mughal dependency under the Emperor Akbar, administered by the Ahmadabad Subah. In 1735, when the empire began to disintegrate, a Mughal officer and military adventurer, Sher Khan Babi, expelled the Mughal governor and asserted his independence. From that time until Indian independence his descendents ruled the state as nawabs. In 1947 the Nawab of Junagadh tried to acceed to the new nation of Pakistan but the Hindu majority in the state objected and Junagadh was absorbed by the Republic of India.

Junagadh first entered into treaty relations with the British in 1807 and maintained a close and friendly association with the Raj.

In 1924 this relationship was formalized when Junagadh was placed under an Agent to the Governor General in the western India States. In 1935 the state comprised 3,337 square miles with a population of 545,152, four-fifths of whom were Hindus.

**RULERS**

Rasul Muhammad Khan,
AH1309-1329/VS1948-1968/1891-1911AD
Mahabat Khan III, AH1329-1368/VS1968-2005/1911-1948AD

## PRINCELY STATE

### MILLED COINAGE

**DOKDO ("Ek Paisa" / "1 Dokdo") KM# 43 Composition:** Copper **Ruler:** Rasul Muhammad Khan AH1309-1329/VS1948-1968/1891-1911AD **Obverse:** Inscription: Perso-Arabic "Ek paisa Junagadh Riiyaasat (government)" **Reverse:** Inscription: "Devanagari-Shri Sorath Sarkaar" **Note:** Struck at Junagadh.

| Date | Mintage | Good | VG | F | VF | XF |
|---|---|---|---|---|---|---|
| AH1325/VS1963 | — | 4.50 | 6.50 | 10.00 | 15.00 | 25.00 |

**DOKDO ("Ek Paisa" / "1 Dokdo") KM# 44.1 Composition:** Copper **Ruler:** Rasul Muhammad Khan AH1309-1329/VS1948-1968/1891-1911AD **Obverse:** Inscription: Perso-Arabic Ek paisa Junagadh Riiyaasat (government) **Reverse:** Inscription: Devanagari-Shri Sorath Sarkaar; date without rosettes **Note:** Struck at Junagadh.

| Date | Mintage | Good | VG | F | VF | XF |
|---|---|---|---|---|---|---|
| VS1963(1906) | — | 1.25 | 2.00 | 3.00 | 4.50 | 7.50 |
| VS1964(1907) | — | — | — | — | — | — |

**DOKDO ("Ek Paisa" / "1 Dokdo") KM# 46.1 Composition:** Copper **Ruler:** Rasul Muhammad Khan AH1309-1329/VS1948-1968/1891-1911AD **Obverse:** Inscription: Perso-Arabic Ek paisa Junagadh Riiyaasat (government) **Reverse:** Inscription: Devanagari-Shri Sorath Sarkaar **Note:** Struck at Junagadh.

| Date | Mintage | Good | VG | F | VF | XF |
|---|---|---|---|---|---|---|
| ND | — | 1.75 | 2.75 | 4.00 | 6.50 | 11.50 |

**DOKDO ("Ek Paisa" / "1 Dokdo") KM# 46.2 Composition:** Copper **Ruler:** Rasul Muhammad Khan AH1309-1329/VS1948-1968/1891-1911AD **Obverse:** Inscription: Perso-Arabic Ek paisa Junagadh Riiyaasat (government) **Reverse:** Inscription: Devanagari-Shri Sorath Sarkaar; stars between inscriptions **Note:** Struck at Junagadh.

| Date | Mintage | Good | VG | F | VF | XF |
|---|---|---|---|---|---|---|
| ND | — | 1.75 | 2.75 | 4.00 | 6.50 | 11.50 |

**DOKDO ("Ek Paisa" / "1 Dokdo") KM# 44.2 Composition:** Copper **Ruler:** Rasul Muhammad Khan AH1309-1329/VS1948-1968/1891-1911AD **Obverse:** Inscription: Perso-Arabic Ek paisa Junagadh Riiyaasat (government) **Reverse:** Inscription: Devanagari-Shri Sorath Sarkaar; date with annulets **Note:** Struck at Junagadh.

| Date | Mintage | Good | VG | F | VF | XF |
|---|---|---|---|---|---|---|
| VS1964(1907) | — | 1.25 | 2.00 | 3.00 | 4.50 | 7.50 |

**DOKDO ("Ek Paisa" / "1 Dokdo") KM# 44.3 Composition:** Copper **Ruler:** Rasul Muhammad Khan AH1309-1329/VS1948-1968/1891-1911AD **Obverse:** Inscription: Perso-Arabic Ek paisa Junagadh Riiyaasat (government) **Reverse:** Inscription: Devanagari-Shri Sorath Sarkaar; date between solid stars **Note:** Struck at Junagadh.

| Date | Mintage | Good | VG | F | VF | XF |
|---|---|---|---|---|---|---|
| VS1964(1907) | — | 1.25 | 2.00 | 3.00 | 4.50 | 7.50 |

**DOKDO ("Ek Paisa" / "1 Dokdo") KM# 44.3a Composition:** Copper **Ruler:** Rasul Muhammad Khan AH1309-1329/VS1948-1968/1891-1911AD **Obverse:** Inscription: Perso-Arabic Ek paisa Junagadh Riiyaasat (government) **Reverse:** Inscription: Devanagari-Shri Sorath Sarkaar; solid star only to left of date **Note:** Struck at Junagadh.

| Date | Mintage | Good | VG | F | VF | XF |
|---|---|---|---|---|---|---|
| VS1964(1907) | — | 2.50 | 4.00 | 6.00 | 10.00 | 16.50 |

**DOKDO ("Ek Paisa" / "1 Dokdo") KM# 44.4 Composition:** Copper **Ruler:** Rasul Muhammad Khan AH1309-1329/VS1948-1968/1891-1911AD **Obverse:** Inscription: Perso-Arabic Ek paisa Junagadh Riiyaasat (government) **Reverse:** Inscription: Devanagari-Shri Sorath Sarkaar; date with outlined stars **Note:** Struck at Junagadh.

| Date | Mintage | Good | VG | F | VF | XF |
|---|---|---|---|---|---|---|
| VS1964(1907) | — | 1.25 | 2.00 | 3.00 | 4.50 | 7.50 |

**DOKDO ("Ek Paisa" / "1 Dokdo") KM# 45.1 Composition:** Copper **Ruler:** Rasul Muhammad Khan AH1309-1329/VS1948-1968/1891-1911AD **Obverse:** Inscription: Perso-Arabic Ek paisa Junagadh Riiyaasat (government) **Reverse:** Inscription: Devanagari-Shri Sorath Sarkaar; date between rosettes **Note:** Struck at Junagadh.

| Date | Mintage | Good | VG | F | VF | XF |
|---|---|---|---|---|---|---|
| VS1964(1907) | — | 0.50 | 0.85 | 1.25 | 1.75 | 3.00 |
| VS1965(1908) | — | 0.50 | 0.85 | 1.25 | 1.75 | 3.00 |
| VS1966(1909) | — | 0.50 | 0.85 | 1.25 | 1.75 | 3.00 |
| VS1967(1910) | — | 0.75 | 0.50 | 2.50 | 3.50 | 6.00 |

**DOKDO ("Ek Paisa" / "1 Dokdo") KM# 45.2 Composition:** Copper **Ruler:** Rasul Muhammad Khan AH1309-1329/VS1948-1968/1891-1911AD **Obverse:** Inscription: Perso-Arabic Ek paisa Junagadh Riiyaasat (government) **Reverse:** Inscription: Devanagari-Shri Sorath Sarkaar; date divided by space in legend **Note:** Struck at Junagadh.

| Date | Mintage | Good | VG | F | VF | XF |
|---|---|---|---|---|---|---|
| VS1966(1909) | — | 0.75 | 1.50 | 2.50 | 3.50 | 6.00 |

**DOKDO ("Ek Paisa" / "1 Dokdo") KM# 45.3 Composition:** Copper **Ruler:** Rasul Muhammad Khan AH1309-1329/VS1948-1968/1891-1911AD **Obverse:** Inscription: Perso-Arabic Ek paisa Junagadh Riiyaasat (government) **Reverse:** Inscription: Devanagari-Shri Sorath Sarkaar; date upside down in legend **Note:** Struck at Junagadh.

| Date | Mintage | Good | VG | F | VF | XF |
|---|---|---|---|---|---|---|
| VS1966(1909) | — | 1.75 | 2.75 | 4.00 | 6.50 | 11.50 |

**DOKDO KM# 61 Weight:** 11.5400 g. **Composition:** Gold **Ruler:** Mahabat Khan III AH1329-1368/VS1968-2005/1911-1948AD **Obverse:** "Shri Divan" in Devanagari below

| Date | Mintage | Good | VG | F | VF | XF |
|---|---|---|---|---|---|---|
| AH1325(1907) Rare | — | — | — | — | — | — |

**DOKDO KM# 63 Composition:** Copper **Ruler:** Mahabat Khan III AH1329-1368/VS1968-2005/1911-1948AD

| Date | Mintage | VG | F | VF | XF | Unc |
|---|---|---|---|---|---|---|
| VS1985(1928) | — | 16.50 | 25.00 | 40.00 | 65.00 | — |
| VS1990(1933) | — | 16.50 | 25.00 | 40.00 | 65.00 | — |

**2 DOKDA KM# 48 Composition:** Copper **Ruler:** Rasul Muhammad Khan AH1309-1329/VS1948-1968/1891-1911AD **Obverse:** Inscription: Perso-Arabic Ek paisa Junagadh Riiyaasat (government) **Reverse:** Inscription: Devanagari-Shri Sorath Sarkaar **Note:** Struck at Junagadh.

| Date | Mintage | Good | VG | F | VF | XF |
|---|---|---|---|---|---|---|
| VS1964(1907) | — | 7.50 | 12.50 | 20.00 | 30.00 | 50.00 |

**KORI KM# 52 Weight:** 4.6000 g. **Composition:** Silver **Ruler:** Rasul Muhammad Khan AH1309-1329/VS1948-1968/1891-1911AD

| Date | Mintage | VG | F | VF | XF | Unc |
|---|---|---|---|---|---|---|
| VS1966(1909) | — | 17.50 | 25.00 | 35.00 | 50.00 | — |

**GOLD KORI KM# 58 Composition:** Gold **Ruler:** Rasul Muhammad Khan AH1309-1329/VS1948-1968/1891-1911AD **Obverse:** Inscription: Perso-Arabic Nawab Bahadur Muhammad Khanji **Reverse:** Date, mint name **Note:** 4.02-4.77 grams

| Date | Mintage | VG | F | VF | XF | Unc |
|---|---|---|---|---|---|---|
| AH1325/VS1963 | — | — | — | 500 | 850 | 1,250 |

**MOHUR KM# 60 Weight:** 11.5400 g. **Composition:** Gold **Ruler:** Rasul Muhammad Khan AH1309-1329/VS1948-1968/1891-1911AD **Obverse:** Inscription: Perso-Arabic Nawab Bahadur Muhammad Khanji **Reverse:** Date, mint name

| Date | Mintage | VG | F | VF | XF | Unc |
|---|---|---|---|---|---|---|
| AH1325/VS1963 | — | — | — | — | 2,000 | 2,800 |

# KISHANGARH

The maharajas of Kishangarh, a small state in northwest India, in the vicinity of Ajmer, belonged to the Rathor Rajputs. The town of Kishangarh, which gave its name to the state, was founded in 1611 and was itself named after Kishen Singh, the first ruler. The maharajas succeeded in reaching terms with Akbar in the late 16th century, and again in 1818 with the British. In 1949 the state was merged into Rajasthan.

**RULERS**

Sardul Singh, VS1936-1957/1879-1900AD
Madan Singh, VS1957-1983/1900-1926AD
Yaghyanarayan Singh, VS1983-1995/1926-1938AD
Sumer Singh, VS1995-2000/1938-1949AD

**MINT**

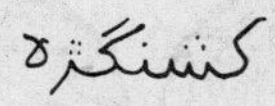

**Kishangarh**

**Mint mark:**
Symbol on reverse: Jhar

## PRINCELY STATE

### ANONYMOUS HAMMERED "DUMP" COINAGE

First Series

**1/8 RUPEE Y# 9 Weight:** 1.3500 g. **Composition:** Silver **Obverse:** Inscription: Nagari "Chadi" (silver) **Reverse:** Jhar

| Date | Mintage | VG | F | VF | XF | Unc |
|---|---|---|---|---|---|---|
| ND(ca.1902-38) | — | 40.00 | 65.00 | 100 | 150 | — |

**1/4 RUPEE Y# 10 Weight:** 2.7000 g. **Composition:** Silver **Obverse:** Inscription: Nagari "Chadi" (silver) **Reverse:** Jhar

| Date | Mintage | VG | F | VF | XF | Unc |
|---|---|---|---|---|---|---|
| ND(ca.1902-38) | — | 40.00 | 65.00 | 100 | 150 | — |

**1/2 RUPEE Y# 11 Weight:** 5.4000 g. **Composition:** Silver **Obverse:** Inscription: Nagari "Chadi" (silver) **Reverse:** Jhar

| Date | Mintage | VG | F | VF | XF | Unc |
|---|---|---|---|---|---|---|
| ND(ca.1902-38) | — | 40.00 | 65.00 | 100 | 150 | — |
| ND(ca. 1902-38) | — | 40.00 | 65.00 | 100 | 150 | — |

**RUPEE** **Y# 12** **Composition:** Silver **Obverse:** Inscription: Nagari "Chadi" (silver) **Reverse:** Jhar **Note:** 10.85-11.05 grams

| Date | Mintage | VG | F | VF | XF | Unc |
|---|---|---|---|---|---|---|
| ND(ca.1902-38) | — | 25.00 | 40.00 | 60.00 | 90.00 | — |

## ANONYMOUS HAMMERED "DUMP" COINAGE

Second Series

Denominations in Nagari, Persian and "merchants numerals", in Annas on obverse.

**2 ANNAS** **Y# 13** **Weight:** 1.3200 g. **Composition:** Silver **Reverse:** Jhar

| Date | Mintage | VG | F | VF | XF | Unc |
|---|---|---|---|---|---|---|
| ND(ca.1902-38) | — | 15.00 | 25.00 | 40.00 | 60.00 | — |

**4 ANNAS** **Y# 14** **Weight:** 2.6200 g. **Composition:** Silver **Reverse:** Jhar

| Date | Mintage | VG | F | VF | XF | Unc |
|---|---|---|---|---|---|---|
| ND(ca.1902-38) | — | 12.50 | 20.00 | 30.00 | 50.00 | — |

**8 ANNAS** **Y# 15** **Weight:** 5.3500 g. **Composition:** Silver **Reverse:** Jhar

| Date | Mintage | VG | F | VF | XF | Unc |
|---|---|---|---|---|---|---|
| ND(ca.1902-38) | — | 15.00 | 25.00 | 40.00 | 60.00 | — |

## HAMMERED "DUMP" COINAGE

1900-1926AD

**1/4 RUPEE** **Y# B3** **Weight:** 2.7000 g. **Composition:** Silver **Obverse:** Inscription: Edward (VII)... **Reverse:** Jhar; inscription: Madan Singh...

| Date | Mintage | VG | F | VF | XF | Unc |
|---|---|---|---|---|---|---|
| ND(1902) | — | 12.50 | 20.00 | 28.50 | 40.00 | — |

**1/2 RUPEE** **Y# A3** **Weight:** 5.4000 g. **Composition:** Silver **Obverse:** Inscription: Empress Victoria... **Reverse:** Jhar; inscription: Madan Singh...

| Date | Mintage | VG | F | VF | XF | Unc |
|---|---|---|---|---|---|---|
| ND(1900-01) | — | 40.00 | 65.00 | 100 | 145 | — |

**1/2 RUPEE** **Y# 3** **Weight:** 5.4000 g. **Composition:** Silver **Obverse:** Inscription: Edward (VII)... **Reverse:** Jhar; inscription: Madan Singh...

| Date | Mintage | VG | F | VF | XF | Unc |
|---|---|---|---|---|---|---|
| 1902 | — | 12.50 | 20.00 | 28.00 | 40.00 | — |

**RUPEE** **Y# C3** **Weight:** 10.8000 g. **Composition:** Silver **Obverse:** Inscription: Empress Victoria... **Reverse:** Jhar; inscription: Madan Singh...

| Date | Mintage | VG | F | VF | XF | Unc |
|---|---|---|---|---|---|---|
| ND(1900-01) | — | — | — | — | — | — |

**MOHUR** **Y# D3** **Weight:** 10.9000 g. **Composition:** Gold **Obverse:** Inscription: Empress Victoria... **Reverse:** Jhar; inscription: Madan Singh...

| Date | Mintage | VG | F | VF | XF | Unc |
|---|---|---|---|---|---|---|
| ND(1900-01) | — | 200 | 300 | 550 | 900 | — |

## HAMMERED "DUMP" COINAGE

1926-1938AD

**1/4 RUPEE** **Y# 4** **Weight:** 2.7000 g. **Composition:** Silver **Obverse:** Inscription: George (V)... **Reverse:** Jhar; inscription: Yaghyanarayan...

| Date | Mintage | VG | F | VF | XF | Unc |
|---|---|---|---|---|---|---|
| ND(1926-38) | — | 12.50 | 20.00 | 28.50 | 40.00 | — |

**1/2 RUPEE** **Y# 5** **Weight:** 5.4000 g. **Composition:** Silver **Obverse:** Inscription: George (V)... **Reverse:** Jhar; inscription: Yaghyanarayan...

| Date | Mintage | VG | F | VF | XF | Unc |
|---|---|---|---|---|---|---|
| ND(1926-38) | — | 12.50 | 20.00 | 28.50 | 40.00 | — |

**RUPEE** **Y# 6** **Weight:** 10.8000 g. **Composition:** Silver **Obverse:** Inscription: George (V)... **Reverse:** Jhar; inscription: Yaghyanarayan...

| Date | Mintage | VG | F | VF | XF | Unc |
|---|---|---|---|---|---|---|
| ND(1926-38) | — | 18.50 | 31.50 | 42.50 | 60.00 | — |

**NAZARANA RUPEE** **Y# 6a** **Composition:** Silver **Obverse:** Inscription: George (V)... **Reverse:** Jhar; inscription: Yaghyanarayan... **Note:** 10.70-10.80 grams

| Date | Mintage | VG | F | VF | XF | Unc |
|---|---|---|---|---|---|---|
| ND(1926-38) | — | 60.00 | 100 | 140 | 200 | — |

**1/2 MOHUR** **Y# 7** **Composition:** Gold **Obverse:** Inscription: George (V)... **Reverse:** Jhar; inscription: Yaghyanarayan... **Note:** Ca. 5.50 grams

| Date | Mintage | VG | F | VF | XF | Unc |
|---|---|---|---|---|---|---|
| ND(1926-38) | — | 135 | 225 | 550 | 850 | — |

**MOHUR** **Y# 8** **Composition:** Gold **Obverse:** Inscription: George (V)... **Reverse:** Jhar; inscription: Yaghyanarayan... **Note:** Ca. 11.00 grams

| Date | Mintage | VG | F | VF | XF | Unc |
|---|---|---|---|---|---|---|
| ND(1926-38) | — | 185 | 300 | 500 | 800 | — |

# KUTCH

State located in northwest India, consisting of a peninsula north of the Gulf of Kutch.

The rulers of Kutch were Jareja Rajputs who, coming from Tatta in Sind, conquered Kutch in the 14th or 15th centuries. The capital city of Bhuj is thought to date from the mid-16th century. In 1617, after Akbar's conquest of Gujerat and the fall of the Gujerat sultans, the Kutch ruler, Rao Bharmal I (1586-1632) visited Jahangir and established a relationship which was sufficiently warm as to leave Kutch virtually independent throughout the Mughal period. Early in the 19th century internal disorder and the existence of rival claimants to the throne resulted in British intrusion into the state's affairs. Rao Bharmalji II was deposed in favor of Rao Desalji II who proved much more amenable to the Government of India's wishes. He and his successors continued to rule in a manner considered by the British to be most enlightened and, as a result, Maharao Khengarji III was created a Knight Grand Commander of the Indian Empire. In view of its geographical isolation Kutch came under the direct control of the Central Government at India's independence.

First coinage was struck in 1617AD.

**RULERS**

Khengarji III, VS1932-1999/1875-1942AD

M(a)-ha-ra-o Sri Khen-ga-r-ji

माहाराउ खेंगारजी

Ma-ha-ra-o Khen-ga-r-ji

माहाराजाधिराज मिरजा महाराओश्री

Ma-ha-ra-ja Dhi-ra-j Mi-r-ja M(a)-ha-ra-o Sri

खेंगारजी बहादुरकछभुज

Khen-ga-r-ji B(a)-ha-du-r K(a)-chh-bhu-j

मिरजामहाराओश्री खेंगारजी

Mi-r-jan M(a)-ha-ra-o Sri Khen-ga-r-ji

महाराओश्री खेंगारजी

M(a)-ha-ra-o Sri Khen-ga-r-ji

महाराजाधिराजमिरजा महाराउ

M(a)-ha-ra-ja Dhi-ra-j Mi-r-jan M(a)-ha-ra-o

श्री खेंगारजी बहादुर

Sri-Khen-ga-r-ji B(a)-ha-du-r

श्री खेंगारजी सवाई बहादुर

Sri Khen-ga-r-ji Sa-va-I B(a)-ha-du-r

महाराउश्री खेंगारजी क कछभुज

M(a)-ha-ra-o Sri Khen-ga-r-ji K(a)-chchh-bhu-j

Vijayarajji

VS1999-2004/1942-1947AD

विजयराजजी

Vi-j(a)-y(a)-ra-j-ji

महाराओश्री विजयराजजी

M(a)-ha-ra-o Sri Vi-j(a)-y(a)-ra-j-ji K(a)-chchh 2000

Madanasinhji

VS2004- /1947- AD

मदनसिंहजी

M(a)-d(a)-n(a)-sin-h-ji

Pragmalji III & Maharani Pritidevi, VS2048-/1991AD-

**MINT**

भुज or بهوج

Bhuj (Devanagari) (Persian)

## PRINCELY STATE

## MEDALLIC COINAGE

In the last years of its coinage history, Kutch struck some non-circulating coins which state denomination. At least one was a pattern which wasn't approved for circulation strikes and the others were probably presentation pieces.

**2-1/2 KORI** **KM# M1** **Weight:** 6.9350 g. **Composition:** 0.9370 Silver .2089 oz. ASW **Ruler:** Madanasinghji VS2004-05/1947-48AD

| Date | Mintage | VG | F | VF | XF | Unc |
|---|---|---|---|---|---|---|
| VS1984 Rare | — | — | — | — | — | — |
| VS1984 Rare | — | — | — | — | — | — |

**5 KORI** **Composition:** Silver **Ruler:** Madanasinghji VS2004-05/1947-48AD **Obverse:** Large bust of Khengarji III left **Reverse:** Inscription: George V...

| Date | Mintage | F | VF | XF | Unc | BU |
|---|---|---|---|---|---|---|
| VS1998(0) | — | — | — | — | — | — |

**5 KORI** **KM# M2** **Composition:** Silver **Ruler:** Madanasinghji VS2004-05/1947-48AD **Obverse:** Small bust of Khengarji III left **Reverse:** Inscription: George V...

| Date | Mintage | VG | F | VF | XF | Unc |
|---|---|---|---|---|---|---|
| VS1985 | — | — | — | — | 450 | 600 |

**5 KORI** **KM# M3** **Composition:** Silver **Ruler:** Madanasinghji VS2004-05/1947-48AD **Obverse:** Large bust of Khengarji III left **Reverse:** Inscription: George V...

| Date | Mintage | VG | F | VF | XF | Unc |
|---|---|---|---|---|---|---|
| VS1985 | — | — | — | — | 450 | 600 |

**10 KORI** **KM# M4** **Composition:** Silver **Ruler:** Madanasinghji VS2004-05/1947-48AD

| Date | Mintage | VG | F | VF | XF | Unc |
|---|---|---|---|---|---|---|
| VS1998/1941 Rare | — | — | — | — | — | — |

**10 KORI** **KM# M4a** **Composition:** Gold **Ruler:** Madanasinghji VS2004-05/1947-48AD

| Date | Mintage | Good | VG | F | VF | XF |
|---|---|---|---|---|---|---|
| VS1998/1941 Rare | — | — | — | — | — | — |

**10 KORI** **KM# M6** **Composition:** Silver **Ruler:** Madanasinghji VS2004-05/1947-48AD **Obverse:** Small bust of Khengarji III left

| Date | Mintage | VG | F | VF | XF | Unc |
|---|---|---|---|---|---|---|
| VS1998/1942 Rare | — | — | — | — | — | — |

**10 KORI** **KM# M6a** **Composition:** Gold **Ruler:** Madanasinghji VS2004-05/1947-48AD **Obverse:** Small bust of Khengarji III left

| Date | Mintage | VG | F | VF | XF | Unc |
|---|---|---|---|---|---|---|
| VS1998/1942 Rare | — | — | — | — | — | — |

**GOLD KORI** **KM# M7** **Weight:** 7.3600 g. **Composition:** Gold **Ruler:** Madanasinghji VS2004-05/1947-48AD **Note:** Coronation of Madanasinghji.

| Date | Mintage | VG | F | VF | XF | Unc |
|---|---|---|---|---|---|---|
| VS2004/1947 | — | — | — | — | 450 | 650 |

**GOLD KORI** **KM# M9** **Weight:** 7.3600 g. **Composition:** Gold **Ruler:** Pragmalji III & Maharani Prittdevi VS2048-/1991AD- **Note:** Coronation of Pragmalji III and Maharani Pritidevi.

| Date | Mintage | VG | F | VF | XF | Unc |
|---|---|---|---|---|---|---|
| VS2048/1991 | — | — | — | — | 450 | 650 |

**MOHUR** **KM# M8** **Weight:** 18.7300 g. **Composition:** Gold **Ruler:** Madanasinghji VS2004-05/1947-48AD **Reverse:** Turreted gateway **Note:** Coronation of Maharani Pritidevi

| Date | Mintage | VG | F | VF | XF | Unc |
|---|---|---|---|---|---|---|
| VS2004/1947 | 30 | — | — | — | 3,500 | 5,000 |

## MILLED COINAGE

### Regal Issues - Second Series

**KORI** **Y# 35.1** **Weight:** 4.7000 g. **Composition:** 0.6100 Silver .0921 oz. ASW **Ruler:** Khengarji III VS1932-98/1875-1942AD **Obverse:** Inscription: Victoria, Empress of India **Reverse:** Open crescent

| Date | Mintage | Good | VG | F | VF | XF |
|---|---|---|---|---|---|---|
| 1901/VS1957 | — | 1.25 | 3.00 | 4.50 | 6.50 | 10.00 |

**5 KORI** **Y# 37.6** **Weight:** 13.8700 g. **Composition:** 0.9370 Silver .4178 oz. ASW **Ruler:** Khengarji III VS1932-98/1875-1942AD **Obverse:** Inscription: Victoria, Empress of India

| Date | Mintage | Good | VG | F | VF | XF |
|---|---|---|---|---|---|---|
| 1899/VS1955 | — | — | 6.50 | 10.00 | 15.00 | 22.50 |
| 1899/VS1956 | — | — | 6.50 | 10.00 | 15.00 | 22.50 |
| 1901/VS1957 | — | 7.00 | 17.50 | 25.00 | 35.00 | 50.00 |

## MILLED COINAGE

### Regal Issues - Third Series

**TRAMBIYO** **Y# 38** **Weight:** 4.0000 g. **Composition:** Copper **Ruler:** Khengarji III VS1932-98/1875-1942AD **Obverse:** Inscription: Edward VII...

| Date | Mintage | Good | VG | F | VF | XF |
|---|---|---|---|---|---|---|
| 1908/VS1965 | — | 0.60 | 1.50 | 2.50 | 3.50 | 4.50 |
| 1909/VS1965 | — | 0.25 | 0.60 | 1.00 | 1.50 | 2.50 |
| 1909/VS1966 | — | 0.25 | 0.60 | 1.00 | 1.50 | 2.00 |
| 1910/VS1966 | — | 0.85 | 1.65 | 2.75 | 4.25 | 6.00 |

**DOKDO** **Y# 39** **Weight:** 8.0000 g. **Composition:** Copper **Ruler:** Khengarji III VS1932-98/1875-1942AD **Obverse:** Inscription: Edward VII...

| Date | Mintage | Good | VG | F | VF | XF |
|---|---|---|---|---|---|---|
| 1909/VS1965 | — | 0.30 | 0.75 | 1.25 | 1.50 | 2.00 |
| 1909/VS1966 | — | 0.30 | 0.75 | 1.25 | 1.50 | 2.00 |

**1-1/2 DOKDA** **Y# 40** **Weight:** 12.0000 g. **Composition:** Copper **Ruler:** Khengarji III VS1932-98/1875-1942AD **Obverse:** Inscription: Edward VII... **Size:** 23 mm.

| Date | Mintage | Good | VG | F | VF | XF |
|---|---|---|---|---|---|---|
| 1909/VS1965 | — | 30.00 | 60.00 | 100 | 115 | 150 |

**3 DOKDA** **Y# 41** **Weight:** 24.0000 g. **Composition:** Copper **Ruler:** Khengarji III VS1932-98/1875-1942AD **Obverse:** Inscription: Edward VII...

| Date | Mintage | Good | VG | F | VF | XF |
|---|---|---|---|---|---|---|
| 1909/VS1965 | — | 30.00 | 60.00 | 100 | 115 | 150 |

**5 KORI** **Y# 45** **Weight:** 13.8700 g. **Composition:** 0.9370 Silver .4178 oz. ASW **Ruler:** Khengarji III VS1932-98/1875-1942AD **Obverse:** Inscription: Edward VII...

| Date | Mintage | Good | VG | F | VF | XF |
|---|---|---|---|---|---|---|
| 1902/VS1959 | — | 60.00 | 120 | 185 | 250 | 375 |
| 1903/VS1960 | — | 60.00 | 120 | 185 | 250 | 375 |
| 1904/VS1961 | — | 60.00 | 120 | 185 | 250 | 375 |
| 1905/VS1962 | — | 60.00 | 120 | 185 | 250 | 375 |
| 1906/VS1963 | — | 60.00 | 120 | 185 | 250 | 375 |
| 1907/VS1964 | — | 60.00 | 120 | 185 | 250 | 375 |
| 1908/VS1965 | — | 50.00 | 100 | 150 | 235 | 350 |
| 1909/VS1966 | — | 50.00 | 100 | 150 | 235 | 350 |

## MILLED COINAGE

### Regal Issues - Fourth Series

**TRAMBIYO** **Y# 46** **Weight:** 4.0000 g. **Composition:** Copper **Ruler:** Khengarji III VS1932-98/1875-1942AD **Obverse:** Inscription: George V...

| Date | Mintage | Good | VG | F | VF | XF |
|---|---|---|---|---|---|---|
| 1919/VS1976 | — | 0.10 | 0.30 | 0.50 | 0.75 | 1.00 |
| 1920/VS1976 | — | 0.10 | 0.30 | 0.50 | 0.75 | 1.50 |
| 1920/VS1977 | — | 0.10 | 0.30 | 0.50 | 0.75 | 1.50 |

**TRAMBIYO** **Y# 54** **Weight:** 4.0000 g. **Composition:** Copper **Ruler:** Khengarji III VS1932-98/1875-1942AD **Obverse:** Inscription: George V...

| Date | Mintage | Good | VG | F | VF | XF |
|---|---|---|---|---|---|---|
| 1928/VS1984 | — | 0.25 | 0.60 | 1.00 | 2.00 | 3.00 |
| 1928/VS1985 | — | 0.10 | 0.30 | 0.50 | 0.75 | 1.00 |

**DOKDO** **Y# 47** **Weight:** 8.0000 g. **Composition:** Copper **Ruler:** Khengarji III VS1932-98/1875-1942AD **Obverse:** Inscription: George V...

| Date | Mintage | Good | VG | F | VF | XF |
|---|---|---|---|---|---|---|
| 1920/VS1976 | — | 0.25 | 0.60 | 1.00 | 1.25 | 2.00 |
| 1920/VS1977 | — | 0.25 | 0.60 | 1.00 | 1.25 | 2.00 |

**DOKDO** **Y# 55** **Weight:** 8.0000 g. **Composition:** Copper **Ruler:** Khengarji III VS1932-98/1875-1942AD **Obverse:** Inscription: George V...

| Date | Mintage | Good | VG | F | VF | XF |
|---|---|---|---|---|---|---|
| 1922/VS1982 (sic) | — | 0.50 | 1.25 | 1.75 | 2.50 | 3.50 |
| 1928/VS1984 | — | 0.25 | 0.60 | 1.00 | 1.25 | 1.50 |
| 1929/VS1985 | — | 0.25 | 0.60 | 1.00 | 1.25 | 1.50 |

**1-1/2 DOKDA** **Y# 48** **Weight:** 12.0000 g. **Composition:** Copper **Ruler:** Khengarji III VS1932-98/1875-1942AD **Obverse:** Inscription: George V...

| Date | Mintage | Good | VG | F | VF | XF |
|---|---|---|---|---|---|---|
| 1926/VS1982 | — | 0.35 | 0.90 | 1.50 | 2.50 | 3.00 |

**1-1/2 DOKDA** **Y# 56** **Weight:** 12.0000 g. **Composition:** Copper **Ruler:** Khengarji III VS1932-98/1875-1942AD **Obverse:** Inscription: George V...

| Date | Mintage | Good | VG | F | VF | XF |
|---|---|---|---|---|---|---|
| 1928/VS1985 | — | 0.20 | 0.50 | 0.75 | 1.00 | 1.50 |
| 1929/VS1985 | — | 0.20 | 0.50 | 0.75 | 1.00 | 1.50 |
| 1929/VS1986 | — | 0.20 | 0.50 | 0.75 | 1.00 | 1.50 |
| 1931/VS1987 | — | 0.20 | 0.50 | 0.75 | 1.00 | 1.50 |
| 1931/VS1988 | — | 0.20 | 0.50 | 0.75 | 1.00 | 1.50 |
| 1932/VS1988 | — | 0.40 | 1.00 | 1.50 | 2.50 | 4.00 |
| 1932/VS1989 | — | 0.20 | 0.50 | 0.75 | 1.00 | 1.50 |

**3 DOKDA** **Y# 49** **Weight:** 24.0000 g. **Composition:** Copper **Ruler:** Khengarji III VS1932-98/1875-1942AD **Obverse:** Inscription: George V...

| Date | Mintage | Good | VG | F | VF | XF |
|---|---|---|---|---|---|---|
| 1926/VS1982 | — | 0.60 | 1.50 | 2.50 | 3.50 | 4.50 |

**3 DOKDA** **Y# 57** **Weight:** 24.0000 g. **Composition:** Copper **Ruler:** Khengarji III VS1932-98/1875-1942AD **Obverse:** Inscription: George V...

| Date | Mintage | Good | VG | F | VF | XF |
|---|---|---|---|---|---|---|
| 1928/VS1985 | — | 0.25 | 0.60 | 1.00 | 1.50 | 2.25 |
| 1929/VS1985 | — | 0.25 | 0.60 | 1.00 | 1.50 | 2.25 |
| 1929/VS1986 | — | 0.25 | 0.60 | 1.00 | 1.50 | 2.25 |
| 1930/VS1987 | — | 0.25 | 0.60 | 1.00 | 1.50 | 2.25 |
| 1931/VS1987 | — | 0.25 | 0.60 | 1.00 | 1.50 | 2.25 |
| 1934/VS1990 | — | 0.25 | 0.60 | 1.00 | 1.50 | 2.25 |
| 1934/VS1991 | — | 0.25 | 0.60 | 1.00 | 1.50 | 2.25 |
| 1935/VS1992 | — | 0.25 | 0.60 | 1.00 | 1.50 | 2.25 |

**1/2 KORI** **Y# 58** **Weight:** 2.3500 g. **Composition:** 0.6010 Silver .0460 oz. ASW **Ruler:** Khengarji III VS1932-98/1875-1942AD **Obverse:** Inscription: George V...

| Date | Mintage | Good | VG | F | VF | XF |
|---|---|---|---|---|---|---|
| 1928/VS1985 | — | 0.75 | 2.00 | 3.00 | 4.00 | 7.00 |

**KORI** **Y# 51** **Weight:** 4.7000 g. **Composition:** 0.6010 Silver .0921 oz. ASW **Ruler:** Khengarji III VS1932-98/1875-1942AD **Obverse:** Inscription: George V...

| Date | Mintage | VG | F | VF | XF | Unc |
|---|---|---|---|---|---|---|
| 1913/VS1970 | — | 0.75 | 2.00 | 3.00 | 4.00 | 7.00 |
| 1923/VS1979 | — | 0.75 | 2.00 | 3.00 | 4.00 | 7.00 |
| 1923/VS1980 | — | 0.75 | 2.00 | 3.00 | 4.00 | 7.00 |
| 1927/VS1984 | — | 1.00 | 2.50 | 3.50 | 5.00 | 8.00 |

**KORI** **Y# 59** **Weight:** 4.7000 g. **Composition:** 0.6010 Silver .0921 oz. ASW **Ruler:** Khengarji III VS1932-98/1875-1942AD **Obverse:** Inscription: George V...

| Date | Mintage | VG | F | VF | XF | Unc |
|---|---|---|---|---|---|---|
| 1928/VS1985 | — | 1.00 | 2.50 | 3.50 | 5.00 | 8.00 |
| 1929/VS1985 | — | 1.00 | 2.50 | 3.50 | 5.00 | 8.00 |
| 1931/VS1987 | — | 2.75 | 6.50 | 10.00 | 15.00 | 22.50 |
| 1931/VS1988 | — | 1.00 | 2.50 | 3.00 | 5.00 | 8.00 |
| 1932/VS1988 | — | 1.00 | 2.50 | 3.00 | 5.00 | 8.00 |
| 1932/VS1989 | — | 1.00 | 2.50 | 3.00 | 5.00 | 8.00 |
| 1933/VS1989 | — | 1.00 | 2.50 | 3.00 | 5.00 | 8.00 |
| 1933/VS1990 | — | 1.00 | 2.50 | 3.00 | 5.00 | 8.00 |
| 1934/VS1990 | — | 1.00 | 2.50 | 3.00 | 5.00 | 8.00 |
| 1934/VS1991 | — | 1.00 | 2.50 | 3.00 | 5.00 | 8.00 |
| 1935/VS1991 | — | 1.00 | 2.50 | 3.00 | 5.00 | 8.00 |

| Date | Mintage | VG | F | VF | XF | Unc |
|---|---|---|---|---|---|---|
| 1935/VS1992 | — | 1.00 | 2.50 | 3.00 | 5.00 | 8.00 |
| 1936/VS1992 | — | 1.25 | 3.00 | 4.50 | 6.50 | 10.00 |

**2-1/2 KORI** **Y# 52** **Weight:** 6.9350 g. **Composition:** 0.9370 Silver .2089 oz. ASW **Ruler:** Khengarji III VS1932-98/1875-1942AD **Obverse:** Inscription: George V...

| Date | Mintage | VG | F | VF | XF | Unc |
|---|---|---|---|---|---|---|
| 1916/VS1973 | — | 1.50 | 4.00 | 6.00 | 9.00 | 13.50 |
| 1917/VS1973 | — | 1.50 | 4.00 | 6.00 | 9.00 | 13.50 |
| 1917/VS1974 | — | 1.50 | 4.00 | 6.00 | 9.00 | 13.50 |
| 1918/VS1974 | — | 1.50 | 4.00 | 6.00 | 9.00 | 13.50 |
| 1919/VS1975 | — | 1.50 | 4.00 | 6.00 | 9.00 | 13.50 |
| 1922/VS1978 | — | 1.50 | 4.00 | 6.00 | 9.00 | 13.50 |
| 1922/VS1979 | — | 1.50 | 4.00 | 6.00 | 9.00 | 13.50 |
| 1924/VS1981 | — | 1.50 | 4.00 | 6.00 | 9.00 | 13.50 |
| 1926/VS1983 | — | 1.50 | 4.00 | 6.00 | 9.00 | 13.50 |

**2-1/2 KORI** **Y# 52a** **Weight:** 6.9350 g. **Composition:** 0.9370 Silver .2089 oz. ASW **Ruler:** Khengarji III VS1932-98/1875-1942AD **Obverse:** Inscription: George V... **Reverse:** Smaller legend

| Date | Mintage | VG | F | VF | XF | Unc |
|---|---|---|---|---|---|---|
| 1927/VS1984 | — | 2.00 | 5.00 | 7.00 | 10.00 | 15.00 |
| 1928/VS1985 | — | 1.50 | 4.00 | 6.00 | 9.00 | 13.50 |
| 1930/VS1986 | — | 1.50 | 4.00 | 6.00 | 9.00 | 13.50 |
| 1930/VS1987 | — | 1.50 | 4.00 | 6.00 | 9.00 | 13.50 |
| 1932/VS1988 | — | 1.50 | 4.00 | 6.00 | 9.00 | 13.50 |
| 1932/VS1989 | — | 1.50 | 4.00 | 6.00 | 9.00 | 13.50 |
| 1933/VS1989 | — | 1.50 | 4.00 | 6.00 | 9.00 | 13.50 |
| 1933/VS1990 | — | 1.50 | 4.00 | 6.00 | 9.00 | 13.50 |
| 1934/VS1990 | — | 1.50 | 4.00 | 6.00 | 9.00 | 13.50 |
| 1934/VS1991 | — | 1.50 | 4.00 | 6.00 | 9.00 | 13.50 |
| 1935/VS1991 | — | 1.50 | 4.00 | 6.00 | 9.00 | 13.50 |
| 1935/VS1992 | — | 1.50 | 4.00 | 6.00 | 9.00 | 13.50 |

**5 KORI** **Y# 53** **Weight:** 13.8700 g. **Composition:** 0.9370 Silver .4178 oz. ASW **Ruler:** Khengarji III VS1932-98/1875-1942AD **Obverse:** Inscription: George V... **Note:** 5 Kori coins were issued with reeded edges until 1925AD, which is when the security edge was introduced. 1924 and 1926 dates exist with lettered edges.

| Date | Mintage | VG | F | VF | XF | Unc |
|---|---|---|---|---|---|---|
| 1913/VS1970 | — | 2.75 | 6.50 | 10.00 | 15.00 | 22.50 |
| 1915/VS1972 | — | 2.75 | 6.50 | 10.00 | 15.00 | 22.50 |
| 1916/VS1973 | — | 2.75 | 6.50 | 10.00 | 15.00 | 22.50 |
| 1916/VS1975 (Sic) | — | 5.00 | 12.50 | 18.50 | 25.00 | 35.00 |
| 1917/VS1973 | — | 2.75 | 6.50 | 10.00 | 15.00 | 22.50 |
| 1917/VS1974 | — | 2.75 | 6.50 | 10.00 | 15.00 | 22.50 |
| 1918/VS1974 | — | 2.75 | 6.50 | 10.00 | 15.00 | 22.50 |
| 1918/VS1975 | — | 2.75 | 6.50 | 10.00 | 15.00 | 22.50 |
| 1919/VS1975 | — | 2.75 | 6.50 | 10.00 | 15.00 | 22.50 |
| 1919/VS1976 | — | 12.50 | 25.00 | 37.50 | 50.00 | 70.00 |
| 1920/VS1977 | — | 3.00 | 7.50 | 11.50 | 16.50 | 25.00 |
| 1921/VS1977 | — | 2.75 | 6.50 | 10.00 | 15.00 | 22.50 |
| 1921/VS1978 | — | 2.75 | 6.50 | 10.00 | 15.00 | 22.50 |
| 1922/VS1974 (Sic) | — | — | — | — | — | — |
| 1922/VS1978 | — | 2.75 | 6.50 | 10.00 | 15.00 | 22.50 |
| 1922/VS1979 | — | 2.75 | 6.50 | 10.00 | 15.00 | 22.50 |
| 1922/VS1982 (Sic) | — | 3.00 | 7.50 | 12.50 | 18.50 | 27.50 |
| 1923/VS1979 | — | 2.75 | 6.50 | 10.00 | 15.00 | 22.50 |
| 1924/VS1978 (Sic) | — | 10.00 | 20.00 | 31.50 | 42.50 | 60.00 |
| 1924/VS1980 | — | 2.75 | 6.50 | 10.00 | 15.00 | 22.50 |
| 1924/VS1981 | — | 2.75 | 6.50 | 10.00 | 15.00 | 22.50 |
| 1925/VS1982 | — | 2.75 | 6.50 | 10.00 | 15.00 | 22.50 |
| 1926/VS1978 (Sic) | — | 5.00 | 12.50 | 18.50 | 25.00 | 35.00 |
| 1926/VS1982 | — | 2.75 | 6.50 | 10.00 | 15.00 | 22.50 |
| 1926/VS1893 | — | 2.75 | 6.50 | 10.00 | 15.00 | 22.50 |
| 1927/VS1984 | — | 7.00 | 17.50 | 25.00 | 35.00 | 50.00 |
| 1927/VS1984 Proof | — | Value: 275 | | | | |

**5 KORI** **Y# 53a** **Weight:** 13.8700 g. **Composition:** 0.9370 Silver .4178 oz. ASW **Ruler:** Khengarji III VS1932-98/1875-1942AD **Obverse:** Inscription: George V...; smaller legend **Reverse:** Smaller legend

| Date | Mintage | VG | F | VF | XF | Unc |
|---|---|---|---|---|---|---|
| 1928/VS1985 | — | 6.00 | 15.00 | 21.50 | 30.00 | 40.00 |
| 1929/VS1986 | — | 2.75 | 6.50 | 10.00 | 15.00 | 22.50 |
| 1930/VS1986 | — | 2.75 | 6.50 | 10.00 | 15.00 | 22.50 |
| 1930/VS1987 | — | 2.75 | 6.50 | 10.00 | 15.00 | 22.50 |
| 1931/VS1987 | — | 2.75 | 6.50 | 10.00 | 15.00 | 22.50 |
| 1931/VS1988 | — | 2.75 | 6.50 | 10.00 | 15.00 | 22.50 |
| 1932/VS1988 | — | 2.75 | 6.50 | 10.00 | 15.00 | 22.50 |
| 1932/VS1989 | — | 2.75 | 6.50 | 10.00 | 15.00 | 22.50 |
| 1933/VS1989 | — | 2.75 | 6.50 | 10.00 | 15.00 | 22.50 |
| 1933/VS1990 | — | 2.75 | 6.50 | 10.00 | 15.00 | 22.50 |
| 1934/VS1990 | — | 2.75 | 6.50 | 10.00 | 15.00 | 22.50 |
| 1934/VS1991 | — | 2.75 | 6.50 | 10.00 | 15.00 | 22.50 |
| 1935/VS1991 | — | 2.75 | 6.50 | 10.00 | 15.00 | 22.50 |
| 1935/VS1992 | — | 2.75 | 6.50 | 10.00 | 15.00 | 22.50 |
| 1936/VS1992 | — | 2.75 | 6.50 | 10.00 | 15.00 | 22.50 |

## MILLED COINAGE

### Regal Issues - Fifth Series

**3 DOKDA** **Y# 63** **Weight:** 24.0000 g. **Composition:** Copper **Ruler:** Khengarji III VS1932-98/1875-1942AD **Obverse:** Inscription: Edward VIII...

| Date | Mintage | Good | VG | F | VF | XF |
|---|---|---|---|---|---|---|
| 1936/VS1993 | — | 1.25 | 3.00 | 5.00 | 7.50 | 10.00 |

**KORI** **Y# 65** **Weight:** 4.7000 g. **Composition:** 0.6010 Silver .0921 oz. ASW **Ruler:** Khengarji III VS1932-98/1875-1942AD **Obverse:** Inscription: Edward VIII...

| Date | Mintage | VG | F | VF | XF | Unc |
|---|---|---|---|---|---|---|
| 1936/VS1992 | — | 1.25 | 3.00 | 4.50 | 6.50 | 10.00 |
| 1936/VS1993 | — | 1.25 | 3.00 | 4.50 | 6.50 | 10.00 |

**2-1/2 KORI** **Y# 66** **Weight:** 6.9350 g. **Composition:** 0.9370 Silver .2089 oz. ASW **Ruler:** Khengarji III VS1932-98/1875-1942AD **Obverse:** Inscription: Edward VIII...

| Date | Mintage | VG | F | VF | XF | Unc |
|---|---|---|---|---|---|---|
| 1936/VS1992 | — | 5.00 | 11.50 | 17.50 | 23.50 | 32.50 |
| 1936/VS1993 | — | 5.00 | 11.50 | 17.50 | 23.50 | 32.50 |

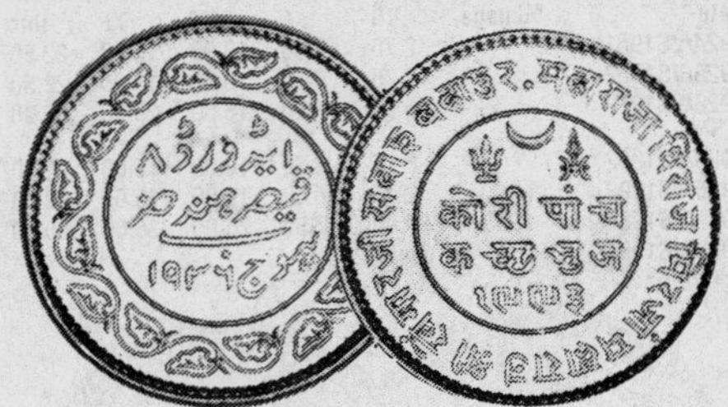

**5 KORI** Y# 67 **Weight:** 13.8700 g. **Composition:** 0.9370 Silver .4178 oz. ASW **Ruler:** Khengarji III VS1932-98/1875-1942AD **Obverse:** Inscription: Edward VIII...

| Date | Mintage | VG | F | VF | XF | Unc |
|---|---|---|---|---|---|---|
| 1936/VS1992 | — | 2.00 | 5.00 | 7.00 | 10.00 | 15.00 |
| 1936/VS1993 | — | 2.00 | 5.00 | 7.00 | 10.00 | 15.00 |

## MILLED COINAGE

Regal Issues - Sixth Series

**TRAMBIYO** Y# 76 **Composition:** Copper **Ruler:** Vijayarajji VS1998-2004/1942-47AD **Obverse:** Inscription: George VI

| Date | Mintage | VG | F | VF | XF | Unc |
|---|---|---|---|---|---|---|
| 1943/VS2000 | — | 0.10 | 0.25 | 0.50 | 1.00 | 1.50 |
| 1944/VS2000 | — | 0.10 | 0.25 | 0.50 | 1.00 | 1.50 |

**DHINGLO (1/16 Kori = 1-1/2 Dokda)** Y# 77 **Composition:** Copper **Ruler:** Vijayarajji VS1998-2004/1942-47AD **Obverse:** Inscription: George VI

| Date | Mintage | VG | F | VF | XF | Unc |
|---|---|---|---|---|---|---|
| 1943/VS2000 | — | 0.10 | 0.25 | 0.40 | 0.65 | 1.00 |
| 1944/VS2000 | — | 0.10 | 0.25 | 0.40 | 0.65 | 1.00 |
| 1947/VS2004 | — | 0.10 | 0.25 | 0.40 | 0.65 | 1.00 |
| 1948/VS2004 | — | 0.20 | 0.50 | 1.00 | 2.00 | 3.50 |

**DHABU (1/8 Kori)** Y# 83 **Composition:** Copper **Ruler:** Madanasinghji VS2004-05/1947-48AD **Subject:** Victory for Indian Independence

| Date | Mintage | VG | F | VF | XF | Unc |
|---|---|---|---|---|---|---|
| VS2004/1947 | — | 0.30 | 0.75 | 1.25 | 1.75 | 3.00 |

**DHABU (1/8 Kori = 3 Dokda)** Y# 78 **Composition:** Copper **Ruler:** Vijayarajji VS1998-2004/1942-47AD **Obverse:** Inscription: George VI

| Date | Mintage | VG | F | VF | XF | Unc |
|---|---|---|---|---|---|---|
| 1943/VS1999 | — | 0.10 | 0.25 | 0.40 | 0.65 | 1.00 |
| 1943/VS2000 | — | 0.10 | 0.25 | 0.40 | 0.65 | 1.00 |
| 1944/VS2000 | — | 0.10 | 0.25 | 0.40 | 0.65 | 1.00 |
| 1947/VS2004 | — | 0.10 | 0.25 | 0.40 | 0.65 | 1.00 |

**PAYALO (1/4 Kori)** Y# 79 **Composition:** Copper **Ruler:** Vijayarajji VS1998-2004/1942-47AD **Obverse:** Inscription: George VI

| Date | Mintage | VG | F | VF | XF | Unc |
|---|---|---|---|---|---|---|
| 1943/VS1999 | — | 0.30 | 0.75 | 1.00 | 1.50 | 2.50 |
| 1943/VS2000 | — | 0.30 | 0.75 | 1.00 | 1.50 | 2.50 |
| 1944/VS2000 | — | 0.30 | 0.75 | 1.00 | 1.50 | 2.50 |
| 1944/VS2001 | — | 0.30 | 0.75 | 1.00 | 1.50 | 2.50 |
| 1945/VS2001 | — | 0.15 | 0.35 | 0.50 | 0.75 | 1.25 |
| 1945/VS2002 | — | 0.15 | 0.35 | 0.50 | 0.75 | 1.25 |
| 1946/VS2002 | — | 0.15 | 0.35 | 0.50 | 0.75 | 1.25 |
| 1946/VS2003 | — | 0.15 | 0.35 | 0.50 | 0.75 | 1.25 |
| 1947/VS2003 | — | 0.30 | 0.75 | 1.00 | 1.50 | 2.50 |

**ADHIO (1/2 Kori)** Y# 80 **Composition:** Copper **Ruler:** Vijayarajji VS1998-2004/1942-47AD **Obverse:** Inscription: George VI

| Date | Mintage | VG | F | VF | XF | Unc |
|---|---|---|---|---|---|---|
| 1943/VS1999 | — | 0.60 | 1.50 | 1.75 | 2.00 | 3.50 |
| 1943/VS2000 | — | 0.60 | 1.50 | 1.75 | 2.00 | 3.50 |
| 1944/VS2001 | — | 0.60 | 1.25 | 1.50 | 1.75 | 3.00 |
| 1945/VS2001 | — | 0.60 | 1.50 | 1.75 | 2.00 | 3.50 |
| 1945/VS2002 | — | 0.60 | 1.50 | 1.75 | 2.00 | 3.50 |
| 1946/VS2002 | — | 0.60 | 1.50 | 1.75 | 2.00 | 3.50 |

**3 DOKDA** Y# 71 **Weight:** 24.0000 g. **Composition:** Copper **Ruler:** Khengarji III VS1932-98/1875-1942AD **Obverse:** Inscription: George VI

| Date | Mintage | Good | VG | F | VF | XF |
|---|---|---|---|---|---|---|
| 1937/VS1993 | — | 0.35 | 0.90 | 1.50 | 2.00 | 3.00 |

**KORI** Y# 73 **Weight:** 4.7000 g. **Composition:** 0.6010 Silver .0921 oz. ASW **Ruler:** Khengarji III VS1932-98/1875-1942AD **Obverse:** Inscription: George VI

| Date | Mintage | VG | F | VF | XF | Unc |
|---|---|---|---|---|---|---|
| 1937/VS1993 | — | 1.25 | 3.00 | 4.50 | 6.50 | 10.00 |
| 1937/VS1994 | — | 1.25 | 3.00 | 4.50 | 6.50 | 10.00 |
| 1938/VS1995 | — | 1.25 | 3.00 | 4.50 | 6.50 | 10.00 |
| 1939/VS1995 | — | 1.25 | 3.00 | 4.50 | 6.50 | 10.00 |
| 1939/VS1996 | — | 1.25 | 3.00 | 4.50 | 6.50 | 10.00 |
| 1940/VS1996 | — | 1.25 | 3.00 | 4.50 | 6.50 | 10.00 |

**KORI** Y# 81 **Weight:** 4.7000 g. **Composition:** 0.6010 Silver .0921 oz. ASW **Ruler:** Vijayarajji VS1998-2004/1942-47AD **Obverse:** Inscription: George VI

| Date | Mintage | VG | F | VF | XF | Unc |
|---|---|---|---|---|---|---|
| 1942/VS1999 | — | 1.00 | 2.50 | 3.50 | 5.00 | 8.00 |
| 1943/VS1999 | — | 1.00 | 2.50 | 3.50 | 5.00 | 8.00 |
| 1943/VS2000 | — | 1.00 | 2.50 | 3.50 | 5.00 | 8.00 |
| 1944/VS2000 | — | 1.00 | 2.50 | 3.50 | 5.00 | 8.00 |
| 1944/VS2001 | — | 1.00 | 2.50 | 3.50 | 5.00 | 8.00 |

**KORI** Y# A81 **Weight:** 4.6600 g. **Composition:** Silver **Ruler:** Vijayarajji VS1998-2004/1942-47AD **Obverse:** Inscription: George VI **Note:** Similar to Y#51.

| Date | Mintage | VG | F | VF | XF | Unc |
|---|---|---|---|---|---|---|
| 1942/VS1998 Rare | — | — | — | — | — | — |

**KORI** Y# 84 **Weight:** 4.7000 g. **Composition:** 0.6010 Silver .0921 oz. ASW **Ruler:** Madanasinghji VS2004-05/1947-48AD **Subject:** Victory for Indian Independence

| Date | Mintage | VG | F | VF | XF | Unc |
|---|---|---|---|---|---|---|
| VS2004/1947 | — | — | 5.00 | 7.00 | 10.00 | 15.00 |

**2-1/2 KORI** Y# 74 **Weight:** 6.9350 g. **Composition:** 0.9370 Silver .2089 oz. ASW **Ruler:** Khengarji III VS1932-98/1875-1942AD **Obverse:** Inscription: George VI

| Date | Mintage | VG | F | VF | XF | Unc |
|---|---|---|---|---|---|---|
| 1937/VS1993 | — | 2.00 | 5.00 | 7.00 | 10.00 | 15.00 |

**5 KORI** Y# 75 **Weight:** 13.8700 g. **Composition:** 0.9370 Silver .4178 oz. ASW **Ruler:** Khengarji III VS1932-98/1875-1942AD **Obverse:** Inscription: George VI

| Date | Mintage | VG | F | VF | XF | Unc |
|---|---|---|---|---|---|---|
| 1936/VS1993 | — | 3.00 | 7.50 | 11.50 | 16.50 | 25.00 |
| 1937/VS1993 | — | 2.75 | 6.50 | 10.00 | 15.00 | 22.50 |
| 1937/VS1994 | — | 2.75 | 6.50 | 10.00 | 15.00 | 22.50 |
| 1938/VS1994 | — | 2.75 | 6.50 | 10.00 | 15.00 | 22.50 |
| 1938/VS1995 | — | 2.75 | 6.50 | 10.00 | 15.00 | 22.50 |
| 1941/VS1997 | — | 4.00 | 10.00 | 15.00 | 21.50 | 30.00 |
| 1941/VS1998 | — | 2.75 | 6.50 | 10.00 | 15.00 | 22.50 |

**5 KORI** Y# 82 **Weight:** 13.8700 g. **Composition:** 0.9370 Silver .4178 oz. ASW **Ruler:** Vijayarajji VS1998-2004/1942-47AD **Obverse:** Inscription: George VI

| Date | Mintage | VG | F | VF | XF | Unc |
|---|---|---|---|---|---|---|
| 1942/VS1998 | — | 2.75 | 6.50 | 10.00 | 15.00 | 22.50 |
| 1942/VS1999 | — | 2.75 | 6.50 | 10.00 | 15.00 | 22.50 |

**5 KORI** Y# 85 **Weight:** 13.8700 g. **Composition:** 0.9370 Silver .4178 oz. ASW **Ruler:** Madanasinghji VS2004-05/1947-48AD **Subject:** Victory for Indian Independence

| Date | Mintage | VG | F | VF | XF | Unc |
|---|---|---|---|---|---|---|
| VS2004/1947 | — | — | 80.00 | 125 | 170 | 240 |

**10 KORI** Y# 82A **Weight:** 17.3900 g. **Composition:** Silver **Ruler:** Vijayarajji VS1998-2004/1942-47AD **Obverse:** Inscription: George VI

| Date | Mintage | VG | F | VF | XF | Unc |
|---|---|---|---|---|---|---|
| 1943/VS1999 Rare | — | — | — | — | — | — |

## LUNAVADA

This small state in the Panch Mahal district of western India was ruled by Solanki Rajputs who claimed descent from Sidraj Jaisingh, the ruler of Anhalwara Patan and Gujerat. The rulers, or maharanas, traced their sovereignty to the early decades of the 15th century. At different times the State was feudatory to either Baroda or Sindhia.

### PRINCELY STATE

#### HAMMERED 'DUMP' COINAGE

**PAISA** KM# 12 (KM7) **Composition:** Copper **Ruler:** Wakhat Singhji VS1924-1986/1867-1929AD **Obverse:** Lotus Blossom **Reverse:** Persian legend **Note:** Round, weight varies 6.5-8.3 grams.

| Date | Mintage | Good | VG | F | VF | XF |
|---|---|---|---|---|---|---|
| ND(ca.1911) | — | 2.50 | 4.00 | 5.50 | 8.50 | — |
| VS1968(1911) | — | 2.50 | 4.00 | 5.50 | 8.50 | — |

## MAKRAI

The rajas of Makrai belong to a very ancient Gond family whose title, Raja Hatiyarai, had been conferred upon them by the emperors of Delhi. This small state of some forty-five villages struggled with varying degrees of success against the Poona Peshwa, Sindhia and the Pindaris before passing under British protection in the 19th century.

**RULER**

Raja Bharat Shah, 1886-1920AD

### PRINCELY STATE

#### HAMMERED 'DUMP' COINAGE

**PAISA** KM# 1 **Composition:** Copper **Ruler:** Raja Bharat Shah 1886-1920AD **Obverse:** Katar **Reverse:** Hindi legend "Shri/Mak/Rai" **Note:** Weight varies 9-11 grams.

| Date | Mintage | Good | VG | F | VF | XF |
|---|---|---|---|---|---|---|
| ND(1886-1920) | — | 2.50 | 4.00 | 6.00 | 9.00 | — |

**PAISA** KM# 2 **Composition:** Copper **Ruler:** Raja Bharat Shah 1886-1920AD **Obverse:** Katar **Reverse:** Hindi legend "Shri/Mak/Rai" **Note:** Square, weight varies 9-11 grams.

| Date | Mintage | Good | VG | F | VF | XF |
|---|---|---|---|---|---|---|
| ND(1886-1920) | — | 3.50 | 6.00 | 9.00 | 13.50 | — |

## MEWAR

State located in Rajputana, northwest India. Capital: Udaipur.

The rulers of Mewar were universally regarded as the highest ranking Rajput house in India. The maharana of Mewar was looked upon as the representative of Rama, the ancient king of Ayodhya - and the family who were Sesodia Rajputs of the Gehlot clan, traced its descent through Rama to Kanak Sen who ruled in the 2nd century. The clan is believed to have migrated to Chitor from Gujarat sometime in the 8th century.

None of the indigenous rulers of India resisted the Muslim invasions into India with greater tenacity than the Rajputs of Mewar. It was their proud boast that they had never permitted a daughter to go into the Mughal harem. Three times the fortress and town of Chitor had fallen to Muslim invaders, to Alauddin Khilji (1303), to Bahadur Shah of Gujarat (1534) and to Akbar (1568). Each time Chitor gradually recovered but the last was the most traumatic experience of all. Rather than to submit to the Mughal onslaught, the women burned themselves on funeral pyres in a fearful rite called jauhar, and the men fell on the swords of the invaders.

After the sacking of Chitor the rana, Udai Singh, retired to the Aravali hills where he founded Udaipur, the capital after 1570. Udai Singh's son, Partab, refused to submit to the Mughal and recovered most of the territory lost in 1568. In the early 19th century Mewar suffered much at the hands of Marathas - Holkar, Sindhia and the Pindaris - until, in 1818, the State came under British supervision. In April 1948 Mewar was merged into Rajasthan and the maharana became governor Maharaj pramukh of the new province.

**RULERS**

Fatteh Singh, VS1941-1986/1884-1929AD
Bhupal Singh, VS1987-2005/1930-1948AD

**MINTS**

Bhilwara بھیلو ارا

Chitor चितोड़

Chitarkot चित्रकूट

Udaipur उदयपुर

**NOTE:** All Mewar coinage is struck without ruler's name, and is largely undated. Certain types were generally struck over several reigns.

**UDAIPUR MINT**

**Swarupshahi Series**

Legend: Dosit Landhan "Friendship with London".

Struck at the Udaipur Mint between ca. 1858-1920AD. Many die varieties exist.

### PRINCELY STATE

#### MILLED COINAGE

**1/16 RUPEE** Y# 7.1 **Weight:** 0.6500 g. **Composition:** Silver **Series:** Swarupshahi **Obverse:** Inscription: Chitarkot/Udaipur **Note:** Struck at Udaipor Mint. Round.

| Date | Mintage | VG | F | VF | XF | Unc |
|---|---|---|---|---|---|---|
| ND(1858-1920) | — | 2.50 | 3.50 | 5.00 | 8.00 | — |

**1/16 RUPEE** Y# 7.2 **Weight:** 0.6500 g. **Composition:** Silver **Obverse:** Inscription: Chitarkot/Udaipur **Size:** 8-10 mm. **Note:** Struck at Udaipor Mint; Swarupshahi Series. Irregular shape.

| Date | Mintage | VG | F | VF | XF | Unc |
|---|---|---|---|---|---|---|
| ND(1858-1920) | — | 3.00 | 4.50 | 6.50 | 10.00 | — |

**1/16 RUPEE** Y# 18 **Weight:** 0.9500 g. **Composition:** Silver **Ruler:** Fatteh Singh VS1941-1986/1884-1929AD **Obverse:** Inscription: Chitarkot/Udaipur **Reverse:** Inscription: Dosti Lundhun (Friendship with London)

| Date | Mintage | VG | F | VF | XF | Unc |
|---|---|---|---|---|---|---|
| VS1985(1928) | 3,262,000 | 0.75 | 2.00 | 3.00 | 4.00 | 7.00 |

**1/8 RUPEE** Y# 8 **Weight:** 1.3000 g. **Composition:** Silver **Series:** Swarupshahi **Obverse:** Inscription: Chitarkot/Udaipur **Size:** 11-12 mm. **Note:** Struck at Udaipor Mint.

| Date | Mintage | VG | F | VF | XF | Unc |
|---|---|---|---|---|---|---|
| ND(1858-1920) | — | 3.00 | 4.50 | 6.50 | 10.00 | — |

**1/8 RUPEE** Y# 19 **Weight:** 1.3600 g. **Composition:** Silver **Ruler:** Fatteh Singh VS1941-1986/1884-1929AD **Obverse:** Inscription: Chitarkot/Udaipur **Reverse:** Inscription: Dosti Lundhun (Friendship with London)

| Date | Mintage | VG | F | VF | XF | Unc |
|---|---|---|---|---|---|---|
| VS1985(1928) | 800,000 | 1.00 | 2.50 | 3.50 | 5.00 | 8.00 |

**1/4 RUPEE** Y# 9 **Weight:** 2.6000 g. **Composition:** Silver **Series:** Swarupshahi **Obverse:** Inscription: Chitarkot/Udaipur **Note:** Struck at Udaipor Mint.

| Date | Mintage | VG | F | VF | XF | Unc |
|---|---|---|---|---|---|---|
| ND(1858-1920) | — | 2.50 | 3.50 | 5.00 | 8.00 | — |

**1/4 RUPEE** Y# 20 **Weight:** 2.7200 g. **Composition:** Silver **Ruler:** Fatteh Singh VS1941-1986/1884-1929AD **Obverse:** Inscription: Chitarkot/Udaipur **Reverse:** Inscription: Dosti Lundhun (Friendship with London)

| Date | Mintage | VG | F | VF | XF | Unc |
|---|---|---|---|---|---|---|
| VS1985(1928) | 839,000 | 1.25 | 3.00 | 4.00 | 6.50 | 10.00 |

**1/2 RUPEE** Y# 10 **Composition:** Silver **Series:** Swarupshahi **Obverse:** Inscription: Chitarkot/Udaipur **Note:** Struck at Udaipor Mint; 5.20-5.40 grams.

| Date | Mintage | VG | F | VF | XF | Unc |
|---|---|---|---|---|---|---|
| ND(1858-1920) | — | 3.00 | 4.50 | 6.50 | 10.00 | — |

**1/2 RUPEE** Y# 21 **Weight:** 5.4600 g. **Composition:** Silver **Ruler:** Fatteh Singh VS1941-1986/1884-1929AD **Obverse:** Inscription: Chitarkot/Udaipur **Reverse:** Inscription: Dosti Lundhun (Friendship with London)

| Date | Mintage | VG | F | VF | XF | Unc |
|---|---|---|---|---|---|---|
| VS1985(1928) | 648,000 | 1.65 | 4.00 | 6.00 | 9.00 | 14.00 |

**1/2 RUPEE** Y# 21a **Composition:** Gold **Ruler:** Fatteh Singh VS1941-1986/1884-1929AD **Obverse:** Inscription: Chitarkot/Udaipur **Reverse:** Inscription: Dosti Lundhun (Friendship with London) **Note:** 5.35-5.70 grams.

| Date | Mintage | VG | F | VF | XF | Unc |
|---|---|---|---|---|---|---|
| VS1985(1928) Proof | — | Value: 1,000 | | | | |

**RUPEE** Y# 11 **Composition:** Silver **Series:** Swarupshahi **Obverse:** Inscription: Chitarkot/Udaipur **Note:** Struck at Udaipor Mint; 10.75-10.85 grams.

| Date | Mintage | VG | F | VF | XF | Unc |
|---|---|---|---|---|---|---|
| ND(1858-1920) | — | 4.00 | 6.00 | 9.00 | 14.00 | — |

**RUPEE** Y# 22.1 **Weight:** 10.8600 g. **Composition:** Silver **Ruler:** Fatteh Singh VS1941-1986/1884-1929AD **Obverse:** Thin legends, inscription: Chitarkot/Udaipur **Reverse:** Inscription: Dosti Lundhun (Friendship with London)

| Date | Mintage | VG | F | VF | XF | Unc |
|---|---|---|---|---|---|---|
| VS1985(1928) | 14,906,000 | 2.00 | 5.00 | 7.00 | 10.00 | 15.00 |

**RUPEE** Y# 22.2 **Weight:** 10.8600 g. **Composition:** Silver **Ruler:** Fatteh Singh VS1941-1986/1884-1929AD **Obverse:** Thick legends, inscription: Chitarkot/Udaipur **Reverse:** Inscription: Dosti Lundhun (Friendship with London)

| Date | Mintage | VG | F | VF | XF | Unc |
|---|---|---|---|---|---|---|
| VS1985(1928) | Inc. above | 6.00 | 15.00 | 20.00 | 30.00 | 45.00 |

**RUPEE** Y# 22a **Composition:** Gold **Ruler:** Fatteh Singh VS1941-1986/1884-1929AD **Obverse:** Inscription: Chitarkot/Udaipur **Reverse:** Inscription: Dosti Lundhun (Friendship with London)

| Date | Mintage | VG | F | VF | XF | Unc |
|---|---|---|---|---|---|---|
| VS1985(1928) Proof | — | Value: 1,500 | | | | |

**1/8 MOHUR** Y# B12 **Weight:** 1.3500 g. **Composition:** Gold **Series:** Swarupshahi **Obverse:** Inscription: Chitarkot/Udaipur **Note:** Struck at Udaipor Mint.

| Date | Mintage | VG | F | VF | XF | Unc |
|---|---|---|---|---|---|---|
| ND(1858-1920) | — | — | 150 | 225 | 400 | 600 |

**1/4 MOHUR** Y# A12 **Composition:** Gold **Series:** Swarupshahi **Obverse:** Inscription: Chitarkot/Udaipur **Note:** Struck at Udaipor Mint; 2.70-2.75 grams.

| Date | Mintage | VG | F | VF | XF | Unc |
|---|---|---|---|---|---|---|
| ND(1858-1920) | — | — | 150 | 300 | 500 | 750 |

**1/2 MOHUR** Y# C12 **Weight:** 5.4000 g. **Composition:** Gold **Series:** Swarupshahi **Obverse:** Inscription: Chitarkot/Udaipur **Note:** Struck at Udaipor Mint.

| Date | Mintage | VG | F | VF | XF | Unc |
|---|---|---|---|---|---|---|
| ND(1858-1920) | — | — | 150 | 300 | 500 | 750 |

**MOHUR** Y# 12 **Weight:** 10.9500 g. **Composition:** Gold **Series:** Swarupshahi **Obverse:** Inscription: Chitarkot/Udaipur **Note:** Struck at Udaipor Mint.

| Date | Mintage | VG | F | VF | XF | Unc |
|---|---|---|---|---|---|---|
| ND(1858-1920) | — | — | 165 | 225 | 350 | 525 |

**1/4 ANNA** Y# 15 **Weight:** 2.2000 g. **Composition:** Copper **Ruler:** Bhupal Singh VS1987-2005/1930-1948 **Obverse:** Inscription: Chitarkot/Udaipur

| Date | Mintage | F | VF | XF | Unc | BU |
|---|---|---|---|---|---|---|
| VS1999(1942) | — | 0.50 | 0.85 | 1.25 | 2.00 | — |

**1/2 ANNA** Y# 16.1 **Weight:** 3.5000 g. **Composition:** Copper **Ruler:** Bhupal Singh VS1987-2005/1930-1948 **Obverse:** Large inscription: Chitarkot/Udaipur

| Date | Mintage | F | VF | XF | Unc | BU |
|---|---|---|---|---|---|---|
| VS1999(1942) | — | 0.50 | 0.85 | 1.25 | 2.00 | — |

**1/2 ANNA** Y# 16.2 **Weight:** 3.5000 g. **Composition:** Copper **Ruler:** Bhupal Singh VS1987-2005/1930-1948 **Obverse:** Small inscription: Chitarkot/Udaipur

| Date | Mintage | F | VF | XF | Unc | BU |
|---|---|---|---|---|---|---|
| VS1999(1942) | — | 0.50 | 0.85 | 1.25 | 2.00 | — |

**ANNA** Y# 17 **Weight:** 4.3000 g. **Composition:** Copper **Ruler:** Bhupal Singh VS1987-2005/1930-1948 **Obverse:** Inscription: Chitarkot/Udaipur

| Date | Mintage | F | VF | XF | Unc | BU |
|---|---|---|---|---|---|---|
| VS2000(1943) | — | 0.60 | 1.00 | 1.25 | 2.50 | — |

**PIE** Y# 13 **Weight:** 2.5000 g. **Composition:** Copper **Ruler:** Fatteh Singh VS1941-1986/1884-1929AD **Obverse:** Inscription: Chitor, date **Reverse:** Inscription: Udaipur **Note:** Struck at Udaipur Mint.

| Date | Mintage | Good | VG | F | VF | XF |
|---|---|---|---|---|---|---|
| VS1975 | — | 7.50 | 12.50 | 18.50 | 27.50 | — |

**PIE** Y# 14 **Weight:** 2.1000 g. **Composition:** Copper **Ruler:** Fatteh Singh VS1941-1986/1884-1929AD **Obverse:** Inscription: Chitor, date **Reverse:** Inscription: Udaipur **Note:** Struck at Udaipur Mint.

| Date | Mintage | Good | VG | F | VF | XF |
|---|---|---|---|---|---|---|
| VS1978 | — | 6.00 | 10.00 | 15.00 | 22.50 | — |

## LOCAL COINAGE

Umarda

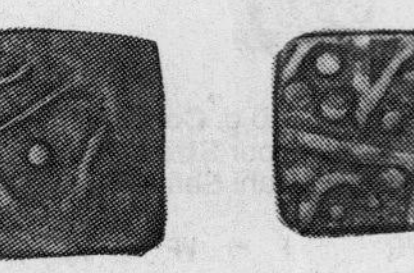

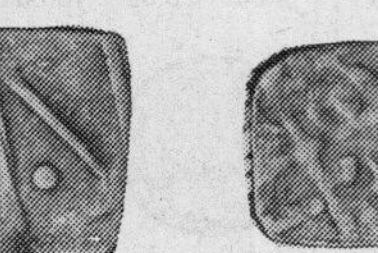

**1/2 PAISA** Y# 24 **Composition:** Copper **Note:** Varieties exist.

| Date | Mintage | Good | VG | F | VF | XF |
|---|---|---|---|---|---|---|
| ND(1938-1941) | — | 0.75 | 1.25 | 1.75 | 2.50 | — |

## PATTERNS

Including off metal strikes

| KM# | Date | Mintage | Identification | Mkt Val |
|---|---|---|---|---|
| Pn1 | 1985(1928) | — | 1/16 Rupee. Silver. Inscription: Chitor, Udaipur. | — |

| KM# | Date | Mintage | Identification | Mkt Val |
|---|---|---|---|---|
| Pn2 | 1985(1928) | — | 1/8 Rupee. Silver. Inscription: Chitor, Udaipur. | — |

| KM# | Date | Mintage | Identification | Mkt Val |
|---|---|---|---|---|
| Pn5 | 1985(1928) | — | 1/2 Rupee. Silver. Inscription: Chitor, Udaipur. | — |

| KM# | Date | Mintage | Identification | Mkt Val |
|---|---|---|---|---|
| Pn6 | 1985(1928) | — | Rupee. Silver. Inscription: Chitor, Udaipur. | — |
| Pn3 | 1985(1928) | — | 1/4 Rupee. Gold. Inscription: Chitarkot, Udaipur. KM20. | 750 |

| KM# | Date | Mintage | Identification | Mkt Val |
|---|---|---|---|---|
| Pn4 | 1985(1928) | — | 1/4 Rupee. Silver. Inscription: Chitor, Udaipur. | — |

# RAJKOT

State located in north central Kathiawar, west India.

The thakurs of Rajkot were Jareja Rajputs and related to the ruling houses of Kutch and Nawanagar. The founder, Jareja Vibhaji was a grandson of Jam Sataji of Nawanagar. After Maratha defeat Rajkot became a tributary to the British and in February 1948 the State was absorbed into Saurashtra.

**RULERS**

Dharmendra Singhji, 1930-1948

## PRINCELY STATE

### MEDALLIC COINAGE

**MOHUR** KM# M1 **Weight:** 7.8800 g. **Composition:** Gold **Ruler:** Dharmendra Singhji 1930-1948AD **Obverse:** Sunrise **Reverse:** Arms

| Date | Mintage | F | VF | XF | Unc | BU |
|---|---|---|---|---|---|---|
| 1945 | 54 | — | — | 300 | 500 | — |

**Note:** Mintage figure is from original records, restrikes exist

**MOHUR** KM# M1a **Composition:** Silver **Ruler:** Dharmendra Singhji 1930-1948AD **Obverse:** Sunrise **Reverse:** Arms

| Date | Mintage | F | VF | XF | Unc | BU |
|---|---|---|---|---|---|---|
| 1945 Restrike | 1,000 | — | — | 10.00 | 15.00 | — |

**Note:** Although originally considered a quasi legitimate issue by some authorities, the silver pieces were produced in recent times for the collector market.

## RATLAM

State located northwest of Indore in Madhya Pradesh.

The rajas of Ratlam were Rathor Rajputs, descendants of the younger branch of the Jodhpur ruling family. Ratlam became the premier Rajput state in western Malwa. The founder, Ratan Singh, received the territory as a grant from Shah Jahan in 1631. Before Maratha collapse some 15% of the state's annual revenue went to Sindhia as tribute. Under British protection it was supervised by the Central India Agency and in 1948 Ratlam became a district of Madhya Bharat.

**RULERS**

Ranjit Singh, VS1921-1950/1864-1893AD

**MINT**

Ratlam

**NOTE:** For 1 Paisa previously listed here refer to Banswara-IPS.

## PRINCELY STATE

### MILLED COINAGE

WW II Emergency Issues

**PAISA KM# 25 Composition:** Copper **Ruler:** Ranjit Singh VS1921-1950/1864-1893AD **Obverse:** Hannman walking left **Note:** Thin, crude restrike of KM#24.

| Date | Mintage | VG | F | VF | XF | Unc |
|---|---|---|---|---|---|---|
| VS1947(1890) | — | 0.65 | 1.00 | 1.75 | — | — |

**Note:** Restruck ca.1942-1945AD

## REWA

State located in eastern north-central India.

The rulers of Rewa were Baghela Rajputs of the Solanki clan who probably migrated from Anhilwara Patan in Gujarat about the 11th century. Arriving in Bundelkhand they carved out for themselves a substantial kingdom, which remained independent until 1597, when they were obliged to become Mughal tributaries under Akbar. With Mughal decline Rewa began to move once more towards independence, this time under the nominal suzerainty of the Peshwa. In 1812 the raja of Rewa, Jai Singh Deo was coerced into a treaty with the British and, failing to observe its conditions, was forced to yield to British control in 1813-1814. In 1948 Rewa was merged into Vindhya Pradesh.

**RULERS**

Venkat Raman Singh, VS1937-1975/1880-1918AD
Gulab Singh, VS1975-2003/1918-1946AD

## PRINCELY STATE

### MILLED COINAGE

**1/2 MOHUR KM# 33 Composition:** Gold **Ruler:** Gulab Singh VS1975-2003/1918-1946AD **Obverse:** Arms **Note:** Accession; Weight varies 4.40-5.40 grams.

| Date | Mintage | VG | F | VF | XF | Unc |
|---|---|---|---|---|---|---|
| VS1975(1918) | — | 200 | 300 | 425 | 600 | — |

**MOHUR KM# 35 Composition:** Gold **Ruler:** Gulab Singh VS1975-2003/1918-1946AD **Obverse:** Arms **Note:** Accession; Weight varies 10.70-11.71 grams.

| Date | Mintage | VG | F | VF | XF | Unc |
|---|---|---|---|---|---|---|
| VS1975(1918) | — | 165 | 225 | 425 | 600 | — |

**MOHUR KM# 36 Composition:** Gold **Ruler:** Gulab Singh VS1975-2003/1918-1946AD **Obverse:** Arms **Note:** Weight varies 10.70-11.71 grams.

| Date | Mintage | VG | F | VF | XF | Unc |
|---|---|---|---|---|---|---|
| VS1975(1918) | — | 165 | 225 | 425 | 600 | — |

**MOHUR KM# 38 Weight:** 11.3600 g. **Composition:** Gold **Ruler:** Gulab Singh VS1975-2003/1918-1946AD **Obverse:** Arms with plain border banner below penant supporters **Note:** Weight varies 10.70-11.71 grams.

| Date | Mintage | VG | F | VF | XF | Unc |
|---|---|---|---|---|---|---|
| VS1976(1919) | — | 225 | 385 | 550 | 800 | — |

**MOHUR KM# 40 Weight:** 8.8000 g. **Composition:** Gold **Ruler:** Gulab Singh VS1975-2003/1918-1946AD **Obverse:** Arms **Note:** Reduced weight.

| Date | Mintage | VG | F | VF | XF | Unc |
|---|---|---|---|---|---|---|
| VS1977(1920) | — | 175 | 265 | 385 | 650 | — |

**1/2 RUPEE KM# 29 Composition:** Silver **Ruler:** Gulab Singh VS1975-2003/1918-1946AD **Note:** Accession; thin flan.

| Date | Mintage | VG | F | VF | XF | Unc |
|---|---|---|---|---|---|---|
| VS1975(1918) | — | 18.50 | 31.50 | 42.50 | 60.00 | — |

**RUPEE KM# 31 Composition:** Silver **Ruler:** Gulab Singh VS1975-2003/1918-1946AD **Obverse:** Arms **Note:** Accession; thick flan.

| Date | Mintage | VG | F | VF | XF | Unc |
|---|---|---|---|---|---|---|
| VS1975(1918) | — | 20.00 | 35.00 | 55.00 | 90.00 | — |

## SAILANA

This small state in west-central India, of slightly over one hundred square miles had once been part of Ratlam, but about 1709 it asserted its independence under the leadership of Pratab Singh, the second son of Chhatrasal. The town of Sailana was founded in 1730 by Jai Singh's successor, and from that date the state was named after it. Due to its small size and vulnerability, Sailana was obliged to become tributary to Sindhia to ensure its survival. In 1819 this payment was limited to one-third of the state's revenues. Later, under agreements of 1840 and 1860, the tribute went to the British for the support of British Indian troops in the region. Barmawal was feudatory to Sailana.

**LOCAL RULERS**

Jaswant Singh, 1895-1919AD
Dilip Singh Bahadur, 1919-1948

## PRINCELY STATE

### MILLED COINAGE

Regal Issues

**1/4 ANNA KM# 15 Composition:** Copper **Ruler:** Jaswant Singh 1890-1919AD **Obverse:** Bust of King Edward VII right

| Date | Mintage | VG | F | VF | XF | Unc |
|---|---|---|---|---|---|---|
| 1908 | 224,000 | 5.00 | 12.50 | 25.00 | 50.00 | 100 |
| 1908 Proof | — | Value: 175 | | | | |

**1/4 ANNA KM# 16 Composition:** Copper **Ruler:** Jaswant Singh 1890-1919AD **Obverse:** Bust of King George V left

| Date | Mintage | VG | F | VF | XF | Unc |
|---|---|---|---|---|---|---|
| 1912 | 224,000 | 1.25 | 3.50 | 6.50 | 12.50 | 25.00 |
| 1912 Proof | — | Value: 175 | | | | |

## TONK

**Tunk**

State located partially in Rajputana and in central India. Tonk was founded in 1806 by Amir Khan (d. 1834), the Pathan Pindari leader who received the territory from Holkar. Amir Khan caused great havoc in Central India by his lightning raids into neighboring states. In 1817 he was forced into submission by the East India Company and remained under British control until India's independence. In March 1948 Tonk was incorporated into Rajasthan.

**RULERS**

Muhammad Ibrahim Ali Khan, AH1284-1349/1868-1930AD
Muhammad Sa'adat Ali Khan, AH1349-1368/1930-1949AD

**MINT MARKS**

Sironj سرونج

Tonk تونک

Flower (on all)

Leaf (several forms)

Beginning with the reign of Muhammad Ibrahim Ali Khan, most coins have both AD and AH dates. Coins with both dates fully legible are worth about 20% more than listed prices. Coins with one date fully legible are worth prices shown. Coins with both dates off are of little value.

There are many minor and major variations of type, varying with location of date, orientation of leaf, arrangement of legend. Although these fall into easily distinguished patterns, they are strictly for the specialist and are omitted here.

The Tonk rupee was known as the "Chanwarshahi".

**TONK MINT**

NOTE: All coins with both AH and AD dates clearly readable command about a 50 percent premium.

## PRINCELY STATE

### HAMMERED "DUMP" COINAGE

**1/2 PAISA** **Y# A24** **Weight:** 5.4000 g. **Composition:** Copper **Ruler:** Muhammad Ibrahim Ali Khan AH1284-1349 / 1868-1930AD **Obverse:** Inscription: George V... **Reverse:** Inscription: Muhammad Ibrahim Ali Khan... **Note:** Struck at Tonk Mint.

| Date | Mintage | Good | VG | F | VF | XF |
|---|---|---|---|---|---|---|
| AH13(46) | — | 3.00 | 6.00 | 10.00 | 15.00 | — |

**PAISA** **Y# 24.1** **Weight:** 7.3000 g. **Composition:** Copper **Ruler:** Muhammad Ibrahim Ali Khan AH1284-1349 / 1868-1930AD **Obverse:** Inscription: George V... **Reverse:** Inscription: Muhammad Ibrahim Ali Khan... **Note:** Struck at Tonk Mint.

| Date | Mintage | Good | VG | F | VF | XF |
|---|---|---|---|---|---|---|
| AH1329 | — | 1.25 | 2.25 | 3.50 | 5.50 | — |
| AH1329(sic) | — | 1.25 | 2.25 | 3.50 | 5.50 | — |
| 1911(sic) | — | 1.25 | 2.25 | 3.50 | 5.50 | — |
| AH1329(sic) | — | 1.25 | 2.25 | 3.50 | 5.50 | — |
| AH1330 | — | 1.25 | 2.25 | 3.50 | 5.50 | — |

**PAISA** **Y# 24.2** **Weight:** 5.0000 g. **Composition:** Copper **Ruler:** Muhammad Ibrahim Ali Khan AH1284-1349 / 1868-1930AD **Obverse:** Inscription: George V... **Reverse:** Inscription: Muhammad Ibrahim Ali Khan... **Note:** Struck at Tonk Mint. Reduced weight.

| Date | Mintage | Good | VG | F | VF | XF |
|---|---|---|---|---|---|---|
| AH1335(1917) | — | 1.25 | 2.25 | 3.50 | 5.50 | — |
| AH(13)38(1924) | — | 1.25 | 2.25 | 3.50 | 5.50 | — |
| AH1342(1924) | — | 1.00 | 1.75 | 2.50 | 4.50 | — |
| AH1344(1925) | — | 1.00 | 1.75 | 2.50 | 4.50 | — |
| AH1344(1925) | — | 1.00 | 1.75 | 2.50 | 4.50 | — |
| AH1345(1926) | — | 1.00 | 1.75 | 2.50 | 4.50 | — |
| AH134x(1928) | — | 1.00 | 1.75 | 2.50 | 4.50 | — |

**1/4 ANNA** **Y# A25.1** **Weight:** 8.3000 g. **Composition:** Copper **Ruler:** Muhammad Ibrahim Ali Khan AH1284-1349 / 1868-1930AD **Obverse:** Inscription: George V... **Reverse:** Inscription: Muhammad Ibrahim Ali Khan... **Note:** Struck at Tonk Mint.

| Date | Mintage | Good | VG | F | VF | XF |
|---|---|---|---|---|---|---|
| AH1335(1917) | — | 1.25 | 2.25 | 3.50 | 5.50 | — |
| AH1336(1917) | — | 1.25 | 2.25 | 3.50 | 5.50 | — |

**1/4 ANNA** **Y# A25.2** **Weight:** 5.4000 g. **Composition:** Copper **Ruler:** Muhammad Ibrahim Ali Khan AH1284-1349 / 1868-1930AD **Obverse:** Inscription: George V... **Reverse:** Inscription: Muhammad Ibrahim Ali Khan... **Note:** Struck at Tonk Mint. Reduced weight.

| Date | Mintage | Good | VG | F | VF | XF |
|---|---|---|---|---|---|---|
| AH1336(1917) | — | 1.00 | 1.75 | 2.50 | 4.50 | — |

**1/8 RUPEE** **Y# 25** **Composition:** Silver **Ruler:** Muhammad Ibrahim Ali Khan AH1284-1349 / 1868-1930AD **Obverse:** Inscription: George V... **Reverse:** Inscription: Muhammad Ibrahim Ali Khan... **Note:** Struck at Tonk Mint. 1.34-1.45 grams.

| Date | Mintage | Good | VG | F | VF | XF |
|---|---|---|---|---|---|---|
| AH1340(1922) | — | 2.75 | 6.50 | 10.00 | 15.00 | 22.50 |
| AH1346(1928) | — | 2.75 | 6.50 | 10.00 | 15.00 | 22.50 |

**1/8 RUPEE** **Y# 30** **Composition:** Silver **Ruler:** Muhammad Sa'adat Ali Khan AH1349-1368 / 1930-1949AD **Obverse:** Inscription: George V... **Reverse:** Inscription: Muhammad Sa'adat Ali Khan... **Note:** Struck at Tonk Mint. 1.34-1.45 grams.

| Date | Mintage | VG | F | VF | XF | Unc |
|---|---|---|---|---|---|---|
| AH1351(1932) | — | 4.00 | 6.50 | 10.00 | 15.00 | — |
| AH1352(1933) | — | 4.00 | 6.50 | 10.00 | 15.00 | — |
| AH1353(1934) | — | 4.00 | 6.50 | 10.00 | 15.00 | — |

**1/4 RUPEE** **Y# 26** **Composition:** Silver **Ruler:** Muhammad Ibrahim Ali Khan AH1284-1349 / 1868-1930AD **Obverse:** Inscription: George V... **Reverse:** Inscription: Muhammad Ibrahim Ali Khan... **Note:** Struck at Tonk Mint. 2.68-2.90 grams.

| Date | Mintage | VG | F | VF | XF | Unc |
|---|---|---|---|---|---|---|
| AH1346(1928) | — | 6.50 | 10.00 | 15.00 | 22.50 | — |

**1/2 RUPEE** **Y# 27** **Composition:** Silver **Ruler:** Muhammad Ibrahim Ali Khan AH1284-1349 / 1868-1930AD **Obverse:** Inscription: George V... **Reverse:** Inscription: Muhammad Ibrahim Ali Khan... **Note:** Struck at Tonk Mint. 5.35-5.80 grams.

| Date | Mintage | VG | F | VF | XF | Unc |
|---|---|---|---|---|---|---|
| AH1346(1928) | — | 11.50 | 17.50 | 23.50 | 32.50 | — |

**RUPEE** **Y# 28** **Composition:** Silver **Ruler:** Muhammad Ibrahim Ali Khan AH1284-1349 / 1868-1930AD **Obverse:** Inscription: George V... **Reverse:** Inscription: Muhammad Ibrahim Ali Khan... **Note:** Struck at Tonk Mint. 10.70-11.60 grams.

| Date | Mintage | VG | F | VF | XF | Unc |
|---|---|---|---|---|---|---|
| AH1329(1911) | — | 5.50 | 8.50 | 13.50 | 20.00 | — |
| AH1330(1912) | — | 5.50 | 8.50 | 13.50 | 20.00 | — |
| AH1341(1923) | — | 5.50 | 8.50 | 13.50 | 20.00 | — |
| AH1342(1923) | — | 5.50 | 8.50 | 13.50 | 20.00 | — |
| AH1342(1924) | — | 5.50 | 8.50 | 13.50 | 20.00 | — |
| AH1343(1924) | — | 5.50 | 8.50 | 13.50 | 20.00 | — |
| AH1343(1925) | — | 5.50 | 8.50 | 13.50 | 20.00 | — |
| AH1344(1925) | — | 5.50 | 8.50 | 13.50 | 20.00 | — |
| AH1344(1926) | — | 5.50 | 8.50 | 13.50 | 20.00 | — |
| AH1345(1926) | — | 5.50 | 8.50 | 13.50 | 20.00 | — |
| AH1346(1926) | — | 5.50 | 8.50 | 13.50 | 20.00 | — |
| AH1346(1927) | — | 5.50 | 8.50 | 13.50 | 20.00 | — |
| AH1347(1928) | — | 5.50 | 8.50 | 13.50 | 20.00 | — |
| AH1348(1928) | — | 5.50 | 8.50 | 13.50 | 20.00 | — |
| AH1348(1929) | — | 5.50 | 8.50 | 13.50 | 20.00 | — |
| AH134x(1930) | — | 5.50 | 8.50 | 13.50 | 20.00 | — |

### MILLED COINAGE

**PICE (Paisa)** **KM# 29** **Composition:** Copper **Ruler:** Muhammad Sa'adat Ali Khan AH1349-1368 / 1930-1949AD **Obverse:** Arms **Reverse:** Leaf

| Date | Mintage | VG | F | VF | XF | Unc |
|---|---|---|---|---|---|---|
| AH1350//1932 | 640,000 | 0.20 | 0.50 | 1.00 | 2.00 | 3.50 |

**PICE (Paisa)** **KM# 29a** **Composition:** Copper **Ruler:** Muhammad Sa'adat Ali Khan AH1349-1368 / 1930-1949AD **Obverse:** Arms **Reverse:** Leaf

| Date | Mintage | VG | F | VF | XF | Unc |
|---|---|---|---|---|---|---|
| AH1350//1932 | 640,000 | — | 0.25 | 0.50 | 1.00 | 1.75 |

## TRAVANCORE

State located in extreme southwest India. A mint was established in ME965/1789-1790AD.

The region of Travancore had a lengthy history before being annexed by the Vijayanagar kingdom. With Vijayanagar's defeat at the battle of Talikota in 1565, Travancore passed under Muslim control until the late 18th century, when it merged as a state in its own right under Raja Martanda Varma. At this time the raja allied himself with British interests as a protection against the Muslim dynasty of Mysore. In 1795 the raja of Travancore officially accepted a subsidiary alliance with the East India Company, and remained within the orbit of British influence from then until India's independence.

**RULERS**

Rama Varma VI, ME1062-1101/1885-1924AD
Bala Rama Varma II, ME1101-1126/1924-1949AD

**DATING**

ME dates are of the Malabar Era. Add 824 or 825 to the ME date for the AD date. (i.e., ME1112 plus 824-825 = 1936-1937AD).

## PRINCELY STATE

### MILLED COINAGE

**CASH** **KM# 40** **Weight:** 0.6500 g. **Composition:** Copper **Ruler:** Rama Varma VI ME1062-1101 / 1885-1924AD **Obv. Legend:** CASH 1

| Date | Mintage | VG | F | VF | XF | Unc |
|---|---|---|---|---|---|---|
| ND(1901) | — | — | 9.00 | 15.00 | 22.50 | 35.00 |

**CASH** **KM# 46** **Weight:** 0.6500 g. **Composition:** Copper **Ruler:** Rama Varma VI ME1062-1101 / 1885-1924AD **Obverse:** Sankha (conch shell) in 6-pointed star **Note:** Thick

| Date | Mintage | VG | F | VF | XF | Unc |
|---|---|---|---|---|---|---|
| ND(1901-10) | — | — | 0.50 | 0.70 | 1.00 | 1.50 |

**Note:** Refer to Bala Rama Varma II listings for thin variety, KM#57

**4 CASH** **KM# 41** **Composition:** Copper **Ruler:** Rama Varma VI ME1062-1101 / 1885-1924AD **Obverse:** RV monogram **Obv. Legend:** CASH FOUR **Reverse:** Sankha (conch shell) in sprays

| Date | Mintage | VG | F | VF | XF | Unc |
|---|---|---|---|---|---|---|
| ND(1901-10) | — | 1.25 | 3.00 | 5.00 | 7.00 | 10.00 |

**4 CASH** **KM# 47** **Composition:** Copper **Ruler:** Rama Varma VI ME1062-1101 / 1885-1924AD **Obverse:** RV monogram **Obv. Legend:** FOUR CASH **Reverse:** Malayalam "Oru Kasu" (One Cash)

| Date | Mintage | VG | F | VF | XF | Unc |
|---|---|---|---|---|---|---|
| ND(1906-35) | — | 0.40 | 1.00 | 1.75 | 2.50 | 3.50 |
| ND(1906-35) Proof | — | Value: 65.00 | | | | |

**4 CASH** **KM# 58** **Composition:** Bronze **Ruler:** Bala Rama Varma II ME1101-1126 / 1924-1949AD **Obverse:** BRV monogram **Reverse:** Sankha (conch shell) in sprays

| Date | Mintage | VG | F | VF | XF | Unc |
|---|---|---|---|---|---|---|
| ND(1938-49) | — | 0.25 | 0.60 | 1.00 | 1.50 | 2.25 |

**8 CASH** KM# 42 **Composition:** Copper **Ruler:** Rama Varma VI ME1062-1101 / 1885-1924AD **Obverse:** RV monogram **Obv. Legend:** CASH EIGHT **Reverse:** Sankha (conch shell) in sprays

| Date | Mintage | VG | F | VF | XF | Unc |
|---|---|---|---|---|---|---|
| ND(1901-10) | — | 1.75 | 4.50 | 7.00 | 10.00 | 15.00 |

**8 CASH** KM# 48 **Composition:** Copper **Ruler:** Rama Varma VI ME1062-1101 / 1885-1924AD **Obverse:** RV monogram **Obv. Legend:** EIGHT CASH **Reverse:** Sankha (conch shell) in sprays

| Date | Mintage | VG | F | VF | XF | Unc |
|---|---|---|---|---|---|---|
| ND(1906-35) | — | 0.50 | 1.35 | 2.25 | 3.00 | 5.00 |
| ND(1906-35) Proof | — | Value: 75.00 | | | | |

**8 CASH** KM# 59 **Composition:** Bronze **Ruler:** Bala Rama Varma II ME1101-1126 / 1924-1949AD **Obverse:** BRV monogram **Reverse:** Sankha (conch shell) in sprays

| Date | Mintage | VG | F | VF | XF | Unc |
|---|---|---|---|---|---|---|
| ND(1938-49) | — | 0.35 | 0.85 | 1.50 | 2.25 | 3.00 |

**CHUCKRAM** KM# 43 **Composition:** Copper **Ruler:** Rama Varma VI ME1062-1101 / 1885-1924AD **Obverse:** RV monogram **Obv. Legend:** CHUCKRAM ONE **Reverse:** Sankha (conch shell) in sprays

| Date | Mintage | VG | F | VF | XF | Unc |
|---|---|---|---|---|---|---|
| ND(1901-10) | — | 1.75 | 4.50 | 7.00 | 10.00 | 15.00 |

**CHUCKRAM** KM# 49 **Composition:** Copper **Ruler:** Rama Varma VI ME1062-1101 / 1885-1924AD **Obverse:** RV monogram **Obv. Legend:** ONE CHUCKRAM **Reverse:** Sankha (conch shell) in sprays

| Date | Mintage | VG | F | VF | XF | Unc |
|---|---|---|---|---|---|---|
| ND(1906-35) | — | 0.50 | 1.35 | 2.25 | 3.00 | 4.50 |

**CHUCKRAM** KM# 60 **Composition:** Bronze **Ruler:** Bala Rama Varma II ME1101-1126 / 1924-1949AD **Obverse:** Bust of Bala Rama Barma II right **Reverse:** Sankha (conch shell) in sprays

| Date | Mintage | VG | F | VF | XF | Unc |
|---|---|---|---|---|---|---|
| ME1114(1938) | — | 0.50 | 1.25 | 2.25 | 3.50 | 5.00 |
| ND(1939-49)(1939) | — | 0.60 | 1.00 | 1.50 | 2.50 | — |

**CHUCKRAM** KM# 60a **Composition:** Bronze **Ruler:** Bala Rama Varma II ME1101-1126 / 1924-1949AD **Obverse:** Bust of Bala Rama Barma II right **Reverse:** Sankha (conch shell) in sprays

| Date | Mintage | VG | F | VF | XF | Unc |
|---|---|---|---|---|---|---|
| ND(1939-49) Prooflike; restrike | — | — | — | — | — | 5,000 |

**2 CHUCKRAMS** KM# 44 **Composition:** Silver **Ruler:** Rama Varma VI ME1062-1101 / 1885-1924AD **Obverse:** RV monogram **Obv. Legend:** CHS. 2 **Reverse:** Sankha (conch shell) in sprays

| Date | Mintage | VG | F | VF | XF | Unc |
|---|---|---|---|---|---|---|
| ND(1901) | — | 1.75 | 4.50 | 7.00 | 10.00 | 15.00 |

**2 CHUCKRAMS** KM# 50 **Composition:** Silver **Ruler:** Rama Varma VI ME1062-1101 / 1885-1924AD **Obverse:** RV monogram **Obv. Legend:** 2 CHS. **Reverse:** Sankha (conch shell) in sprays

| Date | Mintage | VG | F | VF | XF | Unc |
|---|---|---|---|---|---|---|
| ND(1906-28) | — | 0.75 | 2.00 | 3.50 | 5.00 | 7.00 |

**FANAM** KM# 45 **Composition:** Silver **Ruler:** Rama Varma VI ME1062-1101 / 1885-1924AD **Obverse:** RV monogram **Obv. Legend:** FANAM ONE **Reverse:** Sankha (conch shell) in sprays **Edge:** Plain **Note:** Edge varieties exist.

| Date | Mintage | VG | F | VF | XF | Unc |
|---|---|---|---|---|---|---|
| ND(1901) | — | 1.35 | 3.50 | 6.00 | 8.50 | 12.00 |

**FANAM** KM# 51 **Composition:** 0.9500 Silver **Ruler:** Rama Varma VI ME1062-1101 / 1885-1924AD **Reverse:** Sankha (conch shell) in sprays

| Date | Mintage | VG | F | VF | XF | Unc |
|---|---|---|---|---|---|---|
| ME1087(1911) | 1,100,000 | 1.25 | 3.00 | 5.00 | 7.00 | 10.00 |
| ME1087 (1911) | 1,100,000 | 1.35 | 3.00 | 5.00 | 7.00 | 10.00 |
| ME1096 (1920) | 350,000 | 1.35 | 3.50 | 6.00 | 8.50 | 12.00 |
| ME1096(1911) | 350,000 | 1.35 | 3.50 | 6.00 | 8.50 | 12.00 |
| ME1099 (1923) | 350,000 | 1.35 | 3.50 | 6.00 | 8.50 | 12.00 |
| ME1100 (1924) | 700,000 | 1.35 | 3.50 | 6.00 | 8.50 | 12.00 |
| ME1103 (1927) | 700,000 | 1.35 | 3.50 | 6.00 | 8.50 | 12.00 |

**FANAM** KM# 54 **Composition:** Silver **Ruler:** Rama Varma VI ME1062-1101 / 1885-1924AD **Obverse:** RV monogram **Obv. Legend:** ONE FANAM **Reverse:** Sankha (conch shell) in sprays **Edge:** Plain

| Date | Mintage | VG | F | VF | XF | Unc |
|---|---|---|---|---|---|---|
| ND(1911) | — | 4.00 | 10.00 | 17.50 | 25.00 | 35.00 |

**FANAM** KM# 55 **Composition:** Silver **Ruler:** Rama Varma VI ME1062-1101 / 1885-1924AD **Obverse:** RV monogram **Obv. Legend:** FANAM ONE **Reverse:** Sankha (conch shell) in sprays **Edge:** Reeded

| Date | Mintage | VG | F | VF | XF | Unc |
|---|---|---|---|---|---|---|
| ND(1911) | — | 1.25 | 3.00 | 5.00 | 7.00 | 10.00 |

**FANAM** KM# 61 **Composition:** Silver **Ruler:** Bala Rama Varma II ME1101-1126 / 1924-1949AD **Obv. Legend:** BALA RAMA VARMA-TRAVENCORE **Reverse:** Sankha (conch shell) in sprays

| Date | Mintage | VG | F | VF | XF | Unc |
|---|---|---|---|---|---|---|
| ME1112(1937) | 350,000 | 1.25 | 3.00 | 5.00 | 7.00 | 10.00 |

**FANAM** KM# 65 **Composition:** 0.5000 Silver **Ruler:** Bala Rama Varma II ME1101-1126 / 1924-1949AD **Obv. Legend:** BALA RAMA VARMA-TRAVENCORE **Reverse:** Sankha (conch shell) in sprays

| Date | Mintage | VG | F | VF | XF | Unc |
|---|---|---|---|---|---|---|
| ME1116(1941) | 2,096,000 | 0.35 | 0.90 | 1.50 | 2.00 | 3.00 |
| ME1116(1941) Proof | — | Value: 50.00 | | | | |
| ME1118(1942) | 4,157,000 | 0.35 | 0.90 | 1.50 | 2.00 | 3.00 |
| ME1118(1942) Proof | — | Value: 50.00 | | | | |
| ME1119(1946) | 1,925,000 | 0.50 | 1.25 | 2.25 | 3.50 | 5.00 |

**1/4 RUPEE** KM# 52 **Weight:** 2.7200 g. **Composition:** 0.9500 Silver .0831 oz. ASW **Ruler:** Rama Varma VI ME1062-1101 / 1885-1924AD **Obv. Legend:** RAMA VURMA-TRAVENCORE **Reverse:** Sankha (conch shell) in sprays

| Date | Mintage | VG | F | VF | XF | Unc |
|---|---|---|---|---|---|---|
| ME1082 (1906) | — | 2.50 | 6.00 | 10.00 | 14.00 | 20.00 |
| ME1083 (1907) | — | 2.50 | 6.00 | 10.00 | 14.00 | 20.00 |
| ME1085 (1909) | — | 2.50 | 6.00 | 10.00 | 14.00 | 20.00 |
| ME1086 (1910) | — | 2.50 | 6.00 | 10.00 | 14.00 | 20.00 |
| ME1087 (1911) | 400,000 | 1.75 | 4.50 | 7.00 | 10.00 | 15.00 |
| ME1096 (1920) | — | 1.25 | 3.00 | 5.00 | 7.00 | 10.00 |
| ME1099 (1923) | — | 1.25 | 3.00 | 5.00 | 7.00 | 10.00 |
| ME1100 (1924) | — | 1.25 | 3.00 | 5.00 | 7.00 | 10.00 |
| ME1103 (1927) | 200,000 | 1.25 | 3.00 | 5.00 | 7.00 | 10.00 |
| ME1106 (1930) | 200,000 | 1.25 | 3.00 | 5.00 | 7.00 | 10.00 |

**1/4 RUPEE** KM# 62 **Composition:** Silver **Ruler:** Bala Rama Varma II ME1101-1126 / 1924-1949AD **Obv. Legend:** BALA RAMA VARMA-TRAVENCORE

| Date | Mintage | VG | F | VF | XF | Unc |
|---|---|---|---|---|---|---|
| ME1112(1936) | 200,000 | 1.75 | 4.50 | 7.00 | 10.00 | 15.00 |

**1/4 RUPEE** KM# 66 **Composition:** 0.5000 Silver **Ruler:** Bala Rama Varma II ME1101-1126 / 1924-1949AD **Obv. Legend:** BALA RAMA VARMA-TRAVENCORE

| Date | Mintage | VG | F | VF | XF | Unc |
|---|---|---|---|---|---|---|
| ME1116(1941) | 126,000 | 0.90 | 2.25 | 3.75 | 5.50 | 8.00 |
| ME1116(1941) Proof | — | Value: 65.00 | | | | |
| ME1118(1942) | — | 1.50 | 4.00 | 7.00 | 10.00 | 15.00 |

**1/2 RUPEE** KM# 53 **Weight:** 5.4400 g. **Composition:** 0.9500 Silver .1662 oz. ASW **Ruler:** Rama Varma VI ME1062-1101 / 1885-1924AD **Reverse:** Legend shorter on bottom

| Date | Mintage | VG | F | VF | XF | Unc |
|---|---|---|---|---|---|---|
| ME1084 (1908) | — | 3.50 | 8.50 | 14.00 | 20.00 | 28.00 |
| ME1085 (1909) | — | 3.50 | 8.50 | 14.00 | 20.00 | 28.00 |
| ME1086 (1910) | — | 3.50 | 8.50 | 14.00 | 20.00 | 28.00 |
| ME1087 (1911) | 300,000 | 2.50 | 6.00 | 10.00 | 14.00 | 20.00 |
| ME1103 (1927) | 100,000 | 3.00 | 7.50 | 12.50 | 17.50 | 25.00 |
| ME1106 (1930) | 100,000 | 3.00 | 7.50 | 12.50 | 17.50 | 25.00 |
| ME1107 (1931) | 800,000 | 2.50 | 6.00 | 10.00 | 14.00 | 20.00 |

| Date | Mintage | VG | F | VF | XF | Unc |
|---|---|---|---|---|---|---|
| ND(1928-49)(1928) | — | Value: 40.00 | | | | |

**Note:** Refer to Rama Varma VI listings for thick variety, KM#46

**1/2 RUPEE** KM# 57 **Weight:** 0.4800 g. **Composition:** Copper **Ruler:** Bala Rama Varma II ME1101-1126 / 1924-1949AD **Obverse:** Sankha (conch shell) in 6-pointed star **Reverse:** Malayalam "Oru Kasu" (one cash) **Note:** Thin

| Date | Mintage | F | VF | XF | Unc | BU |
|---|---|---|---|---|---|---|
| ND(1928-49) | — | — | 0.15 | 0.25 | 0.35 | 0.50 |
| ND(1928-49)(1928) | — | Value: 40.00 | | | | |

**Note:** Refer to Rama Varma VI listings for thick variety, KM#46

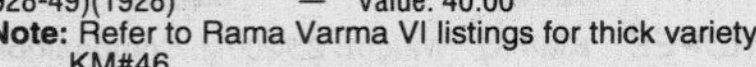

**1/2 RUPEE** KM# 63 **Composition:** Silver **Ruler:** Bala Rama Varma II ME1101-1126 / 1924-1949AD **Obv. Legend:** BALA RAMA VARMA-TRAVENCORE

| Date | Mintage | VG | F | VF | XF | Unc |
|---|---|---|---|---|---|---|
| ME1112(1937) | 200,000 | 3.50 | 8.50 | 14.00 | 20.00 | 28.50 |

**1/2 CHITRA RUPEE** KM# 64 **Composition:** Silver **Ruler:** Bala Rama Varma II ME1101-1126 / 1924-1949AD **Obv. Legend:** BALA RAMA VARMA-TRAVENCORE **Edge:** Reeded

| Date | Mintage | VG | F | VF | XF | Unc |
|---|---|---|---|---|---|---|
| ME1114 (1938-39) | — | 2.50 | 6.00 | 10.00 | 14.00 | 20.00 |

**1/2 CHITRA RUPEE** KM# 67 **Composition:** 0.5000 Silver **Ruler:** Bala Rama Varma II ME1101-1126 / 1924-1949AD **Obv. Legend:** BALA RAMA VARMA-TRAVENCORE **Edge:** Security

| Date | Mintage | VG | F | VF | XF | Unc |
|---|---|---|---|---|---|---|
| ME1116(1941) | 1,600,000 | 1.25 | 3.00 | 5.00 | 7.00 | 10.00 |
| ME1118/6(194 | 1,111,000 | 1.50 | 4.00 | 7.00 | 10.00 | 15.00 |
| ME1118(1942) | Inc. above | 1.25 | 3.00 | 5.00 | 7.00 | 10.00 |
| ME1118(1942) Proof | — | Value: 75.00 | | | | |
| ME1121(1946) | 200,000 | 1.25 | 3.00 | 5.00 | 7.00 | 10.00 |

## TULABHARAM MEDALLIC COINAGE

These presentation coins were struck prior to the weighing in ceremony of the Maharajah. The balance of his weight in these gold coins were distributed amongst the learned Brahmins and are referred to as Tulabhara Kasu. The legend reads "Sri Patmanabha", the National Deity.

**1/4 PAGODA** KM# M10 **Weight:** 1.2800 g. **Composition:** Gold 0 **Obverse:** Inscription: Tamil in three lines in sprays **Reverse:** Sankha (conch shell) in sprays

| Date | Mintage | VG | F | VF | XF | Unc |
|---|---|---|---|---|---|---|
| ND(1870-1931) | — | — | 55.00 | 85.00 | 120 | 175 |

**1/4 PAGODA** KM# M9 **Weight:** 0.6400 g. **Composition:** Gold 0 **Obverse:** Inscription: Tamil in three lines in sprays **Reverse:** Sankha (conch shell) in sprays **Note:** 10.9-12.7 millimeters.

| Date | Mintage | VG | F | VF | XF | Unc |
|---|---|---|---|---|---|---|
| ND(1870-1931) | — | — | 45.00 | 65.00 | 90.00 | 135 |

**1/4 PAGODA** KM# M12 **Weight:** 5.0900 g. **Composition:** Gold 0 **Obverse:** Inscription: Tamil in three lines in sprays **Reverse:** Sankha (conch shell) in sprays **Note:** 20.0-23.9 millimeters.

| Date | Mintage | VG | F | VF | XF | Unc |
|---|---|---|---|---|---|---|
| ND(1870-1931) | — | — | 125 | 210 | 300 | 425 |

**1/4 PAGODA** KM# M11 **Weight:** 2.5400 g. **Composition:** Gold 0 **Obverse:** Inscription: Tamil in three lines in sprays **Reverse:** Sankha (conch shell) in sprays **Note:** Uniface

| Date | Mintage | VG | F | VF | XF | Unc |
|---|---|---|---|---|---|---|
| ND(1870-1931) | — | — | 85.00 | 140 | 200 | 285 |

## PATTERNS

Including off metal strikes

| KM# | Date | Mintage | Identification | Mkt Val |
|---|---|---|---|---|
| Pn3 | 1086(1909) | — | 1/4 Rupee. Bronze. KM#52 | 75.00 |

# TRIPURA

**Hill Tipperah**

Tripura was a Hindu Kingdom consisting of a strip of the fertile plains east of Bengal, and a large tract of hill territory beyond, which had a reputation for providing wild elephants.

At times when Bengal was weak, Tripura rose to prominence and extended its rule into the plains, but when Bengal was strong the kingdom consisted purely of the hill area, which was virtually impregnable and not of enough economic worth to encourage the Muslims to conquer it. In this way Tripura was able to maintain its full independence until the 19th century.

The origins of the Kingdom are veiled in legend, but the first coins were struck during the reign of Ratna Manikya (1464-89) and copied the weight and fabric of the contemporary issues of the Sultans of Bengal. He also copied the lion design that had appeared on certain rare tangkas of Nasir-ud-din Mahmud Shah I dated AH849 (1445AD). In other respects the designs were purely Hindu, and the lion was retained on most of the later issues as a national emblem.

Tripura rose to a political zenith during the 16th century, while Muslim rule in Bengal was weak, and several coins were struck to commemorate successful military campaigns from Chittagong in the south to Sylhetin the north. These conquests were not sustained, and in the early 17th century the Mughal army was able to inflict severe defeats on Tripura, which was forced to pay tribute.

In about 1733AD all the territory in the plains was annexed by the Mughals, and the Raja merely managed his estate there as a zemindar, although he still retained control as independent King of his hill territory.

The situation remained unchanged when the British took over the administrationof Bengalin 1765, and it was only in 1871 that the British appointed an agent in the hills, and began to assist the Maharaja in the administration of his hill territory, which became known as the State of Hill Tipperah.

After the middle of the 18th century, coins were not struck for monetary reasons, but merely for ceremonial use at coronations and other ceremonies, and to keep up the treasured right of coinage.

The coins of Tripura are unusual in that the majority have the name of the King together with that of his Queen, and is the only coinage in the world where this was done consistently.

In common with most other Hindu coinages of northeast India, the coins bear fixed dates. Usually the date used was that of the coronation ceremony, but during the 16th century, coins which were struck with a design commemorating a particular event, bore the date of that event, which can be useful as a historical source, where other written evidence is virtually non-existent.

All modern Tripura coins were presentation pieces, more medallic than monetary in nature. They were struck in very limited numbers and although not intended for local circulation as money, they are often encountered in worn condition.

**RULERS**

**Radha Kishore Manikya**
**TE1306-1319/1896-1909AD**
**Queens of Radha Kishore**
**Queen Ratnamanjari**
**Queen Tulsivati**
**Virendra Kishore Manikya**
**TE1319-1333/1909-1923AD**
**Queen of Virendra Kishore**
**Queen Prabhavati**
**Vira Vikrama Kishore Manikya**
**TE1333-1357/1923-1947AD**
**Queens of Vira Vikrama Kishore Manikya**
**Queen Kanchan Prabha**

**Queen Kirti Mani**

**DATING**

While the early coinage is dated in the Saka Era (SE) the later issues are dated in the Tripurabda era (TE). Toconvert, TE date plus 590 = AD date. The dates appear to be accession years.

# PRINCELY STATE

## MEDALLIC COINAGE

**MOHUR** KM# 396 **Composition:** Gold **Ruler:** Virendra Kishore Manikya TE1319-1333/1909-1923AD **Rev. Legend:** With "Queen Prabhavati" **Edge:** Milled

| Date | Mintage | VG | F | VF | XF | Unc |
|---|---|---|---|---|---|---|
| TE1319(1909) Rare | — | — | — | — | — | — |

**RUPEE** KM# 406 **Composition:** Silver **Ruler:** Vira Vikrama Kishore Manikya TE1333-1357/1923-1947AD **Obverse:** Bust of Vira Vikrama Kishore left **Reverse:** Rampant lion left **Edge:** Milled **Note:** 11.30-11.90 grams. Varieties exist.

| Date | Mintage | VG | F | VF | XF | Unc |
|---|---|---|---|---|---|---|
| TE1337(1930) | — | 20.00 | 30.00 | 45.00 | 65.00 | 110 |

**RUPEE** KM# 409 **Composition:** Silver **Ruler:** Vira Vikrama Kishore Manikya TE1333-1357/1923-1947AD **Obverse:** Rampant lion left **Rev. Legend:** With "Sri Srimati Maharani Kanchan Prabha Maha Devi" **Edge:** Milled

| Date | Mintage | VG | F | VF | XF | Unc |
|---|---|---|---|---|---|---|
| TE1338(1931) | — | 35.00 | 50.00 | 85.00 | 125 | 200 |
| TE1341(1934) | — | 17.50 | 27.50 | 37.50 | 60.00 | 100 |

**RUPEE** KM# 408 **Composition:** Silver **Ruler:** Vira Vikrama Kishore Manikya TE1333-1357/1923-1947AD **Rev. Legend:** With "Queen Kirti Mani"

| Date | Mintage | VG | F | VF | XF | Unc |
|---|---|---|---|---|---|---|
| TE1341(1934)(1934) | — | 50.00 | 85.00 | 125 | 200 | 350 |

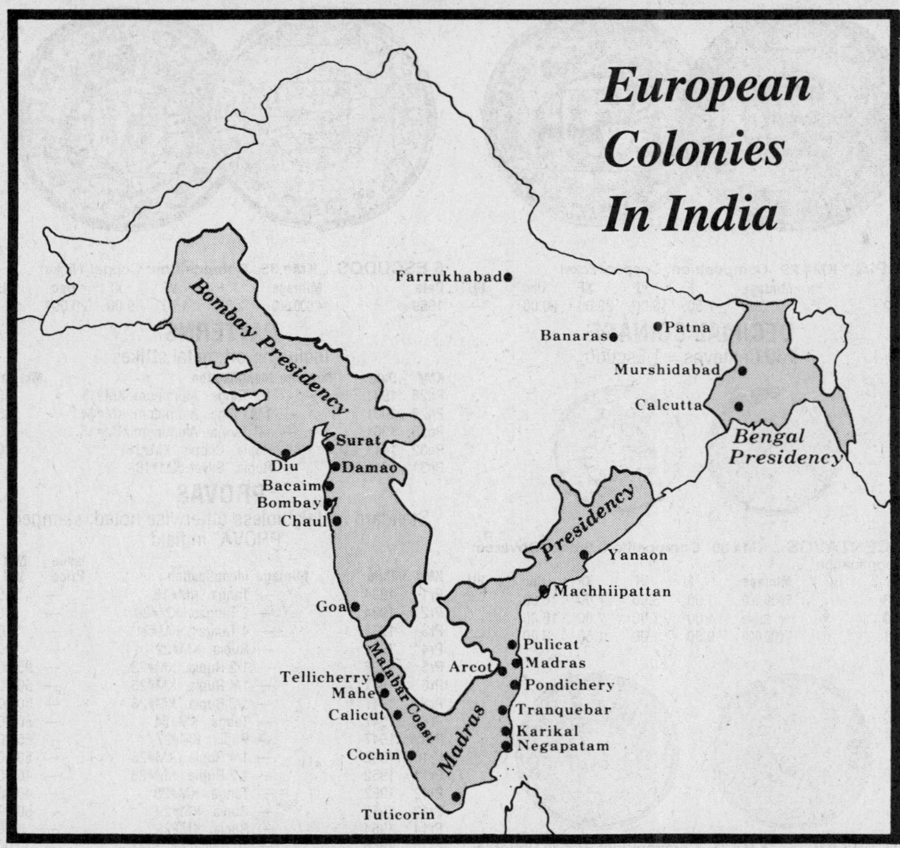


Vasco da Gama, the Portuguese explorer, first visited India in 1498. Portugal seized control of a number of islands and small enclaves on the west coast of India, and for the next hundred years enjoyed a monopoly on trade. With the arrival of powerful Dutch and English fleets in the first half of the 17th century, Portuguese power in the area declined until virtually all of India that remained under Portuguese control were the west coast enclaves of Goa, Damao and Diu. They were forcibly annexed by India in 1962.

**RULERS**
Portuguese, until 1961

**DENOMINATION**
The denomination of most copper coins appears in numerals on the reverse, though 30 Reis is often given as "1/2 T", and 60 Reis as "T" (T = Tanga). The silver coins have the denomination in words, usually on the obverse until 1850, then on the reverse.

**MONETARY SYSTEM**
960 Reis = 16 Tanga = 1 Rupia

# PORTUGUESE COLONY

## COLONIAL COINAGE

**1/12 TANGA** **KM# 13** **Composition:** Bronze **Obverse:** Carlos I bust right **Note:** Roman numeral dating.

| Date | Mintage | F | VF | XF | Unc | BU |
|---|---|---|---|---|---|---|
| 1901 | 960,000 | 6.00 | 12.00 | 28.00 | 55.00 | — |
| 1901 Prooflike | — | — | — | — | — | — |
| 1903 | 960,000 | 6.00 | 12.00 | 28.00 | 55.00 | — |

**1/8 TANGA** **KM# 14** **Composition:** Bronze **Obverse:** Carlos I, roman numeral dating

| Date | Mintage | F | VF | XF | Unc | BU |
|---|---|---|---|---|---|---|
| 1901 | 960,000 | 7.00 | 15.00 | 32.00 | 70.00 | — |
| 1901 Prooflike | — | — | — | — | — | — |
| 1903 | 960,000 | 7.00 | 15.00 | 32.00 | 70.00 | — |

**1/4 TANGA (15 Reis)** **KM# 15** **Composition:** Bronze **Obverse:** Carlos I **Note:** Roman numeral dating.

| Date | Mintage | F | VF | XF | Unc | BU |
|---|---|---|---|---|---|---|
| 1901 | 800,000 | 7.50 | 16.00 | 35.00 | 75.00 | — |
| 1901 Prooflike | — | — | — | — | 200 | — |
| 1903 | 800,000 | 7.50 | 16.00 | 35.00 | 75.00 | — |

**1/2 TANGA (30 Reis)** **KM# 16** **Composition:** Bronze **Obverse:** Carlos I **Note:** Roman numeral dating.

| Date | Mintage | F | VF | XF | Unc | BU |
|---|---|---|---|---|---|---|
| 1901 | 800,000 | 8.00 | 17.50 | 37.50 | 80.00 | — |
| 1901 Prooflike | — | — | — | — | 225 | — |
| 1903 | 800,000 | 8.00 | 17.50 | 37.50 | 80.00 | — |

**TANGA** **KM# 28** **Composition:** Bronze

| Date | Mintage | F | VF | XF | Unc | BU |
|---|---|---|---|---|---|---|
| 1952 | 9,600,000 | 1.00 | 4.00 | 9.00 | 20.00 | — |

**TANGA (60 Reis)** **KM# 19** **Composition:** Bronze

| Date | Mintage | F | VF | XF | Unc | BU |
|---|---|---|---|---|---|---|
| 1934 | 100,000 | 25.00 | 70.00 | 230 | 500 | — |

**TANGA (60 Reis)** **KM# 24** **Composition:** Bronze **Obverse:** Denomination

| Date | Mintage | F | VF | XF | Unc | BU |
|---|---|---|---|---|---|---|
| 1947 | 1,000,000 | 2.00 | 7.00 | 15.00 | 30.00 | — |

**2 TANGAS** **KM# 20** **Composition:** Copper-Nickel

| Date | Mintage | F | VF | XF | Unc | BU |
|---|---|---|---|---|---|---|
| 1934 | 150,000 | 10.00 | 20.00 | 180 | 400 | — |

**4 TANGAS** **KM# 21** **Composition:** Copper-Nickel

| Date | Mintage | F | VF | XF | Unc | BU |
|---|---|---|---|---|---|---|
| 1934 | 100,000 | 20.00 | 60.00 | 200 | 450 | — |

**1/4 RUPIA** **KM# 25** **Composition:** Copper-Nickel **Obverse:** Denomination

| Date | Mintage | F | VF | XF | Unc | BU |
|---|---|---|---|---|---|---|
| 1947 | 800,000 | 5.00 | 10.00 | 20.00 | 40.00 | — |
| 1952 | 4,000,000 | 2.00 | 4.00 | 12.00 | 25.00 | — |

**1/2 RUPIA** **KM# 23** **Weight:** 6.0000 g. **Composition:** 0.8350 Silver .1610 oz. ASW

| Date | Mintage | F | VF | XF | Unc | BU |
|---|---|---|---|---|---|---|
| 1936 | 100,000 | 18.00 | 30.00 | 50.00 | 100 | — |

**1/2 RUPIA** **KM# 26** **Composition:** Copper-Nickel **Obverse:** Denomination

| Date | Mintage | F | VF | XF | Unc | BU |
|---|---|---|---|---|---|---|
| 1947 | 600,000 | 7.00 | 15.00 | 30.00 | 60.00 | — |
| 1952 | 2,000,000 | 2.00 | 5.00 | 12.00 | 25.00 | — |

**RUPIA** KM# 17 **Weight:** 11.6600 g. **Composition:** 0.9170 Silver .3438 oz. ASW **Obverse:** Carlos I

| Date | Mintage | F | VF | XF | Unc | BU |
|---|---|---|---|---|---|---|
| 1903 | 200,000 | 8.00 | 16.00 | 32.00 | 65.00 | — |
| 1904 | 100,000 | 9.00 | 18.00 | 35.00 | 70.00 | — |

**RUPIA** KM# 18 **Weight:** 11.6600 g. **Composition:** 0.9170 Silver .3438 oz. ASW

| Date | Mintage | F | VF | XF | Unc | BU |
|---|---|---|---|---|---|---|
| 1912/1 | 300,000 | 75.00 | 150 | 275 | 500 | — |
| 1912/1 Proof | — | Value: 1,250 | | | | |
| 1912 | Inc. above | 35.00 | 75.00 | 150 | 285 | — |

**RUPIA** KM# 22 **Weight:** 12.0000 g. **Composition:** 0.9170 Silver .3536 oz. ASW

| Date | Mintage | F | VF | XF | Unc | BU |
|---|---|---|---|---|---|---|
| 1935 | 300,000 | 7.50 | 15.00 | 28.00 | 55.00 | — |

**RUPIA** KM# 27 **Weight:** 12.0000 g. **Composition:** 0.5000 Silver .1929 oz. ASW

| Date | Mintage | F | VF | XF | Unc | BU |
|---|---|---|---|---|---|---|
| 1947 | 900,000 | 7.50 | 15.00 | 30.00 | 60.00 | — |

**RUPIA** KM# 29 **Composition:** Copper-Nickel

| Date | Mintage | F | VF | XF | Unc | BU |
|---|---|---|---|---|---|---|
| 1952 | 1,000,000 | 7.50 | 15.00 | 30.00 | 60.00 | — |

## DECIMAL COINAGE

100 Centavos = 1 Escudo

**10 CENTAVOS** KM# 30 **Composition:** Bronze **Obverse:** Denomination

| Date | Mintage | F | VF | XF | Unc | BU |
|---|---|---|---|---|---|---|
| 1958 | 5,000,000 | 1.00 | 3.00 | 7.00 | 16.00 | — |
| 1959 | Inc. above | 1.00 | 3.00 | 7.00 | 16.00 | — |
| 1961 | 1,000,000 | 0.50 | 1.00 | 1.50 | 3.00 | — |

**30 CENTAVOS** KM# 31 **Composition:** Bronze **Obverse:** Denomination

| Date | Mintage | F | VF | XF | Unc | BU |
|---|---|---|---|---|---|---|
| 1958 | 5,000,000 | 0.75 | 2.50 | 7.00 | 16.00 | — |
| 1959 | Inc. above | 2.50 | 7.00 | 15.00 | 30.00 | — |

**60 CENTAVOS** KM# 32 **Composition:** Copper-Nickel

| Date | Mintage | F | VF | XF | Unc | BU |
|---|---|---|---|---|---|---|
| 1958 | 5,000,000 | 2.00 | 4.00 | 10.00 | 20.00 | — |
| 1959 | Inc. above | 1.25 | 2.50 | 6.50 | 13.50 | — |

**ESCUDO** KM# 33 **Composition:** Copper-Nickel

| Date | Mintage | F | VF | XF | Unc | BU |
|---|---|---|---|---|---|---|
| 1958 | 6,000,000 | 1.25 | 2.50 | 7.50 | 16.00 | — |
| 1959 | Inc. above | 1.25 | 2.50 | 6.50 | 13.50 | — |

**3 ESCUDOS** KM# 34 **Composition:** Copper-Nickel

| Date | Mintage | F | VF | XF | Unc | BU |
|---|---|---|---|---|---|---|
| 1958 | 5,000,000 | 2.50 | 5.00 | 12.00 | 22.00 | — |
| 1959 | Inc. above | 2.50 | 4.50 | 9.00 | 18.00 | — |

**6 ESCUDOS** KM# 35 **Composition:** Copper-Nickel

| Date | Mintage | F | VF | XF | Unc | BU |
|---|---|---|---|---|---|---|
| 1959 | 4,000,000 | 2.50 | 4.50 | 9.00 | 20.00 | — |

## PATTERNS

Including off metal strikes

| KM# | Date | Mintage | Identification | Mkt Val |
|---|---|---|---|---|
| Pn28 | 1901 | — | 1/2 Tanga. Aluminum. KM#13 | 135 |
| Pn29 | 1901 | — | 1/8 Tanga. Aluminum. KM#14 | 135 |
| Pn30 | 1901 | — | 1/4 Tanga. Aluminum. KM#15 | 135 |
| Pn32 | 1911 | — | Rupia. Copper. KM#18 | 700 |
| Pn31 | 1911 | — | Rupia. Silver. KM#18 | — |

## PROVAS

Standard metals unless otherwise noted; stamped "PROVA" in field

| KM# | Date | Mintage | Identification | Issue Price | Mkt Val |
|---|---|---|---|---|---|
| Pr1 | 1934 | — | Tanga. KM#19 | — | 325 |
| Pr2 | 1934 | — | 2 Tangas. KM#20 | — | 335 |
| Pr3 | 1934 | — | 4 Tangas. KM#21 | — | 340 |
| Pr4 | 1935 | — | Rupia. KM#22 | — | 140 |
| Pr5 | 1936 | — | 1/2 Rupia. KM#23 | — | 95.00 |
| Pr6 | 1947 | — | 1/4 Rupia. KM#25 | — | 50.00 |
| Pr7 | 1947 | — | 1/2 Rupia. KM#26 | — | 50.00 |
| Pr8 | 1947 | — | Tanga. KM#24 | — | 50.00 |
| Pr9 | 1947 | — | Rupia. KM#27 | — | 85.00 |
| Pr10 | 1952 | — | 1/4 Rupia. KM#25 | — | 50.00 |
| Pr11 | 1952 | — | 1/2 Rupia. KM#26 | — | 40.00 |
| Pr12 | 1952 | — | Tanga. KM#28 | — | 40.00 |
| Pr13 | 1952 | — | Rupia. KM#29 | — | 50.00 |
| Pr14 | 1954 | — | Rupia. KM#29 | — | 250 |
| Pr15 | 1958 | — | 10 Centavos. KM#30 | — | 30.00 |
| Pr16 | 1958 | — | 30 Centavos. KM#31 | — | 40.00 |
| Pr17 | 1958 | — | 60 Centavos. KM#32 | — | 40.00 |
| Pr18 | 1958 | — | Escudo. KM#33 | — | 45.00 |
| Pr19 | 1958 | — | 3 Escudos. KM#34 | — | 45.00 |
| Pr20 | 1959 | — | 10 Centavos. KM#30 | — | 40.00 |
| Pr21 | 1959 | — | 30 Centavos. KM#31 | — | 40.00 |
| Pr22 | 1959 | — | 60 Centavos. KM#32 | — | 40.00 |
| Pr23 | 1959 | — | Escudo. KM#33 | — | 40.00 |
| Pr24 | 1959 | — | 3 Escudos. KM#34 | — | 40.00 |
| Pr25 | 1959 | — | 6 Escudos. KM#35 | — | 40.00 |
| Pr26 | 1961 | — | 10 Centavos. KM#30 | — | 35.00 |
| Pr27 | 1961 | — | 10 Centavos. Nickel-Brass. Incuse N; KM#30 | — | 45.00 |

# INDIA-BRITISH

The civilization of India, which began about 2500 B.C., flourished under a succession of empires - notably those of the Mauryas, the Kushans, the Guptas, the Delhi Sultans and the Mughals – until undermined in the 18th and 19th centuries by European colonial powers.

The Portuguese were the first to arrive, off Calicut in May 1498. It wasn't until 1612, after the Portuguese and Spanish power had begun to wane, that the British East India Company established its initial settlement at Surat. Britain could not have chosen a more propitious time as the central girdle of petty states, and the southern Vijayanagar Empire were crumbling and ripe for foreign exploitation. By the end of the century, English traders were firmly established in Bombay, Madras, Calcutta and lesser places elsewhere, and Britain was implementing its announced policy to create such civil and military institutions as may be the foundation of secure English domination for all time'. By 1757, following the successful conclusion of a war of colonial rivalry with France during which the military victories of Robert Clive, a young officer with the British East India Company, made him a powerful man in India, the British were firmly settled in India not only as traders but as conquerors. During the next 60 years, the British East India Company acquired dominion over most of India by bribery and force, and governed it directly or through puppet princelings.

As a result of the Sepoy Mutiny of 1857-58, a large-scale mutiny among Indian soldiers of the Bengal army, control of the government of India was transferred from the East India Company to the British Crown. At this point in world history, India was the brightest jewel in the British imperial diadem, but even then a movement for greater Indian representation in government presaged the Indian Empire's twilight hour less than a century later-it would pass into history on Aug. 15, 1947.

### COLONIAL COINAGE

This section lists the coins of British India from the reign of William IV (1835) to the reign of George VI (1947). The issues are divided into two main parts:

Coins struck under the authority of the East India Company (E.I.C.) from 1835 until the trading monopoly of the E.I.C. was abolished in 1853. From August 2, 1858 the property and powers of the Company were transferred to the British Crown. From November 1, 1858 to November 1, 1862 the coins continued to bear the design and inscription of the Company.

Coins struck under the authority of the Crown (Regal issues) from 1862 until 1947.

The first regal issues bear the date 1862 and were struck with the date 1862 unchanged until 1874. From then onward all coins bear the year date.

The copper coins dated 1862 have been tentatively attributed by their size to the mint of issue. The silver coins dated 1862 have been attributed to various years of issue by their characteristic marks according to mint records.

In 1877 Queen Victoria was proclaimed Empress of India and the title of the obverse legend was changed accordingly.

For a detailed account of the work of the various mints and the numerous die varieties the general collector and specialist should refer to *The Coins of the British Commonwealth of Nations*, to the end of the reign of King George VI – 1952, Part 4, India, Vol. 1 and 2, by F. Pridmore, Spink, 1980.

### RULERS

British until 1947

### MINT MARKS

The coins of British India were struck at the following mints, indicated in the catalogue by either capital letters after the date when the actual letter appears on the coins or small letters in () designating the mint of issue. Plain dates indicate Royal Mint strikes.

B – Bombay, 1835-1947
C or CM – Calcutta, 1835-1947
I – Bombay, 1918-1919
L – Lahore, 1943-1945
P – Pretoria, South Africa, 1943-1944

In 1947 British rule came to an end and India was divided into two self-governing countries, India and Pakistan. In 1971 Bangladash seceded from Pakistan. All are now independent republics and although they are still members of the British Commonwealth of Nations, their coinages do not belong to the British India series.

### MONETARY SYSTEM

3 Pies = 1 Pice (Paisa)
4 Pice = 1 Anna
16 Annas = 1 Rupee
15 Rupees = 1 Mohur

The transition from the coins of the Moslem monetary system began with the silver pattern Rupees of William IV, 1834, issued by the East India Company, with the value on the reverse, given in English, Bengali, Persian and Nagari characters. This coinage was struck for several years, as dated, except for the currency, Rupee, which was struck from 1835-1840, all dated 1835.

The portrait coins issued by the East India Company for Victoria show two different head designs on the obverse, which are called Type I and Type II. The coins with Type I head have a continuous obverse legend and were struck from 1840 to 1851. The coins with the Type II head have a divided obverse legend and were struck from 1850 (Calcutta) until 1862. The date on the coins remained unchanged: The Rupee, 1/2 Rupee and 1/4 Rupee are dated 1840. Noticeable differences in the ribbon designs of the English vs. Indian obverses exist.

Type I coins have on the reverse a dot after the date those of Type II have no dot, except for some rare 1/4 Rupees and 2 Annas. The latter are mules, struck from reverse dies of the preceding issue.

### KING GEORGE VI: First and Second Heads

While King George VI's First Head is engraved in somewhat higher relief than his second head on all denominations from the 1/12 Anna to the Rupee, an easier way of distinguishing between the two types is that on the First Head the two *fleurs de lis* on the royal crown are larger and extend upward to touch the beaded crest at the top of the crown, while the two *fleurs de lis* on the crown of the Second Head are smaller and extend upward to touch only the line on the crown below the beaded crest.

### ENGRAVER INITIALS

The following initials appear on the obverse on the truncation:
S incuse (Type I).
WW raised or incuse (Type II).
WWS or SWW (Type II).
WWB raised (Type II).

### Proof and Proof-like restrikes

Original proofs are similar to early English Specimen strikes with wire edges and matte finish busts, arms, etc. Restrikes of most of the coins minted from the period 1835 were regularly supplied until this practice was discontinued on July 1, 1970.

Early proof restrikes are found with slight hairlining from polishing of the old dies. Bust, field, arms, etc. are of even smoothness.

Modern proof-like (P/L) restrikes are usually heavily hairlined from excessive polishing of the old dies and have a glassy, varnished or proof-like appearance. Many are common while some are quite scarce including some unusual mulings. These listings are indicated by **P/L-R** after the date and mint mark, for example; "1907(s) P/L R".

# BRITISH COLONIAL

## MILLED COINAGE

**1/12 ANNA** KM# 483 **Composition:** Copper **Obv. Legend:** VICTORIA EMPRESS

| Date | Mintage | F | VF | XF | Unc | BU |
|---|---|---|---|---|---|---|
| 1901(c) | 21,345,000 | 0.35 | 0.75 | 1.75 | 4.00 | — |
| 1901(c) Proof | — | Value: 50.00 | | | | |
| 1901(c) P/L-R | — | — | — | — | 20.00 | — |

**1/12 ANNA** KM# 483b **Composition:** Silver

| Date | Mintage | F | VF | XF | Unc | BU |
|---|---|---|---|---|---|---|
| 1901(c) P/L-R | — | — | — | — | 75.00 | — |

**1/12 ANNA** KM# 483c **Composition:** Gold

| Date | Mintage | F | VF | XF | Unc | BU |
|---|---|---|---|---|---|---|
| 1901(c) P/L-R | — | — | — | — | 400 | — |

**1/12 ANNA** KM# 497 **Composition:** Copper **Obv. Legend:** EDWARD VII KING & EMPEROR **Note:** Thick planchets.

| Date | Mintage | F | VF | XF | Unc | BU |
|---|---|---|---|---|---|---|
| 1903(c) | 7,883,000 | 0.35 | 1.25 | 6.00 | 15.00 | — |
| 1903(c) Proof | — | Value: 60.00 | | | | |
| 1903(c) P/L-R | — | — | — | — | 20.00 | — |
| 1904(c) | 16,506,000 | 0.25 | 1.00 | 4.00 | 12.00 | — |
| 1904(c) Proof | — | Value: 60.00 | | | | |
| 1904(c) P/L-R | — | — | — | — | 20.00 | — |
| 1905(c) | 13,060,000 | 0.25 | 1.00 | 4.00 | 12.00 | — |
| 1905(c) P/L-R | — | — | — | — | 20.00 | — |
| 1906(c) | 9,072,000 | 0.25 | 1.00 | 4.00 | 12.00 | — |
| 1906(c) Proof | — | Value: 60.00 | | | | |
| 1906(c) P/L-R | — | — | — | — | 20.00 | — |

**1/12 ANNA** KM# 497a **Composition:** Silver

| Date | Mintage | F | VF | XF | Unc | BU |
|---|---|---|---|---|---|---|
| 1904(c) P/L-R | — | — | — | — | 75.00 | — |
| 1905(c) P/L-R | — | — | — | — | 75.00 | — |

**1/12 ANNA** KM# 498 **Composition:** Bronze **Obv. Legend:** EDWARD VII KING & EMPEROR **Note:** Thin planchet.

| Date | Mintage | F | VF | XF | Unc | BU |
|---|---|---|---|---|---|---|
| 1906(c) | 2,184,000 | 0.35 | 0.75 | 5.00 | 15.00 | — |
| 1906(c) Proof | — | Value: 50.00 | | | | |
| 1907(c) | 20,985,000 | 0.25 | 0.50 | 3.00 | 9.00 | — |
| 1907(c) Proof | — | Value: 50.00 | | | | |
| 1907(c) P/L-R | — | — | — | — | 20.00 | — |
| 1908(c) | 22,036,000 | 0.25 | 0.50 | 3.00 | 9.00 | — |
| 1908(c) Proof | — | Value: 50.00 | | | | |
| 1908(c) P/L-R | — | — | — | — | 20.00 | — |
| 1909(c) | 12,316,000 | 0.25 | 0.50 | 3.00 | 9.00 | — |
| 1909(c) P/L-R | — | — | — | — | 20.00 | — |
| 1910(c) | 23,520,000 | 0.25 | 0.50 | 3.00 | 9.00 | — |
| 1910(c) P/L-R | — | — | — | — | 20.00 | — |

**1/12 ANNA** KM# 498a **Composition:** Aluminum

| Date | Mintage | F | VF | XF | Unc | BU |
|---|---|---|---|---|---|---|
| 1909(c) Proof | — | Value: 75.00 | | | | |

**1/12 ANNA** KM# 509 **Composition:** Bronze **Obv. Legend:** GEORGE V KING EMPEROR

| Date | Mintage | F | VF | XF | Unc | BU |
|---|---|---|---|---|---|---|
| 1912(c) | 25,938,000 | 0.50 | 0.75 | 1.50 | 4.50 | — |
| 1912(c) Proof | — | Value: 50.00 | | | | |
| 1912(c) P/L-R | — | — | — | — | 20.00 | — |
| 1913(c) | 16,149,000 | 0.25 | 0.50 | 1.00 | 3.00 | — |
| 1913(c) Proof | — | Value: 40.00 | | | | |
| 1913(c) P/L-R Restrike; prooflike | — | — | — | — | 20.00 | — |
| 1914(c) | 19,814,000 | 0.25 | 0.50 | 0.75 | 2.00 | — |
| 1914(c) Proof | — | Value: 40.00 | | | | |
| 1914(c) P/L-R | — | — | — | — | 20.00 | — |
| 1915(c) | 20,563,000 | 0.25 | 0.50 | 0.75 | 2.00 | — |
| 1915(c) Proof | — | Value: 40.00 | | | | |
| 1915(c) P/L-R | — | — | — | — | 20.00 | — |
| 1916(c) | 14,438,000 | 0.25 | 0.50 | 0.75 | 2.00 | — |
| 1916(c) Proof | — | Value: 40.00 | | | | |
| 1916(c) P/L-R | — | — | — | — | 20.00 | — |
| 1917(c) | 35,174,000 | 0.25 | 0.50 | 0.75 | 2.00 | — |
| 1917(c) Proof | — | Value: 40.00 | | | | |
| 1917(c) P/L-R | — | — | — | — | 20.00 | — |
| 1918(c) | 24,192,000 | 0.25 | 0.50 | 0.75 | 2.00 | — |
| 1918(c) Proof | — | Value: 40.00 | | | | |
| 1918(c) P/L-R | — | — | — | — | 20.00 | — |
| 1919(c) | 17,472,000 | 0.25 | 0.50 | 0.75 | 2.00 | — |
| 1919(c) Proof | — | Value: 40.00 | | | | |
| 1919(c) P/L-R | — | — | — | — | 20.00 | — |
| 1920(c) | 39,878,000 | 0.25 | 0.50 | 0.75 | 2.00 | — |
| 1920(c) Proof | — | Value: 40.00 | | | | |
| 1920(c) P/L-R | — | — | — | — | 20.00 | — |
| 1921(c) | 19,334,000 | 0.25 | 0.50 | 0.75 | 2.00 | — |
| 1921(c) Proof | — | Value: 40.00 | | | | |
| 1921(c) P/L-R | — | — | — | — | 20.00 | — |
| 1923(c) | 8,429,000 | 0.25 | 0.50 | 0.75 | 2.00 | — |
| 1923(c) Proof | — | Value: 40.00 | | | | |
| 1923(b) | 8,717,000 | 0.25 | 0.50 | 0.75 | 2.00 | — |
| 1923(b) Proof | — | Value: 40.00 | | | | |
| 1924(c) | 7,200,000 | 0.50 | 0.75 | 1.50 | 4.50 | — |
| 1924(c) Proof | — | Value: 40.00 | | | | |
| 1924(b) | 9,869,000 | 0.25 | 0.50 | 0.75 | 2.00 | — |
| 1924(b) Proof | — | Value: 40.00 | | | | |
| 1924(b) P/L-R | — | — | — | — | 20.00 | — |
| 1925(c) | 5,818,000 | 0.50 | 0.75 | 1.50 | 4.50 | — |
| 1925(c) Proof | — | Value: 40.00 | | | | |
| 1925(b) | 6,415,000 | 0.50 | 0.75 | 1.50 | 4.50 | — |
| 1925(b) Proof | — | Value: 40.00 | | | | |
| 1925(b) P/L-R | — | — | — | — | 20.00 | — |
| 1926(c) | 4,147,000 | 0.50 | 0.75 | 1.50 | 4.50 | — |
| 1926(c) Proof | — | Value: 40.00 | | | | |
| 1926(b) | 15,464,000 | 0.25 | 0.50 | 0.75 | 2.00 | — |
| 1926(b) Proof | — | Value: 40.00 | | | | |
| 1926(b) P/L-R | — | — | — | — | 20.00 | — |
| 1927(c) | 6,662,000 | 0.50 | 0.75 | 1.50 | 4.50 | — |
| 1927(c) Proof | — | Value: 40.00 | | | | |
| 1927(b) | 6,788,000 | 0.50 | 0.75 | 1.50 | 4.50 | — |
| 1927(b) Proof | — | Value: 40.00 | | | | |
| 1927(b) P/L-R | — | — | — | — | 20.00 | — |
| 1928(c) | 8,064,000 | 0.25 | 0.50 | 0.75 | 2.00 | — |
| 1928(c) Proof | — | Value: 40.00 | | | | |
| 1928(b) | 6,135,000 | 0.50 | 0.75 | 1.50 | 4.50 | — |
| 1928(b) Proof | — | Value: 40.00 | | | | |
| 1928(b) P/L-R | — | — | — | — | 20.00 | — |
| 1929(c) | 15,130,000 | 0.25 | 0.50 | 0.75 | 2.00 | — |
| 1929(c) Proof | — | Value: 40.00 | | | | |
| 1929(c) P/L-R | — | — | — | — | 20.00 | — |
| 1930(c) | 13,498,000 | 0.25 | 0.50 | 0.75 | 2.00 | — |
| 1930(c) Proof | — | Value: 40.00 | | | | |
| 1930(c) P/L-R | — | — | — | — | 20.00 | — |
| 1931(c) | 18,278,000 | 0.25 | 0.50 | 0.75 | 2.00 | — |
| 1931(c) Proof | — | Value: 40.00 | | | | |
| 1931(c) P/L-R | — | — | — | — | 20.00 | — |
| 1932(c) | 23,213,000 | 0.25 | 0.50 | 0.75 | 2.00 | — |
| 1932(c) Proof | — | Value: 40.00 | | | | |
| 1932(c) P/L-R | — | — | — | — | 20.00 | — |
| 1933(c) | 16,896,000 | 0.25 | 0.50 | 0.75 | 2.00 | — |
| 1933(c) Proof | — | Value: 40.00 | | | | |
| 1933(c) P/L-R | — | — | — | — | 20.00 | — |
| 1934(c) | 17,146,000 | 0.25 | 0.50 | 0.75 | 2.00 | — |
| 1934(c) Proof | — | Value: 40.00 | | | | |
| 1934(c) P/L-R | — | — | — | — | 20.00 | — |
| 1935(c) | 19,142,000 | 0.25 | 0.50 | 0.75 | 2.00 | — |
| 1935(c) Proof | — | Value: 40.00 | | | | |
| 1935(c) P/L-R | — | — | — | — | 20.00 | — |
| 1936(c) | 23,213,000 | 0.25 | 0.50 | 0.75 | 2.00 | — |
| 1936(b) | 12,887,000 | 0.25 | 0.50 | 0.75 | 2.00 | — |
| 1936(b) P/L-R | — | — | — | — | 20.00 | — |

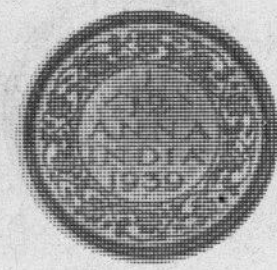

**1/12 ANNA** **KM# 526** **Composition:** Bronze **Obv. Legend:** GEORGE VI KING EMPEROR **Note:** First head.

| Date | Mintage | F | VF | XF | Unc | BU |
|---|---|---|---|---|---|---|
| 1938(c) Proof | — | Value: 35.00 | | | | |
| 1939(c) | 3,571,000 | 0.50 | 0.75 | 1.50 | 4.50 | — |
| 1939(b) | 17,407,000 | 0.25 | 0.50 | 1.00 | 2.50 | — |

**1/12 ANNA** **KM# 527** **Composition:** Bronze **Obv. Legend:** GEORGE VI KING EMPEPOR **Note:** Second head.

| Date | Mintage | F | VF | XF | Unc | BU |
|---|---|---|---|---|---|---|
| 1938(c) P/L-R | — | — | — | — | 20.00 | — |
| 1939(c) | 5,245,000 | 0.25 | 0.50 | 1.00 | 2.50 | — |
| 1939(c) Proof | — | Value: 35.00 | | | | |
| 1939(b) | 31,306,000 | 0.25 | 0.50 | 0.75 | 2.00 | — |
| 1939(b) Proof | — | Value: 35.00 | | | | |
| 1939(b) P/L-R | — | — | — | — | 20.00 | — |
| 1941(b) | 6,137,000 | 0.25 | 0.50 | 0.75 | 2.00 | — |
| 1942(b) | 6,124,000 | 0.50 | 0.75 | 1.50 | 4.50 | — |
| 1942(b) Proof | — | Value: 35.00 | | | | |
| 1942(b) P/L-R | — | — | — | — | 20.00 | — |

**1/2 PICE** **KM# 484** **Composition:** Copper **Obv. Legend:** VICTORIA EMPRESS

| Date | Mintage | F | VF | XF | Unc | BU |
|---|---|---|---|---|---|---|
| 1901(c) | 16,057,000 | 1.00 | 1.75 | 3.50 | 8.50 | — |
| 1901(c) Proof | — | Value: 50.00 | | | | |
| 1901(c) P/L-R | — | — | — | — | 20.00 | — |

**1/2 PICE** **KM# 484b** **Composition:** Silver

| Date | Mintage | F | VF | XF | Unc | BU |
|---|---|---|---|---|---|---|
| 1901(c) P/L-R | — | — | — | — | 75.00 | — |

**1/2 PICE** **KM# 484c** **Composition:** Gold

| Date | Mintage | F | VF | XF | Unc | BU |
|---|---|---|---|---|---|---|
| 1901(c) P/L-R | — | — | — | — | 700 | — |

**1/2 PICE** **KM# 499** **Composition:** Copper **Obv. Legend:** EDWARD VII KING & EMPEROR

| Date | Mintage | F | VF | XF | Unc | BU |
|---|---|---|---|---|---|---|
| 1903(c) | 5,376,000 | 0.75 | 1.50 | 5.00 | 15.00 | — |
| 1903(c) Proof | — | Value: 45.00 | | | | |
| 1903(c) P/L-R | — | — | — | — | 20.00 | — |
| 1904(c) | 8,464,000 | 0.75 | 1.50 | 5.00 | 15.00 | — |
| 1904(c) Proof | — | Value: 45.00 | | | | |
| 1904(c) P/L-R | — | — | — | — | 20.00 | — |
| 1905(c) | 8,922,000 | 0.75 | 1.50 | 5.00 | 15.00 | — |
| 1905(c) P/L-R | — | — | — | — | 20.00 | — |
| 1906(c) | 6,346,000 | 0.75 | 1.50 | 5.00 | 15.00 | — |
| 1906(c) Proof | — | Value: 45.00 | | | | |
| 1906(c) P/L-R | — | — | — | — | 20.00 | — |

**1/2 PICE** **KM# 500c** **Composition:** Silver

| Date | Mintage | F | VF | XF | Unc | BU |
|---|---|---|---|---|---|---|
| 1903(c) P/L-R | — | — | — | — | 75.00 | — |
| 1904(c) P/L-R | — | — | — | — | 75.00 | — |
| 1905(c) P/L-R | — | — | — | — | 75.00 | — |

**1/2 PICE** **KM# 500** **Composition:** Bronze **Obv. Legend:** EDWARD VII KING & EMPEROR **Note:** Thinner planchets.

| Date | Mintage | F | VF | XF | Unc | BU |
|---|---|---|---|---|---|---|
| 1904(c) Proof | — | Value: 45.00 | | | | |
| 1906(c) | 5,860,000 | 0.75 | 1.50 | 4.50 | 12.50 | — |
| 1906(c) Proof | — | Value: 45.00 | | | | |
| 1907(c) | 8,060,000 | 0.75 | 1.50 | 4.50 | 12.50 | — |
| 1907(c) Proof | — | Value: 45.00 | | | | |
| 1907(c) P/L-R | — | — | — | — | 20.00 | — |
| 1908(c) | 10,035,000 | 0.75 | 1.50 | 4.50 | 12.50 | — |
| 1908(c) Proof | — | Value: 45.00 | | | | |
| 1908(c) P/L-R | — | — | — | — | 20.00 | — |
| 1909(c) | 8,493,000 | 0.75 | 1.50 | 4.50 | 12.50 | — |
| 1909(c) P/L-R | — | — | — | — | 20.00 | — |
| 1910(c) | 17,408,000 | 0.75 | 1.50 | 4.50 | 12.50 | — |

**1/2 PICE** **KM# 500b** **Composition:** Nickel

| Date | Mintage | F | VF | XF | Unc | BU |
|---|---|---|---|---|---|---|
| 1904(c) Proof | — | Value: 100 | | | | |

**1/2 PICE** **KM# 500a** **Composition:** Aluminum

| Date | Mintage | F | VF | XF | Unc | BU |
|---|---|---|---|---|---|---|
| 1909(c) Proof | — | Value: 100 | | | | |

**1/2 PICE** **KM# 510** **Composition:** Bronze **Obv. Legend:** GEORGE V KING EMPEROR

| Date | Mintage | F | VF | XF | Unc | BU |
|---|---|---|---|---|---|---|
| 1912(c) | 12,911,000 | 0.25 | 0.50 | 0.75 | 3.00 | — |
| 1912(c) Proof | — | Value: 40.00 | | | | |
| 1912(c) P/L-R | — | — | — | — | 20.00 | — |
| 1913(c) | 10,897,000 | 0.25 | 0.50 | 0.75 | 3.00 | — |
| 1913(c) Proof | — | Value: 40.00 | | | | |
| 1913(c) P/L-R | — | — | — | — | 20.00 | — |
| 1914(c) | 4,877,000 | 0.15 | 0.30 | 0.50 | 2.50 | — |
| 1914(c) Proof | — | Value: 40.00 | | | | |
| 1914(c) P/L-R | — | — | — | — | 20.00 | — |
| 1915(c) | 9,830,000 | 0.15 | 0.30 | 0.50 | 2.50 | — |
| 1915(c) Proof | — | Value: 40.00 | | | | |
| 1915(c) P/L-R | — | — | — | — | 20.00 | — |
| 1916(c) | 5,734,000 | 0.15 | 0.30 | 0.50 | 2.50 | — |
| 1916(c) Proof | — | Value: 40.00 | | | | |
| 1916(c) P/L-R | — | — | — | — | 20.00 | — |
| 1917(c) | 15,296,000 | 0.15 | 0.30 | 0.50 | 2.50 | — |
| 1917(c) Proof | — | Value: 40.00 | | | | |
| 1917(c) P/L-R | — | — | — | — | 20.00 | — |
| 1918(c) | 6,244,000 | 0.15 | 0.30 | 0.50 | 2.50 | — |
| 1918(c) Proof | — | Value: 40.00 | | | | |
| 1918(c) P/L-R | — | — | — | — | 20.00 | — |
| 1919(c) | 11,162,000 | 0.15 | 0.30 | 0.50 | 2.50 | — |
| 1919(c) Proof | — | Value: 40.00 | | | | |
| 1919(c) P/L-R | — | — | — | — | 20.00 | — |
| 1920(c) | 4,493,000 | 0.15 | 0.30 | 0.50 | 2.50 | — |
| 1920(c) Proof | — | Value: 40.00 | | | | |
| 1920(c) P/L-R | — | — | — | — | 20.00 | — |
| 1921(c) | 6,234,000 | 0.15 | 0.30 | 0.50 | 2.50 | — |
| 1921(c) Proof | — | Value: 40.00 | | | | |
| 1921(c) P/L-R | — | — | — | — | 20.00 | — |
| 1922(c) | 6,336,000 | 0.15 | 0.30 | 0.50 | 2.50 | — |
| 1922(c) Proof | — | Value: 40.00 | | | | |
| 1922(c) P/L-R | — | — | — | — | 20.00 | — |
| 1923(c) | 7,411,000 | 0.15 | 0.30 | 0.50 | 2.50 | — |
| 1923(c) Proof | — | Value: 40.00 | | | | |
| 1923(c) P/L-R | — | — | — | — | 20.00 | — |
| 1924(c) | 9,523,000 | 0.15 | 0.30 | 0.50 | 2.50 | — |
| 1924(c) Proof | — | Value: 40.00 | | | | |
| 1924(c) P/L-R | — | — | — | — | 20.00 | — |
| 1925(c) | 3,981,000 | 0.50 | 0.75 | 1.50 | 4.50 | — |
| 1925(c) Proof | — | Value: 40.00 | | | | |
| 1925(c) P/L-R | — | — | — | — | 20.00 | — |
| 1926(c) | 7,885,000 | 0.15 | 0.30 | 0.50 | 2.50 | — |
| 1926(c) Proof | — | Value: 40.00 | | | | |
| 1926(c) P/L-R | — | — | — | — | 20.00 | — |
| 1927(c) | 5,888,000 | 0.15 | 0.30 | 0.50 | 2.50 | — |
| 1927(c) Proof | — | Value: 40.00 | | | | |
| 1927(c) P/L-R | — | — | — | — | 20.00 | — |
| 1928(c) | 5,456,000 | 0.15 | 0.30 | 0.50 | 2.50 | — |
| 1928(c) Proof | — | Value: 40.00 | | | | |
| 1928(c) P/L-R | — | — | — | — | 20.00 | — |
| 1929(c) | 7,654,000 | 0.15 | 0.30 | 0.50 | 2.50 | — |
| 1929(c) Proof | — | Value: 40.00 | | | | |
| 1929(c) P/L-R | — | — | — | — | 20.00 | — |
| 1930(c) | 7,181,000 | 0.15 | 0.30 | 0.50 | 2.50 | — |
| 1930(c) Proof | — | Value: 40.00 | | | | |
| 1930(c) P/L-R | — | — | — | — | 20.00 | — |
| 1931(c) | 8,794,000 | 0.15 | 0.30 | 0.50 | 2.50 | — |
| 1931(c) Proof | — | Value: 40.00 | | | | |
| 1931(c) P/L-R | — | — | — | — | 20.00 | — |
| 1932(c) | 5,440,000 | 0.15 | 0.30 | 0.50 | 2.50 | — |
| 1932(c) Proof | — | Value: 40.00 | | | | |
| 1932(c) P/L-R | — | — | — | — | 20.00 | — |
| 1933(c) | 9,242,000 | 0.15 | 0.30 | 0.50 | 2.50 | — |
| 1933(c) Proof | — | Value: 40.00 | | | | |
| 1933(c) P/L-R | — | — | — | — | 20.00 | — |
| 1934(c) | 8,947,000 | 0.15 | 0.30 | 0.50 | 2.50 | — |
| 1934(c) Proof | — | Value: 40.00 | | | | |
| 1934(c) P/L-R | — | — | — | — | 20.00 | — |
| 1935(c) | 15,501,000 | 0.15 | 0.30 | 0.50 | 2.50 | — |
| 1935(c) Proof | — | Value: 40.00 | | | | |
| 1935(c) P/L-R | — | — | — | — | 20.00 | — |
| 1936(c) | 26,726,000 | 0.10 | 0.25 | 0.40 | 1.25 | — |
| 1936(c) P/L-R | — | — | — | — | 20.00 | — |

**1/2 PICE** **KM# 528** **Composition:** Bronze **Obverse:** First head; high relief **Obv. Legend:** GEORGE VI KING EMPEROR **Note:** Calcutta Mint issues have no mint mark. Mumbai (Bombay) Mint issues have a small dot below the date.

| Date | Mintage | F | VF | XF | Unc | BU |
|---|---|---|---|---|---|---|
| 1938(c) Proof | — | Value: 30.00 | | | | |
| 1938(c) P/L-R | — | — | — | — | 25.00 | — |
| **Note:** Calcutta Mint reported 11,161,000 mintage for 1938 but only proof and modern prooflike restrikes are known | | | | | | |
| 1939(c) | 17,357,000 | 0.15 | 0.40 | 0.60 | 1.75 | — |
| 1939(c) Proof | — | Value: 30.00 | | | | |
| 1939(b) | 9,343,000 | 0.20 | 0.45 | 0.85 | 3.50 | — |
| 1939(b) Proof | — | Value: 30.00 | | | | |
| 1939(b) P/L-R | — | — | — | — | 25.00 | — |
| 1940(c) | 23,770,000 | 0.15 | 0.40 | 0.65 | 1.75 | — |
| 1940(c) Proof | — | Value: 30.00 | | | | |
| 1940(c) P/L-R | — | — | — | — | 25.00 | — |

**1/2 PICE** **KM# 529** **Composition:** Bronze **Obverse:** Second head; low relief **Obv. Legend:** GEORGE VI KING EMPEROR

| Date | Mintage | F | VF | XF | Unc | BU |
|---|---|---|---|---|---|---|
| 1942(b) Proof | — | Value: 50.00 | | | | |
| 1942(b) P/L-R | — | — | — | — | 35.00 | — |

**1/4 ANNA** **KM# 486b** **Composition:** Silver

| Date | Mintage | F | VF | XF | Unc | BU |
|---|---|---|---|---|---|---|
| 1901(c) P/L-R | — | — | — | — | 75.00 | — |

**1/4 ANNA** **KM# 486c** **Composition:** Gold

| Date | Mintage | F | VF | XF | Unc | BU |
|---|---|---|---|---|---|---|
| 1901(c) P/L-R | — | — | — | — | 750 | — |

**1/4 ANNA** **KM# 501** **Composition:** Copper **Obv. Legend:** EDWARD VII KING & EMPEROR

| Date | Mintage | F | VF | XF | Unc | BU |
|---|---|---|---|---|---|---|
| 1903(c) | 105,974,000 | 0.35 | 1.75 | 7.50 | 35.00 | — |
| 1903(c) Proof | — | Value: 50.00 | | | | |
| 1903(c) P/L-R | — | — | — | — | 25.00 | — |
| 1904(c) | 104,595,000 | 0.35 | 1.75 | 7.50 | 35.00 | — |
| 1904(c) Proof | — | Value: 50.00 | | | | |
| 1904(c) P/L-R | — | — | — | — | 25.00 | — |
| 1905(c) | 130,058,000 | 0.35 | 1.75 | 7.50 | 35.00 | — |
| 1905(c) Proof | — | Value: 50.00 | | | | |
| 1905(c) P/L-R | — | — | — | — | 25.00 | — |
| 1906(c) | 47,229,000 | 0.35 | 1.75 | 7.50 | 35.00 | — |
| 1906(c) Proof | — | Value: 50.00 | | | | |

**1/4 ANNA** **KM# 501b** **Composition:** Silver

| Date | Mintage | F | VF | XF | Unc | BU |
|---|---|---|---|---|---|---|
| 1903(c) P/L-R | — | — | — | — | 100 | — |
| 1904(c) P/L-R | — | — | — | — | 100 | — |
| 1905(c) P/L-R | — | — | — | — | 100 | — |

**1/4 ANNA** **KM# 501a** **Composition:** Nickel

| Date | Mintage | F | VF | XF | Unc | BU |
|---|---|---|---|---|---|---|
| 1906(c) Proof | — | Value: 150 | | | | |

**1/4 ANNA** **KM# 502** **Composition:** Bronze **Obv. Legend:** EDWARD VII KING & EMPEROR **Note:** Thinner planchet.

| Date | Mintage | F | VF | XF | Unc | BU |
|---|---|---|---|---|---|---|
| 1906(c) | 115,786,000 | 0.35 | 1.25 | 6.50 | 30.00 | — |
| 1906(c) Proof | — | Value: 40.00 | | | | |
| 1907(c) | 234,682,000 | 0.35 | 1.25 | 6.50 | 30.00 | — |
| 1907(c) Proof | — | Value: 40.00 | | | | |
| 1907(c) P/L-R | — | — | — | — | 20.00 | — |
| 1908(c) | 58,066,000 | 0.35 | 1.25 | 6.50 | 30.00 | — |
| 1908(c) Proof | — | Value: 40.00 | | | | |
| 1908(c) P/L-R | — | — | — | — | 20.00 | — |
| 1909(c) | 29,966,000 | 0.35 | 1.25 | 6.50 | 30.00 | — |
| 1909(c) Proof | — | Value: 40.00 | | | | |
| 1909(c) P/L-R | — | — | — | — | 20.00 | — |
| 1910(c) | 47,265,000 | 0.35 | 1.25 | 6.50 | 30.00 | — |
| 1910(c) P/L-R | — | — | — | — | 20.00 | — |

**1/4 ANNA** **KM# 502a** **Composition:** Aluminum

| Date | Mintage | VG | F | VF | XF | Unc |
|---|---|---|---|---|---|---|
| 1908(c) Proof | — | Value: 150 | | | | |

**1/4 ANNA** KM# 511 **Composition:** Bronze **Obverse:** Type I **Obv. Legend:** GEORGE V KING EMPEROR **Note:** Calcutta Mint issues have no mint mark. Mumbai (Bombay) Mint issues have a small dot below the date. The pieces dated 1911, like the other coins with that date, show the "Pig" elephant.

| Date | Mintage | F | VF | XF | Unc | BU |
|---|---|---|---|---|---|---|
| 1911(c) | 55,918,000 | 0.75 | 2.00 | 5.00 | 20.00 | — |
| 1911(c) Proof | — | Value: 55.00 | | | | |
| 1911(c) P/L-R | — | — | — | — | 20.00 | — |

**1/4 ANNA** KM# 512 **Composition:** Bronze **Obverse:** Type II **Obv. Legend:** GEORGE V KING EMPEROR

| Date | Mintage | F | VF | XF | Unc | BU |
|---|---|---|---|---|---|---|
| 1912(c) | 107,456,000 | 0.20 | 0.40 | 1.00 | 4.00 | — |
| 1912(c) Proof | — | Value: 35.00 | | | | |
| 1912(c) P/L-R | — | — | — | — | 20.00 | — |
| 1913(c) | 82,061,000 | 0.25 | 0.50 | 1.25 | 4.50 | — |
| 1913(c) Proof | — | Value: 35.00 | | | | |
| 1913(c) P/L-R | — | — | — | — | 20.00 | — |
| 1914(c) | 40,576,000 | 0.50 | 0.75 | 1.50 | 3.50 | — |
| 1914(c) Proof | — | Value: 35.00 | | | | |
| 1914(c) P/L-R | — | — | — | — | 20.00 | — |
| 1916(c) | 1,632,000 | 3.50 | 7.00 | 12.00 | 25.00 | — |
| 1916(c) Proof | — | Value: 50.00 | | | | |
| 1917(c) | 69,370,000 | 0.20 | 0.40 | 0.80 | 3.50 | — |
| 1917(c) Proof | — | Value: 35.00 | | | | |
| 1917(c) P/L-R | — | — | — | — | 20.00 | — |
| 1918(c) | 84,045,000 | 0.20 | 0.40 | 0.80 | 3.50 | — |
| 1918(c) Proof | — | Value: 35.00 | | | | |
| 1918(c) P/L-R | — | — | — | — | 20.00 | — |
| 1919(c) | 212,467,000 | 0.20 | 0.40 | 0.80 | 3.50 | — |
| 1919(c) Proof | — | Value: 35.00 | | | | |
| 1919(c) P/L-R | — | — | — | — | 20.00 | — |
| 1920(c) | 96,019,000 | 0.20 | 0.40 | 0.80 | 3.50 | — |
| 1920(c) Proof | — | Value: 35.00 | | | | |
| 1920(c) P/L-R | — | — | — | — | 20.00 | — |
| 1921(c) Proof | — | Value: 35.00 | | | | |
| 1924(b) | 16,322,000 | 0.20 | 0.40 | 0.80 | 3.50 | — |
| 1924(b) Proof | — | Value: 35.00 | | | | |
| 1925(c) | 14,598,000 | 0.20 | 0.40 | 0.80 | 3.50 | — |
| 1925(b) | 14,588,000 | 0.20 | 0.40 | 0.80 | 3.50 | — |
| 1925(b) Proof | — | Value: 35.00 | | | | |
| 1926(c) | 17,389,000 | 0.20 | 0.40 | 0.80 | 3.50 | — |
| 1926(c) Proof | — | Value: 35.00 | | | | |
| 1926(b) | 16,073,000 | 0.20 | 0.40 | 0.80 | 3.50 | — |
| 1926(b) Proof | — | Value: 35.00 | | | | |
| 1926(b) P/L-R | — | — | — | — | 20.00 | — |
| 1927(c) | 6,925,000 | 0.50 | 0.75 | 1.50 | 4.50 | — |
| 1927(c) Proof | — | Value: 35.00 | | | | |
| 1927(b) | 12,440,000 | 0.20 | 0.40 | 0.80 | 3.50 | — |
| 1927(b) Proof | — | Value: 35.00 | | | | |
| 1927(b) P/L-R | — | — | — | — | 20.00 | — |
| 1928(c) | 257,779,000 | 0.20 | 0.40 | 0.80 | 3.50 | — |
| 1928(c) Proof | — | Value: 35.00 | | | | |
| 1928(b) | 10,057,000 | 0.20 | 0.40 | 0.80 | 3.50 | — |
| 1928(b) Proof | — | Value: 35.00 | | | | |
| 1928(b) P/L-R | — | — | — | — | 20.00 | — |
| 1929(c) | 61,542,000 | 0.20 | 0.40 | 0.80 | 3.50 | — |
| 1929(c) Proof | — | Value: 35.00 | | | | |
| 1929(c) P/L-R | — | — | — | — | 20.00 | — |
| 1930(c) | 40,698,000 | 0.20 | 0.40 | 0.80 | 3.50 | — |
| 1930(c) Proof | — | Value: 35.00 | | | | |
| 1930(b) | 9,646,000 | 0.50 | 0.75 | 1.50 | 4.50 | — |
| 1930(b) Proof | — | Value: 35.00 | | | | |
| 1930(b) P/L-R | — | — | — | — | 20.00 | — |
| 1931(c) | 6,835,000 | 0.50 | 0.75 | 1.50 | 4.50 | — |
| 1931(c) Proof | — | Value: 35.00 | | | | |
| 1931(c) P/L-R | — | — | — | — | 20.00 | — |
| 1933(c) | 40,230,000 | 0.20 | 0.40 | 0.80 | 3.50 | — |
| 1933(c) Proof | — | Value: 35.00 | | | | |
| 1933(c) P/L-R | — | — | — | — | 20.00 | — |
| 1934(c) | 80,506,000 | 0.20 | 0.40 | 0.80 | 3.50 | — |
| 1934(c) Proof | — | Value: 35.00 | | | | |
| 1934(c) P/L-R | — | — | — | — | 20.00 | — |
| 1935(c) | 92,595,000 | 0.20 | 0.40 | 0.80 | 3.50 | — |
| 1935(c) Proof | — | Value: 35.00 | | | | |
| 1935(c) P/L-R | — | — | — | — | 20.00 | — |
| 1936(c) | 227,501,000 | 0.20 | 0.40 | 0.80 | 3.50 | — |
| 1936(b) | 61,926,000 | 0.20 | 0.40 | 0.80 | 3.50 | — |
| 1936(b) Proof | — | Value: 35.00 | | | | |
| 1936(b) P/L-R | — | — | — | — | 20.00 | — |

**1/4 ANNA** KM# 530 **Composition:** Bronze **Obverse:** First head; high relief **Obv. Legend:** GEORGE VI KING EMPEROR

| Date | Mintage | F | VF | XF | Unc | BU |
|---|---|---|---|---|---|---|
| 1938(c) | 33,792,000 | 0.25 | 0.40 | 0.75 | 2.00 | — |
| 1938(c) Proof | — | Value: 35.00 | | | | |
| 1938(b) | 16,796,000 | 0.50 | 0.75 | 1.50 | 4.50 | — |
| 1938(b) P/L-R | — | — | — | — | 30.00 | — |
| 1939(c) | 78,279,000 | 0.30 | 0.50 | 1.00 | 2.50 | — |
| 1939(c) Proof | — | Value: 35.00 | | | | |
| 1939(b) | 60,171,000 | 0.30 | 0.50 | 1.00 | 3.50 | — |
| 1939(b) Proof | — | Value: 35.00 | | | | |
| 1939(b) P/L-R | — | — | — | — | 30.00 | — |
| 1940(b) | 116,721,000 | 0.35 | 0.75 | 1.50 | 3.50 | — |

**1/4 ANNA** KM# 531 **Composition:** Bronze **Obverse:** Second head; low relief **Obv. Legend:** GEORGE VI KING EMPEROR

| Date | Mintage | F | VF | XF | Unc | BU |
|---|---|---|---|---|---|---|
| 1940(c) | 140,410,000 | 0.30 | 0.50 | 1.00 | 3.50 | — |
| 1940(c) Proof | — | Value: 35.00 | | | | |
| 1940(b) | — | 0.30 | 0.50 | 1.00 | 3.50 | — |
| **Note:** Mintage included in KM#530 | | | | | | |
| 1940(b) P/L-R | — | — | — | — | 25.00 | — |
| 1941(c) | 121,107,000 | 0.30 | 0.50 | 1.00 | 3.50 | — |
| 1941(c) P/L-R | — | — | — | — | 25.00 | — |
| 1941(b) | 1,446,000 | 0.40 | 0.90 | 2.00 | 6.00 | — |
| 1942(c) | 34,298,000 | 0.30 | 0.50 | 1.00 | 3.50 | — |
| 1942(b) | 8,768,000 | 0.30 | 0.50 | 1.00 | 3.50 | — |
| 1942(b) P/L-R | — | — | — | — | 25.00 | — |

## PICE

**NOTE:** There are three types of the crown, which is on the obverse at the top. These are shown below and are designated as (RC) Round Crown, (HC) High Crown, and (FC) Flat Crown. Calcutta Mint issues have no mint mark. The issues from the other mints have the mint mark below the date as following: Lahore, raised "L"; Pretoria, small round dot; Bombay, diamond dot or "large" round dot. On the Bombay issues dated 1944 the mint mark appears to be a large dot over a diamond.

Round Crown (RC)

High Crown (HC)

Flat Crown (FC)

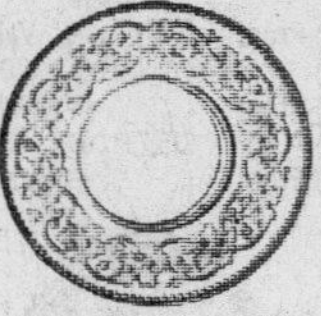

**PICE** KM# 532 **Composition:** Bronze **Obverse:** Small date, small legends

| Date | Mintage | F | VF | XF | Unc | BU |
|---|---|---|---|---|---|---|
| 1943(b) (RC) diamond | 164,659 | 0.30 | 0.50 | 1.00 | 3.50 | — |

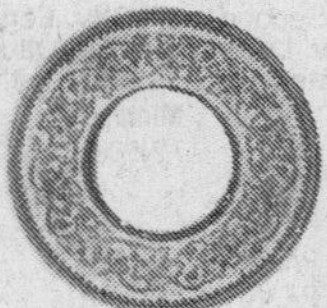

**PICE** KM# 533 **Composition:** Bronze **Obverse:** Large date, large legends

| Date | Mintage | F | VF | XF | Unc | BU |
|---|---|---|---|---|---|---|
| 1943(b) (HC) large dot | — | 0.15 | 0.35 | 0.65 | 1.25 | — |
| 1943(p) (HC) small dot | 98,997,000 | 0.15 | 0.35 | 0.65 | 1.25 | — |
| 1944(c) (HC) | — | 0.15 | 0.35 | 0.65 | 1.25 | — |
| 1944(c) (HC) Proof | — | Value: 25.00 | | | | |
| 1944(b) (HC) large dot | 195,354,000 | 0.15 | 0.35 | 0.65 | 1.25 | — |
| 1944(b) (HC) diamond | — | 0.20 | 0.40 | 0.75 | 2.00 | — |
| 1944(b) (FC) large dot | — | 0.20 | 0.40 | 0.75 | 2.00 | — |
| 1944(b) P/L-R | — | — | — | — | 20.00 | — |
| 1944(p) (HC) small dot | 141,003,000 | 0.20 | 0.40 | 0.75 | 2.00 | — |
| 1944L (HC) | 29,802,000 | 0.20 | 0.40 | 0.80 | 3.50 | — |
| 1945(c) (FC) | 156,322,000 | 0.15 | 0.35 | 0.65 | 1.25 | — |
| 1945(b) (FC) diamond | 237,197,000 | 0.15 | 0.35 | 0.65 | 1.25 | — |
| 1945(b) (FC) large dot | Inc. above | 0.15 | 0.35 | 0.65 | 1.25 | — |
| 1945(b) P/L-R | — | — | — | — | 20.00 | — |
| 1945L (FC) | 238,825,000 | 0.15 | 0.35 | 0.65 | 1.25 | — |
| 1947(c) (HC) | 153,702,000 | 0.15 | 0.35 | 0.65 | 1.25 | — |
| 1947(b) (HC) diamond | 43,654,000 | 0.20 | 0.40 | 0.80 | 3.50 | — |
| 1947(b) Proof | — | Value: 25.00 | | | | |
| 1947 P/L-R | — | — | — | — | 20.00 | — |

**1/2 ANNA** KM# 503 **Composition:** Copper **Obverse:** Head of Edward VII **Reverse:** Similar to KM#487

| Date | Mintage | F | VF | XF | Unc | BU |
|---|---|---|---|---|---|---|
| 1904(c) Proof | — | Value: 2,000 | | | | |

**1/2 ANNA** KM# 534 **Composition:** Copper-Nickel **Obv. Legend:** GEORGE VI KING EMPERPOR **Rev. Legend:** • INDIA •

| Date | Mintage | F | VF | XF | Unc | BU |
|---|---|---|---|---|---|---|
| 1940(c) Proof | — | Value: 325 | | | | |
| 1940(c) P/L-R | — | — | — | — | 50.00 | — |

**1/2 ANNA** KM# 534a **Composition:** Gold

| Date | Mintage | F | VF | XF | Unc | BU |
|---|---|---|---|---|---|---|
| 1940(c) P/L-R | — | — | — | — | 250 | — |

Calcutta Mint struck this denomination each year 1942-1945, denoted by a dot before and after the word "INDIA" on the reverse. Bombay Mint struck only with the dates 1942 and 1945, denoted by "INDIA" without dots before and after. Calcutta also issued proof coins each year while Bombay issued none. However, Bombay later produced proof-like restrikes using old dies from both Bombay and Calcutta indiscriminately; they are all attributed here to Bombay. Source: Pridmore.

**1/2 ANNA** KM# 534b.2 **Composition:** Nickel-Brass **Rev. Legend:** • INDIA •

| Date | Mintage | F | VF | XF | Unc | BU |
|---|---|---|---|---|---|---|
| 1942(c) | 159,000,000 | 0.10 | 0.25 | 0.50 | 2.00 | — |
| 1942(c) Proof | — | Value: 30.00 | | | | |
| 1943(c) | 437,760,000 | 0.10 | 0.25 | 0.50 | 2.00 | — |

| Date | Mintage | F | VF | XF | Unc | BU |
|---|---|---|---|---|---|---|
| 1943(c) Proof | — | Value: 40.00 | | | | |
| 1944(c) | 514,800,000 | 0.10 | 0.25 | 0.50 | 2.00 | — |
| 1944(c) Proof | — | Value: 40.00 | | | | |
| 1945(c) | 215,732,000 | 0.10 | 0.25 | 0.50 | 2.00 | — |
| 1945(c) Proof | — | Value: 40.00 | | | | |

**1/2 ANNA KM# 534b.1 Composition:** Nickel-Brass **Obverse:** Second head **Obv. Legend:** GEORGE VI KING EMPEROR **Rev. Legend:** INDIA (without dots) **Note:** Bombay Mint issues dated 1942-1945 are without a date before and after India.

| Date | Mintage | F | VF | XF | Unc | BU |
|---|---|---|---|---|---|---|
| 1942(b) | 7,945,000 | 0.30 | 0.50 | 1.00 | 3.50 | — |
| 1942(b) P/L-R | — | — | — | — | 40.00 | — |
| 1943(b) P/L-R | — | — | — | — | 40.00 | — |
| 1944(b) P/L-R | — | — | — | — | 40.00 | — |
| 1945(b) P/L-R | — | — | — | — | 25.00 | — |

The Calcutta Mint continued to issue this denomination with the dot before and after INDIA in 1946 and 1947. Bombay also struck in 1946 and 1947, the 1946 issue denoted by a small dot in the center of the dashes before and after the date on the reverse (as well as a dot before and after INDIA, like Calcutta); the characteristics of the 1947 Bombay issue have not been determined but are thought also to resemble the 1946 issue. This denomination is also reported to have been struck in a quantity of 50,829,000 pieces in 1946 at the new Lahore Mint but no way of distinguishing this issue has been found. The proof issue in 1946 was struck by Bombay, not Calcutta. Source: Pridmore.

**1/2 ANNA KM# 535.1 Composition:** Copper-Nickel

| Date | Mintage | F | VF | XF | Unc | BU |
|---|---|---|---|---|---|---|
| 1946(b) | 48,744,000 | 0.10 | 0.25 | 0.50 | 2.00 | — |
| 1946(b) Proof | — | Value: 30.00 | | | | |
| 1946(b) P/L-R | — | — | — | — | 25.00 | — |
| 1947(b) P/L-R | — | — | — | — | 50.00 | — |

**1/2 ANNA KM# 535.2 Composition:** Copper-Nickel

| Date | Mintage | F | VF | XF | Unc | BU |
|---|---|---|---|---|---|---|
| 1946(c) | 75,159,000 | 0.15 | 0.30 | 0.50 | 2.50 | — |
| 1947(c) | 126,392,000 | 0.10 | 0.20 | 0.45 | 1.25 | — |
| 1947(c) Proof | — | Value: 40.00 | | | | |
| 1947(c) P/L-R | — | — | — | — | 25.00 | — |

**ANNA KM# 504 Composition:** Copper-Nickel **Obv. Legend:** EDWARD VII KING & EMPEROR **Note:** Struck only at the Mumbai (Bombay) Mint. Small incuse "B" mint mark in the space below the cross pattee of the crown on the obverse.

| Date | Mintage | F | VF | XF | Unc | BU |
|---|---|---|---|---|---|---|
| 1906B | 200,000 | 20.00 | 50.00 | 125 | 300 | — |
| 1907B | 37,256,000 | 0.50 | 1.25 | 2.00 | 5.00 | — |
| 1907B Proof | — | Value: 60.00 | | | | |
| 1908B | 22,536,000 | 0.50 | 1.25 | 2.00 | 5.00 | — |
| 1908B Proof | — | Value: 60.00 | | | | |
| 1909B | 24,800,000 | 0.50 | 1.25 | 2.00 | 5.00 | — |
| 1909B Proof | — | Value: 60.00 | | | | |
| 1910B | 40,200,000 | 0.50 | 1.25 | 2.00 | 5.00 | — |
| 1910B Proof | — | Value: 60.00 | | | | |

**ANNA KM# 513 Composition:** Copper-Nickel **Obv. Legend:** GEORGE VI KING EMPEROR **Note:** Until 1920, all were struck at the Mumbai (Bombay) Mint without mint mark. From 1923 on, the Bombay Mint issues have a small, raised bead or dot below the date. Calcutta Mint issues hve no mint mark.

| Date | Mintage | F | VF | XF | Unc | BU |
|---|---|---|---|---|---|---|
| 1912(b) | 39,400,000 | 0.40 | 1.00 | 2.50 | 6.00 | — |
| 1912 Proof | — | Value: 50.00 | | | | |
| 1913(b) | 39,776,000 | 0.40 | 1.00 | 2.50 | 6.00 | — |
| 1913 Proof | — | Value: 50.00 | | | | |
| 1914(b) | 48,000,000 | 0.25 | 0.50 | 1.75 | 4.00 | — |
| 1914 Proof | — | Value: 50.00 | | | | |
| 1915(b) | 7,670,000 | 0.40 | 1.00 | 2.50 | 6.00 | — |
| 1915 Proof | — | Value: 50.00 | | | | |
| 1916(b) | 39,087,000 | 0.25 | 0.50 | 1.75 | 4.00 | — |
| 1917(b) | 58,067,000 | 0.25 | 0.50 | 1.75 | 4.00 | — |
| 1917 Proof | — | Value: 50.00 | | | | |
| 1918(b) | 80,692,000 | 0.25 | 0.50 | 1.75 | 4.00 | — |
| 1918(b) Proof | — | Value: 50.00 | | | | |
| 1919(b) | 122,795,000 | 0.25 | 0.50 | 1.75 | 4.00 | — |
| 1919(b) Proof | — | Value: 50.00 | | | | |
| 1919(c) Proof | — | Value: 50.00 | | | | |
| 1920(b) | 9,264,000 | 0.25 | 0.50 | 1.75 | 4.50 | — |
| 1920(b) Proof | — | Value: 50.00 | | | | |
| 1923(b) | 7,125,000 | 0.25 | 0.50 | 1.75 | 4.50 | — |
| 1923(b) Proof | — | Value: 50.00 | | | | |
| 1924(c) | 16,640,000 | 0.25 | 0.50 | 1.75 | 4.00 | — |
| 1924(c) Proof | — | Value: 50.00 | | | | |
| 1924(b) | 17,285,000 | 0.25 | 0.50 | 2.00 | 5.00 | — |
| 1924(b) Proof | — | Value: 50.00 | | | | |
| 1924(b) P/L-R | — | — | — | — | 20.00 | — |
| 1925(c) | 22,388,000 | 0.25 | 0.50 | 2.00 | 5.00 | — |
| 1925(c) Proof | — | Value: 50.00 | | | | |
| 1925(b) | 11,763,000 | 0.25 | 0.50 | 2.00 | 5.00 | — |
| 1925(b) Proof | — | Value: 50.00 | | | | |
| 1925(b) P/L-R | — | — | — | — | 20.00 | — |
| 1926(c) | 13,440,000 | 0.25 | 0.50 | 2.00 | 5.00 | — |
| 1926(c) Proof | — | Value: 50.00 | | | | |
| 1926(b) | 8,088,000 | 0.25 | 0.50 | 2.00 | 5.00 | — |
| 1926(b) Proof | — | Value: 50.00 | | | | |
| 1926(b) P/L-R | — | — | — | — | 20.00 | — |
| 1927(c) | 6,296,000 | 0.40 | 1.00 | 2.50 | 6.00 | — |
| 1927(c) Proof | — | Value: 50.00 | | | | |
| 1927(b) | 12,953,000 | 0.25 | 0.50 | 2.00 | 5.00 | — |
| 1927(b) Proof | — | Value: 50.00 | | | | |
| 1927(b) P/L-R | — | — | — | — | 20.00 | — |
| 1928(c) | 29,568,000 | 1.00 | 1.75 | 3.50 | 8.50 | — |
| 1928(c) Proof | — | Value: 50.00 | | | | |
| 1928(b) | 4,832,000 | 0.25 | 0.50 | 2.00 | 5.00 | — |
| 1928(b) Proof | — | Value: 50.00 | | | | |
| 1928(b) P/L-R | — | — | — | — | 20.00 | — |
| 1929(c) | 42,200,000 | 0.25 | 0.50 | 2.00 | 5.00 | — |
| 1929(c) Proof | — | Value: 50.00 | | | | |
| 1929(c) P/L-R | — | — | — | — | 20.00 | — |
| 1930(c) | 22,816,000 | 0.25 | 0.50 | 2.00 | 5.00 | — |
| 1930(c) Proof | — | Value: 50.00 | | | | |
| 1930(c) P/L-R | — | — | — | — | 20.00 | — |
| 1933(c) | 17,432,000 | 0.25 | 0.50 | 2.00 | 5.00 | — |
| 1933(c) Proof | — | Value: 50.00 | | | | |
| 1933(c) P/L-R | — | — | — | — | 20.00 | — |
| 1934(c) | 34,216,000 | 0.25 | 0.40 | 1.50 | 4.00 | — |
| 1934(c) Proof | — | Value: 50.00 | | | | |
| 1934(c) P/L-R | — | — | — | — | 20.00 | — |
| 1935(c) | 12,952,000 | 0.25 | 0.40 | 1.50 | 4.00 | — |
| 1935(c) Proof | — | Value: 50.00 | | | | |
| 1935(b) | 41,112,000 | 0.25 | 0.40 | 1.50 | 4.00 | — |
| 1935(b) Proof | — | Value: 50.00 | | | | |
| 1935(b) P/L-R | — | — | — | — | 20.00 | — |
| 1936(c) | 21,592,000 | 0.25 | 0.40 | 1.50 | 4.00 | — |
| 1936(b) | 107,136,000 | 0.20 | 0.35 | 1.25 | 3.00 | — |
| 1936(b) Proof | — | Value: 50.00 | | | | |

**ANNA KM# 536 Composition:** Copper-Nickel **Obverse:** First head, high relief **Obv. Legend:** GEORGE VI KING EMPEROR **Note:** Calcutta Mint issues have no mint mark. Bombay Mint issues have a small dot below the date.

| Date | Mintage | VG | F | VF | XF | Unc |
|---|---|---|---|---|---|---|
| 1938(c) | 7,128,000 | — | 0.30 | 0.75 | 1.50 | 5.00 |
| 1938(c) Proof | — | Value: 40.00 | | | | |
| 1938(b) | 3,126,000 | — | 0.40 | 1.00 | 2.00 | 5.00 |
| 1938(b) P/L-R | — | — | — | — | — | 20.00 |
| 1939(c) | 18,192,000 | — | 0.30 | 0.75 | 1.50 | 3.00 |
| 1939(b) | 36,157,000 | — | 0.30 | 0.75 | 1.50 | 3.00 |
| 1939(b) P/L-R | — | — | — | — | — | 20.00 |
| 1940(c) | 60,945,000 | — | 0.30 | 0.75 | 1.50 | 3.00 |
| 1940(c) P/L-R | — | — | — | — | — | 20.00 |
| 1940(b) | — | — | 1.00 | 2.00 | 4.00 | 10.00 |

**ANNA KM# 537 Composition:** Copper-Nickel **Obverse:** Second head, low relief, large crown **Obv. Legend:** GEORGE VI KING EMPEROR **Reverse:** Large "I"

| Date | Mintage | VG | F | VF | XF | Unc |
|---|---|---|---|---|---|---|
| 1940(c) | 76,392,000 | — | 0.10 | 0.25 | 0.50 | 2.00 |
| 1940(c) P/L-R | — | — | — | — | — | 25.00 |
| 1940(b) | 144,712,000 | — | 0.10 | 0.25 | 0.50 | 2.00 |
| 1940(b) P/L-R | — | — | — | — | — | 20.00 |
| 1941(c) | 62,480,000 | — | 0.10 | 0.25 | 0.50 | 2.00 |
| 1941(b) | 40,170,000 | — | 0.15 | 0.40 | 1.00 | 1.50 |
| 1941(b) P/L-R | — | — | — | — | — | 25.00 |

**ANNA KM# 537a Composition:** Nickel-Brass **Obv. Legend:** GEORGE VI KING EMPEROR

| Date | Mintage | VG | F | VF | XF | Unc |
|---|---|---|---|---|---|---|
| 1942(c) | 194,056,000 | — | 0.10 | 0.25 | 0.50 | 2.00 |
| 1942(c) Proof | — | Value: 35.00 | | | | |
| 1942(b) | 103,240,000 | — | 0.15 | 0.40 | 1.00 | 2.50 |
| 1942(b) P/L-R | — | — | — | — | — | 20.00 |
| 1943(c) | 352,256,000 | — | 0.10 | 0.25 | 0.50 | 2.00 |
| 1943(c) Proof | — | Value: 35.00 | | | | |
| 1943(b) | 134,500,000 | — | 0.10 | 0.25 | 0.50 | 2.00 |
| 1943(b) P/L-R | — | — | — | — | — | 20.00 |
| 1944(c) | 457,608,000 | — | 0.10 | 0.25 | 0.50 | 2.00 |
| 1944(c) Proof | — | Value: 35.00 | | | | |
| 1944(b) | 175,208,000 | — | 0.10 | 0.25 | 0.50 | 2.00 |
| 1944(b) P/L-R | — | — | — | — | — | 20.00 |
| 1945(c) | 278,360,000 | — | 0.10 | 0.25 | 0.50 | 2.00 |
| 1945(b) | 61,228,000 | — | 0.20 | 0.40 | 0.80 | 3.50 |

**ANNA KM# 539 Composition:** Copper-Nickel **Obverse:** Second head, low relief, small crown **Obv. Legend:** GEORGE VI KING EMPEROR **Reverse:** Small "I"

| Date | Mintage | VG | F | VF | XF | Unc |
|---|---|---|---|---|---|---|
| 1945(c) | 278,360,000 | — | 0.10 | 0.25 | 0.75 | 2.00 |
| 1945(c) Proof | — | Value: 35.00 | | | | |
| 1945(b) | 61,228,000 | — | 0.10 | 0.25 | 0.75 | 2.00 |
| 1945(b) P/L-R | — | — | — | — | — | 25.00 |

**ANNA KM# 538 Composition:** Copper-Nickel **Obverse:** Second head, low relief, small crown **Obv. Legend:** GEORGE VI KING EMPEROR **Reverse:** Small "I"

| Date | Mintage | F | VF | XF | Unc | BU |
|---|---|---|---|---|---|---|
| 1946(c) | 100,820,000 | 0.10 | 0.15 | 0.35 | 1.50 | — |
| 1946(b) | 82,052,000 | 0.10 | 0.15 | 0.35 | 1.50 | — |
| 1946(b) Proof | — | Value: 40.00 | | | | |
| 1946(b) P/L-R | — | — | — | — | 25.00 | — |
| 1947(c) | 148,656,000 | 0.10 | 0.25 | 0.35 | 1.50 | — |
| 1947(c) Proof | — | Value: 40.00 | | | | |
| 1947(b) | 50,096,000 | 0.10 | 0.25 | 0.50 | 2.00 | — |
| 1947(b) Proof | — | Value: 40.00 | | | | |

**2 ANNAS KM# 488 Weight:** 1.4600 g. **Composition:** 0.9170 Silver .0430 oz. ASW **Obv. Legend:** VICTORIA EMPRESS

| Date | Mintage | F | VF | XF | Unc | BU |
|---|---|---|---|---|---|---|
| 1901C B/II, "C" incuse | 8,944,000 | 1.25 | 2.50 | 5.00 | 10.00 | — |
| 1901C Proof | Inc. above | Value: 35.00 | | | | |
| 1901B B/I, "B" incuse | — | 2.50 | 5.00 | 10.00 | 20.00 | — |
| 1901B B/II, "B" incuse | 1,706,000 | 1.25 | 2.50 | 5.00 | 10.00 | — |
| 1901B Proof | — | Value: 100 | | | | |
| 1901B P/L-R | — | — | — | — | 30.00 | — |

| Date | Mintage | F | VF | XF | Unc | BU |
|---|---|---|---|---|---|---|
| 1901B B/I, "B" raised | — | 2.50 | 5.00 | 10.00 | 20.00 | — |
| 1901B B/II, "B" raised | Inc. above | 1.25 | 2.50 | 5.00 | 10.00 | — |

**2 ANNAS** **KM# 505** **Weight:** 1.4600 g. **Composition:** 0.9170 Silver .0430 oz. ASW **Obverse:** KM#469 **Obv. Legend:** EDWARD VII KING AND EMPEROR **Reverse:** KM#488 **Note:** Mule.

| Date | Mintage | F | VF | XF | Unc | BU |
|---|---|---|---|---|---|---|
| 1903(c) | 4,434,000 | 1.75 | 3.50 | 7.00 | 14.00 | — |
| 1903(c) Proof | — | Value: 65.00 | | | | |
| 1903(c) P/L-R | — | — | — | — | 25.00 | — |
| 1904(c) | 14,632,000 | 1.50 | 3.00 | 6.00 | 12.00 | — |
| 1904(c) Proof | — | Value: 65.00 | | | | |
| 1904(c) P/L-R | — | — | — | — | 25.00 | — |
| 1905(c) | 19,303,000 | 1.50 | 3.00 | 6.00 | 12.00 | — |
| 1905(c) P/L-R | — | — | — | — | 25.00 | — |
| 1906(c) | 13,031,000 | 1.50 | 3.00 | 6.00 | 12.00 | — |
| 1906(c) P/L-R | — | — | — | — | 25.00 | — |
| 1907(c) | 22,145,000 | 1.50 | 3.00 | 6.00 | 12.00 | — |
| 1907(c) Proof | — | Value: 65.00 | | | | |
| 1908(c) | 21,600,000 | 1.50 | 3.00 | 6.00 | 12.00 | — |
| 1908(c) Proof | — | Value: 65.00 | | | | |
| 1908(c) P/L-R | — | — | — | — | 25.00 | — |
| 1909(c) | 6,769,000 | 1.75 | 3.50 | 7.00 | 14.00 | — |
| 1909(c) Proof | — | Value: 65.00 | | | | |
| 1909(c) P/L-R | — | — | — | — | 25.00 | — |
| 1910(c) | 1,604,000 | 1.75 | 3.50 | 7.00 | 14.00 | — |
| 1910(c) Proof | — | Value: 65.00 | | | | |
| 1910(c) P/L-R | — | — | — | — | 25.00 | — |

**2 ANNAS** **KM# 505a** **Composition:** Gold

| Date | Mintage | F | VF | XF | Unc | BU |
|---|---|---|---|---|---|---|
| 1904(c) P/L-R | — | — | — | — | 600 | — |
| 1906(c) P/L-R | — | — | — | — | 600 | — |
| 1910(c) P/L-R | — | — | — | — | 600 | — |

**2 ANNAS** **KM# 514** **Weight:** 1.4600 g. **Composition:** 0.9170 Silver .0430 oz. ASW **Obverse:** Type I **Obv. Legend:** GEORGE V KING EMPEROR

| Date | Mintage | F | VF | XF | Unc | BU |
|---|---|---|---|---|---|---|
| 1911(c) | 16,760,000 | 1.50 | 3.00 | 6.00 | 12.00 | — |
| 1911(c) Proof | — | Value: 75.00 | | | | |
| 1911(c) P/L-R | — | — | — | — | 50.00 | — |

**2 ANNAS** **KM# 515** **Weight:** 1.4600 g. **Composition:** 0.9170 Silver .0430 oz. ASW **Obverse:** Type II **Obv. Legend:** GEORGE V KING EMPEROR

| Date | Mintage | F | VF | XF | Unc | BU |
|---|---|---|---|---|---|---|
| 1912(c) | 7,724,000 | 1.25 | 2.50 | 5.00 | 10.00 | — |
| 1912(c) Proof | — | Value: 50.00 | | | | |
| 1912(b) | 2,462,000 | 1.50 | 3.00 | 6.00 | 12.00 | — |
| 1912(b) Proof | — | Value: 50.00 | | | | |
| 1912(b) P/L-R | — | — | — | — | 25.00 | — |
| 1913(c) | 13,959,000 | 1.25 | 2.50 | 5.00 | 10.00 | — |
| 1913(c) Proof | — | Value: 50.00 | | | | |
| 1913(b) | 5,461,000 | 1.25 | 2.50 | 5.00 | 10.00 | — |
| 1913(b) Proof | — | Value: 50.00 | | | | |
| 1913(b) P/L-R | — | — | — | — | 25.00 | — |
| 1914(c) | 13,622,000 | 1.25 | 2.50 | 5.00 | 10.00 | — |
| 1914(c) Proof | — | Value: 50.00 | | | | |
| 1914(b) | 8,579,000 | 1.25 | 2.50 | 5.00 | 10.00 | — |
| 1914(b) P/L-R | — | — | — | — | 25.00 | — |
| 1915(c) | 5,892,000 | 1.25 | 2.50 | 5.00 | 10.00 | — |
| 1915(c) Proof | — | Value: 50.00 | | | | |
| 1915(b) | 5,943,000 | 1.25 | 2.50 | 5.00 | 10.00 | — |
| 1915(b) P/L-R | — | — | — | — | 25.00 | — |
| 1916(c) | 197,878,000 | 1.25 | 2.00 | 4.00 | 8.00 | — |
| 1916(c) Proof | — | Value: 50.00 | | | | |
| 1916(c) P/L-R | — | — | — | — | 25.00 | — |
| 1917(c) | 25,560,000 | 1.25 | 2.00 | 4.00 | 8.00 | — |
| 1917(c) Proof | — | Value: 50.00 | | | | |
| 1917(c) P/L-R | — | — | — | — | 25.00 | — |

**2 ANNAS** **KM# 516** **Composition:** Copper-Nickel **Obv. Legend:** GEORGE V KING EMPEROR **Note:** Calcutta Mint issues have no mint mark. Bombay Mint issues have a small raised dot on the reverse at the bottom near the rim.

| Date | Mintage | F | VF | XF | Unc | BU |
|---|---|---|---|---|---|---|
| 1918(c) | 53,412,000 | 1.25 | 1.75 | 4.00 | 10.00 | — |
| 1918(c) Proof | — | Value: 50.00 | | | | |
| 1918(b) | 9,191,000 | 1.25 | 1.75 | 4.00 | 10.00 | — |
| 1918(b) Proof | — | Value: 50.00 | | | | |
| 1918(b) P/L-R | — | — | — | — | 20.00 | — |
| 1919(c) | 89,040,000 | 1.25 | 1.75 | 4.00 | 10.00 | — |
| 1919(c) Proof | — | Value: 50.00 | | | | |
| 1919(c) P/L-R | — | — | — | — | 20.00 | — |
| 1920(b) Proof | — | Value: 125 | | | | |
| 1920(c) | 13,520,000 | 1.25 | 1.75 | 4.00 | 10.00 | — |
| 1920(c) Proof | — | Value: 50.00 | | | | |
| 1923(c) | 7,656,000 | 1.25 | 1.75 | 4.00 | 10.00 | — |
| 1923(c) Proof | — | Value: 50.00 | | | | |
| 1923(b) | 6,431,000 | 1.25 | 1.75 | 4.00 | 10.00 | — |
| 1923(b) Proof | — | Value: 50.00 | | | | |
| 1923(b) P/L-R | — | — | — | — | 20.00 | — |
| 1924(c) | 8,384,000 | 1.25 | 1.75 | 4.00 | 10.00 | — |
| 1924(c) Proof | — | Value: 50.00 | | | | |
| 1924(b) | 4,818,000 | 1.50 | 3.00 | 6.00 | 12.00 | — |
| 1924(b) Proof | — | Value: 50.00 | | | | |
| 1924(b) P/L-R | — | — | — | — | 20.00 | — |
| 1925(c) | 10,848,000 | 1.25 | 1.75 | 4.00 | 10.00 | — |
| 1925(c) Proof | — | Value: 50.00 | | | | |
| 1925(b) | 8,348,000 | 1.25 | 1.75 | 4.00 | 10.00 | — |
| 1925(b) Proof | — | Value: 50.00 | | | | |
| 1925(b) P/L-R | — | — | — | — | 220 | — |
| 1926(c) | 8,352,000 | 1.25 | 1.75 | 4.00 | 10.00 | — |
| 1926(c) Proof | — | Value: 50.00 | | | | |
| 1926(b) | 2,927,000 | 1.75 | 3.50 | 7.00 | 14.00 | — |
| 1926(b) Proof | — | Value: 50.00 | | | | |
| 1926(b) P/L-R | — | — | — | — | 20.00 | — |
| 1927(c) | 6,424,000 | 1.25 | 1,375 | 4.00 | 10.00 | — |
| 1927(c) Proof | — | Value: 50.00 | | | | |
| 1927(b) | 4,835,000 | 1.50 | 3.00 | 6.00 | 12.00 | — |
| 1927(b) Proof | — | Value: 50.00 | | | | |
| 1927(b) P/L-R | — | — | — | — | 20.00 | — |
| 1928(c) | 7,352,000 | 1.25 | 1.75 | 4.00 | 10.00 | — |
| 1928(c) Proof | — | Value: 50.00 | | | | |
| 1928(b) | 4,876,000 | 1.50 | 3.00 | 6.00 | 12.00 | — |
| 1928(b) Proof | — | Value: 50.00 | | | | |
| 1928(b) P/L-R | — | — | — | — | 20.00 | — |
| 1929(c) | 13,408,000 | 1.25 | 1.75 | 4.00 | 10.00 | — |
| 1929(c) Proof | — | Value: 50.00 | | | | |
| 1929(c) P/L-R | — | — | — | — | 20.00 | — |
| 1930(c) | 8,888,000 | 1.25 | 1.75 | 4.00 | 10.00 | — |
| 1930(c) Proof | — | Value: 50.00 | | | | |
| 1930(c) P/L-R | — | — | — | — | 20.00 | — |
| 1930(b) | — | 1.25 | 1.75 | 4.00 | 10.00 | — |
| 1933(c) | 4,300,000 | 1.50 | 3.00 | 6.00 | 12.00 | — |
| 1933(c) Proof | — | Value: 50.00 | | | | |
| 1933(c) P/L-R | — | — | — | — | 20.00 | — |
| 1934(c) | 7,016,000 | 1.25 | 1.75 | 4.00 | 10.00 | — |
| 1934(c) Proof | — | Value: 50.00 | | | | |
| 1934(c) P/L-R | — | — | — | — | 20.00 | — |
| 1935(c) | 12,344,000 | 1.25 | 1.75 | 4.00 | 10.00 | — |
| 1935(b) | 21,017,000 | 1.00 | 1.50 | 3.00 | 8.00 | — |
| 1935(b) Proof | — | Value: 50.00 | | | | |
| 1935(b) P/L-R | — | — | — | — | 20.00 | — |
| 1936(b) | 36,295,000 | 1.00 | 1.50 | 3.00 | 8.00 | — |
| 1936(b) Proof | — | Value: 50.00 | | | | |

**2 ANNAS** **KM# 540** **Composition:** Copper-Nickel **Obverse:** First head, high relief **Obv. Legend:** GEORGE VI KING EMPEROR **Note:** Calcutta Mint issues have no mint mark. Bombay Mint issues have a small dot before and after the date.

| Date | Mintage | F | VF | XF | Unc | BU |
|---|---|---|---|---|---|---|
| 1939(c) | 4,148,000 | 1.25 | 3.00 | 6.00 | 15.00 | — |
| 1939(b) | 3,392,000 | 2.00 | 5.00 | 10.00 | 25.00 | — |

**2 ANNAS** **KM# 541** **Composition:** Copper-Nickel **Obverse:** Second head, low relief, large crown **Obv. Legend:** GEORGE VI KING EMPEROR

| Date | Mintage | F | VF | XF | Unc | BU |
|---|---|---|---|---|---|---|
| 1939(c) | Inc. above | 1.25 | 2.00 | 2.50 | 4.00 | — |
| 1939(c) Proof | — | Value: 40.00 | | | | |
| 1939(b) | Inc. above | 0.20 | 0.30 | 0.50 | 1.50 | — |
| 1939(b) Proof | — | Value: 40.00 | | | | |
| 1939(b) P/L-R | — | — | — | — | 25.00 | — |
| 1940(c) | 37,636,000 | 0.20 | 0.30 | 0.50 | 2.00 | — |
| 1940(c) Proof | — | Value: 40.00 | | | | |
| 1940(b) | 50,599,000 | 0.20 | 0.30 | 0.50 | 2.00 | — |
| 1940(b) P/L-R | — | — | — | — | 25.00 | — |
| 1941(c) | 63,456,000 | 0.20 | 0.30 | 0.50 | 1.50 | — |
| 1941(b) | 10,760,000 | 1.25 | 2.00 | 2.50 | 4.00 | — |
| 1941(b) Proof | — | Value: 40.00 | | | | |
| 1941(b) P/L-R | — | — | — | — | 25.00 | — |

**2 ANNAS** **KM# 541a** **Composition:** Nickel-Brass **Obv. Legend:** GEORGE VI KING EMPEROR

| Date | Mintage | F | VF | XF | Unc | BU |
|---|---|---|---|---|---|---|
| 1942(b) Small 4 | 133,000,000 | 0.25 | 0.35 | 0.50 | 2.25 | — |
| 1942(b) Large 4 | Inc. above | 0.20 | 0.35 | 0.50 | 2.25 | — |
| 1943(b) | 343,680,000 | 0.25 | 0.35 | 0.50 | 2.25 | — |
| 1944L | 6,352,000 | 0.50 | 1.25 | 2.00 | 5.00 | — |
| **Note:** On 1944 Lahore issues, a tiny L replaces the decorative stroke in the four quatrefoil angles. | | | | | | |
| 1944(b) Small 4 | 219,700,000 | 0.25 | 0.35 | 0.50 | 2.25 | — |
| 1944(b) Large 4 | Inc. above | 0.25 | 0.35 | 0.50 | 2.25 | — |

**2 ANNAS** **KM# 543** **Composition:** Nickel-Brass **Obverse:** Second head, low relief, large crown **Obv. Legend:** GEORGE VI KING EMPEROR **Reverse:** Small "2"

| Date | Mintage | F | VF | XF | Unc | BU |
|---|---|---|---|---|---|---|
| 1945(c) | 24,260,000 | 0.25 | 0.75 | 1.25 | 2.75 | — |
| 1945(c) Proof | — | Value: 40.00 | | | | |
| 1945(b) | 136,688,000 | 0.25 | 0.35 | 0.50 | 1.50 | — |
| 1945(b) P/L-R | — | — | — | — | 25.00 | — |

**2 ANNAS** **KM# 542** **Composition:** Copper-Nickel **Obverse:** Second head, low relief, small crown **Obv. Legend:** GEORGE VI KING EMPEROR **Reverse:** Small "2"

| Date | Mintage | F | VF | XF | Unc | BU |
|---|---|---|---|---|---|---|
| 1946(c) | 67,267,000 | 0.20 | 0.30 | 0.50 | 2.25 | — |
| 1946(c) | 52,500,000 | 0.20 | 0.30 | 0.50 | 2.25 | — |
| 1946(b) Proof | — | Value: 40.00 | | | | |
| 1946(b) P/L-R | — | — | — | — | 25.00 | — |
| 1946(l) | 25,480,000 | 0.20 | 0.30 | 0.50 | 2.25 | — |
| **Note:** Without "L" mintmark but with small diamond-shaped mark left of "I" on reverse | | | | | | |
| 1947(c) | 57,428,000 | 0.20 | 0.30 | 0.50 | 2.25 | — |
| 1947(b) | 38,908,000 | 0.20 | 0.30 | 0.50 | 2.25 | — |
| 1947(b) Proof | — | Value: 40.00 | | | | |
| 1947(b) P/L-R | — | — | — | — | 25.00 | — |

## 1/4 RUPEE

**NOTE:** The distinguishing features of the 3 busts and 2 reverses are as following:

**BUST A -** The front of dress has 4 panels w/flower at right on bottom panel.

**BUST B -** Front of dress has 3-3/4 panels w/flower at center on incomplete bottom panel.

**BUST C -** Front of dress has 3 panels w/flower at left on bottom panel.

**REVERSE I -** The 2 large petals above the base of the top flower are long and curved downward; long stroke between "1/4".

**REVERSE II -** The 2 large petals above the base of the top flower are short and horizontal; short stroke between "1/4".

**1/4 RUPEE** **KM# 490** **Weight:** 2.9200 g. **Composition:** 0.9170 Silver .0860 oz. ASW **Obverse:** 5 Rupee, KM#476 **Obv. Legend:** VICTORIA EMPRRESS **Reverse:** 1/4 Rupee, KM#470

| Date | Mintage | F | VF | XF | Unc | BU |
|---|---|---|---|---|---|---|
| 1901C C/II, "C" incuse | 4,476,000 | 2.00 | 3.00 | 6.00 | 15.00 | — |
| 1901C Proof | — | Value: 125 | | | | |
| 1901C P/L-R | — | — | — | — | 30.00 | — |

**1/4 RUPEE** **KM# 506** **Weight:** 2.9200 g. **Composition:** 0.9170 Silver .0860 oz. ASW **Obv. Legend:** EDWARD VII KING AND EMPEROR

| Date | Mintage | F | VF | XF | Unc | BU |
|---|---|---|---|---|---|---|
| 1903(c) | 7,060,000 | 1.50 | 3.00 | 8.00 | 20.00 | — |
| 1903(c) Proof | — | Value: 100 | | | | |
| 1903(c) P/L-R | — | — | — | — | 30.00 | — |
| 1904(c) | 10,026,000 | 1.50 | 3.00 | 8.00 | 20.00 | — |
| 1904(c) Proof | — | Value: 100 | | | | |
| 1904(c) P/L-R | — | — | — | — | 30.00 | — |
| 1905(c) | 6,300,000 | 1.50 | 3.00 | 8.00 | 20.00 | — |
| 1905(c) Proof | — | Value: 100 | | | | |
| 1905(c) P/L-R | — | — | — | — | 30.00 | — |
| 1906(c) | 10,672,000 | 1.50 | 3.00 | 8.00 | 20.00 | — |
| 1906(c) P/L-R | — | — | — | — | 30.00 | — |
| 1907(c) | 11,464,000 | 1.50 | 3.00 | 8.00 | 20.00 | — |
| 1907(c) Proof | — | Value: 100 | | | | |
| 1907(c) P/L-R | — | — | — | — | 30.00 | — |
| 1908(c) | 7,084,000 | 1.50 | 3.00 | 8.00 | 20.00 | — |
| 1908(c) Proof | — | Value: 100 | | | | |
| 1908(c) P/L-R | — | — | — | — | 30.00 | — |
| 1909(c) Proof | — | Value: 125 | | | | |
| 1909(c) P/L-R | — | — | — | — | 30.00 | — |
| 1910(c) | 8,024,000 | 1.50 | 3.00 | 8.00 | 20.00 | — |
| 1910(c) Proof | — | Value: 100 | | | | |
| 1910(c) P/L-R | — | — | — | — | 30.00 | — |

**1/4 RUPEE** **KM# 506a** **Composition:** Gold

| Date | Mintage | F | VF | XF | Unc | BU |
|---|---|---|---|---|---|---|
| 1910(c) P/L-R | — | — | — | — | 800 | — |

**1/4 RUPEE** **KM# 517** **Weight:** 2.9200 g. **Composition:** 0.9170 Silver .0860 oz. ASW **Obverse:** Type I **Obv. Legend:** GEORGE V KING EMPEROR

| Date | Mintage | F | VF | XF | Unc | BU |
|---|---|---|---|---|---|---|
| 1911(c) | 2,245,000 | 2.00 | 4.00 | 8.00 | 8.00 | — |
| 1911(c) Proof | — | Value: 90.00 | | | | |
| 1911(c) P/L-R | — | — | — | — | 60.00 | — |

**1/4 RUPEE** **KM# 518** **Weight:** 2.9200 g. **Composition:** 0.9170 Silver .0860 oz. ASW **Obverse:** Type II **Obv. Legend:** GEORGE V KING EMPEROR

| Date | Mintage | F | VF | XF | Unc | BU |
|---|---|---|---|---|---|---|
| 1912(c) | 9,587,000 | 2.00 | 2.75 | 5.00 | 12.00 | — |
| 1912(c) Proof | — | Value: 65.00 | | | | |
| 1912(b) | 2,200,000 | 2.00 | 2.75 | 5.00 | 12.00 | — |
| 1912(b) Proof | — | Value: 65.00 | | | | |
| 1912(b) P/L-R | — | — | — | — | 22.00 | — |
| 1913(c) | 12,686,000 | 2.00 | 2.75 | 5.00 | 12.00 | — |
| 1913(c) Proof | — | Value: 65.00 | | | | |
| 1913(b) | 2,276,000 | 2.00 | 2.75 | 5.00 | 12.00 | — |
| 1913(b) Proof | — | Value: 65.00 | | | | |
| 1913(b) P/L-R | — | — | — | — | 22.00 | — |
| 1914(c) | 1,423,000 | 2.00 | 2.75 | 5.00 | 12.00 | — |
| 1914(c) Proof | — | Value: 65.00 | | | | |
| 1914(b) | 7,949,000 | 2.00 | 2.75 | 5.00 | 10.00 | — |
| 1914(b) P/L-R | — | — | — | — | 22.00 | — |
| 1915(c) | 851,000 | 2.25 | 4.00 | 10.00 | 35.00 | — |
| 1915(c) Proof | — | Value: 65.00 | | | | |
| 1915(b) | 2,096,000 | 2.00 | 2.75 | 5.00 | 12.00 | — |
| 1915(b) P/L-R | — | — | — | — | 22.00 | — |
| 1916(c) | 13,178,000 | 2.00 | 2.75 | 5.00 | 12.00 | — |
| 1916(c) Proof | — | Value: 65.00 | | | | |
| 1916(c) P/L-R | — | — | — | — | 22.00 | — |
| 1917(c) | 21,072,000 | 2.00 | 2.75 | 5.00 | 12.00 | — |
| 1917(c) Proof | — | Value: 65.00 | | | | |
| 1917(c) P/L-R | — | — | — | — | 22.00 | — |
| 1918(c) | 50,575,000 | 2.00 | 2.75 | 5.00 | 12.00 | — |
| 1918(c) Proof | — | Value: 65.00 | | | | |
| 1919(b) | — | 3.50 | 7.50 | 15.00 | 30.00 | — |
| 1919(c) | 26,135,000 | 2.00 | 2.75 | 5.00 | 12.00 | — |
| 1919(c) Proof | — | Value: 65.00 | | | | |
| 1920(b) | — | 3.25 | 6.50 | 12.50 | 25.00 | — |
| 1925(b) | 4,007,000 | 2.00 | 2.75 | 5.00 | 12.00 | — |
| 1925(b) Proof | — | Value: 65.00 | | | | |
| 1925(b) P/L-R | — | — | — | — | 22.00 | — |
| 1926(c) | 8,169,000 | 2.00 | 2.75 | 5.00 | 12.00 | — |
| 1926(c) Proof | — | Value: 65.00 | | | | |
| 1926(c) P/L-R | — | — | — | — | 22.00 | — |
| 1928(b) | 4,023,000 | 2.00 | 2.75 | 5.00 | 12.00 | — |
| 1928(b) Proof | — | Value: 65.00 | | | | |
| 1929(c) | 4,013,000 | 2.00 | 2.75 | 5.00 | 12.00 | — |
| 1929(c) Proof | — | Value: 65.00 | | | | |
| 1929(c) P/L-R | — | — | — | — | 22.00 | — |
| 1930(c) | 3,222,000 | 2.00 | 2.75 | 5.00 | 12.00 | — |
| 1930(c) Proof | — | Value: 65.00 | | | | |
| 1930(c) P/L-R | — | — | — | — | 22.00 | — |
| 1934(c) | 3,946,000 | 2.00 | 2.75 | 5.00 | 10.00 | — |
| 1936(c) | 25,744,000 | 1.25 | 2.25 | 4.00 | 8.00 | — |
| 1936(b) | 9,864,000 | 1.25 | 2.25 | 4.00 | 8.00 | — |
| 1936(b) P/L-R | — | — | — | — | 22.00 | — |

First Head

Second Head (small) Second Head (large)

From 1942 to 1945 the reverse designs of the silver coins change slightly every year. However, a distinct reverse variety occurs on Rupees and 1/4 Rupees dated 1943-44 and on the half Rupee dated 1944, all struck at Bombay. This variety may be distinguished from the other coins by the design of the center bottom flower as illustrated, and is designated as Reverse B.

On the normal common varieties dated 1943-44 the three "scalloped circles" are not connected to each other and the bead in the center is not attached to the nearest circle.

**Obv: First head, reeded edge.**

**NOTE:** Calcutta Mint issues have no mint mark. Bombay coins have a small bead below the lotus flower at the bottom on the reverse, except those dated 1943-1944 with reverse B which have a diamond. Lahore Mint issues have a small "L" in the same position. The nickel coins have a diamond below the date on the reverse.

**1/4 RUPEE** **KM# 544** **Weight:** 2.9200 g. **Composition:** 0.9170 Silver .0860 oz. ASW **Obv. Legend:** GEORGE VI KING EMPEROR

| Date | Mintage | F | VF | XF | Unc | BU |
|---|---|---|---|---|---|---|
| 1938(c) Proof | — | Value: 65.00 | | | | |
| 1938(c) P/L-R | — | — | — | — | 25.00 | — |
| 1939(c) | 3,072,000 | 2.00 | 3.50 | 6.00 | 12.00 | — |
| 1939(c) Proof | — | Value: 65.00 | | | | |
| 1939(b) | 6,770,000 | 2.00 | 3.50 | 5.00 | 10.00 | — |
| 1939(b) P/L-R | — | — | — | — | 25.00 | — |

**1/4 RUPEE** **KM# 544a** **Weight:** 2.9200 g. **Composition:** 0.5000 Silver .0469 oz. ASW **Obv. Legend:** GEORGE VI KING EMPEROR

| Date | Mintage | F | VF | XF | Unc | BU |
|---|---|---|---|---|---|---|
| 1940(b) | 24,635,000 | 2.00 | 3.50 | 5.00 | 10.00 | — |

**1/4 RUPEE** **KM# 545** **Weight:** 2.9200 g. **Composition:** 0.5000 Silver .0469 oz. ASW **Obverse:** Large second head, small rim decoration **Obv. Legend:** GEORGE VI KING EMPEROR **Edge:** Reeded

| Date | Mintage | VG | F | VF | XF | Unc |
|---|---|---|---|---|---|---|
| 1940(c) | 68,675,000 | — | BV | 1.50 | 2.50 | 6.00 |
| 1940(c) Proof | — | Value: 65.00 | | | | |
| 1940(b) | 28,947,000 | — | BV | 1.50 | 2.50 | 6.00 |

**1/4 RUPEE** **KM# 546** **Weight:** 2.9200 g. **Composition:** 0.5000 Silver .0469 oz. ASW **Obverse:** Small second head, large rim decoration **Obv. Legend:** GEORGE VI KING EMPEROR **Edge:** Reeded

| Date | Mintage | F | VF | XF | Unc | BU |
|---|---|---|---|---|---|---|
| 1942(c) | 88,096,000 | BV | 1.50 | 2.25 | 4.50 | — |
| 1943(c) | 90,994,000 | BV | 1.50 | 2.25 | 4.50 | — |

**1/4 RUPEE** **KM# 547** **Weight:** 2.9200 g. **Composition:** 0.5000 Silver .0469 oz. ASW **Obverse:** Small second head, large rim decoration **Obv. Legend:** GEORGE VI KING EMPEROR **Edge:** Security

| Date | Mintage | F | VF | XF | Unc | BU |
|---|---|---|---|---|---|---|
| 1943B | 95,200,000 | BV | 1.50 | 2.25 | 4.50 | — |
| 1943B Proof | — | Value: 60.00 | | | | |
| 1943B Reverse B | Inc. above | BV | 1.50 | 2.25 | 4.50 | — |
| 1943L | 23,700,000 | BV | 1.50 | 2.25 | 4.50 | — |
| 1944B | 170,504,000 | BV | 1.50 | 2.25 | 4.50 | — |
| 1944B Reverse B | Inc. above | BV | 1.50 | 2.25 | 4.50 | — |
| 1944L | 86,400,000 | BV | 1.50 | 2.25 | 4.50 | — |
| 1945(b) Small 5 | 181,648,000 | BV | 1.50 | 2.25 | 4.50 | — |
| 1945(b) Large 5 | Inc. above | 10.00 | 15.00 | 25.00 | 40.00 | — |
| 1945L Small 5 | 29,751,000 | BV | 1.50 | 2.25 | 4.50 | — |
| 1945L Large 5 | Inc. above | BV | 1.00 | 2.00 | 5.00 | — |

**1/4 RUPEE** **KM# 548** **Composition:** Nickel **Obv. Legend:** GEORGE VI KING EMPEROR **Reverse:** Indian tiger **Edge:** Reeded

| Date | Mintage | F | VF | XF | Unc | BU |
|---|---|---|---|---|---|---|
| 1946(b) | 83,600,000 | 0.40 | 0.75 | 1.50 | 5.00 | — |
| 1947(b) | 109,948,000 | 0.40 | 0.75 | 1.50 | 5.00 | — |
| 1947(b) Proof | — | Value: 50.00 | | | | |

**4 ANNAS** **KM# 519** **Composition:** Copper-Nickel **Obv. Legend:** GEORGE V KING EMPEROR • INDIA • **Note:**

Calcutta Mint issues have no mint mark. Bombay Mint issues have a small raised dot on the reverse at the bottom near the rim.

| Date | Mintage | F | VF | XF | Unc | BU |
|---|---|---|---|---|---|---|
| 1919(c) | 18,632 | 2.50 | 5.00 | 10.00 | 20.00 | — |
| 1919(c) Proof | — | Value: 150 | | | | |
| 1919(b) | 7,672,000 | 3.25 | 6.50 | 12.50 | 25.00 | — |
| 1919 P/L-R | — | — | — | — | 25.00 | — |
| 1920(c) | 18,191,000 | 2.50 | 5.00 | 10.00 | 20.00 | — |
| 1920(c) Proof | — | Value: 150 | | | | |
| 1920(b) | 1,666,000 | 3.25 | 6.50 | 12.50 | 25.00 | — |
| 1920(b) Proof | — | Value: 150 | | | | |
| 1920(b) P/L-R | — | — | — | — | 25.00 | — |
| 1921(c) Proof | — | Value: 150 | | | | |
| 1921(c) P/L-R | — | — | — | — | 25.00 | — |
| 1921(b) | 1,219,000 | 3.75 | 7.50 | 15.00 | 30.00 | — |
| 1921(b) Proof | — | — | — | — | 150 | — |

**8 ANNAS** **KM# 520** **Composition:** Copper-Nickel **Obv. Legend:** GEORGE V KING EMPEROR **Note:** Calcutta Mint issues have no mint mark. Bombay Mint issues have a small raised dot on the reverse at the bottom near the rim.

| Date | Mintage | F | VF | XF | Unc | BU |
|---|---|---|---|---|---|---|
| 1919(c) | 2,980,000 | 3.75 | 7.50 | 15.00 | 30.00 | — |
| 1919(c) Proof | — | Value: 150 | | | | |
| 1919(b) | 1,400,000 | 4.00 | 8.50 | 17.50 | 35.00 | — |
| 1919(b) P/L-R | — | — | — | — | 30.00 | — |
| 1920(c) Proof | — | Value: 150 | | | | |
| 1920(c) P/L-R | — | — | — | — | 75.00 | — |
| 1920(b) | 1,000,000 | 12.50 | 25.00 | 50.00 | 100 | — |
| 1920(b) Proof | — | Value: 150 | | | | |
| 1920(b) P/L-R | — | — | — | — | 30.00 | — |

**1/2 RUPEE** **KM# 507** **Weight:** 5.8300 g. **Composition:** 0.9170 Silver .1719 oz. ASW **Obv. Legend:** EDWARD VII KING AND EMPEROR **Note:** Calcutta Mint issues have no mint mark. Bombay Mint issues have a small incuse B in the space below the cross pattee of the crown on the reverse.

| Date | Mintage | F | VF | XF | Unc | BU |
|---|---|---|---|---|---|---|
| 1904(c) Proof | — | Value: 175 | | | | |
| 1904(c) P/L-R | — | — | — | — | 40.00 | — |
| 1905(c) | 823,000 | 3.50 | 10.00 | 25.00 | 50.00 | — |
| 1905(c) P/L-R | — | — | — | — | 40.00 | — |
| 1906(c) | 3,036,000 | 3.50 | 10.00 | 25.00 | 50.00 | — |
| 1906B | 400,000 | 3.75 | 12.50 | 30.00 | 60.00 | — |
| 1906B P/L-R | — | — | — | — | 40.00 | — |
| 1907(c) | 2,786,000 | 3.50 | 10.00 | 25.00 | 50.00 | — |
| 1907(c) Proof | — | Value: 150 | | | | |
| 1907B | 1,856,000 | 3.50 | 10.00 | 25.00 | 50.00 | — |
| 1907B Proof | — | Value: 150 | | | | |
| 1907B P/L-R | — | — | — | — | 40.00 | — |
| 1908(c) | 1,577,000 | 3.50 | 10.00 | 25.00 | 50.00 | — |
| 1908(c) Proof | — | Value: 150 | | | | |
| 1908(c) P/L-R | — | — | — | — | 40.00 | — |
| 1909(c) | 1,569,000 | 3.50 | 10.00 | 25.00 | 50.00 | — |
| 1909(c) Proof | — | Value: 150 | | | | |
| 1909(c) P/L-R | — | — | — | — | 40.00 | — |
| 1909B Proof | — | Value: 450 | | | | |
| 1909B P/L-R | — | — | — | — | 90.00 | — |
| 1910(c) | 3,413,000 | 3.50 | 10.00 | 25.00 | 50.00 | — |
| 1910(c) Proof | — | Value: 150 | | | | |
| 1910B | 809,000 | 3.50 | 10.00 | 25.00 | 50.00 | — |
| 1910B "B" raised | — | 10.00 | 15.00 | 30.00 | 55.00 | — |
| 1910B Proof | — | Value: 150 | | | | |
| 1910B P/L-R | — | — | — | — | 40.00 | — |

**1/2 RUPEE** **KM# 521** **Weight:** 5.8300 g. **Composition:** 0.9170 Silver .1719 oz. ASW **Obverse:** Type I **Obv. Legend:** GEORGE V KING EMPEROR **Note:** Calcutta Mint issues have no mint mark. Bombay Mint issues have a small raised bead or dot in the space below the lotus flower at the bottom of the reverse. The half Rupee dated 1911 like the Rupee and all the other issues of that year has the PIG elephant. It was struck only at the Calcutta Mint.

| Date | Mintage | F | VF | XF | Unc | BU |
|---|---|---|---|---|---|---|
| 1911(c) | 2,293,000 | 2.00 | 6.00 | 12.50 | 30.00 | — |
| 1911(c) Proof | — | Value: 175 | | | | |
| 1911(c) P/L-R | — | — | — | — | 75.00 | — |

**1/2 RUPEE** **KM# 522** **Weight:** 5.8300 g. **Composition:** 0.9170 Silver .1719 oz. ASW **Obverse:** Type II **Obv. Legend:** GEORGE V KING EMPEROR

| Date | Mintage | F | VF | XF | Unc | BU |
|---|---|---|---|---|---|---|
| 1912(c) | 3,390,000 | 2.00 | 6.00 | 12.00 | 28.00 | — |
| 1912(c) Proof | — | Value: 125 | | | | |
| 1912(b) | 1,505,000 | 2.00 | 6.00 | 12.00 | 28.00 | — |
| 1912(b) Proof | — | Value: 125 | | | | |
| 1912(b) P/L-R | — | — | — | — | 22.00 | — |
| 1913(c) | 2,723,000 | 2.00 | 6.00 | 12.00 | 28.00 | — |
| 1913(c) Proof | — | Value: 125 | | | | |
| 1913(b) | 1,825,000 | 2.00 | 6.00 | 12.00 | 28.00 | — |
| 1913(b) Proof | — | Value: 125 | | | | |
| 1913(b) P/L-R | — | — | — | — | 22.00 | — |
| 1914(c) | 1,400,000 | 2.00 | 6.00 | 12.00 | 28.00 | — |
| 1914(c) Proof | — | Value: 125 | | | | |
| 1914(b) | 903,000 | 2.00 | 6.00 | 12.50 | 30.00 | — |
| 1914(b) P/L-R | — | — | — | — | 22.00 | — |
| 1915(c) | 2,804,000 | 2.00 | 6.00 | 12.00 | 28.00 | — |
| 1915(c) Proof | — | Value: 125 | | | | |
| 1916(c) | 3,644,000 | 2.00 | 6.00 | 12.00 | 28.00 | — |
| 1916(c) Proof | — | Value: 125 | | | | |
| 1916(b) | 5,880,000 | 2.00 | 6.00 | 12.00 | 28.00 | — |
| 1917(c) Proof | — | Value: 125 | | | | |
| 1917(b) | 8,822,000 | 2.00 | 6.00 | 12.00 | 28.00 | — |
| 1917(b) Proof | — | Value: 125 | | | | |
| 1918(c) P/L-R | — | — | — | — | 22.00 | — |
| 1918(b) P/L-R | — | — | — | — | 22.00 | — |
| 1918(b) | 10,325,000 | 2.00 | 6.00 | 12.00 | 28.00 | — |
| 1919(b) | 8,958,000 | 2.00 | 6.00 | 12.00 | 28.00 | — |
| 1919(b) Proof | — | Value: 125 | | | | |
| 1919(b) P/L-R | — | — | — | — | 22.00 | — |
| 1919(c) P/L-R | — | — | — | — | 22.00 | — |
| 1921(c) | 5,804,000 | 2.00 | 6.00 | 12.00 | 28.00 | — |
| 1921(c) Proof | — | Value: 125 | | | | |
| 1921(c) P/L-R | — | — | — | — | 22.00 | — |
| 1922(c) | 5,551,000 | 2.00 | 6.00 | 12.00 | 28.00 | — |
| 1922(c) Proof | — | Value: 125 | | | | |
| 1922(b) | 1,037,000 | 2.00 | 6.00 | 12.00 | 28.00 | — |
| 1922(b) Proof | — | Value: 125 | | | | |
| 1922(b) P/L-R | — | — | — | — | 22.00 | — |
| 1923(c) | 3,925,000 | 2.00 | 6.00 | 12.00 | 28.00 | — |
| 1923(c) P/L-R | — | — | — | — | 22.00 | — |
| 1923(b) | 2,076,000 | 2.00 | 6.00 | 12.00 | 28.00 | — |
| 1923(b) Proof | — | Value: 125 | | | | |
| 1923(b) P/L-R | — | — | — | — | 22.00 | — |
| 1924(c) | 4,007,000 | 2.00 | 6.00 | 12.00 | 28.00 | — |
| 1924(c) Proof | — | Value: 125 | | | | |
| 1924(b) | 2,664,000 | 2.00 | 6.00 | 12.00 | 28.00 | — |
| 1924(b) Proof | — | Value: 125 | | | | |
| 1924(b) P/L-R | — | — | — | — | 22.00 | — |
| 1925(c) | 4,119,000 | 2.00 | 6.00 | 12.00 | 28.00 | — |
| 1925(c) Proof | — | Value: 125 | | | | |
| 1925(b) | 1,627,000 | 2.00 | 6.00 | 12.00 | 28.00 | — |
| 1925(b) Proof | — | Value: 125 | | | | |
| 1925(b) P/L-R | — | — | — | — | 22.00 | — |
| 1926(c) | 4,027,000 | 2.00 | 6.00 | 12.00 | 28.00 | — |
| 1926(c) Proof | — | Value: 125 | | | | |
| 1926(b) | 2,011,000 | 2.00 | 6.00 | 12.00 | 28.00 | — |
| 1926(b) Proof | — | Value: 125 | | | | |
| 1926(b) P/L-R | — | — | — | — | 22.00 | — |
| 1927(c) | 2,032,000 | 2.00 | 6.00 | 12.00 | 28.00 | — |
| 1927(c) Proof | — | Value: 125 | | | | |
| 1927(c) P/L-R | — | — | — | — | 22.00 | — |
| 1928(b) | 2,466,000 | 2.00 | 6.00 | 12.00 | 28.00 | — |
| 1928(b) Proof | — | Value: 125 | | | | |
| 1929(c) | 4,050,000 | 2.00 | 6.00 | 12.00 | 28.00 | — |
| 1929(c) Proof | — | Value: 125 | | | | |
| 1929(c) P/L-R | — | — | — | — | 22.00 | — |
| 1930(c) | 2,036,000 | 2.00 | 6.00 | 12.00 | 28.00 | — |
| 1930(c) Proof | — | Value: 125 | | | | |
| 1930(c) P/L-R | — | — | — | — | 22.00 | — |
| 1933/2(c) | 4,056,000 | 5.00 | 10.00 | 25.00 | 50.00 | — |
| 1933(c) | Inc. above | 2.00 | 6.00 | 12.00 | 28.00 | — |
| 1933(c) Proof | — | Value: 75.00 | | | | |
| 1933(c) P/L-R | — | — | — | — | 22.00 | — |
| 1934(c) | 4,056,000 | 2.00 | 6.00 | 12.00 | 28.00 | — |
| 1934(c) Proof | — | Value: 125 | | | | |
| 1934(c) P/L-R | — | — | — | — | 22.00 | — |
| 1936(c) | 16,919,000 | 2.00 | 6.00 | 12.00 | 28.00 | — |
| 1936(b) | 6,693,000 | 2.00 | 6.00 | 12.00 | 28.00 | — |
| 1936(b) P/L-R | — | — | — | — | 22.00 | — |

**Obv: First head, reeded edge.**

**NOTE:** Calcutta Mint issues have no mint mark. Bombay coins dated 1938-43 and 1945 have a bead below the lotus flower at the bottom of the reverse. Specimens dated 1944 with Reverse B have a diamond in the same position. Those dated 1944 with the normal common reverse have either a bead or a diamond. Lahore Mint issues have a small raised "L" in the same position as the Bombay coins. Bombay Mint 1943 coins have either large or small denticles on obverse. The nickel pieces of the last issue have a diamond below the date on the reverse.

**1/2 RUPEE** **KM# 549** **Weight:** 5.8300 g. **Composition:** 0.9170 Silver .1719 oz. ASW **Obverse:** First head **Obv. Legend:** GEORGE VI KING EMPEROR **Edge:** Reeded

| Date | Mintage | F | VF | XF | Unc | BU |
|---|---|---|---|---|---|---|
| 1938(c) Proof | — | Value: 100 | | | | |
| 1938(b) | 2,200,000 | BV | 3.00 | 7.50 | 15.00 | — |
| 1938(b) P/L-R | — | — | — | — | 25.00 | — |
| 1939(c) | 3,300,000 | BV | 3.00 | 7.50 | 15.00 | — |
| 1939(c) Proof | — | Value: 75.00 | | | | |
| 1939(b) | 10,096,000 | BV | 3.00 | 7.50 | 15.00 | — |
| 1939(b) Proof | — | Value: 75.00 | | | | |
| 1939(b) P/L-R | — | — | — | — | 25.00 | — |

**1/2 RUPEE** **KM# A553** **Composition:** Copper-Nickel **Obverse:** KM#552 **Obv. Legend:** GEORGE VI KING EMPEROR **Reverse:** KM#549 **Note:** Mule

| Date | Mintage | F | VF | XF | Unc | BU |
|---|---|---|---|---|---|---|
| 1938(c) P/L-R | — | — | — | — | — | — |

**1/2 RUPEE** **KM# 550** **Weight:** 5.8300 g. **Composition:** 0.9170 Silver .1719 oz. ASW **Obverse:** Large second head, small rim decoration **Obv. Legend:** GEORGE VI KING EMPEROR **Edge:** Reeded

| Date | Mintage | VG | F | VF | XF | Unc |
|---|---|---|---|---|---|---|
| 1939(c) | Inc. above | — | BV | 3.00 | 6.50 | 15.00 |
| 1939(b) | Inc. above | — | BV | 3.00 | 6.50 | 13.50 |

**1/2 RUPEE** **KM# 550a** **Weight:** 5.8300 g. **Composition:** 0.5000 Silver .0937 oz. ASW **Obv. Legend:** GEORGE VI KING EMPEROR

| Date | Mintage | F | VF | XF | Unc | BU |
|---|---|---|---|---|---|---|
| 1940(c) | 32,898,000 | BV | 3.00 | 6.00 | 12.00 | — |
| 1940(c) Proof | — | Value: 75.00 | | | | |
| 1940(b) | 17,811,000 | BV | 3.00 | 6.50 | 13.50 | — |
| 1940(b) P/L-R | — | — | — | — | 25.00 | — |

**1/2 RUPEE** **KM# 551** **Weight:** 5.8300 g. **Composition:** 0.5000 Silver .0937 oz. ASW **Obverse:** Large second head, small rim decoration **Obv. Legend:** GEORGE VI KING EMPEROR **Edge:** Security

| Date | Mintage | VG | F | VF | XF | Unc |
|---|---|---|---|---|---|---|
| 1941(b) | 26,100,000 | — | BV | 2.00 | 5.00 | 12.50 |
| 1942(b) | 61,600,000 | — | BV | 2.00 | 5.00 | 12.50 |

**1/2 RUPEE** KM# 552 **Weight:** 5.8300 g. **Composition:** 0.5000 Silver .0937 oz. ASW **Obverse:** Small second head, large rim decoration **Obv. Legend:** GEORGE VI KING EMPEROR **Reverse:** Denomination and inner circle smaller **Edge:** Security

| Date | Mintage | F | VF | XF | Unc | BU |
|---|---|---|---|---|---|---|
| 1942(b) | Inc. above | BV | 2.00 | 4.50 | 9.00 | — |
| 1943(b) Dot | 90,400,000 | BV | 2.00 | 4.50 | 9.00 | — |
| 1943(b) Proof | — | Value: 75.00 | | | | |
| 1943(b) Diamond | — | BV | 2.00 | 4.50 | 9.00 | — |
| 1943L | 9,000,000 | BV | 2.00 | 4.50 | 9.00 | — |
| 1943L Proof | — | Value: 75.00 | | | | |
| 1944(b) Dot | 46,200,000 | BV | 2.00 | 4.50 | 9.00 | — |
| 1944(b) Diamond | Inc. above | BV | 2.00 | 4.50 | 9.00 | — |
| 1944L | 79,100,000 | BV | 2.00 | 4.50 | 9.00 | — |
| 1944L Proof | — | Value: 75.00 | | | | |
| 1945(b) Small 5 | 32,722,000 | BV | 2.00 | 4.50 | 9.00 | — |
| 1945(b) Large 5 | — | 20.00 | 25.00 | 35.00 | 50.00 | — |
| 1945L Small dot | 79,192,000 | BV | 2.00 | 4.50 | 9.00 | — |
| 1945L Proof | — | Value: 75.00 | | | | |
| 1945L Large dot | Inc. above | 2.50 | 5.00 | 10.00 | 20.00 | — |

**1/2 RUPEE** KM# 553 **Composition:** Nickel **Obv. Legend:** GEORGE VI KING EMPEROR **Reverse:** Indian tiger **Edge:** Reeded

| Date | Mintage | F | VF | XF | Unc | BU |
|---|---|---|---|---|---|---|
| 1946(b) | 47,500,000 | 0.50 | 1.00 | 2.25 | 4.50 | — |
| 1947(b) | 62,724,000 | 0.50 | 1.00 | 2.00 | 4.00 | — |
| 1947(b) Proof | — | Value: 65.00 | | | | |

**RUPEE** KM# 492 **Weight:** 11.6600 g. **Composition:** 0.9170 Silver .3438 oz. ASW **Obv. Legend:** VICTORIA EMPRESS

| Date | Mintage | F | VF | XF | Unc | BU |
|---|---|---|---|---|---|---|
| 1901C C/I, "C" incuse | 72,017,000 | 5.00 | 8.00 | 12.00 | 25.00 | — |
| 1901C Proof | Inc. above | Value: 175 | | | | |
| 1901B A/I, "B" incuse | 130,258,000 | 5.00 | 8.00 | 12.00 | 25.00 | — |
| 1901B Proof | — | Value: 175 | | | | |
| 1901B P/L-R | — | — | — | — | 35.00 | — |
| 1901B C/I, "B" incuse | Inc. above | 5.00 | 8.00 | 12.00 | 25.00 | — |

**RUPEE** KM# 508 **Composition:** Gold **Obv. Legend:** EDWARD VII KING & EMPEROR **Note:** Calcutta Mint issues have no mint mark. Mumbai (Bombay) Mint issues have a small incuse "B" in the space below the cross pattee of the crown on the reverse.

| Date | Mintage | F | VF | XF | Unc | BU |
|---|---|---|---|---|---|---|
| 1903(c) | 49,403,000 | 5.00 | 8.00 | 12.00 | 25.00 | — |
| 1903(c) Proof | — | Value: 350 | | | | |
| 1903B In relief | 52,969 | 5.00 | 8.00 | 12.00 | 25.00 | — |
| 1903B Proof | — | Value: 350 | | | | |
| 1903B Incuse | Inc. above | 5.00 | 8.00 | 12.00 | 25.00 | — |
| 1903B P/L-R | — | — | — | — | 30.00 | — |
| 1904(c) | 58,339,000 | 5.00 | 8.00 | 12.00 | 25.00 | — |
| 1904(c) Proof | — | Value: 350 | | | | |
| 1904B | 101,949,000 | 5.00 | 8.00 | 12.00 | 25.00 | — |
| 1904B Proof | — | Value: 350 | | | | |
| 1904B P/L-R | — | — | — | — | 30.00 | — |
| 1905(c) | 51,258,000 | 5.00 | 8.00 | 12.00 | 25.00 | — |
| 1905(c) Proof | — | Value: 350 | | | | |
| 1905B | 76,202,000 | 5.00 | 8.00 | 12.00 | 25.00 | — |
| 1905B Proof | — | Value: 350 | | | | |
| 1905B P/L-R | — | — | — | — | 30.00 | — |
| 1906(c) | 104,797,000 | 5.00 | 8.00 | 15.00 | 30.00 | — |
| 1906B | 158,953,000 | 5.00 | 8.00 | 15.00 | 30.00 | — |
| 1906B Proof | — | Value: 350 | | | | |
| 1906B P/L-R | — | — | — | — | 30.00 | — |
| 1907(c) | 81,338,000 | 5.00 | 8.00 | 15.00 | 30.00 | — |
| 1907(c) Proof | — | Value: 350 | | | | |
| 1907B | 170,912,000 | 5.00 | 8.00 | 15.00 | 30.00 | — |
| 1907B Proof | — | Value: 350 | | | | |
| 1907B P/L-R | — | — | — | — | 30.00 | — |
| 1908(c) | 20,218,000 | 5.00 | 8.00 | 15.00 | 30.00 | — |
| 1908(c) Proof | — | Value: 350 | | | | |
| 1908B | 10,715,000 | 8.50 | 15.00 | 30.00 | 60.00 | — |
| 1908B Proof | — | Value: 350 | | | | |
| 1908B P/L-R | — | — | — | — | 30.00 | — |
| 1909(c) | 12,759,000 | 5.00 | 8.00 | 15.00 | 30.00 | — |
| 1909(c) Proof | — | Value: 350 | | | | |
| 1909B | 9,539,000 | 8.50 | 15.00 | 30.00 | 60.00 | — |
| 1909B Proof | — | Value: 350 | | | | |
| 1909B P/L-R | — | — | — | — | 30.00 | — |
| 1910(c) | 12,627,000 | 5.00 | 8.00 | 15.00 | 30.00 | — |
| 1910(c) Proof | — | Value: 350 | | | | |
| 1910B | 10,885,000 | 5.00 | 8.00 | 15.00 | 30.00 | — |
| 1910B Proof | — | Value: 350 | | | | |
| 1910B P/L-R | — | — | — | — | 30.00 | — |

**NOTE:** Calcutta Mint issues have no mint mark. Bombay Mint issues have a small raised bead or dot in the space below the lotus flower at the bottom of the reverse.

**Obverse Dies**

Type I

Type II

**Type I -** Obv. die w/elephant with pig-like feet and short tail. Nicknamed "pig rupee".
**Type II -** Obv. die w/redesigned elephant with outlined ear, heavy feet and long tail.

The Rupees dated 1911 were rejected by the public because the elephant, on the Order of the Indian Empire shown on the King's robe, was thought to resemble a pig, an animal considered unclean by most Indians. Out of a total of 9.4 million pieces struck at both mints, only 700,000 were issued, and many of these were withdrawn and melted with unissued pieces. The issues dated 1912 and later have a re-designed elephant.

**RUPEE** KM# 523 **Composition:** Gold **Obverse:** Type I **Obv. Legend:** GEORGE V KING EMPEROR

| Date | Mintage | F | VF | XF | Unc | BU |
|---|---|---|---|---|---|---|
| 1911(c) | 4,300 | 10.00 | 20.00 | 40.00 | 100 | — |
| 1911(c) Proof | — | Value: 600 | | | | |
| 1911(b) | 5,143,000 | 10.00 | 20.00 | 40.00 | 100 | — |
| 1911(b) P/L-R | — | — | — | — | 75.00 | — |

**RUPEE** KM# 524 **Composition:** Gold **Obverse:** Type II **Obv. Legend:** GEORGE V KING EMPEROR

| Date | Mintage | F | VF | XF | Unc | BU |
|---|---|---|---|---|---|---|
| 1912(c) | 45,122,000 | 5.00 | 9.50 | 15.00 | 35.00 | — |
| 1912(c) Proof | — | Value: 500 | | | | |
| 1912(b) | 79,067,000 | 5.00 | 8.00 | 12.50 | 25.00 | — |
| 1912(b) Proof | — | Value: 500 | | | | |
| 1912B P/L-R | — | — | — | — | 30.00 | — |
| 1913(c) | 75,800,000 | 5.00 | 8.00 | 12.50 | 25.00 | — |
| 1913(c) Proof | — | Value: 500 | | | | |
| 1913(b) | 87,466,000 | 5.00 | 8.00 | 12.50 | 25.00 | — |
| 1913(b) Proof | — | Value: 500 | | | | |
| 1913(b) P/L-R | — | — | — | — | 30.00 | — |
| 1914(c) | 33,100,000 | 5.00 | 8.00 | 12.50 | 25.00 | — |
| 1914(c) Proof | — | Value: 500 | | | | |
| 1914(b) | 15,270,000 | 5.00 | 8.00 | 12.50 | 25.00 | — |
| 1914(b) Proof | — | Value: 500 | | | | |
| 1914(b) P/L-R | — | — | — | — | 30.00 | — |
| 1915(c) | 9,900,000 | 8.50 | 15.00 | 30.00 | 60.00 | — |
| 1915(c) Proof | — | Value: 500 | | | | |
| 1915(b) | 5,372,000 | 10.00 | 20.00 | 40.00 | 80.00 | — |
| 1915(b) Proof | — | Value: 500 | | | | |
| 1915(b) P/L-R | — | — | — | — | 30.00 | — |
| 1916(c) | 115,000,000 | 5.00 | 8.00 | 12.50 | 20.00 | — |
| 1916(c) Proof | — | Value: 500 | | | | |
| 1916(b) | 97,900,000 | 5.00 | 8.00 | 12.50 | 20.00 | — |
| 1916(b) Proof | — | — | — | — | — | — |
| 1916(b) P/L-R | — | — | — | — | 30.00 | — |
| 1917(c) | 114,974,000 | 5.00 | 8.00 | 12.50 | 20.00 | — |
| 1917(c) Proof | — | Value: 500 | | | | |
| 1917(b) | 151,583,000 | 5.00 | 8.00 | 12.50 | 20.00 | — |
| 1917(b) Proof | — | Value: 500 | | | | |
| 1917(b) P/L-R | — | — | — | — | 30.00 | — |
| 1918(c) | 205,420,000 | 5.00 | 8.00 | 12.50 | 20.00 | — |
| 1918(c) Proof | — | Value: 500 | | | | |
| 1918(b) | 210,550,000 | 5.00 | 8.00 | 12.50 | 20.00 | — |
| 1918(b) Proof | — | Value: 500 | | | | |
| 1918(b) P/L-R | — | — | — | — | 30.00 | — |
| 1919(c) | 211,206,000 | 5.00 | 8.00 | 12.50 | 20.00 | — |
| 1919(c) Proof | — | Value: 500 | | | | |
| 1919(c) | 226,706,000 | 5.00 | 8.00 | 12.50 | 20.00 | — |
| 1919(b) Proof | — | Value: 500 | | | | |
| 1919(b) P/L-R | — | — | — | — | 30.00 | — |
| 1920(c) | 50,500,000 | 5.00 | 8.00 | 12.50 | 20.00 | — |
| 1920(c) Proof | — | Value: 500 | | | | |
| 1920(b) | 55,937,000 | 5.00 | 8.00 | 12.50 | 20.00 | — |
| 1920(b) Proof | — | Value: 500 | | | | |
| 1920B P/L-R | — | — | — | — | 30.00 | — |
| 1921(b) | 5,115,000 | 12.00 | 22.00 | 45.00 | 125 | — |
| 1921(b) Proof | — | Value: 500 | | | | |
| 1922(b) | 2,051,000 | 12.00 | 22.00 | 45.00 | 125 | — |
| 1922(b) Proof | — | Value: 500 | | | | |
| 1935(c) Proof | — | Value: 500 | | | | |
| 1935(c) P/L-R | — | — | — | — | 125 | — |
| 1936(c) Proof | — | Value: 500 | | | | |

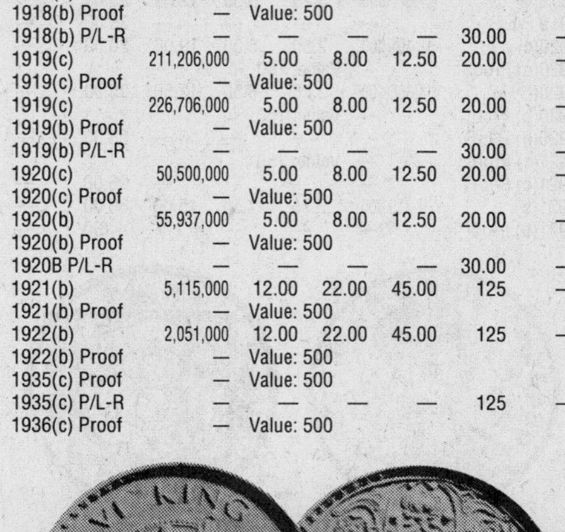

**RUPEE** KM# 554 **Composition:** Gold **Obverse:** First head **Obv. Legend:** GEORGE VI KING EMPEROR **Edge:** Reeded

| Date | Mintage | F | VF | XF | Unc | BU |
|---|---|---|---|---|---|---|
| 1938(c) Proof | — | Value: 275 | | | | |
| 1939(c) Proof | — | Value: 350 | | | | |

**NOTE:** No rupees with the "First Head" were struck for circulation. Those dated 1938-39 were struck in 1940 before the fineness of the silver coins was reduced to .500.

The pieces struck at Calcutta have no mint mark. Bombay issues dated 1938-41 and 1944-45 have a bead below the lotus flower at the bottom of the reverse while those dated 1942-44 have a small diamond mark in the same position. On the specimens dated 1944 with Reverse B the mint mark appears to be a "bead over a diamond". Lahore Mint issues have a small raised "L" in the same position as the Bombay coins. The last issue nickel rupees struck at Bombay have a small diamond below the date on the reverse. The rupees dated 1943 occur with large and small "Second Head" and with

**RUPEE** KM# 555 **Composition:** Gold **Obverse:** Second head, small rim decoration **Obv. Legend:** GEORGE VI KING EMPEROR **Edge:** Reeded

| Date | Mintage | F | VF | XF | Unc | BU |
|---|---|---|---|---|---|---|
| 1938(b) Without dot | 7,352,000 | 7.50 | 11.50 | 16.50 | 27.50 | — |
| 1938(b) Dot | Inc. above | 7.50 | 11.50 | 16.50 | 27.50 | — |
| 1938(b) P/L-R | — | — | — | — | 50.00 | — |
| 1939(b) Dot | 2,450,000 | 150 | 300 | 600 | 1,200 | — |

**RUPEE** KM# A559 **Composition:** Copper-Nickel **Obverse:** KM#557 **Obv. Legend:** GEORGE VI KING EMPEROR **Reverse:** KM#555 **Note:** Mule

| Date | Mintage | F | VF | XF | Unc | BU |
|---|---|---|---|---|---|---|
| 1938(c) P/L-R | — | — | — | — | 150 | — |

**RUPEE** KM# 556 **Weight:** 11.6600 g. **Composition:** 0.5000 Silver .1874 oz. ASW **Obv. Legend:** GEORGE VI KING EMPEROR **Edge:** Security

| Date | Mintage | F | VF | XF | Unc | BU |
|---|---|---|---|---|---|---|
| 1939(b) | — | 200 | 400 | 800 | 1,500 | — |
| 1940(b) | 153,120,000 | BV | 4.00 | 10.00 | 20.00 | — |
| 1941(b) | 111,480,000 | BV | 4.00 | 10.00 | 20.00 | — |
| 1943(b) | — | BV | 4.00 | 10.00 | 20.00 | — |

**Note:** 1943(b) mintage included with KM#557.1.

**RUPEE** KM# 557.1 **Weight:** 11.6600 g. **Composition:** 0.5000 Silver .1874 oz. ASW **Obverse:** Small second head, large rim decoration **Obv. Legend:** GEORGE VI KING EMPEROR **Edge:** Security

| Date | Mintage | F | VF | XF | Unc | BU |
|---|---|---|---|---|---|---|
| 1942(b) Without dot | 7,352,000 | BV | 4.00 | 10.00 | 20.00 | — |
| 1943(b) | 65,995,000 | BV | 4.00 | 10.00 | 20.00 | — |
| 1943(b) Reverse B | Inc. above | BV | 4.00 | 10.00 | 20.00 | — |
| 1944(b) Reverse B | 146,206,000 | BV | 4.00 | 10.00 | 20.00 | — |
| 1944(b) | Inc. above | BV | 4.00 | 10.00 | 20.00 | — |
| 1944L Small L | 91,400,000 | BV | 4.00 | 10.00 | 20.00 | — |
| 1944L Large L | Inc. above | BV | 4.00 | 10.00 | 20.00 | — |
| 1945(b) Small 5 | 142,666,000 | BV | 3.00 | 6.00 | 12.50 | — |
| 1945(b) Large 5 | Inc. above | 30.00 | 35.00 | 45.00 | 60.00 | — |
| 1945(b) Proof | — | — | — | — | — | — |
| 1945L | 118,126,000 | BV | 3.00 | 6.00 | 12.50 | — |

**RUPEE** KM# 557a **Composition:** Copper-Nickel **Obv. Legend:** GEORGE VI KING EMPEROR

| Date | Mintage | F | VF | XF | Unc | BU |
|---|---|---|---|---|---|---|
| 1943(b) P/L-R | — | — | — | — | 125 | — |

**RUPEE** KM# 557.2 **Weight:** 11.6600 g. **Composition:** 0.5000 Silver .1874 oz. ASW **Edge:** Reeded (error)

| Date | Mintage | F | VF | XF | Unc | BU |
|---|---|---|---|---|---|---|
| 1944(b) | — | — | — | — | — | — |
| 1945(b) | — | — | — | — | — | — |

**RUPEE** KM# 559 **Composition:** Nickel **Reverse:** Indian tiger **Edge:** Security

| Date | Mintage | F | VF | XF | Unc | BU |
|---|---|---|---|---|---|---|
| 1947(b) | 118,028,000 | 1.50 | 2.50 | 5.00 | 10.00 | — |
| 1947B Proof | — | Value: 75.00 | | | | |

**Note:** Mumbai (Bombay) issue has diamond mark below date

| Date | Mintage | F | VF | XF | Unc | BU |
|---|---|---|---|---|---|---|
| 1947(l) | 41,911,000 | 1.50 | 3.00 | 6.00 | 12.00 | — |

**Note:** Lahore without privy mark

**15 RUPEES** KM# 525 **Weight:** 7.9881 g. **Composition:** 0.9170 Gold .2354 oz. AGW **Obv. Legend:** GEORGE V KING EMPEROR **Note:** This issue is equal in weight and fineness to the British sovereign.

| Date | Mintage | F | VF | XF | Unc | BU |
|---|---|---|---|---|---|---|
| 1918(b) | 2,110,000 | 200 | 275 | 350 | 475 | — |
| 1918(b) Proof | 12 | Value: 2,500 | | | | |
| 1918(b) P/L-R | — | — | — | — | 500 | — |

## TRADE COINAGE

The Mansfield Commission of 1868 allowed for the admission of British and Australian sovereigns (see Australian section; sovereigns with shield reverse were struck for export to India) as payment for sums due.

The fifth branch of the Royal Mint was established in a section of the Mumbai (Bombay) Mint as of December 21, 1917. This was a war-time measure, its purpose being to strike into sovereigns the gold blanks supplied by the Mumbai and other Indian mints. The Mumbai sovereigns bear the mint mark "I" and were struck from August 15, 1918 to April 22, 1919. The branch mint was closed in May, 1919.

**SOVEREIGN** KM# 525A **Weight:** 7.9881 g. **Composition:** 0.9170 Gold .2354 oz. AGW

| Date | Mintage | F | VF | XF | Unc | BU |
|---|---|---|---|---|---|---|
| 1918I | 1,295,000 | 110 | 125 | 155 | 200 | — |
| 1918I Proof | — | — | — | — | — | — |
| 1918I P/L-R | — | — | — | — | 575 | — |

## BULLION COINAGE

**TOLA** KM# 496A **Weight:** 11.7000 g. **Composition:** 0.9960 Gold .3747 oz. AGW

| Date | Mintage | VG | F | VF | XF | Unc |
|---|---|---|---|---|---|---|
| ND(1931) | — | — | — | BV | 175 | 225 |

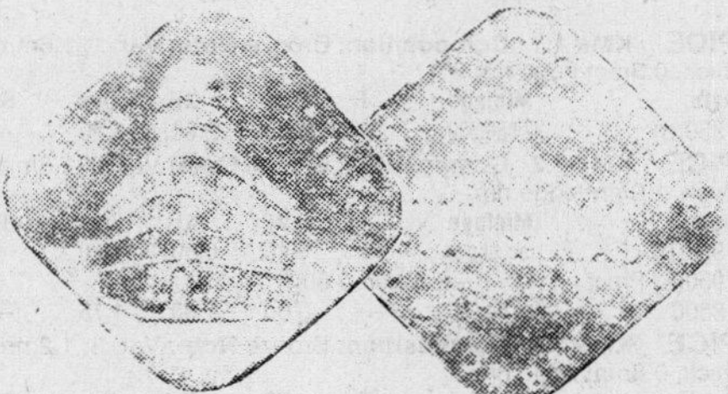

**5 TOLAS** KM# 496B **Weight:** 58.5000 g. **Composition:** 0.9957 Gold 1.8727 oz. AGW

| Date | Mintage | VG | F | VF | XF | Unc |
|---|---|---|---|---|---|---|
| ND(1931) | — | — | — | BV | 850 | 1,100 |

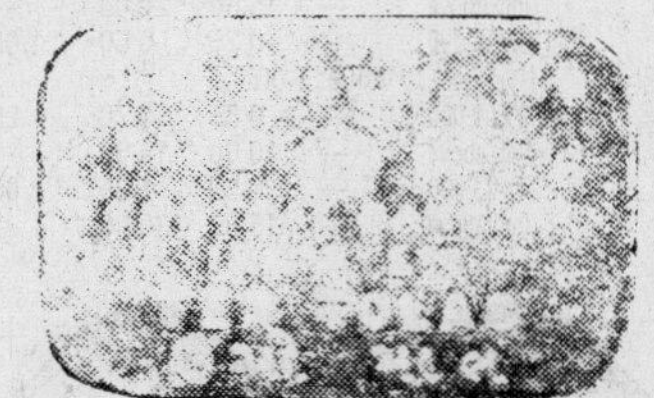

**10 TOLAS** KM# 496C **Weight:** 117.0000 g. **Composition:** 0.9956 Gold 3.7451 oz. AGW **Note:** Uniface.

| Date | Mintage | VG | F | VF | XF | Unc |
|---|---|---|---|---|---|---|
| ND(1921) | — | — | — | BV | 1,800 | 2,100 |

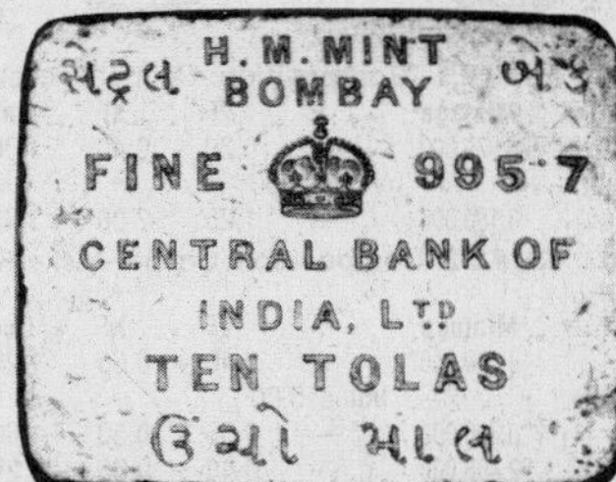


**10 TOLAS** KM# 496D **Composition:** 0.9957 Gold

| Date | Mintage | VG | F | VF | XF | Unc |
|---|---|---|---|---|---|---|
| ND(1922) | — | — | — | BV | 1,800 | 2,100 |

## PATTERNS

Including off metal strikes

P# are in reference to "The Coins of the British Commonwealth of Nation" Part 4, India, Vol. 1 and 2 by F. Pridmore (Spink and Son Ltd., London 1980).

| KM# | Date | Mintage | Identification | Mkt Val |
|---|---|---|---|---|
| Pn66 | 1901 | — | Rupee. Silver. P#1045 | 1,750 |
| Pn68 | 1903 | — | 1/4 Rupee. Silver. With "718.93" countermark. P#1074 | — |
| Pn69 | 1903 | — | Anna. Nickel. P#1053 | 450 |
| Pn70 | 1904 | — | 1/4 Anna. Copper. P#1051 | 750 |
| Pn71 | 1904 | — | Anna. Copper-Nickel. P#1054 | 300 |
| Pn72 | 1904 | — | Anna. Tin. 22 mm. P#1055 | 450 |
| Pn73 | 1904 | — | Anna. Copper-Nickel. 21 mm. P#1056 | 300 |
| Pn74 | 1904 | — | Anna. Copper-Nickel. P#1058 | 300 |
| Pn75 | 1904 | — | Anna. Copper-Nickel. P#1059 | 300 |
| Pn76 | 1904 | — | Anna. Copper-Nickel. P#1060 | 300 |
| Pn77 | 1904 | — | Anna. White Metal. P#1061 | 300 |
| Pn78 | 1904 | — | Anna. Copper-Nickel. P#1062 | 300 |
| Pn79 | 1904 | — | Anna. Copper-Nickel. P#1063 | 300 |
| Pn80 | 1904 | — | 1/4 Rupee. Nickel. P#1075 | 300 |
| Pn81 | 1905 | — | Anna. Copper-Nickel. P#924 | — |
| Pn82 | 1905 | — | Anna. White Metal. P#1057 | 300 |
| Pn83 | 1905 | — | Anna. | 30.00 |
| Pn84 | 1905 | — | Anna. White Metal. Low relief bust; P#1066 | 300 |
| Pn85 | 1905 | — | Anna. White Metal. High relief bust; P#1067 | 300 |
| Pn86 | 1905 | — | Anna. Copper. High relief bust; P#1069 | 300 |
| Pn87 | 1905 | — | Anna. Silver. High relief bust; P#1068 | 300 |
| Pn88 | 1905 | — | Anna. White Metal. Without dot border. P#1070A | 300 |
| Pn89 | 1905 | — | Anna. Copper-Nickel. | — |
| Pn90 | 1905 | — | Anna. Silver. Without dot border. P#1070B | 300 |
| Pn91 | 1906 | — | Anna. White Metal. Raised bar edge. P#1064 | 300 |
| Pn92 | 1906 | — | Anna. White Metal. Double raised bar edge. P#1065 | 300 |
| Pn93 | 1906 | — | Anna. Copper-Nickel. Scalloped planchet; P#1071 | 300 |
| Pn94 | 1906 | — | Rupee. Copper-Nickel. "SPEC-IMEN" divided by crown. Lettered edge. P#1047 | 1,000 |
| Pn95 | 1907 | — | Rupee. Silver. P#1048 | — |
| Pn96 | 1908 | — | 1/2 Anna. Copper-Nickel. | 300 |
| Pn97 | 1908 | — | 1/2 Anna. White Metal. P#1073 | 500 |
| Pn98 | 1909 | — | 1/2 Pice. Aluminum. | 175 |
| Pn99 | 1910 | — | Rupee. Silver. P#1049 | 1,750 |
| Pn100 | 1910 | — | Rupee. Gold. P#1050 | — |
| Pn101 | | — | 2 Annas. Tin. P#1052 | — |
| Pn102 | 1917 | — | 2 Annas. Copper-Nickel. Round; P#1078 | — |
| Pn103 | 1917 | — | 2 Annas. Copper-Nickel. Square; P#1079 | — |
| Pn104 | 1918 | — | 4 Annas. Copper-Nickel. Round with center hole; P#1076 | — |
| Pn105 | 1919 | — | 2 Annas. Copper-Nickel. Eight-lobed planchet; P#1087 | — |
| Pn106 | 1919 | — | 4 Annas. Copper-Nickel. Triangle; P#1077 | — |
| Pn107 | 1921 | — | Anna. Copper-Nickel. P#1080 | 250 |
| Pn108 | 1921 | — | Anna. Copper. P#1081 | 250 |
| Pn109 | 1921 | — | Anna. Gold. P#1082 | — |
| Pn110 | 1929 | — | Anna. Copper-Nickel. P#1083 | 400 |
| Pn111 | 1929 | — | Anna. Copper-Nickel. Wide border; P#1084 | 400 |
| Pn112 | 1937 | — | 2 Annas. Copper-Nickel. P#1093 | 800 |
| Pn113 | 1937 | — | 2 Annas. Copper-Nickel. Serrated circular border. P#1094 | 800 |
| Pn114 | 1938 | — | 1/4 Anna. Bronze. Head of George V | — |
| Pn115 | 1938 | — | 1/2 Anna. Nickel. P#1095 | — |
| Pn116 | 1938 | — | Rupee. Silver. Head of George V | — |
| Pn117 | 1941 | — | Dollar. Silver. P#1088A | 2,500 |
| Pn118 | 1941 | — | Dollar. Silver. Fine milled edge. | 750 |
| Pn119 | 1941 | — | Dollar. Silver. "S" in "RUPEES" 1/2 to left of large "1"; P#1088B | — |
| Pn120 | 1941 | — | Dollar. Silver. P#1089 | 2,500 |
| Pn121 | 1943 | — | Pice. Bronze. P#1091 | 450 |
| Pn122 | 1945 | — | Pie. Bronze. P#1092 | — |
| Pn123 | 1946 | — | Pie. Bronze. Tiger left. P#1090 | — |

## PROOF SETS

| KM# | Date | Mintage | Identification | Mkt Val |
|---|---|---|---|---|
| PS3 | 1904 (5) | — | KM#497, 499, 503, Pn70(2) | 3,000 |
| PS4 | 1904 (3) | — | KM#497, 499, 501(bronze) with "1" countermark on reverse | 3,000 |
| PS5 | 1911(c) (4) | — | KM#514, 517, 521, 523 | 400 |
| PS6 | 1919(c) (8) | — | KM#513, 516, 519-520 (2 each - V.I.P.) | 1,500 |
| PS7 | 1938(C) (6) | — | KM#527-528, 530, 536, 544, 555 | 350 |
| PS8 | 1947(b) (7) | — | KM#533, 535, 538, 542, 548, 553, 559 | 300 |

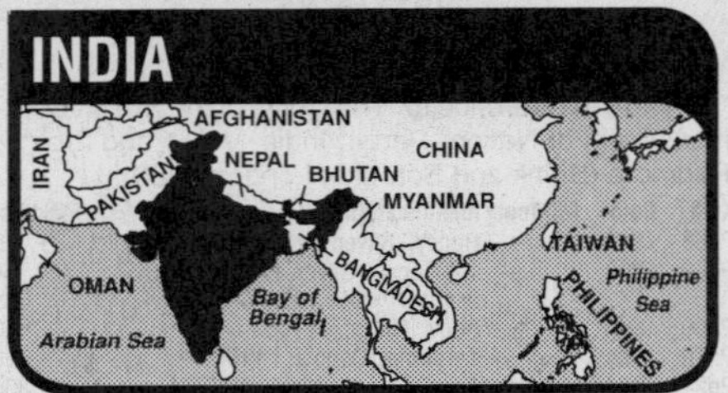


The Republic of India, a subcontinent jutting southward from the mainland of Asia, has an area of 1,269,346 sq. mi. (3,287,590 sq. km.) and a population of over 900 million, second only to that of the People's Republic of China. Capital: New Delhi. India's economy is based on agriculture and industrial activity. Engineering goods, cotton apparel and fabrics, handicrafts, tea, iron and steel are exported.

The people of India have had a continuous civilization since about 2,500 B.C., when an urban culture based on commerce and trade, and to a lesser extent, agriculture, was developed by the inhabitants of the Indus River Valley. The origins of this civilization are uncertain, but it declined about 1,500 B.C., when the region was conquered by the Aryans. Over the following 2,000 years, the Aryans developed a Brahmanic civilization and introduced the caste system. Several successive empires flourished in India over the following centuries, notably those of the Mauryans, Guptas, and Mughals. In the 8th century A.D., the Arabs expanded into western India, bringing with them the Islamic faith. A Muslim dynasty (the Mughal Empire) controlled virtually the entire subcontinent during the period preceding the arrival of the Europeans; an Indo-Islamic style of art and architecture evolved, of which the Taj Mahal is a splendid example.

The Portuguese were the first Europeans to arrive, off Calicut in May 1498. It wasn't until 1612, after Portuguese and Spanish power began to wane, that the British East India Company established its initial settlement at Surat. By the end of the century, English traders were firmly established in Bombay, Madras, and Calcutta, as well as in some parts of the interior, and Britain was implementing a policy to create the civil and military institutions that would insure British dominion over the country. By 1757, following the successful conclusion of a war of colonial rivalry with France, the British were firmly established in India as not only traders, but as conquerors. During the next 60 years, the British East India Company acquired dominion over most of India by intrigue and force, and ruled directly, or through puppet princelings.

The Indian Mutiny (called the first War of Independence by Indian Nationalists) of 1857-58, begun by Indian troops in the service of the British East India Company, revealed the intensity of the growing resentment against British domination. The widespread rebellion against British rule was unsuccessful, but resulted in the transfer of government from the company to the British crown, and was a source of inspiration, to later Indian nationalists. Agitation for representation in the government continued.

Following World War I, in which India sent six million troops to fight at the side of the Allies, Indian nationalism intensified under the banner of the Indian National Congress and the leadership of Mohandas Karamchand Gandhi, who called for non-violent revolt against British authority. The Government of India Act of 1935 proposed a federal status linking the British Indian provinces with the many princely states; in addition, provincial legislatures were to be created. The federal status was never implemented, but the legislatures were created after the election of 1937, with the National Congress winning majorities in most of the provinces.

When Britain declared war on Germany in Sept. 1939, the Viceroy declared India also to be at war with a common enemy. The Congress, however, demanded independence as a condition for cooperation; Britain refused. But as the Japanese advanced into Asia, Britain offered to transfer to Indians power over all but military affairs during the war, and set forth a plan for postwar independence. Congress was willing to accept the wartime transfer of power, but both Congress and the Muslim League rejected Britain's plan for independence; Congress because it did not sufficiently safeguard Indian unity, the Muslims (who wanted a separate Muslim state) because of fears of what would happen to Muslims within a united India.

Early in 1947, Prime Minister Clement Attlee announced that Britain would leave India "by a date not later than June 1948," even though the Hindus and Muslims could not agree among themselves on a plan for self-government. The National Congress, aware that the Muslim League would revolt rather than accept an all-India government, reluctantly agreed to the formation of a separate Muslim state. The Muslim-majority provinces of the North West Frontier. Sindh and West Punjab in the west, and East Bengal in the east were separated from India to form the Muslim state of Pakistan, which became independent on Aug. 14, 1947. India became independent on the following day. Because British India coins dated 1947 were struck until 1950, they can be considered the first coins of Independent India. India became a republic on Jan. 26, 1950.

The Republic of India is a member of the Common-wealth of Nations. The president is the Chief of State. The prime minister is the Head of Government.

**MINT MARKS**

**(Mint marks usually appear directly below the date.)**

B -- Mumbai (Bombay), proof issues only
(B) - Mumbai (Bombay), diamond
C - Ottawa
(1985 25 Paise; 1988 10, 25 & 50 Paise)
(C) - Calcutta, no mint mark
H - Birmingham (1985 Rupee only)
(H) - Hyderabad, star (1963-- )
(Hd) - Hyderabad, diamond split vertically (1953-1960)
(Hy) - Hyderabad, incuse dot in diamond (1960-1968)
(K) - Kremnica, Slovakia, MK in circle
(L) - London, diamond below first date digit
M - Mumbai (Bombay), proof only after 1996
(M) - Mexico City, M beneath O
(N) - Noida, dot
(P) - Pretoria, M in oval
(T) - Taegu (Korea), star below first date digit

From 1950 through 1964 the Republic of India proof coins carry the regular diamond mint mark and can be distinguished from circulation issues only by their proof-like finish. From 1969 proofs carry the capital "B" mint mark. Some Bombay issues after1969 have a "proof-like" appearance although bearing the diamond mint mark of circulation issues. Beginning in 1972 proofs of the larger denominations - 10, 20 and 100 rupees -were partly frosted on their main features, including numerals. From 1975 all proofs were similarly frosted, from the 1 paisa to 100 rupees. Proof-like issues are often erroneously offered as proofs.

**MONETARY SYSTEM**

**(Until 1957)**

4 Pice = 1 Anna
16 Annas = 1 Rupee

# REPUBLIC

## STANDARD COINAGE

**PICE KM# 1.1 Composition:** Bronze **Note:** Var. 1: 1.6mm thick, 0.3mm edge rim.

| Date | Mintage | F | VF | XF | Unc | BU |
|---|---|---|---|---|---|---|
| 1950(B) | 32,080,000 | — | 1.00 | 2.00 | 3.00 | — |

**PICE KM# 1.2 Composition:** Bronze **Note:** Var. 2: 1.6mm thick, 1.0mm edge rim.

| Date | Mintage | F | VF | XF | Unc | BU |
|---|---|---|---|---|---|---|
| 1950(B) | Inc. above | — | 0.40 | 0.80 | 1.50 | — |
| 1950(B) Proof | — | Value: 2.50 | | | | |
| 1950C | 14,000,000 | — | 0.50 | 1.00 | 1.75 | — |

**PICE KM# 1.3 Composition:** Bronze **Note:** Var. 3: 1.2mm thick, 0.8mm edge rim.

| Date | Mintage | F | VF | XF | Unc | BU |
|---|---|---|---|---|---|---|
| 1951(B) | 104,626,000 | — | 0.20 | 0.40 | 0.75 | — |
| 1951(C) | 127,300,000 | — | 0.20 | 0.40 | 0.75 | — |
| 1952(B) | 213,830,000 | — | 0.25 | 0.40 | 0.80 | — |
| 1953(B) | 242,358,000 | — | 0.25 | 0.50 | 1.00 | — |
| 1953(C) | 111,000,000 | — | 0.25 | 0.50 | 1.00 | — |
| 1953(Hd) | Inc. above | — | 15.00 | 20.00 | — | — |
| 1954(B) | 136,758,000 | — | 0.25 | 0.50 | 1.00 | — |
| 1954(B) Proof | — | Value: 5.00 | | | | |
| 1954(C) | 52,600,000 | — | 0.35 | 0.70 | 1.25 | — |
| 1954(Hd) | Inc. above | — | 10.00 | 15.00 | — | — |
| 1955(B) | 24,423,000 | — | 0.50 | 1.25 | 2.00 | — |
| 1955(Hd) | Inc. above | — | 15.00 | 20.00 | — | — |

**1/2 ANNA KM# 2.1 Composition:** Copper-Nickel

| Date | Mintage | F | VF | XF | Unc | BU |
|---|---|---|---|---|---|---|
| 1950(B) | 26,076,000 | — | 0.20 | 0.40 | 1.00 | — |
| 1950(B) Proof | — | Value: 3.00 | | | | |
| 1950(C) | 3,100,000 | — | 1.25 | 2.00 | 3.25 | — |

**1/2 ANNA KM# 2.2 Composition:** Copper-Nickel **Reverse:** Larger date

| Date | Mintage | F | VF | XF | Unc | BU |
|---|---|---|---|---|---|---|
| 1954(B) | 14,000,000 | — | 0.40 | 0.65 | 1.25 | — |
| 1954(B) Proof | — | Value: 5.00 | | | | |
| 1954(C) | 20,800,000 | — | 0.30 | 0.50 | 1.00 | — |
| 1955(B) | 22,488,000 | — | 0.40 | 0.65 | 1.25 | — |

**ANNA KM# 3.1 Composition:** Copper-Nickel

| Date | Mintage | F | VF | XF | Unc | BU |
|---|---|---|---|---|---|---|
| 1950(B) | 9,944,000 | — | 0.45 | 0.75 | 1.50 | — |
| 1950(B) Proof | — | Value: 4.00 | | | | |

**ANNA KM# 3.2 Composition:** Copper-Nickel **Reverse:** Larger date, first Hindi letter varieties

| Date | Mintage | F | VF | XF | Unc | BU |
|---|---|---|---|---|---|---|
| 1954(B) | 20,388,000 | — | 0.35 | 0.60 | 1.25 | — |
| 1954(B) Proof | — | Value: 6.50 | | | | |
| 1955(B) | — | — | 15.00 | 20.00 | 30.00 | — |

**2 ANNAS KM# 4 Composition:** Copper-Nickel

| Date | Mintage | F | VF | XF | Unc | BU |
|---|---|---|---|---|---|---|
| 1950(B) | 7,536,000 | — | 0.75 | 1.50 | 2.50 | — |
| 1950(B) Proof | — | Value: 5.00 | | | | |
| 1954(B) | 10,548,000 | — | 0.75 | 1.50 | 2.50 | — |
| 1954(B) Proof | — | Value: 8.00 | | | | |
| 1955(B) | — | — | 15.00 | 20.00 | 30.00 | — |

**1/4 RUPEE KM# 5.1 Composition:** Nickel **Note:** Var. 1: Large lion.

| Date | Mintage | F | VF | XF | Unc | BU |
|---|---|---|---|---|---|---|
| 1950(B) | 7,650,000 | — | 0.60 | 1.50 | 2.50 | — |
| 1950(B) Proof | — | Value: 5.00 | | | | |
| 1950(C) | 7,800,000 | — | 0.60 | 1.50 | 2.50 | — |
| 1951(B) | 41,439,000 | — | 0.45 | 1.00 | 2.00 | — |
| 1951(C) | 13,500,000 | — | 0.55 | 1.00 | 2.00 | — |
| 1954(B) Proof | — | Value: 6.00 | | | | |
| 1954(C) | 58,300,000 | — | 0.65 | 1.50 | 2.50 | — |
| 1955(B) | 57,936,000 | — | 2.00 | 4.00 | 6.00 | — |

**1/4 RUPEE KM# 5.2 Composition:** Nickel **Note:** Var. 2: Small lion.

| Date | Mintage | F | VF | XF | Unc | BU |
|---|---|---|---|---|---|---|
| 1954(C) | Inc. above | — | 0.40 | 1.00 | 1.75 | — |
| 1955(C) | 28,900,000 | — | 0.40 | 1.00 | 1.75 | — |
| 1956(C) | 22,000,000 | — | 0.70 | 1.25 | 2.00 | — |

**1/2 RUPEE KM# 6.1 Composition:** Nickel **Note:** Var. 1: Large lion.

| Date | Mintage | F | VF | XF | Unc | BU |
|---|---|---|---|---|---|---|
| 1950(B) | 12,352,000 | — | 0.75 | 1.25 | 2.50 | — |
| 1950(B) Proof | — | Value: 5.50 | | | | |
| 1950(C) | 1,100,000 | — | 1.25 | 2.00 | 5.00 | — |
| 1951(B) | 9,239,000 | — | 1.00 | 1.50 | 3.50 | — |
| 1954(B) Proof | — | Value: 8.00 | | | | |
| 1954(C) | 36,300,000 | — | 0.50 | 1.00 | 2.50 | — |
| 1955(B) | 18,977,000 | — | 0.75 | 1.50 | 4.50 | — |

**1/2 RUPEE KM# 6.2 Composition:** Nickel **Obverse:** Dots missing between words **Note:** Var. 2: Small lion.

| Date | Mintage | F | VF | XF | Unc | BU |
|---|---|---|---|---|---|---|
| 1956(C) | 24,900,000 | — | 0.50 | 1.00 | 2.50 | — |

**RUPEE** KM# 7.1 **Composition:** Nickel

| Date | Mintage | F | VF | XF | Unc | BU |
|---|---|---|---|---|---|---|
| 1950(B) | 19,412,000 | — | 1.50 | 2.50 | 4.50 | — |
| 1950(B) Proof | — | Value: 7.00 | | | | |

**RUPEE** KM# 7.2 **Composition:** Nickel **Reverse:** First Hindi letter varieties

| Date | Mintage | F | VF | XF | Unc | BU |
|---|---|---|---|---|---|---|
| 1954(B) | Inc. above | — | 2.00 | 3.00 | 5.50 | — |
| 1954(B) Proof | — | Value: 10.00 | | | | |

## DECIMAL COINAGE

100 Naye Paise = 1 Rupee (1957-63);
100 Paise = 1 Rupee (1964- )

NOTE: The Paisa was at first called "Naya Paisa"(= New Paisa), so that people would distinguish from the old non-decimal Paisa (or Pice, equal to 1/64 Rupee). After 7 years, the word "new" was dropped, and the coin was simply called a "Paisa".

NOTE: Many of the Paisa standard types come with three obverse varieties.

1957-1989

TYPE I: Side lions toothless with 2 to 3 fur rows, dot in wheel center, short squat "D" in "INDIA".

1967-1994

TYPE II: Asoka lion pedestal more imposing. Side lions with 3 or 4 fur rows, more elegant "D" in "INDIA". The shape of the "D" in "INDIA" is the easiest way to distinguish this obverse.

1979-

TYPE III: Similar to obverse I but 2 teeth, 4 to 5 fur rows, bull fatter, without central wheel dot.

NOTE: Paisa standard pieces with mint mark B, 1969 to date, were sturck only in proof.

NOTE: Indian mintage figures are not divided by mint, and often include dates other than the year in which struck. They should be regarded with reserve.

**NAYA PAISA** KM# 8 **Composition:** Bronze

| Date | Mintage | F | VF | XF | Unc | BU |
|---|---|---|---|---|---|---|
| 1957(B) | 618,630,000 | — | 0.30 | 0.50 | 0.85 | — |
| 1957(C) | Inc. above | — | 0.30 | 0.50 | 0.85 | — |
| 1957(Hd) | Inc. above | — | 0.30 | 0.50 | 0.85 | — |
| 1958(B) | 468,630,000 | — | 0.45 | 0.75 | 1.50 | — |
| 1958(Hd) | Inc. above | — | 0.45 | 0.75 | 1.50 | — |
| 1959(B) | 351,120,000 | — | 0.30 | 0.50 | 0.85 | — |
| 1959(C) | Inc. above | — | 0.30 | 0.50 | 0.85 | — |
| 1959(Hd) | Inc. above | — | 0.30 | 0.50 | 0.85 | — |
| 1960(B) | 357,940,000 | — | 0.30 | 0.50 | 0.85 | — |
| 1960(B) Proof | — | Value: 2.00 | | | | |
| 1960(C) | Inc. above | — | 2.25 | 3.50 | 5.00 | — |
| 1960(Hd) | Inc. above | — | 3.25 | 4.00 | 5.00 | — |
| 1961(B) | 573,170,000 | — | 0.30 | 0.50 | 0.85 | — |
| 1961(B) Proof | — | Value: 2.00 | | | | |
| 1961(C) | Inc. above | — | 0.30 | 0.50 | 0.85 | — |
| 1961(Hy) | Inc. above | — | 0.50 | 0.75 | 1.25 | — |
| 1962(B) | — | — | — | — | — | — |

**Note:** 1962(B) has only been found in some of the 1962 uncirculated mint sets; Varieties of the split diamond have been reported

**NAYA PAISA** KM# 8a **Composition:** Nickel-Brass

| Date | Mintage | F | VF | XF | Unc | BU |
|---|---|---|---|---|---|---|
| 1962(B) | 235,103,000 | — | 0.20 | 0.35 | 0.70 | — |
| 1962(B) Proof | — | Value: 1.50 | | | | |
| 1962(C) | Inc. above | — | 0.20 | 0.35 | 0.70 | — |
| 1962(Hy) | Inc. above | — | 0.50 | 0.75 | 1.25 | — |
| 1963(B) | 343,313,000 | — | 0.20 | 0.35 | 0.70 | — |
| 1963(B) Proof | — | Value: 1.50 | | | | |
| 1963(C) | Inc. above | — | 0.25 | 0.50 | 1.00 | — |
| 1963(H) | Inc. above | — | 0.25 | 0.40 | 0.80 | — |

**PAISA** KM# 9 **Composition:** Nickel-Brass **Note:** Type I.

| Date | Mintage | F | VF | XF | Unc | BU |
|---|---|---|---|---|---|---|
| 1964(B) | 539,068,000 | — | 0.20 | 0.35 | 0.60 | — |
| 1964(C) | Inc. above | — | 0.20 | 0.35 | 0.60 | — |
| 1964(H) | Inc. above | — | 0.20 | 0.35 | 0.60 | — |

**PAISA** KM# 9a **Composition:** Bronze

| Date | Mintage | F | VF | XF | Unc | BU |
|---|---|---|---|---|---|---|
| 1964(H) | Inc. above | — | — | — | — | — |

**PAISA** KM# 10.1 **Composition:** Aluminum **Note:** Type I.

| Date | Mintage | F | VF | XF | Unc | BU |
|---|---|---|---|---|---|---|
| 1965(B) | 223,480,000 | — | 0.40 | 0.65 | 1.00 | — |
| 1965(Hy) | Inc. above | — | 0.40 | 0.65 | 1.00 | — |
| 1966(B) | 404,200,000 | — | 0.20 | 0.30 | 0.50 | — |
| 1966(C) | Inc. above | — | 0.30 | 0.50 | 1.00 | — |
| 1966(Hy) | Inc. above | — | 0.20 | 0.30 | 0.50 | — |
| 1967(B) | 450,433,000 | — | 0.20 | 0.30 | 0.50 | — |
| 1967(C) | Inc. above | — | 0.20 | 0.30 | 0.50 | — |
| 1967(Hy) | Inc. above | — | 0.20 | 0.30 | 0.50 | — |
| 1968(B) | 302,720,000 | — | 0.20 | 0.30 | 0.50 | — |
| 1968(C) | Inc. above | — | 0.20 | 0.30 | 0.50 | — |
| 1968(Hy) | Inc. above | — | 0.20 | 0.30 | 0.50 | — |
| 1969(B) | 125,930,000 | — | 1.50 | 2.25 | 3.00 | — |
| 1969B Proof | 9,147 | Value: 1.50 | | | | |
| 1969(H) | Inc. above | — | 3.00 | 4.00 | 5.00 | — |
| 1970(B) | 15,800,000 | — | 2.00 | 2.50 | 5.00 | — |

**Note:** 1970(B) is found only in the uncirculated sets of that year. It has a mirrorlike surface

| Date | Mintage | F | VF | XF | Unc | BU |
|---|---|---|---|---|---|---|
| 1970B Proof | 3,046 | Value: 1.00 | | | | |
| 1971B Proof | 4,375 | Value: 1.00 | | | | |
| 1971(H) | 112,100,000 | — | 0.20 | 0.30 | 0.50 | — |
| 1972(B) | 62,090,000 | — | 0.20 | 0.30 | 0.50 | — |
| 1972B Proof | 7,895 | Value: 1.00 | | | | |
| 1972(H) | Inc. above | — | 0.20 | 0.30 | 0.50 | — |
| 1973B Proof | 7,562 | Value: 1.00 | | | | |
| 1974B Proof | — | Value: 1.00 | | | | |
| 1975B Proof | — | Value: 1.00 | | | | |
| 1976B Proof | — | Value: 1.00 | | | | |
| 1977B Proof | — | Value: 1.00 | | | | |
| 1978B Proof | — | Value: 1.00 | | | | |
| 1979B Proof | — | Value: 1.00 | | | | |
| 1980B Proof | — | Value: 1.00 | | | | |
| 1981B Proof | — | Value: 1.00 | | | | |

**PAISA** KM# 10.2 **Composition:** Aluminum **Note:** Type II.

| Date | Mintage | F | VF | XF | Unc | BU |
|---|---|---|---|---|---|---|
| 1969(C) | Inc. above | — | 2.50 | 3.00 | 4.00 | — |
| 1970(C) | Inc. above | — | 0.40 | 0.65 | 1.00 | — |

**2 NAYE PAISE** KM# 11 **Composition:** Copper-Nickel

| Date | Mintage | F | VF | XF | Unc | BU |
|---|---|---|---|---|---|---|
| 1957(B) | 406,230,000 | — | 0.15 | 0.40 | 0.80 | — |
| 1957(C) | Inc. above | — | 0.15 | 0.40 | 0.80 | — |
| 1958(B) | 245,660,000 | — | 0.15 | 0.40 | 0.80 | — |
| 1958(C) | Inc. above | — | 0.15 | 0.40 | 0.80 | — |
| 1959(B) | 171,445,000 | — | 0.15 | 0.40 | 0.80 | — |
| 1959(C) | Inc. above | — | 0.15 | 0.40 | 0.80 | — |
| 1960(B) | 121,820,000 | — | 0.15 | 0.40 | 0.80 | — |
| 1960(B) Proof | — | Value: 2.00 | | | | |
| 1960(C) | Inc. above | — | 0.20 | 0.40 | 0.80 | — |
| 1961(B) | 190,610,000 | — | 0.20 | 0.40 | 0.80 | — |
| 1961(B) Proof | — | Value: 2.00 | | | | |
| 1961(C) | Inc. above | — | 0.20 | 0.40 | 0.80 | — |
| 1962(B) | 318,181,000 | — | 0.20 | 0.40 | 0.80 | — |
| 1962(B) Proof | — | Value: 1.50 | | | | |
| 1962(C) | Inc. above | — | 0.20 | 0.40 | 0.80 | — |
| 1963(B) | 372,380,000 | — | 0.20 | 0.40 | 0.80 | — |
| 1963(B) Proof | — | Value: 1.50 | | | | |
| 1963(C) | Inc. above | — | 0.20 | 0.40 | 0.80 | — |

**2 PAISE** KM# 12 **Composition:** Copper-Nickel **Note:** Type I.

| Date | Mintage | F | VF | XF | Unc | BU |
|---|---|---|---|---|---|---|
| 1964(B) | 323,504,000 | — | 0.20 | 0.40 | 0.80 | — |
| 1964(C) | Inc. above | — | 0.20 | 0.40 | 0.80 | — |

**2 PAISE** KM# 13.1 **Composition:** Aluminum **Reverse:** 10mm "2" **Note:** Type I. Obv. 1 INDIA starts farther from right lion.

| Date | Mintage | F | VF | XF | Unc | BU |
|---|---|---|---|---|---|---|
| 1965(B) | 175,770,000 | — | 0.20 | 0.40 | 0.80 | — |
| 1965(C) | Inc. above | — | 0.40 | 0.65 | 1.00 | — |
| 1966(B) | 386,795,000 | — | 0.20 | 0.30 | 0.50 | — |
| 1966(C) | Inc. above | — | 0.20 | 0.30 | 0.50 | — |
| 1967(B) | 454,593,000 | — | 0.20 | 0.30 | 0.50 | — |

**2 PAISE** KM# 13.2 **Composition:** Aluminum **Reverse:** 10-1/2mm "2" **Note:** Type 1.

| Date | Mintage | F | VF | XF | Unc | BU |
|---|---|---|---|---|---|---|
| 1967(C) | Inc. above | — | 0.40 | 0.65 | 1.25 | — |

**2 PAISE** KM# 13.3 **Composition:** Aluminum **Reverse:** 10mm "2" **Note:** Type 2.

| Date | Mintage | F | VF | XF | Unc | BU |
|---|---|---|---|---|---|---|
| 1967(B) | — | — | 3.00 | 5.00 | 8.00 | — |

**2 PAISE** KM# 13.5 **Composition:** Aluminum **Reverse:** 11mm "2" **Note:** Type 2.

| Date | Mintage | F | VF | XF | Unc | BU |
|---|---|---|---|---|---|---|
| 1968(B) | 305,205,000 | — | 0.10 | 0.25 | 0.50 | — |
| 1968(C) | Inc. above | — | 0.20 | 0.30 | 0.50 | — |
| 1969(B) | 5,335,000 | — | 2.00 | 3.00 | 5.00 | — |
| 1969B Proof | 9,147 | Value: 1.00 | | | | |
| 1970(B) | — | — | — | — | 5.00 | — |

**Note:** 1970(B) is found only in the uncirculated sets of that year. It has a mirrorlike surface

| Date | Mintage | F | VF | XF | Unc | BU |
|---|---|---|---|---|---|---|
| 1970B Proof | 3,046 | Value: 1.00 | | | | |
| 1970(C) | 79,100,000 | — | 0.20 | 0.30 | 0.50 | — |

| Date | Mintage | F | VF | XF | Unc | BU |
|---|---|---|---|---|---|---|
| 1971B Proof | 4,375 | Value: 1.00 | | | | |
| 1971(C) | 207,900,000 | — | 0.20 | 0.30 | 0.50 | — |

**2 PAISE** **KM# 13.4** **Composition:** Aluminum **Reverse:** 11mm "2" **Note:** Type 1.

| Date | Mintage | F | VF | XF | Unc | BU |
|---|---|---|---|---|---|---|
| 1968(C) | — | — | 6.00 | 8.00 | 10.00 | — |
| 1977(B) | — | — | 0.60 | 1.00 | 1.50 | — |
| 1978(B) | — | — | 0.40 | 0.65 | 1.00 | — |

**2 PAISE** **KM# 13.6** **Composition:** Aluminum **Reverse:** Small date **Note:** Varieties of date size exist.

| Date | Mintage | F | VF | XF | Unc | BU |
|---|---|---|---|---|---|---|
| 1972B Proof | 7,895 | Value: 1.00 | | | | |
| 1972(C) | 261,270,000 | — | 0.20 | 0.30 | 0.50 | — |
| 1972(H) | Inc. above | — | 0.20 | 0.30 | 0.50 | — |
| 1973B Proof | 7,562 | Value: 1.00 | | | | |
| 1973(C) | — | — | 0.15 | 0.25 | 0.50 | — |
| 1973(H) | — | — | 0.15 | 0.25 | 0.50 | — |
| 1974B Proof | — | Value: 1.00 | | | | |
| 1974(C) | — | — | 0.15 | 0.25 | 0.50 | — |
| 1974(H) | — | — | 0.15 | 0.25 | 0.50 | — |
| 1975B Proof | — | Value: 1.00 | | | | |
| 1975(C) | 184,500,000 | — | 0.40 | 0.65 | 1.00 | — |
| 1975(H) | Inc. above | — | 0.15 | 0.25 | 0.50 | — |
| 1976(B) | 68,140,000 | — | 0.15 | 0.25 | 0.50 | — |
| 1976B Proof | — | Value: 1.00 | | | | |
| 1976(H) | — | — | 1.50 | 2.25 | 3.00 | — |
| 1977(B) | 251,955,000 | — | 0.25 | 0.40 | 0.70 | — |
| 1977B Proof | — | Value: 1.00 | | | | |
| 1977(H) | Inc. above | — | 0.15 | 0.25 | 0.50 | — |
| 1978B Proof | — | Value: 1.00 | | | | |
| 1978(H) | 144,010,000 | — | 0.15 | 0.25 | 0.50 | — |
| 1979B Proof | — | Value: 1.00 | | | | |
| 1979(H) | — | — | 0.65 | 1.00 | 1.50 | — |
| 1980B Proof | — | Value: 1.00 | | | | |
| 1981B Proof | — | Value: 1.00 | | | | |

**3 PAISE** **KM# 14.1** **Composition:** Aluminum **Note:** Type 1.

| Date | Mintage | F | VF | XF | Unc | BU |
|---|---|---|---|---|---|---|
| 1964(B) | 138,890,000 | — | 0.20 | 0.40 | 0.70 | — |
| 1964(C) | Inc. above | — | 0.20 | 0.40 | 0.70 | — |
| 1965(B) | 459,825,000 | — | 0.20 | 0.30 | 0.60 | — |
| 1965(C) | Inc. above | — | 0.20 | 0.30 | 0.60 | — |
| 1966(B) | 390,440,000 | — | 0.20 | 0.30 | 0.60 | — |
| 1966(C) | Inc. above | — | 0.20 | 0.30 | 0.60 | — |
| 1966(Hy) | Inc. above | — | 0.20 | 0.30 | 0.60 | — |
| 1967(B) | 167,018,000 | — | 0.20 | 0.30 | 0.60 | — |
| 1967(C) | Inc. above | — | 0.20 | 0.30 | 0.60 | — |
| 1967(H) | Inc. above | — | 0.75 | 1.25 | 2.00 | — |
| 1968(B) | — | — | 3.00 | 4.00 | 6.00 | — |
| 1968(H) | — | — | — | — | — | — |

**3 PAISE** **KM# 14.2** **Composition:** Aluminum **Note:** Type 2.

| Date | Mintage | F | VF | XF | Unc | BU |
|---|---|---|---|---|---|---|
| 1967(C) | — | — | 4.00 | 6.00 | 8.00 | — |
| 1967(H) | Inc. above | — | 4.00 | 6.00 | 8.00 | — |
| 1968(B) | 246,390,000 | — | — | 0.25 | 0.50 | — |
| 1968(C) | Inc. above | — | 0.10 | 0.25 | 0.50 | — |
| 1968(H) | Inc. above | — | 0.20 | 0.35 | 0.60 | — |
| 1969(B) | — | — | 0.10 | 0.25 | 0.50 | — |
| 1969B Proof | 9,147 | Value: 1.00 | | | | |
| 1969(C) | 7,025,000 | — | 0.20 | 0.30 | 0.50 | — |
| 1969(H) | Inc. above | — | 1.75 | 2.50 | 4.00 | — |
| 1970(B) | — | — | — | — | 5.00 | — |
| **Note:** (1970(B) is found only in the uncirculated sets of that year. It has a mirrorlike surface | | | | | | |
| 1970B Proof | 3,046 | Value: 1.00 | | | | |
| 1970(C) | 15,300,000 | — | 0.10 | 0.25 | 0.50 | — |
| 1971B Proof | 4,375 | Value: 1.00 | | | | |
| 1971(C) | 203,100,000 | — | — | 0.25 | 0.50 | — |
| 1971(H) | Inc. above | — | — | 0.25 | 0.50 | — |

**3 PAISE** **KM# 15** **Composition:** Aluminum **Note:** Type 2.

| Date | Mintage | F | VF | XF | Unc | BU |
|---|---|---|---|---|---|---|
| 1972B Proof | 7,895 | Value: 1.00 | | | | |
| 1973B Proof | 7,562 | Value: 1.00 | | | | |
| 1974B Proof | — | Value: 1.00 | | | | |
| 1975B Proof | — | Value: 1.00 | | | | |
| 1976B Proof | — | Value: 1.00 | | | | |
| 1977B Proof | — | Value: 1.00 | | | | |
| 1978B Proof | — | Value: 1.00 | | | | |
| 1979B Proof | — | Value: 1.00 | | | | |
| 1980B Proof | — | Value: 1.00 | | | | |
| 1981B | — | Value: 1.00 | | | | |

**5 NAYE PAISE** **KM# 16** **Composition:** Copper-Nickel

| Date | Mintage | F | VF | XF | Unc | BU |
|---|---|---|---|---|---|---|
| 1957(B) | 227,210,000 | — | 0.25 | 0.45 | 1.00 | — |
| 1957(C) | Inc. above | — | 0.25 | 0.45 | 1.00 | — |
| 1958(B) | 214,320,000 | — | 0.25 | 0.45 | 1.00 | — |
| 1958(C) | Inc. above | — | 0.25 | 0.45 | 1.00 | — |
| 1959(B) | 137,105,000 | — | 0.25 | 0.45 | 1.00 | — |
| 1959(C) | Inc. above | — | 2.50 | 4.00 | 7.00 | — |
| 1960(B) | 93,345,000 | — | 0.25 | 0.45 | 1.00 | — |
| 1960(B) Proof | — | Value: 2.00 | | | | |
| 1960(C) | Inc. above | — | 0.25 | 0.45 | 1.00 | — |
| 1960(Hy) | Inc. above | — | 6.00 | 10.00 | — | — |
| 1961(B) | 197,620,000 | — | 0.25 | 0.45 | 1.00 | — |
| 1961(B) Proof | — | Value: 2.00 | | | | |
| 1961(C) | Inc. above | — | 0.35 | 0.60 | 1.00 | — |
| 1961(Hy) | Inc. above | — | 6.00 | 10.00 | — | — |
| 1962(B) | 224,277,000 | — | 0.25 | 0.45 | 1.00 | — |
| 1962(B) Proof | — | Value: 1.50 | | | | |
| 1962(C) | Inc. above | — | 0.25 | 0.45 | 1.00 | — |
| 1962(Hy) | Inc. above | — | 2.00 | 3.25 | 7.00 | — |
| 1963(B) | 332,600,000 | — | 0.20 | 0.35 | 0.80 | — |
| 1963(B) Proof | — | Value: 1.50 | | | | |
| 1963(C) | Inc. above | — | 2.00 | 3.00 | 6.00 | — |
| 1963(H) | Inc. above | — | 2.00 | 3.25 | 7.00 | — |

**5 PAISE** **KM# 17** **Composition:** Copper-Nickel **Note:** Type 1.

| Date | Mintage | F | VF | XF | Unc | BU |
|---|---|---|---|---|---|---|
| 1964(B) | 156,000,000 | — | 0.40 | 0.60 | 1.00 | — |
| 1964(C) | Inc. above | — | 0.40 | 0.60 | 1.00 | — |
| 1964(H) | Inc. above | — | 6.00 | 10.00 | — | — |
| 1965(B) | 203,855,000 | — | 0.25 | 0.45 | 0.75 | — |
| 1965(C) | Inc. above | — | 0.40 | 0.60 | 1.00 | — |
| 1965(H) | Inc. above | — | 6.00 | 10.00 | — | — |
| 1966(B) | 101,395,000 | — | 0.75 | 1.25 | 2.00 | — |
| 1966(C) | Inc. above | — | 0.40 | 0.60 | 1.00 | — |

6mm Short 5     7mm Tall 5

**5 PAISE** **KM# 18.1** **Composition:** Aluminum **Reverse:** 6mm, short 5 **Note:** Type 1.

| Date | Mintage | F | VF | XF | Unc | BU |
|---|---|---|---|---|---|---|
| 1967(B) | 608,533,000 | — | 0.35 | 0.60 | 1.00 | — |

**5 PAISE** **KM# 18.3** **Composition:** Aluminum **Note:** Type 2.

| Date | Mintage | F | VF | XF | Unc | BU |
|---|---|---|---|---|---|---|
| 1967(H) | — | — | 4.50 | 7.00 | 10.00 | — |
| 1968(B) | — | — | 0.15 | 0.25 | 0.50 | — |
| **Note:** Mintage included in KM18.2 | | | | | | |
| 1968(C) | — | — | 0.15 | 0.25 | 0.50 | — |
| **Note:** Mintage included in KM18.2 | | | | | | |
| 1968(H) | — | — | 0.40 | 0.60 | 1.00 | — |
| **Note:** Mintage included in KM18.2 | | | | | | |
| 1969(B) | 3,740,000 | — | 2.00 | 3.50 | 5.00 | — |
| 1969B Proof | 9,147 | Value: 1.00 | | | | |
| 1970(B) | 39,900,000 | — | 1.25 | 2.00 | 3.50 | — |
| 1970B Proof | 3,046 | Value: 1.00 | | | | |
| 1970(C) | Inc. above | — | 0.25 | 0.35 | 0.60 | — |
| 1970(H) | Inc. above | — | 0.25 | 0.40 | 0.75 | — |
| 1971(B) | — | — | 0.10 | 0.15 | 0.50 | — |
| **Note:** Included with 1971(H) of KM18.2 | | | | | | |
| 1971B Proof | 4,375 | Value: 1.00 | | | | |
| 1971(C) | Inc. above | — | 0.10 | 0.15 | 0.50 | — |
| 1971(H) | — | — | 0.25 | 0.45 | 0.75 | — |

**5 PAISE** **KM# 18.2** **Composition:** Aluminum **Reverse:** 7mm, tall 5

| Date | Mintage | F | VF | XF | Unc | BU |
|---|---|---|---|---|---|---|
| 1967(B) | Inc. above | — | 0.15 | 0.25 | 0.50 | — |
| 1967(C) | Inc. above | — | 0.15 | 0.25 | 0.50 | — |
| 1967(H) | Inc. above | — | 0.15 | 0.25 | 0.50 | — |
| 1968(B) | — | — | 3.50 | 5.00 | 8.50 | — |
| 1968(C) | — | — | 3.50 | 5.00 | 8.50 | — |
| 1968(H) | 666,750,000 | — | 0.75 | 1.25 | 2.00 | — |
| 1971(H) | 499,200,000 | — | 0.10 | 0.25 | 0.50 | — |

**5 PAISE** **KM# 18.6** **Composition:** Aluminum **Note:** Type 2.

| Date | Mintage | F | VF | XF | Unc | BU |
|---|---|---|---|---|---|---|
| 1972(B) | — | — | 0.10 | 0.15 | 0.50 | — |
| **Note:** Mintage included in KM18.4 | | | | | | |
| 1972B Proof | 7,895 | Value: 1.00 | | | | |
| 1972(C) | — | — | 0.10 | 0.15 | 0.50 | — |
| **Note:** Mintage included in KM18.4 | | | | | | |
| 1972(H) | — | — | 3.50 | 5.00 | 7.00 | — |
| 1973(B) | — | — | 0.10 | 0.15 | 0.50 | — |
| 1973B Proof | 7,562 | Value: 1.00 | | | | |
| 1973(C) | — | — | 0.20 | 0.30 | 0.60 | — |
| 1973(H) | — | — | 0.10 | 0.15 | 0.50 | — |
| 1974B Proof | — | Value: 1.00 | | | | |
| 1974(B) | — | — | 0.10 | 0.15 | 0.50 | — |
| 1974(C) | — | — | 0.10 | 0.15 | 0.50 | — |
| 1974(H) | — | — | 0.10 | 0.15 | 0.50 | — |
| 1975(B) | — | — | 0.10 | 0.15 | 0.50 | — |
| 1975B Proof | — | Value: 1.00 | | | | |
| 1975(C) | 289,080,000 | — | 0.20 | 0.30 | 0.60 | — |
| 1975(H) | Inc. above | — | 0.10 | 0.15 | 0.50 | — |
| 1976(B) | 53,205,000 | — | 0.10 | 0.15 | 0.50 | — |
| 1976(C) | — | — | — | 0.10 | 0.20 | — |
| 1976(H) | — | — | 0.10 | 0.15 | 0.50 | — |
| 1977(B) | 257,899,999 | — | 0.10 | 0.15 | 0.50 | — |
| 1977(C) | Inc. above | — | 0.10 | 0.15 | 0.50 | — |
| 1977(H) | Inc. above | — | 0.10 | 0.15 | 0.50 | — |
| 1978(C) | — | — | 0.10 | 0.15 | 0.50 | — |
| 1978(H) | — | — | 0.10 | 0.15 | 0.50 | — |
| 1979(B) | — | — | 0.10 | 0.15 | 0.50 | — |
| 1979(C) | — | — | 0.20 | 0.35 | 0.80 | — |
| 1979(H) | — | — | 0.10 | 0.15 | 0.50 | — |
| 1980(B) | 21,440,000 | — | 0.10 | 0.15 | 0.50 | — |
| 1980B Proof | — | Value: 1.00 | | | | |
| 1980(C) | Inc. above | — | 0.20 | 0.30 | 0.60 | — |
| 1980(H) | Inc. above | — | 0.10 | 0.15 | 0.50 | — |
| 1981B Proof | — | Value: 1.00 | | | | |
| 1981(C) | 4,365,000 | — | 0.10 | 0.15 | 0.50 | — |
| 1981(H) | Inc. above | — | 0.10 | 0.15 | 0.50 | — |
| **Note:** Due to faulty dies, 1981(H) often resembles the non-existent 1981(B). | | | | | | |
| 1982B Proof | 3,499,000 | Value: 1.00 | | | | |
| 1982(C) | Inc. above | — | 0.10 | 0.15 | 0.50 | — |
| 1982(H) | Inc. above | — | 0.10 | 0.15 | 0.50 | — |
| 1983(C) | 3,110,000 | — | 0.25 | 0.50 | 1.00 | — |
| 1983(H) | Inc. above | — | 0.10 | 0.15 | 0.50 | — |
| 1984(C) | — | — | 0.25 | 0.50 | 1.00 | — |
| 1984(H) | Inc. above | — | 0.10 | 0.15 | 0.50 | — |
| **Note:** Due to faulty dies, 1981(H) often resembles the non-existent 1981(B). | | | | | | |

**5 PAISE** **KM# 18.4** **Composition:** Aluminum **Note:** Type 1, new reverse.

| Date | Mintage | F | VF | XF | Unc | BU |
|---|---|---|---|---|---|---|
| 1972(H) | 512,430,000 | — | 0.35 | 0.60 | 1.00 | — |

**5 PAISE** **KM# 18.5** **Composition:** Aluminum **Reverse:** Larger 5

| Date | Mintage | F | VF | XF | Unc | BU |
|---|---|---|---|---|---|---|
| 1973(H) | — | — | 2.50 | 3.50 | 5.50 | — |
| 1977(B) | — | — | 2.00 | 3.00 | 5.00 | — |
| 1978(B) | — | — | 0.75 | 1.25 | 2.00 | — |

**5 PAISE** **KM# 19** **Composition:** Aluminum **Series:** F.A.O. **Subject:** Food and Work For All

| Date | Mintage | F | VF | XF | Unc | BU |
|---|---|---|---|---|---|---|
| 1976(B) | 34,680,000 | — | 0.35 | 0.50 | 1.00 | — |
| 1976B Proof | — | Value: 1.00 | | | | |
| 1976(C) | 60,040,000 | — | 0.35 | 0.50 | 1.00 | — |
| 1976(H) | 60,290,000 | — | 0.35 | 1.00 | 2.00 | — |

**5 PAISE** **KM# 20** **Composition:** Aluminum **Series:** F.A.O. **Subject:** Save For Development

| Date | Mintage | F | VF | XF | Unc | BU |
|---|---|---|---|---|---|---|
| 1977(B) | 20,100,000 | — | 0.30 | 0.50 | 1.00 | — |
| 1977B Proof | 2,224 | Value: 1.25 | | | | |
| 1977(C) | 40,470,000 | — | 0.30 | 0.50 | 1.00 | — |
| 1977(H) | 20,380,000 | — | 2.25 | 3.50 | 5.00 | — |

**5 PAISE** **KM# 21** **Composition:** Aluminum **Series:** F.A.O. **Subject:** Food and Shelter For All

| Date | Mintage | F | VF | XF | Unc | BU |
|---|---|---|---|---|---|---|
| 1978(B) | 28,440,000 | — | 0.35 | 0.50 | 1.00 | — |
| 1978B Proof | — | Value: 1.25 | | | | |
| 1978(C) | 30,870,000 | — | 0.50 | 1.00 | 2.00 | — |
| 1978(H) | 21,100,000 | — | 1.00 | 1.50 | 2.25 | — |

**5 PAISE** **KM# 22** **Composition:** Aluminum **Series:** International Year of the Child

| Date | Mintage | F | VF | XF | Unc | BU |
|---|---|---|---|---|---|---|
| 1979(B) | 39,860,000 | — | 0.35 | 0.50 | 1.00 | — |
| 1979B Proof | — | Value: 1.25 | | | | |
| 1979(C) | 80,370,000 | — | 0.35 | 0.50 | 1.00 | — |
| 1979(H) | 1,100,000 | — | 1.50 | 2.00 | 2.50 | — |

**5 PAISE** **KM# 23** **Composition:** Aluminum **Note:** Weight reduced

| Date | Mintage | F | VF | XF | Unc | BU |
|---|---|---|---|---|---|---|
| 1984(C) | — | — | 6.00 | 8.00 | 10.00 | — |
| 1985(B) | 54,860,000 | — | 6.00 | 8.00 | 10.00 | — |
| 1985(C) | Inc. above | — | 10.00 | 15.00 | 20.00 | — |
| 1985(H) | Inc. above | — | 0.50 | 0.75 | 1.00 | — |
| 1986(C) | — | — | 0.50 | 0.75 | 1.00 | — |
| 1986(H) | — | — | 0.50 | 0.75 | 1.00 | — |
| 1987(C) | — | — | 0.50 | 0.75 | 1.00 | — |
| 1987(H) | — | — | 0.75 | 1.00 | 2.00 | — |
| 1988(C) | — | — | 0.25 | 0.50 | 1.00 | — |
| 1988(H) | — | — | 0.50 | 1.00 | 2.00 | — |
| 1989(C) | — | — | 0.50 | 1.00 | 2.00 | — |
| 1989(H) | — | — | 0.50 | 1.00 | 2.00 | — |
| 1990(C) | — | — | 1.00 | 1.50 | 2.50 | — |
| 1990(H) | — | — | 1.00 | 1.50 | 2.50 | — |
| 1991(C) | — | — | 0.50 | 0.75 | 1.25 | — |
| 1991(H) | — | — | 0.25 | 0.50 | 1.00 | — |
| 1992(B) | — | — | 1.00 | 1.50 | 2.50 | — |
| 1992(H) | — | — | 0.25 | 0.50 | 1.00 | — |
| 1993(C) | — | — | 1.00 | 1.50 | 2.50 | — |
| 1993(H) | — | — | 0.25 | 0.50 | 1.00 | — |
| 1994(H) | — | — | 0.25 | 0.50 | 1.00 | — |

**10 NAYE PAISE** **KM# 24.1** **Composition:** Copper-Nickel **Reverse:** 6.5mm "10"

| Date | Mintage | F | VF | XF | Unc | BU |
|---|---|---|---|---|---|---|
| 1957(B) | 139,655,000 | — | 0.25 | 0.50 | 1.00 | — |
| 1957(C) | Inc. above | — | 0.25 | 0.50 | 1.00 | — |

**10 NAYE PAISE** **KM# 24.2** **Composition:** Copper-Nickel **Reverse:** 7mm "10"

| Date | Mintage | F | VF | XF | Unc | BU |
|---|---|---|---|---|---|---|
| 1958(B) | 123,160,000 | — | 0.25 | 0.50 | 1.00 | — |
| 1958(C) | Inc. above | — | 0.25 | 0.50 | 1.00 | — |
| 1959(B) | 148,570,000 | — | 0.25 | 0.50 | 1.00 | — |
| 1959(C) | Inc. above | — | 0.25 | 0.50 | 1.00 | — |
| 1960(B) | 52,335,000 | — | 0.35 | 0.75 | 2.00 | — |
| 1960(B) Proof | — | Value: 2.00 | | | | |
| 1961(B) | 172,545,000 | — | 0.25 | 0.50 | 1.00 | — |
| 1961(B) Proof | — | Value: 2.00 | | | | |
| 1961(C) | Inc. above | — | 0.25 | 0.50 | 1.00 | — |
| 1961(Hy) | Inc. above | — | 3.50 | 6.50 | 11.50 | — |
| 1962(B) | 172,777,000 | — | 0.25 | 0.50 | 1.00 | — |
| 1962(B) Proof | — | Value: 1.50 | | | | |
| 1962(C) | Inc. above | — | 0.25 | 0.50 | 1.00 | — |
| 1962(Hy) | Inc. above | — | 3.25 | 5.00 | 9.00 | — |
| 1963(B) | 182,834,000 | — | 0.25 | 0.50 | 1.00 | — |
| 1963(B) Proof | — | Value: 1.50 | | | | |
| 1963(C) | Inc. above | — | 0.25 | 0.50 | 1.00 | — |
| 1963(H) | Inc. above | — | 1.00 | 2.50 | 5.00 | — |

**10 PAISE** **KM# 25** **Composition:** Copper-Nickel **Reverse:** 6.5mm "10" **Note:** Type 1.

| Date | Mintage | F | VF | XF | Unc | BU |
|---|---|---|---|---|---|---|
| 1964(B) Open 4 | 84,112,000 | — | 0.20 | 0.50 | 1.00 | — |
| 1964(B) Closed 4 | Inc. above | — | 5.00 | 7.00 | 10.00 | — |
| 1964(C) | Inc. above | — | 0.20 | 0.50 | 1.00 | — |
| 1964(H) | Inc. above | — | 3.00 | 5.00 | 7.00 | — |
| 1965(B) | 253,430,000 | — | 0.20 | 0.50 | 1.00 | — |
| 1965(C) | Inc. above | — | 0.20 | 0.50 | 1.00 | — |
| 1965(Hy) | Inc. above | — | 4.00 | 6.00 | 8.00 | — |
| 1965(H) | Inc. above | — | 3.00 | 5.00 | 7.00 | — |
| 1966(B) | 326,990,000 | — | 0.20 | 0.50 | 1.00 | — |
| 1966(C) | Inc. above | — | 0.20 | 1.00 | 1.00 | — |
| 1966(Hy) | Inc. above | — | 0.40 | 0.75 | 1.25 | — |
| 1967(B) | 59,443,000 | — | 0.40 | 0.75 | 1.25 | — |
| 1967(C) | Inc. above | — | 0.40 | 0.75 | 1.25 | — |
| 1967(H) | Inc. above | — | 3.00 | 5.00 | 7.00 | — |

**10 PAISE** **KM# 26.1** **Composition:** Nickel-Brass **Note:** Type 1.

| Date | Mintage | F | VF | XF | Unc | BU |
|---|---|---|---|---|---|---|
| 1968(H) | 55,940,000 | — | 30.00 | 50.00 | 80.00 | — |

**10 PAISE** **KM# 26.2** **Composition:** Nickel-Brass **Obverse:** Obverse 2 **Reverse:** 6.5mm "10"

| Date | Mintage | F | VF | XF | Unc | BU |
|---|---|---|---|---|---|---|
| 1968(B) | — | — | 0.20 | 0.50 | 1.00 | — |
| **Note:** Mintage included in KM26.1 | | | | | | |
| 1968(C) | — | — | 0.20 | 0.50 | 1.00 | — |
| **Note:** Mintage included in KM26.1 | | | | | | |
| 1968(H) | — | — | 0.20 | 0.50 | 1.00 | — |
| **Note:** Mintage included in KM26.1 | | | | | | |

**10 PAISE** **KM# 26.3** **Composition:** Nickel-Brass **Reverse:** 7mm "10" **Note:** Type 2.

| Date | Mintage | F | VF | XF | Unc | BU |
|---|---|---|---|---|---|---|
| 1969(B) | 65,405,000 | — | 0.20 | 0.50 | 1.00 | — |
| 1969B Proof | 9,147 | Value: 1.50 | | | | |
| 1969(C) | Inc. above | — | 0.20 | 0.50 | 1.00 | — |
| 1969(H) | Inc. above | — | 0.20 | 0.50 | 1.00 | — |
| 1970(B) | 48,400,000 | — | 0.20 | 0.50 | 1.00 | — |
| 1970B Proof | 3,046 | Value: 1.50 | | | | |
| 1970(C) | Inc. above | — | 0.20 | 0.50 | 1.00 | — |
| 1971(B) | 88,800,000 | — | 0.20 | 0.50 | 1.00 | — |
| 1971B Proof | 4,375 | Value: 1.30 | | | | |

**10 PAISE** **KM# 27.1** **Composition:** Aluminum **Reverse:** 9mm "10" **Note:** Type 2.

| Date | Mintage | F | VF | XF | Unc | BU |
|---|---|---|---|---|---|---|
| 1971(B) | 146,100,000 | — | 0.20 | 0.50 | 1.00 | — |
| 1971(C) | Inc. above | — | 0.20 | 0.50 | 1.00 | — |
| 1971(H) | Inc. above | — | 0.50 | 1.00 | 2.00 | — |
| 1972(B) | 735,090,000 | — | 0.20 | 0.35 | 1.00 | — |
| 1972B Proof | 7,895 | Value: 1.30 | | | | |
| 1972(C) | Inc. above | — | 0.20 | 0.50 | 1.00 | — |
| 1973(B) | — | — | 0.20 | 0.50 | 1.00 | — |
| 1973B Proof | 7,567 | Value: 1.30 | | | | |
| 1973(C) | — | — | 0.20 | 0.50 | 1.00 | — |
| 1973(H) | — | — | 0.20 | 0.50 | 1.00 | — |
| 1974(B) | — | — | 0.20 | 0.50 | 1.00 | — |
| 1974(C) | — | — | 0.20 | 0.50 | 1.00 | — |
| 1974(H) | — | — | 2.00 | 3.00 | 5.00 | — |
| 1975(B) | — | — | 1.00 | 2.00 | 3.00 | — |
| 1975(C) | 298,830,000 | — | 1.00 | 2.00 | 3.00 | — |
| 1976(C) | Inc. above | — | 2.00 | 3.00 | 5.00 | — |
| 1977(B) | 25,288,000 | — | 1.00 | 2.00 | 3.00 | — |
| 1977(C) | Inc. above | — | 0.25 | 0.50 | 1.00 | — |
| 1978(B) | 48,215,000 | — | 0.15 | 0.30 | 1.00 | — |
| 1978(C) | Inc. above | — | 0.15 | 0.30 | 1.00 | — |
| 1978(H) | Inc. above | — | 0.15 | 0.30 | 1.00 | — |

**10 PAISE** **KM# 28** **Composition:** Aluminum **Series:** F.A.O.

| Date | Mintage | F | VF | XF | Unc | BU |
|---|---|---|---|---|---|---|
| 1974(B) | 146,070,000 | — | 0.30 | 0.50 | 1.00 | — |
| 1974B Proof | — | Value: 1.00 | | | | |
| 1974(C) | 168,500,000 | — | 0.50 | 1.00 | 2.00 | — |
| 1974(H) | 10,010,000 | — | 3.00 | 4.00 | 6.00 | — |

**10 PAISE** **KM# 29** **Composition:** Aluminum **Series:** F.A.O. **Subject:** Women's Year **Note:** Mint mark is below wheat stalk.

| Date | Mintage | F | VF | XF | Unc | BU |
|---|---|---|---|---|---|---|
| 1975(B) | 69,160,000 | — | 0.30 | 0.50 | 1.00 | — |
| 1975B Proof | — | Value: 1.00 | | | | |
| 1975(C) | 84,820,000 | — | 0.30 | 0.60 | 1.00 | — |

**10 PAISE** **KM# 30** **Composition:** Aluminum **Series:** F.A.O. **Subject:** Ford and Work For All

| Date | Mintage | F | VF | XF | Unc | BU |
|---|---|---|---|---|---|---|
| 1976(B) | 36,040,000 | — | 1.00 | 1.50 | 2.00 | — |
| 1976B Proof | — | Value: 3.00 | | | | |
| 1976(C) | 26,180,000 | — | 2.00 | 3.00 | 5.00 | — |

**10 PAISE** **KM# 31** **Composition:** Aluminum **Series:** F.A.O. **Subject:** Save For Development

| Date | Mintage | F | VF | XF | Unc | BU |
|---|---|---|---|---|---|---|
| 1977(B) | 17,040,000 | — | 0.25 | 0.50 | 1.00 | — |
| 1977B Proof | 2,224 | Value: 1.00 | | | | |
| 1977(C) | 8,020,000 | — | 2.00 | 3.00 | 5.00 | — |

**10 PAISE** **KM# 32** **Composition:** Aluminum **Series:** F.A.O. **Subject:** Food and Shelter For All

| Date | Mintage | F | VF | XF | Unc | BU |
|---|---|---|---|---|---|---|
| 1978(B) | 24,470,000 | — | 0.25 | 0.50 | 1.00 | — |
| 1978B Proof | — | Value: 1.00 | | | | |
| 1978(C) | 26,160,000 | — | 1.00 | 1.50 | 2.00 | — |
| 1978(H) | 12,100,000 | — | 1.00 | 1.50 | 2.00 | — |

**10 PAISE** **KM# 33** **Composition:** Aluminum **Series:** International Year of the Child

| Date | Mintage | F | VF | XF | Unc | BU |
|---|---|---|---|---|---|---|
| 1979(B) | 39,270,000 | — | 0.25 | 0.50 | 1.00 | — |
| 1979B Proof | — | Value: 1.00 | | | | |
| 1979(C) | 61,700,000 | — | 0.50 | 1.00 | 2.50 | — |
| 1979(H) | 2,250,000 | — | 0.60 | 1.00 | 2.50 | — |

**10 PAISE** **KM# 34** **Composition:** Aluminum **Obverse:** KM#32 **Reverse:** KM#33 **Note:** Mule.

| Date | Mintage | F | VF | XF | Unc | BU |
|---|---|---|---|---|---|---|
| 1979(B) | — | — | 5.00 | 7.50 | 10.00 | — |

**10 PAISE** **KM# 27.2** **Composition:** Aluminum **Reverse:** 8mm 10

| Date | Mintage | F | VF | XF | Unc | BU |
|---|---|---|---|---|---|---|
| 1979(B) | — | — | 0.50 | 1.00 | 2.00 | — |
| 1979(C) | — | — | 0.50 | 1.50 | 3.00 | — |
| 1979(H) | — | — | 0.50 | 1.00 | 2.00 | — |
| 1980(C) | — | — | 10.00 | 12.00 | 15.00 | — |

**10 PAISE** **KM# 27.3** **Composition:** Aluminum **Note:** Type 3.

| Date | Mintage | F | VF | XF | Unc | BU |
|---|---|---|---|---|---|---|
| 1980(B) | — | — | 0.20 | 0.50 | 1.00 | — |
| 1980(C) | — | — | 0.20 | 0.50 | 1.00 | — |
| 1980(H) | — | — | 0.20 | 0.50 | 1.00 | — |
| 1981(B) | — | — | 0.20 | 0.50 | 1.00 | — |
| 1981(C) | — | — | 0.20 | 0.50 | 1.00 | — |
| 1982(C) | — | — | 0.20 | 0.50 | 1.00 | — |
| 1982(H) | — | — | 0.20 | 0.50 | 1.00 | — |

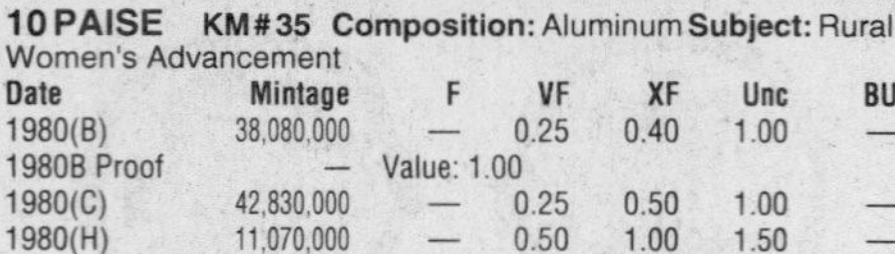

**10 PAISE** **KM# 35** **Composition:** Aluminum **Subject:** Rural Women's Advancement

| Date | Mintage | F | VF | XF | Unc | BU |
|---|---|---|---|---|---|---|
| 1980(B) | 38,080,000 | — | 0.25 | 0.40 | 1.00 | — |
| 1980B Proof | — | Value: 1.00 | | | | |
| 1980(C) | 42,830,000 | — | 0.25 | 0.50 | 1.00 | — |
| 1980(H) | 11,070,000 | — | 0.50 | 1.00 | 1.50 | — |

**10 PAISE** **KM# 36** **Composition:** Aluminum **Subject:** World Food Day

| Date | Mintage | F | VF | XF | Unc | BU |
|---|---|---|---|---|---|---|
| 1981(B) | 83,280,000 | — | 0.25 | 0.40 | 1.00 | — |
| 1981B Proof | — | Value: 1.00 | | | | |
| 1981(C) | 33,930,000 | — | 0.25 | 0.50 | 1.00 | — |

**10 PAISE** **KM# 37** **Composition:** Aluminum **Subject:** IX Asian Games

| Date | Mintage | F | VF | XF | Unc | BU |
|---|---|---|---|---|---|---|
| 1982(B) | — | — | 0.25 | 0.45 | 0.75 | — |
| 1982B Proof | — | Value: 1.00 | | | | |
| 1982(C) | 30,560,000 | — | 0.25 | 0.45 | 0.75 | — |
| 1982(H) | 17,080,000 | — | 0.25 | 0.50 | 1.00 | — |

**10 PAISE** **KM# 38** **Composition:** Aluminum **Subject:** World Food Day

| Date | Mintage | F | VF | XF | Unc | BU |
|---|---|---|---|---|---|---|
| 1982(C) | 2,970,000 | — | 2.50 | 3.50 | 5.00 | — |
| 1982(H) | 11,690,000 | — | 0.50 | 1.00 | 2.00 | — |

**10 PAISE** **KM# 39** **Composition:** Aluminum

| Date | Mintage | F | VF | XF | Unc | BU |
|---|---|---|---|---|---|---|
| 1983(B) | — | — | 0.10 | 0.25 | 0.50 | — |
| 1983(C) | — | — | 0.10 | 0.25 | 0.50 | — |
| 1983(H) | — | — | 0.10 | 0.25 | 0.50 | — |
| 1984(B) | 112,050,000 | — | 0.10 | 0.25 | 0.50 | — |
| 1984(C) | Inc. above | — | 0.25 | 0.50 | 1.00 | — |
| 1984(H) | Inc. above | — | 0.10 | 0.25 | 0.50 | — |
| 1985(B) | 184,655,000 | — | 0.20 | 0.30 | 0.50 | — |
| 1985(C) | Inc. above | — | 0.20 | 0.30 | 0.50 | — |
| 1985(H) | Inc. above | — | 0.20 | 0.30 | 0.50 | — |
| 1986(B) | 298,525,000 | — | 0.10 | 0.15 | 0.30 | — |
| 1986(C) | Inc. above | — | 0.20 | 0.30 | 0.50 | — |
| 1986(H) | Inc. above | — | 0.50 | 1.00 | 1.50 | — |
| 1987(C) | 299,460,000 | — | 0.15 | 0.25 | 0.45 | — |
| 1987(H) | Inc. above | — | 0.15 | 0.25 | 0.45 | — |
| 1988(B) | 264,510,000 | — | 0.10 | 0.15 | 0.30 | — |
| 1988(C) | Inc. above | — | 0.10 | 0.15 | 0.30 | — |
| 1988(H) | Inc. above | — | 1.00 | 1.50 | 2.00 | — |
| 1989(B) | — | — | 0.15 | 0.25 | 0.45 | — |
| 1989(C) | — | — | 0.15 | 0.25 | 0.45 | — |
| 1989(H) | — | — | 0.15 | 0.25 | 0.45 | — |
| 1990(B) | — | — | 0.50 | 0.75 | 1.25 | — |
| 1991(B) | — | — | 0.15 | 0.25 | 0.45 | — |
| 1991(C) | — | — | 0.15 | 0.25 | 0.45 | — |
| 1991(H) | — | — | 0.15 | 0.25 | 0.45 | — |
| 1993(C) | — | — | 0.15 | 0.30 | 0.60 | — |
| 1993(H) | — | — | 0.30 | 0.50 | 0.75 | — |

**10 PAISE** **KM# 40.1** **Composition:** Stainless Steel

| Date | Mintage | F | VF | XF | Unc | BU |
|---|---|---|---|---|---|---|
| 1988C | 183,040,000 | — | 0.10 | 0.15 | 0.25 | — |
| 1988(B) | 4,040,000 | — | 0.25 | 0.40 | 0.75 | — |
| 1988(C) | — | — | 5.00 | 7.00 | 10.00 | — |
| 1988(H) | Inc. above | — | 3.00 | 5.00 | 8.00 | — |
| 1988(N) | — | — | 0.15 | 0.25 | 0.40 | — |
| 1989(B) | — | — | 0.60 | 1.00 | 1.50 | — |
| 1989(C) | — | — | 0.40 | 0.70 | 1.00 | — |
| 1989(H) | — | — | 0.20 | 0.30 | 0.50 | — |
| 1989(N) | — | — | 0.25 | 0.40 | 0.75 | — |
| 1990(B) | — | — | 0.15 | 0.30 | 0.50 | — |
| 1990(C) | — | — | 0.40 | 0.70 | 1.00 | — |
| 1990(H) | — | — | 0.20 | 0.30 | 0.50 | — |
| 1990(N) Small mm | — | — | 0.15 | 0.30 | 0.50 | — |
| 1990(N) Large mm | — | — | 1.25 | 1.75 | 2.50 | — |
| 1991(C) | — | — | 0.15 | 0.30 | 0.50 | — |
| 1991(H) | — | — | 0.15 | 0.30 | 0.50 | — |
| 1991(N) | — | — | 0.15 | 0.30 | 0.50 | — |
| 1992(N) | — | — | 0.30 | 0.60 | 1.00 | — |
| 1993(H) | — | — | 0.15 | 0.30 | 0.50 | — |
| 1996(C) | — | — | 0.15 | 0.30 | 0.50 | — |
| 1996(N) | — | — | 0.15 | 0.30 | 0.50 | — |
| 1997(C) | — | — | 0.15 | 0.30 | 0.50 | — |
| 1997(H) | — | — | 0.20 | 0.30 | 0.50 | — |
| 1998(B) | — | — | 0.25 | 0.40 | 0.70 | — |
| 1998(C) | — | — | 0.25 | 0.40 | 0.70 | — |

**10 PAISE** **KM# 40.2** **Composition:** Stainless Steel **Obverse:** Error: MARAT for BHARAT

| Date | Mintage | F | VF | XF | Unc | BU |
|---|---|---|---|---|---|---|
| 1988(C) | — | — | 1.25 | 2.00 | 3.00 | — |
| 1989(C) | — | — | 7.00 | 10.00 | 15.00 | — |

**20 PAISE** **KM# 41** **Composition:** Nickel-Brass **Reverse:** Lotus Blossom **Note:** Varieties of high and low date exist.

| Date | Mintage | F | VF | XF | Unc | BU |
|---|---|---|---|---|---|---|
| 1968(B) | 10,585,000 | — | 0.50 | 1.00 | 1.50 | — |
| 1968(C) | Inc. above | — | 0.50 | 1.00 | 1.50 | — |
| 1969(B) | 197,940,000 | — | 0.40 | 0.85 | 1.50 | — |
| 1969(C) | — | — | 0.40 | 0.85 | 1.50 | — |
| 1970(B) | Inc. above | — | 0.30 | 0.60 | 1.00 | — |
| 1970(C) | Inc. above | — | 0.30 | 0.60 | 1.00 | — |
| 1970(H) | Inc. above | — | 0.30 | 0.60 | 1.00 | — |
| 1971(B) | 124,200,000 | — | 0.30 | 0.60 | 1.00 | — |

**20 PAISE** **KM# 42.1** **Composition:** Aluminum-Bronze **Subject:** Centennial - Birth of Mahatma Gandhi **Obv. Legend:** .7-.9 from rims

| Date | Mintage | F | VF | XF | Unc | BU |
|---|---|---|---|---|---|---|
| ND(1969)(B) | 45,010 | — | 0.40 | 0.65 | 1.00 | — |
| ND(1969)B Proof | 9,147 | Value: 2.00 | | | | |
| ND(1969)(C) | 45,070,000 | — | 0.50 | 0.80 | 1.50 | — |
| ND(1969)(H) | 3,000,000 | — | 0.75 | 1.50 | 2.50 | — |

**20 PAISE** **KM# 42.2** **Composition:** Aluminum-Bronze **Obv. Legend:** 1.2mm from rim

| Date | Mintage | F | VF | XF | Unc | BU |
|---|---|---|---|---|---|---|
| ND(1969)(B) | — | — | 2.00 | 3.00 | 5.00 | — |
| ND(1969)(C) | — | — | 3.00 | 5.00 | 8.00 | — |

**20 PAISE** **KM# 42.3** **Composition:** Aluminum-Bronze **Note:** Eyes, mustache recut, legends 1.2mm from rim.

| Date | Mintage | F | VF | XF | Unc | BU |
|---|---|---|---|---|---|---|
| ND(1969)(B) | — | — | 0.60 | 1.00 | 1.50 | — |

**Note:** Struck during 1969 and 1970

**20 PAISE** **KM# 43.1** **Composition:** Aluminum-Bronze **Series:** F.A.O. **Subject:** Food For All **Note:** Wide rims.

| Date | Mintage | F | VF | XF | Unc | BU |
|---|---|---|---|---|---|---|
| 1970(B) | 5,160,000 | — | 0.75 | 1.25 | 2.00 | — |
| 1970B Proof | 3,046 | Value: 2.00 | | | | |
| 1970(C) | 5,010,000 | — | 0.75 | 1.25 | 2.00 | — |

**20 PAISE** **KM# 43.2** **Composition:** Aluminum-Bronze **Note:** Narrow rims, lions' fur recut.

| Date | Mintage | F | VF | XF | Unc | BU |
|---|---|---|---|---|---|---|
| 1971(B) | 60,000 | — | 0.70 | 0.90 | 1.25 | — |
| 1971B Proof | 4,375 | Value: 2.00 | | | | |

**20 PAISE** **KM# 45** **Composition:** Aluminum **Series:** F.A.O. **Note:** Similar to 10 Paise, KM#38.

| Date | Mintage | F | VF | XF | Unc | BU |
|---|---|---|---|---|---|---|
| 1982(C) | — | — | 2.00 | 3.25 | 5.00 | — |
| 1982(H) | — | — | 1.00 | 1.50 | 2.50 | — |

**20 PAISE** **KM# 44** **Composition:** Aluminum

| Date | Mintage | F | VF | XF | Unc | BU |
|---|---|---|---|---|---|---|
| 1982(B) | — | — | 0.25 | 0.40 | 1.00 | — |
| 1982(H) | — | — | 0.25 | 0.40 | 1.00 | — |
| 1982(H) Without mm | — | — | 0.25 | 0.40 | 1.00 | — |
| 1983(C) | 28,505,000 | — | 0.25 | 0.40 | 1.00 | — |
| 1983(H) | Inc. above | — | 0.25 | 0.40 | 1.00 | — |
| 1984(C) | Inc. above | — | 0.25 | 0.40 | 1.00 | — |
| 1984(H) | Inc. above | — | 0.25 | 0.40 | 1.00 | — |
| 1985(B) | 84,495,000 | — | 0.25 | 0.40 | 1.00 | — |
| 1985(C) | Inc. above | — | 0.25 | 0.40 | 1.00 | — |
| 1985(H) | Inc. above | — | 0.25 | 0.40 | 1.00 | — |
| 1986(B) | 155,610,000 | — | 0.25 | 0.40 | 0.75 | — |
| 1986(C) | Inc. above | — | 0.15 | 0.30 | 0.75 | — |
| 1986(H) | Inc. above | — | 0.15 | 0.30 | 0.75 | — |
| 1987(C) | — | — | 0.15 | 0.30 | 0.75 | — |
| 1987(H) | 153,073,000 | — | 0.15 | 0.30 | 0.75 | — |
| 1988(B) | 125,048,000 | — | 0.15 | 0.30 | 0.75 | — |
| 1988(C) | Inc. above | — | 0.15 | 0.30 | 0.75 | — |
| 1988(H) | Inc. above | — | 0.35 | 0.60 | 1.00 | — |
| 1989(C) | — | — | 0.35 | 0.60 | 1.00 | — |
| 1989(H) | — | — | 0.15 | 0.25 | 0.75 | — |
| 1990(C) | — | — | 0.35 | 0.60 | 1.00 | — |
| 1990(H) | — | — | 0.15 | 0.25 | 0.75 | — |
| 1991(C) | — | — | 0.15 | 0.25 | 0.75 | — |
| 1991(H) | — | — | 0.15 | 0.25 | 0.75 | — |
| 1992(H) | — | — | 0.15 | 0.25 | 0.75 | — |
| 1994(H) | — | — | 0.15 | 0.25 | 0.75 | — |

**20 PAISE** **KM# 46** **Composition:** Aluminum **Series:** F.A.O. **Subject:** Fisheries

| Date | Mintage | F | VF | XF | Unc | BU |
|---|---|---|---|---|---|---|
| 1983(C) | — | — | 1.00 | 1.50 | 2.50 | — |

**Note:** Mintage included in KM44

| Date | Mintage | F | VF | XF | Unc | BU |
|---|---|---|---|---|---|---|
| 1983(H) | — | — | 1.00 | 1.50 | 2.50 | — |

**Note:** Mintage included in KM44

**25 NAYE PAISE** **KM# 47.1** **Composition:** Nickel

| Date | Mintage | F | VF | XF | Unc | BU |
|---|---|---|---|---|---|---|
| 1957(B) | 5,640,000 | — | 0.75 | 1.25 | 2.00 | — |
| 1957(C) | Inc. above | — | 0.75 | 1.25 | 2.00 | — |
| 1959(B) | 43,080,000 | — | 0.45 | 0.75 | 1.25 | — |
| 1959(C) | Inc. above | — | 0.45 | 0.75 | 1.25 | — |
| 1960(B) | 115,320,000 | — | 0.30 | 0.60 | 1.00 | — |
| 1960(B) Proof | — | Value: 2.00 | | | | |
| 1960(C) | Inc. above | — | 0.30 | 0.60 | 1.00 | — |

**25 NAYE PAISE** **KM# 47.2** **Composition:** Nickel **Reverse:** Large 25

| Date | Mintage | F | VF | XF | Unc | BU |
|---|---|---|---|---|---|---|
| 1961(B) | 109,008,000 | — | 0.30 | 0.60 | 1.00 | — |
| 1961(B) Proof | — | Value: 2.00 | | | | |
| 1961(C) | Inc. above | — | 0.30 | 0.60 | 1.00 | — |
| 1962(B) | 79,242,000 | — | 0.30 | 0.60 | 1.00 | — |
| 1962(B) Proof | — | Value: 2.00 | | | | |
| 1962(C) | Inc. above | — | 0.30 | 0.60 | 1.00 | — |
| 1963(B) | 101,565,000 | — | 0.30 | 0.60 | 1.00 | — |
| 1963(B) Proof | — | Value: 2.00 | | | | |
| 1963(C) | Inc. above | — | 0.30 | 0.60 | 1.00 | — |

**25 PAISE** **KM# 48.1** **Composition:** Nickel **Note:** Type 1, Type 1.

| Date | Mintage | F | VF | XF | Unc | BU |
|---|---|---|---|---|---|---|
| 1964(B) | 85,321,000 | — | 0.30 | 0.60 | 1.25 | — |
| 1964(C) | Inc. above | — | 0.30 | 0.60 | 1.25 | — |

**25 PAISE** **KM# 48.2** **Composition:** Nickel **Note:** Type 1, Reverse 2.

| Date | Mintage | F | VF | XF | Unc | BU |
|---|---|---|---|---|---|---|
| 1965(B) | 143,662,000 | — | 0.30 | 0.60 | 1.00 | — |
| 1965(C) | Inc. above | — | 0.30 | 0.60 | 1.00 | — |
| 1966(B) | 59,040,000 | — | 0.30 | 0.60 | 1.00 | — |
| 1966(C) | Inc. above | — | 0.30 | 0.60 | 1.00 | — |
| 1967(B) | 30,027,000 | — | 4.50 | 6.00 | 8.00 | — |

**25 PAISE** **KM# 48.3** **Composition:** Nickel **Note:** Type 2, Reverse 2.

| Date | Mintage | F | VF | XF | Unc | BU |
|---|---|---|---|---|---|---|
| 1967(C) | — | — | 0.30 | 0.70 | 1.50 | — |

**Note:** Mintage included in KM48.2

| Date | Mintage | F | VF | XF | Unc | BU |
|---|---|---|---|---|---|---|
| 1968(C) | — | — | 1.50 | 2.25 | 3.50 | — |

**Note:** Mintage included in KM48.2

**25 PAISE** **KM# 49.3** **Composition:** Copper-Nickel **Note:** Type 2, 10mm between lion nosetips, 16-16.3mm across field. Bull has three legs.

| Date | Mintage | F | VF | XF | Unc | BU |
|---|---|---|---|---|---|---|
| 1972(C) | — | — | 2.50 | 3.50 | 5.00 | — |

**Note:** Mintage included in KM49.1

| Date | Mintage | F | VF | XF | Unc | BU |
|---|---|---|---|---|---|---|
| 1973(C) | — | — | 0.85 | 1.25 | 2.00 | — |
| 1974(C) | — | — | 0.85 | 1.25 | 2.00 | — |

**25 PAISE** **KM# 49.2** **Composition:** Copper-Nickel **Note:** Type 2, 9mm between lion nosetips, 15mm across field.

| Date | Mintage | F | VF | XF | Unc | BU |
|---|---|---|---|---|---|---|
| 1972(C) | — | — | 0.35 | 0.60 | 1.00 | — |
| 1977(B) | — | — | 0.35 | 0.60 | 1.00 | — |

**Note:** Mintage included in KM49.1

| Date | Mintage | F | VF | XF | Unc | BU |
|---|---|---|---|---|---|---|
| 1977B Proof | — | Value: 1.50 | | | | |

**Note:** Mintage included in KM49.1

| Date | Mintage | F | VF | XF | Unc | BU |
|---|---|---|---|---|---|---|
| 1978(B) | — | — | 3.25 | 5.00 | 7.00 | — |

**Note:** Mintage included in KM49.1

| Date | Mintage | F | VF | XF | Unc | BU |
|---|---|---|---|---|---|---|
| 1979B Proof | — | Value: 1.50 | | | | |

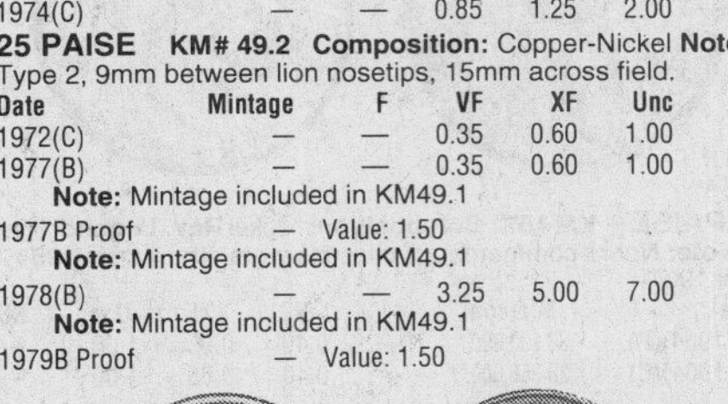

**25 PAISE** **KM# 49.1** **Composition:** Copper-Nickel **Note:** Type 1a, lion with whiskers, faces and wheel redesigned. 1984-86 have edges rounded (local blanks) or flat (Korean blanks).

| Date | Mintage | F | VF | XF | Unc | BU |
|---|---|---|---|---|---|---|
| 1972(B) | 367,640,000 | — | 0.20 | 0.40 | 0.70 | — |
| 1972B Proof | 7,895 | Value: 1.00 | | | | |
| 1972(H) | Inc. above | — | 0.45 | 1.00 | 2.00 | — |
| 1973(B) | — | — | 0.20 | 0.40 | 0.70 | — |
| 1973B Proof | 7,567 | Value: 1.00 | | | | |
| 1973(H) | — | — | 0.35 | 0.60 | 1.00 | — |
| 1974(B) | — | — | 0.20 | 0.40 | 0.70 | — |
| 1974B Proof | — | Value: 1.00 | | | | |
| 1974(H) | — | — | 0.45 | 0.75 | 1.25 | — |
| 1975(B) | 559,980,000 | — | 0.20 | 0.40 | 0.70 | — |
| 1975B Proof | — | Value: 1.00 | | | | |
| 1975(H) | Inc. above | — | 3.00 | 4.00 | 5.00 | — |
| 1976(B) | 30,016,000 | — | 0.60 | 1.00 | 1.50 | — |
| 1976B Proof | Inc. above | Value: 1.00 | | | | |
| 1976(H) | Inc. above | — | 0.60 | 1.00 | 1.50 | — |
| 1977(B) | 270,520,000 | — | 0.20 | 0.40 | 0.70 | — |
| 1977(C) | Inc. above | — | 0.35 | 0.60 | 1.00 | — |
| 1977(H) | Inc. above | — | 0.35 | 0.60 | 1.00 | — |
| 1978B Proof | — | Value: 1.00 | | | | |
| 1978(C) | 131,632,000 | — | 0.25 | 0.40 | 0.70 | — |
| 1978(H) | — | — | 0.25 | 0.40 | 0.70 | — |
| 1979(C) | — | — | 0.50 | 1.00 | 1.50 | — |
| 1979(H) | — | — | 0.50 | 1.00 | 1.50 | — |
| 1980(C) | 6,175,000 | — | 0.25 | 0.40 | 0.70 | — |
| 1980(H) | Inc. above | — | 0.25 | 0.40 | 0.70 | — |
| 1981(B) | 11,048,000 | — | 0.25 | 0.40 | 0.70 | — |
| 1981(C) | Inc. above | — | 1.50 | 2.00 | 2.50 | — |
| 1981(H) | Inc. above | — | 0.45 | 0.75 | 1.25 | — |
| 1982(C) | 38,288,000 | — | 0.45 | 0.75 | 1.25 | — |
| 1983(C) | 137,488,000 | — | 0.45 | 0.75 | 1.25 | — |
| 1984(B) | 98,740,000 | — | 0.45 | 0.75 | 1.25 | — |
| 1984(C) | Inc. above | — | 0.45 | 0.75 | 1.25 | — |
| 1985(B) | 113,872,000 | — | 0.45 | 0.75 | 1.25 | — |
| 1985C | Inc. above | — | 0.15 | 0.25 | 0.50 | — |
| 1985(C) | Inc. above | — | 0.45 | 0.75 | 1.25 | — |
| 1985(H) | Inc. above | — | 0.45 | 0.75 | 1.25 | — |
| 1986(B) | 362,624,000 | — | 0.60 | 0.90 | 1.50 | — |
| 1986(C) | Inc. above | — | 0.60 | 0.90 | 1.50 | — |
| 1986(H) | Inc. above | — | 0.60 | 0.90 | 1.50 | — |
| 1987(C) | 341,160,000 | — | 0.60 | 0.90 | 1.50 | — |
| 1987(H) | Inc. above | — | 0.60 | 0.90 | 1.50 | — |
| 1988(H) | 303,252,000 | — | 0.60 | 0.90 | 1.50 | — |

**25 PAISE** **KM# 49.7** **Composition:** Nickel **Reverse:** Large 25 **Note:** Type 1, lion without whiskers.

| Date | Mintage | F | VF | XF | Unc | BU |
|---|---|---|---|---|---|---|
| 1972(B) | — | — | 8.00 | 12.00 | 18.00 | — |

**25 PAISE** **KM# 49.6** **Composition:** Copper-Nickel **Note:** 9-1/2mm between lion nosetips. Bull has four legs.

| Date | Mintage | F | VF | XF | Unc | BU |
|---|---|---|---|---|---|---|
| 1974(C) | — | — | 0.85 | 1.25 | 2.00 | — |
| 1975(C) | — | — | 0.85 | 1.25 | 2.00 | — |
| 1976(C) | — | — | 2.00 | 3.50 | 5.00 | — |

**25 PAISE** **KM# 49.4** **Composition:** Copper-Nickel **Note:** Type 1b, central lion, bull and horse re-engraved.

| Date | Mintage | F | VF | XF | Unc | BU |
|---|---|---|---|---|---|---|
| 1974(B) | — | — | 2.00 | 5.00 | 6.50 | — |
| 1975(B) | — | — | 5.00 | 7.00 | 12.00 | — |
| 1975(H) | — | — | 1.00 | 3.00 | 5.00 | — |
| 1976(H) | — | — | 6.00 | 8.00 | 15.00 | — |
| 1978(B) | — | — | 2.00 | 3.00 | 5.00 | — |
| 1979(B) | — | — | 2.50 | 5.00 | 7.00 | — |
| 1981(B) | — | — | 4.00 | 6.00 | 8.00 | — |

**25 PAISE** **KM# 50** **Composition:** Copper-Nickel **Subject:** Rural Women's Advancement

| Date | Mintage | F | VF | XF | Unc | BU |
|---|---|---|---|---|---|---|
| 1980(B) | 15,050,000 | — | 0.30 | 0.50 | 1.00 | — |
| 1980B Proof | — | Value: 1.00 | | | | |
| 1980(C) | 8,520,000 | — | 0.50 | 1.00 | 1.50 | — |
| 1980(H) | 10,380,000 | — | 1.00 | 1.50 | 2.00 | — |

**25 PAISE** **KM# 51** **Composition:** Copper-Nickel **Subject:** World Food Day

| Date | Mintage | F | VF | XF | Unc | BU |
|---|---|---|---|---|---|---|
| 1981(B) | 2,170,000 | — | 1.00 | 1.50 | 2.00 | — |
| 1981B Proof | — | Value: 2.00 | | | | |
| 1981(C) | 4,500,000 | — | 1.00 | 1.50 | 2.00 | — |
| 1981(H) | 9,340,000 | — | 1.50 | 2.00 | 3.00 | — |

**25 PAISE** **KM# 52** **Composition:** Copper-Nickel **Subject:** IX Asian Games

| Date | Mintage | F | VF | XF | Unc | BU |
|---|---|---|---|---|---|---|
| 1982(B) | 12,000,000 | — | 0.30 | 0.50 | 1.00 | — |
| 1982B Proof | — | Value: 1.00 | | | | |
| 1982(C) | 12,000,000 | — | 0.30 | 0.50 | 1.00 | — |
| 1982(H) | 330,000 | — | 2.50 | 3.50 | 5.00 | — |

**25 PAISE** **KM# 53.1** **Composition:** Copper-Nickel **Subject:** Forestry **Edge:** Rounded

| Date | Mintage | F | VF | XF | Unc | BU |
|---|---|---|---|---|---|---|
| 1985(B) | — | — | 1.50 | 2.00 | 2.75 | — |

**Note:** Mintage included in KM49.1

| Date | Mintage | F | VF | XF | Unc | BU |
|---|---|---|---|---|---|---|
| 1985(H) | — | — | 5.00 | 7.00 | 10.00 | — |

**Note:** Mintage included in KM49.1

**25 PAISE** **KM# 53.2** **Composition:** Copper-Nickel **Edge:** Flat

| Date | Mintage | F | VF | XF | Unc | BU |
|---|---|---|---|---|---|---|
| 1985(B) | — | — | 5.00 | 7.00 | 10.00 | — |
| 1985(C) | — | — | 3.00 | 5.00 | 7.00 | — |

**25 PAISE** **KM# 49.5** **Composition:** Copper-Nickel **Note:** Type 3.

| Date | Mintage | F | VF | XF | Unc | BU |
|---|---|---|---|---|---|---|
| 1986(B) | — | — | 0.15 | 0.30 | 1.00 | — |
| 1986(C) | — | — | 0.45 | 0.75 | 1.25 | — |
| 1986(H) | — | — | 0.45 | 0.75 | 1.25 | — |
| 1987(B) | — | — | 0.15 | 0.30 | 1.00 | — |
| 1987(C) | — | — | 0.25 | 0.40 | 1.50 | — |
| 1987(C) Long 7 | — | — | 0.25 | 0.40 | 1.50 | — |
| 1988(B) | — | — | 0.20 | 0.35 | 1.25 | — |
| 1988(C) 8's 1.3mm tall | — | — | 0.45 | 0.75 | 2.00 | — |
| 1988(C) 8's 1.8mm tall | — | — | 0.45 | 0.75 | 2.00 | — |
| 1988(H) | — | — | 0.45 | 1.00 | 1.75 | — |
| 1989(B) | — | — | 0.45 | 1.00 | 1.75 | — |
| 1989(C) | — | — | 2.00 | 2.50 | 3.00 | — |
| 1990(B) | — | — | 2.00 | 3.50 | 7.00 | — |

**25 PAISE** **KM# 54** **Composition:** Stainless Steel **Note:** Varieties of date size exist.

| Date | Mintage | F | VF | XF | Unc | BU |
|---|---|---|---|---|---|---|
| 1988C | 305,280,000 | — | 0.10 | 0.20 | 0.40 | — |
| 1988(B) | — | — | 0.45 | 0.75 | 1.25 | — |
| 1988(C) | 18,920,000 | — | 3.50 | 5.00 | 8.00 | — |
| 1988(H) | — | — | 6.00 | 8.00 | 10.00 | — |
| 1988(N) | Inc. above | — | 0.45 | 0.75 | 1.25 | — |
| 1989(B) | — | — | 0.65 | 1.00 | 1.50 | — |
| 1989(C) | — | — | 0.65 | 1.00 | 1.50 | — |
| 1989(H) | — | — | 1.00 | 2.00 | 3.00 | — |
| 1989(N) | — | — | 0.15 | 0.30 | 0.50 | — |
| 1990(B) | — | — | 0.25 | 0.50 | 1.00 | — |
| 1990(C) | — | — | 0.25 | 0.50 | 1.00 | — |
| 1990(H) | — | — | 0.25 | 0.40 | 0.70 | — |
| 1990(N) Large mm | — | — | 0.40 | 0.65 | 1.00 | — |
| 1991(B) | — | — | 0.25 | 0.40 | 0.70 | — |
| 1991(C) | — | — | 0.25 | 0.40 | 0.70 | — |
| 1991(H) | — | — | 0.25 | 0.40 | 0.70 | — |
| 1991(N) | — | — | 0.25 | 0.40 | 0.70 | — |
| 1992(B) | — | — | 0.25 | 0.40 | 0.70 | — |
| 1992(C) | — | — | 1.00 | 2.00 | 3.00 | — |
| 1992(H) | — | — | 1.00 | 2.00 | 3.00 | — |
| 1992(N) | — | — | 0.50 | 1.00 | 2.00 | — |
| 1993(B) | — | — | 0.50 | 1.00 | 2.00 | — |
| 1993(C) | — | — | 0.50 | 1.00 | 2.00 | — |
| 1993(H) | — | — | 2.00 | 3.00 | 5.00 | — |
| 1993(N) | — | — | 0.50 | 0.70 | 1.00 | — |
| 1994(B) | — | — | 0.15 | 0.30 | 0.50 | — |
| 1994(C) | — | — | 0.10 | 0.20 | 0.40 | — |
| 1994(H) | — | — | 0.10 | 0.20 | 0.40 | — |
| 1994(N) | — | — | 0.10 | 0.20 | 0.40 | — |
| 1995(B) | — | — | 0.10 | 0.20 | 0.40 | — |
| 1995(C) | — | — | 0.25 | 0.50 | 1.00 | — |
| 1995(H) | — | — | 0.10 | 0.20 | 0.40 | — |
| 1995(N) | — | — | 0.10 | 0.20 | 0.40 | — |
| 1996(B) | — | — | 0.10 | 0.20 | 0.40 | — |
| 1996(C) | — | — | 0.10 | 0.20 | 0.40 | — |
| 1996(H) | — | — | 0.10 | 0.20 | 0.40 | — |
| 1996(N) | — | — | 0.10 | 0.20 | 0.35 | — |
| 1997(B) | — | — | 0.10 | 0.20 | 0.40 | — |
| 1997(C) | — | — | 0.10 | 0.20 | 0.40 | — |
| 1997(H) | — | — | 0.50 | 1.00 | 2.00 | — |
| 1997(N) | — | — | 0.10 | 0.20 | 0.40 | — |
| 1998(B) | — | — | 0.10 | 0.20 | 0.40 | — |
| 1998(C) | — | — | 0.10 | 0.20 | 0.40 | — |
| 1998(H) | — | — | 0.10 | 0.20 | 0.40 | — |
| 1998(N) | — | — | 0.10 | 0.20 | 0.40 | — |
| 1999(B) | — | — | 0.10 | 0.20 | 0.40 | — |
| 1999(C) | — | — | 0.10 | 0.20 | 0.40 | — |
| 1999(H) | — | — | 0.10 | 0.20 | 0.40 | — |
| 1999(N) | — | — | 0.10 | 0.20 | 0.40 | — |
| 2000(B) | — | — | 0.10 | 0.20 | 0.40 | — |
| 2000(C) | — | — | 0.10 | 0.20 | 0.40 | — |
| 2000(H) | — | — | 0.10 | 0.20 | 0.40 | — |
| 2000(N) | — | — | 0.10 | 0.20 | 0.40 | — |
| 2001(B) | — | — | 0.10 | 0.20 | 0.40 | — |
| 2001(C) | — | — | 0.10 | 0.20 | 0.40 | — |

**50 NAYE PAISE** **KM# 55** **Composition:** Nickel

| Date | Mintage | F | VF | XF | Unc | BU |
|---|---|---|---|---|---|---|
| 1960(B) | 11,224,000 | — | 1.00 | 1.50 | 2.50 | — |
| 1960(B) Proof | — | Value: 3.00 | | | | |
| 1960(C) | Inc. above | — | 0.50 | 1.25 | 2.00 | — |
| 1961(B) | 45,992,000 | — | 0.25 | 0.60 | 1.25 | — |
| 1961(B) Proof | — | Value: 3.00 | | | | |
| 1961(C) | Inc. above | — | 0.25 | 0.60 | 1.25 | — |
| 1962(B) | 64,227,999 | — | 0.25 | 0.60 | 1.25 | — |
| 1962(B) Proof | — | Value: 3.00 | | | | |
| 1962(C) | Inc. above | — | 0.25 | 0.60 | 1.25 | — |
| 1963(B) | 58,168,000 | — | 0.25 | 0.60 | 1.25 | — |
| 1963(B) Proof | — | Value: 3.00 | | | | |
| 1963(C) | Inc. above | — | 1.00 | 1.50 | 2.50 | — |

**50 PAISE** **KM# 56** **Composition:** Nickel **Subject:** Death of Jawaharlal Nehru **Rev. Legend:** English

| Date | Mintage | F | VF | XF | Unc | BU |
|---|---|---|---|---|---|---|
| ND(1964)(B) | 21,900,000 | — | 0.40 | 0.65 | 1.00 | — |
| ND(1964)B Proof | — | Value: 2.50 | | | | |
| ND(1964)(C) | 7,160,000 | — | 0.75 | 1.50 | 2.75 | — |

**50 PAISE** **KM# 57** **Composition:** Nickel **Rev. Legend:** Hindi **Note:** Nehru commemorative issues were struck from 1964 until 1967.

| Date | Mintage | F | VF | XF | Unc | BU |
|---|---|---|---|---|---|---|
| ND(1964)(B) | 36,190,000 | — | 0.40 | 0.65 | 1.00 | — |
| ND(1964)(C) | 28,350,000 | — | 0.40 | 0.65 | 1.00 | — |

**50 PAISE** **KM# 58.1** **Composition:** Nickel **Note:** Obverse 1, Reverse 1.

| Date | Mintage | F | VF | XF | Unc | BU |
|---|---|---|---|---|---|---|
| 1964(C) | 23,361,000 | — | 0.50 | 1.00 | 1.75 | — |
| 1967(B) | 19,267,000 | — | 0.50 | 1.00 | 1.75 | — |

**Note:** Varieties of 1967(B) reverse edges exist, half teeth and the scarce full teeth

**50 PAISE** **KM# 58.2** **Composition:** Nickel **Note:** Obverse 2, Reverse 2.

| Date | Mintage | F | VF | XF | Unc | BU |
|---|---|---|---|---|---|---|
| 1967(C) | — | — | 0.60 | 1.00 | 1.50 | — |
| 1968(B) | 28,076,000 | — | 0.25 | 0.60 | 1.00 | — |

**Note:** A scarce 1968(b) variety exists with crude obverse, no whiskers, thick horsetail

| Date | Mintage | F | VF | XF | Unc | BU |
|---|---|---|---|---|---|---|
| 1968(C) | Inc. above | — | 0.25 | 0.60 | 1.00 | — |
| 1969(B) | 59,388,000 | — | 0.25 | 0.60 | 1.00 | — |
| 1969(C) | Inc. above | — | 0.35 | 0.75 | 1.25 | — |
| 1970(B) | Inc. above | — | 0.35 | 0.75 | 1.25 | — |
| 1970(C) | Inc. above | — | 0.25 | 0.60 | 1.00 | — |
| 1971(C) | 57,900,000 | — | 0.25 | 0.50 | 0.85 | — |

**50 PAISE** **KM# 59** **Composition:** Nickel **Subject:** Centennial - Birth of Mahatma Gandhi **Note:** Struck during 1969 and 1970.

| Date | Mintage | F | VF | XF | Unc | BU |
|---|---|---|---|---|---|---|
| ND(1969)(B) | 10,260,000 | — | 0.25 | 0.50 | 1.00 | — |
| ND(1969)B Proof | 9,147 | Value: 2.00 | | | | |
| ND(1969)(C) | 12,100,000 | — | 0.25 | 0.50 | 1.00 | — |

**50 PAISE** **KM# 58.3** **Composition:** Nickel **Note:** Obverse 1, Reverse 2.

| Date | Mintage | F | VF | XF | Unc | BU |
|---|---|---|---|---|---|---|
| 1970(B) | — | — | 1.00 | 2.00 | 3.00 | — |

**Note:** Included 1969

| Date | Mintage | F | VF | XF | Unc | BU |
|---|---|---|---|---|---|---|
| 1970B Proof | 3,046 | Value: 2.00 | | | | |
| 1971B Proof | 4,375 | Value: 2.00 | | | | |

**50 PAISE** **KM# 61** **Composition:** Copper-Nickel **Reverse:** Lettering spaced out **Note:** Type 2.

| Date | Mintage | F | VF | XF | Unc | BU |
|---|---|---|---|---|---|---|
| 1972(B) | — | — | 0.35 | 0.60 | 1.00 | — |
| 1972(C) | — | — | 0.35 | 0.60 | 1.00 | — |
| 1973(B) | — | — | 0.35 | 0.60 | 1.00 | — |
| 1973(C) | — | — | 2.00 | 3.50 | 6.00 | — |

**50 PAISE** **KM# 60** **Composition:** Copper-Nickel **Subject:** 25th Anniversary of Independence

| Date | Mintage | F | VF | XF | Unc | BU |
|---|---|---|---|---|---|---|
| ND(1972)(B) | 43,800,000 | — | 0.30 | 0.50 | 1.00 | — |
| ND(1972)B Proof | 7,895 | Value: 2.00 | | | | |
| ND(1972)(C) | 40,080,000 | — | 0.45 | 0.75 | 1.50 | — |

**50 PAISE** **KM# 62** **Composition:** Copper-Nickel **Series:** F.A.O. **Subject:** Grow More Food

| Date | Mintage | F | VF | XF | Unc | BU |
|---|---|---|---|---|---|---|
| 1973(B) | 28,720,000 | — | 0.30 | 0.50 | 1.00 | — |
| 1973B Proof | 11,000 | Value: 2.00 | | | | |
| 1973(C) | 40,100,000 | — | 0.30 | 0.50 | 1.00 | — |

**50 PAISE** **KM# 63** **Composition:** Copper-Nickel **Reverse:** Lettering close **Note:** Type 2.

| Date | Mintage | F | VF | XF | Unc | BU |
|---|---|---|---|---|---|---|
| 1974(B) | — | — | 0.25 | 0.50 | 1.00 | — |
| 1974B Proof | — | Value: 2.00 | | | | |
| 1974(C) | — | — | 0.35 | 0.75 | 1.50 | — |
| 1975(B) | 225,880,000 | — | 0.25 | 0.50 | 1.00 | — |
| 1975B Proof | — | Value: 2.00 | | | | |
| 1975(C) | Inc. above | — | 0.25 | 0.50 | 1.00 | — |
| 1975(H) | — | — | 0.75 | 1.25 | 2.00 | — |
| 1976(B) | 99,564,000 | — | 0.25 | 0.50 | 1.00 | — |
| 1976B Proof | Inc. above | Value: 2.00 | | | | |
| 1976(C) | Inc. above | — | 0.35 | 0.75 | 1.50 | — |
| 1976(H) | Inc. above | — | 0.75 | 1.25 | 2.00 | — |
| 1977(B) | 97,272,000 | — | 0.25 | 0.50 | 1.00 | — |
| 1977B Proof | Inc. above | Value: 2.00 | | | | |
| 1977(C) | Inc. above | — | 0.40 | 0.75 | 1.50 | — |
| 1977(H) | Inc. above | — | 0.40 | 0.75 | 1.50 | — |
| 1978B Proof | 25,648,000 | Value: 2.00 | | | | |
| 1978(C) | — | — | 0.25 | 0.50 | 1.00 | — |
| 1979B Proof | — | Value: 2.00 | | | | |
| 1980(B) | — | — | 0.25 | 0.50 | 1.00 | — |
| 1980B Proof | — | Value: 2.00 | | | | |
| 1980(C) | — | — | 5.00 | 8.00 | 12.00 | — |
| 1981B Proof | — | Value: 2.00 | | | | |
| 1983(C) | 62,634,000 | — | 5.00 | 8.00 | 12.00 | — |

**50 PAISE** **KM# 64** **Composition:** Copper-Nickel **Subject:** National Integration

| Date | Mintage | F | VF | XF | Unc | BU |
|---|---|---|---|---|---|---|
| 1982(B) | 9,804,000 | — | 0.40 | 0.75 | 1.25 | — |
| 1982B Proof | — | Value: 3.00 | | | | |
| 1982(C) | Inc. above | — | 10.00 | 15.00 | 20.00 | — |

**50 PAISE** **KM# 65** **Composition:** Copper-Nickel **Note:** Type 3.

| Date | Mintage | F | VF | XF | Unc | BU |
|---|---|---|---|---|---|---|
| 1984(B) | 61,548,000 | — | 0.25 | 0.50 | 0.85 | — |
| 1984(C) | Inc. above | — | 1.00 | 1.50 | 2.50 | — |
| 1984(H) | — | — | 2.00 | 3.00 | 5.00 | — |
| 1985(B) | 210,964,000 | — | 0.25 | 0.50 | 0.85 | — |
| 1985(C) | Inc. above | — | 0.25 | 0.50 | 0.85 | — |
| 1985(H) | Inc. above | — | 1.00 | 1.50 | 3.00 | — |
| 1985(T) | Inc. above | — | 0.20 | 0.30 | 0.65 | — |
| 1986(C) | 117,576,000 | — | 0.50 | 1.00 | 2.00 | — |
| 1987(B) | — | — | 0.25 | 0.50 | 0.85 | — |
| 1987(C) | 145,140,000 | — | 0.25 | 0.50 | 0.85 | — |
| 1987(H) | Inc. above | — | 0.40 | 0.75 | 1.50 | — |
| 1988(B) | 149,092,000 | — | 0.25 | 0.50 | 0.85 | — |
| 1988(C) | Inc. above | — | 1.00 | 1.50 | 3.00 | — |
| 1988(H) | Inc. above | — | 1.00 | 1.50 | 2.50 | — |
| 1989(B) | — | — | 0.50 | 1.00 | 2.00 | — |
| 1989(C) | — | — | 0.50 | 1.00 | 2.00 | — |
| 1990(B) | — | — | 2.00 | 4.00 | 7.00 | — |

**50 PAISE** **KM# 66** **Composition:** Copper-Nickel **Subject:** Golden Jubilee of Reserve Bank of India

| Date | Mintage | F | VF | XF | Unc | BU |
|---|---|---|---|---|---|---|
| ND(1985)(B) | — | — | 0.50 | 0.85 | 1.75 | — |
| **Note:** Mintage included in KM65 | | | | | | |
| ND(1985)B Proof | — | Value: 15.00 | | | | |
| **Note:** Mintage included in KM680 | | | | | | |
| ND(1985)(C) | — | — | 2.00 | 3.00 | 5.00 | — |
| ND(1985)(H) | — | — | 0.75 | 1.25 | 2.50 | — |
| **Note:** Mintage included in KM65 | | | | | | |

**50 PAISE** **KM# 67.1** **Composition:** Copper-Nickel **Subject:** Death of Indira Gandhi

| Date | Mintage | F | VF | XF | Unc | BU |
|---|---|---|---|---|---|---|
| ND(1985)(B) | — | — | 0.20 | 0.40 | 1.00 | — |
| **Note:** Mintage included in KM65 | | | | | | |
| ND(1985)B Proof | — | Value: 17.50 | | | | |
| **Note:** Mintage included in KM65 | | | | | | |
| ND(1985)(C) | — | — | 0.20 | 0.40 | 1.00 | — |
| **Note:** Mintage included in KM65 | | | | | | |
| ND(1985)(H) | — | — | 0.65 | 1.00 | 1.50 | — |
| **Note:** Mintage included in KM65 | | | | | | |

**50 PAISE** **KM# 67.2** **Composition:** Copper-Nickel **Obverse:** KM#68 **Reverse:** KM#67 **Note:** Mule.

| Date | Mintage | F | VF | XF | Unc | BU |
|---|---|---|---|---|---|---|
| ND(1985)(C) | — | — | 35.00 | 50.00 | 80.00 | — |

**50 PAISE** **KM# 68.2** **Composition:** Copper-Nickel **Obverse:** KM#67 **Reverse:** KM#68 **Note:** Mule.

| Date | Mintage | F | VF | XF | Unc | BU |
|---|---|---|---|---|---|---|
| 1986(C) | — | — | 50.00 | 70.00 | 100 | — |

**50 PAISE** **KM# 68.1** **Composition:** Copper-Nickel **Series:** F.A.O. **Subject:** Fisheries

| Date | Mintage | F | VF | XF | Unc | BU |
|---|---|---|---|---|---|---|
| 1986(B) | — | — | 0.30 | 0.50 | 1.00 | — |
| **Note:** Mintage included in KM65 | | | | | | |
| 1986B Proof | — | Value: 15.00 | | | | |
| **Note:** Mintage included in KM65 | | | | | | |
| 1986(C) | — | — | 2.00 | 3.00 | 5.00 | — |
| 1986(H) | — | — | 2.00 | 3.00 | 5.00 | — |
| **Note:** Mintage included in KM65 | | | | | | |

**50 PAISE** **KM# 69** **Composition:** Stainless Steel **Subject:** Parliament Building in New Delhi

| Date | Mintage | F | VF | XF | Unc | BU |
|---|---|---|---|---|---|---|
| 1988C | 272,160,000 | — | 0.20 | 0.30 | 0.50 | — |
| 1988(B) | — | — | 0.20 | 0.40 | 0.75 | — |
| 1988(C) | 2,195,000 | — | 6.00 | 9.00 | 14.00 | — |
| 1988(H) | Inc. above | — | 6.00 | 9.00 | 14.00 | — |
| 1988(N) | — | — | 0.20 | 0.40 | 0.75 | — |
| 1989(B) | — | — | 0.20 | 0.40 | 0.75 | — |
| 1989(C) | — | — | 1.50 | 3.00 | 5.00 | — |
| 1989(H) | — | — | 0.50 | 1.00 | 2.00 | — |
| 1989(N) | — | — | 0.15 | 0.50 | 1.00 | — |
| 1990(B) | — | — | 0.15 | 0.50 | 1.00 | — |
| 1990(C) | — | — | 0.50 | 1.00 | 2.00 | — |
| 1990(H) | — | — | 0.15 | 0.50 | 1.00 | — |
| 1990(N) Small mm | — | — | 0.15 | 0.50 | 1.00 | — |
| 1990(N) Large mm | — | — | 0.15 | 0.50 | 1.00 | — |
| 1991(B) | — | — | 0.15 | 0.50 | 1.00 | — |
| 1991(C) | — | — | 0.15 | 0.50 | 1.00 | — |
| 1991(H) | — | — | 0.15 | 0.25 | 0.50 | — |
| 1991(N) | — | — | 0.10 | 0.35 | 0.60 | — |
| 1992(B) | — | — | 0.10 | 0.35 | 0.60 | — |
| 1992(C) | — | — | 0.50 | 1.00 | 2.00 | — |
| 1992(H) | — | — | 0.10 | 0.35 | 0.60 | — |
| 1992(N) | — | — | 0.10 | 0.35 | 0.60 | — |
| 1993(C) | — | — | 0.50 | 1.00 | 2.00 | — |
| 1993(N) | — | — | 0.10 | 0.35 | 0.60 | — |
| 1994(B) | — | — | 0.10 | 0.35 | 0.60 | — |
| 1994(C) | — | — | 0.50 | 1.00 | 2.00 | — |
| 1994(H) | — | — | 0.10 | 0.35 | 0.60 | — |
| 1994(N) | — | — | 0.10 | 0.35 | 0.60 | — |
| 1995(B) | — | — | 0.10 | 0.20 | 0.35 | — |
| 1995(C) | — | — | 0.50 | 1.00 | 2.00 | — |
| 1995(H) | — | — | 0.20 | 0.30 | 0.50 | — |
| 1995(N) | — | — | 0.10 | 0.20 | 0.35 | — |
| 1996(B) | — | — | 0.10 | 0.20 | 0.35 | — |
| 1996(C) | — | — | 0.10 | 0.20 | 0.35 | — |
| 1996(H) | — | — | 0.10 | 0.20 | 0.35 | — |
| 1996(N) | — | — | 0.10 | 0.20 | 0.35 | — |
| 1997(B) | — | — | 0.10 | 0.20 | 0.35 | — |
| 1997(C) | — | — | 0.10 | 0.20 | 0.35 | — |
| 1997(H) | — | — | 2.00 | 3.00 | 5.00 | — |
| 1997(N) | — | — | 0.10 | 0.20 | 0.35 | — |
| 1998(B) | — | — | 0.10 | 0.20 | 0.35 | — |
| 1998(C) | — | — | 0.10 | 0.20 | 0.35 | — |
| 1998(H) | — | — | 1.00 | 1.50 | 3.00 | — |
| 1998(N) | — | — | 0.10 | 0.20 | 0.35 | — |
| 1999(B) | — | — | 0.15 | 0.25 | 0.50 | — |
| 1999(C) | — | — | 0.15 | 0.25 | 0.50 | — |
| 1999(H) | — | — | 0.15 | 0.25 | 0.50 | — |
| 1999(N) | — | — | 0.15 | 0.25 | 0.50 | — |
| 2000(B) | — | — | 0.15 | 0.25 | 0.50 | — |
| 2000(C) | — | — | 0.15 | 0.25 | 0.50 | — |
| 2000(H) | — | — | 0.15 | 0.25 | 0.50 | — |
| 2000(N) | — | — | 0.15 | 0.25 | 0.50 | — |
| 2001(B) | — | — | 0.15 | 0.25 | 0.50 | — |
| 2001(C) | — | — | 0.15 | 0.25 | 0.50 | — |
| 2001(N) | — | — | 0.15 | 0.25 | 0.50 | — |

**50 PAISE** **KM# 70** **Composition:** Stainless Steel **Subject:** 50th Anniversary of Independence

| Date | Mintage | F | VF | XF | Unc | BU |
|---|---|---|---|---|---|---|
| 1997(B) | — | — | 0.25 | 0.40 | 0.75 | — |
| 1997(C) | — | — | 0.25 | 0.40 | 0.75 | — |
| 1997(H) | — | — | 0.25 | 0.40 | 0.75 | — |
| 1997(M) Proof | — | Value: 15.00 | | | | |
| 1997(N) | — | — | 0.25 | 0.40 | 0.75 | — |

**RUPEE KM# 75.1 Weight:** 10.0000 g. **Composition:** Nickel **Note:** Obverse 1.

| Date | Mintage | F | VF | XF | Unc | BU |
|---|---|---|---|---|---|---|
| 1962(C) | 3,689,000 | — | 1.00 | 2.00 | 3.00 | — |

**RUPEE KM# 76 Weight:** 10.0000 g. **Composition:** Nickel **Subject:** Death of Jawaharlal Nehru **Note:** Nehru commemorative issues were struck until 1967.

| Date | Mintage | F | VF | XF | Unc | BU |
|---|---|---|---|---|---|---|
| ND(1964)(B) | 10,010,000 | — | 0.65 | 1.00 | 2.00 | — |
| ND(1964)B Proof | — | Value: 5.00 | | | | |
| ND(1964)(C) | 10,020,000 | — | 0.65 | 1.00 | 2.00 | — |

**RUPEE KM# 77 Weight:** 10.0000 g. **Composition:** Nickel **Subject:** Centennial - Birth of Mahatma Gandhi **Note:** Struck during 1969 and 1970.

| Date | Mintage | F | VF | XF | Unc | BU |
|---|---|---|---|---|---|---|
| ND(1969)(B) | 5,180,000 | — | 0.70 | 1.25 | 2.00 | — |
| ND(1969)B Proof | 9,147 | Value: 3.00 | | | | |
| ND(1969)(C) | 6,690,000 | — | 1.00 | 1.50 | 2.50 | — |

**RUPEE KM# 75.2 Weight:** 10.0000 g. **Composition:** Nickel **Reverse:** Smaller date and denomination

| Date | Mintage | F | VF | XF | Unc | BU |
|---|---|---|---|---|---|---|
| 1970(B) | Inc. above | — | 3.50 | 5.00 | 7.00 | — |
| 1970B Proof | 3,046 | Value: 3.00 | | | | |
| 1971B Proof | 4,375 | Value: 3.00 | | | | |
| 1972B Proof | 7,895,000 | Value: 2.50 | | | | |
| 1973B Proof | 7,567 | Value: 2.50 | | | | |
| 1974B Proof | — | Value: 2.50 | | | | |

**RUPEE KM# 78.1 Weight:** 8.0000 g. **Composition:** Copper-Nickel

| Date | Mintage | F | VF | XF | Unc | BU |
|---|---|---|---|---|---|---|
| 1975(B) | 98,850,000 | — | 0.40 | 0.85 | 1.50 | — |
| 1975B Proof | — | Value: 2.50 | | | | |
| 1975(C) | — | — | 6.50 | 8.00 | 10.00 | — |
| 1976(B) | 161,895,000 | — | 0.35 | 0.75 | 1.50 | — |
| 1976B Proof | Inc. above | Value: 2.50 | | | | |
| 1977(B) | 177,105,000 | — | 0.35 | 0.75 | 1.50 | — |
| 1977B Proof | Inc. above | Value: 2.50 | | | | |
| 1978(B) | 127,348,000 | — | 0.40 | 0.80 | 1.50 | — |
| 1978B Proof | Inc. above | Value: 2.50 | | | | |
| 1978(C) | Inc. above | — | 0.50 | 1.00 | 1.75 | — |
| 1979(C) | — | — | 8.00 | 11.00 | 15.00 | — |

**RUPEE KM# 78.2 Weight:** 8.0000 g. **Composition:** Copper-Nickel **Note:** Type 2.

| Date | Mintage | F | VF | XF | Unc | BU |
|---|---|---|---|---|---|---|
| 1975(C) | — | — | 0.40 | 0.85 | 1.50 | — |
| **Note:** Mintage included in KM78.1 | | | | | | |
| 1976(C) | — | — | 0.50 | 1.25 | 2.25 | — |
| **Note:** Mintage included in KM78.1 | | | | | | |

**RUPEE KM# 78.3 Weight:** 8.0000 g. **Composition:** Copper-Nickel **Note:** Type 3. Border varieties of long vs. short teeth on 1981 reverse and 1982 obverse.

| Date | Mintage | F | VF | XF | Unc | BU |
|---|---|---|---|---|---|---|
| 1979(B) | — | — | 0.35 | 0.60 | 1.00 | — |
| 1979B Proof | — | Value: 2.50 | | | | |
| 1979(C) | — | — | 0.40 | 0.75 | 1.50 | — |
| 1980(B) | 84,768,000 | — | 0.35 | 0.60 | 1.00 | — |
| 1980B Proof | — | Value: 2.50 | | | | |
| 1980(C) | Inc. above | — | 0.40 | 0.75 | 1.25 | — |
| 1981(B) | 82,458,000 | — | 0.35 | 0.60 | 1.00 | — |
| 1981B Proof | — | Value: 2.50 | | | | |
| 1981(C) | Inc. above | — | 0.40 | 0.75 | 1.25 | — |
| 1982(B) | 116,811,000 | — | 0.40 | 0.75 | 1.25 | — |

**RUPEE KM# 79.1 Weight:** 6.0000 g. **Composition:** Copper-Nickel **Edge:** Security **Note:** Lions' hair and ears on 1984(B)-1989(B) issues vary from others.

| Date | Mintage | F | VF | XF | Unc | BU |
|---|---|---|---|---|---|---|
| 1983(B) | 32,490,000 | — | 0.30 | 0.50 | 1.00 | — |
| 1983(C) | Inc. above | — | 0.30 | 0.50 | 1.00 | — |
| 1984(B) | 152,378,000 | — | 0.25 | 0.40 | 0.75 | — |
| 1984(C) | Inc. above | — | 0.25 | 0.40 | 0.75 | — |
| 1984(H) | Inc. above | — | 1.50 | 2.25 | 3.00 | — |
| 1985(B) | 444,516,000 | — | 0.25 | 0.40 | 0.75 | — |
| 1985(C) | Inc. above | — | 0.25 | 0.40 | 0.75 | — |
| 1985H | Inc. above | — | 0.25 | 0.40 | 0.75 | — |
| 1985(L) | Inc. above | — | 0.25 | 0.40 | 0.75 | — |
| 1986(B) | 1,396,074,000 | — | 0.25 | 0.40 | 0.75 | — |
| 1986(C) | Inc. above | — | 0.25 | 0.40 | 0.75 | — |
| 1986(H) | Inc. above | — | 1.50 | 2.25 | 3.00 | — |
| 1987(B) | 685,502,000 | — | 0.25 | 0.40 | 0.75 | — |
| 1987(C) | Inc. above | — | 0.25 | 0.40 | 0.75 | — |
| 1987(H) | Inc. above | — | 0.25 | 0.40 | 0.75 | — |
| 1988(B) | 240,447,000 | — | 0.75 | 1.25 | 2.00 | — |
| 1988(C) | Inc. above | — | 0.25 | 0.40 | 0.75 | — |
| 1988(H) | Inc. above | — | 0.40 | 0.75 | 1.25 | — |
| 1989(B) | — | — | 1.50 | 2.25 | 3.00 | — |
| 1989(C) | — | — | 0.25 | 0.45 | 0.75 | — |
| 1989(H) | — | — | 0.25 | 0.45 | 0.75 | — |
| 1990(C) | — | — | 1.50 | 2.25 | 3.00 | — |
| 1990(H) | — | — | 0.25 | 0.45 | 0.75 | — |

**RUPEE KM# 80 Weight:** 6.0000 g. **Composition:** Copper-Nickel **Subject:** Youth Year **Edge:** Security

| Date | Mintage | F | VF | XF | Unc | BU |
|---|---|---|---|---|---|---|
| 1985(B) | — | — | 0.35 | 0.60 | 1.25 | — |
| **Note:** Mintage included in KM79.1 | | | | | | |
| 1985(C) | — | — | 0.50 | 1.00 | 2.00 | — |
| **Note:** Mintage included in KM79.1 | | | | | | |
| 1985(C) Proof | — | Value: 10.00 | | | | |
| **Note:** Mintage included in KM79.1 | | | | | | |
| 1985(H) | — | — | 2.00 | 3.00 | 5.00 | — |

**RUPEE KM# 81 Weight:** 6.0000 g. **Composition:** Copper-Nickel **Series:** F.A.O. **Reverse:** Small Farmers

| Date | Mintage | F | VF | XF | Unc | BU |
|---|---|---|---|---|---|---|
| 1987(B) | 234,223,000 | — | 0.35 | 0.60 | 1.25 | — |
| 1987B Proof | — | Value: 5.00 | | | | |
| 1987(C) | Inc. above | — | 0.50 | 1.00 | 2.00 | — |
| 1987(H) | 191,120,000 | — | 1.50 | 3.00 | 4.00 | — |

**RUPEE KM# 82 Weight:** 6.0000 g. **Composition:** Copper-Nickel **Series:** F.A.O. **Reverse:** Rainfed Farming

| Date | Mintage | F | VF | XF | Unc | BU |
|---|---|---|---|---|---|---|
| 1988(B) | — | — | 1.00 | 1.50 | 3.00 | — |
| **Note:** Mintage included in KM79.1 | | | | | | |
| 1988(C) | — | — | 1.00 | 2.00 | 4.00 | — |
| 1988(H) | — | — | 3.00 | 5.00 | 8.00 | — |

**RUPEE KM# 79.2 Weight:** 6.0000 g. **Composition:** Copper-Nickel **Obverse:** Horse in pedestal shorter, more detailed

| Date | Mintage | F | VF | XF | Unc | BU |
|---|---|---|---|---|---|---|
| 1988(B) | — | — | 1.00 | 1.50 | 2.50 | — |
| 1989(N) | — | — | 1.00 | 1.50 | 2.50 | — |
| 1990(N) | — | — | 1.00 | 1.50 | 2.50 | — |

**RUPEE KM# 79.3 Weight:** 6.0000 g. **Composition:** Copper-Nickel **Obverse:** Lions' chest hairs restyled

| Date | Mintage | F | VF | XF | Unc | BU |
|---|---|---|---|---|---|---|
| 1988(B) | — | — | 0.25 | 0.50 | 1.00 | — |
| 1989(B) | — | — | 0.25 | 0.50 | 1.00 | — |
| 1990(B) | — | — | 0.25 | 0.50 | 1.00 | — |

**RUPEE KM# 79.4 Weight:** 6.0000 g. **Composition:** Copper-Nickel **Obverse:** Similar to 79.1 **Edge:** Milled **Note:** Traces of security edge and/or mostly smooth edges are frequently encountered, especially for 1989. 1989-1991(c) is a variety with bulging eyes on side lions and irregular straight hair on central lion.

| Date | Mintage | F | VF | XF | Unc | BU |
|---|---|---|---|---|---|---|
| 1989(B) | — | — | 10.00 | 15.00 | 20.00 | — |
| 1989(C) | — | — | 5.00 | 7.00 | 11.00 | — |
| 1989(H) | — | — | 10.00 | 15.00 | 20.00 | — |
| 1990(C) | — | — | 0.35 | 0.50 | 1.00 | — |
| 1990(H) | — | — | 0.50 | 0.75 | 1.50 | — |
| 1991(C) | — | — | 0.35 | 0.50 | 1.00 | — |

**RUPEE** **KM# 83** **Weight:** 6.0000 g. **Composition:** Copper-Nickel **Subject:** 100th Anniversary of Nehru's Birth

| Date | Mintage | F | VF | XF | Unc | BU |
|---|---|---|---|---|---|---|
| 1989(B) | — | — | 0.25 | 0.50 | 1.00 | — |
| 1989B Proof | — | Value: 5.00 | | | | |
| 1989(C) | — | — | 1.00 | 2.00 | 3.00 | — |
| 1989(H) | — | — | 1.00 | 2.00 | 3.00 | — |

**RUPEE** **KM# 84** **Weight:** 6.0000 g. **Composition:** Copper-Nickel **Series:** F.A.O. **Subject:** Food and Environment

| Date | Mintage | F | VF | XF | Unc | BU |
|---|---|---|---|---|---|---|
| 1989(B) | — | — | 1.00 | 2.00 | 3.50 | — |
| 1989(H) | — | — | 5.00 | 8.00 | 10.00 | — |

**RUPEE** **KM# 87.1** **Weight:** 6.0000 g. **Composition:** Copper-Nickel **Subject:** SAARC Year - Care for the Girl Child

| Date | Mintage | F | VF | XF | Unc | BU |
|---|---|---|---|---|---|---|
| 1990(B) | — | — | 0.40 | 0.80 | 2.00 | — |

**RUPEE** **KM# 79.5** **Weight:** 6.0000 g. **Composition:** Copper-Nickel **Obverse:** Lions similar to KM#79.3

| Date | Mintage | F | VF | XF | Unc | BU |
|---|---|---|---|---|---|---|
| 1990(C) | — | — | 0.50 | 1.00 | 2.00 | — |
| 1990(B) | — | — | 0.35 | 0.60 | 1.00 | — |
| 1991(B) | — | — | 0.20 | 0.35 | 0.85 | — |
| 1991(H) | — | — | 0.35 | 0.60 | 1.00 | — |

**RUPEE** **KM# 87.2** **Weight:** 6.0000 g. **Composition:** Copper-Nickel **Edge:** Milled **Note:** Edge varieties exist.

| Date | Mintage | F | VF | XF | Unc | BU |
|---|---|---|---|---|---|---|
| 1990(B) | — | — | 0.50 | 1.25 | 3.00 | — |
| 1990(H) | — | — | 0.50 | 1.25 | 3.00 | — |

**RUPEE** **KM# 85** **Weight:** 6.0000 g. **Composition:** Copper-Nickel **Subject:** Dr. Ambedkar

| Date | Mintage | F | VF | XF | Unc | BU |
|---|---|---|---|---|---|---|
| 1990(B) | — | — | 0.20 | 0.75 | 1.50 | — |
| 1990(H) | — | — | 0.40 | 1.25 | 2.50 | — |

**RUPEE** **KM# 86** **Weight:** 6.0000 g. **Composition:** Copper-Nickel **Subject:** 15th Anniversary of I.C.D.S.

| Date | Mintage | F | VF | XF | Unc | BU |
|---|---|---|---|---|---|---|
| ND(1990)(B) | — | — | 0.20 | 0.75 | 1.50 | — |
| ND(1990)(H) | — | — | 0.40 | 1.25 | 2.50 | — |

**RUPEE** **KM# 88** **Weight:** 6.0000 g. **Composition:** Copper-Nickel **Series:** F.A.O. **Reverse:** Farming Scene

| Date | Mintage | F | VF | XF | Unc | BU |
|---|---|---|---|---|---|---|
| 1990(C) | — | — | 3.00 | 5.00 | 8.00 | — |
| **Note:** 1990(C) is seldom well struck | | | | | | |
| 1990(H) | — | — | 5.00 | 7.00 | 10.00 | — |

**RUPEE** **KM# 89** **Weight:** 6.0000 g. **Composition:** Copper-Nickel **Subject:** Rajiv Gandhi **Note:** Edge varieties exist.

| Date | Mintage | F | VF | XF | Unc | BU |
|---|---|---|---|---|---|---|
| ND(1991)(B) | — | — | 0.35 | 0.75 | 1.50 | — |
| **Note:** The Bombay mint mark occasionally resembles the Noida mm | | | | | | |
| ND(1991)(H) | — | — | 0.40 | 1.00 | 2.00 | — |

**RUPEE** **KM# 90** **Weight:** 6.0000 g. **Composition:** Copper-Nickel **Subject:** Commonwealth Parliamentary Conference

| Date | Mintage | F | VF | XF | Unc | BU |
|---|---|---|---|---|---|---|
| 1991(B) | — | — | 0.35 | 0.75 | 1.50 | — |
| 1991(B) Prooflike | — | — | — | — | 3.00 | — |
| 1991B Proof | — | Value: 5.00 | | | | |

**RUPEE** **KM# 91** **Weight:** 6.0000 g. **Composition:** Copper-Nickel **Subject:** Tourism Year

| Date | Mintage | F | VF | XF | Unc | BU |
|---|---|---|---|---|---|---|
| 1991(B) | — | — | 0.35 | 0.75 | 1.50 | — |
| 1991(H) | — | — | 0.60 | 1.25 | 2.50 | — |
| 1991(B) Prooflike | — | — | — | — | 3.00 | — |
| 1991B Proof | — | Value: 5.00 | | | | |

**RUPEE** **KM# 93** **Composition:** Copper-Nickel **Subject:** Quit India **Edge:** Milled

| Date | Mintage | F | VF | XF | Unc | BU |
|---|---|---|---|---|---|---|
| ND(1992)(B) | — | — | 0.50 | 1.00 | 2.00 | — |
| ND(1992)(C) | — | — | 1.00 | 3.00 | 6.00 | — |
| ND(1992)(H) | — | — | 2.00 | 3.50 | 8.00 | — |

**RUPEE** **KM# 94** **Composition:** Copper-Nickel **Series:** World Food Day

| Date | Mintage | F | VF | XF | Unc | BU |
|---|---|---|---|---|---|---|
| 1992(C) | — | — | 1.50 | 2.50 | 4.50 | — |

**RUPEE** **KM# 92.1** **Composition:** Stainless Steel **Note:** Milled edge, sometimes faint.

| Date | Mintage | F | VF | XF | Unc | BU |
|---|---|---|---|---|---|---|
| 1992(B) | — | — | 0.20 | 0.30 | 0.60 | — |
| 1992(H) | — | — | 0.20 | 0.30 | 0.60 | — |
| 1993(B) | — | — | 0.20 | 0.30 | 0.60 | — |
| **Note:** Two mintmark varieties exist for 1993(B) and 1994(B) | | | | | | |
| 1993(C) | — | — | 0.20 | 0.30 | 0.60 | — |
| 1993(H) | — | — | 0.20 | 0.30 | 0.60 | — |
| 1993(N) | — | — | 0.20 | 0.30 | 0.60 | — |
| 1994(B) | — | — | 0.15 | 0.25 | 0.50 | — |
| **Note:** Two mintmark varieties exist for 1993(B) and 1994(B) | | | | | | |
| 1994(C) | — | — | 0.15 | 0.25 | 0.50 | — |
| 1994(H) | — | — | 0.15 | 0.25 | 0.50 | — |
| 1994(N) | — | — | 0.15 | 0.25 | 0.50 | — |
| 1995(B) | — | — | 0.15 | 0.25 | 0.50 | — |
| 1995(C) | — | — | 0.15 | 0.25 | 0.50 | — |
| 1995(H) | — | — | 0.15 | 0.25 | 0.50 | — |
| 1995(N) | — | — | 0.15 | 0.25 | 0.50 | — |
| 1996(H) | — | — | 1.00 | 1.50 | 2.50 | — |

**RUPEE** **KM# 95** **Composition:** Copper-Nickel **Subject:** Inter Parliamentary Union Conference

| Date | Mintage | F | VF | XF | Unc | BU |
|---|---|---|---|---|---|---|
| 1993(B) | — | — | 0.50 | 1.25 | 3.00 | — |

**RUPEE** **KM# 96** **Composition:** Stainless Steel **Subject:** International Year of the Family

| Date | Mintage | F | VF | XF | Unc | BU |
|---|---|---|---|---|---|---|
| 1994(B) | — | — | 0.40 | 0.75 | 2.00 | — |

**RUPEE** **KM# 97.1** **Composition:** Stainless Steel **Subject:** Eighth World Tamil Conference **Obverse:** Asoka column **Reverse:** St. Thiruvalluvar

| Date | Mintage | F | VF | XF | Unc | BU |
|---|---|---|---|---|---|---|
| 1995(B) | — | — | 0.50 | 1.00 | 1.50 | — |
| 1995(H) | — | — | 0.70 | 1.25 | 2.00 | — |
| 1995(N) | — | — | 0.50 | 1.00 | 1.75 | — |

**RUPEE** **KM# 97.2** **Composition:** Stainless Steel **Edge:** Plain

| Date | Mintage | F | VF | XF | Unc | BU |
|---|---|---|---|---|---|---|
| 1995(H) | — | — | 4.00 | 7.00 | 10.00 | — |
| 1995(N) | — | — | 4.00 | 7.00 | 10.00 | — |

**RUPEE** **KM# 92.2** **Composition:** Stainless Steel **Edge:** Plain starting in 1996

| Date | Mintage | F | VF | XF | Unc | BU |
|---|---|---|---|---|---|---|
| 1995(B) | — | — | 1.00 | 1.50 | 2.50 | — |
| 1995(H) | — | — | 1.00 | 1.50 | 2.50 | — |
| 1995(N) | — | — | 1.00 | 1.50 | 2.50 | — |
| 1996(B) | — | — | 0.15 | 0.35 | 0.60 | — |
| 1996(C) | — | — | 0.15 | 0.35 | 0.60 | — |
| 1996(H) | — | — | 0.15 | 0.35 | 0.60 | — |
| 1996(N) | — | — | 0.15 | 0.35 | 0.60 | — |
| 1997(B) | — | — | 0.15 | 0.35 | 0.60 | — |
| 1997(C) | — | — | 0.15 | 0.35 | 0.60 | — |
| 1997(H) | — | — | 1.50 | 2.00 | 3.00 | — |
| 1997(M) | — | — | 0.15 | 0.35 | 0.50 | — |
| 1997(N) | — | — | 0.15 | 0.35 | 0.50 | — |
| 1998(B) | — | — | 0.15 | 0.35 | 0.50 | — |
| 1998(C) | — | — | 0.15 | 0.35 | 0.50 | — |
| 1998(H) | — | — | 0.15 | 0.35 | 0.50 | — |
| 1998(K) | — | — | 0.15 | 0.35 | 0.50 | — |
| 1998(N) | — | — | 0.15 | 0.35 | 0.50 | — |
| 1999(B) | — | — | 0.15 | 0.35 | 0.50 | — |
| 1999(K) | — | — | 0.15 | 0.30 | 0.45 | — |
| 1999(N) | — | — | 0.15 | 0.30 | 0.45 | — |
| 1999(C) | — | — | 0.15 | 0.35 | 0.50 | — |
| 1999(H) | — | — | 0.15 | 0.35 | 0.50 | — |
| 2000(B) | — | — | 0.15 | 0.30 | 0.45 | — |
| 2000(K) | — | — | 0.15 | 0.30 | 0.45 | — |
| 2000(C) | — | — | 0.15 | 0.30 | 0.45 | — |
| 2000(H) | — | — | 0.15 | 0.30 | 0.45 | — |
| 2000(N) | — | — | 0.15 | 0.30 | 0.45 | — |
| 2001(B) | — | — | 0.15 | 0.30 | 0.45 | — |
| 2001(C) | — | — | 0.15 | 0.30 | 0.45 | — |
| 2001(C) | — | — | 0.15 | 0.30 | 0.45 | — |
| 2001(H) | — | — | 0.15 | 0.30 | 0.45 | — |
| 2001(K) | — | — | 0.15 | 0.30 | 0.45 | — |
| 2001(N) | — | — | 0.15 | 0.30 | 0.45 | — |

**RUPEE** **KM# 98** **Composition:** Stainless Steel **Reverse:** Port Blair Jail **Note:** Variation exist.

| Date | Mintage | F | VF | XF | Unc | BU |
|---|---|---|---|---|---|---|
| 1997(B) | — | — | 0.30 | 0.50 | 0.80 | — |
| 1997(C) | — | — | 0.30 | 0.50 | 0.80 | — |
| 1997(H) | — | — | 0.30 | 0.50 | 0.80 | — |
| 1997(N) | — | — | 0.40 | 0.60 | 1.00 | — |

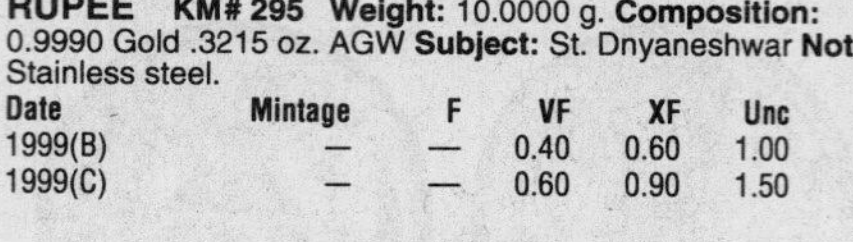

**RUPEE** **KM# 295** **Weight:** 10.0000 g. **Composition:** 0.9990 Gold .3215 oz. AGW **Subject:** St. Dnyaneshwar **Note:** Stainless steel.

| Date | Mintage | F | VF | XF | Unc | BU |
|---|---|---|---|---|---|---|
| 1999(B) | — | — | 0.40 | 0.60 | 1.00 | — |
| 1999(C) | — | — | 0.60 | 0.90 | 1.50 | — |

## 2 RUPEES

### 2 Rupee Obverses

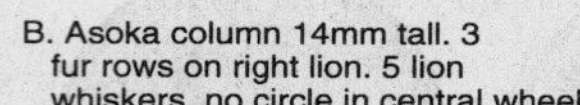

A. Asoka column 15mm tall. 5 fur rows on right lion. No lion whiskers, circle in central wheel.

B. Asoka column 14mm tall. 3 fur rows on right lion. 5 lion whiskers, no circle in central wheel.

C. Asoka column 13mm tall. 4 fur rows on right lion. No dot in central wheel.

D. Asoka column 13mm tall. 4 fur rows. Recut chest on central lion. Dot in central wheel.

E. Asoka column 13mm tall. No fur rows on right lion. 2 whiskers on central lion.

**NOTE:** Obverses C and D include both 4.5 x 5mm and 5 x 5.5mm numeral 2 varieties.

**2 RUPEES** **KM# 120** **Composition:** Copper-Nickel **Subject:** IX Asian Games

| Date | Mintage | F | VF | XF | Unc | BU |
|---|---|---|---|---|---|---|
| 1982(B) | 12,720,000 | — | 0.35 | 0.50 | 1.25 | — |
| 1982B Proof | Inc. above | Value: 2.50 | | | | |
| 1982(C) | Inc. above | — | 0.35 | 0.50 | 1.25 | — |

**2 RUPEES** **KM# 121.1** **Composition:** Copper-Nickel **Subject:** National Integration **Obverse:** Asoka column 14mm tall **Reverse:** Small date

| Date | Mintage | F | VF | XF | Unc | BU |
|---|---|---|---|---|---|---|
| 1982(B) | — | — | 0.30 | 1.00 | 1.75 | — |
| **Note:** Mintage included in KM120 | | | | | | |
| 1982B Proof | — | Value: 3.50 | | | | |
| 1982(C) | — | — | 0.30 | 1.00 | 2.25 | — |
| **Note:** Mintage included in KM120 | | | | | | |

**2 RUPEES** **KM# 122** **Composition:** Copper-Nickel **Subject:** Golden Jubilee of Reserve Bank of India

| Date | Mintage | F | VF | XF | Unc | BU |
|---|---|---|---|---|---|---|
| ND(1985)(B) Proof | — | Value: 60.00 | | | | |

**2 RUPEES** **KM# 121.2** **Composition:** Copper-Nickel **Obverse:** Asoka column 15mm tall **Reverse:** Large date

| Date | Mintage | F | VF | XF | Unc | BU |
|---|---|---|---|---|---|---|
| 1990(B) | — | — | 0.40 | 1.00 | 2.25 | — |
| 1990(C) | — | — | 0.40 | 1.00 | 2.25 | — |
| 1990(H) | — | — | 0.80 | 3.00 | 5.00 | — |

**2 RUPEES** **KM# 123** **Composition:** Copper-Nickel **Subject:** Tourism **Note:** Similar to 1 Rupee, KM#91.

| Date | Mintage | F | VF | XF | Unc | BU |
|---|---|---|---|---|---|---|
| 1991 Prooflike | — | — | — | — | 6.00 | — |
| 1991 Proof | — | Value: 10.00 | | | | |

**2 RUPEES** **KM# 121.4** **Composition:** Copper-Nickel **Obverse:** B

| Date | Mintage | F | VF | XF | Unc | BU |
|---|---|---|---|---|---|---|
| 1992(B) | — | — | 0.30 | 0.50 | 1.00 | — |
| 1993(B) | — | — | 0.30 | 0.50 | 1.00 | — |
| 1994(B) | — | — | 0.30 | 0.50 | 1.00 | — |
| 1994(H) | — | — | 2.75 | 5.00 | 6.50 | — |
| 1994(N) | — | — | 2.75 | 5.00 | 6.50 | — |
| 1995(B) | — | — | 0.30 | 0.50 | 1.00 | — |
| 1995(H) | — | — | 3.00 | 5.50 | 8.00 | — |
| 1995(N) | — | — | 0.30 | 0.50 | 1.00 | — |
| 1996(B) | — | — | 2.50 | 4.00 | 6.00 | — |
| 1996(B-H) | — | — | 5.00 | 10.00 | 15.00 | — |
| 1996(N) | — | — | 0.30 | 0.50 | 1.00 | — |
| 1997(B) | — | — | 0.30 | 0.50 | 1.00 | — |
| 1998(N) | — | — | 0.30 | 0.50 | 1.00 | — |

**2 RUPEES** **KM# 121.3** **Composition:** Copper-Nickel **Obverse:** Asoka column 15mm tall **Size:** 26 mm. **Note:** Reduced size.

| Date | Mintage | F | VF | XF | Unc | BU |
|---|---|---|---|---|---|---|
| 1992(B) | — | — | 2.50 | 4.00 | 7.00 | — |
| 1992(C) | — | — | 0.30 | 0.50 | 1.00 | — |
| 1992(H) | — | — | 0.40 | 1.00 | 1.50 | — |
| 1993(C) | — | — | 0.40 | 1.25 | 2.00 | — |
| 1993(H) | — | — | 0.35 | 0.60 | 1.25 | — |
| 1994(C) | — | — | 0.40 | 1.25 | 2.00 | — |
| 1994(H) | — | — | 0.35 | 0.80 | 1.50 | — |
| 1995(B) | — | — | 2.50 | 4.00 | 7.00 | — |
| 1995(C) | — | — | 0.30 | 0.50 | 1.00 | — |
| 1995(H) | — | — | 0.30 | 0.50 | 1.00 | — |
| 1996(C) | — | — | 0.30 | 0.50 | 1.00 | — |
| 1996(H) | — | — | 0.30 | 0.50 | 1.00 | — |
| 1997(C) | — | — | 0.30 | 0.50 | 1.00 | — |
| 1997(H) | — | — | 0.30 | 0.50 | 1.00 | — |
| 1998(C) | — | — | 0.30 | 0.50 | 1.00 | — |
| 1999(C) | — | — | 0.30 | 0.50 | 1.00 | — |
| 2000(C) | — | — | 0.30 | 0.50 | 1.00 | — |

**2 RUPEES KM# 124.1 Composition:** Copper-Nickel **Subject:** Small Family Happy Family

| Date | Mintage | F | VF | XF | Unc | BU |
|---|---|---|---|---|---|---|
| 1993(B) | — | — | 0.50 | 0.90 | 1.50 | — |

**2 RUPEES KM# 124.2 Composition:** Copper-Nickel **Obverse:** A

| Date | Mintage | F | VF | XF | Unc | BU |
|---|---|---|---|---|---|---|
| 1993(H) | — | — | 2.00 | 3.00 | 5.00 | — |

**2 RUPEES KM# 125.1 Composition:** Copper-Nickel **Series:** World Food Day **Subject:** Bio Diversity

| Date | Mintage | F | VF | XF | Unc | BU |
|---|---|---|---|---|---|---|
| 1993(B) | — | — | 0.50 | 0.90 | 1.50 | — |

**2 RUPEES KM# 125.2 Composition:** Copper-Nickel **Obverse:** A

| Date | Mintage | F | VF | XF | Unc | BU |
|---|---|---|---|---|---|---|
| 1993(H) | — | — | 2.00 | 3.00 | 5.00 | — |

**2 RUPEES KM# 126.1 Composition:** Copper-Nickel **Series:** F.A.O. **Subject:** Water For Life

| Date | Mintage | F | VF | XF | Unc | BU |
|---|---|---|---|---|---|---|
| 1994(B) | — | — | 0.60 | 1.10 | 2.00 | — |
| 1994(C) | — | — | 1.00 | 2.00 | 4.00 | — |
| 1994(H) | — | — | 2.00 | 4.50 | 11.00 | — |

**2 RUPEES KM# 126.2 Composition:** Copper-Nickel **Obverse:** B

| Date | Mintage | F | VF | XF | Unc | BU |
|---|---|---|---|---|---|---|
| 1994(B) | — | — | — | — | — | — |

**2 RUPEES KM# 127.1 Composition:** Copper-Nickel **Subject:** Globalizing Indian Agriculture - Agriexpo 95 **Obverse:** A **Reverse:** Steerhead in wreath of two stalks of wheat

| Date | Mintage | F | VF | XF | Unc | BU |
|---|---|---|---|---|---|---|
| 1995(B) | — | — | 0.60 | 1.25 | 2.00 | — |
| 1995(C) | — | — | 1.00 | 3.00 | 6.00 | — |

**2 RUPEES KM# 127.2 Composition:** Copper-Nickel **Obverse:** B

| Date | Mintage | F | VF | XF | Unc | BU |
|---|---|---|---|---|---|---|
| 1995(B) | — | — | 3.00 | 5.00 | 10.00 | — |

**2 RUPEES KM# 127.3 Composition:** Copper-Nickel **Obverse:** C

| Date | Mintage | F | VF | XF | Unc | BU |
|---|---|---|---|---|---|---|
| 1995(B) | — | — | — | — | — | — |

**2 RUPEES KM# 128 Composition:** Copper-Nickel **Subject:** Eighth World Tamil Conference **Obverse:** Asoka column 13mm tall **Reverse:** St. Thiruvalluvar

| Date | Mintage | F | VF | XF | Unc | BU |
|---|---|---|---|---|---|---|
| 1995(B) | — | — | 0.60 | 1.00 | 1.75 | — |

**2 RUPEES KM# 129.1 Composition:** Copper-Nickel **Subject:** Sardar Vallabhbhai Patel **Obverse:** A **Reverse:** Portrait of Patel

| Date | Mintage | F | VF | XF | Unc | BU |
|---|---|---|---|---|---|---|
| 1995(B) | — | — | 2.50 | 4.00 | 7.00 | — |
| 1996M Proof | — | Value: 8.00 | | | | |

**2 RUPEES KM# 121.5 Composition:** Copper-Nickel **Obverse:** C

| Date | Mintage | F | VF | XF | Unc | BU |
|---|---|---|---|---|---|---|
| 1995(B) | — | — | 2.50 | 4.00 | 6.00 | — |
| 1996(B) | — | — | 0.30 | 0.50 | 1.00 | — |
| 1996(H) | — | — | 0.30 | 0.50 | 1.00 | — |
| 1997(B) | — | — | 0.30 | 0.50 | 1.00 | — |
| 1997(H) | — | — | 0.30 | 0.50 | 1.00 | — |
| 1997(T) | — | — | 0.30 | 0.50 | 1.00 | — |
| 1998(B) | — | — | 0.30 | 0.50 | 1.00 | — |
| 1998(H) | — | — | 0.30 | 0.50 | 1.00 | — |
| 1998(P) | — | — | 0.30 | 0.50 | 1.00 | — |
| 1998(T) | — | — | 0.30 | 0.50 | 1.00 | — |
| 1999(B) | — | — | 0.30 | 0.50 | 1.00 | — |
| 1999(H) | — | — | 0.30 | 0.50 | 1.00 | — |
| 1999(Ld) | — | — | 0.30 | 0.50 | 1.00 | — |
| 1999(N) | — | — | 0.30 | 0.50 | 1.00 | — |
| 1999(C) | — | — | 0.30 | 0.50 | 1.00 | — |
| 2000(B) | — | — | 0.30 | 0.50 | 1.00 | — |
| 2000(C) | — | — | 0.30 | 0.50 | 1.00 | — |
| 2000(H) | — | — | 0.30 | 0.50 | 1.00 | — |
| 2000(N) | — | — | 0.30 | 0.50 | 1.00 | — |
| 2000(R) | — | — | 0.30 | 0.50 | 1.00 | — |
| 2001(B) | — | — | 0.30 | 0.50 | 1.00 | — |
| 2001(C) | — | — | 0.30 | 0.50 | 1.00 | — |
| 2001(N) | — | — | 0.30 | 0.50 | 1.00 | — |
| 2001(H) | — | — | 0.30 | 0.50 | 1.00 | — |

**2 RUPEES KM# 129.2 Composition:** Copper-Nickel **Obverse:** B

| Date | Mintage | F | VF | XF | Unc | BU |
|---|---|---|---|---|---|---|
| 1996(N) | — | — | 1.00 | 1.50 | 3.00 | — |

**2 RUPEES KM# 129.3 Composition:** Copper-Nickel **Obverse:** C

| Date | Mintage | F | VF | XF | Unc | BU |
|---|---|---|---|---|---|---|
| 1996(B) | — | — | 2.00 | 3.00 | 5.00 | — |
| 1996(H) | — | — | 0.40 | 0.70 | 1.25 | — |

**2 RUPEES KM# 129.4 Composition:** Copper-Nickel **Obverse:** D

| Date | Mintage | F | VF | XF | Unc | BU |
|---|---|---|---|---|---|---|
| 1996(B) | — | — | 0.40 | 0.70 | 1.25 | — |
| 1996(C) | — | — | 0.30 | 0.60 | 1.00 | — |

**2 RUPEES KM# 129.5 Composition:** Copper-Nickel

| Date | Mintage | F | VF | XF | Unc | BU |
|---|---|---|---|---|---|---|
| 1996(B) | — | — | 30.00 | 40.00 | 65.00 | — |

**Note:** This type exists with and without die damage below ashoka column

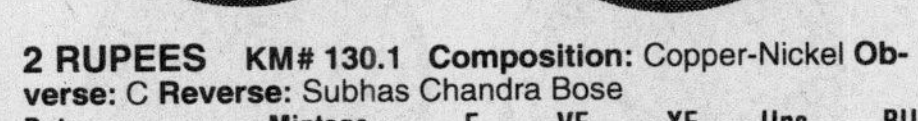

**2 RUPEES KM# 130.1 Composition:** Copper-Nickel **Obverse:** C **Reverse:** Subhas Chandra Bose

| Date | Mintage | F | VF | XF | Unc | BU |
|---|---|---|---|---|---|---|
| 1996(C) | — | — | 10.00 | 12.00 | 15.00 | — |
| 1997(B) | — | — | 0.60 | 0.90 | 1.25 | — |
| 1997(C) | — | — | 0.60 | 0.90 | 1.25 | — |
| 1997(H) | — | — | 1.50 | 2.50 | 4.00 | — |
| 1997(M) Proof | — | Value: 3.25 | | | | |

**2 RUPEES KM# 130.2 Composition:** Copper-Nickel **Obverse:** B

| Date | Mintage | F | VF | XF | Unc | BU |
|---|---|---|---|---|---|---|
| 1997(N) | — | — | 1.00 | 2.00 | 3.50 | — |
| 1997(H) | — | — | 0.60 | 0.90 | 1.25 | — |

**2 RUPEES KM# 131.1 Composition:** Copper-Nickel **Obverse:** C **Reverse:** Sri Aurobindo

| Date | Mintage | F | VF | XF | Unc | BU |
|---|---|---|---|---|---|---|
| 1998(B) | — | — | 0.60 | 0.90 | 1.50 | — |
| 1998(N) | — | — | 1.00 | 1.50 | 3.00 | — |
| 1998(C) | — | — | 1.00 | 1.50 | 3.00 | — |
| 1998(M) Proof | — | Value: 3.50 | | | | |

**2 RUPEES KM# 121.6 Composition:** Copper-Nickel **Obverse:** D

| Date | Mintage | F | VF | XF | Unc | BU |
|---|---|---|---|---|---|---|
| 1998(B) | — | — | 0.30 | 0.50 | 1.00 | — |
| 1998(H) | — | — | 0.30 | 0.50 | 1.00 | — |
| 1999(B) | — | — | 0.75 | 1.00 | 1.50 | — |
| 2000(B) | — | — | 0.75 | 1.00 | 1.50 | — |

**2 RUPEES KM# 131.2 Composition:** Copper-Nickel **Obverse:** D

| Date | Mintage | F | VF | XF | Unc | BU |
|---|---|---|---|---|---|---|
| 1998(B) | — | — | 3.00 | 5.00 | 8.00 | — |

**2 RUPEES KM# 296.1 Composition:** Copper-Nickel **Obverse:** A **Reverse:** Deshbandhu Chittaranjan Das

| Date | Mintage | F | VF | XF | Unc | BU |
|---|---|---|---|---|---|---|
| 1998(C) | — | — | 10.00 | 15.00 | 25.00 | — |

**2 RUPEES KM# 296.2 Composition:** Copper-Nickel **Obverse:** B

| Date | Mintage | F | VF | XF | Unc | BU |
|---|---|---|---|---|---|---|
| 1998(N) | — | — | 3.00 | 4.00 | 6.00 | — |

**2 RUPEES KM# 296.3 Composition:** Copper-Nickel **Obverse:** C, 7mm, edge flat

| Date | Mintage | F | VF | XF | Unc | BU |
|---|---|---|---|---|---|---|
| 1998(C) | — | — | 4.00 | 6.00 | 8.00 | — |

**2 RUPEES KM# 296.4 Composition:** Copper-Nickel **Note:** 5-6mm, edge flat.

| Date | Mintage | F | VF | XF | Unc | BU |
|---|---|---|---|---|---|---|
| 1998(C) | — | — | 6.00 | 8.00 | 12.00 | — |

**2 RUPEES KM# 296.5 Composition:** Copper-Nickel **Note:** 3-5mm, edge flat.

| Date | Mintage | F | VF | XF | Unc | BU |
|---|---|---|---|---|---|---|
| 1998(C) | — | — | 3.00 | 4.00 | 6.00 | — |

**2 RUPEES KM# 296.6 Composition:** Copper-Nickel **Obverse:** D **Note:** 3-5mm, edge flat.

| Date | Mintage | F | VF | XF | Unc | BU |
|---|---|---|---|---|---|---|
| 1998(C) | — | — | 0.75 | 1.25 | 2.00 | — |

**2 RUPEES KM# 290 Composition:** Copper-Nickel **Obverse:** C **Reverse:** Chhatrapati Shivaji

| Date | Mintage | F | VF | XF | Unc | BU |
|---|---|---|---|---|---|---|
| 1999(B) | — | — | 0.75 | 1.25 | 2.00 | — |
| 1999(N) | — | — | 0.75 | 1.25 | 2.00 | — |
| 1999(C) | — | — | 0.75 | 1.25 | 2.00 | — |

**2 RUPEES KM# 291 Composition:** Copper-Nickel **Subject:** Supreme Court: 50 Years **Obverse:** C; Lion column above

denomination **Reverse:** Wheel above lion column **Edge:** Plain, eleven sided

| Date | Mintage | F | VF | XF | Unc | BU |
|---|---|---|---|---|---|---|
| 2000(B) | — | — | 0.75 | 1.25 | 2.00 | — |
| 2000(C) | — | — | 0.75 | 1.25 | 2.00 | — |

**5 RUPEES** **KM# 150** **Composition:** Copper-Nickel **Subject:** Death of Indira Gandhi

| Date | Mintage | F | VF | XF | Unc | BU |
|---|---|---|---|---|---|---|
| ND(1985)(B) | 59,288,000 | — | 0.75 | 1.50 | 3.00 | — |
| ND(1985)B Proof | Inc. above | Value: 27.50 | | | | |
| ND(1985)(H) | Inc. above | — | 3.50 | 6.00 | 15.00 | — |

**5 RUPEES** **KM# 151** **Composition:** Copper-Nickel **Subject:** Centennial - Nehru's Birth

| Date | Mintage | F | VF | XF | Unc | BU |
|---|---|---|---|---|---|---|
| 1989(B) | — | — | 1.00 | 2.00 | 3.00 | — |
| **Note:** Short rim teeth. | | | | | | |
| 1989(B) | — | — | 2.00 | 3.00 | 4.50 | — |
| **Note:** Long rim teeth. | | | | | | |
| 1989B Proof | — | Value: 25.00 | | | | |
| 1989(H) | — | — | 3.50 | 6.00 | 15.00 | — |

**5 RUPEES** **KM# 152** **Composition:** Copper-Nickel **Subject:** Commonwealth Parliamentary Conference **Note:** Similar to 1 Rupee, KM#90.

| Date | Mintage | F | VF | XF | Unc | BU |
|---|---|---|---|---|---|---|
| 1991(B) Prooflike | — | — | — | — | 10.00 | — |
| 1991B Proof | — | Value: 20.00 | | | | |

**5 RUPEES** **KM# 153** **Composition:** Copper-Nickel **Subject:** Tourism **Note:** Similar to 1 Rupee, KM#91.

| Date | Mintage | F | VF | XF | Unc | BU |
|---|---|---|---|---|---|---|
| 1991(B) Prooflike | — | — | — | — | 10.00 | — |
| 1991B Proof | — | Value: 20.00 | | | | |

**5 RUPEES** **KM# 154.1** **Composition:** Copper-Nickel **Edge:** Security

| Date | Mintage | F | VF | XF | Unc | BU |
|---|---|---|---|---|---|---|
| 1992(B) | — | — | 0.20 | 0.75 | 1.50 | — |
| 1992(C) | — | — | 0.20 | 0.75 | 1.50 | — |
| 1992(H) | — | — | 0.20 | 0.75 | 1.50 | — |
| 1993(B) | — | — | 0.20 | 0.75 | 1.50 | — |
| 1993(C) | — | — | 0.20 | 0.75 | 1.50 | — |
| 1994(B) | — | — | 0.20 | 0.75 | 1.50 | — |
| 1994(C) | — | — | 0.20 | 0.75 | 1.50 | — |
| 1994(H) | — | — | 0.20 | 0.75 | 1.50 | — |
| 1995(B) | — | — | 0.20 | 0.75 | 1.50 | — |
| 1995(C) | — | — | 0.20 | 0.75 | 1.50 | — |
| 1995(H) | — | — | 0.20 | 0.75 | 1.50 | — |
| 1995(N) | — | — | 0.20 | 0.75 | 1.50 | — |
| 1996(B) | — | — | 0.20 | 0.50 | 1.00 | — |
| 1996(C) | — | — | 0.20 | 0.50 | 1.00 | — |
| 1996(H) | — | — | 0.20 | 0.50 | 1.00 | — |
| 1996(N) | — | — | 0.20 | 0.50 | 1.00 | — |
| 1997(B) | — | — | 0.20 | 0.50 | 1.00 | — |
| 1997(C) | — | — | 0.20 | 0.50 | 1.00 | — |
| 1997(H) | — | — | 0.20 | 0.50 | 1.00 | — |
| 1997(N) | — | — | 0.20 | 0.50 | 1.00 | — |
| 1998(B) | — | — | 0.20 | 0.50 | 1.00 | — |
| 1998(C) | — | — | 0.20 | 0.50 | 1.00 | — |
| 1998(H) | — | — | 0.25 | 0.50 | 1.00 | — |
| 1998(N) | — | — | 0.25 | 0.50 | 1.00 | — |
| 1999(C) | — | — | 0.25 | 0.50 | 1.00 | — |
| 1999(H) | — | — | 0.25 | 0.50 | 1.00 | — |

| Date | Mintage | F | VF | XF | Unc | BU |
|---|---|---|---|---|---|---|
| 1999(N) | — | — | 0.25 | 0.50 | 1.00 | — |
| 1999(R) | — | — | 0.25 | 0.50 | 1.00 | — |
| 2000(C) | — | — | 0.25 | 0.50 | 1.00 | — |
| 2000(H) | — | — | 0.50 | 1.00 | 2.00 | — |
| 2000(R) | — | — | 0.25 | 0.50 | 1.00 | — |
| 2000(N) | — | — | 0.25 | 0.50 | 1.00 | — |
| 2001(C) | — | — | 0.25 | 0.50 | 1.00 | — |
| 2001(N) | — | — | 0.25 | 0.50 | 1.00 | — |

**5 RUPEES** **KM# 155** **Composition:** Copper-Nickel **Subject:** World of Work **Edge:** Security

| Date | Mintage | F | VF | XF | Unc | BU |
|---|---|---|---|---|---|---|
| ND(1994)(B) | — | — | 0.75 | 1.00 | 1.75 | — |
| ND(1994)B Proof | — | Value: 5.00 | | | | |
| ND(1994)(H) | — | — | 1.50 | 2.25 | 4.00 | — |
| ND(1994)(N) | — | — | 1.00 | 1.50 | 3.00 | — |

**5 RUPEES** **KM# 156** **Composition:** Copper-Nickel **Series:** 50 Years - United Nations

| Date | Mintage | F | VF | XF | Unc | BU |
|---|---|---|---|---|---|---|
| 1995(B) | — | — | 0.75 | 1.00 | 1.75 | — |
| 1995(N) | — | — | 1.00 | 1.50 | 3.00 | — |

**5 RUPEES** **KM# 157** **Composition:** Copper-Nickel **Series:** 50th Anniversary - F.A.O. **Obverse:** Asoka column **Reverse:** Hand clutching stalks of wheat

| Date | Mintage | F | VF | XF | Unc | BU |
|---|---|---|---|---|---|---|
| 1995(B) | — | — | 0.75 | 1.00 | 1.75 | — |
| 1995(H) | — | — | 1.50 | 3.00 | 5.00 | — |
| 1995(N) | — | — | 1.00 | 1.50 | 3.00 | — |

**5 RUPEES** **KM# 158** **Composition:** Copper-Nickel **Subject:** Eighth World Tamil Conference **Obverse:** Asoka column **Reverse:** St. Thiruvalluvar

| Date | Mintage | F | VF | XF | Unc | BU |
|---|---|---|---|---|---|---|
| 1995(B) | — | — | 0.75 | 1.00 | 1.75 | — |

**5 RUPEES** **KM# 159** **Composition:** Copper-Nickel **Subject:** Mother's Health is Child's Health

| Date | Mintage | F | VF | XF | Unc | BU |
|---|---|---|---|---|---|---|
| 1996(B) | — | — | 0.75 | 1.00 | 1.50 | — |
| 1996(H) | — | — | 0.75 | 1.00 | 1.50 | — |
| 1996(N) | — | — | 1.00 | 1.50 | 2.25 | — |

**5 RUPEES** **KM# 154.2** **Composition:** Copper-Nickel **Edge:** Milled

| Date | Mintage | F | VF | XF | Unc | BU |
|---|---|---|---|---|---|---|
| 1996(C) | — | — | 8.00 | 10.00 | 15.00 | — |
| 1998(H) | — | — | 8.00 | 10.00 | 15.00 | — |
| 2000(C) | — | — | 8.00 | 10.00 | 15.00 | — |

**5 RUPEES** **KM# 160** **Composition:** Copper-Nickel **Subject:** 2nd International Crop Science Conference **Note:** This conference was never held.

| Date | Mintage | F | VF | XF | Unc | BU |
|---|---|---|---|---|---|---|
| 1996(C) | 11,000 | — | 15.00 | 17.00 | 20.00 | — |

**5 RUPEES** **KM# 154.3** **Composition:** Copper-Nickel **Edge:** Plain

| Date | Mintage | F | VF | XF | Unc | BU |
|---|---|---|---|---|---|---|
| 1998(H) Error | — | — | 5.00 | 10.00 | 15.00 | — |

**5 RUPEES** **KM# 154.4** **Composition:** Copper Nickel **Obverse:** similar to KM#121.5

| Date | Mintage | F | VF | XF | Unc | BU |
|---|---|---|---|---|---|---|
| 1998(B) | — | — | 0.25 | 0.50 | 1.00 | — |
| 1999(B) | — | — | 0.25 | 0.50 | 1.00 | — |
| 2000(B) | — | — | 0.25 | 0.50 | 1.00 | — |
| 2001(B) | — | — | 0.25 | 0.50 | 1.00 | — |

**10 RUPEES** **KM# 185** **Weight:** 15.0000 g. **Composition:** 0.8000 Silver .3858 oz. ASW **Subject:** Centennial - Mahatma Gandhi's Birth **Note:** Struck during 1969 and 1970.

| Date | Mintage | F | VF | XF | Unc | BU |
|---|---|---|---|---|---|---|
| ND(1969)(B) | 3,160,000 | — | — | 4.00 | 6.00 | — |
| ND(1969)B Proof | 9,147 | Value: 8.50 | | | | |
| ND(1969)(C) | 100,000 | — | — | 7.00 | 10.00 | — |

**10 RUPEES** **KM# 186** **Weight:** 15.0000 g. **Composition:** 0.8000 Silver .3858 oz. ASW **Series:** F.A.O.

| Date | Mintage | F | VF | XF | Unc | BU |
|---|---|---|---|---|---|---|
| 1970(B) | 300,000 | — | — | 4.00 | 7.50 | — |
| 1970B Proof | 3,046 | Value: 9.00 | | | | |
| 1970(C) | 100,000 | — | — | 6.00 | 10.00 | — |
| 1971(B) | — | — | — | 6.00 | 10.00 | — |
| 1971B Proof | 1,594 | Value: 10.00 | | | | |

**10 RUPEES** **KM# 187** **Weight:** 22.5000 g. **Composition:** 0.5000 Silver .3617 oz. ASW **Subject:** 25th Anniversary of Independence

| Date | Mintage | F | VF | XF | Unc | BU |
|---|---|---|---|---|---|---|
| ND(1972)(B) | 1,000,000 | — | — | — | 7.00 | — |
| ND(1972)B Proof | 7,895 | Value: 9.50 | | | | |

**10 RUPEES** **KM# 187a** **Composition:** Copper-Nickel

| Date | Mintage | F | VF | XF | Unc | BU |
|---|---|---|---|---|---|---|
| ND(1972)(B) | — | — | — | — | 6.00 | — |
| ND(1972)(C) | — | — | — | — | 6.00 | — |

**Note:** Rim thinner, inner flag circle missing on Calcutta issues

**10 RUPEES** **KM# 188** **Weight:** 22.3000 g. **Composition:** 0.5000 Silver .3585 oz. ASW **Series:** F.A.O.

| Date | Mintage | F | VF | XF | Unc | BU |
|---|---|---|---|---|---|---|
| 1973(B) | 64,000 | — | — | — | 6.50 | — |
| 1973B Proof | 15,000 | Value: 9.50 | | | | |

**10 RUPEES** **KM# 189** **Composition:** Copper-Nickel **Series:** F.A.O.

| Date | Mintage | F | VF | XF | Unc | BU |
|---|---|---|---|---|---|---|
| 1974(B) | 65,000 | — | — | 2.00 | 4.50 | — |
| 1974B Proof | 12,000 | Value: 7.00 | | | | |

**10 RUPEES** **KM# 190** **Composition:** Copper-Nickel **Series:** F.A.O. **Subject:** Women's Year

| Date | Mintage | F | VF | XF | Unc | BU |
|---|---|---|---|---|---|---|
| 1975(B) | 49,000 | — | — | 2.00 | 4.50 | — |
| 1975B Proof | 2,531 | Value: 8.50 | | | | |

**10 RUPEES** **KM# 191** **Composition:** Copper-Nickel **Series:** F.A.O. **Subject:** Food and Work For All

| Date | Mintage | F | VF | XF | Unc | BU |
|---|---|---|---|---|---|---|
| 1976(B) | 49,000 | — | — | 2.00 | 4.50 | — |
| 1976B Proof | 3,400 | Value: 8.50 | | | | |

**10 RUPEES** **KM# 192** **Composition:** Copper-Nickel **Series:** F.A.O. **Subject:** Save For Development

| Date | Mintage | F | VF | XF | Unc | BU |
|---|---|---|---|---|---|---|
| 1977(B) | 20,000 | — | — | 2.00 | 4.50 | — |
| 1977B Proof | 5,969 | Value: 8.50 | | | | |

**10 RUPEES** **KM# 193** **Composition:** Copper-Nickel **Series:** F.A.O. **Subject:** Food and Shelter For All

| Date | Mintage | F | VF | XF | Unc | BU |
|---|---|---|---|---|---|---|
| 1978(B) | 25,000 | — | — | 2.00 | 4.50 | — |
| 1978B Proof | — | Value: 8.50 | | | | |

**10 RUPEES** **KM# 194** **Composition:** Copper-Nickel **Series:** International Year of the Child

| Date | Mintage | F | VF | XF | Unc | BU |
|---|---|---|---|---|---|---|
| 1979(B) | — | — | — | 2.50 | 5.00 | — |
| 1979B Proof | — | Value: 9.50 | | | | |

**10 RUPEES** **KM# 195** **Composition:** Copper-Nickel **Subject:** Rural Women's Advancement

| Date | Mintage | F | VF | XF | Unc | BU |
|---|---|---|---|---|---|---|
| 1980(B) | — | — | — | 2.50 | 5.00 | — |
| 1980B Proof | — | Value: 9.50 | | | | |

**10 RUPEES** **KM# 196** **Composition:** Copper-Nickel **Series:** World Food Day

| Date | Mintage | F | VF | XF | Unc | BU |
|---|---|---|---|---|---|---|
| 1981(B) | — | — | — | 2.50 | 5.00 | — |
| 1981B Proof | — | Value: 9.50 | | | | |

**10 RUPEES** **KM# 197** **Composition:** Copper-Nickel **Subject:** IX Asian Games

| Date | Mintage | F | VF | XF | Unc | BU |
|---|---|---|---|---|---|---|
| 1982(B) | — | — | — | 2.50 | 5.00 | — |
| 1982B Proof | — | Value: 9.50 | | | | |

**10 RUPEES** **KM# 198** **Composition:** Copper-Nickel **Subject:** National Integration

| Date | Mintage | F | VF | XF | Unc | BU |
|---|---|---|---|---|---|---|
| 1982(B) | — | — | — | — | 6.00 | — |
| 1982B Proof | — | Value: 10.00 | | | | |

**10 RUPEES** **KM# 199** **Composition:** Copper-Nickel **Subject:** Golden Jubilee - Reserve Bank of India

| Date | Mintage | F | VF | XF | Unc | BU |
|---|---|---|---|---|---|---|
| ND(1985)(B) | — | — | — | — | 65.00 | — |
| ND(1985)B Proof | — | Value: 75.00 | | | | |

**10 RUPEES** **KM# 200** **Composition:** Copper-Nickel **Subject:** Youth Year **Note:** Similar to 1 Rupee, KM#80.

| Date | Mintage | F | VF | XF | Unc | BU |
|---|---|---|---|---|---|---|
| 1985(C) | — | — | — | — | 10.00 | — |
| 1985(C) Proof | — | Value: 30.00 | | | | |

**10 RUPEES** **KM# 201** **Composition:** Copper-Nickel **Subject:** Commonwealth Parliamentary Conference **Note:** Similar to 1 Rupee, KM#90.

| Date | Mintage | F | VF | XF | Unc | BU |
|---|---|---|---|---|---|---|
| 1991(B) Prooflike | — | — | — | — | 10.00 | — |
| 1991B Proof | — | Value: 20.00 | | | | |

**10 RUPEES** **KM# 202** **Composition:** Copper-Nickel **Subject:** Quit India **Note:** Similar to 1 Rupee, KM#93.

| Date | Mintage | F | VF | XF | Unc | BU |
|---|---|---|---|---|---|---|
| 1992(B) Proof | — | Value: 10.00 | | | | |

**10 RUPEES** **KM# 203** **Composition:** Copper-Nickel **Subject:** 100th Anniversary - Birth of Patel **Note:** Similar to 2 Rupee, KM#129.

| Date | Mintage | F | VF | XF | Unc | BU |
|---|---|---|---|---|---|---|
| 1996(B) | — | — | — | — | 8.00 | — |
| 1996M Proof | — | Value: 12.00 | | | | |

**10 RUPEES** **KM# 204** **Composition:** Copper-Nickel **Subject:** Subhas Chandra Bose **Note:** Similar to 2 Rupees, KM#130.

| Date | Mintage | F | VF | XF | Unc | BU |
|---|---|---|---|---|---|---|
| 1997(C) | — | — | — | — | 8.00 | — |
| 1997M Proof | — | Value: 12.00 | | | | |

**10 RUPEES** **KM# 205** **Composition:** Copper-Nickel **Subject:** Sri Aurobindo **Note:** Similar to 2 Rupees, KM#131.

| Date | Mintage | F | VF | XF | Unc | BU |
|---|---|---|---|---|---|---|
| 1998(B) | — | — | — | — | 8.00 | — |
| 1998M Proof | — | Value: 12.00 | | | | |

**20 RUPEES** **KM# 240** **Weight:** 30.0000 g. **Composition:** 0.5000 Silver .4823 oz. ASW **Series:** F.A.O.

| Date | Mintage | F | VF | XF | Unc | BU |
|---|---|---|---|---|---|---|
| 1973(B) | 64,000 | — | — | — | 8.00 | — |
| 1973B Proof | 12,000 | Value: 12.50 | | | | |

**20 RUPEES** **KM# 241** **Composition:** Copper-Nickel **Subject:** Death of Indira Gandhi

| Date | Mintage | F | VF | XF | Unc | BU |
|---|---|---|---|---|---|---|
| ND(1985)(B) | — | — | — | — | 12.50 | — |
| ND(1985)B Proof | — | Value: 50.00 | | | | |

**20 RUPEES** **KM# 242** **Composition:** Copper-Nickel **Series:** F.A.O. **Subject:** Fisheries

| Date | Mintage | F | VF | XF | Unc | BU |
|---|---|---|---|---|---|---|
| 1986(B) | — | — | — | — | 10.00 | — |
| 1986B Proof | — | Value: 20.00 | | | | |

**20 RUPEES** **KM# 243** **Composition:** Copper-Nickel **Series:** F.A.O. **Subject:** Small Farmers

| Date | Mintage | F | VF | XF | Unc | BU |
|---|---|---|---|---|---|---|
| 1987(B) | — | — | — | — | 10.00 | — |
| 1987B Proof | — | Value: 20.00 | | | | |

**20 RUPEES** **KM# 244** **Composition:** Copper-Nickel **Subject:** 100th Anniversary of Nehru's Birth

| Date | Mintage | F | VF | XF | Unc | BU |
|---|---|---|---|---|---|---|
| 1989(B) | — | — | — | — | 10.00 | — |
| 1989B Proof | — | Value: 20.00 | | | | |

**50 RUPEES** **KM# 255** **Weight:** 34.7000 g. **Composition:** 0.5000 Silver .5578 oz. ASW **Series:** F.A.O.

| Date | Mintage | F | VF | XF | Unc | BU |
|---|---|---|---|---|---|---|
| 1974(B) | 82,000 | — | — | — | 8.00 | — |
| 1974B Proof | 13,000 | Value: 12.50 | | | | |

**50 RUPEES** **KM# 256** **Weight:** 34.7000 g. **Composition:** 0.5000 Silver .5578 oz. ASW **Series:** F.A.O. **Subject:** Women's Year

| Date | Mintage | F | VF | XF | Unc | BU |
|---|---|---|---|---|---|---|
| 1975(B) | 65,000 | — | — | — | 11.50 | — |
| 1975B Proof | 2,691 | Value: 20.00 | | | | |

**50 RUPEES** **KM# 257** **Weight:** 34.7000 g. **Composition:** 0.5000 Silver .5578 oz. ASW **Series:** F.A.O. **Subject:** Food and Work For All

| Date | Mintage | F | VF | XF | Unc | BU |
|---|---|---|---|---|---|---|
| 1976(B) | 42,000 | — | — | — | 12.50 | — |
| 1976B Proof | 3,385 | Value: 20.00 | | | | |

**50 RUPEES** **KM# 258** **Weight:** 34.7000 g. **Composition:** 0.5000 Silver .5578 oz. ASW **Series:** F.A.O. **Subject:** Save For Development

| Date | Mintage | F | VF | XF | Unc | BU |
|---|---|---|---|---|---|---|
| 1977(B) | 26,000 | — | — | — | 12.50 | — |
| 1977B Proof | 2,544 | Value: 20.00 | | | | |

**50 RUPEES** **KM# 259** **Weight:** 34.7000 g. **Composition:** 0.5000 Silver .5578 oz. ASW **Series:** F.A.O. **Subject:** Food and Shelter For All

| Date | Mintage | F | VF | XF | Unc | BU |
|---|---|---|---|---|---|---|
| 1978(B) | 25,000 | — | — | — | 12.50 | — |
| 1978B Proof | — | Value: 20.00 | | | | |

**50 RUPEES** **KM# 260** **Weight:** 34.7000 g. **Composition:** 0.5000 Silver .5578 oz. ASW **Series:** International Year of the Child

| Date | Mintage | F | VF | XF | Unc | BU |
|---|---|---|---|---|---|---|
| 1979(B) | — | — | — | — | 12.50 | — |
| 1979B Proof | — | Value: 20.00 | | | | |

**50 RUPEES** **KM# 261** **Composition:** Copper-Nickel **Subject:** Quit India **Note:** Similar to 1 Rupee, KM#93.

| Date | Mintage | F | VF | XF | Unc | BU |
|---|---|---|---|---|---|---|
| 1992(B) | — | — | — | — | 12.50 | — |

**50 RUPEES** **KM# 262** **Composition:** Copper-Nickel **Subject:** International Labor Organizations **Note:** Similar to 100 Rupees, KM#287.

| Date | Mintage | F | VF | XF | Unc | BU |
|---|---|---|---|---|---|---|
| ND(1994) | — | — | — | — | 15.00 | — |
| ND(1994) Proof | — | Value: 20.00 | | | | |

**50 RUPEES** **KM# 263** **Composition:** Copper-Nickel **Subject:** 100th Anniversary - Birth of Patel **Note:** Similar to 2 Rupees, KM#129.

| Date | Mintage | F | VF | XF | Unc | BU |
|---|---|---|---|---|---|---|
| 1996(B) | — | — | — | — | 15.00 | — |
| 1996M Proof | — | Value: 30.00 | | | | |

**50 RUPEES** **KM# 264** **Composition:** Copper-Nickel **Subject:** Subhas Chandra Bose **Note:** Similar to 2 Rupees, KM#130.

| Date | Mintage | F | VF | XF | Unc | BU |
|---|---|---|---|---|---|---|
| 1997(C) | — | — | — | — | 15.00 | — |
| 1997(C) Proof | — | Value: 45.00 | | | | |

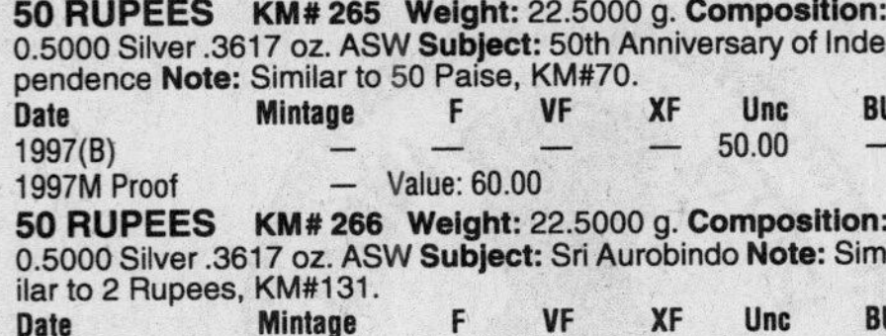

**50 RUPEES** **KM# 265** **Weight:** 22.5000 g. **Composition:** 0.5000 Silver .3617 oz. ASW **Subject:** 50th Anniversary of Independence **Note:** Similar to 50 Paise, KM#70.

| Date | Mintage | F | VF | XF | Unc | BU |
|---|---|---|---|---|---|---|
| 1997(B) | — | — | — | — | 50.00 | — |
| 1997M Proof | — | Value: 60.00 | | | | |

**50 RUPEES** **KM# 266** **Weight:** 22.5000 g. **Composition:** 0.5000 Silver .3617 oz. ASW **Subject:** Sri Aurobindo **Note:** Similar to 2 Rupees, KM#131.

| Date | Mintage | F | VF | XF | Unc | BU |
|---|---|---|---|---|---|---|
| 1998(B) | — | — | — | — | 15.00 | — |
| 1998M Proof | — | Value: 30.00 | | | | |

**100 RUPEES** **KM# 275** **Weight:** 35.0000 g. **Composition:** 0.5000 Silver .5627 oz. ASW **Subject:** Rural Women's Advancement

| Date | Mintage | F | VF | XF | Unc | BU |
|---|---|---|---|---|---|---|
| 1980(B) | 21,000 | — | — | — | 18.50 | — |
| 1980B Proof | 5,811 | Value: 27.50 | | | | |

**100 RUPEES** **KM# 276** **Weight:** 35.0000 g. **Composition:** 0.5000 Silver .5627 oz. ASW **Series:** World Food Day

| Date | Mintage | F | VF | XF | Unc | BU |
|---|---|---|---|---|---|---|
| 1981(B) | 22,000 | — | — | — | 18.50 | — |
| 1981B Proof | 2,950 | Value: 28.50 | | | | |

**100 RUPEES** **KM# 277** **Weight:** 29.1600 g. **Composition:** 0.9250 Silver .8673 oz. ASW **Series:** International Year of the Child

| Date | Mintage | F | VF | XF | Unc | BU |
|---|---|---|---|---|---|---|
| 1981 (1983)B Proof | — | Value: 27.50 | | | | |

**100 RUPEES** **KM# 278** **Weight:** 35.0000 g. **Composition:** 0.5000 Silver .5627 oz. ASW **Subject:** IX Asian Games

| Date | Mintage | F | VF | XF | Unc | BU |
|---|---|---|---|---|---|---|
| 1982(B) | — | — | — | — | 17.50 | — |
| 1982B Proof | — | Value: 27.50 | | | | |

**100 RUPEES** **KM# 279** **Weight:** 35.0000 g. **Composition:** 0.5000 Silver .5627 oz. ASW **Subject:** National Integration

| Date | Mintage | F | VF | XF | Unc | BU |
|---|---|---|---|---|---|---|
| 1982(B) | — | — | — | — | 25.00 | — |
| 1982B Proof | — | Value: 35.00 | | | | |

**100 RUPEES** **KM# 280** **Weight:** 35.0000 g. **Composition:** 0.5000 Silver .5627 oz. ASW **Subject:** Golden Jubilee - Reserve Bank of India

| Date | Mintage | F | VF | XF | Unc | BU |
|---|---|---|---|---|---|---|
| 1985(B) | — | — | — | — | 75.00 | — |
| 1985B Proof | — | Value: 85.00 | | | | |

**100 RUPEES** **KM#281** **Weight:** 35.0000 g. **Composition:** 0.5000 Silver .5627 oz. ASW **Subject:** Death of Indira Gandhi

| Date | Mintage | F | VF | XF | Unc | BU |
|---|---|---|---|---|---|---|
| ND(1985)(B) | — | — | — | — | 30.00 | — |
| ND(1985)B Proof | — | Value: 70.00 | | | | |

**100 RUPEES** **KM#282** **Weight:** 35.0000 g. **Composition:** 0.5000 Silver .5627 oz. ASW **Subject:** Youth Year **Note:** Similar to 1 Rupee, KM#80.

| Date | Mintage | F | VF | XF | Unc | BU |
|---|---|---|---|---|---|---|
| 1985(C) | 16,000 | — | — | — | 30.00 | — |
| 1985(C) Proof | 6,267 | Value: 50.00 | | | | |

**100 RUPEES** **KM#283** **Weight:** 35.0000 g. **Composition:** 0.5000 Silver .5627 oz. ASW **Series:** F.A.O. **Subject:** Fisheries

| Date | Mintage | F | VF | XF | Unc | BU |
|---|---|---|---|---|---|---|
| 1986(B) | — | — | — | — | 30.00 | — |
| 1986B Proof | — | Value: 50.00 | | | | |

**100 RUPEES** **KM#284** **Weight:** 35.0000 g. **Composition:** 0.5000 Silver .5627 oz. ASW **Series:** F.A.O. **Subject:** Small Farmers

| Date | Mintage | F | VF | XF | Unc | BU |
|---|---|---|---|---|---|---|
| 1987(B) | — | — | — | — | 30.00 | — |
| 1987B Proof | — | Value: 50.00 | | | | |

**100 RUPEES** **KM#285** **Weight:** 35.0000 g. **Composition:** 0.5000 Silver .5627 oz. ASW **Subject:** 100th Anniversary of Nehru's Birth

| Date | Mintage | F | VF | XF | Unc | BU |
|---|---|---|---|---|---|---|
| 1989(B) | — | — | — | — | 30.00 | — |
| 1989B Proof | — | Value: 50.00 | | | | |

**100 RUPEES** **KM#286** **Weight:** 35.0000 g. **Composition:** 0.5000 Silver .5627 oz. ASW **Subject:** Quit India **Note:** Similar to 1 Rupee, KM#93.

| Date | Mintage | F | VF | XF | Unc | BU |
|---|---|---|---|---|---|---|
| 1992(B) | — | — | — | — | 25.00 | — |

**100 RUPEES** **KM#287** **Weight:** 35.0000 g. **Composition:** 0.5000 Silver .5627 oz. ASW **Subject:** World of Work

| Date | Mintage | F | VF | XF | Unc | BU |
|---|---|---|---|---|---|---|
| ND(1994) | — | — | — | — | 25.00 | — |
| ND(1994) Proof | — | Value: 40.00 | | | | |

**100 RUPEES** **KM#288** **Weight:** 35.0000 g. **Composition:** 0.5000 Silver .5627 oz. ASW **Subject:** 100th Anniversary - Birth of Patel **Note:** Similar to 2 Rupees, KM#129.

| Date | Mintage | F | VF | XF | Unc | BU |
|---|---|---|---|---|---|---|
| 1996(B) | — | — | — | — | 50.00 | — |
| 1996M Proof | — | Value: 70.00 | | | | |

**100 RUPEES** **KM#289** **Weight:** 35.0000 g. **Composition:** 0.5000 Silver .5627 oz. ASW **Subject:** Subhas Chandra Bose **Note:** Similar to 2 Rupees, KM#130.

| Date | Mintage | F | VF | XF | Unc | BU |
|---|---|---|---|---|---|---|
| 1997(C) | — | — | — | — | 35.00 | — |

**100 RUPEES** **KM#292** **Weight:** 35.0000 g. **Composition:** 0.5000 Silver .5627 oz. ASW **Subject:** Sri Aurobindo **Note:** Similar to 2 Rupees, KM#131.

| Date | Mintage | F | VF | XF | Unc | BU |
|---|---|---|---|---|---|---|
| 1998(B) | — | — | — | — | 30.00 | — |
| 1998M Proof | — | Value: 50.00 | | | | |

## PATTERNS

Including off metal strikes

| KM# | Date | Mintage | Identification | Mkt Val |
|---|---|---|---|---|
| Pn1 | 1946 | — | 1/4 Rupee. Nickel. KM#548. | — |
| Pn2 | 1946 | — | 1/2 Rupee. Nickel. KM#553. | — |
| Pn3 | 1946 | — | Rupee. Nickel. KM#559. | — |
| Pn4 | 1947 | — | 1/4 Rupee. Copper-Nickel. | — |
| Pn5 | 1947 | — | 1/2 Rupee. Copper-Nickel. | — |
| Pn6 | 1947 | — | Rupee. Copper-Nickel. | — |
| Pn7 | 1947 | — | Rupee. Set of Pn1-3. | 1,500 |
| Pn8 | 1949 | — | Pice. Bronze. | — |
| Pn9 | 1949 | — | Anna. Copper-Nickel. | — |
| Pn10 | 1949 | — | 2 Annas. Copper-Nickel. Profile peacock left. | — |
| Pn11 | 1949 | — | 2 Annas. Copper-Nickel. Facing displayed peacock. | — |
| Pn12 | 1949 | — | 1/4 Rupee. Nickel. | — |
| Pn13 | 1949 | — | 1/2 Rupee. Nickel. Worker with finished background. | — |
| Pn14 | 1949 | — | 1/2 Rupee. Nickel. Worker with plain background. | — |
| Pn15 | 1949 | — | Rupee. Nickel. Standing figure. | — |
| Pn16 | 1949 | — | Rupee. Nickel. Similar to Pn9. | — |
| Pn17 | 1964 | — | Paisa. Copper. Half thickness and weight. | — |

## PIEFORTS

| KM# | Date | Mintage | Identification | Mkt Val |
|---|---|---|---|---|
| P1 | 1981 | — | 100 Rupees. KM#277 | 250 |

## MINT SETS

| KM# | Date | Mintage | Identification | Issue Price | Mkt Val |
|---|---|---|---|---|---|
| MS3 | 1962(B) (6) | — | KM#8a, 11, 16, 24.2, 47.2, 55 | 1.50 | 5.00 |
| MS4 | 1962(B) (7) | — | KM#8a, 11, 16, 24.2, 47.2, 55, 75.1(C) | 3.60 | 8.00 |
| MS6 | 1967(B) (8) | — | KM#10.1, 13.1, 14.1, 18.1, 25, 48.2, 58.1, 75.1 (1962 dated Rupee) | 1.00 | 15.00 |
| MS5 | ND(1964)(B) (2) | — | KM#56, 76 | 1.00 | 3.75 |
| MS7 | ND(1969)(B) (4) | 25,281 | KM#42.1, 59, 77, 185 Blue plastic case | 2.50 | 10.00 |
| MS8 | 1970(B) (8) | — | KM#10.1, 13.5, 14.2, 18.3, 26.3, 41, 58.2, 75.2 Brown vinyl case | 1.00 | 18.00 |
| MS9 | 1970(B) (2) | 22,999 | KM#43.1, 186 | 2.00 | 9.00 |
| MS10 | 1971(B) (2) | 9,987 | KM#43.2, 186 | — | 8.50 |
| MS11 | 1972(B) (2) | 43,121 | KM#60, 187 | 2.00 | 7.00 |
| MS11a | 1972(B (2) | — | KM#60, 187a | 2.00 | 7.50 |
| MS12 | 1973(B) (2) | 48,670 | KM#188, 240 | — | 15.00 |
| MS13 | 1974(B) (2) | 50,219 | KM#189, 255 | 10.00 | 12.50 |
| MS14 | 1975(B) (2) | 40,279 | KM#190, 256 | 12.00 | 13.50 |
| MS15 | 1976(B) (2) | 25,105 | KM#191, 257 | 12.00 | 16.00 |
| MS16 | 1977(B) (2) | 17,071 | KM#192, 258 | 12.00 | 16.00 |
| MS17 | 1978(B) (2) | 15,041 | KM#193, 259 | 10.00 | 16.00 |
| MS18 | 1979(B) (2) | — | KM#194, 260 | — | 16.50 |
| MS19 | 1980(B) (2) | — | KM#195, 275 | — | 21.50 |
| MS20 | 1981(B) (2) | — | KM#196, 276 | — | 21.50 |
| MS21 | 1982(B) (2) | — | KM#197, 278 | — | 21.50 |
| MS22 | 1985(B) (2) | — | KM#199, 280 | 48.00 | 140 |
| MS23 | ND(1985)(B) (2) | — | KM#241, 281 | 43.00 | 100 |
| MS24 | ND(1985)(C) (2) | — | KM#200, 282 | — | 40.00 |
| MS25 | 1986 (2) | — | KM#242, 283 | 45.00 | 100 |
| MS26 | 1987(B) (2) | — | KM#243, 284 | 45.00 | 40.00 |
| MS27 | 1989(B) (2) | — | KM#244, 285 | 40.00 | 40.00 |
| MS28 | 1989(B) (2) | — | KM#83, 285 | 50.00 | 45.00 |
| MS29 | 1991(B) (2) | — | KM#152, 201 | — | 18.00 |
| MS30 | 1991(B) (3) | — | KM#90, 152, 201 | — | 20.00 |
| MS31 | 1991(B) (2) | — | KM#123, 153 | — | 20.00 |
| MS32 | 1991(B) (3) | — | KM#91, 123, 153 | — | 22.00 |

| KM# | Date | Mintage | Identification | Issue Price | Mkt Val |
|---|---|---|---|---|---|
| MS33 | 1992(B) (4) | — | KM#92.1, 202, 261, 286 | — | 45.00 |
| MS34 | 1994(B) (3) | — | KM#155, 262, 287 | — | 45.00 |
| MS35 | 1996(M) (3) | — | KM#203, 263, 288 | — | 50.00 |
| MS36 | 1996(M) (2) | — | KM#263, 288 | 65.00 | 45.00 |
| MS37 | 1997(C) (3) | — | KM#204, 264, 289 | — | 50.00 |
| MS38 | 1997(B) (2) | — | KM#70, 265 | 50.00 | 40.00 |
| MS39 | 1998(B) (4) | — | KM#131.1, 205, 266, 292 | — | 55.00 |

## PROOF SETS

| KM# | Date | Mintage | Identification | Issue Price | Mkt Val |
|---|---|---|---|---|---|
| PS1 | 1950(B) (7) | — | KM#1.2, 2.1, 3.1, 4, 5.1, 6.1, 7.1 | 8.40 | 30.00 |
| PS2 | 1954(B) (7) | — | KM#1.3, 2.2, 3.2, 4, 5.1, 6.1, 7.2 | 8.40 | 50.00 |
| PS3 | 1960(B) (6) | — | KM#8, 11, 16, 24.2, 47.1, 55 | 7.00 | 30.00 |
| PS4 | 1961(B) (6) | — | KM#8, 11, 16, 24.2, 47.2, 55 | 7.00 | 40.00 |
| PS5 | 1962(B) (7) | — | KM#8, 11, 16, 24.2, 47.2, 55, 75.1 | 8.40 | 40.00 |
| PS7 | 1963(B) (6) | — | KM#8a, 11, 16, 24.2, 47.2, 55, 75.1 | 7.00 | 30.00 |
| PS8 | 1963(B) (7) | — | KM#8a, 11, 16, 24.2, 47.2, 55, 75.1 | 8.40 | 25.00 |
| PS6 | 1962(B) (7) | — | KM#8a, 11, 16, 24.1, 47.2, 55, 75.1 | 8.40 | 35.00 |
| PS9 | ND(1964)(B) (2) | — | KM#56, 76 | 5.00 | 7.50 |
| PS10 | 1969B (9) | 9,097 | KM#10.1, 13.5, 14.2, 18.3, 26.3, 42.1, 59, 77, 185 | 15.25 | 15.00 |
| PS12 | 1971B (9) | 4,161 | KM#10.1, 13.5, 14.2, 18.3, 26.3, 43.2, 58.3, 75.2, 186 | 15.25 | 15.00 |
| PS11 | 1970B (9) | 2,900 | KM#10.1, 13.5, 14.2, 18.3, 26.3, 43.1, 58.3, 75.2, 186 | 15.25 | 15.00 |
| PS13 | 1972B (9) | 7,701 | KM#10.1, 13.6, 15, 18.6, 27.1, 49.1, 60, 75.2, 187 | 15.25 | 15.00 |
| PS14 | 1973B (10) | 7,563 | KM#10.1, 13.5, 15, 18.6, 27.1, 49.1, 62, 75.1, 188, 240 | 26.00 | 25.00 |
| PS15 | 1973B (9) | 3,326 | KM#10.1, 13.6, 15, 18.6, 27.1, 49.1, 62, 75.2, 188 | 15.25 | 15.00 |
| PS17 | 1974B (10) | 9,138 | KM#10.1, 13.6, 15, 18.6, 28, 49.1, 63, 75.2, 189, 255 | 29.00 | 22.00 |
| PS16 | 1973B (2) | 2,408 | KM#188, 240 | 17.50 | 22.00 |
| PS18 | 1974B (2) | 1,712 | KM#189, 255 | 7.50 | 20.00 |
| PS19 | 1975B (10) | 2,370 | KM#10.1, 13.6, 15, 18.6, 29, 49.1, 63, 78.1 | 35.00 | 30.00 |
| PS20 | 1975B (2) | 160 | KM#190, 256 | 22.00 | 27.50 |
| PS21 | 1976B (10) | 3,209 | KM#10.1, 13.6, 15, 19, 30, 49.1, 63, 78.1, 191, 257 | 35.00 | 30.00 |
| PS22 | 1976B (2) | 190 | KM#191, 257 | 22.00 | 27.50 |
| PS23 | 1977B (10) | 2,222 | KM#10.1, 13.6, 15, 20, 31, 63, 78.1, 192, 258 | 35.00 | 30.00 |
| PS24 | 1977B (2) | — | KM#192, 258 | — | 27.50 |
| PS25 | 1978B (10) | 1,390 | KM#10.1, 13.6, 15, 21, 32, 49.1, 63, 78.1, 193, 259 | 35.00 | 30.00 |
| PS26 | 1978B (2) | — | KM#193, 259 | — | 27.50 |
| PS27 | 1979B (10) | — | KM#10.1, 13.6, 15, 22, 33, 49.2, 63, 78.3, 194, 260 | — | 35.00 |
| PS28 | 1979B (2) | — | KM#194, 260 | — | 28.00 |
| PS29 | 1980B (4) | — | KM#35, 50, 195, 275 | — | 40.00 |
| PS30 | 1980B (2) | — | KM#195, 275 | — | 35.00 |
| PS31 | 1981B (4) | — | KM#36, 51, 196, 276 | — | 40.00 |
| PS32 | 1981B (2) | — | KM#196, 276 | — | 35.00 |
| PS-A33 | 1982B (4) | — | KM#64, 121.1, 198, 279 | — | 52.50 |
| PS-A34 | 1982B (2) | — | KM#198, 279 | — | 45.00 |
| PS33 | 1982B (4) | — | KM#52, 120, 197, 278 | 48.00 | 40.00 |
| PS34 | 1982B (2) | — | KM#197, 278 | 38.00 | 35.00 |
| PS35 | 1985B (4) | — | KM#66, 122, 199, 280 | 98.00 | 235 |
| PS37 | ND(1985)B (4) | — | KM#67.1, 150, 241, 281 | 88.00 | 150 |
| PS36 | 1985B (2) | — | KM#199, 280 | 58.00 | 160 |
| PS38 | ND(1985)B (2) | — | KM#241, 281 | 48.00 | 120 |
| PS39 | 1985(C) (3) | — | KM#80, 200, 282 | — | 70.00 |
| PS40 | 1986B (3) | — | KM#68.1, 242, 283 | 70.00 | 130 |
| PS41 | 1986B (2) | — | KM#242, 283 | 50.00 | 120 |
| PS42 | 1987B (3) | — | KM#81, 243, 284 | 65.00 | 75.00 |
| PS43 | 1987B (2) | — | KM#243, 284 | 60.00 | 70.00 |
| PS44 | 1989B (4) | — | KM#83, 151, 244, 285 | 90.00 | 100 |
| PS45 | 1989B (2) | — | KM#244, 285 | 65.00 | 70.00 |
| PS46 | 1991(B) (3) | — | KM#90, 152, 201 | — | 45.00 |
| PS47 | 1991(B) (3) | — | KM#91, 123, 153 | — | 35.00 |
| PS48 | ND(1994) (3) | — | KM#155, 262, 287 | 18.75 | 55.00 |
| PS49 | ND(1994) (2) | — | KM#262, 287 | 18.05 | 50.00 |
| PS50 | 1996M (4) | — | KM#129, 203, 263, 288 | 110 | 85.00 |
| PS51 | 1996M (2) | — | KM#263, 288 | 100 | 75.00 |
| PS52 | 1997(C) (3) | — | KM#24, 264, 289 | — | 75.00 |
| PS53 | 1997M (2) | — | KM#70, 265 | 75.00 | 60.00 |
| PS54 | 1998M (4) | — | KM#131.1, 205, 266, 290 | — | 95.00 |

# INDONESIA

The Republic of Indonesia, the world's largest archipelago, extends for more than 3,000 miles (4,827 km.) along the equator from the mainland of southeast Asia to Australia. The 17,508 islands comprising the archipelago have a combined area of 788,425 sq. mi. (1,919,440 sq.km.) and a population of 205 million, including East Timor. On August 30, 1999, the Timorese majority voted for independence. The Inter FET (International Forces for East Timor) is now in charge of controlling the chaotic situation. Capitol: Jakarta. Petroleum, timber, rubber, and coffee are exported.

Had Columbus succeeded in reaching the fabled Spice Islands, he would have found advanced civilizations a millennium old, and temples still ranked among the finest examples of ancient art. During the opening centuries of the Christian era, the islands were influenced by Hindu priests and traders who spread their culture and religion. Moslem invasions began in the 13th century, fragmenting the island kingdoms into small states which were unable to resist Western colonial infiltration. Portuguese traders established posts in the 16th century, but they were soon outnumbered by the Dutch who arrived in 1596 and gradually asserted control over the islands comprising present-day Indonesia. Dutch dominance, interrupted by British incursions during the Napoleonic Wars, established the Netherlands East Indies as one of the richest colonial possessions in the world.

The Indonesian independence movement, which began between the two world wars, was encouraged by the Japanese during their 3 1/2-year occupation during World War II. Indonesia proclaimed its independence on Aug. 17,1945, three days after the surrender of Japan and full sovereignty. On Dec. 27, 1949, after four years of guerilla warfare including two large scale campaigns by the Dutch in an effort to reassert control, complete independence was established. Rebellions in Bandung and on the Molluccan Islands occurred in 1950. During the reign of President Mohammad Achmad Sukarno (1950-67) the new Republic not only held together but started to develop. West Irian, formerly Netherlands New Guinea, came under the administration of Indonesia on May 1, 1963. In 1965, the army staged an anti-communist coup in which thousands perished.

On November 28, 1975 the Portuguese Province of Timor, an overseas province occupying the eastern half of the East Indian island of Timor, attained independence as the People's Democratic Republic of East Timor. On December 5, 1975 the government of the People's Democratic Republic was seized by a guerrilla faction sympathetic to the Indonesian territorial claim to East Timor which ousted the constitutional government and replaced it with the Provisional Government of East Timor. On July 17, 1976, the Provisional Government enacted a law that dissolved the free republic and made East Timor the 27th province of Indonesia.

The VOC (United East India Company) struck coins and emergency issues for the Indonesian Archipelago and for the islands at various mints in the Netherlands and the islands. In 1798 the VOC was subsumed by the Dutch government, which issued VOC type transitional and regal types during the Batavian Republic and the Kingdom of the Netherlands until independence. The British issued a coinage during the various occupations by the British East Indian Company, 1811-24. Modern coinage issued by the Republic of Indonesia includes separate series for West Irian and for the Riau Archipelago, an area of small islands between Singapore and Sumatra.

**MONETARY SYSTEM**

100 Sen = 1 Rupiah

# REPUBLIC

## STANDARD COINAGE

100 Sen = 1 Rupiah

**SEN KM# 7 Composition:** Aluminum

| Date | Mintage | F | VF | XF | Unc | BU |
|---|---|---|---|---|---|---|
| 1952(u) | 100,000 | — | 0.25 | 0.50 | 1.00 | — |

**5 SEN KM# 5 Composition:** Aluminum

| Date | Mintage | F | VF | XF | Unc | BU |
|---|---|---|---|---|---|---|
| 1951(u) | — | — | 0.10 | 0.25 | 0.50 | — |
| 1954 | — | — | 0.10 | 0.25 | 0.50 | — |

**10 SEN KM# 6 Composition:** Aluminum

| Date | Mintage | F | VF | XF | Unc | BU |
|---|---|---|---|---|---|---|
| 1951(u) | — | — | 0.15 | 0.25 | 0.45 | — |
| 1954 | 50,000,000 | — | 0.15 | 0.25 | 0.45 | — |

**10 SEN KM# 12 Composition:** Aluminum

| Date | Mintage | F | VF | XF | Unc | BU |
|---|---|---|---|---|---|---|
| 1957 | 50,224,000 | — | 0.25 | 0.50 | 1.00 | — |

**25 SEN KM# 8 Composition:** Aluminum

| Date | Mintage | F | VF | XF | Unc | BU |
|---|---|---|---|---|---|---|
| 1952(u) | 200,000,000 | — | 0.10 | 0.20 | 0.40 | — |

**25 SEN KM# 11 Composition:** Aluminum

| Date | Mintage | F | VF | XF | Unc | BU |
|---|---|---|---|---|---|---|
| 1955 | 25,767,000 | — | 0.10 | 0.20 | 0.40 | — |
| 1957 | 99,752,000 | — | 0.10 | 0.20 | 0.40 | — |

**50 SEN KM# 9 Composition:** Copper-Nickel

| Date | Mintage | F | VF | XF | Unc | BU |
|---|---|---|---|---|---|---|
| 1952(u) | 100,000,000 | — | 0.15 | 0.25 | 0.45 | — |

**50 SEN KM# 10.1 Composition:** Copper-Nickel

| Date | Mintage | F | VF | XF | Unc | BU |
|---|---|---|---|---|---|---|
| 1954 | 1,290,000 | — | 1.00 | 2.25 | 4.50 | — |
| 1955 | 15,000,000 | — | 0.15 | 0.25 | 0.45 | — |

**50 SEN KM# 10.2 Composition:** Copper-Nickel **Reverse:** Different head, larger lettering

| Date | Mintage | F | VF | XF | Unc | BU |
|---|---|---|---|---|---|---|
| 1957 | 24,977,000 | — | 0.15 | 0.25 | 0.45 | — |

**50 SEN KM# 13 Composition:** Aluminum

| Date | Mintage | F | VF | XF | Unc | BU |
|---|---|---|---|---|---|---|
| 1958 | 100,000,000 | — | 0.15 | 0.25 | 0.50 | — |

**50 SEN KM# 14 Composition:** Aluminum **Reverse:** Modified eagle

| Date | Mintage | F | VF | XF | Unc | BU |
|---|---|---|---|---|---|---|
| 1959 | 100,000,000 | — | 0.15 | 0.25 | 0.50 | — |
| 1961 | 128,528,000 | — | 0.15 | 0.25 | 0.50 | — |

**RUPIAH KM# 20 Composition:** Aluminum **Reverse:** Fantail flycatcher, denomination

| Date | Mintage | F | VF | XF | Unc | BU |
|---|---|---|---|---|---|---|
| 1970 | 136,010,000 | — | — | 0.15 | 0.25 | — |

**2 RUPIAH KM# 21 Composition:** Aluminum

| Date | Mintage | F | VF | XF | Unc | BU |
|---|---|---|---|---|---|---|
| 1970 | 139,230,000 | — | — | 0.15 | 0.25 | — |

**5 RUPIAH KM# 22 Composition:** Aluminum **Reverse:** Black drongo, denomination

| Date | Mintage | F | VF | XF | Unc | BU |
|---|---|---|---|---|---|---|
| 1970 | 448,000,000 | — | 0.15 | 0.30 | 0.65 | — |

**5 RUPIAH KM# 37 Composition:** Aluminum **Subject:** Family planning program

| Date | Mintage | F | VF | XF | Unc | BU |
|---|---|---|---|---|---|---|
| 1974 | 447,910,000 | — | 0.10 | 0.15 | 0.25 | — |

**5 RUPIAH KM# 43 Composition:** Aluminum **Subject:** Family planning program

| Date | Mintage | F | VF | XF | Unc | BU |
|---|---|---|---|---|---|---|
| 1979 | 413,200,000 | — | 0.10 | 0.15 | 0.25 | — |
| 1995 | 6,420,000 | — | 0.20 | 0.30 | 0.60 | — |
| 1996 | — | — | 0.20 | 0.30 | 0.60 | — |

**10 RUPIAH KM# 33 Composition:** Copper-Nickel **Series:** F.A.O.

| Date | Mintage | F | VF | XF | Unc | BU |
|---|---|---|---|---|---|---|
| 1971 | 286,360,000 | — | 0.10 | 0.20 | 0.40 | — |

**10 RUPIAH KM# 38 Composition:** Brass-Clad Steel **Subject:** National saving program

| Date | Mintage | F | VF | XF | Unc | BU |
|---|---|---|---|---|---|---|
| 1974 | 222,910,000 | — | 0.10 | 0.20 | 0.40 | — |

**10 RUPIAH KM# 44 Composition:** Aluminum **Series:** F.A.O.

| Date | Mintage | F | VF | XF | Unc | BU |
|---|---|---|---|---|---|---|
| 1979 | 285,670,000 | — | 0.10 | 0.20 | 0.40 | — |

**25 RUPIAH KM# 34 Composition:** Copper-Nickel **Reverse:** Victoria crowned pigeon, denomination

| Date | Mintage | F | VF | XF | Unc | BU |
|---|---|---|---|---|---|---|
| 1971 | 1,221,610,000 | — | 0.10 | 0.20 | 0.40 | — |

**25 RUPIAH KM# 55 Composition:** Aluminum **Reverse:** Nutmeg plant

| Date | Mintage | F | VF | XF | Unc | BU |
|---|---|---|---|---|---|---|
| 1991 | 30,000,000 | — | — | 0.40 | 0.85 | — |
| 1992 | 64,000,000 | — | — | 0.40 | 0.85 | — |
| 1993 | 20,000,000 | — | — | 0.40 | 0.85 | — |
| 1994 | 250,000,000 | — | — | 0.25 | 0.60 | — |
| 1995 | 184,480,000 | — | — | 0.25 | 0.60 | — |
| 1996 | — | — | — | 0.25 | 0.60 | — |

**50 RUPIAH KM# 35 Composition:** Copper-Nickel **Reverse:** Greater bird of paradise, denomination

| Date | Mintage | F | VF | XF | Unc | BU |
|---|---|---|---|---|---|---|
| 1971 | 1,035,435,000 | — | 0.10 | 0.20 | 0.50 | — |

**50 RUPIAH KM# 52 Composition:** Aluminum-Bronze **Reverse:** Komodo dragon lizard

| Date | Mintage | F | VF | XF | Unc | BU |
|---|---|---|---|---|---|---|
| 1991 | 67,000,000 | — | 0.10 | 0.20 | 0.50 | — |
| 1992 | 70,000,000 | — | 0.10 | 0.20 | 0.50 | — |
| 1993 | 120,000,000 | — | 0.10 | 0.20 | 0.40 | — |
| 1994 | 300,000,000 | — | 0.10 | 0.20 | 0.40 | — |
| 1995 | 591,880,000 | — | 0.10 | 0.20 | 0.40 | — |
| 1996 | — | — | 0.10 | 0.20 | 0.50 | — |
| 1997 | 150,000 | — | 0.10 | 0.20 | 0.50 | — |
| 1998 | 150,000 | — | 0.10 | 0.20 | 0.50 | — |

**50 RUPIAH KM# 60 Composition:** Aluminum **Obverse:** National arms **Reverse:** Denomination and black-naped oriole

| Date | Mintage | F | VF | XF | Unc | BU |
|---|---|---|---|---|---|---|
| 1999 | — | — | — | — | 0.40 | — |
| 2001 | — | — | — | — | 0.30 | — |

**100 RUPIAH KM# 36 Composition:** Copper-Nickel

| Date | Mintage | F | VF | XF | Unc | BU |
|---|---|---|---|---|---|---|
| 1973 | 252,868,000 | — | 0.30 | 0.60 | 1.50 | — |

**100 RUPIAH KM# 42 Composition:** Copper-Nickel **Subject:** Forestry for prosperity

| Date | Mintage | F | VF | XF | Unc | BU |
|---|---|---|---|---|---|---|
| 1978 | 907,773,000 | — | 0.25 | 0.50 | 1.35 | — |

**100 RUPIAH KM# 53 Composition:** Aluminum-Bronze **Subject:** Cow racing

| Date | Mintage | F | VF | XF | Unc | BU |
|---|---|---|---|---|---|---|
| 1991 | 94,000,000 | — | — | 0.30 | 0.65 | — |
| 1992 | 120,000,000 | — | — | 0.30 | 0.60 | — |
| 1993 | 300,000,000 | — | — | 0.30 | 0.60 | — |

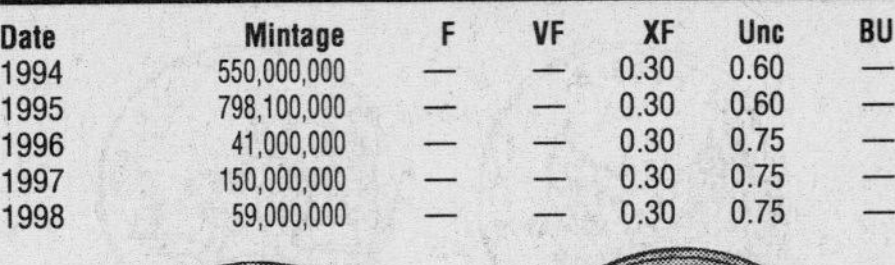

| Date | Mintage | F | VF | XF | Unc | BU |
|---|---|---|---|---|---|---|
| 1994 | 550,000,000 | — | — | 0.30 | 0.60 | — |
| 1995 | 798,100,000 | — | — | 0.30 | 0.60 | — |
| 1996 | 41,000,000 | — | — | 0.30 | 0.75 | — |
| 1997 | 150,000,000 | — | — | 0.30 | 0.75 | — |
| 1998 | 59,000,000 | — | — | 0.30 | 0.75 | — |

**100 RUPIAH** **KM# 61** **Composition:** Aluminum **Obverse:** National arms **Reverse:** Denomination and palm cockatoo

| Date | Mintage | F | VF | XF | Unc | BU |
|---|---|---|---|---|---|---|
| 1999 | — | — | — | — | 0.65 | — |
| 2000 | — | — | — | — | 0.65 | — |
| 2001 | — | — | — | — | 0.60 | — |

**200 RUPIAH** **KM# 23** **Weight:** 8.0000 g. **Composition:** 0.9990 Silver .2569 oz. ASW **Subject:** 25th anniversary of independence **Reverse:** Great bird of paradise

| Date | Mintage | F | VF | XF | Unc | BU |
|---|---|---|---|---|---|---|
| 1970 Proof | 5,100 | Value: 16.50 | | | | |

**250 RUPIAH** **KM# 24** **Weight:** 10.0000 g. **Composition:** 0.9990 Silver .3212 oz. ASW **Subject:** 25th anniversary of independence **Obverse:** Manjusri statue from Temple of Tumpang

| Date | Mintage | F | VF | XF | Unc | BU |
|---|---|---|---|---|---|---|
| 1970 Proof | 5,000 | Value: 18.50 | | | | |

**500 RUPIAH** **KM# 25** **Weight:** 20.0000 g. **Composition:** 0.9990 Silver .6424 oz. ASW **Subject:** 25th anniversary of independence **Obverse:** Similar to 10,000 Rupiah, KM#30 **Reverse:** Wayang dancer

| Date | Mintage | F | VF | XF | Unc | BU |
|---|---|---|---|---|---|---|
| 1970 Proof | 4,800 | Value: 30.00 | | | | |

**500 RUPIAH** **KM# 54** **Composition:** Aluminum-Bronze **Reverse:** Jasmine

| Date | Mintage | F | VF | XF | Unc | BU |
|---|---|---|---|---|---|---|
| 1991 | 71,000,000 | — | — | — | 2.50 | — |
| 1992 | 100,000,000 | — | — | — | 2.50 | — |
| 1993 | — | — | — | — | 2.50 | — |
| 1994 | — | — | — | — | 2.50 | — |

**500 RUPIAH** **KM# 59** **Composition:** Aluminum-Bronze **Obverse:** National emblem **Reverse:** Denomination

| Date | Mintage | F | VF | XF | Unc | BU |
|---|---|---|---|---|---|---|
| 1997 | — | — | — | — | 2.25 | — |
| 2000 | — | — | — | — | 2.00 | — |
| 2001 | — | — | — | — | 2.00 | — |

**750 RUPIAH** **KM# 26** **Weight:** 30.0000 g. **Composition:** 0.9990 Silver .9636 oz. ASW **Subject:** 25th Anniversary of Independence **Obverse:** Similar to 20,000 Rupiah, KM#31 **Reverse:** Garuda bird

| Date | Mintage | F | VF | XF | Unc | BU |
|---|---|---|---|---|---|---|
| 1970 Proof | 4,950 | Value: 42.50 | | | | |

**1000 RUPIAH** **KM# 27** **Weight:** 40.0000 g. **Composition:** 0.9990 Silver 1.2848 oz. ASW **Subject:** 25th anniversary of independence - Gen. Sudirman **Obverse:** Similar to 25,000 Rupiah, KM#32 **Reverse:** Similar to 750 Rupiah, KM#26

| Date | Mintage | F | VF | XF | Unc | BU |
|---|---|---|---|---|---|---|
| 1970 Proof | 4,250 | Value: 55.00 | | | | |

**1000 RUPIAH** **KM# 56** **Ring Composition:** Copper-Nickel **Center Composition:** Brass **Reverse:** Palm tree

| Date | Mintage | F | VF | XF | Unc | BU |
|---|---|---|---|---|---|---|
| 1993 | 5,000,000 | — | — | — | 3.25 | — |
| 1994 | 6,000,000 | — | — | — | 3.25 | — |
| 1995 | 19,900,000 | — | — | — | 3.25 | — |
| 1996 | — | — | — | — | 3.25 | — |
| 1997 | — | — | — | — | 3.25 | — |
| 2000 | — | — | — | — | 3.25 | — |

**2000 RUPIAH** **KM# 28** **Weight:** 4.9300 g. **Composition:** 0.9000 Gold .1426 oz. AGW **Subject:** 25th anniversary of independence **Reverse:** Great bird of paradise

| Date | Mintage | F | VF | XF | Unc | BU |
|---|---|---|---|---|---|---|
| 1970 Proof | 2,970 | Value: 110 | | | | |

**2000 RUPIAH** **KM# 39** **Weight:** 25.6500 g. **Composition:** 0.5000 Silver .4123 oz. ASW **Subject:** Conservation series **Reverse:** Javan tiger

| Date | Mintage | F | VF | XF | Unc | BU |
|---|---|---|---|---|---|---|
| 1974 | 43,000 | — | — | — | 10.00 | — |

**2000 RUPIAH** **KM# 39a** **Weight:** 28.2800 g. **Composition:** 0.9250 Silver .8411 oz. ASW **Subject:** Conservation series **Reverse:** Javan tiger

| Date | Mintage | F | VF | XF | Unc | BU |
|---|---|---|---|---|---|---|
| 1974 Proof | 18,000 | Value: 16.00 | | | | |

**5000 RUPIAH** **KM# 29** **Weight:** 12.3400 g. **Composition:** 0.9000 Gold .3571 oz. AGW **Subject:** 25th anniversary of independence **Obverse:** Manjusri statue from Temple of Tumpang **Reverse:** Similar to 2,000 Rupiah, KM#28

| Date | Mintage | F | VF | XF | Unc | BU |
|---|---|---|---|---|---|---|
| 1970 Proof | 2,150 | Value: 245 | | | | |

**5000 RUPIAH** **KM# 40** **Weight:** 32.0000 g. **Composition:** 0.5000 Silver .5144 oz. ASW **Subject:** Conservation series **Obverse:** Similar to 100,000 Rupiah, KM#41 **Reverse:** Orangutan

| Date | Mintage | F | VF | XF | Unc | BU |
|---|---|---|---|---|---|---|
| 1974 | 43,000 | — | — | — | 12.50 | — |

**5000 RUPIAH** **KM# 40a** **Weight:** 35.0000 g. **Composition:** 0.9250 Silver 1.0409 oz. ASW **Subject:** Conservation series **Obverse:** Similar to 100,000 Rupiah, KM#41 **Reverse:** Orangutan

| Date | Mintage | F | VF | XF | Unc | BU |
|---|---|---|---|---|---|---|
| 1974 Proof | 17,000 | Value: 20.00 | | | | |

**10000 RUPIAH** KM# 30 **Weight:** 24.6800 g. **Composition:** 0.9000 Gold .7142 oz. AGW **Subject:** 25th anniversary of independence **Obverse:** Wayang dancer **Reverse:** Similar to 2,000 Rupiah, KM#28

| Date | Mintage | F | VF | XF | Unc | BU |
|---|---|---|---|---|---|---|
| 1970 Proof | 1,440 | Value: 525 | | | | |

**10000 RUPIAH** KM# 45 **Weight:** 19.4400 g. **Composition:** 0.9250 Silver .5782 oz. ASW **Subject:** Wildlife **Reverse:** Babi rusa (wild pig)

| Date | Mintage | F | VF | XF | Unc | BU |
|---|---|---|---|---|---|---|
| 1987 Proof | 25,000 | Value: 50.00 | | | | |

**10000 RUPIAH** KM# 50 **Weight:** 19.4400 g. **Composition:** 0.9250 Silver .5782 oz. ASW **Series:** Save the Child **Reverse:** Playing badminton

| Date | Mintage | F | VF | XF | Unc | BU |
|---|---|---|---|---|---|---|
| 1990 Proof | 20,000 | Value: 50.00 | | | | |

**20000 RUPIAH** KM# 31 **Weight:** 49.3700 g. **Composition:** 0.9000 Gold 1.4391 oz. AGW **Subject:** 25th anniversary of independence **Obverse:** Garuda bird **Reverse:** Similar to 2,000 Rupiah, KM#28

| Date | Mintage | F | VF | XF | Unc | BU |
|---|---|---|---|---|---|---|
| 1970 Proof | 1,285 | — | — | — | 1,100 | — |

**25000 RUPIAH** KM# 32 **Weight:** 61.7100 g. **Composition:** 0.9000 Gold 1.7858 oz. AGW **Subject:** 25th anniversary of independence **Obverse:** Gen. Sudirman **Reverse:** Similar to 20,000 Rupiah, KM#31

| Date | Mintage | F | VF | XF | Unc | BU |
|---|---|---|---|---|---|---|
| 1970 Proof | 970 | Value: 1,250 | | | | |

**100000 RUPIAH** KM# 41 **Weight:** 33.4370 g. **Composition:** 0.9000 Gold .9676 oz. AGW **Subject:** Conservation series **Reverse:** Komodo dragon lizard

| Date | Mintage | F | VF | XF | Unc | BU |
|---|---|---|---|---|---|---|
| 1974 | 5,333 | — | — | — | 400 | — |
| 1974 Proof | 1,369 | Value: 550 | | | | |

**125000 RUPIAH** KM# 47 **Weight:** 8.0000 g. **Composition:** 0.9580 Gold .2465 oz. AGW **Subject:** Museum of Struggle '45

| Date | Mintage | F | VF | XF | Unc | BU |
|---|---|---|---|---|---|---|
| 1990 Proof | 16,000 | Value: 115 | | | | |

**150000 RUPIAH** KM# 62 **Weight:** 6.2200 g. **Composition:** 0.9990 Gold **Subject:** For the children of the world **Reverse:** Boy playing at horseback riding

| Date | Mintage | F | VF | XF | Unc | BU |
|---|---|---|---|---|---|---|
| 1999 Proof | 200 | Value: 200 | | | | |

**200000 RUPIAH** KM# 46 **Weight:** 10.0000 g. **Composition:** 0.9170 Gold .2947 oz. AGW **Subject:** Wildlife **Reverse:** Javan rhinoceros

| Date | Mintage | F | VF | XF | Unc | BU |
|---|---|---|---|---|---|---|
| 1987 Proof | 5,000 | Value: 300 | | | | |

**200000 RUPIAH** KM# 51 **Weight:** 10.0000 g. **Composition:** 0.9170 Gold .2947 oz. AGW **Series:** Save the Children **Reverse:** Balinese dancer

| Date | Mintage | F | VF | XF | Unc | BU |
|---|---|---|---|---|---|---|
| 1990 Proof | 3,000 | Value: 300 | | | | |

**250000 RUPIAH** KM# 48 **Weight:** 17.0000 g. **Composition:** 0.9580 Gold .5238 oz. AGW **Subject:** 45 years - Indonesian archipelago **Obverse:** Similar to 125,000 Rupiah, KM#47

| Date | Mintage | F | VF | XF | Unc | BU |
|---|---|---|---|---|---|---|
| 1990 Proof | 16,000 | Value: 235 | | | | |

**300000 RUPIAH** KM# 57 **Weight:** 17.0000 g. **Composition:** 0.9583 Gold .5238 oz. AGW **Subject:** 50th anniversary of independence **Obverse:** National emblem **Reverse:** Presidential talk show

| Date | Mintage | F | VF | XF | Unc | BU |
|---|---|---|---|---|---|---|
| 1995 Sets only | 3,000 | — | — | — | 800 | — |

**750000 RUPIAH** KM# 49 **Weight:** 45.0000 g. **Composition:** 0.9580 Gold 1.3866 oz. AGW **Subject:** 45 years - arms of generation 1945 **Obverse:** Simlar to 125,000 Rupiah, KM#47

| Date | Mintage | F | VF | XF | Unc | BU |
|---|---|---|---|---|---|---|
| 1990 Proof | 16,000 | — | — | — | 625 | — |

**850000 RUPIAH** KM# 58 **Weight:** 50.0000 g. **Composition:** 0.9583 Gold 1.5405 oz. AGW **Subject:** 50th anniversary of independence **Obverse:** National emblem **Reverse:** President Soeharto's portrait

| Date | Mintage | F | VF | XF | Unc | BU |
|---|---|---|---|---|---|---|
| 1995 Sets only | 3,000 | — | — | — | 2,200 | — |

## MEDALLIC COINAGE

**25 RUPIAH** KM# M1 **Composition:** Gold **Subject:** Prince Diponegoro

| Date | Mintage | F | VF | XF | Unc | BU |
|---|---|---|---|---|---|---|
| ND(1952)(u) | 36,000 | — | — | 125 | 200 | — |

## PATTERNS

Including off metal strikes

| KM# | Date | Mintage | Identification | Mkt Val |
|---|---|---|---|---|

| KM# | Date | Mintage | Identification | Mkt Val |
|---|---|---|---|---|
| Pn1 | 1951 | — | 25 Sen. Aluminum. | 275 |
| Pn2 | 1955 | — | 50 Sen. Raised SPECIMEN. 2 known. | 325 |

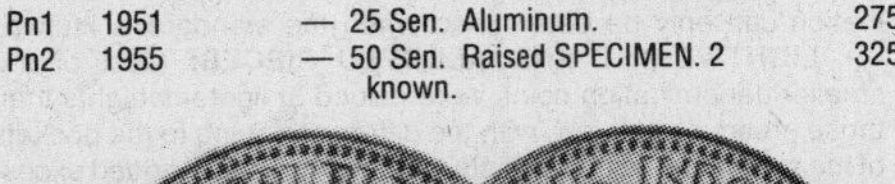

| KM# | Date | Mintage | Identification | Mkt Val |
|---|---|---|---|---|
| Pn3 | 1963 | — | 2-1/2 Rupiah. Aluminum. | 150 |
| Pn4 | 1970 | — | Rupiah. Bronze. KM20. | 125 |
| Pn5 | 1970 | — | 2 Rupiah. Copper. KM21. | 125 |
| Pn6 | 1970 | — | 2 Rupiah. Bronze. KM20. | 125 |
| Pn7 | 1970 | — | 25 Rupiah. Bronze. | — |
| Pn8 | 1973 | — | 100 Rupiah. Aluminum. | 150 |
| Pn9 | 1979 | — | 10 Rupiah. Copper-Nickel. | — |
| Pn10 | 1990 | — | 125000 Rupiah. Gold-plated base metal. KM#47. | — |
| Pn11 | 1990 | — | 250000 Rupiah. Gold-plated base metal. KM#48. | — |
| Pn12 | 1990 | — | 750000 Rupiah. Gold-plated base metal. KM#49. | — |
| Pn13 | 1991 | — | 500 Rupiah. Copper-Nickel. | — |
| Pn14 | 1992 | — | 500 Rupiah. Bronze. | — |
| Pn15 | 1993 | — | 50 Rupiah. Copper-Nickel. | — |
| Pn16 | 1993 | — | 100 Rupiah. Copper-Nickel. | — |

## MINT SETS

| KM# | Date | Mintage | Identification | Issue Price | Mkt Val |
|---|---|---|---|---|---|
| MS1 | Mixed dates (14) | — | KM5-6 (1951, 1954), 7-9 (1952), 10.1 (1955), 10.2 (1957), 11 (1955, 1957), 12 (1957), 14 (1961) | — | 18.00 |
| MS2 | Mixed dates (9) | — | KM20-21 (1970), 33-35 (1971), 36 (1973), 37-38 (1974), 42 (1978) | 2.40 | 6.50 |
| MS3 | 1970 (3) | — | KM20-22 | — | 1.50 |
| MS4 | 1971 (3) | — | KM33-35 | — | 1.50 |

## PROOF SETS

| KM# | Date | Mintage | Identification | Issue Price | Mkt Val |
|---|---|---|---|---|---|
| PS1 | 1970 (10) | 970 | KM23-32 | 490 | 3,400 |
| PS2 | 1970 (5) | 4,250 | KM23-27 | 50.00 | 170 |
| PS3 | 1974 (2) | 30,000 | KM39a-40a | 50.00 | 36.00 |
| PS4 | 1990 (3) | 15,750 | KM47-49 | 755 | 975 |
| PS5 | 1990 (2) | — | KM50-51 | — | 350 |
| PS6 | 1995 (2) | 3,000 | KM57-58 | 2,975 | 3,000 |

# IRIAN BARAT

**(West Irian, Irian Jaya, Netherlands New Guinea)**

A province of Indonesia comprising the western half of the island of New Guinea. A special set of coins dated 1962 were issued in 1964,were recalled December 31, 1971 and are no longer legal tender.

## INDONESIAN PROVINCE

## STANDARD COINAGE

No inscription on edge

**SEN** KM# 5 **Composition:** Aluminum **Edge:** Plain

| Date | Mintage | F | VF | XF | Unc | BU |
|---|---|---|---|---|---|---|
| 1962 | — | 0.25 | 0.50 | 1.00 | 2.00 | — |

**5 SEN** KM# 6 **Composition:** Aluminum **Edge:** Plain

| Date | Mintage | F | VF | XF | Unc | BU |
|---|---|---|---|---|---|---|
| 1962 | — | 0.25 | 0.50 | 1.25 | 2.25 | — |

**10 SEN** KM# 7 **Composition:** Aluminum **Edge:** Plain

| Date | Mintage | F | VF | XF | Unc | BU |
|---|---|---|---|---|---|---|
| 1962 | — | 0.25 | 0.50 | 1.25 | 2.25 | — |

**25 SEN** KM# 8.1 **Composition:** Aluminum **Edge:** Reeded

| Date | Mintage | F | VF | XF | Unc | BU |
|---|---|---|---|---|---|---|
| 1962 | — | — | — | — | — | — |

**25 SEN** KM# 8.2 **Composition:** Aluminum **Reverse:** Different style "5"

| Date | Mintage | F | VF | XF | Unc | BU |
|---|---|---|---|---|---|---|
| 1962 | — | 0.75 | 1.50 | 2.50 | 4.50 | — |

**50 SEN** KM# 9 **Composition:** Aluminum **Edge:** Reeded

| Date | Mintage | F | VF | XF | Unc | BU |
|---|---|---|---|---|---|---|
| 1962 | — | 0.85 | 1.60 | 3.00 | 7.00 | — |

## PATTERNS

Including off metal strikes

| KM# | Date | Mintage | Identification | Mkt Val |
|---|---|---|---|---|

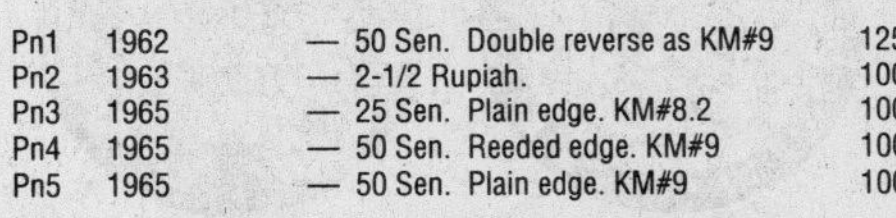

| KM# | Date | Mintage | Identification | Mkt Val |
|---|---|---|---|---|
| Pn1 | 1962 | — | 50 Sen. Double reverse as KM#9 | 125 |
| Pn2 | 1963 | — | 2-1/2 Rupiah. | 100 |
| Pn3 | 1965 | — | 25 Sen. Plain edge. KM#8.2 | 100 |
| Pn4 | 1965 | — | 50 Sen. Reeded edge. KM#9 | 100 |
| Pn5 | 1965 | — | 50 Sen. Plain edge. KM#9 | 100 |

| KM# | Date | Mintage | Identification | Mkt Val |
|---|---|---|---|---|
| Pn6 | 1965//1962 | — | 50 Sen. As KM#9. | 150 |

# RIAU ARCHIPELAGO

A group of 3,214 islands off the tip of the Malay Peninsula. Coins were issued near the end of 1963 (although dated 1962) and recalled as worthless on Sept. 30, 1964. They were legal tender from Oct. 15, 1963 to July 1, 1964.

**INSCRIPTION ON EDGE**
**KEPULAUAN RIAU**

## INDONESIAN PROVINCE

## STANDARD COINAGE

**SEN** KM# 5 **Composition:** Aluminum

| Date | Mintage | F | VF | XF | Unc | BU |
|---|---|---|---|---|---|---|
| 1962 | — | 0.35 | 0.75 | 1.25 | 2.50 | — |

**5 SEN** KM# 6 **Composition:** Aluminum

| Date | Mintage | F | VF | XF | Unc | BU |
|---|---|---|---|---|---|---|
| 1962 | — | 0.30 | 0.60 | 1.50 | 3.00 | — |

**10 SEN** KM# 7 **Composition:** Aluminum

| Date | Mintage | F | VF | XF | Unc | BU |
|---|---|---|---|---|---|---|
| 1962 | — | 0.35 | 0.70 | 1.75 | 3.50 | — |

**25 SEN** KM# 8.1 **Composition:** Aluminum **Reverse:** "25" style similar to Irian Barat, KM#8.1

| Date | Mintage | F | VF | XF | Unc | BU |
|---|---|---|---|---|---|---|
| 1962 | — | — | — | — | — | — |

**25 SEN** KM# 8.2 **Composition:** Aluminum **Reverse:** Different style "5"

| Date | Mintage | F | VF | XF | Unc | BU |
|---|---|---|---|---|---|---|
| 1962 | — | 0.85 | 1.60 | 2.75 | 5.50 | — |

**50 SEN** KM# 9 **Composition:** Aluminum **Reverse:** 17 laurel leaves

| Date | Mintage | F | VF | XF | Unc | BU |
|---|---|---|---|---|---|---|
| 1962 | — | 1.00 | 2.00 | 3.50 | 10.00 | — |

# IRAN

The Islamic Republic of Iran, located between the Caspian Sea and the Persian Gulf in southwestern Asia, has an area of 636,296 sq. mi. (1,648,000 sq. km.) and a population of 40 million. Capital: Tehran. Although predominantly an agricultural state, Iran depends heavily on oil for foreign exchange. Crude oil, carpets and agricultural products are exported.

Iran (historically known as Persia until 1931AD) is one of the world's most ancient and resilient nations. Strategically astride the lower land gate to Asia, it has been conqueror and conquered, sovereign nation and vassal state, ever emerging from its periods of glory or travail with its culture and political individuality intact. Iran (Persia) was a powerful empire under Cyrus the Great (600-529 B.C.), its borders extending from the Indus to the Nile. It has also been conquered by the predatory empires of antique and recent times - Assyrian, Medean, Macedonian, Seljuq, Turk, Mongol - and more recently been coveted by Russia, the Third Reich and Great Britain. Revolts against the absolute power of the Persian shahs resulted in the establishment of a constitutional monarchy in1906.

With 4,000 troops, Reza Khan marched on the capital arriving in Tehran in the early morning of Feb. 22,1921. The government was taken over with hardly a shot and Zia ad-Din was set up as premier, but the real power was with Reza Khan, although he was officially only the minister of war. In 1923, Reza Khan appointed himself prime minister and summoned the "majlis." Who eventually gave him military powers and he became independent of the shah's authority. In 1925 Reza Khan Pahlavi was elected Shah of Persia. A few weeks later his eldest son, Shahpur Mohammed Reza was appointed Crown Prince and was crowned on April 25, 1926.

In 1931 the Kingdom of Persia became known as the Kingdom of Iran. In 1979 the monarchy was toppled and an Islamic Republic proclaimed.

**TITLES**

دار الخلافة

Dar al-Khilafat

**RULERS**

**Qajar Dynasty**

مظفر الدين

Muzaffar al-Din Shah, AH1313-1324/1896-1907AD

محمد علی

Muhammad Ali Shah, AH1324-1327/1907-1909AD

سلطان احمد

Sultan Ahmad Shah, AH1327-1344/1909-1925AD

**Pahlavi Dynasty**

رضا

Reza Shah, as prime minister, SH1302-1304/1923-1925AD as Shah, SH1304-1320/1925-1941AD

محمد رضا

Mohammad Reza Pahlavi, Shah SH1320-1358/1941-1979AD

جمهوری اسلامی ایران

Islamic Republic, SH1358-/1979-AD

**MINTNAME**

Tehran طهران

Tiflis

**MINT MARKS**

H - Heaton (Birmingham)
L - Leningrad (St. Petersburg)

**COIN DATING**

Iranian coins were dated according to the Moslem lunar calendar until March 21, 1925 (AD), when dating was switched to a new calendar based on the solar year, indicated by the notation SH. The monarchial calendar system was adopted in 1976 = MS2535 and was abandoned in 1978 = MS2537. The previously used solar year calendar was restored at that time.

**MONETARY SYSTEM**

1825-1931
(AH1241-1344, SH1304-09)

50 Dinars = 1 Shahi
20 Shahis = 1 Kran (Qiran)
10 Krans = 1 Toman

**NOTE:** From AD1830-34 (AH1245-50) the gold Toman was known as a 'Keshwarsetan.'

1932-Date (SH1310-Date)

5 Dinars = 1 Shahi
20 Shahis = 1 Rial (100 Dinars)
10 Rials = 1 Toman

**NOTE:** The Toman ceased to be an official unit in 1932, but continues to be applied in popular usage. Thus, 135 Rials' is always expressed as 13 Toman, 5 Rials'. The term Rial' is often used in conversation, as well as either Kran' or Ezar' (short for Hazar = 1000) is used.

**NOTE:** The Law of 18 March 1930 fixed the gold Pahlavi at 20 Rials. No gold coins were struck. The Law of 13 March1932 divided the Pahlavi into 100 Rials, instead of 20. The Rial's weight was reduced from 0.3661 grams of pure gold to 0.0732. Since 1937 gold has been allowed to float and the Pahlavi is quoted daily in Rials in the marketplaces.

**KINGDOM**

NOTE: Other mints also produced local Falus, for which examples were not available to illustrate. Still other mints operated only or largely at earlier dates. These include Damavand, Damghan, Darabjird, Fa'Farafad, Kangan, Ra', Semnan, Tus, Tuy and others.

**SILVER AND GOLD COINAGE**

The precious metal monetary system of Qajar Persia prior to the reforms of 1878 was the direct descendant of the Mongol system introduced by Ghazan Mahmud in 1297AD, and was the last example of a medieval islamic coinage. It is not a modern system, and cannot be understood as such. It is not possible to list types, dates, and mints as for other countries, both because of the nature of the coinage, and because very little research has been done on the series. The following comments should help elucidate its nature.

**STANDARDS:** The weight of the primary silver and gold coins was set by law and was expressed in terms of the Mesqal (about 4.61 g) and the Nokhod (24 Nokhod = 1 Mesqal). The primary silver coin was the Rupee from AH1211-1212, the Riyal from AH1212-1241, and the Gheran from AH1241-1344. The standard gold coin was the Toman. Currently the price of gold is quoted in Mesqals.

**DENOMINATIONS:** In addition to the primary denominations, noted in the last

paragraph, fractional pieces were coined, valued at one-eighth, one-fourth, and one-half the primary denomination, usually in much smaller quantities. These were ordinarily struck from the same dies as the larger pieces, sometimes on broad, thin flans, sometimes on thick, dumpy flans. On the smaller coins, the denomination can best be determined only by weighing the coin. The denomination is almost never expressed on the coin!

**DEVALUATIONS:** From time to time, the standard for silver and gold was reduced, and the old coin recalled and replaced with lighter coin, the difference going to the government coffers. The effect was that of a devaluation of the primary silver and gold coins, or inversely regarded, an increase in the price of silver and gold. The durations of each standard varied from about 2 to 20 years. The standards are given for each ruler, as the denomination can only be determined when the standard is known.

**LIGHTWEIGHT AND ALLOYED PIECES:** Most of the smaller denomination coins were issued at lighter weights than those prescribed by law, with the difference going to the pockets of the mintmasters. Other mints, notably Hamadan, added excessive amounts of alloy to the coins, and some mintmasters lost their heads as a result. Discrepancies in weight of as much as 15 percent and more are observed, with the result that it is often quite impossible to determine the denomination of a coin!

**OVERSIZE COINS:** Occasionally, multiples of the primary denominations were produced, usually on special occasions for presentation by the Shah to his favorites. These 'coins' did not circulate (except as bullion), and were usually worn as ornaments. They were the 'NCLT's' of their day.

**MINTS & EPITHETS:** Qajar coinage was struck at 34 mints (plus at least a dozen others striking only copper Falus), which are listed previously, with drawings of the mintnames in Persian, as they appear on the coins. However, the Persian script admits of infinite variation and stylistic whimsy, so the forms given are only guides, and not absolute. Only a knowledge of the script will assure correct reading. In addition to the city name, most mintnames were given identifying epithets, which occasionally appear in lieu of the mintname, particularly at Iravan and Mashhad.

**TYPES:** There were no types in the modern sense, but the arrangement of the legends and the ornamental borders were frequently changed. These changes do not coincide with changes in standards, and cannot be used to determine the mint, which must be found by actually reading the reverse inscriptions.

**ARRANGEMENT**

The following listings are arranged first by ruler, with various standards explained. Then, the coins are listed by denomination within each reign. For each denomination, one or more pieces, when available, are illustrated, with the mint and date noted beneath each photo. For each type, a date range is given, but this range indicates the years during which the particular type was current, and does not imply that every year of the interval is known on actual coins. Because dates were carelessly engraved, and old dies were used until they wore out or broke, we occasionally find coins of a particular type dated before or after the indicated interval. Such coins command no premium. No attempt has been made to determine which mints actually exist for which types.

**KRAN STANDARD**
AH1293-1344, SH1304-1309,
1876-1931AD
50 Dinars = 1 Shahi
1000 Dinars = 20 Shahis = 1 Kran (Qiron)
10 Krans = 1 Toman

**Special Gold Issue**
AH1337/1918-1919AD
1 Ashrafi (= 1 Toman)
SH1305-1309/1927-1931AD

Toman replaced by Pahlavi (light standard). Relationship of Pahlavi to Kran not known.

**NOTE:** Dated reverse dies lacking the ruler's name were not discarded at the end of a reign (especially from Nasir al-Din to Muzaffar al-Din), but remained in use until broken or worn out. Sometimes the old date was scratched out or changed, but often the die was used with the old date unaltered. Some dies with date below wreath retained the old date but had the new date engraved among the lion's legs.

**SHAHI SEFID**
(White Shahi)

Called the White (i.e. silver) Shahi to distinguish it from the Black or Copper Shahi, the Shahi Sefid was actually worth 3 Shahis (150 Dinars) or 3-1/8 Shahis (156-1/4 Dinars). It was used primarily for distribution on New Year's Day (now RUZ) as good-luck gifts. Since 1926 special privately struck tokens, having no monetary value, have been used instead of coins. The Shahi Sefid was broader, but much thinner than the 1/4 Kran (Rob'I), worth 250 Dinars.

# KINGDOM

## Anonymous Ruler

## MILLED COINAGE

**50 DINARS** **KM# 961** **Composition:** Copper-Nickel

| Date | Mintage | F | VF | XF | Unc |
|---|---|---|---|---|---|
| AH1319 | 12,000,000 | 0.75 | 1.50 | 4.00 | 8.00 |
| AH1321 | 10,000,000 | 0.75 | 1.50 | 4.00 | 8.00 |
| AH1326 | 8,000,000 | 1.25 | 2.50 | 10.00 | 20.00 |
| AH1332 | 6,000,000 | 1.00 | 2.00 | 5.00 | 12.50 |
| AH1337 | 7,000,000 | 0.75 | 1.50 | 3.50 | 7.50 |

**50 DINARS** **KM# 1091** **Composition:** Copper-Nickel

| Date | Mintage | F | VF | XF | Unc |
|---|---|---|---|---|---|
| SH1305 | 11,000,000 | 0.80 | 2.00 | 5.00 | 12.50 |
| SH1307 | 2,500,000 | 0.80 | 2.00 | 5.00 | 12.50 |

**SHAHI SEFID (White Shahi)** **KM# 1007** **Weight:** 0.0691 g. **Composition:** 0.9000 Silver .0200 oz. ASW **Obv. Legend:** "Sahib al-Zaman"

| Date | Mintage | VG | F | VF | XF | Unc |
|---|---|---|---|---|---|---|
| AH1326 | — | 40.00 | 60.00 | 125 | 175 | — |

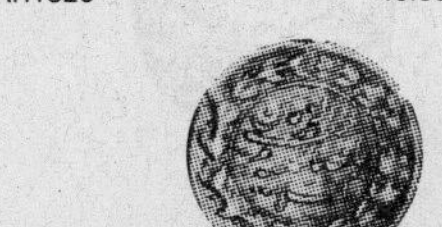

**SHAHI SEFID (White Shahi)** **KM# 1049** **Weight:** 0.0691 g. **Composition:** 0.9000 Silver .0200 oz. ASW **Rev. Legend:** "Sahib-al-Zaman"

| Date | Mintage | VG | F | VF | XF | Unc |
|---|---|---|---|---|---|---|
| ND(1913-24) | — | 5.00 | 10.00 | 20.00 | 40.00 | — |
| AH1332 | — | 5.00 | 10.00 | 18.00 | 35.00 | — |
| **Note:** Included in KM#1032 | | | | | | |
| AH1333 | — | 5.00 | 10.00 | 20.00 | 40.00 | — |
| **Note:** Included in KM#1047 | | | | | | |
| AH1337 | — | 5.00 | 10.00 | 20.00 | 40.00 | — |
| **Note:** Included in KM#1047 | | | | | | |
| AH1341 | 3,000 | 10.00 | 15.00 | 25.00 | 50.00 | — |
| AH1342 | — | 10.00 | 15.00 | 25.00 | 50.00 | — |
| **Note:** Included in KM#1047 | | | | | | |

**100 DINARS** **KM# 962** **Composition:** Copper-Nickel

| Date | Mintage | F | VF | XF | Unc |
|---|---|---|---|---|---|
| AH1319 | 9,000,000 | 0.75 | 1.50 | 4.00 | 8.00 |
| AH1321/19 | 5,000,000 | 4.00 | 6.00 | 11.50 | 30.00 |
| AH1321 | Inc. above | 0.75 | 1.50 | 4.00 | 8.00 |
| AH1326 | 6,000,000 | 1.50 | 2.50 | 6.00 | 15.00 |
| AH1332 | 5,000,000 | 1.00 | 2.00 | 5.00 | 12.50 |
| AH1337 | 6,500,000 | 0.75 | 1.50 | 3.00 | 6.50 |

**100 DINARS** **KM# 1092** **Composition:** Copper-Nickel

| Date | Mintage | F | VF | XF | Unc |
|---|---|---|---|---|---|
| SH1305 | 4,500,000 | 1.00 | 1.50 | 3.50 | 10.00 |
| SH1307 | 3,750,000 | 1.00 | 1.50 | 3.50 | 10.00 |

**1/4 KRAN (Rob'i = 5 Shahis)** **KM# 1093** **Weight:** 1.1513 g. **Composition:** 0.9000 Silver .0333 oz. ASW **Note:** 8,000 reported struck in SH1305, but that year not yet found and presumed not to exist.

| Date | Mintage | VG | F | VF | XF | Unc |
|---|---|---|---|---|---|---|
| SH1304 | Est. 24,000 | 7.50 | 20.00 | 50.00 | 85.00 | — |

**500 DINARS (10 Shahis = 1/2 Kran)** **KM# 1094** **Weight:** 2.3025 g. **Composition:** 0.9000 Silver .0666 oz. ASW

| Date | Mintage | F | VF | XF | Unc |
|---|---|---|---|---|---|
| SH1304 | — | 450 | 525 | 700 | 1,000 |

**1000 DINARS (Kran, Qiran)** **KM# 1095** **Weight:** 4.6050 g. **Composition:** 0.9000 Silver .1332 oz. ASW

| Date | Mintage | F | VF | XF | Unc |
|---|---|---|---|---|---|
| SH1304 | 2,573,000 | 3.00 | 5.00 | 10.00 | 20.00 |
| SH1305 | 2,265,000 | 4.00 | 7.00 | 12.50 | 25.00 |

**2000 DINARS (2 Krans)** **KM# 1096** **Weight:** 9.2100 g. **Composition:** 0.9000 Silver .2665 oz. ASW **Reverse:** Date below lion

| Date | Mintage | F | VF | XF | Unc |
|---|---|---|---|---|---|
| SH1304 | 11,920,000 | 6.00 | 10.00 | 15.00 | 35.00 |
| SH1305 | 9,785,000 | 5.00 | 8.00 | 12.00 | 25.00 |

**5000 DINARS (5 Krans)** **KM# 1097** **Weight:** 23.0251 g. **Composition:** 0.9000 Silver .6662 oz. ASW **Note:** Cross reference Dav.#292.

| Date | Mintage | F | VF | XF | Unc |
|---|---|---|---|---|---|
| SH1304 | 500,000 | 10.00 | 15.00 | 30.00 | 80.00 |
| SH1305 | 1,363,000 | 12.00 | 20.00 | 37.50 | 90.00 |

## REFORM COINAGE

5 Dinars = 1 Shahi; 100 Dinars = 1 Rial;
100 Rials = 1 Pahlavi

The pahlavi was made equal in weight to the British sovereign. It was originally valued at 100 Rials, but has always fluctuated with market prices of gold and silver.

**DINAR** **KM# 1121** **Composition:** Bronze

| Date | Mintage | F | VF | XF | Unc |
|---|---|---|---|---|---|
| SH1310 | 10,000,000 | 8.00 | 15.00 | 30.00 | 60.00 |

**2 DINARS** **KM# 1122** **Composition:** Bronze

| Date | Mintage | F | VF | XF | Unc |
|---|---|---|---|---|---|
| SH1310 | 5,000,000 | 7.00 | 15.00 | 35.00 | 70.00 |

**5 DINARS** **KM# 1123** **Composition:** Copper-Nickel

| Date | Mintage | F | VF | XF | Unc |
|---|---|---|---|---|---|
| SH1310 | 3,750,000 | 10.00 | 20.00 | 50.00 | 150 |

**5 DINARS** **KM# 1123a** **Composition:** Copper

| Date | Mintage | F | VF | XF | Unc |
|---|---|---|---|---|---|
| SH1314 | 480,000 | 100 | 225 | 400 | — |

**5 DINARS** **KM# 1138** **Composition:** Aluminum-Bronze

| Date | Mintage | F | VF | XF | Unc |
|---|---|---|---|---|---|
| SH1315 | 5,665,000 | 2.50 | 4.00 | 10.00 | 20.00 |
| SH1316 | Inc. above | 0.40 | 0.75 | 1.50 | 5.00 |
| SH1317 | 13,025,000 | 0.40 | 0.75 | 1.50 | 5.00 |
| SH1318 | — | 0.40 | 0.75 | 1.50 | 5.00 |
| SH1319 | — | 0.40 | 0.75 | 1.50 | 5.00 |
| SH1320 | — | 0.40 | 0.75 | 1.50 | 4.00 |
| SH1321 | — | 0.40 | 0.75 | 1.50 | 5.00 |

**10 DINARS** **KM# 1124** **Weight:** 4.0000 g. **Composition:** Copper-Nickel **Note:** Struck at Berlin.

| Date | Mintage | F | VF | XF | Unc |
|---|---|---|---|---|---|
| SH1310 | 3,750,000 | 9.00 | 18.00 | 35.00 | 125 |

**10 DINARS** **KM# 1124a** **Weight:** 3.2000 g. **Composition:** Copper **Note:** Struck at Tehran.

| Date | Mintage | F | VF | XF | Unc |
|---|---|---|---|---|---|
| SH1314 | 11,350,000 | 11.50 | 20.00 | 45.00 | 125 |

**10 DINARS** **KM# 1139** **Composition:** Aluminum-Bronze

| Date | Mintage | F | VF | XF | Unc |
|---|---|---|---|---|---|
| SH1315 | 6,195,000 | 2.00 | 5.00 | 15.00 | 25.00 |
| SH1316 | Inc. above | 0.80 | 1.50 | 4.00 | 10.00 |
| SH1317 | 17,120,000 | 0.40 | 0.80 | 2.00 | 6.00 |

| Date | Mintage | F | VF | XF | Unc |
|---|---|---|---|---|---|
| SH1318 | — | 0.40 | 0.80 | 2.00 | 6.00 |
| SH1319 | — | 0.40 | 0.80 | 2.00 | 6.00 |
| SH1320 | — | 0.40 | 0.80 | 2.00 | 6.00 |
| SH1321 | — | 0.45 | 1.00 | 2.50 | 6.00 |

**25 DINARS KM# 1125 Composition:** Copper-Nickel

| Date | Mintage | F | VF | XF | Unc |
|---|---|---|---|---|---|
| SH1310 | 750,000 | 18.00 | 35.00 | 75.00 | 200 |

**25 DINARS KM# 1125a Composition:** Copper

| Date | Mintage | F | VF | XF | Unc |
|---|---|---|---|---|---|
| SH1314 | 1,152,000 | 30.00 | 60.00 | 85.00 | 250 |

**25 DINARS KM# 1140 Composition:** Aluminum-Bronze

| Date | Mintage | F | VF | XF | Unc |
|---|---|---|---|---|---|
| SH1326 | — | 3.00 | 6.00 | 15.00 | 30.00 |
| SH1327 | — | 10.00 | 15.00 | 30.00 | 60.00 |
| SH1329 | — | 4.00 | 7.00 | 20.00 | 40.00 |

**25 DINARS KM# 1141 Composition:** Aluminum-Bronze **Obverse:** 25 Dinars, KM#1140 **Reverse:** 1 Rial, KM#1143 **Note:** Mule

| Date | Mintage | F | VF | XF | Unc |
|---|---|---|---|---|---|
| SH1329 | — | 100 | 150 | 250 | 400 |

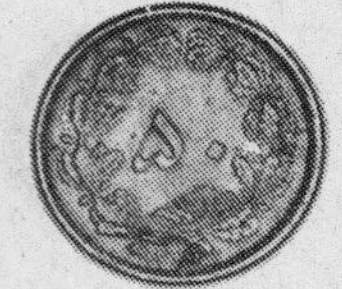

**50 DINARS KM# 1142 Composition:** Aluminum-Bronze

| Date | Mintage | F | VF | XF | Unc |
|---|---|---|---|---|---|
| SH1315 | 15,968,000 | 3.00 | 4.50 | 10.00 | 35.00 |
| SH1316 | 34,200,000 | 1.25 | 2.50 | 6.00 | 20.00 |
| SH1317 | 17,314,000 | 0.60 | 1.50 | 4.00 | 15.00 |
| SH1318 | — | 0.60 | 1.50 | 4.00 | 15.00 |
| SH1319 | — | 1.50 | 2.50 | 6.00 | 20.00 |
| SH1320 | — | 0.75 | 1.50 | 3.00 | 10.00 |
| SH1321/0 | — | 0.75 | 1.50 | 3.00 | 15.00 |
| SH1322/10 | — | 0.75 | 1.50 | 3.00 | 15.00 |
| SH1322/12 | — | 0.75 | 1.50 | 3.00 | 10.00 |
| SH1322/0 | — | 0.75 | 1.50 | 3.00 | 10.00 |
| SH1322/1 | — | 0.75 | 1.50 | 3.00 | 10.00 |
| SH1331 | 8,162,000 | 3.50 | 4.50 | 10.00 | 25.00 |
| SH1332 | 22,892,000 | 2.00 | 3.00 | 5.00 | 10.00 |

**50 DINARS KM# 1142a Composition:** Copper

| Date | Mintage | F | VF | XF | Unc |
|---|---|---|---|---|---|
| SH1322 | — | 2.00 | 4.00 | 7.00 | 12.00 |
| SH1322/0 | — | 2.00 | 6.00 | 9.00 | 15.00 |

**50 DINARS KM# 1156 Composition:** Aluminum-Bronze **Note:** Reduced thickness.

| Date | Mintage | F | VF | XF | Unc |
|---|---|---|---|---|---|
| SH1332 | — | 25.00 | 30.00 | 40.00 | 50.00 |
| SH1333 | 4,036,000 | 0.75 | 1.50 | 2.50 | 8.00 |
| SH1334 | 1,370,000 | 0.75 | 1.50 | 4.00 | 10.00 |
| SH1335 | 926,000 | 0.75 | 1.50 | 2.50 | 8.00 |
| SH1336 | — | 1.00 | 1.25 | 2.00 | 8.00 |

**Note:** Mint reports record 126,500 in SH1337 and 20,000 in SH1338; these were probably dated SH1336

| Date | Mintage | F | VF | XF | Unc |
|---|---|---|---|---|---|
| SH1342 | 800,000 | 0.60 | 1.00 | 1.75 | 6.00 |
| SH1343 | 1,400,000 | 0.60 | 1.00 | 1.75 | 6.00 |
| SH1344 | 1,600,000 | 0.35 | 0.65 | 1.25 | 5.00 |
| SH1345 | 1,690,000 | 0.35 | 0.65 | 1.25 | 5.00 |
| SH1346 | — | 0.20 | 0.25 | 0.50 | 2.00 |

**Note:** Mintage report seems excessive for this and all SH1346 coinage

| Date | Mintage | F | VF | XF | Unc |
|---|---|---|---|---|---|
| SH1347 | 2,000,000 | 0.20 | 0.25 | 0.50 | 2.00 |
| SH1348 | 1,500,000 | 0.20 | 0.25 | 0.50 | 2.00 |
| SH1349 | 360,000 | 2.00 | 3.00 | 4.50 | 12.50 |
| SH1350 | — | 0.30 | 0.50 | 0.75 | 2.00 |
| SH1351 | — | 0.30 | 0.50 | 0.75 | 2.00 |
| SH1353 | 60,000 | 0.30 | 0.50 | 0.75 | 2.00 |
| SH1354 | 16,000 | 0.75 | 1.25 | 2.00 | 5.00 |

**50 DINARS KM# 1156a Composition:** Brass-Coated Steel

| Date | Mintage | F | VF | XF | Unc |
|---|---|---|---|---|---|
| MS2535 | 27,000 | 0.80 | 1.00 | 2.00 | 3.00 |
| MS2536 | — | 1.00 | 1.50 | 2.50 | 4.00 |
| MS2537 | — | 1.00 | 1.50 | 2.50 | 4.00 |
| SH1357 | — | 1.00 | 2.00 | 3.50 | 6.00 |
| SH1358 | — | 3.00 | 4.00 | 6.00 | 10.00 |

**10 SHAHIS KM# 1126.2 Composition:** Copper **Edge:** Plain

| Date | Mintage | F | VF | XF | Unc |
|---|---|---|---|---|---|
| SH1314 | Inc. above | 5.00 | 7.00 | 15.00 | 40.00 |

**10 SHAHIS KM# 1126.1 (KM1126) Composition:** Copper **Edge:** Reeded

| Date | Mintage | F | VF | XF | Unc |
|---|---|---|---|---|---|
| SH1314 Small date | 15,714,000 | 3.00 | 4.00 | 12.50 | 30.00 |
| SH1314 Large date | Inc. above | 3.00 | 4.00 | 12.50 | 30.00 |

**1/4 RIAL KM# 1127 Weight:** 1.2500 g. **Composition:** 0.8280 Silver .0332 oz. ASW

| Date | Mintage | F | VF | XF | Unc |
|---|---|---|---|---|---|
| SH1315 | 600,000 | 1.00 | 1.25 | 1.75 | 4.00 |

**Note:** The second "1" is often short, so that the date looks like 1305

## Nasir al-Din Shah
### AH1264-1313/1848-96AD
### MILLED COINAGE

**SHAHI SEFID (White Shahi) KM# 891 Composition:** Copper-Nickel Clad Brass **Obv. Legend:** "Nasir al-Din" (KM# 889) **Rev. Legend:** "Shahib al-zaman" (obverse of KM#1001)

| Date | Mintage | VG | F | VF | XF | Unc |
|---|---|---|---|---|---|---|
| ND(1908-09) | — | 25.00 | 50.00 | 75.00 | 125 | — |

## Muzaffar al-Din Shah
### AH1313-24/1896-1907AD
### MILLED COINAGE

**SHAHI SEFID (White Shahi) KM# 965 Weight:** 0.0691 g. **Composition:** 0.9000 Silver .0200 oz. ASW **Obv. Legend:** "Muzaffar al-Din Shah"

| Date | Mintage | VG | F | VF | XF | Unc |
|---|---|---|---|---|---|---|
| ND(1895-1903) | — | 4.00 | 8.00 | 20.00 | 40.00 | — |

**Note:** Some undated issues show traces of an old date (usually AH1301 or AH1303) below wreath on reverse; these are worth slightly more than other undated issues

| Date | Mintage | VG | F | VF | XF | Unc |
|---|---|---|---|---|---|---|
| AH1313 Rare | — | — | — | — | — | — |
| AH1314 | — | 10.00 | 20.00 | 40.00 | 75.00 | — |
| AH1315 | — | 10.00 | 20.00 | 40.00 | 75.00 | — |
| AH1316 | — | 10.00 | 20.00 | 40.00 | 75.00 | — |
| AH1317 | — | 15.00 | 25.00 | 50.00 | 100 | — |
| AH1318 | — | 8.00 | 15.00 | 30.00 | 60.00 | — |
| AH8310 | — | 8.00 | 15.00 | 30.00 | 60.00 | — |

**Note:** Error for 1318

| Date | Mintage | VG | F | VF | XF | Unc |
|---|---|---|---|---|---|---|
| AH1319 | — | 8.00 | 15.00 | 30.00 | 60.00 | — |
| AH1039 | — | 15.00 | 25.00 | 50.00 | 100 | — |

**Note:** Error for 1319

| Date | Mintage | VG | F | VF | XF | Unc |
|---|---|---|---|---|---|---|
| AH1320 | 150,000 | 8.00 | 15.00 | 30.00 | 60.00 | — |

**SHAHI SEFID (White Shahi) KM# 966 Weight:** 0.0691 g. **Composition:** 0.9000 Silver .0200 oz. ASW **Reverse:** Denomination omitted

| Date | Mintage | VG | F | VF | XF | Unc |
|---|---|---|---|---|---|---|
| ND(1901) | — | 25.00 | 50.00 | 80.00 | 165 | — |
| AH1319 Rare | — | — | — | — | — | — |

**Note:** A number of varieties and mulings of KM#965 and KM#966 with other denominations, especially 1/4 Krans and 500 Dinar pieces, are reported; these command a premium over others of the same types; a total of 58,000 pieces were reported struck in AH1322, 1323 and 1324, but none are known with those dates; the specimens were either struck from old dies or were undated types.

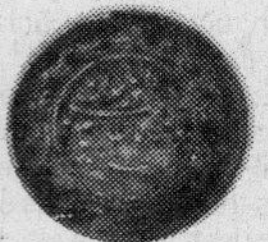

**SHAHI SEFID (White Shahi) KM# 967 Weight:** 0.0691 g. **Composition:** 0.9000 Silver .0200 oz. ASW **Obv. Legend:** "Muzaffar al-Din Shah" **Rev. Legend:** "Sahib al-Zaman" **Note:** Thick and thin lettering varieties exist.

| Date | Mintage | VG | F | VF | XF | Unc |
|---|---|---|---|---|---|---|
| ND(1903-06) | — | 25.00 | 50.00 | 85.00 | 165 | — |

**1/4 KRAN (Rob'i = 5 Shahis) KM# 968 Weight:** 1.1513 g. **Composition:** 0.9000 Silver .0333 oz. ASW **Obv. Legend:** "Muzaffar al-din Shah" **Note:** 300 specimens reportedly struck in AH1322, but none known to exist.

| Date | Mintage | VG | F | VF | XF | Unc |
|---|---|---|---|---|---|---|
| ND(1896-1901) | — | 3.00 | 8.00 | 15.00 | 28.00 | — |
| AH1314 | — | 30.00 | 50.00 | 100 | 200 | — |
| AH1316 | — | 6.00 | 12.50 | 20.00 | 35.00 | — |
| AH1318 | — | 15.00 | 25.00 | 50.00 | 85.00 | — |
| AH1319 | — | 12.50 | 20.00 | 35.00 | 65.00 | — |

ناصرالدين شاه قاجار السلطان

السلطان صاحبقران ناصرالدين شاه قاجار

**First Nasir al-din legend Second Nasir al-din legend with *Sahibqiran* added**

**Forms of the denomination:**

**500 DINARS:** ۵۰۰ دینار

or پانصد دینار

ده شاهی

**500 DINARS (10 Shahis = 1/2 Kran) KM# 969 Weight:** 2.3025 g. **Composition:** 0.9000 Silver .0666 oz. ASW **Obv. Legend:** "Muzaffar al-din", 500 Dinars **Reverse:** Date amidst legs, arranged variously **Note:** Some reverse dies were previously used under Nasir al-Din and show traces of old date beneath wreath on reverse.

| Date | Mintage | VG | F | VF | XF | Unc |
|---|---|---|---|---|---|---|
| ND(1895-1905) | — | 5.00 | 10.00 | 20.00 | 35.00 | — |
| AH1298 (sic) | — | 50.00 | 100 | 150 | 250 | — |

**Note:** The 1298 is an "undated" variety showing 1298 of the dies previous user

| Date | Mintage | VG | F | VF | XF | Unc |
|---|---|---|---|---|---|---|
| AH1313 | — | 25.00 | 40.00 | 75.00 | 150 | — |
| AH1314 | — | 10.00 | 20.00 | 40.00 | 100 | — |
| AH1315 | — | 25.00 | 40.00 | 75.00 | 150 | — |
| AH1316 | — | 25.00 | 40.00 | 75.00 | 150 | — |
| AH1317 | — | — | — | — | — | — |

**Note:** Reported, not confirmed

| Date | Mintage | VG | F | VF | XF | Unc |
|---|---|---|---|---|---|---|
| AH1318 | — | 15.00 | 30.00 | 50.00 | 125 | — |
| AH1319 | — | 12.50 | 20.00 | 40.00 | 100 | — |
| AH1322 | — | 10.00 | 20.00 | 30.00 | 50.00 | — |

**500 DINARS (10 Shahis = 1/2 Kran)** **KM# 977** **Weight:** 2.3025 g. **Composition:** 0.9000 Silver .0666 oz. ASW **Obverse:** Bust of Muzaffar al-Din Shah

| Date | Mintage | VG | F | VF | XF | Unc |
|---|---|---|---|---|---|---|
| AH1323 | 130,000 | 15.00 | 20.00 | 35.00 | 80.00 | — |

**Forms of the denomination:**

**1000 DINARS:** یکهزار دینار

**1 KRAN:** یکقران

**1000 DINARS (Kran, Qiran)** **KM# 972** **Weight:** 4.6050 g. **Composition:** 0.9000 Silver .1332 oz. ASW **Obverse:** Crown added above legend **Reverse:** Date amidst lion's legs

| Date | Mintage | F | VF | XF | Unc |
|---|---|---|---|---|---|
| AH1317 | — | 100 | 175 | 250 | — |
| AH1318 | — | 100 | 175 | 250 | — |
| AH1319 | — | 150 | 225 | 350 | — |
| AH1322 | — | 75.00 | 150 | 225 | — |

**1000 DINARS (Kran, Qiran)** **KM# 978** **Weight:** 4.6050 g. **Composition:** 0.9000 Silver .1332 oz. ASW **Obverse:** Bust of Muzaffer al-Din Shah, date below sprays

| Date | Mintage | F | VF | XF | Unc |
|---|---|---|---|---|---|
| AH1323 | 125,000 | 20.00 | 30.00 | 65.00 | 125 |

**Forms of the denomination:**

**2 KRANS:** دو قران

**2000 DINARS:** دو هزار دینار

**2000 DINARS (2 Krans)** **KM# 974** **Weight:** 9.2100 g. **Composition:** 0.9000 Silver .2665 oz. ASW **Obverse:** Crown added **Reverse:** Position of date amidst legs varies **Rev. Legend:** "2000 Dinars" **Note:** Blundered dates exist.

| Date | Mintage | F | VF | XF | Unc |
|---|---|---|---|---|---|
| AH1312 | — | 75.00 | 100 | 200 | — |
| AH1314 | — | 25.00 | 40.00 | 100 | 200 |
| AH1315 | — | 18.50 | 27.50 | 65.00 | 150 |
| AH1316 | — | 15.00 | 25.00 | 50.00 | 110 |
| AH1317 | — | 15.00 | 25.00 | 50.00 | 110 |
| AH1318 | — | 10.00 | 20.00 | 35.00 | 90.00 |
| AH1319 | — | 10.00 | 20.00 | 35.00 | 90.00 |
| AH1320 | 13,959,000 | 10.00 | 20.00 | 35.00 | 75.00 |

**2000 DINARS (2 Krans)** **KM# 975** **Weight:** 9.2100 g. **Composition:** 0.9000 Silver .2665 oz. ASW **Reverse:** Position of digits varies between lion's legs **Rev. Legend:** 2 Krans

| Date | Mintage | F | VF | XF | Unc |
|---|---|---|---|---|---|
| AH1320 | Inc. above | 12.50 | 20.00 | 40.00 | 100 |
| AH1321 | *18,108,000 | 15.00 | 22.50 | 45.00 | 100 |
| **Note:** In blundered form as 13201 | | | | | |
| AH1322 | 8,640,000 | 8.00 | 15.00 | 30.00 | 80.00 |

**2000 DINARS (2 Krans)** **KM# 979** **Weight:** 9.2100 g. **Composition:** 0.9000 Silver .2665 oz. ASW **Obverse:** Bust of Muzaffer al-Din Shah, date below sprays

| Date | Mintage | F | VF | XF | Unc |
|---|---|---|---|---|---|
| AH1322 | — | 15.00 | 30.00 | 60.00 | 120 |
| **Note:** Mintage inluded in AH1322 above | | | | | |
| AH'13' | — | 60.00 | 100 | 200 | — |
| **Note:** 23 of 1323 filled in or never punched | | | | | |
| AH13233 | — | 45.00 | 85.00 | 190 | — |
| **Note:** Error | | | | | |

**5000 DINARS (5 Krans)** **KM# 976** **Weight:** 23.0251 g. **Composition:** 0.9000 Silver .6662 oz. ASW **Obv. Legend:** "Muzaffar al-din Shah" **Note:** Cross reference Dav.#288.

| Date | Mintage | F | VF | XF | Unc |
|---|---|---|---|---|---|
| AH1320 | 250,000 | 8.00 | 11.50 | 18.50 | 30.00 |
| **Note:** Actual mintage must be considerably greater | | | | | |

**5000 DINARS (5 Krans)** **KM# 980** **Weight:** 23.0251 g. **Composition:** 0.9000 Silver .6662 oz. ASW **Subject:** Royal Birthday **Note:** Cross reference Dav.#287.

| Date | Mintage | F | VF | XF | Unc |
|---|---|---|---|---|---|
| AH1322 | — | 400 | 550 | 800 | 1,200 |

**5000 DINARS (5 Krans)** **KM# 981** **Weight:** 23.0251 g. **Composition:** 0.9000 Silver .6662 oz. ASW **Obverse:** Without additional inscriptions flanking head **Note:** Cross reference Dav.#289.

| Date | Mintage | F | VF | XF | Unc |
|---|---|---|---|---|---|
| AH1324 | 3,040 | 700 | 1,000 | 1,750 | — |

## MILLED GOLD COINAGE

Modern imitations exist of many types, particularly the small 1/5, 1/2, and 1 Toman coins. These are usually underweight (or rarely overweight), and are sold in the bazaars at a small premium over bullion. They are usually crude and probably not intended to deceive collectors, but some are sold for jewelry and some are dated outside the reign of the ruler whose name or portrait they bear. A few deceptive counterfeits are known of the large 10 Toman pieces.

**2000 DINARS (1/5 Toman)** **KM# 986** **Weight:** 0.6520 g. **Composition:** 0.9000 Gold .0188 oz. AGW **Obv. Legend:** "Mazaffar-al-Din Shah" **Reverse:** Lion and sun

| Date | Mintage | F | VF | XF | Unc |
|---|---|---|---|---|---|
| AH9301 Error for 1319 | — | 125 | 175 | 275 | 400 |

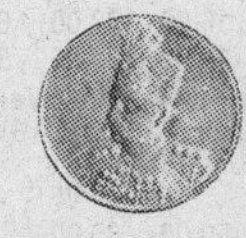

**2000 DINARS (1/5 Toman)** **KM# 991** **Weight:** 0.5749 g. **Composition:** 0.9000 Gold .0166 oz. AGW **Obverse:** Bust of Muzaffar al-Din Shah

| Date | Mintage | F | VF | XF | Unc |
|---|---|---|---|---|---|
| ND | — | 75.00 | 135 | 200 | 300 |

**2000 DINARS (1/5 Toman)** **KM# 992** **Weight:** 0.5749 g. **Composition:** 0.9000 Gold .0166 oz. AGW **Obverse:** Date and denomination added

| Date | Mintage | F | VF | XF | Unc |
|---|---|---|---|---|---|
| AH1319 | — | 50.00 | 100 | 150 | 250 |
| AH1322 | — | 50.00 | 100 | 150 | 250 |
| AH1323 | — | 50.00 | 100 | 150 | 250 |
| AH1324 | — | 50.00 | 100 | 150 | 250 |

**2000 DINARS (1/5 Toman)** **KM# 922** **Weight:** 0.6520 g. **Composition:** 0.9000 Gold .0188 oz. AGW **Note:** Mule. Reverse: KM#923, reverse: KM#991.

| Date | Mintage | F | VF | XF | Unc |
|---|---|---|---|---|---|
| AH1295 (sic) | — | — | — | — | — |

**5000 DINARS (1/2 Toman)** **KM# 994** **Weight:** 1.4372 g. **Composition:** 0.9000 Gold .0416 oz. AGW **Obverse:** Bust of Muzaffar right

| Date | Mintage | F | VF | XF | Unc |
|---|---|---|---|---|---|
| AH1316 | — | 25.00 | 50.00 | 70.00 | 135 |
| AH1318 | — | 25.00 | 50.00 | 75.00 | 150 |
| AH1319 | — | 30.00 | 60.00 | 100 | 200 |
| AH1320 | — | 30.00 | 60.00 | 100 | 200 |
| AH1321 | — | 30.00 | 60.00 | 100 | 200 |
| AH1322 | — | 30.00 | 60.00 | 100 | 200 |
| AH1323 | — | 25.00 | 50.00 | 75.00 | 150 |
| AH1324 | — | 25.00 | 50.00 | 75.00 | 150 |

**TOMAN** **KM# 995** **Weight:** 2.8744 g. **Composition:** 0.9000 Gold .0832 oz. AGW **Obverse:** Bust of Muzaffer 1/2 right, accession date, AH1314 above left

| Date | Mintage | F | VF | XF | Unc |
|---|---|---|---|---|---|
| AH1316 | — | 50.00 | 90.00 | 140 | 225 |
| AH1318 | — | 45.00 | 75.00 | 125 | 200 |
| AH1319 | — | 60.00 | 100 | 160 | 250 |
| AH1321 | — | 60.00 | 100 | 160 | 250 |

**2 TOMANS** **KM# 996** **Weight:** 5.7488 g. **Composition:** 0.9000 Gold .1663 oz. AGW **Obverse:** Bust of Muzaffer 1/2 left, date at left **Rev. Legend:** "Muzaffer al-Din Shah"

| Date | Mintage | F | VF | XF | Unc |
|---|---|---|---|---|---|
| AH1322 | — | 250 | 400 | 750 | 1,500 |

**2 TOMANS** **KM# 997** **Weight:** 5.7488 g. **Composition:** 0.9000 Gold .1663 oz. AGW **Subject:** Royal Birthday **Obverse:** Bust with legend at left and right **Rev. Legend:** "Muzaffer al-Din Shah"

| Date | Mintage | F | VF | XF | Unc |
|---|---|---|---|---|---|
| AH1322 | — | 150 | 300 | 600 | 1,250 |

## Muhammad Ali Shah
### AH1324-27/1907-09AD

### MILLED COINAGE

**SHAHI SEFID (White Shahi)** KM# 1006 **Weight:** 0.0691 g. **Composition:** 0.9000 Silver .0200 oz. ASW **Obv. Legend:** "Muhammad Ali Shah"

| Date | Mintage | VG | F | VF | XF | Unc |
|---|---|---|---|---|---|---|
| AH1325 | — | 15.00 | 30.00 | 60.00 | 110 | — |
| AH1326 | — | 10.00 | 16.00 | 32.00 | 65.00 | — |
| AH1327 | — | 8.00 | 12.00 | 25.00 | 52.00 | — |

**SHAHI SEFID (White Shahi)** KM# 1008 **Weight:** 0.0691 g. **Composition:** 0.9000 Silver .0200 oz. ASW **Obverse:** KM#1006 **Reverse:** Obverse of KM#1007

| Date | Mintage | VG | F | VF | XF | Unc |
|---|---|---|---|---|---|---|
| ND(1909-10) | — | 30.00 | 50.00 | 80.00 | 150 | — |

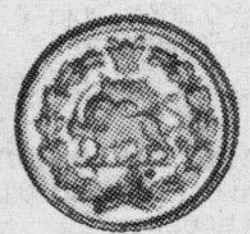

**1/4 KRAN (Rob'i = 5 Shahis)** KM# 1009 **Weight:** 1.1513 g. **Composition:** 0.9000 Silver .0333 oz. ASW **Obv. Legend:** "Muhammad Ali Shah"

| Date | Mintage | VG | F | VF | XF | Unc |
|---|---|---|---|---|---|---|
| AH1325 | — | 20.00 | 30.00 | 50.00 | 100 | — |
| AH1326 | — | 7.50 | 15.00 | 27.50 | 40.00 | — |
| AH1327 | — | 5.00 | 10.00 | 20.00 | 35.00 | — |

**500 DINARS (10 Shahis = 1/2 Kran)** KM# 1010 **Weight:** 2.3025 g. **Composition:** 0.9000 Silver .0666 oz. ASW **Obv. Legend:** "Muhammad Ali Shah"

| Date | Mintage | VG | F | VF | XF | Unc |
|---|---|---|---|---|---|---|
| AH1325 | 218,000 | 20.00 | 40.00 | 75.00 | 160 | — |
| AH1326 | 218,000 | 15.00 | 25.00 | 50.00 | 110 | — |
| AH1336 Error for 1326 | Inc. above | 20.00 | 35.00 | 60.00 | 125 | — |

**500 DINARS (10 Shahis = 1/2 Kran)** KM# 1014 **Weight:** 2.3025 g. **Composition:** 0.9000 Silver .0666 oz. ASW **Obverse:** KM#1013; date **Reverse:** KM#1010; date

| Date | Mintage | VG | F | VF | XF | Unc |
|---|---|---|---|---|---|---|
| AH1325 | — | 75.00 | 125 | 175 | 320 | — |
| AH1326 | — | 60.00 | 100 | 150 | 240 | — |

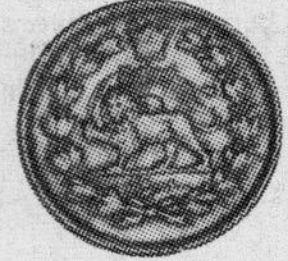

**500 DINARS (10 Shahis = 1/2 Kran)** KM# 1013 **Weight:** 2.3025 g. **Composition:** 0.9000 Silver .0666 oz. ASW **Obverse:** Bust of Muhammad Ali Shah, date below sprays

| Date | Mintage | VG | F | VF | XF | Unc |
|---|---|---|---|---|---|---|
| AH1326 Mintage included in KM#1010 | — | 20.00 | 40.00 | 85.00 | 150 | — |
| AH1327 | — | 20.00 | 40.00 | 85.00 | 150 | — |

**1000 DINARS (Kran, Qiran)** KM# 1011 **Weight:** 4.6050 g. **Composition:** 0.9000 Silver .1332 oz. ASW **Obv. Legend:** "Muhammad Ali Shah"

| Date | Mintage | F | VF | XF | Unc |
|---|---|---|---|---|---|
| AH1325 | 289,000 | 150 | 300 | 600 | — |
| AH1326 | 289,000 | 150 | 300 | 600 | — |

**1000 DINARS (Kran, Qiran)** KM# 1015 **Weight:** 4.6050 g. **Composition:** 0.9000 Silver .1332 oz. ASW **Obverse:** Bust of Muhammad Ali Shah, date below sprays

| Date | Mintage | F | VF | XF | Unc |
|---|---|---|---|---|---|
| AH1326 | — | 45.00 | 70.00 | 150 | 375 |
| Note: Mintage included in KM#1011 | | | | | |
| AH1327/6 | — | — | — | — | — |
| AH1327 | — | 40.00 | 60.00 | 125 | 350 |

**1000 DINARS (Kran, Qiran)** KM# 1016 **Weight:** 4.6050 g. **Composition:** 0.9000 Silver .1332 oz. ASW **Obverse:** KM#1015; date **Reverse:** KM#1011; date

| Date | Mintage | F | VF | XF | Unc |
|---|---|---|---|---|---|
| AH1326 | — | 125 | 200 | 350 | — |
| Note: Mintage included in KM#1011 | | | | | |

**2000 DINARS (2 Krans)** KM# 1012 **Weight:** 9.2100 g. **Composition:** 0.9000 Silver .2665 oz. ASW **Obv. Legend:** "Muhammad Ali Shah" **Reverse:** 2 Krans

| Date | Mintage | F | VF | XF | Unc |
|---|---|---|---|---|---|
| AH1325 | 3,076,000 | 15.00 | 25.00 | 50.00 | 100 |
| AH1326 | 3,069,000 | 7.50 | 11.50 | 20.00 | 50.00 |
| AH1327 | — | 7.50 | 11.50 | 20.00 | 50.00 |

**2000 DINARS (2 Krans)** KM# 1017 **Weight:** 9.2100 g. **Composition:** 0.9000 Silver .2665 oz. ASW **Obverse:** Portrait of Muhammad Ali Shah

| Date | Mintage | F | VF | XF | Unc |
|---|---|---|---|---|---|
| AH1326 | — | 1,500 | 2,000 | 2,500 | — |
| Note: Mintage included in KM#1012 | | | | | |

**5000 DINARS (5 Krans)** KM# 1018 **Weight:** 23.0251 g. **Composition:** 0.9000 Silver .6662 oz. ASW **Obverse:** Bust of Muhammad Ali Shah, date below sprays **Note:** Cross reference Dav.#290.

| Date | Mintage | F | VF | XF | Unc |
|---|---|---|---|---|---|
| AH1327 | — | 575 | 850 | 1,750 | — |
| Note: Obverse always weakly struck with little detail in head and face | | | | | |

### MILLED GOLD COINAGE

Modern imitations exist of many types, particularly the small 1/5, 1/2, and 1 Toman coins. These are usually underweight (or rarely overweight), and are sold in the bazaars at a small premium over bullion. They are usually crude and probably not intended to deceive collectors, but some are sold for jewelry and some are dated outside the reign of the ruler whose name or portrait they bear. A few deceptive counterfeits are known of the large 10 Toman pieces.

**2000 DINARS (1/5 Toman)** KM# 1024 **Weight:** 0.5749 g. **Composition:** 0.9000 Gold .0166 oz. AGW **Obverse:** Bust of Muhammad Ali Shah turned half left, divided date **Reverse:** Legend in wreath

| Date | Mintage | F | VF | XF | Unc |
|---|---|---|---|---|---|
| AH1326 | — | 100 | 190 | 270 | 475 |
| AH1327 | — | 100 | 190 | 270 | 475 |

**5000 DINARS (1/2 Toman)** KM# 1021 **Weight:** 1.4372 g. **Composition:** 0.9000 Gold .0416 oz. AGW **Obv. Legend:** Muhammad Ali Shah **Reverse:** Lion and sun

| Date | Mintage | F | VF | XF | Unc |
|---|---|---|---|---|---|
| AH1324 | — | 100 | 150 | 250 | 400 |
| AH1325 | — | 150 | 225 | 350 | 450 |

**5000 DINARS (1/2 Toman)** KM# 1025 **Weight:** 1.4372 g. **Composition:** 0.9000 Gold .0416 oz. AGW **Obverse:** Bust of Muhammad 1/2 left **Rev. Legend:** "Muhammad Ali Shah"

| Date | Mintage | F | VF | XF | Unc |
|---|---|---|---|---|---|
| AH1326 | — | 125 | 200 | 300 | 450 |
| AH1362 Error for 1326 | — | 150 | 250 | 350 | 525 |
| AH1327 | — | 125 | 200 | 300 | 450 |

**TOMAN** KM# 1022 **Weight:** 2.8744 g. **Composition:** 0.9000 Gold .0832 oz. AGW **Obv. Legend:** "Muhammad Ali Shah" **Reverse:** Lion and sun

| Date | Mintage | F | VF | XF | Unc |
|---|---|---|---|---|---|
| AH1324 | — | 250 | 450 | 675 | 900 |

**TOMAN** KM# 1026 **Weight:** 2.8744 g. **Composition:** 0.9000 Gold .0832 oz. AGW **Obverse:** Bust of Muhammad 1/2 left, AH1326 **Reverse:** Legend in closed wreath **Rev. Legend:** "Muhammad Ali Shah"

| Date | Mintage | F | VF | XF | Unc |
|---|---|---|---|---|---|
| AH1327 | — | 200 | 350 | 500 | 750 |

## Sultan Ahmad Shah
### AH1327-44/1909-25AD

### MILLED COINAGE

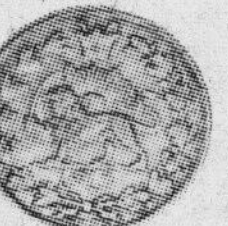

**SHAHI SEFID (White Shahi)** KM# 1031 **Weight:** 0.0691 g. **Composition:** 0.9000 Silver .0200 oz. ASW **Obv. Legend:** "Ahmad Shah" **Reverse:** Date below wreath

| Date | Mintage | VG | F | VF | XF | Unc |
|---|---|---|---|---|---|---|
| AH1328 | — | 3.00 | 5.00 | 10.00 | 20.00 | — |
| AH1329 | — | 3.00 | 6.00 | 12.00 | 25.00 | — |
| AH1330 | 189,000 | 2.00 | 4.00 | 10.00 | 20.00 | — |

**SHAHI SEFID (White Shahi)** **KM# 1032** **Weight:** 0.0691 g. **Composition:** 0.9000 Silver .0200 oz. ASW **Reverse:** Date amidst lion's legs

| Date | Mintage | VG | F | VF | XF | Unc |
|---|---|---|---|---|---|---|
| AH1332 | 10,000 | 20.00 | 30.00 | 50.00 | 85.00 | — |

**SHAHI SEFID (White Shahi)** **KM# 1033** **Weight:** 0.0691 g. **Composition:** 0.9000 Silver .0200 oz. ASW **Obv. Legend:** "Ahmad Shah" **Rev. Legend:** "Sahib-al-Zaman"

| Date | Mintage | VG | F | VF | XF | Unc |
|---|---|---|---|---|---|---|
| ND(1913-15) | — | 40.00 | 60.00 | 125 | 200 | — |

**SHAHI SEFID (White Shahi)** **KM# 1047** **Weight:** 0.0691 g. **Composition:** 0.9000 Silver .0200 oz. ASW **Note:** Varieties exist.

| Date | Mintage | VG | F | VF | XF | Unc |
|---|---|---|---|---|---|---|
| AH1333 | 78,000 | 2.00 | 5.00 | 10.00 | 20.00 | — |
| AH1334 | 6,000 | 4.00 | 12.00 | 20.00 | 40.00 | — |
| AH1335 | 73,000 | 3.00 | 8.00 | 15.00 | 30.00 | — |
| AH1335//1337 | Inc. above | 20.00 | 40.00 | 80.00 | 165 | — |
| AH1337 | 76,000 | 3.00 | 8.00 | 15.00 | 30.00 | — |
| AH1337//1337 | — | 20.00 | 40.00 | 75.00 | 150 | — |
| AH1339 | 10,000 | 4.00 | 12.00 | 20.00 | 40.00 | — |
| AH1342 | 20,000 | 4.00 | 12.00 | 20.00 | 40.00 | — |

**SHAHI SEFID (White Shahi)** **KM# 1048** **Weight:** 0.0691 g. **Composition:** 0.9000 Silver .0200 oz. ASW **Obverse:** KM#1047 **Rev. Legend:** "Sahib-al-Zaman"

| Date | Mintage | VG | F | VF | XF | Unc |
|---|---|---|---|---|---|---|
| AH1335 | — | 30.00 | 50.00 | 80.00 | 150 | — |

**Note:** Mintage included in KM#1047 of AH1335

**SHAHI SEFID (White Shahi)** **KM# 1050** **Weight:** 0.6908 g. **Composition:** 0.9000 Silver .0200 oz. ASW **Obverse:** KM#1047 dated AH1339 **Reverse:** Similar to KM#1049 with AH1341 between lion's legs, AH1327 below wreath

| Date | Mintage | VG | F | VF | XF | Unc |
|---|---|---|---|---|---|---|
| AH1339//1341 & 1327 | — | 30.00 | 50.00 | 80.00 | 150 | — |

**Note:** Numerous silver Nouruz tokens, some with dates SH1328-1346, are available in Tehran for a fraction of the price of true Shahis

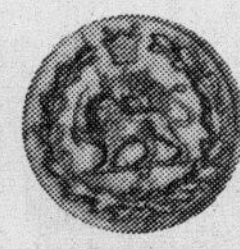

**1/4 KRAN (Rob'i = 5 Shahis)** **KM# 1035** **Weight:** 1.1513 g. **Composition:** 0.9000 Silver .0333 oz. ASW **Obv. Legend:** "Ahmad Shah"

| Date | Mintage | VG | F | VF | XF | Unc |
|---|---|---|---|---|---|---|
| AH1327 | — | 3.00 | 5.00 | 10.00 | 20.00 | — |
| AH1328 | — | 2.00 | 4.00 | 7.50 | 15.00 | — |
| AH1329 | 130,000 | 7.50 | 12.50 | 20.00 | 40.00 | — |
| AH1330 | 156,000 | 2.00 | 4.00 | 7.50 | 15.00 | — |
| AH1331 | 30,000 | — | — | — | — | — |

**Note:** Reported, not confirmed.

| Date | Mintage | VG | F | VF | XF | Unc |
|---|---|---|---|---|---|---|
| AH1313 Error for 1331 | Inc. above | — | — | — | — | — |

**Note:** Reported, not confirmed.

**1/4 KRAN (Rob'i = 5 Shahis)** **KM# 1052** **Weight:** 1.1513 g. **Composition:** 0.9000 Silver .0333 oz. ASW **Obverse:** KM#1051 **Obv. Legend:** "Ahmad Shah" **Reverse:** KM#1009 **Note:** Mule

| Date | Mintage | VG | F | VF | XF | Unc |
|---|---|---|---|---|---|---|
| ND(1909-10) | — | 20.00 | 40.00 | 60.00 | 115 | — |
| AH1327 | — | 30.00 | 60.00 | 125 | 175 | — |

**1/4 KRAN (Rob'i = 5 Shahis)** **KM# 1051** **Weight:** 1.1513 g. **Composition:** 0.9000 Silver .0333 oz. ASW **Obv. Legend:** "Ahmad Shah" **Reverse:** Date amidst legs

| Date | Mintage | VG | F | VF | XF | Unc |
|---|---|---|---|---|---|---|
| AH1332 | 252,000 | 2.00 | 5.00 | 10.00 | 20.00 | — |
| AH1333 | Inc. above | 3.00 | 6.00 | 12.00 | 25.00 | — |
| AH1334 | 70,000 | 5.00 | 10.00 | 20.00 | 50.00 | — |
| AH1335 | 260,000 | 2.00 | 4.00 | 8.00 | 15.00 | — |
| AH1336 | 160,000 | 2.00 | 4.00 | 8.00 | 15.00 | — |
| AH1337 | 80,000 | 3.00 | 6.00 | 12.00 | 25.00 | — |
| AH1339 | 28,000 | 4.00 | 9.00 | 15.00 | 30.00 | — |
| AH1341 | 22,000 | 5.00 | 12.00 | 20.00 | 40.00 | — |
| AH1342 | 110,000 | 3.00 | 6.00 | 12.00 | 25.00 | — |
| AH1343 | 186,000 | 2.00 | 4.00 | 8.00 | 15.00 | — |

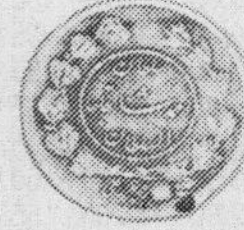

**1/4 KRAN (Rob'i = 5 Shahis)** **KM# 1053** **Weight:** 1.1513 g. **Composition:** 0.9000 Silver .0333 oz. ASW **Obverse:** KM#1051, date below wreath

| Date | Mintage | VG | F | VF | XF | Unc |
|---|---|---|---|---|---|---|
| AH1334 Mintage included with KM#1051 | — | 40.00 | 75.00 | 150 | 250 | — |

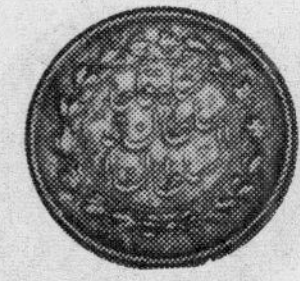

**500 DINARS (10 Shahis = 1/2 Kran)** **KM# 1036** **Weight:** 2.3025 g. **Composition:** 0.9000 Silver .0666 oz. ASW **Obv. Legend:** "Ahmad Shah"

| Date | Mintage | VG | F | VF | XF | Unc |
|---|---|---|---|---|---|---|
| AH1327 | — | 3.00 | 5.00 | 12.50 | 20.00 | — |
| AH1328 | — | 3.00 | 5.00 | 12.50 | 20.00 | — |
| AH1329 | 44,000 | 6.00 | 10.00 | 20.00 | 40.00 | — |
| AH1330 | 627,000 | 3.00 | 5.00 | 12.50 | 20.00 | — |

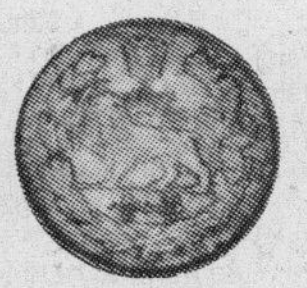

**500 DINARS (10 Shahis = 1/2 Kran)** **KM# 1054** **Weight:** 2.3025 g. **Composition:** 0.9000 Silver .0666 oz. ASW **Obverse:** Portrait of Ahmad Shah, date below sprays

| Date | Mintage | VG | F | VF | XF | Unc |
|---|---|---|---|---|---|---|
| AH1331 | — | 1.50 | 3.00 | 6.00 | 15.00 | — |

**Note:** Mintage included in AH1330 above

| Date | Mintage | VG | F | VF | XF | Unc |
|---|---|---|---|---|---|---|
| AH1332 | 560,000 | 1.00 | 2.00 | 5.00 | 10.00 | — |
| AH1333 | 292,000 | 1.00 | 2.00 | 5.00 | 10.00 | — |
| AH1334 | 65,000 | 1.50 | 3.00 | 6.00 | 12.00 | — |
| AH1335 | 150,000 | 4.00 | 8.00 | 15.00 | 30.00 | — |
| AH1336 | 240,000 | 2.50 | 4.00 | 8.00 | 20.00 | — |
| AH1339 | — | 10.00 | 17.50 | 25.00 | 40.00 | — |
| AH1343 | 160,000 | 3.00 | 6.00 | 10.00 | 25.00 | — |

**Note:** 10,000 reported struck in AH1337 probably dated AH1336

**500 DINARS (10 Shahis = 1/2 Kran)** **KM# 1055** **Weight:** 2.3025 g. **Composition:** 0.9000 Silver .0666 oz. ASW **Obverse:** Date **Reverse:** Date

| Date | Mintage | VG | F | VF | XF | Unc |
|---|---|---|---|---|---|---|
| AH1332 | — | 15.00 | 30.00 | 50.00 | 90.00 | — |

**Note:** Mintage included in KM#1054

**1000 DINARS (Kran, Qiran)** **KM# 1038** **Weight:** 4.6050 g. **Composition:** 0.9000 Silver .1332 oz. ASW **Obv. Legend:** "Sultan Ahmad Shah"

| Date | Mintage | F | VF | XF | Unc |
|---|---|---|---|---|---|
| AH1327 | — | 15.00 | 25.00 | 40.00 | 70.00 |
| AH1328 | — | 4.00 | 8.00 | 15.00 | 40.00 |
| AH1329 | 3,000,000 | 4.00 | 8.00 | 15.00 | 40.00 |
| AH1330 | — | 4.00 | 8.00 | 15.00 | 40.00 |

**1000 DINARS (Kran, Qiran)** **KM# 1037** **Weight:** 4.6050 g. **Composition:** 0.9000 Silver .1332 oz. ASW **Obverse:** KM#1038 **Reverse:** KM#1011 **Note:** Traditional issue.

| Date | Mintage | F | VF | XF | Unc |
|---|---|---|---|---|---|
| AH1326 (sic) Rare | — | — | — | — | — |

**1000 DINARS (Kran, Qiran)** **KM# 1056** **Weight:** 4.6050 g. **Composition:** 0.9000 Silver .1332 oz. ASW **Obverse:** Bust of Ahmad Shah, date below sprays

| Date | Mintage | F | VF | XF | Unc |
|---|---|---|---|---|---|
| AH1331 | 1,310,000 | 5.00 | 8.00 | 25.00 | 40.00 |
| AH1332 | 1,891,000 | 3.00 | 5.00 | 12.50 | 30.00 |
| AH1333 | 2,179,000 | 7.50 | 12.00 | 25.00 | 40.00 |
| AH1334 | 1,273,000 | 3.00 | 5.00 | 12.50 | 25.00 |
| AH1335 | 2,162,000 | 3.00 | 5.00 | 12.50 | 25.00 |
| AH1336 | 1,412,000 | 3.50 | 6.00 | 15.00 | 30.00 |
| AH1337 | 3,330,000 | 3.00 | 5.00 | 12.50 | 25.00 |
| AH1339 | 35,000 | 12.50 | 25.00 | 55.00 | 90.00 |
| AH1330 Error for 1340 | — | 30.00 | 65.00 | 125 | 175 |
| AH1340 | 28,000 | 15.00 | 30.00 | 60.00 | 100 |
| AH1341 | 170,000 | 8.00 | 15.00 | 35.00 | 60.00 |
| AH1342 | 255,000 | 3.00 | 6.00 | 20.00 | 30.00 |
| AH1343 | 1,345,000 | 3.00 | 6.00 | 20.00 | 30.00 |
| AH1344 | 2,978,000 | 4.00 | 6.00 | 20.00 | 35.00 |

**1000 DINARS (Kran, Qiran)** **KM# 1059** **Weight:** 4.6050 g. **Composition:** 0.9000 Silver .1332 oz. ASW **Subject:** 10th Year of Reign

| Date | Mintage | F | VF | XF | Unc |
|---|---|---|---|---|---|
| AH1337 | 975,000 | 25.00 | 40.00 | 75.00 | 150 |

**2000 DINARS (2 Krans)** **KM# 1040** **Weight:** 9.2100 g. **Composition:** 0.9000 Silver .2665 oz. ASW **Obv. Legend:** "Ahmad Shah" **Reverse:** Date below wreath, "2 Krans"

| Date | Mintage | F | VF | XF | Unc |
|---|---|---|---|---|---|
| AH1327 | — | 4.50 | 7.00 | 12.00 | 30.00 |

**Note:** Mintage included in KM#1328

| Date | Mintage | F | VF | XF | Unc |
|---|---|---|---|---|---|
| AH1328 | 30,000,000 | 4.50 | 7.00 | 12.00 | 20.00 |
| AH1329 | 29,250,000 | 4.50 | 7.00 | 12.00 | 20.00 |

**2000 DINARS (2 Krans)** **KM# 1041** **Weight:** 9.2100 g. **Composition:** 0.9000 Silver .2665 oz. ASW **Reverse:** Date below wreath, "2000 Dinars", fierce triangular face on lion

| Date | Mintage | F | VF | XF | Unc |
|---|---|---|---|---|---|
| AH1330 | 2,901,000 | 5.00 | 8.00 | 15.00 | 35.00 |

**2000 DINARS (2 Krans)** **KM# 1043** **Weight:** 9.2100 g. **Composition:** 0.9000 Silver .2665 oz. ASW **Obv. Legend:** "Ahmad Shah" **Reverse:** Date amidst legs, "2000 Dinars"

| Date | Mintage | F | VF | XF | Unc |
|---|---|---|---|---|---|
| AH1330 | — | 4.00 | 7.00 | 10.00 | 30.00 |
| **Note:** Mintage included in KM#1041 | | | | | |
| AH1331 | 13,412,000 | 5.00 | 10.00 | 17.00 | 40.00 |

**2000 DINARS (2 Krans)** **KM# 1057** **Weight:** 9.2100 g. **Composition:** 0.9000 Silver .2665 oz. ASW **Obverse:** Bust of Ahmad Shah, date below sprays

| Date | Mintage | F | VF | XF | Unc |
|---|---|---|---|---|---|
| AH1331 | — | 6.00 | 12.50 | 25.00 | 50.00 |
| **Note:** Mintage included in KM#1043 | | | | | |
| AH1332 | 12,926,000 | 5.00 | 7.50 | 15.00 | 30.00 |
| AH1333 | Inc. above | 5.00 | 7.50 | 15.00 | 30.00 |
| AH1334 | 4,299,000 | 5.00 | 7.50 | 15.00 | 30.00 |
| AH1335 | 9,777,000 | 5.00 | 7.50 | 15.00 | 30.00 |
| AH1336 | 5,401,000 | 5.00 | 7.50 | 15.00 | 30.00 |
| AH1337 | 2,951,000 | 5.00 | 7.50 | 15.00 | 30.00 |
| AH1339 | 1,085,000 | 6.00 | 12.50 | 25.00 | 50.00 |
| AH1330 Error for 1340 | — | 50.00 | 100 | 150 | 250 |
| **Note:** Mintage included in KM#1043 | | | | | |
| AH1340 | 254,000 | 9.00 | 15.00 | 30.00 | 65.00 |
| AH1341 | 4,460,000 | 5.00 | 7.50 | 15.00 | 30.00 |
| AH1342 | 2,245,000 | 5.00 | 8.00 | 20.00 | 35.00 |
| AH1343 | 5,205,000 | 5.00 | 8.00 | 20.00 | 35.00 |
| AH1344/34 | 12,354 | 7.00 | 12.00 | 25.00 | 55.00 |
| AH1344 | Inc. above | 6.00 | 10.00 | 20.00 | 40.00 |

**2000 DINARS (2 Krans)** **KM# 1060** **Weight:** 9.2100 g. **Composition:** 0.9000 Silver .2665 oz. ASW **Subject:** 10th Anniversary of Reign

| Date | Mintage | F | VF | XF | Unc |
|---|---|---|---|---|---|
| AH1337 | 3,508,000 | 25.00 | 40.00 | 100 | 225 |

**5000 DINARS (5 Krans)** **KM# 1058** **Weight:** 23.0251 g. **Composition:** 0.9000 Silver .6662 oz. ASW **Obverse:** Portrait of Ahmad Shah, date below sprays **Note:** Beware of altered date AH1331 specimens. 9,000 reported minted in AH1336, probably dated earlier. Cross reference Dav.#291.

| Date | Mintage | F | VF | XF | Unc |
|---|---|---|---|---|---|
| AH1331 | — | 60.00 | 150 | 250 | 500 |
| AH1332 | 3,000,000 | 8.00 | 12.00 | 30.00 | 85.00 |
| AH1333 | 667,000 | 10.00 | 15.00 | 35.00 | 90.00 |
| AH1334 | 443,000 | 10.00 | 15.00 | 35.00 | 90.00 |
| AH1335 | 1,884,000 | 10.00 | 15.00 | 35.00 | 90.00 |
| AH1337 | 165,000 | 12.00 | 25.00 | 55.00 | 110 |
| AH1339 | 90,000 | 20.00 | 30.00 | 60.00 | 125 |
| AH1340 | 303,000 | 12.00 | 25.00 | 55.00 | 110 |
| AH1341 | 757,000 | 10.00 | 15.00 | 35.00 | 90.00 |
| AH1342/32 | 546,000 | 10.00 | 15.00 | 35.00 | 90.00 |
| AH1342 | Inc. above | 10.00 | 15.00 | 35.00 | 90.00 |
| AH1343 | 935,000 | 10.00 | 15.00 | 35.00 | 90.00 |
| AH1344/34 | 2,284,000 | 10.00 | 15.00 | 30.00 | 85.00 |
| AH1344 | Inc. above | 15.00 | 20.00 | 40.00 | 95.00 |

## CLANDESTINE COINAGE

**1000 DINARS** **KM# 1039** **Composition:** Silver **Note:** KM#1039 differs from KM#1038 in that it is about 1 milimeter broader and has a much thicker rim and more clearly defined denticles. Struck in Germany, without Iranian authorization, for circulation in western Iran during World War I. Also, the lion lacks the triangular face and fierce expression of KM#1038 and the point of the Talwar (scimitar) does not touch the sunburst as it does on Tehran issues.

| Date | Mintage | F | VF | XF | Unc |
|---|---|---|---|---|---|
| AH1330 (sic) | — | — | 7.00 | 18.00 | 30.00 |
| AH1330 (sic) Rare | — | — | — | — | — |

**2000 DINARS** **KM# 1042** **Composition:** Silver **Reverse:** Lion's face has friendly expression

| Date | Mintage | F | VF | XF | Unc |
|---|---|---|---|---|---|
| AH1330 (sic) | — | 4.00 | 7.00 | 10.00 | 27.00 |
| **Note:** See general note for KM#1039 | | | | | |

## MILLED GOLD COINAGE

Modern imitations exist of many types, particularly the small 1/5, 1/2, and 1 Toman coins. These are usually underweight (or rarely overweight), and are sold in the bazaars at a small premium over bullion. They are usually crude and probably not intended to deceive collectors, but some are sold for jewelry and some are dated outside the reign of the ruler whose name or portrait they bear. A few deceptive counterfeits are known of the large 10 Toman pieces.

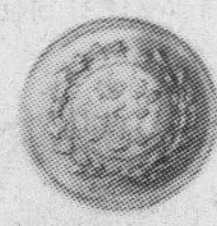

**2000 DINARS (1/5 Toman)** **KM# 1066** **Weight:** 0.5749 g. **Composition:** 0.9000 Gold .0166 oz. AGW **Obv. Legend:** "Ahmad Shah" **Reverse:** Lion and sun

| Date | Mintage | F | VF | XF | Unc |
|---|---|---|---|---|---|
| AH1328 | — | 100 | 175 | 250 | 500 |
| AH1329 | — | 70.00 | 125 | 200 | 325 |
| AH1330 | — | — | — | — | — |

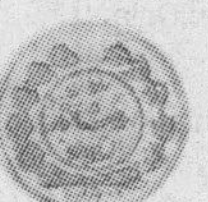

**2000 DINARS (1/5 Toman)** **KM# 1070** **Weight:** 0.5749 g. **Composition:** 0.9000 Gold .0166 oz. AGW **Obverse:** Bust of Ahmad Shah **Rev. Legend:** "Ahmad Shah"

| Date | Mintage | F | VF | XF | Unc |
|---|---|---|---|---|---|
| AH1332 | — | 20.00 | 35.00 | 60.00 | 130 |
| AH1333 | — | 15.00 | 30.00 | 55.00 | 115 |
| AH1334 | — | 15.00 | 30.00 | 40.00 | 75.00 |

| Date | Mintage | F | VF | XF | Unc |
|---|---|---|---|---|---|
| AH1335 | — | 12.50 | 25.00 | 35.00 | 50.00 |
| AH1337 | — | 12.50 | 25.00 | 35.00 | 50.00 |
| AH1339 | — | 15.00 | 30.00 | 40.00 | 75.00 |
| AH1340 | — | 17.00 | 35.00 | 50.00 | 90.00 |
| AH1341 | — | 15.00 | 30.00 | 40.00 | 75.00 |
| AH1342 | — | 15.00 | 30.00 | 40.00 | 75.00 |
| AH1343 | — | 15.00 | 30.00 | 40.00 | 60.00 |

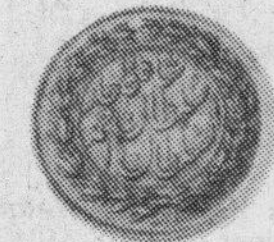

**5000 DINARS (1/2 Toman)** **KM# 1067** **Weight:** 1.4372 g. **Composition:** 0.9000 Gold .0416 oz. AGW **Obv. Legend:** "Ahmad Shah" **Reverse:** Lion and sun

| Date | Mintage | F | VF | XF | Unc |
|---|---|---|---|---|---|
| AH1328 | — | 60.00 | 125 | 200 | 275 |
| AH1329 | — | 60.00 | 100 | 150 | 200 |
| AH1330 | — | 60.00 | 100 | 175 | 225 |

**5000 DINARS (1/2 Toman)** **KM# 1071** **Weight:** 1.4372 g. **Composition:** 0.9000 Gold .0416 oz. AGW **Obverse:** Bust of Ahmad Shah divides date **Rev. Legend:** "Ahmad Shah"

| Date | Mintage | F | VF | XF | Unc |
|---|---|---|---|---|---|
| AH1331 | — | 50.00 | 100 | 150 | 300 |
| AH1332 | — | 40.00 | 60.00 | 100 | 150 |
| AH1333 | — | 25.00 | 40.00 | 75.00 | 125 |
| AH1334 | — | 25.00 | 30.00 | 40.00 | 70.00 |
| AH1335 | — | 25.00 | 30.00 | 40.00 | 70.00 |
| AH1336 | — | 25.00 | 35.00 | 50.00 | 90.00 |
| AH1337 | — | 25.00 | 30.00 | 40.00 | 70.00 |
| AH1339 | — | 25.00 | 35.00 | 60.00 | 110 |
| AH1340 | — | 25.00 | 35.00 | 60.00 | 110 |
| AH1341 | — | 25.00 | 30.00 | 45.00 | 90.00 |
| AH1342 | — | 25.00 | 30.00 | 45.00 | 90.00 |
| AH1343 | — | 25.00 | 30.00 | 45.00 | 90.00 |

**5000 DINARS (1/2 Toman)** **KM# 1072** **Weight:** 1.4372 g. **Composition:** 0.9000 Gold .0416 oz. AGW **Obverse:** KM#1071 **Rev. Legend:** "Sahib al-Zaman"

| Date | Mintage | F | VF | XF | Unc |
|---|---|---|---|---|---|
| AH1340 | — | 100 | 150 | 250 | 400 |

**TOMAN** **KM# 1068** **Weight:** 2.8744 g. **Composition:** 0.9000 Gold .0832 oz. AGW **Obv. Legend:** "Ahmad Shah", AH1328-1332 **Reverse:** Lion and sun

| Date | Mintage | F | VF | XF | Unc |
|---|---|---|---|---|---|
| AH1329 | — | 200 | 300 | 500 | 750 |

**TOMAN** **KM# 1073** **Weight:** 2.8744 g. **Composition:** 0.9000 Gold .0832 oz. AGW **Obverse:** KM#1074 **Reverse:** Ahmad Shah Pattern 2 Toman **Note:** The reverse die used was of an unadopted pattern.

| Date | Mintage | F | VF | XF | Unc |
|---|---|---|---|---|---|
| AH1332 | — | 300 | 600 | 900 | 1,500 |
| AH1333 | — | 300 | 600 | 900 | 1,500 |

**TOMAN** **KM# 1074** **Weight:** 2.8744 g. **Composition:** 0.9000 Gold .0832 oz. AGW **Obverse:** Bust of Ahmad Shah 1/2 left **Rev. Legend:** "Ahmad Shah"

| Date | Mintage | F | VF | XF | Unc |
|---|---|---|---|---|---|
| AH1334 | — | 45.00 | 60.00 | 100 | 175 |
| AH1335 | — | 45.00 | 70.00 | 100 | 175 |
| AH1337 | — | 45.00 | 60.00 | 100 | 175 |
| AH1339 | — | 45.00 | 70.00 | 100 | 175 |
| AH1340 | — | 45.00 | 70.00 | 100 | 175 |
| AH1341 | — | 40.00 | 50.00 | 90.00 | 150 |
| AH1342 | — | 40.00 | 50.00 | 90.00 | 150 |
| AH1343 | — | 40.00 | 50.00 | 90.00 | 150 |

**5 TOMANS** **KM# 1075** **Weight:** 14.3720 g. **Composition:** 0.9000 Gold .4159 oz. AGW **Obv. Legend:** "Ahmad Shah" **Reverse:** Lion and sun **Note:** A number of gold medals of 5 Toman weight were struck between 1297 and 1326. These bear a couplet which clearly indicates that they are medals awarded by the Shah for bravery.

| Date | Mintage | F | VF | XF | Unc |
|---|---|---|---|---|---|
| AH1332/1 | — | 1,100 | 1,600 | 2,000 | 2,700 |
| AH1334/2/1 | — | 1,100 | 1,600 | 2,000 | 2,700 |

**10 TOMANS** **KM# 1076** **Weight:** 28.7440 g. **Composition:** 0.9000 Gold .8317 oz. AGW **Obverse:** Bust of Ahmad Shah **Obv. Legend:** "Ahmad Shah"

| Date | Mintage | F | VF | XF | Unc |
|---|---|---|---|---|---|
| AH1331 | — | 2,400 | 4,350 | 6,500 | 8,500 |
| AH1334 Rare | — | — | — | — | — |
| AH1337//1334 | — | — | — | 6,500 | 8,500 |

**Note:** The date on the AH1334 reverse die was not changed for use as the reverse to the 1337 issue

**10 TOMANS** **KM# 1077** **Weight:** 28.7440 g. **Composition:** 0.9000 Gold .8317 oz. AGW **Obverse:** Bust of Ahmad Shah **Reverse:** Lion and sun

| Date | Mintage | F | VF | XF | Unc |
|---|---|---|---|---|---|
| AH1337 | — | 1,850 | 3,000 | 4,500 | 5,500 |

**ASHRAFI** **KM# 1080** **Composition:** Gold **Obverse:** Bust of Ahmad Shah **Reverse:** Lion and sun

| Date | Mintage | F | VF | XF | Unc |
|---|---|---|---|---|---|
| AH1337 Rare | — | — | — | — | — |

**2 ASHRAFI** **KM# A1081** **Composition:** Gold **Obverse:** Bust of Ahmad Shah **Reverse:** Lion and sun

| Date | Mintage | F | VF | XF | Unc |
|---|---|---|---|---|---|
| AH1337 Rare | — | — | — | — | — |

**5 ASHRAFI** **KM# 1081** **Composition:** Gold **Obverse:** Bust of Ahmad Shah **Reverse:** Lion and sun

| Date | Mintage | F | VF | XF | Unc |
|---|---|---|---|---|---|
| AH1337 Rare | — | — | — | — | — |

**10 ASHRAFI** **KM# 1082** **Composition:** Gold **Obverse:** Bust of Ahmad Shah **Reverse:** Lion and sun

| Date | Mintage | F | VF | XF | Unc |
|---|---|---|---|---|---|
| AH1337 Rare | — | — | — | — | — |

# Reza Shah
## AH1344-1360/1923-41AD
## MILLED COINAGE

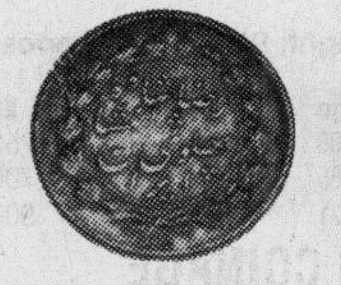

**500 DINARS (10 Shahis = 1/2 Kran)** **KM# 1098** **Weight:** 2.3025 g. **Composition:** 0.9000 Silver .0666 oz. ASW **Obv. Legend:** "Reza Shah"

| Date | Mintage | F | VF | XF | Unc |
|---|---|---|---|---|---|
| SH1305 | 10,000 | 75.00 | 125 | 200 | 400 |

**500 DINARS (10 Shahis = 1/2 Kran)** **KM# 1102** **Weight:** 2.3025 g. **Composition:** 0.9000 Silver .0666 oz. ASW **Obverse:** Bust of Reza Shah, "Julius 1304" left, date below

| Date | Mintage | F | VF | XF | Unc |
|---|---|---|---|---|---|
| SH1306 | 5,000 | 40.00 | 60.00 | 85.00 | 120 |
| SH1307 | 46,000 | 4.50 | 7.50 | 15.00 | 30.00 |
| SH1308 | 464,000 | 4.50 | 7.50 | 15.00 | 30.00 |

**Note:** Some of the coins reported in SH1308 were dated 1307

**1000 DINARS (Kran, Qiran)** **KM# 1099** **Weight:** 4.6050 g. **Composition:** 0.9000 Silver .1332 oz. ASW **Obv. Legend:** "Reza Shah"

| Date | Mintage | F | VF | XF | Unc |
|---|---|---|---|---|---|
| SH1305 | — | 3.00 | 5.00 | 10.00 | 20.00 |

**Note:** Mintage included in KM#1095

| Date | Mintage | F | VF | XF | Unc |
|---|---|---|---|---|---|
| SH1306/5 | 3,130,000 | 5.00 | 8.00 | 15.00 | 25.00 |
| SH1306 | Inc. above | 3.00 | 5.00 | 10.00 | 20.00 |

**1000 DINARS (Kran, Qiran)** **KM# 1103** **Weight:** 4.6050 g. **Composition:** 0.9000 Silver .1332 oz. ASW **Obverse:** Bust of Reza Shah, date below sprays

| Date | Mintage | F | VF | XF | Unc |
|---|---|---|---|---|---|
| SH1306 | — | 4.00 | 8.00 | 15.00 | 30.00 |

**Note:** Mintage included in KM#1099

| Date | Mintage | F | VF | XF | Unc |
|---|---|---|---|---|---|
| SH1307 | 4,300,000 | 4.00 | 6.00 | 10.00 | 20.00 |
| SH1308 | 603,000 | 4.00 | 6.00 | 10.00 | 20.00 |

**2000 DINARS (2 Krans)** **KM# 1100** **Weight:** 9.2100 g. **Composition:** 0.9000 Silver .2665 oz. ASW **Obv. Legend:** "Reza Shah" **Reverse:** Date below wreath

| Date | Mintage | F | VF | XF | Unc |
|---|---|---|---|---|---|
| SH1305 | — | 5.00 | 10.00 | 20.00 | 30.00 |
| SH1306 | 9,380,000 | 4.00 | 7.00 | 12.50 | 25.00 |

**2000 DINARS (2 Krans)** **KM# 1104** **Weight:** 9.2100 g. **Composition:** 0.9000 Silver .2665 oz. ASW **Obverse:** Bust of Reza Shah, "Julus 1304" at left, date below

| Date | Mintage | F | VF | XF | Unc |
|---|---|---|---|---|---|
| SH1306 | — | 4.00 | 6.00 | 12.50 | 25.00 |

**Note:** Mintage included in KM#1100

| Date | Mintage | F | VF | XF | Unc |
|---|---|---|---|---|---|
| SH1306 Proof | — | Value: 375 | | | |
| SH1306H | 11,714,000 | 3.00 | 5.00 | 10.00 | 20.00 |
| SH1306L | 7,500,000 | 3.00 | 5.00 | 8.00 | 18.00 |
| SH1307 | 11,146,000 | 3.00 | 6.00 | 15.00 | 25.00 |
| SH1308 | 1,611,000 | 4.00 | 10.00 | 20.00 | 30.00 |

**2000 DINARS (2 Krans)** **KM# 1105** **Weight:** 9.2100 g. **Composition:** 0.9000 Silver .2665 oz. ASW **Obverse:** KM#1104 **Reverse:** KM#1057 **Note:** Mule.

| Date | Mintage | F | VF | XF | Unc |
|---|---|---|---|---|---|
| SH1306 | — | — | — | — | — |

**Note:** Reported, not confirmed

**5000 DINARS (5 Krans)** **KM# 1101** **Weight:** 23.0251 g. **Composition:** 0.9000 Silver .6662 oz. ASW **Obv. Legend:** "Reza Shah" **Note:** Cross reference Dav.#293.

| Date | Mintage | F | VF | XF | Unc |
|---|---|---|---|---|---|
| SH1305 | — | 10.00 | 15.00 | 35.00 | 100 |

**Note:** Mintage included in KM#1097

| Date | Mintage | F | VF | XF | Unc |
|---|---|---|---|---|---|
| SH1306 | 3,186,000 | 10.00 | 15.00 | 30.00 | 85.00 |

**5000 DINARS (5 Krans)** **KM# 1106** **Weight:** 23.0251 g. **Composition:** 0.9000 Silver .6662 oz. ASW **Obverse:** Portrait of Reza Shah, "Julus 1304" at left, date below **Note:** Cross reference Dav.#294. Mint marks located as on 2000 Dinars, KM#1104.

| Date | Mintage | F | VF | XF | Unc |
|---|---|---|---|---|---|
| SH1306 | — | 9.00 | 12.50 | 20.00 | 37.50 |

**Note:** Mintage including in KM#1101

| Date | Mintage | F | VF | XF | Unc |
|---|---|---|---|---|---|
| SH1306 Proof | — | Value: 400 | | | |

| Date | Mintage | F | VF | XF | Unc |
|---|---|---|---|---|---|
| SH1306H | 4,711,000 | 6.00 | 10.00 | 17.50 | 32.50 |
| SH1306L | 3,000,000 | 6.00 | 7.50 | 30.00 | 45.00 |
| SH1307 | 3,928,000 | 6.00 | 7.50 | 15.00 | 30.00 |
| SH1308 | 584,000 | 12.50 | 25.00 | 50.00 | 100 |

**5000 DINARS (5 Krans)** **KM# 1107** **Weight:** 23.0251 g. **Composition:** 0.9000 Silver .6662 oz. ASW **Obverse:** KM#1106 **Reverse:** KM#1058 **Note:** Mule.

| Date | Mintage | F | VF | XF | Unc |
|---|---|---|---|---|---|
| SH1306 | — | — | — | — | — |

**Note:** Reported, not confirmed

## MILLED GOLD COINAGE

Modern imitations exist of many types, particularly the small 1/5, 1/2, and 1 Toman coins. These are usually underweight (or rarely overweight), and are sold in the bazaars at a small premium over bullion. They are usually crude and probably not intended to deceive collectors, but some are sold for jewelry and some are dated outside the reign of the ruler whose name or portrait they bear. A few deceptive counterfeits are known of the large 10 Toman pieces.

**PAHLAVI** **KM# 1108** **Weight:** 2.8744 g. **Composition:** Gold .0832 oz. AGW **Subject:** Reza's First New Year Celebration **Obverse:** Reza type legend **Reverse:** Lion and sun

| Date | Mintage | F | VF | XF | Unc |
|---|---|---|---|---|---|
| SH1305 | — | 125 | 200 | 300 | 450 |

**PAHLAVI** **KM# 1111** **Weight:** 1.9180 g. **Composition:** Gold .0555 oz. AGW

| Date | Mintage | F | VF | XF | Unc |
|---|---|---|---|---|---|
| SH1305 | 5,000 | 70.00 | 100 | 175 | 275 |

**PAHLAVI** **KM# 1114** **Weight:** 2.8744 g. **Composition:** Gold .0832 oz. AGW

| Date | Mintage | F | VF | XF | Unc |
|---|---|---|---|---|---|
| SH1306 | 21,000 | 45.00 | 65.00 | 85.00 | 125 |
| SH1307 | 5,000 | 60.00 | 85.00 | 120 | 180 |
| SH1308 | 989 | 80.00 | 100 | 160 | 275 |

**2 PAHLAVI** **KM# 1112** **Weight:** 3.8360 g. **Composition:** Gold .1110 oz. AGW

| Date | Mintage | F | VF | XF | Unc |
|---|---|---|---|---|---|
| SH1305 | 1,134 | 325 | 500 | 750 | 1,000 |

**2 PAHLAVI** **KM# 1115** **Weight:** 3.8360 g. **Composition:** Gold .1110 oz. AGW

| Date | Mintage | F | VF | XF | Unc |
|---|---|---|---|---|---|
| SH1306 | 2,494 | 60.00 | 90.00 | 150 | 250 |
| SH1307 | 7,000 | 60.00 | 90.00 | 150 | 230 |
| SH1308 | 789 | 75.00 | 115 | 200 | 285 |

**5 PAHLAVI** **KM# 1113** **Weight:** 9.5900 g. **Composition:** Gold .2775 oz. AGW

| Date | Mintage | F | VF | XF | Unc |
|---|---|---|---|---|---|
| SH1305 | 271 | 500 | 700 | 950 | 2,000 |

**5 PAHLAVI** **KM# 1116** **Weight:** 9.5900 g. **Composition:** Gold .2775 oz. AGW

| Date | Mintage | F | VF | XF | Unc |
|---|---|---|---|---|---|
| SH1306 | 909 | 400 | 550 | 750 | 1,000 |
| SH1307 | 785 | 375 | 500 | 700 | 900 |
| SH1308 | 121 | 450 | 600 | 900 | 1,400 |

## REFORM COINAGE

5 Dinars = 1 Shahi; 100 Dinars = 1 Rial; 100 Rials = 1 Pahlavi

The pahlavi was made equal in weight to the British sovereign. It was originally valued at 100 Rials, but has always fluctuated with market prices of gold and silver.

**1/2 RIAL** **KM# 1128** **Weight:** 2.5000 g. **Composition:** 0.8280 Silver .0665 oz. ASW **Rev. Legend:** "Reza Shah" **Note:** All 1/2 Rials dated SH1311-1315 are recut dies, usually from SH1310.

| Date | Mintage | F | VF | XF | Unc |
|---|---|---|---|---|---|
| SH1310 | 2,000,000 | 1.00 | 3.00 | 6.00 | 15.00 |
| SH1311 | — | 30.00 | 40.00 | 50.00 | 90.00 |
| SH1312 | — | 1.00 | 3.00 | 5.00 | 14.00 |
| SH1313 | 1,945,000 | 1.50 | 3.00 | 6.00 | 15.00 |
| SH1314 | 100,000 | 3.00 | 9.00 | 20.00 | 40.00 |
| SH1315 | 800,000 | 2.00 | 4.00 | 9.00 | 20.00 |

**2 RIALS** **KM# 1130** **Weight:** 10.0000 g. **Composition:** 0.8280 Silver .2662 oz. ASW **Obv. Legend:** "Reza Shah" **Note:** All coins dated SH1311-13 cut or punched over SH1310.

| Date | Mintage | F | VF | XF | Unc |
|---|---|---|---|---|---|
| SH1310 | 6,145,000 | 2.00 | 5.00 | 10.00 | 25.00 |
| SH1311 | 8,838,000 | 2.00 | 5.00 | 10.00 | 22.00 |
| SH1312 | 19,175,000 | 2.00 | 5.00 | 10.00 | 20.00 |
| SH1313 | 4,015,000 | 2.00 | 7.00 | 15.00 | 32.00 |

**2 RIALS** **KM# 1158** **Composition:** Copper-Nickel **Obv. Legend:** "Muhammad Reza Shah Pahlavi"

| Date | Mintage | F | VF | XF | Unc |
|---|---|---|---|---|---|
| SH1331 | 5,335,000 | 1.25 | 3.00 | 7.00 | 20.00 |
| SH1332 | 6,870,000 | 1.00 | 2.00 | 4.00 | 8.00 |
| SH1333 | 13,668,000 | 0.15 | 0.75 | 2.00 | 7.00 |
| SH1334 | 7,185,000 | 0.15 | 0.75 | 2.00 | 7.00 |
| SH1335 | 2,400,000 | 0.15 | 0.75 | 3.00 | 12.50 |
| SH1336 | 325,000 | 15.00 | 25.00 | 40.00 | 75.00 |

**5 RIALS** **KM# 1131** **Weight:** 25.0000 g. **Composition:** 0.8280 Silver .6655 oz. ASW **Obv. Legend:** "Reza Shah" **Note:** Most coins dated SH1311-13 are cut or punched over SH1310.

| Date | Mintage | F | VF | XF | Unc |
|---|---|---|---|---|---|
| SH1310 | 5,471,000 | 7.50 | 8.00 | 12.00 | 20.00 |
| SH1311 | 4,527,000 | 7.50 | 8.00 | 12.00 | 20.00 |
| SH1312/0 | 5,502,000 | 7.50 | 10.00 | 15.00 | 25.00 |
| SH1312 | Inc. above | 7.50 | 8.00 | 12.00 | 20.00 |
| SH1313 | 1,208,000 | 7.50 | 10.00 | 15.00 | 25.00 |

**1/2 PAHLAVI** **KM# 1132** **Weight:** 4.0680 g. **Composition:** 0.9000 Gold .1177 oz. AGW **Obverse:** Bust of Reza Shah

| Date | Mintage | F | VF | XF | Unc |
|---|---|---|---|---|---|
| SH1310 | 696 | 75.00 | 150 | 275 | 375 |
| SH1311 | 286 | 75.00 | 175 | 300 | 400 |
| SH1312 | 892 | 75.00 | 150 | 250 | 350 |
| SH1313 | 531 | 75.00 | 175 | 300 | 400 |
| SH1314 | — | 75.00 | 175 | 300 | 400 |
| SH1315 | 1,042 | 75.00 | 175 | 275 | 375 |

**PAHLAVI** **KM# 1133** **Weight:** 8.1360 g. **Composition:** 0.9000 Gold .2354 oz. AGW **Obverse:** Bust of Reza Shah

| Date | Mintage | F | VF | XF | Unc |
|---|---|---|---|---|---|
| SH1310 | 304 | 300 | 500 | 850 | 1,200 |

# Muhammad Reza Pahlavi Shah

### AH1360-1397/1941-79AD

## REFORM COINAGE

5 Dinars = 1 Shahi; 100 Dinars = 1 Rial; 100 Rials = 1 Pahlavi

The pahlavi was made equal in weight to the British sovereign. It was originally valued at 100 Rials, but has always fluctuated with market prices of gold and silver.

**RIAL** **KM# 1143** **Weight:** 1.6000 g. **Composition:** 0.6000 Silver .0308 oz. ASW **Obv. Legend:** "Muhammad Reza Shah Pahlavi"

| Date | Mintage | F | VF | XF | Unc |
|---|---|---|---|---|---|
| SH1322 | — | 0.50 | 1.00 | 2.00 | 5.00 |
| SH1323/3 | — | — | — | — | — |
| SH1323 | — | 0.50 | 1.00 | 2.00 | 5.00 |
| SH1324/3 | — | — | — | — | — |
| SH1324 | — | 0.50 | 1.00 | 2.00 | 5.00 |
| SH1424 Error for 1324 | — | — | — | — | — |
| SH1325 | — | 0.75 | 1.50 | 2.00 | 5.00 |
| SH1326 | 567,000 | 35.00 | 40.00 | 50.00 | 100 |
| SH1327 | 5,795,000 | 1.50 | 2.50 | 4.00 | 8.00 |
| SH1328 | 1,565,000 | 1.50 | 2.50 | 4.00 | 8.00 |
| SH1329 | 144,000 | 35.00 | 40.00 | 50.00 | 100 |
| SH1330 | — | 2.00 | 3.00 | 5.00 | 15.00 |

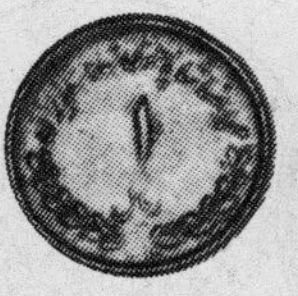

**RIAL** **KM# 1157** **Composition:** Copper-Nickel **Obv. Legend:** "Muhammad Reza Shah Pahlavi"

| Date | Mintage | F | VF | XF | Unc |
|---|---|---|---|---|---|
| SH(13)31 | 4,735,000 | 1.00 | 2.00 | 5.00 | 15.00 |
| SH(13)32 | 3 | 4.00 | 8.00 | 15.00 | 30.00 |
| **Note:** Much rarer than mintage would indicate | | | | | |
| SH(13)33 | 16,405,000 | 0.60 | 1.00 | 2.00 | 5.00 |
| SH(13)34 | 8,980,000 | 0.60 | 1.00 | 2.00 | 5.00 |
| SH(13)35 | 8,910,000 | 0.50 | 1.00 | 1.00 | 5.00 |
| SH(13)36 | 4,450,000 | 1.00 | 2.00 | 8.00 | 20.00 |

**RIAL** **KM# 1171** **Weight:** 2.0000 g. **Composition:** Copper-Nickel **Obv. Legend:** "Muhammad Reza Pahlavi"

| Date | Mintage | F | VF | XF | Unc |
|---|---|---|---|---|---|
| SH1337 | 8,005,000 | 0.50 | 1.00 | 2.00 | 5.00 |

**RIAL** **KM# 1171a** **Weight:** 1.7500 g. **Composition:** Copper-Nickel **Note:** Date varieties exist.

| Date | Mintage | F | VF | XF | Unc |
|---|---|---|---|---|---|
| SH1338 | 14,940,000 | 0.10 | 0.20 | 0.40 | 3.00 |
| SH1339 | 8,400,000 | 0.25 | 0.50 | 1.00 | 4.00 |
| SH1340 | 8,490,000 | 0.25 | 0.50 | 1.00 | 4.00 |
| SH1341 | 8,680,000 | 0.25 | 0.50 | 1.00 | 4.00 |
| SH1342 | 13,332,000 | 0.10 | 0.20 | 0.40 | 3.00 |
| SH1343 | 14,746,000 | 0.10 | 0.15 | 0.25 | 2.00 |
| SH1344 | 12,050,000 | 0.10 | 0.20 | 0.50 | 3.50 |
| SH1345 | 13,786,000 | 0.10 | 0.15 | 0.20 | 2.00 |
| SH1346 | 155,321,000 | 0.10 | 0.15 | 0.20 | 2.00 |
| SH1347 | 20,664,000 | 0.10 | 0.15 | 0.25 | 3.00 |
| SH1348 | 22,960,000 | 0.10 | 0.15 | 0.20 | 2.00 |
| SH1349 | 19,918,000 | 0.10 | 0.15 | 0.20 | 2.00 |
| SH1350 | 24,248,000 | 0.10 | 0.20 | 0.65 | 2.00 |
| SH1351/0 | 21,825,000 | 0.10 | 0.25 | 0.40 | 3.00 |
| SH1351 | Inc. above | 0.10 | 0.15 | 0.20 | 2.00 |
| SH1352 | 31,449,000 | 0.10 | 0.15 | 0.20 | 2.00 |
| SH1353 Large date | 33,700,000 | 0.10 | 0.20 | 0.25 | 3.00 |
| SH1353 Small date | Inc. above | 0.10 | 0.15 | 0.20 | 2.00 |
| SH1354 | — | 0.10 | 0.15 | 0.20 | 2.00 |
| MS2536 | — | 0.10 | 0.15 | 0.25 | 3.00 |

**RIAL** **KM# 1183** **Composition:** Copper-Nickel **Series:** F.A.O **Obv. Legend:** "Muhammad Reza Shah Pahlavi"

| Date | Mintage | F | VF | XF | Unc |
|---|---|---|---|---|---|
| SH1350 | 2,770,000 | 0.10 | 0.15 | 0.25 | 1.00 |
| SH1351 | 8,605,000 | 0.10 | 0.15 | 0.25 | 1.00 |
| SH1353 | 2,000,000 | 0.50 | 0.80 | 1.25 | 2.00 |
| SH1354 | 1,000,000 | 0.50 | 0.80 | 1.25 | 2.00 |

**RIAL** **KM# 1205** **Composition:** Copper-Nickel **Subject:** 50th Anniversary of Pahlavi Rule

| Date | Mintage | F | VF | XF | Unc |
|---|---|---|---|---|---|
| MS2535 | 61,945,000 | 0.50 | 1.00 | 1.50 | 2.50 |

**RIAL** **KM# 1172** **Composition:** Copper-Nickel **Obverse:** "Aryamehr" added to legend **Obv. Legend:** "Muhammad Reza Shah Pahlavi"

| Date | Mintage | F | VF | XF | Unc |
|---|---|---|---|---|---|
| MS2536 | 71,150,000 | 0.10 | 0.15 | 0.25 | 2.00 |
| MS2537 | — | 0.10 | 0.15 | 0.25 | 2.00 |
| MS2537/6537 Error 2/6 | — | — | — | — | 6.00 |
| SH1357/6 | — | 0.25 | 0.50 | 0.75 | 5.00 |
| SH1357 | — | 0.25 | 0.50 | 0.75 | 3.00 |

**2 RIALS** **KM# 1144** **Weight:** 3.2000 g. **Composition:** 0.6000 Silver .0617 oz. ASW **Obv. Legend:** "Muhammad Reza Shah Pahlavi"

| Date | Mintage | F | VF | XF | Unc |
|---|---|---|---|---|---|
| SH1322 | — | 0.50 | 1.00 | 3.50 | 7.00 |
| SH1323/2 | — | 10.00 | 20.00 | 30.00 | 50.00 |
| SH1323 | — | 0.50 | 1.00 | 3.00 | 6.00 |
| SH1324 | — | 0.50 | 1.00 | 3.00 | 6.00 |
| SH1325 | — | 1.25 | 3.00 | 5.00 | 11.00 |
| SH1326 | 187,000 | 50.00 | 60.00 | 75.00 | 125 |
| SH1327 | 3,140,000 | 1.50 | 3.00 | 5.00 | 12.50 |
| SH1328 | 1,198,000 | 2.50 | 4.50 | 7.50 | 16.00 |
| SH1329 | — | 65.00 | 80.00 | 100 | 150 |
| SH1330 | — | 5.00 | 8.00 | 12.50 | 30.00 |

**2 RIALS** **KM# 1173** **Composition:** Copper-Nickel **Obv. Legend:** "Muhammad Reza Pahlavi"

| Date | Mintage | F | VF | XF | Unc |
|---|---|---|---|---|---|
| SH1338 | 17,610,000 | 0.10 | 0.25 | 0.75 | 4.00 |
| SH1339 | 8,575,000 | 0.10 | 0.25 | 0.50 | 4.00 |
| SH1340 | 5,668,000 | 0.10 | 0.25 | 0.50 | 4.00 |
| SH1341 | 5,820,000 | 0.10 | 0.25 | 0.75 | 4.00 |
| SH1342 | 8,570,000 | 0.10 | 0.25 | 0.50 | 4.00 |
| SH1343 | 11,250,000 | 0.10 | 0.25 | 0.50 | 3.00 |
| SH1344 | 5,155,000 | 0.10 | 0.25 | 0.50 | 4.00 |
| SH1345 | 2,267,000 | 0.15 | 0.30 | 1.00 | 5.00 |
| SH1346 | 92,792,000 | — | 0.10 | 0.20 | 4.00 |
| SH1347 | 10,300,000 | — | 0.10 | 1.00 | 6.00 |
| SH1348 | 9,319,000 | 0.20 | 0.45 | 1.10 | 4.00 |
| SH1349 | 9,895,000 | 0.20 | 0.40 | 1.00 | 4.00 |
| SH1350 | 9,545,000 | 0.15 | 0.35 | 1.00 | 4.00 |
| SH1351 | 13,305,000 | 0.15 | 0.35 | 1.00 | 3.00 |
| SH1352 | 15,910,000 | — | 0.10 | 0.20 | 3.00 |
| SH1353 | 28,477,000 | — | 0.10 | 0.20 | 3.00 |
| SH1354/3 | — | 0.20 | 0.40 | 1.00 | 5.00 |
| SH1354 | 41,700,000 | — | 0.10 | 0.20 | 3.00 |
| MS2536 | 54,725,000 | — | 0.10 | 0.20 | 3.00 |

**2 RIALS** **KM# 1206** **Composition:** Copper-Nickel **Subject:** 50th Anniversary of Pahlavi

| Date | Mintage | F | VF | XF | Unc |
|---|---|---|---|---|---|
| MS2535 | 59,568,000 | 0.25 | 0.50 | 1.00 | 2.50 |

**2 RIALS** **KM# 1174** **Composition:** Copper-Nickel **Obverse:** "Aryamehr" added to legend **Obv. Legend:** "Muhammad Reza Pahlavi"

| Date | Mintage | F | VF | XF | Unc |
|---|---|---|---|---|---|
| MS2536 | Inc. above | 0.25 | 0.50 | 1.00 | 4.00 |
| MS2537 | — | 0.25 | 0.50 | 1.00 | 4.00 |
| SH1357 | — | 0.25 | 0.50 | 1.00 | 4.00 |

**5 RIALS** **KM# 1145** **Weight:** 8.0000 g. **Composition:** 0.6000 Silver .1543 oz. ASW **Obv. Legend:** "Muhammad Reza Shah Pahlavi"

| Date | Mintage | F | VF | XF | Unc |
|---|---|---|---|---|---|
| SH1322 | — | 1.00 | 2.00 | 3.50 | 6.00 |
| SH1323 | — | 1.00 | 2.50 | 3.50 | 6.00 |
| SH1324 | — | 1.00 | 2.00 | 4.50 | 10.00 |
| SH1325 | — | 1.00 | 2.00 | 3.50 | 6.00 |
| SH1326 | 61,000 | 60.00 | 70.00 | 85.00 | 140 |
| SH1327 | 836,000 | 2.00 | 5.00 | 7.50 | 20.00 |
| SH1328 | 282,000 | 2.50 | 10.00 | 20.00 | 40.00 |
| SH1329 | — | 75.00 | 85.00 | 100 | 175 |

**5 RIALS** **KM# 1159** **Composition:** Copper-Nickel **Obv. Legend:** "Muhammad Reza Shah Pahlavi"

| Date | Mintage | F | VF | XF | Unc |
|---|---|---|---|---|---|
| SH1331 | 3,660,000 | 0.50 | 2.00 | 5.00 | 20.00 |
| SH1332 | 16,350,000 | 0.25 | 1.00 | 3.00 | 10.00 |
| SH1333 | 6,582,000 | 0.25 | 1.00 | 3.00 | 10.00 |
| SH1334 | 300,000 | 10.00 | 15.00 | 25.00 | 50.00 |
| SH1336 | 1,410,000 | 0.50 | 2.00 | 5.00 | 20.00 |

**5 RIALS** **KM# 1175** **Weight:** 7.0000 g. **Composition:** Copper-Nickel **Obv. Legend:** "Muhammad Reza Shah Pahlavi"

| Date | Mintage | F | VF | XF | Unc |
|---|---|---|---|---|---|
| SH1337 | 3,660,000 | 1.00 | 2.50 | 7.50 | 22.50 |
| SH1338 | 10,467,000 | 0.50 | 2.50 | 8.00 | 20.00 |

**5 RIALS** **KM# 1175a** **Weight:** 5.0000 g. **Composition:** Copper-Nickel

| Date | Mintage | F | VF | XF | Unc |
|---|---|---|---|---|---|
| SH1338 | Inc. above | 0.25 | 0.40 | 1.50 | 5.00 |
| SH1339 | 3,980,000 | 0.25 | 0.40 | 1.50 | 5.00 |
| SH1340 | 3,814,000 | 0.25 | 0.40 | 1.50 | 5.00 |
| SH1341 | 2,332,000 | 0.25 | 0.40 | 1.50 | 5.00 |
| SH1342 | 7,838,000 | 0.25 | 0.40 | 1.00 | 4.00 |
| SH1343 | 9,484,000 | 0.25 | 0.40 | 1.00 | 4.00 |
| SH1344 | 3,468,000 | 0.25 | 0.40 | 1.00 | 4.00 |
| SH1345 | 6,092,000 | 0.25 | 0.40 | 1.00 | 4.00 |
| SH1346/36 | 74,781,000 | 0.25 | 0.40 | 1.50 | 5.00 |
| SH1346 | Inc. above | 0.25 | 0.40 | 1.00 | 4.00 |

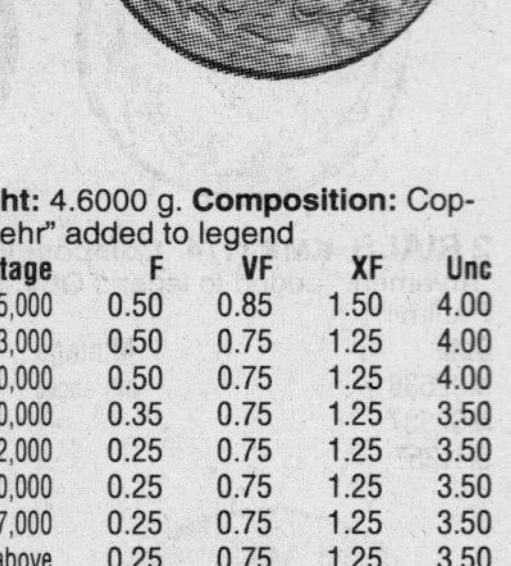

**5 RIALS** KM# 1176 **Weight:** 4.6000 g. **Composition:** Copper-Nickel **Obverse:** "Aryamehr" added to legend

| Date | Mintage | F | VF | XF | Unc |
|---|---|---|---|---|---|
| SH1347 | 7,745,000 | 0.50 | 0.85 | 1.50 | 4.00 |
| SH1348 | 9,193,000 | 0.50 | 0.75 | 1.25 | 4.00 |
| SH1349 | 7,300,000 | 0.50 | 0.75 | 1.25 | 4.00 |
| SH1350 | 10,160,000 | 0.35 | 0.75 | 1.25 | 3.50 |
| SH1351 | 20,582,000 | 0.25 | 0.75 | 1.25 | 3.50 |
| SH1352 | 23,590,000 | 0.25 | 0.75 | 1.25 | 3.50 |
| SH1353 | 28,367,000 | 0.25 | 0.75 | 1.25 | 3.50 |
| SH1353 Large date | Inc. above | 0.25 | 0.75 | 1.25 | 3.50 |
| SH1354 | 27,294,000 | 0.25 | 0.75 | 1.25 | 3.50 |
| MS2536 | 47,906,000 | 0.20 | 0.50 | 1.25 | 3.50 |
| MS2537 | — | 0.35 | 0.65 | 1.25 | 3.50 |
| SH1357 | — | 0.50 | 0.75 | 1.25 | 3.50 |

**5 RIALS** KM# 1207 **Composition:** Copper-Nickel **Subject:** 50th Anniversary of Pahlavi Rule

| Date | Mintage | F | VF | XF | Unc |
|---|---|---|---|---|---|
| MS2535 | 37,144,000 | 0.25 | 0.50 | 1.25 | 3.50 |

**10 RIALS** KM# 1146 **Weight:** 16.0000 g. **Composition:** 0.6000 Silver .3086 oz. ASW **Obv. Legend:** "Muhammad Reza Shah Pahlavi" **Note:** Counterfeits are known dated SH1322.

| Date | Mintage | F | VF | XF | Unc |
|---|---|---|---|---|---|
| SH1323/2 | — | 2.00 | 3.50 | 7.00 | 20.00 |
| SH1323 | — | 2.00 | 3.00 | 5.00 | 12.00 |
| SH1324 | — | 2.00 | 3.00 | 5.00 | 15.00 |
| SH1325 | — | 2.00 | 3.00 | 6.00 | 17.50 |
| SH1326 | — | 100 | 125 | 150 | 225 |

**10 RIALS** KM# 1177 **Weight:** 12.0000 g. **Composition:** Copper-Nickel **Obv. Legend:** "Muhammad Reza Shah Pahlavi"

| Date | Mintage | F | VF | XF | Unc |
|---|---|---|---|---|---|
| SH1333 | | | | | |
| SH1335 | 6,225,000 | 0.50 | 2.00 | 4.00 | 9.00 |
| SH1336 | 4,415,000 | 1.00 | 3.00 | 7.50 | 15.00 |
| SH1337 | 715,000 | 3.00 | 6.00 | 9.00 | 20.00 |
| SH1338 | 1,210,000 | 0.50 | 2.00 | 6.00 | 14.00 |
| SH1339 | 2,775,000 | 0.50 | 2.00 | 4.00 | 9.00 |
| SH1340 | 3,660,000 | 0.50 | 2.00 | 4.00 | 9.00 |
| SH1341 | 744,000 | 20.00 | 35.00 | 50.00 | 75.00 |
| SH1343 | 6,874,000 | 0.50 | 2.00 | 4.00 | 9.00 |

**10 RIALS** KM# 1177a **Weight:** 9.0000 g. **Composition:** Copper-Nickel **Note:** Thin flan.

| Date | Mintage | F | VF | XF | Unc |
|---|---|---|---|---|---|
| SH1341 | — | 0.35 | 1.00 | 2.50 | 5.00 |
| **Note:** Mintage included in KM#1177 | | | | | |
| SH1342 | 3,763,000 | 0.35 | 1.00 | 2.00 | 4.00 |
| SH1343 | — | 0.35 | 0.75 | 1.50 | 2.50 |
| **Note:** Mintage included in KM#1177 | | | | | |
| SH1344 | 1,627,000 | 0.35 | 0.75 | 1.50 | 2.50 |

**10 RIALS** KM# 1178 **Composition:** Copper-Nickel **Obv. Legend:** "Muhammad Reza Shah Pahlavi" **Reverse:** Value in words

| Date | Mintage | F | VF | XF | Unc |
|---|---|---|---|---|---|
| SH1345 | 1,699,000 | 0.50 | 0.60 | 2.00 | 5.00 |
| SH1346 | 38,897,000 | 0.40 | 0.50 | 1.00 | 4.00 |
| SH1347 | 8,220,000 | 0.40 | 0.65 | 1.50 | 8.00 |
| SH1348 | 7,156,000 | 0.40 | 0.50 | 1.00 | 4.00 |
| SH1349 | 7,397,000 | 0.40 | 0.50 | 1.00 | 4.00 |
| SH1350 | 8,972,000 | 0.40 | 0.50 | 1.00 | 4.00 |
| SH1351 | 9,912,000 | 0.40 | 0.50 | 1.00 | 4.00 |
| SH1352 | 28,776,000 | 0.50 | 2.00 | 4.50 | 7.00 |

**10 RIALS** KM# 1182 **Composition:** Copper-Nickel **Series:** F.A.O

| Date | Mintage | F | VF | XF | Unc |
|---|---|---|---|---|---|
| SH1348 | 150,000 | 0.25 | 0.50 | 1.00 | 3.50 |

**10 RIALS** KM# 1179 **Composition:** Copper-Nickel **Reverse:** Value in numerals

| Date | Mintage | F | VF | XF | Unc |
|---|---|---|---|---|---|
| SH1352 | Inc. above | 0.30 | 0.60 | 1.00 | 4.00 |
| SH1353 | 22,234,000 | 0.30 | 0.60 | 1.00 | 3.00 |
| SH1354 | 23,482,000 | 0.30 | 0.60 | 1.00 | 4.00 |
| MS2536 | 24,324,000 | 0.30 | 0.60 | 1.00 | 3.00 |
| MS2537 | — | 0.30 | 0.60 | 1.00 | 4.00 |
| SH1357 | — | 0.30 | 1.00 | 1.50 | 4.00 |

**10 RIALS** KM# 1208 **Composition:** Copper-Nickel **Subject:** 50th Anniversary of Pahlavi Rule

| Date | Mintage | F | VF | XF | Unc |
|---|---|---|---|---|---|
| MS2535 | 29,859,000 | 0.25 | 0.50 | 0.75 | 3.00 |

**20 RIALS** KM# 1180 **Composition:** Copper-Nickel **Obv. Legend:** "Muhammad Reza Shah Pahlavi" **Reverse:** Value in words

| Date | Mintage | F | VF | XF | Unc |
|---|---|---|---|---|---|
| SH1350 | 2,349,000 | 0.25 | 1.00 | 3.00 | 6.00 |
| SH1351 | 11,416,000 | 0.25 | 0.85 | 1.00 | 3.00 |
| SH1352 | 7,172,000 | 0.25 | 0.85 | 1.25 | 5.00 |

**20 RIALS** KM# 1181 **Composition:** Copper-Nickel **Reverse:** Value in numerals **Note:** Varieties exist in date size.

| Date | Mintage | F | VF | XF | Unc |
|---|---|---|---|---|---|
| SH1352 | — | 0.25 | 0.75 | 1.00 | 3.50 |
| **Note:** Mintage included in KM#1180 | | | | | |
| SH1353 | 12,601,000 | 0.25 | 0.75 | 1.00 | 3.75 |
| SH1354 | 16,246,000 | 0.25 | 0.75 | 1.00 | 4.00 |
| MS2536 | — | 0.40 | 0.75 | 1.00 | 4.00 |
| MS2537 | — | 0.50 | 0.75 | 1.00 | 4.00 |
| SH1357 | — | 0.50 | 1.00 | 1.50 | 5.00 |

**20 RIALS** KM# 1196 **Composition:** Copper-Nickel **Subject:** 7th Asian Games

| Date | Mintage | F | VF | XF | Unc |
|---|---|---|---|---|---|
| SH1353 | Inc. above | 0.75 | 1.50 | 2.50 | 4.50 |

**20 RIALS** KM# 1209 **Composition:** Copper-Nickel **Subject:** 50th Anniversary of Pahlavi Rule

| Date | Mintage | F | VF | XF | Unc |
|---|---|---|---|---|---|
| MS2535 | — | 0.50 | 1.00 | 2.00 | 4.50 |

**20 RIALS** KM# 1211 **Composition:** Copper-Nickel **Series:** F.A.O

| Date | Mintage | F | VF | XF | Unc |
|---|---|---|---|---|---|
| MS2535 | 10,000,000 | 0.50 | 1.00 | 2.00 | 4.50 |
| MS2536 | 23,370,000 | 0.50 | 1.00 | 3.00 | 5.50 |

**20 RIALS** KM# 1214 **Composition:** Copper-Nickel **Subject:** 50th Anniversary of Bank Melli

| Date | Mintage | F | VF | XF | Unc |
|---|---|---|---|---|---|
| SH1357 | — | 4.00 | 5.00 | 7.00 | 13.50 |

**20 RIALS** **KM# 1215** **Composition:** Copper-Nickel **Series:** F.A.O

| Date | Mintage | F | VF | XF | Unc |
|---|---|---|---|---|---|
| SH1357 | 5,000,000 | 0.50 | 0.75 | 2.00 | 6.00 |

**25 RIALS** **KM# 1184** **Weight:** 7.5000 g. **Composition:** 0.9990 Silver .2409 oz. ASW **Subject:** 2500th Anniversary of Persian Empire **Note:** Column head from Artaxerxes' Palace in Susa

| Date | Mintage | F | VF | XF | Unc |
|---|---|---|---|---|---|
| SH1350(1971) Proof | 18,000 | Value: 10.00 | | | |

**1/4 PAHLAVI** **KM# 1160** **Weight:** 2.0340 g. **Composition:** 0.9000 Gold .0589 oz. AGW **Obverse:** Bust of Muhammad Reza Pahlavi

| Date | Mintage | F | VF | XF | Unc |
|---|---|---|---|---|---|
| SH1332 | 41,000 | BV | 35.00 | 45.00 | 60.00 |
| SH1333 | 7,000 | 35.00 | 45.00 | 100 | 150 |
| SH1334 | — | BV | 35.00 | 60.00 | 100 |
| SH1335 | 41,000 | BV | 35.00 | 45.00 | 60.00 |
| SH1336 Rare | — | — | — | — | — |

**1/4 PAHLAVI** **KM# 1160a** **Weight:** 2.0340 g. **Composition:** 0.9000 Gold .0589 oz. AGW **Note:** Thinner and broader.

| Date | Mintage | F | VF | XF | Unc |
|---|---|---|---|---|---|
| SH1336 | 7,000 | 150 | 350 | 750 | 1,250 |
| SH1337 | 33,000 | — | BV | 22.00 | 30.00 |
| SH1338 | 136,000 | — | BV | 22.00 | 30.00 |
| SH1339 | 156,000 | — | BV | 22.00 | 30.00 |
| SH1340 | 60,000 | — | BV | 22.00 | 30.00 |
| SH1342 | 80,000 | — | BV | 22.00 | 30.00 |
| SH1343 | 40,000 | — | BV | 22.00 | 30.00 |
| **Note:** Reported, not confirmed | | | | | |
| SH1344 | 30,000 | — | 30.00 | 35.00 | 55.00 |
| SH1345 | 40,000 | — | BV | 22.00 | 30.00 |
| SH1346 | 30,000 | — | BV | 22.00 | 30.00 |
| SH1347 | 60,000 | — | BV | 22.00 | 30.00 |
| SH1348 | 60,000 | — | BV | 22.00 | 30.00 |
| SH1349 | 80,000 | — | BV | 22.00 | 30.00 |
| SH1350 | 80,000 | — | BV | 22.00 | 30.00 |
| SH1351 | 103,000 | — | BV | 22.00 | 30.00 |
| SH1353 | — | — | BV | 22.00 | 30.00 |

**1/4 PAHLAVI** **KM# 1198** **Weight:** 2.0340 g. **Composition:** 0.9000 Gold .0589 oz. AGW **Obverse:** "Aryamehr" added to legend

| Date | Mintage | F | VF | XF | Unc |
|---|---|---|---|---|---|
| SH1354 | 106,000 | — | BV | 22.00 | 30.00 |
| SH1355 | 186,000 | — | BV | 22.00 | 30.00 |
| MS2536 | — | — | BV | 22.00 | 30.00 |
| MS2537 | — | — | BV | 22.00 | 30.00 |
| SH1358 | — | BV | 35.00 | 75.00 | 115 |

**50 RIALS** **KM# 1185** **Weight:** 15.0000 g. **Composition:** 0.9990 Silver .4818 oz. ASW **Subject:** 2500th Anniversary of Persian Empire **Note:** Walking griffin with ram antlers

| Date | Mintage | F | VF | XF | Unc |
|---|---|---|---|---|---|
| SH1350(1971) Proof | 18,000 | Value: 15.00 | | | |

**1/2 PAHLAVI** **KM# 1147** **Weight:** 4.0680 g. **Composition:** 0.9000 Gold .1177 oz. AGW **Obv. Legend:** "Muhammad Reza Shah"

| Date | Mintage | F | VF | XF | Unc |
|---|---|---|---|---|---|
| SH1320 | — | 150 | 350 | 750 | 1,250 |
| SH1321 | — | BV | 100 | 200 | 300 |
| SH1322 | — | — | BV | 40.00 | 50.00 |
| SH1323 | 76,000 | — | BV | 40.00 | 50.00 |
| SH1324 | — | — | — | — | — |
| **Note:** Reported, not confirmed | | | | | |

**1/2 PAHLAVI** **KM# 1149** **Weight:** 4.0680 g. **Composition:** 0.9000 Gold .1177 oz. AGW **Obverse:** High relief head of Muhammad Reza Pahlavi

| Date | Mintage | F | VF | XF | Unc |
|---|---|---|---|---|---|
| SH1324 | — | BV | 40.00 | 50.00 | 60.00 |
| SH1325 | — | BV | 40.00 | 50.00 | 60.00 |
| SH1326 | 36,000 | BV | 50.00 | 65.00 | 110 |
| SH1327 | 36,000 | BV | 50.00 | 65.00 | 110 |
| SH1328 | — | BV | 60.00 | 75.00 | 130 |
| SH1329 | 75 | — | 250 | 400 | 750 |
| SH1330 | 98,000 | — | — | — | 1,350 |

**1/2 PAHLAVI** **KM# 1161** **Weight:** 4.0680 g. **Composition:** 0.9000 Gold .1177 oz. AGW **Obverse:** Low relief head

| Date | Mintage | F | VF | XF | Unc |
|---|---|---|---|---|---|
| SH1330 | — | BV | 40.00 | 50.00 | 55.00 |
| **Note:** Mintage included in KM#1149 | | | | | |
| SH1332 | — | — | 300 | 450 | 750 |
| SH1333 | — | BV | 55.00 | 70.00 | 100 |
| SH1334 | — | — | 55.00 | 70.00 | 100 |
| SH1335 | — | — | BV | 45.00 | 55.00 |
| SH1336 | 132,000 | — | BV | 45.00 | 55.00 |
| SH1337 | 102,000 | — | BV | 40.00 | 50.00 |
| SH1338 | 140,000 | — | BV | 40.00 | 50.00 |
| SH1339 | 142,000 | — | BV | 40.00 | 50.00 |
| SH1340 | 439,000 | — | BV | 40.00 | 50.00 |
| SH1342 | 40,000 | — | BV | 40.00 | 50.00 |
| SH1343 | — | — | — | — | — |
| **Note:** Reported, not confirmed | | | | | |
| SH1344 | 30,000 | BV | 65.00 | 75.00 | 110 |
| SH1345 | 40,000 | — | BV | 45.00 | 50.00 |
| SH1346 | 40,000 | — | BV | 45.00 | 50.00 |
| SH1347 | 50,000 | — | BV | 45.00 | 50.00 |
| SH1348 | 40,000 | — | BV | 45.00 | 50.00 |
| SH1349 | 80,000 | — | BV | 45.00 | 50.00 |
| SH1350 | 80,000 | — | BV | 45.00 | 50.00 |
| SH1351 | 103,000 | — | BV | 45.00 | 50.00 |
| SH1352 | 67,000 | — | BV | 45.00 | 50.00 |
| SH1353 | — | — | BV | 45.00 | 50.00 |

**1/2 PAHLAVI** **KM# 1199** **Weight:** 4.0680 g. **Composition:** 0.9000 Gold .1177 oz. AGW **Obverse:** "Aryamehr" added to legend

| Date | Mintage | F | VF | XF | Unc |
|---|---|---|---|---|---|
| SH1354 | 37,000 | — | BV | 45.00 | 50.00 |
| SH1355 | 153,000 | — | BV | 45.00 | 50.00 |
| MS2536 | — | — | BV | 45.00 | 50.00 |
| MS2537 | — | — | BV | 45.00 | 50.00 |
| SH1358 | — | — | — | 275 | 375 |

**75 RIALS** **KM# 1186** **Weight:** 22.5000 g. **Composition:** 0.9990 Silver .7227 oz. ASW **Subject:** 2500th Anniversary of Persian Empire **Obverse:** Similar to 200 Rials, KM#1188 **Note:** Stone of Cyrus II

| Date | Mintage | F | VF | XF | Unc |
|---|---|---|---|---|---|
| SH1350(1971) Proof | 18,000 | Value: 16.50 | | | |

**100 RIALS** **KM# 1187.1** **Weight:** 30.0000 g. **Composition:** 0.9990 Silver .9636 oz. ASW **Subject:** 2500th Anniversary of Persian Empire **Obverse:** Similar to 200 Rials, KM#1188 **Reverse:** Polished field below ruins **Note:** Palace of Darius I and pillars of reception hall in Persepolis

| Date | Mintage | F | VF | XF | Unc |
|---|---|---|---|---|---|
| SH1350(1971) Proof | 18,000 | Value: 25.00 | | | |

**100 RIALS** **KM# 1187.2** **Weight:** 30.0000 g. **Composition:** 0.9990 Silver .9636 oz. ASW **Reverse:** Frosted field below ruins

| Date | Mintage | F | VF | XF | Unc |
|---|---|---|---|---|---|
| SH1350(1971) Proof | Inc. above | Value: 25.00 | | | |

**PAHLAVI** **KM# 1148** **Weight:** 8.1360 g. **Composition:** 0.9000 Gold .2354 oz. AGW **Obv. Legend:** "Muhammad Reza Shah"

| Date | Mintage | F | VF | XF | Unc |
|---|---|---|---|---|---|
| SH1320 | — | 250 | 600 | 1,250 | 1,750 |
| **Note:** Possibly a pattern | | | | | |
| SH1321 | — | — | — | 1,750 | 2,500 |
| **Note:** Possibly a pattern | | | | | |
| SH1322 | — | — | BV | 80.00 | 110 |
| SH1323 | 311,000 | — | BV | 80.00 | 110 |
| SH1324 | — | — | BV | 80.00 | 110 |

**PAHLAVI** **KM# 1150** **Weight:** 8.1360 g. **Composition:** 0.9000 Gold .2354 oz. AGW **Obverse:** High relief head of Muhammad Reza Pahlavi

| Date | Mintage | F | VF | XF | Unc |
|---|---|---|---|---|---|
| SH1324 | — | BV | 90.00 | 100 | 120 |
| SH1325 | — | BV | 90.00 | 100 | 120 |
| SH1326 | 151,000 | BV | 90.00 | 100 | 120 |
| SH1327 | 20,000 | BV | 90.00 | 100 | 120 |
| SH1328 | 4,000 | BV | 125 | 185 | 260 |
| SH1329 | 4,000 | BV | 125 | 185 | 260 |
| SH1330 | 48,000 | BV | 125 | 185 | 260 |

**PAHLAVI** **KM# 1162** **Weight:** 8.1360 g. **Composition:** 0.9000 Gold .2354 oz. AGW **Obverse:** Low relief head

| Date | Mintage | F | VF | XF | Unc |
|---|---|---|---|---|---|
| SH1330 | — | — | BV | 80.00 | 110 |
| SH1331 | — | — | 500 | 800 | 1,200 |
| SH1332 | — | — | 500 | 800 | 1,200 |
| SH1333 | — | BV | 100 | 120 | 160 |
| SH1334 | — | BV | 100 | 120 | 160 |
| SH1335 | — | — | BV | 80.00 | 110 |
| SH1336 | 453,000 | — | BV | 80.00 | 110 |
| SH1337 | 665,000 | — | BV | 80.00 | 110 |
| SH1338 | 776,000 | — | BV | 80.00 | 110 |
| SH1339 | 847,000 | — | BV | 80.00 | 110 |
| SH1340 | 528,000 | — | BV | 80.00 | 110 |
| SH1342 | 20,000 | — | BV | 80.00 | 110 |
| SH1343 | 10,000 | — | — | — | — |
| **Note:** Reported, not confirmed | | | | | |
| SH1344 | — | BV | 110 | 110 | 160 |
| SH1345 | 20,000 | — | BV | 80.00 | 110 |
| SH1346 | 30,000 | — | BV | 80.00 | 110 |
| SH1347 | 40,000 | — | BV | 80.00 | 110 |
| SH1348 | 70,000 | — | BV | 80.00 | 110 |
| SH1349 | 70,000 | — | BV | 80.00 | 110 |
| SH1350 | 60,000 | — | BV | 80.00 | 110 |
| SH1351 | 100,000 | — | BV | 80.00 | 110 |
| SH1352 | 320,000 | — | BV | 80.00 | 110 |
| SH1353 | — | — | BV | 80.00 | 110 |

**PAHLAVI** **KM# 1200** **Weight:** 8.1360 g. **Composition:** 0.9000 Gold .2354 oz. AGW **Obverse:** "Aryamehr" added to legend

| Date | Mintage | F | VF | XF | Unc |
|---|---|---|---|---|---|
| SH1354 | 21,000 | — | BV | 80.00 | 110 |
| SH1355 | 203,000 | — | BV | 80.00 | 110 |
| MS2536 | — | — | BV | 80.00 | 110 |
| MS2537 | — | — | BV | 80.00 | 110 |
| SH1358 | — | — | 125 | 200 | 300 |

**200 RIALS** **KM# 1188** **Weight:** 60.0000 g. **Composition:** 0.9990 Silver 1.9273 oz. ASW **Subject:** 2500th Anniversary of Persian Empire **Obverse:** Conjoined bust of royal couple left **Note:** Imperial couple.

| Date | Mintage | F | VF | XF | Unc |
|---|---|---|---|---|---|
| SH1350(1971) Proof | 23,000 | Value: 42.50 | | | |

**2-1/2 PAHLAVI** **KM# A1163** **Weight:** 20.3400 g. **Composition:** 0.9000 Gold .5885 oz. AGW **Obverse:** Bust of Mohammad Reza Pahlavi **Reverse:** Lion

| Date | Mintage | F | VF | XF | Unc |
|---|---|---|---|---|---|
| SH1338 | — | — | — | — | — |

**2-1/2 PAHLAVI** **KM# 1163** **Weight:** 20.3400 g. **Composition:** 0.9000 Gold .5885 oz. AGW **Reverse:** Three-line inscription, date below

| Date | Mintage | F | VF | XF | Unc |
|---|---|---|---|---|---|
| SH1339 | 1,682 | BV | 200 | 225 | 255 |
| SH1340 | 2,788 | BV | 200 | 225 | 255 |
| SH1342 | 30 | — | — | — | — |
| SH1347 | 2,000 | — | — | — | — |
| **Note:** Reported, not confirmed | | | | | |
| SH1348 | 3,000 | BV | 200 | 225 | 255 |
| SH1349 | 3,000 | — | — | — | — |
| **Note:** Reported, not confirmed | | | | | |
| SH1350 | 2,000 | BV | 200 | 225 | 255 |
| SH1351 | 2,500 | BV | 200 | 225 | 255 |
| SH1352 | 3,000 | BV | 200 | 225 | 255 |
| SH1353 | — | BV | 200 | 225 | 255 |

**2-1/2 PAHLAVI** **KM# 1201** **Weight:** 20.3400 g. **Composition:** 0.9000 Gold .5885 oz. AGW **Obverse:** "Aryamehr" added to legend **Edge:** Reeded **Size:** 30 mm.

| Date | Mintage | F | VF | XF | Unc |
|---|---|---|---|---|---|
| SH1354 | 18,000 | — | BV | 200 | 235 |
| SH1355 | 16,000 | — | BV | 200 | 235 |
| MS2536 | — | — | BV | 200 | 235 |
| MS2537 | — | — | BV | 200 | 235 |
| SH1358 Rare | — | — | — | — | — |

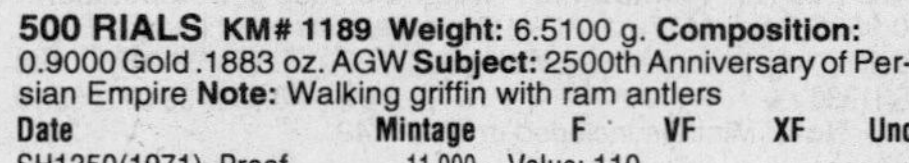

**500 RIALS** **KM# 1189** **Weight:** 6.5100 g. **Composition:** 0.9000 Gold .1883 oz. AGW **Subject:** 2500th Anniversary of Persian Empire **Note:** Walking griffin with ram antlers

| Date | Mintage | F | VF | XF | Unc |
|---|---|---|---|---|---|
| SH1350(1971) Proof | 11,000 | Value: 110 | | | |

**5 PAHLAVI** **KM# 1164** **Weight:** 40.6799 g. **Composition:** 0.9000 Gold 1.1772 oz. AGW **Obverse:** Bust of Muhammad Reza Pahlavi **Reverse:** Lion

| Date | Mintage | F | VF | XF | Unc |
|---|---|---|---|---|---|
| SH1339 | 2,225 | BV | 400 | 450 | 500 |
| SH1340 | 2,430 | BV | 400 | 450 | 500 |
| SH1342 | 20 | — | — | — | — |
| SH1347 | 500 | — | — | — | — |
| **Note:** Reported, not confirmed | | | | | |
| SH1348 | 2,000 | BV | 400 | 450 | 500 |
| SH1349 | 700 | — | — | — | — |
| **Note:** Reported, not confirmed | | | | | |
| SH1350 | 2,000 | BV | 400 | 450 | 500 |
| SH1351 | 2,500 | BV | 400 | 450 | 500 |
| SH1352 | 2,100 | BV | 400 | 450 | 500 |
| SH1353 | — | BV | 400 | 450 | 500 |

**5 PAHLAVI** **KM# 1202** **Weight:** 40.6799 g. **Composition:** 0.9000 Gold 1.1772 oz. AGW **Obverse:** "Aryamehr" added to legend

| Date | Mintage | F | VF | XF | Unc |
|---|---|---|---|---|---|
| SH1354 | 10,000 | — | BV | 425 | 485 |
| SH1355 | 17,000 | — | BV | 425 | 485 |
| MS2536 | — | — | BV | 425 | 485 |
| MS2537 | — | — | BV | 425 | 485 |
| SH1358 | — | — | 550 | 700 | 900 |

**750 RIALS** **KM# 1190** **Weight:** 9.7700 g. **Composition:** 0.9000 Gold .2827 oz. AGW **Subject:** 2500th Anniversary of Persian Empire **Note:** Stone of Cyrus II

| Date | Mintage | F | VF | XF | Unc |
|---|---|---|---|---|---|
| SH1350(1971) Proof | 10,000 | Value: 135 | | | |

**1000 RIALS** **KM# 1191.1** **Weight:** 13.0300 g. **Composition:** 0.9000 Gold .3770 oz. AGW **Subject:** 2500th Anniversary of Persian Empire **Reverse:** Polished fields below ruins **Note:** Palace of Darius I and pillars of reception hall in Persepolis

| Date | Mintage | F | VF | XF | Unc |
|---|---|---|---|---|---|
| SH1350(1971) Proof | 10,000 | Value: 200 | | | |

**1000 RIALS** **KM# 1191.2** **Weight:** 13.0300 g. **Composition:** 0.9000 Gold .3770 oz. AGW **Subject:** 2500th Anniversary of Persian Empire **Reverse:** Frosted fields below ruins

| Date | Mintage | F | VF | XF | Unc |
|---|---|---|---|---|---|
| SH1350(1971) Proof | Inc. above | Value: 200 | | | |

World Coin News
FROM THE PUBLISHERS OF THE STANDARD CATALOG OF WORLD COINS
Vol. 29, No. 3 March 2002 U.S. $3.50/Canada $4.50

## Viking dollar makes waves

By Dave Harper

The United States Mint won the Coin of the Year Award for its commemorative silver dollar dated 2000 honoring Leif Ericson.

An international panel of judges made the selection in the second round of COTY voting from a field of 10 coins that survived the first round of balloting that concluded in December.

On the obverse, the .900 fine silver dollar features a profile of the Viking mariner who may have visited the New World almost 500 years before Christopher Columbus. The reverse shows a Viking longship.

The award will be given at a time and place agreeable to the U.S. Mint. It might be in April at the Mint Directors Conference in Osaka, Japan, or it might be at the American Numismatic Association convention in July in New York City. Both events have hosted award ceremonies in previous years.

This is the fourth time since the creation of COTY by *World Coin News* that a coin from the United States has been voted this international honor.

The United States won the very first Coin of the Year Award with the 1982 George Washington commemorative half dollar. That award was given in a special ceremony held in 1984.

Also winning were the 1983 U.S. Olympic silver dollar, which received its recognition in 1985 and the 1986 Statue of Liberty $5 gold piece, which took the

COTY/Page 69

The U.S. Mint's commemorative silver dollar featuring Leif Ericson was selected by an international panel of judges as *World Coin News'* Coin of the Year.

*Inside:*

Queen's jubilee

A number of mints are producing commemoratives honoring the 50th anniversary of the reign of Queen Elizabeth II.

(See page 4)

Euro chances

What are your odds when calling heads or tails with euro coins? Richard Giedroyc reports on the results found by two Polish scientists.

(See page 10)

Propaganda leaflets

The U.S. military has been dropping nearly as many leaflets in Afghanistan as there are citizens. Herbert A. Friedman looks at the psychology and strategy involved.

(See page 28)

## Mints announce 2002 coins

A number of mints announced their 2002 commemorative releases at the World Money Fair Feb. 1-3 in Basel, Switzerland.

Martin Peeters, a Netherlands member of the Worldwide Bimetallic Collectors Club, said in the club's e-mail newsletter that the Australian Mint will release a $50 commemorati... coin to mark the Battl... The British Royal ...

2-pound coins to celebrate the 17th Commonwealth Games in Manchester, England.

Peeters said that there was strong public interest in purchasing euro coins, but mints only had them available for display, not for sale. That included euro currency from San Marino and the ... which have not appeared yet. ... said it will release only ...d 2-euro sets March 1.

## Chinese calendar saluted

The Royal Canadian Mint is selling its 2002 Year of the Horse hologram coin designed by Canadian artist Harvey Chan.

The $150, 18-karat gold coin is the third in the Chinese lunar calendar series and features the holographic image of a horse in repose.

The coin is priced at $388.88 ($254.45 U.S.) and has a limited mintage of 6,888. The obverse portrays an effigy of Queen Elizabeth II by Dora de Pédery-Hunt.

The Chinese lunar calendar follows a 12-year cycle, with a different animal associated with each year in the cycle. Chinese astrology ascribes character traits to each animal, and people are said to share the traits of the animals associated with the year of their birth. The Chinese New Year begins on Feb. 12 and the 2002 calendar year is the year 4699 in the Chinese calendar.

Other animals in the Chinese year cycle are the rat, ox, tiger, rabbit, dragon, snake, horse, sheep, monkey, rooster, dog and pig.

For more information, contact the Mint at (800) 267-1871; e-mail, service@mint.ca; Web site, www.rcmint.ca.

The Royal Canadian Mint released this holographic gold coin recognizing the Year of the Horse.

*1-year*
(12 issues)
**$27.98**

**Save over $14**
***off the cover price***

**For Faster Credit Card Service,**
***Call Toll-Free 800-258-0929***
**Offer WCABA8JJ**
Mon.-Fri. 7 am-8 pm; Sat. 8 am-2 pm, CST

## *The leading publication solely devoted to world currency for 29 years*

**World Coin News** brings you:

- **Columnists** including award winning authors Don Bailey & Alan Herbert
- **News** on the latest releases from the world's mints
- **Major worldwide auction** previews & results
- **Extensive calendar** of events for shows & auctions
- **Contact information** for new release mints or authorized sellers
- **Ads** from the world's dealers to help you look for the best buys

***and much more!***

Offer WCABA8JJ

*1-year*
(12 issues)
**$25.98**

**Save over $20**
***off the cover price***

**For Faster Credit Card Service,**
***Call Toll-Free 800-258-0929***
**Offer CMABA8JJ**
Mon.-Fri. 7 am-8 pm; Sat. 8 am-2 pm, CST

# Coins®

Each month **Coins** gives you:

- **Expert tips** on how to get the best value for your collecting dollar
- **Feature articles** ranging from earliest U.S. coins through modern issues
- **Monthly show calendar**
- **The MOST U.S. coin price guide pages, including two double issues:**

  **May** adds an U.S. paper money price guide.

  **November** brings you a Canadian and Mexican coin price guide
- **Monthly Coin Clinic** column
- **Monthly 50 states quarter** section

***plus more!***

Offer CMABA8JJ

# Yes, I want to subscribe!

❑ **1-year** (12 issues) of **World Coin News** for **$27.98.**
❑ Enclosed is my check or money order
(payable to World Coins)
Please charge my credit card:
❑ VISA ❑ DISCOVER-NOVUS
❑ MASTERCARD ❑ AMEX
Card #: ____________________
Exp.: ____________________
Signature ____________________
**Name** ____________________
**Address** ____________________
**City** ____________________
**State** __________ **Zip** ____________________
**Phone** **(for order verification)** ____________________
**E-mail** ____________________

Send this slip and payment to:
**World Coin News** ***www.collect.com***
Offer WCABA8JJ, 700 E. State St., Iola, WI 54990-0001

**For Faster Credit Card Service,**
***Call Toll-Free 800-258-0929***
**Offer WCABA8JJ** Mon.-Fri. 7 am-8 pm; Sat. 8 am-2 pm, CST

World Coin News
FROM THE PUBLISHERS OF THE STANDARD CATALOG OF WORLD COINS
Vol. 29, No. 2 February 2002 U.S. $3.50/Canada $4.50

New euros invade America

Inside: World Cup coins · Tokens from Vulcan · Tajikistan's currency

Service medals set record

Coins mark Year of Horse

*1-year*
(12 issues)
$27[98]

***Save over $14***
***off the cover price***

# Yes, I want to subscribe!

❑ **1-year** (12 issues) of **Coins** magazine for **$25.98.**
❑ Enclosed is my check or money order
(payable to Coins)
Please charge my credit card:
❑ VISA ❑ DISCOVER-NOVUS
❑ MASTERCARD ❑ AMEX
Card #: ____________________
Exp.: ____________________
Signature ____________________
**Name** ____________________
**Address** ____________________
**City** ____________________
**State** __________ **Zip** ____________________
**Phone** (for order verification) ____________________
**E-mail** ____________________

Send this slip and payment to:
**Coins** magazine ***www.collect.com***
Offer CMABA8JJ, 700 E. State St., Iola, WI 54990-0001

**For Faster Credit Card Service,**
***Call Toll-Free 800-258-0929***
**Offer CMABA8JJ** Mon.-Fri. 7 am-8 pm; Sat. 8 am-2 pm, CST

***Save over $20***
***off the cover price***

**10 PAHLAVI** KM# 1210 **Weight:** 81.3598 g. **Composition:** 0.9000 Gold 2.3544 oz. AGW **Subject:** 50th Anniversary of Pahlavi Rule

| Date | Mintage | F | VF | XF | Unc |
|---|---|---|---|---|---|
| MS2535 | — | — | — | 850 | 1,000 |

**10 PAHLAVI** KM# 1212 **Weight:** 81.3598 g. **Composition:** 0.9000 Gold 2.3544 oz. AGW **Subject:** Centenary of Reza Shah's Birth

| Date | Mintage | F | VF | XF | Unc |
|---|---|---|---|---|---|
| MS2536 | — | — | — | 850 | 1,000 |

**10 PAHLAVI** KM# 1213 **Weight:** 81.3598 g. **Composition:** 0.9000 Gold 2.3544 oz. AGW **Obverse:** "Aryamehr" added to legend

| Date | Mintage | F | VF | XF | Unc |
|---|---|---|---|---|---|
| MS2537 | — | — | — | 850 | 1,000 |
| SH1358 | — | — | — | 1,500 | 2,000 |

**2000 RIALS** KM# 1192 **Weight:** 26.0600 g. **Composition:** 0.9000 Gold .7541 oz. AGW **Subject:** 2500th Anniversary of Persian Empire **Note:** Imperial couple

| Date | Mintage | F | VF | XF | Unc |
|---|---|---|---|---|---|
| SH1350(1971) Proof | 9,805 | Value: 400 | | | |

# ISLAMIC REPUBLIC

## MILLED COINAGE

**50 DINARS** KM# 1231 **Composition:** Brass Clad Steel **Obverse:** Without crown

| Date | Mintage | F | VF | XF | Unc |
|---|---|---|---|---|---|
| SH1358 | — | — | 6.50 | 8.00 | 12.00 |

**RIAL** KM# 1232 **Composition:** Copper-Nickel

| Date | Mintage | F | VF | XF | Unc |
|---|---|---|---|---|---|
| SH1358 | — | — | 0.25 | 0.75 | 1.75 |
| SH1359 | — | — | 0.25 | 0.75 | 1.75 |
| SH1360 | — | — | 0.25 | 0.75 | 1.75 |
| SH1361 | — | — | 0.25 | 0.75 | 1.75 |
| SH1362 | — | — | 0.25 | 0.75 | 1.75 |
| SH1363 | — | — | — | — | — |
| **Note:** Reported, not confirmed | | | | | |
| SH1364 | — | — | 0.25 | 0.75 | 1.75 |
| SH1365 | — | — | 0.15 | 0.65 | 1.25 |
| SH1366 | — | — | 0.15 | 0.65 | 1.25 |
| SH1367 | — | — | 0.15 | 0.65 | 1.25 |

**RIAL** KM# 1245 **Composition:** Bronze Clad Steel **Subject:** World Jerusalem Day **Reverse:** Mosque of Omar

| Date | Mintage | F | VF | XF | Unc |
|---|---|---|---|---|---|
| SH1359 | — | — | 0.50 | 1.50 | 2.50 |

**RIAL** KM# 1263 **Composition:** Brass **Reverse:** Mount Damavand

| Date | Mintage | F | VF | XF | Unc |
|---|---|---|---|---|---|
| SH1371 | — | — | 2.50 | 5.00 | 10.00 |

**2 RIALS** KM# 1233 **Composition:** Copper-Nickel

| Date | Mintage | F | VF | XF | Unc |
|---|---|---|---|---|---|
| SH1358 | — | — | 0.60 | 1.25 | 3.50 |
| SH1359 | — | — | 0.50 | 1.25 | 3.50 |
| SH1360 | — | — | 0.50 | 1.25 | 3.50 |
| SH1361 | — | — | 0.50 | 1.00 | 3.00 |
| SH1362 | — | — | 0.35 | 0.75 | 2.75 |
| SH1363 | — | — | 0.50 | 1.00 | 3.00 |
| SH1364 | — | — | 0.35 | 0.75 | 2.75 |
| SH1365 | — | — | 0.25 | 0.75 | 2.50 |
| SH1366 | — | — | 0.25 | 0.75 | 2.50 |
| SH1367 | — | — | 0.25 | 0.75 | 2.50 |

**5 RIALS** KM# 1234 **Composition:** Copper-Nickel **Note:** Date varieties exist.

| Date | Mintage | F | VF | XF | Unc |
|---|---|---|---|---|---|
| SH1358 | — | — | 0.75 | 1.25 | 3.50 |
| SH1359 | — | — | 0.75 | 1.25 | 3.50 |
| SH1360 | — | — | 0.75 | 1.25 | 3.50 |
| SH1361 | — | — | 0.75 | 1.25 | 3.50 |
| SH1362 | — | — | 0.75 | 1.25 | 3.50 |
| SH1363 | — | — | 0.75 | 1.25 | 3.50 |
| SH1364 | — | — | 0.75 | 1.25 | 3.50 |
| SH1365 | — | — | 0.75 | 1.25 | 3.50 |
| SH1366 | — | — | 0.75 | 1.25 | 3.50 |
| SH1367 | — | — | 0.75 | 1.25 | 3.50 |
| SH1368 | — | — | 0.75 | 1.25 | 3.50 |

**5 RIALS** KM# 1258 **Composition:** Brass **Reverse:** Tomb of Hafez

| Date | Mintage | F | VF | XF | Unc |
|---|---|---|---|---|---|
| SH1371 | — | — | 0.50 | 1.25 | 3.00 |
| SH1372 | — | — | 0.50 | 1.25 | 3.00 |
| SH1373 | — | — | 0.50 | 1.25 | 3.00 |
| SH1375 | — | — | 0.50 | 1.25 | 3.00 |
| SH1376 | — | — | 0.50 | 1.25 | 3.00 |

**10 RIALS** KM# 1235.1 **Composition:** Copper-Nickel

| Date | Mintage | F | VF | XF | Unc |
|---|---|---|---|---|---|
| SH1358 | — | — | 1.00 | 2.50 | 4.50 |
| SH1358 Large date | — | — | 1.00 | 2.50 | 4.50 |
| SH1359 | — | — | 1.00 | 2.50 | 4.50 |
| SH1360 | — | — | 1.00 | 2.50 | 4.50 |
| SH1361 | — | — | 1.00 | 2.00 | 4.00 |

**10 RIALS** KM# 1243 **Composition:** Copper-Nickel **Subject:** 1st Anniversary of Revolution

| Date | Mintage | F | VF | XF | Unc |
|---|---|---|---|---|---|
| SH1358 | — | — | 1.50 | 2.50 | 4.50 |

**10 RIALS** KM# 1249 **Weight:** 6.9700 g. **Composition:** Copper-Nickel **Subject:** Moslem Unity **Edge:** Reeded

| Date | Mintage | F | VF | XF | Unc |
|---|---|---|---|---|---|
| SH1361 | — | — | 1.50 | 2.50 | 4.50 |

**10 RIALS** KM# 1235.2 **Composition:** Copper-Nickel **Reverse:** Redesigned wreath **Note:** Date varieties exist.

| Date | Mintage | F | VF | XF | Unc |
|---|---|---|---|---|---|
| SH1361 | — | — | 1.00 | 2.00 | 4.00 |
| SH1362 | — | — | 1.00 | 2.00 | 4.00 |
| SH1363 | — | — | 1.00 | 2.00 | 4.00 |
| SH1364 | — | — | 0.90 | 1.50 | 4.00 |
| SH1365 | — | — | 0.90 | 1.50 | 4.00 |
| SH1366 | — | — | 0.90 | 1.50 | 4.00 |
| SH1366 Small date | — | — | 0.90 | 1.50 | 4.00 |
| SH1367 | — | — | 0.65 | 1.50 | 3.00 |

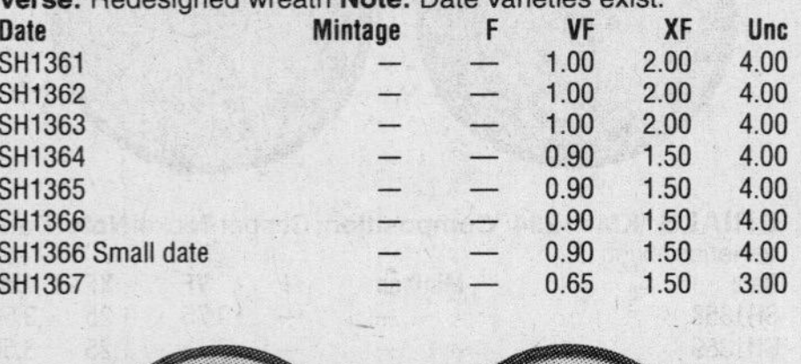

**10 RIALS** KM# 1253.1 **Weight:** 3.0200 g. **Composition:** Copper-Nickel **Subject:** World Jerusalem Day **Obverse:** Small denomination numerals **Edge:** Plain

| Date | Mintage | F | VF | XF | Unc |
|---|---|---|---|---|---|
| SH1368 | — | — | 1.00 | 2.00 | 4.00 |

**10 RIALS** KM# 1253.2 **Weight:** 3.0200 g. **Composition:** Copper-Nickel **Obverse:** Large denomination numerals

| Date | Mintage | F | VF | XF | Unc |
|---|---|---|---|---|---|
| SH1368 | — | — | 1.00 | 2.00 | 4.00 |

**10 RIALS** KM# 1259 **Composition:** Aluminum-Bronze **Reverse:** Tomb of Ferdousi

| Date | Mintage | F | VF | XF | Unc |
|---|---|---|---|---|---|
| SH1371 | — | — | 1.00 | 2.00 | 3.75 |
| SH1372 | — | — | 1.00 | 2.00 | 3.75 |
| SH1373 | — | — | 1.00 | 2.00 | 3.75 |
| SH1374 | — | — | 1.00 | 2.00 | 3.75 |
| SH1376 | — | — | 1.00 | 2.00 | 3.75 |

**20 RIALS** KM# 1244 **Composition:** Copper-Nickel **Subject:** 1400th Anniversary of Mohammed's Flight

| Date | Mintage | F | VF | XF | Unc |
|---|---|---|---|---|---|
| SH1358 | — | — | 2.50 | 3.50 | 5.00 |

**20 RIALS** KM# 1236 **Composition:** Copper-Nickel **Note:** Date varieties exist.

| Date | Mintage | F | VF | XF | Unc |
|---|---|---|---|---|---|
| SH1358 | — | — | 1.00 | 1.75 | 4.50 |
| SH1359 | — | — | 1.00 | 1.75 | 4.50 |
| SH1360 | — | — | 1.00 | 1.75 | 4.50 |
| SH1361 | — | — | 1.00 | 1.75 | 4.50 |
| SH1362 | — | — | 1.00 | 1.75 | 4.50 |
| SH1363 | — | — | 1.00 | 1.75 | 4.50 |
| SH1364 | — | — | 1.00 | 1.75 | 4.50 |
| SH1365 | — | — | 1.00 | 1.75 | 4.50 |
| SH1366 | — | — | 1.00 | 1.75 | 4.50 |
| SH1367 | — | — | 1.00 | 1.75 | 4.50 |

**20 RIALS** KM# 1246 **Composition:** Copper-Nickel **Subject:** 2nd Anniversary of Islamic Revolution

| Date | Mintage | F | VF | XF | Unc |
|---|---|---|---|---|---|
| SH1359 | — | — | 2.50 | 3.50 | 5.00 |

**20 RIALS** KM# 1247 **Composition:** Copper-Nickel **Subject:** 3rd Anniversary of Islamic Revolution

| Date | Mintage | F | VF | XF | Unc |
|---|---|---|---|---|---|
| SH1360 | — | — | 2.50 | 3.50 | 5.00 |

**20 RIALS** KM# 1251 **Composition:** Copper-Nickel **Subject:** Islamic Banking Week

| Date | Mintage | F | VF | XF | Unc |
|---|---|---|---|---|---|
| SH1367 | — | — | 2.50 | 3.50 | 5.00 |

**20 RIALS** KM# 1254.2 **Composition:** Copper-Nickel **Reverse:** Redesigned thick wreath **Note:** 1.70 milimeters thick.

| Date | Mintage | F | VF | XF | Unc |
|---|---|---|---|---|---|
| SH1368 | — | — | 2.50 | 3.50 | 5.00 |

**20 RIALS** KM# 1254.1 **Composition:** Copper-Nickel **Subject:** 8 Years of Sacred Defense **Obverse:** Twenty-two dots around rim **Note:** 2.00 milimeters thick.

| Date | Mintage | F | VF | XF | Unc |
|---|---|---|---|---|---|
| SH1368 | — | — | 2.50 | 3.50 | 5.00 |

**50 RIALS** KM# 1237.1 **Composition:** Aluminum-Bronze **Subject:** Oil and Agriculture **Reverse:** Map in relief **Edge:** Lettered **Note:** Two varieties of edge lettering exist.

| Date | Mintage | F | VF | XF | Unc |
|---|---|---|---|---|---|
| SH1359 | — | — | 2.00 | 3.50 | 8.00 |
| SH1360 | — | — | 2.00 | 3.50 | 8.00 |
| SH1361 | — | — | 2.00 | 3.50 | 8.00 |
| SH1362 | — | — | 2.00 | 3.50 | 8.00 |
| SH1364 | — | — | 2.00 | 3.50 | 8.00 |
| SH1365 | — | — | 2.00 | 3.50 | 8.00 |

**50 RIALS** KM# 1237.2 **Composition:** Aluminum-Bronze **Reverse:** Map incuse

| Date | Mintage | F | VF | XF | Unc |
|---|---|---|---|---|---|
| SH1366 | — | — | 4.00 | 6.00 | 9.00 |
| SH1367 | — | — | — | 4.50 | 7.00 |
| SH1368 | — | — | — | 4.50 | 7.00 |

**50 RIALS** KM# 1252 **Composition:** Copper-Nickel **Subject:** 10th Anniversary of Revolution

| Date | Mintage | F | VF | XF | Unc |
|---|---|---|---|---|---|
| SH1367 | — | — | 3.00 | 5.00 | 7.50 |

**50 RIALS** KM# 1237.1a **Composition:** Copper-Nickel **Edge:** Lettered

| Date | Mintage | F | VF | XF | Unc |
|---|---|---|---|---|---|
| SH1368 | — | — | 2.00 | 3.50 | 7.50 |
| SH1369 | — | — | 2.00 | 3.50 | 7.50 |
| SH1370 | — | — | 2.00 | 3.50 | 7.50 |

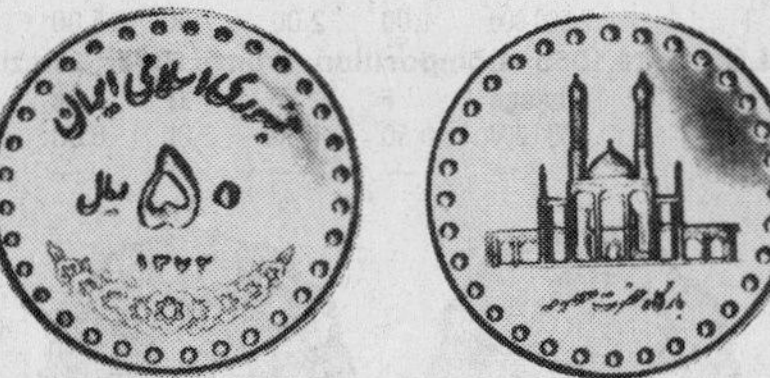

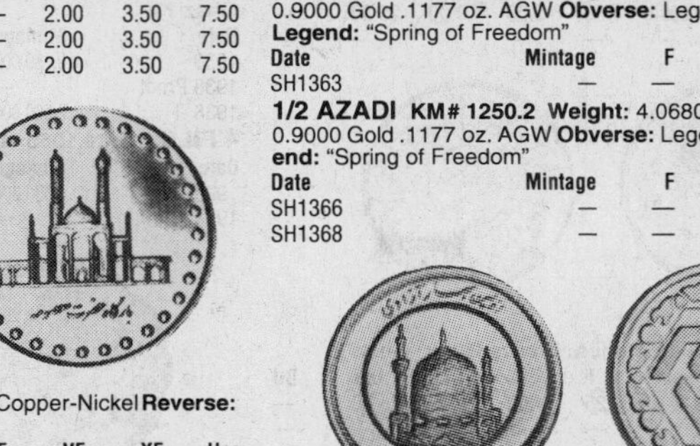

**50 RIALS KM#1260 Composition:** Copper-Nickel **Reverse:** Shrine of Hazrat Masumah

| Date | Mintage | F | VF | XF | Unc |
|---|---|---|---|---|---|
| SH1371 | — | — | 2.50 | 3.50 | 5.00 |
| SH1372 | — | — | 2.50 | 3.50 | 5.00 |
| SH1373 | — | — | 2.50 | 3.50 | 5.00 |
| SH1374 | — | — | 2.50 | 3.50 | 5.00 |
| SH1375 | — | — | 2.50 | 3.50 | 5.00 |
| SH1377 | — | — | 2.50 | 3.50 | 5.00 |

**100 RIALS KM# 1261.1 Composition:** Copper-Nickel **Obverse:** Thin denomination, numerals **Reverse:** Shrine of Imam Reza

| Date | Mintage | F | VF | XF | Unc |
|---|---|---|---|---|---|
| SH1371 | — | — | — | — | 6.50 |

**100 RIALS KM# 1261.2 Composition:** Copper-Nickel **Obverse:** Thick denomination, numerals

| Date | Mintage | F | VF | XF | Unc |
|---|---|---|---|---|---|
| SH1372 | — | — | — | — | 6.50 |
| SH1373 | — | — | — | — | 6.50 |
| SH1375 | — | — | — | — | 6.50 |

**250 RIALS KM# 1262 Ring Composition:** Brass **Center Composition:** Copper-Nickel **Reverse:** Stylized flower

| Date | Mintage | F | VF | XF | Unc |
|---|---|---|---|---|---|
| SH1372 | — | — | — | — | 7.50 |
| SH1373 | — | — | — | — | 7.50 |
| SH1374 | — | — | — | — | 7.50 |
| SH1375 | — | — | — | — | 7.50 |
| SH1376 | — | — | — | — | 7.50 |

## BULLION COINAGE

Issued by the National Bank of Iran

**1/4 AZADI KM# 1238 Weight:** 2.0339 g. **Composition:** 0.9000 Gold .0588 oz. AGW **Obv. Legend:** "1st Spring of Freedom"

| Date | Mintage | F | VF | XF | Unc |
|---|---|---|---|---|---|
| SH1358 | — | — | — | — | 175 |

**1/2 AZADI KM# 1239 Weight:** 4.0680 g. **Composition:** 0.9000 Gold .1177 oz. AGW **Obv. Legend:** "1st Spring of Freedom"

| Date | Mintage | F | VF | XF | Unc |
|---|---|---|---|---|---|
| SH1358 | — | — | — | — | 100 |

**1/2 AZADI KM# 1250.1 Weight:** 4.0680 g. **Composition:** 0.9000 Gold .1177 oz. AGW **Obverse:** Legend shortened **Obv. Legend:** "Spring of Freedom"

| Date | Mintage | F | VF | XF | Unc |
|---|---|---|---|---|---|
| SH1363 | — | — | — | — | 100 |

**1/2 AZADI KM# 1250.2 Weight:** 4.0680 g. **Composition:** 0.9000 Gold .1177 oz. AGW **Obverse:** Legend larger **Obv. Legend:** "Spring of Freedom"

| Date | Mintage | F | VF | XF | Unc |
|---|---|---|---|---|---|
| SH1366 | — | — | — | — | 100 |
| SH1368 | — | — | — | — | 100 |

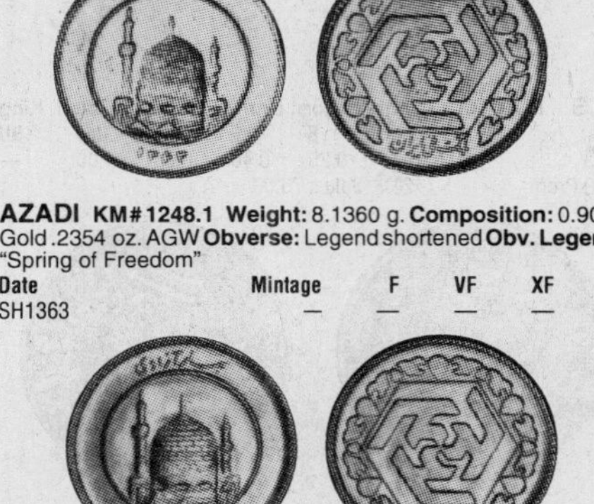

**AZADI KM# 1240 Weight:** 8.1360 g. **Composition:** 0.9000 Gold .2354 oz. AGW **Obv. Legend:** "1st Spring of Freedom"

| Date | Mintage | F | VF | XF | Unc |
|---|---|---|---|---|---|
| SH1358 | — | — | — | — | 125 |

**AZADI KM# 1248.1 Weight:** 8.1360 g. **Composition:** 0.9000 Gold .2354 oz. AGW **Obverse:** Legend shortened **Obv. Legend:** "Spring of Freedom"

| Date | Mintage | F | VF | XF | Unc |
|---|---|---|---|---|---|
| SH1363 | — | — | — | — | 120 |

**AZADI KM# 1248.2 Weight:** 8.1360 g. **Composition:** 0.9000 Gold .2354 oz. AGW **Obverse:** Legend larger **Obv. Legend:** "Spring of Freedom"

| Date | Mintage | F | VF | XF | Unc |
|---|---|---|---|---|---|
| SH1364 | — | — | — | — | 120 |
| SH1365 | — | — | — | — | 120 |
| SH1366 | — | — | — | — | 120 |
| SH1367 | — | — | — | — | 120 |
| SH1368 | — | — | — | — | 120 |
| SH1369 | — | — | — | — | 120 |
| SH1370 | — | — | — | — | 120 |

**AZADI KM# 1264 Weight:** 8.1360 g. **Composition:** 0.9000 Gold .2354 oz. AGW **Obverse:** The Central Bank of Islamic Republic of Iran **Reverse:** Portrait above date

| Date | Mintage | F | VF | XF | Unc |
|---|---|---|---|---|---|
| SH1370 | — | — | — | — | 125 |
| SH1373 | — | — | — | — | 125 |
| SH1374 | — | — | — | — | 125 |
| SH1375 | — | — | — | — | 125 |

**2-1/2 AZADI KM# 1241 Weight:** 20.3400 g. **Composition:** 0.9000 Gold .5885 oz. AGW **Obv. Legend:** "1st Spring of Freedom"

| Date | Mintage | F | VF | XF | Unc |
|---|---|---|---|---|---|
| SH1358 | 6 | — | — | — | 900 |

**Note:** A mintage of 6 pieces is reported, but more exist

**5 AZADI KM# 1242 Weight:** 40.6800 g. **Composition:** 0.9000 Gold 1.1770 oz. AGW **Obv. Legend:** "1st Spring of Freedom"

| Date | Mintage | F | VF | XF | Unc |
|---|---|---|---|---|---|
| SH1358 | — | — | — | — | 2,200 |

## PATTERNS

Including off metal strikes

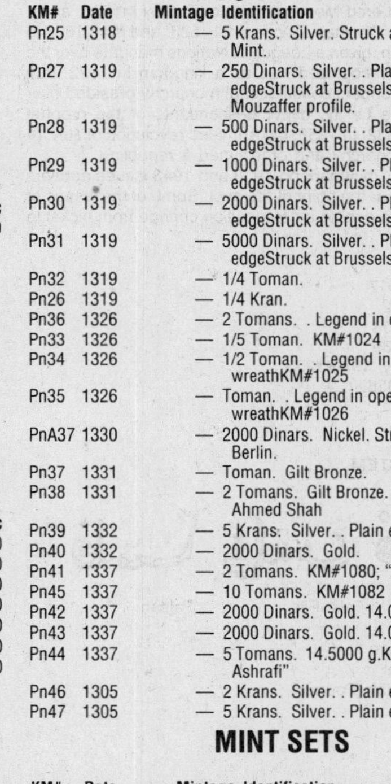

| KM# | Date | Mintage | Identification | Mkt Val |
|---|---|---|---|---|
| Pn25 | 1318 | — | 5 Krans. Silver. Struck at Paris Mint. | 1,750 |
| Pn27 | 1319 | — | 250 Dinars. Silver. . Plain edgeStruck at Brussels Mint. Mouzaffer profile. | 550 |
| Pn28 | 1319 | — | 500 Dinars. Silver. . Plain edgeStruck at Brussels Mint. | 700 |
| Pn29 | 1319 | — | 1000 Dinars. Silver. . Plain edgeStruck at Brussels Mint. | 700 |
| Pn30 | 1319 | — | 2000 Dinars. Silver. . Plain edgeStruck at Brussels Mint. | 800 |
| Pn31 | 1319 | — | 5000 Dinars. Silver. . Plain edgeStruck at Brussels Mint. | 1,750 |
| Pn32 | 1319 | — | 1/4 Toman. | 300 |
| Pn26 | 1319 | — | 1/4 Kran. | — |
| Pn36 | 1326 | — | 2 Tomans. . Legend in open wreath | — |
| Pn33 | 1326 | — | 1/5 Toman. KM#1024 | 300 |
| Pn34 | 1326 | — | 1/2 Toman. . Legend in open wreathKM#1025 | 300 |
| Pn35 | 1326 | — | Toman. . Legend in open wreathKM#1026 | 375 |
| PnA37 | 1330 | — | 2000 Dinars. Nickel. Struck at Berlin. | — |
| Pn37 | 1331 | — | Toman. Gilt Bronze. | 300 |
| Pn38 | 1331 | — | 2 Tomans. Gilt Bronze. Portrait of Ahmed Shah | 350 |
| Pn39 | 1332 | — | 5 Krans. Silver. . Plain edge | 1,000 |
| Pn40 | 1332 | — | 2000 Dinars. Gold. | — |
| Pn41 | 1337 | — | 2 Tomans. KM#1080; "2 Ashrafi" | — |
| Pn45 | 1337 | — | 10 Tomans. KM#1082 | — |
| Pn42 | 1337 | — | 2000 Dinars. Gold. 14.0000 g. | 5,000 |
| Pn43 | 1337 | — | 2000 Dinars. Gold. 14.0000 g. | 5,000 |
| Pn44 | 1337 | — | 5 Tomans. 14.5000 g.KM#1081; "5 Ashrafi" | 3,500 |
| Pn46 | 1305 | — | 2 Krans. Silver. . Plain edge | 2,500 |
| Pn47 | 1305 | — | 5 Krans. Silver. . Plain edge | 2,500 |

## MINT SETS

| KM# | Date | Mintage | Identification | Issue Price | Mkt Val |
|---|---|---|---|---|---|
| MS1 | SH1342 (1963) (4) | — | KM#1171a, 1173, 1175a, 1177a | 2.00 | 15.00 |
| MS2 | SH1343 (1964) (4) | — | KM#1171a, 1173, 1175a, 1177a | 2.00 | 11.50 |
| MS3 | SH1348 (1969) (5) | — | KM#1156, 1171a, 1173, 1176, 1178 | 2.00 | 17.00 |
| MS4 | SH1350 (1971) (5) | — | KM#1156, 1171a, 1173, 1176, 1178 | 2.00 | 17.00 |
| MS5 | SH1353 (1974) (6) | — | KM#1156, 1171a, 1173, 1176, 1179, 1181 | 2.00 | 19.00 |
| MS6 | SH1354 (1975) (6) | — | KM#1156, 1171a, 1173, 1176, 1179, 1181 | 2.00 | 22.00 |
| MS7 | MS2535 (1976) (6) | — | KM#1156a, 1205-1209 | 2.50 | 21.50 |
| MS8 | MS2536 (1977) (6) | — | KM#1156a, 1172-1173, 1176, 1179, 1181 | 2.50 | 20.00 |
| MS9 | SH1358 (1989) (8) | — | KM#1243-1244 dated 1358; 1246 dated 1359; 1247 dated 1360; 1252 dated 1367; 1253.1, 1253.2, 1254.1 dated 1368 | — | 40.00 |
| MS10 | SH1366 (1989) (7) | — | KM#1232-1234, 1236 dated 1366; 1235.2, 1237.2 dated 1367; 1237.1a dated 1368 | — | 25.00 |
| MS11 | SH1371 (1993) (5) | — | KM#1258-1262 | — | 25.00 |

## PROOF SETS

| KM# | Date | Mintage | Identification | Issue Price | Mkt Val |
|---|---|---|---|---|---|
| PS1 | SH1306(1927) | 20 | KM#1104, 1106 (Two each type) | — | 1,700 |
| PS2 | SH1350(1971) (9) | 9,805 | KM#1184-1192 | 261 | 960 |
| PS3 | SH1350(1971) (5) | 18,100 | KM#1184-1188 | 59.50 | 115 |

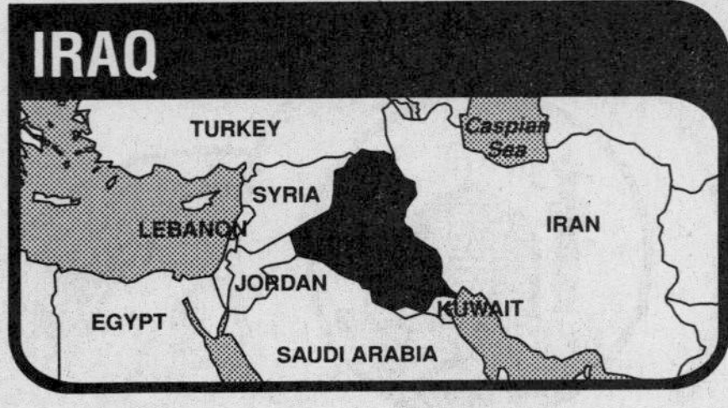


The Republic of Iraq, historically known as Mesopotamia, is located in the Near East and is bordered by Kuwait, Iran, Turkey, Syria, Jordan and Saudi Arabia. It has area of 167,925 sq. mi. (434,920 sq. km.) and a population of 14 million. Capital: Baghdad. The economy of Iraq is based on agriculture and petroleum. Crude oil accounted for 94 percent of the exports before the war with Iran began in 1980.

Mesopotamia was the site of a number of flourishing civilizations of antiquity - Sumeria, Assyria, Babylonia, Parthia, Persia and the Biblical cities of Ur, Ninevehand and Babylon. Desired because of its favored location, which embraced the fertile alluvial plains of the Tigris and Euphrates Rivers, Mesopotamia - 'land between the rivers'- was conquered by Cyrus the Great of Persia, Alexander of Macedonia and by Arabs who made the legendary city of Baghdad the capital of the ruling caliphate. Suleiman the Magnificent conquered Mesopotamia for Turkey in1534, and it formed part of the Ottoman Empire until 1623, and from 1638 to 1917. Great Britain, given a League of Nations mandate over the territory in 1920, recognized Iraq as a kingdom in 1922. Iraq became an independent constitutional monarchy presided over by the Hashemite family, direct descendants of the prophet Mohammed, in 1932. In 1958, the army-led revolution of July 14 overthrew the monarchy and proclaimed a republic.

**NOTE:** The 'I' mintmark on 1938 and 1943 issues appears on the obverse near the point of the bust. Some of the issues of 1938 have a dot to denote a composition change from nickel to copper-nickel.

**RULERS**

Ottoman, until 1917
British, 1921-1922
Faisal I, 1921-1933
Ghazi I, 1933-1939
Faisal II, Regency, 1939-1953
As King, 1953-1958

**MINT MARKS**

I – Bombay

**MONETARY SYSTEM**

Falus, Fulus — Fals, Fils — Falsan

50 Fils = 1 Dirham
200 Fils = 1 Riyal
1000 Fils = 1 Dinar (Pound)

**TITLES**

العراق

Al-Iraq

المملكة العراقية

Al-Mamlaka(t) al-Iraqiya(t)

الجمهورية العرقية

Al-Jumhuriya(t) al-Iraqiya(t)

# KINGDOM OF IRAQ

## DECIMAL COINAGE

**FILS KM# 95 Composition:** Bronze **Ruler:** Faisal I

| Date | Mintage | F | VF | XF | Unc | BU |
|---|---|---|---|---|---|---|
| 1931 | 4,000,000 | 1.00 | 3.00 | 10.00 | 25.00 | — |
| 1931 Proof | — | — | — | — | — | — |
| 1933 | 6,000,000 | 1.00 | 3.00 | 10.00 | 25.00 | — |
| 1933 Proof | — | — | — | — | — | — |

**FILS KM# 102 Composition:** Bronze **Ruler:** Ghazi I

| Date | Mintage | F | VF | XF | Unc | BU |
|---|---|---|---|---|---|---|
| 1936 | 3,000,000 | 1.25 | 4.00 | 10.00 | 25.00 | — |
| 1936 Proof | — | — | — | — | — | — |
| 1938 | 36,000,000 | 0.25 | 0.50 | 1.00 | 3.00 | — |
| 1938 -I | 3,000,000 | 0.50 | 2.00 | 5.00 | 15.00 | — |
| 1938 Proof | — | — | — | — | — | — |

**FILS KM# 109 Composition:** Bronze **Ruler:** Faisal II, King

| Date | Mintage | F | VF | XF | Unc | BU |
|---|---|---|---|---|---|---|
| 1953 | 41,000,000 | 0.25 | 0.40 | 0.60 | 1.00 | — |
| 1953 Proof | 200 | Value: 75.00 | | | | |

**2 FILS KM# 96 Composition:** Bronze **Ruler:** Faisal I

| Date | Mintage | F | VF | XF | Unc | BU |
|---|---|---|---|---|---|---|
| 1931 | 2,500,000 | 1.25 | 3.50 | 10.00 | 25.00 | — |
| 1931 Proof | — | — | — | — | — | — |
| 1933 | 1,000,000 | 1.50 | 4.00 | 15.00 | 35.00 | — |
| 1933 Proof | — | — | — | — | — | — |

**2 FILS KM# 110 Composition:** Bronze **Ruler:** Faisal II, King

| Date | Mintage | F | VF | XF | Unc | BU |
|---|---|---|---|---|---|---|
| 1953 | 500,000 | 0.50 | 1.00 | 3.00 | 12.50 | — |
| 1953 Proof | 200 | Value: 100 | | | | |

**4 FILS KM# 97 Composition:** Nickel **Ruler:** Faisal I

| Date | Mintage | F | VF | XF | Unc | BU |
|---|---|---|---|---|---|---|
| 1931 | 4,500,000 | 1.50 | 4.00 | 15.00 | 50.00 | — |
| 1931 Proof | — | — | — | — | — | — |
| 1933 | 6,500,000 | 1.50 | 4.00 | 15.00 | 50.00 | — |
| 1933 Proof | — | — | — | — | — | — |

**4 FILS KM# 105 Composition:** Nickel **Ruler:** Ghazi I

| Date | Mintage | F | VF | XF | Unc | BU |
|---|---|---|---|---|---|---|
| 1938 | 1,000,000 | 1.00 | 2.00 | 6.00 | 15.00 | — |
| 1938 Proof | — | — | — | — | — | — |
| 1939 | 1,000,000 | 1.25 | 2.50 | 10.00 | 30.00 | — |
| 1939 Proof | — | — | — | — | — | — |

**4 FILS KM# 105a Composition:** Copper-Nickel **Ruler:** Ghazi I

| Date | Mintage | F | VF | XF | Unc | BU |
|---|---|---|---|---|---|---|
| 1938 | 2,750,000 | 0.75 | 1.00 | 2.00 | 6.00 | — |
| 1938 Proof | — | — | — | — | — | — |
| 1938 -I | 2,500,000 | 1.00 | 2.00 | 7.50 | 15.00 | — |

**4 FILS KM# 105b Composition:** Bronze **Ruler:** Ghazi I

| Date | Mintage | F | VF | XF | Unc | BU |
|---|---|---|---|---|---|---|
| 1938 | 8,000,000 | 0.50 | 1.00 | 2.00 | 6.00 | — |
| 1938 Proof | — | — | — | — | — | — |

**4 FILS KM# 107 Composition:** Bronze **Ruler:** Faisal II, Regency

| Date | Mintage | F | VF | XF | Unc | BU |
|---|---|---|---|---|---|---|
| 1943 -I | 1,500,000 | 2.00 | 3.00 | 7.00 | 15.00 | — |

**4 FILS KM# 111 Composition:** Copper-Nickel **Ruler:** Faisal II, Regency

| Date | Mintage | F | VF | XF | Unc | BU |
|---|---|---|---|---|---|---|
| 1953 | 20,750,000 | 0.50 | 0.75 | 1.00 | 2.50 | — |
| 1953 Proof | 200 | Value: 75.00 | | | | |

**10 FILS KM# 98 Composition:** Nickel **Ruler:** Faisal I

| Date | Mintage | F | VF | XF | Unc | BU |
|---|---|---|---|---|---|---|
| 1931 | 2,400,000 | 2.00 | 5.00 | 16.50 | 50.00 | — |
| 1931 Proof | — | — | — | — | — | — |
| 1933 | 2,200,000 | 2.00 | 5.00 | 16.50 | 50.00 | — |
| 1933 Proof | — | — | — | — | — | — |

**10 FILS KM# 103 Composition:** Nickel **Ruler:** Ghazi I

| Date | Mintage | F | VF | XF | Unc | BU |
|---|---|---|---|---|---|---|
| 1937 | 400,000 | 3.00 | 5.00 | 16.50 | 50.00 | — |
| 1937 Proof | — | — | — | — | — | — |
| 1938 | 600,000 | 2.50 | 4.00 | 10.00 | 35.00 | — |
| 1938 Proof | — | — | — | — | — | — |

**10 FILS KM# 103a Composition:** Copper-Nickel **Ruler:** Ghazi I

| Date | Mintage | F | VF | XF | Unc | BU |
|---|---|---|---|---|---|---|
| 1938 | 1,100,000 | 1.00 | 2.00 | 4.00 | 10.00 | — |
| 1938 Proof | — | — | — | — | — | — |
| 1938 -I | 1,500,000 | 1.50 | 2.50 | 6.00 | 15.00 | — |

**10 FILS KM# 103b Composition:** Bronze **Ruler:** Ghazi I

| Date | Mintage | F | VF | XF | Unc | BU |
|---|---|---|---|---|---|---|
| 1938 | 8,250,000 | 0.50 | 1.00 | 2.50 | 6.50 | — |
| 1938 Proof | — | — | — | — | — | — |

**10 FILS KM# 108 Composition:** Bronze **Ruler:** Faisal II, Regency

| Date | Mintage | F | VF | XF | Unc | BU |
|---|---|---|---|---|---|---|
| 1943 -I | 1,500,000 | 3.00 | 7.00 | 20.00 | 50.00 | — |

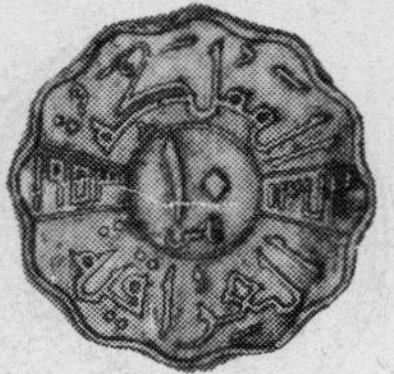

**10 FILS** **KM# 112** **Composition:** Copper-Nickel **Ruler:** Faisal II, Regency

| Date | Mintage | F | VF | XF | Unc | BU |
|---|---|---|---|---|---|---|
| 1953 | 11,400,000 | 0.50 | 0.75 | 1.00 | 2.50 | — |
| 1953 Proof | 200 | Value: 75.00 | | | | |

**20 FILS** **KM# 99** **Weight:** 3.6000 g. **Composition:** 0.5000 Silver .0579 oz. ASW **Ruler:** Faisal I

| Date | Mintage | F | VF | XF | Unc | BU |
|---|---|---|---|---|---|---|
| 1931 | 1,500,000 | 2.50 | 9.00 | 25.00 | 75.00 | — |
| 1931 Proof | — | — | — | — | — | — |
| 1933 | 1,100,000 | 2.50 | 9.00 | 25.00 | 75.00 | — |
| 1933 Proof | — | — | — | — | — | — |
| 1933 (error) 1252 | Inc. above | 20.00 | 60.00 | 100 | 200 | — |

**20 FILS** **KM# 106** **Weight:** 3.6000 g. **Composition:** 0.5000 Silver .0579 oz. ASW **Ruler:** Ghazi I

| Date | Mintage | F | VF | XF | Unc | BU |
|---|---|---|---|---|---|---|
| 1938 | 1,200,000 | 2.00 | 3.50 | 8.00 | 22.00 | — |
| 1938 -I | 1,350,000 | 2.00 | 4.00 | 9.00 | 26.00 | — |

**20 FILS** **KM# 113** **Weight:** 3.6000 g. **Composition:** 0.5000 Silver .0579 oz. ASW **Ruler:** Faisal II, King

| Date | Mintage | F | VF | XF | Unc | BU |
|---|---|---|---|---|---|---|
| 1953 | 250,000 | 25.00 | 45.00 | 70.00 | 140 | — |
| 1953 Proof | 200 | Value: 300 | | | | |

**20 FILS** **KM# 116** **Weight:** 2.8000 g. **Composition:** 0.5000 Silver .0450 oz. ASW **Ruler:** Faisal II, King

| Date | Mintage | F | VF | XF | Unc | BU |
|---|---|---|---|---|---|---|
| 1955 | 4,000,000 | 1.50 | 3.00 | 5.00 | 10.00 | — |
| 1955 Proof | — | Value: 80.00 | | | | |

**50 FILS** **KM# 100** **Weight:** 9.0000 g. **Composition:** 0.5000 Silver .1447 oz. ASW **Ruler:** Faisal I

| Date | Mintage | F | VF | XF | Unc | BU |
|---|---|---|---|---|---|---|
| 1931 | 8,800,000 | 3.00 | 10.00 | 28.00 | 80.00 | — |
| 1931 Proof | — | — | — | — | — | — |
| 1933 | 800,000 | 6.00 | 15.00 | 35.00 | 100 | — |
| 1933 Proof | — | — | — | — | — | — |

**50 FILS** **KM# 104** **Weight:** 9.0000 g. **Composition:** 0.5000 Silver .1447 oz. ASW **Ruler:** Ghazi I

| Date | Mintage | F | VF | XF | Unc | BU |
|---|---|---|---|---|---|---|
| 1937 | 1,200,000 | 2.50 | 7.00 | 10.00 | 30.00 | — |
| 1937 Proof | — | — | — | — | — | — |
| 1938 | 5,300,000 | 2.00 | 4.00 | 8.00 | 25.00 | — |
| 1938 Proof | — | — | — | — | — | — |
| 1938 -I | 7,500,000 | 2.00 | 4.00 | 8.00 | 25.00 | — |

**50 FILS** **KM# 114** **Weight:** 9.0000 g. **Composition:** 0.5000 Silver .1447 oz. ASW **Ruler:** Faisal II, King

| Date | Mintage | F | VF | XF | Unc | BU |
|---|---|---|---|---|---|---|
| 1953 | 560,000 | 50.00 | 100 | 150 | 250 | — |
| 1953 Proof | 200 | Value: 450 | | | | |

**50 FILS** **KM# 117** **Weight:** 7.0000 g. **Composition:** 0.5000 Silver .1126 oz. ASW **Ruler:** Faisal II, King

| Date | Mintage | F | VF | XF | Unc | BU |
|---|---|---|---|---|---|---|
| 1955 | 12,000,000 | 2.50 | 4.00 | 6.00 | 11.50 | — |
| 1955 Proof | — | Value: 80.00 | | | | |

**100 FILS** **KM# 115** **Weight:** 10.0000 g. **Composition:** 0.9000 Silver .2893 oz. ASW **Ruler:** Faisal II, King

| Date | Mintage | F | VF | XF | Unc | BU |
|---|---|---|---|---|---|---|
| 1953 | 1,200,000 | 5.00 | 7.50 | 20.00 | 50.00 | — |
| 1953 Proof | 200 | Value: 250 | | | | |

**100 FILS** **KM# 118** **Weight:** 10.0000 g. **Composition:** 0.5000 Silver .1607 oz. ASW **Ruler:** Faisal II, King

| Date | Mintage | F | VF | XF | Unc | BU |
|---|---|---|---|---|---|---|
| 1955 | 1,000,000 | — | 700 | 1,000 | 1,500 | — |
| 1955 Proof | — | Value: 300 | | | | |

**RIYAL (200 Fils)** **KM# 101** **Weight:** 20.0000 g. **Composition:** 0.5000 Silver .3215 oz. ASW **Ruler:** Faisal I **Note:** Dav. #255.

| Date | Mintage | F | VF | XF | Unc | BU |
|---|---|---|---|---|---|---|
| 1932 | 500,000 | 7.50 | 15.00 | 35.00 | 350 | — |
| 1932 Proof | Est. 20 | Value: 1,600 | | | | |

# REPUBLIC

## DECIMAL COINAGE

**FILS** **KM# 119** **Composition:** Bronze

| Date | Mintage | F | VF | XF | Unc | BU |
|---|---|---|---|---|---|---|
| 1959 | 72,000,000 | 0.15 | 0.25 | 0.50 | 1.00 | — |
| 1959 Proof | 400 | Value: 30.00 | | | | |

**5 FILS** **KM# 120** **Composition:** Copper-Nickel

| Date | Mintage | F | VF | XF | Unc | BU |
|---|---|---|---|---|---|---|
| 1959 | 30,000,000 | 0.15 | 0.25 | 0.50 | 1.00 | — |
| 1959 Proof | 400 | Value: 30.00 | | | | |

**5 FILS** **KM# 125** **Composition:** Copper-Nickel

| Date | Mintage | F | VF | XF | Unc | BU |
|---|---|---|---|---|---|---|
| 1967 | 17,000,000 | 0.15 | 0.25 | 0.35 | 0.50 | — |
| 1971 | 15,000,000 | 0.15 | 0.25 | 0.35 | 0.50 | — |

**5 FILS** **KM# 125a** **Composition:** Stainless Steel

| Date | Mintage | F | VF | XF | Unc | BU |
|---|---|---|---|---|---|---|
| 1971 | 2,000,000 | 0.20 | 0.30 | 0.50 | 0.75 | — |
| 1974 | 15,000,000 | 0.10 | 0.15 | 0.25 | 0.35 | — |
| 1975 | 94,800,000 | 0.10 | 0.15 | 0.25 | 0.35 | — |
| 1980 | 20,160,000 | 0.10 | 0.15 | 0.25 | 0.35 | — |
| 1981 | 29,840,000 | 0.10 | 0.15 | 0.25 | 0.35 | — |

**5 FILS** **KM# 141** **Composition:** Stainless Steel **Series:** F.A.O

| Date | Mintage | F | VF | XF | Unc | BU |
|---|---|---|---|---|---|---|
| 1975 | 2,000,000 | 0.10 | 0.15 | 0.25 | 0.50 | — |

**5 FILS** **KM# 159** **Composition:** Stainless Steel
**Reverse :** Babylon - Ruins

| Date | Mintage | F | VF | XF | Unc | BU |
|---|---|---|---|---|---|---|
| 1982 | — | 0.10 | 0.15 | 0.25 | 0.50 | — |

**5 FILS** **KM# 159a** **Composition:** Copper-Nickel

| Date | Mintage | F | VF | XF | Unc | BU |
|---|---|---|---|---|---|---|
| 1982 Proof | — | Value: 3.00 | | | | |

**10 FILS** **KM# 121** **Composition:** Copper-Nickel

| Date | Mintage | F | VF | XF | Unc | BU |
|---|---|---|---|---|---|---|
| 1959 | 24,000,000 | 0.25 | 0.35 | 0.65 | 1.50 | — |
| 1959 Proof | 400 | Value: 30.00 | | | | |

**10 FILS** **KM# 126** **Composition:** Copper-Nickel

| Date | Mintage | F | VF | XF | Unc | BU |
|---|---|---|---|---|---|---|
| 1967 | 13,400,000 | 0.20 | 0.30 | 0.60 | 1.25 | — |
| 1971 | 12,000,000 | 0.20 | 0.30 | 0.60 | 1.25 | — |

**10 FILS** **KM# 126a** **Composition:** Stainless Steel

| Date | Mintage | F | VF | XF | Unc | BU |
|---|---|---|---|---|---|---|
| 1971 | 1,550,000 | 0.25 | 0.35 | 0.65 | 1.50 | — |
| 1974 | 12,000,000 | 0.20 | 0.30 | 0.50 | 1.00 | — |
| 1975 | 52,456,000 | 0.20 | 0.30 | 0.50 | 1.00 | — |
| 1979 | 13,800,000 | 0.20 | 0.30 | 0.50 | 1.00 | — |
| 1980 | 11,264,000 | 0.20 | 0.30 | 0.50 | 1.00 | — |
| 1981 | 63,736,000 | 0.20 | 0.30 | 0.50 | 1.00 | — |

**10 FILS** **KM# 142** **Composition:** Stainless Steel **Series:** F.A.O

| Date | Mintage | F | VF | XF | Unc | BU |
|---|---|---|---|---|---|---|
| 1975 | 1,000,000 | 0.15 | 0.25 | 0.50 | 0.75 | — |

**10 FILS** **KM# 160** **Composition:** Stainless Steel
**Reverse:** Babylon - Ishtar Gate

| Date | Mintage | F | VF | XF | Unc | BU |
|---|---|---|---|---|---|---|
| 1982 | — | — | — | — | 0.75 | — |

**10 FILS** **KM# 160a** **Composition:** Copper-Nickel

| Date | Mintage | F | VF | XF | Unc | BU |
|---|---|---|---|---|---|---|
| 1982 Proof | — | Value: 3.00 | | | | |

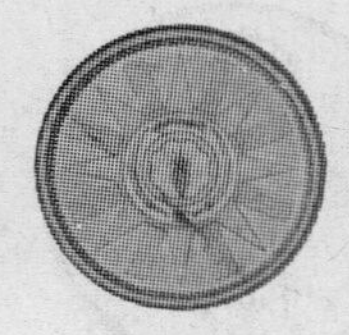

**25 FILS** **KM# 122** **Weight:** 2.5000 g. **Composition:** 0.5000 Silver .0401 oz. ASW

| Date | Mintage | F | VF | XF | Unc | BU |
|---|---|---|---|---|---|---|
| 1959 | 12,000,000 | 0.50 | 0.75 | 1.50 | 3.00 | — |
| 1959 Proof | 400 | Value: 40.00 | | | | |

**25 FILS** **KM# 127** **Composition:** Copper-Nickel

| Date | Mintage | F | VF | XF | Unc | BU |
|---|---|---|---|---|---|---|
| 1969 | 6,000,000 | 0.20 | 0.30 | 0.50 | 1.00 | — |
| 1970 | 6,000,000 | 0.20 | 0.30 | 0.50 | 1.00 | — |
| 1972 | 12,000,000 | 0.20 | 0.30 | 0.50 | 1.00 | — |
| 1975 | 48,000,000 | 0.20 | 0.30 | 0.50 | 1.00 | — |
| 1981 | 60,000,000 | 0.20 | 0.30 | 0.50 | 1.00 | — |

**25 FILS** **KM# 161** **Composition:** Copper-Nickel
**Reverse:** Babylon - Lion

| Date | Mintage | F | VF | XF | Unc | BU |
|---|---|---|---|---|---|---|
| 1982 | — | — | — | — | 1.25 | — |
| 1982 Proof | — | Value: 4.00 | | | | |

**50 FILS** **KM# 123** **Weight:** 5.0000 g. **Composition:** 0.5000 Silver .0803 oz. ASW

| Date | Mintage | F | VF | XF | Unc | BU |
|---|---|---|---|---|---|---|
| 1959 | 24,000,000 | 0.75 | 1.25 | 2.00 | 4.50 | — |
| 1959 Proof | 400 | Value: 80.00 | | | | |

**50 FILS** **KM# 128** **Composition:** Copper-Nickel

| Date | Mintage | F | VF | XF | Unc | BU |
|---|---|---|---|---|---|---|
| 1969 | 12,000,000 | 0.25 | 0.35 | 0.65 | 1.25 | — |
| 1970 | 12,000,000 | 0.25 | 0.35 | 0.65 | 1.25 | — |
| 1972 | 12,000,000 | 0.25 | 0.35 | 0.65 | 1.25 | — |
| 1975 | 36,000,000 | 0.25 | 0.35 | 0.65 | 1.25 | — |
| 1979 | 1,500,000 | 0.25 | 0.35 | 0.65 | 1.75 | — |
| 1980 | 23,520,000 | 0.25 | 0.35 | 0.65 | 1.25 | — |
| 1981 | 138,995,000 | 0.25 | 0.35 | 0.65 | 1.00 | — |
| 1990 | — | 0.25 | 0.35 | 0.65 | 1.00 | — |

**50 FILS** **KM# 162** **Composition:** Copper-Nickel
**Reverse:** Babylon - Bull

| Date | Mintage | F | VF | XF | Unc | BU |
|---|---|---|---|---|---|---|
| 1982 | — | 0.25 | 0.50 | 0.75 | 2.50 | — |
| 1982 Proof | — | Value: 6.00 | | | | |

**100 FILS** **KM# 124** **Weight:** 10.0000 g. **Composition:** 0.5000 Silver .1607 oz. ASW

| Date | Mintage | F | VF | XF | Unc | BU |
|---|---|---|---|---|---|---|
| 1959 | 6,000,000 | 2.00 | 3.00 | 4.50 | 9.00 | — |
| 1959 Proof | 400 | Value: 150 | | | | |

**100 FILS** **KM# 129** **Composition:** Copper-Nickel

| Date | Mintage | F | VF | XF | Unc | BU |
|---|---|---|---|---|---|---|
| 1970 | 6,000,000 | 0.35 | 0.50 | 0.75 | 1.50 | — |
| 1972 | 6,000,000 | 0.35 | 0.50 | 0.75 | 1.50 | — |
| 1975 | 12,000,000 | 0.35 | 0.50 | 0.75 | 1.50 | — |
| 1979 | 1,000,000 | 0.35 | 0.75 | 1.50 | 3.00 | — |

**250 FILS** **KM# 130** **Composition:** Nickel **Series:** F.A.O
**Subject:** Agrarian Reform Day

| Date | Mintage | F | VF | XF | Unc | BU |
|---|---|---|---|---|---|---|
| 1970 | 500,000 | — | 1.50 | 3.00 | 6.00 | — |
| 1970 Proof | 1,000 | Value: 14.50 | | | | |

**Note:** Edge inscription w/FAO-250-repeated three times, relief and incuse varieties reported

**250 FILS** **KM# 131** **Composition:** Nickel **Subject:** 1st Anniversary Peace with Kurds

| Date | Mintage | F | VF | XF | Unc | BU |
|---|---|---|---|---|---|---|
| 1971 | 500,000 | — | 1.50 | 3.00 | 6.00 | — |
| 1971 Proof | 1,000 | Value: 14.50 | | | | |

**250 FILS** **KM# 135** **Composition:** Nickel **Subject:** Silver Jublilee of Al Baath Party

| Date | Mintage | F | VF | XF | Unc | BU |
|---|---|---|---|---|---|---|
| 1972 | 250,000 | — | 1.50 | 3.00 | 6.00 | — |

**250 FILS** **KM# 136** **Composition:** Nickel **Subject:** 25th Anniversary of Central Bank

| Date | Mintage | F | VF | XF | Unc | BU |
|---|---|---|---|---|---|---|
| 1972 | 250,000 | — | 1.50 | 3.00 | 6.00 | — |

**250 FILS** **KM# 138** **Composition:** Nickel **Subject:** Oil Nationalization

| Date | Mintage | F | VF | XF | Unc | BU |
|---|---|---|---|---|---|---|
| 1973 | 260,000 | — | 1.50 | 3.00 | 6.50 | — |
| 1973 Proof | 5,000 | Value: 12.00 | | | | |

**250 FILS** **KM# 144** **Composition:** Nickel **Subject:** International Year of the Child

| Date | Mintage | F | VF | XF | Unc | BU |
|---|---|---|---|---|---|---|
| 1979 Proof | 10,000 | Value: 8.00 | | | | |

**250 FILS** **KM# 146** **Composition:** Copper-Nickel **Subject:** 1st Anniversary of Hussein as President

| Date | Mintage | F | VF | XF | Unc | BU |
|---|---|---|---|---|---|---|
| 1980 | — | — | 1.00 | 2.00 | 5.00 | — |

**250 FILS** **KM# 147** **Composition:** Copper-Nickel

| Date | Mintage | F | VF | XF | Unc | BU |
|---|---|---|---|---|---|---|
| 1980 | — | — | 1.00 | 2.00 | 5.00 | — |
| 1981 | 25,568,000 | — | 1.00 | 2.00 | 5.00 | — |
| 1990 | — | — | 1.00 | 2.00 | 5.00 | — |

**250 FILS** **KM# 152** **Composition:** Copper-Nickel **Subject:** World Food Day

| Date | Mintage | F | VF | XF | Unc | BU |
|---|---|---|---|---|---|---|
| 1981 | 46,432,000 | — | 1.00 | 2.00 | 4.00 | — |

**250 FILS** **KM# 155** **Composition:** Copper-Nickel **Subject:** Nonaligned Nations Baghdad Conference

| Date | Mintage | F | VF | XF | Unc | BU |
|---|---|---|---|---|---|---|
| 1982 | — | — | 1.00 | 2.00 | 5.00 | — |

**250 FILS** **KM# 163** **Composition:** Copper-Nickel **Reverse:** Babylon - Top of Hammurabi Stele

| Date | Mintage | F | VF | XF | Unc | BU |
|---|---|---|---|---|---|---|
| 1982 | — | — | 1.00 | 2.00 | 4.50 | — |
| 1982 Proof | — | Value: 8.00 | | | | |

**500 FILS** **KM# 132** **Composition:** Nickel **Subject:** 50th Anniversary of Iraqi Army

| Date | Mintage | F | VF | XF | Unc | BU |
|---|---|---|---|---|---|---|
| 1971 | 100,000 | — | 2.50 | 4.50 | 10.00 | — |
| 1971 Proof | 5,000 | Value: 15.00 | | | | |

**500 FILS** **KM# 139** **Composition:** Nickel **Subject:** Oil Nationalization

| Date | Mintage | F | VF | XF | Unc | BU |
|---|---|---|---|---|---|---|
| 1973 | 260,000 | — | 2.50 | 4.50 | 10.00 | — |
| 1973 Proof | 5,000 | Value: 15.00 | | | | |

**500 FILS** **KM# 165** **Weight:** 9.0800 g. **Composition:** Nickel **Obverse:** Denomination: "500 Fals"

| Date | Mintage | F | VF | XF | Unc | BU |
|---|---|---|---|---|---|---|
| 1982 | — | — | 2.50 | 4.00 | 7.00 | — |

**500 FILS** **KM# 165a** **Composition:** Nickel **Obverse:** Denomination: "500 Falsan" **Note:** Reduced weight, 8.98 g.

| Date | Mintage | F | VF | XF | Unc | BU |
|---|---|---|---|---|---|---|
| 1982 | — | — | 20.00 | 35.00 | 85.00 | — |

**500 FILS** **KM# 168** **Weight:** 9.0800 g. **Composition:** Nickel **Obverse:** Denomination: "500 Fals" **Reverse:** Babylon - Lion of Babylon

| Date | Mintage | F | VF | XF | Unc | BU |
|---|---|---|---|---|---|---|
| 1982 | — | — | 2.00 | 3.50 | 8.00 | — |
| 1982 Proof | — | Value: 12.50 | | | | |

**500 FILS** **KM# 168a** **Weight:** 9.0800 g. **Composition:** Nickel **Obverse:** Denomination: "500 Falsan"

| Date | Mintage | F | VF | XF | Unc | BU |
|---|---|---|---|---|---|---|
| 1982 | — | — | 15.00 | 25.00 | 75.00 | — |

**DINAR** **KM# 133** **Weight:** 31.0000 g. **Composition:** 0.9000 Silver .8971 oz. ASW **Subject:** 50th Anniversary of Iraqi Army **Obverse:** Similar to 500 Fils, KM#132

| Date | Mintage | F | VF | XF | Unc | BU |
|---|---|---|---|---|---|---|
| 1971 | 20,000 | — | — | — | 22.50 | — |
| 1971 Proof | — | Value: 40.00 | | | | |

**DINAR** **KM# 137** **Weight:** 31.0000 g. **Composition:** 0.5000 Silver .4983 oz. ASW **Subject:** 25th Anniversary of Central Bank **Obverse:** Similar to 250 Fils, KM#136

| Date | Mintage | F | VF | XF | Unc | BU |
|---|---|---|---|---|---|---|
| 1972 | 50,000 | — | — | — | 20.00 | — |
| 1972 Proof | — | Value: 35.00 | | | | |

**DINAR** **KM# 140** **Weight:** 31.0000 g. **Composition:** 0.5000 Silver .4983 oz. ASW **Subject:** Oil Nationalization

| Date | Mintage | F | VF | XF | Unc | BU |
|---|---|---|---|---|---|---|
| 1973 | 60,000 | — | — | — | 20.00 | — |
| 1973 Proof | 5,000 | Value: 37.50 | | | | |

**DINAR** **KM# 143** **Weight:** 31.0000 g. **Composition:** 0.9000 Silver .8971 oz. ASW **Subject:** Inauguaration of Tharthat-Euphrates Canal

| Date | Mintage | F | VF | XF | Unc | BU |
|---|---|---|---|---|---|---|
| 1977 Proof | 7,000 | Value: 40.00 | | | | |

**DINAR** **KM# 145** **Weight:** 31.0000 g. **Composition:** 0.9000 Silver .8971 oz. ASW **Subject:** International Year of the Child

| Date | Mintage | F | VF | XF | Unc | BU |
|---|---|---|---|---|---|---|
| 1979 Proof | 5,000 | Value: 47.50 | | | | |

**Note:** KM#145 is commonly found impaired. Value listed is for unimpaired Proof

**DINAR** **KM# 148** **Weight:** 30.5300 g. **Composition:** 0.9000 Silver .8835 oz. ASW **Subject:** 15thCentury of Hegira

| Date | Mintage | F | VF | XF | Unc | BU |
|---|---|---|---|---|---|---|
| 1980 Proof | 25,000 | Value: 50.00 | | | | |

**Note:** KM#148 is commonly found impaired. Value listed is for unimpaired Proof

**DINAR** **KM# 149** **Composition:** Nickel **Subject:** Battle of Qadissyiat **Reverse:** Bust of Saddam Hussein left

| Date | Mintage | F | VF | XF | Unc | BU |
|---|---|---|---|---|---|---|
| 1980 | — | — | — | 3.50 | 8.00 | — |
| 1980 Proof | — | Value: 12.50 | | | | |

**DINAR** **KM# 153** **Composition:** Nickel **Subject:** 50th Anniversary of Iraq Air Force **Reverse:** Bust of Saddam Hussein left

| Date | Mintage | F | VF | XF | Unc | BU |
|---|---|---|---|---|---|---|
| 1981 | — | — | — | 3.50 | 8.00 | — |

**DINAR** **KM# 170** **Composition:** Nickel **Subject:** Circulation Coinage

| Date | Mintage | F | VF | XF | Unc | BU |
|---|---|---|---|---|---|---|
| 1981 | — | — | — | — | 6.50 | — |

**DINAR** **KM# 156** **Composition:** Nickel **Subject:** Non-aligned Nations Baghdad Conference

| Date | Mintage | F | VF | XF | Unc | BU |
|---|---|---|---|---|---|---|
| 1982 | — | — | — | 3.50 | 8.00 | — |

**DINAR** **KM# 164** **Composition:** Nickel **Reverse:** Tower of Babylon

| Date | Mintage | F | VF | XF | Unc | BU |
|---|---|---|---|---|---|---|
| 1982 | — | — | — | 3.50 | 8.00 | — |
| 1982 Proof | — | Value: 12.50 | | | | |

**5 DINARS** **KM# 134** **Weight:** 13.5700 g. **Composition:** 0.9170 Gold .4001 oz. AGW **Subject:** 50th Anniversary of Iraqi Army

| Date | Mintage | F | VF | XF | Unc | BU |
|---|---|---|---|---|---|---|
| 1971 | 20,000 | — | — | — | 225 | — |
| 1971 Proof | — | Value: 250 | | | | |

**5 DINARS** **KM# 171** **Composition:** Bronze **Obverse:** Denomination and legend **Reverse:** Two swords rched above palm tree

| Date | Mintage | F | VF | XF | Unc | BU |
|---|---|---|---|---|---|---|
| 1990 | — | — | — | — | — | — |

**Note:** Not released to circulation

**10 DINARS** **KM# 172** **Composition:** Bronze **Obverse:** Denomination and legend **Reverse:** Two swords rched above palm tree

| Date | Mintage | F | VF | XF | Unc | BU |
|---|---|---|---|---|---|---|
| 1990 | — | — | — | — | — | — |

**Note:** Not released to circulation

**50 DINARS** **KM# 166** **Weight:** 13.7000 g. **Composition:** 0.9170 Gold .4037 oz. AGW **Subject:** International Year of the Child

| Date | Mintage | F | VF | XF | Unc | BU |
|---|---|---|---|---|---|---|
| 1979 Proof | 10,000 | Value: 280 | | | | |
| 1979 Impaired Proof - BV + 10% | Inc. above | — | — | — | — | — |

**50 DINARS** **KM# 150** **Weight:** 13.0000 g. **Composition:** 0.9170 Gold .3832 oz. AGW **Subject:** 1th Century of Hegira

| Date | Mintage | F | VF | XF | Unc | BU |
|---|---|---|---|---|---|---|
| 1980 Proof | 13,000 | Value: 225 | | | | |
| 1980 Impaired Proof BV + 10% | Inc. above | — | — | — | — | — |

**50 DINARS** **KM# 173** **Weight:** 16.9650 g. **Composition:** 0.9170 Gold .5002 oz. AGW **Subject:** 1st Anniversary of Hussein as President

| Date | Mintage | F | VF | XF | Unc | BU |
|---|---|---|---|---|---|---|
| 1980 Proof | — | Value: 375 | | | | |

**50 DINARS** **KM# 157** **Weight:** 13.7000 g. **Composition:** 0.9170 Gold .4040 oz. AGW **Subject:** Nonaligned Nations Baghdad Conference

| Date | Mintage | F | VF | XF | Unc | BU |
|---|---|---|---|---|---|---|
| 1982 Proof | 10,000 | Value: 225 | | | | |

**100 DINARS** KM# 167 **Weight:** 26.0000 g. **Composition:** 0.9170 Gold .7665 oz. AGW **Subject:** International Year of the Child

| Date | Mintage | F | VF | XF | Unc | BU |
|---|---|---|---|---|---|---|
| 1979 Impaired Proof - BV + 10% | Inc. above | — | — | — | — | — |
| 1979 Proof | 10,000 | Value: 450 | | | | |

**100 DINARS** KM# 151 **Weight:** 26.0000 g. **Composition:** 0.9170 Gold .7665 oz. AGW **Subject:** 15th Century of Hegira

| Date | Mintage | F | VF | XF | Unc | BU |
|---|---|---|---|---|---|---|
| 1980 Proof | 14,000 | Value: 400 | | | | |
| 1980 Impaired Proof - BV + 10% | Inc. above | — | — | — | — | — |

**100 DINARS** KM# 174 **Weight:** 33.9300 g. **Composition:** 0.9170 Gold 1.0003 oz. AGW **Subject:** 1st Anniversary of Hussein as President

| Date | Mintage | F | VF | XF | Unc | BU |
|---|---|---|---|---|---|---|
| 1980 Proof | — | Value: 725 | | | | |

**100 DINARS** KM# 158 **Weight:** 33.9300 g. **Composition:** 0.9170 Gold 1.0003 oz. AGW **Subject:** Nonaligned Nations Baghdad Conference

| Date | Mintage | F | VF | XF | Unc | BU |
|---|---|---|---|---|---|---|
| 1982 Proof | 10,000 | Value: 400 | | | | |

## MEDALLIC COINAGE

**500 FILS** KM# M1 **Weight:** 37.5000 g. **Composition:** 0.5000 Silver .6028 oz. ASW **Subject:** 1st Anniversary of the Republic **Obverse:** Bust of General Abdul Karim Kassem

| Date | Mintage | F | VF | XF | Unc | BU |
|---|---|---|---|---|---|---|
| 1959 | 500,000 | — | 6.50 | 12.50 | 22.50 | — |
| 1959 Proof | — | Value: 50.00 | | | | |

**50 DINARS** KM# M3 **Weight:** 16.9650 g. **Composition:** 0.9170 Gold .5002 oz. AGW **Subject:** 1st Anniversary of Hussein as President **Obverse:** Bust 3/4 left above Legend **Reverse:** Arabic legend

| Date | Mintage | F | VF | XF | Unc | BU |
|---|---|---|---|---|---|---|
| 1980 Proof | 10,000 | Value: 300 | | | | |

**100 DINARS** KM# M2 **Weight:** 38.0000 g. **Composition:** 0.9170 Gold 1.1200 oz. AGW **Subject:** Battle of Gadissyiat **Obverse:** Bust of Saddam Hussein

| Date | Mintage | F | VF | XF | Unc | BU |
|---|---|---|---|---|---|---|
| 1980 | — | — | — | — | 550 | — |

## PATTERNS

Including off metal strikes

| KM# | Date | Mintage | Identification | Mkt Val |
|---|---|---|---|---|
| Pn1 | 1935 | — | 20 Fils. KM106. | 450 |
| Pn2 | 1935 | — | 50 Fils. KM104. | 450 |
| Pn3 | 1936 | — | 2 Fils. KM96. | 250 |
| Pn4 | 1936 | — | 4 Fils. KM105. | 275 |
| Pn5 | 1936 | — | 10 Fils. KM103. | 325 |
| Pn6 | 1936 | — | 20 Fils. KM106. | 425 |
| Pn7 | 1936 | — | 50 Fils. KM104. | 450 |

## PROOF SETS

| KM# | Date | Mintage | Identification | Issue Price | Mkt Val |
|---|---|---|---|---|---|
| PS1 | 1953 (7) | 200 | KM109-115 | — | 1,325 |
| PS2 | 1955 (3) | — | KM116-118 | — | 500 |
| PS3 | 1959 (6) | 400 | KM119-124 | — | 360 |
| PS4 | 1959 (7) | — | KM119-124, plus medallic crown (M1) | — | 400 |
| PS5 | 1973 (3) | 5,000 | KM138-140 | — | 62.00 |
| PS6 | 1982 (7) | — | KM159a-160a, 161-164, 168 | — | 50.00 |

# IRELAND REPUBLIC

The Republic of Ireland, which occupies five-sixths of the island of Ireland located in the Atlantic Ocean west of Great Britain, has an area of 27,136 sq. mi. (70,280 sq. km.) and a population of 4.3 million. Capital: Dublin. Agriculture and dairy farming are the principal industries. Meat, livestock, dairy products and textiles are exported.

A race of tall, red-haired Celts from Gaul arrived in Ireland about 400 B.C., assimilated the native Erainn and Picts, and established a Gaelic civilization. After the arrival of St. Patrick in 432AD, Ireland evolved into a center of Latin learning, which sent missionaries to Europe and possibly North America. In 1154, Pope Adrian IV gave all of Ireland to English King Henry II to administer as a Papal fief. Because of the enactment of anti-Catholic laws and the awarding of vast tracts of Irish land to Protestant absentee landowners, English control did not become reasonably absolute until 1800 when England and Ireland became the 'United Kingdom of Great Britain and Ireland'. Religious freedom was restored to the Irish in 1829, but agitation for political autonomy continued until the Irish Free State was established as a dominion on Dec. 6, 1921.Ireland proclaimed itself a republic on April 18, 1949. The government, however, does not use the term 'Republic of Ireland', which tacitly acknowledges the partitioning of the island into Ireland and Northern Ireland, but refers to the country simply as 'Ireland'.

**RULERS**

British, until 1921

**MONETARY SYSTEM**

**(1928-1971)**

4 Farthings = 1 Penny
12 Pence = 1 Shilling
2 Shillings = 1 Florin
20 Shillings = 1 Pound

**NOTE:** This section has been renumbered to segregate the coinage of the Irish Free State from the earlier crown coinage of Ireland.

# IRISH FREE STATE

## STERLING COINAGE

**FARTHING** KM# 1 **Composition:** Bronze **Obv. Legend:** SAORSTAT EIREANN = Irish Free State **Reverse:** European woodcock

| Date | Mintage | F | VF | XF | Unc | BU |
|---|---|---|---|---|---|---|
| 1928 | 300,000 | 0.50 | 1.50 | 4.50 | 10.00 | — |
| 1928 Proof | 6,001 | Value: 15.00 | | | | |
| 1930 | 288,000 | 0.75 | 1.50 | 4.50 | 16.50 | — |
| 1931 | 192,000 | 4.50 | 8.00 | 15.00 | 35.00 | — |
| 1931 Proof | — | — | — | — | — | — |
| 1932 | 192,000 | 5.00 | 10.00 | 18.00 | 45.00 | — |
| 1933 | 480,000 | 0.75 | 1.50 | 4.00 | 16.50 | — |
| 1935 | 192,000 | 5.00 | 8.00 | 15.00 | 35.00 | — |
| 1936 | 192,000 | 5.00 | 8.00 | 16.50 | 37.50 | — |
| 1937 | 480,000 | 0.50 | 1.50 | 3.00 | 14.50 | — |

**1/2 PENNY** KM# 2 **Composition:** Bronze **Obv. Legend:** SAORSTATE EIREANN = Irish Free State **Reverse:** Sow with piglets

| Date | Mintage | F | VF | XF | Unc | BU |
|---|---|---|---|---|---|---|
| 1928 | 2,880,000 | 0.75 | 2.00 | 5.00 | 14.00 | — |
| 1928 Proof | 6,001 | Value: 15.00 | | | | |
| 1933 | 720,000 | 5.00 | 15.00 | 80.00 | 750 | — |
| 1935 | 960,000 | 2.00 | 6.00 | 50.00 | 275 | — |
| 1937 | 960,000 | 1.00 | 3.00 | 15.00 | 35.00 | — |

**PENNY** KM# 3 **Composition:** Bronze **Obv. Legend:** SAORSTATE EIREANN = Irish Free State **Reverse:** Hen with chicks

| Date | Mintage | F | VF | XF | Unc | BU |
|---|---|---|---|---|---|---|
| 1928 | 9,000,000 | 0.50 | 1.00 | 4.00 | 20.00 | — |
| 1928 Proof | 6,001 | Value: 18.50 | | | | |
| 1931 | 2,400,000 | 1.00 | 2.00 | 12.00 | 50.00 | — |
| 1931 Proof | — | Value: 1,500 | | | | |
| 1933 | 1,680,000 | 1.00 | 2.50 | 20.00 | 125 | — |
| 1935 | 5,472,000 | 0.50 | 1.00 | 8.00 | 32.00 | — |
| 1937 | 5,400,000 | 0.50 | 1.00 | 15.00 | 70.00 | — |
| 1937 Proof | — | Value: 12.50 | | | | |

**3 PENCE** KM# 4 **Composition:** Nickel **Obv. Legend:** SAORSTATE EIREANN = Irish Free State **Reverse:** Hare

| Date | Mintage | F | VF | XF | Unc | BU |
|---|---|---|---|---|---|---|
| 1928 | 1,500,000 | 0.50 | 1.00 | 3.50 | 10.00 | — |
| 1928 Proof | 6,001 | Value: 20.00 | | | | |
| 1933 | 320,000 | 3.00 | 10.00 | 75.00 | 400 | — |
| 1934 | 800,000 | 1.00 | 2.00 | 12.50 | 70.00 | — |
| 1935 | 240,000 | 3.00 | 8.00 | 35.00 | 225 | — |

**6 PENCE** KM# 5 **Composition:** Nickel **Obv. Legend:** SAORSTATE EIREANN = Irish Free State **Reverse:** Irish wolf-hound

| Date | Mintage | F | VF | XF | Unc | BU |
|---|---|---|---|---|---|---|
| 1928 | 3,201,000 | 0.50 | 1.00 | 5.00 | 17.50 | — |
| 1928 Proof | 6,001 | Value: 25.00 | | | | |
| 1934 | 600,000 | 1.00 | 2.00 | 18.00 | 120 | — |
| 1935 | 520,000 | 1.00 | 3.00 | 30.00 | 320 | — |

**SHILLING** KM# 6 **Weight:** 5.6552 g. **Composition:** 0.7500 Silver .1364 oz. ASW **Obv. Legend:** SAORSTAT EIREANN = Irish Free State **Reverse:** Bull

| Date | Mintage | F | VF | XF | Unc | BU |
|---|---|---|---|---|---|---|
| 1928 | 2,700,000 | 1.50 | 5.00 | 10.00 | 22.50 | — |
| 1928 Proof | 6,001 | Value: 27.50 | | | | |
| 1930 | 460,000 | 5.00 | 25.00 | 150 | 550 | — |
| 1930 | — | Value: 1,200 | | | | |
| 1931 | 400,000 | 4.50 | 18.00 | 90.00 | 225 | — |
| 1933 | 300,000 | 5.00 | 20.00 | 100 | 325 | — |
| 1935 | 400,000 | 2.00 | 7.00 | 25.00 | 85.00 | — |
| 1937 | 100,000 | 12.00 | 65.00 | 500 | 2,000 | — |

**FLORIN** KM# 7 **Weight:** 11.3104 g. **Composition:** 0.7500 Silver .2727 oz. ASW **Obv. Legend:** SAORSTAT EIREANN = Irish Free State **Reverse:** Salmon

| Date | Mintage | F | VF | XF | Unc | BU |
|---|---|---|---|---|---|---|
| 1928 | 2,025,000 | 3.00 | 7.00 | 15.00 | 40.00 | — |
| 1928 Proof | 6,001 | Value: 42.50 | | | | |
| 1930 | 330,000 | 6.50 | 25.00 | 135 | 400 | — |
| 1931 | 200,000 | 8.00 | 35.00 | 225 | 500 | — |
| 1933 | 300,000 | 5.00 | 25.00 | 195 | 575 | — |
| 1934 | 150,000 | 10.00 | 60.00 | 325 | 750 | — |
| 1934 Proof | — | Value: 2,750 | | | | |
| 1935 | 390,000 | 5.00 | 17.50 | 65.00 | 185 | — |
| 1937 | 150,000 | 10.00 | 35.00 | 210 | 750 | — |

**1/2 CROWN** KM# 8 **Weight:** 14.1380 g. **Composition:** 0.7500 Silver .3409 oz. ASW **Obv. Legend:** SAORSTAT EIREANN = Irish Free State **Reverse:** Close O and I in COROIN, 8 tufts in horse's tail, with 156 beads in border **Note:** Irish hunter.

| Date | Mintage | F | VF | XF | Unc | BU |
|---|---|---|---|---|---|---|
| 1928 | 2,160,000 | 3.50 | 10.00 | 20.00 | 45.00 | — |
| 1928 Proof | 6,001 | Value: 55.00 | | | | |
| 1930 | 352,000 | 4.50 | 20.00 | 125 | 400 | — |
| 1931 | 160,000 | 9.00 | 30.00 | 250 | 650 | — |
| 1933 | 336,000 | 4.50 | 20.00 | 125 | 400 | — |
| 1934 | 480,000 | 4.00 | 15.00 | 40.00 | 150 | — |
| 1937 | 40,000 | 65.00 | 150 | 750 | 1,750 | — |

# IRELAND
## (Republic)

## STERLING COINAGE

**FARTHING** KM# 9 **Composition:** Bronze **Obv. Legend:** EIRE = Ireland **Reverse:** European woodcock

| Date | Mintage | F | VF | XF | Unc | BU |
|---|---|---|---|---|---|---|
| 1939 | 786,000 | 0.50 | 1.00 | 2.00 | 7.50 | — |
| 1939 Proof | — | Value: 815 | | | | |
| 1940 | 192,000 | 2.00 | 4.00 | 8.00 | 20.00 | — |
| 1941 | 480,000 | 0.50 | 0.75 | 2.00 | 6.50 | — |
| 1943 | 480,000 | 0.50 | 0.75 | 2.00 | 6.50 | — |
| 1944 | 480,000 | 0.75 | 1.25 | 3.00 | 10.00 | — |
| 1946 | 480,000 | 0.50 | 0.75 | 2.00 | 6.00 | — |
| 1946 Proof | — | — | — | — | — | — |
| 1949 | 192,000 | 0.75 | 3.00 | 6.00 | 18.00 | — |
| 1949 Proof | — | Value: 300 | | | | |
| 1953 | 192,000 | 0.25 | 0.50 | 1.25 | 3.00 | — |
| 1953 Proof | — | Value: 300 | | | | |
| 1959 | 192,000 | 0.25 | 0.50 | 1.25 | 3.00 | — |
| 1966 | 96,000 | 0.35 | 0.75 | 1.50 | 3.50 | — |

**1/2 PENNY** KM# 10 **Composition:** Bronze **Obv. Legend:** EIRE = Ireland **Reverse:** Sow with piglets

| Date | Mintage | F | VF | XF | Unc | BU |
|---|---|---|---|---|---|---|
| 1939 | 240,000 | 10.00 | 17.50 | 60.00 | 200 | — |
| 1939 Proof | — | Value: 1,000 | | | | |
| 1940 | 1,680,000 | 1.00 | 4.50 | 40.00 | 150 | — |
| 1941 | 2,400,000 | 0.20 | 0.50 | 2.50 | 20.00 | — |
| 1942 | 6,931,000 | 0.10 | 0.25 | 1.50 | 8.00 | — |
| 1943 | 2,669,000 | 0.20 | 0.50 | 3.00 | 22.00 | — |
| 1946 | 720,000 | 1.00 | 2.50 | 15.00 | 60.00 | — |
| 1949 | 1,344,000 | 0.10 | 0.25 | 1.50 | 12.50 | — |
| 1949 Proof | — | — | — | — | — | — |
| 1953 | 2,400,000 | 0.10 | 0.15 | 0.25 | 1.00 | — |
| 1953 Proof | — | Value: 400 | | | | |
| 1964 | 2,160,000 | 0.10 | 0.15 | 0.25 | 1.00 | — |
| 1965 | 1,440,000 | 0.10 | 0.15 | 0.75 | 2.00 | — |
| 1966 | 1,680,000 | 0.10 | 0.15 | 0.25 | 1.00 | — |
| 1967 | 1,200,000 | 0.10 | 0.15 | 0.25 | 1.00 | — |

**PENNY** KM# 11 **Composition:** Bronze **Obv. Legend:** EIRE = Ireland **Reverse:** Hen with chicks

| Date | Mintage | F | VF | XF | Unc | BU |
|---|---|---|---|---|---|---|
| 1940 | 312,000 | 3.00 | 10.00 | 65.00 | 225 | — |
| 1941 | 4,680,000 | 0.25 | 0.50 | 8.00 | 50.00 | — |
| 1942 | 17,520,000 | 0.25 | 0.50 | 2.00 | 11.50 | — |
| 1943 | 3,360,000 | 0.75 | 1.50 | 7.50 | 45.00 | — |
| 1946 | 4,800,000 | 0.25 | 0.50 | 3.00 | 20.00 | — |
| 1948 | 4,800,000 | 0.25 | 0.50 | 3.00 | 8.00 | — |
| 1949 | 4,080,000 | 0.25 | 0.50 | 3.00 | 8.00 | — |
| 1949 Proof | — | Value: 600 | | | | |
| 1950 | 2,400,000 | 0.25 | 0.50 | 3.50 | 12.50 | — |
| 1950 Proof | — | Value: 600 | | | | |
| 1952 | 2,400,000 | 0.25 | 0.50 | 2.00 | 6.00 | — |
| 1962 | 1,200,000 | 0.75 | 2.50 | 3.50 | 12.50 | — |
| 1962 Proof | — | Value: 175 | | | | |
| 1963 | 9,600,000 | 0.20 | 0.40 | 0.75 | 2.00 | — |
| 1963 Proof | — | Value: 175 | | | | |
| 1964 | 6,000,000 | 0.20 | 0.40 | 0.75 | 1.50 | — |
| 1964 Proof | — | — | — | — | — | — |
| 1965 | 11,160,000 | 0.20 | 0.40 | 0.75 | 1.50 | — |
| 1966 | 6,000,000 | 0.20 | 0.40 | 0.75 | 1.50 | — |
| 1967 | 2,400,000 | 0.20 | 0.40 | 0.75 | 1.50 | — |
| 1968 | 21,000,000 | 0.20 | 0.40 | 0.75 | 1.50 | — |
| 1968 Proof | — | Value: 350 | | | | |

**Note:** Varieties exist

**3 PENCE** KM# 12 **Composition:** Nickel **Obv. Legend:** EIRE = Ireland **Reverse:** Hare

| Date | Mintage | F | VF | XF | Unc | BU |
|---|---|---|---|---|---|---|
| 1939 | 64,000 | 10.00 | 20.00 | 70.00 | 525 | — |
| 1939 Proof | — | Value: 1,500 | | | | |
| 1940 | 720,000 | 1.50 | 3.00 | 12.50 | 50.00 | — |

**3 PENCE** KM# 12a **Composition:** Copper-Nickel **Obv. Legend:** EIRE = Ireland **Reverse:** Hare

| Date | Mintage | F | VF | XF | Unc | BU |
|---|---|---|---|---|---|---|
| 1942 | 4,000,000 | 0.25 | 0.75 | 6.00 | 30.00 | — |
| 1942 Proof | — | Value: 350 | | | | |
| 1943 | 1,360,000 | 0.50 | 2.00 | 15.00 | 80.00 | — |
| 1943 Proof | — | — | — | — | — | — |
| 1946 | 800,000 | 1.00 | 2.00 | 10.00 | 45.00 | — |
| 1946 Proof | — | Value: 200 | | | | |
| 1948 | 1,600,000 | 1.00 | 2.00 | 35.00 | 125 | — |
| 1949 | 1,200,000 | 0.25 | 0.50 | 3.00 | 25.00 | — |
| 1949 Proof | — | Value: 200 | | | | |
| 1950 | 1,600,000 | 0.25 | 0.50 | 3.00 | 20.00 | — |
| 1950 Proof | — | Value: 400 | | | | |
| 1953 | 1,600,000 | 0.25 | 0.50 | 2.00 | 10.00 | — |
| 1956 | 1,200,000 | 0.25 | 0.50 | 2.00 | 8.00 | — |
| 1961 | 2,400,000 | 0.15 | 0.25 | 0.50 | 6.00 | — |
| 1962 | 3,200,000 | 0.15 | 0.25 | 0.50 | 8.00 | — |
| 1963 | 4,000,000 | 0.15 | 0.25 | 0.50 | 2.50 | — |
| 1964 | 4,000,000 | 0.10 | 0.15 | 0.25 | 1.50 | — |
| 1965 | 3,600,000 | 0.10 | 0.15 | 0.25 | 1.50 | — |
| 1966 | 4,000,000 | 0.10 | 0.15 | 0.25 | 1.00 | — |
| 1967 | 2,400,000 | 0.10 | 0.15 | 0.25 | 1.00 | — |
| 1968 | 4,000,000 | 0.10 | 0.15 | 0.25 | 1.00 | — |
| 1968 Proof | — | — | — | — | — | — |

**6 PENCE** KM# 13 **Composition:** Nickel **Obv. Legend:** EIRE = Ireland **Reverse:** Irish wolf-hound

| Date | Mintage | F | VF | XF | Unc | BU |
|---|---|---|---|---|---|---|
| 1939 | 876,000 | 0.75 | 2.00 | 8.00 | 55.00 | — |
| 1939 Proof | — | Value: 1,150 | | | | |
| 1940 | 1,120,000 | 0.75 | 2.00 | 6.00 | 45.00 | — |

**6 PENCE** KM# 13a **Composition:** Copper-Nickel **Obv. Legend:** EIRE = Ireland **Reverse:** Irish wolf-hound

| Date | Mintage | F | VF | XF | Unc | BU |
|---|---|---|---|---|---|---|
| 1942 | 1,320,000 | 0.50 | 1.00 | 5.00 | 40.00 | — |
| 1945 | 400,000 | 2.00 | 8.00 | 50.00 | 160 | — |

| Date | Mintage | F | VF | XF | Unc | BU |
|---|---|---|---|---|---|---|
| 1946 | 720,000 | 2.00 | 10.00 | 100 | 450 | — |
| 1947 | 800,000 | 1.00 | 12.00 | 30.00 | 70.00 | — |
| 1948 | 800,000 | 1.00 | 1.50 | 10.00 | 55.00 | — |
| 1949 | 600,000 | 1.50 | 3.50 | 15.00 | 65.00 | — |
| 1950 | 800,000 | 1.00 | 3.00 | 12.00 | 60.00 | — |
| 1952 | 800,000 | 0.50 | 1.00 | 5.00 | 20.00 | — |
| 1952 Proof | — | Value: 175 | | | | |
| 1953 | 800,000 | 0.50 | 1.00 | 5.00 | 18.00 | — |
| 1955 | 600,000 | 1.00 | 2.50 | 8.00 | 20.00 | — |
| 1956 | 600,000 | 0.75 | 2.00 | 4.00 | 15.00 | — |
| 1958 | 600,000 | 1.00 | 2.50 | 6.00 | 65.00 | — |
| 1958 | — | Value: 350 | | | | |
| 1959 | 2,000,000 | 0.25 | 0.50 | 3.00 | 15.00 | — |
| 1960 | 2,020,000 | 0.25 | 0.50 | 2.00 | 12.00 | — |
| 1961 | 3,000,000 | 0.25 | 0.25 | 1.00 | 6.50 | — |
| 1962 | 4,000,000 | 0.25 | 0.75 | 4.00 | 60.00 | — |
| 1963 | 4,000,000 | 0.15 | 0.25 | 0.50 | 3.00 | — |
| 1964 | 6,000,000 | 0.15 | 0.25 | 0.50 | 3.00 | — |
| 1966 | 2,000,000 | 0.15 | 0.25 | 0.50 | 1.50 | — |
| 1967 | 4,000,000 | 0.15 | 0.25 | 0.50 | 1.50 | — |
| 1968 | 8,000,000 | 0.15 | 0.25 | 0.50 | 1.50 | — |
| 1969 | 2,000,000 | 0.15 | 0.25 | 0.50 | 1.50 | — |

**SHILLING** **KM# 14** **Weight:** 5.6552 g. **Composition:** 0.7500 Silver .1364 oz. ASW **Obv. Legend:** EIRE = Ireland **Reverse:** Bull

| Date | Mintage | F | VF | XF | Unc | BU |
|---|---|---|---|---|---|---|
| 1939 | 1,140,000 | 2.50 | 4.50 | 12.50 | 32.50 | — |
| 1939 Proof | — | Value: 775 | | | | |
| 1940 | 580,000 | 3.00 | 5.00 | 15.00 | 40.00 | — |
| 1941 | 300,000 | 4.00 | 12.00 | 22.50 | 45.00 | — |
| 1942 | 286,000 | 4.00 | 7.50 | 15.00 | 40.00 | — |

**SHILLING** **KM# 14a** **Composition:** Copper-Nickel **Obv. Legend:** EIRE = Ireland **Reverse:** Bull

| Date | Mintage | F | VF | XF | Unc | BU |
|---|---|---|---|---|---|---|
| 1951 | 2,000,000 | 0.25 | 0.50 | 2.50 | 15.00 | — |
| 1951 Proof | — | Value: 500 | | | | |
| 1954 | 3,000,000 | 0.25 | 0.50 | 2.50 | 11.50 | — |
| 1954 Proof | — | — | — | — | — | — |
| 1955 | 1,000,000 | 1.00 | 2.00 | 5.00 | 15.00 | — |
| 1955 Proof | — | — | — | — | — | — |
| 1959 | 2,000,000 | 0.25 | 0.50 | 4.00 | 35.00 | — |
| 1962 | 4,000,000 | 0.25 | 0.50 | 1.00 | 7.00 | — |
| 1963 | 4,000,000 | 0.25 | 0.50 | 1.00 | 3.00 | — |
| 1964 | 4,000,000 | 0.25 | 0.50 | 1.00 | 2.00 | — |
| 1966 | 3,000,000 | 0.25 | 0.50 | 1.00 | 2.00 | — |
| 1968 | 4,000,000 | 0.25 | 0.50 | 1.00 | 3.00 | — |

**FLORIN** **KM# 15** **Weight:** 11.3104 g. **Composition:** 0.7500 Silver .2727 oz. ASW **Obv. Legend:** EIRE = Ireland **Reverse:** Salmon

| Date | Mintage | F | VF | XF | Unc | BU |
|---|---|---|---|---|---|---|
| 1939 | 1,080,000 | 2.00 | 5.00 | 18.00 | 40.00 | — |
| 1939 Proof | — | Value: 800 | | | | |
| 1940 | 670,000 | 3.00 | 6.00 | 20.00 | 45.00 | — |
| 1941 | 400,000 | 3.00 | 8.00 | 22.50 | 55.00 | — |
| 1941 Proof | — | Value: 800 | | | | |
| 1942 | 109,000 | 5.00 | 15.00 | 25.00 | 50.00 | — |
| 1943 | — | 1,200 | 2,000 | 4,000 | 8,000 | — |

**Note:** Approximately 35 known

**FLORIN** **KM# 15a** **Composition:** Copper-Nickel **Obv. Legend:** EIRE = Ireland **Reverse:** Salmon

| Date | Mintage | F | VF | XF | Unc | BU |
|---|---|---|---|---|---|---|
| 1951 | 1,000,000 | 1.00 | 2.00 | 6.00 | 16.00 | — |
| 1951 Proof | — | Value: 600 | | | | |
| 1954 | 1,000,000 | 1.00 | 2.00 | 6.00 | 18.00 | — |
| 1954 Proof | — | Value: 450 | | | | |
| 1955 | 1,000,000 | 1.00 | 2.00 | 5.00 | 15.00 | — |
| 1955 Proof | — | Value: 450 | | | | |
| 1959 | 2,000,000 | 0.50 | 1.00 | 2.50 | 10.00 | — |
| 1961 | 2,000,000 | 0.50 | 1.00 | 7.00 | 22.00 | — |
| 1962 | 2,400,000 | 0.50 | 1.00 | 2.00 | 10.00 | — |
| 1963 | 3,000,000 | 0.25 | 0.50 | 0.75 | 4.00 | — |
| 1964 | 4,000,000 | 0.25 | 0.50 | 0.75 | 2.00 | — |
| 1965 | 2,000,000 | 0.25 | 0.50 | 0.75 | 2.00 | — |
| 1966 | 3,625,000 | 0.25 | 0.50 | 0.75 | 2.00 | — |
| 1968 | 1,000,000 | 0.25 | 0.35 | 1.00 | 4.50 | — |

**1/2 CROWN** **KM# 16** **Weight:** 14.1380 g. **Composition:** 0.7500 Silver .3409 oz. ASW **Obv. Legend:** EIRE = Ireland **Reverse:** Normal spacing between O and I in COROIN, 7 tufts in horse's tail, with 151 beads in border **Note:** Irish hunter.

| Date | Mintage | F | VF | XF | Unc | BU |
|---|---|---|---|---|---|---|
| 1939 | 888,000 | 3.00 | 8.00 | 17.50 | 55.00 | — |
| 1939 Proof | — | Value: 800 | | | | |
| 1940 | 752,000 | 3.00 | 8.00 | 15.00 | 50.00 | — |
| 1941 | 320,000 | 4.00 | 12.50 | 30.00 | 75.00 | — |
| 1942 | 286,000 | 4.00 | 12.50 | 25.00 | 50.00 | — |

**1/2 CROWN** **KM# 16a** **Composition:** Copper-Nickel **Obv. Legend:** EIRE = Ireland **Reverse:** Normal spacing between O and I in COROIN, 7 tufts in horse's tail, with 151 beads in border **Note:** Irish hunter.

| Date | Mintage | F | VF | XF | Unc | BU |
|---|---|---|---|---|---|---|
| 1951 | 800,000 | 1.50 | 3.00 | 10.00 | 35.00 | — |
| 1951 Proof | — | Value: 600 | | | | |
| 1954 | 400,000 | 2.00 | 4.00 | 15.00 | 50.00 | — |
| 1954 Proof | — | Value: 500 | | | | |
| 1955 | 1,080,000 | 1.00 | 2.00 | 6.00 | 25.00 | — |
| 1955 Proof | — | Value: 200 | | | | |
| 1959 | 1,600,000 | 1.00 | 1.75 | 3.00 | 12.50 | — |
| 1961 | 1,600,000 | 1.00 | 1.75 | 3.50 | 20.00 | — |
| 1961 Proof | — | — | — | — | — | — |
| 1962 | 3,200,000 | 0.50 | 1.00 | 2.50 | 12.50 | — |
| 1962 Proof | — | — | — | — | — | — |
| 1963 | 2,400,000 | 0.50 | 1.00 | 2.00 | 7.50 | — |
| 1964 | 3,200,000 | 0.50 | 1.00 | 2.00 | 6.00 | — |
| 1966 | 700,000 | 0.75 | 1.50 | 3.00 | 6.00 | — |
| 1967 | 2,000,000 | 0.50 | 1.00 | 2.00 | 6.00 | — |

**Note:** 1967 exists struck with a polished reverse die. Estimated value is $15.00 in uncirculated

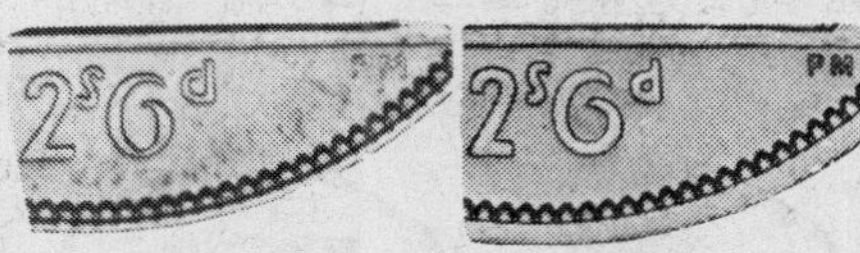

**1/2 CROWN** **KM# 17** **Composition:** Copper-Nickel **Obverse:** KM#16a **Reverse:** KM#8. **Note:** Mule.

| Date | Mintage | VG | F | VF | XF | Unc |
|---|---|---|---|---|---|---|
| 1961 | Inc. above | — | 8.00 | 25.00 | 200 | — |

**10 SHILLING** **KM# 18** **Weight:** 18.1400 g. **Composition:** 0.8330 Silver .4858 oz. ASW **Subject:** 50th Anniversary of Easter Uprising

| Date | Mintage | F | VF | XF | Unc | BU |
|---|---|---|---|---|---|---|
| 1966 | Est. 2,000,000 | — | — | 4.50 | 9.00 | — |

**Note:** Approximately 1.270 melted down

| Date | Mintage | F | VF | XF | Unc | BU |
|---|---|---|---|---|---|---|
| 1966 Proof | 20,000 | Value: 17.50 | | | | |

## DECIMAL COINAGE

100 Pence = 1 Pound (Punt)

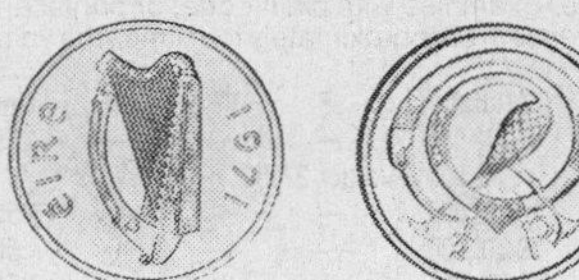

**1/2 PENNY** **KM# 19** **Composition:** Bronze **Reverse:** Stylized bird

| Date | Mintage | F | VF | XF | Unc | BU |
|---|---|---|---|---|---|---|
| 1971 | 100,500,000 | — | — | 0.10 | 0.30 | — |
| 1971 Proof | 50,000 | Value: 1.00 | | | | |
| 1975 | 10,500,000 | — | — | 0.10 | 0.30 | — |
| 1976 | 5,464,000 | — | — | 0.10 | 0.30 | — |
| 1978 | 20,302,000 | — | — | — | 0.25 | — |
| 1980 | 20,616,000 | — | — | — | 0.25 | — |

| Date | Mintage | F | VF | XF | Unc | BU |
|---|---|---|---|---|---|---|
| 1982 | 9,660,000 | — | — | — | 0.30 | — |
| 1985 | 2,784,000 | — | — | — | — | — |
| 1986 | Est. 12,250 | — | — | — | — | — |

**Note:** This mintage figure represents a surplus of coins minted for Polished Standard Specimen Sets (Proof Sets) later released into circulation. The entire surplus was presumably remelted due to demonitization of this denomination Jan. 1, 1987.

| Date | Mintage | F | VF | XF | Unc | BU |
|---|---|---|---|---|---|---|
| 1986 Proof | 6,750 | Value: 12.50 | | | | |

**PENNY** **KM# 20** **Composition:** Bronze **Reverse:** Stylized bird

| Date | Mintage | F | VF | XF | Unc | BU |
|---|---|---|---|---|---|---|
| 1971 | 100,500,000 | — | — | 0.10 | 0.20 | — |
| 1971 Proof | 50,000 | Value: 1.25 | | | | |
| 1974 | 10,000,000 | — | — | 0.10 | 0.25 | — |
| 1975 | 10,000,000 | — | — | 0.10 | 0.25 | — |
| 1976 | 38,164,000 | — | — | 0.10 | 0.20 | — |
| 1978 | 25,746,000 | — | — | 0.10 | 0.20 | — |
| 1979 | 21,766,000 | — | — | 0.10 | 0.20 | — |
| 1980 | 86,712,000 | — | — | 0.10 | 0.20 | — |
| 1982 | 54,189,000 | — | — | 0.10 | 0.20 | — |
| 1985 | 19,242,000 | — | — | 0.10 | 0.20 | — |
| 1986 | 36,584,000 | — | — | 0.10 | 0.20 | — |
| 1986 Proof | 6,750 | Value: 1.25 | | | | |
| 1988 | 56,772,000 | — | — | 0.10 | 0.20 | — |

**PENNY** **KM# 20a** **Composition:** Copper Plated Steel

| Date | Mintage | F | VF | XF | Unc | BU |
|---|---|---|---|---|---|---|
| 1990 | 65,099,000 | — | — | 0.10 | 0.15 | — |
| 1992 | 25,643,000 | — | — | 0.10 | 0.15 | — |
| 1993 | 10,000,000 | — | — | 0.10 | 0.15 | — |
| 1994 | 45,800,000 | — | — | 0.10 | 0.15 | — |
| 1995 | 70,836,000 | — | — | 0.10 | 0.15 | — |
| 1996 | — | — | — | 0.10 | 0.15 | — |
| 1998 | — | — | — | 0.10 | 0.15 | — |
| 2000 | — | — | — | 0.10 | 0.15 | — |

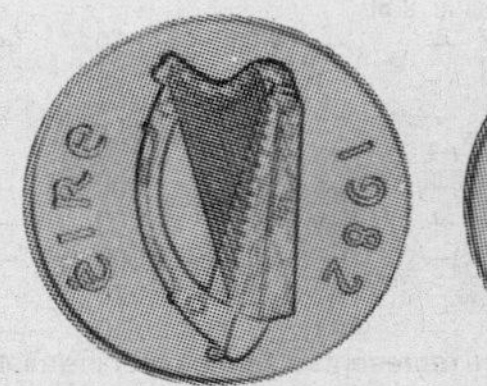

**2 PENCE** **KM# 21** **Composition:** Bronze **Reverse:** Stylized bird

| Date | Mintage | F | VF | XF | Unc | BU |
|---|---|---|---|---|---|---|
| 1971 | 75,500,000 | — | — | 0.10 | 1.00 | — |
| 1971 Proof | 50,000 | Value: 1.50 | | | | |
| 1975 | 20,010,000 | — | — | 0.10 | 0.30 | — |
| 1976 | 5,414,000 | — | — | 0.10 | 0.50 | — |
| 1978 | 12,000,000 | — | — | 0.10 | 0.30 | — |
| 1979 | 32,373,000 | — | — | 0.10 | 0.30 | — |
| 1980 | 59,828,000 | — | — | 0.10 | 0.30 | — |
| 1982 | 30,435,000 | — | — | 0.10 | 0.30 | — |
| 1985 | 14,469,000 | — | — | 0.10 | 0.30 | — |
| 1986 | 23,865,000 | — | — | 0.10 | 0.30 | — |
| 1986 Proof | 6,750 | Value: 1.50 | | | | |
| 1988 | 35,868,000 | — | — | 0.10 | 0.30 | — |

**2 PENCE** **KM# 21a** **Composition:** Copper Plated Steel

| Date | Mintage | F | VF | XF | Unc | BU |
|---|---|---|---|---|---|---|
| 1990 | 34,284,000 | — | — | 0.10 | 0.25 | — |
| 1992 | 10,215,000 | — | — | 0.10 | 0.25 | — |
| 1995 | 55,459,000 | — | — | 0.10 | 0.25 | — |
| 1996 | — | — | — | 0.10 | 0.25 | — |
| 1998 | — | — | — | 0.10 | 0.25 | — |
| 2000 | — | — | — | 0.10 | 0.25 | — |

**5 PENCE** **KM# 22** **Composition:** Copper-Nickel **Reverse:** Bull right

| Date | Mintage | F | VF | XF | Unc | BU |
|---|---|---|---|---|---|---|
| 1969 | 5,000,000 | — | 0.10 | 0.15 | 1.00 | — |
| 1970 | 10,000,000 | — | — | 0.10 | 0.50 | — |
| 1971 | 8,000,000 | — | — | 0.10 | 0.50 | — |
| 1971 Proof | 50,000 | Value: 2.00 | | | | |
| 1974 | 7,000,000 | — | — | 0.10 | 0.50 | — |
| 1975 | 10,000,000 | — | — | 0.10 | 0.50 | — |

| Date | Mintage | F | VF | XF | Unc | BU |
|---|---|---|---|---|---|---|
| 1976 | 20,616,000 | — | — | 0.10 | 0.50 | — |
| 1978 | 28,536,000 | — | — | 0.10 | 0.50 | — |
| 1980 | 22,190,000 | — | — | 0.10 | 0.50 | — |
| 1982 | 24,404,000 | — | — | 0.10 | 0.50 | — |
| 1985 | 4,202,000 | — | — | 0.10 | 0.50 | — |
| 1986 | 15,298,000 | — | 0.10 | 0.15 | 1.00 | — |
| 1986 Proof | 6,750 | Value: 2.00 | | | | |
| 1990 | 7,547,000 | — | — | 0.10 | 0.50 | — |

**5 PENCE** **KM# 28** **Composition:** Copper-Nickel **Reverse:** Bull left **Note:** Reduced size: 18.5mm.

| Date | Mintage | F | VF | XF | Unc | BU |
|---|---|---|---|---|---|---|
| 1992 | 74,526,000 | — | — | 0.10 | 0.40 | — |
| 1993 | 89,109,000 | — | — | 0.10 | 0.40 | — |
| 1994 | 31,058,000 | — | — | 0.10 | 0.40 | — |
| 1995 | 14,667,000 | — | — | 0.10 | 0.40 | — |
| 1996 | 158,546,000 | — | — | 0.10 | 0.40 | — |
| 1998 | 63,247,000 | — | — | 0.10 | 0.40 | — |
| 2000 | — | — | — | 0.10 | 0.40 | — |

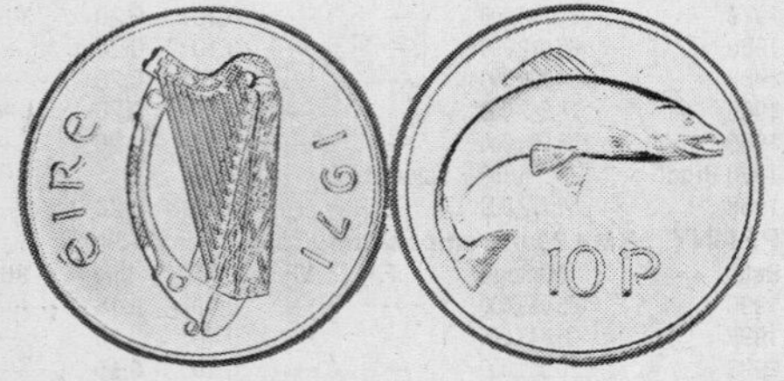

**10 PENCE** **KM# 23** **Composition:** Copper-Nickel **Reverse:** Salmon right

| Date | Mintage | F | VF | XF | Unc | BU |
|---|---|---|---|---|---|---|
| 1969 | 27,000,000 | — | — | 0.40 | 1.25 | — |
| 1971 | 4,000,000 | — | — | 0.40 | 1.25 | — |
| 1971 Proof | 50,000 | Value: 2.50 | | | | |
| 1973 | 2,500,000 | — | — | 0.40 | 1.50 | — |
| 1974 | 7,500,000 | — | — | 0.35 | 1.25 | — |
| 1975 | 15,000,000 | — | — | 0.35 | 1.25 | — |
| 1976 | 9,433,000 | — | — | 0.35 | 1.25 | — |
| 1978 | 30,905,000 | — | — | 0.25 | 1.00 | — |
| 1980 | 44,605,000 | — | — | 0.25 | 1.00 | — |
| 1982 | 7,374,000 | — | — | 0.25 | 1.00 | — |
| 1985 | 4,099,999 | — | — | 0.25 | 1.25 | — |
| 1986 | Est. 4,250 | — | 2.00 | 5.00 | 16.50 | — |

**Note:** This mintage figure represents a surplus of coins minted for Polished Standard Specimen Sets (Proof Sets), later released into circulation

| Date | Mintage | F | VF | XF | Unc | BU |
|---|---|---|---|---|---|---|
| 1986 Proof | 6,750 | Value: 16.50 | | | | |

**10 PENCE** **KM# 29** **Composition:** Copper-Nickel **Reverse:** Salmon left **Note:** Reduced size. 22.0mm.

| Date | Mintage | F | VF | XF | Unc | BU |
|---|---|---|---|---|---|---|
| 1993 | 80,061,000 | — | — | — | 0.75 | — |
| 1994 | 58,510,000 | — | — | — | 0.75 | — |
| 1995 | 15,781,000 | — | — | — | 0.75 | — |
| 1996 | 18,402,000 | — | — | — | 0.75 | — |
| 1997 | 10,033,000 | — | — | — | 0.75 | — |
| 1998 | 10,000,000 | — | — | — | 0.75 | — |
| 1999 | 24,500,000 | — | — | — | 0.75 | — |
| 2000 | — | — | — | — | 0.75 | — |

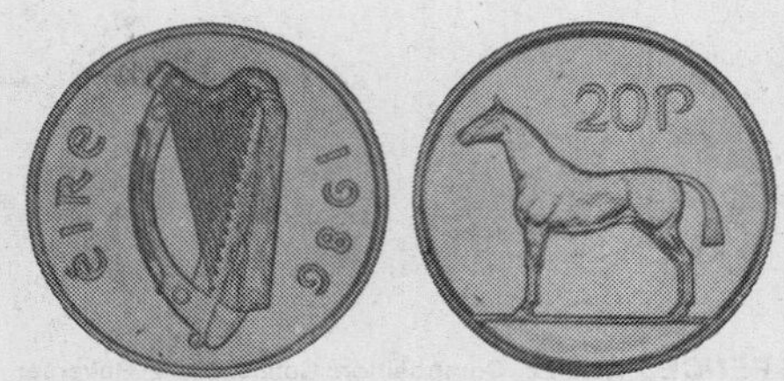

**20 PENCE** **KM# 25** **Composition:** Copper-Nickel **Reverse:** Irish Hunter

| Date | Mintage | F | VF | XF | Unc | BU |
|---|---|---|---|---|---|---|
| 1986 | 50,430,000 | — | — | 0.50 | 1.50 | — |
| 1986 Proof | 6,750 | Value: 3.50 | | | | |
| 1988 | 20,661,000 | — | — | 0.50 | 1.50 | — |
| 1992 | 14,761,000 | — | — | 0.50 | 1.50 | — |

| Date | Mintage | F | VF | XF | Unc | BU |
|---|---|---|---|---|---|---|
| 1994 | 11,086,000 | — | — | 0.50 | 1.50 | — |
| 1995 | 18,160,000 | — | — | 0.50 | 1.50 | — |
| 1996 | 29,291,000 | — | — | 0.50 | 1.50 | — |
| 1998 | 25,024,000 | — | — | 0.50 | 1.50 | — |
| 1999 | 11,000,000 | — | — | 0.50 | 1.50 | — |
| 2000 | — | — | — | 0.50 | 1.50 | — |

**50 PENCE** **KM# 24** **Composition:** Copper-Nickel **Reverse:** Woodcock

| Date | Mintage | F | VF | XF | Unc | BU |
|---|---|---|---|---|---|---|
| 1970 | 9,000,000 | — | — | 1.50 | 4.00 | — |
| 1971 | 600,000 | — | 1.00 | 2.00 | 6.00 | — |
| 1971 Proof | 50,000 | Value: 3.50 | | | | |
| 1974 | 1,000,000 | — | 1.00 | 2.00 | 7.00 | — |
| 1975 | 2,000,000 | — | — | 1.50 | 4.00 | — |
| 1976 | 3,000,000 | — | — | 1.25 | 3.00 | — |
| 1977 | 4,800,000 | — | — | 1.25 | 3.00 | — |
| 1978 | 4,500,000 | — | — | 1.25 | 3.00 | — |
| 1979 | 4,000,000 | — | — | 1.25 | 3.00 | — |
| 1981 | 6,000,000 | — | — | 1.00 | 2.00 | — |
| 1982 | 2,000,000 | — | — | 1.25 | 3.00 | — |
| 1983 | 7,000,000 | — | — | 1.00 | 1.75 | — |
| 1986 | 3,250 | — | 3.00 | 6.00 | 18.50 | — |

**Note:** This circulation mintage figure represents a surplus of coins minted for Polished Standard Specimen Sets (Proof Sets), later released into circulation

| Date | Mintage | F | VF | XF | Unc | BU |
|---|---|---|---|---|---|---|
| 1986 Proof | 6,750 | Value: 18.50 | | | | |
| 1988 | Est. 12,000,000 | — | — | 1.00 | 1.75 | — |
| 1996 | 6,000,000 | — | — | 1.00 | 1.75 | — |
| 1997 | 6,000,000 | — | — | 1.00 | 1.75 | — |
| 1998 | 22,955,000 | — | — | 1.00 | 1.75 | — |
| 1999 | 10,000,000 | — | — | 1.00 | 1.75 | — |
| 2000 | — | — | — | 1.00 | 1.75 | — |

**50 PENCE** **KM# 26** **Composition:** Copper-Nickel **Subject:** Dublin Millennium

| Date | Mintage | F | VF | XF | Unc | BU |
|---|---|---|---|---|---|---|
| 1988 | 5,000,000 | — | — | — | 2.50 | — |
| 1988 Proof | 50,000 | Value: 15.00 | | | | |

**PUNT (Pound)** **KM# 27** **Composition:** Copper-Nickel **Reverse:** Red Deer **Note:** The normal KM27 was struck with an engrailed edge. Examples with plain edge, or partial engrailing command a premium of approximately four times the values listed here.

| Date | Mintage | F | VF | XF | Unc | BU |
|---|---|---|---|---|---|---|
| 1990 | 62,292,000 | — | — | — | 7.50 | — |
| 1990 Proof | 42,000 | Value: 27.50 | | | | |
| 1994 | 14,925,000 | — | — | — | 7.50 | — |
| 1995 | 10,215,000 | — | — | — | 7.50 | — |
| 1996 | 9,230,000 | — | — | — | 7.50 | — |
| 1998 | 22,955,000 | — | — | — | 7.50 | — |
| 1999 | 10,000,000 | — | — | — | 7.50 | — |
| 2000 | — | — | — | — | 7.50 | — |

**PUNT (Pound)** **KM# 30** **Weight:** 28.0000 g. **Composition:** 0.9250 Silver .8328 oz. ASW **Subject:** 50th Anniversary - United Nations **Obverse:** Harp **Rev. Legend:** Dove and UN logo

| Date | Mintage | F | VF | XF | Unc | BU |
|---|---|---|---|---|---|---|
| ND(1995) Proof | — | Value: 40.00 | | | | |

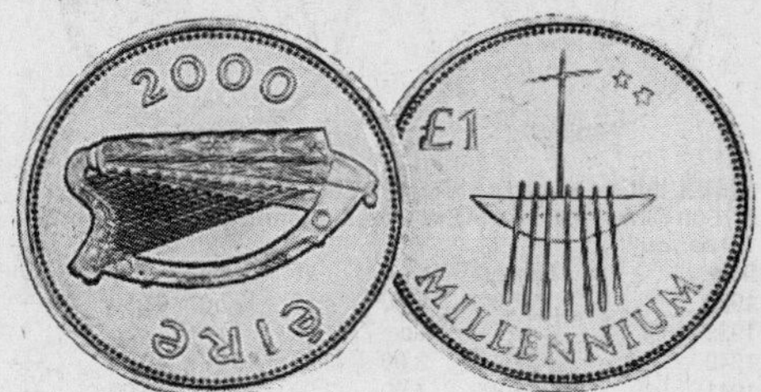

**PUNT (Pound)** **KM# 31** **Composition:** Copper-Nickel **Subject:** Dublin Millennium **Obverse:** Harp **Rev. Legend:** Stylized ancient ship **Note:** Struck at Sandyford.

| Date | Mintage | F | VF | XF | Unc | BU |
|---|---|---|---|---|---|---|
| 2000 | — | — | — | — | 7.50 | — |

## MEDALLIC COINAGE

European Currency Unit - ECU

**5 ECU** **KM# M1** **Weight:** 10.0000 g. **Composition:** 0.9250 Silver .974 oz. ASW **Subject:** EEC Council Meeting in Dublin

| Date | Mintage | F | VF | XF | Unc | BU |
|---|---|---|---|---|---|---|
| 1990 Proof | 20,000 | Value: 25.00 | | | | |

**5 ECU** **KM# M2** **Weight:** 28.0000 g. **Composition:** 0.9250 Silver .8328 oz. ASW **Subject:** EEC Council Meeting in Dublin

| Date | Mintage | F | VF | XF | Unc | BU |
|---|---|---|---|---|---|---|
| 1990 Proof | 20,000 | Value: 40.00 | | | | |

**50 ECU** KM# M3 **Weight:** 15.0000 g. **Composition:** 0.9170 Gold .4421 oz. AGW **Subject:** EEC Council Meeting in Dublin

| Date | Mintage | F | VF | XF | Unc | BU |
|---|---|---|---|---|---|---|
| 1990 Proof | 5,000 | Value: 450 | | | | |

## PATTERNS

Including off metal strikes

| KM# | Date | Mintage | Identification | Mkt Val |
|---|---|---|---|---|
| Pn2 | 1938 | — | 1/2 Crown. KM16. | — |
| Pn3 | 1985 | — | 20 Pence. Km25. | — |
| Pn1 | 1985 | — | Penny. KM11. | 15,000 |

## PROVAS

Public Morbiducci Series

| KM# | Date | Mintage | Identification | Mkt Val |
|---|---|---|---|---|
| Pr3 | 1927 | — | Penny. Silvered Bronze. | 8,000 |
| Pr4 | 1927 | 4 | 3 Pence. Nickel. | 5,000 |
| Pr5 | 1927 | 4 | 6 Pence. Nickel. | 5,000 |
| Pr6 | 1927 | 5 | Shilling. Silver. | 5,000 |
| Pr7 | 1927 | 4 | Florin. Silver. | 6,500 |
| Pr8 | 1927 | 5 | 1/2 Crown. Silver. | 8,500 |
| Pr8a | 1927 | — | 1/2 Crown. Copper. | — |

**Note:** This series exists in other than standard metals

## PIEFORTS

| KM# | Date | Mintage | Identification | Mkt Val |
|---|---|---|---|---|
| P1 | 2000 | — | Punt. Silver. 20.0000 g. Stylized ancient ship. as KM#31 | 40.00 |

## MINT SETS

| KM# | Date | Mintage | Identification | Issue Price | Mkt Val |
|---|---|---|---|---|---|
| MS1 | 1966 (8) | 96,000 | KM9-11, 12a-16a | — | 20.00 |
| MS2 | Various dates (6) | — | KM19-21(1971), 22 (1970), 23(1969), 24(1970) | — | 6.50 |
| MS3 | 1971 (6) | — | KM19-24 | 1.50 | 9.00 |
| MS4 | 1978 (6) | — | KM19-24 | — | 5.00 |
| MS5 | 1982 (6) | — | KM19-24 | — | 5.00 |
| MS6 | 1996 (7) | — | KM20a-21a, 24-25, 27-29 | — | 12.50 |
| MS7 | 1998 (7) | — | KM20a-21a, 25-25, 27-29 | — | 12.50 |
| MS8 | 2000 (7) | — | KM20a-21a, 24-25, 28-29, 31 | — | 12.50 |

## PROOF SETS

| KM# | Date | Mintage | Identification | Issue Price | Mkt Val |
|---|---|---|---|---|---|
| PS1 | 1928 (8) | 6,001 | KM1-8 | — | 200 |
| PS2 | 1966 (2) | — | KM18(2) | — | 40.00 |
| PS3 | 1971 (6) | 50,000 | KM19-24 | 4.40 | 12.50 |
| PS4 | 1986 (7) | 6,750 | KM19-25 | — | 55.00 |
| PS5 | 1990 (3) | — | KMM1-M3 | — | 500 |

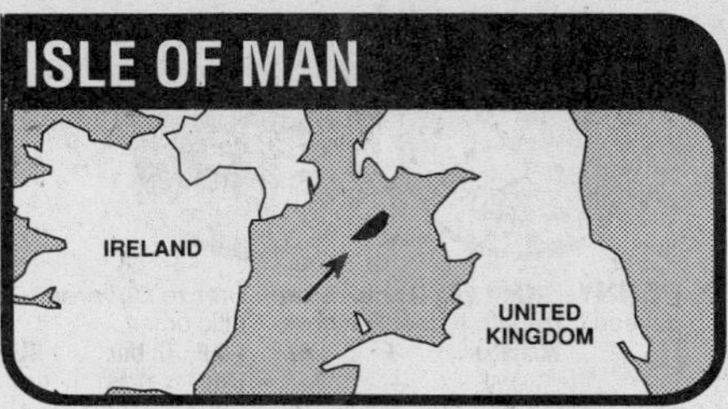


The Isle of Man, a dependency of the British Crown located in the Irish Sea equidistant from Ireland, Scotland and England, has an area of 227 sq. mi. (588 sq. km.) and a population of 68,000. Capital: Douglas. Agriculture, dairy farming, fishing and tourism are the chief industries.

The prevalence of prehistoric artifacts and monuments on the island give evidence that its' mild, almost sub-tropical climate was enjoyed by mankind before the dawn of history. Vikings came to the Isle of Man during the 9th century and remained until ejected by the Scottish in 1266. The island came under the protection of the British Crown in 1288, and in 1406 was granted, in perpetuity, to the earls of Derby, from whom it was inherited, 1736, by the Duke of Atholl. The British Crown purchased the rights and title in 1765; the remaining privileges of the Atholl family were transferred to the crown in 1829. The Isle of Man is ruled by its own legislative council and the House of Keys, one of the oldest legislative assemblies in the world. Acts of Parliament passed in London do not affect the island unless it is specifically mentioned.

**RULERS**

James Murray, Duke of Atholl, 1736-1765
British Commencing 1765

**MINT MARKS**

PM - Pobjoy Mint

**PRIVY MARKS**

(a) - Big Apple - 1988
(at) - Angel Blowing Trumpet – 1997

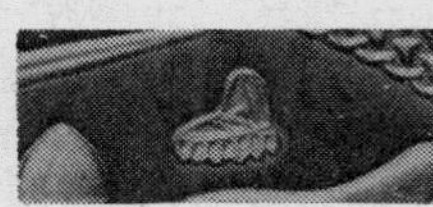

(b) - Baby Crib - 1982
(ba) - Basel Bugle - 1990
(bb) - Big Ben - 1987-1988
(br) - Brooklyn Bridge - 1989
(bs) - Teddy Bear in Stocking - 1996
(c) - Chicago Water Tower CICF - 1990-1991
(cc) - Christmas cracker - 1991
(d) - St. Paul's Cathedral - 1989
(f) - FUN logo - 1988
(fl) - Fleur de Lis - 1990
(fr) - Frauenkirche - Munich Numismata - 1990-1991
(fw) - Fairy w/magic wand - 1999
(h) - Horse - Hong Kong Int. - 1990
(l) - Statue of Liberty - 1987
(lc) - Lion crowned - 1989
(m) - Queen mother's portrait - 1980
(ma) - Maple leaf - CNA - 1990
(mt) - Mistletoe - Christmas - 1987, 1989
(ns) - North Star - 1994
(p) - Carrier Pigeon - Basel - 1988-1989
(pi) - Pine tree - 1986
(pt) - Partridge in a pear tree - 1988
(py) - Poppy - 1995
(s) - Bridge - SINPEX - 1987
(sb) - Soccer ball - 1982
(sc) - Santa Claus - 1995
(sg) - Sleigh - Christmas - 1990
(SL) - St. Louis Arch - 1987
(ss) - Sailing Ship - Sydney - 1988
(t) - Stylized triskelion - 1979
(tb) - Tower Bridge - 1990
(ti) - TICC logo - Tokyo - 1990
(v) - Viking ship - 1990
(vw) - Viking ship in wreath - 1986
(w) - Stylized triskelion - 1985
(x) - Snowman - 1998

**PRIVY LETTERS**

A - ANA - 1985-1992
C - Coinex, London - 1985-1989
D.M.I.H.E. - Ideal Home Exhibit, London, 1980
D.M.I.H.E.N. - Ideal Home Exhibit, Manchester, 1980
F - FUN - 1987
H - Hong Kong Expo - 1985
L - Long Beach - 1985-1987
T - Torex, Toronto - 1986
U - Uncirculated - 1988, 1990, 1994, 1995
X - Ameripex - 1986

# CROWN COLONY

## DECIMAL COINAGE

5 New Pence = 1 Shilling; 25 New Pence = 1 Crown; 100 New Pence = 1 Pound

**1/2 NEW PENNY** KM# 19 **Composition:** Bronze **Obverse:** Bust of Queen Elizabeth II right **Reverse:** St. James' Weed; Cushaq; Ragwort

| Date | Mintage | F | VF | XF | Unc | BU |
|---|---|---|---|---|---|---|
| 1971 | 495,000 | — | — | 0.10 | 0.25 | — |
| 1971 Proof | 10,000 | Value: 1.50 | | | | |
| 1972 | 1,000 | — | — | — | 20.00 | — |
| 1973 | 1,000 | — | — | — | 20.00 | — |
| 1974 | 1,000 | — | — | — | 20.00 | — |
| 1975 | 825,000 | — | — | 0.10 | 0.15 | — |

**1/2 NEW PENNY** KM# 19a **Weight:** 2.1000 g. **Composition:** 0.9250 Silver .0624 oz. ASW **Obverse:** Bust of Queen Elizabeth II right **Reverse:** St. James' Weed; Cushaq; Ragwort

| Date | Mintage | F | VF | XF | Unc | BU |
|---|---|---|---|---|---|---|
| 1975 | 20,000 | — | — | — | 2.50 | — |

**1/2 NEW PENNY** KM# 19b **Weight:** 4.0000 g. **Composition:** 0.9500 Platinum .12214 oz. APW **Obverse:** Bust of Queen Elizabeth II right **Reverse:** St. James' Weed; Cushaq; Ragwort

| Date | Mintage | F | VF | XF | Unc | BU |
|---|---|---|---|---|---|---|
| 1975 Proof | 600 | Value: 100 | | | | |

**1/2 PENNY** KM# 32 **Composition:** Bronze **Obverse:** Bust of Queen Elizabeth II right **Reverse:** Atlantic herring

| Date | Mintage | F | VF | XF | Unc | BU |
|---|---|---|---|---|---|---|
| 1976 | 600,000 | — | — | 0.10 | 0.25 | — |
| 1978 | — | — | — | 0.10 | 0.25 | — |
| 1978 Proof | — | Value: 1.00 | | | | |
| 1979(t) AA | — | — | — | 0.10 | 0.25 | — |
| 1979(t) AB | — | — | — | 0.10 | 0.25 | — |

**1/2 PENNY** KM# 32a **Weight:** 2.1000 g. **Composition:** 0.9250 Silver .0624 oz. ASW **Obverse:** Bust of Queen Elizabeth II right

| Date | Mintage | F | VF | XF | Unc | BU |
|---|---|---|---|---|---|---|
| 1976 | 20,000 | — | — | — | 2.00 | — |
| 1978 | 10,000 | — | — | — | 2.00 | — |
| 1979 (t) Proof | 10,000 | Value: 2.50 | | | | |

**1/2 PENNY** KM# 32b **Weight:** 4.0000 g. **Composition:** 0.9500 Platinum .1221 oz. APW **Obverse:** Bust of Queen Elizabeth II right

| Date | Mintage | F | VF | XF | Unc | BU |
|---|---|---|---|---|---|---|
| 1976 Proof | 600 | Value: 100 | | | | |
| 1978 Proof | 600 | Value: 100 | | | | |
| 1979 (t) Proof | 500 | Value: 100 | | | | |

**1/2 PENNY** KM# 40 **Composition:** Bronze **Series:** F.A.O. **Obverse:** Bust of Queen Elizabeth II right

| Date | Mintage | F | VF | XF | Unc | BU |
|---|---|---|---|---|---|---|
| 1977 PM on reverse | 700,000 | — | — | 0.10 | 0.25 | — |
| 1977 Without PM on reverse | Inc. above | — | — | — | 5.00 | — |

**1/2 PENNY** KM# 40a **Weight:** 2.1000 g. **Composition:** 0.9250 Silver .0624 oz. ASW **Obverse:** Bust of Queen Elizabeth II right

| Date | Mintage | F | VF | XF | Unc | BU |
|---|---|---|---|---|---|---|
| 1977 Proof | 10,000 | Value: 4.00 | | | | |

**1/2 PENNY** KM# 58 **Composition:** Bronze **Obverse:** Bust of Queen Elizabeth II right **Reverse:** Atlantic herring

| Date | Mintage | F | VF | XF | Unc | BU |
|---|---|---|---|---|---|---|
| 1980 AA | — | — | — | 0.10 | 0.25 | — |
| 1980 AB | — | — | — | 0.10 | 0.25 | — |
| 1980 Proof | — | Value: 1.00 | | | | |
| 1981 AA | — | — | — | 0.10 | 0.25 | — |
| 1982 AA | — | — | — | 0.10 | 0.25 | — |
| 1982 (b) | — | — | — | 0.10 | 0.25 | — |
| 1982 (b) Proof | 25,000 | Value: 1.00 | | | | |
| 1983 AA | — | — | — | 0.10 | 0.25 | — |

**1/2 PENNY** KM# 58a **Weight:** 2.1000 g. **Composition:** 0.5000 Silver .0337 oz. ASW **Obverse:** Bust of Queen Elizabeth II right

| Date | Mintage | F | VF | XF | Unc | BU |
|---|---|---|---|---|---|---|
| 1980 Proof | 10,000 | Value: 4.00 | | | | |

**1/2 PENNY** KM# 58c **Weight:** 3.5500 g. **Composition:** 0.9170 Gold .1046 oz. AGW **Obverse:** Bust of Queen Elizabeth II right **Reverse:** Atlantic Herring

| Date | Mintage | F | VF | XF | Unc | BU |
|---|---|---|---|---|---|---|
| 1980 Proof | — | Value: 65.00 | | | | |
| 1982 (b) Proof | 500 | Value: 65.00 | | | | |
| 1983 Proof | — | Value: 65.00 | | | | |

**1/2 PENNY** KM# 58d **Weight:** 4.0000 g. **Composition:** 0.9500 Platinum .1221 oz. APW **Obverse:** Bust of Queen Elizabeth II right

| Date | Mintage | F | VF | XF | Unc | BU |
|---|---|---|---|---|---|---|
| 1980 Proof | 500 | Value: 100 | | | | |
| 1982 (b) Proof | 500 | Value: 100 | | | | |
| 1983 Proof | — | Value: 100 | | | | |

**1/2 PENNY** KM# 72.1 **Weight:** 4.0000 g. **Composition:** 0.9500 Bronze .1221 oz. **Series:** F.A.O **Obverse:** Bust of Queen Elizabeth II right

| Date | Mintage | F | VF | XF | Unc | BU |
|---|---|---|---|---|---|---|
| 1981 | — | — | — | — | 0.10 | — |

**1/2 PENNY** KM# 72.2 **Weight:** 4.0000 g. **Composition:** 0.9500 Bronze .1221 oz. **Obverse:** Bust of Queen Elizabeth II right **Reverse:** World Food Day, 16-10-81

| Date | Mintage | F | VF | XF | Unc | BU |
|---|---|---|---|---|---|---|
| 1981 | 10,000 | — | 2.00 | 5.00 | 10.00 | — |

**1/2 PENNY** KM# 58b **Weight:** 2.1000 g. **Composition:** 0.9250 Silver .0624 oz. ASW **Obverse:** Bust of Queen Elizabeth II right

| Date | Mintage | F | VF | XF | Unc | BU |
|---|---|---|---|---|---|---|
| 1982 Proof | 10,000 | Value: 4.00 | | | | |
| 1983 Proof | 5,000 | Value: 5.00 | | | | |

**1/2 PENNY** KM# 111 **Weight:** 4.0000 g. **Composition:** 0.9500 Bronze .1221 oz. **Subject:** Quincentenary of the College of Arms **Obverse:** Bust of Queen Elizabeth II right **Reverse:** Fuchsia blossom

| Date | Mintage | F | VF | XF | Unc | BU |
|---|---|---|---|---|---|---|
| 1984 AA | — | — | — | — | 0.10 | — |

**1/2 PENNY** KM# 111a **Weight:** 2.1000 g. **Composition:** 0.9250 Silver .0625 oz. ASW **Obverse:** Bust of Queen Elizabeth II right

| Date | Mintage | F | VF | XF | Unc | BU |
|---|---|---|---|---|---|---|
| 1984 Proof | — | Value: 5.00 | | | | |

**1/2 PENNY** KM# 111b **Weight:** 3.5500 g. **Composition:** 0.9170 Gold .1046 oz. AGW **Obverse:** Bust of Queen Elizabeth II right **Reverse:** Fuchsia blossom on garnished and scrolled shield

| Date | Mintage | F | VF | XF | Unc | BU |
|---|---|---|---|---|---|---|
| 1984 Proof | 150 | Value: 125 | | | | |

**1/2 PENNY** KM# 142 **Composition:** Bronze **Obverse:** Bust of Queen Elizabeth II right

| Date | Mintage | F | VF | XF | Unc | BU |
|---|---|---|---|---|---|---|
| 1985(w) AA | — | — | — | — | 0.10 | — |
| 1985 Proof | 50,000 | Value: 2.00 | | | | |

**1/2 PENNY** KM# 142a **Obverse:** Bust of Queen Elizabeth II right

| Date | Mintage | F | VF | XF | Unc | BU |
|---|---|---|---|---|---|---|
| 1985 Proof | 10,000 | Value: 3.00 | | | | |

**1/2 PENNY** KM# 142b **Weight:** 3.5500 g. **Composition:** 0.9170 Gold .1046 oz. AGW **Obverse:** Bust of Queen Elizabeth II right

| Date | Mintage | F | VF | XF | Unc | BU |
|---|---|---|---|---|---|---|
| 1985 Proof | 300 | Value: 85.00 | | | | |

**1/2 PENNY** KM# 142c **Weight:** 4.0000 g. **Composition:** 0.9500 Platinum .1221 oz. APW **Obverse:** Bust of Queen Elizabeth II right

| Date | Mintage | F | VF | XF | Unc | BU |
|---|---|---|---|---|---|---|
| 1985 Proof | 200 | Value: 100 | | | | |

**NEW PENNY** KM# 20 **Composition:** Bronze **Obverse:** Bust of Queen Elizabeth II right **Reverse:** Celtic cross

| Date | Mintage | F | VF | XF | Unc | BU |
|---|---|---|---|---|---|---|
| 1971 | 100,000 | — | — | 0.10 | 0.35 | — |
| 1971 Proof | 10,000 | Value: 2.00 | | | | |
| 1972 | 1,000 | — | — | — | 20.00 | — |
| 1973 | 1,000 | — | — | — | 20.00 | — |
| 1974 | 1,000 | — | — | — | 20.00 | — |
| 1975 | 855,000 | — | — | 0.10 | 0.20 | — |

**NEW PENNY** KM# 20a **Weight:** 4.2000 g. **Composition:** 0.9250 Silver .1249 oz. ASW **Obverse:** Bust of Queen Elizabeth II right

| Date | Mintage | F | VF | XF | Unc | BU |
|---|---|---|---|---|---|---|
| 1975 | 20,000 | — | — | — | 5.00 | — |

**NEW PENNY** KM# 20b **Weight:** 8.0000 g. **Composition:** 0.9500 Platinum .2443 oz. APW **Obverse:** Bust of Queen Elizabeth II right

| Date | Mintage | F | VF | XF | Unc | BU |
|---|---|---|---|---|---|---|
| 1975 Proof | 600 | Value: 200 | | | | |

**PENNY** KM# 33 **Composition:** Bronze **Obverse:** Bust of Queen Elizabeth II right **Reverse:** Loaghtyn sheep

| Date | Mintage | F | VF | XF | Unc | BU |
|---|---|---|---|---|---|---|
| 1976 | 900,000 | — | — | 0.20 | 0.75 | — |
| 1977 | 1,000,000 | — | — | 0.20 | 0.75 | — |
| 1978 | — | — | — | 0.20 | 0.75 | — |
| 1978 Proof | — | Value: 1.25 | | | | |
| 1979 AA(t) | — | — | — | 0.20 | 0.75 | — |
| 1979 AB(t) | — | — | — | 0.20 | 0.75 | — |
| 1979 AC(t) | — | — | — | 0.20 | 0.75 | — |
| 1979 AD | — | — | — | 0.20 | 0.75 | — |
| 1979 AE | — | — | — | 0.20 | 0.75 | — |

**PENNY** KM# 33a **Weight:** 4.2000 g. **Composition:** 0.9250 Silver .1249 oz. ASW **Obverse:** Bust of Queen Elizabeth II right

| Date | Mintage | F | VF | XF | Unc | BU |
|---|---|---|---|---|---|---|
| 1976 | 20,000 | — | — | — | 4.00 | — |
| 1977 Proof | 10,000 | Value: 5.00 | | | | |
| 1978 | 10,000 | — | — | — | 4.00 | — |
| 1979 (t) Proof | 10,000 | Value: 5.00 | | | | |

**PENNY** KM# 33b **Weight:** 8.0000 g. **Composition:** 0.9500 Platinum .2443 oz. APW **Obverse:** Bust of Queen Elizabeth II right **Reverse:** Loaghtyn sheep

| Date | Mintage | F | VF | XF | Unc | BU |
|---|---|---|---|---|---|---|
| 1976 Proof | 600 | Value: 200 | | | | |
| 1978 Proof | 600 | Value: 200 | | | | |
| 1979 (t) Proof | 500 | Value: 200 | | | | |

**PENNY** KM# 59 **Composition:** Bronze **Obverse:** Bust of Queen Elizabeth II right **Reverse:** Manx cat

| Date | Mintage | F | VF | XF | Unc | BU |
|---|---|---|---|---|---|---|
| 1980 AA | — | — | — | 0.20 | 0.75 | — |
| 1980 AB | — | — | — | 0.20 | 0.75 | — |
| 1980 AC | — | — | — | 0.20 | 0.75 | — |
| 1980 Proof | — | Value: 1.50 | | | | |
| 1981 AA | — | — | — | 0.20 | 0.75 | — |
| 1982 AA | — | — | — | 0.20 | 0.75 | — |
| 1982 (b) | — | — | — | 0.20 | 0.75 | — |
| 1982 (b) Proof | 25,000 | Value: 1.50 | | | | |
| 1983 AA | — | — | — | 0.20 | 0.75 | — |
| 1983 AB | — | — | — | 0.20 | 0.75 | — |

**PENNY** KM# 59a **Weight:** 4.2000 g. **Composition:** 0.5000 Silver .0675 oz. ASW **Obverse:** Bust of Queen Elizabeth II right

| Date | Mintage | F | VF | XF | Unc | BU |
|---|---|---|---|---|---|---|
| 1980 Proof | 10,000 | Value: 5.00 | | | | |
| 1980 AD | — | — | — | — | — | — |

**PENNY** KM# 59c **Weight:** 7.1000 g. **Composition:** 0.9170 Gold .2093 oz. AGW **Obverse:** Bust of Queen Elizabeth II right **Reverse:** Manx cat

| Date | Mintage | F | VF | XF | Unc | BU |
|---|---|---|---|---|---|---|
| 1980 Proof | 300 | Value: 125 | | | | |
| 1982 (b) Proof | 500 | Value: 125 | | | | |
| 1983 Proof | — | Value: 125 | | | | |

**PENNY** KM# 59d **Weight:** 8.0000 g. **Composition:** 0.9500 Platinum .2443 oz. APW **Obverse:** Bust of Queen Elizabeth II right

| Date | Mintage | F | VF | XF | Unc | BU |
|---|---|---|---|---|---|---|
| 1980 Proof | 500 | Value: 200 | | | | |
| 1982 (b) Proof | 500 | Value: 200 | | | | |
| 1983 Proof | — | Value: 200 | | | | |

**PENNY** KM# 59b **Weight:** 4.2000 g. **Composition:** 0.9250 Silver .0675 oz. ASW **Obverse:** Bust of Queen Elizabeth II right

| Date | Mintage | F | VF | XF | Unc | BU |
|---|---|---|---|---|---|---|
| 1981 Proof | — | Value: 5.00 | | | | |
| 1982 (b) Proof | 10,000 | Value: 5.00 | | | | |
| 1983 Proof | 5,000 | Value: 5.00 | | | | |

**PENNY** KM# 112 **Composition:** Bronze **Subject:** Quincentenary of the College of Arms **Obverse:** Bust of Queen Elizabeth II right **Reverse:** Shag bird on tilting shield

| Date | Mintage | F | VF | XF | Unc | BU |
|---|---|---|---|---|---|---|
| 1984 AA | — | — | — | 0.10 | 0.25 | — |

**PENNY** KM# 112a **Weight:** 4.2000 g. **Composition:** 0.9250 Silver .0675 oz. ASW **Obverse:** Bust of Queen Elizabeth II right

| Date | Mintage | F | VF | XF | Unc | BU |
|---|---|---|---|---|---|---|
| 1984 Proof | — | Value: 5.00 | | | | |

**PENNY** KM# 112b **Weight:** 7.1000 g. **Composition:** 0.9170 Gold .2093 oz. AGW **Obverse:** Bust of Queen Elizabeth II right **Reverse:** Puffin

| Date | Mintage | F | VF | XF | Unc | BU |
|---|---|---|---|---|---|---|
| 1984 Proof | 150 | Value: 250 | | | | |

**PENNY** KM# 143a **Weight:** 4.2000 g. **Composition:** 0.9250 Silver .0675 oz. ASW **Obverse:** Head of Queen Elizabeth II right

| Date | Mintage | F | VF | XF | Unc | BU |
|---|---|---|---|---|---|---|
| 1985 Proof | 10,000 | Value: 3.00 | | | | |

**PENNY** KM# 143b **Weight:** 7.1000 g. **Composition:** 0.9170 Gold .2093 oz. AGW **Obverse:** Head of Queen Elizabeth II right

| Date | Mintage | F | VF | XF | Unc | BU |
|---|---|---|---|---|---|---|
| 1985 Proof | 300 | Value: 175 | | | | |

**PENNY** KM# 143c **Weight:** 8.0000 g. **Composition:** 0.9500 Platinum .2443 oz. APW **Obverse:** Head of Queen Elizabeth II right

| Date | Mintage | F | VF | XF | Unc | BU |
|---|---|---|---|---|---|---|
| 1985 Proof | 200 | Value: 200 | | | | |

**PENNY** KM# 143 **Composition:** Bronze **Obverse:** Head of Queen Elizabeth II right

| Date | Mintage | F | VF | XF | Unc | BU |
|---|---|---|---|---|---|---|
| 1985 (W) AA | — | — | — | 0.10 | 0.25 | — |
| 1985 | — | — | — | 0.10 | 0.30 | — |
| 1985 Proof | 50,000 | Value: 2.00 | | | | |
| 1986 AA | — | — | — | 0.10 | 0.25 | — |
| 1987 AA | — | — | — | 0.10 | 0.25 | — |
| 1987 AB | — | — | — | 0.10 | 0.30 | — |
| 1987 AC | — | — | — | 0.10 | 0.30 | — |

**PENNY** KM# 207 **Composition:** Bronze **Obverse:** Head of Queen Elizabeth II right **Reverse:** Precision Tools

| Date | Mintage | F | VF | XF | Unc | BU |
|---|---|---|---|---|---|---|
| 1988 AA | — | — | — | — | 0.20 | — |
| 1988 AB | — | — | — | 0.10 | 0.30 | — |
| 1988 AC | — | — | — | 0.10 | 0.30 | — |
| 1988 AD | — | — | — | 0.10 | 0.30 | — |
| 1989 AA | — | — | — | — | 0.20 | — |
| 1989 AB | — | — | — | 0.10 | 0.30 | — |
| 1989 AC | — | — | — | 0.10 | 0.30 | — |
| 1989 AD | — | — | — | 0.10 | 0.30 | — |
| 1989 AE | — | — | — | 0.10 | 0.30 | — |
| 1990 AA | — | — | — | — | 0.20 | — |
| 1991 AA | — | — | — | — | 0.20 | — |
| 1991 AE | — | — | — | — | 0.20 | — |
| 1992 | — | — | — | — | 0.20 | — |
| 1993 AA | — | — | — | — | 0.20 | — |
| 1994 AA | — | — | — | — | 0.20 | — |
| 1995 AA | — | — | — | — | 0.20 | — |

**PENNY** **KM# 588** **Composition:** Bronze Plated Steel **Subject:** Sports **Obverse:** Head of Queen Elizabeth II right **Reverse:** Rugby ball

| Date | Mintage | F | VF | XF | Unc | BU |
|---|---|---|---|---|---|---|
| 1996 AA | — | — | — | — | 0.20 | — |

**PENNY** **KM# 588a** **Weight:** 4.2000 g. **Composition:** 0.9250 Silver .0675 oz. ASW **Subject:** Sports **Obverse:** Head of Queen Elizabeth II right **Reverse:** Rugby ball

| Date | Mintage | F | VF | XF | Unc | BU |
|---|---|---|---|---|---|---|
| 1996 Proof | — | Value: 10.00 | | | | |

**PENNY** **KM# 823** **Composition:** Bronze Plated Steel **Obverse:** Rank-Broadley portrait of Queen Elizabeth II **Reverse:** Rugby ball, denomination

| Date | Mintage | F | VF | XF | Unc | BU |
|---|---|---|---|---|---|---|
| 1998 AA | — | — | — | — | 0.20 | — |

**PENNY** **KM# 1036** **Weight:** 3.5300 g. **Composition:** Bronze Plated Steel **Obverse:** Queen's portrait **Reverse:** Ruins **Edge:** Plain

| Date | Mintage | F | VF | XF | Unc | BU |
|---|---|---|---|---|---|---|
| 2000 AA | — | — | — | — | 0.25 | — |

**2 NEW PENCE** **KM# 21** **Composition:** Bronze **Obverse:** Bust of Queen Elizabeth II right **Reverse:** Falcons

| Date | Mintage | F | VF | XF | Unc | BU |
|---|---|---|---|---|---|---|
| 1971 | 100,000 | — | — | 0.20 | 0.75 | — |
| 1971 Proof | 10,000 | Value: 2.50 | | | | |
| 1972 | 1,000 | — | — | — | 20.00 | — |
| 1973 | 1,000 | — | — | — | 20.00 | — |
| 1974 | 1,000 | — | — | — | 20.00 | — |
| 1975 | 725,000 | — | — | 0.20 | 0.75 | — |

**2 NEW PENCE** **KM# 21a** **Weight:** 8.4000 g. **Composition:** 0.9250 Silver .2498 oz. ASW **Obverse:** Bust of Queen Elizabeth II right

| Date | Mintage | F | VF | XF | Unc | BU |
|---|---|---|---|---|---|---|
| 1975 | 20,000 | — | — | — | 5.00 | — |

**2 NEW PENCE** **KM# 21b** **Weight:** 16.0000 g. **Composition:** 0.9500 Platinum .4887 oz. APW **Obverse:** Bust of Queen Elizabeth II right **Reverse:** Falcons

| Date | Mintage | F | VF | XF | Unc | BU |
|---|---|---|---|---|---|---|
| 1975 Proof | 600 | Value: 375 | | | | |

**2 PENCE** **KM# 34** **Composition:** Bronze **Obverse:** Bust of Queen Elizabeth II right **Reverse:** Manx Shearwater

| Date | Mintage | F | VF | XF | Unc | BU |
|---|---|---|---|---|---|---|
| 1976 | 800,000 | — | — | 0.20 | 0.50 | — |
| 1977 | 1,000,000 | — | — | 0.20 | 0.50 | — |
| 1978 | — | — | — | — | 0.50 | — |
| 1978 Proof | — | Value: 1.25 | | | | |
| 1979 AA(t) | 10,000 | — | — | 0.20 | 0.50 | — |
| 1979 AB(t) | — | — | — | 0.20 | 0.50 | — |
| 1979 AC(t) | — | — | — | 0.20 | 0.50 | — |
| 1979 AD(t) | — | — | — | 0.20 | 0.50 | — |
| 1979 AE(t) | — | — | — | 0.20 | 0.50 | — |
| 1979 AF(t) | — | — | — | 0.20 | 0.50 | — |
| 1979 AG(t) | — | — | — | 0.20 | 0.50 | — |
| 1979 AH(t) | — | — | — | 0.20 | 0.50 | — |

**2 PENCE** **KM# 34a** **Weight:** 8.4000 g. **Composition:** 0.9250 Silver .2498 oz. ASW **Obverse:** Bust of Queen Elizabeth II right

| Date | Mintage | F | VF | XF | Unc | BU |
|---|---|---|---|---|---|---|
| 1976 | 20,000 | — | — | — | 5.00 | — |
| 1977 Proof | 10,000 | Value: 6.00 | | | | |
| 1978 | 10,000 | — | — | — | 6.00 | — |
| 1979 (t) Proof | 10,000 | Value: 6.00 | | | | |

**2 NEW PENCE** **KM# 34b** **Weight:** 16.0000 g. **Composition:** 0.9500 Platinum .4887 oz. APW **Obverse:** Bust of Queen Elizabeth II right **Reverse:** Manx Shearwater

| Date | Mintage | F | VF | XF | Unc | BU |
|---|---|---|---|---|---|---|
| 1976 Proof | 600 | Value: 375 | | | | |
| 1977 Proof | 600 | Value: 375 | | | | |
| 1978 Proof | — | Value: 375 | | | | |
| 1979 (t) Proof | 500 | Value: 375 | | | | |

**2 PENCE** **KM# 60** **Composition:** Bronze **Obverse:** Bust of Queen Elizabeth II right **Reverse:** Red-billed chough

| Date | Mintage | F | VF | XF | Unc | BU |
|---|---|---|---|---|---|---|
| 1980 AA | — | — | — | 0.20 | 0.50 | — |
| 1980 AB | — | — | — | 0.20 | 0.50 | — |
| 1980 AC | — | — | — | 0.20 | 0.50 | — |
| 1980 AD | — | — | — | 0.20 | 0.50 | — |
| 1980 Proof | — | Value: 1.25 | | | | |
| 1981 AA | — | — | — | 0.20 | 0.50 | — |
| 1981 AB | — | — | — | 0.20 | 0.50 | — |
| 1982 AA | — | — | — | 0.20 | 0.50 | — |
| 1982 (b) | — | — | — | 0.20 | 0.50 | — |
| 1982 (b) Proof | 25,000 | Value: 1.25 | | | | |
| 1983 AA | — | — | — | 0.20 | 0.50 | — |
| 1983 AB | — | — | — | 0.20 | 0.50 | — |
| 1983 AC | — | — | — | 0.20 | 0.50 | — |
| 1983 AD | — | — | — | 0.20 | 0.50 | — |
| 1983 AE | — | — | — | 0.20 | 0.50 | — |

**2 PENCE** **KM# 60a** **Weight:** 8.4000 g. **Composition:** 0.5000 Silver .1350 oz. ASW **Obverse:** Bust of Queen Elizabeth II right

| Date | Mintage | F | VF | XF | Unc | BU |
|---|---|---|---|---|---|---|
| 1980 Proof | 10,000 | Value: 5.00 | | | | |

**2 PENCE** **KM# 60b** **Weight:** 8.4000 g. **Composition:** 0.9250 Silver .2498 oz. ASW **Obverse:** Bust of Queen Elizabeth II right

| Date | Mintage | F | VF | XF | Unc | BU |
|---|---|---|---|---|---|---|
| 1981 Proof | | | | | | |
| 1982 (b) Proof | 10,000 | Value: 5.00 | | | | |
| 1983 Proof | 5,000 | Value: 6.00 | | | | |

**2 PENCE** **KM# 60c** **Weight:** 14.2000 g. **Composition:** 0.9170 Gold .4186 oz. AGW **Obverse:** Bust of Queen Elizabeth II right **Reverse:** Manx Shearwater

| Date | Mintage | F | VF | XF | Unc | BU |
|---|---|---|---|---|---|---|
| 1980 Proof | 300 | Value: 225 | | | | |
| 1982 (b) Proof | 500 | Value: 225 | | | | |
| 1983 Proof | — | Value: 225 | | | | |

**2 NEW PENCE** **KM# 60d** **Weight:** 16.0000 g. **Composition:** 0.9500 Platinum .4887 oz. APW **Obverse:** Bust of Queen Elizabeth II right

| Date | Mintage | F | VF | XF | Unc | BU |
|---|---|---|---|---|---|---|
| 1980 Proof | 500 | Value: 375 | | | | |
| 1982 (b) Proof | 500 | Value: 375 | | | | |
| 1983 Proof | — | Value: 375 | | | | |

**2 PENCE** **KM# 113** **Composition:** Bronze **Subject:** Quincentenary of the College of Arms **Obverse:** Bust of Queen Elizabeth II right **Reverse:** Peregrine falcon on ornamented shield

| Date | Mintage | F | VF | XF | Unc | BU |
|---|---|---|---|---|---|---|
| 1984 AA | — | — | — | 0.20 | 0.50 | — |

**2 PENCE** **KM# 113b** **Weight:** 14.2000 g. **Composition:** 0.9170 Gold .4185 oz. AGW **Obverse:** Bust of Queen Elizabeth II right **Reverse:** Falcon

| Date | Mintage | F | VF | XF | Unc | BU |
|---|---|---|---|---|---|---|
| 1984 Proof | 150 | Value: 450 | | | | |

**2 PENCE** **KM# 144** **Composition:** Bronze **Obverse:** Head of Queen Elizabeth II right

| Date | Mintage | F | VF | XF | Unc | BU |
|---|---|---|---|---|---|---|
| 1985(W) AA | — | — | — | 0.20 | 0.50 | — |
| 1985(W) AB | — | — | — | 0.20 | 0.50 | — |
| 1985 Proof | 50,000 | Value: 3.00 | | | | |
| 1986 AA | — | — | — | 0.20 | 0.50 | — |
| 1986 AB | — | — | — | 0.20 | 0.50 | — |
| 1986 AC | — | — | — | 0.20 | 0.50 | — |
| 1986 AD | — | — | — | 0.20 | 0.50 | — |
| 1987 AA | — | — | — | 0.20 | 0.50 | — |
| 1987 AB | — | — | — | 0.20 | 0.50 | — |
| 1987 AC | — | — | — | 0.20 | 0.50 | — |
| 1987 AD | — | — | — | 0.20 | 0.50 | — |

**2 PENCE** **KM# 144b** **Weight:** 14.2000 g. **Composition:** 0.9170 Gold .4185 oz. AGW **Obverse:** Head of Queen Eliabeth II right

| Date | Mintage | F | VF | XF | Unc | BU |
|---|---|---|---|---|---|---|
| 1985 Proof | 300 | Value: 325 | | | | |

**2 PENCE** **KM# 144c** **Weight:** 16.0000 g. **Composition:** 0.9500 Platinum APW **Obverse:** Had of Queen Elizabeth II right

| Date | Mintage | F | VF | XF | Unc | BU |
|---|---|---|---|---|---|---|
| 1985 Proof | 200 | Value: 375 | | | | |

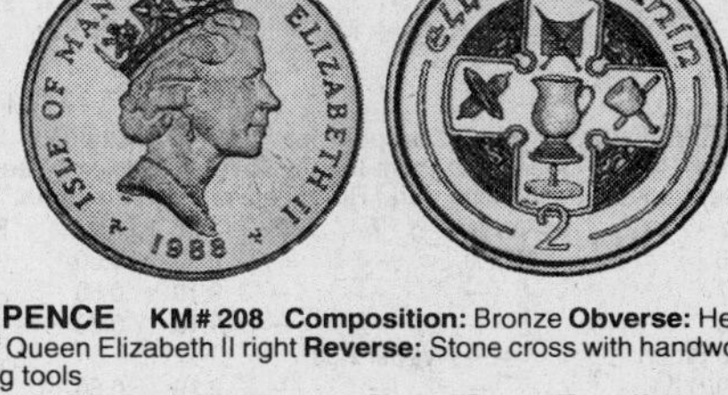

**2 PENCE** **KM# 208** **Composition:** Bronze **Obverse:** Head of Queen Elizabeth II right **Reverse:** Stone cross with handworking tools

| Date | Mintage | F | VF | XF | Unc | BU |
|---|---|---|---|---|---|---|
| 1988 AA | — | — | — | — | 0.30 | — |
| 1988 AB | — | — | — | 0.10 | 0.30 | — |
| 1988 AC | — | — | — | 0.10 | 0.30 | — |
| 1988 AD | — | — | — | 0.10 | 0.30 | — |
| 1989 AA | — | — | — | — | 0.30 | — |
| 1989 AB | — | — | — | 0.10 | 0.30 | — |
| 1989 AC | — | — | — | 0.10 | 0.30 | — |
| 1990 AA | — | — | — | — | 0.30 | — |
| 1991 AA | — | — | — | — | 0.30 | — |
| 1992 AA | — | — | — | — | 0.30 | — |
| 1993 AA | — | — | — | — | 0.30 | — |
| 1994 AA | — | — | — | — | 0.30 | — |
| 1995 AA | — | — | — | — | 0.30 | — |

**2 PENCE** **KM# 589** **Composition:** Bronze Clad Steel **Subject:** Sports **Obverse:** Head of Queen Elizabeth II right **Reverse:** Bicyclists

| Date | Mintage | F | VF | XF | Unc | BU |
|---|---|---|---|---|---|---|
| 1996 | — | — | — | — | 0.20 | — |

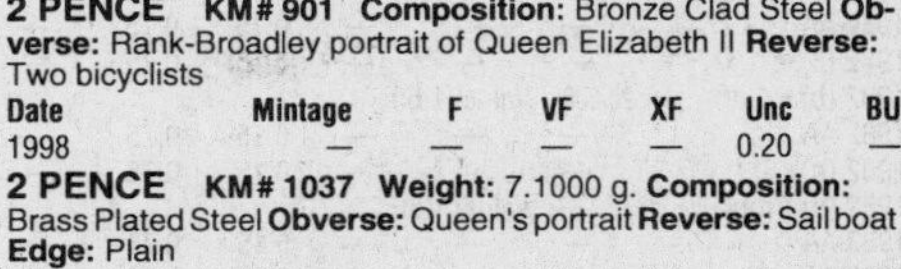

**2 PENCE** **KM# 901** **Composition:** Bronze Clad Steel **Obverse:** Rank-Broadley portrait of Queen Elizabeth II **Reverse:** Two bicyclists

| Date | Mintage | F | VF | XF | Unc | BU |
|---|---|---|---|---|---|---|
| 1998 | — | — | — | — | 0.20 | — |

**2 PENCE** **KM# 1037** **Weight:** 7.1000 g. **Composition:** Brass Plated Steel **Obverse:** Queen's portrait **Reverse:** Sailboat **Edge:** Plain

| Date | Mintage | F | VF | XF | Unc | BU |
|---|---|---|---|---|---|---|
| 2000 AA | — | — | — | — | 0.40 | — |

**5 NEW PENCE** **KM# 22** **Composition:** Copper-Nickel **Obverse:** Bust of Queen Elizabeth II right **Reverse:** Tower of Refuge

| Date | Mintage | F | VF | XF | Unc | BU |
|---|---|---|---|---|---|---|
| 1971 | 100,000 | — | — | 0.10 | 0.50 | — |
| 1971 Proof | 10,000 | Value: 2.50 | | | | |
| 1972 | 1,000 | — | — | — | 25.00 | — |
| 1973 | 1,000 | — | — | — | 25.00 | — |
| 1974 | 1,000 | — | — | — | 25.00 | — |
| 1975 | 1,400,000 | — | — | 0.10 | 0.25 | — |

**5 NEW PENCE** **KM# 22a** **Weight:** 6.5000 g. **Composition:** 0.9250 Silver .1933 oz. ASW **Obverse:** Bust of Queen Elizabeth II right

| Date | Mintage | F | VF | XF | Unc | BU |
|---|---|---|---|---|---|---|
| 1975 | 20,000 | — | — | — | 5.00 | — |

**5 NEW PENCE** **KM# 22b** **Weight:** 12.5000 g. **Composition:** 0.9500 Platinum .3818 oz. APW **Obverse:** Bust of Queen Elizabeth II right **Reverse:** Tower of Refuge

| Date | Mintage | F | VF | XF | Unc | BU |
|---|---|---|---|---|---|---|
| 1975 Proof | 600 | Value: 300 | | | | |

**5 PENCE** **KM# 35.1** **Composition:** Copper-Nickel **Obverse:** Bust of Queen Elizabeth II right **Reverse:** Laxey wheel **Note:** Lady Isabella; Mint mark: PM on obverse and reverse.

| Date | Mintage | F | VF | XF | Unc | BU |
|---|---|---|---|---|---|---|
| 1976 | 800,000 | — | — | 0.10 | 0.60 | — |
| 1977 | — | — | — | 0.10 | 0.60 | — |
| 1978 | — | — | — | 0.10 | 0.60 | — |
| 1978 Proof | — | Value: 1.50 | | | | |
| 1979(t) AA | — | — | — | 0.10 | 0.60 | — |

**5 PENCE** **KM# 35.1a** **Weight:** 6.5000 g. **Composition:** 0.9250 Silver .1933 oz. ASW **Obverse:** Bust of Queen Elizabeth II right

| Date | Mintage | F | VF | XF | Unc | BU |
|---|---|---|---|---|---|---|
| 1976 | 20,000 | — | — | — | 5.50 | — |
| 1977 Proof | 10,000 | Value: 5.50 | | | | |
| 1978 | 10,000 | — | — | — | 5.50 | — |
| 1979(t) AA Proof | 10,000 | Value: 5.50 | | | | |

**5 PENCE** **KM# 35.1b** **Weight:** 12.5000 g. **Composition:** 0.9500 Platinum .3818 oz. APW **Obverse:** Bust of Queen Elizabeth II right **Reverse:** Laxey wheel

| Date | Mintage | F | VF | XF | Unc | BU |
|---|---|---|---|---|---|---|
| 1976 Proof | 600 | Value: 300 | | | | |
| 1978 Proof | 600 | Value: 300 | | | | |
| 1979 Proof | 500 | Value: 300 | | | | |

**5 PENCE** **KM# 35.2** **Composition:** Copper-Nickel **Obverse:** Bust of Queen Elizabeth II right **Note:** Mint mark: PM on obverse only.

| Date | Mintage | F | VF | XF | Unc | BU |
|---|---|---|---|---|---|---|
| 1976 | Inc. above | — | — | 0.15 | 0.75 | — |

**5 PENCE** **KM# 61** **Composition:** Copper-Nickel **Obverse:** Bust of Queen Elizabeth II right **Reverse:** Loagthyn sheep

| Date | Mintage | F | VF | XF | Unc | BU |
|---|---|---|---|---|---|---|
| 1979 AA | — | — | — | 0.15 | 0.75 | — |
| 1979 AA | — | — | — | 0.15 | 0.75 | — |
| 1980 AA | — | — | — | 0.15 | 0.75 | — |
| 1980 AB | — | — | — | 0.15 | 0.75 | — |
| 1980 AC | — | — | — | 0.15 | 0.75 | — |
| 1980 Proof | — | Value: 1.50 | | | | |
| 1980 AA | — | — | — | 0.15 | 0.75 | — |
| 1980 AB | — | — | — | 0.15 | 0.75 | — |
| 1980 AC | — | — | — | 0.15 | 0.75 | — |
| 1981 AA | — | — | — | 0.15 | 0.75 | — |
| 1981 AA | — | — | — | 0.15 | 0.75 | — |
| 1982 AA | — | — | — | 0.15 | 0.75 | — |
| 1982 (b) | — | — | — | 0.15 | 0.75 | — |
| 1982 (b) Proof | 25,000 | Value: 1.50 | | | | |
| 1982 AA | — | — | — | 0.15 | 0.75 | — |
| 1982 (b) | — | — | — | 0.15 | 0.75 | — |
| 1982 (b) Proof | — | Value: 1.50 | | | | |
| 1983 AA | — | — | — | 0.15 | 0.75 | — |
| 1983 AA | — | — | — | 0.15 | 1.50 | — |

**5 PENCE** **KM# 61a** **Weight:** 6.5000 g. **Composition:** 0.5000 Silver .1045 oz. ASW **Obverse:** Bust of Queen Elizabeth II right

| Date | Mintage | F | VF | XF | Unc | BU |
|---|---|---|---|---|---|---|
| 1980 Proof | 10,000 | Value: 5.00 | | | | |

**5 PENCE** **KM# 61c** **Weight:** 11.0000 g. **Composition:** 0.9170 Gold .3243 oz. AGW **Obverse:** Bust of Queen Elizabeth II right **Reverse:** Loagthyn sheep

| Date | Mintage | F | VF | XF | Unc | BU |
|---|---|---|---|---|---|---|
| 1980 Proof | 300 | Value: 180 | | | | |
| 1982 (b) Proof | 500 | Value: 180 | | | | |
| 1983 Proof | — | Value: 180 | | | | |

**5 PENCE** **KM# 61d** **Weight:** 12.5000 g. **Composition:** 0.9500 Platinum .3818 oz. APW **Obverse:** Bust of Queen Elizabeth II right

| Date | Mintage | F | VF | XF | Unc | BU |
|---|---|---|---|---|---|---|
| 1980 Proof | 500 | Value: 300 | | | | |
| 1982 Proof | 500 | Value: 300 | | | | |
| 1983 Proof | — | Value: 300 | | | | |

**5 PENCE** **KM# 61b** **Weight:** 6.5000 g. **Composition:** 0.9250 Silver .1933 oz. ASW **Obverse:** Bust of Queen Elizabeth II right

| Date | Mintage | F | VF | XF | Unc | BU |
|---|---|---|---|---|---|---|
| 1981 Proof | — | Value: 5.00 | | | | |
| 1982 Proof | 10,000 | Value: 5.00 | | | | |
| 1983 Proof | 5,000 | Value: 5.00 | | | | |

**5 PENCE** **KM# 114** **Composition:** Copper-Nickel **Subject:** Quincentenary of the College of Arms **Obverse:** Bust of Queen Elizabeth II right **Reverse:** Cushag

| Date | Mintage | F | VF | XF | Unc | BU |
|---|---|---|---|---|---|---|
| 1984 AA | — | — | — | 0.10 | 0.50 | — |

**5 PENCE** **KM# 114a** **Weight:** 6.5000 g. **Composition:** 0.9250 Silver .1933 oz. ASW **Obverse:** Bust of Queen Elizabeth II right

| Date | Mintage | F | VF | XF | Unc | BU |
|---|---|---|---|---|---|---|
| 1984 Proof | — | Value: 5.00 | | | | |

**5 PENCE** **KM# 114b** **Weight:** 11.0000 g. **Composition:** 0.9170 Gold .3242 oz. AGW **Obverse:** Bust of Queen Elizabeth II right **Reverse:** Cushag

| Date | Mintage | F | VF | XF | Unc | BU |
|---|---|---|---|---|---|---|
| 1984 Proof | 150 | Value: 400 | | | | |

**5 PENCE** **KM# 145** **Composition:** Copper-Nickel **Obverse:** Head of Queen Elizabeth II right

| Date | Mintage | F | VF | XF | Unc | BU |
|---|---|---|---|---|---|---|
| 1985(w) AA | — | — | — | 0.10 | 0.50 | — |
| 1985 Proof | 50,000 | Value: 3.00 | | | | |
| 1986 AA | — | — | — | 0.10 | 0.50 | — |
| 1986 AB | — | — | — | 0.10 | 0.50 | — |
| 1986 AC | — | — | — | 0.10 | 0.50 | — |
| 1986 AD | — | — | — | 0.10 | 0.50 | — |
| 1987 AA | — | — | — | 0.10 | 0.50 | — |

**5 PENCE** **KM# 145a** **Weight:** 6.5000 g. **Composition:** 0.9250 Silver .1933 oz. ASW **Obverse:** Head of Queen Elizabeth II right

| Date | Mintage | F | VF | XF | Unc | BU |
|---|---|---|---|---|---|---|
| 1985 Proof | 10,000 | Value: 8.00 | | | | |

**5 PENCE** **KM# 145b** **Weight:** 11.0000 g. **Composition:** 0.9170 Gold .3242 oz. AGW **Obverse:** Head of Queen Elizabeth II right

| Date | Mintage | F | VF | XF | Unc | BU |
|---|---|---|---|---|---|---|
| 1985 Proof | 300 | Value: 180 | | | | |

**5 PENCE** **KM# 145c** **Weight:** 12.5000 g. **Composition:** 0.9500 Platinum .3818 oz. APW **Obverse:** Head of Queen Elizabeth II right

| Date | Mintage | F | VF | XF | Unc | BU |
|---|---|---|---|---|---|---|
| 1985 Proof | 200 | Value: 300 | | | | |

**5 PENCE** **KM# 209.1** **Composition:** Copper-Nickel **Obverse:** Head of Queen Elizabeth II right **Reverse:** Windsurfing

| Date | Mintage | F | VF | XF | Unc | BU |
|---|---|---|---|---|---|---|
| 1988 AA | — | — | — | — | 0.50 | — |
| 1989 AA | — | — | — | — | 0.50 | — |
| 1990 | — | — | — | — | 0.50 | — |

**5 PENCE** **KM# 209.2** **Composition:** Copper-Nickel **Obverse:** Head of Queen Elizabeth II right **Note:** Reduced size: 18mm.

| Date | Mintage | F | VF | XF | Unc | BU |
|---|---|---|---|---|---|---|
| 1990 AA | — | — | — | — | 0.50 | — |
| 1991 AA | — | — | — | — | 0.50 | — |
| 1991 AB | — | — | — | — | 0.50 | — |
| 1992 AA | — | — | — | — | 0.50 | — |
| 1993 AA | — | — | — | — | 0.50 | — |

**5 PENCE** **KM# 392** **Composition:** Copper-Nickel **Obverse:** Head of Queen Elizabeth II right **Reverse:** Golf clubs and ball

| Date | Mintage | F | VF | XF | Unc | BU |
|---|---|---|---|---|---|---|
| 1994 | — | — | — | — | 0.50 | — |
| 1995 | — | — | — | — | 0.50 | — |

**5 PENCE** **KM# 392a** **Weight:** 3.2500 g. **Composition:** 0.9250 Silver .0967 oz. ASW **Obverse:** Head of Queen Elizabeth II right

| Date | Mintage | F | VF | XF | Unc | BU |
|---|---|---|---|---|---|---|
| 1994 Proof | Est. 25,000 | Value: 10.00 | | | | |

**5 PENCE** **KM# 392b** **Weight:** 3.2500 g. **Composition:** 0.9170 Gold .0958 oz. AGW **Obverse:** Head of Queen Elizabeth II right **Reverse:** Golf clubs and ball

| Date | Mintage | F | VF | XF | Unc | BU |
|---|---|---|---|---|---|---|
| 1994 Proof | 10,000 | Value: 70.00 | | | | |

**5 PENCE** **KM# 392c** **Weight:** 3.2500 g. **Composition:** 0.9500 Platinum .0992 oz. APW

| Date | Mintage | F | VF | XF | Unc | BU |
|---|---|---|---|---|---|---|
| 1994 Proof | 3,500 | Value: 85.00 | | | | |

**5 PENCE** **KM# 590** **Composition:** Copper-Nickel **Subject:** Sports **Obverse:** Head of Queen Elizabeth II right **Reverse:** Golfer

| Date | Mintage | F | VF | XF | Unc | BU |
|---|---|---|---|---|---|---|
| 1996 AA | — | — | — | — | 0.50 | — |

**5 PENCE** **KM# 590a** **Weight:** 3.2500 g. **Composition:** 0.9250 Silver .0967 oz. ASW **Subject:** Sports **Obverse:** Head of Queen Elizabeth II right **Reverse:** Golfer

| Date | Mintage | F | VF | XF | Unc | BU |
|---|---|---|---|---|---|---|
| 1996 Proof | — | Value: 10.00 | | | | |

**5 PENCE** **KM# 902** **Composition:** Copper-Nickel **Obverse:** Rank-Broadley portrait of Queen Elizabeth II **Reverse:** Golfer in action

| Date | Mintage | F | VF | XF | Unc | BU |
|---|---|---|---|---|---|---|
| 1998 AA | — | — | — | — | 0.50 | — |

**5 PENCE** **KM# 1038** **Weight:** 3.2400 g. **Composition:** Copper-Nickel **Obverse:** Queen's portrait **Reverse:** Gaut's Cross **Edge:** Reeded

| Date | Mintage | F | VF | XF | Unc | BU |
|---|---|---|---|---|---|---|
| 2000 AC | — | — | — | — | 0.75 | — |

**10 NEW PENCE** **KM# 23** **Composition:** Copper-Nickel **Obverse:** Bust of Queen Elizabeth II right **Reverse:** Triskelion

| Date | Mintage | F | VF | XF | Unc | BU |
|---|---|---|---|---|---|---|
| 1971 | 100,000 | — | — | 0.20 | 0.50 | — |
| 1971 Proof | 10,000 | Value: 3.50 | | | | |
| 1972 | 1,000 | — | — | — | 25.00 | — |
| 1973 | 1,000 | — | — | — | 25.00 | — |
| 1974 | 1,000 | — | — | — | 25.00 | — |
| 1975 | 1,500,000 | — | — | 0.20 | 0.40 | — |

**10 NEW PENCE** **KM# 23a** **Weight:** 13.0000 g. **Composition:** 0.9250 Silver .3866 oz. ASW **Obverse:** Bust of Queen Elizabeth II right

| Date | Mintage | F | VF | XF | Unc | BU |
|---|---|---|---|---|---|---|
| 1975 | 20,000 | — | — | — | 10.00 | — |

**10 NEW PENCE** **KM# 23b** **Weight:** 25.0000 g. **Composition:** 0.9500 Platinum .7636 oz. APW **Obverse:** Bust of Queen Elizabeth II right **Reverse:** Triskelion

| Date | Mintage | F | VF | XF | Unc | BU |
|---|---|---|---|---|---|---|
| 1975 Proof | 600 | Value: 580 | | | | |

**10 PENCE** **KM# 36.1** **Composition:** Copper-Nickel **Obverse:** Bust of Queen Elizabeth II right **Reverse:** Triskelion **Note:** Mintmark: PM on obverse and reverse.

| Date | Mintage | F | VF | XF | Unc | BU |
|---|---|---|---|---|---|---|
| 1976 | 2,800,000 | — | — | 0.20 | 0.80 | — |
| 1977 | — | — | — | 0.20 | 0.80 | — |
| 1978 | — | — | — | 0.20 | 0.80 | — |
| 1978 Proof | — | Value: 2.00 | | | | |
| 1979(t) AA | — | — | — | 0.20 | 0.80 | — |
| 1979(t) AB | — | — | — | 0.20 | 0.80 | — |

**10 PENCE** **KM# 36.1a** **Weight:** 13.0000 g. **Composition:** 0.9250 Silver .3866 oz. ASW **Obverse:** Bust of Queen Elizabeth II right

| Date | Mintage | F | VF | XF | Unc | BU |
|---|---|---|---|---|---|---|
| 1976 | 20,000 | — | — | — | 10.00 | — |
| 1977 Proof | 10,000 | Value: 10.00 | | | | |
| 1978 | 10,000 | — | — | — | 10.00 | — |
| 1979 (t) Proof | 10,000 | Value: 10.00 | | | | |

**10 PENCE** **KM# 36.1b** **Weight:** 25.0000 g. **Composition:** 0.9500 Platinum .7636 oz. APW **Obverse:** Bust of Queen Elizabeth II right **Reverse:** Triskelion

| Date | Mintage | F | VF | XF | Unc | BU |
|---|---|---|---|---|---|---|
| 1976 Proof | 600 | Value: 580 | | | | |
| 1978 Proof | 600 | Value: 580 | | | | |
| 1979 (t) Proof | 500 | Value: 580 | | | | |

**10 PENCE** **KM# 36.2** **Composition:** Copper-Nickel **Obverse:** Bust of Queen Elizabeth II right **Note:** Mintmark: PM on obverse only.

| Date | Mintage | F | VF | XF | Unc | BU |
|---|---|---|---|---|---|---|
| 1976 | Inc. above | — | — | 0.20 | 1.00 | — |

**10 PENCE** **KM# 62** **Composition:** Copper-Nickel **Obverse:** Bust of Queen Elizabeth II right **Reverse:** Gyrfalcon

| Date | Mintage | F | VF | XF | Unc | BU |
|---|---|---|---|---|---|---|
| 1980 AA | — | — | — | 0.25 | 1.00 | — |
| 1980 AB | — | — | — | 0.25 | 1.00 | — |
| 1980 Proof | — | Value: 2.00 | | | | |
| 1981 AA | — | — | — | 0.25 | 1.00 | — |
| 1982 AA | — | — | — | 0.25 | 1.00 | — |
| 1982 AB | — | — | — | 0.25 | 1.00 | — |
| 1982 AB(b) | — | — | — | 0.25 | 1.00 | — |
| 1982 AC | — | — | — | 0.25 | 1.00 | — |
| 1982 AD | — | — | — | 0.25 | 1.00 | — |
| 1982 (b) Proof | 25,000 | Value: 2.00 | | | | |
| 1983 AA | — | — | — | 0.25 | 1.00 | — |
| 1983 AB | — | — | — | 0.25 | 1.00 | — |
| 1983 AC | — | — | — | 0.25 | 1.00 | — |
| 1983 AD | — | — | — | 0.25 | 1.00 | — |

**10 PENCE** **KM# 62a** **Weight:** 13.0000 g. **Composition:** 0.5000 Silver .2090 oz. ASW **Obverse:** Bust of Queen Elizabeth II right

| Date | Mintage | F | VF | XF | Unc | BU |
|---|---|---|---|---|---|---|
| 1980 Proof | 10,000 | Value: 10.00 | | | | |

**10 PENCE** **KM# 62c** **Weight:** 22.0000 g. **Composition:** 0.9170 Gold .6486 oz. AGW **Obverse:** Bust of Queen Elizabeth II right **Reverse:** Falcon

| Date | Mintage | F | VF | XF | Unc | BU |
|---|---|---|---|---|---|---|
| 1980 Proof | 300 | Value: 350 | | | | |
| 1982 (b) Proof | 500 | Value: 350 | | | | |
| 1983 Proof | — | Value: 350 | | | | |

**10 PENCE** **KM# 62d** **Weight:** 25.0000 g. **Composition:** 0.9500 Platinum .7636 oz. APW **Obverse:** Bust of Queen Elizabeth II right

| Date | Mintage | F | VF | XF | Unc | BU |
|---|---|---|---|---|---|---|
| 1980 Proof | 500 | Value: 580 | | | | |
| 1982 (b) Proof | 500 | Value: 580 | | | | |
| 1983 Proof | — | Value: 580 | | | | |

**10 PENCE** **KM# 62b** **Weight:** 13.0000 g. **Composition:** 0.9250 Silver .3866 oz. ASW **Obverse:** Bust of Queen Elizabeth II right

| Date | Mintage | F | VF | XF | Unc | BU |
|---|---|---|---|---|---|---|
| 1981 Proof | — | Value: 10.00 | | | | |
| 1982 Proof | 10,000 | Value: 10.00 | | | | |
| 1983 Proof | 5,000 | Value: 12.50 | | | | |

**10 PENCE** **KM# 115** **Composition:** Copper-Nickel **Subject:** Quincentenary of the College of Arms **Obverse:** Bust of Queen Elizabeth II right **Reverse:** Loagthyn ram

| Date | Mintage | F | VF | XF | Unc | BU |
|---|---|---|---|---|---|---|
| 1984 AA | — | — | — | 0.20 | 0.80 | — |
| 1984 AB | — | — | — | 0.20 | 0.80 | — |
| 1984 AC | — | — | — | 0.20 | 0.80 | — |
| 1984 AD | — | — | — | 0.20 | 0.80 | — |
| 1984 AE | — | — | — | 0.20 | 0.80 | — |
| 1984 AF | — | — | — | 0.20 | 0.80 | — |
| 1984 AG | — | — | — | 0.20 | 0.80 | — |

**10 PENCE** **KM# 115a** **Composition:** Silver **Obverse:** Bust of Queen Elizabeth II right

| Date | Mintage | F | VF | XF | Unc | BU |
|---|---|---|---|---|---|---|
| 1984 Proof | — | Value: 10.00 | | | | |

**10 PENCE** **KM# 115b** **Weight:** 22.0000 g. **Composition:** 0.9170 Gold .6484 oz. AGW **Obverse:** Bust of Queen Elizabeth II right **Reverse:** Loagthyn ram

| Date | Mintage | F | VF | XF | Unc | BU |
|---|---|---|---|---|---|---|
| 1984 Proof | 150 | Value: 700 | | | | |

**10 PENCE** **KM# 146** **Composition:** Copper-Nickel **Obverse:** Head of Queen Elizabeth II right

| Date | Mintage | F | VF | XF | Unc | BU |
|---|---|---|---|---|---|---|
| 1985(w) AA | — | — | — | 0.20 | 0.80 | — |
| 1985(w) AB | — | — | — | 0.20 | 0.80 | — |
| 1985 Proof | 50,000 | Value: 3.00 | | | | |
| 1986 AA | — | — | — | 0.20 | 0.80 | — |
| 1987 AA | — | — | — | 0.20 | 0.80 | — |

**10 PENCE** **KM# 146a** **Weight:** 13.0000 g. **Composition:** 0.9250 Silver .3866 oz. ASW **Obverse:** Head of Queen Elizabeth II right

| Date | Mintage | F | VF | XF | Unc | BU |
|---|---|---|---|---|---|---|
| 1985 Proof | 10,000 | Value: 18.00 | | | | |

**10 PENCE** **KM# 146b** **Weight:** 22.0000 g. **Composition:** 0.9170 Gold .6484 oz. AGW **Obverse:** Head of Queen Elizabeth II right

| Date | Mintage | F | VF | XF | Unc | BU |
|---|---|---|---|---|---|---|
| 1985 Proof | 300 | Value: 500 | | | | |

**10 PENCE** **KM# 146c** **Weight:** 25.0000 g. **Composition:** 0.9500 Platinum .7636 oz. APW **Obverse:** Head of Queen Elizabeth II right

| Date | Mintage | F | VF | XF | Unc | BU |
|---|---|---|---|---|---|---|
| 1985 Proof | 200 | Value: 600 | | | | |

**10 PENCE** **KM# 210** **Composition:** Copper-Nickel **Obverse:** Head of Queen Elizabeth II right **Reverse:** Island and portcullis on globe

| Date | Mintage | F | VF | XF | Unc | BU |
|---|---|---|---|---|---|---|
| 1988 AA | — | — | — | — | 0.75 | — |
| 1989 AA | — | — | — | — | 0.75 | — |
| 1990 | — | — | — | — | 0.75 | — |
| 1991 | — | — | — | — | 0.75 | — |
| 1992 | — | — | — | — | 0.75 | — |

**10 PENCE** **KM# 337** **Composition:** Copper-Nickel **Obverse:** Head of Queen Elizabeth II right **Reverse:** Triskeles symbol **Note:** Varieties exist.

| Date | Mintage | F | VF | XF | Unc | BU |
|---|---|---|---|---|---|---|
| 1992 AA | — | — | — | — | 0.75 | — |
| 1992 AB | — | — | — | — | 0.75 | — |
| 1992 AC | — | — | — | — | 0.75 | — |
| 1993 AA | — | — | — | — | 0.75 | — |
| 1994 AA | — | — | — | — | 0.75 | — |
| 1995 AA | — | — | — | — | 0.75 | — |

**10 PENCE** **KM# 337a** **Weight:** 8.0457 g. **Composition:** 0.9250 Silver .2392 oz. ASW **Obverse:** Head of Queen Elizabeth II right

| Date | Mintage | F | VF | XF | Unc | BU |
|---|---|---|---|---|---|---|
| 1992 Proof | — | Value: 13.50 | | | | |

**10 PENCE** **KM# 337b** **Weight:** 13.6158 g. **Composition:** 0.9170 Gold .4013 oz. AGW **Obverse:** Head of Queen Elizabeth II right **Reverse:** Triskeles symbol

| Date | Mintage | F | VF | XF | Unc | BU |
|---|---|---|---|---|---|---|
| 1992 Proof | — | Value: 285 | | | | |

**10 PENCE** **KM# 337c** **Weight:** 15.4725 g. **Composition:** 0.9500 Platinum .4725 oz. APW **Obverse:** Head of Queen Elizabeth II right

| Date | Mintage | F | VF | XF | Unc | BU |
|---|---|---|---|---|---|---|
| 1992 Proof | — | Value: 400 | | | | |

**10 PENCE** **KM# 591** **Composition:** Copper-Nickel **Subject:** Sports **Obverse:** Head of Queen Elizabeth II right **Reverse:** Sailboat

| Date | Mintage | F | VF | XF | Unc | BU |
|---|---|---|---|---|---|---|
| 1996 AA | — | — | — | — | 1.00 | — |

**10 PENCE** **KM# 591a** **Weight:** 8.0457 g. **Composition:** 0.9250 Silver .2392 oz. ASW **Subject:** Sports **Obverse:** Head of Queen Elizabeth II right **Reverse:** Sailboat

| Date | Mintage | F | VF | XF | Unc | BU |
|---|---|---|---|---|---|---|
| 1996 Proof | — | Value: 22.50 | | | | |

**10 PENCE** **KM# 903** **Composition:** Copper-Nickel **Obverse:** Rank-Broadley portrait of Queen Elizabeth II **Reverse:** Sailboat

| Date | Mintage | F | VF | XF | Unc | BU |
|---|---|---|---|---|---|---|
| 1998 | — | — | — | — | 1.00 | — |

**10 PENCE** **KM# 1039** **Weight:** 6.5500 g. **Composition:** Copper-Nickel **Obverse:** Queen's portrait **Reverse:** St. German's Cathedral **Edge:** Reeded

| Date | Mintage | F | VF | XF | Unc | BU |
|---|---|---|---|---|---|---|
| 2000 AA | — | — | — | — | 1.00 | — |

**20 PENCE** **KM# 90** **Composition:** Copper-Nickel **Subject:** Medieval Norse History **Obverse:** Bust of Queen Elizabeth II right

| Date | Mintage | F | VF | XF | Unc | BU |
|---|---|---|---|---|---|---|
| 1982 AA | 30,000 | — | — | 0.35 | 1.00 | — |
| 1982 AB | — | — | — | 0.35 | 1.00 | — |
| 1982 AB(b) | — | — | 0.50 | 1.00 | 5.00 | — |
| 1982 AC | — | — | — | 0.35 | 1.00 | — |
| 1982 AD | — | — | — | 0.35 | 1.00 | — |
| 1982 (b) Proof | 25,000 | Value: 6.00 | | | | |
| 1982 BB Proof | — | Value: 1.00 | | | | |
| 1983 AA | — | — | — | 0.35 | 1.00 | — |

**20 PENCE** **KM# 90a** **Weight:** 6.0000 g. **Composition:** 0.9250 Silver .1784 oz. ASW **Subject:** Medieval Norse History **Obverse:** Head of Queen Elizabeth II right

| Date | Mintage | F | VF | XF | Unc | BU |
|---|---|---|---|---|---|---|
| 1982 Proof | 15,000 | Value: 10.00 | | | | |
| 1982 (b) Proof | 10,000 | Value: 10.00 | | | | |
| 1983 Proof | 5,000 | Value: 15.00 | | | | |

**20 PENCE** **KM# 90b** **Weight:** 10.0000 g. **Composition:** 0.9170 Gold .2948 oz. AGW **Subject:** Medieval Norse History **Obverse:** Bust of Queen Elizabeth II right

| Date | Mintage | F | VF | XF | Unc | BU |
|---|---|---|---|---|---|---|
| 1982 Proof | 1,500 | Value: 180 | | | | |
| 1982 (b) Proof | 500 | Value: 180 | | | | |
| 1983 Proof | — | Value: 180 | | | | |

**20 PENCE** **KM# 90c** **Weight:** 11.3000 g. **Composition:** 0.9500 Platinum .3452 oz. APW **Subject:** Medieval Norse History **Obverse:** Bust of Queen Elizabeth II right

| Date | Mintage | F | VF | XF | Unc | BU |
|---|---|---|---|---|---|---|
| 1982 Proof | 250 | Value: 275 | | | | |
| 1982 (b) Proof | 500 | Value: 275 | | | | |
| 1983 Proof | — | Value: 275 | | | | |

**20 PENCE** **KM# 116** **Composition:** Copper-Nickel **Subject:** Quincentenary of the College of Arms **Obverse:** Bust of Queen Elizabeth II right **Reverse:** Atlantic herring

| Date | Mintage | F | VF | XF | Unc | BU |
|---|---|---|---|---|---|---|
| 1984 AA | — | — | — | 0.35 | 1.00 | — |

**20 PENCE** **KM# 116a** **Composition:** Silver **Subject:** Quincentenary of the College of Arms **Obverse:** Bust of Queen Elizabeth II right **Reverse:** Atlantic herring

| Date | Mintage | F | VF | XF | Unc | BU |
|---|---|---|---|---|---|---|
| 1984 Proof | — | Value: 20.00 | | | | |

**20 PENCE** **KM# 116b** **Weight:** 5.0000 g. **Composition:** 0.9170 Gold .1474 oz. AGW **Subject:** Quincentenary of the College of Arms **Obverse:** Bust of Queen Elizabeth II right **Reverse:** Atlantic herring

| Date | Mintage | F | VF | XF | Unc | BU |
|---|---|---|---|---|---|---|
| 1984 Proof | 150 | Value: 175 | | | | |

**20 PENCE** **KM# 147** **Composition:** Copper-Nickel **Obverse:** Head of Queen Elizabeth II right **Reverse:** Atlantic herring

| Date | Mintage | F | VF | XF | Unc | BU |
|---|---|---|---|---|---|---|
| 1985(w) AA | — | — | — | 0.35 | 1.00 | — |
| 1985 Proof | 50,000 | Value: 3.00 | | | | |
| 1986 AA | — | — | — | 0.35 | 1.00 | — |
| 1986 AB | — | — | — | 0.35 | 1.00 | — |
| 1986 AC | — | — | — | 0.35 | 1.00 | — |
| 1987 AA | — | — | — | 0.35 | 1.00 | — |

**20 PENCE** **KM# 147a** **Weight:** 5.0000 g. **Composition:** 0.9250 Silver .1487 oz. ASW **Obverse:** Head of Queen Elizabeth II right **Reverse:** Atlantic herring

| Date | Mintage | F | VF | XF | Unc | BU |
|---|---|---|---|---|---|---|
| 1985 Proof | 10,000 | Value: 8.00 | | | | |

**20 PENCE** **KM# 147b** **Weight:** 5.0000 g. **Composition:** 0.9170 Gold .1474 oz. AGW **Obverse:** Head of Queen Elizabeth II right **Reverse:** Atlantic herring

| Date | Mintage | F | VF | XF | Unc | BU |
|---|---|---|---|---|---|---|
| 1985 Proof | 300 | Value: 100 | | | | |

**20 PENCE** **KM# 147c** **Weight:** 5.0000 g. **Composition:** 0.9500 Platinum .1527 oz. APW **Obverse:** Head of Queen Elizabeth II right **Obv. Legend:** Atlantic herring

| Date | Mintage | F | VF | XF | Unc | BU |
|---|---|---|---|---|---|---|
| 1985 Proof | 200 | Value: 120 | | | | |

**20 PENCE** **KM# 211** **Composition:** Copper-Nickel **Obverse:** Head of Queen Elizabeth II right **Reverse:** Farm combine harverster

| Date | Mintage | F | VF | XF | Unc | BU |
|---|---|---|---|---|---|---|
| 1988 AA | — | — | — | — | 1.00 | — |
| 1989 AA | — | — | — | — | 1.00 | — |
| 1990 AA | — | — | — | — | 1.00 | — |
| 1991 AA | — | — | — | — | 1.00 | — |
| 1992 AA | — | — | — | — | 1.00 | — |
| 1993 AA | — | — | — | — | 1.00 | — |

**20 PENCE** **KM# 391** **Composition:** Copper-Nickel **Obverse:** Head of Queen Elizabeth II right **Reverse:** Farm combine harverster **Note:** Obverse and reverse design revised with border.

| Date | Mintage | F | VF | XF | Unc | BU |
|---|---|---|---|---|---|---|
| 1993 AA | — | — | — | — | 1.00 | — |
| 1994 AA | — | — | — | — | 1.00 | — |
| 1995 AA | — | — | — | — | 1.00 | — |

**20 PENCE** **KM# 592** **Composition:** Copper-Nickel **Subject:** Sports **Obverse:** Head of Queen Elizabeth II right **Reverse:** Race cars

| Date | Mintage | F | VF | XF | Unc | BU |
|---|---|---|---|---|---|---|
| 1996 AA | — | — | — | — | 1.25 | — |

**20 PENCE** **KM# 904** **Composition:** Copper-Nickel **Obverse:** Rank-Broadley portrait of Queen Elizabeth II **Reverse:** Race cars

| Date | Mintage | F | VF | XF | Unc | BU |
|---|---|---|---|---|---|---|
| 1998 AA | — | — | — | — | 1.25 | — |

**20 PENCE** **KM# 1040** **Weight:** 4.9100 g. **Composition:** Copper-Nickel **Subject:** Rushen Abbey **Obverse:** Queen's portrait **Reverse:** Monk writing **Edge:** Plain, seven sided

| Date | Mintage | F | VF | XF | Unc | BU |
|---|---|---|---|---|---|---|
| 2000 AA | — | — | — | — | 1.50 | — |

**50 NEW PENCE** **KM# 24** **Composition:** Copper-Nickel **Obverse:** Bust of Queen Elizabeth II right **Reverse:** Viking ship sailing right

| Date | Mintage | F | VF | XF | Unc | BU |
|---|---|---|---|---|---|---|
| 1971 | 100,000 | — | — | 0.75 | 1.50 | — |
| 1971 Proof | 10,000 | Value: 7.50 | | | | |
| 1972 | 1,000 | — | — | — | 30.00 | — |
| 1973 | 1,000 | — | — | — | 30.00 | — |
| 1974 | 1,000 | — | — | — | 30.00 | — |
| 1975 | 227,000 | — | — | 0.75 | 1.50 | — |

**50 NEW PENCE** **KM# 24a** **Weight:** 15.5000 g. **Composition:** 0.9250 Silver .4610 oz. ASW **Obverse:** Bust of Queen Elizabeth II right **Reverse:** Viking ship sailing right

| Date | Mintage | F | VF | XF | Unc | BU |
|---|---|---|---|---|---|---|
| 1975 | 20,000 | — | — | — | 12.50 | — |

**50 NEW PENCE** **KM# 24b** **Weight:** 30.4000 g. **Composition:** 0.9500 Platinum .9286 oz. APW **Obverse:** Bust of Queen Elizabeth II right **Reverse:** Viking ship sailing right

| Date | Mintage | F | VF | XF | Unc | BU |
|---|---|---|---|---|---|---|
| 1975 Proof | 600 | Value: 650 | | | | |

**50 PENCE** **KM# 39** **Composition:** Copper-Nickel **Obverse:** Bust of Queen Elizabeth II right **Reverse:** Viking ship sailing left

| Date | Mintage | F | VF | XF | Unc | BU |
|---|---|---|---|---|---|---|
| 1976 | 250,000 | — | — | 0.75 | 2.00 | — |
| 1977 | 50,000 | — | — | 0.75 | 2.50 | — |
| 1978 | 25,000 | — | — | 0.75 | 2.50 | — |
| 1978 Proof | — | Value: 3.50 | | | | |
| 1979 (t)AA | — | — | — | 0.75 | 3.00 | — |

**50 PENCE** **KM# 39a** **Weight:** 15.5000 g. **Composition:** 0.9250 Silver .4610 oz. ASW **Obverse:** Bust of Queen Elizabeth II right **Reverse:** Viking ship sailing left

| Date | Mintage | F | VF | XF | Unc | BU |
|---|---|---|---|---|---|---|
| 1976 | 20,000 | — | — | — | 12.50 | — |
| 1977 Proof | 10,000 | Value: 12.50 | | | | |
| 1978 | 10,000 | — | — | — | 12.50 | — |
| 1979 (t) Proof | 10,000 | Value: 12.50 | | | | |

**50 PENCE** **KM# 39b** **Weight:** 30.4000 g. **Composition:** 0.9500 Platinum .9286 oz. APW **Obverse:** Bust of Queen Elizabeth II right **Reverse:** Viking ship sailing left

| Date | Mintage | F | VF | XF | Unc | BU |
|---|---|---|---|---|---|---|
| 1976 Proof | 600 | Value: 650 | | | | |
| 1978 Proof | 600 | Value: 650 | | | | |
| 1979 (t) Proof | 500 | Value: 650 | | | | |

**50 PENCE** **KM# 51.1** **Composition:** Copper-Nickel **Subject:** Manx Day of Tynwald, July 5 **Obverse:** Bust of Queen Elizabeth II right **Reverse:** Ship **Edge:** Upright with obverse on top **Edge Lettering:** H.M.Q.E. II ROYAL VISIT I.OM. JULY 5, 1979

| Date | Mintage | F | VF | XF | Unc | BU |
|---|---|---|---|---|---|---|
| 1979 AA | 50,000 | — | — | — | 5.00 | — |
| 1979 AB | — | — | — | — | 5.00 | — |

**50 PENCE** **KM# 51.2** **Composition:** Copper-Nickel **Obverse:** Bust of Queen Elizabeth II right **Reverse:** Ship **Edge:** Lettering upright with reverse on top

| Date | Mintage | F | VF | XF | Unc | BU |
|---|---|---|---|---|---|---|
| 1979 AA | — | — | — | — | 5.00 | — |
| 1979 AB | — | — | — | — | 5.00 | — |

**50 PENCE** **KM# 51.3** **Composition:** Copper-Nickel **Obverse:** Bust of Queen Elizabeth II right **Reverse:** Ship **Note:** Inscription not centered in flat sections.

| Date | Mintage | F | VF | XF | Unc | BU |
|---|---|---|---|---|---|---|
| 1979 AA | — | — | — | — | 5.00 | — |
| 1979 AB | — | — | — | — | 5.00 | — |

**50 PENCE** **KM# 51a** **Weight:** 15.5000 g. **Composition:** 0.9250 Silver .4610 oz. ASW **Obverse:** Bust of Queen Elizabeth II right **Reverse:** Ship

| Date | Mintage | F | VF | XF | Unc | BU |
|---|---|---|---|---|---|---|
| 1979 | 10,000 | — | — | — | 10.00 | — |
| 1979 Proof | 5,000 | Value: 15.00 | | | | |

**50 PENCE** **KM# 51b** **Weight:** 30.4000 g. **Composition:** 0.9500 Platinum .9286 oz. APW **Subject:** Manx Millenium of Tynwald **Obverse:** Bust of Queen Elizabeth II right **Reverse:** Ship **Edge:** H.M.Q.E. II ROYAL VISIT I.O.M. JULY 5, 1979

| Date | Mintage | F | VF | XF | Unc | BU |
|---|---|---|---|---|---|---|
| 1979 Proof | 500 | Value: 650 | | | | |

**50 PENCE** **KM# 53** **Composition:** Copper-Nickel **Obverse:** Bust of Queen Elizabeth II right **Reverse:** Odin's raven, Point of Ayre lighthouse

| Date | Mintage | F | VF | XF | Unc | BU |
|---|---|---|---|---|---|---|
| 1979 AA | — | — | — | — | 3.00 | — |
| 1979 AB | — | — | — | — | 3.00 | — |

**50 PENCE** **KM# 53a** **Weight:** 15.5000 g. **Composition:** 0.9250 Silver .4610 oz. ASW **Obverse:** Bust of Queen Elizabeth II right **Reverse:** Odin's Raven, Point of Ayre lighhouse

| Date | Mintage | F | VF | XF | Unc | BU |
|---|---|---|---|---|---|---|
| 1979 | — | — | — | — | 10.00 | — |
| 1979 Proof | — | Value: 15.00 | | | | |

**50 PENCE** **KM# 71b** **Weight:** 26.0000 g. **Composition:** 0.9170 Gold .7666 oz. AGW **Subject:** Christmas 1980 **Obverse:** Bust of Queen Elizabeth II right **Reverse:** Carriage

| Date | Mintage | F | VF | XF | Unc | BU |
|---|---|---|---|---|---|---|
| 1980 Proof | 250 | Value: 500 | | | | |

**50 PENCE** **KM# 70d** **Weight:** 30.4000 g. **Composition:** 0.9500 Platinum .9286 oz. APW **Obverse:** Bust of Queen Elizabeth II right **Reverse:** Viking longship

| Date | Mintage | F | VF | XF | Unc | BU |
|---|---|---|---|---|---|---|
| 1980 Proof | 500 | Value: 750 | | | | |
| 1982 (b) Proof | 500 | Value: 750 | | | | |
| 1983 Proof | — | Value: 750 | | | | |

**50 PENCE** **KM# 71c** **Weight:** 30.4000 g. **Composition:** 0.9500 Platinum .9286 oz. APW **Obverse:** Bust of Queen Elizabeth II right **Reverse:** Carriage

| Date | Mintage | F | VF | XF | Unc | BU |
|---|---|---|---|---|---|---|
| 1980 Proof | 50 | Value: 775 | | | | |

**50 PENCE** **KM# 71** **Composition:** Copper-Nickel **Subject:** Christmas 1980 **Obverse:** Bust of Queen Elizabeth II right **Reverse:** Carriage

| Date | Mintage | F | VF | XF | Unc | BU |
|---|---|---|---|---|---|---|
| 1980 AA | 30,000 | — | — | — | 2.50 | — |
| 1980 AB | — | — | — | — | 2.50 | — |
| 1980 AD | — | — | — | — | 2.50 | — |

**50 PENCE** **KM# 71a** **Weight:** 15.5000 g. **Composition:** 0.9250 Silver .4610 oz. ASW **Obverse:** Bust of Queen Elizabeth II right **Reverse:** Carriage

| Date | Mintage | F | VF | XF | Unc | BU |
|---|---|---|---|---|---|---|
| 1980 Proof | 5,000 | Value: 12.50 | | | | |

**50 PENCE KM# 70 Composition:** Copper-Nickel **Obverse:** Bust of Queen Elizabeth II right **Reverse:** Viking longship

| Date | Mintage | F | VF | XF | Unc | BU |
|---|---|---|---|---|---|---|
| 1980 AA | 10,000 | — | — | 0.75 | 2.00 | — |
| 1980 AB | — | — | — | 0.75 | 2.00 | — |
| 1980 Proof | — | Value: 2.50 | | | | |
| 1981 AA | — | — | — | 0.75 | 2.00 | — |
| 1982 AC | — | — | — | 0.75 | 2.00 | — |
| 1982 (b) | — | — | — | 0.75 | 2.00 | — |
| 1982 (b) Proof | 25,000 | Value: 2.50 | | | | |
| 1983 AA | — | — | — | 0.75 | 2.00 | — |
| 1984 AA | — | — | — | 0.75 | 2.00 | — |

**50 PENCE KM# 57 Weight:** 15.5000 g. **Composition:** 0.9250 Silver .4610 oz. ASW **Obverse:** Bust of Queen Elizabeth II right **Reverse:** Carriage **Note:** Mule.

| Date | Mintage | F | VF | XF | Unc | BU |
|---|---|---|---|---|---|---|
| 1980 | — | — | — | — | — | — |

**50 PENCE KM# 69 Weight:** 15.5000 g. **Composition:** 0.9250 Silver .4610 oz. ASW **Obverse:** Bust of Queen Elizabeth II right **Edge Lettering:** ODINS RAVEN VIKING EXHIBN NEW YORK 1980

| Date | Mintage | F | VF | XF | Unc | BU |
|---|---|---|---|---|---|---|
| 1980 AA | 20,000 | — | — | — | 4.00 | — |

**50 PENCE KM# 69a Weight:** 15.5000 g. **Composition:** 0.9250 Silver .4610 oz. ASW **Obverse:** Bust of Queen Elizabeth II right

| Date | Mintage | F | VF | XF | Unc | BU |
|---|---|---|---|---|---|---|
| 1980 | — | — | — | — | 15.00 | — |
| 1980 Proof | 5,000 | Value: 20.00 | | | | |

**50 PENCE KM# 69b Weight:** 26.0000 g. **Composition:** 0.9170 Gold .7666 oz. AGW **Obverse:** Bust of Queen Elizabeth II right **Edge Lettering:** ODINS RAVEN VIKING EXHIBN NEW YORK 1980

| Date | Mintage | F | VF | XF | Unc | BU |
|---|---|---|---|---|---|---|
| 1980 | 250 | — | — | — | 500 | — |

**50 PENCE KM# 69c Weight:** 30.4000 g. **Composition:** 0.9500 Platinum .9286 oz. APW **Obverse:** Bust of Queen Elizabeth II right

| Date | Mintage | F | VF | XF | Unc | BU |
|---|---|---|---|---|---|---|
| 1980 Proof | 50 | Value: 775 | | | | |

**50 PENCE KM# 70a Weight:** 15.5000 g. **Composition:** 0.5000 Silver .2491 oz. ASW **Obverse:** Bust of Queen Elizabeth II right **Reverse:** Viking longship

| Date | Mintage | F | VF | XF | Unc | BU |
|---|---|---|---|---|---|---|
| 1980 Proof | 10,000 | Value: 10.00 | | | | |
| 1982 (b) Proof | 10,000 | Value: 15.00 | | | | |

**50 PENCE KM# 70c Weight:** 26.0000 g. **Composition:** 0.9170 Gold .7666 oz. AGW **Obverse:** Bust of Queen Elizabeth II right **Reverse:** Viking longship

| Date | Mintage | F | VF | XF | Unc | BU |
|---|---|---|---|---|---|---|
| 1980 Proof | 300 | Value: 500 | | | | |
| 1982 (b) Proof | 500 | Value: 500 | | | | |
| 1983 Proof | — | Value: 500 | | | | |

**50 PENCE KM# 83 Composition:** Copper-Nickel **Subject:** Tourist Trophy Motorcycle Races **Obverse:** Bust of Queen Elizabeth II right **Reverse:** Motorcyclist - Joey Dunlop

| Date | Mintage | F | VF | XF | Unc | BU |
|---|---|---|---|---|---|---|
| 1981 AA | 30,000 | — | — | — | 3.00 | — |
| 1981 AB | Inc. above | — | — | — | 3.00 | — |

**50 PENCE KM# 84 Composition:** Copper-Nickel **Subject:** Christmas 1981 **Obverse:** Bust of Queen Elizabeth II right **Reverse:** Manx Nickey boat

| Date | Mintage | F | VF | XF | Unc | BU |
|---|---|---|---|---|---|---|
| 1981 AA | 30,000 | — | — | — | 3.00 | — |
| 1981 AB | Inc. above | — | — | — | 3.00 | — |
| 1981 Proof | — | Value: 7.50 | | | | |

**50 PENCE KM# 83a Weight:** 15.5000 g. **Composition:** 0.9250 Silver .4610 oz. ASW **Subject:** Tourist Trophy Motorcycle Races **Obverse:** Bust of Queen Elizabeth II right **Reverse:** Motorcyclist - Joey Dunlop

| Date | Mintage | F | VF | XF | Unc | BU |
|---|---|---|---|---|---|---|
| 1981 Proof | 5,000 | Value: 15.00 | | | | |

**50 PENCE KM# 84a Weight:** 15.5000 g. **Composition:** 0.9250 Silver .4610 oz. ASW **Subject:** Christmas 1981 **Obverse:** Bust of Queen Elizabeth II right **Reverse:** Manx Nickey boat

| Date | Mintage | F | VF | XF | Unc | BU |
|---|---|---|---|---|---|---|
| 1981 Proof | 5,000 | Value: 12.50 | | | | |

**50 PENCE KM# 83b Weight:** 26.0000 g. **Composition:** 0.9170 Gold .7666 oz. AGW **Subject:** Tourist Trophy Motorcycle Races **Obverse:** Bust of Queen Elizabeth II right **Reverse:** Motorcyclist - Joey Dunlop

| Date | Mintage | F | VF | XF | Unc | BU |
|---|---|---|---|---|---|---|
| 1981 Proof | 250 | Value: 500 | | | | |

**50 PENCE KM# 84b Weight:** 26.0000 g. **Composition:** 0.9170 Gold .7666 oz. AGW **Subject:** Christmas 1981 **Obverse:** Bust of Queen Elizabeth II right **Reverse:** Manx Nickey boat

| Date | Mintage | F | VF | XF | Unc | BU |
|---|---|---|---|---|---|---|
| 1981 Proof | 250 | Value: 550 | | | | |

**50 PENCE KM# 83c Weight:** 30.4000 g. **Composition:** 0.9500 Platinum .9286 oz. APW **Subject:** Tourist Trophy Motorcycle Races **Obverse:** Bust of Queen Elizabeth II right **Reverse:** Motorcyclist - Joey Dunlop

| Date | Mintage | F | VF | XF | Unc | BU |
|---|---|---|---|---|---|---|
| 1981 Proof | 50 | Value: 775 | | | | |

**50 PENCE KM# 84c Weight:** 30.4000 g. **Composition:** 0.9500 Platinum .9286 oz. APW **Subject:** Christmas 1981 **Obverse:** Bust of Queen Elizabeth II right **Reverse:** Manx Nickey boat

| Date | Mintage | F | VF | XF | Unc | BU |
|---|---|---|---|---|---|---|
| 1981 Proof | — | Value: 775 | | | | |

**50 PENCE KM# 70b Weight:** 15.5000 g. **Composition:** 0.9250 Silver .4610 oz. ASW **Obverse:** Bust of Queen Elizabeth II right **Reverse:** Viking longship

| Date | Mintage | F | VF | XF | Unc | BU |
|---|---|---|---|---|---|---|
| 1981 Proof | — | Value: 17.50 | | | | |
| 1983 Proof | 5,000 | Value: 17.50 | | | | |

**50 PENCE KM# 101 Composition:** Copper-Nickel **Subject:** Tourist Trophy Motorcycle Races **Obverse:** Bust of Queen Elizabeth II right **Reverse:** Motorcyclist

| Date | Mintage | F | VF | XF | Unc | BU |
|---|---|---|---|---|---|---|
| 1982 | 30,000 | — | — | — | 3.00 | — |
| 1982 Proof | — | Value: 7.50 | | | | |

**50 PENCE KM# 102 Composition:** Copper-Nickel **Subject:** Christmas 1982 **Obverse:** Bust of Queen Elizabeth II right **Reverse:** Victorian carolers around tree, Castle Rushen in background

| Date | Mintage | F | VF | XF | Unc | BU |
|---|---|---|---|---|---|---|
| 1982 AA | 30,000 | — | — | — | 2.50 | — |
| 1982 AB | Inc. above | — | — | — | 2.50 | — |
| 1982 D | Inc. above | — | — | — | 2.50 | — |
| 1982 Proof | 250 | Value: 7.50 | | | | |

**50 PENCE KM# 101a Weight:** 15.5000 g. **Composition:** 0.9250 Silver .4610 oz. ASW **Subject:** Tourist Trophy Motorcycle Races **Obverse:** Bust of Queen Elizabeth II right **Reverse:** Motorcyclist

| Date | Mintage | F | VF | XF | Unc | BU |
|---|---|---|---|---|---|---|
| 1982 Proof | 5,000 | Value: 15.00 | | | | |

**50 PENCE KM# 101b Weight:** 26.0000 g. **Composition:** 0.9170 Gold .7666 oz. AGW **Subject:** Tourist Trophy Motorcycle Races **Obverse:** Bust of Queen Elizabeth II right **Reverse:** Motorcyclist

| Date | Mintage | F | VF | XF | Unc | BU |
|---|---|---|---|---|---|---|
| 1982 Proof | 250 | Value: 550 | | | | |

**50 PENCE KM# 102a Weight:** 15.5000 g. **Composition:** 0.9250 Silver .4610 oz. ASW **Subject:** Christmas 1982 **Obverse:** Bust of Queen Elizabeth II right **Reverse:** Victorian carolers around tree, Castle Rushen in background

| Date | Mintage | F | VF | XF | Unc | BU |
|---|---|---|---|---|---|---|
| 1982 Proof | 5,000 | Value: 12.50 | | | | |

**50 PENCE KM# 101c Weight:** 30.4000 g. **Composition:** 0.9500 Platinum .9286 oz. APW **Subject:** Tourist Trophy Motorcycle Races **Obverse:** Bust of Queen Elizabeth II right **Reverse:** Motorcyclist

| Date | Mintage | F | VF | XF | Unc | BU |
|---|---|---|---|---|---|---|
| 1982 Proof | 50 | Value: 775 | | | | |

**50 PENCE KM# 102b Weight:** 26.0000 g. **Composition:** 0.9170 Gold .7666 oz. AGW **Subject:** Christmas 1982 **Obverse:** Bust of Queen Elizabeth II right **Reverse:** Victorian carolers around tree, Castle Rushen in background

| Date | Mintage | F | VF | XF | Unc | BU |
|---|---|---|---|---|---|---|
| 1982 Proof | 250 | Value: 500 | | | | |

**50 PENCE KM# 102c Weight:** 30.4000 g. **Composition:** 0.9500 Platinum .9286 oz. APW **Subject:** Christmast 1982 **Obverse:** Bust of Queen Elizabeth II right **Reverse:** Victorian carolers around tree, Castle Rushen in background

| Date | Mintage | F | VF | XF | Unc | BU |
|---|---|---|---|---|---|---|
| 1982 Proof | 50 | Value: 775 | | | | |

**50 PENCE KM# 107 Composition:** Copper-Nickel **Subject:** Christmas 1983 **Obverse:** Bust of Queen Elizabeth II right **Reverse:** Ford Model T driving left

| Date | Mintage | F | VF | XF | Unc | BU |
|---|---|---|---|---|---|---|
| 1983 AA | — | — | — | — | 4.00 | — |
| 1983 AC | 30,000 | — | — | — | 4.00 | — |

**50 PENCE KM# 108 Composition:** Copper-Nickel **Subject:** Tourist Trophy Motorcycle Races **Obverse:** Bust of Queen Elizabeth II right **Reverse:** Motorcyclist - Ron Haslam

| Date | Mintage | F | VF | XF | Unc | BU |
|---|---|---|---|---|---|---|
| 1983 AA | 30,000 | — | — | — | 3.00 | — |
| 1983 AB | Inc. above | — | — | — | 3.00 | — |
| 1983 AC | Inc. above | — | — | — | 3.00 | — |
| 1983 AD | Inc. above | — | — | — | 3.00 | — |

**50 PENCE KM# 107a Weight:** 15.5000 g. **Composition:** 0.9250 Silver .4610 oz. ASW **Series:** Christmas 1983 **Obverse:** Bust of Queen Elizabeth II right **Reverse:** Ford Model T driving left

| Date | Mintage | F | VF | XF | Unc | BU |
|---|---|---|---|---|---|---|
| 1983 Proof | 5,000 | Value: 12.50 | | | | |

**50 PENCE KM# 107b Weight:** 26.0000 g. **Composition:** 0.9170 Gold .7666 oz. AGW **Subject:** Christmas 1983 **Obverse:** Bust of Queen Elizabeth II right **Reverse:** Ford Model T driving left

| Date | Mintage | F | VF | XF | Unc | BU |
|---|---|---|---|---|---|---|
| 1983 Proof | 250 | Value: 500 | | | | |

**50 PENCE KM# 108a Weight:** 15.5000 g. **Composition:** 0.9250 Silver .4610 oz. ASW **Obverse:** Bust of Queen Elizabeth II right **Reverse:** Motorcyclist - Ron Haslam **Edge Lettering:** Tourist Trophy Motorcycle Races

| Date | Mintage | F | VF | XF | Unc | BU |
|---|---|---|---|---|---|---|
| 1983 Proof | 5,000 | Value: 15.00 | | | | |

**50 PENCE KM# 107c Weight:** 30.4000 g. **Composition:** 0.9500 Platinum .9286 oz. APW **Subject:** Christmas 1983 **Obverse:** Bust of Queen Elizabeth II right **Reverse:** Ford Model T driving left

| Date | Mintage | F | VF | XF | Unc | BU |
|---|---|---|---|---|---|---|
| 1983 Proof | 50 | Value: 775 | | | | |

**50 PENCE KM# 108b Weight:** 26.0000 g. **Composition:** 0.9170 Gold .7666 oz. AGW **Subject:** Tourist Trophy Motorcycle Races **Obverse:** Bust of Queen Elizabeth II right **Reverse:** Motorcyclist - Ron Haslam

| Date | Mintage | F | VF | XF | Unc | BU |
|---|---|---|---|---|---|---|
| 1983 Proof | 250 | Value: 500 | | | | |

**50 PENCE KM# 108c Weight:** 30.4000 g. **Composition:** 0.9500 Platinum .9286 oz. APW **Subject:** Tourist Trophy Motorcycle Races **Obverse:** Bust of Queen Elizabeth II right **Reverse:** Motorcyclist - Ron Haslam

| Date | Mintage | F | VF | XF | Unc | BU |
|---|---|---|---|---|---|---|
| 1983 Proof | 50 | Value: 775 | | | | |

**50 PENCE** **KM# 125** **Composition:** Copper-Nickel **Subject:** Quincentenary of the College of Arms **Obverse:** Bust of Queen Elziabeth II right **Reverse:** Viking longship on shield

| Date | Mintage | F | VF | XF | Unc | BU |
|---|---|---|---|---|---|---|
| 1984 AA | — | — | — | — | 2.00 | — |

**50 PENCE** **KM# 126** **Composition:** Copper-Nickel **Subject:** Tourist Trophy Motorcycle Races **Obverse:** Bust of Queen Elizabeth II right **Reverse:** Two motorcyclists - Mike Bodine

| Date | Mintage | F | VF | XF | Unc | BU |
|---|---|---|---|---|---|---|
| 1984 AA | 30,000 | — | — | — | 2.25 | — |

**50 PENCE** **KM# 127** **Composition:** Copper-Nickel **Subject:** Christmas 1984 **Obverse:** Bust of Queen Elizabeth II right **Reverse:** The "Sutherland" train

| Date | Mintage | F | VF | XF | Unc | BU |
|---|---|---|---|---|---|---|
| 1984 AA | — | — | — | — | 2.50 | — |
| 1984 AB | — | — | — | — | 2.50 | — |
| 1984 AC | — | — | — | — | 2.50 | — |
| 1984 Proof | — | Value: 7.50 | | | | |

**50 PENCE** **KM# 125a** **Weight:** 15.5000 g. **Composition:** 0.9250 Silver .4610 oz. ASW **Subject:** Quincentenary ofthe College of Arms **Obverse:** Bust of Queen Elizabeth II right **Reverse:** Viking longship on shield

| Date | Mintage | F | VF | XF | Unc | BU |
|---|---|---|---|---|---|---|
| 1984 Proof | — | Value: 15.00 | | | | |

**50 PENCE** **KM# 126a** **Weight:** 15.5000 g. **Composition:** 0.9250 Silver .4610 oz. ASW **Subject:** Tourist Trophy Motorcyle Races **Obverse:** Bust of Queen Elizabeth II right **Reverse:** Two motorcyclist - Mike Bodine

| Date | Mintage | F | VF | XF | Unc | BU |
|---|---|---|---|---|---|---|
| 1984 Proof | 5,000 | Value: 15.00 | | | | |

**50 PENCE** **KM# 125b** **Weight:** 26.0000 g. **Composition:** 0.9170 Gold .7666 oz. AGW **Subject:** Quincentenary of the College of Arms **Obverse:** Bust of Queen Elizabeth II right **Reverse:** Viking longship on shield

| Date | Mintage | F | VF | XF | Unc | BU |
|---|---|---|---|---|---|---|
| 1984 Proof | 150 | Value: 500 | | | | |

**50 PENCE** **KM# 126b** **Weight:** 26.0000 g. **Composition:** 0.9170 Gold .7666 oz. AGW **Subject:** Tourist Trophy Motorcycle Races **Obverse:** Bust of Queen Elizabeth II right **Reverse:** Two motorcyclist - Mike Bodine

| Date | Mintage | F | VF | XF | Unc | BU |
|---|---|---|---|---|---|---|
| 1984 Proof | 250 | Value: 500 | | | | |

**50 PENCE** **KM# 126c** **Weight:** 30.4000 g. **Composition:** 0.9500 Platinum .9286 oz. APW **Subject:** Tourist Trophy Motorcycle Races **Obverse:** Bust of Queen Elizabeth II right **Reverse:** Two motorcyclist - Mike Bodine

| Date | Mintage | F | VF | XF | Unc | BU |
|---|---|---|---|---|---|---|
| 1984 Proof | 50 | Value: 775 | | | | |

**50 PENCE** **KM# 127a** **Weight:** 15.5000 g. **Composition:** 0.9250 Silver .4610 oz. ASW **Subject:** Christmas 1984 **Obverse:** Bust of Queen Elizabeth II right **Reverse:** The "Sutherland" train

| Date | Mintage | F | VF | XF | Unc | BU |
|---|---|---|---|---|---|---|
| 1984 Proof | — | Value: 25.00 | | | | |

**50 PENCE** **KM# 127b** **Weight:** 26.0000 g. **Composition:** 0.9170 Gold .7666 oz. AGW **Subject:** Christmas 1984 **Obverse:** Bust of Queen Elizabeth II right **Reverse:** The "Sutherland" train

| Date | Mintage | F | VF | XF | Unc | BU |
|---|---|---|---|---|---|---|
| 1984 Proof | 250 | Value: 500 | | | | |

**50 PENCE** **KM# 127c** **Weight:** 30.4000 g. **Composition:** 0.9500 Platinum .9286 oz. APW **Subject:** Christmas 1984 **Obverse:** Bust of Queen Elizabeth II right **Reverse:** The "Sutherland" train

| Date | Mintage | F | VF | XF | Unc | BU |
|---|---|---|---|---|---|---|
| 1984 Proof | — | Value: 750 | | | | |

**50 PENCE** **KM# 148** **Composition:** Copper-Nickel **Obverse:** Head of Queen Elizabeth II right **Reverse:** Viking ship on shield

| Date | Mintage | F | VF | XF | Unc | BU |
|---|---|---|---|---|---|---|
| 1985(w) AA | — | — | — | — | 2.00 | — |
| 1985(w) AB | — | — | — | — | 2.00 | — |
| 1985 (w) Proof | 50,000 | Value: 4.00 | | | | |
| 1986 AA | — | — | — | — | 2.00 | — |
| 1986 AB | — | — | — | — | 2.00 | — |
| 1987 AA | — | — | — | — | 2.00 | — |

**50 PENCE** **KM# 158** **Composition:** Copper-Nickel **Subject:** Christmas 1985 **Obverse:** Head of Queen Elizabeth II right **Reverse:** de Havilland dragon DH84

| Date | Mintage | F | VF | XF | Unc | BU |
|---|---|---|---|---|---|---|
| 1985 AA | — | — | — | — | 3.50 | — |
| 1985 AB | — | — | — | — | 3.50 | — |
| 1985 BB | — | — | — | — | 3.50 | — |
| 1985 Proof | — | Value: 9.50 | | | | |

**50 PENCE** **KM# 158a** **Weight:** 15.5000 g. **Composition:** 0.9250 Silver .4610 oz. ASW **Subject:** Christmas 1985 **Obverse:** Head of Queen Elizabeth II right **Reverse:** de Havilland Dragon DH84

| Date | Mintage | F | VF | XF | Unc | BU |
|---|---|---|---|---|---|---|
| 1985 Proof | 5,000 | Value: 20.00 | | | | |

**50 PENCE** **KM# 158b** **Weight:** 26.0000 g. **Composition:** 0.9170 Gold .7666 oz. AGW **Subject:** Christmas 1985 **Obverse:** Head of Queen Elizabeth II right **Reverse:** de Havilland Dragon DH84

| Date | Mintage | F | VF | XF | Unc | BU |
|---|---|---|---|---|---|---|
| 1985 Proof | Est. 250 | Value: 500 | | | | |

**50 PENCE** **KM# 148a** **Weight:** 15.5000 g. **Composition:** 0.9250 Silver .4610 oz. ASW **Obverse:** Head of Queen Elizabeth II right **Reverse:** Viking ship on shield

| Date | Mintage | F | VF | XF | Unc | BU |
|---|---|---|---|---|---|---|
| 1985 Proof | Est. 10,000 | Value: 15.00 | | | | |

**50 PENCE** **KM# 158c** **Weight:** 30.4000 g. **Composition:** 0.9500 Platinum .9286 oz. APW **Subject:** Christmas 1985 **Obverse:** Head of Queen Elizabeth II right **Reverse:** de Havilland Dragon DH84

| Date | Mintage | F | VF | XF | Unc | BU |
|---|---|---|---|---|---|---|
| 1985 Proof | — | Value: 750 | | | | |

**50 PENCE** **KM# 148b** **Weight:** 26.0000 g. **Composition:** 0.9170 Gold .7666 oz. AGW **Obverse:** Head of Queen Elizabeth II right **Reverse:** Viking ship on shield

| Date | Mintage | F | VF | XF | Unc | BU |
|---|---|---|---|---|---|---|
| 1985 Proof | Est. 300 | Value: 500 | | | | |

**50 PENCE** **KM# 148c** **Weight:** 30.4000 g. **Composition:** 0.9500 Platinum .9286 oz. APW **Obverse:** Head of Queen Elizabeth II right **Reverse:** Viking ship on shield

| Date | Mintage | F | VF | XF | Unc | BU |
|---|---|---|---|---|---|---|
| 1985 Proof | Est. 200 | Value: 750 | | | | |

**50 PENCE** **KM# 172** **Composition:** Copper-Nickel **Subject:** Christmas 1986 **Obverse:** Head of Queen Elizabeth II right **Reverse:** Horsedrawn tram

| Date | Mintage | F | VF | XF | Unc | BU |
|---|---|---|---|---|---|---|
| 1986 AA | — | — | — | — | 3.50 | — |
| 1986 AB | — | — | — | — | 3.50 | — |
| 1986 Proof | — | Value: 9.50 | | | | |

**50 PENCE** **KM# 172a** **Weight:** 15.5000 g. **Composition:** 0.9250 Silver .4610 oz. ASW **Subject:** Christmas 1986 **Obverse:** Head of Queen Elizabeth II right **Reverse:** Horsedrawn tram

| Date | Mintage | F | VF | XF | Unc | BU |
|---|---|---|---|---|---|---|
| 1986 Proof | Est. 5,000 | Value: 20.00 | | | | |

**50 PENCE** **KM# 172b** **Weight:** 26.0000 g. **Composition:** 0.9170 Gold .7666 oz. AGW **Subject:** Christmas 1986 **Obverse:** Head of Queen Elizabeth II right **Reverse:** Horsedrawn tram

| Date | Mintage | F | VF | XF | Unc | BU |
|---|---|---|---|---|---|---|
| 1986 Proof | — | Value: 500 | | | | |

**50 PENCE** **KM# 190** **Composition:** Copper-Nickel **Subject:** Christmas 1987 **Obverse:** Head of Queen Elizabeth II right **Reverse:** Thorneycroft bus

| Date | Mintage | F | VF | XF | Unc | BU |
|---|---|---|---|---|---|---|
| 1987 AA | Est. 30,000 | — | — | — | 2.50 | — |
| 1987 D | — | — | — | — | 2.50 | — |
| 1987 Proof | — | Value: 7.50 | | | | |

**50 PENCE** **KM# 190a** **Weight:** 15.5000 g. **Composition:** 0.9250 Silver .4610 oz. ASW **Subject:** Christmas 1987 **Obverse:** Head of Queen Elizabeth II right **Reverse:** Thorneycroft bus

| Date | Mintage | F | VF | XF | Unc | BU |
|---|---|---|---|---|---|---|
| 1987 Proof | Est. 5,000 | Value: 20.00 | | | | |

**50 PENCE** **KM# 190b** **Weight:** 26.0000 g. **Composition:** 0.9170 Gold .7666 oz. AGW **Subject:** Christmas 1987 **Obverse:** Head of Queen Elizabeth II right **Reverse:** Thorneycroft bus

| Date | Mintage | F | VF | XF | Unc | BU |
|---|---|---|---|---|---|---|
| 1987 Proof | Est. 250 | Value: 500 | | | | |

**50 PENCE** **KM# 190c** **Weight:** 30.4000 g. **Composition:** 0.9500 Platinum .9286 oz. APW **Subject:** Christmas 1987 **Obverse:** Head of Queen Elizabeth II right **Reverse:** Thorneycroft bus

| Date | Mintage | F | VF | XF | Unc | BU |
|---|---|---|---|---|---|---|
| 1987 Proof | Est. 50 | Value: 775 | | | | |

**50 PENCE** **KM# 212** **Composition:** Copper-Nickel **Obverse:** Head of Queen Elizabeth II right **Reverse:** Computer

| Date | Mintage | F | VF | XF | Unc | BU |
|---|---|---|---|---|---|---|
| 1988 AA | — | — | — | — | 2.50 | — |
| 1989 AA | — | — | — | — | 2.50 | — |
| 1990 AA | — | — | — | — | 2.50 | — |
| 1991 | — | — | — | — | 2.50 | — |
| 1992 | — | — | — | — | 2.50 | — |
| 1993 AA | — | — | — | — | 2.50 | — |
| 1994 AA | — | — | — | — | 2.50 | — |
| 1995 AA | — | — | — | — | 2.50 | — |

**50 PENCE** **KM# 244** **Composition:** Copper-Nickel **Subject:** Christmas 1988 **Obverse:** Head of Queen Elizabeth II right **Reverse:** Motorbike and side car

| Date | Mintage | F | VF | XF | Unc | BU |
|---|---|---|---|---|---|---|
| 1988 AA | — | — | — | — | 2.50 | — |
| 1988 BA | — | — | — | — | 2.50 | — |
| 1988 Proof | — | Value: 6.50 | | | | |

**50 PENCE** **KM# 244a** **Weight:** 15.5000 g. **Composition:** 0.9250 Silver .4610 oz. ASW **Subject:** Christmas 1988 **Obverse:** Head of Queen Elizabeth II right **Reverse:** Motorbike and side car

| Date | Mintage | F | VF | XF | Unc | BU |
|---|---|---|---|---|---|---|
| 1988 Proof | — | Value: 20.00 | | | | |

**50 PENCE** **KM# 244b** **Weight:** 26.0000 g. **Composition:** 0.9170 Gold .7666 oz. AGW **Subject:** Christmas 1988 **Obverse:** Head of Queen Elizabeth II right **Reverse:** Motorbike and side car

| Date | Mintage | F | VF | XF | Unc | BU |
|---|---|---|---|---|---|---|
| 1988 Proof | — | Value: 500 | | | | |

**50 PENCE** **KM# 244c** **Weight:** 30.4000 g. **Composition:** 0.9500 Platinum .9286 oz. APW **Subject:** Christmas 1988 **Obverse:** Head of Queen Elizabeth II right **Reverse:** Motorbike and side car

| Date | Mintage | F | VF | XF | Unc | BU |
|---|---|---|---|---|---|---|
| 1988 Proof | — | Value: 800 | | | | |

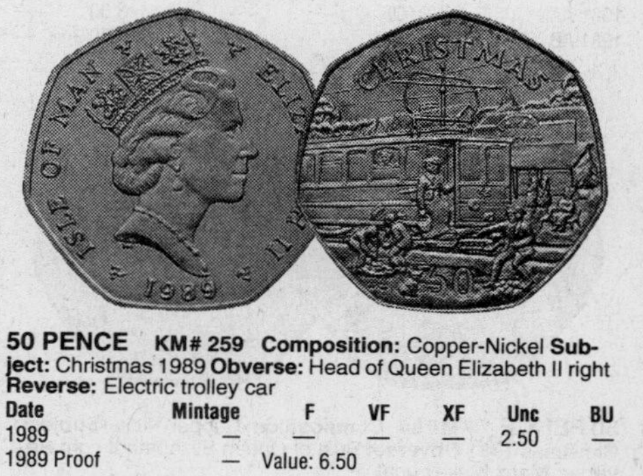

**50 PENCE** **KM# 259** **Composition:** Copper-Nickel **Subject:** Christmas 1989 **Obverse:** Head of Queen Elizabeth II right **Reverse:** Electric trolley car

| Date | Mintage | F | VF | XF | Unc | BU |
|---|---|---|---|---|---|---|
| 1989 | — | — | — | — | 2.50 | — |
| 1989 Proof | — | Value: 6.50 | | | | |

**50 PENCE KM# 259a Weight:** 15.5000 g. **Composition:** 0.9250 Silver .4610 oz. ASW **Subject:** Christmas 1989 **Obverse:** Head of Queen Elizabeth II right **Reverse:** Electric trolly car

| Date | Mintage | F | VF | XF | Unc | BU |
|---|---|---|---|---|---|---|
| 1989 Proof | — | Value: 40.00 | | | | |

**50 PENCE KM# 259b Weight:** 26.0000 g. **Composition:** 0.9170 Gold .7666 oz. AGW **Subject:** Christmas 1989 **Obverse:** Head of Queen Elizabeth II right **Reverse:** Electric trolley car

| Date | Mintage | F | VF | XF | Unc | BU |
|---|---|---|---|---|---|---|
| 1989 Proof | — | Value: 835 | | | | |

**50 PENCE KM# 259c Weight:** 30.4000 g. **Composition:** 0.9500 Platinum .9286 oz. APW **Subject:** Christmas 1989 **Obverse:** Head of Queen Elizabeth II right **Reverse:** Electric trolley car

| Date | Mintage | F | VF | XF | Unc | BU |
|---|---|---|---|---|---|---|
| 1989 Proof | — | Value: 1,170 | | | | |

**50 PENCE KM# 282 Composition:** Copper-Nickel **Subject:** Christmas 1990 **Obverse:** Head of Queen Elizabeth II right **Reverse:** Oceanliner

| Date | Mintage | F | VF | XF | Unc | BU |
|---|---|---|---|---|---|---|
| 1990 AA | — | — | — | — | 2.50 | — |
| 1990 AB | — | — | — | — | 2.50 | — |
| 1990 Proof | 30,000 | Value: 6.50 | | | | |

**50 PENCE KM# 282a Weight:** 15.5000 g. **Composition:** 0.9250 Silver .4610 oz. ASW **Subject:** Christmas 1990 **Obverse:** Head of Queen Elizabeth II right **Reverse:** Oceanliner

| Date | Mintage | F | VF | XF | Unc | BU |
|---|---|---|---|---|---|---|
| 1990 Proof | 5,000 | Value: 40.00 | | | | |

**50 PENCE KM# 282b Weight:** 26.0000 g. **Composition:** 0.9170 Gold .7666 oz. AGW **Subject:** Christmas 1990 **Obverse:** Head of Queen Elizabeth II right **Reverse:** Oceanliner

| Date | Mintage | F | VF | XF | Unc | BU |
|---|---|---|---|---|---|---|
| 1990 Proof | 250 | Value: 800 | | | | |

**50 PENCE KM# 282c Weight:** 30.4000 g. **Composition:** 0.9500 Platinum .9286 oz. APW **Subject:** Christmas 1990 **Obverse:** Oceanliner

| Date | Mintage | F | VF | XF | Unc | BU |
|---|---|---|---|---|---|---|
| 1990 Proof | 50 | Value: 1,100 | | | | |

**50 PENCE KM# 303 Composition:** Copper-Nickel **Subject:** Christmas 1991 **Obverse:** Head of Queen Elizabeth II right **Reverse:** Nativity scene

| Date | Mintage | F | VF | XF | Unc | BU |
|---|---|---|---|---|---|---|
| 1991 | — | — | — | — | 2.50 | — |
| 1991 Proof | 30,000 | Value: 6.50 | | | | |

**50 PENCE KM# 303a Weight:** 15.5000 g. **Composition:** 0.9250 Silver .4610 oz. ASW **Subject:** Christmas 1991 **Obverse:** Head of Queen Elizabeth II right **Reverse:** Nativity scene

| Date | Mintage | F | VF | XF | Unc | BU |
|---|---|---|---|---|---|---|
| 1991 Proof | 5,000 | Value: 40.00 | | | | |

**50 PENCE KM# 303b Weight:** 26.0000 g. **Composition:** 0.9170 Gold .7666 oz. AGW **Subject:** Christmas 1991 **Obverse:** Head of Queen Elizabeth II right **Reverse:** Nativity scene

| Date | Mintage | F | VF | XF | Unc | BU |
|---|---|---|---|---|---|---|
| 1991 Proof | 250 | Value: 685 | | | | |

**50 PENCE KM# 303c Weight:** 30.4000 g. **Composition:** 0.9500 Platinum .9286 oz. APW **Subject:** Christmas 1991 **Obverse:** Head of Queen Elizabeth II right **Reverse:** Nativity scene

| Date | Mintage | F | VF | XF | Unc | BU |
|---|---|---|---|---|---|---|
| 1991 Proof | 50 | Value: 860 | | | | |

**50 PENCE KM# 335 Composition:** Copper-Nickel **Subject:** Christmas 1992 **Obverse:** Head of Queen Elizabeth II right **Reverse:** Newspaper boy hawking the Manx Mercury

| Date | Mintage | F | VF | XF | Unc | BU |
|---|---|---|---|---|---|---|
| 1992 AA | — | — | — | — | 2.50 | — |
| 1992 Proof | — | Value: 6.50 | | | | |

**50 PENCE KM# 335a Weight:** 15.5000 g. **Composition:** 0.9250 Silver .4610 oz. ASW **Subject:** Christmas 1992 **Obverse:** Head of Queen Elizabeth II right **Reverse:** Newspaper boy hawking the Manx Mercury

| Date | Mintage | F | VF | XF | Unc | BU |
|---|---|---|---|---|---|---|
| 1992 Proof | 5,000 | Value: 40.00 | | | | |

**50 PENCE KM# 356 Composition:** Copper-Nickel **Subject:** Christmas 1993 **Obverse:** Head of Queen Elizabeth II right **Reverse:** Framed nativity scene

| Date | Mintage | F | VF | XF | Unc | BU |
|---|---|---|---|---|---|---|
| 1993 AA | — | — | — | — | 2.50 | — |
| 1993 D | — | — | — | — | 2.50 | — |
| 1993 Proof | 30,000 | Value: 6.50 | | | | |

**50 PENCE KM# 356a Weight:** 15.5000 g. **Composition:** 0.9250 Silver .4610 oz. ASW **Subject:** Christmas 1993 **Obverse:** Head of Queen Elizabeth II right **Reverse:** Framed nativity scene

| Date | Mintage | F | VF | XF | Unc | BU |
|---|---|---|---|---|---|---|
| 1993 Proof | Est. 5,000 | Value: 40.00 | | | | |

**50 PENCE KM# 356b Weight:** 26.0000 g. **Composition:** 0.9170 Gold .7666 oz. AGW **Subject:** Christmas 1993 **Obverse:** Head of Queen Elizabeth II right **Reverse:** Framed nativity scene

| Date | Mintage | F | VF | XF | Unc | BU |
|---|---|---|---|---|---|---|
| 1993 Proof | Est. 250 | Value: 685 | | | | |

**50 PENCE KM# 356c Weight:** 30.4000 g. **Composition:** 0.950 Platinum .9286 oz. APW **Subject:** Christmas 1993 **Obverse:** Head of Queen Elizabeth II right **Reverse:** Framed nativity scene

| Date | Mintage | F | VF | XF | Unc | BU |
|---|---|---|---|---|---|---|
| 1993 Proof | Est. 50 | Value: 860 | | | | |

**50 PENCE KM# 425 Composition:** Copper-Nickel **Subject:** Christmas 1994 **Obverse:** Head of Queen Elizabeth II right **Reverse:** Two young boys with pole

| Date | Mintage | F | VF | XF | Unc | BU |
|---|---|---|---|---|---|---|
| 1994 AA | — | — | — | — | 2.50 | — |

**50 PENCE KM# 425a Weight:** 15.5000 g. **Composition:** 0.9250 Silver .4610 oz. ASW **Subject:** Christmas 1994 **Obverse:** Head of Queen Elizabeth II right **Reverse:** Two young boys with pole

| Date | Mintage | F | VF | XF | Unc | BU |
|---|---|---|---|---|---|---|
| 1994 Proof | — | Value: 40.00 | | | | |

**50 PENCE KM# 456a Weight:** 15.5000 g. **Composition:** 0.9250 Silver .4610 oz. ASW **Subject:** Legislative Building Centenary **Obverse:** Head of Queen Elizabeth II right **Reverse:** Building

| Date | Mintage | F | VF | XF | Unc | BU |
|---|---|---|---|---|---|---|
| 1994 Proof | — | Value: 40.00 | | | | |

**50 PENCE KM# 456 Composition:** Copper-Nickel **Subject:** Legislative Building Centenary **Obverse:** Head of Queen Elizabeth II right **Reverse:** Building

| Date | Mintage | F | VF | XF | Unc | BU |
|---|---|---|---|---|---|---|
| 1994 AA | — | — | — | — | 3.00 | — |

**50 PENCE KM# 521 Composition:** Copper-Nickel **Subject:** Christmas 1995 **Obverse:** Head of Queen Elizabeth II right **Reverse:** Sledding

| Date | Mintage | F | VF | XF | Unc | BU |
|---|---|---|---|---|---|---|
| 1995 AA | Est. 30,000 | — | — | — | 2.50 | — |

**50 PENCE KM# 521a Weight:** 15.5000 g. **Composition:** 0.9250 Silver .4610 oz. ASW **Subject:** Christmas 1995 **Obverse:** Head of Queen Elizabeth II right **Reverse:** Sledding

| Date | Mintage | F | VF | XF | Unc | BU |
|---|---|---|---|---|---|---|
| 1995 Proof | Est. 5,000 | Value: 40.00 | | | | |

**50 PENCE KM# 521b Weight:** 26.0000 g. **Composition:** 0.9170 Gold .7666 oz. AGW **Subject:** Christmas 1995 **Obverse:** Head of Queen Elizabeth II right **Reverse:** Sledding

| Date | Mintage | F | VF | XF | Unc | BU |
|---|---|---|---|---|---|---|
| 1995 Proof | Est. 250 | Value: 650 | | | | |

**50 PENCE KM# 593 Composition:** Copper-Nickel **Subject:** Sports **Obverse:** Head of Queen Elizabeth II right **Reverse:** Motorcyclists

| Date | Mintage | F | VF | XF | Unc | BU |
|---|---|---|---|---|---|---|
| 1996 AA | — | — | — | — | 3.00 | — |

**50 PENCE KM# 694 Composition:** Copper-Nickel **Subject:** Christmas 1996 **Obverse:** Head of Queen Elizabeth II right **Reverse:** Choir boys throwing snowballs

| Date | Mintage | F | VF | XF | Unc | BU |
|---|---|---|---|---|---|---|
| 1996 AA | Est. 30,000 | — | — | — | 2.75 | — |

**50 PENCE KM# 694a Weight:** 15.5000 g. **Composition:** 0.9250 Silver .4610 oz. ASW **Subject:** Christmas 1996 **Obverse:** Head of Queen Elizabeth II right **Reverse:** Throwing snowballs

| Date | Mintage | F | VF | XF | Unc | BU |
|---|---|---|---|---|---|---|
| 1996 Proof | Est. 5,000 | Value: 40.00 | | | | |

**50 PENCE KM# 694b Weight:** 26.0000 g. **Composition:** 0.9170 Gold .7666 oz. AGW **Subject:** Christmas 1996 **Obverse:** Head of Queen Elizabeth II right **Reverse:** Throwing snowballs

| Date | Mintage | F | VF | XF | Unc | BU |
|---|---|---|---|---|---|---|
| 1996 Proof | Est. 250 | Value: 650 | | | | |

**50 PENCE KM# 794 Composition:** Copper-Nickel **Subject:** Christmas 1997 **Obverse:** Head of Queen Elizabeth II right **Reverse:** Cameo of T.E. Brown with montage of his literary characters

| Date | Mintage | F | VF | XF | Unc | BU |
|---|---|---|---|---|---|---|
| 1997 | Est. 30,000 | — | — | — | 2.75 | — |

**50 PENCE KM# 794a Weight:** 8.0000 g. **Composition:** 0.9250 Silver .2379 oz. ASW **Subject:** Christmas 1987 **Obverse:** Head of Queen Elizabeth II right **Reverse:** Cameo of T.E. Brown with montage of his literacy characters

| Date | Mintage | F | VF | XF | Unc | BU |
|---|---|---|---|---|---|---|
| 1997 Proof | Est. 5,000 | Value: 40,00 | | | | |

**50 PENCE KM# 794b Weight:** 8.0000 g. **Composition:** 0.9160 Gold .2356 oz. AGW **Subject:** Christmas 1997 **Obverse:** Head of Queen Elizabeth II right **Reverse:** Cameo of T.E. Brown with montage of his literacy characters

| Date | Mintage | F | VF | XF | Unc | BU |
|---|---|---|---|---|---|---|
| 1997 Proof | 250 | Value: 650 | | | | |

**50 PENCE** **KM# 806** **Composition:** Copper-Nickel **Obverse:** Head of Queen Elizabeth II right **Reverse:** Two motorcycle racers

| Date | Mintage | F | VF | XF | Unc | BU |
|---|---|---|---|---|---|---|
| 1997 AA | — | — | — | — | 3.50 | — |

**50 PENCE** **KM# 806a** **Weight:** 8.0000 g. **Composition:** 0.9250 Silver .2379 oz. ASW **Obverse:** Head of Queen Elizabeth II right **Reverse:** Two motorcycle racers

| Date | Mintage | F | VF | XF | Unc | BU |
|---|---|---|---|---|---|---|
| 1997 Proof | 5,000 | Value: 35.00 | | | | |

**50 PENCE** **KM# 806b** **Weight:** 8.0000 g. **Composition:** 0.9999 Gold .2572 oz. AGW **Obverse:** Head of Queen Elizabeth II right **Reverse:** Two motorcycle racers

| Date | Mintage | F | VF | XF | Unc | BU |
|---|---|---|---|---|---|---|
| 1997 Proof | Est. 250 | Value: 650 | | | | |

**50 PENCE** **KM# 905** **Composition:** Copper-Nickel **Obverse:** Rank-Broadley portrait of Queen Elizabeth II **Reverse:** Motorcyclists

| Date | Mintage | F | VF | XF | Unc | BU |
|---|---|---|---|---|---|---|
| 1998 AA | — | — | — | — | 3.00 | — |

**50 PENCE** **KM# 908** **Composition:** Copper-Nickel **Subject:** Christmas 1998 **Obverse:** Head of Queen Elizabeth II right **Reverse:** Kitchen scene

| Date | Mintage | F | VF | XF | Unc | BU |
|---|---|---|---|---|---|---|
| 1998 | Est. 30,000 | — | — | — | 3.00 | — |

**50 PENCE** **KM# 908a** **Weight:** 8.0000 g. **Composition:** 0.9250 Silver .2379 oz. ASW **Subject:** Christmas 1998 **Obverse:** Head of Queen Elizabeth II right **Reverse:** Kitchen scene

| Date | Mintage | F | VF | XF | Unc | BU |
|---|---|---|---|---|---|---|
| 1998 Proof | 5,000 | Value: 35.00 | | | | |

**50 PENCE** **KM# 908b** **Weight:** 8.0000 g. **Composition:** 0.9167 Gold .2358 oz. AGW **Subject:** Christmas 1998 **Obverse:** Head of Queen Elizabeth II right **Reverse:** Kitchen scene

| Date | Mintage | F | VF | XF | Unc | BU |
|---|---|---|---|---|---|---|
| 1998 Proof | 250 | Value: 650 | | | | |

**50 PENCE** **KM# 993** **Composition:** Copper-Nickel **Obverse:** Rank-Broadley portrait of Queen Elizabeth II **Reverse:** Motorcycle racer above denomination

| Date | Mintage | F | VF | XF | Unc | BU |
|---|---|---|---|---|---|---|
| 1999 | — | — | — | — | 3.00 | — |

**50 PENCE** **KM# 993a** **Weight:** 8.0000 g. **Composition:** 0.9250 Silver .2379 oz. ASW **Obverse:** Rank-Broadley portrait of Queen Elizabeth II **Reverse:** Motorcycle racer above denomination

| Date | Mintage | F | VF | XF | Unc | BU |
|---|---|---|---|---|---|---|
| 1999 Proof | Est. 5,000 | Value: 35.00 | | | | |

**50 PENCE** **KM# 993b** **Weight:** 8.0000 g. **Composition:** 0.9160 Gold .2356 oz. AGW **Obverse:** Rank-Broadley portrait of Queen Elizabeth II **Reverse:** Motorcycle racer above denomination

| Date | Mintage | F | VF | XF | Unc | BU |
|---|---|---|---|---|---|---|
| 1999 Proof | Est. 250 | Value: 650 | | | | |

**50 PENCE** **KM# 1011** **Composition:** Copper-Nickel **Subject:** Christmas 1999 **Obverse:** Rank-Broadley portrait of Queen Elizabeth II **Reverse:** Tree decorating scene

| Date | Mintage | F | VF | XF | Unc | BU |
|---|---|---|---|---|---|---|
| 1999 AA | Est. 30,000 | — | — | — | 3.00 | — |

**50 PENCE** **KM# 1011a** **Weight:** 8.0000 g. **Composition:** 0.9250 Silver .2379 oz. ASW **Subject:** Christmas 1999 **Obverse:** Rank-Broadley portrait of Queen Elizabeth II **Reverse:** Tree decorating scene

| Date | Mintage | F | VF | XF | Unc | BU |
|---|---|---|---|---|---|---|
| 1999 Proof | Est. 5,000 | Value: 35.00 | | | | |

**50 PENCE** **KM# 1011b** **Weight:** 8.0000 g. **Composition:** 0.9160 Gold .2356 oz. AGW **Subject:** Christmas 1999 **Obverse:** Rank-Broadley portrait of Queen Elizabeth II **Reverse:** Tree decorating scene

| Date | Mintage | F | VF | XF | Unc | BU |
|---|---|---|---|---|---|---|
| 1999 Proof | Est. 250 | Value: 650 | | | | |

**50 PENCE** **KM# 1041** **Weight:** 7.9400 g. **Composition:** Copper-Nickel **Obverse:** Queen's portrait **Reverse:** Stylized crucifix **Edge:** Plain, seven sided

| Date | Mintage | F | VF | XF | Unc | BU |
|---|---|---|---|---|---|---|
| 2000 AA | — | — | — | — | 2.25 | — |

**50 PENCE** **KM# 1050** **Weight:** 8.0000 g. **Composition:** Copper-Nickel **Obverse:** Queen's portrait **Reverse:** Dr. John Kelly translating the bible into Manx **Edge:** Plain, seven sided **Size:** 27.3 mm.

| Date | Mintage | F | VF | XF | Unc | BU |
|---|---|---|---|---|---|---|
| 2000 | 30,000 | — | — | — | 8.00 | — |

**50 PENCE** **KM# 1050a** **Weight:** 8.0000 g. **Composition:** 0.9250 Silver .2379 oz. ASW

| Date | Mintage | F | VF | XF | Unc | BU |
|---|---|---|---|---|---|---|
| 2000 Proof | 5,000 | Value: 34.00 | | | | |

**50 PENCE** **KM# 1050b** **Weight:** 8.0000 g. **Composition:** 0.9160 Gold .2356 oz. AGW

| Date | Mintage | F | VF | XF | Unc | BU |
|---|---|---|---|---|---|---|
| 2000 Proof | 250 | Value: 645 | | | | |

**50 PENCE** **KM# 1105** **Weight:** 8.0000 g. **Composition:** Copper-Nickel **Subject:** Christmas **Obverse:** Queen's portrait **Reverse:** Postman and children **Edge:** Plain, seven sided **Size:** 27.3 mm.

| Date | Mintage | F | VF | XF | Unc | BU |
|---|---|---|---|---|---|---|
| 2001 | 30,000 | — | — | — | 10.00 | — |

**50 PENCE** **KM# 1105a** **Weight:** 8.0000 g. **Composition:** 0.9250 Silver .2379 oz. ASW **Edge:** Plain, seven sided **Size:** 27.3 mm.

| Date | Mintage | F | VF | XF | Unc | BU |
|---|---|---|---|---|---|---|
| 2001 Proof | 5,000 | Value: 34.00 | | | | |

**50 PENCE** **KM# 1105b** **Weight:** 8.0000 g. **Composition:** 0.9167 Gold .2358 oz. AGW **Edge:** Plain, seven sided **Size:** 27.3 mm.

| Date | Mintage | F | VF | XF | Unc | BU |
|---|---|---|---|---|---|---|
| 2001 Proof | 250 | Value: 645 | | | | |

**1/2 SOVEREIGN (1/2 Pound)** **KM# 15** **Weight:** 3.9940 g. **Composition:** 0.9170 Gold .1177 oz. AGW **Subject:** 200th Anniversary of Acquistion **Obverse:** Bust of Queen Elizabeth II right

| Date | Mintage | F | VF | XF | Unc | BU |
|---|---|---|---|---|---|---|
| 1965 | 1,500 | — | — | — | 55.00 | — |

**1/2 SOVEREIGN (1/2 Pound)** **KM# 15a** **Weight:** 4.0000 g. **Composition:** 0.9800 Gold .1260 oz. AGW **Subject:** 200th Anniersary of Acquistion **Obverse:** Bust of Queen Elizabeth II right

| Date | Mintage | F | VF | XF | Unc | BU |
|---|---|---|---|---|---|---|
| 1965 Proof | 1,000 | Value: 60.00 | | | | |

**1/2 SOVEREIGN (1/2 Pound)** **KM# 26** **Weight:** 3.9813 g. **Composition:** 0.9170 Gold .1173 oz. AGW **Obverse:** Bust of Queen Elizabeth II right

| Date | Mintage | F | VF | XF | Unc | BU |
|---|---|---|---|---|---|---|
| 1973 | 14,000 | — | — | — | 60.00 | — |
| 1973 Proof | 1,250 | Value: 65.00 | | | | |
| 1974 | 6,566 | — | — | — | 60.00 | — |
| 1974 Proof | 2,500 | Value: 65.00 | | | | |
| 1975 | 1,956 | — | — | — | 60.00 | — |
| 1975 Proof | — | Value: 65.00 | | | | |
| 1976 | 2,558 | — | — | — | 60.00 | — |
| 1976 Proof | — | Value: 65.00 | | | | |
| 1977 | — | — | — | — | 60.00 | — |
| 1977 Proof | 1,250 | Value: 70.00 | | | | |
| 1978 Proof | 1,250 | Value: 70.00 | | | | |
| 1979 (t) | 8,000 | — | — | — | 60.00 | — |
| 1979 (t) Proof | 30,000 | Value: 65.00 | | | | |
| 1980 (m) Proof | 7,500 | Value: 65.00 | | | | |
| 1980 (v) Proof | — | Value: 65.00 | | | | |
| 1982 (b) | 40,000 | — | — | — | 60.00 | — |
| 1982 (b) Proof | 30,000 | Value: 65.00 | | | | |

**1/2 SOVEREIGN (1/2 Pound)** **KM# 85** **Weight:** 3.9813 g. **Composition:** 0.9170 Gold .1173 oz. AGW **Subject:** Wedding of Prince Charles and Lady Diana **Obverse:** Bust of Queen Elizabeth II right **Reverse:** Portraits of Royal Couple, joined shields

| Date | Mintage | F | VF | XF | Unc | BU |
|---|---|---|---|---|---|---|
| 1981 Proof | 30,000 | Value: 100 | | | | |

**1/2 SOVEREIGN (1/2 Pound)** **KM# 260** **Weight:** 3.9813 g. **Composition:** 0.9170 Gold .1173 oz. AGW **Obverse:** Bust of Queen Elizabeth II right **Note:** Similar to 5 Pounds, KM#263.

| Date | Mintage | F | VF | XF | Unc | BU |
|---|---|---|---|---|---|---|
| 1984 | 20 | — | — | — | 200 | — |
| 1984 Proof | 20 | Value: 250 | | | | |

**1/2 SOVEREIGN (1/2 Pound)** **KM# 264** **Weight:** 3.9813 g. **Composition:** 0.9170 Gold .1173 oz. AGW **Obverse:** Head of Queen Elizabeth II right **Note:** Similar to 1 Pound, KM#265.

| Date | Mintage | F | VF | XF | Unc | BU |
|---|---|---|---|---|---|---|
| 1988 Proof | 5,879 | Value: 85.00 | | | | |

**SOVEREIGN (Pound)** **KM# 16** **Weight:** 7.9881 g. **Composition:** 0.9170 Gold .2355 oz. AGW **Subject:** 200th Anniversary of Acquistion **Obverse:** Bust of Queen Elizabeth II right

| Date | Mintage | F | VF | XF | Unc | BU |
|---|---|---|---|---|---|---|
| 1965 | 2,000 | — | — | — | 115 | — |

**SOVEREIGN (Pound)** **KM# 16a** **Weight:** 8.0000 g. **Composition:** 0.9800 Gold .2520 oz. AGW **Subject:** 200th Anniversary of Acquistion **Obverse:** Bust of Queen Elizabeth II right

| Date | Mintage | F | VF | XF | Unc | BU |
|---|---|---|---|---|---|---|
| 1965 Proof | 1,000 | Value: 125 | | | | |

**SOVEREIGN (Pound)** **KM# 27** **Weight:** 7.9627 g. **Composition:** 0.9170 Gold .2347 oz. AGW **Obverse:** Bust of Queen Elizabeth II right

| Date | Mintage | F | VF | XF | Unc | BU |
|---|---|---|---|---|---|---|
| 1973 | 40,000 | — | — | — | 110 | — |
| 1973 Proof | 1,250 | Value: 125 | | | | |
| 1974 | 8,604 | — | — | — | 115 | — |
| 1974 Proof | 2,500 | Value: 125 | | | | |
| 1975 | 956 | — | — | — | 140 | — |
| 1975 Proof | — | Value: 135 | | | | |
| 1976 | 1,238 | — | — | — | 120 | — |
| 1976 Proof | — | Value: 130 | | | | |
| 1977 | — | — | — | — | 120 | — |
| 1977 Proof | 1,250 | Value: 130 | | | | |
| 1978 Proof | 1,250 | Value: 130 | | | | |
| 1979 AA (t) | 10,000 | — | — | — | 110 | — |
| 1979 D (t) | — | — | — | — | 110 | — |
| 1979 (t) Proof | 30,000 | Value: 120 | | | | |
| 1980 D (m) Proof | 5,000 | Value: 120 | | | | |
| 1980 (v) Proof | — | Value: 120 | | | | |
| 1982 (b) | 30,000 | — | — | — | 110 | — |
| 1982 (b) Proof | 40,000 | Value: 120 | | | | |

**SOVEREIGN (Pound)** **KM# 44** **Composition:** Virenium **Obverse:** Bust of Queen Elizabeth II right

| Date | Mintage | F | VF | XF | Unc | BU |
|---|---|---|---|---|---|---|
| 1978 AA | — | — | — | — | 3.00 | — |
| 1978 AB | — | — | — | — | 3.00 | — |
| 1978 AC | — | — | — | — | 2.50 | — |
| 1978 AD | 3,780 | — | — | — | 7.50 | — |
| 1978 BB | — | — | — | — | — | — |
| 1978 BC Proof | 150,000 | Value: 3.50 | | | | |
| 1979 AA(t) | — | — | — | — | 2.50 | — |
| 1979 AB(t) | — | — | — | — | 2.50 | — |
| 1979 AC(t) | — | — | — | — | 2.50 | — |
| 1979 BB(t) Proof | — | Value: 3.50 | | | | |
| 1979 (t) Crossed oars | — | — | — | — | 2.50 | — |
| 1980 AA DMIHE | 30,000 | — | — | — | 2.50 | — |
| 1980 AA DMIHEN | — | — | — | — | 2.50 | — |
| 1980 AA TT | — | — | — | — | 2.50 | — |
| 1980 AB DMIHE | — | — | — | — | 2.50 | — |
| 1980 AB DHIHEN | — | — | — | — | 2.50 | — |
| 1980 AB TT | — | — | — | — | 5.50 | — |
| 1980 AC DMIHE | 100,000 | — | — | — | 2.50 | — |
| 1980 Proof | 5,000 | Value: 10.00 | | | | |

| Date | Mintage | F | VF | XF | Unc | BU |
|---|---|---|---|---|---|---|
| 1980 AA | — | — | — | — | 2.50 | — |
| 1980 AB | — | — | — | — | 2.50 | — |
| 1980 AC | — | — | — | — | 2.50 | — |
| 1981 AA | — | — | — | — | 2.50 | — |

**SOVEREIGN (Pound)** **KM# 44a** **Weight:** 4.6000 g. **Composition:** 0.9250 Silver .1368 oz. ASW **Obverse:** Bust of Queen Elizabeth II right

| Date | Mintage | F | VF | XF | Unc | BU |
|---|---|---|---|---|---|---|
| 1978 | — | — | — | — | 8.00 | — |
| 1978 D Proof | 100,000 | Value: 8.00 | | | | |
| 1979 D(t) Proof | 75,000 | Value: 15.00 | | | | |
| 1980 Proof | 75,000 | Value: 8.00 | | | | |
| 1981 Proof | — | Value: 8.00 | | | | |
| 1982 (b) Proof | 1,000 | Value: 35.00 | | | | |

**SOVEREIGN (Pound)** **KM# 44b** **Weight:** 9.0000 g. **Composition:** 0.9500 Platinum .2749 oz. APW **Obverse:** Bust of Queen Elizabeth II right

| Date | Mintage | F | VF | XF | Unc | BU |
|---|---|---|---|---|---|---|
| 1978 Proof | 1,000 | Value: 200 | | | | |
| 1979 Proof | — | Value: 200 | | | | |
| 1980 Proof | 1,000 | Value: 200 | | | | |
| 1982 (b) Proof | 100 | Value: 250 | | | | |

**SOVEREIGN (Pound)** **KM# 44c** **Weight:** 7.9627 g. **Composition:** 0.9170 Gold .2347 oz. AGW **Obverse:** Bust of Queen Elizabeth II right

| Date | Mintage | F | VF | XF | Unc | BU |
|---|---|---|---|---|---|---|
| 1980 Proof | 5,000 | Value: 125 | | | | |
| 1980 T.T. Proof | 300 | Value: 225 | | | | |
| 1982 (b) | 250 | — | — | — | 225 | — |
| 1982 (b) Proof | 750 | Value: 200 | | | | |

**SOVEREIGN (Pound)** **KM# 44d** **Weight:** 4.6000 g. **Composition:** 0.5000 Silver .0739 oz. ASW **Obverse:** Bust of Queen Elizabeth II right

| Date | Mintage | F | VF | XF | Unc | BU |
|---|---|---|---|---|---|---|
| 1980 Proof | 10,000 | Value: 15.00 | | | | |

**SOVEREIGN (Pound)** **KM# 86** **Weight:** 7.9627 g. **Composition:** 0.9170 Gold .2347 oz. AGW **Subject:** Wedding of Prince Charles and Lady Diana **Obverse:** Bust of Queen Elizabeth II right **Reverse:** Portraits of Royal Couple, joined shields

| Date | Mintage | F | VF | XF | Unc | BU |
|---|---|---|---|---|---|---|
| 1981 Proof | 40,000 | Value: 150 | | | | |

**SOVEREIGN (Pound)** **KM# 109** **Composition:** Virenium **Obverse:** Bust of Queen Elizabeth II right **Reverse:** Peel

| Date | Mintage | F | VF | XF | Unc | BU |
|---|---|---|---|---|---|---|
| 1983 AA | — | — | — | — | 3.50 | — |

**SOVEREIGN (Pound)** **KM# 109a** **Weight:** 4.6000 g. **Composition:** 0.9250 Silver .1368 oz. ASW **Obverse:** Bust of Queen Elizabeth II right **Reverse:** Peel

| Date | Mintage | F | VF | XF | Unc | BU |
|---|---|---|---|---|---|---|
| 1983 Proof | — | Value: 20.00 | | | | |

**SOVEREIGN (Pound)** **KM# 109b** **Weight:** 9.5000 g. **Composition:** 0.3740 Gold .1142 oz. AGW **Obverse:** Bust of Queen Elizabeth II right **Reverse:** Peel

| Date | Mintage | F | VF | XF | Unc | BU |
|---|---|---|---|---|---|---|
| 1983 Proof | — | Value: 75.00 | | | | |

**SOVEREIGN (Pound)** **KM# 109c** **Weight:** 7.9627 g. **Composition:** 0.9170 Gold .2347 oz. AGW **Obverse:** Bust of Queen Elizabeth II right **Reverse:** Peel

| Date | Mintage | F | VF | XF | Unc | BU |
|---|---|---|---|---|---|---|
| 1983 Proof | — | Value: 150 | | | | |

**SOVEREIGN (Pound)** **KM# 109d** **Weight:** 9.0000 g. **Composition:** 0.9500 Platinum .2749 oz. APW **Obverse:** Bust of Queen Elizabeth II right **Reverse:** Peel

| Date | Mintage | F | VF | XF | Unc | BU |
|---|---|---|---|---|---|---|
| 1983 Proof | — | Value: 200 | | | | |

**SOVEREIGN (Pound)** **KM# 128** **Composition:** Virenium **Obverse:** Bust of Queen Elizaeth II right **Reverse:** Castletown

| Date | Mintage | F | VF | XF | Unc | BU |
|---|---|---|---|---|---|---|
| 1984 D | — | — | — | — | 4.00 | — |
| 1984 AA | — | — | — | — | 4.00 | — |

**SOVEREIGN (Pound)** **KM# 128a** **Weight:** 4.6000 g. **Composition:** 0.9250 Silver .1368 oz. ASW **Obverse:** Bust of Queen Elizabeth II right **Reverse:** Castletown

| Date | Mintage | F | VF | XF | Unc | BU |
|---|---|---|---|---|---|---|
| 1984 | — | — | — | — | 10.00 | — |
| 1984 D Proof | — | Value: 20.00 | | | | |

**SOVEREIGN (Pound)** **KM# 128b** **Weight:** 9.5000 g. **Composition:** 0.3740 Gold .1142 oz. AGW **Obverse:** Bust of Queen Elizabeth II right **Reverse:** Castletown

| Date | Mintage | F | VF | XF | Unc | BU |
|---|---|---|---|---|---|---|
| 1984 Proof | 4,950 | Value: 75.00 | | | | |

**SOVEREIGN (Pound)** **KM# 128c** **Weight:** 7.9627 g. **Composition:** 0.9170 Gold .2347 oz. AGW **Obverse:** Bust of Queen Elizabeth II right **Reverse:** Castletown

| Date | Mintage | F | VF | XF | Unc | BU |
|---|---|---|---|---|---|---|
| 1984 Proof | 950 | Value: 150 | | | | |

**SOVEREIGN (Pound)** **KM# 261** **Weight:** 7.9627 g. **Composition:** 0.9170 Gold .2347 oz. AGW **Obverse:** Bust of Queen Elizabeth II right **Reverse:** Four crowned shields

| Date | Mintage | F | VF | XF | Unc | BU |
|---|---|---|---|---|---|---|
| 1984 | 20 | — | — | — | 350 | — |
| 1984 Proof | 20 | Value: 450 | | | | |

**SOVEREIGN (Pound)** **KM# 128d** **Weight:** 9.0000 g. **Composition:** 0.9500 Platinum .2749 oz. APW **Obverse:** Bust of Queen Elizabeth II right **Reverse:** Castletown

| Date | Mintage | F | VF | XF | Unc | BU |
|---|---|---|---|---|---|---|
| 1984 Proof | — | Value: 200 | | | | |

**SOVEREIGN (Pound)** **KM# 135** **Weight:** 4.6000 g. **Composition:** 0.9250 Silver .1368 oz. ASW **Obverse:** Bust of Queen Elizabeth II right **Reverse:** Ramsey

| Date | Mintage | F | VF | XF | Unc | BU |
|---|---|---|---|---|---|---|
| 1985 D | — | — | — | — | 10.00 | — |
| 1985 D Proof | Est. 5,000 | Value: 22.50 | | | | |

**SOVEREIGN (Pound)** **KM# 135b** **Weight:** 7.9627 g. **Composition:** 0.9170 Gold .2347 oz. AGW **Obverse:** Bust of Queeen Elizabeth II right **Reverse:** Ramsey

| Date | Mintage | F | VF | XF | Unc | BU |
|---|---|---|---|---|---|---|
| 1985 Proof | Est. 150 | Value: 175 | | | | |

**SOVEREIGN (Pound)** **KM# 135c** **Weight:** 9.0000 g. **Composition:** 0.9500 Platinum .2749 oz. APW **Obverse:** Bust of Queen Elizabeth II right **Reverse:** Ramsey

| Date | Mintage | F | VF | XF | Unc | BU |
|---|---|---|---|---|---|---|
| 1985 Proof | Est. 550 | Value: 200 | | | | |

**SOVEREIGN (Pound)** **KM# 136** **Weight:** 4.6000 g. **Composition:** 0.9250 Silver .1368 oz. ASW **Obverse:** Bust of Queen Elizabeth II right **Reverse:** Douglas

| Date | Mintage | F | VF | XF | Unc | BU |
|---|---|---|---|---|---|---|
| 1986 AA | — | — | — | — | 10.00 | — |
| 1986 D Proof | — | Value: 25.00 | | | | |

**SOVEREIGN (Pound)** **KM# 136b** **Weight:** 7.9627 g. **Composition:** 0.9170 Gold .2347 oz. AGW **Obverse:** Bust of Queen Elizabeth II right **Reverse:** Douglas

| Date | Mintage | F | VF | XF | Unc | BU |
|---|---|---|---|---|---|---|
| 1986 Proof | — | Value: 150 | | | | |

**SOVEREIGN (Pound)** **KM# 136c** **Weight:** 9.0000 g. **Composition:** 0.9500 Platinum .2749 oz. APW **Obverse:** Bust of Queen Elizabeth II right **Reverse:** Douglas

| Date | Mintage | F | VF | XF | Unc | BU |
|---|---|---|---|---|---|---|
| 1986 Proof | — | Value: 200 | | | | |

**SOVEREIGN (Pound)** **KM# 151** **Composition:** Virenium **Obverse:** Head of Queen Elizabeth II right **Reverse:** Ramsey

| Date | Mintage | F | VF | XF | Unc | BU |
|---|---|---|---|---|---|---|
| 1985 | — | — | — | — | 3.50 | — |
| 1985 Proof | 25,000 | Value: 6.00 | | | | |

**SOVEREIGN (Pound)** **KM# 151a** **Weight:** 4.6000 g. **Composition:** 0.9250 Silver .1368 oz. ASW **Obverse:** Head of Queen Elizabeth II right **Reverse:** Ramsey

| Date | Mintage | F | VF | XF | Unc | BU |
|---|---|---|---|---|---|---|
| 1985 Proof | — | Value: 35.00 | | | | |

**SOVEREIGN (Pound)** **KM# 175** **Composition:** Virenium **Obverse:** Head of Queen Elizabeth II right **Reverse:** Douglas

| Date | Mintage | F | VF | XF | Unc | BU |
|---|---|---|---|---|---|---|
| 1986 | — | — | — | — | 3.50 | — |
| 1986 Proof | 25,000 | Value: 6.00 | | | | |

**SOVEREIGN (Pound)** **KM# 182** **Composition:** Virenium **Obverse:** Head of Queen Elizabeth II right

| Date | Mintage | F | VF | XF | Unc | BU |
|---|---|---|---|---|---|---|
| 1987 AA | — | — | — | — | 3.50 | — |

**SOVEREIGN (Pound)** **KM# 265** **Weight:** 7.9627 g. **Composition:** 0.9170 Gold .2347 oz. AGW **Obverse:** Head of Queen Elizabeth II right **Reverse:** Four crowned shields

| Date | Mintage | F | VF | XF | Unc | BU |
|---|---|---|---|---|---|---|
| 1988 | 5,876 | — | — | — | 125 | — |
| 1988 Proof | 1,600 | Value: 150 | | | | |

**SOVEREIGN (Pound)** **KM# 213** **Composition:** Virenium **Obverse:** Head of Queen Elizabeth II right **Reverse:** Telecommunicator

| Date | Mintage | F | VF | XF | Unc | BU |
|---|---|---|---|---|---|---|
| 1988 AA | — | — | — | — | 3.50 | — |
| 1988 BB | — | — | — | — | 3.50 | — |
| 1988 D | — | — | — | — | 3.50 | — |
| 1989 AA | — | — | — | — | 3.50 | — |
| 1990 AA | — | — | — | — | 3.50 | — |
| 1991 AA | — | — | — | — | 3.50 | — |
| 1992 AB | — | — | — | — | 3.50 | — |
| 1993 AA | — | — | — | — | 3.50 | — |
| 1994 AA | — | — | — | — | 3.50 | — |
| 1995 AA | — | — | — | — | 3.50 | — |

**SOVEREIGN (Pound)** **KM# 213a** **Weight:** 4.6000 g. **Composition:** 0.9250 Silver .1368 oz. ASW **Obverse:** Head of Queen Elizabeth II right **Reverse:** Telecommunicator

| Date | Mintage | F | VF | XF | Unc | BU |
|---|---|---|---|---|---|---|
| 1988 Proof | — | Value: 10.00 | | | | |
| 1989 Proof | — | Value: 10.00 | | | | |
| 1990 Proof | — | Value: 10.00 | | | | |
| 1991 Proof | — | Value: 10.00 | | | | |
| 1992 Proof | — | Value: 10.00 | | | | |

**SOVEREIGN (Pound)** **KM# 594a** **Weight:** 4.6000 g. **Composition:** 0.9250 Silver .1368 oz. ASW **Subject:** Sports **Obverse:** Head of Queen Elizabeth II right **Reverse:** Cricket equipment

| Date | Mintage | F | VF | XF | Unc | BU |
|---|---|---|---|---|---|---|
| 1996 Proof | — | Value: 25.00 | | | | |

**SOVEREIGN (Pound)** **KM# 594** **Composition:** Nickel-Brass **Subject:** Sports **Obverse:** Head of Queen Elizabeth II right **Reverse:** Cricket equipment

| Date | Mintage | F | VF | XF | Unc | BU |
|---|---|---|---|---|---|---|
| 1996 AA | — | — | — | — | 4.00 | — |

**SOVEREIGN (Pound)** **KM# 655** **Composition:** Virenium **Subject:** Douglas Centenary **Obverse:** Head of Queen Elizabeth II right **Reverse:** City arms

| Date | Mintage | F | VF | XF | Unc | BU |
|---|---|---|---|---|---|---|
| 1996 AA | — | — | — | — | 4.00 | — |

**SOVEREIGN (Pound)** **KM# 655a** **Weight:** 9.5000 g. **Composition:** 0.9250 Silver .2825 oz. ASW **Subject:** Douglas Centenary **Obverse:** Head of Queen Elizabeth II right **Reverse:** City arms

| Date | Mintage | F | VF | XF | Unc | BU |
|---|---|---|---|---|---|---|
| 1996 Proof | 25,000 | Value: 15.00 | | | | |

**SOVEREIGN (Pound)** **KM# 655b** **Weight:** 9.5000 g. **Composition:** 0.9160 Gold .2798 oz. AGW **Subject:** Douglas Centenary **Obverse:** Head of Queen Elizabeth II right **Reverse:** City arms

| Date | Mintage | F | VF | XF | Unc | BU |
|---|---|---|---|---|---|---|
| 1996 Proof | Est. 10,000 | Value: 175 | | | | |

**SOVEREIGN (Pound)** **KM# 906** **Composition:** Virenium **Obverse:** Rank-Broadley portrait of Queen Elizabeth II **Reverse:** Cricket equipment

| Date | Mintage | F | VF | XF | Unc | BU |
|---|---|---|---|---|---|---|
| 1998 AA | — | — | — | — | 4.00 | — |

**SOVEREIGN (Pound)** **KM# 1042** **Weight:** 9.5000 g. **Composition:** Brass **Subject:** Millennium Bells **Obverse:** Queen's portrait **Reverse:** Trikeles and three bells **Edge:** Reeded and plain sections

| Date | Mintage | F | VF | XF | Unc | BU |
|---|---|---|---|---|---|---|
| 2000 AA | — | — | — | — | 4.00 | — |

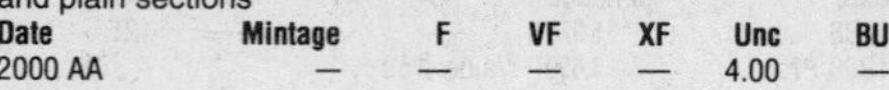

**2 POUNDS** **KM# 28** **Weight:** 15.9253 g. **Composition:** 0.9170 Gold .4695 oz. AGW **Obverse:** Bust of Queen Elizabeth II right

| Date | Mintage | F | VF | XF | Unc | BU |
|---|---|---|---|---|---|---|
| 1973 | 3,612 | — | — | — | 200 | — |
| 1973 Proof | 1,250 | Value: 225 | | | | |
| 1974 | 1,257 | — | — | — | 200 | — |
| 1974 Proof | 2,500 | Value: 220 | | | | |
| 1975 | 456 | — | — | — | 200 | — |
| 1975 Proof | — | Value: 220 | | | | |
| 1976 | 578 | — | — | — | 200 | — |
| 1976 Proof | — | Value: 220 | | | | |
| 1977 | — | — | — | — | 200 | — |
| 1977 Proof | 1,250 | Value: 225 | | | | |
| 1978 Proof | 1,250 | Value: 225 | | | | |
| 1979 (t) | 2,000 | — | — | — | 200 | — |
| 1979 (t) Proof | 30,000 | Value: 215 | | | | |
| 1980 (m) Proof | 2,000 | Value: 220 | | | | |
| 1982 (b) | 15,000 | — | — | — | 200 | — |
| 1982 (b) Proof | 5,000 | Value: 220 | | | | |

**2 POUNDS** **KM# 87** **Weight:** 15.9253 g. **Composition:** 0.9170 Gold .4695 oz. AGW **Subject:** Wedding of Prince Charles and Lady Diana **Obverse:** Bust of Queen Elizabeth II right **Reverse:** Portraits of Royal Couple, joined shields

| Date | Mintage | F | VF | XF | Unc | BU |
|---|---|---|---|---|---|---|
| 1981 Proof | 5,000 | Value: 275 | | | | |

**2 POUNDS** **KM# 129** **Composition:** Virenium **Obverse:** Similar to KM#28 **Reverse:** Tower of Refuge and Manx Shearwater in flight

| Date | Mintage | F | VF | XF | Unc | BU |
|---|---|---|---|---|---|---|
| 1984PM Reported, not confirmed | — | — | — | — | — | — |

**2 POUNDS** **KM# 129a** **Center Composition:** Silver **Obverse:** Bust of Queen Elizabeth II right **Reverse:** Tower of Refuge and Manx Shearwater in flight

| Date | Mintage | F | VF | XF | Unc | BU |
|---|---|---|---|---|---|---|
| 1984PM Reported, not confirmed | — | — | — | — | — | — |

**2 POUNDS** **KM# 262** **Weight:** 15.9200 g. **Composition:** 0.9170 Gold .4695 oz. AGW **Obverse:** Bust of Queen Elizabeth II right **Reverse:** Four crowned shields **Note:** Similar to 5 Pounds, KM#263

| Date | Mintage | F | VF | XF | Unc | BU |
|---|---|---|---|---|---|---|
| 1984 | 20 | — | — | — | 650 | — |
| 1984 Proof | 20 | Value: 800 | | | | |

**2 POUNDS** **KM# 149** **Composition:** Virenium **Obverse:** Head of Queen Elizabeth II right **Reverse:** Tower of Refuge and Manx Shearwater in flight

| Date | Mintage | F | VF | XF | Unc | BU |
|---|---|---|---|---|---|---|
| 1985 Reported, not confirmed | — | — | — | — | — | — |

**2 POUNDS** **KM# 149a** **Center Composition:** Silver **Obverse:** Head of Queen Elizabeth II right **Reverse:** Tower of Refuge and Manx Shearwater in flight

| Date | Mintage | F | VF | XF | Unc | BU |
|---|---|---|---|---|---|---|
| 1985 Reported, not confirmed | — | — | — | — | — | — |

**2 POUNDS** **KM# 167** **Composition:** Virenium **Obverse:** Head of Queen Elizabeth II right **Reverse:** Tower of Refuge and Manx Shearwater in flight

| Date | Mintage | F | VF | XF | Unc | BU |
|---|---|---|---|---|---|---|
| 1986 (VW) | — | — | — | — | 6.50 | — |
| 1986 Proof | — | Value: 8.50 | | | | |
| 1987 AA | — | — | — | — | 6.50 | — |

**2 POUNDS** **KM# 214** **Composition:** Virenium **Obverse:** Head of Queen Elizabeth II right **Reverse:** Manx Airlines

| Date | Mintage | F | VF | XF | Unc | BU |
|---|---|---|---|---|---|---|
| 1988 AA | — | — | — | — | 6.50 | — |
| 1988 D | — | — | — | — | 6.50 | — |
| 1989 | — | — | — | — | 6.50 | — |
| 1990 AA | — | — | — | — | 6.50 | — |
| 1991 AA | — | — | — | — | 6.50 | — |
| 1992 AA | — | — | — | — | 6.50 | — |

**2 POUNDS** **KM# 257a** **Center Weight:** 9.3000 g. **Center Composition:** 0.9250 Silver .2766 oz. ASW **Obverse:** Head of Queen Elizabeth II right **Reverse:** Manx Airlines Dirigible

| Date | Mintage | F | VF | XF | Unc | BU |
|---|---|---|---|---|---|---|
| 1989 Reported, not confirmed | — | — | — | — | — | — |

**2 POUNDS** **KM# 257b** **Weight:** 15.9400 g. **Composition:** 0.9170 Gold .4730 oz. AGW **Obverse:** Head of Queen Elizabeth II right **Reverse:** Manx Airlines Dirigible

| Date | Mintage | F | VF | XF | Unc | BU |
|---|---|---|---|---|---|---|
| 1989 Reported, not confirmed | — | — | — | — | — | — |

**2 POUNDS** **KM# 257c** **Center Weight:** 18.0000 g. **Center Composition:** 0.9500 Platinum .5498 oz. APW **Obverse:** Head of Queen Elizabeth II right **Reverse:** Manx Airlines Dirigible

| Date | Mintage | F | VF | XF | Unc | BU |
|---|---|---|---|---|---|---|
| 1989 Reported, not confirmed | — | — | — | — | — | — |

**Note:** Most recalled by government. Few actually issued

**2 POUNDS** **KM# 344** **Composition:** Virenium **Subject:** World Champion - Nigel Mansell **Obverse:** Head of Queen Elizabeth II right **Reverse:** Race driver

| Date | Mintage | F | VF | XF | Unc | BU |
|---|---|---|---|---|---|---|
| 1993 | — | — | — | — | 6.50 | — |

**2 POUNDS** **KM# 398** **Composition:** Virenium **Subject:** Indycar World Series Champion - Nigel Mansell **Obverse:** Head of Queen Elizabeth II right **Reverse:** Two racecars

| Date | Mintage | F | VF | XF | Unc | BU |
|---|---|---|---|---|---|---|
| 1994 AA | — | — | — | — | 7.50 | — |

**2 POUNDS** **KM# 465** **Composition:** Virenium **Subject:** 50th Anniversary - VE and VJ Day **Obverse:** Head of Queen Elizabeth II right

| Date | Mintage | F | VF | XF | Unc | BU |
|---|---|---|---|---|---|---|
| 1995 | — | — | — | — | 7.00 | — |

**2 POUNDS** **KM# 595** **Composition:** Virenium **Subject:** Sports **Obverse:** Head of Queen Elizabeth II right **Reverse:** Racing cars

| Date | Mintage | F | VF | XF | Unc | BU |
|---|---|---|---|---|---|---|
| 1996 AA | — | — | — | — | 7.00 | — |

**2 POUNDS** **KM# 844** **Ring Composition:** Brass **Center Composition:** Copper-Nickel **Obverse:** Head of Queen Elizabeth II right **Reverse:** Racecars

| Date | Mintage | F | VF | XF | Unc | BU |
|---|---|---|---|---|---|---|
| 1997 AA | — | — | — | — | 8.00 | — |

**2 POUNDS** **KM# 858** **Ring Composition:** Brass **Center Composition:** Copper-Nickel **Obverse:** Rank-Broadley portrait of Queen Elizabeth II **Reverse:** Three racecars

| Date | Mintage | F | VF | XF | Unc | BU |
|---|---|---|---|---|---|---|
| 1998 AA | — | — | — | — | 8.00 | — |

**2 POUNDS** **KM# 1043** **Ring Weight:** 12.0000 g. **Ring Composition:** Brass **Center Composition:** Copper-Nickel **Subject:** Thorwald's Cross **Obverse:** Queen's portrait **Reverse:** Ancient drawing **Edge:** Reeded

| Date | Mintage | F | VF | XF | Unc | BU |
|---|---|---|---|---|---|---|
| 2000 AA | — | — | — | — | 7.50 | — |

**5 POUNDS** **KM# 17** **Weight:** 39.9403 g. **Composition:** 0.9170 Gold 1.1776 oz. AGW **Subject:** 200th Anniversary of Acquisition **Obverse:** Bust of Queen Elizabeth II right

| Date | Mintage | F | VF | XF | Unc | BU |
|---|---|---|---|---|---|---|
| 1965 | 500 | — | — | — | 540 | — |

**5 POUNDS** **KM# 17a** **Center Weight:** 39.9500 g. **Center Composition:** 0.9800 Gold 1.2588 oz. AGW **Subject:** 200th Anniversary of Acquisition **Obverse:** Bust of Queen Elizabeth II right

| Date | Mintage | F | VF | XF | Unc | BU |
|---|---|---|---|---|---|---|
| 1965 Proof | 1,000 | Value: 575 | | | | |

**5 POUNDS** **KM# 29** **Center Weight:** 39.8134 g. **Center Composition:** 0.9170 Gold 1.1739 oz. AGW **Obverse:** Bust of Queen Elizabeth II right

| Date | Mintage | F | VF | XF | Unc | BU |
|---|---|---|---|---|---|---|
| 1973 | 3,035 | — | — | — | 450 | — |
| 1973 Proof | 1,250 | Value: 600 | | | | |
| 1974 | 481 | — | — | — | 600 | — |
| 1974 Proof | 2,500 | Value: 475 | | | | |
| 1975 | 306 | — | — | — | 600 | — |
| 1975 Proof | — | Value: 500 | | | | |
| 1976 | 370 | — | — | — | 600 | — |
| 1976 Proof | — | Value: 500 | | | | |
| 1977 | — | — | — | — | 475 | — |
| 1977 Proof | 1,250 | Value: 600 | | | | |
| 1978 Proof | 1,250 | Value: 600 | | | | |
| 1979 (t) | 1,000 | — | — | — | 600 | — |
| 1979 (t) Proof | 1,000 | Value: 600 | | | | |
| 1980 (m) | 250 | — | — | — | 650 | — |
| 1982 (b) | 10,000 | — | — | — | 450 | — |
| 1982 (b) Proof | 500 | Value: 600 | | | | |

**5 POUNDS** **KM# 89** **Center Weight:** 39.8134 g. **Center Composition:** 0.9170 Gold 1.1739 oz. AGW **Subject:** Wedding of Prince Charles and Lady Diana **Obverse:** Bust of Queen Elizabeth II right **Reverse:** Portraits of Royal Couple, joined shields

| Date | Mintage | F | VF | XF | Unc | BU |
|---|---|---|---|---|---|---|
| 1981 Proof | 1,000 | Value: 650 | | | | |

**5 POUNDS** **KM# 88** **Center Composition:** Virenium **Obverse:** Bust of Queen Elizabeth II right **Reverse:** Compass showing geographic location

| Date | Mintage | F | VF | XF | Unc | BU |
|---|---|---|---|---|---|---|
| 1981 AA | — | — | — | — | 10.00 | — |
| 1981 AB | — | — | — | — | 10.00 | — |
| 1981 AC | — | — | — | — | 10.00 | — |
| 1981 Proof | 30,000 | Value: 12.00 | | | | |
| 1982 Proof | — | Value: 12.00 | | | | |
| 1983 AA | — | — | — | — | 20.00 | — |
| 1984 AC | — | — | — | — | 10.00 | — |

**5 POUNDS** **KM# 88a** **Center Weight:** 23.5000 g. **Center Composition:** 0.9250 Silver .6989 oz. ASW **Obverse:** Bust of Queen Elizabeth II right **Reverse:** Compass showing geographic location

| Date | Mintage | F | VF | XF | Unc | BU |
|---|---|---|---|---|---|---|
| 1981 Proof | 500 | Value: 40.00 | | | | |
| 1982 (b) Proof | 1,000 | Value: 35.00 | | | | |
| 1983 Proof | 5,000 | Value: 25.00 | | | | |

**5 POUNDS** **KM# 88b** **Center Weight:** 39.9000 g. **Center Composition:** 0.9170 Gold 1.1764 oz. AGW **Obverse:** Bust of Queen Elizabeth II right **Reverse:** Compass showing geographic location

| Date | Mintage | F | VF | XF | Unc | BU |
|---|---|---|---|---|---|---|
| 1981 Proof | 1,000 | Value: 625 | | | | |
| 1982 (b) Proof | 250 | Value: 650 | | | | |
| 1982 (b) Proof | 750 | Value: 650 | | | | |
| 1983 Proof | — | Value: 650 | | | | |

**5 POUNDS** **KM# 88c** **Center Weight:** 45.5000 g. **Center Composition:** 0.9500 Platinum 1.3898 oz. APW **Obverse:** Bust of Queen Elizabeth II right **Reverse:** Compass showing geographic location

| Date | Mintage | F | VF | XF | Unc | BU |
|---|---|---|---|---|---|---|
| 1981 Proof | 500 | Value: 800 | | | | |
| 1982 (b) Proof | 100 | Value: 1,100 | | | | |
| 1983 Proof | — | Value: 1,000 | | | | |

**5 POUNDS** **KM# 134** **Center Composition:** Virenium **Subject:** Quincentenery of the College of Arms **Obverse:** Bust of Queen Elizabeth II right

| Date | Mintage | F | VF | XF | Unc | BU |
|---|---|---|---|---|---|---|
| 1984 AA | — | — | — | — | 10.00 | — |
| 1984 BB | — | — | — | — | 10.00 | — |

**5 POUNDS** **KM# 134a** **Center Weight:** 23.5000 g. **Center Composition:** 0.9250 Silver .6989 oz. ASW **Subject:** Quincentenery of the College of Arms **Obverse:** Bust of Queen Elizabeth II right

| Date | Mintage | F | VF | XF | Unc | BU |
|---|---|---|---|---|---|---|
| 1984 Proof | — | Value: 40.00 | | | | |

**5 POUNDS** **KM# 134b** **Center Weight:** 39.9000 g. **Center Composition:** 0.9170 Gold 1.1759 oz. AGW **Subject:** Quincentenery of the College of Arms **Obverse:** Bust of Queen Elizabeth II right

| Date | Mintage | F | VF | XF | Unc | BU |
|---|---|---|---|---|---|---|
| 1984 Proof | 150 | Value: 750 | | | | |

**5 POUNDS** **KM# 134c** **Center Weight:** 45.5000 g. **Center Composition:** 0.9500 Platinum 1.3898 oz. APW **Subject:** Quincentenery of the College of Arms **Obverse:** Bust of Queen Elizabeth II right

| Date | Mintage | F | VF | XF | Unc | BU |
|---|---|---|---|---|---|---|
| 1984 Proof | — | Value: 1,100 | | | | |

**5 POUNDS** **KM# 263** **Center Weight:** 39.8300 g. **Center Composition:** 0.9170 Gold 1.1740 oz. AGW **Obverse:** Bust of Queen Elizabeth II right **Reverse:** Four crowned shields

| Date | Mintage | F | VF | XF | Unc | BU |
|---|---|---|---|---|---|---|
| 1984 | 20 | — | — | — | 1,250 | — |
| 1984 Proof | 20 | Value: 1,650 | | | | |

**5 POUNDS** **KM# 150** **Center Composition:** Virenium **Obverse:** Head of Queen Elizabeth II right **Reverse:** Similar to KM#134 with sports privy mark

| Date | Mintage | F | VF | XF | Unc | BU |
|---|---|---|---|---|---|---|
| 1985 AA(w) | — | — | — | — | 10.00 | — |
| 1985 Proof | 25,000 | Value: 10.00 | | | | |
| 1986 AA | — | — | — | — | 10.00 | — |
| 1987 AA | — | — | — | — | 10.00 | — |

**5 POUNDS** **KM# 150a** **Center Weight:** 23.5000 g. **Center Composition:** 0.9250 Silver .6989 oz. ASW **Obverse:** Head of Queen Elizabeth II right

| Date | Mintage | F | VF | XF | Unc | BU |
|---|---|---|---|---|---|---|
| 1985 Proof | Est. 5,000 | Value: 40.00 | | | | |

**5 POUNDS** **KM# 150b** **Center Weight:** 39.9000 g. **Center Composition:** 0.9170 Gold 1.1759 oz. AGW **Obverse:** Viking ship on shield

| Date | Mintage | F | VF | XF | Unc | BU |
|---|---|---|---|---|---|---|
| 1985 Proof | Est. 150 | Value: 750 | | | | |

**5 POUNDS** **KM# 150c** **Center Weight:** 45.5000 g. **Center Composition:** 0.9500 Platinum 1.3898 oz. APW **Obverse:** Head of Queen Elizabeth II right

| Date | Mintage | F | VF | XF | Unc | BU |
|---|---|---|---|---|---|---|
| 1985 Proof | Est. 100 | Value: 1,200 | | | | |

**5 POUNDS** **KM# 215** **Center Composition:** Virenium **Obverse:** Head of Queen Elizabeth II right **Reverse:** Lobster fishing boat

| Date | Mintage | F | VF | XF | Unc | BU |
|---|---|---|---|---|---|---|
| 1988 AA | — | — | — | — | 10.00 | — |
| 1989 AA | — | — | — | — | 10.00 | — |
| 1990 AA | — | — | — | — | 10.00 | — |
| 1992 AA | — | — | — | — | 10.00 | — |

**5 POUNDS** **KM# 336** **Center Composition:** Virenium **Subject:** World Champion - Nigel Mansell **Obverse:** Head of Queen Elizabeth II right **Reverse:** Race driver

| Date | Mintage | F | VF | XF | Unc | BU |
|---|---|---|---|---|---|---|
| 1993 AA | — | — | — | — | 12.50 | — |

**5 POUNDS** **KM# 399** **Center Composition:** Virenium **Subject:** Indycar World Series Champion - Nigel Mansell **Obverse:** Head of Queen Elizabeth II right **Reverse:** 2 race cars

| Date | Mintage | F | VF | XF | Unc | BU |
|---|---|---|---|---|---|---|
| 1994 AA | — | — | — | — | 15.00 | — |

**5 POUNDS** **KM# 466** **Center Composition:** Virenium **Subject:** 50th Anniversary - End of World War II **Obverse:** Head of Queen Elizabeth II right **Reverse:** Winston Churchill

| Date | Mintage | F | VF | XF | Unc | BU |
|---|---|---|---|---|---|---|
| 1995 | — | — | — | — | 15.00 | — |

**5 POUNDS** **KM# 466a** **Center Weight:** 23.5000 g. **Center Composition:** 0.9250 Silver .6989 oz. ASW **Subject:** 50th Anniversary - End of World War II **Obverse:** Head of Queen Elizabeth II right **Reverse:** Winston Churchill

| Date | Mintage | F | VF | XF | Unc | BU |
|---|---|---|---|---|---|---|
| 1995 Proof | — | Value: 40.00 | | | | |

**5 POUNDS** **KM# 466b** **Center Weight:** 39.8300 g. **Center Composition:** 0.9170 Gold 1.1759 oz. AGW **Subject:** 50th Anniversary - End of World War II **Obverse:** Head of Queen Elizabeth II right **Reverse:** Winston Churchill

| Date | Mintage | F | VF | XF | Unc | BU |
|---|---|---|---|---|---|---|
| 1995 Proof | Est. 850 | Value: 750 | | | | |

**5 POUNDS** **KM# 587** **Center Composition:** Virenium **Subject:** European Soccer Championships **Obverse:** Head of Queen Elizabeth II right **Reverse:** Players

| Date | Mintage | F | VF | XF | Unc | BU |
|---|---|---|---|---|---|---|
| 1996 AA | — | — | — | — | 16.00 | — |

**5 POUNDS** **KM# 587a** **Center Weight:** 23.5000 g. **Center Composition:** 0.9250 Silver .6989 oz. ASW **Subject:** European Soccer Championships **Obverse:** Head of Queen Elizabeth II right **Reverse:** Players

| Date | Mintage | F | VF | XF | Unc | BU |
|---|---|---|---|---|---|---|
| 1996 Proof | Est. 5,000 | Value: 40.00 | | | | |

**5 POUNDS** **KM# 587b** **Center Weight:** 39.0830 g. **Center Composition:** 0.9160 Gold 1.1510 oz. AGW **Subject:** European Soccer Championships **Obverse:** Head of Queen Elizabeth II right **Reverse:** Players

| Date | Mintage | F | VF | XF | Unc | BU |
|---|---|---|---|---|---|---|
| 1996 Proof | Est. 850 | Value: 900 | | | | |

**5 POUNDS** **KM# 769** **Center Composition:** Virenium **Subject:** 50th Anniversary - Queen Elizabeth and Prince Philip **Obverse:** Bust of Queen Elizabeth II right **Reverse:** Current portrait of Queen Elizabeth and Prince Philip

| Date | Mintage | F | VF | XF | Unc | BU |
|---|---|---|---|---|---|---|
| 1997 | — | — | — | — | 16.50 | — |

**5 POUNDS** **KM# 769a** **Center Weight:** 23.5000 g. **Center Composition:** 0.9250 Silver .6989 oz. ASW **Subject:** 50th Anniversary - Queen Elizabeth and Prince Philip **Obverse:** Bust of Queen Elizabeth II right **Reverse:** Current portrait of Queen Elizabeth and Prince Philip

| Date | Mintage | F | VF | XF | Unc | BU |
|---|---|---|---|---|---|---|
| 1997 Proof | Est. 5,000 | Value: 40.00 | | | | |

**5 POUNDS** **KM# 769b** **Center Weight:** 39.8300 g. **Center Composition:** 0.9167 Gold 1.1740 oz. AGW **Subject:** 50th Anniversary - Queen Elizabeth and Prince Philip **Obverse:** Bust of Queen Elizabeth II right **Obv. Legend:** Current portrait of Queen Elizabeth and Prince Philip

| Date | Mintage | F | VF | XF | Unc | BU |
|---|---|---|---|---|---|---|
| 1997 Proof | Est. 850 | Value: 900 | | | | |

**5 POUNDS** **KM# 912** **Center Composition:** Virenium **Subject:** 50th Birthday - Prince Charles **Obverse:** Rank-Broadley portrait of Queen Elizabeth II **Reverse:** Portrait of Prince Charles

| Date | Mintage | F | VF | XF | Unc | BU |
|---|---|---|---|---|---|---|
| 1998 | — | — | — | — | 16.50 | — |

**5 POUNDS** **KM# 912a** **Center Weight:** 23.5000 g. **Center Composition:** 0.9250 Silver .6989 oz. ASW **Subject:** 50th Birthday - Prince Charles **Obverse:** Rank-Broadley portrait of Queen Elizabeth II **Reverse:** Portrait of Prince Charles

| Date | Mintage | F | VF | XF | Unc | BU |
|---|---|---|---|---|---|---|
| 1998 Proof | Est. 5,000 | Value: 50.00 | | | | |

**5 POUNDS** **KM# 912b** **Center Weight:** 39.8300 g. **Center Composition:** 0.9167 Gold 1.1740 oz. AGW **Subject:** 50th Birthday - Prince Charles **Obverse:** Rank-Broadley portrait Queen Elizabeth II **Reverse:** Portrait of Prince Charles

| Date | Mintage | F | VF | XF | Unc | BU |
|---|---|---|---|---|---|---|
| 1998 Proof | Est. 850 | Value: 885 | | | | |

**5 POUNDS** **KM# 991** **Center Composition:** Virenium **Subject:** Soccer **Obverse:** Rank-Broadley portrait of Queen Elizabeth II **Reverse:** Two soccer players

| Date | Mintage | F | VF | XF | Unc | BU |
|---|---|---|---|---|---|---|
| 1998 AA | — | — | — | — | 16.50 | — |

**5 POUNDS** **KM# 943** **Center Composition:** Virenium **Subject:** 175th Anniversary of the RN LI **Obverse:** Head of Queen Elizabeth II right **Reverse:** Lifeboat at sea

| Date | Mintage | F | VF | XF | Unc | BU |
|---|---|---|---|---|---|---|
| 1999 | — | — | — | — | 15.50 | — |

**5 POUNDS** **KM# 943a** **Center Weight:** 23.5000 g. **Center Composition:** 0.9250 Silver .6989 oz. ASW **Subject:** 175th Anniversary of the RN LI **Obverse:** Head of Queen Elizabeth II right **Reverse:** Lifeboat at sea

| Date | Mintage | F | VF | XF | Unc | BU |
|---|---|---|---|---|---|---|
| 1999 Proof | Est. 10,000 | Value: 50.00 | | | | |

**5 POUNDS** **KM# 943b** **Center Weight:** 39.8300 g. **Center Composition:** 0.9167 Gold 1.1739 oz. AGW **Subject:** 175th Anniversary of the RN LI **Obverse:** Head of Queen Elizabeth II right **Reverse:** Lifeboat at sea

| Date | Mintage | F | VF | XF | Unc | BU |
|---|---|---|---|---|---|---|
| 1999 Proof | 850 | Value: 885 | | | | |

**5 POUNDS** **KM# 1044** **Weight:** 20.1000 g. **Composition:** Virenium **Subject:** St. Patrick's Hymn **Obverse:** Queen's portrait **Reverse:** Stylized cross design **Edge:** Reeded and plain sections

| Date | Mintage | F | VF | XF | Unc | BU |
|---|---|---|---|---|---|---|
| 2000 AA | — | — | — | — | 16.50 | — |

**10 POUNDS** **KM# 345** **Weight:** 10.0000 g. **Composition:** 0.9250 Silver .2973 oz. ASW **Subject:** Indycar World Series Champion - Nigel Mansell **Obverse:** Head of Queen Elizabeth II right **Reverse:** Race driver **Note:** Similar to 5 Pounds, KM#336

| Date | Mintage | F | VF | XF | Unc | BU |
|---|---|---|---|---|---|---|
| 1993 Proof | Est. 20,000 | Value: 35.00 | | | | |

**10 POUNDS** **KM# 400** **Weight:** 10.0000 g. **Composition:** 0.9250 Silver .2973 oz. ASW **Subject:** Indycar World Series Champion - Nigel Mansell **Obverse:** Head of Queen Elizabeth II right **Reverse:** Two race cars **Note:** Similar to 5 Pounds, KM#399

| Date | Mintage | F | VF | XF | Unc | BU |
|---|---|---|---|---|---|---|
| 1994 Proof | Est. 20,000 | Value: 35.00 | | | | |

**25 POUNDS** **KM# 346** **Weight:** 28.2800 g. **Composition:** 0.9250 Silver .8411 oz. ASW **Subject:** World Champion - Nigel Mansell **Obverse:** Bust of Queen Elizabeth II right **Reverse:** Two race cars

| Date | Mintage | F | VF | XF | Unc | BU |
|---|---|---|---|---|---|---|
| 1993 Proof | Est. 15,000 | Value: 50.00 | | | | |

**50 POUNDS** **KM# 347** **Weight:** 6.2200 g. **Composition:** 0.9990 Gold .2000 oz. AGW **Subject:** World Champion - Nigel Mansell **Obverse:** Head of Queen Elizabeth II right **Reverse:** Two race cars **Note:** Similar to 5 Pounds, KM#336

| Date | Mintage | F | VF | XF | Unc | BU |
|---|---|---|---|---|---|---|
| 1993 Proof | Est. 5,000 | Value: 150 | | | | |

**50 POUNDS** **KM# 401** **Weight:** 6.2200 g. **Composition:** 0.9990 Gold .2000 oz. AGW **Subject:** Indycar World Series Champion - Nigel Mansell **Obverse:** Head of Queen Elizabeth II right **Reverse:** Two race cars **Note:** Similar to 5 Pounds, KM#399

| Date | Mintage | F | VF | XF | Unc | BU |
|---|---|---|---|---|---|---|
| 1994 Proof | Est. 5,000 | Value: 150 | | | | |

## CROWN SERIES

Pobjoy Mint Key

Pobjoy Mint: (M) MATTE - Normal circulation strike. (U) SPECIAL UNCIRCULATED - Polished or proof-like in appearance, slightly frosted features. (P) PROOF - The highest quality obtainable having mirror-like fields and frosted features.

**CROWN (25 Pence)** **KM# 25** **Composition:** Copper-Nickel **Subject:** 25th Wedding Anniversary **Obverse:** Bust of Queen Elizabeth II right **Rev. Designer:** Stuart Devlin **Note:** Struck at the Royal Canadian Mint.

| Date | Mintage | F | VF | XF | Unc | BU |
|---|---|---|---|---|---|---|
| 1972 | 70,000 | — | — | — | 3.00 | — |

**CROWN (25 Pence)** **KM# 25a** **Weight:** 28.2800 g. **Composition:** 0.9250 Silver .8411 oz. ASW **Obverse:** Bust of Queen Elizabeth II right **Rev. Designer:** Stuart Devlin **Note:** Struck at the Royal Canadian Mint.

| Date | Mintage | F | VF | XF | Unc | BU |
|---|---|---|---|---|---|---|
| 1972 Proof | 15,000 | Value: 10.00 | | | | |

**CROWN (25 Pence)** **KM# 31** **Composition:** Copper-Nickel **Obverse:** Bust of Queen Elizabeth II right **Reverse:** Manx cat

| Date | Mintage | F | VF | XF | Unc | BU |
|---|---|---|---|---|---|---|
| 1975 | 35,000 | — | — | — | 3.00 | — |

**CROWN (25 Pence)** **KM# 31a** **Weight:** 28.2800 g. **Composition:** 0.9250 Silver .8411 oz. ASW **Obverse:** Bust of Queen Elizabeth II right **Reverse:** Manx cat

| Date | Mintage | F | VF | XF | Unc | BU |
|---|---|---|---|---|---|---|
| 1975 | — | — | — | — | 9.00 | — |
| 1975 Proof | 30,000 | Value: 13.50 | | | | |

**1/25 CROWN** **KM# 235** **Weight:** 1.2441 g. **Composition:** 0.9990 Gold .0400 oz. AGW **Obverse:** Bust Queen Elizabeth II right **Reverse:** Manx cat

| Date | Mintage | F | VF | XF | Unc | BU |
|---|---|---|---|---|---|---|
| 1988 | 40,000 | — | — | — | 175 | — |
| 1988 Proof | 5,000 | Value: 178 | | | | |

**1/25 CROWN KM# 252 Weight:** 1.2441 g. **Composition:** 0.9990 Gold .0400 oz. AGW **Obverse:** Bust Queen Elizabeth II **Reverse:** Persian cat

| Date | Mintage | F | VF | XF | Unc | BU |
|---|---|---|---|---|---|---|
| 1989 | — | — | — | — | 50.00 | — |
| 1989 Proof | — | Value: 52.00 | | | | |

**1/25 CROWN KM# 467 Weight:** 1.2441 g. **Composition:** 0.9995 Platinum .0400 oz. APW **Obverse:** Bust of Queen Elizabeth II right **Reverse:** Persian cat

| Date | Mintage | F | VF | XF | Unc | BU |
|---|---|---|---|---|---|---|
| 1989 | — | — | — | — | 60.00 | — |
| 1989 Proof | — | Value: 62.00 | | | | |

**1/25 CROWN KM# 277 Weight:** 1.2441 g. **Composition:** 0.9990 Gold .0400 oz. AGW **Obverse:** Bust of Queen Elizabeth II **Reverse:** Alley cat

| Date | Mintage | F | VF | XF | Unc | BU |
|---|---|---|---|---|---|---|
| 1990 | — | — | — | — | 50.00 | — |
| 1990 Proof | — | Value: 52.00 | | | | |

**1/25 CROWN KM# 294 Weight:** 1.2441 g. **Composition:** 0.9990 Gold .0400 oz. AGW **Obverse:** Bust of Queen Elizabeth II right **Reverse:** Norwegian cat

| Date | Mintage | F | VF | XF | Unc | BU |
|---|---|---|---|---|---|---|
| 1991 | — | — | — | — | 50.00 | — |
| 1991 Proof | — | Value: 52.00 | | | | |

**1/25 CROWN KM# 322 Weight:** 1.2441 g. **Composition:** 0.9990 Gold .0400 oz. AGW **Subject:** America's Cup **Obverse:** Bust of Queen Elizabeth II right **Reverse:** Sailboat

| Date | Mintage | F | VF | XF | Unc | BU |
|---|---|---|---|---|---|---|
| 1992 Proof like | 50,000 | — | — | — | — | — |

**1/25 CROWN KM# 328 Weight:** 1.2441 g. **Composition:** 0.9990 Gold .0400 oz. AGW **Obverse:** Bust of Queen Elizabeth II right **Reverse:** Siamese cat

| Date | Mintage | F | VF | XF | Unc | BU |
|---|---|---|---|---|---|---|
| 1992 | — | — | — | — | 45.00 | — |
| 1992 Proof | — | Value: 47.00 | | | | |

**1/25 CROWN KM# 338 Weight:** 1.2441 g. **Composition:** 0.9990 Gold .0400 oz. AGW **Subject:** Year of the Cockerel **Obverse:** Bust of Queen Elizabeth II right **Reverse:** Cockerel in inner circle

| Date | Mintage | F | VF | XF | Unc | BU |
|---|---|---|---|---|---|---|
| 1993 Proof | Est. 25,000 | Value: 40.00 | | | | |

**1/25 CROWN KM# 349 Weight:** 1.2441 g. **Composition:** 0.9990 Gold .0400 oz. AGW **Obverse:** Bust of Queen Elizabeth II right **Reverse:** Maine Coon cat

| Date | Mintage | F | VF | XF | Unc | BU |
|---|---|---|---|---|---|---|
| 1993 | — | — | — | — | 45.00 | — |
| 1993 Proof | — | Value: 47.00 | | | | |

**1/25 CROWN KM# 376 Weight:** 1.2441 g. **Composition:** 0.9990 Gold .0400 oz. AGW **Obverse:** Bust of Queen Elizabeth II right **Reverse:** Japanese Bobtail cat

| Date | Mintage | F | VF | XF | Unc | BU |
|---|---|---|---|---|---|---|
| 1994 | — | — | — | — | 40.00 | — |
| 1994 Proof | — | Value: 42.00 | | | | |

**1/25 CROWN KM# 402 Weight:** 1.2441 g. **Composition:** 0.9990 Gold .0400 oz. AGW **Obverse:** Bust of Queen Elizabeth II right **Reverse:** Pekingese Dog

| Date | Mintage | F | VF | XF | Unc | BU |
|---|---|---|---|---|---|---|
| 1994 Proof | Est. 25,000 | Value: 50.00 | | | | |

**1/25 CROWN KM# 473 Weight:** 1.2441 g. **Composition:** 0.9995 Platinum .0400 oz. APW **Obverse:** Bust of Queen Elizabeth II right **Reverse:** Japanese Bobtail cat

| Date | Mintage | F | VF | XF | Unc | BU |
|---|---|---|---|---|---|---|
| 1994 | — | — | — | — | 60.00 | — |
| 1994 Proof | — | Value: 62.00 | | | | |

**1/25 CROWN KM# 442 Weight:** 1.2441 g. **Composition:** 0.9990 Gold .0400 oz. AGW **Obverse:** Bust of Queen Elizabeth II right **Reverse:** Turkish cat

| Date | Mintage | F | VF | XF | Unc | BU |
|---|---|---|---|---|---|---|
| 1995 U | — | — | — | — | 40.00 | — |
| 1995 Proof | — | Value: 42.00 | | | | |

**1/25 CROWN KM# 449 Weight:** 1.2441 g. **Composition:** 0.9990 Gold .0400 oz. AGW **Subject:** Year of the Pig **Obverse:** Bust of Queen Elizabeth II right **Reverse:** Sow with piglets

| Date | Mintage | F | VF | XF | Unc | BU |
|---|---|---|---|---|---|---|
| 1995 Proof | Est. 25,000 | Value: 45.00 | | | | |

**1/25 CROWN KM# 478 Weight:** 1.2441 g. **Composition:** 0.9995 Platinum .0400 oz. APW **Obverse:** Bust of Queen Elizabeth II right **Reverse:** Turkish cat

| Date | Mintage | F | VF | XF | Unc | BU |
|---|---|---|---|---|---|---|
| 1995 | — | — | — | — | 50.00 | — |
| 1995 Proof | — | Value: 52.00 | | | | |

**1/25 CROWN KM# 597 Weight:** 1.2441 g. **Composition:** 0.9990 Gold .0400 oz. AGW **Series:** Flower Fairies **Obverse:** Bust of Queen Elizabeth II right **Reverse:** Orchis

| Date | Mintage | F | VF | XF | Unc | BU |
|---|---|---|---|---|---|---|
| 1996 Proof | Est. 25,000 | Value: 40.00 | | | | |

**1/25 CROWN KM# 598 Weight:** 1.2441 g. **Composition:** 0.9990 Gold .0400 oz. AGW **Series:** Flower Fairies **Obverse:** Bust of Queen Elizabeth II right **Reverse:** Rose

| Date | Mintage | F | VF | XF | Unc | BU |
|---|---|---|---|---|---|---|
| 1996 Proof | Est. 25,000 | Value: 40.00 | | | | |

**1/25 CROWN KM# 599 Weight:** 1.2441 g. **Composition:** 0.9990 Gold .0400 oz. AGW **Series:** Flower Fairies **Obverse:** Bust of Queen Elizabeth II right **Reverse:** Fuchsia

| Date | Mintage | F | VF | XF | Unc | BU |
|---|---|---|---|---|---|---|
| 1996 Proof | Est. 25,000 | Value: 40.00 | | | | |

**1/25 CROWN KM# 600 Weight:** 1.2441 g. **Composition:** 0.9990 Gold .0400 oz. AGW **Series:** Flower Fairies **Obverse:** Bust of Queen Elizabeth II right **Reverse:** Pinks **Note:**

| Date | Mintage | F | VF | XF | Unc | BU |
|---|---|---|---|---|---|---|
| 1996 Proof | Est. 25,000 | Value: 40.00 | | | | |

**1/25 CROWN KM# 613 Weight:** 1.2441 g. **Composition:** 0.9990 Gold .0400 oz. AGW **Obverse:** Bust of Queen Elizabeth II right **Reverse:** Burmese cat **Note:** #621a.

| Date | Mintage | F | VF | XF | Unc | BU |
|---|---|---|---|---|---|---|
| 1996 U | — | — | — | — | 40.00 | — |
| 1996 Proof | — | Value: 42.00 | | | | |

**1/25 CROWN KM# 614 Weight:** 1.2441 g. **Composition:** 0.9995 Platinum .0400 oz. APW **Obverse:** Bust of Queen Elizabeth II right **Reverse:** Burmese cat

| Date | Mintage | F | VF | XF | Unc | BU |
|---|---|---|---|---|---|---|
| 1996 | — | — | — | — | 50.00 | — |
| 1996 Proof | — | Value: 52.00 | | | | |

**1/25 CROWN KM# 728 Weight:** 1.2441 g. **Composition:** 0.9990 Gold .0400 oz. AGW **Subject:** Year of the Rat **Obverse:** Bust of Queen Elizabeth II right **Reverse:** Rat **Note:** Similar to 1 Crown, KM#732.

| Date | Mintage | F | VF | XF | Unc | BU |
|---|---|---|---|---|---|---|
| 1996 Proof | — | — | — | — | — | — |

**Note:** Entire series purchased by one buyer; Mintage, disposition, and market value unknown

**1/25 CROWN KM# 721 Weight:** 1.2441 g. **Composition:** 0.9990 Gold .0400 oz. AGW **Subject:** Year of the Ox **Obverse:** Bust of Queen Elizabeth II right **Reverse:** Ox laying down

| Date | Mintage | F | VF | XF | Unc | BU |
|---|---|---|---|---|---|---|
| 1997 Proof | Est. 20,000 | Value: 40.00 | | | | |

**1/25 CROWN KM# 735 Weight:** 1.2441 g. **Composition:** 0.9990 Gold .0400 oz. AGW **Series:** Flower Fairies **Obverse:** Bust of Queen Elizabeth II right **Reverse:** Candytuft

| Date | Mintage | F | VF | XF | Unc | BU |
|---|---|---|---|---|---|---|
| 1997 Proof | Est. 25,000 | Value: 40.00 | | | | |

**1/25 CROWN KM# 735a Weight:** 1.2504 g. **Composition:** 0.9950 Platinum .0400 oz. APW **Series:** Flower Fairies **Obverse:** Bust of Queen Elizabeth II right **Reverse:** Candytuft

| Date | Mintage | F | VF | XF | Unc | BU |
|---|---|---|---|---|---|---|
| 1997 Proof | Est. 7,500 | Value: 50.00 | | | | |

**1/25 CROWN KM# 736 Weight:** 1.2441 g. **Composition:** 0.9999 Gold .0400 oz. AGW **Series:** Flower Fairies **Obverse:** Bust of Queen Elizabeth II right **Reverse:** Snowdrop

| Date | Mintage | F | VF | XF | Unc | BU |
|---|---|---|---|---|---|---|
| 1997 Proof | Est. 25,000 | Value: 40.00 | | | | |

**1/25 CROWN KM# 736a Weight:** 1.2504 g. **Composition:** 0.9950 Platinum .0400 oz. APW **Series:** Flower Fairies **Obverse:** Bust of Queen Elizabeth II right **Reverse:** Snowdrop

| Date | Mintage | F | VF | XF | Unc | BU |
|---|---|---|---|---|---|---|
| 1997 Proof | Est. 7,500 | Value: 50.00 | | | | |

**1/25 CROWN KM# 737 Weight:** 1.2441 g. **Composition:** 0.9999 Gold .0400 oz. AGW **Series:** Flower Fairies **Obverse:** Bust of Queen Elizabeth II right **Reverse:** Tulip

| Date | Mintage | F | VF | XF | Unc | BU |
|---|---|---|---|---|---|---|
| 1997 Proof | Est. 25,000 | Value: 40.00 | | | | |

**1/25 CROWN KM# 737a Weight:** 1.2504 g. **Composition:** 0.9950 Platinum .0400 oz. APW **Series:** Flower Fairies **Obverse:** Bust of Queen Elizabeth II right **Reverse:** Tulip

| Date | Mintage | F | VF | XF | Unc | BU |
|---|---|---|---|---|---|---|
| 1997 Proof | Est. 7,500 | Value: 50.00 | | | | |

**1/25 CROWN KM# 738 Weight:** 1.2441 g. **Composition:** 0.9999 Gold .0400 oz. AGW **Series:** Flower Fairies **Obverse:** Bust of Queen Elizabeth II right **Reverse:** Jasmine

| Date | Mintage | F | VF | XF | Unc | BU |
|---|---|---|---|---|---|---|
| 1997 Proof | Est. 25,000 | Value: 40.00 | | | | |

**1/25 CROWN KM# 738a Weight:** 1.2504 g. **Composition:** 0.9950 Platinum .0400 oz. APW **Series:** Flower Fairies **Obverse:** Bust of Queen Elizabeth II right **Reverse:** Jasmine

| Date | Mintage | F | VF | XF | Unc | BU |
|---|---|---|---|---|---|---|
| 1997 Proof | Est. 7,500 | Value: 50.00 | | | | |

**1/25 CROWN KM# 770 Weight:** 1.2440 g. **Composition:** 0.9999 Gold .0400 oz. AGW **Obverse:** Bust of Queen Elizabeth II right **Reverse:** Long-Haired-Smoke cat **Note:** Similar to 1 Crown, KM#774.

| Date | Mintage | F | VF | XF | Unc | BU |
|---|---|---|---|---|---|---|
| 1997 | — | — | — | — | 40.00 | — |
| 1997 Proof | — | Value: 42.00 | | | | |

**1/25 CROWN KM# 770a Weight:** 1.2440 g. **Composition:** 0.9999 Platinum .0400 oz. APW **Obverse:** Bust of Queen Elizabeth II right **Reverse:** Long-Haired-Smoke cat

| Date | Mintage | F | VF | XF | Unc | BU |
|---|---|---|---|---|---|---|
| 1997 | — | — | — | — | 50.00 | — |
| 1997 Proof | — | Value: 52.00 | | | | |

**1/25 CROWN KM# 789 Weight:** 1.2440 g. **Composition:** 0.9999 Gold .0400 oz. AGW **Subject:** History of the Cat **Obverse:** Bust of Queen Elizabeth II right **Reverse:** Cat stalking a spider

| Date | Mintage | F | VF | XF | Unc | BU |
|---|---|---|---|---|---|---|
| 1997 Proof | Est. 25,000 | Value: 45.00 | | | | |

**1/25 CROWN KM# 812 Weight:** 1.2441 g. **Composition:** 0.9999 Gold .0400 oz. AGW **Subject:** Year of the Tiger **Obverse:** Bust of Queen Elizabeth II right **Reverse:** Tiger

| Date | Mintage | F | VF | XF | Unc | BU |
|---|---|---|---|---|---|---|
| 1998 Proof | Est. 20,000 | Value: 45.00 | | | | |

**1/25 CROWN KM# 828 Weight:** 1.2441 g. **Composition:** 0.9999 Gold .0400 oz. AGW **Series:** Flower Fairies **Obverse:** Bust of Queen Elizabeth II right **Reverse:** Standing fairy, lavender

| Date | Mintage | F | VF | XF | Unc | BU |
|---|---|---|---|---|---|---|
| 1998 Proof | Est. 25,000 | Value: 45.00 | | | | |

**1/25 CROWN KM# 828a Weight:** 1.2441 g. **Composition:** 0.9995 Platinum .0400 oz. APW **Series:** Flower Fairies **Obverse:** Bust of Queen Elizabeth II right **Reverse:** Fairy standing, lavender

| Date | Mintage | F | VF | XF | Unc | BU |
|---|---|---|---|---|---|---|
| 1998 Proof | Est. 7,500 | Value: 55.00 | | | | |

**1/25 CROWN KM# 829 Weight:** 1.2441 g. **Composition:** 0.9999 Gold .0400 oz. AGW **Series:** Flower Fairies **Obverse:** Bust of Queen Elizabeth II right **Reverse:** Two fairies, sweet pea

| Date | Mintage | F | VF | XF | Unc | BU |
|---|---|---|---|---|---|---|
| 1998 Proof | Est. 25,000 | Value: 45.00 | | | | |

**1/25 CROWN KM# 829a Weight:** 1.2441 g. **Composition:** 0.9995 Platinum .0400 oz. APW **Series:** Flower Fairies **Obverse:** Bust of Queen Elizabeth II right **Reverse:** Two fairies, sweet pea

| Date | Mintage | F | VF | XF | Unc | BU |
|---|---|---|---|---|---|---|
| 1998 Proof | Est. 7,500 | Value: 55.00 | | | | |

**1/25 CROWN KM# 830 Weight:** 1.2441 g. **Composition:** 0.9999 Gold .0400 oz. AGW **Series:** Flower Fairies **Obverse:** Bust of Queen Elizabeth II right **Reverse:** Two fairies, sweet pea

| Date | Mintage | F | VF | XF | Unc | BU |
|---|---|---|---|---|---|---|
| 1998 Proof | — | — | — | — | 45.00 | — |

**1/25 CROWN KM# 830a Weight:** 1.2441 g. **Composition:** 0.9995 Platinum .0400 oz. APW **Series:** Flower Fairies **Obverse:** Bust of Queen Elizabeth II right **Reverse:** Two fairies, sweet pea

| Date | Mintage | F | VF | XF | Unc | BU |
|---|---|---|---|---|---|---|
| 1998 Proof | Est. 30,000 | Value: 55.00 | | | | |

**1/25 CROWN KM# 831 Weight:** 1.2441 g. **Composition:** 0.9999 Gold .0400 oz. AGW **Series:** Flower Fairies **Obverse:** Bust of Queen Elizabeth II right **Reverse:** Fairy standing, daffodil

| Date | Mintage | F | VF | XF | Unc | BU |
|---|---|---|---|---|---|---|
| 1998 Proof | Est. 25,000 | Value: 45.00 | | | | |

**1/25 CROWN KM# 831a Weight:** 1.2441 g. **Composition:** 0.9995 Platinum .0400 oz. APW **Series:** Flower Fairies **Obverse:** Bust of Queen Elizabeth II right **Reverse:** Fairy standing, daffodil

| Date | Mintage | F | VF | XF | Unc | BU |
|---|---|---|---|---|---|---|
| 1998 Proof | Est. 7,500 | Value: 55.00 | | | | |

**1/25 CROWN KM# 853 Weight:** 1.2440 g. **Composition:** 0.9999 Gold .0400 oz. AGW **Obverse:** Bust of Queen Elizabeth II right **Reverse:** Birman cat **Note:** Similar to 1/5 Crown, KM#857.

| Date | Mintage | F | VF | XF | Unc | BU |
|---|---|---|---|---|---|---|
| 1998 | — | — | — | — | 40.00 | — |
| 1998 Proof | 1,000 | Value: 42.00 | | | | |

**1/25 CROWN KM# 853a Weight:** 1.2440 g. **Composition:** 0.9995 Platinum .0400 oz. APW **Obverse:** Bust of Queen Elizabeth II right **Reverse:** Birman cat

| Date | Mintage | F | VF | XF | Unc | BU |
|---|---|---|---|---|---|---|
| 1998 Proof | — | Value: 50.00 | | | | |

**1/25 CROWN KM# 859 Weight:** 1.2440 g. **Composition:** 0.9999 Gold .0400 oz. AGW **Subject:** History of the Cat **Obverse:** Bust of Queen Elizabeth II right **Reverse:** Egyptian Mau cat with earring

| Date | Mintage | F | VF | XF | Unc | BU |
|---|---|---|---|---|---|---|
| 1998 Proof | Est. 25,000 | Value: 45.00 | | | | |

**1/25 CROWN KM# 948 Weight:** 1.2440 g. **Composition:** 0.9999 Gold .0400 oz. AGW **Subject:** Year of the Rabbit **Obverse:** Bust of Queen Elizabeth II right **Reverse:** Two rabbits

| Date | Mintage | F | VF | XF | Unc | BU |
|---|---|---|---|---|---|---|
| 1999 Proof | Est. 20,000 | Value: 45.00 | | | | |

**1/25 CROWN KM# 958 Weight:** 1.2440 g. **Composition:** 0.9999 Gold .0400 oz. AGW **Obverse:** Bust of Queen Elizabeth II right **Reverse:** British Blue cat

| Date | Mintage | F | VF | XF | Unc | BU |
|---|---|---|---|---|---|---|
| 1999 | — | — | — | — | 40.00 | — |
| 1999 Proof | — | Value: 42.00 | | | | |
| 1999 U Y2K | 20,000 | — | — | — | 40.00 | — |

**1/25 CROWN KM# 958a Weight:** 1.2441 g. **Composition:** 0.9995 Platinum .0400 oz. APW **Obverse:** Bust of Queen Elizabeth II right **Reverse:** British Blue cat

| Date | Mintage | F | VF | XF | Unc | BU |
|---|---|---|---|---|---|---|
| 1999 Proof | — | Value: 50.00 | | | | |

**1/25 CROWN** **KM# 1052** **Weight:** 1.2400 g. **Composition:** 0.9999 Gold .0399 oz. AGW **Obverse:** Bust of Queen Elizabeth II right **Reverse:** Scottish fold kitten **Edge:** Reeded **Size:** 13.92 mm.

| Date | Mintage | F | VF | XF | Unc | BU |
|---|---|---|---|---|---|---|
| 2000 | — | — | — | — | 32.00 | — |
| 2000 Proof | — | Value: 45.00 | | | | |

**1/25 CROWN** **KM# 1052a** **Weight:** 1.2441 g. **Composition:** 0.9995 Platinum .0400 oz. APW

| Date | Mintage | F | VF | XF | Unc | BU |
|---|---|---|---|---|---|---|
| 2000 | — | — | — | — | 41.00 | — |

**1/25 CROWN** **KM# 1012** **Weight:** 1.2440 g. **Composition:** 0.9999 Gold .0400 oz. AGW **Subject:** Year of the Dragon **Obverse:** Bust of Queen Elizabeth II right **Reverse:** Dragon, Chinese characters **Note:** Similar to 1/5 Crown, KM#1012.

| Date | Mintage | F | VF | XF | Unc | BU |
|---|---|---|---|---|---|---|
| 2000 Proof | Est. 20,000 | Value: 45.00 | | | | |

**1/25 CROWN** **KM# 1058** **Weight:** 1.2400 g. **Composition:** 0.9999 Gold .0399 oz. AGW **Subject:** Year of the Snake **Obverse:** Queen's portrait **Reverse:** Snake **Edge:** Reeded **Size:** 13.92 mm.

| Date | Mintage | F | VF | XF | Unc | BU |
|---|---|---|---|---|---|---|
| 2001 Proof | 20,000 | Value: 49.50 | | | | |

**1/25 CROWN** **KM# 1067** **Weight:** 1.2441 g. **Composition:** 0.9999 Gold .0400 oz. AGW **Subject:** Somali Kittens **Obverse:** Queen's portrait **Reverse:** Two kittens **Edge:** Reeded **Size:** 13.9 mm.

| Date | Mintage | F | VF | XF | Unc | BU |
|---|---|---|---|---|---|---|
| 2001 | — | — | — | — | 32.00 | — |
| 2001 Proof | 1,000 | Value: 50.00 | | | | |

**1/25 CROWN** **KM# 1067a** **Weight:** 1.2441 g. **Composition:** 0.9995 Platinum .0400 oz. APW **Edge:** Reeded **Size:** 13.9 mm.

| Date | Mintage | F | VF | XF | Unc | BU |
|---|---|---|---|---|---|---|
| 2001 | — | — | — | — | 60.00 | — |

**1/25 CROWN** **KM# 1086** **Weight:** 1.2441 g. **Composition:** 0.9999 Gold .0400 oz. AGW **Subject:** Harry Potter **Obverse:** Queen's portrait **Reverse:** Boy with magic wand **Edge:** Reeded **Size:** 13.9 mm.

| Date | Mintage | F | VF | XF | Unc | BU |
|---|---|---|---|---|---|---|
| 2001 Proof | 10,000 | Value: 49.50 | | | | |

**1/25 CROWN** **KM# 1088** **Weight:** 1.2441 g. **Composition:** 0.9999 Gold .0400 oz. AGW **Series:** Harry Potter **Subject:** Journey to Hogwarts **Obverse:** Queen's portrait **Reverse:** Boat full of children going to castle **Edge:** Reeded **Size:** 13.9 mm.

| Date | Mintage | F | VF | XF | Unc | BU |
|---|---|---|---|---|---|---|
| 2001 Proof | 10,000 | Value: 49.50 | | | | |

**1/25 CROWN** **KM# 1090** **Weight:** 1.2441 g. **Composition:** 0.9999 Gold .0400 oz. AGW **Series:** Harry Potter **Subject:** First Quidditch **Obverse:** Queen's portrait **Reverse:** Harry flying a broom **Edge:** Reeded **Size:** 13.9 mm.

| Date | Mintage | F | VF | XF | Unc | BU |
|---|---|---|---|---|---|---|
| 2001 Proof | 10,000 | Value: 49.50 | | | | |

**1/25 CROWN** **KM# 1092** **Weight:** 1.2441 g. **Composition:** 0.9999 Gold .0400 oz. AGW **Series:** Harry Potter **Subject:** Birth of Norbert **Obverse:** Queen's portrait **Edge:** Reeded **Size:** 13.9 mm.

| Date | Mintage | F | VF | XF | Unc | BU |
|---|---|---|---|---|---|---|
| 2001 Proof | 10,000 | Value: 49.50 | | | | |

**1/25 CROWN** **KM# 1094** **Weight:** 1.2441 g. **Composition:** 0.9999 Gold .0400 oz. AGW **Series:** Harry Potter **Subject:** School **Obverse:** Queen's portrait **Reverse:** Harry in Potions class **Edge:** Reeded **Size:** 13.9 mm.

| Date | Mintage | F | VF | XF | Unc | BU |
|---|---|---|---|---|---|---|
| 2001 Proof | 10,000 | Value: 49.50 | | | | |

**1/25 CROWN** **KM# 1096** **Weight:** 1.2441 g. **Composition:** 0.9999 Gold .0400 oz. AGW **Series:** Harry Potter **Subject:** Keys **Obverse:** Queen's portrait **Reverse:** Harry catching a flying key **Edge:** Reeded **Size:** 13.9 mm.

| Date | Mintage | F | VF | XF | Unc | BU |
|---|---|---|---|---|---|---|
| 2001 Proof | 10,000 | Value: 49.50 | | | | |

**1/25 CROWN** **KM# 1098** **Weight:** 1.2441 g. **Composition:** 0.9999 Gold .0400 oz. AGW **Subject:** Year of the Horse **Obverse:** Queen's portrait **Reverse:** Two horses **Edge:** Reeded **Size:** 13.9 mm.

| Date | Mintage | F | VF | XF | Unc | BU |
|---|---|---|---|---|---|---|
| 2002 Proof | 20,000 | Value: 49.50 | | | | |

**1/10 CROWN** **KM# 236** **Weight:** 3.1100 g. **Composition:** 0.9990 Gold .1000 oz. AGW **Obverse:** Bust of Queen Elizabeth II right **Reverse:** Manx cat

| Date | Mintage | F | VF | XF | Unc | BU |
|---|---|---|---|---|---|---|
| 1988 | 12,000 | — | — | — | 100 | — |
| 1988 Proof | 5,000 | Value: 102 | | | | |

**1/10 CROWN** **KM# 253** **Weight:** 3.1100 g. **Composition:** 0.9990 Gold .1000 oz. AGW **Obverse:** Bust of Queen Elizabeth II right **Reverse:** Persian cat

| Date | Mintage | F | VF | XF | Unc | BU |
|---|---|---|---|---|---|---|
| 1989 | — | — | — | — | 85.00 | — |
| 1989 Proof | — | Value: 87.00 | | | | |

**1/10 CROWN** **KM# 468** **Weight:** 3.1100 g. **Composition:** 0.9995 Platinum .1000 oz. APW **Obverse:** Bust of Queen Elizabeth II right **Reverse:** Persian cat

| Date | Mintage | F | VF | XF | Unc | BU |
|---|---|---|---|---|---|---|
| 1989 | — | — | — | — | 100 | — |
| 1989 Proof | — | Value: 102 | | | | |

**1/10 CROWN** **KM# 278** **Weight:** 3.1100 g. **Composition:** 0.9990 Gold .1000 oz. AGW **Obverse:** Bust of Queen Elizabeth II right **Reverse:** Alley cat **Note:** Similar to 1 Crown, KM#281.

| Date | Mintage | F | VF | XF | Unc | BU |
|---|---|---|---|---|---|---|
| 1990 | — | — | — | — | 75.00 | — |
| 1990 Proof | — | Value: 77.00 | | | | |

**1/10 CROWN** **KM# 295** **Weight:** 3.1100 g. **Composition:** 0.9990 Gold .1000 oz. AGW **Obverse:** Bust of Queen Elizabeth II right **Reverse:** Norwegian cat **Note:** Similar to 1 Crown, KM#292.

| Date | Mintage | F | VF | XF | Unc | BU |
|---|---|---|---|---|---|---|
| 1991 | — | — | — | — | 75.00 | — |
| 1991 Proof | — | Value: 77.00 | | | | |

**1/10 CROWN** **KM# 323** **Weight:** 3.1100 g. **Composition:** 0.9990 Gold .1000 oz. AGW **Subject:** America's Cup **Obverse:** Sailboat

| Date | Mintage | F | VF | XF | Unc | BU |
|---|---|---|---|---|---|---|
| 1992 Proof like | 25,000 | — | — | — | 125 | — |

**1/10 CROWN** **KM# 323a** **Weight:** 3.1100 g. **Composition:** 0.9995 Platinum .1000 oz. APW **Subject:** America's Cup **Obverse:** Bust of Queen Elizabeth II right **Reverse:** Sailboat

| Date | Mintage | F | VF | XF | Unc | BU |
|---|---|---|---|---|---|---|
| 1992 Proof like | 5,000 | — | — | — | 200 | — |

**1/10 CROWN** **KM# 329** **Weight:** 3.1100 g. **Composition:** 0.9990 Gold .1000 oz. AGW **Obverse:** Bust of Queen Elizabeth II right **Reverse:** Siamese cat **Note:** Similar to 1 Crown, KM#334.

| Date | Mintage | F | VF | XF | Unc | BU |
|---|---|---|---|---|---|---|
| 1992 | — | — | — | — | 65.00 | — |
| 1992 Proof | — | Value: 67.00 | | | | |

**1/10 CROWN** **KM# 339** **Weight:** 3.1100 g. **Composition:** 0.9990 Gold .1000 oz. AGW **Subject:** Year of the Cockerel **Obverse:** Bust of Queen Elizabeth II right **Reverse:** Cockerel in inner circle

| Date | Mintage | F | VF | XF | Unc | BU |
|---|---|---|---|---|---|---|
| 1993 Proof | Est. 20,000 | Value: 85.00 | | | | |

**1/10 CROWN** **KM# 350** **Weight:** 3.1100 g. **Composition:** 0.9990 Gold .1000 oz. AGW **Obverse:** Bust of Queen Elizabeth II right **Reverse:** Maine Coon cat **Note:** Similar to 1 Crown, KM#355.

| Date | Mintage | F | VF | XF | Unc | BU |
|---|---|---|---|---|---|---|
| 1993 | — | — | — | — | 65.00 | — |
| 1993 Proof | — | Value: 67.00 | | | | |

**1/10 CROWN** **KM# 377** **Weight:** 3.1100 g. **Composition:** 0.9990 Gold .1000 oz. AGW **Obverse:** Bust of Queen Elizabeth II right **Reverse:** Japanese Bobtail cat

| Date | Mintage | F | VF | XF | Unc | BU |
|---|---|---|---|---|---|---|
| 1994 | — | — | — | — | 60.00 | — |
| 1994 Proof | — | Value: 62.00 | | | | |

**1/10 CROWN** **KM# 403** **Weight:** 3.1100 g. **Composition:** 0.9990 Gold .1000 oz. AGW **Obverse:** Bust of Queen Elizabeth II right **Reverse:** Pekingese dog

| Date | Mintage | F | VF | XF | Unc | BU |
|---|---|---|---|---|---|---|
| 1994 Proof | 20,000 | Value: 95.00 | | | | |

**1/10 CROWN** **KM# 474** **Weight:** 3.1100 g. **Composition:** 0.9995 Platinum .1000 oz. APW **Obverse:** Bust of Queen Elizabeth II right **Reverse:** Japanese Bobtail cat

| Date | Mintage | F | VF | XF | Unc | BU |
|---|---|---|---|---|---|---|
| 1994 | — | — | — | — | 100 | — |
| 1994 Proof | — | Value: 102 | | | | |

**1/10 CROWN** **KM# 443** **Weight:** 3.1100 g. **Composition:** 0.9990 Gold .1000 oz. AGW **Obverse:** Bust of Queen Elizabeth II right **Reverse:** Turkish cat

| Date | Mintage | F | VF | XF | Unc | BU |
|---|---|---|---|---|---|---|
| 1995 | — | — | — | — | 60.00 | — |
| 1995 Proof | — | Value: 62.00 | | | | |

**1/10 CROWN** **KM# 450** **Weight:** 3.1100 g. **Composition:** 0.9990 Gold .1000 oz. AGW **Subject:** Year of the Pig **Obverse:** Bust of Queen Elizabeth II right **Reverse:** Sow with piglets

| Date | Mintage | F | VF | XF | Unc | BU |
|---|---|---|---|---|---|---|
| 1995 Proof | Est. 20,000 | Value: 95.00 | | | | |

**1/10 CROWN** **KM# 479** **Weight:** 3.1100 g. **Composition:** 0.9995 Platinum .1000 oz. APW **Obverse:** Bust of Queen Elizabeth II right **Reverse:** Turkish cat

| Date | Mintage | F | VF | XF | Unc | BU |
|---|---|---|---|---|---|---|
| 1995 | — | — | — | — | 100 | — |
| 1995 Proof | — | Value: 102 | | | | |

**1/10 CROWN** **KM# 601** **Weight:** 3.1100 g. **Composition:** 0.9990 Gold .1000 oz. AGW **Series:** Flower Fairies **Obverse:** Bust of Queen Elizabeth II right **Reverse:** Orchis

| Date | Mintage | F | VF | XF | Unc | BU |
|---|---|---|---|---|---|---|
| 1996 Proof | Est. 20,000 | Value: 90.00 | | | | |

**1/10 CROWN** **KM# 602** **Weight:** 3.1100 g. **Composition:** 0.9990 Gold .1000 oz. AGW **Series:** Flower Fairies **Obverse:** Bust of Queen Elizabeth II right **Reverse:** Rose

| Date | Mintage | F | VF | XF | Unc | BU |
|---|---|---|---|---|---|---|
| 1996 Proof | Est. 20,000 | Value: 90.00 | | | | |

**1/10 CROWN** **KM# 603** **Weight:** 3.1100 g. **Composition:** 0.9990 Gold .1000 oz. AGW **Series:** Flower Fairies **Obverse:** Bust of Queen Elizabeth II right **Reverse:** Fuchsia

| Date | Mintage | F | VF | XF | Unc | BU |
|---|---|---|---|---|---|---|
| 1996 Proof | Est. 20,000 | Value: 90.00 | | | | |

**1/10 CROWN** **KM# 604** **Weight:** 3.1100 g. **Composition:** 0.9990 Gold .1000 oz. AGW **Obverse:** Bust of Queen Elizabeth II right **Reverse:** Pinks

| Date | Mintage | F | VF | XF | Unc | BU |
|---|---|---|---|---|---|---|
| 1996 Proof | Est. 20,000 | Value: 90.00 | | | | |

**1/10 CROWN** **KM# 615** **Weight:** 3.1100 g. **Composition:** 0.9990 Gold .1000 oz. AGW **Obverse:** Bust of Queen Elizabeth II right **Reverse:** Burmese cat

| Date | Mintage | F | VF | XF | Unc | BU |
|---|---|---|---|---|---|---|
| 1996 | — | — | — | — | 60.00 | — |
| 1996 Proof | — | Value: 62.00 | | | | |

**1/10 CROWN** **KM# 616** **Weight:** 3.1100 g. **Composition:** 0.9995 Platinum .1000 oz. APW **Obverse:** Bust of Queen Elizabeth II right **Reverse:** Burmese cat

| Date | Mintage | F | VF | XF | Unc | BU |
|---|---|---|---|---|---|---|
| 1996 | — | — | — | — | 100 | — |
| 1996 Proof | — | Value: 102 | | | | |

**1/10 CROWN** **KM# 729** **Weight:** 3.1100 g. **Composition:** 0.9990 Gold .1000 oz. AGW **Subject:** Year of the Rat **Obverse:** Bust of Queen Elizabeth II right **Reverse:** Rat

| Date | Mintage | F | VF | XF | Unc | BU |
|---|---|---|---|---|---|---|
| 1996 Proof | — | — | — | — | — | — |

**Note:** Entire series purchased by one buyer. Mintage, disposition and market value unknown

**1/10 CROWN** **KM# 722** **Weight:** 3.1100 g. **Composition:** 0.9990 Gold .1000 oz. AGW **Subject:** Year of the Ox **Obverse:** Bust of Queen Elizabeth II right **Reverse:** Ox laying down

| Date | Mintage | F | VF | XF | Unc | BU |
|---|---|---|---|---|---|---|
| 1997 Proof | Est. 15,000 | Value: 90.00 | | | | |

**1/10 CROWN** **KM# 743** **Weight:** 3.1100 g. **Composition:** 0.9990 Gold .1000 oz. AGW **Series:** Flower Fairies **Obverse:** Bust of Queen Elizabeth II right **Reverse:** Candytuft

| Date | Mintage | F | VF | XF | Unc | BU |
|---|---|---|---|---|---|---|
| 1997 Proof | Est. 20,000 | Value: 80.00 | | | | |

**1/10 CROWN** **KM# 743a** **Weight:** 3.1259 g. **Composition:** 0.9950 Platinum .1000 oz. APW **Series:** Flower Fairies **Obverse:** Bust of Queen Elizabeth II right **Reverse:** Candytuft

| Date | Mintage | F | VF | XF | Unc | BU |
|---|---|---|---|---|---|---|
| 1997 Proof | Est. 5,000 | Value: 80.00 | | | | |

**1/10 CROWN** **KM# 744** **Weight:** 3.1103 g. **Composition:** 0.9999 Gold .1000 oz. AGW **Obverse:** Bust of Queen Elizabeth II right **Reverse:** Snowdrop

| Date | Mintage | F | VF | XF | Unc | BU |
|---|---|---|---|---|---|---|
| 1997 Proof | Est. 20,000 | Value: 80.00 | | | | |

**1/10 CROWN** **KM# 744a** **Weight:** 3.1259 g. **Composition:** 0.9950 Platinum .1000 oz. APW **Series:** Flower Fairies **Obverse:** Bust of Queen Elizabeth II right **Reverse:** Snowdrop

| Date | Mintage | F | VF | XF | Unc | BU |
|---|---|---|---|---|---|---|
| 1997 Proof | Est. 5,000 | Value: 85.00 | | | | |

**1/10 CROWN** **KM# 745** **Weight:** 3.1103 g. **Composition:** 0.9999 Gold .1000 oz. AGW **Series:** Flower Fairies **Obverse:** Bust of Queen Elizabeth II right **Reverse:** Tulip

| Date | Mintage | F | VF | XF | Unc | BU |
|---|---|---|---|---|---|---|
| 1997 Proof | Est. 20,000 | Value: 80.00 | | | | |

**1/10 CROWN** **KM# 745a** **Weight:** 3.1259 g. **Composition:** 0.9950 Platinum .1000 oz. APW **Series:** Flower Fairies **Obverse:** Bust of Queen Elizabeth II right **Reverse:** Tulip

| Date | Mintage | F | VF | XF | Unc | BU |
|---|---|---|---|---|---|---|
| 1997 Proof | Est. 5,000 | Value: 85.00 | | | | |

**1/10 CROWN** **KM# 746** **Weight:** 3.1103 g. **Composition:** 0.9999 Gold .1000 oz. AGW **Series:** Flower Fairies **Obverse:** Bust of Queen Elizabeth II right **Reverse:** Jasmine

| Date | Mintage | F | VF | XF | Unc | BU |
|---|---|---|---|---|---|---|
| 1997 Proof | Est. 20,000 | Value: 80.00 | | | | |

**1/10 CROWN** **KM# 746a** **Weight:** 3.1259 g. **Composition:** 0.9950 Platinum .1000 oz. APW **Series:** Flower Fairies **Obverse:** Bust of Queen Elizabeth II right **Reverse:** Jasmine

| Date | Mintage | F | VF | XF | Unc | BU |
|---|---|---|---|---|---|---|
| 1997 Proof | Est. 5,000 | Value: 85.00 | | | | |

**1/10 CROWN** **KM# 771** **Weight:** 3.1100 g. **Composition:** 0.9999 Gold .1000 oz. AGW **Obverse:** Bust of Queen Elizabeth II right **Reverse:** Long-Haired-Smoke cat

| Date | Mintage | F | VF | XF | Unc | BU |
|---|---|---|---|---|---|---|
| 1997 | — | — | — | — | 60.00 | — |
| 1997 Proof | — | Value: 62.00 | | | | |

**1/10 CROWN** **KM# 771a** **Weight:** 3.1100 g. **Composition:** 0.9995 Platinum .1000 oz. APW **Obverse:** Bust of Queen Elizabeth II right **Reverse:** Long-Haired-Smoke cat

| Date | Mintage | F | VF | XF | Unc | BU |
|---|---|---|---|---|---|---|
| 1997 | — | — | — | — | 100 | — |
| 1997 Proof | — | Value: 102 | | | | |

**1/10 CROWN** **KM# 790** **Weight:** 3.1100 g. **Composition:** 0.9999 Gold .1000 oz. AGW **Subject:** History of the Cat **Obverse:** Bust of Queen Elizabeth II right **Reverse:** Cat stalking a spider

| Date | Mintage | F | VF | XF | Unc | BU |
|---|---|---|---|---|---|---|
| 1997 Proof | Est. 20,000 | Value: 90.00 | | | | |

**1/10 CROWN** **KM# 813** **Weight:** 3.1100 g. **Composition:** 0.9999 Gold .1000 oz. AGW **Subject:** Year of the Tiger **Obverse:** Bust of Queen Elizabeth II right **Reverse:** Tiger

| Date | Mintage | F | VF | XF | Unc | BU |
|---|---|---|---|---|---|---|
| 1998 Proof | Est. 15,000 | Value: 90.00 | | | | |

**1/10 CROWN** **KM# 832** **Weight:** 3.1100 g. **Composition:** 0.9999 Gold .1000 oz. AGW **Series:** Flower Fairies **Obverse:** Bust of Queen Elizabeth II right **Reverse:** Standing fairy, lavender

| Date | Mintage | F | VF | XF | Unc | BU |
|---|---|---|---|---|---|---|
| 1998 Proof | Est. 20,000 | Value: 90.00 | | | | |

**1/10 CROWN** **KM# 832a** **Weight:** 3.1100 g. **Composition:** 0.9995 Platinum .1000 oz. APW **Series:** Flower Fairies **Obverse:** Bust of Queen Elizabeth II right **Reverse:** Standing fairy, lavender

| Date | Mintage | F | VF | XF | Unc | BU |
|---|---|---|---|---|---|---|
| 1998 Proof | Est. 5,000 | Value: 100 | | | | |

**1/10 CROWN** **KM# 833** **Weight:** 3.1100 g. **Composition:** 0.9999 Gold .1000 oz. AGW **Series:** Flower Fairies **Obverse:** Bust of Queen Elizabeth II right **Reverse:** Two fairies, Sweet Pea

| Date | Mintage | F | VF | XF | Unc | BU |
|---|---|---|---|---|---|---|
| 1998 Proof | Est. 20,000 | Value: 90.00 | | | | |

**1/10 CROWN** **KM# 833a** **Weight:** 3.1100 g. **Composition:** 0.9995 Platinum .1000 oz. APW **Series:** Flower Fairies **Obverse:** Bust of Queen Elizabeth II right **Reverse:** Two fairies, Sweet Pea

| Date | Mintage | F | VF | XF | Unc | BU |
|---|---|---|---|---|---|---|
| 1998 Proof | Est. 5,000 | Value: 100 | | | | |

**1/10 CROWN** **KM# 834** **Weight:** 3.1100 g. **Composition:** 0.9999 Gold .1000 oz. AGW **Obverse:** Bust of Queen Elizabeth II right **Reverse:** Fairy looking into flower, White Bindweed

| Date | Mintage | F | VF | XF | Unc | BU |
|---|---|---|---|---|---|---|
| 1998 Proof | Est. 20,000 | Value: 90.00 | | | | |

**1/10 CROWN** **KM# 834a** **Weight:** 3.1100 g. **Composition:** 0.9995 Platinum .1000 oz. APW **Series:** Flower Fairies **Obverse:** Bust of Queen Elizabeth II right **Reverse:** Fairy looking into flower, White Bindweed

| Date | Mintage | F | VF | XF | Unc | BU |
|---|---|---|---|---|---|---|
| 1998 Proof | Est. 5,000 | Value: 100 | | | | |

**1/10 CROWN** **KM# 835** **Weight:** 3.1100 g. **Composition:** 0.9999 Gold .1000 oz. AGW **Series:** Flower Fairies **Obverse:** Bust of Queen Elizabeth II right **Reverse:** Fairy standing with flower, Daffodil

| Date | Mintage | F | VF | XF | Unc | BU |
|---|---|---|---|---|---|---|
| 1998 Proof | Est. 20,000 | Value: 90.00 | | | | |

**1/10 CROWN** **KM# 835a** **Weight:** 3.1100 g. **Composition:** 0.9995 Platinum .1000 oz. APW **Obverse:** Bust of Queen Elizabeth II right **Reverse:** Fairy standing with flower, daffodil **Rev. Legend:** Flower Fairies

| Date | Mintage | F | VF | XF | Unc | BU |
|---|---|---|---|---|---|---|
| 1998 Proof | Est. 5,000 | Value: 100 | | | | |

**1/10 CROWN** **KM# 854** **Weight:** 3.1100 g. **Composition:** 0.9999 Gold .1000 oz. AGW **Obverse:** Bust of Queen Elizabeth II right **Reverse:** Birman cat

| Date | Mintage | F | VF | XF | Unc | BU |
|---|---|---|---|---|---|---|
| 1998 | — | — | — | — | 65.00 | — |
| 1998 Proof | 1,000 | Value: 70.00 | | | | |

**1/10 CROWN** **KM# 854a** **Weight:** 3.1100 g. **Composition:** 0.9995 Platinum .1000 oz. APW **Obverse:** Bust of Queen Elizabeth II right **Reverse:** Birman cat

| Date | Mintage | F | VF | XF | Unc | BU |
|---|---|---|---|---|---|---|
| 1998 Proof | — | Value: 100 | | | | |

**1/10 CROWN** **KM# 860** **Weight:** 3.1100 g. **Composition:** 0.9999 Gold .1000 oz. AGW **Subject:** History of the Cat **Obverse:** Bust of Queen Elizabeth II right **Reverse:** Egyptian Mau cat with earring

| Date | Mintage | F | VF | XF | Unc | BU |
|---|---|---|---|---|---|---|
| 1998 Proof | Est. 20,000 | Value: 90.00 | | | | |

**1/10 CROWN** **KM# 949** **Weight:** 3.1100 g. **Composition:** 0.9999 Gold .1000 oz. AGW **Subject:** Year of the Rabbit **Obverse:** Bust of Queen Elizabeth II right **Reverse:** Two rabbits

| Date | Mintage | F | VF | XF | Unc | BU |
|---|---|---|---|---|---|---|
| 1999 Proof | — | Value: 90.00 | | | | |

**1/10 CROWN** **KM# 960** **Weight:** 3.1100 g. **Composition:** 0.9999 Gold .1000 oz. AGW **Obverse:** Bust of Queen Elizabeth II right **Reverse:** British Blue cat cleaning its paw

| Date | Mintage | F | VF | XF | Unc | BU |
|---|---|---|---|---|---|---|
| 1999 | — | — | — | — | 70.00 | — |
| 1999 Proof | — | Value: 90.00 | | | | |
| 1999 U Y2K | 20,000 | — | — | — | 70.00 | — |

**1/10 CROWN** **KM# 960a** **Weight:** 3.1104 g. **Composition:** 0.9995 Platinum .1000 oz. APW **Obverse:** Bust of Queen Elizabeth II right **Reverse:** British Blue cat cleaning its paw

| Date | Mintage | F | VF | XF | Unc | BU |
|---|---|---|---|---|---|---|
| 1999 Proof | — | Value: 100 | | | | |

**1/10 CROWN** **KM# 1053** **Weight:** 3.1100 g. **Composition:** 0.9999 Gold .1000 oz. AGW **Obverse:** Bust of Queen Elizabeth II right **Reverse:** Scottish kitten playing with world **Edge:** Reeded **Size:** 17.95 mm.

| Date | Mintage | F | VF | XF | Unc | BU |
|---|---|---|---|---|---|---|
| 2000 | — | — | — | — | 70.00 | — |
| 2000 Proof | — | Value: 90.00 | | | | |

**1/10 CROWN** **KM# 1053a** **Weight:** 3.1104 g. **Composition:** 0.9995 Platinum .1000 oz. APW **Reverse:** Scottish kitten playing with the world

| Date | Mintage | F | VF | XF | Unc | BU |
|---|---|---|---|---|---|---|
| 2000 | — | — | — | — | 78.00 | — |

**1/10 CROWN** **KM# 1013** **Weight:** 3.1100 g. **Composition:** 0.9999 Gold .1000 oz. AGW **Subject:** Year of the Dragon **Obverse:** Bust of Queen Elizabeth II right **Reverse:** Dragon, Chinese characters

| Date | Mintage | F | VF | XF | Unc | BU |
|---|---|---|---|---|---|---|
| 2000 Proof | Est. 15,000 | Value: 90.00 | | | | |

**1/10 CROWN** **KM# 1059** **Weight:** 3.1100 g. **Composition:** 0.9999 Gold .1000 oz. AGW **Subject:** Year of the Snake **Obverse:** Queen's portrait **Reverse:** Snake **Edge:** Reeded **Size:** 17.95 mm.

| Date | Mintage | F | VF | XF | Unc | BU |
|---|---|---|---|---|---|---|
| 2001 Proof | 15,000 | Value: 95.00 | | | | |

**1/10 CROWN** **KM# 1068** **Weight:** 3.1100 g. **Composition:** 0.9999 Gold .1000 oz. AGW **Obverse:** Queen's portrait **Reverse:** Somali kittens **Edge:** Reeded **Size:** 18 mm.

| Date | Mintage | F | VF | XF | Unc | BU |
|---|---|---|---|---|---|---|
| 2001 | — | — | — | — | 70.00 | — |
| 2001 Proof | 1,000 | Value: 95.00 | | | | |

**1/10 CROWN** **KM# 1068a** **Weight:** 3.1100 g. **Composition:** 0.9995 Platinum .1000 oz. APW **Reverse:** Somali kittens **Edge:** Reeded **Size:** 18 mm.

| Date | Mintage | F | VF | XF | Unc | BU |
|---|---|---|---|---|---|---|
| 2001 | — | — | — | — | 130 | — |

**1/10 CROWN** **KM# 1099** **Weight:** 3.1100 g. **Composition:** 0.9999 Gold .1000 oz. AGW **Subject:** Year of the Horse **Obverse:** Queen's portrait **Reverse:** Two horses **Edge:** Reeded **Size:** 17.95 mm.

| Date | Mintage | F | VF | XF | Unc | BU |
|---|---|---|---|---|---|---|
| 2002 Proof | 15,000 | Value: 95.00 | | | | |

**1/5 CROWN** **KM# 237** **Weight:** 6.2200 g. **Composition:** 0.9990 Gold .2000 oz. AGW **Obverse:** Bust of Queen Elizabeth II right **Reverse:** Manx cat

| Date | Mintage | F | VF | XF | Unc | BU |
|---|---|---|---|---|---|---|
| 1988 | 6,750 | — | — | — | 200 | — |
| 1988 Proof | 5,000 | Value: 202 | | | | |

**1/5 CROWN** **KM# 254** **Weight:** 6.2200 g. **Composition:** 0.9990 Gold .2000 oz. AGW **Obverse:** Bust of Queen Elizabeth II right **Reverse:** Persian cat

| Date | Mintage | F | VF | XF | Unc | BU |
|---|---|---|---|---|---|---|
| 1989 | — | — | — | — | 150 | — |
| 1989 Proof | — | Value: 152 | | | | |

**1/5 CROWN** **KM# 274** **Weight:** 6.2200 g. **Composition:** 0.9990 Gold .2000 oz. AGW **Obverse:** Bust of Queen Elizabeth II right **Reverse:** George Washington

| Date | Mintage | F | VF | XF | Unc | BU |
|---|---|---|---|---|---|---|
| 1989 Proof | Est. 5,000 | Value: 180 | | | | |

**1/5 CROWN** **KM# 469** **Weight:** 6.2200 g. **Composition:** 0.9990 Platinum .2000 oz. APW **Obverse:** Bust of Queen Elizabeth II right **Reverse:** Persian cat

| Date | Mintage | F | VF | XF | Unc | BU |
|---|---|---|---|---|---|---|
| 1989 | — | — | — | — | 165 | — |
| 1989 Proof | — | Value: 167 | | | | |

**1/5 CROWN** **KM# 268** **Weight:** 6.2200 g. **Composition:** 0.9990 Gold .2000 oz. AGW **Subject:** 150th Anniversary of "Penny Black" Stamp **Obverse:** Bust of Queen Elizabeth II right **Reverse:** Penny Black Stamp

| Date | Mintage | F | VF | XF | Unc | BU |
|---|---|---|---|---|---|---|
| 1990 Proof | Est. 5,000 | Value: 210 | | | | |

**1/5 CROWN** **KM# 279.1** **Weight:** 6.2200 g. **Composition:** 0.9990 Gold .2000 oz. AGW **Obverse:** Bust of Queen Elizabeth II right **Reverse:** Alley cat

| Date | Mintage | F | VF | XF | Unc | BU |
|---|---|---|---|---|---|---|
| 1990 | — | — | — | — | 125 | — |
| 1990 Proof | — | Value: 127 | | | | |

**1/5 CROWN** **KM# 279.2** **Weight:** 6.2200 g. **Composition:** 0.9990 Gold .2000 oz. AGW **Obverse:** Bust of Queen Elizabeth II right **Reverse:** Dies claiming platinum metal content **Note:** Error.

| Date | Mintage | F | VF | XF | Unc | BU |
|---|---|---|---|---|---|---|
| 1990 | 467 | — | — | — | 400 | — |

**1/5 CROWN** **KM# 306** **Weight:** 6.2200 g. **Composition:** 0.9990 Gold .2000 oz. AGW **Obverse:** Bust of Queen Elizabeth II right **Reverse:** Queen Mother with two daughters

| Date | Mintage | F | VF | XF | Unc | BU |
|---|---|---|---|---|---|---|
| 1990 Proof | — | Value: 200 | | | | |

**1/5 CROWN** **KM# 306a** **Weight:** 6.2200 g. **Composition:** 0.9990 Platinum .2000 oz. APW **Obverse:** Bust of Queen Elizabeth II right **Reverse:** Queen Mother with 2 daughters

| Date | Mintage | F | VF | XF | Unc | BU |
|---|---|---|---|---|---|---|
| 1990 Proof | — | Value: 300 | | | | |

**1/5 CROWN** **KM# 472** **Weight:** 6.2200 g. **Composition:** 0.9990 Platinum .2000 oz. APW **Obverse:** Bust of Queen Elizabeth II right **Reverse:** Alley cat

| Date | Mintage | F | VF | XF | Unc | BU |
|---|---|---|---|---|---|---|
| 1990 | — | — | — | — | 165 | — |
| 1990 Proof | — | Value: 167 | | | | |

**1/5 CROWN** **KM# 819** **Weight:** 6.2200 g. **Composition:** 0.9990 Gold .2000 oz. AGW **Subject:** Soccer **Obverse:** Bust of Queen Elizabeth II right **Reverse:** Milano

| Date | Mintage | F | VF | XF | Unc | BU |
|---|---|---|---|---|---|---|
| 1990 Proof | Est. 500 | Value: 115 | | | | |

**1/5 CROWN** **KM# 819a** **Weight:** 6.2200 g. **Composition:** 0.9990 Platinum .2000 oz. APW **Subject:** Soccer **Obverse:** Bust of Queen Elizabeth II right **Reverse:** Milano

| Date | Mintage | F | VF | XF | Unc | BU |
|---|---|---|---|---|---|---|
| 1990 Proof | Est. 250 | Value: 150 | | | | |

**1/5 CROWN** **KM# 820** **Weight:** 6.2200 g. **Composition:** 0.9990 Gold .2000 oz. AGW **Subject:** Soccer **Obverse:** Bust of Queen Elizabeth II right **Reverse:** Torino

| Date | Mintage | F | VF | XF | Unc | BU |
|---|---|---|---|---|---|---|
| 1990 Proof | Est. 500 | Value: 115 | | | | |

**1/5 CROWN** **KM# 820a** **Weight:** 6.2200 g. **Composition:** 0.9990 Platinum .2000 oz. APW **Subject:** Soccer **Obverse:** Bust of Queen Elizabeth II right **Reverse:** Torino

| Date | Mintage | F | VF | XF | Unc | BU |
|---|---|---|---|---|---|---|
| 1990 Proof | Est. 250 | Value: 150 | | | | |

**1/5 CROWN** **KM# 821** **Weight:** 6.2200 g. **Composition:** 0.9990 Gold .2000 oz. AGW **Subject:** Soccer **Obverse:** Bust of Queen Elizabeth II right **Reverse:** Bologna

| Date | Mintage | F | VF | XF | Unc | BU |
|---|---|---|---|---|---|---|
| 1990 Proof | Est. 500 | Value: 115 | | | | |

**1/5 CROWN** **KM# 821a** **Weight:** 6.2200 g. **Composition:** 0.9990 Platinum .2000 oz. APW **Subject:** Soccer **Obverse:** Bust of Queen Elizabeth II right **Reverse:** Bologna

| Date | Mintage | F | VF | XF | Unc | BU |
|---|---|---|---|---|---|---|
| 1990 | Est. 250 | Value: 150 | | | | |

**1/5 CROWN** **KM# 822** **Weight:** 6.2200 g. **Composition:** 0.9990 Gold .2000 oz. AGW **Subject:** Soccer **Obverse:** Bust of Queen Elizabeth II right **Reverse:** Palermo

| Date | Mintage | F | VF | XF | Unc | BU |
|---|---|---|---|---|---|---|
| 1990 Proof | Est. 500 | Value: 115 | | | | |

**1/5 CROWN** **KM# 822a** **Weight:** 6.2200 g. **Composition:** 0.9990 Platinum .2000 oz. APW **Subject:** Soccer **Obverse:** Bust of Queen Elizabeth II right **Reverse:** Palermo

| Date | Mintage | F | VF | XF | Unc | BU |
|---|---|---|---|---|---|---|
| 1990 | Est. 250 | Value: 150 | | | | |

**1/5 CROWN** **KM# 290** **Weight:** 6.2200 g. **Composition:** 0.9990 Gold .2000 oz. AGW **Subject:** 100th Anniversary - American Numismatic Association **Obverse:** Bust of Queen Elizabeth II right **Reverse:** Coins

| Date | Mintage | F | VF | XF | Unc | BU |
|---|---|---|---|---|---|---|
| 1991 Proof | 100 | Value: 185 | | | | |

**1/5 CROWN** **KM# 296** **Weight:** 6.2200 g. **Composition:** 0.9990 Gold .2000 oz. AGW **Obverse:** Bust of Queen Elizabeth II right **Reverse:** Norwegian cat with bushy tail

| Date | Mintage | F | VF | XF | Unc | BU |
|---|---|---|---|---|---|---|
| 1991 | — | — | — | — | 115 | — |
| 1991 Proof | — | Value: 117 | | | | |

**1/5 CROWN** **KM# 302** **Weight:** 6.2200 g. **Composition:** 0.9990 Gold .2000 oz. AGW **Subject:** America's Cup **Obverse:** Bust of Queen Elizabeth II right **Reverse:** Sail boat

| Date | Mintage | F | VF | XF | Unc | BU |
|---|---|---|---|---|---|---|
| 1991 Proof | Est. 250 | Value: 190 | | | | |

**1/5 CROWN** **KM# 324** **Weight:** 6.2200 g. **Composition:** 0.9990 Gold .2000 oz. AGW **Subject:** America's Cup **Obverse:** Bust of Queen Elizabeth II right **Reverse:** Sailboat

| Date | Mintage | F | VF | XF | Unc | BU |
|---|---|---|---|---|---|---|
| 1992 Proof like | 10,000 | — | — | — | 120 | — |

**1/5 CROWN** **KM# 330** **Weight:** 6.2200 g. **Composition:** 0.9990 Gold .2000 oz. AGW **Obverse:** Bust of Queen Elizabeth II right **Reverse:** Siamese cat

| Date | Mintage | F | VF | XF | Unc | BU |
|---|---|---|---|---|---|---|
| 1992 | — | — | — | — | 115 | — |
| 1992 Proof | — | Value: 117 | | | | |

**1/5 CROWN** **KM# 340** **Weight:** 6.2200 g. **Composition:** 0.9990 Gold .2000 oz. AGW **Subject:** Year of the Cockerel **Obverse:** Bust of Queen Elizabeth II right **Reverse:** Cockerel in inner circle

| Date | Mintage | F | VF | XF | Unc | BU |
|---|---|---|---|---|---|---|
| 1993 Proof | Est. 10,000 | Value: 165 | | | | |

**1/5 CROWN** **KM# 351** **Weight:** 6.2200 g. **Composition:** 0.9990 Gold .2000 oz. AGW **Obverse:** Bust of Queen Elizabeth II right **Reverse:** Maine Coon cat

| Date | Mintage | F | VF | XF | Unc | BU |
|---|---|---|---|---|---|---|
| 1993 | — | — | — | — | 125 | — |
| 1993 Proof | — | Value: 127 | | | | |

**1/5 CROWN** **KM# 365** **Weight:** 6.2200 g. **Composition:** 0.9990 Gold .2000 oz. AGW **Subject:** World Cup Soccer - Type I **Obverse:** Bust of Queen Elizabeth II right **Reverse:** Player in foreground kicking ball

| Date | Mintage | F | VF | XF | Unc | BU |
|---|---|---|---|---|---|---|
| 1994 Proof | Est. 5,000 | Value: 160 | | | | |

**1/5 CROWN** **KM# 367** **Weight:** 6.2200 g. **Composition:** 0.9990 Gold .2000 oz. AGW **Subject:** World Cup Soccer - Type II **Obverse:** Bust of Queen Elizabeth II right **Obv. Legend:** Three players

| Date | Mintage | F | VF | XF | Unc | BU |
|---|---|---|---|---|---|---|
| 1994 Proof | Est. 5,000 | Value: 160 | | | | |

**1/5 CROWN** **KM# 369** **Weight:** 6.2200 g. **Composition:** 0.9990 Gold .2000 oz. AGW **Subject:** World Cup Soccer - Type III **Obverse:** Bust of Queen Eliabeth II right **Reverse:** Player with knee bent, 2nd player in background

| Date | Mintage | F | VF | XF | Unc | BU |
|---|---|---|---|---|---|---|
| 1994 Proof | Est. 5,000 | Value: 160 | | | | |

**1/5 CROWN** **KM# 371** **Weight:** 6.2200 g. **Composition:** 0.9990 Gold .2000 oz. AGW **Subject:** World Cup Soccer - Type IV **Obverse:** Bust of Queen Elizabeth II right **Reverse:** Three players with one kicking ball.

| Date | Mintage | F | VF | XF | Unc | BU |
|---|---|---|---|---|---|---|
| 1994 Proof | Est. 5,000 | Value: 160 | | | | |

**1/5 CROWN** **KM# 373** **Weight:** 6.2200 g. **Composition:** 0.9990 Gold .2000 oz. AGW **Subject:** World Cup Soccer - Type V **Obverse:** Bust of Queen Elizabeth II right **Reverse:** Goalie catching ball in hand

| Date | Mintage | F | VF | XF | Unc | BU |
|---|---|---|---|---|---|---|
| 1994 Proof | Est. 5,000 | Value: 160 | | | | |

**1/5 CROWN** **KM# 375** **Weight:** 6.2200 g. **Composition:** 0.9990 Gold .2000 oz. AGW **Subject:** World Cup Soccer - Type VI **Obverse:** Bust of Queen Elizabeth II right **Reverse:** Two players kicking at ball

| Date | Mintage | F | VF | XF | Unc | BU |
|---|---|---|---|---|---|---|
| 1994 Proof | Est. 5,000 | Value: 160 | | | | |

**1/5 CROWN** **KM# 378** **Weight:** 6.2200 g. **Composition:** 0.9990 Gold .2000 oz. AGW **Obverse:** Bust of Queen Elizabeth II right **Reverse:** Japanese Bobtail cat

| Date | Mintage | F | VF | XF | Unc | BU |
|---|---|---|---|---|---|---|
| 1994 | — | — | — | — | 90.00 | — |
| 1994 Proof | — | Value: 92.00 | | | | |

**1/5 CROWN** **KM# 383** **Weight:** 6.2200 g. **Composition:** 0.9990 Gold .2000 oz. AGW **Series:** Preserve Planet Earth **Obverse:** Bust of Queen Elizabeth II right **Reverse:** Woolly mammoth

| Date | Mintage | F | VF | XF | Unc | BU |
|---|---|---|---|---|---|---|
| 1994 Proof | Est. 5,000 | Value: 160 | | | | |

**1/5 CROWN** **KM# 389** **Weight:** 6.2200 g. **Composition:** 0.9990 Gold .2000 oz. AGW **Series:** Preserve Planet Earth **Obverse:** Bust of Queen Elizabeth II right **Reverse:** Mother and pup gray seals

| Date | Mintage | F | VF | XF | Unc | BU |
|---|---|---|---|---|---|---|
| 1994 Proof | 5,000 | Value: 160 | | | | |

**1/5 CROWN** **KM# 390** **Weight:** 6.2200 g. **Composition:** 0.9990 Gold .2000 oz. AGW **Series:** Preserve Planet Earth **Obverse:** Bust of Queen Elizabeth II right **Reverse:** Two deer

| Date | Mintage | F | VF | XF | Unc | BU |
|---|---|---|---|---|---|---|
| 1994 Proof | 5,000 | Value: 160 | | | | |

**1/5 CROWN** **KM# 404** **Weight:** 6.2200 g. **Composition:** 0.9990 Gold .2000 oz. AGW **Obverse:** Bust of Queen Elizabeth II right **Reverse:** Pekingese dog

| Date | Mintage | F | VF | XF | Unc | BU |
|---|---|---|---|---|---|---|
| 1994 Proof | 10,000 | Value: 170 | | | | |

**1/5 CROWN** **KM# 409** **Weight:** 6.2200 g. **Composition:** 0.9990 Gold .2000 oz. AGW **Series:** Man in Flight **Obverse:** Bust of Queen Elizabeth II right **Reverse:** Manned glider, Otto Lilienthal

| Date | Mintage | F | VF | XF | Unc | BU |
|---|---|---|---|---|---|---|
| 1994 Proof | Est. 5,000 | Value: 170 | | | | |

**1/5 CROWN** **KM# 410** **Weight:** 6.2200 g. **Composition:** 0.9990 Gold .2000 oz. AGW **Series:** Man in Flight **Obverse:** Bust of Queen Elizabeth II right **Reverse:** Dirigible, Ferdinand von Zeppelin

| Date | Mintage | F | VF | XF | Unc | BU |
|---|---|---|---|---|---|---|
| 1994 Proof | Est. 5,000 | Value: 170 | | | | |

**1/5 CROWN** **KM# 411** **Weight:** 6.2200 g. **Composition:** 0.9990 Gold .2000 oz. AGW **Series:** Man in Flight **Obverse:** Bust of Queen Elizabeth II right **Reverse:** Bust of Louis Bleriot behind plane flying across channel

| Date | Mintage | F | VF | XF | Unc | BU |
|---|---|---|---|---|---|---|
| 1994 Proof | Est. 5,000 | Value: 170 | | | | |

**1/5 CROWN** **KM# 412** **Weight:** 6.2200 g. **Composition:** 0.9990 Gold .2000 oz. AGW **Series:** Man in Flight **Obverse:** Bust of Queen Elizabeth II right **Reverse:** Plane flying above ocean, Alcock and Brown

| Date | Mintage | F | VF | XF | Unc | BU |
|---|---|---|---|---|---|---|
| 1994 Proof | Est. 5,000 | Value: 170 | | | | |

**1/5 CROWN** **KM# 413** **Weight:** 6.2200 g. **Composition:** 0.9990 Gold .2000 oz. AGW **Series:** Man in Flight **Subject:** First England to Australia Flight **Obverse:** Bust of Queen Elizabeth II right **Reverse:** Biplane flying

| Date | Mintage | F | VF | XF | Unc | BU |
|---|---|---|---|---|---|---|
| 1994 Proof | Est. 5,000 | Value: 170 | | | | |

**1/5 CROWN** **KM# 414** **Weight:** 6.2200 g. **Composition:** 0.9990 Gold .2000 oz. AGW **Series:** Man in Flight **Subject:** 60th Anniversary of Airmail **Obverse:** Bust of Queen Elizabeth II right **Reverse:** Plane flying left above inscription

| Date | Mintage | F | VF | XF | Unc | BU |
|---|---|---|---|---|---|---|
| 1994 Proof | Est. 5,000 | Value: 170 | | | | |

**1/5 CROWN** **KM# 415** **Weight:** 6.2200 g. **Composition:** 0.9990 Gold .2000 oz. AGW **Series:** Man in Flight **Subject:** 50th Anniversary of International Civil Aviation Organization **Obverse:** Bust of Queen Elizabeth II right **Reverse:** Trademark of ICAO

| Date | Mintage | F | VF | XF | Unc | BU |
|---|---|---|---|---|---|---|
| 1994 Proof | Est. 5,000 | Value: 170 | | | | |

**1/5 CROWN** **KM# 416** **Weight:** 6.2200 g. **Composition:** 0.9990 Gold .2000 oz. AGW **Series:** Man in Flight **Subject:** First Concrode Flight **Obverse:** Bust of Queen Elizabeth II right **Reverse:** Concorde waiting at airport

| Date | Mintage | F | VF | XF | Unc | BU |
|---|---|---|---|---|---|---|
| 1994 Proof | Est. 5,000 | Value: 170 | | | | |

**1/5 CROWN** **KM# 475** **Weight:** 6.2200 g. **Composition:** 0.9990 Platinum .2000 oz. APW **Obverse:** Bust of Queen Elizabeth II right **Reverse:** Japanese Bobtail cat

| Date | Mintage | F | VF | XF | Unc | BU |
|---|---|---|---|---|---|---|
| 1994 | — | — | — | — | 125 | — |
| 1994 Proof | — | Value: 130 | | | | |

**1/5 CROWN** **KM# 429** **Weight:** 6.2200 g. **Composition:** 0.9990 Gold .2000 oz. AGW **Series:** Man in Flight **Obverse:** Bust of Queen Elizabeth II right **Reverse:** Wright Brothers airplane in flight

| Date | Mintage | F | VF | XF | Unc | BU |
|---|---|---|---|---|---|---|
| 1995 Proof | Est. 5,000 | Value: 170 | | | | |

**1/5 CROWN** **KM# 426** **Weight:** 6.2200 g. **Composition:** 0.9990 Gold .2000 oz. AGW **Series:** Man in Flight **Obverse:** Bust of Queen Elizabeth II right **Reverse:** Icarus' wings melting

| Date | Mintage | F | VF | XF | Unc | BU |
|---|---|---|---|---|---|---|
| 1995 Proof | Est. 5,000 | Value: 170 | | | | |

**1/5 CROWN** **KM# 427** **Weight:** 6.2200 g. **Composition:** 0.9990 Gold .2000 oz. AGW **Series:** Man in Flight **Obverse:** Bust of Queen Elizabeth II right **Reverse:** Leonardo Da Vinci and aircraft design

| Date | Mintage | F | VF | XF | Unc | BU |
|---|---|---|---|---|---|---|
| 1995 Proof | Est. 5,000 | Value: 170 | | | | |

**1/5 CROWN** **KM# 428** **Weight:** 6.2200 g. **Composition:** 0.9990 Gold .2000 oz. AGW **Series:** Man in Flight **Obverse:** Bust of Queen Elizabeth II right **Reverse:** Montgolfier Brothers balloon in flight

| Date | Mintage | F | VF | XF | Unc | BU |
|---|---|---|---|---|---|---|
| 1995 Proof | Est. 5,000 | Value: 170 | | | | |

**1/5 CROWN** **KM# 430** **Weight:** 6.2200 g. **Composition:** 0.9990 Gold .2000 oz. AGW **Series:** Man in Flight **Subject:** 1st Flight Tokyo to Paris by Abe and Kawachi **Obverse:** Bust of Queen Elizabeth II right **Reverse:** Two busts above airplane in flight

| Date | Mintage | F | VF | XF | Unc | BU |
|---|---|---|---|---|---|---|
| 1995 Proof | Est. 5,000 | Value: 170 | | | | |

**1/5 CROWN** **KM# 431** **Weight:** 6.2200 g. **Composition:** 0.9990 Gold .2000 oz. AGW **Series:** Man in Flight **Subject:** FW109, First Diesel Powered Aircraft **Obverse:** Bust of Queen Elizabeth II right **Reverse:** Airplane on ground

| Date | Mintage | F | VF | XF | Unc | BU |
|---|---|---|---|---|---|---|
| 1995 Proof | Est. 5,000 | Value: 170 | | | | |

**1/5 CROWN** **KM# 432** **Weight:** 6.2200 g. **Composition:** 0.9990 Gold .2000 oz. AGW **Series:** Man in Flight **Subject:** ME262, First Jet Aircraft **Obverse:** Bust of Queen Elizabeth II right **Reverse:** Jet flying into clouds

| Date | Mintage | F | VF | XF | Unc | BU |
|---|---|---|---|---|---|---|
| 1995 Proof | Est. 5,000 | Value: 170 | | | | |

**1/5 CROWN** **KM# 433** **Weight:** 6.2200 g. **Composition:** 0.9990 Gold .2000 oz. AGW **Series:** Man in Flight **Subject:** 25th Anniversary of Boeing 747 **Obverse:** Bust of Queen Elizabeth II right **Reverse:** Jumbo jet in flight

| Date | Mintage | F | VF | XF | Unc | BU |
|---|---|---|---|---|---|---|
| 1995 Proof | Est. 5,000 | Value: 170 | | | | |

**1/5 CROWN** **KM# 444** **Weight:** 6.2200 g. **Composition:** 0.9990 Gold .2000 oz. AGW **Obverse:** Bust of Queen Elizabeth II right **Reverse:** Turkish cat

| Date | Mintage | F | VF | XF | Unc | BU |
|---|---|---|---|---|---|---|
| 1995 | — | — | — | — | 90.00 | — |
| 1995 Proof | — | Value: 92.00 | | | | |

**1/5 CROWN** **KM# 451** **Weight:** 6.2200 g. **Composition:** 0.9990 Gold .2000 oz. AGW **Subject:** Year of the Pig **Obverse:** Bust of Queen Elizabeth II right **Reverse:** Sow and piglets

| Date | Mintage | F | VF | XF | Unc | BU |
|---|---|---|---|---|---|---|
| 1995 Proof | Est. 10,000 | Value: 170 | | | | |

**1/5 CROWN** **KM# 457** **Weight:** 6.2200 g. **Composition:** 0.9990 Gold .2000 oz. AGW **Subject:** 95th Birthday of Queen Mother **Obverse:** Bust of Queen Elizabeth II right **Reverse:** Bust of Queen Mother

| Date | Mintage | F | VF | XF | Unc | BU |
|---|---|---|---|---|---|---|
| 1995 Proof | Est. 5,000 | Value: 170 | | | | |

**1/5 CROWN** **KM# 459** **Weight:** 6.2200 g. **Composition:** 0.9990 Gold .2000 oz. AGW **Series:** Preserve Planet Earth **Obverse:** Bust of Queen Elizabeth II right **Reverse:** Otter

| Date | Mintage | F | VF | XF | Unc | BU |
|---|---|---|---|---|---|---|
| 1995 Proof | Est. 5,000 | Value: 170 | | | | |

**1/5 CROWN** **KM# 460** **Weight:** 6.2200 g. **Composition:** 0.9990 Gold .2000 oz. AGW **Series:** Preserve Planet Earth **Obverse:** Bust of Queen Elizabeth II right **Reverse:** Egret Birds

| Date | Mintage | F | VF | XF | Unc | BU |
|---|---|---|---|---|---|---|
| 1995 Proof | Est. 5,000 | Value: 170 | | | | |

**1/5 CROWN** **KM# 480** **Weight:** 6.2200 g. **Composition:** 0.9990 Platinum .2000 oz. APW **Obverse:** Bust of Queen Elizabeth II right **Reverse:** Turkish cat

| Date | Mintage | F | VF | XF | Unc | BU |
|---|---|---|---|---|---|---|
| 1995 | — | — | — | — | 125 | — |
| 1995 Proof | — | Value: 130 | | | | |

**1/5 CROWN** **KM# 483** **Weight:** 6.2200 g. **Composition:** 0.9990 Gold .2000 oz. AGW **Series:** Aircraft of WWII **Obverse:** Bust of Queen Elizabeth II right **Reverse:** Hawker Hurricane

| Date | Mintage | F | VF | XF | Unc | BU |
|---|---|---|---|---|---|---|
| 1995 Proof | Est. 5,000 | Value: 185 | | | | |

**1/5 CROWN** **KM# 484** **Weight:** 6.2200 g. **Composition:** 0.9990 Gold .2000 oz. AGW **Series:** Aircraft of World War II **Obverse:** Bust of Queen Elizabeth II right **Reverse:** P. 51 Munstang

| Date | Mintage | F | VF | XF | Unc | BU |
|---|---|---|---|---|---|---|
| 1995 Proof | Est. 5,000 | Value: 185 | | | | |

**1/5 CROWN** **KM# 485** **Weight:** 6.2200 g. **Composition:** 0.9990 Gold .2000 oz. AGW **Series:** Aircraft of World War II **Obverse:** Bust of Queen Elizabeth II right **Reverse:** Letrov S328

| Date | Mintage | F | VF | XF | Unc | BU |
|---|---|---|---|---|---|---|
| 1995 Proof | Est. 5,000 | Value: 185 | | | | |

**1/5 CROWN** **KM# 486** **Weight:** 6.2200 g. **Composition:** 0.9990 Gold .2000 oz. AGW **Series:** Aircraft of World War II **Obverse:** Bust of Queen Elizabeth II right **Reverse:** Messerschmitt ME262

| Date | Mintage | F | VF | XF | Unc | BU |
|---|---|---|---|---|---|---|
| 1995 Proof | Est. 5,000 | Value: 185 | | | | |

**1/5 CROWN** **KM# 487** **Weight:** 6.2200 g. **Composition:** 0.9990 Gold .2000 oz. AGW **Series:** Aircraft of World War II **Obverse:** Bust of Queen Elizabeth II right **Reverse:** JU87 Stuka

| Date | Mintage | F | VF | XF | Unc | BU |
|---|---|---|---|---|---|---|
| 1995 Proof | Est. 5,000 | Value: 185 | | | | |

**1/5 CROWN** **KM# 488** **Weight:** 6.2200 g. **Composition:** 0.9990 Gold .2000 oz. AGW **Series:** Aircraft of World War II **Obverse:** Bust of Queen Elizabeth II right **Reverse:** MIG 3

| Date | Mintage | F | VF | XF | Unc | BU |
|---|---|---|---|---|---|---|
| 1995 Proof | Est. 5,000 | Value: 185 | | | | |

**1/5 CROWN** **KM# 489** **Weight:** 6.2200 g. **Composition:** 0.9990 Gold .2000 oz. AGW **Series:** Aircraft of World War II **Obverse:** Bust of Queen Elizabeth II right **Reverse:** Nakajima Ki-49 Donryu

| Date | Mintage | F | VF | XF | Unc | BU |
|---|---|---|---|---|---|---|
| 1995 Proof | Est. 5,000 | Value: 185 | | | | |

**1/5 CROWN** **KM# 490** **Weight:** 6.2200 g. **Composition:** 0.9990 Gold .2000 oz. AGW **Series:** Aircraft of World War II **Obverse:** Bust of Queen Elizabeth II right **Reverse:** Vickers Wellington

| Date | Mintage | F | VF | XF | Unc | BU |
|---|---|---|---|---|---|---|
| 1995 Proof | Est. 5,000 | Value: 185 | | | | |

**1/5 CROWN** **KM# 491** **Weight:** 6.2200 g. **Composition:** 0.9990 Gold .2000 oz. AGW **Series:** Aircraft of World War II **Obverse:** Bust of Queen Elizabeth II right **Reverse:** Spitfire

| Date | Mintage | F | VF | XF | Unc | BU |
|---|---|---|---|---|---|---|
| 1995 Proof | Est. 5,000 | Value: 185 | | | | |

**1/5 CROWN** **KM# 492** **Weight:** 6.2200 g. **Composition:** 0.9990 Gold .2000 oz. AGW **Series:** Aircraft of World War II **Obverse:** Bust of Queen Elizabeth II right **Reverse:** Fokker G. 1a

| Date | Mintage | F | VF | XF | Unc | BU |
|---|---|---|---|---|---|---|
| 1995 Proof | Est. 5,000 | Value: 185 | | | | |

**1/5 CROWN** **KM# 493** **Weight:** 6.2200 g. **Composition:** 0.9990 Gold .2000 oz. AGW **Series:** Aircraft of World War II **Obverse:** Bust of Queen Elizabeth II right **Reverse:** Commonwealth Boomerang CA-13

| Date | Mintage | F | VF | XF | Unc | BU |
|---|---|---|---|---|---|---|
| 1995 Proof | Est. 5,000 | Value: 185 | | | | |

**1/5 CROWN** **KM# 494** **Weight:** 6.2200 g. **Composition:** 0.9990 Gold .2000 oz. AGW **Series:** Aircraft of World War II **Obverse:** Bust of Queen Elizabeth II right **Reverse:** Briston Blenheim 142M

| Date | Mintage | F | VF | XF | Unc | BU |
|---|---|---|---|---|---|---|
| 1995 Proof | Est. 5,000 | Value: 185 | | | | |

**1/5 CROWN** **KM# 495** **Weight:** 6.2200 g. **Composition:** 0.9990 Gold .2000 oz. AGW **Series:** Aircraft of World War II **Obverse:** Bust of Queen Elizabeth II right **Reverse:** Mitsubishi Zero

| Date | Mintage | F | VF | XF | Unc | BU |
|---|---|---|---|---|---|---|
| 1995 Proof | Est. 5,000 | Value: 185 | | | | |

**1/5 CROWN** **KM# 496** **Weight:** 6.2200 g. **Composition:** 0.9990 Gold .2000 oz. AGW **Series:** Aircraft of World War II **Obverse:** Bust of Queen Elizabeth II right **Reverse:** Heinkel HE111

| Date | Mintage | F | VF | XF | Unc | BU |
|---|---|---|---|---|---|---|
| 1995 Proof | Est. 5,000 | Value: 185 | | | | |

**1/5 CROWN** **KM# 497** **Weight:** 6.2200 g. **Composition:** 0.9990 Gold .2000 oz. AGW **Series:** Aircraft of World War II **Obverse:** Bust of Queen Elizabeth II right **Reverse:** Boulton Paul P82 Defiant

| Date | Mintage | F | VF | XF | Unc | BU |
|---|---|---|---|---|---|---|
| 1995 Proof | Est. 5,000 | Value: 185 | | | | |

**1/5 CROWN** **KM# 498** **Weight:** 6.2200 g. **Composition:** 0.9990 Gold .2000 oz. AGW **Series:** Aircraft of World War II **Obverse:** Bust of Queen Elizabeth II right **Reverse:** Boeing B289 - Enola Gay

| Date | Mintage | F | VF | XF | Unc | BU |
|---|---|---|---|---|---|---|
| 1995 Proof | Est. 5,000 | Value: 185 | | | | |

**1/5 CROWN** **KM# 499** **Weight:** 6.2200 g. **Composition:** 0.9990 Gold .2000 oz. AGW **Series:** Aircraft of World War II **Obverse:** Bust of Queen Elizabeth II right **Reverse:** Douglas DC-3 (C47)

| Date | Mintage | F | VF | XF | Unc | BU |
|---|---|---|---|---|---|---|
| 1995 Proof | Est. 5,000 | Value: 185 | | | | |

**1/5 CROWN** **KM# 500** **Weight:** 6.2200 g. **Composition:** 0.9990 Gold .2000 oz. AGW **Series:** Aircraft of World War II **Obverse:** Bust of Queen Elizabeth II right **Reverse:** Fairey Swordfish

| Date | Mintage | F | VF | XF | Unc | BU |
|---|---|---|---|---|---|---|
| 1995 Proof | Est. 5,000 | Value: 185 | | | | |

**1/5 CROWN** **KM# 501** **Weight:** 6.2200 g. **Composition:** 0.9990 Gold .2000 oz. AGW **Series:** Aircraft of World War II **Obverse:** Bust of Queen Elizabeth II right **Reverse:** Curtiss P40

| Date | Mintage | F | VF | XF | Unc | BU |
|---|---|---|---|---|---|---|
| 1995 Proof | Est. 5,000 | Value: 185 | | | | |

**1/5 CROWN** **KM# 523** **Weight:** 6.2200 g. **Composition:** 0.9990 Gold .2000 oz. AGW **Subject:** America's Cup **Obverse:** Bust of Queen Elizabeth II right **Reverse:** Two sailing boats

| Date | Mintage | F | VF | XF | Unc | BU |
|---|---|---|---|---|---|---|
| 1995 Proof | Est. 5,000 | Value: 125 | | | | |

**1/5 CROWN** **KM# 525** **Weight:** 6.2200 g. **Composition:** 0.9999 Gold .2000 oz. AGW **Series:** Inventions of the Modern World **Obverse:** Bust of Queen Elizabeth II right **Reverse:** Cameo of Tsai Lun, paper and tree

| Date | Mintage | F | VF | XF | Unc | BU |
|---|---|---|---|---|---|---|
| 1995 Proof | Est. 5,000 | Value: 165 | | | | |

**1/5 CROWN** **KM# 527** **Weight:** 6.2200 g. **Composition:** 0.9999 Gold .2000 oz. AGW **Series:** Inventions of the Modern World **Obverse:** Bust of Queen Elizabeth II right **Reverse:** Cameo of Chang Heng and Seismograph

| Date | Mintage | F | VF | XF | Unc | BU |
|---|---|---|---|---|---|---|
| 1995 Proof | Est. 5,000 | Value: 165 | | | | |

**1/5 CROWN** **KM# 529** **Weight:** 6.2200 g. **Composition:** 0.9999 Gold .2000 oz. AGW **Series:** Inventions of the Modern World **Obverse:** Bust of Queen Elizabeth II right **Reverse:** Cameo of Tsu Chung Chih and compass cart

| Date | Mintage | F | VF | XF | Unc | BU |
|---|---|---|---|---|---|---|
| 1995 Proof | Est. 5,000 | Value: 165 | | | | |

**1/5 CROWN** **KM# 531** **Weight:** 6.2200 g. **Composition:** 0.9999 Gold .2000 oz. AGW **Series:** Inventions of the Modern World **Obverse:** Bust of Queen Elizabeth II right **Reverse:** Cameo of Pi Sheng and movable type

| Date | Mintage | F | VF | XF | Unc | BU |
|---|---|---|---|---|---|---|
| 1995 Proof | Est. 5,000 | Value: 165 | | | | |

**1/5 CROWN** **KM# 533** **Weight:** 6.2200 g. **Composition:** 0.9999 Gold .2000 oz. AGW **Series:** Inventions of the Modern World **Obverse:** Bust of Queen Elizabeth II right **Reverse:** Cameo of Charles Babbage and first computer

| Date | Mintage | F | VF | XF | Unc | BU |
|---|---|---|---|---|---|---|
| 1995 Proof | Est. 5,000 | Value: 165 | | | | |

**1/5 CROWN** **KM# 535** **Weight:** 6.2200 g. **Composition:** 0.9999 Gold .2000 oz. AGW **Series:** Inventions of the Modern World **Obverse:** Bust of Queen Elizabeth II right **Reverse:** Cameo of Fox Talbot, photography

| Date | Mintage | F | VF | XF | Unc | BU |
|---|---|---|---|---|---|---|
| 1995 Proof | Est. 5,000 | Value: 165 | | | | |

**1/5 CROWN** **KM# 537** **Weight:** 6.2200 g. **Composition:** 0.9999 Gold .2000 oz. AGW **Series:** Inventions of the Modern World **Obverse:** Bust of Queen Elizabeth II right **Reverse:** Cameo of Rudolf Diesel, diesel engine

| Date | Mintage | F | VF | XF | Unc | BU |
|---|---|---|---|---|---|---|
| 1995 Proof | Est. 5,000 | Value: 165 | | | | |

**1/5 CROWN** **KM# 539** **Weight:** 6.2200 g. **Composition:** 0.9999 Gold .2000 oz. AGW **Series:** Inventions of the Modern World **Obverse:** Bust of Queen Elizabeth II right **Reverse:** Cameo of Wilhelm K. Roentgen and x-ray of hand

| Date | Mintage | F | VF | XF | Unc | BU |
|---|---|---|---|---|---|---|
| 1995 Proof | Est. 5,000 | Value: 165 | | | | |

**1/5 CROWN** **KM# 541** **Weight:** 6.2200 g. **Composition:** 0.9999 Gold .2000 oz. AGW **Series:** Inventions of the Modern World **Obverse:** Bust of Queen Elizabeth II right **Reverse:** Cameo of Guglielmo Marconi and radio equipment

| Date | Mintage | F | VF | XF | Unc | BU |
|---|---|---|---|---|---|---|
| 1995 Proof | Est. 5,000 | Value: 165 | | | | |

**1/5 CROWN** **KM# 543** **Weight:** 6.2200 g. **Composition:** 0.9999 Gold .2000 oz. AGW **Series:** Inventions of the Modern World **Obverse:** Bust of Queen Elizabeth II right **Reverse:** Cameo of John L. Baird and television equipment

| Date | Mintage | F | VF | XF | Unc | BU |
|---|---|---|---|---|---|---|
| 1995 Proof | Est. 5,000 | Value: 165 | | | | |

**1/5 CROWN** **KM# 545** **Weight:** 6.2200 g. **Composition:** 0.9999 Gold .2000 oz. AGW **Series:** Inventions of the Modern World **Obverse:** Bust of Queen Elizabeth II right **Reverse:** Cameo of Alexander Fleming and microscope

| Date | Mintage | F | VF | XF | Unc | BU |
|---|---|---|---|---|---|---|
| 1995 Proof | Est. 5,000 | Value: 165 | | | | |

**1/5 CROWN** **KM# 547** **Weight:** 6.2200 g. **Composition:** 0.9999 Gold .2000 oz. AGW **Series:** Inventions of the Modern World **Obverse:** Bust of Queen Elizabeth II right **Reverse:** Cameo of Lazlo Biro and ball point pen

| Date | Mintage | F | VF | XF | Unc | BU |
|---|---|---|---|---|---|---|
| 1995 Proof | Est. 5,000 | Value: 165 | | | | |

**1/5 CROWN** **KM# 549** **Weight:** 6.2200 g. **Composition:** 0.9999 Gold .2000 oz. AGW **Series:** Inventions of the Modern World **Obverse:** Bust of Queen Elizabeth II right **Reverse:** Cameo of Wernher von Braun and rocket

| Date | Mintage | F | VF | XF | Unc | BU |
|---|---|---|---|---|---|---|
| 1996 Proof | Est. 5,000 | Value: 165 | | | | |

**1/5 CROWN** **KM# 550** **Weight:** 6.2200 g. **Composition:** 0.9999 Gold .2000 oz. AGW **Series:** Inventions of the Modern World **Obverse:** Bust of Queen Elizabeth II right **Reverse:** Cameo of Thomas Edison, electricity

| Date | Mintage | F | VF | XF | Unc | BU |
|---|---|---|---|---|---|---|
| 1996 Proof | Est. 5,000 | Value: 165 | | | | |

**1/5 CROWN** **KM# 551** **Weight:** 6.2200 g. **Composition:** 0.9999 Gold .2000 oz. AGW **Series:** Inventions of the Modern World **Obverse:** Bust of Queen Elizabeth II right **Reverse:** Compass

| Date | Mintage | F | VF | XF | Unc | BU |
|---|---|---|---|---|---|---|
| 1996 Proof | Est. 5,000 | Value: 165 | | | | |

**1/5 CROWN** **KM# 552** **Weight:** 6.2200 g. **Composition:** 0.9999 Gold .2000 oz. AGW **Series:** Inventions of the Modern World **Obverse:** Bust of Queen Elizabeth II right **Reverse:** Cameo of Michael Faraday, electricity

| Date | Mintage | F | VF | XF | Unc | BU |
|---|---|---|---|---|---|---|
| 1996 Proof | Est. 5,000 | Value: 165 | | | | |

**1/5 CROWN** **KM# 553** **Weight:** 6.2200 g. **Composition:** 0.9999 Gold .2000 oz. AGW **Series:** Inventions of the Modern World **Obverse:** Bust of Queen Elizabeth II right **Reverse:** Cameo of Emile Berliner and gramophone

| Date | Mintage | F | VF | XF | Unc | BU |
|---|---|---|---|---|---|---|
| 1996 Proof | Est. 5,000 | Value: 165 | | | | |

**1/5 CROWN** **KM# 554** **Weight:** 6.2200 g. **Composition:** 0.9999 Gold .2000 oz. AGW **Series:** Inventions of the Modern World **Obverse:** Bust of Queen Elizabeth II right **Reverse:** Cameo of Alexander Graham Bell, voice transmission

| Date | Mintage | F | VF | XF | Unc | BU |
|---|---|---|---|---|---|---|
| 1996 Proof | Est. 5,000 | Value: 165 | | | | |

**1/5 CROWN** **KM# 561** **Weight:** 6.2200 g. **Composition:** 0.9999 Gold .2000 oz. AGW **Series:** 1996 Summer Olympics - Atlanta **Obverse:** Bust of Queen Elizabeth II right **Reverse:** Hurdler

| Date | Mintage | F | VF | XF | Unc | BU |
|---|---|---|---|---|---|---|
| 1996 Proof | Est. 5,000 | Value: 165 | | | | |

**1/5 CROWN** **KM# 562** **Weight:** 6.2200 g. **Composition:** 0.9999 Gold .2000 oz. AGW **Series:** 1996 Summer Olympics - Atlanta **Obverse:** Bust of Queen Elizabeth II right **Reverse:** Runners

| Date | Mintage | F | VF | XF | Unc | BU |
|---|---|---|---|---|---|---|
| 1996 Proof | Est. 5,000 | Value: 165 | | | | |

**1/5 CROWN** **KM# 563** **Weight:** 6.2200 g. **Composition:** 0.9999 Gold .2000 oz. AGW **Series:** 1996 Summer Olympics - Atlanta **Obverse:** Bust of Queen Elizabeth II right **Reverse:** Sailing

| Date | Mintage | F | VF | XF | Unc | BU |
|---|---|---|---|---|---|---|
| 1996 Proof | Est. 5,000 | Value: 165 | | | | |

**1/5 CROWN** **KM# 564** **Weight:** 6.2200 g. **Composition:** 0.9999 Gold .2000 oz. AGW **Series:** 1996 Summer Olympics - Atlanta **Obverse:** Bust of Queen Elizabeth II right **Reverse:** Swimmers

| Date | Mintage | F | VF | XF | Unc | BU |
|---|---|---|---|---|---|---|
| 1996 Proof | Est. 5,000 | Value: 165 | | | | |

**1/5 CROWN** **KM# 565** **Weight:** 6.2200 g. **Composition:** 0.9999 Gold .2000 oz. AGW **Series:** 1996 Summer Olympics - Atlanta **Obverse:** Bust of Queen Elizabeth II right **Reverse:** Equestrian

| Date | Mintage | F | VF | XF | Unc | BU |
|---|---|---|---|---|---|---|
| 1996 Proof | Est. 5,000 | Value: 165 | | | | |

**1/5 CROWN** **KM# 566** **Weight:** 6.2200 g. **Composition:** 0.9999 Gold .2000 oz. AGW **Series:** 1996 Summer Olympics - Atlanta **Obverse:** Bust of Queen Elizabeth II right **Reverse:** Cyclists and Nike

| Date | Mintage | F | VF | XF | Unc | BU |
|---|---|---|---|---|---|---|
| 1996 Proof | Est. 5,000 | Value: 165 | | | | |

**1/5 CROWN** **KM# 573** **Weight:** 6.2200 g. **Composition:** 0.9990 Gold .2000 oz. AGW **Series:** Bicentennial of Robert Burns **Obverse:** Bust of Queen Elizabeth II right **Reverse:** Seated

| Date | Mintage | F | VF | XF | Unc | BU |
|---|---|---|---|---|---|---|
| 1996 Proof | Est. 5,000 | Value: 165 | | | | |

**1/5 CROWN** **KM# 574** **Weight:** 6.2200 g. **Composition:** 0.9990 Gold .2000 oz. AGW **Series:** Bicentennial of Robert Burns **Obverse:** Bust of Queen Elizabeth II right **Reverse:** Pirate ships

| Date | Mintage | F | VF | XF | Unc | BU |
|---|---|---|---|---|---|---|
| 1996 Proof | Est. 5,000 | Value: 165 | | | | |

**1/5 CROWN** **KM# 575** **Weight:** 6.2200 g. **Composition:** 0.9990 Gold .2000 oz. AGW **Series:** Bicentennial of Robert Burns **Obverse:** Bust of Queen Elizabeth II right **Reverse:** Auld Lang Syne

| Date | Mintage | F | VF | XF | Unc | BU |
|---|---|---|---|---|---|---|
| 1996 Proof | Est. 5,000 | Value: 165 | | | | |

**1/5 CROWN** **KM# 576** **Weight:** 6.2200 g. **Composition:** 0.9990 Gold .2000 oz. AGW **Series:** Bicentennial of Robert Burns **Obverse:** Bust of Queen Elizabeth II right **Reverse:** Edinburgh Castle

| Date | Mintage | F | VF | XF | Unc | BU |
|---|---|---|---|---|---|---|
| 1996 Proof | Est. 5,000 | Value: 165 | | | | |

**1/5 CROWN** **KM# 581** **Weight:** 6.2200 g. **Composition:** 0.9990 Gold .2000 oz. AGW **Subject:** Queen's Birthday **Obverse:** Bust of Queen Elizabeth II right **Reverse:** Flowers

| Date | Mintage | F | VF | XF | Unc | BU |
|---|---|---|---|---|---|---|
| 1996 Proof | Est. 5,000 | Value: 165 | | | | |

**1/5 CROWN** **KM# 583** **Weight:** 6.2200 g. **Composition:** 0.9990 Gold .2000 oz. AGW **Subject:** Preserve Planet Earth **Obverse:** Bust of Queen Elizabeth II right **Reverse:** Killer whale

| Date | Mintage | F | VF | XF | Unc | BU |
|---|---|---|---|---|---|---|
| 1996 Proof | Est. 5,000 | Value: 165 | | | | |

**1/5 CROWN** **KM# 584** **Weight:** 6.2200 g. **Composition:** 0.9990 Gold .2000 oz. AGW **Subject:** Preserve Planet Earth **Obverse:** Bust of Queen Elizabeth II right **Reverse:** Razorbill feeding chick

| Date | Mintage | F | VF | XF | Unc | BU |
|---|---|---|---|---|---|---|
| 1996 Proof | Est. 5,000 | Value: 165 | | | | |

**1/5 CROWN KM# 605 Weight:** 6.2200 g. **Composition:** 0.9990 Gold .2000 oz. AGW **Series:** Flower Fairies **Obverse:** Bust of Queen Elizabeth II right **Reverse:** Orchis

| Date | Mintage | F | VF | XF | Unc | BU |
|---|---|---|---|---|---|---|
| 1996 Proof | Est. 5,000 | Value: 170 | | | | |

**1/5 CROWN KM# 606 Weight:** 6.2200 g. **Composition:** 0.9990 Gold .2000 oz. AGW **Series:** Flower Fairies **Obverse:** Bust of Queen Elizabeth II right **Reverse:** Rose

| Date | Mintage | F | VF | XF | Unc | BU |
|---|---|---|---|---|---|---|
| 1996 Proof | Est. 5,000 | Value: 170 | | | | |

**1/5 CROWN KM# 607 Weight:** 6.2200 g. **Composition:** 0.9990 Gold .2000 oz. AGW **Series:** Flower Fairies **Obverse:** Bust of Queen Elizabeth II right **Reverse:** Fuchsia

| Date | Mintage | F | VF | XF | Unc | BU |
|---|---|---|---|---|---|---|
| 1996 Proof | Est. 5,000 | Value: 170 | | | | |

**1/5 CROWN KM# 608 Weight:** 6.2200 g. **Composition:** 0.9990 Gold .2000 oz. AGW **Series:** Flower Fairies **Obverse:** Bust of Queen Elizabeth II right **Reverse:** Pinks

| Date | Mintage | F | VF | XF | Unc | BU |
|---|---|---|---|---|---|---|
| 1996 Proof | Est. 5,000 | Value: 170 | | | | |

**1/5 CROWN KM# 617 Weight:** 6.2200 g. **Composition:** 0.9990 Gold .2000 oz. AGW **Obverse:** Bust of Queen Elizabeth II right **Reverse:** Burmese cat

| Date | Mintage | F | VF | XF | Unc | BU |
|---|---|---|---|---|---|---|
| 1996 | — | — | — | — | 90.00 | — |
| 1996 Proof | — | Value: 92.00 | | | | |

**1/5 CROWN KM# 618 Weight:** 6.2200 g. **Composition:** 0.9990 Platinum .2000 oz. APW **Obverse:** Bust of Queen Elizabeth II right **Reverse:** Burmese cat

| Date | Mintage | F | VF | XF | Unc | BU |
|---|---|---|---|---|---|---|
| 1996 | — | — | — | — | 125 | — |
| 1996 Proof | — | Value: 130 | | | | |

**1/5 CROWN KM# 625 Weight:** 6.2200 g. **Composition:** 0.9990 Gold .2000 oz. AGW **Obverse:** Bust of Queen Elizabeth II right **Reverse:** Portrait of Ferdinand Magellan, map and ship

| Date | Mintage | F | VF | XF | Unc | BU |
|---|---|---|---|---|---|---|
| 1996 Proof | Est. 5,000 | Value: 165 | | | | |

**1/5 CROWN KM# 628 Weight:** 6.2200 g. **Composition:** 0.9990 Gold .2000 oz. AGW **Obverse:** Bust of Queen Elizabeth II right **Reverse:** Portrait of Sir Francis Drake, map and ship

| Date | Mintage | F | VF | XF | Unc | BU |
|---|---|---|---|---|---|---|
| 1996 Proof | Est. 5,000 | Value: 165 | | | | |

**1/5 CROWN KM# 631 Weight:** 6.2200 g. **Composition:** 0.9990 Gold .2000 oz. AGW **Series:** European Football Championship **Obverse:** Bust of Queen Elizabeth II right **Reverse:** Romania vs Bulgaria

| Date | Mintage | F | VF | XF | Unc | BU |
|---|---|---|---|---|---|---|
| 1996 Proof | Est. 5,000 | Value: 165 | | | | |

**1/5 CROWN KM# 634 Weight:** 6.2200 g. **Composition:** 0.9990 Gold .2000 oz. AGW **Series:** European Football Championship **Obverse:** Bust of Queen Elizabeth II right **Reverse:** Czech Rep. vs Italy

| Date | Mintage | F | VF | XF | Unc | BU |
|---|---|---|---|---|---|---|
| 1996 Proof | Est. 5,000 | Value: 165 | | | | |

**1/5 CROWN KM# 637 Weight:** 6.2200 g. **Composition:** 0.9990 Gold .2000 oz. AGW **Series:** European Football Championship **Obverse:** Bust of Queen Elizabeth II right **Reverse:** Germany vs Russia

| Date | Mintage | F | VF | XF | Unc | BU |
|---|---|---|---|---|---|---|
| 1996 Proof | Est. 5,000 | Value: 165 | | | | |

**1/5 CROWN KM# 640 Weight:** 6.2200 g. **Composition:** 0.9990 Gold .2000 oz. AGW **Series:** European Football Championship **Obverse:** Bust of Queen Elizabeth II right **Reverse:** Spain vs France

| Date | Mintage | F | VF | XF | Unc | BU |
|---|---|---|---|---|---|---|
| 1996 Proof | Est. 5,000 | Value: 165 | | | | |

**1/5 CROWN KM# 643 Weight:** 6.2200 g. **Composition:** 0.9990 Gold .2000 oz. AGW **Series:** European Football Championship **Obverse:** Bust of Queen Elizabeth II right **Reverse:** Turkey vs Croatia

| Date | Mintage | F | VF | XF | Unc | BU |
|---|---|---|---|---|---|---|
| 1996 Proof | Est. 5,000 | Value: 165 | | | | |

**1/5 CROWN KM# 646 Weight:** 6.2200 g. **Composition:** 0.9990 Gold .2000 oz. AGW **Series:** Eurpean Football Championship **Obverse:** Bust of Queen Elizabeth II right **Reverse:** Denmark vs Portugal

| Date | Mintage | F | VF | XF | Unc | BU |
|---|---|---|---|---|---|---|
| 1996 Proof | Est. 5,000 | Value: 165 | | | | |

**1/5 CROWN KM# 649 Weight:** 6.2200 g. **Composition:** 0.9990 Gold .2000 oz. AGW **Series:** European Football Championship **Obverse:** Bust of Queen Elizabeth II right **Reverse:** Scotland vs England

| Date | Mintage | F | VF | XF | Unc | BU |
|---|---|---|---|---|---|---|
| 1996 Proof | Est. 5,000 | Value: 165 | | | | |

**1/5 CROWN KM# 652 Weight:** 6.2200 g. **Composition:** 0.9990 Gold .2000 oz. AGW **Series:** European Football Championship **Obverse:** Bust of Queen Elizabeth II right **Reverse:** Holland vs Switzerland

| Date | Mintage | F | VF | XF | Unc | BU |
|---|---|---|---|---|---|---|
| 1996 Proof | Est. 5,000 | Value: 165 | | | | |

**1/5 CROWN KM# 656 Weight:** 6.2200 g. **Composition:** 0.9990 Gold .2000 oz. AGW **Series:** European Football Championship **Obverse:** Bust of Queen Elizabeth II right **Reverse:** Winner, Germany

| Date | Mintage | F | VF | XF | Unc | BU |
|---|---|---|---|---|---|---|
| 1996 Proof | Est. 5,000 | Value: 165 | | | | |

**1/5 CROWN KM# 659 Weight:** 6.2200 g. **Composition:** 0.9990 Gold .2000 oz. AGW **Series:** Legend of King Arthur **Obverse:** Bust of Queen Elizabeth II right **Reverse:** King Arthur with sword, orb

| Date | Mintage | F | VF | XF | Unc | BU |
|---|---|---|---|---|---|---|
| 1996 Proof | Est. 5,000 | Value: 165 | | | | |

**1/5 CROWN KM# 660 Weight:** 6.2200 g. **Composition:** 0.9990 Gold .2000 oz. AGW **Series:** Legend of King Arthur **Obverse:** Bust of Queen Elizabeth II right **Reverse:** Queen Guinevere

| Date | Mintage | F | VF | XF | Unc | BU |
|---|---|---|---|---|---|---|
| 1996 Proof | Est. 5,000 | Value: 165 | | | | |

**1/5 CROWN KM# 661 Weight:** 6.2200 g. **Composition:** 0.9990 Gold .2000 oz. AGW **Series:** Legend of King Arthur **Obverse:** Bust of Queen Elizabeth II right **Reverse:** Sir Lancelot

| Date | Mintage | F | VF | XF | Unc | BU |
|---|---|---|---|---|---|---|
| 1996 Proof | Est. 5,000 | Value: 165 | | | | |

**1/5 CROWN KM# 662 Weight:** 6.2200 g. **Composition:** 0.9990 Gold .2000 oz. AGW **Series:** Legend of King Arthur **Obverse:** Bust of Queen Elizabeth II right **Reverse:** Merlin

| Date | Mintage | F | VF | XF | Unc | BU |
|---|---|---|---|---|---|---|
| 1996 Proof | Est. 5,000 | Value: 165 | | | | |

**1/5 CROWN KM# 663 Weight:** 6.2200 g. **Composition:** 0.9990 Gold .2000 oz. AGW **Series:** Legend of King Arthur **Obverse:** Bust of Queen Elizabeth II right **Reverse:** Camelot Castle

| Date | Mintage | F | VF | XF | Unc | BU |
|---|---|---|---|---|---|---|
| 1996 Proof | Est. 5,000 | Value: 165 | | | | |

**1/5 CROWN KM# 664 Weight:** 6.2200 g. **Composition:** 0.9990 Platinum .2000 oz. APW **Series:** Legend of King Arthur **Obverse:** Bust of Queen Elizabeth II right **Reverse:** King Arthur with sword, orb

| Date | Mintage | F | VF | XF | Unc | BU |
|---|---|---|---|---|---|---|
| 1996 Proof | Est. 5,000 | Value: 185 | | | | |

**1/5 CROWN KM# 665 Weight:** 6.2200 g. **Composition:** 0.9990 Platinum .2000 oz. APW **Series:** Legend of King Arthur **Obverse:** Bust of Queen Elizabeth II right **Reverse:** Queen Guinevere

| Date | Mintage | F | VF | XF | Unc | BU |
|---|---|---|---|---|---|---|
| 1996 Proof | Est. 5,000 | Value: 185 | | | | |

**1/5 CROWN KM# 666 Weight:** 6.2200 g. **Composition:** 0.9990 Platinum .2000 oz. APW **Series:** Legend of King Arthur **Obverse:** Bust of Queen Elizabeth II right **Reverse:** Sir Lancelot

| Date | Mintage | F | VF | XF | Unc | BU |
|---|---|---|---|---|---|---|
| 1996 Proof | Est. 5,000 | Value: 185 | | | | |

**1/5 CROWN KM# 667 Weight:** 6.2200 g. **Composition:** 0.9990 Platinum .2000 oz. APW **Series:** Legend of King Arthur **Obverse:** Bust of Queen Elizabeth II right **Reverse:** Merlin

| Date | Mintage | F | VF | XF | Unc | BU |
|---|---|---|---|---|---|---|
| 1996 Proof | Est. 5,000 | Value: 185 | | | | |

**1/5 CROWN KM# 668 Weight:** 6.2200 g. **Composition:** 0.9990 Platinum .2000 oz. APW **Series:** Legend of King Arthur **Obverse:** Bust of Queen Elizabeth II right **Reverse:** Camelot Castle

| Date | Mintage | F | VF | XF | Unc | BU |
|---|---|---|---|---|---|---|
| 1996 Proof | Est. 5,000 | Value: 185 | | | | |

**1/5 CROWN KM# 730 Weight:** 6.2200 g. **Composition:** 0.9990 Gold .2000 oz. AGW **Subject:** Year of the Rat **Obverse:** Bust of Queen Elizabeth II right **Reverse:** Rat

| Date | Mintage | F | VF | XF | Unc | BU |
|---|---|---|---|---|---|---|
| 1996 Proof | — | — | — | — | — | — |

**Note:** Entire series purchased by one buyer. Mintage, disposition and market value unknown

**1/5 CROWN KM# 766 Weight:** 6.2200 g. **Composition:** 0.9999 Gold .2000 oz. AGW **Subject:** Fridtjof Nansen 1861-1930 **Obverse:** Bust of Queen Elizabeth II right **Reverse:** Portrait, map and ship "The Fram"

| Date | Mintage | F | VF | XF | Unc | BU |
|---|---|---|---|---|---|---|
| 1997 Proof | Est. 5,000 | Value: 175 | | | | |

**1/5 CROWN KM# 723 Weight:** 6.2200 g. **Composition:** 0.9990 Gold .2000 oz. AGW **Subject:** Year of the Ox **Obverse:** Bust of Queen Elizabeth II right **Reverse:** Ox laying down

| Date | Mintage | F | VF | XF | Unc | BU |
|---|---|---|---|---|---|---|
| 1997 Proof | Est. 12,000 | Value: 170 | | | | |

**1/5 CROWN KM# 751 Weight:** 6.2200 g. **Composition:** 0.9990 Gold .2000 oz. AGW **Series:** Flower Faries **Obverse:** Bust of Queen Elizabeth II right **Reverse:** Candytuft

| Date | Mintage | F | VF | XF | Unc | BU |
|---|---|---|---|---|---|---|
| 1997 Proof | Est. 5,000 | Value: 165 | | | | |

**1/5 CROWN KM# 751a Weight:** 6.2518 g. **Composition:** 0.9950 Platinum .2000 oz. APW **Series:** Flower Faries **Obverse:** Bust of Queen Elizabeth II right **Reverse:** Candytuft

| Date | Mintage | F | VF | XF | Unc | BU |
|---|---|---|---|---|---|---|
| 1997 Proof | Est. 2,500 | Value: 175 | | | | |

**1/5 CROWN KM# 752 Weight:** 6.2200 g. **Composition:** 0.9999 Gold .2000 oz. AGW **Series:** Flower Faries **Obverse:** Bust of Queen Elizabeth II right **Reverse:** Snowdrop

| Date | Mintage | F | VF | XF | Unc | BU |
|---|---|---|---|---|---|---|
| 1997 Proof | Est. 5,000 | Value: 165 | | | | |

**1/5 CROWN KM# 752a Weight:** 6.2518 g. **Composition:** 0.9950 Platinum .2000 oz. APW **Series:** Flower Faries **Obverse:** Bust of Queen Elizabeth II right **Reverse:** Snowdrop

| Date | Mintage | F | VF | XF | Unc | BU |
|---|---|---|---|---|---|---|
| 1997 Proof | Est. 2,500 | Value: 175 | | | | |

**1/5 CROWN KM# 753 Weight:** 6.2200 g. **Composition:** 0.9999 Gold .2000 oz. AGW **Series:** Flower Faries **Obverse:** Bust of Queen Elizabeth II right **Reverse:** Tulip

| Date | Mintage | F | VF | XF | Unc | BU |
|---|---|---|---|---|---|---|
| 1997 Proof | Est. 5,000 | Value: 165 | | | | |

**1/5 CROWN KM# 753a Weight:** 6.2518 g. **Composition:** 0.9950 Platinum .2000 oz. APW **Series:** Flower Faries **Obverse:** Bust of Queen Elizabeth II right **Reverse:** Tulip

| Date | Mintage | F | VF | XF | Unc | BU |
|---|---|---|---|---|---|---|
| 1997 Proof | Est. 2,500 | Value: 175 | | | | |

**1/5 CROWN KM# 754 Weight:** 6.2200 g. **Composition:** 0.9999 Gold .2000 oz. AGW **Series:** Flower Faries **Obverse:** Bust of Queen Elizabeth II right **Reverse:** Jasmine

| Date | Mintage | F | VF | XF | Unc | BU |
|---|---|---|---|---|---|---|
| 1997 Proof | Est. 5,000 | Value: 165 | | | | |

**1/5 CROWN KM# 754a Weight:** 6.2518 g. **Composition:** 0.9950 Platinum .2000 oz. APW **Series:** Flower Faries **Obverse:** Bust of Queen Elizabeth II right **Reverse:** Jasmine

| Date | Mintage | F | VF | XF | Unc | BU |
|---|---|---|---|---|---|---|
| 1997 Proof | Est. 2,500 | Value: 175 | | | | |

**1/5 CROWN KM# 763 Weight:** 6.2200 g. **Composition:** 0.9999 Gold .2000 oz. AGW **Subject:** Leiv Eiricksson 999-1001 **Obverse:** Bust of Queen Elizabeth II right **Reverse:** Portrait and Viking ship with map sail

| Date | Mintage | F | VF | XF | Unc | BU |
|---|---|---|---|---|---|---|
| 1997 Proof | Est. 5,000 | Value: 175 | | | | |

**1/5 CROWN KM# 772 Weight:** 6.2200 g. **Composition:** 0.9999 Gold .2000 oz. AGW **Obverse:** Bust of Queen Elizabeth II right **Reverse:** Long-Haired-Smoke cat

| Date | Mintage | F | VF | XF | Unc | BU |
|---|---|---|---|---|---|---|
| 1997 | — | — | — | — | 90.00 | — |
| 1997 Proof | — | Value: 92.00 | | | | |

**1/5 CROWN KM# 772a Weight:** 6.2200 g. **Composition:** 0.9999 Platinum .2000 oz. APW **Obverse:** Bust of Queen Elizabeth II right **Reverse:** Long-Haired-Smoke cat

| Date | Mintage | F | VF | XF | Unc | BU |
|---|---|---|---|---|---|---|
| 1997 | — | — | — | — | 125 | — |
| 1997 Proof | — | Value: 130 | | | | |

**1/5 CROWN KM# 776 Weight:** 6.2200 g. **Composition:** 0.9999 Gold .2000 oz. AGW **Subject:** History of the Cat **Obverse:** Bust of Queen Elizabeth II right **Reverse:** Cat stalking a spider

| Date | Mintage | F | VF | XF | Unc | BU |
|---|---|---|---|---|---|---|
| 1997 Proof | Est. 7,500 | Value: 165 | | | | |

**1/5 CROWN KM# 781 Weight:** 6.2200 g. **Composition:** 0.9999 Gold .2000 oz. AGW **Subject:** 90th Anniversary of the TT - 1907 **Obverse:** Bust of Queen Elizabeth II right **Reverse:** 1907 winner Charlie Collier

| Date | Mintage | F | VF | XF | Unc | BU |
|---|---|---|---|---|---|---|
| 1997 Proof | Est. 5,000 | Value: 165 | | | | |

**1/5 CROWN KM# 783 Weight:** 6.2200 g. **Composition:** 0.9999 Gold .2000 oz. AGW **Subject:** 90th Anniversary of the TT - 1907 **Obverse:** Bust of Queen Elizabeth II right **Reverse:** 1937 winner Omobono Tenni

| Date | Mintage | F | VF | XF | Unc | BU |
|---|---|---|---|---|---|---|
| 1997 Proof | Est. 5,000 | Value: 165 | | | | |

**1/5 CROWN KM# 785 Weight:** 6.2200 g. **Composition:** 0.9999 Gold .2000 oz. AGW **Subject:** 90th Anniversary of the TT - 1907 **Obverse:** Bust of Queen Elizabeth II right **Reverse:** 1957 winner Bob McIntyre

| Date | Mintage | F | VF | XF | Unc | BU |
|---|---|---|---|---|---|---|
| 1997 Proof | Est. 5,000 | Value: 165 | | | | |

**1/5 CROWN KM# 787 Weight:** 6.2200 g. **Composition:** 0.9999 Gold .2000 oz. AGW **Subject:** 90th Anniversary of the TT - 1907 **Obverse:** Bust of Queen Elizabeth II right **Reverse:** 1967 winner Mike Hailwood

| Date | Mintage | F | VF | XF | Unc | BU |
|---|---|---|---|---|---|---|
| 1997 Proof | Est. 5,000 | Value: 165 | | | | |

**1/5 CROWN KM# 792 Weight:** 6.2200 g. **Composition:** 0.9999 Gold .2000 oz. AGW **Subject:** Golden Wedding Anniversary of Queen Elizabeth II and Prince Philip **Obverse:** Bust of Queen Elizabeth II right **Reverse:** Wedding portrait

| Date | Mintage | F | VF | XF | Unc | BU |
|---|---|---|---|---|---|---|
| 1997 Proof | Est. 3,500 | Value: 165 | | | | |

**1/5 CROWN** **KM# 798** **Weight:** 6.2200 g. **Composition:** 0.9999 Gold .2000 oz. AGW **Series:** Year 2000 **Subject:** Birth of Christ **Obverse:** Bust of Queen Elizabeth II right **Reverse:** Madonna and child with angels

| Date | Mintage | F | VF | XF | Unc | BU |
|---|---|---|---|---|---|---|
| 1997 Proof | Est. 2,000 | Value: 165 | | | | |

**1/5 CROWN** **KM# 800** **Weight:** 6.2200 g. **Composition:** 0.9999 Gold .2000 oz. AGW **Series:** Year 2000 **Subject:** Fall of the Roman Empire 476 **Obverse:** Bust of Queen Elizabeth II right **Reverse:** Barbarian defeating Roman soldier

| Date | Mintage | F | VF | XF | Unc | BU |
|---|---|---|---|---|---|---|
| 1997 Proof | Est. 2,000 | Value: 165 | | | | |

**1/5 CROWN** **KM# 802** **Weight:** 6.2200 g. **Composition:** 0.9999 Gold .2000 oz. AGW **Series:** Year 2000 **Subject:** Flight of Mohammed 622 **Obverse:** Bust of Queen Elizabeth II right **Reverse:** Arabs and camels at an oasis

| Date | Mintage | F | VF | XF | Unc | BU |
|---|---|---|---|---|---|---|
| 1997 Proof | Est. 2,000 | Value: 165 | | | | |

**1/5 CROWN** **KM# 804** **Weight:** 6.2200 g. **Composition:** 0.9999 Gold .2000 oz. AGW **Series:** Year 2000 **Subject:** Norman Conquest 1066 **Obverse:** Bust of Queen Elizabeth II right **Reverse:** William the Conqueror rallying his troops

| Date | Mintage | F | VF | XF | Unc | BU |
|---|---|---|---|---|---|---|
| 1997 Proof | Est. 2,000 | Value: 165 | | | | |

**1/5 CROWN** **KM# 807** **Weight:** 6.2200 g. **Composition:** 0.9999 Gold .2000 oz. AGW **Series:** World Cup Soccer **Obverse:** Bust of Queen Elizabeth II right **Reverse:** Team captains in pre-game handshake

| Date | Mintage | F | VF | XF | Unc | BU |
|---|---|---|---|---|---|---|
| 1998 Proof | Est. 5,000 | Value: 165 | | | | |

**1/5 CROWN** **KM# 814** **Weight:** 6.2200 g. **Composition:** 0.9999 Gold .2000 oz. AGW **Series:** Year of the Tiger **Obverse:** Bust of Queen Elizabeth II right **Reverse:** Tiger

| Date | Mintage | F | VF | XF | Unc | BU |
|---|---|---|---|---|---|---|
| 1998 Proof | Est. 12,000 | Value: 165 | | | | |

**1/5 CROWN** **KM# 824** **Weight:** 6.2200 g. **Composition:** 0.9999 Gold .2000 oz. AGW **Obverse:** Bust of Queen Elizabeth II right **Reverse:** Portrait Marco Polo, caravan and palace

| Date | Mintage | F | VF | XF | Unc | BU |
|---|---|---|---|---|---|---|
| 1998 Proof | Est. 5,000 | Value: 165 | | | | |

**1/5 CROWN** **KM# 826** **Weight:** 6.2200 g. **Composition:** 0.9999 Gold .2000 oz. AGW **Obverse:** Bust of Queen Elizabeth II right **Reverse:** Portrait Vasco da Gama, ship and African map

| Date | Mintage | F | VF | XF | Unc | BU |
|---|---|---|---|---|---|---|
| 1998 Proof | Est. 5,000 | Value: 165 | | | | |

**1/5 CROWN** **KM# 836** **Weight:** 6.2200 g. **Composition:** 0.9999 Gold .2000 oz. AGW **Series:** Flower Fairies **Obverse:** Bust of Queen Elizabeth II right **Reverse:** Standing fairy, lavender

| Date | Mintage | F | VF | XF | Unc | BU |
|---|---|---|---|---|---|---|
| 1998 Proof | Est. 5,000 | Value: 165 | | | | |

**1/5 CROWN** **KM# 836a** **Weight:** 6.2200 g. **Composition:** 0.9999 Platinum .2000 oz. APW **Series:** Flower Fairies **Obverse:** Bust of Queen Elizabeth II right **Reverse:** Standing fairy, lavender

| Date | Mintage | F | VF | XF | Unc | BU |
|---|---|---|---|---|---|---|
| 1998 Proof | Est. 2,500 | Value: 200 | | | | |

**1/5 CROWN** **KM# 837** **Weight:** 6.2200 g. **Composition:** 0.9999 Gold .2000 oz. AGW **Series:** Flower Fairies **Obverse:** Bust of Queen Elizabeth II right **Reverse:** Two fairies, sweet pea

| Date | Mintage | F | VF | XF | Unc | BU |
|---|---|---|---|---|---|---|
| 1998 Proof | Est. 5,000 | Value: 165 | | | | |

**1/5 CROWN** **KM# 837a** **Weight:** 6.2200 g. **Composition:** 0.9999 Platinum .2000 oz. APW **Series:** Flower Fairies **Obverse:** Bust of Queen Elizabeth II right **Reverse:** Two fairies, sweet pea

| Date | Mintage | F | VF | XF | Unc | BU |
|---|---|---|---|---|---|---|
| 1998 Proof | Est. 2,500 | Value: 200 | | | | |

**1/5 CROWN** **KM# 838** **Weight:** 6.2200 g. **Composition:** 0.9999 Gold .2000 oz. AGW **Series:** Flower Fairies **Obverse:** Bust of Queen Elizabeth II right **Reverse:** Fairy looking into flower, White Bindweed

| Date | Mintage | F | VF | XF | Unc | BU |
|---|---|---|---|---|---|---|
| 1998 Proof | Est. 5,000 | Value: 165 | | | | |

**1/5 CROWN** **KM# 838a** **Weight:** 6.2200 g. **Composition:** 0.9999 Platinum .2000 oz. APW **Series:** Flower Fairies **Obverse:** Bust of Queen Elizabeth II right **Reverse:** Fairy looking into flower, White Bindweed

| Date | Mintage | F | VF | XF | Unc | BU |
|---|---|---|---|---|---|---|
| 1998 Proof | Est. 2,500 | Value: 200 | | | | |

**1/5 CROWN** **KM# 839** **Weight:** 6.2200 g. **Composition:** 0.9999 Gold .2000 oz. AGW **Series:** Flower Fairies **Obverse:** Bust of Queen Elizabeth II right **Reverse:** Fairy standing, daffodil

| Date | Mintage | F | VF | XF | Unc | BU |
|---|---|---|---|---|---|---|
| 1998 Proof | Est. 5,000 | Value: 165 | | | | |

**1/5 CROWN** **KM# 839a** **Weight:** 6.2200 g. **Composition:** 0.9999 Platinum .2000 oz. APW **Series:** Flower Fairies **Obverse:** Bust of Queen Elizabeth II right **Reverse:** Fairy standing, daffodil

| Date | Mintage | F | VF | XF | Unc | BU |
|---|---|---|---|---|---|---|
| 1998 Proof | Est. 2,500 | Value: 200 | | | | |

**1/5 CROWN** **KM# 845** **Weight:** 6.2200 g. **Composition:** 0.9999 Gold .2000 oz. AGW **Series:** Winter Olympics - Nagano **Obverse:** Bust of Queen Elizabeth II right **Reverse:** Ski jumper

| Date | Mintage | F | VF | XF | Unc | BU |
|---|---|---|---|---|---|---|
| 1998 Proof | Est. 5,000 | Value: 165 | | | | |

**1/5 CROWN** **KM# 846** **Weight:** 6.2200 g. **Composition:** 0.9999 Gold .2000 oz. AGW **Series:** Winter Olympics - Nagano **Obverse:** Bust of Queen Elizabeth II right **Reverse:** Slalom skier

| Date | Mintage | F | VF | XF | Unc | BU |
|---|---|---|---|---|---|---|
| 1998 Proof | Est. 5,000 | Value: 165 | | | | |

**1/5 CROWN** **KM# 847** **Weight:** 6.2200 g. **Composition:** 0.9999 Gold .2000 oz. AGW **Series:** Winter Olympics - Nagano **Obverse:** Bust of Queen Elizabeth II right **Reverse:** Figure skaters, Olympic torch

| Date | Mintage | F | VF | XF | Unc | BU |
|---|---|---|---|---|---|---|
| 1998 | Est. 5,000 | Value: 165 | | | | |

**1/5 CROWN** **KM# 848** **Weight:** 6.2200 g. **Composition:** 0.9999 Gold .2000 oz. AGW **Series:** Winter Olympics - Nagano **Obverse:** Bust of Queen Elizabeth II right **Reverse:** Figure skater, speed skater and skier

| Date | Mintage | F | VF | XF | Unc | BU |
|---|---|---|---|---|---|---|
| 1998 Proof | Est. 5,000 | Value: 165 | | | | |

**1/5 CROWN** **KM# 855** **Weight:** 6.2200 g. **Composition:** 0.9999 Gold .2000 oz. AGW **Obverse:** Bust of Queen Elizabeth II right **Reverse:** Birman cat

| Date | Mintage | F | VF | XF | Unc | BU |
|---|---|---|---|---|---|---|
| 1998 Proof | 1,000 | Value: 90.00 | | | | |

**1/5 CROWN** **KM# 855a** **Weight:** 6.2200 g. **Composition:** 0.9995 Platinum .2000 oz. APW **Obverse:** Bust of Queen Elizabeth II right **Reverse:** Birman cat

| Date | Mintage | F | VF | XF | Unc | BU |
|---|---|---|---|---|---|---|
| 1998 Proof | — | Value: 130 | | | | |

**1/5 CROWN** **KM# 861** **Weight:** 6.2200 g. **Composition:** 0.9999 Gold .2000 oz. AGW **Series:** History of the Cat **Obverse:** Bust of Queen Elizabeth II right **Reverse:** Egyptian Mau cat with earring

| Date | Mintage | F | VF | XF | Unc | BU |
|---|---|---|---|---|---|---|
| 1998 Proof | Est. 7,500 | Value: 170 | | | | |

**1/5 CROWN** **KM# 871** **Weight:** 6.2200 g. **Composition:** 0.9999 Gold .2000 oz. AGW **Subject:** 125th Anniversary of the Steam Railway **Obverse:** Bust of Queen Elizabeth II right **Reverse:** "The General"

| Date | Mintage | F | VF | XF | Unc | BU |
|---|---|---|---|---|---|---|
| 1998 Proof | Est. 5,000 | Value: 170 | | | | |

**1/5 CROWN** **KM# 873** **Weight:** 6.2200 g. **Composition:** 0.9999 Gold .2000 oz. AGW **Subject:** 125th Anniversary of the Steam Railway **Obverse:** Bust of Queen Elizabeth II right **Reverse:** "The Rocket" and portrait

| Date | Mintage | F | VF | XF | Unc | BU |
|---|---|---|---|---|---|---|
| 1998 Proof | Est. 5,000 | Value: 170 | | | | |

**1/5 CROWN** **KM# 875** **Weight:** 6.2200 g. **Composition:** 0.9999 Gold .2000 oz. AGW **Subject:** 125th Anniversary of the Steam Railway **Obverse:** Bust of Queen Elizabeth II right **Reverse:** Orient Express parlor car interior view

| Date | Mintage | F | VF | XF | Unc | BU |
|---|---|---|---|---|---|---|
| 1998 Proof | Est. 5,000 | Value: 170 | | | | |

**1/5 CROWN** **KM# 877** **Weight:** 6.2200 g. **Composition:** 0.9999 Gold .2000 oz. AGW **Subject:** 125th Anniversary of the Steam Railway **Obverse:** Bust of Queen Elizabeth II right **Reverse:** Mount Pilatus railway

| Date | Mintage | F | VF | XF | Unc | BU |
|---|---|---|---|---|---|---|
| 1998 Proof | Est. 5,000 | Value: 170 | | | | |

**1/5 CROWN** **KM# 879** **Weight:** 6.2200 g. **Composition:** 0.9999 Gold .2000 oz. AGW **Subject:** 125th Anniversary of the Steam Railway **Obverse:** Bust of Queen Elizabeth II right **Reverse:** No. 1 Sutherland locomotive

| Date | Mintage | F | VF | XF | Unc | BU |
|---|---|---|---|---|---|---|
| 1998 Proof | Est. 5,000 | Value: 170 | | | | |

**1/5 CROWN** **KM# 881** **Weight:** 6.2200 g. **Composition:** 0.9999 Gold .2000 oz. AGW **Subject:** 125th Anniversary of the Steam Railway **Obverse:** Bust of Queen Elizabeth II right **Reverse:** "Flying Scotsman"

| Date | Mintage | F | VF | XF | Unc | BU |
|---|---|---|---|---|---|---|
| 1998 Proof | Est. 5,000 | Value: 170 | | | | |

**1/5 CROWN** **KM# 883** **Weight:** 6.2200 g. **Composition:** 0.9999 Gold .2000 oz. AGW **Subject:** 125th Anniversary of the Steam Railway **Obverse:** Bust of Queen Elizabeth II right **Reverse:** Mallard locomotive

| Date | Mintage | F | VF | XF | Unc | BU |
|---|---|---|---|---|---|---|
| 1998 Proof | Est. 5,000 | Value: 170 | | | | |

**1/5 CROWN** **KM# 885** **Weight:** 6.2200 g. **Composition:** 0.9999 Gold .2000 oz. AGW **Subject:** 125th Anniversary of the Steam Railway **Obverse:** Bust of Queen Elizabeth II right **Reverse:** The Big Boy locomotive

| Date | Mintage | F | VF | XF | Unc | BU |
|---|---|---|---|---|---|---|
| 1998 Proof | Est. 5,000 | Value: 170 | | | | |

**1/5 CROWN** **KM# 887** **Weight:** 6.2200 g. **Composition:** 0.9999 Gold .2000 oz. AGW **Series:** Year 2000 **Obverse:** Bust of Queen Elizabeth II right **Reverse:** American Independence 1776

| Date | Mintage | F | VF | XF | Unc | BU |
|---|---|---|---|---|---|---|
| 1998 Proof | Est. 2,000 | Value: 170 | | | | |

**1/5 CROWN** **KM# 889** **Weight:** 6.2200 g. **Composition:** 0.9999 Gold .2000 oz. AGW **Series:** Year 2000 **Obverse:** Bust of Queen Elizabeth II right **Reverse:** French Revolution 1789

| Date | Mintage | F | VF | XF | Unc | BU |
|---|---|---|---|---|---|---|
| 1998 Proof | Est. 2,000 | Value: 170 | | | | |

**1/5 CROWN** **KM# 891** **Weight:** 6.2200 g. **Composition:** 0.9999 Gold .2000 oz. AGW **Series:** Year 2000 **Obverse:** Bust of Queen Elizabeth II right **Reverse:** Reformation of the Church 1517

| Date | Mintage | F | VF | XF | Unc | BU |
|---|---|---|---|---|---|---|
| 1998 Proof | Est. 2,000 | Value: 170 | | | | |

**1/5 CROWN** **KM# 893** **Weight:** 6.2200 g. **Composition:** 0.9999 Gold .2000 oz. AGW **Series:** Year 2000 **Obverse:** Bust of Queen Elizabeth II right **Reverse:** 400th Anniversary of the Renaissance

| Date | Mintage | F | VF | XF | Unc | BU |
|---|---|---|---|---|---|---|
| 1998 Proof | Est. 2,000 | Value: 170 | | | | |

**1/5 CROWN** **KM# 895** **Weight:** 6.2200 g. **Composition:** 0.9999 Gold .2000 oz. AGW **Subject:** 125th Anniversary of the Steam Railway **Obverse:** Bust of Queen Elizabeth II right **Reverse:** Ocean wave and sea gull

| Date | Mintage | F | VF | XF | Unc | BU |
|---|---|---|---|---|---|---|
| 1998 Proof | Est. 5,000 | Value: 170 | | | | |

**1/5 CROWN** **KM# 913** **Weight:** 6.2200 g. **Composition:** 0.9999 Gold .2000 oz. AGW **Subject:** Battle of Waterloo 1815 **Obverse:** Bust of Queen Elizabeth II right **Reverse:** Wellington on horse

| Date | Mintage | F | VF | XF | Unc | BU |
|---|---|---|---|---|---|---|
| 1999 Proof | Est. 2,000 | Value: 170 | | | | |

**1/5 CROWN** **KM# 984** **Weight:** 6.2200 g. **Composition:** 0.9999 Gold .2000 oz. AGW **Subject:** Founding of the UN - Millennium **Obverse:** Bust of Queen Elizabeth II right **Reverse:** UN Building, logo

| Date | Mintage | F | VF | XF | Unc | BU |
|---|---|---|---|---|---|---|
| 2000 Proof | Est. 2,000 | Value: 170 | | | | |

**1/5 CROWN** **KM# 985** **Weight:** 6.2200 g. **Composition:** 0.9999 Gold .2000 oz. AGW **Subject:** 1st Man on the Moon - Millennium **Obverse:** Bust of Queen Elizabeth II right **Reverse:** Landing scene, date

| Date | Mintage | F | VF | XF | Unc | BU |
|---|---|---|---|---|---|---|
| 2000 Proof | Est. 2,000 | Value: 170 | | | | |

**1/5 CROWN** **KM# 915** **Weight:** 6.2200 g. **Composition:** 0.9999 Gold .2000 oz. AGW **Subject:** U.S. Civil War **Obverse:** Bust of Queen Elizabeth II right **Reverse:** Cameos of Lee and Grant, flags, sword and drum

| Date | Mintage | F | VF | XF | Unc | BU |
|---|---|---|---|---|---|---|
| 1999 Proof | Est. 2,000 | Value: 170 | | | | |

**1/5 CROWN** **KM# 917** **Weight:** 6.2200 g. **Composition:** 0.9999 Gold .2000 oz. AGW **Subject:** Bolshevik Revolution 1917 **Obverse:** Bust of Queen Elizabeth II right **Reverse:** Lenin above the Aurora

| Date | Mintage | F | VF | XF | Unc | BU |
|---|---|---|---|---|---|---|
| 1999 Proof | Est. 2,000 | Value: 170 | | | | |

**1/5 CROWN** **KM# 987** **Weight:** 6.2200 g. **Composition:** 0.9999 Gold .2000 oz. AGW **Subject:** Fall of the Berlin Wall -

Millennium **Obverse:** Bust of Queen Elizabeth II right **Reverse:** Crowds surrounding wall

| Date | Mintage | F | VF | XF | Unc | BU |
|---|---|---|---|---|---|---|
| 2000 Proof | Est. 2,000 | Value: 170 | | | | |

**1/5 CROWN KM# 989 Weight:** 6.2200 g. **Composition:** 0.9999 Gold .2000 oz. AGW **Subject:** Millennium 2000 - The Future **Obverse:** Bust of Queen Elizabeth II right **Reverse:** International space station

| Date | Mintage | F | VF | XF | Unc | BU |
|---|---|---|---|---|---|---|
| 2000 Proof | Est. 2,000 | Value: 170 | | | | |

**1/5 CROWN KM# 919 Weight:** 6.2200 g. **Composition:** 0.9999 Gold .2000 oz. AGW **Subject:** Armistice Day 1918 **Obverse:** Bust of Queen Elizabeth II right **Reverse:** Biplane above tank

| Date | Mintage | F | VF | XF | Unc | BU |
|---|---|---|---|---|---|---|
| 1999 Proof | Est. 2,000 | Value: 170 | | | | |

**1/5 CROWN KM# 921 Weight:** 6.2200 g. **Composition:** 0.9999 Gold .2000 oz. AGW **Series:** Summer Olympics - Sydney **Obverse:** Bust of Queen Elizabeth II right **Reverse:** Three javelin throwers

| Date | Mintage | F | VF | XF | Unc | BU |
|---|---|---|---|---|---|---|
| 1999 Proof | Est. 5,000 | Value: 170 | | | | |

**1/5 CROWN KM# 923 Weight:** 6.2200 g. **Composition:** 0.9999 Gold .2000 oz. AGW **Series:** Summer Olympics - Sydney **Obverse:** Bust of Queen Elizabeth II right **Reverse:** Female diver

| Date | Mintage | F | VF | XF | Unc | BU |
|---|---|---|---|---|---|---|
| 1999 Proof | Est. 5,000 | Value: 170 | | | | |

**1/5 CROWN KM# 925 Weight:** 6.2200 g. **Composition:** 0.9999 Gold .2000 oz. AGW **Series:** Summer Olympics - Sydney **Obverse:** Bust of Queen Elizabeth II right **Reverse:** Sailboat

| Date | Mintage | F | VF | XF | Unc | BU |
|---|---|---|---|---|---|---|
| 1999 Proof | Est. 5,000 | Value: 170 | | | | |

**1/5 CROWN KM# 927 Weight:** 6.2200 g. **Composition:** 0.9999 Gold .2000 oz. AGW **Series:** Summer Olympics - Sydney **Obverse:** Bust of Queen Elizabeth II right **Reverse:** Two runners

| Date | Mintage | F | VF | XF | Unc | BU |
|---|---|---|---|---|---|---|
| 1999 Proof | Est. 5,000 | Value: 170 | | | | |

**1/5 CROWN KM# 929 Weight:** 6.2200 g. **Composition:** 0.9999 Gold .2000 oz. AGW **Series:** Summer Olympics - Sydney **Obverse:** Bust of Queen Elizabeth II right **Reverse:** Two hurdlers

| Date | Mintage | F | VF | XF | Unc | BU |
|---|---|---|---|---|---|---|
| 1999 Proof | Est. 5,000 | Value: 170 | | | | |

**1/5 CROWN KM# 931 Weight:** 6.2200 g. **Composition:** 0.9999 Gold .2000 oz. AGW **Series:** World Cup Rugby 1999 **Obverse:** Bust of Queen Elizabeth II right **Reverse:** Bust of William Webb Ellis

| Date | Mintage | F | VF | XF | Unc | BU |
|---|---|---|---|---|---|---|
| 1999 Proof | Est. 5,000 | Value: 170 | | | | |

**1/5 CROWN KM# 933 Weight:** 6.2200 g. **Composition:** 0.9999 Gold .2000 oz. AGW **Series:** World Cup Rugby 1999 **Obverse:** Bust of Queen Elizabeth II right **Reverse:** Rugby scrum

| Date | Mintage | F | VF | XF | Unc | BU |
|---|---|---|---|---|---|---|
| 1999 Proof | Est. 5,000 | Value: 170 | | | | |

**1/5 CROWN KM# 935 Weight:** 6.2200 g. **Composition:** 0.9999 Gold .2000 oz. AGW **Series:** World Cup Rugby 1999 **Obverse:** Bust of Queen Elizabeth II right **Reverse:** Player running for catch

| Date | Mintage | F | VF | XF | Unc | BU |
|---|---|---|---|---|---|---|
| 1999 Proof | Est. 5,000 | Value: 170 | | | | |

**1/5 CROWN KM# 937 Weight:** 6.2200 g. **Composition:** 0.9999 Gold .2000 oz. AGW **Series:** World Cup Rugby 1999 **Obverse:** Bust of Queen Elizabeth II right **Reverse:** Goal kick

| Date | Mintage | F | VF | XF | Unc | BU |
|---|---|---|---|---|---|---|
| 1999 Proof | Est. 5,000 | Value: 170 | | | | |

**1/5 CROWN KM# 939 Weight:** 6.2200 g. **Composition:** 0.9999 Gold .2000 oz. AGW **Series:** World Cup Rugby 1999 **Obverse:** Bust of Queen Elizabeth II right **Reverse:** Tackled ball carrier

| Date | Mintage | F | VF | XF | Unc | BU |
|---|---|---|---|---|---|---|
| 1999 Proof | Est. 5,000 | Value: 170 | | | | |

**1/5 CROWN KM# 941 Weight:** 6.2200 g. **Composition:** 0.9999 Gold .2000 oz. AGW **Series:** World Cup Rugby 1999 **Obverse:** Bust of Queen Elizabeth II right **Reverse:** Player leaping for catch

| Date | Mintage | F | VF | XF | Unc | BU |
|---|---|---|---|---|---|---|
| 1999 Proof | Est. 5,000 | Value: 170 | | | | |

**1/5 CROWN KM# 950 Weight:** 6.2200 g. **Composition:** 0.9999 Gold .2000 oz. AGW **Series:** Year of the Rabbit **Obverse:** Bust of Queen Elizabeth II right **Reverse:** Two rabbits

| Date | Mintage | F | VF | XF | Unc | BU |
|---|---|---|---|---|---|---|
| 1999 Proof | Est. 12,000 | Value: 170 | | | | |

**1/5 CROWN KM# 954 Weight:** 6.2200 g. **Composition:** 0.9999 Gold .2000 oz. AGW **Obverse:** Bust of Queen Elizabeth II right **Reverse:** Portrait Sir Walter Raleigh, ship and dates

| Date | Mintage | F | VF | XF | Unc | BU |
|---|---|---|---|---|---|---|
| 1999 Proof | Est. 5,000 | Value: 170 | | | | |

**1/5 CROWN KM# 956 Weight:** 6.2200 g. **Composition:** 0.9999 Gold .2000 oz. AGW **Obverse:** Bust of Queen Elizabeth II right **Reverse:** Portrait Robert Falcon Scott and compass

| Date | Mintage | F | VF | XF | Unc | BU |
|---|---|---|---|---|---|---|
| 1999 Proof | Est. 5,000 | Value: 170 | | | | |

**1/5 CROWN KM# 962 Weight:** 6.2200 g. **Composition:** 0.9999 Gold .2000 oz. AGW **Subject:** British Blue Cat **Obverse:** Bust of Queen Elizabeth II right **Reverse:** Cat cleaning paw

| Date | Mintage | F | VF | XF | Unc | BU |
|---|---|---|---|---|---|---|
| 1999 | — | — | — | — | 90.00 | — |
| 1999 Proof | — | Value: 92.00 | | | | |
| 1999 U Y2K | Est. 5,000 | — | — | — | 100 | — |

**1/5 CROWN KM# 962a Weight:** 6.2200 g. **Composition:** 0.9995 Platinum .2000 oz. APW **Subject:** British Blue Cat **Obverse:** Bust of Queen Elizabeth II right **Reverse:** Cat cleaning paw

| Date | Mintage | F | VF | XF | Unc | BU |
|---|---|---|---|---|---|---|
| 1999 Proof | — | Value: 130 | | | | |

**1/5 CROWN KM# 975 Weight:** 6.2200 g. **Composition:** 0.9999 Gold .2000 oz. AGW **Series:** The Life and Times of the Queen Mother **Obverse:** Bust of Queen Elizabeth II right **Reverse:** Child in chair

| Date | Mintage | F | VF | XF | Unc | BU |
|---|---|---|---|---|---|---|
| 1999 Proof | Est. 5,000 | Value: 170 | | | | |

**1/5 CROWN KM# 977 Weight:** 6.2200 g. **Composition:** 0.9999 Gold .2000 oz. AGW **Series:** The Life and Times of the Queen Mother **Obverse:** Bust of Queen Elizabeth II right **Reverse:** Engagement portrait

| Date | Mintage | F | VF | XF | Unc | BU |
|---|---|---|---|---|---|---|
| 1999 Proof | Est. 5,000 | Value: 170 | | | | |

**1/5 CROWN KM# 979 Weight:** 6.2200 g. **Composition:** 0.9999 Gold .2000 oz. AGW **Series:** The Life and Times of the Queen Mother **Obverse:** Bust of Queen Elizabeth II right **Reverse:** Honeymoon departure

| Date | Mintage | F | VF | XF | Unc | BU |
|---|---|---|---|---|---|---|
| 1999 Proof | Est. 5,000 | Value: 170 | | | | |

**1/5 CROWN KM# 994 Weight:** 6.2200 g. **Composition:** 0.9999 Gold .2000 oz. AGW **Subject:** The Wedding of HRH Prince Edward **Obverse:** Queen's portrait

**Reverse:** Portrait of Prince Edward

| Date | Mintage | F | VF | XF | Unc | BU |
|---|---|---|---|---|---|---|
| 1999 Proof | Est. 5,000 | Value: 170 | | | | |

**1/5 CROWN KM# 995 Weight:** 6.2200 g. **Composition:** 0.9999 Gold .2000 oz. AGW **Series:** The Life and Times of the Queen Mother **Subject:** The Wedding of HRH The Prince Edward **Obverse:** Bust of Queen Elizabeth II right **Reverse:** Head of Prince Edward

| Date | Mintage | F | VF | XF | Unc | BU |
|---|---|---|---|---|---|---|
| 1999 Proof | Est. 5,000 | Value: 170 | | | | |

**1/5 CROWN KM# 997 Weight:** 6.2200 g. **Composition:** 0.9999 Gold .2000 oz. AGW **Series:** The Life and Times of the Queen Mother **Subject:** The Wedding of HRH The Prince Edward **Obverse:** Bust of Queen Elizabeth II right **Reverse:** Head of Sophie Rhys-Jones

| Date | Mintage | F | VF | XF | Unc | BU |
|---|---|---|---|---|---|---|
| 1999 Proof | Est. 5,000 | Value: 170 | | | | |

**1/5 CROWN KM# 999 Weight:** 6.2200 g. **Composition:** 0.9999 Gold .2000 oz. AGW **Subject:** 30th Anniversary of First Man on the Moon **Obverse:** Bust of Queen Elizabeth II right **Reverse:** Apollo XI, two moon walkers, date

| Date | Mintage | F | VF | XF | Unc | BU |
|---|---|---|---|---|---|---|
| 1999 Proof | Est. 2,000 | Value: 170 | | | | |

**1/5 CROWN KM# 1001 Weight:** 6.2200 g. **Composition:** 0.9999 Gold .2000 oz. AGW **Subject:** 30th Anniversary of First Man on the Moon **Obverse:** Bust of Queen Elizabeth II right **Reverse:** Mariner IX, 1971, space craft orbiting Mars

| Date | Mintage | F | VF | XF | Unc | BU |
|---|---|---|---|---|---|---|
| 1999 Proof | Est. 2,000 | Value: 170 | | | | |

**1/5 CROWN KM# 1003 Weight:** 6.2200 g. **Composition:** 0.9999 Gold .2000 oz. AGW **Subject:** 30th Anniversary of First Man on the Moon **Obverse:** Bust of Queen Elizabeth II right **Reverse:** Apollo-Soyuz link-up

| Date | Mintage | F | VF | XF | Unc | BU |
|---|---|---|---|---|---|---|
| 1999 Proof | Est. 2,000 | Value: 170 | | | | |

**1/5 CROWN KM# 1005 Weight:** 6.2200 g. **Composition:** 0.9999 Gold .2000 oz. AGW **Subject:** 30th Anniversary of First Man on the Moon **Obverse:** Bust of Queen Elizabeth II right **Reverse:** Viking Mars Lander, 1978

| Date | Mintage | F | VF | XF | Unc | BU |
|---|---|---|---|---|---|---|
| 1999 Proof | Est. 2,000 | Value: 170 | | | | |

**1/5 CROWN KM# 1007 Weight:** 6.2200 g. **Composition:** 0.9999 Gold .2000 oz. AGW **Subject:** 30th Anniversary of First Man on the Moon **Obverse:** Bust of Queen Elizabeth II right **Reverse:** Shuttle Columbia, 1981

| Date | Mintage | F | VF | XF | Unc | BU |
|---|---|---|---|---|---|---|
| 1999 Proof | Est. 2,000 | Value: 170 | | | | |

**1/5 CROWN KM# 1009 Weight:** 6.2200 g. **Composition:** 0.9999 Gold .2000 oz. AGW **Subject:** 30th Anniversary of First Man on the Moon **Obverse:** Bust of Queen Elizabeth II right **Reverse:** Mars Pathfinder, 1997

| Date | Mintage | F | VF | XF | Unc | BU |
|---|---|---|---|---|---|---|
| 1999 Proof | Est. 2,000 | Value: 170 | | | | |

**1/5 CROWN KM# 1054 Weight:** 6.2200 g. **Composition:** 0.9999 Gold .2000 oz. AGW **Obverse:** Bust of Queen Elizabeth II right **Reverse:** Scottish kitten **Edge:** Reeded **Size:** 22 mm.

| Date | Mintage | F | VF | XF | Unc | BU |
|---|---|---|---|---|---|---|
| 2000 | — | — | — | — | 109 | — |
| 2000 Proof | — | Value: 175 | | | | |

**1/5 CROWN KM# 1046 Weight:** 6.2200 g. **Composition:** 0.9999 Gold .2000 oz. AGW **Obverse:** Queen's portrait **Reverse:** Prince William's portrait **Edge:** Reeded

| Date | Mintage | F | VF | XF | Unc | BU |
|---|---|---|---|---|---|---|
| 2000 Proof | 5,000 | Value: 175 | | | | |

**1/5 CROWN KM# 1048 Weight:** 6.2200 g. **Composition:** 0.9999 Gold .2000 oz. AGW **Reverse:** Queen Mother's portrait with insert pearl

| Date | Mintage | F | VF | XF | Unc | BU |
|---|---|---|---|---|---|---|
| 2000 Proof | 2,000 | Value: 175 | | | | |

**1/5 CROWN KM# 1054a Weight:** 6.2200 g. **Composition:** 0.9995 Platinum .2000 oz. APW **Reverse:** Scottish kitten

| Date | Mintage | F | VF | XF | Unc | BU |
|---|---|---|---|---|---|---|
| 2000 | — | — | — | — | 188 | — |

**1/5 CROWN KM# 1014 Weight:** 6.2200 g. **Composition:** 0.9999 Gold .2000 oz. AGW **Subject:** Year of the Dragon **Obverse:** Bust of Queen Elizabeth II right **Reverse:** Dragon, Chinese characters

| Date | Mintage | F | VF | XF | Unc | BU |
|---|---|---|---|---|---|---|
| 2000 Proof | Est. 12,000 | Value: 170 | | | | |

**1/5 CROWN KM# 1060 Weight:** 6.2200 g. **Composition:** 0.9999 Gold .2000 oz. AGW **Subject:** Year of the Snake **Obverse:** Queen's portrait **Reverse:** Snake **Edge:** Reeded **Size:** 22 mm.

| Date | Mintage | F | VF | XF | Unc | BU |
|---|---|---|---|---|---|---|
| 2001 Proof | 12,000 | Value: 175 | | | | |

**1/5 CROWN KM# 1069 Weight:** 6.2200 g. **Composition:** 0.9999 Gold .2000 oz. AGW **Subject:** Somali Kittens **Obverse:** Queen's portrait **Reverse:** Two kittens **Edge:** Reeded **Size:** 22 mm.

| Date | Mintage | F | VF | XF | Unc | BU |
|---|---|---|---|---|---|---|
| 2001 | — | — | — | — | 110 | — |
| 2001 Proof | 1,000 | Value: 175 | | | | |

**1/5 CROWN KM# 1069a Weight:** 6.2200 g. **Composition:** 0.9995 Platinum .2000 oz. APW **Reverse:** Somali kittens **Edge:** Reeded **Size:** 22 mm.

| Date | Mintage | F | VF | XF | Unc | BU |
|---|---|---|---|---|---|---|
| 2001 | — | — | — | — | 200 | — |

**1/5 CROWN KM# 1074 Weight:** 6.2200 g. **Composition:** 0.9999 Gold .2000 oz. AGW **Subject:** Queen Mother **Obverse:** Queen's portrait **Reverse:** 1948 Silver wedding anniversary **Edge:** Reeded **Size:** 22 mm.

| Date | Mintage | F | VF | XF | Unc | BU |
|---|---|---|---|---|---|---|
| 2001 Proof | 5,000 | Value: 175 | | | | |

**1/5 CROWN KM# 1075 Weight:** 6.2200 g. **Composition:** 0.9999 Gold .2000 oz. AGW **Subject:** Queen Mother **Obverse:** Queen's portrait **Reverse:** 1948 holding baby Prince Charles **Edge:** Reeded **Size:** 22 mm.

| Date | Mintage | F | VF | XF | Unc | BU |
|---|---|---|---|---|---|---|
| 2001 Proof | 5,000 | Value: 175 | | | | |

**1/5 CROWN KM# 1078 Weight:** 6.2200 g. **Composition:** 0.9999 Gold .2000 oz. AGW **Subject:** Martin Frobisher **Obverse:** Queen's portrait **Reverse:** Portrait, ship and map **Edge:** Reeded **Size:** 22 mm.

| Date | Mintage | F | VF | XF | Unc | BU |
|---|---|---|---|---|---|---|
| 2001 Proof | 5,000 | Value: 175 | | | | |

**1/5 CROWN KM# 1079 Weight:** 6.2200 g. **Composition:** 0.9999 Gold .2000 oz. AGW **Subject:** Ronald Amundsen **Obverse:** Queen's portrait **Reverse:** Portrait, ship and dirigible **Edge:** Reeded **Size:** 22 mm.

| Date | Mintage | F | VF | XF | Unc | BU |
|---|---|---|---|---|---|---|
| 2001 Proof | 5,000 | Value: 175 | | | | |

**1/5 CROWN KM# 1082 Weight:** 6.2200 g. **Composition:** 0.9999 Gold .2000 oz. AGW **Subject:** Queen's 75th Birthday **Obverse:** Queen's portrait **Reverse:** Flower bouquet with a tiny diamond mounted on the bow of the ribbon **Edge:** Reeded **Size:** 22 mm.

| Date | Mintage | F | VF | XF | Unc | BU |
|---|---|---|---|---|---|---|
| 2001 Proof | 2,000 | Value: 299 | | | | |

**1/5 CROWN KM# 1100 Weight:** 6.2200 g. **Composition:** 0.9999 Gold .2000 oz. AGW **Subject:** Year of the Horse **Obverse:** Queen's portrait **Reverse:** Two horses **Edge:** Reeded **Size:** 22 mm.

| Date | Mintage | F | VF | XF | Unc | BU |
|---|---|---|---|---|---|---|
| 2002 Proof | 12,000 | Value: 175 | | | | |

**1/4 CROWN KM# 669 Ring Weight:** 3.8880 g. **Ring Composition:** 0.9950 Platinum .1244 oz. APW **Center Weight:** 3.8880 g. **Center Composition:** 0.9990 Gold .1249 oz. AGW **Series:** Legend of King Arthur **Obverse:** Bust of Queen Elizabeth II right **Reverse:** King Arthur with sword and orb

| Date | Mintage | F | VF | XF | Unc | BU |
|---|---|---|---|---|---|---|
| 1996 Proof | Est. 5,000 | Value: 195 | | | | |

**1/4 CROWN KM# 670 Ring Weight:** 3.8880 g. **Ring Composition:** 0.9950 Platinum .1244 oz. APW **Center Weight:**

3.8880 g. **Center Composition:** 0.9990 Gold .1249 oz. AGW **Series:** Legend of King Arthur **Obverse:** Bust of Queen Elizabeth II right **Reverse:** Queen Guinevere

| Date | Mintage | F | VF | XF | Unc | BU |
|---|---|---|---|---|---|---|
| 1996 Proof | Est. 5,000 | Value: 195 | | | | |

**1/4 CROWN** **KM# 671** **Ring Weight:** 3.8880 g. **Ring Composition:** 0.9950 Platinum .1244 oz. APW **Center Weight:** 3.8880 g. **Center Composition:** 0.9990 Gold .1249 oz. AGW **Series:** Legend of King Arthur **Obverse:** Bust of Queen Elizabeth II right **Reverse:** Sir Lancelot

| Date | Mintage | F | VF | XF | Unc | BU |
|---|---|---|---|---|---|---|
| 1996 Proof | Est. 5,000 | Value: 195 | | | | |

**1/4 CROWN** **KM# 672** **Ring Weight:** 3.8880 g. **Ring Composition:** 0.9950 Platinum .1244 oz. APW **Center Weight:** 3.8880 g. **Center Composition:** 0.9990 Gold .1249 oz. AGW **Series:** Legend of King Arthur **Obverse:** Bust of Queen Elizabeth II right **Reverse:** Merlin

| Date | Mintage | F | VF | XF | Unc | BU |
|---|---|---|---|---|---|---|
| 1996 Proof | Est. 5,000 | Value: 195 | | | | |

**1/4 CROWN** **KM# 673** **Ring Weight:** 3.8880 g. **Ring Composition:** 0.9950 Platinum .1244 oz. APW **Center Weight:** 3.8880 g. **Center Composition:** 0.9990 Gold .1249 oz. AGW **Series:** Legend of King Arthur **Obverse:** Bust of Queen Elizabeth II right **Reverse:** Camelot Castle

| Date | Mintage | F | VF | XF | Unc | BU |
|---|---|---|---|---|---|---|
| 1996 Proof | Est. 5,000 | Value: 195 | | | | |

**1/4 CROWN** **KM# 674** **Center Weight:** 3.8880 g. **Center Composition:** 0.9950 Platinum .1244 oz. APW **Series:** Legend of King Arthur **Obverse:** Bust of Queen Elizabeth II right **Reverse:** King Arthur with sword and orb

| Date | Mintage | F | VF | XF | Unc | BU |
|---|---|---|---|---|---|---|
| 1996 Proof | Est. 5,000 | Value: 195 | | | | |

**1/4 CROWN** **KM# 675** **Center Weight:** 3.8880 g. **Center Composition:** 0.9950 Platinum .1244 oz. APW **Series:** Legend of King Arthur **Obverse:** Bust of Queen Elizabeth II right **Reverse:** Queen Guinevere

| Date | Mintage | F | VF | XF | Unc | BU |
|---|---|---|---|---|---|---|
| 1996 Proof | Est. 5,000 | Value: 195 | | | | |

**1/4 CROWN** **KM# 676** **Center Weight:** 3.8880 g. **Center Composition:** 0.9950 Platinum .1244 oz. APW **Series:** Legend of King Arthur **Obverse:** Bust of Queen Elizabeth II right **Reverse:** Sir Lancelot

| Date | Mintage | F | VF | XF | Unc | BU |
|---|---|---|---|---|---|---|
| 1996 Proof | Est. 5,000 | Value: 195 | | | | |

**1/4 CROWN** **KM# 677** **Center Weight:** 3.8880 g. **Center Composition:** 0.9950 Platinum .1244 oz. APW **Series:** Legend of King Arthur **Obverse:** Bust of Queen Elizabeth II right **Reverse:** Merlin

| Date | Mintage | F | VF | XF | Unc | BU |
|---|---|---|---|---|---|---|
| 1996 Proof | Est. 5,000 | Value: 195 | | | | |

**1/4 CROWN** **KM# 678** **Center Weight:** 3.8880 g. **Center Composition:** 0.9950 Platinum .1244 oz. APW **Series:** Legend of King Arthur **Obverse:** Bust of Queen Elizabeth II right **Reverse:** Camelot Castle

| Date | Mintage | F | VF | XF | Unc | BU |
|---|---|---|---|---|---|---|
| 1996 Proof | Est. 5,000 | Value: 195 | | | | |

**1/2 CROWN** **KM# 187** **Weight:** 15.5500 g. **Composition:** 0.9990 Gold .5000 oz. AGW **Subject:** U. S. Constitution **Obverse:** Bust of Queen Elizabeth II right **Reverse:** Bust of American presidents

| Date | Mintage | F | VF | XF | Unc | BU |
|---|---|---|---|---|---|---|
| 1987 Proof | 12,000 | Value: 375 | | | | |

**1/2 CROWN** **KM# 187a** **Weight:** 15.5500 g. **Composition:** 0.9990 Platinum .5000 oz. APW **Subject:** U. S. Constitution **Obverse:** Bust of Queen Elizabeth II right **Reverse:** Bust of American presidents

| Date | Mintage | F | VF | XF | Unc | BU |
|---|---|---|---|---|---|---|
| 1987 Proof | 250 | Value: 600 | | | | |

**1/2 CROWN** **KM# 238** **Weight:** 15.5500 g. **Composition:** 0.9990 Gold .5000 oz. AGW **Obverse:** Bust of Queen Elizabeth II right **Reverse:** Manx cat

| Date | Mintage | F | VF | XF | Unc | BU |
|---|---|---|---|---|---|---|
| 1988 | 6,375 | — | — | — | 235 | — |
| 1988 Proof | 5,000 | Value: 255 | | | | |

**1/2 CROWN** **KM# 286** **Weight:** 16.4000 g. **Composition:** 0.9480 Gold .5000 oz. AGW **Subject:** Australian Bicentennial **Obverse:** Bust of Queen Elizabeth II right **Reverse:** Cockatoo

| Date | Mintage | F | VF | XF | Unc | BU |
|---|---|---|---|---|---|---|
| 1988 Proof | Est. 7,500 | Value: 250 | | | | |

**1/2 CROWN** **KM# 287** **Weight:** 16.4000 g. **Composition:** 0.9480 Gold .5000 oz. AGW **Subject:** Australian Bicentennial **Obverse:** Bust of Queen Elizabeth II right **Reverse:** Koala

| Date | Mintage | F | VF | XF | Unc | BU |
|---|---|---|---|---|---|---|
| 1988 Proof | Est. 7,500 | Value: 250 | | | | |

**1/2 CROWN** **KM# 288** **Weight:** 16.4000 g. **Composition:** 0.9480 Gold .5000 oz. AGW **Subject:** Australian Bicentennial **Obverse:** Bust of Queen Elizabeth II right **Reverse:** Duckbill platypus

| Date | Mintage | F | VF | XF | Unc | BU |
|---|---|---|---|---|---|---|
| 1988 Proof | Est. 7,500 | Value: 250 | | | | |

**1/2 CROWN** **KM# 289** **Weight:** 16.4000 g. **Composition:** 0.9480 Gold .5000 oz. AGW **Subject:** Australian Bicentennial **Obverse:** Bust of Queen Elizabeth II right **Reverse:** Kangaroo

| Date | Mintage | F | VF | XF | Unc | BU |
|---|---|---|---|---|---|---|
| 1988 Proof | Est. 7,500 | Value: 250 | | | | |

**1/2 CROWN** **KM# 359** **Weight:** 15.5500 g. **Composition:** 0.9990 Platinum .5000 oz. APW **Subject:** Australian Bicentennial **Obverse:** Bust of Queen Elizabeth II right **Reverse:** Cockatoo

| Date | Mintage | F | VF | XF | Unc | BU |
|---|---|---|---|---|---|---|
| 1988 Proof | — | Value: 450 | | | | |

**1/2 CROWN** **KM# 360** **Weight:** 15.5500 g. **Composition:** 0.9990 Platinum .5000 oz. APW **Subject:** Australian Bicentennial **Obverse:** Bust of Queen Elizabeth II right **Reverse:** Koala

| Date | Mintage | F | VF | XF | Unc | BU |
|---|---|---|---|---|---|---|
| 1988 Proof | — | Value: 450 | | | | |

**1/2 CROWN** **KM# 361** **Weight:** 15.5500 g. **Composition:** 0.9990 Platinum .5000 oz. APW **Subject:** Australian Bicentennial **Obverse:** Bust of Queen Elizabeth II right **Reverse:** Duckbill platypus

| Date | Mintage | F | VF | XF | Unc | BU |
|---|---|---|---|---|---|---|
| 1988 Proof | — | Value: 450 | | | | |

**1/2 CROWN** **KM# 362** **Weight:** 15.5500 g. **Composition:** 0.9990 Platinum .5000 oz. APW **Subject:** Australian Bicentennial **Obverse:** Bust of Queen Elizabeth II right **Reverse:** Kangaroo

| Date | Mintage | F | VF | XF | Unc | BU |
|---|---|---|---|---|---|---|
| 1988 Proof | — | Value: 450 | | | | |

**1/2 CROWN** **KM# 363** **Weight:** 15.5500 g. **Composition:** 0.9990 Platinum .5000 oz. APW **Subject:** Australian Bicentennial **Obverse:** Bust of Queen Elizabeth II right **Reverse:** Dingo Dog

| Date | Mintage | F | VF | XF | Unc | BU |
|---|---|---|---|---|---|---|
| 1988 Proof | — | Value: 450 | | | | |

**1/2 CROWN** **KM# 255** **Weight:** 16.4000 g. **Composition:** 0.9480 Gold .5000 oz. AGW **Obverse:** Bust of Queen Elizabeth II right **Reverse:** Persian cat

| Date | Mintage | F | VF | XF | Unc | BU |
|---|---|---|---|---|---|---|
| 1989 | — | — | — | — | 300 | — |
| 1989 Proof | — | Value: 305 | | | | |

**1/2 CROWN** **KM# 470** **Weight:** 15.5500 g. **Composition:** 0.9990 Platinum .5000 oz. APW **Obverse:** Bust of Queen Elizabeth II right **Reverse:** Persian cat

| Date | Mintage | F | VF | XF | Unc | BU |
|---|---|---|---|---|---|---|
| 1989 | — — | — | — | — | BV+20% | — |

**1/2 CROWN** **KM# 280** **Weight:** 16.4000 g. **Composition:** 0.9480 Gold .5000 oz. AGW **Obverse:** Bust of Queen Elizabeth II right **Reverse:** Alley cat

| Date | Mintage | F | VF | XF | Unc | BU |
|---|---|---|---|---|---|---|
| 1990 | — | — | — | — | 300 | — |
| 1990 Proof | — | Value: 310 | | | | |

**1/2 CROWN** **KM# 297** **Weight:** 15.5500 g. **Composition:** 0.9990 Gold .5000 oz. AGW **Obverse:** Bust of Queen Elizabeth II right **Reverse:** Norwegian cat

| Date | Mintage | F | VF | XF | Unc | BU |
|---|---|---|---|---|---|---|
| 1991 | — | — | — | — | 250 | — |
| 1991 Proof | — | Value: 260 | | | | |

**1/2 CROWN** **KM# 325** **Center Weight:** 15.5500 g. **Center Composition:** 0.9990 Gold .5000 oz. AGW **Subject:** America's Cup **Obverse:** Bust of Queen Elizabeth II right **Reverse:** Sailboat

| Date | Mintage | F | VF | XF | Unc | BU |
|---|---|---|---|---|---|---|
| 1992 Proof like | 2,000 | — | — | — | 345 | — |

**1/2 CROWN** **KM# 331** **Weight:** 15.5500 g. **Composition:** 0.9990 Gold .5000 oz. AGW **Obverse:** Bust of Queen Elizabeth II right **Reverse:** Siamese cat

| Date | Mintage | F | VF | XF | Unc | BU |
|---|---|---|---|---|---|---|
| 1992 | — | — | — | — | 250 | — |
| 1992 Proof | — | Value: 260 | | | | |

**1/2 CROWN** **KM# 341** **Weight:** 15.5500 g. **Composition:** 0.9990 Gold .5000 oz. AGW **Subject:** Year of the Rooster **Obverse:** Bust of Queen Elizabeth II right **Reverse:** Cockerel in inner circle

| Date | Mintage | F | VF | XF | Unc | BU |
|---|---|---|---|---|---|---|
| 1993 Proof | Est. 5,000 | Value: 365 | | | | |

**1/2 CROWN** **KM# 352** **Weight:** 15.5500 g. **Composition:** 0.9990 Gold .5000 oz. AGW **Obverse:** Bust of Queen Elizabeth II right **Reverse:** Maine coon cat

| Date | Mintage | F | VF | XF | Unc | BU |
|---|---|---|---|---|---|---|
| 1993 | — | — | — | — | 225 | — |
| 1993 Proof | — | Value: 235 | | | | |

**1/2 CROWN** **KM# 379** **Weight:** 15.5500 g. **Composition:** 0.9990 Gold .5000 oz. AGW **Obverse:** Bust of Queen Elizabeth II right **Reverse:** Japanese bobtail cat

| Date | Mintage | F | VF | XF | Unc | BU |
|---|---|---|---|---|---|---|
| 1994 | — | — | — | — | 225 | — |
| 1994 Proof | — | Value: 235 | | | | |

**1/2 CROWN** **KM# 405** **Weight:** 15.5500 g. **Composition:** 0.9990 Gold .5000 oz. AGW **Obverse:** Bust of Queen Elizabeth II right **Reverse:** Pekingese dog

| Date | Mintage | F | VF | XF | Unc | BU |
|---|---|---|---|---|---|---|
| 1994 Proof | 5,000 | Value: 360 | | | | |

**1/2 CROWN** **KM# 476** **Weight:** 15.5500 g. **Composition:** 0.9990 Platinum .5000 oz. APW **Obverse:** Bust of Queen Elizabeth II right **Reverse:** Japanese bobtail cat

| Date | Mintage | F | VF | XF | Unc | BU |
|---|---|---|---|---|---|---|
| 1994 Proof | — | — | — | — | — | — |

**1/2 CROWN** **KM# 445** **Weight:** 15.5500 g. **Composition:** 0.9990 Gold .5000 oz. AGW **Obverse:** Bust of Queen Elizabeth II right **Reverse:** Turkish cat looking back

| Date | Mintage | F | VF | XF | Unc | BU |
|---|---|---|---|---|---|---|
| 1995 U | — | — | — | — | 225 | — |
| 1995 Proof | — | Value: 235 | | | | |

**1/2 CROWN** **KM# 452** **Weight:** 15.5500 g. **Composition:** 0.9990 Gold .5000 oz. AGW **Subject:** Year of the Pig **Obverse:** Bust of Queen Elizabeth II right **Reverse:** Sow with piglets

| Date | Mintage | F | VF | XF | Unc | BU |
|---|---|---|---|---|---|---|
| 1995 Proof | Est. 5,000 | Value: 360 | | | | |

**1/2 CROWN** **KM# 481** **Weight:** 15.5500 g. **Composition:** 0.9990 Platinum .5000 oz. APW **Obverse:** Bust of Queen Elizabeth II right **Reverse:** Turkish cat

| Date | Mintage | F | VF | XF | Unc | BU |
|---|---|---|---|---|---|---|
| 1995 Proof | — | — | — | — | — | — |

**1/2 CROWN** **KM# 731** **Center Weight:** 15.5517 g. **Center Composition:** 0.9999 Gold .5000 oz. AGW **Subject:** Year of the Rat **Obverse:** Bust of Queen Elizabeth II right **Reverse:** Rat

| Date | Mintage | F | VF | XF | Unc | BU |
|---|---|---|---|---|---|---|
| 1996 Proof | — | — | — | — | — | — |

**1/2 CROWN** **KM# 619** **Weight:** 15.5500 g. **Composition:** 0.9990 Gold .5000 oz. AGW **Obverse:** Bust of Queen Elizabeth II right **Reverse:** Burmese cat

| Date | Mintage | F | VF | XF | Unc | BU |
|---|---|---|---|---|---|---|
| 1996 U | — | — | — | — | 225 | — |
| 1996 Proof | — | Value: 235 | | | | |

**1/2 CROWN** **KM# 620** **Weight:** 15.5500 g. **Composition:** 0.9990 Platinum .5000 oz. APW **Obverse:** Bust of Queen Elizabeth II right **Reverse:** Burmese cat

| Date | Mintage | F | VF | XF | Unc | BU |
|---|---|---|---|---|---|---|
| 1996 U | — | — | — | — | —BV+20% | — |

**1/2 CROWN** **KM# 724** **Weight:** 15.5517 g. **Composition:** 0.9999 Gold .5000 oz. AGW **Subject:** Year of the Ox **Obverse:** Bust of Queen Elizabeth II right **Reverse:** Ox laying down

| Date | Mintage | F | VF | XF | Unc | BU |
|---|---|---|---|---|---|---|
| 1996 Proof | Est. 6,000 | Value: 360 | | | | |

**1/2 CROWN** **KM# 767a** **Weight:** 15.5500 g. **Composition:** 0.9990 Silver .5 oz. ASW **Obverse:** Bust of Queen Elizabeth II right **Reverse:** Portrait of Fridtjof Nansen, map and ship "The Fram" **Note:** Similar to 1 Crown, KM#768

| Date | Mintage | F | VF | XF | Unc | BU |
|---|---|---|---|---|---|---|
| 1997 Proof | — | Value: 30.00 | | | | |

**1/2 CROWN** **KM# 764** **Weight:** 15.5517 g. **Composition:** 0.9999 Gold .5000 oz. AGW **Obverse:** Bust of Queen Elizabeth II right **Reverse:** Portrait of Leiv Eiriksson and Viking ship with map sail

| Date | Mintage | F | VF | XF | Unc | BU |
|---|---|---|---|---|---|---|
| 1997 Proof | Est. 2,500 | Value: 360 | | | | |

**1/2 CROWN** **KM# 767** **Weight:** 15.5517 g. **Composition:** 0.9999 Gold .5000 oz. AGW **Obverse:** Bust of Queen Elizabeth II right **Reverse:** Portrait of Fridtjof Nansen, map and ship "The Fram"

| Date | Mintage | F | VF | XF | Unc | BU |
|---|---|---|---|---|---|---|
| 1997 Proof | Est. 2,500 | Value: 360 | | | | |

**1/2 CROWN** **KM# 773** **Weight:** 15.5517 g. **Composition:** 0.9999 Gold .5000 oz. AGW **Obverse:** Bust of Queen Elizabeth II right **Reverse:** Long-Haired-Smoke cat

| Date | Mintage | F | VF | XF | Unc | BU |
|---|---|---|---|---|---|---|
| 1997 | — | — | — | — | 195 | — |
| 1997 Proof | — | Value: 200 | | | | |

**1/2 CROWN** **KM# 791** **Weight:** 15.5517 g. **Composition:** 0.9999 Gold .5000 oz. AGW **Subject:** History of the Cat **Obverse:** Bust of Queen Elizabeth II right **Reverse:** Cat stalking a spider

| Date | Mintage | F | VF | XF | Unc | BU |
|---|---|---|---|---|---|---|
| 1997 Proof | Est. 2,500 | Value: 360 | | | | |

**1/2 CROWN** **KM# 815** **Weight:** 15.5000 g. **Composition:** 0.9999 Gold .5000 oz. AGW **Subject:** Year of the Tiger **Obverse:** Bust of Queen Elizabeth II right **Reverse:** Tiger

| Date | Mintage | F | VF | XF | Unc | BU |
|---|---|---|---|---|---|---|
| 1998 Proof | Est. 6,000 | Value: 345 | | | | |

**1/2 CROWN** **KM# 856** **Weight:** 15.5517 g. **Composition:** 0.9999 Gold .5000 oz. AGW **Obverse:** Bust of Queen Elizabeth II right **Reverse:** Birman cat

| Date | Mintage | F | VF | XF | Unc | BU |
|---|---|---|---|---|---|---|
| 1998 | — | — | — | — | 195 | — |
| 1998 Proof | 1,000 | Value: 200 | | | | |

**1/2 CROWN** **KM# 856a** **Weight:** 15.5517 g. **Composition:** 0.9995 Platinum .5000 oz. APW **Obverse:** Bust of Queen Elizabeth II right **Reverse:** Birman cat

| Date | Mintage | F | VF | XF | Unc | BU |
|---|---|---|---|---|---|---|
| 1998 Reported not confirmed | — | — | — | — | — | — |

**1/2 CROWN** **KM# 862** **Weight:** 15.5517 g. **Composition:** 0.9999 Gold .5000 oz. AGW **Subject:** History of the Cat **Obverse:** Bust of Queen Elizabeth II right **Reverse:** Egyptain Mau cat with earring

| Date | Mintage | F | VF | XF | Unc | BU |
|---|---|---|---|---|---|---|
| 1998 Proof | Est. 250 | Value: 375 | | | | |

**1/2 CROWN** **KM# 951** **Weight:** 15.5517 g. **Composition:** 0.9999 Gold .5000 oz. AGW **Subject:** Year of the Rabbit **Obverse:** Bust of Queen Elizabeth II right **Reverse:** Two rabbits

| Date | Mintage | F | VF | XF | Unc | BU |
|---|---|---|---|---|---|---|
| 1999 Proof | Est. 6,000 | Value: 345 | | | | |

**1/2 CROWN** **KM# A994** **Ring Weight:** 9.0000 g. **Ring Composition:** 0.9999 Gold .2893 oz. AGW **Center Composition:** Titanium **Subject:** Millennium **Obverse:** Rank-Broadley portrait of Queen Elizabeth II **Reverse:** 24-hour clock with world globe center

| Date | Mintage | F | VF | XF | Unc | BU |
|---|---|---|---|---|---|---|
| 2000 Proof | 10,000 | Value: 175 | | | | |

**1/2 CROWN** **KM# 964** **Weight:** 15.5517 g. **Composition:** 0.9999 Gold .5000 oz. AGW **Subject:** British Blue cat **Obverse:** Bust of Queen Elizabeth II right **Reverse:** Cat cleaning paw

| Date | Mintage | F | VF | XF | Unc | BU |
|---|---|---|---|---|---|---|
| 1999 | — | — | — | — | 195 | — |
| 1999 Proof | — | Value: 200 | | | | |

**1/2 CROWN** **KM# 964a** **Weight:** 15.5518 g. **Composition:** 0.9995 Platinum .5000 oz. APW **Subject:** British Blue cat **Obverse:** Bust of Queen Elizabeth II right **Reverse:** Cat cleaning paw

| Date | Mintage | F | VF | XF | Unc | BU |
|---|---|---|---|---|---|---|
| 1999 Reported, not confirmed | — | — | — | — | — | — |

**1/2 CROWN** **KM# 1084** **Ring Weight:** 9.0000 g. **Ring Composition:** 0.9990 Gold .2891 oz. AGW **Center Weight:** 2.0000 g. **Center Composition:** 0.9900 Titanium **Subject:** Greenwich Meridian Time Clock **Obverse:** Queen's portrait **Reverse:** Greenwich Meridian Line on map clock face **Edge:** Reeded **Size:** 32.25 mm.

| Date | Mintage | F | VF | XF | Unc | BU |
|---|---|---|---|---|---|---|
| 2000 Proof | 10,000 | Value: 200 | | | | |

**1/2 CROWN** **KM# 1055** **Weight:** 15.5517 g. **Composition:** 0.9999 Gold .5000 oz. AGW **Subject:** Scottish Fold Kitten **Obverse:** Bust of Queen Elizabeth II right **Reverse:** Kitten playing with world **Edge:** Reeded **Size:** 30 mm.

| Date | Mintage | F | VF | XF | Unc | BU |
|---|---|---|---|---|---|---|
| 2000 | — | — | — | — | 250 | — |
| 2000 Proof | — | Value: 350 | | | | |

**1/2 CROWN** **KM# 1015** **Weight:** 15.5517 g. **Composition:** 0.9999 Gold .5000 oz. AGW **Subject:** Year of the Dragon **Obverse:** Bust of Queen Elizabeth II right **Reverse:** Dragon, Chinese characters

| Date | Mintage | F | VF | XF | Unc | BU |
|---|---|---|---|---|---|---|
| 2000 Proof | Est. 6,000 | Value: 345 | | | | |

**1/2 CROWN** **KM# 1061** **Weight:** 15.5517 g. **Composition:** 0.9999 Gold .5000 oz. AGW **Subject:** Year of the Snake **Obverse:** Queen's portrait **Reverse:** Snake **Edge:** Reeded **Size:** 30 mm.

| Date | Mintage | F | VF | XF | Unc | BU |
|---|---|---|---|---|---|---|
| 2001 Proof | 6,000 | Value: 340 | | | | |

**1/2 CROWN** **KM# 1070** **Weight:** 15.5517 g. **Composition:** 0.9999 Gold .5000 oz. AGW **Subject:** Somali Kittens **Obverse:** Queen's portrait **Reverse:** Two kittens **Edge:** Reeded **Size:** 30 mm.

| Date | Mintage | F | VF | XF | Unc | BU |
|---|---|---|---|---|---|---|
| 2001 | — | — | — | — | 250 | — |
| 2001 Proof | 1,000 | Value: 340 | | | | |

**1/2 CROWN** **KM# 1071** **Weight:** 15.5517 g. **Composition:** 0.9995 Platinum .5000 oz. APW **Subject:** Somali Kittens **Obverse:** Queen's portrait **Reverse:** Two kittens **Edge:** Reeded **Size:** 27 mm.

| Date | Mintage | F | VF | XF | Unc | BU |
|---|---|---|---|---|---|---|
| 2001 | — | — | — | — | 450 | — |

**1/2 CROWN** **KM# 1101** **Weight:** 15.5500 g. **Composition:** 0.9999 Gold .4999 oz. AGW **Subject:** Year of the Horse **Obverse:** Queen's portrait **Reverse:** Two horses **Edge:** Reeded **Size:** 30 mm.

| Date | Mintage | F | VF | XF | Unc | BU |
|---|---|---|---|---|---|---|
| 2002 Proof | 6,000 | Value: 340 | | | | |

**CROWN** **KM# 18** **Composition:** Copper-Nickel **Obverse:** Bust of Queen Elizabeth II right **Reverse:** Manx cat

| Date | Mintage | F | VF | XF | Unc | BU |
|---|---|---|---|---|---|---|
| 1970 | 150,000 | — | — | — | 7.50 | — |

**CROWN** **KM# 18a** **Weight:** 28.2800 g. **Composition:** 0.9250 Silver .8411 oz. ASW **Obverse:** Bust of Queen Elizabeth II right **Reverse:** Manx cat

| Date | Mintage | F | VF | XF | Unc | BU |
|---|---|---|---|---|---|---|
| 1970 Proof | 11,000 | Value: 16.50 | | | | |

**CROWN** **KM# 30** **Composition:** Copper-Nickel **Subject:** Centenary - Birth of Winston Churchill **Obverse:** Bust of Queen Elizabeth II right **Reverse:** Bust of Winston Churchill **Note:** Most of this issue are double die

| Date | Mintage | F | VF | XF | Unc | BU |
|---|---|---|---|---|---|---|
| 1974 | 45,000 | — | — | — | 2.50 | — |

**CROWN** **KM# 30a** **Weight:** 28.2800 g. **Composition:** 0.9250 Silver .8411 oz. ASW **Obverse:** Bust of Queen Elizabeth II right **Reverse:** Bust of Winston Churchill

| Date | Mintage | F | VF | XF | Unc | BU |
|---|---|---|---|---|---|---|
| 1974 | — | — | — | — | 8.00 | — |
| 1974 Proof | 30,000 | Value: 9.50 | | | | |

**CROWN** **KM# 37** **Composition:** Copper-Nickel **Subject:** Bicentenary of American Independence **Obverse:** Bust of Queen Elizabeth II right **Reverse:** Bust of George Washington left **Note:** Doubled die strike exists.

| Date | Mintage | F | VF | XF | Unc | BU |
|---|---|---|---|---|---|---|
| 1976 | 50,000 | — | — | — | 2.50 | — |

**CROWN** KM# 37a **Weight:** 28.2800 g. **Composition:** 0.9250 Silver .8411 oz. ASW **Subject:** Bicentenary of American Independence **Obverse:** Bust of Queen Elizabeth II right **Reverse:** Bust of George Washington left

| Date | Mintage | F | VF | XF | Unc | BU |
|---|---|---|---|---|---|---|
| 1976 | — | — | — | — | 8.00 | — |
| 1976 Proof | 30,000 | Value: 10.00 | | | | |

**CROWN** KM# 38 **Composition:** Copper-Nickel **Obverse:** Bust of Queen Elizabeth II right **Reverse:** Horse drawn tram **Note:** Doubled die strike exists.

| Date | Mintage | F | VF | XF | Unc | BU |
|---|---|---|---|---|---|---|
| 1976 | 50,000 | — | — | — | 7.50 | — |

**CROWN** KM# 38a **Weight:** 28.2800 g. **Composition:** 0.9250 Silver .8411 oz. ASW **Obverse:** Bust of Queen Elizabeth II right **Reverse:** Horse drawn tram

| Date | Mintage | F | VF | XF | Unc | BU |
|---|---|---|---|---|---|---|
| 1976 | — | — | — | — | 12.50 | — |
| 1976 Proof | 30,000 | Value: 15.00 | | | | |

**CROWN** KM# 41a **Weight:** 28.2800 g. **Composition:** 0.9250 Silver .8411 oz. ASW **Subject:** Silver Jubilee **Obverse:** Bust of Queen Elizabeth II right **Reverse:** Triskles at center, three St. Edward's crowns around

| Date | Mintage | F | VF | XF | Unc | BU |
|---|---|---|---|---|---|---|
| ND(1977) | — | — | — | — | 8.00 | — |
| ND(1977) Proof | 30,000 | Value: 10.00 | | | | |
| ND(1977) | — | — | — | — | 8.00 | — |
| ND(1977) Proof | 30,000 | Value: 10.00 | | | | |

**CROWN** KM# 41 **Composition:** Copper-Nickel **Subject:** Silver Jubilee **Obverse:** Bust of Queen Elizabeth II right **Reverse:** Triskles at center, three St. Edward's Crowns around

| Date | Mintage | F | VF | XF | Unc | BU |
|---|---|---|---|---|---|---|
| ND(1977) | — | — | — | — | 4.50 | — |
| ND(1977) | — | — | — | — | 4.50 | — |

**CROWN** KM# 42 **Composition:** Copper-Nickel **Subject:** Queen's Jubilee Appeal **Obverse:** Bust of Queen Elizabeth II right **Reverse:** Crown

| Date | Mintage | F | VF | XF | Unc | BU |
|---|---|---|---|---|---|---|
| 1977 | — | — | — | — | 2.50 | — |

**Note:** Wide and narrow rims exist

**CROWN** KM# 42a **Weight:** 28.2800 g. **Composition:** 0.9250 Silver .8411 oz. ASW **Subject:** Queen's Jubilee Appeal **Obverse:** Bust of Queen Elizabeth II right **Reverse:** Crown

| Date | Mintage | F | VF | XF | Unc | BU |
|---|---|---|---|---|---|---|
| 1977 | 70,000 | — | — | — | 8.00 | — |
| 1977 Proof | 30,000 | Value: 10.00 | | | | |

**CROWN** KM# 43 **Composition:** Copper-Nickel **Subject:** 25th Anniversary of Coronation **Obverse:** Bust of Queen Elizabeth II right **Reverse:** Male and female peregrine falcons **Note:** For mule of Isle of Man obverse with Ascension Island KM#1 reverse, refer to Ascension Island listings.

| Date | Mintage | F | VF | XF | Unc | BU |
|---|---|---|---|---|---|---|
| 1978 | — | — | — | — | 5.00 | — |
| 1978 Proof | — | Value: 7.50 | | | | |

**CROWN** KM# 43a **Weight:** 28.2800 g. **Composition:** 0.9250 Silver .8411 oz. ASW **Subject:** 25th Anniversary of Coronation **Obverse:** Bust of Queen Elizabeth II right **Reverse:** Male and female peregrine falcons

| Date | Mintage | F | VF | XF | Unc | BU |
|---|---|---|---|---|---|---|
| 1978 | 70,000 | — | — | — | 10.00 | — |
| 1978 Proof | 30,000 | Value: 15.00 | | | | |

**CROWN** KM# 45 **Composition:** Copper-Nickel **Subject:** 30th Anniversary of Manx Coinage **Obverse:** Bust of Queen Elizabeth II right **Reverse:** Nine different coins in circle

| Date | Mintage | F | VF | XF | Unc | BU |
|---|---|---|---|---|---|---|
| 1979 | — | — | — | — | 3.00 | — |
| 1979 Proof | — | Value: 7.50 | | | | |

**CROWN** KM# 49 **Weight:** 28.2800 g. **Composition:** Copper-Nickel **Subject:** Millennium of Tynwald **Obverse:** Bust of Queen Elizabeth II right **Reverse:** Royalist soldier and English Man-of-War

| Date | Mintage | F | VF | XF | Unc | BU |
|---|---|---|---|---|---|---|
| 1979 | 100,000 | — | — | — | 6.50 | — |

**CROWN** KM# 45a **Weight:** 28.2800 g. **Composition:** 0.9250 Silver .8411 oz. ASW **Subject:** 300th Anniversary of Manx Coinage **Obverse:** Bust of Queen Elizabeth II right **Reverse:** Nine coins in circle

| Date | Mintage | F | VF | XF | Unc | BU |
|---|---|---|---|---|---|---|
| 1979 | 70,000 | — | — | — | 10.00 | — |
| 1979 Proof | 30,000 | Value: 12.00 | | | | |

**CROWN** KM# 46 **Composition:** Copper-Nickel **Subject:** Millennium of Tynwald **Obverse:** Bust of Queen Elizabeth II right **Reverse:** Viking longship, Godred Cravan

| Date | Mintage | F | VF | XF | Unc | BU |
|---|---|---|---|---|---|---|
| 1979 | 100,000 | — | — | — | 3.50 | — |

**CROWN** KM# 46a **Weight:** 28.2800 g. **Composition:** 0.9250 Silver .8411 oz. ASW **Subject:** Millennium of Tynwald **Obverse:** Bust of Queen Elizabeth II right **Reverse:** Viking longship, Godfred Cravan

| Date | Mintage | F | VF | XF | Unc | BU |
|---|---|---|---|---|---|---|
| 1979 | 25,000 | — | — | — | 12.00 | — |
| 1979 Proof | 10,000 | Value: 15.00 | | | | |

**CROWN** KM# 46b **Weight:** 43.0000 g. **Composition:** 0.9170 Gold 1.2678 oz. AGW **Subject:** Millennium of Tynwald **Obverse:** Bust of Queen Elizabeth II right **Reverse:** Viking longship

| Date | Mintage | F | VF | XF | Unc | BU |
|---|---|---|---|---|---|---|
| 1979 Proof | 300 | Value: 700 | | | | |

**CROWN** KM# 46c **Weight:** 52.0000 g. **Composition:** 0.9500 Platinum 1.5884 oz. APW **Subject:** Millennium of Tynwald **Obverse:** Bust of Queen Elizabeth II right **Reverse:** Viking longship

| Date | Mintage | F | VF | XF | Unc | BU |
|---|---|---|---|---|---|---|
| 1979 Proof | 100 | Value: 1,200 | | | | |

**CROWN** KM# 47 **Composition:** Copper-Nickel **Subject:** Millennium of Tynwald **Obverse:** Bust of Queen Elizabeth II right **Reverse:** Englsih cog, Castle Rushen

| Date | Mintage | F | VF | XF | Unc | BU |
|---|---|---|---|---|---|---|
| 1979 | 100,000 | — | — | — | 6.50 | — |

**CROWN** KM# 47a **Weight:** 28.2800 g. **Composition:** 0.9250 Silver .8411 oz. ASW **Subject:** Millennium of Tynwald **Obverse:** Bust of Queen Elizabeth II right **Reverse:** Englsih cog, Castle Rushen

| Date | Mintage | F | VF | XF | Unc | BU |
|---|---|---|---|---|---|---|
| 1979 | 25,000 | — | — | — | 9.00 | — |
| 1979 Proof | 10,000 | Value: 12.50 | | | | |

**CROWN** KM# 47b **Weight:** 43.0000 g. **Composition:** 0.9170 Gold 1.2678 oz. AGW **Subject:** Millennium of Tynwald **Obverse:** Bust of Queen Elizabeth II right **Reverse:** English cog, Castle Rushen

| Date | Mintage | F | VF | XF | Unc | BU |
|---|---|---|---|---|---|---|
| 1979 Proof | 300 | Value: 700 | | | | |

**CROWN** KM# 47c **Weight:** 52.0000 g. **Composition:** 0.9500 Platinum 1.5884 oz. APW **Subject:** Millennium of Tynwald **Obverse:** Bust of Queen Elizabeth II right **Reverse:** English cog, Castle Rushen

| Date | Mintage | F | VF | XF | Unc | BU |
|---|---|---|---|---|---|---|
| 1979 Proof | 100 | Value: 1,200 | | | | |

**CROWN** **KM# 48** **Composition:** Copper-Nickel **Subject:** Millennium of Tynwald **Obverse:** Bust of Queen Elizabeth II right **Reverse:** Flemish carrack, St. Michael Island

| Date | Mintage | F | VF | XF | Unc | BU |
|---|---|---|---|---|---|---|
| 1979 | 100,000 | — | — | — | 6.50 | — |

**CROWN** **KM# 48a** **Weight:** 28.2800 g. **Composition:** 0.9250 Silver .8411 oz. ASW **Subject:** Millennium of Tynwald **Obverse:** Bust of Queen Elizabeth II right **Reverse:** Flemish carrack, St. Michael Island

| Date | Mintage | F | VF | XF | Unc | BU |
|---|---|---|---|---|---|---|
| 1979 | 25,000 | — | — | — | 9.00 | — |
| 1979 Proof | 10,000 | Value: 12.50 | | | | |

**CROWN** **KM# 48b** **Weight:** 43.0000 g. **Composition:** 0.9170 Gold 1.2678 oz. AGW **Subject:** Millennium of Tynwald **Obverse:** Bust of Queen Elizabeth II right **Reverse:** Flemish carrack, St. Michael Island

| Date | Mintage | F | VF | XF | Unc | BU |
|---|---|---|---|---|---|---|
| 1979 Proof | 300 | Value: 700 | | | | |

**CROWN** **KM# 48c** **Weight:** 52.0000 g. **Composition:** 0.9500 Platinum 1.5884 oz. APW **Subject:** Millennium of Tynwald **Obverse:** Bust of Queen Elizabeth II right **Reverse:** Flemish carrack, St. Michael Island

| Date | Mintage | F | VF | XF | Unc | BU |
|---|---|---|---|---|---|---|
| 1979 Proof | 100 | Value: 1,200 | | | | |

**CROWN** **KM# 49a** **Weight:** 28.2800 g. **Composition:** 0.9250 Silver .8411 oz. ASW **Subject:** Millennium of Tynwald **Obverse:** Bust of Queen Elizabeth II right **Reverse:** Royalist soldier and English Man-of-War

| Date | Mintage | F | VF | XF | Unc | BU |
|---|---|---|---|---|---|---|
| 1979 | 25,000 | — | — | — | 9.00 | — |
| 1979 Proof | 10,000 | Value: 12.50 | | | | |

**CROWN** **KM# 49b** **Weight:** 43.0000 g. **Composition:** 0.9170 Gold 1.2678 oz. AGW **Subject:** Millennium of Tynwald **Obverse:** Bust of Queen Elizabeth II right **Reverse:** Royalist soldier and English Man-of-War

| Date | Mintage | F | VF | XF | Unc | BU |
|---|---|---|---|---|---|---|
| 1979 Proof | 300 | Value: 700 | | | | |

**CROWN** **KM# 49c** **Weight:** 52.0000 g. **Composition:** 0.9500 Platinum 1.5884 oz. APW **Subject:** Millennium of Tynwald **Obverse:** Bust of Queen Elizabeth II right **Reverse:** Royalist soldier and English Man-of-War

| Date | Mintage | F | VF | XF | Unc | BU |
|---|---|---|---|---|---|---|
| 1979 Proof | 100 | Value: 1,200 | | | | |

**CROWN** **KM# 50** **Weight:** 28.2800 g. **Composition:** Copper-Nickel **Subject:** Millennium of Tynwald **Obverse:** Bust of Queen Elizabeth II right **Reverse:** Lifeboat and Sir William Hillory portrait

| Date | Mintage | F | VF | XF | Unc | BU |
|---|---|---|---|---|---|---|
| 1979 | 100,000 | — | — | — | 6.50 | — |

**CROWN** **KM# 50a** **Weight:** 28.2800 g. **Composition:** 0.9250 Silver .8411 oz. ASW **Subject:** Millennium of Tynwald **Obverse:** Bust of Queen Elizabeth II right **Reverse:** Lifeboat and Sir William Hillory portrait

| Date | Mintage | F | VF | XF | Unc | BU |
|---|---|---|---|---|---|---|
| 1979 | 25,000 | — | — | — | 9.00 | — |
| 1979 Proof | 10,000 | Value: 12.50 | | | | |

**CROWN** **KM# 50b** **Weight:** 43.0000 g. **Composition:** 0.9170 Gold 1.2678 oz. AGW **Subject:** Millennium of Tynwald **Obverse:** Bust of Queen Elizabeth II right **Reverse:** Lifeboat and Sir William Hillory portrait

| Date | Mintage | F | VF | XF | Unc | BU |
|---|---|---|---|---|---|---|
| 1979 Proof | 300 | Value: 700 | | | | |

**CROWN** **KM# 50c** **Weight:** 52.0000 g. **Composition:** 0.9500 Platinum 1.5884 oz. APW **Subject:** Millennium of Tynwald **Obverse:** Bust of Queen Elizabeth II right **Reverse:** Lifeboat and Sir William Hillory portrait

| Date | Mintage | F | VF | XF | Unc | BU |
|---|---|---|---|---|---|---|
| 1979 Proof | 100 | Value: 1,200 | | | | |

**CROWN** **KM# 63** **Composition:** Copper-Nickel **Subject:** Derby Bicentennial **Obverse:** Bust of Queen Elizabeth II right **Reverse:** Men racing horse

| Date | Mintage | F | VF | XF | Unc | BU |
|---|---|---|---|---|---|---|
| 1980 | 100,000 | — | — | — | 4.00 | — |

**CROWN** **KM# 63a** **Weight:** 28.2800 g. **Composition:** 0.9250 Silver .8411 oz. ASW **Subject:** Derby Bicentennial **Obverse:** Bust of Queen Elizabeth II right **Reverse:** Men racing horse

| Date | Mintage | F | VF | XF | Unc | BU |
|---|---|---|---|---|---|---|
| 1980 | 35,000 | — | — | — | 8.50 | — |
| 1980 Proof | 20,000 | Value: 12.50 | | | | |

**CROWN** **KM# 63b** **Weight:** 52.0000 g. **Composition:** 0.9500 Platinum 1.5884 oz. APW **Subject:** Derby Bicentennial **Obverse:** Bust of Queen Elizabeth II right **Reverse:** Men racing horse

| Date | Mintage | F | VF | XF | Unc | BU |
|---|---|---|---|---|---|---|
| 1980 Proof | 500 | Value: 1,000 | | | | |

**CROWN** **KM# 63c** **Weight:** 43.0000 g. **Composition:** 0.9170 Gold 1.2678 oz. AGW **Subject:** Derby Bicentennial **Obverse:** Bust of Queen Elizabeth II right **Reverse:** Men racing horse

| Date | Mintage | F | VF | XF | Unc | BU |
|---|---|---|---|---|---|---|
| 1980 Proof | — | Value: 700 | | | | |

**CROWN** **KM# 64** **Composition:** Copper-Nickel **Subject:** 1980 Winter Olympics - Lake Placid **Obverse:** Bust of Queen Elizabeth II right **Reverse:** Skier at top

| Date | Mintage | F | VF | XF | Unc | BU |
|---|---|---|---|---|---|---|
| 1980 | 100,000 | — | — | — | 3.00 | — |
| 1980 Proof like | — | — | — | — | 7.50 | — |

**CROWN** **KM# 64a** **Weight:** 28.2800 g. **Composition:** 0.9250 Silver .8411 oz. ASW **Subject:** 1980 Winter Olympics - Lake Placid **Obverse:** Bust of Queen Elizabeth II right **Reverse:** Skier at top

| Date | Mintage | F | VF | XF | Unc | BU |
|---|---|---|---|---|---|---|
| 1980 Matte | — | — | — | — | 16.50 | — |
| 1980 Proof | 10,000 | Value: 17.50 | | | | |

**CROWN** **KM# 64b** **Weight:** 39.8000 g. **Composition:** 0.9170 Gold 1.1735 oz. AGW **Subject:** 1980 Winter Olympics - Lake Placid **Obverse:** Bust of Queen Elizabeth II right **Reverse:** Skier at top

| Date | Mintage | F | VF | XF | Unc | BU |
|---|---|---|---|---|---|---|
| 1980 | 1,500 | — | — | — | 650 | — |
| 1980 Proof | 500 | Value: 675 | | | | |

**CROWN** **KM# 64c** **Weight:** 52.0000 g. **Composition:** 0.9500 Platinum 1.5884 oz. APW **Subject:** 1980 Winter Olympics - Lake Placid **Obverse:** Bust of Queen Elizabeth II right **Reverse:** Skier at top

| Date | Mintage | F | VF | XF | Unc | BU |
|---|---|---|---|---|---|---|
| 1980 Proof | 100 | Value: 1,200 | | | | |

**CROWN** **KM# 65** **Composition:** Copper-Nickel **Subject:** 1980 Summer Olympics - Moscow **Obverse:** Bust of Queen Elizabeth II right **Reverse:** Runner at top

| Date | Mintage | F | VF | XF | Unc | BU |
|---|---|---|---|---|---|---|
| 1980 | 30,000 | — | — | — | 3.00 | — |
| 1980 Proof like | — | — | — | — | 7.50 | — |

**CROWN** **KM# 65a** **Weight:** 28.2800 g. **Composition:** 0.9250 Silver .8411 oz. ASW **Subject:** 1980 Summer Olympics - Moscow **Obverse:** Bust of Queen Elizabeth II right **Reverse:** Runner at top

| Date | Mintage | F | VF | XF | Unc | BU |
|---|---|---|---|---|---|---|
| 1980 | — | — | — | — | 16.50 | — |
| 1980 Proof | 10,000 | Value: 17.50 | | | | |

**CROWN** **KM# 65b** **Weight:** 39.8000 g. **Composition:** 0.9170 Gold 1.1735 oz. AGW **Subject:** 1980 Summer Olympics - Moscow **Obverse:** Bust of Queen Elizabeth II right **Reverse:** Runner at top

| Date | Mintage | F | VF | XF | Unc | BU |
|---|---|---|---|---|---|---|
| 1980 | 1,500 | — | — | — | 650 | — |

**CROWN** **KM# 65c** **Weight:** 52.0000 g. **Composition:** 0.9500 Platinum 1.5884 oz. APW **Subject:** 1980 Summer Olympics - Moscow **Obverse:** Bust of Queen Elizabeth II right **Reverse:** Runner at top

| Date | Mintage | F | VF | XF | Unc | BU |
|---|---|---|---|---|---|---|
| 1980 Proof | 100 | Value: 1,200 | | | | |

**CROWN** **KM# 66** **Composition:** Copper-Nickel **Subject:** 1980 Summer Olympics - Moscow **Obverse:** Bust of Queen Elizabeth II right **Reverse:** Javelin thrower at top

| Date | Mintage | F | VF | XF | Unc | BU |
|---|---|---|---|---|---|---|
| 1980 | 30,000 | — | — | — | 3.00 | — |
| 1980 Proof like | — | — | — | — | 7.50 | — |

**CROWN** **KM# 66a** **Weight:** 28.2800 g. **Composition:** 0.9250 Silver .8411 oz. ASW **Subject:** 1980 Summer Olympics - Moscow **Obverse:** Bust of Queen Elizabeth II right **Reverse:** Javelin thrower at top

| Date | Mintage | F | VF | XF | Unc | BU |
|---|---|---|---|---|---|---|
| 1980 Matte | — | — | — | — | 16.50 | — |
| 1980 Proof | 10,000 | Value: 17.50 | | | | |

**CROWN** **KM# 66b** **Weight:** 39.8000 g. **Composition:** 0.9170 Gold 1.1735 oz. AGW **Subject:** 1980 Summer Olympics - Moscow **Obverse:** Bust of Queen Elizabeth II right **Reverse:** Javelin thrower at top

| Date | Mintage | F | VF | XF | Unc | BU |
|---|---|---|---|---|---|---|
| 1980 | 1,500 | — | — | — | 650 | — |

**CROWN** **KM# 66c** **Weight:** 52.0000 g. **Composition:** 0.9500 Platinum 1.5884 oz. APW **Subject:** 1980 Summer Olympics - Moscow **Obverse:** Bust of Queen Elizabeth II right **Reverse:** Javelin thrower at top

| Date | Mintage | F | VF | XF | Unc | BU |
|---|---|---|---|---|---|---|
| 1980 Proof | 100 | Value: 1,200 | | | | |

**CROWN** **KM# 67** **Composition:** Copper-Lead Alloy **Subject:** 1980 Summer Olympics - Moscow **Obverse:** Bust of Queen Elizabeth II right **Reverse:** Judo match at top

| Date | Mintage | F | VF | XF | Unc | BU |
|---|---|---|---|---|---|---|
| 1980 | 30,000 | — | — | — | 3.00 | — |
| 1980 Prooflike | — | — | — | — | 7.50 | — |

**CROWN** **KM# 67a** **Weight:** 28.2800 g. **Composition:** 0.9250 Silver .8411 oz. ASW **Subject:** 1980 Summer Olympics - Moscow **Obverse:** Bust of Queen Elizabeth II right **Reverse:** Judo match at top

| Date | Mintage | F | VF | XF | Unc | BU |
|---|---|---|---|---|---|---|
| 1980 Matte | — | — | — | — | 16.50 | — |
| 1980 Proof | 10,000 | Value: 17.50 | | | | |

**CROWN** **KM# 67b** **Weight:** 39.8000 g. **Composition:** 0.9170 Gold 1.1735 oz. AGW **Subject:** 1980 Summer Olympics - Moscow **Obverse:** Bust of Queen Elizabeth II right **Reverse:** Judo match at top

| Date | Mintage | F | VF | XF | Unc | BU |
|---|---|---|---|---|---|---|
| 1980 | 1,500 | — | — | — | 650 | — |

**CROWN** **KM# 67c** **Weight:** 52.0000 g. **Composition:** 0.9500 Platinum 1.5884 oz. APW **Subject:** 1980 Summer Olympics - Moscow **Obverse:** Bust of Queen Elizabeth II right **Reverse:** Judo match at top

| Date | Mintage | F | VF | XF | Unc | BU |
|---|---|---|---|---|---|---|
| 1980 Proof | 100 | Value: 1,200 | | | | |

**CROWN** **KM# 68** **Composition:** Copper-Nickel **Subject:** 80th Birthday of Queen Mother **Obverse:** Bust of Queen Elizabeth II right **Reverse:** Bust of Queen Mother

| Date | Mintage | F | VF | XF | Unc | BU |
|---|---|---|---|---|---|---|
| 1980 | 100,000 | — | — | — | 4.50 | — |

**CROWN** **KM# 68a** **Weight:** 28.2800 g. **Composition:** 0.5000 Silver .4546 oz. ASW **Subject:** 80th Birthday of Queen Mother **Obverse:** Bust of Queen Elizabeth II right **Reverse:** Bust of Queen Mother

| Date | Mintage | F | VF | XF | Unc | BU |
|---|---|---|---|---|---|---|
| 1980 | 50,000 | — | — | — | 10.00 | — |

**CROWN** **KM# 68b** **Weight:** 28.2800 g. **Composition:** 0.9250 Silver .8411 oz. ASW **Subject:** 80th Birthday of Queen Mother **Obverse:** Bust of Queen Elizabeth II right **Reverse:** Bust of Queen Mother

| Date | Mintage | F | VF | XF | Unc | BU |
|---|---|---|---|---|---|---|
| 1980 Proof | 30,000 | Value: 15.00 | | | | |

**CROWN** **KM# 68c** **Weight:** 5.0000 g. **Composition:** 0.3740 Gold .0601 oz. AGW **Subject:** 80th Birthday of Queen Mother **Obverse:** Bust of Queen Elizabeth II right **Reverse:** Bust of Queen Mother

| Date | Mintage | F | VF | XF | Unc | BU |
|---|---|---|---|---|---|---|
| 1980 | 50,000 | — | — | — | 75.00 | — |

**CROWN** **KM# 68d** **Weight:** 7.9600 g. **Composition:** 0.9170 Gold .2347 oz. AGW **Subject:** 80th Birthday of Queen Mother **Obverse:** Bust of Queen Elizabeth II right **Reverse:** Bust of Queen Mother

| Date | Mintage | F | VF | XF | Unc | BU |
|---|---|---|---|---|---|---|
| 1980 | 1,000 | — | — | — | 150 | — |

**CROWN** **KM# 73** **Composition:** Copper-Nickel **Subject:** Duke of Edinburgh Awared Scheme **Obverse:** Bust of Queen Elizabeth II right **Reverse:** Prince Philip, Duke of Edinburgh bust facing.

| Date | Mintage | F | VF | XF | Unc | BU |
|---|---|---|---|---|---|---|
| 1981 | 50,000 | — | — | — | 2.50 | — |

**CROWN** **KM# 75** **Composition:** Copper-Nickel **Subject:** Duke of Edinburgh Awared Scheme **Obverse:** Bust of Queen Elizabeth II right **Reverse:** Caring for the bedridden, hiking, swimming

| Date | Mintage | F | VF | XF | Unc | BU |
|---|---|---|---|---|---|---|
| 1981 | 50,000 | — | — | — | 2.50 | — |

**CROWN** **KM# 75a** **Weight:** 28.2800 g. **Composition:** 0.9250 Silver .8411 oz. ASW **Subject:** Duke of Edinburgh Awared Scheme **Obverse:** Bust of Queen Elizabeth II right **Reverse:** Caring for the bedridden, hiking, swimming

| Date | Mintage | F | VF | XF | Unc | BU |
|---|---|---|---|---|---|---|
| 1981 | 20,000 | — | — | — | 10.00 | — |
| 1981 Proof | 15,000 | Value: 12.00 | | | | |

**CROWN** **KM# 73a** **Weight:** 28.2800 g. **Composition:** 0.9250 Silver .8411 oz. ASW **Subject:** Duke of Edinburgh Awared Scheme **Obverse:** Bust of Queen Elizabeth II right **Reverse:** Prince Philip, Duke of Edinburgh bust facing.

| Date | Mintage | F | VF | XF | Unc | BU |
|---|---|---|---|---|---|---|
| 1981 | 20,000 | — | — | — | 10.00 | — |
| 1981 Proof | 15,000 | Value: 12.50 | | | | |

**CROWN** **KM# 73b** **Weight:** 5.1000 g. **Composition:** 0.3740 Gold 0.613 oz. AGW **Subject:** Duke of Edinburgh Awared Scheme **Obverse:** Bust of Queen Elizabeth II right **Reverse:** Prince Philip, Duke of Edinburgh bust facing.

| Date | Mintage | F | VF | XF | Unc | BU |
|---|---|---|---|---|---|---|
| 1981 Proof | 10,000 | Value: 85.00 | | | | |

**CROWN** **KM# 73c** **Weight:** 7.9600 g. **Composition:** 0.9170 Gold .2347 oz. AGW **Subject:** Duke of Edinburgh Awared Scheme **Obverse:** Bust of Queen Elizabeth II right **Reverse:** Prince Philip, Duke of Edinburgh bust facing.

| Date | Mintage | F | VF | XF | Unc | BU |
|---|---|---|---|---|---|---|
| 1981 Proof | 1,000 | Value: 150 | | | | |

**CROWN** **KM# 73d** **Weight:** 52.0000 g. **Composition:** 0.9500 Platinum 1.5884 oz. APW **Subject:** Duke of Edinburgh Awared Scheme **Obverse:** Bust of Queen Elizabeth II right **Reverse:** Prince Philip, Duke of Edinburgh bust facing.

| Date | Mintage | F | VF | XF | Unc | BU |
|---|---|---|---|---|---|---|
| 1981 Proof | 100 | Value: 1,100 | | | | |

**CROWN** **KM# 74** **Composition:** Copper-Nickel **Subject:** Duke of Edinburgh Awared Scheme **Obverse:** Bust of Queen Elizabeth II right **Reverse:** Monogram within garter

| Date | Mintage | F | VF | XF | Unc | BU |
|---|---|---|---|---|---|---|
| 1981 | 50,000 | — | — | — | 2.50 | — |

**CROWN** **KM# 74a** **Weight:** 28.2800 g. **Composition:** 0.9250 Silver .8411 oz. ASW **Subject:** Duke of Edinburgh Awared Scheme **Obverse:** Bust of Queen Elizabeth II right **Reverse:** Monogram within garter

| Date | Mintage | F | VF | XF | Unc | BU |
|---|---|---|---|---|---|---|
| 1981 | 20,000 | — | — | — | 10.00 | — |
| 1981 | 15,000 | Value: 12.00 | | | | |

**Note:** Proof

**CROWN** **KM# 74b** **Weight:** 5.1000 g. **Composition:** 0.3740 Gold .0613 oz. AGW **Subject:** Duke of Edinburgh Awared Scheme **Obverse:** Bust of Queen Elizabeth II right **Reverse:** Monogram within garter

| Date | Mintage | F | VF | XF | Unc | BU |
|---|---|---|---|---|---|---|
| 1981 Proof | 10,000 | Value: 85.00 | | | | |

**CROWN** **KM# 74c** **Weight:** 7.9600 g. **Composition:** 0.9170 Gold .2347 oz. AGW **Subject:** Duke of Edinburgh Awared Scheme **Obverse:** Bust of Queen Elizabeth II right **Reverse:** Monogram within garter

| Date | Mintage | F | VF | XF | Unc | BU |
|---|---|---|---|---|---|---|
| 1981 Proof | 1,000 | Value: 150 | | | | |

**CROWN** **KM# 74d** **Weight:** 52.0000 g. **Composition:** 0.9500 Platinum 1.5884 oz. APW **Subject:** Duke of Edinburgh Awared Scheme **Obverse:** Bust of Queen Elizabeth II right **Reverse:** Monogram within garter

| Date | Mintage | F | VF | XF | Unc | BU |
|---|---|---|---|---|---|---|
| 1981 Proof | 100 | Value: 1,150 | | | | |

**CROWN** **KM# 75b** **Weight:** 5.1000 g. **Composition:** 0.3740 Gold .0613 oz. AGW **Subject:** Duke of Edinburgh Awared Scheme **Obverse:** Bust of Queen Elizabeth II right **Reverse:** Caring for the bedridden, hiking, swimming

| Date | Mintage | F | VF | XF | Unc | BU |
|---|---|---|---|---|---|---|
| 1981 Proof | 10,000 | Value: 85.00 | | | | |

**CROWN** **KM# 75c** **Weight:** 7.9600 g. **Composition:** 0.9170 Gold .2347 oz. AGW **Subject:** Duke of Edinburgh Awared Scheme **Obverse:** Bust of Queen Elizabeth II right **Reverse:** Caring for the bedridden, hiking, swimming

| Date | Mintage | F | VF | XF | Unc | BU |
|---|---|---|---|---|---|---|
| 1981 Proof | 1,000 | Value: 150 | | | | |

**CROWN** **KM# 75d** **Weight:** 52.0000 g. **Composition:** 0.9500 Platinum 1.5884 oz. APW **Subject:** Duke of Edinburgh Awared Scheme **Obverse:** Bust of Queen Elizabeth II right **Reverse:** Caring for the bedridden, hiking, swimming

| Date | Mintage | F | VF | XF | Unc | BU |
|---|---|---|---|---|---|---|
| 1981 Proof | 100 | Value: 1,100 | | | | |

**CROWN** **KM# 76** **Composition:** Copper-Nickel **Subject:** Duke of Edinburgh Awared Scheme **Obverse:** Bust of Queen Elizabeth II right **Reverse:** Rock climbing, sailing, motorcycling

| Date | Mintage | F | VF | XF | Unc | BU |
|---|---|---|---|---|---|---|
| 1981 | 50,000 | — | — | — | 2.50 | — |

**CROWN** **KM# 76a** **Weight:** 28.2800 g. **Composition:** 0.9250 Silver .8411 oz. ASW **Subject:** Duke of Edinburgh Awared Scheme **Obverse:** Bust of Queen Elizabeth II right **Reverse:** Rock climbing, sailing, motorcycling

| Date | Mintage | F | VF | XF | Unc | BU |
|---|---|---|---|---|---|---|
| 1981 | 20,000 | — | — | — | 10.00 | — |
| 1981 Proof | 15,000 | Value: 12.00 | | | | |

**CROWN** **KM# 76b** **Weight:** 5.1000 g. **Composition:** 0.3740 Gold .0613 oz. AGW **Subject:** Duke of Edinburgh Awared Scheme **Obverse:** Bust of Queen Elizabeth II right **Reverse:** Rock climbing, sailing, motorcycling

| Date | Mintage | F | VF | XF | Unc | BU |
|---|---|---|---|---|---|---|
| 1981 Proof | 10,000 | Value: 85.00 | | | | |

**CROWN** **KM# 76c** **Weight:** 7.9600 g. **Composition:** 0.9170 Gold .2347 oz. AGW **Subject:** Duke of Edinburgh Awared Scheme **Obverse:** Bust of Queen Elizabeth II right **Reverse:** Rock climbing, sailing, motorcycling

| Date | Mintage | F | VF | XF | Unc | BU |
|---|---|---|---|---|---|---|
| 1981 Proof | 1,000 | Value: 150 | | | | |

**CROWN** **KM# 76d** **Weight:** 52.0000 g. **Composition:** 0.9500 Platinum 1.5884 oz. APW **Subject:** Duke of Edinburgh Awared Scheme **Obverse:** Bust of Queen Elizabeth II right **Reverse:** Rock climbing, sailing, motorcycling

| Date | Mintage | F | VF | XF | Unc | BU |
|---|---|---|---|---|---|---|
| 1981 Proof | 100 | Value: 1,150 | | | | |

**CROWN** **KM# 77** **Composition:** Copper-Nickel **Subject:** International Year of Disabled **Obverse:** Bust of Queen Elizabeth II right **Reverse:** Braille and bust of Louis Braille

| Date | Mintage | F | VF | XF | Unc | BU |
|---|---|---|---|---|---|---|
| 1981 Prooflike | — | — | — | — | 5.00 | — |

**CROWN** **KM# 77a** **Weight:** 28.2800 g. **Composition:** 0.9250 Silver .8411 oz. ASW **Subject:** International Year of Disabled **Obverse:** Bust of Queen Elizabeth II right **Reverse:** Braille and bust of Louis Braille

| Date | Mintage | F | VF | XF | Unc | BU |
|---|---|---|---|---|---|---|
| 1981 | 20,000 | — | — | — | 10.00 | — |
| 1981 Proof | 15,000 | Value: 14.00 | | | | |

**CROWN** **KM# 77b** **Weight:** 5.1000 g. **Composition:** 0.3740 Gold .0613 oz. AGW **Subject:** International Year of Disabled **Obverse:** Bust of Queen Elizabeth II right **Reverse:** Braille and bust of Louis Braille

| Date | Mintage | F | VF | XF | Unc | BU |
|---|---|---|---|---|---|---|
| 1981 Proof | 10,000 | Value: 100 | | | | |

**CROWN** **KM# 77c** **Weight:** 7.9600 g. **Composition:** 3917.0000 Gold .2347 oz. AGW **Subject:** International Year of Disabled **Obverse:** Bust of Queen Elizabeth II right **Reverse:** Braille and bust of Louis Braille

| Date | Mintage | F | VF | XF | Unc | BU |
|---|---|---|---|---|---|---|
| 1981 Proof | 1,000 | Value: 165 | | | | |

**CROWN** **KM# 77d** **Weight:** 52.0000 g. **Composition:** 0.9500 Platinum 1.5884 oz. APW **Subject:** International Year of Disabled **Obverse:** Bust of Queen Elizabeth II right **Reverse:** Braille and bust of Louis Braille

| Date | Mintage | F | VF | XF | Unc | BU |
|---|---|---|---|---|---|---|
| 1981 Proof | 100 | Value: 1,150 | | | | |

**CROWN** **KM# 78** **Composition:** Copper-Nickel **Subject:** International Year of Disabled **Obverse:** Bust of Queen Elizabeth II right **Reverse:** Beethoven, violin and music score

| Date | Mintage | F | VF | XF | Unc | BU |
|---|---|---|---|---|---|---|
| 1981 | 50,000 | — | — | — | 2.50 | — |
| 1981 Prooflike | — | — | — | — | — | — |

**CROWN** **KM# 78a** **Weight:** 28.2800 g. **Composition:** 0.9250 Silver .8411 oz. ASW **Subject:** International Year of Disabled **Obverse:** Bust of Queen Elizabeth II right **Reverse:** Beethoven, violin and music score

| Date | Mintage | F | VF | XF | Unc | BU |
|---|---|---|---|---|---|---|
| 1981 | 20,000 | — | — | — | 12.00 | — |
| 1981 Proof | 15,000 | Value: 16.50 | | | | |

**CROWN** **KM# 78b** **Weight:** 5.1000 g. **Composition:** 0.3740 Gold .0613 oz. AGW **Subject:** International Year of Disabled **Obverse:** Bust of Queen Elizabeth II right **Reverse:** Beethoven, violin and music score

| Date | Mintage | F | VF | XF | Unc | BU |
|---|---|---|---|---|---|---|
| 1981 Proof | 10,000 | Value: 100 | | | | |

**CROWN** **KM# 78c** **Weight:** 7.9600 g. **Composition:** 0.9170 Gold .2347 oz. AGW **Subject:** International Year of Disabled **Obverse:** Bust of Queen Elizabeth II right **Reverse:** Beethoven, violin and music score

| Date | Mintage | F | VF | XF | Unc | BU |
|---|---|---|---|---|---|---|
| 1981 Proof | 1,000 | Value: 165 | | | | |

**CROWN** **KM# 78d** **Weight:** 52.0000 g. **Composition:** 0.9500 Platinum 1.5884 oz. APW **Subject:** International Year of Disabled **Obverse:** Bust of Queen Elizabeth II right **Reverse:** Beethoven, violin and music score

| Date | Mintage | F | VF | XF | Unc | BU |
|---|---|---|---|---|---|---|
| 1981 Proof | 100 | Value: 1,150 | | | | |

**CROWN** **KM# 79** **Composition:** Copper-Nickel **Subject:** International Year of Disabled **Obverse:** Bust of Queen Elizabeth II right **Reverse:** Sir Douglas Bader

| Date | Mintage | F | VF | XF | Unc | BU |
|---|---|---|---|---|---|---|
| 1981 | 50,000 | — | — | — | 2.50 | — |
| 1981 Prooflike | — | — | — | — | 5.00 | — |

**CROWN** **KM# 79a** **Weight:** 28.2800 g. **Composition:** 0.9250 Silver .8411 oz. ASW **Subject:** International Year of Disabled **Obverse:** Bust of Queen Elizabeth II right **Reverse:** Sir Douglas Bader

| Date | Mintage | F | VF | XF | Unc | BU |
|---|---|---|---|---|---|---|
| 1981 | 20,000 | — | — | — | 10.00 | — |
| 1981 Proof | 15,000 | Value: 14.00 | | | | |

**CROWN** **KM# 79b** **Weight:** 5.1000 g. **Composition:** 0.3740 Gold 0.613 oz. AGW **Subject:** International Year of Disabled **Obverse:** Bust of Queen Elizabeth II right **Reverse:** Sir Douglas Bader

| Date | Mintage | F | VF | XF | Unc | BU |
|---|---|---|---|---|---|---|
| 1981 Proof | 10,000 | Value: 100 | | | | |

**CROWN** **KM# 79c** **Weight:** 7.9600 g. **Composition:** 0.9170 Gold .2347 oz. AGW **Subject:** International Year of Disabled **Obverse:** Bust of Queen Elizabeth II right **Reverse:** Sir Douglas Bader

| Date | Mintage | F | VF | XF | Unc | BU |
|---|---|---|---|---|---|---|
| 1981 Proof | 1,000 | Value: 165 | | | | |

**CROWN** **KM# 79d** **Weight:** 52.0000 g. **Composition:** 0.9500 Platinum 1.5884 oz. APW **Subject:** International Year of Disabled **Obverse:** Bust of Queen Elizabeth II right **Reverse:** Sir Douglas Bader

| Date | Mintage | F | VF | XF | Unc | BU |
|---|---|---|---|---|---|---|
| 1981 Proof | 100 | Value: 1,150 | | | | |

**CROWN** **KM# 80** **Composition:** Copper-Nickel **Subject:** International Year of Disabled **Obverse:** Bust of Queen Elizabeth II right **Reverse:** Sir Francis Chichester and sailing boat

| Date | Mintage | F | VF | XF | Unc | BU |
|---|---|---|---|---|---|---|
| 1981 | 50,000 | — | — | — | 2.50 | — |
| 1981 Proof like | — | — | — | — | 5.00 | — |

**CROWN** **KM# 80a** **Weight:** 28.2800 g. **Composition:** 0.9250 Silver .8411 oz. ASW **Subject:** International Year of Disabled **Obverse:** Bust of Queen Elizabeth II right **Reverse:** Sir Francis Chichester and sailing boat

| Date | Mintage | F | VF | XF | Unc | BU |
|---|---|---|---|---|---|---|
| 1981 | 20,000 | — | — | — | 14.00 | — |
| 1981 Proof | 15,000 | Value: 20.00 | | | | |

**CROWN** **KM# 80b** **Weight:** 5.1000 g. **Composition:** 0.3740 Gold .0613 oz. AGW **Subject:** International Year of Disabled **Obverse:** Bust of Queen Elizabeth II right **Reverse:** Sir Francis Chichester and sailing boat

| Date | Mintage | F | VF | XF | Unc | BU |
|---|---|---|---|---|---|---|
| 1981 Proof | 10,000 | Value: 100 | | | | |

**CROWN** **KM# 80c** **Weight:** 7.9600 g. **Composition:** 0.9170 Gold .2347 oz. AGW **Subject:** International Year of Disabled **Obverse:** Bust of Queen Elizabeth II right **Reverse:** Sir Francis Chichester and sailing boat

| Date | Mintage | F | VF | XF | Unc | BU |
|---|---|---|---|---|---|---|
| 1981 Proof | 1,000 | Value: 165 | | | | |

**CROWN** **KM# 80d** **Weight:** 52.0000 g. **Composition:** 0.9500 Platinum 1.5884 oz. APW **Subject:** International Year of Disabled **Obverse:** Bust of Queen Elizabeth II right **Reverse:** Sir Francis Chichester and sailing boat

| Date | Mintage | F | VF | XF | Unc | BU |
|---|---|---|---|---|---|---|
| 1981 Proof | 100 | Value: 1,150 | | | | |

**CROWN** **KM# 81** **Composition:** Copper-Nickel **Subject:** Wedding of Prince Charles and Lady Diana **Obverse:** Bust of Queen Elizabeth II right **Reverse:** Coats of arms

| Date | Mintage | F | VF | XF | Unc | BU |
|---|---|---|---|---|---|---|
| 1981 | 50,000 | — | — | — | 2.25 | — |

**CROWN** **KM# 81a** **Weight:** 28.2800 g. **Composition:** 0.9250 Silver .8411 oz. ASW **Subject:** Wedding of Prince Charles and Lady Diana **Obverse:** Bust of Queen Elizabeth II right **Reverse:** Coats of arms

| Date | Mintage | F | VF | XF | Unc | BU |
|---|---|---|---|---|---|---|
| 1981 | 20,000 | — | — | — | 12.00 | — |
| 1981 Proof | 15,000 | Value: 15.00 | | | | |

**CROWN** **KM# 81b** **Weight:** 5.1000 g. **Composition:** 0.3740 Gold .0613 oz. AGW **Subject:** Wedding of Prince Charles and Lady Diana **Obverse:** Bust of Queen Elizabeth II right **Reverse:** Coats of arms

| Date | Mintage | F | VF | XF | Unc | BU |
|---|---|---|---|---|---|---|
| 1981 Proof | 10,000 | Value: 85.00 | | | | |

**CROWN** **KM# 81c** **Weight:** 7.9600 g. **Composition:** 0.9170 Gold .2347 oz. AGW **Subject:** Wedding of Prince Charles and Lady Diana **Obverse:** Bust of Queen Elizabeth II right **Reverse:** Coats of arms

| Date | Mintage | F | VF | XF | Unc | BU |
|---|---|---|---|---|---|---|
| 1981 Proof | 1,000 | Value: 150 | | | | |

**CROWN** **KM# 81d** **Weight:** 52.0000 g. **Composition:** 0.9500 Platinum 1.5884 oz. APW **Subject:** Wedding of Prince Charles and Lady Diana **Obverse:** Bust of Queen Elizabeth II right **Reverse:** Coats of arms

| Date | Mintage | F | VF | XF | Unc | BU |
|---|---|---|---|---|---|---|
| 1981 Proof | 100 | Value: 1,150 | | | | |

**CROWN** **KM# 82** **Composition:** Copper-Nickel **Subject:** Wedding of Prince Charles and Lady Diana **Obverse:** Bust of Queen Elizabeth II right **Reverse:** Heads of Prince Charles and Lady Diana

| Date | Mintage | F | VF | XF | Unc | BU |
|---|---|---|---|---|---|---|
| 1981 | 50,000 | — | — | — | 2.25 | — |

**CROWN** **KM# 82a** **Weight:** 28.2800 g. **Composition:** 0.9250 Silver .8411 oz. ASW **Subject:** Wedding of Prince Charles and Lady Diana **Obverse:** Bust of Queen Elizabeth II right **Reverse:** Heads of Prince Charles and Lady Diana

| Date | Mintage | F | VF | XF | Unc | BU |
|---|---|---|---|---|---|---|
| 1981 | 20,000 | — | — | — | 12.00 | — |
| 1981 | 15,000 | Value: 15.00 | | | | |

**CROWN** **KM# 82b** **Weight:** 5.1000 g. **Composition:** 0.3740 Gold .0613 oz. AGW **Subject:** Wedding of Prince Charles and Lady Diana **Obverse:** Bust of Queen Elizabeth II right **Reverse:** Heads of Prince Charles and Lady Diana

| Date | Mintage | F | VF | XF | Unc | BU |
|---|---|---|---|---|---|---|
| 1981 Proof | 10,000 | Value: 85.00 | | | | |

**CROWN** **KM# 82c** **Weight:** 7.9600 g. **Composition:** 0.9170 Gold .2347 oz. AGW **Subject:** Wedding of Prince Charles and Lady Diana **Obverse:** Bust of Queen Elizabeth II right **Reverse:** Heads of Prince Charles and Lady Diana

| Date | Mintage | F | VF | XF | Unc | BU |
|---|---|---|---|---|---|---|
| 1981 Proof | 1,000 | Value: 150 | | | | |

**CROWN** **KM# 82d** **Weight:** 52.0000 g. **Composition:** 0.9500 Platinum 1.5884 oz. APW **Subject:** Wedding of Prince Charles and Lady Diana **Obverse:** Bust of Queen Elizabeth II right **Reverse:** Heads of Prince Charles and Lady Diana

| Date | Mintage | F | VF | XF | Unc | BU |
|---|---|---|---|---|---|---|
| 1981 Proof | — | Value: 1,250 | | | | |

**CROWN** **KM# 91** **Composition:** Copper-Nickel **Series:** XII World Cup - Spain **Obverse:** Bust of Queen Elizabeth II right **Reverse:** Map, man holding torphy

| Date | Mintage | F | VF | XF | Unc | BU |
|---|---|---|---|---|---|---|
| 1982 | 50,000 | — | — | — | 3.50 | — |

**CROWN** **KM# 91a** **Weight:** 28.2800 g. **Composition:** 0.9250 Silver .8411 oz. ASW **Series:** XII World Cup - Spain **Obverse:** Bust of Queen Elizabeth II right **Reverse:** Map, man holding torphy

| Date | Mintage | F | VF | XF | Unc | BU |
|---|---|---|---|---|---|---|
| 1982 | 20,000 | — | — | — | 16.50 | — |
| 1982 Proof | 15,000 | Value: 24.00 | | | | |

**CROWN** **KM# 91b** **Weight:** 5.1000 g. **Composition:** 0.3740 Gold .0613 oz. AGW **Series:** XII World Cup - Spain **Obverse:** Bust of Queen Elizabeth II right **Reverse:** Map, man holding torphy

| Date | Mintage | F | VF | XF | Unc | BU |
|---|---|---|---|---|---|---|
| 1982 Proof | 40,000 | Value: 75.00 | | | | |

**CROWN** **KM# 91c** **Weight:** 7.9600 g. **Composition:** 0.9170 Gold .2347 oz. AGW **Series:** XII World Cup - Spain **Obverse:** Bust of Queen Elizabeth II right **Reverse:** Map, man holding torphy

| Date | Mintage | F | VF | XF | Unc | BU |
|---|---|---|---|---|---|---|
| 1982 Proof | 4,000 | Value: 150 | | | | |

**CROWN** **KM# 91d** **Weight:** 52.0000 g. **Composition:** 0.9500 Platinum 1.5884 oz. APW **Series:** XII World Cup - Spain **Obverse:** Bust of Queen Elizabeth II right **Reverse:** Map, man holding torphy

| Date | Mintage | F | VF | XF | Unc | BU |
|---|---|---|---|---|---|---|
| 1982 Proof | 100 | Value: 1,100 | | | | |

**CROWN** **KM# 92** **Composition:** Copper-Nickel **Series:** XII World Cup - Spain **Obverse:** Bust of Queen Elizabeth II right **Reverse:** Six country shields

| Date | Mintage | F | VF | XF | Unc | BU |
|---|---|---|---|---|---|---|
| 1982 | 50,000 | — | — | — | 3.50 | — |

**CROWN** **KM# 92a** **Weight:** 28.2800 g. **Composition:** 0.9250 Silver .8411 oz. ASW **Series:** XII World Cup - Spain **Obverse:** Bust of Queen Elizabeth II right **Reverse:** Six country shields

| Date | Mintage | F | VF | XF | Unc | BU |
|---|---|---|---|---|---|---|
| 1982 | 20,000 | — | — | — | 14.50 | — |
| 1982 Proof | 15,000 | Value: 17.50 | | | | |

**CROWN** **KM# 92b** **Weight:** 5.1000 g. **Composition:** 0.3740 Gold .0613 oz. AGW **Series:** XII World Cup - Spain **Obverse:** Bust of Queen Elizabeth II right **Reverse:** Six country shields

| Date | Mintage | F | VF | XF | Unc | BU |
|---|---|---|---|---|---|---|
| 1982 Proof | 40,000 | Value: 75.00 | | | | |

**CROWN** **KM# 92c** **Weight:** 7.9600 g. **Composition:** 0.9170 Gold .2347 oz. AGW **Series:** XII World Cup - Spain **Obverse:** Bust of Queen Elizabeth II right **Reverse:** Six country shields

| Date | Mintage | F | VF | XF | Unc | BU |
|---|---|---|---|---|---|---|
| 1982 Proof | 4,000 | Value: 150 | | | | |

**CROWN** **KM# 92d** **Weight:** 52.0000 g. **Composition:** 0.9500 Platinum 1.5884 oz. APW **Series:** XII World Cup - Spain **Obverse:** Bust of Queen Elizabeth II right **Reverse:** Six country shields

| Date | Mintage | F | VF | XF | Unc | BU |
|---|---|---|---|---|---|---|
| 1982 Proof | 100 | Value: 1,350 | | | | |

**CROWN** **KM# 93** **Composition:** Copper-Nickel **Series:** XII World Cup - Spain **Obverse:** Bust of Queen Elizabeth II right **Reverse:** Three soccer action scenes, all players standing

| Date | Mintage | F | VF | XF | Unc | BU |
|---|---|---|---|---|---|---|
| 1982 | 50,000 | — | — | — | 3.50 | — |
| 1982 (sb) | — | — | — | — | 5.00 | — |

**CROWN** **KM# 93a** **Weight:** 28.2800 g. **Composition:** 0.9250 Silver .8411 oz. ASW **Series:** XII World Cup - Spain **Obverse:** Bust of Queen Elizabeth II right **Reverse:** Three soccer action sceans, all players standing

| Date | Mintage | F | VF | XF | Unc | BU |
|---|---|---|---|---|---|---|
| 1982 | 20,000 | — | — | — | 14.50 | — |
| 1982 Proof | 15,000 | Value: 20.00 | | | | |

**CROWN** **KM# 93b** **Weight:** 5.1000 g. **Composition:** 0.3740 Gold .0613 oz. AGW **Series:** XII World Cup - Spain **Obverse:** Bust of Queen Elizabeth II right **Reverse:** Three soccer action sceans, all players standing

| Date | Mintage | F | VF | XF | Unc | BU |
|---|---|---|---|---|---|---|
| 1982 Proof | 40,000 | Value: 75.00 | | | | |

**CROWN** **KM# 93c** **Weight:** 7.9600 g. **Composition:** 0.9170 Gold .2347 oz. AGW **Series:** XII World Cup - Spain **Obverse:** Bust of Queen Elizabeth II right **Reverse:** Three soccer action sceans, all players standing

| Date | Mintage | F | VF | XF | Unc | BU |
|---|---|---|---|---|---|---|
| 1982 Proof | 4,000 | Value: 150 | | | | |

**CROWN** **KM# 93d** **Weight:** 52.0000 g. **Composition:** 0.9500 Platinum 1.5884 oz. APW **Series:** XII World Cup - Spain

**Obverse:** Bust of Queen Elizabeth II right **Reverse:** Three soccer action sceans, all players standing

| Date | Mintage | F | VF | XF | Unc | BU |
|---|---|---|---|---|---|---|
| 1982 Proof | 100 | Value: 1,100 | | | | |

**CROWN** **KM# 94** **Composition:** Copper-Nickel **Series:** XII World Cup - Spain **Obverse:** Bust of Queen Elizabeth II right **Reverse:** Three soccer action sceans, all players standing

| Date | Mintage | F | VF | XF | Unc | BU |
|---|---|---|---|---|---|---|
| 1982 | 50,000 | — | — | — | 3.50 | — |

**CROWN** **KM# 94a** **Weight:** 28.2800 g. **Composition:** 0.9250 Silver .8411 oz. ASW **Series:** XII World Cup - Spain **Obverse:** Bust of Queen Elizabeth II right **Reverse:** Three soccer action sceans, all players standing

| Date | Mintage | F | VF | XF | Unc | BU |
|---|---|---|---|---|---|---|
| 1982 | 20,000 | — | — | — | 14.50 | — |
| 1982 Proof | 15,000 | Value: 20.00 | | | | |

**CROWN** **KM# 94b** **Weight:** 5.1000 g. **Composition:** 0.3740 Gold .0613 oz. AGW **Series:** XII World Cup - Spain **Obverse:** Bust of Queen Elizabeth II right **Reverse:** Three soccer action sceans, all players standing

| Date | Mintage | F | VF | XF | Unc | BU |
|---|---|---|---|---|---|---|
| 1982 Proof | 40,000 | Value: 75.00 | | | | |

**CROWN** **KM# 94c** **Weight:** 7.9600 g. **Composition:** 0.9170 Gold .2347 oz. AGW **Series:** XII World Cup - Spain **Obverse:** Bust of Queen Elizabeth II right **Reverse:** Three soccer action sceans, all players standing

| Date | Mintage | F | VF | XF | Unc | BU |
|---|---|---|---|---|---|---|
| 1982 Proof | 4,000 | Value: 150 | | | | |

**CROWN** **KM# 94d** **Weight:** 52.0000 g. **Composition:** 0.9500 Platinum 1.5884 oz. APW **Series:** XII World Cup - Spain **Obverse:** Bust of Queen Elizabeth II right **Reverse:** Three soccer action sceans, all players standing

| Date | Mintage | F | VF | XF | Unc | BU |
|---|---|---|---|---|---|---|
| 1982 Proof | 100 | Value: 1,100 | | | | |

**CROWN** **KM# 95** **Composition:** Copper-Nickel **Series:** XII World Cup - Spain **Obverse:** Bust of Queen Elizabeth II right **Reverse:** Six country shields, with 1982 above Italian shield

| Date | Mintage | F | VF | XF | Unc | BU |
|---|---|---|---|---|---|---|
| 1982 | — | — | — | — | 3.50 | — |

**CROWN** **KM# 95a** **Weight:** 28.2800 g. **Composition:** 0.9250 Silver .8411 oz. ASW **Series:** XII World Cup - Spain **Obverse:** Bust of Queen Elizabeth II right **Reverse:** Six country shields, with 1982 above Italian shield

| Date | Mintage | F | VF | XF | Unc | BU |
|---|---|---|---|---|---|---|
| 1982 | — | Value: 20.00 | | | | |

**CROWN** **KM# 95b** **Weight:** 5.1000 g. **Composition:** 0.3740 Gold .0613 oz. AGW **Series:** XII World Cup - Spain **Obverse:** Bust of Queen Elizabeth II right **Reverse:** Six country shields, with 1982 above Italian shield

| Date | Mintage | F | VF | XF | Unc | BU |
|---|---|---|---|---|---|---|
| 1982 Proof | 3,000 | — | — | — | — | — |

**CROWN** **KM# 95c** **Weight:** 7.9600 g. **Composition:** 0.9170 Gold .2347 oz. AGW **Series:** XII World Cup - Spain **Obverse:** Bust of Queen Elizabeth II right **Reverse:** Six country shields, with 1982 above Italian shield

| Date | Mintage | F | VF | XF | Unc | BU |
|---|---|---|---|---|---|---|
| 1982 Proof | — | — | — | — | — | — |

**CROWN** **KM# 95d** **Weight:** 52.0000 g. **Composition:** 0.9500 Platinum 1.5884 oz. APW **Series:** XII World Cup - Spain **Obverse:** Bust of Queen Elizabeth II right **Reverse:** Six country shields, with 1982 above Italian shield

| Date | Mintage | F | VF | XF | Unc | BU |
|---|---|---|---|---|---|---|
| 1982 Proof | — | — | — | — | — | — |

**CROWN** **KM# 96** **Composition:** Copper-Nickel **Series:** Maritime Heritage **Obverse:** Bust of Queen Elizabeth II right **Reverse:** "Mayflower" and cameo of Miles Standish

| Date | Mintage | F | VF | XF | Unc | BU |
|---|---|---|---|---|---|---|
| 1982 | Est. 50,000 | — | — | — | 3.00 | — |
| 1982 Prooflike | Inc. above | — | — | — | — | — |

**CROWN** **KM# 96a** **Weight:** 28.2800 g. **Composition:** 0.9250 Silver .8411 oz. ASW **Series:** Maritime Heritage **Obverse:** Bust of Queen Elizabeth II right **Reverse:** "Mayflower" and cameo of Miles Standish

| Date | Mintage | F | VF | XF | Unc | BU |
|---|---|---|---|---|---|---|
| 1982 | 15,000 | — | — | — | 20.00 | — |
| 1982 Proof | 10,000 | Value: 25.00 | | | | |

**CROWN** **KM# 96b** **Weight:** 5.1000 g. **Composition:** 0.3740 Gold .0613 oz. AGW **Series:** Maritime Heritage **Obverse:** Bust of Queen Elizabeth II right **Reverse:** "Mayflower" and cameo of Miles Standish

| Date | Mintage | F | VF | XF | Unc | BU |
|---|---|---|---|---|---|---|
| 1982 Proof | 22,000 | Value: 75.00 | | | | |

**CROWN** **KM# 96c** **Weight:** 7.9600 g. **Composition:** 0.9170 Gold .2347 oz. AGW **Series:** Maritime Heritage **Obverse:** Bust of Queen Elizabeth II right **Reverse:** "Mayflower" and cameo of Miles Standish

| Date | Mintage | F | VF | XF | Unc | BU |
|---|---|---|---|---|---|---|
| 1982 Proof | 2,000 | Value: 150 | | | | |

**CROWN** **KM# 96d** **Weight:** 52.0000 g. **Composition:** 0.9500 Platinum 1.5884 oz. APW **Series:** Maritime Heritage **Obverse:** Bust of Queen Elizabeth II right **Reverse:** "Mayflower" and cameo of Miles Standish

| Date | Mintage | F | VF | XF | Unc | BU |
|---|---|---|---|---|---|---|
| 1982 Proof | 50 | Value: 1,250 | | | | |

**CROWN** **KM# 97** **Composition:** Copper-Nickel **Series:** Maritime Heritage **Obverse:** Bust of Queen Elizabeth II right **Reverse:** "H.M.S. Bounty" and cameo of Fletcher Christian

| Date | Mintage | F | VF | XF | Unc | BU |
|---|---|---|---|---|---|---|
| 1982 | Est. 50,000 | — | — | — | 3.00 | — |
| 1982 Proof like | Inc. above | — | — | — | — | — |

**CROWN** **KM# 97a** **Weight:** 28.2800 g. **Composition:** 0.9250 Silver .8411 oz. ASW **Series:** Maritime Heritage **Obverse:** Bust of Queen Elizabeth II right **Reverse:** "H.M.S. Bounty" and cameo of Fletcher Christian

| Date | Mintage | F | VF | XF | Unc | BU |
|---|---|---|---|---|---|---|
| 1982 | 15,000 | — | — | — | 20.00 | — |
| 1982 Proof | 10,000 | Value: 25.00 | | | | |

**CROWN** **KM# 97b** **Weight:** 5.1000 g. **Composition:** 0.3740 Gold .0613 oz. AGW **Series:** Maritime Heritage **Obverse:** Bust of Queen Elizabeth II right **Reverse:** "H.M.S. Bounty" and cameo of Fletcher Christian

| Date | Mintage | F | VF | XF | Unc | BU |
|---|---|---|---|---|---|---|
| 1982 Proof | 22,000 | Value: 75.00 | | | | |

**CROWN** **KM# 97c** **Weight:** 7.9600 g. **Composition:** 0.9170 Gold .2347 oz. AGW **Series:** Maritime Heritage **Obverse:** Bust of Queen Elizabeth II right **Reverse:** "H.M.S. Bounty" and cameo of Fletcher Christian

| Date | Mintage | F | VF | XF | Unc | BU |
|---|---|---|---|---|---|---|
| 1982 Proof | 2,000 | Value: 150 | | | | |

**CROWN** **KM# 97d** **Weight:** 52.0000 g. **Composition:** 0.9500 Platinum 1.5884 oz. APW **Series:** Maritime Heritage **Obverse:** Bust of Queen Elizabeth II right **Reverse:** "H.M.S. Bounty" and cameo of Fletcher Christian

| Date | Mintage | F | VF | XF | Unc | BU |
|---|---|---|---|---|---|---|
| 1982 Proof | 50 | Value: 1,250 | | | | |

**CROWN** **KM# 98** **Composition:** Copper-Nickel **Series:** Maritime Heritage **Obverse:** Bust of Queen Elizabeth II right **Reverse:** "H.M.S. Victory" and cameo of John Quilliam

| Date | Mintage | F | VF | XF | Unc | BU |
|---|---|---|---|---|---|---|
| 1982 | Est. 50,000 | — | — | — | 3.00 | — |
| 1982 Prooflike | Inc. above | — | — | — | — | — |

**CROWN** **KM# 98a** **Weight:** 28.2800 g. **Composition:** 0.9250 Silver .8411 oz. ASW **Series:** Maritime Heritage **Obverse:** Bust of Queen Elizabeth II right **Reverse:** "H.M.S. Victory" and cameo of John Quilliam

| Date | Mintage | F | VF | XF | Unc | BU |
|---|---|---|---|---|---|---|
| 1982 | 15,000 | — | — | — | 20.00 | — |
| 1982 Proof | 10,000 | Value: 25.00 | | | | |

**CROWN** **KM# 98b** **Weight:** 5.1000 g. **Composition:** 0.3740 Gold .0613 oz. AGW **Series:** Maritime Heritage **Obverse:** Bust of Queen Elizabeth II right **Reverse:** "H.M.S. Victory" and cameo of John Quilliam

| Date | Mintage | F | VF | XF | Unc | BU |
|---|---|---|---|---|---|---|
| 1982 Proof | 22,000 | Value: 75.00 | | | | |

**CROWN** **KM# 98c** **Weight:** 7.9600 g. **Composition:** 0.9170 Gold .2347 oz. AGW **Series:** Maritime Heritage **Obverse:** Bust of Queen Elizabeth II right **Reverse:** "H.M.S. Victory" and cameo of John Quilliam

| Date | Mintage | F | VF | XF | Unc | BU |
|---|---|---|---|---|---|---|
| 1982 Proof | 2,000 | Value: 150 | | | | |

**CROWN** **KM# 98d** **Weight:** 52.0000 g. **Composition:** 0.9500 Platinum 1.5884 oz. APW **Series:** Maritime Heritage **Obverse:** Bust of Queen Elizabeth II right **Reverse:** "H.M.S. Victory" and cameo of John Quilliam

| Date | Mintage | F | VF | XF | Unc | BU |
|---|---|---|---|---|---|---|
| 1982 Proof | 50 | Value: 1,250 | | | | |

**CROWN** **KM# 99** **Composition:** Copper-Nickel **Series:** Maritime Heritage **Obverse:** Bust of Queen Elizabeth II right **Reverse:** P.S. Mona's "Queen II" and cameo of Capt. William Cain

| Date | Mintage | F | VF | XF | Unc | BU |
|---|---|---|---|---|---|---|
| 1982 | Est. 50,000 | — | — | — | 3.00 | — |
| 1982 Prooflike | Inc. above | — | — | — | — | — |

**CROWN** **KM# 99a** **Weight:** 28.2800 g. **Composition:** 0.9250 Silver .8411 oz. ASW **Series:** Maritime Heritage **Obverse:** Bust of Queen Elizabeth II right **Reverse:** P.S. Mona's "Queen II" and cameo of Capt. William Cain

| Date | Mintage | F | VF | XF | Unc | BU |
|---|---|---|---|---|---|---|
| 1982 | 15,000 | — | — | — | 20.00 | — |
| 1982 Proof | 10,000 | Value: 25.00 | | | | |

**CROWN** **KM# 99b** **Weight:** 5.1000 g. **Composition:** 0.3740 Gold .0613 oz. AGW **Series:** Maritime Heritage **Obverse:** Bust of Queen Elizabeth II right **Reverse:** P.S. Mona's "Queen II" and cameo of Capt. William Cain

| Date | Mintage | F | VF | XF | Unc | BU |
|---|---|---|---|---|---|---|
| 1982 Proof | 22,000 | Value: 75.00 | | | | |

**CROWN** **KM# 99c** **Weight:** 7.9600 g. **Composition:** 0.9170 Gold .2347 oz. AGW **Series:** Maritime Heritage **Obverse:** Bust of Queen Elizabeth II right **Reverse:** P.S. Mona's "Queen II" and cameo of Capt. William Cain

| Date | Mintage | F | VF | XF | Unc | BU |
|---|---|---|---|---|---|---|
| 1982 Proof | 2,000 | Value: 150 | | | | |

**CROWN** **KM# 99d** **Weight:** 52.0000 g. **Composition:** 0.9500 Platinum 1.5884 oz. APW **Series:** Maritime Heritage **Obverse:** Bust of Queen Elizabeth II right **Reverse:** P.S. Mona's "Queen II" and cameo of Capt. William Cain

| Date | Mintage | F | VF | XF | Unc | BU |
|---|---|---|---|---|---|---|
| 1982 Proof | 50 | Value: 1,250 | | | | |

**CROWN** **KM# 103** **Composition:** Copper-Nickel **Series:** Manned Flight **Obverse:** Bust of Queen Elizabeth II right **Reverse:** Hot air ballon

| Date | Mintage | F | VF | XF | Unc | BU |
|---|---|---|---|---|---|---|
| 1983 | 50,000 | — | — | — | 3.75 | — |
| 1983 DMIHE | — | — | — | — | 15.00 | — |

**CROWN** **KM# 103a** **Weight:** 28.2800 g. **Composition:** 0.9250 Silver .8411 oz. ASW **Series:** Manned Flight **Obverse:** Bust of Queen Elizabeth II right **Reverse:** Hot air ballon

| Date | Mintage | F | VF | XF | Unc | BU |
|---|---|---|---|---|---|---|
| 1983 | 15,000 | — | — | — | 20.00 | — |
| 1983 | 11,000 | Value: 25.00 | | | | |

**CROWN** **KM# 103b** **Weight:** 5.1000 g. **Composition:** 0.3740 Gold .0613 oz. AGW **Series:** Manned Flight **Obverse:** Bust of Queen Elizabeth II right **Reverse:** Hot air ballon

| Date | Mintage | F | VF | XF | Unc | BU |
|---|---|---|---|---|---|---|
| 1983 Proof | 5,500 | Value: 100 | | | | |

**CROWN** **KM# 103c** **Weight:** 7.9600 g. **Composition:** 0.9170 Gold .2347 oz. AGW **Series:** Manned Flight **Obverse:** Bust of Queen Elizabeth II right **Reverse:** Hot air ballon

| Date | Mintage | F | VF | XF | Unc | BU |
|---|---|---|---|---|---|---|
| 1983 Proof | 500 | Value: 175 | | | | |

**CROWN** **KM# 103d** **Weight:** 52.0000 g. **Composition:** 0.9500 Platinum 1.5884 oz. APW **Series:** Manned Flight **Obverse:** Bust of Queen Elizabeth II right **Reverse:** Hot air ballon

| Date | Mintage | F | VF | XF | Unc | BU |
|---|---|---|---|---|---|---|
| 1983 Proof | 50 | Value: 1,250 | | | | |

**CROWN** **KM# 104** **Composition:** Copper-Nickel **Series:** Manned Flight **Obverse:** Bust of Queen Elizabeth II right **Reverse:** Biplane

| Date | Mintage | F | VF | XF | Unc | BU |
|---|---|---|---|---|---|---|
| 1983 | 50,000 | — | — | — | 3.75 | — |
| 1983 DMIHE | — | — | — | — | 15.00 | — |

**CROWN** **KM# 104a** **Weight:** 28.2800 g. **Composition:** 0.9250 Silver .8411 oz. ASW **Series:** Manned Flight **Obverse:** Bust of Queen Elizabeth II right **Reverse:** Biplane

| Date | Mintage | F | VF | XF | Unc | BU |
|---|---|---|---|---|---|---|
| 1983 | 15,000 | — | — | — | 20.00 | — |
| 1983 Proof | 11,000 | Value: 25.00 | | | | |

**CROWN** **KM# 104b** **Weight:** 5.1000 g. **Composition:** 0.3740 Gold .0613 oz. AGW **Series:** Manned Flight **Obverse:** Bust of Queen Elizabeth II right **Reverse:** Biplane

| Date | Mintage | F | VF | XF | Unc | BU |
|---|---|---|---|---|---|---|
| 1983 Proof | 5,500 | Value: 100 | | | | |

**CROWN** KM# 104c **Weight:** 7.9600 g. **Composition:** 0.9170 Gold .2347 oz. AGW **Series:** Manned Flight **Obverse:** Bust of Queen Elizabeth II right **Reverse:** Biplane

| Date | Mintage | F | VF | XF | Unc | BU |
|---|---|---|---|---|---|---|
| 1983 Proof | 500 | Value: 175 | | | | |

**CROWN** KM# 104d **Weight:** 52.0000 g. **Composition:** 0.9500 Platinum 1.5884 oz. APW **Series:** Manned Flight **Obverse:** Bust of Queen Elizabeth II right **Reverse:** Biplane

| Date | Mintage | F | VF | XF | Unc | BU |
|---|---|---|---|---|---|---|
| 1983 Proof | 50 | Value: 1,500 | | | | |

**CROWN** KM# 105 **Composition:** Copper-Nickel **Series:** Manned Flight **Obverse:** Bust of Queen Elizabeth II right **Reverse:** Jet

| Date | Mintage | F | VF | XF | Unc | BU |
|---|---|---|---|---|---|---|
| 1983 | 50,000 | — | — | — | 3.75 | — |
| 1983 DMIHE | — | — | — | — | 15.00 | — |

**CROWN** KM# 105a **Weight:** 28.2800 g. **Composition:** 0.9250 Silver .8411 oz. ASW **Series:** Manned Flight **Obverse:** Bust of Queen Elizabeth II right **Reverse:** Jet

| Date | Mintage | F | VF | XF | Unc | BU |
|---|---|---|---|---|---|---|
| 1983 | 15,000 | — | — | — | 20.00 | — |
| 1983 Proof | 11,000 | Value: 25.00 | | | | |

**CROWN** KM# 105b **Weight:** 5.1000 g. **Composition:** 0.3740 Gold .0613 oz. AGW **Series:** Manned Flight **Obverse:** Bust of Queen Elizabeth II right **Reverse:** Jet

| Date | Mintage | F | VF | XF | Unc | BU |
|---|---|---|---|---|---|---|
| 1983 Proof | 5,500 | Value: 100 | | | | |

**CROWN** KM# 105c **Weight:** 7.9600 g. **Composition:** 0.9170 Gold .2347 oz. AGW **Series:** Manned Flight **Obverse:** Bust of Queen Elizabeth II right **Reverse:** Jet

| Date | Mintage | F | VF | XF | Unc | BU |
|---|---|---|---|---|---|---|
| 1983 Proof | 500 | Value: 175 | | | | |

**CROWN** KM# 105d **Weight:** 52.0000 g. **Composition:** 0.9500 Platinum 1.5884 oz. APW **Series:** Manned Flight **Obverse:** Bust of Queen Elizabeth II right **Reverse:** Jet

| Date | Mintage | F | VF | XF | Unc | BU |
|---|---|---|---|---|---|---|
| 1983 Proof | 50 | Value: 1,500 | | | | |

**CROWN** KM# 106 **Composition:** Copper-Nickel **Series:** Manned Flight **Obverse:** Bust of Queen Elizabeth II right **Reverse:** Space Shuttle

| Date | Mintage | F | VF | XF | Unc | BU |
|---|---|---|---|---|---|---|
| 1983 | 50,000 | — | — | — | 3.75 | — |
| 1983 DMIHE | — | — | — | — | 15.00 | — |

**CROWN** KM# 106a **Weight:** 28.2800 g. **Composition:** 0.9250 Silver .8411 oz. ASW **Series:** Manned Flight **Obverse:** Bust of Queen Elizabeth II right **Reverse:** Space shuttle

| Date | Mintage | F | VF | XF | Unc | BU |
|---|---|---|---|---|---|---|
| 1983 | 15,000 | — | — | — | 12.00 | — |
| 1983 Proof | 11,000 | Value: 20.00 | | | | |

**CROWN** KM# 106b **Weight:** 5.1000 g. **Composition:** 0.3740 Gold .0613 oz. AGW **Series:** Manned Flight **Obverse:** Bust of Queen Elizabeth II right **Reverse:** Space shuttle

| Date | Mintage | F | VF | XF | Unc | BU |
|---|---|---|---|---|---|---|
| 1983 Proof | 5,500 | Value: 100 | | | | |

**CROWN** KM# 106c **Weight:** 7.9600 g. **Composition:** 0.9170 Gold .2347 oz. AGW **Series:** Manned Flight **Obverse:** Bust of Queen Elizabeth II right **Reverse:** Space shuttle

| Date | Mintage | F | VF | XF | Unc | BU |
|---|---|---|---|---|---|---|
| 1983 Proof | 500 | Value: 175 | | | | |

**CROWN** KM# 106d **Weight:** 52.0000 g. **Composition:** 0.9500 Platinum 1.5884 oz. APW **Series:** Manned Flight **Obverse:** Bust of Queen Elizabeth II right **Reverse:** Space Shuttle

| Date | Mintage | F | VF | XF | Unc | BU |
|---|---|---|---|---|---|---|
| 1983 Proof | 50 | Value: 1,500 | | | | |

**CROWN** KM# 117e **Composition:** Silver Clad Copper-Nickel **Series:** 1984 Olympics **Obverse:** Bust of Queen Elizabeth II right **Reverse:** Figure skaters Jayne Torvill and Christopher Dean

| Date | Mintage | F | VF | XF | Unc | BU |
|---|---|---|---|---|---|---|
| 1984 | 20,000 | — | — | — | 20.00 | — |

**CROWN** KM# 118e **Composition:** Silver Clad Copper-Nickel **Series:** 1984 Olympics **Obverse:** Bust of Queen Elizabeth II right **Reverse:** Runners

| Date | Mintage | F | VF | XF | Unc | BU |
|---|---|---|---|---|---|---|
| 1984 | 20,000 | — | — | — | 20.00 | — |

**CROWN** KM# 117 **Composition:** Copper-Nickel **Series:** 1984 Olympics **Obverse:** Bust of Queen Elizabeth II right **Reverse:** Figure skaters Jayne Torvill and Christopher Dean

| Date | Mintage | F | VF | XF | Unc | BU |
|---|---|---|---|---|---|---|
| 1984 | 50,000 | — | — | — | 3.50 | — |
| 1984 Proof | — | Value: 8.50 | | | | |

**CROWN** KM# 117a **Weight:** 28.2800 g. **Composition:** 0.9250 Silver .8411 oz. ASW **Series:** 1984 Olympics **Obverse:** Bust of Queen Elizabeth II right **Reverse:** Figure Skaters Jayne Torvill and Christopher Dean

| Date | Mintage | F | VF | XF | Unc | BU |
|---|---|---|---|---|---|---|
| 1984 Proof | 15,000 | Value: 30.00 | | | | |

**CROWN** KM# 117b **Weight:** 5.1000 g. **Composition:** 0.3740 Gold .0613 oz. AGW **Series:** 1984 Olympics **Obverse:** Bust of Queen Elizabeth II right **Reverse:** Figure skaters Jayne Torvill and Christopher Dean

| Date | Mintage | F | VF | XF | Unc | BU |
|---|---|---|---|---|---|---|
| 1984 Proof | 10,000 | Value: 75.00 | | | | |

**CROWN** KM# 117c **Weight:** 7.9600 g. **Composition:** 0.9170 Gold .2347 oz. AGW **Series:** 1984 Olympics **Obverse:** Bust of Queen Elizabeth II right **Reverse:** Figure skaters Jayne Torvill and Christopher Dean

| Date | Mintage | F | VF | XF | Unc | BU |
|---|---|---|---|---|---|---|
| 1984 Proof | 1,000 | Value: 150 | | | | |

**CROWN** KM# 117d **Weight:** 52.0000 g. **Composition:** 0.9500 Platinum 1.5884 oz. APW **Series:** 1984 Olympics **Obverse:** Bust of Queen Elizabeth II right **Reverse:** Figure skaters Jayne Torvill and Christopher Dean

| Date | Mintage | F | VF | XF | Unc | BU |
|---|---|---|---|---|---|---|
| 1984 Proof | 100 | Value: 1,500 | | | | |

**CROWN** KM# 118 **Composition:** Copper-Nickel **Series:** 1984 Olympics **Obverse:** Bust of Queen Elizabeth II right **Reverse:** Runners

| Date | Mintage | F | VF | XF | Unc | BU |
|---|---|---|---|---|---|---|
| 1984 | 50,000 | — | — | — | 3.50 | — |
| 1984 Proof | — | Value: 8.50 | | | | |

**CROWN** KM# 118a **Weight:** 28.2800 g. **Composition:** 0.9250 Silver .8411 oz. ASW **Series:** 1984 Olympics **Obverse:** Bust of Queen Elizabeth II right **Reverse:** Runners

| Date | Mintage | F | VF | XF | Unc | BU |
|---|---|---|---|---|---|---|
| 1984 Proof | 15,000 | Value: 30.00 | | | | |

**CROWN** KM# 118b **Weight:** 5.1000 g. **Composition:** 0.3740 Gold .0613 oz. AGW **Series:** 1984 Olympics **Obverse:** Bust of Queen Elizabeth II right **Reverse:** Runners

| Date | Mintage | F | VF | XF | Unc | BU |
|---|---|---|---|---|---|---|
| 1984 Proof | 10,000 | Value: 75.00 | | | | |

**CROWN** KM# 118c **Weight:** 7.9600 g. **Composition:** 0.9170 Gold .2347 oz. AGW **Series:** 1984 Olympics **Obverse:** Bust of Queen Elizabeth II right **Reverse:** Runners

| Date | Mintage | F | VF | XF | Unc | BU |
|---|---|---|---|---|---|---|
| 1984 Proof | 1,000 | Value: 150 | | | | |

**CROWN** KM# 118d **Weight:** 52.0000 g. **Composition:** 0.9500 Platinum 1.5884 oz. APW **Series:** 1984 Olympics **Obverse:** Bust of Queen Elizabeth II right **Reverse:** Runners

| Date | Mintage | F | VF | XF | Unc | BU |
|---|---|---|---|---|---|---|
| 1984 Proof | 100 | Value: 1,500 | | | | |

**CROWN** KM# 119 **Composition:** Copper-Nickel **Series:** 1984 Olympics **Obverse:** Bust of Queen Elizabeth II right **Reverse:** Gymnastics

| Date | Mintage | F | VF | XF | Unc | BU |
|---|---|---|---|---|---|---|
| 1984 | 50,000 | — | — | — | 3.50 | — |
| 1984 Proof | — | Value: 8.50 | | | | |

**CROWN** KM# 119a **Weight:** 28.2800 g. **Composition:** 0.9250 Silver .8411 oz. ASW **Series:** 1984 Olympics **Obverse:** Bust of Queen Elizabeth II right **Reverse:** Gymnastics

| Date | Mintage | F | VF | XF | Unc | BU |
|---|---|---|---|---|---|---|
| 1984 Proof | 15,000 | Value: 30.00 | | | | |

**CROWN** KM# 119b **Weight:** 5.1000 g. **Composition:** 0.3740 Gold .0613 oz. AGW **Series:** 1984 Olympics **Obverse:** Bust of Queen Elizabeth II right **Reverse:** Gymnastics

| Date | Mintage | F | VF | XF | Unc | BU |
|---|---|---|---|---|---|---|
| 1984 Proof | 10,000 | Value: 75.00 | | | | |

**CROWN** KM# 119c **Weight:** 7.9600 g. **Composition:** 0.9170 Gold .2347 oz. AGW **Series:** 1984 Olympics **Obverse:** Bust of Queen Elizabeth II right **Reverse:** Gymnastics

| Date | Mintage | F | VF | XF | Unc | BU |
|---|---|---|---|---|---|---|
| 1984 Proof | 1,000 | Value: 150 | | | | |

**CROWN** KM# 119d **Weight:** 52.0000 g. **Composition:** 0.9500 Platinum 1.5884 oz. APW **Series:** 1984 Olympics **Obverse:** Bust of Queen Elizabeth II right **Reverse:** Gymnastics

| Date | Mintage | F | VF | XF | Unc | BU |
|---|---|---|---|---|---|---|
| 1984 Proof | 100 | Value: 1,500 | | | | |

**CROWN** KM# 120 **Composition:** Copper-Nickel **Series:** 1984 Olympics **Obverse:** Bust of Queen Elizabeth II right **Reverse:** Equestrian

| Date | Mintage | F | VF | XF | Unc | BU |
|---|---|---|---|---|---|---|
| 1984 | 50,000 | — | — | — | 3.50 | — |
| 1984 Proof | — | Value: 8.50 | | | | |

**CROWN** KM# 120a **Weight:** 28.2800 g. **Composition:** 0.9250 Silver .8411 oz. ASW **Series:** 1984 Olympics **Obverse:** Bust of Queen Elizabeth II right **Reverse:** Equestiran

| Date | Mintage | F | VF | XF | Unc | BU |
|---|---|---|---|---|---|---|
| 1984 Proof | 15,000 | Value: 30.00 | | | | |

**CROWN** KM# 120b **Weight:** 5.1000 g. **Composition:** 0.3740 Gold .0613 oz. AGW **Series:** 1984 Olympics **Obverse:** Bust of Queen Elizabeth II right **Reverse:** Equestrian

| Date | Mintage | F | VF | XF | Unc | BU |
|---|---|---|---|---|---|---|
| 1984 Proof | 10,000 | Value: 75.00 | | | | |

**CROWN** KM# 120c **Weight:** 7.9600 g. **Composition:** 0.9170 Gold .2347 oz. AGW **Series:** 1984 Olympics **Obverse:** Bust of Queen Elizabeth II right **Reverse:** Equestrian

| Date | Mintage | F | VF | XF | Unc | BU |
|---|---|---|---|---|---|---|
| 1984 Proof | 1,000 | Value: 150 | | | | |

**CROWN** KM# 120d **Weight:** 52.0000 g. **Composition:** 0.9500 Platinum 1.5884 oz. APW **Series:** 1984 Olympics **Obverse:** Bust of Queen Elizabeth II right **Reverse:** Equestiran

| Date | Mintage | F | VF | XF | Unc | BU |
|---|---|---|---|---|---|---|
| 1984 Proof | 100 | Value: 1,500 | | | | |

**CROWN** KM# 121 **Composition:** Copper-Nickel **Subject:** Quincentenary **Obverse:** Bust of Queen Elizabeth II right **Reverse:** The college of arms

| Date | Mintage | F | VF | XF | Unc | BU |
|---|---|---|---|---|---|---|
| 1984 | — | — | — | — | 2.50 | — |
| 1984 Proof like | — | — | — | — | — | — |

**CROWN** KM# 121a **Weight:** 28.2800 g. **Composition:** 0.9250 Silver .8411 oz. ASW **Subject:** Quincentenary **Obverse:** Bust of Queen Elizabeth II right **Reverse:** The college of arms

| Date | Mintage | F | VF | XF | Unc | BU |
|---|---|---|---|---|---|---|
| 1984 | — | — | — | — | 12.00 | — |
| 1984 Proof | — | Value: 18.00 | | | | |

**CROWN** KM# 121b **Weight:** 5.1000 g. **Composition:** 0.3740 Gold .0613 oz. AGW **Subject:** Quincentenary **Obverse:** Bust of Queen Elizabeth II right **Reverse:** The college of arms

| Date | Mintage | F | VF | XF | Unc | BU |
|---|---|---|---|---|---|---|
| 1984 Proof | 10,000 | Value: 75.00 | | | | |

**CROWN** KM# 121c **Weight:** 7.9600 g. **Composition:** 0.9170 Gold .2347 oz. AGW **Subject:** Quincentenary **Obverse:** Bust of Queen Elizabeth II right **Reverse:** The college of arms

| Date | Mintage | F | VF | XF | Unc | BU |
|---|---|---|---|---|---|---|
| 1984 Proof | 1,000 | Value: 150 | | | | |

**CROWN** KM# 121d **Weight:** 52.0000 g. **Composition:** 0.9500 Platinum 1.5884 oz. APW **Subject:** Quincentenary **Obverse:** Bust of Queen Elizabeth II right **Reverse:** The college of arms

| Date | Mintage | F | VF | XF | Unc | BU |
|---|---|---|---|---|---|---|
| 1984 Proof | — | Value: 1,100 | | | | |

**CROWN** KM# 122 **Composition:** Copper-Nickel **Subject:** Quincentenary **Obverse:** Bust of Queen Elizabeth II right **Reverse:** The college of arms

| Date | Mintage | F | VF | XF | Unc | BU |
|---|---|---|---|---|---|---|
| 1984 | — | — | — | — | 4.50 | — |
| 1984 Prooflike | — | — | — | — | — | — |

**CROWN** KM# 122a **Weight:** 28.2800 g. **Composition:** 0.9250 Silver .8411 oz. ASW **Subject:** Quincentenary **Obverse:** Bust of Queen Elizabeth II right **Reverse:** The college of arms

| Date | Mintage | F | VF | XF | Unc | BU |
|---|---|---|---|---|---|---|
| 1984 | — | — | — | — | 12.00 | — |
| 1984 Proof | — | Value: 18.00 | | | | |

**CROWN** KM# 122b **Weight:** 5.1000 g. **Composition:** 0.3740 Gold .0613 oz. AGW **Subject:** Quincentenary **Obverse:** Bust of Queen Elizabeth II right **Reverse:** The college of arms

| Date | Mintage | F | VF | XF | Unc | BU |
|---|---|---|---|---|---|---|
| 1984 Proof | 10,000 | Value: 75.00 | | | | |

**CROWN** KM# 122c **Weight:** 7.9600 g. **Composition:** 0.9170 Gold .2347 oz. AGW **Subject:** Quincentenary **Obverse:** Bust of Queen Elizabeth II right **Reverse:** The college of arms

| Date | Mintage | F | VF | XF | Unc | BU |
|---|---|---|---|---|---|---|
| 1984 Proof | 1,000 | Value: 150 | | | | |

**CROWN KM# 122d Weight:** 52.0000 g. **Composition:** 0.9500 Platinum 1.5884 oz. APW **Subject:** Quincentenary **Obverse:** Bust of Queen Elizabeth II right **Reverse:** The college of arms

| Date | Mintage | F | VF | XF | Unc | BU |
|---|---|---|---|---|---|---|
| 1984 Proof | — | Value: 1,100 | | | | |

**CROWN KM# 123 Composition:** Copper-Nickel **Subject:** Quincentenary **Obverse:** Bust of Queen Elizabeth II right **Reverse:** The college of arms

| Date | Mintage | F | VF | XF | Unc | BU |
|---|---|---|---|---|---|---|
| 1984 | — | — | — | — | 4.50 | — |
| 1984 Prooflike | — | — | — | — | — | — |

**CROWN KM# 123a Weight:** 28.2800 g. **Composition:** 0.9250 Silver .8411 oz. ASW **Subject:** Quincentenary **Obverse:** Bust of Queen Elizabeth II right **Reverse:** The college of arms

| Date | Mintage | F | VF | XF | Unc | BU |
|---|---|---|---|---|---|---|
| 1984 | — | — | — | — | 12.00 | — |
| 1984 Proof | — | Value: 18.00 | | | | |

**CROWN KM# 123b Weight:** 5.1000 g. **Composition:** 0.3740 Gold .0613 oz. AGW **Subject:** Quincentenary **Obverse:** Bust of Queen Elizabeth II right **Reverse:** The college of arms

| Date | Mintage | F | VF | XF | Unc | BU |
|---|---|---|---|---|---|---|
| 1984 Proof | 10,000 | Value: 75.00 | | | | |

**CROWN KM# 123c Weight:** 7.9600 g. **Composition:** 0.9170 Gold .2347 oz. AGW **Subject:** Quincentenary **Obverse:** Bust of Queen Elizabeth II right **Reverse:** The college of arms

| Date | Mintage | F | VF | XF | Unc | BU |
|---|---|---|---|---|---|---|
| 1984 Proof | 1,000 | Value: 150 | | | | |

**CROWN KM# 123d Weight:** 52.0000 g. **Composition:** 0.9500 Platinum 1.5884 oz. APW **Subject:** Quincentenary **Obverse:** Bust of Queen Elizabeth II right **Reverse:** The college of arms

| Date | Mintage | F | VF | XF | Unc | BU |
|---|---|---|---|---|---|---|
| 1984 Proof | — | Value: 1,100 | | | | |

**CROWN KM# 124 Composition:** Copper-Nickel **Subject:** Quincentenary **Obverse:** Bust of Queen Elizabeth II right **Reverse:** The college of arms

| Date | Mintage | F | VF | XF | Unc | BU |
|---|---|---|---|---|---|---|
| 1984 | — | — | — | — | 4.50 | — |
| 1984 Proof like | — | — | — | — | — | — |

**CROWN KM# 124a Weight:** 28.2800 g. **Composition:** 0.9250 Silver .8411 oz. ASW **Subject:** Quincentenary **Obverse:** Bust of Queen Elizabeth II right **Reverse:** The college of arms

| Date | Mintage | F | VF | XF | Unc | BU |
|---|---|---|---|---|---|---|
| 1984 | — | — | — | — | 12.00 | — |
| 1984 Proof | — | Value: 18.00 | | | | |

**CROWN KM# 124b Weight:** 5.1000 g. **Composition:** 0.3740 Gold .0613 oz. AGW **Subject:** Quincentenary **Obverse:** Bust of Queen Elizabeth II right **Reverse:** The college of arms

| Date | Mintage | F | VF | XF | Unc | BU |
|---|---|---|---|---|---|---|
| 1984 Proof | 10,000 | Value: 75.00 | | | | |

**CROWN KM# 124c Weight:** 7.9600 g. **Composition:** 0.9170 Gold .2347 oz. AGW **Subject:** Quincentenary **Obverse:** Bust of Queen Elizabeth II right **Reverse:** The college of arms

| Date | Mintage | F | VF | XF | Unc | BU |
|---|---|---|---|---|---|---|
| 1984 Proof | 1,000 | Value: 150 | | | | |

**CROWN KM# 124d Weight:** 52.0000 g. **Composition:** 0.9500 Platinum 1.5884 oz. APW **Subject:** Quincentenary **Obverse:** Bust of Queen Elizabeth II right **Reverse:** The college of arms

| Date | Mintage | F | VF | XF | Unc | BU |
|---|---|---|---|---|---|---|
| 1984 Proof | — | Value: 1,100 | | | | |

**CROWN KM# 130 Composition:** Copper-Nickel **Subject:** 30th Commonwealth Parliamentary Conference **Obverse:** Bust of Queen Elizabeth II right **Reverse:** Queen Elizabeth II and Prince Philip **Rev. Legend:** Celtic uncial script

| Date | Mintage | F | VF | XF | Unc | BU |
|---|---|---|---|---|---|---|
| 1984 | — | — | — | — | 3.00 | — |

**CROWN KM# 130a Weight:** 28.2800 g. **Composition:** 0.9250 Silver .8411 oz. ASW **Subject:** 30th Commonwealth Parliamentary Conference **Obverse:** Bust of Queen Elizabeth II right **Reverse:** Queen Elizabeth II and prince Philip **Rev. Legend:** Celtic uncial script

| Date | Mintage | F | VF | XF | Unc | BU |
|---|---|---|---|---|---|---|
| 1984 | — | — | — | — | 15.00 | — |
| 1984 Proof | — | Value: 20.00 | | | | |

**CROWN KM# 130b Weight:** 5.1000 g. **Composition:** 0.3740 Gold .0613 oz. AGW **Subject:** 30th Commonwealth Parliamentary Conference **Obverse:** Bust of Queen Elizabeth II right **Reverse:** Queen Elizabeth II and Prince Philip **Rev. Legend:** Celtic uncial script

| Date | Mintage | F | VF | XF | Unc | BU |
|---|---|---|---|---|---|---|
| 1984 Proof | 10,000 | Value: 75.00 | | | | |

**CROWN KM# 130c Weight:** 7.9600 g. **Composition:** 0.9170 Gold .2347 oz. AGW **Subject:** 30th Commonwealth Parliamentary Conference **Obverse:** Bust of Queen Elizabeth II right **Reverse:** Queen Elizabeth II and Prince Philip **Rev. Legend:** Celtic uncial script

| Date | Mintage | F | VF | XF | Unc | BU |
|---|---|---|---|---|---|---|
| 1984 Proof | 1,000 | Value: 150 | | | | |

**CROWN KM# 130d Weight:** 52.0000 g. **Composition:** 0.9500 Platinum 1.5884 oz. APW **Subject:** 30th Commonwealth Parliamentary Conference **Obverse:** Bust of Queen Elizabeth II right **Reverse:** Queen Elizabeth Ii and Prince Philip **Rev. Legend:** Celtic uncial script

| Date | Mintage | F | VF | XF | Unc | BU |
|---|---|---|---|---|---|---|
| 1984 Proof | — | Value: 1,100 | | | | |

**CROWN KM# 131 Composition:** Copper-Nickel **Subject:** 30th Commonwealth Parliamentary Conference **Obverse:** Bust of Queen Elizabeth II right **Reverse:** Throne, shield and sword

| Date | Mintage | F | VF | XF | Unc | BU |
|---|---|---|---|---|---|---|
| 1984 | — | — | — | — | 3.00 | — |

**CROWN KM# 131a Weight:** 28.2800 g. **Composition:** 0.9250 Silver .8411 oz. ASW **Subject:** 30th Commonwealth Parliamentary Conference **Obverse:** Bust of Queen Elizabeth II right **Reverse:** Throne, sceptre and shield

| Date | Mintage | F | VF | XF | Unc | BU |
|---|---|---|---|---|---|---|
| 1984 | — | — | — | — | 15.00 | — |
| 1984 Proof | — | Value: 20.00 | | | | |

**CROWN KM# 131b Weight:** 5.1000 g. **Composition:** 0.3740 Gold .0613 oz. AGW **Subject:** 30th Commonwealth Parliamentary Conference **Obverse:** Bust of Queen Elizabeth II right **Reverse:** Throne, sceptre and shield

| Date | Mintage | F | VF | XF | Unc | BU |
|---|---|---|---|---|---|---|
| 1984 Proof | 10,000 | Value: 75.00 | | | | |

**CROWN KM# 131c Weight:** 7.9600 g. **Composition:** 0.9170 Gold .2347 oz. AGW **Subject:** 30th Commonwealth Parliamentary Conference **Obverse:** Bust of Queen Elizabeth II right **Reverse:** Throne, sceptre and shield

| Date | Mintage | F | VF | XF | Unc | BU |
|---|---|---|---|---|---|---|
| 1984 Proof | 1,000 | Value: 150 | | | | |

**CROWN KM# 131d Weight:** 52.0000 g. **Composition:** 0.9500 Platinum 1.5884 oz. APW **Subject:** 30th Commonwealth Parliamentary Conference **Obverse:** Bust of Queen Elizabeth II right **Reverse:** Throne, shield and sword

| Date | Mintage | F | VF | XF | Unc | BU |
|---|---|---|---|---|---|---|
| 1984 Proof | — | Value: 1,100 | | | | |

**CROWN KM# 132 Composition:** Copper-Nickel **Subject:** 30th Commonwealth Parliamentary Conference **Obverse:** Bust of Queen Elizabeth II right **Reverse:** Princess Anne

| Date | Mintage | F | VF | XF | Unc | BU |
|---|---|---|---|---|---|---|
| 1984 | — | — | — | — | 3.00 | — |

**CROWN KM# 132a Weight:** 28.2800 g. **Composition:** 0.9250 Silver .8411 oz. ASW **Subject:** 30th Commonwealth Parliamentary Conference **Obverse:** Bust of Queen Elizabeth II right **Reverse:** Princess Anne

| Date | Mintage | F | VF | XF | Unc | BU |
|---|---|---|---|---|---|---|
| 1984 | — | — | — | — | 15.00 | — |
| 1984 Proof | — | Value: 20.00 | | | | |

**CROWN KM# 132b Weight:** 5.1000 g. **Composition:** 0.3740 Gold .0613 oz. AGW **Subject:** 30th Commonwealth Parliamentary Conference **Obverse:** Bust of Queen Elizabeth II right **Reverse:** Princess Anne

| Date | Mintage | F | VF | XF | Unc | BU |
|---|---|---|---|---|---|---|
| 1984 Proof | 10,000 | Value: 75.00 | | | | |

**CROWN KM# 132c Weight:** 7.9600 g. **Composition:** 0.9170 Gold .2347 oz. AGW **Subject:** 30th Commonwealth Parliamentary Conference **Obverse:** Bust of Queen Elizabeth II right **Reverse:** Princess Anne

| Date | Mintage | F | VF | XF | Unc | BU |
|---|---|---|---|---|---|---|
| 1984 Proof | 1,000 | Value: 150 | | | | |

**CROWN KM# 132d Weight:** 52.0000 g. **Composition:** 0.9500 Platinum 1.5884 oz. APW **Subject:** 30th Commonwealth Parliamentary Conference **Obverse:** Bust of Queen Elizabeth II right **Reverse:** Priness Anne

| Date | Mintage | F | VF | XF | Unc | BU |
|---|---|---|---|---|---|---|
| 1984 Proof | — | Value: 1,100 | | | | |

**CROWN KM# 133 Composition:** Copper-Nickel **Subject:** 30th Commonwealth Parliamentary Conference **Obverse:** Bust of Queen Elizabeth II right **Reverse:** Conference tent

| Date | Mintage | F | VF | XF | Unc | BU |
|---|---|---|---|---|---|---|
| 1984 | — | — | — | — | 3.00 | — |

**CROWN KM# 133a Weight:** 28.2800 g. **Composition:** 0.9250 Silver .8411 oz. ASW **Subject:** 30th Commonwealth Parliamentary Conference **Obverse:** Bust of Queen Elizabeth II right **Reverse:** Conference tent

| Date | Mintage | F | VF | XF | Unc | BU |
|---|---|---|---|---|---|---|
| 1984 | — | — | — | — | 15.00 | — |
| 1984 Proof | — | Value: 20.00 | | | | |

**CROWN KM# 133b Weight:** 5.1000 g. **Composition:** 0.3740 Gold .0613 oz. AGW **Subject:** 30th Commonwealth Parliamentary Conference **Obverse:** Bust of Queen Elizabeth II right **Reverse:** Conference tent

| Date | Mintage | F | VF | XF | Unc | BU |
|---|---|---|---|---|---|---|
| 1984 Proof | 10,000 | Value: 75.00 | | | | |

**CROWN KM# 133c Weight:** 7.9600 g. **Composition:** 0.9170 Gold .2347 oz. AGW **Subject:** 30th Commonwealth Parliamentary Conference **Obverse:** Bust of Queen Elizabeth II right **Reverse:** Conference tent

| Date | Mintage | F | VF | XF | Unc | BU |
|---|---|---|---|---|---|---|
| 1984 Proof | 1,000 | Value: 150 | | | | |

**CROWN KM# 133d Weight:** 52.0000 g. **Composition:** 0.9500 Platinum 1.5884 oz. APW **Subject:** 30th Commonwealth Parliamentary Conference **Obverse:** Bust of Queen Elizabeth II right **Reverse:** Conference tent

| Date | Mintage | F | VF | XF | Unc | BU |
|---|---|---|---|---|---|---|
| 1984 Proof | — | Value: 1,100 | | | | |

**CROWN KM# 220 Composition:** Copper-Nickel **Obverse:** Bust of Queen Elizabeth II right **Reverse:** Queen Mother and Princesses Elizabeth and Margaret

| Date | Mintage | F | VF | XF | Unc | BU |
|---|---|---|---|---|---|---|
| 1985 | Est. 50,000 | — | — | — | 2.50 | — |
| 1990 | — | — | — | — | 2.50 | — |

**CROWN KM# 220b Weight:** 28.2800 g. **Composition:** 0.9250 Silver .8411 oz. ASW **Obverse:** Bust of Queen Elizabeth II right **Reverse:** Queen Mother and Princesses Elizabeth and Margaret

| Date | Mintage | F | VF | XF | Unc | BU |
|---|---|---|---|---|---|---|
| 1985 Proof | Est. 15,000 | Value: 25.00 | | | | |
| 1990 Proof | — | Value: 28.00 | | | | |

**CROWN** **KM# 216** **Composition:** Copper-Nickel **Obverse:** Bust of Queen Elizabeth II right **Reverse:** Queen Mother as a young girl

| Date | Mintage | F | VF | XF | Unc | BU |
|---|---|---|---|---|---|---|
| 1985 | Est. 50,000 | — | — | — | 2.50 | — |

**CROWN** **KM# 216a** **Composition:** Silver Clad Copper-Nickel **Obverse:** Bust of Queen Elizabeth II right **Reverse:** Queen Mother as a young girl

| Date | Mintage | F | VF | XF | Unc | BU |
|---|---|---|---|---|---|---|
| 1985 Proof | Est. 20,000 | Value: 10.00 | | | | |

**CROWN** **KM# 216b** **Weight:** 28.2800 g. **Composition:** 0.9250 Silver .8411 oz. ASW **Obverse:** Bust of Queen Elizabeth II right **Reverse:** Queen Mother as a young girl

| Date | Mintage | F | VF | XF | Unc | BU |
|---|---|---|---|---|---|---|
| 1985 Proof | Est. 15,000 | Value: 25.00 | | | | |

**CROWN** **KM# 216c** **Weight:** 5.1000 g. **Composition:** 0.3740 Gold .0613 oz. AGW **Obverse:** Bust of Queen Elizabeth II right **Reverse:** Queen Mother as a young girl

| Date | Mintage | F | VF | XF | Unc | BU |
|---|---|---|---|---|---|---|
| 1985 Proof | Est. 10,000 | Value: 75.00 | | | | |

**CROWN** **KM# 216d** **Weight:** 7.9600 g. **Composition:** 0.9170 Gold .2347 oz. AGW **Obverse:** Bust of Queen Elizabeth II right **Reverse:** Queen Mother as a young girl

| Date | Mintage | F | VF | XF | Unc | BU |
|---|---|---|---|---|---|---|
| 1985 Proof | Est. 1,000,000 | Value: 150 | | | | |

**CROWN** **KM# 216e** **Weight:** 52.0000 g. **Composition:** 0.9500 Platinum 1.5884 oz. APW **Obverse:** Bust of Queen Elizabeth II right **Reverse:** Queen Mother as a young girl

| Date | Mintage | F | VF | XF | Unc | BU |
|---|---|---|---|---|---|---|
| 1985 Proof | Est. 100 | Value: 1,100 | | | | |

**CROWN** **KM# 217** **Composition:** Copper-Nickel **Obverse:** Bust of Queen Elizabeth II right **Reverse:** Portrait of King George VI and Elizabeth

| Date | Mintage | F | VF | XF | Unc | BU |
|---|---|---|---|---|---|---|
| 1985 | Est. 50,000 | — | — | — | 2.50 | — |

**CROWN** **KM# 217a** **Composition:** Silver Clad Copper-Nickel **Obverse:** Bust of Queen Elizabeth II right **Reverse:** Portrait of King George VI and Elizabeth

| Date | Mintage | F | VF | XF | Unc | BU |
|---|---|---|---|---|---|---|
| 1985 Proof | Est. 20,000 | Value: 10.00 | | | | |

**CROWN** **KM# 217b** **Weight:** 28.2800 g. **Composition:** 0.9250 Silver .8411 oz. ASW **Obverse:** Bust of Queen Elizabeth II right **Reverse:** Portrait of King George VI and Elizabeth

| Date | Mintage | F | VF | XF | Unc | BU |
|---|---|---|---|---|---|---|
| 1985 Proof | Est. 15,000 | Value: 25.00 | | | | |

**CROWN** **KM# 217c** **Weight:** 5.1000 g. **Composition:** 0.3740 Gold .0613 oz. AGW **Obverse:** Bust of Queen Elizabeth II right **Reverse:** Portrait of King George VI and Elizabeth

| Date | Mintage | F | VF | XF | Unc | BU |
|---|---|---|---|---|---|---|
| 1985 Proof | Est. 10,000 | Value: 75.00 | | | | |

**CROWN** **KM# 217d** **Weight:** 7.9600 g. **Composition:** 0.9170 Gold .2347 oz. AGW **Obverse:** Bust of Queen Elizabeth II right **Reverse:** Portrait of King George VI and Elizabeth

| Date | Mintage | F | VF | XF | Unc | BU |
|---|---|---|---|---|---|---|
| 1985 Proof | Est. 1,000 | Value: 150 | | | | |

**CROWN** **KM# 217e** **Weight:** 52.0000 g. **Composition:** 0.9500 Platinum 1.5884 oz. APW **Obverse:** Bust of Queen Elizabeth II right **Reverse:** Portrait of King George VI and Elizabeth

| Date | Mintage | F | VF | XF | Unc | BU |
|---|---|---|---|---|---|---|
| 1985 Proof | Est. 100 | Value: 1,100 | | | | |

**CROWN** **KM# 218** **Composition:** Copper-Nickel **Obverse:** Bust of Queen Elizabeth II right **Reverse:** Wedding portrait of King George VI and Elizabeth

| Date | Mintage | F | VF | XF | Unc | BU |
|---|---|---|---|---|---|---|
| 1985 | Est. 50,000 | — | — | — | 2.50 | — |

**CROWN** **KM# 218a** **Composition:** Silver Clad Copper-Nickel **Obverse:** Bust of Queen Elizabeth II right **Reverse:** Wedding portrait of King George VI and Elizabeth

| Date | Mintage | F | VF | XF | Unc | BU |
|---|---|---|---|---|---|---|
| 1985 Proof | Est. 20,000 | Value: 10.00 | | | | |

**CROWN** **KM# 218c** **Weight:** 5.1000 g. **Composition:** 0.3740 Gold .0613 oz. AGW **Obverse:** Bust of Queen Elizabeth II right **Reverse:** Wedding portrait of King George VI and Elizabeth

| Date | Mintage | F | VF | XF | Unc | BU |
|---|---|---|---|---|---|---|
| 1985 Proof | Est. 10,000 | Value: 75.00 | | | | |

**CROWN** **KM# 218b** **Weight:** 28.2800 g. **Composition:** 0.9250 Silver .8411 oz. ASW **Obverse:** Bust of Queen Elizabeth II right **Reverse:** Wedding portrait of King George VI and Elizabeth

| Date | Mintage | F | VF | XF | Unc | BU |
|---|---|---|---|---|---|---|
| 1985 Proof | Est. 15,000 | Value: 25.00 | | | | |

**CROWN** **KM# 218d** **Weight:** 7.9600 g. **Composition:** 0.9170 Gold .2347 oz. AGW **Obverse:** Bust of Queen Elizabeth II right **Reverse:** Wedding portrait of King George VI and Elizabeth

| Date | Mintage | F | VF | XF | Unc | BU |
|---|---|---|---|---|---|---|
| 1985 Proof | Est. 1,000 | Value: 150 | | | | |

**CROWN** **KM# 218e** **Weight:** 52.0000 g. **Composition:** 0.9500 Platinum 1.5884 oz. APW **Obverse:** Bust of Queen Elizabeth II right **Reverse:** Wedding portrait of King George VI and Elizabeth

| Date | Mintage | F | VF | XF | Unc | BU |
|---|---|---|---|---|---|---|
| 1985 Proof | Est. 100 | Value: 1,100 | | | | |

**CROWN** **KM# 219** **Composition:** Copper-Nickel **Obverse:** Bust of Queen Elizabeth II right **Reverse:** Queen Mother and Princess Elizabeth

| Date | Mintage | F | VF | XF | Unc | BU |
|---|---|---|---|---|---|---|
| 1985 | Est. 50,000 | — | — | — | 2.50 | — |

**CROWN** **KM# 219a** **Composition:** Silver Clad Copper-Nickel **Obverse:** Bust of Queen Elizabeth II right **Reverse:** Queen Mother and Princess Elizabeth

| Date | Mintage | F | VF | XF | Unc | BU |
|---|---|---|---|---|---|---|
| 1985 Proof | Est. 20,000 | Value: 10.00 | | | | |

**CROWN** **KM# 219b** **Weight:** 28.2800 g. **Composition:** 0.9250 Silver .8411 oz. ASW **Obverse:** Bust of Queen Elizabeth II right **Reverse:** Queen Mother and Princess Elizabeth

| Date | Mintage | F | VF | XF | Unc | BU |
|---|---|---|---|---|---|---|
| 1985 Proof | Est. 15,000 | Value: 25.00 | | | | |

**CROWN** **KM# 219c** **Weight:** 5.1000 g. **Composition:** 0.3740 Gold .0613 oz. AGW **Obverse:** Bust of Queen Elizabeth II right **Reverse:** Queen Mother and Princess Elizabeth

| Date | Mintage | F | VF | XF | Unc | BU |
|---|---|---|---|---|---|---|
| 1985 Proof | Est. 10,000 | Value: 75.00 | | | | |

**CROWN** **KM# 219d** **Weight:** 7.9600 g. **Composition:** 0.9170 Gold .2347 oz. AGW **Obverse:** Bust of Queen Elizabeth II right **Reverse:** Queen Mother and Princess Elizabeth

| Date | Mintage | F | VF | XF | Unc | BU |
|---|---|---|---|---|---|---|
| 1985 Proof | Est. 1,000 | Value: 150 | | | | |

**CROWN** **KM# 219e** **Weight:** 52.0000 g. **Composition:** 0.9500 Platinum 1.5884 oz. APW **Obverse:** Bust of Queen Elizabeth II right **Reverse:** Queen Mother and Princess Elizabeth

| Date | Mintage | F | VF | XF | Unc | BU |
|---|---|---|---|---|---|---|
| 1985 Proof | Est. 100 | Value: 1,100 | | | | |

**CROWN** **KM# 220a** **Composition:** Silver Clad Copper-Nickel **Obverse:** Bust of Queen Elizabeth II right **Reverse:** Queen Mother and Princesses Elizabeth and Margaret

| Date | Mintage | F | VF | XF | Unc | BU |
|---|---|---|---|---|---|---|
| 1985 Proof | Est. 20,000 | Value: 10.00 | | | | |

**CROWN** **KM# 220c** **Weight:** 5.1000 g. **Composition:** 0.3740 Gold .0613 oz. AGW **Obverse:** Bust of Queen Elizabeth II right **Reverse:** Queen Mother and Princesses Elizabeth and Margaret

| Date | Mintage | F | VF | XF | Unc | BU |
|---|---|---|---|---|---|---|
| 1985 Proof | Est. 10,000 | Value: 75.00 | | | | |

**CROWN** **KM# 220d** **Weight:** 7.9600 g. **Composition:** 0.9170 Gold .2347 oz. AGW **Obverse:** Bust of Queen Elizabeth II right **Reverse:** Queen Mother and Princess Elizabeth and Margaret

| Date | Mintage | F | VF | XF | Unc | BU |
|---|---|---|---|---|---|---|
| 1985 Proof | Est. 1,000 | Value: 150 | | | | |

**CROWN** **KM# 220e** **Weight:** 52.0000 g. **Composition:** 0.9500 Platinum 1.5884 oz. APW **Obverse:** Bust of Queen Elizabeth II right **Reverse:** Queen Mother and Princess Elizabeth and Margaret

| Date | Mintage | F | VF | XF | Unc | BU |
|---|---|---|---|---|---|---|
| 1985 Proof | Est. 100 | Value: 1,100 | | | | |

**CROWN** **KM# 221** **Composition:** Copper-Nickel **Subject:** 85th Birthday of Queen Mother **Obverse:** Bust of Queen Elizabeth II right **Reverse:** Queen Mother

| Date | Mintage | F | VF | XF | Unc | BU |
|---|---|---|---|---|---|---|
| 1985 | Est. 50,000 | — | — | — | 2.50 | — |

**CROWN** **KM# 221a** **Composition:** Silver Clad Copper-Nickel **Subject:** 85th Birthday of Queen Mother **Obverse:** Bust of Queen Elizabeth II right **Reverse:** Queen Mother

| Date | Mintage | F | VF | XF | Unc | BU |
|---|---|---|---|---|---|---|
| 1985 Proof | Est. 20,000 | Value: 10.00 | | | | |

**CROWN** **KM# 221b** **Weight:** 28.2800 g. **Composition:** 0.9250 Silver .8411 oz. ASW **Subject:** 85th Birthday of Queen Mother **Obverse:** Bust of Queen Elizabeth II right **Reverse:** Queen Mother

| Date | Mintage | F | VF | XF | Unc | BU |
|---|---|---|---|---|---|---|
| 1985 Proof | Est. 15,000 | Value: 25.00 | | | | |

**CROWN** **KM# 221c** **Weight:** 5.1000 g. **Composition:** 0.3740 Gold .0613 oz. AGW **Subject:** 85th Birthday of Queen Mother **Obverse:** Bust of Queen Elizabeth II right **Reverse:** Queen Mother

| Date | Mintage | F | VF | XF | Unc | BU |
|---|---|---|---|---|---|---|
| 1985 Proof | Est. 10,000 | Value: 75.00 | | | | |

**CROWN** **KM# 221d** **Weight:** 7.9600 g. **Composition:** 0.9170 Gold .2347 oz. AGW **Subject:** 85th Birthday fo Queen Mother **Obverse:** Bust of Queen Elizabeth II right **Reverse:** Queen Mother

| Date | Mintage | F | VF | XF | Unc | BU |
|---|---|---|---|---|---|---|
| 1985 Proof | Est. 1,000,000 | Value: 150 | | | | |

**CROWN** **KM# 221e** **Weight:** 52.0000 g. **Composition:** 0.9500 Platinum 1.5884 oz. APW **Subject:** 85th Birthday fo Queen Mother **Obverse:** Bust of Queen Elizabeth II right **Reverse:** Queen Mother

| Date | Mintage | F | VF | XF | Unc | BU |
|---|---|---|---|---|---|---|
| 1985 Proof | Est. 100 | Value: 1,100 | | | | |

**CROWN** **KM# 164a** **Composition:** Silver Clad Copper-Nickel **Series:** World Cup Soccer - Mexico **Obverse:** Bust of Queen Elizabeth II right **Reverse:** Globe

| Date | Mintage | F | VF | XF | Unc | BU |
|---|---|---|---|---|---|---|
| 1986 | Est. 20,000 | Value: 10.00 | | | | |
| 1989 | — | — | — | — | 80.00 | — |

**CROWN** **KM# 165a** **Composition:** Silver Clad Copper-Nickel **Series:** World Cup Soccer - Mexico **Obverse:** Bust of Queen Elizabeth II right **Reverse:** Flags

| Date | Mintage | F | VF | XF | Unc | BU |
|---|---|---|---|---|---|---|
| 1986 | Est. 20,000 | Value: 10.00 | | | | |
| 1989 | — | — | — | — | 80.00 | — |

**CROWN** **KM# 160** **Composition:** Copper-Nickel **Series:** World Cup Soccer - Mexico **Obverse:** Bust of Queen Elizabeth II right **Reverse:** Map and two players

| Date | Mintage | F | VF | XF | Unc | BU |
|---|---|---|---|---|---|---|
| 1986 | Est. 50,000 | — | — | — | 2.50 | — |

**CROWN** **KM# 160a** **Composition:** Silver Clad Copper-Nickel **Series:** World Cup Soccer - Mexico **Obverse:** Bust of Queen Elizabeth II right **Reverse:** Map and two players

| Date | Mintage | F | VF | XF | Unc | BU |
|---|---|---|---|---|---|---|
| 1986 Proof | Est. 20,000 | Value: 10.00 | | | | |

**CROWN KM# 160b Weight:** 28.2800 g. **Composition:** 0.9250 Silver .8411 oz. ASW **Series:** World Cup Soccer - Mexico **Obverse:** Bust of Queen Elizabeth II right **Reverse:** Map and two players

| Date | Mintage | F | VF | XF | Unc | BU |
|---|---|---|---|---|---|---|
| 1986 Proof | Est. 15,000 | Value: 17.50 | | | | |

**CROWN KM# 160c Weight:** 5.1000 g. **Composition:** 0.3740 Gold .0613 oz. AGW **Series:** World Cup Soccer - Mexico **Obverse:** Bust of Queen Elizabeth II right **Reverse:** Map and two players

| Date | Mintage | F | VF | XF | Unc | BU |
|---|---|---|---|---|---|---|
| 1986 Proof | Est. 10,000 | Value: 75.00 | | | | |

**CROWN KM# 160d Weight:** 7.9600 g. **Composition:** 0.9170 Gold .2347 oz. AGW **Series:** World Cup Soccer - Mexico **Obverse:** Bust of Queen Elizabeth II right **Reverse:** Map and two players

| Date | Mintage | F | VF | XF | Unc | BU |
|---|---|---|---|---|---|---|
| 1986 Proof | Est. 1,000 | Value: 150 | | | | |

**CROWN KM# 160e Weight:** 52.0000 g. **Composition:** 0.9500 Platinum 1.5884 oz. APW **Series:** World Cup Soccer - Mexico **Obverse:** Bust of Queen Elizabeth II right **Reverse:** Map and two players

| Date | Mintage | F | VF | XF | Unc | BU |
|---|---|---|---|---|---|---|
| 1986 Proof | Est. 200 | Value: 1,100 | | | | |

**CROWN KM# 161 Composition:** Copper-Nickel **Series:** World Cup Soccer - Mexico **Obverse:** Bust of Queen Elizabeth II right **Reverse:** Three players

| Date | Mintage | F | VF | XF | Unc | BU |
|---|---|---|---|---|---|---|
| 1986 | Est. 50,000 | — | — | — | 2.50 | — |

**CROWN KM# 161a Composition:** Silver Clad Copper-Nickel **Series:** World Cup Soccer - Mexico **Obverse:** Bust of Queen Elizabeth II right **Reverse:** Three players

| Date | Mintage | F | VF | XF | Unc | BU |
|---|---|---|---|---|---|---|
| 1986 Proof | Est. 20,000 | Value: 10.00 | | | | |

**CROWN KM# 161b Weight:** 28.2800 g. **Composition:** 0.9250 Silver .8411 oz. ASW **Series:** World Cup Soccer - Mexico **Obverse:** Bust of Queen Elizabeth II right **Reverse:** Three players

| Date | Mintage | F | VF | XF | Unc | BU |
|---|---|---|---|---|---|---|
| 1986 Proof | Est. 15,000 | Value: 17.50 | | | | |

**CROWN KM# 161c Weight:** 5.1000 g. **Composition:** 0.3740 Gold .0613 oz. AGW **Series:** World Cup Soccer - Mexico **Obverse:** Bust of Queen Elizabeth II right **Reverse:** Three players

| Date | Mintage | F | VF | XF | Unc | BU |
|---|---|---|---|---|---|---|
| 1986 Proof | Est. 10,000 | Value: 75.00 | | | | |

**CROWN KM# 161d Weight:** 7.9600 g. **Composition:** 0.9170 Gold .2347 oz. AGW **Series:** World Cup Soccer - Mexico **Obverse:** Bust of Queen Elizabeth II right **Reverse:** Three players

| Date | Mintage | F | VF | XF | Unc | BU |
|---|---|---|---|---|---|---|
| 1986 Proof | Est. 1,000 | Value: 150 | | | | |

**CROWN KM# 162 Composition:** Copper-Nickel **Series:** World Cup Soccer - Mexico **Obverse:** Bust of Queen Elizabeth II right **Reverse:** Two players

| Date | Mintage | F | VF | XF | Unc | BU |
|---|---|---|---|---|---|---|
| 1986 | Est. 50,000 | — | — | — | 2.50 | — |

**CROWN KM# 161e Weight:** 52.0000 g. **Composition:** 0.9500 Platinum 1.5884 oz. APW **Series:** World Cup Soccer - Mexico **Obverse:** Bust of Queen Elizabeth II right **Reverse:** Three players

| Date | Mintage | F | VF | XF | Unc | BU |
|---|---|---|---|---|---|---|
| 1986 Proof | Est. 200 | Value: 1,100 | | | | |

**CROWN KM# 162a Composition:** Silver Clad Copper-Nickel **Series:** World Cup Soccer - Mexico **Obverse:** Bust of Queen Elizabeth II right **Reverse:** Two players

| Date | Mintage | F | VF | XF | Unc | BU |
|---|---|---|---|---|---|---|
| 1986 Proof | Est. 20,000 | Value: 10.00 | | | | |

**CROWN KM# 162b Weight:** 28.2800 g. **Composition:** 0.9250 Silver .8411 oz. ASW **Series:** World Cup Soccer - Mexico **Obverse:** Bust of Queen Elizabeth II right **Reverse:** Two players

| Date | Mintage | F | VF | XF | Unc | BU |
|---|---|---|---|---|---|---|
| 1986 Proof | Est. 15,000 | Value: 17.50 | | | | |

**CROWN KM# 162c Weight:** 5.1000 g. **Composition:** 0.3740 Gold .0613 oz. AGW **Series:** World Cup Soccer - Mexico **Obverse:** Bust of Queen Elizabeth II right **Reverse:** Two players

| Date | Mintage | F | VF | XF | Unc | BU |
|---|---|---|---|---|---|---|
| 1986 Proof | Est. 10,000 | Value: 75.00 | | | | |

**CROWN KM# 162d Weight:** 7.9600 g. **Composition:** 0.9170 Gold .2347 oz. AGW **Series:** World Cup Soccer - Mexico **Obverse:** Bust of Queen Elizabeth II right **Reverse:** Two players

| Date | Mintage | F | VF | XF | Unc | BU |
|---|---|---|---|---|---|---|
| 1986 Proof | Est. 1,000 | Value: 150 | | | | |

**CROWN KM# 162e Weight:** 52.0000 g. **Composition:** 0.9500 Platinum 1.5884 oz. APW **Series:** World Cup Soccer - Mexico **Obverse:** Bust of Queen Elizabeth II right **Reverse:** Two players

| Date | Mintage | F | VF | XF | Unc | BU |
|---|---|---|---|---|---|---|
| 1986 Proof | Est. 200 | Value: 1,100 | | | | |

**CROWN KM# 163 Composition:** Copper-Nickel **Series:** World Cup Soccer - Mexico **Obverse:** Bust of Queen Elizabeth II right **Reverse:** Net and two players

| Date | Mintage | F | VF | XF | Unc | BU |
|---|---|---|---|---|---|---|
| 1986 | Est. 50,000 | — | — | — | 2.50 | — |

**CROWN KM# 163a Composition:** Silver Clad Copper-Nickel **Series:** World Cup Soccer - Mexico **Obverse:** Bust of Queen Elizabeth II right **Reverse:** Net and two players

| Date | Mintage | F | VF | XF | Unc | BU |
|---|---|---|---|---|---|---|
| 1986 Proof | Est. 20,000 | Value: 10.00 | | | | |

**CROWN KM# 163b Weight:** 28.2800 g. **Composition:** 0.9250 Silver .8411 oz. ASW **Series:** World Cup Soccer - Mexico **Obverse:** Bust of Queen Elizabeth II right **Reverse:** Net and two players

| Date | Mintage | F | VF | XF | Unc | BU |
|---|---|---|---|---|---|---|
| 1986 Proof | Est. 15,000 | Value: 17.50 | | | | |

**CROWN KM# 163c Weight:** 5.1000 g. **Composition:** 0.3740 Gold .0613 oz. AGW **Series:** World Cup Soccer - Mexico **Obverse:** Bust of Queen Elizabeth II right **Reverse:** Net and two players

| Date | Mintage | F | VF | XF | Unc | BU |
|---|---|---|---|---|---|---|
| 1986 Proof | Est. 10,000 | Value: 75.00 | | | | |

**CROWN KM# 163d Weight:** 7.9600 g. **Composition:** 0.9170 Gold .2347 oz. AGW **Series:** World Cup Soccer - Mexico **Obverse:** Bust of Queen Elizabeth II right **Reverse:** Net and two players

| Date | Mintage | F | VF | XF | Unc | BU |
|---|---|---|---|---|---|---|
| 1986 Proof | Est. 1,000 | Value: 150 | | | | |

**CROWN KM# 163e Weight:** 52.0000 g. **Composition:** 0.9500 Platinum 1.5884 oz. APW **Series:** World Cup Soccer - Mexico **Obverse:** Bust of Queen Elizabeth II right **Reverse:** Net and two players

| Date | Mintage | F | VF | XF | Unc | BU |
|---|---|---|---|---|---|---|
| 1986 Proof | Est. 200 | Value: 1,100 | | | | |

**CROWN KM# 164 Composition:** Copper-Nickel **Series:** World Cup Soccer - Mexico **Obverse:** Bust of Queen Elizabeth II right **Reverse:** Globe

| Date | Mintage | F | VF | XF | Unc | BU |
|---|---|---|---|---|---|---|
| 1986 | Est. 50,000 | — | — | — | 2.50 | — |

**CROWN KM# 164b Weight:** 28.2800 g. **Composition:** 0.9250 Silver .8411 oz. ASW **Series:** World Cup Soccer - Mexico **Obverse:** Bust of Queen Elizabeth II right **Reverse:** Globe

| Date | Mintage | F | VF | XF | Unc | BU |
|---|---|---|---|---|---|---|
| 1986 Proof | Est. 15,000 | Value: 17.50 | | | | |

**CROWN KM# 164c Weight:** 5.1000 g. **Composition:** 0.3740 Gold .0613 oz. AGW **Series:** World Cup Soccer - Mexico **Obverse:** Bust of Queen Elizabeth II right **Reverse:** Globe

| Date | Mintage | F | VF | XF | Unc | BU |
|---|---|---|---|---|---|---|
| 1986 Proof | Est. 10,000 | Value: 75.00 | | | | |

**CROWN KM# 164d Weight:** 7.9600 g. **Composition:** 0.9170 Gold .2347 oz. AGW **Series:** World Cup Soccer - Mexico **Obverse:** Bust of Queen Elizabeth II right **Reverse:** Globe

| Date | Mintage | F | VF | XF | Unc | BU |
|---|---|---|---|---|---|---|
| 1986 Proof | Est. 1,000 | Value: 150 | | | | |

**CROWN KM# 164e Weight:** 52.0000 g. **Composition:** 0.9500 Platinum 1.5884 oz. APW **Series:** World Cup Soccer - Mexico **Obverse:** Bust of Queen Elizabeth II right **Reverse:** Globe

| Date | Mintage | F | VF | XF | Unc | BU |
|---|---|---|---|---|---|---|
| 1986 Proof | Est. 200 | Value: 1,100 | | | | |

**CROWN KM# 165 Composition:** Copper-Nickel **Series:** World Cup Soccer - Mexico **Obverse:** Bust of Queen Elizabeth II right **Reverse:** Flags

| Date | Mintage | F | VF | XF | Unc | BU |
|---|---|---|---|---|---|---|
| 1986 | Est. 50,000 | — | — | — | 2.50 | — |

**CROWN KM# 165b Weight:** 28.2800 g. **Composition:** 0.9250 Silver .8411 oz. ASW **Series:** World Cup Soccer - Mexico **Obverse:** Bust of Queen Elizabeth II right **Reverse:** Flags

| Date | Mintage | F | VF | XF | Unc | BU |
|---|---|---|---|---|---|---|
| 1986 Proof | Est. 15,000 | Value: 17.50 | | | | |

**CROWN KM# 165c Weight:** 5.1000 g. **Composition:** 0.3740 Gold .0613 oz. AGW **Series:** World Cup Soccer - Mexico **Obverse:** Bust of Queen Elizabeth II right **Reverse:** Flags

| Date | Mintage | F | VF | XF | Unc | BU |
|---|---|---|---|---|---|---|
| 1986 Proof | Est. 10,000 | Value: 75.00 | | | | |

**CROWN KM# 165d Weight:** 7.9600 g. **Composition:** 0.9170 Gold .2347 oz. AGW **Series:** World Cup Soccer - Mexico **Obverse:** Bust of Queen Elizabeth II right **Reverse:** Flags

| Date | Mintage | F | VF | XF | Unc | BU |
|---|---|---|---|---|---|---|
| 1986 Proof | Est. 1,000 | Value: 150 | | | | |

**CROWN KM# 165e Weight:** 52.0000 g. **Composition:** 0.9500 Platinum 1.5884 oz. APW **Series:** World Cup Soccer - Mexico **Obverse:** Bust of Queen Elizabeth II right **Reverse:** Flags

| Date | Mintage | F | VF | XF | Unc | BU |
|---|---|---|---|---|---|---|
| 1986 Proof | Est. 200 | Value: 1,100 | | | | |

**CROWN KM# 173 Composition:** Copper-Nickel **Subject:** Prince Andrew's Wedding **Obverse:** Bust of Queen Elizabeth II right **Reverse:** Portraits

| Date | Mintage | F | VF | XF | Unc | BU |
|---|---|---|---|---|---|---|
| 1986 | Est. 50,000 | — | — | — | 4.00 | — |
| 1986 Prooflike | — | — | — | — | — | — |

**CROWN KM# 173a Composition:** Silver Clad Copper-Nickel **Subject:** Prince Andrew's Wedding **Obverse:** Bust of Queen Elizabeth II right **Reverse:** Portraits

| Date | Mintage | F | VF | XF | Unc | BU |
|---|---|---|---|---|---|---|
| 1986 Proof | Est. 20,000 | Value: 12.00 | | | | |

**CROWN KM# 173b Weight:** 28.2800 g. **Composition:** 0.9250 Silver .8411 oz. ASW **Subject:** Prince Andrew's Wedding **Obverse:** Bust of Queen Elizabeth II right **Reverse:** Portraits

| Date | Mintage | F | VF | XF | Unc | BU |
|---|---|---|---|---|---|---|
| 1986 | Est. 20,000 | — | — | — | 15.00 | — |
| 1986 Proof | Est. 15,000 | Value: 18.00 | | | | |

**CROWN KM# 173c Weight:** 5.1000 g. **Composition:** 0.3740 Gold .0613 oz. AGW **Subject:** Prince Andrew's Wedding **Obverse:** Bust of Queen Elizabeth II right **Reverse:** Portraits

| Date | Mintage | F | VF | XF | Unc | BU |
|---|---|---|---|---|---|---|
| 1986 Proof | Est. 10,000 | Value: 65.00 | | | | |

**CROWN KM# 173d Weight:** 7.9600 g. **Composition:** 0.9170 Gold .2347 oz. AGW **Subject:** Prince Andrew's Wedding **Obverse:** Bust of Queen Elizabeth II right **Reverse:** Portraits

| Date | Mintage | F | VF | XF | Unc | BU |
|---|---|---|---|---|---|---|
| 1986 Proof | Est. 1,000 | Value: 150 | | | | |

**CROWN KM# 173e Weight:** 52.0000 g. **Composition:** 0.9500 Platinum 1.5884 oz. APW **Subject:** Prince Andrew's Wedding **Obverse:** Bust of Queen Elizabeth II right **Reverse:** Portraits

| Date | Mintage | F | VF | XF | Unc | BU |
|---|---|---|---|---|---|---|
| 1986 Proof | Est. 100 | Value: 1,200 | | | | |

**CROWN KM# 174 Composition:** Copper-Nickel **Subject:** Prince Andrew's Wedding **Obverse:** Bust of Queen Elizabeth II right **Reverse:** Coat of Arms

| Date | Mintage | F | VF | XF | Unc | BU |
|---|---|---|---|---|---|---|
| 1986 | Est. 50,000 | — | — | — | 4.00 | — |
| 1986 Prooflike | — | — | — | — | — | — |

**CROWN KM# 174a Composition:** Silver Clad Copper-Nickel **Subject:** Prince Andrew's Wedding **Obverse:** Bust of Queen Elizabeth II right **Reverse:** Coat of Arms

| Date | Mintage | F | VF | XF | Unc | BU |
|---|---|---|---|---|---|---|
| 1986 Proof | Est. 20,000 | Value: 12.00 | | | | |

**CROWN KM# 174b Weight:** 28.2800 g. **Composition:** 0.9250 Silver .8411 oz. ASW **Subject:** Prince Andrew's Wedding **Obverse:** Bust of Queen Elizabeth II right **Reverse:** Coat of Arms

| Date | Mintage | F | VF | XF | Unc | BU |
|---|---|---|---|---|---|---|
| 1986 | Est. 20,000 | — | — | — | 15.00 | — |
| 1986 Proof | Est. 15,000 | Value: 18.00 | | | | |

**CROWN** **KM# 174c** **Weight:** 5.1000 g. **Composition:** 0.3740 Gold .0613 oz. AGW **Subject:** Prince Andrew's Wedding **Obverse:** Bust of Queen Elizabeth II right **Reverse:** Coat of Arms

| Date | Mintage | F | VF | XF | Unc | BU |
|---|---|---|---|---|---|---|
| 1986 Proof | Est. 10,000 | Value: 75.00 | | | | |

**CROWN** **KM# 174d** **Weight:** 7.9600 g. **Composition:** 0.9170 Gold .2347 oz. AGW **Subject:** Prince Andrew's Wedding **Obverse:** Bust of Queen Elizabeth II right **Reverse:** Coat of Arms

| Date | Mintage | F | VF | XF | Unc | BU |
|---|---|---|---|---|---|---|
| 1986 Proof | Est. 1,000 | Value: 150 | | | | |

**CROWN** **KM# 174e** **Weight:** 52.0000 g. **Composition:** 0.9500 Platinum 1.5884 oz. APW **Subject:** Prince Andrew's Wedding **Obverse:** Bust of Queen Elizabeth II right **Reverse:** Coat of Arms

| Date | Mintage | F | VF | XF | Unc | BU |
|---|---|---|---|---|---|---|
| 1986 Proof | Est. 100 | Value: 1,200 | | | | |

**CROWN** **KM# 176** **Composition:** Copper-Nickel **Subject:** United States Constitution **Obverse:** Bust of Queen Elizabeth II right **Reverse:** Statue of Liberty surrounded by bust of presidents

| Date | Mintage | F | VF | XF | Unc | BU |
|---|---|---|---|---|---|---|
| 1987 Prooflike | — | — | — | — | — | — |

**CROWN** **KM# 176a** **Weight:** 31.1000 g. **Composition:** 0.9990 Palladium 1.0000 oz. **Subject:** United States Constitution Bicentennial **Obverse:** Bust of Queen Elizabeth II right **Reverse:** Statue of Liberty surrounded by bust of presidents

| Date | Mintage | F | VF | XF | Unc | BU |
|---|---|---|---|---|---|---|
| 1987 Proof | Est. 25,000 | Value: 750 | | | | |

**CROWN** **KM# 176b** **Weight:** 31.1000 g. **Composition:** 0.9950 Platinum 1.0000 oz. APW **Subject:** United States Constitution Bicentennial **Obverse:** Bust of Queen Elizabeth II right **Reverse:** Statue of Liberty surrounded by bust of presidents

| Date | Mintage | F | VF | XF | Unc | BU |
|---|---|---|---|---|---|---|
| 1987 Proof | Est. 1,000 | Value: 800 | | | | |

**CROWN** **KM# 179** **Composition:** Copper-Nickel **Series:** Americ'a Cup **Obverse:** Bust of Queen Elizabeth II right **Reverse:** Kookaburra III and map

| Date | Mintage | F | VF | XF | Unc | BU |
|---|---|---|---|---|---|---|
| 1987 | 50,000 | — | — | — | 3.00 | — |
| 1987 Prooflike | — | — | — | — | 8.00 | — |

**CROWN** **KM# 179b** **Weight:** 28.2800 g. **Composition:** 0.9250 Silver .8411 oz. ASW **Series:** America's Cup **Obverse:** Bust of Queen Elizabeth II right **Reverse:** Kookaburra III and map

| Date | Mintage | F | VF | XF | Unc | BU |
|---|---|---|---|---|---|---|
| 1987 | Est. 20,000 | — | — | — | 26.50 | — |
| 1987 Proof | Est. 15,000 | Value: 40.00 | | | | |

**CROWN** **KM# 179c** **Weight:** 31.1030 g. **Composition:** 0.9990 Palladium 1.0000 oz. **Series:** America's Cup **Obverse:** Bust of Queen Elizabeth II right **Reverse:** Kookaburra III and map

| Date | Mintage | F | VF | XF | Unc | BU |
|---|---|---|---|---|---|---|
| 1987 Proof | 1,000 | Value: 750 | | | | |

**CROWN** **KM# 183** **Composition:** Copper-Nickel **Series:** America's Cup **Obverse:** Bust of Queen Elizabeth II right **Reverse:** Saiboats and cup

| Date | Mintage | F | VF | XF | Unc | BU |
|---|---|---|---|---|---|---|
| 1987 | 50,000 | — | — | — | 3.00 | — |
| 1987 Prooflike | — | — | — | — | 8.00 | — |

**CROWN** **KM# 183b** **Weight:** 28.2800 g. **Composition:** 0.9250 Silver .8411 oz. ASW **Series:** America's Cup **Obverse:** Bust of Queen Elizabeth II right **Reverse:** Sailboats and cup

| Date | Mintage | F | VF | XF | Unc | BU |
|---|---|---|---|---|---|---|
| 1987 | Est. 20,000 | — | — | — | 26.50 | — |
| 1987 Proof | Est. 15,000 | Value: 40.00 | | | | |

**CROWN** **KM# 183c** **Weight:** 31.1030 g. **Composition:** 0.9990 Palladium 1.0000 oz. **Series:** America's Cup **Obverse:** Bust of Queen Elizabeth II right **Reverse:** Sailboats and cup

| Date | Mintage | F | VF | XF | Unc | BU |
|---|---|---|---|---|---|---|
| 1987 Proof | 1,000 | Value: 600 | | | | |

**CROWN** **KM# 184** **Composition:** Copper-Nickel **Series:** America's Cup **Obverse:** Bust of Queen Elizabeth II right **Reverse:** Statue of Liberty and sailboats

| Date | Mintage | F | VF | XF | Unc | BU |
|---|---|---|---|---|---|---|
| 1987 | 50,000 | — | — | — | 3.00 | — |
| 1987 Prooflike | — | — | — | — | 8.00 | — |

**CROWN** **KM# 184b** **Weight:** 28.2800 g. **Composition:** 0.9250 Silver .8411 oz. ASW **Series:** Americ'a Cup **Obverse:** Bust of Queen Elizabeth II right **Reverse:** Statue of Liberty and sailboats

| Date | Mintage | F | VF | XF | Unc | BU |
|---|---|---|---|---|---|---|
| 1987 | Est. 20,000 | — | — | — | 26.50 | — |
| 1987 Proof | Est. 15,000 | Value: 40.00 | | | | |

**CROWN** **KM# 184c** **Weight:** 31.1030 g. **Composition:** 0.9990 Palladium 1.0000 oz. **Series:** America's Cup **Obverse:** Bust of Queen Elizabeth II right **Reverse:** Statue of Liberty and sailboats

| Date | Mintage | F | VF | XF | Unc | BU |
|---|---|---|---|---|---|---|
| 1987 Proof | 1,000 | Value: 750 | | | | |

**CROWN** **KM# 185b** **Weight:** 28.2800 g. **Composition:** 0.9250 Silver .8411 oz. ASW **Series:** America's Cup **Obverse:** Bust of Queen Elizabeth II right **Reverse:** Bust of George Steers and sailboat

| Date | Mintage | F | VF | XF | Unc | BU |
|---|---|---|---|---|---|---|
| 1987 | Est. 20,000 | — | — | — | 26.50 | — |
| 1987 Proof | Est. 15,000 | Value: 40.00 | | | | |

**CROWN** **KM# 185** **Composition:** Copper-Nickel **Series:** America's Cup **Obverse:** Bust of Queen Elizabeth II right **Reverse:** Portrait George Steers and sailboat

| Date | Mintage | F | VF | XF | Unc | BU |
|---|---|---|---|---|---|---|
| 1987 | 50,000 | — | — | — | 3.00 | — |
| 1987 Prooflike | — | — | — | — | 8.00 | — |

**CROWN** **KM# 185c** **Weight:** 31.1030 g. **Composition:** 0.9990 Palladium 1.0000 oz. **Series:** America's Cup **Obverse:** Bust of Queen Elizabeth II right **Reverse:** Bust of George Steers and sailboat

| Date | Mintage | F | VF | XF | Unc | BU |
|---|---|---|---|---|---|---|
| 1987 Proof | 1,000 | Value: 750 | | | | |

**CROWN** **KM# 186** **Composition:** Copper-Nickel **Series:** America's Cup **Obverse:** Bust of Queen Elizabeth II right **Reverse:** Bust of Sir Thomas Lipton and sailboat

| Date | Mintage | F | VF | XF | Unc | BU |
|---|---|---|---|---|---|---|
| 1987 | 50,000 | — | — | — | 3.00 | — |
| 1987 Prooflike | — | — | — | — | 8.00 | — |

**CROWN** **KM# 186b** **Weight:** 28.2800 g. **Composition:** 0.9250 Silver .8411 oz. ASW **Series:** America's Cup **Obverse:** Bust of Queen Elizabeth II right **Reverse:** Bust of Sir Thomas Lipton and sailboat

| Date | Mintage | F | VF | XF | Unc | BU |
|---|---|---|---|---|---|---|
| 1987 | Est. 20,000 | — | — | — | 26.50 | — |
| 1987 Proof | Est. 15,000 | Value: 40.00 | | | | |

**CROWN** **KM# 186c** **Weight:** 31.1030 g. **Composition:** 0.9990 Palladium 1.0000 oz. **Series:** America's Cup **Obverse:** Bust of Queen Elizabeth II right **Reverse:** Bust of Sir Thomas LIpton and sailboat

| Date | Mintage | F | VF | XF | Unc | BU |
|---|---|---|---|---|---|---|
| 1987 Proof | 1,000 | Value: 750 | | | | |

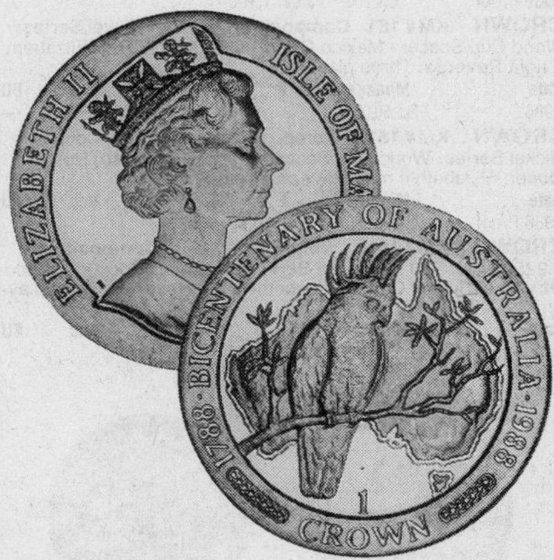


**CROWN** **KM# 222** **Composition:** Copper-Nickel **Subject:** Australian Bicentennial **Obverse:** Bust of Queen Elizabeth II right **Reverse:** Cockatoo

| Date | Mintage | F | VF | XF | Unc | BU |
|---|---|---|---|---|---|---|
| 1988 | — | — | — | — | 9.00 | — |
| 1988 Proof | 500 | Value: 15.00 | | | | |

**CROWN** **KM# 223** **Composition:** Copper-Nickel **Subject:** Australian Bicentennial **Obverse:** Bust of Queen Elizabeth II right **Reverse:** Koala

| Date | Mintage | F | VF | XF | Unc | BU |
|---|---|---|---|---|---|---|
| 1988 | — | — | — | — | 9.00 | — |
| 1988 Proof | 500 | Value: 15.00 | | | | |

**CROWN** **KM# 224** **Composition:** Copper-Nickel **Subject:** Australian Bicentennial **Obverse:** Bust of Queen Elizabeth II right **Reverse:** Dicklbill platypus

| Date | Mintage | F | VF | XF | Unc | BU |
|---|---|---|---|---|---|---|
| 1988 | — | — | — | — | 9.00 | — |
| 1988 Proof | 500 | Value: 15.00 | | | | |

**CROWN** **KM# 225** **Composition:** Copper-Nickel **Subject:** Australian Bicentennial **Obverse:** Bust of Queen Elizabeth II right **Reverse:** Kangaroo

| Date | Mintage | F | VF | XF | Unc | BU |
|---|---|---|---|---|---|---|
| 1988 | — | — | — | — | 9.00 | — |
| 1988 Proof | 500 | Value: 15.00 | | | | |

**CROWN** **KM# 226** **Composition:** Copper-Nickel **Subject:** Australian Bicentennial **Obverse:** Bust of Queen Elizabeth II right **Reverse:** Dingo

| Date | Mintage | F | VF | XF | Unc | BU |
|---|---|---|---|---|---|---|
| 1988 | — | — | — | — | 9.00 | — |

**CROWN** **KM# 227** **Composition:** Copper-Nickel **Subject:** Australian Bicentennial **Obverse:** Bust of Queen Elizabeth II right **Reverse:** Tasmanian devil

| Date | Mintage | F | VF | XF | Unc | BU |
|---|---|---|---|---|---|---|
| 1988 | — | — | — | — | 9.00 | — |

**CROWN** **KM# 228** **Composition:** Copper-Nickel **Series:** Steam Navigation **Obverse:** Bust of Queen Elizabeth II right **Reverse:** Patrick Miller's Number One

| Date | Mintage | F | VF | XF | Unc | BU |
|---|---|---|---|---|---|---|
| 1988 | — | — | — | — | 3.50 | — |

**CROWN** **KM# 229** **Composition:** Copper-Nickel **Series:** Steam Navigation **Obverse:** Bust of Queen Elizabeth II right **Reverse:** Sirius

| Date | Mintage | F | VF | XF | Unc | BU |
|---|---|---|---|---|---|---|
| 1988 | — | — | — | — | 3.50 | — |

**CROWN** **KM# 230** **Composition:** Copper-Nickel **Series:** Steam Navigation **Obverse:** Bust of Queen Elizabeth II right **Reverse:** Chaperon

| Date | Mintage | F | VF | XF | Unc | BU |
|---|---|---|---|---|---|---|
| 1988 | — | — | — | — | 3.50 | — |

**CROWN** **KM# 231** **Composition:** Copper-Nickel **Series:** Steam Navigation **Obverse:** Bust of Queen Elizabeth II right **Reverse:** Mauretania

| Date | Mintage | F | VF | XF | Unc | BU |
|---|---|---|---|---|---|---|
| 1988 | — | — | — | — | 3.50 | — |

**CROWN** **KM# 232** **Composition:** Copper-Nickel **Series:** Steam Navigation **Obverse:** Bust of Queen Elizabeth II right **Reverse:** Queen Mary

| Date | Mintage | F | VF | XF | Unc | BU |
|---|---|---|---|---|---|---|
| 1988 | — | — | — | — | 3.50 | — |

**CROWN** **KM# 233** **Composition:** Copper-Nickel **Series:** Steam Navigation **Obverse:** Bust of Queen Elizabeth II right **Reverse:** Queen Elizabeth II

| Date | Mintage | F | VF | XF | Unc | BU |
|---|---|---|---|---|---|---|
| 1988 | — | — | — | — | 3.50 | — |

**CROWN** **KM# 234** **Weight:** 31.1000 g. **Composition:** 0.9990 Silver 1.0000 oz. ASW **Obverse:** Bust of Queen Elizabeth II right **Reverse:** Manx cat

| Date | Mintage | F | VF | XF | Unc | BU |
|---|---|---|---|---|---|---|
| 1988 Proof | 15,000 | Value: 15.00 | | | | |

**CROWN** **KM# 239** **Weight:** 31.1000 g. **Composition:** 0.9990 Gold 1.0000 oz. AGW **Obverse:** Bust of Queen Elizabeth II right **Reverse:** Manx cat

| Date | Mintage | F | VF | XF | Unc | BU |
|---|---|---|---|---|---|---|
| 1988 U | 4,300 | — | — | — | 500 | — |
| 1988 Proof | 5,000 | Value: 510 | | | | |

**CROWN** **KM# 245** **Composition:** Copper-Nickel **Obverse:** Bust of Queen Elizabeth II right **Reverse:** Manx cat

| Date | Mintage | F | VF | XF | Unc | BU |
|---|---|---|---|---|---|---|
| 1988 | — | — | — | — | 10.00 | — |
| 1988 Proof | 250 | Value: 25.00 | | | | |

**CROWN** **KM# 314** **Weight:** 31.1000 g. **Composition:** 0.9990 Silver 1.0000 oz. ASW **Subject:** Australian Bicentennial **Obverse:** Bust of Queen Elizabeth II right **Reverse:** Cockatoo

| Date | Mintage | F | VF | XF | Unc | BU |
|---|---|---|---|---|---|---|
| 1988 Proof | — | Value: 175 | | | | |

**CROWN** **KM# 315** **Weight:** 31.1000 g. **Composition:** 0.9990 Silver 1.0000 oz. ASW **Subject:** Australian Bicentennial **Obverse:** Bust of Queen Elizabeth II right **Reverse:** Koala

| Date | Mintage | F | VF | XF | Unc | BU |
|---|---|---|---|---|---|---|
| 1988 Proof | — | Value: 175 | | | | |

**CROWN** **KM# 316** **Weight:** 31.1000 g. **Composition:** 0.9990 Silver 1.0000 oz. ASW **Subject:** Australian Bicentennial **Obverse:** Bust of Queen Elizabeth II right **Reverse:** Duckbill platypus

| Date | Mintage | F | VF | XF | Unc | BU |
|---|---|---|---|---|---|---|
| 1988 Proof | — | Value: 175 | | | | |

**CROWN** **KM# 317** **Weight:** 31.1000 g. **Composition:** 0.9999 Silver 1.0000 oz. ASW **Subject:** Australian Bicentennial **Obverse:** Bust of Queen Elizabeth II right **Reverse:** Kangaroo

| Date | Mintage | F | VF | XF | Unc | BU |
|---|---|---|---|---|---|---|
| 1988 Proof | — | Value: 175 | | | | |

**CROWN** **KM# 318** **Weight:** 31.1000 g. **Composition:** 0.9999 Silver 1.0000 oz. ASW **Subject:** Australian Bicentennial **Obverse:** Bust of Queen Elizabeth II right **Reverse:** Dingo

| Date | Mintage | F | VF | XF | Unc | BU |
|---|---|---|---|---|---|---|
| 1988 Proof | — | Value: 175 | | | | |

**CROWN** **KM# 319** **Weight:** 31.1000 g. **Composition:** 0.9999 Silver 1.0000 oz. ASW **Subject:** Australian Bicentennial **Obverse:** Bust of Queen Elizabeth II right **Reverse:** Tasmanian Devil

| Date | Mintage | F | VF | XF | Unc | BU |
|---|---|---|---|---|---|---|
| 1988 Proof | — | Value: 175 | | | | |

**CROWN** **KM# 240** **Composition:** Copper-Nickel **Series:** Mutiny on the Bounty **Obverse:** Bust of Queen Elizabeth II right **Reverse:** Captain Bligh and Elizabeth Betham

| Date | Mintage | F | VF | XF | Unc | BU |
|---|---|---|---|---|---|---|
| 1989 | — | — | — | — | 3.25 | — |
| 1989 Prooflike | — | — | — | — | 15.00 | — |

**CROWN** **KM# 240a** **Weight:** 28.2800 g. **Composition:** 0.9250 Silver .8411 oz. ASW **Series:** Mutiny on the Bounty **Obverse:** Bust of Queen Elizabeth II right **Reverse:** Captain Bligh and Elizabeth Betham

| Date | Mintage | F | VF | XF | Unc | BU |
|---|---|---|---|---|---|---|
| 1989 Proof | — | Value: 45.00 | | | | |

**CROWN** **KM# 241** **Composition:** Copper-Nickel **Series:** Mutiny on the Bounty **Obverse:** Bust of Queen Elizabeth II right **Reverse:** H.M.S. Bounty

| Date | Mintage | F | VF | XF | Unc | BU |
|---|---|---|---|---|---|---|
| 1989 | — | — | — | — | 7.50 | — |
| 1989 Prooflike | — | — | — | — | 15.00 | — |

**CROWN** **KM# 241a** **Weight:** 28.2800 g. **Composition:** 0.9250 Silver .8411 oz. ASW **Series:** Mutiny on the Bounty **Obverse:** Bust of Queen Elizabeth II right **Reverse:** H.M.S. Bounty

| Date | Mintage | F | VF | XF | Unc | BU |
|---|---|---|---|---|---|---|
| 1989 Proof | — | Value: 45.00 | | | | |

**CROWN** **KM# 242** **Composition:** Copper-Nickel **Series:** Mutiny on the Bounty **Obverse:** Bust of Queen Elizabeth II right **Reverse:** Captain Bligh and crew set afloat

| Date | Mintage | F | VF | XF | Unc | BU |
|---|---|---|---|---|---|---|
| 1989 | — | — | — | — | 7.50 | — |
| 1989 Prooflike | — | — | — | — | 15.00 | — |

**CROWN** **KM# 242a** **Weight:** 28.2800 g. **Composition:** 0.9250 Silver .8411 oz. ASW **Series:** Mutiny on the Bounty **Obverse:** Bust of Queen Elizabeth II right **Reverse:** Captain Bligh and crew set afloat

| Date | Mintage | F | VF | XF | Unc | BU |
|---|---|---|---|---|---|---|
| 1989 Proof | — | Value: 45.00 | | | | |

**CROWN** **KM# 243** **Composition:** Copper-Nickel **Series:** Muntiny on the Bounty **Obverse:** Bust of Queen Elizabeth II right **Reverse:** Pitcairn Island

| Date | Mintage | F | VF | XF | Unc | BU |
|---|---|---|---|---|---|---|
| 1989 | — | — | — | — | 7.50 | — |
| 1989 Prooflike | — | — | — | — | 15.00 | — |

**CROWN** **KM# 243a** **Weight:** 28.2800 g. **Composition:** 0.9250 Silver .8411 oz. ASW **Series:** Mutiny on the Bounty **Obverse:** Bust of Queen Elizabeth II right **Reverse:** Pitcairn Island

| Date | Mintage | F | VF | XF | Unc | BU |
|---|---|---|---|---|---|---|
| 1989 Proof | — | Value: 45.00 | | | | |

**CROWN** **KM# 246** **Composition:** Copper-Nickel **Obverse:** Bust of Queen Elizabeth II right **Reverse:** Washington crossing the Delaware

| Date | Mintage | F | VF | XF | Unc | BU |
|---|---|---|---|---|---|---|
| 1989 | — | — | — | — | 2.75 | — |
| 1989 Proof | — | Value: 9.00 | | | | |

**CROWN** **KM# 246a** **Weight:** 28.2800 g. **Composition:** 0.9250 Silver .8411 oz. ASW **Obverse:** Bust of Queen Elizabeth II right **Reverse:** Washington crossing the Delaware

| Date | Mintage | F | VF | XF | Unc | BU |
|---|---|---|---|---|---|---|
| 1989 Proof | — | Value: 22.50 | | | | |

**CROWN** **KM# 247** **Composition:** Copper-Nickel **Subject:** George Washington Inauguration **Obverse:** Bust of Queen Elizabeth II right **Reverse:** Head of George Washington

| Date | Mintage | F | VF | XF | Unc | BU |
|---|---|---|---|---|---|---|
| 1989 | — | — | — | — | 2.75 | — |
| 1989 Proof | — | Value: 9.00 | | | | |

**CROWN** **KM# 247a** **Weight:** 28.2800 g. **Composition:** 0.9250 Silver .8411 oz. ASW **Subject:** George Washington Inauguration **Obverse:** Bust of Queen Elizabeth II right **Reverse:** Head of George Washington

| Date | Mintage | F | VF | XF | Unc | BU |
|---|---|---|---|---|---|---|
| 1989 Proof | — | Value: 22.50 | | | | |

**CROWN** **KM# 248** **Composition:** Copper-Nickel **Subject:** George Washington Inauguration **Obverse:** Bust of Queen Elizabeth II right **Reverse:** Cameo of George Washington with two eagles surrounding

| Date | Mintage | F | VF | XF | Unc | BU |
|---|---|---|---|---|---|---|
| 1989 | — | — | — | — | 2.75 | — |
| 1989 Proof | — | Value: 9.00 | | | | |

**CROWN** **KM# 248a** **Weight:** 28.2800 g. **Composition:** 0.9250 Silver .8411 oz. ASW **Subject:** George Washington Inauguration **Obverse:** Bust of Queen Elizabeth II right **Reverse:** Cameo of George Washinton with two eagles surrounding

| Date | Mintage | F | VF | XF | Unc | BU |
|---|---|---|---|---|---|---|
| 1989 Proof | — | Value: 22.50 | | | | |

**CROWN** **KM# 249** **Composition:** Copper-Nickel **Subject:** George Washington Inauguration **Obverse:** Bust of Queen Elizabeth II right **Reverse:** George Washington taking oath

| Date | Mintage | F | VF | XF | Unc | BU |
|---|---|---|---|---|---|---|
| 1989 | — | — | — | — | 2.75 | — |
| 1989 Proof | — | Value: 9.00 | | | | |

**CROWN** **KM# 249a** **Weight:** 28.2800 g. **Composition:** 0.9250 Silver .8411 oz. ASW **Subject:** George Washington Inauguration **Obverse:** Bust of Queen Elizabeth II right **Reverse:** George Washington taking oath

| Date | Mintage | F | VF | XF | Unc | BU |
|---|---|---|---|---|---|---|
| 1989 Proof | — | Value: 22.50 | | | | |

**CROWN** **KM# 250** **Composition:** Copper-Nickel **Obverse:** Bust of Queen Elizabeth II right **Reverse:** Persian cat

| Date | Mintage | F | VF | XF | Unc | BU |
|---|---|---|---|---|---|---|
| 1989 | — | — | — | — | 9.00 | — |
| 1989 Proof | 250 | Value: 32.00 | | | | |

**CROWN** **KM# 251** **Weight:** 31.1000 g. **Composition:** 0.9990 Silver 1.0000 oz. ASW **Obverse:** Bust of Queen Elizabeth II right **Reverse:** Persian cat

| Date | Mintage | F | VF | XF | Unc | BU |
|---|---|---|---|---|---|---|
| 1989 Proof | — | Value: 28.00 | | | | |

**CROWN** **KM# 256** **Weight:** 31.1000 g. **Composition:** 0.9990 Gold 1.0000 oz. AGW **Obverse:** Bust of Queen Elizabeth II right **Reverse:** Persian cat

| Date | Mintage | F | VF | XF | Unc | BU |
|---|---|---|---|---|---|---|
| 1989 | — | — | — | — | 450 | — |
| 1989 Proof | — | Value: 460 | | | | |

**CROWN** **KM# 273** **Composition:** Copper-Nickel **Subject:** Royal Visit **Obverse:** Bust of Queen Elizabeth II right

| Date | Mintage | F | VF | XF | Unc | BU |
|---|---|---|---|---|---|---|
| 1989 | Est. 50,000 | — | — | — | 4.00 | — |

**CROWN** **KM# 273a** **Weight:** 31.1000 g. **Composition:** 0.9990 Silver 1.0000 oz. ASW **Subject:** Royal Visit **Obverse:** Bust of Queen Elizabeth II right

| Date | Mintage | F | VF | XF | Unc | BU |
|---|---|---|---|---|---|---|
| 1989 Proof | Est. 20,000 | Value: 35.00 | | | | |

**CROWN** **KM# 273b** **Weight:** 31.1000 g. **Composition:** 0.9990 Gold 1.0000 oz. AGW **Subject:** Royal Visit **Obverse:** Bust of Queen Elizabeth II right

| Date | Mintage | F | VF | XF | Unc | BU |
|---|---|---|---|---|---|---|
| 1989 Proof | Est. 7,500 | Value: 685 | | | | |

**CROWN** **KM# 471** **Weight:** 31.1035 g. **Composition:** 0.9995 Platinum .9995 oz. APW **Obverse:** Bust of Queen Elizabeth II right **Reverse:** Persian cat

| Date | Mintage | F | VF | XF | Unc | BU |
|---|---|---|---|---|---|---|
| 1989 | — | — | — | — | BV+20% | — |
| | — | | | | | |

**CROWN** **KM# 267** **Composition:** Copper-Nickel **Subject:** 150th Anniverwary of "Penny Black" Stamp **Obverse:** Bust of Queen Elizabeth II right **Reverse:** Stamp **Note:** Struck in "pearl black" Copper-Nickel.

| Date | Mintage | F | VF | XF | Unc | BU |
|---|---|---|---|---|---|---|
| 1990 | — | — | — | — | 9.00 | — |
| 1990 Proof | 50,000 | Value: 16.50 | | | | |

**CROWN** **KM# 267a** **Weight:** 28.2800 g. **Composition:** 0.9250 Silver .8411 oz. ASW **Subject:** 150th Anniverwary of "Penny Black" Stamp **Obverse:** Bust of Queen Elizabeth II right **Reverse:** Stamp

| Date | Mintage | F | VF | XF | Unc | BU |
|---|---|---|---|---|---|---|
| 1990 Proof | 30,000 | Value: 30.00 | | | | |

**CROWN** **KM# 267b** **Weight:** 31.1000 g. **Composition:** 0.9170 Gold 1.0000 oz. AGW **Subject:** 150th Anniverwary of "Penny Black" Stamp **Obverse:** Bust of Queen Elizabeth II right **Reverse:** Stamp

| Date | Mintage | F | VF | XF | Unc | BU |
|---|---|---|---|---|---|---|
| 1990 Proof | Est. 1,000 | Value: 685 | | | | |

**CROWN** **KM# 267c** **Weight:** 52.0000 g. **Composition:** 0.9500 Platinum 1.5884 oz. APW **Subject:** 150th Anniverwary of "Penny Black" Stamp **Obverse:** Bust of Queen Elizabeth II right **Reverse:** Stamp

| Date | Mintage | F | VF | XF | Unc | BU |
|---|---|---|---|---|---|---|
| 1990 Proof | Est. 50 | Value: 1,350 | | | | |

**CROWN** **KM# 269** **Composition:** Copper-Nickel **Series:** Soccer **Obverse:** Bust of Queen Elizabeth II right **Reverse:** Milano

| Date | Mintage | F | VF | XF | Unc | BU |
|---|---|---|---|---|---|---|
| 1990 | — | — | — | — | 3.25 | — |

**CROWN** **KM# 269a** **Weight:** 28.2800 g. **Composition:** 0.9250 Silver .8411 oz. ASW **Series:** Soccer **Obverse:** Bust of Queen Elizabeth II right **Reverse:** Milano

| Date | Mintage | F | VF | XF | Unc | BU |
|---|---|---|---|---|---|---|
| 1990 Proof | Est. 30,000 | Value: 20.00 | | | | |

**CROWN** **KM# 269b** **Weight:** 6.2200 g. **Composition:** 0.9990 Gold .2000 oz. AGW **Series:** Soccer **Obverse:** Bust of Queen Elizabeth II right **Reverse:** Milano

| Date | Mintage | F | VF | XF | Unc | BU |
|---|---|---|---|---|---|---|
| 1990 Proof | Est. 500 | Value: 200 | | | | |

**CROWN** **KM# 269c** **Weight:** 6.2230 g. **Composition:** 0.9990 Platinum .2000 oz. APW **Series:** Soccer **Obverse:** Bust of Queen Elizabeth II right **Reverse:** Milano

| Date | Mintage | F | VF | XF | Unc | BU |
|---|---|---|---|---|---|---|
| 1990 Proof | Est. 100 | Value: 250 | | | | |

**CROWN** **KM# 270** **Composition:** Copper-Nickel **Series:** Soccer **Obverse:** Bust of Queen Elizabeth II right **Reverse:** Torino

| Date | Mintage | F | VF | XF | Unc | BU |
|---|---|---|---|---|---|---|
| 1990 | — | — | — | — | 6.00 | — |

**CROWN** **KM# 270a** **Weight:** 28.2800 g. **Composition:** 0.9250 Silver .8411 oz. ASW **Series:** Soccer **Obverse:** Bust of Queen Elizabeth II right **Reverse:** Torino

| Date | Mintage | F | VF | XF | Unc | BU |
|---|---|---|---|---|---|---|
| 1990 Proof | Est. 30,000 | Value: 20.00 | | | | |

**CROWN** **KM# 270b** **Weight:** 6.2200 g. **Composition:** 0.9990 Gold .2000 oz. AGW **Series:** Soccer **Obverse:** Bust of Queen Elizabeth II right **Reverse:** Torino

| Date | Mintage | F | VF | XF | Unc | BU |
|---|---|---|---|---|---|---|
| 1990 Proof | Est. 500 | Value: 200 | | | | |

**CROWN** **KM# 270c** **Weight:** 6.2230 g. **Composition:** 0.9990 Platinum .2000 oz. APW **Series:** Soccer **Obverse:** Bust of Queen Elizabeth II right **Reverse:** Torino

| Date | Mintage | F | VF | XF | Unc | BU |
|---|---|---|---|---|---|---|
| 1990 Proof | Est. 100 | Value: 250 | | | | |

**CROWN** **KM# 271** **Composition:** Copper-Nickel **Series:** Soccer **Obverse:** Bust of Queen Elizabeth II right **Reverse:** Bologna

| Date | Mintage | F | VF | XF | Unc | BU |
|---|---|---|---|---|---|---|
| 1990 | — | — | — | — | 6.00 | — |

**CROWN** **KM# 271a** **Weight:** 28.2800 g. **Composition:** 0.9250 Silver .8411 oz. ASW **Series:** Soccer **Obverse:** Bust of Queen Elizabeth II right **Reverse:** Bologna

| Date | Mintage | F | VF | XF | Unc | BU |
|---|---|---|---|---|---|---|
| 1990 Proof | Est. 30,000 | Value: 30.00 | | | | |

**CROWN** **KM# 271b** **Weight:** 6.2200 g. **Composition:** 0.9990 Gold .2000 oz. AGW **Series:** Soccer **Obverse:** Bust of Queen Elizabeth II right **Reverse:** Bologna

| Date | Mintage | F | VF | XF | Unc | BU |
|---|---|---|---|---|---|---|
| 1990 Proof | Est. 500 | Value: 200 | | | | |

**CROWN** **KM# 271c** **Weight:** 6.2230 g. **Composition:** 0.9990 Platinum .2000 oz. APW **Series:** Soccer **Obverse:** Bust of Queen Elizabeth II right **Reverse:** Bologna

| Date | Mintage | F | VF | XF | Unc | BU |
|---|---|---|---|---|---|---|
| 1990 Proof | Est. 100 | Value: 250 | | | | |

**CROWN** **KM# 272** **Composition:** Copper-Nickel **Series:** Soccer **Obverse:** Bust of Queen Elizabeth II right **Reverse:** Palermo

| Date | Mintage | F | VF | XF | Unc | BU |
|---|---|---|---|---|---|---|
| 1990 | — | — | — | — | 6.00 | — |

**CROWN** **KM# 272a** **Weight:** 28.2800 g. **Composition:** 0.9250 Silver .8411 oz. ASW **Series:** Soccer **Obverse:** Bust of Queen Elizabeth II right **Reverse:** Palermo

| Date | Mintage | F | VF | XF | Unc | BU |
|---|---|---|---|---|---|---|
| 1990 Proof | Est. 30,000 | Value: 20.00 | | | | |

**CROWN** **KM# 272b** **Weight:** 6.2200 g. **Composition:** 0.9990 Gold .2000 oz. AGW **Series:** Soccer **Obverse:** Bust of Queen Elizabeth II right **Reverse:** Palermo

| Date | Mintage | F | VF | XF | Unc | BU |
|---|---|---|---|---|---|---|
| 1990 Proof | Est. 500 | Value: 200 | | | | |

**CROWN** **KM# 272c** **Weight:** 6.2230 g. **Composition:** 0.9990 Platinum .2000 oz. APW **Series:** Soccer **Obverse:** Bust of Queen Elizabeth II right **Reverse:** Palermo

| Date | Mintage | F | VF | XF | Unc | BU |
|---|---|---|---|---|---|---|
| 1990 Proof | Est. 100 | Value: 250 | | | | |

**CROWN** **KM# 275** **Composition:** Copper-Nickel **Obverse:** Bust of Queen Elizabeth II right **Reverse:** Alley cat

| Date | Mintage | F | VF | XF | Unc | BU |
|---|---|---|---|---|---|---|
| 1990 | — | — | — | — | 9.00 | — |
| 1990 Proof | 250 | Value: 35.00 | | | | |

**CROWN** **KM# 276** **Weight:** 31.1000 g. **Composition:** 0.9990 Silver 1.000 oz. ASW **Obverse:** Bust of Queen Elizabeth II right **Reverse:** Alley cat

| Date | Mintage | F | VF | XF | Unc | BU |
|---|---|---|---|---|---|---|
| 1990 Proof | — | Value: 28.00 | | | | |

**CROWN** **KM# 281** **Weight:** 31.1000 g. **Composition:** 0.9990 Gold 1.000 oz. AGW **Obverse:** Bust of Queen Elizabeth II right **Reverse:** Alley cat

| Date | Mintage | F | VF | XF | Unc | BU |
|---|---|---|---|---|---|---|
| 1990 | — | — | — | — | 500 | — |
| 1990 Proof | — | Value: 510 | | | | |

**CROWN** **KM# 283** **Composition:** Copper-Nickel **Obverse:** Bust of Queen Elizabeth II right **Reverse:** Sir Winston Churchill with cigar

| Date | Mintage | F | VF | XF | Unc | BU |
|---|---|---|---|---|---|---|
| 1990 | — | — | — | — | 3.25 | — |

**CROWN** **KM# 283a** **Weight:** 28.2800 g. **Composition:** 0.9250 Silver .8411 oz. ASW **Obverse:** Bust of Queen Elizabeth II right **Reverse:** Sir Winston Churchill with cigar

| Date | Mintage | F | VF | XF | Unc | BU |
|---|---|---|---|---|---|---|
| 1990 Proof | Est. 25,000 | Value: 50.00 | | | | |

**CROWN** **KM# 283b** **Weight:** 6.2230 g. **Composition:** 0.9990 Gold .2000 oz. AGW **Obverse:** Bust of Queen Elizabeth II right **Reverse:** Sir Winston Churchill with cigar

| Date | Mintage | F | VF | XF | Unc | BU |
|---|---|---|---|---|---|---|
| 1990 Proof | Est. 500 | Value: 200 | | | | |

**CROWN** **KM# 283c** **Weight:** 6.2230 g. **Composition:** 0.9990 Platinum .2000 oz. APW **Obverse:** Bust of Queen Elizabeth II right **Reverse:** Sir Winston Churchill with cigar

| Date | Mintage | F | VF | XF | Unc | BU |
|---|---|---|---|---|---|---|
| 1990 Proof | Est. 100 | Value: 250 | | | | |

**CROWN** **KM# 284** **Composition:** Copper-Nickel **Obverse:** Bust of Queen Elizabeth II right **Reverse:** Sir Winston Churchill in garter robes

| Date | Mintage | F | VF | XF | Unc | BU |
|---|---|---|---|---|---|---|
| 1990 | — | — | — | — | 3.25 | — |

**CROWN** **KM# 284a** **Weight:** 28.2800 g. **Composition:** 0.9250 Silver .8411 oz. ASW **Obverse:** Bust of Queen Elizabeth II right **Reverse:** Sir Winston Churchill in garter robes

| Date | Mintage | F | VF | XF | Unc | BU |
|---|---|---|---|---|---|---|
| 1990 Proof | Est. 25,000 | Value: 50.00 | | | | |

**CROWN** **KM# 284b** **Weight:** 6.2230 g. **Composition:** 0.9990 Gold .2000 oz. AGW **Obverse:** Bust of Queen Elizabeth II right **Reverse:** Sir Winston Churchill in garter robes

| Date | Mintage | F | VF | XF | Unc | BU |
|---|---|---|---|---|---|---|
| 1990 Proof | Est. 500 | Value: 200 | | | | |

**CROWN** **KM# 284c** **Weight:** 6.2230 g. **Composition:** 0.9990 Platinum .2000 oz. APW **Obverse:** Bust of Queen Elizabeth II right **Reverse:** Sir Winston Churchill in garter robes

| Date | Mintage | F | VF | XF | Unc | BU |
|---|---|---|---|---|---|---|
| 1990 Proof | Est. 100 | Value: 250 | | | | |

**CROWN** **KM# 320** **Composition:** Copper Nickel **Subject:** America's Cup - San Diego **Reverse:** Cameo of sailing ship above two modern sailboats **Rev. Legend:** AMERICA'S CUP CHALLENGE

| Date | Mintage | F | VF | XF | Unc | BU |
|---|---|---|---|---|---|---|
| 1991 | Est. 125 | — | — | — | 30.00 | |

**CROWN** **KM# 291** **Composition:** Copper-Nickel **Subject:** 100th Anniversary - American Numismatic Association **Obverse:** Bust of Queen Elizabeth II right **Reverse:** Circle of coins

| Date | Mintage | F | VF | XF | Unc | BU |
|---|---|---|---|---|---|---|
| 1991 | — | — | — | — | 4.50 | — |

**CROWN** **KM# 291a** **Weight:** 28.2800 g. **Composition:** 0.9250 Silver .8411 oz. ASW **Subject:** 100th Anniversary - American Numismatic Association **Obverse:** Bust of Queen Elizabeth II right **Reverse:** Circle of coins

| Date | Mintage | F | VF | XF | Unc | BU |
|---|---|---|---|---|---|---|
| 1991 Proof | — | Value: 22.00 | | | | |

**CROWN** **KM# 292** **Composition:** Copper-Nickel **Obverse:** Bust of Queen Elizabeth II right **Reverse:** Norwegian cat

| Date | Mintage | F | VF | XF | Unc | BU |
|---|---|---|---|---|---|---|
| 1991 | — | — | — | — | 9.00 | — |
| 1991 Proof | 15 | — | — | — | — | — |

**CROWN** **KM# 293** **Weight:** 31.1000 g. **Composition:** 0.9990 Silver 1.0000 oz. ASW **Obverse:** Bust of Queen Elizabeth II right **Reverse:** Norwegian cat

| Date | Mintage | F | VF | XF | Unc | BU |
|---|---|---|---|---|---|---|
| 1991 Proof | 50,000 | Value: 28.00 | | | | |

**CROWN** **KM# 298** **Weight:** 31.1000 g. **Composition:** 0.9990 Gold 1.0000 oz. AGW **Obverse:** Bust of Queen Elizabeth II right **Reverse:** Norwegian cat

| Date | Mintage | F | VF | XF | Unc | BU |
|---|---|---|---|---|---|---|
| 1991 | — | — | — | — | 435 | — |
| 1991 Proof | — | Value: 445 | | | | |

**CROWN** **KM# 304** **Composition:** Copper-Nickel **Subject:** 10th Wedding Anniversary **Obverse:** Bust of Queen Elizabeth II right **Reverse:** Head of Prince Charles

| Date | Mintage | F | VF | XF | Unc | BU |
|---|---|---|---|---|---|---|
| 1991 | — | — | — | — | 3.75 | — |

**CROWN** **KM# 304a** **Weight:** 28.2800 g. **Composition:** 0.9250 Silver .8411 oz. ASW **Subject:** 10th Wedding Anniversary **Obverse:** Bust of Queen Elizabeth II right **Reverse:** Head of Prince Charles

| Date | Mintage | F | VF | XF | Unc | BU |
|---|---|---|---|---|---|---|
| 1991 Proof | — | Value: 40.00 | | | | |

**CROWN** **KM# 304b** **Weight:** 6.2200 g. **Composition:** 0.9990 Gold .2000 oz. AGW **Subject:** 10th Wedding Anniversary **Obverse:** Bust of Queen Elizabeth II right **Reverse:** Head of Prince Charles

| Date | Mintage | F | VF | XF | Unc | BU |
|---|---|---|---|---|---|---|
| 1991 Proof | — | Value: 165 | | | | |

**CROWN** **KM# 305** **Composition:** Copper-Nickel **Subject:** 10th Wedding Anniversary **Obverse:** Bust of Queen Elizabeth II right **Reverse:** Head of Princess Diana

| Date | Mintage | F | VF | XF | Unc | BU |
|---|---|---|---|---|---|---|
| 1991 | — | — | — | — | 3.75 | — |

**CROWN** **KM# 305a** **Weight:** 28.2800 g. **Composition:** 0.9250 Silver .8411 oz. ASW **Subject:** 10th Wedding Anniversary **Obverse:** Bust of Queen Elizabeth II right **Reverse:** Head of Princess Diana

| Date | Mintage | F | VF | XF | Unc | BU |
|---|---|---|---|---|---|---|
| 1991 Proof | — | Value: 40.00 | | | | |

**CROWN** **KM# 305b** **Weight:** 6.2200 g. **Composition:** 0.9990 Gold .2000 oz. AGW **Subject:** 10th Wedding Anniversary **Obverse:** Bust of Queen Elizabeth II right **Reverse:** Head of Princess Diana

| Date | Mintage | F | VF | XF | Unc | BU |
|---|---|---|---|---|---|---|
| 1991 Proof | — | Value: 165 | | | | |

**CROWN** **KM# 310** **Composition:** Copper-Nickel **Series:** Discovery of America **Obverse:** Bust of Queen Elizabeth II right **Reverse:** John Casement and train engine

| Date | Mintage | F | VF | XF | Unc | BU |
|---|---|---|---|---|---|---|
| 1992 | — | — | — | — | 3.75 | — |
| 1992 Proof | — | Value: 12.00 | | | | |

**CROWN** **KM# 310a** **Weight:** 28.2800 g. **Composition:** 0.9250 Silver .8411 oz. ASW **Series:** Discovery of America **Obverse:** Bust of Queen Elizabeth II right **Reverse:** John Casement and train engine

| Date | Mintage | F | VF | XF | Unc | BU |
|---|---|---|---|---|---|---|
| 1992 Proof | — | Value: 45.00 | | | | |

**CROWN** **KM# 311** **Composition:** Copper-Nickel **Series:** Discovery of America **Obverse:** Bust of Queen Elizabeth II right **Reverse:** Dan Casement and train engine

| Date | Mintage | F | VF | XF | Unc | BU |
|---|---|---|---|---|---|---|
| 1992 | — | — | — | — | 3.75 | — |
| 1992 Proof | — | Value: 12.00 | | | | |

**CROWN** **KM# 311a** **Weight:** 28.2800 g. **Composition:** 0.9250 Silver .8411 oz. ASW **Series:** Discovery of America **Obverse:** Bust of Queen Elizabeth II right **Reverse:** Dan Casement and train engine

| Date | Mintage | F | VF | XF | Unc | BU |
|---|---|---|---|---|---|---|
| 1992 Proof | — | Value: 45.00 | | | | |

**CROWN** **KM# 312** **Composition:** Copper-Nickel **Series:** Discovery of America **Obverse:** Bust of Queen Elizabeth II right **Reverse:** Promontory Point, Utah

| Date | Mintage | F | VF | XF | Unc | BU |
|---|---|---|---|---|---|---|
| 1992 | — | — | — | — | 3.75 | — |
| 1992 Proof | — | Value: 10.00 | | | | |

**CROWN** **KM# 312a** **Weight:** 28.2800 g. **Composition:** 0.9250 Silver .8411 oz. ASW **Series:** Discovery of America **Obverse:** Bust of Queen Elizabeth II right **Reverse:** Promontory Point, Utah

| Date | Mintage | F | VF | XF | Unc | BU |
|---|---|---|---|---|---|---|
| 1992 Proof | — | Value: 45.00 | | | | |

**CROWN** **KM# 313** **Composition:** Copper-Nickel **Series:** Discovery of America **Obverse:** Bust of Queen Elizabeth II right **Reverse:** Flags of United States and Isle of Man

| Date | Mintage | F | VF | XF | Unc | BU |
|---|---|---|---|---|---|---|
| 1992 | — | — | — | — | 3.75 | — |
| 1992 Proof | — | Value: 10.00 | | | | |

**CROWN** **KM# 313a** **Weight:** 28.2800 g. **Composition:** 0.9250 Silver .8411 oz. ASW **Series:** Discovery of America **Obverse:** Bust of Queen Elizabeth II right **Reverse:** Flags of United States and Isle of Man

| Date | Mintage | F | VF | XF | Unc | BU |
|---|---|---|---|---|---|---|
| 1992 Proof | — | Value: 25.00 | | | | |

**CROWN** **KM# 326** **Composition:** Copper-Nickel **Subject:** America's Cup - San Diego **Obverse:** Bust of Queen Elizabeth II right **Reverse:** Sailboat

| Date | Mintage | F | VF | XF | Unc | BU |
|---|---|---|---|---|---|---|
| 1992 | — | — | — | — | 4.75 | — |
| 1992 Proof | — | Value: 12.50 | | | | |

**CROWN** **KM# 326a** **Weight:** 28.2800 g. **Composition:** 0.9250 Silver .8411 oz. ASW **Subject:** America's Cup - San Diego **Obverse:** Bust of Queen Elizabeth II right **Reverse:** Sailboat

| Date | Mintage | F | VF | XF | Unc | BU |
|---|---|---|---|---|---|---|
| 1992 Proof | 25,000 | — | — | — | 60.00 | — |

**CROWN** **KM# 326b** **Weight:** 31.0300 g. **Composition:** 0.9990 Gold 1.0000 oz. AGW **Subject:** America's Cup - San Diego **Obverse:** Bust of Queen Elizabeth II right **Reverse:** Sailboat

| Date | Mintage | F | VF | XF | Unc | BU |
|---|---|---|---|---|---|---|
| 1992 Proof | — | — | — | — | 800 | — |

**CROWN** **KM# 332** **Composition:** Copper-Nickel **Obverse:** Bust of Queen Elizabeth II right **Reverse:** Seated siamese cat

| Date | Mintage | F | VF | XF | Unc | BU |
|---|---|---|---|---|---|---|
| 1992 | — | — | — | — | 10.00 | — |

**CROWN** **KM# 333** **Weight:** 31.1000 g. **Composition:** 0.9990 Silver 1.0000 oz. ASW **Obverse:** Bust of Queen Elizabeth II right **Reverse:** Seated siamese cat

| Date | Mintage | F | VF | XF | Unc | BU |
|---|---|---|---|---|---|---|
| 1992 Proof | 50,000 | Value: 28.00 | | | | |

**CROWN** **KM# 334** **Weight:** 31.1000 g. **Composition:** 0.9990 Gold 1.0000 oz. AGW **Obverse:** Bust of Queen Elizabeth II right **Reverse:** Seated siamese cat

| Date | Mintage | F | VF | XF | Unc | BU |
|---|---|---|---|---|---|---|
| 1992 | — | — | — | — | 425 | — |
| 1992 Proof | — | Value: 435 | | | | |

**CROWN** **KM# 342** **Weight:** 31.1000 g. **Composition:** 0.9990 Gold 1.0000 oz. AGW **Subject:** Year of the Cockerel **Obverse:** Bust of Queen Elizabeth II right **Reverse:** Cockerel in inner circle

| Date | Mintage | F | VF | XF | Unc | BU |
|---|---|---|---|---|---|---|
| 1993 Proof | Est. 2,500 | Value: 750 | | | | |

**CROWN** **KM# 353** **Composition:** Copper-Nickel **Obverse:** Bust of Queen Elizabeth II right **Reverse:** Mine coon cat

| Date | Mintage | F | VF | XF | Unc | BU |
|---|---|---|---|---|---|---|
| 1993 | — | — | — | — | 8.50 | — |

**CROWN** **KM# 354** **Weight:** 31.1000 g. **Composition:** 0.9990 Silver 1.0000 oz. ASW **Obverse:** Bust of Queen Elizabeth II right **Reverse:** Maine coon cat

| Date | Mintage | F | VF | XF | Unc | BU |
|---|---|---|---|---|---|---|
| 1993 Proof | 50,000 | Value: 28.00 | | | | |

**CROWN** **KM# 355** **Weight:** 31.1000 g. **Composition:** 0.9990 Gold 1.0000 oz. AGW **Obverse:** Bust of Queen Elizabeth II right **Reverse:** Maine coon cat

| Date | Mintage | F | VF | XF | Unc | BU |
|---|---|---|---|---|---|---|
| 1993 | — | — | — | — | 425 | — |
| 1993 Proof | — | Value: 435 | | | | |

**CROWN KM# 357 Composition:** Copper-Nickel **Series:** Preserve Planet Earth **Obverse:** Bust of Queen Elizabeth II right **Reverse:** Iguanodon

| Date | Mintage | F | VF | XF | Unc | BU |
|---|---|---|---|---|---|---|
| 1993 | — | — | — | — | 8.50 | — |

**CROWN KM# 358 Composition:** Copper-Nickel **Series:** Preserve Planet Earth **Obverse:** Bust of Queen Elizabeth II right **Reverse:** Diplodocus

| Date | Mintage | F | VF | XF | Unc | BU |
|---|---|---|---|---|---|---|
| 1993 | — | — | — | — | 8.50 | — |

**CROWN KM# 364 Composition:** Copper-Nickel **Series:** World Cup Soccer **Obverse:** Bust of Queen Elizabeth II right **Reverse:** Two players

| Date | Mintage | F | VF | XF | Unc | BU |
|---|---|---|---|---|---|---|
| 1994 | — | — | — | — | 6.00 | — |

**CROWN KM# 364a Weight:** 28.2800 g. **Composition:** 0.9250 Silver .8411 oz. ASW **Series:** World Cup Soccer **Obverse:** Bust of Queen Elizabeth II right **Reverse:** Two players

| Date | Mintage | F | VF | XF | Unc | BU |
|---|---|---|---|---|---|---|
| 1994 Proof | Est. 30,000 | Value: 35.00 | | | | |

**CROWN KM# 366 Composition:** Copper-Nickel **Series:** World Cup Soccer **Obverse:** Bust of Queen Elizabeth II right **Reverse:** Three players

| Date | Mintage | F | VF | XF | Unc | BU |
|---|---|---|---|---|---|---|
| 1994 | — | — | — | — | 6.00 | — |

**CROWN KM# 366a Weight:** 28.2800 g. **Composition:** 0.9250 Silver .8411 oz. ASW **Series:** World Cup Soccer **Obverse:** Bust of Queen Elizabeth II right **Reverse:** Three players

| Date | Mintage | F | VF | XF | Unc | BU |
|---|---|---|---|---|---|---|
| 1994 Proof | Est. 30,000 | Value: 35.00 | | | | |

**CROWN KM# 368 Composition:** Copper-Nickel **Series:** World Cup Soccer **Obverse:** Bust of Queen Elizabeth II right **Reverse:** One player with knee bent with second player in background

| Date | Mintage | F | VF | XF | Unc | BU |
|---|---|---|---|---|---|---|
| 1994 | — | — | — | — | 6.00 | — |

**CROWN KM# 368a Weight:** 28.2800 g. **Composition:** 0.9250 Silver .8411 oz. ASW **Series:** World Cup Soccer **Obverse:** Bust of Queen Elizabeth II right **Reverse:** One player with knee bent, second player in background

| Date | Mintage | F | VF | XF | Unc | BU |
|---|---|---|---|---|---|---|
| 1994 Proof | Est. 30,000 | Value: 35.00 | | | | |

**CROWN KM# 370 Composition:** Copper-Nickel **Series:** World Cup Soccer **Obverse:** Bust of Queen Elizabeth II right **Reverse:** Three players, one kicking ball

| Date | Mintage | F | VF | XF | Unc | BU |
|---|---|---|---|---|---|---|
| 1994 | — | — | — | — | 6.00 | — |

**CROWN KM# 370a Weight:** 28.2800 g. **Composition:** 0.9250 Silver .8411 oz. ASW **Series:** World Cup Soccer **Obverse:** Bust of Queen Elizabeth II right **Reverse:** Three players, one kicking ball

| Date | Mintage | F | VF | XF | Unc | BU |
|---|---|---|---|---|---|---|
| 1994 Proof | Est. 30,000 | Value: 35.00 | | | | |

**CROWN KM# 372 Composition:** Copper-Nickel **Series:** World Cup Soccer **Obverse:** Bust of Queen Elizabeth II right **Reverse:** Two players, one with ball in hand

| Date | Mintage | F | VF | XF | Unc | BU |
|---|---|---|---|---|---|---|
| 1994 | — | — | — | — | 6.00 | — |

**CROWN KM# 372a Weight:** 28.2800 g. **Composition:** 0.9250 Silver .8411 oz. ASW **Series:** World Cup Soccer **Obverse:** Bust of Queen Elizabeth II right **Reverse:** Two players, one with ball in hand

| Date | Mintage | F | VF | XF | Unc | BU |
|---|---|---|---|---|---|---|
| 1994 Proof | Est. 30,000 | Value: 35.00 | | | | |

**CROWN KM# 374 Composition:** Copper-Nickel **Series:** World Cup Soccer **Obverse:** Bust of Queen Elizabeth II right **Reverse:** Two players kicking ball right

| Date | Mintage | F | VF | XF | Unc | BU |
|---|---|---|---|---|---|---|
| 1994 | — | — | — | — | 6.00 | — |

**CROWN KM# 374a Weight:** 28.2800 g. **Composition:** 0.9250 Silver .8411 oz. ASW **Series:** World Cup Soccer **Obverse:** Bust of Queen Elizabeth II right **Reverse:** Two players kicking ball right

| Date | Mintage | F | VF | XF | Unc | BU |
|---|---|---|---|---|---|---|
| 1994 Proof | Est. 30,000 | Value: 35.00 | | | | |

**CROWN KM# 380 Composition:** Copper-Nickel **Obverse:** Bust of Queen Elizabeth II right **Reverse:** Japanese bobtail cat

| Date | Mintage | F | VF | XF | Unc | BU |
|---|---|---|---|---|---|---|
| 1994 | — | — | — | — | 7.50 | — |

**CROWN KM# 381 Weight:** 31.1000 g. **Composition:** 0.9990 Silver 1.0000 oz. ASW **Obverse:** Bust of Queen Elizabeth II right **Reverse:** Japanese bobtail cat

| Date | Mintage | F | VF | XF | Unc | BU |
|---|---|---|---|---|---|---|
| 1994 Proof | — | Value: 28.00 | | | | |

**CROWN KM# 382 Weight:** 31.1000 g. **Composition:** 0.9990 Gold 1.0000 oz. AGW **Obverse:** Bust of Queen Elizabeth II right **Reverse:** Japanese bobtail cat

| Date | Mintage | F | VF | XF | Unc | BU |
|---|---|---|---|---|---|---|
| 1994 | — | — | — | — | 400 | — |
| 1994 Proof | — | Value: 410 | | | | |

**CROWN KM# 384 Composition:** Copper-Nickel **Series:** Preserve Planet Earth **Obverse:** Bust of Queen Elizabeth II right **Reverse:** Wooly mammoth

| Date | Mintage | F | VF | XF | Unc | BU |
|---|---|---|---|---|---|---|
| 1994 | — | — | — | — | 8.50 | — |

**CROWN KM# 384a Weight:** 28.2800 g. **Composition:** 0.9250 Silver .8411 oz. ASW **Series:** Preserve Planet Earth **Obverse:** Bust of Queen Elizabeth II right **Reverse:** Wooly mammoth

| Date | Mintage | F | VF | XF | Unc | BU |
|---|---|---|---|---|---|---|
| 1994 Proof | Est. 30,000 | Value: 35.00 | | | | |

**CROWN** **KM# 385** **Composition:** Copper-Nickel **Series:** Preserve Planet Earth **Obverse:** Bust of Queen Elizabeth II right **Reverse:** Four red-necked wallaby

| Date | Mintage | F | VF | XF | Unc | BU |
|---|---|---|---|---|---|---|
| 1994 | — | — | — | — | 9.00 | — |

**CROWN** **KM# 385a** **Weight:** 28.2800 g. **Composition:** 0.9250 Silver .8411 oz. ASW **Series:** Preserve Planet Earth **Obverse:** Bust of Queen Elizabeth II right **Reverse:** Four red-necked wallaby

| Date | Mintage | F | VF | XF | Unc | BU |
|---|---|---|---|---|---|---|
| 1994 Proof | Est. 30,000 | Value: 35.00 | | | | |

**CROWN** **KM# 386** **Composition:** Copper-Nickel **Series:** Preserve Planet Earth **Obverse:** Bust of Queen Elizabeth II right **Reverse:** Grey seal mother and pup

| Date | Mintage | F | VF | XF | Unc | BU |
|---|---|---|---|---|---|---|
| 1994 | — | — | — | — | 9.00 | — |

**CROWN** **KM# 386a** **Weight:** 28.2800 g. **Composition:** 0.9250 Silver .8411 oz. ASW **Series:** Preserve Planet Earth **Obverse:** Bust of Queen Elizabeth II right **Reverse:** Grey seal mother and pup

| Date | Mintage | F | VF | XF | Unc | BU |
|---|---|---|---|---|---|---|
| 1994 Proof | Est. 30,000 | Value: 35.00 | | | | |

**CROWN** **KM# 387** **Composition:** Copper-Nickel **Series:** Preserve Planet Earth **Obverse:** Bust of Queen Elizabeth II right **Reverse:** Two fallow deer

| Date | Mintage | F | VF | XF | Unc | BU |
|---|---|---|---|---|---|---|
| 1994 | — | — | — | — | 9.00 | — |

**CROWN** **KM# 387a** **Weight:** 28.2800 g. **Composition:** 0.9250 Silver .8411 oz. ASW **Series:** Preserve Planet Earth **Obverse:** Bust of Queen Elizabeth II right **Reverse:** Two fallow deer

| Date | Mintage | F | VF | XF | Unc | BU |
|---|---|---|---|---|---|---|
| 1994 Proof | Est. 30,000 | Value: 35.00 | | | | |

**CROWN** **KM# 406** **Composition:** Copper-Nickel **Obverse:** Bust of Queen Elizabeth II right **Reverse:** Pekingese dog

| Date | Mintage | F | VF | XF | Unc | BU |
|---|---|---|---|---|---|---|
| 1994 | — | — | — | — | 8.00 | — |

**CROWN** **KM# 407** **Weight:** 31.1000 g. **Composition:** 0.9990 Silver 1.000 oz. ASW **Obverse:** Bust of Queen Elizabeth II right **Reverse:** Pekingese dog

| Date | Mintage | F | VF | XF | Unc | BU |
|---|---|---|---|---|---|---|
| 1994 Proof | — | Value: 40.00 | | | | |

**CROWN** **KM# 408** **Weight:** 31.1000 g. **Composition:** 0.9990 Gold 1.000 oz. AGW **Obverse:** Bust of Queen Elizabeth II right **Reverse:** Pekingese dog

| Date | Mintage | F | VF | XF | Unc | BU |
|---|---|---|---|---|---|---|
| 1994 Proof | Est. 5,000 | Value: 700 | | | | |

**CROWN** **KM# 417** **Composition:** Copper-Nickel **Series:** Man in Flight **Obverse:** Bust of Queen Elizabeth II right **Reverse:** Otto Lilienthal

| Date | Mintage | F | VF | XF | Unc | BU |
|---|---|---|---|---|---|---|
| 1994 | — | — | — | — | 7.00 | — |

**CROWN** **KM# 417a** **Weight:** 28.2800 g. **Composition:** 0.9250 Silver .8411 oz. ASW **Series:** Man in Flight **Obverse:** Bust of Queen Elizabeth II right **Reverse:** Otto Lilienthal

| Date | Mintage | F | VF | XF | Unc | BU |
|---|---|---|---|---|---|---|
| 1994 Proof | Est. 30,000 | Value: 40.00 | | | | |

**CROWN** **KM# 418** **Composition:** Copper-Nickel **Series:** Man in Flight **Obverse:** Bust of Queen Elizabeth II right **Reverse:** Ferdinand von Zeppelin

| Date | Mintage | F | VF | XF | Unc | BU |
|---|---|---|---|---|---|---|
| 1994 | — | — | — | — | 8.00 | — |

**CROWN** **KM# 419** **Composition:** Copper-Nickel **Series:** Man in Flight **Obverse:** Bust of Queen Elizabeth II right **Reverse:** Louis Bleriot

| Date | Mintage | F | VF | XF | Unc | BU |
|---|---|---|---|---|---|---|
| 1994 | — | — | — | — | 8.00 | — |

**CROWN** **KM# 419a** **Weight:** 28.2800 g. **Composition:** 0.9250 Silver .8411 oz. ASW **Series:** Man in Flight **Obverse:** Bust of Queen Elizabeth II right **Reverse:** Louis Bleriot

| Date | Mintage | F | VF | XF | Unc | BU |
|---|---|---|---|---|---|---|
| 1994 Proof | Est. 30,000 | Value: 40.00 | | | | |

**CROWN** **KM# 420** **Composition:** Copper-Nickel **Series:** Man in Flight **Obverse:** Bust of Queen Elizabeth II right **Reverse:** Alcock and Brown

| Date | Mintage | F | VF | XF | Unc | BU |
|---|---|---|---|---|---|---|
| 1994 | — | — | — | — | 8.00 | — |

**CROWN** **KM# 420a** **Weight:** 28.2800 g. **Composition:** 0.9250 Silver .8411 oz. ASW **Series:** Man in Flight **Obverse:** Bust of Queen Elizabeth II right **Reverse:** Alcock and Brown

| Date | Mintage | F | VF | XF | Unc | BU |
|---|---|---|---|---|---|---|
| 1994 Proof | Est. 30,000 | Value: 40.00 | | | | |

**CROWN** **KM# 421** **Composition:** Copper-Nickel **Series:** Man in Flight **Obverse:** Bust of Queen Elizabeth II right **Reverse:** First England to Australia flight

| Date | Mintage | F | VF | XF | Unc | BU |
|---|---|---|---|---|---|---|
| 1994 | — | — | — | — | 8.00 | — |

**CROWN** **KM# 421a** **Weight:** 28.2800 g. **Composition:** 0.9250 Silver .8411 oz. ASW **Series:** Man in Flight **Obverse:** Bust of Queen Elizabeth II right **Reverse:** First England to Australia flight

| Date | Mintage | F | VF | XF | Unc | BU |
|---|---|---|---|---|---|---|
| 1994 Proof | Est. 30,000 | Value: 40.00 | | | | |

**CROWN** **KM# 422** **Composition:** Copper-Nickel **Series:** Man in Flight **Subject:** 60th Anniersary of Airmail **Obverse:** Bust of Queen Elizabeth II right **Reverse:** Airplane

| Date | Mintage | F | VF | XF | Unc | BU |
|---|---|---|---|---|---|---|
| 1994 | — | — | — | — | 8.00 | — |

**CROWN** **KM# 422a** **Weight:** 28.2800 g. **Composition:** 0.9250 Silver .8411 oz. ASW **Series:** Man in Flight **Subject:** 60th Anniversary of Airmail **Obverse:** Bust of Queen Elizabeth II right **Reverse:** Airplane

| Date | Mintage | F | VF | XF | Unc | BU |
|---|---|---|---|---|---|---|
| 1994 Proof | Est. 30,000 | Value: 40.00 | | | | |

**CROWN** **KM# 423** **Composition:** Copper-Nickel **Series:** Man in Flight **Subject:** 50th Anniversary of International Civil Aviation Organization **Obverse:** Bust of Queen Elizabeth II right **Reverse:** Emblem

| Date | Mintage | F | VF | XF | Unc | BU |
|---|---|---|---|---|---|---|
| 1994 | — | — | — | — | 8.00 | — |

**CROWN** **KM# 423a** **Weight:** 28.2800 g. **Composition:** 0.9250 Silver .8411 oz. ASW **Series:** Man in Flight **Subject:** 50th Anniersary of International Civil Aviation Organization **Obverse:** Bust of Queen Elizabeth II right **Reverse:** Emblem

| Date | Mintage | F | VF | XF | Unc | BU |
|---|---|---|---|---|---|---|
| 1994 Proof | Est. 30,000 | Value: 40.00 | | | | |

**CROWN** **KM# 424** **Composition:** Copper-Nickel **Series:** Man in Flight **Subject:** 25th Anniversary of First Concorde Flight **Obverse:** Bust of Queen Elizabeth II right **Reverse:** Concorde

| Date | Mintage | F | VF | XF | Unc | BU |
|---|---|---|---|---|---|---|
| 1994 | — | — | — | — | 8.00 | — |

**CROWN** **KM# 424a** **Weight:** 28.2800 g. **Composition:** 0.9250 Silver .8411 oz. ASW **Series:** Man in Flight **Subject:** 25th Anniersary of First Concorde Flight **Obverse:** Bust of Queen Elizabeth II right **Reverse:** Concorde

| Date | Mintage | F | VF | XF | Unc | BU |
|---|---|---|---|---|---|---|
| 1994 Proof | Est. 30,000 | Value: 40.00 | | | | |

**CROWN** **KM# 477** **Weight:** 31.1035 g. **Composition:** 0.9995 Platinum .9995 oz. APW **Obverse:** Bust of Queen Elizabeth II right **Reverse:** Japanese bobtail cat

| Date | Mintage | F | VF | XF | Unc | BU |
|---|---|---|---|---|---|---|
| 1994 | — | — | — | — | BV+20% | — |

**CROWN** **KM# 695** **Composition:** Copper-Nickel **Series:** Normandy Invasion **Obverse:** Bust of Queen Elizabeth II right **Reverse:** Troop ship and landing craft

| Date | Mintage | F | VF | XF | Unc | BU |
|---|---|---|---|---|---|---|
| 1994 | — | — | — | — | 6.50 | — |

**CROWN** **KM# 695a** **Weight:** 28.2800 g. **Composition:** 0.9250 Silver .8411 oz. ASW **Series:** Normandy Invasion **Obverse:** Bust of Queen Elizabeth II right **Reverse:** Troop ship and landing craft

| Date | Mintage | F | VF | XF | Unc | BU |
|---|---|---|---|---|---|---|
| 1994 Proof | Est. 30,000 | Value: 26.50 | | | | |

**CROWN** **KM# 696** **Composition:** Copper-Nickel **Series:** Normandy Invasion **Obverse:** Bust of Queen Elizabeth II right **Reverse:** American troops landing

| Date | Mintage | F | VF | XF | Unc | BU |
|---|---|---|---|---|---|---|
| 1994 | — | — | — | — | 6.50 | — |

**CROWN** **KM# 696a** **Weight:** 28.2800 g. **Composition:** 0.9250 Silver .8411 oz. ASW **Series:** Normandy Invasion **Obverse:** Bust of Queen Elizabeth II right **Reverse:** American troops landing

| Date | Mintage | F | VF | XF | Unc | BU |
|---|---|---|---|---|---|---|
| 1994 Proof | Est. 30,000 | Value: 26.50 | | | | |

**CROWN** **KM# 697** **Composition:** Copper-Nickel **Series:** Normandy Invasion **Obverse:** Bust of Queen Elizabeth II right **Reverse:** American soldier behind rock

| Date | Mintage | F | VF | XF | Unc | BU |
|---|---|---|---|---|---|---|
| 1994 | — | — | — | — | 6.50 | — |

**CROWN** **KM#697a** **Weight:** 28.2800 g. **Composition:** 0.9250 Silver .8411 oz. ASW **Series:** Normandy Invasion **Obverse:** Bust of Queen Elizabeth II right **Reverse:** American soldier behind rock

| Date | Mintage | F | VF | XF | Unc | BU |
|---|---|---|---|---|---|---|
| 1994 Proof | Est. 30,000 | Value: 26.50 | | | | |

**CROWN** **KM# 698** **Composition:** Copper-Nickel **Series:** Normandy Invasion **Obverse:** Bust of Queen Elizabeth II right **Reverse:** German machine gun nest

| Date | Mintage | F | VF | XF | Unc | BU |
|---|---|---|---|---|---|---|
| 1994 | — | — | — | — | 6.50 | — |

**CROWN** **KM# 698a** **Weight:** 28.2800 g. **Composition:** 0.9250 Silver .8411 oz. ASW **Series:** Normandy Invasion **Obverse:** Bust of Queen Elizabeth II right **Reverse:** German machine gun nest

| Date | Mintage | F | VF | XF | Unc | BU |
|---|---|---|---|---|---|---|
| 1994 Proof | Est. 30,000 | Value: 26.50 | | | | |

**CROWN** **KM# 699** **Composition:** Copper-Nickel **Series:** Normandy Invasion **Obverse:** Bust of Queen Elizabeth II right **Reverse:** British troops landing

| Date | Mintage | F | VF | XF | Unc | BU |
|---|---|---|---|---|---|---|
| 1994 | — | — | — | — | 6.50 | — |

**CROWN** **KM# 699a** **Weight:** 28.2800 g. **Composition:** 0.9250 Silver .8411 oz. ASW **Series:** Normandy Invasion **Obverse:** Bust of Queen Elizabeth II right **Reverse:** British troops landing

| Date | Mintage | F | VF | XF | Unc | BU |
|---|---|---|---|---|---|---|
| 1994 Proof | Est. 30,000 | Value: 26.50 | | | | |

**CROWN** **KM# 700** **Composition:** Copper-Nickel **Series:** Normandy Invasion **Obverse:** Bust of Queen Elizabeth II right **Reverse:** General Eisenhower facing left

| Date | Mintage | F | VF | XF | Unc | BU |
|---|---|---|---|---|---|---|
| 1994 | — | — | — | — | 6.50 | — |

**CROWN** **KM# 700a** **Weight:** 28.2800 g. **Composition:** 0.9250 Silver .8411 oz. ASW **Series:** Normandy Invasion **Obverse:** Bust of Queen Elizabeth II right **Reverse:** General Eisenhower facing left

| Date | Mintage | F | VF | XF | Unc | BU |
|---|---|---|---|---|---|---|
| 1994 Proof | Est. 30,000 | Value: 26.50 | | | | |

**CROWN** **KM# 701** **Composition:** Copper-Nickel **Series:** Normandy Invasion **Obverse:** Bust of Queen Elizabeth II right **Reverse:** General Omar Bradley looking right

| Date | Mintage | F | VF | XF | Unc | BU |
|---|---|---|---|---|---|---|
| 1994 | — | — | — | — | 6.50 | — |

**CROWN** **KM# 701a** **Weight:** 28.2800 g. **Composition:** 0.9250 Silver .8411 oz. ASW **Series:** Normandy Invasion **Obverse:** Bust of Queen Elizabeth II right **Reverse:** General Omar Bradley looking right

| Date | Mintage | F | VF | XF | Unc | BU |
|---|---|---|---|---|---|---|
| 1994 Proof | Est. 30,000 | Value: 26.50 | | | | |

**CROWN** **KM# 702** **Composition:** Copper-Nickel **Series:** Normandy Invasion **Obverse:** Bust of Queen Elizabeth II right **Reverse:** General Montgomery facing left

| Date | Mintage | F | VF | XF | Unc | BU |
|---|---|---|---|---|---|---|
| 1994 | — | — | — | — | 6.50 | — |

**CROWN** **KM# 702a** **Weight:** 28.2800 g. **Composition:** 0.9250 Silver .8411 oz. ASW **Series:** Normandy Invasion **Obverse:** Bust of Queen Elizabeth II right **Reverse:** General Montgomery facing left

| Date | Mintage | F | VF | XF | Unc | BU |
|---|---|---|---|---|---|---|
| 1994 Proof | Est. 30,000 | Value: 26.50 | | | | |

**CROWN** **KM# 703** **Weight:** 6.2200 g. **Composition:** 0.9999 Gold .2000 oz. AGW **Series:** Normandy Invasion **Obverse:** Bust of Queen Elizabeth II right **Reverse:** Troop ship and landing craft

| Date | Mintage | F | VF | XF | Unc | BU |
|---|---|---|---|---|---|---|
| 1994 Proof | Est. 5,000 | Value: 165 | | | | |

**CROWN** **KM# 704** **Weight:** 6.2200 g. **Composition:** 0.9999 Gold .2000 oz. AGW **Series:** Normandy Invasion **Obverse:** Bust of Queen Elizabeth II right **Reverse:** American troops landing

| Date | Mintage | F | VF | XF | Unc | BU |
|---|---|---|---|---|---|---|
| 1994 Proof | Est. 5,000 | Value: 165 | | | | |

**CROWN** **KM# 705** **Weight:** 6.2200 g. **Composition:** 0.9999 Gold .2000 oz. AGW **Series:** Normandy Invasion **Obverse:** Bust of Queen Elizabeth II right **Reverse:** American soldier behind rock

| Date | Mintage | F | VF | XF | Unc | BU |
|---|---|---|---|---|---|---|
| 1994 Proof | Est. 5,000 | Value: 165 | | | | |

**CROWN** **KM# 706** **Weight:** 6.2200 g. **Composition:** 0.9999 Gold .2000 oz. AGW **Series:** Normandy Invasion **Obverse:** Bust of Queen Elizabeth II right **Reverse:** German machine gun nest

| Date | Mintage | F | VF | XF | Unc | BU |
|---|---|---|---|---|---|---|
| 1994 Proof | Est. 5,000 | Value: 165 | | | | |

**CROWN** **KM# 707** **Weight:** 6.2200 g. **Composition:** 0.9999 Gold .2000 oz. AGW **Series:** Normandy Invasion **Obverse:** Bust of Queen Elizabeth II right **Reverse:** British troops landing

| Date | Mintage | F | VF | XF | Unc | BU |
|---|---|---|---|---|---|---|
| 1994 Proof | Est. 5,000 | Value: 165 | | | | |

**CROWN** **KM# 708** **Weight:** 6.2200 g. **Composition:** 0.9999 Gold .2000 oz. AGW **Series:** Normandy Invasion **Obverse:** Bust of Queen Elizabeth II right **Reverse:** General Eisenhower facing left

| Date | Mintage | F | VF | XF | Unc | BU |
|---|---|---|---|---|---|---|
| 1994 Proof | Est. 5,000 | Value: 165 | | | | |

**CROWN** **KM# 709** **Weight:** 6.2200 g. **Composition:** 0.9999 Gold .2000 oz. AGW **Series:** Normandy Invasion **Obverse:** Bust of Queen Elizabeth II right **Reverse:** General Omar Bradley facing right

| Date | Mintage | F | VF | XF | Unc | BU |
|---|---|---|---|---|---|---|
| 1994 Proof | Est. 5,000 | Value: 165 | | | | |

**CROWN** **KM# 710** **Weight:** 6.2200 g. **Composition:** 0.9999 Gold .2000 oz. AGW **Series:** Normandy Invasion **Obverse:** Bust of Queen Elizabeth II right **Reverse:** General Montgomery facing left

| Date | Mintage | F | VF | XF | Unc | BU |
|---|---|---|---|---|---|---|
| 1994 Proof | Est. 5,000 | Value: 165 | | | | |

**CROWN** **KM# 520** **Composition:** Copper-Nickel **Series:** Aircraft of WW II **Obverse:** Bust of Queen Elizabeth II right **Reverse:** Curtiss P-40 Tomahawk

| Date | Mintage | F | VF | XF | Unc | BU |
|---|---|---|---|---|---|---|
| 1995 | — | — | — | — | 5.50 | — |

**CROWN** **KM# 520a** **Weight:** 28.2800 g. **Composition:** 0.9250 Silver .8411 oz. ASW **Series:** Aircraft of WW II **Obverse:** Bust of Queen Elizabeth II right **Reverse:** Curtiss P-40 Tomahawk

| Date | Mintage | F | VF | XF | Unc | BU |
|---|---|---|---|---|---|---|
| 1995 Proof | Est. 30,000 | Value: 30.00 | | | | |

**CROWN** **KM# 548** **Composition:** Copper-Nickel **Series:** Inventions of the Modern World **Obverse:** Bust of Queen Elizabeth II right **Reverse:** Cameo of Lazlo Bird, ball point pen

| Date | Mintage | F | VF | XF | Unc | BU |
|---|---|---|---|---|---|---|
| 1995 | — | — | — | — | 5.00 | — |

**CROWN** **KM# 546** **Composition:** Copper-Nickel **Series:** Inventions of the Modern World **Obverse:** Bust of Queen Elizabeth II right **Reverse:** Cameo of Alexander Fleming and microscope

| Date | Mintage | F | VF | XF | Unc | BU |
|---|---|---|---|---|---|---|
| 1995 | — | — | — | — | 5.00 | — |

**CROWN** **KM# 544** **Composition:** Copper-Nickel **Series:** Inventions of the Modern World **Obverse:** Bust of Queen Elizabeth II right **Reverse:** Cameo L. Baird and television equipment

| Date | Mintage | F | VF | XF | Unc | BU |
|---|---|---|---|---|---|---|
| 1995 | — | — | — | — | 5.00 | — |

**CROWN** **KM# 530** **Composition:** Copper-Nickel **Series:** Inventions of the Modern World **Obverse:** Bust of Queen Elizabeth II right **Reverse:** Cameo of Tsu Chung Chih and compass cart

| Date | Mintage | F | VF | XF | Unc | BU |
|---|---|---|---|---|---|---|
| 1995 | — | — | — | — | 5.00 | — |

**CROWN** **KM# 532** **Composition:** Copper-Nickel **Series:** Inventions of the Modern World **Obverse:** Bust of Queen Elizabeth II right **Reverse:** Cameo of Pi Sheng and movable type

| Date | Mintage | F | VF | XF | Unc | BU |
|---|---|---|---|---|---|---|
| 1995 | — | — | — | — | 5.00 | — |

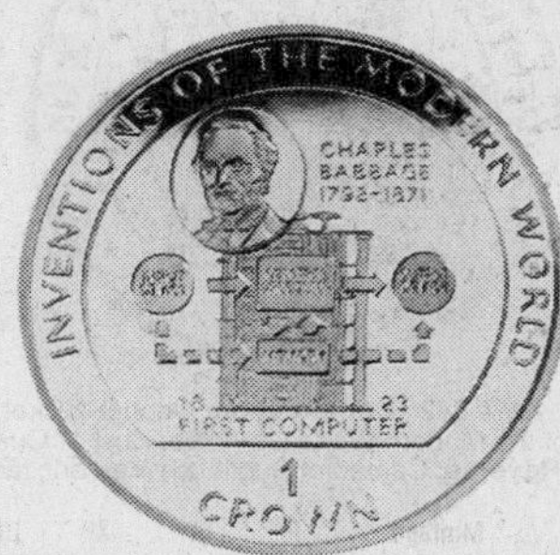


**CROWN** **KM# 534** **Composition:** Copper-Nickel **Series:** Inventions of the Modern World **Obverse:** Bust of Queen Elizabeth II right **Reverse:** Cameo of Charles Babbage and 1st computer

| Date | Mintage | F | VF | XF | Unc | BU |
|---|---|---|---|---|---|---|
| 1995 | — | — | — | — | 5.00 | — |

**CROWN** **KM# 536** **Composition:** Copper-Nickel **Series:** Inventions of the Modern World **Obverse:** Bust of Queen Elizabeth II right **Reverse:** Cameo of Fox Talbot, photography

| Date | Mintage | F | VF | XF | Unc | BU |
|---|---|---|---|---|---|---|
| 1995 | — | — | — | — | 5.00 | — |

**CROWN** **KM# 538** **Composition:** Copper-Nickel **Series:** Inventions of the Modern World **Obverse:** Bust of Queen Elizabeth II right **Reverse:** Cameo Rudolf Diesel and engine

| Date | Mintage | F | VF | XF | Unc | BU |
|---|---|---|---|---|---|---|
| 1995 | — | — | — | — | 5.00 | — |

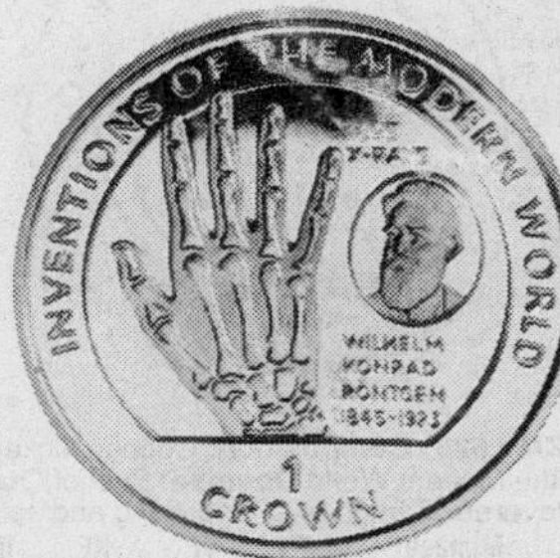


**CROWN** **KM# 540** **Composition:** Copper-Nickel **Series:** Inventions of the Modern World **Obverse:** Bust of Queen Elizabeth II right **Reverse:** Cameo of Wilhelm K. Roentgern, x-ray

| Date | Mintage | F | VF | XF | Unc | BU |
|---|---|---|---|---|---|---|
| 1995 | — | — | — | — | 5.00 | — |

**CROWN** **KM# 542** **Composition:** Copper-Nickel **Series:** Inventions of the Modern World **Obverse:** Bust of Queen Elizabeth II right **Reverse:** Cameo of Guglielmo Marconi, radio equipment

| Date | Mintage | F | VF | XF | Unc | BU |
|---|---|---|---|---|---|---|
| 1995 | — | — | — | — | 5.00 | — |

**CROWN** **KM# 524** **Composition:** Copper-Nickel **Series:** America's Cup **Obverse:** Bust of Queen Elizabeth II right **Reverse:** Sail boats

| Date | Mintage | F | VF | XF | Unc | BU |
|---|---|---|---|---|---|---|
| 1995 | — | — | — | — | 5.00 | — |

**CROWN** **KM# 526** **Composition:** Copper-Nickel **Series:** Inventions of the Modern World **Obverse:** Bust of Queen Elizabeth II right **Reverse:** Cameo Tsai Lun, paper and tree

| Date | Mintage | F | VF | XF | Unc | BU |
|---|---|---|---|---|---|---|
| 1995 | — | — | — | — | 5.00 | — |

**CROWN** **KM# 528** **Composition:** Copper-Nickel **Series:** Inventions of the Modern World **Obverse:** Bust of Queen Elizabeth II right **Reverse:** Cameo of Chang Heng and seismograph

| Date | Mintage | F | VF | XF | Unc | BU |
|---|---|---|---|---|---|---|
| 1995 | — | — | — | — | 5.00 | — |

**CROWN** **KM# 524a** **Weight:** 28.2800 g. **Composition:** 0.9250 Silver .8411 oz. ASW **Series:** America's Cup **Obverse:** Bust of Queen Elizabeth II right **Reverse:** Sail Boats

| Date | Mintage | F | VF | XF | Unc | BU |
|---|---|---|---|---|---|---|
| 1995 Proof | Est. 30,000 | Value: 50.00 | | | | |

**CROWN** **KM# 526a** **Weight:** 28.2800 g. **Composition:** 0.9250 Silver .8411 oz. ASW **Series:** Inventions of the Modern World **Obverse:** Bust of Queen Elizabeth II right **Reverse:** Cameo of Tsai Lun, paper and tree

| Date | Mintage | F | VF | XF | Unc | BU |
|---|---|---|---|---|---|---|
| 1995 Proof | Est. 30,000 | Value: 40.00 | | | | |

**CROWN** **KM# 528a** **Weight:** 28.2800 g. **Composition:** 0.9250 Silver .8411 oz. ASW **Series:** Inventions of the Modern World **Obverse:** Bust of Queen Elizabeth II right **Reverse:** Cameo of Chang Heng and seismograph

| Date | Mintage | F | VF | XF | Unc | BU |
|---|---|---|---|---|---|---|
| 1995 Proof | Est. 30,000 | Value: 40.00 | | | | |

**CROWN** **KM# 530a** **Weight:** 28.2800 g. **Composition:** 0.9250 Silver .8411 oz. ASW **Series:** Inventions of the Modern World **Obverse:** Bust of Queen Elizabeth II right **Reverse:** Cameo of Tsu Chung Chih and compass car

| Date | Mintage | F | VF | XF | Unc | BU |
|---|---|---|---|---|---|---|
| 1995 Proof | Est. 30,000 | Value: 40.00 | | | | |

**CROWN** **KM# 532a** **Weight:** 28.2800 g. **Composition:** 0.9250 Silver .8411 oz. ASW **Series:** Inventions of the Modern World **Obverse:** Bust of Queen Elizabeth II right **Reverse:** Cameo of Pi Sheng and movable type

| Date | Mintage | F | VF | XF | Unc | BU |
|---|---|---|---|---|---|---|
| 1995 Proof | Est. 30,000 | Value: 40.00 | | | | |

**CROWN** **KM# 534a** **Weight:** 28.2800 g. **Composition:** 0.9250 Silver .8411 oz. ASW **Series:** Inventions of the Modern World **Obverse:** Bust of Queen Elizabeth II right **Reverse:** Cameo of Charles Babbage and first computer

| Date | Mintage | F | VF | XF | Unc | BU |
|---|---|---|---|---|---|---|
| 1995 Proof | Est. 30,000 | Value: 40.00 | | | | |

**CROWN** **KM# 536a** **Weight:** 28.2800 g. **Composition:** 0.9250 Silver .8411 oz. ASW **Series:** Inventions of the Modern World **Obverse:** Bust of Queen Elizabeth II right **Reverse:** Cameo of Fox Talbot, photography

| Date | Mintage | F | VF | XF | Unc | BU |
|---|---|---|---|---|---|---|
| 1995 Proof | Est. 30,000 | Value: 40.00 | | | | |

**CROWN** **KM# 538a** **Weight:** 28.2800 g. **Composition:** 0.9250 Silver .8411 oz. ASW **Series:** Inventions of the Modern World **Obverse:** Bust of Queen Elizabeth II right **Reverse:** Cameo of Rudolf Diesel and engine

| Date | Mintage | F | VF | XF | Unc | BU |
|---|---|---|---|---|---|---|
| 1995 Proof | Est. 30,000 | Value: 40.00 | | | | |

**CROWN** **KM# 540a** **Weight:** 28.2800 g. **Composition:** 0.9250 Silver .8411 oz. ASW **Series:** Inventions of the Modern World **Obverse:** Bust of Queen Elizabeth II right **Reverse:** Cameo of Wilhelm K. Roentgen, x-ray

| Date | Mintage | F | VF | XF | Unc | BU |
|---|---|---|---|---|---|---|
| 1995 Proof | Est. 30,000 | Value: 40.00 | | | | |

**CROWN** **KM# 542a** **Weight:** 28.2800 g. **Composition:** 0.9250 Silver .8411 oz. ASW **Series:** Inventions of the Modern World **Obverse:** Bust of Queen Elizabeth II right **Reverse:** Cameo of Guglielmo Marconi and radio equipment

| Date | Mintage | F | VF | XF | Unc | BU |
|---|---|---|---|---|---|---|
| 1995 Proof | Est. 30,000 | Value: 40.00 | | | | |

**CROWN** **KM# 544a** **Weight:** 28.2800 g. **Composition:** 0.9250 Silver .8411 oz. ASW **Series:** Inventions of the Modern World **Obverse:** Bust of Queen Elizabeth II right **Reverse:** Cameo of John L. Baird and television equipment

| Date | Mintage | F | VF | XF | Unc | BU |
|---|---|---|---|---|---|---|
| 1995 Proof | Est. 30,000 | Value: 40.00 | | | | |

**CROWN** **KM# 546a** **Weight:** 28.2800 g. **Composition:** 0.9250 Silver .8411 oz. ASW **Series:** Inventions of the Modern World **Obverse:** Bust of Queen Elizabeth II right **Reverse:** Cameo of Alexander Fleming and microscope

| Date | Mintage | F | VF | XF | Unc | BU |
|---|---|---|---|---|---|---|
| 1995 Proof | Est. 30,000 | — | — | — | 40.00 | — |

**CROWN** **KM# 548a** **Weight:** 28.2800 g. **Composition:** 0.9250 Silver .8411 oz. ASW **Series:** Inventions of the Modern World **Obverse:** Bust of Queen Elizabeth II right **Reverse:** Cameo of Lazlo Bird, ball point pen

| Date | Mintage | F | VF | XF | Unc | BU |
|---|---|---|---|---|---|---|
| 1995 Proof | Est. 30,000 | Value: 40.00 | | | | |

**CROWN** **KM# 434** **Composition:** Copper-Nickel **Series:** Man in Flight **Obverse:** Bust of Queen Elizabeth II right **Reverse:** Icarus' wings melting

| Date | Mintage | F | VF | XF | Unc | BU |
|---|---|---|---|---|---|---|
| 1995 Proof | — | Value: 7.50 | | | | |

**CROWN** **KM# 434a** **Weight:** 28.2800 g. **Composition:** 0.9250 Silver .8411 oz. ASW **Series:** Man in Flight **Obverse:** Bust of Queen Elizabeth II right **Reverse:** Icarus' wings melting

| Date | Mintage | F | VF | XF | Unc | BU |
|---|---|---|---|---|---|---|
| 1995 Proof | Est. 30,000 | Value: 37.50 | | | | |

**CROWN** **KM# 435** **Composition:** Copper-Nickel **Series:** Man in Flight **Obverse:** Bust of Queen Elizabeth II right **Reverse:** Leonardo Da Vinci and aircraft design

| Date | Mintage | F | VF | XF | Unc | BU |
|---|---|---|---|---|---|---|
| 1995 Proof | — | Value: 6.50 | | | | |

**CROWN** **KM# 435a** **Weight:** 28.2800 g. **Composition:** 0.9250 Silver .8411 oz. ASW **Series:** Man in Flight **Obverse:** Bust of Queen Elizabeth II right **Reverse:** Leonardo da Vinci and aircraft design

| Date | Mintage | F | VF | XF | Unc | BU |
|---|---|---|---|---|---|---|
| 1995 Proof | Est. 30,000 | Value: 37.50 | | | | |

**CROWN** **KM# 436** **Composition:** Copper-Nickel **Series:** Man in Flight **Obverse:** Bust of Queen Elizabeth II right **Reverse:** Montgolfier Brothers' balloon

| Date | Mintage | F | VF | XF | Unc | BU |
|---|---|---|---|---|---|---|
| 1995 Proof | — | Value: 7.50 | | | | |

**CROWN** **KM# 436a** **Weight:** 28.2800 g. **Composition:** 0.9250 Silver .8411 oz. ASW **Series:** Man in Flight **Obverse:** Bust of Queen Elizabeth II right **Reverse:** Montgolfier brothers' balloon

| Date | Mintage | F | VF | XF | Unc | BU |
|---|---|---|---|---|---|---|
| 1995 Proof | Est. 30,000 | Value: 35.00 | | | | |

**CROWN** **KM# 437** **Composition:** Copper-Nickel **Series:** Man in Flight **Obverse:** Bust of Queen Elizabeth II right **Reverse:** Wright Brothers' airplane

| Date | Mintage | F | VF | XF | Unc | BU |
|---|---|---|---|---|---|---|
| 1995 Proof | — | Value: 6.50 | | | | |

**CROWN** **KM# 437a** **Weight:** 28.2800 g. **Composition:** 0.9250 Silver .8411 oz. ASW **Series:** Man in Flight **Obverse:** Bust of Queen Elizabeth II right **Reverse:** Wright brothers' airplane

| Date | Mintage | F | VF | XF | Unc | BU |
|---|---|---|---|---|---|---|
| 1995 Proof | Est. 30,000 | Value: 38.50 | | | | |

**CROWN** **KM# 438** **Composition:** Copper-Nickel **Series:** Man in Flight **Subject:** First Flight Toyko to Paris **Obverse:** Bust of Queen Elizabeth II right **Reverse:** Heads of Abe and Kawachi over airplane

| Date | Mintage | F | VF | XF | Unc | BU |
|---|---|---|---|---|---|---|
| 1995 Proof | — | Value: 6.50 | | | | |

**CROWN** **KM# 438a** **Weight:** 28.2800 g. **Composition:** 0.9250 Silver .8411 oz. ASW **Series:** Man in Flight **Subject:** First

Flight Tokyo to Paris **Obverse:** Bust of Queen Elizabeth II right **Reverse:** Heads of Abe and Kawachi above plane

| Date | Mintage | F | VF | XF | Unc | BU |
|---|---|---|---|---|---|---|
| 1995 Proof | Est. 30,000 | Value: 40.00 | | | | |

**CROWN KM# 439.1 Composition:** Copper-Nickel **Series:** Man in Flight **Obverse:** Bust of Queen Elizabeth II right **Reverse:** FW190, first diesel powered aircraft

| Date | Mintage | F | VF | XF | Unc | BU |
|---|---|---|---|---|---|---|
| 1995 Proof | 500 | Value: 12.50 | | | | |

**ROWN KM# 439.1a Weight:** 28.2800 g. **Composition:** .9250 Silver .8411 oz. ASW **Series:** Man in Flight **Obverse:** Bust Queen Elizabeth II right **Reverse:** First diesel powered aircraft

| te | Mintage | F | VF | XF | Unc | BU |
|---|---|---|---|---|---|---|
| 95 Proof | Est. 30,000 | Value: 40.00 | | | | |

**CROWN KM# 439.2 Composition:** Copper-Nickel **Series:** Man in Flight **Obverse:** Bust of Queen Elizabeth II right **Reverse:** FW190 BMW injection aero engine

| Date | Mintage | F | VF | XF | Unc | BU |
|---|---|---|---|---|---|---|
| 1995 | — | — | — | — | 6.50 | — |

**CROWN KM# 440.1 Composition:** Copper-Nickel **Series:** Man in Flight **Obverse:** Bust of Queen Elizabeth II right **Reverse:** ME262, first jet aircraft 1941

| Date | Mintage | F | VF | XF | Unc | BU |
|---|---|---|---|---|---|---|
| 1995 Proof | 500 | Value: 12.50 | | | | |

**CROWN KM# 440.1a Weight:** 28.2800 g. **Composition:** 0.9250 Silver .8411 oz. ASW **Series:** Man in Flight **Obverse:** Bust of Queen Elizabeth II right **Reverse:** ME262, first jet aircraft 1941

| Date | Mintage | F | VF | XF | Unc | BU |
|---|---|---|---|---|---|---|
| 1995 Proof | Est. 30,000 | Value: 40.00 | | | | |

**CROWN KM# 440.2 Composition:** Copper-Nickel **Series:** Man in Flight **Obverse:** Bust of Queen Elizabeth II right **Reverse:** Jet powered aircraft 1942

| Date | Mintage | F | VF | XF | Unc | BU |
|---|---|---|---|---|---|---|
| 1995 | — | — | — | — | 6.50 | — |

**CROWN KM# 441 Composition:** Copper-Nickel **Series:** Man in Flight **Subject:** 25th Anniversary of Boeing 747 **Obverse:** Bust of Queen Elizabeth II right **Reverse:** Boeing 747

| Date | Mintage | F | VF | XF | Unc | BU |
|---|---|---|---|---|---|---|
| 1995 Proof | — | Value: 6.50 | | | | |

**CROWN KM# 441a Weight:** 28.2800 g. **Composition:** 0.9250 Silver .8411 oz. ASW **Series:** Man in Flight **Subject:** 25th Anniversary of Boeing 747 **Obverse:** Bust of Queen Elizabeth II right **Reverse:** Boeing 747

| Date | Mintage | F | VF | XF | Unc | BU |
|---|---|---|---|---|---|---|
| 1995 Proof | Est. 30,000 | Value: 38.50 | | | | |

**CROWN KM# 446 Composition:** Copper-Nickel **Obverse:** Bust of Queen Elizabeth II right **Reverse:** Turkish cat

| Date | Mintage | F | VF | XF | Unc | BU |
|---|---|---|---|---|---|---|
| 1995 | — | — | — | — | 7.50 | — |

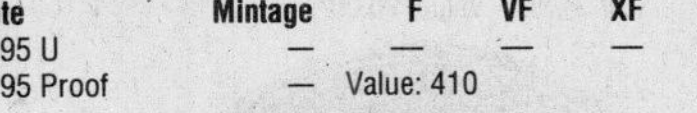

**CROWN KM# 447 Weight:** 31.1000 g. **Composition:** 0.9990 Silver 1.0000 oz. ASW **Obverse:** Bust of Queen Elizabeth II right **Reverse:** Turkish cat

| Date | Mintage | F | VF | XF | Unc | BU |
|---|---|---|---|---|---|---|
| 1995 Proof | — | Value: 28.00 | | | | |

**CROWN KM# 448 Weight:** 31.1000 g. **Composition:** 0.9990 Gold 1.0000 oz. AGW **Obverse:** Bust of Queen Elizabeth II right **Reverse:** Turkish cat

| Date | Mintage | F | VF | XF | Unc | BU |
|---|---|---|---|---|---|---|
| 1995 U | — | — | — | — | 400 | — |
| 1995 Proof | — | Value: 410 | | | | |

**CROWN KM# 453 Composition:** Copper-Nickel **Subject:** Year of the Pig **Obverse:** Bust of Queen Elizabeth II right **Reverse:** Mother pig with piglets

| Date | Mintage | F | VF | XF | Unc | BU |
|---|---|---|---|---|---|---|
| 1995 | — | — | — | — | 8.50 | — |

**CROWN KM# 454 Weight:** 31.1035 g. **Composition:** 0.9990 Silver 1.0000 oz. ASW **Subject:** Year of the Pig **Obverse:** Bust of Queen Elizabeth II right **Reverse:** Mother pig with piglets

| Date | Mintage | F | VF | XF | Unc | BU |
|---|---|---|---|---|---|---|
| 1995 Proof | — | Value: 40.00 | | | | |

**CROWN KM# 455 Weight:** 31.1035 g. **Composition:** 0.9990 Gold 1.0000 oz. AGW **Subject:** Year of the Pig **Obverse:** Bust of Queen Elizabeth II right **Reverse:** Mother pig with piglets

| Date | Mintage | F | VF | XF | Unc | BU |
|---|---|---|---|---|---|---|
| 1995 Proof | Est. 2,500 | Value: 700 | | | | |

**CROWN KM# 458 Composition:** Copper-Nickel **Subject:** 95th Birthday of Queen Mother **Obverse:** Bust of Queen Elizabeth II right **Reverse:** Bust of Queen Mother

| Date | Mintage | F | VF | XF | Unc | BU |
|---|---|---|---|---|---|---|
| 1995 | — | — | — | — | 5.00 | — |

**CROWN KM# 458a Weight:** 28.2800 g. **Composition:** 0.9250 Silver .8411 oz. ASW **Subject:** 95th Birthday of Queen Mother **Obverse:** Bust of Queen Elizabeth II right **Reverse:** Bust of Queen Mother

| Date | Mintage | F | VF | XF | Unc | BU |
|---|---|---|---|---|---|---|
| 1995 Proof | Est. 30,000 | Value: 35.00 | | | | |

**CROWN KM# 461 Composition:** Copper-Nickel **Series:** Preserve Planet Earth **Obverse:** Bust of Queen Elizabeth II right **Reverse:** European otter

| Date | Mintage | F | VF | XF | Unc | BU |
|---|---|---|---|---|---|---|
| 1995 | — | — | — | — | 8.50 | — |

**CROWN KM# 461a Weight:** 28.2800 g. **Composition:** 0.9250 Silver .8411 oz. ASW **Series:** Preserve Planet Earth **Obverse:** Bust of Queen Elizabeth II right **Reverse:** European otter

| Date | Mintage | F | VF | XF | Unc | BU |
|---|---|---|---|---|---|---|
| 1995 Proof | Est. 30,000 | Value: 40.00 | | | | |

**CROWN KM# 462 Composition:** Copper-Nickel **Series:** Preserve Planet Earth **Obverse:** Bust of Queen Elizabeth II right **Reverse:** Egrets

| Date | Mintage | F | VF | XF | Unc | BU |
|---|---|---|---|---|---|---|
| 1995 | — | — | — | — | 8.50 | — |

**CROWN KM# 462a Weight:** 28.2800 g. **Composition:** 0.9250 Silver .8411 oz. ASW **Series:** Preserve Planet Earth **Obverse:** Bust of Queen Elizabeth II right **Reverse:** Egrets

| Date | Mintage | F | VF | XF | Unc | BU |
|---|---|---|---|---|---|---|
| 1995 Proof | Est. 30,000 | Value: 40.00 | | | | |

**CROWN KM# 482 Weight:** 31.1035 g. **Composition:** 0.9995 Platinum .9995 oz. APW **Obverse:** Bust of Queen Elizabeth II right **Reverse:** Turkish cat

| Date | Mintage | F | VF | XF | Unc | BU |
|---|---|---|---|---|---|---|
| 1995 | — | — | — | — | BV+20% | — |

—

**CROWN** **KM# 502** **Composition:** Copper-Nickel **Series:** Aircraft of WW II **Obverse:** Bust of Queen Elizabeth II right **Reverse:** Hawker Hurricane

| Date | Mintage | F | VF | XF | Unc | BU |
|---|---|---|---|---|---|---|
| 1995 | — | — | — | — | 5.50 | — |

**CROWN** **KM# 502a** **Weight:** 28.2800 g. **Composition:** 0.9250 Silver .8411 oz. ASW **Series:** Aircraft of WW II **Obverse:** Bust of Queen Elizabeth II right **Reverse:** Hawker Hurricane

| Date | Mintage | F | VF | XF | Unc | BU |
|---|---|---|---|---|---|---|
| 1995 Proof | Est. 30,000 | Value: 30.00 | | | | |

**CROWN** **KM# 503** **Composition:** Copper-Nickel **Series:** Aircraft of WW II **Obverse:** Bust of Queen Elizabeth II right **Reverse:** P-51 Mustang

| Date | Mintage | F | VF | XF | Unc | BU |
|---|---|---|---|---|---|---|
| 1995 | — | — | — | — | — | — |

**CROWN** **KM# 503a** **Weight:** 28.2800 g. **Composition:** 0.9250 Silver .8411 oz. ASW **Series:** Aircraft of WW II **Obverse:** Bust of Queen Elizabeth II right **Reverse:** P-51 Mustang

| Date | Mintage | F | VF | XF | Unc | BU |
|---|---|---|---|---|---|---|
| 1995 Proof | — | Value: 30.00 | | | | |

**CROWN** **KM# 504** **Composition:** Copper-Nickel **Series:** Aircraft of WW II **Obverse:** Bust of Queen Elizabeth II right **Reverse:** Letov 5328

| Date | Mintage | F | VF | XF | Unc | BU |
|---|---|---|---|---|---|---|
| 1995 | — | — | — | — | 5.50 | — |

**CROWN** **KM# 504a** **Weight:** 28.2800 g. **Composition:** 0.9250 Silver .8411 oz. ASW **Series:** Aircraft of WW II **Obverse:** Bust of Queen Elizabeth II right **Reverse:** Letov 5328

| Date | Mintage | F | VF | XF | Unc | BU |
|---|---|---|---|---|---|---|
| 1995 Proof | Est. 30,000 | Value: 30.00 | | | | |

**CROWN** **KM# 505** **Composition:** Copper-Nickel **Series:** Aircraft of WW II **Obverse:** Bust of Queen Elizabeth II right **Reverse:** Messerschmitt ME262

| Date | Mintage | F | VF | XF | Unc | BU |
|---|---|---|---|---|---|---|
| 1995 | — | — | — | — | 5.50 | — |

**CROWN** **KM# 505a** **Weight:** 28.2800 g. **Composition:** 0.9250 Silver .8411 oz. ASW **Series:** Aircraft of WW II **Obverse:** Bust of Queen Elizabeth II right **Reverse:** Messerschmitt ME262

| Date | Mintage | F | VF | XF | Unc | BU |
|---|---|---|---|---|---|---|
| 1995 Proof | Est. 30,000 | Value: 30.00 | | | | |

**CROWN** **KM# 506** **Composition:** Copper-Nickel **Series:** Aircraft of WW II **Obverse:** Bust of Queen Elizabeth II right **Reverse:** JU87 Stuka

| Date | Mintage | F | VF | XF | Unc | BU |
|---|---|---|---|---|---|---|
| 1995 | — | — | — | — | 5.50 | — |

**CROWN** **KM# 506a** **Weight:** 28.2800 g. **Composition:** 0.9250 Silver .8411 oz. ASW **Series:** Aircraft of WW II **Obverse:** Bust of Queen Elizabeth II right **Reverse:** JU87 Stuka

| Date | Mintage | F | VF | XF | Unc | BU |
|---|---|---|---|---|---|---|
| 1995 Proof | Est. 30,000 | Value: 30.00 | | | | |

**CROWN** **KM# 507** **Composition:** Copper-Nickel **Series:** Aircraft of WW II **Obverse:** Bust of Queen Elizabeth II right **Reverse:** MIG 3

| Date | Mintage | F | VF | XF | Unc | BU |
|---|---|---|---|---|---|---|
| 1995 | — | — | — | — | 5.50 | — |

**CROWN** **KM# 507a** **Weight:** 28.2800 g. **Composition:** 0.9250 Silver .8411 oz. ASW **Series:** Aircraft of WW II **Obverse:** Bust of Queen Elizabeth II right **Reverse:** MIG 3

| Date | Mintage | F | VF | XF | Unc | BU |
|---|---|---|---|---|---|---|
| 1995 Proof | Est. 30,000 | Value: 30.00 | | | | |

**CROWN** **KM# 508** **Composition:** Copper-Nickel **Series:** Aircraft of WW II **Obverse:** Bust of Queen Elizabeth II right **Reverse:** Nakajima KI-49 Donryu

| Date | Mintage | F | VF | XF | Unc | BU |
|---|---|---|---|---|---|---|
| 1995 | — | — | — | — | 5.50 | — |

**CROWN** **KM# 508a** **Weight:** 28.2800 g. **Composition:** 0.9250 Silver .8411 oz. ASW **Series:** Aircraft of WW II **Obverse:** Bust of Queen Elizabeth II right **Reverse:** Nakajima KI-49 Donryu

| Date | Mintage | F | VF | XF | Unc | BU |
|---|---|---|---|---|---|---|
| 1995 Proof | Est. 30,000 | Value: 30.00 | | | | |

**CROWN** **KM# 509** **Composition:** Copper-Nickel **Series:** Aircraft of WW II **Obverse:** Bust of Queen Elizabeth II right **Reverse:** Vickers Wellington

| Date | Mintage | F | VF | XF | Unc | BU |
|---|---|---|---|---|---|---|
| 1995 | — | — | — | — | 5.50 | — |

**CROWN** **KM# 509a** **Weight:** 28.2800 g. **Composition:** 0.9250 Silver .8411 oz. ASW **Series:** Aircraft of WW II **Obverse:** Bust of Queen Elizabeth II right **Reverse:** Vickers Wellington

| Date | Mintage | F | VF | XF | Unc | BU |
|---|---|---|---|---|---|---|
| 1995 Proof | Est. 30,000 | Value: 30.00 | | | | |

**CROWN** **KM# 510** **Composition:** Copper-Nickel **Series:** Aircraft of WW II **Obverse:** Bust of Queen Elizabeth II right **Reverse:** Supermarine Spitfire

| Date | Mintage | F | VF | XF | Unc | BU |
|---|---|---|---|---|---|---|
| 1995 (py) | — | — | — | — | 5.50 | — |
| 1995 | — | — | — | — | 5.50 | — |

**CROWN** **KM# 510a** **Weight:** 28.2800 g. **Composition:** 0.9250 Silver .8411 oz. ASW **Series:** Aircraft of WW II **Obverse:** Bust of Queen Elizabeth II right **Reverse:** Supermarine Spitfire

| Date | Mintage | F | VF | XF | Unc | BU |
|---|---|---|---|---|---|---|
| 1995 Proof | Est. 30,000 | Value: 30.00 | | | | |

**CROWN** **KM# 511** **Composition:** Copper-Nickel **Series:** Aircraft of WW II **Obverse:** Bust of Queen Elizabeth II right **Reverse:** Fokker G.1a

| Date | Mintage | F | VF | XF | Unc | BU |
|---|---|---|---|---|---|---|
| 1995 | — | — | — | — | 5.50 | — |

**CROWN** **KM# 511a** **Weight:** 28.2800 g. **Composition:** 0.9250 Silver .8411 oz. ASW **Series:** Aircraft of WW II **Obverse:** Bust of Queen Elizabeth II right **Reverse:** Fokker G.1a

| Date | Mintage | F | VF | XF | Unc | BU |
|---|---|---|---|---|---|---|
| 1995 Proof | Est. 30,000 | Value: 30.00 | | | | |

**CROWN** **KM# 512** **Composition:** Copper-Nickel **Series:** Aircraft of WW II **Obverse:** Bust of Queen Elizabeth II right **Reverse:** Commonwealth Boomerang CA-13

| Date | Mintage | F | VF | XF | Unc | BU |
|---|---|---|---|---|---|---|
| 1995 | — | — | — | — | 5.50 | — |

**CROWN** **KM# 512a** **Weight:** 28.2800 g. **Composition:** 0.9250 Silver .8411 oz. ASW **Series:** Aircraft of WW II **Obverse:** Bust of Queen Elizabeth II right **Reverse:** Boomerang CA-13

| Date | Mintage | F | VF | XF | Unc | BU |
|---|---|---|---|---|---|---|
| 1995 Proof | Est. 30,000 | Value: 30.00 | | | | |

**CROWN** **KM# 513** **Composition:** Copper-Nickel **Series:** Aircraft of WW II **Obverse:** Bust of Queen Elizabeth II right **Reverse:** Bristol Blenheim 142

| Date | Mintage | F | VF | XF | Unc | BU |
|---|---|---|---|---|---|---|
| 1995 | — | — | — | — | 5.50 | — |

**CROWN** **KM# 513a** **Weight:** 28.2800 g. **Composition:** 0.9250 Silver .8411 oz. ASW **Series:** Aircraft of WW II **Obverse:** Bust of Queen Elizabeth II right **Reverse:** Bristol Blenheim 142

| Date | Mintage | F | VF | XF | Unc | BU |
|---|---|---|---|---|---|---|
| 1995 Proof | Est. 30,000 | Value: 30.00 | | | | |

**CROWN** **KM# 514** **Composition:** Copper-Nickel **Series:** Aircraft of WW II **Obverse:** Bust of Queen Elizabeth II right **Reverse:** Mitsubishi Zero

| Date | Mintage | F | VF | XF | Unc | BU |
|---|---|---|---|---|---|---|
| 1995 | — | — | — | — | 5.50 | — |

**CROWN** **KM# 514a** **Weight:** 28.2800 g. **Composition:** 0.9250 Silver .8411 oz. ASW **Series:** Aircraft of WW II **Obverse:** Bust of Queen Elizabeth II right **Reverse:** Mitsubishi Zero

| Date | Mintage | F | VF | XF | Unc | BU |
|---|---|---|---|---|---|---|
| 1995 Proof | Est. 30,000 | Value: 30.00 | | | | |

**CROWN** **KM# 515** **Composition:** Copper-Nickel **Series:** Aircraft of WW II **Obverse:** Bust of Queen Elizabeth II right **Reverse:** Heinkel HE 111

| Date | Mintage | F | VF | XF | Unc | BU |
|---|---|---|---|---|---|---|
| 1995 | — | — | — | — | 5.50 | — |

**CROWN** **KM# 515a** **Weight:** 28.2800 g. **Composition:** 0.9250 Silver .8411 oz. ASW **Series:** Aircraft of WW II **Obverse:** Bust of Queen Elizabeth II right **Reverse:** Heinkel HE 111

| Date | Mintage | F | VF | XF | Unc | BU |
|---|---|---|---|---|---|---|
| 1995 Proof | Est. 30,000 | Value: 30.00 | | | | |

**CROWN** **KM# 516** **Composition:** Copper-Nickel **Series:** Aircraft of WW II **Obverse:** Bust of Queen Elizabeth II right **Reverse:** Boulton Paul P.82 Defiant

| Date | Mintage | F | VF | XF | Unc | BU |
|---|---|---|---|---|---|---|
| 1995 | — | — | — | — | 5.50 | — |

**CROWN** **KM# 516a** **Weight:** 28.2800 g. **Composition:** 0.9250 Silver .8411 oz. ASW **Series:** Aircraft of WW II **Obverse:** Bust of Queen Elizabeth II right **Reverse:** Boulton Paul P.82 Defiant

| Date | Mintage | F | VF | XF | Unc | BU |
|---|---|---|---|---|---|---|
| 1995 Proof | Est. 30,000 | Value: 30.00 | | | | |

**CROWN** **KM# 517** **Composition:** Copper-Nickel **Series:** Aircraft of WW II **Obverse:** Bust of Queen Elizabeth II right **Reverse:** Boeing B-29 Enola Gay

| Date | Mintage | F | VF | XF | Unc | BU |
|---|---|---|---|---|---|---|
| 1995 | — | — | — | — | 5.50 | — |

**CROWN** **KM# 517a** **Weight:** 28.2800 g. **Composition:** 0.9250 Silver .8411 oz. ASW **Series:** Aircraft of WW II **Obverse:** Bust of Queen Elizabeth II right **Reverse:** Boeing B-29 Enola Gay

| Date | Mintage | F | VF | XF | Unc | BU |
|---|---|---|---|---|---|---|
| 1995 Proof | Est. 30,000 | Value: 30.00 | | | | |

**CROWN** **KM# 518** **Composition:** Copper-Nickel **Series:** Aircraft of WW II **Obverse:** Bust of Queen Elizabeth II right **Reverse:** Douglas DC-3 (C-47) Dakota

| Date | Mintage | F | VF | XF | Unc | BU |
|---|---|---|---|---|---|---|
| 1995 | — | — | — | — | 5.50 | — |

**CROWN** **KM#518a** **Weight:** 28.2800 g. **Composition:** 0.9250 Silver .8411 oz. ASW **Series:** Aircraft of WW II **Obverse:** Bust of Queen Elizabeth II right **Reverse:** Douglas DC-3 (C-47) Dakota

| Date | Mintage | F | VF | XF | Unc | BU |
|---|---|---|---|---|---|---|
| 1995 Proof | Est. 30,000 | Value: 30.00 | | | | |

**CROWN** **KM# 519** **Composition:** Copper-Nickel **Series:** Aircraft of WW II **Obverse:** Bust of Queen Elizabeth II right **Reverse:** Fairey Swordfish

| Date | Mintage | F | VF | XF | Unc | BU |
|---|---|---|---|---|---|---|
| 1995 | — | — | — | — | 5.50 | — |

**CROWN** **KM# 519a** **Weight:** 28.2800 g. **Composition:** 0.9250 Silver .8411 oz. ASW **Series:** Aircraft of WW II **Obverse:** Bust of Queen Elizabeth II right **Reverse:** Fairey Swordfish

| Date | Mintage | F | VF | XF | Unc | BU |
|---|---|---|---|---|---|---|
| 1995 Proof | Est. 30,000 | Value: 30.00 | | | | |

**CROWN** **KM# 555** **Composition:** Copper-Nickel **Series:** Inventions of the Modern World **Obverse:** Bust of Queen Elizabeth II right **Reverse:** Cameo of Wernher von Braun and rocket

| Date | Mintage | F | VF | XF | Unc | BU |
|---|---|---|---|---|---|---|
| 1996 | — | — | — | — | 5.00 | — |

**CROWN** **KM# 555a** **Weight:** 28.2800 g. **Composition:** 0.9250 Silver .8411 oz. ASW **Series:** Inventions of the Modern World **Obverse:** Bust of Queen Elizabeth II right **Reverse:** Cameo of Wernher von Braun and rocket

| Date | Mintage | F | VF | XF | Unc | BU |
|---|---|---|---|---|---|---|
| 1996 Proof | Est. 30,000 | Value: 40.00 | | | | |

**CROWN** **KM# 556** **Composition:** Copper-Nickel **Series:** Inventions of the Modern World **Obverse:** Bust of Queen Elizabeth II right **Reverse:** Cameo of Thomas Edison, electricity

| Date | Mintage | F | VF | XF | Unc | BU |
|---|---|---|---|---|---|---|
| 1996 | — | — | — | — | 5.00 | — |

**CROWN** **KM# 556a** **Weight:** 28.2800 g. **Composition:** 0.9250 Silver .8411 oz. ASW **Series:** Inventions of the Modern World **Obverse:** Bust of Queen Elizabeth II right **Reverse:** Cameo of Thomas Edison, electricity

| Date | Mintage | F | VF | XF | Unc | BU |
|---|---|---|---|---|---|---|
| 1996 Proof | — | — | — | — | 40.00 | — |

**CROWN** **KM# 557a** **Weight:** 28.2800 g. **Composition:** 0.9250 Silver .8411 oz. ASW **Series:** Inventions of the Modern World **Obverse:** Bust of Queen Elizabeth II right **Reverse:** Compass

| Date | Mintage | F | VF | XF | Unc | BU |
|---|---|---|---|---|---|---|
| 1996 Proof | — | Value: 40.00 | | | | |

**CROWN** **KM# 558.1** **Composition:** Copper-Nickel **Series:** Inventions of the Modern World **Obverse:** Bust of Queen Elizabeth II right **Reverse:** Cameo of Michael Faraday, electricity

| Date | Mintage | F | VF | XF | Unc | BU |
|---|---|---|---|---|---|---|
| 1996 | — | — | — | — | 5.00 | — |

**CROWN** **KM# 558.2** **Composition:** Copper-Nickel **Series:** Inventions of the Modern World **Obverse:** Bust of Queen Elizabeth II right **Reverse:** Cameo of Michael Faraday, electricity. Error legend: EXRERIMENTAL

| Date | Mintage | F | VF | XF | Unc | BU |
|---|---|---|---|---|---|---|
| 1996 | — | — | — | — | 12.50 | — |

**CROWN** **KM# 558.2a** **Weight:** 28.2800 g. **Composition:** 0.9250 Silver .8411 oz. ASW **Series:** Inventions of the Modern World **Obverse:** Bust of Queen Elizabeth II right **Reverse:** Cameo of Michael Faraday, electricity. Error legend: EXRERIMENTAL

| Date | Mintage | F | VF | XF | Unc | BU |
|---|---|---|---|---|---|---|
| 1996 Proof | Est. 30,000 | Value: 40.00 | | | | |

**CROWN** **KM# 559** **Composition:** Copper-Nickel **Series:** Inventions of the Modern World **Obverse:** Bust of Queen Elizabeth II right **Reverse:** Emile Berliner, gramophone

| Date | Mintage | F | VF | XF | Unc | BU |
|---|---|---|---|---|---|---|
| 1996 | — | — | — | — | 5.00 | — |

**CROWN** **KM# 560** **Composition:** Copper-Nickel **Series:** Inventions of the Modern World **Obverse:** Bust of Queen Elizabeth II right **Reverse:** Cameo of Alexander Graham Bell, voice transmission

| Date | Mintage | F | VF | XF | Unc | BU |
|---|---|---|---|---|---|---|
| 1996 | — | — | — | — | 5.00 | — |

**CROWN** **KM# 560a** **Weight:** 28.2800 g. **Composition:** 0.9250 Silver .8411 oz. ASW **Series:** Inventions of the Modern World **Obverse:** Bust of Queen Elizabeth II right **Reverse:** Cameo of Alexander Graham Bell, voice transmission

| Date | Mintage | F | VF | XF | Unc | BU |
|---|---|---|---|---|---|---|
| 1996 Proof | 30,000 | Value: 40.00 | | | | |

**CROWN** **KM# 567** **Composition:** Copper-Nickel **Series:** 1996 Summer Olympics - Atlanta **Obverse:** Bust of Queen Elizabeth II right **Reverse:** Hurdler

| Date | Mintage | F | VF | XF | Unc | BU |
|---|---|---|---|---|---|---|
| 1996 | — | — | — | — | 6.00 | — |

**CROWN** **KM# 567a** **Weight:** 28.2800 g. **Composition:** 0.9250 Silver .8411 oz. ASW **Series:** 1996 Summer Olympics - Atlanta **Obverse:** Bust of Queen Elizabeth II right **Reverse:** Hurdler

| Date | Mintage | F | VF | XF | Unc | BU |
|---|---|---|---|---|---|---|
| 1996 Proof | Est. 30,000 | Value: 35.00 | | | | |

**CROWN** **KM# 568** **Composition:** Copper-Nickel **Series:** 1996 Summer Olympics - Atlanta **Obverse:** Bust of Queen Elizabeth II right **Reverse:** Runners

| Date | Mintage | F | VF | XF | Unc | BU |
|---|---|---|---|---|---|---|
| 1996 | — | — | — | — | 6.00 | — |

**CROWN** **KM# 568a** **Weight:** 28.2800 g. **Composition:** 0.9250 Silver .8411 oz. ASW **Series:** 1996 Summer Olympics - Atlanta **Obverse:** Bust of Queen Elizabeth II right **Reverse:** Runners

| Date | Mintage | F | VF | XF | Unc | BU |
|---|---|---|---|---|---|---|
| 1996 Proof | Est. 30,000 | Value: 35.00 | | | | |

**CROWN** **KM# 569** **Composition:** Copper-Nickel **Series:** 1996 Summer Olympics - Atlanta **Obverse:** Bust of Queen Elizabeth II right **Reverse:** Sailing

| Date | Mintage | F | VF | XF | Unc | BU |
|---|---|---|---|---|---|---|
| 1996 | — | — | — | — | 6.00 | — |

**CROWN** **KM# 569a** **Weight:** 28.2800 g. **Composition:** 0.9250 Silver .8411 oz. ASW **Series:** 1996 Summer Olympics - Atlanta **Obverse:** Bust of Queen Elizabeth II right **Reverse:** Sailing

| Date | Mintage | F | VF | XF | Unc | BU |
|---|---|---|---|---|---|---|
| 1996 Proof | Est. 30,000 | Value: 35.00 | | | | |

**CROWN** **KM# 570** **Composition:** Copper-Nickel **Series:** 1996 Summer Olympics - Atlanta **Obverse:** Bust of Queen Elizabeth II right **Reverse:** Swimming

| Date | Mintage | F | VF | XF | Unc | BU |
|---|---|---|---|---|---|---|
| 1996 | — | — | — | — | 6.00 | — |

**CROWN** **KM# 570a** **Weight:** 28.2800 g. **Composition:** 0.9250 Silver .8411 oz. ASW **Series:** 1996 Summer Olympics - Atlanta **Obverse:** Bust of Queen Elizabeth II right **Reverse:** Swimming

| Date | Mintage | F | VF | XF | Unc | BU |
|---|---|---|---|---|---|---|
| 1996 Proof | Est. 30,000 | Value: 35.00 | | | | |

**CROWN** **KM# 571** **Composition:** Copper-Nickel **Series:** 1996 Summer Olympics - Atlanta **Obverse:** Bust of Queen Elizabeth II right **Reverse:** Equestrian

| Date | Mintage | F | VF | XF | Unc | BU |
|---|---|---|---|---|---|---|
| 1996 | — | — | — | — | 6.00 | — |

**CROWN** **KM# 571a** **Weight:** 28.2800 g. **Composition:** 0.9250 Silver .8411 oz. ASW **Series:** 1996 Summer Olympics - Atlanta **Obverse:** Bust of Queen Elizabeth II right **Reverse:** Equestrian

| Date | Mintage | F | VF | XF | Unc | BU |
|---|---|---|---|---|---|---|
| 1996 Proof | Est. 30,000 | Value: 35.00 | | | | |

**CROWN** **KM# 572** **Composition:** Copper-Nickel **Series:** 1996 Summer Olympics - Atlanta **Obverse:** Bust of Queen Elizabeth II right **Reverse:** Cyclists and nike

| Date | Mintage | F | VF | XF | Unc | BU |
|---|---|---|---|---|---|---|
| 1996 | — | — | — | — | 6.00 | — |

**CROWN** **KM# 572a** **Weight:** 28.2800 g. **Composition:** 0.9250 Silver .8411 oz. ASW **Series:** 1996 Summer Olympics - Atlanta **Obverse:** Bust of Queen Elizabeth II right **Reverse:** Cyclists and nike

| Date | Mintage | F | VF | XF | Unc | BU |
|---|---|---|---|---|---|---|
| 1996 Proof | Est. 30,000 | Value: 35.00 | | | | |

**CROWN** **KM# 577** **Composition:** Copper-Nickel **Series:** Bicentenary of Robert Burns **Obverse:** Bust of Queen Elizabeth II right **Reverse:** Burns seated

| Date | Mintage | F | VF | XF | Unc | BU |
|---|---|---|---|---|---|---|
| 1996 | — | — | — | — | 5.00 | — |

**CROWN** **KM# 577a** **Weight:** 28.2800 g. **Composition:** 0.9250 Silver .8411 oz. ASW **Series:** Bicentenary of Robert Burns **Obverse:** Bust of Queen Elizabeth II right **Reverse:** Burns seated

| Date | Mintage | F | VF | XF | Unc | BU |
|---|---|---|---|---|---|---|
| 1996 Proof | Est. 30,000 | Value: 40.00 | | | | |

**CROWN** **KM# 578** **Composition:** Copper-Nickel **Series:** Bicentenary of Robert Burns **Obverse:** Bust of Queen Elizabeth II right **Reverse:** Pirate ship

| Date | Mintage | F | VF | XF | Unc | BU |
|---|---|---|---|---|---|---|
| 1996 | — | — | — | — | 5.00 | — |

**CROWN** **KM# 578a** **Weight:** 28.2800 g. **Composition:** 0.9250 Silver .8411 oz. ASW **Series:** Bicentenary of Robert Burns **Obverse:** Bust of Queen Elizabeth II right **Reverse:** Pirate ship

| Date | Mintage | F | VF | XF | Unc | BU |
|---|---|---|---|---|---|---|
| 1996 Proof | Est. 30,000 | Value: 40.00 | | | | |

**CROWN** **KM# 579** **Composition:** Copper-Nickel **Series:** Bicentenary of Robert Burns **Obverse:** Bust of Queen Elizabeth II right **Reverse:** Auld Lang Syne

| Date | Mintage | F | VF | XF | Unc | BU |
|---|---|---|---|---|---|---|
| 1996 | — | — | — | — | 5.00 | — |

**CROWN** **KM# 579a** **Weight:** 28.2800 g. **Composition:** 0.9250 Silver .8411 oz. ASW **Series:** Bicentenary of Robert Burns **Obverse:** Bust of Queen Elizabeth II right **Reverse:** Auld Lang Syne

| Date | Mintage | F | VF | XF | Unc | BU |
|---|---|---|---|---|---|---|
| 1996 Proof | Est. 30,000 | Value: 40.00 | | | | |

**CROWN** KM# 580 **Composition:** Copper-Nickel **Series:** Bicentenary of Robert Burns **Obverse:** Bust of Queen Elizabeth II right **Reverse:** Edinburgh Castle

| Date | Mintage | F | VF | XF | Unc | BU |
|---|---|---|---|---|---|---|
| 1996 | — | — | — | — | 5.00 | — |

**CROWN** KM# 580a **Weight:** 28.2800 g. **Composition:** 0.9250 Silver .8411 oz. ASW **Series:** Bicentenary of Robert Burns **Obverse:** Bust of Queen Elizabeth II right **Reverse:** Edinburgh Castle

| Date | Mintage | F | VF | XF | Unc | BU |
|---|---|---|---|---|---|---|
| 1996 Proof | Est. 30,000 | Value: 40.00 | | | | |

**CROWN** KM# 582 **Weight:** 28.2800 g. **Composition:** 0.9250 Silver .8411 oz. ASW **Subject:** 70th Birthday of Queen Elizabeth II **Obverse:** Bust of Queen Elizabeth II right **Reverse:** Flowers

| Date | Mintage | F | VF | XF | Unc | BU |
|---|---|---|---|---|---|---|
| 1996 | — | — | — | — | 6.00 | — |

**CROWN** KM# 582a **Weight:** 28.2800 g. **Composition:** 0.9250 Silver .8411 oz. ASW **Subject:** 70th Birthday of Queen Elizabeth II **Obverse:** Bust of Queen Elizabeth II right **Reverse:** Flowers

| Date | Mintage | F | VF | XF | Unc | BU |
|---|---|---|---|---|---|---|
| 1996 Proof | Est. 30,000 | Value: 40.00 | | | | |

**CROWN** KM# 585 **Composition:** Copper-Nickel **Series:** Preserve Planet Earth **Obverse:** Bust of Queen Elizabeth II right **Reverse:** Killer whale

| Date | Mintage | F | VF | XF | Unc | BU |
|---|---|---|---|---|---|---|
| 1996 | — | — | — | — | 8.50 | — |

**CROWN** KM# 585a **Weight:** 28.2800 g. **Composition:** 0.9250 Silver .8411 oz. ASW **Series:** Preserve Planet Earth **Obverse:** Bust of Queen Elizabeth II right **Reverse:** Killer whale

| Date | Mintage | F | VF | XF | Unc | BU |
|---|---|---|---|---|---|---|
| 1996 Proof | Est. 30,000 | Value: 40.00 | | | | |

**CROWN** KM# 586 **Composition:** Copper-Nickel **Series:** Preserve Planet Earth **Obverse:** Bust of Queen Elizabeth II right **Reverse:** Razorbill feeding chick

| Date | Mintage | F | VF | XF | Unc | BU |
|---|---|---|---|---|---|---|
| 1996 | — | — | — | — | 8.50 | — |

**CROWN** KM# 586a **Weight:** 28.2800 g. **Composition:** 0.9250 Silver .8411 oz. ASW **Series:** Preserve Planet Earth **Obverse:** Bust of Queen Elizabeth II right **Reverse:** Razorbill feeding check

| Date | Mintage | F | VF | XF | Unc | BU |
|---|---|---|---|---|---|---|
| 1996 Proof | Est. 30,000 | Value: 40.00 | | | | |

**CROWN** KM# 609 **Composition:** Copper-Nickel **Series:** Flower Fairies **Obverse:** Bust of Queen Elizabeth II right **Reverse:** Orchis

| Date | Mintage | F | VF | XF | Unc | BU |
|---|---|---|---|---|---|---|
| 1996 | — | — | — | — | 5.00 | — |

**CROWN** KM# 609a **Weight:** 28.2800 g. **Composition:** 0.9250 Silver .8411 oz. ASW **Series:** Flower Fairies **Obverse:** Bust of Queen Elizabeth II right **Reverse:** Orchis

| Date | Mintage | F | VF | XF | Unc | BU |
|---|---|---|---|---|---|---|
| 1996 Proof | Est. 30,000 | Value: 40.00 | | | | |

**CROWN** KM# 610 **Composition:** Copper-Nickel **Series:** Flower Fairies **Obverse:** Bust of Queen Elizabeth II right **Reverse:** Rose

| Date | Mintage | F | VF | XF | Unc | BU |
|---|---|---|---|---|---|---|
| 1996 | — | — | — | — | 5.00 | — |

**CROWN** KM# 610a **Weight:** 28.2800 g. **Composition:** 0.9250 Silver .8411 oż. ASW **Series:** Flower Fairies **Obverse:** Bust of Queen Elizabeth II right **Reverse:** Rose

| Date | Mintage | F | VF | XF | Unc | BU |
|---|---|---|---|---|---|---|
| 1996 Proof | Est. 30,000 | Value: 40.00 | | | | |

**CROWN** KM# 611 **Composition:** Copper-Nickel **Series:** Flower Fairies **Obverse:** Bust of Queen Elizabeth II right **Reverse:** Fuchsia

| Date | Mintage | F | VF | XF | Unc | BU |
|---|---|---|---|---|---|---|
| 1996 | — | — | — | — | 5.00 | — |

**CROWN** KM# 611a **Weight:** 28.2800 g. **Composition:** 0.9250 Silver .8411 oz. ASW **Series:** Flower Fairies **Obverse:** Bust of Queen Elizabeth II right **Reverse:** Fuchsia

| Date | Mintage | F | VF | XF | Unc | BU |
|---|---|---|---|---|---|---|
| 1996 Proof | Est. 30,000 | Value: 40.00 | | | | |

**CROWN** KM# 612 **Composition:** Copper-Nickel **Series:** Flower Fairies **Obverse:** Bust of Queen Elizabeth II right **Reverse:** Pinks

| Date | Mintage | F | VF | XF | Unc | BU |
|---|---|---|---|---|---|---|
| 1996 | — | — | — | — | 5.00 | — |

**CROWN** KM# 612a **Weight:** 28.2800 g. **Composition:** 0.9250 Silver .8411 oz. ASW **Series:** Flower Fairies **Obverse:** Bust of Queen Elizabeth II right **Reverse:** Pinks

| Date | Mintage | F | VF | XF | Unc | BU |
|---|---|---|---|---|---|---|
| 1996 Proof | Est. 30,000 | Value: 40.00 | | | | |

**CROWN** KM# 621 **Composition:** Copper-Nickel **Obverse:** Bust of Queen Elizabeth II right **Reverse:** Burmese cat

| Date | Mintage | F | VF | XF | Unc | BU |
|---|---|---|---|---|---|---|
| 1996 | — | — | — | — | 10.00 | — |

**CROWN** KM# 621a **Weight:** 31.1035 g. **Composition:** 0.9990 Silver 1.000 oz. ASW **Obverse:** Bust of Queen Elizabeth II right **Reverse:** Burmese cat

| Date | Mintage | F | VF | XF | Unc | BU |
|---|---|---|---|---|---|---|
| 1996 Proof | Est. 50,000 | Value: 40.00 | | | | |

**CROWN** KM# 621b **Weight:** 31.1000 g. **Composition:** 0.9990 Gold 1.0000 oz. AGW **Obverse:** Bust of Queen Elizabeth II right **Reverse:** Burmese cat

| Date | Mintage | F | VF | XF | Unc | BU |
|---|---|---|---|---|---|---|
| 1996 U | — | — | — | — | 400 | — |
| 1996 Proof | — | Value: 410 | | | | |

**CROWN** KM# 624 **Weight:** 31.1035 g. **Composition:** 0.9995 Platinum .9995 oz. APW **Obverse:** Bust of Queen Elizabeth II right **Reverse:** Burmese cat

| Date | Mintage | F | VF | XF | Unc | BU |
|---|---|---|---|---|---|---|
| 1996 | — | — | — | — | BV+20% | — |

**CROWN** KM# 626 **Composition:** Copper-Nickel **Obverse:** Bust of Queen Elizabeth II right **Reverse:** Bust of Ferdinand Magellan, map and ship

| Date | Mintage | F | VF | XF | Unc | BU |
|---|---|---|---|---|---|---|
| 1996 | — | — | — | — | 7.50 | — |

**CROWN** KM# 626a **Weight:** 28.2800 g. **Composition:** 0.9250 Silver .8411 oz. ASW **Obverse:** Bust of Queen Elizabeth II right **Reverse:** Bust of Ferdinand Magellan, map and ship

| Date | Mintage | F | VF | XF | Unc | BU |
|---|---|---|---|---|---|---|
| 1996 Proof | Est. 30,000 | Value: 40.00 | | | | |

**CROWN** KM# 629 **Composition:** Copper-Nickel **Obverse:** Bust of Queen Elizabeth II right **Reverse:** Bust of Sir Francis Drake, map and ship

| Date | Mintage | F | VF | XF | Unc | BU |
|---|---|---|---|---|---|---|
| 1996 | — | — | — | — | 7.50 | — |

**CROWN** KM# 629a **Weight:** 28.2800 g. **Composition:** 0.9250 Silver .8411 oz. ASW **Obverse:** Bust of Queen Elizabeth II right **Reverse:** Bust of Sir Francis Drake, map and ship

| Date | Mintage | F | VF | XF | Unc | BU |
|---|---|---|---|---|---|---|
| 1996 Proof | Est. 30,000 | Value: 40.00 | | | | |

**CROWN** KM# 632 **Composition:** Copper-Nickel **Series:** European Football Championship **Obverse:** Bust of Queen Elizabeth II right **Reverse:** Romania vs Bulgaria

| Date | Mintage | F | VF | XF | Unc | BU |
|---|---|---|---|---|---|---|
| 1996 | — | — | — | — | 7.00 | — |

**CROWN** KM# 632a **Weight:** 28.2800 g. **Composition:** 0.9250 Silver .8411 oz. ASW **Series:** European Football Championship **Obverse:** Bust of Queen Elizabeth II right **Reverse:** Romania vs Bulgaria

| Date | Mintage | F | VF | XF | Unc | BU |
|---|---|---|---|---|---|---|
| 1996 Proof | Est. 30,000 | Value: 40.00 | | | | |

**CROWN** KM# 635 **Composition:** Copper-Nickel **Series:** European Football Championship **Obverse:** Bust of Queen Elizabeth II right **Reverse:** Czech Repulic vs Itay

| Date | Mintage | F | VF | XF | Unc | BU |
|---|---|---|---|---|---|---|
| 1996 | — | — | — | — | 7.00 | — |

**CROWN** KM# 635a **Weight:** 28.2800 g. **Composition:** 0.9250 Silver .8411 oz. ASW **Series:** European Football Championship **Obverse:** Bust of Queen Elizabeth II right **Reverse:** Czech Republic vs Italy

| Date | Mintage | F | VF | XF | Unc | BU |
|---|---|---|---|---|---|---|
| 1996 Proof | Est. 30,000 | Value: 40.00 | | | | |

**CROWN** KM# 638 **Composition:** Copper-Nickel **Series:** European Football Championship **Obverse:** Bust of Queen Elizabeth II right **Reverse:** Germany vs Russia

| Date | Mintage | F | VF | XF | Unc | BU |
|---|---|---|---|---|---|---|
| 1996 | — | — | — | — | 7.00 | — |

**CROWN** KM# 638a **Weight:** 28.2800 g. **Composition:** 0.9250 Silver .8411 oz. ASW **Series:** European Football Championship **Obverse:** Bust of Queen Elizabeth II right **Reverse:** Germany vs Russia

| Date | Mintage | F | VF | XF | Unc | BU |
|---|---|---|---|---|---|---|
| 1996 Proof | Est. 30,000 | Value: 40.00 | | | | |

**CROWN** KM# 641 **Composition:** Copper-Nickel **Series:** European Football Championship **Obverse:** Bust of Queen Elizabeth II right **Reverse:** Spain vs France

| Date | Mintage | F | VF | XF | Unc | BU |
|---|---|---|---|---|---|---|
| 1996 | — | — | — | — | 7.00 | — |

**CROWN** KM# 641a **Weight:** 28.2800 g. **Composition:** 0.9250 Silver .8411 oz. ASW **Series:** European Football Championship **Obverse:** Bust of Queen Elizabeth II right **Reverse:** Spain vs France

| Date | Mintage | F | VF | XF | Unc | BU |
|---|---|---|---|---|---|---|
| 1996 Proof | Est. 30,000 | Value: 40.00 | | | | |

**CROWN** KM# 644 **Composition:** Copper-Nickel **Series:** European Football Championship **Obverse:** Bust of Queen Elizabeth II right **Reverse:** Turkey vs Croatia

| Date | Mintage | F | VF | XF | Unc | BU |
|---|---|---|---|---|---|---|
| 1996 | — | — | — | — | 7.00 | — |

**CROWN** KM# 644a **Weight:** 28.2800 g. **Composition:** 0.9250 Silver .8411 oz. ASW **Series:** European Football Championship **Obverse:** Bust of Queen Elizabeth II right **Reverse:** Turkey vs Croatia

| Date | Mintage | F | VF | XF | Unc | BU |
|---|---|---|---|---|---|---|
| 1996 Proof | Est. 30,000 | Value: 40.00 | | | | |

**CROWN** KM# 647 **Composition:** Copper-Nickel **Series:** European Football Championship **Obverse:** Bust of Queen Elizabeth II right **Reverse:** Denmark vs Portugal

| Date | Mintage | F | VF | XF | Unc | BU |
|---|---|---|---|---|---|---|
| 1996 | — | — | — | — | 6.00 | — |

**CROWN** KM# 647a **Weight:** 28.2800 g. **Composition:** 0.9250 Silver .8411 oz. ASW **Series:** European Football Championship **Obverse:** Bust of Queen Elizabeth II right **Reverse:** Denmark vs Portugal

| Date | Mintage | F | VF | XF | Unc | BU |
|---|---|---|---|---|---|---|
| 1996 Proof | Est. 30,000 | Value: 40.00 | | | | |

**CROWN** KM# 650 **Composition:** Copper-Nickel **Series:** European Football Championship **Obverse:** Bust of Queen Elizabeth II right **Reverse:** Scotland vs England

| Date | Mintage | F | VF | XF | Unc | BU |
|---|---|---|---|---|---|---|
| 1996 | — | — | — | — | 7.00 | — |

**CROWN** KM# 650a **Weight:** 28.2800 g. **Composition:** 0.9250 Silver .8411 oz. ASW **Series:** European Football Championship **Obverse:** Bust of Queen Elizabeth II right **Reverse:** Scotland vs England

| Date | Mintage | F | VF | XF | Unc | BU |
|---|---|---|---|---|---|---|
| 1996 Proof | Est. 30,000 | Value: 40.00 | | | | |

**CROWN** KM# 653 **Composition:** Copper-Nickel **Series:** European Football Championship **Obverse:** Bust of Queen Elizabeth II right **Reverse:** Holland vs Switzerland

| Date | Mintage | F | VF | XF | Unc | BU |
|---|---|---|---|---|---|---|
| 1996 | — | — | — | — | 7.00 | — |

**CROWN** KM# 653a **Weight:** 28.2800 g. **Composition:** 0.9250 Silver .8411 oz. ASW **Series:** European Football Championship **Obverse:** Bust of Queen Elizabeth II right **Reverse:** Holland vs Switzerland

| Date | Mintage | F | VF | XF | Unc | BU |
|---|---|---|---|---|---|---|
| 1996 Proof | Est. 30,000 | Value: 40.00 | | | | |

**CROWN** KM# 657 **Composition:** Copper-Nickel **Series:** European Football Championship **Obverse:** Bust of Queen Elizabeth II right **Reverse:** German shield, winner

| Date | Mintage | F | VF | XF | Unc | BU |
|---|---|---|---|---|---|---|
| 1996 | — | — | — | — | 7.00 | — |

**CROWN** KM# 657a **Weight:** 28.2800 g. **Composition:** 0.9250 Silver .8411 oz. ASW **Series:** European Football Championship **Obverse:** Bust of Queen Elizabeth II right **Reverse:** German shield, winner

| Date | Mintage | F | VF | XF | Unc | BU |
|---|---|---|---|---|---|---|
| 1996 Proof | Est. 30,000 | Value: 40.00 | | | | |

**CROWN** KM# 679 **Composition:** Copper-Nickel **Series:** Legend of King Arthur **Obverse:** Bust of Queen Elizabeth II right **Reverse:** King Arthur with Sword and orb

| Date | Mintage | F | VF | XF | Unc | BU |
|---|---|---|---|---|---|---|
| 1996 | Est. 30,000 | — | — | — | 9.00 | — |

**CROWN** **KM# 679a** **Weight:** 28.2800 g. **Composition:** 0.9250 Silver .8411 oz. ASW **Series:** Legend of King Arthur **Obverse:** Bust of Queen Elizabeth II right **Reverse:** King Arthur with sword and orb

| Date | Mintage | F | VF | XF | Unc | BU |
|---|---|---|---|---|---|---|
| 1996 Proof | Est. 30,000 | Value: 22.50 | | | | |

**CROWN** **KM# 680** **Composition:** Copper-Nickel **Series:** Legend of King Arthur **Obverse:** Bust of Queen Elizabeth II right **Reverse:** Queen Guinevere

| Date | Mintage | F | VF | XF | Unc | BU |
|---|---|---|---|---|---|---|
| 1996 | — | — | — | — | 9.00 | — |

**CROWN** **KM# 680a** **Weight:** 28.2800 g. **Composition:** 0.9250 Silver .8411 oz. ASW **Series:** Legend of King Arthur **Obverse:** Bust of Queen Elizabeth II right **Reverse:** Queen Guinevere

| Date | Mintage | F | VF | XF | Unc | BU |
|---|---|---|---|---|---|---|
| 1996 Proof | Est. 30,000 | Value: 22.50 | | | | |

**CROWN** **KM# 681** **Composition:** Copper-Nickel **Series:** Legend of King Arthur **Obverse:** Bust of Queen Elizabeth II right **Reverse:** Sir Lancelot

| Date | Mintage | F | VF | XF | Unc | BU |
|---|---|---|---|---|---|---|
| 1996 | — | — | — | — | 9.00 | — |

**CROWN** **KM# 681a** **Weight:** 28.2800 g. **Composition:** 0.9250 Silver .8411 oz. ASW **Series:** Legend of King Arthur **Obverse:** Bust of Queen Elizabeth II right **Reverse:** Sir Lancelot

| Date | Mintage | F | VF | XF | Unc | BU |
|---|---|---|---|---|---|---|
| 1996 Proof | Est. 30,000 | Value: 22.50 | | | | |

**CROWN** **KM# 682** **Composition:** Copper-Nickel **Series:** Legend of King Arthur **Obverse:** Bust of Queen Elizabeth II right **Reverse:** Merlin

| Date | Mintage | F | VF | XF | Unc | BU |
|---|---|---|---|---|---|---|
| 1996 | — | — | — | — | 9.00 | — |

**CROWN** **KM# 682a** **Weight:** 28.2800 g. **Composition:** 0.9250 Silver .8411 oz. ASW **Series:** Legend of King Arthur **Obverse:** Bust of Queen Elizabeth II right **Reverse:** Merlin

| Date | Mintage | F | VF | XF | Unc | BU |
|---|---|---|---|---|---|---|
| 1996 Proof | Est. 30,000 | Value: 22.50 | | | | |

**CROWN** **KM# 683** **Composition:** Copper-Nickel **Series:** Legend of King Arthur **Obverse:** Bust of Queen Elizabeth II right **Reverse:** Camelot Castle

| Date | Mintage | F | VF | XF | Unc | BU |
|---|---|---|---|---|---|---|
| 1996 | — | — | — | — | 9.00 | — |

**CROWN** **KM# 683a** **Weight:** 28.2800 g. **Composition:** 0.9250 Silver .8411 oz. ASW **Series:** Legend of King Arthur **Obverse:** Bust of Queen Elizabeth II right **Reverse:** Camelot Castle

| Date | Mintage | F | VF | XF | Unc | BU |
|---|---|---|---|---|---|---|
| 1996 Proof | Est. 30,000 | Value: 25.00 | | | | |

**CROWN** **KM# 732** **Composition:** Copper-Nickel **Subject:** Year of the Rat **Obverse:** Bust of Queen Elizabeth II right **Reverse:** Rat

| Date | Mintage | F | VF | XF | Unc | BU |
|---|---|---|---|---|---|---|
| 1996 | — | — | — | — | 7.50 | — |

**CROWN** **KM# 732a** **Weight:** 28.2800 g. **Composition:** 0.9250 Silver .8411 oz. ASW **Subject:** Year of the Rat **Obverse:** Bust of Queen Elizabeth II right **Reverse:** Rat

| Date | Mintage | F | VF | XF | Unc | BU |
|---|---|---|---|---|---|---|
| 1996 Proof | — | — | — | — | — | — |

**Note:** Entire silver issue purchased by one buyer. Mintage, disposition and market value unknown

**CROWN** **KM# 733** **Weight:** 31.1035 g. **Composition:** 0.9999 Gold 1.0000 oz. AGW **Subject:** Year of the Rat **Obverse:** Bust of Queen Elizabeth II right **Reverse:** Rat

| Date | Mintage | F | VF | XF | Unc | BU |
|---|---|---|---|---|---|---|
| 1996 Proof | — | — | — | — | — | — |

**Note:** Entire gold issue purchased by one buyer. Mintage, disposition and market value unknown

**CROWN** **KM# 725** **Composition:** Copper-Nickel **Subject:** Year of the Ox **Obverse:** Bust of Queen Elizabeth II right **Reverse:** Ox laying down

| Date | Mintage | F | VF | XF | Unc | BU |
|---|---|---|---|---|---|---|
| 1997 | — | — | — | — | 8.00 | — |

**CROWN** **KM# 725a** **Weight:** 28.2800 g. **Composition:** 0.9250 Silver .8411 oz. ASW **Subject:** Year of the Ox **Obverse:** Bust of Queen Elizabeth II right **Reverse:** Ox laying down

| Date | Mintage | F | VF | XF | Unc | BU |
|---|---|---|---|---|---|---|
| 1997 Proof | Est. 30,000 | Value: 40.00 | | | | |

**CROWN** **KM# 726** **Weight:** 31.1035 g. **Composition:** 0.9999 Gold 1.0000 oz. AGW **Subject:** Year of the Ox **Obverse:** Bust of Queen Elizabeth II right **Reverse:** Ox laying down

| Date | Mintage | F | VF | XF | Unc | BU |
|---|---|---|---|---|---|---|
| 1997 Proof | Est. 2,000 | Value: 700 | | | | |

**CROWN** **KM# 759** **Composition:** Copper-Nickel **Series:** Flower Fairies **Obverse:** Bust of Queen Elizabeth II right **Reverse:** Candytuft

| Date | Mintage | F | VF | XF | Unc | BU |
|---|---|---|---|---|---|---|
| 1997 | — | — | — | — | 7.50 | — |

**CROWN** **KM# 759a** **Weight:** 28.2800 g. **Composition:** 0.9250 Silver .8411 oz. ASW **Series:** Flower Fairies **Obverse:** Bust of Queen Elizabeth II right **Reverse:** Candytuft

| Date | Mintage | F | VF | XF | Unc | BU |
|---|---|---|---|---|---|---|
| 1997 Proof | Est. 30,000 | Value: 40.00 | | | | |

**CROWN** **KM# 760** **Composition:** Copper-Nickel **Series:** Flower Fairies **Obverse:** Bust of Queen Elizabeth II right **Reverse:** Snowdrop

| Date | Mintage | F | VF | XF | Unc | BU |
|---|---|---|---|---|---|---|
| 1997 | — | — | — | — | 7.50 | — |

**CROWN** **KM# 760a** **Weight:** 28.2800 g. **Composition:** 0.9250 Silver .8411 oz. ASW **Series:** Flower Fairies **Obverse:** Bust of Queen Elizabeth II right **Reverse:** Snowdrop

| Date | Mintage | F | VF | XF | Unc | BU |
|---|---|---|---|---|---|---|
| 1997 Proof | Est. 30,000 | Value: 40.00 | | | | |

**CROWN** **KM# 761** **Composition:** Copper-Nickel **Series:** Flower Fairies **Obverse:** Bust of Queen Elizabeth II right **Reverse:** Tulip

| Date | Mintage | F | VF | XF | Unc | BU |
|---|---|---|---|---|---|---|
| 1997 | — | — | — | — | 7.50 | — |

**CROWN** **KM# 761a** **Weight:** 28.2800 g. **Composition:** 0.9250 Silver .8411 oz. ASW **Series:** Flower Fairies **Obverse:** Bust of Queen Elizabeth II right **Reverse:** Tulip

| Date | Mintage | F | VF | XF | Unc | BU |
|---|---|---|---|---|---|---|
| 1997 Proof | Est. 30,000 | Value: 40.00 | | | | |

**CROWN** **KM# 762** **Composition:** Copper-Nickel **Series:** Flower Fairies **Obverse:** Bust of Queen Elizabeth II right **Reverse:** Jasmine

| Date | Mintage | F | VF | XF | Unc | BU |
|---|---|---|---|---|---|---|
| 1997 | — | — | — | — | 7.50 | — |

**CROWN** **KM# 762a** **Weight:** 28.2800 g. **Composition:** 0.9250 Silver .8411 oz. ASW **Series:** Flower Fairies **Obverse:** Bust of Queen Elizabeth II right **Reverse:** Jasmine

| Date | Mintage | F | VF | XF | Unc | BU |
|---|---|---|---|---|---|---|
| 1997 Proof | Est. 30,000 | Value: 40.00 | | | | |

**CROWN** **KM# 765** **Composition:** Copper-Nickel **Obverse:** Bust of Queen Elizabeth II right **Reverse:** Levi Eiriksson 999-1001, viking ship with map sail

| Date | Mintage | F | VF | XF | Unc | BU |
|---|---|---|---|---|---|---|
| 1997 | — | — | — | — | 7.50 | — |

**CROWN** **KM# 765a** **Weight:** 28.2800 g. **Composition:** 0.9250 Silver .8411 oz. ASW **Obverse:** Bust of Queen Elizabeth II right **Reverse:** Levi Eiriksson 999-1001, viking ship with map sail

| Date | Mintage | F | VF | XF | Unc | BU |
|---|---|---|---|---|---|---|
| 1997 Proof | Est. 30,000 | Value: 40.00 | | | | |

**CROWN** **KM# 768** **Composition:** Copper-Nickel **Obverse:** Bust of Queen Elizabeth II right **Reverse:** Bust of Fridtjof Nansen, map and his ship "The Fram"

| Date | Mintage | F | VF | XF | Unc | BU |
|---|---|---|---|---|---|---|
| 1997 | — | — | — | — | 7.50 | — |

**CROWN** **KM# 768a** **Weight:** 28.2800 g. **Composition:** 0.9250 Silver .8411 oz. ASW **Obverse:** Bust of Queen Elizabeth II right **Reverse:** Bust of Fridtjof Nansen, map and his ship "The Fram"

| Date | Mintage | F | VF | XF | Unc | BU |
|---|---|---|---|---|---|---|
| 1997 Proof | Est. 30,000 | Value: 40.00 | | | | |

**CROWN** **KM# 774** **Composition:** Copper-Nickel **Obverse:** Bust of Queen Elizabeth II right **Reverse:** Long-Haired-Smoke cat

| Date | Mintage | F | VF | XF | Unc | BU |
|---|---|---|---|---|---|---|
| 1997 | — | — | — | — | 8.00 | — |

**CROWN** **KM# 774a** **Weight:** 31.1035 g. **Composition:** 0.9999 Silver 1.0000 oz. ASW **Obverse:** Bust of Queen Elizabeth II right **Reverse:** Long-Haired-Smoke cat

| Date | Mintage | F | VF | XF | Unc | BU |
|---|---|---|---|---|---|---|
| 1997 Proof | Est. 50,000 | Value: 40.00 | | | | |

**CROWN** **KM# 774b** **Weight:** 31.1035 g. **Composition:** 0.9999 Gold 1.0000 oz. AGW **Obverse:** Bust of Queen Elizabeth II right **Reverse:** Long-Haired-Smoke cat

| Date | Mintage | F | VF | XF | Unc | BU |
|---|---|---|---|---|---|---|
| 1997 | — | — | — | — | 400 | — |
| 1997 Proof | — | Value: 410 | | | | |

**CROWN** **KM# 777** **Weight:** 28.2800 g. **Composition:** 0.9250 Silver .8411 oz. ASW **Series:** History of the Cat **Obverse:** Bust of Queen Elizabeth II right **Reverse:** Ancestry of Felidae, evolution of the cat

| Date | Mintage | F | VF | XF | Unc | BU |
|---|---|---|---|---|---|---|
| 1997 Proof | Est. 10,000 | Value: 40.00 | | | | |

**CROWN** **KM# 778** **Weight:** 28.2800 g. **Composition:** 0.9250 Silver .8411 oz. ASW **Series:** History of the Cat **Obverse:** Bust of Queen Elizabeth II right **Reverse:** Felis Silvestris Grampia, snarling cat

| Date | Mintage | F | VF | XF | Unc | BU |
|---|---|---|---|---|---|---|
| 1997 Proof | Est. 10,000 | Value: 40.00 | | | | |

**CROWN** **KM# 779** **Weight:** 28.2800 g. **Composition:** 0.9250 Silver .8411 oz. ASW **Series:** History of the Cat **Obverse:** Bust of Queen Elizabeth II right **Reverse:** Mayalurus Iriomotensis, cat walking left

| Date | Mintage | F | VF | XF | Unc | BU |
|---|---|---|---|---|---|---|
| 1997 Proof | Est. 10,000 | Value: 40.00 | | | | |

**CROWN** **KM# 780** **Weight:** 28.2800 g. **Composition:** 0.9250 Silver .8411 oz. ASW **Series:** History of the Cat **Obverse:** Bust of Queen Elizabeth II right **Reverse:** Ancient Egyptian Goddess Bast and artifacts

| Date | Mintage | F | VF | XF | Unc | BU |
|---|---|---|---|---|---|---|
| 1997 Proof | Est. 10,000 | Value: 40.00 | | | | |

**CROWN** **KM# 782** **Composition:** Copper-Nickel **Subject:** 90th Anniversary of the TT **Obverse:** Bust of Queen Elizabeth II right **Reverse:** 1907 winner Charlie Collier

| Date | Mintage | F | VF | XF | Unc | BU |
|---|---|---|---|---|---|---|
| 1997 | — | — | — | — | 8.50 | — |

**CROWN** **KM# 782a** **Weight:** 28.2800 g. **Composition:** 0.9250 Silver .8411 oz. ASW **Subject:** 90th Anniversary of the TT **Obverse:** Bust of Queen Elizabeth II right **Reverse:** 1907 winnter Charlie Collier

| Date | Mintage | F | VF | XF | Unc | BU |
|---|---|---|---|---|---|---|
| 1997 Proof | Est. 30,000 | Value: 42.50 | | | | |

**CROWN** **KM# 784** **Composition:** Copper-Nickel **Subject:** 90th Anniversary of the TT **Obverse:** Bust of Queen Elizabeth II right **Reverse:** 1937 winner Omobono Tenni

| Date | Mintage | F | VF | XF | Unc | BU |
|---|---|---|---|---|---|---|
| 1997 | — | — | — | — | 8.50 | — |

**CROWN** **KM# 784a** **Weight:** 28.2800 g. **Composition:** 0.9250 Silver .8411 oz. ASW **Subject:** 90th Anniversary of the TT **Obverse:** Bust of Queen Elizabeth II right **Reverse:** 1937 winner Omobono Tenni

| Date | Mintage | F | VF | XF | Unc | BU |
|---|---|---|---|---|---|---|
| 1997 Proof | Est. 30,000 | Value: 42.50 | | | | |

**CROWN** **KM# 786** **Composition:** Copper-Nickel **Subject:** 90th Anniversary of the TT **Obverse:** Bust of Queen Elizabeth II right **Reverse:** 1957 winner Bob McIntyre

| Date | Mintage | F | VF | XF | Unc | BU |
|---|---|---|---|---|---|---|
| 1997 | — | — | — | — | 8.50 | — |

**CROWN** **KM# 786a** **Weight:** 28.2800 g. **Composition:** 0.9250 Silver .8411 oz. ASW **Subject:** 90th Anniversary of the TT **Obverse:** Bust of Queen Elizabeth II right **Reverse:** 1957 winner Bob McIntyre

| Date | Mintage | F | VF | XF | Unc | BU |
|---|---|---|---|---|---|---|
| 1997 Proof | Est. 30,000 | Value: 42.50 | | | | |

**CROWN** **KM# 788** **Composition:** Copper-Nickel **Subject:** 90th Anniversary of the TT **Obverse:** Bust of Queen Elizabeth II right **Reverse:** 1967 winner Mike Hailwood

| Date | Mintage | F | VF | XF | Unc | BU |
|---|---|---|---|---|---|---|
| 1997 | — | — | — | — | 8.50 | — |

**CROWN** KM# 788a **Weight:** 28.2800 g. **Composition:** 0.9250 Silver .8411 oz. ASW **Subject:** 90th Anniversary of the TT **Obverse:** Bust of Queen Elizabeth II right **Reverse:** 1967 winner Mike Hailwood

| Date | Mintage | F | VF | XF | Unc | BU |
|---|---|---|---|---|---|---|
| 1997 Proof | Est. 30,000 | Value: 42.50 | | | | |

**CROWN** KM# 793 **Composition:** Copper-Nickel **Subject:** 50th Wedding Anniversary of Queen Elizabeth II and Prince Philip **Obverse:** Bust of Queen Elizabeth II right **Reverse:** Wedding portrait

| Date | Mintage | F | VF | XF | Unc | BU |
|---|---|---|---|---|---|---|
| 1997 | — | — | — | — | 8.00 | — |

**CROWN** KM# 793a **Weight:** 28.2800 g. **Composition:** 0.9250 Gold Clad Silver .8411 oz. **Subject:** 50th Wedding Anniversary of Queen Elizabeth II and Prince Philip **Obverse:** Bust of Queen Elizabeth II right **Reverse:** Wedding portrait

| Date | Mintage | F | VF | XF | Unc | BU |
|---|---|---|---|---|---|---|
| 1997 Proof | Est. 10,000 | Value: 40.00 | | | | |

**CROWN** KM# 799 **Composition:** Copper-Nickel **Series:** Year 2000 **Subject:** Birth of Christ **Obverse:** Bust of Queen Elizabeth II right **Reverse:** Madonna and child with angels

| Date | Mintage | F | VF | XF | Unc | BU |
|---|---|---|---|---|---|---|
| 1997 | — | — | — | — | 7.50 | — |

**CROWN** KM# 799a **Weight:** 28.2800 g. **Composition:** 0.9250 Silver .8411 oz. ASW **Series:** Year 2000 **Subject:** Birth of Christ **Obverse:** Bust of Queen Elizabeth II right **Reverse:** Madonna and child with angels

| Date | Mintage | F | VF | XF | Unc | BU |
|---|---|---|---|---|---|---|
| 1997 Proof | Est. 10,000 | Value: 50.00 | | | | |

**CROWN** KM# 803 **Composition:** Copper-Nickel **Series:** Year 2000 **Subject:** Flight of Mohammed 622 **Obverse:** Bust of Queen Elizabeth II right **Reverse:** Arabs and camels at oasis

| Date | Mintage | F | VF | XF | Unc | BU |
|---|---|---|---|---|---|---|
| 1997 | — | — | — | — | 7.50 | — |

**CROWN** KM# 801 **Composition:** Copper-Nickel **Series:** Year 2000 **Subject:** Fall of the Roman Empire 476 **Obverse:** Bust of Queen Elizabeth II right **Reverse:** Barbarian defeating soldier

| Date | Mintage | F | VF | XF | Unc | BU |
|---|---|---|---|---|---|---|
| 1997 | — | — | — | — | 7.50 | — |

**CROWN** KM# 801a **Weight:** 28.2800 g. **Composition:** 0.9250 Silver .8411 oz. ASW **Series:** Year 2000 **Subject:** Fall of the Roman Empire 476 **Obverse:** Bust of Queen Elizabeth II right **Reverse:** Barbarian defeating soldier

| Date | Mintage | F | VF | XF | Unc | BU |
|---|---|---|---|---|---|---|
| 1997 Proof | Est. 10,000 | Value: 50.00 | | | | |

**CROWN** KM# 803a **Weight:** 28.2800 g. **Composition:** 0.9250 Silver .8411 oz. ASW **Series:** Year 2000 **Subject:** Flight of Mohammed 622 **Obverse:** Bust of Queen Elizabeth II right **Reverse:** Arabs and camels at oasis

| Date | Mintage | F | VF | XF | Unc | BU |
|---|---|---|---|---|---|---|
| 1997 Proof | Est. 10,000 | Value: 50.00 | | | | |

**CROWN** KM# 805 **Composition:** Copper-Nickel **Series:** Year 2000 **Subject:** Norman Conquest 1066 **Obverse:** Bust of Queen Elizabeth II right **Reverse:** William the Conqueror rallying his troops

| Date | Mintage | F | VF | XF | Unc | BU |
|---|---|---|---|---|---|---|
| 1997 | — | — | — | — | 7.50 | — |

**CROWN** KM# 805a **Weight:** 28.2800 g. **Composition:** 0.9250 Silver .8411 oz. ASW **Series:** Year 2000 **Subject:** Norman Conquest 1066 **Obverse:** Bust of Queen Elizabeth II right **Reverse:** William the Conqueror rallying his troops

| Date | Mintage | F | VF | XF | Unc | BU |
|---|---|---|---|---|---|---|
| 1997 Proof | Est. 10,000 | Value: 50.00 | | | | |

**CROWN** KM# 808 **Composition:** Copper-Nickel **Series:** World Cup Soccer **Obverse:** Bust of Queen Elizabeth II right **Reverse:** Goalie blocking a shot

| Date | Mintage | F | VF | XF | Unc | BU |
|---|---|---|---|---|---|---|
| 1998 | — | — | — | — | 7.50 | — |

**CROWN** KM# 808a **Weight:** 28.2800 g. **Composition:** 0.9250 Silver .8411 oz. ASW **Series:** World Cup Soccer **Obverse:** Bust of Queen Elizabeth II right **Reverse:** Goalie blocking a shot

| Date | Mintage | F | VF | XF | Unc | BU |
|---|---|---|---|---|---|---|
| 1998 Proof | Est. 30,000 | Value: 45.00 | | | | |

**CROWN** KM# 809 **Composition:** Copper-Nickel **Series:** World Cup Soccer **Obverse:** Bust of Queen Elizabeth II right **Reverse:** Two soccer players kicking ball

| Date | Mintage | F | VF | XF | Unc | BU |
|---|---|---|---|---|---|---|
| 1998 | — | — | — | — | 7.50 | — |

**CROWN** KM# 809a **Weight:** 28.2800 g. **Composition:** 0.9250 Silver .8411 oz. ASW **Series:** World Cup Soccer **Obverse:** Bust of Queen Elizabeth II right **Reverse:** Two soccer players kicking ball

| Date | Mintage | F | VF | XF | Unc | BU |
|---|---|---|---|---|---|---|
| 1998 Proof | Est. 30,000 | Value: 45.00 | | | | |

**CROWN** KM# 810 **Composition:** Copper-Nickel **Series:** World Cup Soccer **Obverse:** Bust of Queen Elizabeth II right **Reverse:** Two soccer players heading the ball

| Date | Mintage | F | VF | XF | Unc | BU |
|---|---|---|---|---|---|---|
| 1998 | — | — | — | — | 7.50 | — |

**CROWN** KM# 810a **Weight:** 28.2800 g. **Composition:** 0.9250 Silver .8411 oz. ASW **Series:** World Cup Soccer **Obverse:** Bust of Queen Elizabeth II right **Reverse:** Two soccer players heading the ball

| Date | Mintage | F | VF | XF | Unc | BU |
|---|---|---|---|---|---|---|
| 1998 Proof | Est. 30,000 | Value: 45.00 | | | | |

**CROWN** KM# 811 **Composition:** Copper-Nickel **Series:** World Cup Soccer **Obverse:** Bust of Queen Elizabeth II right **Reverse:** Three soccer players

| Date | Mintage | F | VF | XF | Unc | BU |
|---|---|---|---|---|---|---|
| 1998 | — | — | — | — | 7.50 | — |

**CROWN** KM# 811a **Weight:** 28.2800 g. **Composition:** 0.9250 Silver .8411 oz. ASW **Series:** World Cup Soccer **Obverse:** Bust of Queen Elizabeth II right **Reverse:** Three soccer players

| Date | Mintage | F | VF | XF | Unc | BU |
|---|---|---|---|---|---|---|
| 1998 Proof | Est. 30,000 | Value: 45.00 | | | | |

**CROWN** KM# 816 **Composition:** Copper-Nickel **Subject:** Year of the Tiger **Obverse:** Bust of Queen Elizabeth II right **Reverse:** Tiger

| Date | Mintage | F | VF | XF | Unc | BU |
|---|---|---|---|---|---|---|
| 1998 | — | — | — | — | 8.00 | — |

**CROWN** KM# 816a **Weight:** 28.2800 g. **Composition:** 0.9250 Silver .8411 oz. ASW **Subject:** Year of the Tiger **Obverse:** Bust of Queen Elizabeth II right **Reverse:** Tiger

| Date | Mintage | F | VF | XF | Unc | BU |
|---|---|---|---|---|---|---|
| 1998 Proof | Est. 30,000 | Value: 45.00 | | | | |

**CROWN** KM# 817 **Weight:** 31.1035 g. **Composition:** 0.9999 Gold 1.0000 oz. AGW **Subject:** Year of the Tiger **Obverse:** Bust of Queen Elizabeth II right **Reverse:** Tiger

| Date | Mintage | F | VF | XF | Unc | BU |
|---|---|---|---|---|---|---|
| 1998 Proof | Est. 2,000 | Value: 650 | | | | |

**CROWN** **KM# 825** **Composition:** Copper-Nickel **Obverse:** Bust of Queen Elizabeth II right **Reverse:** Bust of Marco Polo right, caravan and palace

| Date | Mintage | F | VF | XF | Unc | BU |
|---|---|---|---|---|---|---|
| 1998 | — | — | — | — | 7.50 | — |

**CROWN** **KM# 825a** **Weight:** 28.2800 g. **Composition:** 0.9250 Silver .8411 oz. ASW **Obverse:** Bust of Queen Elizabeth II right **Reverse:** Bust of Marco Polo right, caravan and palace

| Date | Mintage | F | VF | XF | Unc | BU |
|---|---|---|---|---|---|---|
| 1998 Proof | Est. 30,000 | Value: 47.50 | | | | |

**CROWN** **KM# 827 (KM826)** **Composition:** Copper-Nickel **Obverse:** Bust of Queen Elizabeth II right **Reverse:** Bust of Vasco da Gama, ship and African map

| Date | Mintage | F | VF | XF | Unc | BU |
|---|---|---|---|---|---|---|
| 1998 | — | — | — | — | 7.50 | — |

**CROWN** **KM# 827a (KM826a)** **Weight:** 28.2800 g. **Composition:** 0.9250 Silver .8411 oz. ASW **Obverse:** Bust of Queen Elizabeth II right **Reverse:** Bust of Vasco da Gama, ship and African map

| Date | Mintage | F | VF | XF | Unc | BU |
|---|---|---|---|---|---|---|
| 1998 Proof | Est. 30,000 | Value: 47.50 | | | | |

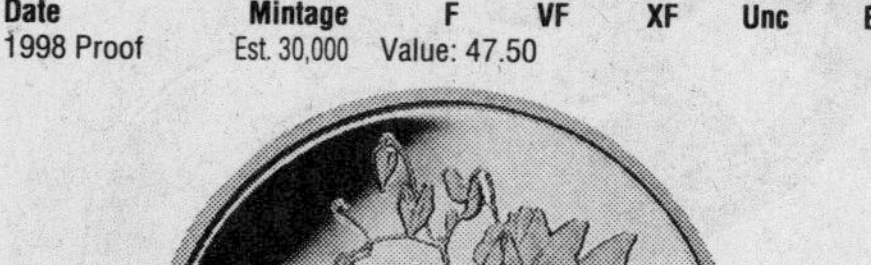

**CROWN** **KM# 840** **Composition:** Copper-Nickel **Series:** Flower Fairies **Obverse:** Bust of Queen Elizabeth II right **Reverse:** Lavender, fairy standing

| Date | Mintage | F | VF | XF | Unc | BU |
|---|---|---|---|---|---|---|
| 1998 | — | — | — | — | 7.50 | — |

**CROWN** **KM# 840a** **Weight:** 28.2800 g. **Composition:** 0.9250 Silver .8411 oz. ASW **Series:** Flower Fairies **Obverse:** Bust of Queen Elizabeth II right **Reverse:** Lavender, fairy standing

| Date | Mintage | F | VF | XF | Unc | BU |
|---|---|---|---|---|---|---|
| 1998 Proof | Est. 30,000 | Value: 47.50 | | | | |

**CROWN** **KM# 841** **Composition:** Copper-Nickel **Series:** Flower Fairies **Obverse:** Bust of Queen Elizabeth II right **Reverse:** Sweet pea, two fairies

| Date | Mintage | F | VF | XF | Unc | BU |
|---|---|---|---|---|---|---|
| 1998 | — | — | — | — | 7.50 | — |

**CROWN** **KM# 841a** **Weight:** 28.2800 g. **Composition:** 0.9250 Silver .8411 oz. ASW **Series:** Flower Fairies **Obverse:** Bust of Queen Elizabeth II right **Reverse:** Sweet pea, two fairies

| Date | Mintage | F | VF | XF | Unc | BU |
|---|---|---|---|---|---|---|
| 1998 Proof | Est. 30,000 | Value: 47.50 | | | | |

**CROWN** **KM# 842** **Composition:** Copper-Nickel **Series:** Flower Fairies **Obverse:** Bust of Queen Elizabeth II right **Reverse:** White bindweed, fairy looking into flower

| Date | Mintage | F | VF | XF | Unc | BU |
|---|---|---|---|---|---|---|
| 1998 | — | — | — | — | 7.50 | — |

**CROWN** **KM# 842a** **Weight:** 28.2800 g. **Composition:** 0.9250 Silver .8411 oz. ASW **Series:** Flower Fairies **Obverse:** Bust of Queen Elizabeth II right **Reverse:** White bindweed, fairy looking into flower

| Date | Mintage | F | VF | XF | Unc | BU |
|---|---|---|---|---|---|---|
| 1998 Proof | Est. 30,000 | Value: 47.50 | | | | |

**CROWN** **KM# 843** **Composition:** Copper-Nickel **Series:** Flower Fairies **Obverse:** Bust of Queen Elizabeth II right **Reverse:** Daffodil, fairy standing with flower

| Date | Mintage | F | VF | XF | Unc | BU |
|---|---|---|---|---|---|---|
| 1998 | — | — | — | — | 7.50 | — |

**CROWN** **KM# 843a** **Weight:** 28.2800 g. **Composition:** 0.9250 Silver .8411 oz. ASW **Series:** Flower Fairies **Obverse:** Bust of Queen Elizabeth II right **Reverse:** Daffodil, fairy standing with flower

| Date | Mintage | F | VF | XF | Unc | BU |
|---|---|---|---|---|---|---|
| 1998 Proof | Est. 20,000 | Value: 47.50 | | | | |

**CROWN** **KM# 849** **Composition:** Copper-Nickel **Series:** Winter Olympics - Nagano **Obverse:** Bust of Queen Elizabeth II right **Reverse:** Bobsled

| Date | Mintage | F | VF | XF | Unc | BU |
|---|---|---|---|---|---|---|
| 1998 | — | — | — | — | 7.50 | — |

**CROWN** **KM# 849a** **Weight:** 28.2800 g. **Composition:** 0.9250 Silver .8411 oz. ASW **Series:** Winter Olympics - Nagano **Obverse:** Bust of Queen Elizabeth II right **Reverse:** Bobsled

| Date | Mintage | F | VF | XF | Unc | BU |
|---|---|---|---|---|---|---|
| 1998 Proof | Est. 30,000 | Value: 47.50 | | | | |

**CROWN** **KM# 850** **Composition:** Copper-Nickel **Series:** Winter Olympics - Nagano **Obverse:** Bust of Queen Elizabeth II right **Reverse:** Cross-country skier

| Date | Mintage | F | VF | XF | Unc | BU |
|---|---|---|---|---|---|---|
| 1998 | — | — | — | — | 7.50 | — |

**CROWN** **KM# 850a** **Weight:** 28.2800 g. **Composition:** 0.9250 Silver .8411 oz. ASW **Series:** Winter Olympics - Nagano **Obverse:** Bust of Queen Elizabeth II right **Reverse:** Cross-country skier

| Date | Mintage | F | VF | XF | Unc | BU |
|---|---|---|---|---|---|---|
| 1998 Proof | Est. 30,000 | Value: 47.50 | | | | |

**CROWN** **KM# 851** **Composition:** Copper-Nickel **Series:** Winter Olympics - Nagano **Obverse:** Bust of Queen Elizabeth II right **Reverse:** Two hockey players

| Date | Mintage | F | VF | XF | Unc | BU |
|---|---|---|---|---|---|---|
| 1998 | — | — | — | — | 7.50 | — |

**CROWN** **KM# 851a** **Weight:** 28.2800 g. **Composition:** 0.9250 Silver .8411 oz. ASW **Series:** Winter Olympics - Nagano **Obverse:** Bust of Queen Elizabeth II right **Reverse:** Two hockey players

| Date | Mintage | F | VF | XF | Unc | BU |
|---|---|---|---|---|---|---|
| 1998 Proof | Est. 30,000 | Value: 47.50 | | | | |

**CROWN** **KM# 852** **Composition:** Copper-Nickel **Series:** Winter Olympics - Nagano **Obverse:** Bust of Queen Elizabeth II right **Reverse:** Two speed skaters

| Date | Mintage | F | VF | XF | Unc | BU |
|---|---|---|---|---|---|---|
| 1998 | — | — | — | — | 7.50 | — |

**CROWN** **KM# 852a** **Weight:** 28.2800 g. **Composition:** 0.9250 Silver .8411 oz. ASW **Series:** Winter Olympics - Nagano **Obverse:** Bust of Queen Elizabeth II right **Reverse:** Two speed skaters

| Date | Mintage | F | VF | XF | Unc | BU |
|---|---|---|---|---|---|---|
| 1998 Proof | Est. 30,000 | Value: 47.50 | | | | |

**CROWN** **KM# 857** **Composition:** Copper-Nickel **Obverse:** Bust of Queen Elizabeth II right **Reverse:** Birman cat

| Date | Mintage | F | VF | XF | Unc | BU |
|---|---|---|---|---|---|---|
| 1998 | — | — | — | — | 8.00 | — |
| 1998 Proof | — | Value: 15.00 | | | | |

**CROWN** **KM# 857a** **Weight:** 31.1035 g. **Composition:** 0.9999 Silver 1.0000 oz. ASW **Obverse:** Bust of Queen Elizabeth II right **Reverse:** Birman cat

| Date | Mintage | F | VF | XF | Unc | BU |
|---|---|---|---|---|---|---|
| 1998 Proof | Est. 50,000 | Value: 47.50 | | | | |

**CROWN** **KM# 857b** **Weight:** 31.1035 g. **Composition:** 0.9999 Gold 1.0000 oz. AGW **Obverse:** Bust of Queen Elizabeth II right **Reverse:** Birman cat

| Date | Mintage | F | VF | XF | Unc | BU |
|---|---|---|---|---|---|---|
| 1998 | — | — | — | — | 400 | — |
| 1998 Proof | 1,000 | Value: 410 | | | | |

**CROWN** **KM# 872** **Composition:** Copper-Nickel **Subject:** 125th Anniversary of the Steam Railway **Obverse:** Bust of Queen Elizabeth II right **Reverse:** The General locomotive

| Date | Mintage | F | VF | XF | Unc | BU |
|---|---|---|---|---|---|---|
| 1998 | — | — | — | — | 10.00 | — |

**CROWN** **KM# 872a** **Weight:** 28.2800 g. **Composition:** 0.9250 Silver .8410 oz. ASW **Subject:** 125th Anniversary of the Steam Railway **Obverse:** Bust of Queen Elizabeth II right **Reverse:** "The General"

| Date | Mintage | F | VF | XF | Unc | BU |
|---|---|---|---|---|---|---|
| 1998 Proof | Est. 30,000 | Value: 47.50 | | | | |

**CROWN** **KM# 874** **Composition:** Copper-Nickel **Subject:** 125th Anniversary of the Steam Railway **Obverse:** Bust of Queen Elizabeth II right **Reverse:** The Rocket locomotive and portrtait

| Date | Mintage | F | VF | XF | Unc | BU |
|---|---|---|---|---|---|---|
| 1998 | — | — | — | — | 10.00 | — |

**CROWN** **KM# 874a** **Weight:** 28.2800 g. **Composition:** 0.9250 Silver .8410 oz. ASW **Subject:** 125th Anniversary of the Steam Railway **Obverse:** Bust of Queen Elizabeth II right **Reverse:** "The Rocket" and portrait

| Date | Mintage | F | VF | XF | Unc | BU |
|---|---|---|---|---|---|---|
| 1998 Proof | Est. 30,000 | Value: 47.50 | | | | |

**CROWN** **KM# 876** **Composition:** Copper-Nickel **Subject:** 125th Anniversary of the Steam Railway **Obverse:** Bust of Queen Elizabeth II right **Reverse:** Orient Express parlor car interior view

| Date | Mintage | F | VF | XF | Unc | BU |
|---|---|---|---|---|---|---|
| 1998 | — | — | — | — | 10.00 | — |

**CROWN** **KM# 876a** **Weight:** 28.2800 g. **Composition:** 0.9250 Silver .8410 oz. ASW **Subject:** 125th Anniversary of the Steam Railway **Obverse:** Bust of Queen Elizabeth II right **Reverse:** Orient Express parlor car interior view

| Date | Mintage | F | VF | XF | Unc | BU |
|---|---|---|---|---|---|---|
| 1998 Proof | Est. 30,000 | Value: 47.50 | | | | |

**CROWN** **KM# 878** **Composition:** Copper-Nickel **Subject:** 125th Anniversary of the Steam Railway **Obverse:** Bust of Queen Elizabeth II right **Reverse:** Mount Pilatus Railway

| Date | Mintage | F | VF | XF | Unc | BU |
|---|---|---|---|---|---|---|
| 1998 | — | — | — | — | 10.00 | — |

**CROWN** **KM# 878a** **Weight:** 28.2800 g. **Composition:** 0.9250 Silver .8410 oz. ASW **Subject:** 125th Anniversary of the Steam Railway **Obverse:** Bust of Queen Elizabeth II right **Reverse:** Mount Pilatus Railway

| Date | Mintage | F | VF | XF | Unc | BU |
|---|---|---|---|---|---|---|
| 1998 Proof | Est. 30,000 | Value: 47.50 | | | | |

**CROWN** **KM# 880** **Composition:** Copper-Nickel **Subject:** 125th Anniversary of the Steam Railway **Obverse:** Bust of Queen Elizabeth II right **Reverse:** No. 1 Sutherland locomotive

| Date | Mintage | F | VF | XF | Unc | BU |
|---|---|---|---|---|---|---|
| 1998 | — | — | — | — | 10.00 | — |

**CROWN** **KM# 880a** **Weight:** 28.2800 g. **Composition:** 0.9250 Silver .8410 oz. ASW **Subject:** 125th Anniversary of the Steam Railway **Obverse:** Bust of Queen Elizabeth II right **Reverse:** No. 1 Sutherland locomotive

| Date | Mintage | F | VF | XF | Unc | BU |
|---|---|---|---|---|---|---|
| 1998 Proof | Est. 30,000 | Value: 47.50 | | | | |

**CROWN** **KM# 882** **Composition:** Copper-Nickel **Subject:** 125th Anniversary of the Steam Railway **Obverse:** Bust of Queen Elizabeth II right **Reverse:** "Flying Scotsman" locomotive

| Date | Mintage | F | VF | XF | Unc | BU |
|---|---|---|---|---|---|---|
| 1998 | — | — | — | — | 10.00 | — |

**CROWN** **KM# 882a** **Weight:** 28.2800 g. **Composition:** 0.9250 Silver .8410 oz. ASW **Subject:** 125th Anniversary of the Steam Railway **Obverse:** Bust of Queen Elizabeth II right **Reverse:** "Flying Scotsman"

| Date | Mintage | F | VF | XF | Unc | BU |
|---|---|---|---|---|---|---|
| 1998 Proof | Est. 30,000 | Value: 47.50 | | | | |

**CROWN** **KM# 884** **Composition:** Copper-Nickel **Subject:** 125th Anniversary of the Steam Railway **Obverse:** Bust of Queen Elizabeth II right **Reverse:** The Mallard locomotive

| Date | Mintage | F | VF | XF | Unc | BU |
|---|---|---|---|---|---|---|
| 1998 | — | — | — | — | 10.00 | — |

**CROWN** **KM# 884a** **Weight:** 28.2800 g. **Composition:** 0.9250 Silver .8410 oz. ASW **Subject:** 125th Anniversary of the Steam Railway **Obverse:** Bust of Queen Elizabeth II right **Reverse:** The Mallard locomotive

| Date | Mintage | F | VF | XF | Unc | BU |
|---|---|---|---|---|---|---|
| 1998 Proof | Est. 30,000 | Value: 47.50 | | | | |

**CROWN** **KM# 886** **Composition:** Copper-Nickel **Subject:** 125th Anniversary of the Steam Railway **Obverse:** Bust of Queen Elizabeth II right **Reverse:** The Big Boy locomotive

| Date | Mintage | F | VF | XF | Unc | BU |
|---|---|---|---|---|---|---|
| 1998 | — | — | — | — | 10.00 | — |

**CROWN** **KM# 886a** **Weight:** 28.2800 g. **Composition:** 0.9250 Silver .8410 oz. ASW **Subject:** 125th Anniversary of the Steam Railway **Obverse:** Bust of Queen Elizabeth II right **Reverse:** The Big Boy locomotive

| Date | Mintage | F | VF | XF | Unc | BU |
|---|---|---|---|---|---|---|
| 1998 Proof | Est. 30,000 | Value: 47.50 | | | | |

**CROWN** **KM# 888** **Composition:** Copper-Nickel **Series:** Year 2000 **Obverse:** Bust of Queen Elizabeth II right **Reverse:** American Independence 1776

| Date | Mintage | F | VF | XF | Unc | BU |
|---|---|---|---|---|---|---|
| 1998 | — | — | — | — | 7.50 | — |

**CROWN** **KM# 888a** **Weight:** 28.2800 g. **Composition:** 0.9250 Silver .8410 oz. ASW **Series:** Year 2000 **Obverse:** Bust of Queen Elizabeth II right **Reverse:** American Independence 1776

| Date | Mintage | F | VF | XF | Unc | BU |
|---|---|---|---|---|---|---|
| 1998 Proof | Est. 30,000 | Value: 28.50 | | | | |

**CROWN** **KM# 890** **Composition:** Copper-Nickel **Series:** Year 2000 **Obverse:** Bust of Queen Elizabeth II right **Reverse:** French Revolution 1789

| Date | Mintage | F | VF | XF | Unc | BU |
|---|---|---|---|---|---|---|
| 1998 | — | — | — | — | 7.50 | — |

**CROWN** **KM# 890a** **Weight:** 28.2800 g. **Composition:** 0.9250 Silver .8410 oz. ASW **Series:** Year 2000 **Obverse:** Bust of Queen Elizabeth II right **Reverse:** French Revolution 1789

| Date | Mintage | F | VF | XF | Unc | BU |
|---|---|---|---|---|---|---|
| 1998 Proof | Est. 30,000 | Value: 28.50 | | | | |

**CROWN** **KM# 892** **Composition:** Copper-Nickel **Series:** Year 2000 **Obverse:** Bust of Queen Elizabeth II right **Reverse:** Reformation of the Church 1517

| Date | Mintage | F | VF | XF | Unc | BU |
|---|---|---|---|---|---|---|
| 1998 | — | — | — | — | 7.50 | — |

**CROWN** **KM# 892a** **Weight:** 28.2800 g. **Composition:** 0.9250 Silver .8410 oz. ASW **Series:** Year 2000 **Obverse:** Bust of Queen Elizabeth II right **Reverse:** Reformation of the church 1517

| Date | Mintage | F | VF | XF | Unc | BU |
|---|---|---|---|---|---|---|
| 1998 Proof | Est. 30,000 | Value: 28.50 | | | | |

**CROWN** **KM# 894** **Composition:** Copper-Nickel **Series:** Year 2000 **Obverse:** Bust of Queen Elizabeth II right **Reverse:** 400th Anniversary of the Renaissance

| Date | Mintage | F | VF | XF | Unc | BU |
|---|---|---|---|---|---|---|
| 1998 | — | — | — | — | 7.50 | — |

**CROWN** **KM# 894a** **Weight:** 28.2800 g. **Composition:** 0.9250 Silver .8410 oz. ASW **Series:** Year 2000 **Obverse:** Bust of Queen Elizabeth II right **Reverse:** 400th Anniversary of the Renaissance

| Date | Mintage | F | VF | XF | Unc | BU |
|---|---|---|---|---|---|---|
| 1998 Proof | Est. 30,000 | Value: 28.50 | | | | |

**CROWN** **KM# 896** **Composition:** Copper-Nickel **Series:** Year of the Ocean **Obverse:** Bust of Queen Elizabeth II right **Reverse:** Basking shark

| Date | Mintage | F | VF | XF | Unc | BU |
|---|---|---|---|---|---|---|
| 1998 | — | — | — | — | 8.50 | — |

**CROWN** **KM# 896a** **Weight:** 28.2800 g. **Composition:** 0.9250 Silver .8410 oz. ASW **Series:** Year of the Ocean **Obverse:** Bust of Queen Elizabeth II right **Reverse:** Basking shark

| Date | Mintage | F | VF | XF | Unc | BU |
|---|---|---|---|---|---|---|
| 1998 Proof | Est. 30,000 | Value: 47.50 | | | | |

**CROWN** **KM# 897** **Composition:** Copper-Nickel **Series:** Year of the Ocean **Obverse:** Bust of Queen Elizabeth II right **Reverse:** Humpback whale

| Date | Mintage | F | VF | XF | Unc | BU |
|---|---|---|---|---|---|---|
| 1998 | — | — | — | — | 8.50 | — |

**CROWN** **KM# 897a** **Weight:** 28.2800 g. **Composition:** 0.9250 Silver .8410 oz. ASW **Series:** Year of the Ocean **Obverse:** Bust of Queen Elizabeth II right **Reverse:** Humpback whale

| Date | Mintage | F | VF | XF | Unc | BU |
|---|---|---|---|---|---|---|
| 1998 Proof | Est. 30,000 | Value: 47.50 | | | | |

**CROWN** **KM# 898** **Composition:** Copper-Nickel **Series:** Year of the Ocean **Obverse:** Bust of Queen Elizabeth II right **Reverse:** Penguins and seals

| Date | Mintage | F | VF | XF | Unc | BU |
|---|---|---|---|---|---|---|
| 1998 | — | — | — | — | 8.50 | — |

**CROWN** **KM# 898a** **Weight:** 28.2800 g. **Composition:** 0.9250 Silver .8410 oz. ASW **Series:** Year of the Ocean **Obverse:** Bust of Queen Elizabeth II right **Reverse:** Penguins and seals

| Date | Mintage | F | VF | XF | Unc | BU |
|---|---|---|---|---|---|---|
| 1998 Proof | Est. 30,000 | Value: 47.50 | | | | |

**CROWN** **KM# 899** **Composition:** Copper-Nickel **Series:** Year of the Ocean **Obverse:** Bust of Queen Elizabeth II right **Reverse:** Sailboats

| Date | Mintage | F | VF | XF | Unc | BU |
|---|---|---|---|---|---|---|
| 1998 | — | — | — | — | 8.50 | — |

**CROWN** **KM# 899a** **Weight:** 28.2800 g. **Composition:** 0.9250 Silver .8410 oz. ASW **Series:** Year of the Ocean **Obverse:** Bust of Queen Elizabeth II right **Reverse:** Sailboats

| Date | Mintage | F | VF | XF | Unc | BU |
|---|---|---|---|---|---|---|
| 1998 Proof | Est. 30,000 | Value: 47.50 | | | | |

**CROWN** **KM# A984** **Composition:** Copper-Nickel **Subject:** Founding of the UN 1945 **Obverse:** Bust of Queen Elizabeth II right **Reverse:** UN Building and logo

| Date | Mintage | F | VF | XF | Unc | BU |
|---|---|---|---|---|---|---|
| 2000 | — | — | — | — | 8.50 | — |

**CROWN** **KM# 914** **Composition:** Copper-Nickel **Subject:** Battle of Waterloo 1815 **Obverse:** Bust of Queen Elizabeth II right **Reverse:** Wellington on horse

| Date | Mintage | F | VF | XF | Unc | BU |
|---|---|---|---|---|---|---|
| 1999 | — | — | — | — | 7.50 | — |

**CROWN** **KM# 914a** **Weight:** 28.2800 g. **Composition:** 0.9250 Silver .8410 oz. ASW **Subject:** Battle of Waterloo 1815 **Obverse:** Bust of Queen Elizabeth II right **Reverse:** Wellington on horse

| Date | Mintage | F | VF | XF | Unc | BU |
|---|---|---|---|---|---|---|
| 1999 Proof | Est. 10,000 | Value: 50.00 | | | | |

**CROWN** **KM# 984a** **Weight:** 28.2800 g. **Composition:** 0.9250 Silver .8410 oz. ASW **Subject:** Founding of the UN 1945 **Obverse:** Bust of Queen Elizabeth II right **Reverse:** UN building and logo

| Date | Mintage | F | VF | XF | Unc | BU |
|---|---|---|---|---|---|---|
| 2000 Proof | — | Value: 50.00 | | | | |

**CROWN** **KM# 916** **Composition:** Copper-Nickel **Subject:** American Civil War 1865 **Obverse:** Bust of Queen Elizabeth II right **Reverse:** Cameos of Grant and Lee, swords, flag and drum

| Date | Mintage | F | VF | XF | Unc | BU |
|---|---|---|---|---|---|---|
| 1999 | — | — | — | — | 7.50 | — |

**CROWN** **KM# 986** **Composition:** Copper-Nickel **Subject:** First Man on the Moon **Obverse:** Bust of Queen Elizabeth II right **Reverse:** Astronauts on moon and flag

| Date | Mintage | F | VF | XF | Unc | BU |
|---|---|---|---|---|---|---|
| 2000 | — | — | — | — | 7.50 | — |

**CROWN** **KM# 916a** **Weight:** 28.2800 g. **Composition:** 0.9250 Silver .8410 oz. ASW **Subject:** American Civil War 1865 **Obverse:** Bust of Queen Elizabeth II right **Reverse:** Cameos of Grant and Lee, swords, flag and drum

| Date | Mintage | F | VF | XF | Unc | BU |
|---|---|---|---|---|---|---|
| 1999 Proof | Est. 10,000 | Value: 50.00 | | | | |

**CROWN** **KM# 986a** **Weight:** 28.2800 g. **Composition:** 0.9250 Silver .8410 oz. ASW **Subject:** First Man on the Moon **Obverse:** Bust of Queen Elizabeth II right **Reverse:** Astronauts on moon and flag

| Date | Mintage | F | VF | XF | Unc | BU |
|---|---|---|---|---|---|---|
| 2000 Proof | Est. 10,000 | Value: 50.00 | | | | |

**CROWN** **KM# 918** **Composition:** Copper-Nickel **Subject:** Russian Revolution 1917 **Obverse:** Bust of Queen Elizabeth II right **Reverse:** Lenin above the Aurora

| Date | Mintage | F | VF | XF | Unc | BU |
|---|---|---|---|---|---|---|
| 1999 | — | — | — | — | 7.50 | — |

**CROWN** **KM# 988** **Composition:** Copper-Nickel **Subject:** Fall of Berlin Wall 1989 **Obverse:** Bust of Queen Elizabeth II right **Reverse:** Crowds around wall

| Date | Mintage | F | VF | XF | Unc | BU |
|---|---|---|---|---|---|---|
| 2000 | — | — | — | — | 7.50 | — |

**CROWN** **KM# 988a** **Weight:** 28.2800 g. **Composition:** 0.9250 Silver .8410 oz. ASW **Subject:** Fall of Berlin Wall 1989 **Obverse:** Bust of Queen Elizabeth II right **Reverse:** Crowds around wall

| Date | Mintage | F | VF | XF | Unc | BU |
|---|---|---|---|---|---|---|
| 2000 Proof | Est. 10,000 | Value: 50.00 | | | | |

**CROWN KM# 918a Weight:** 28.2800 g. **Composition:** 0.9250 Silver .8410 oz. ASW **Subject:** Russian Revolution 1917 **Obverse:** Bust of Queen Elizabeth II right **Reverse:** Lenin above the Aurora

| Date | Mintage | F | VF | XF | Unc | BU |
|---|---|---|---|---|---|---|
| 1999 Proof | Est. 10,000 | Value: 50.00 | | | | |

**CROWN KM# 920 Composition:** Copper-Nickel **Subject:** World War I Armistice Day 1918 **Obverse:** Bust of Queen Elizabeth II right **Reverse:** Biplane above tank

| Date | Mintage | F | VF | XF | Unc | BU |
|---|---|---|---|---|---|---|
| 1999 | — | — | — | — | 7.50 | — |

**CROWN KM# 990 Composition:** Copper-Nickel **Subject:** Millennium 2000 - The Future **Obverse:** Bust of Queen Elizabeth II right **Reverse:** International Space Station

| Date | Mintage | F | VF | XF | Unc | BU |
|---|---|---|---|---|---|---|
| 2000 | — | — | — | — | 7.50 | — |

**CROWN KM# 920a Weight:** 28.2800 g. **Composition:** 0.9250 Silver .8410 oz. ASW **Subject:** World War I Armistice Day 1918 **Obverse:** Bust of Queen Elizabeth II right **Reverse:** Biplane above tank

| Date | Mintage | F | VF | XF | Unc | BU |
|---|---|---|---|---|---|---|
| 1999 Proof | Est. 10,000 | Value: 50.00 | | | | |

**CROWN KM# 990a Weight:** 28.2800 g. **Composition:** 0.9250 Silver .8410 oz. ASW **Subject:** Millennium 2000 - The Future **Obverse:** Bust of Queen Elizabeth II right **Reverse:** International Space Station

| Date | Mintage | F | VF | XF | Unc | BU |
|---|---|---|---|---|---|---|
| 2000 Proof | Est. 10,000 | Value: 50.00 | | | | |

**CROWN KM# 922 Composition:** Copper-Nickel **Series:** Summer Olympics - Sydney **Obverse:** Bust of Queen Elizabeth II right **Reverse:** Three javelin throwers

| Date | Mintage | F | VF | XF | Unc | BU |
|---|---|---|---|---|---|---|
| 1999 | — | — | — | — | 7.50 | — |

**CROWN KM# 922a Weight:** 28.2800 g. **Composition:** 0.9250 Silver .8410 oz. ASW **Series:** Summer Olympics - Sydney **Obverse:** Bust of Queen Elizabeth II right **Reverse:** Three Javelin throwers

| Date | Mintage | F | VF | XF | Unc | BU |
|---|---|---|---|---|---|---|
| 1999 Proof | Est. 10,000 | Value: 50.00 | | | | |

**CROWN KM# 924 Composition:** Copper-Nickel **Series:** Summer Olympics - Sydney **Obverse:** Bust of Queen Elizabeth II right **Reverse:** Diver and map of Australia

| Date | Mintage | F | VF | XF | Unc | BU |
|---|---|---|---|---|---|---|
| 1999 | — | — | — | — | 7.50 | — |

**CROWN KM# 924a Weight:** 28.2800 g. **Composition:** 0.9250 Silver .8410 oz. ASW **Series:** Summer Olympics - Sydney **Obverse:** Bust of Queen Elizabeth II right **Reverse:** Diver and map of Australia

| Date | Mintage | F | VF | XF | Unc | BU |
|---|---|---|---|---|---|---|
| 1999 Proof | Est. 10,000 | Value: 50.00 | | | | |

**CROWN KM# 926 Composition:** Copper-Nickel **Series:** Summer Olympics - Sydney **Obverse:** Bust of Queen Elizabeth II right **Reverse:** Sailboat and Sydney Opera House

| Date | Mintage | F | VF | XF | Unc | BU |
|---|---|---|---|---|---|---|
| 1999 | — | — | — | — | 7.50 | — |

**CROWN KM# 926a Weight:** 28.2800 g. **Composition:** 0.9250 Silver .8410 oz. ASW **Series:** Summer Olympics - Sydney **Obverse:** Bust of Queen Elizabeth II right **Reverse:** Sailboat and Sydney Opera House

| Date | Mintage | F | VF | XF | Unc | BU |
|---|---|---|---|---|---|---|
| 1999 Proof | Est. 10,000 | Value: 50.00 | | | | |

**CROWN KM# 928 Composition:** Copper-Nickel **Series:** Summer Olympics - Sydney **Obverse:** Bust of Queen Elizabeth II right **Reverse:** Two runenrs, one with torch

| Date | Mintage | F | VF | XF | Unc | BU |
|---|---|---|---|---|---|---|
| 1999 | — | — | — | — | 7.50 | — |

**CROWN KM# 928a Weight:** 28.2800 g. **Composition:** 0.9250 Silver .8410 oz. ASW **Series:** Summer Olympics - Sydney **Obverse:** Bust of Queen Elizabeth II right **Reverse:** Two runners, one with torch

| Date | Mintage | F | VF | XF | Unc | BU |
|---|---|---|---|---|---|---|
| 1999 Proof | Est. 10,000 | Value: 50.00 | | | | |

**CROWN KM# 930 Composition:** Copper-Nickel **Series:** Summer Olympics - Sydney **Obverse:** Bust of Queen Elizabeth II right **Reverse:** Hurdlers and Sydney Opera House

| Date | Mintage | F | VF | XF | Unc | BU |
|---|---|---|---|---|---|---|
| 1999 | — | — | — | — | 7.50 | — |

**CROWN KM# 930a Weight:** 28.2800 g. **Composition:** 0.9250 Silver .8410 oz. ASW **Series:** Summer Olympics - Sydney **Obverse:** Bust of Queen Elizabeth II right **Reverse:** Hurdlers and Sydney Opera House

| Date | Mintage | F | VF | XF | Unc | BU |
|---|---|---|---|---|---|---|
| 1999 Proof | Est. 10,000 | Value: 50.00 | | | | |

**CROWN KM# 932 Composition:** Copper-Nickel **Series:** World Cup Rugby 1999 **Obverse:** Bust of Queen Elizabeth II right **Reverse:** Bust of William Web Elliss with players behind

| Date | Mintage | F | VF | XF | Unc | BU |
|---|---|---|---|---|---|---|
| 1999 | — | — | — | — | 8.00 | — |

**CROWN KM# 932a Weight:** 28.2800 g. **Composition:** 0.9250 Silver .8410 oz. ASW **Series:** World Cup Rugby 1999 **Obverse:** Bust of Queen Elizabeth II right **Reverse:** Bust of William Web Ellis and player behind

| Date | Mintage | F | VF | XF | Unc | BU |
|---|---|---|---|---|---|---|
| 1999 Proof | Est. 10,000 | Value: 50.00 | | | | |

**CROWN KM# 934 Composition:** Copper-Nickel **Series:** World Cup Rugby 1999 **Obverse:** Bust of Queen Elizabeth II right **Reverse:** Rugby scrum

| Date | Mintage | F | VF | XF | Unc | BU |
|---|---|---|---|---|---|---|
| 1999 | — | — | — | — | 8.00 | — |

**CROWN KM# 934a Weight:** 28.2800 g. **Composition:** 0.9250 Silver .8410 oz. ASW **Series:** World Cup Rugby 1999 **Obverse:** Bust of Queen Elizabeth II right **Reverse:** Rugby scrum

| Date | Mintage | F | VF | XF | Unc | BU |
|---|---|---|---|---|---|---|
| 1999 Proof | Est. 10,000 | Value: 50.00 | | | | |

**CROWN KM# 936 Composition:** Copper-Nickel **Series:** World Cup Rugby 1999 **Obverse:** Bust of Queen Elizabeth II right **Reverse:** Player catching ball

| Date | Mintage | F | VF | XF | Unc | BU |
|---|---|---|---|---|---|---|
| 1999 | — | — | — | — | 8.00 | — |

**CROWN KM# 936a Weight:** 28.2800 g. **Composition:** 0.9250 Silver .8410 oz. ASW **Series:** World Cup Rugby 1999 **Obverse:** Bust of Queen Elizabeth II right **Reverse:** Player catching ball

| Date | Mintage | F | VF | XF | Unc | BU |
|---|---|---|---|---|---|---|
| 1999 Proof | Est. 10,000 | Value: 50.00 | | | | |

**CROWN** **KM# 938** **Composition:** Copper-Nickel **Series:** World Cup Rugby 1999 **Obverse:** Bust of Queen Elizabeth II right **Reverse:** Goal kick

| Date | Mintage | F | VF | XF | Unc | BU |
|---|---|---|---|---|---|---|
| 1999 | — | — | — | — | 8.00 | — |

**CROWN** **KM# 938a** **Weight:** 28.2800 g. **Composition:** 0.9250 Silver .8410 oz. ASW **Series:** World Cup Rugby 1999 **Obverse:** Bust of Queen Elizabeth II right **Reverse:** Goal kick

| Date | Mintage | F | VF | XF | Unc | BU |
|---|---|---|---|---|---|---|
| 1999 Proof | Est. 10,000 | Value: 50.00 | | | | |

**CROWN** **KM# 940** **Composition:** Copper-Nickel **Series:** World Cup Rugby 1999 **Obverse:** Bust of Queen Elizabeth II right **Reverse:** Ball runner being tackled

| Date | Mintage | F | VF | XF | Unc | BU |
|---|---|---|---|---|---|---|
| 1999 | — | — | — | — | 8.00 | — |

**CROWN** **KM# 940a** **Weight:** 28.2800 g. **Composition:** 0.9250 Silver .8410 oz. ASW **Series:** World Cup Rugby 1999 **Obverse:** Bust of Queen Elizabeth II right **Reverse:** Ball runner being tackled

| Date | Mintage | F | VF | XF | Unc | BU |
|---|---|---|---|---|---|---|
| 1999 Proof | Est. 10,000 | Value: 50.00 | | | | |

**CROWN** **KM# 942** **Composition:** Copper-Nickel **Series:** World Cup Rugby 1999 **Obverse:** Bust of Queen Elizabeth II right **Reverse:** Player jumping for catch

| Date | Mintage | F | VF | XF | Unc | BU |
|---|---|---|---|---|---|---|
| 1999 | — | — | — | — | 8.00 | — |

**CROWN** **KM# 942a** **Weight:** 28.2800 g. **Composition:** 0.9250 Silver .8410 oz. ASW **Series:** World Cup Rugby 1999 **Obverse:** Bust of Queen Elizabeth II right **Reverse:** Player jumping for catch

| Date | Mintage | F | VF | XF | Unc | BU |
|---|---|---|---|---|---|---|
| 1999 Proof | Est. 10,000 | Value: 50.00 | | | | |

**CROWN** **KM# 952** **Composition:** Copper-Nickel **Subject:** Year of the Rabbit **Obverse:** Bust of Queen Elizabeth II right **Reverse:** Two rabbits, Chinese characters

| Date | Mintage | F | VF | XF | Unc | BU |
|---|---|---|---|---|---|---|
| 1999 | — | — | — | — | 8.00 | — |

**CROWN** **KM# 952a** **Weight:** 28.2800 g. **Composition:** 0.9250 Silver .8410 oz. ASW **Subject:** Year of the Rabbit **Obverse:** Bust of Queen Elizabeth II right **Reverse:** Two rabbits, Chinese characters

| Date | Mintage | F | VF | XF | Unc | BU |
|---|---|---|---|---|---|---|
| 1999 Proof | Est. 10,000 | Value: 50.00 | | | | |

**CROWN** **KM# 952b** **Weight:** 31.1035 g. **Composition:** 0.9999 Gold .9999 oz. AGW **Subject:** Year of the Rabbit **Obverse:** Bust of Queen Elizabeth II right **Reverse:** Two rabbits, Chinese characters

| Date | Mintage | F | VF | XF | Unc | BU |
|---|---|---|---|---|---|---|
| 1999 Proof | Est. 2,000 | Value: 650 | | | | |

**CROWN** **KM# 955** **Composition:** Copper-Nickel **Obverse:** Bust of Queen Elizabeth II right **Reverse:** Bust of Sir Walter Raleigh, map of America and ship

| Date | Mintage | F | VF | XF | Unc | BU |
|---|---|---|---|---|---|---|
| 1999 | — | — | — | — | 8.50 | — |

**CROWN** **KM# 955a** **Weight:** 28.2800 g. **Composition:** 0.9250 Silver .8410 oz. ASW **Obverse:** Bust of Queen Elizabeth II right **Reverse:** Bust of Sir Walter Raleigh, map of America and ship

| Date | Mintage | F | VF | XF | Unc | BU |
|---|---|---|---|---|---|---|
| 1999 Proof | Est. 10,000 | Value: 50.00 | | | | |

**CROWN** **KM# 957** **Composition:** Copper-Nickel **Obverse:** Bust of Queen Elizabeth II right **Reverse:** Compass, bust of Robert Falcon Scott and men pulling sled

| Date | Mintage | F | VF | XF | Unc | BU |
|---|---|---|---|---|---|---|
| 1999 | — | — | — | — | 8.50 | — |

**CROWN** **KM# 957a** **Weight:** 28.2800 g. **Composition:** 0.9250 Silver .8410 oz. ASW **Obverse:** Bust of Queen Elizabeth II right **Reverse:** Compass, bust of Robert Falcon Scott and men pulling sled

| Date | Mintage | F | VF | XF | Unc | BU |
|---|---|---|---|---|---|---|
| 1999 Proof | Est. 10,000 | Value: 50.00 | | | | |

**CROWN** **KM# 966** **Composition:** Copper-Nickel **Obverse:** Bust of Queen Elizabeth II right **Reverse:** British blue cat cleaning its paws

| Date | Mintage | F | VF | XF | Unc | BU |
|---|---|---|---|---|---|---|
| 1999 | — | — | — | — | 8.50 | — |

**CROWN** **KM# 967** **Weight:** 31.1035 g. **Composition:** 0.9990 Silver 1.0000 oz. ASW **Obverse:** Bust of Queen Elizabeth II right **Reverse:** British blue cat cleaning its paws

| Date | Mintage | F | VF | XF | Unc | BU |
|---|---|---|---|---|---|---|
| 1999 Proof | Est. 50,000 | Value: 50.00 | | | | |

**CROWN** **KM# 968** **Weight:** 31.1035 g. **Composition:** 0.9990 Gold 1.0000 oz. AGW **Obverse:** Bust of Queen Elizabeth II right **Reverse:** British blue cat cleaning its paws

| Date | Mintage | F | VF | XF | Unc | BU |
|---|---|---|---|---|---|---|
| 1999 | — | — | — | — | 400 | — |
| 1999 Proof | — | Value: 410 | | | | |

**CROWN** **KM# 976** **Composition:** Copper-Nickel **Series:** The Life and Times of the Queen Mother **Obverse:** Bust of Queen Elizabeth II right **Reverse:** Child in chair

| Date | Mintage | F | VF | XF | Unc | BU |
|---|---|---|---|---|---|---|
| 1999 | — | — | — | — | 7.50 | — |

**CROWN** **KM# 976a** **Weight:** 28.2800 g. **Composition:** 0.9250 Silver .8410 oz. ASW **Series:** The Life and Times of the Queen Mother **Obverse:** Bust of Queen Elizabeth II right **Reverse:** Child in chair

| Date | Mintage | F | VF | XF | Unc | BU |
|---|---|---|---|---|---|---|
| 1999 Proof | Est. 10,000 | Value: 50.00 | | | | |

**CROWN** **KM# 978** **Composition:** Copper-Nickel **Series:** The Life and Times of the Queen Mother **Obverse:** Bust of Queen Elizabeth II right **Reverse:** Royal engagement portrait

| Date | Mintage | F | VF | XF | Unc | BU |
|---|---|---|---|---|---|---|
| 1999 | — | — | — | — | 7.50 | — |

**CROWN** **KM# 978a** **Weight:** 28.2800 g. **Composition:** 0.9250 Silver .8410 oz. ASW **Series:** The Life and Times of the Queen Mother **Obverse:** Bust of Queen Elizabeth II right **Reverse:** Royal engagement portrait

| Date | Mintage | F | VF | XF | Unc | BU |
|---|---|---|---|---|---|---|
| 1999 Proof | Est. 10,000 | Value: 50.00 | | | | |

**CROWN** **KM# 980** **Composition:** Copper-Nickel **Series:** The Life and Times of the Queen Mother **Obverse:** Bust of Queen Elizabeth II right **Reverse:** Wedding portrait

| Date | Mintage | F | VF | XF | Unc | BU |
|---|---|---|---|---|---|---|
| 1999 | — | — | — | — | 7.50 | — |

**CROWN** **KM# 980a** **Weight:** 28.2800 g. **Composition:** 0.9250 Silver .8410 oz. ASW **Series:** The Life and Times of the

Queen Mother **Obverse:** Bust of Queen Elizabeth II right **Reverse:** Wedding portrait

| Date | Mintage | F | VF | XF | Unc | BU |
|---|---|---|---|---|---|---|
| 1999 Proof | Est. 10,000 | Value: 50.00 | | | | |

**CROWN** **KM# 982** **Composition:** Copper-Nickel **Subject:** The Life and Times of the Queen Mother **Obverse:** Queen's portrait **Reverse:** Honeymoon departure

| Date | Mintage | F | VF | XF | Unc | BU |
|---|---|---|---|---|---|---|
| 1999 | — | — | — | — | 7.50 | — |

**CROWN** **KM# 982a** **Weight:** 28.2800 g. **Composition:** 0.9250 Silver .8410 oz. ASW **Series:** The Life and Times of the Queen Mother **Obverse:** Bust of Queen Elizabeth II right **Reverse:** Honeymoon departure

| Date | Mintage | F | VF | XF | Unc | BU |
|---|---|---|---|---|---|---|
| 1999 Proof | Est. 10,000 | Value: 50.00 | | | | |

**CROWN** **KM# 996** **Composition:** Copper-Nickel **Subject:** The Wedding of HRH The Prince Edward **Obverse:** Bust of Queen Elizabeth II right **Reverse:** Head of Prince Edward right

| Date | Mintage | F | VF | XF | Unc | BU |
|---|---|---|---|---|---|---|
| 1999 | — | — | — | — | 8.00 | — |

**CROWN** **KM# 996a** **Weight:** 28.2800 g. **Composition:** 0.9250 Silver .8410 oz. ASW **Subject:** The Wedding of HRH The Prince Edward **Obverse:** Bust of Queen Elizabeth II right **Reverse:** Head of Prince Edward right

| Date | Mintage | F | VF | XF | Unc | BU |
|---|---|---|---|---|---|---|
| 1999 Proof | Est. 10,000 | Value: 50.00 | | | | |

**CROWN** **KM# 998** **Composition:** Copper-Nickel **Subject:** The Wedding of HRH The Prince Edward **Obverse:** Bust of Queen Elizabeth II right **Reverse:** Head of Sophie Rhys-Jones left

| Date | Mintage | F | VF | XF | Unc | BU |
|---|---|---|---|---|---|---|
| 1999 | — | — | — | — | 8.00 | — |

**CROWN** **KM# 998a** **Weight:** 28.2800 g. **Composition:** 0.9250 Silver .8410 oz. ASW **Subject:** The Wedding of HRH The Prince Edward **Obverse:** Bust of Queen Elizabeth II right **Reverse:** Head of Sophie Rhys-Jones left

| Date | Mintage | F | VF | XF | Unc | BU |
|---|---|---|---|---|---|---|
| 1999 Proof | Est. 10,000 | Value: 50.00 | | | | |

**CROWN** **KM# 1000** **Composition:** Copper-Nickel **Subject:** 30th Anniversary of First Man on the Moon **Obverse:** Bust of Queen Elizabeth II right **Reverse:** Apollo XI, 1969 and moon walkers

| Date | Mintage | F | VF | XF | Unc | BU |
|---|---|---|---|---|---|---|
| 1999 | — | — | — | — | 7.50 | — |

**CROWN** **KM# 1000a** **Weight:** 28.2800 g. **Composition:** 0.9250 Silver .8410 oz. ASW **Subject:** 30th Anniversary of First Man on the Moon **Obverse:** Bust of Queen Elizabeth II right **Reverse:** Apollo XI, 1969 and two moon walkers

| Date | Mintage | F | VF | XF | Unc | BU |
|---|---|---|---|---|---|---|
| 1999 Proof | Est. 10,000 | Value: 50.00 | | | | |

**CROWN** **KM# 1002** **Composition:** Copper-Nickel **Subject:** 30th Anniversary of First Man on the Moon **Obverse:** Bust of Queen Elizabeth II right **Reverse:** Mariner IX, 1971 and orbiting Mars

| Date | Mintage | F | VF | XF | Unc | BU |
|---|---|---|---|---|---|---|
| 1999 | — | — | — | — | 7.50 | — |

**CROWN** **KM# 1002a** **Weight:** 28.2800 g. **Composition:** 0.9250 Silver .8410 oz. ASW **Subject:** 30th Anniversary of First Man on the Moon **Obverse:** Bust of Queen Elizabeth II right **Reverse:** Mariner IX, 1971 and orbiting Mars

| Date | Mintage | F | VF | XF | Unc | BU |
|---|---|---|---|---|---|---|
| 1999 | Est. 10,000 | Value: 50.00 | | | | |

**CROWN** **KM# 1004** **Composition:** Copper-Nickel **Subject:** 30th Anniversary of First Man on the Moon **Obverse:** Bust of Queen Elizabeth II right **Reverse:** Apollo-Soyuz link-up, 1975

| Date | Mintage | F | VF | XF | Unc | BU |
|---|---|---|---|---|---|---|
| 1999 | — | — | — | — | 7.50 | — |

**CROWN** **KM# 1004a** **Weight:** 28.2800 g. **Composition:** 0.9250 Silver .8410 oz. ASW **Subject:** 30th Anniversary of First Man on the Moon **Obverse:** Bust of Queen Elizabeth II right **Reverse:** Apollo-Soyuz link-up, 1975

| Date | Mintage | F | VF | XF | Unc | BU |
|---|---|---|---|---|---|---|
| 1999 Proof | Est. 10,000 | Value: 50.00 | | | | |

**CROWN** **KM# 1006** **Composition:** Copper-Nickel **Subject:** 30th Anniversary of First Man on the Moon **Obverse:** Bust of Queen Elizabeth II right **Reverse:** Viking Mars Lander, 1978

| Date | Mintage | F | VF | XF | Unc | BU |
|---|---|---|---|---|---|---|
| 1999 | — | — | — | — | 7.50 | — |

**CROWN** **KM# 1006a** **Weight:** 28.2800 g. **Composition:** 0.9250 Silver .8410 oz. ASW **Subject:** 30th Anniversary of First Man on the Moon **Obverse:** Bust of Queen Elizabeth II right **Reverse:** Viking Mars lander, 1978

| Date | Mintage | F | VF | XF | Unc | BU |
|---|---|---|---|---|---|---|
| 1999 Proof | Est. 10,000 | Value: 50.00 | | | | |

**CROWN** **KM# 1008** **Composition:** Copper-Nickel **Subject:** 30th Anniversary of First Man on the Moon **Obverse:** Bust of Queen Elizabeth II right **Reverse:** Shuttle oribiter Columbia, 1981

| Date | Mintage | F | VF | XF | Unc | BU |
|---|---|---|---|---|---|---|
| 1999 | — | — | — | — | 7.50 | — |

**CROWN** **KM# 1008a** **Weight:** 28.2800 g. **Composition:** 0.9250 Silver .8410 oz. ASW **Subject:** 30th Anniversary of First Man on the Moon **Obverse:** Bust of Queen Elizabeth II right **Reverse:** Shuttle oribiter Columbia, 1981

| Date | Mintage | F | VF | XF | Unc | BU |
|---|---|---|---|---|---|---|
| 1999 Proof | Est. 10,000 | Value: 50.00 | | | | |

**CROWN** **KM# 1010** **Composition:** Copper-Nickel **Subject:** 30th Anniversary of First Man on the Moon **Obverse:** Bust of Queen Elizabeth II right **Reverse:** Mars Pathfinder, 1997

| Date | Mintage | F | VF | XF | Unc | BU |
|---|---|---|---|---|---|---|
| 1999 | — | — | — | — | 7.50 | — |

**CROWN** **KM# 1010a** **Weight:** 28.2800 g. **Composition:** 0.9250 Silver .8410 oz. ASW **Subject:** 30th Anniversary of First Man on the Moon **Obverse:** Bust of Queen Elizabeth II right **Reverse:** Mars Pathfinder, 1997

| Date | Mintage | F | VF | XF | Unc | BU |
|---|---|---|---|---|---|---|
| 1999 Proof | Est. 10,000 | Value: 50.00 | | | | |

**CROWN** **KM# 1057** **Weight:** 31.1035 g. **Composition:** 0.9999 Gold 1.0000 oz. AGW **Subject:** Scottish Fold Kitten **Obverse:** Bust of Queen Elizabeth II right **Reverse:** Kitten playing with world **Edge:** Reeded **Size:** 32.7 mm.

| Date | Mintage | F | VF | XF | Unc | BU |
|---|---|---|---|---|---|---|
| 2000 | — | — | — | — | 470 | — |
| 2000 Proof | — | Value: 650 | | | | |

**CROWN** **KM# 1047** **Weight:** 28.2800 g. **Composition:** Copper-Nickel **Obverse:** Queen's portrait **Reverse:** Prince William's portrait **Edge:** Reeded

| Date | Mintage | F | VF | XF | Unc | BU |
|---|---|---|---|---|---|---|
| 2000 | — | — | — | — | 10.00 | — |

**CROWN** **KM# 1047a** **Weight:** 28.2800 g. **Composition:** 0.9250 Silver .8410 oz. ASW

| Date | Mintage | F | VF | XF | Unc | BU |
|---|---|---|---|---|---|---|
| 2000 Proof | 10,000 | Value: 47.50 | | | | |

**CROWN** **KM# 1049** **Composition:** Copper-Nickel **Obverse:** Queen's portrait **Reverse:** Queen Mother's portrait

| Date | Mintage | F | VF | XF | Unc | BU |
|---|---|---|---|---|---|---|
| 2000 | — | — | — | — | 10.00 | — |

**CROWN** **KM# 1049a** **Weight:** 28.2800 g. **Composition:** 0.9250 Silver .8410 oz. ASW

| Date | Mintage | F | VF | XF | Unc | BU |
|---|---|---|---|---|---|---|
| 2000 Proof | 10,000 | Value: 47.50 | | | | |

**CROWN** **KM# 1019** **Weight:** 28.2800 g. **Composition:** Copper-Nickel **Subject:** Millenium **Obverse:** Queen's portrait **Reverse:** MM Monogram **Edge:** Reeded **Size:** 38.6 mm.

| Date | Mintage | F | VF | XF | Unc | BU |
|---|---|---|---|---|---|---|
| 2000 | — | — | — | — | 10.00 | — |

**CROWN** **KM# 1019a** **Weight:** 28.2800 g. **Composition:** 0.9250 Silver .8410 oz. ASW **Subject:** Millenium

| Date | Mintage | F | VF | XF | Unc | BU |
|---|---|---|---|---|---|---|
| 2000 Proof | 10,000 | Value: 47.50 | | | | |

**CROWN** **KM# 1055a** **Weight:** 6.2200 g. **Composition:** 0.9995 Platinum .2000 oz. APW

| Date | Mintage | F | VF | XF | Unc | BU |
|---|---|---|---|---|---|---|
| 2000 | — | — | — | — | 383 | — |

**CROWN** **KM# 1051** **Weight:** 28.2800 g. **Composition:** 0.9250 Silver .8410 oz. ASW **Subject:** Millennium-Meridian **Obverse:** Queen's portrait **Reverse:** Old Royal Observatory clock face with an embedded brass strip from the original Prime meridan **Edge:** Reeded **Size:** 38.6 mm.

| Date | Mintage | F | VF | XF | Unc | BU |
|---|---|---|---|---|---|---|
| 2000 Proof | 10,000 | Value: 47.50 | | | | |

**CROWN KM# 1056 Composition:** Copper-Nickel **Subject:** Scottish Fold Kitten **Obverse:** Queen's portrait **Reverse:** Kitten playing with world **Edge:** Reeded **Size:** 38.6 mm.

| Date | Mintage | F | VF | XF | Unc | BU |
|---|---|---|---|---|---|---|
| 2000 | — | — | — | — | 10.00 | — |

**CROWN KM# 1056a Weight:** 31.1035 g. **Composition:** 0.9999 Silver 1.000 oz. ASW

| Date | Mintage | F | VF | XF | Unc | BU |
|---|---|---|---|---|---|---|
| 2000 Proof | 50,000 | Value: 47.50 | | | | |

**CROWN KM# 1016 Composition:** Copper-Nickel **Subject:** Year of the Dragon **Obverse:** Bust of Queen Elizabeth II right **Reverse:** Dragon

| Date | Mintage | F | VF | XF | Unc | BU |
|---|---|---|---|---|---|---|
| 2000 | — | — | — | — | 8.50 | — |

**CROWN KM# 1016a Weight:** 28.2800 g. **Composition:** 0.9250 Silver .8410 oz. ASW **Subject:** Year of the Dragon **Obverse:** Bust of Queen Elizabeth II right **Reverse:** Dragon

| Date | Mintage | F | VF | XF | Unc | BU |
|---|---|---|---|---|---|---|
| 2000 Proof | Est. 30,000 | Value: 50.00 | | | | |

**CROWN KM# 1017 Weight:** 31.1035 g. **Composition:** 0.9999 Gold 1.0000 oz. AGW **Subject:** Year of the Dragon **Obverse:** Bust of Queen Elizabeth II right **Reverse:** Dragon

| Date | Mintage | F | VF | XF | Unc | BU |
|---|---|---|---|---|---|---|
| 2000 Proof | Est. 2,000 | Value: 650 | | | | |

**CROWN KM# 1062 Weight:** 28.2800 g. **Composition:** Copper-Nickel **Subject:** Year of the Snake **Obverse:** Queen's portrait **Reverse:** Snake **Edge:** Reeded **Size:** 38.6 mm.

| Date | Mintage | F | VF | XF | Unc | BU |
|---|---|---|---|---|---|---|
| 2001 | — | — | — | — | 10.00 | — |

**CROWN KM# 1062a Weight:** 28.2800 g. **Composition:** 0.9250 Silver .8410 oz. ASW

| Date | Mintage | F | VF | XF | Unc | BU |
|---|---|---|---|---|---|---|
| 2001 Proof | 30,000 | Value: 47.50 | | | | |

**CROWN KM# 1063 Weight:** 31.1035 g. **Composition:** 0.9999 Gold 1.0000 oz. AGW **Subject:** Year of the Snake **Obverse:** Queen's portrait **Reverse:** Snake **Edge:** Reeded **Size:** 32.7 mm.

| Date | Mintage | F | VF | XF | Unc | BU |
|---|---|---|---|---|---|---|
| 2001 Proof | 2,000 | Value: 650 | | | | |

**CROWN KM# 1072 Weight:** 28.2800 g. **Composition:** Copper-Nickel **Subject:** Somali Kittens **Obverse:** Queen's portrait **Reverse:** Two kittens **Edge:** Reeded **Size:** 38.6 mm.

| Date | Mintage | F | VF | XF | Unc | BU |
|---|---|---|---|---|---|---|
| 2001 | — | — | — | — | 10.00 | — |

**CROWN KM# 1072a Weight:** 31.1035 g. **Composition:** 0.9990 Silver 1.0000 oz. ASW **Edge:** Reeded **Size:** 38.6 mm.

| Date | Mintage | F | VF | XF | Unc | BU |
|---|---|---|---|---|---|---|
| 2001 Proof | 50,000 | Value: 47.50 | | | | |

**CROWN KM# 1073 Weight:** 31.1035 g. **Composition:** 0.9999 Gold 1.0000 oz. AGW **Subject:** Somali Kittens **Obverse:** Queen's portrait **Reverse:** Two kittens **Edge:** Reeded **Size:** 32.7 mm.

| Date | Mintage | F | VF | XF | Unc | BU |
|---|---|---|---|---|---|---|
| 2001 | — | — | — | — | 470 | — |
| 2001 Proof | 1,000 | Value: 650 | | | | |

**CROWN KM# 1076 Weight:** 28.2800 g. **Composition:** Copper-Nickel **Subject:** Queen Mother **Obverse:** Queen's portrait **Reverse:** 1948 Silver wedding anniversary **Edge:** Reeded **Size:** 38.6 mm.

| Date | Mintage | F | VF | XF | Unc | BU |
|---|---|---|---|---|---|---|
| 2001 | — | — | — | — | 10.00 | — |

**CROWN KM# 1076a Weight:** 28.2800 g. **Composition:** 0.9250 Silver .8410 oz. ASW **Edge:** Reeded **Size:** 38.6 mm.

| Date | Mintage | F | VF | XF | Unc | BU |
|---|---|---|---|---|---|---|
| 2001 Proof | 10,000 | Value: 47.50 | | | | |

**CROWN KM# 1077 Composition:** Copper-Nickel **Subject:** Queen Mother **Obverse:** Queen's portrait **Reverse:** 1948 holding baby Prince Charles **Edge:** Reeded **Size:** 38.6 mm.

| Date | Mintage | F | VF | XF | Unc | BU |
|---|---|---|---|---|---|---|
| 2001 | — | — | — | — | 10.00 | — |

**CROWN KM# 1077a Weight:** 28.2800 g. **Composition:** 0.9250 Silver .8410 oz. ASW **Edge:** Reeded **Size:** 38.6 mm.

| Date | Mintage | F | VF | XF | Unc | BU |
|---|---|---|---|---|---|---|
| 2001 Proof | 10,000 | Value: 47.50 | | | | |

**CROWN KM# 1080 Composition:** Copper-Nickel **Subject:** Martin Frobisher **Obverse:** Queen's portrait **Reverse:** Portrait, ship and map **Edge:** Reeded **Size:** 38.6 mm.

| Date | Mintage | F | VF | XF | Unc | BU |
|---|---|---|---|---|---|---|
| 2001 | — | — | — | — | 10.00 | — |

**CROWN KM# 1080a Weight:** 28.2800 g. **Composition:** 0.9250 Silver .8410 oz. ASW **Edge:** Reeded **Size:** 38.6 mm.

| Date | Mintage | F | VF | XF | Unc | BU |
|---|---|---|---|---|---|---|
| 2001 Proof | 10,000 | Value: 47.50 | | | | |

**CROWN KM# 1081 Composition:** Copper-Nickel **Subject:** Roald Amundsen **Obverse:** Queen's portrait **Reverse:** Portrait, ship and dirigible **Edge:** Reeded **Size:** 38.6 mm.

| Date | Mintage | F | VF | XF | Unc | BU |
|---|---|---|---|---|---|---|
| 2001 | — | — | — | — | 10.00 | — |

**CROWN KM# 1081a Weight:** 28.2800 g. **Composition:** 0.9250 Silver .8410 oz. ASW **Edge:** Reeded **Size:** 38.6 mm.

| Date | Mintage | F | VF | XF | Unc | BU |
|---|---|---|---|---|---|---|
| 2001 Proof | 10,000 | Value: 47.50 | | | | |

**CROWN KM# 1085 Weight:** 28.2800 g. **Composition:** Copper-Nickel **Subject:** Joey Dunlop (1952-2000) **Obverse:** Queen Elizabeth's portrait **Reverse:** Motorcycle racer **Edge:** Reeded **Size:** 38.6 mm.

| Date | Mintage | F | VF | XF | Unc | BU |
|---|---|---|---|---|---|---|
| 2001 Black finish | — | — | — | — | 10.00 | — |

**CROWN KM# 1085a Weight:** 28.2800 g. **Composition:** 0.9250 Silver .8410 oz. ASW **Edge:** Reeded **Size:** 38.6 mm.

| Date | Mintage | F | VF | XF | Unc | BU |
|---|---|---|---|---|---|---|
| 2001 Proof | 10,000 | Value: 47.50 | | | | |

**CROWN KM# 1083 Weight:** 28.2800 g. **Composition:** Copper-Nickel **Subject:** Queen's 75th Birthday **Obverse:** Queen's portrait **Reverse:** Flower bouquet **Edge:** Reeded **Size:** 38.6 mm.

| Date | Mintage | F | VF | XF | Unc | BU |
|---|---|---|---|---|---|---|
| 2001 | — | — | — | — | 14.00 | — |

**CROWN KM# 1083a Weight:** 28.2800 g. **Composition:** 0.9250 Silver .8410 oz. ASW **Edge:** Reeded **Size:** 38.6 mm.

| Date | Mintage | F | VF | XF | Unc | BU |
|---|---|---|---|---|---|---|
| 2001 Proof | 10,000 | Value: 49.00 | | | | |

**CROWN KM# 1087 Weight:** 28.2800 g. **Composition:** Copper-Nickel **Subject:** Harry Potter **Obverse:** Queen's portrait **Reverse:** Boy with magic wand **Edge:** Reeded **Size:** 38.6 mm.

| Date | Mintage | F | VF | XF | Unc | BU |
|---|---|---|---|---|---|---|
| 2001 | — | — | — | — | 10.00 | — |

**CROWN KM# 1087a Weight:** 28.2800 g. **Composition:** 0.9250 Silver .8410 oz. ASW **Edge:** Reeded **Size:** 38.6 mm.

| Date | Mintage | F | VF | XF | Unc | BU |
|---|---|---|---|---|---|---|
| 2001 Proof | 15,000 | Value: 47.50 | | | | |

**CROWN KM# 1089 Weight:** 28.2800 g. **Composition:** Copper-Nickel **Series:** Harry Potter **Subject:** Journey to Hogwarts **Obverse:** Queen's portrait **Reverse:** Boat full of children going to castle **Edge:** Reeded **Size:** 38.6 mm.

| Date | Mintage | F | VF | XF | Unc | BU |
|---|---|---|---|---|---|---|
| 2001 | — | — | — | — | 10.00 | — |

**CROWN KM# 1089a Weight:** 28.2800 g. **Composition:** 0.9250 Silver .8410 oz. ASW **Edge:** Reeded **Size:** 38.6 mm.

| Date | Mintage | F | VF | XF | Unc | BU |
|---|---|---|---|---|---|---|
| 2001 Proof | 15,000 | Value: 47.50 | | | | |

**CROWN KM# 1091 Composition:** Copper-Nickel **Series:** Harry Potter **Subject:** First Quidditch Match **Obverse:** Queen's portrait **Reverse:** Harry flying a broom

| Date | Mintage | F | VF | XF | Unc | BU |
|---|---|---|---|---|---|---|
| 2001 | — | — | — | — | 10.00 | — |

**CROWN KM# 1091a Weight:** 28.2800 g. **Composition:** 0.9250 Silver .8410 oz. ASW **Series:** Harry Potter

| Date | Mintage | F | VF | XF | Unc | BU |
|---|---|---|---|---|---|---|
| 2001 Proof | 15,000 | Value: 47.50 | | | | |

**CROWN KM# 1093 Composition:** Copper-Nickel **Series:** Harry Potter **Subject:** Birth of Norbert **Obverse:** Queen's portrait **Reverse:** Hagrid children watching Norbert hatch

| Date | Mintage | F | VF | XF | Unc | BU |
|---|---|---|---|---|---|---|
| 2001 | — | — | — | — | 10.00 | — |

**CROWN KM# 1093a Weight:** 28.2800 g. **Composition:** 0.9250 Silver .8410 oz. ASW **Series:** Harry Potter

| Date | Mintage | F | VF | XF | Unc | BU |
|---|---|---|---|---|---|---|
| 2001 Proof | 15,000 | Value: 47.50 | | | | |

**CROWN KM# 1095 Composition:** Copper-Nickel **Series:** Harry Potter **Subject:** School **Obverse:** Queen's portrait **Reverse:** Harry in Potions class

| Date | Mintage | F | VF | XF | Unc | BU |
|---|---|---|---|---|---|---|
| 2001 | — | — | — | — | 10.00 | — |

**CROWN KM# 1095a Weight:** 28.2800 g. **Composition:** 0.9250 Silver .8410 oz. ASW **Series:** Harry Potter

| Date | Mintage | F | VF | XF | Unc | BU |
|---|---|---|---|---|---|---|
| 2001 Proof | 15,000 | Value: 47.50 | | | | |

**CROWN KM# 1097 Composition:** Copper-Nickel **Series:** Harry Potter **Subject:** Keys **Obverse:** Queen's portrait **Reverse:** Harry catching a flying key

| Date | Mintage | F | VF | XF | Unc | BU |
|---|---|---|---|---|---|---|
| 2001 | — | — | — | — | 10.00 | — |

**CROWN KM# 1097a Weight:** 28.2800 g. **Composition:** 0.9250 Silver .8410 oz. ASW **Series:** Harry Potter

| Date | Mintage | F | VF | XF | Unc | BU |
|---|---|---|---|---|---|---|
| 2001 Proof | 15,000 | Value: 47.50 | | | | |

**CROWN KM# 1102 Weight:** 28.2800 g. **Composition:** Copper-Nickel **Subject:** Year of the Horse **Obverse:** Queen's portrait **Reverse:** Two horses **Size:** 38.6 mm.

| Date | Mintage | F | VF | XF | Unc | BU |
|---|---|---|---|---|---|---|
| 2002 | — | — | — | — | 10.00 | — |

**CROWN KM# 1102a Weight:** 28.2800 g. **Composition:** 0.9250 Silver .8410 oz. ASW **Edge:** Reeded **Size:** 38.6 mm.

| Date | Mintage | F | VF | XF | Unc | BU |
|---|---|---|---|---|---|---|
| 2002 Proof | 30,000 | Value: 47.50 | | | | |

**CROWN KM# 1103 Weight:** 31.1000 g. **Composition:** 0.9999 Gold .9998 oz. AGW **Subject:** Year of the Horse

| Date | Mintage | F | VF | XF | Unc | BU |
|---|---|---|---|---|---|---|
| 2002 Proof | 2,000 | Value: 650 | | | | |

**5 CROWN KM# 177 Weight:** 155.5500 g. **Composition:** 0.9990 Silver 5.0000 oz. ASW **Subject:** Bicentennial of U.S. Constitution **Obverse:** Bust of Queen Elizabeth II right **Reverse:** Bust of U.S. Presidents **Size:** 65 mm. **Note:** Illustration reduced.

| Date | Mintage | F | VF | XF | Unc | BU |
|---|---|---|---|---|---|---|
| 1987 Proof | 9,000 | Value: 65.00 | | | | |

**5 CROWN KM# 180 Weight:** 155.5500 g. **Composition:** 0.9990 Silver 5.0000 oz. ASW **Series:** America's Cup **Obverse:** Bust of Queen Elizabeth II right **Reverse:** Sailboats and trophy **Size:** 65 mm. **Note:** Illustration reduced.

| Date | Mintage | F | VF | XF | Unc | BU |
|---|---|---|---|---|---|---|
| 1987 Proof | 6,000 | Value: 90.00 | | | | |

**5 CROWN KM# 299 Weight:** 155.5500 g. **Composition:** 0.9990 Silver 5.0000 oz. ASW **Series:** America's Cup **Obverse:** Bust of Queen Elizabeth II right **Reverse:** Sailboats and Statue of Liberty **Size:** 65 mm. **Note:** Illustration reduced.

| Date | Mintage | F | VF | XF | Unc | BU |
|---|---|---|---|---|---|---|
| 1987 Proof | 200 | Value: 220 | | | | |

**5 CROWN** **KM# 308** **Weight:** 155.5500 g. **Composition:** 0.9990 Silver 5.0000 oz. ASW **Series:** America's Cup **Obverse:** Bust of Queen Elizabeth II right **Reverse:** Three sailboats and map **Size:** 65 mm. **Note:** Illustration reduced.

| Date | Mintage | F | VF | XF | Unc | BU |
|---|---|---|---|---|---|---|
| 1987 Proof | — | Value: 350 | | | | |

**5 CROWN** **KM# 206** **Weight:** 155.5500 g. **Composition:** 0.9990 Silver 5.0000 oz. ASW **Subject:** Steam Navigation **Obverse:** Bust of Queen Elizabeth II right **Reverse:** R.M.S. Queen Mary **Size:** 65 mm. **Note:** Illustration reduced.

| Date | Mintage | F | VF | XF | Unc | BU |
|---|---|---|---|---|---|---|
| 1988 | — | — | — | — | 150 | — |

**5 CROWN** **KM# 285** **Weight:** 155.5500 g. **Composition:** 0.9990 Silver 5.0000 oz. ASW **Subject:** Australian Bicentennial **Obverse:** Bust of Queen Elizabeth II right **Reverse:** Kangaroo

| Date | Mintage | F | VF | XF | Unc | BU |
|---|---|---|---|---|---|---|
| 1988 Proof | — | Value: 150 | | | | |

**5 CROWN** **KM# 321** **Weight:** 155.5500 g. **Composition:** 0.9990 Silver 5.0000 oz. ASW **Series:** America's Cup **Obverse:** Bust of Queen Elizabeth II right **Reverse:** Cameo of sailing ship above 2 modern sailboats

| Date | Mintage | F | VF | XF | Unc | BU |
|---|---|---|---|---|---|---|
| 1991 Proof | Est. 15 | — | — | — | — | — |

**5 CROWN** **KM# 327** **Weight:** 155.5500 g. **Composition:** 0.9990 Silver 5.0000 oz. ASW **Series:** Americ'a Cup **Obverse:** Bust of Queen Elizabeth II right **Reverse:** Sailboat

| Date | Mintage | F | VF | XF | Unc | BU |
|---|---|---|---|---|---|---|
| 1992 | — | — | — | — | 150 | — |

**5 CROWN** **KM# 348** **Weight:** 155.5500 g. **Composition:** 0.9990 Silver 5.0000 oz. ASW **Obverse:** Bust of Queen Elizabeth II right **Reverse:** Siamese cat **Size:** 65 mm. **Note:** Illustration reduced.

| Date | Mintage | F | VF | XF | Unc | BU |
|---|---|---|---|---|---|---|
| 1992 Proof | — | Value: 225 | | | | |

**5 CROWN** **KM# 689** **Weight:** 155.5175 g. **Composition:** 0.9990 Silver 5.0000 oz. ASW **Series:** Legend of King Arthur **Obverse:** Bust of Queen Elizabeth II right **Reverse:** King Arthur with sword and orb

| Date | Mintage | F | VF | XF | Unc | BU |
|---|---|---|---|---|---|---|
| 1996 Proof | Est. 999 | Value: 75.00 | | | | |

**5 CROWN** **KM# 690** **Weight:** 155.5175 g. **Composition:** 0.9990 Silver 5.0000 oz. ASW **Series:** Legend of King Arthur **Obverse:** Bust of Queen Elizabeth II right **Reverse:** Queen Guinevere

| Date | Mintage | F | VF | XF | Unc | BU |
|---|---|---|---|---|---|---|
| 1996 Proof | Est. 999 | Value: 75.00 | | | | |

**5 CROWN** **KM# 691** **Weight:** 155.5175 g. **Composition:** 0.9990 Silver 5.0000 oz. ASW **Series:** Legend of King Arthur **Obverse:** Bust of Queen Elizabeth II right **Reverse:** Sir Lancelot

| Date | Mintage | F | VF | XF | Unc | BU |
|---|---|---|---|---|---|---|
| 1996 | Est. 999 | Value: 75.00 | | | | |

**5 CROWN** **KM# 692** **Weight:** 155.5175 g. **Composition:** 0.9990 Silver 5.0000 oz. ASW **Series:** Legend of King Arthur **Obverse:** Bust of Queen Elizabeth II right **Reverse:** Merlin

| Date | Mintage | F | VF | XF | Unc | BU |
|---|---|---|---|---|---|---|
| 1996 | Est. 999 | Value: 85.00 | | | | |

**5 CROWN** **KM# 693** **Weight:** 155.5175 g. **Composition:** 0.9990 Silver 5.0000 oz. ASW **Series:** Legend of King Arthur **Obverse:** Bust of Queen Elizabeth II right **Reverse:** Camelot Castle

| Date | Mintage | F | VF | XF | Unc | BU |
|---|---|---|---|---|---|---|
| 1996 | Est. 999 | Value: 100 | | | | |

**5 CROWN** **KM# 734** **Weight:** 155.5175 g. **Composition:** 0.9999 Gold 5.0000 oz. AGW **Subject:** Year of the Rat **Obverse:** Bust of Queen Elizabeth II right **Reverse:** Rat

| Date | Mintage | F | VF | XF | Unc | BU |
|---|---|---|---|---|---|---|
| 1996 Proof | — | — | — | — | — | — |

**Note:** Entire series purchased by one buyer. Mintage, disposition, and market value unknown

**5 CROWN** **KM# 727** **Weight:** 155.5175 g. **Composition:** 0.9999 Gold 5.0000 oz. AGW **Subject:** Year of the Ox **Obverse:** Bust of Queen Elizabeth II right **Reverse:** Ox laying down

| Date | Mintage | F | VF | XF | Unc | BU |
|---|---|---|---|---|---|---|
| 1997 Proof | Est. 250 | — | — | — | — | — |

**5 CROWN** **KM# 818** **Weight:** 155.5175 g. **Composition:** 0.9999 Gold 5.0000 oz. AGW **Subject:** Year of the Tiger **Obverse:** Bust of Queen Elizabeth II right **Reverse:** Tiger

| Date | Mintage | F | VF | XF | Unc | BU |
|---|---|---|---|---|---|---|
| 1998 Proof | Est. 250 | — | — | — | — | — |

**5 CROWN** **KM# 953** **Weight:** 155.5175 g. **Composition:** 0.9999 Gold 5.0000 oz. AGW **Subject:** Year of the Rabbit **Obverse:** Bust of Queen Elizabeth II right **Reverse:** Two rabbits

| Date | Mintage | F | VF | XF | Unc | BU |
|---|---|---|---|---|---|---|
| 1999 Proof | Est. 250 | Value: 3,225 | | | | |

**5 CROWN** **KM# 1018** **Weight:** 155.5175 g. **Composition:** 0.9999 Gold 5.0000 oz. AGW **Subject:** Year of the Dragon **Obverse:** Bust of Queen Elizabeth II right **Reverse:** Dragon, Chinese characters

| Date | Mintage | F | VF | XF | Unc | BU |
|---|---|---|---|---|---|---|
| 2000 Proof | Est. 250 | — | — | — | — | — |

**5 CROWN** **KM# 1064** **Weight:** 155.5175 g. **Composition:** 0.9999 Gold 5.0000 oz. AGW **Subject:** Year of the Snake **Obverse:** Queen's portrait **Reverse:** Snake **Edge:** Reeded **Size:** 65 mm.

| Date | Mintage | F | VF | XF | Unc | BU |
|---|---|---|---|---|---|---|
| 2001 Proof | 250 | — | — | — | — | — |

**5 CROWN** **KM# 1104** **Weight:** 155.5100 g. **Composition:** 0.9999 Gold 4.9993 oz. AGW **Subject:** Year of the Horse **Obverse:** Queen's portrait **Reverse:** Two horses **Edge:** Reeded **Size:** 65 mm.

| Date | Mintage | F | VF | XF | Unc | BU |
|---|---|---|---|---|---|---|
| 2002 Proof | 250 | Value: 3,000 | | | | |

**10 CROWN** **KM# 181** **Weight:** 311.0350 g. **Composition:** 0.9990 Silver 10.0000 oz. ASW **Series:** America's Cup **Obverse:** Bust of Queen Elizabeth II right **Reverse:** Sailboats and Statue of Liberty **Size:** 75 mm. **Note:** Illustration reduced.

| Date | Mintage | F | VF | XF | Unc | BU |
|---|---|---|---|---|---|---|
| 1987 Proof | 2,000 | Value: 125 | | | | |

**10 CROWN** **KM# 188** **Weight:** 311.0350 g. **Composition:** 0.9990 Silver 10.0000 oz. ASW **Subject:** Bicentenary of America's Constitution **Obverse:** Bust of Queen Elizabeth II right **Reverse:** Bust of Presidents **Size:** 75 mm. **Note:** Illustration reduced.

| Date | Mintage | F | VF | XF | Unc | BU |
|---|---|---|---|---|---|---|
| 1987 Proof | 6,000 | Value: 110 | | | | |

**10 CROWN** **KM# 300** **Weight:** 311.0350 g. **Composition:** 0.9990 Silver 10.0000 oz. ASW **Series:** America's Cup **Obverse:** Bust of Queen Elizabeth II right **Reverse:** Sailboats and trophy **Size:** 75 mm. **Note:** Illustration reduced.

| Date | Mintage | F | VF | XF | Unc | BU |
|---|---|---|---|---|---|---|
| 1987 Proof | 69 | Value: 350 | | | | |

**10 CROWN** **KM# 309** **Weight:** 311.0350 g. **Composition:** 0.9990 Silver 10.0000 oz. ASW **Series:** America's Cup **Obverse:** Bust of Queen Elizabeth II right **Reverse:** Three sailboats and map **Size:** 75 mm. **Note:** Illustration reduced.

| Date | Mintage | F | VF | XF | Unc | BU |
|---|---|---|---|---|---|---|
| 1987 Proof | — | Value: 525 | | | | |

**10 CROWN** **KM# 258** **Weight:** 311.0350 g. **Composition:** 0.9990 Silver 10.0000 oz. ASW **Subject:** Australian Bicentennial **Obverse:** Bust of Queen Elizabeth II right **Reverse:** Koala **Size:** 75 mm. **Note:** Illustration reduced.

| Date | Mintage | F | VF | XF | Unc | BU |
|---|---|---|---|---|---|---|
| 1988 Proof | Est. 13,000 | Value: 150 | | | | |

**10 CROWN** **KM# 992** **Weight:** 311.0350 g. **Composition:** 0.9990 Silver 10.0000 oz. ASW **Obverse:** Bust of Queen Elizabeth II right **Reverse:** Siamese cat

| Date | Mintage | F | VF | XF | Unc | BU |
|---|---|---|---|---|---|---|
| 1992 Proof | — | Value: 300 | | | | |

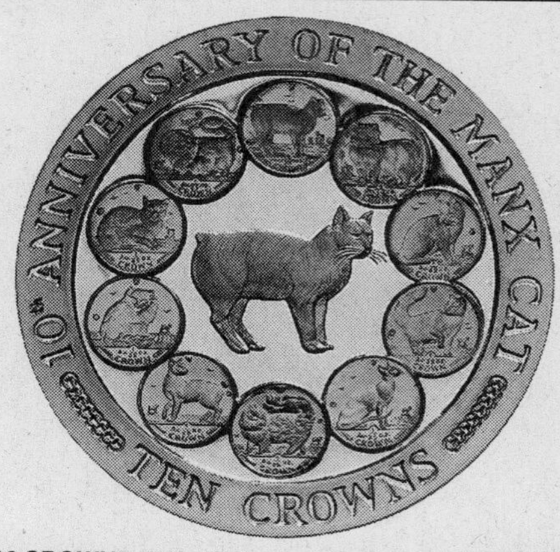


**10 CROWN** **KM# 775** **Weight:** 311.0300 g. **Composition:** 0.9250 Silver 9.2499 oz. ASW **Subject:** 10th Anniversary of the Manx Cat **Obverse:** Bust of Queen Elizabeth II right **Reverse:** Cat within inlaid circle of ten, cat coin designs **Size:** 75 mm. **Note:** Illustraiton reduced.

| Date | Mintage | F | VF | XF | Unc | BU |
|---|---|---|---|---|---|---|
| 1997 Proof | Est. 1,997 | Value: 350 | | | | |

## GOLD BULLION COINAGE

### Angel Series

**1/20 ANGEL** **KM# 166** **Weight:** 1.6970 g. **Composition:** 0.9170 Gold .0500 oz. AGW **Obverse:** Bust of Queen Elizabeth II right **Reverse:** Archangel Michael

| Date | Mintage | F | VF | XF | Unc | BU |
|---|---|---|---|---|---|---|
| 1986 | — | — | — | — | 45.00 | — |
| 1986 (pi) Proof | 5,000 | Value: 60.00 | | | | |
| 1987 | — | — | — | — | 45.00 | — |
| 1987 Proof | — | Value: 60.00 | | | | |

**1/20 ANGEL** **KM# 193** **Weight:** 1.6970 g. **Composition:** 0.9170 Gold .0500 oz. AGW **Obverse:** Bust of Queen Elizabeth II right **Reverse:** Archangel Michael

| Date | Mintage | F | VF | XF | Unc | BU |
|---|---|---|---|---|---|---|
| 1988 | — | — | — | — | 35.00 | — |
| 1988 (pi) | — | — | — | — | 50.00 | — |
| 1989 (h) Proof | Est. 5,000 | Value: 60.00 | | | | |
| 1989 (mt) Proof | 3,000 | Value: 60.00 | | | | |
| 1990 (sg) Proof | Est. 3,000 | Value: 60.00 | | | | |
| 1991 (cc) Proof | 1,000 | Value: 60.00 | | | | |
| 1992 (cb) Proof | 1,000 | Value: 60.00 | | | | |
| 1993 Proof | Est. 1,000 | Value: 60.00 | | | | |

**1/20 ANGEL** **KM# 393** **Weight:** 1.5551 g. **Composition:** 0.9999 Gold .0500 oz. AGW **Obverse:** Bust of Queen Elizabeth II right **Reverse:** Archangel Michael

| Date | Mintage | F | VF | XF | Unc | BU |
|---|---|---|---|---|---|---|
| 1994 (ns) Proof | — | Value: 50.00 | | | | |
| 1995 (sc) Proof | — | Value: 60.00 | | | | |
| 1996 (bs) Proof | Est. 1,000 | Value: 60.00 | | | | |
| 1997 (at) Proof | Est. 1,000 | Value: 60.00 | | | | |
| 1998 (x) Proof | Est. 1,000 | Value: 60.00 | | | | |
| 1999 (fw) Proof | Est. 1,000 | Value: 60.00 | | | | |
| 2000 (ch) Proof | Est. 1,000 | Value: 60.00 | | | | |

**1/20 ANGEL** **KM# 1106** **Weight:** 1.5552 g. **Composition:** 0.9999 Gold .0500 oz. AGW **Obverse:** Queen's new portrait **Reverse:** St. Michael slaying dragon, three crown privy mark at right **Edge:** Reeded **Size:** 15 mm.

| Date | Mintage | F | VF | XF | Unc | BU |
|---|---|---|---|---|---|---|
| 2001 (3c) Proof | 1,000 | Value: 62.00 | | | | |

**1/10 ANGEL** **KM# 138** **Weight:** 3.3900 g. **Composition:** 0.9170 Gold .1000 oz. AGW **Obverse:** Bust of Queen Elizabeth II right **Reverse:** Archangel Michael

| Date | Mintage | F | VF | XF | Unc | BU |
|---|---|---|---|---|---|---|
| 1984 Proof | 5,000 | Value: 75.00 | | | | |

**1/10 ANGEL** KM# 140 **Weight:** 3.3900 g. **Composition:** 0.9170 Gold .1000 oz. AGW **Obverse:** Bust of Queen Elizabeth II right **Reverse:** Archangel Michael

| Date | Mintage | F | VF | XF | Unc | BU |
|---|---|---|---|---|---|---|
| 1985 Proof | 3,000 | Value: 75.00 | | | | |
| 1985 | 8,000 | — | — | — | 65.00 | — |
| 1986 | — | — | — | — | 65.00 | — |
| 1986 Proof | — | Value: 75.00 | | | | |
| 1987 | — | — | — | — | 65.00 | — |
| 1987 Proof | — | Value: 75.00 | | | | |

**1/10 ANGEL** KM# 159 **Weight:** 3.3900 g. **Composition:** 0.9170 Gold .1000 oz. AGW **Obverse:** Bust of Queen Elizabeth II right **Reverse:** Archangel Michael

| Date | Mintage | F | VF | XF | Unc | BU |
|---|---|---|---|---|---|---|
| 1985 A | 1,000 | — | — | — | 90.00 | — |
| 1985 C | 1,000 | — | — | — | 90.00 | — |
| 1985 H | 1,000 | — | — | — | 90.00 | — |
| 1985 L | 1,000 | — | — | — | 90.00 | — |
| 1985 | 5,000 | — | — | — | 65.00 | — |
| 1986 A | 1,000 | — | — | — | 90.00 | — |
| 1986 T | 1,000 | — | — | — | 90.00 | — |
| 1986 X | 1,000 | — | — | — | 90.00 | — |
| 1987 A | 1,000 | — | — | — | 90.00 | — |
| 1987 F Proof | 1,000 | Value: 95.00 | | | | |
| 1987 L | 1,000 | — | — | — | 90.00 | — |
| 1987 (mt) Proof | 3,000 | Value: 90.00 | | | | |
| 1988 A Proof | 1,000 | Value: 90.00 | | | | |

**1/10 ANGEL** KM# 194 **Weight:** 3.3900 g. **Composition:** 0.9170 Gold .1000 oz. AGW **Obverse:** Bust of Queen Elizabeth II right **Reverse:** Archangel Michael

| Date | Mintage | F | VF | XF | Unc | BU |
|---|---|---|---|---|---|---|
| 1988 | — | — | — | — | 65.00 | — |
| 1989 A Proof | 250 | Value: 100 | | | | |
| 1990 A Proof | 1,000 | Value: 90.00 | | | | |
| 1991 A Proof | 400 | Value: 95.00 | | | | |
| **Note:** 299 pieces have been melted | | | | | | |
| 1992 A | 100 | — | — | — | 120 | — |

**1/10 ANGEL** KM# 394 **Weight:** 3.1103 g. **Composition:** 0.9999 Gold .1000 oz. AGW **Obverse:** Bust of Queen Elizabeth II right **Reverse:** Archangel Michael

| Date | Mintage | F | VF | XF | Unc | BU |
|---|---|---|---|---|---|---|
| 1994 Proof | — | Value: 75.00 | | | | |

**1/4 ANGEL** KM# 152.1 **Weight:** 8.4830 g. **Composition:** 0.9170 Gold .2500 oz. AGW **Obverse:** Bust of Queen Elizabeth II right **Reverse:** Archangel Michael

| Date | Mintage | F | VF | XF | Unc | BU |
|---|---|---|---|---|---|---|
| 1985 | 2,117 | — | — | — | 110 | — |
| 1985 Proof | 51 | Value: 175 | | | | |
| 1986 L | 1,000 | — | — | — | 110 | — |
| 1986 Proof | — | Value: 125 | | | | |

**1/4 ANGEL** KM# 152.2 **Weight:** 8.4830 g. **Composition:** 0.9170 Gold .2500 oz. AGW **Obverse:** Bust of Queen Elizabeth II right **Reverse:** Archangel Michael

| Date | Mintage | F | VF | XF | Unc | BU |
|---|---|---|---|---|---|---|
| 1987 | — | — | — | — | 110 | — |
| 1987 Proof | — | Value: 125 | | | | |
| 1987 (s) Proof | 1,000 | Value: 125 | | | | |
| 1987 (SL) Proof | 568 | Value: 125 | | | | |
| 1987 (bb) Proof | 1,000 | Value: 125 | | | | |

**1/4 ANGEL** KM# 195 **Weight:** 8.4830 g. **Composition:** 0.9170 Gold .2500 oz. AGW **Obverse:** Bust of Queen Elizabeth II right **Reverse:** Archangel Michael

| Date | Mintage | F | VF | XF | Unc | BU |
|---|---|---|---|---|---|---|
| 1988 | — | — | — | — | 150 | — |
| 1988 (f) Proof | 1,000 | Value: 200 | | | | |
| 1988 (p) Proof | 1,000 | Value: 200 | | | | |
| 1988 (ss) Proof | 1,000 | Value: 200 | | | | |
| 1989 C (d) Proof | 1,000 | Value: 200 | | | | |
| 1989 (p) Proof | 500 | Value: 200 | | | | |
| 1989 (hk) Proof | 1,000 | Value: 200 | | | | |
| 1989 (y) | — | — | — | — | 150 | — |
| 1990 (ba) Proof | 1,000 | Value: 200 | | | | |
| **Note:** 513 pieces melted | | | | | | |
| 1990 (c) Proof | 250 | Value: 220 | | | | |
| 1990 (fl) | 1,000 | — | — | — | 150 | — |

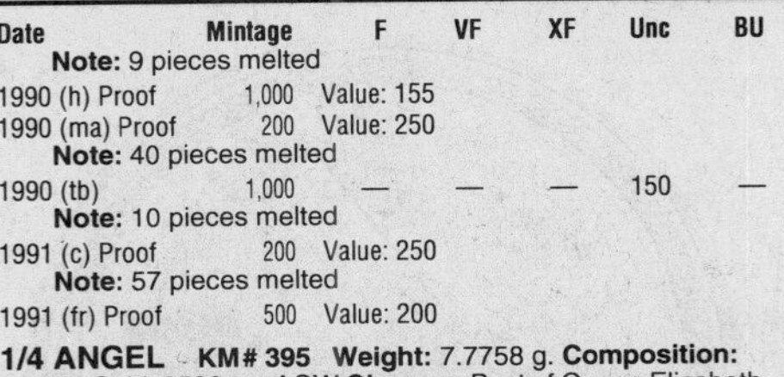

| Date | Mintage | F | VF | XF | Unc | BU |
|---|---|---|---|---|---|---|
| **Note:** 9 pieces melted | | | | | | |
| 1990 (h) Proof | 1,000 | Value: 155 | | | | |
| 1990 (ma) Proof | 200 | Value: 250 | | | | |
| **Note:** 40 pieces melted | | | | | | |
| 1990 (tb) | 1,000 | — | — | — | 150 | — |
| **Note:** 10 pieces melted | | | | | | |
| 1991 (c) Proof | 200 | Value: 250 | | | | |
| **Note:** 57 pieces melted | | | | | | |
| 1991 (fr) Proof | 500 | Value: 200 | | | | |

**1/4 ANGEL** KM# 395 **Weight:** 7.7758 g. **Composition:** 0.9999 Gold .2500 oz. AGW **Obverse:** Bust of Queen Elizabeth II right **Reverse:** Archangel Michael

| Date | Mintage | F | VF | XF | Unc | BU |
|---|---|---|---|---|---|---|
| 1994 Proof | — | Value: 165 | | | | |

**1/4 ANGEL** KM# 1065 **Ring Weight:** 3.8880 g. **Ring Composition:** 0.9995 Platinum .1244 oz. APW **Center Weight:** 3.8880 g. **Center Composition:** 0.9999 Gold .1249 oz. AGW **Obverse:** Queen's portrait **Reverse:** Archangel Michael **Edge:** Reeded **Size:** 22 mm.

| Date | Mintage | F | VF | XF | Unc | BU |
|---|---|---|---|---|---|---|
| 1995 Proof | — | Value: 250 | | | | |

**1/2 ANGEL** KM# 155 **Weight:** 16.9380 g. **Composition:** 0.9170 Gold .5000 oz. AGW **Obverse:** Bust of Queen Elizabeth II right **Reverse:** Archangel Michael

| Date | Mintage | F | VF | XF | Unc | BU |
|---|---|---|---|---|---|---|
| 1985 | 1,776 | — | — | — | 185 | — |
| 1985 Proof | 51 | Value: 275 | | | | |
| 1986 | — | — | — | — | 185 | — |
| 1986 Proof | 3,000 | Value: 225 | | | | |
| 1987 | — | — | — | — | 185 | — |
| 1987 Proof | — | Value: 225 | | | | |

**1/2 ANGEL** KM# 196 **Weight:** 16.9380 g. **Composition:** 0.9170 Gold .5000 oz. AGW **Obverse:** Bust of Queen Elizabeth II right **Reverse:** Archangel Michael

| Date | Mintage | F | VF | XF | Unc | BU |
|---|---|---|---|---|---|---|
| 1988 | — | — | — | — | 185 | — |

**1/2 ANGEL** KM# 396 **Weight:** 15.5517 g. **Composition:** 0.9999 Gold .5000 oz. AGW **Obverse:** Bust of Queen Elizabeth II right **Reverse:** Archangel Michael

| Date | Mintage | F | VF | XF | Unc | BU |
|---|---|---|---|---|---|---|
| 1994 Proof | — | Value: 250 | | | | |

**ANGEL** KM# 139 **Weight:** 33.9300 g. **Composition:** 0.9170 Gold 1.0000 oz. AGW **Obverse:** Bust of Queen Elizabeth II right **Reverse:** Archangel Michael

| Date | Mintage | F | VF | XF | Unc | BU |
|---|---|---|---|---|---|---|
| 1984 Proof | 3,000 | Value: 450 | | | | |

**ANGEL** KM# 141 **Weight:** 33.9300 g. **Composition:** 0.9170 Gold 1.0000 oz. AGW **Obverse:** Bust of Queen Elizabeth II right **Reverse:** Archangel Michael

| Date | Mintage | F | VF | XF | Unc | BU |
|---|---|---|---|---|---|---|
| 1985 Proof like | — | — | — | — | — | — |
| 1985 | 28,000 | — | — | — | 350 | — |
| 1985 Proof | 3,000 | Value: 400 | | | | |
| 1986 | — | — | — | — | 350 | — |
| 1986 Proof | — | Value: 400 | | | | |
| 1987 | — | — | — | — | 350 | — |
| 1987 Proof | — | Value: 400 | | | | |

**ANGEL** KM# 191 **Weight:** 33.9300 g. **Composition:** 0.9170 Gold 1.0000 oz. AGW **Subject:** Hong Kong Coin Show **Obverse:** Bust of Queen Elizabeth II right **Reverse:** Archangel Michael

| Date | Mintage | F | VF | XF | Unc | BU |
|---|---|---|---|---|---|---|
| 1987 Proof | 1,000 | Value: 500 | | | | |

**ANGEL** KM# 197 **Weight:** 33.9300 g. **Composition:** 0.9170 Gold 1.0000 oz. AGW **Obverse:** Bust of Queen Elizabeth II right **Reverse:** Archangel Michael

| Date | Mintage | F | VF | XF | Unc | BU |
|---|---|---|---|---|---|---|
| 1988 | — | — | — | — | 375 | — |
| 1988 (ss) Proof | 1,000 | Value: 450 | | | | |

**ANGEL** KM# 397 **Weight:** 31.1035 g. **Composition:** 0.9999 Gold 1.0000 oz. AGW **Obverse:** Bust of Queen Elizabeth II right **Reverse:** Archangel Michael

| Date | Mintage | F | VF | XF | Unc | BU |
|---|---|---|---|---|---|---|
| 1994 Proof | — | Value: 450 | | | | |

**ANGEL** KM# 522 **Weight:** 31.1035 g. **Composition:** 0.9999 Gold 1.0000 oz. AGW **Obverse:** Bust of Queen Elizabeth II right **Reverse:** Archangel Michael

| Date | Mintage | F | VF | XF | Unc | BU |
|---|---|---|---|---|---|---|
| 1995 Proof | — | Value: 450 | | | | |

**5 ANGEL** **KM# 156** **Weight:** 169.6680 g. **Composition:** 0.9170 Gold 5.0000 oz. AGW **Obverse:** Bust of Queen Elizabeth II right **Reverse:** Archangel Michael

| Date | Mintage | F | VF | XF | Unc | BU |
|---|---|---|---|---|---|---|
| 1985 | 104 | — | — | — | 1,950 | — |
| 1985 Proof | 90 | Value: 2,000 | | | | |
| 1986 | 89 | — | — | — | 1,950 | — |
| 1986 Proof | 250 | Value: 2,000 | | | | |
| 1987 | 150 | — | — | — | 1,950 | — |
| 1987 Proof | 27 | Value: 2,150 | | | | |

**5 ANGEL** **KM# 198** **Weight:** 169.6680 g. **Composition:** 0.9170 Gold 5.0000 oz. AGW **Obverse:** Bust of Queen Elizabeth II right **Reverse:** Archangel Michael

| Date | Mintage | F | VF | XF | Unc | BU |
|---|---|---|---|---|---|---|
| 1988 | 250 | — | — | — | 1,950 | — |

**10 ANGEL** **KM# 157** **Weight:** 339.3350 g. **Composition:** 0.9170 Gold 10.0000 oz. AGW **Obverse:** Bust of Queen Elizabeth II right **Reverse:** Archangel Michael

| Date | Mintage | F | VF | XF | Unc | BU |
|---|---|---|---|---|---|---|
| 1985 | 79 | — | — | — | 3,750 | — |
| 1985 Proof | 68 | Value: 3,800 | | | | |
| 1986 | 47 | — | — | — | 3,800 | — |
| 1986 Proof | 250 | Value: 3,800 | | | | |
| 1987 | 150 | — | — | — | 3,750 | — |
| 1987 Proof | 30 | Value: 3,950 | | | | |

**10 ANGEL** **KM# 199** **Weight:** 339.3350 g. **Composition:** 0.9170 Gold 10.0000 oz. AGW **Obverse:** Bust of Queen Elizabeth II right **Reverse:** Archangel Michael

| Date | Mintage | F | VF | XF | Unc | BU |
|---|---|---|---|---|---|---|
| 1988 Proof | 250 | Value: 3,800 | | | | |

**15 ANGEL** **KM# 189** **Weight:** 508.9575 g. **Composition:** 0.9170 Gold 15.0000 oz. AGW **Obverse:** Bust of Queen Elizabeth II right **Reverse:** Archangel Michael

| Date | Mintage | F | VF | XF | Unc | BU |
|---|---|---|---|---|---|---|
| 1987 | 150 | — | — | — | 5,500 | — |
| 1987 Proof | 18 | Value: 7,500 | | | | |

**15 ANGEL** **KM# 200** **Weight:** 508.9575 g. **Composition:** 0.9170 Gold 15.0000 oz. AGW **Obverse:** Bust of Queen Elizabeth II right **Reverse:** Archangel Michael

| Date | Mintage | F | VF | XF | Unc | BU |
|---|---|---|---|---|---|---|
| 1988 Proof | — | Value: 7,500 | | | | |

**20 ANGEL** **KM# 201** **Weight:** 678.6720 g. **Composition:** 0.9170 Gold 20.0000 oz. AGW **Obverse:** Bust of Queen Elizabeth II right **Reverse:** Archangel Michael **Size:** 75.2 mm. **Note:** Illustration reduced.

| Date | Mintage | F | VF | XF | Unc | BU |
|---|---|---|---|---|---|---|
| 1988 | 250 | — | — | — | 8,500 | — |
| 1988 Proof | 100 | Value: 9,000 | | | | |

**20 ANGEL** **KM# 201a** **Composition:** Gilt Silver **Obverse:** Bust of Queen Elizabeth II right **Reverse:** Archangel Michael

| Date | Mintage | F | VF | XF | Unc | BU |
|---|---|---|---|---|---|---|
| 1988 | — | — | — | — | — | — |

**25 ANGEL** **KM# 301** **Weight:** 848.2750 g. **Composition:** 0.9170 Gold 25.0000 oz. AGW **Obverse:** Bust of Queen Elizabeth II right **Reverse:** Archangel Michael

| Date | Mintage | F | VF | XF | Unc | BU |
|---|---|---|---|---|---|---|
| 1989 | — | — | — | — | 11,500 | — |

## GOLD BULLION COINAGE

### Sovereign Series

**1/5 SOVEREIGN** **KM# 969** **Weight:** 1.0000 g. **Composition:** 0.9999 Gold .0321 oz. AGW **Obverse:** Bust of Queen Elizabeth II right **Reverse:** Triskeles

| Date | Mintage | F | VF | XF | Unc | BU |
|---|---|---|---|---|---|---|
| 1999 | — | — | — | — | BV+40% | — |

**1/2 SOVEREIGN** **KM# 970** **Weight:** 2.5000 g. **Composition:** 0.9999 Gold .0804 oz. AGW **Obverse:** Bust of Queen Elizabeth II right **Reverse:** Triskeles

| Date | Mintage | F | VF | XF | Unc | BU |
|---|---|---|---|---|---|---|
| 1999 | — | — | — | — | BV+30% | — |

**3/4 SOVEREIGN** **KM# 971** **Weight:** 3.5000 g. **Composition:** 0.9999 Gold .1125 oz. AGW **Obverse:** Bust of Queen Elizabeth II right **Reverse:** Triskeles

| Date | Mintage | F | VF | XF | Unc | BU |
|---|---|---|---|---|---|---|
| 1999 | — | — | — | — | BV+25% | — |

**SOVEREIGN** **KM# 972** **Weight:** 5.0000 g. **Composition:** 0.9999 Gold .1607 oz. AGW **Obverse:** Bust of Queen Elizabeth II right **Reverse:** Triskeles

| Date | Mintage | F | VF | XF | Unc | BU |
|---|---|---|---|---|---|---|
| 1999 | — | — | — | — | BV+20% | — |

**2 SOVEREIGNS** **KM# 973** **Weight:** 10.0000 g. **Composition:** 0.9999 Gold .3215 oz. AGW **Obverse:** Bust of Queen Elizabeth II right **Reverse:** Triskeles

| Date | Mintage | F | VF | XF | Unc | BU |
|---|---|---|---|---|---|---|
| 1999 | — | — | — | — | — | — |

**5 SOVEREIGNS** **KM# 974** **Weight:** 31.1035 g. **Composition:** 0.9999 Gold .9999 oz. AGW **Obverse:** Bust of Queen Elizabeth II right **Reverse:** Triskeles

| Date | Mintage | F | VF | XF | Unc | BU |
|---|---|---|---|---|---|---|
| 1999 | — | — | — | — | BV+5% | — |

## GOLD BULLION COINAGE

### Platina Series

**1/25 PLATINA** **KM# 944** **Weight:** 1.2447 g. **Composition:** 0.7500 White Gold .0300 oz. AGW **Obverse:** Bust of Queen Elizabeth II right **Reverse:** Crowned arms

| Date | Mintage | F | VF | XF | Unc | BU |
|---|---|---|---|---|---|---|
| 1999 Proof | Est. 10,000 | Value: 40.00 | | | | |

**1/10 PLATINA** **KM# 945** **Weight:** 3.1103 g. **Composition:** 0.7500 White Gold .0750 oz. AGW **Obverse:** Bust of Queen Elizabeth II right **Reverse:** Crowned arms

| Date | Mintage | F | VF | XF | Unc | BU |
|---|---|---|---|---|---|---|
| 1999 Proof | Est. 7,500 | Value: 75.00 | | | | |

**1/5 PLATINA** **KM# 946** **Weight:** 6.2200 g. **Composition:** 0.7500 White Gold .1500 oz. AGW **Obverse:** Bust of Queen Elizabeth II right **Reverse:** Crowned arms

| Date | Mintage | F | VF | XF | Unc | BU |
|---|---|---|---|---|---|---|
| 1999 Proof | Est. 5,000 | Value: 135 | | | | |

**1/2 PLATINA** **KM# 947** **Weight:** 15.5517 g. **Composition:** 0.7500 White Gold .3750 oz. AGW **Obverse:** Bust of Queen Elizabeth II right **Reverse:** Crowned arms

| Date | Mintage | F | VF | XF | Unc | BU |
|---|---|---|---|---|---|---|
| 1999 Proof | Est. 3,500 | Value: 255 | | | | |

## PLATINUM BULLION COINAGE

Noble Series

**1/20 NOBLE KM# 266 Weight:** 1.5551 g. **Composition:** 0.9995 Platinum .0500 oz. APW **Obverse:** Bust of Queen Elizabeth II right **Reverse:** Ship with hologramsail

| Date | Mintage | F | VF | XF | Unc | BU |
|---|---|---|---|---|---|---|
| 1989 Proof | 10,000 | Value: 65.00 | | | | |
| 1992 | — | — | — | — | 60.00 | — |

**1/10 NOBLE KM# 137 Weight:** 3.1100 g. **Composition:** 0.9995 Platinum .1000 oz. APW **Obverse:** Bust of Queen Elizabeth II right **Reverse:** Ship with hologramsail

| Date | Mintage | F | VF | XF | Unc | BU |
|---|---|---|---|---|---|---|
| 1984 | — | — | — | — | 90.00 | — |
| 1984 Proof | 5,000 | Value: 95.00 | | | | |

**1/10 NOBLE KM# 153 Weight:** 3.1100 g. **Composition:** 0.9995 Platinum .1000 oz. APW **Obverse:** Bust of Queen Elizabeth II right **Reverse:** Ship with hologramsail

| Date | Mintage | F | VF | XF | Unc | BU |
|---|---|---|---|---|---|---|
| 1985 | 99,000 | — | — | — | 90.00 | — |
| 1985 Proof | 5,000 | Value: 95.00 | | | | |
| 1986 | — | — | — | — | 90.00 | — |
| 1986 Proof | 5,000 | Value: 95.00 | | | | |
| 1987 | — | — | — | — | 90.00 | — |
| 1987 Proof | 5,000 | Value: 95.00 | | | | |

**1/10 NOBLE KM# 202 Weight:** 3.1100 g. **Composition:** 0.9995 Platinum .1000 oz. APW **Obverse:** Bust of Queen Elizabeth II right **Reverse:** Ship with hologramsail

| Date | Mintage | F | VF | XF | Unc | BU |
|---|---|---|---|---|---|---|
| 1988 | 5,000 | — | — | — | 90.00 | — |
| 1989 | 5,000 | — | — | — | 90.00 | — |

**1/4 NOBLE KM# 168 Weight:** 7.7757 g. **Composition:** 0.9995 Platinum .2500 oz. APW **Obverse:** Bust of Queen Elizabeth II right **Reverse:** Ship with hologramsail

| Date | Mintage | F | VF | XF | Unc | BU |
|---|---|---|---|---|---|---|
| 1986 Proof | 2,015 | Value: 160 | | | | |
| 1987 Proof | 3,250 | Value: 160 | | | | |
| 1987 (1) Proof | 750 | Value: 170 | | | | |

**1/4 NOBLE KM# 203 Weight:** 7.7757 g. **Composition:** 0.9995 Platinum .2500 oz. APW **Obverse:** Bust of Queen Elizabeth II right **Reverse:** Ship with hologramsail

| Date | Mintage | F | VF | XF | Unc | BU |
|---|---|---|---|---|---|---|
| 1988 | — | — | — | — | 160 | — |
| 1988 (a) | 100 | — | — | — | 180 | — |
| 1988 (p) Proof | 1,000 | Value: 160 | | | | |
| 1988 (bb) Proof | 1,000 | Value: 160 | | | | |
| 1989 (br) Proof | 250 | Value: 175 | | | | |
| 1989 (p) Proof | 500 | Value: 170 | | | | |
| 1990 (ba) Proof | 1,000 | Value: 160 | | | | |
| 1990 (ti) Proof | Est. 1,000 | Value: 160 | | | | |

**1/4 NOBLE KM# 1066 Ring Weight:** 3.8880 g. **Ring Composition:** 0.9999 Gold .1249 oz. AGW **Center Weight:** 0.9995 g. **Center Composition:** 0.1244 Platinum APW **Obverse:** Queen's portrait **Reverse:** Viking ship **Edge:** Reeded **Size:** 22 mm.

| Date | Mintage | F | VF | XF | Unc | BU |
|---|---|---|---|---|---|---|
| 1995 Proof | — | Value: 250 | | | | |

**1/4 NOBLE KM# 717 Weight:** 7.7757 g. **Composition:** 0.9995 Platinum .2500 oz. APW **Obverse:** Bust of Queen Elizabeth II right **Reverse:** Ship with hologramsail

| Date | Mintage | F | VF | XF | Unc | BU |
|---|---|---|---|---|---|---|
| 1996 Proof | Est. 10,000 | Value: 165 | | | | |

**1/2 NOBLE KM# 169 Weight:** 15.5514 g. **Composition:** 0.9995 Platinum .5000 oz. APW **Obverse:** Bust of Queen Elizabeth II right **Reverse:** Ship with hologramsail

| Date | Mintage | F | VF | XF | Unc | BU |
|---|---|---|---|---|---|---|
| 1986 Proof | 15 | Value: 500 | | | | |
| 1987 Proof | 3,000 | Value: 320 | | | | |

**1/2 NOBLE KM# 204 Weight:** 15.5514 g. **Composition:** 0.9995 Platinum .5000 oz. APW **Obverse:** Bust of Queen Elizabeth II right **Reverse:** Ship with hologramsail

| Date | Mintage | F | VF | XF | Unc | BU |
|---|---|---|---|---|---|---|
| 1988 Proof | 3,000 | Value: 320 | | | | |
| 1989 Proof | 3,000 | Value: 320 | | | | |

**NOBLE KM# 110 Weight:** 31.1030 g. **Composition:** 0.9995 Platinum .9991 oz. APW **Obverse:** Bust of Queen Elizabeth II right **Reverse:** Ship with hologramsail

| Date | Mintage | F | VF | XF | Unc | BU |
|---|---|---|---|---|---|---|
| 1983 | 1,700 | — | — | — | 575 | — |
| 1983 Proof | 94 | Value: 750 | | | | |
| 1984 | — | — | — | — | 575 | — |
| 1984 Proof | 2,000 | Value: 600 | | | | |

**NOBLE KM# 154 Weight:** 31.1030 g. **Composition:** 0.9995 Platinum .9991 oz. APW **Obverse:** Bust of Queen Elizabeth II right **Reverse:** Ship with hologramsail

| Date | Mintage | F | VF | XF | Unc | BU |
|---|---|---|---|---|---|---|
| 1985 | — | — | — | — | 575 | — |
| 1985 Proof | 3,000 | Value: 585 | | | | |
| 1986 | — | — | — | — | 575 | — |
| 1986 Proof | 3,000 | Value: 585 | | | | |
| 1987 | — | — | — | — | 575 | — |
| 1987 Proof | 3,000 | Value: 585 | | | | |

**NOBLE KM# 205 Weight:** 31.1030 g. **Composition:** 0.9995 Platinum .9991 oz. APW **Obverse:** Bust of Queen Elizabeth II right **Reverse:** Ship with hologramsail

| Date | Mintage | F | VF | XF | Unc | BU |
|---|---|---|---|---|---|---|
| 1988 Proof | 3,000 | Value: 580 | | | | |
| 1989 Proof | 3,000 | Value: 580 | | | | |

**5 NOBLE KM# 170 Weight:** 155.5140 g. **Composition:** 0.9995 Platinum 5.0000 oz. APW **Obverse:** Bust of Queen Elizabeth II right **Reverse:** Ship with hologramsail

| Date | Mintage | F | VF | XF | Unc | BU |
|---|---|---|---|---|---|---|
| 1986 Proof | 15 | Value: 4,000 | | | | |
| 1987 Proof | 11 | Value: 3,500 | | | | |
| 1988 Proof | — | Value: 5,400 | | | | |

**10 NOBLE KM# 171 Weight:** 311.0280 g. **Composition:** 0.9995 Platinum 10.0000 oz. APW **Obverse:** Bust of Queen Elizabeth II right **Reverse:** Ship with hologramsail **Note:** Illustration reduced. Actual size: 63mm.

| Date | Mintage | F | VF | XF | Unc | BU |
|---|---|---|---|---|---|---|
| 1986 Proof | 15 | Value: 8,000 | | | | |
| 1987 Proof | 11 | Value: 7,500 | | | | |
| 1988 Proof | — | Value: 10,000 | | | | |

## TRADE COINAGE

Ecu Series

**15 ECUS** KM# 711 **Weight:** 10.0000 g. **Composition:** 0.9250 Silver .2974 oz. ASW **Obverse:** Bust of Queen Elizabeth II right **Reverse:** Manx cat on shield

| Date | Mintage | F | VF | XF | Unc | BU |
|---|---|---|---|---|---|---|
| 1994 | Est. 30,000 | — | — | — | 40.00 | — |

**15 ECUS** KM# 714 **Weight:** 10.0000 g. **Composition:** 0.9250 Silver .2974 oz. ASW **Subject:** 50th Anniversary of United Nations **Obverse:** Bust of Queen Elizabeth II right **Reverse:** Blacksmith

| Date | Mintage | F | VF | XF | Unc | BU |
|---|---|---|---|---|---|---|
| 1995 Proof | Est. 30,000 | Value: 42.50 | | | | |

**25 ECUS** KM# 712 **Weight:** 19.2000 g. **Composition:** 0.9250 Silver .5710 oz. ASW **Subject:** 50th Anniversary of United Nations **Obverse:** Bust of Queen Elizabeth II right **Reverse:** Viking boat on helmeted shield

| Date | Mintage | F | VF | XF | Unc | BU |
|---|---|---|---|---|---|---|
| 1994 | Est. 15,000 | — | — | — | 52.50 | — |

**25 ECUS** KM# 715 **Weight:** 19.2000 g. **Composition:** 0.9250 Silver .5710 oz. ASW **Subject:** 50th Anniversary of United Nations **Obverse:** Bust of Queen Elizabeth II right **Reverse:** Ram's head shield

| Date | Mintage | F | VF | XF | Unc | BU |
|---|---|---|---|---|---|---|
| 1995 Proof | Est. 15,000 | Value: 55.00 | | | | |

**75 ECUS** KM# 713 **Weight:** 6.2200 g. **Composition:** 0.9990 Gold .2000 oz. AGW **Obverse:** Bust of Queen Elizabeth II right **Reverse:** Triskeles on crowned shield

| Date | Mintage | F | VF | XF | Unc | BU |
|---|---|---|---|---|---|---|
| 1994 | Est. 2,000 | — | — | — | 190 | — |

**75 ECUS** KM# 716 **Weight:** 6.2200 g. **Composition:** 0.9990 Gold .2000 oz. AGW **Obverse:** Bust of Queen Elizabeth II right **Reverse:** Falcons on shield

| Date | Mintage | F | VF | XF | Unc | BU |
|---|---|---|---|---|---|---|
| 1995 Proof | Est. 2,000 | Value: 200 | | | | |

## TRADE COINAGE

### Sterling Euro Series

**10 EURO** KM# 718 **Weight:** 10.0000 g. **Composition:** 0.9250 Silver .2974 oz. ASW **Subject:** Spain - 10 years Membership E.C. **Obverse:** Bust of Queen Elizabeth II right **Reverse:** Head of De Falla and opera scene

| Date | Mintage | F | VF | XF | Unc | BU |
|---|---|---|---|---|---|---|
| 1996 Proof | Est. 30,000 | Value: 40.00 | | | | |

**10 EURO** KM# 795 **Weight:** 10.0000 g. **Composition:** 0.9250 Silver .2974 oz. ASW **Subject:** 200th Anniversary Birth of Franza Schubert **Obverse:** Bust of Queen Elizabeth II right **Reverse:** Head of Schubert and piano recital scene

| Date | Mintage | F | VF | XF | Unc | BU |
|---|---|---|---|---|---|---|
| 1997 Proof | Est. 30,000 | Value: 40.00 | | | | |

**10 EURO** KM# 796 **Weight:** 10.0000 g. **Composition:** 0.9250 Silver .2974 oz. ASW **Obverse:** Bust of Queen Elizabeth II right **Reverse:** Bust of Jan Sweelinck and organ player

| Date | Mintage | F | VF | XF | Unc | BU |
|---|---|---|---|---|---|---|
| 1997 Proof | Est. 30,000 | Value: 40.00 | | | | |

**10 EURO** KM# 909 **Weight:** 10.0000 g. **Composition:** 0.9250 Silver .2974 oz. ASW **Subject:** 125th Anniversary of the Isle of Man Railway **Obverse:** Bust of Queen Elizabeth II right **Reverse:** Old steam train

| Date | Mintage | F | VF | XF | Unc | BU |
|---|---|---|---|---|---|---|
| 1998 Proof | Est. 30,000 | Value: 40.00 | | | | |

**10 EURO** KM# 910 **Weight:** 10.0000 g. **Composition:** 0.9250 Silver .2974 oz. ASW **Subject:** Myths and Legends - Manannan **Obverse:** Bust of Queen Elizabeth II right **Reverse:** Warrior riding horse

| Date | Mintage | F | VF | XF | Unc | BU |
|---|---|---|---|---|---|---|
| 1998 Proof | Est. 30,000 | Value: 40.00 | | | | |

**15 EURO** KM# 719 **Weight:** 19.2000 g. **Composition:** 0.9250 Silver .5710 oz. ASW **Subject:** First Performance - La Boheme **Obverse:** Bust of Queen Elizabeth II right **Reverse:** Head of Puccini and scene

| Date | Mintage | F | VF | XF | Unc | BU |
|---|---|---|---|---|---|---|
| 1996 Proof | Est. 15,000 | Value: 75.00 | | | | |

**50 EURO** KM# 720 **Weight:** 6.2200 g. **Composition:** 0.9999 Gold .1999 oz. AGW **Subject:** 125th Anniversary of Aida-Verdi **Obverse:** Bust of Queen Elizabeth II right

| Date | Mintage | F | VF | XF | Unc | BU |
|---|---|---|---|---|---|---|
| 1996 Proof | Est. 2,000 | Value: 165 | | | | |

**50 EURO** KM# 797 **Weight:** 6.2200 g. **Composition:** 0.9999 Gold .1999 oz. AGW **Obverse:** Bust of Queen Elizabeth II right **Reverse:** Head of Thomas Moore and harp player

| Date | Mintage | F | VF | XF | Unc | BU |
|---|---|---|---|---|---|---|
| 1997 Proof | Est. 2,000 | Value: 165 | | | | |

**50 EURO** KM# 911 **Weight:** 6.2200 g. **Composition:** 0.9999 Gold .1999 oz. AGW **Subject:** St. George **Obverse:** Bust of Queen Elizabeth II right **Reverse:** Rider spearing dragon as captive damsel watches

| Date | Mintage | F | VF | XF | Unc | BU |
|---|---|---|---|---|---|---|
| 1998 Proof | Est. 2,000 | Value: 175 | | | | |

## PIEFORTS

| KM# | Date | Mintage | Identification | Mkt Val |
|---|---|---|---|---|
| P4 | 1983 | 4,950 | Pound. Silver. KM109. | 35.00 |
| P5 | 1983 | 4,950 | Pound. Silver. KM127 | 35.00 |
| P6 | 1983 | 4,950 | Pound. Silver. KM130 | 40.00 |
| P7 | 1983 | 4,950 | Pound. Silver. KM131 | 40.00 |
| P8 | 1984 | 1,000 | Pound. 0.3740 Gold. | 125 |
| P9 | 1984 | 250 | Pound. 0.9170 Gold. | 350 |
| P10 | 1985 | 4,950 | Pound. Silver. | 40.00 |
| P11 | 1985 | 950 | Pound. 0.3740 Gold. | 125 |
| P12 | 1985 | 250 | Pound. 0.9170 Gold. | 350 |
| P13 | 1985 | 50 | Pound. Platinum. | 450 |

## WW I P.O.W. TOKEN COINAGE

Issued ca. 1914-18 at Knockaloe Internment Camp, Peel for German prisoners of war.

**6 PENCE** **KM# Tn22** **Composition:** Brass **Obverse:** PEEL **Reverse:** 6d in sprays

| Date | Mintage | F | VF | XF | Unc | BU |
|---|---|---|---|---|---|---|
| ND | — | 60.00 | 100 | — | — | — |

## WW II P.O.W TOKEN COINAGE

Issued in 1941 at Onchan Internment camp for German prisoners of war.

**1/2 PENNY** **KM# Tn23** **Composition:** Brass

| Date | Mintage | F | VF | XF | Unc | BU |
|---|---|---|---|---|---|---|
| ND | 2,000 | 17.50 | 35.00 | 75.00 | 160 | — |

**PENNY** **KM# Tn24** **Composition:** Brass

| Date | Mintage | F | VF | XF | Unc | BU |
|---|---|---|---|---|---|---|
| ND | 20,000 | 6.00 | 15.00 | 35.00 | 75.00 | — |

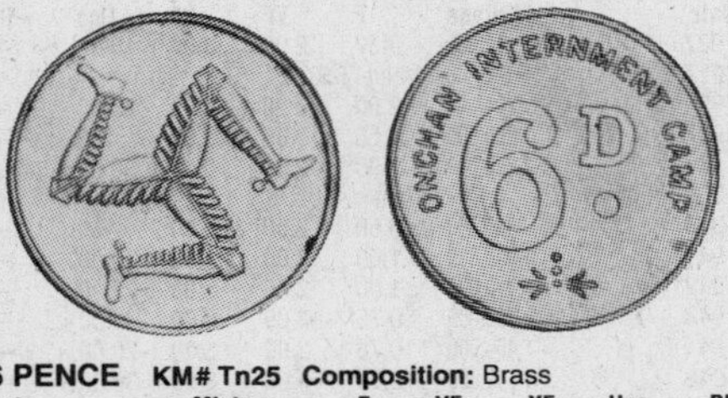

**6 PENCE** **KM# Tn25** **Composition:** Brass

| Date | Mintage | F | VF | XF | Unc | BU |
|---|---|---|---|---|---|---|
| ND | 2,500 | 12.00 | 28.00 | 60.00 | 130 | — |

## PATTERNS

Including off metal strikes

| KM# | Date | Mintage | Identification | Mkt Val |
|---|---|---|---|---|
| Pn20 | 1987 | 30 | 1/2 Crown. Silver. | 300 |
| Pn21 | 1989 | — | Crown. Copper-Nickel. Black finish, first penny postage stamp. | — |
| Pn23 | 1992 | — | 5 Pounds. Nigell Mansell, KM336. | — |

## MINT SETS

| KM# | Date | Mintage | Identification | Issue Price | Mkt Val |
|---|---|---|---|---|---|
| MS1 | 1965 (3) | 1,500 | KM15-17 | — | 700 |
| MS2 | 1971 (6) | 50,000 | KM19-24 | 3.00 | 3.00 |
| MS3 | 1973 (4) | 2,500 | KM26-29 | 760 | 820 |
| MS4 | 1974 (4) | 250 | KM26-29 | — | 975 |
| MS5 | 1975 (6) | 20,000 | KM19-24 | — | 3.00 |
| MS6 | 1975 (6) | 20,000 | KM19a-24a | 56.50 | 40.00 |
| MS7 | 1975 (4) | 200 | KM26-29 | — | 1,000 |
| MS8 | 1976 (6) | 20,000 | KM32-34, 35.1,36.2, 39 | — | 4.00 |
| MS9 | 1976 (6) | 20,000 | KM32a-34a, 35.1a-36.1a, 39a | — | 37.50 |
| MS10 | 1976 (4) | — | KM26-29 | — | 980 |
| MS11 | 1977 (6) | 50,000 | KM33-34, 35.1-36.1, 39-40 | — | 4.00 |
| MS12 | 1977 (4) | 180 | KM26-29 | — | 850 |
| MS13 | 1978 (6) | 10,000 | KM32a-34a, 35.1a-36.1a, 39a | — | 50.00 |
| MS14 | 1978 (6) | — | KM32-34, 35.1-36.1, 39 | — | 4.00 |
| MS15 | 1979 (6) | — | KM32-34, 35.1-36.1, 39 | — | 5.00 |
| MS16 | 1979 (4) | — | KM26-29 | — | 970 |
| MS17 | 1980 (6) | 30,000 | KM58-62, 70 | — | 5.00 |
| MS18 | 1981 (6) | — | KM58-62, 70 | — | 5.00 |
| MS19 | 1982 | — | | — | 6.00 |
| MS20 | 1983 (9) | — | KM58-62, 70, 88, 90, 109 | — | 27.50 |
| MS21 | 1983 (6) | — | KM58-62, 70 | — | 5.00 |
| MS22 | 1989 (9) | — | KM207-208, 209.1, 210-215 | — | 25.00 |
| MS23 | 1990 (9) | — | KM207-208, 209.1, 210-215 | 25.00 | 25.00 |
| MS24 | 1992 (9) | — | KM207-208, 209.2, 210-215 | 25.00 | 25.00 |
| MS25 | 1994 (9) | — | KM207-208, 212-213, 337, 391-392, 398-399 | 25.00 | 25.00 |
| MS26 | 1995 (9) | — | KM207-208, 212-213, 337, 391-392, 465-466 | — | — |
| MS27 | 1996 (9) | — | KM587-595 | — | 25.00 |
| MS28 | 1997 (5) | 5,000 | KM770-773, 774b | — | 785 |

## PROOF SETS

| KM# | Date | Mintage | Identification | Issue Price | Mkt Val |
|---|---|---|---|---|---|
| PS1 | 1965 (3) | 1,000 | KM15a-17a | — | 750 |
| PS2 | 1971 (6) | 10,000 | KM19-24 | 20.00 | 12.50 |
| PS3 | 1973 (4) | 1,250 | KM26-29 | 950 | 1,025 |
| PS4 | 1974 (4) | 2,500 | KM26-29 | 900 | 885 |
| PS6 | 1975 (4) | — | KM26-29 | — | 920 |
| PS5 | 1975 (6) | 600 | KM19b-24b | 1,175 | 2,200 |
| PS8 | 1976 (4) | — | KM26-29 | — | 920 |
| PS7 | 1976 (6) | 600 | KM32b-34b, 35.1b-36.1b, 39b | — | 2,200 |
| PS9 | 1977 (6) | 10,000 | KM33a-34a, 35.1a-36.1a, 39a, 40a | — | 35.00 |
| PS10 | 1977 (4) | 1,250 | KM26-29 | — | 1,025 |
| PS11 | 1978 (7) | — | KM32-36, 39, 44 | — | 15.00 |
| PS12 | 1978 (7) | 600 | KM32b-34b, 35.1b-36.1b, 39b, 44b | — | 24.00 |
| PS13 | 1979 (7) | 10,000 | KM32a-34a, 35.1a-36.1a, 39a, 44a | 110 | 50.00 |
| PS14 | 1979 (7) | 500 | KM32b-34b, 35.1b, 36.1b, 39b, 44b | 2,765 | 2,400 |
| PS15 | 1979 (4) | 1,000 | KM26-29 | — | 1,000 |
| PSA16 | 1980 (7) | — | KM44, 58-62, 70 | — | 20.00 |
| PS16 | 1980 (7) | 10,000 | KM44d, 58a-62a, 70a | — | 50.00 |
| PS17 | 1980 (7) | — | KM44c, 58c-62c, 70c | — | 170 |
| PS18 | 1980 (7) | 300 | KM44b, 58d-62d, 70d | — | 1,575 |
| PSA19 | 1981 (7) | — | KM44a, 59b-62b, 70b, 88a, | — | — |
| PS19 | 1982 (9) | 1,000 | KM44a, 58b-62b, 70a, 88a, 90a | — | 130 |
| PS20 | 1982 (9) | 250 | KM44c, 58b-62b, 88b, 90b | — | 1,050 |
| PS21 | 1982 (9) | 100 | KM44b, 58c-62c, 88c, 90c | — | 2,570 |
| PSA22 | 1982 (8) | — | KM44a, 59b-62b, 70a, 88a, 90a | — | — |
| PS22 | 1982 (7) | 25,000 | KM58-62, 70, 90 | — | 15.00 |
| PS23 | 1982 (7) | 9,000 | KM58b-62b, 70a, 90a | — | 60.00 |
| PS24 | 1982 (7) | 250 | KM58c-62c, 70c, 90b | — | 245 |
| PS25 | 1982 (7) | 400 | KM58d-62d, 70d, 90c | — | 1,720 |
| PS26 | 1983 (7) | — | KM58d-62d, 90a, 109a | — | 1,585 |
| PS27 | 1983 (7) | — | KM58b-62b, 90b, 109b | — | 290 |
| PS28 | 1983 (7) | — | KM58c-62c, 90c, 109c | — | 1,370 |
| PSA29 | 1983 (9) | — | KM59b-62b, 70b, 88a, 90a, 109a | — | — |
| PS29 | 1985 (9) | 25,000 | KM142-148, 150-151 | 36.00 | 36.00 |
| PS30 | 1985 (9) | 5,000 | KM135, 142a-148a, 150a | 120 | 120 |
| PS31 | 1985 (9) | 150 | KM135b, 142b-148b, 150b | 3,240 | 2,800 |
| PS32 | 1985 (9) | 100 | KM135c, 142c-148c, 150c | 3,600 | 3,850 |
| PS33 | 1985 (7) | 25,000 | KM142-148 | 20.00 | 20.00 |
| PS34 | 1985 (7) | 5,000 | KM142a-148a | 72.00 | 72.00 |
| PS35 | 1985 (7) | 150 | KM142b-148b | 2,160 | 1,875 |
| PS36 | 1985 (7) | 100 | KM142c-148c | 2,400 | 2,450 |
| PS37 | 1985 (6) | 51 | KM140-141, 152.1, 155-157 | — | 6,750 |
| PS38 | 1986 (7) | 17 | KM140-141, 152.1, 155-157, 166 | — | 6,700 |
| PS39 | 1986 (6) | 15 | KM153-154, 168-171 | — | 13,350 |
| PS-A40 | 1983-1986 (4) | — | KM109a, 128a, 135-136 | — | — |
| PS40 | 1986 (4) | 2,000 | KM153-154, 168-169 | 1,950 | 1,350 |
| PS41 | 1986 (5) | 2,500 | KM140-141, 152.1, 155, 166 | — | 900 |
| PS42 | 1987 (4) | — | KM176a, 177, 187-188 | — | 1,150 |
| PS43 | 1987 (6) | 30 | KM140-141, 152.2, 155-157 | — | 6,950 |
| PS44 | 1987 (5) | — | KM140-141, 152.2, 155, 166 | — | 900 |
| PS45 | 1987 (4) | 3,000 | KM140-141, 152.2, 155 | — | 850 |
| PS46 | 1987 (6) | 11 | KM153-154, 168-169, 170-171 | — | 12,575 |
| PS47 | 1987 (4) | 2,500 | KM153-154, 168-169 | — | 1,325 |
| PS48 | 1988 (5) | 611 | KM235-239 | — | 1,250 |
| PS49 | 1988 (4) | 500 | KM222-225 | — | 35.00 |
| PS50 | 1988 (4) | 7,500 | KM286-289 | — | 1,400 |
| PS51 | 1996 (5) | 500 | KM613, 615, 617, 619, 621b | — | 845 |
| PS52 | 1998 (5) | 1,000 | KM853-856, 857b | — | 815 |
| PS53 | 1999 (5) | 1,000 | KM958, 960, 962, 964, 968 | 1,300 | 835 |
| PS54 | 2000 (5) | 1,000 | KM1052-1055, 1057 | 1,300 | 1,300 |
| PS55 | 2001 (5) | 1,000 | KM#1067-1070, 1073 | — | 1,310 |

## PROOF-LIKE SETS (PL)

| KM# | Date | Mintage | Identification | Issue Price | Mkt Val |
|---|---|---|---|---|---|
| PL1 | 1980 (4) | — | KM64-67 | — | 20.00 |
| PL2 | 1981 (4) | — | KM77-80 | — | 25.00 |
| PL3 | 1982 (4) | 50,000 | KM96-99 | — | 60.00 |
| PL4 | 1984 (4) | — | KM121-124 | — | 20.00 |
| PL5 | 1986 (2) | — | KM173-174 | — | 16.00 |
| PL6 | 1989 (6) | 50,000 | KM240-243 | — | 60.00 |

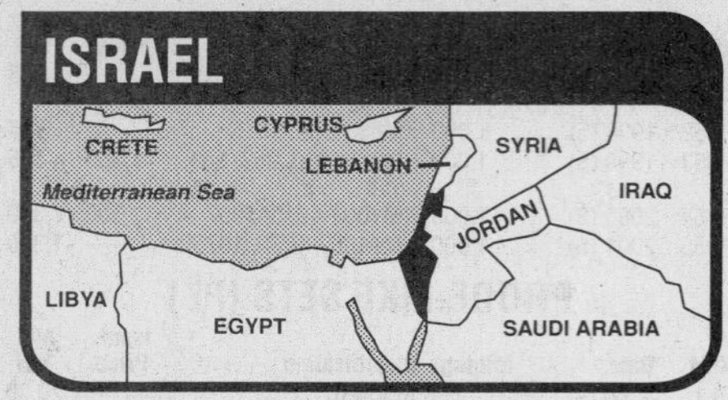


The state of Israel, a Middle Eastern republic at the eastern end of the Mediterranean Sea, bounded by Lebanon on the north, Syria on the northeast, Jordan on the east, and Egypt on the southwest, has an area of 9,000sq. mi. (20,770 sq. km.) and a population of 4.9 million. Capital: Jerusalem. Finished diamonds, chemicals, citrus, textiles, and minerals are exported.

**HEBREW COIN DATING**

Modern Israel's coins carry Hebrew dating formed from a combination of the 22 consonant letters of the Hebrew alphabet and read from right to left. The Jewish calendar dates back more than 5700 years; but five millenniums are assumed in the dating of coins (until 1981). Thus, the year 5735 (1975AD) appears as 735, with the first two characters from the right indicating the number of years in hundreds; tav (400), plus shin (300). The next is lamedh (30), followed by a separation mark which has the appearance of double quotation marks, then heh (5).

The separation mark - generally similar to a single quotation mark through 5718 (1958 AD), and like a double quotation mark thereafter - serves the purpose of indicating that the letters form a number, not a word, and on some issues can be confused with the character yodh (10), which in a stylized rendering can appear similar, although slightly larger and thicker. The separation mark does not appear in either form on a few commemorative issues.

The Jewish New Year falls in September or October by Christian calendar reckoning. Where dual dating is encountered, with but a few exceptions the Hebrew dating on the coins of modern Israel is 3760 years greater than the Christian dating; 5735 is equivalent to 1975AD, with the 5000 assumed until 1981, when full dates appear on the coins. These exceptions are most of the Hanukka coins, (Feast of Lights), the Bank of Israel gold 50 Pound commemorative of 5725 (1964AD) and others. In such special instances the differential from Christian dating is 3761 years, except in the instance of the 5720 Chanuka Pound, which is dated 1960AD, as is the issue of 5721, an arrangement reflecting the fact that the events fall early in the Jewish year and late in the Christian.

The Star of David is not a mint mark. It appears only on some coins sold by the Israel Government Coins and Medals Corporation Ltd. Which is owned by the Israel government, and is a division of the Prime Minister's office and sole distributor to collectors. The Star of David was first used in 1971 on the science coin to signify that it was minted in Jerusalem, but was later used by different mint facilities.

| | | |
|---|---|---|
| 1948 | תש"ח | (5)708 |
| 1949 | תשט | (5)709 |
| 1952 | תש"ב | (5)712 |
| 1954 | תש"ד | (5)714 |
| 1955 | תשט'ו | (5)715 |
| 1957 | תש"ד | (5)717 |
| 1958 | תש"ח | (5)718 |
| 1958 | תשי"ח | (5)718 |
| 1959 | תשיט | (5)719 |
| 1959 | תשי"ט | (5)719 |
| 1960 | תש"ך | (5)720 |
| 1960 | תשר | (5)720 |
| 1961 | תשכ"א | (5)721 |
| 1962 | תשכ"ב | (5)722 |
| 1963 | תשכ"ג | (5)723 |
| 1964 | תשכ"ד | (5)724 |
| 1965 | תשכ"ה | (5)725 |
| 1966 | תשכ"ו | (5)726 |
| 1967 | תשכ"ז | (5)727 |
| 1968 | תשכ"ח | (5)728 |
| 1969 | תשכ"ט | (5)729 |
| 1970 | תש"ל | (5)730 |
| 1971 | תשל"א | (5)731 |
| 1972 | תשל"ב | (5)732 |
| 1973 | תשל"ג | (5)733 |
| 1974 | תשל"ד | (5)734 |
| 1975 | תשל"ה | (5)735 |
| 1976 | תשל"ו | (5)736 |
| 1977 | תשל"ז | (5)737 |
| 1978 | תשל"ח | (5)738 |
| 1979 | תשל"ט | (5)739 |
| 1980 | תש"ם | (5)740 |
| 1981 | תשמ"א | (5)741 |
| 1981 | התשמ"א | 5741 |
| 1982 | התשמ"ב | 5742 |
| 1983 | התשמ"ג | 5743 |
| 1984 | התשמ"ד | 5744 |
| 1985 | התשמ"ה | 5745 |
| 1986 | התשמ"ו | 5746 |
| 1987 | התשמ"ז | 5747 |
| 1988 | התשמ"ח | 5748 |
| 1989 | התשמ"ט | 5749 |
| 1990 | התש"ן | 5750 |
| 1991 | התשנ"א | 5751 |
| 1992 | התשנ"ב | 5752 |
| 1993 | התשנ"ג | 5753 |
| 1994 | התשנ"ד | 5754 |
| 1995 | התשנ"ה | 5755 |
| 1996 | התשנ"ו | 5756 |
| 1997 | התשנ"ז | 5757 |
| 1998 | התשנ"ח | 5758 |
| 1999 | התשנ"ט | 5759 |
| 2000 | התש"ס | 5760 |
| 2001 | התשס"א | 5761 |
| 2002 | התשס"ב | 5762 |
| 2003 | התשס"ג | 5763 |
| 2004 | התשס"ד | 5764 |

**MINT MARKS**
(o) - Ottawa
(s) - San Francisco
None – Jerusalem

(M) MATTE -Normal circulation strike or a dull finish produced by sandblasting special uncirculated (polish finish) or proof quality dies.

(U) SPECIAL UNCIRCULATED - Polished or proof-like in appearance without any frosted features.

(P) PROOF - The highest quality obtainable having mirror-like fields and frosted features.

**MONETARY SYSTEM**
1000 Mils = 1 Pound

# PALESTINE

## MIL COINAGE

**MIL** KM# 1 **Composition:** Bronze

| Date | Mintage | F | VF | XF | Unc | BU |
|---|---|---|---|---|---|---|
| 1927 | 10,000 | 0.50 | 2.00 | 3.00 | 15.00 | — |
| 1927 Proof | 66 | Value: 650 | | | | |
| 1935 | 704,000 | 2.00 | 3.00 | 5.00 | 25.00 | — |
| 1937 | 1,200,000 | 1.50 | 2.00 | 10.00 | 100 | — |
| 1939 | 3,700,000 | 1.00 | 2.00 | 10.00 | 30.00 | — |
| 1939 Proof | — | Value: 400 | | | | |
| 1940 | 396,000 | 6.50 | 12.50 | 50.00 | 150 | — |
| 1941 | 1,920,000 | 1.00 | 2.00 | 5.00 | 20.00 | — |
| 1942 | 4,480,000 | 1.00 | 2.00 | 5.00 | 25.00 | — |
| 1943 | 2,800,000 | 0.75 | 2.00 | 5.00 | 35.00 | — |
| 1944 | 1,400,000 | 0.75 | 2.00 | 5.00 | 20.00 | — |
| 1946 | 1,632,000 | 2.00 | 4.00 | 8.00 | 30.00 | — |
| 1946 Proof | — | Value: 500 | | | | |
| 1947 | 2,880,000 | — | — | — | 10,000 | — |

**Note:** Only 5 known. The entire issue was to be melted down

**2 MILS** KM# 2 **Composition:** Bronze

| Date | Mintage | F | VF | XF | Unc | BU |
|---|---|---|---|---|---|---|
| 1927 | 5,000,000 | 2.00 | 3.00 | 5.00 | 30.00 | — |
| 1927 Proof | 66 | Value: 700 | | | | |
| 1941 | 1,600,000 | 1.00 | 2.00 | 6.00 | 40.00 | — |
| 1941 Proof | — | Value: 400 | | | | |
| 1942 | 2,400,000 | 1.00 | 2.50 | 10.00 | 40.00 | — |
| 1945 | 960,000 | 2.00 | 5.00 | 20.00 | 150 | — |
| 1946 | 960,000 | 4.00 | 10.00 | 30.00 | 175 | — |
| 1947 | 480,000 | — | — | — | — | — |

**Note:** The entire issue was melted down

**5 MILS** KM# 3 **Composition:** Copper-Nickel

| Date | Mintage | F | VF | XF | Unc | BU |
|---|---|---|---|---|---|---|
| 1927 | 10,000,000 | 0.75 | 2.00 | 5.00 | 30.00 | — |
| 1927 Proof | 66 | Value: 550 | | | | |
| 1934 | 500,000 | 6.50 | 12.50 | 50.00 | 175 | — |
| 1935 | 2,700,000 | 0.75 | 2.00 | 7.00 | 60.00 | — |
| 1939 | 2,000,000 | 0.75 | 2.00 | 5.00 | 30.00 | — |
| 1939 Proof | — | Value: 425 | | | | |
| 1941 | 400,000 | 10.00 | 20.00 | 35.00 | 175 | — |
| 1941 Proof | — | Value: 375 | | | | |
| 1946 | 1,000,000 | 2.00 | 4.00 | 8.00 | 30.00 | — |
| 1946 Proof | — | Value: 450 | | | | |
| 1947 | 1,000,000 | — | — | — | — | — |

**Note:** The entire issue was melted down

**5 MILS** KM# 3a **Composition:** Bronze

| Date | Mintage | F | VF | XF | Unc | BU |
|---|---|---|---|---|---|---|
| 1942 | 2,700,000 | 1.50 | 2.00 | 8.00 | 60.00 | — |
| 1944 | 1,000,000 | 2.00 | 5.00 | 10.00 | 60.00 | — |

**10 MILS** **KM# 4** **Composition:** Copper-Nickel

| Date | Mintage | F | VF | XF | Unc | BU |
|---|---|---|---|---|---|---|
| 1927 | 5,000,000 | 2.00 | 6.00 | 10.00 | 50.00 | — |
| 1927 Proof | 66 | Value: 575 | | | | |
| 1933 | 500,000 | 4.00 | 8.00 | 65.00 | 220 | — |
| 1933 Proof | — | Value: 350 | | | | |
| 1934 | 500,000 | 5.00 | 12.00 | 85.00 | 400 | — |
| 1934 Proof | — | Value: 375 | | | | |
| 1935 | 1,150,000 | 1.00 | 10.00 | 35.00 | 250 | — |
| 1935 Proof | — | Value: 425 | | | | |
| 1937 | 750,000 | 2.00 | 5.00 | 15.00 | 150 | — |
| 1937 Proof | — | Value: 425 | | | | |
| 1939 | 1,000,000 | 1.00 | 5.00 | 15.00 | 100 | — |
| 1939 Proof | — | Value: 350 | | | | |
| 1940 | 1,500,000 | 1.00 | 5.00 | 15.00 | 100 | — |
| 1940 Proof | — | Value: 350 | | | | |
| 1941 | 400,000 | 6.00 | 15.00 | 50.00 | 200 | — |
| 1941 Proof | — | Value: 350 | | | | |
| 1942 | 600,000 | 4.00 | 10.00 | 30.00 | 175 | — |
| 1946 | 1,000,000 | 2.00 | 15.00 | 25.00 | 75.00 | — |
| 1946 Proof | — | Value: 300 | | | | |
| 1947 | 1,000,000 | — | — | — | — | — |

**Note:** The entire issue was melted down

**10 MILS** **KM# 4a** **Composition:** Bronze

| Date | Mintage | F | VF | XF | Unc | BU |
|---|---|---|---|---|---|---|
| 1942 | 1,000,000 | 4.00 | 5.00 | 15.00 | 100 | — |
| 1943 | 1,000,000 | 7.00 | 10.00 | 20.00 | 125 | — |

**20 MILS** **KM# 5** **Composition:** Copper-Nickel

| Date | Mintage | F | VF | XF | Unc | BU |
|---|---|---|---|---|---|---|
| 1927 | 1,500,000 | 7.00 | 12.00 | 35.00 | 100 | — |
| 1927 Proof | 66 | Value: 800 | | | | |
| 1933 | 250,000 | 10.00 | 20.00 | 50.00 | 320 | — |
| 1934 | 125,000 | 40.00 | 70.00 | 175 | 500 | — |
| 1934 Proof | — | — | — | — | — | — |
| 1935 | 575,000 | 5.00 | 15.00 | 50.00 | 225 | — |
| 1940 | 200,000 | 10.00 | 15.00 | 50.00 | 350 | — |
| 1940 Proof | — | Value: 500 | | | | |
| 1941 | 100,000 | 50.00 | 75.00 | 150 | 700 | — |
| 1941 Proof | — | Value: 1,200 | | | | |

**20 MILS** **KM# 5a** **Composition:** Bronze

| Date | Mintage | F | VF | XF | Unc | BU |
|---|---|---|---|---|---|---|
| 1942 | 1,100,000 | 6.00 | 12.00 | 30.00 | 175 | — |
| 1944 | 1,000,000 | 20.00 | 50.00 | 80.00 | 200 | — |

**50 MILS** **KM# 6** **Weight:** 5.8319 g. **Composition:** 0.7200 Silver .1350 oz. ASW

| Date | Mintage | F | VF | XF | Unc | BU |
|---|---|---|---|---|---|---|
| 1927 | 8,000,000 | 3.50 | 10.00 | 15.00 | 110 | — |
| 1927 Proof | 66 | Value: 775 | | | | |
| 1931 | 500,000 | 12.00 | 30.00 | 75.00 | 400 | — |
| 1933 | 1,000,000 | 5.00 | 10.00 | 25.00 | 125 | — |
| 1934 | 399,000 | 10.00 | 25.00 | 50.00 | 125 | — |
| 1935 | 5,600,000 | 4.00 | 5.00 | 10.00 | 50.00 | — |
| 1939 | 3,000,000 | 4.00 | 6.00 | 12.00 | 40.00 | — |
| 1939 Proof | — | Value: 275 | | | | |
| 1940 | 2,000,000 | 5.00 | 20.00 | 30.00 | 75.00 | — |
| 1940 Proof | — | Value: 150 | | | | |
| 1942 | 5,000,000 | 4.00 | 6.00 | 12.00 | 60.00 | — |

**50 MILS** **KM# 7** **Weight:** 11.6638 g. **Composition:** 0.7200 Silver .2700 oz. ASW

| Date | Mintage | F | VF | XF | Unc | BU |
|---|---|---|---|---|---|---|
| 1927 | 2,000,000 | 5.00 | 10.00 | 25.00 | 150 | — |
| 1927 Proof | 66 | Value: 850 | | | | |
| 1931 | 250,000 | 40.00 | 75.00 | 175 | 1,000 | — |
| 1931 Proof | — | Value: 1,400 | | | | |
| 1933 | 500,000 | 15.00 | 30.00 | 100 | 500 | — |
| 1934 | 200,000 | 60.00 | 85.00 | 175 | 600 | — |
| 1935 | 2,850,000 | 5.00 | 10.00 | 20.00 | 100 | — |
| 1939 | 1,500,000 | 6.00 | 12.00 | 25.00 | 120 | — |
| 1939 Proof | — | Value: 250 | | | | |
| 1940 | 1,000,000 | 8.50 | 15.00 | 25.00 | 110 | — |
| 1942 | 2,500,000 | 8.50 | 15.00 | 25.00 | 90.00 | — |

## TOKEN COINAGE

**SOUVENIR MIL** **KM# Tn1** **Composition:** Bronze

| Date | Mintage | F | VF | XF | Unc | BU |
|---|---|---|---|---|---|---|
| 1927 | — | — | 100 | 175 | 300 | — |

**Note:** This souvenir which incorporates an appropriate reproduction of a 1927 1 Mil coin of Palestine was privately created for sale to pilgrims as a souvenir of their visit tothe Holyland. The Arabic translates to "Souvenir fo the Holy Land." It is not known who produced them nor how many were produced

# STATE OF ISRAEL

## MIL COINAGE

**25 MILS** **KM# 8** **Composition:** Aluminum

| Date | Mintage | F | VF | XF | Unc | BU |
|---|---|---|---|---|---|---|
| JE5708 (1948) | 43,000 | — | 75.00 | 200 | 850 | — |
| JE5709 (1949) open link | 650,000 | — | 25.00 | 75.00 | 150 | — |
| JE5709 (1949) closed link | — | — | 10.00 | 15.00 | 25.00 | — |

**Note:** KM#8 was released April 6, 1949

## REFORM COINAGE

1000 Prutah = 1 Lirah

NOTE: The 1949 Prutah coins, except for the 100 and 500 Prutah values, occur with and without a small pearl under the bar connecting the wreath on the reverse. Only the 50 and 100 Prutah coins were issued in 5709. All later coins were struck with frozen dates.

**PRUTA** **KM# 9** **Composition:** Aluminum **Obverse:** Anchor

| Date | Mintage | F | VF | XF | Unc | BU |
|---|---|---|---|---|---|---|
| JE5709 (1949) With pearl | 2,685,000 | — | 0.50 | 1.00 | 2.00 | — |
| JE5709 (1949) Without pearl | 2,500,000 | — | 1.00 | 2.50 | 10.00 | — |
| JE5709 (1949) Proof | 20,000 | Value: 500 | | | | |

**5 PRUTAH** **KM# 10** **Composition:** Bronze **Obverse:** 4-stringed lyre

| Date | Mintage | F | VF | XF | Unc | BU |
|---|---|---|---|---|---|---|
| JE5709 (1949) With pearl | 5,045,000 | — | 0.50 | 1.00 | 2.50 | — |
| JE5709 (1949) Proof | 25,000 | Value: 500 | | | | |
| JE5709 (1949) Without pearl | 5,000,000 | — | 0.50 | 2.00 | 10.00 | — |

**10 PRUTAH** **KM# 20** **Composition:** Aluminum **Obverse:** Ceremonial jug

| Date | Mintage | F | VF | XF | Unc | BU |
|---|---|---|---|---|---|---|
| JE5717 (1957) | 1,000,000 | — | 0.35 | 0.75 | 2.50 | — |

**10 PRUTAH** **KM# 11** **Composition:** Bronze **Obverse:** Amphora

| Date | Mintage | F | VF | XF | Unc | BU |
|---|---|---|---|---|---|---|
| JE5709 (1949) With pearl | 7,448,000 | — | 0.75 | 2.50 | 30.00 | — |
| JE5709 (1949) Proof | 20,000 | Value: 500 | | | | |
| JE5709 (1949) Without pearl | 7,500,000 | — | 0.50 | 1.00 | 4.00 | — |

**10 PRUTAH** **KM# 17** **Composition:** Aluminum **Obverse:** Ceremonial pitcher

| Date | Mintage | F | VF | XF | Unc | BU |
|---|---|---|---|---|---|---|
| JE5712 (1952) | 26,042,000 | — | 0.35 | 0.75 | 2.50 | — |

**10 PRUTAH** **KM#20a** **Composition:** Copper Electroplated Aluminum **Obverse:** Ceremonial pitcher

| Date | Mintage | F | VF | XF | Unc | BU |
|---|---|---|---|---|---|---|
| JE5717 (1957) | 1,088,000 | — | 0.35 | 0.75 | 2.50 | — |

**25 PRUTAH** **KM# 12** **Composition:** Copper-Nickel **Obverse:** Grapes

| Date | Mintage | F | VF | XF | Unc | BU |
|---|---|---|---|---|---|---|
| JE5709 (1949) With pearl | 10,520,000 | — | 0.50 | 0.75 | 2.00 | — |
| JE5709 (1949) Proof | 20,000 | Value: 500 | | | | |
| JE5709 (1949) Without pearl | 2,500,000 | — | 10.00 | 20.00 | 50.00 | — |

**25 PRUTAH** **KM# 12a** **Composition:** Nickel-Clad Steel **Obverse:** Grapes

| Date | Mintage | F | VF | XF | Unc | BU |
|---|---|---|---|---|---|---|
| JE5714 (1954) | 3,697,000 | — | 0.50 | 1.00 | 3.00 | — |

**50 PRUTAH** **KM# 13.1** **Composition:** Copper-Nickel **Obverse:** Grape leaves **Edge:** Reeded

| Date | Mintage | F | VF | XF | Unc | BU |
|---|---|---|---|---|---|---|
| JE5709 (1949) With pearl | 12,040,000 | — | 5.00 | 10.00 | 25.00 | — |
| JE5709 (1949) Proof | 20,000 | Value: 500 | | | | |
| JE5709 (1949) Without pearl | Inc. above | — | 1.00 | 2.00 | 4.50 | — |
| JE5714 (1954) | 250,000 | — | 10.00 | 17.50 | 35.00 | — |

**50 PRUTAH** **KM# 13.2** **Composition:** Copper-Nickel **Obverse:** Grape leaves **Edge:** Plain

| Date | Mintage | F | VF | XF | Unc | BU |
|---|---|---|---|---|---|---|
| JE5714 (1954) | 4,500,000 | — | 0.50 | 1.00 | 3.00 | — |

**50 PRUTAH** **KM# 13.2a** **Composition:** Nickel-Clad Steel **Obverse:** Grape leaves **Edge:** Plain

| Date | Mintage | F | VF | XF | Unc | BU |
|---|---|---|---|---|---|---|
| JE5714 (1954) | 17,774,000 | — | 0.50 | 1.00 | 3.00 | — |

**100 PRUTAH** **KM# 14** **Composition:** Copper-Nickel **Obverse:** Date palm

| Date | Mintage | F | VF | XF | Unc | BU |
|---|---|---|---|---|---|---|
| JE5709 (1949) | 6,062,000 | — | 0.75 | 1.25 | 3.50 | — |
| JE5709 (1949) Proof | 20,000 | Value: 500 | | | | |
| JE5715 (1949) | 5,868,000 | — | 1.00 | 1.50 | 4.00 | — |

**100 PRUTAH** **KM# 18** **Composition:** Nickel-Clad Steel **Obverse:** Date palm **Reverse:** Large wreath, close to edge **Size:** 25.6 mm. **Note:** Reduced size, Bern die.

| Date | Mintage | F | VF | XF | Unc | BU |
|---|---|---|---|---|---|---|
| JE5714 (1954) | 700,000 | — | 1.00 | 1.50 | 3.00 | — |

**100 PRUTAH** **KM# 19** **Composition:** Nickel-Coated Steel **Obverse:** Date palm **Reverse:** Small wreath, away from edge **Size:** 25.6 mm. **Note:** Reduced size, Utrecht die.

| Date | Mintage | F | VF | XF | Unc | BU |
|---|---|---|---|---|---|---|
| JE5714 (1954) | 20,000 | — | 300 | 450 | 1,000 | — |

**250 PRUTAH** **KM# 15** **Composition:** Copper-Nickel **Obverse:** Barley spears

| Date | Mintage | F | VF | XF | Unc | BU |
|---|---|---|---|---|---|---|
| JE5709 (1949) With pearl | 1,496,000 | — | 2.50 | 10.00 | 20.00 | — |
| JE5709 (1949) Without pearl | 524,000 | — | 1.00 | 2.00 | 5.00 | — |

**250 PRUTAH** **KM# 15a** **Weight:** 14.4000 g. **Composition:** 0.5000 Silver .2315 oz. ASW **Obverse:** Barley spears

| Date | Mintage | F | VF | XF | Unc | BU |
|---|---|---|---|---|---|---|
| JE5709 (1949) H | 44,000 | — | 4.00 | 6.50 | 11.50 | — |

**Note:** Not placed into circulation

**500 PRUTAH** **KM# 16** **Weight:** 25.5000 g. **Composition:** 0.5000 Silver .4099 oz. ASW **Obverse:** Pomegranates **Note:** Dav. #257.

| Date | Mintage | F | VF | XF | Unc | BU |
|---|---|---|---|---|---|---|
| JE5709 (1949) | 34,000 | — | 8.50 | 12.50 | 25.00 | — |

**Note:** Not placed into circulation

## REFORM COINAGE

100 Agorot = 1 Lirah

Commencing January 1, 1958-1980

**AGORAH** **KM# 24.1** **Composition:** Aluminum

| Date | Mintage | F | VF | XF | Unc | BU |
|---|---|---|---|---|---|---|
| JE5720 (1960) "Lamed" wtih serif | 12,768,000 | — | 5.00 | 10.00 | 20.00 | — |
| JE5720 (1960) "Lamed" without lower serif | Inc. above | — | 10.00 | 20.00 | 100 | — |
| JE5720 (1960) Large date | 300 | — | 150 | 300 | 750 | — |
| JE5721 (1961) | 19,262,000 | — | 0.50 | 2.00 | 5.00 | — |
| JE5721 (1961) Thick date | Inc. above | — | 5.00 | 15.00 | 100 | — |
| JE5721 (1961) Wide date | Inc. above | — | 5.00 | 15.00 | 100 | — |
| JE5722 (1962) Large date | 14,500,000 | — | 0.10 | 0.40 | 0.75 | — |
| JE5722 (1962) Small date, small serifs | Inc. above | — | 5.00 | 10.00 | 20.00 | — |
| JE5723 (1963) Coin turn | 14,804,000 | — | 0.10 | 0.40 | 0.75 | — |
| JE5723 (1963) Metal turn | 10,000 | — | 4.00 | 9.00 | 20.00 | — |
| JE5724 (1964) | 27,552,000 | — | — | — | 0.75 | — |
| JE5725 (1965) | 20,708,000 | — | — | — | 0.25 | — |
| JE5726 (1966) | 10,165,000 | — | — | — | 0.25 | — |
| JE5727 (1967) | 6,781,000 | — | — | — | 0.25 | — |
| JE5728 (1968) | 20,899,000 | — | — | — | 0.25 | — |
| JE5729 (1969) | 22,120,000 | — | — | — | 0.25 | — |
| JE5730 (1970) | 17,748,000 | — | — | — | 0.25 | — |
| JE5731 (1971) | 10,290,000 | — | — | — | 0.25 | — |
| JE5732 (1972) | 24,512,000 | — | — | — | 0.25 | — |
| JE5733 (1973) | 20,496,000 | — | — | — | 0.25 | — |
| JE5734 (1974) | 42,080,000 | — | — | — | 0.25 | — |
| JE5735 (1975) | 1,574,000 | — | — | — | 0.25 | — |
| JE5736 (1976) | 4,512,000 | — | — | — | 0.25 | — |
| JE5737 (1977) | 9,680,000 | — | — | — | 0.25 | — |
| JE5738 (1978) | 8,864,000 | — | — | — | 0.25 | — |
| JE5739 (1979) | 4,048,000 | — | — | — | 0.25 | — |
| JE5740 (1980) | 2,600,000 | — | — | — | 1.00 | — |

**AGORAH** **KM# 24.2** **Composition:** Aluminum **Obverse:** Star of David in field

| Date | Mintage | F | VF | XF | Unc | BU |
|---|---|---|---|---|---|---|
| JE5731 (1971) | 175,000 | — | — | — | 1.00 | — |
| JE5732 (1972) | 100,000 | — | — | — | 1.00 | — |
| JE5734 (1974) | 100,000 | — | — | — | 1.00 | — |
| JE5735 (1975) | 100,000 | — | — | — | 1.00 | — |
| JE5736 (1976) | 70,000 | — | — | — | 1.00 | — |
| JE5737 (1977) | 60,000 | — | — | — | 1.00 | — |
| JE5738 (1978) | 57,000 | — | — | — | 1.00 | — |
| JE5739 (1979) | 50,000 | — | — | — | 1.00 | — |

**AGORAH** **KM# 63** **Composition:** Aluminum **Subject:** 25th Anniversary of Independence **Note:** Struck for sets only

| Date | Mintage | F | VF | XF | Unc | BU |
|---|---|---|---|---|---|---|
| JE5733 (1973) | 100,000 | — | — | — | 1.00 | — |

**AGORAH** **KM# 96** **Composition:** Nickel **Subject:** 25th Anniversary - Bank of Israel **Note:** Struck for sets only

| Date | Mintage | F | VF | XF | Unc | BU |
|---|---|---|---|---|---|---|
| JE5740 (1980) | 35,000 | — | — | — | 2.00 | — |

**5 AGOROT** **KM# 25** **Composition:** Aluminum-Bronze

| Date | Mintage | F | VF | XF | Unc | BU |
|---|---|---|---|---|---|---|
| JE5720 (1960) | 8,019,000 | — | 5.00 | 10.00 | 25.00 | — |
| JE5721 (1961) Sharp, flat date | 15,090,000 | — | 0.25 | 0.50 | 1.50 | — |
| JE5721 (1961) I.C.I. issue; high date with serifs | 5,000,000 | — | 10.00 | 20.00 | 75.00 | — |
| JE5722 (1962) Large date | 11,198,000 | — | 0.25 | 0.50 | 1.00 | — |
| JE5722 (1962) Small date | Inc. above | — | 5.00 | 10.00 | 25.00 | — |
| JE5723 (1963) | 1,429,000 | — | 0.25 | 0.50 | 1.25 | — |
| JE5724 (1964) | 21,000 | — | 12.00 | 145 | 450 | — |
| JE5725 (1965) | 201,000 | — | — | 0.10 | 0.25 | — |
| JE5726 (1966) | 291,000 | — | — | 0.10 | 0.25 | — |
| JE5727 (1967) | 2,195,000 | — | — | 0.10 | 0.25 | — |
| JE5728 (1968) | 4,019,999 | — | — | 0.10 | 0.25 | — |
| JE5729 (1969) | 2,200,000 | — | — | 0.10 | 0.25 | — |
| JE5730 (1970) | 4,003,999 | — | — | 0.10 | 0.25 | — |
| JE5731 (1971) | 14,010,000 | — | — | 0.10 | 0.25 | — |
| JE5732 (1972) | 9,005,000 | — | — | 0.10 | 0.25 | — |
| JE5733 (1973) | 25,720,000 | — | — | 0.10 | 0.25 | — |
| JE5734 (1974) | 10,470,000 | — | — | 0.10 | 0.25 | — |
| JE5735 (1975) | 10,232,000 | — | — | 0.10 | 0.25 | — |
| JE5736 (1976) | — | — | — | 0.10 | 0.25 | — |
| JE5737 (1977) | — | — | — | 0.10 | 0.25 | — |

**5 AGOROT** **KM# 25a** **Composition:** Aluminum-Bronze **Obverse:** Star of David in field

| Date | Mintage | F | VF | XF | Unc | BU |
|---|---|---|---|---|---|---|
| JE5731 (1971) | 126,000 | — | — | — | 1.00 | — |
| JE5732 (1972) | 69,000 | — | — | — | 1.00 | — |

**5 AGOROT** **KM# 64** **Composition:** Copper-Nickel **Subject:** 25th Anniversary of Independence

| Date | Mintage | F | VF | XF | Unc | BU |
|---|---|---|---|---|---|---|
| JE5733 (1973) In sets only | 100,000 | — | — | — | 1.50 | — |

**5 AGOROT** **KM# 25c** **Composition:** Aluminum-Bronze **Obverse:** Star of David in field

| Date | Mintage | F | VF | XF | Unc | BU |
|---|---|---|---|---|---|---|
| JE5734 (1974) In sets only | 93,000 | — | — | — | 1.00 | — |
| JE5735 (1975) In sets only | 62,000 | — | — | — | 1.00 | — |
| JE5736 (1976) In sets only | — | — | — | — | 1.00 | — |
| JE5737 (1977) In sets only | 60,000 | — | — | — | 1.00 | — |
| JE5738 (1978) | 128 | — | — | — | 1.00 | — |
| JE5739 (1979) | 18,000 | — | — | — | 1.00 | — |

**5 AGOROT** **KM# 25b** **Composition:** Aluminum **Obverse:** Star of David in field

| Date | Mintage | F | VF | XF | Unc | BU |
|---|---|---|---|---|---|---|
| JE5736 (1976) (M) | 13,156,000 | — | — | 0.10 | 0.50 | — |
| JE5737 (1977) (M) | 16,800,000 | — | — | 0.10 | 0.50 | — |
| JE5737 (1977)(o) | 15,000,000 | — | — | 0.10 | 0.50 | — |
| JE5738 (1978) (M) | 21,480,000 | — | — | 0.10 | 0.50 | — |
| JE5738 (1978)(o) (U) | 38,760,000 | — | — | 0.10 | 0.50 | — |
| JE5739 (1979) (M) | 12,836,000 | — | — | 0.10 | 0.50 | — |

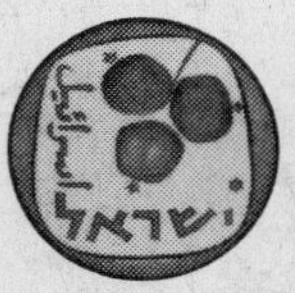

**5 AGOROT** **KM# 97** **Composition:** Nickel **Subject:** 25th Anniversary - Bank of Israel **Note:** Struck for sets only

| Date | Mintage | F | VF | XF | Unc | BU |
|---|---|---|---|---|---|---|
| JE5740 (1980) | 35,000 | — | — | — | 2.00 | — |

**10 AGOROT** **KM# 26** **Composition:** Aluminum-Bronze

| Date | Mintage | F | VF | XF | Unc | BU |
|---|---|---|---|---|---|---|
| JE5720 (1960) | 14,397,000 | — | 0.50 | 1.00 | 10.00 | — |
| JE5721 (1961) | 12,821,000 | — | 0.50 | 1.00 | 6.00 | — |
| JE5721 (1961) | Inc. above | — | 25.00 | 80.00 | 325 | — |
| **Note:** "Fatha" in Arabic, legend: "Israel" | | | | | | |
| JE5722 (1962) Large date, thick letters | 8,845,000 | — | 0.25 | 0.50 | 1.00 | — |
| JE5722 (1962) Small date, thin letters | Inc. above | — | 5.00 | 10.00 | 20.00 | — |
| JE5723 (1963) | 3,931,000 | — | 0.25 | 0.50 | 1.00 | — |
| JE5724 (1964) Large date | 3,612,000 | — | 0.25 | 0.50 | 1.00 | — |
| JE5724 (1964) Small date | Inc. above | — | 10.00 | 20.00 | 50.00 | — |
| JE5725 (1965) | 201,000 | — | — | 0.20 | 0.25 | — |
| JE5726 (1966) | 7,276,000 | — | — | 0.10 | 0.25 | — |
| JE5727 (1967) | 6,426,000 | — | — | 0.10 | 0.25 | — |
| JE5728 (1968) | 4,825,000 | — | — | 0.10 | 0.25 | — |
| JE5729 (1969) | 6,810,000 | — | — | 0.10 | 0.25 | — |
| JE5730 (1970) | 6,131,000 | — | — | 0.10 | 0.25 | — |
| JE5731 (1971) | 6,810,000 | — | — | 0.10 | 0.25 | — |
| JE5732 (1972) | 19,653,000 | — | — | 0.10 | 0.25 | — |
| JE5733 (1973) | 16,205,000 | — | — | 0.10 | 0.25 | — |
| JE5734 (1974) | 22,040,000 | — | — | 0.10 | 0.25 | — |
| JE5735 (1975) | 25,135,000 | — | — | 0.10 | 0.25 | — |
| JE5736 (1976) | 54,870,000 | — | — | 0.10 | 0.25 | — |
| JE5737 (1977) | 27,886,000 | — | — | 0.10 | 0.25 | — |

**10 AGOROT** **KM# 26a** **Composition:** Aluminum-Bronze **Obverse:** Star of David in field

| Date | Mintage | F | VF | XF | Unc | BU |
|---|---|---|---|---|---|---|
| JE5731 (1971) | 175,000 | — | — | — | 0.25 | — |
| JE5732 (1972) | 100,000 | — | — | — | 0.25 | — |

**10 AGOROT** **KM# 65** **Composition:** Copper-Nickel **Subject:** 25th Anniversary of Independence

| Date | Mintage | F | VF | XF | Unc | BU |
|---|---|---|---|---|---|---|
| JE5733 (1973) In sets only | 100,000 | — | — | — | 1.00 | — |

**10 AGOROT** **KM# 26c** **Composition:** Copper-Nickel **Obverse:** Star of David in field

| Date | Mintage | F | VF | XF | Unc | BU |
|---|---|---|---|---|---|---|
| JE5734 (1974) In sets only | 100,000 | — | — | — | 1.00 | — |
| JE5735 (1975) In sets only | 100,000 | — | — | — | 1.00 | — |
| JE5736 (1976) In sets only | 70,000 | — | — | — | 1.00 | — |
| JE5737 (1977) In sets only | 60,000 | — | — | — | 1.00 | — |
| JE5738 (1978) In sets only | 57,000 | — | — | — | 1.00 | — |
| JE5739 (1979) In sets only | — | — | — | — | 1.00 | — |

**10 AGOROT** **KM# 26b** **Composition:** Aluminum **Obverse:** Star of David in field

| Date | Mintage | F | VF | XF | Unc | BU |
|---|---|---|---|---|---|---|
| JE5737 (1977)(o) (U) | 30,100,000 | — | — | 0.10 | 0.25 | — |
| JE5738 (1978) (M) | 24,050,000 | — | — | 0.10 | 0.25 | — |
| JE5738 (1978)(o) (U) | 104,336,000 | — | — | 0.10 | 0.25 | — |
| JE5739 (1979) | 22,201,000 | — | — | 0.10 | 0.25 | — |
| JE5740 (1980) | 4,752,000 | — | — | 0.10 | 0.25 | — |

**Note:** Most of the 5740 dated coins were melted down before being issued

**10 AGOROT** **KM# 98** **Composition:** Nickel **Subject:** 25th Anniversary - Bank of Israel **Note:** Struck for sets only.

| Date | Mintage | F | VF | XF | Unc | BU |
|---|---|---|---|---|---|---|
| JE5740 (1980) | 35,000 | — | — | — | 2.00 | — |

**25 AGOROT** **KM# 27** **Composition:** Aluminum-Bronze

| Date | Mintage | F | VF | XF | Unc | BU |
|---|---|---|---|---|---|---|
| JE5720 (1960) | 4,391,000 | — | 0.25 | 0.50 | 3.00 | — |
| JE5721 (1961) | 5,009,000 | — | 0.10 | 0.20 | 1.00 | — |
| JE5722 (1962) | 882,000 | — | 0.15 | 0.30 | 1.00 | — |
| JE5723 (1963) | 194,000 | — | 0.50 | 1.00 | 5.00 | — |
| JE5724 (1964) Five trial pieces only | — | — | — | — | — | — |
| JE5725 (1965) | 187,000 | — | 0.10 | 0.20 | 0.50 | — |
| JE5726 (1966) | 320,000 | — | — | 0.10 | 0.40 | — |
| JE5727 (1967) | 325,000 | — | — | 0.10 | 0.40 | — |
| JE5728 (1968) | 445,000 | — | — | 0.10 | 0.40 | — |
| JE5729 (1969) | 432,000 | — | — | 0.10 | 0.40 | — |
| JE5730 (1970) | 417,000 | — | — | 0.10 | 0.40 | — |
| JE5731 (1971) | 500,000 | — | — | 0.10 | 0.40 | — |
| JE5732 (1972) | 1,883,000 | — | — | 0.10 | 0.40 | — |
| JE5733 (1973) | 3,370,000 | — | — | 0.10 | 0.40 | — |
| JE5734 (1974) | 2,320,000 | — | — | 0.10 | 0.40 | — |
| JE5735 (1975) | 3,968,000 | — | — | 0.10 | 0.40 | — |
| JE5736 (1976) | 3,901,000 | — | — | 0.10 | 0.40 | — |
| JE5737 (1977) | 1,832,000 | — | — | 0.10 | 0.40 | — |
| JE5738 (1978) | 12,200,000 | — | — | 0.10 | 0.40 | — |
| JE5739 (1979) | 10,842,000 | — | — | 0.10 | 0.40 | — |

**25 AGOROT** **KM# 27a** **Composition:** Aluminum-Bronze **Obverse:** Star of David in field

| Date | Mintage | F | VF | XF | Unc | BU |
|---|---|---|---|---|---|---|
| JE5731 (1971) | 126,000 | — | — | — | 0.40 | — |
| JE5732 (1972) | 69,000 | — | — | — | 0.40 | — |

**25 AGOROT** **KM# 66** **Composition:** Copper-Nickel **Subject:** 25th Anniversary of Independence **Note:** Struck for sets only.

| Date | Mintage | F | VF | XF | Unc | BU |
|---|---|---|---|---|---|---|
| JE5733 (1973) | 100,000 | — | — | — | 1.50 | — |

**25 AGOROT** **KM# 27b** **Composition:** Copper-Nickel **Obverse:** Star of David in field **Note:** Struck for sets only.

| Date | Mintage | F | VF | XF | Unc | BU |
|---|---|---|---|---|---|---|
| JE5734 (1974) | 93,000 | — | — | — | 1.00 | — |
| JE5735 (1975) | 62,000 | — | — | — | 1.00 | — |
| JE5736 (1976) | — | — | — | — | 1.00 | — |
| JE5737 (1977) | 60,000 | — | — | — | 1.00 | — |
| JE5738 (1978) | 57,000 | — | — | — | 1.00 | — |
| JE5739 (1979) | 32,000 | — | — | — | 1.00 | — |

**25 AGOROT** **KM# 99** **Composition:** Nickel **Subject:** 25th Anniversary - Bank of Israel **Note:** Struck for sets only.

| Date | Mintage | F | VF | XF | Unc | BU |
|---|---|---|---|---|---|---|
| JE5740 (1980) | 35,000 | — | — | — | 2.00 | — |

**1/2 LIRAH** **KM# 36.1** **Composition:** Copper-Nickel

| Date | Mintage | F | VF | XF | Unc | BU |
|---|---|---|---|---|---|---|
| JE5723 (1963) Large animals | 5,607,000 | — | 0.50 | 2.00 | 5.00 | — |
| JE5723 (1963) Small animals | Inc. above | — | 3.00 | 15.00 | 30.00 | — |
| JE5724 (1964) | 3,762,000 | — | 0.10 | 0.75 | 2.00 | — |
| JE5725 (1965) | 1,551,000 | — | 0.10 | 0.15 | 1.00 | — |
| JE5726 (1966) | 2,139,000 | — | 0.10 | 0.15 | 0.50 | — |
| JE5727 (1967) | 1,942,000 | — | 0.10 | 0.15 | 0.50 | — |
| JE5728 (1968) | 1,183,000 | — | 0.10 | 0.15 | 0.50 | — |
| JE5729 (1969) | 450,000 | — | 0.10 | 0.20 | 0.60 | — |
| JE5730 (1970) | 1,000,999 | — | 0.10 | 0.20 | 0.60 | — |
| JE5731 (1971) | 500,000 | — | 0.10 | 0.20 | 0.60 | — |
| JE5732 (1972) | 421,000 | — | 0.10 | 0.20 | 0.60 | — |
| JE5733 (1973) | 3,225,000 | — | 0.10 | 0.15 | 0.50 | — |
| JE5734 (1974) | 4,275,000 | — | 0.10 | 0.15 | 0.50 | — |
| JE5735 (1975) | 11,066,000 | — | 0.10 | 0.15 | 0.50 | — |
| JE5736 (1976) | 4,959,000 | — | 0.10 | 0.15 | 0.50 | — |
| JE5737 (1977) | 4,983,000 | — | 0.10 | 0.15 | 0.50 | — |
| JE5738 (1978) | 14,325,000 | — | 0.10 | 0.15 | 0.50 | — |
| JE5739 (1979) | 21,391,000 | — | 0.10 | 0.15 | 0.50 | — |

**1/2 LIRAH** **KM# 36.2** **Composition:** Copper-Nickel **Obverse:** Star of David in field **Note:** Stuck for sets only.

| Date | Mintage | F | VF | XF | Unc | BU |
|---|---|---|---|---|---|---|
| JE5731 (1971) | 175,000 | — | — | — | 1.00 | — |
| JE5732 (1972) | 100,000 | — | — | — | 1.00 | — |
| JE5734 (1974) | 100,000 | — | — | — | 1.00 | — |
| JE5735(1975) | 100,000 | — | — | — | 1.00 | — |
| JE5736 (1976) | 70,000 | — | — | — | 1.00 | — |
| JE5737 (1977) | 60,000 | — | — | — | 1.00 | — |
| JE5738 (1978) | 57,000 | — | — | — | 1.00 | — |
| JE5739 (1979) | 50,000 | — | — | — | 1.00 | — |

**1/2 LIRAH** **KM# 67** **Composition:** Copper-Nickel **Subject:** 25th Anniversary of Independence **Note:** Struck for sets only.

| Date | Mintage | F | VF | XF | Unc | BU |
|---|---|---|---|---|---|---|
| JE5733 (1973) | 100,000 | — | — | — | 1.50 | — |

**1/2 LIRAH** **KM# 100** **Composition:** Nickel **Subject:** 25th Anniversary - Bank of Israel **Note:** Struck for sets only.

| Date | Mintage | F | VF | XF | Unc | BU |
|---|---|---|---|---|---|---|
| JE5740 (1980) | 35,000 | — | — | — | 3.00 | — |

**LIRAH** **KM# 101** **Composition:** Nickel **Subject:** 25th Anniversary - Bank of Israel **Note:** Struck for sets only.

| Date | Mintage | F | VF | XF | Unc | BU |
|---|---|---|---|---|---|---|
| JE5740 (1980) | 35,000 | — | — | — | 4.00 | — |

**LIRAH** **KM# 22** **Composition:** Copper-Nickel **Subject:** Hanukkah - Law Is Light

| Date | Mintage | F | VF | XF | Unc | BU |
|---|---|---|---|---|---|---|
| JE5719-1958 Proof | 5,000 | Value: 28.00 | | | | |
| JE5719 1958 | 150,000 | — | — | — | 2.00 | — |
| JE5719 1958 | 5,000 | Value: 28.00 | | | | |

**LIRAH** **KM# 37** **Composition:** Copper-Nickel

| Date | Mintage | F | VF | XF | Unc | BU |
|---|---|---|---|---|---|---|
| JE5723 (1963) Large animals | 4,212,000 | — | 0.50 | 1.50 | 3.00 | — |
| JE5723 (1963) Large animals | 4,212,000 | — | 0.50 | 1.50 | 3.00 | — |
| JE5723 (1963) Small animals | Inc. above | — | 1.00 | 10.00 | 20.00 | — |
| JE5724 (1964) Only ten trial pieces struck | — | — | — | — | — | — |
| JE5725 (1965) | 166,000 | — | 0.25 | 0.50 | 1.25 | — |
| JE5725 (1965) | 166,000 | — | 0.25 | 0.50 | 1.25 | — |
| JE5726 (1966) | 290,000 | — | 0.25 | 0.50 | 1.25 | — |
| JE5726 (1966) | 290,000 | — | 0.25 | 0.50 | 1.25 | — |
| JE5727 (1967) | 180,000 | — | 0.25 | 0.50 | 1.25 | — |
| JE5727 (19697) | 180,000 | — | 0.25 | 0.50 | 1.25 | — |

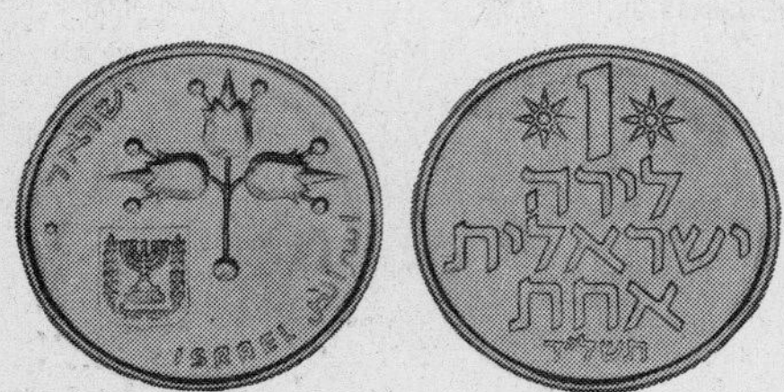


**LIRAH** **KM# 47.1** **Composition:** Copper-Nickel

| Date | Mintage | F | VF | XF | Unc | BU |
|---|---|---|---|---|---|---|
| JE5727 (1967) | 3,830,000 | — | 0.10 | 0.25 | 1.00 | — |
| JE5728 (1968) | 3,932,000 | — | 0.10 | 0.25 | 1.00 | — |
| JE5729 (1969) | 12,484,000 | — | 0.10 | 0.25 | 0.75 | — |
| JE5730 (1970) | 4,794,000 | — | 0.10 | 0.25 | 0.75 | — |
| JE5731 (1971) | 2,993,000 | — | 0.10 | 0.25 | 0.75 | — |
| JE5732 (1972) | 2,489,000 | — | 0.10 | 0.25 | 0.75 | — |
| JE5733 (1973) | 10,265,000 | — | 0.10 | 0.25 | 0.75 | — |
| JE5734 (1974) | 6,287,000 | — | 0.10 | 0.25 | 0.75 | — |
| JE5735 (1975) | 13,225,000 | — | 0.10 | 0.25 | 0.75 | — |
| JE5736 (1976) | 4,268,000 | — | 0.10 | 0.25 | 0.75 | — |
| JE5737 (1977) | 11,129,000 | — | 0.10 | 0.25 | 0.75 | — |
| JE5738 (1978) | 61,752,000 | — | 0.10 | 0.25 | 0.75 | — |
| JE5739 (1979) | 34,815,000 | — | 0.10 | 0.25 | 0.75 | — |
| JE5740 (1980) | 10,840,000 | — | 0.10 | 0.25 | 0.75 | — |

**Note:** Most of the 5740 dated coins were melted down before being issued

**LIRAH** **KM# 47.2** **Composition:** Copper-Nickel **Obverse:** Star of David in field **Note:** Struck for sets only.

| Date | Mintage | F | VF | XF | Unc | BU |
|---|---|---|---|---|---|---|
| JE5731 (1971) | 126,000 | — | — | — | 1.50 | — |
| JE5732 (1972) | 69,000 | — | — | — | 1.50 | — |
| JE5734 (1974) | 93,000 | — | — | — | 1.50 | — |
| JE5735 (1975) | 62,000 | — | — | — | 1.50 | — |
| JE5736 (1976) | — | — | — | — | 1.50 | — |
| JE5737 (1977) | Inc. above | — | — | — | 1.50 | — |
| JE5738 (1978) | Inc. above | — | — | — | 1.50 | — |
| JE5739 (1979) | — | — | — | — | 1.50 | — |

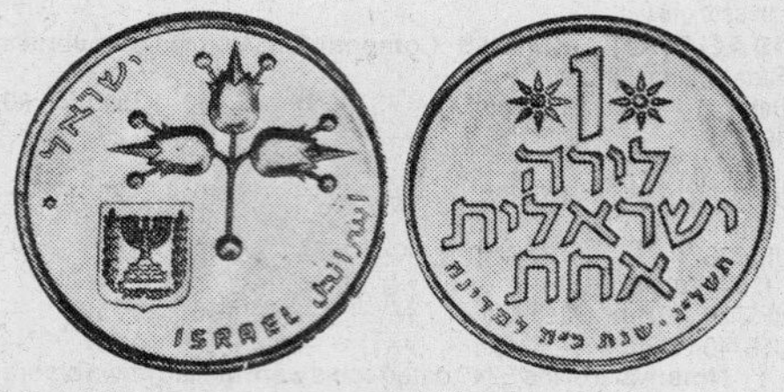


**LIRAH** **KM# 68** **Composition:** Copper-Nickel **Subject:** 25th Anniversary of Independence **Note:** Struck for sets only.

| Date | Mintage | F | VF | XF | Unc | BU |
|---|---|---|---|---|---|---|
| JE5733 (1973) | 100,000 | — | — | — | 2.00 | — |

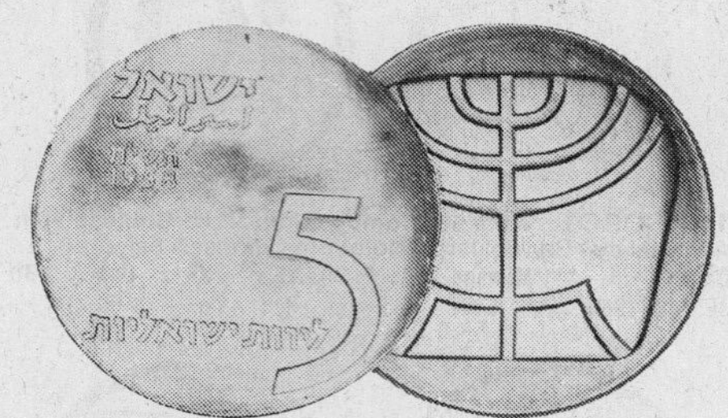

**5 LIROT** **KM# 21** **Weight:** 25.0000 g. **Composition:** 0.9000 Silver .7234 oz. ASW **Subject:** 10th Anniversary of Independence **Reverse:** Menorah **Note:** Dav. #258

| Date | Mintage | F | VF | XF | Unc | BU |
|---|---|---|---|---|---|---|
| JE5718-1958 | 98,000 | — | — | — | 10.00 | 15.00 |
| JE5718-1958 Frosted Proof | 2,000 | Value: 275 | | | | |

**5 LIROT** **KM# 23** **Composition:** Copper-Nickel **Subject:** 11th Anniversary of Independence **Reverse:** Ingathering of exiles **Note:** Dav. #259.

| Date | Mintage | F | VF | XF | Unc | BU |
|---|---|---|---|---|---|---|
| JE5719-1959 | 27,000 | — | — | — | 15.00 | 17.50 |
| JE5719-1959 Proof | 4,682 | Value: 35.00 | | | | |

**5 LIROT** **KM# 90** **Composition:** Copper-Nickel

| Date | Mintage | F | VF | XF | Unc | BU |
|---|---|---|---|---|---|---|
| JE5738 (1978) | 8,350,000 | — | 0.35 | 0.70 | 3.00 | — |
| JE5739 (1979) | 37,646,000 | — | 0.35 | 0.60 | 2.00 | — |

**5 LIROT** **KM# 90a** **Composition:** Copper-Nickel **Obverse:** Star of David in field **Note:** Struck for sets only.

| Date | Mintage | F | VF | XF | Unc | BU |
|---|---|---|---|---|---|---|
| JE5739 (1979) | — | — | — | — | 2.00 | — |

**5 LIROT** **KM# 102** **Composition:** Nickel **Subject:** 25th Anniversary - Bank of Israel **Note:** Struck for sets only.

| Date | Mintage | F | VF | XF | Unc | BU |
|---|---|---|---|---|---|---|
| JE5740 (1980) | 35,000 | — | — | — | 6.00 | — |

## COMMEMORATIVE COINAGE

NOTE: All proof commemoratives with the exception of the 1 and 5 Lirot issues of 1958 and the gold 100 Lirot Jerusalem 1968 issues are distinguished from the uncirculated editions by the presence of the Hebrew letter "mem".

**1/2 LIRAH** **KM# 31** **Composition:** Copper-Nickel **Subject:** Feast of Purim

| Date | Mintage | F | VF | XF | Unc | BU |
|---|---|---|---|---|---|---|
| JE5721 (1961) | 20,000 | — | — | — | 6.00 | — |
| JE5721 (1961) Proof | 4,901 | Value: 18.50 | | | | |
| JE5722 (1962) | 20,000 | — | — | — | 5.00 | — |
| JE5722 (1962) Proof | 9,894 | Value: 11.50 | | | | |

**LIRAH** **KM# 28** **Composition:** Copper-Nickel **Subject:** Hanukkah - 50th Anniversary of Deganya

| Date | Mintage | F | VF | XF | Unc | BU |
|---|---|---|---|---|---|---|
| JE5720-1960 | 49,000 | — | — | — | 6.00 | — |
| JE5720-1960 | 49,000 | — | — | — | 6.00 | — |
| JE5720-1960 Proof | 4,702 | Value: 20.00 | | | | |

**LIRAH KM# 32 Composition:** Copper-Nickel **Subject:** Hanukkah **Reverse:** Henrietta Szold

| Date | Mintage | F | VF | XF | Unc | BU |
|---|---|---|---|---|---|---|
| JE5720-1960 | 17,000 | — | — | — | 17.50 | — |
| JE5720-1960 Proof | 3,000 | Value: 90.00 | | | | |

**LIRAH KM# 34 Composition:** Copper-Nickel **Subject:** Hanukkah **Reverse:** Death of a Hasmonean Hero

| Date | Mintage | F | VF | XF | Unc | BU |
|---|---|---|---|---|---|---|
| JE5721 | 19,000 | — | — | — | 9.00 | — |
| JE5721 Proof | 9,324 | Value: 12.50 | | | | |

**LIRAH KM# 38 Composition:** Copper-Nickel **Subject:** Hanukkah **Reverse:** Italian lamp

| Date | Mintage | F | VF | XF | Unc | BU |
|---|---|---|---|---|---|---|
| JE5722-1962 | 9,560 | — | — | — | 15.00 | — |
| JE5722-1962 Proof | 5,941 | Value: 25.00 | | | | |

**LIRAH KM# 42 Composition:** Copper-Nickel **Subject:** Hanukkah **Reverse:** 18th Century North African lamp

| Date | Mintage | F | VF | XF | Unc | BU |
|---|---|---|---|---|---|---|
| JE5723-1963 | 9,928 | — | — | — | 12.50 | — |
| JE5723-1963 Proof | 5,412 | Value: 25.00 | | | | |

**5 LIROT KM# 29 Weight:** 25.0000 g. **Composition:** 0.9000 Silver .7234 oz. ASW **Subject:** 12th Anniversary of Independence **Reverse:** Dr. Theodor Herzl **Note:** Dav. #29.

| Date | Mintage | F | VF | XF | Unc | BU |
|---|---|---|---|---|---|---|
| JE5720-1960 | 34,000 | — | — | — | 14.00 | — |
| JE5720-1960 Proof | 4,827 | Value: 35.00 | | | | |

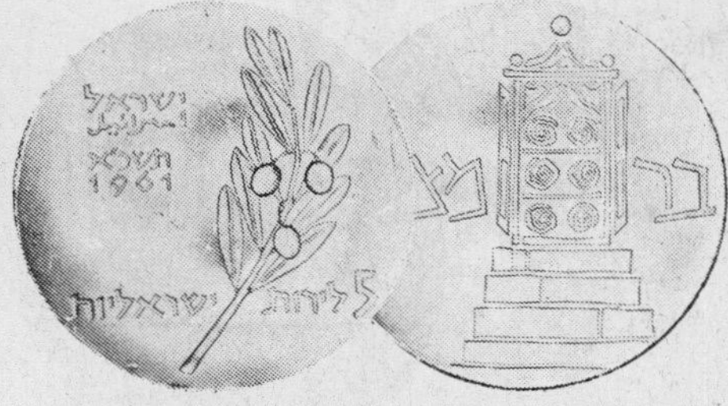

**5 LIROT KM# 33 Weight:** 25.0000 g. **Composition:** 0.9000 Silver .7234 oz. ASW **Subject:** 13th Anniversary of Independence **Reverse:** Bar Mitzvah **Note:** Dav. #261

| Date | Mintage | F | VF | XF | Unc | BU |
|---|---|---|---|---|---|---|
| JE5721-1961 | 19,000 | — | — | — | 32.50 | — |
| JE5721-1961 Proof | 4,455 | Value: 55.00 | | | | |

**5 LIROT KM# 35 Weight:** 25.0000 g. **Composition:** 0.9000 Silver .7234 oz. ASW **Subject:** 14th Anniversary of Independence **Reverse:** Negev Industrialization **Note:** Dav. #262,

| Date | Mintage | F | VF | XF | Unc | BU |
|---|---|---|---|---|---|---|
| JE5722-1962 | 10,000 | — | — | — | 27.50 | — |
| JE5722-1962 Proof | 4,960 | Value: 45.00 | | | | |

**5 LIROT KM# 39 Weight:** 25.0000 g. **Composition:** 0.9000 Silver .7234 oz. ASW **Subject:** 15th Anniversary of Independence **Reverse:** Seafaring **Note:** Dav. #263.

| Date | Mintage | F | VF | XF | Unc | BU |
|---|---|---|---|---|---|---|
| JE5723-1963 | 5,960 | — | — | — | 185 | — |
| JE5723-1963 Proof | 4,495 | Value: 220 | | | | |

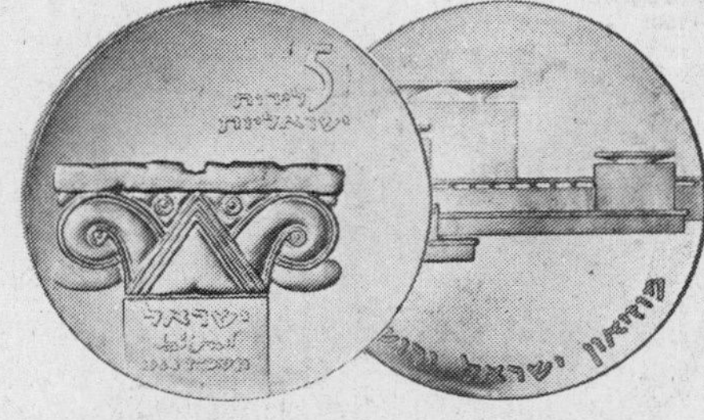

**5 LIROT KM# 43 Weight:** 25.0000 g. **Composition:** 0.9000 Silver .7234 oz. ASW **Subject:** 16th Anniversary of Independence **Reverse:** Israel Museum **Note:** Dav. #264.

| Date | Mintage | F | VF | XF | Unc | BU |
|---|---|---|---|---|---|---|
| JE5724-1964 | 11,000 | — | — | — | 25.00 | — |
| JE5724-1964 Proof | 4,421 | Value: 45.00 | | | | |

**5 LIROT KM# 45 Weight:** 25.0000 g. **Composition:** 0.9000 Silver .7234 oz. ASW **Subject:** 17th Anniversary of Independence **Reverse:** Knesset Building **Note:** Dav. #265.

| Date | Mintage | F | VF | XF | Unc | BU |
|---|---|---|---|---|---|---|
| JE5725-1965 | 25,000 | — | — | — | 14.00 | — |
| JE5725-1965 Proof | 7,537 | Value: 18.00 | | | | |

**5 LIROT KM# 46 Weight:** 25.0000 g. **Composition:** 0.9000 Silver .7234 oz. ASW **Subject:** 18th Anniversary of Independence **Reverse:** Israel lives on **Note:** Dav. #266.

| Date | Mintage | F | VF | XF | Unc | BU |
|---|---|---|---|---|---|---|
| JE5726-1966 | 32,000 | — | — | — | 9.00 | — |
| JE5726-1966 Proof | 10,000 | Value: 12.00 | | | | |

**5 LIROT KM# 48 Weight:** 25.0000 g. **Composition:** 0.9000 Silver .7234 oz. ASW **Subject:** 19th Anniversary of Independence **Reverse:** Port of Eilat **Note:** Dav. #267.

| Date | Mintage | F | VF | XF | Unc | BU |
|---|---|---|---|---|---|---|
| JE5727-1967 | 30,000 | — | — | — | 10.00 | — |
| JE5727-1967 Proof | 7,680 | Value: 17.50 | | | | |

**5 LIROT KM# 69.1 Weight:** 20.0000 g. **Composition:** 0.7500 Silver .4823 oz. ASW **Subject:** Hanukkah **Reverse:** Russian Lamp

| Date | Mintage | F | VF | XF | Unc | BU |
|---|---|---|---|---|---|---|
| JE5733-1972 | 75,000 | — | — | — | 5.50 | — |

**5 LIROT KM# 69.2 Weight:** 20.0000 g. **Composition:** 0.7500 Silver .4823 oz. ASW **Subject:** Hanukkah **Reverse:** Russian Lamp **Edge:** Reeded

| Date | Mintage | F | VF | XF | Unc | BU |
|---|---|---|---|---|---|---|
| JE5733-1972 Proof | 22,000 | Value: 7.50 | | | | |

**5 LIROT** KM# 75.1 **Weight:** 20.0000 g. **Composition:** 0.5000 Silver .3215 oz. ASW **Subject:** Hanukkah **Reverse:** Babylonian lamp **Edge:** Plain

| Date | Mintage | F | VF | XF | Unc | BU |
|---|---|---|---|---|---|---|
| JE5734-1973 | 95,000 | — | — | — | 5.50 | — |

**5 LIROT** KM# 75.2 **Weight:** 20.0000 g. **Composition:** 0.5000 Silver .3215 oz. ASW **Subject:** Hanukkah **Reverse:** Babylonian lamp **Edge:** Reeded

| Date | Mintage | F | VF | XF | Unc | BU |
|---|---|---|---|---|---|---|
| JE5734-1973 Proof | 45,000 | Value: 7.50 | | | | |

**10 LIROT** KM# 49 **Weight:** 26.0000 g. **Composition:** 0.9000 Silver .7524 oz. ASW **Subject:** Victory Commemorative **Note:** Dav. #268

| Date | Mintage | F | VF | XF | Unc | BU |
|---|---|---|---|---|---|---|
| JE5727-1967 | 234,000 | — | — | — | 10.00 | — |

**10 LIROT** KM# 49a **Weight:** 26.0000 g. **Composition:** 0.9350 Silver .7816 oz. ASW **Subject:** Victory Commemorative **Note:** Dav. #268

| Date | Mintage | F | VF | XF | Unc | BU |
|---|---|---|---|---|---|---|
| JE5727-1967 Proof | 50,000 | Value: 12.00 | | | | |

**10 LIROT** KM# 51 **Weight:** 26.0000 g. **Composition:** 0.9000 Silver .7524 oz. ASW **Subject:** 20th Anniversary of Independence **Reverse:** Jerusalem Reunification **Note:** Dav. #269.

| Date | Mintage | F | VF | XF | Unc | BU |
|---|---|---|---|---|---|---|
| JE5728-1968 | 50,000 | — | — | — | 10.00 | — |
| JE5728-1968(1968) Proof | 20,000 | Value: 12.00 | | | | |

**10 LIROT** KM# 53.1 **Weight:** 26.0000 g. **Composition:** 0.9000 Silver .7524 oz. ASW **Subject:** 21st Anniversary of Independence **Reverse:** Shalom **Note:** Struck at the U.S. Mint(s).

| Date | Mintage | F | VF | XF | Unc | BU |
|---|---|---|---|---|---|---|
| JE5729-1969 | 40,000 | — | — | — | 10.00 | — |

**10 LIROT** KM# 53.2 **Weight:** 26.0000 g. **Composition:** 0.9000 Silver .7524 oz. ASW **Subject:** 21st Anniversary of Independence **Reverse:** K A F to right of helmet

| Date | Mintage | F | VF | XF | Unc | BU |
|---|---|---|---|---|---|---|
| JE5729-1969 | 20,000 | — | — | — | 12.00 | — |
| **Note:** Jerusalem Mint | | | | | | |
| JE5729-1969 Proof | 20,000 | Value: 11.00 | | | | |
| **Note:** U.S. Mint(s) | | | | | | |

**10 LIROT** KM# 56.2 **Weight:** 26.0000 g. **Composition:** 0.9000 Silver .7524 oz. ASW **Subject:** Pidyon Haben **Edge:** Reeded **Note:** Struck at the San Francisco Mint.

| Date | Mintage | F | VF | XF | Unc | BU |
|---|---|---|---|---|---|---|
| JE5730-1970 Proof | 15,000 | Value: 12.00 | | | | |

**10 LIROT** KM# 55 **Weight:** 26.0000 g. **Composition:** 0.9000 Silver .7524 oz. ASW **Subject:** 22nd Anniversary of Independence **Reverse:** Mikveh Israel Centenary

| Date | Mintage | F | VF | XF | Unc | BU |
|---|---|---|---|---|---|---|
| JE5730-1970 | 48,000 | — | — | — | 9.00 | — |
| JE5730-1970(1970) Proof | 22,000 | Value: 12.00 | | | | |

**10 LIROT** KM# 56.1 **Weight:** 26.0000 g. **Composition:** 0.9000 Silver .7524 oz. ASW **Subject:** Pidyon Haben **Edge:** Plain

| Date | Mintage | F | VF | XF | Unc | BU |
|---|---|---|---|---|---|---|
| JE5730-1970 | 49,000 | — | — | — | 10.00 | — |

**10 LIROT** KM# 59.2 **Weight:** 26.0000 g. **Composition:** 0.9000 Silver .7524 oz. ASW **Obverse:** Legend away from rim, open "Mem" **Note:** Berne die.

| Date | Mintage | F | VF | XF | Unc | BU |
|---|---|---|---|---|---|---|
| JE5731-1971 Proof | 80 | Value: 650 | | | | |

**10 LIROT** KM# 57.1 **Weight:** 26.0000 g. **Composition:** 0.9000 Silver .7524 oz. ASW **Subject:** Pidyon Haben **Edge:** Plain

| Date | Mintage | F | VF | XF | Unc | BU |
|---|---|---|---|---|---|---|
| JE5731-1971 | 30,000 | — | — | — | 10.00 | — |

**10 LIROT** KM# 57.2 **Weight:** 26.0000 g. **Composition:** 0.9000 Silver .7524 oz. ASW **Subject:** Pidyon Haben **Edge:** Reeded

| Date | Mintage | F | VF | XF | Unc | BU |
|---|---|---|---|---|---|---|
| JE5731-1971 Proof | 14,000 | Value: 12.00 | | | | |

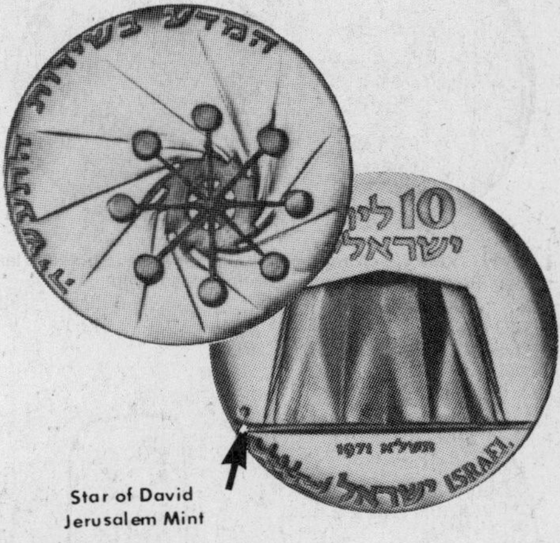

Star of David
Jerusalem Mint

**10 LIROT** KM# 58 **Weight:** 26.0000 g. **Composition:** 0.9000 Silver .7524 oz. ASW **Subject:** 23rd Anniversary of Independence **Reverse:** Science and Industry

| Date | Mintage | F | VF | XF | Unc | BU |
|---|---|---|---|---|---|---|
| JE5731-1971 | 30,000 | — | — | — | 10.00 | — |
| **Note:** Struck at the Utrecht Mint | | | | | | |
| JE5731-1971 Star | 23,000 | — | — | — | 10.00 | — |

| Date | Mintage | F | VF | XF | Unc | BU |
|---|---|---|---|---|---|---|
| **Note:** Struck at the Jerusalem Mint | | | | | | |
| JE5731-1971 Proof | 18,000 | Value: 12.00 | | | | |

**10 LIROT** **KM# 59.1** **Weight:** 26.0000 g. **Composition:** 0.9000 Silver .7524 oz. ASW **Subject:** Let My People Go **Obverse:** Legend on rim, closed "Mem"

| Date | Mintage | F | VF | XF | Unc | BU |
|---|---|---|---|---|---|---|
| JE5731-1971 | 73,000 | — | — | — | 10.00 | — |
| JE5731-1971(1971) Proof | 20,000 | Value: 12.00 | | | | |

**10 LIROT** **KM# 61.1** **Weight:** 26.0000 g. **Composition:** 0.9000 Silver .7524 oz. ASW **Subject:** Pidyon Haben **Edge:** Plain

| Date | Mintage | F | VF | XF | Unc | BU |
|---|---|---|---|---|---|---|
| JE5732-1972 With star | 30,000 | — | — | — | 10.00 | — |
| JE5732-1972(1972) Without star | 15,000 | — | — | — | 12.00 | — |

**10 LIROT** **KM# 61.2** **Weight:** 26.0000 g. **Composition:** 0.9000 Silver .7524 oz. ASW **Subject:** Pidyon Haben **Edge:** Reeded

| Date | Mintage | F | VF | XF | Unc | BU |
|---|---|---|---|---|---|---|
| JE5732-1972 Proof | 12,000 | Value: 12.00 | | | | |

**10 LIROT** **KM# 62** **Weight:** 26.0000 g. **Composition:** 0.9000 Silver .7524 oz. ASW **Subject:** 24th Anniversary of Independence **Reverse:** Aviation **Edge:** Lettered

| Date | Mintage | F | VF | XF | Unc | BU |
|---|---|---|---|---|---|---|
| JE5732-1972 | 50,000 | — | — | — | 10.00 | — |
| JE5732-1972(1972) Proof | 15,000 | Value: 12.50 | | | | |

**10 LIROT** **KM# 70.1** **Weight:** 26.0000 g. **Composition:** 0.9000 Silver .7524 oz. ASW **Subject:** Pidyon Haben **Edge:** Plain

| Date | Mintage | F | VF | XF | Unc | BU |
|---|---|---|---|---|---|---|
| JE5733-1973 | 101,000 | — | — | — | 10.00 | — |

**10 LIROT** **KM# 70.2** **Weight:** 26.0000 g. **Composition:** 0.9000 Silver .7524 oz. ASW **Subject:** Pidyon Haben **Edge:** Reeded

| Date | Mintage | F | VF | XF | Unc | BU |
|---|---|---|---|---|---|---|
| JE5733-1973 Proof | 15,000 | Value: 12.00 | | | | |

**10 LIROT** **KM# 71** **Weight:** 26.0000 g. **Composition:** 0.9000 Silver .7524 oz. ASW **Subject:** 25th Anniversary of Independence **Edge:** Lettered

| Date | Mintage | F | VF | XF | Unc | BU |
|---|---|---|---|---|---|---|
| JE5733-1973 | 124,000 | — | — | — | 10.00 | — |
| JE5733-1973 Proof | 41,000 | Value: 12.00 | | | | |

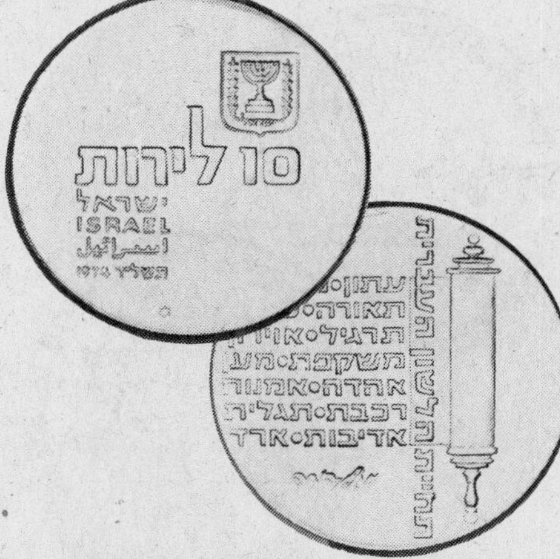


**10 LIROT** **KM# 77** **Weight:** 26.0000 g. **Composition:** 0.9000 Silver .7524 oz. ASW **Subject:** 26th Anniversary of Independence **Edge:** Lettered

| Date | Mintage | F | VF | XF | Unc | BU |
|---|---|---|---|---|---|---|
| JE5734-1974 | 127,000 | — | — | — | 9.00 | — |
| JE5734-1974 Proof | 50,000 | Value: 11.00 | | | | |

**10 LIROT** **KM# 76.1** **Weight:** 26.0000 g. **Composition:** 0.9000 Silver .7524 oz. ASW **Subject:** Pidyon Haben **Edge:** Plain

| Date | Mintage | F | VF | XF | Unc | BU |
|---|---|---|---|---|---|---|
| JE5734-1974 | 109,000 | — | — | — | 10.00 | — |

**10 LIROT** **KM# 76.2** **Weight:** 26.0000 g. **Composition:** 0.9000 Silver .7524 oz. ASW **Subject:** Pidyon Haben **Edge:** Reeded

| Date | Mintage | F | VF | XF | Unc | BU |
|---|---|---|---|---|---|---|
| JE5734-1974 Proof | 44,000 | Value: 12.00 | | | | |

**10 LIROT** **KM# 78.1** **Weight:** 26.0000 g. **Composition:** 0.9000 Silver .7524 oz. ASW **Subject:** Hanukkah **Reverse:** Damascus lamp **Edge:** Plain

| Date | Mintage | F | VF | XF | Unc | BU |
|---|---|---|---|---|---|---|
| JE5735-1974 | 74,000 | — | — | — | 5.50 | — |

**10 LIROT** **KM# 78.2** **Weight:** 26.0000 g. **Composition:** 0.9000 Silver .7524 oz. ASW **Subject:** Hanukkah **Reverse:** Damascus lamp **Edge:** Reeded

| Date | Mintage | F | VF | XF | Unc | BU |
|---|---|---|---|---|---|---|
| JE5735-1974 Proof | 59,000 | Value: 7.50 | | | | |

**10 LIROT** **KM# 84.2** **Weight:** 26.0000 g. **Composition:** 0.9000 Silver .7524 oz. ASW **Subject:** Hanukkah **Reverse:** Holland lamp **Edge:** Reeded

| Date | Mintage | F | VF | XF | Unc | BU |
|---|---|---|---|---|---|---|
| JE5736-1975 Proof | 34,000 | Value: 8.00 | | | | |

**10 LIROT** **KM# 84.1** **Weight:** 26.0000 g. **Composition:** 0.9000 Silver .7524 oz. ASW **Subject:** Hanukkah **Reverse:** Holland lamp **Edge:** Plain

| Date | Mintage | F | VF | XF | Unc | BU |
|---|---|---|---|---|---|---|
| JE5736-1975 | 44,000 | — | — | — | 6.00 | — |

**10 LIROT** KM# 87.1 **Weight:** 20.0000 g. **Composition:** 0.5000 Silver .3215 oz. ASW **Subject:** Bicentennial - American Independence **Reverse:** U.S. Hanukkah lamp **Edge:** Plain

| Date | Mintage | F | VF | XF | Unc | BU |
|---|---|---|---|---|---|---|
| JE5737-1976 | 25,000 | — | — | — | 11.00 | — |

**10 LIROT** KM# 87.2 **Weight:** 20.0000 g. **Composition:** 0.5000 Silver .3215 oz. ASW **Subject:** Bicentennial - American Independence **Reverse:** U.S. Hanukkah lamp **Edge:** Reeded

| Date | Mintage | F | VF | XF | Unc | BU |
|---|---|---|---|---|---|---|
| JE5737-1976 Proof | 20,000 | Value: 13.00 | | | | |

**10 LIROT** KM# 91.1 **Composition:** Copper-Nickel **Subject:** Hanukkah **Reverse:** Jerusalem lamp **Edge:** Plain

| Date | Mintage | F | VF | XF | Unc | BU |
|---|---|---|---|---|---|---|
| JE5738-1977 | 46,000 | — | — | — | 3.00 | — |

**10 LIROT** KM# 91.3 **Composition:** Copper-Nickel **Subject:** Hanukkah **Reverse:** Jerusalem lamp **Edge:** Reeded **Note:** Closed style "mem".

| Date | Mintage | F | VF | XF | Unc | BU |
|---|---|---|---|---|---|---|
| JE5738-1977 Proof | Inc. above | Value: 11.00 | | | | |

**10 LIROT** KM# 91.2 **Composition:** Copper-Nickel **Subject:** Hanukkah **Reverse:** Jerusalem lamp **Edge:** Reeded **Note:** Open style "mem."

| Date | Mintage | F | VF | XF | Unc | BU |
|---|---|---|---|---|---|---|
| JE5738-1977 Proof | 30,000 | Value: 6.50 | | | | |

**20 LIROT** KM# 30 **Weight:** 7.9880 g. **Composition:** 0.9170 Gold .2355 oz. AGW **Subject:** 100th Anniversity - Birth of Dr. Theodor Herzl

| Date | Mintage | F | VF | XF | Unc | BU |
|---|---|---|---|---|---|---|
| JE5720-1960 | 10,000 | — | — | — | 160 | — |

**25 LIROT** KM# 79.1 **Weight:** 26.0000 g. **Composition:** 0.9350 Silver .7816 oz. ASW **Subject:** 1st Anniversary - Death of David Ben Gurion **Edge:** Plain

| Date | Mintage | F | VF | XF | Unc | BU |
|---|---|---|---|---|---|---|
| JE5735-1974 | 99,000 | — | — | — | 11.00 | — |

**25 LIROT** KM# 79.2 **Weight:** 26.0000 g. **Composition:** 0.9350 Silver .7816 oz. ASW **Subject:** 1st Anniversary - Death of David Ben Gurion **Edge:** Reeded

| Date | Mintage | F | VF | XF | Unc | BU |
|---|---|---|---|---|---|---|
| JE5735-1974 Proof | 64,000 | Value: 13.00 | | | | |

**25 LIROT** KM# 80.2 **Weight:** 26.0000 g. **Composition:** 0.9000 Silver .7524 oz. ASW **Subject:** Pidyon Haben **Edge:** Reeded

| Date | Mintage | F | VF | XF | Unc | BU |
|---|---|---|---|---|---|---|
| JE5735-1975 Proof | 49,000 | Value: 13.00 | | | | |

**25 LIROT** KM# 80.1 **Weight:** 26.0000 g. **Composition:** 0.9000 Silver .7524 oz. ASW **Subject:** Pidyon Haben **Edge:** Plain

| Date | Mintage | F | VF | XF | Unc | BU |
|---|---|---|---|---|---|---|
| JE5735-1975 | 62,000 | — | — | — | 11.00 | — |

**25 LIROT** KM# 81 **Weight:** 30.0000 g. **Composition:** 0.8000 Silver .7717 oz. ASW **Subject:** 25th Anniversary of Israel Bond Program **Edge:** Lettered

| Date | Mintage | F | VF | XF | Unc | BU |
|---|---|---|---|---|---|---|
| JE5735-1975 | 49,000 | — | — | — | 10.00 | — |
| JE5735-1975 Proof | 40,000 | Value: 12.00 | | | | |

**25 LIROT** KM# 85 **Weight:** 26.0000 g. **Composition:** 0.9000 Silver .7534 oz. ASW **Subject:** 28th Anniversary of Independence **Reverse:** Strength **Edge:** Lettered

| Date | Mintage | F | VF | XF | Unc | BU |
|---|---|---|---|---|---|---|
| JE5736-1976 | 38,000 | — | — | — | 9.00 | — |
| JE5736-1976 Proof | 27,000 | Value: 11.00 | | | | |

**25 LIROT** KM# 86.1 **Weight:** 30.0000 g. **Composition:** 0.8000 Silver .7717 oz. ASW **Subject:** Pidyon Haben **Edge:** Plain

| Date | Mintage | F | VF | XF | Unc | BU |
|---|---|---|---|---|---|---|
| JE5736-1976 | 37,000 | — | — | — | 10.00 | — |

**25 LIROT** KM# 86.2 **Weight:** 30.0000 g. **Composition:** 0.8000 Silver .7717 oz. ASW **Subject:** Pidyon Haben **Edge:** Reeded

| Date | Mintage | F | VF | XF | Unc | BU |
|---|---|---|---|---|---|---|
| JE5736-1976 Proof | 29,000 | Value: 12.00 | | | | |

**25 LIROT** KM# 88 **Weight:** 20.0000 g. **Composition:** 0.5000 Silver .3215 oz. ASW **Subject:** 29th Anniversary of Independence **Reverse:** Brotherhood **Edge:** Lettered

| Date | Mintage | F | VF | XF | Unc | BU |
|---|---|---|---|---|---|---|
| JE5737-1977 | 37,000 | — | — | — | 9.00 | — |
| JE5737-1977 Proof | 27,000 | Value: 11.00 | | | | |

**25 LIROT** **KM# 89.1** **Weight:** 26.0000 g. **Composition:** 0.9000 Silver .7534 oz. ASW **Subject:** Pidyon Haben **Edge:** Plain

| Date | Mintage | F | VF | XF | Unc | BU |
|---|---|---|---|---|---|---|
| JE5737-1977 | 32,000 | — | — | — | 10.00 | — |

**25 LIROT** **KM# 89.2** **Weight:** 26.0000 g. **Composition:** 0.9000 Silver .7534 oz. ASW **Subject:** Pidyon Haben **Edge:** Reeded

| Date | Mintage | F | VF | XF | Unc | BU |
|---|---|---|---|---|---|---|
| JE5737-1977 Proof | 19,000 | Value: 12.00 | | | | |

**25 LIROT** **KM# 94.2** **Weight:** 26.0000 g. **Composition:** 0.9000 Silver .7534 oz. ASW **Subject:** Hanukkah **Reverse:** French lamp **Edge:** Reeded

| Date | Mintage | F | VF | XF | Unc | BU |
|---|---|---|---|---|---|---|
| JE5739-1978 Proof | 22,000 | Value: 8.00 | | | | |

**25 LIROT** **KM# 94.1** **Weight:** 26.0000 g. **Composition:** 0.9000 Silver .7534 oz. ASW **Subject:** Hanukkah **Reverse:** French lamp **Edge:** Plain

| Date | Mintage | F | VF | XF | Unc | BU |
|---|---|---|---|---|---|---|
| JE5739-1978 | 36,000 | — | — | — | 5.00 | — |

**50 LIROT** **KM# 40** **Weight:** 13.3400 g. **Composition:** 0.9170 Gold .3933 oz. AGW **Subject:** 10th Anniversary - Death of Weizmann

| Date | Mintage | F | VF | XF | Unc | BU |
|---|---|---|---|---|---|---|
| JE5723-1962 Without "mem," Proof | 10 | — | — | — | — | — |
| JE5723-1962 Proof | 6,202 | Value: 225 | | | | |

**50 LIROT** **KM# 44** **Weight:** 13.3400 g. **Composition:** 0.9170 Gold .3933 oz. AGW **Subject:** 10th Anniversary - Bank of Israel

| Date | Mintage | F | VF | XF | Unc | BU |
|---|---|---|---|---|---|---|
| JE5725-1964 | 6,014 | — | — | — | 250 | — |
| JE5725-1964 Proof | 841 | Value: 3,200 | | | | |

**50 LIROT** **KM# 72** **Weight:** 7.0000 g. **Composition:** 0.9000 Gold .2025 oz. AGW **Subject:** 25th Anniversary of Independence

| Date | Mintage | F | VF | XF | Unc | BU |
|---|---|---|---|---|---|---|
| JE5733-1973 Proof | 28,000 | Value: 100 | | | | |

**50 LIROT** **KM# 92.1** **Weight:** 20.0000 g. **Composition:** 0.5000 Silver .3215 oz. ASW **Subject:** 30th Anniversary of Independence **Reverse:** Loyalty **Edge:** Plain

| Date | Mintage | F | VF | XF | Unc | BU |
|---|---|---|---|---|---|---|
| JE5738-1978 | 40,000 | — | — | — | 9.00 | — |

**50 LIROT** **KM# 92.2** **Weight:** 20.0000 g. **Composition:** 0.5000 Silver .3215 oz. ASW **Subject:** 30th Anniversary of Independence **Reverse:** Loyalty **Edge:** Reeded

| Date | Mintage | F | VF | XF | Unc | BU |
|---|---|---|---|---|---|---|
| JE5738-1978 Proof | 22,000 | Value: 10.00 | | | | |

**50 LIROT** **KM# 95** **Weight:** 20.0000 g. **Composition:** 0.5000 Silver .3215 oz. ASW **Subject:** 31st Anniverdary of Independence **Reverse:** Motherhood **Edge:** Lettered

| Date | Mintage | F | VF | XF | Unc | BU |
|---|---|---|---|---|---|---|
| JE5739-1979 | 24,000 | — | — | — | 10.00 | — |
| JE5739-1979 Proof | 16,000 | Value: 12.00 | | | | |

**100 LIROT** **KM# 41** **Weight:** 26.6800 g. **Composition:** 0.9170 Gold .7866 oz. AGW **Subject:** 10th Anniverdary - Death of Weizmann

| Date | Mintage | F | VF | XF | Unc | BU |
|---|---|---|---|---|---|---|
| JE5723-1962 Proof | 6,203 | Value: 400 | | | | |
| JE5723-1962 Proof | 10 | — | — | — | — | — |

**100 LIROT** **KM# 50** **Weight:** 26.6800 g. **Composition:** 0.9170 Gold .7866 oz. AGW **Subject:** Victory Commemorative

| Date | Mintage | F | VF | XF | Unc | BU |
|---|---|---|---|---|---|---|
| JE5727-1967 Proof | 9,004 | Value: 350 | | | | |

**100 LIROT** **KM# 52** **Weight:** 25.0000 g. **Composition:** 0.8000 Gold .6430 oz. AGW **Subject:** 20th Anniversary - Jerusalem Reunification

| Date | Mintage | F | VF | XF | Unc | BU |
|---|---|---|---|---|---|---|
| JE5728-1968 Proof | 13,000 | Value: 300 | | | | |

**100 LIROT** **KM# 54** **Weight:** 25.0000 g. **Composition:** 0.8000 Gold .6430 oz. AGW **Subject:** 21st Anniversary of Independence **Reverse:** Shalom

| Date | Mintage | F | VF | XF | Unc | BU |
|---|---|---|---|---|---|---|
| JE5729-1969 Proof | 13,000 | Value: 300 | | | | |

**100 LIROT** **KM# 60** **Weight:** 22.0000 g. **Composition:** 0.9000 Gold .6366 oz. AGW **Subject:** Let My People Go

| Date | Mintage | F | VF | XF | Unc | BU |
|---|---|---|---|---|---|---|
| JE5731-1971 Proof | 9,956 | Value: 275 | | | | |

**100 LIROT** **KM# 73** **Weight:** 13.5000 g. **Composition:** 0.9000 Gold .3906 oz. AGW **Subject:** 25th Anniversary of Independence

| Date | Mintage | F | VF | XF | Unc | BU |
|---|---|---|---|---|---|---|
| JE5733-1973 Proof | 28,000 | Value: 175 | | | | |

**100 LIROT** **KM# 103.1** **Weight:** 20.0000 g. **Composition:** 0.5000 Silver .3215 oz. ASW **Subject:** Hanukkah **Reverse:** Egyptian lamp **Edge:** Plain

| Date | Mintage | F | VF | XF | Unc | BU |
|---|---|---|---|---|---|---|
| JE5750-1979 | 32,000 | — | — | — | 8.50 | — |

**100 LIROT** **KM# 103.2** **Weight:** 20.0000 g. **Composition:** 0.5000 Silver .3215 oz. ASW **Subject:** Hanukkah **Reverse:** Egyptian lamp **Edge:** Reeded

| Date | Mintage | F | VF | XF | Unc | BU |
|---|---|---|---|---|---|---|
| JE5750-1979 Proof | 19,000 | Value: 11.50 | | | | |

**200 LIROT** **KM# 74** **Weight:** 27.0000 g. **Composition:** 0.9000 Gold .7813 oz. AGW **Subject:** 25th Anniversary of Independence

| Date | Mintage | F | VF | XF | Unc | BU |
|---|---|---|---|---|---|---|
| JE5733-1973 Proof | 18,000 | Value: 320 | | | | |

**200 LIROT** **KM# 82** **Weight:** 28.0000 g. **Composition:** 0.9000 Gold .8102 oz. AGW **Subject:** 1st Anniversary - Death of David Ben Gurion

| Date | Mintage | F | VF | XF | Unc | BU |
|---|---|---|---|---|---|---|
| JE5734-1974 Proof | 48,000 | Value: 325 | | | | |

**200 LIROT** **KM# 83** **Weight:** 20.0000 g. **Composition:** 0.9000 Gold .5787 oz. AGW **Subject:** 25th Anniversary of Israel Bond Program

| Date | Mintage | F | VF | XF | Unc | BU |
|---|---|---|---|---|---|---|
| JE5735-1975 Proof | 31,000 | Value: 225 | | | | |

**200 LIROT** **KM# 104** **Weight:** 26.0000 g. **Composition:** 0.9000 Silver .7534 oz. ASW **Subject:** 32nd Anniversary of Independence **Reverse:** Egyptian and Israeli Peace Treaty **Edge:** Lettered

| Date | Mintage | F | VF | XF | Unc | BU |
|---|---|---|---|---|---|---|
| JE5740-1980 | 20,000 | — | — | — | 10.00 | — |
| JE5740-1980 Proof | 13,000 | Value: 15.00 | | | | |

**1000 LIROT** **KM# 93** **Weight:** 12.0000 g. **Composition:** 0.9000 Gold .3473 oz. AGW **Subject:** 30th Anniversary of Independence **Reverse:** Tree of Life

| Date | Mintage | F | VF | XF | Unc | BU |
|---|---|---|---|---|---|---|
| JE5738-1978 Proof | 12,000 | Value: 175 | | | | |

**5000 LIROT** **KM# 105** **Weight:** 17.2800 g. **Composition:** 0.9000 Gold .50000 oz. AGW **Subject:** 32nd Anniversary of independence **Reverse:** Egyptian & Israeli Peace Tready

| Date | Mintage | F | VF | XF | Unc | BU |
|---|---|---|---|---|---|---|
| JE5740-1980 Proof | 6,382 | Value: 250 | | | | |

## REFORM COINAGE

10 Old Agorot = 1 New Agorah;
100 New Agorot = 1 Sheqel

Commencing February 24, 1980-1985

**NEW AGORAH** **KM# 106** **Composition:** Aluminum **Obverse:** Date palm

| Date | Mintage | F | VF | XF | Unc | BU |
|---|---|---|---|---|---|---|
| JE5740 (1980) | 200,000,000 | — | — | — | 0.10 | — |
| **Note:** 110 million coins were reportedly melted down | | | | | | |
| JE5741 (1981) | 1,000,000 | — | — | 0.10 | 0.20 | — |
| JE5742 (1982) | 1,000,000 | — | — | 0.10 | 0.20 | — |

**5 NEW AGOROT** **KM# 107** **Composition:** Aluminum **Obverse:** Menorah

| Date | Mintage | F | VF | XF | Unc | BU |
|---|---|---|---|---|---|---|
| JE5740-(1980) | 69,532,000 | — | — | — | 0.10 | — |
| JE5741 (1981) | 1,000,000 | — | — | 0.10 | 0.20 | — |
| JE5742 (1982) | 5,000,000 | — | — | — | 0.10 | — |

**10 NEW AGOROT** **KM# 108** **Composition:** Bronze **Obverse:** Pomegranate

| Date | Mintage | F | VF | XF | Unc | BU |
|---|---|---|---|---|---|---|
| JE5740 (1980) | 167,932,000 | — | — | — | 0.10 | — |
| **Note:** 70.200 million coins were reportedly melted down | | | | | | |
| JE5741 (1981) | 241,160,000 | — | — | — | 0.10 | — |
| JE5742 (1982) | 23,000,000 | — | — | — | 0.10 | — |
| JE5743 (1983) | 2,500,000 | — | — | 0.10 | 0.15 | — |
| JE5744 (1984) | 500,000 | — | — | 0.10 | 0.20 | — |

**1/2 SHEQEL** **KM# 109** **Composition:** Copper-Nickel

| Date | Mintage | F | VF | XF | Unc | BU |
|---|---|---|---|---|---|---|
| JE5740 (1980) | 52,308,000 | — | — | 0.25 | 0.50 | — |
| JE5741 (1981) | 53,272,000 | — | — | 0.25 | 0.50 | — |
| JE5742 (1982) | 18,808,000 | — | — | 0.25 | 0.50 | — |
| JE5743 (1983) | 250,000 | — | — | 0.35 | 0.70 | — |
| JE5744 (1984) | 250,000 | — | — | 0.35 | 0.70 | — |

**1/2 SHEQEL** **KM# 121** **Weight:** 7.2000 g. **Composition:** 0.8500 Silver .1967 oz. ASW **Series:** Holyland Sites **Reverse:** Gumran Caves

| Date | Mintage | F | VF | XF | Unc | BU |
|---|---|---|---|---|---|---|
| JE5742-1982 | 15,000 | — | — | — | 10.00 | — |

**1/2 SHEQEL** **KM# 126** **Weight:** 7.2000 g. **Composition:** 0.8500 Silver .1967 oz. ASW **Series:** Holyland Sites **Reverse:** Herodion Ruins

| Date | Mintage | F | VF | XF | Unc | BU |
|---|---|---|---|---|---|---|
| JE5743-1983 | 11,000 | — | — | — | 10.00 | — |

**1/2 SHEQEL** **KM# 140** **Weight:** 7.2000 g. **Composition:** 0.8500 Silver .1967 oz. ASW **Series:** Holyland Sites **Reverse:** Kidron Valley

| Date | Mintage | F | VF | XF | Unc | BU |
|---|---|---|---|---|---|---|
| JE5744-1984 | 7,538 | — | — | — | 16.00 | — |

**1/2 SHEQEL** **KM# 152** **Weight:** 7.2000 g. **Composition:** 0.8500 Silver .1967 oz. ASW **Series:** Holyland Sites **Reverse:** Capernaum

| Date | Mintage | F | VF | XF | Unc | BU |
|---|---|---|---|---|---|---|
| JE5745-1985 | 6,010 | — | — | — | 16.50 | — |

**SHEQEL KM# 110.1 Weight:** 14.4000 g. **Composition:** 0.8500 Silver .3935 oz. ASW **Subject:** Hanukkah **Reverse:** Corfu lamp **Edge:** Plain

| Date | Mintage | F | VF | XF | Unc | BU |
|---|---|---|---|---|---|---|
| JE5740-1980 | 24,000 | — | — | — | 10.00 | — |

**SHEQEL KM# 110.2 Weight:** 14.4000 g. **Composition:** 0.8500 Silver .3935 oz. ASW **Subject:** Hanukkah **Reverse:** Corfu lamp **Edge:** Reeded

| Date | Mintage | F | VF | XF | Unc | BU |
|---|---|---|---|---|---|---|
| JE5740-1980 Proof | 15,000 | Value: 15.00 | | | | |

**SHEQEL KM# 111 Composition:** Copper-Nickel **Reverse:** Chalice

| Date | Mintage | F | VF | XF | Unc | BU |
|---|---|---|---|---|---|---|
| JE5741(1981) | 154,540,000 | — | — | 0.65 | 0.85 | — |
| JE5742 (1982) | 15,850,000 | — | — | 0.65 | 0.85 | — |
| JE5743 (1983) | 26,360,000 | — | — | 0.65 | 0.85 | — |
| JE5744 (1984) | 32,205,000 | — | — | 0.65 | 0.85 | — |
| JE5745 (1985) | 500,000 | — | — | 1.00 | 4.00 | — |

**SHEQEL KM# 116.1 Weight:** 14.4000 g. **Composition:** 0.8500 Silver .3935 oz. ASW **Subject:** Hanukkah **Reverse:** Polish lamp **Edge:** Plain

| Date | Mintage | F | VF | XF | Unc | BU |
|---|---|---|---|---|---|---|
| JE5742 -1981 | 16,000 | — | — | — | 10.00 | — |

**SHEQEL KM# 116.2 Weight:** 14.4000 g. **Composition:** 0.8500 Silver .3935 oz. ASW **Subject:** Hanukkah **Reverse:** Polish lamp **Edge:** Reeded

| Date | Mintage | F | VF | XF | Unc | BU |
|---|---|---|---|---|---|---|
| JE5742 -1981 Proof | 11,000 | Value: 16.50 | | | | |

**SHEQEL KM# 122 Weight:** 14.4000 g. **Composition:** 0.8500 Silver .3935 oz. ASW **Series:** Holyland Sites **Reverse:** Qumran Caves

| Date | Mintage | F | VF | XF | Unc | BU |
|---|---|---|---|---|---|---|
| JE5743-1982 Proof | 9,000 | Value: 20.00 | | | | |

**SHEQEL KM# 123 Weight:** 14.4000 g. **Composition:** 0.8500 Silver .3935 oz. ASW **Subject:** Hanukkah **Reverse:** Yeman lamp

| Date | Mintage | F | VF | XF | Unc | BU |
|---|---|---|---|---|---|---|
| JE5743-1982(1982) | 14,000 | — | — | — | 13.50 | — |

**SHEQEL KM# 129 Weight:** 14.4000 g. **Composition:** 0.8500 Silver .3935 oz. ASW **Subject:** Hanukkah **Reverse:** Prague lamp

| Date | Mintage | F | VF | XF | Unc | BU |
|---|---|---|---|---|---|---|
| JE5743-1983 | 13,000 | — | — | — | 12.00 | — |

**SHEQEL KM# 128 Weight:** 14.4000 g. **Composition:** 0.8500 Silver .3935 oz. ASW **Series:** Holyland Sites **Reverse:** Herodion Ruins

| Date | Mintage | F | VF | XF | Unc | BU |
|---|---|---|---|---|---|---|
| JE5744-1983 Proof | 10,000 | Value: 22.00 | | | | |

**SHEQEL KM# 127 Weight:** 14.4000 g. **Composition:** 0.8500 Silver .3935 oz. ASW **Subject:** 35th Anniversary - State of Israel **Reverse:** Valour

| Date | Mintage | F | VF | XF | Unc | BU |
|---|---|---|---|---|---|---|
| JE5743-1983 | 15,000 | — | — | — | 12.50 | — |

**SHEQEL KM# 135 Weight:** 14.4000 g. **Composition:** 0.8500 Silver .3935 oz. ASW **Subject:** 36th Anniversary - State of Israel **Reverse:** Kinsmen

| Date | Mintage | F | VF | XF | Unc | BU |
|---|---|---|---|---|---|---|
| JE5744-1984 | 18,000 | — | — | — | 15.00 | — |

**SHEQEL KM# 141 Weight:** 14.4000 g. **Composition:** 0.8500 Silver .3935 oz. ASW **Series:** Holyland Sites **Reverse:** Kidron Valley

| Date | Mintage | F | VF | XF | Unc | BU |
|---|---|---|---|---|---|---|
| JE5745-1984 Proof | 6,798 | Value: 30.00 | | | | |

**SHEQEL KM# 144 Weight:** 14.4000 g. **Composition:** 0.8500 Silver .3935 oz. ASW **Subject:** Hanukkah **Reverse:** Theresianstadt lamp

| Date | Mintage | F | VF | XF | Unc | BU |
|---|---|---|---|---|---|---|
| JE5745-1984 | 11,000 | — | — | — | 15.00 | — |

**SHEQEL KM# 148 Weight:** 14.4000 g. **Composition:** 0.8500 Silver .3935 oz. ASW **Subject:** 36th Anniversary of independence **Reverse:** Scientific Acheivement

| Date | Mintage | F | VF | XF | Unc | BU |
|---|---|---|---|---|---|---|
| JE5745-1985 | 8,520 | — | — | — | 14.50 | — |

**SHEQEL KM# 155 Weight:** 14.4000 g. **Composition:** 0.8500 Silver .3935 oz. ASW **Reverse:** Ancient ship

| Date | Mintage | F | VF | XF | Unc | BU |
|---|---|---|---|---|---|---|
| JE5745-1985 Proof Like | 13,000 | — | — | — | 20.00 | — |

**SHEQEL KM# 153 Weight:** 14.4000 g. **Composition:** 0.8500 Silver .3935 oz. ASW **Series:** Holyland Sites **Reverse:** Capernaum

| Date | Mintage | F | VF | XF | Unc | BU |
|---|---|---|---|---|---|---|
| JE5746-1985 Proof | 6,010 | Value: 22.00 | | | | |

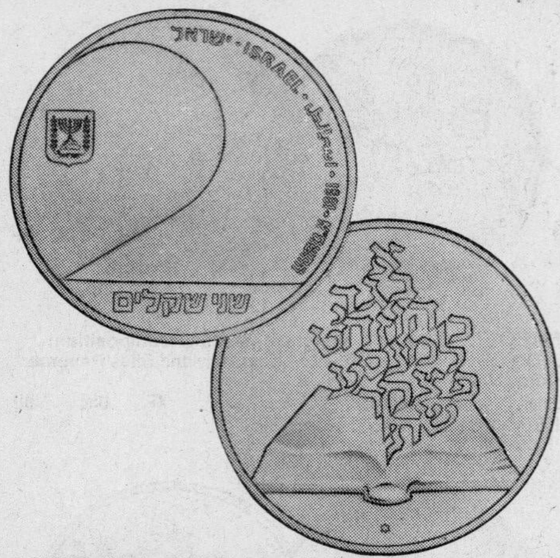

**2 SHEQALIM KM# 112 Weight:** 28.8000 g. **Composition:** 0.8250 Silver .7639 oz. ASW **Subject:** 33rd Anniversary of independence **Reverse:** People of the Book **Edge:** Lettered

| Date | Mintage | F | VF | XF | Unc | BU |
|---|---|---|---|---|---|---|
| JE5741-1981 | 16,000 | — | — | — | 12.50 | — |
| JE5741-1981 Proof | 11,000 | Value: 20.00 | | | | |

**2 SHEQALIM KM# 117 Weight:** 28.8000 g. **Composition:** 0.8500 Silver .7871 oz. ASW **Subject:** 34th Anniversary of Independence **Reverse:** Baron Edmond de Rothschild **Edge:** Lettered

| Date | Mintage | F | VF | XF | Unc | BU |
|---|---|---|---|---|---|---|
| JE5742-1982 | 13,000 | — | — | — | 15.00 | — |
| JE5742-1982 Proof | 9,506 | Value: 25.00 | | | | |

**2 SHEQALIM KM# 124 Weight:** 28.8000 g. **Composition:** 0.8500 Silver .7871 oz. ASW **Subject:** Hanukkah **Reverse:** Yemen lamp

| Date | Mintage | F | VF | XF | Unc | BU |
|---|---|---|---|---|---|---|
| JE5743-1982 Proof | 8,996 | Value: 27.50 | | | | |

**2 SHEQALIM KM# 130 Weight:** 28.8000 g. **Composition:** 0.8500 Silver .7871 oz. ASW **Subject:** 35th Anniversary of independence **Reverse:** Valour; similar to 1 Shequel, KM#127

| Date | Mintage | F | VF | XF | Unc | BU |
|---|---|---|---|---|---|---|
| JE5743-1983 Proof | 10,000 | Value: 22.50 | | | | |

**2 SHEQALIM KM# 131 Weight:** 28.8000 g. **Composition:** 0.8500 Silver .7871 oz. ASW **Subject:** Hanukkah **Reverse:** Prague lamp

| Date | Mintage | F | VF | XF | Unc | BU |
|---|---|---|---|---|---|---|
| JE5744-1983 Proof | 11,000 | Value: 22.50 | | | | |

**2 SHEQALIM KM# 145 Weight:** 28.8000 g. **Composition:** 0.8500 Silver .7871 oz. ASW **Subject:** Hanukkah **Reverse:** Theresianstadt lamp

| Date | Mintage | F | VF | XF | Unc | BU |
|---|---|---|---|---|---|---|
| JE5745-1984 Proof | 10,000 | Value: 28.00 | | | | |

**2 SHEQALIM KM# 136 Weight:** 28.8000 g. **Composition:** 0.8500 Silver .7871 oz. ASW **Subject:** 36th Anniversary of independence **Reverse:** Kinsmen

| Date | Mintage | F | VF | XF | Unc | BU |
|---|---|---|---|---|---|---|
| JE5744-1984 Proof | 8,526 | Value: 25.00 | | | | |

**2 SHEQALIM KM# 149 Weight:** 28.8000 g. **Composition:** 0.8500 Silver .7871 oz. ASW **Subject:** 37th Anniversary of Independence **Reverse:** Scientific achievement

| Date | Mintage | F | VF | XF | Unc | BU |
|---|---|---|---|---|---|---|
| JE5745-1985 Proof | 8,330 | Value: 28.00 | | | | |

**5 SHEQALIM KM# 118 Composition:** Aluminum-Bronze **Series:** Cornucopiae

| Date | Mintage | F | VF | XF | Unc | BU |
|---|---|---|---|---|---|---|
| JE5742 (1982) | 30,000,000 | — | — | 0.75 | 1.25 | — |
| JE5743 (1983) | 994,000 | — | — | 1.00 | 2.00 | — |
| JE5744 (1984) | 17,389,000 | — | — | 0.75 | 1.25 | — |
| JE5745 (1985) | 250,000 | — | — | 1.00 | 2.50 | — |

**5 SHEQALIM KM# 125 Weight:** 8.6300 g. **Composition:** 0.9000 Gold .2497 oz. AGW **Series:** Holyland Sites **Reverse:** Gumran Caves

| Date | Mintage | F | VF | XF | Unc | BU |
|---|---|---|---|---|---|---|
| JE5743-1982 Proof | 4,927 | Value: 170 | | | | |

**5 SHEQALIM** **KM# 132** **Weight:** 0.8630 g. **Composition:** 0.9000 Gold .2497 oz. AGW **Series:** Holyland Sites **Reverse:** Herodion Ruins

| Date | Mintage | F | VF | XF | Unc | BU |
|---|---|---|---|---|---|---|
| JE5744-1983 Proof | 4,346 | Value: 170 | | | | |

**5 SHEQALIM** **KM# 142** **Weight:** 8.6300 g. **Composition:** 0.9000 Gold .2497 oz. AGW **Series:** Holyland Sites **Reverse:** Kidron Valley

| Date | Mintage | F | VF | XF | Unc | BU |
|---|---|---|---|---|---|---|
| JE5745 -1984 Proof | 2,601 | Value: 370 | | | | |

**5 SHEQALIM** **KM# 154** **Weight:** 8.6300 g. **Composition:** 0.9000 Gold .2497 oz. AGW **Series:** Holyland Sites **Reverse:** Capernaum

| Date | Mintage | F | VF | XF | Unc | BU |
|---|---|---|---|---|---|---|
| JE5746-1985 Proof | 2,633 | Value: 275 | | | | |

**10 SHEQALIM** **KM# 113** **Weight:** 17.2800 g. **Composition:** 0.9000 Gold .5000 oz. AGW **Subject:** 33rd Anniversary of independence **Reverse:** People of the book

| Date | Mintage | F | VF | XF | Unc | BU |
|---|---|---|---|---|---|---|
| JE5741-1981 Proof | 5,673 | Value: 250 | | | | |

**10 SHEQALIM** **KM# 120** **Weight:** 17.2800 g. **Composition:** 0.9000 Gold .5000 oz. AGW **Subject:** 34th Anniversary of Independence **Reverse:** Baron Edmond de Rothschild

| Date | Mintage | F | VF | XF | Unc | BU |
|---|---|---|---|---|---|---|
| JE5742-1982 Proof | 4,875 | Value: 250 | | | | |

**10 SHEQALIM** **KM# 119** **Composition:** Copper-Nickel **Obverse:** Ancient Galley

| Date | Mintage | F | VF | XF | Unc | BU |
|---|---|---|---|---|---|---|
| JE5742 (1982) | 36,084,000 | — | — | 0.75 | 1.25 | — |
| JE5743 (1983) | 17,851,000 | — | — | 0.75 | 1.25 | — |
| JE5744 (1984) | 31,950,000 | — | — | 0.75 | 1.25 | — |
| JE5745 (1985) | 25,864,000 | — | — | 0.50 | 0.75 | — |

**10 SHEQALIM** **KM# 134** **Composition:** Copper-Nickel **Subject:** Hanukkah

| Date | Mintage | F | VF | XF | Unc | BU |
|---|---|---|---|---|---|---|
| JE5744 (1983) | 2,000,000 | — | — | 1.00 | 1.50 | — |
| JE5744 (1984) | — | — | — | 1.00 | 1.50 | — |

**10 SHEQALIM** **KM# 133** **Weight:** 17.2800 g. **Composition:** 0.9000 Gold .5000 oz. AGW **Subject:** 35th Anniversary of Independence **Reverse:** Valour

| Date | Mintage | F | VF | XF | Unc | BU |
|---|---|---|---|---|---|---|
| JE5743-1983 Proof | 3,650 | Value: 340 | | | | |

**10 SHEQALIM** **KM# 138** **Weight:** 17.2800 g. **Composition:** 0.9000 Gold .5000 oz. AGW **Subject:** 36th Anniversary of Independence **Reverse:** Kinsmen

| Date | Mintage | F | VF | XF | Unc | BU |
|---|---|---|---|---|---|---|
| JE5744-1984 Proof | 3,798 | Value: 360 | | | | |

**10 SHEQALIM** **KM# 137** **Composition:** Copper-Nickel **Obverse:** Head of Theodor Herzl left

| Date | Mintage | F | VF | XF | Unc | BU |
|---|---|---|---|---|---|---|
| JE5744 (1984) | 2,003,000 | — | — | 1.00 | 1.50 | — |

**10 SHEQALIM** **KM# 150** **Weight:** 17.2800 g. **Composition:** 0.9000 Gold .5000 oz. AGW **Subject:** 37th Anniversary of Independence **Reverse:** Schientific Achievement

| Date | Mintage | F | VF | XF | Unc | BU |
|---|---|---|---|---|---|---|
| JE5745-1985 Proof | 3,240 | Value: 375 | | | | |

**25 SHEQEL** **KM# 114.1** **Weight:** 26.0000 g. **Composition:** 0.9000 Silver .7524 oz. ASW **Subject:** 100th Anniversary - Birth of Zeev Jabotinsky

| Date | Mintage | F | VF | XF | Unc | BU |
|---|---|---|---|---|---|---|
| JE5740-1980 | 14,000 | — | — | — | 15.00 | — |

**25 SHEQEL** **KM# 114.2** **Weight:** 26.0000 g. **Composition:** 0.9000 Silver .7524 oz. ASW **Subject:** 100th Anniversary - Birth of Zeev Jabotinsky **Edge:** Reeded

| Date | Mintage | F | VF | XF | Unc | BU |
|---|---|---|---|---|---|---|
| JE5740-1980 Proof | 12,000 | Value: 25.00 | | | | |

**50 SHEQALIM** **KM# 139** **Composition:** Aluminum-Bronze **Obverse:** Ancient coin

| Date | Mintage | F | VF | XF | Unc | BU |
|---|---|---|---|---|---|---|
| JE5744 (1984) | 13,994,000 | — | — | 0.50 | 1.00 | — |
| JE5745 (1985) | 1,000,000 | — | — | 0.75 | 1.50 | — |

**50 SHEQALIM** **KM# 147** **Composition:** Aluminum-Bronze **Obverse:** Head of David Ben Guirion left

| Date | Mintage | F | VF | XF | Unc | BU |
|---|---|---|---|---|---|---|
| JE5745 (1985) | 1,000,000 | — | — | 1.00 | 1.50 | — |

**100 SHEQALIM** **KM# 143** **Composition:** Copper-Nickel

| Date | Mintage | F | VF | XF | Unc | BU |
|---|---|---|---|---|---|---|
| JE5744 (1984) | 30,028,000 | — | — | 1.00 | 2.00 | — |
| JE5745 (1985) | 19,638,000 | — | — | 1.00 | 2.00 | — |

**100 SHEQALIM** **KM# 146** **Composition:** Copper-Nickel **Subject:** Hanukkah

| Date | Mintage | F | VF | XF | Unc | BU |
|---|---|---|---|---|---|---|
| JE5745 (1984) | 2,000,000 | — | — | 1.25 | 2.25 | — |
| JE5745 (1985) | — | — | — | 1.25 | 2.25 | — |

**100 SHEQALIM** KM# 151 **Composition:** Copper-Nickel **Obverse:** Head of Zeev Jabotinsky

| Date | Mintage | F | VF | XF | Unc | BU |
|---|---|---|---|---|---|---|
| JE5745 (1985) | 2,000,000 | — | — | 1.25 | 2.25 | — |

**500 SHEQEL** KM# 115 **Weight:** 17.2800 g. **Composition:** 0.9000 Gold .5000 oz. AGW **Subject:** 100th Anniversary - Birth of Zeev Jabotinsky

| Date | Mintage | F | VF | XF | Unc | BU |
|---|---|---|---|---|---|---|
| JE5740-1980 Proof | 7,471 | Value: 240 | | | | |

## REFORM COINAGE

10 Sheqalim = 1 Agorah;
1000 Sheqalim = 1 New Sheqel

September 4, 1985

**AGORAH** KM# 156 **Composition:** Aluminum-Bronze

| Date | Mintage | F | VF | XF | Unc | BU |
|---|---|---|---|---|---|---|
| JE5745 (1985) | 58,144,000 | — | — | — | 0.50 | — |
| JE5746 (1986) | 95,272,000 | — | — | — | 0.50 | — |
| JE5747 (1987) | 1,080,000 | — | — | — | 0.50 | — |
| JE5748 (1988) | 15,768,000 | — | — | — | 0.50 | — |
| JE5749 (1989) | 10,801,000 | — | — | — | 0.50 | — |
| JE5750 (1990) | 4,968,000 | — | — | — | 0.50 | — |
| JE5751 (1991) In sets only | 10,000 | — | — | — | 1.00 | — |
| JE5754 (1994) | 8,000 | — | — | — | 0.50 | — |
| JE5755 (1995) | 10,000 | — | — | — | 0.50 | — |
| JE5756 (1996) | — | — | — | — | 0.50 | — |

**AGORAH** KM# 171 **Composition:** Aluminum-Bronze **Subject:** Hanukkah

| Date | Mintage | F | VF | XF | Unc | BU |
|---|---|---|---|---|---|---|
| JE5747 (1986) | 1,004,000 | — | — | 0.15 | 0.75 | — |
| JE5748 (1987) | 540,000 | — | — | 0.15 | 0.75 | — |
| JE5748 (1988) | 504,000 | — | — | 0.15 | 0.75 | — |
| JE5749 (1988) | Inc. above | — | — | 0.15 | 0.75 | — |
| JE5750 (1989) | 2,160,000 | — | — | 0.15 | 0.75 | — |
| JE5751 (1990) | 4,968,000 | — | — | 0.15 | 0.75 | — |
| JE5752 (1991) | — | — | — | 0.15 | 0.75 | — |
| JE5756 (1996) | — | — | — | 0.15 | 0.75 | — |

**AGORAH** KM# 193 **Composition:** Nickel **Subject:** 40th Anniversary of Independence

| Date | Mintage | F | VF | XF | Unc | BU |
|---|---|---|---|---|---|---|
| JE5748 (1988) | 504,000 | — | — | — | 0.25 | — |

**5 AGOROT** KM# 157 **Composition:** Aluminum-Bronze

| Date | Mintage | F | VF | XF | Unc | BU |
|---|---|---|---|---|---|---|
| JE5745 (1985) | 34,504,000 | — | — | 0.10 | 0.15 | — |
| JE5746 (1986) | 12,384,000 | — | — | 0.10 | 0.15 | — |
| JE5747 (1987) | 14,257,000 | — | — | 0.10 | 0.15 | — |
| JE5748 (1988) | 9,360,000 | — | — | 0.10 | 0.15 | — |
| JE5749 (1989) | 4,896,000 | — | — | 0.10 | 0.15 | — |
| JE5750 (1990) | 576,000 | — | — | 0.10 | 0.15 | — |
| JE5751 (1991) | 4,464,000 | — | — | 0.10 | 0.15 | — |
| JE5752 (1992) | — | — | — | 0.10 | 0.15 | — |
| JE5753 (1993) | 8,000 | — | — | 0.10 | 0.15 | — |
| JE5754 (1994) | 8,000 | — | — | 0.10 | 0.15 | — |
| JE5755 (1995) | 7,500 | — | — | 0.10 | 0.15 | — |
| JE5757 (1997) | — | — | — | 0.10 | 0.15 | — |
| JE5758 (1998) | — | — | — | 0.10 | 0.15 | — |

**5 AGOROT** KM# 172 **Composition:** Aluminum-Bronze **Subject:** Hanukkah

| Date | Mintage | F | VF | XF | Unc | BU |
|---|---|---|---|---|---|---|
| JE5747 (1986) | 1,004,000 | — | — | 0.10 | 0.30 | — |
| JE5748 (1987) | 536,000 | — | — | 0.10 | 0.30 | — |
| JE5749 (1988) | 504,000 | — | — | 0.10 | 0.30 | — |
| JE5750 (1989) | 2,016,000 | — | — | 0.10 | 0.30 | — |
| JE5751 (1990) | 1,488,000 | — | — | 0.10 | 0.30 | — |
| JE5752 (1991) | — | — | — | 0.10 | 0.30 | — |
| JE5753 (1992) | 960,000 | — | — | 0.10 | 0.30 | — |
| JE5753 (1993) | 12,000 | — | — | 0.10 | 0.30 | — |
| JE5754 (1994) | 12,000 | — | — | 0.10 | 0.30 | — |
| JE5755 (1995) | — | — | — | 0.10 | 0.30 | — |
| JE5756 (1996) | — | — | — | 0.10 | 0.30 | — |
| JE5757 (1997) | — | — | — | 0.10 | 0.30 | — |

**5 AGOROT** KM# 194 **Composition:** Nickel **Subject:** 40th Anniversary of Independence

| Date | Mintage | F | VF | XF | Unc | BU |
|---|---|---|---|---|---|---|
| JE5748 (1988) | 504,000 | — | — | — | 0.30 | — |

**10 AGOROT** KM# 158 **Composition:** Aluminum-Bronze

| Date | Mintage | F | VF | XF | Unc | BU |
|---|---|---|---|---|---|---|
| JE5745 (1985) | 45,000,000 | — | — | 0.10 | 0.20 | — |
| JE5746 (1986) | 92,754,000 | — | — | 0.10 | 0.20 | — |
| JE5747 (1987) | 19,351,000 | — | — | 0.10 | 0.20 | — |
| JE5748 (1988) | 8,640,000 | — | — | 0.10 | 0.20 | — |
| JE5749 (1989) | 420,000 | — | — | 0.10 | 0.20 | — |
| JE5750 (1990) | 2,376,000 | — | — | 0.10 | 0.20 | — |
| JE5751 (1991) | 59,425,000 | — | — | 0.10 | 0.20 | — |

**Note:** Exist with 6mm or 7mm long date; thick or thin letters; and 7mm or 7.5mm value 10

| Date | Mintage | F | VF | XF | Unc | BU |
|---|---|---|---|---|---|---|
| JE5752 (1992) | — | — | — | 0.10 | 0.20 | — |
| JE5753 (1993) | 25,920,000 | — | — | 0.10 | 0.20 | — |
| JE5754 (1994) | — | — | — | 0.10 | 0.20 | — |
| JE5755 (1995) | — | — | — | 0.10 | 0.20 | — |
| JE5756 | — | — | — | 0.10 | 0.20 | — |
| JE5757 (1997) | — | — | — | 0.10 | 0.20 | — |
| JE5758 | — | — | — | 0.10 | 0.20 | — |
| JE5759 (1999) | — | — | — | 0.10 | 0.20 | — |

**10 AGOROT** KM# 173 **Composition:** Aluminum-Bronze **Subject:** Hanukkah

| Date | Mintage | F | VF | XF | Unc | BU |
|---|---|---|---|---|---|---|
| JE5747 (1986) | 1,004,000 | — | — | 0.10 | 0.40 | — |
| JE5748 (1987) | 834,000 | — | — | 0.10 | 0.40 | — |
| JE5749 (1988) | 798,000 | — | — | 0.10 | 0.40 | — |
| JE5750 (1989) | 2,052,000 | — | — | 0.10 | 0.40 | — |
| JE5751 (1990) | 1,488,000 | — | — | 0.10 | 0.40 | — |
| JE5752 (1991) | — | — | — | 0.10 | 0.40 | — |
| JE5753 (1992) | 1,404,000 | — | — | 0.10 | 0.40 | — |
| JE5754 (1993) | 12,000 | — | — | 0.10 | 0.40 | — |
| JE5755 (1994) | 12,000 | — | — | 0.10 | 0.40 | — |
| JE5756 (1995) | — | — | — | 0.10 | 0.40 | — |
| JE5757 (1996) | — | — | — | 0.10 | 0.40 | — |
| JE5758 (1997) | — | — | — | 0.10 | 0.40 | — |

**10 AGOROT** KM# 195 **Composition:** Nickel **Subject:** 40th Anniversary of Independence

| Date | Mintage | F | VF | XF | Unc | BU |
|---|---|---|---|---|---|---|
| JE5748 (1988) | 504,000 | — | — | — | 0.40 | — |

**1/2 NEW SHEQEL** KM# 159 **Composition:** Aluminum-Bronze

| Date | Mintage | F | VF | XF | Unc | BU |
|---|---|---|---|---|---|---|
| JE5745 (1985) | 20,328,000 | — | — | 0.35 | 0.75 | — |
| JE5746 (1986) | 4,392,000 | — | — | 0.35 | 0.75 | — |
| JE5747 (1987) | 144,000 | — | — | 0.35 | 2.00 | — |
| JE5748 (1988) In sets only | 20,000 | — | — | — | 3.00 | — |
| JE5749 (1989) | 756,000 | — | — | 0.35 | 0.75 | — |
| JE5750 (1990) | 648,000 | — | — | 0.35 | 0.75 | — |
| JE5751 (1991) | 288,000 | — | — | 0.35 | 0.75 | — |
| JE5752 (1992) | — | — | — | 0.35 | 0.75 | — |
| JE5753 (1992) | 5,184,000 | — | — | 0.35 | 0.75 | — |
| JE5754 (1993) | 8,000 | — | — | 0.35 | 0.75 | — |
| JE5755 (1994) | 8,000 | — | — | 0.35 | 0.75 | — |
| JE5755 (1995) | 10,000 | — | — | 0.35 | 0.75 | — |
| JE5757 (1997) | — | — | — | 0.35 | 0.75 | — |
| JE5758 (1998) | — | — | — | 0.35 | 0.75 | — |
| JE5759 (1999) | — | — | — | 0.35 | 0.75 | — |

**1/2 NEW SHEQEL** KM# 167 **Composition:** Aluminum-Bronze **Reverse:** Baron Edmund de Rothschild

| Date | Mintage | F | VF | XF | Unc | BU |
|---|---|---|---|---|---|---|
| JE5746 (1986) | 2,000,000 | — | — | 0.50 | 1.50 | — |

**1/2 NEW SHEQEL** KM# 168 **Weight:** 7.2000 g. **Composition:** 0.8500 Silver .1967 oz. ASW **Series:** Holyland Sites **Reverse:** Akko

| Date | Mintage | F | VF | XF | Unc | BU |
|---|---|---|---|---|---|---|
| JE5747-1986 | 6,224 | — | — | — | 12.50 | — |

**1/2 NEW SHEQEL** KM# 174 **Composition:** Aluminum-Bronze **Subject:** Hanukkah

| Date | Mintage | F | VF | XF | Unc | BU |
|---|---|---|---|---|---|---|
| JE5747 (1986) | 1,004,000 | — | — | 0.35 | 0.85 | — |
| JE5748 (1987) | 532,000 | — | — | 0.35 | 0.85 | — |
| JE5749 (1988) | 504,000 | — | — | 0.35 | 0.85 | — |
| JE5750 (1989) | 2,016,000 | — | — | 0.35 | 0.85 | — |

| Date | Mintage | F | VF | XF | Unc | BU |
|---|---|---|---|---|---|---|
| JE5751 (1990) | 960,000 | — | — | 0.35 | 0.85 | — |
| JE5752 (1991) | — | — | — | 0.35 | 0.85 | — |
| JE5753 (1992) | 304,000 | — | — | 0.35 | 0.85 | — |
| JE5754 (1993) | 12,000 | — | — | 0.35 | 0.85 | — |
| JE5755 (1994) | 12,000 | — | — | 0.35 | 0.85 | — |
| JE5756 (1995) | — | — | — | 0.35 | 0.85 | — |
| JE5757 (1996) | — | — | — | 0.35 | 0.85 | — |
| JE5758 (1997) | — | — | — | 0.35 | 0.85 | — |

**1/2 NEW SHEQEL** **KM# 180** **Weight:** 7.2000 g. **Composition:** 0.8500 Silver .1967 oz. ASW **Series:** Holyland Sites **Reverse:** Jericho

| Date | Mintage | F | VF | XF | Unc | BU |
|---|---|---|---|---|---|---|
| JE5747--1987 | 7,590 | — | — | — | 13.50 | — |

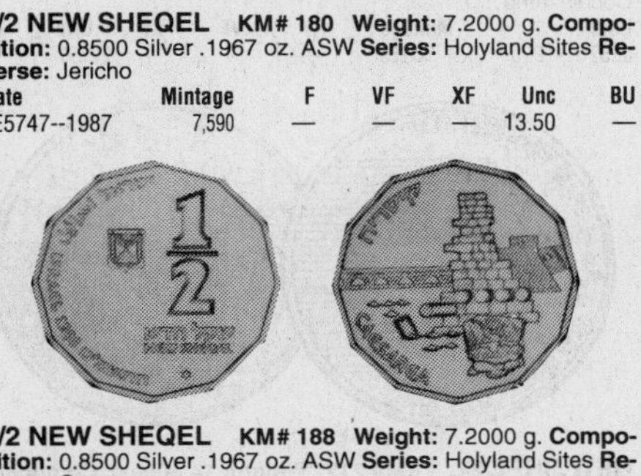

**1/2 NEW SHEQEL** **KM# 188** **Weight:** 7.2000 g. **Composition:** 0.8500 Silver .1967 oz. ASW **Series:** Holyland Sites **Reverse:** Caesarea

| Date | Mintage | F | VF | XF | Unc | BU |
|---|---|---|---|---|---|---|
| JE5749-1988 | 5,865 | — | — | — | 15.00 | — |

**1/2 NEW SHEQEL** **KM# 196** **Composition:** Nickel **Subject:** 40th Anniversary of Independence

| Date | Mintage | F | VF | XF | Unc | BU |
|---|---|---|---|---|---|---|
| JE5748 (1988) | 500,000 | — | — | — | 0.50 | — |

**1/2 NEW SHEQEL** **KM# 202** **Weight:** 7.2000 g. **Composition:** 0.8500 Silver .1967 oz. ASW **Reverse:** Jaffa Harbor

| Date | Mintage | F | VF | XF | Unc | BU |
|---|---|---|---|---|---|---|
| JE5750-1989 | 4,940 | — | — | — | 24.00 | — |

**1/2 NEW SHEQEL** **KM# 209** **Weight:** 7.2000 g. **Composition:** 0.8500 Silver .1967 oz. ASW **Reverse:** Sea of Galilee sites, map

| Date | Mintage | F | VF | XF | Unc | BU |
|---|---|---|---|---|---|---|
| JE5751-1990 | 4,346 | — | — | — | 25.00 | — |

**1/2 NEW SHEQEL** **KM# 303** **Composition:** Copper-Aluminum-Nickel **Series:** Hanukka **Obverse:** Denomination **Reverse:** Theresienstadt lamp **Note:** Struck for sets only.

| Date | Mintage | F | VF | XF | Unc | BU |
|---|---|---|---|---|---|---|
| JE5754 (1993) | 12,000 | — | — | — | 8.00 | — |

**1/2 NEW SHEQEL** **KM# 304** **Composition:** Copper-Aluminum-Nickel **Series:** Hanukka **Obverse:** Denomination **Reverse:** Early American lamp **Note:** Struck for sets only.

| Date | Mintage | F | VF | XF | Unc | BU |
|---|---|---|---|---|---|---|
| JE5755 (1994) | 12,000 | — | — | — | 8.00 | — |

**1/2 NEW SHEQEL** **KM# 305** **Composition:** Copper-Aluminum-Nickel **Series:** Hanukka **Obverse:** Denomination **Reverse:** 14th century French lamp **Note:** Struck for sets only.

| Date | Mintage | F | VF | XF | Unc | BU |
|---|---|---|---|---|---|---|
| JE5756 (1995) | 7,500 | — | — | — | 10.00 | — |

**1/2 NEW SHEQEL** **KM# 318** **Composition:** Copper-Aluminum-Nickel **Series:** Hanukka **Obverse:** Denomination **Reverse:** Russian lamp **Note:** Struck for sets only.

| Date | Mintage | F | VF | XF | Unc | BU |
|---|---|---|---|---|---|---|
| JE5757 (1996) | — | — | — | — | 8.00 | — |

**1/2 NEW SHEQEL** **KM# 314** **Composition:** Copper-Aluminum-Nickel **Series:** Hanukka **Obverse:** Denomination **Reverse:** English lamp **Note:** Struck for sets only.

| Date | Mintage | F | VF | XF | Unc | BU |
|---|---|---|---|---|---|---|
| JE5758 (1997) | 10,000 | — | — | — | 8.00 | — |

**1/2 NEW SHEQEL** **KM# 331** **Composition:** Copper-Aluminum-Nickel **Series:** Hanukka **Obverse:** Denomination **Reverse:** Menorah **Note:** Struck for sets only.

| Date | Mintage | F | VF | XF | Unc | BU |
|---|---|---|---|---|---|---|
| JE5759 (1998) | — | — | — | — | 8.00 | — |

**1/2 NEW SHEQEL** **KM# 324** **Composition:** Bronze **Subject:** High Tech in Israel **Obverse:** Cypruss trees, demonimation **Reverse:** Mosaic bouquet **Note:** Struck for sets only.

| Date | Mintage | F | VF | XF | Unc | BU |
|---|---|---|---|---|---|---|
| JE5760 (1999) | — | — | — | — | 8.00 | — |

**1/2 NEW SHEQEL** **KM# 332** **Composition:** Copper-Aluminum-Nickel **Reverse:** Jerusalem Hanukkah lamp **Note:** Struck for sets only.

| Date | Mintage | F | VF | XF | Unc | BU |
|---|---|---|---|---|---|---|
| JE5760 (1999) | — | — | — | — | 8.00 | — |

**NEW SHEQEL** **KM# 231a** **Weight:** 3.4600 g. **Composition:** 0.9000 Gold .1001 oz. AGW **Series:** Wildlife **Reverse:** Roe and Lily

| Date | Mintage | F | VF | XF | Unc | BU |
|---|---|---|---|---|---|---|
| JE5752 | 2,000 | Value: 125 | | | | |

**NEW SHEQEL** **KM# 163** **Composition:** Copper-Nickel **Subject:** Hanukkah

| Date | Mintage | F | VF | XF | Unc | BU |
|---|---|---|---|---|---|---|
| JE5746 (1985) | 1,056,000 | — | — | 0.65 | 1.50 | — |
| JE5747 (1986) | 1,004,000 | — | — | 0.65 | 1.50 | — |
| JE5748 (1987) | 534,000 | — | — | 0.65 | 1.50 | — |
| JE5749 (1988) | 504,000 | — | — | 0.65 | 1.50 | — |
| JE5750 (1989) | 2,052,000 | — | — | 0.65 | 1.50 | — |
| JE5751 (1990) | 1,104,000 | — | — | 0.65 | 1.50 | — |
| JE5752 (1991) | — | — | — | 0.65 | 1.50 | — |
| JE5753 (1992) | 922,000 | — | — | 0.65 | 1.50 | — |
| JE5754 (1993) | 12,000 | — | — | 0.65 | 1.50 | — |
| JE5755 (1994) | 12,000 | — | — | 0.65 | 1.50 | — |
| JE5756 (1995) | 7,500 | — | — | 0.65 | 1.50 | — |
| JE5757 (1996) | — | — | — | 0.65 | 1.50 | — |
| JE5758 (1997) | — | — | — | 0.65 | 1.50 | — |

**NEW SHEQEL** **KM# 161** **Weight:** 14.4000 g. **Composition:** 0.8500 Silver .3935 oz. ASW **Subject:** Hanukkah **Reverse:** Ashkenaz lamp

| Date | Mintage | F | VF | XF | Unc | BU |
|---|---|---|---|---|---|---|
| JE5745-1985 | 9,460 | — | — | — | 14.00 | — |

**NEW SHEQEL** **KM# 160** **Composition:** Copper-Nickel

| Date | Mintage | F | VF | XF | Unc | BU |
|---|---|---|---|---|---|---|
| JE5745 (1985) | 29,088,000 | — | — | 0.65 | 1.50 | — |
| JE5746 (1986) | 20,960,000 | — | — | 0.65 | 1.50 | — |
| JE5747 (1987) | 216,000 | — | — | 0.65 | 3.00 | — |
| JE5748 (1988) | 20,376,000 | — | — | 0.65 | 1.50 | — |
| JE5749 (1989) | 8,706,000 | — | — | 0.65 | 1.50 | — |
| JE5750 (1990) | 756,000 | — | — | 0.65 | 1.50 | — |
| JE5751 (1991) | 1,152,000 | — | — | 0.65 | 1.50 | — |
| JE5752 (1992) | — | — | — | 0.65 | 1.50 | — |
| JE5753 (1993) | 8,640,000 | — | — | 0.65 | 1.50 | — |
| JE5754 (1994) | 8,000 | — | — | 0.65 | 1.50 | — |
| JE5755 (1995) | 10,000 | — | — | 0.65 | 1.50 | — |

**NEW SHEQEL** **KM# 169** **Weight:** 14.4000 g. **Composition:** 0.8500 Silver .3935 oz. ASW **Series:** Holyland Sites **Reverse:** Akko

| Date | Mintage | F | VF | XF | Unc | BU |
|---|---|---|---|---|---|---|
| JE5747-1986 Proof | 6,117 | Value: 22.00 | | | | |

**NEW SHEQEL** **KM# 175** **Weight:** 14.4000 g. **Composition:** 0.8500 Silver .3935 oz. ASW **Subject:** Hanukkah **Reverse:** Algerian lamp

| Date | Mintage | F | VF | XF | Unc | BU |
|---|---|---|---|---|---|---|
| JE5747-1986 | 8,227 | — | — | — | 18.00 | — |

**NEW SHEQEL** **KM# 164** **Weight:** 14.4000 g. **Composition:** 0.8500 Silver .3935 oz. ASW **Subject:** 38th Anniversary of Independence **Reverse:** Tribute to the arts

| Date | Mintage | F | VF | XF | Unc | BU |
|---|---|---|---|---|---|---|
| JE5746-1986 | 8,010 | — | — | — | 15.00 | — |

**NEW SHEQEL** **KM# 183** **Weight:** 14.4000 g. **Composition:** 0.8500 Silver .3935 oz. ASW **Subject:** Hanukkah **Reverse:** English lamp

| Date | Mintage | F | VF | XF | Unc | BU |
|---|---|---|---|---|---|---|
| JE5748-1987 | 7,810 | — | — | — | 20.00 | — |

**NEW SHEQEL** **KM# 181** **Weight:** 14.4000 g. **Composition:** 0.8500 Silver .3935 oz. ASW **Series:** Holyland Sites **Reverse:** Jericho

| Date | Mintage | F | VF | XF | Unc | BU |
|---|---|---|---|---|---|---|
| JE5748-1987 Proof | 8,196 | Value: 25.00 | | | | |

**NEW SHEQEL** **KM# 177** **Weight:** 14.4000 g. **Composition:** 0.8500 Silver .3935 oz. ASW **Subject:** 20th Anniversary - United Jerusalem

| Date | Mintage | F | VF | XF | Unc | BU |
|---|---|---|---|---|---|---|
| JE5747-1987 | 8,107 | — | — | — | 15.00 | — |

**NEW SHEQEL** **KM# 189** **Weight:** 14.4000 g. **Composition:** 0.8500 Silver .3935 oz. ASW **Series:** Holyland Sites **Reverse:** Caesarea

| Date | Mintage | F | VF | XF | Unc | BU |
|---|---|---|---|---|---|---|
| JE5749-1988 Proof | 6,560 | Value: 32.00 | | | | |

**NEW SHEQEL** **KM# 191** **Weight:** 14.4000 g. **Composition:** 0.8500 Silver .3935 oz. ASW **Subject:** Hanukkah **Reverse:** Tunisian lamp

| Date | Mintage | F | VF | XF | Unc | BU |
|---|---|---|---|---|---|---|
| JE5749-1988 | 6,688 | — | — | — | 22.50 | — |

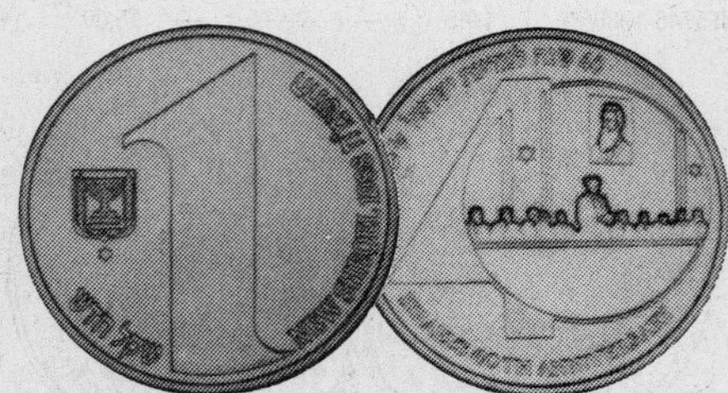

**NEW SHEQEL** **KM# 185** **Weight:** 14.4000 g. **Composition:** 0.8500 Silver .3935 oz. ASW **Subject:** 40th Anniversary of Independence

| Date | Mintage | F | VF | XF | Unc | BU |
|---|---|---|---|---|---|---|
| JE5748-1988 | 8,990 | — | — | — | 13.50 | — |

**NEW SHEQEL** **KM# 197** **Composition:** Nickel **Subject:** 40th Anniversary of Independence

| Date | Mintage | F | VF | XF | Unc | BU |
|---|---|---|---|---|---|---|
| JE5748 (1988) | 504,000 | — | — | — | 1.75 | — |

**NEW SHEQEL** **KM# 198** **Composition:** Nickel **Reverse:** Maimonides

| Date | Mintage | F | VF | XF | Unc | BU |
|---|---|---|---|---|---|---|
| JE5748 (1988) | 980,000 | — | — | — | 1.75 | — |

**NEW SHEQEL** **KM# 199** **Weight:** 14.4000 g. **Composition:** 0.8500 Silver .3935 oz. ASW **Subject:** 41th Anniversary of Independence

| Date | Mintage | F | VF | XF | Unc | BU |
|---|---|---|---|---|---|---|
| JE5749-1989 | 6,249 | — | — | — | 20.00 | — |

**NEW SHEQEL** **KM# 205** **Weight:** 14.4000 g. **Composition:** 0.8500 Silver .3935 oz. ASW **Subject:** Hanukkah **Reverse:** Persian lamp

| Date | Mintage | F | VF | XF | Unc | BU |
|---|---|---|---|---|---|---|
| JE5750-1989 | 6,171 | — | — | — | 20.00 | — |

**NEW SHEQEL** **KM# 203** **Weight:** 14.4000 g. **Composition:** 0.8500 Silver .3935 oz. ASW **Reverse:** Jaffa Harbor

| Date | Mintage | F | VF | XF | Unc | BU |
|---|---|---|---|---|---|---|
| JE5750-1989 Proof | 5,844 | Value: 35.00 | | | | |

**NEW SHEQEL** **KM# 210** **Weight:** 14.4000 g. **Composition:** 0.8500 Silver .3935 oz. ASW **Reverse:** Sea of Galilee sites, map

| Date | Mintage | F | VF | XF | Unc | BU |
|---|---|---|---|---|---|---|
| JE5751-1990 Proof | 4,735 | Value: 40.00 | | | | |

**NEW SHEQEL** **KM# 215** **Weight:** 14.4000 g. **Composition:** 0.8500 Silver .3935 oz. ASW **Subject:** Hanukkah **Reverse:** Cochin lamp

| Date | Mintage | F | VF | XF | Unc | BU |
|---|---|---|---|---|---|---|
| JE5751-1990 | 5,259 | — | — | — | 22.50 | — |

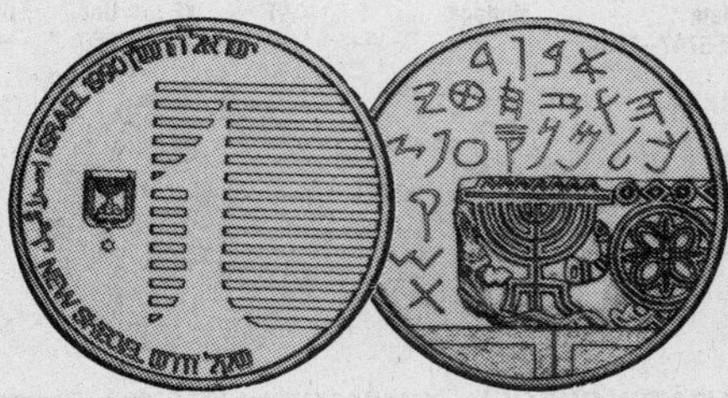


**NEW SHEQEL** **KM# 212** **Weight:** 14.4000 g. **Composition:** 0.8500 Silver .3935 oz. ASW **Subject:** 42th Anniversary of Independence **Reverse:** Archaeology

| Date | Mintage | F | VF | XF | Unc | BU |
|---|---|---|---|---|---|---|
| JE5750-1990 | 5,509 | — | — | — | 22.50 | — |

**NEW SHEQEL** **KM# 218** **Weight:** 14.4000 g. **Composition:** 0.9250 Silver .4282 oz. ASW **Subject:** 43th Anniversary of independence **Reverse:** Immigration to Israel

| Date | Mintage | F | VF | XF | Unc | BU |
|---|---|---|---|---|---|---|
| JE5751-1991 | Est. 15,000 | — | — | — | 20.00 | — |

**NEW SHEQEL** **KM# 220** **Weight:** 14.4000 g. **Composition:** 0.9250 Silver .4282 oz. ASW **Subject:** Flora and Fauna **Reverse:** Cedar trees and dove **Note:** Similar to 2 New Sheqalim, KM#221.

| Date | Mintage | F | VF | XF | Unc | BU |
|---|---|---|---|---|---|---|
| JE5751-1991 | 4,125 | — | — | — | 25.00 | — |

**NEW SHEQEL** **KM# 342** **Weight:** 3.4600 g. **Composition:** 0.9000 Gold .1001 oz. AGW **Subject:** Flora and Fauna **Reverse:** Cedar trees and dove **Note:** Similar to 2 New Sheqalim, KM#221.

| Date | Mintage | F | VF | XF | Unc | BU |
|---|---|---|---|---|---|---|
| JE5751-1991 Proof | 2,515 | Value: 125 | | | | |

**NEW SHEQEL** **KM# 223** **Weight:** 14.4000 g. **Composition:** 0.9250 Silver .4282 oz. ASW **Series:** Judaic **Reverse:** Kiddush cup

| Date | Mintage | F | VF | XF | Unc | BU |
|---|---|---|---|---|---|---|
| JE5751-1991 | 4,876 | — | — | — | 25.00 | — |

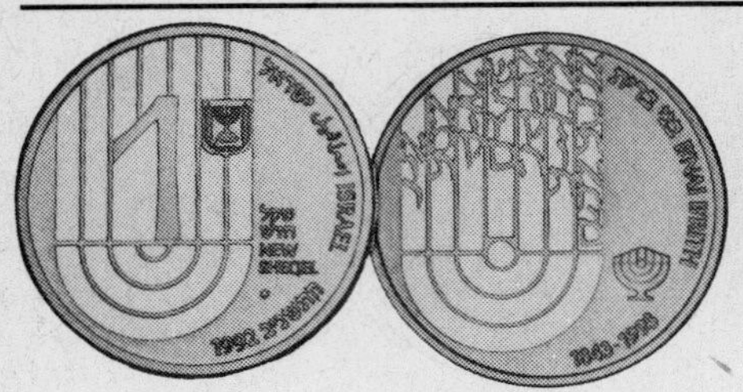


**NEW SHEQEL** **KM# 234** **Weight:** 14.4000 g. **Composition:** 0.9250 Silver .4282 oz. ASW **Series:** Judaic **Note:** B'nai B'rith.

| Date | Mintage | F | VF | XF | Unc | BU |
|---|---|---|---|---|---|---|
| JE5752-1992 | 4,034 | — | — | — | 25.00 | — |

**NEW SHEQEL** **KM# 343** **Weight:** 3.4600 g. **Composition:** 0.9000 Gold .1001 oz. AGW **Series:** Wildlife **Reverse:** Roe and lily

| Date | Mintage | F | VF | XF | Unc | BU |
|---|---|---|---|---|---|---|
| JE5752-1992 Proof | 2,000 | Value: 125 | | | | |

**NEW SHEQEL** **KM# 225** **Weight:** 14.4000 g. **Composition:** 0.9250 Silver .4282 oz. ASW **Subject:** 44th Anniversary of Independence **Reverse:** Israeli law

| Date | Mintage | F | VF | XF | Unc | BU |
|---|---|---|---|---|---|---|
| JE5752-1992 | 4,047 | — | — | — | 35.00 | — |

**NEW SHEQEL** **KM# 238** **Weight:** 14.4000 g. **Composition:** 0.9250 Silver .4282 oz. ASW **Series:** Judaic **Reverse:** Shabbat candles

| Date | Mintage | F | VF | XF | Unc | BU |
|---|---|---|---|---|---|---|
| JE5752-1992 | 5,564 | — | — | — | 25.00 | — |

**NEW SHEQEL** **KM# 240** **Weight:** 14.4000 g. **Composition:** 0.9250 Silver .4282 oz. ASW **Subject:** 45th Anniversary of Independence **Reverse:** Tourism

| Date | Mintage | F | VF | XF | Unc | BU |
|---|---|---|---|---|---|---|
| JE5753-1993 | 6,985 | — | — | — | 22.50 | — |

**NEW SHEQEL** **KM# 250** **Weight:** 14.4000 g. **Composition:** 0.9250 Silver .4282 oz. ASW **Series:** Judaic **Reverse:** Havdalah spicebox

| Date | Mintage | F | VF | XF | Unc | BU |
|---|---|---|---|---|---|---|
| JE5753-1993 | 3,288 | — | — | — | 25.00 | — |

**NEW SHEQEL** **KM# 243** **Weight:** 14.4000 g. **Composition:** 0.9250 Silver .4282 oz. ASW **Series:** Wildlife **Reverse:** A young hart

| Date | Mintage | F | VF | XF | Unc | BU |
|---|---|---|---|---|---|---|
| JE5753-1993 | 3,761 | — | — | — | 25.00 | — |

**NEW SHEQEL** **KM# 244** **Weight:** 3.4600 g. **Composition:** 0.9000 Gold .1001 oz. AGW **Series:** Wildlife **Reverse:** A young hart

| Date | Mintage | F | VF | XF | Unc | BU |
|---|---|---|---|---|---|---|
| JE5753-1993 Proof | 1,679 | Value: 125 | | | | |

**NEW SHEQEL** **KM# 247** **Weight:** 14.4000 g. **Composition:** 0.9250 Silver .4282 oz. ASW **Note:** Revolt and Heroism.

| Date | Mintage | F | VF | XF | Unc | BU |
|---|---|---|---|---|---|---|
| JE5753-1993 | 4,642 | — | — | — | 25.00 | — |

**NEW SHEQEL** **KM# 252** **Weight:** 14.4000 g. **Composition:** 0.9250 Silver .4282 oz. ASW **Subject:** Enviroment **Reverse:** Globe in flower

| Date | Mintage | F | VF | XF | Unc | BU |
|---|---|---|---|---|---|---|
| JE5754-1994 | 3,490 | — | — | — | 25.00 | — |

**NEW SHEQEL** **KM# 256** **Weight:** 14.4000 g. **Composition:** 0.9250 Silver .4282 oz. ASW **Series:** Biblical **Reverse:** Abraham's willingness to sacrifice Isaac

| Date | Mintage | F | VF | XF | Unc | BU |
|---|---|---|---|---|---|---|
| JE5754-1994 | 5,000 | — | — | — | 25.00 | — |

**NEW SHEQEL** **KM# 259** **Weight:** 14.4000 g. **Composition:** 0.9250 Silver .4282 oz. ASW **Obverse:** Palm tree **Reverse:** Leopard

| Date | Mintage | F | VF | XF | Unc | BU |
|---|---|---|---|---|---|---|
| JE5754-1994 | 3,286 | — | — | — | 25.00 | — |

**NEW SHEQEL** **KM# 260** **Weight:** 3.4600 g. **Composition:** 0.9000 Gold .1001 oz. AGW **Obverse:** Palm tree **Reverse:** Leopard

| Date | Mintage | F | VF | XF | Unc | BU |
|---|---|---|---|---|---|---|
| JE5754-1994 | 1,355 | — | — | — | 170 | — |

**NEW SHEQEL** **KM# 160a** **Composition:** Nickel Clad Steel

| Date | Mintage | F | VF | XF | Unc | BU |
|---|---|---|---|---|---|---|
| JE5754 (1994) | — | — | — | — | 1.00 | — |
| JE5754 (1994)(o) | — | — | — | — | 1.00 | — |
| JE5755 (1995) | — | — | — | — | 1.00 | — |
| JE5755 (1995)(o) | — | — | — | — | 1.00 | — |
| JE5756 (1996)(o) | — | — | — | — | 1.00 | — |
| JE5757 (1997) | — | — | — | — | 1.00 | — |
| JE5758 (1998) | — | — | — | — | 1.00 | — |
| JE5759 (1999) | — | — | — | — | 1.00 | — |

**NEW SHEQEL** **KM# 263** **Weight:** 14.4000 g. **Composition:** 0.9250 Silver .4282 oz. ASW **Subject:** Medicine

| Date | Mintage | F | VF | XF | Unc | BU |
|---|---|---|---|---|---|---|
| JE5755-1995 | 3,468 | — | — | — | 25.00 | — |

**NEW SHEQEL** **KM# 267** **Weight:** 14.4000 g. **Composition:** 0.9250 Silver .4282 oz. ASW **Subject:** 50th anniversary - Defeat of Nazi Germany

| Date | Mintage | F | VF | XF | Unc | BU |
|---|---|---|---|---|---|---|
| JE5755-1995 Proof Like | 3,450 | — | — | — | 32.00 | — |

**NEW SHEQEL** **KM# 271** **Weight:** 14.4000 g. **Composition:** 0.9250 Silver .4282 oz. ASW **Series:** F.A.O.

| Date | Mintage | F | VF | XF | Unc | BU |
|---|---|---|---|---|---|---|
| JE5755-1995 Proof Like | Est. 5,000 | — | — | — | 30.00 | — |

**NEW SHEQEL** **KM# 274** **Weight:** 14.4000 g. **Composition:** 0.9250 Silver .4327 oz. ASW **Reverse:** Fox and vineyard

| Date | Mintage | F | VF | XF | Unc | BU |
|---|---|---|---|---|---|---|
| JE5755-1995 | Est. 4,500 | — | — | — | 25.00 | — |

**NEW SHEQEL** **KM# 275** **Weight:** 3.4600 g. **Composition:** 0.9000 Gold .1001 oz. AGW **Reverse:** Fox and vineyard

| Date | Mintage | F | VF | XF | Unc | BU |
|---|---|---|---|---|---|---|
| JE5755-1995 Proof | Est. 2,000 | Value: 125 | | | | |

**NEW SHEQEL** **KM# 278** **Weight:** 14.4000 g. **Composition:** 0.9250 Silver .4282 oz. ASW **Subject:** Peace Treaty with Jordan

| Date | Mintage | F | VF | XF | Unc | BU |
|---|---|---|---|---|---|---|
| JE5755-1995 | Est. 6,000 | — | — | — | 30.00 | — |

**NEW SHEQEL** **KM# 287** **Weight:** 14.4000 g. **Composition:** 0.9250 Silver .4282 oz. ASW **Subject:** Port of Caesarea **Reverse:** Ancient ship

| Date | Mintage | F | VF | XF | Unc | BU |
|---|---|---|---|---|---|---|
| JE5755-1995 | Est. 5,000 | — | — | — | 25.00 | — |

**NEW SHEQEL** **KM# 281** **Weight:** 14.4000 g. **Composition:** 0.9250 Silver .4282 oz. ASW **Subject:** Solomon's Judgment **Note:** Similar to 10 New Sheqalim, KM#283.

| Date | Mintage | F | VF | XF | Unc | BU |
|---|---|---|---|---|---|---|
| JE5755-1995 | Est. 5,000 | — | — | — | 25.00 | — |

**NEW SHEQEL** **KM# 284** **Weight:** 14.4000 g. **Composition:** 0.9250 Silver .4282 oz. ASW **Subject:** Jerusalem's Third Millennium **Note:** Similar to 30 New Sheqalim, KM#286.

| Date | Mintage | F | VF | XF | Unc | BU |
|---|---|---|---|---|---|---|
| JE5756-1996 | Est. 5,000 | — | — | — | 35.00 | — |

**NEW SHEQEL** **KM# 294** **Weight:** 14.4000 g. **Composition:** 0.9250 Silver .4282 oz. ASW **Obverse:** Similar to 10 New Sheqalim, KM#296 **Reverse:** Miriam and the women

| Date | Mintage | F | VF | XF | Unc | BU |
|---|---|---|---|---|---|---|
| JE5756-1996 | Est. 4,500 | — | — | — | 25.00 | — |

**NEW SHEQEL** **KM# 297** **Weight:** 14.4000 g. **Composition:** 0.9250 Silver .4282 oz. ASW **Obverse:** National arms and denomination **Reverse:** Head of Yitzhak Rabin left

| Date | Mintage | F | VF | XF | Unc | BU |
|---|---|---|---|---|---|---|
| JE5756-1996 BU | Est. 5,300 | — | — | — | — | 25.00 |

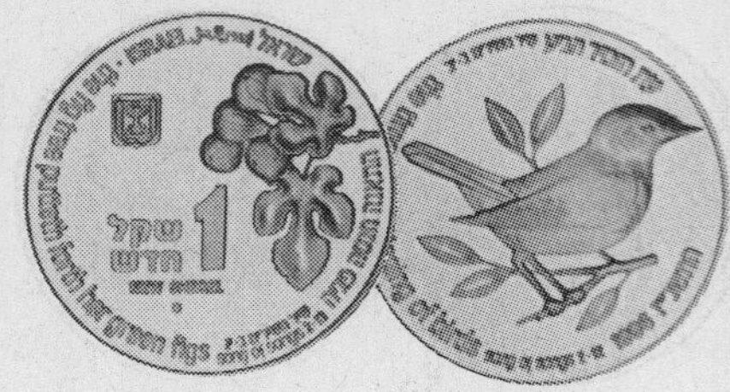

**NEW SHEQEL** **KM# 290** **Weight:** 14.4000 g. **Composition:** 0.9250 Silver .4282 oz. ASW **Reverse:** Nightingale

| Date | Mintage | F | VF | XF | Unc | BU |
|---|---|---|---|---|---|---|
| JE5756-1996 Proof | Est. 3,500 | Value: 25.00 | | | | |

**NEW SHEQEL** **KM# 291** **Weight:** 3.4600 g. **Composition:** 0.9000 Gold .1001 oz. AGW **Reverse:** Nightingale

| Date | Mintage | F | VF | XF | Unc | BU |
|---|---|---|---|---|---|---|
| JE5756 Proof | Est. 1,500 | Value: 120 | | | | |

**NEW SHEQEL** **KM# 307** **Weight:** 3.4600 g. **Composition:** 0.9000 Gold .1001 oz. AGW **Obverse:** Pomegranates and denomination **Reverse:** Lion **Edge:** Reeded

| Date | Mintage | F | VF | XF | Unc | BU |
|---|---|---|---|---|---|---|
| JE5757-1997 Proof | 1,500 | Value: 120 | | | | |

**NEW SHEQEL** **KM# 306** **Weight:** 14.4000 g. **Composition:** 0.9250 Silver .4282 oz. ASW **Obverse:** Pomegranates and denomination **Reverse:** Lion

| Date | Mintage | F | VF | XF | Unc | BU |
|---|---|---|---|---|---|---|
| JE5757-1997 | 3,500 | — | — | — | 27.50 | — |

**NEW SHEQEL** **KM# 300** **Weight:** 14.4000 g. **Composition:** 0.9250 Silver .4282 oz. ASW **Subject:** First Zionist Congress Centennial **Obverse:** Denomination **Reverse:** Portrait of Herzl

| Date | Mintage | F | VF | XF | Unc | BU |
|---|---|---|---|---|---|---|
| JE5757-1997 | 5,000 | — | — | — | 25.00 | — |

**NEW SHEQEL** **KM# 310** **Weight:** 14.4300 g. **Composition:** 0.9250 Silver .4291 oz. ASW **Subject:** 50th Anniversary of Independence **Obverse:** Denominaton **Reverse:** Flag

| Date | Mintage | F | VF | XF | Unc | BU |
|---|---|---|---|---|---|---|
| JE5758-1998 Proof like | Est. 10,000 | — | — | — | 25.00 | — |

**NEW SHEQEL** **KM# 316** **Weight:** 14.4300 g. **Composition:** 0.9250 Silver .4291 oz. ASW **Subject:** Noah's Ark **Obverse:** Dove, rainbow and denomination **Reverse:** Noah releasing dove

| Date | Mintage | F | VF | XF | Unc | BU |
|---|---|---|---|---|---|---|
| JE5758-1998 Proof like | Est. 4,500 | — | — | — | 25.00 | — |

**NEW SHEQEL** **KM# 320** **Weight:** 14.4300 g. **Composition:** 0.9250 Silver .4291 oz. ASW **Obverse:** Cypress trees, denomination **Reverse:** Stork

| Date | Mintage | F | VF | XF | Unc | BU |
|---|---|---|---|---|---|---|
| JE5758 (1998) | — | — | — | — | 25.00 | — |

**NEW SHEQEL** **KM# 321** **Weight:** 3.4600 g. **Composition:** 0.9000 Gold .1001 oz. AGW **Obverse:** Cypress trees, denomination **Reverse:** Stork

| Date | Mintage | F | VF | XF | Unc | BU |
|---|---|---|---|---|---|---|
| JE5758 (1998) Proof | Est. 1,500 | Value: 120 | | | | |

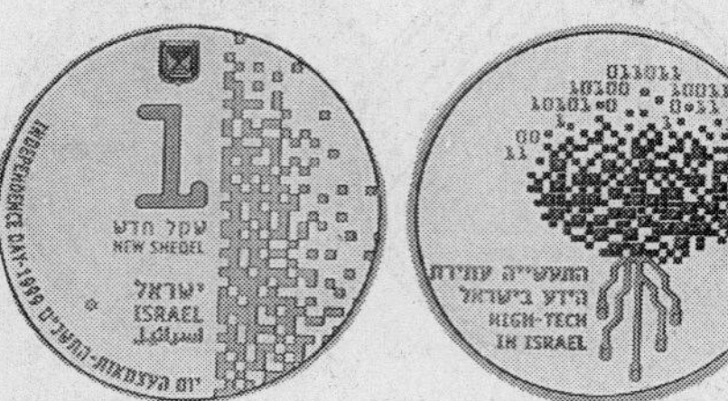

**NEW SHEQEL** **KM# 325** **Weight:** 14.4000 g. **Composition:** 0.9250 Silver .4282 oz. ASW **Subject:** High-Tech in Israel **Obverse:** Denominaton and mosaic **Reverse:** Mosaic bouquet

| Date | Mintage | F | VF | XF | Unc | BU |
|---|---|---|---|---|---|---|
| JE5759 (1999) Prooflike | Est. 2,500 | — | — | — | 27.50 | — |

**NEW SHEQEL** **KM# 333** **Weight:** 14.4000 g. **Composition:** 0.9250 Silver .4282 oz. ASW **Series:** Biblical **Reverse:** Abraham looking at the stars

| Date | Mintage | F | VF | XF | Unc | BU |
|---|---|---|---|---|---|---|
| JE5760-1999 Prooflike | — | — | — | — | 25.00 | — |

**NEW SHEQEL** **KM# 336** **Weight:** 14.4000 g. **Composition:** 0.9250 Silver .4282 oz. ASW **Subject:** Independence Day

**Obverse:** Denomination **Reverse:** Arch above inscription **Edge:** Plain **Size:** 30 mm.

| Date | Mintage | F | VF | XF | Unc | BU |
|---|---|---|---|---|---|---|
| JE5161-2000 Prooflike | — | — | — | — | 25.00 | — |

**NEW SHEQEL KM# 339 Weight:** 14.4000 g. **Composition:** 0.9250 Silver .4282 oz. ASW **Subject:** Joseph and His Brothers **Obverse:** Denomination **Reverse:** Joseph standing before kneeling figures **Edge:** Plain

| Date | Mintage | F | VF | XF | Unc | BU |
|---|---|---|---|---|---|---|
| JE5761-2000 Prooflike | — | — | — | — | 28.00 | — |

**NEW SHEQEL KM# 328 Weight:** 14.4000 g. **Composition:** 0.9250 Silver .4282 oz. ASW **Subject:** The Millenium Coin **Obverse:** Denomination, olive branch **Reverse:** Year 2000 motif incorporating dove with olive branch

| Date | Mintage | F | VF | XF | Unc | BU |
|---|---|---|---|---|---|---|
| JE5760-1999 Prooflike | Est. 2,000 | — | — | — | 30.00 | — |

**NEW SHEQEL KM# 344 Weight:** 14.4000 g. **Composition:** 0.9250 Silver .4282 oz. ASW **Subject:** Independence Day and Education **Obverse:** Denomination **Reverse:** Pomegranate full of symbols **Edge:** Plain **Size:** 30 mm.

| Date | Mintage | F | VF | XF | Unc | BU |
|---|---|---|---|---|---|---|
| 2001 Prooflike | 3,000 | — | — | — | 30.00 | — |

**NEW SHEQEL KM# 347 Weight:** 14.4000 g. **Composition:** 0.9250 Silver .4282 oz. ASW **Obverse:** Shittah tree **Reverse:** Ibex **Edge:** Plain **Size:** 30 mm.

| Date | Mintage | F | VF | XF | Unc | BU |
|---|---|---|---|---|---|---|
| 2001 Prooflike | — | — | — | — | 25.00 | — |

**NEW SHEQEL KM# 348 Weight:** 3.4600 g. **Composition:** 0.9000 Gold .1001 oz. AGW **Obverse:** Shittah tree **Reverse:** Ibex **Edge:** Reeded **Size:** 18 mm.

| Date | Mintage | F | VF | XF | Unc | BU |
|---|---|---|---|---|---|---|
| 2001 Proof | — | Value: 110 | | | | |

**NEW SHEQEL KM# 231 Weight:** 14.4000 g. **Composition:** 0.9250 Silver .4282 oz. ASW **Series:** Wildlife **Reverse:** Roe and lily

| Date | Mintage | F | VF | XF | Unc | BU |
|---|---|---|---|---|---|---|
| JE5752-1992 | 4,105 | — | — | — | 22.50 | — |

**2 NEW SHEQALIM KM# 162 Weight:** 28.8000 g. **Composition:** 0.8500 Silver .7871 oz. ASW **Subject:** Hanukkah **Reverse:** Ashkanaz lamp

| Date | Mintage | F | VF | XF | Unc | BU |
|---|---|---|---|---|---|---|
| JE5745-1985 Proof | 9,225 | Value: 25.00 | | | | |

**2 NEW SHEQALIM KM# 176 Weight:** 28.8000 g. **Composition:** 0.8500 Silver .7871 oz. ASW **Subject:** Hanukkah **Reverse:** Algerian lamp

| Date | Mintage | F | VF | XF | Unc | BU |
|---|---|---|---|---|---|---|
| JE5746-1986 Proof | 8,343 | Value: 25.00 | | | | |

**2 NEW SHEQALIM KM# 165 Weight:** 28.8000 g. **Composition:** 0.8500 Silver .7871 oz. ASW **Subject:** 38th Anniversary of Independence **Reverse:** Tribute to the arts

| Date | Mintage | F | VF | XF | Unc | BU |
|---|---|---|---|---|---|---|
| JE5746-1986 Proof | 7,344 | Value: 25.00 | | | | |

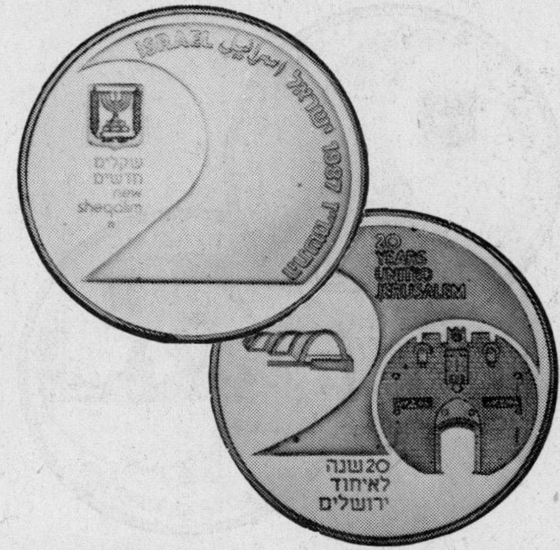


**2 NEW SHEQALIM KM# 178 Weight:** 28.8000 g. **Composition:** 0.8500 Silver .7871 oz. ASW **Subject:** 20th Anniversary - United Jerusalem

| Date | Mintage | F | VF | XF | Unc | BU |
|---|---|---|---|---|---|---|
| JE5747-1987 Proof | 7,788 | Value: 25.00 | | | | |

**2 NEW SHEQALIM KM# 184 Weight:** 28.8000 g. **Composition:** 0.8500 Silver .7871 oz. ASW **Subject:** Hanukkah **Reverse:** English lamp

| Date | Mintage | F | VF | XF | Unc | BU |
|---|---|---|---|---|---|---|
| JE5747-1987 Proof | 8,039 | Value: 28.00 | | | | |

**2 NEW SHEQALIM KM# 192 Weight:** 28.8000 g. **Composition:** 0.8500 Silver .7871 oz. ASW **Subject:** Hanukkah **Reverse:** Tunisian lamp

| Date | Mintage | F | VF | XF | Unc | BU |
|---|---|---|---|---|---|---|
| JE5748-1988 Proof | 7,110 | Value: 30.00 | | | | |

**2 NEW SHEQALIM** **KM# 186** **Weight:** 28.8000 g. **Composition:** 0.8500 Silver .7871 oz. ASW **Subject:** 40th Anniversary of Independence

| Date | Mintage | F | VF | XF | Unc | BU |
|---|---|---|---|---|---|---|
| JE5748-1988 Proof | 9,100 | Value: 25.00 | | | | |

**2 NEW SHEQALIM** **KM# 216** **Weight:** 28.8000 g. **Composition:** 0.8500 Silver .7871 oz. ASW **Subject:** Hanukkah **Reverse:** Cochin lamp

| Date | Mintage | F | VF | XF | Unc | BU |
|---|---|---|---|---|---|---|
| JE5750-1990 Proof | 5,383 | Value: 42.00 | | | | |

**2 NEW SHEQALIM** **KM# 224** **Weight:** 28.8000 g. **Composition:** 0.9250 Silver .8565 oz. ASW **Series:** Judaic **Reverse:** Kiddush cup

| Date | Mintage | F | VF | XF | Unc | BU |
|---|---|---|---|---|---|---|
| JE5751-1991 Proof | 6,575 | Value: 35.00 | | | | |

**2 NEW SHEQALIM** **KM# 200** **Weight:** 28.8000 g. **Composition:** 0.8500 Silver .7871 oz. ASW **Subject:** 41st Aniversary of Independence

| Date | Mintage | F | VF | XF | Unc | BU |
|---|---|---|---|---|---|---|
| JE5749-1989 Proof | 7,062 | Value: 32.00 | | | | |

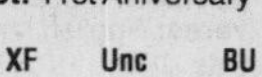
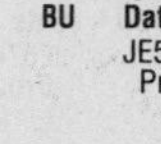
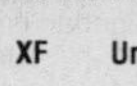

**2 NEW SHEQALIM** **KM# 213** **Weight:** 28.8000 g. **Composition:** 0.8500 Silver .7871 oz. ASW **Subject:** 42nd Aniversary of Independence **Reverse:** Archaeology

| Date | Mintage | F | VF | XF | Unc | BU |
|---|---|---|---|---|---|---|
| JE5750-1990 Proof | 5,457 | Value: 45.00 | | | | |

**2 NEW SHEQALIM** **KM# 221** **Weight:** 28.8000 g. **Composition:** 0.9250 Silver .8565 oz. ASW **Reverse:** Cedar trees and dove **Note:** Flora and Fauna.

| Date | Mintage | F | VF | XF | Unc | BU |
|---|---|---|---|---|---|---|
| JE5751-1991 Proof | 5,005 | Value: 45.00 | | | | |

**2 NEW SHEQALIM** **KM# 206** **Weight:** 28.8000 g. **Composition:** 0.8500 Silver .7871 oz. ASW **Subject:** Hanukkah **Reverse:** Persian lamp

| Date | Mintage | F | VF | XF | Unc | BU |
|---|---|---|---|---|---|---|
| JE5749-1989 Proof | 6,282 | Value: 30.00 | | | | |

**2 NEW SHEQALIM** **KM# 219** **Weight:** 28.8000 g. **Composition:** 0.9250 Silver .8565 oz. ASW **Subject:** 43nd Aniversary of independence **Reverse:** Immigration to Israel

| Date | Mintage | F | VF | XF | Unc | BU |
|---|---|---|---|---|---|---|
| JE5751-1991 Proof | 6,693 | Value: 40.00 | | | | |

**2 NEW SHEQALIM** **KM# 228** **Weight:** 28.8000 g. **Composition:** 0.9250 Silver .8565 oz. ASW **Subject:** IX Paralympic Games

| Date | Mintage | F | VF | XF | Unc | BU |
|---|---|---|---|---|---|---|
| JE5752-1992 Proof | 3,718 | Value: 47.50 | | | | |

**2 NEW SHEQALIM** **KM# 232** **Weight:** 28.8000 g. **Composition:** 0.9250 Silver .8565 oz. ASW **Series:** Wildlife **Reverse:** Rose and lily

| Date | Mintage | F | VF | XF | Unc | BU |
|---|---|---|---|---|---|---|
| JE5752-1992 Proof | 4,724 | Value: 45.00 | | | | |

**2 NEW SHEQALIM** **KM# 226** **Weight:** 28.8000 g. **Composition:** 0.9250 Silver .8565 oz. ASW **Subject:** 44th Anniversary of Independence **Reverse:** Israeli law

| Date | Mintage | F | VF | XF | Unc | BU |
|---|---|---|---|---|---|---|
| JE5752-1992 Proof | 4,486 | Value: 47.50 | | | | |

**2 NEW SHEQALIM** **KM# 239** **Weight:** 28.8000 g. **Composition:** 0.9250 Silver .8565 oz. ASW **Series:** Judaic **Reverse:** Shabbat candles

| Date | Mintage | F | VF | XF | Unc | BU |
|---|---|---|---|---|---|---|
| JE5752-1992 Proof | 4,975 | Value: 35.00 | | | | |

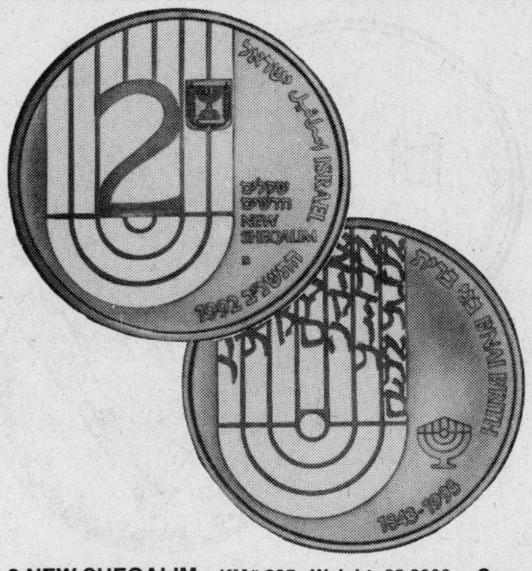


**2 NEW SHEQALIM** **KM# 235** **Weight:** 28.8000 g. **Composition:** 0.9250 Silver .8565 oz. ASW **Note:** B'nai B'rith.

| Date | Mintage | F | VF | XF | Unc | BU |
|---|---|---|---|---|---|---|
| JE5752-1992 Proof | 4,622 | Value: 40.00 | | | | |

**2 NEW SHEQALIM** **KM# 251** **Weight:** 28.8000 g. **Composition:** 0.9250 Silver .8565 oz. ASW **Series:** Judaic **Reverse:** Havdalah spicebox

| Date | Mintage | F | VF | XF | Unc | BU |
|---|---|---|---|---|---|---|
| JE5753-1993 Proof | 4,750 | Value: 35.00 | | | | |

**2 NEW SHEQALIM** **KM# 241** **Weight:** 28.8000 g. **Composition:** 0.9250 Silver .8565 oz. ASW **Series:** Judaic **Subject:** 45th Anniversary of Independence **Reverse:** Tourism

| Date | Mintage | F | VF | XF | Unc | BU |
|---|---|---|---|---|---|---|
| JE5753-1993 Proof | 4,570 | Value: 42.00 | | | | |

**2 NEW SHEQALIM** **KM# 245** **Weight:** 28.8000 g. **Composition:** 0.9250 Silver .8565 oz. ASW **Series:** Wildlife **Reverse:** A young hart

| Date | Mintage | F | VF | XF | Unc | BU |
|---|---|---|---|---|---|---|
| JE5753-1993 Proof | 5,382 | Value: 45.00 | | | | |

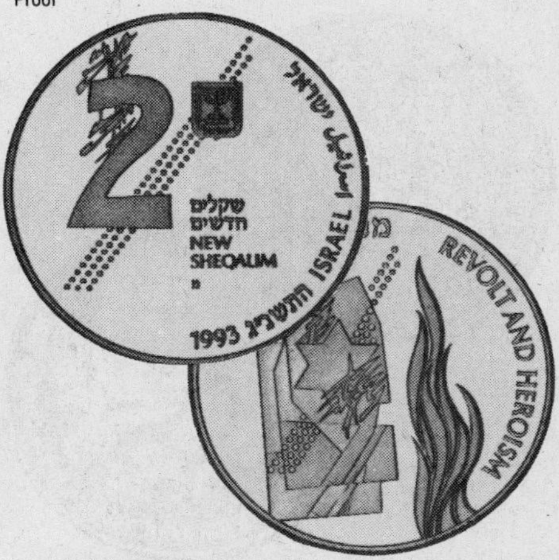


**2 NEW SHEQALIM** **KM# 248** **Weight:** 28.8000 g. **Composition:** 0.9250 Silver .8565 oz. ASW **Subject:** Revolt and Heroism

| Date | Mintage | F | VF | XF | Unc | BU |
|---|---|---|---|---|---|---|
| JE5753-1993 Proof | 4,994 | Value: 35.00 | | | | |

**2 NEW SHEQALIM** **KM# 253** **Weight:** 28.8000 g. **Composition:** 0.9250 Silver .8565 oz. ASW **Subject:** Environment **Reverse:** World globe and flower

| Date | Mintage | F | VF | XF | Unc | BU |
|---|---|---|---|---|---|---|
| JE5754-1994 | 4,272 | — | — | — | 42.00 | — |

**2 NEW SHEQALIM** **KM# 257** **Weight:** 28.8000 g. **Composition:** 0.9250 Silver .8565 oz. ASW **Series:** Biblical **Reverse:** Abrahams' willingness to sacrifice Isaac

| Date | Mintage | F | VF | XF | Unc | BU |
|---|---|---|---|---|---|---|
| JE5754-1994 Proof | 5,000 | Value: 40.00 | | | | |

**2 NEW SHEQALIM** **KM# 261** **Weight:** 28.8000 g. **Composition:** 0.9250 Silver .8565 oz. ASW **Obverse:** Palm tree **Reverse:** Leopard

| Date | Mintage | F | VF | XF | Unc | BU |
|---|---|---|---|---|---|---|
| JE5754-1994 Proof | 4,283 | Value: 40.00 | | | | |

**2 NEW SHEQALIM** **KM# 264** **Weight:** 28.8000 g. **Composition:** 0.9250 Silver .8565 oz. ASW **Subject:** Medicine

| Date | Mintage | F | VF | XF | Unc | BU |
|---|---|---|---|---|---|---|
| JE5755-1995 Proof | 3,698 | Value: 45.00 | | | | |

**2 NEW SHEQALIM** **KM# 268** **Weight:** 28.8000 g. **Composition:** 0.9250 Silver .8565 oz. ASW **Subject:** 50th Anniversary - Defeat of Nazi Germany

| Date | Mintage | F | VF | XF | Unc | BU |
|---|---|---|---|---|---|---|
| JE5755-1995 Proof | 5,808 | Value: 42.00 | | | | |

**2 NEW SHEQALIM** **KM# 272** **Weight:** 28.8000 g. **Composition:** 0.9250 Silver .8565 oz. ASW **Series:** F.A.O.

| Date | Mintage | F | VF | XF | Unc | BU |
|---|---|---|---|---|---|---|
| JE5755-1995 Proof | Est. 4,500 | Value: 42.00 | | | | |

**2 NEW SHEQALIM** **KM# 282** **Weight:** 28.8000 g. **Composition:** 0.9250 Silver .8565 oz. ASW **Series:** Biblical **Subject:** Solom's Judgment **Note:** Similar to 10 New Sheqel, KM#283.

| Date | Mintage | F | VF | XF | Unc | BU |
|---|---|---|---|---|---|---|
| JE5755-1995 Proof | Est. 5,000 | Value: 40.00 | | | | |

**2 NEW SHEQALIM** **KM# 288** **Weight:** 28.8000 g. **Composition:** 0.9250 Silver .8565 oz. ASW **Reverse:** Ancient ship **Note:** Port of Caesarea.

| Date | Mintage | F | VF | XF | Unc | BU |
|---|---|---|---|---|---|---|
| JE5755-1995 Proof | Est. 5,000 | Value: 40.00 | | | | |

**2 NEW SHEQALIM** **KM# 279** **Weight:** 28.8000 g. **Composition:** 0.9250 Silver .8565 oz. ASW **Subject:** Peace Treaty with Jordan **Note:** Similar to 1 New Sheqel, KM#178.

| Date | Mintage | F | VF | XF | Unc | BU |
|---|---|---|---|---|---|---|
| JE5755-1995 Proof | Est. 5,000 | Value: 40.00 | | | | |

**2 NEW SHEQALIM** **KM# 276** **Weight:** 28.8000 g. **Composition:** 0.9250 Silver .8565 oz. ASW **Series:** Wildlife **Reverse:** Fox and vineyard **Note:** Similar to 1 New Sheqel, KM#274.

| Date | Mintage | F | VF | XF | Unc | BU |
|---|---|---|---|---|---|---|
| JE5755-1995 Proof | Est. 4,500 | Value: 40.00 | | | | |

**2 NEW SHEQALIM** **KM# 295** **Weight:** 28.8000 g. **Composition:** 0.9250 Silver .8565 oz. ASW **Reverse:** Miriam and the women **Note:** Similar to 10 New Sheqalim, KM#296.

| Date | Mintage | F | VF | XF | Unc | BU |
|---|---|---|---|---|---|---|
| JE5756-1996 Proof | Est. 4,500 | Value: 45.00 | | | | |

**2 NEW SHEQALIM** **KM# 292** **Weight:** 28.8000 g. **Composition:** 0.9250 Silver .8565 oz. ASW **Reverse:** Nightingale bird

| Date | Mintage | F | VF | XF | Unc | BU |
|---|---|---|---|---|---|---|
| JE5756-1996 Proof | Est. 3,500 | Value: 45.00 | | | | |

**2 NEW SHEQALIM** **KM# 298** **Weight:** 28.8000 g. **Composition:** 0.9250 Silver .8565 oz. ASW **Obverse:** National arms and denomination **Reverse:** Head of Yitzhak Rabin left

| Date | Mintage | F | VF | XF | Unc | BU |
|---|---|---|---|---|---|---|
| JE5756-1996 Proof | Est. 5,300 | Value: 42.50 | | | | |

**2 NEW SHEQALIM KM# 301 Weight:** 28.8000 g. **Composition:** 0.9250 Silver .8565 oz. ASW **Subject:** First Zionist Congress Centennial **Obverse:** Denomination **Reverse:** Portrait of Herzl

| Date | Mintage | F | VF | XF | Unc | BU |
|---|---|---|---|---|---|---|
| JE5757-1997 Proof | 5,000 | Value: 42.50 | | | | |

**2 NEW SHEQALIM KM# 308 Weight:** 28.8000 g. **Composition:** 0.9250 Silver .8565 oz. ASW **Obverse:** Pomegrantes and denomination **Reverse:** Lion **Note:** Lions den.

| Date | Mintage | F | VF | XF | Unc | BU |
|---|---|---|---|---|---|---|
| JE5757-1997 Proof | 3,500 | Value: 45.00 | | | | |

**2 NEW SHEQALIM KM# 322 Weight:** 28.8000 g. **Composition:** 0.9250 Silver .8565 oz. ASW **Obverse:** Cypress tree, denomination **Reverse:** Stork

| Date | Mintage | F | VF | XF | Unc | BU |
|---|---|---|---|---|---|---|
| JE5758 (1998) Proof | — | Value: 45.00 | | | | |

**2 NEW SHEQALIM KM# 317 Weight:** 28.8000 g. **Composition:** 0.9250 Silver .8565 oz. ASW **Subject:** Noah's Ark **Obverse:** Dove, rainbow and denomination **Reverse:** Noah releasing dove

| Date | Mintage | F | VF | XF | Unc | BU |
|---|---|---|---|---|---|---|
| JE5758-1998 Proof | Est. 4,500 | Value: 45.00 | | | | |

**2 NEW SHEQALIM KM# 311 Weight:** 28.8000 g. **Composition:** 0.9250 Silver .8565 oz. ASW **Series:** Judaic **Subject:** 50th Anniversary of Independence **Obverse:** Denomination **Reverse:** Flag

| Date | Mintage | F | VF | XF | Unc | BU |
|---|---|---|---|---|---|---|
| JE5758-1998 Proof | Est. 10,000 | Value: 40.00 | | | | |

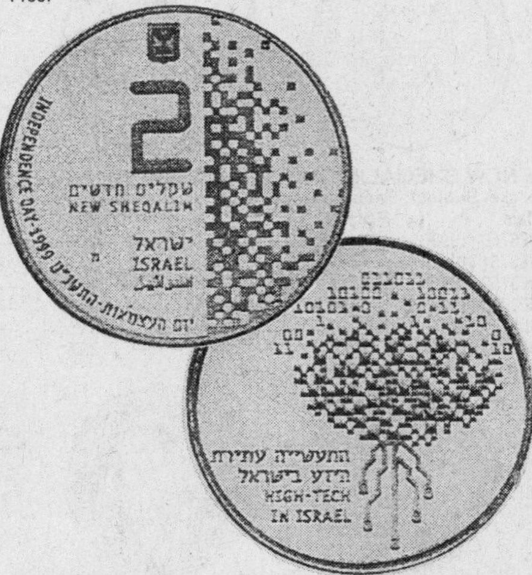

**2 NEW SHEQALIM KM# 326 Weight:** 28.8000 g. **Composition:** 0.9250 Silver .8565 oz. ASW **Subject:** High Tech in Israel **Obverse:** Denomination and mosaic **Reverse:** Mosaic bouquet

| Date | Mintage | F | VF | XF | Unc | BU |
|---|---|---|---|---|---|---|
| JE5759 (1999) Proof | 6,000 | Value: 45.00 | | | | |

**2 NEW SHEQALIM KM# 334 Weight:** 28.8000 g. **Composition:** 0.9250 Silver .8565 oz. ASW **Series:** Biblical **Reverse:** Abraham looking to stars

| Date | Mintage | F | VF | XF | Unc | BU |
|---|---|---|---|---|---|---|
| JE5760-1999 Proof | — | Value: 45.00 | | | | |

**2 NEW SHEQALIM KM# 329 Weight:** 28.8000 g. **Composition:** 0.9250 Silver .8565 oz. ASW **Obverse:** Denomination, olive branch **Reverse:** Year 2000 motif incorporating dove with olive branch **Note:** The Millennium coin.

| Date | Mintage | F | VF | XF | Unc | BU |
|---|---|---|---|---|---|---|
| JE5760-1999 Proof | — | Value: 45.00 | | | | |

**2 NEW SHEQALIM KM# 337 Weight:** 28.8000 g. **Composition:** 0.9250 Silver .8565 oz. ASW **Subject:** Independence Day **Obverse:** Denomination **Reverse:** Arch above inscription **Edge:** Plain **Size:** 38.7 mm.

| Date | Mintage | F | VF | XF | Unc | BU |
|---|---|---|---|---|---|---|
| JE5761-2000 Proof | — | Value: 45.00 | | | | |

**2 NEW SHEQALIM KM# 340 Weight:** 28.8000 g. **Composition:** 0.9250 Silver .8565 oz. ASW **Subject:** Joseph and His Brothers **Obverse:** Denomination **Reverse:** Joseph standing before kneeling figures **Edge:** Reeded **Size:** 38.7 mm.

| Date | Mintage | F | VF | XF | Unc | BU |
|---|---|---|---|---|---|---|
| JE5761-2000 Proof | — | Value: 45.00 | | | | |

**2 NEW SHEQALIM KM# 345 Weight:** 28.8000 g. **Composition:** 0.9250 Silver .8564 oz. ASW **Subject:** Independence Day and Education **Obverse:** Denomination **Reverse:** Pomegranate full of symbols **Edge:** Reeded **Size:** 38.7 mm.

| Date | Mintage | F | VF | XF | Unc | BU |
|---|---|---|---|---|---|---|
| 2001 Proof | 3,000 | Value: 45.00 | | | | |

**2 NEW SHEQALIM** **KM# 349** **Weight:** 28.8000 g. **Composition:** 0.9250 Silver .8564 oz. ASW **Obverse:** Shittah tree **Reverse:** Ibex **Edge:** Reeded **Size:** 38.7 mm.

| Date | Mintage | F | VF | XF | Unc | BU |
|---|---|---|---|---|---|---|
| 2001 Prooflike | — | — | — | — | 45.00 | — |

**5 NEW SHEQALIM** **KM# 170** **Weight:** 8.6300 g. **Composition:** 0.9000 Gold .2497 oz. AGW **Series:** Holyland Sites **Reverse:** Akko **Note:** Similar to 1 New Sheqel, KM#169.

| Date | Mintage | F | VF | XF | Unc | BU |
|---|---|---|---|---|---|---|
| JE5746-1986 Proof | 2,800 | Value: 225 | | | | |

**5 NEW SHEQALIM** **KM# 182** **Weight:** 8.6300 g. **Composition:** 0.9000 Gold .2497 oz. AGW **Series:** Holyland Sites **Reverse:** Jericho

| Date | Mintage | F | VF | XF | Unc | BU |
|---|---|---|---|---|---|---|
| JE5747-1987 Proof | 4,000 | Value: 185 | | | | |

**5 NEW SHEQALIM** **KM# 190** **Weight:** 8.6300 g. **Composition:** 0.9000 Gold .2497 oz. AGW **Series:** Holyland Sites **Reverse:** Caesarea

| Date | Mintage | F | VF | XF | Unc | BU |
|---|---|---|---|---|---|---|
| JE5748-1988 Proof | 3,454 | Value: 210 | | | | |

**5 NEW SHEQALIM** **KM# 204** **Weight:** 8.6300 g. **Composition:** 0.9000 Gold .2497 oz. AGW **Series:** Holyland Sites **Reverse:** Jaffa Harbor

| Date | Mintage | F | VF | XF | Unc | BU |
|---|---|---|---|---|---|---|
| JE5749-1989 Proof | 2,402 | Value: 250 | | | | |

**5 NEW SHEQALIM** **KM# 207** **Composition:** Copper-Nickel

| Date | Mintage | F | VF | XF | Unc | BU |
|---|---|---|---|---|---|---|
| JE5750 (1990) | 15,000,000 | — | — | — | 3.75 | — |
| JE5751 (1991) | 324,000 | — | — | — | 3.75 | — |
| JE5752 (1992) | — | — | — | — | 3.75 | — |
| JE5753 (1993) | 8,000 | — | — | — | 3.75 | — |
| JE5754 (1994) | 8,000 | — | — | — | 3.75 | — |
| JE5755 (1995) | 10,000 | — | — | — | 3.75 | — |
| JE5757 (1997) | — | — | — | — | 3.75 | — |
| JE5758 (1998) | — | — | — | — | 3.75 | — |
| JE5759 (1999) | — | — | — | — | 3.75 | — |

**5 NEW SHEQALIM** **KM# 208** **Composition:** Copper-Nickel **Reverse:** Bust of Levi Eshkol

| Date | Mintage | F | VF | XF | Unc | BU |
|---|---|---|---|---|---|---|
| JE5750 (1990) | 1,500,000 | — | — | — | 5.00 | — |

**5 NEW SHEQALIM** **KM# 217** **Composition:** Copper-Nickel **Subject:** Hanukka **Reverse:** Ancient column

| Date | Mintage | F | VF | XF | Unc | BU |
|---|---|---|---|---|---|---|
| JE5750 (1990) | 500,000 | — | — | — | 3.75 | — |
| JE5751 (1991) | — | — | — | — | 3.75 | — |
| JE5752 (1992) | 501,000 | — | — | — | 3.75 | — |
| JE5753 (1993) | 12,000 | — | — | — | 3.75 | — |
| JE5754 (1994) | 12,000 | — | — | — | 3.75 | — |
| JE5755 (1995) | 7,500 | — | — | — | 3.75 | — |

**5 NEW SHEQALIM** **KM# 211** **Weight:** 8.6300 g. **Composition:** 0.9000 Gold .2497 oz. AGW **Series:** Holyland Sites **Reverse:** Sea of Galilee map

| Date | Mintage | F | VF | XF | Unc | BU |
|---|---|---|---|---|---|---|
| JE5750-1990 Proof | 1,935 | Value: 320 | | | | |

**5 NEW SHEQALIM** **KM# 222** **Weight:** 8.6300 g. **Composition:** 0.9000 Gold .2497 oz. AGW **Obverse:** 2 cedar trees, denomination **Reverse:** Dove and tree trunk in legend **Note:** Flora and Fauna

| Date | Mintage | F | VF | XF | Unc | BU |
|---|---|---|---|---|---|---|
| JE5751-1991 Proof | 2,000 | Value: 260 | | | | |

**5 NEW SHEQALIM** **KM# 236** **Weight:** 8.6300 g. **Composition:** 0.9000 Gold .2497 oz. AGW **Reverse:** Stylized design with inscription **Note:** B'nai B'rith

| Date | Mintage | F | VF | XF | Unc | BU |
|---|---|---|---|---|---|---|
| JE5752 Proof | 2,305 | Value: 260 | | | | |

**5 NEW SHEQALIM** **KM# 237** **Composition:** Copper-Nickel **Reverse:** Bust of Chaim Weizmann

| Date | Mintage | F | VF | XF | Unc | BU |
|---|---|---|---|---|---|---|
| JE5752-1992 | 1,501,000 | — | — | — | 5.00 | — |
| JE5753-1993 | — | — | — | — | 5.00 | — |

**5 NEW SHEQALIM** **KM# 229** **Weight:** 8.6300 g. **Composition:** 0.9000 Gold .2497 oz. AGW **Subject:** IX Paralympic Games

| Date | Mintage | F | VF | XF | Unc | BU |
|---|---|---|---|---|---|---|
| JE5752-1992 Proof | 1,629 | Value: 375 | | | | |

**5 NEW SHEQALIM** **KM# 233** **Weight:** 8.6300 g. **Composition:** 0.9000 Gold .2497 oz. AGW **Series:** Wildlife **Obverse:** Lily **Reverse:** Roe

| Date | Mintage | F | VF | XF | Unc | BU |
|---|---|---|---|---|---|---|
| JE5752-1992 Proof | 2,150 | Value: 225 | | | | |

**5 NEW SHEQALIM** **KM# 246** **Weight:** 8.6300 g. **Composition:** 0.9000 Gold .2497 oz. AGW **Series:** Wildlife **Reverse:** A young hart

| Date | Mintage | F | VF | XF | Unc | BU |
|---|---|---|---|---|---|---|
| JE5753-1993 Proof | 1,782 | Value: 235 | | | | |

**5 NEW SHEQALIM** **KM# 254** **Weight:** 8.6300 g. **Composition:** 0.9000 Gold .2497 oz. AGW **Subject:** Enviroment **Reverse:** World globe in flower

| Date | Mintage | F | VF | XF | Unc | BU |
|---|---|---|---|---|---|---|
| JE5754-1994 Proof | 1,407 | Value: 240 | | | | |

**5 NEW SHEQALIM** **KM# 265** **Weight:** 8.6300 g. **Composition:** 0.9000 Gold .2497 oz. AGW **Subject:** Medicine

| Date | Mintage | F | VF | XF | Unc | BU |
|---|---|---|---|---|---|---|
| JE5755-1995 Proof | 1,155 | Value: 325 | | | | |

**5 NEW SHEQALIM** **KM# 277** **Weight:** 8.6300 g. **Composition:** 0.9000 Gold .2497 oz. AGW **Reverse:** Fox and vineyard **Note:** Similar to 1 New Sheqalim, KM#274.

| Date | Mintage | F | VF | XF | Unc | BU |
|---|---|---|---|---|---|---|
| JE5755-1995 Proof | Est. 2,000 | Value: 220 | | | | |

**5 NEW SHEQALIM** **KM# 293** **Weight:** 8.6300 g. **Composition:** 0.9000 Gold .2497 oz. AGW **Reverse:** Nightingale **Note:** Similar to 1 New Sheqalim, KM#290.

| Date | Mintage | F | VF | XF | Unc | BU |
|---|---|---|---|---|---|---|
| JE5756-1996 Proof | Est. 1,500 | Value: 240 | | | | |

**5 NEW SHEQALIM** **KM# 309** **Weight:** 8.6300 g. **Composition:** 0.9000 Gold .2497 oz. AGW **Obverse:** Pomegranates and denominaton **Reverse:** Lion

| Date | Mintage | F | VF | XF | Unc | BU |
|---|---|---|---|---|---|---|
| JE5757-1997 Proof | 1,500 | Value: 240 | | | | |

**5 NEW SHEQALIM** **KM# 323** **Weight:** 8.6300 g. **Composition:** 0.9000 Gold .2497 oz. AGW **Obverse:** Cypress tree **Reverse:** Stork

| Date | Mintage | F | VF | XF | Unc | BU |
|---|---|---|---|---|---|---|
| JE5758 (1998) Proof | — | Value: 240 | | | | |

**5 NEW SHEQALIM** **KM# 350** **Weight:** 8.6300 g. **Composition:** 0.9000 Gold .2497 oz. AGW **Obverse:** Shittah tree **Reverse:** Ibex **Edge:** Reeded **Size:** 22 mm.

| Date | Mintage | F | VF | XF | Unc | BU |
|---|---|---|---|---|---|---|
| 2001 Proof | — | Value: 225 | | | | |

**10 NEW SHEQALIM** **KM# 166** **Weight:** 17.2800 g. **Composition:** 0.9000 Gold .5000 oz. AGW **Subject:** 38th Anniversary of Independence **Reverse:** Tribute to the arts

| Date | Mintage | F | VF | XF | Unc | BU |
|---|---|---|---|---|---|---|
| JE5746-1986 Proof | 2,485 | Value: 460 | | | | |

**10 NEW SHEQALIM** **KM# 179** **Weight:** 17.2800 g. **Composition:** 0.9000 Gold .5000 oz. AGW **Subject:** 39th Anniversary - United Jerusalem

| Date | Mintage | F | VF | XF | Unc | BU |
|---|---|---|---|---|---|---|
| JE5747-1987 Proof | 3,200 | Value: 325 | | | | |

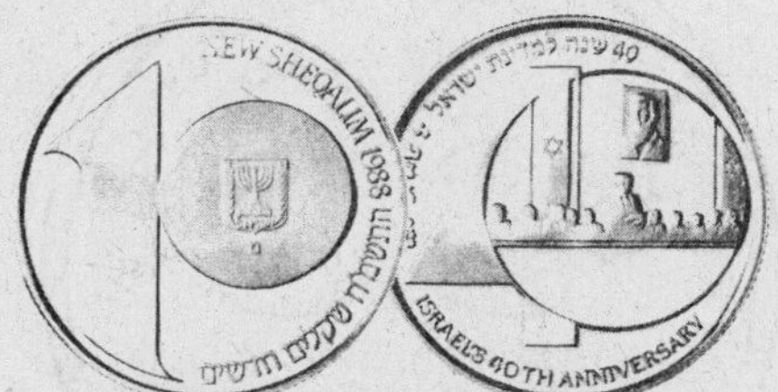

**10 NEW SHEQALIM** **KM# 187** **Weight:** 17.2800 g. **Composition:** 0.9000 Gold .5000 oz. AGW **Subject:** 40th Anniversary of Independence

| Date | Mintage | F | VF | XF | Unc | BU |
|---|---|---|---|---|---|---|
| JE5748-1988 Proof | Est. 4,575 | Value: 245 | | | | |

**10 NEW SHEQALIM** **KM# 201** **Weight:** 17.2800 g. **Composition:** 0.9000 Gold .5000 oz. AGW **Subject:** 41th Anniversary of Independence **Reverse:** Gazelle in forest, legend at left

| Date | Mintage | F | VF | XF | Unc | BU |
|---|---|---|---|---|---|---|
| JE5749-1989 Proof | 2,743 | Value: 335 | | | | |

**10 NEW SHEQALIM** **KM# 214** **Weight:** 17.2800 g. **Composition:** 0.9000 Gold .5000 oz. AGW **Subject:** 42nd Anniversary of Independence **Reverse:** Archaeology

| Date | Mintage | F | VF | XF | Unc | BU |
|---|---|---|---|---|---|---|
| JE5750-1990 Proof | 1,815 | Value: 550 | | | | |

**10 NEW SHEQALIM** **KM# 230** **Weight:** 17.2800 g. **Composition:** 0.9000 Gold .5000 oz. AGW **Subject:** 43rd Anniversary of Independence **Reverse:** Immigration to Israel

| Date | Mintage | F | VF | XF | Unc | BU |
|---|---|---|---|---|---|---|
| JE5751-1991 Proof | 2,236 | Value: 385 | | | | |

**10 NEW SHEQALIM** **KM# 227** **Weight:** 17.2800 g. **Composition:** 0.9000 Gold .5000 oz. AGW **Subject:** 44th Anniversary of Independence **Reverse:** Israeli law **Note:** Edge varieties exist.

| Date | Mintage | F | VF | XF | Unc | BU |
|---|---|---|---|---|---|---|
| JE5752-1992 Proof | 2,125 | Value: 650 | | | | |

**10 NEW SHEQALIM** **KM# 249** **Weight:** 17.2800 g. **Composition:** 0.9000 Gold .5000 oz. AGW **Obverse:** State emblem, denomination and legend **Reverse:** Tourism **Note:** Revolt and Heroism.

| Date | Mintage | F | VF | XF | Unc | BU |
|---|---|---|---|---|---|---|
| JE5753-1993 Proof | 1,583 | Value: 425 | | | | |

**10 NEW SHEQALIM** **KM# 242** **Weight:** 17.2800 g. **Composition:** 0.9000 Gold .5000 oz. AGW **Subject:** 45th Anniversary of Independence **Reverse:** Tourism

| Date | Mintage | F | VF | XF | Unc | BU |
|---|---|---|---|---|---|---|
| JE5753-1993 Proof | 1,944 | Value: 350 | | | | |

**10 NEW SHEQALIM** **KM# 255** **Weight:** 17.2800 g. **Composition:** 0.9000 Gold .5000 oz. AGW **Subject:** Enviroment **Reverse:** World globe in flower

| Date | Mintage | F | VF | XF | Unc | BU |
|---|---|---|---|---|---|---|
| JE5754-1994 Proof | 1,482 | Value: 400 | | | | |

**10 NEW SHEQALIM** **KM# 258** **Weight:** 17.2800 g. **Composition:** 0.9000 Gold .5000 oz. AGW **Reverse:** Abraham's willingness to sacrifice Isaac

| Date | Mintage | F | VF | XF | Unc | BU |
|---|---|---|---|---|---|---|
| JE5754-1994 Proof | Est. 2,000 | Value: 375 | | | | |

**10 NEW SHEQALIM** **KM# 262** **Center Weight:** 8.6300 g. **Center Composition:** 0.9000 Gold .2497 oz. AGW **Obverse:** Palm tree **Reverse:** Leopard

| Date | Mintage | F | VF | XF | Unc | BU |
|---|---|---|---|---|---|---|
| JE5754-1994 Proof | 1,535 | Value: 240 | | | | |

**10 NEW SHEQALIM** **KM# 283** **Weight:** 17.2800 g. **Composition:** 0.9000 Gold .5000 oz. AGW **Subject:** Solomon's Judgement

| Date | Mintage | F | VF | XF | Unc | BU |
|---|---|---|---|---|---|---|
| JE5755(1995) Proof | Est. 2,000 | Value: 375 | | | | |

**10 NEW SHEQALIM** **KM# 266** **Weight:** 17.2800 g. **Composition:** 0.9000 Gold .5000 oz. AGW **Subject:** Medicine

| Date | Mintage | F | VF | XF | Unc | BU |
|---|---|---|---|---|---|---|
| JE5755-1995 Proof | 1,230 | Value: 450 | | | | |

**10 NEW SHEQALIM** **KM# 269** **Weight:** 16.9600 g. **Composition:** 0.9170 Gold .4998 oz. AGW **Subject:** 50th Anniversary - Defeat of Nazi Germany

| Date | Mintage | F | VF | XF | Unc | BU |
|---|---|---|---|---|---|---|
| JE5755-1995 Proof | 1,742 | Value: 380 | | | | |

**10 NEW SHEQALIM** **KM# 270** **Ring Composition:** Nickel Bonded Steel **Center Composition:** Aureate Bonded Bronze

| Date | Mintage | F | VF | XF | Unc | BU |
|---|---|---|---|---|---|---|
| JE5755 (1995) | Est. 18,000 | — | — | — | 7.00 | — |

**10 NEW SHEQALIM** **KM# 273** **Ring Composition:** Nickel Bonded Steel **Center Composition:** Aureate Bonded Bronze **Reverse:** Bust of Golda Meir

| Date | Mintage | F | VF | XF | Unc | BU |
|---|---|---|---|---|---|---|
| JE5755 (1995) | 1,500,000 | — | — | — | 10.00 | — |

**10 NEW SHEQALIM** **KM# 280** **Weight:** 16.9600 g. **Composition:** 0.9170 Gold .4998 oz. AGW **Subject:** Peace Treaty with Jordan

| Date | Mintage | F | VF | XF | Unc | BU |
|---|---|---|---|---|---|---|
| JE5755-1995 Proof | Est. 1,500 | Value: 400 | | | | |

**10 NEW SHEQALIM** **KM# 289** **Weight:** 16.9600 g. **Composition:** 0.9170 Gold .4998 oz. AGW **Reverse:** Port of Caesarea, ancient ship **Note:** Similar to 1 New Sheqalim, KM#287.

| Date | Mintage | F | VF | XF | Unc | BU |
|---|---|---|---|---|---|---|
| JE5755-1995 Proof | Est. 1,700 | Value: 385 | | | | |

**10 NEW SHEQALIM** **KM# 285** **Weight:** 16.9600 g. **Composition:** 0.9170 Gold .4998 oz. AGW **Subject:** Jerusalem's Third Millennium **Note:** Similar to 30 New Sheqalim, KM#286.

| Date | Mintage | F | VF | XF | Unc | BU |
|---|---|---|---|---|---|---|
| JE5756-1996 Proof | Est. 1,996 | Value: 380 | | | | |

**10 NEW SHEQALIM** **KM# 296** **Weight:** 17.2800 g. **Composition:** 0.9000 Gold .5000 oz. AGW **Reverse:** Miriam and the women

| Date | Mintage | F | VF | XF | Unc | BU |
|---|---|---|---|---|---|---|
| JE5756-1996 Proof | Est. 1,500 | Value: 400 | | | | |

**10 NEW SHEQALIM** **KM# 302** **Weight:** 17.2800 g. **Composition:** 0.9000 Gold .5000 oz. AGW **Subject:** First Zionist Congress Centennial **Obverse:** Denomination **Reverse:** Portrait of Herzl

| Date | Mintage | F | VF | XF | Unc | BU |
|---|---|---|---|---|---|---|
| JE5757-1997 Proof | 1,500 | Value: 400 | | | | |

**10 NEW SHEQALIM** **KM# 315** **Ring Composition:** Nickel Bonded Steel **Center Composition:** Aureate **Subject:** Hannukah **Obverse:** Denomination **Reverse:** Palm tree and baskets

| Date | Mintage | F | VF | XF | Unc | BU |
|---|---|---|---|---|---|---|
| JE5757 (1997) | 10,000 | — | — | — | 7.00 | — |

**10 NEW SHEQALIM** **KM# 312** **Weight:** 15.5500 g. **Composition:** 0.9990 Gold .4994 oz. AGW **Subject:** 50th Anniversary of Independence **Obverse:** Denomination **Reverse:** Flag

| Date | Mintage | F | VF | XF | Unc | BU |
|---|---|---|---|---|---|---|
| JE5758 (1998) Proof | Est. 3,000 | Value: 360 | | | | |

**10 NEW SHEQALIM** **KM# 319** **Weight:** 17.2800 g. **Composition:** 0.9000 Gold .5000 oz. AGW **Subject:** Noah's Ark **Obverse:** Rainbow, dove, denomination **Reverse:** Noah releasing dove from ark

| Date | Mintage | F | VF | XF | Unc | BU |
|---|---|---|---|---|---|---|
| JE5758 (1998) Proof | Est. 1,500 | Value: 400 | | | | |

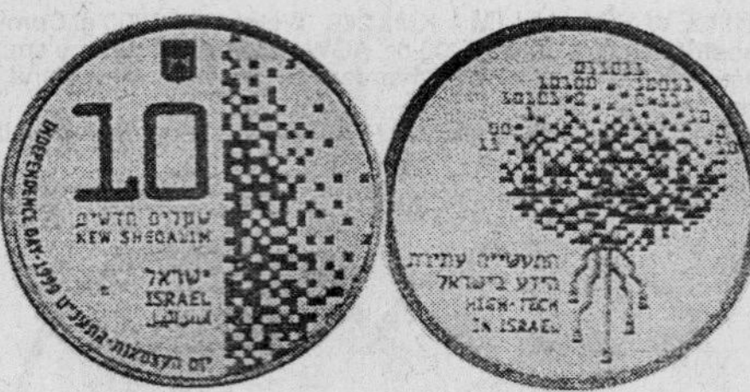


**10 NEW SHEQALIM** **KM# 327** **Weight:** 16.9600 g. **Composition:** 0.9170 Gold .5000 oz. AGW **Subject:** High-Tech in Israel **Obverse:** Denomination and mosaic **Reverse:** Mosaic bouquet

| Date | Mintage | F | VF | XF | Unc | BU |
|---|---|---|---|---|---|---|
| JE5759 (1999) Proof | 2,000 | Value: 600 | | | | |

**10 NEW SHEQALIM** **KM# 330** **Weight:** 16.9600 g. **Composition:** 0.9170 Gold .5000 oz. AGW **Subject:** The Millennium Coin **Obverse:** Denomination, olive branch **Reverse:** Year 2000 motif incorporating dove with olive branch

| Date | Mintage | F | VF | XF | Unc | BU |
|---|---|---|---|---|---|---|
| JE5760-1999 Proof | Est. 2,000 | Value: 400 | | | | |

**10 NEW SHEQALIM** **KM# 338** **Weight:** 16.9600 g. **Composition:** 0.9170 Gold .5000 oz. AGW **Subject:** Love Thy Neighbor **Obverse:** Gates of Jerusalem **Reverse:** Back of gate; arch above inscription **Edge:** Reeded

| Date | Mintage | F | VF | XF | Unc | BU |
|---|---|---|---|---|---|---|
| JE5760-2000 Proof | — | Value: 400 | | | | |

**10 NEW SHEQALIM** **KM# 341** **Weight:** 16.9600 g. **Composition:** 0.9170 Gold .5000 oz. AGW **Series:** Biblical **Obverse:** Denomination **Reverse:** Joseph standing before kneeling figures. **Edge:** Reeded **Size:** 30 mm.

| Date | Mintage | F | VF | XF | Unc | BU |
|---|---|---|---|---|---|---|
| JE5761-2000 Proof | 1,000 | Value: 400 | | | | |

**10 NEW SHEQALIM** **KM# 346** **Weight:** 16.9600 g. **Composition:** 0.9170 Gold .5000 oz. AGW **Subject:** Independence Day and Education **Obverse:** Denomination **Reverse:** Pomegranate full of symbols **Edge:** Reeded **Size:** 30 mm.

| Date | Mintage | F | VF | XF | Unc | BU |
|---|---|---|---|---|---|---|
| 2001 Proof | 1,200 | Value: 430 | | | | |

**20 NEW SHEQALIM** **KM# 299** **Weight:** 31.1035 g. **Composition:** 0.9990 Gold 1.0000 oz. AGW **Obverse:** Arms above denomination **Reverse:** Head of Yitzhak Rabin left

| Date | Mintage | F | VF | XF | Unc | BU |
|---|---|---|---|---|---|---|
| JE5756-1996 Proof | 1,999 | Value: 1,000 | | | | |

**20 NEW SHEQALIM** **KM# 313** **Weight:** 31.1035 g. **Composition:** 0.9990 Gold 1.0000 oz. AGW **Subject:** 50th Anniversary of Independence **Obverse:** Denomination **Reverse:** Flag

| Date | Mintage | F | VF | XF | Unc | BU |
|---|---|---|---|---|---|---|
| JE5758-1998 Proof | Est. 3,000 | Value: 600 | | | | |

**30 NEW SHEQALIM** **KM# 286** **Weight:** 155.5175 g. **Composition:** 0.9990 Silver 5.0000 oz. ASW **Subject:** Jerusalem's Third Millennium **Note:** Illustration reduced. Actual size: 65mm.

| Date | Mintage | F | VF | XF | Unc | BU |
|---|---|---|---|---|---|---|
| JE5756-1996 Proof | Est. 4,000 | Value: 175 | | | | |

## PATTERNS

| KM# | Date | Mintage | Identification | Mkt Val |
|---|---|---|---|---|
| Pn1 | 1960 | — | Agorah. 8 fat and wide grains. Large 9.50mm 1 and date. | — |
| Pn2 | 1960 | — | Agorah. 8 thin and narrow grains. Small 9.00mm 1 and large date. | — |
| Pn3 | 1960 | — | Agorah. 8 thin and narrow grains. Large 9.50mm 1 and date. | — |

## PIEFORTS

| KM# | Date | Mintage | Identification | Mkt Val |
|---|---|---|---|---|
| P1 | 5741-1981 | 30,217 | New Agorah. Copper-Nickel. KM106. | 1.25 |
| P2 | 5741 | 30,217 | 5 New Agorot. Copper-Nickel. KM107. | 1.50 |
| P3 | 5741-1981 | 30,217 | 10 New Agorot. Bronze. KM108. | 2.00 |
| P4 | 5741-1981 | 30,217 | 1/2 Sheqel. KM109. | 2.50 |
| P5 | 5741-1981 | 30,217 | Sheqel. KM111. | 3.50 |
| **Note:** P1-5 were struck at the Bern Mint | | | | |
| P6 | 5742-1982 | 18,735 | New Agorah. Copper-Nickel. KM106 | 3.00 |
| P7 | 5742-1982 | 19,735 | 5 New Agorot. Copper-Nickel. KM107. | 3.00 |
| P8 | 5742-1982 | 18,735 | 10 New Agorot. KM108. | 3.00 |
| P9 | 5742-1982 | 21,735 | 1/2 Sheqel. KM109. | 4.50 |
| P10 | 5742-1982 | 19,735 | Sheqel. KM111. | 4.50 |
| P11 | 5742-1982 | 20,735 | 5 Sheqalim. KM118. | 7.00 |
| P15 | 5743-1983 | 17,177 | 1/2 Sheqel. KM109. | 2.00 |
| P17 | 5743-1983 | 17,177 | 5 Sheqalim. KM118. | 2.50 |
| P14 | 5743-1983 | 17,177 | 10 New Agorot. KM108. | 2.00 |
| P18 | 5743-1983 | 17,177 | 10 Sheqalim. KM119. | 3.50 |
| P16 | 5743-1983 | 17,177 | Sheqel. KM111. | 2.00 |
| P21 | 5744-1984 | 15,572 | 10 New Agorot. KM108. | 2.00 |
| P22 | 5744-1984 | 15,572 | 1/2 Sheqel. KM109. | 2.00 |
| P23 | 5744-1984 | 15,572 | Sheqel. KM111. | 2.00 |
| P24 | 5744-1984 | 15,572 | 5 Sheqalim. KM118. | 2.50 |
| P25 | 5744-1984 | 15,572 | 10 Sheqalim. KM119. | 3.50 |
| **Note:** P6-25 were struck at the Rome Mint | | | | |
| P26 | 5745-1985 | 14,768 | Sheqel. KM111. | 2.00 |
| P27 | 5745-1985 | 14,768 | 5 Sheqalim. KM118. | 2.00 |
| P28 | 5745-1985 | 14,768 | 10 Sheqalim. KM119. | 2.50 |
| P29 | 5745-1985 | 14,768 | 50 Sheqalim. KM139. | 3.00 |
| P30 | 5745-1985 | 14,768 | 100 Sheqalim. KM143. | 3.00 |
| **Note:** P26-30 were struck at the Bern Mint | | | | |
| P31 | 5746-1986 | 12,665 | Agorah. KM156. | 1.00 |
| P32 | 5746-1986 | 12,665 | Agorah. KM157. | 2.00 |
| P33 | 5746-1986 | 12,665 | 10 Agorot. KM158. | 2.00 |
| P34 | 5746-1986 | 12,665 | 1/2 New Sheqel. KM159. | 3.00 |
| P35 | 5746-1986 | 12,665 | New Sheqel. KM160. | 3.00 |
| **Note:** P31-35 were struck at the Paris Mint | | | | |
| P36 | 5747-1987 | 11,529 | Agorah. KM156. | 1.00 |
| P37 | 5747-1987 | 11,529 | 5 Agorot. KM157. | 2.00 |
| P38 | 5747-1987 | 11,529 | 10 Agorot. KM158. | 2.00 |
| P39 | 5747-1987 | 11,529 | 1/2 New Sheqel. KM159. | 3.00 |
| P40 | 5747-1987 | 11,529 | New Sheqel. KM160. | 3.00 |
| P41 | 5748-1988 | 12,027 | 5 Agorot. KM194. | 2.00 |
| PA41 | 5748-1988 | — | Agorah. KM193. | — |
| P42 | 5748-1988 | 12,027 | 10 Agorot. KM195. | 2.00 |
| P43 | 5748-1988 | 12,027 | 1/2 New Sheqel. KM196. | 3.00 |
| P44 | 5748-1988 | 12,027 | New Sheqel. KM197. | 3.00 |
| **Note:** P36-44 were struck at the Stuttgart Mint | | | | |
| P45 | 5749-1989 | 9,622 | Agorah. KM156. | 1.00 |
| P46 | 5749-1989 | 9,622 | 5 Agorot. KM157. | 2.00 |
| P47 | 5749-1989 | 9,622 | 10 Agorot. KM155. | 2.00 |
| P48 | 5749-1989 | 9,622 | 1/2 New Sheqel. KM159. | 3.00 |
| P49 | 5749-1989 | 9,622 | New Sheqel. KM160. | 3.00 |
| P50 | 5750-1990 | — | Agorah. Bronze. KM156. | 1.00 |
| P51 | 5750-1990 | — | 5 Agorot. Bronze. KM157. | 2.00 |
| P52 | 5750-1990 | — | 10 Agorot. Bronze. KM158. | 2.00 |
| P53 | 5750-1990 | — | 1/2 New Sheqel. Bronze. KM159. | 3.00 |
| P54 | 5750-1990 | — | New Sheqel. KM160. | 3.00 |
| P55 | 5750-1990 | — | 5 New Sheqalim. KM207. | 6.00 |
| P56 | 5751-1991 | — | Agorah. KM156. | — |
| P57 | 5751-1991 | — | 5 Agorot. KM157. | — |
| P58 | 5751-1991 | — | 10 Agorot. KM158. | — |
| P59 | 5751-1991 | — | 1/2 New Sheqel. KM159. | — |
| P60 | 5751-1991 | — | New Sheqel. KM160. | — |
| P61 | 5751 | — | 5 New Sheqalim. KM207. | — |
| P62 | 5752-1992 | — | Agorah. KM156. | — |
| P63 | 5752-1992 | — | 5 Agorot. KM157. | — |
| P64 | 5752-1992 | — | 10 Agorot. KM158. | — |
| P65 | 5752-1992 | — | 1/2 New Sheqel. KM159. | — |
| P66 | 5752-1992 | — | New Sheqel. KM160. | — |
| P67 | 5752-1992 | — | 5 New Sheqalim. KM207. | — |
| P68 | 5753-1993 | 8,000 | Agorah. KM156. | — |
| P69 | 5753-1993 | 8,000 | 5 Agorot. KM157. | — |
| P70 | 5753-1993 | 8,000 | 10 Agorot. KM158. | — |
| P71 | 5753-1993 | 8,000 | 1/2 New Sheqel. KM159. | — |
| P72 | 5753-1993 | 8,000 | New Sheqel. KM160. | — |
| P73 | 5753-1993 | 8,000 | 5 New Sheqalim. KM161. | — |
| P74 | 5754-1994 | 8,000 | Agorah. KM156. | — |
| P75 | 5754-1994 | 8,000 | 5 Agorot. KM157. | — |
| P76 | 5754-1994 | 8,000 | 10 Agorot. KM158. | — |
| P77 | 5754-1994 | 8,000 | 1/2 New Sheqel. KM159. | — |
| P78 | 5754-1994 | 8,000 | 1/2 New Sheqel. Bronze. KM306. | — |
| P79 | 5754-1994 | 8,000 | New Sheqel. KM160. | — |
| P80 | 5754-1994 | 8,000 | 5 New Sheqalim. KM207. | — |
| P81 | 5755-1995 | 10,000 | Agorah. KM156. | — |
| P82 | 5755-1995 | 10,000 | 5 Agorot. KM157. | — |
| P83 | 5755-1995 | 10,000 | 10 Agorot. KM158. | — |
| P84 | 5755-1995 | 10,000 | 1/2 New Sheqel. KM159. | — |
| P85 | 5755-1995 | 10,000 | 1/2 New Sheqel. Bronze. KM307. | — |
| P86 | 5755-1995 | 10,000 | New Sheqel. KM160. | — |
| P87 | 5755-1995 | 10,000 | 5 New Sheqalim. KM207. | — |
| P88 | 5755-1995 | 10,000 | 10 New Sheqalim. KM270. | — |

## MINT SETS

| KM# | Date | Mintage | Identification | Issue Price | Mkt Val |
|---|---|---|---|---|---|
| MSA1 | 1949 (10) | — | KM8-12, 13.1, 14, 15, 15a, 16, in puffin tin. | — | 195 |
| MS1 | 1927 (14) | — | KM1-7 two each | — | 1,750 |
| MS2 | 1962 (16) | 4,000 | KM12a, 13.2a, 17-20, 20a, 24.1, 25-27 | 18.50 | 75.00 |
| MS3 | 1963 (18) | 7,000 | As MS2 with KM#36.1, 37 in presentation holder. | 22.50 | 50.00 |
| MS4 | 1963 (6) | 200 | KM24.1, 25-26 (1962), 27, 36.1, 37 (white folder) | 2.50 | 140 |
| MS5 | 1963 (6) | 2,000 | KM#24.1, 25, 26, 27, 36.1, 37 (plain white card) | 2.50 | 125 |
| MS6 | 1963 (6) | 10,000 | KM#24.1 with inverted reverse, KM#25, 26, 27, 36.1, 37 (card with map). | 2.60 | 35.00 |
| MS7 | 1963 (6) | 10,544 | KM#24.1, 25, 26, 27, 36.1, 37 (card with map) - issued in 1964. | 2.60 | 12.00 |
| MS8 | 1965 (6) | 153,424 | KM24.1, 25-27, 36.1, 37 | 3.50 | 3.00 |
| MS9 | 1966 (6) | 114,714 | KM24.1, 25-27, 36.1, 37 | 3.50 | 3.00 |
| MS10 | 1967 (6) | 128,124 | KM24.1, 25-27, 36.1, 37 (card) | 3.50 | 3.00 |
| MS11 | 1968 (6) | 184,552 | KM24.1, 25-27, 36.1, 47.1 (card) | 3.50 | 3.00 |
| MS12 | 1969 (6) | 158,052 | KM24.1, 25-27, 36.1, 47.1 (card) | 3.50 | 3.50 |
| MS13 | 1970 (6) | 60,045 | KM24.1, 25-27, 36.1, 47.1, in red wallet | 3.75 | 4.00 |
| MS13a | 1970 (6) | 64,800 | KM24.1, 25-27, 36.1, 47.1(card) | 3.75 | 4.00 |
| MS14 | 1971 (6) | 32,543 | KM24.1, 25-27, 36.1, 47.1, in blue wallet | 3.50 | 4.00 |
| MS14a | 1971 (6) | 125,921 | KM24.1, 25-27, 36.1, 47.1, with Star of David, in pink plastic case | 3.00 | 3.00 |
| MS15 | 1972 (6) | 21,486 | KM24.1, 25-27, 36.1, 47.1, in violet wallet | 3.00 | 5.00 |
| MS15a | 1972 (6) | 68,513 | KM24.1, 25-27, 36.1, 47.1, with Star of David, in violet plastic case | 3.50 | 3.00 |
| MS16 | 1973 (6) | 97,107 | KM63-68, in blue plastic case | 3.50 | 4.00 |
| MS23 | 1979 (7) | — | KM#24.2, 25c, 26c, 27b, 36.2, 47.2, 90a. | — | 5.00 |

## MINT SETS NON-STANDARD METALS

| KM# | Date | Mintage | Identification | Issue Price | Mkt Val |
|---|---|---|---|---|---|
| MS17 | 1974 (6) | 92,868 | KM24.1, 25a-27a, 36.1, 47.1, in brown plastic case | 3.50 | 3.00 |
| MS18 | 1975 (6) | 61,686 | KM#24.1, 25a, 26a, 27a, 36.2, 47.2 in brown plastic case. | 3.50 | 5.00 |
| MS19 | 1976 (6) | 64,654 | KM84-89, in green plastic case | 3.50 | 4.00 |
| MS20 | 1977 (6) | 37,208 | KM#24.1, 25a, 26a, 27a, 36.2, 47.2. | 3.50 | 4.00 |
| MS21 | 1977 (6) | 57,200 | As KM#20. | 3.50 | 5.00 |
| MS22 | 1979 (7) | 31,590 | KM#24.1, 25b, 26b, 27, 36.1, 47.1, 90, plastic booklet. | 1.80 | 5.00 |
| MS24 | 1980 (7) | — | KM#24.1, 26b, 47.1, 106, 107, 108, 109. | 3.50 | 10.00 |
| MSA24 | mixed date set (7) | — | KM#24.1, 25, 26, 27, 36.1, 47.1, 90. | — | 5.00 |
| MS25 | 1980 (7) | 31,348 | KM96-102 | 13.00 | 15.00 |
| MS26 | 1982 (7) | 30,000 | KM106-109, 111, 118-119 | 3.50 | 8.00 |
| MS27 | 1982 (6) | 18,735 | KM106-109, 111, 118 piefors | 11.00 | 18.00 |
| MS28 | 1983 (7) | 17,177 | KM106-109, 11, 118-119 pieforts | 11.00 | 20.00 |
| MS28a | 1983 (5) | 17,478 | KM108-109, 111, 118-119 | 3.50 | 8.00 |
| MS29 | 1984 (9) | 13,403 | KM108-109, 111, 118-119, 134, 137, 143 | 4.50 | 10.00 |
| MS29a | 1984 (7) | 15,572 | KM106-109, 111, 118-119 pieforts | 10.00 | 20.00 |
| MS30 | 1985 (8) | 15,224 | KM111, 118-119, 139-140, 143, 146, 151 | 4.50 | 15.00 |
| MS31 | 1985 (5) | 14,768 | KM111, 118-119, 139,143 pieforts | 10.00 | 16.00 |
| MS32 | 1985 (5) | 7,760 | KM156-160 | 10.00 | 30.00 |
| MS33 | 1986 (5) | 12,665 | KM156-160, pieforts | 12.00 | 25.00 |
| MS34 | 1986 (12) | 14,305 | KM156-160, 163, 167, 171-174 mixed dates | 9.00 | 12.00 |
| MS35 | 1986 (5) | — | KM163, 171-174 | — | 6.00 |
| MS36 | 1987 (10) | 11,094 | KM156-160, 163, 171-174 mixed dates | 10.00 | — |
| MS37 | 1987 (5) | 30,000 | KM163, 171-174 | 6.50 | 6.00 |
| MS38 | 1987 (5) | 11,529 | KM156-160 pieforts | 18.00 | 25.00 |
| MS39 | 1988 (6) | — | KM156-60, 198, green holder | 7.50 | 7.50 |
| MS40 | 1988 (5) | 12,027 | KM193-197, pieforts | — | 25.00 |
| MS41 | 1988 (5) | 15,000 | KM193-197, blue holder | 6.50 | 8.50 |
| MS42 | 1988 (5) | 20,000 | KM163, 171-174 | 8.00 | 10.00 |
| MS43 | 1989 (10) | 9,716 | KM156-160, 163, 171-174 | 7.00 | 12.00 |
| MS44 | 1989 (5) | 15,000 | KM156-160, pieforts | 15.00 | 25.00 |
| MS45 | 1989 (5) | 7,562 | KM163, 171-174 | 5.00 | 10.00 |
| MS46 | 1990 (6) | 12,000 | KM156-160, 207 | 8.00 | 10.00 |
| MS47 | 1990 (6) | 10,000 | KM156-160, 207, pieforts | 15.00 | 30.00 |
| MS48 | 1990 (6) | 7,929 | KM163, 171-174, 217 | 8.00 | 8.00 |
| MS49 | 1991 (7) | 6,746 | KM208 (5750), 156-160, 207 (5751) | 10.00 | 20.00 |
| MS50 | 1991 (6) | 6,617 | KM156-160, 207, pieforts | 15.00 | 25.00 |
| MS51 | 1991 (5) | 6,886 | KM163, 172-174, 217 | 8.00 | 8.00 |
| MS52 | 1992 (6) | 8,000 | KM156-160, 207 | 15.00 | 15.00 |
| MS53 | Mixed date (7) | 8,000 | KM134, 147, 151, 167, 198, 208, 237 | 15.00 | 15.00 |
| MS54 | 1992 (5) | 8,000 | KM157-160, 207 | 8.00 | 10.00 |
| MS55 | 1992 (5) | 8,000 | KM163, 172-174, 217 | 9.50 | 8.00 |
| MS56 | 1993 (6) | 8,000 | KM156-160, 207, pieforts | 15.00 | 35.00 |
| MS57 | 1993 (6) | 12,000 | KM163, 172-174, 217, 303 | 16.00 | 20.00 |
| MS58 | 1993-94 (5) | 8,000 | KM157-160, 207 | 14.50 | 18.00 |
| MS59 | 1994 (6) | 12,000 | KM163, 172-174, 217, 304 | 17.00 | 20.00 |
| MS60 | 1994 (7) | 8,000 | KM156-160, 207, P78 | 17.00 | 20.00 |
| MS61 | 1995 (7) | 7,500 | KM157-159, 163, 217, 270, 305 | 29.00 | 35.00 |
| MS62 | 1995 (8) | 10,000 | KM156-160, 207, 270, P85 | 33.00 | 35.00 |
| MS63 | 1996 (6) | — | KM163, 172-174, 217, 318 | — | 20.00 |
| MS64 | 1997 (7) | 10,000 | KM163, 172-174, 217, 314-315 | — | 35.00 |

## OFFICIALLY ASSEMBLED HISTORICAL SETS

| KM# | Date | Mintage | Identification | Issue Price | Mkt Val |
|---|---|---|---|---|---|
| HS1 | 1927-55 (7) | 18,000 | The coin and Moon Set, KM1, 10, 12-15, 17, plus medal | 15.00 | 15.00 |
| HS2 | 1948-1985 (9) | 26,000 | KM#11, 13, 14, 27, 36, 47, 107, 108, 109 plus a medal. | 15.00 | 15.00 |

## PROOF SETS

| KM# | Date | Mintage | Identification | Issue Price | Mkt Val |
|---|---|---|---|---|---|
| PS1 | 1927 (14) | 34 | KM1-7 two each, original case | — | 7,500 |
| PS2 | 1927 (7) | 4 | KM1-7 original case | — | 5,000 |
| PS3 | 1996 (2) | — | KM294-295 | — | 65.00 |
| PS4 | 1996 (3) | — | KM294-296 | — | 450 |

## SPECIAL SELECT SETS

| KM# | Date | Mintage | Identification | Issue Price | Mkt Val |
|---|---|---|---|---|---|
| SS1 | 1949 (10) | 300 | KM8-12with pearl ,13.1 with pearl, 14-15 with pearl, 15 without pearl, 16 in two piece heavy plastic case (light blue molded bottom and a clear swivel top) | — | 250 |

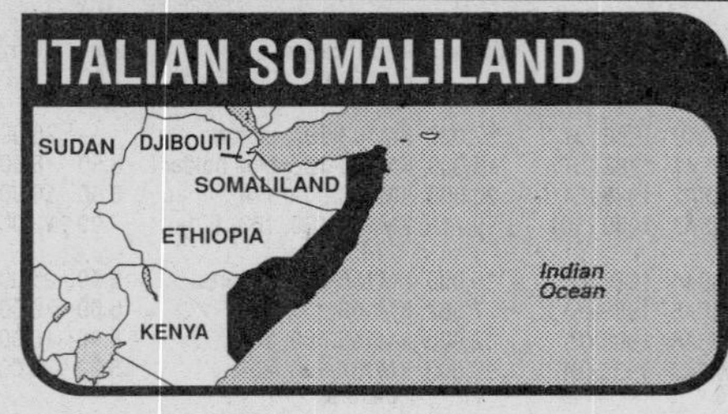


Italian Somaliland, a former Italian Colony in East Africa, extended south from Ras Asir to Kenya. Area: 178,218 sq. miles (461,585 sq. km). Capital: Mogadisho. In 1885, Italy obtained commercial concessions in the area of the sultan of Zanzibar, and in 1905 purchased the coast from Warshek to Brava. The Italians then extended their occupation inward. Cession of the Jubaland Province by Britain in 1924, and seizure of the sultanates of Obbia and Mejertein in 1925-27 brought direct Italian administration over the whole territory. Italian dominance continued until WW II. British troops occupied Italian Somaliland in 1941. Britain administered the colony until 1950 when it became a UN trust territory administered by Italy. On July 1, 1960. Italian Somaliland united with British Somaliland to form the Independent Somali Democratic Republic.

**TITLES**

الصومال الايطليانية

Al-Somal Al-Italiyaniya(t)

**MONETARY SYSTEM**

100 Bese = 1 Rupia

# ITALIAN POSSESSION

## STANDARD COINAGE

100 Bese = 1 Rupia

**BESA** KM# 1 **Composition:** Bronze

| Date | Mintage | F | VF | XF | Unc | BU |
|---|---|---|---|---|---|---|
| 1909R | 2,000,000 | 10.00 | 20.00 | 40.00 | 145 | — |
| 1910R | 500,000 | 10.00 | 20.00 | 40.00 | 145 | — |
| 1913R | 200,000 | 15.00 | 30.00 | 90.00 | 300 | — |
| 1921R | 500,000 | 12.50 | 22.50 | 45.00 | 175 | — |

**2 BESE** KM# 2 **Composition:** Bronze

| Date | Mintage | F | VF | XF | Unc | BU |
|---|---|---|---|---|---|---|
| 1909R | 500,000 | 12.50 | 25.00 | 65.00 | 250 | — |
| 1910R | 250,000 | 12.50 | 25.00 | 65.00 | 275 | — |
| 1913R | 300,000 | 15.00 | 30.00 | 90.00 | 300 | — |
| 1921R | 600,000 | 12.50 | 25.00 | 65.00 | 235 | — |
| 1923R | 1,500,000 | 12.50 | 22.50 | 60.00 | 230 | — |
| 1924R | Inc. above | 12.50 | 20.00 | 55.00 | 220 | — |

**4 BESE** KM# 3 **Composition:** Bronze

| Date | Mintage | F | VF | XF | Unc | BU |
|---|---|---|---|---|---|---|
| 1909R | 250,000 | 18.00 | 35.00 | 90.00 | 375 | — |
| 1910R | 250,000 | 18.00 | 35.00 | 90.00 | 385 | — |
| 1913R | 50,000 | 35.00 | 85.00 | 250 | 650 | — |
| 1921R | 200,000 | 20.00 | 40.00 | 100 | 400 | — |

| Date | Mintage | F | VF | XF | Unc | BU |
|---|---|---|---|---|---|---|
| 1923R | 1,000,000 | 20.00 | 40.00 | 100 | 400 | — |
| 1924R | Inc. above | 20.00 | 50.00 | 110 | 420 | — |

**1/4 RUPIA** KM# 4 **Weight:** 2.9160 g. **Composition:** 0.9170 Silver .0859 oz. ASW

| Date | Mintage | F | VF | XF | Unc | BU |
|---|---|---|---|---|---|---|
| 1910R | 400,000 | 12.50 | 25.00 | 70.00 | 175 | — |
| 1913R | 100,000 | 35.00 | 65.00 | 150 | 275 | — |

**1/2 RUPIA** KM# 5 **Weight:** 5.8319 g. **Composition:** 0.9170 Silver .1719 oz. ASW

| Date | Mintage | F | VF | XF | Unc | BU |
|---|---|---|---|---|---|---|
| 1910R | 400,000 | 20.00 | 40.00 | 90.00 | 200 | — |
| 1912R | 100,000 | 22.50 | 45.00 | 100 | 220 | — |
| 1913R | 100,000 | 22.50 | 45.00 | 100 | 220 | — |
| 1915R | 50,000 | 35.00 | 75.00 | 200 | 400 | — |
| 1919R | 200,000 | 20.00 | 40.00 | 90.00 | 200 | — |

**RUPIA** KM# 6 **Weight:** 11.6638 g. **Composition:** 0.9170 Silver .3437 oz. ASW

| Date | Mintage | F | VF | XF | Unc | BU |
|---|---|---|---|---|---|---|
| 1910R | 300,000 | 25.00 | 55.00 | 110 | 200 | — |
| 1912R | 600,000 | 25.00 | 55.00 | 110 | 200 | — |
| 1913R | 300,000 | 25.00 | 50.00 | 100 | 220 | — |
| 1914R | 300,000 | 25.00 | 50.00 | 100 | 185 | — |
| 1915R | 250,000 | 25.00 | 50.00 | 100 | 185 | — |
| 1919R | 400,000 | 25.00 | 50.00 | 100 | 185 | — |
| 1920R | 1,300,000 | 500 | 900 | 2,000 | 3,500 | — |
| 1921R | 940,000 | 950 | 2,150 | 3,350 | 5,750 | — |

## REFORM COINAGE

100 Centesimi = 1 Lira

**5 LIRE** KM# 7 **Weight:** 6.0000 g. **Composition:** 0.8350 Silver .1611 oz. ASW

| Date | Mintage | F | VF | XF | Unc | BU |
|---|---|---|---|---|---|---|
| 1925R | 400,000 | 65.00 | 125 | 225 | 350 | — |

**10 LIRE** KM# 8 **Weight:** 12.0000 g. **Composition:** 0.8350 Silver .3221 oz. ASW

| Date | Mintage | F | VF | XF | Unc | BU |
|---|---|---|---|---|---|---|
| 1925R | 100,000 | 100 | 200 | 300 | 485 | — |

## PROVAS

| KM# | Date | Mintage | Identification | Mkt Val |
|---|---|---|---|---|
| Pr1 | 1909R | — | Besa. Bronze. | 250 |
| Pr2 | 1909R | — | 2 Bese. Bronze. | 300 |
| Pr3 | 1909R | — | 4 Bese. Bronze. | 400 |
| Pr4 | 1909R | — | 4 Bese. Silver. | — |
| Pr5 | 1910R | — | 4 Bese. Nickel. | — |

| KM# | Date | Mintage | Identification | Mkt Val |
|---|---|---|---|---|
| Pr6 | 1910R | — | 1/4 Rupia. Silver. | 400 |

| KM# | Date | Mintage | Identification | Mkt Val |
|---|---|---|---|---|
| Pr7 | 1910R | — | 1/2 Rupia. Silver. | 375 |

| KM# | Date | Mintage | Identification | Mkt Val |
|---|---|---|---|---|
| Pr8 | 1910R | — | Rupia. Silver. | 400 |
| Pr9 | 1915R | — | 1/2 Rupia. Silver. 1 ANNO/DI GUERRA flanks crown. | — |
| Pr10 | 1915R | — | Rupia. Silver. 1 ANNO/DI GUERRA flanks crown. | — |
| Pr13 | 1925R | — | 10 Lire. Silver. PROVA. | 1,000 |
| Pr14 | 1925R | — | 10 Lire. Silver. PROVA DI STAMPA. | 850 |
| Pr11 | 1925R | — | 5 Lire. Silver. PROVA. | 800 |
| Pr12 | 1925R | — | 5 Lire. Silver. PROVA DI STAMPA. | 700 |

## TRIAL STRIKES

| KM# | Date | Mintage | Identification | Mkt Val |
|---|---|---|---|---|
| TS2 | 1909 | — | 2 Bese. Lead. | — |
| TS1 | 1909 | — | Besa. Pewter. | 375 |
| TS3 | 1910 | — | 4 Bese. Pewter. | 750 |

# ITALY

The Italian Republic, a 700-mile-long peninsula extending into the heart of the Mediterranean Sea, has an area of 116,304 sq. mi. (301,230 sq. km.) and a population of 60 million. Capital: Rome. The economy centers around agriculture, manufacturing, forestry and fishing. Machinery, textiles, clothing and motor vehicles are exported.

From the fall of Rome until modern times, 'Italy' was little more than a geographical expression. Although nominally included in the Empire of Charlemagne and the Holy Roman Empire, it was in reality divided into a number of independent states and kingdoms presided over by wealthy families, soldiers of fortune or hereditary rulers. The 19th century unification movement fostered by Mazzini, Garibaldi and Cavour attained fruition in 1860-70 with the creation of the Kingdom of Italy and the installation of Victor Emmanuel, king of Sardinia, as king of Italy. Benito Mussolini came to power during the post-World War I period of economic and political unrest, and installed a Fascist dictatorship with a figurehead king as titular Head of State. Mussolini entered Italy into the German-Japanese anti-comitern pact (Tri-Partite Pact) and withdrew from the League of Nations. The war did not go well for Italy and Germany was forced to assist Italy in its failed invasion of Greece. The Allied invasion of Sicily on July 10, 1943 and bombings of Rome brought the Fascist council to a no vote of confidence on July 23, 1943. Mussolini was arrested but soon escaped and set up a government in Salo. Rome fell to the Allied forces in June, 1944 and the country was allowed the status of cobelligerent against Germany. The Germans held northern Italy for another year. Mussolini was eventually captured and executed by partisans.

Following the defeat of the Axis powers, the Italian monarchy was dissolved by plebiscite, and the Italian Republic proclaimed.

## KINGDOM

### DECIMAL COINAGE

**CENTESIMO** **KM# 35** **Composition:** Copper **Ruler:** Vittorio Emanuele III

| Date | Mintage | F | VF | XF | Unc | BU |
|---|---|---|---|---|---|---|
| 1902R | 26,000 | 165 | 450 | 850 | 1,650 | — |
| 1903R | 5,655,000 | 1.00 | 2.00 | 4.00 | 18.00 | — |
| 1904/0R | 14,626,000 | 2.00 | 3.00 | 7.50 | 22.00 | — |
| 1904R | Inc. above | 1.00 | 2.00 | 4.00 | 10.00 | — |
| 1905/0R | 8,531,000 | 2.00 | 3.00 | 7.50 | 22.00 | — |
| 1905R | Inc. above | 1.00 | 2.00 | 4.00 | 10.00 | — |
| 1908R | 3,859,000 | 1.00 | 2.00 | 4.00 | 10.00 | — |

**CENTESIMO** **KM# 40** **Composition:** Copper **Ruler:** Vittorio Emanuele III

| Date | Mintage | F | VF | XF | Unc | BU |
|---|---|---|---|---|---|---|
| 1908R | 57,000 | 150 | 225 | 450 | 850 | — |
| 1909R | 3,539,000 | 1.00 | 2.00 | 4.00 | 10.00 | — |
| 1910R | 3,599,000 | 1.00 | 2.00 | 4.00 | 10.00 | — |
| 1911R | 700,000 | 5.00 | 10.00 | 15.00 | 28.00 | — |
| 1912R | 3,995,000 | 1.00 | 2.00 | 4.00 | 10.00 | — |
| 1913R | 3,200,000 | 1.00 | 2.00 | 4.00 | 10.00 | — |
| 1914R | 11,585,000 | 1.00 | 2.00 | 4.00 | 10.00 | — |
| 1915R | 9,757,000 | 1.00 | 2.00 | 4.00 | 10.00 | — |
| 1916R | 9,845,000 | 1.00 | 2.00 | 4.00 | 10.00 | — |

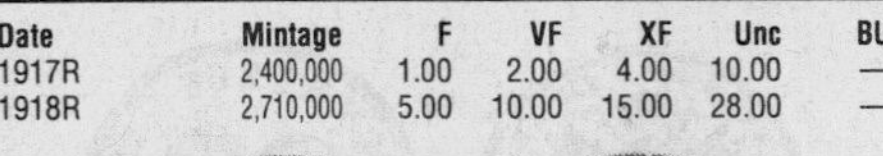

| Date | Mintage | F | VF | XF | Unc | BU |
|---|---|---|---|---|---|---|
| 1917R | 2,400,000 | 1.00 | 2.00 | 4.00 | 10.00 | — |
| 1918R | 2,710,000 | 5.00 | 10.00 | 15.00 | 28.00 | — |

**2 CENTESIMI** **KM# 38** **Composition:** Copper **Ruler:** Vittorio Emanuele III

| Date | Mintage | F | VF | XF | Unc | BU |
|---|---|---|---|---|---|---|
| 1903R | 5,000,000 | 0.60 | 1.50 | 4.00 | 15.00 | — |
| 1905R | 1,260,000 | 4.00 | 8.50 | 18.00 | 35.00 | — |
| 1906R | 3,145,000 | 0.60 | 1.50 | 3.50 | 8.00 | — |
| 1907R | 230,000 | 25.00 | 50.00 | 75.00 | 165 | — |
| 1908R | 1,518,000 | 1.00 | 2.50 | 5.00 | 18.00 | — |

**2 CENTESIMI** **KM# 41** **Composition:** Copper **Ruler:** Vittorio Emanuele III

| Date | Mintage | F | VF | XF | Unc | BU |
|---|---|---|---|---|---|---|
| 1908 | 298,000 | 9.00 | 15.00 | 25.00 | 90.00 | — |
| 1909 | 2,419,000 | 0.60 | 1.50 | 3.00 | 16.50 | — |
| 1910 | 590,000 | 2.00 | 4.00 | 9.00 | 32.00 | — |
| 1911 | 2,777,000 | 0.60 | 1.50 | 3.00 | 16.50 | — |
| 1912 | 840,000 | 0.60 | 2.00 | 5.00 | 17.50 | — |
| 1914 | 1,648,000 | 0.50 | 1.30 | 2.00 | 16.50 | — |
| 1915 | 4,860,000 | 0.50 | 1.30 | 2.50 | 16.50 | — |
| 1916 | 1,540,000 | 0.50 | 1.30 | 2.00 | 16.50 | — |
| 1917 | 3,638,000 | 0.50 | 1.30 | 2.00 | 16.50 | — |

**5 CENTESIMI** **KM# 42** **Composition:** Copper **Ruler:** Vittorio Emanuele III

| Date | Mintage | F | VF | XF | Unc | BU |
|---|---|---|---|---|---|---|
| 1908R | 824,000 | 10.00 | 25.00 | 50.00 | 145 | — |
| 1909R | 1,734,000 | 0.75 | 1.75 | 3.50 | 18.00 | — |
| 1912R | 743,000 | 1.75 | 3.00 | 6.00 | 35.00 | — |
| 1913R Dot after D | 1,964,000 | 4.00 | 10.00 | 18.00 | 55.00 | — |
| 1913R Without dot after D | Inc. above | 40.00 | 75.00 | 150 | 250 | — |
| 1915R | 1,038,000 | 3.50 | 7.50 | 12.50 | 35.00 | — |
| 1918R | 4,242,000 | 0.75 | 1.75 | 3.50 | 16.50 | — |

**5 CENTESIMI** **KM# 59** **Composition:** Copper **Ruler:** Vittorio Emanuele III

| Date | Mintage | F | VF | XF | Unc | BU |
|---|---|---|---|---|---|---|
| 1919R | 13,208,000 | 0.75 | 2.00 | 3.00 | 12.00 | — |
| 1920R | 33,372,000 | 0.30 | 0.75 | 2.00 | 5.50 | — |
| 1921R | 80,111,000 | 0.30 | 0.75 | 2.00 | 5.50 | — |
| 1922R | 42,914,000 | 0.30 | 0.75 | 2.00 | 5.50 | — |
| 1923R | 29,614,000 | 0.30 | 0.75 | 2.00 | 5.50 | — |
| 1924R | 20,352,000 | 0.30 | 0.75 | 2.00 | 5.50 | — |
| 1925R | 40,460,000 | 0.30 | 0.75 | 2.00 | 5.50 | — |
| 1926R | 21,158,000 | 0.30 | 0.75 | 2.00 | 5.50 | — |
| 1927R | 15,800,000 | 0.30 | 0.75 | 2.00 | 5.50 | — |
| 1928R | 16,090,000 | 0.30 | 0.75 | 2.00 | 5.50 | — |
| 1929R | 29,000,000 | 0.30 | 0.75 | 2.00 | 5.50 | — |
| 1930R | 22,694,000 | 0.30 | 0.75 | 2.00 | 5.50 | — |
| 1931R | 20,000,000 | 0.30 | 0.75 | 2.00 | 5.50 | — |
| 1932R | 11,456,000 | 0.30 | 0.75 | 2.00 | 5.50 | — |
| 1933R | 20,720,000 | 0.30 | 0.75 | 2.00 | 5.50 | — |
| 1934R | 16,000,000 | 0.30 | 0.75 | 2.00 | 5.50 | — |
| 1935R | 11,000,000 | 0.30 | 0.75 | 2.00 | 5.50 | — |
| 1936R | 9,462,000 | 0.30 | 0.75 | 2.00 | 5.50 | — |
| 1937R | 972,000 | 4.00 | 8.00 | 12.50 | 27.50 | — |

**5 CENTESIMI** **KM# 73** **Composition:** Copper **Ruler:** Vittorio Emanuele III

| Date | Mintage | F | VF | XF | Unc | BU |
|---|---|---|---|---|---|---|
| 1936R Yr. XIV | Inc. above | 2.00 | 4.00 | 9.00 | 18.50 | — |
| 1937R Yr. XV | 7,207,000 | 0.30 | 0.75 | 1.00 | 3.50 | — |
| 1938R Yr. XVI | 24,000,000 | 0.20 | 0.65 | 1.00 | 3.50 | — |
| 1939R Yr. XVII | 22,000,000 | 0.20 | 0.65 | 1.00 | 3.50 | — |

**5 CENTESIMI** **KM# 73a** **Composition:** Aluminum-Bronze **Ruler:** Vittorio Emanuele III

| Date | Mintage | F | VF | XF | Unc | BU |
|---|---|---|---|---|---|---|
| 1939R Yr. XVII | 1,000,000 | 0.30 | 0.75 | 1.25 | 3.50 | — |
| 1940R Yr. XVIII | 9,630,000 | 0.30 | 0.75 | 1.00 | 3.50 | — |
| 1941R Yr. XIX | 16,340,000 | 0.30 | 0.75 | 1.00 | 3.50 | — |
| 1942R Yr. XX | 25,200,000 | 0.30 | 0.75 | 1.25 | 3.50 | — |
| 1943R Yr. XXI | 13,922,000 | 2.00 | 5.00 | 10.00 | 22.00 | — |

**10 CENTESIMI** **KM# 43** **Composition:** Copper **Ruler:** Vittorio Emanuele III **Note:** Similar to 5 Centesimi, KM#42.

| Date | Mintage | F | VF | XF | Unc | BU |
|---|---|---|---|---|---|---|
| 1908R Rare | — | — | — | — | — | — |

**10 CENTESIMI** **KM# 51** **Composition:** Copper **Ruler:** Vittorio Emanuele III **Subject:** 50th anniversary of kingdom

| Date | Mintage | F | VF | XF | Unc | BU |
|---|---|---|---|---|---|---|
| 1911R | 2,000,000 | 3.50 | 6.50 | 12.50 | 40.00 | — |

**10 CENTESIMI** **KM# 60** **Composition:** Copper **Ruler:** Vittorio Emanuele III

| Date | Mintage | F | VF | XF | Unc | BU |
|---|---|---|---|---|---|---|
| 1919R | 986,000 | 20.00 | 35.00 | 50.00 | 110 | — |
| 1920R | 37,995,000 | 0.50 | 1.25 | 4.00 | 11.50 | — |
| 1921R | 66,510,000 | 0.50 | 1.25 | 4.00 | 11.50 | — |
| 1922R | 45,217,000 | 0.50 | 1.25 | 4.00 | 11.50 | — |
| 1923R | 31,529,000 | 0.50 | 1.25 | 4.00 | 11.50 | — |
| 1924R | 35,312,000 | 0.50 | 1.25 | 4.00 | 11.50 | — |
| 1925R | 22,370,000 | 0.50 | 1.25 | 4.00 | 11.50 | — |
| 1926R | 25,190,000 | 0.50 | 1.25 | 4.00 | 11.50 | — |
| 1927R | 22,673,000 | 0.50 | 1.25 | 4.00 | 11.50 | — |
| 1928R | 15,680,000 | 0.50 | 2.00 | 7.50 | 22.00 | — |
| 1929R | 15,593,000 | 0.50 | 1.25 | 4.00 | 11.50 | — |
| 1930R | 17,115,000 | 0.50 | 1.25 | 4.00 | 11.50 | — |
| 1931R | 10,750,000 | 0.50 | 1.25 | 4.00 | 11.50 | — |
| 1932R | 5,678,000 | 1.25 | 2.50 | 7.50 | 22.00 | — |
| 1933R | 10,250,000 | 0.50 | 1.25 | 4.00 | 11.50 | — |
| 1934R | 18,300,000 | 0.50 | 1.25 | 4.00 | 11.50 | — |
| 1935R | 10,500,000 | 0.50 | 1.25 | 4.00 | 11.50 | — |
| 1936R | 8,770,000 | 0.50 | 1.50 | 4.50 | 13.50 | — |
| 1937R | 5,500,000 | 0.50 | 1.50 | 4.50 | 13.50 | — |

**10 CENTESIMI** **KM# 74** **Composition:** Copper **Ruler:** Vittorio Emanuele III

| Date | Mintage | F | VF | XF | Unc | BU |
|---|---|---|---|---|---|---|
| 1936R Yr. XIV | Inc. above | 0.75 | 1.50 | 3.00 | 13.50 | — |
| 1937R Yr. XV | 7,212,000 | 0.25 | 0.75 | 1.50 | 4.50 | — |
| 1938R Yr. XVI | 18,750,000 | 0.25 | 0.75 | 1.50 | 4.50 | — |
| 1939R Yr. XVII | 24,750,000 | 0.25 | 0.75 | 1.50 | 4.50 | — |

**10 CENTESIMI** **KM# 74a** **Composition:** Aluminum-Bronze **Ruler:** Vittorio Emanuele III

| Date | Mintage | F | VF | XF | Unc | BU |
|---|---|---|---|---|---|---|
| 1939R Yr. XVII | 750,000 | 0.50 | 1.50 | 2.00 | 4.50 | — |
| 1940R Yr. XVIII | 23,355,000 | 0.20 | 0.60 | 1.00 | 4.50 | — |
| 1941R Yr. XIX | 27,050,000 | 0.20 | 0.60 | 1.00 | 4.50 | — |

| Date | Mintage | F | VF | XF | Unc | BU |
|---|---|---|---|---|---|---|
| 1942R Yr. XX | 18,100,000 | 0.20 | 0.60 | 1.00 | 4.50 | — |
| 1943R Yr. XXI | 25,400,000 | 0.25 | 0.60 | 2.00 | 5.50 | — |

**20 CENTESIMI** **KM# 44** **Composition:** Nickel **Ruler:** Vittorio Emanuele III

| Date | Mintage | F | VF | XF | Unc | BU |
|---|---|---|---|---|---|---|
| 1908R | 14,315,000 | 0.50 | 1.00 | 3.00 | 11.50 | — |
| 1909R | 19,280,000 | 0.50 | 1.00 | 3.00 | 11.50 | — |
| 1910R | 21,887,000 | 0.50 | 1.00 | 3.00 | 11.50 | — |
| 1911R | 13,671,000 | 0.50 | 1.00 | 3.00 | 11.50 | — |
| 1912R | 21,040,000 | 0.50 | 1.00 | 3.00 | 11.50 | — |
| 1913R | 20,729,000 | 0.50 | 1.00 | 3.00 | 11.50 | — |
| 1914R | 14,308,000 | 0.50 | 1.00 | 3.00 | 11.50 | — |
| 1919R | 3,475,000 | 1.00 | 3.50 | 10.00 | 28.00 | — |
| 1920R | 27,284,000 | 0.50 | 1.00 | 3.00 | 11.50 | — |
| 1921R | 50,372,000 | 0.50 | 1.00 | 3.00 | 11.50 | — |
| 1922R | 17,134,000 | 0.50 | 1.00 | 3.00 | 11.50 | — |
| 1926R | 500 | — | — | — | 175 | — |
| 1927R | 100 | — | — | — | 245 | — |
| 1928R | 50 | — | — | — | 285 | — |
| 1929R | 50 | — | — | — | 285 | — |
| 1930R | 50 | — | — | — | 285 | — |
| 1931R | 50 | — | — | — | 285 | — |
| 1932R | 50 | — | — | — | 285 | — |
| 1933R | 50 | — | — | — | 285 | — |
| 1934R | 50 | — | — | — | 285 | — |
| 1935R | 50 | — | — | — | 285 | — |

**20 CENTESIMI** **KM# 58** **Composition:** Copper-Nickel **Ruler:** Vittorio Emanuele III **Edge:** Plain and reeded **Note:** Overstruck on KM#28.

| Date | Mintage | F | VF | XF | Unc | BU |
|---|---|---|---|---|---|---|
| 1918R | 43,097,000 | 0.50 | 1.00 | 4.00 | 10.00 | — |
| 1919R | 33,432,000 | 0.50 | 1.00 | 4.00 | 10.00 | — |
| 1920R | 923,000 | 3.00 | 5.00 | 10.00 | 32.00 | — |

**20 CENTESIMI** **KM# 75** **Composition:** Nickel **Ruler:** Vittorio Emanuele III **Size:** 21.5 mm.

| Date | Mintage | F | VF | XF | Unc | BU |
|---|---|---|---|---|---|---|
| 1936R Yr. XIV | 117,000 | 20.00 | 45.00 | 95.00 | 200 | — |
| 1937R Yr. XV | 50 | — | — | — | 375 | — |
| 1938R Yr. XVII | 20 | — | — | — | 500 | — |

**20 CENTESIMI** **KM# 75a** **Composition:** Stainless Steel **Ruler:** Vittorio Emanuele III **Edge:** Plain **Size:** 22.5 mm. **Note:** Magnetic.

| Date | Mintage | F | VF | XF | Unc | BU |
|---|---|---|---|---|---|---|
| 1939R Yr. XVII | 10,462,000 | 2.00 | 6.00 | 14.00 | 38.00 | — |
| 1940R Yr. XVIII | 35,350,000 | 1.40 | 3.50 | 10.00 | 28.00 | — |
| 1942R Yr. XX | 48,500,000 | 1.40 | 3.50 | 10.00 | 30.00 | — |

**20 CENTESIMI** **KM# 75b** **Composition:** Stainless Steel **Ruler:** Vittorio Emanuele III **Edge:** Reeded **Size:** 21.8 mm. **Note:** Magnetic.

| Date | Mintage | F | VF | XF | Unc | BU |
|---|---|---|---|---|---|---|
| 1939R Yr. XVII | Inc. above | — | — | — | — | — |
| 1939R Yr. XVIII | Inc. above | 0.35 | 0.70 | 2.00 | 8.00 | — |
| 1940R Yr. XVIII | Inc. above | 0.20 | 0.40 | 1.40 | 4.50 | — |
| 1941R Yr. XIX | 97,300,000 | 0.20 | 0.40 | 1.40 | 4.50 | — |
| 1942R Yr. XX | Inc. above | 0.25 | 0.50 | 1.00 | 4.00 | — |
| 1943R Yr. XXI | 18,453,000 | 0.35 | 0.70 | 1.75 | 5.50 | — |

**20 CENTESIMI** **KM# 75d** **Composition:** Stainless Steel **Ruler:** Vittorio Emanuele III **Edge:** Reeded **Size:** 21.8 mm. **Note:** Non-magnetic.

| Date | Mintage | F | VF | XF | Unc | BU |
|---|---|---|---|---|---|---|
| 1939R Yr. XVII | Inc. above | 0.35 | 0.70 | 2.00 | 8.00 | — |
| 1939R Yr. XVIII | 25,300,000 | 0.35 | 1.00 | 2.75 | 8.00 | — |
| 1940R Yr. XVIII | Inc. above | 0.20 | 0.40 | 1.40 | 4.50 | — |

**20 CENTESIMI** **KM# 75c** **Composition:** Stainless Steel **Ruler:** Vittorio Emanuele III **Edge:** Plain **Size:** 22.5 mm. **Note:** Non-magnetic.

| Date | Mintage | F | VF | XF | Unc | BU |
|---|---|---|---|---|---|---|
| 1939R Yr. XVII | Inc. above | 2.00 | 6.00 | 14.00 | 38.00 | — |

**25 CENTESIMI** **KM# 36** **Composition:** Nickel **Ruler:** Vittorio Emanuele III

| Date | Mintage | F | VF | XF | Unc | BU |
|---|---|---|---|---|---|---|
| 1902R | 7,773,000 | 15.00 | 35.00 | 65.00 | 150 | — |
| 1903R | 5,895,000 | 12.50 | 25.00 | 45.00 | 120 | — |

**50 CENTESIMI** **KM# 61.1** **Composition:** Nickel **Ruler:** Vittorio Emanuele III **Edge:** Plain

| Date | Mintage | F | VF | XF | Unc | BU |
|---|---|---|---|---|---|---|
| 1919R | 3,700,000 | 2.50 | 5.00 | 20.00 | 55.00 | — |
| 1920R | 29,450,000 | 0.75 | 1.50 | 3.00 | 20.00 | — |
| 1921R | 16,849,000 | 0.75 | 1.50 | 3.00 | 20.00 | — |
| 1924R | 599,000 | 50.00 | 100 | 285 | 650 | — |
| 1925R | 24,884,000 | 1.50 | 2.50 | 8.00 | 25.00 | — |
| 1926R | 500 | — | — | — | 300 | — |
| 1927R | 100 | — | — | — | 400 | — |
| 1928R | 50 | — | — | — | 500 | — |

**50 CENTESIMI** **KM# 61.2** **Composition:** Nickel **Ruler:** Vittorio Emanuele III **Edge:** Reeded

| Date | Mintage | F | VF | XF | Unc | BU |
|---|---|---|---|---|---|---|
| 1919R | Inc. above | 2.50 | 6.25 | 12.50 | 110 | — |
| 1920R | Inc. above | 2.50 | 6.25 | 12.50 | 110 | — |
| 1921R | Inc. above | 2.50 | 6.25 | 12.50 | 110 | — |
| 1924R | Inc. above | 25.00 | 50.00 | 85.00 | 285 | — |
| 1925R | Inc. above | 2.00 | 4.00 | 10.00 | 55.00 | — |
| 1929R | 50 | — | — | — | 385 | — |
| 1930R | 50 | — | — | — | 385 | — |
| 1931R | 50 | — | — | — | 385 | — |
| 1932R | 50 | — | — | — | 385 | — |
| 1933R | 50 | — | — | — | 385 | — |
| 1934R | 50 | — | — | — | 385 | — |
| 1935R | 50 | — | — | — | 385 | — |

**50 CENTESIMI** **KM# 76** **Composition:** Nickel **Ruler:** Vittorio Emanuele III

| Date | Mintage | F | VF | XF | Unc | BU |
|---|---|---|---|---|---|---|
| 1936R Yr. XIV | 118,000 | 17.50 | 40.00 | 90.00 | 185 | — |
| 1937R Yr. XV | 50 | — | — | — | 385 | — |
| 1938R Yr. XVII | 20 | — | — | — | 550 | — |

**50 CENTESIMI** **KM# 76b** **Composition:** Stainless Steel **Ruler:** Vittorio Emanuele III **Note:** Magnetic.

| Date | Mintage | F | VF | XF | Unc | BU |
|---|---|---|---|---|---|---|
| 1939R Yr. XVII | Inc. above | 0.35 | 0.75 | 2.00 | 8.00 | — |
| 1940R Yr. XVIII | Inc. above | 0.25 | 0.60 | 1.50 | 5.00 | — |
| 1941R Yr. XIX | 58,100,000 | 0.25 | 0.60 | 1.50 | 5.00 | — |
| 1942R Yr. XX | 26,450,000 | 0.25 | 0.60 | 1.50 | 5.00 | — |
| 1943R Yr. XXI | 361,000 | 25.00 | 45.00 | 75.00 | 165 | — |

**50 CENTESIMI** **KM# 76a** **Composition:** Stainless Steel **Ruler:** Vittorio Emanuele III **Note:** Non-magnetic.

| Date | Mintage | F | VF | XF | Unc | BU |
|---|---|---|---|---|---|---|
| 1939R Yr. XVII | 9,373,000 | 0.35 | 0.75 | 2.00 | 8.00 | — |
| 1939R Yr. XVIII | 10,005,000 | 0.35 | 0.75 | 2.00 | 8.00 | — |
| 1940R Yr. XVIII | 19,005,000 | 0.25 | 0.60 | 1.50 | 5.00 | — |

**LIRA** **KM# 32** **Weight:** 5.0000 g. **Composition:** 0.8350 Silver .1342 oz. ASW **Ruler:** Vittorio Emanuele III

| Date | Mintage | F | VF | XF | Unc | BU |
|---|---|---|---|---|---|---|
| 1901R | 2,590,000 | 5.00 | 12.50 | 40.00 | 220 | — |
| 1902R | 4,084,000 | 3.50 | 7.50 | 30.00 | 200 | — |
| 1905R | 700,000 | 30.00 | 60.00 | 175 | 750 | — |
| 1906R | 4,665,000 | 3.50 | 5.00 | 20.00 | 110 | — |
| 1907R | 8,472,000 | 2.50 | 4.50 | 20.00 | 110 | — |

**LIRA** **KM# 45** **Weight:** 5.0000 g. **Composition:** 0.8350 Silver .1342 oz. ASW **Ruler:** Vittorio Emanuele III

| Date | Mintage | F | VF | XF | Unc | BU |
|---|---|---|---|---|---|---|
| 1908R | 2,212,000 | 20.00 | 40.00 | 120 | 450 | — |
| 1909R | 3,475,000 | 3.50 | 7.50 | 35.00 | 220 | — |
| 1910R | 5,525,000 | 2.50 | 5.00 | 25.00 | 150 | — |
| 1912R | 5,865,000 | 2.50 | 4.00 | 15.00 | 80.00 | — |
| 1913R | 16,177,000 | 2.00 | 3.50 | 9.00 | 45.00 | — |

**LIRA** **KM# 57** **Weight:** 5.0000 g. **Composition:** 0.8350 Silver .1342 oz. ASW **Ruler:** Vittorio Emanuele III

| Date | Mintage | F | VF | XF | Unc | BU |
|---|---|---|---|---|---|---|
| 1915R | 5,229,000 | 2.75 | 4.00 | 20.00 | 80.00 | — |
| 1916R | 1,835,000 | 5.00 | 10.00 | 30.00 | 135 | — |
| 1917R | 9,744,000 | 2.75 | 4.00 | 12.50 | 55.00 | — |

**LIRA** **KM# 62** **Composition:** Nickel **Ruler:** Vittorio Emanuele III

| Date | Mintage | F | VF | XF | Unc | BU |
|---|---|---|---|---|---|---|
| 1922R | 82,267,000 | 0.60 | 1.00 | 7.00 | 22.00 | — |
| 1923R | 20,175,000 | 0.60 | 1.00 | 7.00 | 22.00 | — |
| 1924R Closed 2 | 29,288,000 | 0.60 | 1.00 | 7.00 | 22.00 | — |
| 1926R | 500 | — | — | — | 250 | — |
| 1927R | 100 | — | — | — | 350 | — |
| 1928R | 19,996,000 | 1.00 | 2.00 | 15.00 | 45.00 | — |
| 1929R | 50 | — | — | — | 385 | — |
| 1930R | 50 | — | — | — | 385 | — |
| 1931R | 50 | — | — | — | 385 | — |
| 1932R | 50 | — | — | — | 385 | — |
| 1933R | 50 | — | — | — | 385 | — |
| 1934R | 50 | — | — | — | 385 | — |
| 1935R | 50 | — | — | — | 385 | — |

**LIRA** **KM# 77** **Composition:** Nickel **Ruler:** Vittorio Emanuele III

| Date | Mintage | F | VF | XF | Unc | BU |
|---|---|---|---|---|---|---|
| 1936R Yr. XIV | 119,000 | 15.00 | 35.00 | 70.00 | 145 | — |
| 1937R Yr. XV | 50 | — | — | — | 400 | — |
| 1938R XVII | 20 | — | — | — | 550 | — |

**LIRA** **KM# 77b** **Composition:** Stainless Steel **Ruler:** Vittorio Emanuele III **Note:** Magnetic.

| Date | Mintage | F | VF | XF | Unc | BU |
|---|---|---|---|---|---|---|
| 1939R Yr. XVII | Inc. above | 0.40 | 1.50 | 4.00 | 15.00 | — |
| 1939R Yr. XVIII | Inc. above | 0.35 | 0.75 | 1.50 | 6.50 | — |
| 1940R Yr. XVIII | Inc. above | 0.30 | 0.60 | 1.25 | 5.50 | — |
| 1941R Yr. XIX | 8,550,000 | 0.50 | 1.75 | 5.00 | 17.50 | — |
| 1942R Yr. XX | 5,700,000 | 0.35 | 0.75 | 1.50 | 6.50 | — |
| 1943R Yr. XXI | 11,500,000 | 10.00 | 20.00 | 35.00 | 85.00 | — |

**LIRA** **KM# 77a** **Composition:** Stainless Steel **Ruler:** Vittorio Emanuele III **Note:** Non-magnetic.

| Date | Mintage | F | VF | XF | Unc | BU |
|---|---|---|---|---|---|---|
| 1939R Yr. XVII | 10,034,000 | 0.40 | 1.50 | 4.00 | 15.00 | — |
| 1939R Yr. XVIII | 15,977,000 | 0.35 | 0.75 | 1.50 | 6.50 | — |
| 1940R Yr. XVIII | 25,997,000 | 0.30 | 0.60 | 1.25 | 5.50 | — |

**2 LIRE** KM# 33 **Weight:** 10.0000 g. **Composition:** 0.8350 Silver .2684 oz. ASW **Ruler:** Vittorio Emanuele III

| Date | Mintage | F | VF | XF | Unc | BU |
|---|---|---|---|---|---|---|
| 1901R | 72,000 | 200 | 400 | 1,450 | 3,200 | — |
| 1902R | 549,000 | 50.00 | 100 | 320 | 1,000 | — |
| 1903R | 54,000 | 300 | 500 | 1,800 | 5,500 | — |
| 1904R | 157,000 | 125 | 250 | 800 | 1,500 | — |
| 1905R | 1,643,000 | 10.00 | 20.00 | 85.00 | 450 | — |
| 1906R | 970,000 | 12.50 | 25.00 | 130 | 450 | — |
| 1907R | 1,245,000 | 10.00 | 20.00 | 85.00 | 450 | — |

**2 LIRE** KM# 46 **Weight:** 10.0000 g. **Composition:** 0.8350 Silver .2684 oz. ASW **Ruler:** Vittorio Emanuele III

| Date | Mintage | F | VF | XF | Unc | BU |
|---|---|---|---|---|---|---|
| 1908R | 2,283,000 | 6.00 | 15.00 | 85.00 | 325 | — |
| 1910R | 719,000 | 25.00 | 50.00 | 200 | 650 | — |
| 1911R | 535,000 | 30.00 | 60.00 | 225 | 900 | — |
| 1912R | 2,166,000 | 6.00 | 15.00 | 85.00 | 325 | — |

**2 LIRE** KM# 52 **Weight:** 10.0000 g. **Composition:** 0.8350 Silver .2684 oz. ASW **Ruler:** Vittorio Emanuele III **Subject:** 50th anniversary of kingdom

| Date | Mintage | F | VF | XF | Unc | BU |
|---|---|---|---|---|---|---|
| 1911R | 1,000,000 | 12.50 | 25.00 | 70.00 | 185 | — |

**2 LIRE** KM# 55 **Weight:** 10.0000 g. **Composition:** 0.8350 Silver .2684 oz. ASW **Ruler:** Vittorio Emanuele III

| Date | Mintage | F | VF | XF | Unc | BU |
|---|---|---|---|---|---|---|
| 1914R | 10,390,000 | 4.00 | 6.00 | 12.00 | 50.00 | — |
| 1915R | 7,948,000 | 4.00 | 6.00 | 12.00 | 50.00 | — |
| 1916R | 10,923,000 | 4.00 | 6.00 | 12.00 | 50.00 | — |
| 1917R | 6,123,000 | 6.00 | 12.50 | 25.00 | 65.00 | — |

**2 LIRE** KM# 63 **Composition:** Nickel **Ruler:** Vittorio Emanuele III

| Date | Mintage | F | VF | XF | Unc | BU |
|---|---|---|---|---|---|---|
| 1923R | 32,260,000 | 1.00 | 2.50 | 6.00 | 22.00 | — |
| 1924R | 45,051,000 | 1.00 | 2.50 | 6.00 | 22.00 | — |
| 1925R | 14,628,000 | 1.00 | 2.50 | 6.00 | 32.00 | — |
| 1926R | 5,101,000 | 5.00 | 10.00 | 50.00 | 165 | — |
| 1927R | 1,632,000 | 25.00 | 50.00 | 100 | 325 | — |
| 1928R | 50 | — | — | — | 425 | — |
| 1929R | 50 | — | — | — | 425 | — |
| 1930R | 50 | — | — | — | 425 | — |
| 1931R | 50 | — | — | — | 425 | — |
| 1932R | 50 | — | — | — | 425 | — |
| 1933R | 50 | — | — | — | 425 | — |
| 1934R | 50 | — | — | — | 425 | — |
| 1935R | 50 | — | — | — | 425 | — |

**2 LIRE** KM# 78 **Composition:** Nickel **Ruler:** Vittorio Emanuele III

| Date | Mintage | F | VF | XF | Unc | BU |
|---|---|---|---|---|---|---|
| 1936R Yr. XIV | 120,000 | 22.50 | 50.00 | 100 | 225 | — |
| 1937R Yr. XV | 50 | — | — | — | 425 | — |
| 1939R Yr. XVII | 20 | — | — | — | 600 | — |

**2 LIRE** KM# 78b **Composition:** Stainless Steel **Ruler:** Vittorio Emanuele III **Note:** Magnetic.

| Date | Mintage | F | VF | XF | Unc | BU |
|---|---|---|---|---|---|---|
| 1939R Yr. XVII | Inc. above | 0.60 | 1.75 | 5.00 | 17.00 | — |
| 1939R Yr. XVIII | Inc. above | 0.40 | 0.90 | 2.50 | 10.00 | — |
| 1940R Yr. XVIII | Inc. above | 0.40 | 0.90 | 2.00 | 5.50 | — |
| 1941R Yr. XIX | 1,865,000 | 0.50 | 1.50 | 3.00 | 11.50 | — |
| 1942R Yr. XX | 2,450,000 | 40.00 | 80.00 | 160 | 350 | — |
| 1943R Yr. XXI | 600,000 | 20.00 | 40.00 | 100 | 225 | — |

**2 LIRE** KM# 78a **Composition:** Stainless Steel **Ruler:** Vittorio Emanuele III **Note:** Non-magnetic.

| Date | Mintage | F | VF | XF | Unc | BU |
|---|---|---|---|---|---|---|
| 1939R Yr. XVII | 2,900,000 | 0.60 | 1.75 | 5.00 | 17.00 | — |
| 1939R Yr. XVIII | 4,873,000 | 0.40 | 0.90 | 2.50 | 10.00 | — |
| 1940R Yr. XVIII | 5,742,000 | 0.40 | 0.90 | 2.00 | 5.50 | — |

**5 LIRE** KM# 34 **Weight:** 25.0000 g. **Composition:** 0.9000 Silver .7234 oz. ASW **Ruler:** Vittorio Emanuele III

| Date | Mintage | F | VF | XF | Unc | BU |
|---|---|---|---|---|---|---|
| 1901R | 114 | — | — | 15,000 | 20,000 | — |

**5 LIRE** KM# 53 **Weight:** 25.0000 g. **Composition:** 0.9000 Silver .7234 oz. ASW **Ruler:** Vittorio Emanuele III **Subject:** 50th anniversary of kingdom

| Date | Mintage | F | VF | XF | Unc | BU |
|---|---|---|---|---|---|---|
| 1911R | 60,000 | 150 | 300 | 500 | 1,000 | — |

**5 LIRE** KM# 56 **Weight:** 25.0000 g. **Composition:** 0.9000 Silver .7234 oz. ASW **Ruler:** Vittorio Emanuele III

| Date | Mintage | F | VF | XF | Unc | BU |
|---|---|---|---|---|---|---|
| 1914R | 273,000 | 500 | 850 | 2,500 | 4,500 | — |

**5 LIRE** KM# 67.1 **Weight:** 5.0000 g. **Composition:** 0.8350 Silver .1342 oz. ASW **Ruler:** Vittorio Emanuele III **Edge Lettering:** *FERT*

| Date | Mintage | F | VF | XF | Unc | BU |
|---|---|---|---|---|---|---|
| 1926R | 5,405,000 | 5.00 | 15.00 | 35.00 | 175 | — |
| 1927R | 92,887,000 | 1.50 | 3.00 | 7.00 | 25.00 | — |
| 1928R | 9,908,000 | 6.00 | 15.00 | 45.00 | 200 | — |
| 1929R | 33,803,000 | 2.00 | 4.00 | 8.00 | 28.00 | — |
| 1930R | 19,525,000 | 2.00 | 4.00 | 10.00 | 30.00 | — |
| 1931R | 50 | — | — | — | 450 | — |
| 1932R | 50 | — | — | — | 450 | — |
| 1933R | 50 | — | — | — | 450 | — |
| 1934R | 50 | — | — | — | 450 | — |
| 1935R | 50 | — | — | — | 450 | — |

**5 LIRE** KM# 67.2 **Weight:** 5.0000 g. **Composition:** 0.8350 Silver .1342 oz. ASW **Ruler:** Vittorio Emanuele III **Edge Lettering:** **FERT**

| Date | Mintage | F | VF | XF | Unc | BU |
|---|---|---|---|---|---|---|
| 1927R | Inc. above | 2.00 | 4.00 | 8.00 | 38.00 | — |
| 1928R | Inc. above | 10.00 | 20.00 | 50.00 | 220 | — |
| 1929R | Inc. above | 3.00 | 6.00 | 12.00 | 45.00 | — |

**5 LIRE** KM# 79 **Weight:** 5.0000 g. **Composition:** 0.8350 Silver .1342 oz. ASW **Ruler:** Vittorio Emanuele III

| Date | Mintage | F | VF | XF | Unc | BU |
|---|---|---|---|---|---|---|
| 1936R Yr. XIV | 1,016,000 | 10.00 | 20.00 | 40.00 | 110 | — |
| 1937R Yr. XV | 100,000 | 15.00 | 30.00 | 60.00 | 150 | — |
| 1938R Yr. XVIII | 20 | — | — | — | 600 | — |
| 1939R Yr. XVIII | 20 | — | — | — | 600 | — |
| 1940R Yr. XIX | 20 | — | — | — | 600 | — |
| 1941R Yr. XX | 20 | — | — | — | 600 | — |

**10 LIRE** KM# 47 **Weight:** 3.2258 g. **Composition:** 0.9000 Gold .0933 oz. AGW **Ruler:** Vittorio Emanuele III **Size:** 18 mm.

| Date | Mintage | F | VF | XF | Unc | BU |
|---|---|---|---|---|---|---|
| 1910R Rare | — | — | — | — | — | — |
| **Note:** All but one piece melted | | | | | | |
| 1912R | 6,796 | 700 | 1,250 | 2,000 | 3,500 | — |
| 1926R | 40 | — | — | 6,000 | 9,000 | — |
| 1927R | 30 | — | — | 5,000 | 7,000 | — |

**10 LIRE** **KM# 68.1** **Weight:** 10.0000 g. **Composition:** 0.8350 Silver .2684 oz. ASW **Ruler:** Vittorio Emanuele III **Edge Lettering:** *FERT*

| Date | Mintage | F | VF | XF | Unc | BU |
|---|---|---|---|---|---|---|
| 1926R | 1,748,000 | 65.00 | 135 | 275 | 600 | — |
| 1927R | 44,801,000 | 6.00 | 12.00 | 30.00 | 70.00 | — |
| 1928R | 6,652,000 | 20.00 | 55.00 | 125 | 300 | — |
| 1929R | 6,800,000 | 30.00 | 65.00 | 150 | 350 | — |
| 1930R | 3,668,000 | 60.00 | 125 | 250 | 500 | — |
| 1931R | 50 | — | — | — | 750 | — |
| 1932R | 50 | — | — | — | 750 | — |
| 1933R | 50 | — | — | — | 750 | — |
| 1934R | 50 | — | — | — | 750 | — |

**10 LIRE** **KM# 68.2** **Weight:** 10.0000 g. **Composition:** 0.8350 Silver .2684 oz. ASW **Ruler:** Vittorio Emanuele III **Edge Lettering:** **FERT**

| Date | Mintage | F | VF | XF | Unc | BU |
|---|---|---|---|---|---|---|
| 1927R | Inc. above | 10.00 | 20.00 | 40.00 | 90.00 | — |
| 1928R | Inc. above | 75.00 | 150 | 300 | 600 | — |
| 1929R | Inc. above | 20.00 | 55.00 | 125 | 275 | — |

**10 LIRE** **KM# 80** **Weight:** 10.0000 g. **Composition:** 0.8350 Silver .2684 oz. ASW **Ruler:** Vittorio Emanuele III

| Date | Mintage | F | VF | XF | Unc | BU |
|---|---|---|---|---|---|---|
| 1936R Yr. XIV | 619,000 | 15.00 | 30.00 | 60.00 | 125 | — |
| 1937R Yr. XV | 50 | — | — | — | 675 | — |
| 1938R Yr. XVII | 20 | — | — | — | 850 | — |
| 1939R Yr. XVIII | 20 | — | — | — | 850 | — |
| 1940R Yr. XIX | 20 | — | — | — | 850 | — |
| 1941R Yr. XX | 20 | — | — | — | 850 | — |

**20 LIRE** **KM# 37.1** **Weight:** 6.4516 g. **Composition:** 0.9000 Gold .1867 oz. AGW **Ruler:** Vittorio Emanuele III

| Date | Mintage | F | VF | XF | Unc | BU |
|---|---|---|---|---|---|---|
| 1902R | 181 | — | 8,000 | 15,000 | 20,000 | — |
| 1903R | 1,800 | 350 | 700 | 1,200 | 1,800 | — |
| 1905R | 8,715 | 250 | 400 | 650 | 900 | — |
| 1908R Rare | — | — | — | — | — | — |

**20 LIRE** **KM# 37.2** **Weight:** 6.4516 g. **Composition:** 0.9000 Gold .1867 oz. AGW **Ruler:** Vittorio Emanuele III **Obverse:** Small anchor at bottom indicates gold in coin is from Eritrea

| Date | Mintage | F | VF | XF | Unc | BU |
|---|---|---|---|---|---|---|
| 1902R | 115 | 4,500 | 10,000 | 20,000 | 30,000 | — |

**20 LIRE** **KM# 48** **Weight:** 6.4516 g. **Composition:** 0.9000 Gold .1867 oz. AGW **Ruler:** Vittorio Emanuele III **Obverse:** Uniformed bust

| Date | Mintage | F | VF | XF | Unc | BU |
|---|---|---|---|---|---|---|
| 1910R | Est. 33,000 | — | — | — | 30,000 | — |
| **Note:** Six pieces currently known to exist | | | | | | |
| 1912R | 59,000 | 275 | 400 | 750 | 1,100 | — |
| 1926R | 40 | — | — | 5,000 | 8,000 | — |
| 1927R | 30 | — | — | — | 10,000 | — |

**20 LIRE** **KM# 64** **Weight:** 6.4516 g. **Composition:** 0.9000 Gold .1867 oz. AGW **Ruler:** Vittorio Emanuele III **Subject:** 1st anniversary of Fascist government

| Date | Mintage | F | VF | XF | Unc | BU |
|---|---|---|---|---|---|---|
| 1923R | 20,000 | 200 | 350 | 650 | 850 | — |

**20 LIRE** **KM# 69** **Weight:** 15.0000 g. **Composition:** 0.8000 Silver .3858 oz. ASW **Ruler:** Vittorio Emanuele III

| Date | Mintage | F | VF | XF | Unc | BU |
|---|---|---|---|---|---|---|
| 1927R Yr. V | 100 | — | — | 4,000 | 5,500 | — |
| 1927R Yr. VI | 3,518,000 | 40.00 | 80.00 | 200 | 500 | — |
| 1928R Yr. VI | 2,487,000 | 65.00 | 100 | 320 | 625 | — |
| 1929R Yr. VII | 50 | — | — | — | 1,750 | — |
| 1930R Yr. VIII | 50 | — | — | — | 1,750 | — |
| 1931R Yr. IX | 50 | — | — | — | 1,750 | — |
| 1932R Yr. X | 50 | — | — | — | 1,750 | — |
| 1933R Yr. XI | 50 | — | — | — | 1,750 | — |
| 1934R Yr. XII | 50 | — | — | — | 1,750 | — |

**20 LIRE** **KM# 70** **Weight:** 20.0000 g. **Composition:** 0.6000 Silver .3858 oz. ASW **Ruler:** Vittorio Emanuele III **Subject:** 10th anniversary - end of World War I **Note:** Similar 20 and 100 Lire pieces struck in gold, silver and silvered brass are modern fantasies.

| Date | Mintage | F | VF | XF | Unc | BU |
|---|---|---|---|---|---|---|
| 1928R | — | 65.00 | 125 | 275 | 700 | — |

**20 LIRE** **KM# 81** **Weight:** 20.0000 g. **Composition:** 0.8000 Silver .5145 oz. ASW **Ruler:** Vittorio Emanuele III

| Date | Mintage | F | VF | XF | Unc | BU |
|---|---|---|---|---|---|---|
| 1936R Yr. XIV | 10,000 | 250 | 500 | 1,000 | 2,000 | — |
| 1937R Yr. XV | 50 | — | — | — | 2,500 | — |
| 1938R Yr. XVII | 20 | — | — | — | 3,000 | — |
| 1939R Yr. XVIII | 20 | — | — | — | 3,000 | — |
| 1940R Yr. XIX | 20 | — | — | — | 3,250 | — |
| 1941R Yr. XX | 20 | — | — | — | 3,250 | — |

**50 LIRE** **KM# 49** **Weight:** 16.1290 g. **Composition:** 0.9000 Gold .4667 oz. AGW **Ruler:** Vittorio Emanuele III

| Date | Mintage | F | VF | XF | Unc | BU |
|---|---|---|---|---|---|---|
| 1910R Rare | 2,096 | — | — | — | — | — |
| 1912R | 11,000 | 350 | 650 | 1,150 | 1,750 | — |
| 1926R | 40 | — | — | — | 15,000 | — |
| 1927R | 30 | — | — | — | 18,000 | — |

**50 LIRE** **KM# 54** **Weight:** 16.1290 g. **Composition:** 0.9000 Gold .4667 oz. AGW **Ruler:** Vittorio Emanuele III **Subject:** 50th anniversary of kingdom

| Date | Mintage | F | VF | XF | Unc | BU |
|---|---|---|---|---|---|---|
| 1911R | 20,000 | 300 | 500 | 750 | 1,450 | — |

**50 LIRE** **KM# 71** **Weight:** 4.3995 g. **Composition:** 0.9000 Gold .1273 oz. AGW **Ruler:** Vittorio Emanuele III

| Date | Mintage | F | VF | XF | Unc | BU |
|---|---|---|---|---|---|---|
| 1931R Yr. IX | 32,000 | 90.00 | 125 | 155 | 250 | — |
| 1931R Yr. X | Inc. above | 200 | 300 | 400 | 600 | — |
| 1932R Yr. X | 12,000 | 200 | 300 | 400 | 600 | — |
| 1933R Yr. XI | 6,463 | 300 | 400 | 600 | 800 | — |

**50 LIRE** **KM# 82** **Weight:** 4.3995 g. **Composition:** 0.9000 Gold .1273 oz. AGW **Ruler:** Vittorio Emanuele III

| Date | Mintage | F | VF | XF | Unc | BU |
|---|---|---|---|---|---|---|
| 1936R | 790 | 1,000 | 2,000 | 4,000 | 6,000 | — |

**100 LIRE** **KM# 39** **Weight:** 32.2580 g. **Composition:** 0.9000 Gold .9334 oz. AGW **Ruler:** Vittorio Emanuele III

| Date | Mintage | F | VF | XF | Unc | BU |
|---|---|---|---|---|---|---|
| 1903R | 916 | 1,800 | 3,500 | 7,000 | 9,500 | — |
| 1905R | 1,012 | 1,500 | 2,700 | 5,500 | 7,500 | — |

**100 LIRE** **KM# 50** **Weight:** 32.2580 g. **Composition:** 0.9000 Gold .9334 oz. AGW **Ruler:** Vittorio Emanuele III

| Date | Mintage | F | VF | XF | Unc | BU |
|---|---|---|---|---|---|---|
| 1910R Rare | 2,013 | — | — | — | — | — |
| 1912R | 4,946 | — | 1,800 | 3,000 | 4,500 | — |
| 1926R | 40 | — | 13,000 | 18,000 | 23,000 | — |
| 1927R | 30 | — | 15,000 | 20,000 | 25,000 | — |

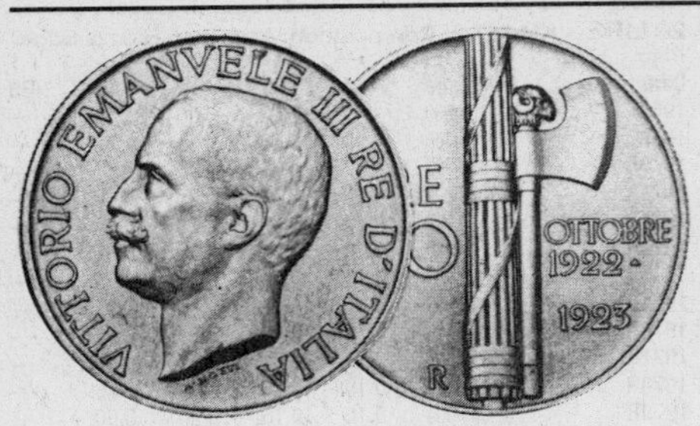


**100 LIRE** **KM# 65** **Weight:** 32.2580 g. **Composition:** 0.9000 Gold .9334 oz. AGW **Ruler:** Vittorio Emanuele III **Subject:** 1st anniversary of Fascist government

| Date | Mintage | F | VF | XF | Unc | BU |
|---|---|---|---|---|---|---|
| 1923R Matte finish | 20,000 | 750 | 1,000 | 1,500 | 3,000 | — |
| 1923R Bright finish, rare | — | — | — | — | — | — |

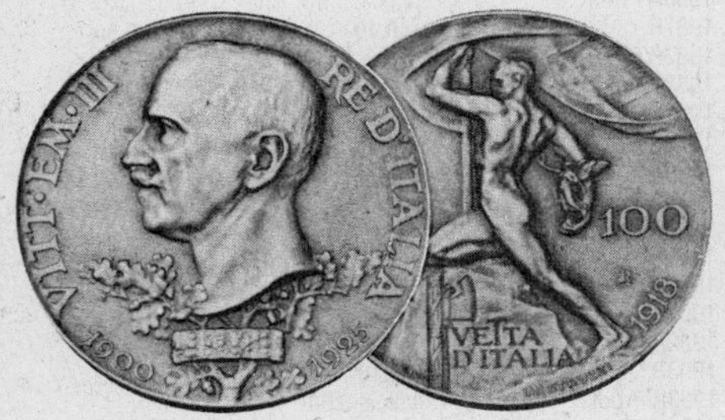


**100 LIRE** **KM# 66** **Weight:** 32.2580 g. **Composition:** 0.9000 Gold .9334 oz. AGW **Ruler:** Vittorio Emanuele III **Subject:** 25th year of reign, 10th anniversary - World War I entry

| Date | Mintage | F | VF | XF | Unc | BU |
|---|---|---|---|---|---|---|
| 1925R Matte finish | 5,000 | 1,000 | 1,500 | 3,000 | 5,000 | — |
| 1925R Bright finish, rare | — | — | — | — | — | — |

**100 LIRE** **KM#72** **Weight:** 8.7990 g. **Composition:** 0.9000 Gold .2546 oz. AGW **Ruler:** Vittorio Emanuele III

| Date | Mintage | F | VF | XF | Unc | BU |
|---|---|---|---|---|---|---|
| 1931R Yr. IX | 34,000 | 150 | 250 | 350 | 525 | — |
| 1931R Yr. X | Inc. above | 150 | 250 | 375 | 600 | — |
| 1932R Yr. X | 9,081 | 150 | 250 | 375 | 600 | — |
| 1933R Yr. XI | 6,464 | 175 | 275 | 425 | 725 | — |

**100 LIRE** **KM#83** **Weight:** 8.7990 g. **Composition:** 0.9000 Gold .2546 oz. AGW **Ruler:** Vittorio Emanuele III

| Date | Mintage | F | VF | XF | Unc | BU |
|---|---|---|---|---|---|---|
| 1936R | 812 | 1,250 | 2,500 | 4,000 | 7,000 | — |

**100 LIRE** **KM#84** **Weight:** 5.1900 g. **Composition:** 0.9000 Gold .1502 oz. AGW **Ruler:** Vittorio Emanuele III

| Date | Mintage | F | VF | XF | Unc | BU |
|---|---|---|---|---|---|---|
| 1937R Yr. XVI | 249 | — | 6,000 | 12,000 | 18,000 | — |
| 1940R Yr. XVIII, rare | 2 | — | — | — | — | — |

# REPUBLIC

## DECIMAL COINAGE

**LIRA** **KM# 87** **Composition:** Aluminum

| Date | Mintage | F | VF | XF | Unc | BU |
|---|---|---|---|---|---|---|
| 1946R | 104,000 | 10.00 | 30.00 | 65.00 | 125 | — |
| 1947R | 12,000 | 60.00 | 140 | 250 | 450 | — |
| 1948R | 9,000,000 | 0.40 | 1.00 | 3.00 | 12.00 | — |
| 1949R | 13,200,000 | 0.40 | 1.00 | 2.50 | 10.00 | — |
| 1950R | 1,942,000 | 1.00 | 2.00 | 6.00 | 17.50 | — |

**LIRA** **KM# 91** **Composition:** Aluminum **Note:** The 1968-1969 and 1982-1999 dates were issued in sets only.

| Date | Mintage | F | VF | XF | Unc | BU |
|---|---|---|---|---|---|---|
| 1951R | 3,680,000 | 0.20 | 0.50 | 1.00 | 8.00 | — |
| 1952R | 2,720,000 | 0.20 | 0.50 | 1.00 | 5.00 | — |
| 1953R | 2,800,000 | 0.20 | 0.50 | 1.00 | 3.00 | — |
| 1954R | 41,040,000 | 0.10 | 0.25 | 0.50 | 1.85 | — |
| 1955R | 32,640,000 | 0.10 | 0.25 | 0.50 | 1.85 | — |
| 1956R | 1,840,000 | 0.20 | 0.50 | 4.00 | 15.00 | — |
| 1957R | 7,440,000 | 0.10 | 0.25 | 0.50 | 2.00 | — |
| 1958R | 5,280,000 | 0.10 | 0.25 | 0.50 | 2.00 | — |
| 1959R | 1,680,000 | 0.10 | 0.25 | 0.50 | 2.00 | — |
| 1968R | 100,000 | — | — | — | 17.00 | — |
| 1969R | 310,000 | — | — | — | 5.00 | — |
| 1970R | 1,011,000 | — | — | — | 2.50 | — |
| 1980R | 1,500,000 | — | — | — | 1.50 | — |
| 1981R | 500,000 | — | — | — | 1.50 | — |
| 1982R | 85,000 | — | — | — | 2.50 | — |
| 1983R | 76,000 | — | — | — | 6.00 | — |
| 1984R | 77,000 | — | — | — | 4.00 | — |
| 1985R | 73,000 | — | — | — | 2.00 | — |
| 1985R Proof | 20,000 | Value: 4.00 | | | | |
| 1986R | — | — | — | — | 2.00 | — |
| 1986R Proof | — | Value: 4.00 | | | | |
| 1987R | 177,000 | — | — | — | 2.50 | — |
| 1987R Proof | — | Value: 4.50 | | | | |
| 1988R | 77,000 | — | — | — | 2.00 | — |
| 1988R Proof | — | Value: 4.50 | | | | |
| 1989R | — | — | — | — | 2.00 | — |
| 1989R Proof | — | Value: 4.50 | | | | |
| 1990R | — | — | — | — | 2.00 | — |
| 1990R Proof | — | Value: 4.50 | | | | |
| 1991R | — | — | — | — | 2.00 | — |
| 1991R Proof | — | Value: 4.50 | | | | |
| 1992R | — | — | — | — | 2.00 | — |
| 1992R Proof | — | Value: 4.50 | | | | |
| 1993R | — | — | — | — | 2.00 | — |
| 1993R Proof | — | Value: 4.50 | | | | |
| 1994R | — | — | — | — | 2.00 | — |
| 1995R | — | — | — | — | 2.00 | — |
| 1996R | — | — | — | — | 2.00 | — |
| 1997R | — | — | — | — | 2.00 | — |
| 1998R | — | — | — | — | 2.00 | — |
| 1999R | — | — | — | — | 2.00 | — |

**LIRA** **KM# 204** **Weight:** 14.6000 g. **Composition:** 0.8350 Silver .3919 oz. ASW **Series:** History of the Lira **Subject:** Lira of 1901, KM#32 **Obverse:** King's head right within inner circle **Reverse:** Heraldic eagle design **Edge:** Reeded and plain

| Date | Mintage | F | VF | XF | Unc | BU |
|---|---|---|---|---|---|---|
| 1999R | — | — | — | — | 30.00 | — |

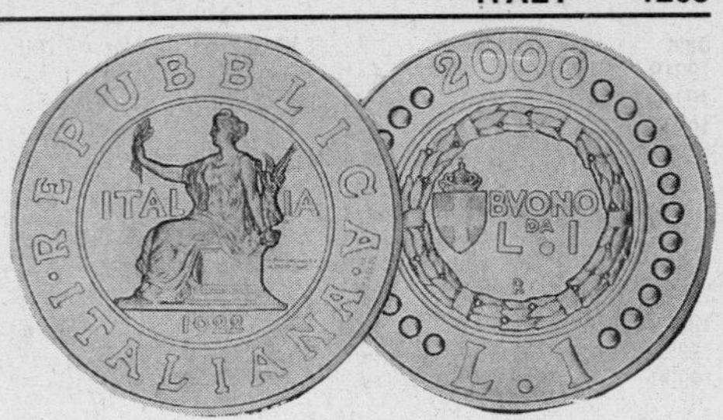


**LIRA** **KM# 206** **Weight:** 14.6000 g. **Composition:** 0.8350 Silver .3919 oz. ASW **Series:** History of the Lira **Subject:** Lira of 1922, KM#62 **Obverse:** Seated allegorical figure **Reverse:** Crowned arms and denomination **Edge:** Reeded and plain sections **Size:** 34 mm.

| Date | Mintage | F | VF | XF | Unc | BU |
|---|---|---|---|---|---|---|
| 2000 | — | — | — | — | 25.00 | — |

**LIRA** **KM# 207** **Weight:** 14.6000 g. **Composition:** 0.8350 Silver .3919 oz. ASW **Series:** History of the Lire **Subject:** Lira of 1936, KM#77 **Obverse:** Portrait of Vittorio Emanuele III **Reverse:** Eagle in front of fasces **Edge:** Reeded and plain sections **Size:** 34 mm.

| Date | Mintage | F | VF | XF | Unc | BU |
|---|---|---|---|---|---|---|
| 2000 | — | — | — | — | 25.00 | — |

**2 LIRE** **KM# 88** **Composition:** Aluminum

| Date | Mintage | F | VF | XF | Unc | BU |
|---|---|---|---|---|---|---|
| 1946R | 123,000 | 7.50 | 20.00 | 50.00 | 110 | — |
| 1947R | 12,000 | 65.00 | 150 | 275 | 475 | — |
| 1948R | 7,200,000 | 0.50 | 1.50 | 3.00 | 9.00 | — |
| 1949R | 1,350,000 | 5.00 | 12.00 | 25.00 | 50.00 | — |
| 1950R | 2,640,000 | 0.60 | 1.75 | 4.00 | 13.50 | — |

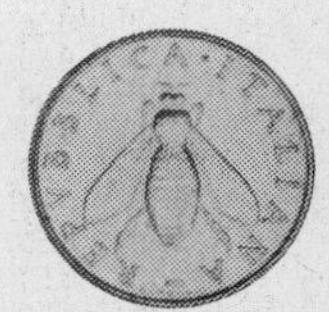

**2 LIRE** **KM# 94** **Composition:** Aluminum **Note:** The 1968-1969 and 1982-1999 dates were issued in sets only.

| Date | Mintage | F | VF | XF | Unc | BU |
|---|---|---|---|---|---|---|
| 1953R | 4,125,000 | 0.25 | 0.50 | 0.75 | 4.00 | — |
| 1954R | 22,500,000 | 0.25 | 0.50 | 0.75 | 2.00 | — |
| 1955R | 2,750,000 | 0.25 | 0.50 | 0.75 | 3.50 | — |
| 1956R | 1,500,000 | 1.00 | 3.00 | 5.00 | 15.00 | — |
| 1957R | 6,313,000 | 0.25 | 0.50 | 0.75 | 2.50 | — |
| 1958R | 125,000 | 20.00 | 60.00 | 140 | 200 | — |
| 1959R | 2,000,000 | 0.25 | 0.50 | 0.75 | 2.50 | — |
| 1968R | 100,000 | — | — | — | 15.00 | — |
| 1969R | 310,000 | — | — | — | 4.00 | — |
| 1970R | 1,140,000 | — | — | — | 2.50 | — |
| 1980R | 500,000 | — | — | — | 1.00 | — |
| 1981R | 500,000 | — | — | — | 1.00 | — |
| 1982R | 85,000 | — | — | — | 2.50 | — |
| 1983R | 76,000 | — | — | — | 6.00 | — |
| 1984R | 77,000 | — | — | — | 4.00 | — |
| 1985R | 73,000 | — | — | — | 1.00 | — |
| 1985R Proof | 20,000 | Value: 3.50 | | | | |
| 1986R | — | — | — | — | 1.00 | — |
| 1986R Proof | — | Value: 3.50 | | | | |
| 1987R | 177,000 | — | — | — | 1.50 | — |
| 1987R Proof | — | Value: 4.00 | | | | |
| 1988R | 77,000 | — | — | — | 1.00 | — |
| 1988R Proof | — | Value: 4.50 | | | | |
| 1989R | — | — | — | — | 1.00 | — |
| 1989R Proof | — | Value: 4.50 | | | | |
| 1990R | — | — | — | — | 1.00 | — |
| 1990R Proof | — | Value: 4.50 | | | | |

| Date | Mintage | F | VF | XF | Unc | BU |
|---|---|---|---|---|---|---|
| 1991R | — | — | — | — | 1.00 | — |
| 1991R Proof | — | Value: 4.50 | | | | |
| 1992R | — | — | — | — | 1.00 | — |
| 1992R Proof | — | Value: 4.50 | | | | |
| 1993R | — | — | — | — | 1.00 | — |
| 1993R Proof | — | Value: 4.50 | | | | |
| 1994R | — | — | — | — | 1.00 | — |
| 1995R | — | — | — | — | 1.00 | — |
| 1996R | — | — | — | — | 1.00 | — |
| 1997R | — | — | — | — | 1.00 | — |
| 1998R | — | — | — | — | 1.00 | — |
| 1999R | — | — | — | — | 1.00 | — |

**5 LIRE** **KM# 89** **Composition:** Aluminum

| Date | Mintage | F | VF | XF | Unc | BU |
|---|---|---|---|---|---|---|
| 1946R | 81,000 | 100 | 200 | 300 | 600 | — |
| 1947R | 17,000 | 125 | 275 | 425 | 750 | — |
| 1948R | 25,125,000 | 0.50 | 1.50 | 5.00 | 15.00 | — |
| 1949R | 71,100,000 | 0.30 | 0.75 | 2.00 | 10.00 | — |
| 1950 | 114,790,000 | 0.30 | 0.75 | 2.00 | 10.00 | — |

**5 LIRE** **KM# 92** **Composition:** Aluminum

| Date | Mintage | F | VF | XF | Unc | BU |
|---|---|---|---|---|---|---|
| 1951R | 40,260,000 | 0.10 | 0.25 | 0.50 | 3.00 | — |
| 1952R | 57,400,000 | 0.10 | 0.25 | 0.50 | 4.00 | — |
| 1953R | 196,200,000 | 0.10 | 0.25 | 0.50 | 2.00 | — |
| 1954R | 436,400,000 | 0.10 | 0.25 | 0.50 | 1.50 | — |
| 1955R | 159,000,000 | 0.10 | 0.25 | 0.50 | 2.00 | — |
| 1956R | 400,000 | 15.00 | 50.00 | 250 | 800 | — |
| 1966R | 1,200,000 | 0.25 | 0.50 | 1.00 | 1.50 | — |
| 1967R | 10,600,000 | 0.10 | 0.25 | 0.50 | 1.00 | — |
| 1968R | 7,500,000 | — | — | 0.10 | 0.75 | — |
| 1969R | 7,910,000 | — | — | 0.10 | 0.75 | — |
| 1969R Inverted 1 (die break at base of 1) | 969,000 | 1.00 | 2.00 | 4.00 | 22.50 | — |
| 1970R | 3,200,000 | — | — | 0.10 | 0.75 | — |
| 1971R | 8,600,000 | — | — | 0.10 | 0.75 | — |
| 1972R | 16,400,000 | — | — | 0.10 | 0.50 | — |
| 1973R | 28,800,000 | — | — | 0.10 | 0.50 | — |
| 1974R | 6,600,000 | — | — | 0.10 | 0.50 | — |
| 1975R | 7,000,000 | — | — | 0.10 | 0.50 | — |
| 1976R | 8,800,000 | — | — | 0.10 | 0.50 | — |
| 1977R | 6,700,000 | — | — | 0.10 | 0.50 | — |
| 1978R | 3,600,000 | — | — | 0.10 | 0.50 | — |
| 1979R | 4,200,000 | — | — | 0.10 | 0.50 | — |
| 1980R | 3,663,000 | — | — | 0.10 | 0.50 | — |
| 1981R | 7,788,000 | — | — | 0.10 | 0.50 | — |
| 1982R | 855,000 | — | — | 0.10 | 0.50 | — |
| 1983R | 14,020,000 | — | — | 0.10 | 0.50 | — |
| 1984R | 122,000 | — | — | 0.10 | 0.50 | — |
| 1985R | 3,000,000 | — | — | 0.10 | 0.50 | — |
| 1985R Proof | 20,000 | Value: 2.50 | | | | |
| 1986R | 5,000,000 | — | — | 0.10 | 0.50 | — |
| 1986R Proof | — | Value: 2.50 | | | | |
| 1987R | 7,000,000 | — | — | 0.10 | 0.50 | — |
| 1987R Proof | — | Value: 2.50 | | | | |
| 1988R | 5,000,000 | — | — | 0.10 | 0.50 | — |
| 1988R Proof | — | Value: 2.50 | | | | |
| 1989R Coin rotation | — | — | — | 0.10 | 0.50 | — |
| 1989R Medal rotation | — | — | — | — | 10.00 | — |
| 1989R Proof | — | Value: 2.50 | | | | |
| 1990R | — | — | — | 0.10 | 0.50 | — |
| 1990R Proof | — | Value: 2.50 | | | | |
| 1991R | — | — | — | 0.10 | 0.50 | — |
| 1991R Proof | — | Value: 2.50 | | | | |
| 1992R | — | — | — | 0.10 | 0.50 | — |
| 1992R Proof | — | Value: 2.50 | | | | |
| 1993R | — | — | — | 0.10 | 0.50 | — |
| 1993R Proof | — | Value: 2.50 | | | | |
| 1994R | — | — | — | 0.10 | 0.50 | — |
| 1995R | — | — | — | 0.10 | 0.50 | — |
| 1996R | — | — | — | 0.10 | 0.50 | — |
| 1997R | — | — | — | 0.10 | 0.50 | — |
| 1998R | — | — | — | 0.10 | 0.50 | — |
| 1999R | — | — | — | 0.10 | 0.50 | — |

**10 LIRE** **KM# 90** **Composition:** Aluminum

| Date | Mintage | F | VF | XF | Unc | BU |
|---|---|---|---|---|---|---|
| 1946R | 101,000 | 50.00 | 100 | 175 | 285 | — |
| 1947R | 12,000 | 200 | 600 | 1,200 | 1,850 | — |
| 1948R | 14,400,000 | 1.00 | 4.00 | 25.00 | 65.00 | — |
| 1949R | 49,500,000 | 0.50 | 1.00 | 3.00 | 15.00 | — |
| 1950R | 53,311,000 | 0.50 | 1.00 | 3.00 | 15.00 | — |

**10 LIRE** **KM# 93** **Composition:** Aluminum

| Date | Mintage | F | VF | XF | Unc | BU |
|---|---|---|---|---|---|---|
| 1951R | 96,600,000 | 0.10 | 0.25 | 2.00 | 10.00 | — |
| 1952R | 105,150,000 | 0.10 | 0.25 | 1.50 | 8.00 | — |
| 1953R | 151,500,000 | 0.10 | 0.25 | 1.00 | 6.00 | — |
| 1954R | 95,250,000 | 0.50 | 1.00 | 5.00 | 40.00 | — |
| 1955R | 274,950,000 | 0.10 | 0.15 | 1.00 | 3.00 | — |
| 1956R | 76,650,000 | 0.10 | 0.25 | 1.25 | 6.00 | — |
| 1965R | 1,050,000 | 0.25 | 0.50 | 1.50 | 8.00 | — |
| 1966R | 16,500,000 | 0.10 | 0.25 | 1.00 | 3.00 | — |
| 1967R | 29,450,000 | 0.10 | 0.25 | 1.00 | 2.00 | — |
| 1968R | 32,200,000 | — | — | 0.10 | 0.75 | — |
| 1969R | 23,710,000 | — | — | 0.10 | 0.75 | — |
| 1970R | 14,100,000 | — | — | 0.10 | 0.75 | — |
| 1971R | 23,550,000 | — | — | 0.10 | 0.75 | — |
| 1972R | 61,300,000 | — | — | 0.10 | 0.50 | — |
| 1973R | 145,800,000 | — | — | 0.10 | 0.50 | — |
| 1974R | 85,000,000 | — | — | 0.10 | 0.50 | — |
| 1975R | 76,800,000 | — | — | 0.10 | 0.50 | — |
| 1976R | 82,000,000 | — | — | 0.10 | 0.50 | — |
| 1977R | 80,750,000 | — | — | 0.10 | 0.50 | — |
| 1978R | 43,800,000 | — | — | 0.10 | 0.50 | — |
| 1979R | 98,000,000 | — | — | 0.10 | 0.50 | — |
| 1980R | 81,109,000 | — | — | 0.10 | 0.50 | — |
| 1981R | 46,967,000 | — | — | 0.10 | 0.50 | — |
| 1982R | 45,986,000 | — | — | 0.10 | 0.50 | — |
| 1983R | 15,110,000 | — | — | 0.10 | 0.50 | — |
| 1984R | 11,122,000 | — | — | 0.10 | 0.50 | — |
| 1985R | 15,000,000 | — | — | 0.10 | 0.50 | — |
| 1985R Proof | 20,000 | Value: 3.50 | | | | |
| 1986R | 16,000,000 | — | — | 0.10 | 0.50 | — |
| 1986R Proof | — | Value: 3.50 | | | | |
| 1987R | 13,000,000 | — | — | 0.10 | 0.50 | — |
| 1987R Proof | — | Value: 3.50 | | | | |
| 1988R | 13,000,000 | — | — | 0.10 | 0.50 | — |
| 1988R Proof | — | Value: 3.50 | | | | |
| 1989R | — | — | — | 0.10 | 0.50 | — |
| 1989R Proof | — | Value: 3.50 | | | | |
| 1990R | — | — | — | 0.10 | 0.50 | — |
| 1990R Proof | — | Value: 3.50 | | | | |
| 1991R | — | — | — | 0.10 | 0.50 | — |
| 1991R Proof | — | Value: 3.50 | | | | |
| 1992R | — | — | — | 0.10 | 0.50 | — |
| 1992R Proof | — | Value: 3.50 | | | | |
| 1993R | — | — | — | 0.10 | 0.50 | — |
| 1993R Proof | — | Value: 3.50 | | | | |
| 1994R | — | — | — | 0.10 | 0.50 | — |
| 1995R | — | — | — | 0.10 | 0.50 | — |
| 1996R | — | — | — | 0.10 | 0.50 | — |
| 1997R | — | — | — | 0.10 | 0.50 | — |
| 1998R | — | — | — | 0.10 | 0.50 | — |
| 1999R | — | — | — | 0.10 | 0.50 | — |

**20 LIRE** **KM# 97.1** **Composition:** Aluminum-Bronze

| Date | Mintage | F | VF | XF | Unc | BU |
|---|---|---|---|---|---|---|
| 1957R Serifed 7 | Est. 60,075,000 | 0.20 | 0.40 | 2.00 | 10.00 | — |
| 1957R Plain 7 | Inc. above | 0.20 | 0.40 | 2.00 | 10.00 | — |
| 1958R | 80,550,000 | 0.20 | 0.40 | 2.00 | 10.00 | — |
| 1959R | 4,005,000 | 0.50 | 1.25 | 5.00 | 50.00 | — |

**20 LIRE** **KM# 97.2** **Composition:** Aluminum-Bronze **Edge:** Plain

| Date | Mintage | F | VF | XF | Unc | BU |
|---|---|---|---|---|---|---|
| 1968R | 100,000 | — | 2.50 | 5.00 | 35.00 | — |
| 1969R | 16,735,000 | 0.10 | 0.15 | 0.25 | 1.00 | — |
| 1970R | 31,500,000 | 0.10 | 0.15 | 0.25 | 0.65 | — |
| 1971R | 12,375,000 | 0.10 | 0.15 | 0.25 | 1.00 | — |
| 1972R | 34,400,000 | 0.10 | 0.15 | 0.25 | 0.65 | — |
| 1973R | 20,000,000 | 0.10 | 0.15 | 0.25 | 0.65 | — |
| 1974R | 17,000,000 | 0.10 | 0.15 | 0.20 | 0.65 | — |
| 1975R | 25,000,000 | 0.10 | 0.15 | 0.20 | 0.65 | — |
| 1976R | 15,000,000 | 0.10 | 0.15 | 0.20 | 0.65 | — |
| 1977R | 10,000,000 | 0.10 | 0.15 | 0.20 | 0.65 | — |
| 1978R | 8,415,000 | 0.10 | 0.15 | 0.20 | 0.65 | — |
| 1979R | 32,000,000 | 0.10 | 0.15 | 0.20 | 0.50 | — |
| 1980R | 61,795,000 | 0.10 | 0.15 | 0.20 | 0.50 | — |
| 1981R | 68,557,000 | 0.10 | 0.15 | 0.20 | 0.50 | — |
| 1982R | 44,774,000 | 0.10 | 0.15 | 0.20 | 0.50 | — |
| 1983R | 15,110,000 | 0.10 | 0.15 | 0.20 | 0.50 | — |
| 1984R | 5,122,000 | 0.10 | 0.15 | 0.20 | 0.50 | — |
| 1985R | 15,000,000 | 0.10 | 0.15 | 0.20 | 0.50 | — |
| 1985R Proof | 20,000 | Value: 3.50 | | | | |
| 1986R | 13,000,000 | 0.10 | 0.15 | 0.20 | 0.50 | — |
| 1986R Proof | — | Value: 3.50 | | | | |
| 1987R | 8,234,000 | 0.10 | 0.15 | 0.20 | 0.50 | — |
| 1987R Proof | — | Value: 3.50 | | | | |
| 1988R | 13,000,000 | 0.10 | 0.15 | 0.20 | 0.50 | — |
| 1988R Proof | — | Value: 3.50 | | | | |
| 1989R | — | 0.10 | 0.15 | 0.20 | 0.50 | — |
| 1989R Proof | — | Value: 3.50 | | | | |
| 1990R | — | 0.10 | 0.15 | 0.20 | 0.50 | — |
| 1990R Proof | — | Value: 3.50 | | | | |
| 1991R | — | 0.10 | 0.15 | 0.20 | 0.50 | — |
| 1991R Proof | — | Value: 3.50 | | | | |
| 1992R | — | 0.10 | 0.15 | 0.20 | 0.50 | — |
| 1992R Proof | — | Value: 3.50 | | | | |
| 1993R | — | 0.10 | 0.15 | 0.20 | 0.50 | — |
| 1993R Proof | — | Value: 3.50 | | | | |
| 1994R | — | 0.10 | 0.15 | 0.20 | 0.50 | — |
| 1995R | — | 0.10 | 0.15 | 0.20 | 3.50 | — |
| 1996R | — | 0.10 | 0.15 | 0.20 | 3.50 | — |
| 1997R | — | 0.10 | 0.15 | 0.20 | 3.50 | — |
| 1998R | — | 0.10 | 0.15 | 0.20 | 3.50 | — |
| 1999R | — | 0.10 | 0.15 | 0.20 | 3.50 | — |

**50 LIRE** **KM# 95** **Composition:** Stainless Steel

| Date | Mintage | F | VF | XF | Unc | BU |
|---|---|---|---|---|---|---|
| 1954R | 17,600,000 | 1.00 | 3.00 | 20.00 | 75.00 | — |
| 1955R | 70,500,000 | 0.50 | 1.50 | 10.00 | 40.00 | — |
| 1956R | 69,400,000 | 0.50 | 1.50 | 10.00 | 40.00 | — |
| 1957R | 8,925,000 | 2.00 | 4.00 | 25.00 | 120 | — |
| 1958R | 825,000 | 4.00 | 10.00 | 50.00 | 200 | — |
| 1959R | 8,800,000 | 0.50 | 1.50 | 15.00 | 80.00 | — |
| 1960R | 2,025,000 | 2.00 | 4.00 | 20.00 | 100 | — |
| 1961R | 11,100,000 | 0.50 | 1.50 | 10.00 | 40.00 | — |
| 1962R | 17,700,000 | 0.50 | 1.50 | 10.00 | 40.00 | — |
| 1963R | 31,600,000 | 0.20 | 0.75 | 2.50 | 20.00 | — |
| 1964R | 37,900,000 | 0.20 | 0.75 | 2.50 | 18.00 | — |
| 1965R | 25,300,000 | 0.20 | 0.50 | 1.50 | 12.00 | — |
| 1966R | 27,400,000 | 0.20 | 0.40 | 0.80 | 8.00 | — |
| 1967R | 28,000,000 | 0.20 | 0.40 | 0.80 | 6.00 | — |
| 1968R | 17,800,000 | 0.20 | 0.30 | 0.50 | 1.50 | — |
| 1969R | 23,010,000 | 0.20 | 0.30 | 0.50 | 1.50 | — |
| 1970R | 21,411,000 | 0.10 | 0.20 | 0.50 | 1.50 | — |
| 1971R | 33,410,000 | 0.10 | 0.20 | 0.50 | 1.50 | — |
| 1972R | 39,000,000 | 0.10 | 0.20 | 0.50 | 1.50 | — |
| 1973R | 48,700,000 | 0.10 | 0.20 | 0.50 | 1.50 | — |
| 1974R | 65,100,000 | 0.10 | 0.20 | 0.35 | 1.00 | — |
| 1975R | 87,000,000 | 0.10 | 0.15 | 0.25 | 0.75 | — |
| 1976R | 180,600,000 | 0.10 | 0.15 | 0.25 | 0.75 | — |
| 1977R | 293,800,000 | 0.10 | 0.15 | 0.25 | 0.75 | — |
| 1978R | 416,808,000 | 0.10 | 0.15 | 0.25 | 0.75 | — |
| 1979R | 256,630,000 | 0.10 | 0.15 | 0.25 | 0.75 | — |
| 1980R | — | 0.10 | 0.15 | 0.25 | 0.75 | — |
| 1981R | — | 0.10 | 0.15 | 0.25 | 0.75 | — |
| 1982R | — | 0.10 | 0.15 | 0.25 | 0.75 | — |
| 1983R | — | 0.10 | 0.15 | 0.25 | 0.75 | — |
| 1984R | — | 0.10 | 0.15 | 0.25 | 0.75 | — |
| 1985R | — | 0.10 | 0.15 | 0.25 | 0.75 | — |
| 1985R Proof | 20,000 | Value: 3.50 | | | | |
| 1986R | — | 0.10 | 0.15 | 0.25 | 0.75 | — |
| 1986R Proof | — | Value: 3.50 | | | | |
| 1987R | 14,682,000 | 0.10 | 0.15 | 0.25 | 0.75 | — |
| 1987R Proof | — | Value: 3.50 | | | | |
| 1988R | 20,000,000 | 0.10 | 0.15 | 0.25 | 0.75 | — |
| 1988R Proof | — | Value: 3.50 | | | | |
| 1989R | — | 0.10 | 0.15 | 0.25 | 0.75 | — |
| 1989R Proof | — | Value: 3.50 | | | | |

**50 LIRE** **KM# 95a** **Composition:** Stainless Steel **Note:** Reduced size.

| Date | Mintage | F | VF | XF | Unc | BU |
|---|---|---|---|---|---|---|
| 1990R | 3,600,000,000 | — | — | — | 0.35 | — |
| 1991R | — | — | — | — | 0.35 | — |
| 1991R Proof | — | Value: 4.00 | | | | |
| 1992R | — | — | — | — | 0.35 | — |
| 1992R Proof | — | Value: 4.00 | | | | |
| 1993R | — | — | — | — | 0.35 | — |
| 1993R Proof | — | Value: 4.00 | | | | |
| 1994R | — | — | — | — | 0.35 | — |
| 1995R | — | — | — | — | 0.35 | — |

**50 LIRE** **KM# 183** **Composition:** Copper Nickel

| Date | Mintage | F | VF | XF | Unc | BU |
|---|---|---|---|---|---|---|
| 1996R | — | — | — | — | 0.35 | — |
| 1996R Proof | — | Value: 4.00 | | | | |
| 1997R | — | — | — | — | 0.35 | — |
| 1998R Proof | — | Value: 4.00 | | | | |
| 1999R | — | — | — | — | 0.35 | — |

**100 LIRE** **KM# 96** **Composition:** Stainless Steel

| Date | Mintage | F | VF | XF | Unc | BU |
|---|---|---|---|---|---|---|
| 1955R | 8,600,000 | 1.00 | 3.00 | 20.00 | 185 | — |
| 1956R | 99,800,000 | 0.25 | 1.00 | 4.00 | 50.00 | — |
| 1957R | 90,600,000 | 0.25 | 1.50 | 15.00 | 150 | — |
| 1958R | 25,640,000 | 0.25 | 1.50 | 15.00 | 150 | — |
| 1959R | 19,500,000 | 0.25 | 1.50 | 12.00 | 120 | — |
| 1960R | 20,700,000 | 0.25 | 1.50 | 10.00 | 100 | — |
| 1961R | 11,860,000 | 0.25 | 1.50 | 10.00 | 100 | — |
| 1962R | 21,700,000 | 0.20 | 0.50 | 3.00 | 40.00 | — |
| 1963R | 33,100,000 | 0.20 | 0.50 | 2.00 | 30.00 | — |
| 1964R | 31,300,000 | 0.20 | 0.50 | 1.50 | 20.00 | — |
| 1965R | 37,000,000 | 0.20 | 0.50 | 1.50 | 20.00 | — |
| 1966R | 52,500,000 | 0.15 | 0.25 | 1.00 | 15.00 | — |
| 1967R | 23,700,000 | 0.15 | 0.25 | 1.00 | 15.00 | — |
| 1968R | 34,200,000 | 0.15 | 0.25 | 0.50 | 3.00 | — |
| 1969R | 27,710,000 | 0.15 | 0.25 | 0.50 | 3.00 | — |
| 1970R | 25,011,000 | 0.15 | 0.25 | 0.50 | 3.00 | — |
| 1971R | 25,910,000 | 0.15 | 0.25 | 0.50 | 3.00 | — |
| 1972R | 31,170,000 | 0.15 | 0.25 | 0.50 | 3.00 | — |
| 1973R | 30,780,000 | 0.15 | 0.25 | 0.50 | 5.00 | — |
| 1974R | 83,880,000 | 0.15 | 0.25 | 0.35 | 0.85 | — |
| 1975R | 106,650,000 | 0.15 | 0.25 | 0.35 | 0.85 | — |
| 1976R | 160,020,000 | 0.15 | 0.25 | 0.35 | 0.85 | — |
| 1977R | 253,980,000 | 0.15 | 0.25 | 0.35 | 0.85 | — |
| 1978R | 343,626,000 | 0.15 | 0.25 | 0.35 | 0.85 | — |
| 1979R | 187,913,000 | 0.15 | 0.25 | 0.35 | 0.85 | — |
| 1980R | — | 0.15 | 0.25 | 0.35 | 0.85 | — |
| 1981R | — | 0.15 | 0.25 | 0.35 | 0.85 | — |
| 1982R | — | 0.15 | 0.25 | 0.35 | 0.85 | — |
| 1983R | — | 0.15 | 0.25 | 0.35 | 0.85 | — |
| 1984R | — | 0.15 | 0.25 | 0.35 | 0.85 | — |
| 1985R | — | 0.15 | 0.25 | 0.35 | 0.85 | — |
| 1985R Proof | 20,000 | Value: 4.50 | | | | |
| 1986R | — | 0.15 | 0.25 | 0.35 | 0.85 | — |
| 1986R Proof | — | Value: 4.50 | | | | |
| 1987R | 25,000,000 | 0.15 | 0.25 | 0.35 | 0.85 | — |
| 1987R Proof | — | Value: 4.50 | | | | |
| 1988R | 23,000,000 | 0.15 | 0.25 | 0.85 | 1.00 | — |
| 1988R Proof | — | Value: 4.50 | | | | |
| 1989R | — | 0.15 | 0.25 | 0.85 | 1.00 | — |
| 1989R Proof | — | Value: 4.50 | | | | |

**100 LIRE** **KM# 102** **Composition:** Stainless Steel **Subject:** 100th anniversary - birth of Guglielmo Marconi

| Date | Mintage | F | VF | XF | Unc | BU |
|---|---|---|---|---|---|---|
| ND(1974)R | 50,000,000 | 0.15 | 0.25 | 0.35 | 1.50 | — |

**100 LIRE** **KM# 106** **Composition:** Stainless Steel **Series:** F.A.O.

| Date | Mintage | F | VF | XF | Unc | BU |
|---|---|---|---|---|---|---|
| 1979R | 100,000,000 | 0.15 | 0.25 | 0.50 | 1.50 | — |

**100 LIRE** **KM# 108** **Composition:** Stainless Steel **Subject:** Centennial of Livorno Naval Academy

| Date | Mintage | F | VF | XF | Unc | BU |
|---|---|---|---|---|---|---|
| ND(1981)R | 40,000,000 | 0.15 | 0.25 | 0.35 | 1.50 | — |

**100 LIRE** **KM# 127** **Weight:** 8.0000 g. **Composition:** 0.8350 Silver .2148 oz. ASW **Subject:** 900th anniversary - University of Bologna

| Date | Mintage | F | VF | XF | Unc | BU |
|---|---|---|---|---|---|---|
| 1988R | 44,000 | — | — | — | 18.00 | — |
| 1988R Proof | 13,000 | Value: 28.00 | | | | |

**100 LIRE** **KM# 96a** **Composition:** Stainless Steel **Note:** Reduced size.

| Date | Mintage | F | VF | XF | Unc | BU |
|---|---|---|---|---|---|---|
| 1990R | 3,560,000,000 | — | — | — | 0.50 | — |
| 1990R Proof | — | Value: 4.50 | | | | |
| 1991R | — | — | — | — | 0.50 | — |
| 1991R Proof | — | Value: 4.50 | | | | |
| 1992R | — | — | — | — | 0.50 | — |
| 1992R Proof | — | Value: 4.50 | | | | |

**100 LIRE** **KM# 171** **Weight:** 4.5000 g. **Composition:** 835.0000 Silver .1208 oz. ASW **Subject:** 100th anniversary - Bank of Italy **Reverse:** Printing press **Note:** Both uncirculated and proof versions were issued in sets only.

| Date | Mintage | F | VF | XF | Unc | BU |
|---|---|---|---|---|---|---|
| ND(1993)R | — | — | — | — | 20.00 | — |
| ND(1993)R Proof | — | Value: 35.00 | | | | |

**100 LIRE** **KM# 159** **Composition:** Copper Nickel

| Date | Mintage | F | VF | XF | Unc | BU |
|---|---|---|---|---|---|---|
| 1993R | — | — | — | — | 0.75 | — |
| 1993R Proof | — | Value: 5.00 | | | | |
| 1994R | — | — | — | — | 0.75 | — |
| 1994R Proof | — | Value: 5.00 | | | | |
| 1996R | — | — | — | — | 0.75 | — |
| 1997R | — | — | — | — | 0.75 | — |
| 1998R | — | — | — | — | 0.75 | — |
| 1999R | — | — | — | — | 0.75 | — |

**100 LIRE** **KM# 180** **Weight:** 4.5000 g. **Composition:** 835.0000 Silver .1208 oz. ASW **Series:** F.A.O. **Reverse:** Logo and denomination

| Date | Mintage | F | VF | XF | Unc | BU |
|---|---|---|---|---|---|---|
| ND(1995)R | — | — | — | — | 0.75 | — |

**200 LIRE** **KM# 105** **Composition:** Aluminum-Bronze

| Date | Mintage | F | VF | XF | Unc | BU |
|---|---|---|---|---|---|---|
| 1977R | 15,900,000 | 0.20 | 0.25 | 0.35 | 1.25 | — |
| 1978R | 461,034,000 | 0.20 | 0.25 | 0.35 | 1.25 | — |
| 1979R | 212,745,000 | 0.20 | 0.25 | 0.35 | 1.25 | — |
| 1980R | — | 0.20 | 0.25 | 0.35 | 1.25 | — |
| 1981R | — | 0.20 | 0.25 | 0.35 | 1.25 | — |
| 1982R | — | 0.20 | 0.25 | 0.35 | 1.25 | — |
| 1983R | — | 0.20 | 0.25 | 0.35 | 1.25 | — |
| 1984R | — | 0.20 | 0.25 | 0.35 | 1.25 | — |
| 1985R | — | 0.20 | 0.25 | 0.35 | 1.25 | — |
| 1985R Proof | 20,000 | Value: 4.00 | | | | |
| 1986R | — | 0.20 | 0.25 | 0.35 | 1.25 | — |
| 1986R Proof | — | Value: 4.00 | | | | |
| 1987R | 26,180,000 | 0.20 | 0.25 | 0.35 | 1.25 | — |
| 1987R Proof | — | Value: 4.00 | | | | |
| 1988R | 37,000,000 | 0.20 | 0.25 | 0.35 | 1.25 | — |
| 1988R Proof | — | Value: 4.00 | | | | |
| 1991R | — | 0.20 | 0.25 | 0.35 | 1.25 | — |
| 1991R Proof | — | Value: 4.00 | | | | |
| 1995R | — | 0.20 | 0.25 | 0.35 | 1.25 | — |
| 1996R | — | 0.20 | 0.25 | 0.35 | 1.25 | — |
| 1997R | — | 0.20 | 0.25 | 0.35 | 1.25 | — |
| 1998R | — | 0.20 | 0.25 | 0.35 | 1.25 | — |

**200 LIRE** **KM# 107** **Composition:** Aluminum-Bronze **Series:** F.A.O. **Subject:** International Women's Year

| Date | Mintage | F | VF | XF | Unc | BU |
|---|---|---|---|---|---|---|
| 1980R | 50,000,000 | 0.20 | 0.25 | 0.35 | 1.25 | — |

**200 LIRE** **KM# 109** **Composition:** Aluminum-Bronze **Subject:** World Food Day

| Date | Mintage | F | VF | XF | Unc | BU |
|---|---|---|---|---|---|---|
| 1981R | 50,000,000 | 0.20 | 0.25 | 0.35 | 1.25 | — |

**200 LIRE** **KM# 128** **Weight:** 5.0000 g. **Composition:** 0.8350 Silver .1342 oz. ASW **Subject:** 900th anniversary - University of Bologna **Obverse:** Similar to 100 Lire, KM#127

| Date | Mintage | F | VF | XF | Unc | BU |
|---|---|---|---|---|---|---|
| 1988R | 68,000 | — | — | — | 20.00 | — |
| 1988R Proof | 13,000 | Value: 30.00 | | | | |

**200 LIRE** **KM# 130** **Composition:** Bronzital **Subject:** Taranto Naval Yards

| Date | Mintage | F | VF | XF | Unc | BU |
|---|---|---|---|---|---|---|
| ND(1989)R | 50,000,000 | — | — | — | 1.25 | — |
| ND(1989)R Proof | — | Value: 4.00 | | | | |

**200 LIRE** **KM# 133** **Weight:** 5.0000 g. **Composition:** 0.8350 Silver .1342 oz. ASW **Subject:** Soccer **Reverse:** Ball on world globe

| Date | Mintage | F | VF | XF | Unc | BU |
|---|---|---|---|---|---|---|
| 1989R | 86,000 | — | — | — | 11.50 | — |
| 1989R Proof | 28,000 | Value: 16.50 | | | | |

**200 LIRE** **KM# 138** **Weight:** 5.0000 g. **Composition:** 0.8350 Silver .1342 oz. ASW **Subject:** Christopher Columbus **Obverse:** Similar to KM#139 **Reverse:** Coat of arms and dolphins

| Date | Mintage | F | VF | XF | Unc | BU |
|---|---|---|---|---|---|---|
| 1989R | 75,000 | — | — | — | 13.50 | — |
| 1989R Proof | 25,000 | Value: 22.50 | | | | |

**200 LIRE** **KM# 135** **Composition:** Bronzital **Subject:** State Council building

| Date | Mintage | F | VF | XF | Unc | BU |
|---|---|---|---|---|---|---|
| ND(1990)R | — | — | — | — | 1.25 | — |
| ND(1990)R Proof | — | Value: 4.00 | | | | |

**200 LIRE** **KM# 142** **Weight:** 9.0000 g. **Composition:** 0.8350 Silver .2416 oz. ASW **Subject:** Italian flora and fauna

| Date | Mintage | F | VF | XF | Unc | BU |
|---|---|---|---|---|---|---|
| 1991R | 57,000 | — | — | — | 15.00 | — |
| 1991R Proof | 10,000 | Value: 25.00 | | | | |

**200 LIRE** **KM# 151** **Composition:** Aluminum-Bronze **Subject:** Genoa Stamp Exposition

| Date | Mintage | F | VF | XF | Unc | BU |
|---|---|---|---|---|---|---|
| 1992R | 110,000,000 | — | — | — | 1.35 | — |
| 1992R Proof | — | Value: 4.00 | | | | |

**200 LIRE** **KM# 155** **Composition:** Aluminum-Bronze **Subject:** 70th anniversary of military aviation

| Date | Mintage | F | VF | XF | Unc | BU |
|---|---|---|---|---|---|---|
| 1993R | — | — | — | — | 1.35 | — |

**200 LIRE** **KM# 172** **Weight:** 5.0000 g. **Composition:** 0.8350 Silver .1343 oz. ASW **Subject:** 100th anniversary - Bank of Italy **Reverse:** Hammered minting scene **Note:** Both uncirculated and proof versions were issued in sets only.

| Date | Mintage | F | VF | XF | Unc | BU |
|---|---|---|---|---|---|---|
| ND(1993)R | 52,000 | — | — | — | 25.00 | — |
| ND(1993)R Proof | 10,000 | Value: 40.00 | | | | |

**200 LIRE** **KM# 164** **Composition:** Aluminum-Bronze **Subject:** 180th anniversary - Carabinieri

| Date | Mintage | F | VF | XF | Unc | BU |
|---|---|---|---|---|---|---|
| ND(1994)R | — | — | — | — | 1.35 | — |

**200 LIRE** **KM# 184** **Composition:** Brass **Subject:** Centennial - Customs Service Academy **Obverse:** 2 large buildings **Reverse:** Shield above denomination, hat and sword

| Date | Mintage | F | VF | XF | Unc | BU |
|---|---|---|---|---|---|---|
| ND(1996)R | — | — | — | — | 1.00 | — |

**200 LIRE** **KM# 188** **Composition:** Brass **Subject:** Centennial - Italian Naval League **Reverse:** League seal

| Date | Mintage | F | VF | XF | Unc | BU |
|---|---|---|---|---|---|---|
| ND(1997)R | 36,000 | — | — | — | 65.00 | — |
| ND(1997)R Proof | 7,695 | Value: 95.00 | | | | |

**200 LIRE** **KM# 218** **Weight:** 5.0000 g. **Composition:** Aluminum-Bronze **Ruler:** Umberto II **Subject:** The Carabinieri, Protectors of Art Heritage **Obverse:** Allegorical portrait **Reverse:** Flaming bomb and David statue **Edge:** Reeded **Size:** 24 mm.

| Date | Mintage | F | VF | XF | Unc | BU |
|---|---|---|---|---|---|---|
| ND(1999) | — | — | — | — | 1.50 | — |

**500 LIRE** **KM# 98** **Weight:** 11.0000 g. **Composition:** 0.8350 Silver .2953 oz. ASW **Edge:** Lettered **Edge Lettering:** Dates in raised lettering

| Date | Mintage | F | VF | XF | Unc | BU |
|---|---|---|---|---|---|---|
| 1958R | 24,240,000 | — | BV | 4.00 | 8.00 | — |
| 1958R Prooflike | Inc. above | — | — | — | 30.00 | — |
| 1959R | 19,360,000 | — | BV | 4.00 | 8.00 | — |
| 1959R Prooflike | Inc. above | — | — | — | 30.00 | — |
| 1960R | 24,080,000 | — | BV | 4.00 | 8.00 | — |
| 1960R Prooflike | Inc. above | — | — | — | 30.00 | — |
| 1961R | 6,560,000 | — | BV | 10.00 | 25.00 | — |
| 1961R Prooflike | Inc. above | — | — | — | 50.00 | — |
| 1964R | 4,880,000 | — | BV | 4.50 | 10.00 | — |
| 1964R Prooflike | Inc. above | — | — | — | 30.00 | — |
| 1965R | 3,120,000 | — | BV | 4.50 | 10.00 | — |
| 1965R Prooflike | Inc. above | — | — | — | 30.00 | — |
| 1966R | 13,120,000 | — | BV | 3.25 | 5.00 | — |
| **Note:** Varieties exist | | | | | | |
| 1966R Prooflike | Inc. above | — | — | — | 25.00 | — |
| 1967R | 2,480,000 | — | BV | 3.25 | 5.00 | — |
| 1967R Prooflike | Inc. above | — | — | — | 25.00 | — |
| 1968R | 100,000 | — | — | — | 110 | — |
| 1968R Prooflike | Inc. above | — | — | — | 120 | — |
| 1969R | 310,000 | — | — | — | 15.00 | — |
| 1969R Prooflike | Inc. above | — | — | — | 30.00 | — |
| 1970R | 1,140,000 | — | — | — | 12.50 | — |
| 1970R Prooflike | Inc. above | — | — | — | 25.00 | — |
| 1980R | 500,000 | — | — | — | 15.00 | — |
| 1980R Prooflike | Inc. above | — | — | — | 25.00 | — |
| 1981R | 500,000 | — | — | — | 16.50 | — |
| 1981R Prooflike | Inc. above | — | — | — | 30.00 | — |
| 1982R | 115,000 | — | — | — | 16.50 | — |
| 1982R Prooflike | Inc. above | — | — | — | 30.00 | — |
| 1983R | 76,000 | — | — | — | 165 | — |
| 1984R | 77,000 | — | — | — | 60.00 | — |
| 1985R | 73,000 | — | — | — | 30.00 | — |
| 1985R Proof | 15,000 | Value: 60.00 | | | | |
| 1986R | 95,000 | — | — | — | 35.00 | — |
| 1986R Proof | Inc. above | Value: 60.00 | | | | |
| 1987R | 60,000 | — | — | — | 40.00 | — |
| 1987R Proof | 15,000 | Value: 65.00 | | | | |
| 1988R | 55,000 | — | — | — | 150 | — |
| 1988R Proof | 10,000 | Value: 185 | | | | |
| 1989R | 60,000 | — | — | — | 65.00 | — |
| 1989R Proof | 10,000 | Value: 85.00 | | | | |
| 1990R | 60,000 | — | — | — | 75.00 | — |
| 1990R Proof | 10,000 | Value: 75.00 | | | | |
| 1991R | — | — | — | — | 65.00 | — |
| 1991R Proof | — | Value: 85.00 | | | | |
| 1992R | — | — | — | — | 35.00 | — |

| Date | Mintage | F | VF | XF | Unc | BU |
|---|---|---|---|---|---|---|
| 1992R Proof | — | Value: 60.00 | | | | |
| 1993R | — | — | — | — | 35.00 | — |
| 1993R Proof | — | Value: 60.00 | | | | |
| 1994R | — | — | — | — | 35.00 | — |
| 1995R | — | — | — | — | 35.00 | — |
| 1996R | — | — | — | — | 35.00 | — |
| 1997R | — | — | — | — | 35.00 | — |
| 1998R | — | — | — | — | 35.00 | — |

**500 LIRE** **KM# 99** **Weight:** 11.0000 g. **Composition:** 0.8350 Silver .2953 oz. ASW **Subject:** Italian Unification Centennial

| Date | Mintage | F | VF | XF | Unc | BU |
|---|---|---|---|---|---|---|
| ND(1961)R | 27,120,000 | — | BV | 3.00 | 6.50 | — |
| ND(1961)R Prooflike | Inc. above | — | — | — | 25.00 | — |

**500 LIRE** **KM# 100** **Weight:** 11.0000 g. **Composition:** 0.8350 Silver .2953 oz. ASW **Subject:** 700th anniversary - birth of Dante Alighieri

| Date | Mintage | F | VF | XF | Unc | BU |
|---|---|---|---|---|---|---|
| 1965R | 4,272,000 | — | BV | 4.00 | 8.50 | — |
| 1965R Proof | Inc. above | Value: 15.00 | | | | |

**500 LIRE** **KM# 103** **Weight:** 11.0000 g. **Composition:** 0.8350 Silver .2953 oz. ASW **Subject:** 100th anniversary - birth of Guglielmo Marconi

| Date | Mintage | F | VF | XF | Unc | BU |
|---|---|---|---|---|---|---|
| ND(1974)R | 670,000 | — | — | — | 17.50 | — |
| ND(1974)R Proof | Inc. above | Value: 35.00 | | | | |

**500 LIRE** **KM# 104** **Weight:** 11.0000 g. **Composition:** 0.8350 Silver .2953 oz. ASW **Subject:** 500th anniversary - birth of Michelangelo

| Date | Mintage | F | VF | XF | Unc | BU |
|---|---|---|---|---|---|---|
| 1975R | 286,000 | — | — | — | 20.00 | — |
| 1975R Proof | Inc. above | Value: 50.00 | | | | |

**500 LIRE** **KM# 110** **Weight:** 11.0000 g. **Composition:** 0.8350 Silver .2953 oz. ASW **Subject:** 200th Anniversary - Death of Virgil

| Date | Mintage | F | VF | XF | Unc | BU |
|---|---|---|---|---|---|---|
| 1981R (1982) | 341,000 | — | — | — | 20.00 | — |
| 1981R (1982) Proof | Inc. above | Value: 28.00 | | | | |

**500 LIRE** **KM# 111** **Center Composition:** Bronzital **Note:** Acmonital ring.

| Date | Mintage | F | VF | XF | Unc | BU |
|---|---|---|---|---|---|---|
| 1982R | 200,000,000 | — | 0.40 | 0.60 | 2.00 | — |
| **Note:** Obverse portrait varieties exist | | | | | | |
| 1983R | 230,000,000 | — | 0.40 | 0.60 | 2.00 | — |
| 1984R | — | — | 0.40 | 0.60 | 2.00 | — |
| 1985R | — | — | 0.40 | 0.60 | 2.00 | — |
| 1985R Proof | 20,000 | Value: 15.00 | | | | |
| 1986R | — | — | 0.40 | 0.60 | 2.00 | — |
| 1986R Proof | — | Value: 12.50 | | | | |
| 1987R | 200,000,000 | — | 0.40 | 0.60 | 2.00 | — |
| 1987R Proof | — | Value: 20.00 | | | | |
| 1988R | 142,000,000 | — | 0.40 | 0.60 | 2.00 | — |
| 1988R Proof | — | Value: 25.00 | | | | |
| 1989R | — | — | 0.40 | 0.60 | 2.00 | — |
| 1989R Proof | — | Value: 20.00 | | | | |
| 1990R | — | — | 0.40 | 0.60 | 2.00 | — |
| 1990R Proof | — | Value: 20.00 | | | | |
| 1991R | — | — | 0.40 | 0.60 | 2.00 | — |
| 1991R Proof | — | Value: 20.00 | | | | |
| 1992R | — | — | 0.40 | 0.60 | 2.00 | — |
| **Note:** Obverse portrait varieties exist | | | | | | |
| 1992R Proof | — | Value: 20.00 | | | | |
| 1995R | — | — | — | 0.60 | 2.00 | — |

**500 LIRE** **KM# 112** **Weight:** 11.0000 g. **Composition:** 0.8350 Silver .2953 oz. ASW **Subject:** 100th anniversary - death of Giuseppe Garibaldi

| Date | Mintage | F | VF | XF | Unc | BU |
|---|---|---|---|---|---|---|
| 1982R (1983) | 193,000 | — | — | — | 20.00 | — |
| 1982R (1983) Proof | Inc. above | Value: 32.00 | | | | |

**500 LIRE** **KM# 113** **Weight:** 11.0000 g. **Composition:** 0.8350 Silver .2953 oz. ASW **Subject:** Galileo Galilei

| Date | Mintage | F | VF | XF | Unc | BU |
|---|---|---|---|---|---|---|
| ND(1983)R | 198,000 | — | — | — | 20.00 | — |
| ND(1983)R Proof | Inc. above | Value: 32.00 | | | | |

**500 LIRE** **KM# 114** **Weight:** 11.0000 g. **Composition:** 0.8350 Silver .2953 oz. ASW **Subject:** Los Angeles Olympics

| Date | Mintage | F | VF | XF | Unc | BU |
|---|---|---|---|---|---|---|
| 1984 | 193,000 | — | — | — | 22.50 | — |

**500 LIRE** **KM# 115** **Weight:** 11.0000 g. **Composition:** 0.8350 Silver .2953 oz. ASW **Subject:** First Italian president of Common Market

| Date | Mintage | F | VF | XF | Unc | BU |
|---|---|---|---|---|---|---|
| 1985R | 103,000 | — | — | — | 60.00 | — |
| 1985R Proof | 29,000 | Value: 85.00 | | | | |

**500 LIRE** **KM# 116** **Weight:** 11.0000 g. **Composition:** 0.8350 Silver .2953 oz. ASW **Subject:** Duino College

| Date | Mintage | F | VF | XF | Unc | BU |
|---|---|---|---|---|---|---|
| 1985R | 126,000 | — | — | — | 20.00 | — |
| 1985R Proof | — | Value: 37.50 | | | | |

**500 LIRE** **KM# 117** **Weight:** 11.0000 g. **Composition:** 0.8350 Silver .2953 oz. ASW **Subject:** European Year of Music

| Date | Mintage | F | VF | XF | Unc | BU |
|---|---|---|---|---|---|---|
| 1985R | 96,000 | — | — | — | 20.00 | — |
| 1985R Proof | Inc. above | Value: 35.00 | | | | |

**500 LIRE** **KM# 118** **Weight:** 11.0000 g. **Composition:** 0.8350 Silver .2953 oz. ASW **Subject:** Etruscan culture

| Date | Mintage | F | VF | XF | Unc | BU |
|---|---|---|---|---|---|---|
| 1985R | 104,000 | — | — | — | 20.00 | — |
| 1985R Proof | Inc. above | Value: 35.00 | | | | |

**500 LIRE** **KM# 123** **Weight:** 11.0000 g. **Composition:** 0.8350 Silver .2953 oz. ASW **Subject:** 200th anniversary - birth of Alessandro Manzoni

| Date | Mintage | F | VF | XF | Unc | BU |
|---|---|---|---|---|---|---|
| 1985R | 89,000 | — | — | — | 45.00 | — |
| 1985R Proof | 20,000 | Value: 65.00 | | | | |

**500 LIRE** **KM# 119** **Weight:** 11.0000 g. **Composition:** 0.8350 Silver .2953 oz. ASW **Subject:** Soccer championship - Mexico

| Date | Mintage | F | VF | XF | Unc | BU |
|---|---|---|---|---|---|---|
| 1986R | 91,000 | — | — | — | 20.00 | — |
| 1986R Proof | 21,000 | Value: 36.50 | | | | |

**500 LIRE** **KM# 120** **Weight:** 11.0000 g. **Composition:** 0.8350 Silver .2953 oz. ASW **Subject:** Year of Peace

| Date | Mintage | F | VF | XF | Unc | BU |
|---|---|---|---|---|---|---|
| 1986R | 90,000 | — | — | — | 20.00 | — |
| 1986R Proof | 19,000 | Value: 36.50 | | | | |

**500 LIRE** **KM# 124** **Weight:** 11.0000 g. **Composition:** 0.8350 Silver .2953 oz. ASW **Subject:** 600th anniversary - birth of Donatello

| Date | Mintage | F | VF | XF | Unc | BU |
|---|---|---|---|---|---|---|
| 1986R | 60,000 | — | — | — | 60.00 | — |
| 1986R Proof | 20,000 | Value: 90.00 | | | | |

**500 LIRE** **KM# 121** **Weight:** 11.0000 g. **Composition:** 0.8350 Silver .2953 oz. ASW **Subject:** Year of the Family

| Date | Mintage | F | VF | XF | Unc | BU |
|---|---|---|---|---|---|---|
| 1987R | 85,000 | — | — | — | 27.50 | — |
| 1987R Proof | 20,000 | Value: 50.00 | | | | |

**500 LIRE** **KM# 122** **Weight:** 11.0000 g. **Composition:** 0.8350 Silver .2953 oz. ASW **Subject:** World Athletic Championships

| Date | Mintage | F | VF | XF | Unc | BU |
|---|---|---|---|---|---|---|
| 1987R | 80,000 | — | — | — | 22.50 | — |
| 1987R Proof | 20,000 | Value: 50.00 | | | | |

**500 LIRE** **KM# 132** **Weight:** 11.0000 g. **Composition:** 0.8350 Silver .2953 oz. ASW **Subject:** Giacomo Leopardi

| Date | Mintage | F | VF | XF | Unc | BU |
|---|---|---|---|---|---|---|
| 1987R | 58,000 | — | — | — | 70.00 | — |
| 1987R Proof | 10,000 | Value: 135 | | | | |

**500 LIRE** **KM# 125** **Weight:** 11.0000 g. **Composition:** 0.8350 Silver .2953 oz. ASW **Subject:** Summer Olympics - Seoul

| Date | Mintage | F | VF | XF | Unc | BU |
|---|---|---|---|---|---|---|
| 1988R | 70,000 | — | — | — | 27.50 | — |
| 1988R Proof | 13,000 | Value: 42.50 | | | | |

**500 LIRE** **KM# 126** **Weight:** 11.0000 g. **Composition:** 0.8350 Silver .2953 oz. ASW **Subject:** 40th anniversary of constitution

| Date | Mintage | F | VF | XF | Unc | BU |
|---|---|---|---|---|---|---|
| ND(1988)R | 67,000 | — | — | — | 27.50 | — |
| ND(1988)R Proof | 13,000 | Value: 40.00 | | | | |

**500 LIRE** **KM# 129** **Weight:** 11.0000 g. **Composition:** 0.8350 Silver .2953 oz. ASW **Subject:** 900th anniversary - University of Bologna **Obverse:** Similar to 100 Lire, KM#127

| Date | Mintage | F | VF | XF | Unc | BU |
|---|---|---|---|---|---|---|
| 1988R | 68,000 | — | — | — | 40.00 | — |
| 1988R Proof | 13,000 | Value: 70.00 | | | | |

**500 LIRE** **KM# 144** **Weight:** 11.0000 g. **Composition:** 0.8350 Silver .2953 oz. ASW **Subject:** 100th anniversary - death of Giovanni Bosco

| Date | Mintage | F | VF | XF | Unc | BU |
|---|---|---|---|---|---|---|
| 1988R | 51,000 | — | — | — | 100 | — |
| 1988R Proof | 9,000 | Value: 130 | | | | |

**500 LIRE** **KM# 131** **Weight:** 11.0000 g. **Composition:** 0.8350 Silver .2953 oz. ASW **Subject:** Fight against cancer

| Date | Mintage | F | VF | XF | Unc | BU |
|---|---|---|---|---|---|---|
| 1989R | 46,000 | — | — | — | 75.00 | — |
| 1989R Proof | 13,000 | Value: 135 | | | | |

**500 LIRE** **KM# 134** **Weight:** 11.0000 g. **Composition:** 0.8350 Silver .2953 oz. ASW **Subject:** Soccer **Reverse:** Map of Italy on world globe

| Date | Mintage | F | VF | XF | Unc | BU |
|---|---|---|---|---|---|---|
| 1989R | 88,000 | — | — | — | 27.50 | — |
| 1989R | 28,000 | Value: 32.50 | | | | |

**500 LIRE** **KM# 139** **Weight:** 11.0000 g. **Composition:** 0.8350 Silver .2953 oz. ASW **Subject:** Christopher Columbus **Reverse:** Ships in dock

| Date | Mintage | F | VF | XF | Unc | BU |
|---|---|---|---|---|---|---|
| 1989R | 75,000 | — | — | — | 32.50 | — |
| 1989R Proof | 25,000 | Value: 45.00 | | | | |

**500 LIRE** **KM# 145** **Weight:** 11.0000 g. **Composition:** 0.8350 Silver .2953 oz. ASW **Subject:** 350th anniversary - death of Tommaso Campanella

| Date | Mintage | F | VF | XF | Unc | BU |
|---|---|---|---|---|---|---|
| 1989R | 51,000 | — | — | — | 85.00 | — |
| 1989R Proof | 9,260 | Value: 125 | | | | |

**500 LIRE** **KM# 136** **Weight:** 11.0000 g. **Composition:** 0.8350 Silver .2953 oz. ASW **Subject:** Soccer

| Date | Mintage | F | VF | XF | Unc | BU |
|---|---|---|---|---|---|---|
| 1990R | 86,000 | — | — | — | 25.00 | — |
| 1990R Proof | 28,000 | Value: 42.50 | | | | |

**500 LIRE** **KM# 137** **Weight:** 11.0000 g. **Composition:** 0.8350 Silver .2953 oz. ASW **Subject:** Italian presidency of the E.E.C. Council

| Date | Mintage | F | VF | XF | Unc | BU |
|---|---|---|---|---|---|---|
| 1990R | 54,000 | — | — | — | 25.00 | — |
| 1990R Proof | 10,000 | Value: 45.00 | | | | |

**500 LIRE** **KM# 140** **Weight:** 11.0000 g. **Composition:** 0.8350 Silver .2953 oz. ASW **Subject:** Columbus - discovery of America

| Date | Mintage | F | VF | XF | Unc | BU |
|---|---|---|---|---|---|---|
| 1990R | 75,000 | — | — | — | 27.50 | — |
| 1990R Proof | 25,000 | Value: 42.50 | | | | |

**500 LIRE** **KM# 146** **Weight:** 11.0000 g. **Composition:** 0.8350 Silver .2953 oz. ASW **Subject:** 500th anniversary - birth of Tizian

| Date | Mintage | F | VF | XF | Unc | BU |
|---|---|---|---|---|---|---|
| 1990R | 62,000 | — | — | — | 60.00 | — |
| 1990R Proof | 9,450 | Value: 100 | | | | |

**500 LIRE** **KM# 143** **Weight:** 15.0000 g. **Composition:** 0.8350 Silver .4027 oz. ASW **Subject:** Italian flora and fauna

| Date | Mintage | F | VF | XF | Unc | BU |
|---|---|---|---|---|---|---|
| 1991R | 50,000 | — | — | — | 40.00 | — |
| 1991R Proof | 9,500 | Value: 55.00 | | | | |

**500 LIRE** **KM# 147** **Weight:** 15.0000 g. **Composition:** 0.8350 Silver .4027 oz. ASW **Subject:** 2,100th anniversary of Ponte Milvio

| Date | Mintage | F | VF | XF | Unc | BU |
|---|---|---|---|---|---|---|
| 1991R | 59,000 | — | — | — | 30.00 | — |
| 1991R Proof | 14,000 | Value: 42.50 | | | | |

**500 LIRE** **KM# 141** **Weight:** 11.0000 g. **Composition:** 0.8350 Silver .2953 oz. ASW **Subject:** 250th anniversary - death of Antonio Vivaldi

| Date | Mintage | F | VF | XF | Unc | BU |
|---|---|---|---|---|---|---|
| ND(1991)R | 55,000 | — | — | — | 65.00 | — |
| ND(1991)R Proof | 11,000 | Value: 110 | | | | |

**500 LIRE** **KM# 148** **Weight:** 11.0000 g. **Composition:** 0.8350 Silver .2953 oz. ASW **Subject:** Discovery of America **Reverse:** Old map

| Date | Mintage | F | VF | XF | Unc | BU |
|---|---|---|---|---|---|---|
| 1991R | 75,000 | — | — | — | 30.00 | — |
| 1991R Proof | 25,000 | Value: 50.00 | | | | |

**500 LIRE** **KM# 149** **Weight:** 15.0000 g. **Composition:** 0.8350 Silver .4027 oz. ASW **Subject:** 500th anniversary - death of Lorenzo de' Medici

| Date | Mintage | F | VF | XF | Unc | BU |
|---|---|---|---|---|---|---|
| ND(1992)R | 50,000 | — | — | — | 30.00 | — |
| ND(1992)R Proof | 10,000 | Value: 50.00 | | | | |

**500 LIRE** **KM# 150** **Weight:** 11.0000 g. **Composition:** 0.8350 Silver .2953 oz. ASW **Subject:** Christopher Columbus

| Date | Mintage | F | VF | XF | Unc | BU |
|---|---|---|---|---|---|---|
| 1992R | 67,000 | — | — | — | 30.00 | — |
| 1992R Proof | 18,000 | Value: 55.00 | | | | |

**500 LIRE** **KM# 152** **Weight:** 15.0000 g. **Composition:** 0.8350 Silver .4027 oz. ASW **Subject:** 200th anniversary - birth of Gioacchino Rossini

| Date | Mintage | F | VF | XF | Unc | BU |
|---|---|---|---|---|---|---|
| 1992R | 45,000 | — | — | — | 28.50 | — |
| 1992R Proof | 9,000 | Value: 65.00 | | | | |

**500 LIRE** **KM# 153** **Weight:** 15.0000 g. **Composition:** 0.8350 Silver .4027 oz. ASW **Subject:** Olympics **Reverse:** Buildings and track

| Date | Mintage | F | VF | XF | Unc | BU |
|---|---|---|---|---|---|---|
| 1992R | 67,000 | — | — | — | 27.50 | — |
| 1992R Proof | 12,000 | Value: 47.50 | | | | |

**500 LIRE** **KM# 154** **Weight:** 15.0000 g. **Composition:** 0.8350 Silver .4027 oz. ASW **Subject:** Flora and fauna

| Date | Mintage | F | VF | XF | Unc | BU |
|---|---|---|---|---|---|---|
| 1992R | 8,650 | — | — | — | 40.00 | — |
| 1992R Proof | 6,500 | Value: 60.00 | | | | |

**500 LIRE** **KM# 161** **Weight:** 11.0000 g. **Composition:** 0.8350 Silver .2953 oz. ASW **Subject:** 500th anniversary - death of Piero Della Francesca

| Date | Mintage | F | VF | XF | Unc | BU |
|---|---|---|---|---|---|---|
| 1992R | 52,000 | — | — | — | 65.00 | — |
| 1992R Proof | 9,500 | Value: 110 | | | | |

**500 LIRE** **KM# 156** **Weight:** 15.0000 g. **Composition:** 0.8350 Silver .4027 oz. ASW **Subject:** 2,000th anniversary - death of Horace

| Date | Mintage | F | VF | XF | Unc | BU |
|---|---|---|---|---|---|---|
| 1993R | 50,000 | — | — | — | 30.00 | — |
| 1993R Proof | 10,000 | Value: 50.00 | | | | |

**500 LIRE** **KM# 157** **Weight:** 15.0000 g. **Composition:** 0.8350 Silver .4027 oz. ASW **Subject:** Wildlife protection **Reverse:** Storks and swordfish

| Date | Mintage | F | VF | XF | Unc | BU |
|---|---|---|---|---|---|---|
| 1993R | 36,000 | — | — | — | 40.00 | — |
| 1993R Proof | 10,000 | Value: 55.00 | | | | |

**500 LIRE** **KM# 158** **Weight:** 15.0000 g. **Composition:** 0.8350 Silver .4027 oz. ASW **Subject:** 650th anniversary - University of Pisa

| Date | Mintage | F | VF | XF | Unc | BU |
|---|---|---|---|---|---|---|
| 1993R | 41,000 | — | — | — | 30.00 | — |
| 1993R Proof | 9,080 | Value: 50.00 | | | | |

**500 LIRE** **KM# 160** **Ring Composition:** Stainless Steel **Center Composition:** Brass **Subject:** Centennial - Bank of Italy **Note:** Large and small designer's name, GROSSI, exist.

| Date | Mintage | F | VF | XF | Unc | BU |
|---|---|---|---|---|---|---|
| ND(1993)R | Est. 50,000 | — | — | — | 3.50 | — |
| ND(1993)R Proof | 10,000 | Value: 10.00 | | | | |

**500 LIRE** **KM# 163** **Weight:** 11.0000 g. **Composition:** 0.8350 Silver .2953 oz. ASW **Subject:** 200th anniversary - death of Carolo Goldoni

| Date | Mintage | F | VF | XF | Unc | BU |
|---|---|---|---|---|---|---|
| 1993R | 50,000 | — | — | — | 35.00 | — |
| 1993R Proof | 8,500 | Value: 60.00 | | | | |

**500 LIRE** **KM# 173** **Weight:** 11.0000 g. **Composition:** 0.8350 Silver .2953 oz. ASW **Subject:** Centennial - Bank of Italy **Reverse:** Statues and building **Note:** Both uncirculated and proof versions were offered in sets only.

| Date | Mintage | F | VF | XF | Unc | BU |
|---|---|---|---|---|---|---|
| ND(1993)R | — | — | — | — | 40.00 | — |
| ND(1993)R Proof | — | Value: 75.00 | | | | |

**500 LIRE** **KM# 167** **Ring Composition:** Stainless Steel **Center Composition:** Brass **Subject:** 500th anniversary - publication of mathematical work by Luca Pacioli

| Date | Mintage | F | VF | XF | Unc | BU |
|---|---|---|---|---|---|---|
| ND(1994)R | — | — | — | — | 2.00 | — |

**500 LIRE** **KM# 181** **Ring Composition:** Stainless Steel **Center Composition:** Brass **Subject:** Istituto Nazionale di Statistica **Reverse:** Institute building

| Date | Mintage | F | VF | XF | Unc | BU |
|---|---|---|---|---|---|---|
| ND(1996)R | — | — | — | — | 2.00 | — |

**500 LIRE** **KM# 187** **Ring Composition:** Stainless Steel **Center Composition:** Brass **Subject:** 50th anniversary - National Police Code **Obverse:** Allegorical portrait **Reverse:** Mythological figure above coat of arms

| Date | Mintage | F | VF | XF | Unc | BU |
|---|---|---|---|---|---|---|
| ND(1997)R | — | — | — | — | 2.00 | — |

**500 LIRE** **KM# 193** **Ring Composition:** Stainless Steel **Center Composition:** Aluminum-Bronze **Series:** F.A.O. **Subject:** F.A.O. - 20 years **Obverse:** Allegorical portrait **Reverse:** Hand and grains

| Date | Mintage | F | VF | XF | Unc | BU |
|---|---|---|---|---|---|---|
| ND(1998)R | — | — | — | — | 2.00 | — |

**500 LIRE** **KM# 203** **Ring Weight:** 6.8200 g. **Ring Composition:** Stainless Steel **Center Composition:** Aluminum-Bronze **Subject:** European parliamentary elections **Obverse:** Allegorical portrait **Reverse:** Ballot box **Edge:** Reeded and plain sections **Size:** 25.9 mm.

| Date | Mintage | F | VF | XF | Unc | BU |
|---|---|---|---|---|---|---|
| ND(1999)R | — | — | — | — | — | — |
| ND(2000)R | — | — | — | — | 2.00 | — |

**1000 LIRE** **KM# 101** **Weight:** 14.6000 g. **Composition:** 0.8350 Silver .392 oz. ASW **Subject:** Centennial of Rome as capital

| Date | Mintage | F | VF | XF | Unc | BU |
|---|---|---|---|---|---|---|
| ND(1970)R | 3,011,000 | — | — | — | 16.00 | — |
| ND(1970)R Proof | — | Value: 28.00 | | | | |

**1000 LIRE** **KM# 165** **Weight:** 14.6000 g. **Composition:** 0.8350 Silver .392 oz. ASW **Subject:** 900th anniversary - St. Mark's Basilica

| Date | Mintage | F | VF | XF | Unc | BU |
|---|---|---|---|---|---|---|
| 1994R | — | — | — | — | 32.00 | — |
| 1994R Proof | — | Value: 75.00 | | | | |

**1000 LIRE** **KM# 168** **Weight:** 14.6000 g. **Composition:** 0.8350 Silver .392 oz. ASW **Subject:** Flora and fauna protection

| Date | Mintage | F | VF | XF | Unc | BU |
|---|---|---|---|---|---|---|
| 1994R | — | — | — | — | 30.00 | — |
| 1994R Proof | — | Value: 75.00 | | | | |

**1000 LIRE** **KM# 169** **Weight:** 14.6000 g. **Composition:** 0.8350 Silver .392 oz. ASW **Obverse:** Tintoretto in oval **Reverse:** Collage of his paintings

| Date | Mintage | F | VF | XF | Unc | BU |
|---|---|---|---|---|---|---|
| 1994R | — | — | — | — | 30.00 | — |
| 1994R Proof | — | Value: 55.00 | | | | |

**1000 LIRE** **KM# 185** **Weight:** 14.6000 g. **Composition:** 0.8350 Silver .392 oz. ASW **Subject:** Pietro Mascagni

| Date | Mintage | F | VF | XF | Unc | BU |
|---|---|---|---|---|---|---|
| 1995R | 45,000 | — | — | — | 30.00 | — |
| 1995R Proof | 7,960 | Value: 65.00 | | | | |

**1000 LIRE** **KM# 182** **Weight:** 14.6000 g. **Composition:** 0.8350 Silver .392 oz. ASW **Subject:** Olympics **Reverse:** Torch runner, stadium, denomination

| Date | Mintage | F | VF | XF | Unc | BU |
|---|---|---|---|---|---|---|
| 1996R | — | — | — | — | 35.00 | — |
| 1996R Proof | — | Value: 70.00 | | | | |

**1000 LIRE** **KM# 199** **Weight:** 14.6000 g. **Composition:** 0.8350 Silver .392 oz. ASW **Subject:** Montale commemorative **Note:** Both uncirculated and proof versions were offered in sets only.

| Date | Mintage | F | VF | XF | Unc | BU |
|---|---|---|---|---|---|---|
| 1996R | 45,000 | — | — | — | 32.50 | — |
| 1996R Proof | 8,000 | Value: 65.00 | | | | |

**1000 LIRE** **KM# 200** **Weight:** 14.6000 g. **Composition:** 0.8350 Silver 0.392 oz. ASW **Subject:** Donizetti commemorative **Note:** Both uncirculated and proof versions were offered in sets only.

| Date | Mintage | F | VF | XF | Unc | BU |
|---|---|---|---|---|---|---|
| 1997R | 44,000 | — | — | — | 32.50 | — |
| 1997R Proof | 8,440,000 | Value: 65.00 | | | | |

**1000 LIRE** **KM# 194** **Center Composition:** Copper Nickel **Subject:** European Union **Obverse:** Allegorical portrait **Reverse:** Correct map of Europe

| Date | Mintage | F | VF | XF | Unc | BU |
|---|---|---|---|---|---|---|
| 1997R | — | — | — | — | 5.00 | — |
| 1998R | — | — | — | — | 5.00 | — |
| 1999R | — | — | — | — | 5.00 | — |

**1000 LIRE** **KM# 190** **Center Composition:** Copper Nickel **Subject:** European Union **Obverse:** Allegorical portrait **Reverse:** Error map of European Union showing the old West Germany

| Date | Mintage | F | VF | XF | Unc | BU |
|---|---|---|---|---|---|---|
| 1997R | — | — | — | — | 5.00 | — |

**1000 LIRE** **KM# 201** **Weight:** 14.6000 g. **Composition:** 0.8350 Silver 0.392 oz. ASW **Subject:** Bernini commemorative **Note:** Both uncirculated and proof versions were offered in sets only.

| Date | Mintage | F | VF | XF | Unc | BU |
|---|---|---|---|---|---|---|
| 1998R | — | — | — | — | 32.50 | — |
| 1998R Proof | — | Value: 65.00 | | | | |

**2000 LIRE** **KM# 195** **Weight:** 16.0000 g. **Composition:** 0.8350 Silver .4295 oz. ASW **Subject:** Christian millenium **Obverse:** Leaves and birds sprouting from globe top **Reverse:** Jesus above denomination

| Date | Mintage | F | VF | XF | Unc | BU |
|---|---|---|---|---|---|---|
| 1998R | — | — | — | — | 28.00 | — |
| 1998R Proof | — | Value: 65.00 | | | | |

**2000 LIRE** **KM# 196** **Weight:** 16.0000 g. **Composition:** 0.8350 Silver .4295 oz. ASW **Obverse:** World globe **Reverse:** Creative brain unraveling DNA

| Date | Mintage | F | VF | XF | Unc | BU |
|---|---|---|---|---|---|---|
| 1998R | — | — | — | — | 28.00 | — |
| 1998R Proof | — | Value: 65.00 | | | | |

**2000 LIRE** **KM# 202** **Weight:** 16.0000 g. **Composition:** 0.8350 Silver .4295 oz. ASW **Subject:** National Museum in Rome **Obverse:** Ancient coin **Reverse:** Seated gladiator

| Date | Mintage | F | VF | XF | Unc | BU |
|---|---|---|---|---|---|---|
| 1999R | — | — | — | — | 40.00 | — |

**5000 LIRE** **KM# 170** **Weight:** 18.0000 g. **Composition:** 0.8350 Silver .4832 oz. ASW **Subject:** University of Pisa

| Date | Mintage | F | VF | XF | Unc | BU |
|---|---|---|---|---|---|---|
| 1993R | 42,000 | — | — | — | 35.00 | — |
| 1993R Proof | 8,500 | Value: 90.00 | | | | |

**5000 LIRE** **KM# 175** **Weight:** 18.0000 g. **Composition:** 0.8350 Silver .4832 oz. ASW **Subject:** 600th anniversary - birth of Pisanello

| Date | Mintage | F | VF | XF | Unc | BU |
|---|---|---|---|---|---|---|
| 1995R | 38,000 | — | — | — | 35.00 | — |
| 1995R Proof | 9,000 | Value: 80.00 | | | | |

**5000 LIRE** **KM# 178** **Weight:** 18.0000 g. **Composition:** 0.8350 Silver .4832 oz. ASW **Subject:** Italian presidency of the European Union

| Date | Mintage | F | VF | XF | Unc | BU |
|---|---|---|---|---|---|---|
| 1996R | 38,000 | — | — | — | 40.00 | — |
| 1996R Proof | 7,996,000 | Value: 85.00 | | | | |

**5000 LIRE** **KM# 189** **Weight:** 18.0000 g. **Composition:** 0.8350 Silver .4832 oz. ASW **Subject:** Giovanni Antonio Canal **Obverse:** Portrait and Venice city view **Reverse:** Harbor full of sailboats

| Date | Mintage | F | VF | XF | Unc | BU |
|---|---|---|---|---|---|---|
| ND(1997)R | 36,000 | — | — | — | 37.50 | — |
| ND(1997)R Proof | 7,550,000 | Value: 85.00 | | | | |

**5000 LIRE** **KM# 197** **Weight:** 18.0000 g. **Composition:** 0.8350 Silver .4832 oz. ASW **Subject:** 1999 **Obverse:** Birds sprouting from globe **Reverse:** Saint and merchant with cloth

| Date | Mintage | F | VF | XF | Unc | BU |
|---|---|---|---|---|---|---|
| 1999R | — | — | — | — | 32.50 | — |
| 1999R Proof | — | Value: 55.00 | | | | |

**5000 LIRE** **KM# 198** **Weight:** 18.0000 g. **Composition:** 0.8350 Silver .4832 oz. ASW **Subject:** 1999 **Obverse:** Three birds and nine stars encircle world **Reverse:** Satellite dish and wheels

| Date | Mintage | F | VF | XF | Unc | BU |
|---|---|---|---|---|---|---|
| 1999R | — | — | — | — | 32.50 | — |
| 1999R Proof | — | Value: 55.00 | | | | |

**10000 LIRE** **KM# 166** **Weight:** 22.0000 g. **Composition:** 0.8350 Silver .5907 oz. ASW **Subject:** World Cup Soccer

| Date | Mintage | F | VF | XF | Unc | BU |
|---|---|---|---|---|---|---|
| 1994R | 43,000 | — | — | — | 95.00 | — |
| 1994R Proof | 9,000 | Value: 110 | | | | |

**10000 LIRE** **KM# 174** **Weight:** 22.0000 g. **Composition:** 0.8350 Silver .5907 oz. ASW **Subject:** 40th anniversary - Conference of Messina

| Date | Mintage | F | VF | XF | Unc | BU |
|---|---|---|---|---|---|---|
| 1995R | 42,000 | — | — | — | 65.00 | — |
| 1995R Proof | 8,050 | Value: 95.00 | | | | |

**10000 LIRE** **KM# 179** **Weight:** 22.0000 g. **Composition:** 0.8350 Silver .5907 oz. ASW **Subject:** 50th anniversary of the republic

| Date | Mintage | F | VF | XF | Unc | BU |
|---|---|---|---|---|---|---|
| 1996R | 38,000 | — | — | — | 65.00 | — |
| 1996R Proof | 7,900 | Value: 95.00 | | | | |

**10000 LIRE** **KM# 192** **Weight:** 22.0000 g. **Composition:** 0.8350 Silver .5907 oz. ASW **Subject:** Soccer **Obverse:** Allegorical portrait **Reverse:** Stylized soccer design

| Date | Mintage | F | VF | XF | Unc | BU |
|---|---|---|---|---|---|---|
| 1998R | — | — | — | — | 32.50 | — |
| 1998R Proof | — | Value: 55.00 | | | | |

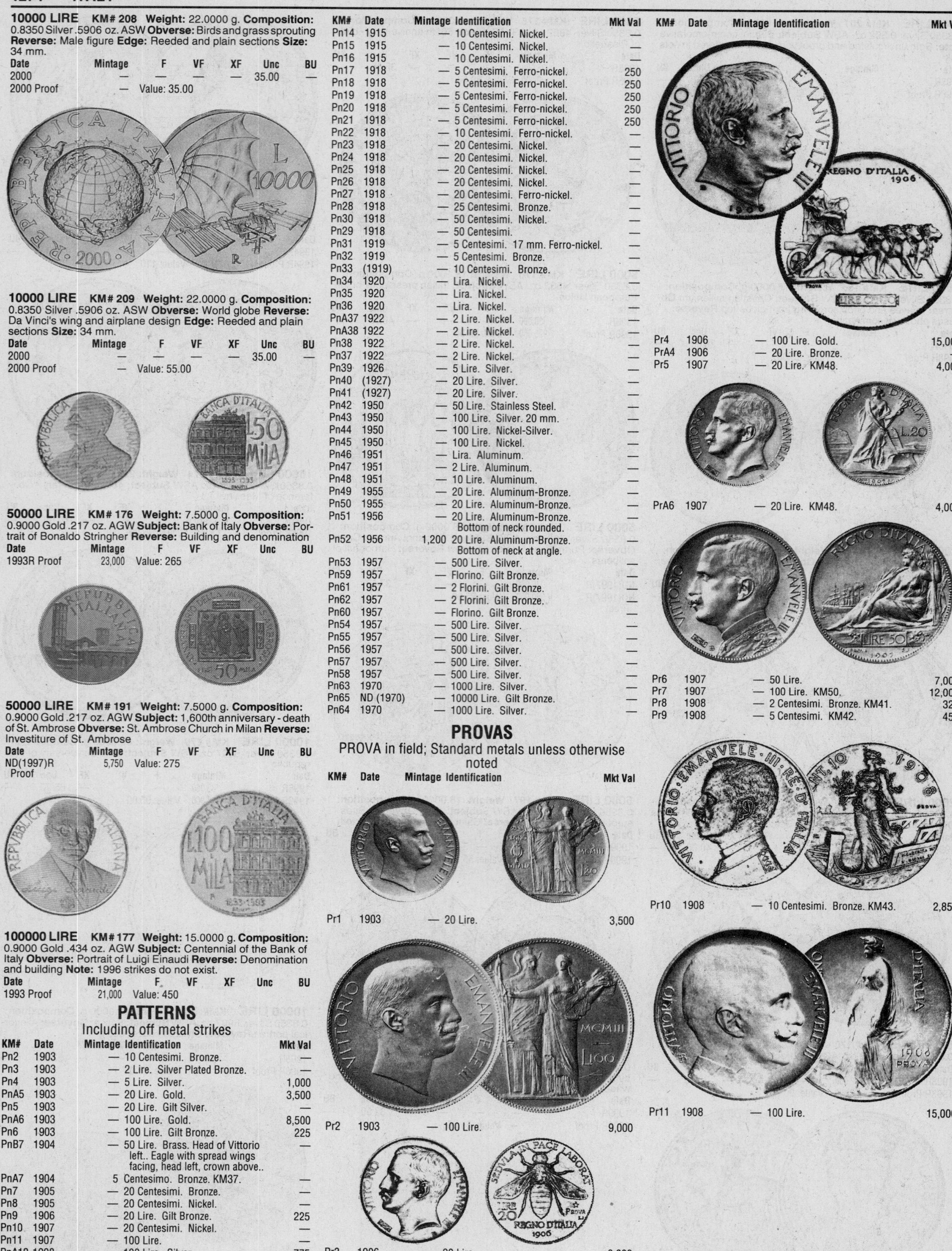

**10000 LIRE** KM# 208 **Weight:** 22.0000 g. **Composition:** 0.8350 Silver .5906 oz. ASW **Obverse:** Birds and grass sprouting **Reverse:** Male figure **Edge:** Reeded and plain sections **Size:** 34 mm.

| Date | Mintage | F | VF | XF | Unc | BU |
|---|---|---|---|---|---|---|
| 2000 | — | — | — | — | 35.00 | — |
| 2000 Proof | — | Value: 35.00 | | | | |

**10000 LIRE** KM# 209 **Weight:** 22.0000 g. **Composition:** 0.8350 Silver .5906 oz. ASW **Obverse:** World globe **Reverse:** Da Vinci's wing and airplane design **Edge:** Reeded and plain sections **Size:** 34 mm.

| Date | Mintage | F | VF | XF | Unc | BU |
|---|---|---|---|---|---|---|
| 2000 | — | — | — | — | 35.00 | — |
| 2000 Proof | — | Value: 55.00 | | | | |

**50000 LIRE** KM# 176 **Weight:** 7.5000 g. **Composition:** 0.9000 Gold .217 oz. AGW **Subject:** Bank of Italy **Obverse:** Portrait of Bonaldo Stringher **Reverse:** Building and denomination

| Date | Mintage | F | VF | XF | Unc | BU |
|---|---|---|---|---|---|---|
| 1993R Proof | 23,000 | Value: 265 | | | | |

**50000 LIRE** KM# 191 **Weight:** 7.5000 g. **Composition:** 0.9000 Gold .217 oz. AGW **Subject:** 1,600th anniversary - death of St. Ambrose **Obverse:** St. Ambrose Church in Milan **Reverse:** Investiture of St. Ambrose

| Date | Mintage | F | VF | XF | Unc | BU |
|---|---|---|---|---|---|---|
| ND(1997)R Proof | 5,750 | Value: 275 | | | | |

**100000 LIRE** KM# 177 **Weight:** 15.0000 g. **Composition:** 0.9000 Gold .434 oz. AGW **Subject:** Centennial of the Bank of Italy **Obverse:** Portrait of Luigi Einaudi **Reverse:** Denomination and building **Note:** 1996 strikes do not exist.

| Date | Mintage | F | VF | XF | Unc | BU |
|---|---|---|---|---|---|---|
| 1993 Proof | 21,000 | Value: 450 | | | | |

## PATTERNS

Including off metal strikes

| KM# | Date | Mintage | Identification | Mkt Val |
|---|---|---|---|---|
| Pn2 | 1903 | — | 10 Centesimi. Bronze. | — |
| Pn3 | 1903 | — | 2 Lire. Silver Plated Bronze. | — |
| Pn4 | 1903 | — | 5 Lire. Silver. | 1,000 |
| PnA5 | 1903 | — | 20 Lire. Gold. | 3,500 |
| Pn5 | 1903 | — | 20 Lire. Gilt Silver. | — |
| PnA6 | 1903 | — | 100 Lire. Gold. | 8,500 |
| Pn6 | 1903 | — | 100 Lire. Gilt Bronze. | 225 |
| PnB7 | 1904 | — | 50 Lire. Brass. Head of Vittorio left.. Eagle with spread wings facing, head left, crown above.. | — |
| PnA7 | 1904 | 5 | Centesimo. Bronze. KM37. | — |
| Pn7 | 1905 | — | 20 Centesimi. Bronze. | — |
| Pn8 | 1905 | — | 20 Centesimi. Nickel. | — |
| Pn9 | 1906 | — | 20 Lire. Gilt Bronze. | 225 |
| Pn10 | 1907 | — | 20 Centesimi. Nickel. | — |
| Pn11 | 1907 | — | 100 Lire. | — |
| PnA12 | 1908 | — | 100 Lire. Silver. | 775 |
| Pn12 | 1908 | — | 100 Lire. Bronze. | 250 |
| Pn13 | 1915 | — | 10 Centesimi. Nickel. | — |
| Pn14 | 1915 | — | 10 Centesimi. Nickel. | — |
| Pn15 | 1915 | — | 10 Centesimi. Nickel. | — |
| Pn16 | 1915 | — | 10 Centesimi. Nickel. | — |
| Pn17 | 1918 | — | 5 Centesimi. Ferro-nickel. | 250 |
| Pn18 | 1918 | — | 5 Centesimi. Ferro-nickel. | 250 |
| Pn19 | 1918 | — | 5 Centesimi. Ferro-nickel. | 250 |
| Pn20 | 1918 | — | 5 Centesimi. Ferro-nickel. | 250 |
| Pn21 | 1918 | — | 5 Centesimi. Ferro-nickel. | 250 |
| Pn22 | 1918 | — | 10 Centesimi. Ferro-nickel. | — |
| Pn23 | 1918 | — | 20 Centesimi. Nickel. | — |
| Pn24 | 1918 | — | 20 Centesimi. Nickel. | — |
| Pn25 | 1918 | — | 20 Centesimi. Nickel. | — |
| Pn26 | 1918 | — | 20 Centesimi. Nickel. | — |
| Pn27 | 1918 | — | 20 Centesimi. Ferro-nickel. | — |
| Pn28 | 1918 | — | 25 Centesimi. Bronze. | — |
| Pn30 | 1918 | — | 50 Centesimi. Nickel. | — |
| Pn29 | 1918 | — | 50 Centesimi. | — |
| Pn31 | 1919 | — | 5 Centesimi. 17 mm. Ferro-nickel. | — |
| Pn32 | 1919 | — | 5 Centesimi. Bronze. | — |
| Pn33 | (1919) | — | 10 Centesimi. Bronze. | — |
| Pn34 | 1920 | — | Lira. Nickel. | — |
| Pn35 | 1920 | — | Lira. Nickel. | — |
| Pn36 | 1920 | — | Lira. Nickel. | — |
| PnA37 | 1922 | — | 2 Lire. Nickel. | — |
| PnA38 | 1922 | — | 2 Lire. Nickel. | — |
| Pn38 | 1922 | — | 2 Lire. Nickel. | — |
| Pn37 | 1922 | — | 2 Lire. Nickel. | — |
| Pn39 | 1926 | — | 5 Lire. Silver. | — |
| Pn40 | (1927) | — | 20 Lire. Silver. | — |
| Pn41 | (1927) | — | 20 Lire. Silver. | — |
| Pn42 | 1950 | — | 50 Lire. Stainless Steel. | — |
| Pn43 | 1950 | — | 100 Lire. Silver. 20 mm. | — |
| Pn44 | 1950 | — | 100 Lire. Nickel-Silver. | — |
| Pn45 | 1950 | — | 100 Lire. Nickel. | — |
| Pn46 | 1951 | — | Lira. Aluminum. | — |
| Pn47 | 1951 | — | 2 Lire. Aluminum. | — |
| Pn48 | 1951 | — | 10 Lire. Aluminum. | — |
| Pn49 | 1955 | — | 20 Lire. Aluminum-Bronze. | — |
| Pn50 | 1955 | — | 20 Lire. Aluminum-Bronze. | — |
| Pn51 | 1956 | — | 20 Lire. Aluminum-Bronze. Bottom of neck rounded. | — |
| Pn52 | 1956 | 1,200 | 20 Lire. Aluminum-Bronze. Bottom of neck at angle. | — |
| Pn53 | 1957 | — | 500 Lire. Silver. | — |
| Pn59 | 1957 | — | Florino. Gilt Bronze. | — |
| Pn61 | 1957 | — | 2 Florini. Gilt Bronze. | — |
| Pn62 | 1957 | — | 2 Florini. Gilt Bronze. | — |
| Pn60 | 1957 | — | Florino. Gilt Bronze. | — |
| Pn54 | 1957 | — | 500 Lire. Silver. | — |
| Pn55 | 1957 | — | 500 Lire. Silver. | — |
| Pn56 | 1957 | — | 500 Lire. Silver. | — |
| Pn57 | 1957 | — | 500 Lire. Silver. | — |
| Pn58 | 1957 | — | 500 Lire. Silver. | — |
| Pn63 | 1970 | — | 1000 Lire. Silver. | — |
| Pn65 | ND (1970) | — | 10000 Lire. Gilt Bronze. | — |
| Pn64 | 1970 | — | 1000 Lire. Silver. | — |

## PROVAS

PROVA in field; Standard metals unless otherwise noted

| KM# | Date | Mintage | Identification | Mkt Val |
|---|---|---|---|---|
| Pr1 | 1903 | — | 20 Lire. | 3,500 |
| Pr2 | 1903 | — | 100 Lire. | 9,000 |
| Pr3 | 1906 | — | 20 Lire. | 9,000 |
| Pr4 | 1906 | — | 100 Lire. Gold. | 15,000 |
| PrA4 | 1906 | — | 20 Lire. Bronze. | — |
| Pr5 | 1907 | — | 20 Lire. KM48. | 4,000 |
| PrA6 | 1907 | — | 20 Lire. KM48. | 4,000 |
| Pr6 | 1907 | — | 50 Lire. | 7,000 |
| Pr7 | 1907 | — | 100 Lire. KM50. | 12,000 |
| Pr8 | 1908 | — | 2 Centesimi. Bronze. KM41. | 325 |
| Pr9 | 1908 | — | 5 Centesimi. KM42. | 450 |
| Pr10 | 1908 | — | 10 Centesimi. Bronze. KM43. | 2,850 |
| Pr11 | 1908 | — | 100 Lire. | 15,000 |

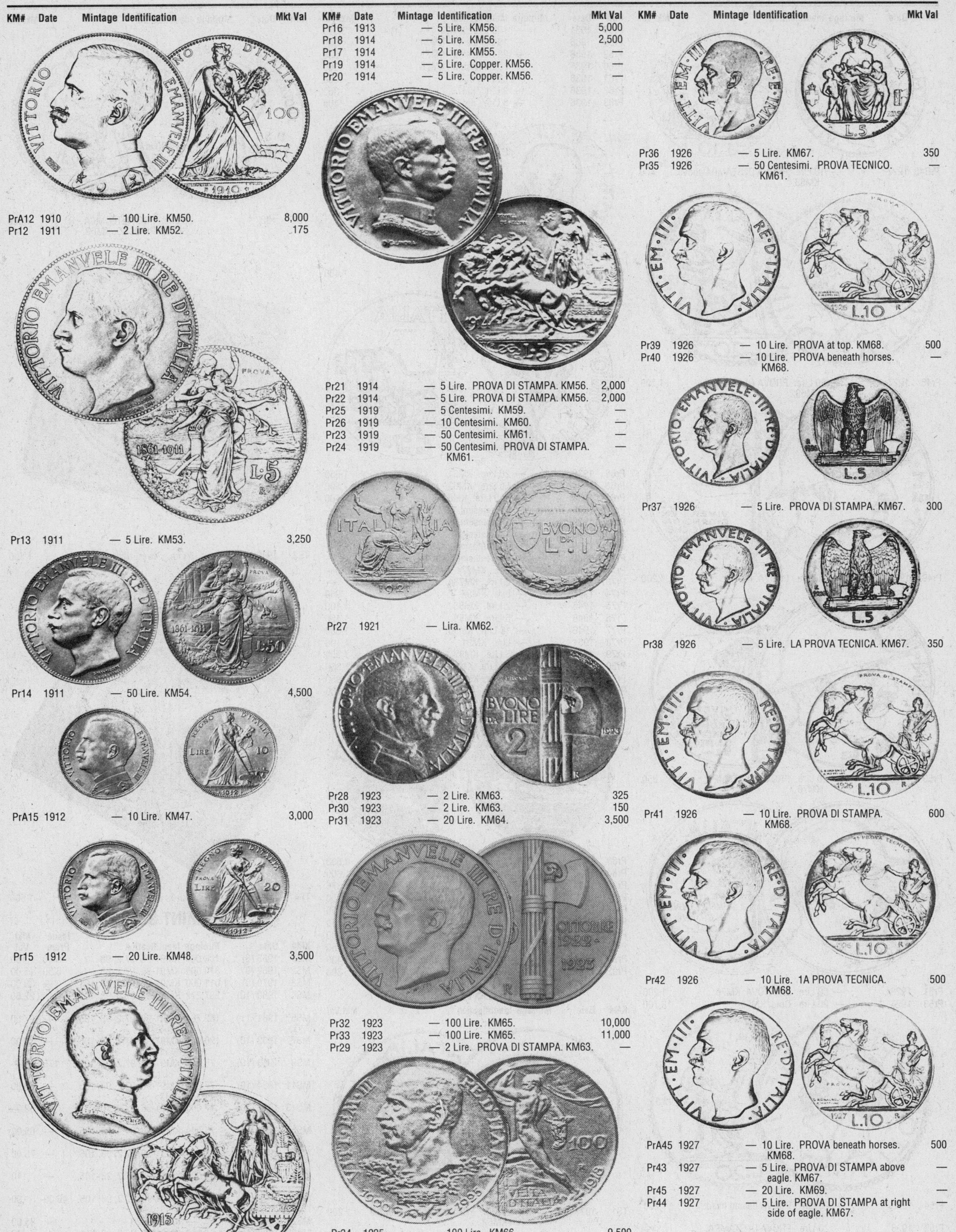

| KM# | Date | Mintage | Identification | Mkt Val |
|---|---|---|---|---|
| PrA12 | 1910 | — | 100 Lire. KM50. | 8,000 |
| Pr12 | 1911 | — | 2 Lire. KM52. | 175 |
| Pr13 | 1911 | — | 5 Lire. KM53. | 3,250 |
| Pr14 | 1911 | — | 50 Lire. KM54. | 4,500 |
| PrA15 | 1912 | — | 10 Lire. KM47. | 3,000 |
| Pr15 | 1912 | — | 20 Lire. KM48. | 3,500 |
| Pr16 | 1913 | — | 5 Lire. KM56. | 5,000 |
| Pr18 | 1914 | — | 5 Lire. KM56. | 2,500 |
| Pr17 | 1914 | — | 2 Lire. KM55. | — |
| Pr19 | 1914 | — | 5 Lire. Copper. KM56. | — |
| Pr20 | 1914 | — | 5 Lire. Copper. KM56. | — |
| Pr21 | 1914 | — | 5 Lire. PROVA DI STAMPA. KM56. | 2,000 |
| Pr22 | 1914 | — | 5 Lire. PROVA DI STAMPA. KM56. | 2,000 |
| Pr25 | 1919 | — | 5 Centesimi. KM59. | — |
| Pr26 | 1919 | — | 10 Centesimi. KM60. | — |
| Pr23 | 1919 | — | 50 Centesimi. KM61. | — |
| Pr24 | 1919 | — | 50 Centesimi. PROVA DI STAMPA. KM61. | — |
| Pr27 | 1921 | — | Lira. KM62. | — |
| Pr28 | 1923 | — | 2 Lire. KM63. | 325 |
| Pr30 | 1923 | — | 2 Lire. KM63. | 150 |
| Pr31 | 1923 | — | 20 Lire. KM64. | 3,500 |
| Pr32 | 1923 | — | 100 Lire. KM65. | 10,000 |
| Pr33 | 1923 | — | 100 Lire. KM65. | 11,000 |
| Pr29 | 1923 | — | 2 Lire. PROVA DI STAMPA. KM63. | — |
| Pr34 | 1925 | — | 100 Lire. KM66. | 9,500 |
| Pr36 | 1926 | — | 5 Lire. KM67. | 350 |
| Pr35 | 1926 | — | 50 Centesimi. PROVA TECNICO. KM61. | — |
| Pr39 | 1926 | — | 10 Lire. PROVA at top. KM68. | 500 |
| Pr40 | 1926 | — | 10 Lire. PROVA beneath horses. KM68. | — |
| Pr37 | 1926 | — | 5 Lire. PROVA DI STAMPA. KM67. | 300 |
| Pr38 | 1926 | — | 5 Lire. LA PROVA TECNICA. KM67. | 350 |
| Pr41 | 1926 | — | 10 Lire. PROVA DI STAMPA. KM68. | 600 |
| Pr42 | 1926 | — | 10 Lire. 1A PROVA TECNICA. KM68. | 500 |
| PrA45 | 1927 | — | 10 Lire. PROVA beneath horses. KM68. | 500 |
| Pr43 | 1927 | — | 5 Lire. PROVA DI STAMPA above eagle. KM67. | — |
| Pr45 | 1927 | — | 20 Lire. KM69. | — |
| Pr44 | 1927 | — | 5 Lire. PROVA DI STAMPA at right side of eagle. KM67. | — |

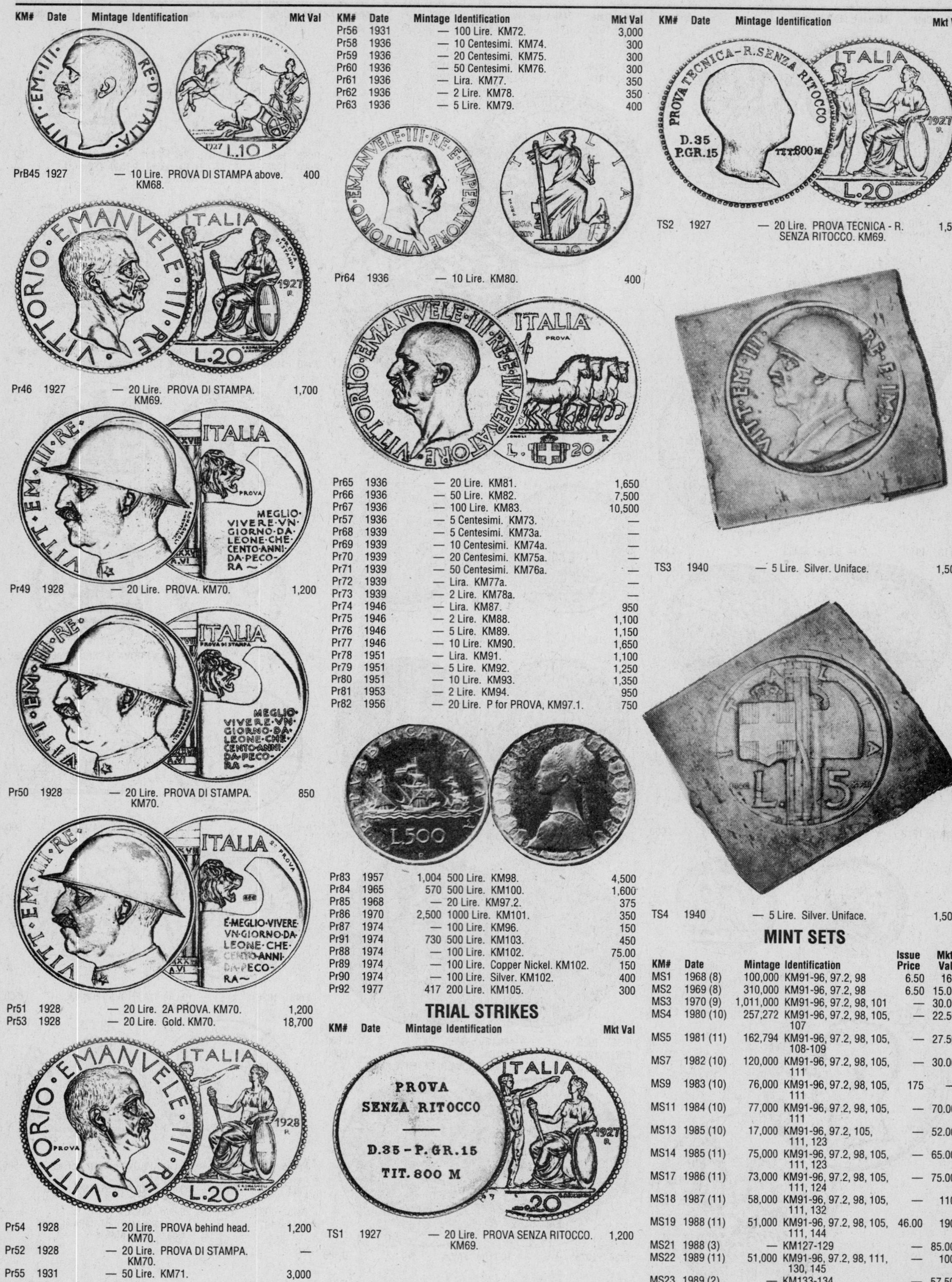

| KM# | Date | Mintage | Identification | Mkt Val |
|---|---|---|---|---|
| PrB45 | 1927 | — | 10 Lire. PROVA DI STAMPA above. KM68. | 400 |
| Pr46 | 1927 | — | 20 Lire. PROVA DI STAMPA. KM69. | 1,700 |
| Pr49 | 1928 | — | 20 Lire. PROVA. KM70. | 1,200 |
| Pr50 | 1928 | — | 20 Lire. PROVA DI STAMPA. KM70. | 850 |
| Pr51 | 1928 | — | 20 Lire. 2A PROVA. KM70. | 1,200 |
| Pr53 | 1928 | — | 20 Lire. Gold. KM70. | 18,700 |
| Pr54 | 1928 | — | 20 Lire. PROVA behind head. KM70. | 1,200 |
| Pr52 | 1928 | — | 20 Lire. PROVA DI STAMPA. KM70. | — |
| Pr55 | 1931 | — | 50 Lire. KM71. | 3,000 |
| Pr56 | 1931 | — | 100 Lire. KM72. | 3,000 |
| Pr58 | 1936 | — | 10 Centesimi. KM74. | 300 |
| Pr59 | 1936 | — | 20 Centesimi. KM75. | 300 |
| Pr60 | 1936 | — | 50 Centesimi. KM76. | 300 |
| Pr61 | 1936 | — | Lira. KM77. | 350 |
| Pr62 | 1936 | — | 2 Lire. KM78. | 350 |
| Pr63 | 1936 | — | 5 Lire. KM79. | 400 |
| Pr64 | 1936 | — | 10 Lire. KM80. | 400 |
| Pr65 | 1936 | — | 20 Lire. KM81. | 1,650 |
| Pr66 | 1936 | — | 50 Lire. KM82. | 7,500 |
| Pr67 | 1936 | — | 100 Lire. KM83. | 10,500 |
| Pr57 | 1936 | — | 5 Centesimi. KM73. | — |
| Pr68 | 1939 | — | 5 Centesimi. KM73a. | — |
| Pr69 | 1939 | — | 10 Centesimi. KM74a. | — |
| Pr70 | 1939 | — | 20 Centesimi. KM75a. | — |
| Pr71 | 1939 | — | 50 Centesimi. KM76a. | — |
| Pr72 | 1939 | — | Lira. KM77a. | — |
| Pr73 | 1939 | — | 2 Lire. KM78a. | — |
| Pr74 | 1946 | — | Lira. KM87. | 950 |
| Pr75 | 1946 | — | 2 Lire. KM88. | 1,100 |
| Pr76 | 1946 | — | 5 Lire. KM89. | 1,150 |
| Pr77 | 1946 | — | 10 Lire. KM90. | 1,650 |
| Pr78 | 1951 | — | Lira. KM91. | 1,100 |
| Pr79 | 1951 | — | 5 Lire. KM92. | 1,250 |
| Pr80 | 1951 | — | 10 Lire. KM93. | 1,350 |
| Pr81 | 1953 | — | 2 Lire. KM94. | 950 |
| Pr82 | 1956 | — | 20 Lire. P for PROVA, KM97.1. | 750 |
| Pr83 | 1957 | 1,004 | 500 Lire. KM98. | 4,500 |
| Pr84 | 1965 | 570 | 500 Lire. KM100. | 1,600 |
| Pr85 | 1968 | — | 20 Lire. KM97.2. | 375 |
| Pr86 | 1970 | 2,500 | 1000 Lire. KM101. | 350 |
| Pr87 | 1974 | — | 100 Lire. KM96. | 150 |
| Pr91 | 1974 | 730 | 500 Lire. KM103. | 450 |
| Pr88 | 1974 | — | 100 Lire. KM102. | 75.00 |
| Pr89 | 1974 | — | 100 Lire. Copper Nickel. KM102. | 150 |
| Pr90 | 1974 | — | 100 Lire. Silver. KM102. | 400 |
| Pr92 | 1977 | 417 | 200 Lire. KM105. | 300 |

## TRIAL STRIKES

| KM# | Date | Mintage | Identification | Mkt Val |
|---|---|---|---|---|
| TS1 | 1927 | — | 20 Lire. PROVA SENZA RITOCCO. KM69. | 1,200 |
| TS2 | 1927 | — | 20 Lire. PROVA TECNICA - R. SENZA RITOCCO. KM69. | 1,500 |
| TS3 | 1940 | — | 5 Lire. Silver. Uniface. | 1,500 |
| TS4 | 1940 | — | 5 Lire. Silver. Uniface. | 1,500 |

## MINT SETS

| KM# | Date | Mintage | Identification | Issue Price | Mkt Val |
|---|---|---|---|---|---|
| MS1 | 1968 (8) | 100,000 | KM91-96, 97.2, 98 | 6.50 | 160 |
| MS2 | 1969 (8) | 310,000 | KM91-96, 97.2, 98 | 6.50 | 15.00 |
| MS3 | 1970 (9) | 1,011,000 | KM91-96, 97.2, 98, 101 | — | 30.00 |
| MS4 | 1980 (10) | 257,272 | KM91-96, 97.2, 98, 105, 107 | — | 22.50 |
| MS5 | 1981 (11) | 162,794 | KM91-96, 97.2, 98, 105, 108-109 | — | 27.50 |
| MS7 | 1982 (10) | 120,000 | KM91-96, 97.2, 98, 105, 111 | — | 30.00 |
| MS9 | 1983 (10) | 76,000 | KM91-96, 97.2, 98, 105, 111 | 175 | — |
| MS11 | 1984 (10) | 77,000 | KM91-96, 97.2, 98, 105, 111 | — | 70.00 |
| MS13 | 1985 (10) | 17,000 | KM91-96, 97.2, 105, 111, 123 | — | 52.00 |
| MS14 | 1985 (11) | 75,000 | KM91-96, 97.2, 98, 105, 111, 123 | — | 65.00 |
| MS17 | 1986 (11) | 73,000 | KM91-96, 97.2, 98, 105, 111, 124 | — | 75.00 |
| MS18 | 1987 (11) | 58,000 | KM91-96, 97.2, 98, 105, 111, 132 | — | 110 |
| MS19 | 1988 (11) | 51,000 | KM91-96, 97.2, 98, 105, 111, 144 | 46.00 | 190 |
| MS21 | 1988 (3) | — | KM127-129 | — | 85.00 |
| MS22 | 1989 (11) | 51,000 | KM91-96, 97.2, 98, 111, 130, 145 | — | 100 |
| MS23 | 1989 (2) | — | KM133-134 | — | 57.50 |

| KM# | Date | Mintage | Identification | Issue Price | Mkt Val |
|---|---|---|---|---|---|
| MS24 | 1989 (2) | — | KM138-139 | — | 57.50 |
| MS25 | 1990 (11) | 52,800 | KM91-94, 95a-96a, 97.2, 98, 111, 135, 146 | — | 90.00 |
| MS26 | 1991 (11) | 64,000 | KM91-94, 95a-96a, 97.2, 98, 105, 111, 141 | 50.00 | 90.00 |
| MS27 | 1991 (2) | — | KM142-143 | — | 60.00 |
| MS28 | 1992 (11) | 52,000 | KM91-94, 95a-96a, 97.2, 98, 111, 151, 161 | 50.00 | 110 |
| MS29 | 1993 (11) | 50,000 | KM91-94, 95a, 97.2, 98, 155, 159, 160, 163 | — | 85.00 |
| MS31 | ND (1993) (3) | — | KM171-173 | 31.00 | 85.00 |
| MS30 | 1994 (11) | — | KM91-94, 95a, 97.2, 98, 159, 164, 167, 169 | — | 175 |
| MS32 | 1995 (11) | — | KM91-94, 95a, 97.2, 98, 105, 111, 180, 185 | — | 150 |
| MS33 | 1996 (11) | — | KM91-94, 97.2, 98, 159, 181, 183-184, 199 | — | 75.00 |
| MS34 | 1997 (12) | — | KM91-94, 97.2, 98, 159, 183, 186-187, 196, 200 | — | 125 |
| MS35 | 1998 (12) | — | KM91-94, 97.2, 98, 105, 159, 183, 193-194, 201 | — | 80.00 |
| MS36 | 1998 (2) | — | KM195-196 | — | 55.00 |
| MS37 | 1999 (2) | — | KM197-198 | — | 65.00 |

## PROOF SETS

| KM# | Date | Mintage | Identification | Issue Price | Mkt Val |
|---|---|---|---|---|---|
| PS1 | 1985 (10) | 5,000 | KM91-96, 97.2, 105, 111, 123 | — | 110 |
| PS2 | 1985 (11) | 15,000 | KM91-96, 97.2, 98, 105, 111, 123 | — | 170 |
| PS3 | 1986 (10) | — | KM91-96, 97.2, 105, 111, 124 | — | 135 |
| PS4 | 1986 (11) | 18,000 | KM91-96, 97.2, 98, 105, 111, 124 | — | 115 |
| PS5 | 1987 (11) | 10,000 | KM91-96, 97.2, 98, 105, 111, 132 | — | 120 |
| PS6 | 1988 (11) | 9,000 | KM91-96, 97.2, 98, 105, 111, 144 | 100 | 235 |
| PS7 | 1988 (3) | — | KM127-129 | — | 135 |
| PS10 | 1989 (2) | — | KM133-134 | — | 90.00 |
| PS8 | 1989 (11) | 9,260 | KM91-96, 97.2, 98, 111, 130, 145 | — | 140 |
| PS11 | 1989 (2) | — | KM138-139 | — | 90.00 |
| PS9 | 1990 (11) | 9,400 | KM91-94, 95a-96a, 97.2, 98, 111, 135, 146 | — | 215 |
| PS12 | 1991 (11) | 11,000 | KM91-94, 95a-96a, 97.2, 98, 105, 111, 141 | 100 | 220 |
| PS13 | 1992 (11) | 9,500 | KM91-94, 95a-96a, 97.2, 98, 111, 151, 161 | 90.00 | 175 |
| PS14 | 1993 (11) | 10,000 | KM91-94, 95a, 97.2, 98, 155, 159, 160, 163 | — | 155 |
| PS15 | ND (1993) (3) | — | KM171-173 | 60.00 | 150 |
| PS16 | 1998 (2) | — | KM195-196 | — | 130 |
| PS17 | 1999 (2) | — | KM197-198 | — | 110 |

# IVORY COAST

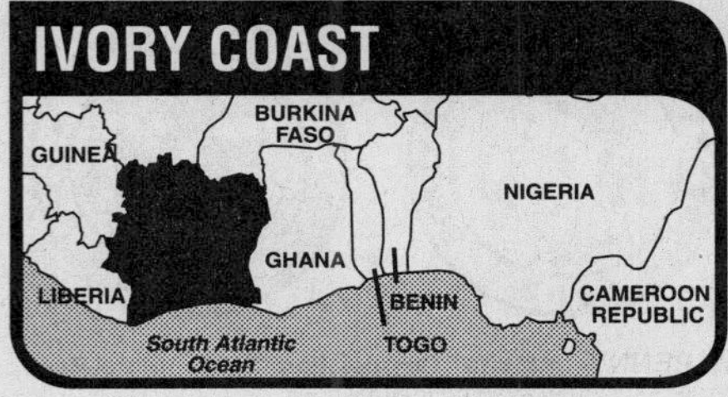


The Republic of the Ivory Coast, (Cote d'Ivoire), a former French Overseas territory located on the south side of the African bulge between Liberia and Ghana, has an area of 124,504 sq. mi. (322,463 sq. km.) and a population of 11.8 million. Capital: Yamoussoukro. The predominantly agricultural economy is one of Africa's most prosperous. Coffee, tropical woods, cocoa, and bananas are exported.

French and Portuguese navigators visited the Ivory Coast in the 15th century. French traders set up establishments in the 19th century, and gradually extended their influence along the coast and inland. The area was organized as a territory in 1893, and from 1904 to 1958 was a constituent unit of the Federation of French West Africa - as a Colony under the Third Republic and an Overseas Territory under the Fourth. In 1958 Ivory Coast became an autonomous republic within the French Community. Independence was attained on Aug. 7, 1960.

## REPUBLIC

### DECIMAL COINAGE

**10 FRANCS** KM# 1 **Weight:** 25.0000 g. **Composition:** 0.9250 Silver .7434 oz. ASW **Note:** Varieties exist in 2.9mm and 3.5mm planchets.

| Date | Mintage | F | VF | XF | Unc | BU |
|---|---|---|---|---|---|---|
| 1966 Proof | — | Value: 55.00 | | | | |

**10 FRANCS** KM# 2 **Weight:** 3.2000 g. **Composition:** 0.9000 Gold .0926 oz. AGW

| Date | Mintage | F | VF | XF | Unc | BU |
|---|---|---|---|---|---|---|
| 1966 Proof | 2,000 | Value: 85.00 | | | | |

**25 FRANCS** KM# 3 **Weight:** 8.0000 g. **Composition:** 0.9000 Gold .2315 oz. AGW

| Date | Mintage | F | VF | XF | Unc | BU |
|---|---|---|---|---|---|---|
| 1966 Proof | 2,000 | Value: 135 | | | | |

**50 FRANCS** KM# 4 **Weight:** 16.0000 g. **Composition:** 0.9000 Gold .4630 oz. AGW **Note:** Similar to 25 Francs, KM#3.

| Date | Mintage | F | VF | XF | Unc | BU |
|---|---|---|---|---|---|---|
| 1966 Proof | 2,000 | Value: 265 | | | | |

**100 FRANCS** KM# 5 **Weight:** 32.0000 g. **Composition:** 0.9000 Gold .9260 oz. AGW **Note:** Similar to the 10 Francs, KM#1.

| Date | Mintage | F | VF | XF | Unc | BU |
|---|---|---|---|---|---|---|
| 1966 Proof | 2,000 | Value: 525 | | | | |

## ESSAIS

Standard metals unless otherwise noted

| KM# | Date | Mintage | Identification | Mkt Val |
|---|---|---|---|---|
| E1 | 1966 | — | 100 Francs. Silver. KM5. | 50.00 |

## PIEFORTS WITH ESSAI

| KM# | Date | Mintage | Identification | Mkt Val |
|---|---|---|---|---|
| PE1 | 1966 | — | 100 Francs. Silver. KM5. | 125 |

## PROOF SETS

| KM# | Date | Mintage | Identification | Issue Price | Mkt Val |
|---|---|---|---|---|---|
| PS1 | 1966 (4) | 2,000 | KM2-5 | — | 1,000 |

# JAMAICA

Jamaica, a member of the British Commonwealth is situated in the Caribbean Sea 90 miles south of Cuba, has an area of 4,244 sq. mi. (10,990 sq. km.) and a population of 2.1 million. Capital: Kingston. The economy is founded chiefly on mining, tourism and agriculture. Aluminum, bauxite, sugar, rum and molasses are exported.

Jamaica was discovered by Columbus on May 3, 1494, and settled by Spain in 1509. The island was captured in1655 by a British naval force under the command of Admiral William Penn, sent by Oliver Cromwell and ceded to Britain by the Treaty of Madrid, 1670. For more than 150 years, the Jamaican economy of sugar, slaves and piracy was one of the most prosperous in the new world. Dissension between the property-oriented island legislature and the home government prompted parliament to establish a crown colony government for Jamaica in 1866. From 1958 to 1961 Jamaica was a member of the West Indies Federation, withdrawing when Jamaican voters rejected the association. The colony attained independence on Aug. 6, 1962. Jamaica is a member of the Commonwealth of Nations. Elizabeth II is the Head of State, as Queen of Jamaica.

In 1758, the Jamaican Assembly authorized stamping a certain amount of Spanish milled coinage. Token coinage by merchants aided the island's monetary supply in the early19th century. Sterling coinage was introduced in Jamaica in 1825, with the additional silver three halfpence under William IV and Victoria. Certain issues of three pence of William IV and Victoria were intended for colonial use, including Jamaica, as were the last dates of three pence for George VI.

There was an extensive token and work tally coinage for Jamaica in the late 19th and early 20th centuries.

A decimal standard currency system was adopted on Sept. 8, 1969.

**RULERS**

British, until 1962

**MINT MARKS**

C - Royal Canadian Mint, Ottawa
H - Heaton
FM - Franklin Mint, U.S.A.**
(fm) - Franklin Mint, U.S.A.*
no mint mark - Royal Mint, London @06*NOTE: @05During 1970 the Franklin Mint produced matte and proof coins (1 cent-1 dollar) using dies similar to/or Royal Mint without the FM mint mark.

**NOTE:** From 1975-1985 the Franklin Mint produced coinage in up to 3 different qualities. Qualities of issue are designated in ( ) after each date and are defined as follows:

**(M) MATTE** - Normal circulation strike or a dull finish produced by sandblasting special uncirculated (polish finish) or proof quality dies.

**(U) SPECIAL UNCIRCULATED** - Polished or proof-like in appearance without any frosted features.

(P) **PROOF** - The highest quality obtainable having mirror-like fields and frosted features.

**MONETARY SYSTEM**

4 Farthings = 1 Penny
12 Pence = 1 Shilling
8 Reales = 6 Shillings, 8 Pence
(Commencing 1969)
100 Cents = 1 Dollar

## BRITISH ADMINISTRATION

### REGULAR COINAGE

**FARTHING** KM# 18 **Composition:** Copper-Nickel **Reverse:** Horizontal shading in arms

| Date | Mintage | F | VF | XF | Unc | BU |
|---|---|---|---|---|---|---|
| 1902 | 144,000 | 2.00 | 4.00 | 15.00 | 45.00 | — |
| 1903 | 144,000 | 2.00 | 4.00 | 15.00 | 45.00 | — |

**FARTHING** **KM# 21** **Composition:** Copper-Nickel **Reverse:** Vertical shading in arms

| Date | Mintage | F | VF | XF | Unc | BU |
|---|---|---|---|---|---|---|
| 1904 | 192,000 | 1.00 | 2.50 | 12.00 | 35.00 | — |
| 1904 Proof | — | Value: 250 | | | | |
| 1905 | 192,000 | 1.00 | 2.50 | 12.00 | 35.00 | — |
| 1906 | 528,000 | 1.00 | 2.00 | 8.00 | 28.00 | — |
| 1907 | 192,000 | 1.00 | 2.50 | 12.00 | 32.00 | — |
| 1909 | 144,000 | 2.00 | 4.00 | 15.00 | 45.00 | — |
| 1910 | 48,000 | 4.00 | 8.00 | 25.00 | 50.00 | — |

**FARTHING** **KM# 24** **Composition:** Copper-Nickel

| Date | Mintage | F | VF | XF | Unc | BU |
|---|---|---|---|---|---|---|
| 1914 | 192,000 | 2.00 | 4.00 | 12.00 | 35.00 | — |
| 1916H | 480,000 | 0.75 | 2.00 | 6.00 | 20.00 | — |
| 1916H Proof | — | Value: 250 | | | | |
| 1918C | 208,000 | 1.00 | 2.00 | 8.00 | 25.00 | — |
| 1918C Proof | — | Value: 225 | | | | |
| 1919C | 401,000 | 0.75 | 2.00 | 6.00 | 20.00 | — |
| 1926 | 240,000 | 1.00 | 2.00 | 8.00 | 25.00 | — |
| 1928 | 480,000 | 0.75 | 2.00 | 6.00 | 20.00 | — |
| 1928 Proof | — | Value: 225 | | | | |
| 1932 | 480,000 | 0.75 | 2.00 | 6.00 | 20.00 | — |
| 1932 Proof | — | — | — | — | — | — |
| 1934 | 480,000 | 0.75 | 2.00 | 6.00 | 20.00 | — |
| 1934 Proof | — | — | — | — | — | — |

**FARTHING** **KM# 27** **Composition:** Copper-Nickel

| Date | Mintage | F | VF | XF | Unc | BU |
|---|---|---|---|---|---|---|
| 1937 | 480,000 | 0.50 | 1.50 | 5.00 | 15.00 | — |
| 1937 Proof | — | Value: 175 | | | | |

**FARTHING** **KM# 30** **Composition:** Copper-Nickel **Obverse:** Larger head

| Date | Mintage | F | VF | XF | Unc | BU |
|---|---|---|---|---|---|---|
| 1938 | 480,000 | 0.20 | 0.40 | 1.50 | 8.50 | — |
| 1938 Proof | — | — | — | — | — | — |
| 1942 | 480,000 | 0.20 | 0.40 | 1.50 | 8.50 | — |
| 1945 | 480,000 | 0.20 | 0.40 | 1.50 | 8.50 | — |
| 1945 Proof | — | Value: 120 | | | | |
| 1947 | 192,000 | 0.35 | 1.50 | 4.00 | 15.00 | — |
| 1947 Proof | — | Value: 120 | | | | |

**FARTHING** **KM# 33** **Composition:** Copper-Nickel **Obverse:** Without AND EMPEROR OF INIDA in legend

| Date | Mintage | F | VF | XF | Unc | BU |
|---|---|---|---|---|---|---|
| 1950 | 288,000 | 0.10 | 0.25 | 0.80 | 3.25 | — |
| 1950 Proof | — | Value: 175 | | | | |
| 1952 | 288,000 | 0.10 | 0.25 | 0.80 | 3.25 | — |
| 1952 Proof | — | Value: 175 | | | | |

**1/2 PENNY** **KM# 19** **Composition:** Copper-Nickel **Reverse:** Horizontal shading in arms

| Date | Mintage | F | VF | XF | Unc | BU |
|---|---|---|---|---|---|---|
| 1902 | 48,000 | 2.00 | 5.00 | 20.00 | 50.00 | — |
| 1903 | 48,000 | 2.00 | 5.00 | 20.00 | 60.00 | — |

**1/2 PENNY** **KM# 22** **Composition:** Copper-Nickel **Reverse:** Vertical shading in arms

| Date | Mintage | F | VF | XF | Unc | BU |
|---|---|---|---|---|---|---|
| 1904 | 48,000 | 1.50 | 5.00 | 25.00 | 70.00 | — |
| 1905 | 48,000 | 1.50 | 5.00 | 25.00 | 70.00 | — |
| 1906 | 432,000 | 0.65 | 1.50 | 7.50 | 25.00 | — |
| 1907 | 504,000 | 0.65 | 1.50 | 7.50 | 25.00 | — |
| 1909 | 144,000 | 0.75 | 2.00 | 10.00 | 40.00 | — |
| 1910 | 144,000 | 0.75 | 2.00 | 10.00 | 40.00 | — |

**1/2 PENNY** **KM# 25** **Composition:** Copper-Nickel

| Date | Mintage | F | VF | XF | Unc | BU |
|---|---|---|---|---|---|---|
| 1914 | 96,000 | 3.00 | 6.00 | 25.00 | 75.00 | — |
| 1916H | 192,000 | 0.35 | 1.50 | 6.00 | 20.00 | — |
| 1918C | 251,000 | 0.35 | 1.50 | 6.00 | 20.00 | — |
| 1918C Proof | — | Value: 200 | | | | |
| 1919C | 312,000 | 0.35 | 1.00 | 5.00 | 20.00 | — |
| 1920 | 480,000 | 0.35 | 1.00 | 5.00 | 20.00 | — |
| 1926 | 240,000 | 0.35 | 1.00 | 5.00 | 30.00 | — |
| 1928 | 120,000 | 0.35 | 1.00 | 5.00 | 20.00 | — |
| 1928 Proof | — | Value: 200 | | | | |

**1/2 PENNY** **KM# 28** **Composition:** Nickel-Brass

| Date | Mintage | F | VF | XF | Unc | BU |
|---|---|---|---|---|---|---|
| 1937 | 960,000 | 0.50 | 1.00 | 3.50 | 12.00 | — |
| 1937 Proof | — | Value: 175 | | | | |

**1/2 PENNY** **KM# 31** **Composition:** Nickel-Brass **Obverse:** Larger head

| Date | Mintage | F | VF | XF | Unc | BU |
|---|---|---|---|---|---|---|
| 1938 | 960,000 | 0.25 | 0.75 | 3.50 | 12.00 | — |
| 1938 Proof | — | Value: 175 | | | | |
| 1940 | 960,000 | 0.25 | 0.75 | 3.50 | 12.00 | — |
| 1940 Proof | — | Value: 175 | | | | |
| 1942 | 960,000 | 0.25 | 0.75 | 3.50 | 12.00 | — |
| 1945 | 960,000 | 0.25 | 0.75 | 3.50 | 12.00 | — |
| 1945 Proof | — | Value: 175 | | | | |
| 1947 | 960,000 | 0.25 | 0.75 | 3.50 | 12.00 | — |
| 1947 Proof | — | Value: 200 | | | | |

**1/2 PENNY** **KM# 34** **Composition:** Nickel-Brass **Obverse:** Without AND EMPEROR OF INIDA in legend

| Date | Mintage | F | VF | XF | Unc | BU |
|---|---|---|---|---|---|---|
| 1950 | 1,440,000 | 0.10 | 0.20 | 0.30 | 3.25 | — |
| 1950 Proof | — | Value: 175 | | | | |
| 1952 | 1,200,000 | 0.10 | 0.20 | 0.30 | 3.25 | — |
| 1952 Proof | — | Value: 175 | | | | |

**1/2 PENNY** **KM# 36** **Composition:** Nickel-Brass

| Date | Mintage | F | VF | XF | Unc | BU |
|---|---|---|---|---|---|---|
| 1955 | 1,440,000 | 0.10 | 0.15 | 0.40 | 2.00 | — |
| 1955 Proof | — | Value: 150 | | | | |
| 1957 | 600,000 | 1.00 | 2.00 | 4.00 | 6.00 | — |
| 1957 Proof | — | — | — | — | — | — |
| 1958 | 960,000 | 0.10 | 0.20 | 0.50 | 2.00 | — |
| 1958 Proof | — | Value: 150 | | | | |
| 1959 | 960,000 | 0.10 | 0.20 | 0.50 | 2.00 | — |
| 1959 Proof | — | — | — | — | — | — |
| 1961 | 480,000 | 0.20 | 0.40 | 1.00 | 4.00 | — |
| 1961 Proof | — | — | — | — | — | — |
| 1962 | 960,000 | 0.10 | 0.15 | 0.30 | 1.75 | — |
| 1962 Proof | — | Value: 150 | | | | |
| 1963 | 960,000 | 0.10 | 0.15 | 0.30 | 1.75 | — |
| 1963 Proof | — | Value: 150 | | | | |

**1/2 PENNY** **KM# 38** **Composition:** Nickel-Brass **Reverse:** New arms

| Date | Mintage | F | VF | XF | Unc | BU |
|---|---|---|---|---|---|---|
| 1964 | 1,440,000 | 0.10 | 0.15 | 0.20 | 0.80 | — |
| 1965 | 1,200,000 | 0.10 | 0.15 | 0.20 | 0.80 | — |
| 1966 | 1,680,000 | 0.10 | 0.15 | 0.20 | 0.80 | — |

**1/2 PENNY** **KM# 41** **Composition:** Copper-Nickel-Zinc **Subject:** Jamaican Coinage Centennial

| Date | Mintage | F | VF | XF | Unc | BU |
|---|---|---|---|---|---|---|
| 1969 | 30,000 | 0.10 | 0.15 | 0.25 | 0.75 | — |
| 1969 Proof | 5,000 | Value: 2.50 | | | | |

**PENNY** **KM# 20** **Composition:** Copper-Nickel **Reverse:** Horizontal shading in arms

| Date | Mintage | F | VF | XF | Unc | BU |
|---|---|---|---|---|---|---|
| 1902 | 60,000 | 2.25 | 6.00 | 25.00 | 70.00 | — |
| 1903 | 60,000 | 2.25 | 6.00 | 25.00 | 70.00 | — |

**PENNY** KM# 23 **Composition:** Copper-Nickel **Reverse:** Vertical shading in arms

| Date | Mintage | F | VF | XF | Unc | BU |
|---|---|---|---|---|---|---|
| 1904 | 24,000 | 10.00 | 20.00 | 50.00 | 125 | — |
| 1904 Proof | — | Value: 250 | | | | |
| 1905 | 48,000 | 2.00 | 4.75 | 22.50 | 60.00 | — |
| 1906 | 156,000 | 1.25 | 2.50 | 12.00 | 45.00 | — |
| 1907 | 108,000 | 1.25 | 2.50 | 12.00 | 45.00 | — |
| 1909 | 144,000 | 1.25 | 2.50 | 12.00 | 45.00 | — |
| 1910 | 144,000 | 1.25 | 2.50 | 12.00 | 45.00 | — |

**PENNY** KM# 26 **Composition:** Copper-Nickel

| Date | Mintage | F | VF | XF | Unc | BU |
|---|---|---|---|---|---|---|
| 1914 | 24,000 | 10.00 | 20.00 | 65.00 | 175 | — |
| 1916H | 24,000 | 10.00 | 20.00 | 60.00 | 175 | — |
| 1918C | 187,000 | 2.00 | 5.00 | 15.00 | 60.00 | — |
| 1918C Proof | — | Value: 200 | | | | |
| 1919C | 251,000 | 1.25 | 4.75 | 12.00 | 50.00 | — |
| 1920 | 360,000 | 0.75 | 2.50 | 9.50 | 32.50 | — |
| 1926 | 240,000 | 0.75 | 2.50 | 9.50 | 35.00 | — |
| 1928 | 360,000 | 0.75 | 2.50 | 9.50 | 35.00 | — |
| 1928 Proof | — | Value: 200 | | | | |

**PENNY** KM# 29 **Composition:** Nickel-Brass

| Date | Mintage | F | VF | XF | Unc | BU |
|---|---|---|---|---|---|---|
| 1937 | 1,200,000 | 1.00 | 1.75 | 3.25 | 12.00 | — |
| 1937 Proof | — | Value: 200 | | | | |

**PENNY** KM# 32 **Composition:** Nickel-Brass **Obverse:** Larger head

| Date | Mintage | F | VF | XF | Unc | BU |
|---|---|---|---|---|---|---|
| 1938 | 1,200,000 | 0.35 | 0.65 | 3.25 | 12.00 | — |
| 1938 Proof | — | Value: 200 | | | | |
| 1940 | 1,200,000 | 0.35 | 0.65 | 3.25 | 12.00 | — |
| 1940 Proof | — | Value: 200 | | | | |
| 1942 | 1,200,000 | 0.35 | 0.65 | 3.25 | 12.00 | — |
| 1942 Proof | — | Value: 200 | | | | |
| 1945 | 1,200,000 | 0.35 | 0.65 | 3.25 | 12.00 | — |
| 1945 Proof | — | Value: 200 | | | | |
| 1947 | 480,000 | 0.35 | 0.65 | 3.25 | 12.00 | — |
| 1947 Proof | — | Value: 200 | | | | |

**PENNY** KM# 35 **Composition:** Nickel-Brass **Obverse:** Without AND EMPEROR OF INDIA in legend

| Date | Mintage | F | VF | XF | Unc | BU |
|---|---|---|---|---|---|---|
| 1950 | 600,000 | 0.20 | 0.35 | 2.00 | 10.00 | — |
| 1950 Proof | — | Value: 200 | | | | |
| 1952 | 725,000 | 0.20 | 0.35 | 2.00 | 10.00 | — |
| 1952 Proof | — | Value: 200 | | | | |

**PENNY** KM# 37 **Composition:** Nickel-Brass

| Date | Mintage | F | VF | XF | Unc | BU |
|---|---|---|---|---|---|---|
| 1953 | 1,200,000 | 0.10 | 0.20 | 0.50 | 1.50 | — |
| 1953 Proof | — | Value: 115 | | | | |
| 1955 | 960,000 | 0.10 | 0.25 | 1.00 | 4.00 | — |
| 1955 Proof | — | Value: 115 | | | | |
| 1957 | 600,000 | 0.10 | 0.25 | 1.00 | 4.00 | — |
| 1957 Proof | — | — | — | — | — | — |
| 1958 | 1,080,000 | 0.10 | 0.20 | 0.30 | 3.00 | — |
| 1958 Proof | — | Value: 100 | | | | |
| 1959 | 1,368,000 | 0.10 | 0.20 | 0.30 | 2.50 | — |
| 1959 Proof | — | — | — | — | — | — |
| 1960 | 1,368,000 | 0.10 | 0.20 | 0.30 | 2.50 | — |
| 1960 Proof | — | — | — | — | — | — |
| 1961 | 1,368,000 | 0.10 | 0.20 | 0.30 | 2.50 | — |
| 1961 Proof | — | — | — | — | — | — |
| 1962 | 1,920,000 | 0.10 | 0.20 | 0.30 | 2.50 | — |
| 1962 Proof | — | Value: 100 | | | | |
| 1963 | 720,000 | 2.00 | 4.00 | 10.00 | 50.00 | — |
| 1963 Proof | — | Value: 100 | | | | |

**PENNY** KM# 39 **Composition:** Nickel-Brass

| Date | Mintage | F | VF | XF | Unc | BU |
|---|---|---|---|---|---|---|
| 1964 | 480,000 | 0.10 | 0.15 | 0.25 | 0.75 | — |
| 1965 | 1,200,000 | 0.10 | 0.15 | 0.20 | 0.35 | — |
| 1966 | 1,200,000 | 0.10 | 0.15 | 0.20 | 0.35 | — |
| 1967 | 2,760,000 | 0.10 | 0.15 | 0.20 | 0.35 | — |

**PENNY** KM# 42 **Composition:** Copper-Nickel-Zinc **Subject:** Jamaican Coinage Centennial

| Date | Mintage | F | VF | XF | Unc | BU |
|---|---|---|---|---|---|---|
| 1969 | 30,000 | 0.10 | 0.15 | 0.30 | 0.75 | — |
| 1969 Proof | 5,000 | Value: 2.50 | | | | |

**5 SHILLING** KM# 40 **Composition:** Copper-Nickel **Subject:** VIII Commonwealth Games

| Date | Mintage | F | VF | XF | Unc | BU |
|---|---|---|---|---|---|---|
| 1966 | 190,000 | — | 2.00 | 3.00 | 5.00 | — |
| 1966 Proof | 20,000 | Value: 6.50 | | | | |

## DECIMAL COINAGE

The Franklin Mint and Royal Mint have both been striking the 1 Cent through 1 Dollar coinage. The 1970 issues were all struck with dies similar to/or Royal Mint without the FM mint mark. The Royual Mint issues have the name JAMAICA extending beyond the native headdress feathers. Those struck after 1970 by the Franklin Mint have the name JAMAICA within the headdress feathers.

**CENT** KM# 45 **Composition:** Bronze **Reverse:** Ackee fruit

| Date | Mintage | F | VF | XF | Unc | BU |
|---|---|---|---|---|---|---|
| 1971 (RM) | 5,625,000 | — | — | 0.10 | 0.25 | — |
| 1969 | 30,200,000 | — | — | 0.10 | 0.25 | — |
| 1969 Proof | 19,000 | Value: 0.50 | | | | |
| 1970 (RM) Small date | 10,000,000 | — | — | 0.10 | 0.25 | — |
| 1970FM (M); Large date | 5,000 | — | — | 0.10 | 0.25 | — |
| 1970FM (P) | 12,000 | Value: 0.50 | | | | |

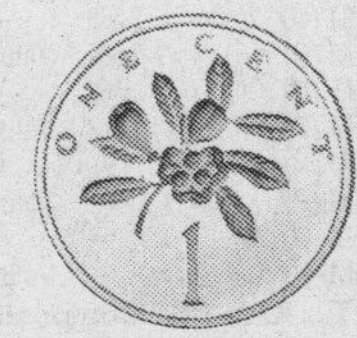


**CENT** KM# 51 **Composition:** Bronze

| Date | Mintage | F | VF | XF | Unc | BU |
|---|---|---|---|---|---|---|
| 1971FM (M) | 4,834 | — | — | 0.10 | 0.25 | — |
| 1971FM (P) | 14,000 | Value: 0.50 | | | | |
| 1972FM (M) | 7,982 | — | — | 0.10 | 0.25 | — |
| 1972FM (P) | 17,000 | Value: 0.50 | | | | |
| 1973FM (M) | 29,000 | — | — | 0.10 | 0.25 | — |
| 1973FM (P) | 28,000 | Value: 0.50 | | | | |
| 1974FM (M) | 28,000 | — | — | 0.10 | 0.25 | — |
| 1974FM (P) | 22,000 | Value: 0.50 | | | | |
| 1975FM (M) | 36,000 | — | — | 0.10 | 0.25 | — |
| 1975FM (U) | 4,683 | — | — | — | 0.25 | — |
| 1975FM (P) | 16,000 | Value: 0.50 | | | | |

**CENT** KM# 52 **Composition:** Bronze **Series:** F.A.O

| Date | Mintage | F | VF | XF | Unc | BU |
|---|---|---|---|---|---|---|
| 1971 | 20,000 | — | — | 0.10 | 0.30 | — |
| 1972 | 5,000,000 | — | — | 0.10 | 0.30 | — |

| Date | Mintage | F | VF | XF | Unc | BU |
|---|---|---|---|---|---|---|
| 1973 | 5,500,000 | — | — | 0.10 | 0.30 | — |
| 1974 | 3,000,000 | — | — | 0.10 | 0.30 | — |

**CENT** **KM# 64** **Composition:** Aluminum **Series:** F.A.O

| Date | Mintage | F | VF | XF | Unc | BU |
|---|---|---|---|---|---|---|
| 1975 | 15,000,000 | — | — | 0.10 | 0.20 | — |
| 1976 | 16,000,000 | — | — | 0.10 | 0.20 | — |
| 1977 | — | — | — | 0.10 | 0.20 | — |
| 1978 | 8,400,000 | — | — | 0.10 | 0.20 | — |
| 1980 | 10,000,000 | — | — | 0.10 | 0.20 | — |
| 1981 | 8,000,000 | — | — | 0.10 | 0.20 | — |
| 1982 | 10,000,000 | — | — | 0.10 | 0.20 | — |
| 1983 | 1,342,000 | — | — | — | 0.15 | — |
| 1984 | 8,704,000 | — | — | — | 0.15 | — |
| 1985 | 5,112,000 | — | — | — | 0.15 | — |
| 1985 Proof | — | Value: 0.50 | | | | |
| 1986 | 17,534,000 | — | — | — | 0.15 | — |
| 1987 | 9,968,000 | — | — | — | 0.15 | — |
| 1987 Proof | — | Value: 0.50 | | | | |
| 1988 Proof | — | Value: 0.50 | | | | |
| 1989 Proof | — | Value: 0.50 | | | | |
| 1990 | — | — | — | — | 0.15 | — |
| 1990 Proof | — | Value: 0.50 | | | | |
| 1991 | — | — | — | — | 0.15 | — |
| 1991 Proof | — | Value: 0.50 | | | | |
| 1992 Proof | — | Value: 0.50 | | | | |
| 1993 Proof | — | Value: 0.50 | | | | |
| 2000 | — | — | — | — | — | — |

**CENT** **KM# 68** **Composition:** Aluminum

| Date | Mintage | F | VF | XF | Unc | BU |
|---|---|---|---|---|---|---|
| 1976FM (M) | 28,000 | — | — | — | 0.15 | — |
| 1976FM (U) | 1,802 | — | — | — | 0.25 | — |
| 1976FM (P) | 24,000 | Value: 0.50 | | | | |
| 1977FM (M) | 28,000 | — | — | — | 0.15 | — |
| 1977FM (U) | 597 | — | — | — | 1.50 | — |
| 1977FM (P) | 10,000 | Value: 0.50 | | | | |
| 1978FM (M) | 28,000 | — | — | — | 0.15 | — |
| 1978FM (U) | 1,282 | — | — | — | 0.40 | — |
| 1978FM (P) | 6,058 | Value: 0.60 | | | | |
| 1979FM (M) | 28,000 | — | — | — | 0.15 | — |
| 1979FM (U) | 2,608 | — | — | — | 0.40 | — |
| 1979FM (P) | 4,049 | Value: 0.60 | | | | |
| 1980FM (M) | 28,000 | — | — | — | 0.15 | — |
| 1980FM (U) | 3,668 | — | — | — | 0.35 | — |
| 1980FM (P) | 2,688 | Value: 0.75 | | | | |
| 1981FM (U) | 482 | — | — | — | 1.50 | — |
| 1981FM (P) | 1,577 | Value: 0.75 | | | | |
| 1982FM (U) | — | — | — | — | 0.35 | — |
| 1982FM (P) | — | Value: 0.75 | | | | |
| 1984FM (U) | — | — | — | — | 0.35 | — |
| 1984FM (P) | — | Value: 0.75 | | | | |

**CENT** **KM# 136** **Composition:** Aluminum **Note:** Mule. 2 obverses of KM#64.

| Date | Mintage | F | VF | XF | Unc | BU |
|---|---|---|---|---|---|---|
| 1982FM | — | — | — | 220 | 250 | — |

**CENT** **KM# 137** **Composition:** Aluminum **Note:** Mule. 2 reverses of KM#64.

| Date | Mintage | F | VF | XF | Unc | BU |
|---|---|---|---|---|---|---|
| 1982FM | — | — | — | 250 | 300 | — |

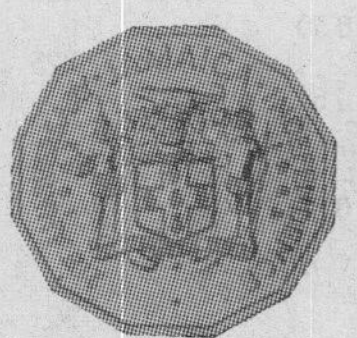

**CENT** **KM# 101** **Composition:** Aluminum **Subject:** 21st Anniversary of Independence

| Date | Mintage | F | VF | XF | Unc | BU |
|---|---|---|---|---|---|---|
| ND(1983)M (U) | — | — | — | — | 0.35 | — |
| ND(1983)FM (P) | — | Value: 0.75 | | | | |

**5 CENTS** **KM# 46** **Composition:** Copper-Nickel **Reverse:** American crocodile

| Date | Mintage | F | VF | XF | Unc | BU |
|---|---|---|---|---|---|---|
| 1969 | 12,008,000 | — | — | 0.10 | 0.50 | — |
| 1969 Proof | 30,000 | Value: 0.65 | | | | |
| 1970FM (M) | 5,000 | — | — | 0.10 | 0.50 | — |
| 1970FM (P) | 12,000 | Value: 0.65 | | | | |
| 1972 | 6,000,000 | — | — | 0.10 | 0.50 | — |
| 1975 | 6,010,000 | — | — | 0.10 | 0.50 | — |
| 1977 | 2,400,000 | — | — | 0.10 | 0.50 | — |
| 1978 | 2,000,000 | — | — | 0.10 | 0.50 | — |
| 1980 | 2,272,000 | — | — | 0.10 | 0.50 | — |
| 1981 | 2,001,000 | — | — | 0.10 | 0.50 | — |
| 1982 | 2,000,000 | — | — | 0.10 | 0.50 | — |
| 1983 | 992,000 | — | — | 0.10 | 0.50 | — |
| 1984 | 3,508,000 | — | — | 0.10 | 0.50 | — |
| 1985 | 4,760,000 | — | — | 0.10 | 0.50 | — |
| 1985 Proof | — | Value: 0.65 | | | | |
| 1986 | 14,504,000 | — | — | 0.10 | 0.50 | — |
| 1987 | 13,166,000 | — | — | 0.10 | 0.50 | — |
| 1987 Proof | — | Value: 0.65 | | | | |
| 1988 | 9,780,000 | — | — | 0.10 | 0.50 | — |
| 1988 Proof | — | Value: 0.65 | | | | |
| 1989 | — | — | — | 0.10 | 0.50 | — |
| 1989 Proof | — | Value: 0.65 | | | | |

**5 CENTS** **KM# 53** **Composition:** Copper-Nickel

| Date | Mintage | F | VF | XF | Unc | BU |
|---|---|---|---|---|---|---|
| 1971FM (M) | 4,834 | — | — | 0.10 | 0.35 | — |
| 1971FM (P) | 14,000 | Value: 0.50 | | | | |
| 1972FM (M) | 7,982 | — | — | 0.10 | 0.35 | — |
| 1972FM (P) | 17,000 | Value: 0.50 | | | | |
| 1973FM (M) | 17,000 | — | — | 0.10 | 0.35 | — |
| 1973FM (P) | 28,000 | Value: 0.50 | | | | |
| 1974FM (M) | 16,000 | — | — | 0.10 | 0.35 | — |
| 1974FM (P) | 22,000 | Value: 0.50 | | | | |
| 1975FM (M) | 6,240 | — | — | 0.10 | 0.35 | — |
| 1975FM (U) | 4,683 | — | — | — | 0.35 | — |
| 1975FM (P) | 16,000 | Value: 0.50 | | | | |
| 1976FM (M) | 5,560 | — | — | 0.10 | 0.35 | — |
| 1976FM (U) | 1,802 | — | — | — | 0.35 | — |
| 1976FM (P) | 24,000 | Value: 0.50 | | | | |
| 1977FM (M) | 5,560 | — | — | 0.10 | 0.40 | — |
| 1977FM (U) | 597 | — | — | — | 1.50 | — |
| 1977FM (P) | 10,000 | Value: 0.50 | | | | |
| 1978FM (M) | 5,560 | — | — | 0.10 | 0.40 | — |
| 1978FM (U) | 1,282 | — | — | — | 0.60 | — |
| 1978FM (P) | 6,058 | Value: 0.75 | | | | |
| 1979FM (M) | 5,560 | — | — | 0.10 | 0.40 | — |
| 1979FM (U) | 2,608 | — | — | — | 0.50 | — |
| 1979FM (P) | 4,049 | Value: 0.75 | | | | |
| 1980FM (M) | 5,560 | — | — | 0.10 | 0.40 | — |
| 1980FM (U) | 3,668 | — | — | — | 0.50 | — |
| 1980FM (P) | 2,688 | Value: 1.00 | | | | |
| 1981FM (U) | 482 | — | — | — | 1.50 | — |
| 1981FM (P) | 1,577 | Value: 1.00 | | | | |
| 1982FM (U) | — | — | — | — | 0.50 | — |
| 1982FM (P) | — | Value: 1.00 | | | | |
| 1984FM (U) | — | — | — | — | 0.50 | — |
| 1984FM (P) | — | Value: 1.00 | | | | |

**5 CENTS** **KM# 102** **Composition:** Copper-Nickel **Subject:** 21st Anniversary of Independence

| Date | Mintage | F | VF | XF | Unc | BU |
|---|---|---|---|---|---|---|
| ND(1983)FM (U) | — | — | — | — | 0.50 | — |
| ND(1983)FM (P) | — | Value: 1.00 | | | | |

**5 CENTS** **KM# 46a** **Composition:** Nickel Plated Steel

| Date | Mintage | F | VF | XF | Unc | BU |
|---|---|---|---|---|---|---|
| 1990 | — | — | — | 0.10 | 0.50 | — |
| 1990 Proof | — | Value: 0.65 | | | | |
| 1991 | — | — | — | 0.10 | 0.50 | — |
| 1991 Proof | — | Value: 0.65 | | | | |
| 1992 | — | — | — | 0.10 | 0.50 | — |
| 1992 Proof | — | Value: 0.65 | | | | |
| 1993 | — | — | — | 0.10 | 0.50 | — |
| 1993 Proof | — | Value: 0.65 | | | | |

**10 CENTS** **KM# 47** **Composition:** Copper-Nickel **Note:** Lignum Vitae

| Date | Mintage | F | VF | XF | Unc | BU |
|---|---|---|---|---|---|---|
| 1969 | 19,508,000 | — | — | 0.10 | 0.50 | — |
| 1969 Proof | 30,000 | Value: 0.75 | | | | |
| 1970FM (M) | 5,000 | — | — | 0.10 | 0.50 | — |
| 1970FM (P) | 12,000 | Value: 0.75 | | | | |
| 1972 | 6,000,000 | — | — | 0.10 | 0.50 | — |
| 1975 | 10,010,000 | — | — | 0.10 | 0.40 | — |
| 1977 | 8,000,000 | — | — | 0.10 | 0.40 | — |
| 1981 | 8,000,000 | — | — | 0.10 | 0.30 | — |
| 1982 | 8,000,000 | — | — | 0.10 | 0.30 | — |
| 1983 | 2,000,000 | — | — | 0.10 | 0.30 | — |
| 1984 | 5,000,000 | — | — | 0.10 | 0.30 | — |
| 1985 | 8,310,000 | — | — | 0.10 | 0.30 | — |
| 1985 Proof | — | Value: 0.75 | | | | |
| 1986 | 21,677,000 | — | — | 0.10 | 0.30 | — |
| 1987 | 29,089,000 | — | — | 0.10 | 0.30 | — |
| 1987 Proof | — | Value: 0.75 | | | | |
| 1988 | 15,660,000 | — | — | 0.10 | 0.30 | — |
| 1988 Proof | — | Value: 0.75 | | | | |
| 1989 | — | — | — | 0.10 | 0.30 | — |
| 1989 Proof | — | Value: 0.75 | | | | |

**10 CENTS** **KM# 54** **Composition:** Copper-Nickel

| Date | Mintage | F | VF | XF | Unc | BU |
|---|---|---|---|---|---|---|
| 1971FM (M) | 4,834 | — | — | 0.10 | 0.35 | — |
| 1971FM (P) | 14,000 | Value: 0.75 | | | | |
| 1972FM (M) | 7,982 | — | — | 0.10 | 0.35 | — |
| 1972FM (P) | 17,000 | Value: 0.75 | | | | |
| 1973FM (M) | 15,000 | — | — | 0.10 | 0.35 | — |
| 1973FM (P) | 28,000 | Value: 0.75 | | | | |
| 1974FM (M) | 14,000 | — | — | 0.10 | 0.35 | — |
| 1974FM (P) | 22,000 | Value: 0.75 | | | | |
| 1975FM (M) | 3,120 | — | — | 0.10 | 0.35 | — |
| 1975FM (U) | 4,683 | — | — | — | 0.35 | — |
| 1975FM (P) | 16,000 | Value: 0.75 | | | | |
| 1976FM (M) | 2,780 | — | — | 0.10 | 0.35 | — |
| 1976FM (U) | 1,802 | — | — | — | 0.35 | — |
| 1976FM (P) | 24,000 | Value: 0.75 | | | | |
| 1977FM (M) | 2,780 | — | — | 0.10 | 0.50 | — |
| 1977FM (U) | 597 | — | — | — | 1.50 | — |
| 1977FM (P) | 10,000 | Value: 0.75 | | | | |
| 1978FM (M) | 2,780 | — | — | 0.10 | 0.50 | — |
| 1978FM (U) | 4,062 | — | — | — | 0.60 | — |
| 1978FM (P) | 6,058 | Value: 1.00 | | | | |
| 1979FM (M) | 2,780 | — | — | 0.10 | 0.50 | — |
| 1979FM (U) | 2,608 | — | — | — | 0.60 | — |
| 1979FM (P) | 4,049 | Value: 1.00 | | | | |
| 1980FM (M) | 2,780 | — | — | 0.10 | 0.50 | — |
| 1980FM (U) | 3,668 | — | — | — | 0.50 | — |
| 1980FM (P) | 2,688 | Value: 1.50 | | | | |
| 1981FM (U) | 482 | — | — | — | 1.50 | — |
| 1981FM (P) | 1,577 | Value: 1.50 | | | | |
| 1982FM (U) | — | — | — | — | 0.50 | — |
| 1982FM (P) | — | Value: 1.50 | | | | |
| 1984FM (U) | — | — | — | — | 0.50 | — |
| 1984FM (P) | — | Value: 1.50 | | | | |

**10 CENTS** **KM# 103** **Composition:** Copper-Nickel **Subject:** 21st Anniversary of Independence

| Date | Mintage | F | VF | XF | Unc | BU |
|---|---|---|---|---|---|---|
| ND(1983)FM (U) | — | — | — | — | 0.50 | — |
| ND(1983)FM (P) | — | Value: 1.50 | | | | |

**10 CENTS** **KM# 47a** **Composition:** Nickel Plated Steel

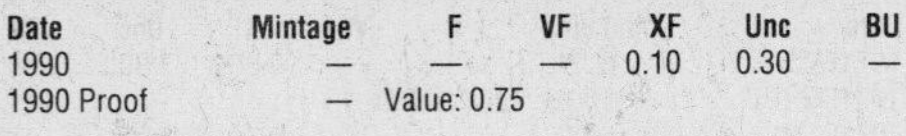

| Date | Mintage | F | VF | XF | Unc | BU |
|---|---|---|---|---|---|---|
| 1990 | — | — | — | 0.10 | 0.30 | — |
| 1990 Proof | — | Value: 0.75 | | | | |

**10 CENTS** **KM# 146.1** **Composition:** Nickel Plated Steel **Note:** Paul Bogle

| Date | Mintage | F | VF | XF | Unc | BU |
|---|---|---|---|---|---|---|
| 1991 | — | — | — | — | 0.50 | — |
| 1991 Proof | — | Value: 1.50 | | | | |
| 1992 | — | — | — | — | 0.50 | — |
| 1992 Proof | — | Value: 1.50 | | | | |
| 1993 | — | — | — | — | 0.50 | — |
| 1993 Proof | — | Value: 1.50 | | | | |
| 1994 | — | — | — | — | 0.50 | — |
| 1994 Proof | — | Value: 1.50 | | | | |

**10 CENTS** **KM# 146.2** **Composition:** Copper Plated Steel **Note:** Reduced size.

| Date | Mintage | F | VF | XF | Unc | BU |
|---|---|---|---|---|---|---|
| 1995 | — | — | — | — | 0.25 | — |
| 2000 | — | — | — | — | — | — |

**20 CENTS** **KM# 48** **Composition:** Copper-Nickel **Reverse:** Mahoe tree

| Date | Mintage | F | VF | XF | Unc | BU |
|---|---|---|---|---|---|---|
| 1969 | 3,758,000 | — | — | 0.20 | 0.75 | — |
| 1969 Proof | 30,000 | Value: 1.00 | | | | |
| 1970FM (M) | 5,000 | — | — | 0.20 | 0.75 | — |
| 1970FM (P) | 12,000 | Value: 1.00 | | | | |
| 1975 | 10,000 | — | — | 0.20 | 0.85 | — |
| 1982 | 1,000,000 | — | — | 0.20 | 0.65 | — |
| 1984 | 2,000,000 | — | — | 0.20 | 0.65 | — |
| 1986 | 2,530,000 | — | — | 0.20 | 0.65 | — |
| 1987 | 5,545,000 | — | — | 0.20 | 0.65 | — |
| 1987 Proof | — | Value: 1.00 | | | | |
| 1988 | 5,016,000 | — | — | 0.20 | 0.65 | — |
| 1988 Proof | — | Value: 1.00 | | | | |
| 1989 | — | — | — | 0.20 | 0.65 | — |
| 1989 Proof | — | Value: 1.00 | | | | |
| 1990 Proof | — | Value: 1.00 | | | | |

**20 CENTS** **KM# 55** **Composition:** Copper-Nickel

| Date | Mintage | F | VF | XF | Unc | BU |
|---|---|---|---|---|---|---|
| 1971FM (M) | 4,834 | — | — | 0.20 | 0.50 | — |
| 1971FM (P) | 14,000 | Value: 1.00 | | | | |
| 1972FM (M) | 7,982 | — | — | 0.20 | 0.50 | — |
| 1972FM (P) | 17,000 | Value: 1.00 | | | | |
| 1973FM (M) | 13,000 | — | — | 0.20 | 0.50 | — |
| 1973FM (P) | 28,000 | Value: 1.00 | | | | |
| 1974FM (M) | 12,000 | — | — | 0.20 | 0.50 | — |
| 1974FM (P) | 22,000 | Value: 1.00 | | | | |
| 1975FM (M) | 1,560 | — | — | 0.20 | 0.50 | — |
| 1975FM (U) | 4,683 | — | — | — | 0.50 | — |
| 1975FM (P) | 16,000 | Value: 1.00 | | | | |
| 1976FM (M) | 1,390 | — | — | 0.20 | 0.50 | — |
| 1976FM (U) | 1,802 | — | — | — | 0.50 | — |
| 1976FM (P) | 24,000 | Value: 1.00 | | | | |

**20 CENTS** **KM# 69** **Composition:** Copper-Nickel **Series:** F.A.O

| Date | Mintage | F | VF | XF | Unc | BU |
|---|---|---|---|---|---|---|
| 1976 | 3,000,000 | — | — | 0.20 | 1.00 | — |
| 1981 | — | — | — | 0.20 | 1.00 | — |
| 1982 Inc. KM#48 | — | — | — | 0.20 | 1.00 | — |
| 1984 | — | — | — | 0.20 | 1.00 | — |
| 1987 | — | — | — | 0.20 | 1.00 | — |

**20 CENTS** **KM# 73** **Composition:** Copper-Nickel

| Date | Mintage | F | VF | XF | Unc | BU |
|---|---|---|---|---|---|---|
| 1977FM (M) | 1,390 | — | — | 0.20 | 0.75 | — |
| 1977FM (U) | 597 | — | — | — | 2.00 | — |
| 1977FM (P) | 10,000 | Value: 1.00 | | | | |
| 1978FM (M) | 1,390 | — | — | 0.20 | 0.75 | — |
| 1978FM (U) | 1,282 | — | — | — | 0.75 | — |
| 1978FM (P) | 6,058 | Value: 1.50 | | | | |
| 1979FM (M) | 1,390 | — | — | 0.20 | 0.75 | — |
| 1979FM (U) | 2,608 | — | — | — | 0.75 | — |
| 1979FM (P) | 4,049 | Value: 1.50 | | | | |
| 1980FM (M) | 1,390 | — | — | 0.20 | 0.60 | — |
| 1980FM (U) | 3,668 | — | — | — | 0.60 | — |
| 1980FM (P) | 2,688 | Value: 2.00 | | | | |
| 1981FM (U) | 482 | — | — | — | 2.00 | — |
| 1981FM (P) | 1,577 | Value: 2.00 | | | | |
| 1982FM (U) | — | — | — | — | 0.60 | — |
| 1982FM (P) | — | Value: 2.00 | | | | |
| 1984FM (U) | — | — | — | — | 0.60 | — |
| 1984FM (P) | — | Value: 2.00 | | | | |

**20 CENTS** **KM# 90** **Composition:** Copper-Nickel **Subject:** World Food Day **Obverse:** JAMAICA more compact

| Date | Mintage | F | VF | XF | Unc | BU |
|---|---|---|---|---|---|---|
| 1981FM (M) | — | — | — | — | 1.50 | — |

**20 CENTS** **KM# 120** **Composition:** Copper-Nickel

| Date | Mintage | F | VF | XF | Unc | BU |
|---|---|---|---|---|---|---|
| 1981 | — | — | — | — | 0.60 | — |
| 1984 | 2,000,000 | — | — | — | 0.60 | — |
| 1985 | 2,988,000 | — | — | — | 0.60 | — |
| 1985 Proof | — | Value: 2.00 | | | | |
| 1986 | 2,530,000 | — | — | — | 0.60 | — |
| 1988 | — | — | — | — | 0.60 | — |

**20 CENTS** **KM# 104** **Composition:** Copper-Nickel **Subject:** 21st Anniversary of Independence

| Date | Mintage | F | VF | XF | Unc | BU |
|---|---|---|---|---|---|---|
| ND(1983)FM (U) | — | — | — | — | 0.60 | — |
| ND(1983)FM (P) | — | Value: 2.00 | | | | |

**25 CENTS** **KM# 49** **Composition:** Copper-Nickel **Reverse:** Streamer-tailed hummingbird

| Date | Mintage | F | VF | XF | Unc | BU |
|---|---|---|---|---|---|---|
| 1969 | 758,000 | — | — | 0.50 | 1.00 | — |
| 1969 Proof | 30,000 | Value: 1.50 | | | | |
| 1970FM (M) | 5,000 | — | — | 0.50 | 1.00 | — |
| 1970FM (P) | 12,000 | Value: 1.50 | | | | |
| 1973 | 160,000 | — | — | 0.50 | 1.00 | — |
| 1975 | 3,110,000 | — | — | 0.50 | 1.00 | — |
| 1982 | 1,000,000 | — | — | 0.50 | 1.00 | — |
| 1984 | 2,002,000 | — | — | 0.50 | 1.00 | — |
| 1985 | 1,999,000 | — | — | 0.50 | 1.00 | — |
| 1985 Proof | — | Value: 1.50 | | | | |
| 1986 | 2,635,000 | — | — | 0.50 | 1.00 | — |
| 1987 | 6,006,000 | — | — | 0.50 | 1.00 | — |
| 1987 Proof | — | Value: 1.50 | | | | |
| 1988 | 3,034,000 | — | — | 0.50 | 1.00 | — |
| 1988 Proof | — | Value: 1.50 | | | | |
| 1989 | — | — | — | 0.50 | 1.00 | — |
| 1989 Proof | — | Value: 1.50 | | | | |
| 1990 Proof | — | Value: 1.50 | | | | |

**25 CENTS** **KM# 56** **Composition:** Copper-Nickel

| Date | Mintage | F | VF | XF | Unc | BU |
|---|---|---|---|---|---|---|
| 1971FM (M) | 4,834 | — | — | 0.50 | 1.00 | — |
| 1971FM (P) | 14,000 | Value: 1.25 | | | | |
| 1972FM (M) | 8,382 | — | — | 0.50 | 1.00 | — |
| 1972FM (P) | 17,000 | Value: 1.25 | | | | |
| 1973FM (M) | 13,000 | — | — | 0.50 | 1.00 | — |
| 1973FM (P) | 28,000 | Value: 1.25 | | | | |
| 1974FM (M) | 12,000 | — | — | 0.50 | 1.00 | — |
| 1974FM (P) | 22,000 | Value: 1.25 | | | | |
| 1975FM (M) | 1,503 | — | — | 0.50 | 1.00 | — |
| 1975FM (U) | 4,683 | — | — | — | 1.00 | — |
| 1975FM (P) | 16,000 | Value: 1.25 | | | | |
| 1976FM (M) | 1,112 | — | — | 0.50 | 1.00 | — |
| 1976FM (U) | 1,802 | — | — | — | 1.00 | — |
| 1976FM (P) | 24,000 | Value: 1.25 | | | | |
| 1977FM (M) | 1,112 | — | — | 0.50 | 1.25 | — |
| 1977FM (U) | 597 | — | — | — | 3.00 | — |
| 1977FM (P) | 10,000 | Value: 1.25 | | | | |
| 1978FM (M) | 1,112 | — | — | 0.50 | 1.25 | — |
| 1978FM (U) | 1,282 | — | — | — | 1.25 | — |
| 1978FM (P) | 6,058 | Value: 2.00 | | | | |
| 1979FM (M) | 1,112 | — | — | 0.50 | 1.25 | — |
| 1979FM (U) | 2,608 | — | — | — | 1.25 | — |
| 1979FM (P) | 4,049 | Value: 2.00 | | | | |
| 1980FM (M) | 1,112 | — | — | 0.50 | 1.00 | — |
| 1980FM (U) | 3,668 | — | — | — | 1.00 | — |
| 1980FM (P) | 2,688 | Value: 3.00 | | | | |
| 1981FM (U) | 482 | — | — | — | 3.00 | — |
| 1981FM (P) | 1,577 | Value: 3.00 | | | | |
| 1982FM (U) | — | — | — | — | 1.00 | — |
| 1982FM (P) | — | Value: 3.00 | | | | |
| 1984FM (U) | — | — | — | — | 1.00 | — |
| 1984FM (P) | — | Value: 3.00 | | | | |

**25 CENTS** **KM# 105** **Composition:** Copper-Nickel **Subject:** 21st Anniversary of Independence

| Date | Mintage | F | VF | XF | Unc | BU |
|---|---|---|---|---|---|---|
| ND(1983)FM (U) | — | — | — | — | 1.50 | — |
| ND(1983)FM (P) | — | Value: 3.00 | | | | |

**25 CENTS** **KM# 154** **Composition:** Copper-Nickel **Subject:** 25th Anniversary - Bank of Jamaica

| Date | Mintage | F | VF | XF | Unc | BU |
|---|---|---|---|---|---|---|
| 1985 | — | — | — | 0.75 | 3.50 | — |

**25 CENTS** **KM# 147** **Composition:** Nickel Plated Steel **Note:** Marcus Garvey

| Date | Mintage | F | VF | XF | Unc | BU |
|---|---|---|---|---|---|---|
| 1991 | — | — | — | — | 1.00 | — |
| 1991 Proof | — | Value: 3.00 | | | | |
| 1992 | — | — | — | — | 1.00 | — |
| 1992 Proof | — | Value: 3.00 | | | | |
| 1993 | — | — | — | — | 1.00 | — |
| 1993 Proof | — | Value: 3.00 | | | | |
| 1994 | — | — | — | — | 1.00 | — |

**25 CENTS** **KM# 167** **Composition:** Copper Plated Steel

| Date | Mintage | F | VF | XF | Unc | BU |
|---|---|---|---|---|---|---|
| 1995 | — | — | — | — | 0.50 | — |
| 1996 | — | — | — | — | 0.50 | — |
| 2000 | — | — | — | — | — | — |

**50 CENTS** **KM# 65** **Composition:** Copper-Nickel **Note:** Marcus Garvey

| Date | Mintage | F | VF | XF | Unc | BU |
|---|---|---|---|---|---|---|
| 1975 | 12,010,000 | — | 0.15 | 0.50 | 1.50 | — |
| 1984 | 2,000,000 | — | 0.15 | 0.50 | 1.50 | — |
| 1985 | 2,119,000 | — | 0.15 | 0.50 | 1.50 | — |
| 1985 Proof | — | Value: 3.00 | | | | |
| 1986 | 3,404,000 | — | 0.15 | 0.50 | 1.50 | — |
| 1987 | 5,545,000 | — | 0.15 | 0.50 | 1.50 | — |
| 1988 | 10,505,000 | — | 0.15 | 0.50 | 1.50 | — |
| 1988 Proof | — | Value: 3.00 | | | | |
| 1989 | — | — | 0.15 | 0.50 | 1.50 | — |
| 1989 Proof | — | Value: 3.00 | | | | |
| 1990 Proof | — | Value: 3.00 | | | | |

**50 CENTS** **KM# 70** **Composition:** Copper-Nickel

| Date | Mintage | F | VF | XF | Unc | BU |
|---|---|---|---|---|---|---|
| 1976FM (M) | 1,112 | — | — | 0.25 | 1.50 | — |
| 1976FM (U) | 1,802 | — | — | — | 1.50 | — |
| 1976FM (P) | 24,000 | Value: 1.50 | | | | |
| 1977FM (M) | 556 | — | — | 0.50 | 3.50 | — |
| 1977FM (U) | 597 | — | — | — | 3.50 | — |
| 1977FM (P) | 10,000 | Value: 1.50 | | | | |
| 1978FM (M) | 556 | — | — | 0.50 | 3.50 | — |
| 1978FM (U) | 1,838 | — | — | — | 2.00 | — |
| 1978FM (P) | 6,058 | Value: 2.50 | | | | |
| 1979FM (M) | 556 | — | — | 0.50 | 3.50 | — |
| 1979FM (U) | 1,282 | — | — | — | 2.50 | — |
| 1979FM (P) | 4,049 | Value: 3.00 | | | | |
| 1980FM (M) | 556 | — | — | 0.50 | 3.50 | — |
| 1980FM (U) | 3,668 | — | — | — | 2.00 | — |
| 1980FM (P) | 2,688 | Value: 3.00 | | | | |
| 1981FM (U) | 482 | — | — | — | 3.50 | — |
| 1981FM (P) | 1,577 | Value: 3.00 | | | | |
| 1982FM (U) | — | — | — | — | 2.00 | — |
| 1982FM (P) | — | Value: 3.00 | | | | |
| 1984FM (U) | — | — | — | — | 2.00 | — |
| 1984FM (P) | — | Value: 3.00 | | | | |

**50 CENTS** **KM# 106** **Composition:** Copper-Nickel **Subject:** 21st Anniversary of Independence

| Date | Mintage | F | VF | XF | Unc | BU |
|---|---|---|---|---|---|---|
| ND(1983)FM (U) | — | — | — | — | 2.00 | — |
| ND(1983)FM (P) | — | Value: 4.00 | | | | |

**50 CENTS** **KM# 132** **Composition:** Copper-Nickel **Subject:** 100th Anniversary - Birth of Marcus Garvey **Obverse:** Arms **Reverse:** Bust of Marcus Garvey right

| Date | Mintage | F | VF | XF | Unc | BU |
|---|---|---|---|---|---|---|
| 1987 Proof | 500 | Value: 3.50 | | | | |

**DOLLAR** **KM# 50** **Composition:** Copper-Nickel **Note:** Sir Alexander Bustamante

| Date | Mintage | F | VF | XF | Unc | BU |
|---|---|---|---|---|---|---|
| 1969 | 47,000 | — | — | 1.00 | 3.00 | — |
| 1969 Proof | 30,000 | Value: 4.50 | | | | |
| 1970FM (M) | 5,000 | — | — | 0.30 | 3.50 | — |
| 1970FM (P) | 14,000 | Value: 4.00 | | | | |

**DOLLAR** **KM# 57** **Composition:** Copper-Nickel **Note:** Similar to KM#50.

| Date | Mintage | F | VF | XF | Unc | BU |
|---|---|---|---|---|---|---|
| 1971FM | 5,024 | — | — | 0.30 | 3.00 | — |
| 1971FM (P) | 15,000 | Value: 4.00 | | | | |
| 1972F (M) | 7,982 | — | — | 0.30 | 2.00 | — |
| 1972FM (P) | 17,000 | Value: 3.00 | | | | |
| 1973FM | 10,000 | — | — | 0.30 | 2.00 | — |
| 1973FM (P) | 28,000 | Value: 3.00 | | | | |
| 1974FM (M) | 8,961 | — | — | 0.30 | 2.00 | — |
| 1974FM (P) | 22,000 | Value: 3.00 | | | | |
| 1975FM (M) | 5,312 | — | — | 0.30 | 2.50 | — |
| 1975FM (U) | 4,683 | — | — | — | 2.50 | — |
| 1975FM (P) | 16,000 | Value: 3.00 | | | | |
| 1976FM (M) | 284 | — | — | — | 17.50 | — |
| 1976FM (U) | 1,802 | — | — | — | 4.00 | — |
| 1976FM (P) | 24,000 | Value: 2.50 | | | | |
| 1977FM (M) | 287 | — | — | — | 17.50 | — |
| 1977FM (U) | 597 | — | — | — | 8.00 | — |
| 1977FM (P) | 10,000 | Value: 4.00 | | | | |
| 1978FM (U) | 1,566 | — | — | — | 4.00 | — |
| 1978FM (P) | 6,058 | Value: 5.00 | | | | |
| 1979FM (M) | 284 | — | — | — | 17.50 | — |
| 1979FM (U) | 2,608 | — | — | — | 4.00 | — |
| 1979FM (P) | 4,049 | Value: 5.00 | | | | |

**DOLLAR** **KM# 84.1** **Composition:** Copper-Nickel **Obverse:** Arms **Reverse:** Bust of Bustamante right

| Date | Mintage | F | VF | XF | Unc | BU |
|---|---|---|---|---|---|---|
| 1980FM (M) | 284 | — | — | — | 20.00 | — |
| 1980FM (U) | 3,668 | — | — | — | 5.00 | — |
| 1980FM (P) | 2,688 | Value: 15.00 | | | | |
| 1981FM (U) | 482 | — | — | — | 8.00 | — |
| 1981FM (P) | 1,577 | Value: 20.00 | | | | |
| 1982FM (U) | — | — | — | — | 4.00 | — |
| 1982FM (P) | — | Value: 20.00 | | | | |

**DOLLAR** **KM# 91** **Composition:** Copper-Nickel **Subject:** World Food Day

| Date | Mintage | F | VF | XF | Unc | BU |
|---|---|---|---|---|---|---|
| ND(1981)FM (U) | — | — | — | — | 7.50 | — |

**DOLLAR** **KM# 96** **Composition:** Copper-Nickel **Subject:** Soccer Games

| Date | Mintage | F | VF | XF | Unc | BU |
|---|---|---|---|---|---|---|
| 1982 | — | — | — | — | 4.50 | — |

**DOLLAR** **KM# 107** **Composition:** Copper-Nickel **Subject:** 21st Anniversary of Independence

| Date | Mintage | F | VF | XF | Unc | BU |
|---|---|---|---|---|---|---|
| ND(1983)FM (U) | 3,710 | — | — | — | 7.50 | — |
| ND(1983)FM (P) | 609 | Value: 20.00 | | | | |

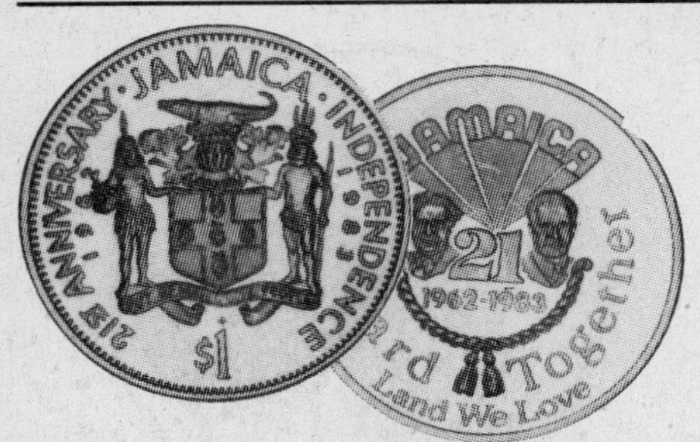


**DOLLAR** **KM# 134** **Composition:** Copper-Nickel **Subject:** 21st Anniversary of Independence

| Date | Mintage | F | VF | XF | Unc | BU |
|---|---|---|---|---|---|---|
| ND(1983)FM (P) | — | Value: 14.00 | | | | |

**DOLLAR** **KM# 113** **Composition:** Copper-Nickel **Subject:** 100th Anniversary - Birth of Bustamante

| Date | Mintage | F | VF | XF | Unc | BU |
|---|---|---|---|---|---|---|
| 1984FM (U) | — | — | — | — | 3.00 | — |
| 1984FM (P) | 268 | Value: 25.00 | | | | |

**DOLLAR** **KM# 84.2** **Composition:** Copper-Nickel **Edge:** Reeded

| Date | Mintage | F | VF | XF | Unc | BU |
|---|---|---|---|---|---|---|
| 1985 | — | — | — | — | 3.00 | — |
| 1985 Proof | — | Value: 7.50 | | | | |
| 1987 Proof | — | Value: 7.50 | | | | |
| 1988 Proof | — | Value: 7.50 | | | | |
| 1989 Proof | — | Value: 7.50 | | | | |
| 1990 | — | — | — | — | 3.00 | — |

**DOLLAR** **KM# 145** **Composition:** Nickel-Brass **Subject:** Sir Alexander Bustamante **Edge:** Reeded over "Bank of Jamaica"

| Date | Mintage | F | VF | XF | Unc | BU |
|---|---|---|---|---|---|---|
| 1990 | — | — | — | — | 2.25 | — |
| 1990 Proof | — | Value: 5.00 | | | | |
| 1991 | — | — | — | — | 2.25 | — |
| 1991 Proof | — | Value: 5.00 | | | | |
| 1992 | — | — | — | — | 2.25 | — |
| 1992 Proof | — | Value: 10.00 | | | | |
| 1993 | — | — | — | — | 2.25 | — |
| 1993 Proof | — | Value: 5.00 | | | | |
| 1994 | — | — | — | — | 2.25 | — |

**DOLLAR** **KM# 145a** **Composition:** Brass Plated Steel **Edge:** Reeded, no inscription

| Date | Mintage | F | VF | XF | Unc | BU |
|---|---|---|---|---|---|---|
| 1993 | — | — | — | — | 2.25 | — |
| 1993 Proof | 500 | Value: 15.00 | | | | |
| 1993 | — | — | — | — | 2.25 | — |
| 1994 | — | — | — | — | 2.25 | — |

**DOLLAR** **KM# 164** **Composition:** Nickel Clad Steel

| Date | Mintage | F | VF | XF | Unc | BU |
|---|---|---|---|---|---|---|
| 1994 | — | — | — | — | 1.00 | — |
| 1995 | — | — | — | — | 1.00 | — |
| 1996 | — | — | — | — | 1.00 | — |
| 2000 | — | — | — | — | — | — |

**5 DOLLARS** **KM# 58** **Weight:** 42.1500 g. **Composition:** 0.9250 Silver 1.2536 oz. ASW **Obverse:** Arms **Reverse:** Norman W. Manley

| Date | Mintage | F | VF | XF | Unc | BU |
|---|---|---|---|---|---|---|
| 1971FM | 4,072 | — | — | — | 12.00 | — |
| 1971FM (P) | 13,000 | Value: 10.00 | | | | |

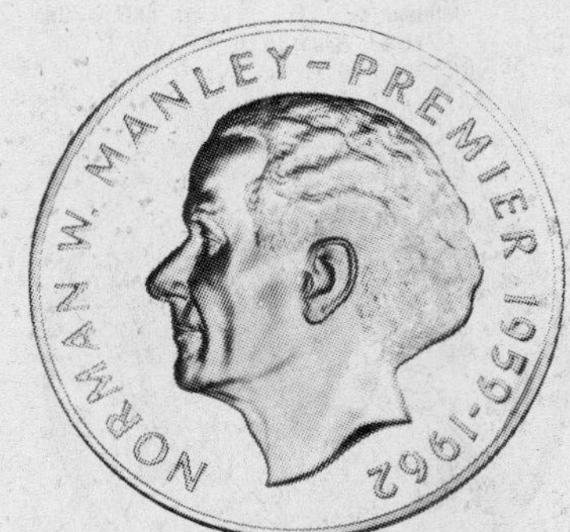


**5 DOLLARS** **KM# 59** **Weight:** 41.4800 g. **Composition:** 0.9250 Silver 1.2336 oz. ASW **Obverse:** Arms

| Date | Mintage | F | VF | XF | Unc | BU |
|---|---|---|---|---|---|---|
| 1972FM | 3,232 | — | — | — | 14.00 | — |
| 1972FM (P) | 21,000 | Value: 12.00 | | | | |
| 1973FM | 6,484 | — | — | — | 12.00 | — |
| 1973FM (P) | 36,000 | Value: 12.00 | | | | |

**5 DOLLARS** **KM# 62** **Weight:** 41.4800 g. **Composition:** 0.9250 Silver 1.2336 oz. ASW **Reverse:** Norman W. Manley

| Date | Mintage | F | VF | XF | Unc | BU |
|---|---|---|---|---|---|---|
| 1974FM (M) | 8,661 | — | — | — | 6.00 | — |
| 1975FM (M) | 65 | — | — | — | — | — |
| 1975FM (U) | 4,683 | — | — | — | 7.00 | — |
| 1976FM (M) | 56 | — | — | — | — | — |
| 1976FM (U) | 1,802 | — | — | — | 8.00 | — |
| 1977FM (M) | 56 | — | — | — | — | — |
| 1977FM (U) | 597 | — | — | — | 12.00 | — |
| 1978FM (U) | 1,338 | — | — | — | 7.00 | — |
| 1979FM (M) | 56 | — | — | — | — | — |
| 1979FM (U) | 2,608 | — | — | — | 6.00 | — |

**5 DOLLARS** **KM# 62a** **Weight:** 37.6000 g. **Composition:** 0.5000 Silver .6044 oz. ASW

| Date | Mintage | F | VF | XF | Unc | BU |
|---|---|---|---|---|---|---|
| 1974FM (P) | 22,000 | Value: 7.50 | | | | |
| 1975FM (P) | 16,000 | Value: 9.00 | | | | |
| 1976FM (P) | 23,000 | Value: 7.50 | | | | |
| 1977FM (P) | 10,000 | Value: 9.00 | | | | |
| 1978FM (P) | 6,058 | Value: 12.00 | | | | |
| 1979FM (P) | 4,049 | Value: 15.00 | | | | |

**5 DOLLARS** **KM# 85.1** **Composition:** Copper-Nickel

| Date | Mintage | F | VF | XF | Unc | BU |
|---|---|---|---|---|---|---|
| 1980FM (M) | 56 | — | — | — | — | — |
| 1980FM (U) | 3,668 | — | — | — | 15.00 | — |
| 1981FM (U) | 482 | — | — | — | 20.00 | — |
| 1982FM (U) | — | — | — | — | 7.50 | — |
| 1984FM (U) | — | — | — | — | 7.50 | — |

**5 DOLLARS** **KM# 85.1a** **Weight:** 18.5600 g. **Composition:** 0.5000 Silver .2983 oz. ASW

| Date | Mintage | F | VF | XF | Unc | BU |
|---|---|---|---|---|---|---|
| 1980FM (P) | 2,688 | Value: 15.00 | | | | |
| 1981FM (P) | 1,577 | Value: 17.00 | | | | |
| 1982FM (P) | 1,040 | Value: 17.00 | | | | |
| 1984FM (P) | 268 | Value: 30.00 | | | | |

**5 DOLLARS** **KM# 108** **Composition:** Copper-Nickel **Subject:** 21st Anniversary of Independence

| Date | Mintage | F | VF | XF | Unc | BU |
|---|---|---|---|---|---|---|
| 1983FM (U) | — | — | — | — | 8.00 | — |

**5 DOLLARS** **KM# 108a** **Weight:** 18.5600 g. **Composition:** 0.5000 Silver .2983 oz. ASW

| Date | Mintage | F | VF | XF | Unc | BU |
|---|---|---|---|---|---|---|
| 1983FM (P) | — | Value: 20.00 | | | | |

**5 DOLLARS** **KM# 85.2** **Weight:** 18.5600 g. **Composition:** 0.5000 Silver .2983 oz. ASW

| Date | Mintage | F | VF | XF | Unc | BU |
|---|---|---|---|---|---|---|
| 1985 | — | — | — | — | 30.00 | — |
| 1987 Proof | — | Value: 30.00 | | | | |
| 1988 Proof | — | Value: 30.00 | | | | |
| 1989 Proof | — | Value: 30.00 | | | | |
| 1990 Proof | 500 | Value: 30.00 | | | | |
| 1991 Proof | — | Value: 30.00 | | | | |
| 1992 Proof | — | Value: 25.00 | | | | |
| 1993 Proof | — | Value: 25.00 | | | | |

**5 DOLLARS** **KM# 157** **Composition:** Nickel Plated Steel **Subject:** Centennial - Birth of Norman Manley

| Date | Mintage | F | VF | XF | Unc | BU |
|---|---|---|---|---|---|---|
| 1993 | — | — | — | — | 2.50 | — |

**5 DOLLARS** **KM# 157a** **Weight:** 18.5000 g. **Composition:** 0.5000 Silver .2984 oz. ASW

| Date | Mintage | F | VF | XF | Unc | BU |
|---|---|---|---|---|---|---|
| 1993 Proof | Est. 2,000 | Value: 40.00 | | | | |

**5 DOLLARS** **KM# 163** **Composition:** Steel **Note:** National Hero - Norman Manley

| Date | Mintage | F | VF | XF | Unc | BU |
|---|---|---|---|---|---|---|
| 1994 | — | — | — | — | 2.50 | — |
| 1995 | — | — | — | — | 2.50 | — |
| 1996 | — | — | — | — | 2.50 | — |
| 2000 | — | — | — | — | — | — |

**10 DOLLARS** KM# 60 **Weight:** 49.2000 g. **Composition:** 0.9250 Silver 1.4632 oz. ASW **Subject:** 10th Anniversary of Independence

| Date | Mintage | F | VF | XF | Unc | BU |
|---|---|---|---|---|---|---|
| ND(1972) | 42,000 | — | — | — | 15.00 | — |
| ND(1972) Proof | 33,000 | Value: 20.00 | | | | |

**10 DOLLARS** KM# 63 **Composition:** Copper-Nickel **Obverse:** Arms

| Date | Mintage | F | VF | XF | Unc | BU |
|---|---|---|---|---|---|---|
| 1974FM (M) | 15,000 | — | — | — | 7.50 | — |

**10 DOLLARS** KM#63a **Weight:** 42.8000 g. **Composition:** 0.9250 Silver 1.2728 oz. ASW

| Date | Mintage | F | VF | XF | Unc | BU |
|---|---|---|---|---|---|---|
| 1974FM (P) | 42,000 | Value: 17.00 | | | | |

**10 DOLLARS** KM# 66 **Composition:** Copper-Nickel **Obverse:** Arms **Reverse:** Christopher Columbus

| Date | Mintage | F | VF | XF | Unc | BU |
|---|---|---|---|---|---|---|
| 1975FM (M) | 30 | — | — | — | — | — |
| 1975FM (U) | 5,758 | — | — | — | 12.00 | — |

**10 DOLLARS** KM#66a **Weight:** 42.8000 g. **Composition:** 0.9250 Silver 1.2728 oz. ASW

| Date | Mintage | F | VF | XF | Unc | BU |
|---|---|---|---|---|---|---|
| 1975FM (P) | 29,000 | Value: 17.00 | | | | |

**10 DOLLARS** KM# 71 **Composition:** Copper-Nickel **Obverse:** Arms **Reverse:** Admiral Horatio Nelson

| Date | Mintage | F | VF | XF | Unc | BU |
|---|---|---|---|---|---|---|
| 1976FM (M) | 27 | — | — | — | — | — |
| 1976FM (U) | 2,302 | — | — | — | 15.00 | — |

**10 DOLLARS** KM#71a **Weight:** 42.8000 g. **Composition:** 0.9250 Silver 1.2728 oz. ASW

| Date | Mintage | F | VF | XF | Unc | BU |
|---|---|---|---|---|---|---|
| 1976FM (P) | 31,000 | Value: 16.00 | | | | |

**10 DOLLARS** KM# 74 **Composition:** Copper-Nickel **Obverse:** Arms **Reverse:** Admiral George Rodney

| Date | Mintage | F | VF | XF | Unc | BU |
|---|---|---|---|---|---|---|
| 1977FM (M) | 27 | — | — | — | — | — |
| 1977FM (U) | 847 | — | — | — | 30.00 | — |

**10 DOLLARS** KM#74a **Weight:** 42.8000 g. **Composition:** 0.9250 Silver 1.2728 oz. ASW

| Date | Mintage | F | VF | XF | Unc | BU |
|---|---|---|---|---|---|---|
| 1977FM (P) | 14,000 | Value: 20.00 | | | | |

**10 DOLLARS** KM# 75 **Composition:** Copper-Nickel **Subject:** Jamaican Unity **Obverse:** Arms

| Date | Mintage | F | VF | XF | Unc | BU |
|---|---|---|---|---|---|---|
| 1978FM (U) | 1,559 | — | — | — | 20.00 | — |

**10 DOLLARS** KM#75a **Weight:** 42.8000 g. **Composition:** 0.9250 Silver 1.2728 oz. ASW

| Date | Mintage | F | VF | XF | Unc | BU |
|---|---|---|---|---|---|---|
| 1978FM (P) | 12,000 | Value: 25.00 | | | | |

**10 DOLLARS** KM# 79 **Composition:** Copper-Nickel **Obverse:** Arms **Reverse:** Homerus Swallowtails

| Date | Mintage | F | VF | XF | Unc | BU |
|---|---|---|---|---|---|---|
| 1979FM (M) | 27 | — | — | — | — | — |
| 1979FM (U) | 2,608 | — | — | — | 30.00 | — |

**10 DOLLARS** KM#79a **Weight:** 42.8000 g. **Composition:** 0.9250 Silver 1.2728 oz. ASW

| Date | Mintage | F | VF | XF | Unc | BU |
|---|---|---|---|---|---|---|
| 1979FM (P) | 8,308 | Value: 35.00 | | | | |

**10 DOLLARS** KM# 80 **Weight:** 22.4500 g. **Composition:** 0.9250 Silver .6677 oz. ASW **Subject:** International Year of the Child

| Date | Mintage | F | VF | XF | Unc | BU |
|---|---|---|---|---|---|---|
| 1979 Proof | 20,000 | Value: 17.00 | | | | |

**10 DOLLARS** KM#86a **Weight:** 22.4500 g. **Composition:** 0.9250 Silver .6677 oz. ASW

| Date | Mintage | F | VF | XF | Unc | BU |
|---|---|---|---|---|---|---|
| 1980FM (P) | 5,394 | Value: 25.00 | | | | |

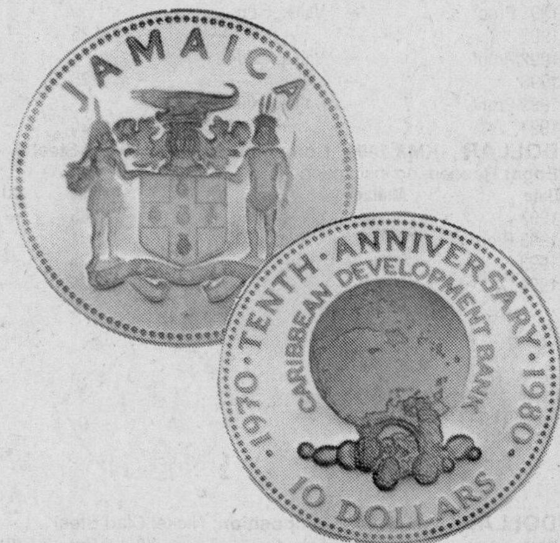


**10 DOLLARS** KM# 87 **Weight:** 30.2800 g. **Composition:** 0.5000 Silver .4868 oz. ASW **Subject:** 10th Anniversary of Caribbean Development Bank

| Date | Mintage | F | VF | XF | Unc | BU |
|---|---|---|---|---|---|---|
| ND(1980)FM (P) | 2,327 | Value: 32.00 | | | | |

**10 DOLLARS** **KM#86** **Composition:** Copper-Nickel **Note:** Streamer-tailed Hummingbirds

| Date | Mintage | F | VF | XF | Unc | BU |
|---|---|---|---|---|---|---|
| 1980FM (M) | 27 | — | — | — | — | — |
| 1980FM (U) | 5,668 | — | — | — | 28.00 | — |

**10 DOLLARS** **KM# 92** **Weight:** 28.2800 g. **Composition:** 0.9250 Silver .8410 oz. ASW **Subject:** Wedding of Prince Charles and Lady Diana

| Date | Mintage | F | VF | XF | Unc | BU |
|---|---|---|---|---|---|---|
| 1981 Proof | 40,000 | Value: 20.00 | | | | |

**10 DOLLARS** **KM# 93** **Composition:** Copper-Nickel **Reverse:** American Crocodile

| Date | Mintage | F | VF | XF | Unc | BU |
|---|---|---|---|---|---|---|
| 1981FM (U) | 804 | — | — | — | 35.00 | — |

**10 DOLLARS** **KM#93a** **Weight:** 22.4500 g. **Composition:** 0.9250 Silver .6677 oz. ASW

| Date | Mintage | F | VF | XF | Unc | BU |
|---|---|---|---|---|---|---|
| 1981FM (P) | 3,216 | Value: 40.00 | | | | |

**10 DOLLARS** **KM# 97** **Composition:** Copper-Nickel **Reverse:** Small Indian Mongoose

| Date | Mintage | F | VF | XF | Unc | BU |
|---|---|---|---|---|---|---|
| 1982FM (U) | — | — | — | — | 25.00 | — |

**10 DOLLARS** **KM#97a** **Weight:** 22.4500 g. **Composition:** 0.9250 Silver .6677 oz. ASW

| Date | Mintage | F | VF | XF | Unc | BU |
|---|---|---|---|---|---|---|
| 1982FM (P) | 1,852 | Value: 40.00 | | | | |

**10 DOLLARS** **KM# 98** **Weight:** 22.4500 g. **Composition:** 0.9250 Silver .6677 oz. ASW **Subject:** Soccer Games

| Date | Mintage | F | VF | XF | Unc | BU |
|---|---|---|---|---|---|---|
| 1982 Proof | 9,775 | Value: 16.50 | | | | |

**10 DOLLARS** **KM# 109** **Composition:** Copper-Nickel **Subject:** 21st Anniversary of Independence

| Date | Mintage | F | VF | XF | Unc | BU |
|---|---|---|---|---|---|---|
| ND(1983)FM (U) | 1,320 | — | — | — | 15.00 | — |

**10 DOLLARS** **KM# 109a** **Weight:** 22.4500 g. **Composition:** 0.9250 Silver .6677 oz. ASW

| Date | Mintage | F | VF | XF | Unc | BU |
|---|---|---|---|---|---|---|
| ND(1983)FM (P) | 1,187 | Value: 25.00 | | | | |

**10 DOLLARS** **KM#111** **Weight:** 22.4500 g. **Composition:** 0.9250 Silver .6677 oz. ASW **Subject:** Royal visit

| Date | Mintage | F | VF | XF | Unc | BU |
|---|---|---|---|---|---|---|
| 1983 | — | Value: 25.00 | | | | |

**10 DOLLARS** **KM# 114** **Composition:** Copper-Nickel **Obverse:** Arms **Reverse:** Blue Marlin

| Date | Mintage | F | VF | XF | Unc | BU |
|---|---|---|---|---|---|---|
| 1984FM (U) | — | — | — | — | 28.00 | — |

**10 DOLLARS** **KM# 114a** **Weight:** 22.4500 g. **Composition:** 0.9350 Silver .6677 oz. ASW

| Date | Mintage | F | VF | XF | Unc | BU |
|---|---|---|---|---|---|---|
| 1984FM (P) | 335 | Value: 70.00 | | | | |

**10 DOLLARS** **KM#115** **Weight:** 22.4500 g. **Composition:** 0.9350 Silver .6677 oz. ASW **Subject:** Decade for Women

| Date | Mintage | F | VF | XF | Unc | BU |
|---|---|---|---|---|---|---|
| 1984 Proof | 1,100 | Value: 30.00 | | | | |
| 1985 Proof | 610 | Value: 42.00 | | | | |

**10 DOLLARS** **KM# 125** **Weight:** 22.4500 g. **Composition:** 0.9350 Silver .6677 oz. ASW **Subject:** Summer Olympics - Sprinter

| Date | Mintage | F | VF | XF | Unc | BU |
|---|---|---|---|---|---|---|
| 1984 Proof | 10,000 | Value: 22.50 | | | | |

**10 DOLLARS** **KM# 123** **Weight:** 22.4500 g. **Composition:** 0.9250 Silver .6677 oz. ASW **Subject:** Year of Youth

| Date | Mintage | F | VF | XF | Unc | BU |
|---|---|---|---|---|---|---|
| 1985 Proof | 1,000 | Value: 40.00 | | | | |

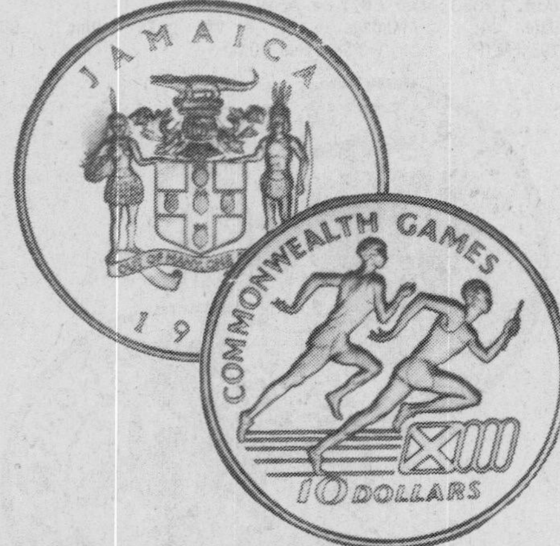


**10 DOLLARS** **KM# 121** **Weight:** 22.4500 g. **Composition:** 0.9350 Silver .6677 oz. ASW **Subject:** XIII Commonwealth Games - Edinburgh

| Date | Mintage | F | VF | XF | Unc | BU |
|---|---|---|---|---|---|---|
| 1986 | 50,000 | — | — | — | 16.50 | — |

**10 DOLLARS** **KM# 121a** **Weight:** 28.2800 g. **Composition:** 0.9250 Silver .8411 oz. ASW

| Date | Mintage | F | VF | XF | Unc | BU |
|---|---|---|---|---|---|---|
| 1986 Proof | 20,000 | Value: 22.50 | | | | |

**10 DOLLARS** **KM# 128** **Weight:** 22.4500 g. **Composition:** 0.9250 Silver .6677 oz. ASW **Subject:** 100th Anniversary - Birth of Marcus Garvey **Reverse:** Marcus Garvey

| Date | Mintage | F | VF | XF | Unc | BU |
|---|---|---|---|---|---|---|
| 1987 Proof | 1,000 | Value: 40.00 | | | | |

**10 DOLLARS** **KM# 133** **Weight:** 22.4500 g. **Composition:** 0.9250 Silver .6677 oz. ASW **Subject:** 25th Anniversary of Independence

| Date | Mintage | F | VF | XF | Unc | BU |
|---|---|---|---|---|---|---|
| 1987 Proof | Est. 500 | Value: 45.00 | | | | |

**10 DOLLARS** **KM# 138** **Composition:** Copper-Nickel **Subject:** Year of the Worker

| Date | Mintage | F | VF | XF | Unc | BU |
|---|---|---|---|---|---|---|
| 1988 | — | — | — | — | 7.00 | — |

**10 DOLLARS** **KM# 138a** **Weight:** 22.4500 g. **Composition:** 0.9250 Silver .6677 oz. ASW

| Date | Mintage | F | VF | XF | Unc | BU |
|---|---|---|---|---|---|---|
| 1988 Proof | Est. 1,000 | Value: 35.00 | | | | |

**10 DOLLARS** **KM# 140** **Composition:** Copper-Nickel **Subject:** Columbus' Discovery of the New World

| Date | Mintage | F | VF | XF | Unc | BU |
|---|---|---|---|---|---|---|
| 1989 | — | — | — | — | 7.00 | — |

**10 DOLLARS** **KM# 140a** **Weight:** 22.4500 g. **Composition:** 0.9250 Silver .6677 oz. ASW

| Date | Mintage | F | VF | XF | Unc | BU |
|---|---|---|---|---|---|---|
| 1989 Proof | Est. 5,500 | Value: 37.50 | | | | |

**10 DOLLARS** **KM# 144** **Composition:** Copper-Nickel **Subject:** Columbus' Arrival in New World

| Date | Mintage | F | VF | XF | Unc | BU |
|---|---|---|---|---|---|---|
| 1990 | — | — | — | — | 7.00 | — |

**10 DOLLARS** **KM# 144a** **Weight:** 22.4500 g. **Composition:** 0.9250 Silver .6677 oz. ASW

| Date | Mintage | F | VF | XF | Unc | BU |
|---|---|---|---|---|---|---|
| 1990 Proof | Est. 11,000 | Value: 35.00 | | | | |

**10 DOLLARS** **KM# 148** **Composition:** Copper-Nickel **Reverse:** Columbus' ship - Pinta

| Date | Mintage | F | VF | XF | Unc | BU |
|---|---|---|---|---|---|---|
| 1991 | — | — | — | — | 7.00 | — |

**10 DOLLARS** **KM# 148a** **Weight:** 22.4500 g. **Composition:** 0.9250 Silver .6677 oz. ASW

| Date | Mintage | F | VF | XF | Unc | BU |
|---|---|---|---|---|---|---|
| 1991 Proof | Est. 5,500 | Value: 40.00 | | | | |

**10 DOLLARS** **KM# 152** **Weight:** 22.4500 g. **Composition:** 0.9250 Silver .6677 oz. ASW **Subject:** 500th Anniversary of Columbus' Arrival

| Date | Mintage | F | VF | XF | Unc | BU |
|---|---|---|---|---|---|---|
| 1992 Proof | 5,500 | Value: 40.00 | | | | |

**10 DOLLARS** **KM# 155** **Weight:** 22.4500 g. **Composition:** 0.9250 Silver .6677 oz. ASW **Subject:** 40th Anniversary - Coronation of Queen Elizabeth II

| Date | Mintage | F | VF | XF | Unc | BU |
|---|---|---|---|---|---|---|
| 1993 Proof | Est. 5,500 | Value: 40.00 | | | | |

**10 DOLLARS** **KM# 161** **Weight:** 28.2800 g. **Composition:** 0.9250 Silver .8411 oz. ASW **Subject:** Royal Visit

| Date | Mintage | F | VF | XF | Unc | BU |
|---|---|---|---|---|---|---|
| 1994 Proof | — | Value: 35.00 | | | | |

**10 DOLLARS** **KM# 168** **Weight:** 20.0000 g. **Composition:** 0.5000 Silver .3215 oz. ASW **Note:** Ernest Hemingway

| Date | Mintage | F | VF | XF | Unc | BU |
|---|---|---|---|---|---|---|
| 1994 | Est. 10,000 | — | — | — | 20.00 | — |

**10 DOLLARS** **KM# 176** **Weight:** 28.2800 g. **Composition:** 0.9250 Silver .8411 oz. ASW **Subject:** Olympic Games **Reverse:** Relay Runner

| Date | Mintage | F | VF | XF | Unc | BU |
|---|---|---|---|---|---|---|
| 1996 Proof | Est. 10,000 | Value: 32.50 | | | | |

**10 DOLLARS** **KM# 181** **Composition:** Stainless Steel **Obverse:** National arms **Reverse:** Portrait of George William Gordon

| Date | Mintage | F | VF | XF | Unc | BU |
|---|---|---|---|---|---|---|
| 1999 | — | — | — | — | 3.00 | — |
| 2000 | — | — | — | — | — | — |

**20 DOLLARS** **KM# 61** **Weight:** 15.7484 g. **Composition:** 0.5000 Gold .2531 oz. AGW **Subject:** 10th Anniversary of Independence

| Date | Mintage | F | VF | XF | Unc | BU |
|---|---|---|---|---|---|---|
| ND(1972) | 30,000 | — | — | — | 90.00 | — |
| ND(1972) Proof | 20,000 | Value: 120 | | | | |

**20 DOLLARS** **KM# 182** **Ring Composition:** Brass **Center Composition:** Copper-Nickel **Obverse:** National arms, denomination above **Reverse:** Marcus Garvey **Edge:** Reeded **Size:** 23 mm.

| Date | Mintage | F | VF | XF | Unc | BU |
|---|---|---|---|---|---|---|
| 2000 | — | — | — | — | 3.00 | — |

**25 DOLLARS** **KM# 76** **Weight:** 136.0800 g. **Composition:** 0.9250 Silver 4.0473 oz. ASW **Subject:** 25th Anniversary of Coronation

| Date | Mintage | F | VF | XF | Unc | BU |
|---|---|---|---|---|---|---|
| ND(1978) | 11,000 | — | — | — | 40.00 | — |
| ND(1978) Proof | 22,000 | Value: 42.00 | | | | |

**25 DOLLARS** **KM# 81** **Weight:** 136.0800 g. **Composition:** 0.9250 Silver 4.0473 oz. ASW **Subject:** 10th Anniversary - Investiture of Prince Charles

| Date | Mintage | F | VF | XF | Unc | BU |
|---|---|---|---|---|---|---|
| ND(1979) | 16,000 | — | — | — | 42.00 | — |
| ND(1979) Proof | 25,000 | Value: 45.00 | | | | |

**25 DOLLARS** **KM# 88** **Weight:** 136.0800 g. **Composition:** 0.5000 Silver 2.1878 oz. ASW **Subject:** 1980 Olympics

| Date | Mintage | F | VF | XF | Unc | BU |
|---|---|---|---|---|---|---|
| 1980 | — | — | — | — | 50.00 | — |
| 1980 Proof | 6,969 | Value: 60.00 | | | | |

**25 DOLLARS** **KM# 94** **Weight:** 136.0800 g. **Composition:** 0.9250 Silver 4.0473 oz. ASW **Subject:** Wedding of Prince Charles and Lady Diana **Obverse:** Bust of Elizabeth II right

| Date | Mintage | F | VF | XF | Unc | BU |
|---|---|---|---|---|---|---|
| 1981 Proof | 6,450 | Value: 80.00 | | | | |

**25 DOLLARS** **KM# 99** **Weight:** 136.0800 g. **Composition:** 0.9250 Silver 4.0473 oz. ASW **Subject:** Soccer Games **Obverse:** Arms

| Date | Mintage | F | VF | XF | Unc | BU |
|---|---|---|---|---|---|---|
| 1982 Proof | 30,000 | Value: 60.00 | | | | |

**25 DOLLARS** **KM# 112** **Weight:** 136.0800 g. **Composition:** 0.9250 Silver 4.0473 oz. ASW **Subject:** Royal Visit

| Date | Mintage | F | VF | XF | Unc | BU |
|---|---|---|---|---|---|---|
| 1983 Proof | — | Value: 60.00 | | | | |

**25 DOLLARS** **KM# 119** **Weight:** 136.0800 g. **Composition:** 0.9250 Silver 4.0473 oz. ASW **Subject:** Humback Whale Protection **Obverse:** Similar to KM#112

| Date | Mintage | F | VF | XF | Unc | BU |
|---|---|---|---|---|---|---|
| 1985 Proof | 2,600 | Value: 100 | | | | |

**25 DOLLARS** **KM#142** **Weight:** 23.3300 g. **Composition:** 0.9250 Silver .6939 oz. ASW **Subject:** World Championship Soccer **Obverse:** Soccer player

| Date | Mintage | F | VF | XF | Unc | BU |
|---|---|---|---|---|---|---|
| 1990 Proof | — | Value: 30.00 | | | | |

**25 DOLLARS** **KM#150** **Weight:** 23.3300 g. **Composition:** 0.9250 Silver .6939 oz. ASW **Subject:** Columbus' Jamaican Landfall of 1494

| Date | Mintage | F | VF | XF | Unc | BU |
|---|---|---|---|---|---|---|
| 1991 Matte | 650 | — | — | — | 60.00 | — |
| 1991 Proof | Est. 25,000 | Value: 40.00 | | | | |

**25 DOLLARS** **KM# 116** **Weight:** 136.0800 g. **Composition:** 0.9250 Silver 4.0473 oz. ASW **Subject:** Summer Olympics - Sprinter

| Date | Mintage | F | VF | XF | Unc | BU |
|---|---|---|---|---|---|---|
| 1984 Proof | 3,300 | Value: 65.00 | | | | |

**25 DOLLARS** **KM# 127** **Weight:** 136.0800 g. **Composition:** 0.9250 Silver 4.0473 oz. ASW **Subject:** World Championship Soccer - Mexico

| Date | Mintage | F | VF | XF | Unc | BU |
|---|---|---|---|---|---|---|
| 1986 | — | — | — | — | 20.00 | — |

**25 DOLLARS** **KM#151** **Weight:** 23.3300 g. **Composition:** 0.9250 Silver .6939 oz. ASW **Subject:** Discovery of America - Landfall

| Date | Mintage | F | VF | XF | Unc | BU |
|---|---|---|---|---|---|---|
| 1992 Matte | 550 | — | — | — | 60.00 | — |
| 1992 Proof | Est. 25,000 | Value: 40.00 | | | | |

**25 DOLLARS** **KM#126** **Weight:** 23.4400 g. **Composition:** 0.9250 Silver .6677 oz. ASW **Subject:** Decade For Women **Note:** Mule. Denomination error for KM#115.

| Date | Mintage | F | VF | XF | Unc | BU |
|---|---|---|---|---|---|---|
| 1984 Proof | — | Value: 200 | | | | |

**25 DOLLARS** **KM#130** **Weight:** 37.7800 g. **Composition:** 0.9250 Silver 1.1236 oz. ASW **Subject:** 25th Anniversary of Independence

| Date | Mintage | F | VF | XF | Unc | BU |
|---|---|---|---|---|---|---|
| 1987 Proof | 1,900 | Value: 45.00 | | | | |

**25 DOLLARS** **KM#159** **Weight:** 23.3300 g. **Composition:** 0.9250 Silver .6939 oz. ASW **Subject:** Olympic Games **Obverse:** Bicyclists

| Date | Mintage | F | VF | XF | Unc | BU |
|---|---|---|---|---|---|---|
| 1992 Proof | 15,000 | Value: 45.00 | | | | |

**25 DOLLARS** **KM#141** **Weight:** 23.3300 g. **Composition:** 0.9250 Silver .6939 oz. ASW **Subject:** Olympics **Obverse:** Relay runners

| Date | Mintage | F | VF | XF | Unc | BU |
|---|---|---|---|---|---|---|
| 1988 Proof | Est. 15,000 | Value: 25.00 | | | | |

**25 DOLLARS** **KM# 160** **Weight:** 23.3300 g. **Composition:** 0.9250 Silver .6939 oz. ASW **Subject:** Olympic Games **Obverse:** Boxers

| Date | Mintage | F | VF | XF | Unc | BU |
|---|---|---|---|---|---|---|
| 1992 Proof | 15,000 | Value: 45.00 | | | | |

**25 DOLLARS** **KM# 165** **Weight:** 28.2000 g. **Composition:** 0.9250 Silver .8386 oz. ASW **Subject:** World Cup Soccer **Obverse:** Soccer player

| Date | Mintage | F | VF | XF | Unc | BU |
|---|---|---|---|---|---|---|
| 1994 | Est. 10,000 | — | — | — | 40.00 | — |

**25 DOLLARS** **KM# 169** **Weight:** 31.4700 g. **Composition:** 0.9250 Silver .9359 oz. ASW **Subject:** Queen Elizabeth's Wedding Anniversary and Queen Mother's Birthday

| Date | Mintage | F | VF | XF | Unc | BU |
|---|---|---|---|---|---|---|
| 1994 Proof | Est. 20,000 | Value: 32.00 | | | | |

**25 DOLLARS** **KM# 166** **Weight:** 28.2000 g. **Composition:** 0.9250 Silver .8386 oz. ASW **Subject:** 25th Anniversary - Caribbean Development Bank

| Date | Mintage | F | VF | XF | Unc | BU |
|---|---|---|---|---|---|---|
| 1995 | Est. 2,000 | — | — | — | 50.00 | — |

**25 DOLLARS** **KM# 170** **Weight:** 28.2800 g. **Composition:** 0.9250 Silver .8411 oz. ASW **Obverse:** Tycho Brahe

| Date | Mintage | F | VF | XF | Unc | BU |
|---|---|---|---|---|---|---|
| 1995 Proof | Est. 10,000 | Value: 40.00 | | | | |

**25 DOLLARS** **KM# 173** **Weight:** 28.2800 g. **Composition:** 0.9250 Silver .8411 oz. ASW **Subject:** U.N. 50th Anniversary **Obverse:** 3 children embracing

| Date | Mintage | F | VF | XF | Unc | BU |
|---|---|---|---|---|---|---|
| ND(1995) Proof | Est. 105,000 | Value: 40.00 | | | | |

**25 DOLLARS** **KM# 174** **Weight:** 28.2800 g. **Composition:** 0.9250 Silver .8411 oz. ASW **Subject:** Endangered Wildlife **Obverse:** Black-billed Amazon Parrots

| Date | Mintage | F | VF | XF | Unc | BU |
|---|---|---|---|---|---|---|
| 1995 Proof | Est. 10,000 | Value: 40.00 | | | | |

**25 DOLLARS** **KM# 177** **Weight:** 28.2800 g. **Composition:** 0.9250 Silver .8411 oz. ASW **Subject:** World Cup Soccer **Obverse:** National arms **Reverse:** Soccer player

| Date | Mintage | F | VF | XF | Unc | BU |
|---|---|---|---|---|---|---|
| 1998 Proof | Est. 10,000 | Value: 40.00 | | | | |

**25 DOLLARS** **KM# 183** **Weight:** 28.2800 g. **Composition:** 0.9250 Silver .8410 oz. ASW **Series:** Olympics **Obverse:** National arms **Reverse:** Two women hurdlers **Edge:** Reeded **Size:** 38.6 mm.

| Date | Mintage | F | VF | XF | Unc | BU |
|---|---|---|---|---|---|---|
| 2000 Proof | 5,500 | — | — | — | 50.00 | — |

**50 DOLLARS** **KM# 171** **Weight:** 28.2800 g. **Composition:** 0.9250 Silver .8411 oz. ASW **Reverse:** Robert Marley

| Date | Mintage | F | VF | XF | Unc | BU |
|---|---|---|---|---|---|---|
| 1995 Proof | 30,000 | Value: 40.00 | | | | |

**50 DOLLARS** **KM# 175** **Weight:** 7.7760 g. **Composition:** 0.5833 Gold .1458 oz. AGW **Reverse:** Queen Mother wedding portrait

| Date | Mintage | F | VF | XF | Unc | BU |
|---|---|---|---|---|---|---|
| 1995 Proof | Est. 5,000 | Value: 90.00 | | | | |

**50 DOLLARS** **KM# 179** **Weight:** 28.2800 g. **Composition:** 0.9250 Silver .8410 oz. ASW **Subject:** 50th Anniversary - University of the West Indies **Obverse:** National amrs **Reverse:** University arms

| Date | Mintage | F | VF | XF | Unc | BU |
|---|---|---|---|---|---|---|
| 1998 Proof | 20,000 | Value: 45.00 | | | | |

**50 DOLLARS** **KM# 184** **Weight:** 28.4500 g. **Composition:** 0.9250 Silver .8461 oz. ASW **Subject:** Millennium **Obverse:** National arms. **Reverse:** Family and radiant sun. **Edge:** Reeded. **Size:** 38.6 mm.

| Date | Mintage | F | VF | XF | Unc | BU |
|---|---|---|---|---|---|---|
| 2002 Proof | 5,000 | Value: 50.00 | | | | |

**100 DOLLARS** **KM# 67** **Weight:** 7.8300 g. **Composition:** 0.9000 Gold .2265 oz. AGW **Reverse:** Christopher Columbus

| Date | Mintage | F | VF | XF | Unc | BU |
|---|---|---|---|---|---|---|
| 1975FM (M) | 100 | — | — | — | 175 | — |
| 1975FM (U) | 10,000 | — | — | — | 100 | — |
| 1975FM (P) | 21,000 | Value: 100 | | | | |

**100 DOLLARS** **KM# 72** **Weight:** 7.8300 g. **Composition:** 0.9000 Gold .2265 oz. AGW **Reverse:** Admiral Horatio Nelson

| Date | Mintage | F | VF | XF | Unc | BU |
|---|---|---|---|---|---|---|
| 1976FM (M) | 100 | — | — | — | 175 | — |
| 1976FM (P) | 8,952 | Value: 110 | | | | |

**100 DOLLARS** **KM# 77** **Weight:** 11.3400 g. **Composition:** 0.9000 Gold .3281 oz. AGW **Subject:** 25th Anniversary of Coronation

| Date | Mintage | F | VF | XF | Unc | BU |
|---|---|---|---|---|---|---|
| ND(1978) | — | — | — | — | 125 | — |
| ND(1978) Proof | 5,835 | Value: 135 | | | | |

**100 DOLLARS** **KM# 82** **Weight:** 11.3400 g. **Composition:** 0.9000 Gold .3281 oz. AGW **Subject:** 10th Anniversary - Investiture of Prince Charles

| Date | Mintage | F | VF | XF | Unc | BU |
|---|---|---|---|---|---|---|
| ND(1979) Proof | 2,891 | Value: 160 | | | | |

**100 DOLLARS** **KM# 110** **Weight:** 7.1300 g. **Composition:** 0.9000 Gold .2063 oz. AGW **Subject:** 21st Anniversary of Independence

| Date | Mintage | F | VF | XF | Unc | BU |
|---|---|---|---|---|---|---|
| ND(1983)FM (P) | 638 | Value: 190 | | | | |

**100 DOLLARS** **KM# 117** **Weight:** 7.1300 g. **Composition:** 0.9000 Gold .2063 oz. AGW **Subject:** 100th Anniversary - Birth of Bustamante

| Date | Mintage | F | VF | XF | Unc | BU |
|---|---|---|---|---|---|---|
| 1984FM (P) | 531 | Value: 150 | | | | |

**100 DOLLARS** **KM# 122** **Weight:** 136.0800 g. **Composition:** 0.9250 Silver 4.0743 oz. ASW **Subject:** World Championship Soccer - Mexico **Obverse:** Similar to KM#149

| Date | Mintage | F | VF | XF | Unc | BU |
|---|---|---|---|---|---|---|
| 1986 Proof | 20,000 | Value: 55.00 | | | | |

**100 DOLLARS** **KM# 129** **Weight:** 11.3400 g. **Composition:** 0.9000 Gold .3281 oz. AGW **Subject:** 100th Anniversary - Birth of Marcus Garvey **Obverse:** National arms **Reverse:** Portrait of Garvey facing

| Date | Mintage | F | VF | XF | Unc | BU |
|---|---|---|---|---|---|---|
| 1987 Proof | 500 | Value: 250 | | | | |

**100 DOLLARS** **KM# 139** **Weight:** 136.0800 g. **Composition:** 0.9250 Silver 4.0473 oz. ASW **Obverse:** Similar to 250 Dollars KM#124 **Reverse:** Streamer-tailed Hummingbird

| Date | Mintage | F | VF | XF | Unc | BU |
|---|---|---|---|---|---|---|
| 1987 Proof | — | Value: 150 | | | | |

**100 DOLLARS** **KM# 135** **Weight:** 136.0800 g. **Composition:** 0.9250 Silver 4.0473 oz. ASW **Subject:** Summer Olympics - Relay Race **Obverse:** Similar to 10 Dollars, KM#111

| Date | Mintage | F | VF | XF | Unc | BU |
|---|---|---|---|---|---|---|
| 1988 Proof | 15,000 | Value: 85.00 | | | | |

**100 DOLLARS** **KM# 143** **Weight:** 136.0800 g. **Composition:** 0.9250 Silver 4.0473 oz. ASW **Subject:** World Championship Soccer **Obverse:** Soccer player

| Date | Mintage | F | VF | XF | Unc | BU |
|---|---|---|---|---|---|---|
| 1990 Proof | — | Value: 150 | | | | |

**100 DOLLARS** **KM# 149** **Weight:** 137.8000 g. **Composition:** 0.9250 Silver 4.0981 oz. ASW **Subject:** Olympics - Boxing **Reverse:** Boxers

| Date | Mintage | F | VF | XF | Unc | BU |
|---|---|---|---|---|---|---|
| 1992 Proof | 10,000 | Value: 95.00 | | | | |

**100 DOLLARS** **KM# 158** **Weight:** 11.3400 g. **Composition:** 0.9000 Gold .3281 oz. AGW **Subject:** Centennial - Birth of Norman Manley

| Date | Mintage | F | VF | XF | Unc | BU |
|---|---|---|---|---|---|---|
| 1993 Proof | 500 | Value: 360 | | | | |

**100 DOLLARS** **KM# 172** **Weight:** 15.9800 g. **Composition:** 0.9990 Gold .5132 oz. AGW **Reverse:** Robert Marley

| Date | Mintage | F | VF | XF | Unc | BU |
|---|---|---|---|---|---|---|
| 1995 Proof | 2,000 | Value: 300 | | | | |

**100 DOLLARS** KM# 178 **Weight:** 15.9800 g. **Composition:** 0.9990 Gold .5132 oz. AGW **Subject:** World Cup Soccer **Obverse:** National arms **Reverse:** Soccer player

| Date | Mintage | F | VF | XF | Unc | BU |
|---|---|---|---|---|---|---|
| 1998 Proof | Est. 500 | Value: 450 | | | | |

**100 DOLLARS** KM# 180 **Weight:** 15.9700 g. **Composition:** 0.9167 Gold .4706 oz. AGW **Subject:** 50th Anniversary - University of the West Indies **Obverse:** National arms **Reverse:** University arms

| Date | Mintage | F | VF | XF | Unc | BU |
|---|---|---|---|---|---|---|
| 1998 Proof | 1,000 | Value: 400 | | | | |

**250 DOLLARS** KM# 78 **Weight:** 43.2200 g. **Composition:** 0.9000 Gold 1.2507 oz. AGW **Subject:** 25th Anniversary of Coronation

| Date | Mintage | F | VF | XF | Unc | BU |
|---|---|---|---|---|---|---|
| ND(1978) Proof | 3,005 | Value: 525 | | | | |

**250 DOLLARS** KM# 83 **Weight:** 43.2200 g. **Composition:** 0.9000 Gold 1.2507 oz. AGW **Subject:** 10th Anniversary - Investiture of Prince Charles

| Date | Mintage | F | VF | XF | Unc | BU |
|---|---|---|---|---|---|---|
| ND(1979) Proof | 1,650 | Value: 600 | | | | |

**250 DOLLARS** KM# 89 **Weight:** 11.3400 g. **Composition:** 0.9000 Gold .3281 oz. AGW **Subject:** 1980 Olympics

| Date | Mintage | F | VF | XF | Unc | BU |
|---|---|---|---|---|---|---|
| 1980 Proof | 902 | Value: 250 | | | | |

**250 DOLLARS** KM# 95 **Weight:** 11.3400 g. **Composition:** 0.9000 Gold .3281 oz. AGW **Subject:** Wedding of Prince Charles and Lady Diana **Obverse:** Elizabeth II

| Date | Mintage | F | VF | XF | Unc | BU |
|---|---|---|---|---|---|---|
| 1981 Proof | 1,491 | Value: 240 | | | | |

**250 DOLLARS** KM# 100 **Weight:** 11.3400 g. **Composition:** 0.9000 Gold .3281 oz. AGW **Subject:** Soccer Games

| Date | Mintage | F | VF | XF | Unc | BU |
|---|---|---|---|---|---|---|
| 1982 Proof | 694 | Value: 270 | | | | |

**250 DOLLARS** KM# 124 **Weight:** 11.3200 g. **Composition:** 0.9000 Gold .3275 oz. AGW **Subject:** Royal Visit

| Date | Mintage | F | VF | XF | Unc | BU |
|---|---|---|---|---|---|---|
| 1983 Proof | 5,000 | Value: 150 | | | | |

**250 DOLLARS** KM# 118 **Weight:** 11.3400 g. **Composition:** 0.9000 Gold .3281 oz. AGW **Subject:** Decade for Women

| Date | Mintage | F | VF | XF | Unc | BU |
|---|---|---|---|---|---|---|
| 1984 Proof | 559 | Value: 250 | | | | |

**250 DOLLARS** KM# 131 **Weight:** 16.0000 g. **Composition:** 0.9000 Gold .4630 oz. AGW **Subject:** 25th Anniversary of Independence

| Date | Mintage | F | VF | XF | Unc | BU |
|---|---|---|---|---|---|---|
| 1987 Proof | 250 | Value: 400 | | | | |

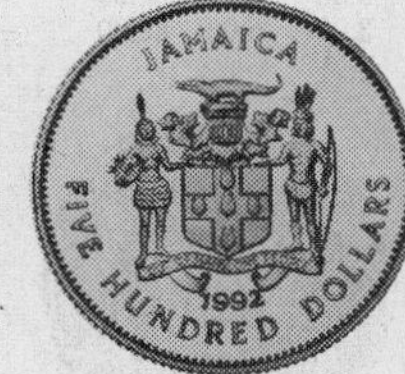

**250 DOLLARS** KM# 153 **Weight:** 11.3400 g. **Composition:** 0.9000 Gold .3281 oz. AGW **Subject:** Columbus Quincentennial **Reverse:** 500 on ships's sail

| Date | Mintage | F | VF | XF | Unc | BU |
|---|---|---|---|---|---|---|
| 1992 Proof | 500 | Value: 500 | | | | |

**250 DOLLARS** KM# 156 **Weight:** 11.3400 g. **Composition:** 0.9000 Gold .3281 oz. AGW **Subject:** 40th Anniversary - Coronation of Queen Elizabeth **Obverse:** Portrait of the queen **Reverse:** Arms

| Date | Mintage | F | VF | XF | Unc | BU |
|---|---|---|---|---|---|---|
| 1993 Proof | Est. 500 | Value: 480 | | | | |

**250 DOLLARS** KM# 162 **Weight:** 47.5400 g. **Composition:** 0.9170 Gold 1.4017 oz. AGW **Subject:** Royal Visit **Obverse:** Coat of arms **Reverse:** Drummer on island map with yacht at right

| Date | Mintage | F | VF | XF | Unc | BU |
|---|---|---|---|---|---|---|
| 1994 Proof | 100 | Value: 1,000 | | | | |

## PIEFORTS

| KM# | Date | Mintage | Identification | Mkt Val |
|---|---|---|---|---|
| P1 | 1979 | — | 10 Dollars. Silver. KM#80 | 65.00 |
| P2 | 1983 | 32 | 250 Dollars. 0.9000 Gold. Design like 10 Dollars, KM#80 | 1,250 |

## MINT SETS

| KM# | Date | Mintage | Identification | Issue Price | Mkt Val |
|---|---|---|---|---|---|
| MS1 | 1969 (2) | 30,000 | KM#41-42 | 0.90 | 2.00 |
| MS2 | 1969 (6) | 30,000 | KM#45-50 | — | 6.50 |
| MS3 | 1970 (6) | 5,000 | KM#45-50 | 16.00 | 6.50 |
| MS4 | 1971 (7) | 4,072 | KM#51, 53-58 | 19.50 | 17.50 |
| MS5 | 1971 (6) | 4,834 | KM#51, 53-57 | — | 8.00 |
| MS6 | 1972 (7) | 2,982 | KM#51, 53-57, 59 | 19.75 | 25.00 |
| MS7 | 1972 (6) | 4,000 | KM#51, 53-57 | 10.00 | 7.00 |
| MS8 | 1973 (7) | 6,404 | KM#51, 53-57, 59 | 19.75 | 20.00 |
| MS9 | 1973 (6) | 3,000 | KM#51, 53-57 | 9.95 | 8.00 |
| MS10 | 1974 (8) | 8,361 | KM#51, 53-57, 59, 63 | 25.00 | 20.00 |
| MS11 | 1975 (8) | 4,683 | KM#51, 53-57, 62, 66 | 27.50 | 20.00 |
| MS12 | 1976 (9) | 1,802 | KM#53-57, 62, 68, 70, 71 | 27.50 | 27.50 |
| MS13 | 1977 (9) | 597 | KM#53-54, 56-57, 62, 68, 70, 73, 74 | 27.50 | 40.00 |
| MS14 | 1978 (9) | 1,282 | KM#53-54, 56-57, 62, 68, 70, 73, 75 | 27.50 | 40.00 |
| MS15 | 1979 (9) | 2,608 | KM#53-54, 56-57, 62, 68, 70, 73, 79 | 27.50 | 40.00 |
| MS16 | 1980 (9) | 3,668 | KM#53-54, 56, 68, 70, 73, 84.1-86 | 30.00 | 30.00 |
| MS17 | 1981 (9) | 482 | KM#53-54, 56, 68, 70, 73, 84.1, 85.1, 93 | 31.00 | 45.00 |
| MS18 | 1982 (9) | — | KM#53-54, 56, 68, 70, 73, 84.1-85.1, 97 | 31.00 | 40.00 |
| MS19 | 1983 (9) | 1,210 | KM#101-109 | 37.00 | 40.00 |
| MS20 | 1984 (9) | — | KM#53-54, 56, 68, 70, 73, 85.1, 113-114 | 37.00 | 35.00 |
| MS21 | 2000 (7) | — | KM#64, 146.2, 163, 164, 167, 181-182 | 25.00 | 27.50 |

## PROOF SETS

| KM# | Date | Mintage | Identification | Issue Price | Mkt Val |
|---|---|---|---|---|---|
| PS1 | 1918C (3) | — | KM#24-26 | — | 600 |
| PS2 | 1928 (3) | 20 | KM#24-26 | — | 600 |
| PS3 | 1937 (3) | — | KM#27-29 | — | 550 |
| PS4 | 1969 (6) | 8,530 | KM#45-50 | 15.00 | 10.00 |
| PS5 | 1969 (2) | 5,000 | KM#41-42 | 2.70 | 7.00 |
| PS6 | 1970 (6) | 11,540 | KM#45-50 | 15.00 | 10.00 |
| PS7 | 1971 (7) | 12,739 | KM#51, 53-58 | 26.50 | 15.00 |
| PS8 | 1971 (6) | 1,048 | KM#51, 53-57 | 15.00 | 10.00 |
| PS9 | 1972 (7) | 16,967 | KM#51, 53-57, 59 | 27.50 | 16.00 |
| PS10 | 1973 (7) | 28,405 | KM#51, 53-57, 59 | 27.50 | 15.00 |
| PS11 | 1974 (8) | 22,026 | KM#51, 53-57, 62a-63a | 50.00 | 30.00 |
| PS12 | 1975 (8) | 15,638 | KM#51, 53-57, 62a, 66a | 55.00 | 35.00 |
| PS13 | 1976 (9) | 22,900 | KM#53-57, 62a, 68, 70, 71a | 55.00 | 40.00 |
| PS14 | 1976 (7) | 1,503 | KM#53-57, 68, 70 | 22.50 | 17.00 |
| PS15 | 1977 | 10,054 | KM#53-54, 56-57, 62a, 68, 70, 73, 74a | 55.00 | 35.00 |
| PS16 | 1978 (9) | 6,058 | KM#53-54, 56-57, 62a, 68, 70, 73, 75a | 59.00 | 40.00 |
| PS17 | 1979 (9) | 4,049 | KM#53-54, 56-57, 62a, 68, 70, 73, 79a | 59.00 | 50.00 |
| PS18 | 1980 (9) | 2,688 | KM#53-54, 56, 68, 70, 73, 84.1, 85.1a, 86a | 90.00 | 60.00 |
| PS19 | 1981 (9) | 1,577 | KM#53-54, 56, 68, 70, 73, 84.1, 85.1a, 93a | 92.00 | 80.00 |
| PS20 | 1982 (9) | — | KM#53-54, 56, 68, 70, 73, 84.1, 85.1a, 97a | 92.00 | 75.00 |
| PS21 | 1983 (9) | 1,210 | KM#101-107, 108a-109a | — | 85.00 |
| PS22 | 1984 (9) | — | KM#53-54, 56, 68, 70, 73, 85.1a, 113, 114a | 92.00 | 75.00 |
| PS23 | 1985 (9) | — | KM#46-47, 49, 64-65, 84.2-85.2, 120, 123 | — | 75.00 |
| PS24 | 1987 (9) | 500 | KM#46-49, 64, 84.2, 85.2, 132, 133 | 90.00 | 75.00 |
| PS25 | 1988 (9) | 500 | KM#46-49, 64-65, 84.2, 85.2, 138a | 115 | 80.00 |
| PS26 | 1989 (9) | 500 | KM#46-49, 64-65, 84.2, 85.2, 140a | 120 | 80.00 |
| PS27 | 1990 (9) | 500 | KM#46a-47a, 48-49, 64-65, 85.2, 144, 145 | 125 | 125 |
| PS28 | 1991 (7) | 500 | KM#46a, 64, 85.2, 145, 146-148 | — | 100 |
| PS29 | 1992 (7) | 500 | KM#46a, 64, 85.2, 145-147, 152 | 138 | 140 |
| PS30 | 1993 (7) | 500 | KM#46a, 64, 85.2, 145a, 146-147, 155 | — | 140 |
| PS31 | 2000 (8) | 500 | KM#64, 146.2, 163, 164, 167, 181-183 | 99.00 | 100 |

## JAPAN

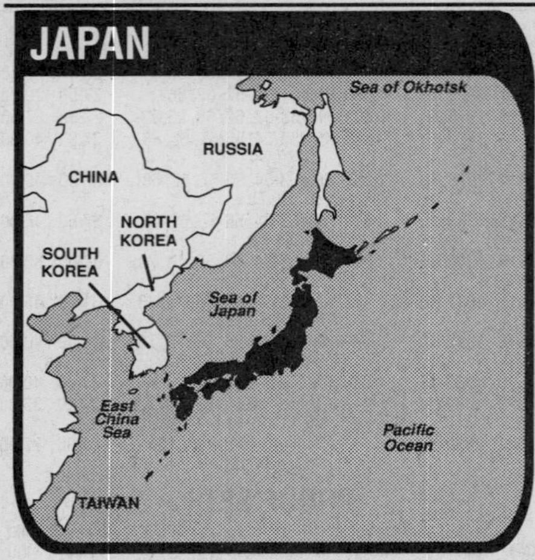


Japan, a constitutional monarchy situated off the east coast of Asia, has an area of 145,809 sq. mi. (377,835 sq. km.) and a population of 123.2 million. Capital: Tokyo. Japan, one of the major industrial nations of the world, exports machinery, motor vehicles, electronics and chemicals.

Japan, founded (so legend holds) in 660 B.C. by a direct descendant of the Sun Goddess, was first brought into contact with the west by a storm-blown Portuguese ship in 1542. European traders and missionaries proceeded to enlarge the contact until the Shogunate, sensing a military threat in the foreign presence, expelled all foreigners and restricted relations with the outside world in the 17th century. After Commodore Perry's U.S. flotilla visited in 1854, Japan rapidly industrialized, abolished the Shogunate and established a parliamentary form of government, and by the end of the 19th century achieved the status of a modern economic and military power. A series of wars with China and Russia, and participation with the allies in World War I, enlarged Japan territorially but brought its interests into conflict with the Far Eastern interests of the United States, Britain and the Netherlands, causing it to align with the Axis Powers for the pursuit of World War II. After its defeat in World War II, General Douglas MacArthur forced Japan to renounce military aggression as a political instrument, and he instituted constitutional democratic self-government. Japan quickly gained a position as an economic world power.

Japanese coinage of concern to this catalog includes those issued for the Ryukyu Islands (also called Liuchu), a chain of islands extending southwest from Japan toward Taiwan (Formosa), before the Japanese government converted the islands into a prefecture under the name Okinawa. Many of the provinces of Japan issued their own definitive coinage under the Shogunate.

**RULERS** Emperors

Years 1-45 明治 or 治明

Yoshihito (Taisho), 1912-1926

Years 1-15 大正 or 正大

Hirohito (Showa), 1926-1989

Years 1-64 昭和 or 和昭

Akihito (Heisei), 1989

Years 1 - 平成

**NOTE:** The personal name of the emperor is followed by the name that he chose for his regnal era.

**MONETARY SYSTEM** Commencing 1870

10 Rin = 1 Sen

100 Sen = 1 Yen

**MONETARY UNITS**

Rin 厘

Sen 銭 Yen 円 or 圓 or 圓

**DATING**

# EMPIRE

## DECIMAL COINAGE

**5 RIN Y# 41 Composition:** Bronze **Ruler:** Yoshihito (Taisho)

| Date | Mintage | F | VF | XF | Unc | BU |
|---|---|---|---|---|---|---|
| Yr.5(1916) | 8,000,000 | 0.50 | 2.00 | 3.50 | 10.00 | — |
| Yr.6(1917) | 5,287,000 | 0.50 | 2.00 | 3.50 | 10.00 | — |
| Yr.7(1918) | 11,661,000 | 0.25 | 1.00 | 2.50 | 7.50 | — |
| Yr.8(1919) | 17,130,000 | 0.25 | 1.00 | 2.50 | 7.50 | — |

**SEN Y# 20 Composition:** Bronze **Ruler:** Mutsuhito (Meiji)

| Date | Mintage | F | VF | XF | Unc | BU |
|---|---|---|---|---|---|---|
| Yr.34(1901) | 5,555,000 | 2.00 | 4.50 | 16.00 | 65.00 | — |
| Yr.35(1902) | 4,444,000 | 5.00 | 10.00 | 25.00 | 145 | — |
| Yr.39(1906) | — | — | — | — | — | — |
| **Note:** None struck for circulation | | | | | | |
| Yr.42(1909) | — | — | — | — | — | — |
| **Note:** None struck for circulation | | | | | | |

**SEN Y# 35 Composition:** Bronze **Ruler:** Yoshihito (Taisho)

| Date | Mintage | F | VF | XF | Unc | BU |
|---|---|---|---|---|---|---|
| Yr.2(1913) | 15,000,000 | 2.00 | 3.00 | 5.00 | 32.00 | — |
| Yr.3(1914) | 10,000,000 | 2.00 | 3.00 | 5.00 | 32.00 | — |
| Yr.4(1915) | 13,000,000 | 2.00 | 3.00 | 5.00 | 32.00 | — |

**SEN Y# 42 Composition:** Bronze

| Date | Mintage | F | VF | XF | Unc | BU |
|---|---|---|---|---|---|---|
| Yr.5(1916) | 19,193,000 | 0.50 | 1.00 | 1.50 | 30.00 | — |
| Yr.6(1917) | 27,183,000 | 0.25 | 0.50 | 1.00 | 25.00 | — |
| Yr.7(1918) | 121,794,000 | 0.25 | 0.50 | 1.00 | 9.50 | — |
| Yr.8(1919) | 209,959,000 | 0.15 | 0.25 | 0.50 | 4.50 | — |
| Yr.9(1920) | 118,829,000 | 0.15 | 0.25 | 0.50 | 4.50 | — |
| Yr.10(1921) | 252,440,000 | 0.15 | 0.25 | 0.50 | 4.50 | — |
| Yr.11(1922) | 253,210,000 | 0.15 | 0.25 | 0.50 | 4.50 | — |
| Yr.12(1923) | 155,500,000 | 0.15 | 0.25 | 0.50 | 5.50 | — |
| Yr.13(1924) | 106,250,000 | 0.15 | 0.25 | 0.50 | 4.50 | — |

**SEN Y# 47 Composition:** Bronze **Ruler:** Hirohito (Showa)

| Date | Mintage | F | VF | XF | Unc | BU |
|---|---|---|---|---|---|---|
| Yr.2(1927) | 26,500,000 | 1.50 | 2.50 | 3.50 | 32.00 | — |
| Yr.4(1929) | 3,000,000 | 3.50 | 7.50 | 15.00 | 45.00 | — |
| Yr.5(1930) | 5,000,000 | 2.50 | 4.50 | 7.50 | 70.00 | — |
| Yr.6(1931) | 25,001,000 | 0.25 | 0.50 | 1.50 | 12.50 | — |
| Yr.7(1932) | 35,066,000 | 0.25 | 0.50 | 1.50 | 9.00 | — |
| Yr.8(1933) | 38,936,000 | 0.15 | 0.25 | 0.50 | 2.50 | — |
| Yr.9(1934) | 100,004,000 | 0.15 | 0.25 | 0.50 | 2.50 | — |
| Yr.10(1935) | 200,009,000 | 0.15 | 0.25 | 0.50 | 1.50 | — |
| Yr.11(1936) | 109,170,000 | 0.15 | 0.25 | 0.50 | 1.50 | — |
| Yr.12(1937) | 133,196,000 | 0.15 | 0.25 | 0.50 | 1.50 | — |
| Yr.13(1938) | 87,649,000 | 0.15 | 0.25 | 0.50 | 1.50 | — |

**SEN Y# 55 Composition:** Bronze

| Date | Mintage | F | VF | XF | Unc | BU |
|---|---|---|---|---|---|---|
| Yr.13(1938) | 113,605,000 | 0.15 | 0.25 | 0.50 | 1.50 | — |

四 
 四

**SEN Y# 56 Composition:** Aluminum

| Date | Mintage | F | VF | XF | Unc | BU |
|---|---|---|---|---|---|---|
| Yr.13(1938) | 45,502,000 | — | 0.25 | 0.50 | 8.50 | — |
| Yr.14(1939) Type A | 444,602,000 | — | 0.50 | 0.75 | 12.00 | — |
| Yr.14(1939) Type B | Inc. above | — | 0.25 | 0.50 | 1.50 | — |
| Yr.15(1940) | 601,110,000 | — | 0.25 | 0.50 | 1.50 | — |

**SEN Y# 59 Weight:** 0.6500 g. **Composition:** Aluminum

| Date | Mintage | F | VF | XF | Unc | BU |
|---|---|---|---|---|---|---|
| Yr.16(1941) | 1,016,620,000 | — | 0.15 | 0.25 | 0.50 | — |
| Yr.17(1942) | 119,709,000 | — | 0.15 | 0.25 | 0.75 | — |
| Yr.18(1943) | 1,163,949,000 | — | 0.15 | 0.25 | 0.50 | — |

**SEN Y# 59a Weight:** 0.5500 g. **Composition:** Aluminum
**Note:** Thinner

| Date | Mintage | F | VF | XF | Unc | BU |
|---|---|---|---|---|---|---|
| Yr.18(1943) | 627,191,000 | — | 0.15 | 0.50 | 1.00 | — |

**SEN KM# 110 Composition:** Reddish Brown Baked Clay

| Date | Mintage | F | VF | XF | Unc | BU |
|---|---|---|---|---|---|---|
| ND(1945) | — | 4.00 | 6.00 | 15.00 | 20.00 | — |

**Note:** Circulated unofficially for a few days before the end of WWII in Central Japan; varieties of color exist

**5 SEN Y# 21 Composition:** Copper-Nickel **Ruler:** Mutsuhito (Meiji)

| Date | Mintage | F | VF | XF | Unc | BU |
|---|---|---|---|---|---|---|
| Yr.34(1901) | 7,124,000 | 7.50 | 15.00 | 25.00 | 125 | — |
| Yr.35(1902) | 2,448,000 | 12.00 | 25.00 | 40.00 | 285 | — |
| Yr.36(1903) | 372,000 | 150 | 250 | 400 | 2,500 | — |
| Yr.37(1904) | 1,628,000 | 20.00 | 35.00 | 75.00 | 400 | — |
| Yr.38(1905) | 6,000,000 | 5.00 | 10.00 | 17.50 | 115 | — |
| Yr.39(1906) | — | — | — | — | — | — |

**Note:** None struck for circulation; Spink-Taisei Hong Kong sale 9-91 BU realized $10,000

**5 SEN** **Y# 43** **Composition:** Copper-Nickel **Ruler:** Yoshihito (Taisho)

| Date | Mintage | F | VF | XF | Unc | BU |
|---|---|---|---|---|---|---|
| Yr.6(1917) | 6,781,000 | 7.50 | 15.00 | 25.00 | 50.00 | — |
| Yr.7(1918) | 9,131,000 | 5.00 | 10.00 | 20.00 | 35.00 | — |
| Yr.8(1919) | 44,980,000 | 3.00 | 6.00 | 12.00 | 20.00 | — |
| Yr.9(1920) | 21,906,000 | 3.00 | 6.00 | 12.00 | 20.00 | — |

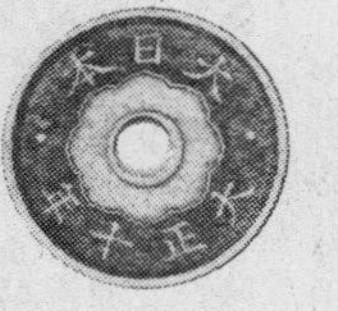

**5 SEN** **Y# 44** **Composition:** Copper-Nickel **Ruler:** Yoshihito (Taisho)

| Date | Mintage | F | VF | XF | Unc | BU |
|---|---|---|---|---|---|---|
| Yr.9(1920) | 100,455,000 | 0.35 | 0.75 | 2.00 | 15.00 | — |
| Yr.10(1921) | 133,020,000 | 0.25 | 0.50 | 1.50 | 5.00 | — |
| Yr.11(1922) | 163,908,000 | 0.25 | 0.50 | 1.50 | 5.00 | — |
| Yr.12(1923) | 80,000,000 | 0.25 | 0.50 | 1.50 | 5.00 | — |

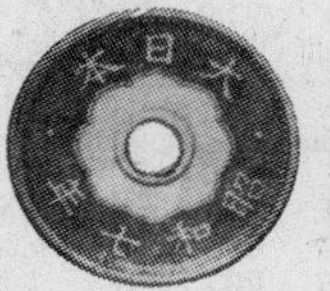

**5 SEN** **Y# 48** **Composition:** Copper-Nickel **Ruler:** Hirohito (Showa)

| Date | Mintage | F | VF | XF | Unc | BU |
|---|---|---|---|---|---|---|
| Yr.7(1932) | 8,000,000 | 0.25 | 0.50 | 1.75 | 7.00 | — |

**5 SEN** **Y# 53** **Composition:** Nickel **Ruler:** Hirohito (Showa)

| Date | Mintage | F | VF | XF | Unc | BU |
|---|---|---|---|---|---|---|
| Yr.8(1933) | 16,150,000 | 0.50 | 1.50 | 3.00 | 5.50 | — |
| Yr.9(1934) | 33,851,000 | 0.50 | 1.00 | 2.00 | 4.50 | — |
| Yr.10(1935) | 13,680,000 | 1.00 | 2.00 | 3.50 | 7.50 | — |
| Yr.11(1936) | 36,321,000 | 0.50 | 1.00 | 2.00 | 4.50 | — |
| Yr.12(1937) | 44,402,000 | 0.50 | 1.00 | 2.00 | 5.50 | — |
| Yr.13(1938) 4 known | 10,000,000 | — | — | — | — | — |

**Note:** Almost entire mintage remelted

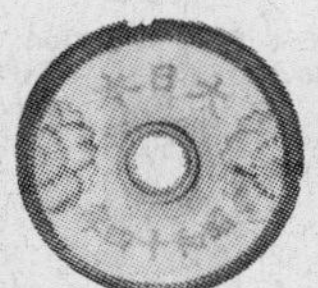
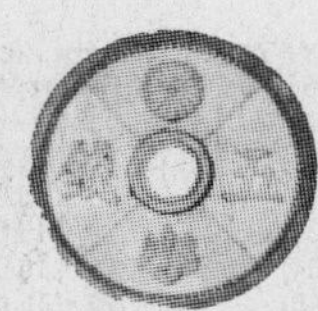

**5 SEN** **Y# 57** **Composition:** Aluminum-Bronze **Ruler:** Hirohito (Showa)

| Date | Mintage | F | VF | XF | Unc | BU |
|---|---|---|---|---|---|---|
| Yr.13(1938) | 400,001,000 | 0.50 | 1.00 | 1.50 | 4.00 | — |
| Yr.14(1939) | 97,903,000 | 0.50 | 1.00 | 1.50 | 4.00 | — |
| Yr.15(1940) | 34,501,000 | 0.50 | 1.00 | 1.50 | 5.00 | — |

**5 SEN** **Y# 60** **Weight:** 1.2000 g. **Composition:** Aluminum **Ruler:** Hirohito (Showa) **Note:** Variety I

| Date | Mintage | F | VF | XF | Unc | BU |
|---|---|---|---|---|---|---|
| Yr.15(1940) | 167,638,000 | — | 0.25 | 1.00 | 3.00 | — |
| Yr.16(1941) | 242,361,000 | — | 0.25 | 0.75 | 2.25 | — |

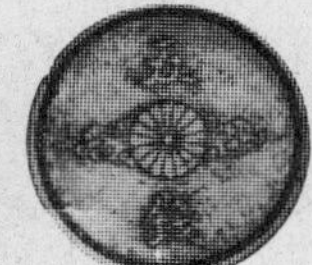

**5 SEN** **Y# 60a** **Weight:** 1.0000 g. **Composition:** Aluminum **Ruler:** Hirohito (Showa) **Note:** Variety 2

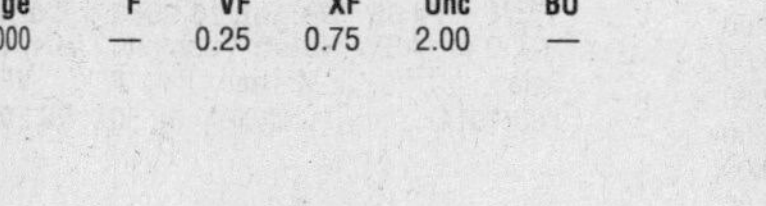

| Date | Mintage | F | VF | XF | Unc | BU |
|---|---|---|---|---|---|---|
| Yr.16(1941) | 478,023,000 | 1.50 | 3.50 | 7.50 | 37.50 | — |
| Yr.17(1942) | Inc. above | — | 0.25 | 0.75 | 1.75 | — |

**5 SEN** **Y# 60b** **Weight:** 0.8000 g. **Composition:** Aluminum **Ruler:** Hirohito (Showa) **Note:** Variety 3

| Date | Mintage | F | VF | XF | Unc | BU |
|---|---|---|---|---|---|---|
| Yr.18(1943) | 276,493,000 | — | 0.25 | 0.75 | 2.00 | — |

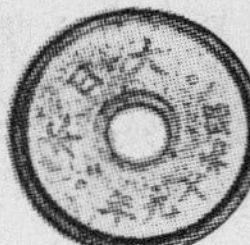
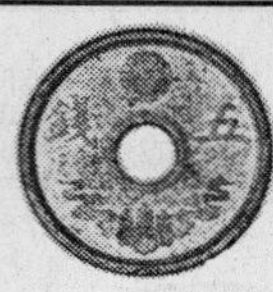

**5 SEN** **Y# 63** **Composition:** Tin-Zinc **Ruler:** Hirohito (Showa)

| Date | Mintage | F | VF | XF | Unc | BU |
|---|---|---|---|---|---|---|
| Yr.19(1944) | 70,003,000 | — | 0.25 | 0.75 | 2.50 | — |

**5 SEN** **Y# 65** **Composition:** Tin-Zinc **Ruler:** Hirohito (Showa)

| Date | Mintage | F | VF | XF | Unc | BU |
|---|---|---|---|---|---|---|
| Yr.20(1945) | 180,008,000 | — | 0.50 | 1.25 | 3.50 | — |
| Yr.21(1946) | Inc. above | — | 0.50 | 1.25 | 3.50 | — |

**5 SEN** **KM# 111** **Composition:** Reddish Brown Baked Clay **Ruler:** Hirohito (Showa)

| Date | Mintage | F | VF | XF | Unc | BU |
|---|---|---|---|---|---|---|
| Yr.201945 | — | 75.00 | 125 | 225 | 300 | — |

**Note:** Not issued for circulation; varieties of color exist

**10 SEN** **Y# 23** **Weight:** 2.6957 g. **Composition:** 0.8000 Silver .0693 oz. ASW **Ruler:** Mutsuhito (Meiji)

| Date | Mintage | F | VF | XF | Unc | BU |
|---|---|---|---|---|---|---|
| Yr.34(1901) | 797,000 | 125 | 175 | 250 | 800 | — |
| Yr.35(1902) | 1,204,000 | 100 | 150 | 200 | 775 | — |
| Yr.37(1904) | 11,106,000 | 4.50 | 7.50 | 10.00 | 35.00 | — |
| Yr.38(1905) | 34,182,000 | 4.50 | 7.50 | 10.00 | 35.00 | — |
| Yr.39(1906) | 4,710,000 | 4.50 | 7.50 | 10.00 | 35.00 | — |

**10 SEN** **Y# 29** **Weight:** 2.2500 g. **Composition:** 0.7200 Silver .0521 oz. ASW **Ruler:** Mutsuhito (Meiji)

| Date | Mintage | F | VF | XF | Unc | BU |
|---|---|---|---|---|---|---|
| Yr.40(1907) | 12,000,000 | 2.50 | 5.00 | 10.00 | 65.00 | — |
| Yr.41(1908) | 12,273,000 | 2.50 | 5.00 | 10.00 | 60.00 | — |
| Yr.42(1909) | 20,279,000 | 1.00 | 3.50 | 5.00 | 27.50 | — |
| Yr.43(1910) | 20,339,000 | 1.00 | 3.50 | 5.00 | 25.00 | — |
| Yr.44(1911) | 38,729,000 | 1.00 | 3.50 | 5.00 | 27.50 | — |
| Yr.45(1912) | 10,755,000 | 1.00 | 3.50 | 5.00 | 30.00 | — |

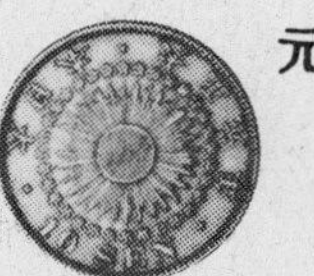
元

**10 SEN** **Y# 36.1** **Weight:** 2.2500 g. **Composition:** 0.7200 Silver .0521 oz. ASW **Ruler:** Yoshihito (Taisho) **Obverse:** Japanese character "first"

| Date | Mintage | F | VF | XF | Unc | BU |
|---|---|---|---|---|---|---|
| Yr.1(1912) | 10,344,000 | 2.50 | 5.00 | 10.00 | 60.00 | — |

**10 SEN** **Y# 36.2** **Weight:** 2.2500 g. **Composition:** 0.7200 Silver **Ruler:** Yoshihito (Taisho)

| Date | Mintage | F | VF | XF | Unc | BU |
|---|---|---|---|---|---|---|
| Yr.2(1913) | 13,321,000 | 1.00 | 2.50 | 5.00 | 12.00 | — |
| Yr.3(1914) | 10,325,000 | 1.00 | 2.50 | 5.00 | 12.00 | — |
| Yr.4(1915) | 16,836,000 | 1.50 | 3.00 | 5.00 | 12.00 | — |
| Yr.5(1916) | 10,324,000 | 1.00 | 2.50 | 4.00 | 12.00 | — |
| Yr.6(1917) | 35,170,000 | 0.75 | 2.00 | 3.00 | 10.00 | — |

**10 SEN** **Y# 45** **Composition:** Copper-Nickel **Ruler:** Yoshihito (Taisho)

| Date | Mintage | F | VF | XF | Unc | BU |
|---|---|---|---|---|---|---|
| Yr.9(1920) | 4,894,000 | 0.50 | 1.00 | 3.00 | 25.00 | — |
| Yr.10(1921) | 61,870,000 | 0.25 | 0.50 | 1.50 | 5.00 | — |
| Yr.11(1922) | 159,770,000 | 0.25 | 0.50 | 1.50 | 5.00 | — |
| Yr.12(1923) | 190,010,000 | 0.25 | 0.50 | 1.50 | 4.50 | — |
| Yr.14(1925) | 54,475,000 | 0.25 | 0.50 | 1.50 | 5.00 | — |
| Yr.15(1926) | 58,675,000 | 0.25 | 0.50 | 1.50 | 5.00 | — |

**10 SEN** **Y# 49** **Composition:** Copper-Nickel **Ruler:** Hirohito (Showa)

| Date | Mintage | F | VF | XF | Unc | BU |
|---|---|---|---|---|---|---|
| Yr.2(1927) | 36,050,000 | 0.25 | 0.50 | 1.50 | 5.00 | — |
| Yr.3(1928) | 41,450,000 | 0.25 | 0.50 | 1.50 | 5.00 | — |
| Yr.4(1929) | 10,000,000 | 0.50 | 1.00 | 2.00 | 25.00 | — |
| Yr.6(1931) | 1,850,000 | 0.75 | 1.50 | 2.50 | 9.00 | — |
| Yr.7(1932) | 23,151,000 | 0.25 | 0.50 | 1.50 | 5.00 | — |

**10 SEN** **Y# 54** **Composition:** Nickel **Ruler:** Hirohito (Showa)

| Date | Mintage | F | VF | XF | Unc | BU |
|---|---|---|---|---|---|---|
| Yr.8(1933) | 14,570,000 | 0.50 | 1.00 | 2.00 | 5.50 | — |
| Yr.9(1934) | 37,351,000 | 0.25 | 0.75 | 1.50 | 4.75 | — |
| Yr.10(1935) | 35,586,000 | 0.30 | 1.00 | 1.75 | 5.25 | — |
| Yr.11(1936) | 77,948,000 | 0.25 | 0.75 | 1.50 | 4.75 | — |
| Yr.12(1937) | 40,001,000 | 0.30 | 1.00 | 1.75 | 5.50 | — |

**10 SEN** **Y# 58** **Composition:** Aluminum-Bronze **Ruler:** Hirohito (Showa)

| Date | Mintage | F | VF | XF | Unc | BU |
|---|---|---|---|---|---|---|
| Yr.13(1938) | 47,077,000 | 0.35 | 0.75 | 1.50 | 4.75 | — |
| Yr.14(1939) | 121,796,000 | 0.25 | 0.50 | 1.00 | 4.50 | — |
| Yr.15(1940) | 16,135,000 | 0.75 | 1.50 | 3.00 | 12.00 | — |

**10 SEN** **Y# 61** **Weight:** 1.5000 g. **Composition:** Aluminum **Ruler:** Hirohito (Showa)

| Date | Mintage | F | VF | XF | Unc | BU |
|---|---|---|---|---|---|---|
| Yr.15(1940) | 575,628,000 | — | 0.20 | 0.35 | 1.50 | — |
| Yr.16(1941) | Inc. above | — | 0.20 | 0.35 | 1.50 | — |

**10 SEN** **Y# 61a** **Weight:** 1.2000 g. **Composition:** Aluminum **Ruler:** Hirohito (Showa)

| Date | Mintage | F | VF | XF | Unc | BU |
|---|---|---|---|---|---|---|
| Yr.16(1941) | 944,947,000 | 0.10 | 0.35 | 0.50 | 2.00 | — |
| Yr.17(1942) | Inc. above | — | 0.20 | 0.35 | 1.50 | — |
| Yr.18(1943) |  | 0.20 | 0.50 | 2.00 | 6.50 | — |

**10 SEN** **Y#61b** **Weight:** 1.0000 g. **Composition:** Aluminum **Ruler:** Hirohito (Showa)

| Date | Mintage | F | VF | XF | Unc | BU |
|---|---|---|---|---|---|---|
| Yr.18(1943) | 756,037,000 | — | 0.20 | 0.35 | 1.50 | — |

**10 SEN** **Y#64** **Composition:** Tin-Zinc **Ruler:** Hirohito (Showa)

| Date | Mintage | F | VF | XF | Unc | BU |
|---|---|---|---|---|---|---|
| Yr.19(1944) | 450,022,000 | — | 0.20 | 0.35 | 1.50 | — |

**10 SEN** **Y#68** **Composition:** Aluminum **Ruler:** Hirohito (Showa)

| Date | Mintage | F | VF | XF | Unc | BU |
|---|---|---|---|---|---|---|
| Yr.20(1945) | 237,590,000 | — | 0.20 | 0.35 | 1.00 | — |
| Yr.21(1946) | Inc. above | — | 0.20 | 0.35 | 1.00 | — |

**10 SEN** **KM#112** **Composition:** Reddish Brown Baked Clay **Ruler:** Hirohito (Showa)

| Date | Mintage | F | VF | XF | Unc | BU |
|---|---|---|---|---|---|---|
| Yr.20(1945) | — | 75.00 | 135 | 245 | 325 | — |

**Note:** Not issued for circulation; varieties of color exist

**20 SEN** **Y#24** **Weight:** 5.3800 g. **Composition:** 0.8000 Silver .1383 oz. ASW **Ruler:** Mutsuhito (Meiji)

| Date | Mintage | F | VF | XF | Unc | BU |
|---|---|---|---|---|---|---|
| Yr.34(1901) | 500,000 | 150 | 225 | 350 | 2,250 | — |
| Yr.37(1904) | 5,250,000 | 5.00 | 10.00 | 20.00 | 70.00 | — |
| Yr.38(1905) | 8,444,000 | 5.00 | 10.00 | 20.00 | 65.00 | — |

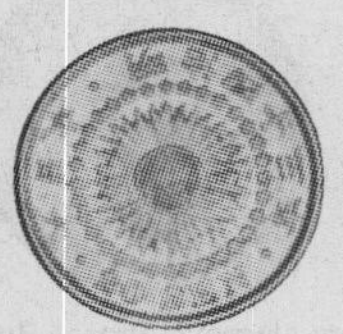

**20 SEN** **Y#30** **Weight:** 4.0500 g. **Composition:** 0.8000 Silver .1042 oz. ASW **Ruler:** Mutsuhito (Meiji)

| Date | Mintage | F | VF | XF | Unc | BU |
|---|---|---|---|---|---|---|
| Yr.39(1906) | 6,555,000 | 7.00 | 13.50 | 25.00 | 200 | — |
| Yr.40(1907) | 20,000,000 | 2.50 | 5.50 | 15.00 | 75.00 | — |
| Yr.41(1908) | 15,000,000 | 2.50 | 5.50 | 15.00 | 75.00 | — |
| Yr.42(1909) | 8,824,000 | 2.50 | 5.50 | 15.00 | 75.00 | — |
| Yr.43(1910) | 21,175,000 | 2.50 | 5.50 | 15.00 | 75.00 | — |
| Yr.44(1911) | 500,000 | 60.00 | 120 | 250 | 1,150 | — |

**50 SEN** **Y#25** **Weight:** 13.5000 g. **Composition:** 0.8000 Silver .3472 oz. ASW **Ruler:** Mutsuhito (Meiji)

| Date | Mintage | F | VF | XF | Unc | BU |
|---|---|---|---|---|---|---|
| Yr.34(1901) | 1,790,000 | 25.00 | 45.00 | 80.00 | 375 | — |
| Yr.35(1902) | 1,023,000 | 50.00 | 85.00 | 150 | 625 | — |
| Yr.36(1903) | 1,503,000 | 30.00 | 50.00 | 90.00 | 425 | — |
| Yr.37(1904) | 5,373,000 | 7.50 | 12.50 | 25.00 | 125 | — |
| Yr.38(1905) | 9,566,000 | 7.50 | 12.50 | 25.00 | 125 | — |

**50 SEN** **Y#31** **Weight:** 10.1000 g. **Composition:** 0.8000 Silver .2597 oz. ASW **Ruler:** Mutsuhito (Meiji)

| Date | Mintage | F | VF | XF | Unc | BU |
|---|---|---|---|---|---|---|
| Yr.39(1906) | 12,478,000 | 4.00 | 8.00 | 25.00 | 225 | — |
| Yr.40(1907) | 24,062,000 | 3.50 | 7.50 | 18.00 | 75.00 | — |
| Yr.41(1908) | 25,470,000 | 3.50 | 7.50 | 18.00 | 75.00 | — |
| Yr.42(1909) | 21,998,000 | 3.50 | 7.50 | 18.00 | 75.00 | — |
| Yr.43(1910) | 15,323,000 | 3.50 | 7.50 | 18.00 | 75.00 | — |
| Yr.44(1911) | 9,900,000 | 3.50 | 7.50 | 18.00 | 75.00 | — |
| Yr.45(1912) | 3,677,000 | 9.00 | 15.00 | 25.00 | 100 | — |

**50 SEN** **Y#37.1** **Weight:** 10.1000 g. **Composition:** 0.8000 Silver .2597 oz. ASW **Ruler:** Yoshihito (Taisho) **Obverse:** Japanese character "first"

| Date | Mintage | F | VF | XF | Unc | BU |
|---|---|---|---|---|---|---|
| Yr.1(1912) | 1,928,000 | 15.00 | 25.00 | 45.00 | 160 | — |

元

**50 SEN** **Y#37.2** **Weight:** 10.1000 g. **Composition:** 0.8000 Silver .2597 oz. ASW **Ruler:** Yoshihito (Taisho)

| Date | Mintage | F | VF | XF | Unc | BU |
|---|---|---|---|---|---|---|
| Yr.2(1913) | 5,910,000 | 5.00 | 10.00 | 22.00 | 60.00 | — |
| Yr.3(1914) | 1,872,000 | 20.00 | 35.00 | 55.00 | 200 | — |
| Yr.4(1915) | 2,011,000 | 17.50 | 30.00 | 50.00 | 160 | — |
| Yr.5(1916) | 8,736,000 | 4.00 | 8.00 | 16.00 | 35.00 | — |
| Yr.6(1917) | 9,963,000 | 4.00 | 8.00 | 16.00 | 35.00 | — |

**50 SEN** **Y#46** **Weight:** 4.9600 g. **Composition:** 0.7200 Silver .1148 oz. ASW **Ruler:** Yoshihito (Taisho)

| Date | Mintage | Good | VG | F | VF | XF |
|---|---|---|---|---|---|---|
| Yr.11(1922) | 76,320,000 | — | — | BV | 1.50 | 5.00 |
| Yr.12(1923) | 185,180,000 | — | — | BV | 1.50 | 3.00 |
| Yr.13(1924) | 78,520,000 | — | — | BV | 1.50 | 3.00 |
| Yr.14(1925) | 47,808,000 | — | — | BV | 1.50 | 3.00 |
| CDYr.15(1926) | 32,572,000 | — | — | BV | 1.50 | 3.00 |

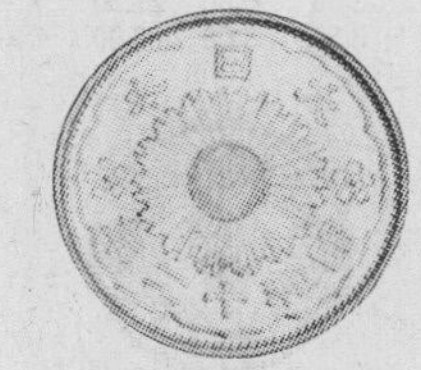

**50 SEN** **Y#50** **Weight:** 4.9600 g. **Composition:** 0.7200 Silver .1148 oz. ASW **Ruler:** Yoshihito (Taisho)

| Date | Mintage | F | VF | XF | Unc | BU |
|---|---|---|---|---|---|---|
| Yr.3(1928) | 38,592,000 | BV | 1.00 | 2.50 | 10.00 | — |
| Yr.4(1929) | 12,568,000 | BV | 1.50 | 5.00 | 30.00 | — |
| Yr.5(1930) | 10,200,000 | BV | 2.00 | 5.50 | 20.00 | — |
| Yr.6(1931) | 27,677,000 | BV | 1.00 | 2.50 | 9.00 | — |
| Yr.7(1932) | 24,132,000 | BV | 1.00 | 2.50 | 9.00 | — |
| Yr.8(1933) | 10,001,000 | BV | 2.00 | 7.00 | 22.00 | — |
| Yr.9(1934) | 20,003,000 | BV | 1.50 | 2.50 | 9.00 | — |
| Yr.10(1935) | 11,738,000 | BV | 1.50 | 2.50 | 9.00 | — |
| Yr.11(1936) | 44,272,000 | BV | 1.50 | 2.50 | 7.00 | — |
| Yr.12(1937) | 48,000,000 | BV | 1.50 | 2.50 | 7.00 | — |
| Yr.13(1938) | 3,600,000 | 50.00 | 75.00 | 125 | 250 | — |

**50 SEN** **Y#67** **Composition:** Brass **Ruler:** Yoshihito (Taisho) **Note:** Varieties exist.

| Date | Mintage | F | VF | XF | Unc | BU |
|---|---|---|---|---|---|---|
| Yr.21(1946) | 268,187,000 | 0.25 | 0.50 | 1.00 | 2.50 | — |
| Yr.22(1947) | Inc. above | — | 650 | 1,000 | 1,700 | — |

**Note:** Not released to circulation

**50 SEN** **Y#69** **Composition:** Brass **Ruler:** Yoshihito (Taisho)

| Date | Mintage | F | VF | XF | Unc | BU |
|---|---|---|---|---|---|---|
| Yr.22(1947) | 849,234,000 | 0.10 | 0.20 | 0.40 | 1.00 | — |
| Yr.23(1948) | Inc. above | 0.10 | 0.20 | 0.40 | 1.00 | — |

**YEN** **Y#A25.3** **Weight:** 26.9568 g. **Composition:** 0.9000 Silver .7800 oz. ASW **Ruler:** Mutsuhito (Meiji)

| Date | Mintage | F | VF | XF | Unc | BU |
|---|---|---|---|---|---|---|
| Yr.34(1901) | 1,256,000 | 15.00 | 30.00 | 50.00 | 160 | — |
| Yr.35(1902) | 668,000 | 25.00 | 50.00 | 75.00 | 225 | — |
| Yr.36(1903) | 5,131,000 | 15.00 | 27.50 | 42.50 | 140 | — |
| Yr.37(1904) | 6,970,000 | 15.00 | 27.50 | 42.50 | 140 | — |
| Yr.38(1905) | 5,031,000 | 15.00 | 27.50 | 42.50 | 140 | — |
| Yr.39(1906) | 3,471,000 | 25.00 | 50.00 | 85.00 | 275 | — |
| Yr.41(1908) | 334,000 | 50.00 | 100 | 150 | 500 | — |
| Yr.45(1912) | 5,000,000 | 12.50 | 25.00 | 42.50 | 120 | — |

**YEN** **Y#38** **Weight:** 26.9568 g. **Composition:** 0.9000 Silver .7800 oz. ASW **Ruler:** Yoshihito (Taisho)

| Date | Mintage | F | VF | XF | Unc | BU |
|---|---|---|---|---|---|---|
| Yr.3(1914) | 11,500,000 | 12.50 | 22.50 | 35.00 | 110 | — |

## REFORM COINAGE

**YEN** **Y# 70** **Composition:** Brass **Ruler:** Hirohito (Showa)

| Date | Mintage | F | VF | XF | Unc | BU |
|---|---|---|---|---|---|---|
| Yr.23(1948) | 451,209,000 | — | 0.25 | 0.50 | 2.00 | — |
| Yr.24(1949) | Inc. above | — | 0.15 | 0.35 | 1.25 | — |
| Yr.25(1950) | Inc. above | — | 0.15 | 0.35 | 1.25 | — |

**YEN** **Y# 74** **Composition:** Aluminum **Ruler:** Hirohito (Showa)

| Date | Mintage | F | VF | XF | Unc | BU |
|---|---|---|---|---|---|---|
| Yr.30(1955) | 381,700,000 | — | — | — | 0.10 | — |
| Yr.31(1956) | 500,900,000 | — | — | — | 0.10 | — |
| Yr.32(1957) | 492,000,000 | — | — | — | 0.10 | — |
| Yr.33(1958) | 374,900,000 | — | — | — | 0.10 | — |
| Yr.34(1959) | 208,600,000 | — | — | — | 0.10 | — |
| Yr.35(1960) | 300,000,000 | — | — | — | 0.10 | — |
| Yr.36(1961) | 432,400,000 | — | — | — | 0.10 | — |
| Yr.37(1962) | 572,000,000 | — | — | — | 0.10 | — |
| Yr.38(1963) | 788,700,000 | — | — | — | 0.10 | — |
| Yr.39(1964) | 1,665,100,000 | — | — | — | 0.10 | — |
| Yr.40(1965) | 1,743,256,000 | — | — | — | 0.10 | — |
| Yr.41(1966) | 807,344,000 | — | — | — | 0.10 | — |
| Yr.42(1967) | 220,600,000 | — | — | — | 0.10 | — |
| Yr.44(1969) | 184,700,000 | — | — | — | 0.10 | — |
| Yr.45(1970) | 556,400,000 | — | — | — | 0.10 | — |
| Yr.46(1971) | 904,950,000 | — | — | — | 0.10 | — |
| Yr.47(1972) | 1,274,950,000 | — | — | — | 0.10 | — |
| Yr.48(1973) | 1,470,000,000 | — | — | — | 0.10 | — |
| Yr.49(1974) | 1,750,000,000 | — | — | — | 0.10 | — |
| Yr.50(1975) | 1,656,150,000 | — | — | — | 0.10 | — |
| Yr.51(1976) | 928,800,000 | — | — | — | 0.10 | — |
| Yr.52(1977) | 895,000,000 | — | — | — | 0.10 | — |
| Yr.53(1978) | 864,000,000 | — | — | — | 0.10 | — |
| Yr.54(1979) | 1,015,000,000 | — | — | — | 0.10 | — |
| Yr.55(1981) | 1,145,000,000 | — | — | — | 0.10 | — |
| Yr.56(1981) | 1,206,000,000 | — | — | — | 0.10 | — |
| Yr.57(1982) | 1,017,000,000 | — | — | — | 0.10 | — |
| Yr.58(1983) | 1,086,000,000 | — | — | — | 0.10 | — |
| Yr.59(1984) | 981,850,000 | — | — | — | 0.10 | — |
| Yr.60(1985) | 837,150,000 | — | — | — | 0.10 | — |
| Yr.61(1985) | 417,960,000 | — | — | — | 0.10 | — |
| Yr.62(1987) | 955,520 | — | — | — | 0.10 | — |
| Yr.62(1987) Proof | 230,000 | Value: 1.50 | | | | |
| Yr.63(1988) | 1,268,842,000 | — | — | — | 0.10 | — |
| Yr.63(1988) Proof | 200,000 | Value: 1.50 | | | | |
| Yr.64(1989) | 116,100,000 | — | — | — | 0.50 | — |

**YEN** **Y# 95.1** **Composition:** Aluminum **Ruler:** Akihito (Heisei) **Obverse:** Small tree **Reverse:** Large 1 on wide ring in center, date below, with Japanese "first" as third character

| Date | Mintage | F | VF | XF | Unc | BU |
|---|---|---|---|---|---|---|
| Yr.1(1989) | 2,366,770,000 | — | — | — | 0.15 | — |
| Yr.1(1989) Proof | 200,000 | Value: 1.50 | | | | |

**YEN** **Y# 95.2** **Composition:** Aluminum **Ruler:** Akihito (Heisei)

| Date | Mintage | F | VF | XF | Unc | BU |
|---|---|---|---|---|---|---|
| Yr.2(1990) | 2,768,753,000 | — | — | — | 0.15 | — |
| Yr.2(1990) Proof | 200,000 | Value: 1.50 | | | | |
| Yr.3(1991) | 2,300,900,000 | — | — | — | 0.15 | — |
| Yr.3(1991) Proof | 220,000 | Value: 1.50 | | | | |
| Yr.4(1992) | 1,298,880,000 | — | — | — | 0.15 | — |
| Yr.4(1992) Proof | 250,000 | Value: 1.50 | | | | |
| Yr.5(1993) | 1,260,990,000 | — | — | — | 0.15 | — |
| Yr.5(1993) Proof | 250,000 | Value: 1.50 | | | | |
| Yr.6(1994) | 1,040,540,000 | — | — | — | 0.15 | — |
| Yr.6(1994) Proof | 227,000 | Value: 1.50 | | | | |
| Yr.7(1995) | 1,041,674,000 | — | — | — | 0.15 | — |
| Yr.7(1995) Proof | 200,000 | Value: 1.50 | | | | |
| Yr.8(1996) | 942,024,000 | — | — | — | 0.15 | — |
| Yr.8(1996) Proof | 189,000 | Value: 1.50 | | | | |
| Yr.9(1997) | 782,874,000 | — | — | — | 0.15 | — |
| Yr.9(1997) Proof | 212,000 | Value: 1.50 | | | | |
| Yr.10(1998) | 452,582,000 | — | — | — | 0.15 | — |
| Yr.10(1998) Proof | 30,000 | Value: 1.50 | | | | |
| Yr.11(1999) | — | — | — | — | 0.15 | — |
| Yr.11(1999) Proof | 270,000 | Value: 1.50 | | | | |
| Yr.12(2000) | — | — | — | — | 0.15 | — |
| Yr.12(2000) Proof | — | Value: 1.50 | | | | |
| Yr.13(2001) | — | — | — | — | — | — |
| Yr.13(2001) Proof | — | — | — | — | — | — |

**5 YEN** **Y# 32** **Weight:** 4.1666 g. **Composition:** 0.9000 Gold .1205 oz. AGW **Ruler:** Mutsuhito (Meiji)

| Date | Mintage | F | VF | XF | Unc | BU |
|---|---|---|---|---|---|---|
| Yr.36(1903) | 21,000 | 900 | 1,000 | 1,350 | 2,250 | — |
| Yr.44(1911) | 59,000 | 850 | 1,000 | 1,300 | 2,150 | — |
| Yr.45(1912) | 59,000 | 850 | 1,000 | 1,300 | 2,150 | — |

**5 YEN** **Y# 39** **Weight:** 4.1666 g. **Composition:** 0.9000 Gold .1205 oz. AGW **Ruler:** Yoshihito (Taisho)

| Date | Mintage | F | VF | XF | Unc | BU |
|---|---|---|---|---|---|---|
| Yr.2(1913) | 40,000 | 750 | 1,000 | 1,250 | 1,850 | — |
| Yr.13(1924) | 76,000 | 650 | 850 | 1,000 | 1,650 | — |

**5 YEN** **Y# 51** **Weight:** 4.1666 g. **Composition:** 0.9000 Gold .1205 oz. AGW **Ruler:** Hirohito (Showa)

| Date | Mintage | F | VF | XF | Unc | BU |
|---|---|---|---|---|---|---|
| Yr.5(1930) | 852,000 | 20,000 | 35,000 | 50,000 | 65,000 | — |

**5 YEN** **Y# 71** **Composition:** Brass **Ruler:** Hirohito (Showa)

| Date | Mintage | F | VF | XF | Unc | BU |
|---|---|---|---|---|---|---|
| Yr.23(1948) | 74,520,000 | — | 0.50 | 0.75 | 12.50 | — |
| Yr.24(1949) | 179,692,000 | — | 0.15 | 0.40 | 8.00 | — |

**5 YEN** **Y# 72** **Composition:** Brass **Ruler:** Hirohito (Showa) **Note:** Old script.

| Date | Mintage | F | VF | XF | Unc | BU |
|---|---|---|---|---|---|---|
| Yr.24(1949) | 111,896,000 | — | 0.15 | 0.25 | 9.00 | — |
| Yr.25(1950) | 181,824,000 | — | 0.15 | 0.25 | 6.50 | — |
| Yr.26(1951) | 197,980,000 | — | 0.15 | 0.25 | 6.50 | — |
| Yr.27(1952) | 55,000,000 | — | 0.30 | 0.60 | 15.00 | — |
| Yr.28(1953) | 45,000,000 | — | 0.30 | 0.60 | 6.50 | — |

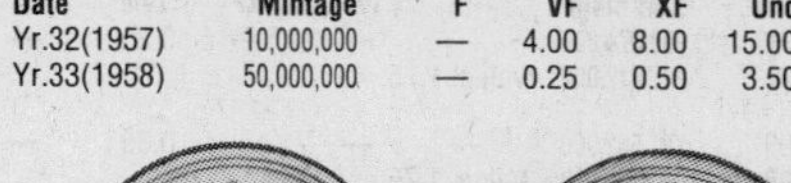

| Date | Mintage | F | VF | XF | Unc | BU |
|---|---|---|---|---|---|---|
| Yr.32(1957) | 10,000,000 | — | 4.00 | 8.00 | 15.00 | — |
| Yr.33(1958) | 50,000,000 | — | 0.25 | 0.50 | 3.50 | — |

**5 YEN** **Y# 72a** **Composition:** Brass **Ruler:** Hirohito (Showa) **Note:** New script.

| Date | Mintage | F | VF | XF | Unc | BU |
|---|---|---|---|---|---|---|
| Yr.34(1959) | 33,000,000 | — | 0.25 | 0.50 | 3.00 | — |
| Yr.35(1960) | 34,800,000 | — | 0.20 | 0.40 | 3.00 | — |
| Yr.36(1961) | 61,000,000 | — | 0.15 | 0.35 | 2.50 | — |
| Yr.37(1962) | 126,700,000 | — | 0.10 | 0.30 | 1.50 | — |
| Yr.38(1963) | 171,800,000 | — | 0.10 | 0.30 | 1.50 | — |
| Yr.39(1964) | 379,700,000 | — | 0.10 | 0.30 | 1.50 | — |
| Yr.40(1965) | 384,200,000 | — | 0.10 | 0.30 | 1.50 | — |
| Yr.41(1966) | 163,100,000 | — | 0.10 | 0.30 | 1.50 | — |
| Yr.42(1967) | 26,000,000 | — | 0.25 | 0.50 | 1.50 | — |
| Yr.43(1968) | 114,000,000 | — | — | 0.10 | 0.15 | — |
| Yr.44(1969) | 240,000,000 | — | — | 0.10 | 0.15 | — |
| Yr.45(1970) | 340,000,000 | — | — | 0.10 | 0.15 | — |
| Yr.46(1971) | 362,050,000 | — | — | 0.10 | 0.15 | — |
| Yr.47(1972) | 562,950,000 | — | — | 0.10 | 0.15 | — |
| Yr.48(1973) | 745,000,000 | — | — | 0.10 | 0.15 | — |
| Yr.49(1974) | 950,000,000 | — | — | 0.10 | 0.15 | — |
| Yr.50(1975) | 970,000,000 | — | — | 0.10 | 0.15 | — |
| Yr.51(1976) | 200,000,000 | — | — | 0.10 | 0.15 | — |
| Yr.52(1977) | 340,000,000 | — | — | 0.10 | 0.15 | — |
| Yr.53(1978) | 318,000,000 | — | — | 0.10 | 0.15 | — |
| Yr.54(1979) | 317,000,000 | — | — | 0.10 | 0.15 | — |
| Yr.55(1980) | 385,000,000 | — | — | 0.10 | 0.15 | — |
| Yr.56(1981) | 95,000,000 | — | — | 0.10 | 0.15 | — |
| Yr.57(1982) | 455,000,000 | — | — | 0.10 | 0.15 | — |
| Yr.58(1983) | 410,000,000 | — | — | 0.10 | 0.15 | — |
| Yr.59(1984) | 202,850,000 | — | — | 0.10 | 0.15 | — |
| Yr.60(1985) | 153,150,000 | — | — | 0.10 | 0.15 | — |
| Yr.61(1986) | 113,960,000 | — | — | 0.10 | 0.15 | — |
| Yr.62(1987) | 631,545,000 | — | — | 0.10 | 0.15 | — |
| Yr.62(1987) Proof | 230,000 | Value: 1.75 | | | | |
| Yr.63(1988) | 368,920,000 | | | | 0.15 | |
| Yr.63(1988) Proof | 200,000 | Value: 1.75 | | | | |
| Yr.64(1989) | 67,332,000 | — | — | — | 0.65 | |

**5 YEN** **Y# 96.1** **Composition:** Brass **Ruler:** Akihito (Heisei) **Obverse:** Inscription and date separated by seed leaf; Japanese character "first" in date **Reverse:** Gear around hole, rice stalk above denomination

| Date | Mintage | F | VF | XF | Unc | BU |
|---|---|---|---|---|---|---|
| Yr.1(1989) | 960,460,000 | — | — | — | 0.35 | — |
| Yr.1(1989) Proof | 200,000 | Value: 1.75 | | | | |

**5 YEN** **Y# 96.2** **Composition:** Brass **Ruler:** Akihito (Heisei)

| Date | Mintage | F | VF | XF | Unc | BU |
|---|---|---|---|---|---|---|
| Yr.2(1990) | 520,753,000 | — | — | — | 0.35 | — |
| Yr.2(1990) Proof | 200,000 | Value: 1.75 | | | | |
| Yr.3(1991) | 516,900,000 | — | — | — | 0.35 | — |
| Yr.3(1991) Proof | 220,000 | Value: 1.75 | | | | |
| Yr.4(1992) | 300,880,000 | — | — | — | 0.35 | — |
| Yr.4(1992) Proof | 250,000 | Value: 1.75 | | | | |
| Yr.5(1993) | 412,990,000 | — | — | — | 0.35 | — |
| Yr.5(1993) Proof | 250,000 | Value: 1.75 | | | | |
| Yr.6(1994) | 197,540,000 | — | — | — | 0.35 | — |
| Yr.6(1994) Proof | 227,000 | Value: 1.75 | | | | |
| Yr.7(1995) | 351,674,000 | — | — | — | 0.35 | — |
| Yr.7(1995) Proof | 200,000 | Value: 1.75 | | | | |
| Yr.8(1996) | 207,024,000 | — | — | — | 0.35 | — |
| Yr.8(1996) Proof | 189,000 | Value: 1.75 | | | | |

| Date | Mintage | F | VF | XF | Unc | BU |
|---|---|---|---|---|---|---|
| Yr.9(1997) | 238,874,000 | — | — | — | 0.35 | — |
| Yr.9(1997) Proof | 212,000 | Value: 1.75 | | | | |
| Yr.10(1998) | 171,582,000 | — | — | — | 0.35 | — |
| Yr.10(1998) Proof | 30,000 | Value: 1.75 | | | | |
| Yr.11(1999) | — | — | — | — | 0.35 | — |
| Yr.11(1999) Proof | 270,000 | Value: 1.75 | | | | |
| Yr.12(2000) | — | Value: 1.75 | | | | |
| Yr.12(2000) Proof | — | — | — | — | — | — |
| Yr.13(2001) | — | — | — | — | — | — |
| Yr.13(2001) Proof | — | — | — | — | — | — |

**10 YEN** Y# 33 **Weight:** 8.3333 g. **Composition:** 0.9000 Gold .2411 oz. AGW **Ruler:** Mutsuhito (Meiji)

| Date | Mintage | F | VF | XF | Unc | BU |
|---|---|---|---|---|---|---|
| Yr.34(1901) | 1,654,000 | 450 | 600 | 750 | 1,250 | — |
| Yr.35(1902) | 3,023,000 | 450 | 600 | 750 | 1,350 | — |
| Yr.36(1903) | 2,902,000 | 450 | 600 | 750 | 1,350 | — |
| Yr.37(1904) | 724,000 | 500 | 800 | 1,250 | 2,500 | — |
| Yr.40(1907) | 157,000 | 500 | 800 | 1,250 | 2,350 | — |
| Yr.41(1908) | 1,160,000 | 450 | 600 | 750 | 1,250 | — |
| Yr.42(1909) | 2,165,000 | 400 | 600 | 750 | 1,200 | — |
| Yr.43(1910) | 8,982 | 7,500 | 1,000 | 15,000 | 25,000 | — |

**10 YEN** Y# 73 **Composition:** Bronze **Ruler:** Hirohito (Showa) **Obverse:** Ancient phoenix temple Hoo-do surrounded by arabesque pattern **Edge:** Reeded

| Date | Mintage | F | VF | XF | Unc | BU |
|---|---|---|---|---|---|---|
| Yr.26(1951) | 101,068,000 | — | 0.20 | 0.35 | 35.00 | — |
| Yr.27(1952) | 486,632,000 | — | 0.20 | 0.35 | 25.00 | — |
| Yr.28(1953) | 466,300,000 | — | 0.20 | 0.35 | 25.00 | — |
| Yr.29(1954) | 520,900,000 | — | 0.20 | 0.35 | 35.00 | — |
| Yr.30(1955) | 123,100,000 | — | 0.20 | 0.35 | 20.00 | — |
| Yr.32(1957) | 50,000,000 | — | 0.25 | 0.65 | 25.00 | — |
| Yr.33(1958) | 25,000,000 | — | 0.40 | 1.00 | 38.00 | — |

**10 YEN** Y# 73a **Composition:** Bronze **Ruler:** Hirohito (Showa) **Edge:** Plain

| Date | Mintage | F | VF | XF | Unc | BU |
|---|---|---|---|---|---|---|
| Yr.34(1959) | 62,400,000 | — | — | 0.20 | 9.00 | — |
| Yr.35(1960) | 225,900,000 | — | — | 0.20 | 1.25 | — |
| Yr.36(1961) | 229,900,000 | — | — | 0.20 | 1.25 | — |
| Yr.37(1962) | 284,200,000 | — | — | 0.20 | 1.25 | — |
| Yr.38(1963) | 411,300,000 | — | — | 0.20 | 0.60 | — |
| Yr.39(1964) | 479,200,000 | — | — | 0.20 | 0.60 | — |
| Yr.40(1965) | 387,600,000 | — | — | 0.20 | 0.60 | — |
| Yr.41(1966) | 395,900,000 | — | — | 0.20 | 0.60 | — |
| Yr.42(1967) | 158,900,000 | — | — | 0.20 | 0.60 | — |
| Yr.43(1968) | 363,600,000 | — | — | 0.20 | 0.40 | — |
| Yr.44(1969) | 414,800,000 | — | — | 0.20 | 0.40 | — |
| Yr.45(1970) | 382,700,000 | — | — | 0.20 | 0.40 | — |
| Yr.46(1971) | 610,050,000 | — | — | 0.20 | 0.40 | — |
| Yr.47(1972) | 634,950,000 | — | — | 0.20 | 0.40 | — |
| Yr.48(1973) | 1,345,000,000 | — | — | 0.20 | 0.35 | — |
| Yr.49(1974) | 1,780,000,000 | — | — | 0.20 | 0.35 | — |
| Yr.50(1975) | 1,280,260,000 | — | — | 0.20 | 0.35 | — |
| Yr.51(1976) | 1,369,740,000 | — | — | 0.20 | 0.35 | — |
| Yr.52(1977) | 1,467,000,000 | — | — | 0.20 | 0.35 | — |
| Yr.53(1978) | 1,435,000,000 | — | — | 0.20 | 0.35 | — |
| Yr.54(1979) | 1,207,000,000 | — | — | 0.20 | 0.35 | — |
| Yr.55(1980) | 1,127,000,000 | — | — | 0.20 | 0.35 | — |
| Yr.56(1981) | 1,369,000,000 | — | — | 0.20 | 0.35 | — |
| Yr.57(1982) | 890,000,000 | — | — | 0.20 | 0.35 | — |
| Yr.58(1983) | 870,000,000 | — | — | 0.20 | 0.35 | — |
| Yr.59(1984) | 533,850,000 | — | — | 0.20 | 0.35 | — |
| Yr.60(1985) | 335,150,000 | — | — | 0.20 | 0.35 | — |
| Yr.61(1986) | 68,960,000 | — | — | 0.25 | 0.75 | — |
| Yr.62(1987) | 165,545,000 | — | — | 0.20 | 0.35 | — |
| Yr.62(1987) Proof | 230,000 | Value: 1.75 | | | | |
| Yr.63(1988) | 617,912,000 | — | — | — | 0.35 | — |
| Yr.63(1988) Proof | 200,000 | Value: 1.75 | | | | |
| Yr.64(1989) | 74,692,000 | — | — | 0.25 | 0.75 | — |

**10 YEN** Y# 97.1 **Composition:** Bronze **Ruler:** Akihito (Heisei) **Reverse:** Japanese character "first" in date

| Date | Mintage | F | VF | XF | Unc | BU |
|---|---|---|---|---|---|---|
| Yr.1(1989) | 666,108,000 | — | — | — | 0.45 | — |
| Yr.1(1989) Proof | 200,000 | Value: 1.75 | | | | |

**10 YEN** Y# 97.2 **Composition:** Bronze **Ruler:** Akihito (Heisei)

| Date | Mintage | F | VF | XF | Unc | BU |
|---|---|---|---|---|---|---|
| Yr.2(1990) | 754,753,000 | — | — | — | 0.45 | — |
| Yr.2(1990) Proof | 200,000 | Value: 1.75 | | | | |
| Yr.3(1991) | 631,900,000 | — | — | — | 0.45 | — |
| Yr.3(1991) Proof | 220,000 | Value: 1.75 | | | | |
| Yr.4(1992) | 537,880,000 | — | — | — | 0.45 | — |
| Yr.4(1992) Proof | 250,000 | Value: 1.75 | | | | |
| Yr.5(1993) | 248,990,000 | — | — | — | 0.45 | — |
| Yr.5(1993) Proof | 250,000 | Value: 1.75 | | | | |
| Yr.6(1994) | 190,540,000 | — | — | — | 0.45 | — |
| Yr.6(1994) Proof | 227,000 | Value: 1.75 | | | | |
| Yr.7(1995) | 248,674,000 | — | — | — | 0.45 | — |
| Yr.7(1995) Proof | 200,000 | Value: 1.75 | | | | |
| Yr.8(1996) | 546,024,000 | — | — | — | 0.45 | — |
| Yr.8(1996) Proof | 189,000 | Value: 1.75 | | | | |
| Yr.9(1997) | 490,874,000 | — | — | — | 0.45 | — |
| Yr.9(1997) Proof | 212,000 | Value: 1.75 | | | | |
| Yr.10(1998) | 409,582,000 | — | — | — | 0.45 | — |
| Yr.10(1998) Proof | 30,000 | Value: 1.75 | | | | |
| Yr.11(1999) | 358,850,000 | — | — | — | 0.45 | — |
| Yr.11(1999) Proof | 270,000 | Value: 1.75 | | | | |
| Yr.12(2000) | — | — | — | — | 0.45 | — |
| Yr.12(2000) Proof | — | Value: 1.75 | | | | |
| Yr.13(2001) | — | — | — | — | — | — |
| Yr.13(2001) Proof | — | — | — | — | — | — |

**20 YEN** Y# 34 **Weight:** 16.6666 g. **Composition:** 0.9000 Gold .4823 oz. AGW **Ruler:** Mutsuhito (Meiji)

| Date | Mintage | F | VF | XF | Unc | BU |
|---|---|---|---|---|---|---|
| Yr.36(1903) Rare | — | — | — | — | — | — |
| Yr.37(1904) | 2,759,000 | 550 | 1,250 | 1,750 | 2,400 | — |
| Yr.38(1905) | 1,045,000 | 550 | 1,250 | 1,750 | 2,400 | — |
| Yr.39(1906) | 1,331,000 | 550 | 1,250 | 1,750 | 2,400 | — |
| Yr.40(1907) | 817,000 | 650 | 1,350 | 2,100 | 2,850 | — |
| Yr.41(1908) | 458,000 | 1,000 | 1,500 | 2,250 | 3,650 | — |
| Yr.42(1909) | 557,000 | 1,000 | 1,500 | 2,250 | 3,750 | — |
| Yr.43(1910) | 2,163,000 | 500 | 1,000 | 1,600 | 2,200 | — |
| Yr.44(1911) | 1,470,000 | 500 | 1,000 | 1,600 | 2,200 | — |
| Yr.45(1912) | 1,272,000 | 525 | 1,100 | 1,700 | 2,300 | — |

**20 YEN** Y# 40.1 **Weight:** 16.6666 g. **Composition:** 0.9000 Gold .4823 oz. AGW **Ruler:** Yoshihito (Taisho) **Obverse:** Japanese character "first" used in date

| Date | Mintage | F | VF | XF | Unc | BU |
|---|---|---|---|---|---|---|
| Yr.1(1912) | 177,000 | 700 | 1,400 | 2,200 | 3,000 | — |

**20 YEN** Y# 40.2 **Weight:** 16.6666 g. **Composition:** 0.9000 Gold .4823 oz. AGW **Ruler:** Yoshihito (Taisho)

| Date | Mintage | F | VF | XF | Unc | BU |
|---|---|---|---|---|---|---|
| Yr.2(1913) | 869,000 | 550 | 1,100 | 1,700 | 2,300 | — |
| Yr.3(1914) | 1,042,000 | 550 | 1,100 | 1,700 | 2,300 | — |
| Yr.4(1915) | 1,509,000 | 550 | 1,100 | 1,700 | 2,300 | — |
| Yr.5(1916) | 2,376,000 | 500 | 1,000 | 1,600 | 2,200 | — |
| Yr.6(1917) | 6,208,000 | 475 | 950 | 1,550 | 2,150 | — |
| Yr.7(1918) | 3,118,000 | 500 | 1,000 | 1,600 | 2,200 | — |
| Yr.8(1919) | 1,531,000 | 500 | 1,000 | 1,600 | 2,200 | — |
| Yr.9(1920) | 370,000 | 600 | 1,300 | 1,800 | 2,650 | — |

**20 YEN** Y# 52 **Weight:** 16.6666 g. **Composition:** 0.9000 Gold .4823 oz. AGW **Ruler:** Hirohito (Showa)

| Date | Mintage | F | VF | XF | Unc | BU |
|---|---|---|---|---|---|---|
| Yr.5(1930) | 11,055,000 | 15,000 | 25,000 | 35,000 | 45,000 | — |
| Yr.6(1931) | 7,526,000 | 17,500 | 27,500 | 37,500 | 47,500 | — |
| Yr.7(1932) Rare | — | — | — | — | — | — |

**50 YEN** Y# 75 **Composition:** Nickel **Ruler:** Hirohito (Showa)

| Date | Mintage | F | VF | XF | Unc | BU |
|---|---|---|---|---|---|---|
| Yr.30(1955) | 63,700,000 | — | 0.75 | 1.50 | 17.50 | — |
| Yr.31(1956) | 91,300,000 | — | 0.75 | 1.00 | 17.50 | — |
| Yr.32(1957) | 39,000,000 | — | 0.75 | 1.50 | 17.50 | — |
| Yr.33(1958) | 18,000,000 | — | 1.00 | 2.50 | 30.00 | — |

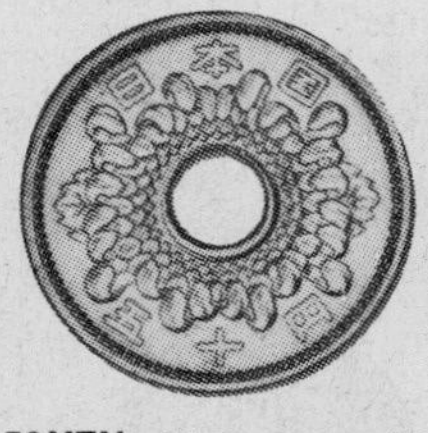

**50 YEN** Y# 76 **Composition:** Nickel **Ruler:** Hirohito (Showa)

| Date | Mintage | F | VF | XF | Unc | BU |
|---|---|---|---|---|---|---|
| Yr.34(1959) | 23,900,000 | — | 1.00 | 2.50 | 17.50 | — |
| Yr.35(1960) | 6,000,000 | — | 12.50 | 22.50 | 40.00 | — |
| Yr.36(1961) | 16,000,000 | — | 2.00 | 4.00 | 20.00 | — |
| Yr.37(1962) | 50,300,000 | — | 0.75 | 1.25 | 5.00 | — |
| Yr.38(1963) | 55,000,000 | — | 0.75 | 1.25 | 5.00 | — |
| Yr.39(1964) | 69,200,000 | — | 0.75 | 1.25 | 4.00 | — |
| Yr.40(1965) | 189,300,000 | — | 0.75 | 1.25 | 3.00 | — |
| Yr.41(1966) | 171,500,000 | — | 0.75 | 1.25 | 2.50 | — |

**50 YEN** Y# 81 **Composition:** Copper-Nickel **Ruler:** Hirohito (Showa)

| Date | Mintage | F | VF | XF | Unc | BU |
|---|---|---|---|---|---|---|
| Yr.42(1967) | 238,400,000 | — | — | 0.75 | 1.00 | — |
| Yr.43(1968) | 200,000,000 | — | — | 0.75 | 1.00 | — |
| Yr.44(1969) | 210,900,000 | — | — | 0.75 | 1.00 | — |
| Yr.45(1970) | 269,800,000 | — | — | 0.75 | 1.00 | — |

| Date | Mintage | F | VF | XF | Unc | BU |
|---|---|---|---|---|---|---|
| Yr.46(1971) | 80,950,000 | — | — | 0.75 | 1.00 | — |
| Yr.47(1972) | 138,980,000 | — | — | 0.75 | 1.00 | — |
| Yr.48(1973) | 200,970,000 | — | — | 0.75 | 1.00 | — |
| Yr.49(1974) | 470,000,000 | — | — | 0.75 | 1.00 | — |
| Yr.50(1975) | 238,120,000 | — | — | 0.75 | 1.00 | — |
| Yr.51(1976) | 241,880,000 | — | — | 0.75 | 1.00 | — |
| Yr.52(1977) | 176,000,000 | — | — | 0.75 | 1.00 | — |
| Yr.53(1978) | 234,000,000 | — | — | 0.75 | 1.00 | — |
| Yr.54(1979) | 110,000,000 | — | — | 0.75 | 1.00 | — |
| Yr.55(1980) | 51,000,000 | — | — | 0.75 | 1.00 | — |
| Yr.56(1981) | 179,000,000 | — | — | 0.75 | 1.00 | — |
| Yr.57(1982) | 30,000,000 | — | — | 0.75 | 1.00 | — |
| Yr.58(1983) | 30,000,000 | — | — | 0.75 | 1.00 | — |
| Yr.59(1984) | 29,850,000 | — | — | 0.75 | 1.00 | — |
| Yr.60(1985) | 10,150,000 | — | — | 0.75 | 1.00 | — |
| Yr.61(1986) | 9,960,000 | — | — | 0.75 | 1.00 | — |
| Yr.62(1987) | 545,000 | — | — | — | 70.00 | — |
| Yr.62(1987) Proof | 230,000 | Value: 75.00 | | | | |
| Yr.63(1988) | 108,912,000 | — | — | — | 1.00 | — |
| Yr.63(1988) Proof | 200,000 | Value: 2.00 | | | | |

**50 YEN** Y# 101.1 **Composition:** Copper-Nickel **Ruler:** Akihito (Heisei) **Obverse:** Japanese character "first" in date

| Date | Mintage | F | VF | XF | Unc | BU |
|---|---|---|---|---|---|---|
| Yr.1(1989) | 244,800,000 | — | — | — | 1.00 | — |
| Yr.1(1989) Proof | 200,000 | Value: 2.00 | | | | |

**50 YEN** Y# 101.2 **Composition:** Copper-Nickel **Ruler:** Akihito (Heisei)

| Date | Mintage | F | VF | XF | Unc | BU |
|---|---|---|---|---|---|---|
| Yr.2(1990) | 274,753,000 | — | — | — | 1.00 | — |
| Yr.2(1990) Proof | 200,000 | Value: 2.00 | | | | |
| Yr.3(1991) | 208,900,000 | — | — | — | 1.00 | — |
| Yr.3(1991) Proof | 220,000 | Value: 2.00 | | | | |
| Yr.4(1992) | 48,880,000 | — | — | — | 1.00 | — |
| Yr.4(1992) Proof | 250,000 | Value: 2.00 | | | | |
| Yr.5(1993) | 50,990,000 | — | — | — | 1.00 | — |
| Yr.5(1993) Proof | 250,000 | Value: 2.00 | | | | |
| Yr.6(1994) | 65,540,000 | — | — | — | 1.00 | — |
| Yr.6(1994) Proof | 227,000 | Value: 2.00 | | | | |
| Yr.7(1995) | 111,674,000 | — | — | — | 1.00 | — |
| Yr.7(1995) Proof | 200,000 | Value: 2.00 | | | | |
| Yr.8(1996) | 82,024,000 | — | — | — | 1.00 | — |
| Yr.8(1996) Proof | 189,000 | Value: 2.00 | | | | |
| Yr.9(1997) | 149,876,000 | — | — | — | 1.00 | — |
| Yr.9(1997) Proof | 212,000 | Value: 2.00 | | | | |
| Yr.10(1998) | 100,582,000 | — | — | — | 1.00 | — |
| Yr.10(1998) Proof | 30,000 | Value: 2.00 | | | | |
| Yr.11(1999) | 58,850,000 | — | — | — | 1.00 | — |
| Yr.11(1999) Proof | 270,000 | Value: 2.00 | | | | |
| Yr.12(2000) | — | — | — | — | 1.00 | — |
| Yr.12(2000) Proof | — | Value: 2.00 | | | | |
| Yr.13(2001) | — | — | — | — | — | — |
| Yr.13(2001) Proof | — | — | — | — | — | — |

**100 YEN** Y# 77 **Weight:** 4.8000 g. **Composition:** 0.6000 Silver .0926 oz. ASW **Ruler:** Hirohito (Showa)

| Date | Mintage | F | VF | XF | Unc | BU |
|---|---|---|---|---|---|---|
| Yr.32(1957) | 30,000,000 | — | 1.50 | 2.50 | 9.00 | — |
| Yr.33(1958) | 70,000,000 | — | 1.50 | 2.50 | 6.00 | — |

**100 YEN** Y# 78 **Weight:** 4.8000 g. **Composition:** 0.6000 Silver .0926 oz. ASW **Ruler:** Hirohito (Showa)

| Date | Mintage | F | VF | XF | Unc | BU |
|---|---|---|---|---|---|---|
| Yr.34(1959) | 110,000,000 | — | 1.50 | 2.50 | 9.00 | — |
| Yr.35(1960) | 50,000,000 | — | 1.50 | 2.50 | 9.00 | — |
| Yr.36(1961) | 15,000,000 | — | 1.50 | 2.50 | 9.00 | — |
| Yr.38(1963) | 45,000,000 | — | 1.50 | 2.50 | 6.00 | — |
| Yr.39(1964) | 10,000,000 | — | 1.75 | 3.50 | 7.50 | — |
| Yr.40(1965) | 62,500,000 | — | 1.50 | 2.50 | 4.00 | — |
| Yr.41(1966) | 97,500,000 | — | 1.50 | 2.50 | 4.00 | — |

**100 YEN** Y# 79 **Weight:** 4.8000 g. **Composition:** 0.6000 Silver .0926 oz. ASW **Ruler:** Hirohito (Showa) **Subject:** 1964 Olympic Games

| Date | Mintage | F | VF | XF | Unc | BU |
|---|---|---|---|---|---|---|
| Yr.39/1964 | 80,000,000 | — | 1.00 | 2.00 | 3.50 | — |

**100 YEN** Y# 82 **Composition:** Copper-Nickel **Ruler:** Hirohito (Showa)

| Date | Mintage | F | VF | XF | Unc | BU |
|---|---|---|---|---|---|---|
| Yr.42(1967) | 432,200,000 | — | — | 1.50 | 2.50 | — |
| **Note:** Varieties exist | | | | | | |
| Yr.43(1968) | 471,000,000 | — | — | 1.50 | 2.50 | — |
| Yr.44(1969) | 323,700,000 | — | — | 1.50 | 2.50 | — |
| Yr.45(1970) | 237,100,000 | — | — | 1.50 | 2.50 | — |
| Yr.46(1971) | 481,050,000 | — | — | 1.50 | 2.50 | — |
| Yr.47(1972) | 468,950,000 | — | — | 1.50 | 2.50 | — |
| Yr.48(1973) | 680,000,000 | — | — | 1.50 | 2.50 | — |
| Yr.49(1974) | 660,000,000 | — | — | 1.50 | 2.50 | — |
| Yr.50(1975) | 437,160,000 | — | — | 1.50 | 2.50 | — |
| Yr.51(1976) | 322,840,000 | — | — | 1.50 | 2.50 | — |
| Yr.52(1977) | 440,000,000 | — | — | 1.50 | 2.50 | — |
| Yr.53(1978) | 292,000,000 | — | — | 1.50 | 2.50 | — |
| Yr.54(1979) | 382,000,000 | — | — | 1.50 | 2.50 | — |
| Yr.55(1980) | 588,000,000 | — | — | 1.50 | 2.50 | — |
| Yr.56(1981) | 348,000,000 | — | — | 1.50 | 2.50 | — |
| Yr.57(1982) | 110,000,000 | — | — | 1.50 | 2.50 | — |
| Yr.58(1983) | 50,000,000 | — | — | 1.50 | 2.50 | — |
| Yr.59(1984) | 41,850,000 | — | — | 1.50 | 2.50 | — |
| Yr.60(1985) | 58,150,000 | — | — | 1.50 | 2.50 | — |
| Yr.61(1986) | 99,960,000 | — | — | 1.50 | 2.50 | — |
| Yr.62(1987) | 193,545,000 | — | — | 1.50 | 2.50 | — |
| Yr.62(1987) Proof | 230,000 | Value: 5.00 | | | | |
| Yr.63(1988) | 362,912,000 | — | — | 1.50 | 2.50 | — |
| Yr.63(1988) Proof | 200,000 | Value: 5.00 | | | | |

**100 YEN** Y# 83 **Composition:** Copper-Nickel **Ruler:** Hirohito (Showa) **Subject:** Osaka Expo '70

| Date | Mintage | F | VF | XF | Unc | BU |
|---|---|---|---|---|---|---|
| Yr.45(1970) | 40,000,000 | — | 2.00 | 3.00 | 5.50 | — |

**100 YEN** Y# 84 **Composition:** Copper-Nickel **Ruler:** Hirohito (Showa) **Subject:** 1972 Winter Olympic Games - Sapporo

| Date | Mintage | F | VF | XF | Unc | BU |
|---|---|---|---|---|---|---|
| Yr.47/1972 | 30,000,000 | — | 2.50 | 4.00 | 6.50 | — |

**100 YEN** Y# 85 **Composition:** Copper-Nickel **Ruler:** Hirohito (Showa) **Subject:** Okinawa Expo '75

| Date | Mintage | F | VF | XF | Unc | BU |
|---|---|---|---|---|---|---|
| Yr.50(1975) | 120,000,000 | — | 1.50 | 2.50 | 3.00 | — |

**100 YEN** Y# 86 **Composition:** Copper-Nickel **Ruler:** Hirohito (Showa) **Subject:** 50th Anniversary of Reign

| Date | Mintage | F | VF | XF | Unc | BU |
|---|---|---|---|---|---|---|
| Yr.51(1976) | 70,000,000 | — | 2.00 | 3.00 | 5.50 | — |

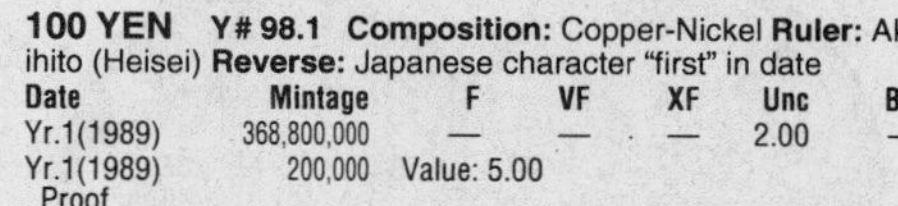

**100 YEN** Y# 98.1 **Composition:** Copper-Nickel **Ruler:** Akihito (Heisei) **Reverse:** Japanese character "first" in date

| Date | Mintage | F | VF | XF | Unc | BU |
|---|---|---|---|---|---|---|
| Yr.1(1989) | 368,800,000 | — | — | — | 2.00 | — |
| Yr.1(1989) Proof | 200,000 | Value: 5.00 | | | | |

**100 YEN** Y# 98.2 **Composition:** Copper-Nickel **Ruler:** Akihito (Heisei)

| Date | Mintage | F | VF | XF | Unc | BU |
|---|---|---|---|---|---|---|
| Yr.2(1990) | 444,753,000 | — | — | — | 2.00 | — |
| Yr.2(1990) Proof | 200,000 | Value: 5.00 | | | | |
| Yr.3(1991) | 374,900,000 | — | — | — | 2.00 | — |
| Yr.3(1991) Proof | 220,000 | Value: 5.00 | | | | |
| Yr.4(1992) | 211,050,000 | — | — | — | 2.00 | — |
| Yr.4(1992) Proof | 250,000 | Value: 5.00 | | | | |
| Yr.5(1993) | 81,990,000 | — | — | — | 2.00 | — |
| Yr.5(1993) Proof | 250,000 | Value: 5.00 | | | | |
| Yr.6(1994) | 81,540,000 | — | — | — | 2.00 | — |
| Yr.6(1994) Proof | 227,000 | Value: 5.00 | | | | |
| Yr.7(1995) | 92,674,000 | — | — | — | 2.00 | — |
| Yr.7(1995) Proof | 200,000 | Value: 5.00 | | | | |
| Yr.8(1996) | 37,024,000 | — | — | — | 2.00 | — |
| Yr.8(1996) Proof | 189,000 | Value: 5.00 | | | | |
| Yr.9(1997) | 271,876,000 | — | — | — | 2.00 | — |
| Yr.9(1997) Proof | 212,000 | Value: 5.00 | | | | |
| Yr.10(1998) | 251,521,000 | — | — | — | 2.00 | — |
| Yr.10(1998) Proof | 30,000 | Value: 5.00 | | | | |
| Yr.11(1999) | 178,850,000 | — | — | — | 2.00 | — |
| Yr.11(1999) Proof | 280,000 | Value: 5.00 | | | | |
| Yr.12(2000) | — | — | — | — | 2.00 | — |
| Yr.12(2000) Proof | — | Value: 5.00 | | | | |
| Yr.13(2001) | — | — | — | — | — | — |
| Yr.13(2001) Proof | — | — | — | — | — | — |

**500 YEN** Y# 87 **Composition:** Copper-Nickel **Ruler:** Hirohito (Showa) **Obverse:** Pawlownia flower

| Date | Mintage | F | VF | XF | Unc | BU |
|---|---|---|---|---|---|---|
| Yr.57(1982) | 300,000,000 | — | — | 7.00 | 9.00 | — |
| Yr.58(1983) | 240,000,000 | — | — | 7.00 | 9.00 | — |
| Yr.59(1984) | 342,850,000 | — | — | 7.00 | 9.00 | — |
| Yr.60(1985) | 97,150,000 | — | — | 7.00 | 9.00 | — |
| Yr.61(1986) | 49,960,000 | — | — | 7.00 | 9.00 | — |
| Yr.62(1987) | 2,545,000 | — | 7.00 | 9.00 | 15.00 | — |
| Yr.62(1987) Proof | 230,000 | Value: 25.00 | | | | |
| Yr.63(1988) | 148,018,000 | — | — | 7.00 | 9.00 | — |
| Yr.63(1988) Proof | 200,000 | Value: 15.00 | | | | |
| Yr.64(1989) | 16,042,000 | — | — | 7.00 | 12.00 | — |

**500 YEN** Y# 88 **Composition:** Copper-Nickel **Ruler:** Hirohito (Showa) **Subject:** 1985 Tsukuba Expo

| Date | Mintage | F | VF | XF | Unc | BU |
|---|---|---|---|---|---|---|
| Yr.60(1985) | 70,000,000 | — | — | 7.00 | 9.00 | — |

**500 YEN** Y# 89 **Composition:** Copper-Nickel **Ruler:** Hirohito (Showa) **Subject:** 100th Anniversary - Governmental Cabinet System

| Date | Mintage | F | VF | XF | Unc | BU |
|---|---|---|---|---|---|---|
| Yr.60(1985) | 70,000,000 | — | — | 7.00 | 9.00 | — |

**500 YEN** Y# 90 **Composition:** Copper-Nickel **Ruler:** Hirohito (Showa) **Subject:** 60 Years of Reign of Hirohito

| Date | Mintage | F | VF | XF | Unc | BU |
|---|---|---|---|---|---|---|
| Yr.61(1986) | 50,000,000 | — | — | 7.00 | 10.00 | — |

**500 YEN** Y# 93 **Composition:** Copper-Nickel **Ruler:** Hirohito (Showa) **Subject:** Opening of Seikan Tunnel

| Date | Mintage | F | VF | XF | Unc | BU |
|---|---|---|---|---|---|---|
| Yr.63(1988) | 20,000,000 | — | — | 8.00 | 12.50 | — |

**500 YEN** Y# 94 **Composition:** Copper-Nickel **Ruler:** Hirohito (Showa) **Subject:** Opening of Seto Bridge

| Date | Mintage | F | VF | XF | Unc | BU |
|---|---|---|---|---|---|---|
| Yr.63(1988) | 20,000,000 | — | — | 8.00 | 12.50 | — |

**500 YEN** Y# 99.1 **Composition:** Copper-Nickel **Ruler:** Hirohito (Showa) **Reverse:** Japanese character "first" in date

| Date | Mintage | F | VF | XF | Unc | BU |
|---|---|---|---|---|---|---|
| Yr.1(1989) | 192,652,000 | — | — | 7.00 | 9.00 | — |
| Yr.1(1989) Proof | 200,000 | Value: 15.00 | | | | |

**500 YEN** Y# 99.2 **Composition:** Copper-Nickel **Ruler:** Hirohito (Showa)

| Date | Mintage | F | VF | XF | Unc | BU |
|---|---|---|---|---|---|---|
| Yr.2(1990) | 159,753,000 | — | — | 7.00 | 9.00 | — |
| Yr.2(1990) Proof | 200,000 | Value: 15.00 | | | | |
| Yr.3(1991) | 169,900,000 | — | — | 7.00 | 9.00 | — |
| Yr.3(1991) Proof | 220,000 | Value: 15.00 | | | | |
| Yr.4(1992) | 87,880,000 | — | — | 7.00 | 9.00 | — |
| Yr.4(1992) Proof | 250,000 | Value: 15.00 | | | | |
| Yr.51993) | 131,990,000 | — | — | 7.00 | 9.00 | — |
| Yr.5(1993) Proof | 250,000 | Value: 15.00 | | | | |
| Yr.6(1994) | 105,545,000 | — | — | 7.00 | 9.00 | — |
| Yr.6(1994) Proof | 227,000 | Value: 15.00 | | | | |
| Yr.7(1995) | 182,665,000 | — | — | — | 9.00 | — |
| Yr.7(1995) Proof | 200,000 | Value: 15.00 | | | | |
| Yr.8(1996) | 99,024,000 | — | — | — | 9.00 | — |
| Yr.8(1996) Proof | 189,000 | Value: 15.00 | | | | |
| Yr.9(1997) | 271,876,000 | — | — | — | 9.00 | — |
| Yr.9(1997) Proof | 212,000 | Value: 15.00 | | | | |
| Yr.10(1998) | 214,578,000 | — | — | — | 9.00 | — |
| Yr.10(1998) Proof | 30,000 | Value: 15.00 | | | | |
| Yr.11(1999) | 164,840,000 | — | — | — | 9.00 | — |
| Yr.11(1999) Proof | 280,000 | Value: 15.00 | | | | |

**500 YEN** Y# 102 **Composition:** Copper-Nickel **Ruler:** Hirohito (Showa) **Subject:** Enthronement of Emperor Akihito

| Date | Mintage | F | VF | XF | Unc | BU |
|---|---|---|---|---|---|---|
| Yr.2(1990) | 30,000,000 | — | — | — | 15.00 | — |

**500 YEN** Y# 106 **Composition:** Copper-Nickel **Ruler:** Hirohito (Showa) **Subject:** 20th Anniversary - Reversion of Okinawa

| Date | Mintage | F | VF | XF | Unc | BU |
|---|---|---|---|---|---|---|
| Yr.4(1992) | 19,953,000 | — | — | — | 17.50 | — |
| Yr.4(1992) Proof | 47,000 | Value: 25.00 | | | | |

**500 YEN** Y# 107 **Composition:** Copper-Nickel **Ruler:** Hirohito (Showa) **Subject:** Royal wedding of Crown Prince

| Date | Mintage | F | VF | XF | Unc | BU |
|---|---|---|---|---|---|---|
| Yr.5(1993) | 29,800,000 | — | — | — | 15.00 | — |
| Yr.5(1993) Proof | 200,000 | Value: 20.00 | | | | |

**500 YEN** Y# 110 **Composition:** Copper-Nickel **Ruler:** Hirohito (Showa) **Subject:** Opening of Kansai International Airport

| Date | Mintage | F | VF | XF | Unc | BU |
|---|---|---|---|---|---|---|
| Yr.6(1994) | 19,900,000 | — | — | — | 17.50 | — |
| Yr.6(1994) Proof | 100,000 | Value: 40.00 | | | | |

**500 YEN** Y# 111 **Composition:** Copper-Nickel **Ruler:** Hirohito (Showa) **Subject:** 12th Asian Games **Reverse:** Runners

| Date | Mintage | F | VF | XF | Unc | BU |
|---|---|---|---|---|---|---|
| Yr.6(1994) | 9,900,000 | — | — | — | 15.00 | — |
| Yr.6(1994) Proof | 100,000 | Value: 30.00 | | | | |

**500 YEN** Y# 112 **Composition:** Copper-Nickel **Ruler:** Hirohito (Showa) **Subject:** 12th Asian Games **Reverse:** Swimmers

| Date | Mintage | F | VF | XF | Unc | BU |
|---|---|---|---|---|---|---|
| Yr.6(1994) | 9,900,000 | — | — | — | 15.00 | — |
| Yr.6(1994) Proof | 100,000 | Value: 30.00 | | | | |

**500 YEN** Y# 113 **Composition:** Copper-Nickel **Ruler:** Hirohito (Showa) **Subject:** 12th Asian Games **Reverse:** Jumper

| Date | Mintage | F | VF | XF | Unc | BU |
|---|---|---|---|---|---|---|
| Yr.6(1994) | 9,900,000 | — | — | — | 15.00 | — |
| Yr.6(1994) Proof | 100,000 | Value: 30.00 | | | | |

**500 YEN** **Y# 114** **Composition:** Copper-Nickel **Ruler:** Hirohito (Showa) **Series:** 1998 Nagano Winter Olympics **Obverse:** Snowboarder **Reverse:** Ptarmigan, denomination, dates

| Date | Mintage | F | VF | XF | Unc | BU |
|---|---|---|---|---|---|---|
| Yr.9(1977) | 19,867,000 | — | — | — | 10.00 | — |
| Yr.9(1977) Proof | 133,000 | Value: 35.00 | | | | |

**500 YEN** **Y# 117** **Composition:** Copper-Nickel **Ruler:** Hirohito (Showa) **Series:** 1998 Nagano Winter Olympics **Obverse:** Bobsledding **Reverse:** Ptarmigan, denomination, dates

| Date | Mintage | F | VF | XF | Unc | BU |
|---|---|---|---|---|---|---|
| Yr.9(1997) | 19,867,000 | — | — | — | 10.00 | — |
| Yr.9(1997) Proof | 133,000 | Value: 35.00 | | | | |

**500 YEN** **Y# 118** **Composition:** Copper-Nickel **Ruler:** Hirohito (Showa) **Series:** 1998 Nagano Winter Olympics **Obverse:** Acrobat skier **Reverse:** Ptarmigan, denomination, dates

| Date | Mintage | F | VF | XF | Unc | BU |
|---|---|---|---|---|---|---|
| Yr.10(1998) | 19,867,000 | — | — | — | 10.00 | — |
| Yr.10(1998) Proof | 133,000 | Value: 35.00 | | | | |

**500 YEN** **Y# 123** **Composition:** Copper-Nickel **Ruler:** Hirohito (Showa) **Subject:** 10th Anniversary of Enthronement **Obverse:** Mt. Fuji and chrysanthemums **Reverse:** Chrysanthemum in wreath

| Date | Mintage | F | VF | XF | Unc | BU |
|---|---|---|---|---|---|---|
| Yr.11(1999) | — | — | — | — | 10.00 | — |
| Yr.11(1999) Proof | — | Value: 30.00 | | | | |

**1000 YEN** **Y# 80** **Weight:** 20.0000 g. **Composition:** 0.9250 Silver .5948 oz. ASW **Ruler:** Hirohito (Showa) **Series:** 1964 Olympic Games **Note:** Dav. #276

| Date | Mintage | F | VF | XF | Unc | BU |
|---|---|---|---|---|---|---|
| Yr.39/1964 | 15,000,000 | — | 20.00 | 30.00 | 50.00 | — |

**5000 YEN** **Y# 100** **Weight:** 15.0000 g. **Composition:** 0.9250 Silver .4461 oz. ASW **Ruler:** Akihito (Heisei) **Subject:** Osaka Exposition

| Date | Mintage | F | VF | XF | Unc | BU |
|---|---|---|---|---|---|---|
| Yr.2/1990 | 10,000,000 | — | — | — | 65.00 | — |

**5000 YEN** **Y# 103** **Weight:** 15.0000 g. **Composition:** 0.9250 Silver .4461 oz. ASW **Ruler:** Akihito (Heisei) **Subject:** Centennial of Parliament

| Date | Mintage | F | VF | XF | Unc | BU |
|---|---|---|---|---|---|---|
| Yr.2(1990) | 5,000,000 | — | — | — | 65.00 | — |

**5000 YEN** **Y# 104** **Weight:** 15.0000 g. **Composition:** 0.9250 Silver .4461 oz. ASW **Ruler:** Akihito (Heisei) **Subject:** Centennial of Judicial System

| Date | Mintage | F | VF | XF | Unc | BU |
|---|---|---|---|---|---|---|
| Yr.2(1990) | 5,000,000 | — | — | — | 65.00 | — |

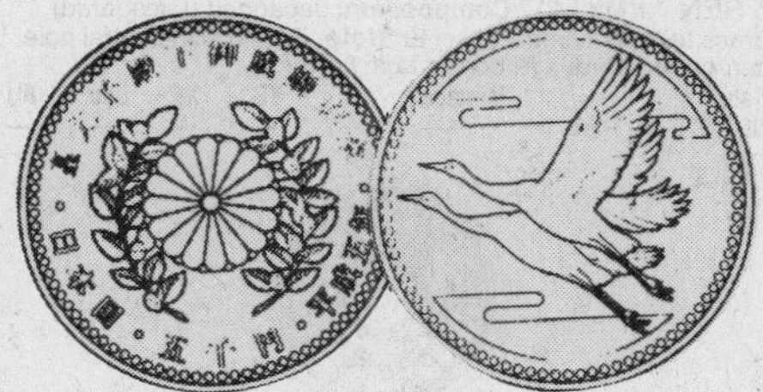

**5000 YEN** **Y# 108** **Weight:** 15.0000 g. **Composition:** 1.0000 Silver .4823 oz. ASW **Ruler:** Akihito (Heisei) **Subject:** Royal wedding of Crown Prince

| Date | Mintage | F | VF | XF | Unc | BU |
|---|---|---|---|---|---|---|
| Yr.5(1993) | 4,800,000 | — | — | — | 70.00 | — |
| Yr.5(1993) Proof | 200,000 | Value: 100 | | | | |

**5000 YEN** **Y# 115** **Weight:** 15.0000 g. **Composition:** 0.9250 Silver .4461 oz. ASW **Ruler:** Akihito (Heisei) **Series:** 1998 Nagano Winter Olympics **Obverse:** Hockey player **Reverse:** Denomination, dates, and Serow

| Date | Mintage | F | VF | XF | Unc | BU |
|---|---|---|---|---|---|---|
| Yr.9(1997) | 4,867,000 | — | — | — | 70.00 | — |
| Yr.9(1997) Proof | 133,000 | Value: 120 | | | | |

**5000 YEN** **Y# 119** **Weight:** 15.0000 g. **Composition:** 0.9250 Silver .4461 oz. ASW **Ruler:** Akihito (Heisei) **Series:** 1998 Nagano Winter Olympics **Obverse:** Biathalon **Reverse:** Denomination, dates, and antelope

| Date | Mintage | F | VF | XF | Unc | BU |
|---|---|---|---|---|---|---|
| Yr.9(1997) | 4,867,000 | — | — | — | 70.00 | — |
| Yr.9(1997) Proof | 133,000 | Value: 120 | | | | |

**5000 YEN** **Y# 120** **Weight:** 15.0000 g. **Composition:** 0.9250 Silver .4461 oz. ASW **Ruler:** Akihito (Heisei) **Series:** 1998 Nagano Winter Olympics **Obverse:** Paralympic skier **Reverse:** Denomination, dates, and antelope

| Date | Mintage | F | VF | XF | Unc | BU |
|---|---|---|---|---|---|---|
| Yr.10(1998) | 4,867,000 | — | — | — | 70.00 | — |
| Yr.10(1998) Proof | 133,000 | Value: 120 | | | | |

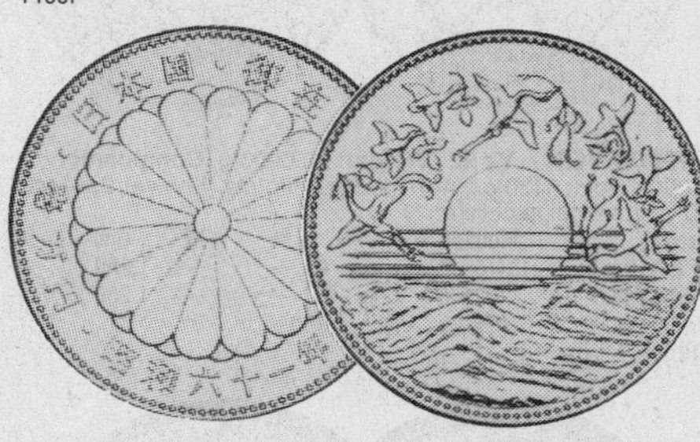

**10000 YEN** **Y# 91** **Weight:** 20.0000 g. **Composition:** 0.9990 Silver .6430 oz. ASW **Ruler:** Hirohito (Showa) **Subject:** 60 Years - Reign of Hirohito

| Date | Mintage | F | VF | XF | Unc | BU |
|---|---|---|---|---|---|---|
| Yr.61(1986) | 10,000,000 | — | — | — | 135 | — |

**10000 YEN** **Y# 116** **Weight:** 15.6000 g. **Composition:** 1.0000 Gold .5022 oz. AGW **Ruler:** Akihito (Heisei) **Series:** 1998 Nagano Winter Olympics **Obverse:** Ski jumper **Reverse:** Denomination, dates, and gentian plant

| Date | Mintage | F | VF | XF | Unc | BU |
|---|---|---|---|---|---|---|
| Yr.9(1997) Proof | 55,000 | Value: 650 | | | | |

**10000 YEN** **Y# 121** **Weight:** 15.6000 g. **Composition:** 1.0000 Gold .5022 oz. AGW **Ruler:** Akihito (Heisei) **Series:** 1998 Nagano Winter Olympics **Obverse:** Figure skater **Reverse:** Denomination, dates, and gentian plant

| Date | Mintage | F | VF | XF | Unc | BU |
|---|---|---|---|---|---|---|
| Yr.9(1997) Proof | 55,000 | Value: 650 | | | | |

**10000 YEN** **Y# 122** **Weight:** 15.6000 g. **Composition:** 1.0000 Gold .5022 oz. AGW **Ruler:** Akihito (Heisei) **Series:** 1998 Nagano Winter Olympics **Obverse:** Speed skater **Reverse:** Denomination, dates, and gentian plant

| Date | Mintage | F | VF | XF | Unc | BU |
|---|---|---|---|---|---|---|
| Yr.10(1998) Proof | 55,000 | Value: 650 | | | | |

**10000 YEN** **Y# 124** **Weight:** 20.0000 g. **Composition:** 1.0000 Gold .6430 oz. AGW **Ruler:** Akihito (Heisei) **Subject:** 15th Anniversary of Enthronement **Obverse:** Chrysanthemum in wreath **Reverse:** Stylized Green Pheasant

| Date | Mintage | F | VF | XF | Unc | BU |
|---|---|---|---|---|---|---|
| Yr.11(1999) Proof | 200,000 | Value: 1,200 | | | | |

**50000 YEN** Y# 109 **Weight:** 18.0000 g. **Composition:** 1.0000 Gold .5788 oz. AGW **Ruler:** Akihito (Heisei) **Subject:** Royal wedding of Crown Prince

| Date | Mintage | F | VF | XF | Unc | BU |
|---|---|---|---|---|---|---|
| Yr.5(1993) | 1,800,000 | — | — | — | 650 | — |
| Yr.5(1993) Proof | 200,000 | Value: 850 | | | | |

**100000 YEN** Y# 92 **Weight:** 20.0000 g. **Composition:** 1.0000 Gold .6430 oz. AGW **Ruler:** Hirohito (Showa) **Subject:** 60 Years - Reign of Hirohito

| Date | Mintage | F | VF | XF | Unc | BU |
|---|---|---|---|---|---|---|
| Yr.61(1986) | 10,000,000 | — | — | — | 1,250 | — |
| Yr.62(1987) | 876,000 | — | — | — | 1,250 | — |
| Yr.62(1987) Proof | 125,000 | Value: 1,350 | | | | |

**100000 YEN** Y# 105 **Weight:** 30.0000 g. **Composition:** 1.0000 Gold .9646 oz. AGW **Ruler:** Akihito (Heisei) **Subject:** Enthronement of Emperor Akihito **Obverse:** Chrysanthemum in wreath **Reverse:** Stylized Green Pheasant

| Date | Mintage | F | VF | XF | Unc | BU |
|---|---|---|---|---|---|---|
| Yr.2(1990) | 1,900,000 | — | — | — | 1,250 | — |
| Yr.2(1990) Proof | 100,000 | Value: 1,350 | | | | |

## PLATINUM BULLION COINAGE

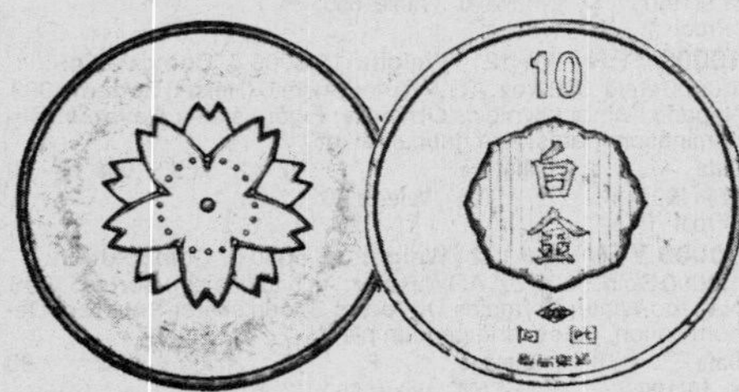

**10 MOMME** KM# 20 **Weight:** 37.4000 g. **Composition:** Platinum APW **Ruler:** Hirohito (Showa)

| Date | Mintage | F | VF | XF | Unc | BU |
|---|---|---|---|---|---|---|
| 1937 | 1,500 | — | — | — | 1,750 | — |

## LEPROSARIUM COINAGE

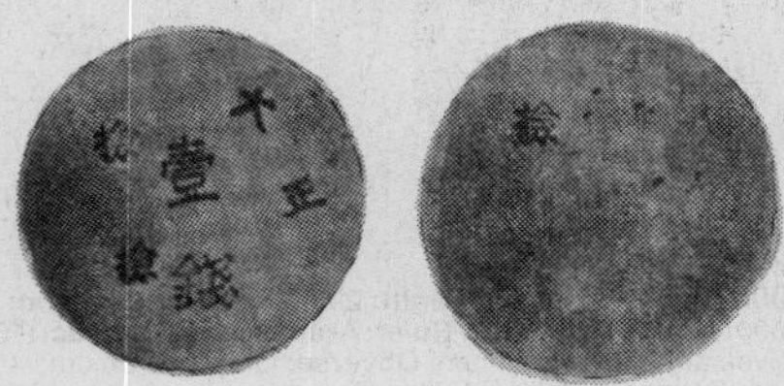

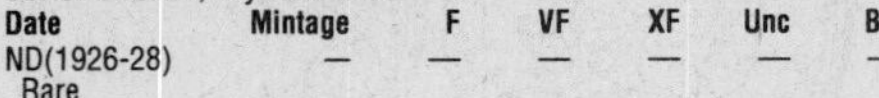

**SEN** KM# L11 **Composition:** Brass **Issuer:** Oshima-Seisho En **Obverse:** Denomination with mulitple stamps **Reverse:** "Ken" symbol = inspection

| Date | Mintage | F | VF | XF | Unc | BU |
|---|---|---|---|---|---|---|
| ND(1912-25) Rare | — | — | — | — | — | — |

**SEN** KM# L20 **Composition:** Japanned (Lacquered) Brass **Issuer:** Tama-Zensei En **Note:** Uniface. Oval with central hole, denomination, rays at border.

| Date | Mintage | F | VF | XF | Unc | BU |
|---|---|---|---|---|---|---|
| ND(1926-28) Rare | — | — | — | — | — | — |

**SEN** KM# L1 **Composition:** Japanned (Lacquered) Brass **Issuer:** Nagashima-Aisei En **Note:** Uniface. Badge of Aisei En above denomination.

| Date | Mintage | F | VF | XF | Unc | BU |
|---|---|---|---|---|---|---|
| ND(1931-48) Rare | — | — | — | — | — | — |

**SEN** KM# L2 **Composition:** Japanned Aluminum **Issuer:** Nagashima-Aisei En

| Date | Mintage | F | VF | XF | Unc | BU |
|---|---|---|---|---|---|---|
| ND(1931-48) | — | — | 450 | 750 | — | — |

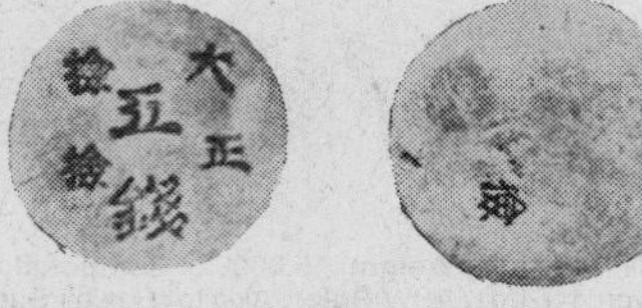

**2 SEN** KM# L12 **Composition:** Brass **Issuer:** Oshima-Seisho En

| Date | Mintage | F | VF | XF | Unc | BU |
|---|---|---|---|---|---|---|
| ND(1912-25) Rare | — | — | — | — | — | — |

**5 SEN** KM# L13 **Composition:** Brass **Issuer:** Oshima-Seisho En

| Date | Mintage | F | VF | XF | Unc | BU |
|---|---|---|---|---|---|---|
| ND(1912-25) Rare | — | — | — | — | — | — |

**5 SEN** KM# L21 **Composition:** Japanned (Lacquered) Brass **Issuer:** Tama-Zensei En **Note:** Round with central hole, perpendicular rays fill border from flower.

| Date | Mintage | F | VF | XF | Unc | BU |
|---|---|---|---|---|---|---|
| ND(1926-28) Rare | — | — | — | — | — | — |

**5 SEN** KM# L3 **Composition:** Japanned (Lacquered) Brass **Issuer:** Nagashima-Aisei En

| Date | Mintage | F | VF | XF | Unc | BU |
|---|---|---|---|---|---|---|
| ND(1931-48) Rare | — | — | — | — | — | — |

**5 SEN** KM# L3a **Composition:** Japanned Aluminum **Issuer:** Nagashima-Aisei En

| Date | Mintage | F | VF | XF | Unc | BU |
|---|---|---|---|---|---|---|
| ND(1931-48) | — | — | 750 | 1,250 | — | — |

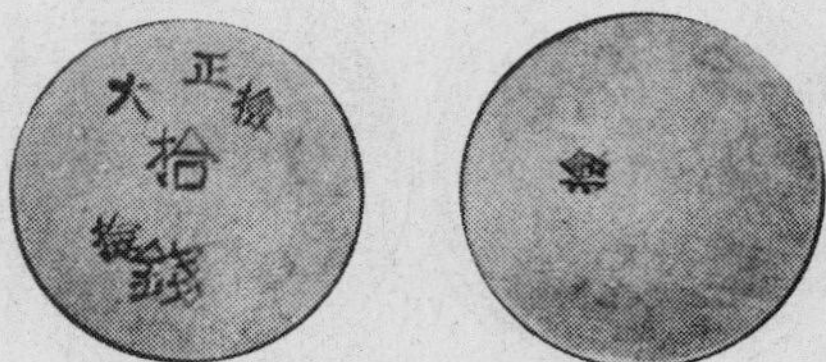

**10 SEN** KM# L14 **Composition:** Brass **Issuer:** Oshima-Seisho En

| Date | Mintage | F | VF | XF | Unc | BU |
|---|---|---|---|---|---|---|
| ND(1912-25) Rare | — | — | — | — | — | — |

**10 SEN** KM# L22 **Composition:** Japanned (Lacquered) Brass **Issuer:** Tama-Zensei En **Note:** Similar to 5 Sen, L21.

| Date | Mintage | F | VF | XF | Unc | BU |
|---|---|---|---|---|---|---|
| ND(1926-28) Rare | — | — | — | — | — | — |

**10 SEN** KM# L4 **Composition:** Japanned (Lacquered) Brass **Issuer:** Nagashima-Aisei En

| Date | Mintage | F | VF | XF | Unc | BU |
|---|---|---|---|---|---|---|
| ND(1931-48) Rare | — | — | — | — | — | — |

**10 SEN** KM# L4a **Composition:** Japanned Aluminum **Issuer:** Nagashima-Aisei En

| Date | Mintage | F | VF | XF | Unc | BU |
|---|---|---|---|---|---|---|
| ND(1931-48) | — | — | 750 | 1,250 | — | — |

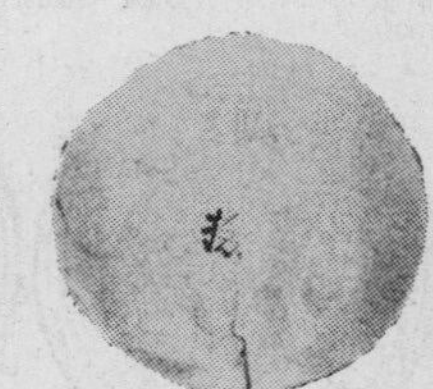

**20 SEN** KM# L15 **Composition:** Brass **Issuer:** Oshima-Seisho En

| Date | Mintage | F | VF | XF | Unc | BU |
|---|---|---|---|---|---|---|
| ND(1912-25) Rare | — | — | — | — | — | — |

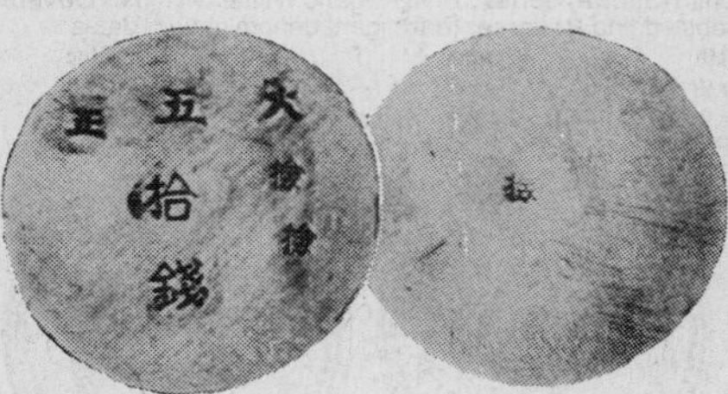

**50 SEN** KM# L16 **Composition:** Brass **Issuer:** Oshima-Seisho En

| Date | Mintage | F | VF | XF | Unc | BU |
|---|---|---|---|---|---|---|
| ND(1912-25) Rare | — | — | — | — | — | — |

**50 SEN** KM# L23 **Composition:** Japanned (Lacquered) Brass **Issuer:** Tama-Zensei En **Note:** Rectangular with center hole. Sunset with ornate border.

| Date | Mintage | F | VF | XF | Unc | BU |
|---|---|---|---|---|---|---|
| ND(1926-28) Rare | — | — | — | — | — | — |

**50 SEN** KM# L5 **Composition:** Japanned (Lacquered) Brass **Issuer:** Nagashima-Aisei En

| Date | Mintage | F | VF | XF | Unc | BU |
|---|---|---|---|---|---|---|
| ND(1931-48) | — | — | 900 | 1,500 | — | — |

**YEN** KM# L6 **Composition:** Brass **Issuer:** Nagashima-Aisei En **Reverse:** Stylized badge of Asei En

| Date | Mintage | F | VF | XF | Unc | BU |
|---|---|---|---|---|---|---|
| ND(1931-48) | — | — | 1,500 | 2,500 | — | — |

## OCCUPATION COINAGE

**SEN Y# 22 Composition:** Aluminum

| Date | Mintage | F | VF | XF | Unc | BU |
|---|---|---|---|---|---|---|
| NE2603(1943) | 233,190,000 | — | 85.00 | 120 | 175 | — |
| NE2604(1944) | 66,810,000 | — | 75.00 | 110 | 150 | — |

**10 SEN Y# A24 Composition:** Tin Alloy **Note:** Previous number: Y#24

| Date | Mintage | F | VF | XF | Unc | BU |
|---|---|---|---|---|---|---|
| NE2603(1943) | 69,490,000 | — | 35.00 | 60.00 | 120 | — |
| NE2604(1944) | 110,510,000 | — | 25.00 | 50.00 | 100 | — |

## PATTERNS

Including off metal strikes

| KM# | Date | Mintage | Identification | Mkt Val |
|---|---|---|---|---|
| Pn31 | NE(1901) | — | Yen. Copper. Yr.34 | 3,250 |
| Pn32 | NE(1901) | — | Yen. Silver. Yr.34 | — |
| Pn33 | NE(1906) | — | 5 Rin. Copper. Yr.39 | 3,250 |
| Pn34 | NE(1908) | — | Sen. Copper. Yr.41 | 3,250 |
| Pn35 | NE(1909) | — | 5 Rin. Copper. Yr.42 | 3,250 |
| Pn37 | NE(1911) | — | Sen. Copper. Yr.44 | 3,250 |
| Pn36 | NE(1911) | — | Sen. Copper. Yr.42 | — |
| Pn38 | NE(1915) | — | Sen. Copper. Yr.4 | 3,250 |
| Pn39 | NE(1916) | — | 5 Rin. Copper. Yr.5 | 3,250 |
| Pn40 | NE(1916) | — | 5 Rin. Copper. Yr.5 | 3,250 |
| Pn41 | NE(1916) | — | Sen. Copper. Yr.5 | 3,250 |
| Pn44 | NE(1916) | — | 5 Sen. Copper-Nickel. Yr.5 | 3,250 |
| Pn42 | NE(1916) | — | Sen. Yr.5 | — |
| Pn43 | NE(1916) | — | Sen. Yr.5 of Taisho | — |
| Pn48 | NE(1918) | — | 50 Sen. Yr.7 | — |
| Pn45 | NE(1918) | — | 10 Sen. Silver. Yr.7 | 8,250 |
| Pn46 | NE(1918) | — | 20 Sen. Silver. Yr.7 | 10,000 |
| Pn47 | NE(1918) | — | 50 Sen. Silver. Yr.7 | 11,000 |
| Pn49 | NE(1919) | — | 10 Sen. Silver. Yr.8 | 7,500 |
| Pn50 | NE(1919) | — | 20 Sen. Silver. Yr.8 | 8,500 |
| Pn51 | NE(1919) | — | 20 Sen. Silver. Yr.8 | 12,500 |
| Pn52 | NE(1920) | — | 25 Sen. Silver. Yr.9 | — |
| Pn53 | NE(1920) | — | 50 Sen. Silver. Yr.9 | — |
| Pn54 | NE(1921) | — | 20 Sen. Silver. Yr.10 | 4,000 |
| Pn55 | NE(1923) | — | 50 Sen. Tin. Yr.12 | 850 |
| Pn56 | NE(1926) | — | 50 Sen. Tin. Yr.15 | 1,650 |
| Pn57 | NE(1927) | — | 50 Sen. Brass. Yr.2 | 625 |
| Pn58 | NE(1927) | — | 50 Sen. Silver. Yr.2 | 3,000 |
| Pn59 | NE(1927) | — | 50 Sen. Brass. Yr.2 | 575 |
| Pn60 | NE(1927) | — | 50 Sen. Silver. Yr.2 | 3,000 |
| Pn61 | NE(1928) | — | 50 Sen. Tin. Yr.3; Y#50 | 400 |
| Pn62 | NE(1933) | — | 5 Sen. Nickel. Yr.8; Y#54 | — |
| Pn63 | NE(1933) | — | 10 Sen. Nickel. Yr.8; Y#53 | — |
| Pn64 | NE(1937) | — | 5 Sen. Brass. Yr.12 | — |
| Pn65 | NE(1937) | — | 10 Sen. Brass. Yr.12 | — |
| Pn66 | NE(1938) | — | Sen. Aluminum. Yr.13 | — |
| Pn67 | NE(1938) | — | 5 Sen. Yr.13 | — |
| Pn68 | NE(1938) | — | 10 Sen. Yr.13 | — |
| Pn69 | NE(1938) | — | 50 Sen. White Metal. Y#50 | 2,500 |
| Pn70 | NE(1943) | — | Sen. Tin Alloy. Occupation issue Y#22 | — |
| Pn71 | NE(1943) | — | Sen. Red Fiber. Occupation issue Y#22 | — |
| Pn72 | NE(1943) | — | 5 Sen. Tin Alloy. Yr. 2603; Y#23 | — |
| PnA73 | NE(1943) | — | 10 Sen. Silver. Yr. 2603; Y#24 | — |
| Pn73 | NE(1945) | — | Sen. Brass. Yr.20; Y#62 | — |
| Pn74 | NE(1945) | — | Sen. White Baked Clay. Yr.20; numerous designs exist. | 150 |
| Pn75 | NE(1945) | — | Sen. Red Baked Clay. Yr.20; numerous designs exist. | 150 |
| Pn76 | NE(1945) | — | 5 Sen. White Baked Clay. Yr.20; numerous designs exist. | 150 |
| Pn77 | NE(1945) | — | 5 Sen. Red Baked Clay. Yr.20; numerous designs exist. | 150 |
| Pn78 | NE(1945) | — | 10 Sen. White Baked Clay. Yr.20; numerous designs exist. | 150 |
| Pn79 | NE(1945) | — | 10 Sen. Red Baked Clay. Yr.20; numerous designs exist. | 150 |
| Pn80 | NE(1946) | — | 10 Sen. Brass. Yr.21; small size; Y#68 | — |
| Pn81 | NE(1950) | — | Yen. Brass. Yr.25; Y#70 | — |
| Pn82 | NE(1950) | — | 10 Yen. Aluminum. Yr.25; Y#73 | — |
| Pn83 | NE(1950) | — | 10 Yen. Copper-Nickel. Yr.25 | 1,000 |
| Pn85 | NE(1951) | — | 10 Yen. Copper-Nickel. Yr.26 | 1,150 |
| Pn84 | NE(1951) | — | 5 Yen. Aluminum. Yr.26; Y#72 | — |
| Pn86 | NE(1958) | — | 5 Yen. Brass. Yr.33 | — |

## MINT SETS

| KM# | Date | Mintage | Identification | Issue Price | Mkt Val |
|---|---|---|---|---|---|
| MS1 | 1969 (5) | 6,162 | Y#72a, 73a, 74, 81, 82 | 1.25 | 650 |
| MS2 | 1970 (6) | 26,000 | Y#72a, 73a, 74, 81-83 | 2.00 | 50.00 |
| MS3 | 1971 (5) | 14,653 | Y#72a, 73a, 74, 81, 82 | 1.60 | 115 |
| MS4 | 1972 (6) | 30,000 | Y#72a, 73a, 74, 81, 82, 84 | 2.90 | 50.00 |
| MS5 | 1975 (5) | 720,000 | Y#72a, 73a, 74, 81, 82 | 2.30 | 5.00 |
| MS10 | 1980 (5) | 520,000 | Y#72a, 73a, 74, 81, 82 | 3.20 | 7.50 |
| MS11 | 1981 (5) | 568,000 | Y#72a, 73a, 74, 81, 82 | 4.00 | 7.50 |
| MS12 | 1982 (6) | 632,000 | Y#72a, 73a, 74, 81, 82, 87 | 6.80 | 9.00 |
| MS13 | 1983 (6) | 502,000 | Y#72a, 73a, 74, 81, 82, 87 | 6.80 | 20.00 |
| MS14 | 1984 (6) | 520,000 | Y#72a, 73a, 74, 81, 82, 87 | 7.40 | 22.50 |
| MS15 | 1985 (7) | 720,000 | Y#72a, 73a, 74, 81, 82, 87, 88 | 8.50 | 20.00 |
| MS16 | 1985 (7) | 100,000 | Y#72a, 73a, 74, 81, 82, 87, 88 | 8.50 | 90.00 |
| MS17 | 1985 (7) | 746,000 | Y#72a, 73a, 74, 81, 82, 87, 89 | 10.50 | 20.00 |
| MS18 | 1986 (7) | 642,000 | Y#72a, 73a, 74, 81, 82, 87, 90 | 15.00 | 20.00 |
| MS19 | 1986 (6) | 517,000 | Y#72a, 73a, 74, 81, 82, 87 | 9.20 | 12.00 |
| MS20 | 1987 (6) | 496,483 | Y#72a, 73a, 74, 81, 82, 87 | 12.00 | 175 |
| MS21 | 1987 (6) | 48,537 | Y#72a, 73a, 74, 81, 82, 87 | 12.00 | 200 |
| MS22 | 1988 (6) | 605,021 | Y#72a, 73a, 74, 81, 82, 87 | 12.40 | 15.00 |
| MS23 | 1988 (6) | 41,979 | Y#72a, 73a, 74, 81, 82, 87 | 12.40 | 20.00 |
| MS24 | 1988 (2) | 400,000 | Y#93-94 | 15.20 | 20.00 |
| MS25 | 1989 (6) | 647,000 | Y#95.1-99.1, 101.1 | 12.80 | 30.00 |
| MS26 | 1990 (6) | 600,000 | Y#95.2-99.2, 101.2 | 2.00 | 25.00 |
| MS27 | 1991 (6) | 600,000 | Y#95.2-99.2, 101.2 | 13.00 | 14.00 |
| MS28 | 1991 (6) | 10,000 | Y#95.2-99.2, 101.2 | 13.60 | 60.00 |
| MS29 | 1991 (6) | 50,000 | Y#95.2-99.2, 101.2 | 13.60 | 24.00 |
| MS30 | 1991 (6) | 40,000 | Y#95.2-99.2, 101.2 | 13.60 | 20.00 |
| MS31 | 1992 (7) | 650,000 | Y#95.2-99.2, 101.2, 106 | 18.40 | 25.00 |
| MS32 | 1992 (6) | 20,000 | Y#95.2-99.2, 101.2 | 13.60 | 30.00 |
| MS33 | 1992 (6) | 50,000 | Y#95.2-99.2, 101.2 | 13.60 | 25.00 |
| MS34 | 1992 (6) | 30,000 | Y#95.2-99.2, 101.2 | 13.60 | 30.00 |
| MS35 | 1993 (7) | 800,000 | Y#95.2-99.2, 101.2, 107 | 22.50 | 32.50 |
| MS36 | 1993 (6) | 70,000 | Y#95.2-99.2, 101.2 | 17.10 | 32.50 |
| MS37 | 1993 (6) | 30,000 | Y#95.2-99.2, 101.2 | 17.10 | 32.50 |
| MS38 | 1993 (6) | 10,000 | Y#95.2-99.2, 101.2 | 17.10 | 45.00 |
| MS39 | 1993 (6) | 30,000 | Y#95.2-99.2, 101.2 | 17.10 | 30.00 |
| MS40 | 1993 (6) | 100,000 | Y#95.2-99.2, 101.2 | 19.80 | 30.00 |
| MS41 | 1994 (6) | 80,000 | Y#95.2-99.2, 101.2 | 19.00 | 32.50 |
| MS42 | 1994 (6) | 20,000 | Y#95.2-99.2, 101.2 | 19.00 | 35.00 |
| MS43 | 1994 (6) | 10,000 | Y#95.2-99.2, 101.2 | 19.00 | 35.00 |
| MS44 | 1994 (6) | 10,000 | Y#95.2-99.2, 101.2 | 19.00 | 125 |
| MS45 | 1994 (6) | 30,000 | Y#95.2-99.2, 101.2 | 19.00 | 32.50 |
| MS46 | 1994 (6) | 800,000 | Y#95.2-99.2, 101.2 | 18.00 | 32.50 |
| MS47 | 1994 (6) | 100,000 | Y#95.2-99.2, 101.2 | 22.00 | 32.50 |
| MS48 | 1994 (6) | 10,000 | Y#95.2-99.2, 101.2 | 19.00 | 35.00 |
| MS49 | 1995 (6) | 80,000 | Y#95.2-99.2, 101.2 | 19.00 | 32.50 |
| MS50 | 1995 (6) | 10,000 | Y#95.2-99.2, 101.2 | 19.00 | 35.00 |
| MS51 | 1995 (6) | 10,000 | Y#95.2-99.2, 101.2 | 19.00 | 35.00 |
| MS52 | 1995 (6) | 10,000 | Y#95.2-99.2, 101.2 | 19.00 | 35.00 |
| MS53 | 1995 (6) | 10,000 | Y#95.2-99.2, 101.2 | 19.00 | 32.50 |
| MS54 | 1995 (6) | 12,000 | Y#95.2-99.2, 101.2 | 19.00 | 32.50 |
| MS55 | 1995 (6) | 600,000 | Y#95.2-99.2, 101.2 | 18.00 | 32.50 |
| MS56 | 1995 (6) | 200,000 | Y#95.2-99.2, 101.2 | 22.00 | 32.50 |
| MS57 | 1995 (6) | 390,000 | Y#95.2-99.2, 101.2 | 19.00 | 30.00 |
| MS58 | 1995 (6) | 192,500 | Y#95.2-99.2, 101.2 | 19.00 | 32.50 |
| MS59 | 1995 (6) | 191,500 | Y#95.2-99.2, 101.2 | 19.00 | 32.50 |
| MS6 | 1976 (5) | 580,000 | Y#72a, 73a, 74, 81, 82 | 2.80 | 5.00 |
| MS60 | 1995 (6) | 177,500 | Y#95.2-99.2, 101.2 | 19.00 | 32.50 |
| MS61 | 1995 (6) | 174,500 | Y#95.2-99.2, 101.2 | 19.00 | 32.50 |
| MS62 | 1995 (6) | 10,000 | Y#95.2-99.2, 101.2 | 18.00 | 32.50 |
| MS63 | 1995 (1) | 20,000 | Y#99.2 | 8.50 | 12.00 |
| MS64 | 1995 (6) | 20,000 | Y#95.2-99.2, 101.2 | 20.00 | 35.00 |
| MS65 | 1996 (6) | 80,000 | Y#95.2-99.2, 101.2 | 17.00 | 35.00 |
| MS66 | 1996 (6) | 10,000 | Y#95.2-99.2, 101.2 | 17.00 | 35.00 |
| MS67 | 1996 (1) | 10,000 | Y#99.2 | 8.00 | 12.00 |
| MS68 | 1996 (6) | 10,000 | Y#95.2-99.2, 101.2 | 19.00 | 35.00 |
| MS69 | 1996 (6) | 10,000 | Y#95.2-99.2, 101.2 | 17.00 | 35.00 |
| MS7 | 1977 (5) | 520,000 | Y#72a, 73a, 74, 81, 82 | 3.00 | 7.50 |
| MS70 | 1996 (6) | 20,000 | Y#95.2-99.2, 101.2 | 17.00 | 35.00 |
| MS71 | 1996 (6) | 8,000 | Y#95.2-99.2, 101.2 | 17.00 | 35.00 |
| MS72 | 1996 (6) | 290,000 | Y#95.2-99.2, 101.2 | 18.00 | 32.50 |
| MS73 | 1996 (6) | 200,000 | Y#95.2-99.2, 101.2 | 20.00 | 35.00 |
| MS74 | 1996 (6) | 100,000 | Y#95.2-99.2, 101.2 | 27.00 | 100 |
| MS75 | 1996 (6) | 321,000 | Y#95.2-99.2, 101.2 | 16.00 | 30.00 |
| MS76 | 1996 (6) | 6,000 | Y#95.2-99.2, 101.2 | 17.00 | 35.00 |
| MS77 | 1997 (1) | 10,000 | Y#101.2 | 8.00 | 12.00 |
| MS78 | 1997 (6) | 10,000 | Y#95.2-99.2, 101.2 | 17.00 | 32.50 |
| MS79 | 1997 (6) | 80,000 | Y#95.2-99.2, 101.2 | 16.00 | 32.50 |
| MS8 | 1978 (5) | 488,000 | Y#72a, 73a, 74, 81, 82 | 3.50 | 7.50 |
| MS80 | 1997 (6) | 10,000 | Y#95.2-99.2, 101.2 | 16.00 | 35.00 |
| MS81 | 1997 (6) | 10,000 | Y#95.2-99.2, 101.2 | 16.00 | 35.00 |
| MS82 | 1997 (6) | 20,000 | Y#95.2-99.2, 101.2 | 16.00 | 35.00 |
| MS83 | 1997 (6) | 10,000 | Y#95.2-99.2, 101.2 | 16.00 | 35.00 |
| MS84 | 1997 (6) | 331,000 | Y#95.2-99.2, 101.2 | 14.00 | 30.00 |
| MS85 | 1997 (6) | 250,000 | Y#95.2-99.2, 101.2 | 15.50 | 35.00 |
| MS86 | 1997 (6) | 8,000 | Y#95.2-99.2, 101.2 | 15.00 | 35.00 |
| MS87 | 1997 | 195,000 | Y#95.2-99.2, 101.2 | 15.50 | 32.50 |
| MS88 | 1997 (6) | 205,000 | Y#95.2-99.2, 101.2 | 15.50 | 32.50 |
| MS89 | 1998 (1) | 10,000 | Y#99.2 | 7.00 | 12.00 |
| MS9 | 1979 (5) | 400,000 | Y#72a, 73a, 74, 81, 82 | 3.80 | 8.50 |
| MS90 | 1998 (6) | 10,000 | Y#95.2-99.2, 101.2 | 16.00 | 35.00 |
| MS91 | 1998 (6) | 81,000 | Y#95.2-99.2, 101.2 | 14.50 | 35.00 |
| MS92 | 1998 (6) | 10,000 | Y#95.2-99.2, 101.2 | 14.50 | 35.00 |
| MS93 | 1998 (6) | 13,000 | Y#95.2-99.2, 101.2 | 14.50 | 35.00 |
| MS94 | 1998 (6) | 257,000 | Y#95.2-99.2, 101.2 | 17.00 | 35.00 |
| MS95 | 1998 (6) | 10,000 | Y#95.2-99.2, 101.2 | 17.00 | 45.00 |
| MS96 | 1998 (6) | 10,000 | Y#95.2-99.2, 101.2 | 17.00 | 45.00 |
| MS97 | 1998 (6) | 10,000 | Y#95.2-99.2, 101.2 | 17.00 | 45.00 |
| MS98 | 1998 (6) | 336,000 | Y#95.2-99.2, 101.2 | 17.50 | 35.00 |
| MS99 | 1998 (6) | 6,000 | Y#95.2-99.2, 101.2 | 18.05 | 35.00 |
| MS100 | 1999 (6) | 20,000 | Y#95.2-99.2, 101.2 | 19.95 | 35.00 |
| MS101 | 1999 (1) | 20,000 | Y#99.2 | 8.55 | 12.00 |
| MS102 | 1999 (6) | 6,000 | Y#95.2-99.2, 101.2 | 1,805 | 45.00 |
| MS103 | 1999 (6) | 80,000 | Y#95.2-99.2, 101.2 | 18.05 | 35.00 |
| MS104 | 1999 (6) | 10,000 | Y#95.2-99.2, 101.2 | 18.05 | 45.00 |
| MS105 | 1999 (6) | 10,000 | Y#95.2-99.2, 101.2 | 18.05 | 45.00 |
| MS106 | 1999 (6) | 10,000 | Y#95.2-99.2, 101.2 | 18.55 | 45.00 |
| MS107 | 1999 (6) | 6,000 | Y#95.2-99.2, 101.2 | 18.55 | 45.00 |
| MS108 | 1999 (6) | 200,000 | Y#95.2-99.2, 101.2 | 18.55 | 35.00 |
| MS109 | 1999 (6) | 250,000 | Y#95.2-99.2, 101.2 | 18.55 | 35.00 |
| MS110 | 1999 (6) | 300,000 | Y#95.2-99.2, 101.2 | 18.55 | 35.00 |
| MS111 | 2000 (5) | 5,000 | Y#95-98, 101 | 11.70 | 23.00 |
| MS112 | 2000 (5) | 65,000 | Y#95-98, 101 | 11.70 | 23.00 |
| MS113 | 2000 (5) | 10,000 | Y#95-98, 101 | 11.70 | 23.00 |
| MS114 | 2000 (5) | 10,000 | Y#95-98, 101 | 11.70 | 23.00 |
| MS115 | 2000 (5) | 10,000 | Y#95-98, 101 | 11.70 | 23.00 |
| MS116 | 2000 (5) | 7,000 | Y#95-98, 101 | 11.70 | 23.00 |
| MS117 | 2000 (5) | 4,000 | Y#95-98, 101 | 11.70 | 23.00 |
| MS118 | 2000 (6) | — | Y#95-98, 101, 123 | 18.00 | 35.00 |
| MS119 | 2000 (2) | — | Y#96, 99 | 9.00 | 17.00 |
| MS120 | 2000 (6) | 200,000 | Y#95-98, 101, 123 | 18.00 | 35.00 |
| MS121 | 2000 (6) | 500,000 | Y#95-98, 101, 123 | 16.20 | 25.00 |
| MS122 | 2000 (6) | 10,000 | Y#95-98, 101, 123 | 18.90 | 35.00 |
| MSA49 | 1994 (1) | 20,000 | Y#99.2 | 9.00 | 15.00 |
| MS123 | 2001 (6) | — | Y#95.2-98.2, 101.2, 125 | — | — |
| MS124 | 2001 (6) | — | Y#95.2-98.2, 101.2, 125 | — | — |
| MS125 | 2001 (6) | — | Y#95.2-98.2, 101.2, 125 | — | — |
| MS126 | 2001 (6) | — | Y#95.2-98.2, 101.2, 125 | — | — |
| MS127 | 2001 (6) | — | Y#95.2-98.2, 101.2, 125 | — | — |

## PROOF SETS

| KM# | Date | Mintage | Identification | Issue Price | Mkt Val |
|---|---|---|---|---|---|
| PS1 | 1987 (6) | 230,000 | Y#72a, 73a, 74, 81, 82, 87 | 37.40 | 150 |
| PS10 | 1994 (6) | 227,000 | Y#95.2-99.2, 101.2 | 72.00 | 75.00 |
| PS11 | 1994 (3) | 100,000 | Y#111-113 | 68.00 | 90.00 |
| PS12 | 1994 (1) | 100,000 | Y#110 | 27.00 | 40.00 |
| PS13 | 1995 (6) | 200,000 | Y#95.2-99.2, 101.2 | 72.00 | 75.00 |
| PS14 | 1996 (6) | 189,000 | Y#95.2-99.2, 101.2 | 103 | 110 |
| PS15 | 1997 (3) | 33,000 | Y#114-116 | 413 | 810 |
| PS16 | 1997 (2) | 100,000 | Y#114-115 | 99.00 | 160 |
| PS17 | 1997 (3) | 33,000 | Y#117, 119, 121 | 406 | 810 |
| PS18 | 1997 (2) | 100,000 | Y#117, 119 | 97.00 | 160 |
| PS19 | 1997 (6) | 1,000 | Y#95.2-99.2, 101.2 | 59.00 | 400 |
| PS2 | 1988 (6) | 200,000 | Y#72a, 73a, 74, 81, 82, 87 | 46.50 | 65.00 |
| PS20 | 1997 (6) | 186,000 | Y#95.2-99.2, 101.2 | 56.00 | 80.00 |
| PS21 | 1997 (6) | 25,000 | Y#95.2-99.2, 101.2 | 56.00 | 110 |
| PS22 | 1998 (3) | 33,000 | Y#118, 120, 122 | 375 | 800 |
| PS23 | 1998 (2) | 100,000 | Y#118, 120 | 90.00 | 120 |
| PS24 | 1998 (6) | 30,000 | Y#95.2-99.2, 101.2 | 59.00 | 85.00 |
| PS25 | 1999 (6) | 70,000 | Y#95.2-99.2, 101.2 | 69.85 | 100 |
| PS26 | 1999 (6) | 50,000 | Y#95.2-99.2, 101.2 | 69.85 | 100 |
| PS27 | 1999 | 150,000 | Y#95.2-99.2, 101.2 | 69.85 | 100 |
| PS3 | 1989 (6) | 200,000 | Y#95.1-99.1, 101.1 | 47.90 | 65.00 |
| PS4 | 1990 (6) | 200,000 | Y#95.1-99.1, 101.1 | 47.90 | 65.00 |
| PS5 | 1991 (6) | 220,000 | Y#95.1-99.1, 101.1 | 58.75 | 65.00 |
| PS6 | 1992 (6) | 250,000 | Y#95.2-99.2, 101.2 | 55.65 | 70.00 |
| PS7 | 1993 (6) | 250,000 | Y#95.2-99.2, 101.2 | 72.00 | 75.00 |
| PS8 | 1993 (3) | 100,000 | Y#107-109 | 100 | 900 |
| PS9 | 1993 (2) | 100,000 | Y#107-108 | 110 | 115 |

# JERSEY

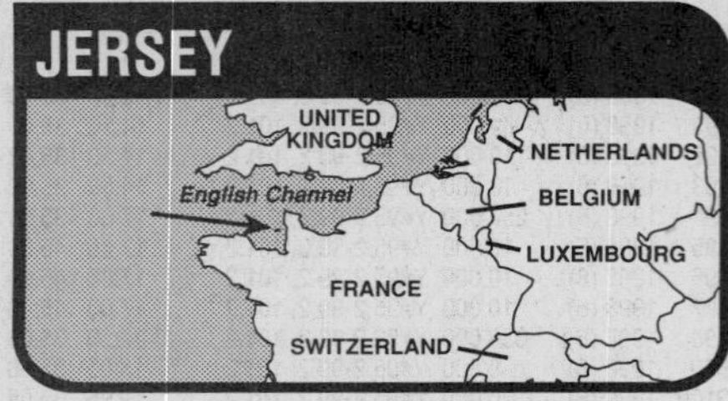


The Bailiwick of Jersey, a British Crown dependency located in the English Channel 12 miles (19 km.) west of Normandy, France, has an area of 45 sq. mi. (117 sq. km.) and a population of 74,000. Capital: St. Helier. The economy is based on agriculture and cattle breeding – the importation of cattle is prohibited to protect the purity of the island's world-famous strain of milch cows.

Jersey was occupied by Neanderthal man by 100,000 B.C., and by Iberians of 2000 B.C. who left their chamber tombs in the island's granite cliffs. Roman legions almost certainly visited the island although they left no evidence of settlement. The country folk of Jersey still speak an archaic form of Norman-French, lingering evidence of the Norman annexation of the island in 933 A.D. Jersey was annexed to England in 1206, 140 years after the Norman Conquest. The dependency is administered by its own laws and customs; laws enacted by the British Parliament do not apply to Jersey unless it is specifically mentioned. During World War II, German troops occupied the island from July1, 1940 until May 9, 1945.

Coins of pre-Roman Gaul and of Rome have been found in abundance on Jersey.

**RULERS**
British

**MINT MARKS**
H - Heaton, Birmingham

**MONETARY SYSTEM**

Commencing 1877

12 Pence = 1 Shilling
5 Shillings = 1 Crown
20 Shillings = 1 Pound
100 New Pence = 1 Pound

## BRITISH DEPENDENCY

### STANDARD COINAGE

**1/24 SHILLING** KM# 9 **Composition:** Bronze

| Date | Mintage | F | VF | XF | Unc | BU |
|---|---|---|---|---|---|---|
| 1909 | 120,000 | 1.00 | 2.50 | 11.50 | 25.00 | — |

**1/24 SHILLING** KM# 11 **Composition:** Bronze

| Date | Mintage | F | VF | XF | Unc | BU |
|---|---|---|---|---|---|---|
| 1911 | 72,000 | 1.00 | 2.50 | 11.50 | 25.00 | — |
| 1913 | 72,000 | 1.00 | 2.50 | 11.50 | 25.00 | — |
| 1923 | 72,000 | 1.00 | 2.50 | 11.50 | 25.00 | — |

**1/24 SHILLING** KM# 13 **Composition:** Bronze

| Date | Mintage | F | VF | XF | Unc | BU |
|---|---|---|---|---|---|---|
| 1923 | 72,000 | 0.75 | 3.00 | 5.50 | 22.50 | — |
| 1923 Proof | — | Value: 550 | | | | |
| 1926 | 120,000 | 0.75 | 2.50 | 4.50 | 20.00 | — |
| 1926 Proof | — | Value: 550 | | | | |

**1/24 SHILLING** KM# 15 **Composition:** Bronze

| Date | Mintage | F | VF | XF | Unc | BU |
|---|---|---|---|---|---|---|
| 1931 | 72,000 | 0.50 | 1.00 | 3.00 | 15.00 | — |
| 1931 Proof | — | Value: 165 | | | | |
| 1933 | 72,000 | 0.50 | 1.00 | 3.00 | 15.00 | — |
| 1933 Proof | — | Value: 165 | | | | |
| 1935 | 72,000 | 0.50 | 1.00 | 3.00 | 15.00 | — |
| 1935 Proof | — | Value: 165 | | | | |

**1/24 SHILLING** KM# 17 **Composition:** Bronze

| Date | Mintage | F | VF | XF | Unc | BU |
|---|---|---|---|---|---|---|
| 1937 | 72,000 | 0.50 | 1.00 | 3.00 | 15.00 | — |
| 1937 Proof | — | Value: 125 | | | | |
| 1946 | 72,000 | 0.50 | 1.00 | 3.00 | 15.00 | — |
| 1946 Proof | — | Value: 125 | | | | |
| 1947 | 72,000 | 0.50 | 1.00 | 3.00 | 15.00 | — |
| 1947 Proof | — | Value: 125 | | | | |

**1/12 SHILLING** KM# 10 **Composition:** Bronze

| Date | Mintage | F | VF | XF | Unc | BU |
|---|---|---|---|---|---|---|
| 1909 | 180,000 | 0.75 | 3.50 | 12.50 | 60.00 | — |

**1/12 SHILLING** KM# 12 **Composition:** Bronze

| Date | Mintage | F | VF | XF | Unc | BU |
|---|---|---|---|---|---|---|
| 1911 | 204,000 | 0.50 | 1.50 | 5.00 | 35.00 | — |
| 1913 | 204,000 | 0.50 | 1.50 | 5.00 | 35.00 | — |
| 1923 | 204,000 | 0.50 | 1.50 | 5.00 | 35.00 | — |

**1/12 SHILLING** KM# 14 **Composition:** Bronze

| Date | Mintage | F | VF | XF | Unc | BU |
|---|---|---|---|---|---|---|
| 1923 | 301,000 | 0.50 | 1.50 | 5.00 | 30.00 | — |
| 1926 | 83,000 | 0.75 | 2.50 | 10.00 | 40.00 | — |

**1/12 SHILLING** KM# 16 **Composition:** Bronze

| Date | Mintage | F | VF | XF | Unc | BU |
|---|---|---|---|---|---|---|
| 1931 | 204,000 | 0.50 | 1.25 | 3.00 | 12.00 | — |
| 1931 Proof | — | Value: 125 | | | | |
| 1933 | 204,000 | 0.50 | 1.25 | 3.00 | 12.00 | — |
| 1933 Proof | — | Value: 125 | | | | |
| 1935 | 204,000 | 0.50 | 1.25 | 3.00 | 12.00 | — |
| 1935 Proof | — | Value: 125 | | | | |

**1/12 SHILLING** KM# 18 **Composition:** Bronze

| Date | Mintage | F | VF | XF | Unc | BU |
|---|---|---|---|---|---|---|
| 1937 | 204,000 | 0.50 | 1.00 | 2.50 | 10.00 | — |
| 1937 Proof | — | Value: 125 | | | | |
| 1946 | 204,000 | 0.50 | 1.00 | 2.50 | 10.00 | — |
| 1946 Proof | — | Value: 125 | | | | |
| 1947 | 444,000 | 0.25 | 0.50 | 1.50 | 7.50 | — |
| 1947 Proof | — | Value: 125 | | | | |

**1/12 SHILLING** KM# 19 **Composition:** Bronze **Subject:** Liberation Commemorataive

| Date | Mintage | F | VF | XF | Unc | BU |
|---|---|---|---|---|---|---|
| 1945 | 1,000,000 | 0.25 | 0.50 | 1.00 | 5.00 | — |
| 1945 Proof | — | Value: 100 | | | | |

**Note:** Struck between 1949-52

**1/12 SHILLING** KM# 20 **Composition:** Bronze **Obverse:** Head of Queen Elizabeth II right

| Date | Mintage | F | VF | XF | Unc | BU |
|---|---|---|---|---|---|---|
| ND | 720,000 | 0.25 | 0.50 | 1.00 | 3.50 | — |
| ND Proof | — | Value: 100 | | | | |

**1/12 SHILLING** KM# 21 **Composition:** Bronze **Obverse:** Head of Queen Elizabeth II right

| Date | Mintage | F | VF | XF | Unc | BU |
|---|---|---|---|---|---|---|
| 1957 | 720,000 | 0.25 | 0.45 | 0.75 | 2.00 | — |
| 1957 Proof | 2,100 | Value: 7.50 | | | | |
| 1964 | 1,200,000 | 0.25 | 0.45 | 0.75 | 1.50 | — |
| 1964 Proof | 20,000 | Value: 2.00 | | | | |

**1/12 SHILLING** **KM# 23** **Composition:** Bronze **Subject:** 300th Anniversary - Accession of King Charles II **Obverse:** Head of Queen Elizabeth II right

| Date | Mintage | F | VF | XF | Unc | BU |
|---|---|---|---|---|---|---|
| ND | 1,200,000 | 0.25 | 0.45 | 0.75 | 1.50 | — |
| ND Proof | 4,200 | Value: 4.00 | | | | |

**1/12 SHILLING** **KM# 24** **Composition:** Bronze **Obverse:** Head of Queen Elizabeth II right **Reverse:** KM#23.

| Date | Mintage | F | VF | XF | Unc | BU |
|---|---|---|---|---|---|---|
| ND Proof | — | Value: 65.00 | | | | |

**1/12 SHILLING** **KM# 26** **Composition:** Bronze **Subject:** Norman Conquest **Obverse:** Head of Queen Elizabeth II right

| Date | Mintage | F | VF | XF | Unc | BU |
|---|---|---|---|---|---|---|
| ND | 1,200,000 | 0.25 | 0.45 | 0.75 | 1.50 | — |
| ND Proof | 30,000 | Value: 2.00 | | | | |

**1/4 SHILLING (3 Pence)** **KM# 22** **Composition:** Nickel-Brass **Obverse:** Head of Queen Elizabeth II right

| Date | Mintage | F | VF | XF | Unc | BU |
|---|---|---|---|---|---|---|
| 1957 | 2,000,000 | 0.10 | 0.15 | 0.50 | 3.00 | — |
| 1957 Proof | 6,300 | Value: 7.50 | | | | |
| 1960 Proof | 4,200 | Value: 8.50 | | | | |

**1/4 SHILLING (3 Pence)** **KM# 25** **Composition:** Nickel-Brass **Obverse:** Head of Queen Elizabeth II right

| Date | Mintage | F | VF | XF | Unc | BU |
|---|---|---|---|---|---|---|
| 1964 | 1,200,000 | 0.10 | 0.15 | 0.20 | 0.75 | — |
| 1964 Proof | 20,000 | Value: 2.00 | | | | |

**1/4 SHILLING (3 Pence)** **KM# 27** **Composition:** Nickel-Brass **Subject:** Norman Conquest **Obverse:** Head of Queen Elizabeth II right

| Date | Mintage | F | VF | XF | Unc | BU |
|---|---|---|---|---|---|---|
| ND | 1,200,000 | 0.10 | 0.15 | 0.35 | 1.25 | — |
| ND Proof | 30,000 | Value: 2.00 | | | | |

**5 SHILLING** **KM# 28** **Composition:** Copper-Nickel **Subject:** Norman Conquest **Obverse:** Head of Queen Elizabeth II right

| Date | Mintage | F | VF | XF | Unc | BU |
|---|---|---|---|---|---|---|
| ND | 300,000 | — | 1.00 | 2.00 | 3.50 | — |
| ND Proof | 30,000 | Value: 6.00 | | | | |

## DECIMAL COINAGE

100 New Pence = 1 Pound

Many of the following coins are also struck in silver, gold, and platinum for collectors

**1/2 NEW PENNY** **KM# 29** **Composition:** Bronze **Obverse:** Bust of Queen Elizabeth II right

| Date | Mintage | F | VF | XF | Unc | BU |
|---|---|---|---|---|---|---|
| 1971 | 3,000,000 | — | — | 0.10 | 0.20 | — |
| 1980 | 200,000 | — | — | 0.10 | 0.20 | — |
| 1980 Proof | 10,000 | Value: 1.35 | | | | |

**1/2 PENNY** **KM# 45** **Composition:** Bronze **Obverse:** Bust of Queen Elizabeth II right

| Date | Mintage | F | VF | XF | Unc | BU |
|---|---|---|---|---|---|---|
| 1981 | 50,000 | — | — | — | 0.10 | — |
| 1981 Proof | 15,000 | Value: 0.90 | | | | |

**NEW PENNY** **KM# 30** **Composition:** Bronze **Obverse:** Bust of Queen Elizabeth II right

| Date | Mintage | F | VF | XF | Unc | BU |
|---|---|---|---|---|---|---|
| 1971 | 4,500,000 | — | — | 0.10 | 0.20 | — |

| Date | Mintage | F | VF | XF | Unc | BU |
|---|---|---|---|---|---|---|
| 1980 | 3,000,000 | — | — | 0.10 | 0.20 | — |
| 1980 Proof | 10,000 | Value: 1.80 | | | | |

**PENNY** **KM# 46** **Composition:** Bronze **Obverse:** Bust of Queen Elizabeth II right

| Date | Mintage | F | VF | XF | Unc | BU |
|---|---|---|---|---|---|---|
| 1981 | 50,000 | — | — | 0.10 | 0.15 | — |
| 1981 Proof | 15,000 | Value: 1.10 | | | | |

**PENNY** **KM# 54** **Composition:** Bronze **Obverse:** Bust of Queen Elizabeth II right **Reverse:** Le Hocq Watch Tower, St. Clement

| Date | Mintage | F | VF | XF | Unc | BU |
|---|---|---|---|---|---|---|
| 1983 | 500,000 | — | — | 0.10 | 0.25 | — |
| 1984 | 1,000,000 | — | — | 0.10 | 0.25 | — |
| 1985 | 1,000,000 | — | — | 0.10 | 0.25 | — |
| 1986 | 2,000,000 | — | — | 0.10 | 0.25 | — |
| 1987 | 1,500,000 | — | — | 0.10 | 0.25 | — |
| 1988 | 1,000,000 | — | — | 0.10 | 0.25 | — |
| 1989 | 1,500,000 | — | — | 0.10 | 0.25 | — |
| 1990 | 2,000 | — | — | 0.10 | 0.25 | — |
| 1992 In sets only | — | — | — | — | 0.50 | — |

**PENNY** **KM# 54a** **Weight:** 4.2000 g. **Composition:** 0.9250 Silver .1249 oz. ASW **Obverse:** Bust of Queen Elizabeth II right **Reverse:** Le Hocq Watch Tower, St. Clement

| Date | Mintage | F | VF | XF | Unc | BU |
|---|---|---|---|---|---|---|
| 1983 Proof | 5,000 | Value: 7.00 | | | | |

**PENNY** **KM# 54b** **Composition:** Copper Plated Steel **Obverse:** Bust of Queen Elizabeth II right **Reverse:** Le Hocq Watch Tower, St. Clement

| Date | Mintage | F | VF | XF | Unc | BU |
|---|---|---|---|---|---|---|
| 1994 | 2,000 | — | — | 0.10 | 0.50 | — |
| 1997 | 320,000 | — | — | 0.10 | 0.50 | — |

**PENNY** **KM# 103** **Composition:** Copper Plated Steel **Obverse:** Rank-Broadley portrait of Queen Elizabeth II

| Date | Mintage | F | VF | XF | Unc | BU |
|---|---|---|---|---|---|---|
| 1998 | 9,300,000 | — | — | 0.10 | 0.50 | — |
| 2000 | — | — | — | 0.10 | 0.50 | — |

**2 NEW PENCE** **KM# 31** **Composition:** Bronze **Obverse:** Bust of Queen Elizabeth II right

| Date | Mintage | F | VF | XF | Unc | BU |
|---|---|---|---|---|---|---|
| 1971 | 2,225,000 | — | — | 0.15 | 0.30 | — |
| 1975 | 750,000 | — | — | 0.15 | 0.40 | — |
| 1980 | 2,000,000 | — | — | 0.15 | 0.30 | — |
| 1980 Proof | 10,000 | Value: 2.25 | | | | |

**2 PENCE** **KM# 47** **Composition:** Bronze **Obverse:** Bust of Queen Elizabeth II right

| Date | Mintage | F | VF | XF | Unc | BU |
|---|---|---|---|---|---|---|
| 1981 | 50,000 | — | — | 0.15 | 0.25 | — |
| 1981 Proof | 15,000 | Value: 1.35 | | | | |

**2 PENCE** **KM# 55** **Composition:** Bronze **Obverse:** Bust of Queen Elizabeth II right **Reverse:** L'Hermitage, St. Helier

| Date | Mintage | F | VF | XF | Unc | BU |
|---|---|---|---|---|---|---|
| 1983 | 800,000 | — | — | 0.15 | 0.25 | — |
| 1984 | 750,000 | — | — | 0.15 | 0.25 | — |
| 1985 | 250,000 | — | — | 0.15 | 0.25 | — |
| 1986 | 1,000,000 | — | — | 0.15 | 0.25 | — |
| 1987 | 2,000,000 | — | — | 0.15 | 0.25 | — |
| 1988 | 750,000 | — | — | 0.15 | 0.25 | — |
| 1989 | 1,000,000 | — | — | 0.15 | 0.25 | — |
| 1990 | 2,600,000 | — | — | 0.15 | 0.25 | — |
| 1997 | 5,500 | — | — | — | 0.50 | — |

**2 PENCE** **KM# 55a** **Weight:** 8.4000 g. **Composition:** 0.9250 Silver .2498 oz. ASW **Obverse:** Bust of Queen Elizabeth II right **Reverse:** L'Hermitage, St. Helier

| Date | Mintage | F | VF | XF | Unc | BU |
|---|---|---|---|---|---|---|
| 1983 Proof | 5,000 | Value: 10.00 | | | | |

**2 PENCE** **KM# 55b** **Composition:** Bronze Clad Steel **Obverse:** Bust of Queen Elizabeth II right **Reverse:** L'Hermitage, St. Helier **Note:** Released into circulation in 1998.

| Date | Mintage | F | VF | XF | Unc | BU |
|---|---|---|---|---|---|---|
| 1992 | — | — | — | 0.15 | 0.50 | — |

**2 PENCE** **KM# 104** **Composition:** Copper Plated Steel **Obverse:** Rank-Broadley portrait of Queen Elizabeth II **Reverse:** L'Hermitage, St. Helier

| Date | Mintage | F | VF | XF | Unc | BU |
|---|---|---|---|---|---|---|
| 1998 | 50,000 | — | — | 0.15 | 0.50 | — |
| 2000 | — | — | — | 0.15 | 0.50 | — |

**5 NEW PENCE** **KM# 32** **Composition:** Copper-Nickel **Obverse:** Bust of Queen Elizabeth II right

| Date | Mintage | F | VF | XF | Unc | BU |
|---|---|---|---|---|---|---|
| 1968 | 3,600,000 | — | 0.15 | 0.25 | 1.00 | — |
| 1980 | 800,000 | — | 0.15 | 0.25 | 1.00 | — |
| 1980 Proof | 10,000 | Value: 2.75 | | | | |

**5 PENCE** **KM# 48** **Composition:** Copper-Nickel **Obverse:** Bust of Queen Elizabeth II right

| Date | Mintage | F | VF | XF | Unc | BU |
|---|---|---|---|---|---|---|
| 1981 | 50,000 | — | 0.15 | 0.25 | 1.00 | — |
| 1981 Proof | 15,000 | Value: 1.80 | | | | |

**5 PENCE** **KM# 56.1** **Composition:** Copper-Nickel **Obverse:** Bust of Queen Elizabeth II right **Reverse:** Seymour Tower, Grouville, L'Avathison

| Date | Mintage | F | VF | XF | Unc | BU |
|---|---|---|---|---|---|---|
| 1983 | 400,000 | — | 0.10 | 0.20 | 1.00 | — |
| 1984 | 300,000 | — | 0.10 | 0.20 | 1.00 | — |
| 1985 | 600,000 | — | 0.10 | 0.20 | 1.00 | — |
| 1986 | 200,000 | — | 0.10 | 0.20 | 1.00 | — |
| 1987 In sets only | — | — | — | — | 0.50 | — |
| 1988 | 400,000 | — | 0.10 | 0.20 | 1.00 | — |
| 1989 | — | — | 0.10 | 0.20 | 1.00 | — |

**5 PENCE** **KM# 56.1a** **Weight:** 6.6000 g. **Composition:** 0.9250 Silver .1963 oz. ASW **Obverse:** Bust of Queen Elizabeth II right **Reverse:** Seymour Tower, Grouville, L'Avathison

| Date | Mintage | F | VF | XF | Unc | BU |
|---|---|---|---|---|---|---|
| 1983 Proof | 5,000 | Value: 10.00 | | | | |

**5 PENCE** **KM# 56.2** **Composition:** Copper-Nickel **Obverse:** Bust of Queen Elizabeth II right **Reverse:** Seymour Tower, Grouville, L'Avathison **Note:** Reduced size.

| Date | Mintage | F | VF | XF | Unc | BU |
|---|---|---|---|---|---|---|
| 1990 | 4,000,000 | — | — | 0.15 | 0.35 | — |
| 1991 | 2,000,000 | — | — | 0.15 | 0.35 | — |
| 1992 | 1,000,000 | — | — | 0.15 | 0.50 | — |
| 1993 | — | — | — | 0.15 | 0.50 | — |
| 1997 In sets only | 5,500 | — | — | — | 1.00 | — |

**5 PENCE** **KM# 105** **Composition:** Copper-Nickel **Obverse:** Rank-Broadley portrait of Queen Elizabeth II

| Date | Mintage | F | VF | XF | Unc | BU |
|---|---|---|---|---|---|---|
| 1998 | 50,000 | — | — | 0.15 | 0.50 | — |
| 2000 | — | — | — | 0.15 | — | — |

**10 NEW PENCE** **KM# 33** **Composition:** Copper-Nickel **Obverse:** Bust of Queen Elizabeth II right

| Date | Mintage | F | VF | XF | Unc | BU |
|---|---|---|---|---|---|---|
| 1968 | 1,500,000 | — | 0.20 | 0.35 | 1.00 | — |
| 1975 | 1,022,000 | — | 0.20 | 0.30 | 0.90 | — |
| 1980 | 1,000,000 | — | 0.20 | 0.30 | 0.75 | — |
| 1980 Proof | 10,000 | Value: 5.50 | | | | |

**10 PENCE** **KM# 49** **Composition:** Copper-Nickel **Obverse:** Bust of Queen Elizabeth II right

| Date | Mintage | F | VF | XF | Unc | BU |
|---|---|---|---|---|---|---|
| 1981 | 50,000 | — | — | 0.30 | 1.00 | — |
| 1981 Proof | 15,000 | Value: 2.25 | | | | |

**10 PENCE** **KM# 57.1** **Composition:** Copper-Nickel **Obverse:** Bust of Queen Elizabeth II right **Reverse:** La Houque Bie, Faldouet, St. Martin

| Date | Mintage | F | VF | XF | Unc | BU |
|---|---|---|---|---|---|---|
| 1983 | 30,000 | — | — | 0.30 | 1.00 | — |
| 1984 | 100,000 | — | — | 0.30 | 1.00 | — |
| 1985 | 100,000 | — | — | 0.30 | 1.00 | — |
| 1986 | 400,000 | — | — | 0.30 | 0.75 | — |
| 1987 | 800,000 | — | — | 0.30 | 0.75 | — |
| 1988 | 650,000 | — | — | 0.30 | 0.75 | — |
| 1989 | 700,000 | — | — | 0.30 | 0.75 | — |
| 1990 | 850,000 | — | — | 0.30 | 0.75 | — |

**10 PENCE** **KM# 57.1a** **Weight:** 13.2000 g. **Composition:** 0.9250 Silver .3926 oz. ASW **Obverse:** Bust of Queen Elizabeth II right **Reverse:** La Houque Bie, Faldouet, St. Martin

| Date | Mintage | F | VF | XF | Unc | BU |
|---|---|---|---|---|---|---|
| 1983 Proof | 5,000 | Value: 15.00 | | | | |

**10 PENCE** **KM# 57.2** **Composition:** Copper-Nickel **Obverse:** Bust of Queen Elizabeth II right **Reverse:** La Houque Bie, Faldouet, St. Martin **Note:** Reduced size.

| Date | Mintage | F | VF | XF | Unc | BU |
|---|---|---|---|---|---|---|
| 1992 | 7,000,000 | — | — | 0.30 | 0.50 | — |
| 1997 In sets only | 5,500 | — | — | — | 1.00 | — |

**20 PENCE** **KM# 53** **Composition:** Copper-Nickel **Subject:** 100th Anniversary of Lighthouse at Corbiere **Obverse:** Bust of Queen Elizabeth II right **Reverse:** Date below lighthouse

| Date | Mintage | F | VF | XF | Unc | BU |
|---|---|---|---|---|---|---|
| 1982 | 200,000 | — | — | 0.50 | 1.50 | — |

**20 PENCE** **KM# 53a** **Weight:** 5.8300 g. **Composition:** 0.9250 Silver .1734 oz. ASW **Subject:** 100th Anniversary of Lighthouse at Corbiere **Obverse:** Bust of Queen Elizabeth II right **Reverse:** Date below lighthouse

| Date | Mintage | F | VF | XF | Unc | BU |
|---|---|---|---|---|---|---|
| 1982 Proof | 1,500 | Value: 15.00 | | | | |

**20 PENCE** **KM# 66** **Composition:** Copper-Nickel **Subject:** 100th Anniversary of Lighthouse at Corbiere **Obverse:** Bust of Queen Elizabeth II right **Reverse:** Date below bust

| Date | Mintage | F | VF | XF | Unc | BU |
|---|---|---|---|---|---|---|
| 1983 | 400,000 | — | — | 0.50 | 1.00 | — |
| 1984 | 250,000 | — | — | 0.50 | 1.00 | — |
| 1986 | 100,000 | — | — | 0.50 | 1.00 | — |
| 1987 | 100,000 | — | — | 0.50 | 1.00 | — |
| 1989 | 100,000 | — | — | 0.50 | 1.00 | — |
| 1990 | 150,000 | — | — | 0.50 | 1.00 | — |
| 1992 In sets only | — | — | — | — | 2.00 | — |
| 1994 | 200,000 | — | — | 0.50 | 1.00 | — |
| 1996 | 250,000 | — | — | 0.50 | 1.00 | — |
| 1997 | 600,000 | — | — | 0.50 | 1.00 | — |
| 1998 | — | — | — | 0.50 | 1.00 | — |

**20 PENCE** **KM# 66a** **Weight:** 5.8300 g. **Composition:** 0.9250 Silver .1734 oz. ASW **Subject:** 100th Anniversary of Lighthouse at Corbiere **Obverse:** Bust of Queen Elizabeth II right **Reverse:** Date below bust

| Date | Mintage | F | VF | XF | Unc | BU |
|---|---|---|---|---|---|---|
| 1983 Proof | 5,000 | Value: 15.00 | | | | |

**20 PENCE** **KM# 107** **Weight:** 5.8300 g. **Composition:** 0.9250 Silver .1734 oz. ASW **Obverse:** Rank-Broadley poertrait of Queen Elizabeth II

| Date | Mintage | F | VF | XF | Unc | BU |
|---|---|---|---|---|---|---|
| 1998 | 90,000 | — | — | 0.50 | 1.00 | — |

**25 PENCE** **KM# 44a** **Weight:** 28.2800 g. **Composition:** 0.9250 Silver .8411 oz. ASW **Subject:** Queen's Silver Jublilee **Obverse:** Bust of Queen Elizabeth II right

| Date | Mintage | F | VF | XF | Unc | BU |
|---|---|---|---|---|---|---|
| ND(1977) Proof | 25,000 | Value: 16.50 | | | | |

**25 PENCE** **KM# 44** **Composition:** Copper-Nickel **Subject:** Queen's Silver Jublilee **Obverse:** Bust of Queen Elizabeth II right

| Date | Mintage | F | VF | XF | Unc | BU |
|---|---|---|---|---|---|---|
| ND(1977) | 262,000 | — | 0.75 | 1.25 | 3.75 | — |

**50 PENCE** **KM# 34** **Composition:** Copper-Nickel **Obverse:** Bust of Queen Elizabeth II right

| Date | Mintage | F | VF | XF | Unc | BU |
|---|---|---|---|---|---|---|
| 1969 | 480,000 | — | — | 0.90 | 1.50 | — |
| 1980 | 100,000 | — | — | 0.90 | 1.50 | — |
| 1980 Proof | 10,000 | Value: 9.00 | | | | |

**50 PENCE** **KM# 35** **Weight:** 5.4200 g. **Composition:** 0.9250 Silver .1612 oz. ASW **Subject:** 25th Wedding Anniversary **Obverse:** Bust of Queen Elizabeth II right

| Date | Mintage | F | VF | XF | Unc | BU |
|---|---|---|---|---|---|---|
| 1972 | 24,000 | — | — | 1.25 | 3.50 | — |
| 1972 Proof | 1,500 | Value: 6.50 | | | | |

**50 PENCE** **KM# 50** **Composition:** Copper-Nickel **Obverse:** Bust of Queen Elizabeth II right

| Date | Mintage | F | VF | XF | Unc | BU |
|---|---|---|---|---|---|---|
| 1981 | 50,000 | — | — | 1.00 | 1.75 | — |
| 1981 Proof | 15,000 | Value: 3.00 | | | | |

**50 PENCE** **KM# 58.1** **Composition:** Copper-Nickel **Obverse:** Bust of Queen Elizabeth II right **Reverse:** Grosnez Castle

| Date | Mintage | F | VF | XF | Unc | BU |
|---|---|---|---|---|---|---|
| 1983 | 50,000 | — | — | 1.00 | 1.75 | — |
| 1984 | 50,000 | — | — | 1.00 | 1.75 | — |
| 1986 | 30,000 | — | — | 1.00 | 1.75 | — |
| 1987 | 150,000 | — | — | 1.00 | 1.75 | — |
| 1988 | 130,000 | — | — | 1.00 | 1.75 | — |
| 1989 | 180,000 | — | — | 1.00 | 1.75 | — |
| 1990 | 370,000 | — | — | 1.00 | 1.75 | — |
| 1992 In sets only | — | — | — | — | 2.50 | — |
| 1994 | 200,000 | — | — | 1.00 | 1.75 | — |
| 1997 In sets only | 5,500 | — | — | — | 2.50 | — |

**50 PENCE** **KM# 58a** **Weight:** 15.5000 g. **Composition:** 0.9250 Silver .4609 oz. ASW **Obverse:** Bust of Queen Elizabeth II right **Reverse:** Grosnez Castle

| Date | Mintage | F | VF | XF | Unc | BU |
|---|---|---|---|---|---|---|
| 1983 Proof | 5,000 | Value: 18.00 | | | | |

**50 PENCE** **KM# 63** **Composition:** Copper-Nickel **Subject:** 40th Anniversary - Liberation of 1945 **Obverse:** Bust of Queen Elizabeth II right

| Date | Mintage | F | VF | XF | Unc | BU |
|---|---|---|---|---|---|---|
| 1985 | 65,000 | — | — | 1.25 | 2.00 | — |

**50 PENCE** **KM# 58.2** **Composition:** Copper-Nickel **Obverse:** Bust of Queen Elizabeth II right **Reverse:** Grosnez Castle **Note:** Small size.

| Date | Mintage | F | VF | XF | Unc | BU |
|---|---|---|---|---|---|---|
| 1997 | 1,500,000 | — | — | — | 2.50 | — |

**50 PENCE** **KM# 108** **Composition:** Copper-Nickel **Obverse:** Rank-Broadley poertrait of Queen Elizabeth II

| Date | Mintage | F | VF | XF | Unc | BU |
|---|---|---|---|---|---|---|
| 1998 | 25,000 | — | — | 1.00 | 2.50 | — |

**POUND** **KM# 36** **Weight:** 10.8400 g. **Composition:** 0.9250 Silver .3224 oz. ASW **Subject:** 25th Wedding Anniversary **Obverse:** Bust of Queen Elizabeth II right

| Date | Mintage | F | VF | XF | Unc | BU |
|---|---|---|---|---|---|---|
| 1972 | 24,000 | — | — | — | 5.00 | — |
| 1972 Proof | 1,500 | Value: 12.00 | | | | |

**POUND** **KM# 51a** **Weight:** 10.4500 g. **Composition:** 0.9250 Silver .3108 oz. ASW **Subject:** Bicentennial - Battle of Jersey **Obverse:** Bust of Queen Elizabeth II right

| Date | Mintage | F | VF | XF | Unc | BU |
|---|---|---|---|---|---|---|
| ND Proof | 10,000 | Value: 15.00 | | | | |

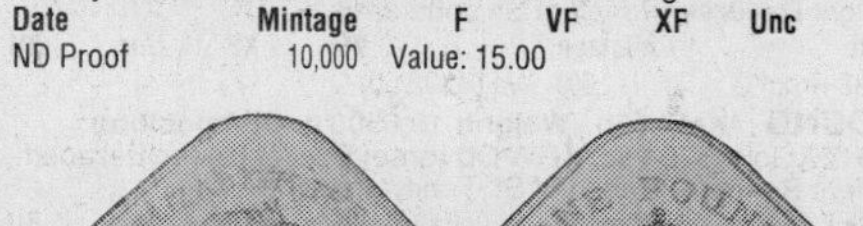

**POUND** **KM# 51** **Composition:** Copper-Nickel **Subject:** Bicentennial - Battle of Jersey **Obverse:** Bust of Queen Elizabeth II right

| Date | Mintage | F | VF | XF | Unc | BU |
|---|---|---|---|---|---|---|
| ND | 200,000 | — | — | 2.00 | 3.25 | — |
| ND Proof | 15,000 | Value: 8.00 | | | | |

**POUND** **KM# 51b** **Weight:** 17.5500 g. **Composition:** 0.9170 Gold .5174 oz. AGW **Subject:** Bicentennial - Battle of Jersey **Obverse:** Bust of Queen Elizabeth II right

| Date | Mintage | F | VF | XF | Unc | BU |
|---|---|---|---|---|---|---|
| ND Proof | 5,000 | Value: 250 | | | | |

**POUND** **KM# 59** **Composition:** Nickel-Brass **Obverse:** Bust of Queen Elizabeth II right **Reverse:** Parish of St. Helier arms

| Date | Mintage | F | VF | XF | Unc | BU |
|---|---|---|---|---|---|---|
| 1983 | 100,000 | — | — | 2.00 | 3.25 | — |

**POUND** **KM# 59a** **Weight:** 11.6800 g. **Composition:** 0.9250 Silver .3474 oz. ASW **Obverse:** Bust of Queen Elizabeth II right **Reverse:** Parish of St. Helier arms

| Date | Mintage | F | VF | XF | Unc | BU |
|---|---|---|---|---|---|---|
| 1983 Proof | 2,500 | Value: 22.50 | | | | |

**POUND** **KM# 59b** **Weight:** 19.6500 g. **Composition:** 0.9170 Gold .5794 oz. AGW **Obverse:** Bust of Queen Elizabeth II right **Reverse:** Parish of St. Helier arms

| Date | Mintage | F | VF | XF | Unc | BU |
|---|---|---|---|---|---|---|
| 1983 Proof | 250 | Value: 250 | | | | |

**Note:** 497 pieces were remelted

**POUND** **KM# 60** **Composition:** Nickel-Brass **Obverse:** Bust of Queen Elizabeth II right **Reverse:** Parish of St. Saviour arms

| Date | Mintage | F | VF | XF | Unc | BU |
|---|---|---|---|---|---|---|
| 1984 | 20,000 | — | — | 2.00 | 3.25 | — |

**POUND** **KM# 60a** **Weight:** 11.6800 g. **Composition:** 0.9250 Silver .3474 oz. ASW **Obverse:** Bust of Queen Elizabeth II right **Reverse:** Parish of St. Saviour arms

| Date | Mintage | F | VF | XF | Unc | BU |
|---|---|---|---|---|---|---|
| 1984 Proof | 2,500 | Value: 22.50 | | | | |

**POUND** **KM# 60b** **Weight:** 19.6500 g. **Composition:** 0.9170 Gold .5794 oz. AGW **Obverse:** Bust of Queen Elizabeth II right **Reverse:** Parish of St. Saviour arms

| Date | Mintage | F | VF | XF | Unc | BU |
|---|---|---|---|---|---|---|
| 1984 Proof | 250 | Value: 275 | | | | |

**POUND** **KM# 61** **Composition:** Nickel-Brass **Obverse:** Bust of Queen Elizabeth II right **Reverse:** Parish of St. Brelade arms

| Date | Mintage | F | VF | XF | Unc | BU |
|---|---|---|---|---|---|---|
| 1984 | 20,000 | — | — | 2.00 | 3.25 | — |

**POUND** **KM# 61a** **Weight:** 11.6800 g. **Composition:** 0.9250 Silver .3474 oz. ASW **Obverse:** Bust of Queen Elizabeth II right **Reverse:** Parish of St. Brelade arms

| Date | Mintage | F | VF | XF | Unc | BU |
|---|---|---|---|---|---|---|
| 1984 Proof | 2,500 | Value: 22.50 | | | | |

**POUND** **KM# 61b** **Weight:** 19.6500 g. **Composition:** 0.9170 Gold .5794 oz. AGW **Obverse:** Bust of Queen Elizabeth II right **Reverse:** Parish of St. Brelade arms

| Date | Mintage | F | VF | XF | Unc | BU |
|---|---|---|---|---|---|---|
| 1984 Proof | 250 | Value: 275 | | | | |

**POUND** **KM# 62b** **Weight:** 19.6500 g. **Composition:** 0.9170 Gold .5794 oz. AGW **Obverse:** Bust of Queen Elizabeth II right **Reverse:** Parish of St. Clement arms

| Date | Mintage | F | VF | XF | Unc | BU |
|---|---|---|---|---|---|---|
| 1985 Proof | 124 | Value: 300 | | | | |

**POUND** **KM# 65b** **Weight:** 19.6500 g. **Composition:** 0.9170 Gold .5794 oz. AGW **Obverse:** Bust of Queen Elizabeth II right **Reverse:** Parish of St. Lawrence arms

| Date | Mintage | F | VF | XF | Unc | BU |
|---|---|---|---|---|---|---|
| 1985 Proof | 108 | Value: 325 | | | | |

**POUND** **KM# 62a** **Weight:** 11.6800 g. **Composition:** 0.9250 Silver .3474 oz. ASW **Obverse:** Bust of Queen Elizabeth II right **Reverse:** Parish of St. Clement arms

| Date | Mintage | F | VF | XF | Unc | BU |
|---|---|---|---|---|---|---|
| 1985 Proof | 2,500 | Value: 22.50 | | | | |

**POUND** **KM# 65a** **Weight:** 11.6800 g. **Composition:** 0.9250 Silver .3474 oz. ASW **Obverse:** Bust of Queen Elizabeth II right **Reverse:** Parish of St. Lawrence arms

| Date | Mintage | F | VF | XF | Unc | BU |
|---|---|---|---|---|---|---|
| 1985 Proof | 2,500 | Value: 22.50 | | | | |

**POUND** **KM# 62** **Composition:** Nickel-Brass **Obverse:** Bust of Queen Elizabeth II right **Reverse:** Parish of St. Clement arms

| Date | Mintage | F | VF | XF | Unc | BU |
|---|---|---|---|---|---|---|
| 1985 | 25,000 | — | — | 2.00 | 3.25 | — |

**POUND** **KM# 65** **Composition:** Nickel-Brass **Obverse:** Bust of Queen Elizabeth II right **Reverse:** Parish of St. Lawrence arms

| Date | Mintage | F | VF | XF | Unc | BU |
|---|---|---|---|---|---|---|
| 1985 | 10,000 | — | — | 2.00 | 3.50 | — |

**POUND** **KM# 68** **Composition:** Nickel-Brass **Obverse:** Bust of Queen Elizabeth II right **Reverse:** Parish of St. Peter arms

| Date | Mintage | F | VF | XF | Unc | BU |
|---|---|---|---|---|---|---|
| 1986 | 10,000 | — | — | 2.00 | 3.25 | — |

**POUND** **KM# 69** **Composition:** Nickel-Brass **Obverse:** Bust of Queen Elizabeth II right **Reverse:** Parish of Grouville arms

| Date | Mintage | F | VF | XF | Unc | BU |
|---|---|---|---|---|---|---|
| 1986 | 10,000 | — | — | 2.00 | 3.25 | — |

**POUND** **KM# 68a** **Weight:** 11.6800 g. **Composition:** 0.9250 Silver .3474 oz. ASW **Obverse:** Bust of Queen Elizabeth II right **Reverse:** Parish of St. Peter arms

| Date | Mintage | F | VF | XF | Unc | BU |
|---|---|---|---|---|---|---|
| 1986 Proof | 2,500 | Value: 22.50 | | | | |

**POUND** **KM# 69a** **Weight:** 11.6800 g. **Composition:** 0.9250 Silver .3474 oz. ASW **Obverse:** Bust of Queen Elizabeth II right **Reverse:** Parish of Grouville arms

| Date | Mintage | F | VF | XF | Unc | BU |
|---|---|---|---|---|---|---|
| 1986 Proof | 2,500 | Value: 22.50 | | | | |

**POUND** **KM# 68b** **Weight:** 19.6500 g. **Composition:** 0.9170 Gold .5794 oz. AGW **Obverse:** Bust of Queen Elizabeth II right **Reverse:** Parish of St. Peter arms

| Date | Mintage | F | VF | XF | Unc | BU |
|---|---|---|---|---|---|---|
| 1986 Proof | 250 | Value: 275 | | | | |

**POUND** **KM# 69b** **Weight:** 19.6500 g. **Composition:** 0.9170 Gold .5794 oz. AGW **Obverse:** Bust of Queen Elizabeth II right **Reverse:** Parish of Grouville arms

| Date | Mintage | F | VF | XF | Unc | BU |
|---|---|---|---|---|---|---|
| 1986 Proof | 250 | Value: 275 | | | | |

**POUND** **KM# 71b** **Weight:** 19.6500 g. **Composition:** 0.9170 Gold .5794 oz. AGW **Obverse:** Bust of Queen Elizabeth II right **Reverse:** Parish of St. Martins arms

| Date | Mintage | F | VF | XF | Unc | BU |
|---|---|---|---|---|---|---|
| 1987 Proof | 250 | Value: 275 | | | | |

**POUND** **KM# 72b** **Weight:** 19.6500 g. **Composition:** 0.9170 Gold .5794 oz. AGW **Obverse:** Bust of Queen Elizabeth II right **Reverse:** Parish of St. Ouen

| Date | Mintage | F | VF | XF | Unc | BU |
|---|---|---|---|---|---|---|
| 1987 Proof | 250 | Value: 285 | | | | |

**POUND** **KM# 71a** **Weight:** 11.6800 g. **Composition:** 0.9250 Silver .3474 oz. ASW **Obverse:** Bust of Queen Elizabeth II right **Reverse:** Parish of St. Martin arms

| Date | Mintage | F | VF | XF | Unc | BU |
|---|---|---|---|---|---|---|
| 1987 Proof | 2,500 | Value: 22.50 | | | | |

**POUND** **KM# 72a** **Weight:** 11.6800 g. **Composition:** 0.9250 Silver .3474 oz. ASW **Obverse:** Bust of Queen Elizabeth II right **Reverse:** Parish of St. Ouen arms

| Date | Mintage | F | VF | XF | Unc | BU |
|---|---|---|---|---|---|---|
| 1987 Proof | 2,500 | Value: 22.50 | | | | |

**POUND** **KM# 71** **Composition:** Nickel-Brass **Obverse:** Bust of Queen Elizabeth II right **Reverse:** Parish of St. Martin arms

| Date | Mintage | F | VF | XF | Unc | BU |
|---|---|---|---|---|---|---|
| 1987 | 10,000 | — | — | 2.00 | 3.50 | — |

**POUND** **KM# 72** **Composition:** Nickel-Brass **Obverse:** Bust of Queen Elizabeth II right **Reverse:** Parish of St. Ouen arms

| Date | Mintage | F | VF | XF | Unc | BU |
|---|---|---|---|---|---|---|
| 1987 | 10,000 | — | — | 2.00 | 3.25 | — |

**POUND** **KM# 73** **Composition:** Nickel-Brass **Obverse:** Bust of Queen Elizabeth II right **Reverse:** Parish of Trinity arms

| Date | Mintage | F | VF | XF | Unc | BU |
|---|---|---|---|---|---|---|
| 1988 | 10,000 | — | — | 2.00 | 4.00 | — |

**POUND** **KM# 74** **Composition:** Nickel-Brass **Obverse:** Bust of Queen Elizabeth II right **Reverse:** Parish of St. John arms

| Date | Mintage | F | VF | XF | Unc | BU |
|---|---|---|---|---|---|---|
| 1988 | 10,000 | — | — | 2.00 | 3.25 | — |

**POUND** **KM# 73a** **Weight:** 11.6800 g. **Composition:** 0.9250 Silver .3474 oz. ASW **Obverse:** Bust of Queen Elizabeth II right **Reverse:** Parish of St. Trinity arms

| Date | Mintage | F | VF | XF | Unc | BU |
|---|---|---|---|---|---|---|
| 1988 Proof | 2,500 | Value: 25.00 | | | | |

**POUND** **KM# 74a** **Weight:** 11.6800 g. **Composition:** 0.9250 Silver .3474 oz. ASW **Obverse:** Bust of Queen Elizabeth II right **Reverse:** Parish of St. John arms

| Date | Mintage | F | VF | XF | Unc | BU |
|---|---|---|---|---|---|---|
| 1988 Proof | 2,500 | Value: 22.50 | | | | |

**POUND** **KM# 73b** **Weight:** 19.6500 g. **Composition:** 0.9170 Gold .5794 oz. AGW **Obverse:** Bust of Queen Elizabeth II right **Reverse:** Parish of St. Trinity arms

| Date | Mintage | F | VF | XF | Unc | BU |
|---|---|---|---|---|---|---|
| 1988 Proof | 250 | Value: 285 | | | | |

**POUND** **KM# 74b** **Weight:** 19.6500 g. **Composition:** 0.9170 Gold .5794 oz. AGW **Obverse:** Bust of Queen Elizabeth II right **Reverse:** Parish of St. John arms

| Date | Mintage | F | VF | XF | Unc | BU |
|---|---|---|---|---|---|---|
| 1988 Proof | 250 | Value: 285 | | | | |

**POUND** **KM# 75b** **Weight:** 19.6500 g. **Composition:** 0.9170 Gold .5794 oz. AGW **Obverse:** Bust of Queen Elizabeth II right **Reverse:** Parish of St. St. Mary's arms

| Date | Mintage | F | VF | XF | Unc | BU |
|---|---|---|---|---|---|---|
| 1989 Proof | 250 | Value: 285 | | | | |

**POUND** **KM# 75a** **Weight:** 11.6800 g. **Composition:** 0.9250 Silver .3474 oz. ASW **Obverse:** Bust of Queen Elizabeth II right **Reverse:** Parish of St. Mary's arms

| Date | Mintage | F | VF | XF | Unc | BU |
|---|---|---|---|---|---|---|
| 1989 Proof | 2,500 | Value: 25.00 | | | | |

**POUND** **KM# 75** **Composition:** Nickel-Brass **Obverse:** Bust of Queen Elizabeth II right **Reverse:** Parish of St. Mary's arms

| Date | Mintage | F | VF | XF | Unc | BU |
|---|---|---|---|---|---|---|
| 1989 | 25,000 | — | — | 2.00 | 3.25 | — |

**POUND** **KM# 84** **Composition:** Nickel-Brass **Obverse:** Bust of Queen Elizabeth II right **Reverse:** Schonner, The Tickler

| Date | Mintage | F | VF | XF | Unc | BU |
|---|---|---|---|---|---|---|
| 1991 | 15,000 | — | — | — | 3.25 | — |

**POUND** **KM# 85** **Composition:** Nickel-Brass **Obverse:** Bust of Queen Elizabeth II right **Reverse:** Sailing ship, Percy Douglas

| Date | Mintage | F | VF | XF | Unc | BU |
|---|---|---|---|---|---|---|
| 1991 | 20,000 | — | — | — | 3.25 | — |

**POUND** **KM# 84a** **Weight:** 11.6800 g. **Composition:** 0.9250 Silver .3474 oz. ASW **Obverse:** Bust of Queen Elizabeth II right **Reverse:** Schooner, The Tickler

| Date | Mintage | F | VF | XF | Unc | BU |
|---|---|---|---|---|---|---|
| 1991 Proof | 3,000 | Value: 21.50 | | | | |

**POUND** **KM# 85a** **Weight:** 11.6800 g. **Composition:** 0.9250 Silver .3474 oz. ASW **Obverse:** Bust of Queen Elizabeth II right **Reverse:** Sailing ship, Percy Douglas

| Date | Mintage | F | VF | XF | Unc | BU |
|---|---|---|---|---|---|---|
| 1991 Proof | 3,000 | Value: 21.50 | | | | |

**POUND** **KM# 84b** **Weight:** 19.6500 g. **Composition:** 0.9170 Gold .5794 oz. AGW **Obverse:** Bust of Queen Elizabeth II right **Reverse:** Schooner, The Tickler

| Date | Mintage | F | VF | XF | Unc | BU |
|---|---|---|---|---|---|---|
| 1991 Proof | Est. 250 | Value: 365 | | | | |

**POUND** **KM# 85b** **Weight:** 19.6500 g. **Composition:** 0.9170 Gold .5794 oz. AGW **Obverse:** Bust of Queen Elizabeth II right **Reverse:** Sailing ship, Percy Douglas

| Date | Mintage | F | VF | XF | Unc | BU |
|---|---|---|---|---|---|---|
| 1991 Proof | 250 | Value: 365 | | | | |

**POUND** **KM# 86b** **Weight:** 19.6500 g. **Composition:** 0.9170 Gold .5794 oz. AGW **Obverse:** Bust of Queen Elizabeth II right **Reverse:** Sailing ship, Hebe

| Date | Mintage | F | VF | XF | Unc | BU |
|---|---|---|---|---|---|---|
| 1992 Proof | Est. 250 | Value: 365 | | | | |

**POUND** **KM# 87b** **Weight:** 19.6500 g. **Composition:** 0.9170 Gold .5794 oz. AGW **Obverse:** Bust of Queen Elizabeth II right **Reverse:** Ornamented coat of arms

| Date | Mintage | F | VF | XF | Unc | BU |
|---|---|---|---|---|---|---|
| 1992 Proof | 250 | Value: 300 | | | | |

**POUND** **KM# 86a** **Weight:** 11.6800 g. **Composition:** 0.9250 Silver .3474 oz. ASW **Obverse:** Bust of Queen Elizabeth II right **Reverse:** Sailing ship, Hebe

| Date | Mintage | F | VF | XF | Unc | BU |
|---|---|---|---|---|---|---|
| 1992 Proof | Est. 3,000 | Value: 21.50 | | | | |

**POUND** **KM# 87a** **Weight:** 11.6800 g. **Composition:** 0.9250 Silver .3474 oz. ASW **Obverse:** Bust of Queen Elizabeth II right **Reverse:** Ornamented coat of arms

| Date | Mintage | F | VF | XF | Unc | BU |
|---|---|---|---|---|---|---|
| 1992 Proof | 3,000 | Value: 21.50 | | | | |

**POUND** **KM# 86** **Composition:** Nickel-Brass **Obverse:** Bust of Queen Elizabeth II right **Reverse:** Sailing ship, Hebe

| Date | Mintage | F | VF | XF | Unc | BU |
|---|---|---|---|---|---|---|
| 1992 | 2,000 | — | — | — | 3.25 | — |

**POUND** **KM# 87** **Composition:** Nickel-Brass **Obverse:** Bust of Queen Elizabeth II right **Reverse:** Ornamented coat of arms

| Date | Mintage | F | VF | XF | Unc | BU |
|---|---|---|---|---|---|---|
| 1992 | 20,000 | — | — | — | 3.50 | — |

**POUND** **KM# 88** **Composition:** Nickel-Brass **Obverse:** Bust of Queen Elizabeth II right **Reverse:** Sailing ship, Gemini

| Date | Mintage | F | VF | XF | Unc | BU |
|---|---|---|---|---|---|---|
| 1993 | — | — | — | — | 3.25 | — |

**POUND** **KM# 90** **Composition:** Nickel-Brass **Obverse:** Bust of Queen Elizabeth II right **Reverse:** Sailing ship, Century

| Date | Mintage | F | VF | XF | Unc | BU |
|---|---|---|---|---|---|---|
| 1993 | — | — | — | — | 3.25 | — |

**POUND** **KM# 88a** **Weight:** 11.6800 g. **Composition:** 0.9250 Silver .3474 oz. ASW **Obverse:** Bust of Queen Elizabeth II right **Reverse:** Sailing ship, Gemini

| Date | Mintage | F | VF | XF | Unc | BU |
|---|---|---|---|---|---|---|
| 1993 Proof | 3,000 | Value: 21.50 | | | | |

**POUND** **KM# 90a** **Weight:** 11.6800 g. **Composition:** 0.9250 Silver .3474 oz. ASW **Obverse:** Bust of Queen Elizabeth II right **Reverse:** Sailing ship, Century

| Date | Mintage | F | VF | XF | Unc | BU |
|---|---|---|---|---|---|---|
| 1993 Proof | Est. 3,000 | Value: 21.50 | | | | |

**POUND** **KM# 88b** **Weight:** 19.6500 g. **Composition:** 0.9170 Gold .5794 oz. AGW **Obverse:** Bust of Queen Elizabeth II right **Reverse:** Sailing ship, Gemini

| Date | Mintage | F | VF | XF | Unc | BU |
|---|---|---|---|---|---|---|
| 1993 Proof | 250 | Value: 375 | | | | |

**POUND** **KM# 90b** **Weight:** 19.6500 g. **Composition:** 0.9170 Gold .5794 oz. AGW **Obverse:** Bust of Queen Elizabeth II right **Reverse:** Sailing ship, Century

| Date | Mintage | F | VF | XF | Unc | BU |
|---|---|---|---|---|---|---|
| 1993 Proof | Est. 250 | Value: 365 | | | | |

**POUND** **KM# 91a** **Weight:** 11.6800 g. **Composition:** 0.9250 Silver .3474 oz. ASW **Obverse:** Bust of Queen Elizabeth II right **Reverse:** Schooner, Resolute

| Date | Mintage | F | VF | XF | Unc | BU |
|---|---|---|---|---|---|---|
| 1994 Proof | 3,000 | Value: 21.50 | | | | |

**POUND** **KM# 91b** **Weight:** 19.6500 g. **Composition:** 0.9170 Gold .5794 oz. AGW **Obverse:** Bust of Queen Elizabeth II right **Reverse:** Schooner, Resolute

| Date | Mintage | F | VF | XF | Unc | BU |
|---|---|---|---|---|---|---|
| 1994 Proof | 250 | Value: 365 | | | | |

**POUND** **KM# 91** **Composition:** Nickel-Brass **Obverse:** Bust of Queen Elizabeth II right **Reverse:** Schooner, Resolute

| Date | Mintage | F | VF | XF | Unc | BU |
|---|---|---|---|---|---|---|
| 1994 | 60,000 | — | — | — | 3.25 | — |
| 1997 | 101,000 | — | — | — | 3.25 | — |

**POUND** **KM# 101** **Composition:** Nickel-Brass **Obverse:** Rank-Broadley portrait of Queen Elizabeth II **Reverse:** Schooner, Resolute **Edge Lettering:** CAESAREA INSULA

| Date | Mintage | F | VF | XF | Unc | BU |
|---|---|---|---|---|---|---|
| 1998 | 174,000 | — | — | — | 3.25 | — |

**SOVEREIGN** **KM# 110** **Weight:** 7.9800 g. **Composition:** 0.9167 Gold .2352 oz. AGW **Subject:** William I - Duke of Normandy **Obverse:** Bust of Queen Elizabeth II right **Reverse:** William seated on throne

| Date | Mintage | F | VF | XF | Unc | BU |
|---|---|---|---|---|---|---|
| 2000 | Est. 2,000 | — | — | — | 125 | — |
| 2000 Proof | Est. 2,000 | Value: 225 | | | | |

**2 POUNDS** **KM# 37** **Weight:** 21.9000 g. **Composition:** 0.9250 Silver .6513 oz. ASW **Subject:** 25th Wedding Anniversary **Obverse:** Similar to 1 Pound, KM#36

| Date | Mintage | F | VF | XF | Unc | BU |
|---|---|---|---|---|---|---|
| 1972 | 24,000 | — | — | — | 11.50 | — |
| 1972 Proof | 1,500 | Value: 25.00 | | | | |

**2 POUNDS** **KM# 52a** **Weight:** 28.2800 g. **Composition:** 0.9250 Silver .8411 oz. ASW **Subject:** Wedding of Prince Charles and Lady Diana **Obverse:** Bust of Queen Elizabeth II right

| Date | Mintage | F | VF | XF | Unc | BU |
|---|---|---|---|---|---|---|
| ND Proof | 35,000 | Value: 16.50 | | | | |

**2 POUNDS** **KM# 52b** **Weight:** 15.9800 g. **Composition:** 0.9170 Gold .4712 oz. AGW **Subject:** Wedding of Prince Charles and Lady Diana **Obverse:** Bust of Queen Elizabeth II right

| Date | Mintage | F | VF | XF | Unc | BU |
|---|---|---|---|---|---|---|
| ND Proof | 1,500 | Value: 225 | | | | |

**2 POUNDS** **KM# 52** **Composition:** Copper-Nickel **Subject:** Wedding of Prince Charles and Lady Diana **Obverse:** Bust of Queen Elizabeth II right

| Date | Mintage | F | VF | XF | Unc | BU |
|---|---|---|---|---|---|---|
| ND | 150,000 | — | — | — | 6.00 | — |

**2 POUNDS** **KM# 64** **Composition:** Copper-Nickel **Subject:** 40th Anniversary of Liberation of 1945 **Obverse:** Bust of Queen Elizabeth II right

| Date | Mintage | F | VF | XF | Unc | BU |
|---|---|---|---|---|---|---|
| 1985 | 20,000 | — | — | — | 6.00 | — |

**2 POUNDS** **KM# 64a** **Weight:** 28.2800 g. **Composition:** 0.9250 Silver .8411 oz. ASW **Subject:** 40th Anniversary of Liberation of 1945 **Obverse:** Bust of Queen Elizabeth II right

| Date | Mintage | F | VF | XF | Unc | BU |
|---|---|---|---|---|---|---|
| 1985 Proof | 2,500 | Value: 35.00 | | | | |

**2 POUNDS** **KM# 64b** **Weight:** 47.5400 g. **Composition:** 0.9170 Gold 1.4011 oz. AGW **Subject:** 40th Anniversary of Liberation of 1945 **Obverse:** Bust of Queen Elizabeth II right

| Date | Mintage | F | VF | XF | Unc | BU |
|---|---|---|---|---|---|---|
| 1985 Proof | 40 | Value: 2,000 | | | | |

**2 POUNDS** **KM# 67.1** **Composition:** Copper-Nickel **Subject:** XIII Commonwealth Games - Edinburgh **Obverse:** Bust of Queen Elizabeth II right **Edge Lettering:** XIII COMMONWEALTH GAMES

| Date | Mintage | F | VF | XF | Unc | BU |
|---|---|---|---|---|---|---|
| 1986 | 50,000 | — | — | — | 6.00 | — |

**2 POUNDS** **KM# 67.1b** **Weight:** 28.2800 g. **Composition:** 0.9250 Silver .8411 oz. ASW **Subject:** XIII Commonwealth Games - Edinburgh **Obverse:** Bust of Queen Elizabeth II right

| Date | Mintage | F | VF | XF | Unc | BU |
|---|---|---|---|---|---|---|
| 1986 Proof | 20,000 | Value: 40.00 | | | | |

**2 POUNDS** **KM# 67.1a** **Weight:** 28.2800 g. **Composition:** 0.5000 Silver .4546 oz. ASW **Subject:** XIII Commonwealth Games - Edinburgh **Obverse:** Bust of Queen Elizabeth II right

| Date | Mintage | F | VF | XF | Unc | BU |
|---|---|---|---|---|---|---|
| 1986 | 20,000 | — | — | — | 20.00 | — |

**2 POUNDS** **KM# 67.2** **Composition:** Copper-Nickel **Subject:** XIII Commonwealth Games - Edinburgh **Obverse:** Bust of Queen Elizabeth II right **Note:** Without edge inscription.

| Date | Mintage | F | VF | XF | Unc | BU |
|---|---|---|---|---|---|---|
| 1986 | 5,000 | — | — | — | 7.50 | — |

**2 POUNDS** **KM# 70a** **Weight:** 28.2800 g. **Composition:** 0.9250 Silver .8411 oz. ASW **Subject:** World Wildlife Fund **Obverse:** Bust of Queen Elizabeth II right **Reverse:** Mauritius pink pigeon

| Date | Mintage | F | VF | XF | Unc | BU |
|---|---|---|---|---|---|---|
| 1987 Proof | 25,000 | Value: 22.50 | | | | |

**2 POUNDS** **KM# 70** **Composition:** Copper-Nickel **Subject:** World Wildlife Fund **Obverse:** Bust of Queen Elizabeth II right **Reverse:** Mauritius pink pigeon

| Date | Mintage | F | VF | XF | Unc | BU |
|---|---|---|---|---|---|---|
| 1987 | 23,000 | — | — | — | 6.50 | — |

**2 POUNDS** **KM# 76** **Composition:** Copper-Nickel **Subject:** Royal Visit **Obverse:** Bust of Queen Elizabeth II right

| Date | Mintage | F | VF | XF | Unc | BU |
|---|---|---|---|---|---|---|
| 1989 | 10,000 | — | — | — | 6.00 | — |

**2 POUNDS** **KM# 76a** **Weight:** 28.3000 g. **Composition:** 0.9250 Silver .8411 oz. ASW **Subject:** Royal Visit **Obverse:** Bust of Queen Elizabeth II right

| Date | Mintage | F | VF | XF | Unc | BU |
|---|---|---|---|---|---|---|
| 1989 Proof | 3,000 | Value: 32.50 | | | | |

**2 POUNDS** **KM# 77** **Weight:** 28.3000 g. **Composition:** 0.9250 Silver .8411 oz. ASW **Subject:** 50th Anniversary - The Battle of Britain **Obverse:** Bust of Queen Elizabeth II right **Reverse:** Spitfire

| Date | Mintage | F | VF | XF | Unc | BU |
|---|---|---|---|---|---|---|
| ND Proof | Est. 10,000 | Value: 40.00 | | | | |

**2 POUNDS** **KM# 83a** **Weight:** 28.3500 g. **Composition:** 0.9250 Silver .8432 oz. ASW **Subject:** 90th Birthday of Queen Mother **Obverse:** Bust of Queen Elizabeth II right

| Date | Mintage | F | VF | XF | Unc | BU |
|---|---|---|---|---|---|---|
| ND Proof | 3,000 | Value: 55.00 | | | | |

**2 POUNDS** **KM# 83b** **Weight:** 15.9800 g. **Composition:** 0.9170 Gold .4708 oz. AGW **Subject:** 90th Birthday of Queen Mother **Obverse:** Bust of Queen Elizabeth II right **Reverse:** Double "E" monogram

| Date | Mintage | F | VF | XF | Unc | BU |
|---|---|---|---|---|---|---|
| ND Proof | 90 | Value: 750 | | | | |

**2 POUNDS** **KM# 83** **Composition:** Copper-Nickel **Subject:** 90th Birthday of Queen Mother **Obverse:** Bust of Queen Elizabeth II right **Reverse:** Double "E" monogram

| Date | Mintage | F | VF | XF | Unc | BU |
|---|---|---|---|---|---|---|
| ND | 10,000 | — | — | — | 7.00 | — |

**2 POUNDS** **KM# 89** **Composition:** Copper-Nickel **Subject:** 40th Anniversary - Coronation of Queen Elizabeth II **Obverse:** Bust of Queen Elizabeth II right

| Date | Mintage | F | VF | XF | Unc | BU |
|---|---|---|---|---|---|---|
| ND | 12,000 | — | — | — | 6.00 | — |

**2 POUNDS** **KM# 89a** **Weight:** 28.2800 g. **Composition:** 0.9250 Silver .8411 oz. ASW **Subject:** 40th Anniversary - Coronation of Queen Elizabeth II **Obverse:** Bust of Queen Elizabeth II right

| Date | Mintage | F | VF | XF | Unc | BU |
|---|---|---|---|---|---|---|
| ND Proof | Est. 10,000 | Value: 55.00 | | | | |

**2 POUNDS** **KM# 92** **Composition:** Copper-Nickel **Subject:** 50th Anniversary of Liberation **Obverse:** Bust of Queen Elizabeth II right

| Date | Mintage | F | VF | XF | Unc | BU |
|---|---|---|---|---|---|---|
| 1995 | 42,000 | — | — | — | 8.00 | — |

**Note:** Also released in special wallet with 1 Pound commemorative banknote (6,000). Market value: $20.00

**2 POUNDS** **KM# 92a** **Weight:** 28.2800 g. **Composition:** 0.9250 Silver .8411 oz. ASW **Subject:** 50th Anniversary of Liberation **Obverse:** Bust of Queen Elizabeth II right

| Date | Mintage | F | VF | XF | Unc | BU |
|---|---|---|---|---|---|---|
| 1995 Proof | 7,000 | Value: 55.00 | | | | |

**2 POUNDS** **KM# 97a** **Weight:** 28.3800 g. **Composition:** 0.9250 Silver .8411 oz. ASW **Subject:** Queen Elizabeth's 70th Birthday **Obverse:** Bust of Queen Elizabeth II right **Reverse:** Flowers

| Date | Mintage | F | VF | XF | Unc | BU |
|---|---|---|---|---|---|---|
| 1996 | Est. 8,000 | — | — | — | 45.00 | — |

**Note:** KM98 and 98a previously listed here, were never produced

**2 POUNDS** **KM# 97** **Composition:** Copper-Nickel **Subject:** Queen Elizabeth's 70th Birthday **Obverse:** Bust of Queen Elizabeth II right **Reverse:** Flowers

| Date | Mintage | F | VF | XF | Unc | BU |
|---|---|---|---|---|---|---|
| 1996 | Est. 20,000 | — | — | — | 8.00 | — |

**2 POUNDS** **KM# 99** **Ring Composition:** Brass **Center Composition:** Copper-Nickel **Obverse:** Bust of Queen Elizabeth II right **Reverse:** Coats of arms circle denomination

| Date | Mintage | F | VF | XF | Unc | BU |
|---|---|---|---|---|---|---|
| 1997 In sets only | 5,500 | — | — | — | 8.50 | — |

**2 POUNDS** **KM# 99a** **Ring Weight:** 12.0000 g. **Ring Composition:** 0.9250 Gold Plated Silver **Center Composition:** Silver **Obverse:** Bust of Queen Elizabeth II right **Reverse:** Coats of arms circle denomination

| Date | Mintage | F | VF | XF | Unc | BU |
|---|---|---|---|---|---|---|
| 1997 Proof | 500 | Value: 65.00 | | | | |

**2 POUNDS** **KM# 102** **Ring Composition:** Brass **Center Composition:** Copper-Nickel **Obverse:** Rank-Broadley portrait of Queen Elizabeth II **Reverse:** Latent image value in circle of arms **Edge Lettering:** CAESARA INSULA

| Date | Mintage | F | VF | XF | Unc | BU |
|---|---|---|---|---|---|---|
| 1998 | 800,000 | — | — | — | 8.00 | — |

**2 POUNDS** **KM# 89b** **Weight:** 5.9800 g. **Composition:** 0.9167 Gold .4709 oz. AGW **Subject:** 40th Anniversary - Coronation of Queen Elizabeth II **Obverse:** Bust of Queen Elizabeth II right

| Date | Mintage | F | VF | XF | Unc | BU |
|---|---|---|---|---|---|---|
| 1998 Proof | Est. 500 | Value: 500 | | | | |

**2 POUNDS 50 PENCE** **KM# 38** **Weight:** 27.6000 g. **Composition:** 0.9250 Silver .8208 oz. ASW **Subject:** 25th Wedding Anniversary **Obverse:** Similar to 1 Pound, KM#36

| Date | Mintage | F | VF | XF | Unc | BU |
|---|---|---|---|---|---|---|
| 1972 | 24,000 | — | — | — | 17.50 | — |
| 1972 Proof | 1,500 | Value: 27.50 | | | | |

**5 POUNDS** **KM# 39** **Weight:** 2.6200 g. **Composition:** 0.9170 Gold .0772 oz. AGW **Subject:** 25th Wedding Anniversary **Obverse:** Bust of Queen Elizabeth II right

| Date | Mintage | F | VF | XF | Unc | BU |
|---|---|---|---|---|---|---|
| 1972 | 8,500 | — | — | — | 37.50 | — |
| 1972 Proof | 1,500 | Value: 60.00 | | | | |

**5 POUNDS** **KM# 78** **Weight:** 155.6000 g. **Composition:** 0.9250 Silver 4.6215 oz. ASW **Subject:** 50th Anniversary - The Battle of Britian **Obverse:** Bust of Queen Elizabeth II right **Reverse:** Spitfire **Note:** Illustration reduce. Actual size: 65mm.

| Date | Mintage | F | VF | XF | Unc | BU |
|---|---|---|---|---|---|---|
| ND Proof | Est. 5,000 | Value: 145 | | | | |

**5 POUNDS** **KM# 100** **Composition:** Copper-Nickel **Subject:** Queen's Golden Wedding Anniversary **Obverse:** Bust of Queen Elizabeth II right **Reverse:** Conjoined busts of royal couple and coat of arms

| Date | Mintage | F | VF | XF | Unc | BU |
|---|---|---|---|---|---|---|
| 1997 | 6,000 | — | — | — | 15.00 | — |

**5 POUNDS** **KM# 100a** **Weight:** 28.2800 g. **Composition:** 0.9250 Silver .8411 oz. ASW **Subject:** Queen's Golden Wedding Anniversary **Obverse:** Bust of Queen Elizabeth II right **Reverse:** Conjoined busts of royal couple and gold plated coat of arms

| Date | Mintage | F | VF | XF | Unc | BU |
|---|---|---|---|---|---|---|
| 1997 Proof | Est. 30,000 | Value: 65.00 | | | | |

**5 POUNDS** **KM# 109** **Weight:** 28.2800 g. **Composition:** 0.9250 Silver .8411 oz. ASW **Subject:** Millennium **Obverse:** Bust of Queen Elizabeth II right **Reverse:** Gold Plated island map on globe

| Date | Mintage | F | VF | XF | Unc | BU |
|---|---|---|---|---|---|---|
| 2000 Proof | 32,000 | Value: 47.50 | | | | |

**10 POUNDS** **KM# 40** **Weight:** 4.6400 g. **Composition:** 0.9170 Gold .1368 oz. AGW **Subject:** 25th Wedding Anniversary **Obverse:** Bust of Queen Elizabeth II right

| Date | Mintage | F | VF | XF | Unc | BU |
|---|---|---|---|---|---|---|
| 1972 | 8,500 | — | — | — | 60.00 | — |
| 1972 Proof | 1,500 | Value: 80.00 | | | | |

**10 POUNDS** **KM# 79** **Weight:** 3.1300 g. **Composition:** 0.9990 Gold .1005 oz. AGW **Subject:** 50th Anniversary - The Battle of Britain **Obverse:** Similar to 50 Pounds, KM#81

| Date | Mintage | F | VF | XF | Unc | BU |
|---|---|---|---|---|---|---|
| ND Proof | Est. 500 | Value: 120 | | | | |

**10 POUNDS** **KM# 93** **Weight:** 3.1300 g. **Composition:** 0.9990 Gold .1005 oz. AGW **Subject:** 50th Anniversary of Liberation **Obverse:** Bust of Queen Elizabeth II right

| Date | Mintage | F | VF | XF | Unc | BU |
|---|---|---|---|---|---|---|
| 1995 Proof sets only | 500 | — | — | — | 85.00 | — |

**20 POUNDS** **KM# 41** **Weight:** 9.2600 g. **Composition:** 0.9170 Gold .2729 oz. AGW **Subject:** 25th Wedding Anniversary **Obverse:** Bust of Queen Elizabeth II right

| Date | Mintage | F | VF | XF | Unc | BU |
|---|---|---|---|---|---|---|
| 1972 | 8,500 | — | — | — | 125 | — |
| 1972 Proof | 1,500 | Value: 165 | | | | |

**25 POUNDS** **KM# 42** **Weight:** 11.9000 g. **Composition:** 0.9170 Gold .3507 oz. AGW **Subject:** 25th Wedding Anniversary **Obverse:** Bust of Queen Elizabeth II right

| Date | Mintage | F | VF | XF | Unc | BU |
|---|---|---|---|---|---|---|
| 1972 | 8,500 | — | — | — | 150 | — |
| 1972 Proof | 1,500 | Value: 220 | | | | |

**25 POUNDS** **KM# 80** **Weight:** 7.8100 g. **Composition:** 0.9990 Gold .2509 oz. AGW **Subject:** 50th Anniversary - The Battle of Britain **Obverse:** Similar to 50 Pounds, KM#81 **Reverse:** Spitfire

| Date | Mintage | F | VF | XF | Unc | BU |
|---|---|---|---|---|---|---|
| 1990 Proof | Est. 500 | Value: 250 | | | | |

**25 POUNDS** **KM# 94** **Weight:** 7.8100 g. **Composition:** 0.9990 Gold .2509 oz. AGW **Subject:** 50th Anniversary of Liberation **Obverse:** Bust of Queen Elizabeth II right

| Date | Mintage | F | VF | XF | Unc | BU |
|---|---|---|---|---|---|---|
| 1995 Proof sets only | 500 | — | — | — | 215 | — |

**50 POUNDS** **KM# 43** **Weight:** 22.6300 g. **Composition:** 0.9170 Gold .6670 oz. AGW **Subject:** 25th Wedding Anniversary **Obverse:** Bust of Queen Elizabeth II right

| Date | Mintage | F | VF | XF | Unc | BU |
|---|---|---|---|---|---|---|
| 1972 | 8,500 | — | — | — | 300 | — |
| 1972 Proof | 1,500 | Value: 375 | | | | |

**50 POUNDS** **KM# 81** **Weight:** 15.6100 g. **Composition:** 0.9990 Gold .5014 oz. AGW **Subject:** 50th Anniversary - Battle of Britain **Obverse:** Bust of Queen Elizabeth II right **Reverse:** Royal Air Force badge dividing dates

| Date | Mintage | F | VF | XF | Unc | BU |
|---|---|---|---|---|---|---|
| ND Proof | Est. 500 | Value: 480 | | | | |

**50 POUNDS** **KM# 95** **Weight:** 15.6100 g. **Composition:** 0.9990 Gold .5014 oz. AGW **Subject:** 50th Anniversary of Liberation **Obverse:** Bust of Queen Elizabeth II right

| Date | Mintage | F | VF | XF | Unc | BU |
|---|---|---|---|---|---|---|
| 1995 Proof sets only | 500 | — | — | — | 435 | — |

**100 POUNDS** KM# 82 **Weight:** 31.2100 g. **Composition:** 0.9990 Gold 1.0025 oz. AGW **Subject:** 50th Anniversary - The Battle of Britain **Obverse:** Bust of Queen Elizabeth II right **Reverse:** Spitfire

| Date | Mintage | F | VF | XF | Unc | BU |
|---|---|---|---|---|---|---|
| ND Proof | Est. 500 | Value: 900 | | | | |

**100 POUNDS** KM# 96 **Weight:** 31.2100 g. **Composition:** 0.9990 Gold 1.0025 oz. AGW **Subject:** 50th Anniversary of Liberation **Obverse:** Bust of Queen Elizabeth II right

| Date | Mintage | F | VF | XF | Unc | BU |
|---|---|---|---|---|---|---|
| 1995 Proof sets only | 500 | — | — | — | 865 | — |

## PIEFORTS

| KM# | Date | Mintage | Identification | Mkt Val |
|---|---|---|---|---|
| P1 | 1982 | 1,500 | 20 Pence. Silver. Date. KM53a. | 30.00 |
| P2 | 1995 | — | 2 Pounds. 0.9250 Silver. KM92a. | 75.00 |

## MINT SETS

| KM# | Date | Mintage | Identification | Issue Price | Mkt Val |
|---|---|---|---|---|---|
| MS1 | 1972 (9) | 8,500 | KM35-43 | 348 | 715 |
| MS2 | 1972 (4) | 15,000 | KM35-38 | 24.00 | 40.00 |
| MS3 | 1983 (7) | 25,000 | KM54-59, 66 | — | 6.00 |
| MS4 | 1987 (7) | — | KM54-55, 56.1-58.1, 66, 71 | — | 6.50 |
| MS5 | 1992 (7) | 6,000 | KM54,55b, 56.2- 57.2, 58.1, 66, 86 | 22.50 | 22.50 |
| MS6 | 1997 (8) | 5,500 | KM54b 55, 56.2-58.2, 66, 91, 99 | — | 28.00 |

## PROOF SETS

| KM# | Date | Mintage | Identification | Issue Price | Mkt Val |
|---|---|---|---|---|---|
| PS1 | 1957 (4) | 1,050 | KM21-22 two each | — | 30.00 |
| PS2.1 | 1960 (4) | 2,100 | KM22- 23 two each | — | 25.00 |
| PS2.2 | 1960 (4) | I.A. | KM22, 24 two each | — | 150 |
| PS3 | 1964 (4) | 10,000 | KM21, 25 two each | — | 8.00 |
| PS4 | 1966 (4) | 15,000 | KM26-27 two each | — | 8.00 |
| PS5 | 1966 (2) | 15,000 | KM28 two pieces | — | 8.00 |
| PS6 | 1972 (9) | 1,500 | KM35-43 | 648 | 975 |
| PS7 | 1980 (6) | 10,000 | KM29-34 | — | 20.00 |
| PS8 | 1981 (7) | 15,000 | KM45-51 | 31.00 | 20.00 |
| PS9 | 1983 (7) | 5,000 | KM54a-55a, 56.1a-57.1a, 58a-59a, 66a | — | 80.00 |
| PS10 | 1990 (4) | 500 | KM79-82 | 1,595 | 1,750 |
| PS11 | 1995 (4) | 500 | KM93-96 | 1,600 | 1,600 |

# JORDAN

The Hashemite Kingdom of Jordan, a constitutional monarchy in southwest Asia, has an area of 37,738 sq. mi.(91,880 sq. km.) and a population of 3.5 million. Capital: Amman. Agriculture and tourism comprise Jordan's economic base. Chief exports are phosphates, tomatoe sand oranges.

Jordan is the Edom and Moab of the time of Moses. It became part of the Roman province of Arabia in 106 A.D., was conquered by the Arabs in 633-36, and was part of the Ottoman Empire from the 16th century until World War I. At that time, the regions presently known as Jordan and Israel were mandated to Great Britain by the League of Nations as Transjordan and Palestine. In 1922 Transjordan was established as the semi-autonomous Emirate of Transjordan, ruled by the Hashemite Prince Abdullah but still nominally a part of the British mandate. The mandate over Transjordan was terminated in 1946, the country becoming the independent Hashemite Kingdom of Transjordan. The kingdom was renamed the Hashemite Kingdom of Jordan in 1950.

NOTE: Several 1964 and 1965 issues were limited to respective quantities of 3,000 and 5,000 examples struck to make up sets for sale to collectors.

**TITLES**

المملكة الاردنية الهاشمية

el-Mamlaka(t) el-Urduniya(t) el-Hashemiya(t)

**RULERS**
Abdullah Ibn Al-Hussein, 1946-1951
Talal Ibn Abdullah, 1951-1952
Hussein Ibn Talal, 1952-1999
Abdullah Ibn Al-Hussein, 1999-

**MONETARY SYSTEM**
100 Fils = 1 Dirham
1000 Fils = 10 Dirhams = 1 Dinar
Commencing 1992
100 Piastres = 1 Dinar

## KINGDOM

## DECIMAL COINAGE

**FIL** KM# 1 **Composition:** Bronze

| Date | Mintage | F | VF | XF | Unc | BU |
|---|---|---|---|---|---|---|
| AH1368(1949) | 350,000 | — | 1.00 | 1.50 | 3.50 | — |
| AH1368(1949) Proof | — | — | — | — | — | — |

**Note:** "FIL" is an error for "FILS," the correct Arabic singular

**FILS** KM# 2 **Composition:** Bronze

| Date | Mintage | F | VF | XF | Unc | BU |
|---|---|---|---|---|---|---|
| AH1368(1949) | Inc. above | — | 0.50 | 0.90 | 2.25 | — |
| AH1368(1949) Proof | 25 | Value: 50.00 | | | | |

**FILS** KM# 8 **Composition:** Bronze

| Date | Mintage | F | VF | XF | Unc | BU |
|---|---|---|---|---|---|---|
| AH1374(1955) | 200,000 | — | 0.35 | 0.50 | 1.00 | — |
| AH1374(1955) Proof | — | — | — | — | — | — |
| AH1379(1959) | 150,000 | — | 0.40 | 0.60 | 1.25 | — |
| AH1379(1959) Proof | — | — | — | — | — | — |
| AH1382(1962) | 200,000 | — | 0.25 | 0.50 | 1.00 | — |
| AH1382(1962) Proof | — | — | — | — | — | — |
| AH1383(1963) | 3,000 | — | 1.50 | 3.00 | 5.00 | — |
| AH1385(1965) | 5,000 | — | 1.00 | 2.00 | 4.00 | — |
| AH1385(1965) Proof | 10,000 | Value: 3.00 | | | | |

**FILS** KM# 14 **Composition:** Bronze **Obverse:** Head of Hussein right

| Date | Mintage | F | VF | XF | Unc | BU |
|---|---|---|---|---|---|---|
| AH1387(1967) | 60,000 | — | 0.15 | 0.25 | 0.75 | — |

**FILS** KM# 35 **Composition:** Bronze

| Date | Mintage | F | VF | XF | Unc | BU |
|---|---|---|---|---|---|---|
| AH1398(1978) | — | — | 0.15 | 0.25 | 0.60 | — |
| AH1398(1978) Proof | 20,000 | Value: 0.75 | | | | |
| AH1404(1984) | 100,000 | — | 0.10 | 0.20 | 0.50 | — |
| AH1406(1986) | — | — | 0.10 | 0.20 | 0.50 | — |
| AH1406(1986) Proof | 5,000 | Value: 0.75 | | | | |

**5 FILS (1/2 Qirsh)** KM# 3 **Composition:** Bronze

| Date | Mintage | F | VF | XF | Unc | BU |
|---|---|---|---|---|---|---|
| AH1368(1949) | 3,300 | — | 0.40 | 0.75 | 1.50 | — |
| AH1368(1949) Proof | 25 | Value: 60.00 | | | | |

**5 FILS (1/2 Qirsh)** KM# 9 **Composition:** Bronze

| Date | Mintage | F | VF | XF | Unc | BU |
|---|---|---|---|---|---|---|
| AH1374(1955) | 3,500,000 | — | 0.35 | 0.50 | 0.75 | — |
| AH1374(1955) Proof | — | — | — | — | — | — |
| AH1380(1960) | 540,000 | — | 0.50 | 0.70 | 1.25 | — |
| AH1380(1960) Proof | — | — | — | — | — | — |
| AH1382(1962) | 250,000 | — | 0.45 | 0.70 | 1.25 | — |
| AH1382(1962) Proof | — | — | — | — | — | — |
| AH1383(1963) | 3,000 | — | — | 4.50 | 7.50 | — |
| AH1384(1964) | 2,500,000 | — | 0.30 | 0.50 | 1.00 | — |
| AH1385(1965) | 5,000 | — | 1.25 | 2.50 | 4.00 | — |
| AH1385(1965) Proof | 10,000 | Value: 5.00 | | | | |
| AH1387(1967) | 2,000,000 | — | 0.10 | 0.20 | 0.40 | — |

**5 FILS (1/2 Qirsh)** KM# 15 **Composition:** Bronze **Obverse:** Head of Hussein right

| Date | Mintage | F | VF | XF | Unc | BU |
|---|---|---|---|---|---|---|
| AH1387(1967) | 800,000 | — | 0.10 | 0.25 | 0.50 | — |
| AH1390(1970) | 1,400,000 | — | — | 0.20 | 0.40 | — |
| AH1392(1972) | 400,000 | — | 0.10 | 0.25 | 0.65 | — |
| AH1394(1974) | 2,000,000 | — | 0.10 | 0.20 | 0.40 | — |
| AH1395(1975) | 9,000,000 | — | 0.10 | 0.15 | 0.30 | — |

**5 FILS (1/2 Qirsh)** **KM# 36** **Composition:** Bronze

| Date | Mintage | F | VF | XF | Unc | BU |
|---|---|---|---|---|---|---|
| AH1398(1978) | 60,200,000 | — | 0.10 | 0.15 | 0.30 | — |
| AH1398(1978) Proof | 20,000 | Value: 1.25 | | | | |
| AH1406(1986) | — | — | 0.10 | 0.15 | 0.30 | — |
| AH1406(1986) Proof | 5,000 | Value: 1.25 | | | | |

**10 FILS (Qirsh, Piastre)** **KM# 4** **Composition:** Bronze

| Date | Mintage | F | VF | XF | Unc | BU |
|---|---|---|---|---|---|---|
| AH1368(1949) | 2,700,000 | — | 0.75 | 1.25 | 2.00 | — |
| AH1368(1949) Proof | 25 | Value: 80.00 | | | | |

**10 FILS (Qirsh, Piastre)** **KM# 10** **Composition:** Bronze

| Date | Mintage | F | VF | XF | Unc | BU |
|---|---|---|---|---|---|---|
| AH1374(1955) | 1,500,000 | — | 0.60 | 1.00 | 2.00 | — |
| AH1374(1955) Proof | — | — | — | — | — | — |
| AH1380(1960) | 60,000 | — | 1.25 | 2.00 | 3.50 | — |
| AH1380(1960) Proof | — | — | — | — | — | — |
| AH1382(1962) | 2,300,000 | — | 0.30 | 0.50 | 1.00 | — |
| AH1382(1962) Proof | — | Value: 50.00 | | | | |
| AH1383(1963) | 1,253,000 | — | 0.30 | 0.50 | 1.00 | — |
| AH1385(1965) | 1,003,000 | — | 0.20 | 0.40 | 1.00 | — |
| AH1385(1965) Proof | 10,000 | Value: 2.00 | | | | |
| AH1387(1967) | 1,000,000 | — | 0.20 | 0.35 | 1.00 | — |

**10 FILS (Qirsh, Piastre)** **KM# 16** **Composition:** Bronze **Obverse:** Head of Hussein right

| Date | Mintage | F | VF | XF | Unc | BU |
|---|---|---|---|---|---|---|
| AH1387(1967) | 500,000 | — | 0.20 | 0.40 | 0.75 | — |
| AH1390(1970) | 1,000,000 | — | 0.20 | 0.35 | 0.60 | — |
| AH1392(1972) | 600,000 | — | 0.20 | 0.40 | 0.75 | — |
| AH1394(1974) | 1,000,000 | — | 0.20 | 0.40 | 0.65 | — |
| AH1395(1975) | 5,000,000 | — | 0.20 | 0.35 | 0.50 | — |

**10 FILS (Qirsh, Piastre)** **KM# 37** **Composition:** Bronze

| Date | Mintage | F | VF | XF | Unc | BU |
|---|---|---|---|---|---|---|
| AH1398(1978) | 30,000,000 | — | 0.10 | 0.15 | 0.40 | — |
| AH1398(1978) Proof | 20,000 | Value: 1.50 | | | | |
| AH1404(1984) | 10,000,000 | — | 0.10 | 0.15 | 0.40 | — |
| AH1406(1986) | — | — | 0.10 | 0.15 | 0.40 | — |
| AH1406(1986) Proof | 5,000 | Value: 1.50 | | | | |
| AH1409(1989) | 8,000 | — | 0.10 | 0.15 | 0.40 | — |

**20 FILS** **KM# 5** **Composition:** Copper-Nickel

| Date | Mintage | F | VF | XF | Unc | BU |
|---|---|---|---|---|---|---|
| AH1368(1949) | 1,570,000 | — | 0.50 | 1.00 | 1.75 | — |
| AH1368(1949) Proof | 25 | Value: 90.00 | | | | |

**20 FILS** **KM# 13** **Composition:** Copper-Nickel

| Date | Mintage | F | VF | XF | Unc | BU |
|---|---|---|---|---|---|---|
| AH1383(1963) | 3,000 | — | 1.50 | 3.00 | 5.00 | — |
| AH1385(1965) | 5,000 | — | 1.50 | 3.00 | 5.00 | — |
| AH1385(1965) Proof | 10,000 | Value: 5.00 | | | | |

**25 FILS (1/4 Dirham)** **KM# 17** **Composition:** Copper-Nickel **Obverse:** Head of Hussein right

| Date | Mintage | F | VF | XF | Unc | BU |
|---|---|---|---|---|---|---|
| AH1387(1967) | 200,000 | — | 0.15 | 0.35 | 0.75 | — |
| AH1390(1970) | 240,000 | — | 0.15 | 0.35 | 0.75 | — |
| AH1394(1974) | 800,000 | — | 0.15 | 0.35 | 0.75 | — |
| AH1395(1975) | 2,000,000 | — | 0.15 | 0.35 | 0.75 | — |
| AH1397(1977) | 1,600,000 | — | 0.15 | 0.35 | 0.75 | — |

**25 FILS (1/4 Dirham)** **KM# 38** **Composition:** Copper-Nickel

| Date | Mintage | F | VF | XF | Unc | BU |
|---|---|---|---|---|---|---|
| AH1398(1978) | — | — | 0.20 | 0.30 | 0.75 | — |
| AH1398(1978) Proof | 20,000 | Value: 2.00 | | | | |
| AH1401(1981) | 2,000,000 | — | 0.20 | 0.30 | 0.75 | — |
| AH1404(1984) | 4,000,000 | — | 0.20 | 0.30 | 0.75 | — |
| AH1406(1986) | — | — | 0.20 | 0.30 | 0.75 | — |
| AH1406(1986) Proof | 5,000 | Value: 2.00 | | | | |
| AH1411(1990) | 5,000,000 | — | 0.20 | 0.30 | 0.75 | — |

**50 FILS (1/2 Dirham)** **KM# 6** **Composition:** Copper-Nickel

| Date | Mintage | F | VF | XF | Unc | BU |
|---|---|---|---|---|---|---|
| AH1368(1949) | 2,500,000 | — | 0.75 | 2.00 | 3.50 | — |
| AH1368(1949) Proof | 25 | Value: 100 | | | | |

**50 FILS (1/2 Dirham)** **KM# 11** **Composition:** Copper-Nickel

| Date | Mintage | F | VF | XF | Unc | BU |
|---|---|---|---|---|---|---|
| AH1374(1955) | 2,500,000 | — | 0.75 | 1.50 | 3.50 | — |
| AH1374(1955) Proof | — | — | — | — | — | — |
| AH1382(1962) | 750,000 | — | 0.85 | 1.00 | 1.50 | — |
| AH1382(1962) Proof | — | — | — | — | — | — |
| AH1383(1963) | 1,003,000 | — | 0.40 | 0.60 | 1.00 | — |
| AH1385(1965) | 1,505,000 | — | 0.40 | 0.60 | 1.00 | — |
| AH1385(1965) Proof | 10,000 | Value: 3.50 | | | | |

**50 FILS (1/2 Dirham)** **KM# 18** **Composition:** Copper-Nickel **Obverse:** Head of Hussein right

| Date | Mintage | F | VF | XF | Unc | BU |
|---|---|---|---|---|---|---|
| AH1387(1967) | 400,000 | — | 0.40 | 0.75 | 1.75 | — |
| AH1390(1970) | 1,000,000 | — | 0.40 | 0.60 | 1.25 | — |
| AH1394(1974) | 1,000,000 | — | 0.40 | 0.60 | 1.25 | — |
| AH1395(1975) | 2,000,000 | — | 0.40 | 0.60 | 1.25 | — |
| AH1397(1977) | 6,000,000 | — | 0.40 | 0.60 | 1.25 | — |

**50 FILS (1/2 Dirham)** **KM# 39** **Composition:** Copper-Nickel

| Date | Mintage | F | VF | XF | Unc | BU |
|---|---|---|---|---|---|---|
| AH1398(1978) | 6,168,000 | — | 0.25 | 0.50 | 1.25 | — |
| AH1398(1978) Proof | 20,000 | Value: 2.50 | | | | |
| AH1400(1980) | — | — | 0.25 | 0.50 | 1.25 | — |
| AH1401(1981) | 5,000,000 | — | 0.25 | 0.50 | 1.25 | — |
| AH1404(1984) | 10,000,000 | — | 0.25 | 0.50 | 1.25 | — |
| AH1406(1986) | — | — | 0.25 | 0.50 | 1.25 | — |
| AH1406(1986) Proof | 5,000 | Value: 2.50 | | | | |
| AH1409(1989) | 6,000,000 | — | 0.25 | 0.50 | 1.25 | — |
| AH1411(1990) | 10,000,000 | — | 0.25 | 0.50 | 1.25 | — |

**100 FILS (Dirham)** KM# 7 **Composition:** Copper-Nickel

| Date | Mintage | F | VF | XF | Unc | BU |
|---|---|---|---|---|---|---|
| AH1368(1949) | 2,000,000 | — | 2.00 | 3.00 | 5.00 | — |
| AH1368(1949) Proof | 25 | Value: 120 | | | | |

**100 FILS (Dirham)** KM# 12 **Composition:** Copper-Nickel

| Date | Mintage | F | VF | XF | Unc | BU |
|---|---|---|---|---|---|---|
| AH1374(1955) | 500,000 | — | 2.00 | 2.50 | 4.00 | — |
| AH1374(1955) Proof | — | — | — | — | — | — |
| AH1382(1962) | 600,000 | — | 1.00 | 1.50 | 3.00 | — |
| AH1382(1962) Proof | — | — | — | — | — | — |
| AH1383(1963) | 3,000 | — | 1.50 | 3.00 | 5.00 | — |
| AH1385(1965) | 405,000 | — | 1.00 | 1.25 | 2.25 | — |
| AH1385(1965) Proof | 10,000 | Value: 4.00 | | | | |

**100 FILS (Dirham)** KM# 19 **Composition:** Copper-Nickel **Obverse:** Head of Hussein right

| Date | Mintage | F | VF | XF | Unc | BU |
|---|---|---|---|---|---|---|
| AH1387(1967) | 175,000 | — | 0.75 | 1.50 | 2.50 | — |
| AH1395(1975) | 2,500,000 | — | 0.40 | 1.00 | 2.00 | — |
| AH1397(1977) | 2,000,000 | — | 0.40 | 1.00 | 2.00 | — |

**100 FILS (Dirham)** KM# 40 **Composition:** Copper-Nickel

| Date | Mintage | F | VF | XF | Unc | BU |
|---|---|---|---|---|---|---|
| AH1398(1978) | 3,000,000 | — | 0.40 | 1.00 | 2.00 | — |
| AH1398(1978) Proof | 20,000 | Value: 3.00 | | | | |
| AH1400(1980) | — | — | 0.40 | 1.00 | 2.00 | — |
| AH1401(1981) | 4,000,000 | — | 0.40 | 1.00 | 2.00 | — |
| AH1404(1984) | 5,000,000 | — | 0.40 | 1.00 | 1.50 | — |
| AH1406(1986) | — | — | 0.40 | 1.00 | 1.50 | — |
| AH1406(1986) Proof | 5,000 | Value: 3.00 | | | | |
| AH1409(1989) | 4,000,000 | — | 0.40 | 1.00 | 1.50 | — |
| AH1411(1990) | 6,000,000 | — | 0.40 | 1.00 | 1.50 | — |

**1/4 DINAR** KM# 20 **Composition:** Copper-Nickel **Series:** F.A.O

| Date | Mintage | F | VF | XF | Unc | BU |
|---|---|---|---|---|---|---|
| AH1389(1969) | 60,000 | — | 2.00 | 3.00 | 5.50 | — |

**1/4 DINAR** KM# 28 **Composition:** Copper-Nickel **Series:** F.A.O

| Date | Mintage | F | VF | XF | Unc | BU |
|---|---|---|---|---|---|---|
| AH1390(1970) | 500,000 | — | 1.00 | 1.50 | 4.00 | — |
| AH1394(1974) | 400,000 | — | 1.00 | 1.50 | 4.00 | — |
| AH1395(1975) | 100,000 | — | 1.00 | 1.50 | 4.00 | — |

**1/4 DINAR** KM# 29 **Weight:** 19.0400 g. **Composition:** 0.9250 Silver .5663 oz. ASW **Subject:** 10th Anniversary - Central Bank of Jordan

| Date | Mintage | F | VF | XF | Unc | BU |
|---|---|---|---|---|---|---|
| AH1394(1974) Proof | 550 | Value: 60.00 | | | | |

**1/4 DINAR** KM# 29a **Composition:** 0.9170 Gold **Subject:** 10th Anniversary - Central Bank of Jordan

| Date | Mintage | F | VF | XF | Unc | BU |
|---|---|---|---|---|---|---|
| AH1394(1974) Proof | 100 | Value: 600 | | | | |

**1/4 DINAR** KM# 30 **Composition:** Copper-Nickel **Subject:** 25th Anniversary of Reign

| Date | Mintage | F | VF | XF | Unc | BU |
|---|---|---|---|---|---|---|
| AH1397(1977) | 200,000 | — | 1.00 | 2.00 | 4.50 | — |

**1/4 DINAR** KM# 41 **Composition:** Copper-Nickel

| Date | Mintage | F | VF | XF | Unc | BU |
|---|---|---|---|---|---|---|
| AH1398(1978) | 200,000 | — | 1.00 | 2.00 | 4.50 | — |
| AH1398(1978) Proof | 20,000 | Value: 5.00 | | | | |
| AH1401(1981) | 800,000 | — | 0.75 | 1.50 | 4.00 | — |
| AH1406(1986) | — | — | 0.75 | 1.50 | 4.00 | — |
| AH1406(1986) Proof | 5,000 | Value: 5.00 | | | | |

**1/2 DINAR** KM# 21 **Weight:** 20.0000 g. **Composition:** 0.9990 Silver .6424 oz. ASW **Reverse:** Al Harraneh Palace

| Date | Mintage | F | VF | XF | Unc | BU |
|---|---|---|---|---|---|---|
| AH1389(1969) Proof | 6,100 | Value: 20.00 | | | | |

**1/2 DINAR** KM# 42 **Composition:** Copper-Nickel **Subject:** 1400th Anniversary of Islam

| Date | Mintage | F | VF | XF | Unc | BU |
|---|---|---|---|---|---|---|
| AH1400(1980) | 2,006,000 | — | 1.50 | 2.50 | 5.00 | — |

**3/4 DINAR** KM# 22 **Weight:** 30.0000 g. **Composition:** 0.9990 Silver .9636 oz. ASW **Obverse:** Similar to 1/2 Dinar, KM#21 **Reverse:** Shrine of the Nativity, Bethlehem

| Date | Mintage | F | VF | XF | Unc | BU |
|---|---|---|---|---|---|---|
| AH1389(1969) Proof | 5,800 | Value: 40.00 | | | | |

**DINAR** **KM# 23** **Weight:** 40.0000 g. **Composition:** 0.9990 Silver 1.2848 oz. ASW **Obverse:** Similar to 1/2 Dinar, KM#21 **Reverse:** Temple Hill, Jerusalem

| Date | Mintage | F | VF | XF | Unc | BU |
|---|---|---|---|---|---|---|
| AH1389(1969) Proof | 6,800 | Value: 60.00 | | | | |

**DINAR** **KM# 47** **Composition:** Nickel-Bronze **Subject:** King Hussein's 50th Birthday

| Date | Mintage | F | VF | XF | Unc | BU |
|---|---|---|---|---|---|---|
| AH1406(1986) | — | — | — | — | 7.50 | — |
| AH1406(1986) Proof | 5,000 | Value: 10.00 | | | | |

**2 DINARS** **KM# 24** **Weight:** 5.5200 g. **Composition:** 0.9000 Gold .1597 oz. AGW **Subject:** Forum in Jerash

| Date | Mintage | F | VF | XF | Unc | BU |
|---|---|---|---|---|---|---|
| AH1389(1969) Proof | 2,425 | Value: 100 | | | | |

**2-1/2 DINARS** **KM# 31** **Weight:** 28.2800 g. **Composition:** 0.9250 Silver .8410 oz. ASW **Subject:** Conservation **Reverse:** Rhim Gazelle

| Date | Mintage | F | VF | XF | Unc | BU |
|---|---|---|---|---|---|---|
| AH1397(1977) | 6,265 | — | — | — | 22.00 | — |
| AH1397(1977) Proof | 5,011 | Value: 28.00 | | | | |

**3 DINARS** **KM# 32** **Weight:** 35.0000 g. **Composition:** 0.9250 Silver 1.0409 oz. ASW **Subject:** Conservation **Obverse:** Similar to 2-1/2 Dinars, KM#31 **Reverse:** Palestine sunbird

| Date | Mintage | F | VF | XF | Unc | BU |
|---|---|---|---|---|---|---|
| AH1397(1977) | 6,263 | — | — | — | 25.00 | — |
| AH1397(1977) Proof | 4,897 | Value: 32.50 | | | | |

**3 DINARS** **KM# 43** **Weight:** 23.3300 g. **Composition:** 0.9250 Silver .6938 oz. ASW **Subject:** International Year of the Child **Obverse:** Similar to 1/4 Dinar, KM#41

| Date | Mintage | F | VF | XF | Unc | BU |
|---|---|---|---|---|---|---|
| AH1401(1981) Proof | 21,000 | Value: 17.50 | | | | |

**5 DINARS** **KM# 25** **Weight:** 13.8200 g. **Composition:** 0.9000 Gold .3999 oz. AGW **Reverse:** Tomb in Petra

| Date | Mintage | F | VF | XF | Unc | BU |
|---|---|---|---|---|---|---|
| AH1389(1969) Proof | 1,950 | Value: 250 | | | | |

**Note:** KM57 and 57a have been relocated to coinages reflecting the monetary reform

**10 DINARS** **KM# 26** **Weight:** 27.6400 g. **Composition:** 0.9000 Gold .7998 oz. AGW **Subject:** Visit of Pope Paul VI

| Date | Mintage | F | VF | XF | Unc | BU |
|---|---|---|---|---|---|---|
| AH1389(1969) Proof | 1,870 | Value: 425 | | | | |

**10 DINARS** **KM# 44** **Weight:** 30.0000 g. **Composition:** 0.9250 Silver .8922 oz. ASW **Reverse:** 15th Century Hijrah calendar

| Date | Mintage | F | VF | XF | Unc | BU |
|---|---|---|---|---|---|---|
| AH1400(1980) Proof | 17,000 | Value: 37.50 | | | | |

**10 DINARS** **KM# 48** **Weight:** 15.2000 g. **Composition:** 0.9250 Silver .4610 oz. ASW **Subject:** King's 50th Birthday

| Date | Mintage | F | VF | XF | Unc | BU |
|---|---|---|---|---|---|---|
| AH1406(1986) Proof | — | Value: 27.50 | | | | |

**10 DINARS** **KM# 72** **Weight:** 31.0000 g. **Composition:** 0.9990 Silver .9957 oz. ASW **Subject:** Millenium and Baptism of Jesus **Obverse:** King's portrait **Reverse:** Baptism scene **Edge:** Reeded **Size:** 40 mm.

| Date | Mintage | F | VF | XF | Unc | BU |
|---|---|---|---|---|---|---|
| AH1420(2000) Matte | — | — | — | — | 45.00 | — |
| AH1420(2000) Proof | — | Value: 55.00 | | | | |

**25 DINARS** KM# 27 **Weight:** 69.1100 g. **Composition:** 0.9000 Gold 1.9999 oz. AGW **Reverse:** Dome of the Rock, Jerusalem

| Date | Mintage | F | VF | XF | Unc | BU |
|---|---|---|---|---|---|---|
| AH1389(1969) Proof | 1,000 | Value: 1,000 | | | | |

**25 DINARS** KM# 33 **Weight:** 15.0000 g. **Composition:** 0.9170 Gold .4422 oz. AGW **Subject:** 25th Anniversary of Reign

| Date | Mintage | F | VF | XF | Unc | BU |
|---|---|---|---|---|---|---|
| ND(AH1397)(1977) FM Proof | 4,724 | Value: 225 | | | | |

**40 DINARS** KM# 45 **Weight:** 14.3100 g. **Composition:** 0.9170 Gold .4216 oz. AGW **Reverse:** 15th Century Hijrah calendar

| Date | Mintage | F | VF | XF | Unc | BU |
|---|---|---|---|---|---|---|
| AH1400(1980) Proof | 9,500 | Value: 325 | | | | |

**50 DINARS** KM# 50 **Weight:** 15.9800 g. **Composition:** 0.9170 Gold .4710 oz. AGW **Subject:** Five Year Plan

| Date | Mintage | F | VF | XF | Unc | BU |
|---|---|---|---|---|---|---|
| AH1396(1976) Proof | 250 | Value: 400 | | | | |

**50 DINARS** KM# 34 **Weight:** 33.4370 g. **Composition:** 0.9000 Gold .9676 oz. AGW **Subject:** Conservation **Reverse:** Houbara bustard

| Date | Mintage | F | VF | XF | Unc | BU |
|---|---|---|---|---|---|---|
| AH1397(1977) | 829 | — | — | — | 450 | — |
| AH1397(1977) Proof | 287 | Value: 750 | | | | |

**50 DINARS** KM# 49 **Weight:** 17.0000 g. **Composition:** 0.9170 Gold .5013 oz. AGW **Subject:** King Husein's 50th Birthday **Note:** Similar to 10 Dinars, KM#48.

| Date | Mintage | F | VF | XF | Unc | BU |
|---|---|---|---|---|---|---|
| AH1405(1985) Proof | 2,000 | Value: 325 | | | | |

**60 DINARS** KM# 46 **Weight:** 17.1700 g. **Composition:** 0.9170 Gold .5062 oz. AGW **Subject:** International Year of the Child **Reverse:** Palace of Culture in Amman

| Date | Mintage | F | VF | XF | Unc | BU |
|---|---|---|---|---|---|---|
| AH1401(1981) Proof | 20,000 | Value: 235 | | | | |

## REFORM COINAGE

100 Piastres = 1 Dinar; 1/2 Qirsh = 1/2 Piastre

**1/4 DINAR** KM# 61 **Composition:** Nickel-Brass **Obverse:** King Hussein facing left **Reverse:** Denomination

| Date | Mintage | F | VF | XF | Unc | BU |
|---|---|---|---|---|---|---|
| AH1416(1995) | — | — | — | — | 3.00 | — |
| AH1417(1996) | — | — | — | — | 3.00 | — |

**1/2 DINAR** KM# 58 **Composition:** Brass **Obverse:** King Hussein facing left

| Date | Mintage | F | VF | XF | Unc | BU |
|---|---|---|---|---|---|---|
| AH1416(1995) | — | — | — | — | 4.00 | — |
| AH1417(1996) | — | — | — | — | 4.00 | — |

**1/2 DINAR** KM# 63 **Ring Composition:** Aluminum-Bronze **Center Composition:** Copper-Nickel **Obverse:** King Hussein facing left **Reverse:** Denomination

| Date | Mintage | F | VF | XF | Unc | BU |
|---|---|---|---|---|---|---|
| AH1417(1996) | — | — | — | — | 8.00 | — |

**DINAR** KM# 51 **Weight:** 15.0000 g. **Composition:** 0.9250 Silver .4461 oz. ASW **Subject:** 40th Year of Reign

| Date | Mintage | F | VF | XF | Unc | BU |
|---|---|---|---|---|---|---|
| AH1413(1992)(1992) | — | Value: 22.00 | | | | |

**DINAR** KM# 52 **Weight:** 8.5000 g. **Composition:** 0.9170 Gold .2505 oz. AGW **Subject:** 40th Year of Reign

| Date | Mintage | F | VF | XF | Unc | BU |
|---|---|---|---|---|---|---|
| AH1413(1992) Proof | — | Value: 185 | | | | |

**DINAR** KM# 62 **Composition:** Brass **Subject:** 50th Anniversary - F.A.O. **Obverse:** King Hussein facing left **Reverse:** F.A.O. logo

| Date | Mintage | F | VF | XF | Unc | BU |
|---|---|---|---|---|---|---|
| AH1415(1994) | — | — | — | — | 10.00 | — |

**DINAR** KM# 59 **Composition:** Brass **Obverse:** King Hussein facing left

| Date | Mintage | F | VF | XF | Unc | BU |
|---|---|---|---|---|---|---|
| AH1416(1995) | — | — | — | — | 8.00 | — |

**DINAR** KM# 68 **Weight:** 31.1035 g. **Composition:** 0.9990 Silver 1.0000 oz. ASW **Subject:** 50 Years - Jordanian Independence **Obverse:** Bust of King Hussein facing left **Reverse:** Portrait of former King Abdullah

| Date | Mintage | F | VF | XF | Unc | BU |
|---|---|---|---|---|---|---|
| ND(1996) Proof | Est. 2,000 | Value: 75.00 | | | | |

**DINAR** KM# 70 **Composition:** Gold **Subject:** 50 Years - Jordanian Independence **Obverse:** Bust of King Hussein facing left **Reverse:** Portrait of former King Abdullah

| Date | Mintage | F | VF | XF | Unc | BU |
|---|---|---|---|---|---|---|
| AH1417(1997) | 400 | — | — | — | 8.00 | — |

**DINAR** KM# 64 **Center Composition:** Brass **Obverse:** Bust of King Hussein facing left **Reverse:** Denomination in ornamented circle

| Date | Mintage | F | VF | XF | Unc | BU |
|---|---|---|---|---|---|---|
| AH1419(1998) | — | — | — | — | 5.50 | — |

**DINAR** KM# 65 **Composition:** Gold **Subject:** Human Rights **Obverse:** Bust of King Hussein facing left **Reverse:** Commemorative legend with denomination in ornamented circle

| Date | Mintage | F | VF | XF | Unc | BU |
|---|---|---|---|---|---|---|
| AH1419(1998) | — | — | — | — | 5.50 | — |

**5 DINARS** **KM# 57** **Composition:** Copper-Nickel **Subject:** UN 50 Years **Obverse:** Bust of King Hussein facing left **Reverse:** Black iris

| Date | Mintage | F | VF | XF | Unc | BU |
|---|---|---|---|---|---|---|
| ND(1995) | — | — | — | — | 10.00 | — |

**5 DINARS** **KM# 57a** **Weight:** 28.2800 g. **Composition:** 0.9250 Silver .8411 oz. ASW **Subject:** UN 50 Years **Obverse:** Bust of King Hussein facing left **Reverse:** Black iris

| Date | Mintage | F | VF | XF | Unc | BU |
|---|---|---|---|---|---|---|
| ND(1995) Proof | 100,000 | Value: 47.50 | | | | |

**5 DINARS** **KM# 66** **Weight:** 28.2800 g. **Composition:** 0.9250 Silver .8411 oz. ASW **Subject:** UNICEF: For the Children of the World **Obverse:** Coinjoined busts of Hussein and Queen Noor **Reverse:** Boy, girl, UNICEF logo

| Date | Mintage | F | VF | XF | Unc | BU |
|---|---|---|---|---|---|---|
| AH1419 - 1999 Proof | 25,000 | Value: 50.00 | | | | |

**5 DINARS** **KM# 71** **Weight:** 28.5000 g. **Composition:** Brass **Subject:** Millennium and Baptism of Jesus **Obverse:** King's portrait **Reverse:** Baptism scene **Edge:** Reeded **Size:** 40 mm.

| Date | Mintage | F | VF | XF | Unc | BU |
|---|---|---|---|---|---|---|
| AH1420 - 2000 Prooflike | 10,000 | — | — | — | 20.00 | — |

**50 DINARS** **KM# 69** **Weight:** 16.9600 g. **Composition:** 0.9166 Gold .4998 oz. AGW **Subject:** 50 Years - Jordanian Independence **Obverse:** King Hussein's portrait **Reverse:** Portrait of former King Abdullah

| Date | Mintage | F | VF | XF | Unc | BU |
|---|---|---|---|---|---|---|
| ND(1969) Proof | Est. 1,000 | Value: 375 | | | | |

**50 DINARS** **KM# 67** **Weight:** 6.2200 g. **Composition:** 0.9990 Gold .1998 oz. AGW **Subject:** UNICEF: For the Children of the World **Obverse:** Conjoined bust of King Hussein and Queen Noor **Reverse:** Boy, girl, UNICEF logo

| Date | Mintage | F | VF | XF | Unc | BU |
|---|---|---|---|---|---|---|
| AH1419 - 1999 Proof | 10,000 | Value: 175 | | | | |

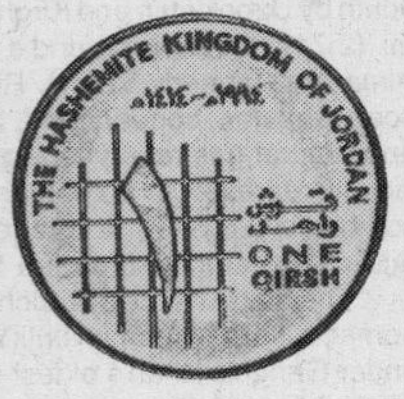

**QIRSH (Piastre)** **KM# 56** **Composition:** Bronze Plated Steel

| Date | Mintage | F | VF | XF | Unc | BU |
|---|---|---|---|---|---|---|
| AH1414 - 1993 | — | — | — | 0.65 | 1.25 | — |
| AH1416 - 1995 | — | — | — | 0.65 | 1.25 | — |

**1/2 QIRSH (1/2 Piastre)** **KM# 60** **Composition:** Copper Plated Steel **Obverse:** Bust of King Hussein facing left **Reverse:** Denomination

| Date | Mintage | F | VF | XF | Unc | BU |
|---|---|---|---|---|---|---|
| AH1416 - 1995 | — | — | — | 0.35 | 0.65 | — |

**2-1/2 PIASTRES** **KM# 53** **Composition:** Stainless Steel

| Date | Mintage | F | VF | XF | Unc | BU |
|---|---|---|---|---|---|---|
| AH1412 - 1991 | — | — | — | 0.75 | 1.50 | — |
| AH1413 - 1992 | — | — | — | 0.75 | 1.50 | — |

**5 PIASTRES** **KM# 54** **Composition:** Nickel Plated Steel

| Date | Mintage | F | VF | XF | Unc | BU |
|---|---|---|---|---|---|---|
| AH1412 - 1991 | — | — | — | 1.00 | 2.00 | — |
| AH1413 - 1992 | — | — | — | 1.00 | 2.00 | — |
| AH1414 - 1993 | — | — | — | 1.00 | 2.00 | — |
| AH1416 - 1995 | — | — | — | 1.00 | 2.00 | — |
| AH1418 - 1998 | — | — | — | 1.00 | 2.00 | — |

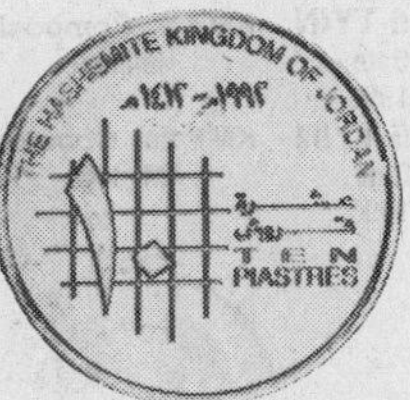

**10 PIASTRES** **KM# 55** **Composition:** Nickel Plated Steel

| Date | Mintage | F | VF | XF | Unc | BU |
|---|---|---|---|---|---|---|
| AH1412 - 1991 | — | — | — | 1.25 | 2.25 | — |
| AH1413 - 1992 | — | — | — | 1.25 | 2.25 | — |
| AH1414 - 1993 | — | — | — | — | — | — |
| AH1414 - 1994 | — | — | — | — | — | — |
| AH1416 - 1995 | — | — | — | 1.25 | 2.25 | — |
| AH1417 - 1996 | — | — | — | 1.25 | 2.25 | — |

## PATTERNS

Including off metal strikes

| KM# | Date | Mintage | Identification | Mkt Val |
|---|---|---|---|---|
| Pn1 | AH1387 | 2 | Fils. Gold. KM14. | — |
| Pn2 | AH1387 | 2 | 5 Fils. Gold. KM15. | — |
| Pn3 | AH1387 | 2 | 10 Fils. Gold. KM16. | — |
| Pn4 | AH1387 | 2 | 25 Fils. Gold. KM17. | — |
| Pn5 | AH1387 | 2 | 50 Fils. Gold. KM18. | 700 |
| Pn6 | AH1387 | 2 | Dirham. Gold. KM19. | 900 |
| Pn7 | AH1395 | 112 | Fils. Gold. As KM14. | 100 |
| Pn8 | AH1395 | 112 | 5 Fils. Gold. As KM15. | 200 |
| Pn9 | AH1395 | 112 | 10 Fils. Gold. As KM16. | 250 |
| Pn10 | AH1395 | 112 | 25 Fils. Gold. As KM17. | 150 |
| Pn12 | AH1395 | 112 | Dirham. Gold. As KM19. | 450 |
| Pn11 | AH1395 | 112 | 50 Fils. Gold. As KM18. | 250 |
| Pn13 | AH1395 | 112 | 1/4 Dinar. Gold. As KM28. | 650 |

## PIEFORTS

| KM# | Date | Mintage | Identification | Mkt Val |
|---|---|---|---|---|
| P1 | AH1981 | 2,050 | 3 Dinars. KM43. | 60.00 |
| P2 | AH1981 | 450 | 60 Dinars. KM46. | 1,350 |
| P3 | AH1985 | 700 | 50 Dinars. KM49. | 700 |
| P4 | AH1992 | — | Dinar. 0.9170 Gold. KM52. | — |
| P5 | AH1996 | — | 50 Dinars. 0.9990 Gold. KM69. | — |

## MINT SETS

| KM# | Date | Mintage | Identification | Issue Price | Mkt Val |
|---|---|---|---|---|---|
| MS1 | 1985 (8) | — | KM35-41, 47 | 10.75 | 15.00 |
| MS2 | Mixed dates (6) | — | KM5 (1949), 8 (1963), 9 (1962), 10-11 (1964), 12 (1962) | — | 10.00 |

## PROOF SETS

| KM# | Date | Mintage | Identification | Issue Price | Mkt Val |
|---|---|---|---|---|---|
| PS1 | 1949 (6) | 25 | KM2-7 | — | 500 |
| PS2 | 1965 (6) | 10,000 | KM8-13 | 14.40 | 17.50 |
| PS3 | 1969 (6) | — | KM21-27 | 396 | 1,900 |
| PS4 | 1969 (6) | — | KM21-26 | — | 900 |
| PS5 | 1969 (4) | — | KM24-27 | — | 1,800 |
| PS6 | 1969 (3) | 5,800 | KM21-23 | 36.00 | 125 |
| PS7 | 1977 (3) | 1,000 | KM31-32, 34 | 780 | 825 |
| PS8 | 1977 (2) | 9,000 | KM31-32 | 60.00 | 65.00 |
| PS9 | 1978 (7) | 20,000 | KM35-41 | 27.00 | 15.00 |
| PS10 | 1980 (2) | — | KM44-45 | 365 | 525 |
| PS11 | 1985 (8) | 5,000 | KM35-41, 47 | 31.00 | 25.00 |

## SPECIMEN SETS (SS)

| KM# | Date | Mintage | Identification | Issue Price | Mkt Val |
|---|---|---|---|---|---|
| SS1 | 1964 (6) | 3,000 | KM8-13 | — | 14.00 |
| SS2 | 1965 (6) | 5,000 | KM8-13 | — | 12.00 |
| SS3 | 1968 (6) | 50 | KM14-19 | — | 300 |
| SS4 | 1968 (6) | 2 | KMPn1-6 | — | — |
| SS5 | 1975 (7) | 112 | KMPn7-13 | — | 2,000 |

# KATANGA

Katanga, the southern province of the former Belgian Congo, had an area of 191,873 sq. mi. (496,951 sq. km.) and was noted for its mineral wealth.

**MONETARY SYSTEM**

100 Centimes = 1 Franc

## DECIMAL COINAGE

**FRANC** **KM# 1** **Composition:** Bronze

| Date | Mintage | F | VF | XF | Unc | BU |
|---|---|---|---|---|---|---|
| 1961 | — | — | 1.00 | 1.75 | 3.50 | — |

**5 FRANCS** **KM# 2** **Composition:** Bronze

| Date | Mintage | F | VF | XF | Unc | BU |
|---|---|---|---|---|---|---|
| 1961 | — | — | 2.00 | 3.75 | 7.50 | — |

**5 FRANCS** **KM# 2a** **Weight:** 13.3300 g. **Composition:** 0.9000 Gold .3857 oz. AGW

| Date | Mintage | F | VF | XF | Unc | BU |
|---|---|---|---|---|---|---|
| 1961 | 20,000 | — | — | — | 200 | — |

# KAZAKHSTAN

The Republic of Kazakhstan (formerly Kazakhstan S.S.R.) is bordered to the west by the Caspian Sea and Russia, to the north by Russia, in the east by the Peoples Republic of China and in the south by Uzbekistan and Kirghizia, it has an area of 1,049,155 sq. mi. (2,717,300 sq. km.) and a population of 16.7 million. Capital: Alma-Ata (formerly Vemy). Rich in mineral resources including coal, tungsten, copper, lead, zinc and manganese with huge oil and natural gas reserves. Agriculture is very important, (it previously represented 20 percent of the total arable acreage of the combined U.S.S.R.) Non-ferrous metallurgy, heavy engineering and chemical industries are leaders in its economy.

The Kazakhs are a branch of the Turkic peoples which led the nomadic life of herdsmen until WW I. In the 13thcentury they came under Genghis Khan's eldest son Jujiand later became a part of the Golden Horde, a western Mongol empire. Around the beginning of the 16th century they were divided into 3 confederacies, known as *zhuz* or hordes, in the steppes of Turkistan. At the end of the 17th century an incursion by the Kalmucks, a remnant of the Oirat Mongol confederacy, resulted in heavy losses on both sides which facilitated Russian penetration. Resistance to Russian settlements varied throughout the 1800's, but by 1900 over 100 million acres were declared Czarist state property and used for a planned peasant colonization. After a revolution in 1905Kazakh deputies were elected. In 1916 the tsarist government ordered mobilization of all males, between19 and 43, for auxiliary service. The Kazakhs rose in defiance which led the governor general of Turkistan to send troops against the rebels. Shortly after the Russian revolution, Kazakh Nationalists asked for full autonomy. The Communist *coup d'etat* of Nov. 1917 led to civil war. In 1919-20 the Red army defeated the "White" Russian forces and occupied Kazakhstan and fought against the Nationalist government formed on Nov. 17, 1917 by Ali Khan Bukey Khan. The Kazakh Autonomous Soviet Socialist Republic was proclaimed on Aug. 26, 1920 within the R.S.F.S.R. Russian and Ukrainian colonization continued while 2 purges in1927 and 1935 quelled any Kazakh feelings of priority in the matters of their country. On Dec. 5, 1936Kazakhstan qualified for full status as an S.S.R. and held its first congress in 1937. Independence was declared on Dec. 16, 1991 and Kazakhstan joined the C.I.S.

**MONETARY SYSTEM**

100 Tyin = 1 Tenge

## REPUBLIC

## DECIMAL COINAGE

**2 TYIN** **KM# 1** **Composition:** Yellow Brass

| Date | Mintage | F | VF | XF | Unc | BU |
|---|---|---|---|---|---|---|
| 1993 | — | — | — | — | 0.45 | — |

**2 TYIN** **KM# 1a** **Composition:** Copper Clad Brass

| Date | Mintage | F | VF | XF | Unc | BU |
|---|---|---|---|---|---|---|
| 1993 | — | — | — | — | 0.45 | — |

**5 TYIN** **KM# 2** **Composition:** Yellow Brass

| Date | Mintage | F | VF | XF | Unc | BU |
|---|---|---|---|---|---|---|
| 1993 | — | — | — | — | 0.60 | — |

**5 TYIN** **KM# 2a** **Composition:** Copper Clad Brass

| Date | Mintage | F | VF | XF | Unc | BU |
|---|---|---|---|---|---|---|
| 1993 | — | — | — | — | 0.60 | — |

**10 TYIN** **KM# 3** **Composition:** Yellow Brass

| Date | Mintage | F | VF | XF | Unc | BU |
|---|---|---|---|---|---|---|
| 1993 | — | — | — | — | 0.80 | — |

**10 TYIN** **KM# 3a** **Composition:** Copper Clad Brass

| Date | Mintage | F | VF | XF | Unc | BU |
|---|---|---|---|---|---|---|
| 1993 | — | — | — | — | 0.80 | — |

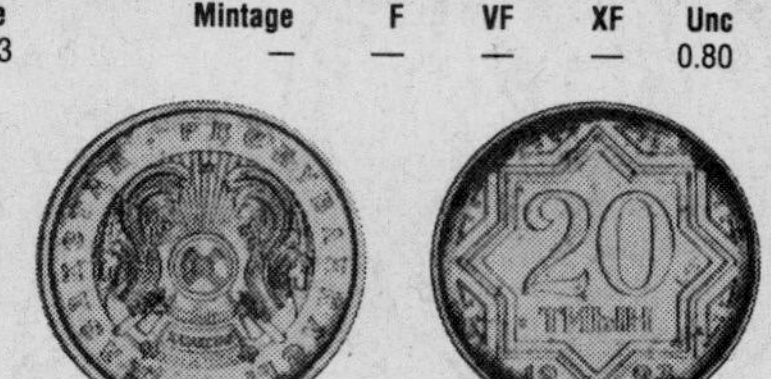

**20 TYIN** **KM# 4** **Composition:** Brass Plated Zinc

| Date | Mintage | F | VF | XF | Unc | BU |
|---|---|---|---|---|---|---|
| 1993 | — | — | — | — | 1.25 | — |

**50 TYIN** **KM# 5** **Composition:** Brass Plated Zinc

| Date | Mintage | F | VF | XF | Unc | BU |
|---|---|---|---|---|---|---|
| 1993 | — | — | — | — | 1.50 | — |

**TENGE** **KM# 6** **Composition:** Copper-Nickel

| Date | Mintage | F | VF | XF | Unc | BU |
|---|---|---|---|---|---|---|
| 1992 | — | — | — | — | 1.00 | — |
| 1993 | — | — | — | — | 0.50 | — |

**TENGE** **KM# 23** **Composition:** Brass **Obverse:** National emblem **Reverse:** Denomination

| Date | Mintage | F | VF | XF | Unc | BU |
|---|---|---|---|---|---|---|
| 1997 | — | — | — | — | 0.50 | — |
| 2000 | — | — | — | — | — | — |

**3 TENGE** **KM# 8** **Composition:** Copper-Nickel

| Date | Mintage | F | VF | XF | Unc | BU |
|---|---|---|---|---|---|---|
| 1993 | — | — | — | — | 0.75 | — |

**5 TENGE** **KM# 9** **Composition:** Copper-Nickel

| Date | Mintage | F | VF | XF | Unc | BU |
|---|---|---|---|---|---|---|
| 1993 | — | — | — | — | 1.25 | — |

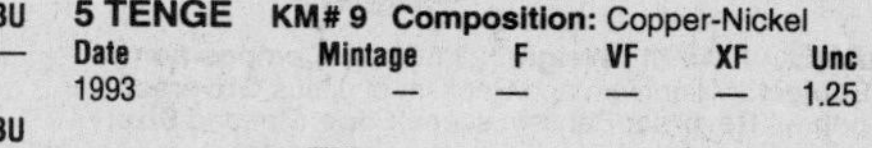

**5 TENGE** **KM# 24** **Composition:** Brass **Obverse:** National emblem **Reverse:** Denomination

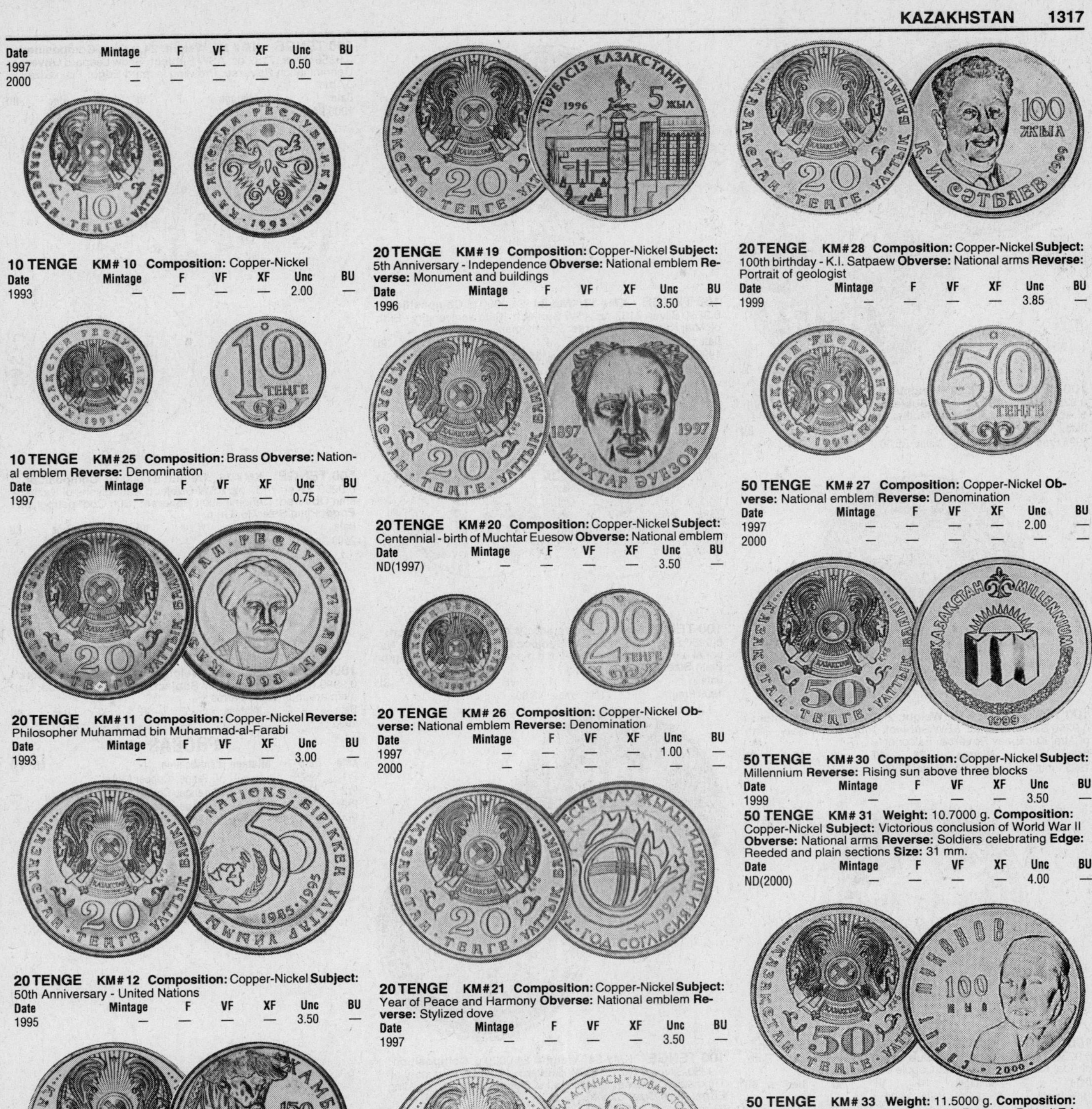

| Date | Mintage | F | VF | XF | Unc | BU |
|---|---|---|---|---|---|---|
| 1997 | — | — | — | — | 0.50 | — |
| 2000 | — | — | — | — | — | — |

**10 TENGE** **KM# 10** **Composition:** Copper-Nickel

| Date | Mintage | F | VF | XF | Unc | BU |
|---|---|---|---|---|---|---|
| 1993 | — | — | — | — | 2.00 | — |

**10 TENGE** **KM# 25** **Composition:** Brass **Obverse:** National emblem **Reverse:** Denomination

| Date | Mintage | F | VF | XF | Unc | BU |
|---|---|---|---|---|---|---|
| 1997 | — | — | — | — | 0.75 | — |

**20 TENGE** **KM# 11** **Composition:** Copper-Nickel **Reverse:** Philosopher Muhammad bin Muhammad-al-Farabi

| Date | Mintage | F | VF | XF | Unc | BU |
|---|---|---|---|---|---|---|
| 1993 | — | — | — | — | 3.00 | — |

**20 TENGE** **KM# 12** **Composition:** Copper-Nickel **Subject:** 50th Anniversary - United Nations

| Date | Mintage | F | VF | XF | Unc | BU |
|---|---|---|---|---|---|---|
| 1995 | — | — | — | — | 3.50 | — |

**20 TENGE** **KM# 18** **Composition:** Copper-Nickel **Subject:** 150th Anniversary - Jambyl **Obverse:** National emblem **Reverse:** Man with stringed instrument

| Date | Mintage | F | VF | XF | Unc | BU |
|---|---|---|---|---|---|---|
| 1996 | — | — | — | — | 3.50 | — |

**20 TENGE** **KM# 19** **Composition:** Copper-Nickel **Subject:** 5th Anniversary - Independence **Obverse:** National emblem **Reverse:** Monument and buildings

| Date | Mintage | F | VF | XF | Unc | BU |
|---|---|---|---|---|---|---|
| 1996 | — | — | — | — | 3.50 | — |

**20 TENGE** **KM# 20** **Composition:** Copper-Nickel **Subject:** Centennial - birth of Muchtar Euesow **Obverse:** National emblem

| Date | Mintage | F | VF | XF | Unc | BU |
|---|---|---|---|---|---|---|
| ND(1997) | — | — | — | — | 3.50 | — |

**20 TENGE** **KM# 26** **Composition:** Copper-Nickel **Obverse:** National emblem **Reverse:** Denomination

| Date | Mintage | F | VF | XF | Unc | BU |
|---|---|---|---|---|---|---|
| 1997 | — | — | — | — | 1.00 | — |
| 2000 | — | — | — | — | — | — |

**20 TENGE** **KM# 21** **Composition:** Copper-Nickel **Subject:** Year of Peace and Harmony **Obverse:** National emblem **Reverse:** Stylized dove

| Date | Mintage | F | VF | XF | Unc | BU |
|---|---|---|---|---|---|---|
| 1997 | — | — | — | — | 3.50 | — |

**20 TENGE** **KM# 22** **Composition:** Copper-Nickel **Subject:** New capital - Astana **Obverse:** National emblem **Reverse:** Flowerlike design

| Date | Mintage | F | VF | XF | Unc | BU |
|---|---|---|---|---|---|---|
| 1998 | — | — | — | — | 3.50 | — |

**20 TENGE** **KM# 28** **Composition:** Copper-Nickel **Subject:** 100th birthday - K.I. Satpaew **Obverse:** National arms **Reverse:** Portrait of geologist

| Date | Mintage | F | VF | XF | Unc | BU |
|---|---|---|---|---|---|---|
| 1999 | — | — | — | — | 3.85 | — |

**50 TENGE** **KM# 27** **Composition:** Copper-Nickel **Obverse:** National emblem **Reverse:** Denomination

| Date | Mintage | F | VF | XF | Unc | BU |
|---|---|---|---|---|---|---|
| 1997 | — | — | — | — | 2.00 | — |
| 2000 | — | — | — | — | — | — |

**50 TENGE** **KM# 30** **Composition:** Copper-Nickel **Subject:** Millennium **Reverse:** Rising sun above three blocks

| Date | Mintage | F | VF | XF | Unc | BU |
|---|---|---|---|---|---|---|
| 1999 | — | — | — | — | 3.50 | — |

**50 TENGE** **KM# 31** **Weight:** 10.7000 g. **Composition:** Copper-Nickel **Subject:** Victorious conclusion of World War II **Obverse:** National arms **Reverse:** Soldiers celebrating **Edge:** Reeded and plain sections **Size:** 31 mm.

| Date | Mintage | F | VF | XF | Unc | BU |
|---|---|---|---|---|---|---|
| ND(2000) | — | — | — | — | 4.00 | — |

**50 TENGE** **KM# 33** **Weight:** 11.5000 g. **Composition:** Copper-Nickel **Obverse:** National arms. **Reverse:** Portrait **Edge:** Reeded and plain sections

| Date | Mintage | F | VF | XF | Unc | BU |
|---|---|---|---|---|---|---|
| 2000 | — | — | — | — | 4.00 | — |

**100 TENGE** KM# 13 **Weight:** 24.0000 g. **Composition:** 0.9250 Silver .7137 oz. ASW **Subject:** 150th anniversary - Birth of Abaj Kunabaev **Reverse:** Mother and child **Edge:** Lettered

| Date | Mintage | F | VF | XF | Unc | BU |
|---|---|---|---|---|---|---|
| 1995 Proof | 6,000 | Value: 35.00 | | | | |

**100 TENGE** KM# 14 **Weight:** 24.0000 g. **Composition:** 0.9250 Silver .7137 oz. ASW **Subject:** 150th anniversary - Birth of Abaj Kunabaev **Reverse:** Falconer

| Date | Mintage | F | VF | XF | Unc | BU |
|---|---|---|---|---|---|---|
| 1995 Proof | 6,000 | Value: 37.50 | | | | |

**100 TENGE** KM# 15 **Weight:** 24.0000 g. **Composition:** 0.9250 Silver .7137 oz. ASW **Subject:** 150th anniversary - Birth of Abaj Kunabaev **Reverse:** Couple on swings

| Date | Mintage | F | VF | XF | Unc | BU |
|---|---|---|---|---|---|---|
| 1995 Proof | 6,000 | Value: 35.00 | | | | |

**100 TENGE** KM# 16 **Weight:** 24.0000 g. **Composition:** 0.9250 Silver .7137 oz. ASW **Subject:** 150th anniversary - Birth of Abaj Kunabaev **Reverse:** Town view

| Date | Mintage | F | VF | XF | Unc | BU |
|---|---|---|---|---|---|---|
| 1995 Proof | 6,000 | Value: 35.00 | | | | |

**100 TENGE** KM# 17 **Weight:** 24.0000 g. **Composition:** 0.9250 Silver .7137 oz. ASW **Subject:** 150th anniversary - Birth of Abaj Kunabaev **Reverse:** Elderly man

| Date | Mintage | F | VF | XF | Unc | BU |
|---|---|---|---|---|---|---|
| 1995 Proof | 6,000 | Value: 35.00 | | | | |

**100 TENGE** KM# 32 **Weight:** 24.0000 g. **Composition:** 0.9250 Silver .7137 oz. ASW **Subject:** Millennium **Obverse:** National arms **Reverse:** Ancient and modern technologies **Edge:** Plain **Size:** 37 mm.

| Date | Mintage | F | VF | XF | Unc | BU |
|---|---|---|---|---|---|---|
| 1999 Proof | 2,000 | Value: 45.00 | | | | |

**100 TENGE** KM# 34 **Weight:** 24.0000 g. **Composition:** 0.9250 Silver .7137 oz. ASW **Subject:** 1500th Anniversary of Turkestan **Obverse:** Denomination **Reverse:** Domed building **Edge:** Plain **Size:** 37 mm.

| Date | Mintage | F | VF | XF | Unc | BU |
|---|---|---|---|---|---|---|
| 2000 Proof | 3,000 | — | — | — | 40.00 | — |

**500 TENGE** KM# 35 **Weight:** 24.0000 g. **Composition:** 0.9250 Silver .7137 oz. ASW **Subject:** Snow Leopard **Obverse:** Denomination **Reverse:** Prowling leopard **Edge:** Plain **Size:** 37 mm.

| Date | Mintage | F | VF | XF | Unc | BU |
|---|---|---|---|---|---|---|
| 2000 Proof | 3,000 | — | — | — | 50.00 | — |

**500 TENGE** KM# 36 **Weight:** 24.0000 g. **Composition:** 0.9250 Silver .7137 oz. ASW **Subject:** Petroglyphs of Kazakhstan **Obverse:** Denomination **Reverse:** "Sun God" petroglyph **Edge:** Plain **Size:** 36.9 mm.

| Date | Mintage | F | VF | XF | Unc | BU |
|---|---|---|---|---|---|---|
| 2000 Proof | 3,000 | — | — | — | 45.00 | — |

**1000 TENGE** KM# 29 **Weight:** 3.1200 g. **Composition:** 0.9999 Gold .1003 oz. AGW **Subject:** Silk Road **Reverse:** Caravan around national arms

| Date | Mintage | F | VF | XF | Unc | BU |
|---|---|---|---|---|---|---|
| 1995 | — | — | — | — | 75.00 | — |

## PROBAS

| KM# | Date | Mintage | Identification | Mkt Val |
|---|---|---|---|---|
| Pr1 | 1992 | — | 50 Tenge. Copper Nickel. | — |
| Pr2 | 1992 | — | 50 Tenge. Copper. | — |
| Pr3 | 1992 | — | 50 Tenge. Brass. | — |
| Pr4 | 1992 | — | 50 Tenge. Aluminum. | — |

# KEELING COCOS

The Territory of Cocos (Keeling) Islands, an Australian territory, comprises a group of 27 coral islands located (see arrow on map of Australia) in the Indian Ocean 1,300 miles northwest of Australia. Only Direction and Home Islands are regularly inhabited. The group has an area of 5.4 sq. mi. and a population of about 569. Calcium, phosphate and coconut products are exported.

The islands were discovered by Capt. William Keeling of the British East India Co. in 1609. Alexander Hare, an English adventurer, established a settlement on one of the southern islands in 1823, but it lasted less than a year. A permanent settlement was established on Direction Island in 1827 by Hare and Capt. John Clunies Ross, a Scot, for the purpose of storing East Indian spices for reshipment to Europe during periods of shortage. When the experiment in spice futures did not develop satisfactorily, Hare left the islands (1829 or 1830), leaving Ross as sole owner. The coral group became a British protectorate in 1856; was attached to the colony of Ceylon in 1878; and was placed under the administration of the Straits Settlements in 1882. In 1903 the group was annexed to the Straits Settlements and incorporated into the colony of Singapore until Nov. of 1955, when it was placed under the administration of Australia.

**RULERS**
British

**MONETARY SYSTEM**
100 Cents = 1 Rupee

## AUSTRALIAN TERRITORY

### DECIMAL COINAGE

**5 CENTS** KM# 1 **Composition:** Bronze

| Date | Mintage | F | VF | XF | Unc | BU |
|---|---|---|---|---|---|---|
| 1977 | — | — | — | 18.00 | 35.00 | — |

**10 CENTS** KM# 2 **Composition:** Bronze

| Date | Mintage | F | VF | XF | Unc | BU |
|---|---|---|---|---|---|---|
| 1977 | — | — | — | 20.00 | 40.00 | — |

**25 CENTS** KM# 3 **Composition:** Bronze

| Date | Mintage | F | VF | XF | Unc | BU |
|---|---|---|---|---|---|---|
| 1977 | — | — | — | 20.00 | 40.00 | — |

**50 CENTS** KM# 4 **Composition:** Bronze

| Date | Mintage | F | VF | XF | Unc | BU |
|---|---|---|---|---|---|---|
| 1977 | — | — | — | 22.00 | 45.00 | — |

**RUPEE** KM# 5 **Composition:** Copper-Nickel

| Date | Mintage | F | VF | XF | Unc | BU |
|---|---|---|---|---|---|---|
| 1977 | — | — | — | 35.00 | 70.00 | — |

**2 RUPEE** KM# 6 **Composition:** Copper-Nickel

| Date | Mintage | F | VF | XF | Unc | BU |
|---|---|---|---|---|---|---|
| 1977 | — | — | — | 35.00 | 70.00 | — |

**5 RUPEE** KM# 7 **Composition:** Copper-Nickel

| Date | Mintage | F | VF | XF | Unc | BU |
|---|---|---|---|---|---|---|
| 1977 | — | — | — | 40.00 | 80.00 | — |

**10 RUPEE** KM# 8 **Weight:** 6.5000 g. **Composition:** 0.9250 Silver .1933 oz. ASW **Subject:** 150th Anniversary - Keeling-Cocos Islands

| Date | Mintage | F | VF | XF | Unc | BU |
|---|---|---|---|---|---|---|
| 1977 | 6,000 | — | — | — | 90.00 | — |
| 1977 Proof | 4,000 | Value: 120 | | | | |

**25 RUPEE** KM# 9 **Weight:** 16.2500 g. **Composition:** 0.9250 Silver .4833 oz. ASW **Subject:** 150th Anniversary - Keeling-Cocos Islands **Note:** Similar to 10 Rupees, KM#9.

| Date | Mintage | F | VF | XF | Unc | BU |
|---|---|---|---|---|---|---|
| 1977 | 6,000 | — | — | — | 135 | — |
| 1977 Proof | 4,000 | Value: 200 | | | | |

**150 RUPEE** KM# 10a **Weight:** 8.4800 g. **Composition:** 0.9160 Gold .2497 oz. AGW

| Date | Mintage | F | VF | XF | Unc | BU |
|---|---|---|---|---|---|---|
| ND(1977) | 2,000 | — | — | — | 275 | — |
| ND(1977) Proof | 2,000 | Value: 375 | | | | |

**150 RUPEE** KM# 10 **Composition:** 0.7500 Gold **Subject:** 150th Anniversary - Keeling-Cocos Islands **Note:** The entire issue of KM#10 was stolen with only 290 pieces being recovered.

| Date | Mintage | F | VF | XF | Unc | BU |
|---|---|---|---|---|---|---|
| ND(1977) | 2,000 | — | — | — | — | — |
| ND(1977) Proof | 2,000 | — | — | — | — | — |

### TOKEN COINAGE

Plastic Ivory

**5 CENTS** KM# Tn1 **Note:** Tn1-Tn7 were all issued with individual serial numbers.

| Date | Mintage | VG | F | VF | XF | Unc |
|---|---|---|---|---|---|---|
| 1913 | 5,000 | 60.00 | 100 | 200 | 350 | — |

**10 CENTS** KM# Tn2

| Date | Mintage | VG | F | VF | XF | Unc |
|---|---|---|---|---|---|---|
| 1913 | 5,000 | 45.00 | 75.00 | 150 | 275 | — |

**25 CENTS** KM# Tn3

| Date | Mintage | VG | F | VF | XF | Unc |
|---|---|---|---|---|---|---|
| 1913 | 5,000 | 20.00 | 30.00 | 60.00 | 100 | — |

**50 CENTS** KM# Tn4

| Date | Mintage | VG | F | VF | XF | Unc |
|---|---|---|---|---|---|---|
| 1913 | 2,000 | 75.00 | 125 | 275 | 500 | — |

**RUPEE** KM# Tn5

| Date | Mintage | VG | F | VF | XF | Unc |
|---|---|---|---|---|---|---|
| 1913 | 2,000 | 25.00 | 40.00 | 75.00 | 125 | — |

**2 RUPEE** KM# Tn6

| Date | Mintage | VG | F | VF | XF | Unc |
|---|---|---|---|---|---|---|
| 1913 | 1,000 | 35.00 | 50.00 | 90.00 | 140 | — |

**5 RUPEE** KM# Tn7

| Date | Mintage | VG | F | VF | XF | Unc |
|---|---|---|---|---|---|---|
| 1913 | 1,000 | 35.00 | 50.00 | 120 | 175 | — |

## TOKEN COINAGE

### Modern Plastic

**CENT** KM# Tn8 **Note:** Aqua color plastic.

| Date | Mintage | F | VF | XF | Unc | BU |
|---|---|---|---|---|---|---|
| 1968 | — | — | — | — | 85.00 | — |

**5 CENTS** KM# Tn9 **Note:** Aqua color plastic.

| Date | Mintage | F | VF | XF | Unc | BU |
|---|---|---|---|---|---|---|
| 1968 | — | — | — | — | 85.00 | — |

**10 CENTS** KM# Tn10 **Note:** Aqua color plastic.

| Date | Mintage | F | VF | XF | Unc | BU |
|---|---|---|---|---|---|---|
| 1968 | — | — | — | — | 90.00 | — |

**25 CENTS** KM# Tn11 **Note:** Aqua color plastic.

| Date | Mintage | F | VF | XF | Unc | BU |
|---|---|---|---|---|---|---|
| 1968 | — | — | — | — | 100 | — |

**50 CENTS** KM# Tn12 **Note:** Aqua color plastic.

| Date | Mintage | F | VF | XF | Unc | BU |
|---|---|---|---|---|---|---|
| 1968 | — | — | — | — | 115 | — |

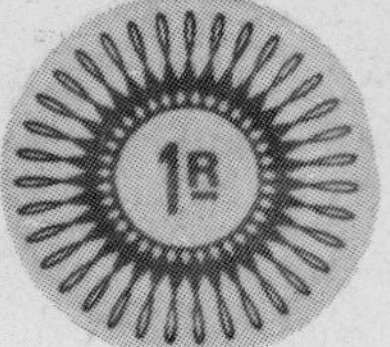

**RUPEE** KM# Tn13 **Note:** Red color plastic.

| Date | Mintage | F | VF | XF | Unc | BU |
|---|---|---|---|---|---|---|
| 1968 | — | — | — | — | 120 | — |

**2 RUPEE** KM# Tn14 **Note:** Red color plastic.

| Date | Mintage | F | VF | XF | Unc | BU |
|---|---|---|---|---|---|---|
| 1968 | — | — | — | — | 130 | — |

**5 RUPEE** KM# Tn15 **Note:** Red color plastic.

| Date | Mintage | F | VF | XF | Unc | BU |
|---|---|---|---|---|---|---|
| 1968 | — | — | — | — | 150 | — |

**10 RUPEE** KM# Tn16 **Note:** Red color plastic.

| Date | Mintage | F | VF | XF | Unc | BU |
|---|---|---|---|---|---|---|
| 1968 | — | — | — | — | 175 | — |

**25 RUPEE** KM# Tn17 **Note:** Red color plastic.

| Date | Mintage | F | VF | XF | Unc | BU |
|---|---|---|---|---|---|---|
| 1968 | — | — | — | — | 200 | — |

## MINT SETS

| KM# | Date | Mintage | Identification | Issue Price | Mkt Val |
|---|---|---|---|---|---|
| MS1 | 1977 (7) | — | KM#1-7 | — | 325 |
| MS2 | 1977 (2) | 6,000 | KM#8-9 | — | 200 |

## PROOF SETS

| KM# | Date | Mintage | Identification | Issue Price | Mkt Val |
|---|---|---|---|---|---|
| PS1 | 1977 (2) | 4,000 | KM#8-9 | 28.00 | 275 |

# KENYA

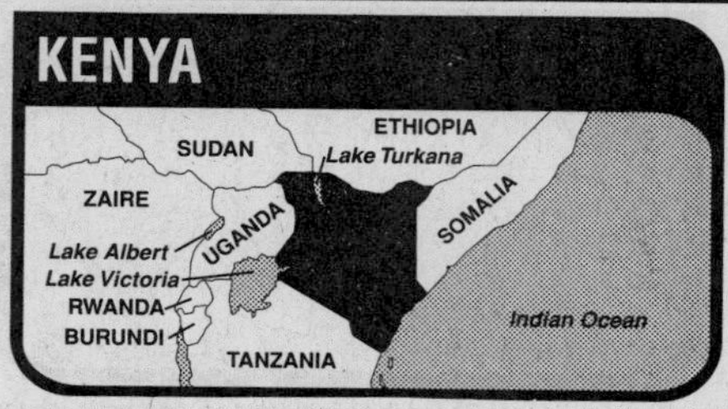


The Republic of Kenya, located on the east coast of Central Africa, has an area of 224,961 sq. mi (582,650 sq. km.) and a population of 20.1 million. Capital: Nairobi. The predominantly agricultural country exports coffee, tea and petroleum products.

The Arabs came to the coast of Kenya in the 8th century and established posts to conduct an ivory and slave trade. The Portuguese, followed in the 16th century. After a lengthy and bitter struggle with the sultans of Zanzibar who controlled much of the southeastern coast of Africa, the Portuguese were driven away (late 17th century) and for many years Kenya was simply a port of call on the route to India. German and British interests in the 19thcentury produced agreements defining their respective spheres of influence. The British sphere was administrated by the Imperial East Africa Co. until 1895, when the British government purchased the company's rights in the East Africa Protectorate which, in 1920, was designated as Kenya Colony and protectorate - the latter being a10-mile wide coastal strip together with Mombasa, Lamuand other small islands nominally retained by the Sultan of Zanzibar. Kenya achieved self-government in June of 1963as a consequence of the 1952-60 Mau Mau terrorist campaign to secure land reforms and political rights for Africans. Independence was attained on Dec. 12, 1963.Kenya became a republic in 1964. It is a member of the Commonwealth of Nations. The president is Chief of State and Head of Government.

Mombasa was a thriving Arabic commercial center when first visited by Portuguese navigator Vasco da Gama in 1498. During the following two centuries Portugal made repeated efforts to capture the island stronghold but was unable to hold it against the assaults of the Muscat Arabs. In 1823 the ruling Mazuri family placed the city under British protection. Britain repudiated the protectorate and it was then seized by Seyyid Said of Oman, 1837, and annexed to Zanzibar. In 1887 the sultan of Zanzibar relinquished the port of Mombasa to British administration. It was occupied by the Imperial British East Africa Company and for the following two decades was the capital of British East Africa.

**RULERS**

British, until 1964

**MONETARY SYSTEM**

100 Cents = 1 Shilling

## REPUBLIC

### STANDARD COINAGE

**5 CENTS** KM# 1 **Composition:** Nickel-Brass **Reverse:** President Jomo Kenyatta bust facing left

| Date | Mintage | F | VF | XF | Unc | BU |
|---|---|---|---|---|---|---|
| 1966 | 28,000,000 | — | 0.25 | 0.50 | 1.00 | — |
| 1966 Proof | 27 | Value: 65.00 | | | | |
| 1967 | 9,600,000 | — | 0.25 | 0.50 | 1.00 | — |
| 1968 | 12,000,000 | — | 0.25 | 0.50 | 1.00 | — |

**5 CENTS** KM# 10 **Composition:** Nickel-Brass **Reverse:** President Jomo Kenyatta bust facing left

| Date | Mintage | F | VF | XF | Unc | BU |
|---|---|---|---|---|---|---|
| 1969 | 800,000 | — | 0.50 | 1.00 | 2.25 | — |
| 1969 Proof | 15 | Value: 100 | | | | |
| 1970 | 10,000,000 | — | 0.15 | 0.25 | 0.50 | — |
| 1971 | 29,680,000 | — | 0.15 | 0.25 | 0.40 | — |
| 1973 Proof | 500 | Value: 15.00 | | | | |
| 1974 | 5,599,000 | — | 0.15 | 0.25 | 0.40 | — |
| 1975 | 28,000,000 | — | 0.15 | 0.25 | 0.40 | — |
| 1978 | 23,168,000 | — | 0.15 | 0.25 | 0.40 | — |

**5 CENTS** **KM# 17** **Composition:** Nickel-Brass **Reverse:** President Arap Moi bust facing right

| Date | Mintage | F | VF | XF | Unc | BU |
|---|---|---|---|---|---|---|
| 1980 | — | — | 0.15 | 0.25 | 0.50 | — |
| 1984 | — | — | 0.15 | 0.25 | 0.75 | — |
| 1986 | — | — | 0.15 | 0.25 | 0.75 | — |
| 1987 | — | — | 0.15 | 0.25 | 0.75 | — |
| 1989 | — | — | 0.15 | 0.25 | 0.50 | — |
| 1990 | — | — | 0.15 | 0.25 | 0.40 | — |
| 1991 | — | — | 0.15 | 0.25 | 0.40 | — |

**10 CENTS** **KM# 2** **Composition:** Nickel-Brass **Reverse:** President Jomo Kenyatta bust facing left

| Date | Mintage | F | VF | XF | Unc | BU |
|---|---|---|---|---|---|---|
| 1966 | 26,000,000 | 0.20 | 0.65 | 1.25 | 2.50 | — |
| 1966 Proof | 27 | Value: 65.00 | | | | |
| 1967 | 7,300,000 | 0.20 | 0.65 | 1.25 | 2.50 | — |
| 1968 | 12,000,000 | 0.20 | 0.65 | 1.25 | 2.50 | — |

**10 CENTS** **KM# 11** **Composition:** Nickel-Brass **Reverse:** President Jomo Kenyatta bust facing left

| Date | Mintage | F | VF | XF | Unc | BU |
|---|---|---|---|---|---|---|
| 1969 | 3,900,000 | — | 0.15 | 0.25 | 0.65 | — |
| 1969 Proof | 15 | Value: 100 | | | | |
| 1970 | 7,200,000 | — | 0.15 | 0.25 | 0.65 | — |
| 1971 | 32,400,000 | — | 0.15 | 0.25 | 0.50 | — |
| 1973 | 3,000,000 | — | 0.15 | 0.25 | 0.75 | — |
| 1973 Proof | 500 | Value: 20.00 | | | | |
| 1974 | 3,000,000 | — | 0.15 | 0.25 | 0.75 | — |
| 1975 | 3,000,000 | — | 0.15 | 0.25 | 0.75 | — |
| 1977 | 45,600,000 | — | 0.15 | 0.25 | 0.50 | — |
| 1978 | 22,600,000 | — | 0.15 | 0.25 | 0.50 | — |

**10 CENTS** **KM# 18** **Composition:** Nickel-Brass **Reverse:** President Arap Moi bust facing right

| Date | Mintage | F | VF | XF | Unc | BU |
|---|---|---|---|---|---|---|
| 1980 | — | — | 0.15 | 0.25 | 1.00 | — |
| 1984 | — | — | 0.15 | 0.25 | 1.25 | — |
| 1986 | — | — | 0.15 | 0.25 | 1.25 | — |
| 1987 | — | — | 0.15 | 0.25 | 1.25 | — |
| 1989 | — | — | 0.15 | 0.25 | 1.00 | — |
| 1990 | — | — | 0.15 | 0.25 | 1.00 | — |
| 1991 | — | — | 0.15 | 0.25 | 0.75 | — |

**10 CENTS** **KM# 18a** **Composition:** Brass Plated Steel **Reverse:** President Arap Moi bust facing right

| Date | Mintage | F | VF | XF | Unc | BU |
|---|---|---|---|---|---|---|
| 1994 | — | — | 0.20 | 0.30 | 1.00 | — |

**10 CENTS** **KM# 31** **Composition:** Brass Plated Steel **Obverse:** Denomination and arms **Reverse:** President Arap Moi bust facing right

| Date | Mintage | F | VF | XF | Unc | BU |
|---|---|---|---|---|---|---|
| 1995 | — | — | 0.10 | 0.20 | 0.40 | — |

**25 CENTS** **KM# 3** **Composition:** Copper-Nickel **Reverse:** President Jomo Kenyatta bust facing left

| Date | Mintage | F | VF | XF | Unc | BU |
|---|---|---|---|---|---|---|
| 1966 | 4,000,000 | 0.30 | 1.00 | 2.00 | 3.50 | — |
| 1966 Proof | 27 | Value: 75.00 | | | | |
| 1967 | 4,000,000 | 0.30 | 1.00 | 2.00 | 3.50 | — |

**25 CENTS** **KM# 12** **Composition:** Copper-Nickel **Reverse:** President Jomo Kenyatta bust facing left

| Date | Mintage | F | VF | XF | Unc | BU |
|---|---|---|---|---|---|---|
| 1969 | 200,000 | 0.50 | 1.00 | 2.50 | 10.00 | — |
| 1969 Proof | 15 | Value: 110 | | | | |
| 1973 Proof | 500 | Value: 18.00 | | | | |

**50 CENTS** **KM# 4** **Composition:** Copper-Nickel **Reverse:** President Jomo Kenyatta bust facing left

| Date | Mintage | F | VF | XF | Unc | BU |
|---|---|---|---|---|---|---|
| 1966 | 4,000,000 | 0.20 | 0.40 | 1.00 | 2.75 | — |
| 1966 Proof | 27 | Value: 75.00 | | | | |
| 1967 | 5,120,000 | 0.20 | 0.40 | 0.85 | 2.25 | — |
| 1968 | 6,000,000 | 0.20 | 0.40 | 0.85 | 2.00 | — |

**50 CENTS** **KM# 13** **Composition:** Copper-Nickel **Reverse:** President Jomo Kenyatta bust facing left

| Date | Mintage | F | VF | XF | Unc | BU |
|---|---|---|---|---|---|---|
| 1969 | 400,000 | 0.40 | 0.80 | 1.50 | 3.00 | — |
| 1969 Proof | 15 | Value: 110 | | | | |
| 1971 | 9,600,000 | — | 0.20 | 0.40 | 0.75 | — |
| 1973 | 3,360,000 | 0.20 | 0.40 | 0.80 | 1.75 | — |
| 1973 Proof | 500 | Value: 18.00 | | | | |
| 1974 | 12,640,000 | — | 0.20 | 0.40 | 0.75 | — |
| 1975 | 8,000,000 | — | 0.20 | 0.40 | 0.75 | — |
| 1977 | 16,000,000 | — | 0.20 | 0.40 | 0.75 | — |
| 1978 | 20,480,000 | — | 0.20 | 0.40 | 0.75 | — |

**50 CENTS** **KM# 19** **Composition:** Copper-Nickel **Reverse:** President Arap Moi bust facing right

| Date | Mintage | F | VF | XF | Unc | BU |
|---|---|---|---|---|---|---|
| 1980 | — | — | 0.15 | 0.25 | 0.75 | — |
| 1989 | — | — | 0.15 | 0.25 | 0.75 | — |
| 1990 | — | — | 0.15 | 0.25 | 0.75 | — |

**50 CENTS** **KM# 19a** **Composition:** Nickel Plated Steel **Reverse:** President Arap Moi bust facing right

| Date | Mintage | F | VF | XF | Unc | BU |
|---|---|---|---|---|---|---|
| 1994 | — | — | 0.25 | 0.35 | 1.00 | — |

**50 CENTS** **KM# 28** **Composition:** Brass Plated Steel **Reverse:** President Arap Moi bust facing right

| Date | Mintage | F | VF | XF | Unc | BU |
|---|---|---|---|---|---|---|
| 1995 | — | — | 0.15 | 0.25 | 0.50 | — |
| 1997 | — | — | 0.15 | 0.25 | 0.50 | — |

**SHILLING** **KM# 5** **Composition:** Copper-Nickel **Reverse:** President Jomo Kenyatta bust facing left

| Date | Mintage | F | VF | XF | Unc | BU |
|---|---|---|---|---|---|---|
| 1966 | 20,000,000 | 0.25 | 0.50 | 1.00 | 3.00 | — |
| 1966 Proof | 27 | Value: 75.00 | | | | |
| 1967 | 4,000,000 | 0.25 | 0.50 | 1.00 | 2.75 | — |
| 1968 | 8,000,000 | 0.20 | 0.40 | 0.80 | 2.25 | — |

**SHILLING** **KM# 14** **Composition:** Copper-Nickel **Reverse:** President Jomo Kenyatta bust facing left

| Date | Mintage | F | VF | XF | Unc | BU |
|---|---|---|---|---|---|---|
| 1969 | 4,000,000 | 0.15 | 0.30 | 0.75 | 2.25 | — |
| 1969 Proof | 15 | Value: 110 | | | | |
| 1971 | 24,000,000 | 0.10 | 0.30 | 0.65 | 2.00 | — |
| 1973 | 2,480,000 | 0.20 | 0.40 | 0.80 | 2.75 | — |
| 1973 Proof | 500 | Value: 20.00 | | | | |
| 1974 | 13,520,000 | 0.10 | 0.30 | 0.65 | 2.00 | — |
| 1975 | 40,856,000 | 0.10 | 0.30 | 0.65 | 2.00 | — |
| 1978 | 20,000,000 | 0.10 | 0.30 | 0.65 | 2.00 | — |

**SHILLING** **KM# 20** **Composition:** Copper-Nickel **Reverse:** President Arap Moi bust facing right

| Date | Mintage | F | VF | XF | Unc | BU |
|---|---|---|---|---|---|---|
| 1980 | — | 0.15 | 0.25 | 0.50 | 1.50 | — |
| 1989 | — | 0.15 | 0.25 | 0.50 | 1.50 | — |

**SHILLING** **KM# 20a** **Composition:** Nickel Plated Steel **Reverse:** President Arap Moi bust facing right

| Date | Mintage | F | VF | XF | Unc | BU |
|---|---|---|---|---|---|---|
| 1994 | — | 0.25 | 0.35 | 0.65 | 1.75 | — |

**SHILLING** **KM# 29** **Composition:** Brass Plated Steel **Reverse:** President Arap Moi bust facing right

| Date | Mintage | F | VF | XF | Unc | BU |
|---|---|---|---|---|---|---|
| 1995 | — | 0.10 | 0.20 | 0.40 | 0.75 | — |
| 1997 | — | 0.10 | 0.20 | 0.40 | 0.75 | — |

**2 SHILLINGS** KM# 6 **Composition:** Copper-Nickel **Reverse:** President Jomo Kenyatta bust facing left

| Date | Mintage | F | VF | XF | Unc | BU |
|---|---|---|---|---|---|---|
| 1966 | 3,000,000 | 1.00 | 2.00 | 3.00 | 7.00 | — |
| 1966 Proof | 27 | Value: 95.00 | | | | |
| 1968 | 1,100,000 | 1.00 | 2.75 | 4.50 | 10.00 | — |

**2 SHILLINGS** KM# 15 **Composition:** Copper-Nickel **Reverse:** President Jomo Kenyatta bust facing left

| Date | Mintage | F | VF | XF | Unc | BU |
|---|---|---|---|---|---|---|
| 1969 | 100,000 | 2.00 | 4.00 | 8.00 | 12.50 | — |
| 1969 Proof | 15 | Value: 120 | | | | |
| 1971 | 1,920,000 | 0.60 | 1.25 | 3.50 | 7.50 | — |
| 1973 Proof | 500 | Value: 25.00 | | | | |

**5 SHILLINGS** KM# 16 **Composition:** Brass **Subject:** 10th anniversary of independence

| Date | Mintage | F | VF | XF | Unc | BU |
|---|---|---|---|---|---|---|
| 1973 | 100,000 | 4.50 | 10.00 | 17.50 | 30.00 | — |
| 1973 Proof | 1,500 | Value: 45.00 | | | | |

**5 SHILLINGS** KM# 23 **Composition:** Copper-Nickel **Reverse:** President Arap Moi bust facing right

| Date | Mintage | F | VF | XF | Unc | BU |
|---|---|---|---|---|---|---|
| 1985 | — | 0.35 | 0.75 | 1.50 | 3.00 | — |

**5 SHILLINGS** KM# 23a **Composition:** Nickel Plated Steel **Reverse:** President Arap Moi bust facing right

| Date | Mintage | F | VF | XF | Unc | BU |
|---|---|---|---|---|---|---|
| 1994 | — | 0.50 | 1.00 | 2.25 | 4.50 | — |

**5 SHILLINGS** KM# 30 **Ring Composition:** Copper-Nickel **Center Composition:** Brass **Reverse:** President Arap Moi bust facing right

| Date | Mintage | F | VF | XF | Unc | BU |
|---|---|---|---|---|---|---|
| 1995 | — | — | — | — | 3.00 | — |
| 1997 | — | — | — | — | 3.00 | — |

**10 SHILLINGS** KM# 27 **Ring Composition:** Brass **Center Composition:** Copper-Nickel **Reverse:** President Arap Moi bust facing right

| Date | Mintage | F | VF | XF | Unc | BU |
|---|---|---|---|---|---|---|
| 1994 | — | — | — | — | 4.50 | — |
| 1995 | — | — | — | — | 4.50 | — |
| 1997 | — | — | — | — | 4.50 | — |

**20 SHILLINGS** KM# 32 **Ring Composition:** Copper-Nickel **Center Composition:** Brass **Obverse:** Denomination above arms **Reverse:** President Arap Moi bust facing right

| Date | Mintage | F | VF | XF | Unc | BU |
|---|---|---|---|---|---|---|
| 1998 | — | — | — | — | 5.00 | — |

**100 SHILLINGS** KM# 7 **Weight:** 7.6000 g. **Composition:** 0.9170 Gold .224 oz. AGW **Subject:** 75th anniversary - birth of President Jomo Kenyatta

| Date | Mintage | F | VF | XF | Unc | BU |
|---|---|---|---|---|---|---|
| 1966 | — | — | — | — | 110 | — |
| 1966 Proof | 7,500 | Value: 135 | | | | |

**200 SHILLINGS** KM# 21 **Weight:** 28.2800 g. **Composition:** 0.9250 Silver .841 oz. ASW **Obverse:** President Moi **Reverse:** Coat of arms

| Date | Mintage | F | VF | XF | Unc | BU |
|---|---|---|---|---|---|---|
| 1979 Proof | Est. 9,500 | Value: 100 | | | | |

**250 SHILLINGS** KM# 8 **Weight:** 19.0000 g. **Composition:** 0.9170 Gold .5602 oz. AGW **Subject:** 75th anniversary - birth of President Jomo Kenyatta

| Date | Mintage | F | VF | XF | Unc | BU |
|---|---|---|---|---|---|---|
| 1966 | — | — | — | — | 250 | — |
| 1966 Proof | 1,000 | Value: 285 | | | | |

**500 SHILLINGS** KM# 9 **Weight:** 38.0000 g. **Composition:** 0.9170 Gold 1.1204 oz. AGW **Subject:** 75th anniversary - birth of President Jomo Kenyatta

| Date | Mintage | F | VF | XF | Unc | BU |
|---|---|---|---|---|---|---|
| 1966 | — | — | — | — | 500 | — |
| 1966 Proof | 500 | Value: 550 | | | | |

**500 SHILLINGS** KM# 24 **Weight:** 28.2800 g. **Composition:** 0.9250 Silver .8410 oz. ASW **Subject:** 10th anniversary of Moi as president

| Date | Mintage | F | VF | XF | Unc | BU |
|---|---|---|---|---|---|---|
| ND(1988) Proof | — | Value: 165 | | | | |

**500 SHILLINGS** KM# 25 **Weight:** 28.3300 g. **Composition:** 0.9250 Silver .8425 oz. ASW **Subject:** 25th anniversary of independence

| Date | Mintage | F | VF | XF | Unc | BU |
|---|---|---|---|---|---|---|
| ND(1988) Proof | — | Value: 185 | | | | |

**1000 SHILLINGS** KM# 26 **Weight:** 28.2800 g. **Composition:** 0.9250 Silver .8351 oz. ASW **Subject:** Silver jubilee of Central Bank

| Date | Mintage | F | VF | XF | Unc | BU |
|---|---|---|---|---|---|---|
| 1991 Proof | — | Value: 275 | | | | |

**3000 SHILLING** KM# 22 **Weight:** 40.0000 g. **Composition:** 0.9170 Gold 1.1787 oz. AGW **Obverse:** President Moi **Reverse:** Coat of arms

| Date | Mintage | F | VF | XF | Unc | BU |
|---|---|---|---|---|---|---|
| 1979 Proof | 2,000 | Value: 750 | | | | |

## MINT SETS

| KM# | Date | Mintage | Identification | Issue Price | Mkt Val |
|---|---|---|---|---|---|
| MS1 | 1966 (3) | — | KM7-9 | — | 865 |

## PROOF SETS

| KM# | Date | Mintage | Identification | Issue Price | Mkt Val |
|---|---|---|---|---|---|
| PS1 | 1966 (6) | 27 | KM1-6 | — | 450 |
| PS2 | 1966 (3) | 500 | KM7-9 | 152 | 975 |
| PS3 | 1969 (6) | 15 | KM10-15 | — | 650 |
| PS4 | 1973 (7) | 500 | KM10-16 | — | 160 |

# KIAU CHAU

Kiau Chau (Kiao Chau, Kiaochow, Kiautscho, now Jiaozhou), a former German trading enclave, including the port of Tsingtao (Qingdao), was located on the Shantung (Shandong) Peninsula of eastern China. Following the murder of two missionaries in Shantung in 1897, Germany occupied Kiaochow Bay, and during subsequent negotiations with the Chinese government obtained a 99 year lease on 177 sq. mi. of land. The enclave was established as a free port in 1899, and a customs house set up to collect tariffs on goods moving to and from the Chinese interior. The Japanese took seige to the port on Aug. 27, 1914 as their first action in World War I to deprive German sea marauders of their east Asian supply and refitting base. Aided by the British forces, the siege ended Nov. 7. Japan retained possession until 1922, when it was restored to China by the Washington Conference on China and naval armaments. It fell again to Japan in 1938, but not before the Chinese had destroyed its manufacturing facilities. It is presently a part of the Peoples Republic of China. The major city is Tsingtao (Qingdao) and is noted for its beer.

**RULERS**

Wilhelm II, 1897-1918
Japanese, 1914-1922, 1938-1945

**MONETARY SYSTEM**

100 Cents = 1 Dollar

## GERMAN OCCUPATION

### STANDARD COINAGE

**5 CENTS** Y# 1 **Composition:** Copper-Nickel **Ruler:** Wilhelm II **Obverse:** German Imperial Eagle **Obv. Legend:** DEUTSCH.KIAUTSHAU GEBIET **Reverse:** Inscription: Kuang-hsü Yüan-pao

| Date | Mintage | F | VF | XF | Unc | BU |
|---|---|---|---|---|---|---|
| 1909 | 610,000 | 50.00 | 75.00 | 120 | 180 | — |
| 1909 Proof | — | Value: 450 | | | | |

**10 CENTS** Y# 2 **Ruler:** Wilhelm II **Obverse:** German Imperial Eagle **Obv. Legend:** DEUTSCH.KIAUTSHAU GEBIET **Reverse:** Inscription: Kuang-hsü Yüan-pao

| Date | Mintage | F | VF | XF | Unc | BU |
|---|---|---|---|---|---|---|
| 1909 | 670,000 | 30.00 | 50.00 | 85.00 | 150 | — |
| 1909 Proof | — | Value: 500 | | | | |

# KIRIBATI

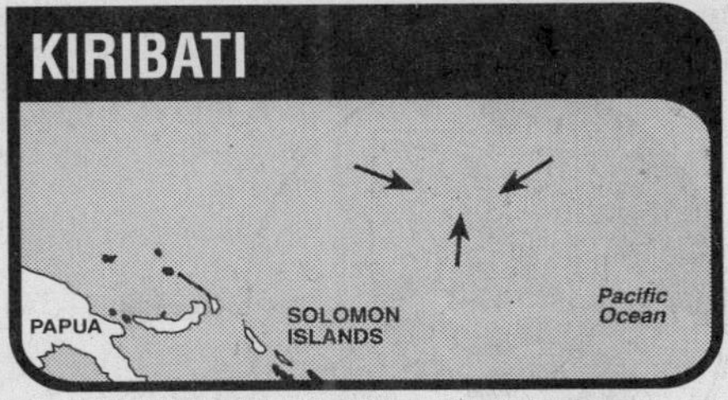


The Republic of Kiribati (formerly the Gilbert Islands), consists of 30 coral atolls and islands spread over more than one million sq. mi. (2,590,000 sq. km.) of the southwest Pacific Ocean, has an area of 332 sq. mi. (717 sq. km.) and a population of 64,200. Capital: Bairiki, on Tarawa. In addition to the Gilbert Islands proper, Kiribati includes Ocean Island, the Central and Southern Line Islands, and the Phoenix Islands, though possession of Canton and Enderbury of the Phoenix Islands is disputed with the United States. Most families engage in subsistence fishing. Copra and phosphates are exported, mostly to Australia and New Zealand.

The Gilbert Islands and the group formerly called the Ellice Islands (now Tuvalu) comprised a single British crown colony, the Gilbert and Ellice Islands.

Spanish mutineers first sighted the islands in 1537, succeeding visits were made by the English navigators John Byron (1764), James Cook (1777), and Thomas Gilbert and John Marshall (1788). An American, Edward Fanning, arrived in 1798. Britain declared a protectorate over the Gilbert and Ellice Islands, and in1915 began the formation of a colony which was completed when the Phoenix Islands were added to the group in 1937. The Central and Southern Line Islands were administratively attached to the Gilbert and Ellice Islands olony in 1972, and remained attached to the Gilberts when Tuvalu was created in 1975. The colony became self-governing in 1971. Kiribati attained independence on July 12, 1979.

**RULERS**

British, until 1979

**MONETARY SYSTEM**

100 Cents = 1 Dollar

## REPUBLIC

### DECIMAL COINAGE

**CENT** KM# 1 **Composition:** Bronze **Subject:** Christmas Island Frigatebird

| Date | Mintage | F | VF | XF | Unc | BU |
|---|---|---|---|---|---|---|
| 1979 | 90,000 | — | — | 0.15 | 0.45 | — |
| 1979 Proof | 10,000 | Value: 1.00 | | | | |
| 1992 | — | — | — | 0.15 | 0.45 | — |

**2 CENTS** KM# 2 **Composition:** Bronze **Subject:** B'abal plant

| Date | Mintage | F | VF | XF | Unc | BU |
|---|---|---|---|---|---|---|
| 1979 | 25,000 | — | — | 0.15 | 0.35 | — |
| 1979 Proof | 10,000 | Value: 1.25 | | | | |
| 1992 | — | — | — | 0.15 | 0.35 | — |

**5 CENTS** KM# 3 **Composition:** Copper-Nickel **Subject:** Tokai lizard

| Date | Mintage | F | VF | XF | Unc | BU |
|---|---|---|---|---|---|---|
| 1979 | 20,000 | — | 0.15 | 0.30 | 1.50 | — |
| 1979 Proof | 10,000 | Value: 2.50 | | | | |

**10 CENTS** KM# 4 **Composition:** Copper-Nickel **Subject:** Bread fruit

| Date | Mintage | F | VF | XF | Unc | BU |
|---|---|---|---|---|---|---|
| 1979 | 20,000 | — | 0.15 | 0.25 | 1.25 | — |
| 1979 Proof | 10,000 | Value: 3.00 | | | | |

**20 CENTS** KM# 5 **Composition:** Copper-Nickel **Subject:** Dolphins

| Date | Mintage | F | VF | XF | Unc | BU |
|---|---|---|---|---|---|---|
| 1979 | 20,000 | — | 0.50 | 1.25 | 5.00 | — |
| 1979 Proof | 10,000 | Value: 7.50 | | | | |

**50 CENTS** KM# 6 **Composition:** Copper-Nickel **Subject:** Panda nut

| Date | Mintage | F | VF | XF | Unc | BU |
|---|---|---|---|---|---|---|
| 1979 | 20,000 | — | 0.50 | 1.00 | 3.00 | — |
| 1979 Proof | 10,000 | Value: 6.50 | | | | |

**DOLLAR** KM# 7 **Composition:** Copper-Nickel **Subject:** Outrigger sailboat

| Date | Mintage | F | VF | XF | Unc | BU |
|---|---|---|---|---|---|---|
| 1979 | 20,000 | — | 0.85 | 1.25 | 4.00 | — |
| 1979 Proof | 10,000 | Value: 8.00 | | | | |

**2 DOLLARS** KM# 14 **Composition:** Nickel-Brass **Subject:** 10th Anniversary of Independence

| Date | Mintage | F | VF | XF | Unc | BU |
|---|---|---|---|---|---|---|
| 1989 | — | — | — | — | 5.00 | — |

**2 DOLLARS** **KM# 21** **Weight:** 10.0000 g. **Composition:** 0.5000 Silver .1607 oz. ASW **Subject:** Titanic sinking **Obverse:** National arms

| Date | Mintage | F | VF | XF | Unc | BU |
|---|---|---|---|---|---|---|
| 1998 Proof | — | Value: 15.00 | | | | |

**5 DOLLARS** **KM# 8** **Weight:** 28.1600 g. **Composition:** 0.5000 Silver .4527 oz. ASW **Subject:** Independence

| Date | Mintage | F | VF | XF | Unc | BU |
|---|---|---|---|---|---|---|
| 1979 | 1,545 | — | — | — | 22.50 | — |

**5 DOLLARS** **KM# 8a** **Weight:** 28.1600 g. **Composition:** 0.9250 Silver .8375 oz. ASW **Subject:** Independence

| Date | Mintage | F | VF | XF | Unc | BU |
|---|---|---|---|---|---|---|
| 1979 Proof | 3,326 | Value: 25.00 | | | | |

**5 DOLLARS** **KM# 10** **Composition:** Copper-Nickel **Subject:** 2nd Anniversary of Independence, and wedding of Prince Charles and Lady Diana

| Date | Mintage | F | VF | XF | Unc | BU |
|---|---|---|---|---|---|---|
| 1981 | 50,000 | — | — | — | 7.00 | — |

**5 DOLLARS** **KM# 10a** **Weight:** 28.6000 g. **Composition:** 0.9250 Silver .8505 oz. ASW **Subject:** 2nd Anniversary of Independence, and wedding of Prince Charles and Lady Diana

| Date | Mintage | F | VF | XF | Unc | BU |
|---|---|---|---|---|---|---|
| 1981 Proof | 25,000 | Value: 21.50 | | | | |

**5 DOLLARS** **KM# 12** **Composition:** Copper-Nickel **Subject:** Royal visit

| Date | Mintage | F | VF | XF | Unc | BU |
|---|---|---|---|---|---|---|
| 1982 | — | — | — | — | 5.00 | — |

**5 DOLLARS** **KM# 12a** **Composition:** Silver **Subject:** Royal visit

| Date | Mintage | F | VF | XF | Unc | BU |
|---|---|---|---|---|---|---|
| 1982 Proof | — | Value: 32.50 | | | | |

**5 DOLLARS** **KM# 19** **Weight:** 31.4700 g. **Composition:** 0.9250 Silver .9359 oz. ASW **Subject:** Discoverer of Kiribati - Capt. John Byron, ship **Obverse:** National arms

| Date | Mintage | F | VF | XF | Unc | BU |
|---|---|---|---|---|---|---|
| 1996 Proof | Est. 15,000 | Value: 50.00 | | | | |

**5 DOLLARS** **KM# 20** **Weight:** 31.4700 g. **Composition:** 0.9250 Silver .9359 oz. ASW **Obverse:** National arms **Reverse:** High diver

| Date | Mintage | F | VF | XF | Unc | BU |
|---|---|---|---|---|---|---|
| 1996 Proof | 40,000 | Value: 30.00 | | | | |

**5 DOLLARS** **KM# 22** **Weight:** 15.5518 g. **Composition:** 0.9250 Silver .4625 oz. ASW **Subject:** Guerra & Paz **Obverse:** Kiribati arms **Reverse:** Dove

| Date | Mintage | F | VF | XF | Unc | BU |
|---|---|---|---|---|---|---|
| ND(1997) Proof | Est. 10,000 | Value: 35.00 | | | | |

**5 DOLLARS** **KM# 23** **Weight:** 15.5518 g. **Composition:** 0.9250 Silver .4625 oz. ASW **Subject:** Powerful empires **Obverse:** Kiribati arms **Reverse:** Helmets and hats

| Date | Mintage | F | VF | XF | Unc | BU |
|---|---|---|---|---|---|---|
| ND(1997) Proof | Est. 10,000 | Value: 35.00 | | | | |

**5 DOLLARS** **KM# 24** **Weight:** 15.5518 g. **Composition:** 0.9250 Silver .4625 oz. ASW **Subject:** Tempora Mutantur **Obverse:** Kiribati arms **Reverse:** Solar system

| Date | Mintage | F | VF | XF | Unc | BU |
|---|---|---|---|---|---|---|
| ND(1997) Proof | Est. 10,000 | Value: 35.00 | | | | |

**5 DOLLARS** **KM# 25** **Weight:** 15.5518 g. **Composition:** 0.9250 Silver .4625 oz. ASW **Subject:** People and monuments - column, compass **Obverse:** Kiribati arms

| Date | Mintage | F | VF | XF | Unc | BU |
|---|---|---|---|---|---|---|
| ND(1997) Proof | Est. 10,000 | Value: 37.50 | | | | |

**5 DOLLARS** **KM# 28** **Weight:** 31.3000 g. **Composition:** 0.9990 Silver 1.0053 oz. ASW **Subject:** 10th Anniversary of Emperor Akihito's Reign **Obverse:** Kinbati arms **Reverse:** Japan's Imperial couple **Edge:** Reeded **Size:** 38.6 mm.

| Date | Mintage | F | VF | XF | Unc | BU |
|---|---|---|---|---|---|---|
| 2000 Proof | 2,000 | Value: 70.00 | | | | |

**10 DOLLARS** **KM# 13** **Weight:** 28.2800 g. **Composition:** 0.9250 Silver .8411 oz. ASW **Subject:** 5th Anniversary of Independence

| Date | Mintage | F | VF | XF | Unc | BU |
|---|---|---|---|---|---|---|
| ND(1984) | — | — | — | — | 85.00 | — |
| ND(1984) Proof | 2,500 | Value: 45.00 | | | | |

**10 DOLLARS** **KM# 13a** **Weight:** 47.5200 g. **Composition:** 0.9170 Gold 1.4012 oz. AGW **Subject:** 5th Anniversary of Independence

| Date | Mintage | F | VF | XF | Unc | BU |
|---|---|---|---|---|---|---|
| ND(1984) Proof | 50 | Value: 1,250 | | | | |

10 DOLLARS KM# 27 Weight: 1.2441 g. Composition: 0.9990 Gold .04 oz. AGW Subject: Titanic Obverse: National arms Reverse: Sinking ships and lifeboats

| Date | Mintage | F | VF | XF | Unc | BU |
|---|---|---|---|---|---|---|
| 1998 Proof | — | Value: 50.00 | | | | |

20 DOLLARS KM# 17 Weight: 31.4700 g. Composition: 0.9250 Silver .9359 oz. ASW Subject: Barcelona Olympics - sailing

| Date | Mintage | F | VF | XF | Unc | BU |
|---|---|---|---|---|---|---|
| 1992 Proof | 40,000 | Value: 28.00 | | | | |

20 DOLLARS KM# 18 Weight: 31.4700 g. Composition: 0.9250 Silver .9359 oz. ASW Subject: Endangered wildlife Reverse: Christmas Island Frigatebird

| Date | Mintage | F | VF | XF | Unc | BU |
|---|---|---|---|---|---|---|
| 1992 Proof | — | Value: 40.00 | | | | |

20 DOLLARS KM# 15 Weight: 31.4700 g. Composition: 0.9250 Silver .9359 oz. ASW Subject: Soccer - World Cup '94

| Date | Mintage | F | VF | XF | Unc | BU |
|---|---|---|---|---|---|---|
| 1993 Proof | Est. 10,000 | Value: 32.50 | | | | |

20 DOLLARS KM# 16 Weight: 31.4700 g. Composition: 0.9250 Silver .9359 oz. ASW Subject: First space walk

| Date | Mintage | F | VF | XF | Unc | BU |
|---|---|---|---|---|---|---|
| 1993 Proof | Est. 15,000 | Value: 32.50 | | | | |

50 DOLLARS KM# 26 Weight: 7.7759 g. Composition: 0.9990 Gold .25 oz. AGW Subject: Tempora Mutantur Obverse: Kiribati arms Reverse: Solar system

| Date | Mintage | F | VF | XF | Unc | BU |
|---|---|---|---|---|---|---|
| ND(1997) Proof | Est. 2,500 | Value: 110 | | | | |

150 DOLLARS KM# 9 Weight: 15.9800 g. Composition: 0.9170 Gold .4711 oz. AGW Subject: Independence - traditional meeting house

| Date | Mintage | F | VF | XF | Unc | BU |
|---|---|---|---|---|---|---|
| 1979 | 422 | — | — | — | 250 | — |
| 1979 Proof | 386 | Value: 275 | | | | |

150 DOLLARS KM# 11 Weight: 15.9800 g. Composition: 0.9170 Gold .4711 oz. AGW Subject: 2nd Anniversary of Independence, and wedding of Prince Charles and Lady Diana

| Date | Mintage | F | VF | XF | Unc | BU |
|---|---|---|---|---|---|---|
| 1981 | 750 | — | — | — | 225 | — |
| 1981 Proof | 1,500 | Value: 250 | | | | |

200 DOLLARS KM# 29 Weight: 31.3000 g. Composition: 0.9990 Gold 1.0053 oz. AGW Subject: 10th Anniversary of Emperor Akihito's Reign Obverse: Kinbati arms Reverse: Japan's Imperial couple Edge: Reeded Size: 35 mm.

| Date | Mintage | F | VF | XF | Unc | BU |
|---|---|---|---|---|---|---|
| 2000 Proof | 500 | Value: 550 | | | | |

## PROOF SETS

| KM# | Date | Mintage | Identification | Issue Price | Mkt Val |
|---|---|---|---|---|---|
| PS1 | 1979 (7) | 10,000 | KM1-7 | 34.00 | 25.00 |
| PS2 | 1981 (2) | — | KM10a, 11 | — | 270 |

# KOREA

Korea, 'Land of the Morning Calm', occupies a mountainous peninsula in northeast Asia bounded by Manchuria, the Yellow Sea and the Sea of Japan.

According to legend, the first Korean dynasty, that of the House of Tangun, ruled from 2333 B.C. to 1122 B.C. It was followed by the dynasty of Kija, a Chinese scholar, which continued until 193 B.C. and brought a high civilization to Korea. The first recorded period in the history of Korea, the period of the Three Kingdoms, lasted from 57 B.C. to 935 A.D. and achieved the first political unification of the peninsula. The Kingdom of Koryo, from which Korea derived its name, was founded in 935 and continued until 1392, when it was superseded by the Yi Dynasty of King Yi. Sung Kye was to last until the Japanese annexation in 1910.

At the end of the 16th century Korea was invaded and occupied for 7 years by Japan, and from 1627 until the late 19th century it was a semi-independent tributary of China. Japan replaced China as the predominant foreign influence at the end of the Sino-Japanese War (1894-95), only to find her position threatened by Russian influence from 1896 to 1904. The Russian threat was eliminated by the Russo-Japanese War (1904-05) and in 1905 Japan established a direct protectorate over Korea. On Aug. 22,1910, the last Korean ruler signed the treaty that annexed Korea to Japan as a government generalcy in the Japanese Empire. Japanese suzerainty was maintained until the end of World War II.

From 1633 to 1891 the monetary system of Korea employed cast coins with a square center hole. Fifty-two agencies were authorized to procure these coins from a lesser number of coin foundries. They exist in thousands of varieties. Seed, or mother coins, were used to make the impressions in the molds in which the regular cash coins were cast. Czarist-Russian Korea experimented with Korean coins when Alexiev of Russia, Korea's Financial Advisor, founded the First Asian Branch of the Russo-Korean Bank on March 1, 1898, and authorized the issuing of a set of new Korean coins with a crowned Russian-style quasi-eagle. British-Japanese opposition and the Russo-Japanese War operated to end the Russian coinage experiment in 1904.

**RULERS**

Yi Hyong (Kojong), 1864-1897
as Emperor Kuang Mu, 1897-1907
Japanese Puppet
Yung Hi (Sunjong), 1907-1910

**DATING**

## KINGDOM

### STANDARD COINAGE

5 FUN KM# 1116 Weight: 17.2000 g. Composition: Copper Ruler: Kuang Mu

| Date | Mintage | F | VF | XF | Unc | BU |
|---|---|---|---|---|---|---|
| 6(1902) | — | 8.00 | 16.00 | 32.00 | 100 | — |

**1/4 YANG** KM# 1117 **Composition:** Copper-Nickel **Ruler:** Kuang Mu **Obverse:** Dragon crowded by small tight circle

| Date | Mintage | F | VF | XF | Unc | BU |
|---|---|---|---|---|---|---|
| 5(1901) | — | 145 | 300 | 500 | 1,100 | — |

# RUSSIAN DOMINATION

## REFORM COINAGE

**CHON** KM# 1121 **Weight:** 6.8000 g. **Composition:** Bronze **Ruler:** Kuang Mu

| Date | Mintage | F | VF | XF | Unc | BU |
|---|---|---|---|---|---|---|
| 2(1902) | 3,001,000 | 1,650 | 3,250 | 5,500 | 8,500 | — |

**5 CHON** KM# 1122 **Weight:** 4.3000 g. **Composition:** Copper-Nickel **Ruler:** Kuang Mu

| Date | Mintage | F | VF | XF | Unc | BU |
|---|---|---|---|---|---|---|
| 6(1902) | 2,800,000 | 1,250 | 2,350 | 4,000 | 6,000 | — |

**1/2 WON** KM# 1123 **Weight:** 13.5000 g. **Composition:** 0.8000 Silver .3473 oz. ASW **Ruler:** Kuang Mu

| Date | Mintage | F | VF | XF | Unc | BU |
|---|---|---|---|---|---|---|
| 5(1901) | 1,831,000 | 2,500 | 5,500 | 9,000 | 14,000 | — |

**Note:** Ponterio & Assoc. Witte Museum sale 8-89 choice BU realized $12,500; Heritage Piedmont sale 6-2000 choice BU realized $18,400

# JAPANESE PROTECTORATE

## REFORM COINAGE

**1/2 CHON** KM# 1124 **Weight:** 3.5600 g. **Composition:** Bronze **Ruler:** Kuang Mu

| Date | Mintage | F | VF | XF | Unc | BU |
|---|---|---|---|---|---|---|
| 10(1906) | 24,000,000 | 3.00 | 10.00 | 25.00 | 90.00 | — |

**1/2 CHON** KM# 1145 **Weight:** 2.1000 g. **Composition:** Bronze **Ruler:** Kuang Mu

| Date | Mintage | F | VF | XF | Unc | BU |
|---|---|---|---|---|---|---|
| 11(1907) Rare | Est. 800,000 | — | — | — | — | — |

**1/2 CHON** KM# 1136 **Weight:** 2.1000 g. **Composition:** Bronze **Ruler:** Yung Hi (Sunjong)

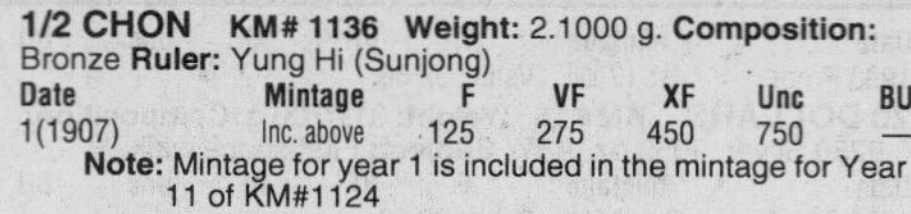

| Date | Mintage | F | VF | XF | Unc | BU |
|---|---|---|---|---|---|---|
| 1(1907) | Inc. above | 125 | 275 | 450 | 750 | — |

**Note:** Mintage for year 1 is included in the mintage for Year 11 of KM#1124

| Date | Mintage | F | VF | XF | Unc | BU |
|---|---|---|---|---|---|---|
| 2(1908) | 21,000,000 | 6.00 | 20.00 | 40.00 | 140 | — |
| 3(1909) | 8,200,000 | 7.00 | 22.00 | 45.00 | 150 | — |
| 4(1910) | 5,070,000 | 85.00 | 200 | 400 | 750 | — |

**CHON** KM# 1125 **Weight:** 7.1300 g. **Composition:** Bronze **Ruler:** Kuang Mu

| Date | Mintage | F | VF | XF | Unc | BU |
|---|---|---|---|---|---|---|
| 9(1905) | 11,800,000 | 9.00 | 15.00 | 30.00 | 100 | — |
| 10(1906) | Inc. above | 6.50 | 12.00 | 25.00 | 100 | — |

**CHON** KM# 1132 **Weight:** 4.2000 g. **Composition:** Bronze **Ruler:** Kuang Mu

| Date | Mintage | F | VF | XF | Unc | BU |
|---|---|---|---|---|---|---|
| 11(1907) | 11,200,000 | 3.50 | 7.50 | 15.00 | 85.00 | — |

**CHON** KM# 1137 **Weight:** 4.2000 g. **Composition:** Bronze **Ruler:** Yung Hi (Sunjong)

| Date | Mintage | F | VF | XF | Unc | BU |
|---|---|---|---|---|---|---|
| 1(1907) | Inc. above | 4.50 | 12.00 | 27.50 | 100 | — |
| 2(1908) | 6,800,000 | 3.00 | 7.00 | 14.00 | 75.00 | — |
| 3(1909) | 9,200,000 | 3.00 | 7.00 | 12.50 | 70.00 | — |
| 4(1910) | 3,500,000 | 4.00 | 11.00 | 23.00 | 90.00 | — |

**5 CHON** KM# 1126 **Weight:** 4.5000 g. **Composition:** Copper-Nickel **Ruler:** Kuang Mu

| Date | Mintage | F | VF | XF | Unc | BU |
|---|---|---|---|---|---|---|
| 9(1905) | 20,000,000 | 7.00 | 20.00 | 40.00 | 80.00 | — |
| 9(1905) Proof | — | Value: 1,500 | | | | |
| 11(1907) | 160,000,000 | 9.00 | 22.00 | 45.00 | 90.00 | — |

**5 CHON** KM# 1138 **Weight:** 4.5000 g. **Composition:** Copper-Nickel **Ruler:** Yung Hi (Sunjong)

| Date | Mintage | F | VF | XF | Unc | BU |
|---|---|---|---|---|---|---|
| 3(1909) | — | 900 | 1,750 | 3,000 | 4,000 | — |

**10 CHON** KM# 1127 **Weight:** 2.7000 g. **Composition:** 0.8000 Silver .0695 oz. ASW **Ruler:** Kuang Mu **Note:** 1.5 milimeters thick.

| Date | Mintage | F | VF | XF | Unc | BU |
|---|---|---|---|---|---|---|
| 10(1906) | 2,000,000 | 15.00 | 25.00 | 50.00 | 100 | — |

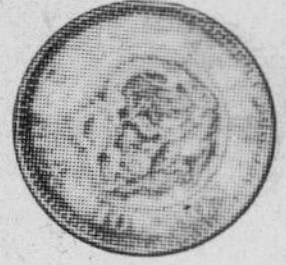

**10 CHON** KM# 1133 **Weight:** 2.2500 g. **Composition:** 0.8000 Silver .0695 oz. ASW **Ruler:** Kuang Mu **Note:** 1.0 milimeters thick.

| Date | Mintage | F | VF | XF | Unc | BU |
|---|---|---|---|---|---|---|
| 11(1907) | 2,400,000 | 15.00 | 25.00 | 60.00 | 120 | — |

**10 CHON** KM# 1139 **Weight:** 2.2500 g. **Composition:** 0.8000 Silver .0578 oz. ASW **Ruler:** Yung Hi (Sunjong)

| Date | Mintage | F | VF | XF | Unc | BU |
|---|---|---|---|---|---|---|
| 2(1908) | 6,300,000 | 12.00 | 20.00 | 35.00 | 75.00 | — |
| 3(1909) Rare | — | — | — | — | — | — |
| 4(1910) | 9,500,000 | 10.00 | 18.00 | 32.00 | 65.00 | — |

**20 CHON** KM# 1128 **Weight:** 5.3900 g. **Composition:** 0.8000 Silver .1386 oz. ASW **Ruler:** Kuang Mu

| Date | Mintage | F | VF | XF | Unc | BU |
|---|---|---|---|---|---|---|
| 9(1905) | 1,000,000 | 30.00 | 70.00 | 120 | 235 | — |
| 9(1905) Proof | — | Value: 2,250 | | | | |
| 10(1906) | 2,500,000 | 25.00 | 50.00 | 100 | 200 | — |
| 10(1906) Proof | — | Value: 1,275 | | | | |

**20 CHON** KM# 1134 **Weight:** 4.0500 g. **Composition:** 0.8000 Silver .1042 oz. ASW **Ruler:** Kuang Mu

| Date | Mintage | F | VF | XF | Unc | BU |
|---|---|---|---|---|---|---|
| 11(1907) | 1,500,000 | 20.00 | 40.00 | 70.00 | 175 | — |

**20 CHON** KM# 1140 **Weight:** 4.0500 g. **Composition:** 0.8000 Silver .1157 oz. ASW **Ruler:** Yung Hi (Sunjong)

| Date | Mintage | F | VF | XF | Unc | BU |
|---|---|---|---|---|---|---|
| 2(1908) | 3,000,000 | 16.50 | 30.00 | 60.00 | 135 | — |
| 3(1909) | 2,000,000 | 16.50 | 30.00 | 60.00 | 135 | — |
| 4(1910) | 2,000,000 | 16.50 | 30.00 | 60.00 | 135 | — |

**1/2 WON** KM# 1129 **Weight:** 13.4800 g. **Composition:** 0.8000 Silver .3467 oz. ASW **Ruler:** Kuang Mu

| Date | Mintage | F | VF | XF | Unc | BU |
|---|---|---|---|---|---|---|
| 9(1905) | 600,000 | 55.00 | 100 | 185 | 385 | — |
| 9(1905) Proof | — | Value: 1,850 | | | | |
| 10(1906) | 1,200,000 | 60.00 | 110 | 200 | 450 | — |

**1/2 WON** KM# 1135 **Weight:** 10.1300 g. **Composition:** 0.8000 Silver .2606 oz. ASW **Ruler:** Kuang Mu

| Date | Mintage | F | VF | XF | Unc | BU |
|---|---|---|---|---|---|---|
| 11(1907) | 1,000,000 | 65.00 | 115 | 225 | 550 | — |

**1/2 WON** KM# 1141 **Weight:** 10.1300 g. **Composition:** 0.8000 Silver .2606 oz. ASW **Ruler:** Yung Hi (Sunjong)

| Date | Mintage | F | VF | XF | Unc | BU |
|---|---|---|---|---|---|---|
| 2(1908) | 1,400,000 | 65.00 | 115 | 215 | 475 | — |

**5 WON** KM# 1142 **Weight:** 4.1666 g. **Composition:** 0.9000 Gold .1206 oz. AGW **Ruler:** Yung Hi (Sunjong)

| Date | Mintage | F | VF | XF | Unc | BU |
|---|---|---|---|---|---|---|
| 2(1908) | 10,000 | 10,000 | 22,750 | 32,000 | 50,000 | — |

**Note:** Heritage Piedmont sale 6-2000 Gem BU realized $86,250

| Date | Mintage | F | VF | XF | Unc | BU |
|---|---|---|---|---|---|---|
| 3(1909) Two known | — | — | — | — | — | — |

**10 WON** KM# 1130 **Weight:** 8.3333 g. **Composition:** 0.9000 Gold .2412 oz. AGW **Ruler:** Kuang Mu

| Date | Mintage | F | VF | XF | Unc | BU |
|---|---|---|---|---|---|---|
| 10(1906) | 5,012 | — | 10,000 | 16,500 | 27,500 | — |

**10 WON** KM# A1130 **Weight:** 8.3333 g. **Composition:** 0.9000 Gold .2412 oz. AGW **Ruler:** Yung Hi (Sunjong)

| Date | Mintage | F | VF | XF | Unc | BU |
|---|---|---|---|---|---|---|
| 3(1909) Two known | — | — | — | — | — | — |

**20 WON** KM# 1131 **Weight:** 16.6666 g. **Composition:** 0.9000 Gold .4823 oz. AGW **Ruler:** Kuang Mu

| Date | Mintage | F | VF | XF | Unc | BU |
|---|---|---|---|---|---|---|
| 10(1906) | 2,506 | — | 22,000 | 35,000 | 60,000 | — |

**20 WON** KM# 1144 **Weight:** 16.6666 g. **Composition:** 0.9000 Gold .4823 oz. AGW **Ruler:** Yung Hi (Sunjong)

| Date | Mintage | F | VF | XF | Unc | BU |
|---|---|---|---|---|---|---|
| 2(1908) Rare | — | — | — | — | — | — |
| 3(1909) Two known | — | — | — | — | — | — |

**Note:** Reported mintages for Year 2 (1908) of 40,000 and Year 3 (1909) of 25,000 exist, but few are know today

## PATTERNS

Including off metal strikes

| KM# | Date | Mintage | Identification | Mkt Val |
|---|---|---|---|---|
| Pn33 | 5 | — | 5 Won. Copper. | — |
| Pn34 | 5 | — | 10 Won. Copper. | — |
| Pn35 | 6 | — | 20 Won. Copper. | — |
| Pn36 | 6 | — | 20 Won. Copper. | — |
| Pn37 | 7 | — | 5 Won. Copper. | — |
| Pn38 | 7 | — | 5 Won. Copper. | — |

# KOREA-NORTH

The Democratic Peoples Republic of Korea, situated in northeastern Asia on the northern half of the Korean peninsula between the Peoples Republic of China and the Republic of Korea, has an area of 46,540 sq. mi. (120,540 sq. km.) and a population of 20 million. Capital: Pyongyang. The economy is based on heavy industry and agriculture. Metals, minerals and farm produce are exported.

Japan replaced China as the predominant foreign influence in Korea in 1895 and annexed the peninsular country in 1910. Defeat in World War II brought an end to Japanese rule. U.S. troops entered Korea from the south and Soviet forces entered from the north. The Cairo conference (1943) had established that Korea should be *free and independent*. The Potsdam conference (1945) set the 38th parallel as the line dividing the occupation forces of the United States and Russia. When Russia refused to permit a U.N. commission designated to supervise reunification elections to enter North Korea, an election was held in South Korea which established the Republic of Korea on Aug. 15,1948. North Korea held an unsupervised election on Aug. 25, 1948, and on Sept. 9, 1948, proclaimed the establishment of the Democratic Peoples Republic of Korea.

**NOTE:** For earlier coinage see Korea.

**MONETARY SYSTEM**

100 Chon = 1 Won

**CIRCULATION RESTRICTIONS**

W/o star:KM#1-4 - General circulation
1 star:KM#5-8 - Issued to visitors from Communist countries.
2 stars:KM#9-12 - Issued to visitors from hard currency countries.

# PEOPLES REPUBLIC

## DECIMAL COINAGE

**CHON** KM# 1 **Composition:** Aluminum

| Date | Mintage | F | VF | XF | Unc | BU |
|---|---|---|---|---|---|---|
| 1959 | — | 0.15 | 0.25 | 0.50 | 1.00 | — |
| 1970 | — | 0.20 | 0.35 | 0.75 | 1.50 | — |

**CHON** KM# 5 **Composition:** Aluminum **Reverse:** Stars in field

| Date | Mintage | F | VF | XF | Unc | BU |
|---|---|---|---|---|---|---|
| 1959 | — | — | — | 0.50 | 1.00 | — |

**CHON** KM# 9 **Composition:** Aluminum **Reverse:** Star left of 1

| Date | Mintage | F | VF | XF | Unc | BU |
|---|---|---|---|---|---|---|
| 1959 | — | — | — | 0.50 | 1.00 | — |

**5 CHON** KM# 2 **Composition:** Aluminum

| Date | Mintage | F | VF | XF | Unc | BU |
|---|---|---|---|---|---|---|
| 1959 | — | 0.50 | 0.75 | 1.00 | 2.00 | — |
| 1974 | — | 0.25 | 0.50 | 1.00 | 2.00 | — |

**5 CHON** KM# 6 **Composition:** Aluminum **Reverse:** Stars in field

| Date | Mintage | F | VF | XF | Unc | BU |
|---|---|---|---|---|---|---|
| 1974 | — | — | — | 1.00 | 2.00 | — |

**5 CHON** KM# 10 **Composition:** Aluminum **Reverse:** Star left of 5

| Date | Mintage | F | VF | XF | Unc | BU |
|---|---|---|---|---|---|---|
| 1974 | — | — | — | 1.00 | 2.00 | — |

**10 CHON** KM# 3 **Composition:** Aluminum

| Date | Mintage | F | VF | XF | Unc | BU |
|---|---|---|---|---|---|---|
| 1959 | — | 0.50 | 0.75 | 1.00 | 2.00 | — |

**10 CHON** KM# 7 **Composition:** Aluminum **Reverse:** Stars in field

| Date | Mintage | F | VF | XF | Unc | BU |
|---|---|---|---|---|---|---|
| 1959 | — | — | — | 1.00 | 2.00 | — |

**10 CHON** KM# 11 **Composition:** Aluminum **Reverse:** Star left of 10

| Date | Mintage | F | VF | XF | Unc | BU |
|---|---|---|---|---|---|---|
| 1959 | — | — | — | 1.00 | 2.00 | — |

**50 CHON** KM# 4 **Composition:** Aluminum

| Date | Mintage | F | VF | XF | Unc | BU |
|---|---|---|---|---|---|---|
| 1978 | — | 0.75 | 1.00 | 1.75 | 3.00 | — |

**50 CHON** KM# 8 **Composition:** Aluminum **Reverse:** Stars in field

| Date | Mintage | F | VF | XF | Unc | BU |
|---|---|---|---|---|---|---|
| 1978 | — | — | — | 1.75 | 3.00 | — |

**50 CHON** KM# 12 **Composition:** Aluminum **Reverse:** Star behind rider

| Date | Mintage | F | VF | XF | Unc | BU |
|---|---|---|---|---|---|---|
| 1978 | — | — | — | 1.75 | 3.00 | — |

**WON** KM# 13 **Composition:** Copper-Nickel **Reverse:** Kim Il Sung's birthplace

| Date | Mintage | F | VF | XF | Unc | BU |
|---|---|---|---|---|---|---|
| 1987 | — | — | — | — | 4.00 | — |
| 1987 Proof | — | Value: 5.00 | | | | |

**WON** KM# 18 **Composition:** Aluminum

| Date | Mintage | F | VF | XF | Unc | BU |
|---|---|---|---|---|---|---|
| 1987 | — | — | — | — | 3.50 | — |

**WON** KM# 14 **Composition:** Copper-Nickel **Reverse:** Kim Il Sung's Arch of Triumph

| Date | Mintage | F | VF | XF | Unc | BU |
|---|---|---|---|---|---|---|
| 1987 | — | — | — | — | 4.00 | — |
| 1987 Proof | — | Value: 5.00 | | | | |

**WON** KM# 15 **Composition:** Copper-Nickel **Reverse:** Kim Il Sung's Tower of Juche

| Date | Mintage | F | VF | XF | Unc | BU |
|---|---|---|---|---|---|---|
| 1987 | — | — | — | — | 4.00 | — |
| 1987 Proof | — | Value: 5.00 | | | | |

**WON** KM# 126 **Composition:** Copper-Nickel **Subject:** Hyonmu **Obverse:** State arms **Reverse:** Mythical creature **Edge:** Reeded **Size:** 32 mm.

| Date | Mintage | F | VF | XF | Unc | BU |
|---|---|---|---|---|---|---|
| 2000 | — | — | — | — | 4.00 | — |

**WON** KM# 127 **Composition:** Copper-Nickel **Subject:** Blue Dragon **Obverse:** State arms **Reverse:** Dragon over mountains **Edge:** Reeded **Size:** 36 mm.

| Date | Mintage | F | VF | XF | Unc | BU |
|---|---|---|---|---|---|---|
| 2000 | — | — | — | — | 4.00 | — |

**WON** KM# 128 **Weight:** 22.0000 g. **Composition:** Copper-Nickel **Subject:** Tiger **Obverse:** Tiger in mountains **Reverse:** Tiger head **Edge:** Plain **Size:** 40 mm.

| Date | Mintage | F | VF | XF | Unc | BU |
|---|---|---|---|---|---|---|
| ND(1998) Proof | 5,000 | — | — | — | 10.00 | — |

**5 WON** KM# 22 **Composition:** Copper-Nickel **Reverse:** Kim Il Sung's Arch of Triumph

| Date | Mintage | F | VF | XF | Unc | BU |
|---|---|---|---|---|---|---|
| 1987 | — | — | — | — | 5.50 | — |
| 1987 Proof | — | Value: 7.50 | | | | |

**5 WON** KM# 23 **Composition:** Copper-Nickel **Reverse:** Kim Il Sung's Tower of Juche

| Date | Mintage | F | VF | XF | Unc | BU |
|---|---|---|---|---|---|---|
| 1987 | — | — | — | — | 5.50 | — |
| 1987 Proof | — | Value: 7.50 | | | | |

**5 WON** KM# 25 **Composition:** Copper-Nickel **Reverse:** Kim Il Sung's birthplace

| Date | Mintage | F | VF | XF | Unc | BU |
|---|---|---|---|---|---|---|
| 1987 | — | — | — | — | 5.50 | — |
| 1987 Proof | — | Value: 7.50 | | | | |

**5 WON** KM# 19 **Composition:** Copper-Nickel **Subject:** World Festival of Youth and Students

| Date | Mintage | F | VF | XF | Unc | BU |
|---|---|---|---|---|---|---|
| 1989 | — | — | — | — | 5.50 | — |
| 1989 Proof | — | Value: 7.50 | | | | |

**5 WON** KM# 92 **Weight:** 12.0000 g. **Composition:** 0.9990 Silver .3854 oz. ASW **Subject:** 50th anniversary of liberation **Reverse:** Teapot in bowl

| Date | Mintage | F | VF | XF | Unc | BU |
|---|---|---|---|---|---|---|
| 1995 In proof sets only | 300 | Value: 40.00 | | | | |

**5 WON** KM# 129 **Weight:** 13.0000 g. **Composition:** Copper Nickel **Subject:** 10th Singapore International Coin Show **Obverse:** State arms. **Reverse:** Multicolor logo. **Edge:** Plain.

| Date | Mintage | F | VF | XF | Unc | BU |
|---|---|---|---|---|---|---|
| 1996 | 1,000 | — | — | — | 10.00 | — |

**5 WON** KM# 130 **Weight:** 27.0000 g. **Composition:** 0.9990 Silver .8672 oz. ASW **Subject:** Kaesong - Sinuiju Railroad **Obverse:** State arms. **Reverse:** Multicolor train. **Edge:** Plain. **Size:** 35 mm.

| Date | Mintage | F | VF | XF | Unc | BU |
|---|---|---|---|---|---|---|
| 1996 | 2,000 | — | — | — | 30.00 | — |

**5 WON** **KM# 131** **Weight:** 27.0000 g. **Composition:** 0.9990 Silver .8672 oz. ASW **Subject:** 1st Beijing International Coin Show **Obverse:** State arms. **Reverse:** Multicolor panda holding logo. **Edge:** Plain. **Size:** 35 mm.

| Date | Mintage | F | VF | XF | Unc | BU |
|---|---|---|---|---|---|---|
| 1996 | 6,000 | — | — | — | 25.00 | — |

**5 WON** **KM# 132** **Weight:** 27.0000 g. **Composition:** 0.9990 Silver .8672 oz. ASW **Subject:** 11th Singapore International Coin Show **Obverse:** State arms. **Reverse:** Multicolor panda holding logo. **Edge:** Plain. **Size:** 35 mm.

| Date | Mintage | F | VF | XF | Unc | BU |
|---|---|---|---|---|---|---|
| 1997 | 1,000 | — | — | — | 25.00 | — |

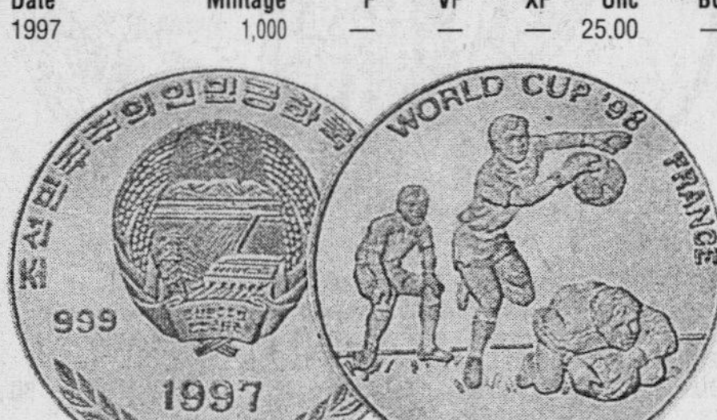


**5 WON** **KM# 133** **Weight:** 27.0000 g. **Composition:** 0.9990 Silver .8672 oz. ASW **Subject:** World Cup Soccer **Obverse:** State arms. **Reverse:** Soccer Players **Edge:** Plain. **Size:** 35 mm.

| Date | Mintage | F | VF | XF | Unc | BU |
|---|---|---|---|---|---|---|
| 1997 | 3,000 | — | — | — | 25.00 | — |

**5 WON** **KM# 100** **Weight:** 26.9400 g. **Composition:** 0.9990 Silver .8644 oz. ASW **Subject:** Olympics **Obverse:** 2 speed skaters

| Date | Mintage | F | VF | XF | Unc | BU |
|---|---|---|---|---|---|---|
| 1997 Proof | 3,000 | Value: 25.00 | | | | |

**5 WON** **KM# 123** **Weight:** 20.0000 g. **Composition:** 0.9990 Silver .6424 oz. ASW **Subject:** History of Seafaring **Obverse:** State arms **Reverse:** Sailing Junk **Edge:** Reeded and plain sections **Size:** 34.3 mm.

| Date | Mintage | F | VF | XF | Unc | BU |
|---|---|---|---|---|---|---|
| 1999 Proof | 5,000 | Value: 30.00 | | | | |

**10 WON** **KM# 65** **Composition:** Copper-Nickel **Subject:** 80th birthday - Kim Il Sung **Reverse:** Kim Il Sung birthplace **Note:** Similar to 50 Won, KM#52.

| Date | Mintage | F | VF | XF | Unc | BU |
|---|---|---|---|---|---|---|
| 1992 | — | — | — | — | 6.00 | — |

**10 WON** **KM# 66** **Composition:** Copper-Nickel **Subject:** 50th birthday - Kim Il Jong **Reverse:** Portrait **Note:** Similar to 50 Won, KM#56.

| Date | Mintage | F | VF | XF | Unc | BU |
|---|---|---|---|---|---|---|
| 1992 | — | — | — | — | 6.00 | — |

**10 WON** **KM# 73** **Composition:** Copper-Nickel **Subject:** 80th birthday - Kim Il Sung **Reverse:** Portrait **Note:** Similar to 50 Won, KM#54.

| Date | Mintage | F | VF | XF | Unc | BU |
|---|---|---|---|---|---|---|
| 1992 | — | — | — | — | 6.00 | — |

**10 WON** **KM# 87** **Composition:** Copper-Nickel **Subject:** Sportsfest **Reverse:** Cartoonlike tiger

| Date | Mintage | F | VF | XF | Unc | BU |
|---|---|---|---|---|---|---|
| 1995 | — | — | — | — | 12.00 | — |

**10 WON** **KM# 87.2** **Weight:** 12.9000 g. **Composition:** Copper Nickel **Subject:** International Sport and Culture Festival **Obverse:** State arms. **Reverse:** Multicolor cartoon cat. **Edge:** Plain. **Size:** 30 mm.

| Date | Mintage | F | VF | XF | Unc | BU |
|---|---|---|---|---|---|---|
| 1995 | — | — | — | — | 6.00 | — |

**10 WON** **KM# 134.1 (KM134)** **Weight:** 12.9000 g. **Composition:** Copper Nickel **Subject:** International Sport and Culture Festival **Obverse:** State arms. **Reverse:** Festival logo. **Edge:** Plain. **Size:** 30 mm.

| Date | Mintage | F | VF | XF | Unc | BU |
|---|---|---|---|---|---|---|
| 1995 | — | — | — | — | 6.00 | — |

**10 WON** **KM# 134.2 (KM134.1)** **Weight:** 12.9000 g. **Composition:** Copper Nickel **Subject:** International Sport and Culture Festival **Obverse:** State arms. **Reverse:** Festival logo with pink flame. **Edge:** Plain. **Size:** 30 mm.

| Date | Mintage | F | VF | XF | Unc | BU |
|---|---|---|---|---|---|---|
| 1995 | — | — | — | — | 6.50 | — |

**10 WON** **KM# 93** **Weight:** 28.0000 g. **Composition:** Silver .8993 oz. ASW **Subject:** 50th anniversary of liberation **Reverse:** Taedong gatehouse

| Date | Mintage | F | VF | XF | Unc | BU |
|---|---|---|---|---|---|---|
| 1995 In proof sets only | 300 | — | — | — | 50.00 | — |

**10 WON** **KM# 105** **Weight:** 31.1035 g. **Composition:** 0.9990 Silver 1 oz. ASW **Subject:** Fauna of Asia - ducks **Obverse:** National arms **Reverse:** Multicolored pair of Mandarin ducks

| Date | Mintage | F | VF | XF | Unc | BU |
|---|---|---|---|---|---|---|
| 1996 Proof | 1,000 | Value: 45.00 | | | | |

**10 WON** **KM# 135** **Weight:** 31.1035 g. **Composition:** 0.9990 Silver 1.0000 oz. ASW **Subject:** Korean Workers' Party **Obverse:** State arms. **Reverse:** Flag and setting sun. **Edge:** Plain. **Size:** 40 mm.

| Date | Mintage | F | VF | XF | Unc | BU |
|---|---|---|---|---|---|---|
| 1996 | 1,000 | — | — | — | 35.00 | — |

**10 WON** **KM# 115** **Weight:** 30.9600 g. **Composition:** 0.9990 Silver .9944 oz. ASW **Subject:** Fauna of Asia **Obverse:** National arms **Reverse:** Multicolored, enameled parrot

| Date | Mintage | F | VF | XF | Unc | BU |
|---|---|---|---|---|---|---|
| 1996 Proof | 1,000 | Value: 75.00 | | | | |

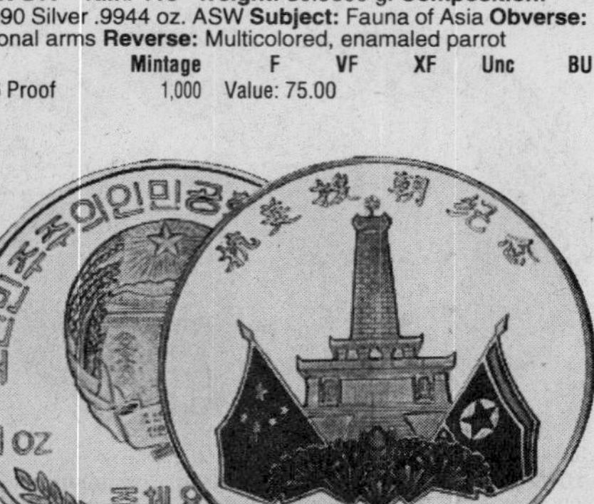

**10 WON** **KM# 120** **Weight:** 30.9600 g. **Composition:** 0.9990 Silver .9944 oz. ASW **Subject:** Korean War **Obverse:** State arms **Reverse:** Multicolored, enameled flags before monument **Edge:** Reeded and plain sections **Size:** 38.6 mm.

| Date | Mintage | F | VF | XF | Unc | BU |
|---|---|---|---|---|---|---|
| 1997 Proof | 20,000 | Value: 35.00 | | | | |

**10 WON** **KM# 124** **Weight:** 30.9500 g. **Composition:** 0.9990 Silver .9940 oz. ASW **Subject:** World of Adventure **Obverse:** State arms **Reverse:** Multicolor sailing scene **Edge:** Segmented reeding **Size:** 40.3 mm.

| Date | Mintage | F | VF | XF | Unc | BU |
|---|---|---|---|---|---|---|
| 1997 Proof | — | Value: 50.00 | | | | |

**10 WON** **KM# 136** **Weight:** 31.1035 g. **Composition:** 0.9990 Silver 1.0000 oz. ASW **Subject:** Chou En Lai Centennial of Birth **Obverse:** State arms. **Reverse:** Chou's portrait. **Edge:** Plain. **Size:** 40 mm.

| Date | Mintage | F | VF | XF | Unc | BU |
|---|---|---|---|---|---|---|
| 1997 | 8,000 | — | — | — | 45.00 | — |

**10 WON** **KM# 137** **Weight:** 31.1035 g. **Composition:** 0.9990 Silver 1.0000 oz. ASW **Subject:** Chinese National Flower **Obverse:** State arms. **Reverse:** Multicolor flower. **Edge:** Plain. **Size:** 40 mm.

| Date | Mintage | F | VF | XF | Unc | BU |
|---|---|---|---|---|---|---|
| 1997 | 8,000 | — | — | — | 10,000 | — |

**10 WON** **KM# 138** **Weight:** 31.1035 g. **Composition:** 0.9990 Silver 1.0000 oz. ASW **Subject:** Giant Panda **Obverse:** State arms. **Reverse:** Multicolor seated panda. **Edge:** Plain. **Size:** 40 mm.

| Date | Mintage | F | VF | XF | Unc | BU |
|---|---|---|---|---|---|---|
| 1997 | 10,000 | — | — | — | 45.00 | — |

**10 WON** **KM# 98** **Weight:** 31.0000 g. **Composition:** 0.9990 Silver .9957 oz. ASW **Subject:** Return of Hong Kong to China **Reverse:** Temple of Heaven above Hong Kong city view

| Date | Mintage | F | VF | XF | Unc | BU |
|---|---|---|---|---|---|---|
| 1997 Proof | 2,000 | Value: 60.00 | | | | |

**10 WON** **KM# 99** **Weight:** 31.0000 g. **Composition:** 0.9990 Silver .9957 oz. ASW **Subject:** Ginseng **Obverse:** State emblem **Reverse:** Enameled ginseng plant including root, leaves, berries

| Date | Mintage | F | VF | XF | Unc | BU |
|---|---|---|---|---|---|---|
| 1997 Proof | 2,000 | Value: 40.00 | | | | |

**10 WON** **KM# 121** **Weight:** 30.9600 g. **Composition:** 0.9990 Silver .9944 oz. ASW **Subject:** Korean War **Obverse:** State arms **Reverse:** Soldier watching bridge bombardment **Edge:** Reeded and plain sections **Size:** 40.3 mm.

| Date | Mintage | F | VF | XF | Unc | BU |
|---|---|---|---|---|---|---|
| 1997 Proof | 20,000 | Value: 35.00 | | | | |

**10 WON** **KM# 101** **Weight:** 30.8800 g. **Composition:** 0.9990 Silver .9918 oz. ASW **Subject:** Shanghai Coin Show **Reverse:** 2 pandas eating bamboo **Note:** Multicolored enamel.

| Date | Mintage | F | VF | XF | Unc | BU |
|---|---|---|---|---|---|---|
| 1997 Proof | 20,000 | Value: 40.00 | | | | |

**10 WON** KM# 102 **Weight:** 30.8800 g. **Composition:** 0.9990 Silver .9918 oz. ASW **Subject:** Year of the Tiger **Reverse:** Tiger on mountain ledge

| Date | Mintage | F | VF | XF | Unc | BU |
|---|---|---|---|---|---|---|
| ND(1998) Proof | 2,000 | Value: 37.50 | | | | |

**10 WON** KM# 110 **Weight:** 30.8800 g. **Composition:** 0.9990 Silver .9918 oz. ASW **Subject:** Korean Folk IV **Obverse:** National arms **Reverse:** Girl on swing

| Date | Mintage | F | VF | XF | Unc | BU |
|---|---|---|---|---|---|---|
| 1998 Proof | 2,000 | Value: 35.00 | | | | |

**10 WON** KM# 111 **Weight:** 30.8800 g. **Composition:** 0.9990 Silver .9918 oz. ASW **Subject:** Korean Folk I **Obverse:** National arms **Reverse:** Two children flying a kite

| Date | Mintage | F | VF | XF | Unc | BU |
|---|---|---|---|---|---|---|
| 1998 Proof | 2,000 | Value: 35.00 | | | | |

**10 WON** KM# 112 **Weight:** 30.8800 g. **Composition:** 0.9990 Silver .9918 oz. ASW **Subject:** Korean Folk II **Obverse:** National arms **Reverse:** Two girls seesawing

| Date | Mintage | F | VF | XF | Unc | BU |
|---|---|---|---|---|---|---|
| 1998 Proof | 2,000 | Value: 35.00 | | | | |

**10 WON** KM# 113 **Weight:** 30.8800 g. **Composition:** 0.9990 Silver .9918 oz. ASW **Subject:** Korean Folk III **Obverse:** National arms **Reverse:** Wrestling

| Date | Mintage | F | VF | XF | Unc | BU |
|---|---|---|---|---|---|---|
| 1998 Proof | 2,000 | Value: 35.00 | | | | |

**10 WON** KM# 114 **Weight:** 30.8800 g. **Composition:** 0.9990 Silver .9918 oz. ASW **Subject:** Korean Folk V **Obverse:** National arms **Reverse:** Three girls jumping rope

| Date | Mintage | F | VF | XF | Unc | BU |
|---|---|---|---|---|---|---|
| 1998 Proof | 2,000 | Value: 35.00 | | | | |

**10 WON** KM# 103 **Weight:** 30.9600 g. **Composition:** 0.9990 Silver .9944 oz. ASW **Subject:** Year of the Rabbitt **Obverse:** National arms **Reverse:** Multicolored rabbit with hearts

| Date | Mintage | F | VF | XF | Unc | BU |
|---|---|---|---|---|---|---|
| 1999 Proof | 5,000 | Value: 40.00 | | | | |

**10 WON** KM# 107 **Weight:** 30.9600 g. **Composition:** 0.9990 Silver .9944 oz. ASW **Subject:** Year of the Rabbitt **Obverse:** National arms **Reverse:** Multicolored rabbits with hearts; same as KM#103 but without legend at top

| Date | Mintage | F | VF | XF | Unc | BU |
|---|---|---|---|---|---|---|
| 1999 Proof | 5,000 | Value: 35.00 | | | | |

**10 WON** KM# 108 **Weight:** 30.9600 g. **Composition:** 0.9990 Silver .9944 oz. ASW **Subject:** Blue dragon **Obverse:** National arms **Reverse:** Dragon flying right over mountains

| Date | Mintage | F | VF | XF | Unc | BU |
|---|---|---|---|---|---|---|
| 1999 Proof | 5,000 | Value: 40.00 | | | | |

**10 WON** KM# 109 **Weight:** 30.9600 g. **Composition:** 0.9990 Silver .9944 oz. ASW **Subject:** Birds of Korea **Obverse:** National arms **Reverse:** Woodpecker on tree limb

| Date | Mintage | F | VF | XF | Unc | BU |
|---|---|---|---|---|---|---|
| 1999 Proof | 3,000 | Value: 40.00 | | | | |

**10 WON** KM# 125 **Weight:** 30.9500 g. **Composition:** 0.9990 Silver .9940 oz. ASW **Subject:** One Korea: 3,000 Years of History **Obverse:** State arms **Reverse:** Radiant map and landmarks **Edge:** Segmented reeding **Size:** 40.3 mm.

| Date | Mintage | F | VF | XF | Unc | BU |
|---|---|---|---|---|---|---|
| 2000 Proof | — | Value: 50.00 | | | | |

**10 WON** KM# 152 **Weight:** 31.0000 g. **Composition:** 0.9990 Silver .9957 oz. ASW **Subject:** Asian Money Fair **Obverse:** State arms. **Reverse:** Two snakes. **Edge:** Reeded and plain sections. **Size:** 39.8 mm.

| Date | Mintage | F | VF | XF | Unc | BU |
|---|---|---|---|---|---|---|
| 2001 Proof | — | Value: 45.00 | | | | |

**10 WON** KM# 153 **Weight:** 31.0000 g. **Composition:** 0.9990 Silver .9957 oz. ASW **Subject:** Tortoise-Serpent **Obverse:** State arms. **Reverse:** Mythical creature. **Edge:** Reeded and plain sections. **Size:** 39.8 mm.

| Date | Mintage | F | VF | XF | Unc | BU |
|---|---|---|---|---|---|---|
| 2001 Proof | — | Value: 45.00 | | | | |

**20 WON** KM# 20 **Weight:** 14.8000 g. **Composition:** 0.9990 Silver .4758 oz. ASW **Subject:** World Festival of Youth and Students

| Date | Mintage | F | VF | XF | Unc | BU |
|---|---|---|---|---|---|---|
| 1989 Proof | — | Value: 25.00 | | | | |

**20 WON** KM# 97 **Weight:** 31.1035 g. **Composition:** 0.9990 Silver 1 oz. ASW **Subject:** Kim Il Sung's death **Obverse:** State emblem **Edge:** Plain.

| Date | Mintage | F | VF | XF | Unc | BU |
|---|---|---|---|---|---|---|
| ND(1994) Proof | 5,000 | Value: 85.00 | | | | |

**20 WON** KM# 74 **Composition:** Copper-Nickel **Subject:** 1998 World Cup Soccer

| Date | Mintage | F | VF | XF | Unc | BU |
|---|---|---|---|---|---|---|
| 1995 Proof | 10,000 | Value: 25.00 | | | | |

**20 WON** KM# 139 **Weight:** 31.1035 g. **Composition:** 0.9990 Silver 1.0000 oz. ASW **Subject:** 50th Anniversary - Korean Workers' Party **Obverse:** State arms. **Reverse:** Monument. **Edge:** Plain. **Size:** 40 mm.

| Date | Mintage | F | VF | XF | Unc | BU |
|---|---|---|---|---|---|---|
| 1995 | — | — | — | — | 35.00 | — |

**20 WON** KM# 94 **Weight:** 50.0000 g. **Composition:** 0.9990 Silver 1.6059 oz. ASW **Subject:** 50th anniversary of liberation **Reverse:** Fairy of Mount Kumgang **Shape:** 50 **Note:** Illustration reduced.

| Date | Mintage | F | VF | XF | Unc | BU |
|---|---|---|---|---|---|---|
| 1995 In proof sets only | 300 | Value: 100 | | | | |

**20 WON** KM# 140 **Weight:** 22.0000 g. **Composition:** Copper Nickel **Subject:** 25th Basel International Coin Show **Obverse:** State arms above phone fax and telex numbers. **Reverse:** Multicolor island and sea scape. **Edge:** Plain. **Size:** 40 mm.

| Date | Mintage | F | VF | XF | Unc | BU |
|---|---|---|---|---|---|---|
| 1996 | 1,000 | — | — | — | 10.00 | — |

**30 WON** KM# 26 **Weight:** 17.0200 g. **Composition:** 0.9990 Silver .5472 oz. ASW **Subject:** Friendship Art Festival

| Date | Mintage | F | VF | XF | Unc | BU |
|---|---|---|---|---|---|---|
| 1989 Proof | — | Value: 35.00 | | | | |

**50 WON** KM# 52 **Weight:** 17.0200 g. **Composition:** 0.9990 Silver .5466 oz. ASW **Subject:** 80th birthday of Kim Il Sung **Reverse:** Kim Il Sung birthplace

| Date | Mintage | F | VF | XF | Unc | BU |
|---|---|---|---|---|---|---|
| 1992 Proof | 1,000 | Value: 40.00 | | | | |

**50 WON** **KM# 54** **Weight:** 17.0200 g. **Composition:** 0.9990 Silver .5466 oz. ASW **Subject:** 80th birthday of Kim Il Sung **Reverse:** Kim Il Sung portrait

| Date | Mintage | F | VF | XF | Unc | BU |
|---|---|---|---|---|---|---|
| 1992 Proof | 1,000 | Value: 45.00 | | | | |

**50 WON** **KM# 56** **Weight:** 17.0200 g. **Composition:** 0.9990 Silver .5466 oz. ASW **Subject:** 50th birthday of Kim Jong Il **Reverse:** Kim Jong Il portrait

| Date | Mintage | F | VF | XF | Unc | BU |
|---|---|---|---|---|---|---|
| 1992 Proof | 5,000 | Value: 45.00 | | | | |

**50 WON** **KM# 88** **Composition:** Copper-Nickel **Subject:** Sportsfest **Reverse:** Wrestlers

| Date | Mintage | F | VF | XF | Unc | BU |
|---|---|---|---|---|---|---|
| 1995 | — | — | — | — | 20.00 | — |

**50 WON** **KM# 141** **Weight:** 12.9000 g. **Composition:** Copper Nickel **Subject:** International Friendship Exhibition **Obverse:** State arms. **Reverse:** Building. **Edge:** Plain. **Size:** 30 mm.

| Date | Mintage | F | VF | XF | Unc | BU |
|---|---|---|---|---|---|---|
| 1995 | — | — | — | — | 7.50 | — |

**50 WON** **KM# 142** **Weight:** 12.9000 g. **Composition:** Copper Nickel **Subject:** May Day Stadium **Obverse:** State arms. **Reverse:** Stadium. **Edge:** Plain. **Size:** 30 mm.

| Date | Mintage | F | VF | XF | Unc | BU |
|---|---|---|---|---|---|---|
| 1995 | — | — | — | — | 7.50 | — |

**100 WON** **KM# 28** **Weight:** 3.1300 g. **Composition:** 0.9990 Gold .1 oz. AGW **Subject:** 40th anniversary of People's Republic

| Date | Mintage | F | VF | XF | Unc | BU |
|---|---|---|---|---|---|---|
| 1988 Proof | — | Value: 75.00 | | | | |

**100 WON** **KM# 70** **Weight:** 7.0000 g. **Composition:** 0.9990 Silver .2248 oz. ASW **Reverse:** 2 adelle penguins, enameled

| Date | Mintage | F | VF | XF | Unc | BU |
|---|---|---|---|---|---|---|
| 1995 Proof | — | Value: 32.00 | | | | |

**100 WON** **KM# 71** **Weight:** 7.0000 g. **Composition:** 0.9990 Silver .2250 oz. ASW **Subject:** 1996 Olympics **Reverse:** Sprinter

| Date | Mintage | F | VF | XF | Unc | BU |
|---|---|---|---|---|---|---|
| 1995 Proof | 30,000 | Value: 20.00 | | | | |

**100 WON** **KM# 72** **Weight:** 7.0000 g. **Composition:** 0.9990 Silver .2250 oz. ASW **Subject:** 1998 World Cup Soccer

| Date | Mintage | F | VF | XF | Unc | BU |
|---|---|---|---|---|---|---|
| 1995 Proof | 30,000 | Value: 20.00 | | | | |

**100 WON** **KM# 104** **Weight:** 7.0000 g. **Composition:** 0.9990 Silver .2250 oz. ASW **Subject:** Aix Galericulata **Obverse:** National arms **Reverse:** Multicolored pair of ducks

| Date | Mintage | F | VF | XF | Unc | BU |
|---|---|---|---|---|---|---|
| 1995 Proof | Est. 30,000 | Value: 30.00 | | | | |

**100 WON** **KM# 122** **Weight:** 7.0000 g. **Composition:** 0.9990 Silver .2248 oz. ASW **Subject:** Robinson Crusoe **Obverse:** State arms **Reverse:** Multicolor row boat scene **Edge:** Plain **Size:** 30 mm.

| Date | Mintage | F | VF | XF | Unc | BU |
|---|---|---|---|---|---|---|
| 1996 Proof | — | Value: 30.00 | | | | |

**200 WON** **KM# 49** **Weight:** 14.9700 g. **Composition:** 0.9990 Silver .5 oz. ASW **Subject:** Olympics **Obverse:** Silver content statement divided by emblem **Reverse:** Equestrian

| Date | Mintage | F | VF | XF | Unc | BU |
|---|---|---|---|---|---|---|
| 1991 Proof | 25,000 | Value: 25.00 | | | | |

**200 WON** **KM# 50** **Weight:** 14.9700 g. **Composition:** 0.9990 Silver .5 oz. ASW **Subject:** Olympics **Obverse:** Silver content statement below emblem **Reverse:** Equestrian

| Date | Mintage | F | VF | XF | Unc | BU |
|---|---|---|---|---|---|---|
| 1991 Proof | Inc. above | Value: 22.50 | | | | |

**200 WON** **KM# 64** **Weight:** 15.0000 g. **Composition:** 0.9990 Silver .481 oz. ASW **Subject:** 1992 Olympics **Reverse:** Runner

| Date | Mintage | F | VF | XF | Unc | BU |
|---|---|---|---|---|---|---|
| 1992 Proof | 25,000 | Value: 20.00 | | | | |

**200 WON** **KM# 95** **Weight:** 8.0000 g. **Composition:** Gold .2569 oz. AGW **Subject:** 50th anniversary of liberation **Reverse:** Turtle ship

| Date | Mintage | F | VF | XF | Unc | BU |
|---|---|---|---|---|---|---|
| 1995 In proof sets only | 300 | Value: 420 | | | | |

**250 WON** **KM# 29** **Weight:** 7.7800 g. **Composition:** 0.9990 Gold .25 oz. AGW **Subject:** 40th anniversary of People's Republic

| Date | Mintage | F | VF | XF | Unc | BU |
|---|---|---|---|---|---|---|
| 1988 Proof | — | Value: 175 | | | | |

**250 WON** **KM# 21** **Weight:** 7.7700 g. **Composition:** 0.9990 Gold .25 oz. AGW **Subject:** World Festival of Youth and Students

| Date | Mintage | F | VF | XF | Unc | BU |
|---|---|---|---|---|---|---|
| 1989 Proof | — | Value: 275 | | | | |

**250 WON** **KM# 116** **Weight:** 20.0000 g. **Composition:** 0.9990 Silver .6464 oz. ASW **Subject:** Millennium **Reverse:** Dragon

| Date | Mintage | F | VF | XF | Unc | BU |
|---|---|---|---|---|---|---|
| 1998//2000 Proof | — | Value: 35.00 | | | | |

**400 WON** **KM# 96** **Weight:** 16.0000 g. **Composition:** Gold .5138 oz. AGW **Subject:** 50th anniversary of liberation **Reverse:** Lake on Mount Baektu

| Date | Mintage | F | VF | XF | Unc | BU |
|---|---|---|---|---|---|---|
| 1995 In proof sets only | 100 | Value: 700 | | | | |

**500 WON** **KM# 39** **Weight:** 27.0000 g. **Composition:** 0.9990 Silver .8681 oz. ASW **Subject:** World Championship Soccer - Mexico '96

| Date | Mintage | F | VF | XF | Unc | BU |
|---|---|---|---|---|---|---|
| 1987 Proof | — | Value: 30.00 | | | | |

**500 WON** **KM# 16** **Weight:** 27.0000 g. **Composition:** 0.9990 Silver .8681 oz. ASW **Subject:** Winter Olympics **Reverse:** Hockey

| Date | Mintage | F | VF | XF | Unc | BU |
|---|---|---|---|---|---|---|
| 1988 Proof | 20,000 | Value: 18.50 | | | | |

**500 WON** **KM# 17** **Weight:** 27.0000 g. **Composition:** 0.9990 Silver .8681 oz. ASW **Subject:** 30th anniversary of Gorch Fock

| Date | Mintage | F | VF | XF | Unc | BU |
|---|---|---|---|---|---|---|
| 1988 Proof | — | Value: 35.00 | | | | |

**500 WON** **KM# 24** **Weight:** 27.0000 g. **Composition:** 0.9990 Silver .8681 oz. ASW **Subject:** World Championship Soccer

| Date | Mintage | F | VF | XF | Unc | BU |
|---|---|---|---|---|---|---|
| 1988 Proof | — | Value: 25.00 | | | | |

**500 WON** **KM# 30** **Weight:** 15.5700 g. **Composition:** 0.9990 Gold .5 oz. AGW **Subject:** 40th anniversary of People's Republic

| Date | Mintage | F | VF | XF | Unc | BU |
|---|---|---|---|---|---|---|
| 1988 Proof | — | Value: 300 | | | | |

**500 WON** **KM# 36** **Weight:** 27.0000 g. **Composition:** 0.9990 Silver .8681 oz. ASW **Series:** F.A.O. **Subject:** Food for all

| Date | Mintage | F | VF | XF | Unc | BU |
|---|---|---|---|---|---|---|
| 1988 Proof | Est. 2,000 | Value: 50.00 | | | | |

**500 WON** **KM# 27** **Weight:** 27.0000 g. **Composition:** 0.9990 Silver .8681 oz. ASW **Subject:** Amerigo Vespucci

| Date | Mintage | F | VF | XF | Unc | BU |
|---|---|---|---|---|---|---|
| 1989 Proof | — | Value: 35.00 | | | | |

**500 WON** **KM# 32** **Weight:** 31.8200 g. **Composition:** 0.9990 Silver 1.0231 oz. ASW **Reverse:** Fairy of Mount Kumgang

| Date | Mintage | F | VF | XF | Unc | BU |
|---|---|---|---|---|---|---|
| 1989 Proof | 2,000 | Value: 50.00 | | | | |

**500 WON** **KM# 33** **Weight:** 27.0000 g. **Composition:** 0.9990 Silver .8682 oz. ASW **Subject:** Calgary Winter Olympics **Reverse:** Figure skater

| Date | Mintage | F | VF | XF | Unc | BU |
|---|---|---|---|---|---|---|
| 1989 Proof | — | Value: 30.00 | | | | |

**500 WON** **KM# 34** **Weight:** 27.0000 g. **Composition:** 0.9990 Silver .8682 oz. ASW **Subject:** Barcelona Summer Olympics **Reverse:** Discus thrower

| Date | Mintage | F | VF | XF | Unc | BU |
|---|---|---|---|---|---|---|
| 1989 Proof | — | Value: 30.00 | | | | |

**500 WON** **KM# 37** **Weight:** 27.0000 g. **Composition:** 0.9990 Silver .8682 oz. ASW **Subject:** World Championship Soccer **Obverse:** Similar to KM#33 **Reverse:** Player kicking ball

| Date | Mintage | F | VF | XF | Unc | BU |
|---|---|---|---|---|---|---|
| 1989 Proof | 15,000 | Value: 50.00 | | | | |

**500 WON** **KM# 38** **Weight:** 27.0000 g. **Composition:** 0.9990 Silver .8682 oz. ASW **Subject:** World Championship Soccer **Reverse:** Goalie

| Date | Mintage | F | VF | XF | Unc | BU |
|---|---|---|---|---|---|---|
| 1989 Proof | — | Value: 27.50 | | | | |

**500 WON** **KM# 40** **Weight:** 31.8200 g. **Composition:** 0.9990 Silver .8682 oz. ASW **Subject:** Olympic table tennis

| Date | Mintage | F | VF | XF | Unc | BU |
|---|---|---|---|---|---|---|
| 1990 Proof | 15,000 | Value: 27.50 | | | | |

**500 WON** **KM# 41** **Weight:** 31.8200 g. **Composition:** 0.9990 Silver .8682 oz. ASW **Subject:** Endangered wildlife **Reverse:** Storks

| Date | Mintage | F | VF | XF | Unc | BU |
|---|---|---|---|---|---|---|
| 1990 Proof | — | Value: 40.00 | | | | |

**500 WON** **KM# 44** **Weight:** 31.1000 g. **Composition:** 0.9990 Silver 1 oz. ASW **Subject:** World Championship Table Tennis **Reverse:** 2 male players

| Date | Mintage | F | VF | XF | Unc | BU |
|---|---|---|---|---|---|---|
| 1991 Proof | 5,000 | Value: 25.00 | | | | |

**500 WON** **KM# 45** **Weight:** 31.1000 g. **Composition:** 0.9990 Silver 1 oz. ASW **Subject:** World Championship Table Tennis **Reverse:** Male player

| Date | Mintage | F | VF | XF | Unc | BU |
|---|---|---|---|---|---|---|
| 1991 Proof | 5,000 | Value: 25.00 | | | | |

**500 WON** **KM# 46** **Weight:** 31.1000 g. **Composition:** 0.9990 Silver 1 oz. ASW **Subject:** World Championship Table Tennis **Reverse:** Female player

| Date | Mintage | F | VF | XF | Unc | BU |
|---|---|---|---|---|---|---|
| 1991 Proof | 5,000 | Value: 25.00 | | | | |

**500 WON** **KM# 47** **Weight:** 31.1000 g. **Composition:** 0.9990 Silver 1 oz. ASW **Subject:** World Championship Table Tennis **Reverse:** Korea unified team

| Date | Mintage | F | VF | XF | Unc | BU |
|---|---|---|---|---|---|---|
| 1991 Proof | 10,000 | Value: 22.50 | | | | |

**500 WON** **KM# 48** **Weight:** 27.0000 g. **Composition:** 0.9990 Silver .8682 oz. ASW **Subject:** First armoured ship

| Date | Mintage | F | VF | XF | Unc | BU |
|---|---|---|---|---|---|---|
| 1991 Proof | Est. 10,000 | Value: 50.00 | | | | |

**500 WON** **KM# 63** **Weight:** 27.0000 g. **Composition:** 0.9990 Silver .8682 oz. ASW **Subject:** Olympics **Reverse:** Women's volleyball

| Date | Mintage | F | VF | XF | Unc | BU |
|---|---|---|---|---|---|---|
| 1991 Proof | 15,000 | Value: 32.50 | | | | |

**500 WON** **KM# 59** **Weight:** 27.0000 g. **Composition:** 0.9990 Silver .8682 oz. ASW **Subject:** Environmental protection **Reverse:** Flowers

| Date | Mintage | F | VF | XF | Unc | BU |
|---|---|---|---|---|---|---|
| 1992 Proof | 1,000 | Value: 55.00 | | | | |

**500 WON** **KM# 144** **Weight:** 27.0000 g. **Composition:** 0.9990 Silver .8672 oz. ASW **Subject:** 1994 World Cup Soccer **Obverse:** State arms. **Reverse:** Three soccer players. **Edge:** Plain. **Size:** 35 mm.

| Date | Mintage | F | VF | XF | Unc | BU |
|---|---|---|---|---|---|---|
| 1992 | — | — | — | — | 30.00 | — |

**500 WON** **KM# 60** **Weight:** 27.0000 g. **Composition:** 0.9990 Silver .8682 oz. ASW **Subject:** 1994 Olympics **Reverse:** Speed skating

| Date | Mintage | F | VF | XF | Unc | BU |
|---|---|---|---|---|---|---|
| 1993 Proof | 1,000 | Value: 35.00 | | | | |

**500 WON** **KM# 61** **Weight:** 27.0000 g. **Composition:** 0.9990 Silver .8682 oz. ASW **Subject:** 1994 Olympics **Reverse:** 2-man bobsled

| Date | Mintage | F | VF | XF | Unc | BU |
|---|---|---|---|---|---|---|
| 1993 Proof | 1,000 | Value: 35.00 | | | | |

**500 WON** **KM# 62.1 (KM62)** **Weight:** 31.1035 g. **Composition:** 0.9990 Silver 1 oz. ASW **Subject:** Prehistoric animals **Obverse:** State arms **Reverse:** Brontosaurus **Edge:** Reeded **Size:** 40.3 mm.

| Date | Mintage | F | VF | XF | Unc | BU |
|---|---|---|---|---|---|---|
| 1993 Proof | — | Value: 45.00 | | | | |

**500 WON** **KM# 145** **Weight:** 31.1035 g. **Composition:** 0.9990 Silver 1.0000 oz. ASW **Subject:** 1994 World Cup Soccer **Obverse:** State arms. **Reverse:** Two players and trophy cup. **Edge:** Plain. **Size:** 40 mm.

| Date | Mintage | F | VF | XF | Unc | BU |
|---|---|---|---|---|---|---|
| 1994 | — | — | — | — | 35.00 | — |

**500 WON** **KM# 146** **Weight:** 17.0000 g. **Composition:** 0.9990 Silver .5460 oz. ASW **Subject:** F.A.O. 50 Years **Obverse:** State arms. **Reverse:** F.A.O. logo. **Edge:** Plain.

| Date | Mintage | F | VF | XF | Unc | BU |
|---|---|---|---|---|---|---|
| 1995 | — | — | — | — | 25.00 | — |

**500 WON** **KM# 143** **Weight:** 31.1035 g. **Composition:** 0.9990 Silver 1.0000 oz. ASW **Subject:** International Sport and Culture Festival **Obverse:** State arms. **Reverse:** Kim Il Jong portrait. **Edge:** Plain. **Size:** 40 mm.

| Date | Mintage | F | VF | XF | Unc | BU |
|---|---|---|---|---|---|---|
| 1995 | — | — | — | — | 35.00 | — |

**500 WON** **KM# 79** **Weight:** 31.1035 g. **Composition:** 0.9990 Silver 1 oz. ASW **Subject:** Fauna of Asia **Reverse:** Owl **Note:** Enameled.

| Date | Mintage | F | VF | XF | Unc | BU |
|---|---|---|---|---|---|---|
| 1995 Proof | 20,000 | Value: 42.50 | | | | |

**Note:**

**500 WON** **KM# 67** **Weight:** 31.1035 g. **Composition:** 0.9990 Silver 1 oz. ASW **Subject:** 1996 Atlanta Olympics **Reverse:** Relay racers

| Date | Mintage | F | VF | XF | Unc | BU |
|---|---|---|---|---|---|---|
| 1995 Proof | 10,0003,000 | Value: 32.50 | | | | |

**500 WON** **KM# 68** **Weight:** 31.1035 g. **Composition:** 0.9990 Silver 1 oz. ASW **Subject:** 1996 Atlanta Olympics **Reverse:** Equestrian

| Date | Mintage | F | VF | XF | Unc | BU |
|---|---|---|---|---|---|---|
| 1995 Proof | 10,0003,000 | Value: 32.50 | | | | |

**500 WON** **KM# 69** **Weight:** 31.1035 g. **Composition:** 0.9990 Silver 1 oz. ASW **Subject:** Fauna of Asia **Reverse:** Tiger **Note:** Enameled.

| Date | Mintage | F | VF | XF | Unc | BU |
|---|---|---|---|---|---|---|
| 1995 Proof | 20,000 | Value: 45.00 | | | | |

**500 WON** **KM# 75** **Weight:** 31.1035 g. **Composition:** 0.9990 Silver 1 oz. ASW **Subject:** 1998 World Cup Soccer

| Date | Mintage | F | VF | XF | Unc | BU |
|---|---|---|---|---|---|---|
| 1995 Proof | 10,000 | Value: 40.00 | | | | |

**500 WON** **KM# 76** **Weight:** 31.1035 g. **Composition:** 0.9990 Silver 1 oz. ASW **Subject:** Fauna of Asia **Reverse:** Panda **Note:** Enameled

| Date | Mintage | F | VF | XF | Unc | BU |
|---|---|---|---|---|---|---|
| 1995 Proof | 20,000 | Value: 37.50 | | | | |

**500 WON** **KM# 77** **Weight:** 31.1035 g. **Composition:** 0.9990 Silver 1 oz. ASW **Subject:** Fauna of Asia **Reverse:** Parrot **Note:** Enameled.

| Date | Mintage | F | VF | XF | Unc | BU |
|---|---|---|---|---|---|---|
| 1995 Proof | 20,000 | Value: 40.00 | | | | |

**500 WON** **KM# 78** **Weight:** 31.1035 g. **Composition:** 0.9990 Silver 1 oz. ASW **Subject:** Fauna of Asia **Reverse:** Eagle **Note:** Enameled.

| Date | Mintage | F | VF | XF | Unc | BU |
|---|---|---|---|---|---|---|
| 1995 Proof | 20,000 | Value: 40.00 | | | | |

**500 WON** **KM# 80** **Weight:** 31.1035 g. **Composition:** 0.9990 Silver 1 oz. ASW **Subject:** Fauna of Asia **Reverse:** 2 Mandarin ducks **Note:** Enameled.

| Date | Mintage | F | VF | XF | Unc | BU |
|---|---|---|---|---|---|---|
| 1995 | 20,000 | Value: 42.50 | | | | |

**500 WON** **KM# 154** **Weight:** 27.0000 g. **Composition:** 0.9990 Silver .8672 oz. ASW **Subject:** First Asian Gymnastic Championship **Obverse:** State arms. **Reverse:** Multicolor panda holding logo. **Edge:** Coarse and finely reeded sections. **Size:** 35.2 mm.

| Date | Mintage | F | VF | XF | Unc | BU |
|---|---|---|---|---|---|---|
| 1996 Proof | — | Value: 60.00 | | | | |

**500 WON** **KM# 89** **Weight:** 31.1035 g. **Composition:** 0.9990 Silver .9969 oz. ASW **Subject:** Olympics **Reverse:** 2 eurythmic gymansts

| Date | Mintage | F | VF | XF | Unc | BU |
|---|---|---|---|---|---|---|
| 1996 | 1,000 | — | — | — | 35.00 | — |

**500 WON** **KM# 90** **Weight:** 31.1035 g. **Composition:** 0.9990 Silver .9969 oz. ASW **Subject:** Olympics **Reverse:** Soccer

| Date | Mintage | F | VF | XF | Unc | BU |
|---|---|---|---|---|---|---|
| 1996 | 30,0001,000 | — | — | — | 42.50 | — |

**500 WON** **KM# 91** **Weight:** 31.1035 g. **Composition:** 0.9990 Silver .9969 oz. ASW **Subject:** Fauna of Asia **Reverse:** Multicolored holographic panda

| Date | Mintage | F | VF | XF | Unc | BU |
|---|---|---|---|---|---|---|
| 1996 Proof | 5,000 | Value: 55.00 | | | | |

**500 WON** **KM# 106** **Weight:** 31.5200 g. **Composition:** 0.9990 Silver 1.0124 oz. ASW **Subject:** Fauna of Asia **Obverse:** National emblem **Reverse:** Multicolored hologram of tiger

| Date | Mintage | F | VF | XF | Unc | BU |
|---|---|---|---|---|---|---|
| 1996 Proof | — | Value: 55.00 | | | | |

**500 WON** **KM# 117** **Weight:** 31.1035 g. **Composition:** 0.9990 Silver 1 oz. ASW **Subject:** Fauna of Asia **Obverse:** National emblem **Reverse:** Multicolored trichogaster leeri fish

| Date | Mintage | F | VF | XF | Unc | BU |
|---|---|---|---|---|---|---|
| 1996 Proof | — | Value: 55.00 | | | | |

**500 WON** **KM# 118** **Weight:** 31.1035 g. **Composition:** 0.9990 Silver 1 oz. ASW **Subject:** Fauna of Asia **Obverse:** National emblem **Reverse:** Multicolored botia macracanthus fish

| Date | Mintage | F | VF | XF | Unc | BU |
|---|---|---|---|---|---|---|
| 1996 Proof | — | Value: 55.00 | | | | |

**500 WON** **KM# 119** **Weight:** 31.1035 g. **Composition:** 0.9990 Silver 1 oz. ASW **Subject:** Fauna of Asia **Obverse:** National emblem **Reverse:** Multicolored long-tailed angelfish

| Date | Mintage | F | VF | XF | Unc | BU |
|---|---|---|---|---|---|---|
| 1996 Proof | — | Value: 55.00 | | | | |

**700 WON** **KM# 147** **Weight:** 31.1035 g. **Composition:** 0.9990 Gold 1.0000 oz. AGW **Subject:** Korean Workers' Party **Obverse:** State arms. **Reverse:** Flag and setting sun. **Edge:** Plain. **Size:** 35 mm.

| Date | Mintage | F | VF | XF | Unc | BU |
|---|---|---|---|---|---|---|
| 1996 | 100 | — | — | — | 750 | — |

**1000 WON** **KM# 31** **Weight:** 31.1300 g. **Composition:** 0.9990 Gold 1 oz. AGW **Subject:** 40th anniversary of People's Republic

| Date | Mintage | F | VF | XF | Unc | BU |
|---|---|---|---|---|---|---|
| 1988 Proof | — | Value: 575 | | | | |

**1000 WON** **KM# 148** **Weight:** 15.5500 g. **Composition:** 0.9990 Gold .4999 oz. AGW **Subject:** Death of Kim Il Sung **Obverse:** State arms. **Reverse:** Portrait. **Edge:** Plain. **Size:** 27 mm.

| Date | Mintage | F | VF | XF | Unc | BU |
|---|---|---|---|---|---|---|
| ND(1994) | — | — | — | — | 400 | — |

**1000 WON** **KM# 149** **Weight:** 31.1035 g. **Composition:** 0.9990 Gold 1.0000 oz. AGW **Subject:** 50th Anniversary - Korean Workers' Party **Obverse:** State arms. **Reverse:** Monument. **Edge:** Plain. **Size:** 35 mm.

| Date | Mintage | F | VF | XF | Unc | BU |
|---|---|---|---|---|---|---|
| 1995 | 1,000 | — | — | — | 600 | — |

**1500 WON** **KM# 58** **Weight:** 8.0000 g. **Composition:** 0.9990 Gold .2572 oz. AGW **Subject:** Olympics **Reverse:** Gymnast

| Date | Mintage | F | VF | XF | Unc | BU |
|---|---|---|---|---|---|---|
| 1990 Proof | Est. 3,000 | Value: 200 | | | | |

**1500 WON** **KM# 42** **Weight:** 15.5500 g. **Composition:** 0.9990 Gold .5 oz. AGW **Subject:** Inter-parliamentary Conference

| Date | Mintage | F | VF | XF | Unc | BU |
|---|---|---|---|---|---|---|
| 1991 Proof | 8001,000 | Value: 400 | | | | |

**1500 WON** **KM# 43** **Weight:** 15.5500 g. **Composition:** 0.9990 Gold .5 oz. AGW **Subject:** Inter-parliamentary Conference

| Date | Mintage | F | VF | XF | Unc | BU |
|---|---|---|---|---|---|---|
| 1991 Proof | 800 | Value: 400 | | | | |

**1500 WON** **KM# 51** **Weight:** 8.0000 g. **Composition:** 0.9990 Gold .2572 oz. AGW **Subject:** Soccer

| Date | Mintage | F | VF | XF | Unc | BU |
|---|---|---|---|---|---|---|
| 1991 Proof | 3,0001,000 | Value: 250 | | | | |

**1500 WON** **KM# 150** **Weight:** 8.0000 g. **Composition:** 0.9990 Gold .2569 oz. AGW **Subject:** Olympics **Obverse:** State arms. **Reverse:** Cyclists racing. **Edge:** Plain. **Size:** 22 mm.

| Date | Mintage | F | VF | XF | Unc | BU |
|---|---|---|---|---|---|---|
| 1993 | 1,000 | — | — | — | 300 | — |

**2000 WON** **KM# 53** **Weight:** 31.1000 g. **Composition:** 0.9990 Gold 1 oz. AGW **Subject:** 80th birthday of Kim Il Sung **Reverse:** Kim Il Sung birthplace

| Date | Mintage | F | VF | XF | Unc | BU |
|---|---|---|---|---|---|---|
| ND(1992) Proof | 500 | Value: 725 | | | | |

**2000 WON** **KM# 55** **Weight:** 31.1000 g. **Composition:** 0.9990 Gold 1 oz. AGW **Subject:** 80th birthday of Kim Il Sung **Reverse:** Portrait of Kim Il Sung

| Date | Mintage | F | VF | XF | Unc | BU |
|---|---|---|---|---|---|---|
| 1992 Proof | 500 | Value: 725 | | | | |

**2000 WON** **KM# 57** **Weight:** 31.1000 g. **Composition:** 0.9990 Gold 1 oz. AGW **Subject:** 50th birthday of Kim Jong Il **Reverse:** Portrait of Kim Jong Il

| Date | Mintage | F | VF | XF | Unc | BU |
|---|---|---|---|---|---|---|
| 1992 Proof | 500 | Value: 725 | | | | |

**2000 WON** **KM# 151** **Weight:** 31.1035 g. **Composition:** 0.9990 Gold 1.0000 oz. AGW **Subject:** Death of Kim Il Sung **Obverse:** State arms. **Reverse:** Kim's portrait. **Edge:** Plain. **Size:** 40 mm.

| Date | Mintage | F | VF | XF | Unc | BU |
|---|---|---|---|---|---|---|
| ND(1994) | — | — | — | — | 600 | — |

**2500 WON** **KM# 35** **Weight:** 15.5500 g. **Composition:** 0.9990 Gold .5 oz. AGW **Subject:** 30th anniversary of Gorch Fock **Obverse:** State emblem **Reverse:** Sailing ship

| Date | Mintage | F | VF | XF | Unc | BU |
|---|---|---|---|---|---|---|
| 1988 Proof | Est. 500 | Value: 350 | | | | |

**2500 WON** **KM# 81** **Weight:** 155.5175 g. **Composition:** 0.9990 Silver 5 oz. ASW **Reverse:** Similar to 500 Won, KM#76 **Size:** 65 mm.

| Date | Mintage | F | VF | XF | Unc | BU |
|---|---|---|---|---|---|---|
| 1995 Proof | 2,500 | Value: 150 | | | | |

**2500 WON** **KM# 82** **Weight:** 155.5175 g. **Composition:** 0.9990 Silver 5 oz. ASW **Reverse:** Similar to 500 Won, KM#69

| Date | Mintage | F | VF | XF | Unc | BU |
|---|---|---|---|---|---|---|
| 1995 Proof | 2,500 | Value: 160 | | | | |

**2500 WON** **KM# 83** **Weight:** 155.5175 g. **Composition:** 0.9990 Silver 5 oz. ASW **Reverse:** Similar to 500 Won, KM#77

| Date | Mintage | F | VF | XF | Unc | BU |
|---|---|---|---|---|---|---|
| 1995 Proof | 2,500 | Value: 155 | | | | |

**2500 WON** **KM# 85** **Weight:** 155.5175 g. **Composition:** 0.9990 Silver 5 oz. ASW **Reverse:** Similar to 500 Won, KM#79

| Date | Mintage | F | VF | XF | Unc | BU |
|---|---|---|---|---|---|---|
| 1995 Proof | 2,500 | Value: 160 | | | | |

**2500 WON** **KM# 86** **Weight:** 155.5175 g. **Composition:** 0.9990 Silver 5 oz. ASW **Reverse:** Similar to 500 Won, KM#80

| Date | Mintage | F | VF | XF | Unc | BU |
|---|---|---|---|---|---|---|
| 1995 Proof | 2,500 | Value: 160 | | | | |

**2500 WON** **KM# 84** **Weight:** 155.5175 g. **Composition:** 0.9990 Silver 5 oz. ASW **Reverse:** Similar to 500 Won, KM#78

| Date | Mintage | F | VF | XF | Unc | BU |
|---|---|---|---|---|---|---|
| 1995 Proof | 2,500 | Value: 155 | | | | |

## PROOF SETS

| KM# | Date | Mintage | Identification | Issue Price | Mkt Val |
|---|---|---|---|---|---|
| PS1 | 1995 (5) | 300 | KM92-96 | — | 1,300 |

# SOUTH KOREA

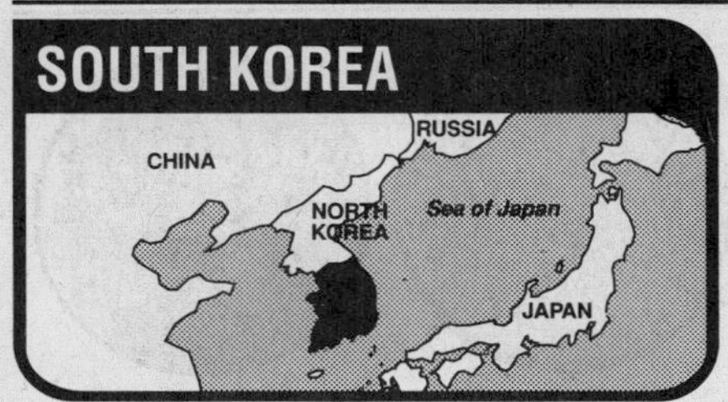


The Republic of Korea, situated in northeastern Asia on the southern half of the Korean peninsula between North Korea and the Korean Strait, has an area of 38,025 sq. mi. (98,480 sq. km.) and a population of 42.5 million. Capital: Seoul. The economy is based on agriculture and light and medium industry. Some of the world's largest oil tankers are built here. Automobiles, plywood, electronics, and textile products are exported.

Japan replaced China as the predominant foreign influence in Korea in 1895 and annexed the peninsular country in 1910. Defeat in World War II brought an end to Japanese rule. U.S. troops entered Korea from the south and Soviet forces entered from the north. The Cairo conference (1943) had established that Korea should be *free and independent.* The Potsdam conference (1945) set the 38th parallel as the line dividing the occupation forces of the United States and Russia. When Russia refused to permit a U.N. commission designated to supervise reunification elections to enter North Korea, an election was held in South Korea on May 10, 1948. By its determination, the Republic of Korea was inaugurated on Aug. 15,1948.

**NOTE:** For earlier coinage see Korea.

**MONETARY SYSTEM**
100 Chon = 1 Hwan

## REPUBLIC

### DECIMAL COINAGE

**10 HWAN** **KM# 1** **Composition:** Bronze **Reverse:** Rose of Sharon

| Date | Mintage | F | VF | XF | Unc | BU |
|---|---|---|---|---|---|---|
| KE4292(1959) | 100,000,000 | 1.00 | 2.00 | 7.00 | 12.00 | — |
| KE4294(1961) | 100,000,000 | 0.20 | 0.35 | 0.75 | 2.50 | — |

**50 HWAN** **KM# 2** **Composition:** Nickel-Brass **Reverse:** Iron clad turtle boat

| Date | Mintage | F | VF | XF | Unc | BU |
|---|---|---|---|---|---|---|
| KE4292(1959) | 24,640,000 | 0.30 | 0.50 | 1.00 | 3.00 | — |
| KE4294(1961) | 20,000,000 | 0.30 | 0.50 | 1.00 | 2.50 | — |

**100 HWAN** **KM# 3** **Composition:** Copper-Nickel **Reverse:** Bust of Rhee Syngman left

| Date | Mintage | F | VF | XF | Unc | BU |
|---|---|---|---|---|---|---|
| KE4292(1959) | — | 1.25 | 1.75 | 2.75 | 6.00 | — |

**Note:** Quantities of KM#1-3 dated 4292 in uncirculated condition were countermarked "SAMPLE" in Korean for distribution to government and banking agencies. See bank samples section at end of listing. KM#3 was withdrawn from circulation June 10, 1962 and melted; KM#1 and KM#2 continued to circulate as 1 Won and 5 Won coins for 13 years respectively until demonitized and withdrawn from circulation March 22, 1975.

## REFORM COINAGE

10 Hwan = 1 Won

**WON** **KM# 4** **Composition:** Brass **Obverse:** Rose of Sharon

| Date | Mintage | F | VF | XF | Unc | BU |
|---|---|---|---|---|---|---|
| 1966 | 7,000,000 | 0.20 | 0.40 | 1.00 | 9.00 | — |
| 1967 | 48,500,000 | — | 0.15 | 0.25 | 1.25 | — |

**WON** **KM# 4a** **Composition:** Aluminum

| Date | Mintage | F | VF | XF | Unc | BU |
|---|---|---|---|---|---|---|
| 1968 | 66,500,000 | — | 0.10 | 0.20 | 0.85 | — |
| 1969 | 85,000,000 | — | — | — | 0.25 | — |
| 1970 | 45,000,000 | — | — | — | 0.25 | — |
| 1974 | 12,000,000 | — | 0.15 | 0.25 | 1.75 | — |
| 1975 | 10,000,000 | — | 0.10 | 0.20 | 0.50 | — |
| 1976 | 20,000,000 | — | — | — | 0.30 | — |
| 1977 | 30,000,000 | — | — | — | 0.30 | — |
| 1978 | 30,000,000 | — | — | — | 0.15 | — |
| 1979 | 30,000,000 | — | — | — | 0.15 | — |
| 1980 | 20,000,000 | — | — | — | 0.15 | — |
| 1981 | 20,000,000 | — | — | — | 0.15 | — |
| 1982 | 30,000,000 | — | — | — | 0.15 | — |
| 1982 Proof | 2,000 | | | | | |

**WON** **KM# 31** **Composition:** Aluminum **Obverse:** Rose of Sharon

| Date | Mintage | F | VF | XF | Unc | BU |
|---|---|---|---|---|---|---|
| 1983 | 40,000,000 | — | — | — | 0.15 | — |
| 1984 | 20,000,000 | — | — | — | 0.15 | — |
| 1985 | 10,000,000 | — | — | — | 0.15 | — |
| 1987 | 10,000,000 | — | — | — | 0.15 | — |
| 1988 | 6,500,000 | — | — | — | 0.15 | — |
| 1989 | 10,000,000 | — | — | — | 0.15 | — |
| 1990 | 6,000,000 | — | — | — | 0.15 | — |
| 1991 | 5,000,000 | — | — | — | 0.15 | — |
| 1995 | 15,000 | — | — | — | 0.15 | — |
| 1996 | 15,000 | — | — | — | 0.15 | — |
| 1997 | 15,000 | — | — | — | 0.15 | — |
| 2001 | — | — | — | — | — | — |

**5 WON** **KM# 5** **Composition:** Bronze **Obverse:** Iron clad turtle boat

| Date | Mintage | F | VF | XF | Unc | BU |
|---|---|---|---|---|---|---|
| 1966 | 4,500,000 | 0.15 | 0.25 | 1.50 | 22.50 | — |
| 1967 | 18,000,000 | 0.15 | 0.25 | 1.00 | 17.50 | — |
| 1968 | 20,000,000 | 0.15 | 0.25 | 1.00 | 17.50 | — |
| 1969 | 25,000,000 | — | 0.10 | 0.25 | 3.25 | — |
| 1970 | 50,000,000 | — | 0.10 | 0.25 | 3.00 | — |

**5 WON** **KM# 5a** **Composition:** Brass **Obverse:** Iron clad turtle boat

| Date | Mintage | F | VF | XF | Unc | BU |
|---|---|---|---|---|---|---|
| 1970 | Inc. above | — | — | 0.10 | 1.25 | — |
| 1971 | 64,038,000 | — | — | — | 0.10 | — |
| 1972 | 60,084,000 | — | — | — | 0.10 | — |
| 1977 | 1,000,000 | — | — | 0.10 | 0.75 | — |
| 1978 | 1,000,000 | — | — | 0.10 | 0.75 | — |
| 1979 | 1,000,000 | — | — | 0.10 | 0.65 | — |
| 1980 | 200,000 | — | 0.25 | 0.50 | 2.50 | — |
| 1981 | 200,000 | — | 0.25 | 0.50 | 1.50 | — |
| 1982 | 200,000 | — | 0.25 | 0.50 | 1.50 | — |
| 1982 Proof | 2,000 | — | — | — | — | — |

**5 WON** **KM# 32** **Composition:** Brass **Obverse:** Iron clad turtle boat

| Date | Mintage | F | VF | XF | Unc | BU |
|---|---|---|---|---|---|---|
| 1983 | 6,000,000 | — | — | 0.10 | 0.25 | — |
| 1987 | 1,000,000 | — | — | 0.10 | 0.25 | — |
| 1988 | 500,000 | — | — | 0.10 | 0.25 | — |
| 1989 | 500,000 | — | — | 0.10 | 0.25 | — |
| 1990 | 600,000 | — | — | 0.10 | 0.25 | — |
| 1991 | 500,000 | — | — | 0.10 | 0.25 | — |
| 1995 | 15,000 | — | — | 0.10 | 0.25 | — |
| 1996 | 15,000 | — | — | 0.10 | 0.25 | — |
| 1997 | 15,000 | — | — | 0.10 | 0.25 | — |
| 2001 | — | — | — | — | — | — |

**10 WON** **KM# 6** **Composition:** Bronze **Obverse:** Pagoda at Pul Guk Temple

| Date | Mintage | F | VF | XF | Unc | BU |
|---|---|---|---|---|---|---|
| 1966 | 10,600,000 | 0.15 | 0.25 | 1.50 | 25.00 | — |
| 1967 | 22,500,000 | 0.15 | 0.25 | 1.50 | 25.00 | — |
| 1968 | 35,000,000 | 0.15 | 0.25 | 1.50 | 18.50 | — |
| 1969 | 46,500,000 | 0.15 | 0.25 | 1.50 | 18.50 | — |
| 1970 | 157,000,000 | 0.15 | 0.25 | 1.50 | 16.50 | — |

**10 WON** **KM# 6a** **Composition:** Brass **Obverse:** Pagoda at Pul Guk Temple

| Date | Mintage | F | VF | XF | Unc | BU |
|---|---|---|---|---|---|---|
| 1970 | Inc. above | — | 0.35 | 1.25 | 13.50 | — |
| 1971 | 220,000,000 | — | — | 0.15 | 1.75 | — |
| 1972 | 270,000,000 | — | — | 0.15 | 1.75 | — |
| 1973 | 30,000,000 | — | 0.10 | 0.35 | 6.50 | — |
| 1974 | 15,000,000 | — | 0.10 | 0.35 | 6.50 | — |
| 1975 | 20,000,000 | — | 0.10 | 0.50 | 11.50 | — |
| 1977 | 1,000,000 | — | 0.10 | 0.35 | 3.50 | — |
| 1978 | 80,000,000 | — | 0.10 | 0.15 | 1.25 | — |
| 1979 | 200,000,000 | — | — | 0.10 | 0.55 | — |
| 1980 | 150,000,000 | — | — | 0.10 | 0.55 | — |
| 1981 | 100,000 | — | 0.25 | 0.75 | 4.50 | — |
| 1982 | 20,000,000 | — | — | 0.10 | 0.60 | — |
| 1982 Proof | 2,000 | — | — | — | — | — |

**10 WON** **KM# 33.1** **Composition:** Brass **Obverse:** Pagoda at Pul Guk Temple

| Date | Mintage | F | VF | XF | Unc | BU |
|---|---|---|---|---|---|---|
| 1983 | 25,000,000 | — | — | 0.10 | 0.35 | — |
| 1985 | 35,000,000 | — | — | 0.10 | 0.35 | — |
| 1986 | 195,000,000 | — | — | 0.10 | 0.35 | — |
| 1987 | 155,000,000 | — | — | 0.10 | 0.35 | — |
| 1988 | 189,000,000 | — | — | 0.10 | 0.35 | — |
| 1989 | 310,000,000 | — | — | 0.10 | 0.35 | — |
| 1990 | 395,000,000 | — | — | 0.10 | 0.35 | — |
| 1991 | 300,000,000 | — | — | 0.10 | 0.35 | — |
| 1992 | 150,000,000 | — | — | 0.10 | 0.35 | — |
| 1993 | 110,000,000 | — | — | 0.10 | 0.35 | — |
| 1994 | 300,000,000 | — | — | 0.10 | 0.35 | — |
| 1995 | 380,000,000 | — | — | 0.10 | 0.35 | — |
| 1996 | 290,000,000 | — | — | 0.10 | 0.35 | — |
| 1997 | 177,000,000 | — | — | 0.10 | 0.35 | — |
| 1999 | — | — | — | 0.10 | 0.35 | — |
| 2000 | — | — | — | 0.10 | 0.35 | — |

**10 WON** **KM# 33.2** **Composition:** Brass **Obverse:** Pagoda at Pul Guk Temple **Reverse:** Thick numbers in denomination

| Date | Mintage | F | VF | XF | Unc | BU |
|---|---|---|---|---|---|---|
| 1991 | — | — | — | 0.10 | 0.35 | — |
| 1997 | — | — | — | 0.10 | 0.35 | — |
| 1998 | — | — | — | 0.10 | 0.35 | — |
| 1999 | — | — | — | 0.10 | 0.35 | — |
| 2001 | — | — | — | — | — | — |

**50 WON** KM# 7 **Weight:** 2.8000 g. **Composition:** 0.9990 Silver .0899 oz. ASW **Obverse:** Yu Kwan-Soon, flag

| Date | Mintage | F | VF | XF | Unc | BU |
|---|---|---|---|---|---|---|
| 4303(1970) Proof | 4,350 | Value: 70.00 | | | | |
| 4304(1971) Rare | — | — | — | — | — | — |

**50 WON** KM# 20 **Composition:** Copper-Nickel **Series:** F.A.O.

| Date | Mintage | F | VF | XF | Unc | BU |
|---|---|---|---|---|---|---|
| 1972 | 6,000,000 | 0.20 | 0.40 | 1.00 | 16.50 | — |
| 1973 | 40,000,000 | — | 0.15 | 0.25 | 3.50 | — |
| 1974 | 25,000,000 | — | 0.15 | 0.25 | 1.50 | — |
| 1977 | 1,000,000 | — | 0.15 | 0.25 | 2.00 | — |
| 1978 | 1,500,000 | — | 0.15 | 0.25 | 1.25 | — |
| 1979 | 20,000,000 | — | 0.10 | 0.20 | 1.25 | — |
| 1980 | 10,000,000 | — | 0.10 | 0.20 | 1.25 | — |
| 1981 | 25,000,000 | — | 0.10 | 0.20 | 1.25 | — |
| 1982 | 40,000,000 | — | 0.10 | 0.20 | 0.75 | — |
| 1982 Proof | 2,000 | — | — | — | — | — |

**50 WON** KM# 34 **Composition:** Copper-Nickel **Series:** F.A.O. **Note:** Die varieties exist

| Date | Mintage | F | VF | XF | Unc | BU |
|---|---|---|---|---|---|---|
| 1983 | 50,000,000 | — | — | 0.10 | 0.45 | — |
| 1984 | 40,000,000 | — | — | 0.10 | 0.45 | — |
| 1985 | 4,000,000 | — | — | 0.10 | 0.45 | — |
| 1987 | 32,000,000 | — | — | 0.10 | 0.45 | — |
| 1988 | 53,000,000 | — | — | 0.10 | 0.45 | — |
| 1989 | 70,000,000 | — | — | 0.10 | 0.45 | — |
| 1990 | 85,000,000 | — | — | 0.10 | 0.35 | — |
| 1991 | 80,000,000 | — | — | 0.10 | 0.35 | — |
| 1992 | 50,000,000 | — | — | 0.10 | 0.35 | — |
| 1993 | 5,000,000 | — | — | 0.10 | 0.35 | — |
| 1994 | 102,000,000 | — | — | 0.10 | 0.35 | — |
| 1995 | 98,000,000 | — | — | 0.10 | 0.35 | — |
| 1996 | 52,000,000 | — | — | 0.10 | 0.35 | — |
| 1997 | 129,000,000 | — | — | 0.10 | 0.35 | — |
| 1998 | — | — | — | 0.10 | 0.35 | — |
| **Note:** Die varieties exist | | | | | | |
| 2001 | — | — | — | — | — | — |

**100 WON** KM# 9 **Composition:** Copper-Nickel

| Date | Mintage | F | VF | XF | Unc | BU |
|---|---|---|---|---|---|---|
| 1970 | 1,500,000 | 0.50 | 0.75 | 1.50 | 18.50 | — |
| 1971 | 13,000,000 | 0.15 | 0.25 | 0.50 | 13.50 | — |
| 1972 | 20,000,000 | — | 0.20 | 0.40 | 11.50 | — |
| 1973 | 80,000,000 | — | 0.15 | 0.30 | 3.00 | — |
| 1974 | 50,000,000 | — | 0.15 | 0.35 | 4.50 | — |
| **Note:** Die varieties exist | | | | | | |
| 1975 | 75,000,000 | — | 0.15 | 0.35 | 6.00 | — |
| **Note:** Die varieties exist | | | | | | |
| 1977 | 30,000,000 | — | 0.15 | 0.35 | 2.25 | — |
| 1978 | 40,000,000 | — | 0.15 | 0.25 | 1.50 | — |
| 1979 | 130,000,000 | — | 0.15 | 0.25 | 1.50 | — |
| 1980 | 60,000,000 | — | 0.15 | 0.25 | 1.50 | — |
| 1981 | 100,000 | — | 0.25 | 0.50 | 4.00 | — |
| 1982 | 50,000,000 | — | 0.15 | 0.25 | 1.25 | — |
| 1982 Proof | 2,000 | — | — | — | — | — |

**100 WON** KM# 8 **Weight:** 5.6000 g. **Composition:** 0.9990 Silver .1798 oz. ASW **Subject:** Admiral Yi Soon-Shin

| Date | Mintage | F | VF | XF | Unc | BU |
|---|---|---|---|---|---|---|
| 4303(1970) Proof | 4,350 | Value: 125 | | | | |

**100 WON** KM# 21 **Composition:** Copper-Nickel **Subject:** 30th Anniersary of Liberation - Yu Kwan Soon

| Date | Mintage | F | VF | XF | Unc | BU |
|---|---|---|---|---|---|---|
| (1975) | 4,998,000 | 0.20 | 0.50 | 0.75 | 2.25 | — |
| (1975) Proof | 2,000 | Value: 125 | | | | |

**100 WON** KM# 24 **Composition:** Copper-Nickel **Subject:** 1st Anniversary of the 5th Republic

| Date | Mintage | F | VF | XF | Unc | BU |
|---|---|---|---|---|---|---|
| 1981 | 4,980,000 | 0.20 | 0.35 | 0.65 | 1.50 | — |
| 1981 Unfrosted, Proof | 18,000 | Value: 25.00 | | | | |
| 1981 Proof | 2,000 | Value: 165 | | | | |

**100 WON** KM# 35.1 **Composition:** Copper-Nickel **Obverse:** Admiral Yi Soon-Shin

| Date | Mintage | F | VF | XF | Unc | BU |
|---|---|---|---|---|---|---|
| 1983 | 8,000,000 | — | 0.15 | 0.25 | 0.60 | — |

**100 WON** KM# 35.2 **Composition:** Copper-Nickel **Obverse:** Admiral Yi Soon-Shin **Reverse:** Modified design

| Date | Mintage | F | VF | XF | Unc | BU |
|---|---|---|---|---|---|---|
| 1984 | 40,000,000 | — | 0.15 | 0.25 | 0.60 | — |
| 1985 | 16,000,000 | — | 0.15 | 0.30 | 1.25 | — |
| 1986 | 131,000,000 | — | 0.15 | 0.25 | 0.60 | — |
| 1987 | 170,000,000 | — | 0.15 | 0.25 | 0.60 | — |
| 1988 | 298,000,000 | — | 0.15 | 0.25 | 0.60 | — |
| 1989 | 250,000,000 | — | 0.15 | 0.25 | 0.60 | — |
| 1990 | 185,000,000 | — | 0.15 | 0.25 | 0.60 | — |
| 1991 | 400,000,000 | — | 0.15 | 0.25 | 0.60 | — |
| 1992 | 425,000,000 | — | 0.15 | 0.25 | 0.60 | — |
| 1993 | 185,000,000 | — | 0.15 | 0.25 | 0.60 | — |
| 1994 | 401,000,000 | — | 0.15 | 0.25 | 0.60 | — |
| 1995 | 228,000,000 | — | 0.15 | 0.25 | 0.60 | — |
| 1996 | 447,000,000 | — | 0.15 | 0.25 | 0.60 | — |
| 1997 | 147,000,000 | — | 0.15 | 0.25 | 0.60 | — |
| 1999 | — | — | 0.15 | 0.25 | 0.60 | — |
| 2000 | — | — | 0.15 | 0.25 | 0.60 | — |
| 2001 | — | — | — | — | — | — |

**200 WON** KM# 10 **Weight:** 11.2000 g. **Composition:** 0.9990 Silver .3596 oz. ASW **Obverse:** Celadon vase

| Date | Mintage | F | VF | XF | Unc | BU |
|---|---|---|---|---|---|---|
| KE4303(1970)(1970) Proof | 4,200 | Value: 115 | | | | |

**250 WON** KM# 11 **Weight:** 14.0000 g. **Composition:** 0.9990 Silver .4497 oz. ASW **Obverse:** Bust of Park Chung-Hee

| Date | Mintage | F | VF | XF | Unc | BU |
|---|---|---|---|---|---|---|
| KE4303(1970)(1970) Proof | 4,100 | Value: 200 | | | | |

**500 WON** KM# 12 **Weight:** 28.0000 g. **Composition:** 0.9990 Silver .8994 oz. ASW **Subject:** Kyongji - Bodhisattva from the Cave Temple

| Date | Mintage | F | VF | XF | Unc | BU |
|---|---|---|---|---|---|---|
| KE4303(1970) Proof | 4,700 | Value: 250 | | | | |

**500 WON** KM# 22 **Composition:** Copper-Nickel **Subject:** 42nd World Shooting Championships

| Date | Mintage | F | VF | XF | Unc | BU |
|---|---|---|---|---|---|---|
| 1978 | 980,000 | 0.35 | 0.75 | 1.50 | 3.50 | — |
| 1978 Unfrosted, proof | 18,000 | Value: 27.50 | | | | |
| 1978 Proof | 2,000 | Value: 220 | | | | |

**500 WON** KM# 27 **Composition:** Copper-Nickel **Obverse:** Manchurian crane

| Date | Mintage | F | VF | XF | Unc | BU |
|---|---|---|---|---|---|---|
| 1982 | 15,000,000 | — | — | 1.00 | 3.75 | — |
| 1982 Proof | 2,000 | — | — | — | — | — |
| 1983 | 64,000,000 | — | — | 1.00 | 2.25 | — |
| 1984 | 70,000,000 | — | — | 1.00 | 2.25 | — |

| Date | Mintage | F | VF | XF | Unc | BU |
|---|---|---|---|---|---|---|
| 1987 | 1,000,000 | — | — | 1.00 | 2.25 | — |
| 1988 | 27,000,000 | — | — | 1.00 | 2.25 | — |
| 1989 | 25,000,000 | — | — | 1.00 | 2.25 | — |
| 1990 | 60,000,000 | — | — | 1.00 | 2.25 | — |
| 1991 | 90,000,000 | — | — | 1.00 | 2.00 | — |
| 1992 | 105,000,000 | — | — | 1.00 | 2.00 | — |
| 1993 | 32,000,000 | — | — | 1.00 | 2.00 | — |
| 1994 | 50,600,000 | — | — | 1.00 | 2.00 | — |
| 1995 | 87,000,000 | — | — | 1.00 | 2.00 | — |
| 1996 | 122,000,000 | — | — | 1.00 | 2.00 | — |
| 1997 | 62,000,000 | — | — | 1.00 | 2.00 | — |
| 2001 | — | — | — | — | — | — |

**1000 WON KM# 13 Weight:** 56.0000 g. **Composition:** 0.9990 Silver 1.7988 oz. ASW **Subject:** U.N. Forces in South Korea **Reverse:** Similar to 200 Won, KM#10

| Date | Mintage | F | VF | XF | Unc | BU |
|---|---|---|---|---|---|---|
| KE4303(1970)(1970) Proof | 4,050 | Value: 425 | | | | |

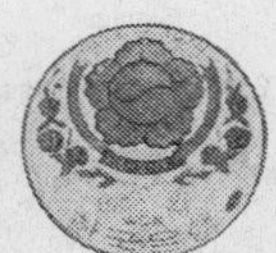

**1000 WON KM# 14.1 Weight:** 3.8700 g. **Composition:** 0.9000 Gold .1119 oz. AGW **Obverse:** Great South Gate in Seoul

| Date | Mintage | F | VF | XF | Unc | BU |
|---|---|---|---|---|---|---|
| KE4303(1970)(1970) Proof | 1,500 | Value: 350 | | | | |

**1000 WON KM# 14.2 Weight:** 3.8700 g. **Composition:** 0.9000 Gold .1119 oz. AGW **Obverse:** Great South Gate in Seoul

| Date | Mintage | F | VF | XF | Unc | BU |
|---|---|---|---|---|---|---|
| KE4303(1970)(1970) Proof | 100 | Value: 1,250 | | | | |

**1000 WON KM# 25 Composition:** Nickel **Subject:** 1st Anniversary of the 5th Republic **Reverse:** Imaginary bird, called Bong-hwang, represents a King

| Date | Mintage | F | VF | XF | Unc | BU |
|---|---|---|---|---|---|---|
| 1981 | 1,880,000 | 1.00 | 1.25 | 1.50 | 4.50 | — |
| 1981 Unfrosted, proof | 18,000 | Value: 27.50 | | | | |
| 1981 Proof | 2,000 | Value: 225 | | | | |

**1000 WON KM# 28 Composition:** Copper-Nickel **Subject:** 1988 Olympics **Obverse:** Dancers

| Date | Mintage | F | VF | XF | Unc | BU |
|---|---|---|---|---|---|---|
| 1982 | 1,980,000 | — | — | 1.25 | 4.00 | — |
| 1982 Unfrosted, proof | 10,000 | Value: 22.50 | | | | |
| 1982 Proof | 10,000 | Value: 37.50 | | | | |

**1000 WON KM# 36 Composition:** Copper-Nickel **Subject:** 1988 Olympics **Obverse:** Drummer (Jangku)

| Date | Mintage | F | VF | XF | Unc | BU |
|---|---|---|---|---|---|---|
| 1983 | 330,000 | — | — | 1.25 | 4.00 | — |
| 1983 Unfrosted, Proof | 56,000 | Value: 12.50 | | | | |
| 1983 Proof | 101,000 | Value: 18.50 | | | | |

**1000 WON KM# 39 Composition:** Copper-Nickel **Subject:** 200 Years of Catholic Church in Korea **Reverse:** Myung Dong Cathedral

| Date | Mintage | F | VF | XF | Unc | BU |
|---|---|---|---|---|---|---|
| 1984 | 572,000 | — | — | 1.25 | 4.00 | — |

**1000 WON KM# 41 Composition:** Copper-Nickel **Subject:** 10th Asian Games **Reverse:** Lion dance

| Date | Mintage | F | VF | XF | Unc | BU |
|---|---|---|---|---|---|---|
| 1986 | 930,000 | — | — | 1.25 | 3.00 | — |
| 1986 Proof | 70,000 | Value: 7.00 | | | | |

**1000 WON KM# 46 Composition:** Copper-Nickel **Subject:** 1988 Olympics **Reverse:** Basketball

| Date | Mintage | F | VF | XF | Unc | BU |
|---|---|---|---|---|---|---|
| 1986 | 560,000 | — | — | — | 4.00 | — |
| 1986 Proof | 140,000 | Value: 8.50 | | | | |

**1000 WON KM# 47 Composition:** Copper-Nickel **Subject:** 1988 Olympics **Reverse:** Tennis

| Date | Mintage | F | VF | XF | Unc | BU |
|---|---|---|---|---|---|---|
| 1987 | 560,000 | — | — | — | 4.00 | — |
| 1987 Proof | 140,000 | Value: 7.50 | | | | |

**1000 WON KM# 48 Composition:** Copper-Nickel **Subject:** 1988 Olympics **Reverse:** Handball

| Date | Mintage | F | VF | XF | Unc | BU |
|---|---|---|---|---|---|---|
| 1987 | 560,000 | — | — | — | 4.00 | — |
| 1987 Proof | 140,000 | Value: 7.50 | | | | |

**1000 WON KM# 49 Composition:** Copper-Nickel **Subject:** 1988 Olympics **Reverse:** Table tennis

| Date | Mintage | F | VF | XF | Unc | BU |
|---|---|---|---|---|---|---|
| 1988 | 560,000 | — | — | — | 4.00 | — |
| 1988 Proof | 140,000 | Value: 7.50 | | | | |

**1000 WON KM# 78 Composition:** Copper-Nickel **Subject:** Taejon International Exposition Kumdori **Reverse:** Mascot of the Expo

| Date | Mintage | F | VF | XF | Unc | BU |
|---|---|---|---|---|---|---|
| 1993 | 590,000 | — | — | — | 4.00 | — |

**1000 WON KM# 87 Composition:** Copper-Nickel **Subject:** 50th Anniversary of U.N.

| Date | Mintage | F | VF | XF | Unc | BU |
|---|---|---|---|---|---|---|
| 1995 | 5,000 | — | — | — | 8.50 | — |

**1000 WON KM# 89 Weight:** 12.0000 g. **Composition:** Brass **Series:** World Cup Soccer **Obverse:** FIFA World Cup logo **Reverse:** Mascot soccer player **Edge:** Reeded **Size:** 32 mm.

| Date | Mintage | F | VF | XF | Unc | BU |
|---|---|---|---|---|---|---|
| 2001 | 102,000 | — | — | — | 7.50 | — |

**2000 WON** **KM# 50** **Composition:** Nickel **Subject:** 1988 Olympics **Reverse:** Boxing

| Date | Mintage | F | VF | XF | Unc | BU |
|---|---|---|---|---|---|---|
| 1986 | 560,000 | — | — | — | 6.50 | — |
| 1986 Proof | 140,000 | Value: 8.50 | | | | |

**2000 WON** **KM# 51** **Composition:** Nickel **Subject:** 1988 Olympics **Reverse:** Tae Kwon Do

| Date | Mintage | F | VF | XF | Unc | BU |
|---|---|---|---|---|---|---|
| 1987 | 560,000 | — | — | — | 5.50 | — |
| 1987 Proof | 140,000 | Value: 8.50 | | | | |

**2000 WON** **KM# 52** **Composition:** Nickel **Subject:** 1988 Olympics **Reverse:** Wrestling

| Date | Mintage | F | VF | XF | Unc | BU |
|---|---|---|---|---|---|---|
| 1987 | 560,000 | — | — | — | 5.50 | — |
| 1987 Proof | 140,000 | Value: 12.50 | | | | |

**2000 WON** **KM# 53** **Composition:** Nickel **Subject:** 1988 Olympics **Reverse:** Weight lifting

| Date | Mintage | F | VF | XF | Unc | BU |
|---|---|---|---|---|---|---|
| 1988 | 560,000 | — | — | — | 5.50 | — |
| 1988 Proof | 140,000 | Value: 8.50 | | | | |

**2000 WON** **KM# 88** **Ring Weight:** 10.7000 g. **Ring Composition:** Copper-Nickel **Center Composition:** Copper-Aluminum-Nickel **Subject:** New Millennium **Obverse:** Astronomical observation instrument **Reverse:** Stylized design **Edge:** Reeded **Size:** 28 mm. **Note:** Korea Minting and Security Printing Corp.

| Date | Mintage | F | VF | XF | Unc | BU |
|---|---|---|---|---|---|---|
| 2000(2000) | — | — | — | — | 9.00 | — |

**2500 WON** **KM# 15.1** **Weight:** 9.6800 g. **Composition:** 0.9000 Gold .2801 oz. AGW **Obverse:** Queen Mother Sunduk

| Date | Mintage | F | VF | XF | Unc | BU |
|---|---|---|---|---|---|---|
| KE4303(1970)(1970) Proof | 1,750 | Value: 500 | | | | |

**2500 WON** **KM# 15.2** **Weight:** 9.6800 g. **Composition:** 0.9000 Gold .2801 oz. AGW **Obverse:** Queen Mother Sunduk

| Date | Mintage | F | VF | XF | Unc | BU |
|---|---|---|---|---|---|---|
| KE4303(1970)(1970) Proof | 100 | Value: 1,500 | | | | |

**5000 WON** **KM# 16.1** **Weight:** 19.3600 g. **Composition:** 0.9000 Gold .5602 oz. AGW **Obverse:** Iron clad turtle boat

| Date | Mintage | F | VF | XF | Unc | BU |
|---|---|---|---|---|---|---|
| KE4303(1970)(1970) Proof | 670 | Value: 1,850 | | | | |

**5000 WON** **KM# 16.2** **Weight:** 19.3600 g. **Composition:** 0.9000 Gold .5602 oz. AGW **Obverse:** Iron clad turtle boat

| Date | Mintage | F | VF | XF | Unc | BU |
|---|---|---|---|---|---|---|
| KE4303(1970)(1970) Proof | 70 | Value: 2,500 | | | | |

**5000 WON** **KM# 23** **Weight:** 23.0000 g. **Composition:** 0.9000 Silver .6655 oz. ASW **Subject:** 42nd World Shooting Championships

| Date | Mintage | F | VF | XF | Unc | BU |
|---|---|---|---|---|---|---|
| 1978 | 80,000 | — | — | — | 32.00 | — |
| 1978 Unfrosted, Proof | 20,000 | Value: 90.00 | | | | |

**5000 WON** **KM# 54** **Weight:** 16.8100 g. **Composition:** 0.9250 Silver .5000 oz. ASW **Subject:** 1988 Olympics **Reverse:** Tiger mascot

| Date | Mintage | F | VF | XF | Unc | BU |
|---|---|---|---|---|---|---|
| 1986 | 92,000 | — | — | — | 8.50 | — |
| 1986 Proof | 235,000 | Value: 10.00 | | | | |

**5000 WON** **KM# 55** **Weight:** 16.8100 g. **Composition:** 0.9250 Silver .5000 oz. ASW **Subject:** 1988 Olympics **Reverse:** Rope pulling

| Date | Mintage | F | VF | XF | Unc | BU |
|---|---|---|---|---|---|---|
| 1986 | 90,000 | — | — | — | 8.50 | — |
| 1986 Proof | 217,000 | Value: 10.00 | | | | |

**5000 WON** **KM# 60** **Weight:** 16.8100 g. **Composition:** 0.9250 Silver .5000 oz. ASW **Subject:** 1988 Olympics **Reverse:** Stadium

| Date | Mintage | F | VF | XF | Unc | BU |
|---|---|---|---|---|---|---|
| 1987 | 73,000 | — | — | — | 10.00 | — |
| 1987 Proof | 199,000 | Value: 12.00 | | | | |

**5000 WON** **KM# 61** **Weight:** 16.8100 g. **Composition:** 0.9250 Silver .5000 oz. ASW **Subject:** 1988 Olympics **Reverse:** Chegi - Kicking

| Date | Mintage | F | VF | XF | Unc | BU |
|---|---|---|---|---|---|---|
| 1987 | 60,000 | — | — | — | 9.00 | — |
| 1987 Proof | 180,000 | Value: 12.00 | | | | |

**5000 WON** **KM# 66** **Weight:** 16.8100 g. **Composition:** 0.9250 Silver .5000 oz. ASW **Subject:** 1988 Olympics **Reverse:** Tae Kwon Do

| Date | Mintage | F | VF | XF | Unc | BU |
|---|---|---|---|---|---|---|
| 1987 | 58,000 | — | — | — | 10.00 | — |
| 1987 Proof | 150,000 | Value: 12.00 | | | | |

**5000 WON** **KM# 67** **Weight:** 16.8100 g. **Composition:** 0.9250 Silver .5000 oz. ASW **Subject:** 1988 Olympics **Reverse:** Girls on swing

| Date | Mintage | F | VF | XF | Unc | BU |
|---|---|---|---|---|---|---|
| 1987 | 60,000 | — | — | — | 9.00 | — |
| 1987 Proof | 147,000 | Value: 12.00 | | | | |

**5000 WON** **KM# 70** **Weight:** 16.8100 g. **Composition:** 0.9250 Silver .5000 oz. ASW **Subject:** 1988 Olympics **Reverse:** Wrestling

| Date | Mintage | F | VF | XF | Unc | BU |
|---|---|---|---|---|---|---|
| 1988 | 59,000 | — | — | — | 10.00 | — |
| 1988 Proof | 136,000 | Value: 12.00 | | | | |

**5000 WON** **KM# 71** **Weight:** 16.8100 g. **Composition:** 0.9250 Silver .5000 oz. ASW **Subject:** 1988 Olympics **Reverse:** Boys spinning top

| Date | Mintage | F | VF | XF | Unc | BU |
|---|---|---|---|---|---|---|
| 1988 | 59,000 | — | — | — | 9.00 | — |
| 1988 Proof | 134,000 | Value: 12.00 | | | | |

**5000 WON** **KM# 79** **Weight:** 16.8100 g. **Composition:** 0.9250 Silver .5000 oz. ASW **Subject:** Taejon International Exposition **Reverse:** Yarn spinners

| Date | Mintage | F | VF | XF | Unc | BU |
|---|---|---|---|---|---|---|
| 1993 | 150,000 | — | — | — | 14.50 | — |

**5000 WON** **KM# 80** **Weight:** 16.8100 g. **Composition:** 0.9250 Silver .5000 oz. ASW **Subject:** Taejon International Exposition **Reverse:** Folk musicians

| Date | Mintage | F | VF | XF | Unc | BU |
|---|---|---|---|---|---|---|
| 1993 | 150,000 | — | — | — | 14.50 | — |

**5000 WON** **KM# 85** **Composition:** Nickel **Subject:** 50th Anniveresary of Liberation from Japan **Obverse:** Kim-Gu

| Date | Mintage | F | VF | XF | Unc | BU |
|---|---|---|---|---|---|---|
| 1995 | 25,000 | — | — | — | 10.00 | — |

**5000 WON** **KM# 96** **Weight:** 22.0000 g. **Composition:** Bronze **Obverse:** Head Office of the Bank of Korea old and new buildings. **Reverse:** 50th Anniversary of the Bank of Korea **Size:** 38 mm.

| Date | Mintage | F | VF | XF | Unc | BU |
|---|---|---|---|---|---|---|
| 2000 | — | — | — | — | — | — |

**10000 WON** **KM# 17.1** **Weight:** 38.7200 g. **Composition:** 0.9000 Gold 1.1205 oz. AGW **Obverse:** Bust of Park Chung-Hee

| Date | Mintage | F | VF | XF | Unc | BU |
|---|---|---|---|---|---|---|
| KE4303(1970)(1970) Proof | 435 | Value: 5,000 | | | | |

**10000 WON** **KM# 17.2** **Weight:** 38.7200 g. **Composition:** 0.9000 Gold 1.1205 oz. AGW **Obverse:** Bust of Park Chung-Hee

| Date | Mintage | F | VF | XF | Unc | BU |
|---|---|---|---|---|---|---|
| KE4303(1970)(1970) Proof | 55 | Value: 6,000 | | | | |

**10000 WON** **KM# 29** **Weight:** 15.0000 g. **Composition:** 0.9000 Silver .4340 oz. ASW **Subject:** 1988 Olympics **Obverse:** Great South Gate, Soul

| Date | Mintage | F | VF | XF | Unc | BU |
|---|---|---|---|---|---|---|
| 1982 | 280,000 | — | — | — | 14.50 | — |
| 1982 Unfrosted, proof | 10,000 | Value: 32.50 | | | | |
| 1982 Proof | 10,000 | Value: 50.00 | | | | |

**10000 WON** **KM# 37** **Weight:** 15.0000 g. **Composition:** 0.9000 Silver .4340 oz. ASW **Subject:** 1988 Olympics **Obverse:** Pavilion of Kyongbok Palace

| Date | Mintage | F | VF | XF | Unc | BU |
|---|---|---|---|---|---|---|
| 1983 | 137,000 | — | — | — | 14.50 | — |
| 1983 Unfrosted, Proof | 56,000 | Value: 25.00 | | | | |
| 1983 Proof | 101,000 | Value: 30.00 | | | | |

**10000 WON** **KM# 40** **Weight:** 23.2600 g. **Composition:** 0.5000 Silver .3739 oz. ASW **Subject:** 200 Years of Catholic Church in Korea

| Date | Mintage | F | VF | XF | Unc | BU |
|---|---|---|---|---|---|---|
| 1984 | 152,000 | — | — | — | 17.50 | — |

**10000 WON** **KM# 42** **Weight:** 23.0000 g. **Composition:** 0.9000 Silver .6655 oz. ASW **Subject:** 10th Asian Gamaes **Obverse:** Similar to 2000 Won, KM#50 **Reverse:** Badminton

| Date | Mintage | F | VF | XF | Unc | BU |
|---|---|---|---|---|---|---|
| 1986 | 130,000 | — | — | — | 14.00 | — |
| 1986 Proof | 70,000 | Value: 24.00 | | | | |

**10000 WON** **KM# 43** **Weight:** 23.0000 g. **Composition:** 0.9000 Silver .6655 oz. ASW **Subject:** 10th Asian Gamaes **Obverse:** Similar to 2000 Won, KM#50 **Reverse:** Soccer

| Date | Mintage | F | VF | XF | Unc | BU |
|---|---|---|---|---|---|---|
| 1986 | 130,000 | — | — | — | 14.00 | — |
| 1986 Proof | 70,000 | Value: 24.00 | | | | |

**10000 WON** **KM# 56** **Weight:** 33.6200 g. **Composition:** 0.9250 Silver 1.0000 oz. ASW **Subject:** 1988 Olympics **Reverse:** Marathon

| Date | Mintage | F | VF | XF | Unc | BU |
|---|---|---|---|---|---|---|
| 1986 | 90,000 | — | — | — | 15.00 | — |
| 1986 Proof | 229,000 | Value: 16.50 | | | | |

**10000 WON** **KM# 57** **Weight:** 33.6200 g. **Composition:** 0.9250 Silver 1.0000 oz. ASW **Subject:** 1988 Olympics **Reverse:** Diving

| Date | Mintage | F | VF | XF | Unc | BU |
|---|---|---|---|---|---|---|
| 1987 | 90,000 | — | — | — | 15.00 | — |
| 1987 Proof | 217,000 | Value: 16.50 | | | | |

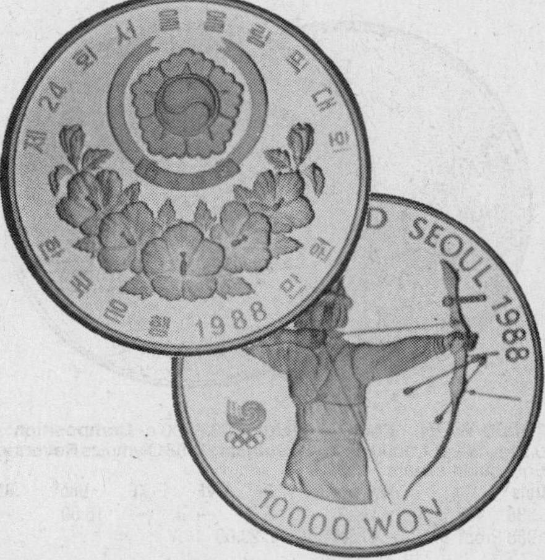


**10000 WON** **KM# 62** **Weight:** 33.6200 g. **Composition:** 0.9250 Silver 1.0000 oz. ASW **Subject:** 1988 Olympics **Reverse:** Archery

| Date | Mintage | F | VF | XF | Unc | BU |
|---|---|---|---|---|---|---|
| 1987 | 60,000 | — | — | — | 17.50 | — |
| 1987 Proof | 182,000 | Value: 16.50 | | | | |
| 1988 | Inc. above | — | — | — | 200 | — |
| 1988 Proof | Inc. above | Value: 90.00 | | | | |

**Note:** 1988 is an error date

**10000 WON** KM# 63 **Weight:** 33.6200 g. **Composition:** 0.9250 Silver 1.0000 oz. ASW **Subject:** 1988 Olympics **Reverse:** Volleyball

| Date | Mintage | F | VF | XF | Unc | BU |
|---|---|---|---|---|---|---|
| 1987 | 72,000 | — | — | — | 16.00 | — |
| 1987 Proof | 188,000 | Value: 17.50 | | | | |

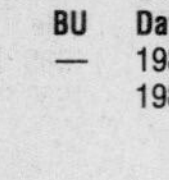

**10000 WON** KM# 74 **Weight:** 33.6200 g. **Composition:** 0.9250 Silver 1.0000 oz. ASW **Subject:** 1988 Olympics **Reverse:** Gymnastics

| Date | Mintage | F | VF | XF | Unc | BU |
|---|---|---|---|---|---|---|
| 1988 | 9,000 | — | — | — | 16.50 | — |
| 1988 Proof | 97,000 | Value: 20.00 | | | | |

**10000 WON** KM# 75 **Weight:** 33.6200 g. **Composition:** 0.9250 Silver 1.0000 oz. ASW **Subject:** 1988 Olympics **Reverse:** Equestrian events

| Date | Mintage | F | VF | XF | Unc | BU |
|---|---|---|---|---|---|---|
| 1988 | 9,000 | — | — | — | 16.50 | — |
| 1988 Proof | 97,000 | Value: 20.00 | | | | |

**10000 WON** KM# 76 **Weight:** 33.6200 g. **Composition:** 0.9250 Silver 1.0000 oz. ASW **Subject:** 1988 Olympics **Reverse:** Cycling

| Date | Mintage | F | VF | XF | Unc | BU |
|---|---|---|---|---|---|---|
| 1988 | 8,700 | — | — | — | 17.50 | — |
| 1988 Proof | 95,000 | Value: 21.50 | | | | |

**10000 WON** KM# 77 **Weight:** 33.6200 g. **Composition:** 0.9250 Silver 1.0000 oz. ASW **Subject:** 1988 Olympics **Reverse:** Soccer

| Date | Mintage | F | VF | XF | Unc | BU |
|---|---|---|---|---|---|---|
| 1988 | 8,700 | — | — | — | 17.50 | — |
| 1988 Proof | 83,000 | Value: 21.50 | | | | |

**10000 WON** KM# 81 **Weight:** 33.6200 g. **Composition:** 0.9250 Silver 1.0000 oz. ASW **Subject:** Taejon International Exposition **Reverse:** Porcelain celadon

| Date | Mintage | F | VF | XF | Unc | BU |
|---|---|---|---|---|---|---|
| 1993 | — | — | — | — | 32.00 | — |

**10000 WON** KM# 86 **Weight:** 23.0000 g. **Composition:** 0.9000 Silver .6655 oz. ASW **Subject:** 50th Anniversary of Liberation from Japan **Obverse:** Ahn Jong-Kun

| Date | Mintage | F | VF | XF | Unc | BU |
|---|---|---|---|---|---|---|
| 1995 | 40,000 | — | — | — | 35.00 | — |

**10000 WON** KM# 84 **Weight:** 22.5000 g. **Composition:** 0.9250 Silver .6691 oz. ASW **Subject:** 50th Anniversary - Republic of Korea **Obverse:** Ahn Jong-Kun **Note:** With multicolor ENAMEL and with GOLD-PLATED center insert.

| Date | Mintage | F | VF | XF | Unc | BU |
|---|---|---|---|---|---|---|
| (1998) | 100,000 | — | — | — | 35.00 | — |

**10000 WON** KM# 93 **Weight:** 31.1035 g. **Composition:** 0.9990 Silver 1.0000 oz. ASW **Series:** World Cup Soccer **Subject:** Daegu Stadium **Obverse:** Multicolor soccer logo **Reverse:** Player controlling te ball **Edge:** Reeded **Size:** 35 mm.

| Date | Mintage | F | VF | XF | Unc | BU |
|---|---|---|---|---|---|---|
| 2001 Proof | 37,000 | Value: 35.00 | | | | |

**10000 WON** KM# 94 **Weight:** 15.5518 g. **Composition:** 0.9990 Gold .5000 oz. AGW **Series:** World Cup Soccer **Obverse:** Soccer logo **Reverse:** World Cup soccer trophy **Edge:** Reeded **Size:** 28 mm.

| Date | Mintage | F | VF | XF | Unc | BU |
|---|---|---|---|---|---|---|
| 2001 Proof | 20,000 | Value: 300 | | | | |

**10000 WON** KM# 90 **Weight:** 31.1035 g. **Composition:** 0.9990 Silver 1.0000 oz. ASW **Series:** World Cup Soccer **Subject:** Gwangju Stadium **Obverse:** Multicolor soccer logo **Reverse:** Player heading the ball **Edge:** Reeded **Size:** 35 mm.

| Date | Mintage | F | VF | XF | Unc | BU |
|---|---|---|---|---|---|---|
| 2001 Proof | 37,000 | Value: 35.00 | | | | |

**10000 WON** KM# 91 **Weight:** 31.1035 g. **Composition:** 0.9990 Silver 1.0000 oz. ASW **Series:** World Sup Soccer **Subject:** Busan Stadium **Obverse:** Multicolor soccer logo **Reverse:** Player kicking the ball **Edge:** Reeded **Size:** 35 mm.

| Date | Mintage | F | VF | XF | Unc | BU |
|---|---|---|---|---|---|---|
| 2001 Proof | 37,000 | Value: 35.00 | | | | |

**10000 WON** KM# 92 **Weight:** 31.1035 g. **Composition:** 0.9990 Silver 1.0000 oz. ASW **Series:** World Cup Soccer **Subject:** Daegu Stadium **Obverse:** Multicolor soccer logo **Reverse:** Player controlling the ball **Edge:** Reeded **Size:** 35 mm.

| Date | Mintage | F | VF | XF | Unc | BU |
|---|---|---|---|---|---|---|
| 2001 Proof | 37,000 | Value: 35.00 | | | | |

**20000 WON** KM# 18.1 **Weight:** 77.4000 g. **Composition:** 0.9000 Gold 2.2398 oz. AGW **Obverse:** Gold Crown - Silla Dynasty **Reverse:** Similar to 5000 Won, KM#16.1

| Date | Mintage | F | VF | XF | Unc | BU |
|---|---|---|---|---|---|---|
| KE4303(1970)(1970) Proof | 382 | Value: 8,750 | | | | |

**20000 WON** KM# 18.2 **Weight:** 77.4000 g. **Composition:** 0.9000 Gold 2.2398 oz. AGW **Obverse:** Gold Crown - Silla Dynasty **Reverse:** Similar to 5000 Won, KM#16.1

| Date | Mintage | F | VF | XF | Unc | BU |
|---|---|---|---|---|---|---|
| KE4303(1970)(1970) Proof | 52 | Value: 10,000 | | | | |

**20000 WON** KM# 26 **Weight:** 23.0000 g. **Composition:** 0.9000 Silver .6655 oz. ASW **Subject:** 1st Anniveresary of the 5th Repulic

| Date | Mintage | F | VF | XF | Unc | BU |
|---|---|---|---|---|---|---|
| 1981 | 80,000 | — | — | — | 35.00 | — |
| 1981 Unfrosted, proof | 18,000 | Value: 40.00 | | | | |
| 1981 Proof | 2,000 | Value: 320 | | | | |

**20000 WON** KM# 30 **Weight:** 23.0000 g. **Composition:** 0.9000 Silver .6655 oz. ASW **Subject:** 1988 Olympics **Obverse:** Flame

| Date | Mintage | F | VF | XF | Unc | BU |
|---|---|---|---|---|---|---|
| 1982 | 180,000 | — | — | — | 26.50 | — |
| 1982 Unfrosted, proof | 10,000 | Value: 50.00 | | | | |
| 1982 Proof | 10,000 | Value: 75.00 | | | | |

**20000 WON** KM# 38 **Weight:** 23.0000 g. **Composition:** 0.9000 Silver .6655 oz. ASW **Subject:** 1988 Olympics **Obverse:** Wrestlers

| Date | Mintage | F | VF | XF | Unc | BU |
|---|---|---|---|---|---|---|
| 1983 | 123,000 | — | — | — | 25.00 | — |
| 1983 Unfrosted, proof | 56,000 | Value: 32.50 | | | | |
| 1983 Proof | 101,000 | Value: 40.00 | | | | |

**20000 WON** KM# 44 **Composition:** 0.9000 Silver **Subject:** 10th Asian Games **Obverse:** Similar to 1000 Won, KM#41 **Reverse:** Runner

| Date | Mintage | F | VF | XF | Unc | BU |
|---|---|---|---|---|---|---|
| 1986 | 130,000 | — | — | — | 30.00 | — |
| 1986 Proof | 70,000 | Value: 40.00 | | | | |

**20000 WON** KM# 45 **Composition:** 0.9000 Silver **Subject:** 10th Asian Games **Obverse:** Similar to 1000 Won, KM#41 **Reverse:** Pul Guk Temple - Kyong Ju City

| Date | Mintage | F | VF | XF | Unc | BU |
|---|---|---|---|---|---|---|
| 1986 | 130,000 | — | — | — | 28.00 | — |
| 1986 Proof | 70,000 | Value: 40.00 | | | | |

**25000 WON** KM# 19.1 **Weight:** 96.8000 g. **Composition:** 0.9000 Gold 2.8012 oz. AGW **Subject:** 10th Asian Games **Obverse:** King Sejong The Great **Reverse:** Similar to 5000 Won, KM#16.1

| Date | Mintage | F | VF | XF | Unc | BU |
|---|---|---|---|---|---|---|
| KE4303(1970)(1970) Proof | 325 | Value: 14,000 | | | | |

**25000 WON** KM# 19.2 **Weight:** 96.8000 g. **Composition:** 0.9000 Gold 2.8012 oz. AGW **Subject:** 10th Asian Games **Obverse:** King Sejong The Great **Reverse:** Similar to 5000 Won, KM#16.1

| Date | Mintage | F | VF | XF | Unc | BU |
|---|---|---|---|---|---|---|
| KE4303(1970)(1970) Proof | 25 | Value: 17,000 | | | | |

**25000 WON** KM# 58 **Weight:** 16.8100 g. **Composition:** 0.9250 Gold .5000 oz. AGW **Subject:** 1988 Olympics **Reverse:** Folk dancing

| Date | Mintage | F | VF | XF | Unc | BU |
|---|---|---|---|---|---|---|
| 1986 | 20,000 | — | — | — | 200 | — |
| 1986 Proof | 111,000 | Value: 215 | | | | |

**25000 WON** KM# 64 **Weight:** 16.8100 g. **Composition:** 0.9250 Gold .5000 oz. AGW **Subject:** 1988 Olympics **Reverse:** Fan dancing

| Date | Mintage | F | VF | XF | Unc | BU |
|---|---|---|---|---|---|---|
| 1987 | 20,000 | — | — | — | 200 | — |
| 1987 Proof | 82,000 | Value: 220 | | | | |

**25000 WON** KM# 68 **Weight:** 16.8100 g. **Composition:** 0.9250 Gold .5000 oz. AGW **Subject:** 1988 Olympics **Reverse:** Kite flying

| Date | Mintage | F | VF | XF | Unc | BU |
|---|---|---|---|---|---|---|
| 1987 | 20,000 | — | — | — | 200 | — |
| 1987 Proof | 79,000 | Value: 225 | | | | |
| 1988 | — | — | — | — | 200 | — |
| 1988 Proof | — | Value: 225 | | | | |

**25000 WON** KM# 72 **Weight:** 16.8100 g. **Composition:** 0.9250 Gold .5000 oz. AGW **Subject:** 1988 Olympics **Reverse:** Korean Seesaw

| Date | Mintage | F | VF | XF | Unc | BU |
|---|---|---|---|---|---|---|
| 1988 | 19,000 | — | — | — | 200 | — |
| 1988 Proof | 62,000 | Value: 225 | | | | |

**25000 WON** KM# 82 **Weight:** 16.8100 g. **Composition:** 0.9250 Gold .5000 oz. AGW **Subject:** Taejon International Exposition **Reverse:** Celestial globe

| Date | Mintage | F | VF | XF | Unc | BU |
|---|---|---|---|---|---|---|
| 1993 | 40,000 | — | — | — | 375 | — |

**30000 WON** **KM# 95** **Weight:** 31.1035 g. **Composition:** 0.9990 Gold 1.0000 oz. AGW **Series:** World Cup Soccer **Obverse:** Soccer logo **Reverse:** Nude soccer player **Edge:** Reeded **Size:** 35 mm.

| Date | Mintage | F | VF | XF | Unc | BU |
|---|---|---|---|---|---|---|
| 2001 Proof | 12,000 | Value: 550 | | | | |

**50000 WON** **KM# 59** **Weight:** 33.6200 g. **Composition:** 0.9250 Gold 1.0000 oz. AGW **Subject:** 1988 Olympics **Reverse:** Turtle boat

| Date | Mintage | F | VF | XF | Unc | BU |
|---|---|---|---|---|---|---|
| 1986 Proof | 30,000 | Value: 375 | | | | |

**50000 WON** **KM# 65** **Weight:** 33.6200 g. **Composition:** 0.9250 Gold 1.0000 oz. AGW **Subject:** 1988 Olympics **Obverse:** Similar to 10,000 Won, KM#62 **Reverse:** Great South Gate

| Date | Mintage | F | VF | XF | Unc | BU |
|---|---|---|---|---|---|---|
| 1987 Proof | 30,000 | Value: 375 | | | | |

**50000 WON** **KM# 69** **Weight:** 33.6200 g. **Composition:** 0.9250 Gold 1.0000 oz. AGW **Subject:** 1988 Olympics **Obverse:** Similar to 10,000 Won, KM#62 **Reverse:** Horse and rider

| Date | Mintage | F | VF | XF | Unc | BU |
|---|---|---|---|---|---|---|
| 1987 Proof | 30,000 | Value: 375 | | | | |

**50000 WON** **KM# 73** **Weight:** 33.6200 g. **Composition:** 0.9250 Gold 1.0000 oz. AGW **Subject:** 1988 Olympics **Obverse:** Similar to 10,000 Won, KM#62 **Reverse:** Pul Guk Temple

| Date | Mintage | F | VF | XF | Unc | BU |
|---|---|---|---|---|---|---|
| 1988 Proof | 30,000 | Value: 375 | | | | |

**50000 WON** **KM# 83** **Weight:** 33.6200 g. **Composition:** 0.9250 Gold 1.0000 oz. AGW **Subject:** Taejon International Exposition **Reverse:** Tower of Great Light

| Date | Mintage | F | VF | XF | Unc | BU |
|---|---|---|---|---|---|---|
| 1993 | 10,000 | — | — | — | 550 | — |

## BANK SAMPLES

Korean

NOTE: Bank samples countermarked in Korean "Sample" have been prepared for government and banking agencies.

| KM# | Date | Mintage | Identification | Issue Price | Mkt Val |
|---|---|---|---|---|---|
| | | | 견 양 | | |
| S1 | 4292 | — | 10 Hwan. Bronze. KM1. | — | 65.00 |
| S2 | 4292 | — | 50 Hwan. Nickel-Brass. KM2. | — | 75.00 |
| S3 | 4292 | — | 100 Hwan. Copper-Nickel. KM3. | — | 90.00 |
| S4 | 1967 | — | Won. Brass. KM4. | — | — |
| S5 | 1975 | — | 100 Won. Copper-Nickel. KM21. | — | — |
| S6 | 1978 | — | 500 Won. Copper-Nickel. KM22. | — | — |
| S7 | 1978 | — | 5000 Won. Silver. KM23. | — | — |
| S8 | 1984 | — | 20000 Won. Silver. KM26. | — | — |
| S9 | 1984 | — | 50000 Won. Silver. KM40. | — | — |

## MINT SETS

| KM# | Date | Mintage | Identification | Issue Price | Mkt Val |
|---|---|---|---|---|---|
| MSA4 | 1988 | — | KM#46-53 | — | 40.00 |
| MS1 | Mixed dates (6) | 75,000 | KM6a(1980), 32, 34, 35.1 (1983), 27, 31 (1984) | — | 60.00 |
| MS2 | 1983 (6) | — | KM27, 31-32, 33.1, 34, 35.1 | — | 60.00 |
| MS3 | 1986 (5) | 130,000 | KM41-45 | 113 | 100 |
| MS4 | 1991 (6) | — | KM27, 31-32, 33.1, 34, 35.2 | — | 12.00 |
| MS5 | 1993 (6) | 10,000 | KM78-83 | 1,180 | 1,200 |
| MS6 | 1993 (5) | 30,000 | KM78-82 | 443 | 450 |
| MS7 | 1993 (4) | 50,000 | KM78-81 | 97.00 | 100 |
| MS8 | 2001 (7) | — | KM#27, 31, 32, 33.2, 34, 35.2, 89 | — | — |

## PROOF SETS

| KM# | Date | Mintage | Identification | Issue Price | Mkt Val |
|---|---|---|---|---|---|
| PS9 | 2001 (6) | 2,002 | KM#90-95 | — | 1,000 |
| PS1 | 1970 (12) | — | KM7-8, 10-13, 14.1-19.1 | 752 | 31,500 |
| PS2 | 1970 (11) | — | KM7-8, 10-13, 14.2-18.2 | — | 22,350 |
| PS3 | 1970 (6) | — | KM7-8, 10-13 | 53.50 | 1,100 |
| PS4 | 1970 (6) | 300 | KM14.1-19.1 | 698 | 32,000 |
| PS5 | 1970 (6) | 25 | KM14.2-19.2 | — | 38,250 |
| PS6 | 1982 (6) | 2,000 | KM4a-6a, 9, 20, 27, (presentation set) | — | 835 |
| PS7 | 1986 (5) | 70,000 | KM41-45 | 170 | 140 |
| PS8 | 1986 (2) | — | KM46, 50 | — | 18.00 |

The State of Kuwait, a constitutional monarchy located on the Arabian Peninsula at the northwestern corner of the Persian Gulf, has an area of 6,880 sq. mi. (17,820 sq. km.) and a population of 1.7 million. Capital: Kuwait. Petroleum, the basis of the economy, provides 95 percent of the exports.

The modern history of Kuwait began with the founding of the city of Kuwait, 1740, by tribesmen who wandered northward from the region of the Qatar Peninsula of eastern Arabia. Fearing that the Turks would take over the sheikhdom, Sheikh Mubarak entered into an agreement with Great Britain, 1899, placing Kuwait under the protection of Britain and empowering Britain to conduct its foreign affairs. Britain terminated the protectorate on June19, 1961, giving Kuwait its independence (by a simple exchange of notes) but agreeing to furnish military aid on request.

Kuwait was invaded and occupied by an army from neighboring Iraq Aug. 2, 1990. Soon thereafter Iraq declared that the country would become a province of Iraq. An international coalition of military forces primarily based in Saudi Arabia led by the United States under terms set by the United Nations, attacked Iraqi military installations to liberate Kuwait. This occurred Jan. 17, 1991. Kuwait City was liberated Feb.27, and a cease-fire was declared Feb. 28. New paper currency was introduced March 24, 1991 to replace earlier notes.

**TITLES**

al-Kuwait

**RULERS**

British Protectorate, until 1961

**LOCAL**

Al Sabah Dynasty

Mubarak Ibn Sabah, 1896-1915
Jabir Ibn Mubarak, 1915-1917
Salim Ibn Mubarak, 1917-1921
Ahmad Ibn Jabir, 1921-1950
Abdullah Ibn Salim, 1950-1965
Sabah Ibn Salim, 1965-1977
Jabir Ibn Ahmad, 1977-

**MONETARY SYSTEM**

1000 Fils = 1 Dinar

# STATE OF KUWAIT

## MODERN COINAGE

**FILS** **KM# 2** **Composition:** Nickel-Brass

| Date | Mintage | F | VF | XF | Unc | BU |
|---|---|---|---|---|---|---|
| AH1380(1960) | 2,000,000 | — | 0.50 | 1.00 | 1.50 | — |
| AH1380(1960) Proof | 60 | Value: 30.00 | | | | |

**FILS** **KM# 9** **Composition:** Nickel-Brass

| Date | Mintage | F | VF | XF | Unc | BU |
|---|---|---|---|---|---|---|
| AH1382(1962) | 500,000 | — | 0.10 | 0.15 | 0.35 | — |
| AH1382(1962) Proof | 60 | Value: 30.00 | | | | |
| AH1384(1964) | 600,000 | — | 0.25 | 0.75 | 1.50 | — |
| AH1385(1965) | 500,000 | — | 0.25 | 0.75 | 1.50 | — |
| AH1386(1966) | 1,875,000 | — | 0.25 | 0.75 | 1.50 | — |
| AH1389(1969) | 375,000 | — | 0.35 | 1.00 | 2.50 | — |
| AH1390(1970) | 500,000 | — | 0.25 | 0.75 | 1.50 | — |
| AH1391(1971) | 500,000 | — | 0.25 | 0.75 | 1.50 | — |
| AH1392(1972) | 500,000 | — | 0.25 | 0.75 | 1.50 | — |
| AH1393(1973) | 375,000 | — | 0.35 | 1.00 | 2.50 | — |
| AH1395(1975) | 500,000 | — | 0.25 | 0.75 | 1.50 | — |

| Date | Mintage | F | VF | XF | Unc | BU |
|---|---|---|---|---|---|---|
| AH1396(1976) | 2,500,000 | — | 0.15 | 0.25 | 0.50 | — |
| AH1397(1977) | 2,500,000 | — | 0.15 | 0.25 | 0.50 | — |
| AH1399(1979) | 1,500,000 | — | 0.15 | 0.25 | 0.50 | — |
| AH1400(1980) | — | — | 0.15 | 0.25 | 0.50 | — |
| AH1403(1983) | — | — | 0.15 | 0.25 | 0.50 | — |
| AH1407(1987) | — | — | 0.15 | 0.25 | 0.50 | — |
| AH1408(1988) | 500,000 | — | 0.15 | 0.25 | 0.50 | — |

**FILS KM# 9a Weight:** 2.4100 g. **Composition:** 0.9250 Silver .0717 oz. ASW

| Date | Mintage | F | VF | XF | Unc | BU |
|---|---|---|---|---|---|---|
| AH1407(1987) Proof | — | Value: 100 | | | | |

**FILS KM# 9b Weight:** 4.0400 g. **Composition:** 0.9170 Gold .1191 oz. AGW

| Date | Mintage | F | VF | XF | Unc | BU |
|---|---|---|---|---|---|---|
| AH1407(1987) Proof | — | — | — | — | — | — |

**5 FILS KM# 3 Composition:** Nickel-Brass

| Date | Mintage | F | VF | XF | Unc | BU |
|---|---|---|---|---|---|---|
| AH1380(1960) | 2,400,000 | — | 0.60 | 1.25 | 2.00 | — |
| AH1380(1960) Proof | 60 | Value: 35.00 | | | | |

**5 FILS KM# 10 Composition:** Nickel-Brass

| Date | Mintage | F | VF | XF | Unc | BU |
|---|---|---|---|---|---|---|
| AH1382(1962) | 1,800,000 | — | 0.10 | 0.20 | 0.45 | — |
| AH1382(1962) Proof | 60 | Value: 35.00 | | | | |
| AH1384(1964) | 600,000 | — | 0.30 | 0.75 | 2.00 | — |
| AH1386(1966) | 1,600,000 | — | 0.20 | 0.35 | 1.00 | — |
| AH1388(1968) | 800,000 | — | 0.30 | 0.75 | 2.25 | — |
| AH1389(1969) | — | — | 0.30 | 0.75 | 2.25 | — |
| AH1389(1969) | 600,000 | — | 0.30 | 0.75 | 2.25 | — |
| AH1390(1970) | 600,000 | — | 0.30 | 0.75 | 2.25 | — |
| AH1391(1971) | 600,000 | — | 0.30 | 0.75 | 2.25 | — |
| AH1392(1972) | 800,000 | — | 0.25 | 0.65 | 1.75 | — |
| AH1393(1973) | 800,000 | — | 0.25 | 0.65 | 1.75 | — |
| AH1394(1974) | 1,200,000 | — | 0.10 | 0.20 | 1.00 | — |
| AH1395(1975) | 5,020,000 | — | 0.10 | 0.20 | 0.50 | — |
| AH1396(1976) | 180,000 | — | 0.35 | 1.00 | 3.00 | — |
| AH1397(1977) | 4,000,000 | — | 0.10 | 0.20 | 0.40 | — |
| AH1399(1979) | 6,700,000 | — | 0.10 | 0.20 | 0.40 | — |
| AH1400(1980) | — | — | 0.10 | 0.20 | 0.40 | — |
| AH1401(1981) | 7,000,000 | — | 0.10 | 0.20 | 0.40 | — |
| AH1403(1983) | — | — | 0.10 | 0.20 | 0.40 | — |
| AH1405(1985) | — | — | 0.10 | 0.20 | 0.40 | — |
| AH1407(1987) | — | — | 0.10 | 0.20 | 0.40 | — |
| AH1408(1988) | 3,000,000 | — | 0.10 | 0.20 | 0.40 | — |
| AH1410(1990) | — | — | 0.10 | 0.20 | 0.40 | — |
| AH1415(1994) | — | — | 0.10 | 0.20 | 0.40 | — |

**Note:** Varieties exist

**5 FILS KM# 10B Weight:** 5.0500 g. **Composition:** 0.9170 Gold .1488 oz. AGW

| Date | Mintage | F | VF | XF | Unc | BU |
|---|---|---|---|---|---|---|
| AH1407(1987) Proof | — | — | — | — | — | — |

**5 FILS KM# 10a Weight:** 3.0100 g. **Composition:** 0.9260 Silver .0895 oz. ASW

| Date | Mintage | F | VF | XF | Unc | BU |
|---|---|---|---|---|---|---|
| AH1407(1987) Proof | — | Value: 100 | | | | |

**10 FILS KM# 4 Composition:** Nickel-Brass

| Date | Mintage | F | VF | XF | Unc | BU |
|---|---|---|---|---|---|---|
| AH1380(1960) | 2,600,000 | — | 0.65 | 1.25 | 2.00 | — |
| AH1380(1960) Proof | 60 | Value: 40.00 | | | | |

**10 FILS KM# 11 Composition:** Nickel-Brass

| Date | Mintage | F | VF | XF | Unc | BU |
|---|---|---|---|---|---|---|
| AH1382(1962) | 1,360,000 | — | 0.15 | 0.25 | 0.65 | — |
| AH1382(1962) Proof | 60 | Value: 40.00 | | | | |
| AH1384(1964) | 800,000 | — | 0.35 | 0.85 | 2.50 | — |
| AH1386(1966) | 1,360,000 | — | 0.30 | 0.75 | 1.75 | — |
| AH1388(1968) | 672,000 | — | 0.35 | 0.85 | 2.50 | — |
| AH1389(1969) | 480,000 | — | 0.50 | 1.00 | 2.75 | — |
| AH1389(1969) | 640,000 | — | 0.35 | 0.85 | 2.50 | — |
| AH1390(1970) | 480,000 | — | 0.50 | 1.00 | 2.75 | — |
| AH1391(1971) | 800,000 | — | 0.35 | 0.85 | 2.50 | — |
| AH1392(1972) | 1,120,000 | — | 0.15 | 0.40 | 2.00 | — |
| AH1393(1973) | 1,440,000 | — | 0.15 | 0.40 | 2.00 | — |
| AH1394(1974) | 1,280,000 | — | 0.15 | 0.40 | 2.00 | — |
| AH1395(1975) | 5,280,000 | — | 0.15 | 0.25 | 0.75 | — |
| AH1396(1976) | 2,400,000 | — | 0.15 | 0.25 | 0.75 | — |
| AH1397(1977) | — | — | 0.15 | 0.25 | 0.75 | — |
| AH1399(1979) | 6,160,000 | — | 0.15 | 0.25 | 0.75 | — |
| AH1400(1980) | — | — | 0.15 | 0.25 | 0.75 | — |
| AH1401(1981) | 8,320,000 | — | 0.15 | 0.25 | 0.75 | — |
| AH1403(1983) | — | — | 0.15 | 0.25 | 0.75 | — |
| AH1405(1985) | — | — | 0.15 | 0.25 | 0.75 | — |
| AH1407(1987) | — | — | 0.15 | 0.25 | 0.75 | — |
| AH1408(1988) | 5,000,000 | — | 0.15 | 0.25 | 0.75 | — |
| AH1410(1990) | — | — | 0.15 | 0.25 | 0.75 | — |

**Note:** Varieties exist

**10 FILS KM# 11b Weight:** 7.6300 g. **Composition:** 0.9170 Gold .2250 oz. AGW

| Date | Mintage | F | VF | XF | Unc | BU |
|---|---|---|---|---|---|---|
| AH1407(1987) Proof | — | — | — | — | — | — |

**10 FILS KM# 11a Weight:** 4.3500 g. **Composition:** 0.9250 Silver .1294 oz. ASW

| Date | Mintage | F | VF | XF | Unc | BU |
|---|---|---|---|---|---|---|
| AH1407(1987) Proof | — | Value: 110 | | | | |

**20 FILS KM# 5 Composition:** Copper-Nickel

| Date | Mintage | F | VF | XF | Unc | BU |
|---|---|---|---|---|---|---|
| AH1380(1960) | 2,000,000 | — | 0.75 | 1.50 | 2.50 | — |
| AH1380(1960) Proof | 60 | Value: 45.00 | | | | |

**20 FILS KM# 12 Composition:** Copper-Nickel

| Date | Mintage | F | VF | XF | Unc | BU |
|---|---|---|---|---|---|---|
| AH1382(1962) | 1,200,000 | — | 0.25 | 0.35 | 0.75 | — |
| AH1382(1962) Proof | 60 | Value: 45.00 | | | | |
| AH1384(1964) | 480,000 | — | 0.50 | 1.00 | 3.00 | — |
| AH1386(1966) | 1,280,000 | — | 0.35 | 0.85 | 2.00 | — |
| AH1388(1968) | 672,000 | — | 0.35 | 0.85 | 2.50 | — |
| AH1389(1969) | 800,000 | — | 0.35 | 0.85 | 2.50 | — |
| AH1389(1969) | 480,000 | — | 0.50 | 1.00 | 3.00 | — |
| AH1390(1970) | 480,000 | — | 0.50 | 1.00 | 3.00 | — |
| AH1391(1971) | 960,000 | — | 0.35 | 0.85 | 2.00 | — |
| AH1392(1972) | 1,440,000 | — | 0.20 | 0.45 | 2.00 | — |
| AH1393(1973) | 1,280,000 | — | 0.20 | 0.45 | 2.00 | — |
| AH1394(1974) | 1,600,000 | — | 0.20 | 0.45 | 1.50 | — |
| AH1395(1975) | 2,400,000 | — | 0.20 | 0.30 | 1.25 | — |
| AH1396(1976) | 3,200,000 | — | 0.20 | 0.30 | 1.25 | — |
| AH1397(1977) | 3,400,000 | — | 0.20 | 0.30 | 1.25 | — |
| AH1399(1979) | 5,520,000 | — | 0.20 | 0.30 | 1.25 | — |
| AH1400(1980) | — | — | 0.20 | 0.30 | 1.00 | — |
| AH1401(1981) | 8,960,000 | — | 0.20 | 0.30 | 1.00 | — |
| AH1403(1983) | — | — | 0.20 | 0.30 | 1.00 | — |
| AH1405(1985) | — | — | 0.20 | 0.30 | 1.00 | — |
| AH1407(1987) | — | — | 0.20 | 0.30 | 1.00 | — |
| AH1408(1988) | 5,000,000 | — | 0.20 | 0.30 | 1.00 | — |
| AH1410(1990) | — | — | 0.20 | 0.30 | 1.00 | — |
| AH1415(1994) | — | — | 0.20 | 0.30 | 1.00 | — |

**Note:** Varieties exist

**20 FILS KM# 12b Weight:** 5.6700 g. **Composition:** 0.9170 Gold .1672 oz. AGW

| Date | Mintage | F | VF | XF | Unc | BU |
|---|---|---|---|---|---|---|
| AH1407(1987) Proof | — | — | — | — | — | — |

**20 FILS KM# 12a Weight:** 3.3700 g. **Composition:** 0.9250 Silver .1002 oz. ASW

| Date | Mintage | F | VF | XF | Unc | BU |
|---|---|---|---|---|---|---|
| AH1407(1987) Proof | — | Value: 110 | | | | |

**50 FILS KM# 6 Composition:** Copper-Nickel

| Date | Mintage | F | VF | XF | Unc | BU |
|---|---|---|---|---|---|---|
| AH1380(1960) | 1,720,000 | — | 0.85 | 1.75 | 2.75 | — |
| AH1380(1960) Proof | 60 | Value: 60.00 | | | | |

**50 FILS KM# 13 Composition:** Copper-Nickel

| Date | Mintage | F | VF | XF | Unc | BU |
|---|---|---|---|---|---|---|
| AH1382(1962) | 900,000 | — | 0.50 | 0.75 | 1.25 | — |
| AH1382(1962) Proof | 60 | Value: 60.00 | | | | |
| AH1384(1964) | 300,000 | — | 0.75 | 1.50 | 4.00 | — |
| AH1386(1966) | 800,000 | — | 0.40 | 0.85 | 2.50 | — |
| AH1388(1968) | 200,000 | — | 1.00 | 2.00 | 6.00 | — |
| AH1389(1969) | 400,000 | — | 0.50 | 1.00 | 3.00 | — |
| AH1389(1969) | 500,000 | — | 0.50 | 1.00 | 3.00 | — |
| AH1390(1970) | 300,000 | — | 0.75 | 1.50 | 4.00 | — |
| AH1391(1971) | 500,000 | — | 0.50 | 1.00 | 3.00 | — |
| AH1392(1972) | 900,000 | — | 0.50 | 0.85 | 2.50 | — |
| AH1393(1973) | 800,000 | — | 0.50 | 0.85 | 2.50 | — |
| AH1394(1974) | 1,000,000 | — | 0.35 | 0.50 | 2.00 | — |
| AH1395(1975) | 1,950,000 | — | 0.35 | 0.50 | 2.00 | — |
| AH1396(1976) | 2,250,000 | — | 0.25 | 0.35 | 2.00 | — |
| AH1397(1977) | 6,000,000 | — | 0.25 | 0.35 | 1.35 | — |
| AH1399(1979) | 6,050,000 | — | 0.25 | 0.35 | 1.35 | — |
| AH1400(1980) | — | — | 0.25 | 0.35 | 1.35 | — |
| AH1401(1981) | 3,000,000 | — | 0.25 | 0.35 | 1.35 | — |
| AH1403(1983) | — | — | 0.25 | 0.35 | 1.35 | — |
| AH1405(1985) | — | — | 0.25 | 0.35 | 1.35 | — |
| AH1407(1987) | 2,000,000 | — | 0.25 | 0.35 | 1.35 | — |
| AH1408(1988) | 3,000,000 | — | 0.25 | 0.35 | 1.35 | — |
| AH1410(1990) | — | — | 0.25 | 0.35 | 1.35 | — |
| AH1413(1992) | — | — | 0.25 | 0.35 | 1.35 | — |
| AH1415(1994) | — | — | 0.25 | 0.35 | 1.35 | — |

**Note:** Varieties exist

| Date | Mintage | F | VF | XF | Unc | BU |
|---|---|---|---|---|---|---|
| AH1417(1997) | — | — | 0.25 | 0.35 | 1.35 | — |

**50 FILS KM# 13b Weight:** 8.5200 g. **Composition:** 0.9170 Gold .2512 oz. AGW

| Date | Mintage | F | VF | XF | Unc | BU |
|---|---|---|---|---|---|---|
| AH1407(1987) Proof | — | — | — | — | — | — |

**50 FILS KM# 13a Weight:** 5.0700 g. **Composition:** 0.9250 Silver .1511 oz. ASW

| Date | Mintage | F | VF | XF | Unc | BU |
|---|---|---|---|---|---|---|
| AH1407(1987) Proof | — | Value: 120 | | | | |

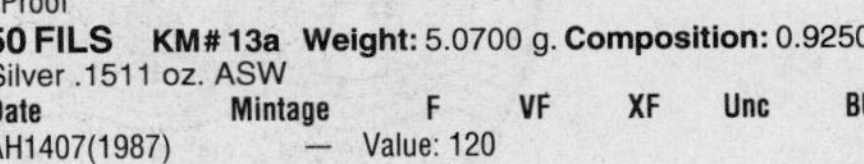

**100 FILS KM# 7 Composition:** Copper-Nickel

| Date | Mintage | F | VF | XF | Unc | BU |
|---|---|---|---|---|---|---|
| AH1380(1960) | 1,260,000 | — | 1.00 | 2.00 | 3.25 | — |
| AH1380(1960) Proof | 60 | Value: 90.00 | | | | |

**100 FILS** **KM# 14** **Composition:** Copper-Nickel

| Date | Mintage | F | VF | XF | Unc | BU |
|---|---|---|---|---|---|---|
| AH1382(1962) | 640,000 | — | 0.50 | 0.65 | 1.50 | — |
| AH1382(1962) Proof | 60 | Value: 90.00 | | | | |
| AH1384(1964) | 160,000 | — | 1.75 | 3.00 | 6.00 | — |
| AH1386(1966) | 640,000 | — | 1.00 | 1.50 | 3.00 | — |
| AH1388(1968) | 160,000 | — | 1.75 | 3.00 | 6.00 | — |
| AH1389(1969) | 320,000 | — | 1.00 | 2.00 | 4.00 | — |
| AH1391(1971) | 240,000 | — | 1.25 | 2.00 | 4.00 | — |
| AH1392(1972) | 400,000 | — | 1.00 | 1.50 | 3.00 | — |
| AH1393(1973) | 480,000 | — | 1.00 | 1.50 | 3.00 | — |
| AH1394(1974) | 480,000 | — | 1.00 | 1.50 | 3.00 | — |
| AH1395(1975) | 3,040,000 | — | 0.50 | 0.75 | 1.75 | — |
| AH1396(1976) | — | — | 0.50 | 0.75 | 1.75 | — |
| AH1397(1977) | 1,600,000 | — | 0.50 | 0.75 | 1.75 | — |
| AH1399(1979) | 3,040,000 | — | 0.50 | 0.75 | 1.75 | — |
| AH1400(1980) | — | — | 0.50 | 0.75 | 1.75 | — |
| AH1401(1981) | 2,960,000 | — | 0.50 | 0.75 | 1.75 | — |
| AH1403(1983) | — | — | 0.50 | 0.75 | 1.75 | — |
| AH1405(1985) | — | — | 0.50 | 0.75 | 1.75 | — |
| AH1407(1987) | 2,000,000 | — | 0.50 | 0.75 | 1.75 | — |
| AH1408(1988) | 2,000,000 | — | 0.50 | 0.75 | 1.75 | — |
| AH1410(1990) | — | — | 0.50 | 0.75 | 1.75 | — |
| AH1415(1994) | — | — | 0.50 | 0.75 | 1.75 | — |

**Note:** Varieties exist

**100 FILS** **KM# 14b** **Weight:** 12.3300 g. **Composition:** 0.9170 Gold .3635 oz. AGW

| Date | Mintage | F | VF | XF | Unc | BU |
|---|---|---|---|---|---|---|
| AH1407(1987) Proof | — | — | — | — | — | — |

**100 FILS** **KM# 14a** **Weight:** 7.3400 g. **Composition:** 0.9250 Silver .2183 oz. ASW

| Date | Mintage | F | VF | XF | Unc | BU |
|---|---|---|---|---|---|---|
| AH1407(1987) Proof | — | Value: 130 | | | | |
| AH1407(1987) Proof | — | Value: 130 | | | | |

**2 DINARS** **KM# 15a** **Weight:** 28.2800 g. **Composition:** 0.9250 Silver .8411 oz. ASW **Subject:** 15th Anninversary of Independence

| Date | Mintage | F | VF | XF | Unc | BU |
|---|---|---|---|---|---|---|
| ND(1976) Proof | 53,000 | Value: 65.00 | | | | |

**2 DINARS** **KM# 15** **Weight:** 28.2800 g. **Composition:** 0.5000 Silver .4546 oz. ASW **Subject:** 15th Anninversary of Independence

| Date | Mintage | F | VF | XF | Unc | BU |
|---|---|---|---|---|---|---|
| ND(1976) | 70,000 | — | — | — | 45.00 | — |

**2 DINARS** **KM# 24** **Weight:** 28.2800 g. **Composition:** 0.9250 Silver .8411 oz. ASW **Subject:** 50th Anniversary - United Nations

| Date | Mintage | F | VF | XF | Unc | BU |
|---|---|---|---|---|---|---|
| ND(1996) Proof | Est. 110,000 | Value: 37.50 | | | | |

**5 DINARS** **KM# 8** **Weight:** 13.5720 g. **Composition:** 0.9170 Gold .4001 oz. AGW

| Date | Mintage | F | VF | XF | Unc | BU |
|---|---|---|---|---|---|---|
| AH1380(1960) | Est. 1,000 | — | — | — | — | — |

**5 DINARS** **KM# 18** **Weight:** 28.2800 g. **Composition:** 0.9250 Silver .8411 oz. ASW **Subject:** 20th Anniversary of Independence **Reverse:** Similar to 100 Dinars, KM#19

| Date | Mintage | F | VF | XF | Unc | BU |
|---|---|---|---|---|---|---|
| ND(1980) Proof | 10,000 | Value: 65.00 | | | | |

**5 DINARS** **KM# 16** **Weight:** 28.2800 g. **Composition:** 0.9250 Silver .8411 oz. ASW **Subject:** 15th Century of the Hijira

| Date | Mintage | F | VF | XF | Unc | BU |
|---|---|---|---|---|---|---|
| AH1401(1981) Proof | 10,000 | Value: 65.00 | | | | |

**5 DINARS** **KM# 20** **Weight:** 33.6250 g. **Composition:** 0.9250 Silver 1.0000 oz. ASW **Subject:** 25th Anniversary of Kuwait Currency **Obverse:** Arabic denomination, buildings, port scene and refinery **Reverse:** English legend, falcon, dhow, building and map on globe

| Date | Mintage | F | VF | XF | Unc | BU |
|---|---|---|---|---|---|---|
| ND(1985) Proof | — | Value: 85.00 | | | | |

**50 DINARS** **KM# 21** **Weight:** 16.9660 g. **Composition:** 0.9170 Gold .5000 oz. AGW **Subject:** 25th Anniversary of Kuwait Independence **Obverse:** Arabic legend, arched design, falcon, tent, dhow and pearl in a shell **Reverse:** Radiant sun, mosque and assembly building, English and Arabic legend

| Date | Mintage | F | VF | XF | Unc | BU |
|---|---|---|---|---|---|---|
| AH1406(1986) Proof | — | Value: 275 | | | | |

**100 DINARS** **KM# 19** **Weight:** 15.9800 g. **Composition:** 0.9170 Gold .4711 oz. AGW **Subject:** 20th Anniversary of Independence

| Date | Mintage | F | VF | XF | Unc | BU |
|---|---|---|---|---|---|---|
| (1980) Proof | 10,000 | Value: 400 | | | | |

**100 DINARS** KM# 17 **Weight:** 15.9800 g. **Composition:** 0.9170 Gold .4711 oz. AGW **Subject:** 15th Century of the Hijira

| Date | Mintage | F | VF | XF | Unc | BU |
|---|---|---|---|---|---|---|
| AH1401(1981) Proof | 10,000 | Value: 375 | | | | |

## MEDALLIC COINAGE

**5 DINARS** KM# M9 **Weight:** 28.2800 g. **Composition:** 0.9250 Silver .8410 oz. ASW **Subject:** 35th Anniversary of National Day **Obverse:** Palace **Reverse:** Flag and building

| Date | Mintage | F | VF | XF | Unc | BU |
|---|---|---|---|---|---|---|
| ND(1985) | — | — | — | — | 65.00 | — |

**5 DINARS** KM# M13 **Weight:** 28.2800 g. **Composition:** 0.9250 Silver .8410 oz. ASW **Subject:** 50th Anniversary of Exporting 1st Oil Shipment **Obverse:** State seal, pump and tankers **Reverse:** Oil well and tanks

| Date | Mintage | F | VF | XF | Unc | BU |
|---|---|---|---|---|---|---|
| ND(1985) | — | — | — | — | 65.00 | — |

**5 DINARS** KM# M6 **Weight:** 33.6250 g. **Composition:** 0.9250 Silver 1.0000 oz. ASW **Subject:** 5th Islamic Summit Conference **Obverse:** Arabic, English and French legend, crescent and minaret. **Reverse:** Arms

| Date | Mintage | F | VF | XF | Unc | BU |
|---|---|---|---|---|---|---|
| ND(1986) Proof | — | — | — | — | — | — |

**5 DINARS** KM# M5 **Weight:** 28.2800 g. **Composition:** 0.9250 Silver .8410 oz. ASW **Subject:** Liberation of Kuwait **Obverse:** Legend in center circle and three inner rings **Reverse:** "Kuwait is free", row of buildings

| Date | Mintage | F | VF | XF | Unc | BU |
|---|---|---|---|---|---|---|
| ND(1991) | — | Value: 65.00 | | | | |
| ND(AH1407) Proof | — | Value: 60.00 | | | | |

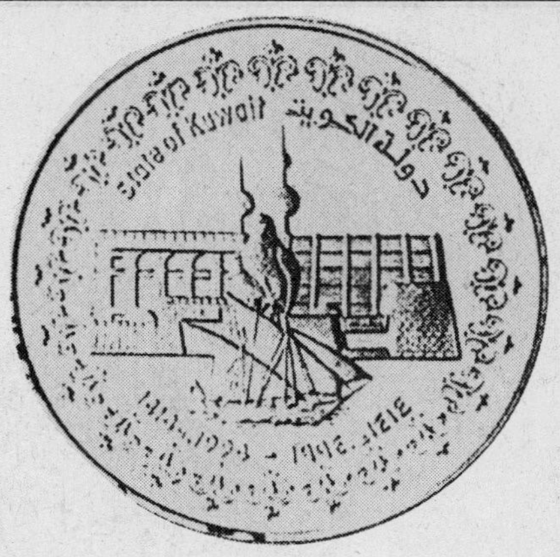

**5 DINARS** KM# M8 **Weight:** 72.5000 g. **Composition:** 0.9250 Silver 2.1561 oz. ASW **Subject:** 25th Anniversary - Central Bank **Obverse:** Falcon, ship and building **Reverse:** Inscription

| Date | Mintage | F | VF | XF | Unc | BU |
|---|---|---|---|---|---|---|
| ND(1994) | — | — | — | — | 120 | — |

**5 DINARS** KM# M11 **Weight:** 28.2800 g. **Composition:** 0.9250 Silver .8410 oz. ASW **Subject:** 5th Liberation Day **Obverse:** State seal **Reverse:** Finger print

| Date | Mintage | F | VF | XF | Unc | BU |
|---|---|---|---|---|---|---|
| AH1406(1996) | — | — | — | — | 65.00 | — |

**5 DINARS** **KM# M15** **Weight:** 28.2800 g. **Composition:** 0.9250 Silver .8410 oz. ASW **Subject:** 30th Anniversary - Kuwait University **Obverse:** Coat of arms

| Date | Mintage | F | VF | XF | Unc | BU |
|---|---|---|---|---|---|---|
| ND(1996) Proof | — | Value: 75.00 | | | | |

**50 DINARS** **KM# M12** **Weight:** 16.9660 g. **Composition:** 0.9170 Gold .5000 oz. AGW **Subject:** 5th Liberation Day **Obverse:** State seal **Reverse:** Finger print

| Date | Mintage | F | VF | XF | Unc | BU |
|---|---|---|---|---|---|---|
| ND(1985) Proof | — | Value: 275 | | | | |

**50 DINARS** **KM# M7** **Weight:** 16.9660 g. **Composition:** 0.9170 Gold .5000 oz. AGW **Subject:** 5th Islamic Summit Conference **Obverse:** Arabic, English and French legend, crescent and minaret **Reverse:** Dhow

| Date | Mintage | F | VF | XF | Unc | BU |
|---|---|---|---|---|---|---|
| ND(1987) Proof | — | Value: 350 | | | | |

**50 DINARS** **KM# M16** **Weight:** 16.9660 g. **Composition:** 0.9170 Gold .5000 oz. AGW **Subject:** 1st Anniversary - Liberation Day **Obverse:** Concentric legends **Reverse:** Building

| Date | Mintage | F | VF | XF | Unc | BU |
|---|---|---|---|---|---|---|
| ND(1991) | — | Value: 275 | | | | |

**50 DINARS** **KM# M10** **Weight:** 16.9660 g. **Composition:** 0.9170 Gold .5000 oz. AGW **Subject:** 35th Anniversary of the National Day **Obverse:** Palace **Reverse:** Flag on builiding

| Date | Mintage | F | VF | XF | Unc | BU |
|---|---|---|---|---|---|---|
| ND(1996) | — | — | — | — | 275 | — |

**50 DINARS** **KM# M14** **Weight:** 16.9660 g. **Composition:** 0.9170 Gold .5000 oz. AGW **Subject:** 50th Anniversary of Exporting 1st Oil Shipment **Obverse:** State seal, pum and tankers **Reverse:** Well and tanks

| Date | Mintage | F | VF | XF | Unc | BU |
|---|---|---|---|---|---|---|
| ND(1996) | — | — | — | — | 275 | — |

## MINT SETS

| KM# | Date | Mintage | Identification | Issue Price | Mkt Val |
|---|---|---|---|---|---|
| MS1 | 1393-94 (6) | — | KM9-14 | 1.75 | 30.00 |

## PROOF SETS

| KM# | Date | Mintage | Identification | Issue Price | Mkt Val |
|---|---|---|---|---|---|
| PS1 | 1961 (6) | 60 | KM2-7 | — | 300 |
| PS2 | 1962 (6) | 60 | KM9-14 | — | 300 |
| PS3 | 1987 (6) | — | KM9a-14a | — | 675 |
| PS4 | 1987 (6) | — | KM9b-14b | — | — |

# KYRGYZSTAN



The Republic of Kyrgyzstan, (formerly Kirghiz S.S.R., a Union Republic of the U.S.S.R.), independent state since Aug. 31, 1991, is a member of the United Nations and of the C.I.S. It was the last state of the Union Republics to declare its sovereignty. Capital: Bishkek (formerly Frunze).

Originally part of the Autonomous Turkestan S.S.R. founded on May 1, 1918, the Kyrgyz ethnic area was established on October 14, 1924 as the Kara-Kirghiz Autonomous Region within the R.S.F.S.R. Then on May25, 1925 the name Kara (black) was dropped. It became an A.S.S.R. on Feb. 1, 1926 and a Union Republic of the U.S.S.R. in 1936. On Dec. 12, 1990, the name was then changed to the Republic of Kyrgyzstan.

**10 SOM** **KM# 1** **Weight:** 28.2800 g. **Composition:** 0.9250 Silver .8411 oz. ASW **Subject:** Millenium of Manas

| Date | Mintage | F | VF | XF | Unc | BU |
|---|---|---|---|---|---|---|
| 1995 Proof | Est. 20,000 | Value: 50.00 | | | | |

**100 SOM** **KM# 2** **Weight:** 6.2200 g. **Composition:** 0.9990 Gold .2000 oz. AGW **Subject:** Millenium of Manas

| Date | Mintage | F | VF | XF | Unc | BU |
|---|---|---|---|---|---|---|
| 1995 Proof | Est. 5,000 | Value: 185 | | | | |

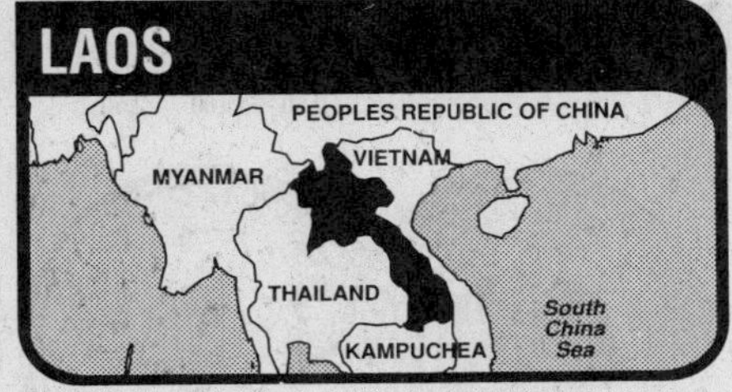


The Lao Peoples Democratic Republic, located on the Indo-Chinese Peninsula between the Socialist Republic of Vietnam and the Kingdom of Thailand, has an area of 91,428 sq. mi. (236,800 km.) and a population of 3.6 million. Capital Vientiane. Agriculture employs 95 per cent of the people. Tin, lumber and coffee are exported.

The first United Kingdom of Lan Xang (Million Elephants) was established in themid-14th century by King Fa Ngum who ruled an area including present Laos, northeastern Thailand, and the southern part of China's Yunnan province from his capital at Luang Prabang. Thailand and Vietnam obtained control over much of the present Lao territory in the 18th century and remained dominant until France established a protectorate over the area in 1893 and incorporated it into the Union of Indo-China. The Independence of Laos was pro-claimed in March of 1945, during the last days of the Japanese occupation of World War II. France reoccupied Laos in 1946, and established it as a constitutional monarchy within the French Union in 1949. In 1953 war erupted between the government and the Pathet Lao, a Communist movement supported by the Vietnamese Communist forces. Peace was declared in 1954 with Laos becoming fully independent in 1955 and the Pathet Lao being permitted to occupy two northern provinces. Civil war broke out again in 1960 with the United States supporting the government of the Kingdom of Laos and the North Vietnamese helping the Communist Pathet Lao, and continued, with intervals of truce and political compromise, until the formation of the Lao Peoples Democratic Republic on Dec. 2, 1975.

**NOTE:** For earlier coinage see French Indo-China.

**RULERS**

Sisavang Vong, 1904-1959
Savang Vatthana, 1959-1975

**MONETARY SYSTEM**

100 Cents = 1 Piastre

**Commencing 1955**

100 Att = 1 Kip

**MINT MARKS**

(a) - Paris, privy marks only
Key - Havana
None - Berlin

NOTE: Private bullion issues previously listed here are now listed in *Unusual World Coins,* 3rd Edition, Krause Publications, Inc., 1992.

# KINGDOM

## STANDARD COINAGE

**10 CENTS** **KM# 4** **Composition:** Aluminum **Ruler:** Sisavang Vong

| Date | Mintage | F | VF | XF | Unc | BU |
|---|---|---|---|---|---|---|
| 1952(a) | 2,000,000 | — | 0.25 | 0.60 | 1.25 | — |

**20 CENTS** **KM# 5** **Composition:** Aluminum **Ruler:** Sisavang Vong

| Date | Mintage | F | VF | XF | Unc | BU |
|---|---|---|---|---|---|---|
| 1952(a) | 3,000,000 | — | 0.35 | 0.75 | 1.50 | — |

**50 CENTS** **KM# 6** **Composition:** Aluminum **Ruler:** Sisavang Vong

| Date | Mintage | F | VF | XF | Unc | BU |
|---|---|---|---|---|---|---|
| 1952(a) | 1,400,000 | — | 0.75 | 1.25 | 2.50 | — |

**1000 KIP** **KM# 7** **Weight:** 10.0000 g. **Composition:** 0.9250 Silver .2973 oz. ASW **Ruler:** Savang Vatthana **Subject:** King Savang Vatthana coronation

| Date | Mintage | F | VF | XF | Unc | BU |
|---|---|---|---|---|---|---|
| 1971 | — | — | — | — | 25.00 | — |
| 1971 Proof | 20,000 | Value: 35.00 | | | | |

**2500 KIP** **KM# 8** **Weight:** 20.0000 g. **Composition:** 0.9250 Silver .5947 oz. ASW **Ruler:** Savang Vatthana **Subject:** King Savang Vatthana coronation

| Date | Mintage | F | VF | XF | Unc | BU |
|---|---|---|---|---|---|---|
| 1971 | — | — | — | — | 35.00 | — |
| 1971 Proof | 20,000 | Value: 45.00 | | | | |

**4000 KIP** **KM# 9** **Weight:** 4.0000 g. **Composition:** 0.9000 Gold .1157 oz. AGW **Ruler:** Savang Vatthana **Subject:** King Savang Vatthana coronation

| Date | Mintage | F | VF | XF | Unc | BU |
|---|---|---|---|---|---|---|
| 1971 Proof | 10,000 | Value: 120 | | | | |

**5000 KIP** **KM# 10** **Weight:** 40.0000 g. **Composition:** 0.9250 Silver 1.1895 oz. ASW **Ruler:** Savang Vatthana **Subject:** King Savang Vatthana coronation **Obverse:** Similar to 2500 Kip, KM#8

| Date | Mintage | F | VF | XF | Unc | BU |
|---|---|---|---|---|---|---|
| 1971 | — | — | — | — | 100 | — |
| 1971 Proof | 20,000 | Value: 125 | | | | |

**5000 KIP** **KM# 16.1** **Weight:** 11.7000 g. **Composition:** 0.9250 Silver .3479 oz. ASW **Ruler:** Savang Vatthana **Subject:** Laotian maiden

| Date | Mintage | F | VF | XF | Unc | BU |
|---|---|---|---|---|---|---|
| 1975 | 400 | — | — | — | 120 | — |
| 1975 Proof | 775 | Value: 125 | | | | |

**5000 KIP** **KM# 16.2** **Weight:** 11.7000 g. **Composition:** 0.9250 Silver .3479 oz. ASW **Ruler:** Savang Vatthana **Subject:** Laotian maiden

| Date | Mintage | F | VF | XF | Unc | BU |
|---|---|---|---|---|---|---|
| ND(1975) | — | — | — | — | 100 | — |

**5000 KIP** **KM# 17** **Weight:** 11.7000 g. **Composition:** 0.9250 Silver .3479 oz. ASW **Ruler:** Savang Vatthana **Subject:** Wat Phra Kio Museum, Vientiane

| Date | Mintage | F | VF | XF | Unc | BU |
|---|---|---|---|---|---|---|
| 1975 | 400 | — | — | — | 120 | — |
| 1975 Proof | 775 | Value: 125 | | | | |

**8000 KIP** **KM# 11** **Weight:** 8.0000 g. **Composition:** 0.9000 Gold .2315 oz. AGW **Ruler:** Savang Vatthana **Subject:** King Savang Vatthana coronation

| Date | Mintage | F | VF | XF | Unc | BU |
|---|---|---|---|---|---|---|
| 1971 Proof | 10,000 | Value: 200 | | | | |

**10000 KIP** **KM#12** **Weight:** 80.0000 g. **Composition:** 0.9250 Silver 2.3791 oz. ASW **Ruler:** Savang Vatthana **Subject:** King Savang Vatthana coronation **Obverse:** Similar to 2500 Kip, KM#8

| Date | Mintage | F | VF | XF | Unc | BU |
|---|---|---|---|---|---|---|
| 1971 | — | — | — | — | 150 | — |
| 1971 Proof | Est. 20,000 | Value: 250 | | | | |

**10000 KIP** **KM# 18** **Weight:** 23.5000 g. **Composition:** 0.9250 Silver .6988 oz. ASW **Ruler:** Savang Vatthana **Subject:** Wat Xieng - Thong Temple

| Date | Mintage | F | VF | XF | Unc | BU |
|---|---|---|---|---|---|---|
| 1975 | 300 | — | — | — | 170 | — |
| 1975 Proof | 650 | Value: 190 | | | | |

**20000 KIP** **KM# 13** **Weight:** 20.0000 g. **Composition:** 0.9000 Gold .5787 oz. AGW **Ruler:** Savang Vatthana **Subject:** King Savang Vatthana coronation

| Date | Mintage | F | VF | XF | Unc | BU |
|---|---|---|---|---|---|---|
| 1971 Proof | Est. 10,000 | Value: 400 | | | | |

**40000 KIP** **KM# 14** **Weight:** 40.0000 g. **Composition:** 0.9000 Gold 1.1575 oz. AGW **Ruler:** Savang Vatthana **Subject:** King Savang Vatthana coronation

| Date | Mintage | F | VF | XF | Unc | BU |
|---|---|---|---|---|---|---|
| 1971 Proof | Est. 10,000 | Value: 700 | | | | |

**50000 KIP** **KM# 19** **Weight:** 3.6000 g. **Composition:** 0.9000 Gold .1041 oz. AGW **Ruler:** Savang Vatthana **Obverse:** Bust of King Savang Vatthana **Reverse:** That Luang Temple

| Date | Mintage | F | VF | XF | Unc | BU |
|---|---|---|---|---|---|---|
| 1975 | 100 | — | — | — | 200 | — |
| 1975 Proof | 175 | Value: 260 | | | | |

**50000 KIP** **KM# 20** **Weight:** 3.6000 g. **Composition:** 0.9000 Gold .1041 oz. AGW **Ruler:** Savang Vatthana **Obverse:** Similar to 5000 Kip, KM#17 **Reverse:** Bust of King Savang Vatthana

| Date | Mintage | F | VF | XF | Unc | BU |
|---|---|---|---|---|---|---|
| 1975 | 100 | — | — | — | 200 | — |
| 1975 Proof | 175 | Value: 260 | | | | |

**80000 KIP** **KM# 15** **Weight:** 80.0000 g. **Composition:** 0.9000 Gold 2.3151 oz. AGW **Ruler:** Savang Vatthana **Subject:** King Savang Vatthana coronation **Obverse:** Similar to 20000 Kip, KM#13

| Date | Mintage | F | VF | XF | Unc | BU |
|---|---|---|---|---|---|---|
| 1971 Proof | — | Value: 1,450 | | | | |

**100000 KIP** **KM# 21** **Weight:** 7.3200 g. **Composition:** 0.9000 Gold .2118 oz. AGW **Ruler:** Savang Vatthana **Obverse:** Bust of King Savang Vatthana **Reverse:** Statue of Buddha

| Date | Mintage | F | VF | XF | Unc | BU |
|---|---|---|---|---|---|---|
| 1975 | 100 | — | — | — | 375 | — |
| 1975 Proof | 100 | Value: 450 | | | | |

## PEOPLES DEMOCRATIC REPUBLIC

### STANDARD COINAGE

100 Att = 1 Kip

**10 ATT** **KM# 22** **Composition:** Aluminum

| Date | Mintage | F | VF | XF | Unc | BU |
|---|---|---|---|---|---|---|
| 1980 | — | — | 0.20 | 0.40 | 0.85 | — |

**20 ATT** **KM# 23** **Composition:** Aluminum

| Date | Mintage | F | VF | XF | Unc | BU |
|---|---|---|---|---|---|---|
| 1980 | — | — | 0.20 | 0.40 | 0.85 | — |

**50 ATT** **KM# 24** **Composition:** Aluminum

| Date | Mintage | F | VF | XF | Unc | BU |
|---|---|---|---|---|---|---|
| 1980 | — | — | 0.45 | 0.90 | 1.50 | — |

**KIP** **KM# 37** **Composition:** Copper-Nickel **Subject:** 10th anniversary of People's Democratic Republic

| Date | Mintage | F | VF | XF | Unc | BU |
|---|---|---|---|---|---|---|
| 1985 | — | — | 0.50 | 1.00 | 2.50 | — |

**5 KIP** **KM# 38** **Composition:** Copper-Nickel **Subject:** 10th anniversary of People's Democratic Republic

| Date | Mintage | F | VF | XF | Unc | BU |
|---|---|---|---|---|---|---|
| 1985 | — | — | 0.75 | 1.50 | 4.00 | — |

**10 KIP** **KM# 39** **Composition:** Copper-Nickel **Subject:** 10th anniversary of People's Democratic Republic

| Date | Mintage | F | VF | XF | Unc | BU |
|---|---|---|---|---|---|---|
| 1985 | — | — | 1.25 | 2.50 | 6.50 | — |

**10 KIP** **KM# 31** **Composition:** Copper-Nickel **Reverse:** 5-masted clipper

| Date | Mintage | F | VF | XF | Unc | BU |
|---|---|---|---|---|---|---|
| 1988 | 30,000 | — | — | — | 9.00 | — |

**10 KIP** **KM# 31a** **Composition:** Nickel Bonded Steel **Reverse:** 5-masted clipper **Size:** 32.5 mm.

| Date | Mintage | F | VF | XF | Unc | BU |
|---|---|---|---|---|---|---|
| 1988 | — | — | — | — | 8.50 | — |

**10 KIP** **KM# 66** **Composition:** Copper **Obverse:** National arms **Reverse:** 5-masted clipper

| Date | Mintage | F | VF | XF | Unc | BU |
|---|---|---|---|---|---|---|
| 1988 | — | — | — | — | 8.50 | — |
| 1988 Proof | 100 | Value: 75.00 | | | | |

**10 KIP** **KM# 30** **Composition:** Copper-Nickel **Subject:** World Soccer Championships - Italy 1990

| Date | Mintage | F | VF | XF | Unc | BU |
|---|---|---|---|---|---|---|
| 1989 | 2,000 | — | — | — | 10.00 | — |

**10 KIP** **KM# 46** **Composition:** Nickel Plated Steel **Series:** Olympics **Reverse:** Bicyclists

| Date | Mintage | F | VF | XF | Unc | BU |
|---|---|---|---|---|---|---|
| 1991 | 5,000 | — | — | — | 13.50 | — |

**10 KIP** **KM# 51** **Composition:** Copper-Nickel **Series:** Endangered wildife **Reverse:** Tigers

| Date | Mintage | F | VF | XF | Unc | BU |
|---|---|---|---|---|---|---|
| 1991 | — | — | — | — | 9.00 | — |

**10 KIP** **KM# 54** **Composition:** Copper **Series:** Endangered wildife **Reverse:** Tigers

| Date | Mintage | F | VF | XF | Unc | BU |
|---|---|---|---|---|---|---|
| 1991 | — | — | — | — | 10.00 | — |

**10 KIP** **KM# 50** **Composition:** Copper-Nickel **Series:** Prehistoric animals **Reverse:** Tyranosaurus rex

| Date | Mintage | F | VF | XF | Unc | BU |
|---|---|---|---|---|---|---|
| 1993 | — | — | — | — | 24.00 | — |

**10 KIP** **KM# 52** **Composition:** Copper-Nickel **Series:** Prehistoric animals **Reverse:** Lufengosaurus

| Date | Mintage | F | VF | XF | Unc | BU |
|---|---|---|---|---|---|---|
| 1994 | — | — | — | — | 24.00 | — |

**10 KIP** **KM# 61** **Composition:** Copper-Nickel **Subject:** 1996 World Food Summit **Obverse:** National emblem **Reverse:** Farmer plowing with ox

| Date | Mintage | F | VF | XF | Unc | BU |
|---|---|---|---|---|---|---|
| 1996 | — | — | — | — | 10.00 | — |

**10 KIP** **KM# 70** **Composition:** Copper Nickel **Series:** XXVII Olympiad **Subject:** Sydney 2000 **Obverse:** National arms **Reverse:** Sail boats, Neptune

| Date | Mintage | F | VF | XF | Unc | BU |
|---|---|---|---|---|---|---|
| 1999 | 10,000 | — | — | — | 7.00 | — |

**20 KIP** **KM# 40** **Composition:** Copper-Nickel **Subject:** 10th anniversary of People's Democratic Republic

| Date | Mintage | F | VF | XF | Unc | BU |
|---|---|---|---|---|---|---|
| 1985 | — | — | 1.50 | 2.50 | 7.00 | — |

**50 KIP** **KM# 25** **Weight:** 38.2000 g. **Composition:** 0.9000 Silver 1.1054 oz. ASW **Subject:** 10th anniversary of People's Democratic Republic **Reverse:** That Ing Hang

| Date | Mintage | F | VF | XF | Unc | BU |
|---|---|---|---|---|---|---|
| 1985 Proof | 2,000 | Value: 45.00 | | | | |

**50 KIP** **KM# 26** **Weight:** 38.2000 g. **Composition:** 0.9000 Silver 1.1054 oz. ASW **Subject:** 10th anniversary of People's Democratic Republic **Reverse:** That Luang

| Date | Mintage | F | VF | XF | Unc | BU |
|---|---|---|---|---|---|---|
| 1985 Proof | 2,000 | Value: 45.00 | | | | |

**50 KIP** **KM# 27** **Weight:** 38.2000 g. **Composition:** 0.9000 Silver 1.1054 oz. ASW **Subject:** 10th anniversary of People's Democratic Republic **Reverse:** Vat Phu

| Date | Mintage | F | VF | XF | Unc | BU |
|---|---|---|---|---|---|---|
| 1985 Proof | 2,000 | Value: 45.00 | | | | |

**50 KIP** **KM# 28** **Weight:** 38.2000 g. **Composition:** 0.9000 Silver 1.1054 oz. ASW **Subject:** 10th anniversary of People's Democratic Republic **Reverse:** Valley of Jars

| Date | Mintage | F | VF | XF | Unc | BU |
|---|---|---|---|---|---|---|
| 1985 Proof | 2,000 | Value: 45.00 | | | | |

**50 KIP** **KM# 41** **Composition:** Copper-Nickel **Subject:** 10th anniversary of People's Democratic Republic

| Date | Mintage | F | VF | XF | Unc | BU |
|---|---|---|---|---|---|---|
| 1985 | — | — | 2.00 | 3.50 | 8.50 | — |

**50 KIP** **KM# 29** **Weight:** 16.0000 g. **Composition:** 0.9990 Silver .5145 oz. ASW **Reverse:** 5-masted sail ship "Prussia"

| Date | Mintage | F | VF | XF | Unc | BU |
|---|---|---|---|---|---|---|
| 1988 Proof | 2,000 | Value: 30.00 | | | | |

**50 KIP** **KM# 32** **Weight:** 12.0000 g. **Composition:** 0.9990 Silver .3855 oz. ASW **Subject:** European Soccer Championship - Germany

| Date | Mintage | F | VF | XF | Unc | BU |
|---|---|---|---|---|---|---|
| 1988 | 5,000 | — | — | — | 32.50 | — |

**50 KIP** **KM# 33** **Weight:** 16.0000 g. **Composition:** 0.9990 Silver .5145 oz. ASW **Subject:** World Soccer Championship - Mexico 86

| Date | Mintage | F | VF | XF | Unc | BU |
|---|---|---|---|---|---|---|
| ND(1988) Proof | 5,000 | Value: 27.50 | | | | |

**50 KIP** **KM# 34** **Weight:** 16.0000 g. **Composition:** 0.9990 Silver .5145 oz. ASW **Subject:** World Soccer Championship - Italy 1990

| Date | Mintage | F | VF | XF | Unc | BU |
|---|---|---|---|---|---|---|
| 1989 Proof | 5,000 | Value: 27.50 | | | | |

**50 KIP** **KM# 35.1** **Weight:** 16.0000 g. **Composition:** 0.9990 Silver .5145 oz. ASW **Series:** Winter Olympics **Subject:** Ice dancing **Note:** Lightly frosted.

| Date | Mintage | F | VF | XF | Unc | BU |
|---|---|---|---|---|---|---|
| 1989 Proof | — | Value: 28.00 | | | | |

**50 KIP** **KM# 35.2** **Weight:** 16.0000 g. **Composition:** 0.9990 Silver .5145 oz. ASW **Series:** Winter Olympics **Subject:** Ice dancing **Note:** Extensive frosting.

| Date | Mintage | F | VF | XF | Unc | BU |
|---|---|---|---|---|---|---|
| 1989 Proof | — | Value: 80.00 | | | | |

**50 KIP** **KM# 36.1** **Weight:** 16.0000 g. **Composition:** 0.9990 Silver .5145 oz. ASW **Series:** Summer Olympics **Subject:** Water polo **Reverse:** Frosted water.

| Date | Mintage | F | VF | XF | Unc | BU |
|---|---|---|---|---|---|---|
| 1989 Proof | 5,000 | Value: 50.00 | | | | |

**50 KIP** **KM# 36.2** **Weight:** 16.0000 g. **Composition:** 0.9990 Silver .5145 oz. ASW **Series:** Summer Olympics **Subject:** Water polo **Reverse:** Unfrosted water.

| Date | Mintage | F | VF | XF | Unc | BU |
|---|---|---|---|---|---|---|
| 1989 Proof | — | Value: 28.00 | | | | |

**50 KIP** **KM# 44** **Weight:** 12.0000 g. **Composition:** 0.9990 Silver .3858 oz. ASW **Subject:** World Cup soccer

| Date | Mintage | F | VF | XF | Unc | BU |
|---|---|---|---|---|---|---|
| 1991 | — | — | — | — | 27.50 | — |

**50 KIP** **KM# 45** **Weight:** 20.0000 g. **Composition:** 0.9990 Silver .644 oz. ASW **Subject:** Wildlife **Reverse:** Tigers

| Date | Mintage | F | VF | XF | Unc | BU |
|---|---|---|---|---|---|---|
| 1991 | 100 | — | — | — | 175 | — |
| 1991 Proof | — | Value: 35.00 | | | | |

**50 KIP** **KM# 47** **Weight:** 20.0000 g. **Composition:** 0.9990 Silver .643 oz. ASW **Subject:** Soccer **Reverse:**.Goalie

| Date | Mintage | F | VF | XF | Unc | BU |
|---|---|---|---|---|---|---|
| 1991 Proof | — | Value: 37.50 | | | | |

**50 KIP** **KM# 48** **Weight:** 20.0000 g. **Composition:** 0.9990 Silver .643 oz. ASW **Subject:** Protection of nature **Reverse:** Elephant

| Date | Mintage | F | VF | XF | Unc | BU |
|---|---|---|---|---|---|---|
| 1993 Proof | — | Value: 37.50 | | | | |

**50 KIP** **KM# 49** **Weight:** 15.9400 g. **Composition:** 0.9990 Silver .5120 oz. ASW **Series:** Prehistoric animals **Reverse:** Sauroctonus

| Date | Mintage | F | VF | XF | Unc | BU |
|---|---|---|---|---|---|---|
| 1993 Proof | — | Value: 35.00 | | | | |

**50 KIP** **KM# 53** **Weight:** 16.0000 g. **Composition:** 0.9990 Silver .5145 oz. ASW **Series:** Prehistoric animals **Reverse:** Elasmosaurus and tylosaurus in combat

| Date | Mintage | F | VF | XF | Unc | BU |
|---|---|---|---|---|---|---|
| 1994 Proof | — | Value: 40.00 | | | | |

**50 KIP** **KM# 56** **Weight:** 20.0000 g. **Composition:** 0.9990 Silver .6424 oz. ASW **Series:** Olympics **Reverse:** Javelin throwers

| Date | Mintage | F | VF | XF | Unc | BU |
|---|---|---|---|---|---|---|
| 1995 Proof | Est. 15,000 | Value: 25.00 | | | | |

**50 KIP** **KM# 57** **Weight:** 20.0000 g. **Composition:** 0.9990 Silver .6424 oz. ASW **Subject:** World Cup soccer **Reverse:** Player and cathedral

| Date | Mintage | F | VF | XF | Unc | BU |
|---|---|---|---|---|---|---|
| 1996 | 100 | — | — | — | 90.00 | — |
| 1996 Proof | 10,000 | Value: 45.00 | | | | |

**50 KIP** **KM# 63** **Weight:** 20.0000 g. **Composition:** 0.9990 Silver .6424 oz. ASW **Series:** XXVII Olympiad **Obverse:** State emblem **Reverse:** Gymnastics

| Date | Mintage | F | VF | XF | Unc | BU |
|---|---|---|---|---|---|---|
| 1996 Proof | — | Value: 45.00 | | | | |

**50 KIP** **KM# 58** **Weight:** 20.0000 g. **Composition:** 0.9990 Silver .6424 oz. ASW **Subject:** World Cup soccer **Reverse:** Stadium, map of France

| Date | Mintage | F | VF | XF | Unc | BU |
|---|---|---|---|---|---|---|
| 1996 Proof | 10,000 | Value: 45.00 | | | | |

**50 KIP** **KM# 62** **Weight:** 20.0000 g. **Composition:** 0.9990 Silver .6424 oz. ASW **Series:** XXVII Olympiad **Obverse:** State emblem **Reverse:** Archer - Diana, goddess of the hunt

| Date | Mintage | F | VF | XF | Unc | BU |
|---|---|---|---|---|---|---|
| 1996 Proof | — | Value: 45.00 | | | | |

**50 KIP** **KM# 64** **Weight:** 15.0000 g. **Composition:** 0.9990 Silver .6423 oz. ASW **Subject:** World of adventure - Leif Ericson **Obverse:** State emblem **Reverse:** Viking longship

| Date | Mintage | F | VF | XF | Unc | BU |
|---|---|---|---|---|---|---|
| 1996 Proof | — | Value: 45.00 | | | | |

**100 KIP** **KM# 42** **Weight:** 3.1500 g. **Composition:** 0.9990 Gold .1012 oz. AGW **Obverse:** Emblem and legend above denomination **Reverse:** 5-masted sail ship "Prussia"

| Date | Mintage | F | VF | XF | Unc | BU |
|---|---|---|---|---|---|---|
| 1988 | 500 | — | — | — | 125 | — |

**100 KIP** **KM# 43** **Weight:** 3.1500 g. **Composition:** 0.9990 Gold .1012 oz. AGW **Subject:** 10th anniversary of People's Democratic Republic **Reverse:** That Louang Temple

| Date | Mintage | F | VF | XF | Unc | BU |
|---|---|---|---|---|---|---|
| 1990 | — | — | — | — | 145 | — |

**500 KIP** **KM# 69** **Weight:** 20.0000 g. **Composition:** 0.9250 Silver .5948 oz. ASW **Subject:** Kouprey **Obverse:** State emblem **Reverse:** Wild bull

| Date | Mintage | F | VF | XF | Unc | BU |
|---|---|---|---|---|---|---|
| 1998 Proof | 10,000 | Value: 50.00 | | | | |

**1000 KIP** **KM# 165** **Weight:** 31.6700 g. **Composition:** 0.9990 Silver 1.0172 oz. ASW **Series:** Endangered wildlife **Obverse:** State emblem **Reverse:** Gibbon

| Date | Mintage | F | VF | XF | Unc | BU |
|---|---|---|---|---|---|---|
| 1996 Proof | — | Value: 60.00 | | | | |

**1000 KIP** **KM# 67** **Weight:** 31.4700 g. **Composition:** 0.9250 Silver .9359 oz. ASW **Series:** Endangered wildlife **Obverse:** State emblem **Reverse:** 2 long-horned saola

| Date | Mintage | F | VF | XF | Unc | BU |
|---|---|---|---|---|---|---|
| 1997 Proof | 15,000 | Value: 40.00 | | | | |

**1200 KIP** **KM# 59** **Composition:** Nickel Bonded Steel **Subject:** Food for all **Reverse:** 3 people harvesting rice

| Date | Mintage | F | VF | XF | Unc | BU |
|---|---|---|---|---|---|---|
| ND(1995) | — | — | — | — | 8.00 | — |

**2000 KIP** **KM# 68** **Weight:** 1.2441 g. **Composition:** 0.9990 Gold .04 oz. AGW **Subject:** That Luang **Obverse:** State emblem **Reverse:** Temple

| Date | Mintage | F | VF | XF | Unc | BU |
|---|---|---|---|---|---|---|
| 1998 Proof | — | Value: 50.00 | | | | |

**3000 KIP** **KM# 72** **Weight:** 20.0000 g. **Composition:** 0.9250 Silver .5948 oz. ASW **Subject:** Retrospection Rabbit

| Date | Mintage | F | VF | XF | Unc | BU |
|---|---|---|---|---|---|---|
| 1999 Proof | — | Value: 50.00 | | | | |

**3000 KIP** **KM# 73** **Weight:** 20.0000 g. **Composition:** 0.9250 Silver .5948 oz. ASW **Subject:** Anticipation Rabbit **Reverse:** Partially gold-plated rabbit

| Date | Mintage | F | VF | XF | Unc | BU |
|---|---|---|---|---|---|---|
| 1999 Proof | — | Value: 50.00 | | | | |

**5000 KIP** **KM# 60** **Weight:** 7.7600 g. **Composition:** 0.5833 Gold .1458 oz. AGW **Series:** Olympics **Reverse:** Two boxers

| Date | Mintage | F | VF | XF | Unc | BU |
|---|---|---|---|---|---|---|
| 1996 | Est. 3,000 | — | — | — | 90.00 | — |

**5000 KIP** **KM# 71** **Weight:** 20.0500 g. **Composition:** 0.9990 Silver .6584 oz. ASW **Series:** XXVII Olympiad **Subject:** Sydney 2000 **Obverse:** State emblem **Reverse:** Sailboats, Neptune

| Date | Mintage | |
|---|---|---|
| | 5,000 | Value: 35.00 |

## ESSAIS

Standard metals unless otherwise noted

| KM# | Date | Mintage | Identification | Issue Price | Mkt Val |
|---|---|---|---|---|---|
| e1 | 1952 | 1,200 | 10 Cents. | — | 20.00 |
| e2 | 1952 | 1,200 | 20 Cents. | — | 22.50 |
| e3 | 1952 | 1,200 | 50 Cents. | — | 22.50 |

## PIEFORTS

| KM# | Date | Mintage | Identification | Issue Price | Mkt Val |
|---|---|---|---|---|---|
| P1 | 1988 | — | 50 Kip. Silver. | — | — |

## PIEFORTS WITH ESSAI

Standard metals unless otherwise noted

Double Thickness

| KM# | Date | Mintage | Identification | Issue Price | Mkt Val |
|---|---|---|---|---|---|
| PE1 | 1952 | 104 | 10 Cents. | — | 50.00 |
| PE2 | 1952 | 104 | 20 Cents. | — | 60.00 |
| PE3 | 1952 | 104 | 50 Cents. | — | 75.00 |

## MINT SETS

| KM# | Date | Mintage | Identification | Issue Price | Mkt Val |
|---|---|---|---|---|---|
| MS1 | 1971 (4) | — | KM7, 8, 10, 12 | — | 300 |
| MS2 | 1975 (6) | 100 | KM16-21 | — | 1,300 |
| MS3 | 1975 (3) | 300 | KM16-18 | — | 420 |

## PROOF SETS

| KM# | Date | Mintage | Identification | Issue Price | Mkt Val |
|---|---|---|---|---|---|
| PS1 | 1971 (5) | 10,000 | KM9, 11, 13-15 | 467 | 2,870 |
| PS2 | 1971 (4) | 20,000 | KM7, 8, 10, 12 | 163 | 450 |
| PS3 | 1975 (6) | — | KM16-21 | — | 1,450 |
| PS4 | 1975 (3) | 650 | KM16-18 | — | 450 |
| PS5 | 1975 (3) | — | KM19-21 | 349 | 960 |
| ps6 | 1985 (4) | 2,000 | KM25-28 | — | 180 |

# LATVIA

The Republic of Latvia, the central Baltic state in east Europe, has an area of 24,749 sq. mi. (43,601 sq. km.) and a population of *2.6 million. Capital: Riga. Livestock raising and manufacturing are the chief industries. Butter, bacon, fertilizers and telephone equipment are exported.

The Latvians, of Aryan descent primarily from the German Order of Livonian Knights, were nomadic tribes-men who settled along the Baltic prior to the 13th century. Ideally situated as a trade route and lacking a central government, conquered in 1561 by Poland and Sweden. Following the third partition of Poland by Austria, Prussia and Russia in 1795, Latvia came under Russian domination and did not experience autonomy until the Russian Revolution of 1917 provided an opportunity for freedom. The Latvian Republic was established on Nov. 18, 1918. The republic was occupied by Soviet troops and annexed to the Soviet Union in 1940. Following the German occupation of 1941-44, it was retaken by Russia and reestablished as a member republic of the Soviet Union. Western countries, including the United States, did not recognize Latvia's incorporation into the Soviet Union.

The coinage issued during the early 20th Century Republic is now obsolete.

Latvia declared their independence from the U.S.S.R. on August 22, 1991.

**MONETARY SYSTEM**

100 Santimu = 1 Lats

# FIRST REPUBLIC
## 1918-1939.
## STANDARD COINAGE

100 Santimu = 1 Lats

**SANTIMS** **KM# 1** **Composition:** Bronze

| Date | Mintage | F | VF | XF | Unc | BU |
|---|---|---|---|---|---|---|
| 1922 | 5,000,000 | 0.65 | 1.40 | 2.75 | 8.00 | — |
| 1923 | 10 | — | — | — | 1,500 | — |
| 1924 | 4,990,000 | 0.65 | 1.40 | 2.75 | 8.00 | — |
| 1926 | 5,000,000 | 0.65 | 1.40 | 2.75 | 8.00 | — |
| 1928 | 5,000,000 | 0.65 | 1.40 | 2.75 | 8.00 | — |
| **Note:** Designer's name below ribbon. | | | | | | |
| 1928 | Inc. above | 2.00 | 5.00 | 10.00 | 32.50 | — |
| **Note:** Without designer's name below ribbon. | | | | | | |
| 1932 | 5,000,000 | 0.65 | 1.40 | 2.75 | 8.00 | — |
| 1932 Proof | — | — | — | — | — | — |
| 1935 | 5,000,000 | 0.65 | 1.40 | 2.75 | 8.00 | — |

**SANTIMS** **KM# 10** **Composition:** Bronze

| Date | Mintage | F | VF | XF | Unc | BU |
|---|---|---|---|---|---|---|
| 1937 | 2,700,000 | 0.65 | 1.40 | 2.75 | 8.00 | — |
| 1938 | 1,900,000 | 0.65 | 1.40 | 2.75 | 10.00 | — |
| 1939 | 3,400,000 | 0.50 | 1.00 | 2.00 | 3.00 | — |
| **Note:** Most were never placed into circulation. | | | | | | |

**2 SANTIMI** **KM# 2** **Composition:** Bronze

| Date | Mintage | F | VF | XF | Unc | BU |
|---|---|---|---|---|---|---|
| 1922 | 10,000,000 | 1.00 | 2.00 | 5.00 | 10.00 | — |
| **Note:** Designer's name below ribbon. | | | | | | |
| 1922 | Inc. above | 5.00 | 10.00 | 17.50 | 35.00 | — |
| **Note:** Without designer's name. | | | | | | |
| 1923 | 2 | — | — | — | 2,000 | — |
| 1926 | 5,000,000 | 0.75 | 1.50 | 4.00 | 9.00 | — |
| 1928 | 5,000,000 | 0.75 | 1.50 | 4.00 | 9.00 | — |

| Date | Mintage | F | VF | XF | Unc | BU |
|---|---|---|---|---|---|---|
| 1932 | 5,000,000 | 0.75 | 1.50 | 4.00 | 9.00 | — |
| 1932 Proof | — | — | — | — | — | — |

**2 SANTIMI** KM# 11.1 **Composition:** Bronze **Size:** 19 mm.

| Date | Mintage | F | VF | XF | Unc | BU |
|---|---|---|---|---|---|---|
| 1937 | 45,000 | 10.00 | 20.00 | 30.00 | 60.00 | — |

**2 SANTIMI** KM# 11.2 **Composition:** Bronze **Size:** 19.5 mm.

| Date | Mintage | F | VF | XF | Unc | BU |
|---|---|---|---|---|---|---|
| 1939 | 5,000,000 | 1.00 | 2.50 | 4.00 | 9.00 | — |

**Note:** Most were never placed in circulation.

**5 SANTIMI** KM# 3 **Composition:** Bronze

| Date | Mintage | F | VF | XF | Unc | BU |
|---|---|---|---|---|---|---|
| 1922 | 15,000,000 | 0.50 | 1.00 | 3.00 | 8.00 | — |
| **Note:** Designer's name below ribbon. | | | | | | |
| 1922 | Inc. above | 3.00 | 6.00 | 10.00 | 20.00 | — |
| **Note:** Without designer's name. | | | | | | |
| 1923 | 2 | — | — | — | 2,250 | — |

**10 SANTIMU** KM# 4 **Composition:** Nickel

| Date | Mintage | F | VF | XF | Unc | BU |
|---|---|---|---|---|---|---|
| 1922 | 15,000,000 | 0.50 | 1.00 | 3.00 | 6.00 | — |

**20 SANTIMU** KM# 5 **Composition:** Nickel

| Date | Mintage | F | VF | XF | Unc | BU |
|---|---|---|---|---|---|---|
| 1922 | 15,000,000 | 0.50 | 1.00 | 3.00 | 8.00 | — |

**50 SANTIMU** KM# 6 **Composition:** Nickel

| Date | Mintage | F | VF | XF | Unc | BU |
|---|---|---|---|---|---|---|
| 1922 | 9,000,000 | 1.00 | 3.00 | 5.00 | 10.00 | — |

**LATS** KM# 7 **Weight:** 5.0000 g. **Composition:** 0.8350 Silver .1342 oz. ASW

| Date | Mintage | F | VF | XF | Unc | BU |
|---|---|---|---|---|---|---|
| 1923 | — | — | — | 900 | — | — |
| 1924 | 10,000,000 | 2.00 | 3.50 | 7.00 | 25.00 | — |

**2 LATI** KM# 8 **Weight:** 10.0000 g. **Composition:** 0.8350 Silver .2684 oz. ASW

| Date | Mintage | F | VF | XF | Unc | BU |
|---|---|---|---|---|---|---|
| 1925 | 6,386,000 | 2.50 | 3.00 | 6.00 | 30.00 | — |
| 1926 | 1,114,000 | 2.50 | 3.50 | 7.00 | 32.50 | — |

**5 LATI** KM# 9 **Weight:** 25.0000 g. **Composition:** 0.8350 Silver .6712 oz. ASW

| Date | Mintage | F | VF | XF | Unc | BU |
|---|---|---|---|---|---|---|
| 1929 | 1,000,000 | 9.00 | 12.00 | 20.00 | 42.50 | — |
| 1929 Proof | — | — | — | — | — | — |
| 1931 | 2,000,000 | 8.00 | 11.50 | 18.00 | 37.50 | — |
| 1931 Proof | — | — | — | — | — | — |
| 1932 | 600,000 | 9.00 | 12.00 | 20.00 | 42.50 | — |
| 1932 Proof | — | — | — | — | — | — |

# MODERN REPUBLIC

## 1991-present.

## STANDARD COINAGE

100 Santimu = 1 Lats

**SANTIMS** KM# 15 **Composition:** Copper Plated Iron

| Date | Mintage | F | VF | XF | Unc | BU |
|---|---|---|---|---|---|---|
| 1992 | — | — | — | — | 0.25 | — |

**2 SANTIMI** KM# 21 **Composition:** Bronze Plated Steel

| Date | Mintage | F | VF | XF | Unc | BU |
|---|---|---|---|---|---|---|
| 1992 | — | — | — | — | 0.50 | — |
| 2000 | — | — | — | — | 0.50 | — |

**5 SANTIMI** KM# 16 **Composition:** Brass

| Date | Mintage | F | VF | XF | Unc | BU |
|---|---|---|---|---|---|---|
| 1992 | — | — | — | — | 0.75 | — |

**10 SANTIMU** KM# 17 **Composition:** Brass

| Date | Mintage | F | VF | XF | Unc | BU |
|---|---|---|---|---|---|---|
| 1992 | — | — | — | — | 1.25 | — |

**20 SANTIMU** KM# 22 **Composition:** Brass

| Date | Mintage | F | VF | XF | Unc | BU |
|---|---|---|---|---|---|---|
| 1992 | — | — | — | — | 1.50 | — |

**50 SANTIMU** KM# 13 **Composition:** Copper-Nickel

| Date | Mintage | F | VF | XF | Unc | BU |
|---|---|---|---|---|---|---|
| 1992 | — | — | — | — | 2.75 | — |

**LATS** KM# 12 **Composition:** Copper-Nickel

| Date | Mintage | F | VF | XF | Unc | BU |
|---|---|---|---|---|---|---|
| 1992 | — | — | — | — | 3.75 | — |

**LATS** KM# 23 **Weight:** 28.2800 g. **Composition:** 0.9250 Silver .8411 oz. ASW **Series:** UN 50th anniversary **Reverse:** Many people holding hands

| Date | Mintage | F | VF | XF | Unc | BU |
|---|---|---|---|---|---|---|
| 1995 Proof | 100,000 | Value: 42.50 | | | | |

**LATS** KM# 39 **Weight:** 15.2000 g. **Composition:** 0.9250 Silver .4520 oz. ASW **Subject:** Millennium **Note:** Button design.

| Date | Mintage | F | VF | XF | Unc | BU |
|---|---|---|---|---|---|---|
| 1999-2000 Proof | 35,000 | Value: 55.00 | | | | |

**LATS** **KM# 44** **Weight:** 20.0000 g. **Composition:** 0.9250 Silver .5948 oz. ASW **Series:** Olympics **Reverse:** 2 cyclists

| Date | Mintage | F | VF | XF | Unc | BU |
|---|---|---|---|---|---|---|
| 1999 Proof | — | Value: 40.00 | | | | |

**LATS** **KM# 45** **Weight:** 31.4700 g. **Composition:** 0.9250 Silver .9359 oz. ASW **Subject:** European mink **Reverse:** Mink on rock

| Date | Mintage | F | VF | XF | Unc | BU |
|---|---|---|---|---|---|---|
| 1999 Proof | — | Value: 50.00 | | | | |

**2 LATI** **KM# 14** **Composition:** Copper-Nickel

| Date | Mintage | F | VF | XF | Unc | BU |
|---|---|---|---|---|---|---|
| 1992 | — | — | — | — | 7.00 | — |

**2 LATI** **KM# 18** **Composition:** Copper-Nickel **Subject:** 75th anniversary - declaration of independence

| Date | Mintage | F | VF | XF | Unc | BU |
|---|---|---|---|---|---|---|
| ND(1993) | 4,000,000 | — | — | — | 7.50 | — |
| ND(1993) Proof | 200,000 | Value: 11.50 | | | | |

**2 LATI** **KM# 38** **Ring Composition:** Copper-Nickel **Center Composition:** Brass **Reverse:** Cow above denomination

| Date | Mintage | F | VF | XF | Unc | BU |
|---|---|---|---|---|---|---|
| 1999 | — | — | — | — | 10.00 | — |

**10 LATU** **KM# 19** **Weight:** 25.1750 g. **Composition:** 0.9250 Silver .7484 oz. ASW **Subject:** 75th anniversary - declaration of independence

| Date | Mintage | F | VF | XF | Unc | BU |
|---|---|---|---|---|---|---|
| ND(1993) Proof | 30,000 | Value: 37.50 | | | | |

**10 LATU** **KM# 24** **Weight:** 31.4700 g. **Composition:** 0.9250 Silver .9359 oz. ASW **Series:** Olympics **Subject:** Canoeing

| Date | Mintage | F | VF | XF | Unc | BU |
|---|---|---|---|---|---|---|
| 1994 Proof | 30,000 | Value: 37.50 | | | | |

**10 LATU** **KM# 25** **Weight:** 31.4700 g. **Composition:** 0.9250 Silver .9359 oz. ASW **Subject:** Julia Maria **Reverse:** 3-masted schooner

| Date | Mintage | F | VF | XF | Unc | BU |
|---|---|---|---|---|---|---|
| 1995 Proof | 20,000 | Value: 45.00 | | | | |

**10 LATU** **KM# 27** **Weight:** 31.4700 g. **Composition:** 0.9250 Silver .9359 oz. ASW **Subject:** 800th anniversary - Reiga **Obverse:** Coat of arms from 1368 **Reverse:** The Great Gould's coat of arms from 1354

| Date | Mintage | F | VF | XF | Unc | BU |
|---|---|---|---|---|---|---|
| 1995 (1997) Proof | — | Value: 50.00 | | | | |

**10 LATU** **KM# 26** **Weight:** 31.4700 g. **Composition:** 0.9250 Silver .9359 oz. ASW **Subject:** Riga 800 **Reverse:** First city seal

| Date | Mintage | F | VF | XF | Unc | BU |
|---|---|---|---|---|---|---|
| 1995 (1996) Proof | Est. 8,000 | Value: 50.00 | | | | |

**10 LATU** **KM# 33** **Weight:** 31.4700 g. **Composition:** 0.9250 Silver .9359 oz. ASW **Series:** Endangered wildlife **Obverse:** National arms **Reverse:** Grieze (corn-crake) bird **Edge:** Lettered **Edge Lettering:** LATVIJAS BANKA \ (2x)

| Date | Mintage | F | VF | XF | Unc | BU |
|---|---|---|---|---|---|---|
| 1996 Proof | 15,000 | Value: 42.50 | | | | |

**10 LATU** **KM# 34** **Weight:** 31.4700 g. **Composition:** 0.9250 Silver .9359 oz. ASW **Subject:** Riga - XVI century **Obverse:** Old coin design above denomination **Reverse:** Old city view

| Date | Mintage | F | VF | XF | Unc | BU |
|---|---|---|---|---|---|---|
| 1996 Proof | — | Value: 50.00 | | | | |

**10 LATU** **KM# 36** **Weight:** 31.3500 g. **Composition:** 0.9990 Silver 1.0069 oz. ASW **Subject:** 800th anniversary of Riga **Obverse:** Old coin design with St. Christopher **Reverse:** Old coin design with city arms **Edge:** Lettered **Edge Lettering:** LATVIJAS REPUBLIKA LATVIJAS BANKA

| Date | Mintage | F | VF | XF | Unc | BU |
|---|---|---|---|---|---|---|
| 1996 Proof | — | Value: 55.00 | | | | |

**10 LATU** **KM# 28** **Weight:** 31.3200 g. **Composition:** 0.9250 Silver .9314 oz. ASW **Obverse:** National arms **Reverse:** 12th-century ship above its sunken remains **Edge:** Lettered **Edge Lettering:** LATIJAS BANKAS

| Date | Mintage | F | VF | XF | Unc | BU |
|---|---|---|---|---|---|---|
| 1997 Proof | 15,000 | Value: 42.50 | | | | |

**10 LATU** KM# 35 **Weight:** 31.4700 g. **Composition:** 0.9250 Silver .9359 oz. ASW **Subject:** Riga - XVII century **Obverse:** Old coin design **Reverse:** Aerial view of walled city

| Date | Mintage | F | VF | XF | Unc | BU |
|---|---|---|---|---|---|---|
| 1997 Proof | — | Value: 50.00 | | | | |

**10 LATU** KM# 29 **Weight:** 1.2441 g. **Composition:** 0.9999 Gold .0400 oz. AGW **Subject:** 800th anniversary - Riga **Obverse:** City arms on old coin design **Reverse:** City arms and ship on old coin design

| Date | Mintage | F | VF | XF | Unc | BU |
|---|---|---|---|---|---|---|
| 1998 Proof | — | Value: 55.00 | | | | |

**10 LATU** KM# 30 **Weight:** 31.4700 g. **Composition:** 0.9250 Silver .9359 oz. ASW **Subject:** 800th anniversary - Riga **Obverse:** National song festival procession **Reverse:** Riga city arms

| Date | Mintage | F | VF | XF | Unc | BU |
|---|---|---|---|---|---|---|
| 1998 Proof | Est. 8,000 | Value: 55.00 | | | | |

**10 LATU** KM# 31 **Weight:** 31.4700 g. **Composition:** 0.9250 Silver .9359 oz. ASW **Subject:** 800th anniversary - Riga **Obverse:** Statue of woman with stars **Reverse:** Lions supporting city arms of Riga

| Date | Mintage | F | VF | XF | Unc | BU |
|---|---|---|---|---|---|---|
| 1998 Proof | Est. 8,000 | Value: 55.00 | | | | |

**10 LATU** KM# 32 **Weight:** 31.4700 g. **Composition:** 0.9250 Silver .9359 oz. ASW **Obverse:** National arms **Reverse:** 1925 Icebreaker "Krisjanis Valdemara"

| Date | Mintage | F | VF | XF | Unc | BU |
|---|---|---|---|---|---|---|
| 1998 Proof | 10,000 | Value: 47.50 | | | | |

**20 LATU** KM# 41 **Weight:** 7.7760 g. **Composition:** 0.5830 Gold .1458 oz. AGW **Reverse:** Sailing ship "Gekronte Ehlendt" **Edge:** Reeded **Note:** Struck at Valcambi.

| Date | Mintage | F | VF | XF | Unc | BU |
|---|---|---|---|---|---|---|
| 1997 Proof | — | Value: 85.00 | | | | |

**20 LATU** KM# 37 **Weight:** 31.4100 g. **Composition:** 0.9210 Silver .9341 oz. ASW **Obverse:** City arms **Reverse:** Melngalvgu **Edge:** Lettered **Edge Lettering:** LATVIJAS REPUBLIKA LATVIJAS BANKA

| Date | Mintage | F | VF | XF | Unc | BU |
|---|---|---|---|---|---|---|
| 1997 Proof | — | Value: 50.00 | | | | |

**20 LATU** KM# 42 **Weight:** 1.2442 g. **Composition:** 0.9990 Gold .0400 oz. AGW **Subject:** Julia Maria **Reverse:** Sailing ship

| Date | Mintage | F | VF | XF | Unc | BU |
|---|---|---|---|---|---|---|
| 1997 Proof | — | Value: 55.00 | | | | |

**20 LATU** KM# 43 **Weight:** 3.1100 g. **Composition:** 0.5830 Gold .0583 oz. AGW **Series:** Olympics **Reverse:** Javelin thrower

| Date | Mintage | F | VF | XF | Unc | BU |
|---|---|---|---|---|---|---|
| 1999 Proof | — | Value: 55.00 | | | | |

**100 LATU** KM# 20 **Weight:** 13.3380 g. **Composition:** 0.8330 Gold .2501 oz. AGW **Subject:** 75th anniversary - declaration of independence

| Date | Mintage | F | VF | XF | Unc | BU |
|---|---|---|---|---|---|---|
| ND(1993) Proof | 5,000 | Value: 225 | | | | |

**100 LATU** KM# 40 **Weight:** 16.2000 g. **Composition:** 0.9990 Gold .5203 oz. AGW **Subject:** Development

| Date | Mintage | F | VF | XF | Unc | BU |
|---|---|---|---|---|---|---|
| 1998 Proof | — | Value: 350 | | | | |

## PATTERNS

Including off metal strikes

| KM# | Date | Mintage | Identification | Mkt Val |
|---|---|---|---|---|
| Pn1 | 1922 | — | 10 Santimu. Silver. KM4. | 225 |
| Pn2 | 1922 | — | 10 Santimu. Aluminum-Bronze. KM4. | 300 |
| Pn3 | 1924 | — | 2 Lati. Silver. | 300 |
| Pn4 | 1938 | — | 2 Santimi. Bronze. KM11.2 | 600 |

## MINT SETS

| KM# | Date | Mintage | Identification | Issue Price | Mkt Val |
|---|---|---|---|---|---|
| MS1 | 1992 (8) | — | KM12-17, 21-22 | — | 25.00 |

## PROOF SETS

| KM# | Date | Mintage | Identification | Issue Price | Mkt Val |
|---|---|---|---|---|---|
| PS1 | ND (1993) (3) | 1,800 | KM18-20 | — | 325 |

# LEBANON

The Republic of Lebanon, situated on the eastern shore of the Mediterranean Sea between Syria and Israel, has an area of 4,015 sq. mi. (10,400 sq. km.) and a population of 3.5 million. Capital: Beirut. The economy is based on agriculture, trade and tourism. Fruit, other foodstuffs and textiles are exported.

Almost at the beginning of recorded history, Lebanon appeared as the well-wooded hinterland of the Phoenicians who exploited its famous forests of cedar. The mountains were a Christian refuge and a Crusader stronghold. Lebanon, the history of which is essentially the same as that of Syria, came under control of the Ottoman Turks early in the 16th century. Following the collapse of the Ottoman Empire after World War I, Lebanon, along with Syria, became a French mandate. The French drew a border around the predominantly Christian Lebanon *Sanjak* or administrative subdivision and on Sept. 1, 1920 proclaimed the area the State of Grand Lebanon (*Etat du Grand Liban*) a republic under French control. France announced the independence of Lebanon on Nov. 26, 1941, but the last British and French troops didn't leave until the end of August 1946.

**TITLES**

الجمهورية اللبنانية

al-Jomhuriya(t) al-Lubnaniya(t)

**MINT MARKS**

(a) - Paris, privy marks only
(u) - Utrecht, privy marks only

**MONETARY SYSTEM**

100 Piastres = 1 Livre (Pound)

## FRENCH PROTECTORATE

### STANDARD COINAGE

**1/2 PIASTRE** KM# 9 **Composition:** Copper-Nickel

| Date | Mintage | F | VF | XF | Unc | BU |
|---|---|---|---|---|---|---|
| 1934(a) | 200,000 | 2.00 | 5.00 | 12.50 | 40.00 | — |
| 1936(a) | 1,200,000 | 1.25 | 3.00 | 7.50 | 25.00 | — |

**1/2 PIASTRE** KM# 9a **Composition:** Zinc

| Date | Mintage | F | VF | XF | Unc | BU |
|---|---|---|---|---|---|---|
| 1941(a) | 1,000,000 | 0.50 | 1.00 | 4.00 | 10.00 | — |

**PIASTRE** KM# 3 **Composition:** Copper-Nickel

| Date | Mintage | F | VF | XF | Unc | BU |
|---|---|---|---|---|---|---|
| 1925(a) | 1,500,000 | 0.50 | 2.00 | 7.50 | 25.00 | — |
| 1931(a) | 300,000 | 1.00 | 4.00 | 12.50 | 45.00 | — |
| 1933(a) | 500,000 | 1.00 | 4.00 | 10.00 | 45.00 | — |
| 1936(a) | 2,200,000 | 0.50 | 1.00 | 6.50 | 20.00 | — |

**PIASTRE** KM# 3a **Composition:** Zinc

| Date | Mintage | F | VF | XF | Unc | BU |
|---|---|---|---|---|---|---|
| 1940(a) | 2,000,000 | 0.50 | 0.75 | 4.00 | 10.00 | — |

**2 PIASTRES** KM# 1 **Composition:** Aluminum-Bronze

| Date | Mintage | F | VF | XF | Unc | BU |
|---|---|---|---|---|---|---|
| 1924(a) | 1,800,000 | 1.25 | 3.00 | 12.50 | 50.00 | — |

**2 PIASTRES** KM# 4 **Composition:** Aluminum-Bronze

| Date | Mintage | F | VF | XF | Unc | BU |
|---|---|---|---|---|---|---|
| 1925(a) | 1,000,000 | 3.00 | 8.00 | 20.00 | 75.00 | — |

**2-1/2 PIASTRES** KM# 10 **Composition:** Aluminum-Bronze

| Date | Mintage | F | VF | XF | Unc | BU |
|---|---|---|---|---|---|---|
| 1940(a) | 1,000,000 | 1.00 | 2.00 | 3.50 | 12.00 | — |

**5 PIASTRES** KM# 2 **Composition:** Aluminum-Bronze

| Date | Mintage | F | VF | XF | Unc | BU |
|---|---|---|---|---|---|---|
| 1924(a) | 1,000,000 | 1.25 | 3.00 | 10.00 | 45.00 | — |

**5 PIASTRES** KM# 5.1 **Composition:** Aluminum-Bronze **Reverse:** Both privy marks to left of "5"

| Date | Mintage | F | VF | XF | Unc | BU |
|---|---|---|---|---|---|---|
| 1925(a) | 1,500,000 | 0.75 | 1.50 | 8.00 | 30.00 | — |

**5 PIASTRES** KM# 5.2 **Composition:** Aluminum-Bronze **Reverse:** Privy marks to left and right of 5 Piastres

| Date | Mintage | F | VF | XF | Unc | BU |
|---|---|---|---|---|---|---|
| 1925(a) | Inc. above | 1.00 | 2.00 | 7.50 | 30.00 | — |
| 1931(a) | 400,000 | 1.50 | 4.00 | 12.50 | 40.00 | — |
| 1933(a) | 500,000 | 1.50 | 4.00 | 12.50 | 40.00 | — |
| 1936(a) | 900,000 | 1.00 | 2.00 | 7.50 | 25.00 | — |
| 1940(a) | 1,000,000 | 0.75 | 1.50 | 5.00 | 15.00 | — |

**10 PIASTRES** KM# 6 **Weight:** 2.0000 g. **Composition:** 0.6800 Silver .0437 oz. ASW

| Date | Mintage | F | VF | XF | Unc | BU |
|---|---|---|---|---|---|---|
| 1929 | 880,000 | 3.00 | 7.00 | 25.00 | 70.00 | — |

**25 PIASTRES** KM# 7 **Weight:** 5.0000 g. **Composition:** 0.6800 Silver .1093 oz. ASW

| Date | Mintage | F | VF | XF | Unc | BU |
|---|---|---|---|---|---|---|
| 1929 | 600,000 | 3.00 | 7.00 | 25.00 | 75.00 | — |
| 1933(a) | 200,000 | 4.50 | 15.00 | 40.00 | 125 | — |
| 1936(a) | 400,000 | 3.50 | 10.00 | 27.50 | 85.00 | — |

**50 PIASTRES** KM# 8 **Weight:** 10.0000 g. **Composition:** 0.6800 Silver .2186 oz. ASW

| Date | Mintage | F | VF | XF | Unc | BU |
|---|---|---|---|---|---|---|
| 1929 | 500,000 | 5.00 | 10.00 | 40.00 | 125 | — |
| 1933(a) | 100,000 | 7.00 | 20.00 | 65.00 | 185 | — |
| 1936(a) | 100,000 | 7.00 | 17.50 | 50.00 | 150 | — |

## WORLD WAR II COINAGE

**1/2 PIASTRE** KM# 11 **Composition:** Brass **Note:** Three varieties known. Usually crudely struck, off-center, etc. Perfectly struck, centered unc. specimens command a considerable premium. Size of letters also vary.

| Date | Mintage | F | VF | XF | Unc | BU |
|---|---|---|---|---|---|---|
| ND(1941) | — | 1.00 | 2.50 | 5.00 | 12.00 | — |

**PIASTRE** KM# 12a **Composition:** Aluminum

| Date | Mintage | F | VF | XF | Unc | BU |
|---|---|---|---|---|---|---|
| ND(1941) | — | — | — | — | — | — |

**PIASTRE** KM# 12 **Composition:** Brass **Note:** Two varieties known. Usually crudely struck, off-center, etc. Perfectly struck, centered unc. specimens command a considerable premium.

| Date | Mintage | F | VF | XF | Unc | BU |
|---|---|---|---|---|---|---|
| ND(1941) | — | 1.00 | 3.00 | 7.50 | 18.00 | — |

**2-1/2 PIASTRES** KM# 13a **Composition:** Aluminum-Bronze

| Date | Mintage | F | VF | XF | Unc | BU |
|---|---|---|---|---|---|---|
| ND(1941) | — | — | 650 | 850 | — | — |

**2-1/2 PIASTRES** KM# 13 **Composition:** Aluminum **Note:** Seven varieties known. Usually crudely struck, off-center, etc. Perfectly struck, centered unc. specimens command a considerable premium.

| Date | Mintage | F | VF | XF | Unc | BU |
|---|---|---|---|---|---|---|
| ND(1941) | — | 1.50 | 3.50 | 8.00 | 20.00 | — |

**5 PIASTRES** KM# A14 **Composition:** Aluminum **Note:** Did not enter circulation in significant numbers.

| Date | Mintage | F | VF | XF | Unc | BU |
|---|---|---|---|---|---|---|
| ND(1941) | — | — | — | 2,000 | 3,000 | — |

# REPUBLIC

## STANDARD COINAGE

**PIASTRE** KM# 19 **Composition:** Aluminum-Bronze

| Date | Mintage | F | VF | XF | Unc | BU |
|---|---|---|---|---|---|---|
| 1955(a) | 4,000,000 | — | 0.10 | 0.20 | 0.35 | — |

**2-1/2 PIASTRES** KM# 20 **Composition:** Aluminum-Bronze

| Date | Mintage | F | VF | XF | Unc | BU |
|---|---|---|---|---|---|---|
| 1955(a) | 5,000,000 | — | 0.10 | 0.25 | 0.50 | — |

**5 PIASTRES** KM# 14 **Composition:** Aluminum

| Date | Mintage | F | VF | XF | Unc | BU |
|---|---|---|---|---|---|---|
| 1952(a) | 3,600,000 | 0.50 | 1.00 | 1.50 | 4.00 | — |

**5 PIASTRES** KM# 18 **Composition:** Aluminum

| Date | Mintage | F | VF | XF | Unc | BU |
|---|---|---|---|---|---|---|
| 1954 | 4,440,000 | 0.10 | 0.30 | 0.50 | 1.25 | — |

**5 PIASTRES** KM# 21 **Composition:** Aluminum-Bronze

| Date | Mintage | F | VF | XF | Unc | BU |
|---|---|---|---|---|---|---|
| 1955(a) | 3,000,000 | 0.10 | 0.20 | 0.30 | 0.50 | — |
| 1961(a) | — | 0.10 | 0.15 | 0.20 | 0.40 | — |

**5 PIASTRES** KM# 25.1 **Composition:** Nickel-Brass

| Date | Mintage | F | VF | XF | Unc | BU |
|---|---|---|---|---|---|---|
| 1968 | 2,000,000 | — | 0.10 | 0.15 | 0.20 | — |
| 1969 | 4,000,000 | — | 0.10 | 0.15 | 0.20 | — |
| 1970 | — | — | 0.10 | 0.15 | 0.25 | — |

**5 PIASTRES** KM# 25.2 **Composition:** Nickel-Brass

| Date | Mintage | F | VF | XF | Unc | BU |
|---|---|---|---|---|---|---|
| 1972(a) | 12,000,000 | — | — | 0.10 | 0.15 | — |
| 1975(a) | — | — | — | 0.10 | 0.15 | — |
| 1980 | — | — | — | 0.10 | 0.15 | — |

**10 PIASTRES** **KM# 15** **Composition:** Aluminum

| Date | Mintage | F | VF | XF | Unc | BU |
|---|---|---|---|---|---|---|
| 1952(a) | 3,600,000 | 0.50 | 1.00 | 5.00 | 15.00 | — |

**10 PIASTRES** **KM# 22** **Composition:** Aluminum-Bronze

| Date | Mintage | F | VF | XF | Unc | BU |
|---|---|---|---|---|---|---|
| 1955 | 2,175,000 | 0.20 | 0.40 | 0.60 | 1.00 | — |

**10 PIASTRES** **KM# 23** **Composition:** Aluminum-Bronze

| Date | Mintage | F | VF | XF | Unc | BU |
|---|---|---|---|---|---|---|
| 1955(a) | 6,000,000 | 0.10 | 0.25 | 0.50 | 0.75 | — |

**10 PIASTRES** **KM# 24** **Composition:** Copper-Nickel

| Date | Mintage | F | VF | XF | Unc | BU |
|---|---|---|---|---|---|---|
| 1961 | 7,000,000 | — | 0.10 | 0.25 | 0.50 | — |
| 1961 Proof | — | — | — | — | — | — |

**10 PIASTRES** **KM# 26** **Composition:** Nickel-Brass

| Date | Mintage | F | VF | XF | Unc | BU |
|---|---|---|---|---|---|---|
| 1968(a) | 2,000,000 | — | 0.10 | 0.15 | 0.25 | — |
| 1969(a) | 5,000,000 | — | — | 0.10 | 0.20 | — |
| 1970(a) | 8,000,000 | — | — | 0.10 | 0.20 | — |
| 1972(a) | 12,000,000 | — | — | 0.10 | 0.20 | — |
| 1975(a) | — | — | — | 0.10 | 0.20 | — |

**25 PIASTRES** **KM# 16.1** **Composition:** Aluminum-Bronze

| Date | Mintage | F | VF | XF | Unc | BU |
|---|---|---|---|---|---|---|
| 1952(u) | 7,200,000 | 0.10 | 0.40 | 0.60 | 1.00 | — |

**25 PIASTRES** **KM# 16.2** **Composition:** Aluminum-Bronze **Note:** Different style of inscription and larger date.

| Date | Mintage | F | VF | XF | Unc | BU |
|---|---|---|---|---|---|---|
| 1961(u) | 5,000,000 | 0.10 | 0.40 | 0.50 | 0.75 | — |

**25 PIASTRES** **KM# 27.1** **Composition:** Nickel-Brass

| Date | Mintage | F | VF | XF | Unc | BU |
|---|---|---|---|---|---|---|
| 1968 | 1,500,000 | 0.10 | 0.15 | 0.25 | 0.50 | — |
| 1969 | 2,500,000 | 0.10 | 0.15 | 0.20 | 0.40 | — |
| 1970 | — | 0.10 | 0.15 | 0.20 | 0.40 | — |
| 1972 | 8,000,000 | 0.10 | 0.15 | 0.20 | 0.30 | — |
| 1975 | — | 0.10 | 0.15 | 0.20 | 0.30 | — |

**25 PIASTRES** **KM# 27.2** **Composition:** Nickel-Brass **Reverse:** Thick, plain 25

| Date | Mintage | F | VF | XF | Unc | BU |
|---|---|---|---|---|---|---|
| 1980 | — | 0.10 | 0.15 | 0.20 | 0.30 | — |

**50 PIASTRES** **KM# 17** **Weight:** 4.9710 g. **Composition:** 0.6000 Silver .0959 oz. ASW

| Date | Mintage | F | VF | XF | Unc | BU |
|---|---|---|---|---|---|---|
| 1952(u) | 7,200,000 | BV | 1.00 | 1.50 | 3.50 | — |

**50 PIASTRES** **KM# 28.1** **Composition:** Nickel

| Date | Mintage | F | VF | XF | Unc | BU |
|---|---|---|---|---|---|---|
| 1968 | 2,000,000 | 0.20 | 0.40 | 0.60 | 1.00 | — |
| 1969 | 3,488,000 | 0.10 | 0.25 | 0.40 | 0.75 | — |
| 1970 | 2,000,000 | 0.10 | 0.25 | 0.40 | 0.50 | — |
| 1971 | 2,000,000 | 0.10 | 0.25 | 0.40 | 0.50 | — |
| 1975 | — | 0.10 | 0.25 | 0.40 | 0.50 | — |
| 1978 | 22,400,000 | 0.10 | 0.25 | 0.40 | 0.50 | — |

**50 PIASTRES** **KM# 28.2** **Composition:** Nickel **Reverse:** Different 50

| Date | Mintage | F | VF | XF | Unc | BU |
|---|---|---|---|---|---|---|
| 1980 | — | 0.10 | 0.25 | 0.40 | 0.50 | — |

**LIVRE** **KM# 29** **Composition:** Nickel **Series:** F.A.O.

| Date | Mintage | F | VF | XF | Unc | BU |
|---|---|---|---|---|---|---|
| 1968 | 300,000 | 0.25 | 0.50 | 1.00 | 3.00 | — |

**LIVRE** **KM# 30** **Composition:** Nickel **Note:** Varieties exist.

| Date | Mintage | F | VF | XF | Unc | BU |
|---|---|---|---|---|---|---|
| 1975 | — | 0.20 | 0.40 | 0.60 | 1.00 | — |
| 1975 Proof | — | — | — | — | — | — |
| 1977 | 8,000,000 | 0.20 | 0.40 | 0.60 | 1.00 | — |
| 1980 | 12,000,000 | 0.20 | 0.40 | 0.60 | 1.00 | — |
| 1981 | — | 0.20 | 0.40 | 0.60 | 1.00 | — |
| 1986 | — | 0.20 | 0.40 | 0.60 | 1.00 | — |

**LIVRE** **KM# 32** **Composition:** Copper-Nickel **Series:** 1980 Winter Olympics **Subject:** Lake Placid

| Date | Mintage | F | VF | XF | Unc | BU |
|---|---|---|---|---|---|---|
| 1980 Proof | 40,000 | Value: 17.50 | | | | |

**5 LIVRES** **KM# 31** **Composition:** Nickel **Series:** F.A.O.

| Date | Mintage | F | VF | XF | Unc | BU |
|---|---|---|---|---|---|---|
| 1978 | 1,000,000 | — | — | — | 2.50 | — |

**10 LIVRES** **KM# 33** **Weight:** 19.0000 g. **Composition:** 0.5000 Silver .3054 oz. ASW **Series:** 1980 Winter Olympics **Subject:** Lake Placid

| Date | Mintage | F | VF | XF | Unc | BU |
|---|---|---|---|---|---|---|
| 1980 Proof | 20,000 | Value: 40.00 | | | | |

**10 LIVRES** **KM# 35** **Composition:** Copper-Nickel **Series:** World Food Day

| Date | Mintage | F | VF | XF | Unc | BU |
|---|---|---|---|---|---|---|
| 1981 | 15,000 | — | — | — | 6.50 | — |

**50 LIVRES** **KM# 37** **Composition:** Stainless Steel **Obverse:** Arabic legend and denomination **Reverse:** French legend and denomination

| Date | Mintage | F | VF | XF | Unc | BU |
|---|---|---|---|---|---|---|
| 1996 | — | — | — | 0.45 | 1.00 | — |

**100 LIVRES** **KM# 38** **Composition:** Copper-Zinc **Obverse:** Arabic legend and denomination **Reverse:** French legend and denomination

| Date | Mintage | F | VF | XF | Unc | BU |
|---|---|---|---|---|---|---|
| 1995 | — | — | — | 0.65 | 1.50 | — |
| 1996 | — | — | — | 0.65 | 1.50 | — |

**250 LIVRES** KM# 36 **Composition:** Brass **Obverse:** Arabic legend and denomination **Reverse:** French legend and denomination

| Date | Mintage | F | VF | XF | Unc | BU |
|---|---|---|---|---|---|---|
| 1995 | — | — | — | 0.75 | 2.00 | — |
| 1996 | — | — | — | 0.75 | 2.00 | — |

**400 LIVRES** KM# 34 **Weight:** 8.0000 g. **Composition:** 0.9000 Gold .2315 oz. AGW **Series:** 1980 Winter Olympics **Subject:** Lake Placid

| Date | Mintage | F | VF | XF | Unc | BU |
|---|---|---|---|---|---|---|
| 1980 Proof | 1,000 | Value: 600 | | | | |

**500 LIVRES** KM# 39 **Composition:** Stainless Steel **Obverse:** Arabic legend and denomination **Reverse:** French legend and denomination

| Date | Mintage | F | VF | XF | Unc | BU |
|---|---|---|---|---|---|---|
| 1995 | — | — | — | 1.00 | 2.50 | — |
| 1996 | — | — | — | 1.00 | 2.50 | — |

## ESSAIS

Standard metals unless otherwise noted

| KM# | Date | Mintage | Identification | Issue Price | Mkt Val |
|---|---|---|---|---|---|
| E1 | 1924 | — | 5 Piastres. KM2. | — | 110 |
| E2 | 1925 | — | Piastre. KM3. | — | 90.00 |
| E3 | 1925 | — | 2 Piastres. KM1. | — | 115 |
| E4 | 1925 | — | 5 Piastres. KM5.1. | — | 90.00 |
| E5 | 1929 | — | Piastre. KM3. | — | 90.00 |
| E6 | 1929 | — | 10 Piastres. KM6. | — | 125 |
| E7 | 1929 | — | 25 Piastres. KM7. | — | 125 |
| E8 | 1929 | — | 50 Piastres. KM8. | — | 125 |

| KM# | Date | Mintage | Identification | Issue Price | Mkt Val |
|---|---|---|---|---|---|
| E9 | 1934 | — | 1/2 Piastre. KM9. | — | 100 |

| KM# | Date | Mintage | Identification | Issue Price | Mkt Val |
|---|---|---|---|---|---|
| E10 | 1940 | — | 2-1/2 Piastres. KM10. | — | 50.00 |
| E11 | 1972 | — | 5 Piastres. KM25. | — | 15.00 |
| E12 | 1972 | — | 10 Piastres. KM26. | — | 15.00 |
| E13 | 1980 | — | 25 Piastres. KM27. | — | 15.00 |
| E15 | 1980 | — | Livre. KM30. | — | 22.50 |
| E14 | 1980 | — | 50 Piastres. KM28. | — | 17.50 |
| E16 | 1981 | — | 10 Livres. KM35. | — | 40.00 |

## PIEFORTS

| KM# | Date | Mintage | Identification | Issue Price | Mkt Val |
|---|---|---|---|---|---|
| P1 | 1980 | 3,000 | Livre. KM32. | 45.00 | 60.00 |
| P2 | 1980 | 3,000 | 10 Livres. KM33. | 95.00 | 125 |
| P3 | 1980 | 750 | 400 Livres. KM34. | — | 1,400 |

# LESOTHO

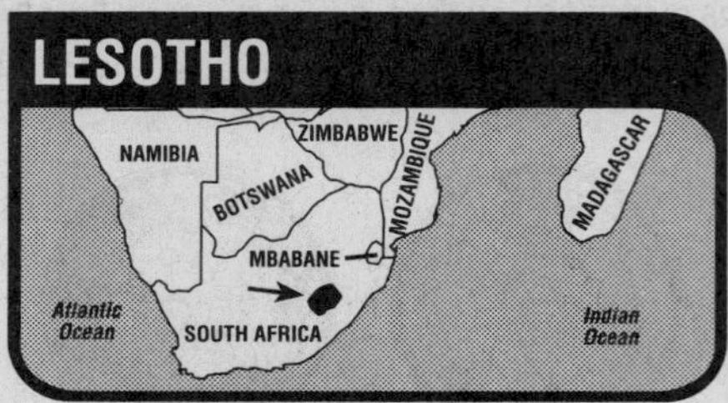


The Kingdom of Lesotho, a constitutional monarchy located within the east-central part of the Republic of South Africa, has an area of 11,720 sq. mi. (30,350 sq. km.) and a population of 1.5 million. Capital: Maseru. The economy is based on subsistence agriculture and live stock raising. Wool, mohair, and cattle are exported.

Lesotho (formerly Basutoland) was sparsely populated until the end of the 16th century. Between the 16th and 19th centuries an influx of refugees from tribal wars led to the development of a distinct Basotho group. During the reign of tribal chief Moshesh I (1823-70), a series of wars with the Orange Free State resulted in the loss of large areas of territory to South Africa. Moshesh appealed to the British for help, and Basutoland was constituted a native state under British protection. In 1871 it was annexed to Cape Colony, but was restored to direct control by the Crown in 1884. From 1884 to 1959 legislative and executive authority was vested in a British High Commissioner. The constitution of 1959 recognized the expressed wish of the people for independence, which was attained on Oct.4, 1966.

Lesotho is a member of the Commonwealth of Nations. The king is Head of State.

**RULERS**

Moshoeshoe II, 1966-1990
Letsie III, 1990-1995
Moshoeshoe II, 1995-

**MONETARY SYSTEM**

100 Licente/Lisente = 1 Maloti/Loti

## KINGDOM

### STANDARD COINAGE

100 Licente/Lisente = 1 Maloti/Loti

**SENTE** KM# 16 **Composition:** Nickel-Brass **Ruler:** Moshoeshoe II **Reverse:** Traditional house

| Date | Mintage | F | VF | XF | Unc | BU |
|---|---|---|---|---|---|---|
| 1979 | 4,500,000 | — | — | 0.15 | 0.40 | — |
| 1979 Proof | 10,000 | Value: 0.65 | | | | |
| 1980 | — | — | — | 0.15 | 0.40 | — |
| 1980 Proof | 10,000 | Value: 0.65 | | | | |
| 1981 Proof | 2,500 | Value: 0.65 | | | | |
| 1983 | — | — | — | 0.15 | 0.40 | — |
| 1985 | — | — | — | 0.15 | 0.40 | — |
| 1989 | — | — | — | 0.15 | 0.40 | — |

**SENTE** KM# 54 **Composition:** Brass **Ruler:** Letsie III

| Date | Mintage | F | VF | XF | Unc | BU |
|---|---|---|---|---|---|---|
| 1992 | — | — | — | 0.15 | 0.75 | — |

**SENTE** KM# 54a **Composition:** Brass Clad Steel **Ruler:** Letsie III

| Date | Mintage | F | VF | XF | Unc | BU |
|---|---|---|---|---|---|---|
| 1992 | — | — | — | — | — | — |

**2 LISENTE** KM# 17 **Composition:** Nickel-Brass **Ruler:** Moshoeshoe II **Reverse:** Steer

| Date | Mintage | F | VF | XF | Unc | BU |
|---|---|---|---|---|---|---|
| 1979 | 3,000,000 | — | — | 0.20 | 0.50 | — |
| 1979 Proof | 10,000 | Value: 1.00 | | | | |
| 1980 | — | — | — | 0.20 | 0.50 | — |
| 1980 Proof | 10,000 | Value: 1.00 | | | | |
| 1981 Proof | 2,500 | Value: 2.00 | | | | |
| 1985 | — | — | — | 0.20 | 0.50 | — |
| 1989 | — | — | — | 0.20 | 0.50 | — |

**2 LISENTE** KM# 55 **Composition:** Brass **Ruler:** Letsie III **Obverse:** National arms **Reverse:** Bull

| Date | Mintage | F | VF | XF | Unc | BU |
|---|---|---|---|---|---|---|
| 1992 | — | — | — | 0.20 | 0.50 | — |

**2 LISENTE** KM# 55a **Weight:** 2.2500 g. **Composition:** Brass Plated Steel **Ruler:** Letsie III **Obverse:** National arms **Reverse:** Bull **Edge:** Plain **Size:** 19.5 mm.

| Date | Mintage | F | VF | XF | Unc | BU |
|---|---|---|---|---|---|---|
| 1992 | — | — | — | 0.20 | 0.50 | — |

**5 LICENTE (Lisente)** KM# 1 **Weight:** 2.8900 g. **Composition:** 0.9000 Silver .0836 oz. ASW **Ruler:** Moshoeshoe II **Subject:** Independence attained

| Date | Mintage | F | VF | XF | Unc | BU |
|---|---|---|---|---|---|---|
| 1966 Proof | 5,000 | Value: 6.00 | | | | |

**5 LICENTE (Lisente)** KM# 18 **Composition:** Nickel-Brass **Ruler:** Moshoeshoe II **Reverse:** Aloe plant

| Date | Mintage | F | VF | XF | Unc | BU |
|---|---|---|---|---|---|---|
| 1979 | 2,700,000 | — | — | 0.25 | 0.60 | — |
| 1979 Proof | 10,000 | Value: 1.25 | | | | |
| 1980 | — | — | — | 0.25 | 0.60 | — |
| 1980 Proof | 10,000 | Value: 1.25 | | | | |
| 1981 Proof | 2,500 | Value: 2.50 | | | | |
| 1989 | — | — | — | 0.25 | 0.60 | — |

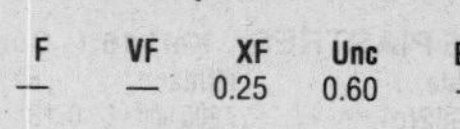

**5 LICENTE (Lisente)** KM# 56 **Composition:** Brass **Ruler:** Letsie III

| Date | Mintage | F | VF | XF | Unc | BU |
|---|---|---|---|---|---|---|
| 1994 | — | — | — | 0.25 | 0.60 | — |

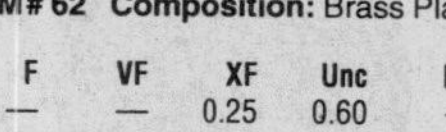

**5 LICENTE (Lisente)** KM# 62 **Composition:** Brass Plated Steel **Ruler:** Letsie III

| Date | Mintage | F | VF | XF | Unc | BU |
|---|---|---|---|---|---|---|
| 1998 | — | — | — | 0.25 | 0.60 | — |

**10 LICENTE (Lisente)** KM# 2 **Weight:** 5.6800 g. **Composition:** 0.9000 Silver .1643 oz. ASW **Ruler:** Moshoeshoe II **Subject:** Independence attained

| Date | Mintage | F | VF | XF | Unc | BU |
|---|---|---|---|---|---|---|
| 1966 Proof | 5,000 | Value: 6.00 | | | | |

**10 LICENTE (Lisente)** **KM# 19** **Composition:** Copper-Nickel **Ruler:** Moshoeshoe II **Reverse:** Angora goat

| Date | Mintage | F | VF | XF | Unc | BU |
|---|---|---|---|---|---|---|
| 1979 | 2,000,000 | — | 0.15 | 0.30 | 0.75 | — |
| 1979 Proof | 10,000 | Value: 1.75 | | | | |
| 1980 | — | — | 0.15 | 0.30 | 0.75 | — |
| 1980 Proof | 10,000 | Value: 1.75 | | | | |
| 1981 Proof | 2,500 | Value: 3.00 | | | | |
| 1983 | — | — | 0.15 | 0.30 | 0.75 | — |
| 1989 | — | — | 0.15 | 0.30 | 0.75 | — |

**10 LICENTE (Lisente)** **KM# 61** **Composition:** Copper-Nickel **Ruler:** Letsie III **Obverse:** National arms **Reverse:** Angora goat

| Date | Mintage | F | VF | XF | Unc | BU |
|---|---|---|---|---|---|---|
| 1992 | — | — | — | — | 0.65 | — |

**10 LICENTE (Lisente)** **KM# 63** **Composition:** Brass Plated Steel **Ruler:** Moshoeshoe II

| Date | Mintage | F | VF | XF | Unc | BU |
|---|---|---|---|---|---|---|
| 1998 | — | — | — | — | 0.65 | — |

**20 LICENTE** **KM# 3.1** **Weight:** 11.2800 g. **Composition:** 0.9000 Silver .3263 oz. ASW **Ruler:** Moshoeshoe II **Subject:** Independence attained **Reverse:** Small 900/1000 at right of date

| Date | Mintage | F | VF | XF | Unc | BU |
|---|---|---|---|---|---|---|
| 1966 Proof | 5,000 | Value: 10.00 | | | | |

**20 LICENTE** **KM# 3.2** **Weight:** 11.2800 g. **Composition:** 0.9000 Silver .3263 oz. ASW **Ruler:** Moshoeshoe II **Subject:** Independence attained **Reverse:** Large 900/1000 at right of date

| Date | Mintage | F | VF | XF | Unc | BU |
|---|---|---|---|---|---|---|
| 1966 Proof | — | Value: 10.00 | | | | |

**20 LICENTE** **KM# 64** **Composition:** Brass Plated Steel **Ruler:** Moshoeshoe II **Reverse:** Flora

| Date | Mintage | F | VF | XF | Unc | BU |
|---|---|---|---|---|---|---|
| 1998 | — | — | — | — | 0.75 | — |

**25 LISENTE** **KM# 20** **Composition:** Copper-Nickel **Ruler:** Moshoeshoe II **Reverse:** Woman in native costume weaving baskets

| Date | Mintage | F | VF | XF | Unc | BU |
|---|---|---|---|---|---|---|
| 1979 | 1,200,000 | — | 0.10 | 0.20 | 1.00 | — |
| 1979 Proof | 10,000 | Value: 2.00 | | | | |
| 1980 | — | — | 0.10 | 0.20 | 1.00 | — |
| 1980 Proof | 10,000 | Value: 2.00 | | | | |
| 1981 Proof | 2,500 | Value: 3.50 | | | | |
| 1985 | — | — | 0.10 | 0.20 | 1.00 | — |
| 1989 | — | — | 0.10 | 0.20 | 1.00 | — |

**50 LICENTE (Lisente)** **KM# 4.1DAV# 38** **Weight:** 28.1000 g. **Composition:** 0.9000 Silver .8131 oz. ASW **Ruler:** Moshoeshoe II **Subject:** Independence attained **Reverse:** Small 900/1000 at right of date

| Date | Mintage | F | VF | XF | Unc | BU |
|---|---|---|---|---|---|---|
| 1966 | — | — | — | — | 10.00 | — |
| 1966 Proof | — | Value: 17.50 | | | | |

**50 LICENTE (Lisente)** **KM# 4.2** **Weight:** 28.1000 g. **Composition:** 0.9000 Silver .8131 oz. ASW **Ruler:** Moshoeshoe II **Subject:** Independence attained **Reverse:** Large 900/1000 at right of date

| Date | Mintage | F | VF | XF | Unc | BU |
|---|---|---|---|---|---|---|
| 1966 | — | — | — | — | 10.00 | — |
| 1966 Proof | 5,000 | Value: 17.50 | | | | |

**50 LICENTE (Lisente)** **KM# 4.3** **Weight:** 28.1000 g. **Composition:** 0.9000 Silver .8131 oz. ASW **Ruler:** Moshoeshoe II **Subject:** Independence attained **Reverse:** Mint mark and fineness below date

| Date | Mintage | F | VF | XF | Unc | BU |
|---|---|---|---|---|---|---|
| 1966 | — | — | — | — | 10.00 | — |
| 1966 Proof | — | Value: 17.50 | | | | |

**50 LICENTE (Lisente)** **KM# 21** **Composition:** Copper-Nickel **Ruler:** Moshoeshoe II **Reverse:** Horse and rider

| Date | Mintage | F | VF | XF | Unc | BU |
|---|---|---|---|---|---|---|
| 1979 | 480,000 | — | 0.35 | 0.50 | 1.25 | — |
| 1979 Proof | 10,000 | Value: 2.50 | | | | |
| 1980 | — | — | 0.35 | 0.50 | 1.25 | — |
| 1980 Proof | 10,000 | Value: 2.50 | | | | |
| 1981 Proof | 2,500 | Value: 4.00 | | | | |
| 1983 | — | — | 0.35 | 0.50 | 1.25 | — |
| 1989 | — | — | 0.35 | 0.50 | 1.25 | — |

**50 LICENTE (Lisente)** **KM# 65** **Composition:** Brass Plated Steel **Ruler:** Moshoeshoe II

| Date | Mintage | F | VF | XF | Unc | BU |
|---|---|---|---|---|---|---|
| 1998 | — | — | — | — | 1.00 | — |

**LOTI** **KM# 5** **Weight:** 3.9940 g. **Composition:** 0.9170 Gold .1177 oz. AGW **Ruler:** Moshoeshoe II **Subject:** Independence attained

| Date | Mintage | F | VF | XF | Unc | BU |
|---|---|---|---|---|---|---|
| 1966 Proof | 3,500 | Value: 70.00 | | | | |

**LOTI** **KM# 8** **Weight:** 3.9940 g. **Composition:** 0.9170 Gold .1177 oz. AGW **Ruler:** Moshoeshoe II **Series:** F.A.O.

| Date | Mintage | F | VF | XF | Unc | BU |
|---|---|---|---|---|---|---|
| 1969 Proof | 3,000 | Value: 65.00 | | | | |

**LOTI** **KM# 22** **Composition:** Copper-Nickel **Ruler:** Moshoeshoe II

| Date | Mintage | F | VF | XF | Unc | BU |
|---|---|---|---|---|---|---|
| 1979 | 1,275,000 | — | 0.65 | 1.25 | 3.00 | — |
| 1979 Proof | 10,000 | Value: 5.00 | | | | |
| 1980 | — | — | 0.75 | 1.50 | 4.00 | — |
| 1980 Proof | 10,000 | Value: 5.00 | | | | |
| 1981 Proof | 2,500 | Value: 7.00 | | | | |
| 1989 | — | — | 0.75 | 1.50 | 4.00 | — |

**LOTI** **KM# 46** **Weight:** 11.3100 g. **Composition:** 0.9250 Silver .3363 oz. ASW **Ruler:** Moshoeshoe II **Subject:** Silver jubilee of King Moshoeshoe II

| Date | Mintage | F | VF | XF | Unc | BU |
|---|---|---|---|---|---|---|
| 1985 Proof | 2,500 | Value: 17.50 | | | | |

**LOTI** **KM# 46a** **Weight:** 18.9800 g. **Composition:** 0.9170 Gold .5626 oz. AGW **Ruler:** Moshoeshoe II **Subject:** Silver jubilee of King Moshoeshoe II

| Date | Mintage | F | VF | XF | Unc | BU |
|---|---|---|---|---|---|---|
| 1985 Proof | 500 | Value: 250 | | | | |

**LOTI** **KM# 60** **Composition:** Copper-Nickel **Ruler:** Letsie III **Series:** 50th anniversary - UN

| Date | Mintage | F | VF | XF | Unc | BU |
|---|---|---|---|---|---|---|
| 1995 | — | — | — | — | 8.00 | — |

**LOTI** **KM# 66** **Composition:** Nickel Plated Steel **Ruler:** Letsie III **Obverse:** Seated king

| Date | Mintage | F | VF | XF | Unc | BU |
|---|---|---|---|---|---|---|
| 1998 | — | — | — | — | 1.50 | — |

**2 MALOTI** **KM# 6** **Weight:** 7.9880 g. **Composition:** 0.9170 Gold .2355 oz. AGW **Ruler:** Moshoeshoe II **Obverse:** Independence attained

| Date | Mintage | F | VF | XF | Unc | BU |
|---|---|---|---|---|---|---|
| 1966 Proof | — | Value: 120 | | | | |

**2 MALOTI** **KM# 9** **Weight:** 7.9880 g. **Composition:** 0.9170 Gold .2355 oz. AGW **Ruler:** Moshoeshoe II **Series:** F.A.O.

| Date | Mintage | F | VF | XF | Unc | BU |
|---|---|---|---|---|---|---|
| 1969 Proof | 3,000 | Value: 120 | | | | |

**2 MALOTI** **KM# 58** **Composition:** Nickel Clad Steel **Ruler:** Moshoeshoe II **Obverse:** National arms **Reverse:** Maize plants

| Date | Mintage | F | VF | XF | Unc | BU |
|---|---|---|---|---|---|---|
| 1996 | — | — | — | — | 2.50 | — |
| 1998 | — | — | — | — | 2.00 | — |

**4 MALOTI** **KM# 7** **Weight:** 15.9760 g. **Composition:** 0.9170 Gold .471 oz. AGW **Ruler:** Moshoeshoe II **Subject:** Independence attained

| Date | Mintage | F | VF | XF | Unc | BU |
|---|---|---|---|---|---|---|
| 1966 Proof | 3,500 | Value: 235 | | | | |

**4 MALOTI** **KM# 10** **Weight:** 15.9760 g. **Composition:** 0.9170 Gold .471 oz. AGW **Ruler:** Moshoeshoe II **Series:** F.A.O.

| Date | Mintage | F | VF | XF | Unc | BU |
|---|---|---|---|---|---|---|
| 1969 Proof | 3,000 | Value: 250 | | | | |

**5 MALOTI** **KM# 59** **Composition:** Nickel Clad Steel **Ruler:** Moshoeshoe II **Obverse:** National arms **Reverse:** 5 wheat ears

| Date | Mintage | F | VF | XF | Unc | BU |
|---|---|---|---|---|---|---|
| 1996 | — | — | — | — | 5.50 | — |
| 1998 | — | — | — | — | 3.50 | — |

**10 MALOTI** **KM# 11** **Weight:** 39.9400 g. **Composition:** 0.9170 Gold 1.1776 oz. AGW **Ruler:** Moshoeshoe II **Series:** F.A.O.

| Date | Mintage | F | VF | XF | Unc | BU |
|---|---|---|---|---|---|---|
| 1969 Proof | 3,000 | Value: 550 | | | | |

**10 MALOTI** **KM# 13** **Weight:** 25.0800 g. **Composition:** 0.9250 Silver .7459 oz. ASW **Ruler:** Moshoeshoe II **Subject:** 10th anniversary of independence

| Date | Mintage | F | VF | XF | Unc | BU |
|---|---|---|---|---|---|---|
| 1976 | 2,300 | — | — | — | 20.00 | — |
| 1976 Proof | 2,100 | Value: 30.00 | | | | |

**10 MALOTI** **KM# 23** **Weight:** 28.2800 g. **Composition:** 0.9250 Silver .8411 oz. ASW **Ruler:** Moshoeshoe II **Subject:** Monument of King Moshoeshoe I

| Date | Mintage | F | VF | XF | Unc | BU |
|---|---|---|---|---|---|---|
| 1979 | 10,000 | — | — | — | 15.00 | — |
| 1979 Proof | 5,000 | Value: 20.00 | | | | |

**10 MALOTI** **KM# 23a** **Weight:** 12.0000 g. **Composition:** 0.5000 Silver .1929 oz. ASW **Ruler:** Moshoeshoe II **Subject:** Monument of King Moshoeshoe I

| Date | Mintage | F | VF | XF | Unc | BU |
|---|---|---|---|---|---|---|
| 1980 | 10,000 | — | — | — | 10.00 | — |
| 1980 Proof | 5,000 | Value: 15.00 | | | | |

**10 MALOTI** **KM# 24** **Weight:** 28.2800 g. **Composition:** 0.9250 Silver .8411 oz. ASW **Ruler:** Moshoeshoe II **Series:** International Year of the Child **Note:** Similar to 15 Maloti, KM#25.

| Date | Mintage | F | VF | XF | Unc | BU |
|---|---|---|---|---|---|---|
| 1979 (1981) | — | — | — | — | 11.50 | — |
| 1979 (1981) Proof | 37,000 | Value: 13.50 | | | | |

**10 MALOTI** **KM# 32** **Weight:** 23.3300 g. **Composition:** 0.9250 Silver .6938 oz. ASW **Ruler:** Moshoeshoe II **Subject:** World Soccer Championship

| Date | Mintage | F | VF | XF | Unc | BU |
|---|---|---|---|---|---|---|
| 1982 Proof | 3,582 | Value: 22.50 | | | | |

**10 MALOTI** **KM# 34** **Weight:** 23.3300 g. **Composition:** 0.9250 Silver .6938 oz. ASW **Ruler:** Moshoeshoe II **Subject:** World Soccer Championship

| Date | Mintage | F | VF | XF | Unc | BU |
|---|---|---|---|---|---|---|
| 1982 Proof | 3,000 | Value: 20.00 | | | | |

**10 MALOTI** **KM# 40** **Weight:** 31.1000 g. **Composition:** 0.5000 Silver .5000 oz. ASW **Ruler:** Moshoeshoe II **Subject:** George Washington **Obverse:** Similar to KM#34 **Reverse:** Washington facing left

| Date | Mintage | F | VF | XF | Unc | BU |
|---|---|---|---|---|---|---|
| 1982 Proof | 7,355 | Value: 17.50 | | | | |

**10 MALOTI** **KM# 41** **Weight:** 31.1000 g. **Composition:** 0.5000 Silver .5000 oz. ASW **Ruler:** Moshoeshoe II **Subject:** George Washington **Obverse:** Similar to KM#34 **Reverse:** Washington on bended knee

| Date | Mintage | F | VF | XF | Unc | BU |
|---|---|---|---|---|---|---|
| 1982 Proof | 4,200 | Value: 17.50 | | | | |

**10 MALOTI** **KM# 42** **Weight:** 31.1000 g. **Composition:** 0.5000 Silver .5000 oz. ASW **Ruler:** Moshoeshoe II **Subject:** George Washington **Obverse:** Similar to KM#34 **Reverse:** Washington crossing the Delaware

| Date | Mintage | F | VF | XF | Unc | BU |
|---|---|---|---|---|---|---|
| 1982 Proof | Est. 15,000 | Value: 17.50 | | | | |

**10 MALOTI** **KM# 49** **Weight:** 23.3300 g. **Composition:** 0.9250 Silver .6939 oz. ASW **Ruler:** Moshoeshoe II **Subject:** Decade for Women

| Date | Mintage | F | VF | XF | Unc | BU |
|---|---|---|---|---|---|---|
| 1985 Proof | 1,000 | Value: 35.00 | | | | |

**10 MALOTI** **KM#50** **Weight:** 28.2800 g. **Composition:** 0.9250 Silver .8411 oz. ASW **Ruler:** Moshoeshoe II **Subject:** Papal visit

| Date | Mintage | F | VF | XF | Unc | BU |
|---|---|---|---|---|---|---|
| 1988 Proof | Est. 15,000 | Value: 45.00 | | | | |

**15 MALOTI** **KM#25** **Weight:** 33.4000 g. **Composition:** 0.9250 Silver .9933 oz. ASW **Ruler:** Moshoeshoe II **Series:** International Year of the Child **Obverse:** Similar to 25 Maloti, KM#35

| Date | Mintage | F | VF | XF | Unc | BU |
|---|---|---|---|---|---|---|
| 1979 | 18,000 | — | — | — | 12.50 | — |
| 1979 Proof | 7,500 | Value: 22.50 | | | | |

**15 MALOTI** **KM# 37** **Composition:** 0.5000 Silver **Ruler:** Moshoeshoe II **Subject:** 15th anniversary of Commonwealth membership **Obverse:** Similar to 50 Maloti, KM#38

| Date | Mintage | F | VF | XF | Unc | BU |
|---|---|---|---|---|---|---|
| 1981 Proof | 2,500 | Value: 30.00 | | | | |

**15 MALOTI** **KM# 53** **Weight:** 12.0000 g. **Composition:** 0.5000 Silver .1929 oz. ASW **Ruler:** Moshoeshoe II **Subject:** 15th anniversary of independence

| Date | Mintage | F | VF | XF | Unc | BU |
|---|---|---|---|---|---|---|
| 1981 Proof | 2,500 | Value: 35.00 | | | | |

**20 MALOTI** **KM# 12** **Weight:** 79.8810 g. **Composition:** 0.9170 Gold 2.3553 oz. AGW **Ruler:** Moshoeshoe II **Series:** F.A.O. **Obverse:** Similar to 10 Maloti, KM#11

| Date | Mintage | F | VF | XF | Unc | BU |
|---|---|---|---|---|---|---|
| 1969 Proof | 3,000 | Value: 1,250 | | | | |

**25 MALOTI** **KM# 35** **Weight:** 16.8200 g. **Composition:** 0.9250 Silver .5003 oz. ASW **Ruler:** Moshoeshoe II **Obverse:** Duke of Edinburgh Youth Awards

| Date | Mintage | F | VF | XF | Unc | BU |
|---|---|---|---|---|---|---|
| 1981 Proof | 5,000 | Value: 35.00 | | | | |

**25 MALOTI** **KM# 44** **Weight:** 28.2800 g. **Composition:** 0.9250 Silver .8411 oz. ASW **Ruler:** Moshoeshoe II **Series:** International Year of Disabled Persons

| Date | Mintage | F | VF | XF | Unc | BU |
|---|---|---|---|---|---|---|
| 1983 | — | — | — | — | 32.50 | — |
| 1983 Proof | — | Value: 55.00 | | | | |

**30 MALOTI** **KM# 30** **Composition:** 0.9250 Silver **Ruler:** Moshoeshoe II **Subject:** Wedding of Prince Charles and Lady Diana

| Date | Mintage | F | VF | XF | Unc | BU |
|---|---|---|---|---|---|---|
| 1981 Proof | 10,000 | Value: 45.00 | | | | |

**50 MALOTI** **KM# 14** **Weight:** 4.5000 g. **Composition:** 0.9000 Gold .1302 oz. AGW **Ruler:** Moshoeshoe II **Subject:** 10th anniversary of independence

| Date | Mintage | F | VF | XF | Unc | BU |
|---|---|---|---|---|---|---|
| ND(1976) | 700 | — | — | — | 125 | — |
| ND(1976) Proof | 1,910 | Value: 115 | | | | |

**50 MALOTI** **KM# 27** **Weight:** 33.6200 g. **Composition:** 0.9250 Silver .9999 oz. ASW **Ruler:** Moshoeshoe II **Subject:** 110th anniversary - death of King Moshoeshoe I

| Date | Mintage | F | VF | XF | Unc | BU |
|---|---|---|---|---|---|---|
| 1980 | 2,500 | — | — | — | 30.00 | — |
| 1980 Proof | 1,400 | Value: 45.00 | | | | |

**50 MALOTI** **KM# 38** **Weight:** 33.6200 g. **Composition:** 0.9250 Silver .9999 oz. ASW **Ruler:** Moshoeshoe II **Subject:** 15th anniversary of Commonwealth membership

| Date | Mintage | F | VF | XF | Unc | BU |
|---|---|---|---|---|---|---|
| 1981 Proof | 5,000 | Value: 40.00 | | | | |

**100 MALOTI** **KM# 15** **Weight:** 9.0000 g. **Composition:** 0.9000 Gold .2604 oz. AGW **Ruler:** Moshoeshoe II **Subject:** 10th anniversary of independence

| Date | Mintage | F | VF | XF | Unc | BU |
|---|---|---|---|---|---|---|
| ND(1976) | 450 | — | — | — | 175 | — |
| ND(1976) Proof | 1,410 | Value: 160 | | | | |

**200 MALOTI** **KM# 45** **Weight:** 15.9800 g. **Composition:** 0.9000 Gold .4624 oz. AGW **Ruler:** Moshoeshoe II **Series:** International Year of Disabled Persons

| Date | Mintage | F | VF | XF | Unc | BU |
|---|---|---|---|---|---|---|
| 1983 | 500 | — | — | — | 400 | — |
| 1983 Proof | 500 | Value: 450 | | | | |

**250 MALOTI** **KM# 26** **Weight:** 33.9300 g. **Composition:** 0.9170 Gold 1 oz. AGW **Ruler:** Moshoeshoe II **Series:** International Year of the Child **Obverse:** Similar to 15 Maloti, KM#25

| Date | Mintage | F | VF | XF | Unc | BU |
|---|---|---|---|---|---|---|
| 1979 | 2,500 | — | — | — | 475 | — |
| 1979 Proof | 2,000 | Value: 525 | | | | |

**250 MALOTI** **KM# 28** **Weight:** 31.1000 g. **Composition:** 0.9170 Gold .917 oz. AGW **Ruler:** Moshoeshoe II **Subject:** 110th anniversary - death of King Moshoeshoe I **Obverse:** Similar to 50 Maloti, KM#27

| Date | Mintage | F | VF | XF | Unc | BU |
|---|---|---|---|---|---|---|
| 1980 | 1,500 | — | — | — | 450 | — |
| 1980 Proof | 3,000 | Value: 475 | | | | |

**250 MALOTI** **KM# 31** **Weight:** 15.9000 g. **Composition:** 0.9170 Gold .4688 oz. AGW **Ruler:** Moshoeshoe II **Subject:** Wedding of Prince Charles and Lady Diana

| Date | Mintage | F | VF | XF | Unc | BU |
|---|---|---|---|---|---|---|
| 1981 | 1,000 | — | — | — | 225 | — |
| 1981 Proof | 1,500 | Value: 275 | | | | |

**250 MALOTI** **KM# 31a** **Weight:** 15.7500 g. **Composition:** 0.9950 Platinum .5039 oz. APW **Ruler:** Moshoeshoe II **Subject:** Wedding of Prince Charles and Lady Diana

| Date | Mintage | F | VF | XF | Unc | BU |
|---|---|---|---|---|---|---|
| 1981 Proof | 200 | Value: 550 | | | | |

**250 MALOTI** **KM# 36** **Weight:** 16.9600 g. **Composition:** 0.9170 Gold .5001 oz. AGW **Ruler:** Moshoeshoe II **Subject:** Duke of Edinburgh Youth Awards

| Date | Mintage | F | VF | XF | Unc | BU |
|---|---|---|---|---|---|---|
| 1981 Proof | 1,500 | Value: 275 | | | | |

**250 MALOTI** KM# 36a **Weight:** 15.7500 g. **Composition:** 0.9950 Platinum .5039 oz. APW **Ruler:** Moshoeshoe II **Subject:** Duke of Edinburgh Youth Awards

| Date | Mintage | F | VF | XF | Unc | BU |
|---|---|---|---|---|---|---|
| 1981 Proof | 200 | Value: 550 | | | | |

**250 MALOTI** KM# 33 **Weight:** 7.1300 g. **Composition:** 0.9000 Gold .2063 oz. AGW **Ruler:** Moshoeshoe II **Subject:** Soccer games

| Date | Mintage | F | VF | XF | Unc | BU |
|---|---|---|---|---|---|---|
| 1982 Proof | 551 | Value: 250 | | | | |

**250 MALOTI** KM# 51 **Weight:** 15.9800 g. **Composition:** 0.9170 Gold .4708 oz. AGW **Ruler:** Moshoeshoe II **Subject:** Papal visit

| Date | Mintage | F | VF | XF | Unc | BU |
|---|---|---|---|---|---|---|
| 1988 Proof | Est. 750 | Value: 500 | | | | |

**500 MALOTI** KM# 29 **Weight:** 33.9300 g. **Composition:** 0.9170 Gold 1 oz. AGW **Ruler:** Moshoeshoe II **Subject:** 110th anniversary - death of King Moshoeshoe I **Obverse:** Similar to 50 Maloti, KM#27

| Date | Mintage | F | VF | XF | Unc | BU |
|---|---|---|---|---|---|---|
| 1980 | 1,500 | — | — | — | 500 | — |
| 1980 Proof | 3,000 | Value: 525 | | | | |

**500 MALOTI** KM# 39 **Weight:** 33.9300 g. **Composition:** 0.9170 Gold 1 oz. AGW **Ruler:** Moshoeshoe II **Subject:** 15th anniversary of commonwealth membership

| Date | Mintage | F | VF | XF | Unc | BU |
|---|---|---|---|---|---|---|
| 1981 Proof | 500 | Value: 550 | | | | |

**500 MALOTI** KM# 39a **Weight:** 31.5000 g. **Composition:** 0.9950 Platinum 1.0078 oz. APW **Ruler:** Moshoeshoe II **Subject:** 15th anniversary of commonwealth membership

| Date | Mintage | F | VF | XF | Unc | BU |
|---|---|---|---|---|---|---|
| 1981 Proof | 200 | Value: 825 | | | | |

**500 MALOTI** KM# 57 **Weight:** 33.9300 g. **Composition:** 0.9166 Gold 1 oz. AGW **Ruler:** Moshoeshoe II **Subject:** Royal wedding **Obverse:** Lesotho arms **Reverse:** Conjoined bust of Diana and Charles

| Date | Mintage | F | VF | XF | Unc | BU |
|---|---|---|---|---|---|---|
| ND(1981) Proof, rare | — | — | — | — | — | — |

**500 MALOTI** KM# 57a **Weight:** 33.4800 g. **Composition:** 0.9995 Platinum 1 oz. APW **Ruler:** Moshoeshoe II **Subject:** Royal wedding **Obverse:** Lesotho arms **Reverse:** Conjoined bust of Diana and Charles

| Date | Mintage | F | VF | XF | Unc | BU |
|---|---|---|---|---|---|---|
| ND(1981) Proof, rare | — | — | — | — | — | — |

## MEDALLIC COINAGE

**10 MALOTI** KM# M1 **Composition:** Copper-Nickel **Ruler:** Moshoeshoe II **Series:** International Games **Reverse:** Field hockey

| Date | Mintage | F | VF | XF | Unc | BU |
|---|---|---|---|---|---|---|
| 1984 Proof | — | Value: 11.00 | | | | |

**10 MALOTI** KM# M2 **Composition:** Copper-Nickel **Ruler:** Moshoeshoe II **Series:** International Games **Reverse:** Hurdler

| Date | Mintage | F | VF | XF | Unc | BU |
|---|---|---|---|---|---|---|
| 1984 Proof | — | Value: 10.00 | | | | |

**25 MALOTI** KM# M3 **Weight:** 28.3500 g. **Composition:** Silver **Ruler:** Moshoeshoe II **Series:** International Games **Reverse:** Hurdler

| Date | Mintage | F | VF | XF | Unc | BU |
|---|---|---|---|---|---|---|
| 1984 Proof | — | Value: 40.00 | | | | |

## PATTERNS

Including off metal strikes

| KM# | Date | Mintage | Identification | Mkt Val |
|---|---|---|---|---|
| Pn1 | 1966 | 2 | 5 Licente. 0.9000 Silver. | — |
| Pn2 | 1966 | 2 | 10 Licente. 0.9000 Silver. | — |
| Pn3 | 1966 | 2 | 20 Licente. 0.9000 Silver. | — |
| Pn4 | 1966 | 2 | 50 Licente. 0.9000 Silver. | — |
| Pn6 | 1966 | 7 | 2 Maloti. 0.9160 Gold. | 500 |
| Pn7 | 1966 | 7 | 4 Maloti. 0.9160 Gold. | 700 |
| Pn8 | 1966 | 7 | 10 Maloti. 0.9160 Gold. | 950 |
| Pn9 | 1966 | 7 | 20 Maloti. 0.9160 Gold. | 1,250 |
| Pn10 | 1979 | 5 | 15 Maloti. Copper-Nickel. KM25. Medallic alignment. | 110 |
| Pn10.2a | 1979 | — | 15 Maloti. 0.9250 Silver. 33.5100 g. | — |
| Pn12 | 1979 | 15 | 250 Maloti. Brass. KM26. | 75.00 |
| Pn13 | 1979 | 5 | 250 Maloti. Copper-Nickel. KM26. Medallic alignment. | 110 |
| Pn11 | 1979 | 15 | 15 Maloti. Copper-Nickel. KM25. Coin alignment. | 80.00 |
| Pn14 | 1979 | 10 | 250 Maloti. Silver. 20.1500 g. KM26. | 115 |
| Pn15 | 1980 | 10 | 50 Maloti. Copper-Nickel. KM27. Medallic alignment. | 125 |
| Pn17 | 1980 | 10 | 250 Maloti. Brass. KM28. Coin alignment. | 110 |
| Pn19 | 1980 | 10 | 500 Maloti. Brass. KM29. Coin alignment. | 110 |
| Pn20 | 1980 | 10 | 500 Maloti. Copper-Nickel. KM29. Medallic alignment. | 110 |
| Pn18 | 1980 | 10 | 250 Maloti. Copper-Nickel. KM28. Medallic alignment. | 100 |
| Pn16 | 1980 | 10 | 50 Maloti. Copper-Nickel. Coin alignment. | 125 |

## PIEFORTS

| KM# | Date | Mintage | Identification | Mkt Val |
|---|---|---|---|---|
| P1 | 1979 | 50 | 10 Maloti. KM24. | 135 |
| P2 | 1981 | — | 250 Maloti. KM31. | 550 |
| P3 | 1983 | — | 25 Maloti. KM4. | 90.00 |
| P4 | 1983 | 100 | 200 Maloti. KM45. | 800 |

## MINT SETS

| KM# | Date | Mintage | Identification | Issue Price | Mkt Val |
|---|---|---|---|---|---|
| MS1 | 1976 (3) | 450 | KM13-15 | 194 | 315 |
| MS2 | 1989 (7) | — | KM16-22 | — | 11.50 |

## PROOF SETS

| KM# | Date | Mintage | Identification | Issue Price | Mkt Val |
|---|---|---|---|---|---|
| PS1 | 1966 (7) | 1,500 | KM1-7 | 301 | 475 |
| PS2 | 1966 (4) | 7 | KMPn6-9 | — | 3,000 |
| PS3 | 1966 (4) | 2 | KMPn1-4 | — | — |
| PS4 | 1966 (4) | 3,500 | KM1, 2, 3.1, 4.1 | 28.00 | 40.00 |
| PS5 | 1966 (3) | 2,000 | KM5-7 | 301 | 430 |
| PSA5 | 1966 (4) | — | KM1, 2, 3.2, 4.2 | 28.00 | 40.00 |
| PS6 | 1969 (5) | 3,000 | KM8-12 | 450 | 2,450 |
| PS7 | 1976 (3) | 1,410 | KM13-15 | 285 | 300 |
| PS8 | 1976 (2) | — | KM14-15 | 270 | 270 |
| PS9 | 1976 (2) | — | KM13-14 | — | 135 |
| PS10 | 1979 (7) | 10,000 | KM16-22 | 34.00 | 15.00 |
| PS11 | 1980 (8) | 10,000 | KM16-22, 23a | 51.00 | 25.00 |
| PS12 | 1981 (8) | 2,500 | KM16-22, 53 | 55.00 | 45.00 |

# LIBERIA

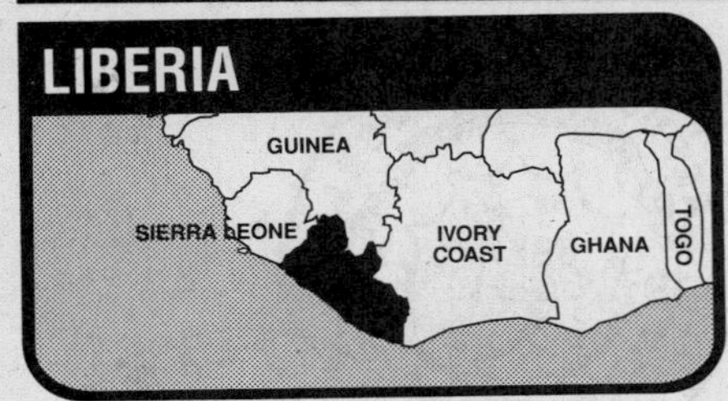


The Republic of Liberia, located on the southern side of the West African bulge between Sierra Leone and Ivory Coast, has an area of 38,250 sq. mi. (111,370 sq. km) and a population of 2.2 million. Capital: Monrovia. The major industries are agriculture, mining and lumbering. Iron ore, diamonds, rubber, coffee and coca are exported.

The Liberian coast was explored and charted by Portuguese navigator Pedro de Cintra in 1461. For the following three centuries Portuguese traders visited the area regularly to trade for gold, slaves and pepper. The modern country of Liberia, Africa's first republic, was settled in1822 by the American Colonization Society as a homeland for American freed slaves, with the U.S. government furnishing funds and assisting in negotiations for procurement of land from the native chiefs. The various settlements united in 1839 to form the Commonwealth of Liberia, and in 1847 established the country as are public with a constitution modeled after that of the United States.

U.S. money was declared legal tender in Liberia in 1943, replacing British West African currency.

Most of the Liberian pattern series, particularly of the1888-90 period are acknowledged to have been 'unofficial' privately sponsored issues, but they are none-the-less avidly collected by many collectors of Liberian coins. The 'K' number designations on these pieces refer to a listing of Liberian patterns compiled and published by Ernst Kraus.

**MINT MARKS**

B - Bern, Switzerland
H - Heaton, Birmingham
(l) - London
(s) - San Francisco, U.S.
FM - Franklin Mint, U.S.A.*
PM - Pobjoy Mint

***NOTE:** From 1975-1985 the Franklin Mint produced coinage in up to 3 different qualities. Qualities of issue are designated in ( ) after each date and are defined as follows:

**(M) MATTE** - Normal circulation strike or a dull finish produced by sandblasting special uncirculated (polish finish) or proof quality dies.

**(U) SPECIAL UNCIRCULATED** - Polished or prooflike in appearance without any frosted features.

**(P) PROOF** - The highest quality obtainable having mirror-like fields and frosted features.

**MONETARY SYSTEM**

100 Cents = 1 Dollar

## REPUBLIC

### STANDARD COINAGE

100 Cents = 1 Dollar

**1/2 CENT** KM# 10 **Composition:** Brass

| Date | Mintage | F | VF | XF | Unc | BU |
|---|---|---|---|---|---|---|
| 1937 | 1,000,000 | 0.10 | 0.25 | 0.40 | 1.00 | — |

**1/2 CENT** KM# 10a **Composition:** Copper-Nickel

| Date | Mintage | F | VF | XF | Unc | BU |
|---|---|---|---|---|---|---|
| 1941 | 250,000 | 0.15 | 0.35 | 0.55 | 1.25 | — |

**CENT** KM# 5 **Composition:** Bronze

| Date | Mintage | F | VF | XF | Unc | BU |
|---|---|---|---|---|---|---|
| 1906H | 180,000 | 4.50 | 10.00 | 22.00 | 50.00 | — |
| 1906H Proof | — | Value: 130 | | | | |

**CENT** KM# 11 **Composition:** Brass

| Date | Mintage | F | VF | XF | Unc | BU |
|---|---|---|---|---|---|---|
| 1937 | 1,000,000 | 0.20 | 0.50 | 1.50 | 6.00 | — |

**CENT** KM# 11a **Composition:** Copper-Nickel

| Date | Mintage | F | VF | XF | Unc | BU |
|---|---|---|---|---|---|---|
| 1941 | 250,000 | 0.50 | 2.50 | 7.50 | 40.00 | — |

**CENT** KM# 13 **Composition:** Bronze

| Date | Mintage | F | VF | XF | Unc | BU |
|---|---|---|---|---|---|---|
| 1960 | 500,000 | — | — | 0.10 | 0.35 | — |
| 1961 | 7,000,000 | — | — | 0.10 | 0.35 | — |
| 1968(l) | 3,000,000 | — | — | 0.10 | 0.35 | — |
| 1968(s) Proof | 14,000 | Value: 1.00 | | | | |
| 1969 Proof | 5,056 | Value: 1.00 | | | | |
| 1970 Proof | 3,464 | Value: 1.00 | | | | |
| 1971 Proof | 3,032 | Value: 1.00 | | | | |
| 1972(d) | 10,000,000 | — | — | 0.10 | 0.35 | — |
| 1972(s) Proof | 4,866 | Value: 1.00 | | | | |
| 1973 Proof | 11,000 | Value: 1.00 | | | | |
| 1974 Proof | 9,362 | Value: 1.00 | | | | |
| 1975 | 5,000,000 | — | — | 0.10 | 0.35 | — |
| 1975 Proof | 4,056 | Value: 1.00 | | | | |
| 1976 Proof | 2,131 | Value: 1.00 | | | | |
| 1977 | 2,500,000 | — | — | 0.10 | 0.35 | — |
| 1977 Proof | 920 | Value: 1.00 | | | | |
| 1978FM Proof | 7,311 | Value: 1.00 | | | | |
| 1983FM | 2,500,000 | — | — | 0.10 | 0.35 | — |
| 1984 | 2,500,000 | — | — | 0.10 | 0.35 | — |

**CENT** KM# 13a **Composition:** Bronze **Edge Lettering:** O.A.U. July 1979

| Date | Mintage | F | VF | XF | Unc | BU |
|---|---|---|---|---|---|---|
| 1979FM Proof | 1,857 | Value: 1.00 | | | | |

**2 CENTS** KM# 6 **Composition:** Bronze

| Date | Mintage | F | VF | XF | Unc | BU |
|---|---|---|---|---|---|---|
| 1906H | 108,000 | 5.00 | 12.00 | 30.00 | 75.00 | — |
| 1906H Proof | — | Value: 160 | | | | |

**2 CENTS** KM# 12 **Composition:** Brass

| Date | Mintage | F | VF | XF | Unc | BU |
|---|---|---|---|---|---|---|
| 1937 | 1,000,000 | 0.15 | 0.35 | 1.00 | 6.00 | — |

**2 CENTS** KM# 12a **Composition:** Copper-Nickel

| Date | Mintage | F | VF | XF | Unc | BU |
|---|---|---|---|---|---|---|
| 1941 | 810,000 | 0.10 | 0.25 | 0.50 | 2.50 | — |
| 1978FM Proof | 7,311 | Value: 2.00 | | | | |

**2 CENTS** KM# 12b **Composition:** Copper-Nickel **Edge Lettering:** O.A.U. July 1979

| Date | Mintage | F | VF | XF | Unc | BU |
|---|---|---|---|---|---|---|
| 1979FM Proof | 1,857 | Value: 2.00 | | | | |

**5 CENTS** KM# 14 **Composition:** Copper-Nickel

| Date | Mintage | F | VF | XF | Unc | BU |
|---|---|---|---|---|---|---|
| 1960 | 1,000,000 | — | 0.10 | 0.15 | 0.50 | — |
| 1961 | 3,200,000 | — | 0.10 | 0.15 | 0.50 | — |
| 1968 Proof | 15,000 | Value: 0.75 | | | | |
| 1969 Proof | 5,056 | Value: 0.75 | | | | |
| 1970 Proof | 3,464 | Value: 1.25 | | | | |
| 1971 Proof | 3,032 | Value: 1.25 | | | | |
| 1972(d) | 3,000,000 | — | 0.10 | 0.15 | 0.35 | — |
| 1972(s) Proof | 4,866 | Value: 0.75 | | | | |
| 1973 Proof | 11,000 | Value: 0.75 | | | | |
| 1974 Proof | 9,362 | Value: 0.75 | | | | |
| 1975 | 3,000,000 | — | 0.10 | 0.15 | 0.35 | — |
| 1975 Proof | 4,056 | Value: 0.75 | | | | |
| 1976 Proof | 2,131 | Value: 0.75 | | | | |
| 1977 | — | — | 0.10 | 0.15 | 0.50 | — |
| 1977 Proof | 920 | Value: 0.75 | | | | |
| 1978FM Proof | 7,311 | Value: 0.75 | | | | |
| 1983FM | 1,000,000 | — | 0.10 | 0.15 | 0.35 | — |
| 1984 | 1,000,000 | — | 0.10 | 0.15 | 0.35 | — |

**5 CENTS** KM# 14a **Composition:** Copper-Nickel **Edge Lettering:** O.A.U. July 1979

| Date | Mintage | F | VF | XF | Unc | BU |
|---|---|---|---|---|---|---|
| 1979FM Proof | 1,857 | Value: 2.00 | | | | |

**5 CENTS** KM# 474 **Weight:** 2.2500 g. **Composition:** Aluminum **Obverse:** National arms **Reverse:** Dragon and denomination **Edge:** Plain **Size:** 26.9 mm.

| Date | Mintage | F | VF | XF | Unc | BU |
|---|---|---|---|---|---|---|
| 2000 | — | — | — | — | 0.75 | — |

**10 CENTS** KM# 7 **Weight:** 2.3200 g. **Composition:** 0.9250 Silver .0690 oz. ASW

| Date | Mintage | F | VF | XF | Unc | BU |
|---|---|---|---|---|---|---|
| 1906H | 35,000 | 5.00 | 12.50 | 32.50 | 100 | — |
| 1906H Proof | — | Value: 250 | | | | |

**10 CENTS** KM# 15 **Weight:** 2.0700 g. **Composition:** 0.9000 Silver .0599 oz. ASW

| Date | Mintage | F | VF | XF | Unc | BU |
|---|---|---|---|---|---|---|
| 1960 | 1,000,000 | BV | 0.75 | 1.25 | 3.00 | — |
| 1961 | 1,200,000 | BV | 0.75 | 1.25 | 3.00 | — |

**10 CENTS** KM# 15a.1 **Weight:** 2.1000 g. **Composition:** Copper-Nickel

| Date | Mintage | F | VF | XF | Unc | BU |
|---|---|---|---|---|---|---|
| 1966 | 2,000,000 | — | 0.15 | 0.25 | 0.50 | — |

**10 CENTS** KM# 15a.2 **Weight:** 1.8000 g. **Composition:** Copper-Nickel

| Date | Mintage | F | VF | XF | Unc | BU |
|---|---|---|---|---|---|---|
| 1968 Proof | 14,000 | Value: 1.25 | | | | |
| 1969 Proof | 5,056 | Value: 1.25 | | | | |
| 1970(d) | 2,500,000 | — | 0.15 | 0.25 | 0.50 | — |
| 1970(s) Proof | 3,464 | Value: 1.50 | | | | |
| 1971 Proof | 3,032 | Value: 1.50 | | | | |
| 1972 Proof | 4,866 | Value: 1.25 | | | | |
| 1973 Proof | 11,000 | Value: 1.00 | | | | |
| 1974 Proof | 9,362 | Value: 1.00 | | | | |
| 1975 | 4,500 | — | 0.15 | 0.20 | 0.35 | — |
| 1975 Proof | 4,056 | Value: 1.00 | | | | |
| 1976 Proof | 2,131 | Value: 1.00 | | | | |
| 1977 | — | — | 0.15 | 0.25 | 0.75 | — |
| 1977 Proof | 920 | Value: 1.00 | | | | |
| 1978FM Proof | 7,311 | Value: 1.00 | | | | |
| 1983FM | 500,000 | — | 0.15 | 0.25 | 0.75 | — |
| 1984FM | 500,000 | — | 0.15 | 0.25 | 0.75 | — |
| 1987 | 10,000,000 | — | 0.15 | 0.25 | 0.75 | — |

**10 CENTS** KM# 15b **Weight:** 1.8000 g. **Composition:** Copper-Nickel **Edge Lettering:** O.A.U. July 1979

| Date | Mintage | F | VF | XF | Unc | BU |
|---|---|---|---|---|---|---|
| 1979FM Proof | 1,857 | Value: 2.00 | | | | |

**25 CENTS** KM# 8 **Weight:** 5.8000 g. **Composition:** 0.9250 Silver .1725 oz. ASW

| Date | Mintage | F | VF | XF | Unc | BU |
|---|---|---|---|---|---|---|
| 1906H | 34,000 | 6.00 | 12.50 | 35.00 | 120 | — |
| 1906H Proof | — | Value: 275 | | | | |

**25 CENTS** KM# 16 **Weight:** 5.1800 g. **Composition:** 0.9000 Silver .1499 oz. ASW

| Date | Mintage | F | VF | XF | Unc | BU |
|---|---|---|---|---|---|---|
| 1960 | 900,000 | BV | 1.50 | 2.00 | 4.50 | — |
| 1961 | 1,200,000 | BV | 1.50 | 2.00 | 4.50 | — |

**25 CENTS** KM# 16a.1 **Weight:** 5.2000 g. **Composition:** Copper-Nickel

| Date | Mintage | F | VF | XF | Unc | BU |
|---|---|---|---|---|---|---|
| 1966 | 800,000 | — | 0.25 | 0.65 | 1.25 | — |

**25 CENTS** KM# 16a.2 **Weight:** 4.8000 g. **Composition:** Copper-Nickel **Note:** 1 and 1.15mm rim varieties exist.

| Date | Mintage | F | VF | XF | Unc | BU |
|---|---|---|---|---|---|---|
| 1968(d) | 1,600,000 | — | 0.25 | 0.50 | 1.00 | — |
| 1968(s) Proof | 14,000 | Value: 1.50 | | | | |
| 1969 Proof | 5,056 | Value: 1.50 | | | | |
| 1970 Proof | 3,464 | Value: 1.75 | | | | |
| 1971 Proof | 3,032 | Value: 1.75 | | | | |
| 1972 Proof | 4,866 | Value: 1.50 | | | | |
| 1973 | 2,000,000 | — | 0.25 | 0.50 | 1.00 | — |
| 1973 Proof | 11,000 | Value: 1.25 | | | | |
| 1974 Proof | 9,362 | Value: 1.25 | | | | |
| 1975 | 1,600,000 | — | 0.25 | 0.50 | 1.00 | — |
| 1975 Proof | 4,056 | Value: 1.25 | | | | |

**25 CENTS** KM# 16a.3 **Weight:** 5.2000 g. **Composition:** Copper-Nickel **Reverse:** Large letters, higher inscription **Note:** Struck in 1988.

| Date | Mintage | F | VF | XF | Unc | BU |
|---|---|---|---|---|---|---|
| 1968 Restrike | 2,400,000 | — | 0.25 | 0.50 | 1.00 | — |

**25 CENTS** KM# 30 **Weight:** 5.2000 g. **Composition:** Copper-Nickel **Series:** F.A.O.

| Date | Mintage | F | VF | XF | Unc | BU |
|---|---|---|---|---|---|---|
| 1976 | 800,000 | — | 0.25 | 0.75 | 1.75 | — |
| 1976 Proof | 2,131 | Value: 4.00 | | | | |
| 1977 Proof | 920 | Value: 5.00 | | | | |
| 1978FM Proof | 7,311 | Value: 2.50 | | | | |

**25 CENTS** KM# 30a **Weight:** 5.2000 g. **Composition:** Copper-Nickel **Edge Lettering:** O.A.U. July 1979

| Date | Mintage | F | VF | XF | Unc | BU |
|---|---|---|---|---|---|---|
| 1979FM Proof | 1,857 | Value: 3.50 | | | | |

**25 CENTS** KM# 16b **Weight:** 4.4600 g. **Composition:** Nickel Clad Steel **Obverse:** Female portrait **Reverse:** Denomination and date **Edge:** Reeded **Size:** 22.9 mm.

| Date | Mintage | F | VF | XF | Unc | BU |
|---|---|---|---|---|---|---|
| 2000 | — | — | — | — | 0.25 | — |

**50 CENTS** KM# 9 **Weight:** 11.6000 g. **Composition:** 0.9250 Silver .3450 oz. ASW

| Date | Mintage | F | VF | XF | Unc | BU |
|---|---|---|---|---|---|---|
| 1906H | 24,000 | 10.00 | 20.00 | 50.00 | 265 | — |
| 1906H Proof | — | Value: 425 | | | | |

**50 CENTS** KM# 17 **Weight:** 10.3700 g. **Composition:** 0.9000 Silver .3001 oz. ASW

| Date | Mintage | F | VF | XF | Unc | BU |
|---|---|---|---|---|---|---|
| 1960 | 1,100,000 | BV | 3.00 | 4.00 | 8.00 | — |
| 1961 | 800,000 | BV | 3.00 | 4.00 | 8.00 | — |

**50 CENTS** KM# 17a.1 **Weight:** 10.4000 g. **Composition:** Copper-Nickel

| Date | Mintage | F | VF | XF | Unc | BU |
|---|---|---|---|---|---|---|
| 1966 | 200,000 | — | 0.75 | 1.00 | 1.50 | — |

**50 CENTS** KM# 17a.2 **Weight:** 8.9000 g. **Composition:** Copper-Nickel

| Date | Mintage | F | VF | XF | Unc | BU |
|---|---|---|---|---|---|---|
| 1968(l) | 1,000,000 | — | 0.60 | 0.80 | 1.50 | — |
| 1968(s) Proof | 14,000 | Value: 1.50 | | | | |
| 1969 Proof | 5,056 | Value: 1.50 | | | | |
| 1970 Proof | 3,464 | Value: 2.50 | | | | |
| 1971 Proof | 3,032 | Value: 2.50 | | | | |
| 1972 Proof | 4,866 | Value: 1.50 | | | | |
| 1973 | 1,000,000 | — | 0.60 | 0.75 | 1.25 | — |
| 1973 Proof | 11,000 | Value: 1.50 | | | | |
| 1974 Proof | 9,362 | Value: 1.50 | | | | |
| 1975 | 800,000 | — | 0.60 | 0.75 | 1.25 | — |
| 1975 Proof | 4,056 | Value: 1.50 | | | | |

**50 CENTS** KM# 31 **Weight:** 8.9000 g. **Composition:** Copper-Nickel

| Date | Mintage | F | VF | XF | Unc | BU |
|---|---|---|---|---|---|---|
| 1976 | 1,000,000 | — | 0.60 | 1.00 | 2.50 | — |
| 1976 Proof | 2,131 | Value: 5.50 | | | | |
| 1977 Proof | 920 | Value: 6.50 | | | | |
| 1978FM Proof | 7,311 | Value: 4.00 | | | | |
| 1987 | 1,800,000 | — | 0.60 | 1.00 | 2.50 | — |

**50 CENTS** KM# 31a **Weight:** 8.9000 g. **Composition:** Copper-Nickel **Edge Lettering:** O.A.U. July 1979

| Date | Mintage | F | VF | XF | Unc | BU |
|---|---|---|---|---|---|---|
| 1979FM Proof | 1,857 | Value: 4.50 | | | | |

**DOLLAR** KM# 18 **Weight:** 20.7400 g. **Composition:** 0.9000 Silver .6001 oz. ASW

| Date | Mintage | F | VF | XF | Unc | BU |
|---|---|---|---|---|---|---|
| 1961 | 200,000 | BV | 4.50 | 6.00 | 12.50 | — |
| 1962 | 1,000,000 | BV | 4.50 | 5.50 | 10.00 | — |

**DOLLAR** KM# 18a.1 **Weight:** 20.7000 g. **Composition:** Copper-Nickel

| Date | Mintage | F | VF | XF | Unc | BU |
|---|---|---|---|---|---|---|
| 1966 | 1,000,000 | — | 1.00 | 1.50 | 2.25 | — |

**DOLLAR** KM# 18a.2 **Weight:** 18.0000 g. **Composition:** Copper-Nickel

| Date | Mintage | F | VF | XF | Unc | BU |
|---|---|---|---|---|---|---|
| 1968(l) | 1,000,000 | — | 1.00 | 1.50 | 2.25 | — |
| 1968(s) Proof | 14,000 | Value: 2.00 | | | | |
| 1969 Proof | 5,056 | Value: 2.00 | | | | |
| 1970(d) | 2,000,000 | — | 1.00 | 1.50 | 3.00 | — |
| 1970(s) Proof | 3,464 | Value: 6.00 | | | | |
| 1971 Proof | 3,032 | Value: 4.50 | | | | |
| 1972 Proof | 4,866 | Value: 4.50 | | | | |
| 1973 Proof | 11,000 | Value: 3.00 | | | | |
| 1974 Proof | 9,362 | Value: 3.00 | | | | |
| 1975 | 400,000 | — | 1.25 | 1.75 | 3.00 | — |
| 1975 Proof | 4,056 | Value: 3.00 | | | | |

**DOLLAR** KM# 32 **Weight:** 18.0000 g. **Composition:** Copper-Nickel

| Date | Mintage | F | VF | XF | Unc | BU |
|---|---|---|---|---|---|---|
| 1976 | 2,000,000 | — | 2.50 | 4.50 | 8.00 | — |
| 1976 Proof | 2,131 | Value: 12.00 | | | | |
| 1977 Proof | 920 | Value: 13.50 | | | | |
| 1978FM Proof | 7,311 | Value: 11.00 | | | | |
| 1987 | 1,500,000 | — | 1.50 | 3.00 | 6.00 | — |

**DOLLAR** KM# 32a **Weight:** 18.0000 g. **Composition:** Copper-Nickel **Edge Lettering:** O.A.U. July 1979

| Date | Mintage | F | VF | XF | Unc | BU |
|---|---|---|---|---|---|---|
| 1979FM Proof | 1,857 | Value: 10.00 | | | | |

**DOLLAR** KM# 98 **Weight:** 18.0000 g. **Composition:** Copper-Nickel **Series:** Preserve Planet Earth **Reverse:** Protoceratops

| Date | Mintage | F | VF | XF | Unc | BU |
|---|---|---|---|---|---|---|
| 1993 | — | — | — | — | 8.00 | — |

**DOLLAR** KM# 109 **Weight:** 28.5200 g. **Composition:** Copper-Nickel **Series:** Preserve Planet Earth **Reverse:** Corythosaurus

| Date | Mintage | F | VF | XF | Unc | BU |
|---|---|---|---|---|---|---|
| 1993 | — | — | — | — | 8.00 | — |

**DOLLAR** KM# 112 **Weight:** 28.5200 g. **Composition:** Copper-Nickel **Series:** Preserve Planet Earth **Reverse:** Atchaeopteryx **Note:** Incorrect spelling.

| Date | Mintage | F | VF | XF | Unc | BU |
|---|---|---|---|---|---|---|
| 1993 | — | — | — | — | 8.00 | — |

**DOLLAR** KM# 101 **Weight:** 18.0000 g. **Composition:** Copper-Nickel **Subject:** Nolan Ryan **Note:** Similar to 10 Dollars, KM#102.

| Date | Mintage | F | VF | XF | Unc | BU |
|---|---|---|---|---|---|---|
| 1993 | — | — | — | — | 8.00 | — |

**DOLLAR** KM# 118 **Weight:** 28.5200 g. **Composition:** Copper-Nickel **Series:** Preserve Planet Earth **Reverse:** Gorillas **Note:** Similar to 10 Dollars, KM#119.

| Date | Mintage | F | VF | XF | Unc | BU |
|---|---|---|---|---|---|---|
| 1994 | — | — | — | — | 8.50 | — |

**DOLLAR** KM# 121 **Weight:** 28.5200 g. **Composition:** Copper-Nickel **Series:** Preserve Planet Earth **Reverse:** Pygmy Hippopotami **Note:** Similar to 10 Dollars, KM#122.

| Date | Mintage | F | VF | XF | Unc | BU |
|---|---|---|---|---|---|---|
| 1994 | — | — | — | — | 8.50 | — |

**DOLLAR** KM# 124 **Weight:** 28.5200 g. **Composition:** Copper-Nickel **Series:** Preserve Planet Earth **Reverse:** Trionyx Turtle **Note:** Similar to 10 Dollars, KM#125.

| Date | Mintage | F | VF | XF | Unc | BU |
|---|---|---|---|---|---|---|
| 1994 | — | — | — | — | 8.50 | — |

**DOLLAR** KM# 131a **Composition:** Gold Plated Copper-Nickel **Note:** Issued in a first day cover.

| Date | Mintage | F | VF | XF | Unc | BU |
|---|---|---|---|---|---|---|
| 1994 | — | — | — | — | 20.00 | — |

**DOLLAR** KM# 115 **Weight:** 28.5200 g. **Composition:** Copper-Nickel **Series:** Preserve Planet Earth **Reverse:** Archaeopteryx **Note:** Correct spelling.

| Date | Mintage | F | VF | XF | Unc | BU |
|---|---|---|---|---|---|---|
| 1994 | — | — | — | — | 8.00 | — |

**DOLLAR** KM# 131 **Weight:** 28.5200 g. **Composition:** Copper-Nickel **Subject:** Centennial - Babe Ruth Sultan of Swat

| Date | Mintage | F | VF | XF | Unc | BU |
|---|---|---|---|---|---|---|
| 1994 | — | — | — | — | 8.00 | — |

**DOLLAR** KM# 139 **Composition:** Copper-Nickel **Subject:** Damon Hill - Formula One Race Car

| Date | Mintage | F | VF | XF | Unc | BU |
|---|---|---|---|---|---|---|
| 1994 Prooflike | — | — | — | — | 7.00 | — |

**DOLLAR** KM# 248 **Composition:** Copper-Nickel **Subject:** Hall of Fame - Roberto Clemente

| Date | Mintage | F | VF | XF | Unc | BU |
|---|---|---|---|---|---|---|
| 1994 | — | — | — | — | 8.00 | — |

**DOLLAR** KM# 249 **Composition:** Copper-Nickel **Subject:** Hall of Fame - Reggie Jackson

| Date | Mintage | F | VF | XF | Unc | BU |
|---|---|---|---|---|---|---|
| 1994 | — | — | — | — | 8.00 | — |

**DOLLAR** KM# 411 **Composition:** Copper-Nickel **Subject:** President Nelson Mandela **Obverse:** National arms **Reverse:** Portrait and gazelle

| Date | Mintage | F | VF | XF | Unc | BU |
|---|---|---|---|---|---|---|
| 1994 | — | — | — | — | 8.50 | — |

**DOLLAR** KM# 133 **Composition:** Copper-Nickel **Series:** Preserve Planet Earth **Reverse:** Leopard; Similar to 10 Dollars, KM#134.

| Date | Mintage | F | VF | XF | Unc | BU |
|---|---|---|---|---|---|---|
| 1995 | — | — | — | — | 8.50 | — |

**DOLLAR** KM# 136 **Composition:** Copper-Nickel **Series:** Preserve Planet Earth **Reverse:** Storks; Similar to 10 Dollars, KM#137

| Date | Mintage | F | VF | XF | Unc | BU |
|---|---|---|---|---|---|---|
| 1995 | — | — | — | — | 8.00 | — |

**DOLLAR** KM# 140 **Composition:** Copper-Nickel **Subject:** Sir Winston Churchill **Reverse:** Similar to 10 Dollars, KM#145

| Date | Mintage | F | VF | XF | Unc | BU |
|---|---|---|---|---|---|---|
| 1995 | — | — | — | — | 6.00 | — |

**DOLLAR** KM# 141 **Composition:** Copper-Nickel **Subject:** President Franklin D. Roosevelt **Reverse:** Similar to 10 Dollars, KM#146

| Date | Mintage | F | VF | XF | Unc | BU |
|---|---|---|---|---|---|---|
| 1995 | — | — | — | — | 6.00 | — |

**DOLLAR** KM# 142 **Composition:** Copper-Nickel **Subject:** General George Patton **Reverse:** Similar to 10 Dollars, KM#147

| Date | Mintage | F | VF | XF | Unc | BU |
|---|---|---|---|---|---|---|
| 1995 | — | — | — | — | 6.00 | — |

**DOLLAR** KM# 143 **Composition:** Copper-Nickel **Subject:** President Harry S. Truman **Reverse:** Similar to 10 Dollars, KM#148

| Date | Mintage | F | VF | XF | Unc | BU |
|---|---|---|---|---|---|---|
| 1995 | — | — | — | — | 6.00 | — |

**DOLLAR** KM# 144 **Composition:** Copper-Nickel **Subject:** President Charles de Gaulle **Reverse:** Similar to 10 Dollars, KM#149

| Date | Mintage | F | VF | XF | Unc | BU |
|---|---|---|---|---|---|---|
| 1995 | — | — | — | — | 6.00 | — |

**DOLLAR** KM# 158 **Composition:** Copper-Nickel **Subject:** Dr. Sun Yat-sen **Reverse:** Similar to 10 Dollars, KM#159

| Date | Mintage | F | VF | XF | Unc | BU |
|---|---|---|---|---|---|---|
| 1995 | — | — | — | — | 6.50 | — |

**DOLLAR** KM# 161 **Composition:** Copper-Nickel **Subject:** General Chiang Kai-shek **Reverse:** Similar to 10 Dollars, KM#162

| Date | Mintage | F | VF | XF | Unc | BU |
|---|---|---|---|---|---|---|
| 1995 | — | — | — | — | 6.50 | — |

**DOLLAR** KM# 164 **Composition:** Copper-Nickel **Subject:** Cairo Conference - Chiang Kai-shek - Roosevelt - Churchill **Reverse:** Similar to 10 Dollars, KM#165

| Date | Mintage | F | VF | XF | Unc | BU |
|---|---|---|---|---|---|---|
| 1995 | — | — | — | — | 6.50 | — |

**DOLLAR** KM# 167 **Composition:** Copper-Nickel **Subject:** 375th Anniversary - Pilgrim Fathers **Reverse:** The "Mayflower"

| Date | Mintage | F | VF | XF | Unc | BU |
|---|---|---|---|---|---|---|
| 1995 | — | — | — | — | 6.00 | — |

**DOLLAR** KM# 168 **Composition:** Copper-Nickel **Subject:** 375th Anniversary - Pilgrim Fathers **Reverse:** First Thanksgiving Scene

| Date | Mintage | F | VF | XF | Unc | BU |
|---|---|---|---|---|---|---|
| 1995 | — | — | — | — | 6.00 | — |

**DOLLAR** KM# 169 **Composition:** Copper-Nickel **Subject:** 375th Anniversary - Pilgrim Fathers **Reverse:** Cape Cod and Pilgrims in skiff

| Date | Mintage | F | VF | XF | Unc | BU |
|---|---|---|---|---|---|---|
| 1995 | — | — | — | — | 6.00 | — |

**DOLLAR** KM# 170 **Composition:** Copper-Nickel **Subject:** 375th Anniversary - Pilgrim Fathers **Reverse:** Pilgrim landing party

| Date | Mintage | F | VF | XF | Unc | BU |
|---|---|---|---|---|---|---|
| 1995 | — | — | — | — | 6.00 | — |

**DOLLAR** KM# 412 **Composition:** Copper-Nickel **Subject:** Nations for Peace **Obverse:** National arms **Reverse:** Paper dolls, UN logo

| Date | Mintage | F | VF | XF | Unc | BU |
|---|---|---|---|---|---|---|
| 1995 | — | — | — | — | 8.50 | — |

**DOLLAR** KM# 128 **Composition:** Copper-Nickel **Subject:** Star Trek **Reverse:** Captains Kirk and Picard **Note:** Similar to 10 Dollars, KM#129.

| Date | Mintage | F | VF | XF | Unc | BU |
|---|---|---|---|---|---|---|
| 1995 | — | — | — | — | 7.50 | — |

**DOLLAR** KM# 207 **Composition:** Copper-Nickel **Subject:** Star Trek **Reverse:** Starships NCC-1701 and NCC-1701D **Note:** Similar to 10 Dollars, KM#208.

| Date | Mintage | F | VF | XF | Unc | BU |
|---|---|---|---|---|---|---|
| 1996 | — | — | — | — | 8.50 | — |

**DOLLAR** KM# 210 **Composition:** Copper-Nickel **Subject:** Star Trek **Reverse:** Scott and McCoy **Note:** Similar to 10 Dollars, KM#211.

| Date | Mintage | F | VF | XF | Unc | BU |
|---|---|---|---|---|---|---|
| 1996 | — | — | — | — | 8.50 | — |

**DOLLAR** KM# 213 **Composition:** Copper-Nickel **Subject:** Star Trek **Reverse:** LaForge and Data **Note:** Similar to 10 Dollars, KM#214.

| Date | Mintage | F | VF | XF | Unc | BU |
|---|---|---|---|---|---|---|
| 1996 | — | — | — | — | 8.50 | — |

**DOLLAR** KM# 216 **Composition:** Copper-Nickel **Subject:** Star Trek **Reverse:** Spock and Uhura **Note:** Similar to 10 Dollars, KM#217.

| Date | Mintage | F | VF | XF | Unc | BU |
|---|---|---|---|---|---|---|
| 1996 | — | — | — | — | 8.50 | — |

**DOLLAR** KM# 219 **Composition:** Copper-Nickel **Subject:** Star Trek **Reverse:** Worf and Dr. Crusher **Note:** Similar to 10 Dollars, KM#220.

| Date | Mintage | F | VF | XF | Unc | BU |
|---|---|---|---|---|---|---|
| 1996 | — | — | — | — | 8.50 | — |

**DOLLAR** **KM# 222** **Composition:** Copper-Nickel **Series:** Preserve Planet Earth **Reverse:** Grey Parrot **Note:** Similar to 10 Dollars, KM#223.

| Date | Mintage | F | VF | XF | Unc | BU |
|---|---|---|---|---|---|---|
| 1996 | — | — | — | — | 8.00 | — |

**DOLLAR** **KM# 225** **Composition:** Copper-Nickel **Series:** Preserve Planet Earth **Reverse:** Love Birds **Note:** Similar to 10 Dollars, KM#226.

| Date | Mintage | F | VF | XF | Unc | BU |
|---|---|---|---|---|---|---|
| 1996 | — | — | — | — | 8.00 | — |

**DOLLAR** **KM# 254** **Composition:** Copper-Nickel **Subject:** Chairman Mao Zedong **Note:** Similar to 10 Dollars, KM#256. Issued in first day cover.

| Date | Mintage | F | VF | XF | Unc | BU |
|---|---|---|---|---|---|---|
| 1996 | 20,000 | — | — | — | 7.50 | — |

**DOLLAR** **KM# 260** **Composition:** Copper-Nickel **Reverse:** Chairman Mao Zedong and President Nixon **Note:** Similar to 10 Dollars, KM#262. Issued in first day cover.

| Date | Mintage | F | VF | XF | Unc | BU |
|---|---|---|---|---|---|---|
| 1996 | 20,000 | — | — | — | 7.50 | — |

**DOLLAR** **KM# 263** **Composition:** Copper-Nickel **Subject:** Pioneers of the West **Reverse:** Daniel Boone **Note:** Similar to 10 Dollars, KM#264.

| Date | Mintage | F | VF | XF | Unc | BU |
|---|---|---|---|---|---|---|
| 1996 | — | — | — | — | 7.50 | — |

**DOLLAR** **KM# 266** **Composition:** Copper-Nickel **Subject:** Pioneers of the West **Reverse:** Davy Crockett **Note:** Similar to 10 Dollars, KM#267.

| Date | Mintage | F | VF | XF | Unc | BU |
|---|---|---|---|---|---|---|
| 1996 | — | — | — | — | 7.50 | — |

**DOLLAR** **KM# 269** **Composition:** Copper-Nickel **Subject:** Pioneers of the West **Reverse:** Jim Bowie **Note:** Similar to 10 Dollars, KM#270.

| Date | Mintage | F | VF | XF | Unc | BU |
|---|---|---|---|---|---|---|
| 1996 | — | — | — | — | 7.50 | — |

**DOLLAR** **KM# 272** **Composition:** Copper-Nickel **Subject:** Pioneers of the West **Reverse:** Kit Carson **Note:** Similar to 10 Dollars, KM#273.

| Date | Mintage | F | VF | XF | Unc | BU |
|---|---|---|---|---|---|---|
| 1996 | — | — | — | — | 7.50 | — |

**DOLLAR** **KM# 275** **Composition:** Copper-Nickel **Subject:** Pioneers of the West **Reverse:** Wild Bill Hickok **Note:** Similar to 10 Dollars, KM#276.

| Date | Mintage | F | VF | XF | Unc | BU |
|---|---|---|---|---|---|---|
| 1996 | — | — | — | — | 7.50 | — |

**DOLLAR** **KM# 278** **Composition:** Copper-Nickel **Subject:** Pioneers of the West **Reverse:** Buffalo Bill **Note:** Similar to 10 Dollars, KM#279.

| Date | Mintage | F | VF | XF | Unc | BU |
|---|---|---|---|---|---|---|
| 1996 | — | — | — | — | 7.50 | — |

**DOLLAR** **KM# 286** **Composition:** Copper-Nickel **Subject:** WWII - Evacuation of Dunkirk **Note:** Similar to 10 Dollars, KM#287.

| Date | Mintage | F | VF | XF | Unc | BU |
|---|---|---|---|---|---|---|
| 1997 | — | — | — | — | 8.50 | — |

**DOLLAR** **KM# 288** **Composition:** Copper-Nickel **Subject:** WWII - Liberation of the Philippines **Note:** Similar to 10 Dollars, KM#289.

| Date | Mintage | F | VF | XF | Unc | BU |
|---|---|---|---|---|---|---|
| 1997 | — | — | — | — | 8.50 | — |

**DOLLAR** **KM# 290** **Composition:** Copper-Nickel **Subject:** WWII - Defense of Stalingrad **Note:** Similar to 10 Dollars, KM#291.

| Date | Mintage | F | VF | XF | Unc | BU |
|---|---|---|---|---|---|---|
| 1997 | — | — | — | — | 8.50 | — |

**DOLLAR** **KM# 292** **Composition:** Copper-Nickel **Subject:** WWII - Arnhem **Note:** Similar to 10 Dollars, KM#293.

| Date | Mintage | F | VF | XF | Unc | BU |
|---|---|---|---|---|---|---|
| 1997 | — | — | — | — | 8.50 | — |

**DOLLAR** **KM# 294** **Composition:** Copper-Nickel **Subject:** WWII - Raid on the Dams **Note:** Similar to 10 Dollars, KM#295.

| Date | Mintage | F | VF | XF | Unc | BU |
|---|---|---|---|---|---|---|
| 1997 | — | — | — | — | 8.50 | — |

**DOLLAR** **KM# 296** **Composition:** Copper-Nickel **Subject:** WWII - West African Campaign **Note:** Similar to 10 Dollars, KM#297.

| Date | Mintage | F | VF | XF | Unc | BU |
|---|---|---|---|---|---|---|
| 1997 | — | — | — | — | 8.50 | — |

**DOLLAR** **KM# 298** **Composition:** Copper-Nickel **Subject:** WWII - North African Campaign **Note:** Similar to 10 Dollars, KM#299.

| Date | Mintage | F | VF | XF | Unc | BU |
|---|---|---|---|---|---|---|
| 1997 | — | — | — | — | 8.50 | — |

**DOLLAR** **KM# 300** **Composition:** Copper-Nickel **Subject:** WWII - The Dieppe Raid **Note:** Similar to 10 Dollars, KM#301.

| Date | Mintage | F | VF | XF | Unc | BU |
|---|---|---|---|---|---|---|
| 1997 | — | — | — | — | 8.50 | — |

**DOLLAR** **KM# 302** **Composition:** Copper-Nickel **Subject:** WWII - Iwo Jima **Note:** Similar to 10 Dollars, KM#303.

| Date | Mintage | F | VF | XF | Unc | BU |
|---|---|---|---|---|---|---|
| 1997 | — | — | — | — | 8.50 | — |

**DOLLAR** **KM# 304** **Composition:** Copper-Nickel **Subject:** WWII - Battle of Britain **Note:** Similar to 10 Dollars, KM#305.

| Date | Mintage | F | VF | XF | Unc | BU |
|---|---|---|---|---|---|---|
| 1997 | — | — | — | — | 8.50 | — |

**DOLLAR** **KM# 306** **Composition:** Copper-Nickel **Subject:** WWII - Liberation of Paris **Note:** Similar to 10 Dollars, KM#307.

| Date | Mintage | F | VF | XF | Unc | BU |
|---|---|---|---|---|---|---|
| 1997 | — | — | — | — | 8.50 | — |

**DOLLAR** **KM# 308** **Composition:** Copper-Nickel **Subject:** WWII - Burma Campaign **Note:** Similar to 10 Dollars, KM#309.

| Date | Mintage | F | VF | XF | Unc | BU |
|---|---|---|---|---|---|---|
| 1997 | — | — | — | — | 8.50 | — |

**DOLLAR** **KM# 310** **Composition:** Copper-Nickel **Subject:** Mahatma Gandhi **Note:** Similar to 10 Dollars, KM#311.

| Date | Mintage | F | VF | XF | Unc | BU |
|---|---|---|---|---|---|---|
| 1997 | — | — | — | — | 8.00 | — |

**DOLLAR** **KM# 324** **Composition:** Copper-Nickel **Subject:** Jurassic Park - Stegosaurus **Obverse:** National arms **Note:** Similar to 10 Dollars, KM#325.

| Date | Mintage | F | VF | XF | Unc | BU |
|---|---|---|---|---|---|---|
| 1997 | — | — | — | — | 9.00 | — |

**DOLLAR** **KM# 327** **Composition:** Copper-Nickel **Subject:** Golden Wedding Anniversary **Obverse:** National arms **Reverse:** E & P initials above 2 shields **Note:** Similar to 10 Dollars, KM#328.

| Date | Mintage | F | VF | XF | Unc | BU |
|---|---|---|---|---|---|---|
| 1997 | — | — | — | — | 7.50 | — |

**DOLLAR** **KM# 330** **Composition:** Copper-Nickel **Subject:** Golden Wedding Anniversary **Obverse:** National arms **Reverse:** Royal couple with horse **Note:** Similar to 10 Dollars, KM#331.

| Date | Mintage | F | VF | XF | Unc | BU |
|---|---|---|---|---|---|---|
| 1997 | — | — | — | — | 7.50 | — |

**DOLLAR** **KM# 333** **Composition:** Copper-Nickel **Subject:** Golden Wedding Anniversary **Obverse:** National arms **Reverse:** Couple with dogs **Note:** Similar to 10 Dollars, KM#334.

| Date | Mintage | F | VF | XF | Unc | BU |
|---|---|---|---|---|---|---|
| 1997 | — | — | — | — | 7.50 | — |

**DOLLAR** **KM# 336** **Composition:** Copper-Nickel **Subject:** Golden Wedding Anniversary **Obverse:** National arms **Reverse:** Royal couple with children **Note:** Similar to 10 Dollars, KM#337.

| Date | Mintage | F | VF | XF | Unc | BU |
|---|---|---|---|---|---|---|
| 1997 | — | — | — | — | 7.50 | — |

**DOLLAR** **KM# 344** **Composition:** Copper-Nickel **Subject:** 150th Anniversary of Independence **Obverse:** National arms **Reverse:** The "Ashmon" **Note:** Similar to 10 Dollars, KM#345.

| Date | Mintage | F | VF | XF | Unc | BU |
|---|---|---|---|---|---|---|
| 1997 | — | — | — | — | 8.50 | — |

**DOLLAR** **KM# 368** **Composition:** Copper-Nickel **Subject:** Star Trek - The Next Generation **Obverse:** National arms **Reverse:** Romulan Warbird **Note:** Similar to 10 Dollars, KM#369.

| Date | Mintage | F | VF | XF | Unc | BU |
|---|---|---|---|---|---|---|
| 1997 | — | — | — | — | 7.50 | — |

**DOLLAR** **KM# 371** **Composition:** Copper-Nickel **Subject:** Star Trek - The Next Generation **Obverse:** National arms **Reverse:** Klingon Attack Cruiser **Note:** Similar to 10 Dollars, KM#372.

| Date | Mintage | F | VF | XF | Unc | BU |
|---|---|---|---|---|---|---|
| 1997 | — | — | — | — | 7.50 | — |

**DOLLAR** **KM# 374** **Composition:** Copper-Nickel **Subject:** Star Trek - The Next Generation **Obverse:** National arms **Reverse:** U.S.S. Enterprise NCC-1701-D **Note:** Similar to 10 Dollars, KM#375.

| Date | Mintage | F | VF | XF | Unc | BU |
|---|---|---|---|---|---|---|
| 1997 | — | — | — | — | 7.50 | — |

**DOLLAR** **KM# 377** **Composition:** Copper-Nickel **Subject:** Star Trek - The Next Generation **Obverse:** National arms **Reverse:** Klingon Bird of Prey **Note:** Similar to 10 Dollars, KM#378.

| Date | Mintage | F | VF | XF | Unc | BU |
|---|---|---|---|---|---|---|
| 1997 | — | — | — | — | 7.50 | — |

**DOLLAR** **KM# 380** **Composition:** Copper-Nickel **Subject:** Star Trek - The Next Generation **Obverse:** National arms **Reverse:** Borg Cube **Note:** Similar to 10 Dollars, KM#381.

| Date | Mintage | F | VF | XF | Unc | BU |
|---|---|---|---|---|---|---|
| 1997 | — | — | — | — | 7.50 | — |

**DOLLAR** **KM# 383** **Composition:** Copper-Nickel **Subject:** Star Trek - The Next Generation **Obverse:** National arms **Reverse:** Ferengi Marauder **Note:** Similar to 10 Dollars, KM#384.

| Date | Mintage | F | VF | XF | Unc | BU |
|---|---|---|---|---|---|---|
| 1997 | — | — | — | — | 7.50 | — |

**DOLLAR** **KM# 313** **Composition:** Copper-Nickel **Subject:** Return of Hong Kong - Dragon **Obverse:** National arms

| Date | Mintage | F | VF | XF | Unc | BU |
|---|---|---|---|---|---|---|
| 1997 | — | — | — | — | 8.50 | — |

**DOLLAR** **KM# 320** **Composition:** Copper-Nickel **Subject:** Fiftieth Anniversary of the Kon-Tiki Expedition **Obverse:** National arms

| Date | Mintage | F | VF | XF | Unc | BU |
|---|---|---|---|---|---|---|
| 1997 | — | — | — | — | 8.50 | — |

**DOLLAR** **KM# 426** **Weight:** 13.9400 g. **Composition:** Copper **Subject:** AZA Species Survival Plan **Obverse:** National arms. **Reverse:** Seated panda eating. **Edge:** Reeded. **Size:** 32 mm.

| Date | Mintage |
|---|---|
| — | |

**DOLLAR** **KM# 386** **Composition:** Copper-Nickel **Subject:** President Ronald Reagan **Obverse:** National arms **Reverse:** Lincoln statue **Note:** Similar to 10 Dollars, KM#387.

| Date | Mintage | F | VF | XF | Unc | BU |
|---|---|---|---|---|---|---|
| 1998 | — | — | — | — | 8.50 | — |

**DOLLAR** **KM# 401** **Composition:** Copper-Nickel **Subject:** Christopher Columbus **Obverse:** National arms **Reverse:** Portrait of Columbus, ship **Note:** Similar to 10 Dollars, KM#402.

| Date | Mintage | F | VF | XF | Unc | BU |
|---|---|---|---|---|---|---|
| 1999 | — | — | — | — | 8.00 | — |

**DOLLAR** **KM# 404** **Composition:** Copper-Nickel **Subject:** Captain Cook **Obverse:** National arms **Reverse:** Portrait, ship and map **Note:** Similar to 10 Dollars, KM#403.

| Date | Mintage | F | VF | XF | Unc | BU |
|---|---|---|---|---|---|---|
| 1999 | — | — | — | — | 8.00 | — |

**DOLLAR** **KM# 407** **Composition:** Copper-Nickel **Subject:** Return of Macao to China **Obverse:** National arms **Reverse:** Dragon and phoenix **Note:** Similar to 10 Dollars, KM#408.

| Date | Mintage | F | VF | XF | Unc | BU |
|---|---|---|---|---|---|---|
| 1999 | — | — | — | — | 8.50 | — |

**DOLLAR** **KM# 413** **Composition:** Copper-Nickel **Subject:** The Wedding of the Prince Edward **Obverse:** National arms **Reverse:** Couple in carriage **Note:** Similar to 10 Dollars, KM#413.

| Date | Mintage | F | VF | XF | Unc | BU |
|---|---|---|---|---|---|---|
| 1999 | — | — | — | — | 8.00 | — |

**DOLLAR** **KM# 442** **Weight:** 28.2800 g. **Composition:** Copper-Nickel **Subject:** Greenwich Meridian **Obverse:** National arms **Reverse:** World landmarks and fireworks **Edge:** Reeded **Size:** 38.6 mm.

| Date | Mintage | F | VF | XF | Unc | BU |
|---|---|---|---|---|---|---|
| 2000 | — | — | — | — | 10.00 | — |

**2 DOLLARS** **KM# 47** **Composition:** Copper-Nickel **Series:** F.A.O. **Subject:** World Fisheries Conference **Reverse:** Longneck croaker fish

| Date | Mintage | F | VF | XF | Unc | BU |
|---|---|---|---|---|---|---|
| 1983 | 100,000 | — | — | — | 12.00 | — |

**2 DOLLARS** **KM# 47a** **Weight:** 28.2800 g. **Composition:** 0.9250 Silver .8411 oz. ASW **Subject:** World Fisheries Conference

| Date | Mintage | F | VF | XF | Unc | BU |
|---|---|---|---|---|---|---|
| 1983 Proof | 20,000 | Value: 52.50 | | | | |

**2 DOLLARS** **KM# 47b** **Weight:** 47.5400 g. **Composition:** Gold **Series:** F.A.O. **Subject:** World Fisheries Conference

| Date | Mintage | F | VF | XF | Unc | BU |
|---|---|---|---|---|---|---|
| 1983 Proof | 600 | Value: 950 | | | | |

**2-1/2 DOLLARS** **KM# 24** **Weight:** 4.1796 g. **Composition:** 0.9000 Gold .1209 oz. AGW **Subject:** Inauguration of President Tolbert

| Date | Mintage | F | VF | XF | Unc | BU |
|---|---|---|---|---|---|---|
| 1972 Proof | — | Value: 80.00 | | | | |

**5 DOLLARS** **KM# 62** **Weight:** 5.0000 g. **Composition:** 0.9000 Gold .1447 oz. AGW **Subject:** 25th Anniversary of Inter-Continental Hotels

| Date | Mintage | F | VF | XF | Unc | BU |
|---|---|---|---|---|---|---|
| ND(1971) Proof | — | — | — | — | — | — |

**5 DOLLARS** **KM# 25** **Weight:** 8.3592 g. **Composition:** 0.9000 Gold .2419 oz. AGW **Subject:** Inauguration of President Tolbert

| Date | Mintage | F | VF | XF | Unc | BU |
|---|---|---|---|---|---|---|
| 1972 Proof | — | Value: 160 | | | | |

**5 DOLLARS** **KM# 29** **Weight:** 34.1000 g. **Composition:** 0.9000 Silver .9868 oz. ASW

| Date | Mintage | F | VF | XF | Unc | BU |
|---|---|---|---|---|---|---|
| 1973 | 500 | — | — | — | 25.00 | — |
| 1973 Proof | 28,000 | Value: 11.50 | | | | |
| 1974 Proof | 20,000 | Value: 11.50 | | | | |
| 1975 Proof | 9,017 | Value: 12.50 | | | | |
| 1976 Proof | 3,683 | Value: 16.50 | | | | |
| 1977 Proof | 1,640 | Value: 18.50 | | | | |
| 1978FM Proof | 7,311 | Value: 13.50 | | | | |

**5 DOLLARS** **KM# 29a** **Weight:** 34.1000 g. **Composition:** 0.9000 Silver .9868 oz. ASW **Edge Lettering:** O.A.U. July 1979

| Date | Mintage | F | VF | XF | Unc | BU |
|---|---|---|---|---|---|---|
| 1979 Proof | 1,857 | Value: 25.00 | | | | |

**5 DOLLARS** **KM# 44** **Composition:** Copper-Nickel **Subject:** Military Memorial

| Date | Mintage | F | VF | XF | Unc | BU |
|---|---|---|---|---|---|---|
| 1982 | 4,000,000 | — | 5.00 | 6.50 | 9.00 | — |
| 1985 | 2,000,000 | — | 5.00 | 6.50 | 9.00 | — |

**5 DOLLARS** **KM# 73** **Weight:** 15.5500 g. **Composition:** 0.9990 Silver .5000 oz. ASW **Subject:** Formula One - Gerhard Berger

| Date | Mintage | F | VF | XF | Unc | BU |
|---|---|---|---|---|---|---|
| 1992 Proof | — | Value: 18.50 | | | | |

**5 DOLLARS** **KM# 76** **Weight:** 15.5500 g. **Composition:** 0.9990 Silver .5000 oz. ASW **Subject:** Formula One - Nigel Mansell

| Date | Mintage | F | VF | XF | Unc | BU |
|---|---|---|---|---|---|---|
| 1992 Proof | Est. 50,000 | Value: 18.50 | | | | |

**5 DOLLARS** **KM# 78** **Weight:** 15.5500 g. **Composition:** 0.9990 Silver .5000 oz. ASW **Subject:** Formula One - Ayrton Senna

| Date | Mintage | F | VF | XF | Unc | BU |
|---|---|---|---|---|---|---|
| 1992 Proof | Est. 50,000 | Value: 18.50 | | | | |

**5 DOLLARS** **KM# 79** **Weight:** 15.5500 g. **Composition:** 0.9990 Silver .5000 oz. ASW **Subject:** Formula One - Riccardo Patrese **Note:** Similar to 10 Dollars, KM#74.

| Date | Mintage | F | VF | XF | Unc | BU |
|---|---|---|---|---|---|---|
| 1992 Proof | Est. 50,000 | Value: 18.50 | | | | |

**5 DOLLARS** **KM# 77** **Weight:** 15.5500 g. **Composition:** 0.9990 Silver .5000 oz. ASW **Subject:** Formula One - Aguri Suzuki **Note:** Similar to 10 Dollars, KM#84.

| Date | Mintage | F | VF | XF | Unc | BU |
|---|---|---|---|---|---|---|
| 1992 Proof | Est. 50,000 | Value: 18.50 | | | | |

**5 DOLLARS** **KM# 80** **Weight:** 15.5500 g. **Composition:** 0.9990 Silver .5000 oz. ASW **Subject:** Formula One - Michael Schumacher **Note:** Similar to 10 Dollars, KM#86.

| Date | Mintage | F | VF | XF | Unc | BU |
|---|---|---|---|---|---|---|
| 1992 Proof | 50,000 | Value: 18.50 | | | | |

**5 DOLLARS** **KM# 81** **Weight:** 15.5500 g. **Composition:** 0.9990 Silver .5000 oz. ASW **Subject:** Formula One - Alain Prost **Note:** Similar to 10 Dollars, KM#87.

| Date | Mintage | F | VF | XF | Unc | BU |
|---|---|---|---|---|---|---|
| 1992 Proof | 50,000 | Value: 18.50 | | | | |

**5 DOLLARS** **KM# 82** **Weight:** 15.5500 g. **Composition:** 0.9990 Silver .5000 oz. ASW **Subject:** Formula One - Ukyo Katayama **Note:** Similar to 10 Dollars, KM#88.

| Date | Mintage | F | VF | XF | Unc | BU |
|---|---|---|---|---|---|---|
| 1992 Proof | 50,000 | Value: 18.50 | | | | |

**5 DOLLARS** **KM# 67** **Weight:** 15.5500 g. **Composition:** 0.9990 Silver .5000 oz. ASW **Subject:** President Bill Clinton **Note:** Similar to 10 Dollars, KM#68.

| Date | Mintage | F | VF | XF | Unc | BU |
|---|---|---|---|---|---|---|
| 1993 Proof | 50,000 | Value: 25.00 | | | | |

**5 DOLLARS** **KM# 97** **Weight:** 15.5500 g. **Composition:** 0.9990 Silver .5000 oz. ASW **Subject:** Chancellor Willy Brandt **Note:** Similar to 10 Dollars, KM#72.

| Date | Mintage | F | VF | XF | Unc | BU |
|---|---|---|---|---|---|---|
| 1993 Proof | — | Value: 18.50 | | | | |

**5 DOLLARS** **KM# 103** **Weight:** 15.5500 g. **Composition:** 0.9990 Silver .5000 oz. ASW **Subject:** President John F. Kennedy **Note:** Similar to 10 Dollars, KM#104.

| Date | Mintage | F | VF | XF | Unc | BU |
|---|---|---|---|---|---|---|
| 1993 Proof | 50,000 | Value: 20.00 | | | | |

**5 DOLLARS** **KM# 179** **Weight:** 15.5500 g. **Composition:** 0.9990 Silver .5000 oz. ASW **Subject:** Formula One - Mika Hakkinen **Reverse:** Similar to 10 Dollars, KM#180

| Date | Mintage | F | VF | XF | Unc | BU |
|---|---|---|---|---|---|---|
| 1995 Proof | 50,000 | Value: 20.00 | | | | |

**5 DOLLARS** **KM# 182** **Weight:** 15.5500 g. **Composition:** 0.9990 Silver .5000 oz. ASW **Subject:** Formula One - Martin Brundle **Reverse:** Similar to 10 Dollars, KM#183

| Date | Mintage | F | VF | XF | Unc | BU |
|---|---|---|---|---|---|---|
| 1995 Proof | Est. 50,000 | Value: 20.00 | | | | |

**5 DOLLARS** **KM# 185** **Weight:** 15.5500 g. **Composition:** 0.9990 Silver .5000 oz. ASW **Subject:** Formula One - Rubens Barrichello **Reverse:** Similar to 10 Dollars, KM#186

| Date | Mintage | F | VF | XF | Unc | BU |
|---|---|---|---|---|---|---|
| 1995 Proof | Est. 50,000 | Value: 20.00 | | | | |

**5 DOLLARS** **KM# 188** **Weight:** 15.5500 g. **Composition:** 0.9990 Silver .5000 oz. ASW **Subject:** Formula One - David Coulthard **Reverse:** Similar to 10 Dollars, KM#189

| Date | Mintage | F | VF | XF | Unc | BU |
|---|---|---|---|---|---|---|
| 1995 Proof | Est. 50,000 | Value: 20.00 | | | | |

**5 DOLLARS** **KM# 191** **Weight:** 15.5500 g. **Composition:** 0.9990 Silver .5000 oz. ASW **Subject:** Formula One - Jean Alesi **Reverse:** Similar to 10 Dollars, KM#192

| Date | Mintage | F | VF | XF | Unc | BU |
|---|---|---|---|---|---|---|
| 1995 Proof | Est. 50,000 | Value: 20.00 | | | | |

**5 DOLLARS** **KM# 195** **Weight:** 15.5500 g. **Composition:** 0.9990 Silver .5000 oz. ASW **Subject:** Formula One - Mark Blundell **Note:** Similar to 10 Dollars, KM#199.

| Date | Mintage | F | VF | XF | Unc | BU |
|---|---|---|---|---|---|---|
| 1996 Proof | 50,000 | Value: 20.00 | | | | |

**5 DOLLARS** **KM# 196** **Weight:** 15.5500 g. **Composition:** 0.9990 Silver .5000 oz. ASW **Subject:** Formula One - Johnny Herbert **Note:** Similar to 10 Dollars, KM#200.

| Date | Mintage | F | VF | XF | Unc | BU |
|---|---|---|---|---|---|---|
| 1996 Proof | 50,000 | Value: 20.00 | | | | |

**5 DOLLARS** **KM# 197** **Weight:** 15.5500 g. **Composition:** 0.9990 Silver .5000 oz. ASW **Subject:** Formula One - Eddie Irvine **Note:** Similar to 10 Dollars, KM#201.

| Date | Mintage | F | VF | XF | Unc | BU |
|---|---|---|---|---|---|---|
| 1996 Proof | 50,000 | Value: 20.00 | | | | |

**5 DOLLARS** **KM# 198** **Weight:** 15.5500 g. **Composition:** 0.9990 Silver .5000 oz. ASW **Subject:** Formula One - Heinz Frentzen **Note:** Similar to 10 Dollars, KM#202.

| Date | Mintage | F | VF | XF | Unc | BU |
|---|---|---|---|---|---|---|
| 1996 Proof | 50,000 | Value: 20.00 | | | | |

**5 DOLLARS** **KM# 228** **Weight:** 15.5500 g. **Composition:** 0.9990 Silver .5000 oz. ASW **Subject:** Formula One - Ayrton Senna **Note:** Similar to 10 Dollars, KM#229.

| Date | Mintage | F | VF | XF | Unc | BU |
|---|---|---|---|---|---|---|
| 1996 Proof | 50,000 | Value: 20.00 | | | | |

**5 DOLLARS** **KM# 255** **Weight:** 15.5500 g. **Composition:** 0.9990 Silver .5000 oz. ASW **Subject:** Chairman Mao Zedong **Note:** Similar to 10 Dollars, KM#256.

| Date | Mintage | F | VF | XF | Unc | BU |
|---|---|---|---|---|---|---|
| 1996 Proof | 20,000 | Value: 20.00 | | | | |

**5 DOLLARS** **KM# 261** **Weight:** 15.5500 g. **Composition:** 0.9990 Silver .5000 oz. ASW **Subject:** Chairman Mao Zedong and President Nixon **Note:** Similar to 10 Dollars, KM#262.

| Date | Mintage | F | VF | XF | Unc | BU |
|---|---|---|---|---|---|---|
| 1996 Proof | 20,000 | Value: 20.00 | | | | |

**5 DOLLARS** **KM# 441** **Weight:** 20.5600 g. **Composition:** Copper Nickel **Obverse:** National arms. **Reverse:** Polar bear. **Edge:** Reeded. **Size:** 38.5 mm.

| Date | Mintage | F | VF | XF | Unc | BU |
|---|---|---|---|---|---|---|
| 1997 | — | — | — | — | 8.50 | — |

**5 DOLLARS** **KM# 452** **Composition:** Copper Nickel **Series:** Diana Princess of Wales **Obverse:** National arms. **Reverse:** Princess Diana facing left.

| Date | Mintage | F | VF | XF | Unc | BU |
|---|---|---|---|---|---|---|
| 1997 | — | — | — | — | — | — |

**5 DOLLARS** **KM# 351** **Composition:** Copper-Nickel **Subject:** Chinese Astrology **Obverse:** Seated Liberty **Reverse:** 2 Rats, Pumpkin

| Date | Mintage | F | VF | XF | Unc | BU |
|---|---|---|---|---|---|---|
| 1997 | Est. 4,000 | — | — | — | 6.50 | — |

**5 DOLLARS** **KM# 352** **Composition:** Copper-Nickel **Subject:** Chinese Astrology **Obverse:** Seated Liberty **Reverse:** Ox

| Date | Mintage | F | VF | XF | Unc | BU |
|---|---|---|---|---|---|---|
| 1997 | Est. 4,000 | — | — | — | 6.50 | — |

**5 DOLLARS** **KM# 353** **Composition:** Copper-Nickel **Subject:** Chinese Astrology **Obverse:** Seated Liberty **Reverse:** Tiger

| Date | Mintage | F | VF | XF | Unc | BU |
|---|---|---|---|---|---|---|
| 1997 | Est. 4,000 | — | — | — | 6.50 | — |

**5 DOLLARS** **KM# 354** **Composition:** Copper-Nickel **Subject:** Chinese Astrology **Obverse:** Seated Liberty **Reverse:** Rabbits

| Date | Mintage | F | VF | XF | Unc | BU |
|---|---|---|---|---|---|---|
| 1997 | Est. 4,000 | — | — | — | 6.50 | — |

**5 DOLLARS** **KM# 355** **Composition:** Copper-Nickel **Subject:** Chinese Astrology **Obverse:** Seated Liberty **Reverse:** Dragon

| Date | Mintage | F | VF | XF | Unc | BU |
|---|---|---|---|---|---|---|
| 1997 | Est. 4,000 | — | — | — | 7.50 | — |

**5 DOLLARS** **KM# 356** **Composition:** Copper-Nickel **Subject:** Chinese Astrology **Obverse:** Seated Liberty **Reverse:** Snake

| Date | Mintage | F | VF | XF | Unc | BU |
|---|---|---|---|---|---|---|
| 1997 | Est. 4,000 | — | — | — | 6.50 | — |

**5 DOLLARS** **KM# 357** **Composition:** Copper-Nickel **Subject:** Chinese Astrology **Obverse:** Seated Liberty **Reverse:** Horse

| Date | Mintage | F | VF | XF | Unc | BU |
|---|---|---|---|---|---|---|
| 1997 | Est. 4,000 | — | — | — | 7.50 | — |

**5 DOLLARS** **KM# 358** **Composition:** Copper-Nickel **Subject:** Chinese Astrology **Obverse:** Seated Liberty **Reverse:** Goat

| Date | Mintage | F | VF | XF | Unc | BU |
|---|---|---|---|---|---|---|
| 1997 | Est. 4,000 | — | — | — | 6.50 | — |

**5 DOLLARS** **KM# 359** **Composition:** Copper-Nickel **Subject:** Chinese Astrology **Obverse:** Seated Liberty **Reverse:** Monkey

| Date | Mintage | F | VF | XF | Unc | BU |
|---|---|---|---|---|---|---|
| 1997 | Est. 4,000 | — | — | — | 6.50 | — |

**5 DOLLARS** **KM# 360** **Composition:** Copper-Nickel **Subject:** Chinese Astrology **Obverse:** Seated Liberty **Reverse:** Rooster

| Date | Mintage | F | VF | XF | Unc | BU |
|---|---|---|---|---|---|---|
| 1997 | Est. 4,000 | — | — | — | 6.50 | — |

**5 DOLLARS** **KM# 361** **Composition:** Copper-Nickel **Subject:** Chinese Astrology **Obverse:** Seated Liberty **Reverse:** Dog

| Date | Mintage | F | VF | XF | Unc | BU |
|---|---|---|---|---|---|---|
| 1997 | Est. 4,000 | — | — | — | 6.50 | — |

**5 DOLLARS** **KM# 362** **Composition:** Copper-Nickel **Subject:** Chinese Astrology **Obverse:** Seated Liberty **Reverse:** Pig

| Date | Mintage | F | VF | XF | Unc | BU |
|---|---|---|---|---|---|---|
| 1997 | Est. 4,000 | — | — | — | 6.50 | — |

**5 DOLLARS** **KM# 445** **Weight:** 25.1000 g. **Composition:** Copper-Nickel **Subject:** Princess Diana **Obverse:** National arms **Reverse:** Diana memorial portrait **Edge:** Reeded **Size:** 38.5 mm.

| Date | Mintage | F | VF | XF | Unc | BU |
|---|---|---|---|---|---|---|
| 1997 Proof | — | Value: 20.00 | | | | |

**5 DOLLARS** **KM# 446** **Weight:** 25.1000 g. **Composition:** Copper-Nickel **Subject:** Diana Series - Lady Spencer **Obverse:** National arms **Reverse:** Young girl's portrait **Edge:** Reeded **Size:** 38.5 mm.

| Date | Mintage | F | VF | XF | Unc | BU |
|---|---|---|---|---|---|---|
| 1997 | — | — | — | — | 15.00 | — |

**5 DOLLARS** **KM# 447** **Weight:** 25.1000 g. **Composition:** Copper-Nickel **Subject:** First TV Interview **Reverse:** Portrait with microphone

| Date | Mintage | F | VF | XF | Unc | BU |
|---|---|---|---|---|---|---|
| 1997 | — | — | — | — | 15.00 | — |

**5 DOLLARS** **KM# 448** **Composition:** Copper-Nickel **Subject:** Diana's Official Portrait **Reverse:** Portrait

| Date | Mintage | F | VF | XF | Unc | BU |
|---|---|---|---|---|---|---|
| 1997 | — | — | — | — | 15.00 | — |

**5 DOLLARS** **KM# 449** **Composition:** Copper-Nickel **Subject:** Wedding Day **Reverse:** Diana in wedding dress

| Date | Mintage | F | VF | XF | Unc | BU |
|---|---|---|---|---|---|---|
| 1997 | — | — | — | — | 15.00 | — |

**5 DOLLARS** **KM# 450** **Composition:** Copper-Nickel **Subject:** "People's Princess" **Reverse:** Formal portrait

| Date | Mintage | F | VF | XF | Unc | BU |
|---|---|---|---|---|---|---|
| 1997 | — | — | — | — | 15.00 | — |

**5 DOLLARS** **KM# 451** **Composition:** Copper-Nickel **Subject:** England's Rose **Reverse:** Diana with bouquet of roses

| Date | Mintage | F | VF | XF | Unc | BU |
|---|---|---|---|---|---|---|
| 1997 | — | — | — | — | 15.00 | — |

**5 DOLLARS** **KM# A452** **Composition:** Copper-Nickel **Subject:** Queen of Hearts **Reverse:** Diana wearing a choker

| Date | Mintage | F | VF | XF | Unc | BU |
|---|---|---|---|---|---|---|
| 1997 | — | — | — | — | 15.00 | — |

**5 DOLLARS** **KM# 453** **Composition:** Copper-Nickel **Subject:** Elegance **Reverse:** Diana wearing a high collar

| Date | Mintage | F | VF | XF | Unc | BU |
|---|---|---|---|---|---|---|
| 1997 | — | — | — | — | 15.00 | — |

**5 DOLLARS** **KM# 454** **Composition:** Copper-Nickel **Subject:** Birth of William **Reverse:** Diana with baby

| Date | Mintage | F | VF | XF | Unc | BU |
|---|---|---|---|---|---|---|
| 1997 | — | — | — | — | 15.00 | — |

**5 DOLLARS** **KM# 455** **Composition:** Copper-Nickel **Subject:** William's Christening **Reverse:** Diana holding baby

| Date | Mintage | F | VF | XF | Unc | BU |
|---|---|---|---|---|---|---|
| 1997 | — | — | — | — | 15.00 | — |

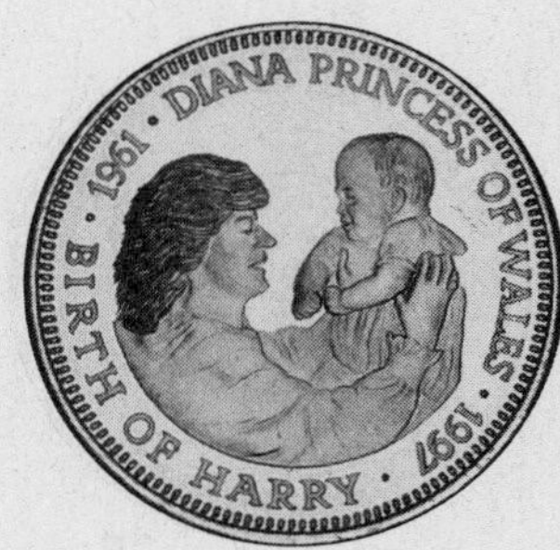


**5 DOLLARS** **KM# 456** **Composition:** Copper-Nickel **Subject:** Birth of Harry **Reverse:** Diana holding Harry.

| Date | Mintage | F | VF | XF | Unc | BU |
|---|---|---|---|---|---|---|
| 1997 | — | — | — | — | 15.00 | — |

**5 DOLLARS** **KM# 457** **Composition:** Copper-Nickel **Subject:** Loving Mother **Reverse:** Diana and her two sons

| Date | Mintage | F | VF | XF | Unc | BU |
|---|---|---|---|---|---|---|
| 1997 | — | — | — | — | 15.00 | — |

**5 DOLLARS** **KM# 458** **Composition:** Copper-Nickel **Subject:** Royal Family **Reverse:** Family portrait

| Date | Mintage | F | VF | XF | Unc | BU |
|---|---|---|---|---|---|---|
| 1997 | — | — | — | — | 15.00 | — |

**5 DOLLARS** **KM# 459** **Composition:** Copper-Nickel **Reverse:** Queen Elizabeth II and Diana

| Date | Mintage | F | VF | XF | Unc | BU |
|---|---|---|---|---|---|---|
| 1997 | — | — | — | — | 15.00 | — |

**5 DOLLARS** **KM# 460** **Composition:** Copper-Nickel **Reverse:** Queen Mother and Diana

| Date | Mintage | F | VF | XF | Unc | BU |
|---|---|---|---|---|---|---|
| 1997 | — | — | — | — | 15.00 | — |

**5 DOLLARS** **KM# 461** **Composition:** Copper-Nickel **Subject:** Visit to Wales **Reverse:** Charles and Diana

| Date | Mintage | F | VF | XF | Unc | BU |
|---|---|---|---|---|---|---|
| 1997 | — | — | — | — | 15.00 | — |

**5 DOLLARS** **KM# 462** **Composition:** Copper-Nickel **Reverse:** Charles and Diana dancing

| Date | Mintage | F | VF | XF | Unc | BU |
|---|---|---|---|---|---|---|
| 1997 | — | — | — | — | 15.00 | — |

**5 DOLLARS** **KM# 463** **Composition:** Copper-Nickel **Subject:** Tour of Japan **Reverse:** Emperor Hirohito and Diana

| Date | Mintage | F | VF | XF | Unc | BU |
|---|---|---|---|---|---|---|
| 1997 | — | — | — | — | 15.00 | — |

**5 DOLLARS** **KM# 464** **Composition:** Copper-Nickel **Obverse:** National arms **Reverse:** Diana reading to child **Size:** 38.5 mm.

| Date | Mintage | F | VF | XF | Unc | BU |
|---|---|---|---|---|---|---|
| 1997 | — | — | — | — | 15.00 | — |

**5 DOLLARS** **KM# 465** **Composition:** Copper-Nickel **Subject:** Charity **Reverse:** Diana with poor child

| Date | Mintage | F | VF | XF | Unc | BU |
|---|---|---|---|---|---|---|
| 1997 | — | — | — | — | 15.00 | — |

**5 DOLLARS** **KM# 466** **Composition:** Copper-Nickel **Reverse:** Diana with sick child

| Date | Mintage | F | VF | XF | Unc | BU |
|---|---|---|---|---|---|---|
| 1997 | — | — | — | — | 15.00 | — |

**5 DOLLARS** **KM# 467** **Composition:** Copper-Nickel **Reverse:** Diana's casket on gun carriage

| Date | Mintage | F | VF | XF | Unc | BU |
|---|---|---|---|---|---|---|
| 1997 | — | — | — | — | 15.00 | — |

**5 DOLLARS** **KM# 339** **Composition:** Copper-Nickel **Subject:** Year of the Tiger **Obverse:** National arms **Reverse:** Tiger with 3 cubs

| Date | Mintage | F | VF | XF | Unc | BU |
|---|---|---|---|---|---|---|
| 1998 (1997) Proof | — | Value: 8.50 | | | | |

**5 DOLLARS** **KM# 363** **Composition:** Copper-Nickel **Subject:** RMS Titanic **Obverse:** Liberian arms **Reverse:** Ship sinking **Note:** Similar to 20 Dollars, KM#364.

| Date | Mintage | F | VF | XF | Unc | BU |
|---|---|---|---|---|---|---|
| 1998 | — | — | — | — | 8.50 | — |

**5 DOLLARS** **KM# 427** **Weight:** 11.1800 g. **Composition:** Copper Nickel **Series:** Millennium 2000 Zodiac **Obverse:** National arms. **Reverse:** Snake. **Edge:** Reeded. **Size:** 31.6 mm.

| Date | Mintage | F | VF | XF | Unc | BU |
|---|---|---|---|---|---|---|
| 2000 | — | — | — | — | 2.50 | — |

**5 DOLLARS** **KM# 429** **Weight:** 11.1800 g. **Composition:** Copper Nickel **Series:** Millennium 2000 Zodiac **Obverse:** National arms. **Reverse:** Ox. **Edge:** Reeded. **Size:** 31.6 mm.

| Date | Mintage | F | VF | XF | Unc | BU |
|---|---|---|---|---|---|---|
| 2000 | — | — | — | — | 2.50 | — |

**5 DOLLARS** **KM# 428** **Weight:** 11.1800 g. **Composition:** Copper Nickel **Series:** Millennium 2000 Zodiac **Obverse:** National arms. **Reverse:** Two rats. **Edge:** Reeded. **Size:** 31.6 mm.

| Date | Mintage | F | VF | XF | Unc | BU |
|---|---|---|---|---|---|---|
| 2000 | — | — | — | — | 2.50 | — |

**5 DOLLARS** **KM# 430** **Weight:** 11.1800 g. **Composition:** Copper Nickel **Series:** Millennium 2000 Zodiac **Obverse:** National arms. **Reverse:** Tiger. **Edge:** Reeded. **Size:** 31.6 mm.

| Date | Mintage | F | VF | XF | Unc | BU |
|---|---|---|---|---|---|---|
| 2000 | — | — | — | — | 2.50 | — |

**5 DOLLARS** **KM# 431** **Weight:** 11.1800 g. **Composition:** Copper Nickel **Series:** Millennium 2000 Zodiac **Obverse:** National arms. **Reverse:** Horse. **Edge:** Reeded. **Size:** 31.6 mm.

| Date | Mintage | F | VF | XF | Unc | BU |
|---|---|---|---|---|---|---|
| 2000 | — | — | — | — | 2.50 | — |

**5 DOLLARS** **KM# 432** **Weight:** 11.1800 g. **Composition:** Copper Nickel **Series:** Millennium 2000 Zodiac **Obverse:** National arms. **Reverse:** Goat. **Edge:** Reeded. **Size:** 31.6 mm.

| Date | Mintage | F | VF | XF | Unc | BU |
|---|---|---|---|---|---|---|
| 2000 | — | — | — | — | 2.50 | — |

**5 DOLLARS** **KM# 433** **Weight:** 11.1800 g. **Composition:** Copper Nickel **Series:** Millennium 2000 Zodiac **Obverse:** National arms. **Reverse:** Monkey. **Edge:** Reeded. **Size:** 31.6 mm.

| Date | Mintage | F | VF | XF | Unc | BU |
|---|---|---|---|---|---|---|
| 2000 | — | — | — | — | 2.50 | — |

**5 DOLLARS** **KM# 434** **Weight:** 11.1800 g. **Composition:** Copper Nickel **Series:** Millennium 2000 Zodiac **Obverse:** National arms. **Reverse:** Rooster. **Edge:** Reeded. **Size:** 31.6 mm.

| Date | Mintage | F | VF | XF | Unc | BU |
|---|---|---|---|---|---|---|
| 2000 | — | — | — | — | 2.50 | — |

**5 DOLLARS** **KM# 436** **Weight:** 11.1800 g. **Composition:** Copper Nickel **Series:** Millennium 2000 Zodiac **Obverse:** National arms. **Reverse:** Pig. **Edge:** Reeded. **Size:** 31.6 mm.

| Date | Mintage | F | VF | XF | Unc | BU |
|---|---|---|---|---|---|---|
| 2000 | — | — | — | — | 2.50 | — |

**5 DOLLARS** **KM# 437** **Weight:** 11.1800 g. **Composition:** Copper Nickel **Series:** Millennium 2000 Zodiac **Obverse:** National arms. **Reverse:** Rabbit. **Edge:** Reeded. **Size:** 31.6 mm.

| Date | Mintage | F | VF | XF | Unc | BU |
|---|---|---|---|---|---|---|
| 2000 | — | — | — | — | 2.50 | — |

**5 DOLLARS** **KM# 438** **Weight:** 11.1800 g. **Composition:** Copper Nickel **Series:** Millennium 2000 Zodiac **Obverse:** National arms. **Reverse:** Dragon. **Edge:** Reeded. **Size:** 31.6 mm.

| Date | Mintage | F | VF | XF | Unc | BU |
|---|---|---|---|---|---|---|
| 2000 | — | — | — | — | 2.50 | — |

**5 DOLLARS** **KM# 494** **Weight:** 8.5000 g. **Composition:** 0.9999 Silver .2733 oz. ASW **Subject:** Soccer **Obverse:** National arms **Reverse:** Soccer player **Edge:** Reeded **Size:** 30 mm.

| Date | Mintage | F | VF | XF | Unc | BU |
|---|---|---|---|---|---|---|
| 2002 Proof | 3,000 | Value: 30.00 | | | | |

**10 DOLLARS** **KM# 63** **Weight:** 11.7200 g. **Composition:** 0.9000 Gold .3391 oz. AGW **Subject:** 25th Anniversary of Inter-Continental Hotels

| Date | Mintage | F | VF | XF | Unc | BU |
|---|---|---|---|---|---|---|
| 1971 Proof | — | — | — | — | — | — |

**10 DOLLARS** **KM# 26** **Weight:** 16.7185 g. **Composition:** 0.9000 Gold .4838 oz. AGW **Subject:** Inauguration of President Tolbert

| Date | Mintage | F | VF | XF | Unc | BU |
|---|---|---|---|---|---|---|
| 1972 Proof | — | Value: 310 | | | | |

**10 DOLLARS** **KM# 53** **Weight:** 23.3300 g. **Composition:** 0.9250 Silver .6939 oz. ASW **Subject:** Decade For Women **Reverse:** Coat of arms, denomination

| Date | Mintage | F | VF | XF | Unc | BU |
|---|---|---|---|---|---|---|
| 1985 Proof | — | Value: 30.00 | | | | |

**10 DOLLARS** **KM# 54** **Weight:** 31.1000 g. **Composition:** 0.9990 Silver 1.0000 oz. ASW **Subject:** President John F. Kennedy

| Date | Mintage | F | VF | XF | Unc | BU |
|---|---|---|---|---|---|---|
| 1988 Proof | 25,000 | Value: 37.50 | | | | |

**10 DOLLARS** **KM# 55** **Weight:** 31.1000 g. **Composition:** 0.9990 Silver 1.0000 oz. ASW **Subject:** President Samuel Kanyon Doe **Note:** Similar to 250 Dollars, KM#56.

| Date | Mintage | F | VF | XF | Unc | BU |
|---|---|---|---|---|---|---|
| 1988 Proof | 25,000 | Value: 37.50 | | | | |

**10 DOLLARS** **KM# 57** **Weight:** 31.1000 g. **Composition:** 0.9990 Silver 1.0000 oz. ASW **Subject:** President George Bush **Note:** Similar to 250 Dollars, KM#58.

| Date | Mintage | F | VF | XF | Unc | BU |
|---|---|---|---|---|---|---|
| 1989 Proof | 25,000 | Value: 37.50 | | | | |

**10 DOLLARS** **KM# 59** **Weight:** 31.1000 g. **Composition:** 0.9990 Silver 1.0000 oz. ASW **Subject:** Emperor Hirohito **Note:** Similar to 250 Dollars, KM#60.

| Date | Mintage | F | VF | XF | Unc | BU |
|---|---|---|---|---|---|---|
| 1989 Proof | 25,000 | Value: 37.50 | | | | |

**10 DOLLARS** KM# 72 **Weight:** 31.1000 g. **Composition:** 0.9990 Silver 1.0000 oz. ASW **Subject:** Chancellor Willy Brandt

| Date | Mintage | F | VF | XF | Unc | BU |
|---|---|---|---|---|---|---|
| 1992 Proof | — | Value: 32.50 | | | | |

**10 DOLLARS** KM# 74 **Weight:** 31.1000 g. **Composition:** 0.9990 Silver 1.0000 oz. ASW **Subject:** Formula One **Reverse:** Riccardo Patrese

| Date | Mintage | F | VF | XF | Unc | BU |
|---|---|---|---|---|---|---|
| 1992 Proof | 25,000 | Value: 40.00 | | | | |

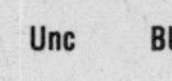

**10 DOLLARS** KM# 75 **Weight:** 31.1000 g. **Composition:** 0.9990 Silver 1.0000 oz. ASW **Subject:** Formula One **Reverse:** Nigel Mansell

| Date | Mintage | F | VF | XF | Unc | BU |
|---|---|---|---|---|---|---|
| 1992 Proof | 25,000 | Value: 40.00 | | | | |

**10 DOLLARS** KM# 83 **Weight:** 31.1000 g. **Composition:** 0.9990 Silver 1.0000 oz. ASW **Subject:** Formula One **Reverse:** Gerhard Berger

| Date | Mintage | F | VF | XF | Unc | BU |
|---|---|---|---|---|---|---|
| 1992 Proof | 25,000 | Value: 40.00 | | | | |

**10 DOLLARS** KM# 84 **Weight:** 31.1000 g. **Composition:** 0.9990 Silver 1.0000 oz. ASW **Subject:** Formula One **Reverse:** Aguri Suzuki

| Date | Mintage | F | VF | XF | Unc | BU |
|---|---|---|---|---|---|---|
| 1992 Proof | 25,000 | Value: 40.00 | | | | |

**10 DOLLARS** KM# 85 **Weight:** 31.1000 g. **Composition:** 0.9990 Silver 1.0000 oz. ASW **Subject:** Formula One **Reverse:** Ayrton Senna

| Date | Mintage | F | VF | XF | Unc | BU |
|---|---|---|---|---|---|---|
| 1992 Proof | 25,000 | Value: 40.00 | | | | |

**10 DOLLARS** KM# 86 **Weight:** 31.1000 g. **Composition:** 0.9990 Silver 1.0000 oz. ASW **Subject:** Formula One **Reverse:** Michael Schumacher

| Date | Mintage | F | VF | XF | Unc | BU |
|---|---|---|---|---|---|---|
| 1992 Proof | 25,000 | Value: 40.00 | | | | |

**10 DOLLARS** KM# 87 **Weight:** 31.1000 g. **Composition:** 0.9990 Silver 1.0000 oz. ASW **Subject:** Formula One **Reverse:** Alain Prost

| Date | Mintage | F | VF | XF | Unc | BU |
|---|---|---|---|---|---|---|
| 1992 Proof | 25,000 | Value: 40.00 | | | | |

**10 DOLLARS** KM# 88 **Weight:** 31.1000 g. **Composition:** 0.9990 Silver 1.0000 oz. ASW **Subject:** Formula One **Reverse:** Ykyo Katayama

| Date | Mintage | F | VF | XF | Unc | BU |
|---|---|---|---|---|---|---|
| 1992 Proof | 25,000 | Value: 40.00 | | | | |

**10 DOLLARS** KM# 68 **Weight:** 31.1000 g. **Composition:** 0.9990 Silver 1.0000 oz. ASW **Subject:** President Bill Clinton

| Date | Mintage | F | VF | XF | Unc | BU |
|---|---|---|---|---|---|---|
| 1993 Proof | 25,000 | Value: 35.00 | | | | |

**10 DOLLARS** KM# 99 **Weight:** 31.1000 g. **Composition:** 0.9990 Silver 1.0000 oz. ASW **Series:** Preserve Planet Earth **Reverse:** Protoceratops

| Date | Mintage | F | VF | XF | Unc | BU |
|---|---|---|---|---|---|---|
| 1993 Proof | 25,000 | Value: 32.50 | | | | |

**10 DOLLARS** KM# 102 **Weight:** 31.1000 g. **Composition:** 0.9990 Silver 1.0000 oz. ASW **Subject:** Baseball Hall of Fame **Reverse:** Nolan Ryan

| Date | Mintage | F | VF | XF | Unc | BU |
|---|---|---|---|---|---|---|
| 1993 Proof | — | Value: 30.00 | | | | |

**10 DOLLARS** KM# 104 **Weight:** 31.1000 g. **Composition:** 0.9990 Silver 1.0000 oz. ASW **Subject:** President John F. Kennedy

| Date | Mintage | F | VF | XF | Unc | BU |
|---|---|---|---|---|---|---|
| 1993 Proof | 25,000 | Value: 40.00 | | | | |

**10 DOLLARS** KM# 110 **Weight:** 31.1000 g. **Composition:** 0.9990 Silver 1.0000 oz. ASW **Series:** Preserve Planet Earth **Reverse:** Corythosaurus

| Date | Mintage | F | VF | XF | Unc | BU |
|---|---|---|---|---|---|---|
| 1993 Proof | 25,000 | Value: 32.50 | | | | |

**10 DOLLARS** KM# 113 **Weight:** 31.1000 g. **Composition:** 0.9990 Silver 1.0000 oz. ASW **Series:** Preserve Planet Earth **Reverse:** Atchaeopteryx **Note:** Incorrect spelling.

| Date | Mintage | F | VF | XF | Unc | BU |
|---|---|---|---|---|---|---|
| 1993 Proof | 25,000 | Value: 32.50 | | | | |

**10 DOLLARS** KM# 116 **Weight:** 31.1000 g. **Composition:** 0.9990 Silver 1.0000 oz. ASW **Series:** Preserve Planet Earth **Reverse:** Archaeopteryx **Note:** Correct spelling.

| Date | Mintage | F | VF | XF | Unc | BU |
|---|---|---|---|---|---|---|
| 1994 Proof | 25,000 | Value: 32.50 | | | | |

**10 DOLLARS** KM# 119 **Weight:** 31.1000 g. **Composition:** 0.9990 Silver 1.0000 oz. ASW **Series:** Preserve Planet Earth **Reverse:** Gorillas

| Date | Mintage | F | VF | XF | Unc | BU |
|---|---|---|---|---|---|---|
| 1994 Proof | 25,000 | Value: 30.00 | | | | |

**10 DOLLARS** KM# 122 **Weight:** 31.1000 g. **Composition:** 0.9990 Silver 1.0000 oz. ASW **Series:** Preserve Planet Earth **Reverse:** Pygmy Hippopotami

| Date | Mintage | F | VF | XF | Unc | BU |
|---|---|---|---|---|---|---|
| 1994 Proof | 25,000 | Value: 30.00 | | | | |

**10 DOLLARS** KM# 125 **Weight:** 31.1000 g. **Composition:** 0.9990 Silver 1.0000 oz. ASW **Series:** Preserve Planet Earth **Reverse:** Nile Soft-shelled Turtle

| Date | Mintage | F | VF | XF | Unc | BU |
|---|---|---|---|---|---|---|
| 1994 Proof | 25,000 | Value: 35.00 | | | | |

**10 DOLLARS** KM# 127 **Weight:** 31.1000 g. **Composition:** 0.9990 Silver 1.0000 oz. ASW **Subject:** President Nelson Mandela

| Date | Mintage | F | VF | XF | Unc | BU |
|---|---|---|---|---|---|---|
| 1994 Proof | 25,000 | Value: 35.00 | | | | |

**10 DOLLARS** KM# 155 **Weight:** 31.1000 g. **Composition:** 0.9990 Silver 1.0000 oz. ASW **Subject:** General Erwin Rommel

| Date | Mintage | F | VF | XF | Unc | BU |
|---|---|---|---|---|---|---|
| 1994 Proof | 25,000 | Value: 40.00 | | | | |

**10 DOLLARS** KM# 156 **Weight:** 31.1000 g. **Composition:** 0.9990 Silver 1.0000 oz. ASW **Subject:** Field Marshall Montgomery

| Date | Mintage | F | VF | XF | Unc | BU |
|---|---|---|---|---|---|---|
| 1994 Proof | 25,000 | Value: 40.00 | | | | |

**10 DOLLARS** KM# 157 **Weight:** 31.1000 g. **Composition:** 0.9990 Silver 1.0000 oz. ASW **Subject:** General Dwight D. Eisenhower

| Date | Mintage | F | VF | XF | Unc | BU |
|---|---|---|---|---|---|---|
| 1994 Proof | 25,000 | Value: 40.00 | | | | |

**10 DOLLARS** KM# 281 **Weight:** 31.1000 g. **Composition:** 0.9990 Silver 1.0000 oz. ASW **Subject:** Baseball Hall of Fame **Reverse:** Reggie Jackson

| Date | Mintage | F | VF | XF | Unc | BU |
|---|---|---|---|---|---|---|
| 1994 Proof | — | Value: 40.00 | | | | |

**10 DOLLARS** **KM# 282** **Weight:** 31.1000 g. **Composition:** 0.9990 Silver 1.0000 oz. ASW **Subject:** Baseball Hall of Fame **Reverse:** Roberto Clemente

| Date | Mintage | F | VF | XF | Unc | BU |
|---|---|---|---|---|---|---|
| 1994 Proof | — | Value: 40.00 | | | | |

**10 DOLLARS** **KM# 137** **Weight:** 31.1000 g. **Composition:** 0.9990 Silver 1.0000 oz. ASW **Series:** Preserve Planet Earth **Reverse:** Storks

| Date | Mintage | F | VF | XF | Unc | BU |
|---|---|---|---|---|---|---|
| 1995 Proof | 25,000 | Value: 30.00 | | | | |

**10 DOLLARS** **KM# 148** **Weight:** 31.1000 g. **Composition:** 0.9990 Silver 1.0000 oz. ASW **Subject:** President Harry S. Truman

| Date | Mintage | F | VF | XF | Unc | BU |
|---|---|---|---|---|---|---|
| 1995 Proof | 25,000 | Value: 40.00 | | | | |

**10 DOLLARS** **KM# 347** **Weight:** 31.1000 g. **Composition:** 0.9990 Silver 1.0000 oz. ASW **Subject:** The History of the Motor Car **Obverse:** National arms **Reverse:** Mercedes-Benz C-Class

| Date | Mintage | F | VF | XF | Unc | BU |
|---|---|---|---|---|---|---|
| 1994 Proof | — | Value: 40.00 | | | | |

**10 DOLLARS** **KM# 145** **Weight:** 31.1000 g. **Composition:** 0.9990 Silver 1.0000 oz. ASW **Subject:** Sir Winston Churchill

| Date | Mintage | F | VF | XF | Unc | BU |
|---|---|---|---|---|---|---|
| 1995 Proof | 25,000 | Value: 40.00 | | | | |

**10 DOLLARS** **KM# 149** **Weight:** 31.1000 g. **Composition:** 0.9990 Silver 1.0000 oz. ASW **Subject:** President Charles de Gaulle

| Date | Mintage | F | VF | XF | Unc | BU |
|---|---|---|---|---|---|---|
| 1995 Proof | 25,000 | Value: 40.00 | | | | |

**10 DOLLARS** **KM# 129** **Weight:** 31.1000 g. **Composition:** 0.9990 Silver 1.0000 oz. ASW **Subject:** Star Trek **Reverse:** Captains Kirk and Picard

| Date | Mintage | F | VF | XF | Unc | BU |
|---|---|---|---|---|---|---|
| 1995 Proof | — | Value: 47.50 | | | | |

**10 DOLLARS** **KM# 146** **Weight:** 31.1000 g. **Composition:** 0.9990 Silver 1.0000 oz. ASW **Subject:** President Franklin D. Roosevelt

| Date | Mintage | F | VF | XF | Unc | BU |
|---|---|---|---|---|---|---|
| 1995 Proof | 25,000 | Value: 40.00 | | | | |

**10 DOLLARS** **KM# 159** **Weight:** 31.1000 g. **Composition:** 0.9990 Silver 1.0000 oz. ASW **Subject:** Dr. Sun Yat Sen

| Date | Mintage | F | VF | XF | Unc | BU |
|---|---|---|---|---|---|---|
| 1995 Proof | 25,000 | Value: 45.00 | | | | |
| 1996 Proof | 25,000 | Value: 45.00 | | | | |

**10 DOLLARS** **KM# 134** **Weight:** 31.1000 g. **Composition:** 0.9990 Silver 1.0000 oz. ASW **Series:** Preserve Planet Earth **Reverse:** Leopard

| Date | Mintage | F | VF | XF | Unc | BU |
|---|---|---|---|---|---|---|
| 1995 Proof | 25,000 | Value: 32.50 | | | | |

**10 DOLLARS** **KM# 147** **Weight:** 31.1000 g. **Composition:** 0.9990 Silver 1.0000 oz. ASW **Subject:** General George Patton

| Date | Mintage | F | VF | XF | Unc | BU |
|---|---|---|---|---|---|---|
| 1995 Proof | 25,000 | Value: 40.00 | | | | |

**10 DOLLARS** **KM# 162** **Weight:** 31.1000 g. **Composition:** 0.9990 Silver 1.0000 oz. ASW **Subject:** General Chiang Kai-shek

| Date | Mintage | F | VF | XF | Unc | BU |
|---|---|---|---|---|---|---|
| 1995 Proof | 25,000 | Value: 45.00 | | | | |
| 1996 Proof | 25,000 | Value: 45.00 | | | | |

**10 DOLLARS** **KM# 165** **Weight:** 31.1000 g. **Composition:** 0.9990 Silver 1.0000 oz. ASW **Subject:** Cairo Conference **Reverse:** Chiang Kai-shek - Roosevelt - Churchill

| Date | Mintage | F | VF | XF | Unc | BU |
|---|---|---|---|---|---|---|
| 1995 Proof | 25,000 | Value: 45.00 | | | | |

**10 DOLLARS** **KM# 171** **Weight:** 31.1000 g. **Composition:** 0.9990 Silver 1.0000 oz. ASW **Subject:** 375th Anniversary - Pilgrim Fathers **Reverse:** The "Mayflower"

| Date | Mintage | F | VF | XF | Unc | BU |
|---|---|---|---|---|---|---|
| 1995 Proof | 25,000 | Value: 40.00 | | | | |

**10 DOLLARS** **KM# 172** **Weight:** 31.1000 g. **Composition:** 0.9990 Silver 1.0000 oz. ASW **Subject:** 375th Anniversary - Pilgrim Fathers **Reverse:** Pilgrims in Skiff

| Date | Mintage | F | VF | XF | Unc | BU |
|---|---|---|---|---|---|---|
| 1995 Proof | 25,000 | Value: 40.00 | | | | |

**10 DOLLARS** **KM# 173** **Weight:** 31.1000 g. **Composition:** 0.9990 Silver 1.0000 oz. ASW **Subject:** 375th Anniversary - Pilgrim Fathers **Reverse:** Pilgrim Landing Party

| Date | Mintage | F | VF | XF | Unc | BU |
|---|---|---|---|---|---|---|
| 1995 Proof | 25,000 | Value: 40.00 | | | | |

**10 DOLLARS** **KM# 174** **Weight:** 31.1000 g. **Composition:** 0.9990 Silver 1.0000 oz. ASW **Subject:** 375th Anniversary - Pilgrim Fathers **Reverse:** First Thanksgiving

| Date | Mintage | F | VF | XF | Unc | BU |
|---|---|---|---|---|---|---|
| 1995 Proof | 25,000 | Value: 40.00 | | | | |

**10 DOLLARS** **KM# 180** **Weight:** 31.1000 g. **Composition:** 0.9990 Silver 1.0000 oz. ASW **Subject:** Formula One **Reverse:** Mika Hakkinen

| Date | Mintage | F | VF | XF | Unc | BU |
|---|---|---|---|---|---|---|
| 1995 Proof | 25,000 | Value: 40.00 | | | | |

**10 DOLLARS** **KM# 183** **Weight:** 31.1000 g. **Composition:** 0.9990 Silver 1.0000 oz. ASW **Subject:** Formula One **Reverse:** Martin Brundle

| Date | Mintage | F | VF | XF | Unc | BU |
|---|---|---|---|---|---|---|
| 1995 Proof | 25,000 | Value: 40.00 | | | | |

**10 DOLLARS** **KM# 186** **Weight:** 31.1000 g. **Composition:** 0.9990 Silver 1.0000 oz. ASW **Subject:** Formula One **Reverse:** Rubens Barrichello

| Date | Mintage | F | VF | XF | Unc | BU |
|---|---|---|---|---|---|---|
| 1995 Proof | 25,000 | Value: 40.00 | | | | |

**10 DOLLARS** **KM# 189** **Weight:** 31.1000 g. **Composition:** 0.9990 Silver 1.0000 oz. ASW **Subject:** Formula One **Reverse:** David Coulthard

| Date | Mintage | F | VF | XF | Unc | BU |
|---|---|---|---|---|---|---|
| 1995 Proof | 25,000 | Value: 40.00 | | | | |

**10 DOLLARS** **KM# 192** **Weight:** 31.1000 g. **Composition:** 0.9990 Silver 1.0000 oz. ASW **Subject:** Formula One **Reverse:** Jean Alesi

| Date | Mintage | F | VF | XF | Unc | BU |
|---|---|---|---|---|---|---|
| 1995 Proof | 25,000 | Value: 40.00 | | | | |

**10 DOLLARS** **KM# 194** **Weight:** 31.1000 g. **Composition:** 0.9990 Silver 1.0000 oz. ASW **Subject:** Nations United for Peace **Reverse:** Logo, paper dolls

| Date | Mintage | F | VF | XF | Unc | BU |
|---|---|---|---|---|---|---|
| 1995 Proof | 25,000 | Value: 37.50 | | | | |

**10 DOLLARS** **KM# 132** **Weight:** 31.1000 g. **Composition:** 0.9990 Silver 1.0000 oz. ASW **Subject:** Centennial - Babe Ruth - Sultan of Swat **Note:** Similar to 1 Dollars, KM#131.

| Date | Mintage | F | VF | XF | Unc | BU |
|---|---|---|---|---|---|---|
| 1995 | — | — | — | — | 42.50 | — |

**10 DOLLARS** **KM# 199** **Weight:** 31.1000 g. **Composition:** 0.9990 Silver 1.0000 oz. ASW **Subject:** Formula One **Reverse:** Mark Blundell

| Date | Mintage | F | VF | XF | Unc | BU |
|---|---|---|---|---|---|---|
| 1996 Proof | 25,000 | Value: 40.00 | | | | |

**10 DOLLARS** **KM# 200** **Weight:** 31.1000 g. **Composition:** 0.9990 Silver 1.0000 oz. ASW **Subject:** Formula One **Reverse:** Johnny Herbert

| Date | Mintage | F | VF | XF | Unc | BU |
|---|---|---|---|---|---|---|
| 1996 Proof | 25,000 | Value: 40.00 | | | | |

**10 DOLLARS** **KM# 211** **Weight:** 31.1000 g. **Composition:** 0.9990 Silver 1.0000 oz. ASW **Subject:** Star Trek **Reverse:** Scott and McCoy

| Date | Mintage | F | VF | XF | Unc | BU |
|---|---|---|---|---|---|---|
| 1996 Proof | 25,000 | Value: 45.00 | | | | |

**10 DOLLARS** **KM# 223** **Weight:** 31.1000 g. **Composition:** 0.9990 Silver 1.0000 oz. ASW **Series:** Preserve Planet Earth **Reverse:** Grey Parrot

| Date | Mintage | F | VF | XF | Unc | BU |
|---|---|---|---|---|---|---|
| 1996 Proof | 25,000 | Value: 40.00 | | | | |

**10 DOLLARS** **KM# 201** **Weight:** 31.1000 g. **Composition:** 0.9990 Silver 1.0000 oz. ASW **Subject:** Formula One **Reverse:** Eddie Irvine

| Date | Mintage | F | VF | XF | Unc | BU |
|---|---|---|---|---|---|---|
| 1996 Proof | 25,000 | Value: 40.00 | | | | |

**10 DOLLARS** **KM# 214** **Weight:** 31.1000 g. **Composition:** 0.9990 Silver 1.0000 oz. ASW **Subject:** Star Trek **Reverse:** LaForge and Data

| Date | Mintage | F | VF | XF | Unc | BU |
|---|---|---|---|---|---|---|
| 1996 Proof | 25,000 | Value: 45.00 | | | | |

**10 DOLLARS** **KM# 226** **Weight:** 31.1000 g. **Composition:** 0.9990 Silver 1.0000 oz. ASW **Series:** Preserve Planet Earth **Reverse:** Love Birds

| Date | Mintage | F | VF | XF | Unc | BU |
|---|---|---|---|---|---|---|
| 1996 Proof | 25,000 | Value: 40.00 | | | | |

**10 DOLLARS** **KM# 202** **Weight:** 31.1000 g. **Composition:** 0.9990 Silver 1.0000 oz. ASW **Subject:** Formula One **Reverse:** Heinz Frentzen

| Date | Mintage | F | VF | XF | Unc | BU |
|---|---|---|---|---|---|---|
| 1996 Proof | 25,000 | Value: 40.00 | | | | |

**10 DOLLARS** **KM# 217** **Weight:** 31.1000 g. **Composition:** 0.9990 Silver 1.0000 oz. ASW **Subject:** Star Trek **Reverse:** Spock and Uhura

| Date | Mintage | F | VF | XF | Unc | BU |
|---|---|---|---|---|---|---|
| 1996 Proof | 25,000 | Value: 45.00 | | | | |

**10 DOLLARS** **KM# 229** **Weight:** 31.1000 g. **Composition:** 0.9990 Silver 1.0000 oz. ASW **Subject:** Formula One **Reverse:** Ayrton Senna

| Date | Mintage | F | VF | XF | Unc | BU |
|---|---|---|---|---|---|---|
| 1996 | 25,000 | Value: 40.00 | | | | |

**10 DOLLARS** **KM# 208** **Weight:** 31.1000 g. **Composition:** 0.9990 Silver 1.0000 oz. ASW **Subject:** Star Trek **Reverse:** Starships NCC-1701 and NCC-1701D

| Date | Mintage | F | VF | XF | Unc | BU |
|---|---|---|---|---|---|---|
| 1996 Proof | 25,000 | Value: 45.00 | | | | |

**10 DOLLARS** **KM# 220** **Weight:** 31.1000 g. **Composition:** 0.9990 Silver 1.0000 oz. ASW **Subject:** Star Trek **Reverse:** Worf and Dr. Crusher

| Date | Mintage | F | VF | XF | Unc | BU |
|---|---|---|---|---|---|---|
| 1996 Proof | 25,000 | Value: 45.00 | | | | |

**10 DOLLARS** **KM# 242** **Weight:** 31.1000 g. **Composition:** 0.9990 Silver 1.0000 oz. ASW **Subject:** President Chiang Ching-kuo

| Date | Mintage | F | VF | XF | Unc | BU |
|---|---|---|---|---|---|---|
| 1996 Proof | 25,000 | Value: 45.00 | | | | |

**10 DOLLARS** **KM# 245** **Weight:** 31.1000 g. **Composition:** 0.9990 Silver 1.0000 oz. ASW **Subject:** President Lee Ten-hui

| Date | Mintage | F | VF | XF | Unc | BU |
|---|---|---|---|---|---|---|
| 1996 Proof | 25,000 | Value: 45.00 | | | | |

**10 DOLLARS** **KM# 256** **Weight:** 31.1000 g. **Composition:** 0.9990 Silver 1.0000 oz. ASW **Subject:** Chairman Mao Zedong **Reverse:** Mao walking

| Date | Mintage | F | VF | XF | Unc | BU |
|---|---|---|---|---|---|---|
| 1996 Proof | 25,000 | Value: 42.50 | | | | |

**10 DOLLARS** **KM# 257** **Weight:** 31.1000 g. **Composition:** 0.9990 Silver 1.0000 oz. ASW **Subject:** Chairman Mao Zedong **Reverse:** Mao with gate of Heavely Peace

| Date | Mintage | F | VF | XF | Unc | BU |
|---|---|---|---|---|---|---|
| 1996 Proof | 25,000 | Value: 42.50 | | | | |

**10 DOLLARS** **KM# 258** **Weight:** 31.1000 g. **Composition:** 0.9990 Silver 1.0000 oz. ASW **Subject:** Chairman Mao Zedong **Reverse:** Mao proclaiming People's Republic

| Date | Mintage | F | VF | XF | Unc | BU |
|---|---|---|---|---|---|---|
| 1996 Proof | 25,000 | Value: 42.50 | | | | |

**10 DOLLARS** **KM# 262** **Weight:** 31.1000 g. **Composition:** 0.9990 Silver 1.0000 oz. ASW **Subject:** Chairman Mao Zedong **Reverse:** Mao and President Nixon

| Date | Mintage | F | VF | XF | Unc | BU |
|---|---|---|---|---|---|---|
| 1996 Proof | 25,000 | Value: 42.50 | | | | |

**10 DOLLARS** **KM# 264** **Weight:** 31.1000 g. **Composition:** 0.9990 Silver 1.0000 oz. ASW **Subject:** Pioneers of the West **Reverse:** Daniel Boone

| Date | Mintage | F | VF | XF | Unc | BU |
|---|---|---|---|---|---|---|
| 1996 Proof | 25,000 | Value: 40.00 | | | | |

**10 DOLLARS** **KM# 267** **Weight:** 31.1000 g. **Composition:** 0.9990 Silver 1.0000 oz. ASW **Subject:** Pioneers of the West **Reverse:** Davy Crockett

| Date | Mintage | F | VF | XF | Unc | BU |
|---|---|---|---|---|---|---|
| 1996 Proof | 25,000 | Value: 40.00 | | | | |

**10 DOLLARS** **KM# 270** **Weight:** 31.1000 g. **Composition:** 0.9990 Silver 1.0000 oz. ASW **Subject:** Pioneers of the West **Reverse:** Jim Bowie

| Date | Mintage | F | VF | XF | Unc | BU |
|---|---|---|---|---|---|---|
| 1996 Proof | 25,000 | Value: 40.00 | | | | |

**10 DOLLARS** **KM# 273** **Weight:** 31.1000 g. **Composition:** 0.9990 Silver 1.0000 oz. ASW **Subject:** Pioneers of the West **Reverse:** Kit Carson

| Date | Mintage | F | VF | XF | Unc | BU |
|---|---|---|---|---|---|---|
| 1996 Proof | 25,000 | Value: 40.00 | | | | |

**10 DOLLARS** **KM# 276** **Weight:** 31.1000 g. **Composition:** 0.9990 Silver 1.0000 oz. ASW **Subject:** Pioneers of the West **Reverse:** Wild Bill Hickok

| Date | Mintage | F | VF | XF | Unc | BU |
|---|---|---|---|---|---|---|
| 1996 Proof | 25,000 | Value: 40.00 | | | | |

**10 DOLLARS** **KM# 279** **Weight:** 31.1000 g. **Composition:** 0.9990 Silver 1.0000 oz. ASW **Subject:** Pioneers of the West **Reverse:** Buffalo Bill

| Date | Mintage | F | VF | XF | Unc | BU |
|---|---|---|---|---|---|---|
| 1996 Proof | 25,000 | Value: 40.00 | | | | |

**10 DOLLARS** **KM# 284** **Weight:** 31.1000 g. **Composition:** 0.9990 Silver 1.0000 oz. ASW **Subject:** Return of Macao to China **Obverse:** National arms **Reverse:** City Views Old and New

| Date | Mintage | F | VF | XF | Unc | BU |
|---|---|---|---|---|---|---|
| 1996 Proof | Est. 6,000 | Value: 50.00 | | | | |

**10 DOLLARS** **KM# 285** **Weight:** 31.1000 g. **Composition:** 0.9990 Silver 1.0000 oz. ASW **Subject:** Return of Hong Kong to China

| Date | Mintage | F | VF | XF | Unc | BU |
|---|---|---|---|---|---|---|
| 1996 Proof | Est. 6,000 | Value: 50.00 | | | | |

**10 DOLLARS** **KM# 287** **Weight:** 31.1000 g. **Composition:** 0.9990 Silver 1.0000 oz. ASW **Series:** WWII **Subject:** Evacuation from Dunkirk **Reverse:** Left, British 1939-45 Star Medal

| Date | Mintage | F | VF | XF | Unc | BU |
|---|---|---|---|---|---|---|
| 1997 Proof | 25,000 | Value: 37.50 | | | | |

**10 DOLLARS** **KM# 289** **Weight:** 31.1000 g. **Composition:** 0.9990 Silver 1.0000 oz. ASW **Series:** WWII **Subject:** Liberation of the Philippines **Reverse:** Right, American Asian-Pacific campaign medal

| Date | Mintage | F | VF | XF | Unc | BU |
|---|---|---|---|---|---|---|
| 1997 Proof | 25,000 | Value: 37.50 | | | | |

**10 DOLLARS** **KM# 291** **Weight:** 31.1000 g. **Composition:** 0.9990 Silver 1.0000 oz. ASW **Series:** WWII **Subject:** Defense of Stalingrad **Reverse:** Left, Soviet Distinguished Combat Medal

| Date | Mintage | F | VF | XF | Unc | BU |
|---|---|---|---|---|---|---|
| 1997 Proof | 25,000 | Value: 37.50 | | | | |

**10 DOLLARS** **KM# 293** **Weight:** 31.1000 g. **Composition:** 0.9990 Silver 1.0000 oz. ASW **Series:** WWII **Subject:** Arnhem **Reverse:** Right, Netherlands Bronze Lion Cross

| Date | Mintage | F | VF | XF | Unc | BU |
|---|---|---|---|---|---|---|
| 1997 Proof | 25,000 | Value: 37.50 | | | | |

**10 DOLLARS** **KM# 295** **Weight:** 31.1000 g. **Composition:** 0.9990 Silver 1.0000 oz. ASW **Series:** WWII **Subject:** Raid on the Dams **Reverse:** Left, British Distinguished Flying Medal

| Date | Mintage | F | VF | XF | Unc | BU |
|---|---|---|---|---|---|---|
| 1997 Proof | 25,000 | Value: 37.50 | | | | |

**10 DOLLARS** **KM# 297** **Weight:** 31.1000 g. **Composition:** 0.9990 Silver 1.0000 oz. ASW **Series:** WWII **Subject:** West African Campaign **Reverse:** Right, WWII Victory Medal

| Date | Mintage | F | VF | XF | Unc | BU |
|---|---|---|---|---|---|---|
| 1997 Proof | 25,000 | Value: 37.50 | | | | |

**10 DOLLARS** **KM# 299** **Weight:** 31.1000 g. **Composition:** 0.9990 Silver 1.0000 oz. ASW **Series:** WWII **Subject:** North African Campaign **Reverse:** Right, British Africa Star Medal

| Date | Mintage | F | VF | XF | Unc | BU |
|---|---|---|---|---|---|---|
| 1997 Proof | 25,000 | Value: 37.50 | | | | |

**10 DOLLARS** **KM# 301** **Weight:** 31.1000 g. **Composition:** 0.9990 Silver 1.0000 oz. ASW **Series:** WWII **Subject:** The Dieppe Raid **Reverse:** Right, British Victoria Cross

| Date | Mintage | F | VF | XF | Unc | BU |
|---|---|---|---|---|---|---|
| 1997 Proof | 25,000 | Value: 37.50 | | | | |

**10 DOLLARS** **KM# 303** **Weight:** 31.1000 g. **Composition:** 0.9990 Silver 1.0000 oz. ASW **Series:** WWII **Subject:** Iwo Jima **Reverse:** Left, Purple Heart Medal

| Date | Mintage | F | VF | XF | Unc | BU |
|---|---|---|---|---|---|---|
| 1997 Proof | 25,000 | Value: 37.50 | | | | |

**10 DOLLARS** **KM# 305** **Weight:** 31.1000 g. **Composition:** 0.9990 Silver 1.0000 oz. ASW **Series:** WWII **Subject:** Battle of Britain **Reverse:** Left, British Distinguished Flying Cross

| Date | Mintage | F | VF | XF | Unc | BU |
|---|---|---|---|---|---|---|
| 1997 Proof | 25,000 | Value: 37.50 | | | | |

**10 DOLLARS** **KM# 307** **Weight:** 31.1000 g. **Composition:** 0.9990 Silver 1.0000 oz. ASW **Series:** WWII **Subject:** Liberation of Paris **Reverse:** Right, Croix de Guerre Medal

| Date | Mintage | F | VF | XF | Unc | BU |
|---|---|---|---|---|---|---|
| 1997 Proof | 25,000 | Value: 37.50 | | | | |

**10 DOLLARS** **KM# 309** **Weight:** 31.1000 g. **Composition:** 0.9990 Silver 1.0000 oz. ASW **Series:** WWII **Subject:** Burma Campaign **Reverse:** Left, British Burma Star Medal

| Date | Mintage | F | VF | XF | Unc | BU |
|---|---|---|---|---|---|---|
| 1997 Proof | 25,000 | Value: 37.50 | | | | |

**10 DOLLARS** KM# 311 **Weight:** 31.1000 g. **Composition:** 0.9990 Silver 1.0000 oz. ASW **Subject:** Mahatma Gandhi **Obverse:** National arms

| Date | Mintage | F | VF | XF | Unc | BU |
|---|---|---|---|---|---|---|
| 1997 Proof | 25,000 | Value: 40.00 | | | | |

**10 DOLLARS** KM# 314 **Weight:** 31.1000 g. **Composition:** 0.9990 Silver 1.0000 oz. ASW **Subject:** Return of Hong Kong **Obverse:** National arms **Reverse:** Dragon

| Date | Mintage | F | VF | XF | Unc | BU |
|---|---|---|---|---|---|---|
| 1997 Proof | 25,000 | Value: 40.00 | | | | |

**10 DOLLARS** KM# 321 **Weight:** 31.1000 g. **Composition:** 0.9990 Silver 1.0000 oz. ASW **Subject:** Fiftieth Anniversary of the Kon-Tiki Expedition **Obverse:** National arms

| Date | Mintage | F | VF | XF | Unc | BU |
|---|---|---|---|---|---|---|
| 1997 Proof | 25,000 | Value: 40.00 | | | | |

**10 DOLLARS** KM# 325 **Weight:** 31.1000 g. **Composition:** 0.9990 Silver 1.0000 oz. ASW **Subject:** Jurassic Park **Obverse:** National arms **Reverse:** Stegosaurus

| Date | Mintage | F | VF | XF | Unc | BU |
|---|---|---|---|---|---|---|
| 1997 Proof | 10,000 | Value: 50.00 | | | | |

**10 DOLLARS** KM# 328 **Weight:** 31.1030 g. **Composition:** 0.9250 Gold Clad Silver .9250 oz. **Subject:** Golden Wedding Anniversary **Obverse:** National arms **Reverse:** E & P initials above 2 shields

| Date | Mintage | F | VF | XF | Unc | BU |
|---|---|---|---|---|---|---|
| 1997 Proof | 10,000 | Value: 50.00 | | | | |

**10 DOLLARS** KM# 331 **Weight:** 31.1030 g. **Composition:** 0.9250 Gold Clad Silver .9250 oz. **Subject:** Golden Wedding Anniversary **Obverse:** National arms **Reverse:** Royal couple with horse

| Date | Mintage | F | VF | XF | Unc | BU |
|---|---|---|---|---|---|---|
| 1997 Proof | 10,000 | Value: 50.00 | | | | |

**10 DOLLARS** KM# 334 **Weight:** 31.1030 g. **Composition:** 0.9250 Gold Clad Silver .9250 oz. **Subject:** Golden Wedding Anniversary **Obverse:** National arms **Reverse:** Royal couple with dogs

| Date | Mintage | F | VF | XF | Unc | BU |
|---|---|---|---|---|---|---|
| 1997 Proof | 10,000 | Value: 50.00 | | | | |

**10 DOLLARS** KM# 337 **Weight:** 31.1030 g. **Composition:** 0.9250 Gold Clad Silver .9250 oz. **Subject:** Golden Wedding Anniversary **Obverse:** National arms **Reverse:** Royal couple with children

| Date | Mintage | F | VF | XF | Unc | BU |
|---|---|---|---|---|---|---|
| 1997 Proof | 10,000 | Value: 50.00 | | | | |

**10 DOLLARS** KM# 345 **Weight:** 31.1035 g. **Composition:** 0.9990 Silver 1.0000 oz. ASW **Subject:** 150th Anniversary - Independence of Liberia **Obverse:** National arms **Reverse:** The "Ashmon"

| Date | Mintage | F | VF | XF | Unc | BU |
|---|---|---|---|---|---|---|
| 1997 Proof | 25,000 | Value: 45.00 | | | | |

**10 DOLLARS** KM# 346 **Composition:** Copper-Nickel **Subject:** Famous Personalities of the World **Obverse:** National arms with blank ribbons **Reverse:** Marilyn Monroe

| Date | Mintage | F | VF | XF | Unc | BU |
|---|---|---|---|---|---|---|
| ND(1997) Proof | — | Value: 15.00 | | | | |

**10 DOLLARS** KM# 348 **Weight:** 31.1035 g. **Composition:** 0.9990 Silver 1.0000 oz. ASW **Subject:** Return of Hong Kong to China **Obverse:** National arms **Reverse:** City View

| Date | Mintage | F | VF | XF | Unc | BU |
|---|---|---|---|---|---|---|
| 1997 Proof | Est. 8,000 | Value: 35.00 | | | | |

**10 DOLLARS** KM# 349 **Weight:** 31.1035 g. **Composition:** 0.9990 Silver 1.0000 oz. ASW **Subject:** Pending Return of Macao to China **Obverse:** National arms **Reverse:** City View

| Date | Mintage | F | VF | XF | Unc | BU |
|---|---|---|---|---|---|---|
| 1997 Proof | Est. 8,000 | Value: 35.00 | | | | |

**10 DOLLARS** **KM#350** **Weight:** 31.1035 g. **Composition:** 0.9990 Silver 1.0000 oz. ASW **Subject:** Diana - The People's Princess **Obverse:** National arms

| Date | Mintage | F | VF | XF | Unc | BU |
|---|---|---|---|---|---|---|
| 1997 Proof | — | Value: 45.00 | | | | |

**10 DOLLARS** **KM#369** **Weight:** 31.1035 g. **Composition:** 0.9990 Silver 1.0000 oz. ASW **Subject:** Star Trek - The Next Generation **Obverse:** National arms **Reverse:** Romulan Warbird

| Date | Mintage | F | VF | XF | Unc | BU |
|---|---|---|---|---|---|---|
| 1997 Proof | 25,000 | Value: 45.00 | | | | |

**10 DOLLARS** **KM#372** **Weight:** 31.1035 g. **Composition:** 0.9990 Silver 1.0000 oz. ASW **Subject:** Star Trek - The Next Generation **Obverse:** National arms **Reverse:** Klingon Attack Cruiser

| Date | Mintage | F | VF | XF | Unc | BU |
|---|---|---|---|---|---|---|
| 1997 Proof | 25,000 | Value: 45.00 | | | | |

**10 DOLLARS** **KM#375** **Weight:** 31.1035 g. **Composition:** 0.9990 Silver 1.0000 oz. ASW **Subject:** Star Trek - The Next Generation **Obverse:** National arms **Reverse:** U.S.S. Enterprise NCC-1701-D

| Date | Mintage | F | VF | XF | Unc | BU |
|---|---|---|---|---|---|---|
| 1997 Proof | 25,000 | Value: 45.00 | | | | |

**10 DOLLARS** **KM#378** **Weight:** 31.1035 g. **Composition:** 0.9990 Silver 1.0000 oz. ASW **Subject:** Star Trek - The Next Generation **Obverse:** National arms **Reverse:** Klingon Bird of Prey

| Date | Mintage | F | VF | XF | Unc | BU |
|---|---|---|---|---|---|---|
| 1997 Proof | 25,000 | Value: 45.00 | | | | |

**10 DOLLARS** **KM#381** **Weight:** 31.1035 g. **Composition:** 0.9990 Silver 1.0000 oz. ASW **Subject:** Star Trek - The Next Generation **Obverse:** National arms **Reverse:** Borg Cube

| Date | Mintage | F | VF | XF | Unc | BU |
|---|---|---|---|---|---|---|
| 1997 Proof | 25,000 | Value: 45.00 | | | | |

**10 DOLLARS** **KM#384** **Weight:** 31.1035 g. **Composition:** 0.9990 Silver 1.0000 oz. ASW **Subject:** Star Trek - The Next Generation **Obverse:** National arms **Reverse:** Ferengi Marauder

| Date | Mintage | F | VF | XF | Unc | BU |
|---|---|---|---|---|---|---|
| 1997 Proof | 25,000 | Value: 45.00 | | | | |

**10 DOLLARS** **KM#387** **Weight:** 31.1035 g. **Composition:** 0.9990 Silver 1.0000 oz. ASW **Subject:** President Ronald Reagan **Obverse:** National arms **Reverse:** Lincoln Statue

| Date | Mintage | F | VF | XF | Unc | BU |
|---|---|---|---|---|---|---|
| 1998 Proof | 25,000 | Value: 50.00 | | | | |

**10 DOLLARS** **KM#402** **Weight:** 31.1035 g. **Composition:** 0.9990 Silver 1.0000 oz. ASW **Subject:** Christopher Columbus **Obverse:** National arms **Reverse:** Portrait, ship

| Date | Mintage | F | VF | XF | Unc | BU |
|---|---|---|---|---|---|---|
| 1999 Proof | 25,000 | Value: 45.00 | | | | |

**10 DOLLARS** **KM#405** **Weight:** 31.1035 g. **Composition:** 0.9990 Silver 1.0000 oz. ASW **Subject:** Captain James Cook **Obverse:** National arms **Reverse:** Portrait, map, ship

| Date | Mintage | F | VF | XF | Unc | BU |
|---|---|---|---|---|---|---|
| 1999 Proof | 25,000 | Value: 45.00 | | | | |

**10 DOLLARS** **KM#408** **Weight:** 31.1035 g. **Composition:** 0.9990 Silver 1.0000 oz. ASW **Subject:** Return of Macao to China **Obverse:** National arms **Reverse:** Dragon and phoenix

| Date | Mintage | F | VF | XF | Unc | BU |
|---|---|---|---|---|---|---|
| 1999 Proof | 25,000 | Value: 50.00 | | | | |

**10 DOLLARS** **KM#414** **Weight:** 31.1035 g. **Composition:** 0.9990 Silver 1.0000 oz. ASW **Subject:** The Wedding of the Prince Edward **Obverse:** National arms **Reverse:** Couple in carriage

| Date | Mintage | F | VF | XF | Unc | BU |
|---|---|---|---|---|---|---|
| 1999 Proof | 10,000 | Value: 50.00 | | | | |

**10 DOLLARS** **KM#424** **Weight:** 15.5517 g. **Composition:** 0.9990 Silver .5000 oz. ASW **Subject:** Liberty **Obverse:** National arms **Reverse:** Conjoined busts of President John F. Kennedy and his son

| Date | Mintage | F | VF | XF | Unc | BU |
|---|---|---|---|---|---|---|
| 1999 Proof | — | Value: 22.50 | | | | |

**10 DOLLARS** **KM# 471** **Weight:** 30.7500 g. **Composition:** 0.9990 Silver .9876 oz. ASW **Subject:** Transrapid-08 Hamburg-Berlin Monorail **Obverse:** National arms **Reverse:** Monorail train car **Edge:** Reeded **Size:** 37.9 mm.

| Date | Mintage | F | VF | XF | Unc | BU |
|---|---|---|---|---|---|---|
| 1999 Proof | — | Value: 35.00 | | | | |

**10 DOLLARS** **KM# 468** **Weight:** 25.0000 g. **Composition:** 0.9250 Silver .7435 oz. ASW **Subject:** The "Mayflower" **Obverse:** National arms **Reverse:** Sail ship **Edge:** Reeded **Size:** 38.7 mm.

| Date | Mintage | F | VF | XF | Unc | BU |
|---|---|---|---|---|---|---|
| 1999 Proof | — | Value: 25.00 | | | | |

**10 DOLLARS** **KM# 469** **Weight:** 20.5000 g. **Composition:** 0.9250 Silver .6097 oz. ASW **Subject:** Millennium **Obverse:** National arms **Reverse:** Millennium Dome **Edge:** Reeded **Size:** 38.6 mm.

| Date | Mintage | F | VF | XF | Unc | BU |
|---|---|---|---|---|---|---|
| 2000 Proof | 2,000 | Value: 40.00 | | | | |

**10 DOLLARS** **KM# 470** **Weight:** 20.5000 g. **Composition:** 0.9250 Silver .6097 oz. ASW **Subject:** Mutiny on the Bounty **Reverse:** Mutineers setting ships officers adrift

| Date | Mintage | F | VF | XF | Unc | BU |
|---|---|---|---|---|---|---|
| 2000 Proof | 2,000 | Value: 40.00 | | | | |

**10 DOLLARS** **KM# 475** **Weight:** 8.4500 g. **Composition:** 0.9990 Silver .2714 oz. ASW **Subject:** General Robert E. Lee **Obverse:** National arms **Reverse:** General Lee on horseback **Edge:** Reeded **Size:** 30.1 mm.

| Date | Mintage | F | VF | XF | Unc | BU |
|---|---|---|---|---|---|---|
| 2000 Proof | — | — | — | — | 17.50 | — |

**10 DOLLARS** **KM# 476** **Weight:** 8.4500 g. **Composition:** 0.9990 Silver .2714 oz. ASW **Subject:** Statue of Liberty **Obverse:** National arms **Reverse:** Statue of Liberty

| Date | Mintage | F | VF | XF | Unc | BU |
|---|---|---|---|---|---|---|
| 2000 Proof | — | — | — | — | 17.50 | — |

**10 DOLLARS** **KM# 492** **Weight:** 3.3930 g. **Composition:** 0.9167 Gold .1000 oz. AGW **Subject:** US Gold Indian Design Copy **Obverse:** Incuse Indian design **Reverse:** Incuse eagle design **Edge:** Reeded **Size:** 16.5 mm.

| Date | Mintage | F | VF | XF | Unc | BU |
|---|---|---|---|---|---|---|
| 2000 | — | — | — | — | 130 | — |

**10 DOLLARS** **KM# 423** **Weight:** 31.1035 g. **Composition:** 0.9990 Silver 1.000 oz. ASW **Subject:** Millennium **Obverse:** Liberty cap, crossed flags of USA and Liberia above Liberian arms **Reverse:** Morgan dollar Liberty portrait

| Date | Mintage | F | VF | XF | Unc | BU |
|---|---|---|---|---|---|---|
| 2000 Proof | Est. 2,000 | Value: 50.00 | | | | |

**10 DOLLARS** **KM# 443** **Weight:** 31.1035 g. **Composition:** 0.9990 Silver 1.0000 oz. ASW **Subject:** Greenwich Meridian **Obverse:** National arms **Reverse:** World landmarks and fireworks **Edge:** Reeded **Size:** 38.6 mm.

| Date | Mintage | F | VF | XF | Unc | BU |
|---|---|---|---|---|---|---|
| 2000 Proof | 25,000 | Value: 47.50 | | | | |

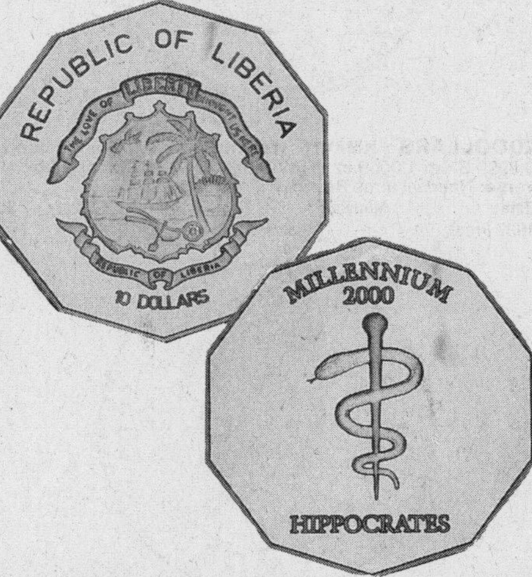


**10 DOLLARS** **KM# 444** **Weight:** 25.0000 g. **Composition:** 0.9250 Silver .7435 oz. ASW **Subject:** Millennium - Hippocrates **Obverse:** National arms **Reverse:** Single snake caduceus **Edge:** Plain, ten-sided **Size:** 36.8 mm.

| Date | Mintage | F | VF | XF | Unc | BU |
|---|---|---|---|---|---|---|
| 2000 Proof | 10,000 | Value: 35.00 | | | | |

**10 DOLLARS** **KM# 493** **Weight:** 770.0000 g. **Composition:** Copper **Subject:** "The Wreck of the Princess Louisa" **Obverse:** National arms. **Reverse:** Sailing ship. **Edge:** Reeded. **Size:** 100 mm. **Note:** Illustration reduced. Actual size 100mm. With an encased glass shard recovered from the wreck site of the Princess Louisa.

| Date | Mintage | F | VF | XF | Unc | BU |
|---|---|---|---|---|---|---|
| 2001 | 2,000 | — | — | — | 200 | — |

**10 DOLLARS** **KM# 491** **Weight:** 25.2500 g. **Composition:** 0.9250 Silver .7509 oz. ASW **Subject:** Illusion **Obverse:** National arms

**Reverse:** Male-female portrait **Edge:** Plain, ten sided **Size:** 36.8 mm.

| Date | Mintage | F | VF | XF | Unc | BU |
|---|---|---|---|---|---|---|
| 2001 Proof | 5,000 | — | — | — | 35.00 | — |



**12 DOLLARS** **KM# 20** **Weight:** 6.0000 g. **Composition:** 0.9000 Gold .1736 oz. AGW **Subject:** 70th Birthday of President Tubman

| Date | Mintage | F | VF | XF | Unc | BU |
|---|---|---|---|---|---|---|
| 1965 Proof | 400 | Value: 125 | | | | |

**15 DOLLARS** **KM# 108** **Weight:** 1.0000 g. **Composition:** 0.9999 Gold .0321 oz. AGW **Series:** Preserve Planet Earth **Reverse:** Compsognathus

| Date | Mintage | F | VF | XF | Unc | BU |
|---|---|---|---|---|---|---|
| 1993 Proof | — | Value: 32.50 | | | | |

**20 DOLLARS** **KM# 19** **Weight:** 18.6500 g. **Composition:** 0.9000 Gold .5397 oz. AGW **Subject:** William Vacanarat Shadrach Tubman

| Date | Mintage | F | VF | XF | Unc | BU |
|---|---|---|---|---|---|---|
| 1964B | 10,000 | — | — | — | 250 | — |

**20 DOLLARS** **KM# 64** **Weight:** 15.8100 g. **Composition:** 0.9000 Gold .8768 oz. AGW **Subject:** 25th Anniversary of Inter-Continental Hotels

| Date | Mintage | F | VF | XF | Unc | BU |
|---|---|---|---|---|---|---|
| 1971 Proof | — | — | — | — | — | — |

**20 DOLLARS** **KM# 27** **Weight:** 33.4370 g. **Composition:** 0.9000 Gold .9675 oz. AGW **Subject:** Inauguration of President Tolbert

| Date | Mintage | F | VF | XF | Unc | BU |
|---|---|---|---|---|---|---|
| 1972 Proof | — | Value: 450 | | | | |

**20 DOLLARS** **KM# 45** **Weight:** 28.2800 g. **Composition:** 0.9250 Silver .8411 oz. ASW **Subject:** Year of the Scout **Obverse:** National arms

| Date | Mintage | F | VF | XF | Unc | BU |
|---|---|---|---|---|---|---|
| 1983 | 10,000 | — | — | — | 30.00 | — |
| 1983 Proof | 10,000 | Value: 48.50 | | | | |

**20 DOLLARS** **KM# 48** **Weight:** 28.2800 g. **Composition:** 0.9250 Silver .8411 oz. ASW **Series:** International Year of Disabled Persons

| Date | Mintage | F | VF | XF | Unc | BU |
|---|---|---|---|---|---|---|
| 1983 | — | — | — | — | 35.00 | — |
| 1983 Proof | — | Value: 50.00 | | | | |

**20 DOLLARS** **KM# 283** **Weight:** 1.2700 g. **Composition:** 0.9990 Gold .0408 oz. AGW **Subject:** Formula One **Reverse:** Damon Hill

| Date | Mintage | F | VF | XF | Unc | BU |
|---|---|---|---|---|---|---|
| 1994 Proof | 25,000 | Value: 65.00 | | | | |

**20 DOLLARS** **KM# 230** **Weight:** 1.2700 g. **Composition:** 0.9990 Gold .0408 oz. AGW **Subject:** Formula One **Reverse:** Ayrton Senna **Note:** Similar to 10 Dollars, KM#229.

| Date | Mintage | F | VF | XF | Unc | BU |
|---|---|---|---|---|---|---|
| 1996 Proof | 15,000 | Value: 65.00 | | | | |

**20 DOLLARS** **KM# 250** **Weight:** 1.2700 g. **Composition:** 0.9990 Gold .0408 oz. AGW **Subject:** Dalai Lama **Note:** Similar to 100 Dollars, KM#252.

| Date | Mintage | F | VF | XF | Unc | BU |
|---|---|---|---|---|---|---|
| 1996 Proof | 15,000 | Value: 65.00 | | | | |

**20 DOLLARS** **KM# 315** **Weight:** 1.2400 g. **Composition:** 0.9990 Gold .0400 oz. AGW **Subject:** Return of Hong Kong to China **Note:** Similar to 10 Dollars, KM#314.

| Date | Mintage | F | VF | XF | Unc | BU |
|---|---|---|---|---|---|---|
| 1997 Proof | — | Value: 65.00 | | | | |

**20 DOLLARS** **KM# 340** **Weight:** 31.1035 g. **Composition:** 0.9990 Silver 1.0000 oz. ASW **Subject:** Year of the Ox **Obverse:** National arms

| Date | Mintage | F | VF | XF | Unc | BU |
|---|---|---|---|---|---|---|
| 1997 Proof | — | Value: 28.50 | | | | |

**20 DOLLARS** **KM# 416** **Weight:** 31.3500 g. **Composition:** 0.9990 Silver 1.0069 oz. ASW **Subject:** Deng Xiaoping **Obverse:** National arms **Reverse:** Portrait, dates

| Date | Mintage | F | VF | XF | Unc | BU |
|---|---|---|---|---|---|---|
| 1997 Proof | — | Value: 27.50 | | | | |

**20 DOLLARS** **KM# 417** **Weight:** 31.4000 g. **Composition:** 0.9990 Silver 1.0085 oz. ASW **Subject:** Princess Diana **Obverse:** National arms **Reverse:** Portrait, dates

| Date | Mintage | F | VF | XF | Unc | BU |
|---|---|---|---|---|---|---|
| 1997 Proof | — | Value: 35.00 | | | | |

**20 DOLLARS** **KM# 341** **Weight:** 31.1035 g. **Composition:** 0.9990 Silver 1.0000 oz. ASW **Subject:** Year of the Tiger **Obverse:** National arms **Reverse:** Tiger in bamboo

| Date | Mintage | F | VF | XF | Unc | BU |
|---|---|---|---|---|---|---|
| 1998 (1997) Proof | — | Value: 25.00 | | | | |

**20 DOLLARS** **KM# 342** **Weight:** 24.9400 g. **Composition:** Silver **Subject:** Year of the Tiger **Obverse:** National arms **Reverse:** Tiger lying in bamboo

| Date | Mintage | F | VF | XF | Unc | BU |
|---|---|---|---|---|---|---|
| 1998 (1997) Proof | — | Value: 37.50 | | | | |

**20 DOLLARS** **KM# 343** **Weight:** 24.9400 g. **Composition:** Silver **Subject:** Year of the Tiger **Obverse:** National arms **Reverse:** Stalking tiger

| Date | Mintage | F | VF | XF | Unc | BU |
|---|---|---|---|---|---|---|
| 1998 (1997) Proof | — | Value: 35.00 | | | | |

**20 DOLLARS** **KM# 364** **Weight:** 31.1035 g. **Composition:** 0.9990 Silver 1.0000 oz. ASW **Subject:** RMS Titanic **Obverse:** National arms **Reverse:** Ship sinking

| Date | Mintage | F | VF | XF | Unc | BU |
|---|---|---|---|---|---|---|
| 1998 Proof | 25,000 | Value: 50.00 | | | | |

**20 DOLLARS** **KM# 389** **Weight:** 31.1035 g. **Composition:** 0.9990 Silver 1.0000 oz. ASW **Subject:** Year of the Rabbit **Obverse:** National arms **Reverse:** Rabbit running left

| Date | Mintage | F | VF | XF | Unc | BU |
|---|---|---|---|---|---|---|
| 1999 Proof | 8,000 | Value: 45.00 | | | | |

**20 DOLLARS** **KM# 390** **Weight:** 31.1035 g. **Composition:** 0.9990 Silver 1.0000 oz. ASW **Subject:** Year of the Rabbit **Obverse:** National arms **Reverse:** Rabbit sitting

| Date | Mintage | F | VF | XF | Unc | BU |
|---|---|---|---|---|---|---|
| 1999 Proof | 8,000 | Value: 45.00 | | | | |

**20 DOLLARS** **KM# 391** **Weight:** 31.1035 g. **Composition:** 0.9990 Silver 1.0000 oz. ASW **Subject:** Year of the Rabbit **Obverse:** National arms **Reverse:** Rabbit running right

| Date | Mintage | F | VF | XF | Unc | BU |
|---|---|---|---|---|---|---|
| 1999 Proof | 8,000 | Value: 45.00 | | | | |

**20 DOLLARS** **KM# 418** **Weight:** 1.2441 g. **Composition:** 0.9999 Gold .0400 oz. AGW **Subject:** Return of Macao to China **Obverse:** National arms **Reverse:** Dragon and phoenix **Note:** Similar to 10 Dollars, KM#408.

| Date | Mintage | F | VF | XF | Unc | BU |
|---|---|---|---|---|---|---|
| 1999 Proof | 25,000 | Value: 55.00 | | | | |

**20 DOLLARS** **KM# 477** **Weight:** 20.0400 g. **Composition:** 0.9990 Silver .6437 oz. ASW **Subject:** Admiral David G. Farragut **Obverse:** National arms **Reverse:** Ferragut's portrait **Edge:** Reeded **Size:** 40.3 mm.

| Date | Mintage | F | VF | XF | Unc | BU |
|---|---|---|---|---|---|---|
| 2000 Proof | Est. 20,000 | — | — | — | 25.00 | — |

**20 DOLLARS** **KM# 478** **Weight:** 20.0400 g. **Composition:** 0.9990 Silver .6437 oz. ASW **Subject:** Surrender of Appomattox **Obverse:** National arms **Reverse:** Surrender signing scene

| Date | Mintage | F | VF | XF | Unc | BU |
|---|---|---|---|---|---|---|
| 2000 Proof | Est. 20,000 | — | — | — | 25.00 | — |

**20 DOLLARS** **KM# 479** **Weight:** 20.0400 g. **Composition:** 0.9990 Silver .6437 oz. ASW **Subject:** Abraham Lincoln **Obverse:** National arms

**Reverse:** Lincoln's portrait

| Date | Mintage | F | VF | XF | Unc | BU |
|---|---|---|---|---|---|---|
| 2000 Proof | Est. 20,000 | — | — | — | 25.00 | — |

**20 DOLLARS** **KM# 480** **Weight:** 20.0400 g. **Composition:** 0.9990 Silver .6437 oz. ASW **Subject:** Montgolfiere Balloon **Obverse:** National arms **Reverse:** First hot air balloon

| Date | Mintage | F | VF | XF | Unc | BU |
|---|---|---|---|---|---|---|
| 2000 Proof | Est. 20,000 | — | — | — | 25.00 | — |

**20 DOLLARS** **KM# 481** **Weight:** 20.0400 g. **Composition:** 0.9990 Silver .6437 oz. ASW **Subject:** Concorde Supersonic Airliner **Obverse:** National arms **Reverse:** Concorde in flight above runway

| Date | Mintage | F | VF | XF | Unc | BU |
|---|---|---|---|---|---|---|
| 2000 Proof | Est. 20,000 | — | — | — | 25.00 | — |

**20 DOLLARS** **KM# 482** **Weight:** 20.0400 g. **Composition:** 0.9990 Silver .6437 oz. ASW **Subject:** Apollo X **Obverse:** National arms

**Reverse:** Rocket launch, space capsule, large X

| Date | Mintage | F | VF | XF | Unc | BU |
|---|---|---|---|---|---|---|
| 2000 Proof | Est. 20,000 | — | — | — | 25.00 | — |

**20 DOLLARS** **KM# 483** **Weight:** 20.0400 g. **Composition:** 0.9990 Silver .6437 oz. ASW **Subject:** Apollo VII **Obverse:** National arms

**Reverse:** Space capsule and three portraits

| Date | Mintage | F | VF | XF | Unc | BU |
|---|---|---|---|---|---|---|
| 2000 Proof | Est. 20,000 | — | — | — | 25.00 | — |

**20 DOLLARS** **KM# 484** **Weight:** 20.0400 g. **Composition:** 0.9990 Silver .6437 oz. ASW **Subject:** STS-1 **Obverse:** National arms **Reverse:** Two portraits with shuttle model

| Date | Mintage | F | VF | XF | Unc | BU |
|---|---|---|---|---|---|---|
| 2000 Proof | Est. 20,000 | — | — | — | 25.00 | — |

**20 DOLLARS** **KM# 485** **Weight:** 20.0400 g. **Composition:** 0.9990 Silver .6437 oz. ASW **Subject:** Skylab I **Obverse:** National arms

**Reverse:** Three portraits below Skylab

| Date | Mintage | F | VF | XF | Unc | BU |
|---|---|---|---|---|---|---|
| 2000 Proof | Est. 20,000 | — | — | — | 25.00 | — |

**20 DOLLARS** **KM# 486** **Weight:** 20.0400 g. **Composition:** 0.9990 Silver .6437 oz. ASW **Series:** Olympics **Obverse:** National arms **Reverse:** Hurdler

| Date | Mintage | F | VF | XF | Unc | BU |
|---|---|---|---|---|---|---|
| 2000 Proof | Est. 20,000 | — | — | — | 25.00 | — |

**20 DOLLARS** **KM# 487** **Weight:** 20.0400 g. **Composition:** 0.9990 Silver .6437 oz. ASW **Series:** Olympics
**Obverse:** National arms
**Reverse:** Equestrian

| Date | Mintage | F | VF | XF | Unc | BU |
|---|---|---|---|---|---|---|
| 2000 Proof | Est. 20,000 | — | — | — | 25.00 | — |

**20 DOLLARS** **KM# 488** **Weight:** 20.0400 g. **Composition:** 0.9990 Silver .6437 oz. ASW **Series:** Olympics **Obverse:** National arms **Reverse:** Two basketball players

| Date | Mintage | F | VF | XF | Unc | BU |
|---|---|---|---|---|---|---|
| 2000 Proof | Est. 20,000 | — | — | — | 25.00 | — |

**20 DOLLARS** **KM# 489** **Weight:** 20.0400 g. **Composition:** 0.9990 Silver .6437 oz. ASW **Series:** Olympics
**Obverse:** National arms **Reverse:** Three cyclists

| Date | Mintage | F | VF | XF | Unc | BU |
|---|---|---|---|---|---|---|
| 2000 Proof | Est. 20,000 | — | — | — | 25.00 | — |

**20 DOLLARS** **KM# 490** **Weight:** 20.0400 g. **Composition:** 0.9990 Silver .6437 oz. ASW **Series:** Olympics **Obverse:** National arms
**Reverse:** Swimmer, cyclist, and speed walker

| Date | Mintage | F | VF | XF | Unc | BU |
|---|---|---|---|---|---|---|
| 2000 Proof | Est. 20,000 | — | — | — | 25.00 | — |

**20 DOLLARS** **KM# 472** **Weight:** 20.1700 g. **Composition:** 0.9990 Silver .6478 oz. ASW **Series:** American History **Obverse:** National arms **Reverse:** The Alamo and defenders **Edge:** Reeded **Size:** 40.3 mm.

| Date | Mintage | F | VF | XF | Unc | BU |
|---|---|---|---|---|---|---|
| 2000 Proof | — | Value: 40.00 | | | | |

**25 DOLLARS** **KM# 21a** **Composition:** 0.9990 Gold

| Date | Mintage | F | VF | XF | Unc | BU |
|---|---|---|---|---|---|---|
| 1965B L Proof | 100 | Value: 400 | | | | |

**25 DOLLARS** **KM# 23** **Composition:** 0.9990 Gold **Subject:** 75th Birthday of President Tubman

| Date | Mintage | F | VF | XF | Unc | BU |
|---|---|---|---|---|---|---|
| ND(1970)B Proof | — | Value: 300 | | | | |

**25 DOLLARS** **KM# 28** **Composition:** 0.9990 Gold **Subject:** Sesquicentennial - Founding of Liberia

| Date | Mintage | F | VF | XF | Unc | BU |
|---|---|---|---|---|---|---|
| ND(1972)B Proof | 3,000 | Value: 300 | | | | |

**25 DOLLARS** **KM# 19a** **Composition:** 0.9990 Gold

| Date | Mintage | F | VF | XF | Unc | BU |
|---|---|---|---|---|---|---|
| 1964B L Proof | 100 | Value: 350 | | | | |

**Note:** Of the total issue, 10,200 were struck of .900 fine gold and bear the "B" mint mark of the Bern Mint below the date, while 100 were struck (restrikes suspected) as proofs of .999 fine gold and are designated by the presence of a small "L" above date

**25 DOLLARS** **KM# 21** **Weight:** 23.3120 g. **Composition:** 0.9000 Gold .6746 oz. AGW **Subject:** 70th Birthday of President Tubman

| Date | Mintage | F | VF | XF | Unc | BU |
|---|---|---|---|---|---|---|
| 1965 | 3,000 | — | — | — | 325 | — |

**25 DOLLARS** **KM# 323** **Weight:** 77.7587 g. **Composition:** 0.9990 Silver 2.5000 oz. ASW **Subject:** 25th Anniversary - Standard Catalog of World Coins **Obverse:** National arms **Reverse:** Children, Globe, World Coins

| Date | Mintage | F | VF | XF | Unc | BU |
|---|---|---|---|---|---|---|
| 1997 Proof | 2,500 | Value: 37.50 | | | | |

**30 DOLLARS** **KM# 22** **Weight:** 15.0000 g. **Composition:** 0.9000 Gold .4340 oz. AGW **Subject:** 70th Birthday of President Tubman

| Date | Mintage | F | VF | XF | Unc | BU |
|---|---|---|---|---|---|---|
| 1965 Proof | 400 | Value: 225 | | | | |

**50 DOLLARS** **KM# 69** **Weight:** 155.5150 g. **Composition:** 0.9990 Silver 5.0000 oz. ASW **Subject:** President Bill Clinton **Note:** Similar to 10 Dollars, KM#68.

| Date | Mintage | F | VF | XF | Unc | BU |
|---|---|---|---|---|---|---|
| 1993 Proof | — | Value: 85.00 | | | | |

**50 DOLLARS** **KM# 251** **Weight:** 3.1103 g. **Composition:** 0.9990 Gold .1000 oz. AGW **Subject:** Dalai Lama **Note:** Similar to 100 Dollars, KM#252.

| Date | Mintage | F | VF | XF | Unc | BU |
|---|---|---|---|---|---|---|
| 1996 Proof | 10,000 | Value: 110 | | | | |

**50 DOLLARS** **KM# 410.1** **Composition:** Copper-Nickel **Obverse:** National arms **Reverse:** Face on Mars with rough texture

| Date | Mintage | F | VF | XF | Unc | BU |
|---|---|---|---|---|---|---|
| 1996 | — | — | — | — | 15.00 | — |

**50 DOLLARS** **KM# 410.2** **Composition:** Copper-Nickel **Obverse:** National arms **Reverse:** Face on Mars with smooth texture

| Date | Mintage | F | VF | XF | Unc | BU |
|---|---|---|---|---|---|---|
| 1996 | — | — | — | — | 15.00 | — |

**50 DOLLARS** **KM# 231** **Weight:** 3.1103 g. **Composition:** 0.9990 Gold .1000 oz. AGW **Subject:** Formula One **Reverse:** Ayrton Senna **Note:** Similar to 10 Dollars, KM#229.

| Date | Mintage | F | VF | XF | Unc | BU |
|---|---|---|---|---|---|---|
| 1996 Proof | 10,000 | Value: 110 | | | | |

**50 DOLLARS** **KM# 316** **Weight:** 3.1103 g. **Composition:** 0.9990 Gold .1000 oz. AGW **Subject:** Return of Hong Kong to China **Note:** Similar to 10 Dollars, KM#314.

| Date | Mintage | F | VF | XF | Unc | BU |
|---|---|---|---|---|---|---|
| 1997 Proof | — | Value: 100 | | | | |

**50 DOLLARS** **KM# 366** **Weight:** 3.1103 g. **Composition:** 0.9990 Gold .1000 oz. AGW **Subject:** RMS Titanic **Obverse:** National arms **Reverse:** Ship sinking **Note:** Similar to 20 Dollars, KM#364.

| Date | Mintage | F | VF | XF | Unc | BU |
|---|---|---|---|---|---|---|
| 1998 Proof | Est. 2,000 | Value: 115 | | | | |

**50 DOLLARS** **KM# 419** **Weight:** 3.1103 g. **Composition:** 0.9990 Gold .1000 oz. AGW **Subject:** Return of Macao to China **Obverse:** National arms **Reverse:** Dragon and phoenix **Note:** Similar to 10 Dollars, KM#408.

| Date | Mintage | F | VF | XF | Unc | BU |
|---|---|---|---|---|---|---|
| 1999 Proof | 10,000 | Value: 100 | | | | |

**100 DOLLARS** **KM# 33** **Weight:** 6.0000 g. **Composition:** 0.9000 Gold .1736 oz. AGW **Subject:** Inauguration of President Tolbert

| Date | Mintage | F | VF | XF | Unc | BU |
|---|---|---|---|---|---|---|
| 1976 Proof | 175 | Value: 225 | | | | |

**100 DOLLARS** **KM# 36** **Weight:** 10.9300 g. **Composition:** 0.9000 Gold .3163 oz. AGW **Subject:** 130th Anniversary of the Republic

| Date | Mintage | F | VF | XF | Unc | BU |
|---|---|---|---|---|---|---|
| 1977FM (U) | 787 | — | — | — | 200 | — |
| 1977FM (P) | 4,250 | Value: 145 | | | | |

**100 DOLLARS** **KM# 37** **Weight:** 10.9300 g. **Composition:** 0.9000 Gold .3163 oz. AGW **Subject:** Organization of African Unity **Reverse:** Summit Conference

| Date | Mintage | F | VF | XF | Unc | BU |
|---|---|---|---|---|---|---|
| 1979FM (P) | 1,656 | Value: 160 | | | | |

**100 DOLLARS** **KM# 38** **Weight:** 11.2000 g. **Composition:** 0.9000 Gold .3241 oz. AGW **Subject:** Organization of African Unity **Reverse:** Elephant

| Date | Mintage | F | VF | XF | Unc | BU |
|---|---|---|---|---|---|---|
| 1979FM (P) | — | Value: 200 | | | | |

**100 DOLLARS** **KM# 50** **Weight:** 10.9300 g. **Composition:** 0.9000 Gold .3163 oz. AGW **Subject:** 5th Anniversary of Government **Reverse:** Leopard

| Date | Mintage | F | VF | XF | Unc | BU |
|---|---|---|---|---|---|---|
| 1985FM (P) | 409 | Value: 450 | | | | |

**100 DOLLARS** **KM# 61** **Weight:** 7.1300 g. **Composition:** 0.9000 Gold .2063 oz. AGW **Series:** Decade For Women **Reverse:** Woman mashing grain

| Date | Mintage | F | VF | XF | Unc | BU |
|---|---|---|---|---|---|---|
| 1985 Proof | 318 | Value: 200 | | | | |

**100 DOLLARS** **KM# 70** **Weight:** 311.0300 g. **Composition:** 0.9990 Silver 10.0000 oz. ASW **Subject:** President Bill Clinton

| Date | Mintage | F | VF | XF | Unc | BU |
|---|---|---|---|---|---|---|
| 1993 Proof | — | Value: 165 | | | | |

**100 DOLLARS** **KM# 100** **Weight:** 6.2200 g. **Composition:** 0.9990 Gold .2000 oz. AGW **Series:** Preserve Planet Earth **Reverse:** Protoceratops

| Date | Mintage | F | VF | XF | Unc | BU |
|---|---|---|---|---|---|---|
| 1993 Proof | Est. 7,500 | Value: 165 | | | | |

**100 DOLLARS** **KM# 111** **Weight:** 6.2200 g. **Composition:** 0.9990 Gold .2000 oz. AGW **Series:** Preserve Planet Earth **Reverse:** Corythosaurus

| Date | Mintage | F | VF | XF | Unc | BU |
|---|---|---|---|---|---|---|
| 1993 Proof | 7,500 | Value: 165 | | | | |

**100 DOLLARS** **KM# 114** **Weight:** 6.2200 g. **Composition:** 0.9990 Gold .2000 oz. AGW **Series:** Preserve Planet Earth **Reverse:** Atchaeopteryx **Note:** Incorrect spelling.

| Date | Mintage | F | VF | XF | Unc | BU |
|---|---|---|---|---|---|---|
| 1993 Proof | Est. 7,500 | Value: 165 | | | | |

**100 DOLLARS** **KM# 117** **Weight:** 6.2200 g. **Composition:** 0.9990 Gold .2000 oz. AGW **Series:** Preserve Planet Earth **Reverse:** Archaeopteryx **Note:** Correct spelling.

| Date | Mintage | F | VF | XF | Unc | BU |
|---|---|---|---|---|---|---|
| 1994 Proof | 7,500 | Value: 165 | | | | |

**100 DOLLARS** **KM# 120** **Weight:** 6.2200 g. **Composition:** 0.9990 Gold .2000 oz. AGW **Series:** Preserve Planet Earth **Reverse:** Gorillas **Note:** Similar to 10 Dollars, KM#120.

| Date | Mintage | F | VF | XF | Unc | BU |
|---|---|---|---|---|---|---|
| 1994 Proof | Est. 7,500 | Value: 165 | | | | |

**100 DOLLARS** **KM# 123** **Weight:** 6.2200 g. **Composition:** 0.9990 Gold .2000 oz. AGW **Series:** Preserve Planet Earth **Reverse:** Pygmy Hippopotami **Note:** Similar to 10 Dollars, KM#122.

| Date | Mintage | F | VF | XF | Unc | BU |
|---|---|---|---|---|---|---|
| 1994 Proof | Est. 7,500 | Value: 165 | | | | |

**100 DOLLARS** **KM# 126** **Weight:** 6.2200 g. **Composition:** 0.9990 Gold .2000 oz. AGW **Series:** Preserve Planet Earth **Reverse:** Trionyx Turtle **Note:** Similar to 10 Dollars, KM#125.

| Date | Mintage | F | VF | XF | Unc | BU |
|---|---|---|---|---|---|---|
| 1994 Proof | Est. 7,500 | Value: 165 | | | | |

**100 DOLLARS** **KM# 130** **Weight:** 6.2200 g. **Composition:** 0.9990 Gold .2000 oz. AGW **Subject:** Star Trek **Reverse:** Captains Kirk and Picard **Note:** Similar to 10 Dollars, KM#129.

| Date | Mintage | F | VF | XF | Unc | BU |
|---|---|---|---|---|---|---|
| 1995 Proof | — | Value: 175 | | | | |

**100 DOLLARS** **KM# 135** **Weight:** 6.2200 g. **Composition:** 0.9990 Gold .2000 oz. AGW **Series:** Preserve Planet Earth **Reverse:** Leopard; Similar to 10 Dollars, KM#134

| Date | Mintage | F | VF | XF | Unc | BU |
|---|---|---|---|---|---|---|
| 1995 Proof | Est. 7,500 | Value: 165 | | | | |

**100 DOLLARS** **KM# 138** **Weight:** 6.2200 g. **Composition:** 0.9990 Gold .2000 oz. AGW **Series:** Preserve Planet Earth **Reverse:** Storks; Similar to 10 Dollars, KM#137

| Date | Mintage | F | VF | XF | Unc | BU |
|---|---|---|---|---|---|---|
| 1995 Proof | Est. 7,500 | Value: 165 | | | | |

**100 DOLLARS** **KM# 150** **Weight:** 6.2200 g. **Composition:** 0.9990 Gold .2000 oz. AGW **Subject:** Sir Winston Churchill **Reverse:** Similar to 10 Dollars, KM#145

| Date | Mintage | F | VF | XF | Unc | BU |
|---|---|---|---|---|---|---|
| 1995 Proof | Est. 7,500 | Value: 125 | | | | |

**100 DOLLARS** **KM# 151** **Weight:** 6.2200 g. **Composition:** 0.9990 Gold .2000 oz. AGW **Subject:** President Franklin D. Roosevelt **Reverse:** Similar to 10 Dollars, KM#146

| Date | Mintage | F | VF | XF | Unc | BU |
|---|---|---|---|---|---|---|
| 1995 Proof | Est. 7,500 | Value: 125 | | | | |

**100 DOLLARS** **KM# 152** **Weight:** 6.2200 g. **Composition:** 0.9990 Gold .2000 oz. AGW **Subject:** General George Patton **Reverse:** Similar to 10 Dollars, KM#147

| Date | Mintage | F | VF | XF | Unc | BU |
|---|---|---|---|---|---|---|
| 1995 Proof | Est. 7,500 | Value: 125 | | | | |

**100 DOLLARS** **KM# 153** **Weight:** 6.2200 g. **Composition:** 0.9990 Gold .2000 oz. AGW **Subject:** President Harry S. Truman **Reverse:** Similar to 10 Dollars, KM#148

| Date | Mintage | F | VF | XF | Unc | BU |
|---|---|---|---|---|---|---|
| 1995 Proof | Est. 7,500 | Value: 125 | | | | |

**100 DOLLARS** **KM# 154** **Weight:** 6.2200 g. **Composition:** 0.9990 Gold .2000 oz. AGW **Subject:** President Chartles de Gaulle **Reverse:** Similar to 10 Dollars, KM#149

| Date | Mintage | F | VF | XF | Unc | BU |
|---|---|---|---|---|---|---|
| 1995 Proof | Est. 7,500 | Value: 125 | | | | |

**100 DOLLARS** **KM# 160** **Weight:** 6.2200 g. **Composition:** 0.9990 Gold .2000 oz. AGW **Subject:** Dr. Sun Yat-sen **Reverse:** Similar to 10 Dollars, KM#159

| Date | Mintage | F | VF | XF | Unc | BU |
|---|---|---|---|---|---|---|
| 1995 Proof | Est. 7,500 | Value: 125 | | | | |

**100 DOLLARS** **KM# 163** **Weight:** 6.2200 g. **Composition:** 0.9990 Gold .2000 oz. AGW **Subject:** General Chiang Kai-shek **Reverse:** Similar to 10 Dollars, KM#162

| Date | Mintage | F | VF | XF | Unc | BU |
|---|---|---|---|---|---|---|
| 1995 Proof | Est. 7,500 | Value: 125 | | | | |

**100 DOLLARS** **KM# 166** **Weight:** 6.2200 g. **Composition:** 0.9990 Gold .2000 oz. AGW **Subject:** Cairo Conference **Reverse:** Chiang Kai-shek - Roosevelt - Churchill

| Date | Mintage | F | VF | XF | Unc | BU |
|---|---|---|---|---|---|---|
| 1995 Proof | Est. 7,500 | Value: 125 | | | | |

**100 DOLLARS** **KM# 175** **Weight:** 6.2200 g. **Composition:** 0.9990 Gold .2000 oz. AGW **Subject:** 375th Anniversary - Pilgrim Fathers **Reverse:** Mayflower; Similar to 10 Dollars, KM#171

| Date | Mintage | F | VF | XF | Unc | BU |
|---|---|---|---|---|---|---|
| 1995 Proof | 7,500 | Value: 120 | | | | |

**100 DOLLARS** **KM# 176** **Weight:** 6.2200 g. **Composition:** 0.9990 Gold .2000 oz. AGW **Subject:** 375th Anniversary - Pilgrim Fathers **Reverse:** Cape Cod and Pilgrims in Skiff

| Date | Mintage | F | VF | XF | Unc | BU |
|---|---|---|---|---|---|---|
| 1995 Proof | 7,500 | Value: 120 | | | | |

**100 DOLLARS** KM# 177 **Weight:** 6.2200 g. **Composition:** 0.9990 Gold .2000 oz. AGW **Subject:** 375th Anniversary - Pilgrim Fathers **Reverse:** Pilgrim Landing Party

| Date | Mintage | F | VF | XF | Unc | BU |
|---|---|---|---|---|---|---|
| 1995 Proof | 7,500 | Value: 120 | | | | |

**100 DOLLARS** KM# 178 **Weight:** 6.2200 g. **Composition:** 0.9990 Gold .2000 oz. AGW **Subject:** 375th Anniversary - Pilgrim Fathers **Reverse:** First Thanksgiving Scene

| Date | Mintage | F | VF | XF | Unc | BU |
|---|---|---|---|---|---|---|
| 1995 Proof | 7,500 | Value: 120 | | | | |

**100 DOLLARS** KM# 209 **Weight:** 6.2200 g. **Composition:** 0.9990 Gold .2000 oz. AGW **Subject:** Star Trek **Reverse:** Starships NCC-1701 and NCC-1701D

| Date | Mintage | F | VF | XF | Unc | BU |
|---|---|---|---|---|---|---|
| 1996 Proof | Est. 7,500 | Value: 150 | | | | |

**100 DOLLARS** KM# 215 **Weight:** 6.2200 g. **Composition:** 0.9990 Gold .2000 oz. AGW **Subject:** Star Trek **Reverse:** LaForge and Data

| Date | Mintage | F | VF | XF | Unc | BU |
|---|---|---|---|---|---|---|
| 1996 Proof | 25,000 | Value: 150 | | | | |

**100 DOLLARS** KM# 252 **Weight:** 6.2200 g. **Composition:** 0.9990 Gold .2000 oz. AGW **Subject:** Dalai Lama

| Date | Mintage | F | VF | XF | Unc | BU |
|---|---|---|---|---|---|---|
| 1996 Proof | Est. 7,500 | Value: 115 | | | | |

**100 DOLLARS** KM# 253 **Weight:** 6.2200 g. **Composition:** 0.9990 Gold .2000 oz. AGW **Subject:** Kin Rama IX of Thailand **Reverse:** King seated on radiant throne

| Date | Mintage | F | VF | XF | Unc | BU |
|---|---|---|---|---|---|---|
| 1996 Proof | Est. 7,500 | Value: 115 | | | | |

**100 DOLLARS** KM# 212 **Weight:** 6.2200 g. **Composition:** 0.9990 Gold .2000 oz. AGW **Subject:** Star Trek **Reverse:** Scott and McCoy

| Date | Mintage | F | VF | XF | Unc | BU |
|---|---|---|---|---|---|---|
| 1996 Proof | 7,500 | Value: 150 | | | | |

**100 DOLLARS** KM# 240 **Weight:** 6.2200 g. **Composition:** 0.9990 Gold .2000 oz. AGW **Subject:** General Chiang Kai-shek **Note:** Similar to 10 Dollars, KM#162.

| Date | Mintage | F | VF | XF | Unc | BU |
|---|---|---|---|---|---|---|
| 1996 Proof | Est. 7,500 | Value: 120 | | | | |

**100 DOLLARS** KM# 218 **Weight:** 6.2200 g. **Composition:** 0.9990 Gold .2000 oz. AGW **Subject:** Star Trek **Reverse:** Spock and Uhura **Note:** Similar to 10 Dollars, KM#217.

| Date | Mintage | F | VF | XF | Unc | BU |
|---|---|---|---|---|---|---|
| 1996 Proof | 25,000 | Value: 150 | | | | |

**100 DOLLARS** KM# 221 **Weight:** 6.2200 g. **Composition:** 0.9990 Gold .2000 oz. AGW **Subject:** Star Trek **Reverse:** Worf and Dr. Crusher **Note:** Similar to 10 Dollars, KM#220.

| Date | Mintage | F | VF | XF | Unc | BU |
|---|---|---|---|---|---|---|
| 1996 Proof | 25,000 | Value: 150 | | | | |

**100 DOLLARS** KM# 224 **Weight:** 6.2200 g. **Composition:** 0.9990 Gold .2000 oz. AGW **Subject:** Preserve Planet Earth **Reverse:** Grey Parrot **Note:** Similar to 10 Dollars, KM#223.

| Date | Mintage | F | VF | XF | Unc | BU |
|---|---|---|---|---|---|---|
| 1996 Proof | 25,000 | Value: 165 | | | | |

**100 DOLLARS** KM# 227 **Weight:** 6.2200 g. **Composition:** 0.9990 Gold .2000 oz. AGW **Subject:** Preserve Planet Earth **Reverse:** Love Birds **Note:** Similar to 10 Dollars, KM#226.

| Date | Mintage | F | VF | XF | Unc | BU |
|---|---|---|---|---|---|---|
| 1996 Proof | 25,000 | Value: 165 | | | | |

**100 DOLLARS** KM# 232 **Weight:** 6.2200 g. **Composition:** 0.9990 Gold .2000 oz. AGW **Subject:** Formula One **Reverse:** Ayrton Senna **Note:** Similar to 10 Dollars, KM#229.

| Date | Mintage | F | VF | XF | Unc | BU |
|---|---|---|---|---|---|---|
| 1996 Proof | 20,000 | Value: 165 | | | | |

**100 DOLLARS** KM# 237 **Weight:** 6.2200 g. **Composition:** 0.9990 Gold .2000 oz. AGW **Subject:** Dr. Sun Yat-sen **Note:** Similar to 10 Dollars, KM#236.

| Date | Mintage | F | VF | XF | Unc | BU |
|---|---|---|---|---|---|---|
| 1996 Proof | Est. 7,500 | Value: 120 | | | | |

**100 DOLLARS** KM# 243 **Weight:** 6.2200 g. **Composition:** 0.9990 Gold .2000 oz. AGW **Subject:** President Chiang Ching-kuo **Note:** Similar to 10 Dollars, KM#242.

| Date | Mintage | F | VF | XF | Unc | BU |
|---|---|---|---|---|---|---|
| 1996 Proof | Est. 7,500 | Value: 120 | | | | |

**100 DOLLARS** KM# 246 **Weight:** 6.2200 g. **Composition:** 0.9990 Gold .2000 oz. AGW **Subject:** President Lee Teng-hui **Note:** Similar to 10 Dollars, KM#245.

| Date | Mintage | F | VF | XF | Unc | BU |
|---|---|---|---|---|---|---|
| 1996 Proof | Est. 7,500 | Value: 120 | | | | |

**100 DOLLARS** KM# 259 **Weight:** 6.2200 g. **Composition:** 0.9990 Gold .2000 oz. AGW **Subject:** Mao Zedong Proclaiming People's Republic **Note:** Similar to 10 Dollars, KM#258.

| Date | Mintage | F | VF | XF | Unc | BU |
|---|---|---|---|---|---|---|
| 1996 Proof | 1,996 | Value: 135 | | | | |

**100 DOLLARS** KM# 312 **Weight:** 6.2200 g. **Composition:** 0.9990 Gold .2000 oz. AGW **Subject:** Mahatma Gandhi **Note:** Similar to 10 Dollars, KM#311.

| Date | Mintage | F | VF | XF | Unc | BU |
|---|---|---|---|---|---|---|
| 1997 Proof | Est. 5,000 | Value: 145 | | | | |

**100 DOLLARS** KM# 317 **Weight:** 6.2200 g. **Composition:** 0.9990 Gold .2000 oz. AGW **Subject:** Return of Hong Kong to China **Note:** Similar to 10 Dollars, KM#314.

| Date | Mintage | F | VF | XF | Unc | BU |
|---|---|---|---|---|---|---|
| 1997 Proof | Est. 5,000 | Value: 145 | | | | |

**100 DOLLARS** KM# 326 **Weight:** 6.2200 g. **Composition:** 0.9990 Gold .2000 oz. AGW **Subject:** Jurassic Park **Obverse:** National arms **Reverse:** Stegosaurus **Note:** Similar to 10 Dollars, KM#325.

| Date | Mintage | F | VF | XF | Unc | BU |
|---|---|---|---|---|---|---|
| 1997 Proof | Est. 2,500 | Value: 175 | | | | |

**100 DOLLARS** KM# 329 **Weight:** 6.2200 g. **Composition:** 0.9990 Gold .2000 oz. AGW **Subject:** Golden Wedding Anniversary **Obverse:** National arms **Reverse:** E & P initials above 2 shields **Note:** Similar to 10 Dollars, KM#328.

| Date | Mintage | F | VF | XF | Unc | BU |
|---|---|---|---|---|---|---|
| 1997 Proof | Est. 3,500 | Value: 175 | | | | |

**100 DOLLARS** KM# 332 **Weight:** 6.2200 g. **Composition:** 0.9990 Gold .2000 oz. AGW **Subject:** Golden Wedding Anniversary **Obverse:** National arms **Reverse:** Royal couple with horse **Note:** Similar to 10 Dollars, KM#331.

| Date | Mintage | F | VF | XF | Unc | BU |
|---|---|---|---|---|---|---|
| 1997 Proof | Est. 3,500 | Value: 175 | | | | |

**100 DOLLARS** KM# 335 **Weight:** 6.2200 g. **Composition:** 0.9990 Gold .2000 oz. AGW **Subject:** Golden Wedding Anniversary **Obverse:** National arms **Reverse:** Royal couple with dogs **Note:** Similar to 10 Dollars, KM#334.

| Date | Mintage | F | VF | XF | Unc | BU |
|---|---|---|---|---|---|---|
| 1997 Proof | Est. 3,500 | Value: 175 | | | | |

**100 DOLLARS** KM# 338 **Weight:** 6.2200 g. **Composition:** 0.9990 Gold .2000 oz. AGW **Subject:** Golden Wedding Anniversary **Obverse:** National arms **Reverse:** Royal couple with children **Note:** Similar to 10 Dollars, KM#337.

| Date | Mintage | F | VF | XF | Unc | BU |
|---|---|---|---|---|---|---|
| 1997 Proof | Est. 3,500 | Value: 175 | | | | |

**100 DOLLARS** KM# 370 **Weight:** 6.2200 g. **Composition:** 0.9990 Gold .2000 oz. AGW **Subject:** Star Trek - The Next Generation **Obverse:** National arms **Reverse:** Romulan Warbird **Note:** Similar to 10 Dollars, KM#369.

| Date | Mintage | F | VF | XF | Unc | BU |
|---|---|---|---|---|---|---|
| 1997 Proof | Est. 7,500 | Value: 150 | | | | |

**100 DOLLARS** KM# 373 **Weight:** 6.2200 g. **Composition:** 0.9990 Gold .2000 oz. AGW **Subject:** Star Trek - The Next Generation **Obverse:** National arms **Reverse:** Klingon Attack Cruiser **Note:** Similar to 10 Dollars, KM#372.

| Date | Mintage | F | VF | XF | Unc | BU |
|---|---|---|---|---|---|---|
| 1997 Proof | Est. 7,500 | Value: 150 | | | | |

**100 DOLLARS** KM# 376 **Weight:** 6.2200 g. **Composition:** 0.9990 Gold .2000 oz. AGW **Subject:** Star Trek - The Next Generation **Obverse:** National arms **Reverse:** U.S.S. Enterprise NCC-1701-D **Note:** Similar to 10 Dollars, KM#375.

| Date | Mintage | F | VF | XF | Unc | BU |
|---|---|---|---|---|---|---|
| 1997 Proof | Est. 7,500 | Value: 150 | | | | |

**100 DOLLARS** KM# 379 **Weight:** 6.2200 g. **Composition:** 0.9990 Gold .2000 oz. AGW **Subject:** Star Trek - The Next Generation **Obverse:** National arms **Reverse:** Klingon Bird of Prey **Note:** Similar to 10 Dollars, KM#378.

| Date | Mintage | F | VF | XF | Unc | BU |
|---|---|---|---|---|---|---|
| 1997 Proof | Est. 7,500 | Value: 150 | | | | |

**100 DOLLARS** KM# 382 **Weight:** 6.2200 g. **Composition:** 0.9990 Gold .2000 oz. AGW **Subject:** Star Trek - The Next Generation **Obverse:** National arms **Reverse:** Borg Cube **Note:** Similar to 10 Dollars, KM#381.

| Date | Mintage | F | VF | XF | Unc | BU |
|---|---|---|---|---|---|---|
| 1997 Proof | Est. 7,500 | Value: 150 | | | | |

**100 DOLLARS** KM# 385 **Weight:** 6.2200 g. **Composition:** 0.9990 Gold .2000 oz. AGW **Subject:** Star Trek - The Next Generation **Obverse:** National arms **Reverse:** Ferengi Marauder **Note:** Similar to 10 Dollars, KM#384.

| Date | Mintage | F | VF | XF | Unc | BU |
|---|---|---|---|---|---|---|
| 1997 Proof | Est. 7,500 | Value: 150 | | | | |

**100 DOLLARS** KM# 473 **Weight:** 6.2200 g. **Composition:** 0.9990 Gold .2000 oz. AGW **Subject:** Princess Diana in Memoriam

| Date | Mintage | F | VF | XF | Unc | BU |
|---|---|---|---|---|---|---|
| 1997 Proof | — | Value: 165 | | | | |

**100 DOLLARS** KM# 322 **Weight:** 6.2200 g. **Composition:** 0.9990 Gold .2000 oz. AGW **Subject:** Fiftieth Anniversary of the Kon-Tiki Expedition **Note:** Similar to 1 Dollar, KM#320.

| Date | Mintage | F | VF | XF | Unc | BU |
|---|---|---|---|---|---|---|
| 1997 Proof | Est. 7,500 | Value: 145 | | | | |

**100 DOLLARS** KM# 365 **Weight:** 6.2200 g. **Composition:** 0.9990 Gold .2000 oz. AGW **Subject:** RMS Titanic **Obverse:** National arms **Reverse:** Ship Sinking **Note:** Similar to 20 Dollars, KM#364.

| Date | Mintage | F | VF | XF | Unc | BU |
|---|---|---|---|---|---|---|
| 1998 Proof | Est. 5,000 | Value: 165 | | | | |

**100 DOLLARS** KM# 388 **Weight:** 6.2200 g. **Composition:** 0.9990 Gold .2000 oz. AGW **Subject:** President Ronald Reagan **Obverse:** National arms **Reverse:** Lincoln Statue **Note:** Similar to 10 Dollars, KM#387.

| Date | Mintage | F | VF | XF | Unc | BU |
|---|---|---|---|---|---|---|
| 1998 Proof | Est. 7,500 | Value: 165 | | | | |

**100 DOLLARS** KM# 403 **Weight:** 6.2200 g. **Composition:** 0.9990 Gold .2000 oz. AGW **Subject:** Christopher Columbus **Obverse:** National arms **Reverse:** Portrait, ship **Note:** Similar to 10 Dollars, KM#402.

| Date | Mintage | F | VF | XF | Unc | BU |
|---|---|---|---|---|---|---|
| 1999 Proof | 10,000 | Value: 175 | | | | |

**100 DOLLARS** KM# 406 **Weight:** 6.2200 g. **Composition:** 0.9990 Gold .2000 oz. AGW **Subject:** Captain James Cook **Obverse:** National arms **Reverse:** Portrait, ship, map **Note:** Similar to 10 Dollars, KM#403.

| Date | Mintage | F | VF | XF | Unc | BU |
|---|---|---|---|---|---|---|
| 1999 Proof | 10,000 | Value: 175 | | | | |

**100 DOLLARS** KM# 409 **Weight:** 6.2200 g. **Composition:** 0.9990 Gold .2000 oz. AGW **Subject:** Return of Macao to China **Obverse:** National arms **Reverse:** Dragon and phoenix **Note:** Similar to 10 Dollars, KM#408.

| Date | Mintage | F | VF | XF | Unc | BU |
|---|---|---|---|---|---|---|
| 1999 Proof | 10,000 | Value: 175 | | | | |

**100 DOLLARS** KM# 415 **Weight:** 6.2200 g. **Composition:** 0.9990 Gold .2000 oz. AGW **Subject:** The Wedding of the Prince **Obverse:** National arms **Reverse:** Couple in carriage **Note:** Similar to 10 Dollars, KM#414.

| Date | Mintage | F | VF | XF | Unc | BU |
|---|---|---|---|---|---|---|
| 1999 Proof | Est. 5,000 | Value: 175 | | | | |

**100 DOLLARS** KM# 392 **Weight:** 6.2200 g. **Composition:** 0.9990 Gold .2000 oz. AGW **Subject:** Year of the Rabbit **Obverse:** National arms **Reverse:** Rabbit running left **Note:** Similar to 20 Dollars, KM#389.

| Date | Mintage | F | VF | XF | Unc | BU |
|---|---|---|---|---|---|---|
| 1999 Proof | 5,000 | Value: 165 | | | | |

**100 DOLLARS** KM# 393 **Weight:** 6.2200 g. **Composition:** 0.9990 Gold .2000 oz. AGW **Subject:** Year of the Rabbit **Obverse:** National arms **Reverse:** Rabbit sitting **Note:** Similar to 20 Dollars, KM#390.

| Date | Mintage | F | VF | XF | Unc | BU |
|---|---|---|---|---|---|---|
| 1999 Proof | 5,000 | Value: 165 | | | | |

**100 DOLLARS** KM# 394 **Weight:** 6.2200 g. **Composition:** 0.9990 Gold .2000 oz. AGW **Subject:** Year of the Rabbit **Obverse:** National arms **Reverse:** Rabbit running right **Note:** Similar to 20 Dollars, KM#391.

| Date | Mintage | F | VF | XF | Unc | BU |
|---|---|---|---|---|---|---|
| 1999 Proof | 5,000 | Value: 165 | | | | |

**150 DOLLARS** KM# 106 **Weight:** 500.0000 g. **Composition:** 0.9990 Silver 16.0756 oz. ASW **Subject:** Preserve Planet Earth **Reverse:** 2 Brachiosauros **Size:** 85 mm. **Note:** Illustration reduced.

| Date | Mintage | F | VF | XF | Unc | BU |
|---|---|---|---|---|---|---|
| 1993 Proof | 121 | Value: 300 | | | | |

**200 DOLLARS** KM# 34 **Weight:** 12.0000 g. **Composition:** 0.9000 Gold .3472 oz. AGW **Subject:** Inauguration of President Tolbert

| Date | Mintage | F | VF | XF | Unc | BU |
|---|---|---|---|---|---|---|
| 1976 Proof | 100 | Value: 350 | | | | |

**200 DOLLARS** KM# 46 **Weight:** 15.9800 g. **Composition:** 0.9170 Gold .4712 oz. AGW **Subject:** Year of the Scout

| Date | Mintage | F | VF | XF | Unc | BU |
|---|---|---|---|---|---|---|
| ND(1983) | — | — | — | — | 325 | — |
| ND(1983) Proof | — | Value: 425 | | | | |

**200 DOLLARS** KM# 49 **Weight:** 15.9800 g. **Composition:** 0.9000 Gold .4624 oz. AGW **Series:** International Year of Disabled Persons

| Date | Mintage | F | VF | XF | Unc | BU |
|---|---|---|---|---|---|---|
| 1983 | 500 | — | — | — | 325 | — |
| 1983 Proof | 500 | Value: 475 | | | | |

**200 DOLLARS** KM# 395 **Weight:** 12.4444 g. **Composition:** 0.9999 Gold .4000 oz. AGW **Subject:** Year of the Rabbit **Obverse:** National arms **Reverse:** Rabbit running left **Note:** Similar to 20 Dollars, KM#389.

| Date | Mintage | F | VF | XF | Unc | BU |
|---|---|---|---|---|---|---|
| 1999 Proof | 1,500 | Value: 325 | | | | |

**200 DOLLARS** KM# 396 **Weight:** 12.4444 g. **Composition:** 0.9999 Gold .4000 oz. AGW **Subject:** Year of the Rabbit **Obverse:** National arms **Reverse:** Rabbit sitting **Note:** Similar to 20 Dollars, KM#390.

| Date | Mintage | F | VF | XF | Unc | BU |
|---|---|---|---|---|---|---|
| 1999 Proof | 1,500 | Value: 325 | | | | |

**200 DOLLARS** KM# 397 **Weight:** 12.4444 g. **Composition:** 0.9999 Gold .4000 oz. AGW **Subject:** Year of the Rabbit **Obverse:** National arms **Reverse:** Rabbit running right **Note:** Similar to 20 Dollars, KM#391.

| Date | Mintage | F | VF | XF | Unc | BU |
|---|---|---|---|---|---|---|
| 1999 Proof | 1,500 | Value: 325 | | | | |

**250 DOLLARS** KM# 52 **Weight:** 15.5000 g. **Composition:** 0.9990 Gold .5000 oz. AGW **Subject:** President John F. Kennedy

| Date | Mintage | F | VF | XF | Unc | BU |
|---|---|---|---|---|---|---|
| 1988 Proof | 5,000 | Value: 350 | | | | |

**250 DOLLARS** KM# 56 **Weight:** 15.5000 g. **Composition:** 0.9990 Gold .5000 oz. AGW **Subject:** President Samuel Kanyon Doe

| Date | Mintage | F | VF | XF | Unc | BU |
|---|---|---|---|---|---|---|
| 1988 Proof | Est. 5,000 | Value: 365 | | | | |

**250 DOLLARS** KM# 58 **Weight:** 15.5000 g. **Composition:** 0.9990 Gold .5000 oz. AGW **Subject:** President George Bush

| Date | Mintage | F | VF | XF | Unc | BU |
|---|---|---|---|---|---|---|
| 1989 Proof | 600 | Value: 365 | | | | |

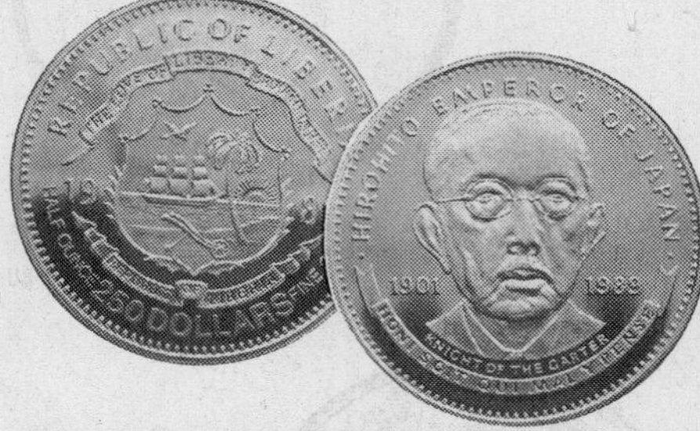

**250 DOLLARS** KM# 60 **Weight:** 15.5000 g. **Composition:** 0.9990 Gold .5000 oz. AGW **Subject:** Emperor Hirohito

| Date | Mintage | F | VF | XF | Unc | BU |
|---|---|---|---|---|---|---|
| 1989 Proof | 600 | Value: 365 | | | | |

**250 DOLLARS** KM# 93 **Weight:** 15.5000 g. **Composition:** 0.9990 Gold .5000 oz. AGW **Subject:** Formula One **Reverse:** Riccardo Patrese; Portrait facing left, car in lower left **Note:** Similar to 10 Dollars, KM#74.

| Date | Mintage | F | VF | XF | Unc | BU |
|---|---|---|---|---|---|---|
| 1992 Proof | Est. 5,000 | Value: 325 | | | | |

**250 DOLLARS** KM# 89 **Weight:** 15.5000 g. **Composition:** 0.9990 Gold .5000 oz. AGW **Subject:** Formula One **Reverse:** Nigel Mansell **Note:** Similar to 10 Dollars, KM#75.

| Date | Mintage | F | VF | XF | Unc | BU |
|---|---|---|---|---|---|---|
| 1992 Proof | Est. 5,000 | Value: 325 | | | | |

**250 DOLLARS** KM# 90 **Weight:** 15.5000 g. **Composition:** 0.9990 Gold .5000 oz. AGW **Subject:** Formula One **Reverse:** Gerhard Berger **Note:** Similar to 10 Dollars, KM#83.

| Date | Mintage | F | VF | XF | Unc | BU |
|---|---|---|---|---|---|---|
| 1992 Proof | Est. 5,000 | Value: 325 | | | | |

**250 DOLLARS** KM# 91 **Weight:** 15.5000 g. **Composition:** 0.9990 Gold .5000 oz. AGW **Subject:** Formula One **Reverse:** Aguri Suzuki; Portrait facing, car in foreground **Note:** Similar to 10 Dollars, KM#84.

| Date | Mintage | F | VF | XF | Unc | BU |
|---|---|---|---|---|---|---|
| 1992 Proof | Est. 5,000 | Value: 325 | | | | |

**250 DOLLARS** KM# 92 **Weight:** 15.5000 g. **Composition:** 0.9990 Gold .5000 oz. AGW **Subject:** Formula One **Reverse:** Ayrton Senna; Portrait facing, car in foreground **Note:** Similar to 10 Dollars, KM#85.

| Date | Mintage | F | VF | XF | Unc | BU |
|---|---|---|---|---|---|---|
| 1992 Proof | Est. 5,000 | Value: 325 | | | | |

**250 DOLLARS** KM# 94 **Weight:** 15.5000 g. **Composition:** 0.9990 Gold .5000 oz. AGW **Subject:** Formula One **Reverse:** Michael Schumacher; Portrait facing left, car at lower left **Note:** Similar to 10 Dollars, KM#86.

| Date | Mintage | F | VF | XF | Unc | BU |
|---|---|---|---|---|---|---|
| 1992 Proof | Est. 5,000 | Value: 325 | | | | |

**250 DOLLARS** KM# 95 **Weight:** 15.5000 g. **Composition:** 0.9990 Gold .5000 oz. AGW **Subject:** Formula One **Reverse:** Alain Prost; Portrait facing left, car in foreground **Note:** Similar to 10 Dollars, KM#87.

| Date | Mintage | F | VF | XF | Unc | BU |
|---|---|---|---|---|---|---|
| 1992 Proof | Est. 5,000 | Value: 325 | | | | |

**250 DOLLARS** KM# 96 **Weight:** 15.5000 g. **Composition:** 0.9990 Gold .5000 oz. AGW **Subject:** Formula One **Reverse:** Ukyo Katayama; Portrait facing, car in foreground **Note:** Similar to 10 Dollars, KM#88.

| Date | Mintage | F | VF | XF | Unc | BU |
|---|---|---|---|---|---|---|
| 1992 Proof | Est. 5,000 | Value: 325 | | | | |

**250 DOLLARS** KM# 71 **Weight:** 15.5000 g. **Composition:** 0.9990 Gold .5000 oz. AGW **Subject:** President Bill Clinton **Reverse:** Portrait right **Note:** Similar to 10 Dollars, KM#68.

| Date | Mintage | F | VF | XF | Unc | BU |
|---|---|---|---|---|---|---|
| 1993 Proof | Est. 5,000 | Value: 325 | | | | |

**250 DOLLARS** KM# 105 **Weight:** 15.5000 g. **Composition:** 0.9990 Gold .5000 oz. AGW **Subject:** President John F. Kennedy **Note:** Similar to 10 Dollars, KM#104.

| Date | Mintage | F | VF | XF | Unc | BU |
|---|---|---|---|---|---|---|
| 1993 Proof | Est. 5,000 | Value: 325 | | | | |

**250 DOLLARS** KM# 181 **Weight:** 15.5000 g. **Composition:** 0.9990 Gold .5000 oz. AGW **Subject:** Formula One **Reverse:** Mika Hakkinen; Similar to 10 Dollars, KM#180

| Date | Mintage | F | VF | XF | Unc | BU |
|---|---|---|---|---|---|---|
| 1995 Proof | Est. 5,000 | Value: 325 | | | | |

**250 DOLLARS** KM# 184 **Weight:** 15.5000 g. **Composition:** 0.9990 Gold .5000 oz. AGW **Subject:** Formula One **Reverse:** Martin Brundle; Similar to 10 Dollars, KM#183

| Date | Mintage | F | VF | XF | Unc | BU |
|---|---|---|---|---|---|---|
| 1995 Proof | Est. 5,000 | Value: 325 | | | | |

**250 DOLLARS** KM# 187 **Weight:** 15.5000 g. **Composition:** 0.9990 Gold .5000 oz. AGW **Subject:** Formula One **Reverse:** Rubens Barricchello; Similar to 10 Dollars, KM#186

| Date | Mintage | F | VF | XF | Unc | BU |
|---|---|---|---|---|---|---|
| 1995 Proof | Est. 5,000 | Value: 325 | | | | |

**250 DOLLARS** KM# 190 **Weight:** 15.5000 g. **Composition:** 0.9990 Gold .5000 oz. AGW **Subject:** Formula One **Reverse:** David Coulthard; Similar to 10 Dollars, KM#189

| Date | Mintage | F | VF | XF | Unc | BU |
|---|---|---|---|---|---|---|
| 1995 Proof | Est. 5,000 | Value: 325 | | | | |

**250 DOLLARS** KM# 193 **Weight:** 15.5000 g. **Composition:** 0.9990 Gold .5000 oz. AGW **Subject:** Formula One **Reverse:** Jean Alesi; Similar to 10 Dollars, KM#192

| Date | Mintage | F | VF | XF | Unc | BU |
|---|---|---|---|---|---|---|
| 1995 Proof | Est. 5,000 | Value: 325 | | | | |

**250 DOLLARS** KM# 203 **Weight:** 15.5000 g. **Composition:** 0.9990 Gold .5000 oz. AGW **Subject:** Formula One **Reverse:** Mark Blundell; Similar to 10 Dollars, KM#199

| Date | Mintage | F | VF | XF | Unc | BU |
|---|---|---|---|---|---|---|
| 1996 Proof | Est. 5,000 | Value: 325 | | | | |

**250 DOLLARS** KM# 204 **Weight:** 15.5000 g. **Composition:** 0.9990 Gold .5000 oz. AGW **Subject:** Formula One **Reverse:** Johnny Herbert **Note:** Similar to 10 Dollars, KM#200.

| Date | Mintage | F | VF | XF | Unc | BU |
|---|---|---|---|---|---|---|
| 1996 Proof | Est. 5,000 | Value: 325 | | | | |

**250 DOLLARS** KM# 205 **Weight:** 15.5000 g. **Composition:** 0.9990 Gold .5000 oz. AGW **Subject:** Formula One **Reverse:** Eddie Irvine **Note:** Similar to 10 Dollars, KM#201.

| Date | Mintage | F | VF | XF | Unc | BU |
|---|---|---|---|---|---|---|
| 1996 Proof | Est. 5,000 | Value: 325 | | | | |

**250 DOLLARS** KM# 206 **Weight:** 15.5000 g. **Composition:** 0.9990 Gold .5000 oz. AGW **Subject:** Formula One **Reverse:** Heinz Frentzen **Note:** Similar to 10 Dollars, KM#202.

| Date | Mintage | F | VF | XF | Unc | BU |
|---|---|---|---|---|---|---|
| 1996 Proof | Est. 5,000 | Value: 325 | | | | |

**250 DOLLARS** KM# 233 **Weight:** 15.5000 g. **Composition:** 0.9990 Gold .5000 oz. AGW **Subject:** Formula One **Reverse:** Ayrton Senna **Note:** Similar to 10 Dollars, KM#229.

| Date | Mintage | F | VF | XF | Unc | BU |
|---|---|---|---|---|---|---|
| 1996 Proof | Est. 5,000 | Value: 325 | | | | |

**250 DOLLARS** KM# 318 **Weight:** 15.5000 g. **Composition:** 0.9990 Gold .5000 oz. AGW **Subject:** Return of Hong Kong **Note:** Similar to 10 Dollars, KM#314.

| Date | Mintage | F | VF | XF | Unc | BU |
|---|---|---|---|---|---|---|
| 1997 Proof | — | Value: 335 | | | | |

**250 DOLLARS** KM# 420 **Weight:** 15.5000 g. **Composition:** 0.9990 Gold .5000 oz. AGW **Subject:** Return of Macao to China **Obverse:** National arms **Reverse:** Dragon and phoenix **Note:** Similar to 10 Dollars, KM#408.

| Date | Mintage | F | VF | XF | Unc | BU |
|---|---|---|---|---|---|---|
| 1999 Proof | Est. 5,000 | Value: 335 | | | | |

**250 DOLLARS** KM# 425 **Weight:** 15.5000 g. **Composition:** 0.9990 Gold .5000 oz. AGW **Subject:** Liberty **Obverse:** National arms **Reverse:** Conjoined busts of President J.F. Kennedy and his son **Note:** Similar to 10 Dollars, KM#424.

| Date | Mintage | F | VF | XF | Unc | BU |
|---|---|---|---|---|---|---|
| 1999 Proof | 375 | Value: 340 | | | | |

**250 DOLLARS** **KM# 439** **Weight:** 15.5517 g. **Composition:** 0.9999 Gold .5000 oz. AGW **Subject:** Taipai, Taiwan Rapid Transit System **Obverse:** National arms above hole* and dragon. **Reverse:** Subway train, logo and tunnel hole.* **Size:** 27 mm. **Note:** Struck at Singapore Mint. *As first done on Albanian coins of 1988.

| Date | Mintage | F | VF | XF | Unc | BU |
|---|---|---|---|---|---|---|
| 1999 Proof | 2,000 | Value: 325 | | | | |

**300 DOLLARS** **KM# 107** **Weight:** 1000.0000 g. **Composition:** 0.9990 Silver 32.1512 oz. ASW **Series:** Preserve Planet Earth **Reverse:** Tyrannosaurus Rex Attaching Triceratops **Size:** 100 mm. **Note:** Illustration reduced.

| Date | Mintage | F | VF | XF | Unc | BU |
|---|---|---|---|---|---|---|
| 1993 Proof | 151 | Value: 700 | | | | |

**300 DOLLARS** **KM# 367** **Weight:** 1000.0000 g. **Composition:** 0.9990 Silver 32.1512 oz. ASW **Subject:** RMS Titanic **Obverse:** National arms **Reverse:** Ship Sinking **Note:** Similar to 20 Dollars, KM#364.

| Date | Mintage | F | VF | XF | Unc | BU |
|---|---|---|---|---|---|---|
| 1998 Proof | Est. 500 | Value: 550 | | | | |

**400 DOLLARS** **KM# 35** **Weight:** 24.0000 g. **Composition:** 0.9000 Gold .6945 oz. AGW **Subject:** Inauguration of President Tolbert

| Date | Mintage | F | VF | XF | Unc | BU |
|---|---|---|---|---|---|---|
| 1976 Proof | 25 | Value: 1,250 | | | | |

**500 DOLLARS** **KM# 234** **Weight:** 31.1035 g. **Composition:** 0.9990 Gold 1.0000 oz. AGW **Subject:** Formula One **Reverse:** Ayrton Senna **Note:** Similar to 10 Dollars, KM#229.

| Date | Mintage | F | VF | XF | Unc | BU |
|---|---|---|---|---|---|---|
| 1996 Proof | Est. 2,500 | Value: 650 | | | | |

**500 DOLLARS** **KM# 421** **Weight:** 31.1035 g. **Composition:** 0.9990 Gold 1.0000 oz. AGW **Subject:** Return of Macao to China **Obverse:** National arms **Reverse:** Dragon and phoenix **Note:** Similar to 10 Dollars, KM#408.

| Date | Mintage | F | VF | XF | Unc | BU |
|---|---|---|---|---|---|---|
| 1999 Proof | Est. 1,000 | Value: 675 | | | | |

**2500 DOLLARS** **KM# 241** **Weight:** 155.5175 g. **Composition:** 0.9990 Gold 5.0000 oz. AGW **Subject:** General Chiang Kai-shek **Note:** Similar to 10 Dollars, KM#162.

| Date | Mintage | F | VF | XF | Unc | BU |
|---|---|---|---|---|---|---|
| 1996 Proof | Est. 250 | Value: 3,000 | | | | |

**2500 DOLLARS** **KM# 235** **Weight:** 155.5175 g. **Composition:** 0.9990 Gold 5.0000 oz. AGW **Subject:** Formula One **Reverse:** Ayrton Senna **Note:** Similar to 10 Dollars, KM#229.

| Date | Mintage | F | VF | XF | Unc | BU |
|---|---|---|---|---|---|---|
| 1996 Proof | Est. 250 | Value: 3,000 | | | | |

**2500 DOLLARS** **KM# 238** **Weight:** 155.5175 g. **Composition:** 0.9990 Gold 5.0000 oz. AGW **Subject:** Dr. Sun Yat-sen **Note:** Similar to 10 Dollars, KM#236.

| Date | Mintage | F | VF | XF | Unc | BU |
|---|---|---|---|---|---|---|
| 1996 Proof | Est. 250 | Value: 3,000 | | | | |

**2500 DOLLARS** **KM# 244** **Weight:** 155.5175 g. **Composition:** 0.9990 Gold 5.0000 oz. AGW **Subject:** President Chiang Ching-kuo **Note:** Similar to 10 Dollars, KM#242.

| Date | Mintage | F | VF | XF | Unc | BU |
|---|---|---|---|---|---|---|
| 1996 Proof | Est. 250 | Value: 3,000 | | | | |

**2500 DOLLARS** **KM# 247** **Weight:** 155.5175 g. **Composition:** 0.9990 Gold 5.0000 oz. AGW **Subject:** President Lee Teng-hui **Note:** Similar to 10 Dollars, KM#245.

| Date | Mintage | F | VF | XF | Unc | BU |
|---|---|---|---|---|---|---|
| 1996 Proof | Est. 250 | Value: 3,000 | | | | |

**2500 DOLLARS** **KM# 319** **Weight:** 155.5175 g. **Composition:** 0.9990 Gold 5.0000 oz. AGW **Subject:** Return of Hong Kong **Note:** Similar to 10 Dollars, KM#314.

| Date | Mintage | F | VF | XF | Unc | BU |
|---|---|---|---|---|---|---|
| 1997 Proof | — | Value: 3,200 | | | | |

**2500 DOLLARS** **KM# 422** **Weight:** 155.5175 g. **Composition:** 0.9990 Gold 5.0000 oz. AGW **Subject:** Return of Macao to China **Obverse:** National arms **Reverse:** Dragon and phoenix **Note:** Similar to 10 Dollars, KM#408.

| Date | Mintage | F | VF | XF | Unc | BU |
|---|---|---|---|---|---|---|
| 1999 Proof | Est. 250 | Value: 3,200 | | | | |

**2500 DOLLARS** **KM# 398** **Weight:** 155.5175 g. **Composition:** 0.9990 Gold 5.0000 oz. AGW **Subject:** Year of the Rabbit **Obverse:** National arms **Reverse:** Rabbit running left **Note:** Similar to 20 Dollars, KM#389.

| Date | Mintage | F | VF | XF | Unc | BU |
|---|---|---|---|---|---|---|
| 1999 Proof | 88 | Value: 3,350 | | | | |

**2500 DOLLARS** **KM# 399** **Weight:** 155.5175 g. **Composition:** 0.9990 Gold 5.0000 oz. AGW **Subject:** Year of the Rabbit **Obverse:** National arms **Reverse:** Rabbit sitting **Note:** Similar to 20 Dollars, KM#390.

| Date | Mintage | F | VF | XF | Unc | BU |
|---|---|---|---|---|---|---|
| 1999 Proof | 88 | Value: 3,350 | | | | |

**2500 DOLLARS** **KM# 400** **Weight:** 155.5175 g. **Composition:** 0.9990 Gold 5.0000 oz. AGW **Subject:** Year of the Rabbit **Obverse:** National arms **Reverse:** Rabbit running right **Note:** Similar to 20 Dollars, KM#391.

| Date | Mintage | F | VF | XF | Unc | BU |
|---|---|---|---|---|---|---|
| 1999 Proof | 88 | Value: 3,350 | | | | |

**2500 DOLLARS** **KM# 440** **Weight:** 155.5175 g. **Composition:** 0.9999 Gold 5.0000 oz. AGW **Subject:** Taipai, Taiwan Rapid Transit System **Obverse:** National arms above dragon. **Reverse:** Dragon around subway train viewing sun with diamond inserts. **Size:** 55 mm. **Note:** Struck at Singapore Mint.

| Date | Mintage | F | VF | XF | Unc | BU |
|---|---|---|---|---|---|---|
| ND(1999) Proof | 50 | — | — | — | — | — |

## MEDALLIC COINAGE

**10 DOLLARS** **KM# M1** **Composition:** Copper-Nickel **Series:** International Games **Reverse:** Weight Lifter

| Date | Mintage | F | VF | XF | Unc | BU |
|---|---|---|---|---|---|---|
| 1984 Proof | — | Value: 11.00 | | | | |

**10 DOLLARS** **KM# M2** **Composition:** Copper-Nickel **Series:** International Games **Reverse:** Basketball

| Date | Mintage | F | VF | XF | Unc | BU |
|---|---|---|---|---|---|---|
| 1984 Proof | — | Value: 10.00 | | | | |

**25 DOLLARS** **KM# M3** **Weight:** 31.3700 g. **Composition:** Silver **Series:** International Games **Reverse:** Basketball

| Date | Mintage | F | VF | XF | Unc | BU |
|---|---|---|---|---|---|---|
| 1984 Proof | — | Value: 100 | | | | |

## PATTERNS

Including off metal strikes

| KM# | Date | Mintage | Identification | Mkt Val |
|---|---|---|---|---|
| Pn55 | 1976 | — | 100 Dollars. Bronze. KM#33. | 250 |
| Pn56 | 1976 | — | 200 Dollars. Bronze. KM#34. | 250 |
| Pn57 | 1976 | — | 400 Dollars. Bronze. KM#35. | 250 |

## PIEFORTS

| KM# | Date | Mintage | Identification | Mkt Val |
|---|---|---|---|---|
| P1 | 1983 | 500 | 2 Dollars. KM#47a. | 75.00 |
| P2 | 1983 | — | 20 Dollars. KM#48. | 100 |
| P3 | 1983 | 100 | 200 Dollars.KM#49. | 800 |

## MINT SETS

| KM# | Date | Mintage | Identification | Issue Price | Mkt Val |
|---|---|---|---|---|---|
| MS1 | 1997 (2) | 4,000 | KM#351-352 | 50.00 | 60.00 |

## PROOF SETS

| KM# | Date | Mintage | Identification | Issue Price | Mkt Val |
|---|---|---|---|---|---|
| PS2 | 1906H (5) | — | KM#5-9 | — | 1,250 |
| PS3 | 1968 (6) | 14,396 | KM#13, 14, 15a.2-18a.2 | 15.25 | 8.00 |
| PS4 | 1969 (6) | 5,056 | KM#13, 14, 15a.2-18a.2 | 15.25 | 8.00 |
| PS5 | 1970 (6) | 3,464 | KM#13, 14, 15a.2-18a.2 | 15.25 | 12.50 |
| PS6 | 1971 (6) | 3,032 | KM#13, 14, 15a.2-18a.2 | 15.25 | 10.00 |
| PS7 | 1972 (6) | 4,866 | KM#13, 14, 15a.2-18a.2 | 15.50 | 9.00 |
| PS8 | 1972 (4) | — | KM#24-27 | — | 1,000 |
| PS9 | 1973 (7) | 10,542 | KM#13, 14, 15a.2-18a.2, 29 | 27.00 | 18.00 |
| PS10 | 1974 (7) | 9,362 | KM#13, 14, 15a.2-18a.2, 29 | 27.00 | 18.00 |
| PS11 | 1975 (7) | 4,056 | KM#13, 14, 15a.2-18a.2, 29 | 31.50 | 20.00 |
| PS12 | 1976 (7) | 2,131 | KM#13, 14, 15a.2, 29-32 | 45.00 | 32.50 |
| PS13 | 1977 (7) | 920 | KM#13, 14, 15a.2, 29-32 | 45.00 | 37.50 |
| PS14 | 1978 (8) | 7,311 | KM#12a, 13, 14, 15a.2, 29-32 | 47.00 | 35.00 |
| PS15 | 1979 (8) | 1,857 | KM#12b, 13a, 14a, 15b, 29a-32a marked O.A.U. July 1979 | 45.00 | 50.00 |
| PS16 | 1997 (3) | — | KM#417, 445, 473 | — | 210 |
| PS17 | 1999 (2) | 375 | KM#424-425 | 345 | 360 |

## LIBYA

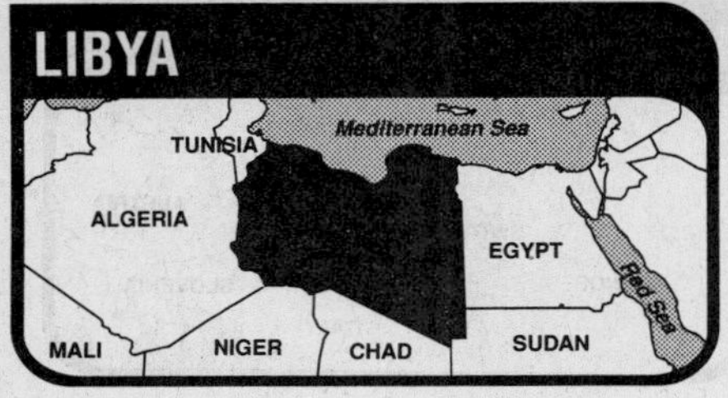


The Socialist People's Libyan Arab Jamahariya, located on the north-central coast of Africa between Tunisia and Egypt, has an area of 679,358 sq. mi. (1,759,540 sq. km.) and a population of 3.9 million. Capital: Tripoli. Crude oil, which accounts for 90 per cent of the export earnings, is the mainstay of the economy.

Libya has been subjected to foreign rule throughout most of its history, various parts of it having been ruled by the Phoenicians, Carthaginians, Vandals, Byzantines, Greeks, Romans, Egyptians, and in the following centuries the Arabs' language, culture and religion were adopted by the indigenous population. Libya was conquered by the Ottoman Turks in 1553, and remained under Turkish domination, becoming a Turkish vilayet in 1835, until it was conquered by Italy and made into a colony in 1911. The name 'Libya', the ancient Greek name for North Africa exclusive of Egypt, was given to the colony by Italy in1934. Libya came under Allied administration after the fall of Tripoli on Jan. 23, 1943, divided into zones of British and French control. On Dec. 24, 1951, in accordance with a United Nations resolution, Libya proclaimed its independence as a constitutional monarchy, thereby becoming the first country to achieve independence through the United Nations. The monarchy was overthrown by a *coup d'etat* on Sept. 1, 1969, and Libya was established as a republic.

**TITLES**

المملكة الليبية

al-Mamlaka(t) al-Libiya(t)

الجمهورية العربية الليبية

al-Jomhuriya(t) al-Arabiya(t) al-Libiya(t)

**RULERS**

Idris I, 1951-1969

**MONETARY SYSTEM**

10 Milliemes = 1 Piastre
100 Piastres = 1 Pound

# MONARCHY

## STANDARD COINAGE

10 Milliemes = 1 Piastre; 100 Piastres = 1 Pound

**MILLIEME** **KM# 1** **Composition:** Bronze **Ruler:** Idris I

| Date | Mintage | F | VF | XF | Unc | BU |
|---|---|---|---|---|---|---|
| ND(1952) | 7,750,000 | — | 0.10 | 0.15 | 0.50 | — |
| ND(1952) Proof | 32 | Value: 75.00 | | | | |

**MILLIEME** **KM# 6** **Composition:** Nickel-Brass **Ruler:** Idris I

| Date | Mintage | F | VF | XF | Unc | BU |
|---|---|---|---|---|---|---|
| AH1385(1965) | 11,000,000 | — | 0.10 | 0.20 | 0.40 | — |

**2 MILLIEMES** **KM# 2** **Composition:** Bronze **Ruler:** Idris I

| Date | Mintage | F | VF | XF | Unc | BU |
|---|---|---|---|---|---|---|
| ND(1952) | 6,650,000 | — | 0.10 | 0.25 | 0.75 | — |
| ND(1952) Proof | 32 | Value: 75.00 | | | | |

**5 MILLIEMES** **KM# 3** **Composition:** Bronze **Ruler:** Idris I

| Date | Mintage | F | VF | XF | Unc | BU |
|---|---|---|---|---|---|---|
| ND(1952) | 7,680,000 | — | 0.15 | 0.35 | 1.00 | — |
| ND(1952) Proof | 32 | Value: 75.00 | | | | |

**5 MILLIEMES** **KM# 7** **Composition:** Nickel-Brass **Ruler:** Idris I

| Date | Mintage | F | VF | XF | Unc | BU |
|---|---|---|---|---|---|---|
| AH1385(1965) | 8,500,000 | — | 0.15 | 0.25 | 0.50 | — |

**PIASTRE** **KM#4** **Composition:** Copper-Nickel **Ruler:** Idris I

| Date | Mintage | F | VF | XF | Unc | BU |
|---|---|---|---|---|---|---|
| ND(1952) | 10,200,000 | — | 0.35 | 0.60 | 1.25 | — |
| ND(1952) Proof | 32 | Value: 100 | | | | |

**10 MILLIEMES** **KM# 8** **Composition:** Copper-Nickel **Ruler:** Idris I

| Date | Mintage | F | VF | XF | Unc | BU |
|---|---|---|---|---|---|---|
| AH1385(1965) | 17,000,000 | — | 0.15 | 0.25 | 0.50 | — |

**2 PIASTRES** **KM# 5** **Composition:** Copper-Nickel **Ruler:** Idris I

| Date | Mintage | F | VF | XF | Unc | BU |
|---|---|---|---|---|---|---|
| ND(1952) | 6,075,000 | — | 0.35 | 0.75 | 1.50 | — |
| ND(1952) Proof | 32 | Value: 125 | | | | |

**20 MILLIEMES** **KM# 9** **Composition:** Copper-Nickel **Ruler:** Idris I

| Date | Mintage | F | VF | XF | Unc | BU |
|---|---|---|---|---|---|---|
| AH1385(1965) | 8,750,000 | — | 0.20 | 0.50 | 2.00 | — |

**50 MILLIEMES** **KM# 10** **Composition:** Copper-Nickel **Ruler:** Idris I

| Date | Mintage | F | VF | XF | Unc | BU |
|---|---|---|---|---|---|---|
| AH1385(1965) | 8,000,000 | — | 0.35 | 0.75 | 3.00 | — |

**100 MILLIEMES** **KM# 11** **Composition:** Copper-Nickel **Ruler:** Idris I

| Date | Mintage | F | VF | XF | Unc | BU |
|---|---|---|---|---|---|---|
| AH1385(1965) | 8,000,000 | — | 0.75 | 1.50 | 4.00 | — |

# SOCIALIST PEOPLE'S REPUBLIC

## STANDARD COINAGE

1000 Dirhams = 1 Dinar

**DIRHAM** **KM# 12** **Composition:** Brass Clad Steel

| Date | Mintage | F | VF | XF | Unc | BU |
|---|---|---|---|---|---|---|
| AH1395(1975) | 20,000,000 | — | 0.25 | 0.50 | 2.00 | — |

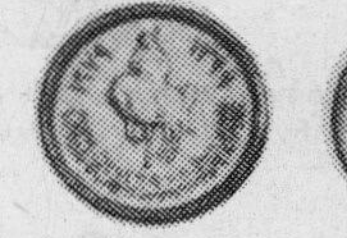

**DIRHAM** **KM# 18** **Composition:** Brass Clad Steel

| Date | Mintage | F | VF | XF | Unc | BU |
|---|---|---|---|---|---|---|
| AH1399(1979) | 1,000,000 | — | 4.00 | 12.00 | 20.00 | — |

**5 DIRHAM** **KM# 13** **Composition:** Brass Clad Steel

| Date | Mintage | F | VF | XF | Unc | BU |
|---|---|---|---|---|---|---|
| AH1395(1975) | 23,000,000 | — | 0.25 | 0.60 | 2.50 | — |

**5 DIRHAM** **KM# 19** **Composition:** Brass Clad Steel

| Date | Mintage | F | VF | XF | Unc | BU |
|---|---|---|---|---|---|---|
| AH1399(1979) | 2,000,000 | — | 3.50 | 10.00 | 18.00 | — |

**10 DIRHAMS** **KM# 14** **Composition:** Copper-Nickel Clad Steel

| Date | Mintage | F | VF | XF | Unc | BU |
|---|---|---|---|---|---|---|
| AH1395(1975) | 52,750,000 | — | 0.25 | 0.65 | 2.75 | — |

**10 DIRHAMS** KM# 20 **Composition:** Copper-Nickel Clad Steel **Size:** 20 mm.

| Date | Mintage | F | VF | XF | Unc | BU |
|---|---|---|---|---|---|---|
| AH1399(1979) | 4,000,000 | — | 3.00 | 9.00 | 15.00 | — |

**20 DIRHAMS** KM# 15 **Composition:** Copper-Nickel Clad Steel

| Date | Mintage | F | VF | XF | Unc | BU |
|---|---|---|---|---|---|---|
| AH1395(1975) | 25,500,000 | — | 0.50 | 1.75 | 5.00 | — |

**20 DIRHAMS** KM# 21 **Composition:** Copper-Nickel Clad Steel

| Date | Mintage | F | VF | XF | Unc | BU |
|---|---|---|---|---|---|---|
| AH1399(1979) | 6,000,000 | — | 3.00 | 9.00 | 15.00 | — |

**50 DIRHAMS** KM# 16 **Composition:** Copper-Nickel

| Date | Mintage | F | VF | XF | Unc | BU |
|---|---|---|---|---|---|---|
| AH1395(1975) | 25,640,000 | — | 1.00 | 2.50 | 7.00 | — |

**50 DIRHAMS** KM# 22 **Composition:** Copper-Nickel

| Date | Mintage | F | VF | XF | Unc | BU |
|---|---|---|---|---|---|---|
| AH1399(1979) | 9,120,000 | — | 2.50 | 6.50 | 12.50 | — |

**100 DIRHAMS** KM# 17 **Composition:** Copper-Nickel

| Date | Mintage | F | VF | XF | Unc | BU |
|---|---|---|---|---|---|---|
| AH1395(1975) | 15,433,000 | — | 1.50 | 3.50 | 9.00 | — |

**100 DIRHAMS** KM# 23 **Composition:** Copper-Nickel

| Date | Mintage | F | VF | XF | Unc | BU |
|---|---|---|---|---|---|---|
| AH1399(1979) | 15,000,000 | — | 2.50 | 6.50 | 12.50 | — |

**5 DINARS** KM# 24 **Weight:** 28.2800 g. **Composition:** 0.9250 Silver .8410 oz. ASW **Subject:** International Year of Disabled Persons

| Date | Mintage | F | VF | XF | Unc | BU |
|---|---|---|---|---|---|---|
| ND(1981) | 20,000 | — | — | — | 65.00 | — |
| ND(1981) Proof | 21,000 | Value: 75.00 | | | | |

**70 DINARS** KM# 25 **Weight:** 15.9800 g. **Composition:** 0.9170 Gold .4712 oz. AGW **Subject:** International Year of Disabled Persons

| Date | Mintage | F | VF | XF | Unc | BU |
|---|---|---|---|---|---|---|
| ND(1981) | 4,000 | — | — | — | 450 | — |
| ND(1981) Proof | 4,000 | Value: 550 | | | | |

## PIEFORTS

| KM# | Date | Mintage | Identification | Mkt Val |
|---|---|---|---|---|
| P1 | 1981 | 2,150 | 5 Dinars. KM24. | 150 |
| P2 | 1981 | 500 | 70 Dinars. KM25. | 1,100 |

## MINT SETS

| KM# | Date | Mintage | Identification | Issue Price | Mkt Val |
|---|---|---|---|---|---|
| MS1 | 1975 (6) | — | KM12-17 | — | 28.00 |

## PROOF SETS

| KM# | Date | Mintage | Identification | Issue Price | Mkt Val |
|---|---|---|---|---|---|
| PS1 | 1952 (5) | 32 | KM1-5 | — | 450 |

# LIECHTENSTEIN

The Principality of Liechtenstein, located in central Europe on the east bank of the Rhine between Austria and Switzerland, has an area of 62 sq. mi. (160 sq. km.) and a population of 27,200. Capital: Vaduz. The economy is based on agriculture and light manufacturing. Canned goods, textiles, ceramics and precision instruments are exported.

The lordships of Schellenburg and Vaduz were merged into the principality of Liechtenstein. It was a member of the Rhine Confederation from 1806 to 1815, and of the German Confederation from 1815 to 1866 when it became independent. Liechtenstein's long and close association with Austria was terminated by World War I. In 1921 it adopted the coinage of Switzerland, and two years later entered into a customs union with the Swiss, who also operated its postal and telegraph systems and represented it in international affairs. The tiny principality abolished its army in 1868 and has avoided involvement in all European wars since that time.

**RULERS**
Prince John II, 1858-1929
Prince Franz I, 1929-1938
Prince Franz Josef II, 1938-1990
Prince Hans Adam II, 1990-

**MINT MARKS**
A - Vienna
B - Bern
M - Munich (restrikes)

**MONETARY SYSTEM**
100 Heller = 1 Krone

## PRINCIPALITY

### REFORM COINAGE

100 Heller = 1 Krone

**KRONE** Y# 2 **Weight:** 5.0000 g. **Composition:** 0.8350 Silver .1342 oz. ASW **Ruler:** Prince John II

| Date | Mintage | F | VF | XF | Unc | BU |
|---|---|---|---|---|---|---|
| 1904 | 75,000 | 10.00 | 15.00 | 20.00 | 35.00 | — |
| 1910 | 45,000 | 10.00 | 15.00 | 20.00 | 35.00 | — |
| 1915 | 75,000 | 10.00 | 15.00 | 20.00 | 35.00 | — |

**2 KRONEN** Y# 3 **Weight:** 10.0000 g. **Composition:** 0.8350 Silver .2684 oz. ASW **Ruler:** Prince John II

| Date | Mintage | F | VF | XF | Unc | BU |
|---|---|---|---|---|---|---|
| 1912 | 50,000 | 12.00 | 20.00 | 35.00 | 65.00 | — |
| 1915 | 38,000 | 15.00 | 25.00 | 40.00 | 75.00 | — |

**5 KRONEN** Y# 4 **Weight:** 24.0000 g. **Composition:** 0.9000 Silver .6944 oz. ASW **Ruler:** Prince John II

| Date | Mintage | F | VF | XF | Unc | BU |
|---|---|---|---|---|---|---|
| 1904 | 15,000 | 55.00 | 90.00 | 150 | 235 | — |
| 1910 | 10,000 | 65.00 | 110 | 185 | 300 | — |
| 1915 | 10,000 | 60.00 | 100 | 165 | 250 | — |

## REFORM COINAGE

100 Rappen = 1 Frank

**1/2 FRANK** Y# 7 **Weight:** 2.5000 g. **Composition:** 0.8350 Silver .0751 oz. ASW **Ruler:** Prince John II **Note:** 15,745 were melted.

| Date | Mintage | F | VF | XF | Unc | BU |
|---|---|---|---|---|---|---|
| 1924 | 30,000 | 65.00 | 125 | 165 | 225 | — |

**FRANK** Y# 8 **Weight:** 5.0000 g. **Composition:** 0.8350 Silver .1342 oz. ASW **Ruler:** Prince John II **Note:** 45,355 were melted.

| Date | Mintage | F | VF | XF | Unc | BU |
|---|---|---|---|---|---|---|
| 1924 | 60,000 | 25.00 | 45.00 | 80.00 | 150 | — |

**2 FRANKEN** Y# 9 **Weight:** 10.0000 g. **Composition:** 0.8350 Silver .2684 oz. ASW **Ruler:** Prince John II **Note:** 41,707 were melted.

| Date | Mintage | F | VF | XF | Unc | BU |
|---|---|---|---|---|---|---|
| 1924 | 50,000 | 40.00 | 90.00 | 150 | 215 | — |

**5 FRANKEN** Y# 10 **Weight:** 25.0000 g. **Composition:** 0.9000 Silver .7234 oz. ASW **Ruler:** Prince John II **Note:** 11,260 were melted.

| Date | Mintage | F | VF | XF | Unc | BU |
|---|---|---|---|---|---|---|
| 1924 | 15,000 | 250 | 350 | 500 | 900 | — |

**10 FRANKEN** Y# 11 **Weight:** 3.2258 g. **Composition:** 0.9000 Gold .0933 oz. AGW **Ruler:** Prince Franz I

| Date | Mintage | F | VF | XF | Unc | BU |
|---|---|---|---|---|---|---|
| 1930 | 2,500 | — | 650 | 850 | 1,200 | — |

**10 FRANKEN** Y# 13 **Weight:** 3.2258 g. **Composition:** 0.9000 Gold .0933 oz. AGW **Ruler:** Prince Franz Josef II

| Date | Mintage | F | VF | XF | Unc | BU |
|---|---|---|---|---|---|---|
| 1946B | 10,000 | — | 150 | 200 | 265 | — |

**10 FRANKEN** Y# 20 **Weight:** 30.0000 g. **Composition:** 0.9000 Silver .8682 oz. ASW **Ruler:** Prince Franz Josef II **Subject:** 50th anniversary of reign **Obverse:** Similar to 50 Franken, Y#21

| Date | Mintage | F | VF | XF | Unc | BU |
|---|---|---|---|---|---|---|
| 1988 Proof | 35,000 | Value: 45.00 | | | | |

**10 FRANKEN** Y# 22 **Weight:** 30.0000 g. **Composition:** 0.9000 Silver .8682 oz. ASW **Ruler:** Prince Hans Adam II **Subject:** Succession of Hans-Adam II

| Date | Mintage | F | VF | XF | Unc | BU |
|---|---|---|---|---|---|---|
| 1990 Proof | 35,000 | Value: 40.00 | | | | |

**20 FRANKEN** Y# 12 **Weight:** 6.4516 g. **Composition:** 0.9000 Gold .1867 oz. AGW **Ruler:** Prince Franz I

| Date | Mintage | F | VF | XF | Unc | BU |
|---|---|---|---|---|---|---|
| 1930 | 2,500 | — | 650 | 850 | 1,500 | — |

**20 FRANKEN** Y# 14 **Weight:** 6.4516 g. **Composition:** 0.9000 Gold .1867 oz. AGW **Ruler:** Prince Franz Josef II

| Date | Mintage | F | VF | XF | Unc | BU |
|---|---|---|---|---|---|---|
| 1946B | 10,000 | — | 125 | 200 | 275 | — |

**25 FRANKEN** Y# 15 **Weight:** 5.6450 g. **Composition:** 0.9000 Gold .1633 oz. AGW **Ruler:** Prince Franz Josef II **Subject:** Franz Josef II and Princess Gina

| Date | Mintage | F | VF | XF | Unc | BU |
|---|---|---|---|---|---|---|
| 1956 | 15,000 | — | — | 200 | 250 | — |

**25 FRANKEN** Y# 18 **Weight:** 5.6450 g. **Composition:** 0.9000 Gold .1633 oz. AGW **Ruler:** Prince Franz Josef II **Subject:** 100th anniversary - National Bank

| Date | Mintage | F | VF | XF | Unc | BU |
|---|---|---|---|---|---|---|
| 1961 | 20,000 | — | — | — | 210 | — |

**50 FRANKEN** Y# 16 **Weight:** 11.2900 g. **Composition:** 0.9000 Gold .3267 oz. AGW **Ruler:** Prince Franz Josef II **Subject:** Franz Josef II and Princess Gina

| Date | Mintage | F | VF | XF | Unc | BU |
|---|---|---|---|---|---|---|
| 1956 | 15,000 | — | — | 300 | 350 | — |

**50 FRANKEN** Y# 19 **Weight:** 11.2900 g. **Composition:** 0.9000 Gold .3267 oz. AGW **Ruler:** Prince Franz Josef II **Subject:** 100th anniversary - National Bank

| Date | Mintage | F | VF | XF | Unc | BU |
|---|---|---|---|---|---|---|
| 1961 | 20,000 | — | — | — | 325 | — |

**50 FRANKEN** Y# 21 **Weight:** 10.0000 g. **Composition:** 0.9000 Gold .2894 oz. AGW **Ruler:** Prince Franz Josef II **Subject:** 50th anniversary of reign

| Date | Mintage | F | VF | XF | Unc | BU |
|---|---|---|---|---|---|---|
| 1988 Proof | 35,000 | Value: 220 | | | | |

**50 FRANKEN** Y# 23 **Weight:** 10.0000 g. **Composition:** 0.9000 Gold .2894 oz. AGW **Ruler:** Prince Hans Adam II **Subject:** Succession of Hans-Adam II

| Date | Mintage | F | VF | XF | Unc | BU |
|---|---|---|---|---|---|---|
| 1990 Proof | 25,000 | Value: 210 | | | | |

**100 FRANKEN** Y# 17 **Weight:** 32.2580 g. **Composition:** 0.9000 Gold .9335 oz. AGW **Ruler:** Prince Franz Josef II **Subject:** Franz Josef II and Princess Gina

| Date | Mintage | F | VF | XF | Unc | BU |
|---|---|---|---|---|---|---|
| 1952 | 4,000 | — | — | 3,000 | 3,600 | — |

## MEDALLIC COINAGE

**20 FRANKEN** KM# M5 **Weight:** 7.0000 g. **Composition:** Gold **Ruler:** Prince Franz Josef II **Subject:** 60th birthday of Franz Joseph II

| Date | Mintage | F | VF | XF | Unc | BU |
|---|---|---|---|---|---|---|
| ND(1966) Proof | — | Value: 100 | | | | |

**20 FRANKEN** KM# M6 **Weight:** 6.9600 g. **Composition:** Gold **Ruler:** Prince Franz Josef II **Subject:** Marriage of Crown Prince Johann Adam and Maria

| Date | Mintage | F | VF | XF | Unc | BU |
|---|---|---|---|---|---|---|
| 1967 Proof | — | Value: 100 | | | | |

## MINT SETS

| KM# | Date | Mintage | Identification | Issue Price | Mkt Val |
|---|---|---|---|---|---|
| MS1 | 1930 (2) | 2,500 | Y11-12 | — | 2,700 |
| MS2 | 1946 (2) | 10,000 | Y13-14 | — | 540 |
| MS3 | 1956 (2) | 15,000 | Y15-16 | — | 600 |
| MS4 | 1961 (2) | 20,000 | Y18-19 | — | 535 |

## PROOF SETS

| KM# | Date | Mintage | Identification | Issue Price | Mkt Val |
|---|---|---|---|---|---|
| PS1 | 1988 (2) | 35,000 | Y20-21 | — | 265 |
| PS2 | 1990 (2) | 25,000 | Y22-23 | — | 250 |

# LITHUANIA

The Republic of Lithuania, southernmost of the Baltic states in east Europe, has an area of 25,174 sq. mi.(65,201 sq. km.) and a population of *3.6 million. Capital: Vilnius. The economy is based on livestock raising and manufacturing. Hogs, cattle, hides and electric motors are exported.

Lithuania emerged as a grand duchy in the 14thcentury. In the 15th century it was a major power of central Europe, stretching from the Baltic to the Black Sea. It was joined with Poland in 1569, but lost Smolensk, Chernigovsk, and the left bank of the river Dnepr Ukraina in 1667.' Following the third partition of Poland by Austria, Prussia and Russia, 1795,Lithuania came under Russian domination and did not regain its independence until shortly before the end of World War I when it declared itself a sovereign republic on Feb. 16, 1918. In fall of 1920, Poland captured Vilna (Vilnius). The republic was occupied by Soviet troops and annexed to the U.S.S.R. in 1940. Following the German occupation of 1941-44, it was retaken by Russia and reestablished as a member republic of the Soviet Union. Western countries, including the United States, did not recognize Lithuania's incorporation into the Soviet Union.

Lithuania declared its independence March 11, 1990and it was recognized by the United States on Sept. 2,1991, followed by the Soviet government in Moscow on Sept. 6. They were seated in the UN General Assembly on Sept. 17, 1991.

## REPUBLIC
### 1918-1940

## STANDARD COINAGE

100 Centas = 1 Litas

**CENTAS** KM# 71 **Composition:** Aluminum-Bronze

| Date | Mintage | F | VF | XF | Unc | BU |
|---|---|---|---|---|---|---|
| 1925 | 5,000,000 | 2.00 | 4.00 | 7.00 | 28.00 | — |

**CENTAS** KM# 79 **Composition:** Bronze

| Date | Mintage | F | VF | XF | Unc | BU |
|---|---|---|---|---|---|---|
| 1936 | 9,995,000 | 2.00 | 3.00 | 6.00 | 26.00 | — |

**2 CENTAI** KM# 80 **Composition:** Bronze

| Date | Mintage | F | VF | XF | Unc | BU |
|---|---|---|---|---|---|---|
| 1936 | 4,951,000 | 3.50 | 5.50 | 10.00 | 40.00 | — |

**5 CENTAI** KM# 72 **Composition:** Aluminum-Bronze

| Date | Mintage | F | VF | XF | Unc | BU |
|---|---|---|---|---|---|---|
| 1925 | 12,000,000 | 2.00 | 3.50 | 7.00 | 20.00 | — |

**5 CENTAI** KM# 81 **Composition:** Bronze

| Date | Mintage | F | VF | XF | Unc | BU |
|---|---|---|---|---|---|---|
| 1936 | 4,800,000 | 2.50 | 4.00 | 9.00 | 35.00 | — |

**10 CENTU** KM# 73 **Composition:** Aluminum-Bronze

| Date | Mintage | F | VF | XF | Unc | BU |
|---|---|---|---|---|---|---|
| 1925 | 12,000,000 | 1.75 | 3.00 | 8.00 | 25.00 | — |

**20 CENTU** KM# 74 **Composition:** Aluminum-Bronze

| Date | Mintage | F | VF | XF | Unc | BU |
|---|---|---|---|---|---|---|
| 1925 | 8,000,000 | 2.00 | 3.50 | 9.00 | 30.00 | — |

**50 CENTU** KM# 75 **Composition:** Aluminum-Bronze

| Date | Mintage | F | VF | XF | Unc | BU |
|---|---|---|---|---|---|---|
| 1925 | 5,000,000 | 5.00 | 7.00 | 15.00 | 40.00 | — |

**LITAS** KM# 76 **Weight:** 2.7000 g. **Composition:** 0.5000 Silver .0434 oz. ASW

| Date | Mintage | F | VF | XF | Unc | BU |
|---|---|---|---|---|---|---|
| 1925 | 5,985,000 | 1.75 | 3.00 | 8.00 | 30.00 | — |
| 1925 Proof | — | Value: 650 | | | | |

**Note:** Struck as proof record specimens by the Royal Mint. Less than 12 are estimated to exist.

**2 LITU** KM# 77 **Weight:** 5.4000 g. **Composition:** 0.5000 Silver .0868 oz. ASW

| Date | Mintage | F | VF | XF | Unc | BU |
|---|---|---|---|---|---|---|
| 1925 | 3,000,000 | 3.50 | 5.50 | 12.00 | 35.00 | — |
| 1925 Proof | — | Value: 650 | | | | |

**Note:** Struck as proof record specimens by the Royal Mint. Less than 12 are estimated to exist.

**5 LITAI** KM# 78 **Weight:** 13.5000 g. **Composition:** 0.5000 Silver .217 oz. ASW

| Date | Mintage | F | VF | XF | Unc | BU |
|---|---|---|---|---|---|---|
| 1925 | 1,000,000 | 4.00 | 8.00 | 18.00 | 60.00 | — |

| Date | Mintage | F | VF | XF | Unc | BU |
|---|---|---|---|---|---|---|
| 1925 Proof | — | Value: 650 | | | | |

**Note:** Struck as proof record specimens by the Royal Mint. Less than 12 are estimated to exist.

**5 LITAI** KM# 82 **Weight:** 9.0000 g. **Composition:** 0.7500 Silver .217 oz. ASW **Obverse:** Designer's initials below bust **Reverse:** Dr. Jonas Basanavicius bust facing left **Edge:** Lettered **Edge Lettering:** TAUTOS GEROVE TAVO GEROVE

| Date | Mintage | F | VF | XF | Unc | BU |
|---|---|---|---|---|---|---|
| 1936 | 2,612,000 | 3.00 | 4.50 | 10.00 | 22.00 | — |

**10 LITU** KM# 83 **Weight:** 18.0000 g. **Composition:** 0.7500 Silver .434 oz. ASW **Reverse:** Grand Duke Vytautas Didysis (Vytautas the Great) bust facing left **Edge:** Lettered **Edge Lettering:** VIENYBEJE TAUTOS JEGA **Note:** A filled-die variety with the knight riding a mare instead of a stallion exists.

| Date | Mintage | F | VF | XF | Unc | BU |
|---|---|---|---|---|---|---|
| 1936 | 720,000 | 7.50 | 13.50 | 22.00 | 55.00 | — |

**10 LITU** KM# 84 **Weight:** 18.0000 g. **Composition:** 0.7500 Silver .434 oz. ASW **Subject:** 20th anniversary of republic **Reverse:** President Smetona head facing left **Edge:** Lettered **Edge Lettering:** VIENYBEJE TAUTOS JEGA

| Date | Mintage | F | VF | XF | Unc | BU |
|---|---|---|---|---|---|---|
| ND(1938) | 170,000 | 15.00 | 20.00 | 30.00 | 85.00 | — |

# MODERN REPUBLIC

## 1991-present

## REFORM COINAGE

100 Centas = 1 Litas

**CENTAS** KM# 85 **Composition:** Aluminum

| Date | Mintage | F | VF | XF | Unc | BU |
|---|---|---|---|---|---|---|
| 1991 | — | — | — | — | 0.25 | — |

**2 CENTAI** KM# 86 **Composition:** Aluminum

| Date | Mintage | F | VF | XF | Unc | BU |
|---|---|---|---|---|---|---|
| 1991 | — | — | — | — | 0.30 | — |

**5 CENTAI** KM# 87 **Composition:** Aluminum

| Date | Mintage | F | VF | XF | Unc | BU |
|---|---|---|---|---|---|---|
| 1991 | — | — | — | — | 0.40 | — |

**10 CENTU** KM# 88 **Composition:** Bronze

| Date | Mintage | F | VF | XF | Unc | BU |
|---|---|---|---|---|---|---|
| 1991 | — | — | — | — | 0.50 | — |

**10 CENTU** KM# 106 **Weight:** 2.6000 g. **Composition:** Brass **Obverse:** Lithuanian knight **Reverse:** Denomination

| Date | Mintage | F | VF | XF | Unc | BU |
|---|---|---|---|---|---|---|
| 1997 | — | — | — | — | 0.40 | — |
| 1998 | — | — | — | — | 0.40 | — |
| 1999 | — | — | — | — | 0.40 | — |
| 2000 | — | — | — | — | 0.40 | — |
| 2000 Proof | 5,000 | Value: 1.00 | | | | |

**20 CENTU** KM# 89 **Composition:** Bronze

| Date | Mintage | F | VF | XF | Unc | BU |
|---|---|---|---|---|---|---|
| 1991 | — | — | — | — | 0.70 | — |
| 1999 | — | — | — | — | 0.70 | — |

**20 CENTU** KM# 107 **Weight:** 4.8000 g. **Composition:** Brass **Obverse:** Lithuanian knight **Reverse:** Denomination

| Date | Mintage | F | VF | XF | Unc | BU |
|---|---|---|---|---|---|---|
| 1997 | — | — | — | — | 0.70 | — |
| 1998 | — | — | — | — | 0.70 | — |
| 1999 | — | — | — | — | 0.70 | — |
| 2000 | — | — | — | — | 0.70 | — |
| 2000 Proof | 5,000 | Value: 1.50 | | | | |

**50 CENTU** KM# 90 **Composition:** Bronze

| Date | Mintage | F | VF | XF | Unc | BU |
|---|---|---|---|---|---|---|
| 1991 | — | — | — | — | 1.00 | — |

**50 CENTU** KM# 108 **Weight:** 6.0000 g. **Composition:** Brass

| Date | Mintage | F | VF | XF | Unc | BU |
|---|---|---|---|---|---|---|
| 1997 | — | — | — | — | 0.85 | — |
| 1998 | — | — | — | — | 1.00 | — |

| Date | Mintage | F | VF | XF | Unc | BU |
|---|---|---|---|---|---|---|
| 1999 | — | — | — | — | 1.00 | — |
| 2000 | — | — | — | — | 1.00 | — |
| 2000 Proof | 5,000 | Value: 2.00 | | | | |

**LITAS** KM# 91 **Composition:** Copper-Nickel

| Date | Mintage | F | VF | XF | Unc | BU |
|---|---|---|---|---|---|---|
| 1991 | — | — | — | — | 2.00 | — |

**LITAS** KM# 109 **Composition:** Copper-Nickel **Subject:** 75th anniversary - Central Bank **Obverse:** Knight and denomination **Reverse:** Portrait

| Date | Mintage | F | VF | XF | Unc | BU |
|---|---|---|---|---|---|---|
| 1997 | 200,000 | — | — | — | 4.00 | — |

**LITAS** KM# 109a **Weight:** 7.7759 g. **Composition:** 0.9990 Gold .25 oz. AGW **Subject:** 75th anniversary - Central Bank **Obverse:** Knight and denomination **Reverse:** Portrait

| Date | Mintage | F | VF | XF | Unc | BU |
|---|---|---|---|---|---|---|
| 1997 Proof | 1,500 | Value: 250 | | | | |

**LITAS** KM# 111 **Composition:** Copper-Nickel **Obverse:** Lithuanian knight **Reverse:** Denomination **Edge:** Reeded

| Date | Mintage | F | VF | XF | Unc | BU |
|---|---|---|---|---|---|---|
| 1998 | — | — | — | — | 2.00 | — |
| 1999 | — | — | — | — | 2.00 | — |
| 2000 | — | — | — | — | 2.00 | — |
| 2000 Proof | 5,000 | Value: 3.00 | | | | |

**LITAS** KM# 117 **Composition:** Copper-Nickel **Subject:** The Baltic Highway **Reverse:** 6 clasped hands **Edge:** Reeded and plain sections

| Date | Mintage | F | VF | XF | Unc | BU |
|---|---|---|---|---|---|---|
| 1999 | 1,000 | — | — | — | 5.00 | — |

**2 LITAI** KM# 92 **Composition:** Copper-Nickel

| Date | Mintage | F | VF | XF | Unc | BU |
|---|---|---|---|---|---|---|
| 1991 | — | — | — | — | 2.75 | — |

**2 LITAI** KM# 112 **Ring Composition:** Brass **Center Composition:** Copper-Nickel **Obverse:** Lithuanian knight **Reverse:** Denomination **Edge:** Segmented reeding

| Date | Mintage | F | VF | XF | Unc | BU |
|---|---|---|---|---|---|---|
| 1998 | — | — | — | — | 2.75 | — |
| 1999 | — | — | — | — | 2.75 | — |
| 2000 | — | — | — | — | 2.75 | — |
| 2000 Proof | 5,000 | Value: 3.75 | | | | |

**5 LITAI** **KM# 93** **Composition:** Copper-Nickel

| Date | Mintage | F | VF | XF | Unc | BU |
|---|---|---|---|---|---|---|
| 1991 | — | — | — | — | 4.50 | |

**5 LITAI** **KM# 113** **Ring Composition:** Copper Nickel **Center Composition:** Brass **Obverse:** Lithuanian knight **Reverse:** Denomination **Edge:** Lettered **Edge Lettering:** PENKI LITAI

| Date | Mintage | F | VF | XF | Unc | BU |
|---|---|---|---|---|---|---|
| 1998 | — | — | — | — | 4.50 | — |
| 1999 | — | — | — | — | 4.50 | — |
| 2000 | — | — | — | — | 4.50 | — |
| 2000 Proof | 5,000 | Value: 5.50 | | | | |

**5 LITAI** **KM# 127** **Subject:** UNICEF - For the Children of the World **Reverse:** Child with pinwheel **Edge:** Lettered **Edge Lettering:** LIETUVOS BANKAS **Size:** 38.6 mm.

| Date | Mintage | F | VF | XF | Unc | BU |
|---|---|---|---|---|---|---|
| 1998 Proof | 25,000 | Value: 30.00 | | | | |

**10 LITU** **KM# 94** **Composition:** Copper-Nickel **Subject:** Darius and Girenas **Edge:** Lettered **Edge Lettering:** SLOVE ATLANTO NUGALETOJAMS

| Date | Mintage | F | VF | XF | Unc | BU |
|---|---|---|---|---|---|---|
| ND(1993)LMK | 10,000 | — | — | — | 42.00 | — |

**10 LITU** **KM# 95** **Composition:** Copper-Nickel **Subject:** Papal visit **Edge:** Lettered **Edge Lettering:** TIKEJIMAS MEILE VILTIS

| Date | Mintage | F | VF | XF | Unc | BU |
|---|---|---|---|---|---|---|
| 1993LMK | 10,000 | — | — | — | 45.00 | — |

**10 LITU** **KM# 96** **Composition:** Copper-Nickel **Subject:** International Song Fest **Edge:** Lettered **Edge Lettering:** SKRISKIT SKAISCIOS DAINOS

| Date | Mintage | F | VF | XF | Unc | BU |
|---|---|---|---|---|---|---|
| 1994LMK Proof | 40,000 | Value: 12.00 | | | | |

**10 LITU** **KM# 97** **Composition:** Copper-Nickel **Subject:** World Sport Games **Edge:** Lettered **Edge Lettering:** LIETUVIAIS ESAME MES GIME

| Date | Mintage | F | VF | XF | Unc | BU |
|---|---|---|---|---|---|---|
| 1995LMK Proof | 10,000 | Value: 12.00 | | | | |

**10 LITU** **KM# 115** **Composition:** Copper-Nickel **Subject:** City of Vilnus **Obverse:** National arms above denomination **Reverse:** Building tops as seen from ground level **Edge:** Lettered **Edge Lettering:** VILNIUS-LIETUVOS SOSTINE

| Date | Mintage | F | VF | XF | Unc | BU |
|---|---|---|---|---|---|---|
| 1998 Proof | 7,500 | Value: 15.00 | | | | |

**10 LITU** **KM# 116** **Composition:** Copper-Nickel **Subject:** City of Kaunas **Obverse:** Lithuanian knight **Reverse:** City arms and buildings **Edge:** Lettered **Edge Lettering:** LAISUAS BUDAMAS, LAISVES NEISSIZADESI

| Date | Mintage | F | VF | XF | Unc | BU |
|---|---|---|---|---|---|---|
| 1999 Proof | 7,500 | Value: 12.00 | | | | |

**10 LITU** **KM# 120** **Weight:** 1.2440 g. **Composition:** 0.9999 Gold .04 oz. AGW **Subject:** Lithuanian gold coinage **Reverse:** Medieval minter

| Date | Mintage | F | VF | XF | Unc | BU |
|---|---|---|---|---|---|---|
| 1999 Proof | 25,000 | Value: 40.00 | | | | |

**50 LITU** **KM# 98** **Weight:** 23.3000 g. **Composition:** 0.9250 Silver .6929 oz. ASW **Subject:** 5th anniversary - independence **Edge:** Lettered **Edge Lettering:** TEGUL MEILE LIETUVOS DEGA MUSU SIRDYSE

| Date | Mintage | F | VF | XF | Unc | BU |
|---|---|---|---|---|---|---|
| ND(1995)LMK Proof | 5,000 | Value: 85.00 | | | | |

**50 LITU** **KM# 99** **Weight:** 23.3000 g. **Composition:** 0.9250 Silver .6929 oz. ASW **Subject:** Mikalojaus K. Ciurlionis **Edge:** Lettered **Edge Lettering:** PASAULIS KAIP DIDELE SIMFONIJA

| Date | Mintage | F | VF | XF | Unc | BU |
|---|---|---|---|---|---|---|
| 1995LMK Proof | 10,000 | Value: 37.50 | | | | |

**50 LITU** **KM# 100** **Weight:** 23.3000 g. **Composition:** 0.9250 Silver .6929 oz. ASW **Subject:** 5th anniversary - Jan. 13 assault **Edge:** Lettered **Edge Lettering:** IR KRAUJU KRIKSTYTI TAMPA VEL GYUYBE

| Date | Mintage | F | VF | XF | Unc | BU |
|---|---|---|---|---|---|---|
| NE(1996) Proof | Est. 10,000 | Value: 37.50 | | | | |

**50 LITU** **KM# 103** **Weight:** 23.3000 g. **Composition:** 0.9250 Silver .6929 oz. ASW **Subject:** Grand Duke Gediminas **Edge:** Lettered **Edge Lettering:** IS PRAEITIES TAVO SUNUS TE STIPRYBE SEMIA

| Date | Mintage | F | VF | XF | Unc | BU |
|---|---|---|---|---|---|---|
| 1996LMK Proof | Est. 10,000 | Value: 37.50 | | | | |

**50 LITU** **KM# 101** **Weight:** 23.3000 g. **Composition:** 0.9250 Silver .6929 oz. ASW **Series:** Olympics **Reverse:** Basketball players **Edge:** Lettered **Edge Lettering:** CITIUS. ALTIUS. FORTIUS.

| Date | Mintage | F | VF | XF | Unc | BU |
|---|---|---|---|---|---|---|
| 1996LMK Proof | Est. 10,000 | Value: 35.00 | | | | |

**50 LITU** KM# 102 **Weight:** 23.3000 g. **Composition:** 0.9250 Silver .6929 oz. ASW **Subject:** King Mindaugas **Edge:** Lettered **Edge Lettering:** IS PRAEITIES TAVO SUNUS TE STIPRYBE SEMIA

| Date | Mintage | F | VF | XF | Unc | BU |
|---|---|---|---|---|---|---|
| 1996LMK Proof | Est. 10,000 | Value: 37.50 | | | | |

**50 LITU** KM# 104 **Weight:** 23.3000 g. **Composition:** 0.9250 Silver .6929 oz. ASW **Subject:** First Lithuanian book **Obverse:** Mounted Lithuanian knight with sword **Reverse:** Page from book **Edge:** Lettered **Edge Lettering:** MARTYNAS MAZVYDAS IMKIT MANE IR SKAITYKIT

| Date | Mintage | F | VF | XF | Unc | BU |
|---|---|---|---|---|---|---|
| 1997 Proof | Est. 5,000 | Value: 40.00 | | | | |

**50 LITU** KM# 105 **Weight:** 23.3000 g. **Composition:** 0.9250 Silver .6929 oz. ASW **Subject:** 600th anniversary - Karaims and Tartars Lithuania **Obverse:** Mounted Lithuanian knight with sword **Reverse:** Karaim castle guard and Tartar warrior **Edge:** Lettered **Edge Lettering:** LIETUVA TEVYNE MUSU

| Date | Mintage | F | VF | XF | Unc | BU |
|---|---|---|---|---|---|---|
| 1997 Proof | Est. 5,000 | Value: 40.00 | | | | |

**50 LITU** KM# 110 **Weight:** 23.3000 g. **Composition:** 0.9250 Silver .6929 oz. ASW **Obverse:** Mounted Lithuanian knight with sword left **Reverse:** Half bust of knight facing and holding sceptre

| Date | Mintage | F | VF | XF | Unc | BU |
|---|---|---|---|---|---|---|
| 1998 Proof | 4,000 | Value: 40.00 | | | | |

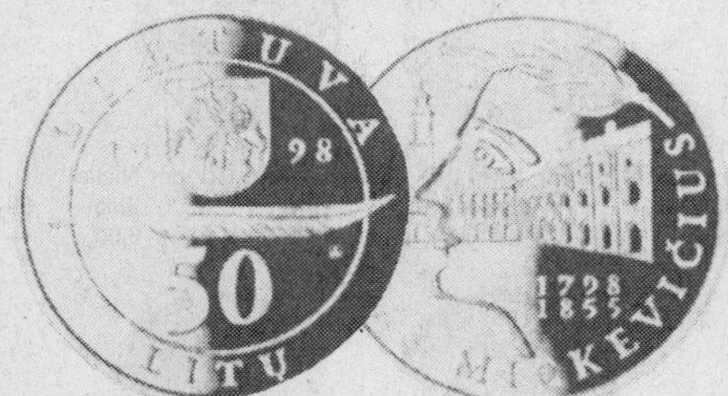

**50 LITU** KM# 114 **Weight:** 23.3000 g. **Composition:** 0.9250 Silver .6929 oz. ASW **Subject:** Adomas Mickevicius **Obverse:** Feather, denomination **Reverse:** Laureated profile of Mickevicius, building

| Date | Mintage | F | VF | XF | Unc | BU |
|---|---|---|---|---|---|---|
| 1998 Proof | Est. 5,000 | Value: 40.00 | | | | |

**50 LITU** KM# 118 **Weight:** 23.1200 g. **Composition:** 0.9250 Silver .6876 oz. ASW **Reverse:** Half bust Grand Duke Kestutis facing **Edge:** Lettered **Edge Lettering:** IS PRAEITIES TAVO SUNVS TE STIPRYBE SEMIA **Size:** 34.1 mm. **Note:** Lithuanian Mint. Grand Duke Kestutis.

| Date | Mintage | F | VF | XF | Unc | BU |
|---|---|---|---|---|---|---|
| 1999 Proof | 2,500 | Value: 42.00 | | | | |

**50 LITU** KM# 119 **Weight:** 28.2800 g. **Composition:** 0.9250 Silver .841 oz. ASW **Obverse:** National arms on stylized bell **Reverse:** Head of Kudirka **Edge:** Lettered **Edge Lettering:** VARDAN TOS LIETUVOS VIENYBE TEZYDI **Size:** 38.6 mm. **Note:** Lithuanian Mint. Vincas Kudrika.

| Date | Mintage | F | VF | XF | Unc | BU |
|---|---|---|---|---|---|---|
| 1999 Proof | 4,000 | Value: 40.00 | | | | |

**50 LITU** KM# 123 **Weight:** 28.2800 g. **Composition:** 0.9250 Silver .841 oz. ASW **Subject:** Baltic Way Highway **Reverse:** 3 pairs of clasped hands **Edge:** Lettered **Edge Lettering:** VILNIUS RYGA TALINAS **Size:** 38.6 mm. **Note:** Lithuanian Mint.

| Date | Mintage | F | VF | XF | Unc | BU |
|---|---|---|---|---|---|---|
| 1999 Proof | 4,000 | Value: 35.00 | | | | |

**50 LITU** KM# 125 **Weight:** 23.3000 g. **Composition:** 0.9250 Silver .6929 oz. ASW **Subject:** Grand Duke Vytautas **Obverse:** National arms above four shields **Reverse:** Crowned portrait holding sword **Edge Lettering:** "IS PRAEITIES TAVO SUNUS TESTIPRYBE SEMIA" **Size:** 34 mm.

| Date | Mintage | F | VF | XF | Unc | BU |
|---|---|---|---|---|---|---|
| 2000 Proof | 2,500 | Value: 20.00 | | | | |

**50 LITU** KM# 121 **Weight:** 28.2800 g. **Composition:** 0.9250 Silver .841 oz. ASW **Subject:** 350th anniversary - the Great Art of Artillery Book **Obverse:** National arms on frame **Reverse:** Old rocket designs **Edge:** Lettered **Edge Lettering:** ARS MAGNA ARTILLERIAE * MDCL

| Date | Mintage | F | VF | XF | Unc | BU |
|---|---|---|---|---|---|---|
| 2000 Proof | 2,000 | Value: 42.00 | | | | |

**50 LITU** KM# 122 **Weight:** 28.2800 g. **Composition:** 0.9250 Silver .841 oz. ASW **Subject:** 10th anniversary of independence **Obverse:** Republic of Lithuania coat of arms **Reverse:** Statue of independence **Edge:** Lettered **Edge Lettering:** LAISVE - AMZINOJI TAUTOS VERTYBE **Size:** 38.6 mm. **Note:** Struck at Lietuvos Monetu Vertybe.

| Date | Mintage | F | VF | XF | Unc | BU |
|---|---|---|---|---|---|---|
| ND(2000) Proof | 3,000 | Value: 45.00 | | | | |

**50 LITU** KM# 124 **Weight:** 28.2800 g. **Composition:** 0.9250 Silver .841 oz. ASW **Series:** XXVII Summer Olympic Games **Obverse:** Republic of Lithuania coat of arms **Reverse:** Man throwing discus, Olympic emblem, year, and SIDNEJUS (Sydney) **Edge:** Lettered **Edge Lettering:** NUGALI STIPRUS DVASIA IR KUNU

| Date | Mintage | F | VF | XF | Unc | BU |
|---|---|---|---|---|---|---|
| 2000 Proof | 4,000 | Value: 40.00 | | | | |

**50 LITU** **KM# 128** **Weight:** 28.2800 g. **Composition:** 0.9250 Silver .841 oz. ASW **Subject:** Millennium **Obverse:** National arms, denomination **Reverse:** Radiant cross, arch **Edge:** Lettered **Edge Lettering:** SALVE NOVUM MILLENNIUM

| Date | Mintage | F | VF | XF | Unc | BU |
|---|---|---|---|---|---|---|
| 2000 Proof | 3,000 | Value: 45.00 | | | | |

**50 LITU** **KM# 129** **Weight:** 28.2800 g. **Composition:** 0.9250 Silver .8410 oz. ASW **Subject:** Motiejus Valancius' 200th Birthday **Obverse:** National arms and church landscape **Reverse:** Bishop's portrait **Edge Lettering:** "LIETUVISKAS ZODIS RASTAS IR TIKEJMAS TAUTOS GYVASTIS" **Size:** 38.6 mm.

| Date | Mintage | F | VF | XF | Unc | BU |
|---|---|---|---|---|---|---|
| 2001 Proof | 2,000 | Value: 50.00 | | | | |

**100 LITU** **KM# 126** **Weight:** 7.7800 g. **Composition:** 0.9999 Gold .2501 oz. AGW **Subject:** Grand Duke Vytautas **Obverse:** Knight on horse **Reverse:** Crowned portrait and sword hilt **Edge Lettering:** "IS PRAEITIES TAVO SUNUS TE STIPRYBE SEMIA" **Size:** 22.3 mm.

| Date | Mintage | F | VF | XF | Unc | BU |
|---|---|---|---|---|---|---|
| 2000 Proof | 2,000 | Value: 125 | | | | |

## PATTERNS

Including off metal strikes

| KM# | Date | Mintage | Identification | Mkt Val |
|---|---|---|---|---|
| Pn3 | 1936 | — | 5 Litai. Silver. Plain edge. Coin struck. | 600 |
| Pn6 | 1936 | — | 10 Litu. Silver. Plain edge. KM83. | 700 |
| Pn4 | 1936 | — | 5 Litai. Silver. Lettered edge. Coin struck. | 600 |
| Pn5 | 1936 | — | 5 Litai. Silver. Designer's name (J. ZIKARAS) below bust. Plain edge. KM82. Medal struck. | 600 |
| Pn7 | 1938 | — | 2 Litai. Brass. Lettered edge. | 550 |
| Pn13 | 1938 | — | 10 Litu. Silver. Coin struck. | 600 |
| Pn8 | 1938 | — | 2 Litai. Silver. Reeded edge. | 650 |
| Pn14 | 1938 | 2 | 10 Litu. Gold. Lettered edge. Medal-struck presentation pieces. | — |
| Pn9 | 1938 | — | 2 Litai. Silver. Lettered edge. | 600 |
| Pn10 | 1938 | — | 2 Litai. Silver. Plain edge. | 600 |
| Pn11 | 1938 | — | 2 Litai. Silver. Plain edge. | 650 |
| Pn12 | 1938 | — | 2 Litai. Silver. Lettered edge. | 650 |
| Pn15 | 1994 | 234 | 50 Litu. Silver. Lettered edge. | — |

## TRIAL STRIKES

| KM# | Date | Mintage | Identification | Mkt Val |
|---|---|---|---|---|
| TS1 | 1925 | — | Centas. Aluminum-Bronze. Uniface. Obverse. | 150 |
| TS3 | 1925 | — | 5 Centai. Aluminum-Bronze. Uniface. Obverse. | 150 |
| TS5 | 1925 | — | 10 Centu. Aluminum-Bronze. Uniface. Obverse. | 175 |
| TS7 | 1925 | — | 20 Centu. Aluminum-Bronze. Uniface. Obverse. | 175 |
| TS9 | 1925 | — | 50 Centu. Aluminum-Bronze. Uniface. Obverse. | 185 |
| TS10 | 1925 | — | 50 Centu. Aluminum-Bronze. Uniface. Reverse. | 185 |
| TS8 | 1925 | — | 20 Centu. Aluminum-Bronze. Uniface. Reverse. | 175 |
| TS6 | 1925 | — | 10 Centu. Aluminum-Bronze. Uniface. Reverse. | 175 |
| TS4 | 1925 | — | 5 Centai. Aluminum-Bronze. Uniface. Reverse. | 150 |
| TS2 | 1925 | — | Centas. Aluminum-Bronze. Uniface. Reverse. | 150 |

## MINT SETS

| KM# | Date | Mintage | Identification | Issue Price | Mkt Val |
|---|---|---|---|---|---|
| MS1 | 1925 (10) | — | KM71-75, 2 of each | — | 950 |
| MS2 | 1991 (9) | 100,000 | KM85-93 | 7.50 | 20.00 |

## PROOF SETS

| KM# | Date | Mintage | Identification | Issue Price | Mkt Val |
|---|---|---|---|---|---|
| PS1 | 2000 (6) | 5,000 | KM106-108, 111-113 | 7.50 | 15.00 |

# LUXEMBOURG

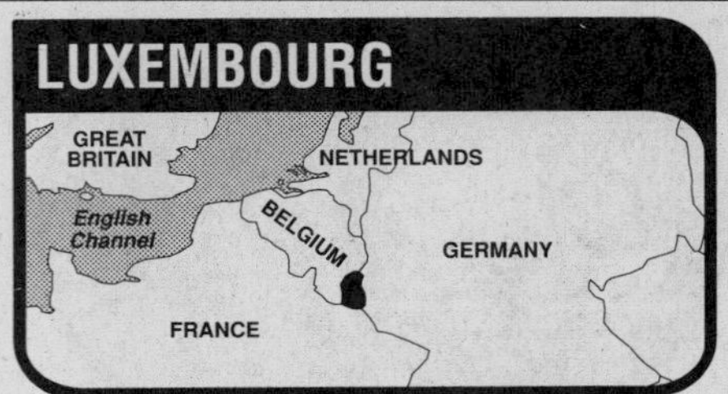


The Grand Duchy of Luxembourg is located in western Europe between Belgium, Germany and France, has an area of 1,103 sq. mi. (2,586 sq. km.) and a population of 377,100. Capital: Luxembourg. The economy is based on steel.

Founded about 963, Luxembourg was a prominent country of the Holy Roman Empire; one of its sovereigns became Holy Roman Emperor as Henry VII, 1308. After being made a duchy by Emperor Charles IV, 1354, Luxembourg passed under the domination of Burgundy, Spain, Austria and France, 1443-1815, regaining autonomy under the Treaty of Vienna, 1815, as a grand duchy in union with the Netherlands, though ostensibly a member of the German Confederation. When Belgium seceded from the Kingdom of the Netherlands, 1830, Luxembourg was forced to cede its greater western section to Belgium. The tiny duchy left the German Confederation in 1867 when the Treaty of London recognized it as an independent state and guaranteed its perpetual neutrality. Luxembourg was occupied by Germany and liberated by American troops in both World Wars.

**RULERS**

Adolphe, 1890-1905
William IV, 1905-1912
Marie Adelaide, 1912-1919
Charlotte, 1919-1964
Jean, 1964-2000
Henri, 2000-

**MINT MARKS**

A - Paris
(b) - Brussels, privy marks only
H - Gunzburg
(u) - Utrecht, privy marks only

**PRIVY MARKS**

Angel's head, two headed eagle - Brussels
Sword, Caduceus - Utrecht (1846-74 although struck at Brussels until 1909)

**NOTE:** Beginning in 1994 the letters "qp" for quality proof appear on Proof coins.

**MONETARY SYSTEM**

100 Centimes = 1 Franc

# DUCHY

## STANDARD COINAGE RESUMED

100 Centimes = 1 Franc

**2-1/2 CENTIMES** **KM# 21** **Composition:** Bronze

| Date | Mintage | F | VF | XF | Unc | BU |
|---|---|---|---|---|---|---|
| 1901(u) | 800,000 | 1.00 | 2.00 | 3.50 | 12.50 | — |
| **Note:** BARTH on reverse | | | | | | |
| 1901(u) | Inc. above | 1.00 | 2.50 | 4.00 | 14.00 | — |
| **Note:** BAPTH on reverse | | | | | | |
| 1908(u) | 400,000 | 1.00 | 2.50 | 4.00 | 14.00 | — |

**5 CENTIMES** **KM# 24** **Composition:** Copper-Nickel

| Date | Mintage | F | VF | XF | Unc | BU |
|---|---|---|---|---|---|---|
| 1901 | 2,000,000 | 0.25 | 0.75 | 1.50 | 6.00 | — |

**5 CENTIMES** **KM# 26** **Composition:** Copper-Nickel

| Date | Mintage | F | VF | XF | Unc | BU |
|---|---|---|---|---|---|---|
| 1908 | 1,500,000 | 0.35 | 1.00 | 1.75 | 7.50 | — |

**5 CENTIMES** KM# 27 **Composition:** Zinc

| Date | Mintage | F | VF | XF | Unc | BU |
|---|---|---|---|---|---|---|
| 1915 | 1,200,000 | 1.00 | 2.50 | 5.50 | 15.00 | — |

**5 CENTIMES** KM# 30 **Composition:** Iron

| Date | Mintage | F | VF | XF | Unc | BU |
|---|---|---|---|---|---|---|
| 1918 | 1,200,000 | 1.00 | 2.50 | 5.00 | 15.00 | — |
| 1921 | 600,000 | 6.00 | 10.00 | 20.00 | 40.00 | — |
| 1922 | 400,000 | 12.00 | 20.00 | 40.00 | 80.00 | — |

**5 CENTIMES** KM# 33 **Composition:** Copper-Nickel

| Date | Mintage | F | VF | XF | Unc | BU |
|---|---|---|---|---|---|---|
| 1924 | 3,000,000 | 0.20 | 0.40 | 0.80 | 4.50 | — |

**5 CENTIMES** KM# 40 **Composition:** Bronze

| Date | Mintage | F | VF | XF | Unc | BU |
|---|---|---|---|---|---|---|
| 1930 | 5,000,000 | 0.10 | 0.25 | 0.60 | 2.50 | — |

**10 CENTIMES** KM# 25 **Composition:** Copper-Nickel

| Date | Mintage | F | VF | XF | Unc | BU |
|---|---|---|---|---|---|---|
| 1901 | 4,000,000 | 0.25 | 0.75 | 1.50 | 7.50 | — |

**10 CENTIMES** KM# 28 **Composition:** Zinc

| Date | Mintage | F | VF | XF | Unc | BU |
|---|---|---|---|---|---|---|
| 1915 | 1,400,000 | 1.25 | 3.00 | 5.00 | 15.00 | — |

**10 CENTIMES** KM# 31 **Composition:** Iron

| Date | Mintage | F | VF | XF | Unc | BU |
|---|---|---|---|---|---|---|
| 1918 | 1,603,000 | 1.50 | 3.50 | 7.50 | 20.00 | — |
| 1921 | 626,000 | 2.00 | 4.50 | 9.00 | 22.50 | — |
| 1923 | 350,000 | 12.00 | 20.00 | 40.00 | 85.00 | — |

**10 CENTIMES** KM# 34 **Composition:** Copper-Nickel

| Date | Mintage | F | VF | XF | Unc | BU |
|---|---|---|---|---|---|---|
| 1924 | 3,500,000 | 0.25 | 0.50 | 1.00 | 4.50 | — |

**10 CENTIMES** KM# 41 **Composition:** Bronze

| Date | Mintage | F | VF | XF | Unc | BU |
|---|---|---|---|---|---|---|
| 1930 | 5,000,000 | 0.10 | 0.25 | 0.75 | 3.00 | — |

**25 CENTIMES** KM# 29 **Composition:** Zinc

| Date | Mintage | F | VF | XF | Unc | BU |
|---|---|---|---|---|---|---|
| 1916 | 800,000 | 1.50 | 3.50 | 7.50 | 15.00 | — |
| 1920 | — | 200 | 400 | 600 | 1,000 | — |

**25 CENTIMES** KM# 32 **Composition:** Iron

| Date | Mintage | F | VF | XF | Unc | BU |
|---|---|---|---|---|---|---|
| 1919 | 804,000 | 2.75 | 5.50 | 11.00 | 30.00 | — |
| 1920 | 800,000 | 2.25 | 4.00 | 8.50 | 25.00 | — |
| 1922 | 600,000 | 2.25 | 4.00 | 8.50 | 25.00 | — |

**25 CENTIMES** KM# 37 **Composition:** Copper-Nickel

| Date | Mintage | F | VF | XF | Unc | BU |
|---|---|---|---|---|---|---|
| 1927 | 2,500,000 | 0.35 | 0.65 | 1.25 | 5.00 | — |

**25 CENTIMES** KM# 42 **Composition:** Bronze

| Date | Mintage | F | VF | XF | Unc | BU |
|---|---|---|---|---|---|---|
| 1930 | 1,000,000 | 0.35 | 0.85 | 1.75 | 6.50 | — |

**25 CENTIMES** KM# 42a.1 **Composition:** Copper-Nickel **Note:** Coin alignment.

| Date | Mintage | F | VF | XF | Unc | BU |
|---|---|---|---|---|---|---|
| 1938 | 2,000,000 | 1.00 | 2.00 | 4.00 | 7.00 | — |

**25 CENTIMES** KM# 42a.2 **Composition:** Copper-Nickel **Note:** Medal alignment.

| Date | Mintage | F | VF | XF | Unc | BU |
|---|---|---|---|---|---|---|
| 1938 | Inc. above | 50.00 | 75.00 | 100 | 200 | — |

**25 CENTIMES** KM# 45 **Composition:** Bronze

| Date | Mintage | F | VF | XF | Unc | BU |
|---|---|---|---|---|---|---|
| 1946 | 1,000,000 | — | 0.15 | 0.25 | 0.75 | — |
| 1947 | 1,000,000 | — | 0.15 | 0.25 | 0.75 | — |

**25 CENTIMES** KM# 45a.2 **Composition:** Aluminum **Note:** Medal alignment.

| Date | Mintage | F | VF | XF | Unc | BU |
|---|---|---|---|---|---|---|
| 1954 | Inc. above | 10.00 | 20.00 | 30.00 | 40.00 | — |
| 1960 | Inc. above | 5.00 | 10.00 | 15.00 | 20.00 | — |
| 1963 | Inc. above | 5.00 | 10.00 | 15.00 | 20.00 | — |
| 1965 | Inc. above | 10.00 | 20.00 | 30.00 | 40.00 | — |
| 1967 | Inc. above | 10.00 | 20.00 | 30.00 | 40.00 | — |

**25 CENTIMES** KM# 45a.1 **Composition:** Aluminum **Note:** Coin alignment.

| Date | Mintage | F | VF | XF | Unc | BU |
|---|---|---|---|---|---|---|
| 1954 | 7,000,000 | — | — | — | 0.10 | — |
| 1957 | 3,020,000 | — | — | — | 0.10 | — |
| 1960 | 3,020,000 | — | — | — | 0.10 | — |
| 1963 | 4,000,000 | — | — | — | 0.10 | — |
| 1965 | 2,000,000 | — | — | — | 0.10 | — |
| 1967 | 3,000,000 | — | — | — | 0.10 | — |
| 1968 | 600,000 | 0.10 | 0.25 | 0.50 | 1.00 | — |
| 1970 | 4,000,000 | — | — | — | 0.10 | — |
| 1972 | 4,000,000 | — | — | — | 0.10 | — |

**25 CENTIMES** KM# 45b **Weight:** 2.9600 g. **Composition:** 0.9250 Silver .088 oz. ASW

| Date | Mintage | F | VF | XF | Unc | BU |
|---|---|---|---|---|---|---|
| 1980 Proof | 3,000 | Value: 12.00 | | | | |

**50 CENTIMES** KM# 43 **Composition:** Nickel

| Date | Mintage | F | VF | XF | Unc | BU |
|---|---|---|---|---|---|---|
| 1930 | 2,000,000 | 0.25 | 0.50 | 1.00 | 5.00 | — |

**FRANC** KM# 35 **Composition:** Nickel

| Date | Mintage | F | VF | XF | Unc | BU |
|---|---|---|---|---|---|---|
| 1924 | 1,000,000 | 0.25 | 0.75 | 1.25 | 8.00 | — |
| 1928 | 2,000,000 | 0.20 | 0.50 | 1.00 | 7.00 | — |
| 1935 | 1,000,000 | 0.25 | 0.75 | 1.25 | 6.00 | — |

**FRANC** KM# 44 **Composition:** Copper-Nickel

| Date | Mintage | F | VF | XF | Unc | BU |
|---|---|---|---|---|---|---|
| 1939 | 5,000,000 | 0.25 | 0.75 | 1.50 | 5.00 | — |

**FRANC** KM# 46.1 **Composition:** Copper-Nickel

| Date | Mintage | F | VF | XF | Unc | BU |
|---|---|---|---|---|---|---|
| 1946 | 4,000,000 | 0.15 | 0.35 | 0.50 | 1.50 | — |
| 1947 | 2,000,000 | 0.20 | 0.40 | 0.75 | 2.00 | — |

**FRANC** **KM# 46.2** **Composition:** Copper-Nickel

| Date | Mintage | F | VF | XF | Unc | BU |
|---|---|---|---|---|---|---|
| 1952 | 5,000,000 | 0.10 | 0.25 | 0.50 | 1.25 | — |
| 1953 | 2,000,000 | 0.10 | 0.25 | 0.50 | 1.00 | — |
| 1955 | 1,000,000 | 0.10 | 0.25 | 0.50 | 1.00 | — |
| 1957 | 2,000,000 | — | 0.10 | 0.25 | 0.50 | — |
| 1960 | 2,000,000 | — | 0.10 | 0.25 | 0.50 | — |
| 1962 | 2,000,000 | — | 0.10 | 0.25 | 0.50 | — |
| 1964 | 2,000,000 | — | 0.10 | 0.25 | 0.50 | — |

**FRANC** **KM# 55** **Composition:** Copper-Nickel

| Date | Mintage | F | VF | XF | Unc | BU |
|---|---|---|---|---|---|---|
| 1965 | 3,000,000 | — | — | 0.10 | 0.20 | — |
| 1966 | 1,000,000 | — | — | 0.10 | 0.20 | — |
| 1968 | 3,000,000 | — | — | 0.10 | 0.20 | — |
| 1970 | 3,000,000 | — | — | 0.10 | 0.20 | — |
| 1972 | 3,000,000 | — | — | 0.10 | 0.20 | — |
| 1973 | 3,000,000 | — | — | 0.10 | 0.20 | — |
| 1976 | 3,000,000 | — | — | 0.10 | 0.20 | — |
| 1977 | 1,000,000 | — | — | 0.10 | 0.20 | — |
| 1978 | 3,000,000 | — | — | 0.10 | 0.20 | — |
| 1979 | 2,000,000 | — | — | 0.10 | 0.20 | — |
| 1980 | 4,000,000 | — | — | 0.10 | 0.20 | — |
| 1981 | 5,000,000 | — | — | 0.10 | 0.20 | — |
| 1982 | 3,000,000 | — | — | 0.10 | 0.20 | — |
| 1983 | 3,000,000 | — | — | 0.10 | 0.20 | — |
| 1984 | 3,000,000 | — | — | 0.10 | 0.20 | — |

**FRANC** **KM# 55a** **Weight:** 4.4700 g. **Composition:** 0.9250 Silver .1329 oz. ASW

| Date | Mintage | F | VF | XF | Unc | BU |
|---|---|---|---|---|---|---|
| 1980 Proof | 3,000 | Value: 20.00 | | | | |

**FRANC** **KM# 46.2a** **Weight:** 4.4500 g. **Composition:** 0.9250 Silver .1323 oz. ASW

| Date | Mintage | F | VF | XF | Unc | BU |
|---|---|---|---|---|---|---|
| 1980 Proof | 3,000 | Value: 20.00 | | | | |

**FRANC** **KM# 59** **Composition:** Copper-Nickel **Reverse:** IML added

| Date | Mintage | F | VF | XF | Unc | BU |
|---|---|---|---|---|---|---|
| 1986 | 3,000,000 | — | — | 0.10 | 0.20 | — |
| 1987 | 3,000,000 | — | — | 0.10 | 0.20 | — |

**FRANC** **KM# 63** **Composition:** Nickel-Steel

| Date | Mintage | F | VF | XF | Unc | BU |
|---|---|---|---|---|---|---|
| 1988 | 10,000,000 | — | — | — | 0.40 | — |
| 1989 | 3,000,000 | — | — | — | 0.40 | — |
| 1990 | 25,010,000 | — | — | — | 0.40 | — |
| 1991 | 10,010,000 | — | — | — | 0.40 | — |
| 1992 In sets only | 10,000 | — | — | — | 0.50 | — |
| 1993 In sets only | 10,000 | — | — | — | 0.50 | — |
| 1994 In sets only | 10,000 | — | — | — | 0.50 | — |
| 1995 In sets only | 10,000 | — | — | — | 0.50 | — |

**2 FRANCS** **KM# 36** **Composition:** Nickel

| Date | Mintage | F | VF | XF | Unc | BU |
|---|---|---|---|---|---|---|
| 1924 | 1,000,000 | 1.00 | 2.25 | 4.00 | 15.00 | — |

**5 FRANCS** **KM# 38** **Weight:** 8.0000 g. **Composition:** 0.6250 Silver .1608 oz. ASW

| Date | Mintage | F | VF | XF | Unc | BU |
|---|---|---|---|---|---|---|
| 1929 | 2,000,000 | BV | 3.00 | 7.00 | 22.50 | — |

**5 FRANCS** **KM# 50** **Composition:** Copper-Nickel

| Date | Mintage | F | VF | XF | Unc | BU |
|---|---|---|---|---|---|---|
| 1949 | 2,000,000 | 0.30 | 0.60 | 1.00 | 2.50 | — |

**5 FRANCS** **KM# 51** **Composition:** Copper-Nickel

| Date | Mintage | F | VF | XF | Unc | BU |
|---|---|---|---|---|---|---|
| 1962 | 2,000,000 | 0.10 | 0.25 | 0.40 | 0.75 | — |

**5 FRANCS** **KM# 56** **Composition:** Copper-Nickel

| Date | Mintage | F | VF | XF | Unc | BU |
|---|---|---|---|---|---|---|
| 1971 | 1,000,000 | — | — | 0.15 | 0.50 | — |
| 1976 | 1,000,000 | — | — | 0.15 | 0.50 | — |
| 1979 | 1,000,000 | — | — | 0.15 | 0.50 | — |
| 1981 | 1,000,000 | — | — | 0.15 | 0.50 | — |

**5 FRANCS** **KM# 51a** **Weight:** 6.7400 g. **Composition:** 0.9250 Silver .2004 oz. ASW

| Date | Mintage | F | VF | XF | Unc | BU |
|---|---|---|---|---|---|---|
| 1980 Proof | 3,000 | Value: 25.00 | | | | |

**5 FRANCS** **KM# 56a** **Weight:** 6.7800 g. **Composition:** 0.9250 Silver .2016 oz. ASW

| Date | Mintage | F | VF | XF | Unc | BU |
|---|---|---|---|---|---|---|
| 1980 Proof | 3,000 | Value: 25.00 | | | | |

**5 FRANCS** **KM# 60.1** **Composition:** Brass **Reverse:** IML added

| Date | Mintage | F | VF | XF | Unc | BU |
|---|---|---|---|---|---|---|
| 1986 | 9,000,000 | — | — | 0.15 | 0.40 | — |
| 1987 | 7,000,000 | — | — | 0.15 | 0.40 | — |
| 1988 | 2,000,000 | — | — | 0.15 | 0.40 | — |

**5 FRANCS** **KM# 60.2** **Composition:** Brass **Reverse:** Larger crown with cross touching rim

| Date | Mintage | F | VF | XF | Unc | BU |
|---|---|---|---|---|---|---|
| 1986 | Inc. above | — | — | 0.15 | 0.40 | — |

**5 FRANCS** **KM# 65** **Composition:** Brass

| Date | Mintage | F | VF | XF | Unc | BU |
|---|---|---|---|---|---|---|
| 1989 | 2,000,000 | — | — | — | 0.60 | — |
| 1990 | 4,010,000 | — | — | — | 0.60 | — |
| 1991 In sets only | 10,000 | — | — | — | 0.75 | — |
| 1992 In sets only | 20,000 | — | — | — | 0.75 | — |
| 1993 In sets only | 18,000 | — | — | — | 0.75 | — |
| 1994 In sets only | 10,000 | — | — | — | 0.75 | — |
| 1995 In sets only | 10,000 | — | — | — | 0.75 | — |

**10 FRANCS** **KM# 39** **Weight:** 13.5000 g. **Composition:** 0.7500 Silver .3255 oz. ASW

| Date | Mintage | F | VF | XF | Unc | BU |
|---|---|---|---|---|---|---|
| 1929 | 1,000,000 | BV | 5.00 | 10.00 | 32.50 | — |

**10 FRANCS** **KM# 57** **Composition:** Nickel

| Date | Mintage | F | VF | XF | Unc | BU |
|---|---|---|---|---|---|---|
| 1971 | 3,000,000 | — | — | 0.30 | 0.60 | — |
| 1972 | 3,000,000 | — | — | 0.30 | 0.60 | — |
| 1974 | 3,000,000 | — | — | 0.30 | 0.60 | — |
| 1976 | 3,000,000 | — | — | 0.30 | 0.60 | — |
| 1977 | 1,000,000 | — | — | 0.30 | 0.60 | — |
| 1978 | 1,000,000 | — | — | 0.30 | 0.60 | — |
| 1979 | 1,000,000 | — | — | 0.30 | 0.60 | — |
| 1980 | 1,000,000 | — | — | 0.30 | 0.60 | — |

**10 FRANCS** **KM# 57a** **Weight:** 8.7900 g. **Composition:** 0.9250 Silver .2614 oz. ASW

| Date | Mintage | F | VF | XF | Unc | BU |
|---|---|---|---|---|---|---|
| 1980 Proof | 3,000 | Value: 28.50 | | | | |

**20 FRANCS** **KM# 47** **Weight:** 8.5000 g. **Composition:** 0.8350 Silver .2282 oz. ASW **Subject:** 600th anniversary - John the Blind

| Date | Mintage | F | VF | XF | Unc | BU |
|---|---|---|---|---|---|---|
| ND(1946) | 100,000 | — | — | 7.00 | 15.00 | — |
| ND(1946) Proof | 100 | Value: 200 | | | | |

**20 FRANCS** **KM# 58** **Composition:** Bronze

| Date | Mintage | F | VF | XF | Unc | BU |
|---|---|---|---|---|---|---|
| 1980 | 3,000,000 | — | — | 0.60 | 1.00 | — |
| 1981 | 3,000,000 | — | — | 0.60 | 1.00 | — |
| 1982 | 3,000,000 | — | — | 0.60 | 1.00 | — |
| 1983 | 2,000,000 | — | — | 0.60 | 1.00 | — |

**20 FRANCS** **KM# 58a** **Weight:** 10.2100 g. **Composition:** 0.9250 Silver .3036 oz. ASW

| Date | Mintage | F | VF | XF | Unc | BU |
|---|---|---|---|---|---|---|
| 1980 Proof | 3,000 | Value: 28.50 | | | | |

**20 FRANCS** **KM# 64** **Weight:** 6.2200 g. **Composition:** 0.9990 Gold .2 oz. AGW **Subject:** 150th anniversary of the grand duchy

| Date | Mintage | F | VF | XF | Unc | BU |
|---|---|---|---|---|---|---|
| ND(1989) Proof | 50,000 | Value: 100 | | | | |

**20 FRANCS** **KM# 67** **Composition:** Bronze

| Date | Mintage | F | VF | XF | Unc | BU |
|---|---|---|---|---|---|---|
| 1990 | 1,110,000 | — | — | — | 2.00 | — |
| 1991 In sets only | 10,000 | — | — | — | 2.50 | — |
| 1992 In sets only | 10,000 | — | — | — | 2.50 | — |
| 1993 In sets only | 10,000 | — | — | — | 2.50 | — |
| 1994 In sets only | 10,000 | — | — | — | 2.50 | — |
| 1995 In sets only | 10,000 | — | — | — | 2.50 | — |

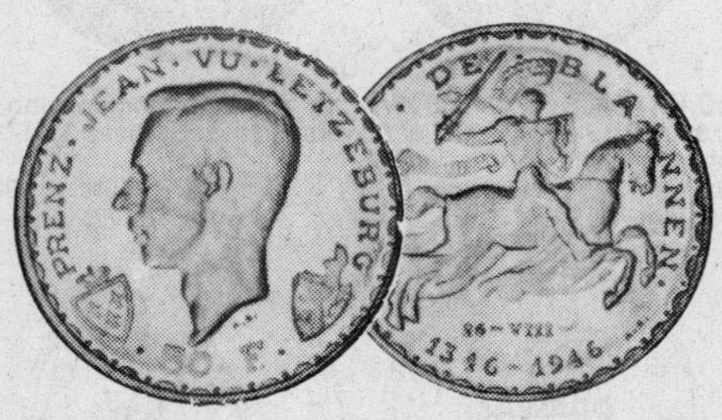

**50 FRANCS** **KM# 48** **Weight:** 12.5000 g. **Composition:** 0.8350 Silver .3356 oz. ASW **Subject:** 600th anniversary - John the Blind

| Date | Mintage | F | VF | XF | Unc | BU |
|---|---|---|---|---|---|---|
| ND(1946) | 100,000 | — | — | 12.50 | 18.00 | — |
| ND(1946) Proof | 100 | Value: 225 | | | | |

**50 FRANCS** **KM# 62** **Composition:** Nickel

| Date | Mintage | F | VF | XF | Unc | BU |
|---|---|---|---|---|---|---|
| 1987 | 3,000,000 | — | — | 1.50 | 3.50 | — |
| 1988 | 1,000,000 | — | — | 1.50 | 3.50 | — |
| 1989 | 1,200,000 | — | — | 1.50 | 3.50 | — |

**50 FRANCS** **KM# 66** **Composition:** Nickel **Note:** Similar to 5 Francs, KM#65.

| Date | Mintage | F | VF | XF | Unc | BU |
|---|---|---|---|---|---|---|
| 1989 | 2,000,000 | — | — | — | 3.50 | — |
| 1990 | 2,010,000 | — | — | — | 3.50 | — |
| 1991 In sets only | 10,000 | — | — | — | 3.50 | — |
| 1992 In sets only | 10,000 | — | — | — | 4.00 | — |
| 1993 In sets only | 10,000 | — | — | — | 4.00 | — |
| 1994 In sets only | 10,000 | — | — | — | 4.00 | — |
| 1995 In sets only | 10,000 | — | — | — | 4.00 | — |

**100 FRANCS** **KM# 49** **Weight:** 25.0000 g. **Composition:** 0.8350 Silver .6711 oz. ASW **Subject:** 600th anniversary - John the Blind

| Date | Mintage | F | VF | XF | Unc | BU |
|---|---|---|---|---|---|---|
| ND(1946) | 98,000 | — | — | 20.00 | 32.50 | — |
| ND(1946) Proof | 100 | Value: 250 | | | | |
| ND(1946) Restrike | 2,000 | — | — | — | 100 | — |

**Note:** Without designer's name

**100 FRANCS** **KM# 52** **Weight:** 18.0000 g. **Composition:** 0.8350 Silver .4832 oz. ASW

| Date | Mintage | F | VF | XF | Unc | BU |
|---|---|---|---|---|---|---|
| 1963 | 50,000 | — | — | 10.00 | 15.00 | — |

**100 FRANCS** **KM# 54** **Weight:** 18.0000 g. **Composition:** 0.8350 Silver .4832 oz. ASW

| Date | Mintage | F | VF | XF | Unc | BU |
|---|---|---|---|---|---|---|
| 1964 | 50,000 | — | — | 7.50 | 12.50 | — |

**100 FRANCS** **KM# 70** **Weight:** 16.1000 g. **Composition:** 0.9250 Silver .4788 oz. ASW **Subject:** 50th anniversary - United Nations

| Date | Mintage | F | VF | XF | Unc | BU |
|---|---|---|---|---|---|---|
| ND(1995) (qp) Proof | 110,000 | Value: 28.50 | | | | |

**250 FRANCS** **KM# 53.1** **Weight:** 25.0000 g. **Composition:** 0.9000 Silver .7234 oz. ASW **Subject:** Millennium of Luxembourg City

| Date | Mintage | F | VF | XF | Unc | BU |
|---|---|---|---|---|---|---|
| ND(1963) | 11,000 | — | — | 25.00 | 40.00 | — |

**250 FRANCS** **KM# 53.2** **Weight:** 25.0000 g. **Composition:** 0.9000 Silver .7234 oz. ASW **Subject:** Millennium of Luxembourg City **Note:** Darkly toned by the mint.

| Date | Mintage | F | VF | XF | Unc | BU |
|---|---|---|---|---|---|---|
| ND(1963) | 8,500 | — | — | 40.00 | 60.00 | — |

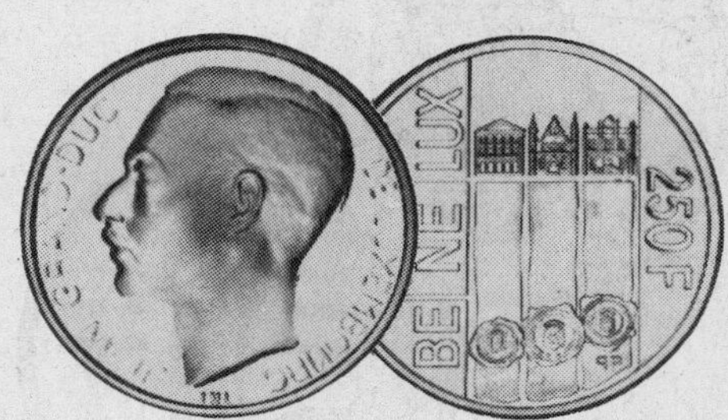

**250 FRANCS** **KM# 68** **Weight:** 18.7500 g. **Composition:** 0.9250 Silver .5577 oz. ASW **Subject:** BE-NE-LUX Treaty

| Date | Mintage | F | VF | XF | Unc | BU |
|---|---|---|---|---|---|---|
| ND(1994) (qp) Proof | 30,000 | Value: 30.00 | | | | |

**500 FRANCS** **KM# 69** **Weight:** 22.8500 g. **Composition:** 0.9250 Silver .6795 oz. ASW **Subject:** 50th anniversary of liberation

| Date | Mintage | F | VF | XF | Unc | BU |
|---|---|---|---|---|---|---|
| ND(1994) | 25,000 | — | — | — | 30.00 | — |
| ND(1994) (qp) Proof | 25,000 | Value: 42.50 | | | | |

**500 FRANCS** KM# 71 **Weight:** 22.8500 g. **Composition:** 0.9250 Silver .6795 oz. ASW **Subject:** Luxembourg - European cultural city

| Date | Mintage | F | VF | XF | Unc | BU |
|---|---|---|---|---|---|---|
| (19)95 (qp) Proof | — | Value: 52.50 | | | | |

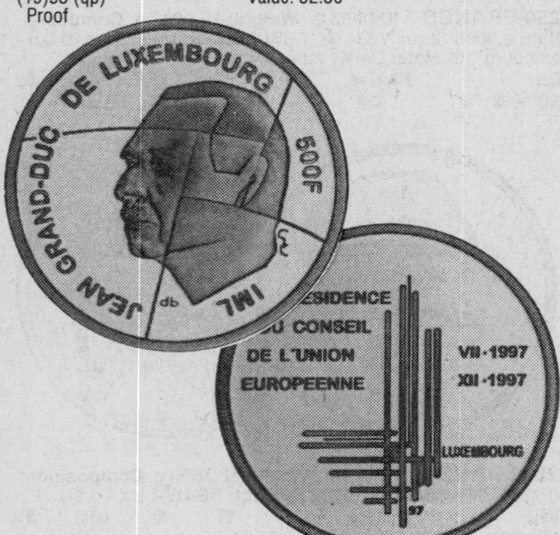


**500 FRANCS** KM# 72 **Weight:** 22.8500 g. **Composition:** 0.9250 Silver .6795 oz. ASW **Subject:** Presidency of the European Community **Obverse:** Segmented portrait **Reverse:** Symbolic design, dates

| Date | Mintage | F | VF | XF | Unc | BU |
|---|---|---|---|---|---|---|
| (19)97 (qp) Proof | 10,000 | Value: 40.00 | | | | |
| (19)97 (qp) Proof | 10,000 | — | — | — | — | — |

**500 FRANCS** KM# 73 **Weight:** 22.8500 g. **Composition:** 0.9250 Silver .6795 oz. ASW **Subject:** 1,300 years of Echternach **Obverse:** Duke's segmented portrait **Reverse:** City seal and anniversary dates

| Date | Mintage | F | VF | XF | Unc | BU |
|---|---|---|---|---|---|---|
| ND(1998) (qp) Proof | — | Value: 40.00 | | | | |

**500 FRANCS** KM# 74 **Weight:** 22.8500 g. **Composition:** 0.9250 Silver .6795 oz. ASW **Subject:** Coronation of Henry III **Obverse:** Portrait **Reverse:** Crowned "H" **Size:** 37 mm.

| Date | Mintage | F | VF | XF | Unc | BU |
|---|---|---|---|---|---|---|
| 2000 (qp) Proof | — | Value: 45.00 | | | | |

## MEDALLIC COINAGE

**20 FRANCS** KM# M1 **Weight:** 6.4516 g. **Composition:** 0.9000 Gold .1867 oz. AGW **Subject:** Marriage commemorative - Prince Jean and Princess Josephine Charlotte

| Date | Mintage | F | VF | XF | Unc | BU |
|---|---|---|---|---|---|---|
| ND(1953)(b) | 26,000 | — | — | 90.00 | 110 | — |

**20 FRANCS** KM# M2 **Composition:** Copper **Subject:** 100th anniversary of Luxembourg

| Date | Mintage | F | VF | XF | Unc | BU |
|---|---|---|---|---|---|---|
| 1963(b) | — | — | — | — | 20.00 | — |

**20 FRANCS** KM# M2a **Composition:** Copper-Nickel **Subject:** 100th anniversary of Luxembourg

| Date | Mintage | F | VF | XF | Unc | BU |
|---|---|---|---|---|---|---|
| 1963(b) | — | — | — | — | 20.00 | — |

**20 FRANCS** KM# M2b **Weight:** 6.4516 g. **Composition:** 0.9000 Gold .1867 oz. AGW **Subject:** 100th anniversary of Luxembourg

| Date | Mintage | F | VF | XF | Unc | BU |
|---|---|---|---|---|---|---|
| 1963(b) | 25,000 | — | — | 75.00 | 95.00 | — |

**20 FRANCS** KM# M4 **Composition:** Bronze .1867 oz. **Subject:** Coronation

| Date | Mintage | F | VF | XF | Unc | BU |
|---|---|---|---|---|---|---|
| 1964(b) | — | — | — | — | 20.00 | — |

**20 FRANCS** KM# M4a **Composition:** Copper-Nickel **Subject:** Coronation

| Date | Mintage | F | VF | XF | Unc | BU |
|---|---|---|---|---|---|---|
| 1964(b) | — | — | — | — | 20.00 | — |

**20 FRANCS** KM# M4b **Composition:** Silver **Subject:** Coronation

| Date | Mintage | F | VF | XF | Unc | BU |
|---|---|---|---|---|---|---|
| 1964(b) | — | — | — | — | 30.00 | — |

**20 FRANCS** KM# M4c **Weight:** 6.4516 g. **Composition:** 0.9000 Gold .1867 oz. AGW **Subject:** Coronation

| Date | Mintage | F | VF | XF | Unc | BU |
|---|---|---|---|---|---|---|
| 1964(b) | 25,000 | — | — | 75.00 | 95.00 | — |

**20 FRANCS** KM# M31 **Weight:** 6.4516 g. **Composition:** 0.9000 Gold .1867 oz. AGW **Subject:** 100th anniversary - death of poet Michel Lentz

| Date | Mintage | F | VF | XF | Unc | BU |
|---|---|---|---|---|---|---|
| 1993 Proof | 500 | Value: 200 | | | | |

**40 FRANCS** KM# M5 **Weight:** 12.9032 g. **Composition:** 0.9000 Gold .3734 oz. AGW **Obverse:** Grand Duchess Charlotte head facing left

| Date | Mintage | F | VF | XF | Unc | BU |
|---|---|---|---|---|---|---|
| 1964(b) | 3,000 | — | — | 185 | 225 | — |

**40 FRANCS** KM# M6 **Weight:** 12.9032 g. **Composition:** 0.9000 Gold .3734 oz. AGW **Obverse:** Prince Felix head facing left

| Date | Mintage | F | VF | XF | Unc | BU |
|---|---|---|---|---|---|---|
| 1964(b) | 3,000 | — | — | 185 | 225 | — |

**40 FRANCS** KM# M7 **Weight:** 12.9032 g. **Composition:** 0.9000 Gold .3734 oz. AGW **Obverse:** Grand Duke Jean head facing left

| Date | Mintage | F | VF | XF | Unc | BU |
|---|---|---|---|---|---|---|
| 1964(b) | 3,000 | — | — | 185 | 225 | — |

**40 FRANCS** KM# M8 **Weight:** 12.9032 g. **Composition:** 0.9000 Gold .3734 oz. AGW **Obverse:** Grand Duchess Josephine Charlotte head facing left

| Date | Mintage | F | VF | XF | Unc | BU |
|---|---|---|---|---|---|---|
| 1964(b) | 3,000 | — | — | 185 | 225 | — |

**40 FRANCS** KM# M9 **Composition:** Copper-Nickel **Subject:** 300th anniversary of patron saint

| Date | Mintage | F | VF | XF | Unc | BU |
|---|---|---|---|---|---|---|
| ND(1966) | — | — | — | — | 10.00 | — |

**40 FRANCS** KM# M9a **Composition:** Silver **Subject:** 300th anniversary of patron saint

| Date | Mintage | F | VF | XF | Unc | BU |
|---|---|---|---|---|---|---|
| ND(1996) | — | — | — | — | 20.00 | — |

**40 FRANCS** KM# M9b **Weight:** 12.9032 g. **Composition:** 0.9000 Gold .3734 oz. AGW **Subject:** 300th anniversary of patron saint (Virgin Mary)

| Date | Mintage | F | VF | XF | Unc | BU |
|---|---|---|---|---|---|---|
| ND(1966) | 5,000 | — | — | 185 | 225 | — |

**40 FRANCS** **KM# M10** **Composition:** Silver **Subject:** 100th anniversary of London Treaty

| Date | Mintage | F | VF | XF | Unc | BU |
|---|---|---|---|---|---|---|
| ND(1967) | — | — | — | — | 20.00 | — |

**40 FRANCS** **KM# M10a** **Composition:** Bronze **Subject:** 100th anniversary of London Treaty

| Date | Mintage | F | VF | XF | Unc | BU |
|---|---|---|---|---|---|---|
| ND(1967) | — | — | — | — | 10.00 | — |

**40 FRANCS** **KM# M10b** **Composition:** Copper-Nickel **Subject:** 100th anniversary of London Treaty

| Date | Mintage | F | VF | XF | Unc | BU |
|---|---|---|---|---|---|---|
| ND(1967) | — | — | — | — | 10.00 | — |

**40 FRANCS** **KM# M10c** **Weight:** 12.9032 g. **Composition:** 0.9000 Gold .3734 oz. AGW **Subject:** 100th anniversary of London Treaty **Obverse:** Henry and Amalia conjoined heads facing left

| Date | Mintage | F | VF | XF | Unc | BU |
|---|---|---|---|---|---|---|
| ND(1967) | 5,000 | — | — | 165 | 200 | — |

**40 FRANCS** **KM# M11** **Weight:** 12.9032 g. **Composition:** 0.9000 Gold .3734 oz. AGW **Subject:** County Henry VII **Reverse:** Prince Henri charging on horseback

| Date | Mintage | F | VF | XF | Unc | BU |
|---|---|---|---|---|---|---|
| 1973 (a) Proof | 5,000 | Value: 245 | | | | |

**40 FRANCS** **KM# M12** **Weight:** 12.9032 g. **Composition:** 0.9000 Gold .3734 oz. AGW **Subject:** 80th birthday of Princes Josephine Charlotte **Reverse:** Fischbach Castle

| Date | Mintage | F | VF | XF | Unc | BU |
|---|---|---|---|---|---|---|
| 1976 (a) Proof | 6,500 | Value: 245 | | | | |

**40 FRANCS** **KM# M13** **Weight:** 12.9032 g. **Composition:** 0.9000 Gold .3734 oz. AGW **Subject:** Silver wedding, 1953-1978

| Date | Mintage | F | VF | XF | Unc | BU |
|---|---|---|---|---|---|---|
| ND(1978) Proof | 3,000 | Value: 275 | | | | |

**40 FRANCS** **KM# M18** **Weight:** 12.9032 g. **Composition:** 0.9000 Gold .3734 oz. AGW **Subject:** Grand Duke Adolph

| Date | Mintage | F | VF | XF | Unc | BU |
|---|---|---|---|---|---|---|
| 1982 Proof | 1,000 | Value: 300 | | | | |

**40 FRANCS** **KM# M19** **Weight:** 12.9032 g. **Composition:** 0.9000 Gold .3734 oz. AGW **Subject:** Grand Duke Guillaume

| Date | Mintage | F | VF | XF | Unc | BU |
|---|---|---|---|---|---|---|
| 1982 Proof | 1,000 | Value: 300 | | | | |

**40 FRANCS** **KM# M20** **Weight:** 12.9032 g. **Composition:** 0.9000 Gold .3734 oz. AGW **Subject:** Grand Duchess Marie - Adelaide

| Date | Mintage | F | VF | XF | Unc | BU |
|---|---|---|---|---|---|---|
| 1982 Proof | 1,000 | Value: 300 | | | | |

**40 FRANCS** **KM# M21** **Weight:** 12.9032 g. **Composition:** 0.9000 Gold .3734 oz. AGW **Subject:** Grand Duchess Charlotte

| Date | Mintage | F | VF | XF | Unc | BU |
|---|---|---|---|---|---|---|
| 1982 Proof | 1,000 | Value: 300 | | | | |

**40 FRANCS** **KM# M22** **Weight:** 12.9032 g. **Composition:** 0.9000 Gold .3734 oz. AGW **Subject:** Grand Duke Jean

| Date | Mintage | F | VF | XF | Unc | BU |
|---|---|---|---|---|---|---|
| 1982 Proof | 1,000 | Value: 300 | | | | |

**40 FRANCS** **KM# M23** **Weight:** 12.9032 g. **Composition:** 0.9000 Gold .3734 oz. AGW **Subject:** Grand Duchess Josephine - Charlotte

| Date | Mintage | F | VF | XF | Unc | BU |
|---|---|---|---|---|---|---|
| 1982 Proof | 1,000 | Value: 300 | | | | |

**40 FRANCS** **KM# M24** **Weight:** 12.9032 g. **Composition:** 0.9000 Gold .3734 oz. AGW **Subject:** Prince Henri

| Date | Mintage | F | VF | XF | Unc | BU |
|---|---|---|---|---|---|---|
| 1982 Proof | 1,000 | Value: 300 | | | | |

**40 FRANCS** **KM# M25** **Weight:** 12.9032 g. **Composition:** 0.9000 Gold .3734 oz. AGW **Subject:** Princess Maria Theresa

| Date | Mintage | F | VF | XF | Unc | BU |
|---|---|---|---|---|---|---|
| 1982 Proof | 1,000 | Value: 300 | | | | |

**40 FRANCS** **KM# M26** **Weight:** 12.9032 g. **Composition:** 0.9000 Gold .3734 oz. AGW **Subject:** Count Henry VII

| Date | Mintage | F | VF | XF | Unc | BU |
|---|---|---|---|---|---|---|
| 1984 Proof | 2,000 | Value: 350 | | | | |

**40 FRANCS** **KM# M27** **Weight:** 12.9032 g. **Composition:** 0.9000 Gold .3734 oz. AGW **Subject:** Visit of Pope John Paul II

| Date | Mintage | F | VF | XF | Unc | BU |
|---|---|---|---|---|---|---|
| 1985 Proof | 1,575 | Value: 400 | | | | |

**40 FRANCS** **KM# M28** **Weight:** 12.9032 g. **Composition:** 0.9000 Gold .3734 oz. AGW **Subject:** Rebuilding of the souvenir monument

| Date | Mintage | F | VF | XF | Unc | BU |
|---|---|---|---|---|---|---|
| 1985 Proof | 200 | Value: 500 | | | | |

**40 FRANCS** **KM# M29** **Weight:** 12.9032 g. **Composition:** 0.9000 Gold .3734 oz. AGW **Subject:** Death of Grand Duchess Charlotte

| Date | Mintage | F | VF | XF | Unc | BU |
|---|---|---|---|---|---|---|
| 1985 Proof | 470 | Value: 450 | | | | |

**40 FRANCS** **KM# M30** **Weight:** 12.9032 g. **Composition:** 0.9000 Gold .3734 oz. AGW **Subject:** 25th anniversary - London Treaty

| Date | Mintage | F | VF | XF | Unc | BU |
|---|---|---|---|---|---|---|
| 1992 Proof | 1,200 | Value: 300 | | | | |

**40 FRANCS** **KM# M32** **Weight:** 12.9032 g. **Composition:** 0.9000 Gold .3734 oz. AGW **Subject:** 40th wedding anniversary, 1953-1993

| Date | Mintage | F | VF | XF | Unc | BU |
|---|---|---|---|---|---|---|
| ND(1993) Proof | 700 | Value: 400 | | | | |

**40 FRANCS** **KM# M33** **Weight:** 12.9032 g. **Composition:** 0.9000 Gold .3734 oz. AGW **Subject:** 30th anniversary of reign, 1964-1994

| Date | Mintage | F | VF | XF | Unc | BU |
|---|---|---|---|---|---|---|
| ND(1994) Proof | 700 | Value: 400 | | | | |

**40 FRANCS** **KM# M34** **Weight:** 12.9032 g. **Composition:** 0.9000 Gold .3734 oz. AGW **Subject:** 100th anniversary - birth of Grand Duchess Charlotte, 1896-1985 **Reverse:** Berg Castle

| Date | Mintage | F | VF | XF | Unc | BU |
|---|---|---|---|---|---|---|
| ND(1996) Proof | 600 | Value: 425 | | | | |

**40 FRANCS** **KM# M35** **Weight:** 12.9032 g. **Composition:** 0.9000 Gold .3734 oz. AGW **Subject:** 550th anniversary - Henri V as count, 1247-1281

| Date | Mintage | F | VF | XF | Unc | BU |
|---|---|---|---|---|---|---|
| ND(1997) Proof | 600 | Value: 425 | | | | |

## ESSAIS

| KM# | Date | Mintage | Identification | Mkt Val |
|---|---|---|---|---|
| E22 | 1901 | — | 5 Centimes. Gold. Adolph. | 1,000 |
| E23 | 1901 | — | 10 Centimes. Gold. Adolph. | 1,000 |
| E24 | 1908 | — | 10 Centimes. Gold. Wilhelm. | 1,000 |
| E25 | 1914 | 100 | 50 Centimes. Copper. | 60.00 |
| E29 | 1914 | 100 | 2 Francs. Copper. | 60.00 |
| E27 | 1914 | 100 | Franc. Copper. | 60.00 |
| E28 | 1914 | — | Franc. Silver. | 45.00 |
| E30 | 1914 | — | 2 Francs. Silver. Restruck after World War I. | 45.00 |
| E26 | 1914 | — | 50 Centimes. Silver. | 45.00 |
| E31 | 1927 | — | 25 Centimes. Gold. | — |
| E32 | 1929 | 50 | 5 Francs. Copper. | 150 |
| E35 | 1929 | 50 | 10 Francs. Copper. | 150 |
| E36 | 1929 | 50 | 10 Francs. Bronze. | 160 |
| E33 | 1929 | 50 | 5 Francs. Bronze. | 160 |
| E34 | 1929 | — | 5 Francs. Gold. | 2,000 |
| EA37 | 1929 | — | 10 Francs. Silver. | 1,200 |
| E38 | 1929 | — | 10 Francs. Gold. | 2,000 |
| E39 | 1939 | — | Franc. Gold. | 1,500 |
| E40 | 1945 | 100 | 25 Centimes. Copper. 25 at top. | 25.00 |
| E41 | 1945 | 100 | 25 Centimes. Copper. 25 at upper right. | 25.00 |
| E42 | 1946 | 100 | 25 Centimes. Copper. | 15.00 |
| E50 | 1946 | 100 | 20 Francs. Copper. | 100 |
| E45 | 1946 | 500 | Franc. Copper. Plain edge. | 15.00 |
| E56 | 1946 | 100 | 100 Francs. Copper. | 150 |
| E53 | 1946 | 100 | 50 Francs. Copper. | 125 |
| E54 | 1946 | 50 | 50 Francs. Silver. | 225 |
| E57 | 1946 | 50 | 100 Francs. Silver. | 325 |
| E46 | 1946 | 100 | Franc. Copper. Milled edge. | 20.00 |
| E51 | 1946 | 50 | 20 Francs. Silver. | 200 |
| E43 | 1946 | 500 | 25 Centimes. Copper. | 15.00 |
| E44 | 1946 | 500 | 25 Centimes. Silver. | 25.00 |
| E52 | 1946 | 25 | 20 Francs. Gold. | 1,200 |
| E47 | 1946 | 500 | Franc. Silver. Plain edge. | 30.00 |
| E58 | 1946 | 25 | 100 Francs. Gold. | 3,000 |
| E55 | 1946 | 25 | 50 Francs. Gold. | 2,000 |
| E48 | 1946 | 100 | Franc. Silver. Milled edge. | 40.00 |
| E49 | 1946 | 100 | Franc. Silver. Small letters. | 40.00 |
| E59 | 1949 | 50 | 5 Francs. Copper. | 50.00 |
| E60 | 1949 | 50 | 5 Francs. Bronze-Aluminum. | 50.00 |
| E61 | 1962 | 50 | 5 Francs. Copper-Nickel. | 30.00 |
| E62 | 1962 | — | 5 Francs. Silver. | 115 |

| KM# | Date | Mintage | Identification | Mkt Val |
|---|---|---|---|---|
| E63 | 1962 | 50 | 5 Francs. Gold. | 1,000 |
| E64 | 1963 | 250 | 20 Francs. Gold. | 200 |
| E65 | 1963 | 50 | 100 Francs. Bronze. | 70.00 |
| E68 | (1963) | — | 250 Francs. Copper-Nickel. | 50.00 |
| E69 | (1963) | 200 | 250 Francs. Bronze. | 50.00 |
| E66 | 1963 | 50 | 100 Francs. Silver. | 60.00 |
| E67 | 1963 | 50 | 100 Francs. Gold. | 1,250 |
| E70 | (1963) | 200 | 250 Francs. Silver. | 85.00 |
| E71 | (1963) | 200 | 250 Francs. Gold. | 1,450 |
| E72 | 1964 | 200 | 20 Francs. Gold. | 200 |
| E73 | 1964 | — | 100 Francs. Copper-Nickel. | 20.00 |
| E74 | 1964 | 200 | 100 Francs. Bronze. | 20.00 |
| E75 | 1964 | 200 | 100 Francs. Silver. | 20.00 |
| E76 | 1964 | 200 | 100 Francs. Gold. | 750 |
| E77 | 1965 | — | Franc. Copper-Nickel. | 15.00 |
| E78 | 1965 | — | Franc. Silver. | 15.00 |
| E79 | 1965 | 200 | Franc. Gold. KM55. | 200 |
| EA80 | 1966 | 100 | 40 Francs. Gold. | 400 |
| EB81 | 1967 | 100 | 40 Francs. Gold. | 400 |
| E82 | 1971 | — | 5 Francs. Copper-Nickel. | 15.00 |
| E85 | 1971 | — | 10 Francs. Copper-Nickel. | 15.00 |
| E86 | 1971 | — | 10 Francs. Silver. | 15.00 |
| E83 | 1971 | — | 5 Francs. Silver. | 15.00 |

| KM# | Date | Mintage | Identification | Mkt Val |
|---|---|---|---|---|
| E84 | 1971 | 250 | 5 Francs. Gold. KM56. | 315 |
| E87 | 1971 | 250 | 10 Francs. Gold. | 325 |
| E88 | 1980 | — | 20 Francs. Bronze. | 20.00 |
| E89 | 1980 | — | 20 Francs. Silver. | 45.00 |
| E90 | 1980 | 500 | 20 Francs. Gold. | 285 |

## PATTERNS

Including off metal strikes

| KM# | Date | Mintage | Identification | Mkt Val |
|---|---|---|---|---|
| Pn13 | 1901 | 100 | 10 Centimes. Copper. Without denomination. | 90.00 |
| Pn8 | 1901 | 100 | 5 Centimes. Copper. Without denomination. | 125 |
| Pn6 | 1901 | — | 2-1/2 Centimes. Copper. | 125 |
| Pn7 | 1901 | 100 | 2-1/2 Centimes. Silver. | 165 |
| Pn9 | 1901 | 100 | 5 Centimes. Copper-Nickel. Without denomination. | 125 |
| Pn14 | 1901 | 100 | 10 Centimes. Copper-Nickel. Without denomination. | 90.00 |
| Pn15 | 1901 | 100 | 10 Centimes. Copper-Nickel. Plain edge. Large letters. | 90.00 |
| Pn10 | 1901 | 100 | 5 Centimes. Copper-Nickel. Without denomination. | — |
| Pn16 | 1901 | 100 | 10 Centimes. Copper-Nickel. Milled edge. Large letters. | 90.00 |
| Pn11 | 1901 | 50 | 5 Centimes. Silver. Without denomination. | 150 |
| Pn12 | 1901 | 20 | 5 Centimes. Gold. Without denomination. | 1,000 |
| Pn17 | 1901 | 50 | 10 Centimes. Silver. Large letters. | 150 |
| Pn18 | 1901 | 20 | 10 Centimes. Gold. Without denomination. | 1,000 |
| Pn19 | | 50 | Franc. Nickel. Head of William. | 150 |
| Pn20 | 1917 | — | 5 Centimes. Copper. Crossed L's. | 150 |
| Pn21 | 1917 | — | 10 Centimes. Copper. | 150 |
| Pn22 | 1923 | 100 | Franc. Aluminum. | 90.00 |
| Pn26 | 1923 | 100 | 2 Francs. Pewter. | 125 |
| Pn27 | 1923 | 100 | 2 Francs. Aluminum. | 120 |
| Pn23 | 1923 | 100 | Franc. Bronze. | 100 |
| Pn24 | 1923 | 100 | Franc. Nickel. | 100 |
| Pn28 | 1923 | 100 | 2 Francs. Bronze. | 115 |
| Pn29 | 1923 | 100 | 2 Francs. Nickel. | 135 |
| Pn25 | 1923 | 100 | Franc. Silver. | 135 |
| Pn30 | 1923 | 100 | 2 Francs. Silver. | 150 |
| Pn31 | 1924 | — | Franc. Aluminum. | 50.00 |
| Pn35 | 1924 | 100 | 2 Francs. Copper. | 100 |
| Pn36 | 1924 | 100 | 2 Francs. Bronze. | 110 |
| Pn32 | 1924 | 100 | Franc. Copper. | 110 |
| Pn33 | 1924 | 100 | Franc. Bronze. | 110 |
| Pn34 | 1924 | 100 | Franc. Silver. | 110 |
| Pn37 | 1930 | — | 5 Centimes. Copper. Crowned value. | 85.00 |

| KM# | Date | Mintage | Identification | Mkt Val |
|---|---|---|---|---|
| Pn39 | 1930 | — | 10 Centimes. Copper. | 125 |
| Pn40 | 1930 | — | 50 Centimes. Copper-Nickel. | 150 |
| Pn41 | 1930 | — | 50 Centimes. Copper-Nickel. | 160 |
| Pn38 | 1930 | — | 5 Centimes. Copper. | 75.00 |
| Pn42 | 1939 | 50 | Franc. Silver. | 100 |
| Pn43 | 1939 | — | Franc. Gold. | 300 |
| Pn44 | 1942 | — | 5 Francs. Zinc. | 100 |
| Pn45 | 1942 | — | 5 Francs. Nickel. | 100 |
| Pn46 | 1947 | 100 | 2 Francs. Copper-Nickel. | 80.00 |
| Pn47 | 1947 | 100 | 5 Francs. Copper-Nickel. | 85.00 |

## PIEFORTS AND PIEFORTS WITH ESSAI

| KM# | Date | Mintage | Identification | Mkt Val |
|---|---|---|---|---|
| PE4 | 1908 | — | 10 Centimes. Gold. | 1,000 |
| P5 | 1927 | 100 | 25 Centimes. Bronze. | 100 |
| P6 | 1938 | 100 | 25 Centimes. Copper-Nickel. | 100 |

## MINT SETS

| KM# | Date | Mintage | Identification | Issue Price | Mkt Val |
|---|---|---|---|---|---|
| MS1 | 1990 (4) | 10,000 | KM63, 65-67 | — | 16.00 |
| MS2 | 1991 (4) | 10,000 | KM63, 65-67 | — | 14.00 |
| MS3 | 1992 (4) | 10,000 | KM63, 65-67 | — | 14.00 |
| MS4 | 1993 (4) | 10,000 | KM63, 65-67 | — | 14.00 |
| MS5 | 1994 (4) | 10,000 | KM63, 65-67 | — | 14.00 |
| MS6 | 1995 (4) | 10,000 | KM63, 65-67 | — | 14.00 |

## PROOF SETS

| KM# | Date | Mintage | Identification | Issue Price | Mkt Val |
|---|---|---|---|---|---|
| PS1 | 1980 (7) | 3,000 | KM45b, 46, 3a, 51a, 55a-58a | — | 160 |

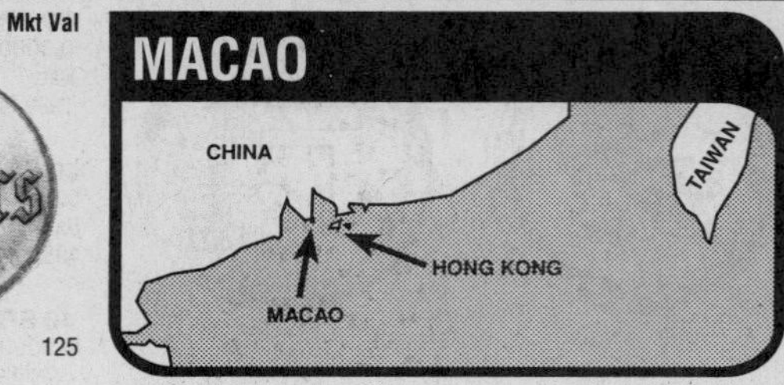


The Province of Macao, a Portuguese overseas province located in the South China Sea 40 miles southwest of Hong Kong, consists of the peninsula of Macao and the islands of Taipa and Coloane. It has an area of 6.2 sq. mi.(16 sq. km.) and a population of 500,000. Capital: Macao. Macao's economy is based on light industry, commerce, tourism, fishing, and gold trading - Macao is one of the entirely free markets for gold in the world. Cement, textiles, fireworks, vegetable oils, and metal products are exported.

Established by the Portuguese in 1557, Macao is the oldest European settlement in the Far East. The Chinese, while agreeing to Portuguese settlement, did not recognize Portuguese sovereign rights and the Portuguese remained largely under control of the Chinese until 1849, when the Portuguese abolished the Chinese customhouse and declared the independence of the port. The Manchu government formally recognized the Portuguese right to *perpetual occupation* of Macao in 1887.

In 1987, Portugal and China agreed that Macao would become a Chinese Territory in 1999. In December of 1999, Macao became a special administrative zone of China.

**RULERS**

Portuguese 1887-1999

**MINT MARKS**

(p) - Pobjoy Mint

(s) - Singapore Mint

**Pobjoy Mint**

**Singapore Mint**

**MONETARY SYSTEM**

100 Avos = 1 Pataca

# PORTUGUESE COLONY

## STANDARD COINAGE

100 Avos = 1 Pataca

**5 AVOS** KM# 1 **Composition:** Bronze

| Date | Mintage | F | VF | XF | Unc | BU |
|---|---|---|---|---|---|---|
| 1952 | 500,000 | — | 3.50 | 15.00 | 30.00 | — |

**5 AVOS** KM# 1a **Composition:** Nickel-Brass

| Date | Mintage | F | VF | XF | Unc | BU |
|---|---|---|---|---|---|---|
| 1967 | 5,000,000 | — | 0.50 | 1.00 | 2.50 | — |

**10 AVOS** KM# 2 **Composition:** Bronze

| Date | Mintage | F | VF | XF | Unc | BU |
|---|---|---|---|---|---|---|
| 1952 | 12,500,000 | — | 0.50 | 1.20 | 4.50 | — |

**10 AVOS** KM# 2a **Composition:** Nickel-Brass

| Date | Mintage | F | VF | XF | Unc | BU |
|---|---|---|---|---|---|---|
| 1967 | 5,525,000 | — | 0.50 | 1.00 | 2.00 | — |
| 1968 | 6,975,000 | — | 0.25 | 1.00 | 2.00 | — |
| 1975 | 20,000,000 | — | 0.10 | 0.50 | 1.50 | — |
| 1976 | Inc. above | — | 0.10 | 0.50 | 1.50 | — |

**10 AVOS** KM# 20 **Composition:** Brass

| Date | Mintage | F | VF | XF | Unc | BU |
|---|---|---|---|---|---|---|
| 1982 | 24,580,000 | — | 0.10 | 0.50 | 1.50 | — |
| 1983 | — | — | 0.10 | 0.50 | 1.50 | — |

| Date | Mintage | F | VF | XF | Unc | BU |
|---|---|---|---|---|---|---|
| 1984 | — | — | 0.25 | 0.75 | 2.50 | — |
| 1985 | — | — | 0.10 | 0.50 | 1.50 | — |
| 1988 | — | — | 0.10 | 0.50 | 1.50 | — |

**10 AVOS** KM# 20a **Weight:** 3.2000 g. **Composition:** 0.9250 Silver .0952 oz. ASW

| Date | Mintage | F | VF | XF | Unc | BU |
|---|---|---|---|---|---|---|
| 1982 Proof | 2,000 | Value: 7.50 | | | | |
| 1983 Proof | 2,500 | Value: 7.50 | | | | |
| 1984 Proof | 2,500 | Value: 7.50 | | | | |
| 1985 Proof | 2,500 | Value: 7.50 | | | | |

**10 AVOS** KM# 20b **Weight:** 4.0000 g. **Composition:** 0.9170 Gold .1179 oz. AGW **Obverse:** Low star

| Date | Mintage | F | VF | XF | Unc | BU |
|---|---|---|---|---|---|---|
| 1982 Proof | 150 | Value: 100 | | | | |

**10 AVOS** KM# 20c **Weight:** 4.5000 g. **Composition:** 0.9500 Platinum .1374 oz. APW

| Date | Mintage | F | VF | XF | Unc | BU |
|---|---|---|---|---|---|---|
| 1982 Proof | 375 | Value: 135 | | | | |

**10 AVOS** KM# 70 **Composition:** Brass

| Date | Mintage | F | VF | XF | Unc | BU |
|---|---|---|---|---|---|---|
| 1993 | — | — | — | — | 0.75 | — |

**20 AVOS** KM# 21 **Composition:** Brass

| Date | Mintage | F | VF | XF | Unc | BU |
|---|---|---|---|---|---|---|
| 1982 | 9,960,000 | — | 0.10 | 0.50 | 1.50 | — |
| 1983 | — | — | 0.10 | 0.50 | 1.50 | — |
| 1984 | — | — | 0.25 | 0.75 | 2.50 | — |
| 1985 | — | — | 0.10 | 0.50 | 1.50 | — |

**20 AVOS** KM# 21a **Weight:** 4.6000 g. **Composition:** 0.9250 Silver .1368 oz. ASW

| Date | Mintage | F | VF | XF | Unc | BU |
|---|---|---|---|---|---|---|
| 1982 Proof | 2,000 | Value: 11.50 | | | | |
| 1983 Proof | 2,500 | Value: 11.50 | | | | |
| 1984 Proof | 2,500 | Value: 11.50 | | | | |
| 1985 Proof | 2,500 | Value: 11.50 | | | | |

**20 AVOS** KM# 21b **Weight:** 5.5000 g. **Composition:** 0.9170 Gold .1621 oz. AGW **Obverse:** Low star

| Date | Mintage | F | VF | XF | Unc | BU |
|---|---|---|---|---|---|---|
| 1982 Proof | 150 | Value: 150 | | | | |

**20 AVOS** KM# 21c **Weight:** 6.2000 g. **Composition:** 0.9500 Platinum .1893 oz. APW

| Date | Mintage | F | VF | XF | Unc | BU |
|---|---|---|---|---|---|---|
| 1982 Proof | 375 | Value: 185 | | | | |

**20 AVOS** KM# 71 **Composition:** Brass

| Date | Mintage | F | VF | XF | Unc | BU |
|---|---|---|---|---|---|---|
| 1993 | — | — | — | — | 1.00 | — |

**50 AVOS** KM# 3 **Composition:** Copper-Nickel

| Date | Mintage | F | VF | XF | Unc | BU |
|---|---|---|---|---|---|---|
| 1952 | 2,560,000 | — | 0.75 | 3.50 | 9.00 | — |

**50 AVOS** KM# 7 **Composition:** Copper-Nickel

| Date | Mintage | F | VF | XF | Unc | BU |
|---|---|---|---|---|---|---|
| 1972 | 1,600,000 | — | 0.50 | 1.50 | 4.00 | — |
| 1973 | 4,840,000 | — | 0.50 | 1.00 | 3.00 | — |

**50 AVOS** KM# 9 **Composition:** Copper-Nickel

| Date | Mintage | F | VF | XF | Unc | BU |
|---|---|---|---|---|---|---|
| 1978 | 3,000,000 | — | 0.50 | 1.50 | 4.00 | — |

**50 AVOS** KM# 22 **Composition:** Brass

| Date | Mintage | F | VF | XF | Unc | BU |
|---|---|---|---|---|---|---|
| 1982 | 16,952,000 | — | 0.50 | 1.00 | 3.00 | — |
| 1983 | — | — | 0.75 | 4.00 | 9.00 | — |
| 1984 | — | — | 0.75 | 3.50 | 7.00 | — |
| 1985 | — | — | 0.50 | 2.00 | 5.00 | — |

**50 AVOS** KM# 22a **Weight:** 5.7000 g. **Composition:** 0.9250 Silver .1695 oz. ASW

| Date | Mintage | F | VF | XF | Unc | BU |
|---|---|---|---|---|---|---|
| 1982 Proof | 2,000 | Value: 13.50 | | | | |
| 1983 Proof | 2,500 | Value: 13.50 | | | | |
| 1984 Proof | 2,500 | Value: 13.50 | | | | |
| 1985 Proof | 2,500 | Value: 13.50 | | | | |

**50 AVOS** KM# 22b **Weight:** 7.4000 g. **Composition:** 0.9170 Gold .2181 oz. AGW **Obverse:** Low star

| Date | Mintage | F | VF | XF | Unc | BU |
|---|---|---|---|---|---|---|
| 1982 Proof | 150 | Value: 175 | | | | |

**50 AVOS** KM# 22c **Weight:** 8.4000 g. **Composition:** 0.9500 Platinum .2565 oz. APW

| Date | Mintage | F | VF | XF | Unc | BU |
|---|---|---|---|---|---|---|
| 1982 Proof | 375 | Value: 245 | | | | |

**50 AVOS** KM# 72 **Composition:** Brass

| Date | Mintage | F | VF | XF | Unc | BU |
|---|---|---|---|---|---|---|
| 1993 | — | — | — | — | 1.50 | — |

**PATACA** KM# 4 **Weight:** 3.0000 g. **Composition:** 0.7200 Silver .0694 oz. ASW

| Date | Mintage | F | VF | XF | Unc | BU |
|---|---|---|---|---|---|---|
| 1952 | 4,500,000 | — | 2.50 | 10.00 | 20.00 | — |

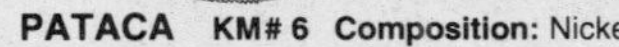

**PATACA** KM# 6 **Composition:** Nickel

| Date | Mintage | F | VF | XF | Unc | BU |
|---|---|---|---|---|---|---|
| 1968 | 5,000,000 | — | 1.00 | 3.00 | 6.50 | — |
| 1975 | 6,000,000 | — | 0.75 | 2.00 | 5.00 | — |

**PATACA** KM# 6a **Composition:** Copper-Nickel

| Date | Mintage | F | VF | XF | Unc | BU |
|---|---|---|---|---|---|---|
| 1980 | — | — | 3.50 | 12.00 | 25.00 | — |

**PATACA** KM# 23.1 **Composition:** Copper-Nickel **Obverse:** High stars

| Date | Mintage | F | VF | XF | Unc | BU |
|---|---|---|---|---|---|---|
| 1982(s) | 6,427,000 | — | 1.00 | 2.00 | 6.00 | — |
| 1983(s) | — | — | 1.50 | 3.50 | 8.00 | — |
| 1984(s) | — | — | 2.00 | 4.50 | 10.00 | — |
| 1985(s) | — | — | 1.50 | 3.50 | 8.00 | — |

**PATACA** KM# 23.1a **Weight:** 9.0000 g. **Composition:** 0.9250 Silver .2677 oz. ASW **Obverse:** High stars

| Date | Mintage | F | VF | XF | Unc | BU |
|---|---|---|---|---|---|---|
| 1982(s) Proof | 2,000 | Value: 17.50 | | | | |
| 1983(s) Proof | 2,500 | Value: 17.50 | | | | |
| 1984(s) Proof | 2,500 | Value: 17.50 | | | | |
| 1985(s) Proof | 2,500 | Value: 17.50 | | | | |

**PATACA** KM# 23.1b **Weight:** 11.6000 g. **Composition:** 0.9170 Gold .342 oz. AGW **Obverse:** High stars

| Date | Mintage | F | VF | XF | Unc | BU |
|---|---|---|---|---|---|---|
| 1982(s) Proof | 150 | Value: 225 | | | | |

**PATACA** KM# 23.1c **Weight:** 13.2000 g. **Composition:** 0.9500 Platinum .4032 oz. APW **Obverse:** High stars

| Date | Mintage | F | VF | XF | Unc | BU |
|---|---|---|---|---|---|---|
| 1982(s) Proof | 375 | Value: 365 | | | | |

**PATACA** KM# 23.2 **Composition:** Copper-Nickel **Obverse:** Low stars

| Date | Mintage | F | VF | XF | Unc | BU |
|---|---|---|---|---|---|---|
| 1982(p) | — | — | 1.00 | 2.00 | 6.00 | — |
| 1983(p) | — | — | 1.50 | 3.50 | 8.00 | — |

**PATACA** KM# 23.2a **Weight:** 5.7000 g. **Composition:** 0.9250 Silver .1695 oz. ASW **Obverse:** Low stars

| Date | Mintage | F | VF | XF | Unc | BU |
|---|---|---|---|---|---|---|
| 1982 Proof | — | Value: 15.00 | | | | |

**PATACA** KM# 57 **Composition:** Copper-Nickel

| Date | Mintage | F | VF | XF | Unc | BU |
|---|---|---|---|---|---|---|
| 1992 | — | — | — | — | 2.50 | — |
| 1998 | — | — | — | — | — | — |

**2 PATACAS** KM# 97 **Composition:** Nickel-Brass **Obverse:** Name and date **Reverse:** Church and Chinese arch **Edge:** Plain, octagonal **Size:** 27.5 mm.

| Date | Mintage | F | VF | XF | Unc | BU |
|---|---|---|---|---|---|---|
| 1998 | — | — | — | — | 3.50 | — |

**5 PATACAS** KM# 5 **Weight:** 15.0000 g. **Composition:** 0.7200 Silver .3472 oz. ASW

| Date | Mintage | F | VF | XF | Unc | BU |
|---|---|---|---|---|---|---|
| 1952 | 900,000 | — | 5.00 | 8.50 | 16.50 | — |

**5 PATACAS** KM# 5a **Weight:** 10.0000 g. **Composition:** 0.9500 Silver .2089 oz. ASW

| Date | Mintage | F | VF | XF | Unc | BU |
|---|---|---|---|---|---|---|
| 1971 | 500,000 | — | 4.00 | 6.50 | 12.50 | — |

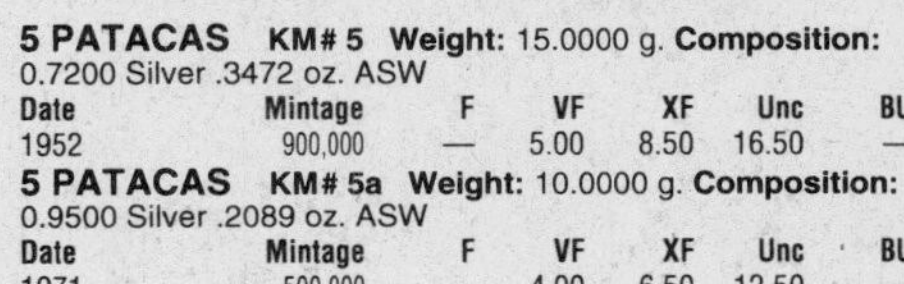

**5 PATACAS** KM# 24.1 **Composition:** Copper-Nickel **Obverse:** High stars **Reverse:** Large dragon

| Date | Mintage | F | VF | XF | Unc | BU |
|---|---|---|---|---|---|---|
| 1982(s) | 1,102,000 | — | 1.00 | 2.00 | 6.00 | — |
| 1983(s) | — | — | 3.50 | 10.00 | 20.00 | — |
| 1984(s) | — | — | 5.00 | 15.00 | 30.00 | — |
| 1985(s) | — | — | 3.50 | 10.00 | 20.00 | — |
| 1988(s) | — | — | 1.00 | 2.00 | 6.00 | — |

**5 PATACAS** KM# 24.1a **Weight:** 10.7000 g. **Composition:** 0.9250 Silver .3182 oz. ASW **Obverse:** High stars **Reverse:** Large dragon

| Date | Mintage | F | VF | XF | Unc | BU |
|---|---|---|---|---|---|---|
| 1982(s) Proof | 2,000 | Value: 32.50 | | | | |
| 1983(s) Proof | 2,500 | Value: 32.50 | | | | |
| 1984(s) Proof | 2,500 | Value: 32.50 | | | | |
| 1985(s) Proof | 2,500 | Value: 32.50 | | | | |

**5 PATACAS** KM# 24.1b **Weight:** 16.3000 g. **Composition:** 0.9170 Gold .4808 oz. AGW **Obverse:** High stars **Reverse:** Large dragon

| Date | Mintage | F | VF | XF | Unc | BU |
|---|---|---|---|---|---|---|
| 1982(s) Proof | 150 | Value: 300 | | | | |

**5 PATACAS** KM# 24.1c **Weight:** 18.4000 g. **Composition:** 0.9500 Platinum .562 oz. APW **Obverse:** High stars **Reverse:** Large dragon

| Date | Mintage | F | VF | XF | Unc | BU |
|---|---|---|---|---|---|---|
| 1982(s) Proof | 375 | Value: 520 | | | | |

**5 PATACAS** KM# 24.2 **Composition:** Copper-Nickel **Obverse:** Low stars **Reverse:** Small dragon

| Date | Mintage | F | VF | XF | Unc | BU |
|---|---|---|---|---|---|---|
| 1982(p) | — | — | 1.00 | 2.00 | 6.00 | — |

**5 PATACAS** KM# 24.2a **Weight:** 10.7000 g. **Composition:** 0.9250 Silver .3182 oz. ASW **Obverse:** Low stars **Reverse:** Small dragon

| Date | Mintage | F | VF | XF | Unc | BU |
|---|---|---|---|---|---|---|
| 1982(p) Proof | — | Value: 25.00 | | | | |

**5 PATACAS** KM# 56 **Composition:** Copper-Nickel

| Date | Mintage | F | VF | XF | Unc | BU |
|---|---|---|---|---|---|---|
| 1992 | — | — | — | — | 6.50 | — |

**10 PATACAS** KM# 83 **Ring Composition:** Brass **Center Composition:** Copper-Nickel **Obverse:** "MACAU" and date **Reverse:** Cathedral and denomination

| Date | Mintage | F | VF | XF | Unc | BU |
|---|---|---|---|---|---|---|
| 1997 | — | — | — | — | 9.50 | — |

**20 PATACAS** KM# 8 **Weight:** 18.0000 g. **Composition:** 0.6500 Silver .3762 oz. ASW

| Date | Mintage | F | VF | XF | Unc | BU |
|---|---|---|---|---|---|---|
| 1974 | 1,000 | — | — | 10.00 | 20.00 | — |

**100 PATACAS** KM# 10 **Weight:** 28.2800 g. **Composition:** 0.9250 Silver .8411 oz. ASW **Subject:** 25th anniversary of Grand Prix

| Date | Mintage | F | VF | XF | Unc | BU |
|---|---|---|---|---|---|---|
| 1978 Proof | 610 | Value: 150 | | | | |

**100 PATACAS** KM# 10a **Composition:** Copper-Nickel **Subject:** 25th anniversary of Grand Prix

| Date | Mintage | F | VF | XF | Unc | BU |
|---|---|---|---|---|---|---|
| 1978 | — | — | — | — | 185 | — |

**100 PATACAS** KM# 11 **Weight:** 28.2800 g. **Composition:** 0.9250 Silver .8411 oz. ASW **Reverse:** Racing car with advertising

| Date | Mintage | F | VF | XF | Unc | BU |
|---|---|---|---|---|---|---|
| 1978 Proof | 5,500 | Value: 70.00 | | | | |

**100 PATACAS** KM# 14 **Weight:** 28.2800 g. **Composition:** 0.9250 Silver .8411 oz. ASW **Subject:** Year of the Goat

| Date | Mintage | F | VF | XF | Unc | BU |
|---|---|---|---|---|---|---|
| 1979(s) Proof | 5,500 | Value: 70.00 | | | | |

**100 PATACAS** KM# 16 **Weight:** 28.2800 g. **Composition:** 0.9250 Silver .8411 oz. ASW **Subject:** Year of the Monkey **Reverse:** Monkey swinging on a rope

| Date | Mintage | F | VF | XF | Unc | BU |
|---|---|---|---|---|---|---|
| 1980 | 1,000 | — | — | — | 65.00 | — |
| 1980 Proof | 2,000 | Value: 75.00 | | | | |

**100 PATACAS** KM# 18 **Weight:** 28.2800 g. **Composition:** 0.9250 Silver .8411 oz. ASW **Subject:** Year of the Cockerel

| Date | Mintage | F | VF | XF | Unc | BU |
|---|---|---|---|---|---|---|
| 1981(p) | 1,000 | — | — | — | 55.00 | — |
| 1981(p) Proof | 1,000 | Value: 70.00 | | | | |

**100 PATACAS** KM# 25 **Weight:** 28.2800 g. **Composition:** 0.9250 Silver .8411 oz. ASW **Subject:** Year of the Dog

| Date | Mintage | F | VF | XF | Unc | BU |
|---|---|---|---|---|---|---|
| 1982(p) | 500 | — | — | — | 60.00 | — |
| 1982(p) Proof | 500 | Value: 75.00 | | | | |
| 1982(s) | 220 | — | — | — | 65.00 | — |
| 1982(s) Proof | 3,500 | Value: 70.00 | | | | |

**100 PATACAS** **KM# 27** **Weight:** 28.2800 g. **Composition:** 0.9250 Silver .8411 oz. ASW **Subject:** Year of the Pig

| Date | Mintage | F | VF | XF | Unc | BU |
|---|---|---|---|---|---|---|
| 1983(s) | 2,500 | — | — | — | 50.00 | — |
| 1983(s) Proof | 2,500 | Value: 65.00 | | | | |

**100 PATACAS** **KM# 29** **Weight:** 28.2800 g. **Composition:** 0.9250 Silver .8411 oz. ASW **Subject:** Year of the Rat

| Date | Mintage | F | VF | XF | Unc | BU |
|---|---|---|---|---|---|---|
| 1984(s) | 2,000 | — | — | — | 55.00 | — |
| 1984(s) Proof | 5,000 | Value: 65.00 | | | | |

**100 PATACAS** **KM# 31** **Weight:** 28.2800 g. **Composition:** 0.9250 Silver .8411 oz. ASW **Subject:** Year of the Ox

| Date | Mintage | F | VF | XF | Unc | BU |
|---|---|---|---|---|---|---|
| 1985(s) | 10,000 | — | — | — | 80.00 | — |
| 1985(s) Proof | 5,000 | Value: 65.00 | | | | |

**100 PATACAS** **KM# 33** **Weight:** 28.2800 g. **Composition:** 0.9250 Silver .8411 oz. ASW **Subject:** Visit of Portugal's President Eanes

| Date | Mintage | F | VF | XF | Unc | BU |
|---|---|---|---|---|---|---|
| 1985(s) | 760 | — | — | — | 90.00 | — |
| 1985(s) Proof | 2,000 | Value: 65.00 | | | | |

**100 PATACAS** **KM# 34** **Weight:** 28.2800 g. **Composition:** 0.9250 Silver .8411 oz. ASW **Subject:** Year of the Tiger

| Date | Mintage | F | VF | XF | Unc | BU |
|---|---|---|---|---|---|---|
| 1986(p) | 760 | — | — | — | 85.00 | — |
| 1986(p) Proof | 3,000 | Value: 65.00 | | | | |

**100 PATACAS** **KM# 36** **Weight:** 28.2800 g. **Composition:** 0.9250 Silver .8411 oz. ASW **Subject:** Year of the Rabbit

| Date | Mintage | F | VF | XF | Unc | BU |
|---|---|---|---|---|---|---|
| 1987(p) | — | — | — | — | 45.00 | — |
| 1987(p) Proof | 5,000 | Value: 60.00 | | | | |

**100 PATACAS** **KM# 38** **Weight:** 28.2800 g. **Composition:** 0.9250 Silver .8411 oz. ASW **Subject:** Year of the Dragon **Reverse:** Dragon walking left **Note:** Similar to 1,000 Patacas, KM#39.

| Date | Mintage | F | VF | XF | Unc | BU |
|---|---|---|---|---|---|---|
| 1988 | — | — | — | — | 50.00 | — |
| 1988 Proof | 5,000 | Value: 65.00 | | | | |

**100 PATACAS** **KM# 40** **Weight:** 28.2800 g. **Composition:** 0.9250 Silver .8411 oz. ASW **Subject:** 35th anniversary of Grand Prix **Reverse:** Racing car, similar to 500 Patacas, KM#42

| Date | Mintage | F | VF | XF | Unc | BU |
|---|---|---|---|---|---|---|
| ND(1988) Proof | 5,000 | Value: 55.00 | | | | |

**100 PATACAS** **KM# 40a** **Composition:** Platinum APW **Subject:** 35th anniversary of Grand Prix **Reverse:** Racing car, similar to 500 Patacas, KM#42

| Date | Mintage | F | VF | XF | Unc | BU |
|---|---|---|---|---|---|---|
| ND(1988) Proof | 10 | Value: 2,750 | | | | |

**100 PATACAS** **KM# 44** **Weight:** 28.2800 g. **Composition:** 0.9250 Silver .8411 oz. ASW **Subject:** Year of the Snake **Reverse:** Coiled snake **Note:** Similar to 1,000 Patacas, KM#45.

| Date | Mintage | F | VF | XF | Unc | BU |
|---|---|---|---|---|---|---|
| 1989(s) | 2,000 | — | — | — | 47.50 | — |
| 1989(s) Proof | 3,000 | Value: 60.00 | | | | |

**100 PATACAS** **KM# 46** **Weight:** 28.2800 g. **Composition:** 0.9250 Silver .8411 oz. ASW **Subject:** Year of the Horse

| Date | Mintage | F | VF | XF | Unc | BU |
|---|---|---|---|---|---|---|
| 1990(s) | 1,000 | — | — | — | 48.50 | — |
| 1990(s) Proof | 3,364 | Value: 75.00 | | | | |

**100 PATACAS** **KM# 48** **Weight:** 28.2800 g. **Composition:** 0.9250 Silver .8411 oz. ASW **Subject:** Year of the Goat **Reverse:** Facing ram **Note:** Similar to KM#51.

| Date | Mintage | F | VF | XF | Unc | BU |
|---|---|---|---|---|---|---|
| 1991(s) | 1,000 | — | — | — | 45.00 | — |
| 1991(s) Proof | Est. 4,000 | Value: 50.00 | | | | |

**100 PATACAS** **KM# 52** **Weight:** 28.2800 g. **Composition:** 0.9250 Silver .8411 oz. ASW **Subject:** Year of the Monkey

| Date | Mintage | F | VF | XF | Unc | BU |
|---|---|---|---|---|---|---|
| 1992(s) | 1,000 | — | — | — | 45.00 | — |
| 1992(s) Proof | Est. 4,000 | Value: 50.00 | | | | |

**100 PATACAS** **KM# 58** **Weight:** 28.2800 g. **Composition:** 0.9250 Silver .8411 oz. ASW **Subject:** Year of the Rooster

| Date | Mintage | F | VF | XF | Unc | BU |
|---|---|---|---|---|---|---|
| 1993 | 500 | — | — | — | 48.50 | — |
| 1993 Proof | Est. 4,000 | Value: 50.00 | | | | |

**100 PATACAS** KM# 62 **Weight:** 28.2800 g. **Composition:** 0.9250 Silver .8411 oz. ASW **Subject:** Macao Grand Prix

| Date | Mintage | F | VF | XF | Unc | BU |
|---|---|---|---|---|---|---|
| ND(1993) Proof | 5,000 | Value: 45.00 | | | | |

**100 PATACAS** KM# 66 **Weight:** 28.2800 g. **Composition:** 0.9250 Silver .8411 oz. ASW **Subject:** Year of the Dog

| Date | Mintage | F | VF | XF | Unc | BU |
|---|---|---|---|---|---|---|
| 1994 | 1,000 | — | — | — | 48.50 | — |
| 1994 Proof | Est. 4,000 | Value: 50.00 | | | | |

**100 PATACAS** KM# 73 **Weight:** 28.2800 g. **Composition:** 0.9250 Silver .8411 oz. ASW **Subject:** Year of the Pig

| Date | Mintage | F | VF | XF | Unc | BU |
|---|---|---|---|---|---|---|
| 1995 | 1,000 | — | — | — | 52.50 | — |
| 1995 Proof | Est. 4,000 | Value: 50.00 | | | | |

**100 PATACAS** KM# 77 **Weight:** 28.2800 g. **Composition:** 0.9250 Silver .8411 oz. ASW **Subject:** Airport

| Date | Mintage | F | VF | XF | Unc | BU |
|---|---|---|---|---|---|---|
| 1995 Proof | 8,000 | Value: 42.50 | | | | |

**100 PATACAS** KM# 79 **Weight:** 28.2800 g. **Composition:** 0.9250 Silver .8411 oz. ASW **Subject:** Year of the Rat

| Date | Mintage | F | VF | XF | Unc | BU |
|---|---|---|---|---|---|---|
| 1996 | 1,000 | — | — | — | 52.50 | — |
| 1996 Proof | Est. 4,000 | Value: 50.00 | | | | |

**100 PATACAS** KM# 84 **Weight:** 28.2800 g. **Composition:** 0.9250 Silver .8411 oz. ASW **Subject:** Year of the Ox **Obverse:** Church facade

| Date | Mintage | F | VF | XF | Unc | BU |
|---|---|---|---|---|---|---|
| 1997 Proof | 4,000 | Value: 50.00 | | | | |

**100 PATACAS** KM# 88 **Weight:** 28.2800 g. **Composition:** 0.9250 Silver .8411 oz. ASW **Subject:** Year of the Tiger **Obverse:** Church facade

| Date | Mintage | F | VF | XF | Unc | BU |
|---|---|---|---|---|---|---|
| 1998 Proof | 5,000 | Value: 50.00 | | | | |

**100 PATACAS** KM# 106 **Weight:** 28.4000 g. **Composition:** 0.9250 Silver .8458 oz. ASW **Subject:** 19th East Asian Insurance Conference **Obverse:** Church facade **Reverse:** Two hands holding world **Edge:** Reeded **Size:** 38.4 mm.

| Date | Mintage | F | VF | XF | Unc | BU |
|---|---|---|---|---|---|---|
| 1998 Proof | Est. 3,000 | — | — | — | 50.00 | — |

**100 PATACAS** **Weight:** 28.2800 g. **Composition:** 0.9250 Silver .8411 oz. ASW **Subject:** Year of the Rabbit **Obverse:** Church facade **Reverse:** Rabbitt **Note:** Similar to 1,000 Patacas, KM#95.

| Date | Mintage | F | VF | XF | Unc | BU |
|---|---|---|---|---|---|---|
| 1999 Proof | Est. 4,000 | Value: 50.00 | | | | |

**100 PATACAS** KM# 96 **Weight:** 31.1035 g. **Composition:** 0.9250 Silver .9250 oz. ASW **Subject:** Macao returns to China **Obverse:** Macao arms **Reverse:** Portuguese and Chinese ships below gold-plated cameo of the Gao Temple

| Date | Mintage | F | VF | XF | Unc | BU |
|---|---|---|---|---|---|---|
| 1999 | Est. 39,000 | — | — | — | 70.00 | — |

**100 PATACAS** KM# 98 **Weight:** 28.2800 g. **Composition:** 0.9250 Silver .8410 oz. ASW **Subject:** Year of the Dragon **Obverse:** Church facade **Reverse:** Dragon **Edge:** Reeded **Size:** 38.6 mm.

| Date | Mintage | F | VF | XF | Unc | BU |
|---|---|---|---|---|---|---|
| 2000 | 1,000 | — | — | — | 40.00 | — |
| 2000 Proof | 4,000 | Value: 55.00 | | | | |

**100 PATACAS** KM# 102 **Weight:** 28.2800 g. **Composition:** 0.9250 Silver .8410 oz. ASW **Subject:** Year of the Snake **Obverse:** Church facade **Reverse:** Snake

| Date | Mintage | F | VF | XF | Unc | BU |
|---|---|---|---|---|---|---|
| 2001 Proof | 4,000 | Value: 55.00 | | | | |

**250 PATACAS** KM# 49 **Weight:** 3.9900 g. **Composition:** 0.9170 Gold .1176 oz. AGW **Subject:** Year of the Goat **Note:** Similar to 1,000 Patacas, KM#51.

| Date | Mintage | F | VF | XF | Unc | BU |
|---|---|---|---|---|---|---|
| 1991 Proof | Est. 2,500 | Value: 110 | | | | |

**250 PATACAS** KM# 53 **Weight:** 3.9900 g. **Composition:** 0.9170 Gold .1176 oz. AGW **Subject:** Year of the Monkey **Note:** Similar to 1,000 Patacas, KM#51.

| Date | Mintage | F | VF | XF | Unc | BU |
|---|---|---|---|---|---|---|
| 1992 Proof | Est. 2,500 | Value: 110 | | | | |

**250 PATACAS** KM# 59 **Weight:** 3.9900 g. **Composition:** 0.9170 Gold .1176 oz. AGW **Subject:** Year of the Rooster **Obverse:** St. Paul's Church **Reverse:** Rooster **Note:** Similar to 1,000 Patacas, KM#58.

| Date | Mintage | F | VF | XF | Unc | BU |
|---|---|---|---|---|---|---|
| 1993 Proof | Est. 2,500 | Value: 110 | | | | |

**250 PATACAS** KM# 67 **Weight:** 3.9900 g. **Composition:** 0.9170 Gold .1176 oz. AGW **Subject:** Year of the Dog **Note:** Similar to 1,000 Patacas, KM#69.

| Date | Mintage | F | VF | XF | Unc | BU |
|---|---|---|---|---|---|---|
| 1994 Proof | Est. 2,500 | Value: 110 | | | | |

**250 PATACAS** KM# 74 **Weight:** 3.9900 g. **Composition:** 0.9170 Gold .1176 oz. AGW **Subject:** Year of the Pig **Obverse:** Building **Reverse:** Pig standing left **Note:** Similar to 100 Patacas, KM#73. In proof sets only.

| Date | Mintage | F | VF | XF | Unc | BU |
|---|---|---|---|---|---|---|
| 1995 Proof | — | Value: 110 | | | | |

**250 PATACAS** KM# 80 **Weight:** 3.9900 g. **Composition:** 0.9170 Gold .1176 oz. AGW **Subject:** Year of the Rat

| Date | Mintage | F | VF | XF | Unc | BU |
|---|---|---|---|---|---|---|
| 1996 | — | Value: 120 | | | | |

**250 PATACAS** KM# 85 **Weight:** 3.9900 g. **Composition:** 0.9170 Gold .1176 oz. AGW **Subject:** Year of the Ox **Note:** Similar to 100 Patacas, KM#84.

| Date | Mintage | F | VF | XF | Unc | BU |
|---|---|---|---|---|---|---|
| 1997 In proof sets only | Est. 2,500 | Value: 115 | | | | |

**250 PATACAS** KM# 89 **Weight:** 3.9900 g. **Composition:** 0.9170 Gold .1176 oz. AGW **Subject:** Year of the Tiger **Note:** Similar to 100 Patacas, KM#88.

| Date | Mintage | F | VF | XF | Unc | BU |
|---|---|---|---|---|---|---|
| 1998 In proof sets only | Est. 2,500 | Value: 115 | | | | |

**250 PATACAS** KM# 93 **Weight:** 3.9900 g. **Composition:** 0.9170 Gold .1176 oz. AGW **Subject:** Year of the Rabbit **Obverse:** Church facade **Reverse:** Rabbit **Note:** Similar to 1,000 Patacas, KM#95.

| Date | Mintage | F | VF | XF | Unc | BU |
|---|---|---|---|---|---|---|
| 1999 In proof sets only | Est. 2,500 | Value: 115 | | | | |

**250 PATACAS** KM# 99 **Weight:** 3.9900 g. **Composition:** 0.9167 Gold .1176 oz. AGW **Subject:** Year of the Dragon **Obverse:** Church facade **Reverse:** Dragon **Edge:** Reeded **Size:** 19.3 mm.

| Date | Mintage | F | VF | XF | Unc | BU |
|---|---|---|---|---|---|---|
| 2000 In Proof sets only | 2,500 | Value: 125 | | | | |

**250 PATACAS** KM# 103 **Weight:** 3.9900 g. **Composition:** 0.9167 Gold .1176 oz. AGW **Subject:** Year of the Snake **Obverse:** Church facade **Reverse:** Snake

| Date | Mintage | F | VF | XF | Unc | BU |
|---|---|---|---|---|---|---|
| 2001 In Proof sets only | 2,500 | Value: 125 | | | | |

**500 PATACAS** **KM# 12** **Weight:** 7.9600 g. **Composition:** 0.9170 Gold .2347 oz. AGW **Subject:** 25th anniversary of Grand Prix **Obverse:** Church facade

| Date | Mintage | F | VF | XF | Unc | BU |
|---|---|---|---|---|---|---|
| 1978 Proof | 550 | Value: 300 | | | | |

**500 PATACAS** **KM# 13** **Weight:** 7.9600 g. **Composition:** 0.9170 Gold .2347 oz. AGW **Reverse:** Racing car without advertising

| Date | Mintage | F | VF | XF | Unc | BU |
|---|---|---|---|---|---|---|
| 1978 Proof | 5,500 | Value: 185 | | | | |

**500 PATACAS** **KM# 15** **Weight:** 7.9600 g. **Composition:** 0.9170 Gold .2347 oz. AGW **Subject:** Year of the Goat

| Date | Mintage | F | VF | XF | Unc | BU |
|---|---|---|---|---|---|---|
| 1979 Proof | 5,500 | Value: 145 | | | | |

**500 PATACAS** **KM# 41** **Weight:** 155.5150 g. **Composition:** 0.9990 Silver 5 oz. ASW **Subject:** 35th anniversary of Grand Prix **Note:** Similar to KM#42.

| Date | Mintage | F | VF | XF | Unc | BU |
|---|---|---|---|---|---|---|
| 1988 Proof | 2,000 | Value: 145 | | | | |

**500 PATACAS** **KM# 42** **Weight:** 7.9881 g. **Composition:** 0.9170 Gold .2354 oz. AGW **Subject:** 35th anniversary of Grand Prix

| Date | Mintage | F | VF | XF | Unc | BU |
|---|---|---|---|---|---|---|
| ND(1988) Proof | 4,500 | Value: 185 | | | | |

**500 PATACAS** **KM# 50** **Weight:** 7.9881 g. **Composition:** 0.9170 Gold .2354 oz. AGW **Subject:** Year of the Goat **Note:** Similar to 1,000 Patacas, KM#51.

| Date | Mintage | F | VF | XF | Unc | BU |
|---|---|---|---|---|---|---|
| 1991 Proof | Est. 2,500 | Value: 185 | | | | |

**500 PATACAS** **KM# 54** **Weight:** 7.9900 g. **Composition:** 0.9170 Gold .2352 oz. AGW **Subject:** Year of the Monkey **Note:** Similar to 1,000 Patacas, KM#51.

| Date | Mintage | F | VF | XF | Unc | BU |
|---|---|---|---|---|---|---|
| 1992 Proof | Est. 2,500 | Value: 200 | | | | |

**500 PATACAS** **KM# 60** **Weight:** 7.9900 g. **Composition:** 0.9170 Gold .2352 oz. AGW **Subject:** Year of the Rooster **Obverse:** St. Paul's Church **Reverse:** Rooster **Note:** Similar to 100 Patacas, KM#58.

| Date | Mintage | F | VF | XF | Unc | BU |
|---|---|---|---|---|---|---|
| 1993 Proof | Est. 2,500 | Value: 200 | | | | |

**500 PATACAS** **KM# 63** **Weight:** 155.6000 g. **Composition:** 0.9990 Silver 5 oz. ASW **Subject:** Macao Grand Prix

| Date | Mintage | F | VF | XF | Unc | BU |
|---|---|---|---|---|---|---|
| 1993 Proof | 2,000 | Value: 145 | | | | |

**500 PATACAS** **KM# 64** **Weight:** 7.9900 g. **Composition:** 0.9170 Gold .2352 oz. AGW **Subject:** Macao Grand Prix

| Date | Mintage | F | VF | XF | Unc | BU |
|---|---|---|---|---|---|---|
| ND(1993) Proof | 4,500 | Value: 185 | | | | |

**500 PATACAS** **KM# 68** **Weight:** 7.9900 g. **Composition:** 0.9170 Gold .2352 oz. AGW **Subject:** Year of the Dog **Note:** Similar to 1,000 Patacas, KM#69.

| Date | Mintage | F | VF | XF | Unc | BU |
|---|---|---|---|---|---|---|
| 1994 Proof | Est. 2,500 | Value: 210 | | | | |

**500 PATACAS** **KM# 75** **Weight:** 7.9900 g. **Composition:** 0.9170 Gold .2352 oz. AGW **Subject:** Year of the Pig **Obverse:** Building **Reverse:** Pig standing left **Note:** Similar to 1,000 Patacas, KM#73.

| Date | Mintage | F | VF | XF | Unc | BU |
|---|---|---|---|---|---|---|
| 1995 In proof sets only | Est. 2,000 | Value: 210 | | | | |

**500 PATACAS** **KM# 81** **Weight:** 7.9900 g. **Composition:** 0.9170 Gold .2352 oz. AGW **Subject:** Year of the Rat

| Date | Mintage | F | VF | XF | Unc | BU |
|---|---|---|---|---|---|---|
| 1996 Proof | — | Value: 210 | | | | |

**500 PATACAS** **KM# 86** **Weight:** 7.9900 g. **Composition:** 0.9170 Gold .2352 oz. AGW **Subject:** Year of the Ox **Note:** Similar to 100 Patacas, KM#84.

| Date | Mintage | F | VF | XF | Unc | BU |
|---|---|---|---|---|---|---|
| 1997 In proof sets only | 2,000 | Value: 225 | | | | |

**500 PATACAS** **KM# 90** **Weight:** 7.9900 g. **Composition:** 0.9170 Gold .2352 oz. AGW **Subject:** Year of the Tiger **Note:** Similar to 100 Patacas, KM#88.

| Date | Mintage | F | VF | XF | Unc | BU |
|---|---|---|---|---|---|---|
| 1998 In proof sets only | 2,500 | Value: 225 | | | | |

**500 PATACAS** **KM# 94** **Weight:** 7.9900 g. **Composition:** 0.9170 Gold .2352 oz. AGW **Subject:** Year of the Rabbit **Obverse:** Church facade **Reverse:** Rabbit **Note:** Similar to 1,000 Patacas, KM#95.

| Date | Mintage | F | VF | XF | Unc | BU |
|---|---|---|---|---|---|---|
| 1999 In proof sets only | Est. 2,500 | Value: 225 | | | | |

**500 PATACAS** **KM# 100** **Weight:** 7.9900 g. **Composition:** 0.9167 Gold .2355 oz. AGW **Subject:** Year of the Dragon **Obverse:** Church facade **Reverse:** Dragon **Edge:** Reeded **Size:** 22.05 mm.

| Date | Mintage | F | VF | XF | Unc | BU |
|---|---|---|---|---|---|---|
| 2000 In Proof sets only | 2,500 | Value: 250 | | | | |

**500 PATACAS** **KM# 104** **Weight:** 7.9900 g. **Composition:** 0.9167 Gold .2355 oz. AGW **Subject:** Year of the Snake **Obverse:** Church facade **Reverse:** Snake

| Date | Mintage | F | VF | XF | Unc | BU |
|---|---|---|---|---|---|---|
| 2001 In Proof sets only | 2,500 | Value: 250 | | | | |

**1000 PATACAS** **KM# 17** **Weight:** 15.9760 g. **Composition:** 0.9170 Gold .4711 oz. AGW **Subject:** Year of the Monkey

| Date | Mintage | F | VF | XF | Unc | BU |
|---|---|---|---|---|---|---|
| 1980 Proof | 5,500 | Value: 385 | | | | |

**1000 PATACAS** **KM# 19** **Weight:** 15.9760 g. **Composition:** 0.9170 Gold .4711 oz. AGW **Subject:** Year of the Cockerel

| Date | Mintage | F | VF | XF | Unc | BU |
|---|---|---|---|---|---|---|
| 1981 | 3,500 | — | — | — | 265 | — |
| 1981 Proof | Inc. above | Value: 300 | | | | |

**1000 PATACAS** **KM# 26** **Weight:** 15.9760 g. **Composition:** 0.9170 Gold .4711 oz. AGW **Subject:** Year of the Dog

| Date | Mintage | F | VF | XF | Unc | BU |
|---|---|---|---|---|---|---|
| 1982 | 256 | — | — | — | 325 | — |
| 1982 Proof | 255 | Value: 470 | | | | |

**1000 PATACAS** **KM# 28** **Weight:** 15.9760 g. **Composition:** 0.9170 Gold .4711 oz. AGW **Subject:** Year of the Pig

| Date | Mintage | F | VF | XF | Unc | BU |
|---|---|---|---|---|---|---|
| 1983 | 400 | — | — | — | 325 | — |
| 1983 Proof | 500 | Value: 450 | | | | |

**1000 PATACAS** **KM# 30** **Weight:** 15.9760 g. **Composition:** 0.9170 Gold .4711 oz. AGW **Subject:** Year of the Rat

| Date | Mintage | F | VF | XF | Unc | BU |
|---|---|---|---|---|---|---|
| 1984 | 2,000 | — | — | — | 275 | — |
| 1984 Proof | 3,000 | Value: 350 | | | | |

**1000 PATACAS** **KM# 32** **Weight:** 15.9760 g. **Composition:** 0.9170 Gold .4711 oz. AGW **Subject:** Year of the Ox

| Date | Mintage | F | VF | XF | Unc | BU |
|---|---|---|---|---|---|---|
| 1985 | 10,000 | — | — | — | 225 | — |
| 1985 Proof | 5,000 | Value: 275 | | | | |

**1000 PATACAS** **KM# 35** **Weight:** 15.9760 g. **Composition:** 0.9170 Gold .4711 oz. AGW **Subject:** Year of the Tiger

| Date | Mintage | F | VF | XF | Unc | BU |
|---|---|---|---|---|---|---|
| 1986(p) | 2,000 | — | — | — | 225 | — |
| 1986(p) Proof | 3,000 | Value: 265 | | | | |

**1000 PATACAS** **KM# 37** **Weight:** 15.9760 g. **Composition:** 0.9170 Gold .4711 oz. AGW **Subject:** Year of the Rabbit

| Date | Mintage | F | VF | XF | Unc | BU |
|---|---|---|---|---|---|---|
| 1987(p) | — | — | — | — | 225 | — |
| 1987(p) Proof | 5,000 | Value: 265 | | | | |

**1000 PATACAS** **KM# 39** **Weight:** 15.9760 g. **Composition:** 0.9170 Gold .4711 oz. AGW **Subject:** Year of the Dragon

| Date | Mintage | F | VF | XF | Unc | BU |
|---|---|---|---|---|---|---|
| 1988 Proof | 5,000 | Value: 265 | | | | |

**1000 PATACAS** KM# 45 **Weight:** 15.9760 g. **Composition:** 0.9170 Gold .4711 oz. AGW **Subject:** Year of the Snake

| Date | Mintage | F | VF | XF | Unc | BU |
|---|---|---|---|---|---|---|
| 1989 | 2,000 | — | — | — | 235 | — |
| 1989 Proof | 3,000 | Value: 300 | | | | |

**1000 PATACAS** KM# 47 **Weight:** 15.9760 g. **Composition:** 0.9170 Gold .4711 oz. AGW **Subject:** Year of the Horse

| Date | Mintage | F | VF | XF | Unc | BU |
|---|---|---|---|---|---|---|
| 1990 | 2,000 | — | — | — | 235 | — |
| 1990 Proof | 3,000 | Value: 300 | | | | |

**1000 PATACAS** KM# 51 **Weight:** 15.9760 g. **Composition:** 0.9170 Gold .4711 oz. AGW **Subject:** Year of the Goat

| Date | Mintage | F | VF | XF | Unc | BU |
|---|---|---|---|---|---|---|
| 1991 | Est. 500 | — | — | — | 375 | — |
| 1991 Proof | Est. 4,500 | Value: 425 | | | | |

**1000 PATACAS** KM# 55 **Weight:** 15.9760 g. **Composition:** 0.9170 Gold .4711 oz. AGW **Subject:** Year of the Monkey

| Date | Mintage | F | VF | XF | Unc | BU |
|---|---|---|---|---|---|---|
| 1992 | Est. 500 | — | — | — | 375 | — |
| 1992 Proof | Est. 4,500 | Value: 425 | | | | |

**1000 PATACAS** KM# 61 **Weight:** 15.9760 g. **Composition:** 0.9170 Gold .4711 oz. AGW **Subject:** Year of the Rooster **Obverse:** St. Paul's Church **Reverse:** Rooster **Note:** Similar to 100 Patacas, KM#58.

| Date | Mintage | F | VF | XF | Unc | BU |
|---|---|---|---|---|---|---|
| 1993 | Est. 500 | — | — | — | 375 | — |
| 1993 Proof | Est. 4,500 | Value: 425 | | | | |

**1000 PATACAS** KM# 69 **Weight:** 15.9760 g. **Composition:** 0.9170 Gold .4711 oz. AGW **Subject:** Year of the Dog

| Date | Mintage | F | VF | XF | Unc | BU |
|---|---|---|---|---|---|---|
| 1994 | Est. 500 | — | — | — | 375 | — |
| 1994 Proof | Est. 4,500 | Value: 425 | | | | |

**1000 PATACAS** KM# 76 **Weight:** 15.9760 g. **Composition:** 0.9170 Gold .4711 oz. AGW **Subject:** Year of the Pig **Obverse:** Building **Reverse:** Pig standing left **Note:** Similar to 100 Patacas, KM#73.

| Date | Mintage | F | VF | XF | Unc | BU |
|---|---|---|---|---|---|---|
| 1995 | Est. 500 | — | — | — | 375 | — |
| 1995 Proof | Est. 4,500 | Value: 425 | | | | |

**1000 PATACAS** KM# 78 **Weight:** 15.9760 g. **Composition:** 0.9170 Gold .4711 oz. AGW **Subject:** Airport **Obverse:** Stylized form **Reverse:** City aerial view **Note:** Similar to 100 Patacas, KM#77.

| Date | Mintage | F | VF | XF | Unc | BU |
|---|---|---|---|---|---|---|
| 1995 Proof | 5,000 | Value: 425 | | | | |

**1000 PATACAS** KM# 82 **Weight:** 15.9760 g. **Composition:** 0.9170 Gold .4711 oz. AGW **Subject:** Year of the Rat

| Date | Mintage | F | VF | XF | Unc | BU |
|---|---|---|---|---|---|---|
| 1996 Proof | — | Value: 450 | | | | |

**1000 PATACAS** KM# 87 **Weight:** 15.9760 g. **Composition:** 0.9170 Gold .4711 oz. AGW **Subject:** Year of the Ox **Note:** Similar to 100 Patacas, KM#84.

| Date | Mintage | F | VF | XF | Unc | BU |
|---|---|---|---|---|---|---|
| 1997 Proof | 5,000 | Value: 500 | | | | |

**1000 PATACAS** KM# 91 **Weight:** 15.9760 g. **Composition:** 0.9170 Gold .4711 oz. AGW **Subject:** Year of the Tiger **Note:** Similar to 100 Patacas, KM#88.

| Date | Mintage | F | VF | XF | Unc | BU |
|---|---|---|---|---|---|---|
| 1998 Proof | 5,000 | Value: 500 | | | | |

**1000 PATACAS** KM# 95 **Weight:** 15.9760 g. **Composition:** 0.9170 Gold .4711 oz. AGW **Subject:** Year of the Rabbit **Obverse:** Church facade **Reverse:** Rabbit **Note:** Similar to 100 Patacas, KM#88.

| Date | Mintage | F | VF | XF | Unc | BU |
|---|---|---|---|---|---|---|
| 1999 Proof | 4,000 | Value: 500 | | | | |

**1000 PATACAS** KM# 101 **Weight:** 15.9760 g. **Composition:** 0.9167 Gold .4709 oz. AGW **Subject:** Year of the Dragon **Obverse:** Church facade **Reverse:** Dragon **Edge:** Reeded **Size:** 28.4 mm.

| Date | Mintage | F | VF | XF | Unc | BU |
|---|---|---|---|---|---|---|
| 2000 | 500 | — | — | — | 400 | — |
| 2000 Proof | 4,000 | Value: 500 | | | | |

**1000 PATACAS** KM# 105 **Weight:** 16.9760 g. **Composition:** 0.9167 Gold .4709 oz. AGW **Subject:** Year of the Snake **Obverse:** Church facade **Reverse:** Snake

| Date | Mintage | F | VF | XF | Unc | BU |
|---|---|---|---|---|---|---|
| 2001 Proof | 4,000 | Value: 500 | | | | |

**10000 PATACAS** KM# 43 **Weight:** 155.5150 g. **Composition:** 0.9990 Gold 5 oz. AGW **Subject:** 35th anniversary of Grand Prix **Note:** Similar to 500 Patacas, KM#42.

| Date | Mintage | F | VF | XF | Unc | BU |
|---|---|---|---|---|---|---|
| 1988 Proof | 500 | Value: 3,000 | | | | |

**10000 PATACAS** KM# 65 **Weight:** 155.5150 g. **Composition:** 0.9990 Gold 5 oz. AGW **Subject:** Macao Grand Prix **Note:** Similar to 500 Patacas, KM#64.

| Date | Mintage | F | VF | XF | Unc | BU |
|---|---|---|---|---|---|---|
| 1993 Proof | 500 | Value: 2,800 | | | | |

## PROVAS

Standard metals

Stamped "PROVA" in field

| KM# | Date | Mintage | Identification | Issue Price | Mkt Val |
|---|---|---|---|---|---|
| Pr1 | 1952 | — | 5 Avos. | — | 20.00 |
| Pr2 | 1952 | — | 10 Avos. | — | 20.00 |
| Pr3 | 1952 | — | 50 Avos. | — | 25.00 |
| Pr4 | 1952 | — | Pataca. | — | 28.00 |
| Pr5 | 1952 | — | 5 Patacas. | — | 32.00 |
| Pr6 | 1967 | — | 5 Avos. | — | 20.00 |
| Pr7 | 1967 | — | 10 Avos. | — | 20.00 |
| Pr8 | 1968 | — | 10 Avos. | — | 20.00 |
| Pr9 | 1968 | — | Pataca. | — | 25.00 |
| Pr10 | 1969 | — | 10 Avos. | — | 10.00 |
| Pr11 | 1971 | — | 5 Patacas. | — | 25.00 |
| Pr12 | 1972 | — | 50 Avos. | — | 20.00 |
| Pr13 | 1973 | — | 50 Avos. | — | 20.00 |
| Pr14 | 1974 | — | 20 Patacas. | — | 35.00 |
| Pr15 | 1975 | — | Pataca. | — | 25.00 |

## PROOF SETS

| KM# | Date | Mintage | Identification | Issue Price | Mkt Val |
|---|---|---|---|---|---|
| PS1 | 1982 (5) | 2,000 | KM20a-24a | — | 82.50 |
| PS1b | 1982 (5) | 150 | KM20b-24b | — | 950 |
| PS1c | 1982 (5) | 375 | KM20c-24c | — | 1,450 |
| PS2 | 1983 (5) | 2,500 | KM20a-24a | 55.00 | 82.50 |
| PS3 | 1984 (5) | 2,500 | KM20a-24a | 55.00 | 82.50 |
| PS4 | 1985 (5) | 2,500 | KM20a-24a | 55.00 | 82.50 |
| PS5 | 1987 (2) | — | KM36-37 | — | 265 |
| PS6 | 1988 (2) | — | KM38-39 | — | 275 |
| PS7 | 1991 (3) | 2,500 | KM49-51 | 775 | 650 |
| PS8 | 1992 (3) | 2,500 | KM53-55 | 825 | 700 |
| PS9 | 1993 (3) | 2,500 | KM59-61 | 830 | 700 |
| PS10 | 1994 (3) | 2,500 | KM67-69 | 825 | 735 |
| PS11 | 1995 (3) | 2,500 | KM74-76 | 825 | 735 |
| PS12 | 1997 (3) | 2,500 | KM85-87 | 849 | 840 |
| PS13 | 1998 (3) | 2,500 | KM89-91 | 855 | 840 |
| PS14 | 1999 (3) | 2,500 | KM93-95 | 850 | 840 |
| PS15 | 2000 (3) | 2,500 | KM#99-101 | 849 | — |
| PS16 | 2001 (3) | 2,500 | KM#103-105 | 849 | — |

The Republic of Macedonia is land-locked, and is bordered in the north by Yugoslavia, to the east by Bulgaria, in the south by Greece and to the west by Albania and has an area of 9,781 sq. mi. (25,713 sq. km.) and a population at the 1991 census was 2,038,847, of which the predominating ethnic groups were Macedonians. The capital is Skopje.

The Slavs settled in Macedonia since the 6th century, who had been Christianized by Byzantium, were conquered by the non-Slav Bulgars in the 7th century and in the9th century formed a Macedo-Bulgarian empire, the western part of which survived until Byzantine conquest in 1014. In the 14th century, it fell to Serbia, and in1355 to the Ottomans. After the Balkan Wars of 1912-13 Turkey was ousted, and Serbia received the greater part of the territory, the balance going to Bulgaria and Greece. In 1918, Yugoslav Macedonia was incorporated into Serbia as 'South Serbia', becoming a republic in the S.F.R. of Yugoslavia. Claims to the historical Macedonian territory have long been a source of contention between Bulgaria and Greece.

On Nov. 20, 1991 parliament promulgated a new constitution, and declared its independence on Nov.20, 1992, but failed to secure EC and US recognition owing to Greek objections to use of the name *Macedonia*. On Dec. 11, 1992, the UN Security Council authorized the expedition of a small peacekeeping force to prevent hostilities spreading into Macedonia.

There is a 120-member single-chamber National Assembly.

# REPUBLIC

## STANDARD COINAGE

**50 DENI** KM# 1 **Composition:** Brass **Obverse:** Seagull flying offshore

| Date | Mintage | F | VF | XF | Unc | BU |
|---|---|---|---|---|---|---|
| 1993 | — | — | 0.10 | 0.20 | 0.50 | — |

**DENAR** KM# 2 **Composition:** Brass **Obverse:** Yugoslavian sheep dog standing left

| Date | Mintage | F | VF | XF | Unc | BU |
|---|---|---|---|---|---|---|
| 1993 | — | — | 0.20 | 0.35 | 1.00 | — |
| 1997 | — | — | 0.20 | 0.35 | 1.00 | — |

**DENAR** KM# 5 **Composition:** Brass **Series:** F.A.O. **Obverse:** Yugoslavian sheep dog

| Date | Mintage | F | VF | XF | Unc | BU |
|---|---|---|---|---|---|---|
| 1995 | 70,000 | — | — | — | 0.75 | — |

**DENAR** KM#5a **Composition:** Copper-Nickel-Zinc **Series:** F.A.O. **Obverse:** Yugoslavian sheep dog

| Date | Mintage | F | VF | XF | Unc | BU |
|---|---|---|---|---|---|---|
| 1995 | — | — | — | — | 0.75 | — |

**DENAR** KM# 8 **Weight:** 15.9800 g. **Composition:** 0.9167 Gold .4709 oz. AGW **Subject:** 5th anniversary - UN membership **Reverse:** Pair of white storks

| Date | Mintage | F | VF | XF | Unc | BU |
|---|---|---|---|---|---|---|
| ND(1996) Proof | 1,500 | Value: 375 | | | | |

**DENAR** KM# 9 **Composition:** Brass **Obverse:** Byzantine coin **Reverse:** Ornamented cross

| Date | Mintage | F | VF | XF | Unc | BU |
|---|---|---|---|---|---|---|
| 2000 | — | — | — | — | 1.25 | — |

**2 DENARI** KM# 3 **Composition:** Brass **Obverse:** Fish above water

| Date | Mintage | F | VF | XF | Unc | BU |
|---|---|---|---|---|---|---|
| 1993 | — | — | 0.25 | 0.50 | 1.25 | — |

**2 DENARI** KM# 6 **Composition:** Brass **Series:** F.A.O. **Obverse:** Fish

| Date | Mintage | F | VF | XF | Unc | BU |
|---|---|---|---|---|---|---|
| 1995 | 70,000 | — | — | — | 1.00 | — |

**2 DENARI** KM# 6a **Composition:** Copper-Nickel-Zinc **Series:** F.A.O. **Obverse:** Fish

| Date | Mintage | F | VF | XF | Unc | BU |
|---|---|---|---|---|---|---|
| 1995 | — | — | — | — | 1.00 | — |

**5 DENARI** KM# 4 **Composition:** Brass **Obverse:** European lynx

| Date | Mintage | F | VF | XF | Unc | BU |
|---|---|---|---|---|---|---|
| 1993 | — | — | 0.35 | 0.75 | 1.75 | — |

**5 DENARI** KM# 7 **Composition:** Brass **Series:** F.A.O. **Obverse:** European lynx

| Date | Mintage | F | VF | XF | Unc | BU |
|---|---|---|---|---|---|---|
| 1995 | 70,000 | — | — | — | 1.25 | — |

**5 DENARI** KM# 7a **Composition:** Copper-Nickel-Zinc **Series:** F.A.O. **Obverse:** European lynx

| Date | Mintage | F | VF | XF | Unc | BU |
|---|---|---|---|---|---|---|
| 1995 | — | — | — | — | 1.25 | — |

## MINT SETS

| KM# | Date | Mintage | Identification | Issue Price | Mkt Val |
|---|---|---|---|---|---|
| MS1 | 1993 (4) | — | KM1-4 | — | 6.50 |
| MS2 | 1995 (3) | — | KM5a-7a | — | 5.50 |

# MADAGASCAR

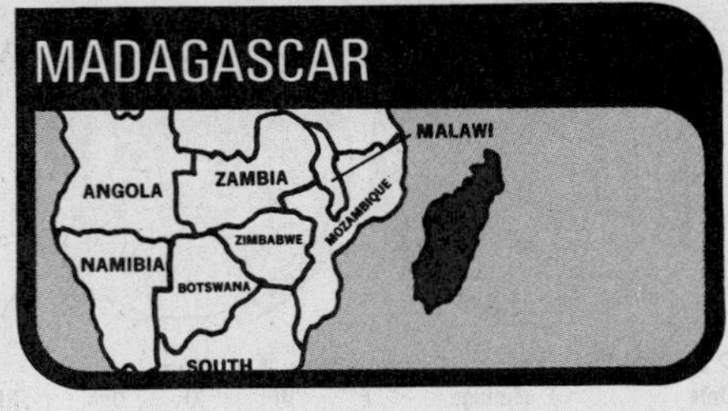


The Democratic Republic of Madagascar, an independent member of the French Community located in the Indian Ocean 250 miles (402 km.) off the southeast coast of Africa, has an area of 226,656 sq. mi. (587,040 sq. km.) and a population of 10 million. Capital: Antananarivo. The economy is primarily agricultural; large bauxite deposits are being developed. Coffee, vanilla, graphite, and rice are exported.

Successive waves of immigrants from south-east Asia, Africa, Arabia and India populated Madagascar beginning about 2,000 years ago. Diago Diaz, a Portuguese navigator, sighted the island of Madagascar on Aug. 10, 1500,when his ship became separated from an India-bound fleet. Attempts at settlement by the British during the reign of Charles I and by the French during the 17th and 18th centuries were of no avail, and the island became a refuge and supply base for Indian Ocean pirates. Despite considerable influence on the island, the British accepted the imposition of a French protectorate in 1886 in return for French recognition of Britain's sphere of influence in Zanzibar. Madagascar was made a French colony in 1896 after absolute control had been established by military force. Britain occupied the island after the fall of France, 1942, to prevent its seizure by the Japanese, returning it to the Free French in 1943. On Oct. 14, 1958, following a decade of intermittent but bitter warfare, Madagascar, as the Malagasy Republic, became an autonomous state within the French Community. On June 27, 1960, it became a sovereign, independent nation, though remaining nominally within the French Community. The Malagasy republic was renamed the Democratic Republic of Madagascar in 1975.

**MONETARY SYSTEM**

100 Centimes = 1 Franc

**MINT MARKS**

(a) - Paris, privy marks only
SA - Pretoria

## FRENCH COLONY

### STANDARD COINAGE

**50 CENTIMES** KM# 1 **Composition:** Bronze

| Date | Mintage | F | VF | XF | Unc | BU |
|---|---|---|---|---|---|---|
| 1943SA | 2,000,000 | 1.50 | 2.50 | 10.00 | 30.00 | — |

**FRANC** KM# 2 **Composition:** Bronze

| Date | Mintage | F | VF | XF | Unc | BU |
|---|---|---|---|---|---|---|
| 1943SA | 5,000,000 | 3.00 | 6.00 | 22.00 | 65.00 | — |

**FRANC** KM# 3 **Composition:** Aluminum

| Date | Mintage | F | VF | XF | Unc | BU |
|---|---|---|---|---|---|---|
| 1948(a) | 7,400,000 | 0.25 | 0.35 | 0.75 | 2.50 | — |
| 1958(a) | 2,600,000 | 0.25 | 0.35 | 0.75 | 2.75 | — |

**2 FRANCS** KM# 4 **Composition:** Aluminum

| Date | Mintage | F | VF | XF | Unc | BU |
|---|---|---|---|---|---|---|
| 1948(a) | 10,000,000 | 0.25 | 0.45 | 0.85 | 2.25 | — |

**5 FRANCS** KM# 5 **Composition:** Aluminum

| Date | Mintage | F | VF | XF | Unc | BU |
|---|---|---|---|---|---|---|
| 1953(a) | 30,012,000 | 0.25 | 0.55 | 1.00 | 2.50 | — |

**10 FRANCS** KM# 6 **Composition:** Aluminum-Bronze

| Date | Mintage | F | VF | XF | Unc | BU |
|---|---|---|---|---|---|---|
| 1953(a) | 25,000,000 | 0.35 | 0.65 | 1.25 | 3.50 | — |

**20 FRANCS** KM# 7 **Composition:** Aluminum-Bronze

| Date | Mintage | F | VF | XF | Unc | BU |
|---|---|---|---|---|---|---|
| 1953(a) | 15,000,000 | 0.75 | 1.50 | 3.00 | 6.50 | — |

## TOKEN COINAGE

**25 CENTIMES** KM# tn1 (prevKMtn1) **Composition:** Aluminum **Issuer:** Societe des Mines d'Or de Andavakoera **Obverse:** Legend of issuer around value **Reverse:** Parakeet head left **Size:** 21 mm.

| Date | Mintage | VG | F | VF | XF | Unc |
|---|---|---|---|---|---|---|
| ND(1920) | — | 10.00 | 20.00 | 50.00 | 120 | — |

**50 CENTIMES** KM# tn2 **Composition:** Aluminum **Issuer:** Societe des Mines d'Or de Andavakoera **Size:** 28 mm. **Note:** Similar to KM#Tn1.

| Date | Mintage | VG | F | VF | XF | Unc |
|---|---|---|---|---|---|---|
| ND(1920) | — | 7.50 | 15.00 | 30.00 | 100 | — |

**FRANC** KM# tn3 **Composition:** Aluminum **Issuer:** Societe des Mines d'Or de Andavakoera **Size:** 32 mm. **Note:** Similar to KM#Tn1.

| Date | Mintage | VG | F | VF | XF | Unc |
|---|---|---|---|---|---|---|
| ND(1920) | — | 9.00 | 18.00 | 35.00 | 100 | — |

# MALAGASY REPUBLIC

## STANDARD COINAGE

5 Francs = 1 Ariary

**FRANC** KM# 8 **Composition:** Stainless Steel

| Date | Mintage | F | VF | XF | Unc | BU |
|---|---|---|---|---|---|---|
| 1965(a) | 1,170,000 | 0.10 | 0.15 | 0.30 | 1.25 | — |
| 1966(a) | — | 0.10 | 0.15 | 0.30 | 1.25 | — |
| 1970(a) | — | 0.10 | 0.15 | 0.30 | 1.25 | — |
| 1974(a) | 1,250,000 | 0.10 | 0.15 | 0.30 | 1.25 | — |
| 1975(a) | 7,355,000 | 0.10 | 0.15 | 0.30 | 1.25 | — |
| 1976(a) | — | 0.10 | 0.15 | 0.30 | 1.25 | — |
| 1977(a) | — | 0.10 | 0.15 | 0.30 | 1.25 | — |
| 1979(a) | — | 0.10 | 0.15 | 0.30 | 1.25 | — |
| 1980(a) | — | 0.15 | 0.20 | 0.40 | 1.45 | — |
| 1981(a) | — | 0.15 | 0.20 | 0.40 | 1.45 | — |
| 1982(a) | — | 0.15 | 0.20 | 0.40 | 1.45 | — |
| 1983(a) | — | 0.15 | 0.20 | 0.40 | 1.45 | — |
| 1986(a) | — | 0.15 | 0.20 | 0.40 | 1.45 | — |
| 1987(a) | — | 0.15 | 0.20 | 0.40 | 1.45 | — |
| 1988(a) | — | 0.15 | 0.20 | 0.40 | 1.45 | — |
| 1989(a) | — | 0.15 | 0.20 | 0.40 | 1.45 | — |
| 1991(a) | — | 0.15 | 0.20 | 0.40 | 1.45 | — |
| 1993(a) | — | 0.15 | 0.20 | 0.40 | 1.45 | — |

**2 FRANCS** KM# 9 **Composition:** Stainless Steel

| Date | Mintage | F | VF | XF | Unc | BU |
|---|---|---|---|---|---|---|
| 1965(a) | 760,000 | 0.15 | 0.25 | 0.50 | 1.50 | — |
| 1970(a) | — | 0.15 | 0.25 | 0.45 | 1.25 | — |
| 1974(a) | 1,250,000 | 0.15 | 0.25 | 0.45 | 1.25 | — |
| 1975(a) | 8,250,000 | 0.15 | 0.25 | 0.45 | 1.25 | — |
| 1976(a) | — | 0.15 | 0.25 | 0.45 | 1.25 | — |
| 1977(a) | — | 0.15 | 0.25 | 0.45 | 1.25 | — |
| 1979(a) | — | 0.15 | 0.25 | 0.45 | 1.25 | — |
| 1980(a) | — | 0.15 | 0.25 | 0.45 | 1.25 | — |
| 1981(a) | — | 0.15 | 0.25 | 0.45 | 1.25 | — |
| 1982(a) | — | 0.15 | 0.25 | 0.45 | 1.25 | — |
| 1983(a) | — | 0.15 | 0.25 | 0.45 | 1.25 | — |
| 1984(a) | — | 0.15 | 0.25 | 0.45 | 1.25 | — |
| 1986(a) | — | 0.15 | 0.25 | 0.45 | 1.25 | — |
| 1987(a) | — | 0.15 | 0.25 | 0.45 | 1.25 | — |
| 1988(a) | — | 0.15 | 0.25 | 0.45 | 1.25 | — |
| 1989(a) | — | 0.15 | 0.25 | 0.45 | 1.25 | — |

**5 FRANCS (Ariary)** KM# 10 **Composition:** Stainless Steel

| Date | Mintage | F | VF | XF | Unc | BU |
|---|---|---|---|---|---|---|
| 1966(a) | — | 0.15 | 0.25 | 0.60 | 1.75 | — |
| 1967(a) | — | 0.15 | 0.25 | 0.60 | 1.75 | — |
| 1968(a) | 7,500,000 | 0.15 | 0.25 | 0.60 | 1.75 | — |
| 1970(a) | — | 0.15 | 0.25 | 0.60 | 1.75 | — |
| 1972(a) | 19,100,000 | 0.15 | 0.25 | 0.60 | 1.75 | — |
| 1976(a) | — | 0.15 | 0.25 | 0.60 | 1.75 | — |
| 1977(a) | — | 0.15 | 0.25 | 0.60 | 1.75 | — |
| 1979(a) | — | 0.15 | 0.25 | 0.60 | 1.75 | — |
| 1980(a) | — | 0.20 | 0.30 | 0.65 | 1.85 | — |
| 1981(a) | — | 0.20 | 0.30 | 0.65 | 1.85 | — |
| 1983(a) | — | 0.20 | 0.30 | 0.65 | 1.85 | — |
| 1984(a) | — | 0.20 | 0.30 | 0.65 | 1.85 | — |
| 1986(a) | — | 0.20 | 0.30 | 0.65 | 1.85 | — |
| 1987(a) | — | 0.20 | 0.30 | 0.65 | 1.85 | — |
| 1988(a) | — | 0.20 | 0.30 | 0.65 | 1.85 | — |
| 1989(a) | — | 0.20 | 0.30 | 0.65 | 1.85 | — |

**10 FRANCS (2 Ariary)** KM# 11 **Composition:** Aluminum-Bronze **Series:** F.A.O.

| Date | Mintage | F | VF | XF | Unc | BU |
|---|---|---|---|---|---|---|
| 1970(a) | 7,000,000 | 0.20 | 0.30 | 0.70 | 2.00 | — |
| 1971(a) | 10,000,000 | 0.20 | 0.30 | 0.70 | 2.00 | — |
| 1972(a) | 5,050,000 | 0.20 | 0.30 | 0.70 | 2.00 | — |
| 1973(a) | 3,000,000 | 0.20 | 0.30 | 0.70 | 2.00 | — |
| 1974(a) | — | 0.20 | 0.30 | 0.70 | 2.00 | — |
| 1975(a) | — | 0.20 | 0.30 | 0.70 | 2.00 | — |
| 1976(a) | 9,500,000 | 0.20 | 0.30 | 0.70 | 2.00 | — |
| 1977(a) | — | 0.20 | 0.30 | 0.70 | 2.00 | — |
| 1978(a) | — | 0.20 | 0.30 | 0.70 | 2.00 | — |
| 1980(a) | — | 0.25 | 0.35 | 0.80 | 2.25 | — |
| 1981(a) | — | 0.25 | 0.35 | 0.80 | 2.25 | — |
| 1982(a) | — | 0.25 | 0.35 | 0.80 | 2.25 | — |
| 1983(a) | — | 0.25 | 0.35 | 0.80 | 2.25 | — |
| 1984(a) | — | 0.25 | 0.35 | 0.80 | 2.25 | — |
| 1986(a) | — | 0.25 | 0.35 | 0.80 | 2.25 | — |
| 1987(a) | 3,200,000 | 0.25 | 0.35 | 0.80 | 2.25 | — |
| 1988(a) | — | 0.25 | 0.35 | 0.80 | 2.25 | — |
| 1989(a) | — | 0.25 | 0.35 | 0.80 | 2.25 | — |

**10 FRANCS (2 Ariary)** KM# 11a **Composition:** Copper Plated Steel **Series:** F.A.O.

| Date | Mintage | F | VF | XF | Unc | BU |
|---|---|---|---|---|---|---|
| 1991 | — | 0.25 | 0.45 | 1.50 | 3.50 | — |

**20 FRANCS (4 Ariary)** KM# 12 **Composition:** Aluminum-Bronze **Series:** F.A.O.

| Date | Mintage | F | VF | XF | Unc | BU |
|---|---|---|---|---|---|---|
| 1970(a) | 4,000,000 | 0.25 | 0.35 | 0.75 | 2.50 | — |
| 1971(a) | 2,000,000 | 0.25 | 0.35 | 0.75 | 2.50 | — |
| 1972(a) | 2,000,000 | 0.30 | 0.40 | 0.80 | 2.75 | — |
| 1973(a) | 3,000,000 | 0.30 | 0.40 | 0.80 | 2.75 | — |
| 1974(a) | — | 0.30 | 0.40 | 0.80 | 2.75 | — |
| 1975(a) | — | 0.30 | 0.40 | 0.80 | 2.75 | — |
| 1976(a) | 2,700,000 | 0.30 | 0.40 | 0.80 | 2.75 | — |
| 1977(a) | — | 0.30 | 0.40 | 0.80 | 2.75 | — |
| 1978(a) | — | 0.30 | 0.40 | 0.80 | 2.75 | — |
| 1979(a) | — | 0.30 | 0.40 | 0.80 | 2.75 | — |
| 1981(a) | — | 0.35 | 0.45 | 0.85 | 3.00 | — |
| 1982(a) | — | 0.35 | 0.45 | 0.85 | 3.00 | — |
| 1983(a) | — | 0.35 | 0.45 | 0.85 | 3.00 | — |
| 1984(a) | — | 0.35 | 0.45 | 0.85 | 3.00 | — |
| 1986(a) | — | 0.35 | 0.45 | 0.85 | 3.00 | — |
| 1987(a) | 5,200,000 | 0.35 | 0.45 | 0.85 | 3.00 | — |
| 1988(a) | — | 0.35 | 0.45 | 0.85 | 3.00 | — |
| 1989(a) | — | 0.35 | 0.45 | 0.85 | 3.00 | — |

# DEMOCRATIC REPUBLIC

## STANDARD COINAGE

5 Francs = 1 Ariary

**5 ARIARY** KM# 17 (KM17.1) **Composition:** Copper Plated Steel **Obverse:** Star above denomination **Reverse:** Rice plant

| Date | Mintage | F | VF | XF | Unc | BU |
|---|---|---|---|---|---|---|
| 1992 | — | 0.65 | 1.25 | 2.25 | 4.00 | — |

**5 ARIARY** **Composition:** Copper Plated Steel **Obverse:** Legend without "DEMOKRATIKA"

| Date | Mintage | F | VF | XF | Unc | BU |
|---|---|---|---|---|---|---|
| 1994 | — | 0.65 | 1.25 | 2.25 | 4.00 | — |

**10 ARIARY** KM# 13 **Composition:** Nickel **Series:** F.A.O **Obverse:** Star above denomination

| Date | Mintage | F | VF | XF | Unc | BU |
|---|---|---|---|---|---|---|
| 1978 | 8,001,000 | 1.50 | 2.75 | 5.00 | 10.00 | — |

**10 ARIARY** KM# 13a **Weight:** 9.0000 g. **Composition:** 0.9250 Silver .2676 oz. ASW

| Date | Mintage | F | VF | XF | Unc | BU |
|---|---|---|---|---|---|---|
| 1978 Proof | 3,800 | Value: 20.00 | | | | |

**10 ARIARY** KM# 13b **Composition:** Copper-Nickel

| Date | Mintage | F | VF | XF | Unc | BU |
|---|---|---|---|---|---|---|
| 1983 | — | 2.00 | 4.00 | 8.00 | 15.00 | — |

**10 ARIARY** KM# 16 **Weight:** 10.0000 g. **Composition:** 0.9170 Gold .2947 oz. AGW **Subject:** World Wildlife Fund **Obverse:** Star above denomination **Reverse:** Ibis

| Date | Mintage | F | VF | XF | Unc | BU |
|---|---|---|---|---|---|---|
| 1988 Proof | Est. 5,000 | Value: 185 | | | | |

**10 ARIARY** KM# 18 **Composition:** Stainless Steel **Obverse:** Star above denomination **Reverse:** Man cutting peat **Note:** Seven-sided.

| Date | Mintage | F | VF | XF | Unc | BU |
|---|---|---|---|---|---|---|
| 1992 | — | 0.75 | 1.50 | 2.75 | 5.00 | — |

**20 ARIARY** KM# 14 **Composition:** Nickel **Series:** F.A.O **Obverse:** Star above denomination **Reverse:** Farmer on tractor discing field

| Date | Mintage | F | VF | XF | Unc | BU |
|---|---|---|---|---|---|---|
| 1978 | 8,001,000 | 2.00 | 4.00 | 8.00 | 16.50 | — |

**20 ARIARY** **KM# 14a** **Weight:** 12.0000 g. **Composition:** 0.9250 Silver .3569 oz. ASW

| Date | Mintage | F | VF | XF | Unc | BU |
|---|---|---|---|---|---|---|
| 1978 Proof | 3,800 | Value: 25.00 | | | | |

**20 ARIARY** **KM# 14b** **Composition:** Copper-Nickel

| Date | Mintage | F | VF | XF | Unc | BU |
|---|---|---|---|---|---|---|
| 1983 | — | 2.50 | 4.50 | 9.00 | 17.50 | — |

**20 ARIARY** **KM# 15** **Weight:** 19.4400 g. **Composition:** 0.9250 Silver .5782 oz. ASW **Subject:** World Wildlife Fund **Obverse:** Star above denomination **Reverse:** Lemur

| Date | Mintage | F | VF | XF | Unc | BU |
|---|---|---|---|---|---|---|
| 1988 Proof | Est. 25,000 | Value: 32.50 | | | | |

**20 ARIARY** **KM# 19 (KM19.1)** **Composition:** Stainless Steel **Obverse:** Star above denomination **Reverse:** Farmer on tractor discing field

| Date | Mintage | F | VF | XF | Unc | BU |
|---|---|---|---|---|---|---|
| 1992 | — | 1.25 | 2.50 | 4.50 | 10.00 | — |

**20 ARIARY** **Composition:** Stainless Steel **Obverse:** Legend without "DEMOKRATIKA"

| Date | Mintage | F | VF | XF | Unc | BU |
|---|---|---|---|---|---|---|
| 1994 | — | 1.25 | 2.50 | 4.50 | 10.00 | — |

**50 ARIARY** **KM# 20 (KM20.1)** **Composition:** Stainless Steel **Obverse:** Star above denomination **Reverse:** Two towering trees

| Date | Mintage | F | VF | XF | Unc | BU |
|---|---|---|---|---|---|---|
| 1992 | — | 2.00 | 3.50 | 6.00 | 12.50 | — |

**50 ARIARY** **Composition:** Stainless Steel **Obverse:** Legend without "DEMOKRATIKA"

| Date | Mintage | F | VF | XF | Unc | BU |
|---|---|---|---|---|---|---|
| 1994 | — | 2.00 | 3.50 | 6.00 | 12.50 | — |

# REPUBLIC OF MADAGASCAR

## Madagaskara Republic

## STANDARD COINAGE

**5 FRANCS (Ariary)** **KM# 21** **Composition:** Stainless Steel **Obverse:** Flower and bank name **Reverse:** Denomination and bovine head

| Date | Mintage | F | VF | XF | Unc | BU |
|---|---|---|---|---|---|---|
| 1996 | — | — | — | — | 2.50 | — |

**10 FRANCS (2 Ariary)** **KM# 22** **Composition:** Copper Plated Steel **Obverse:** Bank name and plant **Reverse:** Value, bovine head

| Date | Mintage | F | VF | XF | Unc | BU |
|---|---|---|---|---|---|---|
| 1996 | — | — | — | — | 3.00 | — |

**5 ARIARY** **KM# 23** **Composition:** Copper Plated Steel **Obverse:** Denomination and bank name **Reverse:** Rice plant

| Date | Mintage | F | VF | XF | Unc | BU |
|---|---|---|---|---|---|---|
| 1994 | — | — | — | — | 2.50 | — |
| 1996 | — | — | — | — | 2.50 | — |

**10 ARIARY** **KM# 27** **Composition:** Nickel Clad Steel **Obverse:** Star above denomination. **Reverse:** Man cutting peat.

| Date | Mintage | F | VF | XF | Unc | BU |
|---|---|---|---|---|---|---|
| 1999 | — | — | — | — | 4.50 | — |

**20 ARIARY** **KM# 24** **Composition:** Nickel Clad Steel **Obverse:** Denomination and new country name **Reverse:** Farmer on tractor discing field

| Date | Mintage | F | VF | XF | Unc | BU |
|---|---|---|---|---|---|---|
| 1994 | — | — | — | — | 6.50 | — |
| 1999 | — | — | — | — | 6.50 | — |

**20 ARIARY** **KM# 26** **Composition:** 0.9250 Silver **Subject:** UNICEF **Reverse:** Child and ring-tailed lemur

| Date | Mintage | F | VF | XF | Unc | BU |
|---|---|---|---|---|---|---|
| 1996 Proof | — | Value: 32.50 | | | | |

**50 ARIARY** **KM# 25** **Composition:** Nickel Clad Steel **Obverse:** Denomination and new country name **Reverse:** Two towering trees

| Date | Mintage | F | VF | XF | Unc | BU |
|---|---|---|---|---|---|---|
| 1994 | — | — | — | — | 8.00 | — |
| 1996 | — | — | — | — | 8.00 | — |

## ESSAIS

Standard metals unless otherwise noted

| KM# | Date | Mintage | Identification | Issue Price | Mkt Val |
|---|---|---|---|---|---|
| e1 | 1948(a) | 2,000 | Franc. Copper-Nickel. KM3. | — | 20.00 |
| e2 | 1948 | 2,000 | 2 Francs. Copper-Nickel. KM4. | — | 25.00 |
| e3 | 1953(a) | 1,200 | 5 Francs. KM5. | — | 15.00 |
| e4 | 1953(a) | 1,200 | 10 Francs. KM6. | — | 20.00 |
| e5 | 1953(a) | 1,200 | 20 Francs. KM7. | — | 25.00 |
| e6 | 1965(a) | — | Franc. KM8. | — | 15.00 |
| e7 | 1965(a) | — | 2 Francs. KM9. | — | 15.00 |
| e8 | 1966(a) | — | 5 Francs. KM10. | — | 15.00 |
| e9 | 1970(a) | — | 10 Francs. KM11. | — | 15.00 |
| e10 | 1970(a) | — | 20 Francs. KM12. | — | 15.00 |

## PIEFORTS WITH ESSAI

Double thickness; Stnadard metals unless otherwise noted

| KM# | Date | Mintage | Identification | Issue Price | Mkt Val |
|---|---|---|---|---|---|
| pe1 | 1948(a) | 104 | Franc. KM3. | — | 75.00 |
| pe2 | 1948(a) | 104 | 2 Francs. KM4. | — | 85.00 |
| pe3 | 1953(a) | 104 | 5 Francs. KM5. | — | 65.00 |
| pe4 | 1953(a) | 104 | 10 Francs. KM6. | — | 70.00 |
| pe5 | 1953(a) | 104 | 20 Francs. KM7. | — | 90.00 |

## "FDC" SETS

| KM# | Date | Mintage | Identification | Issue Price | Mkt Val |
|---|---|---|---|---|---|
| SS1 | 1970 (5) | 1,500 | KM8-12 | 2.75 | 11.50 |

## PROOF SETS

| KM# | Date | Mintage | Identification | Issue Price | Mkt Val |
|---|---|---|---|---|---|
| PS1 | 1978 (2) | 3,800 | KM#13a, 14a | 38.00 | 45.00 |

# MADEIRA ISLANDS

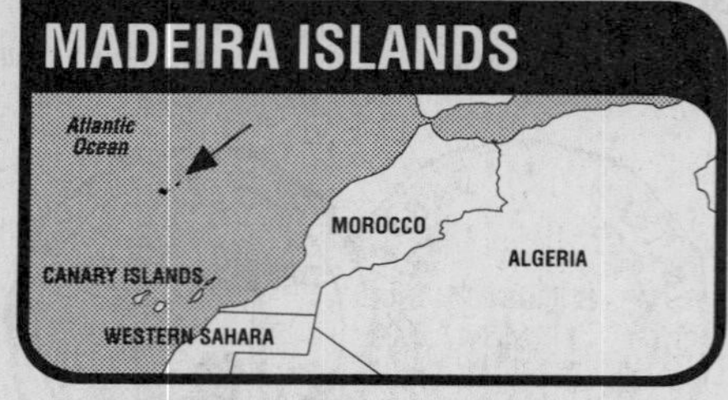


The Madeira Islands, which belong to Portugal, are located 360 miles (492 km.) off the northwest coast of Africa. They have an area of 307 sq. mi. (795 sq. km.) and a population of 270,976. The group consists of two inhabited islands named Madeira and Porto Santo and two groups of uninhabited rocks named Desertas and Selvagens. Capital: Funchal. The two staple products are wine and sugar. Bananas and pineapples are also produced for export.

Although the evidence is insufficient, it is thought that the Phoenicians visited Madeira at an early period. It is also probable that the entire archipelago was explored by Genoese adventurers; an Italian map dated 1351 shows the Madeira Islands quite clearly. The Portuguese navigator Goncalvez Zarco first sighted Porto Santo in 1418, having been driven there by a storm while he was exploring the coast of West Africa. Madeira itself was discovered in 1420. The islands were uninhabited when visited by Zarco, but soon after 1418 Madeira was quickly colonized by Prince Henry the Navigator, aided by the knights of the Order of Christ. British troops occupied the islands in 1801, and again in 1807-14.

**RULERS**
Portuguese

## PORTUGUESE COLONY

### MODERN COINAGE

**25 ESCUDOS** **KM# 4** **Composition:** Copper-Nickel **Subject:** Autonomy of Madeira **Obverse:** Shields of arms over value **Reverse:** Bust of Goncalvez Zarco facing

| Date | Mintage | F | VF | XF | Unc | BU |
|---|---|---|---|---|---|---|
| 1981 | 750,000 | — | — | — | 6.00 | — |

**25 ESCUDOS** **KM# 4a** **Weight:** 11.0000 g. **Composition:** 0.9250 Silver .3272 oz. ASW **Subject:** Autonomy of Madeira **Obverse:** Shields of arms over value **Reverse:** Bust of Goncalvez facing

| Date | Mintage | F | VF | XF | Unc | BU |
|---|---|---|---|---|---|---|
| 1981 Proof | 20,000 | Value: 15.00 | | | | |

**100 ESCUDOS** **KM# 5** **Composition:** Copper-Nickel **Subject:** Autonomy of Madeira **Obverse:** Shields of arms over value **Reverse:** Bust of Goncalvez Zarco facing

| Date | Mintage | F | VF | XF | Unc | BU |
|---|---|---|---|---|---|---|
| 1981 | 250,000 | — | — | 12.00 | — | — |

**100 ESCUDOS** **KM# 5a** **Weight:** 16.5000 g. **Composition:** 0.9250 Silver .4908 oz. ASW **Subject:** Autonomy of Madeira **Obverse:** Shields of arms **Reverse:** Bust of Goncalvez Zarco facing

| Date | Mintage | F | VF | XF | Unc | BU |
|---|---|---|---|---|---|---|
| 1981 Proof | 20,000 | Value: 22.50 | | | | |

### PROVAS

| KM# | Date | Mintage | Identification | Mkt Val |
|---|---|---|---|---|
| Pr1 | 1981 (5) | — | 25 Escudos. KM4. | 30.00 |
| Pr2 | 1981 (5) | — | 100 Escudos. KM5. | 40.00 |

### PROOF SETS

| KM# | Date | Mintage | Identification | Issue Price | Mkt Val |
|---|---|---|---|---|---|
| PS1 | 1981 (2) | 20,000 | KM4a-5a | 42.00 | 37.50 |

# MALAWI

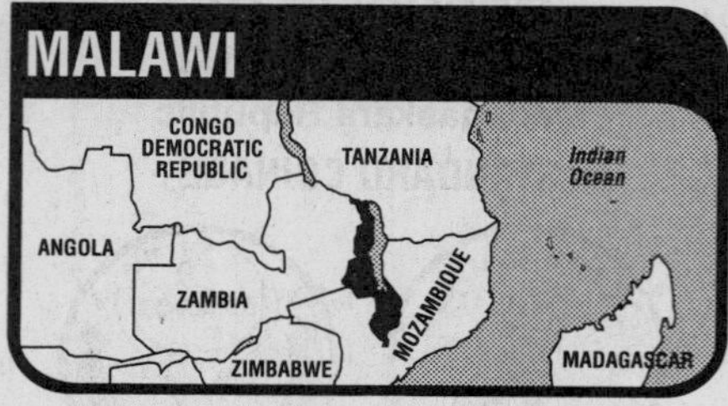


The Republic of Malawi (formerly Nyasaland), located in southeastern Africa to the west of Lake Malawi (Nyasa), has an area of 45,745 sq. mi. (118,480 sq. km.) and a population of 7 million. Capital: Lilongwe. The economy is predominantly agricultural. Tobacco, tea, peanuts and cotton are exported.

Although the Portuguese were the first Europeans to reach the Malawi area, the first meaningful contact was made by missionary-explorer Dr. David Livingstone. He arrived at Lake Malawi on Sept. 16, 1859, and remained to make extensive explorations in the 1860's. Subsequent clashes between settlements of Scottish missionaries and Arab slave traders, and the procurement of development rights by Cecil Rhodes, 1884, stimulated British interest and brought about the establishment of the Nyasaland protectorate in 1891. In 1953 Nyasaland reluctantly joined the Federation of Rhodesia and Nyasaland and, after prolonged protest, was granted self-government within the federation. Nyasaland became the independent nation of Malawi on July 6, 1964, and became a republic two years later. Malawi is a member of the Commonwealth of Nations. The president is the Chief of State and Head of Government.

**NOTE:** For earlier coinage see Rhodesia and Nyasaland.

**MONETARY SYSTEM**
12 Pence = 1 Shilling
2 Shillings = 1 Florin
5 Shillings = 1 Crown
20 Shillings = 1 Pound

## REPUBLIC

### STERLING COINAGE

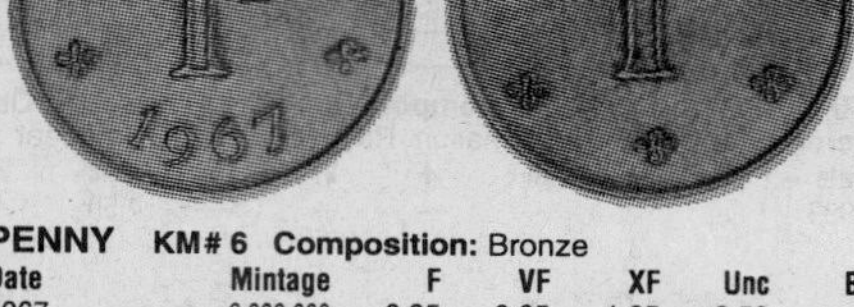


**PENNY** **KM# 6** **Composition:** Bronze

| Date | Mintage | F | VF | XF | Unc | BU |
|---|---|---|---|---|---|---|
| 1967 | 6,000,000 | 0.35 | 0.65 | 1.25 | 2.50 | — |
| 1968 | 3,600,000 | 3.00 | 6.00 | 12.00 | 25.00 | — |

**6 PENCE** **KM# 1** **Composition:** Copper-Nickel-Zinc **Obverse:** Dr. Hastings Kamuzu Banda **Reverse:** Rooster

| Date | Mintage | F | VF | XF | Unc | BU |
|---|---|---|---|---|---|---|
| 1964 | 14,800,000 | 0.25 | 0.50 | 1.00 | 2.50 | — |
| 1964 Proof | 10,000 | Value: 1.50 | | | | |
| 1967 | 6,000,000 | 0.50 | 1.00 | 2.50 | 5.00 | — |

**SCHILLING** **KM# 2** **Composition:** Copper-Nickel-Zinc **Obverse:** Dr. Hastings Kamuzu Banda **Reverse:** Bundled cobs of corn

| Date | Mintage | F | VF | XF | Unc | BU |
|---|---|---|---|---|---|---|
| 1964 | 11,900,000 | 0.35 | 0.65 | 1.25 | 2.50 | — |
| 1964 Proof | 10,000 | Value: 1.50 | | | | |
| 1968 | 3,000,000 | 0.75 | 1.50 | 3.00 | 5.50 | — |

**FLORIN** **KM# 3** **Composition:** Copper-Nickel-Zinc **Obverse:** Dr. Hastings Kamuzu Banda **Reverse:** African elephants

| Date | Mintage | F | VF | XF | Unc | BU |
|---|---|---|---|---|---|---|
| 1964 | 6,500,000 | 0.75 | 1.50 | 3.00 | 5.00 | — |
| 1964 Proof | 10,000 | Value: 3.50 | | | | |

**1/2 CROWN** **KM# 4** **Composition:** Copper-Nickel-Zinc **Obverse:** Dr. Hastings Kamuzu Banda **Reverse:** Arms

| Date | Mintage | F | VF | XF | Unc | BU |
|---|---|---|---|---|---|---|
| 1964 | 6,400,000 | 1.00 | 2.00 | 4.00 | 6.00 | — |
| 1964 Proof | 10,000 | Value: 4.00 | | | | |

**CROWN** **KM# 5** **Composition:** Nickel-Brass **Subject:** Day of the Republic - July 6, 1966

| Date | Mintage | F | VF | XF | Unc | BU |
|---|---|---|---|---|---|---|
| 1966 Proof | 20,000 | Value: 7.50 | | | | |

### DECIMAL COINAGE

100 Tambala = 1 Kwacha

**TAMBALA** **KM# 7.1** **Composition:** Bronze **Obverse:** Dr. Hastings Kamuzu Banda **Reverse:** Rooster

| Date | Mintage | F | VF | XF | Unc | BU |
|---|---|---|---|---|---|---|
| 1971 | 15,000,000 | 0.15 | 0.20 | 0.40 | 0.75 | — |
| 1971 Proof | 4,000 | Value: 1.00 | | | | |
| 1973 | 5,000,000 | 0.15 | 0.20 | 0.40 | 0.75 | — |
| 1974 | 12,500,000 | 0.15 | 0.20 | 0.40 | 0.75 | — |

**TAMBALA** **KM# 7.2** **Composition:** Bronze **Obverse:** Accent mark above "W" in MALAWI

| Date | Mintage | F | VF | XF | Unc | BU |
|---|---|---|---|---|---|---|
| 1975 | — | 0.15 | 0.20 | 0.40 | 0.75 | — |
| 1976 | 10,000,000 | 0.15 | 0.20 | 0.40 | 0.75 | — |
| 1977 | 10,000,000 | 0.15 | 0.20 | 0.40 | 0.75 | — |
| 1979 | 15,000,000 | 0.15 | 0.20 | 0.40 | 0.75 | — |
| 1982 | 15,000,000 | 0.15 | 0.20 | 0.40 | 0.75 | — |

**TAMBALA** **KM# 7.2a** **Composition:** Copper Plated Steel

| Date | Mintage | F | VF | XF | Unc | BU |
|---|---|---|---|---|---|---|
| 1984 | 201,000 | 0.20 | 0.30 | 0.50 | 0.80 | — |
| 1985 | — | 0.20 | 0.30 | 0.50 | 0.80 | — |
| 1985 Proof | 10,000 | Value: 3.00 | | | | |
| 1987 | — | 0.20 | 0.30 | 0.50 | 0.80 | — |
| 1989 | — | 0.20 | 0.30 | 0.50 | 0.80 | — |
| 1991 | — | 0.20 | 0.30 | 0.50 | 0.80 | — |
| 1994 | — | 0.20 | 0.30 | 0.50 | 0.80 | — |

**TAMBALA** **KM# 24** **Composition:** Copper Plated Steel **Obverse:** Portrait of President Bakili Muluzi

| Date | Mintage | F | VF | XF | Unc | BU |
|---|---|---|---|---|---|---|
| 1995 | — | — | — | — | 1.00 | — |

**TAMBALA** **KM# 33** **Composition:** Brass **Obverse:** Arms **Reverse:** 2 fish **Edge:** Plain **Size:** 17.3 mm.

| Date | Mintage | F | VF | XF | Unc | BU |
|---|---|---|---|---|---|---|
| 1995 | — | — | — | — | 1.00 | — |

**2 TAMBALA** **KM# 8.1** **Composition:** Bronze **Obverse:** Dr. Hastings Kamuzu Banda **Reverse:** Paradise Whydah

| Date | Mintage | F | VF | XF | Unc | BU |
|---|---|---|---|---|---|---|
| 1971 | 10,000,000 | 0.25 | 0.40 | 0.75 | 1.50 | — |
| 1971 Proof | 4,000 | Value: 1.75 | | | | |
| 1973 | 5,000,000 | 0.25 | 0.40 | 0.75 | 1.50 | — |
| 1974 | 5,000,000 | 0.25 | 0.40 | 0.75 | 1.50 | — |

**2 TAMBALA** **KM# 8.2** **Composition:** Bronze **Obverse:** Accent mark above "W" in MALAWI

| Date | Mintage | F | VF | XF | Unc | BU |
|---|---|---|---|---|---|---|
| 1975 | — | 0.25 | 0.40 | 0.75 | 1.50 | — |
| 1976 | 5,000,000 | 0.25 | 0.40 | 0.75 | 1.50 | — |
| 1977 | 5,000,000 | 0.25 | 0.40 | 0.75 | 1.50 | — |
| 1979 | 7,637,000 | 0.25 | 0.40 | 0.75 | 1.50 | — |
| 1982 | 15,000,000 | 0.25 | 0.40 | 0.75 | 1.50 | — |

**2 TAMBALA** **KM# 8.2a** **Composition:** Copper Plated Steel

| Date | Mintage | F | VF | XF | Unc | BU |
|---|---|---|---|---|---|---|
| 1984 | 150,000 | 0.30 | 0.50 | 0.85 | 2.00 | — |
| 1985 | — | 0.30 | 0.50 | 0.85 | 2.00 | — |
| 1985 Proof | 10,000 | Value: 4.00 | | | | |
| 1987 | — | 0.30 | 0.50 | 0.85 | 2.00 | — |
| 1989 | — | 0.30 | 0.50 | 0.85 | 2.00 | — |
| 1991 | — | 0.30 | 0.50 | 0.85 | 1.75 | — |
| 1994 | — | 0.30 | 0.50 | 0.85 | 1.75 | — |

**2 TAMBALA** **KM# 25** **Composition:** Copper Plated Steel **Obverse:** Portrait of President Bakili Muluzi

| Date | Mintage | F | VF | XF | Unc | BU |
|---|---|---|---|---|---|---|
| 1995 | — | — | — | — | 1.00 | — |

**2 TAMBALA** **KM# 34** **Composition:** Bronze **Obverse:** National arms **Reverse:** Paradise Whydah bird **Edge:** Plain **Size:** 20.3 mm.

| Date | Mintage | F | VF | XF | Unc | BU |
|---|---|---|---|---|---|---|
| 1995 | — | — | — | — | 1.00 | — |

**5 TAMBALA** **KM# 9.1** **Composition:** Copper-Nickel **Obverse:** Dr. Hastings Kamuzu Banda **Reverse:** Purple heron

| Date | Mintage | F | VF | XF | Unc | BU |
|---|---|---|---|---|---|---|
| 1971 | 7,000,000 | 0.25 | 0.45 | 0.85 | 1.75 | — |
| 1971 Proof | 4,000 | Value: 2.00 | | | | |

**5 TAMBALA** **KM# 9.2** **Composition:** Copper-Nickel **Obverse:** Accent mark above "W" in MALAWI

| Date | Mintage | F | VF | XF | Unc | BU |
|---|---|---|---|---|---|---|
| 1985 Proof | 10,000 | Value: 5.00 | | | | |

**5 TAMBALA** **KM# 9.2a** **Composition:** Nickel Clad Steel

| Date | Mintage | F | VF | XF | Unc | BU |
|---|---|---|---|---|---|---|
| 1989 | — | 0.30 | 0.50 | 0.85 | 2.00 | — |
| 1994 | — | 0.30 | 0.50 | 0.85 | 2.00 | — |

**5 TAMBALA** **KM# 26** **Composition:** Steel **Obverse:** Portrait of President Bakili Muluzi

| Date | Mintage | F | VF | XF | Unc | BU |
|---|---|---|---|---|---|---|
| 1995 | — | — | — | — | 1.50 | — |

**5 TAMBALA** **KM# 32** **Composition:** Steel **Reverse:** Purple heron

| Date | Mintage | F | VF | XF | Unc | BU |
|---|---|---|---|---|---|---|
| 1995 | — | — | — | — | 1.50 | — |

**10 TAMBALA** **KM# 10.1** **Composition:** Copper-Nickel **Obverse:** Dr. Hastings Kamuzu Banda **Reverse:** Bundled cobs of corn

| Date | Mintage | F | VF | XF | Unc | BU |
|---|---|---|---|---|---|---|
| 1971 | 4,000,000 | 0.30 | 0.50 | 1.00 | 2.25 | — |
| 1971 Proof | 4,000 | Value: 2.50 | | | | |

**10 TAMBALA** **KM# 10.2** **Composition:** Copper-Nickel **Obverse:** Accent mark above "W" in MALAWI

| Date | Mintage | F | VF | XF | Unc | BU |
|---|---|---|---|---|---|---|
| 1985 Proof | 10,000 | Value: 6.00 | | | | |
| 1989 | — | 0.40 | 0.80 | 1.50 | 2.75 | — |

**10 TAMBALA** **KM# 10.2a** **Composition:** Nickel Clad Steel

| Date | Mintage | F | VF | XF | Unc | BU |
|---|---|---|---|---|---|---|
| 1989 | — | 0.40 | 0.80 | 1.50 | 2.75 | — |

**10 TAMBALA** **KM# 27** **Composition:** Steel **Obverse:** Portrait of President Bakili Muluzi

| Date | Mintage | F | VF | XF | Unc | BU |
|---|---|---|---|---|---|---|
| 1995 | — | — | — | — | 2.25 | — |

**20 TAMBALA** **KM# 11.1** **Composition:** Copper-Nickel **Obverse:** Dr. Hastings Kamuzu Banda **Reverse:** Elephant cow and calf

| Date | Mintage | F | VF | XF | Unc | BU |
|---|---|---|---|---|---|---|
| 1971 | 3,000,000 | 0.75 | 1.50 | 2.50 | 4.00 | — |
| 1971 Proof | 4,000 | Value: 4.50 | | | | |

**20 TAMBALA** **KM# 11.2** **Composition:** Copper-Nickel **Obverse:** Accent mark above "W" in MALAWI

| Date | Mintage | F | VF | XF | Unc | BU |
|---|---|---|---|---|---|---|
| 1985 Proof | 10,000 | Value: 7.00 | | | | |

**20 TAMBALA** **KM# 11.2a** **Composition:** Nickel Clad Steel

| Date | Mintage | F | VF | XF | Unc | BU |
|---|---|---|---|---|---|---|
| 1989 | — | 0.60 | 1.20 | 2.25 | 3.75 | — |
| 1994 | — | 0.60 | 1.20 | 2.25 | 3.75 | — |

**20 TAMBALA** **KM# 29** **Composition:** Nickel Clad Steel **Obverse:** Portrait of President Bakili Muluzi

| Date | Mintage | F | VF | XF | Unc | BU |
|---|---|---|---|---|---|---|
| 1996 | — | — | — | — | 3.75 | — |

**50 TAMBALA** **KM# 19** **Composition:** Copper-Nickel-Zinc **Obverse:** Dr. Hastings Kamuzu Banda **Reverse:** Arms **Note:** The 1989 date for this coin does not exist.

| Date | Mintage | F | VF | XF | Unc | BU |
|---|---|---|---|---|---|---|
| 1986 | — | 2.00 | 3.00 | 5.00 | 10.00 | — |
| 1994 | — | 2.00 | 3.00 | 5.00 | 10.00 | — |

**50 TAMBALA** **KM# 30** **Composition:** Brass Plated Steel **Obverse:** Portrait of President Bakili Muluzi

| Date | Mintage | F | VF | XF | Unc | BU |
|---|---|---|---|---|---|---|
| 1996 | — | — | — | — | 4.50 | — |

**KWACHA** **KM# 12** **Composition:** Copper-Nickel **Subject:** Decimalization of coinage **Obverse:** Similar to 5 Kwacha, KM#15

| Date | Mintage | F | VF | XF | Unc | BU |
|---|---|---|---|---|---|---|
| 1971 | 20,000 | 1.00 | 2.00 | 3.50 | 6.00 | — |
| 1971 Proof | 4,000 | Value: 6.50 | | | | |

**KWACHA** **KM# 20** **Composition:** Copper-Nickel-Zinc **Obverse:** Dr. Hastings Kamuzu Banda **Reverse:** Rooster

| Date | Mintage | F | VF | XF | Unc | BU |
|---|---|---|---|---|---|---|
| 1992 | — | 1.00 | 2.00 | 3.00 | 5.50 | — |
| 1993 | — | 2.00 | 4.00 | 6.00 | 10.00 | — |

**KWACHA** **KM# 28** **Composition:** Brass **Obverse:** Portrait of President Bakili Muluzi

| Date | Mintage | F | VF | XF | Unc | BU |
|---|---|---|---|---|---|---|
| 1996 | — | — | — | — | 7.00 | — |

**KWACHA** **KM# 282** **Composition:** Brass Plated Steel

| Date | Mintage | F | VF | XF | Unc | BU |
|---|---|---|---|---|---|---|
| 1996 | — | — | — | — | 7.00 | — |

**5 KWACHA** **KM# 15** **Weight:** 28.2800 g. **Composition:** 0.9250 Silver .841 oz. ASW **Subject:** Conservation **Reverse:** Burchell's zebras

| Date | Mintage | F | VF | XF | Unc | BU |
|---|---|---|---|---|---|---|
| 1978 | 4,048 | — | — | — | 17.50 | — |
| 1978 Proof | 3,622 | Value: 32.50 | | | | |

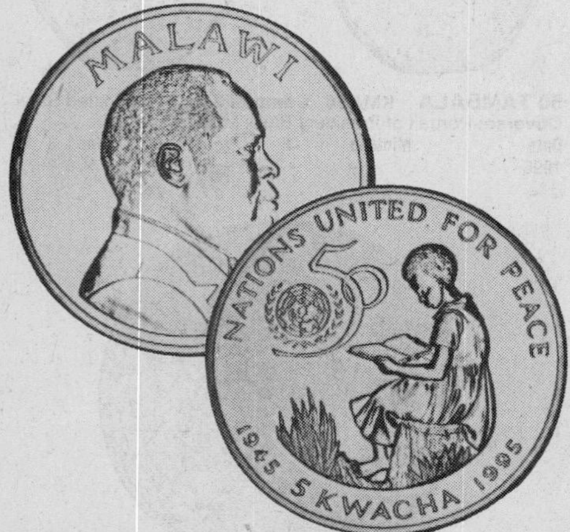

**5 KWACHA** **KM# 23** **Composition:** Copper-Nickel **Subject:** United Nations 50th anniversary **Reverse:** Child reading

| Date | Mintage | F | VF | XF | Unc | BU |
|---|---|---|---|---|---|---|
| ND(1995) | — | — | — | — | 8.50 | — |

**5 KWACHA** **KM# 23a** **Weight:** 28.2800 g. **Composition:** 0.9250 Silver .8410 oz. ASW **Subject:** United Nations 50th anniversary **Reverse:** Child reading

| Date | Mintage | F | VF | XF | Unc | BU |
|---|---|---|---|---|---|---|
| ND(1995) Proof | — | Value: 32.50 | | | | |

**10 KWACHA** **KM# 13** **Weight:** 28.2800 g. **Composition:** 0.9250 Silver .8411 oz. ASW **Subject:** 10th anniversary of independence

| Date | Mintage | F | VF | XF | Unc | BU |
|---|---|---|---|---|---|---|
| 1974 | 7,556 | — | — | — | 11.50 | — |
| 1974 Proof | 4,937 | Value: 17.50 | | | | |

**10 KWACHA** **KM# 14** **Weight:** 28.2800 g. **Composition:** 0.9250 Silver .8411 oz. ASW **Subject:** 10th anniversary of the Reserve Bank **Obverse:** Similar to KM#13.

| Date | Mintage | F | VF | XF | Unc | BU |
|---|---|---|---|---|---|---|
| 1975 | 6,870 | — | — | — | 11.50 | — |
| 1975 Proof | Inc. above | Value: 18.50 | | | | |

**10 KWACHA** **KM# 14a** **Composition:** 0.9000 Gold **Subject:** 10th anniversary of the Reserve Bank

| Date | Mintage | F | VF | XF | Unc | BU |
|---|---|---|---|---|---|---|
| 1975 | — | — | — | — | 1,250 | — |

**10 KWACHA** **KM# 16** **Weight:** 35.0000 g. **Composition:** 0.9250 Silver 1.0409 oz. ASW **Series:** Conservation **Obverse:** Similar to 5 Kwacha, KM#15 **Reverse:** Sable antelope

| Date | Mintage | F | VF | XF | Unc | BU |
|---|---|---|---|---|---|---|
| 1978 | 4,009 | — | — | — | 20.00 | — |
| 1978 Proof | 3,416 | Value: 35.00 | | | | |

**10 KWACHA** **KM# 18** **Weight:** 28.2800 g. **Composition:** 0.9250 Silver .8410 oz. ASW **Subject:** 20th anniversary - Reserve Bank

| Date | Mintage | F | VF | XF | Unc | BU |
|---|---|---|---|---|---|---|
| 1985 Proof | 4,000 | Value: 22.50 | | | | |

**10 KWACHA** **KM#18a** **Weight:** 47.5400 g. **Composition:** 0.9170 Gold 1.4011 oz. AGW **Subject:** 20th anniversary - Reserve Bank **Obverse:** Similar to 250 Kwacha, KM#17 **Reverse:** Eagle

| Date | Mintage | F | VF | XF | Unc | BU |
|---|---|---|---|---|---|---|
| 1985 Proof | 50 | Value: 1,550 | | | | |

**10 KWACHA** **KM# 21** **Weight:** 28.2800 g. **Composition:** 0.9250 Silver .8411 oz. ASW **Series:** Save the Children **Subject:** Fishing

| Date | Mintage | F | VF | XF | Unc | BU |
|---|---|---|---|---|---|---|
| 1992 Proof | 20,000 | Value: 35.00 | | | | |

**20 KWACHA** **KM# 22** **Weight:** 10.0000 g. **Composition:** 0.9170 Gold .2948 oz. AGW **Series:** Save the Children **Subject:** Mother and children

| Date | Mintage | F | VF | XF | Unc | BU |
|---|---|---|---|---|---|---|
| 1992 Proof | Est. 3,000 | Value: 220 | | | | |

**20 KWACHA** **KM# 35** **Weight:** 31.4000 g. **Composition:** 0.9250 Silver .9338 oz. ASW **Subject:** Endangered Wildlife - "The Romans" **Obverse:** National arms **Reverse:** Female elephant with two calves in water **Edge:** Reeded **Size:** 38.6 mm.

| Date | Mintage | F | VF | XF | Unc | BU |
|---|---|---|---|---|---|---|
| 1996 Proof | — | Value: 40.00 | | | | |

**20 KWACHA** **KM# 31** **Weight:** 31.5300 g. **Composition:** 0.9250 Silver .9377 oz. ASW **Subject:** Millennium **Reverse:** People seated below trees, ears of corn, denomination

| Date | Mintage | F | VF | XF | Unc | BU |
|---|---|---|---|---|---|---|
| 1999 Proof | — | Value: 40.00 | | | | |

**250 KWACHA** KM# 17 **Weight:** 33.4370 g. **Composition:** 0.9000 Gold .9676 oz. AGW **Series:** Conservation **Subject:** Nyala

| Date | Mintage | F | VF | XF | Unc | BU |
|---|---|---|---|---|---|---|
| 1978 | 566 | — | — | — | 500 | — |
| 1978 Proof | 208 | Value: 850 | | | | |

## MINT SETS

| KM# | Date | Mintage | Identification | Issue Price | Mkt Val |
|---|---|---|---|---|---|
| MS1 | 1971 (6) | 10,000 | KM7.1-11.1, 12 | 3.30 | 16.50 |
| MS2 | 1978 (2) | — | KM15, 16 | — | 40.00 |

## PROOF SETS

| KM# | Date | Mintage | Identification | Issue Price | Mkt Val |
|---|---|---|---|---|---|
| PS1 | 1964 (4) | 10,000 | KM1-4 | 10.00 | 10.00 |
| PS2 | 1971 (6) | 4,000 | KM7.1-11.1, 12 | 8.70 | 18.50 |
| PS3 | 1978 (2) | — | KM15, 16 | — | 70.00 |
| PS4 | 1985 (5) | 10,000 | KM7.2a-8.2a, 9.2-11.2 | 30.00 | 25.00 |

# MALAYA

Malaya, a former member of the British Commonwealth located in the southern part of the Malay peninsula, consisted of 11 states: the un-federated Malay states of Johore, Kelantan, Kedah, Perlis and Trengganu; the federated Malay states of Negri-Sembilan, Pahang, Perakand Selangor; former members of the Straits Settlements Penang and Malacca. Malaya was occupied by the Japanese during the years 1942-1945. The only local opposition to the Japanese had come mainly from the Chinese Communists who then continued their guerilla operations after the war, finally being defeated in 1956. Malaya was granted full independence on Aug. 31, 1957, and became part of Malaysia in 1963.

**RULERS**
British

**MINT MARKS**
I - Calcutta Mint (1941)
I - Bombay Mint (1945)
No Mint mark - Royal Mint

**MONETARY SYSTEM**
100 Cents = 1 Dollar

## BRITISH COLONY

### STANDARD COINAGE

100 Cents = 1 Dollar

**1/2 CENT** KM# 1 **Composition:** Bronze

| Date | Mintage | F | VF | XF | Unc | BU |
|---|---|---|---|---|---|---|
| 1940 | 6,000,000 | 0.50 | 1.25 | 2.00 | 4.00 | — |
| 1940 Proof | — | Value: 150 | | | | |

**CENT** KM# 2 **Composition:** Bronze

| Date | Mintage | F | VF | XF | Unc | BU |
|---|---|---|---|---|---|---|
| 1939 | 20,000,000 | 0.25 | 0.40 | 0.60 | 1.50 | — |
| 1939 Proof | — | Value: 150 | | | | |
| 1940 | 23,600,000 | 0.25 | 0.40 | 0.60 | 1.50 | — |
| 1940 Proof | — | — | — | — | — | — |
| 1941 I | 33,620,000 | 0.75 | 1.25 | 5.00 | 10.00 | — |

**CENT** KM# 6 **Composition:** Bronze **Note:** Reduced size.

| Date | Mintage | F | VF | XF | Unc | BU |
|---|---|---|---|---|---|---|
| 1943 | 50,000,000 | 0.10 | 0.20 | 0.35 | 0.85 | — |
| 1943 Proof | — | Value: 150 | | | | |
| 1945 | 40,033,000 | 0.10 | 0.20 | 0.35 | 0.85 | — |
| 1945 Proof | — | Value: 150 | | | | |

**5 CENTS** KM# 3 **Weight:** 1.3600 g. **Composition:** 0.7500 Silver .0327 oz. ASW

| Date | Mintage | F | VF | XF | Unc | BU |
|---|---|---|---|---|---|---|
| 1939 | 2,000,000 | 0.50 | 1.00 | 1.50 | 2.50 | — |
| 1939 Proof | — | Value: 250 | | | | |
| 1941 | 4,000,000 | 0.40 | 0.50 | 1.20 | 2.00 | — |
| 1941 Proof | — | Value: 250 | | | | |
| 1941 I | Inc. above | 0.40 | 0.50 | 1.20 | 2.00 | — |

**5 CENTS** KM# 3a **Weight:** 1.3600 g. **Composition:** 0.5000 Silver .0218 oz. ASW

| Date | Mintage | F | VF | XF | Unc | BU |
|---|---|---|---|---|---|---|
| 1943 | 10,000,000 | 0.30 | 0.40 | 0.65 | 1.50 | — |
| 1943 Proof | — | Value: 250 | | | | |
| 1945 | 8,800,000 | 0.30 | 0.40 | 0.65 | 1.50 | — |
| 1945 Proof | — | Value: 250 | | | | |
| 1945 I | 4,600,000 | 0.50 | 0.75 | 1.00 | 2.00 | — |

**5 CENTS** KM# 7 **Composition:** Copper-Nickel

| Date | Mintage | F | VF | XF | Unc | BU |
|---|---|---|---|---|---|---|
| 1948 | 30,000,000 | 0.10 | 0.25 | 0.75 | 2.00 | — |
| 1948 Proof | — | Value: 220 | | | | |
| 1950 | 40,000,000 | 0.10 | 0.25 | 0.75 | 2.00 | — |
| 1950 Proof | — | Value: 220 | | | | |

**10 CENTS** KM# 4 **Weight:** 2.7100 g. **Composition:** 0.7500 Silver .0653 oz. ASW

| Date | Mintage | F | VF | XF | Unc | BU |
|---|---|---|---|---|---|---|
| 1939 | 10,000,000 | 0.75 | 1.00 | 1.25 | 2.50 | — |
| 1939 Proof | — | Value: 280 | | | | |
| 1941 | 17,000,000 | 0.75 | 1.00 | 1.25 | 2.50 | — |
| 1941 Proof | — | Value: 280 | | | | |
| 1941 I Proof, rare | — | — | — | — | — | — |

**10 CENTS** KM# 4a **Weight:** 2.7100 g. **Composition:** 0.5000 Silver .0435 oz. ASW

| Date | Mintage | F | VF | XF | Unc | BU |
|---|---|---|---|---|---|---|
| 1943 | 5,000,000 | 0.75 | 1.00 | 1.50 | 2.50 | — |
| 1943 Proof | — | Value: 280 | | | | |
| 1945 | 3,152,000 | 0.75 | 1.00 | 1.50 | 3.00 | — |
| 1945 I Proof, rare | — | — | — | — | — | — |

**10 CENTS** KM# 8 **Composition:** Copper-Nickel

| Date | Mintage | F | VF | XF | Unc | BU |
|---|---|---|---|---|---|---|
| 1948 | 23,885,000 | 0.15 | 0.30 | 0.75 | 2.25 | — |
| 1948 Proof | — | Value: 280 | | | | |
| 1949 | 26,115,000 | 0.25 | 0.50 | 1.20 | 3.00 | — |
| 1949 Proof | — | Value: 280 | | | | |
| 1950 | 65,000,000 | 0.15 | 0.30 | 0.75 | 2.25 | — |
| 1950 Proof | — | Value: 280 | | | | |

**20 CENTS** KM# 5 **Weight:** 5.4300 g. **Composition:** 0.7500 Silver .1309 oz. ASW

| Date | Mintage | F | VF | XF | Unc | BU |
|---|---|---|---|---|---|---|
| 1939 | 8,000,000 | 1.25 | 1.75 | 2.25 | 4.50 | — |
| 1939 Proof | — | Value: 280 | | | | |

**20 CENTS** KM# 5a **Weight:** 5.4300 g. **Composition:** 0.5000 Silver .0872 oz. ASW

| Date | Mintage | F | VF | XF | Unc | BU |
|---|---|---|---|---|---|---|
| 1943 | 5,000,000 | 1.25 | 1.75 | 2.25 | 4.50 | — |
| 1943 Proof | — | Value: 260 | | | | |
| 1945 | 10,000,000 | 2.00 | 4.00 | 8.00 | 10.00 | — |
| 1945 I Proof, rare | — | — | — | — | — | — |

**20 CENTS** KM# 9 **Composition:** Copper-Nickel

| Date | Mintage | F | VF | XF | Unc | BU |
|---|---|---|---|---|---|---|
| 1948 | 40,000,000 | 0.30 | 0.50 | 1.50 | 4.50 | — |
| 1948 Proof | — | Value: 280 | | | | |
| 1950 | 20,000,000 | 0.30 | 0.50 | 1.50 | 4.50 | — |
| 1950 Proof | — | Value: 280 | | | | |

# MALAYA & BRITISH BORNEO

Malaya & British Borneo, a Currency Commission named the Board of Commissioners of Currency, Malaya and British Borneo, was initiated on Jan. 1, 1952, for the purpose of providing a common currency for use in Johore, Kelantan, Kedah, Perlis, Trengganu, Negri Sembilan, Pahang, Perak, Selangor, Penang, Malacca, Singapore, North Borneo, Sarawak and Brunei.

**RULERS**
British

**MINT MARKS**
KN - King's Norton, Birmingham
H - Heaton, Birmingham
No Mint mark - Royal Mint

**MONETARY SYSTEM**
100 Cents = 1 Dollar

## BRITISH COLONY

### STANDARD COINAGE

100 Cents = 1 Dollar

**CENT** **KM# 5** **Composition:** Bronze

| Date | Mintage | F | VF | XF | Unc | BU |
|---|---|---|---|---|---|---|
| 1956 | 6,250,000 | — | 0.10 | 0.25 | 0.50 | — |
| 1956 Proof | — | Value: 125 | | | | |
| 1957 | 12,500,000 | — | 0.10 | 0.25 | 0.50 | — |
| 1957 Proof | — | — | — | — | — | — |
| 1958 | 5,000,000 | — | 0.10 | 0.25 | 0.50 | — |
| 1958 Proof | — | Value: 125 | | | | |
| 1961 | 10,000,000 | — | 0.10 | 0.20 | 0.50 | — |
| 1961 Proof | — | Value: 125 | | | | |

**CENT** **KM# 6** **Composition:** Bronze

| Date | Mintage | F | VF | XF | Unc | BU |
|---|---|---|---|---|---|---|
| 1962 | 45,000,000 | — | — | 0.10 | 0.35 | — |
| 1962 Proof | Est. 25 | Value: 125 | | | | |

**5 CENTS** **KM# 1** **Composition:** Copper-Nickel

| Date | Mintage | F | VF | XF | Unc | BU |
|---|---|---|---|---|---|---|
| 1953 | 20,000,000 | — | 0.25 | 0.50 | 1.50 | — |
| 1953 Proof | — | Value: 200 | | | | |
| 1957 | 10,000,000 | — | 0.50 | 0.75 | 2.00 | — |
| 1957 Proof | — | — | — | — | — | — |
| 1957H | 10,000,000 | — | 0.50 | 0.75 | 2.00 | — |
| 1957KN | Inc. above | — | 1.25 | 1.75 | 3.00 | — |
| 1958 | 10,000,000 | — | 0.25 | 0.50 | 1.50 | — |
| 1958 Proof | — | Value: 200 | | | | |
| 1958H | 10,000,000 | — | 0.50 | 0.75 | 2.00 | — |
| 1961 | 90,000,000 | — | 0.15 | 0.50 | 1.25 | — |
| 1961 Proof | — | — | — | — | — | — |
| 1961H | 5,000,000 | — | 2.00 | 4.00 | 9.00 | — |
| 1961KN | Inc. above | — | 0.50 | 1.00 | 2.50 | — |

**10 CENTS** **KM# 2** **Composition:** Copper-Nickel

| Date | Mintage | F | VF | XF | Unc | BU |
|---|---|---|---|---|---|---|
| 1953 | 20,000,000 | — | 0.40 | 0.80 | 2.00 | — |
| 1953 Proof | — | Value: 200 | | | | |
| 1956 | 10,000,000 | — | 0.40 | 1.00 | 2.50 | — |
| 1956 Proof | — | Value: 200 | | | | |
| 1957H | 10,000,000 | — | 0.40 | 1.20 | 3.00 | — |
| 1957H Proof | — | Value: 200 | | | | |
| 1957KN | 10,000,000 | — | 0.40 | 1.20 | 3.00 | — |
| 1958 | 10,000,000 | — | 0.40 | 0.80 | 2.00 | — |
| 1958 Proof | — | Value: 200 | | | | |
| 1960 | 10,000,000 | — | 0.40 | 0.80 | 2.00 | — |
| 1960 Proof | — | Value: 200 | | | | |
| 1961 | 60,784,000 | — | 0.20 | 0.50 | 1.00 | — |
| 1961 Proof | — | Value: 200 | | | | |
| 1961H | 69,220,000 | — | 0.20 | 0.50 | 1.00 | — |
| 1961KN | Inc. above | — | 0.50 | 0.80 | 2.75 | — |

**20 CENTS** **KM# 3** **Composition:** Copper-Nickel

| Date | Mintage | F | VF | XF | Unc | BU |
|---|---|---|---|---|---|---|
| 1954 | 10,000,000 | — | 0.80 | 1.50 | 2.50 | — |
| 1954 Proof | — | Value: 220 | | | | |
| 1956 | 5,000,000 | — | 0.75 | 1.25 | 2.00 | — |
| 1956 Proof | — | Value: 220 | | | | |
| 1957H | 2,500,000 | — | 1.20 | 1.80 | 3.00 | — |
| 1957KN | 2,500,000 | — | 1.20 | 1.80 | 4.00 | — |
| 1961 | 32,000,000 | — | 0.50 | 0.75 | 2.00 | — |
| 1961 Proof | — | Value: 200 | | | | |
| 1961H | 23,000,000 | — | 0.75 | 1.25 | 2.25 | — |

**50 CENTS** **KM# 4.1** **Composition:** Copper-Nickel **Edge:** Security

| Date | Mintage | F | VF | XF | Unc | BU |
|---|---|---|---|---|---|---|
| 1954 | 8,000,000 | — | 1.00 | 2.00 | 4.50 | — |
| 1954 Proof | — | Value: 280 | | | | |
| 1955H | 4,000,000 | — | 1.50 | 2.50 | 5.00 | — |
| 1956 | 3,440,000 | — | 1.50 | 2.25 | 5.00 | — |
| 1956 Proof | — | Value: 280 | | | | |
| 1957H | 2,000,000 | — | 1.50 | 2.50 | 5.00 | — |
| 1957KN | 2,000,000 | — | 2.00 | 2.75 | 6.00 | — |
| 1958H | 4,000,000 | — | 1.00 | 1.50 | 5.00 | — |
| 1961 | 17,000,000 | — | 1.00 | 1.50 | 3.50 | — |
| 1961 Proof | — | Value: 280 | | | | |
| 1961H | 4,000,000 | — | 1.50 | 2.50 | 5.00 | — |

**50 CENTS** **KM# 4.2** **Composition:** Copper-Nickel **Note:** Error, without security edge.

| Date | Mintage | F | VF | XF | Unc | BU |
|---|---|---|---|---|---|---|
| 1954 | Inc. above | — | 90.00 | 120 | 300 | — |
| 1957KN | Inc. above | — | 90.00 | 120 | 300 | — |
| 1958H | Inc. above | — | 90.00 | 120 | 300 | — |
| 1961 | Inc. above | — | 90.00 | 120 | 300 | — |
| 1961H | Inc. above | — | 90.00 | 120 | 300 | — |

# MALAY PENINSULA

## KELANTAN

A state in northern Malaysia, colonized by the Javanese in 1300's. It was subject to Thailand from 1780 to 1909.

**TITLES**

كلنتن

Kelantan

خليفة المؤمنين

Khalifa(t) Al-Mu'minin

**SULTANS**
Muhammed IV, 1902-1919

## STATE

### STANDARD COINAGE

**PITIS** **KM# 12** **Composition:** Tin **Obverse:** Arabic legend **Obv. Legend:** Belanjaan Negri Kelantan Adama Mulkahu **Reverse:** Arabic legend **Rev. Legend:** Duriba Fi Dhul Hijja Sanat 1321 **Size:** 24-29 mm.

| Date | Mintage | VG | F | VF | XF | Unc |
|---|---|---|---|---|---|---|
| AH1321 | — | 8.00 | 12.00 | 20.00 | 30.00 | — |

**PITIS** **KM# 15** **Composition:** Tin **Obverse:** Arabic legend **Obv. Legend:** Belanjaan Kerajaan Kelan Tan. **Reverse:** Arabic legend **Rev. Legend:** Duriba Fi Dhul Hijja Sanat 1321

| Date | Mintage | VG | F | VF | XF | Unc |
|---|---|---|---|---|---|---|
| AH1321 | — | 2.00 | 3.00 | 5.00 | 9.00 | — |

**KEPING** **KM# 18** **Composition:** Tin **Obverse:** Arabic legend **Obv. Legend:** Negri Kelantan Satu Keping **Reverse:** Uninscribed, but obverse legend shows through in negative form

| Date | Mintage | VG | F | VF | XF | Unc |
|---|---|---|---|---|---|---|
| AH1323 | — | 15.00 | 25.00 | 40.00 | 60.00 | — |

**10 KEPINGS** **KM# 20** **Composition:** Tin **Obverse:** Arabic legend **Obv. Legend:** Belanjaan Kerajaan Kelantin Sepuloh Keping **Reverse:** Border of diamonds around Arabic legend **Rev. Legend:** Sunia Fi Dhul Hijja Sanat 1321

| Date | Mintage | VG | F | VF | XF | Unc |
|---|---|---|---|---|---|---|
| AH1321 | — | 6.00 | 12.00 | 25.00 | 40.00 | — |

## TRENGGANU

A state in eastern Malaysia on the shore of the south China Sea. Area of dispute between Malacca and Thailand with the latter emerging with possession. Trengganu became a British dependency in 1909.

TITLES

ترغكانو

Khalifa(t) al-Mu'minin

خليفة المؤمنين

Trengganu

**SULTANS**

Zainal Abidin III, 1881-1918
Muhammed, 1918-1920
Sulaiman, 1920-1942

## STATE

### STANDARD COINAGE

**1/4 CENT KM# 17 Composition:** Tin **Ruler:** Zainal Abidin III **Note:** Similar to 1/2 Cent, KM#16.

| Date | Mintage | VG | F | VF | XF | Unc |
|---|---|---|---|---|---|---|
| AH1325 Rare | — | — | — | — | — | — |

**1/2 CENT KM# 16 Composition:** Tin **Ruler:** Zainal Abidin III **Note:** Recast.

| Date | Mintage | VG | F | VF | XF | Unc |
|---|---|---|---|---|---|---|
| AH1322 | — | — | — | — | 15.00 | — |

**1/2 CENT KM# 18 Composition:** Tin **Ruler:** Zainal Abidin III **Note:** Recast. Originals are rare.

| Date | Mintage | VG | F | VF | XF | Unc |
|---|---|---|---|---|---|---|
| AH1325 | — | — | — | — | 15.00 | — |

**CENT KM# 19 Composition:** Tin **Ruler:** Zainal Abidin III

| Date | Mintage | VG | F | VF | XF | Unc |
|---|---|---|---|---|---|---|
| AH1325 | — | 5.00 | 9.00 | 16.00 | 30.00 | — |

**CENT KM# 20 Composition:** Tin **Ruler:** Zainal Abidin III **Note:** Although dated AH1325 (1907), this coin was actually struck in 1920 under Sultan Sulaiman. Authorized mintage was 1 million. Beware of thin lead counterfeits.

| Date | Mintage | VG | F | VF | XF | Unc |
|---|---|---|---|---|---|---|
| AH1325 | — | 5.00 | 9.00 | 16.00 | 30.00 | — |

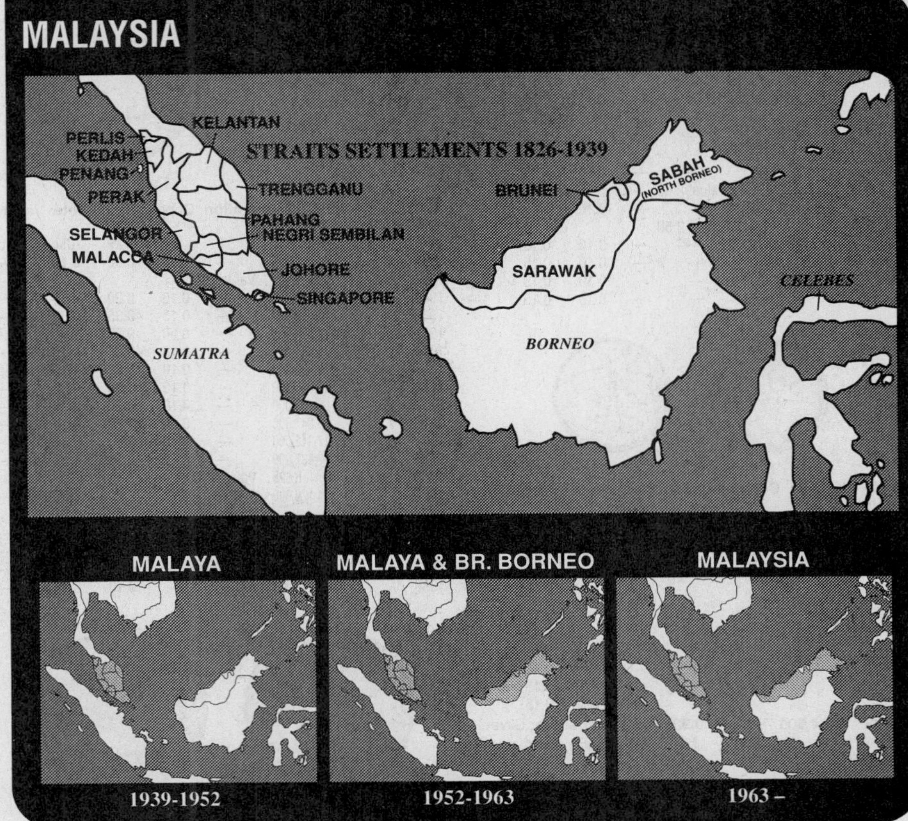


The independent limited constitutional monarchy of Malaysia, which occupies the southern part of the Malay Peninsula in southeast Asia and the northern part of the island of Borneo, has an area of 127,316 sq. mi. (329,750 sq. km.) and a population of 15.4 million. Capital: Kuala Lumpur. The economy is based on agriculture, mining and forestry. Rubber, tin, timber and palm oil are exported.

Malaysia came into being on Sept. 16, 1963, as a federation of Malaya (Johore, Kelantan, Kedah, Perlis, Trengganu, Negri-Sembilan, Pahang, Perak, Selangor, Penang, Malacca), Singapore, Sabah (British North Borneo) and Sarawak. Following two serious racial riots involving Malay and Chinese, Singapore withdrew from the federation on Aug. 9, 1965, to become an independent republic within the British Commonwealth.

**MINT MARKS**

FM - Franklin Mint, U.S.A.

***NOTE:** From 1975-1985 the Franklin Mint produced coinage in up to 3 different qualities. Qualities of issue are designated in ( ) after each date and are defined as follows:

**(M) MATTE** - Normal circulation strike or a dull finish produced by sandblasting special uncirculated (polish finish) or proof quality dies.

**(U) SPECIAL UNCIRCULATED** - Polished or proof-like in appearance without any frosted features.

**(P) PROOF** - The highest quality obtainable having mirror-like fields and frosted features.

**MONETARY SYSTEM**

100 Sen = 1 Ringgit (Dollar)

## REPUBLIC

### STANDARD COINAGE

100 Sen = 1 Ringgit (Dollar)

**SEN KM# 1 Composition:** Bronze **Reverse:** Parliament building **Note:** Varieties exist.

| Date | Mintage | F | VF | XF | Unc | BU |
|---|---|---|---|---|---|---|
| 1967 | 45,000,000 | — | — | 0.10 | 0.15 | — |
| 1967 | 500 | Value: 5.00 | | | | |
| 1968 | 10,500,000 | — | — | 0.10 | 0.15 | — |
| 1970 | 2,535,000 | — | 0.15 | 0.50 | 1.50 | — |
| 1971 | 47,862,000 | — | — | 0.10 | 0.15 | — |
| 1973 | 21,400,000 | — | — | 0.10 | 0.15 | — |
| 1976 | 100 | — | 25.00 | 65.00 | 125 | — |
| 1980FM (P) | 5,000 | Value: 1.00 | | | | |
| 1981FM (P) | 6,628 | Value: 1.00 | | | | |

**SEN KM# 1a Composition:** Copper-Clad Steel

| Date | Mintage | F | VF | XF | Unc | BU |
|---|---|---|---|---|---|---|
| 1973 | Inc. above | — | 0.15 | 0.45 | 0.65 | — |
| 1976 | 27,406,000 | — | — | 0.10 | 0.15 | — |
| 1977 | 21,751,000 | — | — | 0.10 | 0.15 | — |
| 1978 | 30,844,000 | — | — | 0.10 | 0.15 | — |
| 1979 | 15,714,000 | — | — | 0.10 | 0.15 | — |
| 1980 | 16,152,000 | — | — | 0.10 | 0.15 | — |
| 1981 | 24,633,000 | — | — | 0.10 | 0.15 | — |
| 1982 | 37,295,000 | — | — | 0.10 | 0.15 | — |
| 1983 | 19,333,000 | — | — | 0.10 | 0.15 | — |
| 1984 | 26,267,000 | — | — | 0.10 | 0.15 | — |
| 1985 | 52,402,000 | — | — | 0.10 | 0.15 | — |
| 1986 | 48,920,000 | — | — | 0.10 | 0.15 | — |
| 1987 | 35,284,000 | — | — | 0.10 | 0.15 | — |
| 1988 | 56,749,000 | — | — | 0.10 | 0.15 | — |

**SEN KM# 49 Composition:** Bronze Clad Steel **Reverse:** Drum **Note:**

| Date | Mintage | F | VF | XF | Unc | BU |
|---|---|---|---|---|---|---|
| 1989 | 28,429,000 | — | — | — | 0.15 | — |
| 1990 | 102,539,000 | — | — | — | 0.15 | — |
| 1991 | 100,315,000 | — | — | — | 0.15 | — |
| 1992 | 122,824,000 | — | — | — | 0.15 | — |
| 1993 | 153,806,000 | — | — | — | 0.15 | — |
| 1994 | 185,085,000 | — | — | — | 0.15 | — |
| 1995 | 208,611,000 | — | — | — | 0.15 | — |
| 1996 | — | — | — | — | 0.15 | — |
| 1997 | — | — | — | — | 0.15 | — |
| 1998 | — | — | — | — | 0.15 | — |
| 1999 | — | — | — | — | 0.15 | — |

**SEN KM# 49a Weight:** 0.9250 g. **Composition:** Silver

| Date | Mintage | F | VF | XF | Unc | BU |
|---|---|---|---|---|---|---|
| 1992 Proof | — | Value: 15.00 | | | | |

**5 SEN KM# 2 Composition:** Copper-Nickel **Note:** Varieties exist.

| Date | Mintage | F | VF | XF | Unc | BU |
|---|---|---|---|---|---|---|
| 1967 | 75,464,000 | — | — | 0.10 | 0.20 | — |
| 1967 Proof | 500 | Value: 20.00 | | | | |
| 1968 | 74,536,000 | — | — | 0.10 | 0.20 | — |
| 1971 | 16,658,000 | — | — | 0.30 | 0.50 | — |
| 1973 | 102,942,000 | — | — | 0.10 | 0.15 | — |
| 1976 | 65,659,000 | — | — | 0.10 | 0.15 | — |
| 1977 | 10,609,000 | — | — | 0.30 | 0.50 | — |
| 1978 | 50,044,000 | — | — | 0.10 | 0.15 | — |
| 1979 | 38,824,000 | — | — | 0.10 | 0.15 | — |
| 1980 | 33,893,000 | — | — | 0.10 | 0.15 | — |
| 1980FM (P) | 6,628 | Value: 2.00 | | | | |
| 1981 | 51,490,000 | — | — | 0.10 | 0.15 | — |
| 1981FM (P) | — | Value: 2.50 | | | | |
| 1982 | 118,594,000 | — | — | 0.10 | 0.15 | — |
| 1985 | 15,553,000 | — | — | 0.10 | 0.15 | — |
| 1987 | 17,723,000 | — | — | 0.10 | 0.15 | — |
| 1988 | 26,788,000 | — | — | 0.10 | 0.15 | — |

**5 SEN KM# 50 Composition:** Copper-Nickel **Reverse:** Top with string

| Date | Mintage | F | VF | XF | Unc | BU |
|---|---|---|---|---|---|---|
| 1989 | 20,484,000 | — | — | — | 0.15 | — |
| 1990 | 58,909,000 | — | — | — | 0.15 | — |
| 1991 | 46,092,000 | — | — | — | 0.15 | — |
| 1992 | 67,844,000 | — | — | — | 0.15 | — |
| 1993 | 70,703,000 | — | — | — | 0.15 | — |
| 1994 | 83,026,000 | — | — | — | 0.15 | — |
| 1995 | 53,069,000 | — | — | — | 0.15 | — |
| 1996 | — | — | — | — | 0.15 | — |
| 1997 | — | — | — | — | 0.15 | — |
| 1998 | — | — | — | — | 0.15 | — |

**5 SEN KM# 50a Weight:** 0.9250 g. **Composition:** Silver

| Date | Mintage | F | VF | XF | Unc | BU |
|---|---|---|---|---|---|---|
| 1992 Proof | — | Value: 15.00 | | | | |

**10 SEN KM# 3 Composition:** Copper-Nickel **Note:** Varieties exist

| Date | Mintage | F | VF | XF | Unc | BU |
|---|---|---|---|---|---|---|
| 1967 | 106,708,000 | — | 0.10 | 0.15 | 0.30 | — |
| 1967 Proof | 500 | Value: 25.00 | | | | |
| 1968 | 128,292,000 | — | 0.10 | 0.15 | 0.30 | — |
| 1971 | 42,000 | — | 35.00 | 45.00 | 65.00 | — |
| 1973 | 214,832,000 | — | 0.10 | 0.15 | 0.30 | — |
| 1976 | 148,841,000 | — | 0.10 | 0.15 | 0.30 | — |
| 1977 | 52,720,000 | — | 0.10 | 0.15 | 0.30 | — |
| 1978 | 21,162,000 | — | 0.10 | 0.15 | 0.30 | — |
| 1979 | 50,633,000 | — | 0.10 | 0.15 | 0.30 | — |
| 1980 | 51,797,000 | — | 0.10 | 0.15 | 0.30 | — |
| 1980FM (P) | 6,628 | Value: 3.00 | | | | |
| 1981 | 236,639,000 | — | 0.10 | 0.15 | 0.30 | — |
| 1981FM (P) | — | Value: 3.50 | | | | |
| 1982 | 145,639,000 | — | — | 0.10 | 0.25 | — |
| 1983 | 30,832,000 | — | — | 0.10 | 0.25 | — |
| 1988 | 17,852,000 | — | — | 0.10 | 0.25 | — |

**10 SEN KM# 51 Composition:** Copper-Nickel **Reverse:** Ceremonial table

| Date | Mintage | F | VF | XF | Unc | BU |
|---|---|---|---|---|---|---|
| 1989 | 32,392,000 | — | — | — | 0.25 | — |
| 1990 | 132,982,000 | — | — | — | 0.25 | — |
| 1991 | 133,293,000 | — | — | — | 0.25 | — |
| 1992 | 89,919,000 | — | — | — | 0.25 | — |
| 1993 | 44,224,000 | — | — | — | 0.25 | — |
| 1994 | 7,122,000 | — | — | — | 0.25 | — |
| 1995 | 82,217,000 | — | — | — | 0.25 | — |
| 1996 | — | — | — | — | 0.25 | — |
| 1997 | — | — | — | — | 0.25 | — |
| 1998 | — | — | — | — | 0.25 | — |
| 1999 | — | — | — | — | 0.25 | — |

**10 SEN KM# 51a Weight:** 0.9250 g. **Composition:** Silver

| Date | Mintage | F | VF | XF | Unc | BU |
|---|---|---|---|---|---|---|
| 1992 Proof | — | Value: 15.00 | | | | |

**20 SEN KM# 4 Composition:** Copper-Nickel **Note:** Varieties exist.

| Date | Mintage | F | VF | XF | Unc | BU |
|---|---|---|---|---|---|---|
| 1967 | 49,560,000 | — | 0.10 | 0.30 | 0.45 | — |
| 1967 Proof | 500 | Value: 35.00 | | | | |
| 1968 | 40,440,000 | — | 0.10 | 0.30 | 0.45 | — |
| 1969 | 15,000,000 | — | 0.15 | 0.35 | 0.50 | — |
| 1970 | 1,054,000 | — | 0.50 | 0.75 | 1.00 | — |
| 1971 | 9,958,000 | — | 0.15 | 0.35 | 0.50 | — |
| 1973 | 116,075,000 | — | 0.10 | 0.20 | 0.35 | — |
| 1976 | 47,396,000 | — | 0.10 | 0.20 | 0.35 | — |
| 1977 | 66,139,000 | — | 0.10 | 0.20 | 0.35 | — |
| 1978 | 6,847,000 | — | 0.15 | 0.30 | 0.45 | — |
| 1979 | 17,346,000 | — | 0.10 | 0.20 | 0.35 | — |
| 1980 | 32,837,000 | — | 0.10 | 0.20 | 0.35 | — |
| 1980FM (P) | 6,628 | Value: 4.00 | | | | |
| 1981 | 144,128,000 | — | 0.10 | 0.20 | 0.35 | — |
| 1981FM (P) | — | Value: 4.50 | | | | |
| 1982 | 97,905,000 | — | — | 0.10 | 0.25 | — |
| 1983 | 8,105,000 | — | — | 0.10 | 0.25 | — |
| 1987 | 26,225,000 | — | — | 0.10 | 0.25 | — |
| 1988 | 67,218,000 | — | — | 0.10 | 0.25 | — |

**20 SEN KM# 52 Composition:** Copper-Nickel **Reverse:** Basket containing food and utensils

| Date | Mintage | F | VF | XF | Unc | BU |
|---|---|---|---|---|---|---|
| 1989 | 28,945,000 | — | — | — | 0.35 | — |
| 1990 | 56,249,000 | — | — | — | 0.35 | — |
| 1991 | 82,774,000 | — | — | — | 0.35 | — |
| 1992 | 48,975,000 | — | — | — | 0.35 | — |
| 1993 | 55,753,000 | — | — | — | 0.35 | — |
| 1994 | 2,680,000 | — | — | — | 0.35 | — |
| 1997 | — | — | — | — | 0.35 | — |
| 1998 | — | — | — | — | 0.35 | — |

**20 SEN KM# 52a Weight:** 0.9250 g. **Composition:** Silver And Enamel

| Date | Mintage | F | VF | XF | Unc | BU |
|---|---|---|---|---|---|---|
| 1992 Proof | — | Value: 17.50 | | | | |

**50 SEN KM# 5.1 Composition:** Copper-Nickel

| Date | Mintage | F | VF | XF | Unc | BU |
|---|---|---|---|---|---|---|
| 1967 | 15,000,000 | — | 0.25 | 0.50 | 1.00 | — |
| 1967 Proof | 500 | Value: 45.00 | | | | |
| 1968 | 12,000,000 | — | 0.25 | 0.50 | 1.00 | — |
| 1969 | 2,000,000 | — | 0.50 | 0.75 | 1.50 | — |

**50 SEN KM# 5.2 Composition:** Copper-Nickel **Note:** Error with security edge.

| Date | Mintage | F | VF | XF | Unc | BU |
|---|---|---|---|---|---|---|
| 1967 | Inc. above | — | 75.00 | 140 | 240 | — |
| 1968 | Inc. above | — | 75.00 | 140 | 240 | — |
| 1969 | Inc. above | — | 250 | 350 | 550 | — |

**50 SEN KM# 5.3 Composition:** Copper-Nickel **Edge:** Lettered

| Date | Mintage | F | VF | XF | Unc | BU |
|---|---|---|---|---|---|---|
| 1971 | 8,404,000 | — | 0.30 | 0.60 | 1.00 | — |
| 1973 | 50,135,000 | — | 0.25 | 0.50 | 0.75 | — |
| 1976 | — | — | 0.25 | 0.40 | 0.60 | — |
| 1977 | 17,720,000 | — | 0.25 | 0.40 | 0.60 | — |
| 1978 | 11,033,000 | — | 0.25 | 0.40 | 0.60 | — |
| 1979 | 5,361,000 | — | 0.25 | 0.40 | 0.60 | — |
| 1980 | 15,911,000 | — | 0.25 | 0.40 | 0.60 | — |
| 1980FM Proof | 6,628 | Value: 4.50 | | | | |
| 1981 | 22,969,000 | — | — | 0.25 | 0.50 | — |
| 1982 | 20,585,000 | — | — | 0.25 | 0.50 | — |
| 1983 | 11,560,000 | — | — | 0.25 | 0.50 | — |
| 1984 | 10,139,000 | — | — | 0.25 | 0.50 | — |
| 1985 | 7,115,000 | — | — | 0.25 | 0.50 | — |
| 1986 | 8,193,000 | — | — | 0.25 | 0.50 | — |
| 1987 | 7,696,000 | — | — | 0.25 | 0.50 | — |
| 1988 | 26,788,000 | — | — | 0.25 | 0.50 | — |

**50 SEN KM# 5.4 Composition:** Copper-Nickel **Edge:** Plain

| Date | Mintage | F | VF | XF | Unc | BU |
|---|---|---|---|---|---|---|
| 1981FM (P) | — | Value: 8.00 | | | | |

**50 SEN KM# 53 Composition:** Copper-Nickel **Reverse:** Ceremonial kite

| Date | Mintage | F | VF | XF | Unc | BU |
|---|---|---|---|---|---|---|
| 1989 | 6,639,000 | — | — | — | 0.65 | — |
| 1990 | 26,276,000 | — | — | — | 0.65 | — |
| 1991 | 20,721,000 | — | — | — | 0.65 | — |
| 1992 | 15,135,000 | — | — | — | 0.65 | — |
| 1993 | 7,656,000 | — | — | — | 0.65 | — |
| 1994 | 6,566,000 | — | — | — | 0.65 | — |
| 1995 | 1,650,000 | — | — | — | 0.65 | — |
| 1997 | — | — | — | — | 0.65 | — |
| 1998 | — | — | — | — | 0.65 | — |

**50 SEN KM# 53a Weight:** 0.9250 g. **Composition:** Silver

| Date | Mintage | F | VF | XF | Unc | BU |
|---|---|---|---|---|---|---|
| 1992 Proof | — | Value: 20.00 | | | | |

**RINGGIT KM# 7 Composition:** Copper-Nickel **Subject:** 10th Anniversary - Bank Negara

| Date | Mintage | F | VF | XF | Unc | BU |
|---|---|---|---|---|---|---|
| ND(1969) | 1,000,000 | — | 1.00 | 1.50 | 2.75 | — |

**RINGGIT KM# 7a Weight:** 17.0000 g. **Composition:** 0.9250 Silver .5055 oz. ASW

| Date | Mintage | F | VF | XF | Unc | BU |
|---|---|---|---|---|---|---|
| ND(1969) Proof | 1,000 | Value: 275 | | | | |

**RINGGIT KM# 9.1 Composition:** Copper-Nickel

| Date | Mintage | F | VF | XF | Unc | BU |
|---|---|---|---|---|---|---|
| 1971 | 2,000,000 | — | 0.50 | 0.75 | 1.50 | — |
| 1971 Proof | 500 | Value: 800 | | | | |
| 1980 | 472,000 | — | 0.60 | 0.85 | 1.65 | — |
| 1980FM (P) | 6,628 | Value: 8.00 | | | | |
| 1981 | 765,000 | — | 0.60 | 0.85 | 1.65 | — |
| 1982 | 202,000 | — | 0.60 | 0.85 | 1.65 | — |
| 1984 | 355,000 | — | 0.60 | 0.85 | 1.65 | — |
| 1985 | 302,000 | — | 0.60 | 0.85 | 1.65 | — |
| 1986 | 253,000 | — | 0.60 | 0.85 | 1.65 | — |
| 1987 | 177,000 | — | 0.60 | 0.85 | 1.65 | — |

**RINGGIT KM# 12 Composition:** Copper-Nickel **Subject:** Kuala Lumpur Anniversary

| Date | Mintage | F | VF | XF | Unc | BU |
|---|---|---|---|---|---|---|
| 1972 | 500,000 | — | 0.60 | 0.85 | 2.50 | — |
| 1972 Proof | 500 | Value: 350 | | | | |

**RINGGIT** **KM# 13** **Composition:** Copper-Nickel **Subject:** 25th Anniversary - Employee Provident Fund

| Date | Mintage | F | VF | XF | Unc | BU |
|---|---|---|---|---|---|---|
| 1976FM (U) | 500,000 | — | 0.60 | 0.85 | 2.50 | — |
| 1976FM (P) | 7,810 | Value: 18.00 | | | | |

**RINGGIT** **KM# 16** **Composition:** Copper-Nickel **Subject:** 3rd Malaysian 5-Year Plan

| Date | Mintage | F | VF | XF | Unc | BU |
|---|---|---|---|---|---|---|
| ND(1976) | 1,000,000 | — | 0.60 | 0.75 | 2.00 | — |
| ND(1976)FM (P) | 17,000 | Value: 12.00 | | | | |

**RINGGIT** **KM# 22** **Composition:** Copper-Nickel **Subject:** 9th Southeast Asian Games

| Date | Mintage | F | VF | XF | Unc | BU |
|---|---|---|---|---|---|---|
| 1977 | 1,000,000 | — | 0.60 | 0.75 | 2.00 | — |
| 1977FM (P) | 11,000 | Value: 17.50 | | | | |

**RINGGIT** **KM# 25** **Composition:** Copper-Nickel **Subject:** 20th Anniversary of Independence

| Date | Mintage | F | VF | XF | Unc | BU |
|---|---|---|---|---|---|---|
| ND(1977) | 500,000 | — | 0.60 | 0.75 | 2.00 | — |
| ND(1977)FM (P) | 3,100 | Value: 35.00 | | | | |

**RINGGIT** **KM# 26** **Composition:** Copper-Nickel **Subject:** 100th Anniversary of Natural Rubber Production

| Date | Mintage | F | VF | XF | Unc | BU |
|---|---|---|---|---|---|---|
| ND(1977) | 500,000 | — | 0.60 | 0.75 | 2.00 | — |

**RINGGIT** **KM# 27** **Composition:** Copper-Nickel **Subject:** 20th Anniversary of Bank Negara

| Date | Mintage | F | VF | XF | Unc | BU |
|---|---|---|---|---|---|---|
| ND(1979) | 300,000 | — | 0.60 | 0.75 | 2.00 | — |

**RINGGIT** **KM# 27a** **Weight:** 17.0000 g. **Composition:** 0.9250 Silver .5055 oz. ASW

| Date | Mintage | F | VF | XF | Unc | BU |
|---|---|---|---|---|---|---|
| ND(1979) | 8,000 | Value: 16.00 | | | | |
| ND(1979)FM (P) | 6,628 | Value: 25.00 | | | | |

**RINGGIT** **KM# 28** **Composition:** Copper-Nickel **Subject:** 15th Centrury of Hejira

| Date | Mintage | F | VF | XF | Unc | BU |
|---|---|---|---|---|---|---|
| AH1401(1981) | 500,000 | — | 0.60 | 0.75 | 2.00 | — |

**RINGGIT** **KM# 9.2** **Composition:** Copper-Nickel **Edge:** Plain

| Date | Mintage | F | VF | XF | Unc | BU |
|---|---|---|---|---|---|---|
| 1981FM (P) | — | Value: 16.00 | | | | |

**RINGGIT** **KM# 29** **Composition:** Copper-Nickel **Subject:** 4th Malaysian Plan **Note:** Tun Hussein Onn

| Date | Mintage | F | VF | XF | Unc | BU |
|---|---|---|---|---|---|---|
| ND(1981) | 1,000,000 | — | 0.50 | 0.65 | 1.85 | — |
| ND(1981) Proof | 10,000 | Value: 15.00 | | | | |

**RINGGIT** **KM# 32** **Composition:** Copper-Nickel **Subject:** 25th Anniversary of Independence

| Date | Mintage | F | VF | XF | Unc | BU |
|---|---|---|---|---|---|---|
| ND(1982) | 1,500,000 | — | 0.50 | 0.65 | 1.85 | — |
| ND(1982) Proof | 15,000 | Value: 12.00 | | | | |

**RINGGIT** **KM# 36** **Composition:** Copper-Nickel **Subject:** 5th Malaysian 5-Year Plan

| Date | Mintage | F | VF | XF | Unc | BU |
|---|---|---|---|---|---|---|
| ND(1986) | 1,000,000 | — | 0.50 | 0.65 | 1.85 | — |
| ND(1986) Proof | 8,000 | Value: 10.00 | | | | |

**RINGGIT** **KM# 39** **Composition:** Copper-Nickel **Subject:** 35th Annual PATA Conference

| Date | Mintage | F | VF | XF | Unc | BU |
|---|---|---|---|---|---|---|
| ND(1986) | 500,000 | — | 0.50 | 1.00 | 3.50 | — |

**RINGGIT** **KM# 39a** **Weight:** 16.8500 g. **Composition:** 0.5000 Silver .2709 oz. ASW

| Date | Mintage | F | VF | XF | Unc | BU |
|---|---|---|---|---|---|---|
| ND(1986) Proof | 11,000 | Value: 10.00 | | | | |

**RINGGIT** **KM# 43** **Composition:** Copper-Zinc **Subject:** 30th Anniversary of Independence

| Date | Mintage | F | VF | XF | Unc | BU |
|---|---|---|---|---|---|---|
| ND(1987) | 1,000,000 | — | — | 0.60 | 1.75 | — |
| ND(1987) Proof | 20,000 | Value: 10.00 | | | | |

**RINGGIT** **KM# 54** **Composition:** Aluminum-Bronze **Reverse:** Native dagger and scabbard

| Date | Mintage | F | VF | XF | Unc | BU |
|---|---|---|---|---|---|---|
| 1989 | 20,410,000 | — | — | — | 1.75 | — |
| 1990 | 80,102,000 | — | — | — | 1.75 | — |
| 1991 | 169,001,000 | — | — | — | 1.75 | — |
| 1992 | 139,042,000 | — | — | — | 1.75 | — |
| 1993 | 178,894,000 | — | — | — | 1.75 | — |

**RINGGIT** **KM# 54a** **Composition:** 0.9250 Silver

| Date | Mintage | F | VF | XF | Unc | BU |
|---|---|---|---|---|---|---|
| 1992 Proof | — | Value: 20.00 | | | | |

**RINGGIT** **KM# 64** **Composition:** Aluminum-Bronze **Obverse:** Denomination spelled out

| Date | Mintage | F | VF | XF | Unc | BU |
|---|---|---|---|---|---|---|
| 1993 | Inc. above | — | — | — | 2.00 | — |
| 1994 | 36,899,000 | — | — | — | 1.75 | — |
| 1995 | 132,173,000 | — | — | — | 1.75 | — |
| 1996 | — | — | — | — | 1.75 | — |

**RINGGIT** **KM# 65** **Ring Composition:** Nickel-Brass **Center Weight:** 8.1500 g. **Center Composition:** Copper-Nickel **Subject:** Thomas-Uber Cup **Obverse:** City view **Reverse:** Two-handled cup on radiant background **Edge:** Reeded **Size:** 26.5 mm.

| Date | Mintage | F | VF | XF | Unc | BU |
|---|---|---|---|---|---|---|
| 2000 | 2,000 | — | — | — | 7.00 | — |

**5 RINGGIT** **KM# 10** **Composition:** Copper-Nickel

| Date | Mintage | F | VF | XF | Unc | BU |
|---|---|---|---|---|---|---|
| 1971 | 2,000,000 | — | 2.50 | 3.00 | 5.00 | — |
| 1971 Proof | 500 | Value: 850 | | | | |

**5 RINGGIT** **KM# 40** **Weight:** 29.0300 g. **Composition:** 0.5000 Silver .4662 oz. ASW **Subject:** PATA Conference

| Date | Mintage | F | VF | XF | Unc | BU |
|---|---|---|---|---|---|---|
| ND(1986) Proof | 11,000 | Value: 27.50 | | | | |

**5 RINGGIT** **KM# 47** **Composition:** Copper Plated Zinc **Subject:** 15th Southeast Asian Games

| Date | Mintage | F | VF | XF | Unc | BU |
|---|---|---|---|---|---|---|
| 1989 | 500,000 | — | — | — | 6.00 | — |
| 1989 Proof | 50,000 | Value: 12.50 | | | | |

**5 RINGGIT** **KM# 55** **Composition:** Copper Plated Zinc **Subject:** Commonwealth Heads of State Meeting

| Date | Mintage | F | VF | XF | Unc | BU |
|---|---|---|---|---|---|---|
| 1989 | 150,000 | — | — | — | 6.00 | — |
| 1989 Proof | 8,000 | Value: 12.50 | | | | |

**5 RINGGIT** **KM# 59** **Composition:** Copper Plated Zinc **Subject:** 100th Anniversary of Kuala Lumpur

| Date | Mintage | F | VF | XF | Unc | BU |
|---|---|---|---|---|---|---|
| ND(1990) | 100,000 | — | — | — | 6.00 | — |

**5 RINGGIT** **KM# 61** **Composition:** Copper-Zinc-Tin **Series:** World Wildlife Fund **Reverse:** Stylized Milky Stork

| Date | Mintage | F | VF | XF | Unc | BU |
|---|---|---|---|---|---|---|
| ND(1992) | — | — | — | — | 6.00 | — |
| ND(1992) Proof | 3,000 | Value: 15.00 | | | | |

**10 RINGGIT** **KM# 17** **Weight:** 10.8200 g. **Composition:** 0.9250 Silver .3218 oz. ASW **Subject:** 3rd Malaysian 5-Year Plan

| Date | Mintage | F | VF | XF | Unc | BU |
|---|---|---|---|---|---|---|
| ND(1976)FM (U) | 200,000 | — | — | — | 7.00 | — |
| ND(1980)FM (P) | 6,628 | Value: 20.00 | | | | |
| ND(1976)FM (P) | 10,000 | Value: 12.50 | | | | |

**10 RINGGIT** **KM# 44** **Weight:** 10.8200 g. **Composition:** 0.5000 Silver .1740 oz. ASW **Subject:** 30th anniversary of Independence

| Date | Mintage | F | VF | XF | Unc | BU |
|---|---|---|---|---|---|---|
| ND(1987) | 50,000 | — | — | — | 10.00 | — |
| ND(1987) Proof | 10,000 | Value: 20.00 | | | | |

**10 RINGGIT** **KM# 57** **Weight:** 13.6000 g. **Composition:** 0.9250 Silver .4045 oz. ASW **Subject:** Proclamation of Melaka as a Historical City

| Date | Mintage | F | VF | XF | Unc | BU |
|---|---|---|---|---|---|---|
| 1989 Proof | 20,000 | Value: 27.00 | | | | |

**15 RINGGIT** **KM# 19** **Weight:** 28.2800 g. **Composition:** 0.9250 Silver .8411 oz. ASW **Series:** Conservation **Reverse:** Maylasian Gaur

| Date | Mintage | F | VF | XF | Unc | BU |
|---|---|---|---|---|---|---|
| 1976 | 40,000 | — | — | — | 17.50 | — |
| 1976 Proof | 8,113 | Value: 26.50 | | | | |

**15 RINGGIT** **KM# 48** **Weight:** 16.7300 g. **Composition:** 0.9250 Silver .4986 oz. ASW **Subject:** 15th Southeast Asian Games

| Date | Mintage | F | VF | XF | Unc | BU |
|---|---|---|---|---|---|---|
| 1989 Prooflike | 50,000 | — | — | — | — | — |
| 1989 Proof | 20,000 | Value: 25.00 | | | | |

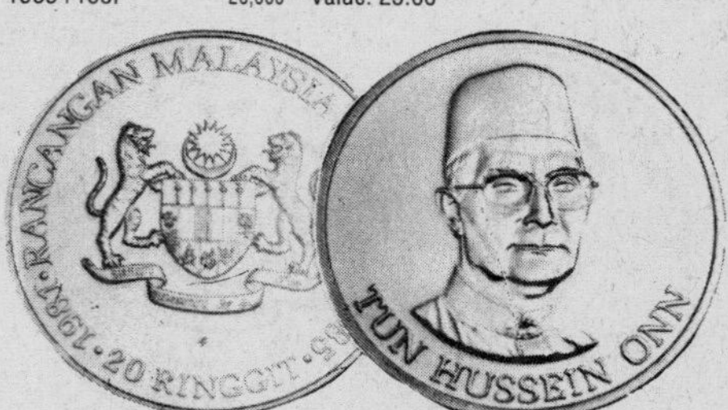


**20 RINGGIT** **KM# 30** **Weight:** 16.2300 g. **Composition:** 0.5000 Silver .2609 oz. ASW **Subject:** 4th Malaysian 5-Year Plan **Reverse:** Tun Hussein Onn

| Date | Mintage | F | VF | XF | Unc | BU |
|---|---|---|---|---|---|---|
| ND(1981)FM (U) | 100,000 | — | — | — | 12.50 | — |
| ND(1981)FM (P) | 5,000 | Value: 27.50 | | | | |

**25 RINGGIT** **KM# 14** **Weight:** 35.0000 g. **Composition:** 0.9250 Silver 1.0409 oz. ASW **Subject:** 25th Anniversary - Employee Provident Fund

| Date | Mintage | F | VF | XF | Unc | BU |
|---|---|---|---|---|---|---|
| 1976FM (U) | 100,000 | — | — | — | 15.00 | — |
| 1976FM (P) | 7,796 | Value: 55.00 | | | | |

**25 RINGGIT** **KM# 20** **Weight:** 35.0000 g. **Composition:** 0.9250 Silver 1.0409 oz. ASW **Series:** Conservation **Obverse:** Similar to 500 Ringgit, KM#21 **Reverse:** Rhinosceros Hornbill

| Date | Mintage | F | VF | XF | Unc | BU |
|---|---|---|---|---|---|---|
| 1976 | 40,000 | — | — | — | 22.50 | — |
| 1976 Proof | 8,008 | Value: 32.50 | | | | |

**25 RINGGIT** **KM# 23** **Weight:** 35.0000 g. **Composition:** 0.9250 Silver 1.0409 oz. ASW **Subject:** 9th Southeast Asian Games

| Date | Mintage | F | VF | XF | Unc | BU |
|---|---|---|---|---|---|---|
| 1977FM (U) | 100,000 | — | — | — | 18.50 | — |
| 1977FM (P) | 5,877 | Value: 37.50 | | | | |
| 1980FM (P) | 5,000 | Value: 47.50 | | | | |

**25 RINGGIT** **KM# 33** **Weight:** 35.0000 g. **Composition:** 0.9250 Silver 1.0409 oz. ASW **Subject:** 25th Anniversary of Independence **Obverse:** Similar to 1 Ringgit, KM#32

| Date | Mintage | F | VF | XF | Unc | BU |
|---|---|---|---|---|---|---|
| ND(1982) | 154,000 | — | — | — | 16.50 | — |
| ND(1982) Proof | 7,000 | Value: 30.00 | | | | |

**25 RINGGIT** **KM# 35** **Weight:** 35.0000 g. **Composition:** 0.5000 Silver .5627 oz. ASW **Subject:** 25th Anniversary of the National Bank

| Date | Mintage | F | VF | XF | Unc | BU |
|---|---|---|---|---|---|---|
| ND(1984) | 98,000 | — | — | — | 16.50 | — |
| ND(1984) Proof | 10,000 | Value: 30.00 | | | | |

**25 RINGGIT** **KM# 41** **Weight:** 23.3300 g. **Composition:** 0.9250 Silver .6939 oz. ASW **Subject:** Women's Decade

| Date | Mintage | F | VF | XF | Unc | BU |
|---|---|---|---|---|---|---|
| ND(1985) Proof | 2,000 | Value: 47.50 | | | | |

**25 RINGGIT** **KM# 37** **Weight:** 35.0000 g. **Composition:** 0.5000 Silver .5627 oz. ASW **Subject:** 5th Malaysian 5-Year Plan

| Date | Mintage | F | VF | XF | Unc | BU |
|---|---|---|---|---|---|---|
| ND(1986) | 80,000 | — | — | — | 17.50 | — |
| ND(1986) Proof | 5,000 | Value: 32.50 | | | | |

**25 RINGGIT** **KM# 56** **Weight:** 21.9000 g. **Composition:** 0.9250 Silver .6527 oz. ASW **Subject:** Commonwealth Heads of State Meeting

| Date | Mintage | F | VF | XF | Unc | BU |
|---|---|---|---|---|---|---|
| 1989 | 30,000 | — | — | — | 17.50 | — |
| 1989 Proof | 8,000 | Value: 32.50 | | | | |

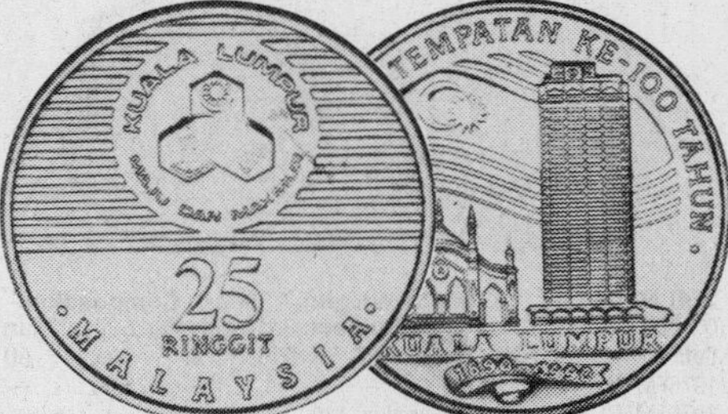


**25 RINGGIT** **KM# 60** **Weight:** 21.9000 g. **Composition:** 0.9250 Silver .6527 oz. ASW **Subject:** 100th Anniversary of Kuala Lumpur

| Date | Mintage | F | VF | XF | Unc | BU |
|---|---|---|---|---|---|---|
| ND(1990) | 25,000 | — | — | — | 17.50 | — |
| ND(1990) Proof | 25,000 | Value: 32.50 | | | | |

**25 RINGGIT** **KM# 62** **Weight:** 21.7700 g. **Composition:** 0.9250 Silver .6474 oz. ASW **Series:** World Wildlife Fund **Subject:** 100th Anniversary of Kuala Lumpur **Reverse:** Reef Fish

| Date | Mintage | F | VF | XF | Unc | BU |
|---|---|---|---|---|---|---|
| ND(1992) Proof | Est. 50,000 | Value: 32.50 | | | | |

**30 RINGGIT** **KM# 46** **Weight:** 22.0000 g. **Composition:** 0.9250 Silver .6557 oz. ASW **Subject:** 30th Anniversary of the National Bank

| Date | Mintage | F | VF | XF | Unc | BU |
|---|---|---|---|---|---|---|
| 1989 | 47,000 | — | — | — | 15.00 | — |
| 1989 Proof | 10,000 | Value: 30.00 | | | | |

**100 RINGGIT** **KM# 11** **Weight:** 18.6600 g. **Composition:** 0.9170 Gold .5502 oz. AGW **Subject:** Prime Minister Abdul Rahman Putra Al-haj

| Date | Mintage | F | VF | XF | Unc | BU |
|---|---|---|---|---|---|---|
| 1971 | 100,000 | — | — | — | 320 | — |
| 1971 Proof | 500 | Value: 900 | | | | |

**200 RINGGIT** **KM# 18** **Weight:** 7.3000 g. **Composition:** 0.9000 Gold .2212 oz. AGW **Subject:** 3rd Malaysian 5-Year Plan

| Date | Mintage | F | VF | XF | Unc | BU |
|---|---|---|---|---|---|---|
| 1976FM (U) | 51,000 | — | — | — | 75.00 | — |
| 1976FM (P) | 3,102 | Value: 110 | | | | |

**200 RINGGIT** **KM# 24** **Weight:** 7.2200 g. **Composition:** 0.9000 Gold .2089 oz. AGW **Subject:** 9th Southeast Asian Games

| Date | Mintage | F | VF | XF | Unc | BU |
|---|---|---|---|---|---|---|
| 1977FM (U) | 12,000 | — | — | — | 90.00 | — |
| 1977FM (P) | 975 | Value: 165 | | | | |

**250 RINGGIT** **KM# 15** **Weight:** 10.1100 g. **Composition:** 0.9000 Gold .2925 oz. AGW **Subject:** 25th Anniversary - Employee Provident Fund

| Date | Mintage | F | VF | XF | Unc | BU |
|---|---|---|---|---|---|---|
| 1976FM (U) | 30,000 | — | — | — | 125 | — |
| 1976FM (P) | 7,706 | Value: 165 | | | | |

**250 RINGGIT** **KM# 42** **Weight:** 8.1000 g. **Composition:** 0.9000 Gold .2344 oz. AGW **Series:** Womens' Decade

| Date | Mintage | F | VF | XF | Unc | BU |
|---|---|---|---|---|---|---|
| 1985 Proof | 1,500 | Value: 230 | | | | |

**250 RINGGIT** **KM# 45** **Weight:** 7.4300 g. **Composition:** 0.9000 Gold .2144 oz. AGW **Subject:** 30th Anniversary of Independence

| Date | Mintage | F | VF | XF | Unc | BU |
|---|---|---|---|---|---|---|
| 1987 | 5,000 | — | — | — | 125 | — |
| 1987 Proof | 2,000 | Value: 165 | | | | |

**250 RINGGIT** **KM# 58** **Weight:** 7.1300 g. **Composition:** 0.9000 Gold .2063 oz. AGW **Subject:** 15th Southeast Asian Games

| Date | Mintage | F | VF | XF | Unc | BU |
|---|---|---|---|---|---|---|
| 1989 Proof | 2,500 | Value: 220 | | | | |

**250 RINGGIT** **KM# 63** **Weight:** 8.6000 g. **Composition:** 0.9000 Gold .2489 oz. AGW **Series:** World Wildlife Fund **Obverse:** Panda above World Wildlife Fund **Reverse:** Clouded Leopard

| Date | Mintage | F | VF | XF | Unc | BU |
|---|---|---|---|---|---|---|
| 1992 Proof | Est. 3,000 | Value: 265 | | | | |

**500 RINGGIT** **KM# 21** **Weight:** 33.4370 g. **Composition:** 0.9000 Gold .9676 oz. AGW **Series:** Conservation **Reverse:** Malayan Tapir

| Date | Mintage | F | VF | XF | Unc | BU |
|---|---|---|---|---|---|---|
| 1976 | 2,894 | — | — | — | 500 | — |
| 1976 Proof | 508 | Value: 650 | | | | |

**500 RINGGIT** **KM# 31** **Weight:** 10.2600 g. **Composition:** 0.9000 Gold .2969 oz. AGW **Subject:** 4th Malaysian 5-Year Plan **Reverse:** Tun Hussein Onn

| Date | Mintage | F | VF | XF | Unc | BU |
|---|---|---|---|---|---|---|
| ND(1981)FM (U) | 20,000 | — | — | — | 200 | — |
| ND(1981)FM (P) | 1,000 | Value: 250 | | | | |

**500 RINGGIT** **KM# 34** **Weight:** 10.2600 g. **Composition:** 0.9000 Gold .2969 oz. AGW **Subject:** 25th Anniversary of Independence **Obverse:** Arms **Reverse:** President upholding dagger **Note:** Similar to 1 Ringgit, KM#32.

| Date | Mintage | F | VF | XF | Unc | BU |
|---|---|---|---|---|---|---|
| 1982 | 20,000 | — | — | — | 210 | — |
| 1982 Proof | 1,000 | Value: 285 | | | | |

**500 RINGGIT** **KM# 38** **Weight:** 10.2600 g. **Composition:** 0.9000 Gold .2969 oz. AGW **Subject:** 5th Malaysian 5-Year Plan

| Date | Mintage | F | VF | XF | Unc | BU |
|---|---|---|---|---|---|---|
| ND(1986) | 10,000 | — | — | — | 220 | — |
| ND(1986) Proof | 1,000 | Value: 325 | | | | |

## PATTERNS

Including off metal strikes

| KM# | Date | Mintage | Identification | Mkt Val |
|---|---|---|---|---|
| Pn1 | ND2602 (1942) | — | 20 Cents. Aluminum. Japanese occupation. | 2,500 |
| Pn2 | ND2602 (1942) | — | 20 Cents. Aluminum. Japanese occupation. | 2,500 |

## MINT SETS

| KM# | Date | Mintage | Identification | Issue Price | Mkt Val |
|---|---|---|---|---|---|
| MS1 | 1967 (5) | 10,000 | KM#1-5.1 | — | 10.00 |
| MS2 | 1973 (5) | 2,000 | KM#1-4, 5.3 | — | 2.50 |
| MS3 | 1980 (6) | 2,000 | KM#1a, 2-4, 5.3 | — | 3.50 |
| MS4 | 1989 (6) | 2,000 | KM#49-54 | — | 4.00 |
| MS5 | 1990 (6) | 2,000 | KM#49-54 | — | 4.00 |

## PROOF SETS

| KM# | Date | Mintage | Identification | Issue Price | Mkt Val |
|---|---|---|---|---|---|
| PS7 | 1980 (9) | 5,000 | KM#1-4, 5.3, 9.1, 17, 23, 27a | 132 | 100 |
| PS4 | 1976 (3) | 2,641 | KM#16-18 | — | 135 |
| PS9 | 1981 (3) | 3,000 | KM#29-31 | — | 320 |
| PS1 | 1967 (5) | 500 | KM#1-5.1 | — | 140 |
| PS2 | 1976 (3) | 508 | KM#19-21 | 808 | 810 |
| PS3 | 1976 (2) | 7,500 | KM#19-20 | — | 60.00 |
| PS5 | 1976 (3) | 1,000 | KM#13-15 | — | 240 |
| PS6 | 1977 (3) | 975 | KM#22-24 | 164 | 220 |
| PS8 | 1981 (6) | — | KM#1-4, 5.4, 9.2 | — | 35.00 |
| PS10 | 1982 (3) | 4,000 | KM#32-34 | — | 325 |
| PS12 | 1986 (2) | 11,000 | KM#39a, 40 | — | 37.50 |
| PS11 | 1986 | 2,000 | KM#36-38 | — | 370 |
| PS13 | 1987 (3) | 1,000 | KM#43-45 | — | 200 |
| PS14 | 1989 (3) | 2,500 | KM#47, 48, 58 | — | 260 |
| PS15 | 1989 (2) | 20,000 | KM#47-48 | — | 37.50 |
| PS16 | 1989 (2) | 15,000 | KM#55-56 | — | 45.00 |
| PS17 | 1992 (6) | 5,000 | KM#49a-54a | — | 100 |
| PS18 | 1992 (3) | 3,000 | KM#61-63 | — | 300 |

# MALDIVE ISLANDS

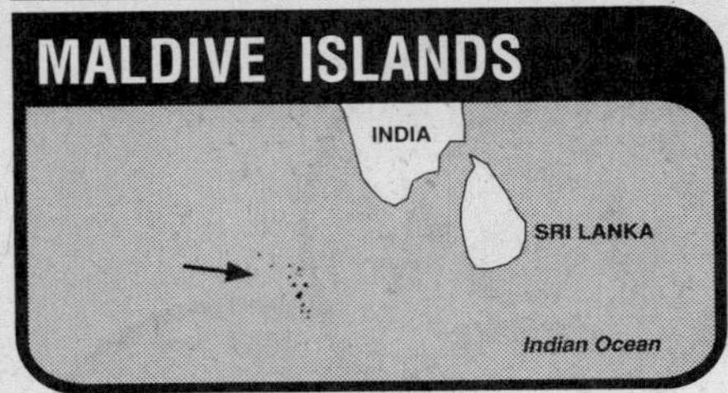


The Republic of Maldives, an archipelago of 2,000 coral islets in the northern Indian Ocean 417 miles (671 km.) west of Ceylon, has an area of 116 sq. mi. (298 sq. km.)and a population of 189,000. Capital: Male. Fishing employs 95 % of the male work force. Dried fish, copra and coir yarn are exported.

The Maldive Islands were visited by Arab traders and converted to Islam in 1153. After being harassed in the16th and 17th centuries by Mopla pirates of the Malabar coast and Portuguese raiders, the Maldivians voluntarily placed themselves under the suzerainty of Ceylon. In 1887 the islands became an internally self-governing British protectorate and a nominal dependency of Ceylon. Traditionally a sultanate, the Maldives became a republic in 1953 but restored the sultanate in 1954. The Sultanate of the Maldive Islands attained complete internal and external autonomy on July 26, 1965, and on Nov. 11,1968, again became a republic.

**RULERS**

Muhammad Imad al-Din V, AH1318-1322/1900-1904AD
Muhammad Shams al-Din III, AH1322-1353/1904-1935AD
Hasan Nur al-Din II, AH1353-1364/1935-1945AD
Abdul-Majid Didi, AH1364-1371/1945-1953AD
First Republic, AH1371-1372/1953-1954AD
Muhammad Farid Didi, AH1372-1388/1954-1968AD
Second Republic, AH1388 to date/1968AD to date*

**MINTNAME**

Mahle (Male) محلى

**MONETARY SYSTEM**

100 Lari = 1 Rupee (Rufiyaa)

## SULTANATE

### STANDARD COINAGE

100 Lari = 1 Rupee (Rufiyaa)

**LARIN** **KM# 41** **Weight:** 0.9000 g. **Composition:** Bronze **Ruler:** Muhammad Shams al-Din III **Note:** Struck at Birmingham, England. Rare mint proof strikes in silver and gold exist.

| Date | Mintage | F | VF | XF | Unc | BU |
|---|---|---|---|---|---|---|
| AH1331 | — | 1.00 | 1.25 | 1.75 | 3.00 | — |

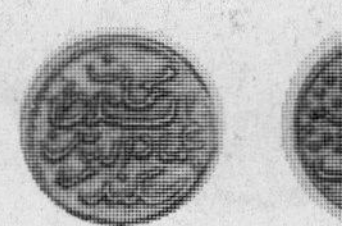

**2 LARIAT** **KM# 39** **Composition:** Copper-Brass **Ruler:** Muhammad Imad al-Din V **Note:** 1.4-2.2 grams. Previously listed date AH1311 is merely poor die cutting of AH1319. Many die varieties exist.

| Date | Mintage | F | VF | XF | Unc | BU |
|---|---|---|---|---|---|---|
| AH1318 | — | 1.50 | 3.50 | 5.00 | 7.50 | — |
| AH1319 | — | 1.50 | 3.50 | 5.00 | 7.50 | — |

**4 LARIAT** **KM# 40.1** **Composition:** Copper-Brass **Ruler:** Muhammad Imad al-Din V **Edge:** Plain or reeded **Note:** 2.5-4.5 grams. Many die varieties exist.

| Date | Mintage | F | VF | XF | Unc | BU |
|---|---|---|---|---|---|---|
| AH1320 | — | 1.50 | 2.50 | 4.50 | 8.00 | — |

**4 LARIAT** **KM# 40.2** **Composition:** Copper-Brass **Ruler:** Muhammad Imad al-Din V **Reverse:** Arabic "Sana(t)" below date **Note:** Silver strikes are most likely presentation pieces.

| Date | Mintage | F | VF | XF | Unc | BU |
|---|---|---|---|---|---|---|
| AH1320 | — | 3.50 | 8.00 | 12.00 | 16.00 | — |

**4 LARIAT** **KM# 42** **Weight:** 3.3000 g. **Composition:** Bronze **Ruler:** Muhammad Shams al-Din III **Note:** Struck at Birmingham, England. Rare mint proof strikes in silver and gold exist.

| Date | Mintage | F | VF | XF | Unc | BU |
|---|---|---|---|---|---|---|
| AH1331 | — | 1.00 | 1.50 | 2.75 | 6.00 | — |

**LAARI** **KM# 43** **Composition:** Bronze **Ruler:** Muhammad Farid Didi **Note:** Similar to Laari, KM#49.

| Date | Mintage | F | VF | XF | Unc | BU |
|---|---|---|---|---|---|---|
| AH1379(1960) | 300,000 | — | 0.15 | 0.25 | 0.50 | — |
| AH1379(1960) Proof | 1,270 | Value: 3.00 | | | | |

**2 LAARI** **KM# 44** **Composition:** Bronze **Ruler:** Muhammad Farid Didi

| Date | Mintage | F | VF | XF | Unc | BU |
|---|---|---|---|---|---|---|
| AH1379(1960) | 600,000 | — | 0.20 | 0.35 | 0.75 | — |
| AH1379(1960) Proof | 1,270 | Value: 3.50 | | | | |

**5 LAARI** **KM# 45** **Composition:** Nickel-Brass **Ruler:** Muhammad Farid Didi

| Date | Mintage | F | VF | XF | Unc | BU |
|---|---|---|---|---|---|---|
| AH1379(1960) | 300,000 | — | 0.25 | 0.40 | 0.75 | — |
| AH1379(1960) Proof | 1,270 | Value: 4.00 | | | | |

**5 LAARI** **KM# 45b** **Composition:** Bronze **Ruler:** Muhammad Farid Didi

| Date | Mintage | F | VF | XF | Unc | BU |
|---|---|---|---|---|---|---|
| AH1379(1960) | — | — | 0.25 | 0.40 | 0.75 | — |

**10 LAARI** **KM# 46** **Composition:** Nickel-Brass **Ruler:** Muhammad Farid Didi

| Date | Mintage | F | VF | XF | Unc | BU |
|---|---|---|---|---|---|---|
| AH1379(1960) | 600,000 | — | 0.50 | 0.75 | 1.50 | — |
| AH1379(1960) Proof | 1,270 | Value: 5.00 | | | | |

**10 LAARI** **KM# 46a** **Composition:** Aluminum **Ruler:** Muhammad Farid Didi **Note:** Similar to 10 Laari, KM#46.

| Date | Mintage | F | VF | XF | Unc | BU |
|---|---|---|---|---|---|---|
| AH1399(1979) | — | — | — | 0.10 | 0.25 | — |
| AH1399(1979) Proof | — | Value: 2.50 | | | | |

**25 LAARI** **KM# 47.1** **Composition:** Nickel-Brass **Ruler:** Muhammad Farid Didi **Edge:** Security

| Date | Mintage | F | VF | XF | Unc | BU |
|---|---|---|---|---|---|---|
| AH1379(1960) | 300,000 | — | 0.60 | 1.00 | 1.50 | — |
| AH1379(1960) Proof | 1,270 | Value: 6.00 | | | | |

**25 LAARI** **KM# 47.2** **Composition:** Nickel-Brass **Ruler:** Muhammad Farid Didi **Edge:** Reeded

| Date | Mintage | F | VF | XF | Unc | BU |
|---|---|---|---|---|---|---|
| AH1379(1960) | — | — | 2.00 | 3.50 | 6.00 | — |

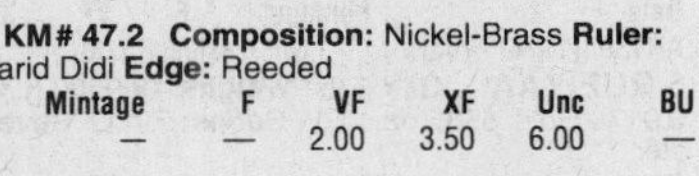

**50 LAARI** **KM# 48.1** **Composition:** Nickel-Brass **Ruler:** Muhammad Farid Didi **Edge:** Security

| Date | Mintage | F | VF | XF | Unc | BU |
|---|---|---|---|---|---|---|
| AH1379(1960) | 300,000 | — | 1.00 | 1.75 | 2.50 | — |
| AH1379(1960) Proof | 1,270 | Value: 8.00 | | | | |

**50 LAARI** **KM# 48.2** **Composition:** Nickel-Brass **Ruler:** Muhammad Farid Didi **Edge:** Reeded

| Date | Mintage | F | VF | XF | Unc | BU |
|---|---|---|---|---|---|---|
| AH1379(1960) | — | — | 3.00 | 5.00 | 8.00 | — |

## REPUBLIC

### MEDALLIC COINAGE

**25 RUFIYAA** **KM# M1** **Composition:** Copper-Nickel **Subject:** International Games - soccer

| Date | Mintage | F | VF | XF | Unc | BU |
|---|---|---|---|---|---|---|
| AH1405(1984) Proof | — | Value: 12.50 | | | | |

**25 RUFIYAA** **KM# M2** **Composition:** Copper-Nickel **Subject:** International Games - swimming

| Date | Mintage | F | VF | XF | Unc | BU |
|---|---|---|---|---|---|---|
| AH1405(1984) Proof | — | Value: 12.50 | | | | |

### STANDARD COINAGE

100 Laari = 1 Rufiyaa

**LAARI** **KM# 49** **Composition:** Aluminum

| Date | Mintage | F | VF | XF | Unc | BU |
|---|---|---|---|---|---|---|
| AH1389(1970) | 500,000 | — | 0.10 | 0.20 | 0.40 | — |
| AH1399(1979) | — | — | 0.10 | 0.20 | 0.40 | — |
| AH1399(1979) Proof | 100,000 | Value: 1.25 | | | | |

**LAARI** **KM# 68** **Composition:** Aluminum **Reverse:** Palm tree

| Date | Mintage | F | VF | XF | Unc | BU |
|---|---|---|---|---|---|---|
| AH1404(1984) | — | — | — | 0.10 | 0.15 | — |
| AH1404(1984) Proof | 2,500 | Value: 2.50 | | | | |

**2 LAARI** **KM# 50** **Composition:** Bronze **Note:** Similar to 2 Laari, KM#44.

| Date | Mintage | F | VF | XF | Unc | BU |
|---|---|---|---|---|---|---|
| AH1389(1970) | 500,000 | — | 0.15 | 0.25 | 0.50 | — |

**2 LAARI** **KM# 50a** **Composition:** Aluminum

| Date | Mintage | F | VF | XF | Unc | BU |
|---|---|---|---|---|---|---|
| AH1399(1979) | — | — | 0.15 | 0.25 | 0.50 | — |
| AH1399(1979) Proof | 100,000 | Value: 1.25 | | | | |

**5 LAARI** **KM# 45a** **Composition:** Aluminum **Note:** Similar to 5 Laari, KM#45.

| Date | Mintage | F | VF | XF | Unc | BU |
|---|---|---|---|---|---|---|
| AH1389(1970) | 300,000 | — | 0.20 | 0.30 | 0.40 | — |
| AH1389(1970) Proof | — | Value: 3.50 | | | | |
| AH1399(1979) | — | — | — | 0.10 | 0.20 | — |
| AH1399(1979) Proof | — | Value: 2.50 | | | | |

**5LAARI** **KM#69** **Composition:** Aluminum **Reverse:** Bonito fish

| Date | Mintage | F | VF | XF | Unc | BU |
|---|---|---|---|---|---|---|
| AH1404(1984) | — | — | — | 0.10 | 0.25 | — |
| AH1404(1984) Proof | 2,500 | Value: 3.00 | | | | |
| AH1411(1990) | — | — | — | 0.10 | 0.25 | — |

**10 LAARI** **KM# 70** **Composition:** Aluminum **Reverse:** Maldivian sailing ship - Dhivehi Odi

| Date | Mintage | F | VF | XF | Unc | BU |
|---|---|---|---|---|---|---|
| AH1404(1984) | — | — | — | 0.10 | 0.20 | — |
| AH1404(1984) Proof | 2,500 | Value: 3.50 | | | | |

**25 LAARI** **KM# 47.3** **Composition:** Nickel-Brass **Note:** Similar to 25 Laari, KM#47.2.

| Date | Mintage | F | VF | XF | Unc | BU |
|---|---|---|---|---|---|---|
| AH1399(1979) | — | — | — | 0.10 | 0.25 | — |
| AH1399(1979) Proof | 100,000 | Value: 3.50 | | | | |

**25 LAARI** **KM# 71** **Composition:** Nickel-Brass **Reverse:** Mosque

| Date | Mintage | F | VF | XF | Unc | BU |
|---|---|---|---|---|---|---|
| AH1404(1984) | — | — | — | 0.15 | 0.45 | — |
| AH1404(1984) Proof | — | Value: 4.00 | | | | |
| AH1411(1990) | — | — | — | 0.15 | 0.45 | — |
| AH1416(1995) | — | — | — | 0.15 | 0.45 | — |

**50 LAARI** **KM# 48.3** **Composition:** Nickel-Brass **Note:** Similar to 50 Laari, KM#48.2.

| Date | Mintage | F | VF | XF | Unc | BU |
|---|---|---|---|---|---|---|
| AH1399(1979) | — | — | 0.10 | 0.20 | 0.40 | — |
| AH1399(1979) Proof | 100,000 | Value: 6.50 | | | | |

**50 LAARI** **KM# 72** **Composition:** Nickel-Brass **Reverse:** Loggerhead sea turtle

| Date | Mintage | F | VF | XF | Unc | BU |
|---|---|---|---|---|---|---|
| AH1404(1984) | — | — | 0.15 | 0.35 | 1.25 | — |
| AH1404(1984) Proof | — | Value: 6.00 | | | | |
| AH1411(1990) | — | — | 0.15 | 0.35 | 1.25 | — |
| AH1415(1994) | — | — | 0.15 | 0.35 | 1.25 | — |

**RUFIYAA** **KM# 73** **Composition:** Copper-Nickel Clad Steel

| Date | Mintage | F | VF | XF | Unc | BU |
|---|---|---|---|---|---|---|
| AH1402(1982) | — | — | 0.20 | 0.50 | 2.00 | — |

**RUFIYAA** **KM# 73a** **Composition:** Copper-Nickel

| Date | Mintage | F | VF | XF | Unc | BU |
|---|---|---|---|---|---|---|
| AH1404(1984) | — | — | 0.20 | 0.50 | 2.00 | — |
| AH1404(1984) Proof | — | Value: 9.00 | | | | |
| AH1411(1990) | — | — | 0.20 | 0.50 | 2.00 | — |
| AH1416(1995) | — | — | 0.20 | 0.50 | 2.00 | — |

**2 RUFIYAA** **KM# 88** **Composition:** Brass **Reverse:** Pacific triton sea shell **Edge:** Lettering over reeding **Edge Lettering:** REPUBLIC OF MALDIVES

| Date | Mintage | F | VF | XF | Unc | BU |
|---|---|---|---|---|---|---|
| AH1415(1995) | — | — | — | — | 5.00 | — |

**5 RUFIYAA** **KM# 55** **Composition:** Copper-Nickel **Series:** F.A.O. **Reverse:** Bonito fish

| Date | Mintage | F | VF | XF | Unc | BU |
|---|---|---|---|---|---|---|
| AH1397(1977) | 15,000 | — | — | 3.50 | 6.50 | — |

**5 RUFIYAA** **KM# 57** **Composition:** Copper-Nickel **Series:** F.A.O. **Reverse:** Spiny lobster

| Date | Mintage | F | VF | XF | Unc | BU |
|---|---|---|---|---|---|---|
| AH1398(1978) | 7,000 | — | — | 4.00 | 7.00 | — |

**5 RUFIYAA** **KM# 57a** **Weight:** 19.1500 g. **Composition:** 0.9250 Silver .5695 oz. ASW **Series:** F.A.O. **Reverse:** Spiny lobster

| Date | Mintage | F | VF | XF | Unc | BU |
|---|---|---|---|---|---|---|
| AH1398(1978) Proof | 1,887 | Value: 25.00 | | | | |

**5 RUFIYAA** **KM# 57b** **Weight:** 18.9500 g. **Composition:** 0.9170 Gold .5585 oz. AGW **Series:** F.A.O. **Reverse:** Spiny lobster

| Date | Mintage | F | VF | XF | Unc | BU |
|---|---|---|---|---|---|---|
| AH1398(1978) Proof | 200 | Value: 600 | | | | |

**10 RUFIYAA** **KM# 59** **Composition:** Copper-Nickel **Series:** F.A.O.

| Date | Mintage | F | VF | XF | Unc | BU |
|---|---|---|---|---|---|---|
| AH1399(1979) | — | — | — | 4.50 | 10.00 | — |

**10 RUFIYAA** **KM# 59a** **Weight:** 25.0000 g. **Composition:** 0.9250 Silver .7435 oz. ASW **Series:** F.A.O.

| Date | Mintage | F | VF | XF | Unc | BU |
|---|---|---|---|---|---|---|
| AH1399(1979) Proof | 3,000 | Value: 17.50 | | | | |

**10 RUFIYAA** **KM# 62** **Composition:** Copper-Nickel **Series:** F.A.O.

| Date | Mintage | F | VF | XF | Unc | BU |
|---|---|---|---|---|---|---|
| AH1400(1980) | — | — | — | 4.00 | 9.00 | — |

**20 RUFIYAA** **KM# 56** **Weight:** 28.2800 g. **Composition:** 0.5000 Silver .4546 oz. ASW **Series:** F.A.O. **Reverse:** Bonito and bluefin tuna

| Date | Mintage | F | VF | XF | Unc | BU |
|---|---|---|---|---|---|---|
| AH1397(1977) | 15,000 | — | — | — | 12.50 | — |

**20 RUFIYAA** **KM# 61** **Weight:** 28.2800 g. **Composition:** 0.9250 Silver .8411 oz. ASW **Series:** International Year of the Child

| Date | Mintage | F | VF | XF | Unc | BU |
|---|---|---|---|---|---|---|
| AH1399(1979) Proof | 12,000 | Value: 14.50 | | | | |

**20 RUFIYAA** **KM# 65** **Composition:** Copper-Nickel **Subject:** World Fisheries Conference

| Date | Mintage | F | VF | XF | Unc | BU |
|---|---|---|---|---|---|---|
| AH1404(1984) | 100,000 | — | — | — | 10.00 | — |

**20 RUFIYAA** **KM# 65a** **Weight:** 28.2800 g. **Composition:** 0.9250 Silver .8411 oz. ASW **Subject:** World Fisheries Conference

| Date | Mintage | F | VF | XF | Unc | BU |
|---|---|---|---|---|---|---|
| AH1404(1984) Proof | 20,000 | Value: 45.00 | | | | |

**20 RUFIYAA** **KM# 74** **Weight:** 19.4400 g. **Composition:** 0.9250 Silver .5782 oz. ASW **Series:** Decade for Women

| Date | Mintage | F | VF | XF | Unc | BU |
|---|---|---|---|---|---|---|
| AH1405(1985) Proof | 500 | Value: 40.00 | | | | |

**25 RUFIYAA** **KM# 58** **Weight:** 28.0500 g. **Composition:** 0.5000 Silver .4509 oz. ASW **Series:** F.A.O. **Reverse:** Sailing ship

| Date | Mintage | F | VF | XF | Unc | BU |
|---|---|---|---|---|---|---|
| AH1398(1978) | 7,140 | — | — | — | 25.00 | — |

**25 RUFIYAA** **KM# 58a** **Weight:** 28.2800 g. **Composition:** 0.9250 Silver .8411 oz. ASW **Series:** F.A.O. **Reverse:** Sailing ship

| Date | Mintage | F | VF | XF | Unc | BU |
|---|---|---|---|---|---|---|
| AH1398(1978) Proof | 2,000 | Value: 37.50 | | | | |

**25 RUFIYAA** **KM# 58b** **Weight:** 28.2500 g. **Composition:** 0.9170 Gold .8326 oz. AGW **Series:** F.A.O. **Reverse:** Sailing ship

| Date | Mintage | F | VF | XF | Unc | BU |
|---|---|---|---|---|---|---|
| AH1398(1978) Proof | 200 | Value: 800 | | | | |

**25 RUFIYAA** **KM# 95** **Composition:** Copper-Nickel **Series:** 50th anniversary - UN **Obverse:** National emblem **Reverse:** UN building and logo

| Date | Mintage | F | VF | XF | Unc | BU |
|---|---|---|---|---|---|---|
| AH1416(1996) | — | — | — | — | 9.50 | — |

**50 RUFIYAA** **KM# 89** **Weight:** 1.2442 g. **Composition:** 0.9999 Gold .04 oz. AGW

| Date | Mintage | F | VF | XF | Unc | BU |
|---|---|---|---|---|---|---|
| AH1415(1995) | Est. 25,000 | — | — | — | 60.00 | — |

**50 RUFIYAA** **KM# 90** **Weight:** 10.0000 g. **Composition:** 0.5000 Silver .1607 oz. ASW **Series:** Olympics **Reverse:** Sailboat

| Date | Mintage | F | VF | XF | Unc | BU |
|---|---|---|---|---|---|---|
| AH1416(1996) | Est. 10,000 | — | — | — | 35.00 | — |

**100 RUFIYAA** **KM# 60** **Weight:** 28.2800 g. **Composition:** 0.8000 Silver .7274 oz. ASW **Series:** F.A.O.

| Date | Mintage | F | VF | XF | Unc | BU |
|---|---|---|---|---|---|---|
| AH1399(1979) | 6,000 | — | — | — | 20.00 | — |

**100 RUFIYAA** **KM# 60a** **Weight:** 28.2800 g. **Composition:** 0.9250 Silver .8411 oz. ASW **Series:** F.A.O.

| Date | Mintage | F | VF | XF | Unc | BU |
|---|---|---|---|---|---|---|
| AH1399(1979) Proof | 8,000 | Value: 22.50 | | | | |

**100 RUFIYAA** **KM# 63** **Weight:** 28.2800 g. **Composition:** 0.8000 Silver .7274 oz. ASW **Series:** F.A.O.

| Date | Mintage | F | VF | XF | Unc | BU |
|---|---|---|---|---|---|---|
| AH1400(1980) | 6,501 | — | — | — | 25.00 | — |

**100 RUFIYAA** **KM# 63a** **Weight:** 28.2800 g. **Composition:** 0.9250 Silver .8411 oz. ASW **Series:** F.A.O.

| Date | Mintage | F | VF | XF | Unc | BU |
|---|---|---|---|---|---|---|
| AH1400(1980) Proof | 3,003 | Value: 45.00 | | | | |

**100 RUFIYAA** **KM# 64** **Weight:** 28.2800 g. **Composition:** 0.9250 Silver .8411 oz. ASW **Subject:** World Food Day **Obverse:** Similar to KM#66

| Date | Mintage | F | VF | XF | Unc | BU |
|---|---|---|---|---|---|---|
| AH1401(1981) | 10,000 | — | — | — | 25.00 | — |
| AH1401(1981) Proof | 5,000 | Value: 40.00 | | | | |

**100 RUFIYAA** **KM# 66** **Weight:** 28.2800 g. **Composition:** 0.9250 Silver .8411 oz. ASW **Series:** International Year of Disabled Persons **Reverse:** Stylized yin and yang symbol

| Date | Mintage | F | VF | XF | Unc | BU |
|---|---|---|---|---|---|---|
| AH1404(1984) | — | — | — | — | 28.00 | — |
| AH1404(1984) Proof | — | Value: 42.00 | | | | |

**100 RUFIYAA** **KM# 75** **Weight:** 15.9800 g. **Composition:** 0.9170 Gold .4712 oz. AGW **Subject:** Opening of Grand Mosque and Islamic Centre

| Date | Mintage | F | VF | XF | Unc | BU |
|---|---|---|---|---|---|---|
| AH1405(1984) Proof | 100 | Value: 600 | | | | |

**100 RUFIYAA** **KM# 67** **Weight:** 15.9800 g. **Composition:** 0.9170 Gold .4712 oz. AGW

| Date | Mintage | F | VF | XF | Unc | BU |
|---|---|---|---|---|---|---|
| AH1404(1984) | 500 | — | — | — | 700 | — |
| AH1404(1984) Proof | 500 | Value: 800 | | | | |

**100 RUFIYAA** **KM# 78** **Weight:** 28.2800 g. **Composition:** 0.9250 Silver .8411 oz. ASW **Subject:** Opening of Grand Mosque and Islamic Centre

| Date | Mintage | F | VF | XF | Unc | BU |
|---|---|---|---|---|---|---|
| AH1405(1984) Proof | 500 | Value: 70.00 | | | | |

**100 RUFIYAA** KM# 76 **Weight:** 28.2800 g. **Composition:** 0.9250 Silver .8411 oz. ASW **Subject:** Commonwealth finance ministers meeting

| Date | Mintage | FVF | XF | Unc | BU |
|---|---|---|---|---|---|
| ND(AH406)(1985) Proof | 300 | Value: 75.00 | | | |

**100 RUFIYAA** KM# 87 **Weight:** 10.0000 g. **Composition:** 0.5000 Silver .1607 oz. ASW **Subject:** Sailing ship "Cutty Sark"

| Date | Mintage | F | VF | XF | Unc | BU |
|---|---|---|---|---|---|---|
| AH1413(1993) Proof | Est. 25,000 | Value: 20.00 | | | | |

**250 RUFIYAA** KM# 82 **Weight:** 31.4700 g. **Composition:** 0.9250 Silver .9359 oz. ASW **Series:** World Football Championship **Reverse:** Soccer ball trailing an inscribed ribbon

| Date | Mintage | F | VF | XF | Unc | BU |
|---|---|---|---|---|---|---|
| AH1410(1990) Proof | — | Value: 22.50 | | | | |

**250 RUFIYAA** KM# 80 **Weight:** 31.4700 g. **Composition:** 0.9250 Silver .9359 oz. ASW **Series:** 1992 Olympics **Subject:** Swimming

| Date | Mintage | F | VF | XF | Unc | BU |
|---|---|---|---|---|---|---|
| AH1410(1990) Proof | — | Value: 22.50 | | | | |

**250 RUFIYAA** KM# 81 **Weight:** 31.4700 g. **Composition:** 0.9250 Silver .9359 oz. ASW **Reverse:** Maldivian sailing ship "Dhivehi Odi"

| Date | Mintage | F | VF | XF | Unc | BU |
|---|---|---|---|---|---|---|
| AH1410(1990) Proof | 15,000 | Value: 28.00 | | | | |

**250 RUFIYAA** KM# 83 **Weight:** 31.4700 g. **Composition:** 0.9250 Silver .9359 oz. ASW **Subject:** World Cup '94 soccer

| Date | Mintage | F | VF | XF | Unc | BU |
|---|---|---|---|---|---|---|
| AH1413(1993) Proof | 25,000 | Value: 36.50 | | | | |

**250 RUFIYAA** KM# 84 **Weight:** 31.4700 g. **Composition:** 0.9250 Silver .9359 oz. ASW **Reverse:** Skylab space station

| Date | Mintage | F | VF | XF | Unc | BU |
|---|---|---|---|---|---|---|
| AH1413(1993) Proof | — | Value: 35.00 | | | | |

**250 RUFIYAA** KM# 85 **Weight:** 31.4700 g. **Composition:** 0.9250 Silver .9359 oz. ASW **Series:** Olympics **Reverse:** Sailing

| Date | Mintage | F | VF | XF | Unc | BU |
|---|---|---|---|---|---|---|
| AH1413(1993) Proof | 25,000 | Value: 27.50 | | | | |

**250 RUFIYAA** KM# 86 **Weight:** 31.4700 g. **Composition:** 0.9250 Silver .9359 oz. ASW **Series:** Endangered wildlife **Reverse:** Turtle

| Date | Mintage | F | VF | XF | Unc | BU |
|---|---|---|---|---|---|---|
| AH1414(1994) Proof | — | Value: 40.00 | | | | |

**250 RUFIYAA** KM# 96 **Weight:** 31.2400 g. **Composition:** 0.9250 Silver .9291 oz. ASW **Subject:** Ibn Battuta **Reverse:** Bust, dhow, and map

| Date | Mintage | F | VF | XF | Unc | BU |
|---|---|---|---|---|---|---|
| AH1416(1995) Proof | — | Value: 37.50 | | | | |

**500 RUFIYAA** KM# 91 **Weight:** 28.2800 g. **Composition:** 0.9250 Silver .8411 oz. ASW **Subject:** 25 years of independence

| Date | Mintage | F | VF | XF | Unc | BU |
|---|---|---|---|---|---|---|
| AH1410(1990) Proof | 1,000 | Value: 65.00 | | | | |

**500 RUFIYAA** KM# 92 **Weight:** 28.2800 g. **Composition:** 0.9250 Silver .8411 oz. ASW **Subject:** 25 years of republic

| Date | Mintage | F | VF | XF | Unc | BU |
|---|---|---|---|---|---|---|
| AH1413(1993) Proof | 500 | Value: 70.00 | | | | |

**1000 RUFIYAA** KM# 93 **Weight:** 15.9800 g. **Composition:** 0.9170 Gold .4712 oz. AGW **Subject:** 25 years of independence

| Date | Mintage | F | VF | XF | Unc | BU |
|---|---|---|---|---|---|---|
| AH1410(1990) Proof | 1,000 | Value: 500 | | | | |

**1000 RUFIYAA** KM# 94 **Weight:** 15.9800 g. **Composition:** 0.9170 Gold .4712 oz. AGW **Subject:** 25 years of republic

| Date | Mintage | F | VF | XF | Unc | BU |
|---|---|---|---|---|---|---|
| AH1413(1993) Proof | 500 | Value: 550 | | | | |

## PATTERNS

Including off metal strikes

| KM# | Date | Mintage | Identification | Mkt Val |
|---|---|---|---|---|
| Pn1 | 1319 (3) | — | Larin. Silver. KM38. | — |
| Pn2 | 1319 (3) | — | 2 Lariat. Silver. KM39. | — |
| Pn3 | 1320 (3) | — | 4 Lariat. Silver. KM40.2. | — |

## PIEFORTS

| KM# | Date | Mintage | Identification | Mkt Val |
|---|---|---|---|---|
| P1 | 1979 (3) | 100 | 20 Rufiyaa. KM61. | 90.00 |
| P2 | 1984 (3) | 100 | 100 Rufiyaa. KM66. | 110 |
| P3 | 1984 (3) | 100 | 100 Rufiyaa. KM67. | 1,000 |

## MINT SETS

| KM# | Date | Mintage | Identification | Issue Price | Mkt Val |
|---|---|---|---|---|---|
| MS1 | 1984 (6) | — | KM68-73 | 8.75 | 12.50 |

## PROOF SETS

| KM# | Date | Mintage | Identification | Issue Price | Mkt Val |
|---|---|---|---|---|---|
| PS2 | 1979 (6) | — | KM45a, 46a, 47.2, 48.2, 49-50 | 30.00 | 18.00 |
| PS1 | 1960 (6) | 1,270 | KM43-48 | — | 30.00 |
| PS3 | 1979 (2) | 3,000 | KM59a, 60a | — | 42.50 |
| PS4 | 1984 (6) | 2,500 | KM68-72, 73a | 30.00 | 28.00 |

# MALI

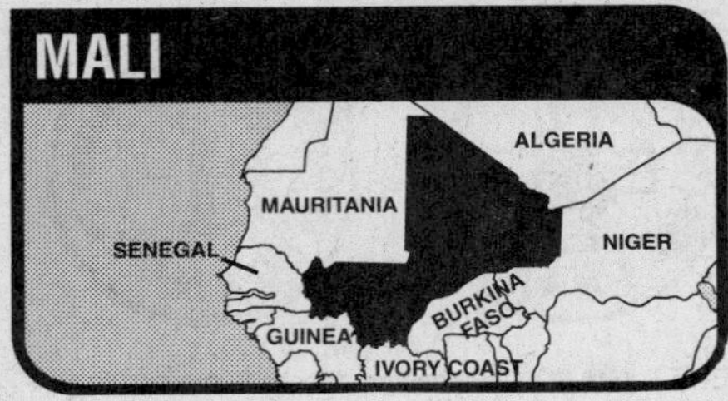


The Republic of Mali, a landlocked country in the interior of West Africa southwest of Algeria, has an area of 482,077 sq. mi. (1,240,000 sq. km.) and a population of 8.1 million. Capital: Bamako. Livestock, fish, cotton and peanuts are exported.

Malians are descendants of the ancient Malinke Kingdom of Mali that controlled the middle Niger from the11th to the 17th centuries. The French penetrated the Sudan (now Mali) about 1880, and established their rule in1898 after subduing fierce native resistance. In 1904 the area became the colony of Upper Senegal-Niger (changed to French Sudan in 1920), and became part of the French Union in 1946. In 1958 French Sudan became the Sudanese Republic with complete internal autonomy. Senegal joined with the Sudanese Republic in 1959 to form the Mali Federation which, in 1960, became a fully independent member of the French Community. Upon Senegal's subsequent withdrawal from the Federation, the Sudanese, on Sept. 22, 1960, proclaimed their nation the fully independent Republic of Mali and severed all ties with France.

**MINT MARKS**

(a) - Paris, privy marks only

## REPUBLIC

### STANDARD COINAGE

**5 FRANCS** **KM# 2** **Composition:** Aluminum

| Date | Mintage | F | VF | XF | Unc | BU |
|---|---|---|---|---|---|---|
| 1961 | — | 0.15 | 0.25 | 0.50 | 1.25 | — |

**10 FRANCS** **KM# 1** **Weight:** 25.0000 g. **Composition:** 0.9000 Silver .7234 oz. ASW **Subject:** Independence

| Date | Mintage | F | VF | XF | Unc | BU |
|---|---|---|---|---|---|---|
| ND(1960) Proof | 10,000 | Value: 32.50 | | | | |

**10 FRANCS** **KM# 3** **Composition:** 0.9000 Aluminum

| Date | Mintage | F | VF | XF | Unc | BU |
|---|---|---|---|---|---|---|
| 1961 | — | 0.50 | 1.00 | 2.00 | 5.00 | — |

**10 FRANCS** **KM# 5** **Weight:** 3.2000 g. **Composition:** 0.9000 Gold .0926 oz. AGW **Subject:** President Modibo Keita **Note:** Similar to 25 Francs, KM#6.

| Date | Mintage | F | VF | XF | Unc | BU |
|---|---|---|---|---|---|---|
| 1967 Proof | — | Value: 85.00 | | | | |

**10 FRANCS** **KM# 11** **Composition:** Aluminum

| Date | Mintage | F | VF | XF | Unc | BU |
|---|---|---|---|---|---|---|
| 1976(a) | 5,000,000 | 1.25 | 2.50 | 4.50 | 12.50 | — |

**10 FRANCS** **KM# 13** **Weight:** 3.2000 g. **Composition:** 0.9000 Gold .0926 oz. AGW **Subject:** Anniversary of Independence **Note:** Similar to 50 Francs, KM#15.

| Date | Mintage | F | VF | XF | Unc | BU |
|---|---|---|---|---|---|---|
| ND Proof, reported not confirmed | — | — | — | — | — | — |

**25 FRANCS** **KM# 4** **Composition:** Aluminum

| Date | Mintage | F | VF | XF | Unc | BU |
|---|---|---|---|---|---|---|
| 1961 | — | 0.35 | 0.65 | 1.50 | 3.50 | — |

**25 FRANCS** **KM# 6** **Weight:** 8.0000 g. **Composition:** 0.9000 Gold .2315 oz. AGW **Subject:** President Modibo Keita

| Date | Mintage | F | VF | XF | Unc | BU |
|---|---|---|---|---|---|---|
| 1967 Proof | — | Value: 145 | | | | |

**25 FRANCS** **KM# 12** **Composition:** Aluminum

| Date | Mintage | F | VF | XF | Unc | BU |
|---|---|---|---|---|---|---|
| 1976(a) | 5,000,000 | 2.50 | 4.00 | 8.00 | 18.00 | — |

**25 FRANCS** **KM# 14** **Weight:** 8.0000 g. **Composition:** 0.9000 Gold .2315 oz. AGW **Subject:** Anniversary of Independence **Note:** Similar to 50 Francs, KM#15.

| Date | Mintage | F | VF | XF | Unc | BU |
|---|---|---|---|---|---|---|
| ND Proof | — | Value: 325 | | | | |

**50 FRANCS** **KM# 7** **Weight:** 16.0000 g. **Composition:** 0.9000 Gold .4630 oz. AGW **Subject:** President Modibo Keita

| Date | Mintage | F | VF | XF | Unc | BU |
|---|---|---|---|---|---|---|
| 1967 Proof | — | Value: 265 | | | | |

**50 FRANCS** **KM# 9** **Composition:** Nickel-Brass **Series:** F.A.O.

| Date | Mintage | F | VF | XF | Unc | BU |
|---|---|---|---|---|---|---|
| 1975(a) | 10,000,000 | 0.25 | 0.50 | 1.00 | 2.50 | — |
| 1977(a) | — | 0.25 | 0.50 | 1.00 | 2.50 | — |

**50 FRANCS** **KM# 15** **Weight:** 16.0000 g. **Composition:** 0.9000 Gold .463 oz. AGW **Subject:** Anniversary of Independence

| Date | Mintage | F | VF | XF | Unc | BU |
|---|---|---|---|---|---|---|
| ND Proof | — | Value: 575 | | | | |

**100 FRANCS** **KM# 8** **Weight:** 32.0000 g. **Composition:** 0.9000 Gold .926 oz. AGW **Subject:** President Modibo Keita

| Date | Mintage | F | VF | XF | Unc | BU |
|---|---|---|---|---|---|---|
| 1967 Proof | — | Value: 500 | | | | |

**100 FRANCS** **KM# 10** **Composition:** Nickel-Brass **Series:** F.A.O.

| Date | Mintage | F | VF | XF | Unc | BU |
|---|---|---|---|---|---|---|
| 1975(a) | 23,000,000 | 0.65 | 1.25 | 2.50 | 5.00 | — |

**100 FRANCS** **KM# 16** **Weight:** 32.0000 g. **Composition:** 0.9000 Gold .926 oz. AGW **Subject:** Anniversary of Independence **Note:** Similar to 50 Francs, KM#15.

| Date | Mintage | F | VF | XF | Unc | BU |
|---|---|---|---|---|---|---|
| ND Proof | — | Value: 950 | | | | |

## ESSAIS

Standard metals unliess otherwise noted

Some essais have surnames stamped (from die) on them. Purpose is unknown.

| KM# | Date | Mintage | Identification | Issue Price | Mkt Val |
|---|---|---|---|---|---|
| E1 | ND1975 | — | 50 Francs. KM9. | — | 17.50 |
| E2 | ND1975 | — | 100 Francs. KM10. | — | 20.00 |
| E3 | ND1976 | — | 10 Francs. KM11. | — | 17.50 |
| E4 | ND1976 | — | 25 Francs. KM12. | — | 20.00 |

## PIEFORTS WITH ESSAIS

Standard metlas unliess otherwise noted

| KM# | Date | Mintage | Identification | Issue Price | Mkt Val |
|---|---|---|---|---|---|
| PE1 | ND1960 | 10 | 10 Francs. KM1. | — | 200 |

## PROOF SETS

| KM# | Date | Mintage | Identification | Issue Price | Mkt Val |
|---|---|---|---|---|---|
| PS1 | 1967 (4) | — | KM5-8 | — | 1,000 |

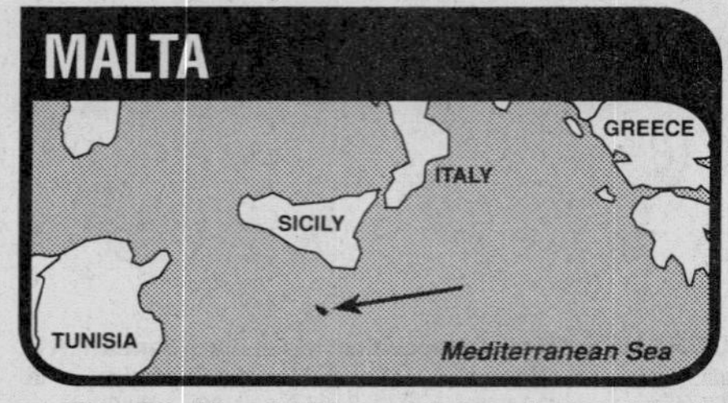


The Republic of Malta, an independent parliamentary democracy within the British Commonwealth, is situated in the Mediterranean Sea between Sicily and North Africa. With the islands of Gozo and Comino, Malta has an area of 124 sq. mi. (320 sq. km.) and a population of 386,000. Capital: Valletta. Malta has no proven mineral resources, an agriculture insufficient to its needs, and a small, but expanding, manufacturing facility. Clothing, textile yarns and fabrics, and knitted wear are exported.

For more than 3,500 years Malta was ruled, in succession by Phoenicians, Carthaginians, Romans, Arabs, Normans, the Knights of Malta, France and Britain. Napoleon seized Malta by treachery in 1798. The French were ousted by a Maltese insurrection assisted by Britain, and in 1814 Malta, of its own free will, became a part of the British Empire. Malta obtained full independence in Sept., 1964; electing to remain within the Commonwealth with the British monarch as the nominal head of state.

Malta became a republic on Dec. 13, 1974, but remained a member of the Commonwealth of Nations. The president is Chief of State. The prime minister is the Head of Government.

**RULERS**

British, until 1964

# REPUBLIC

## DECIMAL COINAGE

10 Mils = 1 Cent; 100 Cents = 1 Pound

**2 MILS** **KM# 5** **Composition:** Aluminum **Obverse:** Maltese cross

| Date | Mintage | F | VF | XF | Unc | BU |
|---|---|---|---|---|---|---|
| 1972 | 30,000 | — | 0.10 | 0.15 | 0.30 | — |
| 1972 Proof | 13,000 | Value: 0.50 | | | | |
| 1976FM (M) | 5,000 | — | — | — | 2.00 | — |
| 1976FM (P) | 26,000 | Value: 0.50 | | | | |
| 1977FM (U) | 5,252 | — | — | — | 1.00 | — |
| 1977FM (P) | 6,884 | Value: 1.00 | | | | |
| 1978FM (U) | 5,252 | — | — | — | 1.00 | — |
| 1978FM (P) | 3,244 | Value: 1.00 | | | | |
| 1979FM (U) | 537 | — | — | — | 3.00 | — |
| 1979FM (P) | 6,577 | Value: 1.00 | | | | |
| 1980FM (U) | 385 | — | — | — | 3.00 | — |
| 1980FM (P) | 3,451 | Value: 1.00 | | | | |
| 1981FM (U) | 444 | — | — | — | 3.00 | — |
| 1981FM (P) | 1,453 | Value: 1.00 | | | | |

**2 MILS** **KM# 54** **Composition:** Aluminum **Subject:** 10th anniversary of decimalization **Obverse:** Maltese cross

| Date | Mintage | F | VF | XF | Unc | BU |
|---|---|---|---|---|---|---|
| 1982FM (U) | 850 | — | — | — | 3.00 | — |
| 1982FM (P) | 1,793 | Value: 1.00 | | | | |

**3 MILS** **KM# 6** **Composition:** Aluminum **Obverse:** Bee and honeycomb

| Date | Mintage | F | VF | XF | Unc | BU |
|---|---|---|---|---|---|---|
| 1972 | — | — | 0.10 | 0.15 | 0.50 | — |
| 1972 Proof | 8,000 | Value: 1.00 | | | | |
| 1976FM (M) | 5,000 | — | — | — | 2.50 | — |
| 1976FM (P) | 26,000 | Value: 1.00 | | | | |
| 1977FM (U) | 5,252 | — | — | — | 1.50 | — |
| 1977FM (P) | 6,884 | Value: 1.25 | | | | |
| 1978FM (U) | 5,252 | — | — | — | 2.50 | — |
| 1978FM (P) | 3,244 | Value: 1.25 | | | | |
| 1979FM (U) | 537 | — | — | — | 5.00 | — |
| 1979FM (P) | 6,577 | Value: 1.25 | | | | |
| 1980FM (U) | 385 | — | — | — | 5.00 | — |
| 1980FM (P) | 3,451 | Value: 1.25 | | | | |
| 1981FM (U) | 449 | — | — | — | 5.00 | — |
| 1981FM (P) | 1,453 | Value: 1.25 | | | | |

**3 MILS** **KM# 55** **Composition:** Aluminum **Subject:** 10th anniversary of decimalization **Obverse:** Bea and honeycomb

| Date | Mintage | F | VF | XF | Unc | BU |
|---|---|---|---|---|---|---|
| 1982FM (U) | 850 | — | — | — | 4.00 | — |
| 1982FM (P) | 1,793 | Value: 1.25 | | | | |

**5 MILS** **KM# 7** **Composition:** Aluminum **Obverse:** Earthen lampstand

| Date | Mintage | F | VF | XF | Unc | BU |
|---|---|---|---|---|---|---|
| 1972 | 4,320,000 | — | 0.10 | 0.15 | 0.40 | — |
| 1972 Proof | 13,000 | Value: 1.00 | | | | |
| 1976FM (M) | 5,000 | — | — | — | 3.00 | — |
| 1976FM (P) | 26,000 | Value: 1.00 | | | | |
| 1977FM (U) | 5,252 | — | — | — | 2.00 | — |
| 1977FM (P) | 6,884 | Value: 1.50 | | | | |
| 1978FM (U) | 5,252 | — | — | — | 2.00 | — |
| 1978FM (P) | 3,244 | Value: 1.50 | | | | |
| 1979FM (U) | 537 | — | — | — | 7.00 | — |
| 1979FM (P) | 6,577 | Value: 1.50 | | | | |
| 1980FM (U) | 385 | — | — | — | 7.00 | — |
| 1980FM (P) | 3,451 | Value: 1.50 | | | | |
| 1981FM (U) | 449 | — | — | — | 7.00 | — |
| 1981FM (P) | 1,453 | Value: 1.50 | | | | |

**5 MILS** **KM# 56** **Composition:** Aluminum **Subject:** 10th anniversary of decimalization **Obverse:** Earthen lampstand

| Date | Mintage | F | VF | XF | Unc | BU |
|---|---|---|---|---|---|---|
| 1982FM (U) | 850 | — | — | — | 5.00 | — |
| 1982FM (P) | 1,793 | Value: 1.50 | | | | |

**CENT** **KM# 8** **Composition:** Bronze **Obverse:** George Cross

| Date | Mintage | F | VF | XF | Unc | BU |
|---|---|---|---|---|---|---|
| 1972 | 5,650,000 | — | 0.10 | 0.15 | 0.40 | — |
| 1972 Proof | 13,000 | Value: 1.25 | | | | |
| 1975 | 1,500,000 | — | 0.10 | 0.20 | 0.50 | — |
| 1976FM (M) | 5,000 | — | — | — | 3.50 | — |
| 1976FM (P) | 26,000 | Value: 1.25 | | | | |
| 1977 | 2,793,000 | — | 0.10 | 0.15 | 0.40 | — |
| 1977FM (U) | 5,252 | — | — | — | 2.50 | — |
| 1977FM (P) | 6,884 | Value: 1.75 | | | | |
| 1978FM (U) | 5,252 | — | — | — | 2.50 | — |
| 1978FM (P) | 3,244 | Value: 1.75 | | | | |
| 1979FM (U) | 537 | — | — | — | 9.00 | — |
| 1979FM (P) | 6,577 | Value: 1.75 | | | | |
| 1980FM (U) | 385 | — | — | — | 9.00 | — |
| 1980FM (P) | 3,451 | Value: 1.75 | | | | |
| 1981FM (U) | 449 | — | — | — | 9.00 | — |
| 1981FM (P) | 1,453 | Value: 1.75 | | | | |
| 1982 | — | — | 0.10 | 0.15 | 0.25 | — |

**CENT** **KM# 57** **Composition:** Bronze **Subject:** 10th anniversary of decimalization **Obverse:** The George Cross military award

| Date | Mintage | F | VF | XF | Unc | BU |
|---|---|---|---|---|---|---|
| 1982FM (U) | 850 | — | — | — | 7.50 | — |
| 1982FM (P) | 1,793 | Value: 1.75 | | | | |

**CENT** **KM# 78** **Composition:** Copper-Zinc **Obverse:** Similar to Lira, KM#82 **Reverse:** Common weasel

| Date | Mintage | F | VF | XF | Unc | BU |
|---|---|---|---|---|---|---|
| 1986 | 21,526,000 | — | 0.15 | 0.25 | 0.50 | — |
| 1986 Proof | 10,000 | Value: 2.00 | | | | |

**CENT** **KM# 93** **Composition:** Copper-Zinc **Reverse:** Common weasel

| Date | Mintage | F | VF | XF | Unc | BU |
|---|---|---|---|---|---|---|
| 1991 | — | — | 0.15 | 0.25 | 0.50 | — |
| 1995 | — | — | 0.15 | 0.25 | 0.50 | — |

**2 CENTS** **KM# 9** **Composition:** Copper-Zinc **Subject:** Penthesilea, Queen of the Amazons

| Date | Mintage | F | VF | XF | Unc | BU |
|---|---|---|---|---|---|---|
| 1972 | 5,640,000 | — | 0.10 | 0.15 | 0.40 | — |
| 1972 Proof | 13,000 | Value: 1.50 | | | | |
| 1976 | 1,000,000 | — | 0.15 | 0.20 | 0.60 | — |
| 1976FM (M) | 2,500 | — | — | — | 4.50 | — |
| 1976FM (P) | 26,000 | Value: 1.50 | | | | |
| 1977 | 6,105,000 | — | 0.10 | 0.15 | 0.40 | — |
| 1977FM (U) | 2,752 | — | — | — | 4.50 | — |
| 1977FM (P) | 6,884 | Value: 2.50 | | | | |
| 1978FM (U) | 2,752 | — | — | — | 4.50 | — |
| 1978FM (P) | 3,244 | Value: 2.50 | | | | |
| 1979FM (U) | 537 | — | — | — | 12.00 | — |
| 1979FM (P) | 6,577 | Value: 2.50 | | | | |
| 1980FM (U) | 385 | — | — | — | 12.00 | — |
| 1980FM (P) | 3,451 | Value: 2.50 | | | | |
| 1981FM (U) | 449 | — | — | — | 12.00 | — |
| 1981FM (P) | 1,453 | Value: 2.50 | | | | |
| 1982 | — | — | 0.10 | 0.15 | 0.30 | — |

**2 CENTS** **KM# 58** **Composition:** Copper-Zinc **Subject:** 10th anniversary of decimalization

| Date | Mintage | F | VF | XF | Unc | BU |
|---|---|---|---|---|---|---|
| 1982FM (U) | 850 | — | — | — | 10.00 | — |
| 1982FM (P) | 1,793 | Value: 2.50 | | | | |

**2 CENTS** **KM# 79** **Composition:** Copper-Zinc **Obverse:** Similar to Lira, KM#82 **Reverse:** Olive branch

| Date | Mintage | F | VF | XF | Unc | BU |
|---|---|---|---|---|---|---|
| 1986 | 280,000 | — | 0.15 | 0.25 | 0.45 | — |
| 1986 Proof | 10,000 | Value: 3.00 | | | | |

**2 CENTS** **KM# 94** **Composition:** Copper-Zinc

| Date | Mintage | F | VF | XF | Unc | BU |
|---|---|---|---|---|---|---|
| 1991 | — | — | 0.15 | 0.25 | 0.45 | — |
| 1992 | — | — | 0.15 | 0.25 | 0.45 | — |
| 1993 | — | — | 0.15 | 0.25 | 0.45 | — |
| 1995 | — | — | — | — | — | — |

**5 CENTS** **KM# 10** **Composition:** Copper-Nickel **Obverse:** Floral altar in the Temple of Hagar Qim

| Date | Mintage | F | VF | XF | Unc | BU |
|---|---|---|---|---|---|---|
| 1972 | 4,180,000 | — | 0.20 | 0.30 | 0.50 | — |
| 1972 Proof | 13,000 | Value: 1.75 | | | | |
| 1976 | 1,009,000 | — | 0.20 | 0.30 | 0.60 | — |
| 1976FM (M) | 2,500 | — | — | — | 5.00 | — |
| 1976FM (P) | 26,000 | Value: 2.00 | | | | |
| 1977 | — | — | 0.20 | 0.30 | 0.50 | — |
| 1977FM (U) | 2,752 | — | — | — | 5.00 | — |
| 1977FM (P) | 6,884 | Value: 3.00 | | | | |
| 1978FM (U) | 2,752 | — | — | — | 5.00 | — |
| 1978FM (P) | 3,244 | Value: 3.00 | | | | |
| 1979FM (U) | 537 | — | — | — | 15.00 | — |
| 1979FM (P) | 6,577 | Value: 3.00 | | | | |
| 1980FM (U) | 385 | — | — | — | 15.00 | — |
| 1980FM (P) | 3,451 | Value: 3.00 | | | | |
| 1981FM (U) | 449 | — | — | — | 15.00 | — |
| 1981FM (P) | 1,453 | Value: 3.00 | | | | |

**5 CENTS** **KM# 59** **Composition:** Copper-Nickel **Subject:** 10th anniversary of decimalization **Obverse:** Floral altar in the Temple of Hagar Qim

| Date | Mintage | F | VF | XF | Unc | BU |
|---|---|---|---|---|---|---|
| 1982FM (U) | 850 | — | — | — | 12.50 | — |
| 1982FM (P) | 1,793 | Value: 3.00 | | | | |

**5 CENTS** **KM# 77** **Composition:** Copper-Nickel **Reverse:** Fresh-water crab

| Date | Mintage | F | VF | XF | Unc | BU |
|---|---|---|---|---|---|---|
| 1986 | 150,000 | — | 0.25 | 0.45 | 1.00 | — |
| 1986 Proof | 10,000 | Value: 3.50 | | | | |

**5 CENTS** **KM# 95** **Composition:** Copper-Nickel **Reverse:** Fresh-water crab

| Date | Mintage | F | VF | XF | Unc | BU |
|---|---|---|---|---|---|---|
| 1991 | — | — | 0.25 | 0.45 | 1.00 | — |
| 1995 | — | — | 0.25 | 0.45 | 1.00 | — |

**10 CENTS** **KM# 11** **Composition:** Copper-Nickel **Obverse:** Barge of the grand master

| Date | Mintage | F | VF | XF | Unc | BU |
|---|---|---|---|---|---|---|
| 1972 | 10,680,000 | — | 0.40 | 0.60 | 1.00 | — |
| 1972 Proof | 13,000 | Value: 2.25 | | | | |
| 1976FM (M) | 1,000 | — | — | — | 6.00 | — |
| 1976FM (P) | 26,000 | Value: 2.50 | | | | |
| 1977FM (U) | 1,252 | — | — | — | 6.00 | — |
| 1977FM (P) | 6,884 | Value: 3.50 | | | | |
| 1978FM (U) | 1,252 | — | — | — | 6.00 | — |
| 1978FM (P) | 3,244 | Value: 3.50 | | | | |
| 1979FM (U) | 537 | — | — | — | 17.50 | — |
| 1979FM (P) | 6,577 | Value: 3.50 | | | | |
| 1980FM (U) | 385 | — | — | — | 15.00 | — |
| 1980FM (P) | 3,451 | Value: 3.50 | | | | |
| 1981FM (U) | 449 | — | — | — | 15.00 | — |
| 1981FM (P) | 1,453 | Value: 3.50 | | | | |

**10 CENTS** **KM# 60** **Composition:** Copper-Nickel **Subject:** 10th anniversary of decimalization **Obverse:** Barge of the grand master

| Date | Mintage | F | VF | XF | Unc | BU |
|---|---|---|---|---|---|---|
| 1982FM (U) | 850 | — | — | — | 14.00 | — |
| 1982FM (P) | 1,793 | Value: 3.50 | | | | |

**10 CENTS** **KM# 76** **Composition:** Copper-Nickel **Reverse:** Dolphin fish

| Date | Mintage | F | VF | XF | Unc | BU |
|---|---|---|---|---|---|---|
| 1986 | 4,188,000 | — | 0.40 | 0.70 | 1.50 | — |
| 1986 Proof | 10,000 | Value: 4.00 | | | | |

**10 CENTS** **KM# 96** **Composition:** Copper-Nickel **Obverse:** Crowned shield **Reverse:** Dolphin fish

| Date | Mintage | F | VF | XF | Unc | BU |
|---|---|---|---|---|---|---|
| 1991 | — | — | 0.40 | 0.70 | 1.50 | — |
| 1992 | — | — | 0.40 | 0.70 | 1.50 | — |
| 1995 | — | — | — | — | — | — |
| 1998 | — | — | — | — | — | — |

**25 CENTS** **KM# 29** **Composition:** Brass **Subject:** 1st anniversary - Republic of Malta

| Date | Mintage | F | VF | XF | Unc | BU |
|---|---|---|---|---|---|---|
| 1975 | 4,750,000 | — | 1.00 | 1.50 | 2.50 | — |
| 1975 Matte proof | — | — | — | — | 150 | — |

**25 CENTS** **KM# 29a** **Composition:** Bronze

| Date | Mintage | F | VF | XF | Unc | BU |
|---|---|---|---|---|---|---|
| 1975 Proof | 6,000 | Value: 12.50 | | | | |

**25 CENTS** **KM# 29b** **Composition:** Copper-Nickel

| Date | Mintage | F | VF | XF | Unc | BU |
|---|---|---|---|---|---|---|
| 1976FM (M) | 300 | — | — | — | 40.00 | — |
| 1976FM (P) | 26,000 | Value: 3.00 | | | | |
| 1977FM (U) | 552 | — | — | — | 20.00 | — |
| 1977FM (P) | 6,884 | Value: 4.50 | | | | |
| 1978FM (U) | 552 | — | — | — | 20.00 | — |
| 1978FM (P) | 3,244 | Value: 4.50 | | | | |
| 1979FM (U) | 537 | — | — | — | 20.00 | — |
| 1979FM (P) | 6,577 | Value: 4.50 | | | | |
| 1980FM (U) | 385 | — | — | — | 20.00 | — |
| 1980FM (P) | 3,451 | Value: 4.50 | | | | |
| 1981FM (U) | 449 | — | — | — | 20.00 | — |
| 1981FM (P) | 1,453 | Value: 4.50 | | | | |

**25 CENTS** **KM# 61** **Composition:** Copper-Nickel **Subject:** 10th anniversary of decimalization

| Date | Mintage | F | VF | XF | Unc | BU |
|---|---|---|---|---|---|---|
| 1982FM (U) | 850 | — | — | — | 15.00 | — |
| 1982FM (P) | 1,793 | Value: 4.50 | | | | |

**25 CENTS** **KM# 80** **Composition:** Copper-Nickel **Reverse:** Ghirlanda flower

| Date | Mintage | F | VF | XF | Unc | BU |
|---|---|---|---|---|---|---|
| 1986 | 3,090,000 | — | 1.00 | 1.80 | 2.50 | — |
| 1986 Proof | 10,000 | Value: 5.00 | | | | |

**25 CENTS** **KM# 97** **Composition:** Copper-Nickel **Obverse:** Crowned shield **Reverse:** Ghirlanda flower

| Date | Mintage | F | VF | XF | Unc | BU |
|---|---|---|---|---|---|---|
| 1991 | — | — | 1.00 | 1.50 | 2.50 | — |
| 1993 | — | — | 1.00 | 1.50 | 2.50 | — |
| 1995 | — | — | 1.00 | 1.50 | 2.50 | — |

**50 CENTS** **KM# 12** **Composition:** Copper-Nickel **Obverse:** Great Siege Monument

| Date | Mintage | F | VF | XF | Unc | BU |
|---|---|---|---|---|---|---|
| 1972 | 5,500,000 | — | 1.75 | 2.00 | 3.50 | — |
| 1972 Proof | 13,000 | Value: 4.50 | | | | |
| 1976FM (M) | 150 | — | — | — | 90.00 | — |
| 1976FM (P) | 26,000 | Value: 5.00 | | | | |
| 1977FM (U) | 402 | — | — | — | 25.00 | — |
| 1977FM (P) | 6,884 | Value: 6.00 | | | | |
| 1978FM (U) | 402 | — | — | — | 25.00 | — |
| 1978FM (P) | 3,244 | Value: 6.00 | | | | |
| 1979FM (U) | 537 | — | — | — | 25.00 | — |
| 1979FM (P) | 6,577 | Value: 6.00 | | | | |
| 1980FM (U) | 385 | — | — | — | 25.00 | — |
| 1980FM (P) | 3,451 | Value: 6.00 | | | | |
| 1981FM (U) | 449 | — | — | — | 25.00 | — |
| 1981FM (P) | 1,453 | Value: 6.00 | | | | |

**50 CENTS** **KM# 62** **Composition:** Copper-Nickel **Subject:** 10th anniversary of decimalization **Obverse:** Great Siege Monument

| Date | Mintage | F | VF | XF | Unc | BU |
|---|---|---|---|---|---|---|
| 1982FM (U) | 850 | — | — | — | 20.00 | — |
| 1982FM (P) | 1,793 | Value: 6.00 | | | | |

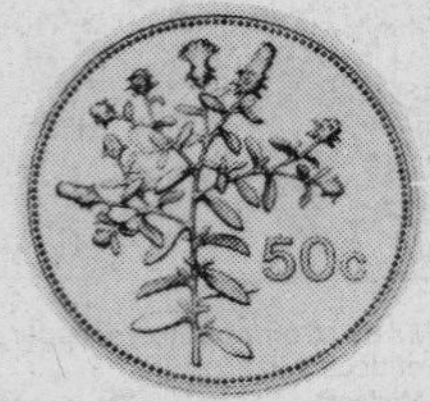


**50 CENTS** **KM# 81** **Composition:** Copper-Nickel **Obverse:** Similar to Lira, KM#82 **Reverse:** Tulliera plant

| Date | Mintage | F | VF | XF | Unc | BU |
|---|---|---|---|---|---|---|
| 1986 | 2,086,000 | — | 1.75 | 2.25 | 4.50 | — |
| 1986 Proof | 10,000 | Value: 7.00 | | | | |

**50 CENTS** **KM# 98** **Composition:** Copper-Nickel **Obverse:** Similar to 5 Cents, KM#95 **Reverse:** Tulliera plant

| Date | Mintage | F | VF | XF | Unc | BU |
|---|---|---|---|---|---|---|
| 1991 | — | — | 1.75 | 2.25 | 4.50 | — |
| 1992 | — | — | 1.75 | 2.25 | 4.50 | — |
| 1995 | — | — | — | — | — | — |

**50 CENTS** **KM# 116** **Composition:** Copper Nickel **Shape:** 8-sided **Size:** 25 mm.

| Date | Mintage | F | VF | XF | Unc | BU |
|---|---|---|---|---|---|---|
| 1995 | — | — | — | — | — | — |

**LIRA** **KM# 13** **Weight:** 10.0000 g. **Composition:** 0.9870 Silver .3173 oz. ASW **Reverse:** Manwel Dimech bust facing left

| Date | Mintage | F | VF | XF | Unc | BU |
|---|---|---|---|---|---|---|
| 1972 | 55,000 | — | — | 4.00 | 7.00 | — |

**LIRA** **KM# 19** **Weight:** 10.0000 g. **Composition:** 0.9870 Silver .3173 oz. ASW **Reverse:** Sir Temi Zammit bust facing left

| Date | Mintage | F | VF | XF | Unc | BU |
|---|---|---|---|---|---|---|
| 1973 | 30,000 | — | — | 4.00 | 7.00 | — |

**LIRA** **KM# 45** **Weight:** 5.6600 g. **Composition:** 0.9250 Silver .1683 oz. ASW **Reverse:** Kelb tal-Fenek, an ancient Maltese dog

| Date | Mintage | F | VF | XF | Unc | BU |
|---|---|---|---|---|---|---|
| 1977 | 66,000 | — | — | 7.00 | 20.00 | — |
| 1977 Proof | 2,500 | Value: 40.00 | | | | |

**LIRA** **KM# 51** **Weight:** 5.6600 g. **Composition:** 0.9250 Silver .1683 oz. ASW **Subject:** Departure of foreign forces

| Date | Mintage | F | VF | XF | Unc | BU |
|---|---|---|---|---|---|---|
| 1979FM (U) | 50,000 | — | — | 4.00 | 7.00 | — |
| 1979FM (P) | 7,871 | Value: 16.50 | | | | |

**LIRA** **KM# 63** **Composition:** Copper-Nickel **Subject:** World Fisheries Conference

| Date | Mintage | F | VF | XF | Unc | BU |
|---|---|---|---|---|---|---|
| ND(1984) | 120,000 | — | — | 4.00 | 7.50 | — |

**LIRA** **KM# 82** **Composition:** Nickel **Reverse:** Merill bird

| Date | Mintage | F | VF | XF | Unc | BU |
|---|---|---|---|---|---|---|
| 1986 | 2,272,000 | — | — | 4.00 | 7.50 | — |
| 1986 Proof | 10,000 | Value: 10.00 | | | | |

**LIRA** **KM# 99** **Composition:** Nickel **Obverse:** Similar to 2 Cents, KM#94

| Date | Mintage | F | VF | XF | Unc | BU |
|---|---|---|---|---|---|---|
| 1991 | — | — | — | 3.50 | 6.00 | — |
| 1994 | — | — | — | — | — | — |
| 1995 | — | — | — | — | — | — |

**2 LIRI** **KM# 14** **Weight:** 20.0000 g. **Composition:** 0.9870 Silver .6347 oz. ASW **Reverse:** Fort St. Angelo

| Date | Mintage | F | VF | XF | Unc | BU |
|---|---|---|---|---|---|---|
| 1972 | 53,000 | — | — | 6.50 | 12.50 | — |

**2 LIRI** **KM# 20** **Weight:** 20.0000 g. **Composition:** 0.9870 Silver .6347 oz. ASW **Obverse:** Similar to KM#14 **Reverse:** Tal-Imdina Gate

| Date | Mintage | F | VF | XF | Unc | BU |
|---|---|---|---|---|---|---|
| 1973 | 30,000 | — | — | 8.00 | 14.50 | — |

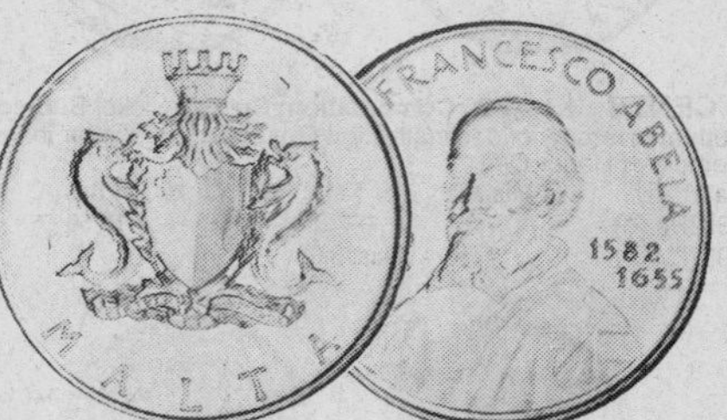


**2 LIRI** **KM# 24** **Weight:** 10.0000 g. **Composition:** 0.9870 Silver .3173 oz. ASW **Reverse:** Giovanni Francesco Abela bust facing forward

| Date | Mintage | F | VF | XF | Unc | BU |
|---|---|---|---|---|---|---|
| 1974 | 25,000 | — | — | 6.50 | 8.50 | — |

**2 LIRI** **KM# 30** **Weight:** 10.0000 g. **Composition:** 0.9870 Silver .3173 oz. ASW **Obverse:** Similar to KM#24 **Reverse:** Similar to KM#31

| Date | Mintage | F | VF | XF | Unc | BU |
|---|---|---|---|---|---|---|
| 1975 | 2,000 | — | — | 8.00 | 15.00 | — |

**2 LIRI** **KM# 31** **Weight:** 10.0000 g. **Composition:** 0.9870 Silver .3173 oz. ASW **Reverse:** Alfonso Maria Galea bust facing left

| Date | Mintage | F | VF | XF | Unc | BU |
|---|---|---|---|---|---|---|
| 1975 | 18,000 | — | — | 6.50 | 8.50 | — |

**2 LIRI** **KM# 40** **Weight:** 10.0000 g. **Composition:** 0.9870 Silver .3173 oz. ASW **Reverse:** Guze Ellul Mercer bust facing right

| Date | Mintage | F | VF | XF | Unc | BU |
|---|---|---|---|---|---|---|
| 1976 | 11,000 | — | — | 8.00 | 10.00 | — |

**2 LIRI** **KM# 46** **Weight:** 11.3100 g. **Composition:** 0.9250 Silver .3363 oz. ASW **Reverse:** Sir Luigi Preziosi bust facing left

| Date | Mintage | F | VF | XF | Unc | BU |
|---|---|---|---|---|---|---|
| 1977 | 15,000 | — | — | — | 9.00 | — |
| 1977 Proof | 3,692 | Value: 12.50 | | | | |

**2 LIRI** **KM# 52** **Weight:** 11.3100 g. **Composition:** 0.9250 Silver .3363 oz. ASW **Series:** World Food Day

| Date | Mintage | F | VF | XF | Unc | BU |
|---|---|---|---|---|---|---|
| 1981 | 1,500 | — | — | — | 15.00 | — |
| 1981 Proof | 12,000 | Value: 10.00 | | | | |

**2 LIRI** **KM# 88** **Weight:** 17.0000 g. **Composition:** 0.9250 Silver .5056 oz. ASW **Subject:** 25th anniversary of Independence

| Date | Mintage | F | VF | XF | Unc | BU |
|---|---|---|---|---|---|---|
| 1989 | 75,000 | — | — | — | 10.00 | — |
| 1989 Proof | 7,500 | Value: 17.50 | | | | |

**4 LIRI** **KM# 25** **Weight:** 20.0000 g. **Composition:** 0.9870 Silver .6347 oz. ASW **Reverse:** Cottonera Gate

| Date | Mintage | F | VF | XF | Unc | BU |
|---|---|---|---|---|---|---|
| 1974 | 24,000 | — | — | 11.50 | 16.50 | — |

**4 LIRI** **KM# 32** **Weight:** 20.0000 g. **Composition:** 0.9870 Silver .6347 oz. ASW **Obverse:** Same as KM#25 **Reverse:** Similar to KM#33

| Date | Mintage | F | VF | XF | Unc | BU |
|---|---|---|---|---|---|---|
| 1975 | 2,000 | — | — | 15.00 | 27.50 | — |

**4 LIRI** **KM# 33** **Weight:** 20.0000 g. **Composition:** 0.9870 Silver .6347 oz. ASW **Reverse:** St. Agatha's Tower at Gammieh

| Date | Mintage | F | VF | XF | Unc | BU |
|---|---|---|---|---|---|---|
| 1975 | 18,000 | — | — | 13.50 | 17.50 | — |

**4 LIRI** **KM# 41** **Weight:** 20.0000 g. **Composition:** 0.9870 Silver .6347 oz. ASW **Reverse:** Fort Manoel Gate

| Date | Mintage | F | VF | XF | Unc | BU |
|---|---|---|---|---|---|---|
| 1976 | 10,000 | — | — | 14.50 | 18.50 | — |

**5 LIRI** **KM# 15** **Weight:** 3.0000 g. **Composition:** 0.9160 Gold .0883 oz. AGW **Reverse:** Hand holding torch, map of Malta

| Date | Mintage | F | VF | XF | Unc | BU |
|---|---|---|---|---|---|---|
| 1972 | 18,000 | — | — | — | 65.00 | — |

**5 LIRI** **KM# 47** **Weight:** 28.2800 g. **Composition:** 0.9250 Silver .8411 oz. ASW **Reverse:** Windmill of Xarolla

| Date | Mintage | F | VF | XF | Unc | BU |
|---|---|---|---|---|---|---|
| 1977 | 15,000 | — | — | — | 22.50 | — |
| 1977 Proof | 3,938 | Value: 37.50 | | | | |

**5 LIRI** **KM# 53** **Weight:** 28.2800 g. **Composition:** 0.9250 Silver .8411 oz. ASW **Subject:** International Youth Conference - UNICEF

| Date | Mintage | F | VF | XF | Unc | BU |
|---|---|---|---|---|---|---|
| 1981 Proof | 11,000 | Value: 15.00 | | | | |

**5 LIRI** **KM# 65** **Weight:** 28.2800 g. **Composition:** 0.9250 Silver .8411 oz. ASW **Series:** International Year of Disabled Persons

| Date | Mintage | F | VF | XF | Unc | BU |
|---|---|---|---|---|---|---|
| 1983 | — | — | — | — | 22.50 | — |
| 1983 Proof | — | Value: 40.00 | | | | |

**5 LIRI** **KM# 67** **Weight:** 20.0000 g. **Composition:** 0.9250 Silver .5949 oz. ASW **Subject:** Maritime history "Strangier" (1813)

| Date | Mintage | F | VF | XF | Unc | BU |
|---|---|---|---|---|---|---|
| 1984 Prooflike | 15,000 | — | — | — | 22.50 | — |

**5 LIRI** **KM# 64** **Weight:** 28.2800 g. **Composition:** 0.9250 Silver .8411 oz. ASW **Subject:** World Fisheries Conference

| Date | Mintage | F | VF | XF | Unc | BU |
|---|---|---|---|---|---|---|
| ND(1984) Proof | 20,000 | Value: 50.00 | | | | |

**5 LIRI** **KM# 68** **Weight:** 20.0000 g. **Composition:** 0.9250 Silver .5949 oz. ASW **Subject:** Maritime history "Tigre" (1839)

| Date | Mintage | F | VF | XF | Unc | BU |
|---|---|---|---|---|---|---|
| 1984 Prooflike | 15,000 | — | — | — | 22.50 | — |

**5 LIRI** **KM# 69** **Weight:** 20.0000 g. **Composition:** 0.9250 Silver .5949 oz. ASW **Subject:** Maritime history "Wignacourt" (1844)

| Date | Mintage | F | VF | XF | Unc | BU |
|---|---|---|---|---|---|---|
| 1984 Prooflike | 15,000 | — | — | — | 22.50 | — |

**5 LIRI** **KM# 70** **Weight:** 20.0000 g. **Composition:** 0.9250 Silver .5949 oz. ASW **Subject:** Maritime history "Providenza" (1848)

| Date | Mintage | F | VF | XF | Unc | BU |
|---|---|---|---|---|---|---|
| 1984 Prooflike | 15,000 | — | — | — | 22.50 | — |

**5 LIRI** **KM# 71** **Weight:** 28.2800 g. **Composition:** 0.9250 Silver .8411 oz. ASW **Series:** Decade for Women

| Date | Mintage | F | VF | XF | Unc | BU |
|---|---|---|---|---|---|---|
| 1984 Proof | 17,000 | Value: 35.00 | | | | |

**5 LIRI** **KM# 72** **Weight:** 20.0000 g. **Composition:** 0.9250 Silver .5949 oz. ASW **Subject:** Maritime history "Malta" (1862)

| Date | Mintage | F | VF | XF | Unc | BU |
|---|---|---|---|---|---|---|
| 1985 Prooflike | 15,000 | — | — | — | 22.50 | — |

**5 LIRI** **KM# 73** **Weight:** 20.0000 g. **Composition:** 0.9250 Silver .5949 oz. ASW **Subject:** Maritime history "Tagliaferro" (1882)

| Date | Mintage | F | VF | XF | Unc | BU |
|---|---|---|---|---|---|---|
| 1985 Prooflike | 15,000 | — | — | — | 22.50 | — |

**5 LIRI** **KM# 74** **Weight:** 20.0000 g. **Composition:** 0.9250 Silver .5949 oz. ASW **Subject:** Maritime history "L'Isle Adam" (1883)

| Date | Mintage | F | VF | XF | Unc | BU |
|---|---|---|---|---|---|---|
| 1985 Prooflike | 15,000 | — | — | — | 22.50 | — |

**5 LIRI** **KM# 75** **Weight:** 20.0000 g. **Composition:** 0.9250 Silver .5949 oz. ASW **Subject:** Maritime history "Maria Dacoutros" (1902)

| Date | Mintage | F | VF | XF | Unc | BU |
|---|---|---|---|---|---|---|
| 1985 Prooflike | 15,000 | — | — | — | 22.50 | — |

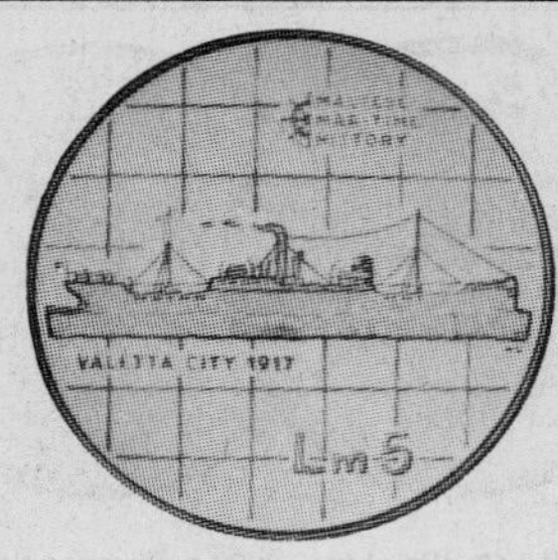


**5 LIRI** **KM# 83** **Weight:** 20.0000 g. **Composition:** 0.9250 Silver .5949 oz. ASW **Subject:** Maritime history "Valetta City" (1917)

| Date | Mintage | F | VF | XF | Unc | BU |
|---|---|---|---|---|---|---|
| 1986 Prooflike | 15,000 | — | — | — | 22.50 | — |

**5 LIRI** **KM# 84** **Weight:** 20.0000 g. **Composition:** 0.9250 Silver .5949 oz. ASW **Subject:** Maritime history "Knight of Malta" (1929)

| Date | Mintage | F | VF | XF | Unc | BU |
|---|---|---|---|---|---|---|
| 1986 Prooflike | 15,000 | — | — | — | 22.50 | — |

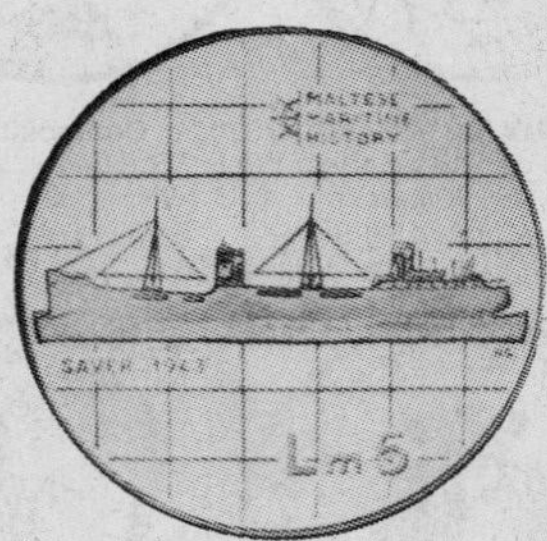


**5 LIRI** **KM# 85** **Weight:** 20.0000 g. **Composition:** 0.9250 Silver .5949 oz. ASW **Subject:** Maritime history "Saver" (1943)

| Date | Mintage | F | VF | XF | Unc | BU |
|---|---|---|---|---|---|---|
| 1986 Prooflike | 15,000 | — | — | — | 22.50 | — |

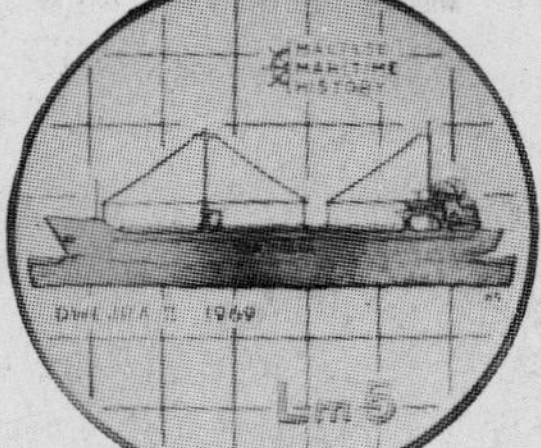


**5 LIRI** **KM# 86** **Weight:** 20.0000 g. **Composition:** 0.9250 Silver .5949 oz. ASW **Subject:** Maritime history "Dwejra II" (1969)

| Date | Mintage | F | VF | XF | Unc | BU |
|---|---|---|---|---|---|---|
| 1986 Prooflike | 15,000 | — | — | — | 22.50 | — |

**5 LIRI** **KM# 87** **Weight:** 28.2800 g. **Composition:** 0.9250 Silver .8411 oz. ASW **Subject:** 20th anniversary - Central Bank of Malta

| Date | Mintage | F | VF | XF | Unc | BU |
|---|---|---|---|---|---|---|
| 1988 | Est. 5,000 | — | — | — | 25.00 | — |
| 1988 Proof | Est. 2,000 | Value: 45.00 | | | | |

**5 LIRI** **KM# 90** **Weight:** 28.6000 g. **Composition:** 0.9250 Silver .8506 oz. ASW **Subject:** Papal visit

| Date | Mintage | F | VF | XF | Unc | BU |
|---|---|---|---|---|---|---|
| 1990 | 500 | — | — | — | 45.00 | — |
| 1990 Proof | 4,000 | Value: 55.00 | | | | |

**5 LIRI** **KM# 91** **Weight:** 28.2800 g. **Composition:** 0.9250 Silver .8411 oz. ASW **Subject:** Entry of Malta to European Economic Community

| Date | Mintage | F | VF | XF | Unc | BU |
|---|---|---|---|---|---|---|
| 1990 | — | — | — | — | 30.00 | — |
| 1990 Proof | Est. 4,000 | Value: 50.00 | | | | |

**5 LIRI** **KM# 92** **Weight:** 28.2800 g. **Composition:** 0.9250 Silver .8411 oz. ASW **Series:** Save the Children

| Date | Mintage | F | VF | XF | Unc | BU |
|---|---|---|---|---|---|---|
| 1991 Proof | 20,000 | Value: 30.00 | | | | |

**5 LIRI** **KM# 100** **Weight:** 28.2800 g. **Composition:** 0.9250 Silver .8411 oz. ASW **Subject:** 50th Anniversary of George Cross Award

| Date | Mintage | F | VF | XF | Unc | BU |
|---|---|---|---|---|---|---|
| 1992 Proof | Est. 10,000 | Value: 37.50 | | | | |

**5 LIRI** **KM# 102** **Weight:** 28.2800 g. **Composition:** 0.9250 Silver .8411 oz. ASW **Subject:** 25th anniversary of Central Bank

| Date | Mintage | F | VF | XF | Unc | BU |
|---|---|---|---|---|---|---|
| ND(1993) | Est. 1,500 | — | — | — | 32.50 | — |
| ND(1993) Proof | Est. 1,500 | Value: 55.00 | | | | |

**5 LIRI** **KM# 106** **Weight:** 28.2800 g. **Composition:** 0.9250 Silver .8411 oz. ASW **Subject:** 400th Anniversary - University of Malta

| Date | Mintage | F | VF | XF | Unc | BU |
|---|---|---|---|---|---|---|
| ND(1993) Proof | Est. 1,000 | Value: 42.50 | | | | |

**5 LIRI** **KM# 107** **Weight:** 28.2800 g. **Composition:** 0.9250 Silver .8411 oz. ASW **Subject:** World Cup soccer

| Date | Mintage | F | VF | XF | Unc | BU |
|---|---|---|---|---|---|---|
| 1993 Proof | Est. 20,000 | Value: 32.50 | | | | |

**5 LIRI** **KM# 108** **Weight:** 31.4700 g. **Composition:** 0.9250 Silver .9359 oz. ASW **Reverse:** Sailing ship "Valletta" and fortress

| Date | Mintage | F | VF | XF | Unc | BU |
|---|---|---|---|---|---|---|
| 1994 Proof | Est. 20,000 | Value: 32.50 | | | | |

**5 LIRI** **KM# 109** **Weight:** 28.2800 g. **Composition:** 0.9250 Silver .8411 oz. ASW **Series:** 50th anniversary - United Nations

| Date | Mintage | F | VF | XF | Unc | BU |
|---|---|---|---|---|---|---|
| 1995 Proof | Est. 125,000 | Value: 30.00 | | | | |

**5 LIRI** **KM# 110** **Weight:** 31.4700 g. **Composition:** 0.9250 Silver .9359 oz. ASW **Series:** Olympic Games **Subject:** Water polo **Obverse:** National arms

| Date | Mintage | F | VF | XF | Unc | BU |
|---|---|---|---|---|---|---|
| 1996 Proof | Est. 35,000 | Value: 28.50 | | | | |

**5 LIRI** **KM# 111** **Weight:** 28.2800 g. **Composition:** 0.9250 Silver .841 oz. ASW **Obverse:** National arms **Reverse:** Bank's pyramid fountain

| Date | Mintage | F | VF | XF | Unc | BU |
|---|---|---|---|---|---|---|
| 1998 Proof | Est. 5,000 | Value: 60.00 | | | | |

**5 LIRI** **KM# 112** **Weight:** 28.2800 g. **Composition:** 0.9250 Silver .841 oz. ASW **Subject:** 200th anniversary - anti-French revolution **Obverse:** National arms **Reverse:** "Blockade" medal of 1798

| Date | Mintage | F | VF | XF | Unc | BU |
|---|---|---|---|---|---|---|
| 1998 Proof | Est. 5,000 | Value: 60.00 | | | | |

**5 LIRI** **KM# 113** **Weight:** 28.3500 g. **Composition:** 0.9250 Silver .8431 oz. ASW **Subject:** Mattia Preti **Obverse:** National arms **Reverse:** Portrait of Preti and John the Baptist

**Edge:** Reeded **Size:** 38.4 mm.

| Date | Mintage | F | VF | XF | Unc | BU |
|---|---|---|---|---|---|---|
| 1999 Proof | Est. 5,000 | — | — | — | 50.00 | — |

**5 LIRI** **KM# 114** **Weight:** 15.0000 g. **Composition:** 0.9250 Silver .4461 oz. ASW **Subject:** Millennium **Obverse:** Two modern gold-plated coin designs **Reverse:** Two ancient gold-plated coin designs and map **Edge:** Plain **Note:** 40x20 milimeters.

| Date | Mintage | F | VF | XF | Unc | BU |
|---|---|---|---|---|---|---|
| 2000 Proof | 32,000 | — | — | — | 50.00 | — |

**10 LIRI** **KM# 16** **Weight:** 6.0000 g. **Composition:** 0.9170 Gold .1767 oz. AGW **Reverse:** Kenur, a Maltese stone charcoal stove

| Date | Mintage | F | VF | XF | Unc | BU |
|---|---|---|---|---|---|---|
| 1972 | 16,000 | — | — | — | 95.00 | — |

**10 LIRI** **KM# 21** **Weight:** 3.0000 g. **Composition:** 0.9170 Gold .0883 oz. AGW **Reverse:** Watchtower

| Date | Mintage | F | VF | XF | Unc | BU |
|---|---|---|---|---|---|---|
| 1973 | 9,078 | — | — | — | 55.00 | — |

**10 LIRI** **KM# 26** **Weight:** 3.0000 g. **Composition:** 0.9170 Gold .0883 oz. AGW **Reverse:** Zerafa flower

| Date | Mintage | F | VF | XF | Unc | BU |
|---|---|---|---|---|---|---|
| 1974 | 9,124 | — | — | — | 55.00 | — |

**10 LIRI** **KM# 34** **Weight:** 3.0000 g. **Composition:** 0.9170 Gold .0883 oz. AGW **Obverse:** Similar to KM#26 **Reverse:** Similar to KM#35

| Date | Mintage | F | VF | XF | Unc | BU |
|---|---|---|---|---|---|---|
| 1975 | 2,000 | — | — | — | 75.00 | — |

**10 LIRI** **KM# 35** **Weight:** 3.0000 g. **Composition:** 0.9170 Gold .0883 oz. AGW **Reverse:** Maltese falcon

| Date | Mintage | F | VF | XF | Unc | BU |
|---|---|---|---|---|---|---|
| 1975 | 6,448 | — | — | — | 90.00 | — |

**10 LIRI** **KM# 42** **Weight:** 3.0000 g. **Composition:** 0.9170 Gold .0883 oz. AGW **Reverse:** Swallow-tail butterfly

| Date | Mintage | F | VF | XF | Unc | BU |
|---|---|---|---|---|---|---|
| 1976 | 4,448 | — | — | — | 100 | — |

**20 LIRI** **KM# 17** **Weight:** 12.0000 g. **Composition:** 0.9170 Gold .3534 oz. AGW **Reverse:** Merill bird

| Date | Mintage | F | VF | XF | Unc | BU |
|---|---|---|---|---|---|---|
| 1972 | 16,000 | — | — | — | 185 | — |

**20 LIRI** **KM# 22** **Weight:** 6.0000 g. **Composition:** 0.9170 Gold .1767 oz. AGW **Reverse:** Dolphins Fountain at Floriana

| Date | Mintage | F | VF | XF | Unc | BU |
|---|---|---|---|---|---|---|
| 1973 | 9,075 | — | — | — | 110 | — |

**20 LIRI** **KM# 27** **Weight:** 6.0000 g. **Composition:** 0.9170 Gold .1767 oz. AGW **Reverse:** Gozo boat

| Date | Mintage | F | VF | XF | Unc | BU |
|---|---|---|---|---|---|---|
| 1974 | 8,700 | — | — | — | 110 | — |

**20 LIRI** **KM# 36** **Weight:** 6.0000 g. **Composition:** 0.9170 Gold .1767 oz. AGW **Obverse:** Similar to KM#27 **Reverse:** Similar to KM#37

| Date | Mintage | F | VF | XF | Unc | BU |
|---|---|---|---|---|---|---|
| 1975 | 2,000 | — | — | — | 150 | — |

**20 LIRI** **KM# 37** **Weight:** 6.0000 g. **Composition:** 0.9170 Gold .1767 oz. AGW **Reverse:** Freshwater crab

| Date | Mintage | F | VF | XF | Unc | BU |
|---|---|---|---|---|---|---|
| 1975 | 5,698 | — | — | — | 125 | — |

**20 LIRI** **KM# 43** **Weight:** 6.0000 g. **Composition:** 0.9170 Gold .1767 oz. AGW **Reverse:** Storm petrel bird

| Date | Mintage | F | VF | XF | Unc | BU |
|---|---|---|---|---|---|---|
| 1976 | 4,098 | — | — | — | 135 | — |

**25 LIRI** **KM# 48** **Weight:** 7.9900 g. **Composition:** 0.9170 Gold .2353 oz. AGW **Subject:** First Gozo coin

| Date | Mintage | F | VF | XF | Unc | BU |
|---|---|---|---|---|---|---|
| 1977 | 4,000 | — | — | — | 125 | — |
| 1977 Proof | 3,249 | Value: 150 | | | | |

**25 LIRI** **KM# 101** **Weight:** 7.9900 g. **Composition:** 0.9170 Gold .2353 oz. AGW **Subject:** 30th anniversary of George Cross award

| Date | Mintage | F | VF | XF | Unc | BU |
|---|---|---|---|---|---|---|
| 1992 Proof | Est. 500 | Value: 185 | | | | |

**50 LIRI** **KM# 18** **Weight:** 30.0000 g. **Composition:** 0.9170 Gold .8836 oz. AGW **Reverse:** Neptune

| Date | Mintage | F | VF | XF | Unc | BU |
|---|---|---|---|---|---|---|
| 1972 | 16,000 | — | — | — | 425 | — |

**50 LIRI** **KM# 23** **Weight:** 15.0000 g. **Composition:** 0.9170 Gold .4418 oz. AGW **Subject:** Auberge de Castille at Valletta

| Date | Mintage | F | VF | XF | Unc | BU |
|---|---|---|---|---|---|---|
| 1973 | 9,075 | — | — | — | 225 | — |

**50 LIRI** **KM# 28** **Weight:** 15.0000 g. **Composition:** 0.9170 Gold .4418 oz. AGW **Subject:** First Maltese coin

| Date | Mintage | F | VF | XF | Unc | BU |
|---|---|---|---|---|---|---|
| 1974 | 8,667 | — | — | — | 225 | — |

**50 LIRI** **KM# 38** **Weight:** 15.0000 g. **Composition:** 0.9170 Gold .4418 oz. AGW **Reverse:** Ornamental stone balcony

| Date | Mintage | F | VF | XF | Unc | BU |
|---|---|---|---|---|---|---|
| 1975 | 2,000 | — | — | — | 325 | — |

**50 LIRI** **KM# 39** **Weight:** 15.0000 g. **Composition:** 0.9170 Gold .4418 oz. AGW **Reverse:** Ornamental stone balcony

| Date | Mintage | F | VF | XF | Unc | BU |
|---|---|---|---|---|---|---|
| 1975 | 5,500 | — | — | — | 225 | — |

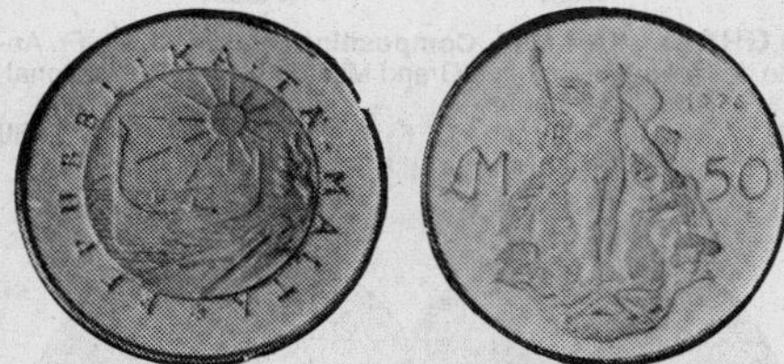

**50 LIRI** **KM# 44** **Weight:** 15.0000 g. **Composition:** 0.9170 Gold .4418 oz. AGW **Reverse:** Ornamental door knocker

| Date | Mintage | F | VF | XF | Unc | BU |
|---|---|---|---|---|---|---|
| 1976 | 3,748 | — | — | — | 225 | — |

**50 LIRI** **KM# 49** **Weight:** 15.9800 g. **Composition:** 0.9170 Gold .4707 oz. AGW **Subject:** Mnara

| Date | Mintage | F | VF | XF | Unc | BU |
|---|---|---|---|---|---|---|
| 1977 | 4,000 | — | — | — | 225 | — |
| 1977 Proof | 846 | Value: 350 | | | | |

**100 LIRI** **KM# 50** **Weight:** 31.9600 g. **Composition:** 0.9170 Gold .9413 oz. AGW **Reverse:** "Les Gavroches" Sculpture

| Date | Mintage | F | VF | XF | Unc | BU |
|---|---|---|---|---|---|---|
| 1977 | 4,000 | — | — | — | 500 | — |
| 1977 Proof | 846 | Value: 650 | | | | |

**100 LIRI** **KM# 66** **Weight:** 15.9800 g. **Composition:** 0.9170 Gold .4709 oz. AGW **Series:** International Year of Disabled Persons

| Date | Mintage | F | VF | XF | Unc | BU |
|---|---|---|---|---|---|---|
| 1983 | 700 | — | — | — | 400 | — |
| 1983 Proof | 600 | Value: 500 | | | | |

**100 LIRI** **KM# 89** **Weight:** 17.0000 g. **Composition:** 0.9170 Gold .5007 oz. AGW **Subject:** 25th anniversary of independence

| Date | Mintage | F | VF | XF | Unc | BU |
|---|---|---|---|---|---|---|
| 1989 | 5,000 | — | — | — | 250 | — |
| 1989 Proof | 2,500 | Value: 300 | | | | |

## EUROPEAN CURRENCY UNIT

ECU

**POUND (2 ECU)** **KM# 103** **Composition:** Copper-Nickel **Subject:** Defense of Europe

| Date | Mintage | F | VF | XF | Unc | BU |
|---|---|---|---|---|---|---|
| 1993 | 25,000 | — | — | — | 12.00 | — |

**5 POUNDS (10 ECU)** **KM# 104** **Weight:** 25.0000 g. **Composition:** 0.9250 Silver .7435 oz. ASW **Subject:** Defense of Europe

| Date | Mintage | F | VF | XF | Unc | BU |
|---|---|---|---|---|---|---|
| 1993 Proof | 35,000 | Value: 30.00 | | | | |

**25 POUNDS (55 ECU)** **KM# 105** **Weight:** 6.7200 g. **Composition:** 0.9000 Gold .1945 oz. AGW **Subject:** Defense of Europe

| Date | Mintage | F | VF | XF | Unc | BU |
|---|---|---|---|---|---|---|
| 1993 Proof | 2,500 | Value: 175 | | | | |

## PIEFORTS

| KM# | Date | Mintage | Identification | Issue Price | Mkt Val |
|---|---|---|---|---|---|
| P1 | 1981 | 177 | 5 Pounds. 0.9250 Silver. KM53. | — | 120 |
| P2 | 1983 | 700 | 5 Pounds. 0.9250 Silver. KM65. | — | 70.00 |
| P3 | 1983 | — | 100 Pounds. 0.9170 Gold. KM66. | — | 800 |
| P3 | 1983 | 150 | 100 Pounds. 0.9170 Gold. KM66. | — | 800 |
| P4 | 1988 | 500 | 100 Pounds. 0.9250 Silver. KM87. | 80.00 | 100 |

## MINT SETS

| KM# | Date | Mintage | Identification | Issue Price | Mkt Val |
|---|---|---|---|---|---|
| MS1 | 1972 (8) | 8,000 | KM5-12 | — | 7.50 |
| MS2 | 1972 (4) | 8,000 | KM15-18 | 210 | 800 |
| MS3 | 1972 (2) | — | KM13-14 | 8.50 | 27.50 |
| MS4 | 1973 (3) | 9,078 | KM21-23 | — | 400 |
| MS5 | 1973 (2) | — | KM19-20 | — | 27.50 |
| MS6 | 1974 (3) | — | KM26-28 | 256 | 400 |
| MS7 | 1974 (2) | — | KM24-25 | 19.60 | 22.50 |
| MS10 | 1975 (2) | — | KM30, 32 | 20.00 | 45.00 |
| MS8 | 1975 (5) | 2,000 | KM30, 32, 34, 36, 38 | 276 | 600 |
| MS9 | 1975 (3) | — | KM34, 36, 38 | 256 | 550 |
| MS-A10 | 1975 (2) | — | KM31, 33 | — | 28.00 |
| MS11 | 1975 (3) | — | KM35, 37, 39 | — | 425 |
| MS12 | 1976 (3) | — | KM42-44 | — | 425 |
| MS13 | 1976 (2) | — | KM40-41 | — | 25.00 |
| MS14 | 1977 (9) | 252 | KM5-12, 29b | — | 60.00 |
| MS15 | 1977 (3) | 4,000 | KM48-50 | 610 | 900 |
| MS16 | 1977 (3) | 15,000 | KM45-47 | 34.50 | 36.50 |
| MS17 | 1978 (9) | 252 | KM5-12, 29b | — | 60.00 |
| MS18 | 1979 (9) | 537 | KM5-12, 29b | — | 110 |
| MS19 | 1980 (9) | 385 | KM5-12, 29b | 11.00 | 110 |
| MS20 | 1981 (9) | 449 | KM5-12, 29b | 13.25 | 110 |
| MS21 | 1982 (9) | 850 | KM54-62 | 13.25 | 120 |
| MS22 | 1984 (4) | 15,000 | KM67-70 | 72.00 | 90.00 |
| MS23 | 1985 (4) | 15,000 | KM72-75 | 72.00 | 90.00 |
| MS24 | 1986 (4) | 15,000 | KM83-86 | 72.00 | 90.00 |

## PROOF SETS

| KM# | Date | Mintage | Identification | Issue Price | Mkt Val |
|---|---|---|---|---|---|
| PS1 | 1972 (8) | 8,000 | KM5-12; plastic case | — | 12.50 |
| PS2 | 1976 (9) | 26,248 | KM5-12, 29b | 27.50 | 15.00 |
| PS3 | 1977 (9) | 6,884 | KM5-12, 29b | 31.50 | 21.50 |
| PS4 | 1977 (3) | 750 | KM48-50 | 909 | 1,150 |
| PS5 | 1977 (3) | 2,500 | KM45-47 | 72.00 | 80.00 |
| PS6 | 1978 (9) | 3,244 | KM5-12, 29b | — | 18.00 |
| PS7 | 1979 (10) | 6,577 | KM5-12, 29b, 51 | 41.50 | 30.00 |
| PS8 | 1980 (9) | 3,451 | KM5-12, 29b | 30.00 | 25.00 |
| PS9 | 1981 (9) | 1,453 | KM5-12, 29b | 25.30 | 45.00 |
| PS10 | 1982 (9) | 1,793 | KM54-62 | 32.00 | 45.00 |
| PS11 | 1986 (7) | 10,000 | KM76-82 | 29.75 | 30.00 |

The Order of Malta, modern successor to the Sovereign Military Hospitaller Order of St. John of Jerusalem (the crusading Knights Hospitallers), derives its sovereignty from grants of extraterritoriality by Italy (1928) and the Vatican City (1953), and from its supranational character as a religious military order owing suzerainty to the Holy See. Its territory is confined to Palazzo Malta on Via Condotti, Villa Malta and the crest of the Aventine Hill, all in the city of Rome. The Order maintains diplomatic relations with about 35 governments, including Italy, Spain, Austria, State of Malta, Portugal, Brazil, Guatemala, Panama, Peru, Iran, Lebanon, Philippines, Liberia, Ethiopia, etc.

The Knights Hospitallers were founded in 1099 just before the crusaders' capture of Jerusalem. Father Gerard (died 1120) was the founder and first rector of the Jerusalem hospital. The headquarters of the Order were successively at Jerusalem 1099-1187; Acre 1187-1291;Cyprus 1291-1310; Rhodes 1310-1522; Malta 1530-1798;Trieste 1798-1799; St. Petersburg 1799-1803; Catania1803-1825; Ferrara 1826-1834; Rome 1834-Present.

The symbolic coins issued by the Order since 1961 are intended to continue the last independent coinage of the Order on Malta in 1798. In traditional tari and scudi denominations, they are issued only in proof condition. They have a theoretical fixed exchange value with the Italian lira, but are not used in commerce.

These medallic issues are perhaps the world's last major symbolic coinage, just as their issuer is the world's last sovereign order of knighthood. Proceeds from the sale of this coinage maintain the Order's hospitals, clinics and leprosariums around the world.

**RULERS**

Ernesto Paterno-Castello di Carcaci,
Lieutenant Grand Master, 1955-1962
Fr. Angelo de Mojana di Cologna, 1962-1988
Fr. Giancarlo Pallavicini, Temporary Grand Master, 1988
Fr. Andreas Bertie, 1988-

**MINT MARKS**

Rome (no mark) 1961
Paris (no mark) 1962
Arezzo (no mark) 1963
Order of Malta Mint in Rome – SMOM in angles of a cross - 1964-

# SOVEREIGN ORDER

## MEDALLIC COINAGE

**10 GRANI** **KM# M17** **Composition:** Bronze **Ruler:** Fr. Angelo de Mojana di Cologna Grand Master

| Date | Mintage | F | VF | XF | Unc | BU |
|---|---|---|---|---|---|---|
| 1967 Proof | 10,000 | Value: 5.00 | | | | |

**10 GRANI** **KM# M29** **Composition:** Bronze **Ruler:** Fr. Angelo de Mojana di Cologna Grand Master

| Date | Mintage | F | VF | XF | Unc | BU |
|---|---|---|---|---|---|---|
| 1969 Proof | 3,000 | Value: 5.50 | | | | |

**10 GRANI** **KM# M35** **Composition:** Bronze **Ruler:** Fr. Angelo de Mojana di Cologna Grand Master

| Date | Mintage | F | VF | XF | Unc | BU |
|---|---|---|---|---|---|---|
| 1970 Proof | 3,000 | Value: 4.50 | | | | |

**10 GRANI** **KM# M40** **Composition:** Bronze **Ruler:** Fr. Angelo de Mojana di Cologna Grand Master **Obv. Legend:** F. ANGELVS DE MOJANA

| Date | Mintage | F | VF | XF | Unc | BU |
|---|---|---|---|---|---|---|
| 1971 Proof | 3,000 | Value: 4.50 | | | | |

**10 GRANI** **KM# M46** **Composition:** Bronze **Ruler:** Fr. Angelo de Mojana di Cologna Grand Master **Subject:** 400th anniversary - Battle of Lepanto **Obverse:** Fr. Petrus de Monte bust facing right

| Date | Mintage | F | VF | XF | Unc | BU |
|---|---|---|---|---|---|---|
| 1971 Proof | 5,000 | Value: 5.00 | | | | |

**10 GRANI** **KM# M48** **Composition:** Bronze **Ruler:** Fr. Angelo de Mojana di Cologna Grand Master **Obverse:** Fr. Angelvs de Mojana bust facing left

| Date | Mintage | F | VF | XF | Unc | BU |
|---|---|---|---|---|---|---|
| 1972 Proof | 3,000 | Value: 4.50 | | | | |
| 1973 Proof | 3,000 | Value: 4.50 | | | | |

**10 GRANI** **KM# M56** **Composition:** Bronze **Ruler:** Fr. Angelo de Mojana di Cologna Grand Master

| Date | Mintage | F | VF | XF | Unc | BU |
|---|---|---|---|---|---|---|
| 1974 Proof | 3,000 | Value: 5.00 | | | | |
| 1975 Proof | 3,000 | Value: 5.00 | | | | |
| 1976 Proof | 3,000 | Value: 5.00 | | | | |
| 1977 Proof | 3,000 | Value: 5.00 | | | | |

**10 GRANI** **KM# M70** **Composition:** Bronze **Ruler:** Fr. Angelo de Mojana di Cologna Grand Master

| Date | Mintage | F | VF | XF | Unc | BU |
|---|---|---|---|---|---|---|
| 1978 Proof | 3,000 | Value: 6.50 | | | | |

**10 GRANI** **KM# M74** **Composition:** Bronze **Ruler:** Fr. Angelo de Mojana di Cologna Grand Master

| Date | Mintage | F | VF | XF | Unc | BU |
|---|---|---|---|---|---|---|
| 1979 Proof | 3,000 | Value: 5.50 | | | | |

**10 GRANI** **KM# M80** **Composition:** Bronze **Ruler:** Fr. Angelo de Mojana di Cologna Grand Master

| Date | Mintage | F | VF | XF | Unc | BU |
|---|---|---|---|---|---|---|
| 1980 Proof | 3,000 | Value: 7.50 | | | | |

**10 GRANI** **KM# M85** **Composition:** Bronze **Ruler:** Fr. Angelo de Mojana di Cologna Grand Master **Series:** International Year of Disabled Persons

| Date | Mintage | F | VF | XF | Unc | BU |
|---|---|---|---|---|---|---|
| 1981 Proof | 3,000 | Value: 8.50 | | | | |

**10 GRANI** **KM# M90** **Composition:** Bronze **Ruler:** Fr. Angelo de Mojana di Cologna Grand Master **Subject:** 20th anniversary of Fr. A. de Mojana

| Date | Mintage | F | VF | XF | Unc | BU |
|---|---|---|---|---|---|---|
| ND(1982) Proof | 2,000 | Value: 7.50 | | | | |

**10 GRANI** **KM# M96** **Composition:** Bronze **Ruler:** Fr. Angelo de Mojana di Cologna Grand Master

| Date | Mintage | F | VF | XF | Unc | BU |
|---|---|---|---|---|---|---|
| 1983 Proof | 2,000 | Value: 7.50 | | | | |

**10 GRANI** **KM# M102** **Composition:** Bronze **Ruler:** Fr. Angelo de Mojana di Cologna Grand Master **Subject:** Piranesi

| Date | Mintage | F | VF | XF | Unc | BU |
|---|---|---|---|---|---|---|
| 1984 Proof | 2,000 | Value: 7.50 | | | | |

**10 GRANI** **KM# M108** **Composition:** Bronze **Ruler:** Fr. Angelo de Mojana di Cologna Grand Master

| Date | Mintage | F | VF | XF | Unc | BU |
|---|---|---|---|---|---|---|
| 1985 Proof | 2,000 | Value: 7.50 | | | | |

**10 GRANI** **KM# M113** **Composition:** Bronze **Ruler:** Fr. Angelo de Mojana di Cologna Grand Master **Reverse:** Grotto of Apparitions at Lourdes

| Date | Mintage | F | VF | XF | Unc | BU |
|---|---|---|---|---|---|---|
| 1986 Proof | 2,000 | Value: 7.50 | | | | |

**10 GRANI** **KM# M118** **Composition:** Bronze **Ruler:** Fr. Angelo de Mojana di Cologna Grand Master **Subject:** 25th anniversary of Fr. A. de Mojana

| Date | Mintage | F | VF | XF | Unc | BU |
|---|---|---|---|---|---|---|
| 1987 Proof | 2,000 | Value: 7.50 | | | | |

**10 GRANI** **KM# M124** **Composition:** Bronze **Ruler:** Fr. Angelo de Mojana di Cologna Grand Master **Obverse:** Fr. A. de Mojana

| Date | Mintage | F | VF | XF | Unc | BU |
|---|---|---|---|---|---|---|
| 1988 Proof | 2,000 | Value: 7.50 | | | | |

**10 GRANI** **KM# M130** **Composition:** Bronze **Ruler:** Fr. Giancarlo Pallavicini Temporary Grand Master **Subject:** Interregnum **Obverse:** Maltese cross **Reverse:** St. John the Baptist

| Date | Mintage | F | VF | XF | Unc | BU |
|---|---|---|---|---|---|---|
| 1988 Proof | 2,000 | Value: 7.50 | | | | |

**10 GRANI** **KM# M136** **Composition:** Bronze **Ruler:** Fr. Andreas Bertie Grand Master **Obverse:** Fr. Andreas Bertie bust facing left

| Date | Mintage | F | VF | XF | Unc | BU |
|---|---|---|---|---|---|---|
| 1988 Proof | Inc. above | Value: 7.50 | | | | |

**10 GRANI** **KM# M142** **Composition:** Bronze **Ruler:** Fr. Andreas Bertie Grand Master

| Date | Mintage | F | VF | XF | Unc | BU |
|---|---|---|---|---|---|---|
| 1989 Proof | 2,000 | Value: 7.50 | | | | |

**10 GRANI** **KM# M148** **Composition:** Bronze **Ruler:** Fr. Andreas Bertie Grand Master

| Date | Mintage | F | VF | XF | Unc | BU |
|---|---|---|---|---|---|---|
| 1990 Proof | 2,000 | Value: 7.50 | | | | |

**10 GRANI** **KM# M153** **Composition:** Bronze **Ruler:** Fr. Andreas Bertie Grand Master **Reverse:** St. John kneeling in prayer

| Date | Mintage | F | VF | XF | Unc | BU |
|---|---|---|---|---|---|---|
| 1991 Proof | 2,000 | Value: 7.50 | | | | |

**10 GRANI** **KM# M158** **Composition:** Bronze **Ruler:** Fr. Andreas Bertie Grand Master

| Date | Mintage | F | VF | XF | Unc | BU |
|---|---|---|---|---|---|---|
| 1992 Proof | 2,000 | Value: 7.50 | | | | |

**10 GRANI** **KM# M164** **Composition:** Bronze **Ruler:** Fr. Andreas Bertie Grand Master

| Date | Mintage | F | VF | XF | Unc | BU |
|---|---|---|---|---|---|---|
| 1993 Proof | 2,000 | Value: 7.50 | | | | |

**10 GRANI** **KM# M170** **Composition:** Bronze **Ruler:** Fr. Andreas Bertie Grand Master

| Date | Mintage | F | VF | XF | Unc | BU |
|---|---|---|---|---|---|---|
| 1994 Proof | 2,000 | Value: 7.50 | | | | |

**10 GRANI** **KM# M176** **Composition:** Bronze **Ruler:** Fr. Andreas Bertie Grand Master

| Date | Mintage | F | VF | XF | Unc | BU |
|---|---|---|---|---|---|---|
| 1994 Proof | 2,000 | Value: 7.50 | | | | |

**2 TARI** **KM# M23.1** **Composition:** Bronze **Ruler:** Fr. Angelo de Mojana di Cologna Grand Master **Series:** F.A.O. **Note:** 1 millimeter thick.

| Date | Mintage | F | VF | XF | Unc | BU |
|---|---|---|---|---|---|---|
| 1968 Proof | 20,000 | Value: 5.50 | | | | |

**2 TARI** **KM# M23.2** **Composition:** Bronze **Ruler:** Fr. Angelo de Mojana di Cologna Grand Master **Series:** F.A.O. **Note:** 2 millimeters thick.

| Date | Mintage | F | VF | XF | Unc | BU |
|---|---|---|---|---|---|---|
| 1968 Proof | Inc. above | Value: 6.00 | | | | |

**9 TARI** **KM# M18** **Weight:** 9.0000 g. **Composition:** 0.9000 Silver .2604 oz. ASW **Ruler:** Fr. Angelo de Mojana di Cologna Grand Master **Obv. Legend:** F. ANGELVS DE MOJANA ...

| Date | Mintage | F | VF | XF | Unc | BU |
|---|---|---|---|---|---|---|
| 1967 Proof | 10,000 | Value: 10.00 | | | | |

**9 TARI** **KM# M30** **Weight:** 9.0000 g. **Composition:** 0.9000 Silver .2604 oz. ASW **Ruler:** Fr. Angelo de Mojana di Cologna Grand Master

| Date | Mintage | F | VF | XF | Unc | BU |
|---|---|---|---|---|---|---|
| 1969 Proof | 3,000 | Value: 10.00 | | | | |

**9 TARI** **KM# M36** **Weight:** 9.0000 g. **Composition:** 0.9000 Silver .2604 oz. ASW **Ruler:** Fr. Angelo de Mojana di Cologna Grand Master **Reverse:** Head of St. John the Baptist

| Date | Mintage | F | VF | XF | Unc | BU |
|---|---|---|---|---|---|---|
| 1970 Proof | 3,000 | Value: 10.00 | | | | |

**9 TARI** **KM# M41** **Weight:** 9.0000 g. **Composition:** 0.9000 Silver .2604 oz. ASW **Ruler:** Fr. Angelo de Mojana di Cologna Grand Master

| Date | Mintage | F | VF | XF | Unc | BU |
|---|---|---|---|---|---|---|
| 1971 Proof | 3,000 | Value: 10.00 | | | | |

**9 TARI** **KM# M47** **Weight:** 9.0000 g. **Composition:** 0.9000 Silver .2604 oz. ASW **Ruler:** Fr. Angelo de Mojana di Cologna Grand Master **Subject:** 400th anniversary - Battle of Lepanto

| Date | Mintage | F | VF | XF | Unc | BU |
|---|---|---|---|---|---|---|
| 1971 Proof | 5,000 | Value: 12.00 | | | | |

**9 TARI** **KM# M49** **Weight:** 9.0000 g. **Composition:** 0.9000 Silver .2604 oz. ASW **Ruler:** Fr. Angelo de Mojana di Cologna Grand Master **Obverse:** Fr. Angelvs de Mojana bust facing left

| Date | Mintage | F | VF | XF | Unc | BU |
|---|---|---|---|---|---|---|
| 1972 Proof | 3,000 | Value: 10.00 | | | | |

**9 TARI** **KM# M53** **Weight:** 9.0000 g. **Composition:** 0.9000 Silver .2604 oz. ASW **Ruler:** Fr. Angelo de Mojana di Cologna Grand Master

| Date | Mintage | F | VF | XF | Unc | BU |
|---|---|---|---|---|---|---|
| 1973 Proof | 3,000 | Value: 10.00 | | | | |

**9 TARI** **KM# M57** **Weight:** 9.0000 g. **Composition:** 0.9000 Silver .2604 oz. ASW **Ruler:** Fr. Angelo de Mojana di Cologna Grand Master

| Date | Mintage | F | VF | XF | Unc | BU |
|---|---|---|---|---|---|---|
| 1974 Proof | 3,000 | Value: 11.50 | | | | |
| 1975 Proof | 3,000 | Value: 11.50 | | | | |
| 1976 Proof | 3,000 | Value: 11.50 | | | | |
| 1977 Proof | 3,000 | Value: 11.50 | | | | |

**9 TARI** **KM# M71** **Weight:** 9.0000 g. **Composition:** 0.9000 Silver .2604 oz. ASW **Ruler:** Fr. Angelo de Mojana di Cologna Grand Master

| Date | Mintage | F | VF | XF | Unc | BU |
|---|---|---|---|---|---|---|
| 1978 Proof | 3,000 | Value: 11.50 | | | | |

**9 TARI** **KM# M75** **Weight:** 9.0000 g. **Composition:** 0.9000 Silver .2604 oz. ASW **Ruler:** Fr. Angelo de Mojana di Cologna Grand Master

| Date | Mintage | F | VF | XF | Unc | BU |
|---|---|---|---|---|---|---|
| 1979 Proof | 3,000 | Value: 11.50 | | | | |

**9 TARI** **KM# M81** **Weight:** 9.0000 g. **Composition:** 0.9000 Silver .2604 oz. ASW **Ruler:** Fr. Angelo de Mojana di Cologna Grand Master

| Date | Mintage | F | VF | XF | Unc | BU |
|---|---|---|---|---|---|---|
| 1980 Proof | 3,000 | Value: 13.50 | | | | |

**9 TARI** **KM# M86** **Weight:** 9.0000 g. **Composition:** 0.9000 Silver .2604 oz. ASW **Ruler:** Fr. Angelo de Mojana di Cologna Grand Master **Series:** International Year of Disabled Persons

| Date | Mintage | F | VF | XF | Unc | BU |
|---|---|---|---|---|---|---|
| 1981 Proof | 3,000 | Value: 18.50 | | | | |

**9 TARI** **KM# M91** **Weight:** 9.0000 g. **Composition:** 0.9000 Silver .2604 oz. ASW **Ruler:** Fr. Angelo de Mojana di Cologna Grand Master **Subject:** 20th anniversary of Fr. A. de Mojana

| Date | Mintage | F | VF | XF | Unc | BU |
|---|---|---|---|---|---|---|
| 1982 Proof | 2,000 | Value: 16.50 | | | | |

**9 TARI** **KM# M97** **Weight:** 9.0000 g. **Composition:** 0.9000 Silver .2604 oz. ASW **Ruler:** Fr. Angelo de Mojana di Cologna Grand Master

| Date | Mintage | F | VF | XF | Unc | BU |
|---|---|---|---|---|---|---|
| 1983 Proof | 2,000 | Value: 16.50 | | | | |

**9 TARI** **KM# M103** **Weight:** 9.0000 g. **Composition:** 0.9000 Silver .2604 oz. ASW **Ruler:** Fr. Angelo de Mojana di Cologna Grand Master

| Date | Mintage | F | VF | XF | Unc | BU |
|---|---|---|---|---|---|---|
| 1984 Proof | 2,000 | Value: 16.50 | | | | |

**9 TARI** **KM# M109** **Weight:** 9.0000 g. **Composition:** 0.9000 Silver .2604 oz. ASW **Ruler:** Fr. Angelo de Mojana di Cologna Grand Master

| Date | Mintage | F | VF | XF | Unc | BU |
|---|---|---|---|---|---|---|
| 1985 Proof | 2,000 | Value: 16.50 | | | | |

**9 TARI** **KM# M114** **Weight:** 9.0000 g. **Composition:** 0.9000 Silver .2604 oz. ASW **Ruler:** Fr. Angelo de Mojana di Cologna Grand Master **Reverse:** Basilica at Lourdes

| Date | Mintage | F | VF | XF | Unc | BU |
|---|---|---|---|---|---|---|
| 1986 Proof | 2,000 | Value: 16.50 | | | | |

**9 TARI** **KM# M119** **Weight:** 9.0000 g. **Composition:** 0.9000 Silver .2604 oz. ASW **Ruler:** Fr. Angelo de Mojana di Cologna Grand Master **Subject:** 25th anniversary of Fr. A. de Mojana

| Date | Mintage | F | VF | XF | Unc | BU |
|---|---|---|---|---|---|---|
| 1987 Proof | 2,000 | Value: 16.50 | | | | |

**9 TARI** **KM# M125** **Weight:** 9.0000 g. **Composition:** 0.9000 Silver .2604 oz. ASW **Ruler:** Fr. Angelo de Mojana di Cologna Grand Master

| Date | Mintage | F | VF | XF | Unc | BU |
|---|---|---|---|---|---|---|
| 1988 Proof | 2,000 | Value: 16.50 | | | | |

**9 TARI** **KM# M131** **Weight:** 9.0000 g. **Composition:** 0.9000 Silver .2604 oz. ASW **Ruler:** Fr. Giancarlo Pallavicini Temporary Grand Master **Subject:** Interregnum **Reverse:** St. John the Baptist

| Date | Mintage | F | VF | XF | Unc | BU |
|---|---|---|---|---|---|---|
| 1988 Proof | — | Value: 16.50 | | | | |

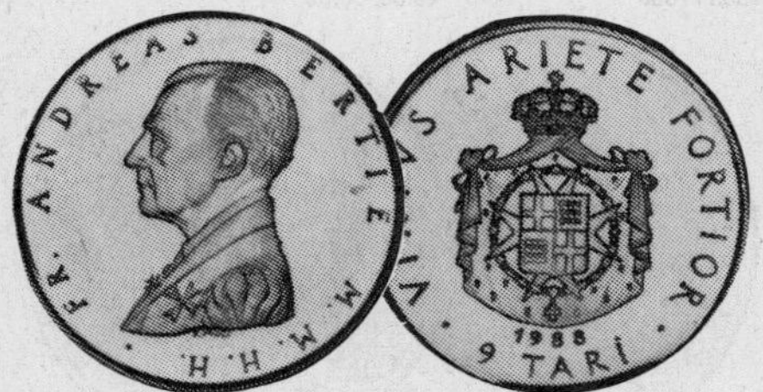

**9 TARI** **KM# M137** **Weight:** 9.0000 g. **Composition:** 0.9000 Silver .2604 oz. ASW **Ruler:** Fr. Andreas Bertie Grand Master **Obverse:** Fr. Andreas Bertie bust facing left

| Date | Mintage | F | VF | XF | Unc | BU |
|---|---|---|---|---|---|---|
| 1988 Proof | — | Value: 16.50 | | | | |

**9 TARI** **KM# M143** **Weight:** 9.0000 g. **Composition:** 0.9000 Silver .2604 oz. ASW **Ruler:** Fr. Andreas Bertie Grand Master

| Date | Mintage | F | VF | XF | Unc | BU |
|---|---|---|---|---|---|---|
| 1989 Proof | 2,000 | Value: 16.50 | | | | |

**9 TARI** **KM# M149** **Weight:** 8.0000 g. **Composition:** 0.9860 Silver .2536 oz. ASW **Ruler:** Fr. Andreas Bertie Grand Master

| Date | Mintage | F | VF | XF | Unc | BU |
|---|---|---|---|---|---|---|
| 1990 Proof | 2,000 | Value: 13.50 | | | | |

**9 TARI** **KM# M154** **Weight:** 8.0000 g. **Composition:** 0.9860 Silver .2536 oz. ASW **Ruler:** Fr. Andreas Bertie Grand Master **Reverse:** St. John welcoming group of people

| Date | Mintage | F | VF | XF | Unc | BU |
|---|---|---|---|---|---|---|
| 1991 Proof | 2,000 | Value: 13.50 | | | | |

**9 TARI** **KM# M159** **Weight:** 8.0000 g. **Composition:** 0.9860 Silver .2536 oz. ASW **Ruler:** Fr. Andreas Bertie Grand Master

| Date | Mintage | F | VF | XF | Unc | BU |
|---|---|---|---|---|---|---|
| 1992 Proof | 2,000 | Value: 13.50 | | | | |

**9 TARI** **KM# M165** **Weight:** 8.0000 g. **Composition:** 0.9860 Silver .2536 oz. ASW **Ruler:** Fr. Andreas Bertie Grand Master

| Date | Mintage | F | VF | XF | Unc | BU |
|---|---|---|---|---|---|---|
| 1993 Proof | 2,000 | Value: 13.50 | | | | |

**9 TARI** **KM# M171** **Weight:** 8.0000 g. **Composition:** 0.9860 Silver .2536 oz. ASW **Ruler:** Fr. Andreas Bertie Grand Master

| Date | Mintage | F | VF | XF | Unc | BU |
|---|---|---|---|---|---|---|
| 1994 Proof | 2,000 | Value: 13.50 | | | | |

**9 TARI** **KM# M177** **Weight:** 8.0000 g. **Composition:** 0.9860 Silver .2536 oz. ASW **Ruler:** Fr. Andreas Bertie Grand Master

| Date | Mintage | F | VF | XF | Unc | BU |
|---|---|---|---|---|---|---|
| 1995 Proof | 2,000 | Value: 13.50 | | | | |

**SCUDO** **KM# M1** **Weight:** 12.0000 g. **Composition:** 0.9860 Silver .3804 oz. ASW **Ruler:** Ernesto Paterno-Castello di Carcaci Lieutenant Grand Master

| Date | Mintage | F | VF | XF | Unc | BU |
|---|---|---|---|---|---|---|
| 1961 Proof | 1,200 | Value: 15.00 | | | | |

**SCUDO** **KM# M5** **Weight:** 12.0000 g. **Composition:** 0.9860 Silver .3804 oz. ASW **Ruler:** Fr. Angelo de Mojana di Cologna Grand Master **Obv. Legend:** F. ANGELVS DE MOJANA ...

| Date | Mintage | F | VF | XF | Unc | BU |
|---|---|---|---|---|---|---|
| 1962 Proof | 200 | Value: 100 | | | | |
| 1963 Proof | 600 | Value: 30.00 | | | | |

**SCUDO** **KM# M9** **Weight:** 12.0000 g. **Composition:** 0.9860 Silver .3804 oz. ASW **Ruler:** Fr. Angelo de Mojana di Cologna Grand Master **Obverse:** F. Angelvs de Mojana

| Date | Mintage | F | VF | XF | Unc | BU |
|---|---|---|---|---|---|---|
| 1964 | 4,000 | — | — | — | 10.00 | — |
| 1964 Proof | 1,000 | Value: 12.50 | | | | |

**SCUDO** **KM# M13** **Weight:** 12.0000 g. **Composition:** 0.9860 Silver .3804 oz. ASW **Ruler:** Fr. Angelo de Mojana di Cologna Grand Master

| Date | Mintage | F | VF | XF | Unc | BU |
|---|---|---|---|---|---|---|
| 1965 Proof | 3,000 | Value: 12.00 | | | | |
| 1966 Proof | 3,000 | Value: 12.00 | | | | |

**SCUDO** **KM# M19** **Weight:** 12.0000 g. **Composition:** 0.9860 Silver .3804 oz. ASW **Ruler:** Fr. Angelo de Mojana di Cologna Grand Master

| Date | Mintage | F | VF | XF | Unc | BU |
|---|---|---|---|---|---|---|
| 1967 Proof | 3,000 | Value: 12.00 | | | | |

**SCUDO** **KM# M24** **Weight:** 12.0000 g. **Composition:** 0.9860 Silver .3804 oz. ASW **Ruler:** Fr. Angelo de Mojana di Cologna Grand Master

| Date | Mintage | F | VF | XF | Unc | BU |
|---|---|---|---|---|---|---|
| 1968 Proof | 3,000 | Value: 12.00 | | | | |

**SCUDO** **KM# M31** **Weight:** 12.0000 g. **Composition:** 0.9860 Silver .3804 oz. ASW **Ruler:** Fr. Angelo de Mojana di Cologna Grand Master

| Date | Mintage | F | VF | XF | Unc | BU |
|---|---|---|---|---|---|---|
| 1969 Proof | 3,000 | Value: 12.00 | | | | |

**SCUDO** **KM# M37** **Weight:** 12.0000 g. **Composition:** 0.9860 Silver .3804 oz. ASW **Ruler:** Fr. Angelo de Mojana di Cologna Grand Master

| Date | Mintage | F | VF | XF | Unc | BU |
|---|---|---|---|---|---|---|
| 1970 Proof | 3,000 | Value: 12.00 | | | | |

**SCUDO** **KM# M42** **Weight:** 12.0000 g. **Composition:** 0.9860 Silver .3804 oz. ASW **Ruler:** Fr. Angelo de Mojana di Cologna Grand Master

| Date | Mintage | F | VF | XF | Unc | BU |
|---|---|---|---|---|---|---|
| 1971 Proof | 3,000 | Value: 12.00 | | | | |

**SCUDO** **KM# M50** **Weight:** 12.0000 g. **Composition:** 0.9860 Silver .3804 oz. ASW **Ruler:** Fr. Angelo de Mojana di Cologna Grand Master

| Date | Mintage | F | VF | XF | Unc | BU |
|---|---|---|---|---|---|---|
| 1972 Proof | 3,000 | Value: 12.00 | | | | |

**SCUDO** **KM# M54** **Weight:** 12.0000 g. **Composition:** 0.9860 Silver .3804 oz. ASW **Ruler:** Fr. Angelo de Mojana di Cologna Grand Master

| Date | Mintage | F | VF | XF | Unc | BU |
|---|---|---|---|---|---|---|
| 1973 Proof | 3,000 | Value: 12.00 | | | | |

**SCUDO** **KM# M58** **Weight:** 12.0000 g. **Composition:** 0.9860 Silver .3804 oz. ASW **Ruler:** Fr. Angelo de Mojana di Cologna Grand Master

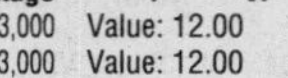

| Date | Mintage | F | VF | XF | Unc | BU |
|---|---|---|---|---|---|---|
| 1974 Proof | 3,000 | Value: 12.00 | | | | |
| 1975 Proof | 3,000 | Value: 12.00 | | | | |

**SCUDO** **KM# M64** **Weight:** 12.0000 g. **Composition:** 0.9860 Silver .3804 oz. ASW **Ruler:** Fr. Angelo de Mojana di Cologna Grand Master

| Date | Mintage | F | VF | XF | Unc | BU |
|---|---|---|---|---|---|---|
| 1976 Proof | 3,000 | Value: 12.00 | | | | |

**SCUDO** **KM# M67** **Weight:** 12.0000 g. **Composition:** 0.9860 Silver .3804 oz. ASW **Ruler:** Fr. Angelo de Mojana di Cologna Grand Master

| Date | Mintage | F | VF | XF | Unc | BU |
|---|---|---|---|---|---|---|
| 1977 Proof | 3,000 | Value: 12.00 | | | | |

**SCUDO** **KM# M72** **Weight:** 12.0000 g. **Composition:** 0.9860 Silver .3804 oz. ASW **Ruler:** Fr. Angelo de Mojana di Cologna Grand Master

| Date | Mintage | F | VF | XF | Unc | BU |
|---|---|---|---|---|---|---|
| 1978 Proof | 3,000 | Value: 12.00 | | | | |

**SCUDO** **KM# M76** **Weight:** 12.0000 g. **Composition:** 0.9860 Silver .3804 oz. ASW **Ruler:** Fr. Angelo de Mojana di Cologna Grand Master **Reverse:** Castle in Magione, Italy

| Date | Mintage | F | VF | XF | Unc | BU |
|---|---|---|---|---|---|---|
| 1979 Proof | 3,000 | Value: 12.00 | | | | |

**SCUDO** **KM# M82** **Weight:** 12.0000 g. **Composition:** 0.9860 Silver .3804 oz. ASW **Ruler:** Fr. Angelo de Mojana di Cologna Grand Master

| Date | Mintage | F | VF | XF | Unc | BU |
|---|---|---|---|---|---|---|
| 1980 Proof | 2,000 | Value: 25.00 | | | | |

**SCUDO** **KM# M87** **Weight:** 12.0000 g. **Composition:** 0.9860 Silver .3804 oz. ASW **Ruler:** Fr. Angelo de Mojana di Cologna Grand Master **Series:** World Food Day

| Date | Mintage | F | VF | XF | Unc | BU |
|---|---|---|---|---|---|---|
| ND(1981) Proof | 2,000 | Value: 28.50 | | | | |

**SCUDO** **KM# M92** **Weight:** 12.0000 g. **Composition:** 0.9860 Silver .3804 oz. ASW **Ruler:** Fr. Angelo de Mojana di Cologna Grand Master **Subject:** 20th anniversary of Fr. A. de Mojana

| Date | Mintage | F | VF | XF | Unc | BU |
|---|---|---|---|---|---|---|
| ND(1982) Proof | 2,000 | Value: 30.00 | | | | |

**SCUDO** **KM# M98** **Weight:** 12.0000 g. **Composition:** 0.9860 Silver .3804 oz. ASW **Ruler:** Fr. Angelo de Mojana di Cologna Grand Master

| Date | Mintage | F | VF | XF | Unc | BU |
|---|---|---|---|---|---|---|
| 1983 Proof | 2,000 | Value: 30.00 | | | | |

**SCUDO** **KM# M104** **Weight:** 12.0000 g. **Composition:** 0.9860 Silver .3804 oz. ASW **Ruler:** Fr. Angelo de Mojana di Cologna Grand Master

| Date | Mintage | F | VF | XF | Unc | BU |
|---|---|---|---|---|---|---|
| 1984 Proof | 2,000 | Value: 15.00 | | | | |

**SCUDO** **KM# M110** **Weight:** 12.0000 g. **Composition:** 0.9860 Silver .3804 oz. ASW **Ruler:** Fr. Angelo de Mojana di Cologna Grand Master

| Date | Mintage | F | VF | XF | Unc | BU |
|---|---|---|---|---|---|---|
| 1985 Proof | 2,000 | Value: 15.00 | | | | |

**SCUDO** **KM# M115** **Weight:** 12.0000 g. **Composition:** 0.9860 Silver .3804 oz. ASW **Ruler:** Fr. Angelo de Mojana di Cologna Grand Master **Obverse:** Similar to 2 Scudi, KM#M116 **Reverse:** Grotto of Apparitions at Lourdes

| Date | Mintage | F | VF | XF | Unc | BU |
|---|---|---|---|---|---|---|
| 1986 Proof | 2,000 | Value: 13.50 | | | | |

**SCUDO** **KM# M120** **Weight:** 12.0000 g. **Composition:** 0.9860 Silver .3804 oz. ASW **Ruler:** Fr. Angelo de Mojana di Cologna Grand Master **Subject:** 25th anniversary of Fr. A. de Mojana

| Date | Mintage | F | VF | XF | Unc | BU |
|---|---|---|---|---|---|---|
| 1987 | 2,000 | — | — | — | 12.50 | — |

**SCUDO** **KM# M126** **Weight:** 12.0000 g. **Composition:** 0.9860 Silver .3804 oz. ASW **Ruler:** Fr. Angelo de Mojana di Cologna Grand Master

| Date | Mintage | F | VF | XF | Unc | BU |
|---|---|---|---|---|---|---|
| 1988 Proof | 2,000 | Value: 12.50 | | | | |

**SCUDO** **KM# M138** **Weight:** 12.0000 g. **Composition:** 0.9860 Silver .3804 oz. ASW **Ruler:** Fr. Andreas Bertie Grand Master **Obverse:** Fr. Andreas Bertie bust facing left

| Date | Mintage | F | VF | XF | Unc | BU |
|---|---|---|---|---|---|---|
| 1988 Proof | 1,000 | Value: 12.50 | | | | |

**SCUDO** **KM# M132** **Weight:** 12.0000 g. **Composition:** 0.9860 Silver .3804 oz. ASW **Ruler:** Fr. Giancarlo Pallavicini Temporary Grand Master **Subject:** Interregnum **Obverse:** Maltese cross with legend SUB. HOC ... **Reverse:** St. John the Baptist

| Date | Mintage | F | VF | XF | Unc | BU |
|---|---|---|---|---|---|---|
| 1988 Proof | Inc. above | Value: 12.50 | | | | |

**SCUDO** **KM# M144** **Weight:** 12.0000 g. **Composition:** 0.9860 Silver .3804 oz. ASW **Ruler:** Fr. Andreas Bertie Grand Master

| Date | Mintage | F | VF | XF | Unc | BU |
|---|---|---|---|---|---|---|
| 1989 Proof | 2,000 | Value: 12.50 | | | | |

**SCUDO** **KM# M150** **Weight:** 12.0000 g. **Composition:** 0.9860 Silver .3804 oz. ASW **Ruler:** Fr. Andreas Bertie Grand Master

| Date | Mintage | F | VF | XF | Unc | BU |
|---|---|---|---|---|---|---|
| 1990 Proof | 2,000 | Value: 12.50 | | | | |

**SCUDO** **KM# M155** **Weight:** 12.0000 g. **Composition:** 0.9860 Silver .3804 oz. ASW **Ruler:** Fr. Andreas Bertie Grand Master **Reverse:** Dome in ornamental frame

| Date | Mintage | F | VF | XF | Unc | BU |
|---|---|---|---|---|---|---|
| 1991 Proof | 2,000 | Value: 12.50 | | | | |

**SCUDO** **KM# M160** **Weight:** 12.0000 g. **Composition:** 0.9860 Silver .3804 oz. ASW **Ruler:** Fr. Andreas Bertie Grand Master

| Date | Mintage | F | VF | XF | Unc | BU |
|---|---|---|---|---|---|---|
| 1992 Proof | 2,000 | Value: 12.50 | | | | |

**SCUDO** **KM# M166** **Weight:** 12.0000 g. **Composition:** 0.9860 Silver .3804 oz. ASW **Ruler:** Fr. Andreas Bertie Grand Master

| Date | Mintage | F | VF | XF | Unc | BU |
|---|---|---|---|---|---|---|
| 1993 Proof | 2,000 | Value: 12.50 | | | | |

**SCUDO** **KM# M172** **Weight:** 12.0000 g. **Composition:** 0.9860 Silver .3804 oz. ASW **Ruler:** Fr. Andreas Bertie Grand Master

| Date | Mintage | F | VF | XF | Unc | BU |
|---|---|---|---|---|---|---|
| 1994 Proof | 2,000 | Value: 12.50 | | | | |

**SCUDO** **KM# M178** **Weight:** 12.0000 g. **Composition:** 0.9860 Silver .3804 oz. ASW **Ruler:** Fr. Andreas Bertie Grand Master

| Date | Mintage | F | VF | XF | Unc | BU |
|---|---|---|---|---|---|---|
| 1995 Proof | 2,000 | Value: 12.50 | | | | |

**SCUDO** **KM# M189** **Weight:** 12.0000 g. **Composition:** 0.9860 Silver .3804 oz. ASW **Ruler:** Fr. Andreas Bertie Grand Master **Obverse:** Portrait left **Reverse:** Oar and wind driven galley **Edge:** Reeded **Size:** 32 mm.

| Date | Mintage | F | VF | XF | Unc | BU |
|---|---|---|---|---|---|---|
| 1997 Proof | — | Value: 15.00 | | | | |

**2 SCUDI** **KM# M2** **Weight:** 24.0000 g. **Composition:** 0.9860 Silver .7608 oz. ASW **Ruler:** Ernesto Paterno-Castello di Carcaci Lieutenant Grand Master

| Date | Mintage | F | VF | XF | Unc | BU |
|---|---|---|---|---|---|---|
| 1961 Proof | 1,200 | Value: 27.50 | | | | |

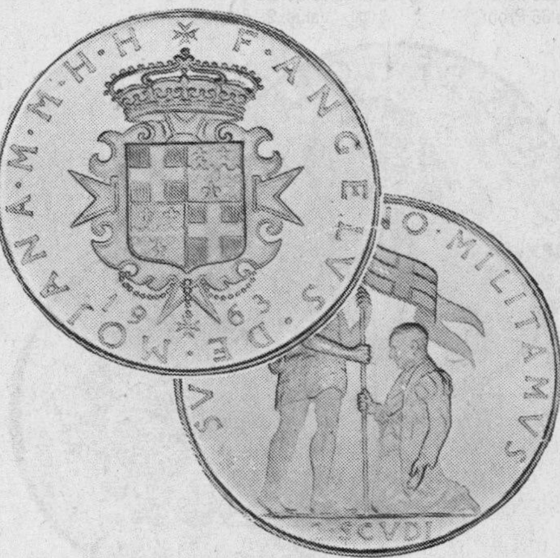

**2 SCUDI** **KM# M6** **Weight:** 24.0000 g. **Composition:** 0.9860 Silver .7608 oz. ASW **Ruler:** Fr. Angelo de Mojana di Cologna Grand Master **Obv. Legend:** F. ANGELVS DE MOJANA ...

| Date | Mintage | F | VF | XF | Unc | BU |
|---|---|---|---|---|---|---|
| 1962 Proof | 200 | Value: 160 | | | | |
| 1963 Proof | 600 | Value: 47.50 | | | | |

**2 SCUDI** **KM# M10** **Weight:** 24.0000 g. **Composition:** 0.9860 Silver .7608 oz. ASW **Ruler:** Fr. Angelo de Mojana di Cologna Grand Master

| Date | Mintage | F | VF | XF | Unc | BU |
|---|---|---|---|---|---|---|
| 1964 | 4,000 | — | — | — | 15.00 | — |
| 1964 Proof | 1,000 | Value: 20.00 | | | | |

**2 SCUDI** KM# M14 **Weight:** 24.0000 g. **Composition:** 0.9860 Silver .7608 oz. ASW **Ruler:** Fr. Angelo de Mojana di Cologna Grand Master

| Date | Mintage | F | VF | XF | Unc | BU |
|---|---|---|---|---|---|---|
| 1965 Proof | 3,000 | Value: 22.50 | | | | |
| 1966 Proof | 3,000 | Value: 22.50 | | | | |

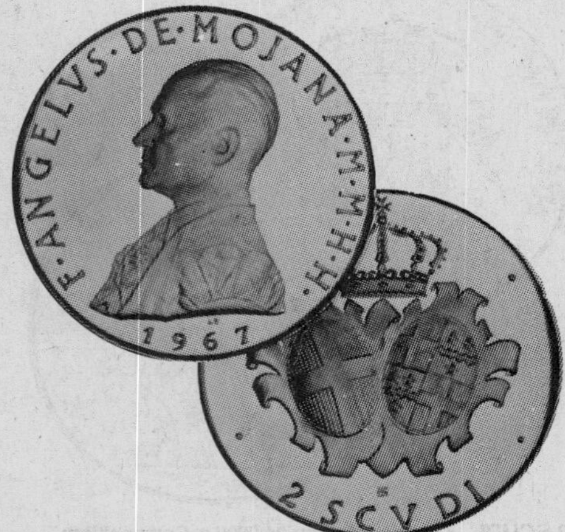


**2 SCUDI** KM# M20 **Weight:** 24.0000 g. **Composition:** 0.9860 Silver .7608 oz. ASW **Ruler:** Fr. Angelo de Mojana di Cologna Grand Master

| Date | Mintage | F | VF | XF | Unc | BU |
|---|---|---|---|---|---|---|
| 1967 Proof | 3,000 | Value: 22.50 | | | | |

**2 SCUDI** KM# M25 **Weight:** 24.0000 g. **Composition:** 0.9860 Silver .7608 oz. ASW **Ruler:** Fr. Angelo de Mojana di Cologna Grand Master

| Date | Mintage | F | VF | XF | Unc | BU |
|---|---|---|---|---|---|---|
| 1968 Proof | 3,000 | Value: 22.50 | | | | |

**2 SCUDI** KM# M32 **Weight:** 24.0000 g. **Composition:** 0.9860 Silver .7608 oz. ASW **Ruler:** Fr. Angelo de Mojana di Cologna Grand Master

| Date | Mintage | F | VF | XF | Unc | BU |
|---|---|---|---|---|---|---|
| 1969 Proof | 3,000 | Value: 22.50 | | | | |

**2 SCUDI** KM# M38 **Weight:** 24.0000 g. **Composition:** 0.9860 Silver .7608 oz. ASW **Ruler:** Fr. Angelo de Mojana di Cologna Grand Master

| Date | Mintage | F | VF | XF | Unc | BU |
|---|---|---|---|---|---|---|
| 1970 Proof | 3,000 | Value: 22.50 | | | | |

**2 SCUDI** KM# M43 **Weight:** 24.0000 g. **Composition:** 0.9860 Silver .7608 oz. ASW **Ruler:** Fr. Angelo de Mojana di Cologna Grand Master

| Date | Mintage | F | VF | XF | Unc | BU |
|---|---|---|---|---|---|---|
| 1971 Proof | 3,000 | Value: 22.50 | | | | |
| 1973 Proof | 3,000 | Value: 22.50 | | | | |

**2 SCUDI** KM# M51 **Weight:** 24.0000 g. **Composition:** 0.9860 Silver .7608 oz. ASW **Ruler:** Fr. Angelo de Mojana di Cologna Grand Master

| Date | Mintage | F | VF | XF | Unc | BU |
|---|---|---|---|---|---|---|
| 1972 Proof | 3,000 | Value: 22.50 | | | | |

**2 SCUDI** KM# M59 **Weight:** 24.0000 g. **Composition:** 0.9860 Silver .7608 oz. ASW **Ruler:** Fr. Angelo de Mojana di Cologna Grand Master

| Date | Mintage | F | VF | XF | Unc | BU |
|---|---|---|---|---|---|---|
| 1974 Proof | 3,000 | Value: 23.50 | | | | |

**2 SCUDI** KM# M60 **Weight:** 24.0000 g. **Composition:** 0.9860 Silver .7608 oz. ASW **Ruler:** Fr. Angelo de Mojana di Cologna Grand Master

| Date | Mintage | F | VF | XF | Unc | BU |
|---|---|---|---|---|---|---|
| 1975 Proof | 3,000 | Value: 22.50 | | | | |

**2 SCUDI** KM# M65 **Weight:** 24.0000 g. **Composition:** 0.9860 Silver .7608 oz. ASW **Ruler:** Fr. Angelo de Mojana di Cologna Grand Master

| Date | Mintage | F | VF | XF | Unc | BU |
|---|---|---|---|---|---|---|
| 1976 Proof | 3,000 | Value: 22.50 | | | | |

**2 SCUDI** KM# M68 **Weight:** 24.0000 g. **Composition:** 0.9860 Silver .7608 oz. ASW **Ruler:** Fr. Angelo de Mojana di Cologna Grand Master

| Date | Mintage | F | VF | XF | Unc | BU |
|---|---|---|---|---|---|---|
| 1977 Proof | 3,000 | Value: 22.50 | | | | |

**2 SCUDI** KM# M73 **Weight:** 24.0000 g. **Composition:** 0.9860 Silver .7608 oz. ASW **Ruler:** Fr. Angelo de Mojana di Cologna Grand Master

| Date | Mintage | F | VF | XF | Unc | BU |
|---|---|---|---|---|---|---|
| 1978 Proof | 3,000 | Value: 27.50 | | | | |

**2 SCUDI** **KM# M77** **Weight:** 24.0000 g. **Composition:** 0.9860 Silver .7608 oz. ASW **Ruler:** Fr. Angelo de Mojana di Cologna Grand Master **Reverse:** Castle in Ipplis Premariacco, Italy

| Date | Mintage | F | VF | XF | Unc | BU |
|---|---|---|---|---|---|---|
| 1979 Proof | 3,000 | Value: 22.50 | | | | |

**2 SCUDI** **KM# M83** **Weight:** 24.0000 g. **Composition:** 0.9860 Silver .7608 oz. ASW **Ruler:** Fr. Angelo de Mojana di Cologna Grand Master

| Date | Mintage | F | VF | XF | Unc | BU |
|---|---|---|---|---|---|---|
| 1980 Proof | 2,000 | Value: 50.00 | | | | |

**2 SCUDI** **KM# M88** **Weight:** 24.0000 g. **Composition:** 0.9860 Silver .7608 oz. ASW **Ruler:** Fr. Angelo de Mojana di Cologna Grand Master **Series:** World Food Day

| Date | Mintage | F | VF | XF | Unc | BU |
|---|---|---|---|---|---|---|
| 1981 Proof | 2,000 | Value: 50.00 | | | | |

**2 SCUDI** **KM# M93** **Weight:** 24.0000 g. **Composition:** 0.9860 Silver .7608 oz. ASW **Ruler:** Fr. Angelo de Mojana di Cologna Grand Master **Subject:** 20th anniversary of Fr. A. de Mojana

| Date | Mintage | F | VF | XF | Unc | BU |
|---|---|---|---|---|---|---|
| ND(1982) Proof | 2,000 | Value: 50.00 | | | | |

**2 SCUDI** **KM# M99** **Weight:** 24.0000 g. **Composition:** 0.9860 Silver .7608 oz. ASW **Ruler:** Fr. Angelo de Mojana di Cologna Grand Master

| Date | Mintage | F | VF | XF | Unc | BU |
|---|---|---|---|---|---|---|
| 1983 Proof | 2,000 | Value: 30.00 | | | | |

**2 SCUDI** **KM# M105** **Weight:** 24.0000 g. **Composition:** 0.9860 Silver .7608 oz. ASW **Ruler:** Fr. Angelo de Mojana di Cologna Grand Master

| Date | Mintage | F | VF | XF | Unc | BU |
|---|---|---|---|---|---|---|
| 1984 Proof | 2,000 | Value: 30.00 | | | | |

**2 SCUDI** **KM# M111** **Weight:** 24.0000 g. **Composition:** 0.9860 Silver .7608 oz. ASW **Ruler:** Fr. Angelo de Mojana di Cologna Grand Master

| Date | Mintage | F | VF | XF | Unc | BU |
|---|---|---|---|---|---|---|
| 1985 Proof | 2,000 | Value: 30.00 | | | | |

**2 SCUDI** **KM# M116** **Weight:** 24.0000 g. **Composition:** 0.9860 Silver .7608 oz. ASW **Ruler:** Fr. Angelo de Mojana di Cologna Grand Master **Reverse:** Grotto of Apparitions at Lourdes

| Date | Mintage | F | VF | XF | Unc | BU |
|---|---|---|---|---|---|---|
| 1986 Proof | 2,000 | Value: 27.50 | | | | |

**2 SCUDI** **KM# M121** **Weight:** 24.0000 g. **Composition:** 0.9860 Silver .7608 oz. ASW **Ruler:** Fr. Angelo de Mojana di Cologna Grand Master **Subject:** 20th anniversary of Fr. A. de Mojana

| Date | Mintage | F | VF | XF | Unc | BU |
|---|---|---|---|---|---|---|
| 1987 Proof | 2,000 | Value: 27.50 | | | | |

**2 SCUDI** **KM# M127** **Weight:** 24.0000 g. **Composition:** 0.9860 Silver .7608 oz. ASW **Ruler:** Fr. Angelo de Mojana di Cologna Grand Master

| Date | Mintage | F | VF | XF | Unc | BU |
|---|---|---|---|---|---|---|
| 1988 Proof | 2,000 | Value: 27.50 | | | | |

**2 SCUDI** **KM# M133** **Weight:** 24.0000 g. **Composition:** 0.9860 Silver .7608 oz. ASW **Ruler:** Fr. Giancarlo Pallavicini Temporary Grand Master **Subject:** Interregnum **Obverse:** Maltese cross with legend SVB. HOC ... **Reverse:** St. John the Baptist

| Date | Mintage | F | VF | XF | Unc | BU |
|---|---|---|---|---|---|---|
| 1988 Proof | Inc. above | Value: 27.50 | | | | |

**2 SCUDI** **KM# M139** **Weight:** 24.0000 g. **Composition:** 0.9860 Silver .7608 oz. ASW **Ruler:** Fr. Andreas Bertie Grand Master **Obverse:** Fr. Andreas Bertie bust facing left

| Date | Mintage | F | VF | XF | Unc | BU |
|---|---|---|---|---|---|---|
| 1988 Proof | 1,000 | Value: 27.50 | | | | |

**2 SCUDI** **KM# M145** **Weight:** 24.0000 g. **Composition:** 0.9860 Silver .7608 oz. ASW **Ruler:** Fr. Andreas Bertie Grand Master **Subject:** John the Baptist

| Date | Mintage | F | VF | XF | Unc | BU |
|---|---|---|---|---|---|---|
| 1989 Proof | 2,000 | Value: 27.50 | | | | |

**2 SCUDI** **KM# M151** **Weight:** 24.0000 g. **Composition:** 0.9860 Silver .7608 oz. ASW **Ruler:** Fr. Andreas Bertie Grand Master

| Date | Mintage | F | VF | XF | Unc | BU |
|---|---|---|---|---|---|---|
| 1990 Proof | 2,000 | Value: 27.50 | | | | |

**2 SCUDI** **KM# M156** **Weight:** 24.0000 g. **Composition:** 0.9860 Silver .7608 oz. ASW **Ruler:** Fr. Andreas Bertie Grand Master **Reverse:** Order of Malta home building

| Date | Mintage | F | VF | XF | Unc | BU |
|---|---|---|---|---|---|---|
| 1991 Proof | 2,000 | Value: 27.50 | | | | |

**2 SCUDI** **KM# M161** **Weight:** 24.0000 g. **Composition:** 0.9860 Silver .7608 oz. ASW **Ruler:** Fr. Andreas Bertie Grand Master

| Date | Mintage | F | VF | XF | Unc | BU |
|---|---|---|---|---|---|---|
| 1992 Proof | 2,000 | Value: 27.50 | | | | |

**2 SCUDI** **KM# M167** **Weight:** 24.0000 g. **Composition:** 0.9860 Silver .7608 oz. ASW **Ruler:** Fr. Andreas Bertie Grand Master

| Date | Mintage | F | VF | XF | Unc | BU |
|---|---|---|---|---|---|---|
| 1993 Proof | 2,000 | Value: 27.50 | | | | |

**2 SCUDI** **KM# M173** **Weight:** 24.0000 g. **Composition:** 0.9860 Silver .7608 oz. ASW **Ruler:** Fr. Andreas Bertie Grand Master

| Date | Mintage | F | VF | XF | Unc | BU |
|---|---|---|---|---|---|---|
| 1994 Proof | 2,000 | Value: 27.50 | | | | |

**2 SCUDI** **KM# M179** **Weight:** 24.0000 g. **Composition:** 0.9860 Silver .7608 oz. ASW **Ruler:** Fr. Andreas Bertie Grand Master

| Date | Mintage | F | VF | XF | Unc | BU |
|---|---|---|---|---|---|---|
| 1995 Proof | 2,000 | Value: 27.50 | | | | |

**3 SCUDI** **KM# M26** **Weight:** 12.0000 g. **Composition:** 0.8000 Silver .3086 oz. ASW **Ruler:** Fr. Angelo de Mojana di Cologna Grand Master **Series:** F.A.O.

| Date | Mintage | F | VF | XF | Unc | BU |
|---|---|---|---|---|---|---|
| 1968 Proof | 20,000 | Value: 15.00 | | | | |

**5 SCUDI** **KM# M3** **Weight:** 4.0000 g. **Composition:** 0.9160 Gold .1179 oz. AGW **Ruler:** Ernesto Paterno-Castello di Carcaci Lieutenant Grand Master

| Date | Mintage | F | VF | XF | Unc | BU |
|---|---|---|---|---|---|---|
| 1961 Proof | 1,200 | Value: 100 | | | | |

**5 SCUDI** **KM# M7** **Weight:** 4.0000 g. **Composition:** 0.9200 Gold .1183 oz. AGW **Ruler:** Fr. Angelo de Mojana di Cologna Grand Master

| Date | Mintage | F | VF | XF | Unc | BU |
|---|---|---|---|---|---|---|
| 1962 Proof | 200 | Value: 325 | | | | |
| 1963 Proof | 600 | Value: 120 | | | | |

**5 SCUDI** **KM# M11** **Weight:** 4.0000 g. **Composition:** 0.9000 Gold .1157 oz. AGW **Ruler:** Fr. Angelo de Mojana di Cologna Grand Master **Obverse:** F. Angelvs de Mojana

| Date | Mintage | F | VF | XF | Unc | BU |
|---|---|---|---|---|---|---|
| 1964 Proof | 1,000 | Value: 100 | | | | |

**5 SCUDI** **KM# M15** **Weight:** 4.0000 g. **Composition:** 0.9000 Gold .1157 oz. AGW **Ruler:** Fr. Angelo de Mojana di Cologna Grand Master

| Date | Mintage | F | VF | XF | Unc | BU |
|---|---|---|---|---|---|---|
| 1965 Proof | 1,000 | Value: 100 | | | | |
| 1966 Proof | 600 | Value: 110 | | | | |

**5 SCUDI** **KM# M21** **Weight:** 4.0000 g. **Composition:** 0.9000 Gold .1157 oz. AGW **Ruler:** Fr. Angelo de Mojana di Cologna Grand Master

| Date | Mintage | F | VF | XF | Unc | BU |
|---|---|---|---|---|---|---|
| 1967 Proof | 1,000 | Value: 100 | | | | |

**5 SCUDI** **KM# M27** **Weight:** 4.0000 g. **Composition:** 0.9000 Gold .1157 oz. AGW **Ruler:** Fr. Angelo de Mojana di Cologna Grand Master

| Date | Mintage | F | VF | XF | Unc | BU |
|---|---|---|---|---|---|---|
| 1968 Proof | 1,000 | Value: 100 | | | | |

**5 SCUDI** **KM# M33.1** **Weight:** 4.0000 g. **Composition:** 0.9000 Gold .1157 oz. AGW **Ruler:** Fr. Angelo de Mojana di Cologna Grand Master

| Date | Mintage | F | VF | XF | Unc | BU |
|---|---|---|---|---|---|---|
| 1969 Proof | 1,000 | Value: 100 | | | | |

**5 SCUDI** **KM# M33.2** **Weight:** 4.0000 g. **Composition:** 0.9000 Gold .1157 oz. AGW **Ruler:** Fr. Angelo de Mojana di Cologna Grand Master

| Date | Mintage | F | VF | XF | Unc | BU |
|---|---|---|---|---|---|---|
| 1970 Proof | 1,000 | Value: 100 | | | | |

**5 SCUDI** **KM# M44** **Weight:** 4.0000 g. **Composition:** 0.9000 Gold .1157 oz. AGW **Ruler:** Fr. Angelo de Mojana di Cologna Grand Master

| Date | Mintage | F | VF | XF | Unc | BU |
|---|---|---|---|---|---|---|
| 1971 Proof | 1,000 | Value: 100 | | | | |
| 1972 Proof | 1,000 | Value: 100 | | | | |
| 1973 Proof | 1,000 | Value: 100 | | | | |
| 1974 Proof | 1,000 | Value: 100 | | | | |
| 1975 Proof | 1,000 | Value: 100 | | | | |

**5 SCUDI** **KM# M66** **Weight:** 4.0000 g. **Composition:** 0.9000 Gold .1157 oz. AGW **Ruler:** Fr. Angelo de Mojana di Cologna Grand Master

| Date | Mintage | F | VF | XF | Unc | BU |
|---|---|---|---|---|---|---|
| 1976 Proof | 1,000 | Value: 100 | | | | |
| 1977 Proof | 1,000 | Value: 100 | | | | |
| 1978 Proof | 1,000 | Value: 100 | | | | |

**5 SCUDI** **KM# M78** **Weight:** 4.0000 g. **Composition:** 0.9000 Gold .1157 oz. AGW **Ruler:** Fr. Angelo de Mojana di Cologna Grand Master

| Date | Mintage | F | VF | XF | Unc | BU |
|---|---|---|---|---|---|---|
| 1979 Proof | 1,000 | Value: 100 | | | | |
| 1980 Proof | 600 | Value: 135 | | | | |
| 1981 Proof | 1,000 | Value: 140 | | | | |

**5 SCUDI** **KM# M94** **Weight:** 4.0000 g. **Composition:** 0.9000 Gold .1157 oz. AGW **Ruler:** Fr. Angelo de Mojana di Cologna Grand Master **Subject:** 20th anniversary of Fr. A. de Mojana

| Date | Mintage | F | VF | XF | Unc | BU |
|---|---|---|---|---|---|---|
| 1982 Proof | 600 | Value: 150 | | | | |

**5 SCUDI** **KM# M100** **Weight:** 4.0000 g. **Composition:** 0.9000 Gold .1157 oz. AGW **Ruler:** Fr. Angelo de Mojana di Cologna Grand Master

| Date | Mintage | F | VF | XF | Unc | BU |
|---|---|---|---|---|---|---|
| 1983 Proof | 600 | Value: 125 | | | | |

**5 SCUDI** **KM# M106** **Weight:** 4.0000 g. **Composition:** 0.9000 Gold .1157 oz. AGW **Ruler:** Fr. Angelo de Mojana di Cologna Grand Master

| Date | Mintage | F | VF | XF | Unc | BU |
|---|---|---|---|---|---|---|
| 1984 Proof | 600 | Value: 125 | | | | |
| 1985 Proof | 600 | Value: 110 | | | | |
| 1986 Proof | 600 | Value: 110 | | | | |

**5 SCUDI** **KM# M122** **Weight:** 4.0000 g. **Composition:** 0.9000 Gold .1157 oz. AGW **Ruler:** Fr. Angelo de Mojana di Cologna Grand Master **Subject:** 25th anniversary of Fr. A. de Mojana

| Date | Mintage | F | VF | XF | Unc | BU |
|---|---|---|---|---|---|---|
| 1987 Proof | 600 | Value: 110 | | | | |

**5 SCUDI** **KM# M128** **Weight:** 4.0000 g. **Composition:** 0.9000 Gold .1157 oz. AGW **Ruler:** Fr. Angelo de Mojana di Cologna Grand Master **Obverse:** Shoulder-length portrait of Fr. A. de Mojana **Reverse:** Similar to KM#M106

| Date | Mintage | F | VF | XF | Unc | BU |
|---|---|---|---|---|---|---|
| 1988 Proof | 600 | Value: 110 | | | | |

**5 SCUDI** **KM# M134** **Weight:** 4.0000 g. **Composition:** 0.9000 Gold .1157 oz. AGW **Ruler:** Fr. Giancarlo Pallavicini Temporary Grand Master **Subject:** Interregnum **Obverse:** Maltese cross with legend SVB. HOC ... **Reverse:** St. John the Baptist

| Date | Mintage | F | VF | XF | Unc | BU |
|---|---|---|---|---|---|---|
| 1988 Proof | Inc. above | Value: 110 | | | | |

**5 SCUDI** **KM# M140** **Weight:** 4.0000 g. **Composition:** 0.9000 Gold .1157 oz. AGW **Ruler:** Fr. Andreas Bertie Grand Master **Obverse:** Fr. Andreas Bertie bust facing left

| Date | Mintage | F | VF | XF | Unc | BU |
|---|---|---|---|---|---|---|
| 1988 Proof | 500 | Value: 110 | | | | |

**5 SCUDI** **KM# M146** **Weight:** 4.0000 g. **Composition:** 0.9000 Gold .1157 oz. AGW **Ruler:** Fr. Andreas Bertie Grand Master

| Date | Mintage | F | VF | XF | Unc | BU |
|---|---|---|---|---|---|---|
| 1989 Proof | 600 | Value: 110 | | | | |
| 1990 Proof | 600 | Value: 110 | | | | |
| 1991 Proof | 600 | Value: 110 | | | | |

**5 SCUDI** **KM# M162** **Weight:** 4.0000 g. **Composition:** 0.9000 Gold .1157 oz. AGW **Ruler:** Fr. Andreas Bertie Grand Master

| Date | Mintage | F | VF | XF | Unc | BU |
|---|---|---|---|---|---|---|
| 1992 Proof | 600 | Value: 110 | | | | |

**5 SCUDI** **KM# M168** **Weight:** 4.0000 g. **Composition:** 0.9000 Gold .1157 oz. AGW **Ruler:** Fr. Andreas Bertie Grand Master

| Date | Mintage | F | VF | XF | Unc | BU |
|---|---|---|---|---|---|---|
| 1993 Proof | 600 | Value: 110 | | | | |

**10 SCUDI** **KM# M4** **Weight:** 8.0000 g. **Composition:** 0.9160 Gold .2358 oz. AGW **Ruler:** Ernesto Paterno-Castello di Carcaci Lieutenant Grand Master

| Date | Mintage | F | VF | XF | Unc | BU |
|---|---|---|---|---|---|---|
| 1961 Proof | 1,200 | Value: 170 | | | | |

**10 SCUDI** **KM# M8** **Weight:** 8.0000 g. **Composition:** 0.9200 Gold .2366 oz. AGW **Ruler:** Fr. Angelo de Mojana di Cologna Grand Master

| Date | Mintage | F | VF | XF | Unc | BU |
|---|---|---|---|---|---|---|
| 1962 Proof | 200 | Value: 500 | | | | |
| 1963 Proof | 600 | Value: 200 | | | | |

**10 SCUDI** **KM# M12** **Weight:** 8.0000 g. **Composition:** 0.9000 Gold .2314 oz. AGW **Ruler:** Fr. Angelo de Mojana di Cologna Grand Master

| Date | Mintage | F | VF | XF | Unc | BU |
|---|---|---|---|---|---|---|
| 1964 Proof | 1,000 | Value: 175 | | | | |

**10 SCUDI** **KM# M16** **Weight:** 8.0000 g. **Composition:** 0.9000 Gold .2314 oz. AGW **Ruler:** Fr. Angelo de Mojana di Cologna Grand Master

| Date | Mintage | F | VF | XF | Unc | BU |
|---|---|---|---|---|---|---|
| 1965 Proof | 1,000 | Value: 175 | | | | |
| 1966 Proof | 600 | Value: 200 | | | | |

**10 SCUDI** **KM# M22** **Weight:** 8.0000 g. **Composition:** 0.9000 Gold .2314 oz. AGW **Ruler:** Fr. Angelo de Mojana di Cologna Grand Master

| Date | Mintage | F | VF | XF | Unc | BU |
|---|---|---|---|---|---|---|
| 1967 Proof | 1,000 | Value: 175 | | | | |

**10 SCUDI** **KM# M28** **Weight:** 8.0000 g. **Composition:** 0.9000 Gold .2314 oz. AGW **Ruler:** Fr. Angelo de Mojana di Cologna Grand Master

| Date | Mintage | F | VF | XF | Unc | BU |
|---|---|---|---|---|---|---|
| 1968 Proof | 1,000 | Value: 175 | | | | |

**10 SCUDI** **KM# M34** **Weight:** 8.0000 g. **Composition:** 0.9000 Gold .2314 oz. AGW **Ruler:** Fr. Angelo de Mojana di Cologna Grand Master

| Date | Mintage | F | VF | XF | Unc | BU |
|---|---|---|---|---|---|---|
| 1969 Proof | 1,000 | Value: 175 | | | | |
| 1970 Proof | 1,000 | Value: 175 | | | | |

**10 SCUDI** **KM# M45** **Weight:** 8.0000 g. **Composition:** 0.9000 Gold .2314 oz. AGW **Ruler:** Fr. Angelo de Mojana di Cologna Grand Master **Obverse:** Bust of Fr. A. de Mojana left **Reverse:** Lamb of God with banner

| Date | Mintage | F | VF | XF | Unc | BU |
|---|---|---|---|---|---|---|
| 1971 Proof | 1,000 | Value: 175 | | | | |

**10 SCUDI** **KM# M52** **Weight:** 8.0000 g. **Composition:** 0.9000 Gold .2314 oz. AGW **Ruler:** Fr. Angelo de Mojana di Cologna Grand Master

| Date | Mintage | F | VF | XF | Unc | BU |
|---|---|---|---|---|---|---|
| 1972 Proof | 1,000 | Value: 175 | | | | |
| 1974 Proof | 1,000 | Value: 175 | | | | |

**10 SCUDI** **KM# M55** **Weight:** 8.0000 g. **Composition:** 0.9000 Gold .2314 oz. AGW **Ruler:** Fr. Angelo de Mojana di Cologna Grand Master

| Date | Mintage | F | VF | XF | Unc | BU |
|---|---|---|---|---|---|---|
| 1973 Proof | 1,000 | Value: 175 | | | | |

**10 SCUDI** **KM# M61** **Weight:** 8.0000 g. **Composition:** 0.9000 Gold .2314 oz. AGW **Ruler:** Fr. Angelo de Mojana di Cologna Grand Master

| Date | Mintage | F | VF | XF | Unc | BU |
|---|---|---|---|---|---|---|
| 1975 Proof | 1,000 | Value: 175 | | | | |
| 1976 Proof | 1,000 | Value: 175 | | | | |

**10 SCUDI** **KM# M69** **Weight:** 8.0000 g. **Composition:** 0.9000 Gold .2314 oz. AGW **Ruler:** Fr. Angelo de Mojana di Cologna Grand Master

| Date | Mintage | F | VF | XF | Unc | BU |
|---|---|---|---|---|---|---|
| 1977 Proof | 1,000 | Value: 175 | | | | |
| 1978 Proof | 1,000 | Value: 175 | | | | |

**10 SCUDI** **KM# M79** **Weight:** 8.0000 g. **Composition:** 0.9000 Gold .2314 oz. AGW **Ruler:** Fr. Angelo de Mojana di Cologna Grand Master

| Date | Mintage | F | VF | XF | Unc | BU |
|---|---|---|---|---|---|---|
| 1979 Proof | 1,000 | Value: 175 | | | | |

**10 SCUDI** **KM# M84** **Weight:** 8.0000 g. **Composition:** 0.9000 Gold .2314 oz. AGW **Ruler:** Fr. Angelo de Mojana di Cologna Grand Master

| Date | Mintage | F | VF | XF | Unc | BU |
|---|---|---|---|---|---|---|
| 1980 Proof | 600 | Value: 275 | | | | |

**10 SCUDI** **KM# M89** **Weight:** 8.0000 g. **Composition:** 0.9000 Gold .2314 oz. AGW **Ruler:** Fr. Angelo de Mojana di Cologna Grand Master **Series:** World Food Day

| Date | Mintage | F | VF | XF | Unc | BU |
|---|---|---|---|---|---|---|
| 1981 Proof | 1,000 | Value: 275 | | | | |

**10 SCUDI** **KM# M95** **Weight:** 8.0000 g. **Composition:** 0.9000 Gold .2314 oz. AGW **Ruler:** Fr. Angelo de Mojana di Cologna Grand Master **Subject:** 20th anniversary of Fr. A. de Mojana

| Date | Mintage | F | VF | XF | Unc | BU |
|---|---|---|---|---|---|---|
| 1982 Proof | 600 | Value: 285 | | | | |

**10 SCUDI** **KM# M101** **Weight:** 8.0000 g. **Composition:** 0.9000 Gold .2314 oz. AGW **Ruler:** Fr. Angelo de Mojana di Cologna Grand Master

| Date | Mintage | F | VF | XF | Unc | BU |
|---|---|---|---|---|---|---|
| 1983 Proof | 600 | Value: 225 | | | | |

**10 SCUDI** **KM# M107** **Weight:** 8.0000 g. **Composition:** 0.9000 Gold .2314 oz. AGW **Ruler:** Fr. Angelo de Mojana di Cologna Grand Master **Reverse:** Altar of Chiesa di Santa Maria al Aventino

| Date | Mintage | F | VF | XF | Unc | BU |
|---|---|---|---|---|---|---|
| 1984 Proof | 600 | Value: 225 | | | | |

**10 SCUDI** **KM# M112** **Weight:** 8.0000 g. **Composition:** 0.9000 Gold .2314 oz. AGW **Ruler:** Fr. Angelo de Mojana di Cologna Grand Master

| Date | Mintage | F | VF | XF | Unc | BU |
|---|---|---|---|---|---|---|
| 1985 Proof | 600 | Value: 225 | | | | |

**10 SCUDI** **KM# M117** **Weight:** 8.0000 g. **Composition:** 0.9000 Gold .2314 oz. AGW **Ruler:** Fr. Angelo de Mojana di Cologna Grand Master

| Date | Mintage | F | VF | XF | Unc | BU |
|---|---|---|---|---|---|---|
| 1986 Proof | 600 | Value: 225 | | | | |

**10 SCUDI** **KM# M123** **Weight:** 8.0000 g. **Composition:** 0.9000 Gold .2314 oz. AGW **Ruler:** Fr. Angelo de Mojana di Cologna Grand Master **Subject:** 25th anniversary of Fr. A. de Mojana

| Date | Mintage | F | VF | XF | Unc | BU |
|---|---|---|---|---|---|---|
| 1987 Proof | — | Value: 225 | | | | |

**10 SCUDI** **KM# M129** **Weight:** 8.0000 g. **Composition:** 0.9000 Gold .2314 oz. AGW **Ruler:** Fr. Angelo de Mojana di Cologna Grand Master **Obverse:** Shoulder-length portrait of Fr. A. Mojana left **Reverse:** Similar to KM#M112

| Date | Mintage | F | VF | XF | Unc | BU |
|---|---|---|---|---|---|---|
| 1988 Proof | 600 | Value: 225 | | | | |

**10 SCUDI** **KM# M135** **Weight:** 8.0000 g. **Composition:** 0.9000 Gold .2314 oz. AGW **Ruler:** Fr. Giancarlo Pallavicini Temporary Grand Master **Subject:** Interregnum **Obverse:** Maltese cross with legend SVB. HOC ... **Reverse:** St. John the Baptist

| Date | Mintage | F | VF | XF | Unc | BU |
|---|---|---|---|---|---|---|
| 1988 Proof | Inc. above | Value: 225 | | | | |

**10 SCUDI** **KM# M141** **Weight:** 8.0000 g. **Composition:** 0.9000 Gold .2314 oz. AGW **Ruler:** Fr. Giancarlo Pallavicini Temporary Grand Master **Obverse:** Fr. Andreas Bertie bust facing left

| Date | Mintage | F | VF | XF | Unc | BU |
|---|---|---|---|---|---|---|
| 1988 Proof | 500 | Value: 225 | | | | |

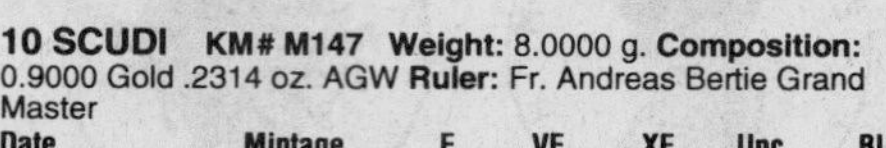

**10 SCUDI** **KM# M147** **Weight:** 8.0000 g. **Composition:** 0.9000 Gold .2314 oz. AGW **Ruler:** Fr. Andreas Bertie Grand Master

| Date | Mintage | F | VF | XF | Unc | BU |
|---|---|---|---|---|---|---|
| 1989 Proof | 600 | Value: 225 | | | | |

**10 SCUDI** **KM# M152** **Weight:** 8.0000 g. **Composition:** 0.9000 Gold .2314 oz. AGW **Ruler:** Fr. Andreas Bertie Grand Master

| Date | Mintage | F | VF | XF | Unc | BU |
|---|---|---|---|---|---|---|
| 1990 Proof | 600 | Value: 225 | | | | |

**10 SCUDI** **KM# M157** **Weight:** 8.0000 g. **Composition:** 0.9000 Gold .2314 oz. AGW **Ruler:** Fr. Andreas Bertie Grand Master **Reverse:** St. John tending the sick

| Date | Mintage | F | VF | XF | Unc | BU |
|---|---|---|---|---|---|---|
| 1991 Proof | 600 | Value: 225 | | | | |

**10 SCUDI** **KM# M163** **Weight:** 8.0000 g. **Composition:** 0.9000 Gold .2314 oz. AGW **Ruler:** Fr. Andreas Bertie Grand Master

| Date | Mintage | F | VF | XF | Unc | BU |
|---|---|---|---|---|---|---|
| 1992 Proof | 600 | Value: 225 | | | | |

**10 SCUDI** **KM# M169** **Weight:** 8.0000 g. **Composition:** 0.9000 Gold .2314 oz. AGW **Ruler:** Fr. Andreas Bertie Grand Master

| Date | Mintage | F | VF | XF | Unc | BU |
|---|---|---|---|---|---|---|
| 1993 Proof | 600 | Value: 225 | | | | |

**10 SCUDI** **KM# M174** **Weight:** 8.0000 g. **Composition:** 0.9000 Gold .2314 oz. AGW **Ruler:** Fr. Andreas Bertie Grand Master

| Date | Mintage | F | VF | XF | Unc | BU |
|---|---|---|---|---|---|---|
| 1994 Proof | 600 | Value: 225 | | | | |

**10 SCUDI** **KM# M180** **Weight:** 8.0000 g. **Composition:** 0.9000 Gold .2314 oz. AGW **Ruler:** Fr. Andreas Bertie Grand Master

| Date | Mintage | F | VF | XF | Unc | BU |
|---|---|---|---|---|---|---|
| 1995 Proof | 600 | Value: 225 | | | | |

**SOVRANO** **KM# M39** **Weight:** 8.0500 g. **Composition:** 0.9000 Gold .2329 oz. AGW **Ruler:** Fr. Angelo de Mojana di Cologna Grand Master **Obverse:** Fr. Angelus de Mojana bust facing left

| Date | Mintage | F | VF | XF | Unc | BU |
|---|---|---|---|---|---|---|
| 1970 Proof | 15,000 | Value: 150 | | | | |

## PROVAS

| KM# | Date | Mintage | Identification | Mkt Val |
|---|---|---|---|---|
| Pr1 | 1961 | — | Scudo. M1. | 30.00 |
| Pr2 | 1961 | — | 2 Scudi. M2. | 60.00 |
| Pr3 | 1961 | — | 5 Scudi. M3. | 125 |
| Pr4 | 1961 | — | 10 Scudi. M4. | 250 |
| Pr5 | 1968 | — | 2 Tari. M23. | 15.00 |
| Pr6 | 1968 | — | 3 Scudi. M26. | 30.00 |

## MINT SETS

| KM# | Date | Mintage | Identification | Issue Price | Mkt Val |
|---|---|---|---|---|---|
| MS1 | 1964 (2) | 4,000 | KMM9, M10 | — | 35.00 |

## PROOF SETS

| KM# | Date | Mintage | Identification | Issue Price | Mkt Val |
|---|---|---|---|---|---|
| PS1 | 1961 (4) | 1,200 | KMM1-M4 | — | 320 |
| PS2 | 1961 (4) | — | KMPr1-4 | — | 535 |
| PS3 | 1962 (4) | 200 | KMM5-M8 | — | 1,100 |
| PS4 | 1963 (4) | 600 | KMM5-M8 | — | 400 |
| PS5 | 1963 (2) | 1,000 | KMM5-M6 | — | 800 |
| PS6 | 1964 (4) | 1,000 | KMM9-M12 | — | 310 |
| PS7 | 1965 (4) | 1,000 | KMM13-M16 | — | 400 |
| PS8 | 1965 (2) | 4,000 | KMM13-M14 | — | 35.00 |
| PS10 | 1966 (2) | 4,000 | KMM13-M14 | — | 35.00 |
| PS9 | 1966 (4) | 600 | KMM13-M16 | — | 350 |
| PS11 | 1967 (4) | 1,000 | KMM19-M22 | 62.50 | 300 |
| PS12 | 1967 (2) | 2,000 | KMM19-M20 | 14.00 | 32.00 |
| PS13 | 1967 (2) | 10,000 | KMM17-M18 | 3.50 | 15.00 |
| PS14 | 1968 (4) | 1,000 | KMM24, M25, M27, M28 | 62.50 | 300 |
| PS15 | 1968 (2) | 2,000 | KMM24-M25 | 14.00 | 32.50 |
| PS16 | 1968 (2) | 20,000 | KMM23, M26 | 3.00 | 17.50 |

| KM# | Date | Mintage | Identification | Issue Price | Mkt Val |
|---|---|---|---|---|---|
| PS17 | 1969 (2) | 1,000 | KMM31, M34 | 75.00 | 300 |
| PS18 | 1969 (2) | 2,000 | KMM31-M32 | 17.00 | 32.50 |
| PS19 | 1969 (2) | 10,000 | KMM29-M30 | 3.00 | 15.00 |
| PS20 | 1970 (4) | 1,000 | KMM33, M34, M37, M38 | 75.00 | 300 |
| PS21 | 1970 (2) | 2,000 | KMM37-M38 | 17.00 | 32.50 |
| PS22 | 1970 (2) | 3,000 | KMM35-M36 | 3.00 | 15.00 |
| PS23 | 1971 (6) | 1,000 | KMM40-M45 | 78.00 | 320 |
| PS24 | 1971 (2) | 2,000 | KMM42-M43 | 17.00 | 32.50 |
| PS25 | 1971 (2) | 2,000 | KMM40-M41 | 3.00 | 15.00 |
| PS26 | 1971 (2) | 5,000 | KMM46-M47 | 5.00 | 17.50 |
| PS27 | 1972 (4) | 1,000 | KMM44, M50-M52 | 82.00 | 300 |
| PS28 | 1972 (2) | 2,000 | KMM50-M51 | 18.00 | 32.50 |
| PS29 | 1972 (2) | 3,000 | KMM49-M50 | 5.00 | 22.50 |
| PS30 | 1973 (6) | 1,000 | KMM43, M44, M48, M53-M55 | 110 | 225 |
| PS31 | 1973 (2) | 2,000 | KMM43, M54 | 12.00 | 32.50 |
| PS32 | 1973 (2) | 3,000 | KMM48, M53 | 6.00 | 15.00 |
| PS33 | 1974 (6) | 1,000 | KMM44, M52, M56-M59 | 170 | 320 |
| PS34 | 1974 (2) | 3,000 | KMM58-M59 | 33.00 | 35.00 |
| PS35 | 1974 (2) | 2,000 | KMM56-M57 | 8.00 | 17.50 |
| PS36 | 1975 (4) | 1,000 | KMM44, M58, M60, M61 | 170 | 310 |
| PS37 | 1975 (2) | 2,000 | KMM58, M60 | 30.00 | 32.50 |
| PS38 | 1975 (2) | 3,000 | KMM56-M57 | 8.00 | 17.50 |
| PS39 | 1976 (4) | 1,000 | KMM61, M64-M66 | 180 | 310 |
| PS40 | 1976 (2) | 2,000 | KMM64-M65 | 35.00 | 33.50 |
| PS41 | 1976 (2) | 3,000 | KMM56-M57 | 10.00 | 17.50 |
| PS42 | 1977 (4) | 1,000 | KMM66-M69 | — | 310 |
| PS43 | 1977 (2) | 2,000 | KMM67-M68 | — | 30.00 |
| PS44 | 1977 (2) | 3,000 | KMM56-M57 | — | 17.50 |
| PS45 | 1978 (4) | 1,000 | KMM66, M69, M72, M73 | — | 310 |
| PS46 | 1978 (2) | 2,000 | KMM72-M73 | — | 30.00 |
| PS47 | 1978 (2) | 3,000 | KMM70-M71 | — | 17.50 |
| PS48 | 1979 (3) | 1,000 | KMM76-M79 | — | 310 |
| PS49 | 1979 (2) | 2,000 | KMM76-M77 | — | 35.00 |
| PS50 | 1979 (2) | 3,000 | KMM74-M75 | — | 15.00 |
| PS51 | 1980 (4) | 600 | KMM78, M82-M84 | — | 385 |
| PS52 | 1980 (2) | 1,400 | KMM82-M83 | — | 40.00 |
| PS53 | 1980 (2) | 3,000 | KMM80-M81 | — | 21.50 |
| PS54 | 1981 (4) | 1,000 | KMM78, M87-M89 | — | 400 |
| PS55 | 1981 (2) | 1,000 | KMM87-M88 | — | 80.00 |
| PS56 | 1981 (2) | 3,000 | KMM85-M86 | — | 27.50 |
| PS57 | 1982 (4) | 600 | KMM92-M95 | — | 525 |
| PS58 | 1982 (2) | 1,400 | KMM92-M93 | — | 80.00 |
| PS59 | 1982 (2) | 2,000 | KMM90-M91 | — | 25.00 |
| PS60 | 1983 (4) | 600 | KMM98-M101 | — | 385 |
| PS61 | 1983 (2) | 1,400 | KMM98-M99 | — | 60.00 |
| PS62 | 1983 (2) | 2,000 | KMM96-M97 | — | 25.00 |
| PS63 | 1984 (4) | 600 | KMM104-M107 | — | 375 |
| PS64 | 1984 (2) | 1,400 | KMM104-M105 | — | 30.00 |
| PS65 | 1984 (2) | 2,000 | KMM102-M103 | — | 25.00 |
| PS66 | 1985 (4) | 600 | KMM106, M110-M112 | — | 375 |
| PS67 | 1985 (2) | 2,000 | KMM110-M111 | — | 45.00 |
| PS68 | 1985 (2) | 2,000 | KMM108-M109 | — | 25.00 |
| PS69 | 1986 (4) | 600 | KMM106, M115-M117 | 200 | 375 |
| PS70 | 1986 (2) | 2,000 | KMM115-M116 | 40.00 | 40.00 |
| PS71 | 1986 (2) | 2,000 | KMM113-M114 | 18.00 | 25.00 |
| PS72 | 1987 (2) | 600 | KMM122-M123 | — | 325 |
| PS73 | 1987 (2) | 2,000 | KMM120-M121 | — | 40.00 |
| PS74 | 1987 (2) | 2,000 | KMM118-M119 | — | 25.00 |
| PS75 | 1988 (2) | 600 | KMM128-M129 | — | 310 |
| PS76 | 1988 (2) | 2,000 | KMM126-M127 | — | 40.00 |
| PS78 | 1988 (2) | — | KMM134-M135 | — | 325 |
| PS82 | 1988 (2) | 1,000 | KMM138-M139 | — | 40.00 |
| PS79 | 1988 (2) | — | KMM132-M133 | — | 40.00 |
| PS80 | 1988 (2) | — | KM130-M131 | — | 25.00 |
| PS81 | 1988 (2) | 500 | KMM140-M141 | — | 325 |
| PS83 | 1988 (2) | — | KMM136-M137 | — | 25.00 |
| PS84 | 1989 (6) | — | KMM142-M147 | — | 400 |
| PS85 | 1989 (2) | — | KMM146-M147 | — | 325 |
| PS86 | 1989 (2) | — | KMM144-M145 | — | 40.00 |
| PS87 | 1989 (2) | — | KMM142-M143 | — | 25.00 |
| PS88 | 1990 (4) | — | KMM146, M150-M152 | — | 375 |
| PS89 | 1990 (2) | — | KMM148-M149 | — | 25.00 |
| PS90 | 1990 (2) | — | KMM150-M151 | — | 40.00 |
| PS91 | 1991 (4) | — | KMM146, M155-M157 | — | 375 |
| PS92 | 1991 (2) | — | KMM153-M154 | — | 25.00 |

## PROOF-LIKE DOLLARS

| KM# | Date | Mintage | Identification | Issue Price | Mkt Val |
|---|---|---|---|---|---|
| PS77 | 1988 (2) | 2,000 | KM124-M125 | — | 25.00 |

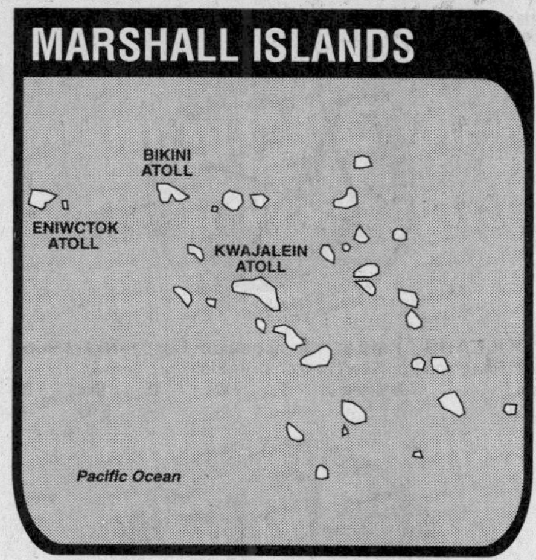


The Republic of the Marshall Islands, an archipelago which is one of the four island groups that make up what is commonly known as Micronesia, consists of 33 coral atolls comprised of over 1,150 islands or islets. It is located east of the Caroline Islands and west-northwest of the Gilbert Islands half way between Hawaii and Australia. The Ratak chain to the east and the Ralik chain to the west comprise a total land area of 70 sq. mi. (181 sq. km.) with a population of 25,000 of which about 10 % includes Americans who work at the Kwajalein Missile Range. Majuro Atoll is the government and commercial center of the Republic.

Very little is known of the history of the islands before the 16th century. It is believed that many countries vessels visited the islands while searching for new trade routes to the East. In 1788, John Marshall, a British sea captain for whom the islands were named, explored them. The Islands have undergone successive domination by the Spanish, Germans, Japanese and Americans. It was the site of some of the fiercest fighting of the entire Pacific theater during World War II. At the conclusion of the war, the United States, under the direction of the United Nations administered the affairs of the Marshall Islands.

A constitutional government was formed on May 1, 1979 with Amata Kabua being elected as the head of the government. On October 1, 1986, the United States notified the United Nations that the Marshall Islands were to be recognized as a separate nation.

The USA dollar is the current monetary system. Recently, the coinage has had limited redemption policies enforced.

**MINT MARKS**

M - Medallic Art Co.
R - Roger Williams Mint, Rhode Island
S - Sunshine Mining Co. Mint, Idaho

# REPUBLIC

## NON-CIRCULATING COLLECTOR COINAGE

The USA dollar is the current monetary system. Recently, the coinage has had limited redemption policies enforced.

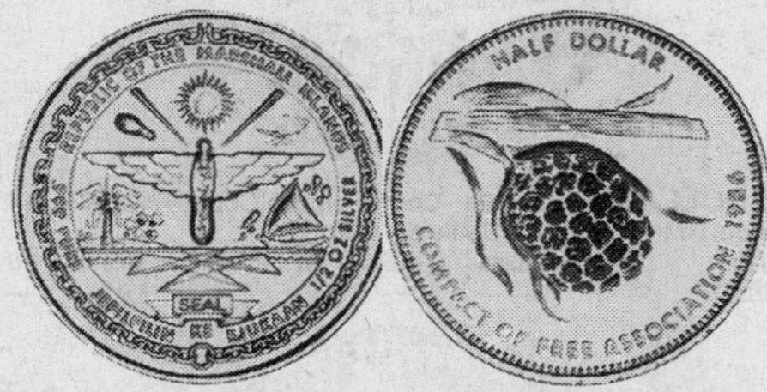


**1/2 DOLLAR** KM# 1 **Weight:** 15.5510 g. **Composition:** 0.9990 Silver .5000 oz. ASW **Reverse:** Pandanus Fruit

| Date | Mintage | F | VF | XF | Unc | BU |
|---|---|---|---|---|---|---|
| 1986 Proof | 10,000 | Value: 12.50 | | | | |

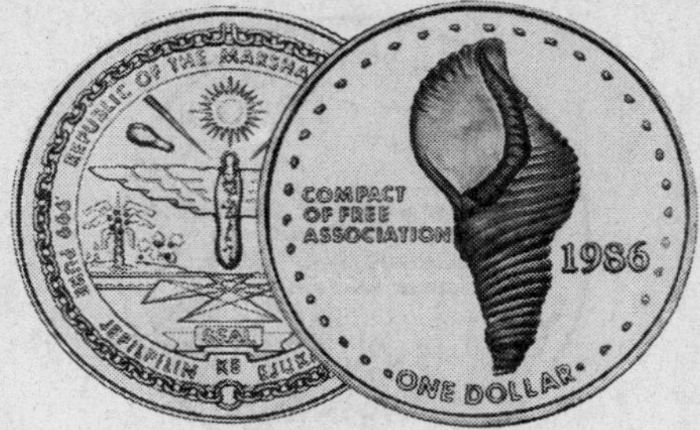


**DOLLAR** KM# 2 **Weight:** 31.1030 g. **Composition:** 0.9990 Silver 1.0000 oz. ASW **Obverse:** Similar to 1/2 Dollar, KM#1 **Reverse:** Triton Shell

| Date | Mintage | F | VF | XF | Unc | BU |
|---|---|---|---|---|---|---|
| 1986 Proof | 10,000 | Value: 25.00 | | | | |

**DOLLAR** KM# 293 **Weight:** 1.5552 g. **Composition:** 0.9990 Gold .0499 oz. AGW **Obverse:** Lion **Note:** Similar to 5 Dollars, KM#295.

| Date | Mintage | F | VF | XF | Unc | BU |
|---|---|---|---|---|---|---|
| 1996 | — | — | — | — | 45.00 | — |

**2-1/2 DOLLARS** KM# 294 **Weight:** 3.1103 g. **Composition:** 0.9990 Gold .0999 oz. AGW **Obverse:** Lion **Note:** Similar to 5 Dollars, KM#295.

| Date | Mintage | F | VF | XF | Unc | BU |
|---|---|---|---|---|---|---|
| 1996 | — | — | — | — | 85.00 | — |

**5 DOLLARS** KM# 6 **Composition:** Copper-Nickel **Subject:** U.S. Space Shuttle - Discovery

| Date | Mintage | F | VF | XF | Unc | BU |
|---|---|---|---|---|---|---|
| 1988 | 756,000 | — | — | — | 3.50 | — |
| 1988M | 431,000 | — | — | — | 4.50 | — |

**5 DOLLARS** KM# 13 **Composition:** Copper-Nickel **Subject:** 20th Anniversary - First Men on the Moon

| Date | Mintage | F | VF | XF | Unc | BU |
|---|---|---|---|---|---|---|
| 1989 | — | — | — | — | 3.50 | — |

**5 DOLLARS** KM# 18 **Composition:** Copper-Nickel **Subject:** 50th Anniversary - Battle of Britain

| Date | Mintage | F | VF | XF | Unc | BU |
|---|---|---|---|---|---|---|
| 1990M | — | — | — | — | 4.50 | — |

**5 DOLLARS** **KM# 33** **Composition:** Copper-Nickel **Subject:** German Unification

| Date | Mintage | F | VF | XF | Unc | BU |
|---|---|---|---|---|---|---|
| 1990M | — | — | — | — | 8.00 | — |

**5 DOLLARS** **KM# 38** **Composition:** Copper-Nickel **Subject:** Dwight David Eisenhower **Obverse:** Similar to KM#6

| Date | Mintage | F | VF | XF | Unc | BU |
|---|---|---|---|---|---|---|
| 1990M | — | — | — | — | 5.00 | — |

**5 DOLLARS** **KM# 35** **Composition:** Copper-Nickel **Subject:** To the Heroes of Pearl Harbor

| Date | Mintage | F | VF | XF | Unc | BU |
|---|---|---|---|---|---|---|
| 1991M | — | — | — | — | 4.00 | — |

**5 DOLLARS** **KM# 37** **Composition:** Copper-Nickel **Subject:** Space Shuttle Columbia

| Date | Mintage | F | VF | XF | Unc | BU |
|---|---|---|---|---|---|---|
| 1991M | — | — | — | — | 5.00 | — |

**5 DOLLARS** **KM# 40** **Composition:** Copper-Nickel **Subject:** To the Heroes of Desert Storm

| Date | Mintage | F | VF | XF | Unc | BU |
|---|---|---|---|---|---|---|
| 1991R | — | — | — | — | 5.50 | — |

**5 DOLLARS** **KM# 81** **Composition:** Copper-Nickel **Subject:** Reaching For New Horizons - Tipnol

| Date | Mintage | F | VF | XF | Unc | BU |
|---|---|---|---|---|---|---|
| 1992R | — | — | — | — | 6.00 | — |

**5 DOLLARS** **KM# 84** **Composition:** Copper-Nickel **Subject:** To the Heroes of the First Air Raid on Tokyo - Doolittle

| Date | Mintage | F | VF | XF | Unc | BU |
|---|---|---|---|---|---|---|
| 1992R | — | — | — | — | 5.50 | — |

**5 DOLLARS** **KM# 87** **Composition:** Copper-Nickel **Subject:** To the Heroes of Corregidor

| Date | Mintage | F | VF | XF | Unc | BU |
|---|---|---|---|---|---|---|
| 1992R | — | — | — | — | 8.00 | — |

**5 DOLLARS** **KM# 90** **Composition:** Copper-Nickel **Subject:** To the Heroes of Battle of Midway

| Date | Mintage | F | VF | XF | Unc | BU |
|---|---|---|---|---|---|---|
| 1992R | — | — | — | — | 8.00 | — |

**5 DOLLARS** **KM# 110** **Composition:** Copper-Nickel **Subject:** Pacific Whales & Dolphins **Reverse:** Humpback Whales

| Date | Mintage | F | VF | XF | Unc | BU |
|---|---|---|---|---|---|---|
| 1993R Prooflike | — | — | — | — | 10.00 | — |

**5 DOLLARS** **KM# 118** **Composition:** Copper-Nickel **Subject:** To the Heroes of the North Atlantic **Reverse:** Submarine

| Date | Mintage | F | VF | XF | Unc | BU |
|---|---|---|---|---|---|---|
| 1993R Prooflike | — | — | — | — | 6.00 | — |

**5 DOLLARS** **KM# 121** **Composition:** Copper-Nickel **Subject:** To the Heroes of Guadalcanal **Reverse:** Marine, Battleship & Airplanes

| Date | Mintage | F | VF | XF | Unc | BU |
|---|---|---|---|---|---|---|
| 1993R Prooflike | — | — | — | — | 6.00 | — |

**5 DOLLARS** **KM# 124** **Composition:** Copper-Nickel **Reverse:** Elvis Presley

| Date | Mintage | F | VF | XF | Unc | BU |
|---|---|---|---|---|---|---|
| 1993R Prooflike | — | — | — | — | 8.00 | — |

**5 DOLLARS** **KM# 126** **Composition:** Copper-Nickel **Subject:** Pacific Whales & Dolphins **Reverse:** Common Dolphin

| Date | Mintage | F | VF | XF | Unc | BU |
|---|---|---|---|---|---|---|
| 1993R Prooflike | — | — | — | — | 10.00 | — |

**5 DOLLARS** **KM# 144** **Composition:** Copper-Nickel **Subject:** Christmas 1993

| Date | Mintage | F | VF | XF | Unc | BU |
|---|---|---|---|---|---|---|
| 1993 | — | — | — | — | 8.50 | — |

**5 DOLLARS KM# 148 Composition:** Copper-Nickel **Subject:** Flight at Kitty Hawk

| Date | Mintage | F | VF | XF | Unc | BU |
|---|---|---|---|---|---|---|
| 1993 | — | — | — | — | 8.50 | — |

**5 DOLLARS KM# 151 Composition:** Copper-Nickel **Subject:** First Men on Moon

| Date | Mintage | F | VF | XF | Unc | BU |
|---|---|---|---|---|---|---|
| 1994 | — | — | — | — | 8.50 | — |

**5 DOLLARS KM# 179 Composition:** Copper-Nickel **Subject:** To the Heroes of D-Day - Normandy Invasion

| Date | Mintage | F | VF | XF | Unc | BU |
|---|---|---|---|---|---|---|
| 1994 | — | — | — | — | 8.50 | — |

**5 DOLLARS KM# 182 Composition:** Copper-Nickel **Subject:** To the Heroes of the Philippines **Reverse:** MacArthur and Staff

| Date | Mintage | F | VF | XF | Unc | BU |
|---|---|---|---|---|---|---|
| 1994 | — | — | — | — | 6.50 | — |

**5 DOLLARS KM# 263 Composition:** Copper-Nickel **Subject:** To the Heroes of the Battle of The Bulge

| Date | Mintage | F | VF | XF | Unc | BU |
|---|---|---|---|---|---|---|
| 1994 | — | — | — | — | 5.50 | — |

**5 DOLLARS KM# 187 Composition:** Copper-Nickel **Subject:** World Cup Soccer

| Date | Mintage | F | VF | XF | Unc | BU |
|---|---|---|---|---|---|---|
| 1994 | — | — | — | — | 5.50 | — |

**5 DOLLARS KM# 260 Composition:** Copper-Nickel **Subject:** Christmas - Cherub

| Date | Mintage | F | VF | XF | Unc | BU |
|---|---|---|---|---|---|---|
| 1994 | — | — | — | — | 5.50 | — |

**5 DOLLARS KM# 270 Composition:** Copper-Nickel **Reverse:** Tornado F. MK 3 - Bomber

| Date | Mintage | F | VF | XF | Unc | BU |
|---|---|---|---|---|---|---|
| 1995 | — | — | — | — | 6.00 | — |

**5 DOLLARS KM# 271 Composition:** Copper-Nickel **Subject:** Christmas **Reverse:** Cherub

| Date | Mintage | F | VF | XF | Unc | BU |
|---|---|---|---|---|---|---|
| 1995 | — | — | — | — | 5.50 | — |

**5 DOLLARS KM# 395 Composition:** Copper-Nickel **Obverse:** State seal **Reverse:** F-80 Shooting Star

| Date | Mintage | F | VF | XF | Unc | BU |
|---|---|---|---|---|---|---|
| 1995 | — | — | — | — | 6.50 | — |

**5 DOLLARS KM# 185 Composition:** Copper-Nickel **Reverse:** F-100 SUper Sabre

| Date | Mintage | F | VF | XF | Unc | BU |
|---|---|---|---|---|---|---|
| 1995 | — | — | — | — | 5.50 | — |

**5 DOLLARS KM# 186 Composition:** Copper-Nickel **Reverse:** F-16 Fighting Falcon

| Date | Mintage | F | VF | XF | Unc | BU |
|---|---|---|---|---|---|---|
| 1995 | — | — | — | — | 5.50 | — |

**5 DOLLARS KM# 216 Composition:** Copper-Nickel **Subject:** Peace - Victory in Europe

| Date | Mintage | F | VF | XF | Unc | BU |
|---|---|---|---|---|---|---|
| 1995 | — | — | — | — | 5.50 | — |

**5 DOLLARS** **KM# 219** **Composition:** Copper-Nickel **Subject:** To the Heroes of the Vietnam War

| Date | Mintage | F | VF | XF | Unc | BU |
|---|---|---|---|---|---|---|
| 1995 | — | — | — | — | 5.50 | — |

**5 DOLLARS** **KM# 222** **Composition:** Copper-Nickel **Reverse:** Elvis Presley

| Date | Mintage | F | VF | XF | Unc | BU |
|---|---|---|---|---|---|---|
| 1995 | — | — | — | — | 9.00 | — |

**5 DOLLARS** **KM# 253** **Composition:** Copper-Nickel **Reverse:** Marilyn Monroe

| Date | Mintage | F | VF | XF | Unc | BU |
|---|---|---|---|---|---|---|
| 1995 | — | — | — | — | 7.00 | — |

**5 DOLLARS** **KM# 257** **Composition:** Copper-Nickel **Series:** 50th Anniversary United Nations **Subject:** Peace

| Date | Mintage | F | VF | XF | Unc | BU |
|---|---|---|---|---|---|---|
| 1995 | — | — | — | — | 5.50 | — |

**5 DOLLARS** **KM# 266** **Composition:** Copper-Nickel **Subject:** Peace - VJ Day

| Date | Mintage | F | VF | XF | Unc | BU |
|---|---|---|---|---|---|---|
| 1995 | — | — | — | — | 5.50 | — |

**5 DOLLARS** **KM# 269** **Composition:** Copper-Nickel **Reverse:** Mirage 2000C Jet Fighter

| Date | Mintage | F | VF | XF | Unc | BU |
|---|---|---|---|---|---|---|
| 1995 | — | — | — | — | 6.00 | — |

**5 DOLLARS** **KM# 225** **Composition:** Copper-Nickel **Subject:** War in the Pacific **Note:** Similar to 10 Dollars, KM#226.

| Date | Mintage | F | VF | XF | Unc | BU |
|---|---|---|---|---|---|---|
| 1995 | — | — | — | — | 9.50 | — |

**5 DOLLARS** **KM# 308** **Composition:** Copper-Nickel **Subject:** Classic Cars **Reverse:** Ford Quadricycle **Note:** Similar to 10 Dollars, KM#309.

| Date | Mintage | F | VF | XF | Unc | BU |
|---|---|---|---|---|---|---|
| 1996 | — | — | — | — | 7.50 | — |

**5 DOLLARS** **KM# 331** **Composition:** Copper-Nickel **Subject:** Steam Locomotive **Reverse:** Big Boy **Note:** Similar to 50 Dollar, KM#292.

| Date | Mintage | F | VF | XF | Unc | BU |
|---|---|---|---|---|---|---|
| 1996 | — | — | — | — | 6.00 | — |

**5 DOLLARS** **KM# 297** **Composition:** Copper-Nickel **Reverse:** Tiger **Note:** Similar to 50 Dollars, KM#299.

| Date | Mintage | F | VF | XF | Unc | BU |
|---|---|---|---|---|---|---|
| 1996 | — | — | — | — | 16.50 | — |

**5 DOLLARS** **KM# 280** **Composition:** Copper-Nickel **Subject:** Year of the Rat

| Date | Mintage | F | VF | XF | Unc | BU |
|---|---|---|---|---|---|---|
| 1996 | — | — | — | — | 8.00 | — |

**5 DOLLARS** **KM# 288** **Composition:** Copper-Nickel **Reverse:** Space Shuttle Columbia

| Date | Mintage | F | VF | XF | Unc | BU |
|---|---|---|---|---|---|---|
| 1996 | — | — | — | — | 5.50 | — |

**5 DOLLARS** **KM# 295** **Weight:** 7.7759 g. **Composition:** 0.9990 Gold .2497 oz. AGW **Obverse:** State seal **Reverse:** Lion

| Date | Mintage | F | VF | XF | Unc | BU |
|---|---|---|---|---|---|---|
| 1996 | — | — | — | — | 200 | — |

**5 DOLLARS** **KM# 300** **Composition:** Copper-Nickel **Reverse:** Elvis Presley

| Date | Mintage | F | VF | XF | Unc | BU |
|---|---|---|---|---|---|---|
| 1996 | — | — | — | — | 9.00 | — |

**5 DOLLARS** **KM# 303** **Composition:** Copper-Nickel **Reverse:** James Dean

| Date | Mintage | F | VF | XF | Unc | BU |
|---|---|---|---|---|---|---|
| 1996 | — | — | — | — | 8.00 | — |

**5 DOLLARS** **KM# 311** **Composition:** Copper-Nickel **Subject:** Classic Cars **Reverse:** Model A Ford

| Date | Mintage | F | VF | XF | Unc | BU |
|---|---|---|---|---|---|---|
| 1996 | — | — | — | — | 7.00 | — |

**5 DOLLARS** **KM# 314** **Composition:** Copper-Nickel **Subject:** Classic Cars **Reverse:** Model T Ford

| Date | Mintage | F | VF | XF | Unc | BU |
|---|---|---|---|---|---|---|
| 1996 | — | — | — | — | 7.00 | — |

**5 DOLLARS** **KM# 317** **Composition:** Copper-Nickel **Subject:** Classic Cars **Reverse:** 1955 Thunderbird

| Date | Mintage | F | VF | XF | Unc | BU |
|---|---|---|---|---|---|---|
| 1996 | — | — | — | — | 8.50 | — |

**5 DOLLARS** **KM# 320** **Composition:** Copper-Nickel **Subject:** Classic Cars **Reverse:** 1964 Mustang

| Date | Mintage | F | VF | XF | Unc | BU |
|---|---|---|---|---|---|---|
| 1996 | — | — | — | — | 8.50 | — |

**5 DOLLARS** **KM# 323** **Composition:** Copper-Nickel **Subject:** Classic Cars **Reverse:** Ford Taurus

| Date | Mintage | F | VF | XF | Unc | BU |
|---|---|---|---|---|---|---|
| 1996 | — | — | — | — | 7.00 | — |

**5 DOLLARS** **KM# 330** **Composition:** Copper-Nickel **Subject:** Steam Locomotive **Reverse:** Pennsylvania K4

| Date | Mintage | F | VF | XF | Unc | BU |
|---|---|---|---|---|---|---|
| 1996 | — | — | — | — | 6.00 | — |

**5 DOLLARS** **KM# 344** **Composition:** Copper-Nickel **Reverse:** Lion

| Date | Mintage | F | VF | XF | Unc | BU |
|---|---|---|---|---|---|---|
| 1996 | — | — | — | — | 15.00 | — |

**5 DOLLARS** **KM# 345** **Composition:** Copper-Nickel **Reverse:** Cheetah

| Date | Mintage | F | VF | XF | Unc | BU |
|---|---|---|---|---|---|---|
| 1996 | — | — | — | — | 15.00 | — |

**5 DOLLARS** **KM# 346** **Composition:** Copper-Nickel **Reverse:** Jaguar

| Date | Mintage | F | VF | XF | Unc | BU |
|---|---|---|---|---|---|---|
| 1996 | — | — | — | — | 15.00 | — |

**5 DOLLARS** **KM# 353** **Composition:** Copper-Nickel **Subject:** Christmas **Reverse:** 20 Angels

| Date | Mintage | F | VF | XF | Unc | BU |
|---|---|---|---|---|---|---|
| 1996 | — | — | — | — | 7.50 | — |

**5 DOLLARS** **KM# 362** **Composition:** Copper-Nickel **Subject:** Year of the Ox **Obverse:** State seal **Reverse:** Stylized Ox

| Date | Mintage | F | VF | XF | Unc | BU |
|---|---|---|---|---|---|---|
| 1997 | — | — | — | — | 7.50 | — |

**5 DOLLARS** **KM# 364** **Composition:** Copper-Nickel **Reverse:** Elvis Presley

| Date | Mintage | F | VF | XF | Unc | BU |
|---|---|---|---|---|---|---|
| 1997 | — | — | — | — | 10.00 | — |

**5 DOLLARS** **KM# 398** **Composition:** Copper-Nickel **Subject:** History's Great Fighting Ships **Obverse:** State seal **Reverse:** USS Constitution

| Date | Mintage | F | VF | XF | Unc | BU |
|---|---|---|---|---|---|---|
| 1997 | — | — | — | — | 6.50 | — |

**5 DOLLARS** **KM# 403** **Composition:** Copper-Nickel **Subject:** Christmas **Obverse:** State seal **Reverse:** 2 Angels

| Date | Mintage | F | VF | XF | Unc | BU |
|---|---|---|---|---|---|---|
| 1997 | — | — | — | — | 6.00 | — |

**5 DOLLARS** **KM# 407** **Composition:** Copper-Nickel **Subject:** Sermon on the Mount **Obverse:** State seal **Reverse:** Jesus Preaching

| Date | Mintage | F | VF | XF | Unc | BU |
|---|---|---|---|---|---|---|
| 1997 | — | — | — | — | 6.00 | — |

**5 DOLLARS** **KM# 369** **Composition:** Copper-Nickel **Subject:** The Last Supper **Obverse:** State seal

| Date | Mintage | F | VF | XF | Unc | BU |
|---|---|---|---|---|---|---|
| 1997 | — | — | — | — | 6.00 | — |

**5 DOLLARS** **KM# 371** **Composition:** Copper-Nickel **Subject:** To the Heroes of the Korean War **Obverse:** State seal **Reverse:** Soldier in poncho

| Date | Mintage | F | VF | XF | Unc | BU |
|---|---|---|---|---|---|---|
| 1997 | — | — | — | — | 6.00 | — |

**5 DOLLARS** **KM# 374** **Composition:** Copper-Nickel **Obverse:** State seal **Reverse:** Gray Wolf

| Date | Mintage | F | VF | XF | Unc | BU |
|---|---|---|---|---|---|---|
| 1997 | — | — | — | — | 12.50 | — |

**5 DOLLARS** **KM# 413** **Composition:** Copper-Nickel **Subject:** Year of the Tiger **Obverse:** State seal **Reverse:** Stylized Tiger

| Date | Mintage | F | VF | XF | Unc | BU |
|---|---|---|---|---|---|---|
| 1998 | — | — | — | — | 5.50 | — |

**5 DOLLARS** **KM# 463** **Composition:** Copper-Nickel **Subject:** History's Great Fighting Ships **Obverse:** State seal **Reverse:** USS Missouri

| Date | Mintage | F | VF | XF | Unc | BU |
|---|---|---|---|---|---|---|
| 1998 | — | — | — | — | 5.50 | — |

**5 DOLLARS** **KM# 464** **Composition:** Copper-Nickel **Subject:** To the Heroes of the Berlin Airlift **Obverse:** State seal **Reverse:** C-54 Landing

| Date | Mintage | F | VF | XF | Unc | BU |
|---|---|---|---|---|---|---|
| 1998 | — | — | — | — | 5.50 | — |

**5 DOLLARS** **KM# 466** **Composition:** Copper-Nickel **Subject:** Classic Cars **Obverse:** State seal **Reverse:** 1912 Chevy Classic Six

| Date | Mintage | F | VF | XF | Unc | BU |
|---|---|---|---|---|---|---|
| 1998 | — | — | — | — | 6.00 | — |

**5 DOLLARS** **KM# 468** **Composition:** Copper-Nickel **Subject:** Classic Cars **Obverse:** State seal **Reverse:** 1931 Chevy Roadster

| Date | Mintage | F | VF | XF | Unc | BU |
|---|---|---|---|---|---|---|
| 1998 | — | — | — | — | 6.00 | — |

**5 DOLLARS** **KM# 470** **Composition:** Copper-Nickel **Subject:** Classic Cars **Obverse:** State seal **Reverse:** Cameo Carrier

| Date | Mintage | F | VF | XF | Unc | BU |
|---|---|---|---|---|---|---|
| 1998 | — | — | — | — | 6.00 | — |

**5 DOLLARS** **KM# 472** **Composition:** Copper-Nickel **Subject:** Classic Cars **Obverse:** State seal **Reverse:** 1957 Chevy Bel Air

| Date | Mintage | F | VF | XF | Unc | BU |
|---|---|---|---|---|---|---|
| 1998 | — | — | — | — | 6.00 | — |

**5 DOLLARS** **KM# 474** **Composition:** Copper-Nickel **Subject:** Classic Cars **Obverse:** State seal **Reverse:** 1957 Chevy Corvette

| Date | Mintage | F | VF | XF | Unc | BU |
|---|---|---|---|---|---|---|
| 1998 | — | — | — | — | 6.00 | — |

**5 DOLLARS** **KM# 476** **Composition:** Copper-Nickel **Subject:** Classic Cars **Obverse:** State seal **Reverse:** 1967 Chevy Camaro

| Date | Mintage | F | VF | XF | Unc | BU |
|---|---|---|---|---|---|---|
| 1998 | — | — | — | — | 6.00 | — |

**5 DOLLARS** **KM# 478** **Composition:** Copper-Nickel **Obverse:** State seal **Reverse:** Babe Ruth - At Bat

| Date | Mintage | F | VF | XF | Unc | BU |
|---|---|---|---|---|---|---|
| 1998 | — | — | — | — | 6.50 | — |

**5 DOLLARS** **KM# 481** **Composition:** Copper-Nickel **Subject:** Christmas **Obverse:** State seal **Reverse:** Angel

| Date | Mintage | F | VF | XF | Unc | BU |
|---|---|---|---|---|---|---|
| 1998 | — | — | — | — | 6.00 | — |

**5 DOLLARS** **KM# 484** **Composition:** Copper-Nickel **Reverse:** Friendship 7 and Discovery blasting off

| Date | Mintage | F | VF | XF | Unc | BU |
|---|---|---|---|---|---|---|
| 1998 | — | — | — | — | 6.00 | — |

**5 DOLLARS** **KM# 486** **Composition:** Copper-Nickel **Subject:** USS United States **Obverse:** National seal **Reverse:** Sailing ship **Edge:** Reeded **Size:** 38.4 mm.

| Date | Mintage | F | VF | XF | Unc | BU |
|---|---|---|---|---|---|---|
| 1998 | — | — | — | — | 10.00 | — |

**5 DOLLARS** **KM# 487** **Composition:** Copper-Nickel **Obverse:** National seal **Reverse:** USS Monitor and Merrimack battle scene **Edge:** Reeded **Size:** 38.4 mm.

| Date | Mintage | F | VF | XF | Unc | BU |
|---|---|---|---|---|---|---|
| 1998 | — | — | — | — | 10.00 | — |

**5 DOLLARS** **KM# 488** **Composition:** Copper-Nickel **Subject:** USS Olympia **Obverse:** National seal **Reverse:** Battleship steaming left **Edge:** Reeded **Size:** 38.4 mm.

| Date | Mintage | F | VF | XF | Unc | BU |
|---|---|---|---|---|---|---|
| 1998 | — | — | — | — | 10.00 | — |

**5 DOLLARS** **KM# 489** **Composition:** Copper-Nickel **Obverse:** National seal **Reverse:** USS Fanning and USS Nicholson **Edge:** Reeded **Size:** 38.4 mm.

| Date | Mintage | F | VF | XF | Unc | BU |
|---|---|---|---|---|---|---|
| 1998 | — | — | — | — | 10.00 | — |

**5 DOLLARS** **KM# 490** **Composition:** Copper-Nickel **Subject:** USS Enterprise **Obverse:** National seal **Reverse:** Two warships **Edge:** Reeded **Size:** 38.4 mm.

| Date | Mintage | F | VF | XF | Unc | BU |
|---|---|---|---|---|---|---|
| 1998 | — | — | — | — | 10.00 | — |

**5 DOLLARS** **KM# 491** **Composition:** Copper-Nickel **Obverse:** National seal **Reverse:** USS New Jersey sailing ship **Edge:** Reeded **Size:** 38.4 mm.

| Date | Mintage | F | VF | XF | Unc | BU |
|---|---|---|---|---|---|---|
| 1998 | — | — | — | — | 10.00 | — |

**5 DOLLARS** **KM# 492** **Composition:** Copper-Nickel **Obverse:** National seal **Reverse:** USS Juneau battleship **Edge:** Reeded **Size:** 38.4 mm.

| Date | Mintage | F | VF | XF | Unc | BU |
|---|---|---|---|---|---|---|
| 1998 | — | — | — | — | 10.00 | — |

**10 DOLLARS** **KM# 147** **Weight:** 11.0000 g. **Composition:** 0.9990 Silver .3533 oz. ASW **Reverse:** Greg Louganis

| Date | Mintage | F | VF | XF | Unc | BU |
|---|---|---|---|---|---|---|
| 1988 Proof | — | Value: 185 | | | | |

**10 DOLLARS** **KM# 41** **Composition:** Brass **Subject:** To the Heroes of Desert Storm

| Date | Mintage | F | VF | XF | Unc | BU |
|---|---|---|---|---|---|---|
| 1991R | — | — | — | — | 8.00 | — |

**10 DOLLARS** **KM# 59** **Composition:** Brass **Reverse:** WWII American P-51 Mustang

| Date | Mintage | F | VF | XF | Unc | BU |
|---|---|---|---|---|---|---|
| 1991S Prooflike | Est. 50,000 | — | — | — | 12.50 | — |

**10 DOLLARS** **KM# 60** **Composition:** Brass **Reverse:** WWII American B-29 Superfortress

| Date | Mintage | F | VF | XF | Unc | BU |
|---|---|---|---|---|---|---|
| 1991S Prooflike | Est. 50,000 | — | — | — | 12.50 | — |

**10 DOLLARS** **KM# 61** **Composition:** Brass **Reverse:** WWII American B-25 Mitchell

| Date | Mintage | F | VF | XF | Unc | BU |
|---|---|---|---|---|---|---|
| 1991S Prooflike | Est. 50,000 | — | — | — | 12.50 | — |

**10 DOLLARS** **KM# 62** **Composition:** Brass **Reverse:** WWII American PBY Catalina

| Date | Mintage | F | VF | XF | Unc | BU |
|---|---|---|---|---|---|---|
| 1991S Prooflike | Est. 50,000 | — | — | — | 12.50 | — |

**10 DOLLARS** **KM# 63** , **Composition:** Brass **Reverse:** WWII German BF 109 Messerschmitt

| Date | Mintage | F | VF | XF | Unc | BU |
|---|---|---|---|---|---|---|
| 1991S Prooflike | Est. 50,000 | — | — | — | 12.50 | — |

**10 DOLLARS** **KM# 64** **Composition:** Brass **Reverse:** WWII British Spitfire

| Date | Mintage | F | VF | XF | Unc | BU |
|---|---|---|---|---|---|---|
| 1991S Prooflike | Est. 50,000 | — | — | — | 12.50 | — |

**10 DOLLARS** **KM# 65** **Composition:** Brass **Reverse:** WWII Japanaese A6M Reisen

| Date | Mintage | F | VF | XF | Unc | BU |
|---|---|---|---|---|---|---|
| 1991S Prooflike | Est. 50,000 | — | — | — | 12.50 | — |

**10 DOLLARS** **KM# 66** **Composition:** Brass **Reverse:** WWII American F6F Hellcat

| Date | Mintage | F | VF | XF | Unc | BU |
|---|---|---|---|---|---|---|
| 1991S Prooflike | Est. 50,000 | — | — | — | 12.50 | — |

**10 DOLLARS** **KM# 67** **Composition:** Brass **Reverse:** WWII Soviet Yak 9

| Date | Mintage | F | VF | XF | Unc | BU |
|---|---|---|---|---|---|---|
| 1991S Prooflike | Est. 50,000 | — | — | — | 12.50 | — |

**10 DOLLARS** **KM# 68** **Composition:** Brass **Reverse:** WWII American B-17 Flying Fortress

| Date | Mintage | F | VF | XF | Unc | BU |
|---|---|---|---|---|---|---|
| 1991S Prooflike | Est. 50,000 | — | — | — | 12.50 | — |

**10 DOLLARS** **KM# 69** **Composition:** Brass **Reverse:** WWII British Hawker Hurricane

| Date | Mintage | F | VF | XF | Unc | BU |
|---|---|---|---|---|---|---|
| 1991S Prooflike | Est. 50,000 | — | — | — | 12.50 | — |

**10 DOLLARS** **KM# 73** **Composition:** Brass **Subject:** To the Heroes of Pearl Harbor **Obverse:** National seal

| Date | Mintage | F | VF | XF | Unc | BU |
|---|---|---|---|---|---|---|
| 1991 Prooflike | — | — | — | — | 12.50 | — |

**10 DOLLARS** **KM# 70** **Composition:** Brass **Reverse:** WWII British Mosquito

| Date | Mintage | F | VF | XF | Unc | BU |
|---|---|---|---|---|---|---|
| 1991S Prooflike | Est. 50,000 | — | — | — | 12.50 | — |

**10 DOLLARS** **KM# 71** **Composition:** Brass **Reverse:** WWII British Lancaster

| Date | Mintage | F | VF | XF | Unc | BU |
|---|---|---|---|---|---|---|
| 1991S Prooflike | Est. 50,000 | — | — | — | 12.50 | — |

**10 DOLLARS** **KM# 96** **Composition:** Brass **Reverse:** WWII American C-47 Skytrain

| Date | Mintage | F | VF | XF | Unc | BU |
|---|---|---|---|---|---|---|
| 1991S Prooflike | Est. 50,000 | — | — | — | 12.50 | — |

**10 DOLLARS** **KM# 98** **Composition:** Brass **Reverse:** WWII American F4U Corsair

| Date | Mintage | F | VF | XF | Unc | BU |
|---|---|---|---|---|---|---|
| 1991S Prooflike | Est. 50,000 | — | — | — | 12.50 | — |

**10 DOLLARS** **KM# 101** **Composition:** Brass **Reverse:** WWII American P-38 Lightning

| Date | Mintage | F | VF | XF | Unc | BU |
|---|---|---|---|---|---|---|
| 1991 Prooflike | Est. 50,000 | — | — | — | 12.50 | — |

**10 DOLLARS** **KM# 103** **Composition:** Brass **Reverse:** WWII Japanese G4M "Betty" Bomber

| Date | Mintage | F | VF | XF | Unc | BU |
|---|---|---|---|---|---|---|
| 1991S Prooflike | Est. 50,000 | — | — | — | 12.50 | — |

**10 DOLLARS** **KM# 107** **Composition:** Brass **Reverse:** WWII Japanese KI-61 Kien "Tony"

| Date | Mintage | F | VF | XF | Unc | BU |
|---|---|---|---|---|---|---|
| 1991S Prooflike | Est. 50,000 | — | — | — | 12.50 | — |

**10 DOLLARS** **KM# 109** **Composition:** Brass **Reverse:** WWII French D.520 Fighter

| Date | Mintage | F | VF | XF | Unc | BU |
|---|---|---|---|---|---|---|
| 1991S Prooflike | Est. 50,000 | — | — | — | 12.50 | — |

**10 DOLLARS** **KM# 125** **Composition:** Brass **Reverse:** WWII German FW 190 Fighters

| Date | Mintage | F | VF | XF | Unc | BU |
|---|---|---|---|---|---|---|
| 1991S Prooflike | Est. 50,000 | — | — | — | 12.50 | — |

**10 DOLLARS** **KM# 131** **Composition:** Brass **Reverse:** WWII American B-24 Liberator

| Date | Mintage | F | VF | XF | Unc | BU |
|---|---|---|---|---|---|---|
| 1991S Prooflike | Est. 50,000 | — | — | — | 12.50 | — |

**10 DOLLARS** **KM# 140** **Composition:** Brass **Reverse:** WWII Italian S.M. 79 Sparviero

| Date | Mintage | F | VF | XF | Unc | BU |
|---|---|---|---|---|---|---|
| 1991S Prooflike | Est. 50,000 | — | — | — | 12.50 | — |

**10 DOLLARS** **KM# 141** **Composition:** Brass **Reverse:** WWII German HE III Bombers

| Date | Mintage | F | VF | XF | Unc | BU |
|---|---|---|---|---|---|---|
| 1991S Prooflike | Est. 50,000 | — | — | — | 12.50 | — |

**10 DOLLARS** **KM# 142** **Composition:** Brass **Reverse:** WWII Sovient IL-2 Shturmovik Ground Attack

| Date | Mintage | F | VF | XF | Unc | BU |
|---|---|---|---|---|---|---|
| 1991S Prooflike | Est. 50,000 | — | — | — | 12.50 | — |

**10 DOLLARS** **KM# 143** **Composition:** Brass **Reverse:** WWII American P-51 Mustang

| Date | Mintage | F | VF | XF | Unc | BU |
|---|---|---|---|---|---|---|
| 1991S Prooflike | Est. 50,000 | — | — | — | 12.50 | — |

**10 DOLLARS** **KM# 82** **Composition:** Brass **Subject:** Legends of Discovery **Reverse:** Santa Maria

| Date | Mintage | F | VF | XF | Unc | BU |
|---|---|---|---|---|---|---|
| 1992R | — | — | — | — | 12.50 | — |

**10 DOLLARS** **KM# 85** **Composition:** Brass **Subject:** First Air Raid on Tokyo **Reverse:** Doolittle

| Date | Mintage | F | VF | XF | Unc | BU |
|---|---|---|---|---|---|---|
| 1992R | — | — | — | — | 12.50 | — |

**10 DOLLARS** **KM# 88** **Composition:** Brass **Subject:** To the Heroes of Corregidor

| Date | Mintage | F | VF | XF | Unc | BU |
|---|---|---|---|---|---|---|
| 1992R | — | — | — | — | 12.50 | — |

**10 DOLLARS** **KM# 91** **Composition:** Brass **Subject:** To the Heroes of Battle of Midway

| Date | Mintage | F | VF | XF | Unc | BU |
|---|---|---|---|---|---|---|
| 1992R | — | — | — | — | 12.50 | — |

**10 DOLLARS** **KM# 119** **Composition:** Brass **Subject:** To the Heroes of the North Atlantic **Reverse:** Submarine

| Date | Mintage | F | VF | XF | Unc | BU |
|---|---|---|---|---|---|---|
| 1993R Prooflike | — | — | — | — | 14.00 | — |

**10 DOLLARS** **KM# 122** **Composition:** Brass **Subject:** To the Heroes of Guadalcanal **Reverse:** Marine, Battleship & Airplanes

| Date | Mintage | F | VF | XF | Unc | BU |
|---|---|---|---|---|---|---|
| 1993R Prooflike | — | — | — | — | 12.50 | — |

**10 DOLLARS** **KM# 127** **Composition:** Brass **Subject:** Pacific Whales & Dolphins **Reverse:** Common Dolphin

| Date | Mintage | F | VF | XF | Unc | BU |
|---|---|---|---|---|---|---|
| 1993R Prooflike | — | — | — | — | 15.00 | — |

**10 DOLLARS** **KM# 129** **Composition:** Brass **Reverse:** Elvis Presley

| Date | Mintage | F | VF | XF | Unc | BU |
|---|---|---|---|---|---|---|
| 1993 Prooflike | — | — | — | — | 15.00 | — |

**10 DOLLARS** **KM# 132** **Composition:** Brass **Subject:** Pacific Whales & Dolphins **Reverse:** Humpback Whales

| Date | Mintage | F | VF | XF | Unc | BU |
|---|---|---|---|---|---|---|
| 1993 | Est. 25,000 | — | — | — | 15.00 | — |

**10 DOLLARS** **KM# 133** **Composition:** Brass **Subject:** Pacific Whales & Dolphins **Reverse:** Risso's Dolphins

| Date | Mintage | F | VF | XF | Unc | BU |
|---|---|---|---|---|---|---|
| 1993 | Est. 25,000 | — | — | — | 15.00 | — |

**10 DOLLARS** **KM# 134** **Composition:** Brass **Subject:** Pacific Whales & Dolphins **Reverse:** Beluga Whales

| Date | Mintage | F | VF | XF | Unc | BU |
|---|---|---|---|---|---|---|
| 1993 | Est. 25,000 | — | — | — | 15.00 | — |

**10 DOLLARS** **KM# 135** **Composition:** Brass **Subject:** Pacific Whales & Dolphins **Reverse:** Hector's Dolphins

| Date | Mintage | F | VF | XF | Unc | BU |
|---|---|---|---|---|---|---|
| 1993 | Est. 25,000 | — | — | — | 15.00 | — |

**10 DOLLARS** **KM# 136** **Composition:** Brass **Subject:** Pacific Whales & Dolphins **Reverse:** Blue Whale

| Date | Mintage | F | VF | XF | Unc | BU |
|---|---|---|---|---|---|---|
| 1993 | Est. 25,000 | — | — | — | 15.00 | — |

**10 DOLLARS** **KM# 137** **Composition:** Brass **Subject:** Pacific Whales & Dolphins **Reverse:** Bottlenose Dolphin

| Date | Mintage | F | VF | XF | Unc | BU |
|---|---|---|---|---|---|---|
| 1993 | Est. 25,000 | — | — | — | 15.00 | — |

**10 DOLLARS** **KM# 138** **Composition:** Brass **Subject:** Pacific Whales & Dolphins **Reverse:** Killer Whale

| Date | Mintage | F | VF | XF | Unc | BU |
|---|---|---|---|---|---|---|
| 1993 | Est. 25,000 | — | — | — | 15.00 | — |

**10 DOLLARS** **KM# 139** **Composition:** Brass **Subject:** Pacific Whales & Dolphins **Reverse:** Baiji Dolphins

| Date | Mintage | F | VF | XF | Unc | BU |
|---|---|---|---|---|---|---|
| 1993 | Est. 25,000 | — | — | — | 15.00 | — |

**10 DOLLARS** **KM# 145** **Composition:** Brass **Subject:** Christmas 1993

| Date | Mintage | F | VF | XF | Unc | BU |
|---|---|---|---|---|---|---|
| 1993 | Est. 25,000 | — | — | — | 12.50 | — |

**10 DOLLARS** **KM# 149** **Composition:** Brass **Subject:** Flight of the Kitty Hawk

| Date | Mintage | F | VF | XF | Unc | BU |
|---|---|---|---|---|---|---|
| 1993 | — | — | — | — | 12.50 | — |

**10 DOLLARS** **KM# 408** **Composition:** Brass **Subject:** Pacific Whales & Dolphins **Reverse:** Indo-Pacific Humpbacked Dolphin

| Date | Mintage | F | VF | XF | Unc | BU |
|---|---|---|---|---|---|---|
| 1993 | Est. 25,000 | — | — | — | 15.00 | — |

**10 DOLLARS** **KM# 409** **Composition:** Brass **Subject:** Pacific Whales & Dolphins **Obverse:** State seal **Reverse:** Long-Snouted Spinner Dolphin

| Date | Mintage | F | VF | XF | Unc | BU |
|---|---|---|---|---|---|---|
| 1993 | Est. 25,000 | — | — | — | 15.00 | — |

**10 DOLLARS** **KM# 410** **Composition:** Brass **Subject:** Pacific Whales & Dolphins **Reverse:** 2 Sperm Whale

| Date | Mintage | F | VF | XF | Unc | BU |
|---|---|---|---|---|---|---|
| 1993 | Est. 25,000 | — | — | — | 15.00 | — |

**10 DOLLARS** **KM# 411** **Composition:** Brass **Subject:** Pacific Whales & Dolphins **Reverse:** Minke Whale

| Date | Mintage | F | VF | XF | Unc | BU |
|---|---|---|---|---|---|---|
| 1993 | Est. 25,000 | — | — | — | 15.00 | — |

**10 DOLLARS** **KM# 152** **Composition:** Brass **Subject:** First Men on the Moon

| Date | Mintage | F | VF | XF | Unc | BU |
|---|---|---|---|---|---|---|
| 1994 | — | — | — | — | 12.50 | — |

**10 DOLLARS** **KM# 155** **Composition:** Brass **Subject:** Mythological Mother Earth

| Date | Mintage | F | VF | XF | Unc | BU |
|---|---|---|---|---|---|---|
| 1994R | — | — | — | — | 15.50 | — |

**10 DOLLARS** **KM# 156** **Composition:** Brass **Reverse:** The Sun

| Date | Mintage | F | VF | XF | Unc | BU |
|---|---|---|---|---|---|---|
| 1994 | — | — | — | — | 15.50 | — |

**10 DOLLARS** **KM# 157** **Composition:** Brass **Reverse:** The Moon

| Date | Mintage | F | VF | XF | Unc | BU |
|---|---|---|---|---|---|---|
| 1994 | — | — | — | — | 15.50 | — |

**10 DOLLARS** **KM# 158** **Composition:** Brass **Reverse:** Pluto

| Date | Mintage | F | VF | XF | Unc | BU |
|---|---|---|---|---|---|---|
| 1994 | — | — | — | — | 15.50 | — |

**10 DOLLARS** **KM# 159** **Composition:** Brass **Reverse:** Mercury

| Date | Mintage | F | VF | XF | Unc | BU |
|---|---|---|---|---|---|---|
| 1994 | — | — | — | — | 15.50 | — |

**10 DOLLARS** **KM# 160** **Composition:** Brass **Reverse:** Venus

| Date | Mintage | F | VF | XF | Unc | BU |
|---|---|---|---|---|---|---|
| 1994 | — | — | — | — | 15.50 | — |

**10 DOLLARS** **KM# 161** **Composition:** Brass **Reverse:** Mars

| Date | Mintage | F | VF | XF | Unc | BU |
|---|---|---|---|---|---|---|
| 1994 | — | — | — | — | 15.50 | — |

**10 DOLLARS** **KM# 162** **Composition:** Brass **Reverse:** Saturn

| Date | Mintage | F | VF | XF | Unc | BU |
|---|---|---|---|---|---|---|
| 1994 | — | — | — | — | 15.50 | — |

**10 DOLLARS** **KM# 163** **Composition:** Brass **Reverse:** Jupiter

| Date | Mintage | F | VF | XF | Unc | BU |
|---|---|---|---|---|---|---|
| 1994 | — | — | — | — | 15.50 | — |

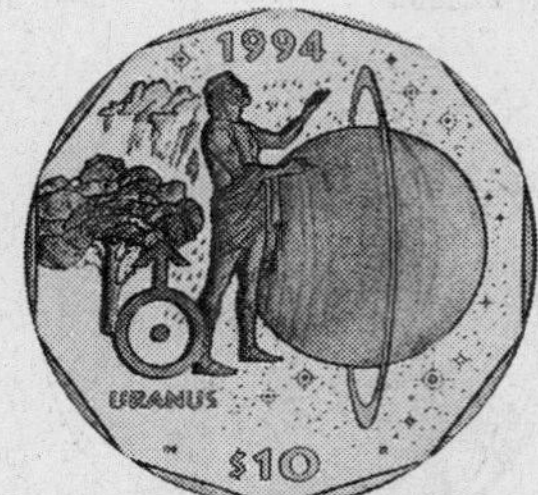


**10 DOLLARS** **KM# 164** **Composition:** Brass **Reverse:** Uranus

| Date | Mintage | F | VF | XF | Unc | BU |
|---|---|---|---|---|---|---|
| 1994 | — | — | — | — | 15.50 | — |

**10 DOLLARS** **KM# 165** **Composition:** Brass **Reverse:** Neptune

| Date | Mintage | F | VF | XF | Unc | BU |
|---|---|---|---|---|---|---|
| 1994 | — | — | — | — | 15.50 | — |

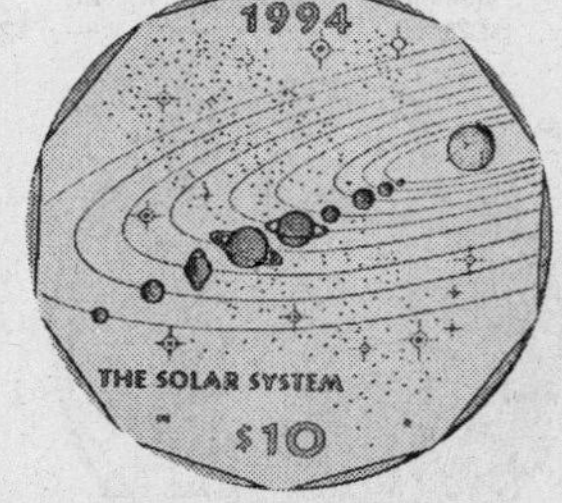


**10 DOLLARS** **KM# 166** **Composition:** Brass **Reverse:** Solar System

| Date | Mintage | F | VF | XF | Unc | BU |
|---|---|---|---|---|---|---|
| 1994 | — | — | — | — | 15.50 | — |

**10 DOLLARS** **KM# 180** **Composition:** Brass **Subject:** To the Heroes of D-Day - Normandy Invasion

| Date | Mintage | F | VF | XF | Unc | BU |
|---|---|---|---|---|---|---|
| 1994 Prooflike | — | — | — | — | 12.50 | — |

**10 DOLLARS** **KM# 183** **Composition:** Brass **Subject:** Heroes of the Philippines **Reverse:** MacArthur and Staff

| Date | Mintage | F | VF | XF | Unc | BU |
|---|---|---|---|---|---|---|
| 1994 Prooflike | — | — | — | — | 12.50 | — |

**10 DOLLARS** **KM# 188** **Composition:** Brass **Subject:** World Cup Soccer

| Date | Mintage | F | VF | XF | Unc | BU |
|---|---|---|---|---|---|---|
| 1994 | — | — | — | — | 12.50 | — |

**10 DOLLARS** **KM# 264** **Composition:** Brass **Reverse:** To the Heroes of the Battle of the Bulge

| Date | Mintage | F | VF | XF | Unc | BU |
|---|---|---|---|---|---|---|
| 1994 Prooflike | — | — | — | — | 12.50 | — |

**10 DOLLARS** **KM# 261** **Composition:** Brass **Subject:** Christmas **Reverse:** Cherub **Note:** Similar to 5 Dollars, KM#271.

| Date | Mintage | F | VF | XF | Unc | BU |
|---|---|---|---|---|---|---|
| 1994 | — | — | — | — | 12.50 | — |

**10 DOLLARS** **KM# 217** **Composition:** Brass **Subject:** Peace - Victory in Europe

| Date | Mintage | F | VF | XF | Unc | BU |
|---|---|---|---|---|---|---|
| 1995 | — | — | — | — | 12.50 | — |

**10 DOLLARS** **KM# 220** **Composition:** Brass **Subject:** To the Heroes of Vietnam

| Date | Mintage | F | VF | XF | Unc | BU |
|---|---|---|---|---|---|---|
| 1995 Prooflike | — | — | — | — | 12.50 | — |

**10 DOLLARS** KM# 223 **Composition:** Brass **Reverse:** Elvis Presley

| Date | Mintage | F | VF | XF | Unc | BU |
|---|---|---|---|---|---|---|
| 1995 | — | — | — | — | 12.50 | — |

**10 DOLLARS** KM# 226 **Composition:** Brass **Subject:** To the Heroes of the War in the Pacific

| Date | Mintage | F | VF | XF | Unc | BU |
|---|---|---|---|---|---|---|
| 1995 Prooflike | — | — | — | — | 12.50 | — |

**10 DOLLARS** KM# 228 **Composition:** Brass **Reverse:** F-14 Tomcat

| Date | Mintage | F | VF | XF | Unc | BU |
|---|---|---|---|---|---|---|
| 1995R | Est. 25,000 | — | — | — | 12.50 | — |

**10 DOLLARS** KM# 229 **Composition:** Brass **Reverse:** F-16 Fighting Falcon

| Date | Mintage | F | VF | XF | Unc | BU |
|---|---|---|---|---|---|---|
| 1995R | Est. 25,000 | — | — | — | 12.50 | — |

**10 DOLLARS** KM# 230 **Composition:** Brass **Reverse:** Me 262A-1a Schwalbe

| Date | Mintage | F | VF | XF | Unc | BU |
|---|---|---|---|---|---|---|
| 1995R | Est. 25,000 | — | — | — | 12.50 | — |

**10 DOLLARS** KM# 231 **Composition:** Brass **Reverse:** F-104 Starfighter

| Date | Mintage | F | VF | XF | Unc | BU |
|---|---|---|---|---|---|---|
| 1995R | Est. 25,000 | — | — | — | 12.50 | — |

**10 DOLLARS** KM# 232 **Composition:** Brass **Reverse:** Mirage 2000C

| Date | Mintage | F | VF | XF | Unc | BU |
|---|---|---|---|---|---|---|
| 1995R | Est. 25,000 | — | — | — | 12.50 | — |

**10 DOLLARS** KM# 233 **Composition:** Brass **Reverse:** F-4 Phantom II

| Date | Mintage | F | VF | XF | Unc | BU |
|---|---|---|---|---|---|---|
| 1995R | Est. 25,000 | — | — | — | 12.50 | — |

**10 DOLLARS** KM# 234 **Composition:** Brass **Reverse:** Sea Harrier

| Date | Mintage | F | VF | XF | Unc | BU |
|---|---|---|---|---|---|---|
| 1995R | Est. 25,000 | — | — | — | 12.50 | — |

**10 DOLLARS** KM# 235 **Composition:** Brass **Reverse:** F-117 Nighthawk

| Date | Mintage | F | VF | XF | Unc | BU |
|---|---|---|---|---|---|---|
| 1995R | Est. 25,000 | — | — | — | 12.50 | — |

**10 DOLLARS** KM# 236 **Composition:** Brass **Reverse:** F-100 Super Sabre

| Date | Mintage | F | VF | XF | Unc | BU |
|---|---|---|---|---|---|---|
| 1995R | Est. 25,000 | — | — | — | 12.50 | — |

**10 DOLLARS** KM# 237 **Composition:** Brass **Reverse:** F-86 Sabre

| Date | Mintage | F | VF | XF | Unc | BU |
|---|---|---|---|---|---|---|
| 1995R | Est. 25,000 | — | — | — | 12.50 | — |

**10 DOLLARS** KM# 238 **Composition:** Brass **Reverse:** MIG-15

| Date | Mintage | F | VF | XF | Unc | BU |
|---|---|---|---|---|---|---|
| 1995R | Est. 25,000 | — | — | — | 12.50 | — |

**10 DOLLARS** KM# 239 **Composition:** Brass **Reverse:** G91R

| Date | Mintage | F | VF | XF | Unc | BU |
|---|---|---|---|---|---|---|
| 1995R | Est. 25,000 | — | — | — | 12.50 | — |

**10 DOLLARS** KM# 240 **Composition:** Brass **Reverse:** SAAB 35 Draken

| Date | Mintage | F | VF | XF | Unc | BU |
|---|---|---|---|---|---|---|
| 1995R | Est. 25,000 | — | — | — | 12.50 | — |

**10 DOLLARS** KM# 241 **Composition:** Brass **Reverse:** Meteor FMK8

| Date | Mintage | F | VF | XF | Unc | BU |
|---|---|---|---|---|---|---|
| 1995R | Est. 25,000 | — | — | — | 12.50 | — |

**10 DOLLARS** KM# 242 **Composition:** Brass **Reverse:** F-105 Thunderbird

| Date | Mintage | F | VF | XF | Unc | BU |
|---|---|---|---|---|---|---|
| 1995R | Est. 25,000 | — | — | — | 12.50 | — |

**10 DOLLARS** KM# 243 **Composition:** Brass **Reverse:** Tornado FMK3

| Date | Mintage | F | VF | XF | Unc | BU |
|---|---|---|---|---|---|---|
| 1995R | Est. 25,000 | — | — | — | 12.50 | — |

**10 DOLLARS** KM# 254 **Composition:** Brass **Reverse:** Marilyn Monroe

| Date | Mintage | F | VF | XF | Unc | BU |
|---|---|---|---|---|---|---|
| 1995 | — | — | — | — | 12.50 | — |

**10 DOLLARS** KM# 258 **Composition:** Brass **Series:** 50th Anniversary United Nations **Subject:** Peace

| Date | Mintage | F | VF | XF | Unc | BU |
|---|---|---|---|---|---|---|
| 1995 | — | — | — | — | 12.50 | — |

**10 DOLLARS** KM# 267 **Composition:** Brass **Subject:** Peace - VJ Day

| Date | Mintage | F | VF | XF | Unc | BU |
|---|---|---|---|---|---|---|
| 1995 | — | — | — | — | 12.50 | — |

**10 DOLLARS** KM# 272 **Composition:** Brass **Subject:** Christmas **Reverse:** Cherub

| Date | Mintage | F | VF | XF | Unc | BU |
|---|---|---|---|---|---|---|
| 1995 | — | — | — | — | 12.50 | — |

**10 DOLLARS** **KM# 282** **Composition:** Brass **Subject:** Freedom / Liberty **Reverse:** Torpedo Boat PT109

| Date | Mintage | F | VF | XF | Unc | BU |
|---|---|---|---|---|---|---|
| 1995 | — | — | — | — | 12.00 | — |

**10 DOLLARS** **KM# 283** **Composition:** Brass **Subject:** Freedom / Liberty **Reverse:** President John F. Kennedy takes Oath of Office

| Date | Mintage | F | VF | XF | Unc | BU |
|---|---|---|---|---|---|---|
| 1995 | — | — | — | — | 12.50 | — |

**10 DOLLARS** **KM# 284** **Composition:** Brass **Subject:** Freedom / Liberty **Reverse:** Peace Corps worker and native

| Date | Mintage | F | VF | XF | Unc | BU |
|---|---|---|---|---|---|---|
| 1995 | — | — | — | — | 12.50 | — |

**10 DOLLARS** **KM# 285** **Composition:** Brass **Subject:** Freedom / Liberty **Reverse:** Battleships under starry sky

| Date | Mintage | F | VF | XF | Unc | BU |
|---|---|---|---|---|---|---|
| 1995 | — | — | — | — | 12.50 | — |

**10 DOLLARS** **KM# 286** **Composition:** Brass **Subject:** Freedom / Liberty **Reverse:** President John F. Kennedy working at desk

| Date | Mintage | F | VF | XF | Unc | BU |
|---|---|---|---|---|---|---|
| 1995 | — | — | — | — | 12.50 | — |

**10 DOLLARS** **KM# 287** **Composition:** Brass **Subject:** Freedom / Liberty **Reverse:** President John F. Kennedy's Eternal Flame

| Date | Mintage | F | VF | XF | Unc | BU |
|---|---|---|---|---|---|---|
| 1995 | — | — | — | — | 12.50 | — |

**10 DOLLARS** **KM# 396** **Composition:** Brass **Subject:** F-16 Fighting Falcon **Obverse:** National seal **Reverse:** Jet fighter

| Date | Mintage | F | VF | XF | Unc | BU |
|---|---|---|---|---|---|---|
| 1995 | Est. 25,000 | — | — | — | 12.00 | — |

**10 DOLLARS** **KM# 289** **Composition:** Brass **Reverse:** Space Shuttle Columbia

| Date | Mintage | F | VF | XF | Unc | BU |
|---|---|---|---|---|---|---|
| 1996 | — | — | — | — | 12.50 | — |

**10 DOLLARS** **KM# 301** **Composition:** Brass **Reverse:** Elvis Presley

| Date | Mintage | F | VF | XF | Unc | BU |
|---|---|---|---|---|---|---|
| 1996 | — | — | — | — | 13.50 | — |

**10 DOLLARS** **KM# 306** **Composition:** Brass **Subject:** Steam Locomotive **Reverse:** Pennsylvania K4

| Date | Mintage | F | VF | XF | Unc | BU |
|---|---|---|---|---|---|---|
| 1996 | Est. 250,000 | — | — | — | 14.00 | — |

**10 DOLLARS** **KM# 307** **Composition:** Brass **Subject:** Steam Locomotive **Reverse:** Big Boy

| Date | Mintage | F | VF | XF | Unc | BU |
|---|---|---|---|---|---|---|
| 1996 | Est. 25,000 | — | — | — | 14.00 | — |

**10 DOLLARS** **KM# 309** **Composition:** Brass **Subject:** Classic Cars **Reverse:** Ford Quadricycle

| Date | Mintage | F | VF | XF | Unc | BU |
|---|---|---|---|---|---|---|
| 1996 Prooflike | — | — | — | — | 12.50 | — |

**10 DOLLARS** **KM# 312** **Composition:** Brass **Subject:** Classic Cars **Reverse:** Model A Ford

| Date | Mintage | F | VF | XF | Unc | BU |
|---|---|---|---|---|---|---|
| 1996 Prooflike | — | — | — | — | 12.50 | — |

**10 DOLLARS** **KM# 321** **Composition:** Brass **Subject:** Classic Cars **Reverse:** 1964 Mustang

| Date | Mintage | F | VF | XF | Unc | BU |
|---|---|---|---|---|---|---|
| 1996 Prooflike | — | — | — | — | 12.50 | — |

**10 DOLLARS** **KM# 336** **Composition:** Brass **Reverse:** Space Shuttle - Challenger

| Date | Mintage | F | VF | XF | Unc | BU |
|---|---|---|---|---|---|---|
| 1996 | — | — | — | — | 12.50 | — |

**10 DOLLARS** **KM# 337** **Composition:** Brass **Reverse:** Space Shuttle - Discovery

| Date | Mintage | F | VF | XF | Unc | BU |
|---|---|---|---|---|---|---|
| 1996 | — | — | — | — | 12.50 | — |

**10 DOLLARS** **KM# 338** **Composition:** Brass **Reverse:** Space Shuttle - Atlantis

| Date | Mintage | F | VF | XF | Unc | BU |
|---|---|---|---|---|---|---|
| 1996 | — | — | — | — | 12.50 | — |

**10 DOLLARS** **KM# 339** **Composition:** Brass **Reverse:** Space Shuttle - Endeavor

| Date | Mintage | F | VF | XF | Unc | BU |
|---|---|---|---|---|---|---|
| 1996 | — | — | — | — | 12.50 | — |

**10 DOLLARS** **KM# 354** **Composition:** Brass **Subject:** Christmas **Reverse:** 2 Angels

| Date | Mintage | F | VF | XF | Unc | BU |
|---|---|---|---|---|---|---|
| 1996 | — | — | — | — | 12.50 | — |

**10 DOLLARS** **KM# 356** **Composition:** Brass **Subject:** Steam Locomotive **Reverse:** DB Class 01

| Date | Mintage | F | VF | XF | Unc | BU |
|---|---|---|---|---|---|---|
| 1996 | — | — | — | — | 14.00 | — |

**10 DOLLARS** **KM# 359** **Composition:** Brass **Subject:** Steam Locomotive **Reverse:** RENFE Class 242

| Date | Mintage | F | VF | XF | Unc | BU |
|---|---|---|---|---|---|---|
| 1996 | — | — | — | — | 14.50 | — |

**10 DOLLARS** **KM# 361** **Composition:** Brass **Subject:** Steam Locomotive **Reverse:** FS Group 691

| Date | Mintage | F | VF | XF | Unc | BU |
|---|---|---|---|---|---|---|
| 1996 | Est. 25,000 | — | — | — | 14.50 | — |

**10 DOLLARS** **KM# 368** **Composition:** Brass **Subject:** Steam Locomotive **Reverse:** SNCF 232. U1

| Date | Mintage | F | VF | XF | Unc | BU |
|---|---|---|---|---|---|---|
| 1996 | Est. 25,000 | — | — | — | 14.50 | — |

**10 DOLLARS** **KM# 378** **Composition:** Brass **Subject:** Steam Locomotive **Reverse:** SAR 520 Class

| Date | Mintage | F | VF | XF | Unc | BU |
|---|---|---|---|---|---|---|
| 1996 | Est. 25,000 | — | — | — | 14.50 | — |

**10 DOLLARS** **KM# 379** **Composition:** Brass **Subject:** Steam Locomotive **Reverse:** Evening Star

| Date | Mintage | F | VF | XF | Unc | BU |
|---|---|---|---|---|---|---|
| 1996 | Est. 25,000 | — | — | — | 14.50 | — |

**10 DOLLARS** **KM# 393** **Composition:** Brass **Subject:** Steam Locomotive **Reverse:** QJ "Advance Forward"

| Date | Mintage | F | VF | XF | Unc | BU |
|---|---|---|---|---|---|---|
| 1996 | Est. 25,000 | — | — | — | 14.50 | — |

**10 DOLLARS** **KM# 394** **Composition:** Brass **Subject:** Steam Locomotive **Obverse:** State seal **Reverse:** Royal Hudson

| Date | Mintage | F | VF | XF | Unc | BU |
|---|---|---|---|---|---|---|
| 1996 | Est. 25,000 | — | — | — | 14.50 | — |

**10 DOLLARS** **KM# 402** **Composition:** Brass **Subject:** Steam Locomotive **Obverse:** State seal **Reverse:** C62 "Swallow"

| Date | Mintage | F | VF | XF | Unc | BU |
|---|---|---|---|---|---|---|
| 1996 | Est. 25,000 | — | — | — | 14.50 | — |

**10 DOLLARS** **KM# 304** **Composition:** Brass **Reverse:** James Dean **Note:** Similar to 5 Dollars, KM#303.

| Date | Mintage | F | VF | XF | Unc | BU |
|---|---|---|---|---|---|---|
| 1996 | — | — | — | — | 13.50 | — |

**10 DOLLARS** **KM# 315** **Composition:** Brass **Subject:** Classic Cars **Reverse:** Model T Ford **Note:** Similar to 5 Dollars, KM#314.

| Date | Mintage | F | VF | XF | Unc | BU |
|---|---|---|---|---|---|---|
| 1996 Prooflike | — | — | — | — | — | — |

**10 DOLLARS** **KM# 318** **Composition:** Brass **Subject:** Classic Cars **Reverse:** 1955 Thunderbird **Note:** Similar to 5 Dollars, KM#317.

| Date | Mintage | F | VF | XF | Unc | BU |
|---|---|---|---|---|---|---|
| 1996 Prooflike | — | — | — | — | 12.50 | — |

**10 DOLLARS** **KM# 324** **Composition:** Brass **Subject:** Classic Cars **Reverse:** Ford Taurus **Note:** Similar to 5 Dollars, KM#323.

| Date | Mintage | F | VF | XF | Unc | BU |
|---|---|---|---|---|---|---|
| 1996 Prooflike | — | — | — | — | 12.50 | — |

**10 DOLLARS** **KM# 347** **Composition:** Brass **Reverse:** Lion **Note:** Similar to 5 Dollars, KM#344.

| Date | Mintage | F | VF | XF | Unc | BU |
|---|---|---|---|---|---|---|
| 1996 | — | — | — | — | 15.00 | — |

**10 DOLLARS** **KM# 348** **Composition:** Brass **Reverse:** Cheetah **Note:** Similar to 5 Dollars, KM#345.

| Date | Mintage | F | VF | XF | Unc | BU |
|---|---|---|---|---|---|---|
| 1996 | — | — | — | — | 15.00 | — |

**10 DOLLARS** **KM# 349** **Composition:** Brass **Reverse:** Jaguar **Note:** Similar to 5 Dollars, KM#346.

| Date | Mintage | F | VF | XF | Unc | BU |
|---|---|---|---|---|---|---|
| 1996 | — | — | — | — | 15.00 | — |

**10 DOLLARS** **KM# 326** **Composition:** Brass **Subject:** Steam Locomotive **Reverse:** Mallard **Note:** Similar to 50 Dollars, KM#296.

| Date | Mintage | F | VF | XF | Unc | BU |
|---|---|---|---|---|---|---|
| 1996 | Est. 25,000 | — | — | — | 14.00 | — |

**10 DOLLARS** **KM# 298** **Composition:** Brass **Reverse:** Tiger **Note:** Similar to 50 Dollars, KM#299.

| Date | Mintage | F | VF | XF | Unc | BU |
|---|---|---|---|---|---|---|
| 1996 | — | — | — | — | 13.50 | — |

**10 DOLLARS** **KM# 372** **Composition:** Brass **Subject:** To the Heroes of the Korean War **Note:** Siimilar to 5 Dollars, KM#371.

| Date | Mintage | F | VF | XF | Unc | BU |
|---|---|---|---|---|---|---|
| 1997 | Est. 25,000 | — | — | — | 12.00 | — |

**10 DOLLARS** **KM# 365** **Composition:** Brass **Reverse:** Elvis Presley **Note:** Similar to 5 Dollars, KM#364.

| Date | Mintage | F | VF | XF | Unc | BU |
|---|---|---|---|---|---|---|
| 1997 | — | — | — | — | 12.50 | — |

**10 DOLLARS** **KM# 381** **Composition:** Brass **Subject:** Twelve Apostles Series **Obverse:** State seal **Reverse:** Andrew

| Date | Mintage | F | VF | XF | Unc | BU |
|---|---|---|---|---|---|---|
| 1997 | Est. 25,000 | — | — | — | 12.00 | — |

**10 DOLLARS** **KM# 382** **Composition:** Brass **Subject:** Twelve Apostles Series **Obverse:** State seal **Reverse:** Bartholomew

| Date | Mintage | F | VF | XF | Unc | BU |
|---|---|---|---|---|---|---|
| 1997 | Est. 25,000 | — | — | — | 12.00 | — |

**10 DOLLARS** **KM# 383** **Composition:** Brass **Subject:** Twelve Apostles Series **Obverse:** State seal **Reverse:** James, Son of Zebedee

| Date | Mintage | F | VF | XF | Unc | BU |
|---|---|---|---|---|---|---|
| 1997 | Est. 25,000 | — | — | — | 12.00 | — |

**10 DOLLARS** **KM# 384** **Composition:** Brass **Subject:** Twelve Apostles Series **Obverse:** State seal **Reverse:** James, Son of Alphaeus

| Date | Mintage | F | VF | XF | Unc | BU |
|---|---|---|---|---|---|---|
| 1997 | Est. 25,000 | — | — | — | 12.00 | — |

**10 DOLLARS** **KM# 385** **Composition:** Brass **Subject:** Twelve Apostles Series **Obverse:** State seal **Reverse:** John

| Date | Mintage | F | VF | XF | Unc | BU |
|---|---|---|---|---|---|---|
| 1997 | Est. 25,000 | — | — | — | 12.00 | — |

**10 DOLLARS** **KM# 386** **Composition:** Brass **Subject:** Twelve Apostles Series **Obverse:** State seal **Reverse:** Paul

| Date | Mintage | F | VF | XF | Unc | BU |
|---|---|---|---|---|---|---|
| 1997 | Est. 25,000 | — | — | — | 12.00 | — |

**10 DOLLARS** **KM# 387** **Composition:** Brass **Subject:** Twelve Apostles Series **Obverse:** State seal **Reverse:** Matthew

| Date | Mintage | F | VF | XF | Unc | BU |
|---|---|---|---|---|---|---|
| 1997 | Est. 25,000 | — | — | — | 12.00 | — |

**10 DOLLARS** **KM# 388** **Composition:** Brass **Subject:** Twelve Apostles Series **Obverse:** State seal **Reverse:** Peter

| Date | Mintage | F | VF | XF | Unc | BU |
|---|---|---|---|---|---|---|
| 1997 | Est. 25,000 | — | — | — | 12.00 | — |

**10 DOLLARS** **KM# 389** **Composition:** Brass **Subject:** Twelve Apostles Series **Obverse:** State seal **Reverse:** Philip

| Date | Mintage | F | VF | XF | Unc | BU |
|---|---|---|---|---|---|---|
| 1997 | Est. 25,000 | — | — | — | 12.00 | — |

**10 DOLLARS** **KM# 390** **Composition:** Brass **Subject:** Twelve Apostles Series **Obverse:** State seal **Reverse:** Simon

| Date | Mintage | F | VF | XF | Unc | BU |
|---|---|---|---|---|---|---|
| 1997 | Est. 25,000 | — | — | — | 12.00 | — |

**10 DOLLARS** **KM# 391** **Composition:** Brass **Subject:** Twelve Apostles Series **Obverse:** State seal **Reverse:** Thaddaeus

| Date | Mintage | F | VF | XF | Unc | BU |
|---|---|---|---|---|---|---|
| 1997 | Est. 25,000 | — | — | — | 12.00 | — |

**10 DOLLARS** **KM# 392** **Composition:** Brass **Subject:** Twelve Apostles Series **Obverse:** State seal **Reverse:** Thomas

| Date | Mintage | F | VF | XF | Unc | BU |
|---|---|---|---|---|---|---|
| 1997 | Est. 25,000 | — | — | — | 12.00 | — |

**10 DOLLARS** **KM# 404** **Composition:** Brass **Subject:** Christmas **Obverse:** State seal **Reverse:** 2 Angels

| Date | Mintage | F | VF | XF | Unc | BU |
|---|---|---|---|---|---|---|
| 1997 | — | — | — | — | 12.00 | — |

**10 DOLLARS** **KM# 406** **Composition:** Brass **Obverse:** National seal **Reverse:** Charing bull elephant

| Date | Mintage | F | VF | XF | Unc | BU |
|---|---|---|---|---|---|---|
| 1997 | — | — | — | — | 13.50 | — |

**10 DOLLARS** **KM# 400** **Composition:** Brass **Obverse:** State seal **Reverse:** Deng Ziaoping

| Date | Mintage | F | VF | XF | Unc | BU |
|---|---|---|---|---|---|---|
| 1997 | — | — | — | — | 12.00 | — |

**10 DOLLARS** **KM# 415** **Composition:** Brass **Subject:** History's Great Fighting Ships **Obverse:** State seal **Reverse:** Viking Longship

| Date | Mintage | F | VF | XF | Unc | BU |
|---|---|---|---|---|---|---|
| 1998 | Est. 25,000 | — | — | — | 12.00 | — |

**10 DOLLARS** **KM# 417** **Composition:** Brass **Subject:** History's Great Fighting Ships **Obverse:** State seal **Reverse:** Greek Trireme

| Date | Mintage | F | VF | XF | Unc | BU |
|---|---|---|---|---|---|---|
| 1998 | Est. 25,000 | — | — | — | 12.00 | — |

**10 DOLLARS** **KM# 419** **Composition:** Brass **Subject:** History's Great Fighting Ships **Obverse:** State seal **Reverse:** Roman Trireme

| Date | Mintage | F | VF | XF | Unc | BU |
|---|---|---|---|---|---|---|
| 1998 | Est. 25,000 | — | — | — | 12.00 | — |

**10 DOLLARS** **KM# 421** **Composition:** Brass **Subject:** History's Great Fighting Ships **Obverse:** State seal **Reverse:** Chinese Ming Treasure Ship

| Date | Mintage | F | VF | XF | Unc | BU |
|---|---|---|---|---|---|---|
| 1998 | Est. 25,000 | — | — | — | 12.00 | — |

**10 DOLLARS** **KM# 423** **Composition:** Brass **Subject:** History's Great Fighting Ships **Obverse:** State seal **Reverse:** Korean Turtle Ship

| Date | Mintage | F | VF | XF | Unc | BU |
|---|---|---|---|---|---|---|
| 1998 | Est. 25,000 | — | — | — | 12.00 | — |

**10 DOLLARS** **KM# 425** **Composition:** Brass **Subject:** History's Great Fighting Ships **Obverse:** State seal **Reverse:** Fijan War Canoe

| Date | Mintage | F | VF | XF | Unc | BU |
|---|---|---|---|---|---|---|
| 1998 | Est. 25,000 | — | — | — | 12.00 | — |

**10 DOLLARS** **KM# 427** **Composition:** Brass **Subject:** History's Great Fighting Ships **Obverse:** State seal **Reverse:** The Bismarck

| Date | Mintage | F | VF | XF | Unc | BU |
|---|---|---|---|---|---|---|
| 1998 | Est. 25,000 | — | — | — | 12.00 | — |

**10 DOLLARS** **KM# 429** **Composition:** Brass **Subject:** History's Great Fighting Ships **Obverse:** State seal **Reverse:** The Graf Spee

| Date | Mintage | F | VF | XF | Unc | BU |
|---|---|---|---|---|---|---|
| 1998 | Est. 25,000 | — | — | — | 12.00 | — |

**10 DOLLARS** **KM# 431** **Composition:** Brass **Subject:** History's Great Fighting Ships **Obverse:** State seal **Reverse:** The Yamato

| Date | Mintage | F | VF | XF | Unc | BU |
|---|---|---|---|---|---|---|
| 1998 | Est. 25,000 | — | — | — | 12.00 | — |

**10 DOLLARS** **KM# 433** **Composition:** Brass **Subject:** History's Great Fighting Ships **Obverse:** State seal **Reverse:** HMS Victory

| Date | Mintage | F | VF | XF | Unc | BU |
|---|---|---|---|---|---|---|
| 1998 | Est. 25,000 | — | — | — | 12.00 | — |

**10 DOLLARS** **KM# 435** **Composition:** Brass **Subject:** History's Great Fighting Ships **Reverse:** HMS Mary Rose

| Date | Mintage | F | VF | XF | Unc | BU |
|---|---|---|---|---|---|---|
| 1998 | Est. 25,000 | — | — | — | 12.00 | — |

**10 DOLLARS** **KM# 437** **Composition:** Brass **Subject:** History's Great Fighting Ships **Reverse:** HMS Dreadnought

| Date | Mintage | F | VF | XF | Unc | BU |
|---|---|---|---|---|---|---|
| 1998 | Est. 25,000 | — | — | — | 12.00 | — |

**10 DOLLARS** **KM# 439** **Composition:** Brass **Subject:** History's Great Fighting Ships **Obverse:** State Seal **Reverse:** HMS Dorsetshire

| Date | Mintage | F | VF | XF | Unc | BU |
|---|---|---|---|---|---|---|
| 1998 | Est. 25,000 | — | — | — | 12.00 | — |

**10 DOLLARS** **KM# 441** **Composition:** Brass **Subject:** History's Great Fighting Ships **Obverse:** State Seal **Reverse:** Nuestra Senora del Rosario

| Date | Mintage | F | VF | XF | Unc | BU |
|---|---|---|---|---|---|---|
| 1998 | Est. 25,000 | — | — | — | 12.00 | — |

**10 DOLLARS** **KM# 443** **Composition:** Brass **Subject:** History's Great Fighting Ships **Obverse:** State Seal **Reverse:** Santisima Trinidad

| Date | Mintage | F | VF | XF | Unc | BU |
|---|---|---|---|---|---|---|
| 1998 | Est. 25,000 | — | — | — | 12.00 | — |

**10 DOLLARS** **KM# 445** **Composition:** Brass **Subject:** History's Great Fighting Ships **Obverse:** State Seal **Reverse:** USS Bonhomme Richard

| Date | Mintage | F | VF | XF | Unc | BU |
|---|---|---|---|---|---|---|
| 1998 | Est. 25,000 | — | — | — | 12.00 | — |

**10 DOLLARS** **KM# 447** **Composition:** Brass **Subject:** History's Great Fighting Ships **Obverse:** State Seal **Reverse:** USS Constellation

| Date | Mintage | F | VF | XF | Unc | BU |
|---|---|---|---|---|---|---|
| 1998 | Est. 25,000 | — | — | — | 12.00 | — |

**10 DOLLARS** **KM# 449** **Composition:** Brass **Subject:** History's Great Fighting Ships **Obverse:** State Seal **Reverse:** USS Hartford

| Date | Mintage | F | VF | XF | Unc | BU |
|---|---|---|---|---|---|---|
| 1998 | Est. 25,000 | — | — | — | 12.00 | — |

**10 DOLLARS** **KM# 451** **Composition:** Brass **Subject:** History's Great Fighting Ships **Obverse:** State Seal **Reverse:** USS Hornet

| Date | Mintage | F | VF | XF | Unc | BU |
|---|---|---|---|---|---|---|
| 1998 | Est. 25,000 | — | — | — | 12.00 | — |

**10 DOLLARS** **KM# 453** **Composition:** Brass **Subject:** History's Great Fighting Ships **Obverse:** State Seal **Reverse:** USS Missouri

| Date | Mintage | F | VF | XF | Unc | BU |
|---|---|---|---|---|---|---|
| 1998 | Est. 25,000 | — | — | — | 12.00 | — |

**10 DOLLARS** **KM# 455** **Composition:** Brass **Subject:** History's Great Fighting Ships **Obverse:** State Seal **Reverse:** USS Tautog

| Date | Mintage | F | VF | XF | Unc | BU |
|---|---|---|---|---|---|---|
| 1998 | Est. 25,000 | — | — | — | 12.00 | — |

**10 DOLLARS** **KM# 457** **Composition:** Brass **Subject:** History's Great Fighting Ships **Obverse:** State Seal **Reverse:** Brederode

| Date | Mintage | F | VF | XF | Unc | BU |
|---|---|---|---|---|---|---|
| 1998 | Est. 25,000 | — | — | — | 12.00 | — |

**10 DOLLARS** **KM# 459** **Composition:** Brass **Subject:** History's Great Fighting Ships **Obverse:** State Seal **Reverse:** Ville de Paris

| Date | Mintage | F | VF | XF | Unc | BU |
|---|---|---|---|---|---|---|
| 1998 | Est. 25,000 | — | — | — | 12.00 | — |

**10 DOLLARS** **KM# 461** **Composition:** Brass **Subject:** History's Great Fighting Ships **Obverse:** State Seal **Reverse:** Galera Veneziana

| Date | Mintage | F | VF | XF | Unc | BU |
|---|---|---|---|---|---|---|
| 1998 | Est. 25,000 | — | — | — | 12.00 | — |

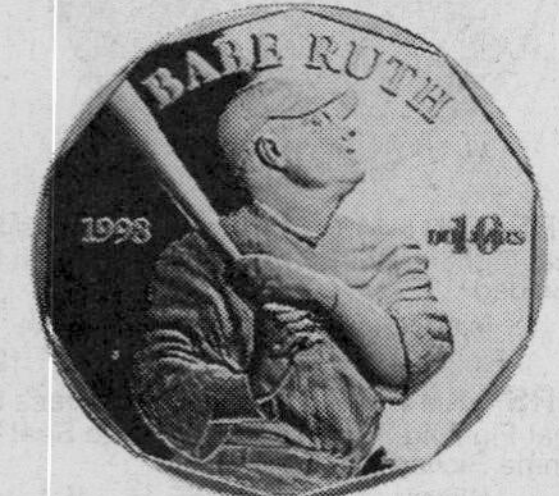


**10 DOLLARS** **KM# 479** **Composition:** Brass **Subject:** Babe Ruth - At Bat **Obverse:** State Seal

| Date | Mintage | F | VF | XF | Unc | BU |
|---|---|---|---|---|---|---|
| 1998 | — | — | — | — | 12.00 | — |

**10 DOLLARS** **KM# 482** **Composition:** Brass **Subject:** Christmas **Obverse:** State Seal **Reverse:** Angel

| Date | Mintage | F | VF | XF | Unc | BU |
|---|---|---|---|---|---|---|
| 1998 | — | — | — | — | 12.00 | — |

**20 DOLLARS** **KM# 3** **Weight:** 3.1100 g. **Composition:** 0.9990 Gold .1000 oz. AGW **Reverse:** Sun

| Date | Mintage | F | VF | XF | Unc | BU |
|---|---|---|---|---|---|---|
| 1986 Proof | Est. 5,000 | Value: 50.00 | | | | |

**20 DOLLARS** **KM# 153** **Weight:** 15.5517 g. **Composition:** 0.9990 Silver .5000 oz. ASW **Subject:** First Men on Moon

| Date | Mintage | F | VF | XF | Unc | BU |
|---|---|---|---|---|---|---|
| 1994 Proof | — | Value: 20.00 | | | | |

**20 DOLLARS** **KM# 189** **Weight:** 15.5517 g. **Composition:** 0.9990 Silver .5000 oz. ASW **Subject:** World Cup Soccer

| Date | Mintage | F | VF | XF | Unc | BU |
|---|---|---|---|---|---|---|
| 1994 Proof | — | Value: 17.50 | | | | |

**20 DOLLARS** **KM# 255** **Weight:** 15.5517 g. **Composition:** 0.9990 Silver .5000 oz. ASW **Subject:** Marilyn Monroe

| Date | Mintage | F | VF | XF | Unc | BU |
|---|---|---|---|---|---|---|
| 1995 Proof | — | Value: 25.00 | | | | |

**20 DOLLARS** **KM# 401** **Weight:** 10.3678 g. **Composition:** 0.9990 Silver .3330 oz. ASW **Subject:** Deng Xiaoping **Obverse:** State seal

| Date | Mintage | F | VF | XF | Unc | BU |
|---|---|---|---|---|---|---|
| 1997 Proof | — | Value: 25.00 | | | | |

**25 DOLLARS** **KM# 20** **Weight:** 33.9600 g. **Composition:** 0.9250 Silver 1.0100 oz. ASW **Subject:** Greg Louganis **Reverse:** Back Dive

| Date | Mintage | F | VF | XF | Unc | BU |
|---|---|---|---|---|---|---|
| 1988 | Est. 280,000 | — | — | — | 75.00 | — |
| 1988 Proof | Est. 350,000 | Value: 110 | | | | |

**25 DOLLARS** **KM# 21** **Weight:** 33.9600 g. **Composition:** 0.9250 Silver 1.0100 oz. ASW **Subject:** Greg Louganis **Reverse:** Twister

| Date | Mintage | F | VF | XF | Unc | BU |
|---|---|---|---|---|---|---|
| 1988 | Est. 280,000 | — | — | — | 80.00 | — |
| 1988 Proof | Est. 350,000 | Value: 110 | | | | |

**25 DOLLARS** **KM# 22** **Weight:** 33.9600 g. **Composition:** 0.9250 Silver 1.0100 oz. ASW **Subject:** Greg Louganis **Reverse:** Jackknife

| Date | Mintage | F | VF | XF | Unc | BU |
|---|---|---|---|---|---|---|
| 1988 | Est. 280,000 | — | — | — | 80.00 | — |
| 1988 Proof | Est. 350,000 | Value: 110 | | | | |

**50 DOLLARS** **KM# 4** **Weight:** 7.7750 g. **Composition:** 0.9990 Gold .2500 oz. AGW **Reverse:** Coconut

| Date | Mintage | F | VF | XF | Unc | BU |
|---|---|---|---|---|---|---|
| 1986 Proof | Est. 5,000 | Value: 125 | | | | |

**50 DOLLARS** **KM# 7** **Weight:** 31.1000 g. **Composition:** 0.9990 Silver 1.0000 oz. ASW **Subject:** John Glenn in Space Orbit

| Date | Mintage | F | VF | XF | Unc | BU |
|---|---|---|---|---|---|---|
| 1989 Proof | Est. 25,000 | Value: 27.50 | | | | |
| 1989S Proof | Inc. above | Value: 23.50 | | | | |

**50 DOLLARS** **KM# 8** **Weight:** 31.1000 g. **Composition:** 0.9990 Silver 1.0000 oz. ASW **Subject:** Neil Armstrong on the Moon **Obverse:** Similar to KM#12

| Date | Mintage | F | VF | XF | Unc | BU |
|---|---|---|---|---|---|---|
| 1989 Proof | Est. 25,000 | Value: 27.50 | | | | |
| 1989S Proof | Inc. above | Value: 23.50 | | | | |

**50 DOLLARS** **KM# 9** **Weight:** 31.1000 g. **Composition:** 0.9990 Silver 1.0000 oz. ASW **Subject:** American Space Station - Skylab **Obverse:** Similar to KM#12

| Date | Mintage | F | VF | XF | Unc | BU |
|---|---|---|---|---|---|---|
| 1989 Proof | Est. 25,000 | Value: 22.50 | | | | |
| 1989S Proof | Inc. above | Value: 20.00 | | | | |

**50 DOLLARS** **KM# 10** **Weight:** 31.1000 g. **Composition:** 0.9990 Silver 1.0000 oz. ASW **Subject:** Apollo - Sojus Joint Mission

| Date | Mintage | F | VF | XF | Unc | BU |
|---|---|---|---|---|---|---|
| 1989 Proof | Est. 25,000 | Value: 27.50 | | | | |
| 1989S Proof | Inc. above | Value: 23.50 | | | | |

**50 DOLLARS** **KM# 11** **Weight:** 31.1000 g. **Composition:** 0.9990 Silver 1.0000 oz. ASW **Subject:** First Space Shuttle Flight

| Date | Mintage | F | VF | XF | Unc | BU |
|---|---|---|---|---|---|---|
| 1989 Proof | Est. 25,000 | Value: 27.50 | | | | |
| 1989S Proof | Inc. above | Value: 23.50 | | | | |

**50 DOLLARS** **KM# 12** **Weight:** 31.1000 g. **Composition:** 0.9990 Silver 1.0000 oz. ASW **Subject:** U.S. Space Shuttle - Discovery

| Date | Mintage | F | VF | XF | Unc | BU |
|---|---|---|---|---|---|---|
| 1989 Proof | Est. 50,000 | Value: 20.00 | | | | |
| 1989S Proof | Inc. above | Value: 18.00 | | | | |

**50 DOLLARS** **KM# 14** **Weight:** 31.1000 g. **Composition:** 0.9990 Silver 1.0000 oz. ASW **Subject:** 20th Anniversary - First Men on the Moon

| Date | Mintage | F | VF | XF | Unc | BU |
|---|---|---|---|---|---|---|
| 1989 Proof | Est. 50,000 | Value: 20.00 | | | | |
| 1989S Proof | Inc. above | Value: 18.00 | | | | |

**50 DOLLARS** **KM# 15** **Weight:** 31.1000 g. **Composition:** 0.9990 Silver 1.0000 oz. ASW **Subject:** First American Space Walk

| Date | Mintage | F | VF | XF | Unc | BU |
|---|---|---|---|---|---|---|
| 1989 Proof | Est. 25,000 | Value: 27.50 | | | | |
| 1989S Proof | Inc. above | Value: 23.50 | | | | |

**50 DOLLARS** **KM# 23** **Weight:** 31.1000 g. **Composition:** 0.9990 Silver 1.0000 oz. ASW **Subject:** First Docking In Space

| Date | Mintage | F | VF | XF | Unc | BU |
|---|---|---|---|---|---|---|
| 1989 Proof | Est. 25,000 | Value: 27.50 | | | | |
| 1989S Proof | Inc. above | Value: 23.50 | | | | |

**50 DOLLARS** **KM# 24** **Weight:** 31.1000 g. **Composition:** 0.9990 Silver 1.0000 oz. ASW **Subject:** First Man-Made Satellite - 1957

| Date | Mintage | F | VF | XF | Unc | BU |
|---|---|---|---|---|---|---|
| 1989 Proof | Est. 25,000 | Value: 22.50 | | | | |
| 1989S Proof | Inc. above | Value: 20.00 | | | | |

**50 DOLLARS** **KM# 25** **Weight:** 31.1000 g. **Composition:** 0.9990 Silver 1.0000 oz. ASW **Subject:** First Man In Space - 1961

| Date | Mintage | F | VF | XF | Unc | BU |
|---|---|---|---|---|---|---|
| 1989 Proof | Est. 25,000 | Value: 27.50 | | | | |
| 1989S Proof | Inc. above | Value: 23.50 | | | | |

**50 DOLLARS** **KM# 26** **Weight:** 31.1000 g. **Composition:** 0.9990 Silver 1.0000 oz. ASW **Subject:** First Woman In Space - 1963

| Date | Mintage | F | VF | XF | Unc | BU |
|---|---|---|---|---|---|---|
| 1989 Proof | Est. 25,000 | Value: 27.50 | | | | |
| 1989S Proof | Inc. above | Value: 23.50 | | | | |

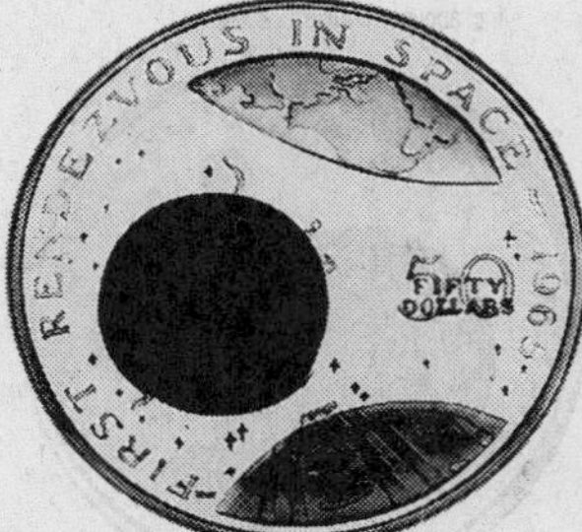


**50 DOLLARS** **KM# 27** **Weight:** 31.1000 g. **Composition:** 0.9990 Silver 1.0000 oz. ASW **Subject:** First Rendezvous In Space - 1965

| Date | Mintage | F | VF | XF | Unc | BU |
|---|---|---|---|---|---|---|
| 1989 Proof | Est. 25,000 | Value: 27.50 | | | | |
| 1989S Proof | Inc. above | Value: 23.50 | | | | |

**50 DOLLARS** **KM# 28** **Weight:** 31.1000 g. **Composition:** 0.9990 Silver 1.0000 oz. ASW **Subject:** First Space Walk - 1965

| Date | Mintage | F | VF | XF | Unc | BU |
|---|---|---|---|---|---|---|
| 1989 Proof | Est. 25,000 | Value: 27.50 | | | | |
| 1989S Proof | Inc. above | Value: 23.50 | | | | |

**50 DOLLARS** **KM# 29** **Weight:** 31.1000 g. **Composition:** 0.9990 Silver 1.0000 oz. ASW **Subject:** First Soft Landing on the Moon - 1966

| Date | Mintage | F | VF | XF | Unc | BU |
|---|---|---|---|---|---|---|
| 1989 Proof | Est. 25,000 | Value: 27.50 | | | | |
| 1989S Proof | Inc. above | Value: 23.50 | | | | |

**50 DOLLARS** **KM# 30** **Weight:** 31.1000 g. **Composition:** 0.9990 Silver 1.0000 oz. ASW **Subject:** First Probe of Venus - 1967

| Date | Mintage | F | VF | XF | Unc | BU |
|---|---|---|---|---|---|---|
| 1989 Proof | Est. 25,000 | Value: 27.50 | | | | |
| 1989S Proof | Inc. above | Value: 23.50 | | | | |

**50 DOLLARS** **KM# 31** **Weight:** 31.1000 g. **Composition:** 0.9990 Silver 1.0000 oz. ASW **Subject:** First Manned Orbit of the Moon - 1968

| Date | Mintage | F | VF | XF | Unc | BU |
|---|---|---|---|---|---|---|
| 1989 Proof | Est. 25,000 | Value: 27.50 | | | | |
| 1989S Proof | Inc. above | Value: 23.50 | | | | |

**50 DOLLARS** **KM# 32** **Weight:** 31.1000 g. **Composition:** 0.9990 Silver 1.0000 oz. ASW **Subject:** First Space Station Crew - 1971

| Date | Mintage | F | VF | XF | Unc | BU |
|---|---|---|---|---|---|---|
| 1989 Proof | Est. 25,000 | Value: 27.50 | | | | |
| 1989S Proof | Inc. above | Value: 23.50 | | | | |

**50 DOLLARS** **KM# 50** **Weight:** 31.1000 g. **Composition:** 0.9990 Silver 1.0000 oz. ASW **Subject:** First Manned Lunar Vehicle - 1971

| Date | Mintage | F | VF | XF | Unc | BU |
|---|---|---|---|---|---|---|
| 1989 Proof | Est. 25,000 | Value: 27.50 | | | | |
| 1989S Proof | Inc. above | Value: 23.50 | | | | |

**50 DOLLARS** **KM# 51** **Weight:** 31.1000 g. **Composition:** 0.9990 Silver 1.0000 oz. ASW **Subject:** First American Satellite - 1958

| Date | Mintage | F | VF | XF | Unc | BU |
|---|---|---|---|---|---|---|
| 1989 Proof | Est. 25,000 | Value: 27.50 | | | | |
| 1989S Proof | Inc. above | Value: 23.50 | | | | |

**50 DOLLARS** **KM# 52** **Weight:** 31.1000 g. **Composition:** 0.9990 Silver 1.0000 oz. ASW **Subject:** First Liquid Fuel Rocket Launch - 1926

| Date | Mintage | F | VF | XF | Unc | BU |
|---|---|---|---|---|---|---|
| 1989 Proof | Est. 25,000 | Value: 27.50 | | | | |
| 1989S Proof | Inc. above | Value: 23.50 | | | | |

**50 DOLLARS** **KM# 53** **Weight:** 31.1000 g. **Composition:** 0.9990 Silver 1.0000 oz. ASW **Subject:** First Untethered Space Walk - 1984

| Date | Mintage | F | VF | XF | Unc | BU |
|---|---|---|---|---|---|---|
| 1989 Proof | Est. 25,000 | Value: 27.50 | | | | |
| 1989S Proof | Inc. above | Value: 23.50 | | | | |

**50 DOLLARS** **KM# 54** **Weight:** 31.1000 g. **Composition:** 0.9990 Silver 1.0000 oz. ASW **Subject:** First Landing on Mars - 1976

| Date | Mintage | F | VF | XF | Unc | BU |
|---|---|---|---|---|---|---|
| 1989 Proof | Est. 25,000 | Value: 27.50 | | | | |
| 1989S Proof | Inc. above | Value: 23.50 | | | | |

**50 DOLLARS** **KM# 55** **Weight:** 31.1000 g. **Composition:** 0.9990 Silver 1.0000 oz. ASW **Subject:** First Flyby of Saturn - 1979

| Date | Mintage | F | VF | XF | Unc | BU |
|---|---|---|---|---|---|---|
| 1989 Proof | Est. 25,000 | Value: 27.50 | | | | |
| 1989S Proof | Inc. above | Value: 23.50 | | | | |

**50 DOLLARS** **KM# 56** **Weight:** 31.1000 g. **Composition:** 0.9990 Silver 1.0000 oz. ASW **Subject:** First Probe Beyond the Solar System - 1983

| Date | Mintage | F | VF | XF | Unc | BU |
|---|---|---|---|---|---|---|
| 1989 Proof | Est. 25,000 | Value: 27.50 | | | | |
| 1989S Proof | Inc. above | Value: 23.50 | | | | |

**50 DOLLARS** **KM# 57** **Weight:** 31.1000 g. **Composition:** 0.9990 Silver 1.0000 oz. ASW **Subject:** First Flyby of Jupiter - 1973

| Date | Mintage | F | VF | XF | Unc | BU |
|---|---|---|---|---|---|---|
| 1989 Proof | Est. 25,000 | Value: 27.50 | | | | |
| 1989S Proof | Inc. above | Value: 23.50 | | | | |

**50 DOLLARS** **KM# 19** **Weight:** 31.1000 g. **Composition:** 0.9990 Silver 1.0000 oz. ASW **Subject:** 50th Anniversary - Battle of Britain

| Date | Mintage | F | VF | XF | Unc | BU |
|---|---|---|---|---|---|---|
| 1990M Proof | Est. 50,000 | Value: 35.00 | | | | |

**50 DOLLARS** **KM# 34** **Weight:** 31.1000 g. **Composition:** 0.9990 Silver 1.0000 oz. ASW **Subject:** German Unification

| Date | Mintage | F | VF | XF | Unc | BU |
|---|---|---|---|---|---|---|
| 1990M Proof | Est. 50,000 | Value: 50.00 | | | | |

**50 DOLLARS** **KM# 39** **Weight:** 31.1000 g. **Composition:** 0.9990 Silver 1.0000 oz. ASW **Subject:** Dwight David Eisenhower

| Date | Mintage | F | VF | XF | Unc | BU |
|---|---|---|---|---|---|---|
| 1990M Proof | Est. 50,000 | Value: 37.50 | | | | |

**50 DOLLARS** **KM# 36** **Weight:** 31.1000 g. **Composition:** 0.9990 Silver 1.0000 oz. ASW **Subject:** Pearl Harbor

| Date | Mintage | F | VF | XF | Unc | BU |
|---|---|---|---|---|---|---|
| 1991M Proof | Est. 50,000 | Value: 27.50 | | | | |

**50 DOLLARS** **KM# 42** **Weight:** 31.1000 g. **Composition:** 0.9990 Silver 1.0000 oz. ASW **Subject:** To the Heroes of Desert Storm

| Date | Mintage | F | VF | XF | Unc | BU |
|---|---|---|---|---|---|---|
| 1991R Proof | — | Value: 22.50 | | | | |

**50 DOLLARS** **KM# 43** **Weight:** 31.1000 g. **Composition:** 0.9990 Silver 1.0000 oz. ASW **Reverse:** WWII American P-51 Mustang

| Date | Mintage | F | VF | XF | Unc | BU |
|---|---|---|---|---|---|---|
| 1991 Proof | Est. 25,000 | Value: 27.50 | | | | |

**50 DOLLARS** **KM# 44** **Weight:** 31.1000 g. **Composition:** 0.9990 Silver 1.0000 oz. ASW **Reverse:** WWII American B-29 Superfortress

| Date | Mintage | F | VF | XF | Unc | BU |
|---|---|---|---|---|---|---|
| 1991M Proof | Est. 25,000 | Value: 27.50 | | | | |

**50 DOLLARS** **KM# 45** **Weight:** 31.1000 g. **Composition:** 0.9990 Silver 1.0000 oz. ASW **Reverse:** WWII German BF-109 Messerschmitt

| Date | Mintage | F | VF | XF | Unc | BU |
|---|---|---|---|---|---|---|
| 1991 Proof | Est. 25,000 | Value: 27.50 | | | | |

**50 DOLLARS** **KM# 46** **Weight:** 31.1000 g. **Composition:** 0.9990 Silver 1.0000 oz. ASW **Reverse:** WWII British Spitfire

| Date | Mintage | F | VF | XF | Unc | BU |
|---|---|---|---|---|---|---|
| 1991M Proof | Est. 25,000 | Value: 27.50 | | | | |

**50 DOLLARS** **KM# 47** **Weight:** 31.1000 g. **Composition:** 0.9990 Silver 1.0000 oz. ASW **Reverse:** WWII American PBY Catalina

| Date | Mintage | F | VF | XF | Unc | BU |
|---|---|---|---|---|---|---|
| 1991M Proof | Est. 25,000 | Value: 25.00 | | | | |

**50 DOLLARS** **KM# 48** **Weight:** 31.1000 g. **Composition:** 0.9990 Silver 1.0000 oz. ASW **Reverse:** WWII Japanese A6M Reisen

| Date | Mintage | F | VF | XF | Unc | BU |
|---|---|---|---|---|---|---|
| 1991M Proof | Est. 25,000 | Value: 27.50 | | | | |

**50 DOLLARS** **KM# 58** **Weight:** 31.1000 g. **Composition:** 0.9990 Silver 1.0000 oz. ASW **Reverse:** WWII American P-40 Warhawk

| Date | Mintage | F | VF | XF | Unc | BU |
|---|---|---|---|---|---|---|
| 1991M Proof | Est. 25,000 | Value: 27.50 | | | | |

**50 DOLLARS** KM# 72 **Weight:** 31.1000 g. **Composition:** 0.9990 Silver 1.0000 oz. ASW **Reverse:** Space Shuttle Columbia - 1981

| Date | Mintage | F | VF | XF | Unc | BU |
|---|---|---|---|---|---|---|
| 1991M Proof | Est. 25,000 | Value: 40.00 | | | | |

**50 DOLLARS** KM# 74 **Weight:** 31.1000 g. **Composition:** 0.9990 Silver 1.0000 oz. ASW **Reverse:** WWII British Hurricane

| Date | Mintage | F | VF | XF | Unc | BU |
|---|---|---|---|---|---|---|
| 1991S Proof | Est. 24,000 | Value: 25.00 | | | | |

**50 DOLLARS** KM# 75 **Weight:** 31.1000 g. **Composition:** 0.9990 Silver 1.0000 oz. ASW **Reverse:** WWII British Mosquito

| Date | Mintage | F | VF | XF | Unc | BU |
|---|---|---|---|---|---|---|
| 1991S Proof | Est. 24,000 | Value: 25.00 | | | | |

**50 DOLLARS** KM# 76 **Weight:** 31.1000 g. **Composition:** 0.9990 Silver 1.0000 oz. ASW **Reverse:** WWII American B-24 Liberator

| Date | Mintage | F | VF | XF | Unc | BU |
|---|---|---|---|---|---|---|
| 1991S Proof | Est. 25,000 | Value: 25.00 | | | | |

**50 DOLLARS** KM# 77 **Weight:** 31.1000 g. **Composition:** 0.9990 Silver 1.0000 oz. ASW **Reverse:** WWII American B-25 Mitchell

| Date | Mintage | F | VF | XF | Unc | BU |
|---|---|---|---|---|---|---|
| 1991S Proof | Est. 25,000 | Value: 27.50 | | | | |

**50 DOLLARS** KM# 78 **Weight:** 31.1000 g. **Composition:** 0.9990 Silver 1.0000 oz. ASW **Reverse:** WWII American C-47 Skytrain

| Date | Mintage | F | VF | XF | Unc | BU |
|---|---|---|---|---|---|---|
| 1991S Proof | Est. 24,000 | Value: 27.50 | | | | |

**50 DOLLARS** KM# 79 **Weight:** 31.1000 g. **Composition:** 0.9990 Silver 1.0000 oz. ASW **Reverse:** WWII American B-17 Flying Fortress

| Date | Mintage | F | VF | XF | Unc | BU |
|---|---|---|---|---|---|---|
| 1991S Proof | Est. 24,000 | Value: 27.50 | | | | |

**50 DOLLARS** KM# 80 **Weight:** 31.1000 g. **Composition:** 0.9990 Silver 1.0000 oz. ASW **Reverse:** WWII American F4U Corsair

| Date | Mintage | F | VF | XF | Unc | BU |
|---|---|---|---|---|---|---|
| 1991S Proof | Est. 24,000 | Value: 27.50 | | | | |

**50 DOLLARS** KM# 93 **Weight:** 31.1000 g. **Composition:** 0.9990 Silver 1.0000 oz. ASW **Reverse:** WWII American P-38 Lightning

| Date | Mintage | F | VF | XF | Unc | BU |
|---|---|---|---|---|---|---|
| 1991S Proof | Est. 25,000 | Value: 27.50 | | | | |

**50 DOLLARS** KM# 94 **Weight:** 31.1000 g. **Composition:** 0.9990 Silver 1.0000 oz. ASW **Reverse:** WWII American F6F Hellcat

| Date | Mintage | F | VF | XF | Unc | BU |
|---|---|---|---|---|---|---|
| 1991S Proof | Est. 24,000 | Value: 25.00 | | | | |

**50 DOLLARS** KM# 95 **Weight:** 31.1000 g. **Composition:** 0.9990 Silver 1.0000 oz. ASW **Reverse:** WWII Japanese G4M "Betty" Bomber

| Date | Mintage | F | VF | XF | Unc | BU |
|---|---|---|---|---|---|---|
| 1991S Proof | Est. 25,000 | Value: 25.00 | | | | |

**50 DOLLARS** KM# 97 **Weight:** 31.1000 g. **Composition:** 0.9990 Silver 1.0000 oz. ASW **Reverse:** WWII Soviet Yak-9

| Date | Mintage | F | VF | XF | Unc | BU |
|---|---|---|---|---|---|---|
| 1991S Proof | Est. 24,000 | Value: 25.00 | | | | |

**50 DOLLARS** KM# 99 **Weight:** 31.1000 g. **Composition:** 0.9990 Silver 1.0000 oz. ASW **Reverse:** WWII Japanese K1-61 Hien "Tony"

| Date | Mintage | F | VF | XF | Unc | BU |
|---|---|---|---|---|---|---|
| 1991S Proof | Est. 25,000 | Value: 25.00 | | | | |

**50 DOLLARS** KM# 100 **Weight:** 31.1000 g. **Composition:** 0.9990 Silver 1.0000 oz. ASW **Reverse:** WWII French D-520 Fighter

| Date | Mintage | F | VF | XF | Unc | BU |
|---|---|---|---|---|---|---|
| 1991S Proof | Est. 25,000 | Value: 25.00 | | | | |

**50 DOLLARS** **KM# 102** **Weight:** 31.1000 g. **Composition:** 0.9990 Silver 1.0000 oz. ASW **Reverse:** WWII German FW 190 Fighters

| Date | Mintage | F | VF | XF | Unc | BU |
|---|---|---|---|---|---|---|
| 1991S Proof | Est. 24,000 | Value: 25.00 | | | | |

**50 DOLLARS** **KM# 104** **Weight:** 31.1000 g. **Composition:** 0.9990 Silver 1.0000 oz. ASW **Reverse:** WWII British Lancaster

| Date | Mintage | F | VF | XF | Unc | BU |
|---|---|---|---|---|---|---|
| 1991S Proof | Est. 25,000 | Value: 25.00 | | | | |

**50 DOLLARS** **KM# 105** **Weight:** 31.1000 g. **Composition:** 0.9990 Silver 1.0000 oz. ASW **Reverse:** WWII Italian S.M. 79 Sparviero Bombers

| Date | Mintage | F | VF | XF | Unc | BU |
|---|---|---|---|---|---|---|
| 1991S Proof | Est. 24,000 | Value: 27.50 | | | | |

**50 DOLLARS** **KM# 106** **Weight:** 31.1000 g. **Composition:** 0.9990 Silver 1.0000 oz. ASW **Reverse:** WWII German HE 111 Bombers

| Date | Mintage | F | VF | XF | Unc | BU |
|---|---|---|---|---|---|---|
| 1991S Proof | Est. 25,000 | Value: 25.00 | | | | |

**50 DOLLARS** **KM# 108** **Weight:** 31.1000 g. **Composition:** 0.9990 Silver 1.0000 oz. ASW **Reverse:** WWII Soviet IL-2 Shturmovik

| Date | Mintage | F | VF | XF | Unc | BU |
|---|---|---|---|---|---|---|
| 1991S Proof | Est. 24,000 | Value: 25.00 | | | | |

**50 DOLLARS** **KM# 83** **Weight:** 31.1000 g. **Composition:** 0.9990 Silver 1.0000 oz. ASW **Subject:** Reaching for the Stars **Reverse:** Greek Ship Argo

| Date | Mintage | F | VF | XF | Unc | BU |
|---|---|---|---|---|---|---|
| 1992R Proof | — | Value: 42.50 | | | | |

**50 DOLLARS** **KM# 86** **Weight:** 31.1000 g. **Composition:** 0.9990 Silver 1.0000 oz. ASW **Subject:** To the Heroes of - First Air Raid on Tokyo - Doolittle

| Date | Mintage | F | VF | XF | Unc | BU |
|---|---|---|---|---|---|---|
| 1992R Proof | — | Value: 45.00 | | | | |

**50 DOLLARS** **KM# 89** **Weight:** 31.1000 g. **Composition:** 0.9990 Silver 1.0000 oz. ASW **Subject:** Heroes of Corregidor

| Date | Mintage | F | VF | XF | Unc | BU |
|---|---|---|---|---|---|---|
| 1992R Proof | — | Value: 45.00 | | | | |

**50 DOLLARS** **KM# 92** **Weight:** 31.1000 g. **Composition:** 0.9990 Silver 1.0000 oz. ASW **Subject:** To the Heroes of - Battle of Midway

| Date | Mintage | F | VF | XF | Unc | BU |
|---|---|---|---|---|---|---|
| 1992R Proof | — | Value: 40.00 | | | | |

**50 DOLLARS** **KM# 111** **Weight:** 31.1000 g. **Composition:** 0.9990 Silver 1.0000 oz. ASW **Subject:** Pacific Whales & Dolphins **Reverse:** Humpback Whale

| Date | Mintage | F | VF | XF | Unc | BU |
|---|---|---|---|---|---|---|
| 1993R Proof | Est. 25,000 | Value: 40.00 | | | | |

**50 DOLLARS** **KM# 112** **Weight:** 31.1000 g. **Composition:** 0.9990 Silver 1.0000 oz. ASW **Reverse:** Risso's Dolphins

| Date | Mintage | F | VF | XF | Unc | BU |
|---|---|---|---|---|---|---|
| 1993R Proof | Est. 25,000 | Value: 40.00 | | | | |

**50 DOLLARS** **KM# 113** **Weight:** 31.1000 g. **Composition:** 0.9990 Silver 1.0000 oz. ASW **Reverse:** Beluga Whale

| Date | Mintage | F | VF | XF | Unc | BU |
|---|---|---|---|---|---|---|
| 1993R Proof | Est. 25,000 | Value: 40.00 | | | | |

**50 DOLLARS** **KM# 114** **Weight:** 31.1000 g. **Composition:** 0.9990 Silver 1.0000 oz. ASW **Reverse:** Hector's Dolphin

| Date | Mintage | F | VF | XF | Unc | BU |
|---|---|---|---|---|---|---|
| 1993R Proof | Est. 25,000 | Value: 40.00 | | | | |

**50 DOLLARS** **KM# 115** **Weight:** 31.1000 g. **Composition:** 0.9990 Silver 1.0000 oz. ASW **Reverse:** Blue Whales

| Date | Mintage | F | VF | XF | Unc | BU |
|---|---|---|---|---|---|---|
| 1993R Proof | Est. 25,000 | Value: 40.00 | | | | |

**50 DOLLARS** **KM# 116** **Weight:** 31.1000 g. **Composition:** 0.9990 Silver 1.0000 oz. ASW **Reverse:** Baiji Dolphins

| Date | Mintage | F | VF | XF | Unc | BU |
|---|---|---|---|---|---|---|
| 1993R Proof | Est. 25,000 | Value: 40.00 | | | | |

**50 DOLLARS** **KM# 117** **Weight:** 31.1000 g. **Composition:** 0,9990 Silver 1.0000 oz. ASW **Reverse:** Killer Whales

| Date | Mintage | F | VF | XF | Unc | BU |
|---|---|---|---|---|---|---|
| 1993R Proof | Est. 25,000 | Value: 40.00 | | | | |

**50 DOLLARS** **KM# 120** **Weight:** 31.1000 g. **Composition:** 0.9990 Silver 1.0000 oz. ASW **Subject:** To the Heroes of the North Atlantic **Reverse:** Submarine

| Date | Mintage | F | VF | XF | Unc | BU |
|---|---|---|---|---|---|---|
| 1993R Proof | — | Value: 60.00 | | | | |

**50 DOLLARS** **KM# 123** **Weight:** 31.1000 g. **Composition:** 0.9990 Silver 1.0000 oz. ASW **Subject:** To the Heroes of Guadalcanal **Reverse:** Marine, Battleship & Airplanes

| Date | Mintage | F | VF | XF | Unc | BU |
|---|---|---|---|---|---|---|
| 1993R Proof | — | Value: 60.00 | | | | |

**50 DOLLARS** **KM# 128** **Weight:** 31.1000 g. **Composition:** 0.9990 Silver 1.0000 oz. ASW **Subject:** Pacific Whales & Dolphins **Reverse:** Common Dolphins

| Date | Mintage | F | VF | XF | Unc | BU |
|---|---|---|---|---|---|---|
| 1993R Proof | — | Value: 40.00 | | | | |

**50 DOLLARS** **KM# 130** **Weight:** 31.1000 g. **Composition:** 0.9990 Silver 1.0000 oz. ASW **Reverse:** Elvis Presley

| Date | Mintage | F | VF | XF | Unc | BU |
|---|---|---|---|---|---|---|
| 1993S Proof | — | Value: 37.50 | | | | |

**50 DOLLARS** **KM# 146** **Weight:** 31.1000 g. **Composition:** 0.9990 Silver 1.0000 oz. ASW **Subject:** Christmas 1993

| Date | Mintage | F | VF | XF | Unc | BU |
|---|---|---|---|---|---|---|
| 1993R Proof | — | Value: 32.50 | | | | |

**50 DOLLARS** **KM# 150** **Weight:** 31.1000 g. **Composition:** 0.9990 Silver 1.0000 oz. ASW **Subject:** Flight of the Kitty Hawk

| Date | Mintage | F | VF | XF | Unc | BU |
|---|---|---|---|---|---|---|
| 1993 Proof | — | Value: 37.50 | | | | |

**50 DOLLARS** **KM# 154** **Weight:** 31.1000 g. **Composition:** 0.9990 Silver 1.0000 oz. ASW **Subject:** First Men on Moon

| Date | Mintage | F | VF | XF | Unc | BU |
|---|---|---|---|---|---|---|
| 1994 Proof | — | Value: 32.50 | | | | |

**50 DOLLARS** **KM# 167** **Weight:** 31.1000 g. **Composition:** 0.9990 Silver 1.0000 oz. ASW **Reverse:** Mythological Mother Earth

| Date | Mintage | F | VF | XF | Unc | BU |
|---|---|---|---|---|---|---|
| 1994 Proof | Est. 25,000 | Value: 30.00 | | | | |

**50 DOLLARS** **KM# 168** **Weight:** 31.1000 g. **Composition:** 0.9990 Silver 1.0000 oz. ASW **Reverse:** Sun

| Date | Mintage | F | VF | XF | Unc | BU |
|---|---|---|---|---|---|---|
| 1994 Proof | Est. 25,000 | Value: 30.00 | | | | |

**50 DOLLARS** **KM# 169** **Weight:** 31.1000 g. **Composition:** 0.9990 Silver 1.0000 oz. ASW **Reverse:** Moon

| Date | Mintage | F | VF | XF | Unc | BU |
|---|---|---|---|---|---|---|
| 1994 Proof | Est. 25,000 | Value: 30.00 | | | | |

**50 DOLLARS** **KM# 170** **Weight:** 31.1000 g. **Composition:** 0.9990 Silver 1.0000 oz. ASW **Reverse:** Pluto

| Date | Mintage | F | VF | XF | Unc | BU |
|---|---|---|---|---|---|---|
| 1994 Proof | Est. 25,000 | Value: 30.00 | | | | |

**50 DOLLARS** **KM# 171** **Weight:** 31.1000 g. **Composition:** 0.9990 Silver 1.0000 oz. ASW **Reverse:** Mercury

| Date | Mintage | F | VF | XF | Unc | BU |
|---|---|---|---|---|---|---|
| 1994 Proof | Est. 25,000 | Value: 30.00 | | | | |

**50 DOLLARS** **KM# 172** **Weight:** 31.1000 g. **Composition:** 0.9990 Silver 1.0000 oz. ASW **Reverse:** Venus

| Date | Mintage | F | VF | XF | Unc | BU |
|---|---|---|---|---|---|---|
| 1994 Proof | Est. 25,000 | Value: 30.00 | | | | |

**50 DOLLARS** **KM# 173** **Weight:** 31.1000 g. **Composition:** 0.9990 Silver 1.0000 oz. ASW **Reverse:** Mars

| Date | Mintage | F | VF | XF | Unc | BU |
|---|---|---|---|---|---|---|
| 1994 Proof | Est. 25,000 | Value: 30.00 | | | | |

**50 DOLLARS** **KM# 174** **Weight:** 31.1000 g. **Composition:** 0.9990 Silver 1.0000 oz. ASW **Reverse:** Saturn

| Date | Mintage | F | VF | XF | Unc | BU |
|---|---|---|---|---|---|---|
| 1994 Proof | Est. 25,000 | Value: 30.00 | | | | |

**50 DOLLARS** **KM# 175** **Weight:** 31.1000 g. **Composition:** 0.9990 Silver 1.0000 oz. ASW **Reverse:** Jupiter

| Date | Mintage | F | VF | XF | Unc | BU |
|---|---|---|---|---|---|---|
| 1994 Proof | Est. 25,000 | Value: 30.00 | | | | |

**50 DOLLARS** **KM# 176** **Weight:** 31.1000 g. **Composition:** 0.9990 Silver 1.0000 oz. ASW **Reverse:** Uranus

| Date | Mintage | F | VF | XF | Unc | BU |
|---|---|---|---|---|---|---|
| 1994 Proof | Est. 25,000 | Value: 30.00 | | | | |

**50 DOLLARS** **KM# 177** **Weight:** 31.1000 g. **Composition:** 0.9990 Silver 1.0000 oz. ASW **Reverse:** Neptune

| Date | Mintage | F | VF | XF | Unc | BU |
|---|---|---|---|---|---|---|
| 1994 Proof | Est. 25,000 | Value: 30.00 | | | | |

**50 DOLLARS** **KM# 178** **Weight:** 31.1000 g. **Composition:** 0.9990 Silver 1.0000 oz. ASW **Reverse:** Solar System

| Date | Mintage | F | VF | XF | Unc | BU |
|---|---|---|---|---|---|---|
| 1994 Proof | Est. 25,000 | Value: 30.00 | | | | |

**50 DOLLARS** **KM# 181** **Weight:** 31.1000 g. **Composition:** 0.9990 Silver 1.0000 oz. ASW **Subject:** To the Heroes of D-Day - Normandy Invasion

| Date | Mintage | F | VF | XF | Unc | BU |
|---|---|---|---|---|---|---|
| 1994 Proof | — | Value: 37.50 | | | | |

**50 DOLLARS** **KM# 184** **Weight:** 31.1000 g. **Composition:** 0.9990 Silver 1.0000 oz. ASW **Subject:** Heroes of the PHilippines **Reverse:** MacArthur and Staff

| Date | Mintage | F | VF | XF | Unc | BU |
|---|---|---|---|---|---|---|
| 1994 Proof | — | Value: 50.00 | | | | |

**50 DOLLARS** **KM# 190** **Weight:** 31.1000 g. **Composition:** 0.9990 Silver 1.0000 oz. ASW **Subject:** World Cup Soccer

| Date | Mintage | F | VF | XF | Unc | BU |
|---|---|---|---|---|---|---|
| 1994 Proof | — | Value: 37.50 | | | | |

**50 DOLLARS** **KM# 262** **Weight:** 31.1000 g. **Composition:** 0.9990 Silver 1.0000 oz. ASW **Subject:** Christmas **Reverse:** Angel

| Date | Mintage | F | VF | XF | Unc | BU |
|---|---|---|---|---|---|---|
| 1994 Proof | — | Value: 35.00 | | | | |

**50 DOLLARS** **KM# 265** **Weight:** 31.1000 g. **Composition:** 0.9990 Silver 1.0000 oz. ASW **Subject:** To the Heroes of - Battle of the Bulge

| Date | Mintage | F | VF | XF | Unc | BU |
|---|---|---|---|---|---|---|
| 1994 Proof | — | Value: 37.50 | | | | |

**50 DOLLARS** **KM# 191** **Weight:** 31.1000 g. **Composition:** 0.9990 Silver 1.0000 oz. ASW **Reverse:** Jet Fighter - F-4 Phantom II

| Date | Mintage | F | VF | XF | Unc | BU |
|---|---|---|---|---|---|---|
| 1995 Proof | 25,000 | Value: 28.50 | | | | |

**50 DOLLARS** **KM# 192** **Weight:** 31.1000 g. **Composition:** 0.9990 Silver 1.0000 oz. ASW **Reverse:** Jet Fighter - F-100 Super Sabre

| Date | Mintage | F | VF | XF | Unc | BU |
|---|---|---|---|---|---|---|
| 1995 Proof | 25,000 | Value: 27.50 | | | | |

**50 DOLLARS** **KM# 193** **Weight:** 31.1000 g. **Composition:** 0.9990 Silver 1.0000 oz. ASW **Reverse:** Jet Fighter - Mirage 2000C

| Date | Mintage | F | VF | XF | Unc | BU |
|---|---|---|---|---|---|---|
| 1995 Proof | 25,000 | Value: 27.50 | | | | |

**50 DOLLARS** **KM# 194** **Weight:** 31.1000 g. **Composition:** 0.9990 Silver 1.0000 oz. ASW **Reverse:** Jet Fighter - F-14 Tomcat

| Date | Mintage | F | VF | XF | Unc | BU |
|---|---|---|---|---|---|---|
| 1995 Proof | 25,000 | Value: 27.50 | | | | |

**50 DOLLARS** **KM# 195** **Weight:** 31.1000 g. **Composition:** 0.9990 Silver 1.0000 oz. ASW **Reverse:** Jet Fighter - F-86 Sabre

| Date | Mintage | F | VF | XF | Unc | BU |
|---|---|---|---|---|---|---|
| 1995 Proof | 25,000 | Value: 27.50 | | | | |

**50 DOLLARS** **KM# 196** **Weight:** 31.1000 g. **Composition:** 0.9990 Silver 1.0000 oz. ASW **Reverse:** Jet Fighter - MIG 15

| Date | Mintage | F | VF | XF | Unc | BU |
|---|---|---|---|---|---|---|
| 1995 Proof | 25,000 | Value: 27.50 | | | | |

**50 DOLLARS** **KM# 197** **Weight:** 31.1000 g. **Composition:** 0.9990 Silver 1.0000 oz. ASW **Reverse:** Jet Fighter - G91R

| Date | Mintage | F | VF | XF | Unc | BU |
|---|---|---|---|---|---|---|
| 1995 Proof | 25,000 | Value: 30.00 | | | | |

**50 DOLLARS** **KM# 198** **Weight:** 31.1000 g. **Composition:** 0.9990 Silver 1.0000 oz. ASW **Reverse:** Jet Fighter - Saab J35 Draken

| Date | Mintage | F | VF | XF | Unc | BU |
|---|---|---|---|---|---|---|
| 1995 Proof | 25,000 | Value: 27.50 | | | | |

**50 DOLLARS** **KM# 199** **Weight:** 31.1000 g. **Composition:** 0.9990 Silver 1.0000 oz. ASW **Reverse:** Jet Fighter - Meteor F.MK8

| Date | Mintage | F | VF | XF | Unc | BU |
|---|---|---|---|---|---|---|
| 1995 Proof | 25,000 | Value: 27.50 | | | | |

**50 DOLLARS** **KM# 200** **Weight:** 31.1000 g. **Composition:** 0.9990 Silver 1.0000 oz. ASW **Reverse:** Jet Fighter - F-105 Thunderchief

| Date | Mintage | F | VF | XF | Unc | BU |
|---|---|---|---|---|---|---|
| 1995 Proof | 25,000 | Value: 27.50 | | | | |

**50 DOLLARS** **KM# 201** **Weight:** 31.1000 g. **Composition:** 0.9990 Silver 1.0000 oz. ASW **Reverse:** Jet Fighter - Tornado F.MK3

| Date | Mintage | F | VF | XF | Unc | BU |
|---|---|---|---|---|---|---|
| 1995 Proof | 25,000 | Value: 27.50 | | | | |

**50 DOLLARS** **KM# 202** **Weight:** 31.1000 g. **Composition:** 0.9990 Silver 1.0000 oz. ASW **Reverse:** Jet Fighter - F-16 Fighting Falcon

| Date | Mintage | F | VF | XF | Unc | BU |
|---|---|---|---|---|---|---|
| 1995 Proof | 25,000 | Value: 27.50 | | | | |

**50 DOLLARS** **KM# 203** **Weight:** 31.1000 g. **Composition:** 0.9990 Silver 1.0000 oz. ASW **Reverse:** Me 262A-la Schwable

| Date | Mintage | F | VF | XF | Unc | BU |
|---|---|---|---|---|---|---|
| 1995 Proof | 25,000 | Value: 27.50 | | | | |

**50 DOLLARS** **KM# 204** **Weight:** 31.1000 g. **Composition:** 0.9990 Silver 1.0000 oz. ASW **Reverse:** Sea Harrier FRS. MK 1

| Date | Mintage | F | VF | XF | Unc | BU |
|---|---|---|---|---|---|---|
| 1995 Proof | 25,000 | Value: 27.50 | | | | |

**50 DOLLARS** **KM# 205** **Weight:** 31.1000 g. **Composition:** 0.9990 Silver 1.0000 oz. ASW **Reverse:** F-117 Nighthawk

| Date | Mintage | F | VF | XF | Unc | BU |
|---|---|---|---|---|---|---|
| 1995 Proof | 25,000 | Value: 28.50 | | | | |

**50 DOLLARS** **KM# 206** **Weight:** 31.1000 g. **Composition:** 0.9990 Silver 1.0000 oz. ASW **Reverse:** MIG - 21MF

| Date | Mintage | F | VF | XF | Unc | BU |
|---|---|---|---|---|---|---|
| 1995 Proof | 25,000 | Value: 28.50 | | | | |

**50 DOLLARS** **KM# 207** **Weight:** 31.1000 g. **Composition:** 0.9990 Silver 1.0000 oz. ASW **Reverse:** F-104 Starfighter

| Date | Mintage | F | VF | XF | Unc | BU |
|---|---|---|---|---|---|---|
| 1995 Proof | 25,000 | Value: 27.50 | | | | |

**50 DOLLARS** **KM# 208** **Weight:** 31.1000 g. **Composition:** 0.9990 Silver 1.0000 oz. ASW **Reverse:** Sukhoi SU-27 UB

| Date | Mintage | F | VF | XF | Unc | BU |
|---|---|---|---|---|---|---|
| 1995 Proof | 25,000 | Value: 28.50 | | | | |

**50 DOLLARS** **KM# 209** **Weight:** 31.1000 g. **Composition:** 0.9990 Silver 1.0000 oz. ASW **Reverse:** F-80 Shooting Star

| Date | Mintage | F | VF | XF | Unc | BU |
|---|---|---|---|---|---|---|
| 1995 Proof | 25,000 | Value: 27.50 | | | | |

**50 DOLLARS** **KM# 210** **Weight:** 31.1000 g. **Composition:** 0.9990 Silver 1.0000 oz. ASW **Reverse:** Swedish Saab JA 37 Viggen

| Date | Mintage | F | VF | XF | Unc | BU |
|---|---|---|---|---|---|---|
| 1995 Proof | 25,000 | Value: 27.50 | | | | |

**50 DOLLARS** **KM# 211** **Weight:** 31.1000 g. **Composition:** 0.9990 Silver 1.0000 oz. ASW **Reverse:** F8U Crusader

| Date | Mintage | F | VF | XF | Unc | BU |
|---|---|---|---|---|---|---|
| 1995 Proof | 25,000 | Value: 27.50 | | | | |

**50 DOLLARS** **KM# 212** **Weight:** 31.1000 g. **Composition:** 0.9990 Silver 1.0000 oz. ASW **Reverse:** Fiat-G91Y Jet Fighter

| Date | Mintage | F | VF | XF | Unc | BU |
|---|---|---|---|---|---|---|
| 1995 Proof | 25,000 | Value: 30.00 | | | | |

**50 DOLLARS** **KM# 213** **Weight:** 31.1000 g. **Composition:** 0.9990 Silver 1.0000 oz. ASW **Reverse:** Mirage FIC

| Date | Mintage | F | VF | XF | Unc | BU |
|---|---|---|---|---|---|---|
| 1995 Proof | Est. 25,000 | Value: 27.50 | | | | |

**50 DOLLARS** **KM# 214** **Weight:** 31.1000 g. **Composition:** 0.9990 Silver 1.0000 oz. ASW **Reverse:** F-15 Eagle

| Date | Mintage | F | VF | XF | Unc | BU |
|---|---|---|---|---|---|---|
| 1995 Proof | Est. 25,000 | Value: 27.50 | | | | |

**50 DOLLARS** **KM#215** **Weight:** 31.1000 g. **Composition:** 0.9990 Silver 1.0000 oz. ASW **Obverse:** State seal **Reverse:** F9F-2 Panther

| Date | Mintage | F | VF | XF | Unc | BU |
|---|---|---|---|---|---|---|
| 1995 Proof | Est. 25,000 | Value: 27.50 | | | | |

**50 DOLLARS** **KM#224** **Weight:** 31.1000 g. **Composition:** 0.9990 Silver 1.0000 oz. ASW **Reverse:** Elvis Presley

| Date | Mintage | F | VF | XF | Unc | BU |
|---|---|---|---|---|---|---|
| 1995 Proof | — | Value: 60.00 | | | | |

**50 DOLLARS** **KM#256** **Weight:** 31.1000 g. **Composition:** 0.9990 Silver 1.0000 oz. ASW **Reverse:** Marilyn Monroe

| Date | Mintage | F | VF | XF | Unc | BU |
|---|---|---|---|---|---|---|
| 1995 Proof | — | Value: 56.00 | | | | |

**50 DOLLARS** **KM#259** **Weight:** 31.1000 g. **Composition:** 0.9990 Silver 1.0000 oz. ASW **Series:** 50th Anniversary United Nations **Subject:** Peace

| Date | Mintage | F | VF | XF | Unc | BU |
|---|---|---|---|---|---|---|
| 1995 Proof | — | Value: 56.00 | | | | |

**50 DOLLARS** **KM#268** **Weight:** 31.1000 g. **Composition:** 0.9990 Silver 1.0000 oz. ASW **Subject:** Peace - VJ Day

| Date | Mintage | F | VF | XF | Unc | BU |
|---|---|---|---|---|---|---|
| 1995 Proof | — | Value: 45.00 | | | | |

**50 DOLLARS** **KM#273** **Weight:** 31.1000 g. **Composition:** 0.9990 Silver 1.0000 oz. ASW **Subject:** Christmas **Reverse:** Cherub

| Date | Mintage | F | VF | XF | Unc | BU |
|---|---|---|---|---|---|---|
| 1995 Proof | — | Value: 35.00 | | | | |

**50 DOLLARS** **KM#274** **Weight:** 31.1000 g. **Composition:** 0.9990 Silver 1.0000 oz. ASW **Subject:** Freedom / Liberty **Reverse:** Torpedo Boat PT-109

| Date | Mintage | F | VF | XF | Unc | BU |
|---|---|---|---|---|---|---|
| 1995 Proof | Est. 25,000 | Value: 56.00 | | | | |

**50 DOLLARS** **KM#275** **Weight:** 31.1000 g. **Composition:** 0.9990 Silver 1.0000 oz. ASW **Subject:** Freedom / Liberty **Reverse:** President John F. Kennedy takes Oath of Office

| Date | Mintage | F | VF | XF | Unc | BU |
|---|---|---|---|---|---|---|
| 1995 Proof | Est. 25,000 | Value: 56.00 | | | | |

**50 DOLLARS** **KM#276** **Weight:** 31.1000 g. **Composition:** 0.9990 Silver 1.0000 oz. ASW **Subject:** Freedom / Liberty **Reverse:** Peace Corps worker and native

| Date | Mintage | F | VF | XF | Unc | BU |
|---|---|---|---|---|---|---|
| 1995 Proof | Est. 25,000 | Value: 56.00 | | | | |

**50 DOLLARS** **KM#367** **Weight:** 31.1000 g. **Composition:** 0.9990 Silver 1.0000 oz. ASW **Obverse:** State seal **Reverse:** F-102A Delta Dagger

| Date | Mintage | F | VF | XF | Unc | BU |
|---|---|---|---|---|---|---|
| 1995 Proof | 25,000 | Value: 27.50 | | | | |

**50 DOLLARS** **KM#397** **Weight:** 31.1000 g. **Composition:** 0.9990 Silver 1.0000 oz. ASW **Obverse:** State seal **Reverse:** B-52 Stratofortress

| Date | Mintage | F | VF | XF | Unc | BU |
|---|---|---|---|---|---|---|
| 1995 Proof | 25,000 | Value: 30.00 | | | | |

**50 DOLLARS** **KM#277** **Weight:** 31.1000 g. **Composition:** 0.9990 Silver 1.0000 oz. ASW **Subject:** Freedom / LIberty **Reverse:** Battleship and freighter

| Date | Mintage | F | VF | XF | Unc | BU |
|---|---|---|---|---|---|---|
| 1995 Proof | Est. 25,000 | Value: 56.00 | | | | |

**50 DOLLARS** **KM#278** **Weight:** 31.1000 g. **Composition:** 0.9990 Silver 1.0000 oz. ASW **Subject:** Freedom / Liberty **Reverse:** President John F. Kennedy working at desk

| Date | Mintage | F | VF | XF | Unc | BU |
|---|---|---|---|---|---|---|
| 1995 Proof | Est. 25,000 | Value: 56.00 | | | | |

**50 DOLLARS** **KM#279** **Weight:** 31.1000 g. **Composition:** 0.9990 Silver 1.0000 oz. ASW **Subject:** Freedom / Liberty **Reverse:** President John F. Kennedy's Eternal Flame

| Date | Mintage | F | VF | XF | Unc | BU |
|---|---|---|---|---|---|---|
| 1995 Proof | Est. 25,000 | Value: 56.00 | | | | |

**50 DOLLARS** **KM#218** **Weight:** 31.1000 g. **Composition:** 0.9990 Silver 1.0000 oz. ASW **Subject:** Victory in Europe **Note:** Similar to 5 Dollars, KM#216.

| Date | Mintage | F | VF | XF | Unc | BU |
|---|---|---|---|---|---|---|
| 1995 Proof | — | Value: 40.00 | | | | |

**50 DOLLARS** **KM#221** **Weight:** 31.1000 g. **Composition:** 0.9990 Silver 1.0000 oz. ASW **Subject:** Vietnam Veterans **Note:** Similar to 5 Dollars, KM#219.

| Date | Mintage | F | VF | XF | Unc | BU |
|---|---|---|---|---|---|---|
| 1995 Proof | — | Value: 32.50 | | | | |

**50 DOLLARS** **KM#227** **Weight:** 31.1000 g. **Composition:** 0.9990 Silver 1.0000 oz. ASW **Subject:** War in the Pacific **Note:** Similar to 10 Dollars, KM#226.

| Date | Mintage | F | VF | XF | Unc | BU |
|---|---|---|---|---|---|---|
| 1995 Proof | — | Value: 32.50 | | | | |

**50 DOLLARS** **KM#313** **Weight:** 31.1000 g. **Composition:** 0.9990 Silver 1.0000 oz. ASW **Subject:** Classic Cars **Reverse:** Model A Ford **Note:** Similar to 10 Dollars, KM#312.

| Date | Mintage | F | VF | XF | Unc | BU |
|---|---|---|---|---|---|---|
| 1996 Proof | — | Value: 37.50 | | | | |

**50 DOLLARS** **KM#340** **Weight:** 31.1000 g. **Composition:** 0.9990 Silver 1.0000 oz. ASW **Reverse:** Space Shuttle Challenger **Note:** Similar to 10 Dollars, KM#336.

| Date | Mintage | F | VF | XF | Unc | BU |
|---|---|---|---|---|---|---|
| 1996 Proof | — | Value: 35.00 | | | | |

**50 DOLLARS** **KM#341** **Weight:** 31.1000 g. **Composition:** 0.9990 Silver 1.0000 oz. ASW **Reverse:** Space Shuttle Discovery **Note:** Similar to 10 Dollars, KM#338.

| Date | Mintage | F | VF | XF | Unc | BU |
|---|---|---|---|---|---|---|
| 1996 Proof | — | Value: 35.00 | | | | |

**50 DOLLARS** **KM#281** **Weight:** 31.1000 g. **Composition:** 0.9990 Silver 1.0000 oz. ASW **Subject:** Year of the Rat **Note:** Similar to 5 Dollars, KM#280.

| Date | Mintage | F | VF | XF | Unc | BU |
|---|---|---|---|---|---|---|
| 1996 Proof | — | Value: 40.00 | | | | |

**50 DOLLARS** **KM#305** **Weight:** 31.1000 g. **Composition:** 0.9990 Silver 1.0000 oz. ASW **Reverse:** James Dean **Note:** Similar to 5 Dollars, KM#303.

| Date | Mintage | F | VF | XF | Unc | BU |
|---|---|---|---|---|---|---|
| 1996 Proof | — | Value: 50.00 | | | | |

**50 DOLLARS** **KM#350** **Weight:** 31.1000 g. **Composition:** 0.9990 Silver 1.0000 oz. ASW **Reverse:** Lion **Note:** Similar to 5 Dollars, KM#344.

| Date | Mintage | F | VF | XF | Unc | BU |
|---|---|---|---|---|---|---|
| 1996 Proof | — | Value: 40.00 | | | | |

**50 DOLLARS** **KM#352** **Weight:** 31.1000 g. **Composition:** 0.9990 Silver 1.0000 oz. ASW **Reverse:** Jaguar **Note:** Similar to 5 Dollars, KM#346.

| Date | Mintage | F | VF | XF | Unc | BU |
|---|---|---|---|---|---|---|
| 1996 Proof | — | Value: 40.00 | | | | |

**50 DOLLARS** KM# 290 **Weight:** 31.1000 g. **Composition:** 0.9990 Silver 1.0000 oz. ASW **Reverse:** Space Shuttle Columbia

| Date | Mintage | F | VF | XF | Unc | BU |
|---|---|---|---|---|---|---|
| 1996 Proof | — | Value: 35.00 | | | | |

**50 DOLLARS** KM# 291 **Weight:** 31.1000 g. **Composition:** 0.9990 Silver 1.0000 oz. ASW **Reverse:** Pennsylvania K4

| Date | Mintage | F | VF | XF | Unc | BU |
|---|---|---|---|---|---|---|
| 1996 Proof | — | Value: 32.50 | | | | |

**50 DOLLARS** KM# 292 **Weight:** 31.1000 g. **Composition:** 0.9990 Silver 1.0000 oz. ASW **Subject:** Steam Locomotive **Reverse:** Big Boy

| Date | Mintage | F | VF | XF | Unc | BU |
|---|---|---|---|---|---|---|
| 1996 Proof | — | Value: 32.50 | | | | |

**50 DOLLARS** KM# 296 **Weight:** 31.1000 g. **Composition:** 0.9990 Silver 1.0000 oz. ASW **Subject:** Steam Locomotive **Reverse:** Mallard

| Date | Mintage | F | VF | XF | Unc | BU |
|---|---|---|---|---|---|---|
| 1996 Proof | — | Value: 32.50 | | | | |

**50 DOLLARS** KM# 299 **Weight:** 31.1000 g. **Composition:** 0.9990 Silver 1.0000 oz. ASW **Reverse:** Tiger

| Date | Mintage | F | VF | XF | Unc | BU |
|---|---|---|---|---|---|---|
| 1996 In set only | — | — | — | — | 40.00 | — |

**50 DOLLARS** KM# 302 **Weight:** 31.1000 g. **Composition:** 0.9990 Silver 1.0000 oz. ASW **Reverse:** Elvis Presley

| Date | Mintage | F | VF | XF | Unc | BU |
|---|---|---|---|---|---|---|
| 1996 Proof | — | Value: 50.00 | | | | |

**50 DOLLARS** KM# 310 **Weight:** 31.1000 g. **Composition:** 0.9990 Silver 1.0000 oz. ASW **Subject:** Classic Cars **Reverse:** Ford Quadricycle

| Date | Mintage | F | VF | XF | Unc | BU |
|---|---|---|---|---|---|---|
| 1996 Proof | — | Value: 37.50 | | | | |

**50 DOLLARS** KM# 316 **Weight:** 31.1000 g. **Composition:** 0.9990 Silver 1.0000 oz. ASW **Subject:** Classic Cars **Reverse:** Model T Ford

| Date | Mintage | F | VF | XF | Unc | BU |
|---|---|---|---|---|---|---|
| 1996 Proof | — | Value: 37.50 | | | | |

**50 DOLLARS** KM# 319 **Weight:** 31.1000 g. **Composition:** 0.9990 Silver 1.0000 oz. ASW **Subject:** Classic Cars **Reverse:** 1955 Thunderbird

| Date | Mintage | F | VF | XF | Unc | BU |
|---|---|---|---|---|---|---|
| 1996 Proof | — | Value: 50.00 | | | | |

**50 DOLLARS** KM# 322 **Weight:** 31.1000 g. **Composition:** 0.9990 Silver 1.0000 oz, ASW **Subject:** Classic Cars **Reverse:** 1964 Mustang

| Date | Mintage | F | VF | XF | Unc | BU |
|---|---|---|---|---|---|---|
| 1996 Proof | — | Value: 40.00 | | | | |

**50 DOLLARS** KM# 325 **Weight:** 31.1000 g. **Composition:** 0.9990 Silver 1.0000 oz. ASW **Subject:** Classic Cars **Reverse:** Ford Taurus

| Date | Mintage | F | VF | XF | Unc | BU |
|---|---|---|---|---|---|---|
| 1996 Proof | — | Value: 32.50 | | | | |

**50 DOLLARS** KM# 327 **Weight:** 31.1000 g. **Composition:** 0.9990 Silver 1.0000 oz. ASW **Subject:** Steam Locomotive **Reverse:** DB Class 01

| Date | Mintage | F | VF | XF | Unc | BU |
|---|---|---|---|---|---|---|
| 1996 Proof | Est. 25,000 | Value: 32.50 | | | | |

**50 DOLLARS** KM# 328 **Weight:** 31.1000 g. **Composition:** 0.9990 Silver 1.0000 oz. ASW **Subject:** Steam Locomotive **Reverse:** Renfe Class 242

| Date | Mintage | F | VF | XF | Unc | BU |
|---|---|---|---|---|---|---|
| 1996 Proof | — | Value: 32.50 | | | | |

**50 DOLLARS** **KM# 329** **Weight:** 31.1000 g. **Composition:** 0.9990 Silver 1.0000 oz. ASW **Subject:** Steam Locomotive **Reverse:** FS Group 691

| Date | Mintage | F | VF | XF | Unc | BU |
|---|---|---|---|---|---|---|
| 1996 Proof | — | Value: 32.50 | | | | |

**50 DOLLARS** **KM# 342** **Weight:** 31.1000 g. **Composition:** 0.9990 Silver 1.0000 oz. ASW **Reverse:** Space Shuttle Atlantis

| Date | Mintage | F | VF | XF | Unc | BU |
|---|---|---|---|---|---|---|
| 1996 Proof | — | Value: 35.00 | | | | |

**50 DOLLARS** **KM# 343** **Weight:** 31.1000 g. **Composition:** 0.9990 Silver 1.0000 oz. ASW **Reverse:** Space Shuttle Endeavor

| Date | Mintage | F | VF | XF | Unc | BU |
|---|---|---|---|---|---|---|
| 1996 Proof | — | Value: 35.00 | | | | |

**50 DOLLARS** **KM# 351** **Weight:** 31.1000 g. **Composition:** 0.9990 Silver 1.0000 oz. ASW **Reverse:** Cheetah

| Date | Mintage | F | VF | XF | Unc | BU |
|---|---|---|---|---|---|---|
| 1996 Proof | — | Value: 40.00 | | | | |

**50 DOLLARS** **KM# 355** **Weight:** 31.1000 g. **Composition:** 0.9990 Silver 1.0000 oz. ASW **Subject:** Christmas **Reverse:** 2 Angels

| Date | Mintage | F | VF | XF | Unc | BU |
|---|---|---|---|---|---|---|
| 1996 Proof | — | Value: 35.00 | | | | |

**50 DOLLARS** **KM# 357** **Weight:** 31.1000 g. **Composition:** 0.9990 Silver 1.0000 oz. ASW **Subject:** Steam Locomotive **Reverse:** SNCF 232.U1

| Date | Mintage | F | VF | XF | Unc | BU |
|---|---|---|---|---|---|---|
| 1996 Proof | — | Value: 40.00 | | | | |

**50 DOLLARS** **KM# 358** **Weight:** 31.1000 g. **Composition:** 0.9990 Silver 1.0000 oz. ASW **Subject:** Steam Locomotive **Reverse:** SAR 520 Class

| Date | Mintage | F | VF | XF | Unc | BU |
|---|---|---|---|---|---|---|
| 1996 Proof | — | Value: 40.00 | | | | |

**50 DOLLARS** **KM# 360** **Weight:** 31.1000 g. **Composition:** 0.9990 Silver 1.0000 oz. ASW **Subject:** Steam Locomotive **Reverse:** Evening Star

| Date | Mintage | F | VF | XF | Unc | BU |
|---|---|---|---|---|---|---|
| 1996 | — | — | — | — | 40.00 | — |

**50 DOLLARS** **KM# 376** **Weight:** 31.1000 g. **Composition:** 0.9990 Silver 1.0000 oz. ASW **Subject:** Steam Locomotive **Reverse:** C62 "Swallow"

| Date | Mintage | F | VF | XF | Unc | BU |
|---|---|---|---|---|---|---|
| 1996 Proof | — | Value: 40.00 | | | | |

**50 DOLLARS** **KM# 377** **Weight:** 31.1000 g. **Composition:** 0.9990 Silver 1.0000 oz. ASW **Subject:** Steam Locomotive **Reverse:** QJ "Advance Forward"

| Date | Mintage | F | VF | XF | Unc | BU |
|---|---|---|---|---|---|---|
| 1996 Proof | — | Value: 40.00 | | | | |

**50 DOLLARS** **KM# 380** **Weight:** 31.1000 g. **Composition:** 0.9990 Silver 1.0000 oz. ASW **Subject:** Steam Locomotive **Reverse:** Royal Hudson

| Date | Mintage | F | VF | XF | Unc | BU |
|---|---|---|---|---|---|---|
| 1996 Proof | — | Value: 40.00 | | | | |

**50 DOLLARS** **KM# 363** **Weight:** 31.1000 g. **Composition:** 0.9990 Silver 1.0000 oz. ASW **Subject:** Year of the Ox **Obverse:** State seal **Reverse:** Stylized Ox

| Date | Mintage | F | VF | XF | Unc | BU |
|---|---|---|---|---|---|---|
| 1997 Proof | — | Value: 57.50 | | | | |

**50 DOLLARS** **KM# 375** **Weight:** 31.1000 g. **Composition:** 0.9990 Silver 1.0000 oz. ASW **Reverse:** Gray Wolf

| Date | Mintage | F | VF | XF | Unc | BU |
|---|---|---|---|---|---|---|
| 1997 Proof | — | Value: 42.50 | | | | |

**50 DOLLARS** **KM# 399** **Weight:** 31.1000 g. **Composition:** 0.9990 Silver 1.0000 oz. ASW **Subject:** History's Great Fightintg Ships **Reverse:** USS Constitution; ship, dates

| Date | Mintage | F | VF | XF | Unc | BU |
|---|---|---|---|---|---|---|
| 1997 Proof | — | Value: 56.00 | | | | |

**50 DOLLARS** **KM# 405** **Weight:** 31.1000 g. **Composition:** 0.9990 Silver 1.0000 oz. ASW **Subject:** Christmas **Reverse:** 2 Angels

| Date | Mintage | F | VF | XF | Unc | BU |
|---|---|---|---|---|---|---|
| 1997 | — | — | — | — | 35.00 | — |

**50 DOLLARS** **KM# 366** **Weight:** 31.1000 g. **Composition:** 0.9990 Silver 1.0000 oz. ASW **Reverse:** Elvis Presley **Note:** Similar to 5 Dollars, KM#362.

| Date | Mintage | F | VF | XF | Unc | BU |
|---|---|---|---|---|---|---|
| 1997 Proof | — | Value: 57.50 | | | | |

**50 DOLLARS** **KM# 370** **Weight:** 31.1000 g. **Composition:** 0.9990 Silver 1.0000 oz. ASW **Subject:** The Last Supper **Note:** Similar to 5 Dollars, KM#369.

| Date | Mintage | F | VF | XF | Unc | BU |
|---|---|---|---|---|---|---|
| 1997 Proof | — | Value: 50.00 | | | | |

**50 DOLLARS** **KM# 373** **Weight:** 31.1000 g. **Composition:** 0.9990 Silver 1.0000 oz. ASW **Subject:** To the Heroes of the Korean War **Note:** Similar to 5 Dollars, KM#371.

| Date | Mintage | F | VF | XF | Unc | BU |
|---|---|---|---|---|---|---|
| 1997 Proof | — | Value: 50.00 | | | | |

**50 DOLLARS** **KM# 467** **Weight:** 31.1000 g. **Composition:** 0.9990 Silver 1.0000 oz. ASW **Subject:** Classic Cars **Obverse:** State seal **Reverse:** 1912 Chevy Classic Six **Note:** Similar to 5 Dollars, KM#466.

| Date | Mintage | F | VF | XF | Unc | BU |
|---|---|---|---|---|---|---|
| 1998 Proof | — | Value: 56.00 | | | | |

**50 DOLLARS** **KM# 469** **Weight:** 31.1000 g. **Composition:** 0.9990 Silver 1.0000 oz. ASW **Subject:** Classic Cars **Obverse:** State seal **Reverse:** 1931 Chevy Roadster **Note:** Similar to 5 Dollars, KM#468.

| Date | Mintage | F | VF | XF | Unc | BU |
|---|---|---|---|---|---|---|
| 1998 Proof | — | Value: 56.00 | | | | |

**50 DOLLARS** **KM# 471** **Weight:** 31.1000 g. **Composition:** 0.9990 Silver 1.0000 oz. ASW **Subject:** Classic Cars **Obverse:** State seal **Reverse:** Cameo Carrier **Note:** Similar to 5 Dollars, KM#470.

| Date | Mintage | F | VF | XF | Unc | BU |
|---|---|---|---|---|---|---|
| 1998 Proof | — | Value: 56.00 | | | | |

**50 DOLLARS** **KM# 473** **Weight:** 31.1000 g. **Composition:** 0.9990 Silver 1.0000 oz. ASW **Subject:** Classic Cars **Obverse:** State seal **Reverse:** 1957 Chevy Bel Air **Note:** Similar to 5 Dollars, KM#472.

| Date | Mintage | F | VF | XF | Unc | BU |
|---|---|---|---|---|---|---|
| 1998 Proof | — | Value: 56.00 | | | | |

**50 DOLLARS** **KM# 475** **Weight:** 31.1000 g. **Composition:** 0.9990 Silver 1.0000 oz. ASW **Subject:** Classic Cars **Obverse:**

State seal **Reverse:** 1957 Chevy Corvette **Note:** Similar to 5 Dollars, KM#474.

| Date | Mintage | F | VF | XF | Unc | BU |
|---|---|---|---|---|---|---|
| 1998 Proof | — | Value: 56.00 | | | | |

**50 DOLLARS** **KM# 477** **Weight:** 31.1000 g. **Composition:** 0.9990 Silver 1.0000 oz. ASW **Subject:** Classic Cars **Obverse:** State seal **Reverse:** 1967 Chevy Camaro **Note:** Similar to 5 Dollars, KM#476.

| Date | Mintage | F | VF | XF | Unc | BU |
|---|---|---|---|---|---|---|
| 1998 Proof | — | Value: 56.00 | | | | |

**50 DOLLARS** **KM# 414** **Weight:** 31.1000 g. **Composition:** 0.9990 Silver 1.0000 oz. ASW **Subject:** Year of the Tiger **Reverse:** Stylized Tiger

| Date | Mintage | F | VF | XF | Unc | BU |
|---|---|---|---|---|---|---|
| 1998 Proof | — | Value: 56.00 | | | | |

**50 DOLLARS** **KM# 416** **Weight:** 31.1000 g. **Composition:** 0.9990 Silver 1.0000 oz. ASW **Subject:** History's Great Fighting Ships **Reverse:** Viking Longship

| Date | Mintage | F | VF | XF | Unc | BU |
|---|---|---|---|---|---|---|
| 1998 Proof | Est. 25,000 | Value: 56.00 | | | | |

**50 DOLLARS** **KM# 418** **Weight:** 31.1000 g. **Composition:** 0.9990 Silver 1.0000 oz. ASW **Subject:** History's Great Fighting Ships **Reverse:** Greek Trireme

| Date | Mintage | F | VF | XF | Unc | BU |
|---|---|---|---|---|---|---|
| 1998 Proof | Est. 25,000 | Value: 56.00 | | | | |

**50 DOLLARS** **KM# 420** **Weight:** 31.1000 g. **Composition:** 0.9990 Silver 1.0000 oz. ASW **Subject:** History's Great Fighting Ships **Reverse:** Roman Trireme

| Date | Mintage | F | VF | XF | Unc | BU |
|---|---|---|---|---|---|---|
| 1998 Proof | Est. 25,000 | Value: 56.00 | | | | |

**50 DOLLARS** **KM# 422** **Weight:** 31.1000 g. **Composition:** 0.9990 Silver 1.0000 oz. ASW **Subject:** History's Great Fighting Ships **Reverse:** Chinese Ming Treasure Ship

| Date | Mintage | F | VF | XF | Unc | BU |
|---|---|---|---|---|---|---|
| 1998 Proof | Est. 25,000 | Value: 56.00 | | | | |

**50 DOLLARS** **KM# 424** **Weight:** 31.1000 g. **Composition:** 0.9990 Silver 1.0000 oz. ASW **Subject:** History's Great Fighting Ships **Reverse:** Korean Turtle Ship

| Date | Mintage | F | VF | XF | Unc | BU |
|---|---|---|---|---|---|---|
| 1998 Proof | Est. 25,000 | Value: 56.00 | | | | |

**50 DOLLARS** **KM# 426** **Weight:** 31.1000 g. **Composition:** 0.9990 Silver 1.0000 oz. ASW **Subject:** History's Great Fighting Ships **Reverse:** Fijan War Canoe

| Date | Mintage | F | VF | XF | Unc | BU |
|---|---|---|---|---|---|---|
| 1998 Proof | Est. 25,000 | Value: 56.00 | | | | |

**50 DOLLARS** **KM# 428** **Weight:** 31.1000 g. **Composition:** 0.9990 Silver 1.0000 oz. ASW **Subject:** History's Great Fighting Ships **Reverse:** The Bismarck

| Date | Mintage | F | VF | XF | Unc | BU |
|---|---|---|---|---|---|---|
| 1998 Proof | Est. 25,000 | Value: 56.00 | | | | |

**50 DOLLARS** **KM# 430** **Weight:** 31.1000 g. **Composition:** 0.9990 Silver 1.0000 oz. ASW **Subject:** History's Great Fighting Ships **Reverse:** The Graf Spee

| Date | Mintage | F | VF | XF | Unc | BU |
|---|---|---|---|---|---|---|
| 1998 Proof | Est. 25,000 | Value: 56.00 | | | | |

**50 DOLLARS** **KM# 432** **Weight:** 31.1000 g. **Composition:** 0.9990 Silver 1.0000 oz. ASW **Subject:** History's Great Fighting Ships **Reverse:** The Yamato

| Date | Mintage | F | VF | XF | Unc | BU |
|---|---|---|---|---|---|---|
| 1998 Proof | Est. 25,000 | Value: 56.00 | | | | |

**50 DOLLARS** **KM# 434** **Weight:** 31.1000 g. **Composition:** 0.9990 Silver 1.0000 oz. ASW **Subject:** History's Great Fighting Ships **Reverse:** HMS Victory

| Date | Mintage | F | VF | XF | Unc | BU |
|---|---|---|---|---|---|---|
| 1998 Proof | Est. 25,000 | Value: 56.00 | | | | |

**50 DOLLARS** **KM# 436** **Weight:** 31.1000 g. **Composition:** 0.9990 Silver 1.0000 oz. ASW **Subject:** History's Great Fighting Ships **Reverse:** HMS Mary Rose

| Date | Mintage | F | VF | XF | Unc | BU |
|---|---|---|---|---|---|---|
| 1998 Proof | Est. 25,000 | Value: 56.00 | | | | |

**50 DOLLARS** **KM# 438** **Weight:** 31.1000 g. **Composition:** 0.9990 Silver 1.0000 oz. ASW **Subject:** History's Great Fighting Ships **Reverse:** HMS Dreadnought

| Date | Mintage | F | VF | XF | Unc | BU |
|---|---|---|---|---|---|---|
| 1998 Proof | Est. 25,000 | Value: 56.00 | | | | |

**50 DOLLARS** **KM# 440** **Weight:** 31.1000 g. **Composition:** 0.9990 Silver 1.0000 oz. ASW **Subject:** History's Great Fighting Ships **Reverse:** HMS Dorsetshire

| Date | Mintage | F | VF | XF | Unc | BU |
|---|---|---|---|---|---|---|
| 1998 Proof | Est. 25,000 | Value: 56.00 | | | | |

**50 DOLLARS** **KM# 442** **Weight:** 31.1000 g. **Composition:** 0.9990 Silver 1.0000 oz. ASW **Subject:** History's Great Fighting Ships **Obverse:** State seal **Reverse:** Spanish Galleon Nuestra Senora del Rosario

| Date | Mintage | F | VF | XF | Unc | BU |
|---|---|---|---|---|---|---|
| 1998 Proof | Est. 25,000 | Value: 56.00 | | | | |

**50 DOLLARS** **KM# 444** **Weight:** 31.1000 g. **Composition:** 0.9990 Silver 1.0000 oz. ASW **Subject:** History's Great Fighting Ships **Obverse:** State seal **Reverse:** Spanish Galleon Santisima Trinidad

| Date | Mintage | F | VF | XF | Unc | BU |
|---|---|---|---|---|---|---|
| 1998 Proof | Est. 25,000 | Value: 56.00 | | | | |

**50 DOLLARS** **KM# 446** **Weight:** 31.1000 g. **Composition:** 0.9990 Silver 1.0000 oz. ASW **Subject:** History's Great Fighting Ships **Obverse:** State seal **Reverse:** USS Bonhomme Richard

| Date | Mintage | F | VF | XF | Unc | BU |
|---|---|---|---|---|---|---|
| 1998 Proof | Est. 25,000 | Value: 56.00 | | | | |

**50 DOLLARS** **KM# 448** **Weight:** 31.1000 g. **Composition:** 0.9990 Silver 1.0000 oz. ASW **Subject:** History's Great Fighting Ships **Obverse:** State seal **Reverse:** USS Constellation

| Date | Mintage | F | VF | XF | Unc | BU |
|---|---|---|---|---|---|---|
| 1998 Proof | Est. 25,000 | Value: 56.00 | | | | |

**50 DOLLARS** **KM# 450** **Weight:** 31.1000 g. **Composition:** 0.9990 Silver 1.0000 oz. ASW **Subject:** History's Great Fighting Ships **Obverse:** State seal **Reverse:** USS Hartford

| Date | Mintage | F | VF | XF | Unc | BU |
|---|---|---|---|---|---|---|
| 1998 Proof | Est. 25,000 | Value: 56.00 | | | | |

**50 DOLLARS** **KM# 452** **Weight:** 31.1000 g. **Composition:** 0.9990 Silver 1.0000 oz. ASW **Subject:** History's Great Fighting Ships **Obverse:** State seal **Reverse:** USS Hornet

| Date | Mintage | F | VF | XF | Unc | BU |
|---|---|---|---|---|---|---|
| 1998 Proof | Est. 25,000 | Value: 56.00 | | | | |

**50 DOLLARS** **KM# 454** **Weight:** 31.1000 g. **Composition:** 0.9990 Silver 1.0000 oz. ASW **Subject:** History's Great Fighting Ships **Obverse:** State seal **Reverse:** USS Missouri

| Date | Mintage | F | VF | XF | Unc | BU |
|---|---|---|---|---|---|---|
| 1998 Proof | Est. 25,000 | Value: 56.00 | | | | |

**50 DOLLARS** **KM# 456** **Weight:** 31.1000 g. **Composition:** 0.9990 Silver 1.0000 oz. ASW **Subject:** History's Great Fighting Ships **Obverse:** State seal **Reverse:** USS Tautog

| Date | Mintage | F | VF | XF | Unc | BU |
|---|---|---|---|---|---|---|
| 1998 Proof | Est. 25,000 | Value: 56.00 | | | | |

**50 DOLLARS** **KM# 458** **Weight:** 31.1000 g. **Composition:** 0.9990 Silver 1.0000 oz. ASW **Subject:** History's Great Fighting Ships **Obverse:** State seal **Reverse:** Dutch Ship Brederode

| Date | Mintage | F | VF | XF | Unc | BU |
|---|---|---|---|---|---|---|
| 1998 Proof | Est. 25,000 | Value: 56.00 | | | | |

**50 DOLLARS** **KM# 460** **Weight:** 31.1000 g. **Composition:** 0.9990 Silver 1.0000 oz. ASW **Subject:** History's Great Fighting Ships **Obverse:** State seal **Reverse:** French Ship Ville de Paris

| Date | Mintage | F | VF | XF | Unc | BU |
|---|---|---|---|---|---|---|
| 1998 Proof | Est. 25,000 | Value: 56.00 | | | | |

**50 DOLLARS** **KM# 462** **Weight:** 31.1000 g. **Composition:** 0.9990 Silver 1.0000 oz. ASW **Subject:** History's Great Fighting Ships **Obverse:** State seal **Reverse:** Italian Ship Galera Veneziana

| Date | Mintage | F | VF | XF | Unc | BU |
|---|---|---|---|---|---|---|
| 1998 Proof | Est. 25,000 | Value: 56.00 | | | | |

**50 DOLLARS** **KM# 465** **Weight:** 31.1000 g. **Composition:** 0.9990 Silver 1.0000 oz. ASW **Subject:** To the Heroes of the Berlin Airlift **Obverse:** State seal **Reverse:** C-54 Landing

| Date | Mintage | F | VF | XF | Unc | BU |
|---|---|---|---|---|---|---|
| 1998 Proof | — | Value: 56.00 | | | | |

**50 DOLLARS** **KM# 480** **Weight:** 31.1000 g. **Composition:** 0.9990 Silver 1.0000 oz. ASW **Subject:** Babe Ruth - At Bat **Obverse:** State seal

| Date | Mintage | F | VF | XF | Unc | BU |
|---|---|---|---|---|---|---|
| 1998 Proof | — | Value: 45.00 | | | | |

**50 DOLLARS** **KM# 483** **Weight:** 31.1000 g. **Composition:** 0.9990 Silver 1.0000 oz. ASW **Subject:** Christmas **Obverse:** State seal **Reverse:** Angel

| Date | Mintage | F | VF | XF | Unc | BU |
|---|---|---|---|---|---|---|
| 1998 Proof | — | Value: 45.00 | | | | |

**50 DOLLARS** **KM# 485** **Weight:** 31.1000 g. **Composition:** 0.9990 Silver 1.0000 oz. ASW **Reverse:** Friendship 7 and Discovery blasting off **Edge:** Reeded

| Date | Mintage | F | VF | XF | Unc | BU |
|---|---|---|---|---|---|---|
| 1998 Proof | — | Value: 56.00 | | | | |

**75 DOLLARS** **KM# 16** **Weight:** 155.6700 g. **Composition:** 0.9990 Silver 5.0055 oz. ASW **Subject:** Greg Louganis - World's Greatest Diver **Note:** Illustration reduced actual size 65mm. An actual mintage of 20 pieces has been reported for KM#16.

| Date | Mintage | F | VF | XF | Unc | BU |
|---|---|---|---|---|---|---|
| 1988 Proof | Est. 175,000 | Value: 800 | | | | |

**100 DOLLARS** **KM# 17** **Weight:** 13.3300 g. **Composition:** 0.5830 Gold .2499 oz. AGW **Subject:** Greg Louganis - World's Greatest Diver **Obverse:** State seal and legend **Reverse:** Diver

| Date | Mintage | F | VF | XF | Unc | BU |
|---|---|---|---|---|---|---|
| 1988 | Est. 280,000 | — | — | — | 275 | — |
| 1988 Proof | Est. 350,000 | Value: 300 | | | | |

**200 DOLLARS** **KM# 5** **Weight:** 31.1030 g. **Composition:** 0.9990 Gold 1.0000 oz. AGW **Reverse:** Stick Chart

| Date | Mintage | F | VF | XF | Unc | BU |
|---|---|---|---|---|---|---|
| 1986 Proof | Est. 5,000 | Value: 425 | | | | |

## MINT SETS

| KM# | Date | Mintage | Identification | Issue Price | Mkt Val |
|---|---|---|---|---|---|
| MS2 | 1988 (4) | — | KM#17, 20-22 | — | 550 |
| MS1 | 1988 (3) | — | KM#20-22 | — | 250 |
| MS3 | 1992R (3) | — | KM#81-83 | 71.00 | 75.00 |
| MS4 | 1992R (3) | — | KM#84-86 | 71.00 | 75.00 |
| MS5 | 1992R (3) | — | KM#87-89 | 71.00 | 75.00 |
| MS6 | 1992R (3) | — | KM#90-92 | 71.00 | 75.00 |
| MS7 | 1992R (3) | — | KM#84, 87, 90 | 17.50 | 20.00 |
| MS8 | 1992R (3) | — | KM#85, 88, 91 | 34.00 | 35.00 |
| MS9 | 1992R (3) | — | KM#86, 89, 92 | 156 | 160 |
| MS10 | 1995 (6) | — | KM#282-287 | 66.00 | 75.00 |
| MS11 | 1998 (24) | 25,000 | KM#415, 417, 419, 421, 423, 425, 427, 429, 431, 433, 435, 437, 439, 441, 443, 445, 447, 449, 451, 453, 455, 457, 459, 461 | 288 | 290 |

## PROOF SETS

| KM# | Date | Mintage | Identification | Issue Price | Mkt Val |
|---|---|---|---|---|---|
| PS1 | 1986 (3) | 5,000 | KM#3-5 | 1,095 | 600 |
| PS2 | 1986 (2) | 10,000 | KM#1-2 | 45.00 | 50.00 |
| PS4 | 1988 (4) | — | KM#17, 20-22 | — | 700 |
| PS3 | 1988 (3) | — | KM#20-22 | — | 375 |
| PS5 | 1991 (3) | — | KM#40-42 | 71.00 | 75.00 |
| PS6 | 1993 (3) | — | KM#124, 129-130 | — | 85.00 |
| PS10 | 1994 (3) | — | KM#263 BU, 264, 265 | — | 75.00 |
| PS7 | 1994 (3) | — | KM#179-180 BU, 181 | 71.00 | 75.00 |
| PS8 | 1994 (3) | — | KM#182 BU, 183 P/L, 184 | 71.00 | 75.00 |
| PS9 | 1994 (3) | — | KM#260 BU, 261, 262 | — | 75.00 |
| PS11 | 1995 (6) | 25,000 | KM#274-279 | — | 340 |
| PS12 | 1995 (3) | — | KM#216 BU, 217, 218 | — | 75.00 |
| PS13 | 1995 (3) | — | KM#219 BU, 220, 221 | — | 75.00 |
| PS14 | 1995 (3) | — | KM#222 BU, 223, 224 | — | 75.00 |
| PS15 | 1995 (3) | — | KM#225 BU, 226, 227 | — | 75.00 |
| PS16 | 1995 (3) | — | KM#253 BU, 254, 255 | — | 95.00 |
| PS17 | 1995 (3) | — | KM#257 BU, 258, 259 | — | 75.00 |
| PS18 | 1995 (3) | — | KM#266 BU, 267, 268 | — | 75.00 |
| PS19 | 1996 (6) | — | KM#308, 311, 314, 317, 320, 323 | 33.00 | 40.00 |
| PS20 | 1996 (6) | — | KM#309, 312, 315, 318, 321, 324 | 66.00 | 80.00 |
| PS21 | 1996 (6) | — | KM#310, 313, 316, 319, 322, 325 | 306 | 325 |
| PS22 | 1996 (3) | — | KM#288-290 | 71.00 | 75.00 |
| PS23 | 1996 (3) | — | KM#297-299 | 71.00 | 78.00 |
| PS24 | 1996 (3) | — | KM#300-302 | 71.00 | 78.00 |
| PS25 | 1996 (3) | — | KM#303-305 | 71.00 | 75.00 |
| PS26 | 1996 (3) | — | KM#308-310 | 71.00 | 75.00 |
| PS27 | 1996 (3) | — | KM#311-313 | 71.00 | 75.00 |
| PS28 | 1996 (3) | — | KM#314-316 | 71.00 | 75.00 |
| PS29 | 1996 (3) | — | KM#317-319 | 71.00 | 75.00 |
| PS30 | 1996 (3) | — | KM#320-322 | 71.00 | 75.00 |
| PS31 | 1996 (4) | — | KM#322-325 | 71.00 | 75.00 |
| PS32 | 1996 (3) | — | KM#353-355 | 71.00 | 75.00 |
| PS33 | 1997 (2) | — | KM#362-363 | 61.00 | 65.00 |
| PS34 | 1997 (3) | — | KM#364-366 | 71.00 | 77.50 |
| PS35 | 1997 (2) | — | KM#369-370 | 61.00 | 62.50 |
| PS36 | 1997 (3) | — | KM#371-373 | 71.00 | 75.00 |
| PS37 | 1997 (2) | — | KM#374-375 | 61.00 | 65.00 |
| PS38 | 1997 (2) | — | KM#398-399 | 61.00 | 62.50 |
| PS39 | 1997 (2) | — | KM#400-401 | — | 37.50 |
| PS40 | 1997 (3) | — | KM#403-405 | 71.00 | 75.00 |
| PS41 | 1998 (24) | — | KM#416, 418, 420, 422, 424, 426, 428, 430, 432, 434, 436, 438, 440, 442, 444, 446, 448, 450, 452, 454, 456, 458, 460, 462 | 1,344 | 1,345 |
| PS42 | 1998 (3) | — | KM#478-480 | 71.00 | 72.00 |
| PS43 | 1998 (3) | — | KM#481-483 | 71.00 | 72.00 |

# MARTINIQUE

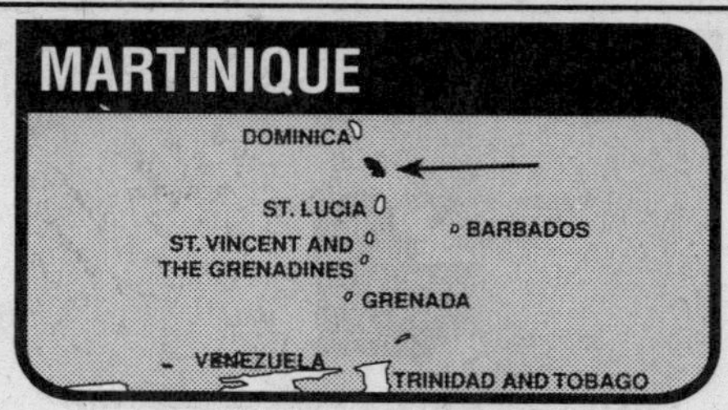


The French Overseas Department of Martinique, located in the Lesser Antilles of the West Indies between Dominica and Saint Lucia, has an area of 425 sq. mi.(1,100 sq. km.) and a population of 290,000. Capital: Fort-de-France. Agriculture and tourism are the major sources of income. Bananas, sugar, and rum are exported.

Christopher Columbus discovered Martinique, probably on June 15, 1502. France took possession on June 25, 1635, and has maintained possession since that time except for three short periods of British occupation during the Napoleonic Wars. A French department since 1946, Martinique voted a reaffirmation of that status in 1958, remaining within the new French Community. Martinique was the birthplace of Napoleon's Empress Josephine, and the site of the eruption of Mt. Pelee in 1902 that claimed 40,000 lives.

The official currency of Martinique is the French franc. The 1897-1922 coinage of the Colony of Martinique is now obsolete.

MONETARY SYSTEM

15 Sols = 1 Escalin

20 Sols = 1 Livre

66 Livres = 4 Escudos = 6400 Reis

## FRENCH COLONY

### DECIMAL COINAGE

**50 CENTIMES** **KM# 40** **Composition:** Copper-Nickel

| Date | Mintage | VG | F | VF | XF | Unc |
|---|---|---|---|---|---|---|
| 1922 | 500,000 | 12.00 | 22.00 | 40.00 | 110 | — |

**FRANC** **KM# 41** **Composition:** Copper-Nickel

| Date | Mintage | VG | F | VF | XF | Unc |
|---|---|---|---|---|---|---|
| 1897 | 300,000 | 18.00 | 30.00 | 60.00 | 140 | — |
| 1922 | 350,000 | 15.00 | 25.00 | 50.00 | 130 | — |

# MAURITANIA

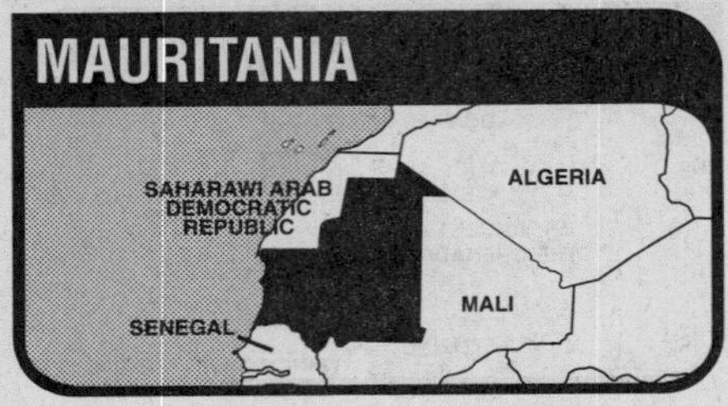


The Islamic Republic of Mauritania, located in northwest Africa bounded by Western Sahara, Mali, Algeria, Senegal and the Atlantic Ocean, has an area of 397,955 sq. mi.(1,030,700 sq. km.) and a population of 1.9 million. Capital: Nouakchott. The economy centers about herding, agriculture, fishing and mining. Iron ore, copper concentrates and fish products are exported.

The indigenous Negroid inhabitants were driven out of Mauritania by Berber invaders of the Islamic faith in the11th century. The Berbers in turn were conquered by Arab invaders, the Beni Hassan, in the 16th century. Arab traders carried on a gainful trade in gum arabic, gold and slaves with Portuguese, Dutch, English and French traders until late in the 19th century when France took control of the area and made it a part of French West Africa, in 1920.Mauritania became a part of the French Union in 1946 and was made an autonomous republic within the new French Community in 1958, when the Islamic Republic of Mauritania was proclaimed. The republic became independent on November 28, 1960, and withdrew from the French Community in 1966.

On June 28, 1973, in a move designed to emphasize its non-alignment with France, Mauritania converted its currency from the old French-supported C.F.A. franc unit to anew unit called the Ouguiya.

**MONETARY SYSTEM**

5 Khoums = 1 Ouguiya

## REPUBLIC

### STANDARD COINAGE

**1/5 OUGUIYA (Khoums)** **KM# 1** **Composition:** Aluminum

| Date | Mintage | VG | F | VF | XF | Unc |
|---|---|---|---|---|---|---|
| AH1393 | 1,000,000 | — | 0.35 | 0.75 | 1.50 | 2.75 |

**OUGUIYA** **KM#2** **Composition:** Copper-Nickel-Aluminum
**Reverse:** Arabic legend in one line

| Date | Mintage | VG | F | VF | XF | Unc |
|---|---|---|---|---|---|---|
| AH1393 | — | — | 5.00 | 10.00 | 17.50 | 30.00 |

**OUGUIYA** **KM#6** **Composition:** Copper-Nickel-Aluminum
**Reverse:** Arabic legend in two lines

| Date | Mintage | VG | F | VF | XF | Unc |
|---|---|---|---|---|---|---|
| AH1394 | — | — | 2.50 | 5.50 | 10.00 | 18.50 |
| AH1401 | — | — | 1.50 | 3.00 | 4.50 | 7.50 |
| AH1403 | — | — | 1.00 | 2.00 | 3.50 | 6.50 |
| AH1406 | — | — | 0.75 | 1.50 | 2.50 | 4.50 |
| AH1407 | — | — | 0.50 | 1.00 | 2.00 | 4.00 |
| AH1410 | — | — | 0.50 | 1.00 | 2.00 | 4.00 |
| AH1414 | — | — | 0.50 | 1.00 | 2.00 | 4.00 |
| AH1416 | — | — | 0.50 | 1.00 | 2.00 | 4.00 |

**5 OUGUIYA** **KM# 3** **Composition:** Copper-Nickel-Aluminum

| Date | Mintage | VG | F | VF | XF | Unc |
|---|---|---|---|---|---|---|
| AH1393 | — | — | 2.50 | 5.50 | 10.00 | 15.00 |
| AH1394 | — | — | 2.50 | 5.50 | 10.00 | 17.50 |
| AH1401 | — | — | 2.00 | 4.00 | 6.00 | 12.50 |
| AH1404 | — | — | 1.50 | 2.50 | 4.50 | 10.00 |
| AH1407 | — | — | 0.75 | 1.50 | 2.50 | 4.50 |
| AH1410 | — | — | 0.50 | 1.00 | 2.00 | 4.00 |
| AH1414 | — | — | 0.50 | 1.00 | 2.00 | 4.00 |
| AH1416 | — | — | 0.50 | 1.00 | 2.00 | 4.00 |
| AH1418 | — | — | 0.50 | 1.00 | 2.00 | 4.00 |

**10 OUGUIYA** **KM# 4** **Composition:** Copper-Nickel

| Date | Mintage | VG | F | VF | XF | Unc |
|---|---|---|---|---|---|---|
| AH1393 | — | — | 2.50 | 5.50 | 10.00 | 17.50 |
| AH1394 | — | — | 2.50 | 5.50 | 10.00 | 17.50 |
| AH1401 | — | — | 2.00 | 5.00 | 7.50 | 15.00 |
| AH1403 | — | — | 1.25 | 2.50 | 4.00 | 8.00 |
| AH1407 | — | — | 1.25 | 2.50 | 4.00 | 8.00 |
| AH1410 | — | — | 0.75 | 1.50 | 2.50 | 4.50 |
| AH1411 | — | — | 0.75 | 1.50 | 2.50 | 4.50 |
| AH1414 | — | — | 0.75 | 1.50 | 2.50 | 4.50 |
| AH1416 | — | — | 0.75 | 1.50 | 2.50 | 4.50 |
| AH1418 | — | — | 0.75 | 1.50 | 2.50 | 4.50 |

**20 OUGUIYA** **KM# 5** **Composition:** Copper-Nickel

| Date | Mintage | VG | F | VF | XF | Unc |
|---|---|---|---|---|---|---|
| AH1393 | — | — | 2.00 | 5.00 | 10.00 | 18.00 |
| AH1394 | — | — | 2.00 | 5.00 | 10.00 | 18.00 |
| AH1403 | — | — | 1.25 | 2.50 | 4.00 | 8.00 |
| AH1407 | — | — | 1.25 | 2.50 | 4.00 | 8.00 |
| AH1410 | — | — | 1.25 | 2.50 | 4.00 | 8.00 |
| AH1414 | — | — | 1.25 | 2.50 | 4.00 | 8.00 |
| AH1416 | — | — | 1.25 | 2.50 | 4.00 | 8.00 |
| AH1418 | — | — | 1.25 | 2.50 | 4.00 | 8.00 |

**500 OUGUIYA** **KM# 7** **Weight:** 26.0800 g. **Composition:** 0.9200 Gold .7714 oz. AGW **Subject:** 15th anniversary of Independence

| Date | Mintage | F | VF | XF | Unc | BU |
|---|---|---|---|---|---|---|
| 1975 (a) | 1,800 | — | — | — | 525 | — |

### MEDALLIC COINAGE

**500 OUGUIYA** **KM# M1.1** **Composition:** Copper-Nickel
**Subject:** International Athletics - Runners **Reverse:** Full baseline

| Date | Mintage | F | VF | XF | Unc | BU |
|---|---|---|---|---|---|---|
| 1984 Proof | — | Value: 14.50 | | | | |

**500 OUGUIYA** **KM# M1.2** **Composition:** Copper-Nickel
**Subject:** International Athletics - Runners **Reverse:** Tapered baseline

| Date | Mintage | F | VF | XF | Unc | BU |
|---|---|---|---|---|---|---|
| 1984 Proof | — | Value: 14.50 | | | | |

**500 OUGUIYA** **KM# M2** **Composition:** Copper-Nickel
**Subject:** International Athletics - Fencing

| Date | Mintage | F | VF | XF | Unc | BU |
|---|---|---|---|---|---|---|
| 1984 Proof | — | Value: 20.00 | | | | |

### MINT SETS

| KM# | Date | Mintage | Identification | Issue Price | Mkt Val |
|---|---|---|---|---|---|
| MS1 | 1973 (10) | — | KM1-5, two each | 20.00 | 150 |

# MAURITIUS

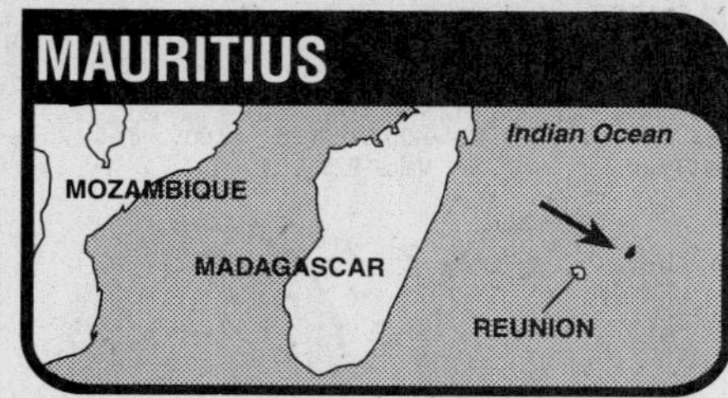


The Republic of Mauritius, a member nation of the British Commonwealth located in the Indian Ocean 500 miles (805 km.) east of Madagascar, has an area of 790 sq. mi. (1,860 sq. km.) and a population of 1 million. Capital: Port Louis. Sugar provides 90 percent of the export revenue.

Cartographic evidence indicates that Arabs and Malays arrived at Mauritius during the Middle Ages. Domingo Fernandez, a Portuguese navigator, visited the island in the early 16th century, but Portugal made no attempt at settlement. The Dutch took possession, and named the island, in 1598. Their colony failed to prosper and was abandoned in 1710. France claimed Mauritius in 1715 and developed a strong and prosperous colony that endured until the island was captured by the British, 1810, during the Napoleonic Wars. British possession was confirmed by the 1814 Treaty of Paris. Mauritius became independent on March 12, 1968. It is a member of the Commonwealth of Nations.

The first coins struck under British auspices for Mauritius were undated (1822) and bore French legends.

**RULERS**
British, until 1968

**MINT MARKS**
H - Heaton, Birmingham
SA - Pretoria Mint

**MONETARY SYSTEM**
100 Cents = 1 Rupee

## REPUBLIC

### STANDARD COINAGE

100 Cents = 1 Rupee

**CENT** **KM# 12** **Composition:** Bronze

| Date | Mintage | F | VF | XF | Unc | BU |
|---|---|---|---|---|---|---|
| 1911 | 1,000,000 | 1.00 | 2.00 | 12.00 | 40.00 | — |
| 1912 | 500,000 | 1.25 | 2.50 | 18.50 | 55.00 | — |
| 1917 | 500,000 | 1.00 | 2.00 | 12.00 | 35.00 | — |
| 1920 | 500,000 | 1.50 | 3.00 | 22.50 | 60.00 | — |
| 1921 | 500,000 | 2.00 | 4.00 | 22.50 | 60.00 | — |
| 1922 | 1,800,000 | 0.75 | 1.50 | 9.00 | 25.00 | — |
| 1923 | 200,000 | 3.00 | 7.00 | 35.00 | 75.00 | — |
| 1924 | 200,000 | 3.00 | 7.00 | 35.00 | 75.00 | — |

**CENT** **KM# 21** **Composition:** Bronze

| Date | Mintage | F | VF | XF | Unc | BU |
|---|---|---|---|---|---|---|
| 1943SA | 520,000 | 0.50 | 1.25 | 4.00 | 10.00 | — |
| 1944SA | 500,000 | 0.50 | 1.25 | 4.00 | 10.00 | — |
| 1945SA | 500,000 | 0.50 | 1.25 | 4.00 | 10.00 | — |
| 1946SA | 500,000 | 0.50 | 1.25 | 4.00 | 10.00 | — |
| 1947SA | 500,000 | 0.50 | 1.25 | 4.00 | 10.00 | — |

**CENT** **KM# 25** **Composition:** Bronze

| Date | Mintage | F | VF | XF | Unc | BU |
|---|---|---|---|---|---|---|
| 1949 | 500,000 | 0.75 | 1.25 | 2.50 | 7.50 | — |
| 1949 Proof | — | Value: 100 | | | | |
| 1952 | 500,000 | 0.75 | 1.25 | 2.50 | 7.50 | — |
| 1952 Proof | — | Value: 100 | | | | |

**CENT** **KM# 31** **Composition:** Bronze

| Date | Mintage | F | VF | XF | Unc | BU |
|---|---|---|---|---|---|---|
| 1953 | 500,000 | 0.10 | 0.25 | 0.50 | 1.50 | — |
| 1953 Proof | — | Value: 75.00 | | | | |
| 1955 | 501,000 | 0.10 | 0.25 | 0.50 | 2.50 | — |
| 1955 Proof | — | Value: 75.00 | | | | |
| 1956 | 500,000 | 0.10 | 0.20 | 0.50 | 2.50 | — |
| 1956 Proof | — | Value: 75.00 | | | | |
| 1957 | 501,000 | 0.10 | 0.20 | 0.50 | 2.50 | — |
| 1959 | 501,000 | 0.10 | 0.20 | 0.50 | 2.50 | — |
| 1959 Proof | — | Value: 75.00 | | | | |
| 1960 | 500,000 | 0.10 | 0.20 | 0.50 | 2.50 | — |
| 1960 Proof | — | Value: 75.00 | | | | |
| 1961 | 500,000 | 0.10 | 0.20 | 0.50 | 2.50 | — |
| 1961 Proof | — | Value: 75.00 | | | | |
| 1962 | 500,000 | 0.10 | 0.20 | 0.50 | 1.50 | — |
| 1962 Proof | — | Value: 50.00 | | | | |
| 1963 | 500,000 | 0.10 | 0.20 | 0.50 | 1.50 | — |
| 1963 Proof | — | Value: 50.00 | | | | |
| 1964 | 1,500,000 | — | 0.10 | 0.20 | 0.50 | — |
| 1964 Proof | — | Value: 50.00 | | | | |
| 1965 | 1,500,000 | — | 0.10 | 0.20 | 0.50 | — |
| 1969 | 500,000 | — | 0.10 | 0.15 | 0.30 | — |
| 1970 | 1,500,000 | — | — | 0.10 | 0.20 | — |
| 1971 | 1,000,000 | — | — | 0.10 | 0.20 | — |
| 1971 Proof | 750 | Value: 17.50 | | | | |
| 1975 | 400,000 | — | — | 0.10 | 0.20 | — |
| 1978 | — | — | — | 0.10 | 0.20 | — |
| 1978 Proof | 9,268 | Value: 1.00 | | | | |

**2 CENTS** **KM# 13** **Composition:** Bronze

| Date | Mintage | F | VF | XF | Unc | BU |
|---|---|---|---|---|---|---|
| 1911 | 500,000 | 2.00 | 4.00 | 15.00 | 40.00 | — |
| 1911 Proof | — | Value: 300 | | | | |
| 1912 | 250,000 | 3.00 | 5.00 | 30.00 | 70.00 | — |
| 1917 | 250,000 | 1.25 | 2.50 | 12.00 | 35.00 | — |
| 1920 | 250,000 | 1.50 | 3.00 | 20.00 | 45.00 | — |
| 1921 | 250,000 | 1.50 | 3.00 | 20.00 | 45.00 | — |
| 1922 | 900,000 | 0.50 | 1.00 | 8.00 | 30.00 | — |
| 1923 | 400,000 | 1.25 | 2.50 | 18.50 | 45.00 | — |
| 1924 | 400,000 | 1.25 | 2.50 | 18.50 | 45.00 | — |

**2 CENTS** **KM# 22** **Composition:** Bronze

| Date | Mintage | F | VF | XF | Unc | BU |
|---|---|---|---|---|---|---|
| 1943SA | 290,000 | 0.75 | 2.00 | 4.00 | 10.00 | — |
| 1944SA | 500,000 | 0.75 | 2.00 | 4.00 | 10.00 | — |
| 1945SA | 250,000 | 0.75 | 2.00 | 4.00 | 10.00 | — |
| 1946SA | 400,000 | 0.75 | 2.00 | 4.00 | 10.00 | — |
| 1947SA | 250,000 | 0.75 | 2.00 | 4.00 | 10.00 | — |

**2 CENTS** **KM# 26** **Composition:** Bronze

| Date | Mintage | F | VF | XF | Unc | BU |
|---|---|---|---|---|---|---|
| 1949 | 250,000 | 0.75 | 1.25 | 2.50 | 6.50 | — |
| 1949 Proof | — | Value: 120 | | | | |
| 1952 | 250,000 | 0.75 | 1.25 | 2.50 | 6.50 | — |
| 1952 Proof | — | Value: 120 | | | | |

**2 CENTS** **KM# 32** **Composition:** Bronze

| Date | Mintage | F | VF | XF | Unc | BU |
|---|---|---|---|---|---|---|
| 1953 | 250,000 | 0.10 | 0.25 | 0.50 | 2.50 | — |
| 1953 Proof | — | Value: 100 | | | | |
| 1954 Proof | — | Value: 300 | | | | |
| 1955 | 501,000 | 0.10 | 0.25 | 0.50 | 2.50 | — |
| 1955 Proof | — | Value: 100 | | | | |
| 1956 | 250,000 | 0.10 | 0.25 | 0.50 | 3.50 | — |
| 1956 Proof | — | Value: 100 | | | | |
| 1957 | 501,000 | 0.10 | 0.25 | 0.50 | 3.50 | — |
| 1959 | 503,000 | 0.10 | 0.25 | 0.50 | 3.50 | — |
| 1959 Proof | — | Value: 100 | | | | |
| 1960 | 250,000 | 0.10 | 0.25 | 0.50 | 3.50 | — |
| 1960 Proof | — | Value: 100 | | | | |
| 1961 | 500,000 | 0.10 | 0.25 | 0.50 | 3.50 | — |
| 1961 Proof | — | Value: 100 | | | | |
| 1962 | 500,000 | 0.10 | 0.25 | 0.50 | 1.50 | — |
| 1962 Proof | — | Value: 75.00 | | | | |
| 1963 | 500,000 | 0.10 | 0.25 | 0.50 | 1.50 | — |
| 1963 Proof | — | Value: 75.00 | | | | |
| 1964 | 1,000,000 | — | 0.10 | 0.25 | 0.50 | — |
| 1964 Proof | — | Value: 50.00 | | | | |
| 1965 | 750,000 | 0.10 | 0.20 | 0.40 | 0.60 | — |
| 1966 | 500,000 | 0.10 | 0.20 | 0.40 | 0.50 | — |
| 1967 | 250,000 | 0.10 | 0.20 | 0.40 | 0.50 | — |
| 1969 | 500,000 | 0.10 | 0.20 | 0.40 | 0.50 | — |
| 1971 | 1,000,000 | — | 0.10 | 0.20 | 0.40 | — |
| 1971 Proof | 750 | Value: 17.50 | | | | |
| 1975 | 5,200,000 | — | — | 0.10 | 0.35 | — |
| 1978 | — | — | — | 0.10 | 0.35 | — |
| 1978 Proof | 9,268 | Value: 1.50 | | | | |

**5 CENTS** **KM# 14** **Composition:** Bronze

| Date | Mintage | F | VF | XF | Unc | BU |
|---|---|---|---|---|---|---|
| 1917 | 600,000 | 2.00 | 4.50 | 27.50 | 80.00 | — |
| 1920 | 200,000 | 2.00 | 4.50 | 32.50 | 100 | — |
| 1921 | 100,000 | 3.00 | 6.50 | 35.00 | 120 | — |
| 1922 | 360,000 | 2.00 | 4.50 | 32.50 | 100 | — |
| 1923 | 400,000 | 3.00 | 6.50 | 35.00 | 120 | — |
| 1924 | 400,000 | 2.00 | 4.50 | 32.50 | 100 | — |

**5 CENTS** **KM# 20** **Composition:** Bronze

| Date | Mintage | F | VF | XF | Unc | BU |
|---|---|---|---|---|---|---|
| 1942SA | 940,000 | 1.50 | 2.50 | 6.50 | 15.00 | — |
| 1944SA | 1,000,000 | 1.25 | 1.75 | 4.00 | 10.00 | — |
| 1945SA | 500,000 | 1.25 | 1.75 | 4.00 | 12.00 | — |

**5 CENTS** **KM# 34** **Composition:** Bronze

| Date | Mintage | F | VF | XF | Unc | BU |
|---|---|---|---|---|---|---|
| 1956 | 201,000 | 0.25 | 0.50 | 0.75 | 5.00 | — |
| 1956 Proof | — | Value: 100 | | | | |
| 1957 | 203,000 | 0.25 | 0.50 | 2.00 | 8.00 | — |
| 1957 Proof | — | Value: 100 | | | | |
| 1959 | 801,000 | 0.25 | 0.50 | 1.00 | 4.00 | — |
| 1959 Proof | — | Value: 75.00 | | | | |
| 1960 | 400,000 | 0.25 | 0.50 | 1.00 | 4.00 | — |

| Date | Mintage | F | VF | XF | Unc | BU |
|---|---|---|---|---|---|---|
| 1960 Proof | — | Value: 75.00 | | | | |
| 1963 | 200,000 | 0.25 | 0.50 | 1.00 | 2.00 | — |
| 1963 Proof | — | Value: 70.00 | | | | |
| 1964 | 600,000 | 0.25 | 0.50 | 1.00 | 2.00 | — |
| 1964 Proof | — | Value: 70.00 | | | | |
| 1965 | 200,000 | 0.25 | 0.50 | 0.75 | 2.00 | — |
| 1966 | 200,000 | 0.25 | 0.50 | 0.75 | 1.50 | — |
| 1967 | 200,000 | 0.25 | 0.50 | 0.75 | 2.00 | — |
| 1969 | 500,000 | 0.10 | 0.15 | 0.25 | 0.50 | — |
| 1970 | 800,000 | 0.10 | 0.15 | 0.25 | 0.50 | — |
| 1971 | 500,000 | 0.10 | 0.15 | 0.25 | 0.50 | — |
| 1971 Proof | 750 | Value: 17.50 | | | | |
| 1975 | 3,700,000 | 0.10 | 0.15 | 0.25 | 0.50 | — |
| 1978 | 8,000,000 | — | 0.10 | 0.20 | 0.50 | — |
| 1978 Proof | 9,268 | Value: 2.00 | | | | |

**10 CENTS** **KM# 24** **Composition:** Copper-Nickel

| Date | Mintage | F | VF | XF | Unc | BU |
|---|---|---|---|---|---|---|
| 1947 | 500,000 | 0.75 | 1.50 | 8.00 | 35.00 | — |
| 1947 Proof | — | Value: 200 | | | | |

**10 CENTS** **KM# 30** **Composition:** Copper-Nickel

| Date | Mintage | F | VF | XF | Unc | BU |
|---|---|---|---|---|---|---|
| 1952 | 250,000 | 0.50 | 0.75 | 1.50 | 6.50 | — |
| 1952 Proof | — | Value: 150 | | | | |

**10 CENTS** **KM# 33** **Composition:** Copper-Nickel

| Date | Mintage | F | VF | XF | Unc | BU |
|---|---|---|---|---|---|---|
| 1954 | 252,000 | 0.20 | 0.35 | 0.75 | 2.50 | — |
| 1954 Proof | — | Value: 150 | | | | |
| 1957 | 250,000 | 0.20 | 0.35 | 0.75 | 2.50 | — |
| 1959 | 253,000 | 0.20 | 0.35 | 0.75 | 2.50 | — |
| 1959 Proof | — | Value: 175 | | | | |
| 1960 | 50,000 | 0.20 | 0.35 | 0.75 | 2.00 | — |
| 1960 Proof | — | Value: 175 | | | | |
| 1963 | 200,000 | 0.15 | 0.30 | 0.60 | 1.50 | — |
| 1963 Proof | — | Value: 175 | | | | |
| 1964 | 200,000 | 0.15 | 0.30 | 0.60 | 1.00 | — |
| 1965 | 200,000 | 0.15 | 0.30 | 0.60 | 1.00 | — |
| 1966 | 200,000 | 0.10 | 0.25 | 0.50 | 0.75 | — |
| 1969 | 200,000 | 0.10 | 0.25 | 0.50 | 0.75 | — |
| 1970 | 500,000 | 0.10 | 0.25 | 0.50 | 0.75 | — |
| 1971 | 300,000 | 0.10 | 0.25 | 0.50 | 0.75 | — |
| 1971 Proof | 750 | Value: 17.50 | | | | |
| 1975 | 6,675,000 | 0.10 | 0.25 | 0.50 | 0.75 | — |
| 1978 | 13,000,000 | 0.10 | 0.25 | 0.50 | 0.75 | — |
| 1978 Proof | 9,268 | Value: 2.50 | | | | |

**1/4 RUPEE** **KM# 15** **Weight:** 2.9200 g. **Composition:** 0.9160 Silver .0816 oz. ASW

| Date | Mintage | F | VF | XF | Unc | BU |
|---|---|---|---|---|---|---|
| 1934 | 400,000 | 2.00 | 7.00 | 20.00 | 60.00 | — |
| 1934 Proof | — | Value: 600 | | | | |
| 1935 | 400,000 | 2.00 | 7.00 | 20.00 | 60.00 | — |
| 1935 Proof | — | Value: 750 | | | | |
| 1936 | 400,000 | 2.00 | 6.00 | 18.00 | 50.00 | — |
| 1936 Proof | — | Value: 650 | | | | |

**1/4 RUPEE** **KM# 18** **Weight:** 2.9200 g. **Composition:** 0.9160 Silver .0816 oz. ASW

| Date | Mintage | F | VF | XF | Unc | BU |
|---|---|---|---|---|---|---|
| 1938 | 2,000,000 | 3.00 | 10.00 | 30.00 | 80.00 | — |
| 1938 Proof | — | Value: 375 | | | | |

**1/4 RUPEE** **KM# 18a** **Weight:** 2.9200 g. **Composition:** 0.5000 Silver .047 oz. ASW

| Date | Mintage | F | VF | XF | Unc | BU |
|---|---|---|---|---|---|---|
| 1946 | 2,000,000 | 7.50 | 20.00 | 40.00 | 100 | — |
| 1946 Proof | — | Value: 400 | | | | |

**1/4 RUPEE** **KM# 27** **Composition:** Copper-Nickel

| Date | Mintage | F | VF | XF | Unc | BU |
|---|---|---|---|---|---|---|
| 1950 | 2,000,000 | 0.50 | 1.00 | 2.00 | 9.50 | — |
| 1950 Proof | — | Value: 175 | | | | |
| 1951 | 1,000,000 | 0.50 | 1.00 | 2.00 | 9.50 | — |
| 1951 Proof | — | Value: 175 | | | | |

**1/4 RUPEE** **KM# 36** **Composition:** Copper-Nickel

| Date | Mintage | F | VF | XF | Unc | BU |
|---|---|---|---|---|---|---|
| 1960 | 1,000,000 | 0.35 | 0.75 | 1.00 | 2.00 | — |
| 1960 Proof | — | Value: 100 | | | | |
| 1964 | 400,000 | 0.25 | 0.50 | 0.75 | 1.50 | — |
| 1964 Proof | — | Value: 100 | | | | |
| 1965 | 400,000 | 0.25 | 0.50 | 0.75 | 1.25 | — |
| 1970 | 400,000 | 0.20 | 0.35 | 0.65 | 1.25 | — |
| 1971 | 540,000 | 0.25 | 0.50 | 0.75 | 1.25 | — |
| 1971 Proof | 750 | Value: 17.50 | | | | |
| 1975 | 8,940,000 | 0.15 | 0.30 | 0.60 | 1.00 | — |
| 1978 | 8,800,000 | 0.15 | 0.30 | 0.60 | 1.00 | — |
| **Note:** Variety exists with lower hole in 8 filled. | | | | | | |
| 1978 Proof | 9,268 | Value: 3.50 | | | | |

**1/2 RUPEE** **KM# 16** **Weight:** 5.8300 g. **Composition:** 0.9160 Silver .1717 oz. ASW

| Date | Mintage | F | VF | XF | Unc | BU |
|---|---|---|---|---|---|---|
| 1934 | 1,000,000 | 2.50 | 5.00 | 15.00 | 50.00 | — |
| 1934 Proof | — | Value: 450 | | | | |

**1/2 RUPEE** **KM# 23** **Weight:** 5.8300 g. **Composition:** 0.5000 Silver .0937 oz. ASW

| Date | Mintage | F | VF | XF | Unc | BU |
|---|---|---|---|---|---|---|
| 1946 | 1,000,000 | 10.00 | 25.00 | 125 | 200 | — |
| 1946 Proof | — | Value: 700 | | | | |

**1/2 RUPEE** **KM# 28** **Composition:** Copper-Nickel

| Date | Mintage | F | VF | XF | Unc | BU |
|---|---|---|---|---|---|---|
| 1950 | 1,000,000 | 0.50 | 1.00 | 1.75 | 7.50 | — |
| 1950 Proof | — | Value: 175 | | | | |
| 1951 | 570,000 | 0.75 | 1.25 | 2.00 | 8.50 | — |
| 1951 Proof | — | Value: 225 | | | | |

**1/2 RUPEE** **KM# 37.1** **Composition:** Copper-Nickel

| Date | Mintage | F | VF | XF | Unc | BU |
|---|---|---|---|---|---|---|
| 1965 | 200,000 | 0.50 | 1.00 | 2.00 | 6.50 | — |
| 1971 | 400,000 | 0.25 | 0.50 | 0.75 | 2.00 | — |
| 1971 Proof | 750 | Value: 22.50 | | | | |
| 1975 | 4,160,000 | 0.25 | 0.50 | 0.75 | 2.00 | — |
| 1978 | 400,000 | 0.25 | 0.50 | 0.75 | 2.00 | — |
| 1978 Proof | 9,268 | Value: 4.00 | | | | |

**1/2 RUPEE** **KM# 37.2** **Composition:** Copper-Nickel **Edge:** Without security feature **Note:** Error.

| Date | Mintage | F | VF | XF | Unc | BU |
|---|---|---|---|---|---|---|
| 1971 | Inc. above | — | — | — | — | — |

**RUPEE** **KM# 17** **Weight:** 11.6600 g. **Composition:** 0.9160 Silver .3434 oz. ASW

| Date | Mintage | F | VF | XF | Unc | BU |
|---|---|---|---|---|---|---|
| 1934 | 1,500,000 | 4.00 | 8.00 | 20.00 | 50.00 | — |
| 1934 Proof | — | Value: 600 | | | | |

**RUPEE** **KM# 19** **Weight:** 11.6600 g. **Composition:** 0.9160 Silver .3434 oz. ASW

| Date | Mintage | F | VF | XF | Unc | BU |
|---|---|---|---|---|---|---|
| 1938 | 200,000 | 10.00 | 20.00 | 60.00 | 175 | — |
| 1938 Proof | — | Value: 550 | | | | |

**RUPEE** **KM# 29.1** **Composition:** Copper-Nickel

| Date | Mintage | F | VF | XF | Unc | BU |
|---|---|---|---|---|---|---|
| 1950 | 1,500,000 | 0.75 | 1.50 | 3.00 | 16.00 | — |
| 1950 Proof | — | Value: 200 | | | | |
| 1951 | 1,000,000 | 0.50 | 1.25 | 2.00 | 12.00 | — |
| 1951 Proof | — | Value: 300 | | | | |

**RUPEE** **KM# 29.2** **Composition:** Copper-Nickel **Edge:** Without security feature **Note:** Error.

| Date | Mintage | F | VF | XF | Unc | BU |
|---|---|---|---|---|---|---|
| 1951 | Inc. above | — | — | — | — | — |

**RUPEE** KM# 35.1 **Composition:** Copper-Nickel

| Date | Mintage | F | VF | XF | Unc | BU |
|---|---|---|---|---|---|---|
| 1956 | 1,000,000 | 0.25 | 0.75 | 1.50 | 7.50 | — |
| 1956 Proof | — | Value: 200 | | | | |
| 1964 | 200,000 | 0.50 | 1.00 | 3.00 | 5.00 | — |
| 1971 | 600,000 | 0.25 | 0.60 | 1.00 | 2.00 | — |
| 1971 Proof | 750 | Value: 45.00 | | | | |
| 1975 | 4,525,000 | 0.25 | 0.60 | 1.00 | 2.00 | — |
| 1978 | 2,000,000 | 0.25 | 0.60 | 1.00 | 2.00 | — |
| 1978 Proof | 9,268 | Value: 5.00 | | | | |

**RUPEE** KM# 35.2 **Composition:** Copper-Nickel **Edge:** Without security feature **Note:** Error.

| Date | Mintage | F | VF | XF | Unc | BU |
|---|---|---|---|---|---|---|
| 1971 | Inc. above | 0.25 | 0.75 | 1.25 | 2.50 | — |

**10 RUPEES** KM# 38 **Composition:** Copper-Nickel **Subject:** Independence **Obverse:** Young Queen Elizabeth **Reverse:** Dodo bird

| Date | Mintage | F | VF | XF | Unc | BU |
|---|---|---|---|---|---|---|
| 1971 | 50,000 | — | 1.50 | 3.00 | 7.50 | — |

**10 RUPEES** KM# 38a **Weight:** 20.0000 g. **Composition:** 0.9250 Silver .5948 oz. ASW **Subject:** Independence **Obverse:** Young Queen Elizabeth **Reverse:** Dodo bird

| Date | Mintage | F | VF | XF | Unc | BU |
|---|---|---|---|---|---|---|
| 1971 Proof | 750 | Value: 125 | | | | |

**10 RUPEES** KM# 46 **Composition:** Copper-Nickel **Subject:** Wedding of Prince Charles and Lady Diana

| Date | Mintage | F | VF | XF | Unc | BU |
|---|---|---|---|---|---|---|
| ND(1981) | — | — | 1.25 | 2.25 | 6.50 | — |

**10 RUPEES** KM# 46a **Weight:** 28.2800 g. **Composition:** 0.9250 Silver .8411 oz. ASW **Subject:** Wedding of Prince Charles and Lady Diana

| Date | Mintage | F | VF | XF | Unc | BU |
|---|---|---|---|---|---|---|
| ND(1981) Proof | 2,090 | Value: 22.50 | | | | |

**10 RUPEES** KM# 48 **Weight:** 28.2800 g. **Composition:** 0.9250 Silver .8411 oz. ASW **Series:** World Food Day **Obverse:** Similar to KM#46

| Date | Mintage | F | VF | XF | Unc | BU |
|---|---|---|---|---|---|---|
| 1981 | 10,000 | — | — | — | 17.50 | — |
| 1981 Proof | 5,000 | Value: 27.50 | | | | |

**25 RUPEES** KM# 40 **Weight:** 25.5000 g. **Composition:** 0.5000 Silver .4099 oz. ASW **Series:** Conservation **Reverse:** Blue swallowtail

| Date | Mintage | F | VF | XF | Unc | BU |
|---|---|---|---|---|---|---|
| 1975 | — | — | — | — | 15.00 | — |

**25 RUPEES** KM# 40a **Weight:** 28.2800 g. **Composition:** 0.9250 Silver .8411 oz. ASW **Series:** Conservation **Reverse:** Blue swallowtail

| Date | Mintage | F | VF | XF | Unc | BU |
|---|---|---|---|---|---|---|
| 1975 | 12 | — | — | — | 100 | — |
| 1975 Proof | 9,869 | Value: 18.50 | | | | |

**25 RUPEES** KM# 43 **Weight:** 28.4000 g. **Composition:** 0.5000 Silver .4565 oz. ASW **Subject:** Queen's silver jubilee

| Date | Mintage | F | VF | XF | Unc | BU |
|---|---|---|---|---|---|---|
| ND(1977) | — | — | — | — | 9.00 | — |

**25 RUPEES** KM# 43a **Weight:** 28.2800 g. **Composition:** 0.9250 Silver .8411 oz. ASW **Subject:** Queen's silver jubilee

| Date | Mintage | F | VF | XF | Unc | BU |
|---|---|---|---|---|---|---|
| ND(1977) Proof | 47,000 | Value: 12.50 | | | | |

**25 RUPEES** KM# 44 **Weight:** 28.2800 g. **Composition:** 0.9250 Silver .8411 oz. ASW **Subject:** 10th anniversary of independence **Obverse:** Similar to 1,000 Rupees, KM#45

| Date | Mintage | F | VF | XF | Unc | BU |
|---|---|---|---|---|---|---|
| 1978 | 20,000 | — | — | — | 12.50 | — |
| 1978 Proof | 5,100 | Value: 25.00 | | | | |

**25 RUPEES** KM# 49 **Weight:** 28.2800 g. **Composition:** 0.9250 Silver .8411 oz. ASW **Series:** International Year of Disabled Persons

| Date | Mintage | F | VF | XF | Unc | BU |
|---|---|---|---|---|---|---|
| 1982 | 11,000 | — | — | — | 18.50 | — |
| 1982 Proof | 10,000 | Value: 23.50 | | | | |

**50 RUPEES** KM# 41 **Weight:** 32.1500 g. **Composition:** 0.5000 Silver .5168 oz. ASW **Series:** Conservation **Obverse:** Similar to 1,000 Rupees, KM#42 **Reverse:** Mauritius Kestrel

| Date | Mintage | F | VF | XF | Unc | BU |
|---|---|---|---|---|---|---|
| 1975 | — | — | — | — | 16.50 | — |

**50 RUPEES** KM# 41a **Weight:** 35.0000 g. **Composition:** 0.9250 Silver 1.0409 oz. ASW **Series:** Conservation **Obverse:** Similar to 1,000 Rupees, KM#42 **Reverse:** Mauritius Kestrel

| Date | Mintage | F | VF | XF | Unc | BU |
|---|---|---|---|---|---|---|
| 1975 | 12 | — | — | — | 125 | — |
| 1975 Proof | 9,513 | Value: 20.00 | | | | |

**200 RUPEES** KM# 39 **Weight:** 15.5600 g. **Composition:** 0.9170 Gold .4587 oz. AGW **Subject:** Independence

| Date | Mintage | F | VF | XF | Unc | BU |
|---|---|---|---|---|---|---|
| 1971 | 2,500 | — | — | — | 200 | — |
| 1971 Proof | 750 | Value: 350 | | | | |

**1000 RUPEES** KM# 42 **Weight:** 33.4370 g. **Composition:** 0.9000 Gold .9676 oz. AGW **Series:** Conservation **Subject:** Mauritius flycatcher

| Date | Mintage | F | VF | XF | Unc | BU |
|---|---|---|---|---|---|---|
| 1975 | 1,966 | — | — | — | 425 | — |
| 1975 Proof | 716 | Value: 600 | | | | |

**1000 RUPEES** KM# 45 **Weight:** 15.9800 g. **Composition:** 0.9170 Gold .4711 oz. AGW **Subject:** 10th anniversary of independence

| Date | Mintage | F | VF | XF | Unc | BU |
|---|---|---|---|---|---|---|
| 1978 | 1,000 | — | — | — | 200 | — |
| 1978 Proof | 1,016 | Value: 250 | | | | |

**1000 RUPEES** KM# 47 **Weight:** 15.9800 g. **Composition:** 0.9170 Gold .4711 oz. AGW **Subject:** Wedding of Prince Charles and Lady Diana

| Date | Mintage | F | VF | XF | Unc | BU |
|---|---|---|---|---|---|---|
| ND(1981) | 28 | — | — | — | 600 | — |
| ND(1981) Proof | 22 | Value: 950 | | | | |

**1000 RUPEES** KM# 50 **Weight:** 15.9800 g. **Composition:** 0.9170 Gold .4711 oz. AGW **Series:** International Year of Disabled Persons

| Date | Mintage | F | VF | XF | Unc | BU |
|---|---|---|---|---|---|---|
| 1982 | 45 | — | — | — | 550 | — |
| 1982 Proof | 48 | Value: 925 | | | | |

## REFORM COINAGE

**CENT** KM# 51 **Composition:** Copper Plated Steel

| Date | Mintage | F | VF | XF | Unc | BU |
|---|---|---|---|---|---|---|
| 1987 | Est. 5,000 | — | — | — | 0.20 | — |
| 1987 Proof | Est. 2,500 | Value: 1.00 | | | | |

**5 CENTS** KM# 52 **Composition:** Copper Plated Steel

| Date | Mintage | F | VF | XF | Unc | BU |
|---|---|---|---|---|---|---|
| 1987 | Est. 5,000 | — | — | — | 0.30 | — |
| 1987 Proof | Est. 2,500 | Value: 2.00 | | | | |
| 1990 | — | — | — | — | 0.30 | — |
| 1991 | — | — | — | — | 0.30 | — |
| 1993 | — | — | — | — | 0.30 | — |
| 1994 | — | — | — | — | 0.30 | — |
| 1996 | — | — | — | — | 0.30 | — |

**20 CENTS** KM# 53 **Composition:** Nickel Plated Steel

| Date | Mintage | F | VF | XF | Unc | BU |
|---|---|---|---|---|---|---|
| 1987 | Est. 5,000 | — | — | — | 0.50 | — |
| 1987 Proof | Est. 2,500 | Value: 3.00 | | | | |
| 1990 | — | — | — | — | 0.50 | — |
| 1991 | — | — | — | — | 0.50 | — |
| 1993 | — | — | — | — | 0.50 | — |
| 1994 | — | — | — | — | 0.50 | — |
| 1995 | — | — | — | — | 0.50 | — |
| 1999 | — | — | — | — | 0.50 | — |

**1/2 RUPEE** KM# 54 **Composition:** Nickel Plated Steel

| Date | Mintage | F | VF | XF | Unc | BU |
|---|---|---|---|---|---|---|
| 1987 | Est. 5,000 | — | — | — | 1.50 | — |
| 1987 Proof | Est. 2,500 | Value: 5.00 | | | | |
| 1990 | — | — | — | — | 1.50 | — |
| 1997 | — | — | — | — | 1.50 | — |
| 1999 | — | — | — | — | 1.50 | — |

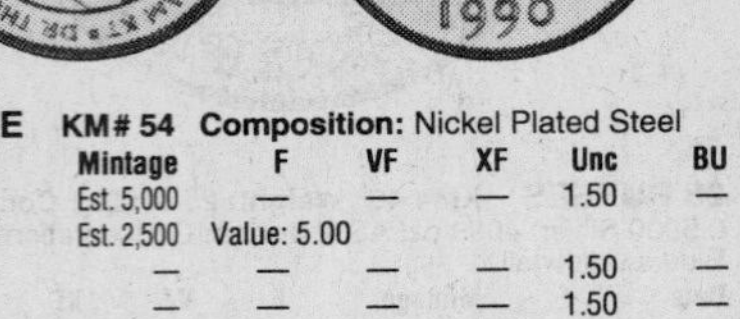

**RUPEE** KM# 55 **Composition:** Copper-Nickel

| Date | Mintage | F | VF | XF | Unc | BU |
|---|---|---|---|---|---|---|
| 1987 | Est. 5,000 | — | — | — | 1.65 | — |
| 1987 Proof | Est. 2,500 | Value: 10.00 | | | | |
| 1990 | — | — | — | — | 1.65 | — |
| 1991 | — | — | — | — | 1.65 | — |
| 1993 | — | — | — | — | 1.65 | — |
| 1994 | — | — | — | — | 1.65 | — |
| 1997 | — | — | — | — | 1.65 | — |

**5 RUPEES** KM# 56 **Composition:** Copper-Nickel

| Date | Mintage | F | VF | XF | Unc | BU |
|---|---|---|---|---|---|---|
| 1987 | Est. 5,000 | — | — | — | 3.00 | — |
| 1987 Proof | Est. 2,500 | Value: 16.00 | | | | |
| 1991 | — | — | — | — | 3.00 | — |
| 1992 | — | — | — | — | 3.00 | — |

**10 RUPEES** KM# 61 **Composition:** Copper-Nickel **Obverse:** Portrait **Reverse:** Sugar cane harvesting

| Date | Mintage | F | VF | XF | Unc | BU |
|---|---|---|---|---|---|---|
| 1997 | — | — | — | — | 4.00 | — |

## GOLD BULLION COINAGE

**100 RUPEES** KM# 57 **Weight:** 3.4120 g. **Composition:** 0.9170 Gold .1 oz. AGW **Obverse:** Similar to 1,000 Rupees, KM#60 **Reverse:** Dodo bird

| Date | Mintage | F | VF | XF | Unc | BU |
|---|---|---|---|---|---|---|
| 1988 | — | — | — | — | 75.00 | — |

**250 RUPEES** KM# 58 **Weight:** 8.5130 g. **Composition:** 0.9170 Gold .25 oz. AGW **Obverse:** Similar to 1,000 Rupees, KM#60 **Reverse:** Dodo bird

| Date | Mintage | F | VF | XF | Unc | BU |
|---|---|---|---|---|---|---|
| 1988 | — | — | — | — | 150 | — |

**500 RUPEES** KM# 59 **Weight:** 17.0250 g. **Composition:** 0.9170 Gold .5 oz. AGW **Obverse:** Similar to 1,000 Rupees, KM#60 **Reverse:** Dodo bird

| Date | Mintage | F | VF | XF | Unc | BU |
|---|---|---|---|---|---|---|
| 1988 | — | — | — | — | 275 | — |

**1000 RUPEES** KM# 60 **Weight:** 34.0500 g. **Composition:** 0.9170 Gold 1 oz. AGW **Reverse:** Dodo bird

| Date | Mintage | F | VF | XF | Unc | BU |
|---|---|---|---|---|---|---|
| 1988 | — | — | — | — | 500 | — |

## PIEFORTS

| KM# | Date | Mintage | Identification | Issue Price | Mkt Val |
|---|---|---|---|---|---|
| P2 | 1981 (10) | — | 1000 Rupees. Gold. KM47. | — | — |
| P3 | 1982 (10) | 1,100 | 25 Rupees. 0.9250 Silver. KM49. | — | 100 |
| P4 | 1982 (10) | — | 1000 Rupees. Gold. KM50. | — | 1,850 |

## MINT SETS

| KM# | Date | Mintage | Identification | Issue Price | Mkt Val |
|---|---|---|---|---|---|
| MS1 | 1987 (6) | 5,000 | KM51-56 | 16.95 | 17.50 |
| MS2 | 1988 (4) | — | KM57-60 | 1,250 | 1,000 |

## PROOF SETS

| KM# | Date | Mintage | Identification | Issue Price | Mkt Val |
|---|---|---|---|---|---|
| PS1 | 1934 (3) | 20 | KM15-17 | — | 2,100 |
| PS2 | 1971 (9) | 750 | KM31-37, 38a, 39 | 200 | 645 |
| PS3 | 1975 (2) | 9,268 | KM40a-41a | 50.00 | 40.00 |
| PS4 | 1978 (7) | 30,000 | KM31-37 | 22.00 | 20.00 |
| PS5 | 1981 (2) | — | KM46a, 47 | — | 975 |
| PS6 | 1987 (6) | 2,500 | KM51-56 | 36.95 | 37.50 |

| Date | Mintage | F | VF | XF | Unc | BU |
|---|---|---|---|---|---|---|
| 1901 | 1,494,000 | 3.00 | 8.00 | 17.50 | 50.00 | — |
| 1901 | 1,494,000 | 3.00 | 8.00 | 17.50 | 50.00 | — |
| 1902/899 | 2,090,000 | 30.00 | 60.00 | 100 | 175 | — |
| 1902 | Inc. above | 2.25 | 4.00 | 10.00 | 40.00 | — |
| 1903 | 8,400,000 | 1.50 | 3.00 | 7.00 | 20.00 | — |
| 1904/3 | 10,250,000 | 1.50 | 10.00 | 20.00 | 55.00 | — |
| 1904 | Inc. above | 1.50 | 3.00 | 7.00 | 25.00 | — |
| 1905 | 3,643,000 | 2.25 | 4.00 | 10.00 | 40.00 | — |

The United States of Mexico, located immediately south of the United States has an area of 759,529 sq. mi. (1,967,183 sq. km.) and an estimated population of 88 million. Capital: Mexico City. The economy is based on agriculture, manufacturing and mining. Oil, cotton, silver, coffee, and shrimp are exported.

Mexico was the site of highly advanced Indian civilizations 1,500 years before conquistador Hernando Cortes conquered the wealthy Aztec empire of Montezuma,1519-21, and founded a Spanish colony which lasted for nearly 300 years. During the Spanish period, Mexico, then called New Spain, stretched from Guatemala to the present states of Wyoming and California, its present northern boundary having been established by the secession of Texas during 1836 and the war of 1846-48 with the United States.

Independence from Spain was declared by Father Miguel Hidalgo on Sept. 16, 1810, (Mexican Independence Day) and was achieved by General Agustin de Iturbide in1821. Iturbide became emperor in 1822 but was deposed when a republic was established a year later. For more than fifty years following the birth of the republic, the political scene of Mexico was characterized by turmoil which saw two emperors (including the unfortunate Maximilian), several dictators and an average of one new government every nine months passing swiftly from obscurity to oblivion. The land, social, economic and labor reforms promulgated by the Reform Constitution of Feb. 5, 1917 established the basis for sustained economic development and participative democracy that have made Mexico one of the most politically stable countries of modern Latin America.

## REPUBLIC
### Second

**MINT MARKS**

A, AS - Alamos
CE - Real de Catorce
CA,CH - Chihuahua
C, Cn, Gn(error) - Culiacan
D, Do - Durango
EoMo - Estado de Mexico
Ga - Guadalajara
GC - Guadalupe y Calvo
G, Go - Guanajuato
H, Ho - Hermosillo
M, Mo - Mexico City
O, OA - Oaxaca
SLP, PI, P, I/P - San Luis Potosi
Z, Zs – Zacatecas

**ASSAYERS INITIALS**

**CULIACAN MINT**

| Initials | Years | Mint Officials |
|---|---|---|
| JQ, Q | 1899-1903 | Jesus S. Quiroz |
| FV, V | 1903 | Francisco Valdez |
| MH, H | 1904 | Merced Hernandez |
| RP, P | 1904-05 | Ramon Ponce de Leon |

**MEXICO CITY MINT**

Because of the great number of assayers for this mint (Mexico City is a much larger mint than any of the others )there is much confusion as to which initial stands for which assayer at any one time. Therefore we feel that it would be of no value to list the assayers.

**ZACATECAS MINT**

| Initials | Years | Mint Officials |
|---|---|---|
| FZ | 1886-1905 | Francisco de P. Zarate |
| FM | 1904-05 | Francisco Mateos |

## DECIMAL COINAGE

100 Centavos = 1 Peso; 5 Pesos = 1 Argentino

**CENTAVO** **KM# 394** **Composition:** Copper **Note:** Struck at Culiacan Mint, mint mark C, Cn. Reduced size; Varieties exist.

| Date | Mintage | F | VF | XF | Unc | BU |
|---|---|---|---|---|---|---|
| 1901 | 220,000 | 15.00 | 22.50 | 35.00 | 65.00 | — |
| 1902 | 320,000 | 15.00 | 22.50 | 50.00 | 90.00 | — |
| 1903 | 536,000 | 7.50 | 12.50 | 20.00 | 50.00 | — |
| 1904/3 | 148,000 | 35.00 | 50.00 | 75.00 | 125 | — |
| 1905 | 110,000 | 100 | 150 | 300 | 550 | — |

**CENTAVO** **KM# 394.1** **Composition:** Copper **Note:** Struck at Mexico City Mint, mint mark M, Mo. Reduced size; Varieties exist.

**5 CENTAVOS** **KM# 400** **Composition:** 0.9030 Silver **Obverse:** Restyled eagle **Note:** Struck at Culiacan Mint, mint mark Cn. Varieties exist.

| Date | Mintage | F | VF | XF | Unc | BU |
|---|---|---|---|---|---|---|
| 1901Cn Q | 148,000 | 1.75 | 2.50 | 4.50 | 15.00 | — |
| 1902Cn Q Narrow C, heavy serifs | 262,000 | 1.75 | 3.00 | 6.00 | 16.50 | — |
| 1902Cn Q Wide C, light serifs | Inc. above | 1.75 | 3.00 | 6.00 | 16.50 | — |
| 1903/1Cn Q | 331,000 | 2.00 | 3.00 | 6.00 | 16.50 | — |
| 1903Cn Q | Inc. above | 1.75 | 2.50 | 4.50 | 15.00 | — |
| 1903/1898Cn V | Inc. above | 3.50 | 4.50 | 9.00 | 22.50 | — |
| 1903Cn V | Inc. above | 1.75 | 2.50 | 4.50 | 15.00 | — |
| 1904Cn H | 352,000 | 1.75 | 2.25 | 5.00 | 16.50 | — |
| 1904Cn H 0/9 | — | 1.75 | 2.50 | 5.00 | 16.50 | — |
| 1904Cn H/C | — | 1.75 | 2.50 | 5.00 | 16.50 | — |

**5 CENTAVOS** **KM# 400.2** **Composition:** 0.9030 Silver **Obverse:** Restyled eagle **Note:** Struck at Mexico City Mint, mint mark Mo.

| Date | Mintage | F | VF | XF | Unc | BU |
|---|---|---|---|---|---|---|
| 1901Mo M | 100,000 | 1.75 | 2.50 | 4.50 | 15.00 | — |
| 1902Mo M | 144,000 | 1.25 | 2.00 | 3.75 | 12.00 | — |
| 1902/1Mo MoM | — | 1.75 | 3.00 | 6.00 | 16.50 | — |
| 1903Mo M | 500,000 | 1.25 | 2.00 | 3.75 | 12.00 | — |
| 1904/804Mo M | 1,090,000 | 1.75 | 3.00 | 6.00 | 16.50 | — |
| 1904/94Mo M | Inc. above | 1.75 | 3.00 | 6.00 | 16.50 | — |
| 1904Mo M | Inc. above | 1.75 | 3.00 | 6.00 | 15.00 | — |
| 1905Mo M | 344,000 | 1.75 | 3.75 | 7.50 | 18.50 | — |

**5 CENTAVOS** **KM# 400.3** **Composition:** 0.9030 Silver **Obverse:** Restyled eagle **Note:** Struck at Zacatecas Mint, mint mark Zs.

| Date | Mintage | F | VF | XF | Unc | BU |
|---|---|---|---|---|---|---|
| 1901Zs Z | 40,000 | 1.75 | 2.50 | 5.00 | 16.50 | — |
| 1902/1Zs Z | 34,000 | 2.00 | 4.50 | 9.00 | 22.50 | — |
| 1902Zs Z | Inc. above | 1.75 | 3.75 | 7.50 | 18.50 | — |
| 1903Zs Z | 217,000 | 1.25 | 2.00 | 5.00 | 12.50 | — |
| 1904Zs Z | 191,000 | 1.75 | 2.50 | 5.00 | 12.50 | — |
| 1904Zs M | Inc. above | 1.75 | 2.50 | 6.00 | 16.50 | — |
| 1905Zs M | 46,000 | 2.00 | 4.50 | 9.00 | 22.50 | — |
| 1905Zs M Repullica - Rare | Inc. above | — | — | — | — | — |

**10 CENTAVOS** **KM# 404** **Weight:** 2.7070 g. **Composition:** 0.9030 Silver .0785 oz. ASW **Obverse:** Restyled eagle **Note:** Struck at Culiacan Mint, mint mark Cn. Varieties exist.

| Date | Mintage | F | VF | XF | Unc | BU |
|---|---|---|---|---|---|---|
| 1901Cn Q | 235,000 | 1.50 | 2.50 | 5.00 | 20.00 | — |
| 1902Cn Q | 186,000 | 1.50 | 2.50 | 5.00 | 20.00 | — |
| 1903Cn Q | 256,000 | 1.50 | 2.50 | 6.00 | 20.00 | — |
| 1903Cn V | Inc. above | 1.50 | 2.50 | 5.00 | 15.00 | — |
| 1904Cn H | 307,000 | 1.50 | 2.50 | 5.00 | 15.00 | — |

**10 CENTAVOS** **KM# 404.2** **Weight:** 2.7070 g. **Composition:** 0.9030 Silver .0785 oz. ASW **Obverse:** Restyled eagle **Note:** Struck at Mexico City Mint, mint mark Mo.

| Date | Mintage | F | VF | XF | Unc | BU |
|---|---|---|---|---|---|---|
| 1901Mo M | 80,000 | 2.50 | 3.50 | 7.00 | 22.50 | — |
| 1902Mo M | 181,000 | 1.50 | 2.50 | 5.00 | 20.00 | — |
| 1903Mo M | 581,000 | 1.50 | 2.50 | 5.00 | 20.00 | — |
| 1904Mo M | 1,266,000 | 1.25 | 2.00 | 4.50 | 18.00 | — |
| 1904Mo MM (Error) | Inc. above | 2.50 | 5.00 | 10.00 | 25.00 | — |
| 1905Mo M | 266,000 | 2.00 | 3.75 | 7.50 | 20.00 | — |

**10 CENTAVOS** **KM# 404.3** **Weight:** 2.7070 g. **Composition:** 0.9030 Silver .0785 oz. ASW **Obverse:** Restyled eagle **Note:** Struck at Zacatecas Mint, mint mark Zs.

| Date | Mintage | F | VF | XF | Unc | BU |
|---|---|---|---|---|---|---|
| 1901Zs Z | 70,000 | 2.50 | 5.00 | 10.00 | 25.00 | — |
| 1902Zs Z | 120,000 | 2.50 | 5.00 | 10.00 | 25.00 | — |
| 1903Zs Z | 228,000 | 1.50 | 3.00 | 10.00 | 20.00 | — |
| 1904Zs Z | 368,000 | 1.50 | 3.00 | 10.00 | 20.00 | — |
| 1904Zs M | Inc. above | 1.50 | 3.00 | 10.00 | 25.00 | — |
| 1905Zs M | 66,000 | 7.50 | 20.00 | 50.00 | 200 | — |

**20 CENTAVOS** **KM# 405** **Weight:** 5.4150 g. **Composition:** 0.9030 Silver .1572 oz. ASW **Obverse:** Restyled eagle **Note:** Struck at Culiacan Mint, mint mark Cn.

| Date | Mintage | F | VF | XF | Unc | BU |
|---|---|---|---|---|---|---|
| 1901Cn Q | 185,000 | 5.00 | 10.00 | 30.00 | 120 | — |
| 1902/802Cn Q | 98,000 | 6.00 | 10.00 | 30.00 | 120 | — |
| 1902Cn Q | Inc. above | 4.00 | 9.00 | 30.00 | 120 | — |
| 1903Cn Q | 93,000 | 4.00 | 9.00 | 30.00 | 120 | — |
| 1904/3Cn H | 258,000 | — | — | — | — | — |
| 1904Cn H | Inc. above | 5.00 | 10.00 | 30.00 | 120 | — |

**20 CENTAVOS** **KM# 405.2** **Weight:** 5.4150 g. **Composition:** 0.9030 Silver .1572 oz. ASW **Obverse:** Restyled eagle **Note:** Struck at Mexico City Mint, mint mark Mo. Varieties exist.

| Date | Mintage | F | VF | XF | Unc | BU |
|---|---|---|---|---|---|---|
| 1901Mo M | 110,000 | 4.00 | 8.00 | 20.00 | 90.00 | — |
| 1902Mo M | 120,000 | 4.00 | 8.00 | 20.00 | 90.00 | — |
| 1903Mo M | 213,000 | 4.00 | 8.00 | 20.00 | 90.00 | — |
| 1904Mo M | 276,000 | 4.00 | 8.00 | 20.00 | 90.00 | — |
| 1905Mo M | 117,000 | 6.50 | 20.00 | 50.00 | 150 | — |

**20 CENTAVOS** **KM# 405.3** **Weight:** 5.4150 g. **Composition:** 0.9030 Silver .1572 oz. ASW **Obverse:** Restyled eagle **Note:** Struck at Zacatecas Mint, mint mark Zs.

| Date | Mintage | F | VF | XF | Unc | BU |
|---|---|---|---|---|---|---|
| 1901/0Zs Z | 130,000 | 25.00 | 50.00 | 100 | 250 | — |
| 1901Zs Z | Inc. above | 5.00 | 10.00 | 20.00 | 100 | — |
| 1902Zs Z | 105,000 | 5.00 | 10.00 | 20.00 | 100 | — |
| 1903Zs Z | 143,000 | 5.00 | 10.00 | 20.00 | 100 | — |
| 1904Zs Z | 246,000 | 5.00 | 10.00 | 20.00 | 100 | — |
| 1904Zs M | Inc. above | 5.00 | 10.00 | 50.00 | 300 | — |
| 1905Zs M | 59,000 | 10.00 | 70.00 | 50.00 | 400 | — |

**PESO** **KM# 409** **Weight:** 27.0730 g. **Composition:** 0.9030 Silver .7860 oz. ASW **Reverse:** Liberty cap **Note:** Struck at Culiacan Mint, mint mark Cn.

| Date | Mintage | F | VF | XF | Unc | BU |
|---|---|---|---|---|---|---|
| 1901Cn JQ | 1,473,000 | 10.00 | 15.00 | 30.00 | 85.00 | — |
| 1902Cn JQ | 1,194,000 | 10.00 | 15.00 | 45.00 | 125 | — |
| 1903Cn JQ | 1,514,000 | 10.00 | 15.00 | 35.00 | 90.00 | — |
| 1903Cn FV | Inc. above | 25.00 | 50.00 | 100 | 225 | — |
| 1904Cn MH | 1,554,000 | 10.00 | 15.00 | 30.00 | 85.00 | — |
| 1904Cn RP | Inc. above | 50.00 | 100 | 150 | 350 | — |
| 1905Cn RP | 598,000 | 25.00 | 50.00 | 100 | 250 | — |

**PESO** **KM# 410.2** **Weight:** 1.6920 g. **Composition:** 0.8750 Gold .0476 oz. AGW **Note:** Struck at Culiacan Mint, mint mark Cn.

| Date | Mintage | F | VF | XF | Unc | BU |
|---|---|---|---|---|---|---|
| 1901/0Cn Q | 2,350 | 65.00 | 100 | 150 | 225 | — |
| 1902Cn Q | 2,480 | 65.00 | 100 | 150 | 225 | — |
| 1902Cn/MoQ/C | Inc. above | 65.00 | 100 | 150 | 225 | — |
| 1904Cn H | 3,614 | 65.00 | 100 | 150 | 225 | — |
| 1904Cn/Mo/ H | Inc. above | 65.00 | 100 | 150 | 250 | — |
| 1905Cn P Reported, not confirmed | 1,000 | — | — | — | — | — |

**PESO** **KM# 410.5** **Weight:** 1.6920 g. **Composition:** 0.8750 Gold .0476 oz. AGW **Note:** Struck at Mexico City Mint, mint mark Mo.

| Date | Mintage | F | VF | XF | Unc | BU |
|---|---|---|---|---|---|---|
| 1901/801Mo M Large date | 8,293 | 40.00 | 60.00 | 90.00 | 185 | — |
| 1901Mo M Small date | Inc. above | 40.00 | 60.00 | 90.00 | 185 | — |
| 1902Mo M Large date | 11,000 | 40.00 | 60.00 | 90.00 | 185 | — |
| 1902Mo M Small date | Inc. above | 40.00 | 60.00 | 90.00 | 185 | — |
| 1903Mo M Large date | 10,000 | 40.00 | 60.00 | 90.00 | 185 | — |
| 1903Mo M Small date | Inc. above | 50.00 | 80.00 | 120 | 200 | — |
| 1904Mo M | 9,845 | 40.00 | 60.00 | 90.00 | 185 | — |
| 1905Mo M | 3,429 | 40.00 | 60.00 | 90.00 | 185 | — |

**PESO** **KM# 409.2** **Weight:** 27.0730 g. **Composition:** 0.9030 Silver .7860 oz. ASW **Reverse:** Liberty cap **Note:** Struck at Mexico City Mint, mint mark Mo. Varieties exist.

| Date | Mintage | F | VF | XF | Unc | BU |
|---|---|---|---|---|---|---|
| 1901Mo AM | 14,505,000 | 9.00 | 11.50 | 20.00 | 70.00 | — |
| 1902/1Mo AM | 16,224,000 | 150 | 300 | 500 | 950 | — |
| 1902Mo AM | Inc. above | 9.00 | 11.50 | 20.00 | 70.00 | — |
| 1903Mo AM | 22,396,000 | 9.00 | 11.50 | 20.00 | 70.00 | — |
| 1903Mo AM (Error) | Inc. above | 1,500 | 2,500 | 3,500 | 7,500 | — |
| 1904Mo AM | 14,935,000 | 9.00 | 11.50 | 20.00 | 70.00 | — |
| 1905Mo AM | 3,557,000 | 15.00 | 25.00 | 55.00 | 125 | — |
| 1908Mo AM | 7,575,000 | 10.00 | 12.50 | 20.00 | 60.00 | — |
| 1908Mo GV | Inc. above | 10.00 | 12.50 | 18.50 | 40.00 | — |
| 1909Mo GV | 2,924,000 | 10.00 | 12.50 | 18.50 | 40.00 | — |

**PESO** **KM# 409.3** **Weight:** 27.0730 g. **Composition:** 0.9030 Silver .7860 oz. ASW **Reverse:** Liberty cap **Note:** Struck at Zacatecas Mint, mint mark Zs. Varieties exist.

| Date | Mintage | F | VF | XF | Unc | BU |
|---|---|---|---|---|---|---|
| 1901Zs AZ | 5,706,000 | 4,000 | 6,500 | 10,000 | — | — |
| 1901Zs FZ | Inc. above | 10.00 | 12.50 | 20.00 | 55.00 | — |
| 1902Zs FZ | 7,134,000 | 10.00 | 12.50 | 20.00 | 55.00 | — |
| 1903/2Zs FZ | 3,080,000 | 12.50 | 15.00 | 50.00 | 125 | — |
| 1903Zs FZ | Inc. above | 10.00 | 12.50 | 20.00 | 65.00 | — |
| 1904Zs FZ | 2,423,000 | 10.00 | 15.00 | 25.00 | 85.00 | — |
| 1904Zs FM | Inc. above | 10.00 | 15.00 | 25.00 | 75.00 | — |
| 1905Zs FM | 995,000 | 20.00 | 40.00 | 60.00 | 150 | — |

**5 PESOS** **KM# 412.6** **Weight:** 8.4600 g. **Composition:** 0.8750 Gold .2380 oz. AGW **Note:** Struck at Mexico City Mint, mint mark Mo.

| Date | Mintage | F | VF | XF | Unc | BU |
|---|---|---|---|---|---|---|
| 1901Mo M | 1,071 | 150 | 300 | 400 | 650 | — |
| 1902Mo M | 1,478 | 150 | 300 | 400 | 650 | — |
| 1903Mo M | 1,162 | 150 | 300 | 400 | 650 | — |
| 1904Mo M | 1,415 | 150 | 300 | 400 | 650 | — |
| 1905Mo M | 563 | 200 | 400 | 550 | 1,500 | — |

**5 PESOS** **KM# 412.2** **Weight:** 8.4600 g. **Composition:** 0.8750 Gold .2380 oz. AGW **Note:** Struck at Culiacan Mint, mint mark Cn.

| Date | Mintage | F | VF | XF | Unc | BU |
|---|---|---|---|---|---|---|
| 1903Cn Q | 1,000 | 150 | 300 | 400 | 750 | — |

**10 PESOS** **KM# 413.7** **Weight:** 16.9200 g. **Composition:** 0.8750 Gold .4760 oz. AGW **Reverse:** Balance scale **Note:** Struck at Mexico City Mint, mint mark Mo.

| Date | Mintage | F | VF | XF | Unc | BU |
|---|---|---|---|---|---|---|
| 1901Mo M | 562 | 350 | 500 | 800 | 1,250 | — |
| 1902Mo M | 719 | 350 | 500 | 800 | 1,250 | — |
| 1903Mo M | 713 | 350 | 500 | 800 | 1,250 | — |
| 1904Mo M | 694 | 350 | 500 | 800 | 1,250 | — |
| 1905Mo M | 401 | 400 | 600 | 950 | 1,500 | — |

**10 PESOS** **KM# 413.2** **Weight:** 16.9200 g. **Composition:** 0.8750 Gold .4760 oz. AGW **Reverse:** Balance scale **Note:** Struck at Culiacan Mint, mint mark Cn.

| Date | Mintage | F | VF | XF | Unc | BU |
|---|---|---|---|---|---|---|
| 1903Cn Q | 774 | 400 | 600 | 1,000 | 1,750 | — |

**20 PESOS** **KM# 414.2** **Weight:** 33.8400 g. **Composition:** 0.8750 Gold .9520 oz. AGW **Reverse:** Balance scale **Note:** Struck at Culiacan Mint, mint mark Cn.

| Date | Mintage | F | VF | XF | Unc | BU |
|---|---|---|---|---|---|---|
| 1901/0Cn Q | 1,496 | — | — | — | — | — |
| 1901Cn Q | Inc. above | 450 | 675 | 950 | 2,000 | — |
| 1902Cn Q | 1,059 | 450 | 675 | 950 | 2,000 | — |
| 1903Cn Q | 1,121 | 450 | 675 | 950 | 2,000 | — |
| 1904Cn H | 4,646 | 450 | 675 | 950 | 2,000 | — |
| 1905Cn P | 1,738 | 500 | 900 | 1,200 | 2,250 | — |

**20 PESOS** **KM# 414.6** **Weight:** 33.8400 g. **Composition:** 0.8750 Gold .9520 oz. AGW **Reverse:** Balance scale **Note:** Struck at Mexico City Mint, mint mark Mo.

| Date | Mintage | F | VF | XF | Unc | BU |
|---|---|---|---|---|---|---|
| 1901Mo M | 29,000 | 400 | 600 | 850 | 1,450 | — |
| 1902Mo M | 38,000 | 400 | 600 | 850 | 1,450 | — |
| 1903/2Mo M | 31,000 | 400 | 600 | 850 | 1,450 | — |
| 1903Mo M | Inc. above | 400 | 600 | 850 | 1,450 | — |
| 1904Mo M | 52,000 | 400 | 600 | 850 | 1,450 | — |
| 1905Mo M | 9,757 | 400 | 600 | 850 | 1,450 | — |

# UNITED STATES

**MINT MARK**

o

M - Mexico City

## DECIMAL COINAGE

**CENTAVO** **KM# 415** **Composition:** Bronze **Size:** 20 mm. **Note:** Struck at Mexico City Mint, mint mark Mo.

| Date | Mintage | F | VF | XF | Unc | BU |
|---|---|---|---|---|---|---|
| 1905 Narrow date | 6,040,000 | 3.25 | 5.75 | 12.50 | 95.00 | — |
| 1905 Wide date | — | 3.25 | 5.75 | 12.50 | 95.00 | — |
| 1906 Narrow date | Est. 67,505,000 | 0.50 | 0.75 | 1.25 | 14.00 | — |

**Note:** 50,000,000 pcs. were struck at the Birmingham Mint

| Date | Mintage | F | VF | XF | Unc | BU |
|---|---|---|---|---|---|---|
| 1906 Wide date | Inc. above | 0.65 | 1.25 | 2.25 | 22.00 | — |
| 1910 Narrow date | 8,700,000 | 1.50 | 2.50 | 6.50 | 90.00 | — |
| 1910 Wide date | — | 1.50 | 2.50 | 6.50 | 90.00 | — |
| 1911 Narrow date | 16,450,000 | 0.60 | 1.00 | 2.75 | 22.50 | — |
| 1911 Wide date | Inc. above | 0.75 | 1.25 | 5.00 | 32.00 | — |
| 1912 | 12,650,000 | 0.75 | 1.25 | 3.00 | 32.00 | — |
| 1913 | 12,850,000 | 0.65 | 1.00 | 2.75 | 33.00 | — |
| 1914 Narrow date | 17,350,000 | 0.60 | 0.85 | 2.50 | 14.50 | — |
| 1914 Wide date | Inc. above | 0.60 | 0.85 | 2.50 | 14.50 | — |
| 1915 | 2,277,000 | 9.00 | 21.50 | 65.00 | 250 | — |
| 1916 | 500,000 | 30.00 | 65.00 | 165 | 1,200 | — |
| 1920 | 1,433,000 | 15.00 | 30.00 | 65.00 | 400 | — |
| 1921 | 3,470,000 | 4.25 | 13.50 | 42.50 | 275 | — |
| 1922 | 1,880,000 | 8.00 | 15.00 | 45.00 | 300 | — |
| 1923 | 4,800,000 | 0.50 | 0.75 | 1.75 | 11.50 | — |
| 1924/3 | 2,000,000 | 50.00 | 140 | 250 | 500 | — |
| 1924 | Inc. above | 4.00 | 10.00 | 20.00 | 225 | — |
| 1925 | 1,550,000 | 3.75 | 9.25 | 20.00 | 215 | — |
| 1926 | 5,000,000 | 0.90 | 1.75 | 3.50 | 26.00 | — |
| 1927/6 | 6,000,000 | 25.00 | 40.00 | 60.00 | 140 | — |
| 1927 | Inc. above | 0.60 | 1.25 | 4.50 | 36.00 | — |
| 1928 | 5,000,000 | 0.60 | 0.80 | 3.25 | 16.50 | — |
| 1929 | 4,500,000 | 0.60 | 0.80 | 1.75 | 18.00 | — |
| 1930 | 7,000,000 | 0.75 | 1.00 | 2.25 | 19.00 | — |
| 1933 | 10,000,000 | 0.25 | 0.35 | 1.75 | 16.50 | — |
| 1934 | 7,500,000 | 0.40 | 0.95 | 3.25 | 35.00 | — |
| 1935 | 12,400,000 | 0.15 | 0.25 | 0.40 | 11.50 | — |
| 1936 | 20,100,000 | 0.15 | 0.20 | 0.30 | 8.00 | — |
| 1937 | 20,000,000 | 0.15 | 0.25 | 0.35 | 3.50 | — |
| 1938 | 10,000,000 | 0.10 | 0.15 | 0.30 | 2.25 | — |
| 1939 | 30,000,000 | 0.10 | 0.20 | 0.30 | 1.25 | — |
| 1940 | 10,000,000 | 0.20 | 0.30 | 0.60 | 6.50 | — |
| 1941 | 15,800,000 | 0.15 | 0.25 | 0.35 | 2.25 | — |
| 1942 | 30,400,000 | 0.15 | 0.20 | 0.30 | 1.25 | — |
| 1943 | 4,310,000 | 0.30 | 0.50 | 0.75 | 9.00 | — |
| 1944 | 5,645,000 | 0.15 | 0.25 | 0.50 | 7.00 | — |
| 1945 | 26,375,000 | 0.10 | 0.15 | 0.25 | 1.00 | — |
| 1946 | 42,135,000 | — | 0.15 | 0.20 | 0.60 | — |
| 1947 | 13,445,000 | — | 0.10 | 0.15 | 0.80 | — |
| 1948 | 20,040,000 | — | 0.15 | 0.30 | 1.10 | — |
| 1949 | 6,235,000 | 0.10 | 0.15 | 0.30 | 1.75 | — |

**Note:** Varieties exist.

**CENTAVO** **KM# 416** **Composition:** Bronze **Size:** 16 mm. **Note:** Zapata Issue. Struck at Mexico City Mint, mint mark Mo. Reduced size.

| Date | Mintage | F | VF | XF | Unc | BU |
|---|---|---|---|---|---|---|
| 1915 | 179,000 | 16.00 | 27.50 | 50.00 | 75.50 | — |

**CENTAVO** **KM# 417** **Composition:** Brass **Size:** 16 mm. **Note:** Struck at Mexico City Mint, mint mark Mo.

| Date | Mintage | F | VF | XF | Unc | BU |
|---|---|---|---|---|---|---|
| 1950 | 12,815,000 | — | 0.15 | 0.30 | 1.75 | 2.00 |
| 1951 | 25,740,000 | — | 0.15 | 0.25 | 0.65 | 1.10 |
| 1952 | 24,610,000 | — | 0.10 | 0.25 | 0.40 | 0.75 |
| 1953 | 21,160,000 | — | 0.10 | 0.25 | 0.40 | 0.85 |
| 1954 | 25,675,000 | — | 0.10 | 0.15 | 0.85 | 1.20 |
| 1955 | 9,820,000 | — | 0.15 | 0.25 | 0.85 | 1.50 |
| 1956 | 11,285,000 | — | 0.15 | 0.25 | 0.80 | 1.45 |
| 1957 | 9,805,000 | — | 0.15 | 0.25 | 0.85 | 1.35 |
| 1958 | 12,155,000 | — | 0.10 | 0.25 | 0.45 | 0.80 |
| 1959 | 11,875,000 | — | 0.10 | 0.25 | 0.75 | 1.25 |
| 1960 | 10,360,000 | — | 0.10 | 0.15 | 0.40 | 0.65 |
| 1961 | 6,385,000 | — | 0.10 | 0.15 | 0.45 | 0.85 |
| 1962 | 4,850,000 | — | 0.10 | 0.15 | 0.55 | 0.90 |
| 1963 | 7,775,000 | — | 0.10 | 0.15 | 0.25 | 0.45 |
| 1964 | 4,280,000 | — | 0.10 | 0.15 | 0.20 | 0.35 |
| 1965 | 2,255,000 | — | 0.10 | 0.15 | 0.25 | 0.40 |
| 1966 | 1,760,000 | — | 0.10 | 0.25 | 0.60 | 0.75 |
| 1967 | 1,290,000 | — | 0.10 | 0.15 | 0.40 | 0.70 |
| 1968 | 1,000,000 | — | 0.10 | 0.20 | 0.85 | 1.25 |
| 1969 | 1,000,000 | — | 0.10 | 0.15 | 0.75 | 1.25 |

**CENTAVO** **KM# 418** **Composition:** Brass **Size:** 13 mm. **Note:** Reduced size.

| Date | Mintage | F | VF | XF | Unc | BU |
|---|---|---|---|---|---|---|
| 1970 | 1,000,000 | — | 0.20 | 0.40 | 1.30 | 1.80 |
| 1972 | 1,000,000 | — | 0.20 | 0.45 | 2.50 | 3.25 |
| 1972/2 | — | — | 0.50 | 1.25 | 3.25 | 5.00 |
| 1973 | 1,000,000 | — | 1.65 | 2.75 | 8.00 | 9.75 |

**2 CENTAVOS** **KM# 419** **Composition:** Bronze **Size:** 25 mm. **Note:** Struck at Mexico City Mint, mint mark Mo.

| Date | Mintage | F | VF | XF | Unc | BU |
|---|---|---|---|---|---|---|
| 1905 | 50,000 | 125 | 275 | 425 | 1,200 | — |
| 1906 Inverted 6 | 9,998,000 | 25.00 | 50.00 | 110 | 375 | — |
| 1906 Wide date | Inc. above | 4.00 | 10.00 | 21.50 | 80.00 | — |
| 1920 | 1,325,000 | 6.50 | 21.50 | 60.00 | 350 | — |
| 1921 | 4,275,000 | 2.50 | 4.75 | 10.00 | 90.00 | — |
| 1922 | — | 225 | 550 | 1,350 | 4,000 | — |
| 1924 | 750,000 | 8.50 | 20.00 | 50.00 | 450 | — |
| 1925 | 3,650,000 | 2.50 | 3.50 | 9.00 | 40.00 | — |
| 1926 | 4,750,000 | 1.00 | 2.25 | 5.50 | 35.00 | — |
| 1927 | 7,250,000 | 0.60 | 1.00 | 4.50 | 22.75 | — |
| 1928 | 3,250,000 | 0.75 | 1.50 | 3.75 | 25.00 | — |
| 1929 | 250,000 | 45.00 | 120 | 500 | 1,000 | — |
| 1935 | 1,250,000 | 4.25 | 9.25 | 22.50 | 200 | — |
| 1939 | 5,000,000 | 0.60 | 0.90 | 2.25 | 20.00 | — |
| 1941 | 3,550,000 | 0.45 | 0.60 | 1.25 | 18.00 | — |

**2 CENTAVOS** **KM# 420** **Composition:** Bronze **Size:** 20 mm. **Note:** Zapata Issue. Struck at Mexico City Mint, mint mark Mo. Reduced size.

| Date | Mintage | F | VF | XF | Unc | BU |
|---|---|---|---|---|---|---|
| 1915 | 487,000 | 6.50 | 9.00 | 13.50 | 65.00 | — |

**5 CENTAVOS** **KM# 421** **Composition:** Nickel **Note:** Struck at Mexico City Mint, mint mark Mo. Varieties exist.

| Date | Mintage | F | VF | XF | Unc | BU |
|---|---|---|---|---|---|---|
| 1905 | 1,420,000 | 6.00 | 9.50 | 22.50 | 290 | — |
| 1906/5 | 10,615,000 | 12.00 | 23.50 | 60.00 | 375 | — |
| 1907 | 4,000,000 | 1.25 | 3.50 | 10.00 | 350 | — |
| 1909 | 2,052,000 | 3.25 | 9.50 | 42.50 | 360 | — |
| 1910 | 6,181,000 | 1.15 | 3.20 | 5.50 | 77.00 | — |
| 1911 Narrow date | 4,487,000 | 0.75 | 3.00 | 5.00 | 85.00 | — |
| 1911 Wide date | Inc. above | 2.50 | 4.25 | 9.00 | 110 | — |
| 1912 Small mint mark | 420,000 | 97.50 | 120 | 210 | 725 | — |
| 1912 Large mint mark | Inc. above | 60.00 | 85.00 | 160 | 575 | — |
| 1913 | 2,035,000 | 1.65 | 3.75 | 9.00 | 100 | — |

**Note:** Wide and narrow dates exist for 1913

| Date | Mintage | F | VF | XF | Unc | BU |
|---|---|---|---|---|---|---|
| 1914 | 2,000,000 | 0.75 | 1.75 | 3.50 | 60.00 | — |

**Note:** 5,000,000 pieces appear to have been struck at the Birmingham Mint in 1914 and all of 1909-1911. The Mexican Mint report does not mention receiving the 1914 dated coins

**5 CENTAVOS** **KM# 422** **Composition:** Bronze **Note:** Struck at Mexico City Mint, mint mark Mo.

| Date | Mintage | F | VF | XF | Unc | BU |
|---|---|---|---|---|---|---|
| 1914 | 2,500,000 | 10.00 | 21.50 | 45.00 | 225 | — |
| 1915 | 11,424,000 | 2.50 | 4.50 | 14.50 | 125 | — |
| 1916 | 2,860,000 | 13.50 | 32.00 | 170 | 690 | — |
| 1917 | 800,000 | 60.00 | 150 | 320 | 820 | — |
| 1918 | 1,332,000 | 28.00 | 70.00 | 175 | 625 | — |
| 1919 | 400,000 | 100 | 190 | 335 | 925 | — |
| 1920 | 5,920,000 | 3.00 | 7.50 | 40.00 | 285 | — |
| 1921 | 2,080,000 | 9.00 | 21.50 | 70.00 | 275 | — |
| 1924 | 780,000 | 35.00 | 80.00 | 235 | 625 | — |
| 1925 | 4,040,000 | 4.75 | 10.00 | 42.50 | 225 | — |
| 1926 | 3,160,000 | 5.50 | 11.00 | 43.50 | 300 | — |
| 1927 | 3,600,000 | 3.25 | 6.75 | 27.50 | 220 | — |
| 1928 Large date | 1,740,000 | 10.00 | 17.50 | 68.00 | 250 | — |
| 1928 Small date | Inc. above | 25.00 | 45.00 | 90.00 | 385 | — |
| 1929 | 2,400,000 | 4.75 | 10.00 | 40.00 | 180 | — |
| 1930 Large oval O in date | 2,600,000 | 4.00 | 7.50 | 27.50 | 210 | — |
| 1930 Small square O in date | Inc. above | 50.00 | 115 | 220 | 565 | — |
| 1931 | — | 475 | 675 | 1,000 | 3,250 | — |
| 1933 | 8,000,000 | 1.25 | 2.00 | 3.25 | 25.00 | — |
| 1934 | 10,000,000 | 1.00 | 1.50 | 2.50 | 22.50 | — |
| 1935 | 21,980,000 | 0.75 | 1.20 | 2.25 | 20.00 | — |

**5 CENTAVOS** **KM# 423** **Composition:** Copper-Nickel **Note:** Struck at Mexico City Mint, mint mark Mo.

| Date | Mintage | F | VF | XF | Unc | BU |
|---|---|---|---|---|---|---|
| 1936 | 46,700,000 | — | 0.65 | 1.25 | 6.50 | 9.00 |
| 1937 | 49,060,000 | — | 0.50 | 1.00 | 6.00 | 9.00 |
| 1938 | 3,340,000 | — | 5.00 | 12.50 | 65.00 | 250 |
| 1940 | 22,800,000 | — | 0.75 | 1.50 | 8.00 | 12.00 |
| 1942 | 7,100,000 | — | 1.50 | 3.20 | 35.00 | 45.00 |

**5 CENTAVOS** **KM# 424** **Ring Composition:** Bronze **Reverse:** "Josefa" Ortiz de Dominguez **Note:** Struck at Mexico City Mint, mint mark Mo.

| Date | Mintage | F | VF | XF | Unc | BU |
|---|---|---|---|---|---|---|
| 1942 | 900,000 | — | 20.00 | 60.00 | 375 | 500 |
| 1943 | 54,660,000 | — | 0.40 | 0.65 | 3.00 | 4.00 |
| 1944 | 53,463,000 | — | 0.25 | 0.35 | 0.75 | 1.00 |
| 1945 | 44,262,000 | — | 0.25 | 0.35 | 0.90 | 1.65 |
| 1946 | 49,054,000 | — | 0.50 | 0.75 | 2.00 | 2.75 |
| 1951 | 50,758,000 | — | 0.60 | 0.85 | 3.00 | 4.75 |
| 1952 | 17,674,000 | — | 1.25 | 2.25 | 9.25 | 11.50 |
| 1953 | 31,568,000 | — | 1.10 | 1.75 | 7.00 | 10.00 |
| 1954 | 58,680,000 | — | 0.40 | 0.75 | 2.75 | 4.00 |
| 1955 | 31,114,000 | — | 1.85 | 2.50 | 10.00 | 14.00 |

**5 CENTAVOS** **KM# 425** **Composition:** Copper-Nickel **Reverse:** White Josefa **Note:** Struck at Mexico City Mint, mint mark Mo.

| Date | Mintage | F | VF | XF | Unc | BU |
|---|---|---|---|---|---|---|
| 1950 | 5,700,000 | — | 0.75 | 1.50 | 6.25 | 8.00 |

**Note:** 5,600,000 pieces struck at Connecticut melted

**5 CENTAVOS** **KM# 426** **Composition:** Brass **Reverse:** White Josefa **Note:** Struck at Mexico City Mint, mint mark Mo.

| Date | Mintage | F | VF | XF | Unc | BU |
|---|---|---|---|---|---|---|
| 1954 Dot | — | — | 9.00 | 32.00 | 325 | 375 |
| 1954 Without dot | — | — | 12.00 | 25.00 | 250 | 290 |
| 1955 | 12,136,000 | — | 0.75 | 1.50 | 9.00 | 12.50 |
| 1956 | 60,216,000 | — | 0.20 | 0.30 | 0.90 | 1.50 |
| 1957 | 55,288,000 | — | 0.15 | 0.20 | 0.90 | 1.50 |
| 1958 | 104,624,000 | — | 0.15 | 0.20 | 0.60 | 1.00 |
| 1959 | 106,000,000 | — | 0.15 | 0.25 | 0.90 | 1.50 |
| 1960 | 99,144,000 | — | 0.10 | 0.15 | 0.50 | 0.75 |
| 1961 | 61,136,000 | — | 0.10 | 0.15 | 0.40 | 0.70 |
| 1962 | 47,232,000 | — | 0.10 | 0.15 | 0.30 | 0.55 |
| 1963 | 156,680,000 | — | — | 0.15 | 0.20 | 0.35 |
| 1964 | 71,168,000 | — | — | 0.15 | 0.20 | 0.40 |
| 1965 | 155,720,000 | — | — | 0.15 | 0.25 | 0.35 |
| 1966 | 124,944,000 | — | — | 0.15 | 0.40 | 0.65 |
| 1967 | 118,816,000 | — | — | 0.15 | 0.25 | 0.40 |
| 1968 | 189,588,000 | — | — | 0.15 | 0.50 | 0.75 |
| 1969 | 210,492,000 | — | — | 0.15 | 0.55 | 0.80 |

**5 CENTAVOS** **KM# 426a** **Composition:** Copper-Nickel **Reverse:** White Josefa **Note:** Struck at Mexico City Mint, mint mark Mo.

| Date | Mintage | F | VF | XF | Unc | BU |
|---|---|---|---|---|---|---|
| 1960 | — | — | 300 | 450 | — | — |
| 1962 | 19 | — | 300 | 450 | — | — |
| 1965 | — | — | 300 | 450 | — | — |

**5 CENTAVOS** **KM# 427** **Composition:** Brass **Reverse:** White Josefa **Size:** 18 mm. **Note:** Due to some minor alloy variations this type is often encountered with a bronze color toning. Reduced size.

| Date | Mintage | F | VF | XF | Unc | BU |
|---|---|---|---|---|---|---|
| 1970 | 163,368,000 | — | 0.10 | 0.15 | 0.35 | 0.45 |
| 1971 | 198,844,000 | — | 0.10 | 0.15 | 0.25 | 0.30 |
| 1972 | 225,000,000 | — | 0.10 | 0.15 | 0.25 | 0.30 |
| 1973 Flat top 3 | 595,070,000 | — | 0.10 | 0.15 | 0.25 | 0.40 |
| 1973 Round top 3 | Inc. above | — | 0.10 | 0.15 | 0.20 | 0.30 |
| 1974 | 401,584,000 | — | 0.10 | 0.15 | 0.30 | 0.40 |
| 1975 | 342,308,000 | — | 0.10 | 0.15 | 0.25 | 0.35 |
| 1976 | 367,524,000 | — | 0.10 | 0.15 | 0.40 | 0.60 |

**10 CENTAVOS** **KM# 428** **Weight:** 2.5000 g. **Composition:** 0.8000 Silver .0643 oz. ASW **Note:** Struck at Mexico City Mint, mint mark Mo.

| Date | Mintage | F | VF | XF | Unc | BU |
|---|---|---|---|---|---|---|
| 1905 | 3,920,000 | — | 5.25 | 7.00 | 35.00 | 50.00 |
| 1906 | 8,410,000 | — | 4.75 | 6.25 | 25.00 | 35.00 |
| 1907/6 | 5,950,000 | — | 45.00 | 115 | 275 | 350 |
| 1907 | Inc. above | — | 5.50 | 7.75 | 35.00 | 42.50 |
| 1909 | 2,620,000 | — | 8.00 | 12.50 | 70.00 | 90.00 |
| 1910/00 | 3,450,000 | — | 10.00 | 32.00 | 75.00 | 100 |
| 1910 | Inc. above | — | 8.00 | 12.50 | 25.00 | 30.00 |
| 1911 Narrow date | 2,550,000 | — | 10.00 | 15.00 | 88.00 | 125 |
| 1911 Wide date | Inc. above | — | 6.00 | 8.50 | 42.50 | 60.00 |
| 1912 | 1,350,000 | — | 9.00 | 16.00 | 120 | 135 |
| 1912 Low 2 | Inc. above | — | 8.00 | 15.00 | 110 | 130 |
| 1913/2 | 1,990,000 | — | 7.50 | 14.00 | 35.00 | 65.00 |
| 1913 | Inc. above | — | 6.00 | 8.50 | 30.00 | 40.00 |
| 1914 | 3,110,000 | — | 4.50 | 5.75 | 13.50 | 20.00 |

**Note:** Wide and narrow dates exist for 1914

**10 CENTAVOS** **KM# 430** **Composition:** Bronze **Note:** Struck at Mexico City Mint, mint mark Mo.

| Date | Mintage | F | VF | XF | Unc | BU |
|---|---|---|---|---|---|---|
| 1919 | 1,232,000 | — | 20.00 | 47.50 | 440 | 525 |
| 1920 | 6,612,000 | — | 12.50 | 38.50 | 400 | 475 |
| 1921 | 2,255,000 | — | 30.00 | 65.00 | 625 | 800 |
| 1935 | 5,970,000 | — | 12.00 | 23.50 | 125 | 175 |

**10 CENTAVOS** **KM# 429** **Weight:** 1.8125 g. **Composition:** 0.8000 Silver .0466 oz. ASW **Size:** 15 mm. **Note:** Struck at Mexico City Mint, mint mark Mo. Reduced size.

| Date | Mintage | F | VF | XF | Unc | BU |
|---|---|---|---|---|---|---|
| 1919 | 8,360,000 | — | 8.00 | 15.00 | 90.00 | 110 |

**10 CENTAVOS** **KM# 431** **Weight:** 1.6600 g. **Composition:** 0.7200 Silver .0384 oz. ASW **Note:** Struck at Mexico City Mint, mint mark Mo.

| Date | Mintage | F | VF | XF | Unc | BU |
|---|---|---|---|---|---|---|
| 1925/15 | 5,350,000 | — | 18.00 | 35.00 | 110 | 125 |
| 1925/3 | Inc. above | — | 18.00 | 35.00 | 115 | 130 |
| 1925 | Inc. above | — | 2.00 | 4.00 | 35.00 | 47.50 |
| 1926/16 | 2,650,000 | — | 25.00 | 55.00 | 160 | 175 |
| 1926 | Inc. above | — | 3.50 | 6.00 | 62.50 | 80.00 |
| 1927 | 2,810,000 | — | 2.25 | 3.00 | 17.50 | 21.50 |
| 1928 | 5,270,000 | — | 1.75 | 2.25 | 12.00 | 14.25 |
| 1930 | 2,000,000 | — | 3.75 | 5.00 | 18.75 | 22.50 |

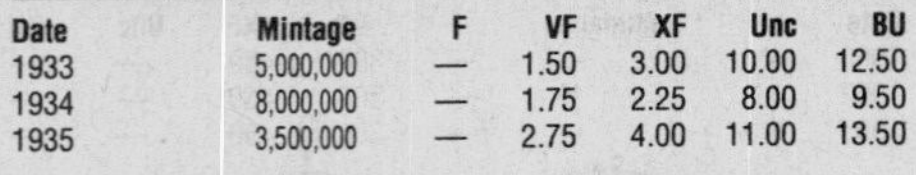

| Date | Mintage | F | VF | XF | Unc | BU |
|---|---|---|---|---|---|---|
| 1933 | 5,000,000 | — | 1.50 | 3.00 | 10.00 | 12.50 |
| 1934 | 8,000,000 | — | 1.75 | 2.25 | 8.00 | 9.50 |
| 1935 | 3,500,000 | — | 2.75 | 4.00 | 11.00 | 13.50 |

**10 CENTAVOS** **KM# 432** **Composition:** Copper-Nickel **Note:** Struck at Mexico City Mint, mint mark Mo.

| Date | Mintage | F | VF | XF | Unc | BU |
|---|---|---|---|---|---|---|
| 1936 | 33,030,000 | — | 0.65 | 2.25 | 8.25 | 10.00 |
| 1937 | 3,000,000 | — | 2.75 | 42.50 | 200 | 250 |
| 1938 | 3,650,000 | — | 1.75 | 5.50 | 60.00 | 75.00 |
| 1939 | 6,920,000 | — | 1.00 | 3.50 | 30.00 | 40.00 |
| 1940 | 12,300,000 | — | 0.40 | 1.00 | 5.00 | 6.50 |
| 1942 | 14,380,000 | — | 0.60 | 1.50 | 7.00 | 8.50 |
| 1945 | 9,558,000 | — | 0.40 | 0.70 | 3.50 | 4.00 |
| 1946 | 46,230,000 | — | 0.25 | 0.45 | 2.25 | 3.10 |

**10 CENTAVOS** **KM# 433** **Composition:** Bronze **Reverse:** Benito Juarez **Note:** Struck at Mexico City Mint, mint mark Mo.

| Date | Mintage | F | VF | XF | Unc | BU |
|---|---|---|---|---|---|---|
| 1955 | 1,818,000 | — | 0.60 | 3.00 | 22.00 | 30.00 |
| 1956 | 5,255,000 | — | 0.50 | 3.00 | 22.00 | 35.00 |
| 1957 | 11,925,000 | — | 0.20 | 0.40 | 5.50 | 8.00 |
| 1959 | 26,140,000 | — | 0.20 | 0.35 | 0.65 | 1.25 |
| 1966 | 5,873,000 | — | 0.15 | 0.25 | 0.65 | 1.50 |

**10 CENTAVOS** **KM# 434.1** **Composition:** Copper-Nickel **Reverse:** Five full rows of kernels, sharp stem, wide date **Note:** Variety I

| Date | Mintage | F | VF | XF | Unc | BU |
|---|---|---|---|---|---|---|
| 1974 | 6,000,000 | — | — | 0.35 | 0.85 | 1.00 |
| 1975 | 5,550,000 | — | 0.10 | 0.35 | 0.85 | 1.75 |
| 1976 | 7,680,000 | — | 0.10 | 0.20 | 0.30 | 0.40 |
| 1977 | 144,650,000 | — | 1.25 | 2.25 | 3.50 | 4.50 |
| 1978 | 271,870,000 | — | — | 1.00 | 1.50 | 2.25 |
| 1979 | 375,660,000 | — | — | 0.50 | 1.00 | 1.75 |
| 1980/79 | 21,290,000 | — | 2.45 | 3.75 | 6.00 | 7.00 |
| 1980 | Inc. above | — | 1.50 | 2.00 | 4.50 | 5.00 |

**10 CENTAVOS** **KM# 434.2** **Composition:** Copper-Nickel **Reverse:** Five full, plus one partial row at left, blunt stem, narrow date **Note:** Variety II

| Date | Mintage | F | VF | XF | Unc | BU |
|---|---|---|---|---|---|---|
| 1974 | Inc. above | — | — | 0.10 | 0.25 | 0.35 |
| 1977 | Inc. above | — | — | 0.10 | 0.30 | 0.35 |
| 1978 | Inc. above | — | — | 0.10 | 0.30 | 0.40 |
| 1979 | Inc. above | — | 0.15 | 0.50 | 1.00 | 2.00 |
| 1980 | Inc. above | — | — | 0.10 | 0.30 | 0.35 |

**10 CENTAVOS** **KM# 434.3** **Composition:** Copper-Nickel **Reverse:** Five full, plus one partial row, blunt stem and wide date **Note:** Variety III

| Date | Mintage | F | VF | XF | Unc | BU |
|---|---|---|---|---|---|---|
| 1980/79 | — | — | — | — | — | — |

**10 CENTAVOS** **KM# 434.4** **Composition:** Copper-Nickel **Reverse:** Five full, plus one partial row, sharp stem and narrow date **Note:** Variety IV

| Date | Mintage | F | VF | XF | Unc | BU |
|---|---|---|---|---|---|---|
| 1979 | — | — | — | — | — | — |

**20 CENTAVOS** **KM# 435** **Weight:** 5.0000 g. **Composition:** 0.8000 Silver .1286 oz. ASW **Note:** Struck at Mexico City Mint, mint mark Mo.

| Date | Mintage | F | VF | XF | Unc | BU |
|---|---|---|---|---|---|---|
| 1905 | 2,565,000 | — | 9.00 | 15.00 | 150 | 175 |
| 1906 | 6,860,000 | — | 7.25 | 14.50 | 60.00 | 80.00 |
| 1907 Straight 7 | 4,000,000 | — | 8.50 | 17.50 | 65.00 | 95.00 |
| 1907 Curved 7 | 5,435,000 | — | 7.50 | 13.50 | 70.00 | 90.00 |
| 1908 | 350,000 | — | 85.00 | 200 | 1,500 | — |
| 1910 | 1,135,000 | — | 9.50 | 15.00 | 80.00 | 95.00 |
| 1911 | 1,150,000 | — | 14.00 | 32.00 | 125 | 150 |
| 1912 | 625,000 | — | 25.00 | 70.00 | 335 | 375 |
| 1913 | 1,000,000 | — | 14.50 | 30.00 | 95.00 | 115 |
| 1914 | 1,500,000 | — | 10.00 | 21.50 | 62.50 | 75.00 |

**20 CENTAVOS** **KM# 436** **Weight:** 3.6250 g. **Composition:** 0.8000 Silver .0932 oz. ASW **Size:** 19 mm. **Note:** Struck at Mexico City Mint, mint mark Mo. Reduced size.

| Date | Mintage | F | VF | XF | Unc | BU |
|---|---|---|---|---|---|---|
| 1919 | 4,155,000 | — | 25.00 | 50.00 | 195 | 245 |

**20 CENTAVOS** **KM# 437** **Composition:** Bronze **Note:** Struck at Mexico City Mint, mint mark Mo.

| Date | Mintage | F | VF | XF | Unc | BU |
|---|---|---|---|---|---|---|
| 1920 | 4,835,000 | — | 40.00 | 110 | 600 | 700 |
| 1935 | 20,000,000 | — | 5.50 | 8.50 | 85.00 | 125 |

**20 CENTAVOS** **KM# 438** **Weight:** 3.3333 g. **Composition:** 0.7200 Silver .0772 oz. ASW **Note:** Struck at Mexico City Mint, mint mark Mo.

| Date | Mintage | F | VF | XF | Unc | BU |
|---|---|---|---|---|---|---|
| 1920 | 3,710,000 | — | 4.75 | 10.00 | 165 | 215 |
| 1921 | 6,160,000 | — | 4.50 | 10.00 | 100 | 145 |
| 1925 | 1,450,000 | — | 8.00 | 17.00 | 125 | 150 |
| 1926/5 | 1,465,000 | — | 18.00 | 45.00 | 325 | 375 |
| 1926 | Inc. above | — | 4.50 | 6.25 | 80.00 | 110 |
| 1927 | 1,405,000 | — | 3.75 | 6.25 | 80.00 | 115 |
| 1928 | 3,630,000 | — | 2.50 | 4.50 | 14.50 | 19.50 |

| Date | Mintage | F | VF | XF | Unc | BU |
|---|---|---|---|---|---|---|
| 1930 | 1,000,000 | — | 3.50 | 6.25 | 22.00 | 30.00 |
| 1933 | 2,500,000 | — | 2.25 | 2.75 | 10.00 | 11.50 |
| 1934 | 2,500,000 | — | 2.25 | 3.00 | 11.00 | 12.50 |
| 1935 | 2,460,000 | — | 2.25 | 2.75 | 10.00 | 11.50 |
| 1937 | 10,000,000 | — | 2.25 | 2.50 | 4.75 | 5.50 |
| 1939 | 8,800,000 | — | 1.75 | 2.00 | 4.00 | 5.00 |
| 1940 | 3,000,000 | — | 1.75 | 2.00 | 3.50 | 5.00 |
| 1941 | 5,740,000 | — | 1.50 | 2.00 | 3.00 | 3.50 |
| 1942 | 12,460,000 | — | 1.50 | 2.00 | 3.25 | 3.80 |
| 1943 | 3,955,000 | — | 2.00 | 2.50 | 3.50 | 4.25 |

**20 CENTAVOS** **KM# 439** **Composition:** Bronze **Note:** Struck at Mexico City Mint, mint mark Mo.

| Date | Mintage | F | VF | XF | Unc | BU |
|---|---|---|---|---|---|---|
| 1943 | 46,350,000 | — | 0.75 | 2.75 | 18.00 | 25.00 |
| 1944 | 83,650,000 | — | 0.40 | 0.65 | 8.00 | 10.00 |
| 1945 | 26,801,000 | — | 1.10 | 3.50 | 9.50 | 12.00 |
| 1946 | 25,695,000 | — | 0.90 | 2.00 | 6.00 | 8.25 |
| 1951 | 11,385,000 | — | 2.50 | 5.50 | 80.00 | 100 |
| 1952 | 6,560,000 | — | 2.50 | 4.50 | 25.00 | 32.50 |
| 1953 | 26,948,000 | — | 0.35 | 0.75 | 7.25 | 11.00 |
| 1954 | 40,108,000 | — | 0.35 | 0.80 | 8.00 | 11.50 |
| 1955 | 16,950,000 | — | 2.50 | 6.00 | 60.00 | 75.00 |

**20 CENTAVOS** **KM# 440** **Composition:** Bronze **Note:** Struck at Mexico City Mint, mint mark Mo.

| Date | Mintage | F | VF | XF | Unc | BU |
|---|---|---|---|---|---|---|
| 1955 Inc. KM#439 | Inc. above | — | 0.65 | 1.50 | 13.50 | 18.50 |
| 1956 | 22,431,000 | — | 0.30 | 0.35 | 3.00 | 5.00 |
| 1957 | 13,455,000 | — | 0.45 | 1.25 | 9.00 | 12.00 |
| 1959 | 6,017,000 | — | 4.00 | 7.50 | 65.00 | 95.00 |
| 1960 | 39,756,000 | — | 0.15 | 0.25 | 0.85 | 1.25 |
| 1963 | 14,869,000 | — | 0.25 | 0.35 | 0.90 | 1.25 |
| 1964 | 28,654,000 | — | 0.25 | 0.40 | 0.90 | 1.25 |
| 1965 | 74,162,000 | — | 0.20 | 0.40 | 0.85 | 1.20 |
| 1966 | 43,745,000 | — | 0.15 | 0.25 | 0.90 | 1.30 |
| 1967 | 46,487,000 | — | 0.20 | 0.55 | 1.20 | 1.50 |
| 1968 | 15,477,000 | — | 0.30 | 0.55 | 1.35 | 1.65 |
| 1969 | 63,647,000 | — | 0.20 | 0.40 | 1.00 | 1.50 |
| 1970 | 76,287,000 | — | 0.15 | 0.20 | 0.90 | 1.30 |
| 1971 | 49,892,000 | — | 0.30 | 0.50 | 1.40 | 1.75 |

**20 CENTAVOS** **KM# 441** **Composition:** Bronze

| Date | Mintage | F | VF | XF | Unc | BU |
|---|---|---|---|---|---|---|
| 1971 Inc. KM#440 | Inc. above | — | 0.20 | 0.35 | 1.75 | 2.35 |
| 1973 | 78,398,000 | — | 0.25 | 0.35 | 0.95 | 1.50 |
| 1974 | 34,200,000 | — | 0.20 | 0.35 | 1.25 | 1.75 |

**20 CENTAVOS** **KM# 442** **Composition:** Copper-Nickel **Reverse:** Francisco Madero

| Date | Mintage | F | VF | XF | Unc | BU |
|---|---|---|---|---|---|---|
| 1974 | 112,000,000 | — | 0.10 | 0.15 | 0.25 | 0.30 |
| 1975 | 611,000,000 | — | 0.10 | 0.15 | 0.30 | 0.35 |
| 1976 | 394,000,000 | — | 0.10 | 0.15 | 0.35 | 0.45 |
| 1977 | 394,350,000 | — | 0.10 | 0.15 | 0.40 | 0.45 |
| 1979 | 524,615,000 | — | 0.10 | 0.15 | 0.30 | 0.40 |

| Date | Mintage | F | VF | XF | Unc | BU |
|---|---|---|---|---|---|---|
| 1979 Doubled die obv. large/small letters | — | — | 1.25 | 2.00 | 4.00 | 8.00 |
| 1980 | 326,500,000 | — | 0.15 | 0.25 | 0.40 | 0.60 |
| 1981 Open 8 | 106,205,000 | — | 0.30 | 0.50 | 1.00 | 2.00 |
| 1981 Closed 8, high date | 248,500,000 | — | 0.30 | 0.50 | 1.00 | 2.00 |
| 1981 Closed 8, low date | — | — | 1.00 | 1.50 | 3.50 | 4.25 |
| 1981/1982 | — | — | 30.00 | 75.00 | 160 | 190 |

**Note:** The 1981/1982 overdate is often mistaken as 1982/1981

| Date | Mintage | F | VF | XF | Unc | BU |
|---|---|---|---|---|---|---|
| 1982 | 286,855,000 | — | 0.40 | 0.60 | 0.90 | 1.10 |
| 1983 Round top 3 | 100,930,000 | — | 0.25 | 0.40 | 1.75 | 2.25 |
| 1983 Flat top 3 | Inc. above | — | 0.25 | 0.50 | 1.25 | 1.75 |
| 1983 Proof | 998 | Value: 15.00 | | | | |

**20 CENTAVOS** **KM# 491** **Composition:** Bronze **Subject:** Olmec Culture

| Date | Mintage | F | VF | XF | Unc | BU |
|---|---|---|---|---|---|---|
| 1983 | 260,000,000 | — | 0.20 | 0.25 | 0.90 | 1.10 |
| 1984 | 180,320,000 | — | 0.20 | 0.25 | 1.50 | 1.70 |

**25 CENTAVOS** **KM# 443** **Weight:** 3.3330 g. **Composition:** 0.3000 Silver .0321 oz. ASW **Note:** Struck at Mexico City Mint, mint mark Mo.

| Date | Mintage | F | VF | XF | Unc | BU |
|---|---|---|---|---|---|---|
| 1950 | 77,060,000 | — | 0.50 | 0.75 | 1.75 | 2.25 |
| 1951 | 41,172,000 | — | 0.50 | 0.75 | 1.60 | 2.00 |
| 1952 | 29,264,000 | — | 0.75 | 1.10 | 1.80 | 2.50 |
| 1953 | 38,144,000 | — | 0.60 | 0.70 | 1.50 | 2.00 |

**25 CENTAVOS** **KM# 444** **Composition:** Copper-Nickel **Reverse:** Francisco Madero

| Date | Mintage | F | VF | XF | Unc | BU |
|---|---|---|---|---|---|---|
| 1964 | 20,686,000 | — | — | 0.15 | 0.25 | 0.40 |
| 1966 Closed beak | 180,000 | — | 0.65 | 1.00 | 2.50 | 3.00 |
| 1966 Open beak | Inc. above | — | 1.75 | 3.50 | 10.00 | 14.00 |

**50 CENTAVOS** **KM# 445** **Weight:** 12.5000 g. **Composition:** 0.8000 Silver .3215 oz. ASW **Note:** Struck at Mexico City Mint, mint mark Mo.

| Date | Mintage | F | VF | XF | Unc | BU |
|---|---|---|---|---|---|---|
| 1905 | 2,446,000 | — | 12.50 | 20.00 | 150 | 225 |
| 1906 Open 9 | 16,966,000 | — | 5.00 | 10.00 | 30.00 | 50.00 |
| 1906 Closed 9 | Inc. above | — | 4.50 | 8.50 | 27.50 | 40.00 |
| 1907 Straight 7 | 18,920,000 | — | 4.50 | 7.25 | 25.00 | 28.50 |
| 1907 Curved 7 | 14,841,000 | — | 5.25 | 8.00 | 25.00 | 28.50 |
| 1908 | 488,000 | — | 65.00 | 150 | 525 | 625 |
| 1912 | 3,736,000 | — | 10.00 | 12.50 | 45.00 | 60.00 |
| 1913/07 | 10,510,000 | — | 30.00 | 70.00 | 225 | 275 |
| 1913/2 | Inc. above | — | 18.00 | 22.50 | 65.00 | 85.00 |
| 1913 | Inc. above | — | 5.50 | 8.50 | 25.00 | 30.00 |
| 1914 | 7,710,000 | — | 6.75 | 13.50 | 30.00 | 40.00 |
| 1916 Narrow date | 480,000 | — | 50.00 | 75.00 | 200 | 290 |
| 1916 Wide date | Inc. above | — | 50.00 | 75.00 | 200 | 290 |
| 1917 | 37,112,000 | — | 5.50 | 8.50 | 20.00 | 22.50 |
| 1918 | 1,320,000 | — | 60.00 | 110 | 250 | 335 |

**50 CENTAVOS** **KM# 446** **Weight:** 9.0625 g. **Composition:** 0.8000 Silver .2331 oz. ASW **Size:** 27 mm. **Note:** Struck at Mexico City Mint, mint mark Mo. Reduced size.

| Date | Mintage | F | VF | XF | Unc | BU |
|---|---|---|---|---|---|---|
| 1918/7 | 2,760,000 | — | 525 | 625 | 1,250 | — |
| 1918 | Inc. above | — | 15.00 | 50.00 | 325 | 400 |
| 1919 | 29,670,000 | — | 7.00 | 16.50 | 100 | 125 |

**50 CENTAVOS** **KM# 447** **Weight:** 8.3333 g. **Composition:** 0.7200 Silver .1929 oz. ASW **Note:** Struck at Mexico City Mint, mint mark Mo.

| Date | Mintage | F | VF | XF | Unc | BU |
|---|---|---|---|---|---|---|
| 1919 | 10,200,000 | — | 8.00 | 18.50 | 87.50 | 110 |
| 1920 | 27,166,000 | — | 6.00 | 8.50 | 65.00 | 80.00 |
| 1921 | 21,864,000 | — | 6.50 | 9.00 | 80.00 | 95.00 |
| 1925 | 3,280,000 | — | 14.00 | 30.00 | 130 | 160 |
| 1937 | 20,000,000 | — | 3.75 | 5.00 | 7.50 | 8.50 |
| 1938 | 100,000 | — | 40.00 | 75.00 | 225 | 300 |
| 1939 | 10,440,000 | — | 5.25 | 7.25 | 14.00 | 16.50 |
| 1942 | 800,000 | — | 5.50 | 7.50 | 15.00 | 17.00 |
| 1943 | 41,512,000 | — | 2.75 | 4.00 | 5.50 | 6.50 |
| 1944 | 55,806,000 | — | 3.00 | 3.75 | 5.50 | 6.50 |
| 1945 | 56,766,000 | — | 3.00 | 3.75 | 6.00 | 6.50 |

**50 CENTAVOS** **KM# 448** **Weight:** 7.9730 g. **Composition:** 0.4200 Silver .1076 oz. ASW **Note:** Struck at Mexico City Mint, mint mark Mo.

| Date | Mintage | F | VF | XF | Unc | BU |
|---|---|---|---|---|---|---|
| 1935 | 70,800,000 | — | 2.20 | 2.75 | 5.00 | 6.00 |

**50 CENTAVOS** **KM# 449** **Weight:** 6.6600 g. **Composition:** 0.3000 Silver .0642 oz. ASW **Reverse:** Cuauhtemoc **Note:** Struck at Mexico City Mint, mint mark Mo.

| Date | Mintage | F | VF | XF | Unc | BU |
|---|---|---|---|---|---|---|
| 1950 | 13,570,000 | — | 1.50 | 1.80 | 3.00 | 4.00 |
| 1951 | 3,650,000 | — | 2.00 | 2.50 | 3.75 | 5.00 |

**50 CENTAVOS** **KM# 450** **Composition:** Bronze **Note:** Struck at Mexico City Mint, mint mark Mo.

| Date | Mintage | F | VF | XF | Unc | BU |
|---|---|---|---|---|---|---|
| 1955 | 3,502,000 | — | 1.20 | 2.20 | 27.50 | 35.00 |
| 1956 | 34,643,000 | — | 0.65 | 1.00 | 3.25 | 4.50 |
| 1957 | 9,675,000 | — | 1.00 | 2.00 | 6.50 | 7.50 |
| 1959 | 4,540,000 | — | 0.35 | 0.50 | 1.50 | 2.00 |

**50 CENTAVOS** **KM# 451** **Composition:** Copper-Nickel

| Date | Mintage | F | VF | XF | Unc | BU |
|---|---|---|---|---|---|---|
| 1964 | 43,806,000 | — | 0.15 | 0.20 | 0.45 | 0.65 |
| 1965 | 14,326,000 | — | 0.20 | 0.25 | 0.45 | 0.65 |
| 1966 | 1,726,000 | — | 0.20 | 0.40 | 1.30 | 1.75 |
| 1967 | 55,144,000 | — | 0.20 | 0.30 | 0.65 | 1.00 |
| 1968 | 80,438,000 | — | 0.15 | 0.30 | 0.65 | 0.80 |
| 1969 | 87,640,000 | — | 0.20 | 0.35 | 0.80 | 1.15 |

**50 CENTAVOS** **KM# 452** **Composition:** Copper-Nickel **Obverse:** Stylized eagle **Note:** Coins dated 1975 and 1976 exist with and without dots in centers of three circles on plumage on reverse. Edge varieties exist.

| Date | Mintage | F | VF | XF | Unc | BU |
|---|---|---|---|---|---|---|
| 1970 | 76,236,000 | — | 0.15 | 0.20 | 0.90 | 1.25 |
| 1971 | 125,288,000 | — | 0.15 | 0.20 | 0.90 | 1.30 |
| 1972 | 16,000,000 | — | 1.25 | 2.00 | 3.00 | 4.75 |
| 1975 Dots | 177,958,000 | — | 0.60 | 1.25 | 3.50 | 6.00 |
| 1975 No dots | Inc. above | — | 0.15 | 0.20 | 0.50 | 0.75 |
| 1976 Dots | 37,480 | — | 0.75 | 1.25 | 5.00 | 6.00 |
| 1976 No dots | Inc. above | — | 0.15 | 0.20 | 0.50 | 0.75 |
| 1977 | 12,410,000 | — | 6.50 | 10.00 | 32.50 | 42.50 |
| 1978 | 85,400,000 | — | 0.15 | 0.25 | 0.50 | 0.75 |
| 1979 Round 2nd 9 in date | 229,000,000 | — | 0.15 | 0.25 | 0.50 | 0.65 |
| 1979 Square 9's in date | Inc. above | — | 0.20 | 0.40 | 1.60 | 2.10 |
| 1980 Narrow date, square 9 | 89,978,000 | — | 0.45 | 0.75 | 1.00 | 2.00 |
| 1980 Wide date, round 9 | 178,188,000 | — | 0.20 | 0.25 | 1.00 | 1.15 |
| 1981 Rectangular 9, narrow date | 142,212,000 | — | 0.50 | 0.75 | 1.75 | 2.50 |
| 1981 Round 9, wide date | Inc. above | — | 0.30 | 0.50 | 1.25 | 1.75 |
| 1982 | 45,474,000 | — | 0.20 | 0.40 | 1.50 | 2.40 |
| 1983 | 90,318,000 | — | 0.50 | 0.75 | 2.25 | 2.85 |
| 1983 Proof | 998 | Value: 15.00 | | | | |

**50 CENTAVOS** **KM# 492** **Composition:** Stainless Steel **Subject:** Palenque Culture **Obverse:** Stylized eagle **Reverse:** Cuauhtemoc

| Date | Mintage | F | VF | XF | Unc | BU |
|---|---|---|---|---|---|---|
| 1983 | 99,540,000 | — | — | 0.30 | 1.50 | 2.50 |
| 1983 Proof | 53 | Value: 165 | | | | |

**PESO** **KM# 453** **Weight:** 27.0700 g. **Composition:** 0.9030 Silver .7859 oz. ASW **Subject:** Caballito **Note:** Struck at Mexico City Mint, mint mark Mo.

| Date | Mintage | F | VF | XF | Unc | BU |
|---|---|---|---|---|---|---|
| 1910 | 3,814,000 | — | 30.00 | 45.00 | 155 | 250 |
| 1911 Long lower left ray on reverse | 1,227,000 | — | 45.00 | 75.00 | 200 | 275 |
| 1911 Short lower left ray on reverse | Inc. above | — | 135 | 225 | 600 | 800 |
| 1912 | 322,000 | — | 95.00 | 200 | 350 | 500 |
| 1913/2 | 2,880,000 | — | 45.00 | 75.00 | 265 | 400 |
| 1913 | Inc. above | — | 45.00 | 70.00 | 170 | 250 |

**Note:** 1913 coins exist with even and unevenly spaced date

| Date | Mintage | F | VF | XF | Unc | BU |
|---|---|---|---|---|---|---|
| 1914 | 120,000 | — | 600 | 950 | 3,000 | — |

**PESO** **KM# 454** **Weight:** 18.1300 g. **Composition:** 0.8000 Silver .4663 oz. ASW **Subject:** Caballito **Note:** Struck at Mexico City Mint, mint mark Mo.

| Date | Mintage | F | VF | XF | Unc | BU |
|---|---|---|---|---|---|---|
| 1918 | 3,050,000 | — | 30.00 | 115 | 1,350 | 2,100 |
| 1919 | 6,151,000 | — | 18.00 | 45.00 | 900 | 1,600 |

**PESO** **KM# 455** **Weight:** 16.6600 g. **Composition:** 0.7200 Silver .3856 oz. ASW **Note:** Struck at Mexico City Mint, mint mark Mo.

| Date | Mintage | F | VF | XF | Unc | BU |
|---|---|---|---|---|---|---|
| 1920/10 | 8,830,000 | — | 50.00 | 90.00 | 320 | — |
| 1920 | Inc. above | — | 6.50 | 18.00 | 150 | 200 |
| 1921 | 5,480,000 | — | 8.00 | 20.00 | 160 | 200 |
| 1922 | 33,620,000 | — | 3.25 | 5.00 | 20.00 | 26.00 |
| 1923 | 35,280,000 | — | 3.25 | 5.00 | 20.00 | 28.00 |
| 1924 | 33,060,000 | — | 3.25 | 5.00 | 20.00 | 26.00 |
| 1925 | 9,160,000 | — | 4.50 | 9.50 | 60.00 | 80.00 |
| 1926 | 28,840,000 | — | 3.25 | 5.00 | 20.00 | 25.00 |
| 1927 | 5,060,000 | — | 5.00 | 10.00 | 55.00 | 80.00 |
| 1932 Open 9 | 50,770,000 | — | 2.75 | 4.00 | 5.00 | 7.00 |
| 1932 Closed 9 | Inc. above | — | 2.75 | 4.00 | 5.00 | 7.00 |
| 1933/2 | 43,920,000 | — | 15.00 | 25.00 | 80.00 | — |
| 1933 | Inc. above | — | 2.75 | 4.00 | 5.00 | 7.00 |
| 1934 | 22,070,000 | — | 3.25 | 4.50 | 9.00 | 10.50 |
| 1935 | 8,050,000 | — | 4.50 | 6.00 | 11.50 | 13.50 |
| 1938 | 30,000,000 | — | 2.75 | 4.00 | 6.00 | 7.50 |
| 1940 | 20,000,000 | — | 2.75 | 3.50 | 5.00 | 6.50 |
| 1943 | 47,662,000 | — | 2.75 | 3.25 | 4.50 | 6.00 |
| 1944 | 39,522,000 | — | 2.75 | 3.50 | 4.50 | 6.00 |
| 1945 | 37,300,000 | — | 2.75 | 3.50 | 4.50 | 6.00 |

**PESO** **KM# 456** **Weight:** 14.0000 g. **Composition:** 0.5000 Silver .2250 oz. ASW **Reverse:** Jose Morelos y Pavon **Note:** Struck at Mexico City Mint, mint mark Mo.

| Date | Mintage | F | VF | XF | Unc | BU |
|---|---|---|---|---|---|---|
| 1947 | 61,460,000 | — | 1.75 | 2.50 | 4.50 | 5.50 |
| 1948 | 22,915,000 | — | 2.25 | 3.50 | 5.50 | 6.50 |
| 1949 | 4,000,000 | — | — | 1,200 | 1,600 | 2,500 |

**Note:** Not released for circulation

| Date | Mintage | F | VF | XF | Unc | BU |
|---|---|---|---|---|---|---|
| 1949 Proof | — | Value: 5,000 | | | | |

**PESO** **KM# 457** **Weight:** 13.3300 g. **Composition:** 0.3000 Silver .1285 oz. ASW **Reverse:** Jose Morelos y Pavon **Note:** Struck at Mexico City Mint, mint mark Mo.

| Date | Mintage | F | VF | XF | Unc | BU |
|---|---|---|---|---|---|---|
| 1950 | 3,287,000 | — | 2.50 | 4.00 | 7.00 | 8.50 |

**PESO** **KM# 458** **Weight:** 16.0000 g. **Composition:** 0.1000 Silver .0514 oz. ASW **Subject:** 100th Anniversary of Constitution **Note:** Struck at Mexico City Mint, mint mark Mo.

| Date | Mintage | F | VF | XF | Unc | BU |
|---|---|---|---|---|---|---|
| 1957 | 500,000 | — | 3.50 | 5.00 | 13.50 | 18.00 |

**PESO** **KM# 459** **Weight:** 16.0000 g. **Composition:** 0.1000 Silver .0514 oz. ASW **Subject:** 100th Anniversary of Constitution **Reverse:** Jose Morelos y Pavon **Note:** Struck at Mexico City Mint, mint mark Mo.

| Date | Mintage | F | VF | XF | Unc | BU |
|---|---|---|---|---|---|---|
| 1957 | 28,273,000 | — | 0.65 | 1.00 | 2.25 | 3.00 |
| 1958 | 41,899,000 | — | 0.65 | 0.85 | 1.85 | 2.50 |
| 1959 | 27,369,000 | — | 1.25 | 2.00 | 5.50 | 7.00 |
| 1960 | 26,259,000 | — | 0.65 | 1.10 | 3.25 | 3.50 |
| 1961 | 52,601,000 | — | 0.50 | 0.90 | 2.25 | 3.00 |
| 1962 | 61,094,000 | — | 0.50 | 0.90 | 2.10 | 2.75 |
| 1963 | 26,394,000 | — | BV | 0.80 | 2.00 | 2.40 |
| 1964 | 15,615,000 | — | BV | 0.75 | 2.00 | 2.40 |
| 1965 | 5,004,000 | — | BV | 0.60 | 1.85 | 2.00 |
| 1966 | 30,998,000 | — | BV | 0.60 | 1.85 | 2.00 |
| 1967 | 9,308,000 | — | BV | 0.60 | 2.75 | 3.50 |

**PESO** **KM# 460** **Composition:** Copper-Nickel **Reverse:** Jose Morelos y Pavon

| Date | Mintage | F | VF | XF | Unc | BU |
|---|---|---|---|---|---|---|
| 1970 Narrow date | 102,715,000 | — | 0.25 | 0.35 | 0.75 | 0.90 |
| 1970 Wide date | Inc. above | — | 1.25 | 2.50 | 8.00 | 10.00 |
| 1971 | 426,222,000 | — | 0.20 | 0.25 | 0.50 | 0.65 |
| 1972 | 120,000,000 | — | 0.20 | 0.25 | 0.40 | 0.65 |
| 1974 | 63,700,000 | — | 0.20 | 0.25 | 0.65 | 0.90 |
| 1975 Tall narrow date | 205,979,000 | — | 0.25 | 0.45 | 1.00 | 1.35 |
| 1975 Short wide date | Inc. above | — | 0.30 | 0.40 | 0.75 | 1.00 |
| 1976 | 94,489,000 | — | 0.15 | 0.20 | 0.50 | 0.75 |
| 1977 Thick date | 94,364,000 | — | 0.25 | 0.45 | 1.00 | 1.25 |
| 1977 Thin date | Inc. above | — | 1.00 | 2.00 | 6.50 | 13.50 |
| 1978 Closed 8 | 208,300,000 | — | 0.20 | 0.30 | 0.65 | 1.15 |
| 1978 Open 8 | 55,140,000 | — | 0.75 | 1.50 | 11.00 | 16.50 |
| 1979 Thin date | 117,884,000 | — | 0.20 | 0.30 | 1.00 | 1.50 |
| 1979 Thick date | Inc. above | — | 0.40 | 0.60 | 1.25 | 1.75 |
| 1980 Closed 8 | 318,800,000 | — | 0.25 | 0.35 | 1.00 | 1.20 |
| 1980 Open 8 | 23,865,000 | — | 0.75 | 1.50 | 9.00 | 12.75 |
| 1981 Closed 8 | 413,349,000 | — | 0.20 | 0.30 | 0.85 | 1.00 |
| 1981 Open 8 | 58,616,000 | — | 0.50 | 1.25 | 7.00 | 8.50 |
| 1982 | 235,000,000 | — | 0.25 | 0.75 | 2.25 | 2.50 |
| 1983 Wide date | 100,000,000 | — | 0.50 | 1.10 | 3.00 | 3.50 |
| 1983 Narrow date | Inc. above | — | 0.30 | 0.45 | 3.25 | 3.75 |
| 1983 Proof | 1,051,000 | Value: 15.00 | | | | |

**PESO** **KM# 496** **Composition:** Stainless Steel **Reverse:** Jose Morelos y Pavon

| Date | Mintage | F | VF | XF | Unc | BU |
|---|---|---|---|---|---|---|
| 1984 | 722,802,000 | — | 0.10 | 0.25 | 0.65 | 0.85 |
| 1985 | 985,000,000 | — | 0.10 | 0.25 | 0.50 | 0.75 |
| 1986 | 740,000,000 | — | 0.10 | 0.25 | 0.50 | 0.75 |
| 1987 | 250,000,000 | — | — | 0.25 | 0.50 | 0.80 |
| 1987 Proof; 2 known | — | Value: 1,250 | | | | |

**2 PESOS** **KM# 461** **Weight:** 1.6666 g. **Composition:** 0.9000 Gold .0482 oz. AGW **Note:** Struck at Mexico City Mint, mint mark Mo.

| Date | Mintage | F | VF | XF | Unc | BU |
|---|---|---|---|---|---|---|
| 1919 | 1,670,000 | — | BV | 25.00 | 32.00 | — |
| 1920 | 4,282,000 | — | BV | 25.00 | 32.00 | — |
| 1944 | 10,000 | 27.50 | 35.00 | 50.00 | 80.00 | — |
| 1945 | Est. 140,000 | — | — | —BV+20% | | — |
| 1946 | 168,000 | 30.00 | 45.00 | 55.00 | 80.00 | — |
| 1947 | 25,000 | 27.50 | 35.00 | 50.00 | 65.00 | — |
| 1948 No specimens known | 45,000 | — | — | — | — | — |

**Note:** During 1951-1972 a total of 4,590,493 pieces were restruck, most likely dated 1945. In 1996 matte restrikes were produced

**2 PESOS** **KM# 462** **Weight:** 26.6667 g. **Composition:** 0.9000 Silver .7717 oz. ASW **Subject:** Centennial of Independence **Note:** Struck at Mexico City Mint, mint mark Mo.

| Date | Mintage | F | VF | XF | Unc | BU |
|---|---|---|---|---|---|---|
| 1921 | 1,278,000 | — | 30.00 | 55.00 | 285 | 425 |

**2-1/2 PESOS** **KM# 463** **Weight:** 2.0833 g. **Composition:** 0.9000 Gold .0602 oz. AGW **Note:** Struck at Mexico City Mint, mint mark Mo.

| Date | Mintage | F | VF | XF | Unc | BU |
|---|---|---|---|---|---|---|
| 1918 | 1,704,000 | — | BV | 28.00 | 45.00 | — |
| 1919 | 984,000 | — | BV | 28.00 | 45.00 | — |
| 1920/10 | 607,000 | — | BV | 55.00 | 100 | — |
| 1920 | Inc. above | — | BV | 28.00 | 45.00 | — |
| 1944 | 20,000 | — | BV | 28.00 | 45.00 | — |
| 1945 | Est. 180,000 | — | — | —BV+18% | | — |
| 1946 | 163,000 | — | BV | 28.00 | 45.00 | — |

| Date | Mintage | F | VF | XF | Unc | BU |
|---|---|---|---|---|---|---|
| 1947 | 24,000 | 200 | 265 | 325 | 400 | — |
| 1948 | 63,000 | BV | 35.00 | 40.00 | 65.00 | — |

**Note:** During 1951-1972 a total of 5,025,087 pieces were restruck, most likely dated 1945. In 1996 matte restrikes were produced

**5 PESOS** **KM# 464** **Weight:** 4.1666 g. **Composition:** 0.9000 Gold .1205 oz. AGW **Note:** Struck at Mexico City Mint, mint mark Mo.

| Date | Mintage | F | VF | XF | Unc | BU |
|---|---|---|---|---|---|---|
| 1905 | 18,000 | 100 | 150 | 200 | 400 | — |
| 1906 | 4,638,000 | — | BV | 50.00 | 70.00 | — |
| 1907 | 1,088,000 | — | BV | 50.00 | 70.00 | — |
| 1910 | 100,000 | BV | 55.00 | 70.00 | 120 | — |
| 1918/7 | 609,000 | BV | 55.00 | 70.00 | 120 | — |
| 1918 | Inc. above | — | BV | 50.00 | 70.00 | — |
| 1919 | 506,000 | — | BV | 50.00 | 70.00 | — |
| 1920 | 2,385,000 | — | BV | 50.00 | 70.00 | — |
| 1955 | Est. 48,000 | — | — | —BV+11% | | — |

**Note:** During 1955-1972 a total of 1,767,645 pieces were restruck, most likely dated 1955. In 1996 matte restrikes were produced

**5 PESOS** **KM# 465** **Weight:** 30.0000 g. **Composition:** 0.9000 Silver .8681 oz. ASW **Reverse:** Head of Cuauhtemoc left **Note:** Struck at Mexico City Mint, mint mark Mo.

| Date | Mintage | F | VF | XF | Unc | BU |
|---|---|---|---|---|---|---|
| 1947 | 5,110,000 | — | BV | 6.25 | 8.75 | 10.00 |
| 1948 | 26,740,000 | — | BV | 6.00 | 8.00 | 9.00 |

**5 PESOS** **KM# 466** **Weight:** 27.7800 g. **Composition:** 0.7200 Silver .06431 oz. ASW **Subject:** Opening of Southern Railroad **Note:** Struck at Mexico City Mint, mint mark Mo.

| Date | Mintage | F | VF | XF | Unc | BU |
|---|---|---|---|---|---|---|
| 1950 | 200,000 | — | 22.50 | 27.50 | 35.00 | 45.00 |

**Note:** It is recorded that 100,000 pieces were melted to be used for the 1968 Mexican Olympic 25 Pesos

**5 PESOS** **KM# 467** **Weight:** 27.7800 g. **Composition:** 0.7200 Silver .6431 oz. ASW **Subject:** Opening of Southern Railroad **Reverse:** Miguel Hidalgo y Costilla **Note:** Struck at Mexico City Mint, mint mark Mo.

| Date | Mintage | F | VF | XF | Unc | BU |
|---|---|---|---|---|---|---|
| 1951 | 4,958,000 | — | BV | 5.75 | 7.00 | 10.00 |
| 1952 | 9,595,000 | — | BV | 5.50 | 6.75 | 9.00 |
| 1953 | 20,376,000 | — | BV | 5.25 | 6.75 | 9.00 |
| 1954 | 30,000 | — | 27.50 | 45.00 | 70.00 | 85.00 |

**5 PESOS** **KM# 468** **Weight:** 27.7800 g. **Composition:** 0.7200 Silver .6431 oz. ASW **Subject:** Bicentennial of Hildago's Birth **Note:** Struck at Mexico City Mint, mint mark Mo.

| Date | Mintage | F | VF | XF | Unc | BU |
|---|---|---|---|---|---|---|
| 1953 | 1,000,000 | — | BV | 5.50 | 7.50 | 10.00 |

**5 PESOS** **KM# 469** **Weight:** 18.0500 g. **Composition:** 0.7200 Silver .4170 oz. ASW **Note:** Struck at Mexico City Mint, mint mark Mo.

| Date | Mintage | F | VF | XF | Unc | BU |
|---|---|---|---|---|---|---|
| 1955 | 4,271,000 | — | 3.25 | 4.00 | 4.75 | 7.00 |
| 1956 | 4,596,000 | — | 3.25 | 4.00 | 4.75 | 7.00 |
| 1957 | 3,464,000 | — | 3.25 | 4.00 | 4.75 | 7.00 |

**5 PESOS** **KM# 470** **Weight:** 18.0500 g. **Composition:** 0.7200 Silver .4170 oz. ASW **Subject:** 100th Anniversary of Constitution **Note:** Struck at Mexico City Mint, mint mark Mo.

| Date | Mintage | F | VF | XF | Unc | BU |
|---|---|---|---|---|---|---|
| 1957 | 200,000 | — | 5.50 | 7.50 | 13.50 | 15.50 |

**5 PESOS** **KM# 471** **Weight:** 27.7800 g. **Composition:** 0.7200 Silver .6431 oz. ASW **Subject:** Centennial of Carranza's Birth **Note:** Struck at Mexico City Mint, mint mark Mo.

| Date | Mintage | F | VF | XF | Unc | BU |
|---|---|---|---|---|---|---|
| 1959 | 1,000,000 | — | BV | 4.50 | 6.50 | 9.50 |

**5 PESOS** **KM# 472** **Composition:** Copper-Nickel **Reverse:** Vicente Guerrero **Note:** Small date, large date varieties.

| Date | Mintage | F | VF | XF | Unc | BU |
|---|---|---|---|---|---|---|
| 1971 | 28,457,000 | — | 0.50 | 0.95 | 2.50 | 3.25 |
| 1972 | 75,000,000 | — | 0.60 | 1.25 | 2.00 | 2.50 |
| 1973 | 19,405,000 | — | 1.25 | 2.10 | 5.00 | 7.50 |
| 1974 | 34,500,000 | — | 0.50 | 0.80 | 1.75 | 2.25 |
| 1976 Small date | 26,121,000 | — | 0.75 | 1.45 | 3.50 | 4.25 |
| 1976 Large date | 121,550,000 | — | 0.35 | 0.50 | 1.50 | 1.75 |
| 1977 | 102,000,000 | — | 0.50 | 0.75 | 1.50 | 2.00 |
| 1978 | 25,700,000 | — | 1.00 | 1.50 | 5.25 | 6.75 |

**5 PESOS** **KM# 485** **Composition:** Copper-Nickel **Subject:** Quetzalcoatl

| Date | Mintage | F | VF | XF | Unc | BU |
|---|---|---|---|---|---|---|
| 1980 | 266,899,999 | — | 0.25 | 0.50 | 1.75 | 2.25 |
| 1981 | 30,500,000 | — | 0.45 | 0.65 | 2.75 | 3.25 |
| 1982 | 20,000,000 | — | 1.50 | 2.35 | 4.25 | 5.25 |
| 1982 Proof | 1,051 | Value: 18.00 | | | | |
| 1983 Proof; 7 known | — | Value: 1,150 | | | | |
| 1984 | 16,300,000 | — | 1.25 | 2.00 | 4.75 | 6.00 |
| 1985 | 76,900,000 | — | 2.25 | 4.00 | 4.50 | 5.25 |

**5 PESOS** **KM# 502** **Composition:** Brass **Subject:** Quetzalcoatl **Note:** Circulation coinage.

| Date | Mintage | F | VF | XF | Unc | BU |
|---|---|---|---|---|---|---|
| 1985 | 30,000,000 | — | — | 0.15 | 0.35 | 0.50 |
| 1987 | 81,900,000 | — | 8.00 | 9.50 | 12.50 | 15.00 |
| 1988 | 76,600,000 | — | — | 0.10 | 0.25 | 0.35 |
| 1988 Proof; 2 known | — | Value: 600 | | | | |

**10 PESOS** KM# 473 **Weight:** 8.3333 g. **Composition:** 0.9000 Gold .2411 oz. AGW **Reverse:** Miguel Hidalgo **Note:** Struck at Mexico City Mint, mint mark Mo.

| Date | Mintage | F | VF | XF | Unc | BU |
|---|---|---|---|---|---|---|
| 1905 | 39,000 | 110 | 125 | 155 | 200 | — |
| 1906 | 2,949,000 | — | BV | 100 | 150 | — |
| 1907 | 1,589,000 | — | BV | 100 | 150 | — |
| 1908 | 890,000 | — | BV | 100 | 150 | — |
| 1910 | 451,000 | — | BV | 100 | 150 | — |
| 1916 | 26,000 | 110 | 120 | 150 | 275 | — |
| 1917 | 1,967,000 | — | BV | 100 | 150 | — |
| 1919 | 266,000 | — | BV | 100 | 150 | — |
| 1920 | 12,000 | 150 | 250 | 400 | 650 | — |
| 1959 | Est. 50,000 | — | — | — | BV+7% | — |

**Note:** *During 1961-1972 a total of 954,983 pieces were restruck, most likely dated 1959. In 1996 matte restrikes were produced

**10 PESOS** KM# 474 **Weight:** 28.8800 g. **Composition:** 0.9000 Silver .8357 oz. ASW **Reverse:** Miguel Hidalgo **Note:** Struck at Mexico City Mint, mint mark Mo.

| Date | Mintage | F | VF | XF | Unc | BU |
|---|---|---|---|---|---|---|
| 1955 | 585,000 | — | BV | 6.00 | 8.75 | 11.50 |
| 1956 | 3,535,000 | — | BV | 5.50 | 8.50 | 12.00 |

**10 PESOS** KM# 475 **Weight:** 28.8800 g. **Composition:** 0.9000 Silver .8357 oz. ASW **Subject:** 100th Anniversary of Constutution **Note:** Struck at Mexico City Mint, mint mark Mo.

| Date | Mintage | F | VF | XF | Unc | BU |
|---|---|---|---|---|---|---|
| 1957 | 100,000 | — | 12.50 | 22.50 | 40.00 | 48.00 |

**10 PESOS** KM# 476 **Weight:** 28.8800 g. **Composition:** 0.9000 Silver .8357 oz. ASW **Subject:** 150th Anniversary - War of Independence **Note:** Struck at Mexico City Mint, mint mark Mo.

| Date | Mintage | F | VF | XF | Unc | BU |
|---|---|---|---|---|---|---|
| 1960 | 1,000,000 | — | BV | 6.00 | 9.00 | 12.00 |

**10 PESOS** KM# 477.1 **Composition:** Copper-Nickel **Reverse:** Miguel Hidalgo **Note:** Thin flan - 1.6mm

| Date | Mintage | F | VF | XF | Unc | BU |
|---|---|---|---|---|---|---|
| 1974 | 3,900,000 | — | 0.50 | 1.00 | 3.50 | 4.25 |
| 1974 Proof | — | Value: 625 | | | | |
| 1975 | 1,000,000 | — | 2.25 | 3.25 | 7.75 | 15.00 |
| 1976 | 74,500,000 | — | 0.25 | 0.75 | 1.75 | 2.25 |
| 1977 | 79,620,000 | — | 0.50 | 1.00 | 2.00 | 3.00 |

**10 PESOS** KM# 477.2 **Composition:** Copper-Nickel **Reverse:** Miguel Hidalgo **Note:** Thick flan - 2.3mm

| Date | Mintage | F | VF | XF | Unc | BU |
|---|---|---|---|---|---|---|
| 1978 | 124,850,000 | — | 0.50 | 0.75 | 2.50 | 2.75 |
| 1979 | 57,200,000 | — | 0.50 | 0.75 | 2.25 | 2.50 |
| 1980 | 55,200,000 | — | 0.50 | 0.75 | 2.50 | 3.75 |
| 1981 | 222,768,000 | — | 0.40 | 0.60 | 2.25 | 2.60 |
| 1982 | 151,770,000 | — | 0.50 | 0.80 | 2.50 | 3.50 |
| 1982 Proof | 1,051 | Value: 18.00 | | | | |
| 1985 | 58,000,000 | — | 1.25 | 1.75 | 5.75 | 7.50 |

**10 PESOS** KM# 512 **Composition:** Stainless Steel **Reverse:** Miguel Hidalgo **Note:** Date varieties exist.

| Date | Mintage | F | VF | XF | Unc | BU |
|---|---|---|---|---|---|---|
| 1985 | 257,000,000 | — | — | 0.15 | 0.50 | 0.75 |
| 1986 | 392,000,000 | — | — | 0.15 | 0.50 | 1.50 |
| 1987 | 305,000,000 | — | — | 0.15 | 0.35 | 0.50 |
| 1988 | 500,300,000 | — | — | 0.15 | 0.25 | 0.35 |
| 1989 | — | — | 0.20 | 0.25 | 0.75 | 1.50 |
| 1990 | — | — | — | 0.25 | 0.75 | 1.25 |
| 1990 Proof; 2 known | — | Value: 500 | | | | |

**20 PESOS** KM# 478 **Weight:** 16.6666 g. **Composition:** 0.9000 Gold .4823 oz. AGW **Note:** Struck at Mexico City Mint, mint mark Mo.

| Date | Mintage | F | VF | XF | Unc | BU |
|---|---|---|---|---|---|---|
| 1917 | 852,000 | — | BV | 155 | 185 | — |
| 1918 | 2,831,000 | — | BV | 155 | 185 | — |
| 1919 | 1,094,000 | — | BV | 155 | 185 | — |
| 1920/10 | 462,000 | — | BV | 160 | 195 | — |
| 1920 | Inc. above | — | BV | 155 | 185 | — |
| 1921/11 | 922,000 | — | BV | 160 | 195 | — |
| 1921/10 | — | — | — | — | — | — |
| 1921 | Inc. above | — | BV | 155 | 185 | — |
| 1959 | Est. 13,000 | — | — | — | — | — |

**Note:** During 1960-1971 a total of 1,158,414 pieces were restruck, most likely dated 1959. In 1996 matte restrikes were produced

**20 PESOS** KM# 486 **Composition:** Copper-Nickel

| Date | Mintage | F | VF | XF | Unc | BU |
|---|---|---|---|---|---|---|
| 1980 | 84,900,000 | — | 0.50 | 0.85 | 2.50 | 3.40 |
| 1981 | 250,573,000 | — | 0.60 | 0.80 | 2.50 | 3.50 |
| 1982 | 236,892,000 | — | 1.00 | 1.75 | 2.75 | 3.85 |
| 1982 Proof | 1,051 | Value: 18.00 | | | | |
| 1983 Proof; 3 known | — | — | — | — | — | — |
| 1984 | 55,000,000 | — | 1.00 | 1.50 | 3.75 | 7.50 |

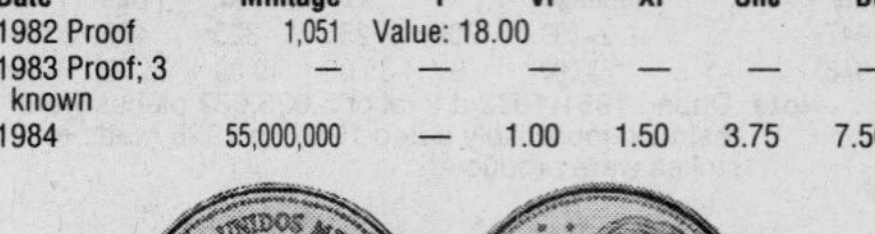

**20 PESOS** KM# 508 **Composition:** Brass **Reverse:** Guadalupe Victoria, First President

| Date | Mintage | F | VF | XF | Unc | BU |
|---|---|---|---|---|---|---|
| 1985 Wide date | 25,000,000 | — | 0.10 | 0.20 | 1.00 | 1.25 |
| 1985 Narrow date | Inc. above | — | 0.10 | 0.25 | 1.50 | 2.00 |
| 1986 | 10,000,000 | — | 1.00 | 1.75 | 5.00 | 6.00 |
| 1988 | 355,200,000 | — | 0.10 | 0.20 | 0.50 | 1.00 |
| 1989 | — | — | 0.15 | 0.30 | 1.50 | 2.00 |
| 1990 | — | — | 0.15 | 0.30 | 1.50 | 2.50 |

**25 PESOS** KM# 479.1 **Weight:** 22.5000 g. **Composition:** 0.7200 Silver .5209 oz. ASW **Note:** Type I, Rings aligned.

| Date | Mintage | F | VF | XF | Unc | BU |
|---|---|---|---|---|---|---|
| 1968 | 27,182,000 | — | BV | 4.00 | 4.75 | 6.00 |

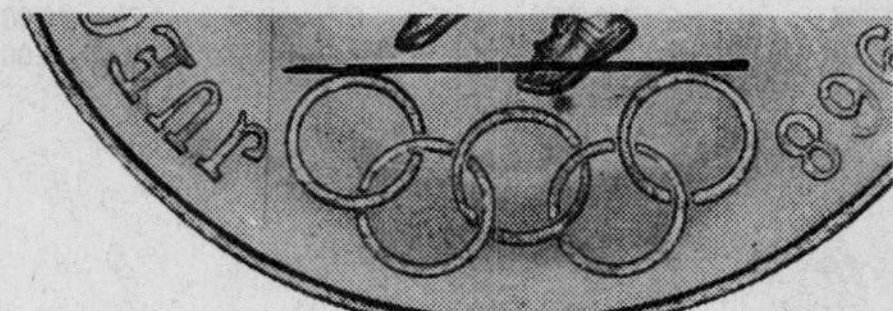

**25 PESOS** KM# 479.2 **Weight:** 22.5000 g. **Composition:** 0.7200 Silver .5209 oz. ASW **Subject:** Summer Olympics - Mexico City **Note:** Type II, center ring low.

| Date | Mintage | F | VF | XF | Unc | BU |
|---|---|---|---|---|---|---|
| 1968 | Inc. above | — | 4.00 | 5.00 | 9.00 | 10.50 |

**25 PESOS** KM# 479.3 **Weight:** 22.5000 g. **Composition:** 0.7200 Silver .5209 oz. ASW **Subject:** Summer Olympics - Mexico City **Note:** Normal tongue and long curved tongue Type III, center rings low. Snake with long curved tongue.

| Date | Mintage | F | VF | XF | Unc | BU |
|---|---|---|---|---|---|---|
| 1968 | Inc. above | — | 4.25 | 5.25 | 9.50 | 11.00 |

**25 PESOS** **KM# 480** **Weight:** 22.5000 g. **Composition:** 0.7200 Silver .5209 oz. ASW **Reverse:** Benito Juarez

| Date | Mintage | F | VF | XF | Unc | BU |
|---|---|---|---|---|---|---|
| 1972 | 2,000,000 | — | — | 4.00 | 5.50 | 6.50 |

**25 PESOS** **KM# 497** **Weight:** 7.7760 g. **Composition:** 0.7200 Silver .1800 oz. ASW **Subject:** 1986 World Cup Soccer Games

| Date | Mintage | F | VF | XF | Unc | BU |
|---|---|---|---|---|---|---|
| 1985 | 354,000 | — | — | — | — | 7.50 |

**25 PESOS** **KM# 503** **Weight:** 8.4060 g. **Composition:** 0.9250 Silver .2450 oz. ASW **Subject:** 1986 World Cup Soccer Games

| Date | Mintage | F | VF | XF | Unc | BU |
|---|---|---|---|---|---|---|
| 1985 Proof | 277,000 | Value: 9.00 | | | | |

**25 PESOS** **KM# 514** **Weight:** 8.4060 g. **Composition:** 0.9250 Silver .2450 oz. ASW **Subject:** 1986 World Cup Soccer Games

| Date | Mintage | F | VF | XF | Unc | BU |
|---|---|---|---|---|---|---|
| 1985 Proof | 234,000 | Value: 9.00 | | | | |

**25 PESOS** **KM# 519** **Weight:** 8.4060 g. **Composition:** 0.9250 Silver .2450 oz. ASW **Subject:** 1986 World Cup Soccer Games

| Date | Mintage | F | VF | XF | Unc | BU |
|---|---|---|---|---|---|---|
| 1986 Proof | — | Value: 9.00 | | | | |

**25 PESOS** **KM# 497a** **Weight:** 8.4060 g. **Composition:** 0.9250 Silver .2450 oz. ASW **Subject:** 1986 World Cup Soccer Games **Reverse:** Without fineness statement

| Date | Mintage | F | VF | XF | Unc | BU |
|---|---|---|---|---|---|---|
| 1986 Proof | — | Value: 9.00 | | | | |

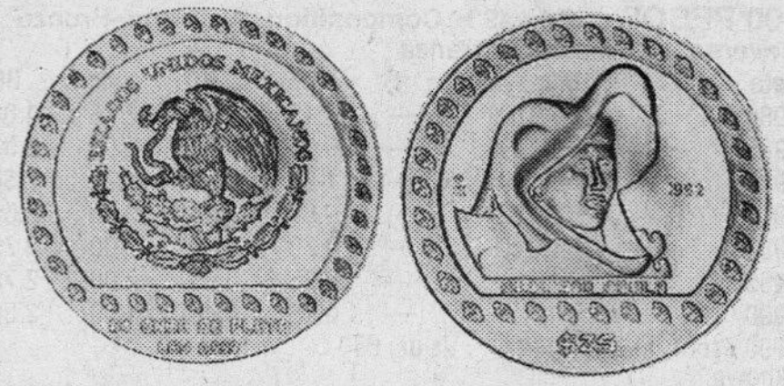

**25 PESOS** **KM# 554** **Weight:** 7.7758 g. **Composition:** 0.9990 Silver .2500 oz. ASW **Reverse:** Eagle warrior

| Date | Mintage | F | VF | XF | Unc | BU |
|---|---|---|---|---|---|---|
| 1992 | 50,000 | — | — | — | 6.50 | — |
| 1992 Proof | 3,000 | Value: 10.50 | | | | |

**50 PESOS** **KM# 481** **Weight:** 41.6666 g. **Composition:** 0.9000 Gold 1.2057 oz. AGW **Subject:** Centennial of Independence **Note:** During 1949-1972 a total of 3,975,654 pieces were restruck, most likely dated 1947. In 1996 matte restrikes were produced. Struck at Mexico City Mint, mint mark Mo.

| Date | Mintage | F | VF | XF | Unc | BU |
|---|---|---|---|---|---|---|
| 1921 | 180,000 | — | — | BV | 450 | — |
| 1922 | 463,000 | — | — | BV | 400 | — |
| 1923 | 432,000 | — | — | BV | 400 | — |
| 1924 | 439,000 | — | — | BV | 400 | — |
| 1925 | 716,000 | — | — | BV | 400 | — |
| 1926 | 600,000 | — | — | BV | 400 | — |
| 1927 | 606,000 | — | — | BV | 400 | — |
| 1928 | 538,000 | — | — | BV | 400 | — |
| 1929 | 458,000 | — | — | BV | 400 | — |
| 1930 | 372,000 | — | — | BV | 400 | — |
| 1931 | 137,000 | — | — | BV | 420 | — |
| 1944 | 593,000 | — | — | BV | 385 | — |
| 1945 | 1,012,000 | — | — | BV | 385 | — |
| 1946 | 1,588,000 | — | — | BV | 385 | — |
| 1947 | 309,000 | — | — | — | BV+3% | — |
| 1947 Specimen | — | — | — | — | — | — |

**Note:** Value, $6,500

**50 PESOS** **KM# 490** **Composition:** Copper-Nickel **Subject:** Coyolxauhqui **Note:** Doubled die examples of 1982 and 1983 dates exist.

| Date | Mintage | F | VF | XF | Unc | BU |
|---|---|---|---|---|---|---|
| 1982 | 222,890,000 | — | 1.00 | 2.50 | 5.00 | 6.25 |
| 1983 | 45,000,000 | — | 1.50 | 3.00 | 6.00 | 6.50 |
| 1983 Proof | 1,051 | Value: 22.00 | | | | |
| 1984 | 73,537,000 | — | 1.00 | 1.35 | 3.50 | 4.00 |
| 1984 Proof; 4 known | — | Value: 750 | | | | |

**50 PESOS** **KM# 495** **Composition:** Copper-Nickel **Subject:** Benito Juarez

| Date | Mintage | F | VF | XF | Unc | BU |
|---|---|---|---|---|---|---|
| 1984 | 94,216,000 | — | 0.65 | 1.25 | 2.75 | 3.50 |
| 1985 | 296,000,000 | — | 0.25 | 0.45 | 1.50 | 2.25 |
| 1986 | 50,000,000 | — | 5.00 | 7.00 | 11.00 | 12.50 |
| 1987 | 210,000,000 | — | 0.25 | 0.45 | 1.00 | 1.25 |
| 1988 | 80,200,000 | — | 6.25 | 9.00 | 12.50 | 14.50 |

**50 PESOS** **KM# 498** **Weight:** 15.5520 g. **Composition:** 0.7200 Silver .3601 oz. ASW **Subject:** 1986 World Cup Soccer Games

| Date | Mintage | F | VF | XF | Unc | BU |
|---|---|---|---|---|---|---|
| 1985 | 347,000 | — | — | — | — | 8.50 |

**50 PESOS** **KM# 504** **Weight:** 16.8310 g. **Composition:** 0.9250 Silver .5000 oz. ASW **Subject:** 1986 World Cup Soccer Games **Reverse:** Without fineness statement

| Date | Mintage | F | VF | XF | Unc | BU |
|---|---|---|---|---|---|---|
| 1985 Proof | 347,000 | Value: 13.50 | | | | |

**50 PESOS** **KM# 515** **Weight:** 16.8310 g. **Composition:** 0.9250 Silver .5000 oz. ASW **Subject:** 1986 World Cup Soccer Games

| Date | Mintage | F | VF | XF | Unc | BU |
|---|---|---|---|---|---|---|
| 1985 Proof | 234,000 | Value: 13.50 | | | | |

**50 PESOS** **KM# 523** **Weight:** 16.8310 g. **Composition:** 0.9250 Silver .5000 oz. ASW **Subject:** 1986 World Cup Soccer Games

| Date | Mintage | F | VF | XF | Unc | BU |
|---|---|---|---|---|---|---|
| 1986 Proof | 190,000 | Value: 13.50 | | | | |

**50 PESOS** **KM# 498a** **Weight:** 16.8310 g. **Composition:** 0.9250 Silver .5000 oz. ASW **Subject:** 1986 World Cup Soccer Games **Reverse:** Without fineness statement

| Date | Mintage | F | VF | XF | Unc | BU |
|---|---|---|---|---|---|---|
| 1986 Proof | 10,000 | Value: 13.50 | | | | |

**50 PESOS** **KM# 532** **Weight:** 15.5500 g. **Composition:** 0.9990 Silver .5000 oz. ASW **Subject:** 50th Anniversary - Nationalization of Oil Industry

| Date | Mintage | F | VF | XF | Unc | BU |
|---|---|---|---|---|---|---|
| ND(1988) | 30,000 | — | — | — | 12.00 | 15.00 |

**50 PESOS** **KM# 495a** **Composition:** Stainless Steel **Subject:** Benito Juarez **Edge:** Plain.

| Date | Mintage | F | VF | XF | Unc | BU |
|---|---|---|---|---|---|---|
| 1988 | 353,300,000 | — | — | 0.20 | 0.75 | 1.50 |
| 1989 | — | — | — | — | — | — |
| 1990 | — | — | — | 0.30 | 1.00 | 2.00 |
| 1991 | — | — | — | — | — | — |
| 1992 | — | — | — | 0.25 | 1.00 | 2.75 |

**50 PESOS** **KM# 555** **Weight:** 15.5517 g. **Composition:** 0.9990 Silver .5000 oz. ASW **Subject:** 50th Anniversary - Nationalization of Oil Industry **Reverse:** Eagle warrior

| Date | Mintage | F | VF | XF | Unc | BU |
|---|---|---|---|---|---|---|
| 1992 | 50,000 | — | — | — | 8.50 | — |
| 1992 Proof | 3,000 | Value: 18.50 | | | | |

**100 PESOS** **KM# 483.1** **Weight:** 27.7700 g. **Composition:** 0.7200 Silver .6429 oz. ASW **Reverse:** Jose Morelos y Pavon **Note:** Low 7's and high 7's.

| Date | Mintage | F | VF | XF | Unc | BU |
|---|---|---|---|---|---|---|
| 1977 Low 7's, sloping shoulder | 5,225,000 | — | BV | 4.00 | 6.00 | 10.00 |
| 1977 High 7's, sloping shoulder | Inc. above | — | BV | 4.00 | 6.00 | 10.50 |

**100 PESOS** **KM# 483.2** **Weight:** 27.7700 g. **Composition:** 0.7200 Silver .6429 oz. ASW **Reverse:** Jose Morelos y Pavon **Note:** Low 7's and high 7's.

| Date | Mintage | F | VF | XF | Unc | BU |
|---|---|---|---|---|---|---|
| 1978 | 9,879,000 | — | BV | 4.00 | 6.50 | 8.50 |
| 1979 | 784,000 | — | BV | 4.00 | 6.50 | 8.50 |
| 1979 Proof | — | Value: 550 | | | | |

**100 PESOS** **KM# 493** **Composition:** Aluminum-Bronze **Reverse:** Venustiano Carranza

| Date | Mintage | F | VF | XF | Unc | BU |
|---|---|---|---|---|---|---|
| 1984 | 227,809,000 | — | 0.45 | 0.60 | 2.75 | 4.00 |
| 1985 | 377,423,000 | — | 0.30 | 0.50 | 2.00 | 3.00 |
| 1986 | 43,000,000 | — | 1.00 | 2.50 | 4.75 | 7.50 |
| 1987 | 165,000,000 | — | 0.60 | 1.25 | 2.50 | 3.50 |
| 1988 | 433,100,000 | — | 0.30 | 0.50 | 2.00 | 2.75 |
| 1989 | — | — | 0.35 | 0.65 | 2.00 | 2.75 |
| 1990 | — | — | 0.15 | 0.40 | 1.50 | 2.50 |
| 1990 Proof; 1 known | — | Value: 650 | | | | |
| 1991 | — | — | 0.15 | 0.25 | 1.00 | 2.50 |
| 1992 | — | — | 0.30 | 0.75 | 1.75 | 3.00 |

**100 PESOS** **KM# 499** **Weight:** 31.1030 g. **Composition:** 0.7200 Silver .7201 oz. ASW **Subject:** 1986 World Cup Soccer Games

| Date | Mintage | F | VF | XF | Unc | BU |
|---|---|---|---|---|---|---|
| 1985 | 302,000 | — | — | — | — | 12.50 |

**100 PESOS** **KM# 499a** **Weight:** 32.6250 g. **Composition:** 0.9250 Silver 1.0000 oz. ASW **Subject:** 1986 World Cup Soccer Games **Reverse:** Without fineness statement

| Date | Mintage | F | VF | XF | Unc | BU |
|---|---|---|---|---|---|---|
| 1985 Proof | 9,006 | Value: 18.50 | | | | |

**100 PESOS** **KM# 505** **Weight:** 32.6250 g. **Composition:** 0.9250 Silver 1.0000 oz. ASW **Subject:** 1986 World Cup Soccer Games **Reverse:** Without fineness statement

| Date | Mintage | F | VF | XF | Unc | BU |
|---|---|---|---|---|---|---|
| 1985 Proof | 9,006 | Value: 18.50 | | | | |

**100 PESOS** **KM# 521** **Weight:** 32.6250 g. **Composition:** 0.9250 Silver 1.0000 oz. ASW **Subject:** 1986 World Cup Soccer Games **Reverse:** Without fineness statement

| Date | Mintage | F | VF | XF | Unc | BU |
|---|---|---|---|---|---|---|
| 1986 Proof | 208,000 | Value: 18.50 | | | | |

**100 PESOS** **KM# 524** **Weight:** 32.6250 g. **Composition:** 0.9250 Silver 1.0000 oz. ASW **Subject:** 1986 World Cup Soccer Games **Reverse:** Without fineness statement

| Date | Mintage | F | VF | XF | Unc | BU |
|---|---|---|---|---|---|---|
| 1986 Proof | 190,000 | Value: 18.50 | | | | |

**100 PESOS** **KM# 537** **Weight:** 32.6250 g. **Composition:** 0.9250 Silver 1.0000 oz. ASW **Subject:** World Wildlife Fund **Reverse:** Monarch butterflies

| Date | Mintage | F | VF | XF | Unc | BU |
|---|---|---|---|---|---|---|
| 1987 Proof | Est. 30,000 | Value: 40.00 | | | | |

**100 PESOS** **KM# 533** **Weight:** 31.1030 g. **Composition:** 0.9990 Silver 1.0000 oz. ASW **Subject:** 50th Anniversary - Nationalization of Oil Industry

| Date | Mintage | F | VF | XF | Unc | BU |
|---|---|---|---|---|---|---|
| 1988 | 10,000 | — | — | — | 28.00 | 35.00 |

**100 PESOS** **KM# 540** **Weight:** 27.0000 g. **Composition:** 0.9250 Silver .8029 oz. ASW **Subject:** Ibero - American Series **Reverse:** Pillars

| Date | Mintage | F | VF | XF | Unc | BU |
|---|---|---|---|---|---|---|
| 1991 Proof | 50,000 | Value: 45.00 | | | | |
| 1992 Proof | 75,000 | Value: 42.00 | | | | |

**100 PESOS** **KM# 539** **Weight:** 33.6250 g. **Composition:** 0.9250 Silver 1.0000 oz. ASW **Subject:** Save the Children

| Date | Mintage | F | VF | XF | Unc | BU |
|---|---|---|---|---|---|---|
| 1991 Proof | 30,000 | Value: 35.00 | | | | |

**100 PESOS** **KM# 566** **Weight:** 31.1035 g. **Composition:** 0.9990 Silver 1.0000 oz. ASW **Subject:** Save the Vaquita Porpoise

| Date | Mintage | F | VF | XF | Unc | BU |
|---|---|---|---|---|---|---|
| 1992 Proof | — | Value: 40.00 | | | | |

**100 PESOS** **KM# 556** **Weight:** 31.1035 g. **Composition:** 0.9990 Silver 1.0000 oz. ASW **Reverse:** Eagle warrior

| Date | Mintage | F | VF | XF | Unc | BU |
|---|---|---|---|---|---|---|
| 1992 | 205,000 | — | — | — | 11.50 | — |
| 1992 | 4,000 | Value: 36.00 | | | | |

**100 PESOS** **KM# 562** **Weight:** 31.1035 g. **Composition:** 0.9990 Silver 1.0000 oz. ASW **Reverse:** Xochipilli - The God of Joy, Music and Dance

| Date | Mintage | F | VF | XF | Unc | BU |
|---|---|---|---|---|---|---|
| 1992 Proof | 4,000 | Value: 36.00 | | | | |

**100 PESOS** **KM# 563** **Weight:** 31.1035 g. **Composition:** 0.9990 Silver 1.0000 oz. ASW **Reverse:** Brasero Efigie - The God of Rain

| Date | Mintage | F | VF | XF | Unc | BU |
|---|---|---|---|---|---|---|
| 1992 Proof | 4,000 | Value: 36.00 | | | | |

**100 PESOS** **KM# 564** **Weight:** 31.1035 g. **Composition:** 0.9990 Silver 1.0000 oz. ASW **Reverse:** Huehueteotl - The God of Fire

| Date | Mintage | F | VF | XF | Unc | BU |
|---|---|---|---|---|---|---|
| 1992 Proof | 4,000 | Value: 36.00 | | | | |

**200 PESOS** **KM# 509** **Composition:** Copper-Nickel **Subject:** 175th Anniversary of Independence

| Date | Mintage | F | VF | XF | Unc | BU |
|---|---|---|---|---|---|---|
| 1985 | 75,000,000 | — | — | 0.25 | 3.25 | 4.75 |

**200 PESOS** **KM# 510** **Composition:** Copper-Nickel **Subject:** 175th Anniversary of 1910 Revolution

| Date | Mintage | F | VF | XF | Unc | BU |
|---|---|---|---|---|---|---|
| 1985 | 98,590,000 | — | — | 0.25 | 3.25 | 4.25 |

**200 PESOS** **KM# 525** **Composition:** Copper-Nickel **Subject:** 1986 World Cup Soccer Games

| Date | Mintage | F | VF | XF | Unc | BU |
|---|---|---|---|---|---|---|
| 1986 | 50,000,000 | — | — | 1.00 | 3.50 | 4.50 |

**200 PESOS** **KM# 526** **Weight:** 62.2060 g. **Composition:** 0.9990 Silver 2.0000 oz. ASW **Subject:** 1986 World Cup Soccer Games

| Date | Mintage | F | VF | XF | Unc | BU |
|---|---|---|---|---|---|---|
| 1986 | 50,000 | — | — | — | 40.00 | 50.00 |

**250 PESOS** **KM# 500.1** **Weight:** 8.6400 g. **Composition:** 0.9000 Gold .2500 oz. AGW **Subject:** 1986 World Cup Soccer Games

| Date | Mintage | F | VF | XF | Unc | BU |
|---|---|---|---|---|---|---|
| 1985 | 100,000 | — | — | — | — | 100 |
| 1986 | — | — | — | — | — | 100 |

**250 PESOS** **KM# 500.2** **Weight:** 8.6400 g. **Composition:** 0.9000 Gold .2500 oz. AGW **Subject:** 1986 World Cup Soccer Games **Reverse:** Without fineness statement

| Date | Mintage | F | VF | XF | Unc | BU |
|---|---|---|---|---|---|---|
| 1985 Proof | 4,506 | Value: 110 | | | | |
| 1986 Proof | — | Value: 135 | | | | |

**250 PESOS** **KM# 506.1** **Weight:** 8.6400 g. **Composition:** 0.9000 Gold .2500 oz. AGW **Subject:** 1986 World Cup Soccer Games

| Date | Mintage | F | VF | XF | Unc | BU |
|---|---|---|---|---|---|---|
| 1985 | 88,000 | — | — | — | — | 110 |

**250 PESOS** **KM# 506.2** **Weight:** 8.6400 g. **Composition:** 0.9000 Gold .2500 oz. AGW **Subject:** 1986 World Cup Soccer Games **Reverse:** Without fineness statement

| Date | Mintage | F | VF | XF | Unc | BU |
|---|---|---|---|---|---|---|
| 1985 Proof | Est. 80,000 | Value: 115 | | | | |

**250 PESOS** **KM# 558** **Weight:** 7.7758 g. **Composition:** 0.9990 Gold .2500 oz. AGW **Subject:** Native Culture **Reverse:** Sculpture of jaguar head

| Date | Mintage | F | VF | XF | Unc | BU |
|---|---|---|---|---|---|---|
| 1992 | 10,000 | — | — | — | 145 | — |
| 1992 Proof | 2,000 | Value: 250 | | | | |

**500 PESOS** **KM# 501.1** **Weight:** 17.2800 g. **Composition:** 0.9000 Gold .5000 oz. AGW **Subject:** 1986 World Cup Soccer Games **Obverse:** Eagle facing left with snake in beak

| Date | Mintage | F | VF | XF | Unc | BU |
|---|---|---|---|---|---|---|
| 1985 | 102,000 | — | — | — | — | 210 |
| 1986 | — | — | — | — | — | 210 |

**500 PESOS** **KM# 501.2** **Weight:** 17.2800 g. **Composition:** 0.9000 Gold .5000 oz. AGW **Subject:** 1986 World Cup Soccer Games **Obverse:** Eagle facing left with snake in beak **Reverse:** Without fineness statement

| Date | Mintage | F | VF | XF | Unc | BU |
|---|---|---|---|---|---|---|
| 1985 Proof | 5,506 | Value: 225 | | | | |
| 1986 Proof | — | Value: 225 | | | | |

**500 PESOS** **KM# 507.1** **Weight:** 17.2800 g. **Composition:** 0.9000 Gold .5000 oz. AGW **Subject:** 1986 World Cup Soccer Games **Obverse:** Eagle facing left with snake in beak

| Date | Mintage | F | VF | XF | Unc | BU |
|---|---|---|---|---|---|---|
| 1985 | — | — | — | — | — | 225 |

**500 PESOS** **KM# 507.2** **Weight:** 17.2800 g. **Composition:** 0.9000 Gold .5000 oz. AGW **Subject:** 1986 World Cup Soccer Games **Obverse:** Eagle facing left with snake in beak **Reverse:** Without fineness statement

| Date | Mintage | F | VF | XF | Unc | BU |
|---|---|---|---|---|---|---|
| 1985 Proof | — | Value: 225 | | | | |

**500 PESOS** **KM# 511** **Weight:** 3334500.0000 g. **Composition:** 0.9250 Silver 1.0000 oz. ASW **Subject:** 17th Anniversary of 1910 Revolution **Obverse:** Eagle facing left with snake in beak

| Date | Mintage | F | VF | XF | Unc | BU |
|---|---|---|---|---|---|---|
| 1985 Proof | 40,000 | Value: 32.50 | | | | |

**500 PESOS** **KM# 529** **Composition:** Copper-Nickel **Reverse:** Francisco Madero

| Date | Mintage | F | VF | XF | Unc | BU |
|---|---|---|---|---|---|---|
| 1986 | 20,000,000 | — | — | 1.00 | 2.50 | 3.00 |
| 1987 | 180,000,000 | — | — | 0.75 | 2.00 | 2.50 |
| 1988 | 230,000,000 | — | — | 0.50 | 2.00 | 2.50 |
| 1988 Proof; 2 known | — | Value: 650 | | | | |
| 1989 | — | — | — | 0.75 | 2.00 | 3.00 |
| 1992 | — | — | — | 1.00 | 2.25 | 3.50 |

**500 PESOS** **KM# 534** **Weight:** 17.2800 g. **Composition:** 0.9000 Gold .5000 oz. AGW **Subject:** 50th Anniversary - Nationalization of Oil Industry **Reverse:** Monument **Note:** Similar to 5000 Pesos, KM#531.

| Date | Mintage | F | VF | XF | Unc | BU |
|---|---|---|---|---|---|---|
| 1988 | — | — | — | — | — | 225 |

**500 PESOS** **KM# 559** **Weight:** 15.5517 g. **Composition:** 0.9990 Gold .5000 oz. AGW **Subject:** Native Culture - Sculpture of Jaguar Head

| Date | Mintage | F | VF | XF | Unc | BU |
|---|---|---|---|---|---|---|
| 1992 | 10,000 | — | — | — | 200 | — |
| 1992 Proof | 2,000 | Value: 400 | | | | |

**1000 PESOS** **KM# 513** **Weight:** 17.2800 g. **Composition:** 0.9000 Gold .5000 oz. AGW **Subject:** 175th Anniversary of Independence

| Date | Mintage | F | VF | XF | Unc | BU |
|---|---|---|---|---|---|---|
| 1985 Proof | — | Value: 325 | | | | |

**1000 PESOS** **KM# 527** **Weight:** 31.1030 g. **Composition:** 0.9990 Gold 1.0000 oz. AGW **Subject:** 1986 World Cup Soccer Games

| Date | Mintage | F | VF | XF | Unc | BU |
|---|---|---|---|---|---|---|
| 1986 | — | — | — | — | — | 550 |

**1000 PESOS** **KM# 536** **Composition:** Aluminum-Bronze **Note:** Juana de Asbaje

| Date | Mintage | F | VF | XF | Unc | BU |
|---|---|---|---|---|---|---|
| 1988 | 229,300,000 | — | 0.85 | 1.25 | 3.75 | 4.25 |
| 1989 | — | — | 0.85 | 1.25 | 3.45 | 4.25 |
| 1990 | — | — | 0.85 | 1.25 | 2.25 | 4.25 |
| 1990 Proof; 2 known | — | Value: 550 | | | | |
| 1991 | — | — | 1.00 | 1.50 | 2.50 | 4.25 |
| 1992 | — | — | 1.00 | 1.50 | 2.25 | 3.50 |

**1000 PESOS** **KM# 535** **Weight:** 34.5590 g. **Composition:** 0.9000 Gold 1.0000 oz. AGW **Subject:** 50th Anniversary - Nationalization of Oil Industry **Reverse:** Portrait of Cardenas **Note:** Similar to 5000 Pesos, KM#531.

| Date | Mintage | F | VF | XF | Unc | BU |
|---|---|---|---|---|---|---|
| 1988 Proof | — | Value: 440 | | | | |

**1000 PESOS** **KM# 560** **Weight:** 31.1035 g. **Composition:** 0.9990 Gold 1.0000 oz. AGW **Subject:** Native Culture **Reverse:** Sculpture of jaguar head

| Date | Mintage | F | VF | XF | Unc | BU |
|---|---|---|---|---|---|---|
| 1992 | 18,000 | — | — | — | 400 | — |
| 1992 Proof | 2,000 | Value: 600 | | | | |

**2000 PESOS** **KM# 528** **Weight:** 62.2000 g. **Composition:** 0.9990 Gold 2.0000 oz. AGW **Subject:** 1986 World Cup Soccer Games

| Date | Mintage | F | VF | XF | Unc | BU |
|---|---|---|---|---|---|---|
| 1986 | — | — | — | — | — | 900 |

**5000 PESOS** **KM# 531** **Composition:** Copper-Nickel **Subject:** 50th Anniversary - Nationalization of Oil Industry

| Date | Mintage | F | VF | XF | Unc | BU |
|---|---|---|---|---|---|---|
| ND(1988) | 50,000,000 | — | — | 4.75 | 7.75 | 10.00 |

**10000 PESOS** **KM# 557** **Weight:** 155.5175 g. **Composition:** 0.9990 Silver 5.0000 oz. ASW **Subject:** Pieora De Tizoc **Reverse:** Native warriors taking female captive **Size:** 64 mm. **Note:** Illustration reduced.

| Date | Mintage | F | VF | XF | Unc | BU |
|---|---|---|---|---|---|---|
| 1992 | 52,000 | — | — | — | 46.00 | — |
| 1992 Proof | 3,005 | Value: 80.00 | | | | |

## REFORM COINAGE

1 New Peso = 1000 Old Pesos

**5 CENTAVOS** **KM# 546** **Composition:** Stainless Steel

| Date | Mintage | F | VF | XF | Unc | BU |
|---|---|---|---|---|---|---|
| 1992 | — | — | — | 0.15 | 0.25 | — |
| 1993 | — | — | — | 0.15 | 0.25 | — |
| 1994 | — | — | — | 0.15 | 0.25 | — |
| 1995 | — | — | — | 0.15 | 0.25 | — |
| 1995 Proof | — | Value: 0.50 | | | | |
| 1996 | — | — | — | 0.15 | 0.25 | — |
| 1997 | — | — | — | 0.15 | 0.25 | — |

**10 CENTAVOS** **KM# 547** **Composition:** Stainless Steel

| Date | Mintage | F | VF | XF | Unc | BU |
|---|---|---|---|---|---|---|
| 1992 | — | — | — | 0.20 | 0.30 | — |
| 1993 | — | — | — | 0.20 | 0.30 | — |
| 1994 | — | — | — | 0.20 | 0.30 | — |
| 1995 | — | — | — | 0.20 | 0.30 | — |
| 1995 Proof | — | Value: 0.60 | | | | |
| 1996 | — | — | — | 0.20 | 0.30 | — |
| 1997 | — | — | — | 0.20 | 0.30 | — |

**20 CENTAVOS** **KM# 548** **Composition:** Aluminum-Bronze

| Date | Mintage | F | VF | XF | Unc | BU |
|---|---|---|---|---|---|---|
| 1992 | — | — | — | 0.25 | 0.35 | — |
| 1993 | — | — | — | 0.25 | 0.35 | — |
| 1994 | — | — | — | 0.25 | 0.35 | — |
| 1995 | — | — | — | 0.25 | 0.35 | — |
| 1995 Proof | — | Value: 0.75 | | | | |
| 1996 | — | — | — | 0.25 | 0.35 | — |

**50 CENTAVOS** **KM# 549** **Composition:** Aluminum-Bronze

| Date | Mintage | F | VF | XF | Unc | BU |
|---|---|---|---|---|---|---|
| 1992 | — | — | — | 0.45 | 0.85 | — |
| 1993 | — | — | — | 0.45 | 0.75 | — |
| 1994 | — | — | — | 0.45 | 0.75 | — |
| 1995 | — | — | — | 0.45 | 0.75 | — |
| 1995 Proof | — | Value: 0.90 | | | | |
| 1996 | — | — | — | 0.45 | 0.75 | — |
| 1997 | — | — | — | 0.45 | 0.75 | — |

**NUEVO PESO** **KM# 550** **Ring Composition:** Stainless Steel **Center Composition:** Aluminum-Bronze

| Date | Mintage | F | VF | XF | Unc | BU |
|---|---|---|---|---|---|---|
| 1992 | — | — | — | 0.60 | 1.25 | — |
| 1993 | — | — | — | 0.60 | 1.25 | — |
| 1994 | — | — | — | 0.60 | 1.25 | — |
| 1995 | — | — | — | 0.60 | 1.25 | — |
| 1995 Proof | — | Value: 2.50 | | | | |

**NUEVO PESO** **KM#644** **Weight:** 7.7700 g. **Composition:** 0.9990 Silver .2496 oz. ASW **Subject:** Eagle Warrior **Obverse:** National arms **Reverse:** Costumed warrior **Edge:** Reeded **Size:** 26.8 mm.

| Date | Mintage | F | VF | XF | Unc | BU |
|---|---|---|---|---|---|---|
| 1993 Proof | — | — | — | — | 11.50 | — |

**NUEVO PESO** **KM#567** **Weight:** 7.7601 g. **Composition:** 0.9990 Silver .2498 oz. ASW **Subject:** Bajorrelieve Del El Tajin

| Date | Mintage | F | VF | XF | Unc | BU |
|---|---|---|---|---|---|---|
| 1993 | 100,000 | — | — | — | 6.50 | — |
| 1993 Proof | 3,000 | Value: 10.50 | | | | |

**NUEVO PESO** **KM#572** **Weight:** 7.7601 g. **Composition:** 0.9990 Silver .2498 oz. ASW **Subject:** Chaac Mool

| Date | Mintage | F | VF | XF | Unc | BU |
|---|---|---|---|---|---|---|
| 1994 Proof | 2,000 | Value: 10.50 | | | | |

**PESO** **KM# 593** **Weight:** 7.7750 g. **Composition:** 0.9990 Silver .2500 oz. ASW **Subject:** Senor De Las Limas **Note:** Similar to 5 Pesos, KM#595.

| Date | Mintage | F | VF | XF | Unc | BU |
|---|---|---|---|---|---|---|
| 1996 | 10,000 | — | — | — | 4.00 | — |
| 1996 Proof | — | Value: 25.00 | | | | |
| 1998 Matte | — | — | — | — | 3.25 | — |

**PESO** **KM#603** **Ring Composition:** Stainless Steel **Center Composition:** Aluminum-Bronze **Note:** Similar to KM#550 but without N.

| Date | Mintage | F | VF | XF | Unc | BU |
|---|---|---|---|---|---|---|
| 1996 | — | — | — | — | 1.25 | — |
| 1998 | — | — | — | — | 1.25 | — |

**PESO** **KM# 617** **Weight:** 7.7759 g. **Composition:** 0.9990 Silver .2500 oz. ASW **Subject:** Disco De La Muerte **Obverse:** Mexican eagle

| Date | Mintage | F | VF | XF | Unc | BU |
|---|---|---|---|---|---|---|
| 1997 | — | — | — | — | 4.00 | — |
| 1997 Proof | — | Value: 10.50 | | | | |
| 1998 Matte | — | — | — | — | 10.50 | — |

**PESO** **KM# 661** **Weight:** 7.7759 g. **Composition:** 0.9990 Silver .2500 oz. ASW **Subject:** Jaguar **Obverse:** National emblem. **Reverse:** Jaguar carving. **Edge:** Reeded. **Size:** 27 mm.

| Date | Mintage | F | VF | XF | Unc | BU |
|---|---|---|---|---|---|---|
| 1998 | — | — | — | — | 4.00 | — |
| 1998 Proof | — | Value: 8.00 | | | | |

**2 NUEVO PESOS** **KM#551** **Ring Composition:** Stainless Steel **Center Composition:** Aluminum-Bronze

| Date | Mintage | F | VF | XF | Unc | BU |
|---|---|---|---|---|---|---|
| 1992 | — | — | — | 1.50 | 2.50 | — |
| 1993 | — | — | — | 1.00 | 2.35 | — |
| 1994 | — | — | — | 1.00 | 2.35 | — |
| 1995 | — | — | — | 1.00 | 2.35 | — |
| 1995 Proof | — | Value: 4.50 | | | | |

**2 NUEVO PESOS** **KM# 645** **Weight:** 15.4200 g. **Composition:** 0.9990 Silver .4953 oz. ASW **Subject:** Eagle Warrior **Obverse:** National arms **Reverse:** Costumed warrior **Edge:** Reeded **Size:** 32.9 mm.

| Date | Mintage | F | VF | XF | Unc | BU |
|---|---|---|---|---|---|---|
| 1993 Proof | — | — | — | — | 23.00 | — |

**2 NUEVO PESOS** **KM# 568** **Weight:** 15.5516 g. **Composition:** 0.9990 Silver .4995 oz. ASW **Subject:** Bajorrelieve Del El Tajin

| Date | Mintage | F | VF | XF | Unc | BU |
|---|---|---|---|---|---|---|
| 1993 | 100,000 | — | — | — | 6.50 | — |
| 1993 Proof | 3,000 | Value: 10.50 | | | | |

**2 NUEVO PESOS** **KM# 573** **Weight:** 15.5516 g. **Composition:** 0.9990 Silver .4995 oz. ASW **Subject:** Chaac Mool

| Date | Mintage | F | VF | XF | Unc | BU |
|---|---|---|---|---|---|---|
| 1994 Matte | 30,000 | — | — | — | 6.50 | — |
| 1994 Proof | 2,000 | Value: 10.50 | | | | |

**2 PESOS** **KM# 594** **Weight:** 15.5517 g. **Composition:** 0.9990 Silver .5000 oz. ASW **Subject:** Senor De Las Limasl **Note:** Similar to 5 Pesos, KM#595.

| Date | Mintage | F | VF | XF | Unc | BU |
|---|---|---|---|---|---|---|
| 1996 | 10,000 | — | — | — | 6.00 | — |
| 1996 Proof | — | Value: 18.50 | | | | |
| 1998 Matte | — | — | — | — | 8.50 | — |

**2 PESOS** **KM# 604** **Ring Composition:** Stainless Steel **Center Composition:** Aluminum-Bronze **Note:** Similar to KM#551, but denomination without N.

| Date | Mintage | F | VF | XF | Unc | BU |
|---|---|---|---|---|---|---|
| 1996 | — | — | — | — | 2.50 | — |
| 1998 | — | — | — | — | 2.50 | — |

**2 PESOS** **KM# 618** **Weight:** 15.5517 g. **Composition:** 0.9990 Silver .5000 oz. ASW **Subject:** Disco De La Muerte **Obverse:** Mexican eagle

| Date | Mintage | F | VF | XF | Unc | BU |
|---|---|---|---|---|---|---|
| 1997 | — | — | — | — | 6.00 | — |
| 1997 Proof | — | Value: 10.50 | | | | |
| 1998 | — | — | — | — | 6.50 | — |

**2 PESOS** **KM# 662** **Weight:** 15.5517 g. **Composition:** 0.9990 Silver .5000 oz. ASW **Subject:** Jaguar **Obverse:** National emblem. **Reverse:** Jaguar carving. **Edge:** Reeded. **Size:** 33 mm.

| Date | Mintage | F | VF | XF | Unc | BU |
|---|---|---|---|---|---|---|
| 1998 | — | — | — | — | 8.00 | — |
| 1998 Proof | — | Value: 16.00 | | | | |

**5 NUEVO PESOS** **KM# 552** **Ring Composition:** Stainless Steel **Center Composition:** Aluminum-Bronze

| Date | Mintage | F | VF | XF | Unc | BU |
|---|---|---|---|---|---|---|
| 1992 | — | — | — | 2.00 | 4.00 | — |
| 1993 | — | — | — | 2.00 | 4.00 | — |
| 1994 | — | — | — | 2.00 | 4.00 | — |
| 1995 Proof | — | Value: 25.00 | | | | |

**5 NUEVO PESOS** **KM# 583** **Weight:** 31.1035 g. **Composition:** 0.9990 Silver .9991 oz. ASW **Subject:** Anciano Con Brasero **Reverse:** Kneeling figure sculpture

| Date | Mintage | F | VF | XF | Unc | BU |
|---|---|---|---|---|---|---|
| 1993 | — | — | — | — | 12.00 | — |
| 1993 Proof | 2,655 | Value: 36.00 | | | | |

**5 NUEVO PESOS** **KM# 646** **Weight:** 31.0500 g. **Composition:** 0.9990 Silver .9973 oz. ASW **Subject:** Eagle Warrior **Obverse:** National arms **Reverse:** Costumed warrior **Edge:** Reeded **Size:** 40 mm.

| Date | Mintage | F | VF | XF | Unc | BU |
|---|---|---|---|---|---|---|
| 1993 Proof | — | — | — | — | 46.00 | — |

**5 NUEVO PESOS** **KM# 647** **Weight:** 31.0000 g. **Composition:** 0.9990 Silver .9957 oz. ASW **Subject:** Xochipilli **Obverse:** National arms **Reverse:** Seated figure sculpture **Edge:** Reeded **Size:** 40 mm.

| Date | Mintage | F | VF | XF | Unc | BU |
|---|---|---|---|---|---|---|
| 1993 Proof | — | — | — | — | 45.00 | — |

**5 NUEVO PESOS** **KM# 648** **Weight:** 31.0000 g. **Composition:** 0.9990 Silver .9957 oz. ASW **Subject:** Brasco Efigie **Obverse:** National arms **Reverse:** Sculpture **Edge:** Reeded. **Size:** 40 mm.

| Date | Mintage | F | VF | XF | Unc | BU |
|---|---|---|---|---|---|---|
| 1993 Proof | — | — | — | — | 45.00 | — |

**5 NUEVO PESOS** **KM# 649** **Weight:** 31.0000 g. **Composition:** 0.9990 Silver .9957 oz. ASW **Subject:** Huchucteotl **Obverse:** National arms **Reverse:** Aztec sculpture **Edge:** Reeded **Size:** 40 mm.

| Date | Mintage | F | VF | XF | Unc | BU |
|---|---|---|---|---|---|---|
| 1993 Proof | — | — | — | — | 45.00 | — |

**5 NUEVO PESOS** **KM# 584** **Weight:** 31.1035 g. **Composition:** 0.9990 Silver .9991 oz. ASW **Subject:** Carita Sonriente **Reverse:** Sculptured head

| Date | Mintage | F | VF | XF | Unc | BU |
|---|---|---|---|---|---|---|
| 1993 | — | — | — | — | 12.00 | — |
| 1993 Proof | 3,000 | Value: 36.00 | | | | |

**5 NUEVO PESOS** **KM# 582** **Weight:** 31.1035 g. **Composition:** 0.9990 Silver .9991 oz. ASW **Subject:** Palma Con Cecodrilo **Obverse:** National emblem **Reverse:** Aerial view of crocodile

| Date | Mintage | F | VF | XF | Unc | BU |
|---|---|---|---|---|---|---|
| 1993 | — | — | — | — | 12.00 | — |
| 1993 Proof | 2,655 | Value: 36.00 | | | | |

**5 NUEVO PESOS** **KM# 569** **Weight:** 31.1035 g. **Composition:** 0.9990 Silver .9991 oz. ASW **Subject:** Bajorrelieve Del El Tajin **Obverse:** Mexican eagle

| Date | Mintage | F | VF | XF | Unc | BU |
|---|---|---|---|---|---|---|
| 1993 | 100,000 | — | — | — | 12.00 | — |
| 1993 Proof | 2,200 | Value: 36.00 | | | | |

**5 NUEVO PESOS** **KM# 574** **Weight:** 31.1035 g. **Composition:** 0.9990 Silver .9991 oz. ASW **Subject:** Chaac Mool **Reverse:** Sculptured head

| Date | Mintage | F | VF | XF | Unc | BU |
|---|---|---|---|---|---|---|
| 1994 Matte | 50,000 | — | — | — | 12.00 | — |
| 1994 Proof | 2,200 | Value: 36.00 | | | | |

**5 NUEVO PESOS** **KM# 575** **Weight:** 31.1035 g. **Composition:** 0.9990 Silver .9991 oz. ASW **Subject:** Chaac Mool **Reverse:** Tomb of Palenque Memorial Stone

| Date | Mintage | F | VF | XF | Unc | BU |
|---|---|---|---|---|---|---|
| 1994 | — | — | — | — | 12.00 | — |
| 1994 Proof | 2,200 | Value: 36.00 | | | | |

**5 NUEVO PESOS** **KM# 577** **Weight:** 31.1035 g. **Composition:** 0.9990 Silver .9991 oz. ASW **Subject:** Mascaron Del Dios Chaac **Reverse:** Elaborately carved wall segment

| Date | Mintage | F | VF | XF | Unc | BU |
|---|---|---|---|---|---|---|
| 1994 | — | — | — | — | 12.00 | — |
| 1994 Proof | 2,200 | Value: 36.00 | | | | |

**5 NUEVO PESOS** **KM# 578** **Weight:** 31.1035 g. **Composition:** 0.9990 Silver .9991 oz. ASW **Subject:** Dintel 26 **Reverse:** 2 seated figures wall carving

| Date | Mintage | F | VF | XF | Unc | BU |
|---|---|---|---|---|---|---|
| 1994 | — | — | — | — | 12.00 | — |
| 1994 Proof | 2,200 | Value: 36.00 | | | | |

**5 NUEVO PESOS** **KM# 588** **Weight:** 27.0000 g. **Composition:** 0.9250 Silver .8030 oz. ASW **Subject:** Environmental Protection **Reverse:** Pacific Ridley Sea Turtle

| Date | Mintage | F | VF | XF | Unc | BU |
|---|---|---|---|---|---|---|
| 1994 Proof | 20,000 | Value: 37.50 | | | | |

**5 NUEVO PESOS** **KM# 657** **Weight:** 31.1710 g. **Composition:** 0.9990 Silver 1.0012 oz. ASW **Series:** Endangered Wildlife **Subject:** Berrendo **Obverse:** National arms past and present **Reverse:** Antelope **Size:** 40 mm.

| Date | Mintage | F | VF | XF | Unc | BU |
|---|---|---|---|---|---|---|
| 2000 | 50,000 | — | — | — | 25.00 | — |

**5 NUEVO PESOS** **KM# 652** **Weight:** 31.1710 g. **Composition:** 0.9990 Silver 1.0012 oz. ASW **Series:** Endangered Wildlife **Subject:** Aguila Real **Obverse:** National arms past and present **Reverse:** Eagle on branch **Size:** 40 mm.

| Date | Mintage | F | VF | XF | Unc | BU |
|---|---|---|---|---|---|---|
| 2000 | 50,000 | — | — | — | 25.00 | — |

**5 NUEVO PESOS** **KM# 655** **Weight:** 31.1710 g. **Composition:** 0.9990 Silver 1.0012 oz. ASW **Series:** Endangered Wildlife **Subject:** Cocodrilo de Rio **Obverse:** National arms past and present **Reverse:** Crocodile **Size:** 40 mm.

| Date | Mintage | F | VF | XF | Unc | BU |
|---|---|---|---|---|---|---|
| 2000 | 50,000 | — | — | — | 25.00 | — |

**5 NUEVO PESOS** **KM# 656** **Weight:** 31.1710 g. **Composition:** 0.9990 Silver 1.0012 oz. ASW **Series:** Endangered Wildlife **Subject:** Nutria de Rio **Obverse:** National arms past and present **Reverse:** Nutria **Size:** 40 mm.

| Date | Mintage | F | VF | XF | Unc | BU |
|---|---|---|---|---|---|---|
| 2000 | 50,000 | — | — | — | 25.00 | — |

**5 NUEVO PESOS** **KM# 653** **Weight:** 31.1710 g. **Composition:** 0.9990 Silver 1.0012 oz. ASW **Subject:** Aguila Arpia **Obverse:** National arms past and present **Reverse:** Harpie Eagle **Size:** 40 mm.

| Date | Mintage | F | VF | XF | Unc | BU |
|---|---|---|---|---|---|---|
| 2001 | 50,000 | — | — | — | 25.00 | — |

**5 NUEVO PESOS** **KM# 654** **Weight:** 31.1710 g. **Composition:** 0.9990 Silver 1.0012 oz. ASW **Series:** Endangered Wildlife **Subject:** Oso Negro **Obverse:** National arms past and present **Reverse:** Black bear **Size:** 40 mm.

| Date | Mintage | F | VF | XF | Unc | BU |
|---|---|---|---|---|---|---|
| 2001 | 50,000 | — | — | — | 25.00 | — |

**5 NUEVO PESOS** **KM# 651** **Weight:** 31.1710 g. **Composition:** 0.9990 Silver 1.0012 oz. ASW **Series:** Endangered Wildlife **Subject:** Manati **Obverse:** National arms past and present **Reverse:** Manati **Edge:** Reeded **Size:** 40 mm.

| Date | Mintage | F | VF | XF | Unc | BU |
|---|---|---|---|---|---|---|
| 2001 | 50,000 | — | — | — | 25.00 | — |

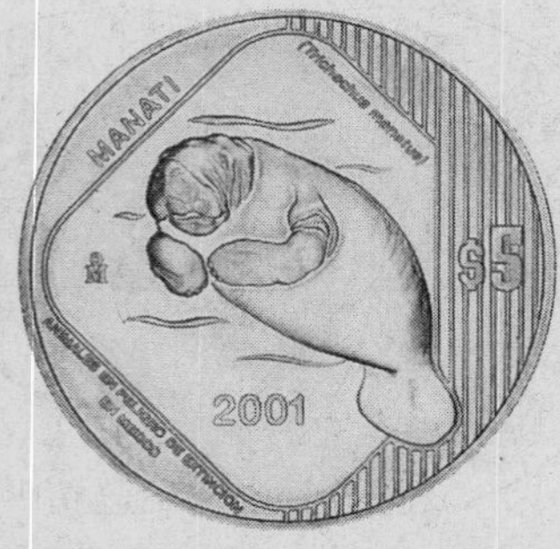


**5 NUEVO PESOS** **KM# 658** **Weight:** 31.1710 g. **Composition:** 0.9990 Silver 1.0012 oz. ASW **Series:** Endangered Wildlife **Subject:** Jaguar **Obverse:** National arms past and present **Reverse:** Jaguar resting **Size:** 40 mm.

| Date | Mintage | F | VF | XF | Unc | BU |
|---|---|---|---|---|---|---|
| 2001 | 50,000 | — | — | — | 25.00 | — |

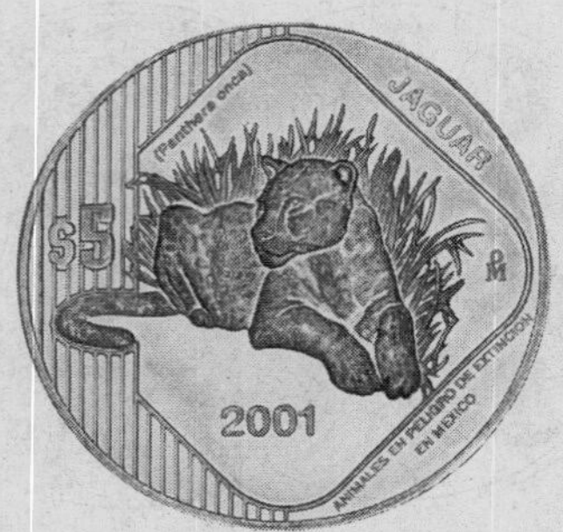


**5 NUEVO PESOS** **KM# 659** **Weight:** 31.1710 g. **Composition:** 0.9990 Silver 1.0012 oz. ASW **Series:** Endangered Wildlife **Subject:** Parrito de las Praderas **Obverse:** National arms past and present **Reverse:** Prairie dog **Size:** 40 mm.

| Date | Mintage | F | VF | XF | Unc | BU |
|---|---|---|---|---|---|---|
| 2001 | 50,000 | — | — | — | 25.00 | — |

**5 NUEVO PESOS** **KM# 660** **Weight:** 31.1710 g. **Composition:** 0.9990 Silver 1.0012 oz. ASW **Series:** Endangered Wildlife **Subject:** Zacatuche **Obverse:** National arms past and present **Reverse:** Rabbit **Size:** 40 mm.

| Date | Mintage | F | VF | XF | Unc | BU |
|---|---|---|---|---|---|---|
| 2001 | 50,000 | — | — | — | 25.00 | — |

**5 PESOS** **KM# 596** **Weight:** 31.1035 g. **Composition:** 0.9990 Silver 1.0000 oz. ASW **Subject:** Hombre Jaguar

| Date | Mintage | F | VF | XF | Unc | BU |
|---|---|---|---|---|---|---|
| 1996 | 30,000 | — | — | — | 13.50 | — |
| 1996 Proof | — | Value: 36.00 | | | | |
| 1998 Matte | — | — | — | — | 10.00 | — |

**5 PESOS** **KM# 595** **Weight:** 31.1035 g. **Composition:** 0.9990 Silver 1.0000 oz. ASW **Subject:** Senor De Las Limas

| Date | Mintage | F | VF | XF | Unc | BU |
|---|---|---|---|---|---|---|
| 1996 | 30,000 | — | — | — | 12.00 | — |
| 1996 Proof | 30,000 | Value: 36.00 | | | | |
| 1998 Matte | — | — | — | — | 16.25 | — |

**5 PESOS** **KM# 597** **Weight:** 31.1035 g. **Composition:** 0.9990 Silver 1.0000 oz. ASW **Subject:** El Luchador

| Date | Mintage | F | VF | XF | Unc | BU |
|---|---|---|---|---|---|---|
| 1996 | 30,000 | — | — | — | 13.50 | — |
| 1996 Proof | — | Value: 36.00 | | | | |
| 1998 Matte | — | — | — | — | 10.00 | — |

**5 PESOS** **KM# 598** **Weight:** 31.1035 g. **Composition:** 0.9990 Silver 1.0000 oz. ASW **Subject:** Hacha Ceremonial

| Date | Mintage | F | VF | XF | Unc | BU |
|---|---|---|---|---|---|---|
| 1996 Proof | 30,000 | Value: 36.00 | | | | |
| 1998 Matte | — | — | — | — | 10.00 | — |

**5 PESOS** **KM# 619** **Weight:** 31.1035 g. **Composition:** 0.9990 Silver 1.0000 oz. ASW **Subject:** Teohituacan - Disco de la Muerte **Obverse:** Eagle and snake

| Date | Mintage | F | VF | XF | Unc | BU |
|---|---|---|---|---|---|---|
| 1997 Proof | Est. 30,000 | Value: 36.00 | | | | |
| 1998 | — | — | — | — | 13.50 | — |

**5 PESOS** **KM# 620** **Weight:** 31.1035 g. **Composition:** 0.9990 Silver 1.0000 oz. ASW **Subject:** Teohituacan - Mascara **Obverse:** Eagle and snake

| Date | Mintage | F | VF | XF | Unc | BU |
|---|---|---|---|---|---|---|
| 1997 Proof | Est. 30,000 | Value: 36.00 | | | | |
| 1998 | — | — | — | — | 13.50 | — |

**5 PESOS** **KM# 621** **Weight:** 31.1035 g. **Composition:** 0.9990 Silver 1.0000 oz. ASW **Subject:** Teohituacan - Vasija **Obverse:** Eagle and snake

| Date | Mintage | F | VF | XF | Unc | BU |
|---|---|---|---|---|---|---|
| 1997 | — | — | — | — | 9.00 | — |
| 1997 Proof | Est. 30,000 | Value: 36.00 | | | | |
| 1998 Matte | — | — | — | — | 13.50 | — |

**5 PESOS** **KM# 622** **Weight:** 31.1035 g. **Composition:** 0.9990 Silver 1.0000 oz. ASW **Subject:** Teohituacan - Jugador of Pelota **Obverse:** Eagle and snake

| Date | Mintage | F | VF | XF | Unc | BU |
|---|---|---|---|---|---|---|
| 1997 | — | — | — | — | 9.00 | — |
| 1997 Proof | Est. 30,000 | Value: 36.50 | | | | |
| 1998 Matte | — | — | — | — | 10.00 | — |

**5 PESOS KM# 629 Weight:** 27.0000 g. **Composition:** 0.9250 Silver .8030 oz. ASW **Subject:** Jarabe Tapatio **Obverse:** Mexican emblem within circle of arms **Reverse:** 2 dancers

| Date | Mintage | F | VF | XF | Unc | BU |
|---|---|---|---|---|---|---|
| 1997 Proof | 20,000 | Value: 30.00 | | | | |

**5 PESOS KM# 605 Ring Composition:** Stainless Steel **Center Composition:** Aluminum-Bronze **Note:** Similar to KM#552 but deonomination without N.

| Date | Mintage | F | VF | XF | Unc | BU |
|---|---|---|---|---|---|---|
| 1997 | — | — | — | — | 5.50 | — |
| 1998 | — | — | — | — | 5.50 | — |

**5 PESOS KM# 663 Weight:** 31.1035 g. **Composition:** 0.9990 Silver 1.0000 oz. ASW **Subject:** Jaguar **Obverse:** National emblem. **Reverse:** Jaguar carving. **Edge:** Reeded. **Size:** 40 mm.

| Date | Mintage | F | VF | XF | Unc | BU |
|---|---|---|---|---|---|---|
| 1998 | — | — | — | — | 18.00 | — |
| 1998 Proof | — | Value: 40.00 | | | | |

**5 PESOS KM# 664 Weight:** 31.1035 g. **Composition:** 0.9990 Silver 1.0000 oz. ASW **Subject:** Sacerdote **Obverse:** National emblem. **Reverse:** Sacerdote sculpture. **Edge:** Reeded. **Size:** 40 mm.

| Date | Mintage | F | VF | XF | Unc | BU |
|---|---|---|---|---|---|---|
| 1998 | — | — | — | — | 18.00 | — |
| 1998 Proof | — | Value: 40.00 | | | | |

**5 PESOS KM# 666 Weight:** 31.1035 g. **Composition:** 0.9990 Silver 1.0000 oz. ASW **Subject:** Serpiente con Craneo **Obverse:** National emblem. **Reverse:** Large sculpture. **Edge:** Reeded. **Size:** 40 mm.

| Date | Mintage | F | VF | XF | Unc | BU |
|---|---|---|---|---|---|---|
| 1998 | — | — | — | — | 18.00 | — |
| 1998 Proof | — | Value: 40.00 | | | | |

**5 PESOS KM# 665 Weight:** 31.1035 g. **Composition:** 0.9990 Silver 1.0000 oz. ASW **Subject:** Quetzalcoatle **Obverse:** National emblem. **Reverse:** Quetzalcoatle sculpture. **Edge:** Reeded. **Size:** 40 mm.

| Date | Mintage | F | VF | XF | Unc | BU |
|---|---|---|---|---|---|---|
| 1998 | — | — | — | — | 18.00 | — |
| 1998 Proof | — | Value: 40.00 | | | | |

**5 PESOS KM# 627 Weight:** 31.1035 g. **Composition:** 0.9990 Silver 1.0000 oz. ASW **Subject:** World Wildlife Fund **Obverse:** Mexican eagle

| Date | Mintage | F | VF | XF | Unc | BU |
|---|---|---|---|---|---|---|
| 1998 Proof | Est. 15,000 | Value: 45.00 | | | | |

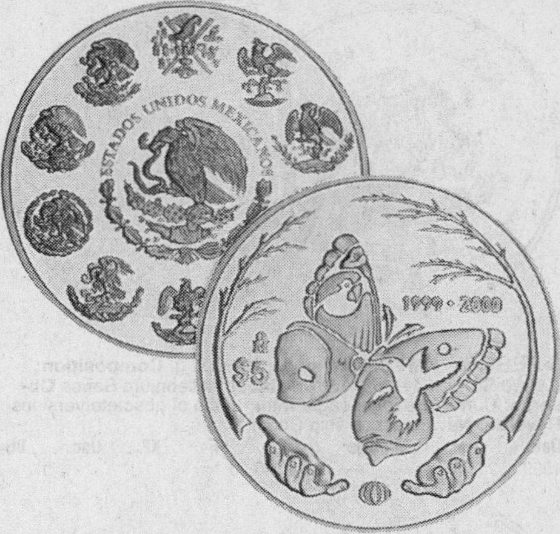


**5 PESOS KM# 630 Weight:** 31.1800 g. **Composition:** 0.9990 Silver 1.0025 oz. ASW **Subject:** Millennium Series **Obverse:** Current national eagle within circle of obsolete versions **Reverse:** Butterfly, dates

| Date | Mintage | F | VF | XF | Unc | BU |
|---|---|---|---|---|---|---|
| 1999-2000 Proof | 75,000 | Value: 30.00 | | | | |

**5 PESOS KM# 631 Weight:** 31.1800 g. **Composition:** 0.9990 Silver 1.0025 oz. ASW **Subject:** Millennium Series **Obverse:** Current national eagle within circle of obsolete versions **Reverse:** Stylized dove/hand of peace

| Date | Mintage | F | VF | XF | Unc | BU |
|---|---|---|---|---|---|---|
| 1999-2000 Proof | 75,000 | Value: 30.00 | | | | |

**5 PESOS KM# 632 Weight:** 31.1800 g. **Composition:** 0.9990 Silver 1.0025 oz. ASW **Subject:** Millennium Series **Obverse:** Current national eagle within circle of obsolete versions **Reverse:** Aztec bird design, denomination

| Date | Mintage | F | VF | XF | Unc | BU |
|---|---|---|---|---|---|---|
| 1999-2000 Proof | 75,000 | Value: 30.00 | | | | |

**5 PESOS** **KM# 635** **Weight:** 19.6000 g. **Composition:** 0.9990 Silver .6411 oz. ASW **Subject:** Millennium Series **Obverse:** Current national eagle within circle of obsolete versions **Reverse:** Naval training ship Cuauhtemoc

| Date | Mintage | F | VF | XF | Unc | BU |
|---|---|---|---|---|---|---|
| 1999 | — | Value: 40.00 | | | | |

**5 PESOS** **KM# 640** **Weight:** 31.1030 g. **Composition:** 0.9990 Silver .9990 oz. ASW **Subject:** UNICEF **Obverse:** National arms **Reverse:** 2 children flying kite **Edge:** Reeded **Size:** 40 mm.

| Date | Mintage | F | VF | XF | Unc | BU |
|---|---|---|---|---|---|---|
| 1999 | — | Value: 42.50 | | | | |

**10 NUEVO PESOS** **KM# 553** **Ring Composition:** Aluminum-Bronze **Center Weight:** 11.1400 g. **Center Composition:** 0.9250 Silver .1666 oz. ASW

| Date | Mintage | F | VF | XF | Unc | BU |
|---|---|---|---|---|---|---|
| 1992 | — | — | — | — | 7.50 | — |
| 1993 | — | — | — | — | 7.50 | — |
| 1994 | — | — | — | — | 7.50 | — |
| 1995 | — | — | — | — | 7.50 | — |

**10 NUEVO PESOS** **KM# 570** **Center Weight:** 115.5175 g. **Center Composition:** 0.9990 Silver 4.9956 oz. ASW **Subject:** Piramide Del El Tajin **Size:** 64 mm. **Note:** Illustration reduced.

| Date | Mintage | F | VF | XF | Unc | BU |
|---|---|---|---|---|---|---|
| 1993 | 50,000 | — | — | — | 46.00 | — |
| 1993 Proof | 3,000 | Value: 78.00 | | | | |

**10 NUEVO PESOS** **KM# 650** **Weight:** 155.3100 g. **Composition:** 0.9990 Silver 4.9883 oz. ASW **Subject:** Piedra de Tizoc **Obverse:** National arms **Reverse:** Warrior capturing woman **Edge:** Reeded **Size:** 64 mm.

| Date | Mintage | F | VF | XF | Unc | BU |
|---|---|---|---|---|---|---|
| 1993 | — | — | — | — | 55.00 | — |

**10 NUEVO PESOS** **KM# 576** **Center Weight:** 115.5175 g. **Center Composition:** 0.9990 Silver 4.9956 oz. ASW **Subject:** Piramide del Castillo **Size:** 64 mm. **Note:** Illustration reduced.

| Date | Mintage | F | VF | XF | Unc | BU |
|---|---|---|---|---|---|---|
| 1994 | 20,000 | — | — | — | 46.50 | — |
| 1994 Proof | 1,000 | Value: 80.00 | | | | |

**10 PESOS** **KM# 599** **Center Weight:** 1555.5175 g. **Center Composition:** 0.9990 Silver 5.0000 oz. ASW **Subject:** Cabeza Olmeca **Size:** 64 mm. **Note:** Illustration reduced.

| Date | Mintage | F | VF | XF | Unc | BU |
|---|---|---|---|---|---|---|
| 1996 Proof | 10,000 | Value: 80.00 | | | | |
| 1998 Matte | — | — | — | — | 46.00 | — |

**10 PESOS** **KM# 606** **Center Weight:** 11.1400 g. **Center Composition:** 0.9250 Silver .1666 oz. ASW **Note:** Similar to KM#553, but denomination without N.

| Date | Mintage | F | VF | XF | Unc | BU |
|---|---|---|---|---|---|---|
| 1996 | — | — | — | — | 7.50 | — |

**10 PESOS** **KM# 623** **Weight:** 1555.5175 g. **Composition:** 0.9990 Silver 5.0000 oz. ASW **Subject:** Piramide Del Sol **Obverse:** Mexican eagle **Size:** 64 mm. **Note:** Illustration reduced.

| Date | Mintage | F | VF | XF | Unc | BU |
|---|---|---|---|---|---|---|
| 1997 | — | — | — | — | 50.00 | — |
| 1997 Proof | 10,000 | Value: 95.00 | | | | |
| 1998 Matte | — | — | — | — | 46.00 | — |

**10 PESOS** **KM# 616** **Ring Composition:** Brass **Center Composition:** Copper-Nickel-Zinc **Subject:** Cabeza Olmeca **Obverse:** National emblem **Reverse:** Aztec design

| Date | Mintage | F | VF | XF | Unc | BU |
|---|---|---|---|---|---|---|
| 1997 | — | — | — | — | 7.50 | — |
| 1998 | — | — | — | — | 7.50 | — |

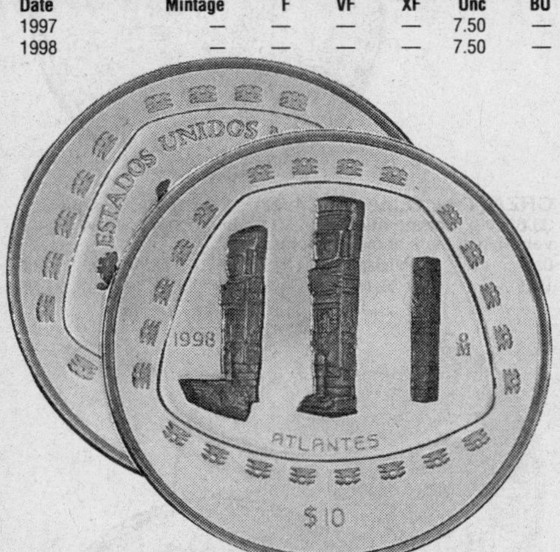

**10 PESOS** **KM# 634** **Weight:** 155.7300 g. **Composition:** 0.9990 Silver 5.0018 oz. ASW **Subject:** Atlantes **Obverse:** National arms **Reverse:** Three curved statues

| Date | Mintage | F | VF | XF | Unc | BU |
|---|---|---|---|---|---|---|
| 1998 | — | — | — | — | 50.00 | — |
| 1998 Proof | — | Value: 95.00 | | | | |

**10 PESOS** **KM# 633** **Weight:** 62.0300 g. **Composition:** 0.9990 Silver 1.9923 oz. ASW **Subject:** Millennium Series **Obverse:** Current national eagle within circle of obsolete versions **Reverse:** Old and modern buildings, dates

| Date | Mintage | F | VF | XF | Unc | BU |
|---|---|---|---|---|---|---|
| 1999-2000 Proof | 75,000 | Value: 60.00 | | | | |

**10 PESOS** **KM# 636** **Ring Composition:** Brass **Center Composition:** Copper-Nickel **Subject:** Millennium Series **Reverse:** Aztec carving

| Date | Mintage | F | VF | XF | Unc | BU |
|---|---|---|---|---|---|---|
| 2000 | — | — | — | — | 7.00 | — |

**20 NUEVO PESOS** **KM# 561** **Ring Composition:** Aluminum-Bronze .2499 oz. **Center Composition:** Silver

| Date | Mintage | F | VF | XF | Unc | BU |
|---|---|---|---|---|---|---|
| 1993 | — | — | — | — | 12.00 | — |
| 1994 | — | — | — | — | 12.00 | — |
| 1995 | — | — | — | — | 12.00 | — |

**20 PESOS** **KM# 641** **Weight:** 6.2210 g. **Composition:** 0.9990 Gold .1998 oz. AGW **Subject:** UNICEF **Obverse:** National arms **Reverse:** Child playing with lasso **Edge:** Reeded **Size:** 21.9 mm.

| Date | Mintage | F | VF | XF | Unc | BU |
|---|---|---|---|---|---|---|
| 1999 | — | — | — | — | 170 | — |

**20 PESOS** **KM# 637** **Ring Composition:** Brass **Center Composition:** Copper-Nickel **Subject:** Xiutecuhtli **Reverse:** Aztec with torch

| Date | Mintage | F | VF | XF | Unc | BU |
|---|---|---|---|---|---|---|
| 2000 | — | — | — | — | 15.00 | — |

**20 PESOS** **KM# 638** **Ring Composition:** Brass **Center Composition:** Copper-Nickel **Subject:** Octavio Paz **Reverse:** Aztec with torch

| Date | Mintage | F | VF | XF | Unc | BU |
|---|---|---|---|---|---|---|
| 2000 | — | — | — | — | 15.00 | — |

**25 NUEVO PESOS** **KM# 585** **Weight:** 7.7758 g. **Composition:** 0.9990 Gold .2500 oz. AGW **Subject:** Hacha Ceremonial **Note:** Similar to 100 New Pesos, KM#587.

| Date | Mintage | F | VF | XF | Unc | BU |
|---|---|---|---|---|---|---|
| 1993 | 16,000 | — | — | — | 145 | — |
| 1993 Proof | 800 | Value: 250 | | | | |

**25 NUEVO PESOS** **KM# 579** **Weight:** 7.7758 g. **Composition:** 0.9990 Gold .2500 oz. AGW **Subject:** Personaje de Jaina **Reverse:** Seated figure

| Date | Mintage | F | VF | XF | Unc | BU |
|---|---|---|---|---|---|---|
| 1994 | 2,000 | — | — | — | 165 | — |
| 1994 Proof | 500 | Value: 300 | | | | |

**25 PESOS** **KM# 600** **Weight:** 7.7758 g. **Composition:** 0.9990 Gold .2500 oz. AGW **Subject:** Sacerdote **Note:** Similar to 100 Pesos, KM#602.

| Date | Mintage | F | VF | XF | Unc | BU |
|---|---|---|---|---|---|---|
| 1996 | 10,000 | — | — | — | 200 | — |
| 1996 Proof | — | Value: 250 | | | | |

**25 PESOS** **KM# 624** **Weight:** 7.7758 g. **Composition:** 0.9990 Gold .2500 oz. AGW **Subject:** Serpiente Emplumada **Obverse:** Mexican eagle **Note:** Similar to 100 Pesos, KM#626.

| Date | Mintage | F | VF | XF | Unc | BU |
|---|---|---|---|---|---|---|
| 1997 | — | — | — | — | 200 | — |
| 1997 Proof | 10,000 | Value: 250 | | | | |

**50 NUEVO PESOS** **KM# 571** **Ring Composition:** Brass **Center Weight:** 34.0000 g. **Center Composition:** 0.9250 Silver .5051 oz. ASW **Subject:** Nino Heroes

| Date | Mintage | F | VF | XF | Unc | BU |
|---|---|---|---|---|---|---|
| 1993 | — | — | — | — | 28.00 | — |
| 1994 | — | — | — | — | 28.00 | — |
| 1995 | — | — | — | — | 28.00 | — |

**50 NUEVO PESOS** **KM# 586** **Weight:** 15.5517 g. **Composition:** 0.9990 Gold .5000 oz. AGW **Subject:** Hacha Ceremonial **Note:** Similar to 100 New Pesos, KM#587.

| Date | Mintage | F | VF | XF | Unc | BU |
|---|---|---|---|---|---|---|
| 1993 | 16,000 | — | — | — | 275 | — |
| 1993 Proof | 500 | Value: 425 | | | | |

**50 NUEVO PESOS** **KM# 580** **Weight:** 15.5517 g. **Composition:** 0.9990 Gold .5000 oz. AGW **Subject:** Personaje de Jaina **Reverse:** Seated figure

| Date | Mintage | F | VF | XF | Unc | BU |
|---|---|---|---|---|---|---|
| 1994 | 1,000 | — | — | — | 300 | — |
| 1994 Proof | 500 | Value: 475 | | | | |

**50 PESOS** **KM# 601** **Weight:** 15.5517 g. **Composition:** 0.9990 Gold .5000 oz. AGW **Subject:** Sacerdote **Note:** Similar to 100 Pesos, KM#602.

| Date | Mintage | F | VF | XF | Unc | BU |
|---|---|---|---|---|---|---|
| 1996 | 10,000 | — | — | — | 375 | — |
| 1996 Proof | — | Value: 425 | | | | |

**50 PESOS** **KM# 608** **Weight:** 15.5517 g. **Composition:** 0.9990 Silver .5000 oz. ASW **Note:** Similar to 50 New Pesos, KM#571 without "N" before denomination.

| Date | Mintage | F | VF | XF | Unc | BU |
|---|---|---|---|---|---|---|
| 1996 | — | — | — | — | 22.00 | — |

**50 PESOS** **KM# 625** **Weight:** 15.5517 g. **Composition:** 0.9990 Gold .5000 oz. AGW **Subject:** Serpiente Emplumada **Obverse:** Mexican eagle **Note:** Similar to 100 Pesos, KM#626.

| Date | Mintage | F | VF | XF | Unc | BU |
|---|---|---|---|---|---|---|
| 1997 | — | — | — | — | 350 | — |
| 1997 Proof | 10,000 | Value: 450 | | | | |

**100 NUEVO PESOS** **KM# 587** **Weight:** 31.1035 g. **Composition:** 0.9990 Gold 1.0000 oz. AGW **Subject:** Hacha Ceremonial

| Date | Mintage | F | VF | XF | Unc | BU |
|---|---|---|---|---|---|---|
| 1993 | 7,158 | — | — | — | 525 | — |
| 1993 Proof | 500 | Value: 650 | | | | |

**100 NUEVO PESOS** **KM# 581** **Weight:** 31.1035 g. **Composition:** 0.9990 Gold 1.0000 oz. AGW **Subject:** Personaje de Jaina

| Date | Mintage | F | VF | XF | Unc | BU |
|---|---|---|---|---|---|---|
| 1994 | 1,000 | — | — | — | 575 | — |
| 1994 Proof | 500 | Value: 700 | | | | |

**100 PESOS** **KM# 602** **Weight:** 31.1035 g. **Composition:** 0.9990 Gold 1.0000 oz. AGW **Subject:** Sacerdote

| Date | Mintage | F | VF | XF | Unc | BU |
|---|---|---|---|---|---|---|
| 1996 | 10,000 | — | — | — | 575 | — |
| 1996 Proof | — | Value: 600 | | | | |

**100 PESOS** **KM# 626** **Weight:** 31.1035 g. **Composition:** 0.9990 Gold 1.0000 oz. AGW **Subject:** Teohituacan - Serpiente Emplumada **Obverse:** Eagle and snake

| Date | Mintage | F | VF | XF | Unc | BU |
|---|---|---|---|---|---|---|
| 1997 | — | — | — | — | 600 | — |
| 1997 Proof | Est. 10,000 | Value: 650 | | | | |

## SILVER BULLION COINAGE

### 1/20 ONZA (1/20 Troy Ounce of Silver) KM# 542

**Weight:** 1.5551 g. **Composition:** 0.9990 Silver .0500 oz. ASW

| Date | Mintage | F | VF | XF | Unc | BU |
|---|---|---|---|---|---|---|
| 1991 | 50,017 | — | — | — | — | 2.45 |
| 1992 | 295,783 | — | — | — | — | 2.45 |
| 1992 Proof | 5,000 | Value: 10.00 | | | | |
| 1993 | 100,000 | — | — | — | — | 2.45 |
| 1993 Proof | — | Value: 10.00 | | | | |
| 1994 | 90,100 | — | — | — | — | 2.45 |
| 1994 Proof | 10,000 | Value: 10.00 | | | | |
| 1995 | 50,000 | — | — | — | — | 2.45 |
| 1995 Proof | 2,000 | Value: 10.00 | | | | |

### 1/20 ONZA (1/20 Troy Ounce of Silver) KM# 609

**Weight:** 1.5551 g. **Composition:** 0.9990 Silver .0500 oz. ASW **Obverse:** Mexican eagle **Reverse:** Winged Victory

| Date | Mintage | F | VF | XF | Unc | BU |
|---|---|---|---|---|---|---|
| 1996 | 50,000 | — | — | — | — | 2.45 |
| 1996 Proof | 1,000 | Value: 10.00 | | | | |
| 1997 | 20,000 | — | — | — | — | 2.45 |
| 1997 Proof | 800 | Value: 10.00 | | | | |
| 1998 | 6,400 | — | — | — | — | 2.45 |
| 1998 Proof | 300 | Value: 10.00 | | | | |
| 1999 Proof | 600 | Value: 10.00 | | | | |
| 2000 Proof | 900 | Value: 10.00 | | | | |
| 2001 | — | — | — | — | — | 2.45 |
| 2001 Proof | — | Value: 10.00 | | | | |

### 1/10 ONZA (1/10 Troy Ounce of Silver) KM# 543

**Weight:** 3.1103 g. **Composition:** 0.9990 Silver .1000 oz. ASW **Obverse:** Mexican eagle **Reverse:** Winged Victory

| Date | Mintage | F | VF | XF | Unc | BU |
|---|---|---|---|---|---|---|
| 1991 | 50,017 | — | — | — | — | 2.55 |
| 1992 | 299,983 | — | — | — | — | 2.55 |
| 1992 Proof | 5,000 | Value: 12.00 | | | | |
| 1993 | 100,000 | — | — | — | — | 2.55 |
| 1993 Proof | — | Value: 12.00 | | | | |
| 1994 | 90,100 | — | — | — | — | 2.55 |
| 1994 Proof | 10,000 | Value: 12.00 | | | | |
| 1995 | 50,000 | — | — | — | — | 2.55 |
| 1995 Proof | 2,000 | Value: 12.00 | | | | |

### 1/10 ONZA (1/10 Troy Ounce of Silver) KM# 610

**Weight:** 3.1103 g. **Composition:** 0.9990 Silver .1000 oz. ASW **Obverse:** Mexican eagle **Reverse:** Winged Victory

| Date | Mintage | F | VF | XF | Unc | BU |
|---|---|---|---|---|---|---|
| 1996 | 50,000 | — | — | — | — | 2.55 |
| 1996 Proof | 1,000 | Value: 12.00 | | | | |
| 1997 | 20,000 | — | — | — | — | 2.55 |
| 1997 Proof | 800 | Value: 12.00 | | | | |
| 1998 | 6,400 | — | — | — | — | 2.55 |
| 1998 Proof | 300 | Value: 12.00 | | | | |
| 1999 Proof | 600 | Value: 12.00 | | | | |
| 2000 Proof | 1,000 | Value: 12.00 | | | | |
| 2001 | — | — | — | — | — | 2.55 |
| 2001 Proof | — | Value: 12.00 | | | | |

### 1/4 ONZA (1/4 Troy Ounce of Silver) KM# 544

**Weight:** 7.7758 g. **Composition:** 0.9990 Silver .2500 oz. ASW **Obverse:** Mexican eagle **Reverse:** Winged Victory

| Date | Mintage | F | VF | XF | Unc | BU |
|---|---|---|---|---|---|---|
| 1991 | 50,017 | — | — | — | — | 4.50 |
| 1992 | 104,000 | — | — | — | — | 4.50 |
| 1992 Proof | 5,000 | Value: 15.00 | | | | |
| 1993 | 86,500 | — | — | — | — | 4.50 |
| 1993 Proof | — | Value: 15.00 | | | | |
| 1994 | 90,100 | — | — | — | — | 4.50 |
| 1994 Proof | 15,000 | Value: 15.00 | | | | |
| 1995 | 50,000 | — | — | — | — | 4.50 |
| 1995 Proof | 2,000 | Value: 15.00 | | | | |

### 1/4 ONZA (1/4 Troy Ounce of Silver) KM# 611

**Weight:** 7.7758 g. **Composition:** 0.9990 Silver .2500 oz. ASW **Obverse:** Mexican eagle **Reverse:** Winged Victory

| Date | Mintage | F | VF | XF | Unc | BU |
|---|---|---|---|---|---|---|
| 1996 | 50,000 | — | — | — | — | 4.50 |
| 1996 Proof | 1,000 | Value: 15.00 | | | | |
| 1997 | 20,000 | — | — | — | — | 4.50 |
| 1997 Proof | 800 | Value: 15.00 | | | | |
| 1998 | 6,400 | — | — | — | — | 4.50 |
| 1998 Proof | 300 | Value: 15.00 | | | | |
| 1999 Proof | 600 | Value: 15.00 | | | | |
| 2000 Proof | 700 | Value: 15.00 | | | | |
| 2001 | — | — | — | — | — | 4.50 |
| 2001 Proof | — | Value: 15.00 | | | | |

### 1/2 ONZA (1/2 Troy Ounce of Silver) KM# 545

**Weight:** 15.5517 g. **Composition:** 0.9990 Silver .5000 oz. ASW **Obverse:** Mexican eagle **Reverse:** Winged Victory

| Date | Mintage | F | VF | XF | Unc | BU |
|---|---|---|---|---|---|---|
| 1991 | 50,618 | — | — | — | — | 6.00 |
| 1992 | 119,000 | — | — | — | — | 6.00 |
| 1992 Proof | 5,000 | Value: 17.50 | | | | |
| 1993 | 71,500 | — | — | — | — | 6.00 |
| 1993 Proof | — | Value: 17.50 | | | | |
| 1994 | 90,100 | — | — | — | — | 6.00 |
| 1994 Proof | 15,000 | Value: 17.50 | | | | |
| 1995 | 50,000 | — | — | — | — | 6.00 |
| 1995 Proof | 2,000 | Value: 17.50 | | | | |

### 1/2 ONZA (1/2 Troy Ounce of Silver) KM# 612

**Weight:** 15.5517 g. **Composition:** 0.9990 Silver .5000 oz. ASW **Obverse:** Mexican eagle **Reverse:** Winged Victory

| Date | Mintage | F | VF | XF | Unc | BU |
|---|---|---|---|---|---|---|
| 1996 | 50,000 | — | — | — | — | 6.00 |
| 1996 Proof | 1,000 | Value: 17.50 | | | | |
| 1997 | 20,000 | — | — | — | — | 6.00 |
| 1997 Proof | 800 | Value: 17.50 | | | | |
| 1998 | 6,400 | — | — | — | — | 6.00 |
| 1998 Proof | 300 | Value: 17.50 | | | | |
| 1999 Proof | 600 | Value: 17.50 | | | | |
| 2000 Proof | 700 | Value: 17.50 | | | | |
| 2001 | — | — | — | — | — | 6.00 |
| 2001 Proof | — | Value: 17.50 | | | | |

### ONZA (Troy Ounce of Silver) KM# M49a

**Weight:** 33.6250 g. **Composition:** 0.9250 Silver 1.0000 oz. ASW **Obverse:** Mint mark above coin press

| Date | Mintage | F | VF | XF | Unc | BU |
|---|---|---|---|---|---|---|
| 1949 | 1,000,000 | — | 10.00 | 12.50 | 17.50 | 27.50 |

### ONZA (Troy Ounce of Silver) KM# M49b.1

**Weight:** 33.6250 g. **Composition:** 0.9250 Silver 1.0000 oz. ASW **Obverse:** Wide spacing between DE MONEDA **Reverse:** Mint mark below balance scale **Note:** Type I

| Date | Mintage | F | VF | XF | Unc | BU |
|---|---|---|---|---|---|---|
| 1978 | 280,000 | — | — | BV | 6.75 | 14.00 |

### ONZA (Troy Ounce of Silver) KM# M49b.2

**Weight:** 33.6250 g. **Composition:** 0.9250 Silver 1.0000 oz. ASW **Obverse:** Close spacing between DE MONEDA **Reverse:** Mint mark below balance scale **Note:** Type II

| Date | Mintage | F | VF | XF | Unc | BU |
|---|---|---|---|---|---|---|
| 1978 | Inc. above | — | — | BV | 6.75 | 12.00 |

### ONZA (Troy Ounce of Silver) KM# M49b.3

**Weight:** 33.6250 g. **Composition:** 0.9250 Silver 1.0000 oz. ASW **Obverse:** Close spacing between DE MONEDA **Reverse:** Left scale pan points to U in UNA **Note:** Type III

| Date | Mintage | F | VF | XF | Unc | BU |
|---|---|---|---|---|---|---|
| 1979 | 4,508,000 | — | — | BV | 6.75 | 13.50 |

**ONZA (Troy Ounce of Silver)** **KM# M49b.4** **Weight:** 33.6250 g. **Composition:** 0.9250 Silver 1.0000 oz. ASW **Obverse:** Close spacing between DE MONEDA **Reverse:** Left scale pan points between U and N of UNA **Note:** Type IV

| Date | Mintage | F | VF | XF | Unc | BU |
|---|---|---|---|---|---|---|
| 1979 | Inc. above | — | — | BV | 6.75 | 13.50 |

**ONZA (Troy Ounce of Silver)** **KM# M49b.5** **Weight:** 33.6250 g. **Composition:** 0.9250 Silver 1.0000 oz. ASW **Obverse:** Close spacing between DE MONEDA **Reverse:** Left scale pan points between U and N of UNA **Note:** Type V

| Date | Mintage | F | VF | XF | Unc | BU |
|---|---|---|---|---|---|---|
| 1980 | 6,104,000 | — | — | BV | 6.75 | 11.00 |
| 1980/70 | Inc. above | — | — | BV | 6.75 | 14.50 |

**ONZA (Troy Ounce of Silver)** **KM# 494.1** **Weight:** 31.1000 g. **Composition:** 0.9990 Silver 1.0000 oz. ASW **Series:** Libertad **Subject:** Libertad

| Date | Mintage | F | VF | XF | Unc | BU |
|---|---|---|---|---|---|---|
| 1982 | 1,050,000 | — | — | — | BV | 12.00 |
| 1983 | 1,002,000 | — | — | — | BV | 12.00 |
| 1983 Proof | 998 | Value: 185 | | | | |
| 1984 | 1,014,000 | — | — | — | BV | 12.00 |
| 1985 | 2,017,000 | — | — | — | BV | 12.00 |
| 1986 | 1,699,000 | — | — | — | BV | 12.50 |
| 1986 Proof | 30,000 | Value: 22.00 | | | | |
| 1987 | 500,000 | — | — | — | BV | 36.50 |
| 1987 Proof | 12,000 | Value: 45.00 | | | | |
| 1988 | 1,500,500 | — | — | BV | BV | 34.00 |
| 1989 | 1,397,000 | — | — | — | BV | 23.00 |
| 1989 Proof | 10,000 | Value: 39.00 | | | | |

**ONZA (Troy Ounce of Silver)** **KM# 494.2** **Weight:** 31.1000 g. **Composition:** 0.9990 Silver 1.0000 oz. ASW **Edge:** Reeded

| Date | Mintage | F | VF | XF | Unc | BU |
|---|---|---|---|---|---|---|
| 1988 Proof | 10,000 | Value: 32.00 | | | | |
| 1990 | 1,200,000 | — | — | — | BV | 12.50 |
| 1990 Proof | 10,000 | Value: 22.00 | | | | |
| 1991 | 1,651,000 | — | — | — | BV | 15.00 |

**ONZA (Troy Ounce of Silver)** **KM# 494.5** **Weight:** 31.1000 g. **Composition:** 0.9990 Silver 1.0000 oz. ASW **Series:** Libertad **Subject:** Libertad **Obverse:** KM#494.3 **Reverse:** KM#494.2 **Edge:** Reeded edge **Note:** Mule

| Date | Mintage | F | VF | XF | Unc | BU |
|---|---|---|---|---|---|---|
| 1991 Proof | 10,000 | Value: 32.00 | | | | |

**ONZA (Troy Ounce of Silver)** **KM# 494.3** **Weight:** 31.1000 g. **Composition:** 0.9990 Silver 1.0000 oz. ASW **Series:** Libertad **Subject:** Libertad **Obverse:** Eight dots below eagle's left talons **Reverse:** Revised design and lettering **Edge:** Reeded edge **Note:** Mule

| Date | Mintage | F | VF | XF | Unc | BU |
|---|---|---|---|---|---|---|
| 1991 | Inc. above | — | — | — | BV | 20.00 |
| 1992 | 2,458,000 | — | — | — | BV | 12.50 |
| 1992 Proof | 10,000 | Value: 32.00 | | | | |

**ONZA (Troy Ounce of Silver)** **KM# 494.4** **Weight:** 31.1000 g. **Composition:** 0.9990 Silver 1.0000 oz. ASW **Series:** Libertad **Subject:** Libertad **Obverse:** Seven dots below eagle's left talons, dull claws on right talon, thick letters **Reverse:** Revised design and lettering **Edge:** Reeded edge **Note:** Mule

| Date | Mintage | F | VF | XF | Unc | BU |
|---|---|---|---|---|---|---|
| 1993 | 1,000,000 | — | — | — | BV | 12.50 |
| 1993 Proof | — | Value: 34.00 | | | | |
| 1994 | 400,000 | — | — | — | BV | 12.50 |
| 1994 Proof | 10,000 | Value: 34.00 | | | | |
| 1995 | 500,000 | — | — | — | BV | 12.50 |
| 1995 Proof | 2,000 | Value: 35.00 | | | | |

**ONZA (Troy Ounce of Silver)** **KM# 613** **Weight:** 33.6250 g. **Composition:** 0.9250 Silver 1.0000 oz. ASW **Obverse:** Mexican eagle **Reverse:** Winged Victory

| Date | Mintage | F | VF | XF | Unc | BU |
|---|---|---|---|---|---|---|
| 1996 | 300,000 | — | — | — | — | 11.50 |
| 1996 Proof | 2,000 | Value: 34.00 | | | | |
| 1997 | 100,000 | — | — | — | — | 13.50 |
| 1997 Proof | 1,500 | Value: 32.50 | | | | |
| 1998 | 67,000 | — | — | — | — | 16.50 |
| 1998 Proof | 500 | Value: 35.00 | | | | |
| 1999 Proof | 600 | Value: 35.00 | | | | |
| 2000 | 340,000 | — | — | — | — | — |
| 2000 | 1,600 | — | — | — | — | — |

**ONZA (Troy Ounce of Silver)** **KM# 639** **Weight:** 31.1000 g. **Composition:** 0.9990 Silver 1.0000 oz. ASW **Series:** Libertad **Subject:** Libertad **Obverse:** Modern Mexican eagle within circle of obsolete versions **Edge:** Reeded edge **Note:** Mule

| Date | Mintage | F | VF | XF | Unc | BU |
|---|---|---|---|---|---|---|
| 2000 | — | — | — | — | — | 10.00 |
| 2000 | — | Value: 35.00 | | | | |

**2 ONZAS (2 Troy Ounces of Silver)** **KM# 614** **Weight:** 62.2070 g. **Composition:** 0.9990 Silver 2.0000 oz. ASW **Series:** Libertad **Obverse:** Mexican eagle **Reverse:** Winged Victory

| Date | Mintage | F | VF | XF | Unc | BU |
|---|---|---|---|---|---|---|
| 1996 | 50,000 | — | — | — | — | 22.00 |
| 1996 Proof | 1,200 | Value: 42.50 | | | | |
| 1997 | 15,000 | — | — | — | — | 20.00 |
| 1997 Proof | 1,300 | Value: 42.50 | | | | |
| 1998 | 7,000 | — | — | — | — | 27.50 |
| 1998 Proof | 400 | Value: 42.50 | | | | |
| 1999 Proof | 280 | Value: 42.50 | | | | |
| 2000 Proof | 500 | Value: 42.50 | | | | |
| 2001 | — | — | — | — | — | 22.50 |
| 2001 Proof | — | Value: 42.50 | | | | |

**5 ONZAS (5 Troy Ounces of Silver)** **KM# 615** **Weight:** 155.5175 g. **Composition:** 0.9990 Silver 5.0000 oz. ASW **Series:** Libertad **Obverse:** Mexican eagle **Reverse:** Winged Victory

| Date | Mintage | F | VF | XF | Unc | BU |
|---|---|---|---|---|---|---|
| 1996 | 20,000 | — | — | — | — | 48.50 |
| 1996 Proof | 1,200 | Value: 75.00 | | | | |
| 1997 | 10,000 | — | — | — | — | 48.50 |
| 1997 Proof | 1,300 | Value: 75.00 | | | | |
| 1998 | 3,500 | — | — | — | — | 48.50 |
| 1998 Proof | 400 | Value: 75.00 | | | | |
| 1999 Proof | 100 | Value: 75.00 | | | | |
| 2000 Proof | 500 | Value: 75.00 | | | | |
| 2001 | — | — | — | — | — | 48.50 |
| 2001 Proof | — | Value: 75.00 | | | | |

## GOLD BULLION COINAGE

**50 PESOS** **KM# 482** **Weight:** 41.6666 g. **Composition:** 0.9000 Gold 1.2057 oz. AGW

| Date | Mintage | F | VF | XF | Unc | BU |
|---|---|---|---|---|---|---|
| 1943 | 89,000 | — | — | — | BV | 525 |

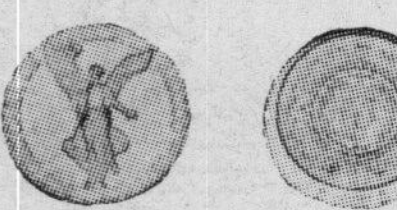

**1/20 ONZA (1/20 Ounce of Pure Gold)** **KM# 530** **Weight:** 1.7500 g. **Composition:** 0.9000 Gold .0500 oz. AGW **Obverse:** Winged Victory **Reverse:** Calendar stone

| Date | Mintage | F | VF | XF | Unc | BU |
|---|---|---|---|---|---|---|
| 1987 | — | — | — | — | — | BV+ 30 |
| 1988 | — | — | — | — | — | BV+30 |

**1/20 ONZA (1/20 Ounce of Pure Gold)** **KM# 589** **Weight:** 1.5551 g. **Composition:** 0.9990 Gold .500 oz. AGW **Obverse:** Winged Victory **Reverse:** Eagle and snake

| Date | Mintage | F | VF | XF | Unc | BU |
|---|---|---|---|---|---|---|
| 1991 | 10,000 | — | — | — | — | BV+30 |
| 1992 | 65,225 | — | — | — | — | BV+30 |
| 1993 | 10,000 | — | — | — | — | BV+30 |
| 1994 | 10,000 | — | — | — | — | BV+30 |
| 2000 | 5,300 | — | — | — | — | — |

**1/20 ONZA (1/20 Ounce of Pure Gold)** **KM# 642** **Weight:** 1.5551 g. **Composition:** 0.9990 Gold .500 oz. AGW **Obverse:** Winged Victory **Reverse:** Teocuitlatl and an Indian working

| Date | Mintage | F | VF | XF | Unc | BU |
|---|---|---|---|---|---|---|
| 2000 Proof | — | Value: 50.00 | | | | |

**1/15 ONZA (1/15 Ounce of Pure Gold)** **KM# 628** **Composition:** 0.9990 Gold **Obverse:** Winged Victory above legend

| Date | Mintage | F | VF | XF | Unc | BU |
|---|---|---|---|---|---|---|
| 1987 | — | — | — | — | — | BV+25 |

**1/10 ONZA (1/10 Ounce of Pure Gold)** **KM# 541** **Weight:** 3.1103 g. **Composition:** 0.9990 Gold .1000 oz. AGW

| Date | Mintage | F | VF | XF | Unc | BU |
|---|---|---|---|---|---|---|
| 1991 | 10,000 | — | — | — | — | BV+20 |
| 1992 | 50,777 | — | — | — | — | BV+20 |
| 1993 | 10,000 | — | — | — | — | BV+20 |
| 1994 | 10,000 | — | — | — | — | — |
| 2000 | 3,500 | — | — | — | — | — |

**1/4 ONZA (1/4 Ounce of Pure Gold)** **KM# 487** **Weight:** 8.6396 g. **Composition:** 0.9000 Gold .2500 oz. AGW **Note:** Similar to KM#488.

| Date | Mintage | F | VF | XF | Unc | BU |
|---|---|---|---|---|---|---|
| 1981 | 313,000 | — | — | — | — | BV+11 |

**1/4 ONZA (1/4 Ounce of Pure Gold)** **KM# 590** **Weight:** 7.7758 g. **Composition:** 0.9990 Gold .2500 oz. AGW **Obverse:** Winged Victory above legend **Reverse:** Eagle and snake

| Date | Mintage | F | VF | XF | Unc | BU |
|---|---|---|---|---|---|---|
| 1991 | 10,000 | — | — | — | — | BV+11 |
| 1992 | 28,106 | — | — | — | — | BV+11 |
| 1993 | 2,500 | — | — | — | — | BV+11 |
| 1994 | 2,500 | — | — | — | — | BV+11 |
| 2000 | 2,500 | — | — | — | — | — |

**1/2 ONZA (1/2 Ounce of Pure Gold)** **KM# 488** **Weight:** 17.2792 g. **Composition:** 0.9000 Gold .5000 oz. AGW

| Date | Mintage | F | VF | XF | Unc | BU |
|---|---|---|---|---|---|---|
| 1981 | 193,000 | — | — | — | — | BV+8 |
| 1989 Proof | 704 | Value: 500 | | | | |

**1/2 ONZA (1/2 Ounce of Pure Gold)** **KM# 591** **Weight:** 15.5517 g. **Composition:** 0.9990 Gold .5000 oz. AGW **Obverse:** Winged Victory above legend **Reverse:** Eagle and snake

| Date | Mintage | F | VF | XF | Unc | BU |
|---|---|---|---|---|---|---|
| 1991 | 10,000 | — | — | — | — | BV+8 |
| 1992 | 25,220 | — | — | — | — | BV+8 |
| 1993 | 2,500 | — | — | — | — | BV+8 |
| 1994 | 2,500 | — | — | — | — | BV+8 |
| 2000 | 1,500 | — | — | — | — | — |

**ONZA (Ounce of Pure Gold)** **KM# 489** **Weight:** 34.5585 g. **Composition:** 0.9000 Gold 1.0000 oz. AGW **Note:** Similar to KM#488.

| Date | Mintage | F | VF | XF | Unc | BU |
|---|---|---|---|---|---|---|
| 1981 | 596,000 | — | — | — | — | BV+3 |
| 1985 | — | — | — | — | — | BV+3 |
| 1988 | — | — | — | — | — | BV+3 |

**ONZA (Ounce of Pure Gold)** **KM# 592** **Weight:** 31.1035 g. **Composition:** 0.9990 Gold 1.0000 oz. AGW **Obverse:** Winged Victory above legend **Reverse:** Eagle and snake

| Date | Mintage | F | VF | XF | Unc | BU |
|---|---|---|---|---|---|---|
| 1991 | 109,193 | — | — | — | — | BV+3 |
| 1992 | 46,281 | — | — | — | — | BV+3 |
| 1993 | 10,000 | — | — | — | — | BV+3 |
| 1995 | 1,000 | — | — | — | — | BV+3 |
| 2000 | 2,730 | — | — | — | — | — |

## PLATINUM BULLION COINAGE

**1/4 ONZA (1/4 Ounce)** **KM# 538** **Weight:** 7.7775 g. **Composition:** 0.9990 Platinum .2500 oz. APW

| Date | Mintage | F | VF | XF | Unc | BU |
|---|---|---|---|---|---|---|
| 1989 | 704 | Value: 300 | | | | |

## MEDALLIC COINAGE

**10 PESOS** **KM# M91a** **Weight:** 8.3333 g. **Composition:** 0.9000 Gold .2411 oz. AGW **Subject:** 200th Anniversary - Birth of Hidalgo

| Date | Mintage | F | VF | XF | Unc | BU |
|---|---|---|---|---|---|---|
| 1953 | — | — | — | — | BV | 110 |

**10 PESOS** **KM# M123a** **Weight:** 8.3333 g. **Composition:** 0.9000 Gold .2411 oz. AGW **Subject:** Centennial of Constitution

| Date | Mintage | F | VF | XF | Unc | BU |
|---|---|---|---|---|---|---|
| 1957 | Est. 73,000 | — | — | — | BV | 110 |

**Note:** Mintage includes #M122a

**20 PESOS** **KM# M92a** **Weight:** 16.6666 g. **Composition:** 0.9000 Gold .4823 oz. AGW **Subject:** 200th Anniversary - Birth of Hidalgo

| Date | Mintage | F | VF | XF | Unc | BU |
|---|---|---|---|---|---|---|
| 1953 | — | — | — | — | BV | 200 |

**50 PESOS** **KM# M122a** **Weight:** 41.6666 g. **Composition:** 0.9000 Gold 1.2057 oz. AGW **Subject:** Centennial of Constitution

| Date | Mintage | F | VF | XF | Unc | BU |
|---|---|---|---|---|---|---|
| 1957 | Inc. M123a | — | — | — | BV | 520 |

## PATTERNS

including off metal strikes

| KM# | Date | Mintage | Identification | Mkt Val |
|---|---|---|---|---|
| Pn170 | 1901 | — | 20 Centavos. Bronze. | 425 |
| Pn171 | 1904 | — | Peso. Aluminum. | — |
| Pn172 | 1906 | — | 2 Centavos. Silver. | — |
| Pn174 | 1907 | — | 50 Centavos. Silver. Incuse lettered edge. | 3,500 |
| Pn173 | 1907 | — | 50 Centavos. Silver. Plain edge. | 4,000 |
| Pn175 | 1907 | — | 50 Centavos. Silver. Raised lettered edge. | 3,500 |
| Pn176 | 1908 | — | 50 Centavos. Silver. Plain edge. | 3,000 |
| Pn177 | 1908 | — | Peso. Silver. Plain edge. | — |
| Pn179 | 1909 | — | Peso. Silver. Incuse lettered edge. | — |
| Pn182 | 1909 | — | Peso. Bronzed Lead. Raised lettered edge. | — |
| Pn183 | 1909 | — | Peso. Silver. Raised lettered edge. | — |
| Pn178 | 1909 | — | Peso. Silver. Plain edge. | 7,000 |
| Pn180 | 1909 | — | Peso. Brass. Incuse lettered edge. | 3,250 |
| Pn181 | 1909 | — | Peso. Brass. Raised lettered edge. | 3,250 |
| Pn185 | 1911 | — | Peso. Silver. Plain edge. | 2,500 |
| Pn186 | 1911 | — | Peso. Bronze. Plain edge. | 2,500 |
| Pn187 | 1911 | — | Peso. Brass. Plain edge. | 2,500 |
| Pn188 | 1914 | — | 5 Centavos. Copper. | 200 |
| Pn189 | 1916 | — | 20 Pesos. Copper. | 1,150 |
| Pn191 | 1936 | — | Peso. Silver. | 3,200 |
| Pn190 | 1936 | — | Centavo. Copper-Nickel. | — |
| Pn192 | 1945 | — | 50 Centavos. Nickel. | 1,250 |
| Pn193 | 1947 | — | Peso. Silver. | 2,500 |
| Pn194 | 1947 | — | Peso. Silver. | 2,500 |
| Pn195 | 1947 | — | 5 Pesos. Silver. | 4,250 |
| Pn196 | 1947 | — | Onza. 0.9250 Silver. | 1,250 |
| Pn197 | 1950 | — | 5 Pesos. Silver. | 1,650 |
| Pn198 | 1951 | 2 | Onza. Silver. | 4,000 |
| Pn199 | 1954 | — | 50 Centavos. Bronze. | — |
| Pn200 | 1954 | — | 50 Centavos. Copper-Nickel. | — |
| Pn201 | 1955 | — | 50 Centavos. Bronze. | 625 |
| Pn202 | 1955 | — | Peso. Copper-Nickel. | 1,800 |
| Pn203 | 1962 | — | 5 Centavos. Copper-Nickel. | 60.00 |
| Pn204 | 1969 | — | Peso. Copper-Nickel. | 2,000 |
| Pn205 | 1969 | — | Peso. Copper-Nickel. | 1,650 |
| Pn206 | 1970 | — | 10 Centavos. Bronze. | 400 |
| Pn207 | 1970 | — | 25 Centavos. Copper-Nickel. | 750 |
| Pn208 | 1973 | — | 10 Pesos. Aluminum-Bronze. | 800 |
| Pn209 | 1974 | — | 10 Pesos. Copper-Nickel. | 600 |
| Pn210 | 1976 | 16 | 100 Pesos. 0.7200 Silver. | — |
| Pn211 | 1978 | — | Onza. Silver. | 3,000 |
| Pn212 | 1978 | — | Onza. 0.9250 Silver. | 2,500 |
| Pn214 | 1978 | — | Onza. 0.9250 Silver. | 2,000 |
| Pn215 | 1978 | — | Onza. 0.9250 Silver. | 1,750 |
| Pn216 | 1979 | — | Onza. 0.9250 Silver. | 2,000 |
| Pn217 | 1979 | — | 20 Pesos. | — |
| Pn218 | 1980 | 8 | 20 Centavos. Copper-Nickel. | — |
| Pn220 | 1980 | — | 10 Pesos. | — |
| Pn219 | 1980 | — | Peso. Brass. | 350 |

| KM# | Date | Mintage | Identification | Mkt Val |
|---|---|---|---|---|
| Pn221 | 1980 | — | 10 Pesos. Bronze. | 750 |
| Pn222 | 1980 | — | 20 Pesos. Copper-Nickel. | 300 |
| Pn223 | 1980 | — | 1/10 Onza. Silver. | 90.00 |
| Pn224 | 1981 | — | 20 Centavos. Copper-Nickel. Small obverse design. | 165 |
| Pn225 | 1981 | — | 20 Centavos. Copper-Nickel. Modified portrait. | 135 |
| Pn226 | 19xx | — | 20 Centavos. Copper. | 350 |
| Pn227 | 1983 | — | 50 Centavos. | 650 |
| Pn228 | 1983 | 12 | Peso. Stainless Steel. | 550 |
| Pn229 | 1983 | — | 5 Pesos. Bronze. | 350 |
| Pn230 | 1983 | — | Onza. Silver. Libertad. | 1,350 |
| Pn232 | | — | 50 Pesos. Gold. | — |
| Pn231 | 1984 | — | 50 Pesos. Copper-Nickel. | 400 |
| Pn233 | 1985 | — | Peso. Copper. | 325 |
| Pn235 | 1986 | — | Peso. Stainless Steel. | 65.00 |
| Pn236 | 1986 | — | 500 Pesos. Stainless Steel. | 500 |
| Pn237 | 1987 | 3 | 100 Pesos. Copper. | — |
| Pn238 | 1987 | 3 | 100 Pesos. Copper-Nickel. | — |
| Pn239 | 1988 | 3 | 100 Pesos. Brass. | — |
| Pn241 | 1988 | — | Onza. Silver. Plain edge. | — |
| Pn240 | 1988 | 3 | 500 Pesos. Aluminum-Brass. | 500 |
| Pn242 | 1990 | — | 50000 Pesos. Copper-Nickel. | 450 |
| Pn243 | 1990 | — | 100000 Pesos. Bronze. | 450 |
| Pn244 | 1991 | — | 100 Pesos. Aluminum. | 275 |
| Pn245 | 1991 | — | 200 Pesos. Aluminum. | 200 |
| Pn246 | 1991 | — | 500 Pesos. Bronze. | 400 |
| Pn247 | 1991 | — | 1000 Pesos. Bronze. | 35.00 |
| Pn248 | 1991 | — | 2000 Pesos. Bronze. | 400 |
| Pn249 | 1991 | — | 2000 Pesos. Steel. | 400 |
| Pn250 | 1991 | — | 2000 Pesos. | 325 |

## TRIAL STRIKES

| KM# | Date | Mintage | Identification | Mkt Val |
|---|---|---|---|---|
| TS15 | 190- | — | 8 Reales. Bronze-Plated Lead. | — |

| KM# | Date | Mintage | Identification | Mkt Val |
|---|---|---|---|---|
| TS16 | 1980 | — | 1/10 Onza. Copper. | 75.00 |
| TS17 | 1980 | — | 1/10 Onza. Silver. | 125 |

## MINT SETS

| KM# | Date | Mintage | Identification | Issue Price | Mkt Val |
|---|---|---|---|---|---|
| MS1 | 1977 (16) | 500 | | — | 500 |
| MSA2 | 1977 (9) | — | 434.1, 434.2, 442, 452, 460 thick date, 460 thin date, 472, 477.1, 483.2, Type II for 3-ring binder | — | 85.00 |
| MS2 | 1978 (9) | 500 | 434.1, 434.2, 442, 452, 460 open 8, 460 closed 8, 472, 477.2, 483.2, Type I flat pack | — | 150 |
| MS3 | 1978 (9) | — | KM434.1, 434.2, 442, 452, 460 open 8, 460 closed 8, 472, 477.2, 483.2, Type II for 3-ring binder | — | 65.00 |
| MS4 | 1979 (8) | — | KM434.2, 442, 452 square 9, 452 round 9, 460 (2), 477.2, 483.2, Type I flat pack | 11.00 | 8.00 |
| MS5 | 1979 (8) | — | KM434.1, 434.2, 442, 452 square 9, 452 round 9, 460, 477.2, 483.2, Type II for 3-ring binder | 11.00 | 9.00 |
| MS6 | 1980 (9) | — | KM434.2, 442, 452 square 9, 452 round 9, 460 open 8, 460 closed 8, 477.2, 485-486 | 4.20 | 11.00 |
| MS7 | 1981 (9) | — | KM442 open 8, 442 closed 8, 452 rectangular 9, 452 round 9, 460 open 8, 460 closed 8, 477.2, 485, 486 | 4.20 | 11.00 |
| MS8 | 1982 (7) | — | KM442, 452, 460, 477.2, 485, 486, 490 | — | 15.00 |
| MS10 | 1983 (11) | — | KM442 (2), 452 (2), 460 (2), 490 (1), 491 (2), 492 (2) for 3-ring plastic set | — | 12.50 |
| MS9 | 1983 (11) | — | KM442 (2), 452 (2), 460 (2), 490 (1), 491 (2), 492 (2), hard case set | — | 12.50 |
| MS11 | 1984 (8) | — | KM485, 486, 490, 491, 493, 495 (2), 496 | — | 17.50 |
| MS12 | 1985 (12) | — | KM477.2, 485, 493 (2), 495 (2), 496, 502, 508, 509, 510, 512 | — | 16.00 |
| MS14 | 1985/1986 (7) | — | KM493, 495, 496, 502, 508, 509, 512 | — | 18.50 |
| MS13 | 1986 (7) | — | KM493, 495, 496, 508, 512, 525, 529 | — | 18.00 |
| MS15 | 1987 (9) | — | KM493, 495 (2), 496, 502 (2), 512, 529 (2) | — | 35.00 |
| MS16 | 1988 (8) | — | KM493, 495a, 502, 508, 512, 529, 531, 536 | — | 20.00 |
| MS17 | 1996 (6) | — | KM546-549, 603-604 | 12.00 | 15.00 |

## PROOF SETS

| KM# | Date | Mintage | Identification | Issue Price | Mkt Val |
|---|---|---|---|---|---|
| PS1 | 1982/1983 (8) | 998 | KM442, 452, 460, 485, 477.2, 486, 490, 494.1 | 495 | 275 |
| PS2 | 1982/1983 (8) | — | KM460, 477.2, 485, 486, 490, 491, 492, PnB169 (in white box with Mo. in gold) | — | — |
| PS3 | 1982/1983 (7) | 23 | KM460, 477.2, 485, 486, 490, 491, 492 (in white box with Mo in gold) | — | 500 |
| PS4 | 1982/1983 (7) | 17 | KM460, 477.2, 485, 486, 490, 491, 492 (in white box ) | — | 500 |
| PS5 | 1982/1983 (7) | 8 | KM460, 477.2, 485, 486, 490, 491, 492 (in white box) | — | 500 |
| PS6 | 1983 (7) | 3 | KM460, 477.2, 485, 486, 490, 491, 492 | — | — |
| PS10 | 1985 (3) | — | KM503-505 (in blue box) | — | 60.00 |
| PS11 | 1985 (2) | — | KM511, 513 | — | 350 |
| PS7 | 1985/1986 (12) | — | KM497a-499a, 503-505, 514-515, 519, 521, 523-524 | — | 250 |
| PS8 | 1985 (4) | — | KM500.2-501.2, 506.2, 507.2 | — | 700 |
| PS9 | 1985 (3) | — | KM499a, 514, 515 (in blue box) | — | 60.00 |
| PS12 | 1989 (3) | 704 | KM488, 494.1, 538, Rainbow | 730 | 850 |
| PS13 | 1992 (5) | 5,000 | KM494.3, 542-545 | — | 87.50 |
| PS14 | 1993 (5) | 5,000 | KM494.4, 542-545 | — | 87.50 |
| PS15 | 1994 (5) | 5,000 | KM494.4, 542-545 | — | 85.00 |
| PS16 | 1995 (7) | — | KM546-550, 552, 553, 555 | 45.00 | 45.00 |

# MEXICO-REVOLUTIONARY

Revolution, 1910-1917

The Mexican independence movement, which is of interest and concern to collectors because of the warfare induced activity of local and state mints, began with the Sept. 16, 1810 march on the capital led by Father Miguel Hidalgo, a well-intentioned man of imagination and courage who proved to be an inept organizer and leader. Hidalgo was captured and executed within 10 months. His revolution, led by such as Morelos, Guerrero and Iturbide, continued and culminated in Mexican independence in 1821. Turbulent years followed. From 1821 to 1877 there were two emperors, several dictators and enough presidents to provide a change of government on the average of once every nine months. Porfirio Diaz, who had the longest tenure of any 19th century dictator in Latin American history, seized power in 1877 and did not relinquish it until 1911.

The final phase of Mexico's lengthy revolutionary period began in 1910 and lasted through the adoption of a liberal constitution and the election of a new congress in 1917. The 1910-1917 revolution was agrarian in character and intended to destroy the regime of Diaz and make Mexico economically and diplomatically independent. The republic experienced a state of upheaval that saw most of the leading figures of the revolution (Villa, Carranza, Obregon, Zapata, Calles) fighting each other at one time or another. Carranza eventually emerged as the most powerful figure of the early revolution. As *de-facto* president in 1916, he convened a constitutional convention, which produced a constitution in which the aims of the revolution were formulized. Obregon, perhaps the ablest general and wiliest politician of the lot, became Mexico's elected president in 1920, bringing the most disastrous but significant decade in Mexico's history to an end.

## AGUASCALIENTES

Aguascalientes is a state in central Mexico. Its coin issues, struck by authority of Pancho Villa, represent his deepest penetration into the Mexican heartland. Lack of silver made it necessary to make all denominations in copper.

## FRANCISCO "PANCHO" VILLA

### REVOLUTIONARY COINAGE

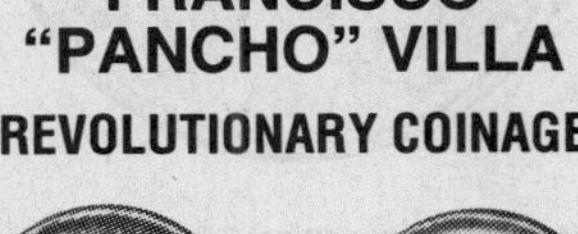

**CENTAVO KM# 601 Composition:** Copper

| Date | Mintage | VG | F | VF | XF | Unc |
|---|---|---|---|---|---|---|
| 1915 Large date, reeded edge | — | 25.00 | 40.00 | 60.00 | 90.00 | — |
| 1915 Large date, plain edge | — | 250 | 350 | 450 | — | — |
| 1915 Small date, reeded edge | — | 20.00 | 30.00 | 50.00 | 75.00 | — |
| 1915 Small date, plain edge | — | 30.00 | 50.00 | 75.00 | 115 | — |

**CENTAVO KM# 601a Composition:** Silver

| Date | Mintage | F | VF | XF | Unc | BU |
|---|---|---|---|---|---|---|
| 1915 Large date | 50 | — | 275 | 450 | — | — |
| 1915 Small date | Inc. above | — | 275 | 450 | — | — |

**2 CENTAVOS KM# 602.1 Composition:** Copper

| Date | Mintage | VG | F | VF | XF | Unc |
|---|---|---|---|---|---|---|
| 1915 Round front 2, plain edge | — | 40.00 | 100 | 200 | 350 | — |

**2 CENTAVOS KM# 602.2 Composition:** Copper

| Date | Mintage | VG | F | VF | XF | Unc |
|---|---|---|---|---|---|---|
| 1915 Square front 2, reeded edge | — | 35.00 | 60.00 | 85.00 | 200 | — |
| 1915 Square front 2, plain edge | — | 40.00 | 70.00 | 100 | 225 | — |

**2 CENTAVOS KM# 602a Composition:** Silver

| Date | Mintage | F | VF | XF | Unc | BU |
|---|---|---|---|---|---|---|
| 1915 | 50 | — | 600 | 1,000 | — | — |

**5 CENTAVOS KM# 603 Composition:** Copper

| Date | Mintage | VG | F | VF | XF | Unc |
|---|---|---|---|---|---|---|
| 1915 Plain edge; Rare | — | — | — | — | — | — |
| 1915 Reeded edge | — | 10.00 | 15.00 | 25.00 | 35.00 | — |

**5 CENTAVOS KM# 604.1 Composition:** Copper **Reverse:** Vertically shaded 5

| Date | Mintage | VG | F | VF | XF | Unc |
|---|---|---|---|---|---|---|
| 1915 Reeded edge | — | 10.00 | 15.00 | 25.00 | 35.00 | — |
| 1915 Plain edge | — | 100 | 150 | 225 | 325 | — |

**5 CENTAVOS KM# 604.2 Composition:** Copper **Reverse:** Horizontally shaded 5

| Date | Mintage | VG | F | VF | XF | Unc |
|---|---|---|---|---|---|---|
| 1915 Reeded edge | — | 15.00 | 20.00 | 35.00 | 50.00 | — |
| 1915 Plain edge | — | 20.00 | 30.00 | 50.00 | 80.00 | — |

**5 CENTAVOS KM# 604a Composition:** Silver

| Date | Mintage | F | VF | XF | Unc | BU |
|---|---|---|---|---|---|---|
| 1915 | 50 | — | 1,000 | 2,000 | — | — |

**20 CENTAVOS** KM# 606 **Composition:** Copper **Obverse:** Blunt winged eagle **Reverse:** With wavy-bottomed 2

| Date | Mintage | VG | F | VF | XF | Unc |
|---|---|---|---|---|---|---|
| 1915 Reeded edge | — | 4.50 | 6.00 | 9.00 | 20.00 | — |

**20 CENTAVOS** KM# 605 **Composition:** Copper **Obverse:** Blunt winged eagle **Reverse:** With flat-bottomed 2

| Date | Mintage | VG | F | VF | XF | Unc |
|---|---|---|---|---|---|---|
| 1915 Reeded edge | — | 4.50 | 6.00 | 9.00 | 22.00 | — |

**20 CENTAVOS** KM# 605a **Composition:** Silver **Obverse:** Blunt winged eagle **Reverse:** With flat-bottomed 2 **Note:** Piedfort.

| Date | Mintage | F | VF | XF | Unc | BU |
|---|---|---|---|---|---|---|
| 1915 Plain edge | 50 | — | 1,200 | 2,000 | — | — |

**20 CENTAVOS** KM# 600 **Composition:** Copper **Obverse:** Pointed winged eagle **Reverse:** With wavy-bottomed 2

| Date | Mintage | VG | F | VF | XF | Unc |
|---|---|---|---|---|---|---|
| 1915 Reeded edge | — | 15.00 | 20.00 | 35.00 | 60.00 | — |

**20 CENTAVOS** KM# 600a **Composition:** Silver **Obverse:** Pointed winged eagle **Reverse:** With wavy-bottomed 2

| Date | Mintage | VG | F | VF | XF | Unc |
|---|---|---|---|---|---|---|
| 1915 | — | 800 | 1,200 | 1,600 | 2,000 | — |

**Note:** Varieties exist with both plain and milled edges and many variations in the shading of the numerals

## CHIHUAHUA

Chihuahua is a northern state of Mexico bordering the U.S. It was the arena that introduced Pancho Villa to the world. Villa, an outlaw, was given a title when asked by Madero to participate in maintaining order during Madero's presidency. After Madero's death in February 1913, Villa became a persuasive leader. Chihuahua was where he made his first coins - the Parral series. The *Army of the North* pesos also came from this state. This coin helped Villa recruit soldiers because of his ability to pay in silver while others were paying in worthless paper money.

## HIDALGO DEL PARRAL

### Fuerzas Constitucionalistas

### REVOLUTIONARY COINAGE

**2 CENTAVOS** KM# 607 **Composition:** Copper

| Date | Mintage | VG | F | VF | XF | Unc |
|---|---|---|---|---|---|---|
| 1913 | — | 2.50 | 4.00 | 8.00 | 15.00 | — |

**2 CENTAVOS** KM# 607a **Composition:** Brass

| Date | Mintage | VG | F | VF | XF | Unc |
|---|---|---|---|---|---|---|
| 1913 | — | 60.00 | 80.00 | 100 | 200 | — |

**50 CENTAVOS** KM# 608 **Composition:** Silver **Edge:** Reeded edge

| Date | Mintage | VG | F | VF | XF | Unc |
|---|---|---|---|---|---|---|
| 1913 | — | 9.00 | 15.00 | 20.00 | 40.00 | — |

**50 CENTAVOS** KM# 609 **Composition:** Silver **Edge:** Plain edge

| Date | Mintage | VG | F | VF | XF | Unc |
|---|---|---|---|---|---|---|
| 1913 | — | 40.00 | 60.00 | 80.00 | 100 | — |

**50 CENTAVOS** KM# 609a **Composition:** Copper **Edge:** Plain edge

| Date | Mintage | VG | F | VF | XF | Unc |
|---|---|---|---|---|---|---|
| 1913 rare | — | — | — | — | — | — |

**PESO** KM# 610 **Composition:** Silver **Reverse:** 1 through PESO and ball, BOLITA

| Date | Mintage | VG | F | VF | XF | Unc |
|---|---|---|---|---|---|---|
| 1913 | — | 900 | 1,200 | 1,800 | 2,000 | — |

**PESO** KM# 611 **Composition:** Silver **Obverse:** Similar to KM#610 **Reverse:** 1 above PESO

| Date | Mintage | VG | F | VF | XF | Unc |
|---|---|---|---|---|---|---|
| 1913 | — | 35.00 | 40.00 | 55.00 | 135 | — |

**Note:** Well struck counterfeits of this coin exist with the dot at the end of the word Peso even with the bottom of the O. On legitimate pieces the dot is slightly higher

## CONSTITUTIONALIST ARMY

### Ejercito Constitucionalista

### REVOLUTIONARY COINAGE

**5 CENTAVOS** KM# 612 **Composition:** Copper **Reverse:** Small rosettes at date

| Date | Mintage | VG | F | VF | XF | Unc |
|---|---|---|---|---|---|---|
| 1914 | — | 20.00 | 30.00 | 50.00 | 80.00 | — |

**5 CENTAVOS** KM# 613 **Composition:** Copper **Reverse:** Large ornamental spear heads at date **Note:** Numerous varieties exist.

| Date | Mintage | VG | F | VF | XF | Unc |
|---|---|---|---|---|---|---|
| 1914 | — | 1.00 | 2.50 | 3.50 | 4.50 | — |
| 1915 | — | 1.00 | 2.50 | 3.50 | 4.50 | — |

**5 CENTAVOS** KM# 613a **Composition:** Brass **Reverse:** Large ornamental spear heads at date **Note:** Numerous varieties exist.

| Date | Mintage | VG | F | VF | XF | Unc |
|---|---|---|---|---|---|---|
| 1914 | — | 2.00 | 3.00 | 6.00 | 8.00 | — |
| 1915 | — | 2.00 | 3.00 | 6.00 | 8.00 | — |

**5 CENTAVOS** KM# 613b **Composition:** Cast Copper **Reverse:** Large ornamental spear heads at date

| Date | Mintage | VG | F | VF | XF | Unc |
|---|---|---|---|---|---|---|
| 1914 | — | 75.00 | 100 | 200 | 250 | — |

**5 CENTAVOS** KM# 614 **Composition:** Copper **Reverse:** Double lined V

| Date | Mintage | VG | F | VF | XF | Unc |
|---|---|---|---|---|---|---|
| 1915 MS | — | 150 | 250 | 325 | 500 | — |
| 1915 SS Unique | — | — | — | — | — | — |

**5 CENTAVOS** KM# 614a **Composition:** Copper **Reverse:** Solid V

| Date | Mintage | VG | F | VF | XF | Unc |
|---|---|---|---|---|---|---|
| 1915 Rare | — | — | — | — | — | — |

**5 CENTAVOS** KM# 614b **Composition:** Copper **Obverse:** KM#614 **Reverse:** Reverse of KM#613 **Note:** Mule.

| Date | Mintage | VG | F | VF | XF | Unc |
|---|---|---|---|---|---|---|
| 1915 | — | — | 350 | — | — | — |

**5 CENTAVOS** KM# 614c **Composition:** Copper **Obverse:** KM#614 **Reverse:** Obverse of KM#612 **Note:** Mule.

| Date | Mintage | VG | F | VF | XF | Unc |
|---|---|---|---|---|---|---|
| 1915 Rare | — | — | — | — | — | — |

**10 CENTAVOS** KM# 615 **Composition:** Copper

| Date | Mintage | VG | F | VF | XF | Unc |
|---|---|---|---|---|---|---|
| 1915 | — | 1.25 | 2.50 | 3.50 | 5.00 | — |

**10 CENTAVOS** KM# 615a **Composition:** Brass

| Date | Mintage | VG | F | VF | XF | Unc |
|---|---|---|---|---|---|---|
| 1915 | — | 1.75 | 5.00 | 15.00 | 20.00 | — |

**Note:** Many varieties exist

# ARMY OF THE NORTH
## Ejercito Del Norte
## REVOLUTIONARY COINAGE

**PESO** **KM# 619** **Composition:** Silver

| Date | Mintage | VG | F | VF | XF | Unc |
|---|---|---|---|---|---|---|
| 1915 | — | 15.00 | 25.00 | 35.00 | 65.00 | — |

**PESO** **KM# 619a** **Composition:** Copper

| Date | Mintage | VG | F | VF | XF | Unc |
|---|---|---|---|---|---|---|
| 1915 | — | 450 | 750 | 1,000 | 1,500 | — |

**PESO** **KM# 619b** **Composition:** Brass **Note:** Uniface obverse

| Date | Mintage | VG | F | VF | XF | Unc |
|---|---|---|---|---|---|---|
| 1915 Rare | — | — | — | — | — | — |

## PATTERNS
### Constitutionalist Army

| KM# | Date | Mintage | Identification | Mkt Val |
|---|---|---|---|---|
| Pn1 | 1913 | — | Peso. Silver. | — |
| Pn4 | 1914 | — | Peso. Silver. | — |

**Note:** Silver or silver plated copper pieces are modern fantasies

| KM# | Date | Mintage | Identification | Mkt Val |
|---|---|---|---|---|
| Pn2.1 | 1914 | — | 50 Centavos. Copper. Reeded edge. | 800 |
| Pn2.2 | 1914 | — | 50 Centavos. Copper. Plain edge. | 1,000 |

**Note:** Specimens exist in silver plated copper

| KM# | Date | Mintage | Identification | Mkt Val |
|---|---|---|---|---|
| Pn3 | 1914 | — | Peso. Copper. | 2,000 |

# DURANGO

A state in north central Mexico. Another area of operation for Pancho Villa. The *Muera Huerta* peso originates in this state. The coins were made in Cuencame under the orders of Generals Cemceros and Contreras.

# CUENCAME
## Muera Huerta (Death to Huerta)
## REVOLUTIONARY COINAGE

**PESO** **KM# 620** **Composition:** Silver **Reverse:** 1914 below UN PESO with 3 stars at each side

| Date | Mintage | VG | F | VF | XF | Unc |
|---|---|---|---|---|---|---|
| 1914 | — | 800 | 1,000 | 1,400 | 2,500 | — |

**PESO** **KM# 621** **Composition:** Silver **Obverse:** Continuous border **Reverse:** Continuous border

| Date | Mintage | VG | F | VF | XF | Unc |
|---|---|---|---|---|---|---|
| 1914 | — | 60.00 | 90.00 | 120 | 200 | — |

**PESO** **KM# 621a** **Composition:** Copper **Obverse:** Continuous border **Reverse:** Continuous border **Note:** Varieties exist.

| Date | Mintage | VG | F | VF | XF | Unc |
|---|---|---|---|---|---|---|
| 1914 | — | 250 | 425 | 650 | 1,200 | — |

**PESO** **KM# 621b** **Composition:** Brass

| Date | Mintage | VG | F | VF | XF | Unc |
|---|---|---|---|---|---|---|
| 1914 | — | — | 600 | 800 | 1,500 | — |

**PESO** **KM# 622** **Composition:** Silver **Obverse:** Dot and dash border **Reverse:** Continuous border

| Date | Mintage | VG | F | VF | XF | Unc |
|---|---|---|---|---|---|---|
| 1914 | — | 60.00 | 100 | 150 | 225 | — |

**Note:** The so-called 20 Pesos gold Muera Huerta pieces are modern fantasies. Refer to Unusual World Coins, 3rd edition, ©1989, Krause Publications, Inc

# ESTADO DE DURANGO
## REVOLUTIONARY COINAGE

**CENTAVO** **KM# 625** **Composition:** Copper

| Date | Mintage | VG | F | VF | XF | Unc |
|---|---|---|---|---|---|---|
| 1914 | — | 2.00 | 3.00 | 5.00 | 7.50 | — |

**CENTAVO** **KM# 625a** **Composition:** Brass

| Date | Mintage | VG | F | VF | XF | Unc |
|---|---|---|---|---|---|---|
| 1914 | — | 9.00 | 15.00 | 20.00 | 30.00 | — |

**CENTAVO** **KM# 625b** **Composition:** Lead

| Date | Mintage | VG | F | VF | XF | Unc |
|---|---|---|---|---|---|---|
| 1914 | — | 20.00 | 40.00 | 65.00 | 90.00 | — |

**CENTAVO** **KM# 625c** **Composition:** Copper **Obverse:** Obverse of KM#625 **Reverse:** Obverse of KM#625

| Date | Mintage | VG | F | VF | XF | Unc |
|---|---|---|---|---|---|---|
| 1914 | — | 25.00 | 50.00 | 80.00 | 125 | — |

**CENTAVO** **KM# 624** **Composition:** Cast Lead **Reverse:** Retrograde N

| Date | Mintage | VG | F | VF | XF | Unc |
|---|---|---|---|---|---|---|
| 1914 | — | 45.00 | 75.00 | 100 | 200 | — |

**CENTAVO** **KM# 626** **Composition:** Copper

| Date | Mintage | VG | F | VF | XF | Unc |
|---|---|---|---|---|---|---|
| 1914 | — | 15.00 | 20.00 | 35.00 | 45.00 | — |

**CENTAVO** **KM# 626a** **Composition:** Brass

| Date | Mintage | VG | F | VF | XF | Unc |
|---|---|---|---|---|---|---|
| 1914 | — | 50.00 | 75.00 | 100 | 250 | — |

**CENTAVO** **KM# 626b** **Composition:** Lead

| Date | Mintage | VG | F | VF | XF | Unc |
|---|---|---|---|---|---|---|
| 1914 | — | 20.00 | 25.00 | 40.00 | 60.00 | — |

**Note:** Varieties in size exist

**CENTAVO** **KM# 627** **Composition:** Copper **Obverse:** Three stars below date **Reverse:** Retrograde N

| Date | Mintage | VG | F | VF | XF | Unc |
|---|---|---|---|---|---|---|
| 1914 | — | 6.00 | 10.00 | 15.00 | 20.00 | — |

**CENTAVO** **KM# 627a** **Composition:** Lead **Obverse:** Three stars below date **Reverse:** Retrograde N

| Date | Mintage | VG | F | VF | XF | Unc |
|---|---|---|---|---|---|---|
| 1914 | — | 20.00 | 30.00 | 40.00 | 50.00 | — |

**CENTAVO** **KM# 628** **Composition:** Aluminum **Obverse:** Eagle on cactus

| Date | Mintage | VG | F | VF | XF | Unc |
|---|---|---|---|---|---|---|
| 1914 | — | 0.65 | 1.00 | 2.00 | 3.00 | — |

**5 CENTAVOS** **KM# 629** **Composition:** Copper **Obv. Legend:** ESTADO DE DURANGO **Reverse:** Large 5

| Date | Mintage | VG | F | VF | XF | Unc |
|---|---|---|---|---|---|---|
| 1914 | — | 1.25 | 2.00 | 4.00 | 7.00 | — |

**5 CENTAVOS** **KM# 630** **Composition:** Copper **Obv. Legend:** E. DE DURANGO **Reverse:** Thin 5

| Date | Mintage | VG | F | VF | XF | Unc |
|---|---|---|---|---|---|---|
| 1914 | — | 125 | 275 | 375 | 600 | — |

**5 CENTAVOS** **KM# 631** **Composition:** Copper **Obv. Legend:** E. DE DURANGO **Reverse:** Thick 5

| Date | Mintage | VG | F | VF | XF | Unc |
|---|---|---|---|---|---|---|
| 1914 | — | 1.25 | 2.00 | 4.00 | 7.50 | — |

**5 CENTAVOS** **KM# 631a** **Composition:** Brass **Obv. Legend:** E. DE DURANGO **Reverse:** Thick 5

| Date | Mintage | VG | F | VF | XF | Unc |
|---|---|---|---|---|---|---|
| 1914 | — | 30.00 | 40.00 | 50.00 | 85.00 | — |

**5 CENTAVOS** **KM# 631b** **Composition:** Lead **Obv. Legend:** E. DE DURANGO **Reverse:** Thick 5

| Date | Mintage | VG | F | VF | XF | Unc |
|---|---|---|---|---|---|---|
| 1914 | — | 45.00 | 70.00 | 100 | 180 | — |

**5 CENTAVOS** **KM# 632** **Composition:** Copper **Obv. Legend:** E. DE DURANGO **Reverse:** Denomination V

| Date | Mintage | VG | F | VF | XF | Unc |
|---|---|---|---|---|---|---|
| 1914 | — | 3.00 | 5.00 | 9.00 | 20.00 | — |

**5 CENTAVOS** **KM# 632a** **Composition:** Lead **Obv. Legend:** E. DE DURANGO **Reverse:** Denomination V

| Date | Mintage | VG | F | VF | XF | Unc |
|---|---|---|---|---|---|---|
| 1914 | — | 50.00 | 75.00 | 100 | 150 | — |

**5 CENTAVOS** **KM# 633** **Composition:** Lead **Obverse:** 3 stars below 1914 **Reverse:** 5 CVS

| Date | Mintage | VG | F | VF | XF | Unc |
|---|---|---|---|---|---|---|
| 1914 | — | — | 400 | 800 | — | — |

**5 CENTAVOS** **KM# 634** **Composition:** Brass

| Date | Mintage | VG | F | VF | XF | Unc |
|---|---|---|---|---|---|---|
| 1914 | — | 0.50 | 1.00 | 2.00 | 3.50 | — |

**5 CENTAVOS** **KM# 634a** **Composition:** Copper

| Date | Mintage | VG | F | VF | XF | Unc |
|---|---|---|---|---|---|---|
| 1914 | — | 75.00 | 100 | 145 | 175 | — |

**Note:** There are numerous varieties of these general types of the Durango 1 and 5 Centavo pieces

## GUERRERO

Guerrero is a state on the southwestern coast of Mexico. It was one of the areas of operation of Zapata and his forces in the south of Mexico. The Zapata forces operated seven different mints in this state. The date ranges were from 1914 to 1917 and denominations from 2 Centavos to 2 Pesos. Some were cast but most were struck and the rarest coin of the group is the Suriana 1915 2 Pesos.

## EMILIANO ZAPATA
### (General Salgado)
### REVOLUTIONARY COINAGE

**2 CENTAVOS** **KM# 638** **Composition:** Copper

| Date | Mintage | VG | F | VF | XF | Unc |
|---|---|---|---|---|---|---|
| 1915 | — | 75.00 | 125 | 175 | 250 | — |

**3 CENTAVOS** **KM# 635** **Composition:** Copper

| Date | Mintage | VG | F | VF | XF | Unc |
|---|---|---|---|---|---|---|
| 1915 | — | 500 | 1,000 | 1,500 | 2,000 | — |

**5 CENTAVOS** **KM# 636** **Composition:** Copper

| Date | Mintage | VG | F | VF | XF | Unc |
|---|---|---|---|---|---|---|
| 1915GRO | — | 800 | 1,200 | 1,800 | 2,600 | — |

**10 CENTAVOS** **KM# 637.1** **Composition:** Copper **Obverse:** Snake head ends at L in REPUBLICA

| Date | Mintage | VG | F | VF | XF | Unc |
|---|---|---|---|---|---|---|
| 1915GRO | — | 600 | 800 | 1,000 | 1,500 | — |

**10 CENTAVOS** **KM# 637.2** **Composition:** Copper **Obverse:** Snake head ends at C in REPUBLICA

| Date | Mintage | VG | F | VF | XF | Unc |
|---|---|---|---|---|---|---|
| 1915GRO | — | 2.00 | 3.00 | 6.50 | 7.50 | — |

**10 CENTAVOS** **KM# 637.2a** **Composition:** Brass **Obverse:** Snake head ends at C in REPUBLICA

| Date | Mintage | VG | F | VF | XF | Unc |
|---|---|---|---|---|---|---|
| 1915GRO | — | 8.00 | 15.00 | 25.00 | 50.00 | — |

**10 CENTAVOS** **KM# 637.2b** **Composition:** Lead **Obverse:** Snake head ends at C in REPUBLICA

| Date | Mintage | VG | F | VF | XF | Unc |
|---|---|---|---|---|---|---|
| 1915GRO | — | 50.00 | 75.00 | 175 | 275 | — |

**10 CENTAVOS** **KM# 637.3** **Composition:** Copper **Obverse:** Snake head ends before A in REPUBLICA **Reverse:** Dot after date

| Date | Mintage | VG | F | VF | XF | Unc |
|---|---|---|---|---|---|---|
| 1915GRO | — | 2.00 | 3.00 | 6.50 | 7.50 | — |

**10 CENTAVOS** **KM# 637.3a** **Composition:** Brass **Obverse:** Snake head ends before A in REPUBLICA **Reverse:** Dot after date

| Date | Mintage | VG | F | VF | XF | Unc |
|---|---|---|---|---|---|---|
| 1915GRO | — | 8.00 | 15.00 | 25.00 | 50.00 | — |

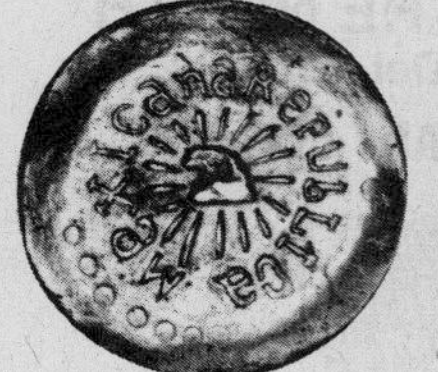

**25 CENTAVOS** **KM# 639** **Composition:** Silver **Obverse:** Cap and rays

| Date | Mintage | VG | F | VF | XF | Unc |
|---|---|---|---|---|---|---|
| 1915 | — | 100 | 200 | 300 | 450 | — |

**50 CENTAVOS** **KM# 640** **Composition:** Silver **Obverse:** Cap and rays

| Date | Mintage | VG | F | VF | XF | Unc |
|---|---|---|---|---|---|---|
| 1915 | — | 900 | 1,500 | 2,100 | 3,000 | — |

**PESO (UN)** **KM# 641a** **Composition:** Copper

| Date | Mintage | Good | VG | F | VF | XF |
|---|---|---|---|---|---|---|
| 1914 | — | — | 100 | 150 | 225 | 900 |

**PESO (UN)** **KM# 641** **Weight:** 0.3000 g. **Composition:** 1.0000 Gold-Silver **Obverse:** Star before UN PESO **Reverse:** Cap and rays

| Date | Mintage | VG | F | VF | XF | Unc |
|---|---|---|---|---|---|---|
| 1914 | — | 15.00 | 25.00 | 35.00 | 65.00 | — |

**Note:** Many die varieties exist

**PESO (UN)** **KM# 642** **Weight:** 0.3000 g. **Composition:** 1.0000 Gold-Silver **Obverse:** Star before and after UN PESO **Reverse:** Cap and rays

| Date | Mintage | VG | F | VF | XF | Unc |
|---|---|---|---|---|---|---|
| 1914 | — | 50.00 | 75.00 | 100 | 150 | — |
| 1915 | — | 600 | 1,000 | 1,500 | 1,800 | — |

**2 PESOS (Dos)** **KM# 643** **Weight:** 0.5950 g. **Composition:** 1.0000 Gold-Silver **Reverse:** Sun and mountains

| Date | Mintage | VG | F | VF | XF | Unc |
|---|---|---|---|---|---|---|
| 1914GRO | — | 12.00 | 20.00 | 32.00 | 60.00 | — |

**Note:** Many varieties exist

**2 PESOS (Dos)** **KM# 643a** **Composition:** Copper

| Date | Mintage | Good | VG | F | VF | XF |
|---|---|---|---|---|---|---|
| 1914 | — | — | — | 600 | 700 | 1,000 |

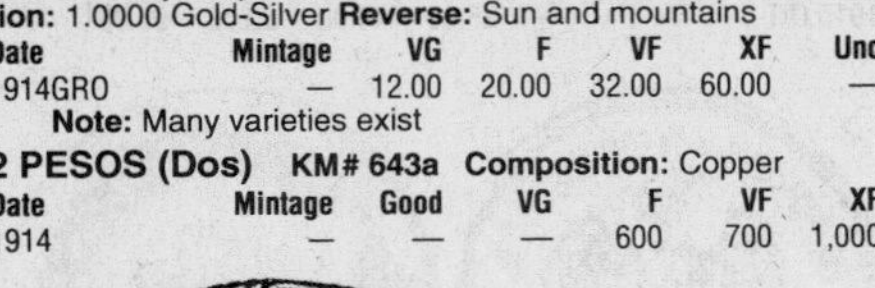

**2 PESOS (Dos)** **KM# 644** **Weight:** 0.5950 g. **Composition:** 1.0000 Gold-Silver **Reverse:** Sun and mountains

| Date | Mintage | VG | F | VF | XF | Unc |
|---|---|---|---|---|---|---|
| 1915GRO | — | 65.00 | 85.00 | 160 | 200 | — |

**2 PESOS (Dos)** **KM# 644a** **Composition:** Copper **Reverse:** Sun and mountains

| Date | Mintage | VG | F | VF | XF | Unc |
|---|---|---|---|---|---|---|
| 1915GRO | — | 400 | 600 | 800 | 1,000 | — |

## ATLIXTAC

### REVOLUTIONARY COINAGE

**10 CENTAVOS** **KM# 645** **Composition:** Copper

| Date | Mintage | VG | F | VF | XF | Unc |
|---|---|---|---|---|---|---|
| 1915 | — | 3.00 | 4.00 | 6.50 | 10.00 | — |

**10 CENTAVOS** **KM# 646** **Composition:** Copper **Obverse:** Stars in legend

| Date | Mintage | VG | F | VF | XF | Unc |
|---|---|---|---|---|---|---|
| 1915 | — | 3.00 | 4.00 | 6.50 | 10.00 | — |

## CACAHUATEPEC

### REVOLUTIONARY COINAGE

**5 CENTAVOS** **KM# 648** **Composition:** Copper

| Date | Mintage | VG | F | VF | XF | Unc |
|---|---|---|---|---|---|---|
| 1917 | — | 12.00 | 25.00 | 40.00 | 75.00 | — |

**20 CENTAVOS** **KM# 649** **Composition:** Silver **Reverse:** Cap and rays above denomination

| Date | Mintage | VG | F | VF | XF | Unc |
|---|---|---|---|---|---|---|
| 1917 | — | 75.00 | 125 | 200 | 250 | — |

**50 CENTAVOS** **KM# 650** **Composition:** Silver **Reverse:** Cap and rays above denomination

| Date | Mintage | VG | F | VF | XF | Unc |
|---|---|---|---|---|---|---|
| 1917 | — | 10.00 | 20.00 | 35.00 | 75.00 | — |

**PESO (UN)** **KM# 651** **Composition:** Silver **Reverse:** Cap and rays

| Date | Mintage | VG | F | VF | XF | Unc |
|---|---|---|---|---|---|---|
| 1917 L.V. Go | — | 1,250 | 2,250 | 3,500 | 5,000 | — |

## CACALOTEPEC

### REVOLUTIONARY COINAGE

**20 CENTAVOS** **KM# 652** **Composition:** Silver **Reverse:** Cap and rays above denomination

| Date | Mintage | VG | F | VF | XF | Unc |
|---|---|---|---|---|---|---|
| 1917 | — | 800 | 1,400 | 1,800 | 2,250 | — |

## CAMPO MORADO

### REVOLUTIONARY COINAGE

**5 CENTAVOS** **KM# 653** **Composition:** Copper

| Date | Mintage | VG | F | VF | XF | Unc |
|---|---|---|---|---|---|---|
| 1915 C.M. | — | 9.00 | 15.00 | 22.50 | 35.00 | — |

**10 CENTAVOS** **KM# 654** **Composition:** Copper

| Date | Mintage | VG | F | VF | XF | Unc |
|---|---|---|---|---|---|---|
| 1915 C.M. GRO | — | 6.00 | 10.00 | 17.50 | 27.50 | — |

**20 CENTAVOS** **KM# 655** **Composition:** Copper

| Date | Mintage | VG | F | VF | XF | Unc |
|---|---|---|---|---|---|---|
| 1915 C.M. GRO | — | 15.00 | 25.00 | 35.00 | 50.00 | — |

**50 CENTAVOS** **KM# 656** **Composition:** Copper **Obverse:** UN PESO effaced below eagle

| Date | Mintage | VG | F | VF | XF | Unc |
|---|---|---|---|---|---|---|
| 1915 C.M. GRO | — | 12.00 | 20.00 | 30.00 | 60.00 | — |

**50 CENTAVOS** **KM# 657** **Composition:** Copper **Note:** Regular obverse.

| Date | Mintage | VG | F | VF | XF | Unc |
|---|---|---|---|---|---|---|
| 1915 C.M. GRO | — | 6.00 | 10.00 | 15.00 | 25.00 | — |

**50 CENTAVOS** **KM# 657a** **Composition:** Base Silver **Note:** Regular obverse.

| Date | Mintage | VG | F | VF | XF | Unc |
|---|---|---|---|---|---|---|
| 1915 C.M. GRO | — | 165 | 275 | 400 | 575 | — |

**PESO (UN)** **KM# 658** **Weight:** 0.3000 g. **Composition:** 1.0000 Gold-Silver **Obverse:** Date below eagle

| Date | Mintage | VG | F | VF | XF | Unc |
|---|---|---|---|---|---|---|
| 1914 Co Mo Gro | — | 450 | 500 | 750 | 900 | — |

**PESO (UN)** **KM# 658a** **Composition:** Brass **Obverse:** Date below eagle

| Date | Mintage | VG | F | VF | XF | Unc |
|---|---|---|---|---|---|---|
| 1914 Co Mo Gro Unique | — | — | — | — | — | — |

**PESO (UN)** **KM# 659** **Weight:** 0.3000 g. **Composition:** 1.0000 Gold-Silver **Reverse:** Date below Liberty cap

| Date | Mintage | VG | F | VF | XF | Unc |
|---|---|---|---|---|---|---|
| 1914 CAMPO Mo | — | 15.00 | 30.00 | 45.00 | 60.00 | — |

**2 PESOS (Dos)** **KM# 660** **Weight:** 0.5950 g. **Composition:** 1.0000 Gold-Silver **Reverse:** Sun over mountains

| Date | Mintage | VG | F | VF | XF | Unc |
|---|---|---|---|---|---|---|
| 1915 Co. Mo. | — | 12.00 | 20.00 | 30.00 | 50.00 | — |

**2 PESOS (Dos)** **KM# 660a** **Composition:** Copper **Reverse:** Sun over mountains

| Date | Mintage | VG | F | VF | XF | Unc |
|---|---|---|---|---|---|---|
| 1915 Co. Mo. | — | — | 600 | 800 | 1,000 | — |

**2 PESOS (Dos)** **KM# 661** **Weight:** 0.5950 g. **Composition:** 1.0000 Gold-Silver **Reverse:** Star before and after Co. Mo

| Date | Mintage | VG | F | VF | XF | Unc |
|---|---|---|---|---|---|---|
| 1915 Co. Mo. | — | 1,200 | 1,500 | 2,000 | 3,000 | — |

**2 PESOS (Dos)** **KM# 662** **Weight:** 0.5950 g. **Composition:** 1.0000 Gold-Silver **Reverse:** Cap and rays

| Date | Mintage | VG | F | VF | XF | Unc |
|---|---|---|---|---|---|---|
| 1915 C. M. GRO | — | 15.00 | 25.00 | 35.00 | 60.00 | — |

**2 PESOS (Dos)** **KM# 662a.1** **Composition:** Copper **Reverse:** Cap and rays

| Date | Mintage | VG | F | VF | XF | Unc |
|---|---|---|---|---|---|---|
| 1915 C. M. GRO | — | — | — | — | 900 | — |

**2 PESOS (Dos)** **KM# 662a.2** **Composition:** Copper **Obverse:** Star between spary and R in REPUBLICA **Reverse:** Cap and rays

| Date | Mintage | VG | F | VF | XF | Unc |
|---|---|---|---|---|---|---|
| 1915 C. M. GRO unique | — | — | — | — | — | — |

# CHILPANCINGO

## REVOLUTIONARY COINAGE

**10 CENTAVOS** **KM# 663** **Composition:** Cast Silver **Reverse:** Sun above denomination

| Date | Mintage | VG | F | VF | XF | Unc |
|---|---|---|---|---|---|---|
| 1914 | — | 700 | 1,000 | 1,200 | 1,500 | — |

**Note:** Counterfeits exist

**20 CENTAVOS** **KM# 664** **Composition:** Cast Silver **Reverse:** Sun above denomination

| Date | Mintage | VG | F | VF | XF | Unc |
|---|---|---|---|---|---|---|
| 1914 | — | 700 | 1,000 | 1,200 | 1,500 | — |

**Note:** Counterfeits exist

# SURIANA

## REVOLUTIONARY COINAGE

**2 PESOS (Dos)** **KM# 665** **Composition:** 1.0000 Gold-Silver .595 oz. **Reverse:** Sun over mountains

| Date | Mintage | VG | F | VF | XF | Unc |
|---|---|---|---|---|---|---|
| 1915 Rare | — | — | — | — | — | — |

**Note:** *Spink America Gerber sale part 2, 6-96 VF realized $16,500

# TAXCO

## REVOLUTIONARY COINAGE

**2 CENTAVOS** **KM# 667** **Composition:** Copper **Obv. Legend:** EDO.DE.GRO

| Date | Mintage | VG | F | VF | XF | Unc |
|---|---|---|---|---|---|---|
| 1915 O/T | — | 25.00 | 40.00 | 60.00 | 90.00 | — |

**5 CENTAVOS** **KM# 668** **Composition:** Copper

| Date | Mintage | VG | F | VF | XF | Unc |
|---|---|---|---|---|---|---|
| 1915 | — | 9.00 | 15.00 | 20.00 | 25.00 | — |

**10 CENTAVOS** **KM# 669** **Composition:** Copper

| Date | Mintage | VG | F | VF | XF | Unc |
|---|---|---|---|---|---|---|
| 1915 | — | 9.00 | 15.00 | 20.00 | 30.00 | — |

**50 CENTAVOS** **KM# 670** **Composition:** Copper **Obverse:** Legend in large letters

| Date | Mintage | VG | F | VF | XF | Unc |
|---|---|---|---|---|---|---|
| 1915 | — | 15.00 | 25.00 | 50.00 | 65.00 | — |

**50 CENTAVOS** **KM# 671** **Composition:** Silver **Reverse:** Sun above denomination

| Date | Mintage | VG | F | VF | XF | Unc |
|---|---|---|---|---|---|---|
| 1915 | — | 20.00 | 30.00 | 40.00 | 70.00 | — |

**PESO (UN)** **KM# 672** **Weight:** 0.3000 g. **Composition:** 1.0000 Gold-Silver **Obverse:** Star before UN PESO **Reverse:** Star before G

| Date | Mintage | VG | F | VF | XF | Unc |
|---|---|---|---|---|---|---|
| 1915 | — | 12.00 | 20.00 | 30.00 | 45.00 | — |

**PESO (UN)** **KM# 672a** **Composition:** Brass **Obverse:** Star before UN PESO **Reverse:** Star before G

| Date | Mintage | VG | F | VF | XF | Unc |
|---|---|---|---|---|---|---|
| 1915 | — | 100 | 200 | 350 | 450 | — |

**PESO (UN)** **KM# 672b** **Composition:** Lead **Obverse:** Star before UN PESO **Reverse:** Star before G

| Date | Mintage | VG | F | VF | XF | Unc |
|---|---|---|---|---|---|---|
| 1915 | — | 50.00 | 100 | 200 | 350 | — |

**PESO (UN)** **KM# 672c** **Composition:** Copper **Obverse:** Star before UN PESO **Reverse:** Star before G

| Date | Mintage | VG | F | VF | XF | Unc |
|---|---|---|---|---|---|---|
| 1915 | — | 100 | 200 | 350 | 450 | — |

**PESO (UN)** **KM# 673** **Weight:** 0.3000 g. **Composition:** 1.0000 Gold-Silver **Obverse:** Star before UN PESO **Reverse:** Without star before G

| Date | Mintage | VG | F | VF | XF | Unc |
|---|---|---|---|---|---|---|
| 1915 | — | 250 | 300 | 400 | 500 | — |

**PESO (UN)** **KM# 674** **Weight:** 0.3000 g. **Composition:** 1.0000 Gold-Silver **Obverse:** Without star before UN PESO **Reverse:** Without star before G

| Date | Mintage | VG | F | VF | XF | Unc |
|---|---|---|---|---|---|---|
| 1915 | — | 75.00 | 150 | 275 | 400 | — |

## PATTERNS

Including off-metal strikes

| KM# | Date | Mintage | Identification | Mkt Val |
|---|---|---|---|---|
| Pn647 | 1914 | — | 2 Pesos. Gold-Silver. 0.3000 g. Atlixtac. | — |

## JALISCO

Jalisco is a state on the west coast of Mexico. The few coins made for this state show that the *Army of the North* did not restrict their operations to the northern border states. The coins were made in Guadalajara under the watchful eye of General Dieguez, commander of this segment of Villa's forces.

## GUADALAJARA

### REVOLUTIONARY COINAGE

**CENTAVO** **KM# 675** **Composition:** Copper **Obverse:** Cap and rays

| Date | Mintage | VG | F | VF | XF | Unc |
|---|---|---|---|---|---|---|
| 1915 | — | 9.50 | 15.00 | 20.00 | 30.00 | — |

**CENTAVO** **KM# 675a** **Composition:** Brass **Obverse:** Cap and rays

| Date | Mintage | VG | F | VF | XF | Unc |
|---|---|---|---|---|---|---|
| 1915 | — | — | — | 300 | 450 | — |

**CENTAVO** **KM# A676** **Composition:** Copper **Obverse:** Cap and rays **Reverse:** Retrograde

| Date | Mintage | VG | F | VF | XF | Unc |
|---|---|---|---|---|---|---|
| 1915 | — | 75.00 | 125 | 250 | 600 | — |

**Note:** Varieties exist.

**2 CENTAVOS** **KM# 676.1** **Composition:** Copper **Obverse:** Cap and rays

| Date | Mintage | VG | F | VF | XF | Unc |
|---|---|---|---|---|---|---|
| 1915 | — | 9.50 | 15.00 | 17.50 | 27.50 | — |

**Note:** Varieties exist.

**2 CENTAVOS** **KM# 676.2** **Composition:** Copper **Obverse:** Retrograde date, smaller Liberty cap and shorter rays

| Date | Mintage | VG | F | VF | XF | Unc |
|---|---|---|---|---|---|---|
| 1915 | — | 125 | 150 | 200 | 300 | — |

**5 CENTAVOS** **KM# 677** **Composition:** Copper **Obverse:** Cap and rays

| Date | Mintage | VG | F | VF | XF | Unc |
|---|---|---|---|---|---|---|
| 1915 | — | 6.50 | 12.00 | 15.00 | 25.00 | — |

**5 CENTAVOS** **KM# 677a** **Composition:** Brass **Obverse:** Cap and rays

| Date | Mintage | VG | F | VF | XF | Unc |
|---|---|---|---|---|---|---|
| 1915 rare | — | — | — | — | — | — |

**10 CENTAVOS** **KM# 678** **Composition:** Copper **Obverse:** Cap and rays above denomination **Reverse:** Arms

| Date | Mintage | VG | F | VF | XF | Unc |
|---|---|---|---|---|---|---|
| 1915 | — | — | — | 1,800 | 2,400 | — |

**PESO** **KM# A678** **Composition:** Copper

| Date | Mintage | VG | F | VF | XF | Unc |
|---|---|---|---|---|---|---|
| 1915 | — | — | — | — | 8,000 | — |

## MEXICO, ESTADO DE

Estado de Mexico is a state in central Mexico that surrounds the Federal District on three sides. The issues by the Zapata forces in this state have two distinctions – the Amecameca pieces are the crudest and the Toluca cardboard piece is the most unusual. General Tenorio authorized the crude incuse Amecameca pieces.

## AMECAMECA

### REVOLUTIONARY COINAGE

**5 CENTAVOS** **KM# 679** **Composition:** Brass **Obv. Legend:** EJERCITO CONVENCIONISTA

| Date | Mintage | VG | F | VF | XF | Unc |
|---|---|---|---|---|---|---|
| ND unique | — | — | — | — | — | — |

**5 CENTAVOS** **KM# 680** **Composition:** Brass **Obverse:** Eagle above RM **Note:** Hand stamped.

| Date | Mintage | VG | F | VF | XF | Unc |
|---|---|---|---|---|---|---|
| ND | — | 100 | 150 | 250 | 350 | — |

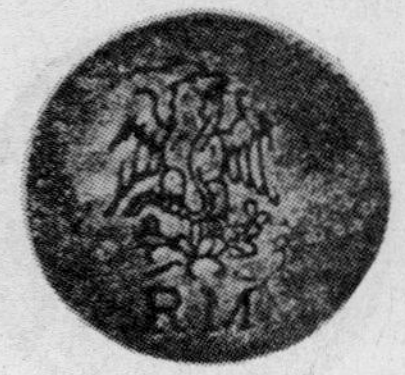

**10 CENTAVOS** **KM# 681** **Composition:** Brass **Obverse:** Eagle above RM **Note:** Hand stamped.

| Date | Mintage | VG | F | VF | XF | Unc |
|---|---|---|---|---|---|---|
| ND | — | 60.00 | 90.00 | 125 | 160 | — |

**Note:** Varieties exist.

**10 CENTAVOS** **KM# 681a** **Composition:** Copper **Obverse:** Eagle above RM **Note:** Hand stamped.

| Date | Mintage | VG | F | VF | XF | Unc |
|---|---|---|---|---|---|---|
| ND | — | 75.00 | 100 | 175 | 250 | — |

**20 CENTAVOS** **KM# 682** **Composition:** Brass **Obverse:** Eagle above RM **Note:** Hand stamped.

| Date | Mintage | VG | F | VF | XF | Unc |
|---|---|---|---|---|---|---|
| ND | — | 15.00 | 22.50 | 35.00 | 60.00 | — |

**Note:** Varieties exist

**20 CENTAVOS** **KM# 682a** **Composition:** Copper **Obverse:** Eagle above RM **Note:** Hand stamped.

| Date | Mintage | VG | F | VF | XF | Unc |
|---|---|---|---|---|---|---|
| ND | — | 25.00 | 50.00 | 175 | 250 | — |

**20 CENTAVOS** **KM# 683** **Composition:** Copper **Obverse:** Eagle over A. D. J.

| Date | Mintage | VG | F | VF | XF | Unc |
|---|---|---|---|---|---|---|
| ND | — | 7.50 | 12.50 | 20.00 | 35.00 | — |

**20 CENTAVOS** **KM# 683a** **Composition:** Brass **Obverse:** Eagle over A. D. J.

| Date | Mintage | VG | F | VF | XF | Unc |
|---|---|---|---|---|---|---|
| ND | — | — | — | 125 | 175 | — |

**25 CENTAVOS** **KM# 684** **Composition:** Brass **Obv. Legend:** EJERCITO CONVENCIONISTA

| Date | Mintage | VG | F | VF | XF | Unc |
|---|---|---|---|---|---|---|
| ND unique | — | — | — | — | — | — |

**25 CENTAVOS** **KM# 685** **Composition:** Copper **Obverse:** Eagle over sprays **Note:** Hand stamped. Many modern counterfeits exist in all metals.

| Date | Mintage | VG | F | VF | XF | Unc |
|---|---|---|---|---|---|---|
| ND | — | 15.00 | 20.00 | 30.00 | 40.00 | — |

**25 CENTAVOS** **KM# 685a** **Composition:** Brass **Obverse:** Eagle over sprays **Note:** Hand stamped

| Date | Mintage | VG | F | VF | XF | Unc |
|---|---|---|---|---|---|---|
| ND | — | — | — | 50.00 | 100 | — |

**25 CENTAVOS** **KM# 685b** **Composition:** Silver **Obverse:** Eagle over sprays **Note:** Hand stamped.

| Date | Mintage | VG | F | VF | XF | Unc |
|---|---|---|---|---|---|---|
| ND | — | — | — | 175 | 250 | — |

**50 CENTAVOS** **KM# 686** **Composition:** Copper **Obverse:** Eagle over sprays **Note:** Hand stamped.

| Date | Mintage | VG | F | VF | XF | Unc |
|---|---|---|---|---|---|---|
| ND | — | 5.00 | 8.00 | 12.00 | 20.00 | — |

**50 CENTAVOS** **KM# 686a** **Composition:** Brass **Obverse:** Eagle over sprays **Note:** Hand stamped.

| Date | Mintage | VG | F | VF | XF | Unc |
|---|---|---|---|---|---|---|
| ND | — | 75.00 | 100 | 150 | 200 | — |

**50 CENTAVOS** **KM# 687** **Composition:** Copper **Note:** Contemporary counterfeit, hand engraved

| Date | Mintage | VG | F | VF | XF | Unc |
|---|---|---|---|---|---|---|
| ND | — | 12.00 | 20.00 | 40.00 | 60.00 | — |

**Note:** KM#687 - ¢ clears top of 5 while KM#686a has the stem of ¢ above the 5

## TENANCINGO, TOWN
### (Distrito Federal Mexico)
### REVOLUTIONARY COINAGE

**2 CENTAVOS** **KM# 688.1** **Composition:** Copper **Reverse:** Without TM below deonomination

| Date | Mintage | VG | F | VF | XF | Unc |
|---|---|---|---|---|---|---|
| 1915 | — | — | — | 350 | 1,500 | |

**2 CENTAVOS** **KM# 688.2** **Composition:** Copper **Reverse:** With TM below deonomination

| Date | Mintage | VG | F | VF | XF | Unc |
|---|---|---|---|---|---|---|
| 1915 | — | — | 200 | 300 | 1,500 | — |

**5 CENTAVOS** **KM# 689.1** **Composition:** Copper **Reverse:** Lined C

| Date | Mintage | VG | F | VF | XF | Unc |
|---|---|---|---|---|---|---|
| 1915 | — | 5.00 | 10.00 | 18.00 | 30.00 | — |

**5 CENTAVOS** **KM# 689.2** **Composition:** Copper **Reverse:** Solid C

| Date | Mintage | VG | F | VF | XF | Unc |
|---|---|---|---|---|---|---|
| 1915 | — | 75.00 | 125 | 300 | 400 | — |

**10 CENTAVOS** **KM# 690.1** **Composition:** Copper **Reverse:** Without dot in C

| Date | Mintage | VG | F | VF | XF | Unc |
|---|---|---|---|---|---|---|
| 1916 | — | 10.00 | 15.00 | 20.00 | 30.00 | |

**10 CENTAVOS** **KM# 690.2** **Composition:** Copper **Reverse:** Dot in C

| Date | Mintage | VG | F | VF | XF | Unc |
|---|---|---|---|---|---|---|
| 1916 | — | 75.00 | 125 | 300 | 400 | — |

**20 CENTAVOS** **KM# 691** **Composition:** Copper

| Date | Mintage | VG | F | VF | XF | Unc |
|---|---|---|---|---|---|---|
| 1915 | — | 25.00 | 40.00 | 55.00 | 75.00 | — |

## TOLUCA, CITY
### (Distrito Federal Mexico)
### REVOLUTIONARY COINAGE

**5 CENTAVOS** **KM# 692.1** **Composition:** Grey Cardboard **Obverse:** Without dot after TOLUCA

| Date | Mintage | VG | F | VF | XF | Unc |
|---|---|---|---|---|---|---|
| 1915 | — | 15.00 | 25.00 | 35.00 | 45.00 | — |

**5 CENTAVOS** **KM# 692.2** **Composition:** Grey Cardboard **Obverse:** Dot after TOLUCA

| Date | Mintage | VG | F | VF | XF | Unc |
|---|---|---|---|---|---|---|
| 1915 | — | 15.00 | 25.00 | 35.00 | 45.00 | — |

### COUNTERMARKED COINAGE

**20 CENTAVOS** **KM# 693.2** **Composition:** Copper **Countermark:** 20 within C **Note:** Countermark on 1 Centavo, KM#394.1.

| CM Date | Host Date | Good | VG | F | VF | XF |
|---|---|---|---|---|---|---|
| (1915) | 1904 | — | 200 | 400 | 800 | 1,000 |

**20 CENTAVOS** **KM# 693.1** **Composition:** Copper **Countermark:** 20 within C **Note:** Countermark on 1 Centavo, KM#415.

| CM Date | Host Date | Good | VG | F | VF | XF |
|---|---|---|---|---|---|---|
| ND(1915) | ND | — | 20.00 | 30.00 | 45.00 | 60.00 |

**Note:** Varieties exist.

**40 CENTAVOS** **KM# 694** **Composition:** Copper **Countermark:** 40 within C **Note:** Countermark on 2 Centavos, KM#419.

| CM Date | Host Date | Good | VG | F | VF | XF |
|---|---|---|---|---|---|---|
| ND(1915) | ND | — | 25.00 | 40.00 | 60.00 | 80.00 |

**Note:** Varieties exist

## MORELOS

Morelos is a state in south central Mexico, adjoining the federal district on the south. It was the headquarters of Emiliano Zapata. His personal quarters were at Tlatizapan in Morelos. The Morelos coins from 2 Centavos to 1 Peso were all copper except one type of 1 Peso in silver. The two operating Zapatista mints in Morelos were Atlihuayan and Tlaltizapan.

## EMILIANO ZAPATA
### (Zapatista)
### REVOLUTIONARY COINAGE

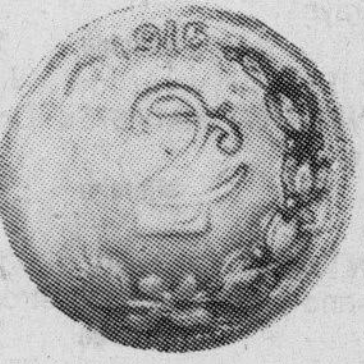

**2 CENTAVOS** **KM# 695** **Composition:** Copper **Obv. Legend:** E.L. DE MORELOS

| Date | Mintage | VG | F | VF | XF | Unc |
|---|---|---|---|---|---|---|
| 1915 | — | 1,000 | 1,400 | 1,800 | 2,250 | — |

**5 CENTAVOS** **KM# 696** **Composition:** Copper **Rev. Legend:** E. DE MOR. 1915

| Date | Mintage | VG | F | VF | XF | Unc |
|---|---|---|---|---|---|---|
| 1915 | — | 300 | 500 | 1,000 | 3,500 | — |

**10 CENTAVOS** **KM# 697** **Composition:** Copper

| Date | Mintage | VG | F | VF | XF | Unc |
|---|---|---|---|---|---|---|
| 1915 | — | 12.00 | 20.00 | 30.00 | 40.00 | — |

**10 CENTAVOS** **KM# 698** **Composition:** Copper **Reverse:** Date effaced from die

| Date | Mintage | VG | F | VF | XF | Unc |
|---|---|---|---|---|---|---|
| ND | — | 12.00 | 20.00 | 35.00 | 55.00 | — |

**10 CENTAVOS** **KM# 699** **Composition:** Copper **Rev. Legend:** E. DE MOR

| Date | Mintage | VG | F | VF | XF | Unc |
|---|---|---|---|---|---|---|
| 1915 | — | 1,000 | 1,500 | 2,000 | 2,500 | — |

**10 CENTAVOS** **KM# 700** **Composition:** Copper **Rev. Legend:** MOR

| Date | Mintage | VG | F | VF | XF | Unc |
|---|---|---|---|---|---|---|
| 1916 | — | 5.00 | 10.00 | 17.50 | 25.00 | — |

**20 CENTAVOS** **KM# 701** **Composition:** Copper

| Date | Mintage | VG | F | VF | XF | Unc |
|---|---|---|---|---|---|---|
| 1915 | — | 9.00 | 15.00 | 25.00 | 35.00 | — |

**50 CENTAVOS** **KM# 702** **Composition:** Copper **Obverse:** MOR beneath eagle **Reverse:** 50C monogram

| Date | Mintage | VG | F | VF | XF | Unc |
|---|---|---|---|---|---|---|
| 1915 | — | 300 | 500 | 900 | 1,300 | — |

**50 CENTAVOS** **KM# 703** **Composition:** Copper **Obverse:** Sprays beneath eagle **Reverse:** 50C monogram

| Date | Mintage | VG | F | VF | XF | Unc |
|---|---|---|---|---|---|---|
| 1915 | — | 12.50 | 17.50 | 30.00 | 42.00 | — |

**Note:** The above exists with a silver and also a brass wash

**50 CENTAVOS** **KM# 703a** **Composition:** Brass **Obverse:** Sprays beneath eagle **Reverse:** 50C monogram

| Date | Mintage | VG | F | VF | XF | Unc |
|---|---|---|---|---|---|---|
| 1915 | — | 100 | 200 | 400 | 600 | — |

**50 CENTAVOS** **KM# 706** **Composition:** Copper **Obverse:** Sprays beneath eagle **Rev. Legend:** REFORMA LIBERTAD JUSTICIA Y LEY

| Date | Mintage | VG | F | VF | XF | Unc |
|---|---|---|---|---|---|---|
| 1915 | — | 350 | 500 | 800 | 1,000 | — |

**50 CENTAVOS** **KM# 704** **Composition:** Copper **Obverse:** MORELOS below eagle

| Date | Mintage | VG | F | VF | XF | Unc |
|---|---|---|---|---|---|---|
| 1916 | — | 12.50 | 17.50 | 27.50 | 35.00 | — |

**PESO (UN)** **KM# 708** **Composition:** Silver **Reverse:** Cap and rays

| Date | Mintage | VG | F | VF | XF | Unc |
|---|---|---|---|---|---|---|
| 1916 | — | 450 | 750 | 1,000 | 1,500 | — |

**PESO (UN)** **KM# 708a** **Composition:** Copper **Reverse:** Cap and rays

| Date | Mintage | VG | F | VF | XF | Unc |
|---|---|---|---|---|---|---|
| 1916 | — | 450 | 750 | 1,000 | 1,500 | — |

## PATTERNS

Including off-metal strikes

| KM# | Date | Mintage | Identification | Issue Price | Mkt Val |
|---|---|---|---|---|---|
| Pn1 | 1915 | — | 50 Centavos. Silver. KM#705. | — | 1,500 |
| Pn2 | 1915 | — | 50 Centavos. Copper. KM#705. | — | 450 |
| Pn3 | 191x | — | Peso. Silver. KM#707. | — | 4,000 |
| Pn4 | 191x | — | Peso. Copper. KM#707a. | — | 4,000 |
| Pn5 | 1916 | — | Peso. Copper. KM#707b. | — | 4,250 |

# OAXACA

Oaxaca is one of the southern states in Mexico. The coins issued in this state represent the most prolific series of the Revolution. Most of the coins bear the portrait of Benito Juarez, have corded or plain edges and were issued by a provisional government in the state. The exceptions are the rectangular 1 and 3 Centavos pieces that begin the series.

## PROVISIONAL GOVERNMENT

### REVOLUTIONARY COINAGE

**CENTAVO (UN)** **KM# 709** **Composition:** Copper **Note:** Rectangular flan.

| Date | Mintage | VG | F | VF | XF | Unc |
|---|---|---|---|---|---|---|
| 1915 | — | 60.00 | 90.00 | 125 | 225 | — |

**CENTAVO (UN)** **KM# 710** **Composition:** Copper **Obverse:** Bust of Juarez left

| Date | Mintage | VG | F | VF | XF | Unc |
|---|---|---|---|---|---|---|
| 1915 | — | 12.00 | 17.50 | 25.00 | 40.00 | — |

**CENTAVO (UN)** **KM# 710a** **Composition:** Brass **Obverse:** Bust of Juarez left

| Date | Mintage | VG | F | VF | XF | Unc |
|---|---|---|---|---|---|---|
| 1915 | — | 50.00 | 100 | 175 | 225 | — |

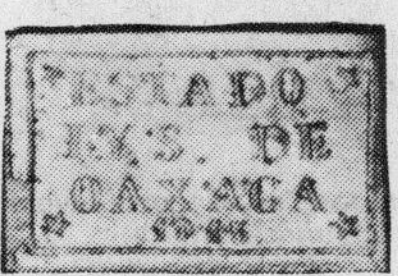


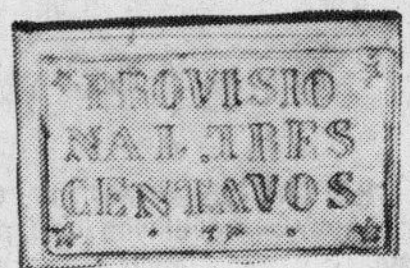


**3 CENTAVOS (Tres)** **KM# 711** **Composition:** Copper **Rev. Legend:** PROVISIO... **Note:** Rectangular flan.

| Date | Mintage | VG | F | VF | XF | Unc |
|---|---|---|---|---|---|---|
| 1915 | — | 60.00 | 100 | 125 | 200 | — |

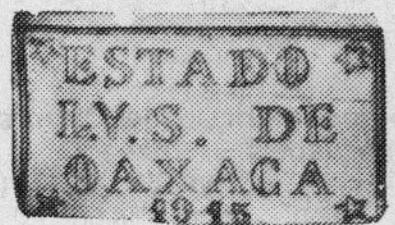


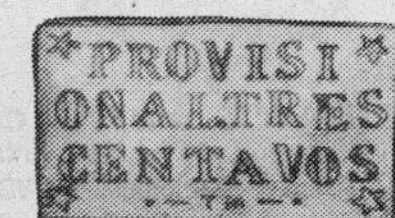


**3 CENTAVOS (Tres)** **KM# 712** **Composition:** Copper **Rev. Legend:** PROVISI... **Note:** Rectangular flan.

| Date | Mintage | VG | F | VF | XF | Unc |
|---|---|---|---|---|---|---|
| 1915 | — | 600 | 1,200 | 1,800 | 3,000 | — |

**3 CENTAVOS (Tres)** **KM# 713.1** **Composition:** Copper **Obverse:** Bust of Juarez left **Reverse:** Without TM below denomination

| Date | Mintage | VG | F | VF | XF | Unc |
|---|---|---|---|---|---|---|
| 1915 | — | 3.00 | 5.00 | 10.00 | 15.00 | — |

**3 CENTAVOS (Tres)** **KM# 713.2** **Composition:** Copper **Reverse:** Without TM below denomination **Edge:** Plain

| Date | Mintage | VG | F | VF | XF | Unc |
|---|---|---|---|---|---|---|
| 1915 | — | — | — | 70.00 | 100 | — |

**3 CENTAVOS (Tres)** **KM# 713.3** **Composition:** Copper **Reverse:** With TM below denomination

| Date | Mintage | VG | F | VF | XF | Unc |
|---|---|---|---|---|---|---|
| 1915 | — | 100 | 150 | 250 | 350 | — |

**3 CENTAVOS (Tres)** **KM# 714** **Composition:** Copper **Reverse:** Small 3

| Date | Mintage | VG | F | VF | XF | Unc |
|---|---|---|---|---|---|---|
| 1915 | — | 6.00 | 9.00 | 14.00 | 20.00 | — |

**5 CENTAVOS** **KM# 715** **Composition:** Copper **Note:** JAN. 15 1915. incuse lettering

| Date | Mintage | VG | F | VF | XF | Unc |
|---|---|---|---|---|---|---|
| 1915 Rare | — | — | — | — | — | — |

**5 CENTAVOS** **KM# 716** **Composition:** Copper **Obverse:** Facing bust of Juarez

| Date | Mintage | VG | F | VF | XF | Unc |
|---|---|---|---|---|---|---|
| 1915 | — | — | — | — | 4,000 | — |

**5 CENTAVOS** **KM# 717** **Composition:** Copper **Obverse:** 2nd bust, low relief with long, pointed truncation

| Date | Mintage | VG | F | VF | XF | Unc |
|---|---|---|---|---|---|---|
| 1915 | — | 1.50 | 3.00 | 4.50 | 7.00 | — |

**5 CENTAVOS** **KM# 718** **Composition:** Copper **Obverse:** 5th bust, heavy with short unfinished lapels

| Date | Mintage | VG | F | VF | XF | Unc |
|---|---|---|---|---|---|---|
| 1915 | — | 1.50 | 2.50 | 4.00 | 6.00 | — |

**5 CENTAVOS** **KM# 719** **Composition:** Copper **Obverse:** 6th bust, curved bottom

| Date | Mintage | VG | F | VF | XF | Unc |
|---|---|---|---|---|---|---|
| 1915 | — | 1.50 | 2.50 | 4.00 | 6.00 | — |

**5 CENTAVOS** **KM# 720** **Composition:** Copper **Obverse:** 7th bust, short truncation with closed lapels

| Date | Mintage | VG | F | VF | XF | Unc |
|---|---|---|---|---|---|---|
| 1915 | — | 1.50 | 3.00 | 4.50 | 7.00 | — |

**5 CENTAVOS** **KM# 721** **Composition:** Copper **Obverse:** 8th bust, short curved truncation

| Date | Mintage | VG | F | VF | XF | Unc |
|---|---|---|---|---|---|---|
| 1915 | — | 1.50 | 2.50 | 4.00 | 6.00 | — |

**10 CENTAVOS** **KM# 722** **Composition:** Copper **Obverse:** 2nd bust, low relief with long, pointed truncation

| Date | Mintage | VG | F | VF | XF | Unc |
|---|---|---|---|---|---|---|
| 1915 | — | 1.50 | 2.50 | 4.00 | 6.00 | — |

**10 CENTAVOS** **KM# 723** **Composition:** Copper **Note:** Obverse and reverse legend retrograde.

| Date | Mintage | VG | F | VF | XF | Unc |
|---|---|---|---|---|---|---|
| 1915 Rare | — | — | — | — | — | — |

**10 CENTAVOS** **KM# 724** **Composition:** Copper **Obverse:** 4th bust, bold, unfinished truncation using 1 Peso obverse die of KM#740

| Date | Mintage | VG | F | VF | XF | Unc |
|---|---|---|---|---|---|---|
| 1915 | — | 3.00 | 5.00 | 7.00 | 9.00 | — |

**10 CENTAVOS** **KM# 725** **Composition:** Copper **Obverse:** 5th bust, heavy with short unfinished lapels centered high

| Date | Mintage | VG | F | VF | XF | Unc |
|---|---|---|---|---|---|---|
| 1915 | — | 1.50 | 2.50 | 4.00 | 6.00 | — |

**10 CENTAVOS** **KM# 726** **Composition:** Copper **Obverse:** 6th bust, curved bottom

| Date | Mintage | VG | F | VF | XF | Unc |
|---|---|---|---|---|---|---|
| 1915 | — | 1.50 | 2.50 | 4.00 | 6.00 | — |

**10 CENTAVOS** **KM# 727.1** **Composition:** Copper **Obverse:** 7th bust, short truncation with closed lapels

| Date | Mintage | VG | F | VF | XF | Unc |
|---|---|---|---|---|---|---|
| 1915 | — | 1.50 | 2.50 | 4.00 | 6.00 | — |

**10 CENTAVOS** **KM# 727.2** **Composition:** Copper **Obverse:** T below bow, M below 1st leaf **Note:** At present, only 4 pieces of this type are known. All are VF or better.

| Date | Mintage | VG | F | VF | XF | Unc |
|---|---|---|---|---|---|---|
| 1915 | — | — | — | 300 | 450 | — |

**10 CENTAVOS** **KM# 727.3** **Composition:** Copper **Obverse:** Counterstamp GV on 7th bust, short truncation with closed lapels **Reverse:** Similar to KM#727.1 **Note:** Letters GV correspond to General Garcia Vigil.

| Date | Mintage | VG | F | VF | XF | Unc |
|---|---|---|---|---|---|---|
| 1915 | — | 100 | 200 | 250 | 350 | — |

**Note:** This counter stamp appears on several different type host 10 cent coins

**20 CENTAVOS** **KM# 728** **Composition:** Silver **Obverse:** 2nd bust, low relief with long pointed truncation

| Date | Mintage | VG | F | VF | XF | Unc |
|---|---|---|---|---|---|---|
| 1915 | — | 500 | 750 | 1,200 | 1,500 | — |

**20 CENTAVOS** **KM# 728a** **Composition:** Copper **Obverse:** 2nd bust, low relief with long pointed truncation

| Date | Mintage | VG | F | VF | XF | Unc |
|---|---|---|---|---|---|---|
| 1915 Rare | — | — | — | — | — | — |

**20 CENTAVOS** **KM# 729.1** **Composition:** Copper **Obverse:** 4th bust, bold unfinished truncation using 1 Peso obverse die

| Date | Mintage | VG | F | VF | XF | Unc |
|---|---|---|---|---|---|---|
| 1915 | — | 1.50 | 3.00 | 4.50 | 7.00 | — |

**20 CENTAVOS** **KM# 729.2** **Composition:** Copper **Counterstamp:** Liberty cap **Obverse:** Counterstamp liberty cap and rays on 4th bust, bold unfinished truncation using 1 Peso obverse die

| Date | Mintage | VG | F | VF | XF | Unc |
|---|---|---|---|---|---|---|
| 1915 | — | 100 | 150 | 200 | 275 | — |

**20 CENTAVOS** **KM# 730** **Composition:** Copper **Obverse:** 5th bust, heavy with short unfinished lapels using 20 Pesos obverse die

| Date | Mintage | VG | F | VF | XF | Unc |
|---|---|---|---|---|---|---|
| 1915 | — | 5.00 | 7.00 | 10.00 | 15.00 | — |

**20 CENTAVOS** **KM# 731.1** **Composition:** Copper **Obverse:** 6th bust, curved bottom

| Date | Mintage | VG | F | VF | XF | Unc |
|---|---|---|---|---|---|---|
| 1915 | — | 1.50 | 2.50 | 4.00 | 6.00 | — |

**20 CENTAVOS** **KM# 731.2** **Composition:** Copper **Note:** Similar to KM#731.1 but with 4th bust.

| Date | Mintage | VG | F | VF | XF | Unc |
|---|---|---|---|---|---|---|
| 1915 Unique | — | — | — | — | — | — |

**20 CENTAVOS** **KM# 732** **Composition:** Copper **Obverse:** 6th bust

| Date | Mintage | VG | F | VF | XF | Unc |
|---|---|---|---|---|---|---|
| 1915 | — | 1.50 | 2.50 | 4.00 | 6.00 | — |

**20 CENTAVOS** **KM# 733** **Composition:** Copper **Obverse:** 7th bust, short truncation with closed lapels

| Date | Mintage | VG | F | VF | XF | Unc |
|---|---|---|---|---|---|---|
| 1915 | — | 1.50 | 3.00 | 4.50 | 7.00 | — |

**50 CENTAVOS** **KM# 734** **Composition:** Silver **Obverse:** 5th bust, heavy, with short unfinished lapels, centered high

| Date | Mintage | VG | F | VF | XF | Unc |
|---|---|---|---|---|---|---|
| 1915 | — | 10.00 | 20.00 | 40.00 | 85.00 | — |

**50 CENTAVOS** **KM# 735** **Composition:** Silver **Obverse:** 6th bust, curved bottom

| Date | Mintage | VG | F | VF | XF | Unc |
|---|---|---|---|---|---|---|
| 1915 | — | 6.00 | 9.00 | 14.00 | 22.50 | — |

**50 CENTAVOS** **KM# 736** **Composition:** Silver **Obverse:** 7th bust, short truncation with closed lapels

| Date | Mintage | VG | F | VF | XF | Unc |
|---|---|---|---|---|---|---|
| 1915 | — | 6.00 | 9.00 | 15.00 | 25.00 | — |

**50 CENTAVOS** **KM# 737** **Composition:** Silver **Obverse:** 8th bust, short truncation with pronounced curve

| Date | Mintage | VG | F | VF | XF | Unc |
|---|---|---|---|---|---|---|
| 1915 | — | 6.50 | 10.00 | 16.00 | 30.00 | — |

**50 CENTAVOS** **KM# 739** **Composition:** Billon **Obverse:** 9th bust, high nearly straight truncation

| Date | Mintage | VG | F | VF | XF | Unc |
|---|---|---|---|---|---|---|
| 1915 | — | — | — | — | 2,000 | — |

**50 CENTAVOS** **KM# 739a** **Composition:** Copper **Obverse:** 9th bust, high nearly straight truncation

| Date | Mintage | VG | F | VF | XF | Unc |
|---|---|---|---|---|---|---|
| 1915 | — | — | — | — | — | — |

**PESO (UN)** **KM# 740.1** **Composition:** Silver **Obverse:** 4th bust, with heavy unfinished truncation

| Date | Mintage | VG | F | VF | XF | Unc |
|---|---|---|---|---|---|---|
| 1915 | — | 3.00 | 5.00 | 8.50 | 14.00 | — |

**PESO (UN)** **KM# 740.2** **Composition:** Silver **Obverse:** 4th bust, with heavy unfinished truncation **Reverse:** TM below bow on wreath

| Date | Mintage | VG | F | VF | XF | Unc |
|---|---|---|---|---|---|---|
| 1915 | — | 150 | 200 | 250 | 350 | — |

**PESO (UN)** **KM# 741** **Composition:** Silver **Obverse:** 5th bust, heavy, with short unfinished lapels, centered high

| Date | Mintage | VG | F | VF | XF | Unc |
|---|---|---|---|---|---|---|
| 1915 | — | 6.00 | 9.00 | 14.00 | 22.50 | — |

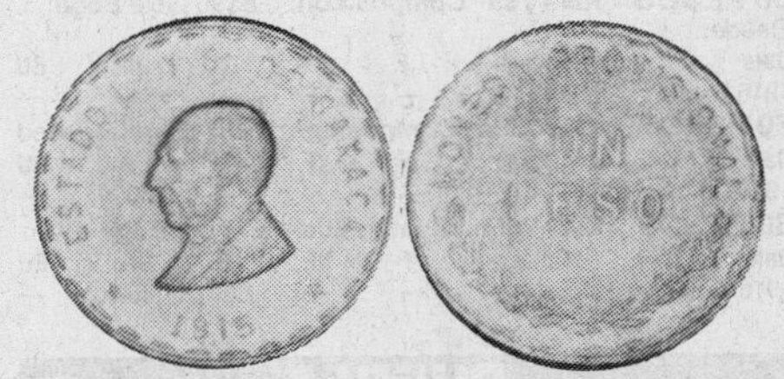

**PESO (UN)** **KM# 742** **Composition:** Silver **Obverse:** 6th bust, curved bottom line

| Date | Mintage | VG | F | VF | XF | Unc |
|---|---|---|---|---|---|---|
| 1915 | — | 6.00 | 9.00 | 14.00 | 22.50 | — |

**PESO (UN)** **KM# 742a** **Composition:** Copper **Obverse:** 6th bust, curved bottom line

| Date | Mintage | VG | F | VF | XF | Unc |
|---|---|---|---|---|---|---|
| 1915 | — | — | — | — | 500 | — |

**PESO (UN)** **KM# 743** **Composition:** Silver **Obverse:** 7th bust, short truncation with closed lapels

| Date | Mintage | VG | F | VF | XF | Unc |
|---|---|---|---|---|---|---|
| 1915 | — | 4.00 | 6.00 | 10.00 | 16.00 | — |

**PESO (UN)** **KM# 743a** **Composition:** Silver **Obverse:** 7th bust, short truncation with closed lapels **Reverse:** TM below bow on wreath

| Date | Mintage | VG | F | VF | XF | Unc |
|---|---|---|---|---|---|---|
| 1915 | — | 35.00 | 75.00 | 150 | 200 | — |

**2 PESOS (Dos)** **KM# 744** **Composition:** Silver **Obverse:** 4th bust, using 1 Peso obverse die

| Date | Mintage | VG | F | VF | XF | Unc |
|---|---|---|---|---|---|---|
| 1915 | — | 12.00 | 20.00 | 25.00 | 35.00 | — |

**2 PESOS (Dos)** **KM# 744a** **Composition:** Copper **Obverse:** 4th bust, using 1 Peso obverse die

| Date | Mintage | VG | F | VF | XF | Unc |
|---|---|---|---|---|---|---|
| 1915 Rare | — | — | — | — | — | — |

**2 PESOS (Dos)** **KM# 745** **Obverse:** 5th bust **Reverse:** Curved bottomed 2 over PESOS **Size:** 22 mm. **Note:** 0.9020 Silver, 0.0100 Gold.

| Date | Mintage | VG | F | VF | XF | Unc |
|---|---|---|---|---|---|---|
| 1915 | — | 12.00 | 20.00 | 27.50 | 37.50 | — |

**2 PESOS (Dos)** **KM# 745a** **Composition:** Copper **Obverse:** 5th bust **Reverse:** Curved bottomed 2 over PESOS

| Date | Mintage | VG | F | VF | XF | Unc |
|---|---|---|---|---|---|---|
| 1915 | — | 50.00 | 75.00 | 110 | 160 | — |

**2 PESOS (Dos)** **KM# A746** **Composition:** Copper **Obverse:** 7th bust, short truncation with closed lapels

| Date | Mintage | VG | F | VF | XF | Unc |
|---|---|---|---|---|---|---|
| 1915 Unique | — | — | — | — | — | — |

**2 PESOS (Dos)** **KM# 746** **Composition:** Silver **Obverse:** 6th bust **Reverse:** 2 PESOS

| Date | Mintage | VG | F | VF | XF | Unc |
|---|---|---|---|---|---|---|
| 1915 | — | 10.00 | 15.00 | 27.50 | 45.00 | — |

**2 PESOS (Dos)** **KM# A747** **Composition:** Silver **Obverse:** 6th bust **Reverse:** Dos PESOS **Note:** Obverse die is free hand engraved.

| Date | Mintage | VG | F | VF | XF | Unc |
|---|---|---|---|---|---|---|
| 1915 | — | — | — | 185 | 275 | — |

**2 PESOS (Dos)** **KM# 746a** **Composition:** Copper **Obverse:** 6th bust **Reverse:** 2PESOS

| Date | Mintage | Good | VG | F | VF | XF |
|---|---|---|---|---|---|---|
| 1915 | — | — | 150 | 200 | 600 | 900 |

**2 PESOS (Dos)** **KM# 747.1** **Composition:** Silver **Obverse:** 6th bust **Reverse:** DOS PESOS

| Date | Mintage | VG | F | VF | XF | Unc |
|---|---|---|---|---|---|---|
| 1915 | — | 10.00 | 15.00 | 25.00 | 40.00 | — |

**2 PESOS (Dos)** **KM# 747.2** **Composition:** Silver **Obverse:** 6th bust, dot after date **Reverse:** DOS PESOS

| Date | Mintage | VG | F | VF | XF | Unc |
|---|---|---|---|---|---|---|
| 1915 | — | 10.00 | 15.00 | 25.00 | 40.00 | — |

**2 PESOS (Dos)** **KM# 747.3** **Composition:** Silver **Obverse:** 6th bust, dot after date, periods after L and S **Reverse:** DOS PESOS

| Date | Mintage | VG | F | VF | XF | Unc |
|---|---|---|---|---|---|---|
| 1915 | — | 10.00 | 15.00 | 25.00 | 40.00 | — |

**2 PESOS (Dos)** KM# 748 **Composition:** 0.9020 Silver **Obverse:** 7th bust, short truncation with closed lapels **Size:** 22 mm.

| Date | Mintage | VG | F | VF | XF | Unc |
|---|---|---|---|---|---|---|
| 1915 | — | 12.00 | 20.00 | 40.00 | 60.00 | — |

**2 PESOS (Dos)** KM# 749 **Composition:** Silver **Obverse:** 10th, small nude bust

| Date | Mintage | VG | F | VF | XF | Unc |
|---|---|---|---|---|---|---|
| 1915 Unique | — | — | — | — | 2,300 | — |

**5 PESOS** KM# 750 **Composition:** 0.1750 Gold **Obverse:** 3rd bust, heavy, with short unfinished lapels

| Date | Mintage | VG | F | VF | XF | Unc |
|---|---|---|---|---|---|---|
| 1915 | — | 150 | 200 | 275 | 375 | — |

**5 PESOS** KM# 750a **Composition:** Copper **Obverse:** 3rd bust, heavy, with short unfinished lapels

| Date | Mintage | VG | F | VF | XF | Unc |
|---|---|---|---|---|---|---|
| 1915 Unique | — | — | — | — | — | — |

**5 PESOS** KM# 751 **Composition:** 0.9020 Silver **Obverse:** 7th bust, short truncation with closed lapels

| Date | Mintage | VG | F | VF | XF | Unc |
|---|---|---|---|---|---|---|
| 1915 | — | 30.00 | 50.00 | 75.00 | 115 | — |

**5 PESOS** KM# 751a **Composition:** Copper **Obverse:** 7th bust, short truncation with closed lapels

| Date | Mintage | VG | F | VF | XF | Unc |
|---|---|---|---|---|---|---|
| 1915 | — | 125 | 200 | 300 | 800 | — |

**10 PESOS** KM# A752 **Composition:** 0.1500 Gold **Obverse:** 4th bust

| Date | Mintage | VG | F | VF | XF | Unc |
|---|---|---|---|---|---|---|
| 1915 Rare | — | — | — | — | — | — |

**10 PESOS** KM# 752 **Composition:** 0.1750 Gold **Obverse:** 5th bust

| Date | Mintage | VG | F | VF | XF | Unc |
|---|---|---|---|---|---|---|
| 1915 | — | 200 | 275 | 375 | 500 | — |

**10 PESOS** KM# 752a **Composition:** Copper **Obverse:** 5th bust

| Date | Mintage | VG | F | VF | XF | Unc |
|---|---|---|---|---|---|---|
| 1915 | — | 300 | 500 | 1,000 | 2,000 | — |

**20 PESOS** KM# A753 **Composition:** 0.1500 Gold **Obverse:** 4th bust

| Date | Mintage | VG | F | VF | XF | Unc |
|---|---|---|---|---|---|---|
| 1915 Unique | — | — | — | — | — | — |

**20 PESOS** KM# 753 **Composition:** 0.1750 Gold **Obverse:** 5th bust, heavy, with short unfinished lapels, centered high

| Date | Mintage | VG | F | VF | XF | Unc |
|---|---|---|---|---|---|---|
| 1915 | — | 400 | 600 | 800 | 1,000 | — |

**20 PESOS** KM# 754 **Composition:** 0.1750 Gold **Obverse:** 7th bust, short truncation with closed lapels

| Date | Mintage | VG | F | VF | XF | Unc |
|---|---|---|---|---|---|---|
| 1915 | — | 200 | 300 | 400 | 625 | — |

**60 PESOS** KM# 755 **Composition:** 0.8590 Gold **Edge:** Reeded

| Date | Mintage | F | VF | XF | Unc | BU |
|---|---|---|---|---|---|---|
| 1916 Rare | — | — | — | — | — | — |

**60 PESOS** KM# 755a **Composition:** Silver **Edge:** Reeded

| Date | Mintage | F | VF | XF | Unc | BU |
|---|---|---|---|---|---|---|
| 1916 | — | — | — | — | 1,800 | — |

**60 PESOS** KM# 755b **Composition:** Copper **Edge:** Plain

| Date | Mintage | F | VF | XF | Unc | BU |
|---|---|---|---|---|---|---|
| 1916 | — | — | — | 1,000 | 1,800 | — |

## PUEBLA

A state of central Mexico. Puebla was a state that occasionally saw Zapata forces active within its boundaries. Also active, and an issuer of coins, was the Madero brigade who issued coins with their name two years after Madero's death. The state issue of 2, 5, 10 and 20 Centavos saw limited circulation and recent hoards have been found of some values.

## CHICONCUAUTLA

### Madero Brigade

### REVOLUTIONARY COINAGE

**10 CENTAVOS** KM# 756 **Composition:** Copper

| Date | Mintage | VG | F | VF | XF | Unc |
|---|---|---|---|---|---|---|
| 1915 | — | 7.50 | 12.50 | 17.50 | 25.00 | — |

**20 CENTAVOS** KM# 757 **Composition:** Copper **Reverse:** TRANSITORIO between rosettes

| Date | Mintage | VG | F | VF | XF | Unc |
|---|---|---|---|---|---|---|
| 1915 | — | 2.50 | 4.00 | 6.50 | 12.00 | — |

**Note:** Varieties exist

**20 CENTAVOS** KM# 758 **Composition:** Copper **Reverse:** TRANSITORIO without rosettes

| Date | Mintage | VG | F | VF | XF | Unc |
|---|---|---|---|---|---|---|
| 1915 | — | 2.50 | 4.00 | 6.50 | 12.00 | — |

## TETELA DEL ORO Y OCAMPO

### REVOLUTIONARY COINAGE

**2 CENTAVOS** KM# 759 **Composition:** Copper

| Date | Mintage | VG | F | VF | XF | Unc |
|---|---|---|---|---|---|---|
| 1915 | — | 12.50 | 20.00 | 28.00 | 45.00 | — |
| 1915 Restrikes | — | 2.00 | 3.00 | 5.00 | 10.00 | — |

**2 CENTAVOS** KM# 760 **Composition:** Copper
**Rev. Legend:** E. DE PU.

| Date | Mintage | VG | F | VF | XF | Unc |
|---|---|---|---|---|---|---|
| 1915 | — | 15.00 | 25.00 | 35.00 | 75.00 | — |

**2 CENTAVOS** KM# 761 **Composition:** Copper
**Rev. Legend:** E. DE PUE.

| Date | Mintage | VG | F | VF | XF | Unc |
|---|---|---|---|---|---|---|
| 1915 | — | 9.00 | 15.00 | 22.50 | 35.00 | — |

**5 CENTAVOS** KM# 762 **Composition:** Copper

| Date | Mintage | VG | F | VF | XF | Unc |
|---|---|---|---|---|---|---|
| 1915 | — | 50.00 | 100 | 150 | 250 | — |

**20 CENTAVOS** **KM# 764** **Composition:** Copper

| Date | Mintage | VG | F | VF | XF | Unc |
|---|---|---|---|---|---|---|
| 1915 | — | 50.00 | 100 | 150 | 225 | — |

## TRIAL STRIKES

| KM# | Date | Mintage | Identification | Mkt Val |
|---|---|---|---|---|
| TS1 | 1915 | — | 10 Centavos. Copper. Uniface, KM#763. | 475 |
| TS2 | 1915 | — | 10 Centavos. Brass. Uniface, KM#763. | 750 |
| TS3 | 1915 | — | 10 Centavos. Copper. KM#761. Eagle. | 1,600 |

# SINALOA

A state along the west coast of Mexico. The cast pieces of this state have been attributed to two people - Generals Rafael Buelna and Juan Carrasco. The cap and rays 8 Reales is usually attributed to General Buelna and the rest of the series to Carrasco. Because of their crude nature it is questionable whether separate series or mints can be determined.

## BUELNA / CARRASCO

### MOLDED OR CAST COINAGE

Revolutionary

**20 CENTAVOS** **KM# 765** **Composition:** Cast Silver **Note:** Sand molded using regular 20 Centavos.

| Date | Mintage | Good | VG | F | VF | XF |
|---|---|---|---|---|---|---|
| ND(1898-1905) | — | 200 | 300 | — | — | — |

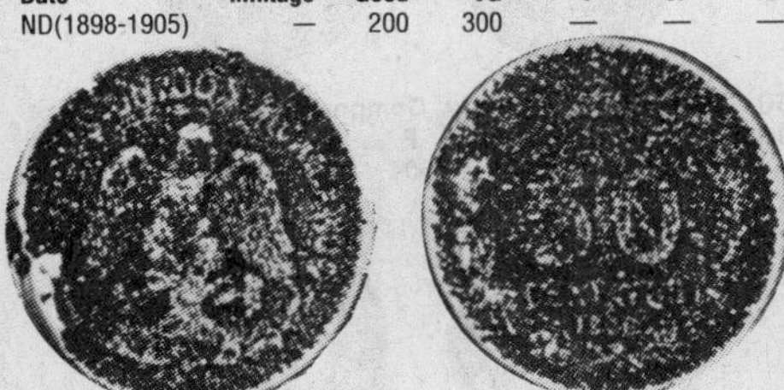

**50 CENTAVOS** **KM# 766** **Composition:** Cast Silver **Note:** Sand molded using regular 50 Centavos, km#445.

| Date | Mintage | Good | VG | F | VF | XF |
|---|---|---|---|---|---|---|
| ND(1905-1918) | — | 200 | 300 | — | — | — |

**PESO** **KM# 768.1** **Composition:** Cast Silver **Note:** Sand molded using regular 8 Reales, KM#377.

| Date | Mintage | Good | VG | F | VF | XF |
|---|---|---|---|---|---|---|
| ND(1824-1897) | — | 17.50 | 35.00 | 45.00 | 55.00 | — |

**PESO** **KM# 768.2** **Composition:** Cast Silver **Countermark:** G.C. **Obverse:** With additional countermark **Note:** Sand molded using regular 8 Reales, KM#377.

| Date | Mintage | Good | VG | F | VF | XF |
|---|---|---|---|---|---|---|
| ND(1824-1897) | — | 25.00 | 45.00 | 100 | 150 | — |

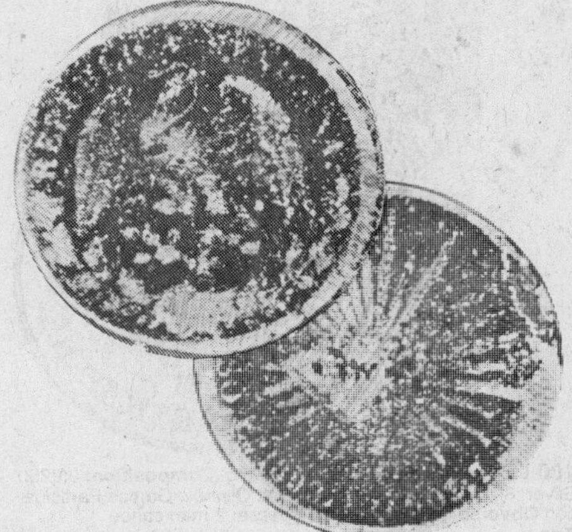

**PESO** **KM# 769** **Composition:** Cast Silver **Countermark:** G.C **Obverse:** With additional countermark **Note:** Sand molded using regular Peso, KM#409.

| Date | Mintage | Good | VG | F | VF | XF |
|---|---|---|---|---|---|---|
| ND(1898-1909) | — | 10.00 | 20.00 | 30.00 | 40.00 | — |

### COUNTERMARKED COINAGE

Revolutionary

These are all crude sand cast coins using regular coins to prepare the mold. Prices below give a range for how much of the original coin from which the mold was prepared is visible.

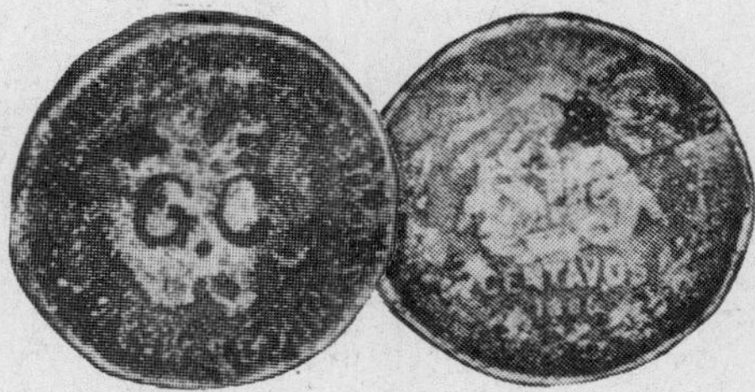

**50 CENTAVOS** **KM# 767** **Composition:** Cast Silver **Countermark:** G.C. **Obverse:** With additional countermark **Note:** Sand molded using regular 50 Centavos, km#445.

| CM Date | Host Date | Good | VG | F | VF | XF |
|---|---|---|---|---|---|---|
| ND | ND(1905-1918) | 200 | 350 | 500 | 600 | — |

**PESO** **KM# 770** **Composition:** Cast Silver **Countermark:** G.C **Obverse:** With additional countermark **Note:** Sand molded using regular Peso, KM#409.

| CM Date | Host Date | Good | VG | F | VF | XF |
|---|---|---|---|---|---|---|
| ND | ND(1898-1909) | 30.00 | 60.00 | 140 | 175 | — |

# MOLDOVA

The Republic of Moldova (formerly the Moldavian S.S.R.) is bordered in the north, east and south by the Ukraine and on the west by Romania. It has an area of 13,000 sq.mi. (33,700 sq.km.) and a population of 4.4 million. The capital is Chisinau. Agricultural products are mainly cereals, grapes, tobacco, sugar beets and fruits. Industry is dominated by food processing, clothing, building materials and agricultural machinery manufacturing.

The historical Romanian principality of Moldova was established in the 14th century. It fell under Turkish suzerainty in the 16th century. From 1812 to 1918 Russians occupied the eastern portion of Moldova, which they named Bessarabia. In March 1918the Bessarabian legislature voted in favor of reunification with Romania. At the Paris Peace Conference in 1920 the union was officially recognized by United States, France, U.K., and Italy a.s.o. The new Soviet government did not accept the union. In 1924, due to Soviet pressure against Romania a Moldavian Autonomous Soviet Socialist Republic (A.S.S.R.) was established within the USSR on border strip that extends east of Nistru River (today it is Transdniestria or Transdniester).

Following the Molotov-Ribbentrop Pact (1939), the Soviet - German agreement which divided Eastern Europe, the Soviet forces reoccupied the region in June 1940 and the Moldavian S.S.R. was proclaimed. The Transdniestria region was transferred to the new republic, while Ukrainian S.S.R. obtained possession of southern part of Bessarabia. The region was liberated by Romanian forces in 1941. The Soviets reconquered the territory in (1944).

A declaration of republican sovereignty was adopted in June 1990 and in Aug. 1991 the area was renamed Moldova, an independent republic. In Dec. 1991Moldova became a member of the C.I.S. In 1992, as a result of Russian involvement, Transdniestria seceded from Moldova. In May 1992 fighting began between Moldavian separatists (Romanians) and rebels aided by contingents of Cossacks and the Russian14th Army. The Moldavian government made several futile requests for United Nations intervention. On July 3, 1992, Russian and Moldavian presidents agreed upon a neutral demarcation line with the withdrawl of Russian forces from Transdniestria. This status will remain until a more feasible constitution is proclaimed.

**RULERS**

Romanian, until 1940

**MONETARY SYSTEM**

100 Bani = 1 Leu

## REPUBLIC

### DECIMAL COINAGE

**BAN** **KM# 1** **Composition:** Aluminum

| Date | Mintage | F | VF | XF | Unc | BU |
|---|---|---|---|---|---|---|
| 1993 | — | — | — | — | 0.20 | — |
| 1995 | — | — | — | — | 0.20 | — |
| 1996 | — | — | — | — | 0.25 | — |

**5 BANI** **KM# 2** **Composition:** Aluminum

| Date | Mintage | F | VF | XF | Unc | BU |
|---|---|---|---|---|---|---|
| 1993 | — | — | — | — | 0.30 | — |
| 1995 | — | — | — | — | 0.30 | — |
| 1996 | — | — | — | — | 0.30 | — |
| 1999 | — | — | — | — | 0.30 | — |
| 2000 | — | — | — | — | 0.30 | — |
| 2001 | — | — | — | — | 0.30 | — |

**10 BANI** **KM# 7** **Composition:** Aluminum

| Date | Mintage | F | VF | XF | Unc | BU |
|---|---|---|---|---|---|---|
| 1995 | — | — | — | — | 0.40 | — |
| 1996 | — | — | — | — | 0.40 | — |
| 1997 | — | — | — | — | 0.40 | — |
| 1998 | — | — | — | — | 0.40 | — |
| 2000 | — | — | — | — | 0.40 | — |
| 2001 | — | — | — | — | 0.40 | — |

**25 BANI** KM# 3 **Composition:** Aluminum

| Date | Mintage | F | VF | XF | Unc | BU |
|---|---|---|---|---|---|---|
| 1993 | — | — | — | — | 0.50 | — |
| 1995 | — | — | — | — | 0.50 | — |
| 1999 | — | — | — | — | 0.50 | — |
| 2000 | — | — | — | — | 0.50 | — |
| 2001 | — | — | — | — | 0.50 | — |

**50 BANI** KM# 4 **Composition:** Aluminum

| Date | Mintage | F | VF | XF | Unc | BU |
|---|---|---|---|---|---|---|
| 1993 | — | — | — | — | 0.75 | — |

**50 BANI** KM# 10 **Composition:** Brass-Clad Steel **Obverse:** Heraldic eagle **Reverse:** Denomination and grape vine

| Date | Mintage | F | VF | XF | Unc | BU |
|---|---|---|---|---|---|---|
| 1997 | — | — | — | — | 1.50 | — |

**LEU** KM# 5 **Composition:** Nickel Clad Steel

| Date | Mintage | F | VF | XF | Unc | BU |
|---|---|---|---|---|---|---|
| 1992 | — | — | — | — | 1.50 | — |

**5 LEI** KM# 6 **Composition:** Nickel Clad Steel

| Date | Mintage | F | VF | XF | Unc | BU |
|---|---|---|---|---|---|---|
| 1993 | — | — | — | — | 3.50 | — |

**100 LEI** KM# 8 **Weight:** 28.2800 g. **Composition:** 0.9250 Silver .8411 oz. ASW **Subject:** 5th Anniversary of Independence **Obverse:** National arms **Reverse:** Flying stork with grapes

| Date | Mintage | F | VF | XF | Unc | BU |
|---|---|---|---|---|---|---|
| 1996 | 20,000 | Value: 55.00 | | | | |

**100 LEI** KM# 9 **Weight:** 28.2800 g. **Composition:** 0.9250 Silver .8411 oz. ASW **Subject:** First Olympic Games Participation **Obverse:** National arms **Reverse:** 2 man canoe

| Date | Mintage | F | VF | XF | Unc | BU |
|---|---|---|---|---|---|---|
| 1996 | 20,000 | Value: 55.00 | | | | |

# MONACO

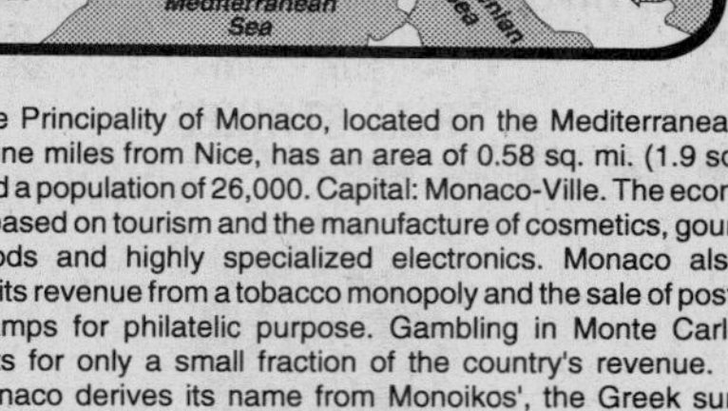

The Principality of Monaco, located on the Mediterranean coast nine miles from Nice, has an area of 0.58 sq. mi. (1.9 sq. km.) and a population of 26,000. Capital: Monaco-Ville. The economy is based on tourism and the manufacture of cosmetics, gourmet foods and highly specialized electronics. Monaco also derives its revenue from a tobacco monopoly and the sale of postage stamps for philatelic purpose. Gambling in Monte Carlo accounts for only a small fraction of the country's revenue.

Monaco derives its name from Monoikos', the Greek surname for Hercules, the mythological strong man who, according to legend, formed the Monacan headland during one of his twelve labors. Monaco has been ruled by the Grimaldi dynasty since 1297 - Prince Rainier III, the present and 31st monarch of Monaco, is still of that line - except for a period during the French Revolution until Napoleon's downfall when the Principality was annexed to France. Since 1865, Monaco has maintained a customs union with France which guarantees its privileged position as long as the royal line remains intact. Under the new constitution proclaimed on December 17, 1962, the Prince shares his power with an 18-member unicameral National Council.

**RULERS**

Albert I, 1889-1922
Louis II, 1922-1949
Rainier III, 1949-

**MINT MARKS**

M - Monaco
A – Paris

**MINT PRIVY MARKS**

(a) - Paris (privy marks only)
(p) - Thunderbolt - Poissy

**MONETARY SYSTEM**

10 Centimes = 1 Decime
10 Decimes = 1 Franc

## PRINCIPALITY

### DECIMAL COINAGE

10 Centimes = 1 Decime; 10 Decimes = 1 Franc

**50 CENTIMES** KM# 110 **Composition:** Aluminum-Bronze

| Date | Mintage | F | VF | XF | Unc | BU |
|---|---|---|---|---|---|---|
| 1924 (p) | 150,000 | 3.50 | 8.00 | 18.00 | 40.00 | — |

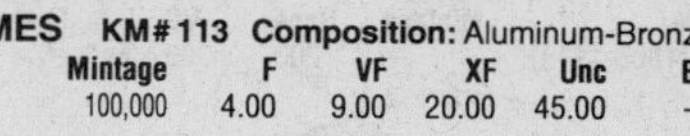

**50 CENTIMES** KM# 113 **Composition:** Aluminum-Bronze

| Date | Mintage | F | VF | XF | Unc | BU |
|---|---|---|---|---|---|---|
| 1926 (p) | 100,000 | 4.00 | 9.00 | 20.00 | 45.00 | — |

**FRANC** KM# 111 **Composition:** Aluminum-Bronze

| Date | Mintage | F | VF | XF | Unc | BU |
|---|---|---|---|---|---|---|
| 1924 (p) | 150,000 | 3.00 | 7.00 | 14.00 | 30.00 | — |

**FRANC** KM# 114 **Composition:** Aluminum-Bronze

| Date | Mintage | F | VF | XF | Unc | BU |
|---|---|---|---|---|---|---|
| 1926 (p) | 100,000 | 4.00 | 9.00 | 16.00 | 35.00 | — |

**FRANC** KM# 120 **Composition:** Aluminum

| Date | Mintage | F | VF | XF | Unc | BU |
|---|---|---|---|---|---|---|
| ND(1943) (a) | 2,500,000 | 0.50 | 1.00 | 2.00 | 4.50 | — |

**FRANC** KM# 120a **Composition:** Aluminum-Bronze

| Date | Mintage | F | VF | XF | Unc | BU |
|---|---|---|---|---|---|---|
| ND(1945) (a) | 1,509,000 | 0.50 | 1.00 | 2.00 | 5.00 | — |

**2 FRANCS** KM# 112 **Composition:** Aluminum-Bronze

| Date | Mintage | F | VF | XF | Unc | BU |
|---|---|---|---|---|---|---|
| 1924 (p) | 75,000 | 8.00 | 14.00 | 30.00 | 70.00 | — |

**2 FRANCS** KM# 115 **Composition:** Aluminum-Bronze

| Date | Mintage | F | VF | XF | Unc | BU |
|---|---|---|---|---|---|---|
| 1926 (p) | 75,000 | 7.00 | 12.00 | 25.00 | 60.00 | — |

**2 FRANCS** KM# 121 **Composition:** Aluminum

| Date | Mintage | F | VF | XF | Unc | BU |
|---|---|---|---|---|---|---|
| ND(1943) (a) | 1,250,000 | 0.75 | 1.50 | 5.00 | 10.00 | — |

**2 FRANCS** KM# 121a **Composition:** Aluminum-Bronze

| Date | Mintage | F | VF | XF | Unc | BU |
|---|---|---|---|---|---|---|
| ND(1945) (a) | 1,080,000 | 0.50 | 1.00 | 2.50 | 6.00 | — |

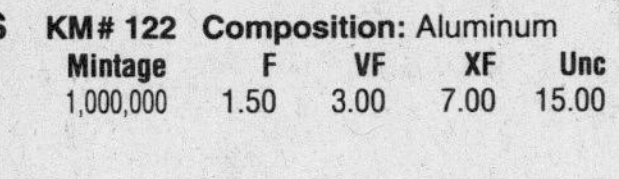

**5 FRANCS** KM# 122 **Composition:** Aluminum

| Date | Mintage | F | VF | XF | Unc | BU |
|---|---|---|---|---|---|---|
| 1945 (a) | 1,000,000 | 1.50 | 3.00 | 7.00 | 15.00 | — |

**10 FRANCS** KM# 123 **Composition:** Copper-Nickel

| Date | Mintage | F | VF | XF | Unc | BU |
|---|---|---|---|---|---|---|
| 1946 (a) | 1,000,000 | 1.50 | 3.00 | 6.00 | 12.50 | — |

**10 FRANCS** KM# 130 **Composition:** Aluminum-Bronze

| Date | Mintage | F | VF | XF | Unc | BU |
|---|---|---|---|---|---|---|
| 1950 (a) | 500,000 | 0.50 | 1.00 | 2.00 | 4.00 | — |
| 1951 (a) | 500,000 | 0.50 | 1.00 | 2.00 | 4.00 | — |

**20 FRANCS (Vingt)** KM# 124 **Composition:** Copper-Nickel

| Date | Mintage | F | VF | XF | Unc | BU |
|---|---|---|---|---|---|---|
| 1947 (a) | 1,000,000 | 2.00 | 4.00 | 8.00 | 20.00 | — |

**20 FRANCS (Vingt)** KM# 131 **Composition:** Aluminum-Bronze

| Date | Mintage | F | VF | XF | Unc | BU |
|---|---|---|---|---|---|---|
| 1950 (a) | 500,000 | 0.65 | 1.25 | 2.50 | 6.00 | — |
| 1951 (a) | 500,000 | 0.65 | 1.25 | 2.50 | 6.00 | — |

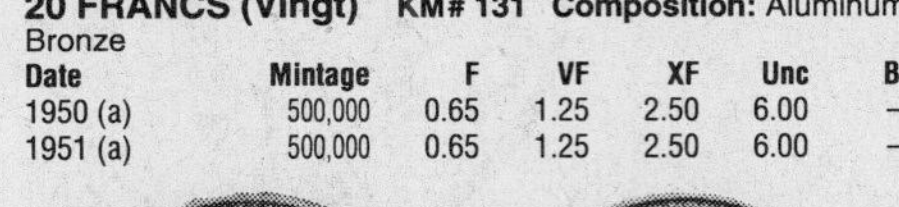

**50 FRANCS (Cinquante)** KM# 132 **Composition:** Aluminum-Bronze

| Date | Mintage | F | VF | XF | Unc | BU |
|---|---|---|---|---|---|---|
| 1950 (a) | 500,000 | 1.50 | 3.00 | 5.00 | 12.00 | — |

**100 FRANCS (Cent)** KM# 105 **Weight:** 32.2580 g. **Composition:** 0.9000 Gold .9335 oz. AGW

| Date | Mintage | F | VF | XF | Unc | BU |
|---|---|---|---|---|---|---|
| 1901A | 15,000 | BV | 420 | 500 | 750 | — |
| 1904A | 10,000 | BV | 420 | 500 | 750 | — |

**100 FRANCS (Cent)** KM# 133 **Composition:** Copper-Nickel

| Date | Mintage | F | VF | XF | Unc | BU |
|---|---|---|---|---|---|---|
| 1950 (a) | 500,000 | 2.00 | 4.00 | 8.00 | 18.00 | — |

**100 FRANCS (Cent)** KM# 134 **Composition:** Copper-Nickel

| Date | Mintage | F | VF | XF | Unc | BU |
|---|---|---|---|---|---|---|
| 1956 (a) | 500,000 | 1.50 | 2.50 | 5.50 | 15.00 | — |

## REFORM COINAGE

100 Old Francs = 1 New Franc

**CENTIME** KM# 155 **Composition:** Stainless Steel

| Date | Mintage | F | VF | XF | Unc | BU |
|---|---|---|---|---|---|---|
| 1976 (a) | 25,000 | — | 0.15 | 0.30 | 4.00 | — |
| 1977 (a) | 25,000 | — | 0.15 | 0.30 | 4.00 | — |
| 1978 (a) | 75,000 | — | 0.15 | 0.30 | 4.00 | — |
| 1979 (a) | 75,000 | — | 0.15 | 0.30 | 4.00 | — |
| 1982 (a) | 10,000 | — | 0.15 | 0.30 | 4.00 | — |
| 1995 (a) | — | — | 0.15 | 0.30 | 4.00 | — |

**5 CENTIMES** KM# 156 **Composition:** Copper-Aluminum-Nickel

| Date | Mintage | F | VF | XF | Unc | BU |
|---|---|---|---|---|---|---|
| 1976 (a) | 25,000 | — | 0.20 | 0.40 | 4.50 | — |
| 1977 (a) | 25,000 | — | 0.20 | 0.40 | 4.50 | — |
| 1978 (a) | 75,000 | — | 0.20 | 0.40 | 4.50 | — |
| 1979 (a) | 75,000 | — | 0.20 | 0.40 | 4.50 | — |
| 1982 (a) | 10,000 | — | 0.20 | 0.40 | 4.50 | — |
| 1995 (a) | — | — | 0.20 | 0.40 | 4.50 | — |

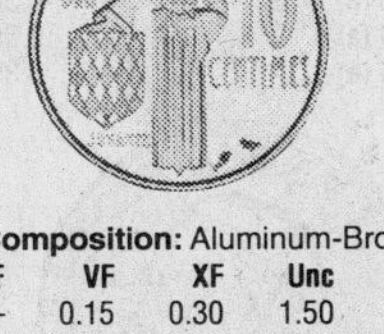

**10 CENTIMES** KM# 142 **Composition:** Aluminum-Bronze

| Date | Mintage | F | VF | XF | Unc | BU |
|---|---|---|---|---|---|---|
| 1962 (a) | 750,000 | — | 0.15 | 0.30 | 1.50 | — |
| 1974 (a) | 179,000 | — | 0.15 | 0.30 | 2.25 | — |
| 1975 (a) | 172,000 | — | 0.15 | 0.30 | 2.25 | — |
| 1976 (a) | 178,000 | — | 0.15 | 0.30 | 2.25 | — |
| 1977 (a) | 172,000 | — | 0.15 | 0.30 | 2.25 | — |
| 1978 (a) | 112,000 | — | 0.15 | 0.30 | 2.50 | — |
| 1979 (a) | 112,000 | — | 0.15 | 0.30 | 2.50 | — |
| 1982 (a) | 100,000 | — | 0.15 | 0.30 | 2.50 | — |
| 1995 (a) | — | — | 0.15 | 0.30 | 2.50 | — |

**20 CENTIMES** KM# 143 **Composition:** Aluminum-Bronze

| Date | Mintage | F | VF | XF | Unc | BU |
|---|---|---|---|---|---|---|
| 1962 (a) | 750,000 | — | 0.25 | 0.50 | 1.75 | — |
| 1974 (a) | 104,000 | — | 0.25 | 0.50 | 2.75 | — |
| 1975 (a) | 97,000 | — | 0.25 | 0.50 | 2.75 | — |
| 1976 (a) | 103,000 | — | 0.25 | 0.50 | 2.75 | — |
| 1977 (a) | 97,000 | — | 0.25 | 0.50 | 2.75 | — |
| 1978 (a) | 81,000 | — | 0.25 | 0.50 | 2.75 | — |
| 1979 (a) | 81,000 | — | 0.25 | 0.50 | 2.75 | — |
| 1982 (a) | 100,000 | — | 0.25 | 0.50 | 2.75 | — |
| 1995 (a) | — | — | 0.25 | 0.50 | 2.75 | — |

**50 CENTIMES** KM# 144 **Composition:** Aluminum-Bronze

| Date | Mintage | F | VF | XF | Unc | BU |
|---|---|---|---|---|---|---|
| 1962 (a) | 375,000 | — | 1.25 | 2.50 | 4.50 | — |

**1/2 FRANC** KM# 145 **Composition:** Nickel

| Date | Mintage | F | VF | XF | Unc | BU |
|---|---|---|---|---|---|---|
| 1965 (a) | 375,000 | 0.30 | 0.60 | 1.25 | 2.50 | — |
| 1968 (a) | 250,000 | 0.30 | 0.60 | 1.25 | 2.50 | — |
| 1974 (a) | 69,000 | 0.35 | 0.70 | 1.50 | 3.50 | — |
| 1975 (a) | 70,000 | 0.35 | 0.70 | 1.50 | 3.50 | — |
| 1976 (a) | 68,000 | 0.35 | 0.70 | 1.50 | 3.50 | — |
| 1977 (a) | 62,000 | 0.35 | 0.70 | 1.50 | 3.50 | — |
| 1978 (a) | 414,000 | 0.30 | 0.60 | 1.25 | 2.75 | — |
| 1979 (a) | 414,000 | 0.30 | 0.60 | 1.25 | 2.75 | — |
| 1982 (a) | 457,000 | 0.30 | 0.60 | 1.25 | 2.75 | — |
| 1989 (a) | — | 0.30 | 0.60 | 1.25 | 2.75 | — |
| 1995 (a) | — | 0.30 | 0.60 | 1.25 | 2.75 | — |

**FRANC** KM# 140 **Composition:** Nickel

| Date | Mintage | F | VF | XF | Unc | BU |
|---|---|---|---|---|---|---|
| 1960 (a) | 500,000 | 0.35 | 0.70 | 1.50 | 3.25 | — |
| 1966 (a) | 175,000 | 0.40 | 0.80 | 1.75 | 4.00 | — |
| 1968 (a) | 250,000 | 0.40 | 0.80 | 1.75 | 4.00 | — |
| 1974 (a) | 194,000 | 0.40 | 0.80 | 1.75 | 4.00 | — |
| 1975 (a) | 195,000 | 0.40 | 0.80 | 1.75 | 4.00 | — |
| 1976 (a) | 193,000 | 0.40 | 0.80 | 1.75 | 4.00 | — |
| 1977 (a) | 188,000 | 0.40 | 0.80 | 1.75 | 4.00 | — |
| 1978 (a) | 783,000 | 0.40 | 0.80 | 1.75 | 3.50 | — |
| 1979 (a) | 783,000 | 0.40 | 0.80 | 1.75 | 3.50 | — |
| 1982 (a) | 525,000 | 0.40 | 0.80 | 1.75 | 3.50 | — |
| 1986 (a) | — | 0.35 | 0.70 | 1.50 | 3.00 | — |
| 1989 (a) | — | 0.35 | 0.70 | 1.50 | 2.75 | — |
| 1995 (a) | — | 0.35 | 0.70 | 1.50 | 2.75 | — |

**2 FRANCS** KM# 157 **Composition:** Nickel

| Date | Mintage | F | VF | XF | Unc | BU |
|---|---|---|---|---|---|---|
| 1979 (a) | 162,000 | 0.60 | 0.85 | 1.75 | 4.00 | — |
| 1981 (a) | 275,000 | 0.60 | 0.85 | 1.75 | 4.00 | — |
| 1982 (a) | 446,000 | 0.60 | 0.85 | 1.75 | 4.00 | — |
| 1995 (a) | — | 0.60 | 0.85 | 1.75 | 4.00 | — |

**2 FRANCS** KM# 166 **Composition:** Nickel **Obverse:** Head left

| Date | Mintage | F | VF | XF | Unc | BU |
|---|---|---|---|---|---|---|
| 1995 (a) | — | 0.60 | 0.85 | 1.75 | 4.00 | — |

**5 FRANCS** KM# 141 **Weight:** 12.0000 g. **Composition:** 0.8350 Silver .3221 oz. ASW

| Date | Mintage | F | VF | XF | Unc | BU |
|---|---|---|---|---|---|---|
| 1960 (a) | 125,000 | — | — | 7.50 | 10.00 | — |
| 1966 (a) | 125,000 | — | — | 7.50 | 10.00 | — |

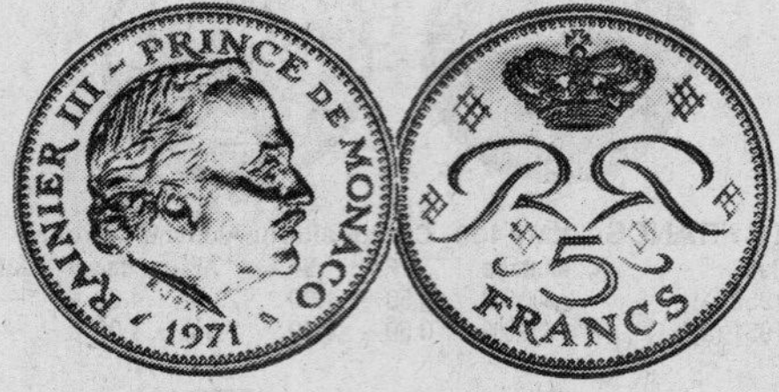


**5 FRANCS** KM# 150 **Composition:** Nickel Clad Copper-Nickel

| Date | Mintage | F | VF | XF | Unc | BU |
|---|---|---|---|---|---|---|
| 1971 (a) | 250,000 | — | 1.50 | 2.50 | 4.50 | — |
| 1974 (a) | 152,000 | — | 1.50 | 2.50 | 4.50 | — |
| 1975 (a) | 8,000 | — | 2.50 | 6.00 | 12.50 | — |
| 1976 (a) | 8,000 | — | 2.50 | 6.00 | 12.50 | — |
| 1977 (a) | 42,000 | — | 2.00 | 5.00 | 10.00 | — |
| 1978 (a) | 22,000 | — | 2.00 | 5.00 | 10.00 | — |
| 1979 (a) | 22,000 | — | 2.00 | 5.00 | 10.00 | — |
| 1982 (a) | 152,000 | — | 2.00 | 5.00 | 10.00 | — |
| 1989 | — | — | 2.00 | 5.00 | 10.00 | — |
| 1995 (a) | — | — | 2.00 | 5.00 | 10.00 | — |

**10 FRANCS** KM# 146 **Weight:** 25.0000 g. **Composition:** 0.9000 Silver .7234 oz. ASW **Subject:** 100th anniversary - Accession of Charles III

| Date | Mintage | F | VF | XF | Unc | BU |
|---|---|---|---|---|---|---|
| 1966 (a) | 38,000 | — | — | — | 21.50 | 27.50 |

**10 FRANCS** KM# 151 **Composition:** Copper-Nickel-Aluminum **Subject:** 25th anniversary of reign

| Date | Mintage | F | VF | XF | Unc | BU |
|---|---|---|---|---|---|---|
| ND(1974) (a) | 25,000 | — | 2.50 | 4.50 | 8.00 | — |

**10 FRANCS** KM# 154 **Composition:** Copper-Nickel-Aluminum

| Date | Mintage | F | VF | XF | Unc | BU |
|---|---|---|---|---|---|---|
| 1975 (a) | 25,000 | — | 2.25 | 3.75 | 8.00 | — |
| 1976 (a) | 16,000 | — | 2.50 | 4.00 | 9.00 | — |
| 1977 (a) | 50,000 | — | 2.25 | 3.25 | 5.50 | — |
| 1978 (a) | 228,000 | — | 2.25 | 3.25 | 5.50 | — |
| 1979 (a) | 228,000 | — | 2.25 | 3.25 | 5.50 | — |
| 1981 (a) | 235,000 | — | 2.25 | 3.25 | 5.50 | — |
| 1982 (a) | 230,000 | — | 2.25 | 3.25 | 5.50 | — |

**10 FRANCS** KM# 160 **Composition:** Copper-Nickel-Aluminum **Obverse:** Princess Grace bust facing left

| Date | Mintage | F | VF | XF | Unc | BU |
|---|---|---|---|---|---|---|
| 1982 (a) | 30,000 | — | — | — | 12.50 | — |

**10 FRANCS** KM# 162 **Composition:** Nickel-Aluminum-Bronze **Subject:** Prince Pierre Foundation

| Date | Mintage | F | VF | XF | Unc | BU |
|---|---|---|---|---|---|---|
| 1989 (a) | — | — | — | — | 6.50 | — |

**10 FRANCS** KM# 163 **Ring Composition:** Aluminum-Bronze **Center Composition:** Steel

| Date | Mintage | F | VF | XF | Unc | BU |
|---|---|---|---|---|---|---|
| 1989 (a) | — | — | — | — | 9.00 | — |
| 1991 (a) | — | — | — | — | 14.00 | — |
| 1992 (a) | — | — | — | — | 12.50 | — |
| 1993 (a) | — | — | — | — | 14.00 | — |
| 1994 (a) | — | — | — | — | 14.00 | — |
| 1995 (a) | — | — | — | — | 9.00 | — |
| 1996 (a) | — | — | — | — | 9.00 | — |
| 1997 (a) | — | — | — | — | 9.00 | — |
| 1998 (a) | — | — | — | — | 9.00 | — |

**20 FRANCS** KM# 165 **Ring Composition:** Nickel **Center Composition:** Copper-Aluminum-Nickel **Reverse:** Prince's palace

| Date | Mintage | F | VF | XF | Unc | BU |
|---|---|---|---|---|---|---|
| 1992 (a) | — | — | — | — | 15.00 | — |
| 1995 (a) | — | — | — | — | 15.00 | — |
| 1997 (a) | — | — | — | — | 15.00 | — |

**50 FRANCS** KM# 152.1 **Weight:** 30.0000 g. **Composition:** 0.9000 Silver .8681 oz. ASW **Subject:** 25th anniversary of reign **Edge:** Commemorative inscription

| Date | Mintage | F | VF | XF | Unc | BU |
|---|---|---|---|---|---|---|
| 1974 (a) | 25,000 | — | — | — | 42.00 | 48.00 |

**50 FRANCS** KM# 152.2 **Weight:** 30.0000 g. **Composition:** 0.9000 Silver .8681 oz. ASW **Edge:** Plain

| Date | Mintage | F | VF | XF | Unc | BU |
|---|---|---|---|---|---|---|
| 1975 (a) | 7,500 | — | — | — | 60.00 | — |
| 1976 (a) | 6,000 | — | — | — | 65.00 | — |

**100 FRANCS** KM# 161 **Weight:** 15.0000 g. **Composition:** 0.9000 Silver .4340 oz. ASW **Subject:** Heir Apparent Prince Albert

| Date | Mintage | F | VF | XF | Unc | BU |
|---|---|---|---|---|---|---|
| 1982 (a) | 30,000 | — | — | — | 75.00 | — |

**100 FRANCS** KM# 164 **Weight:** 15.0000 g. **Composition:** 0.9000 Silver .4340 oz. ASW **Subject:** 40th anniversary of reign

| Date | Mintage | F | VF | XF | Unc | BU |
|---|---|---|---|---|---|---|
| 1989 (a) | 45,000 | — | — | — | 75.00 | — |

## MEDALLIC COINAGE

**10 FRANCS** KM# M1 **Weight:** 25.0000 g. **Composition:** 0.9000 Silver .7234 oz. ASW **Subject:** 10th wedding anniversary

| Date | Mintage | F | VF | XF | Unc | BU |
|---|---|---|---|---|---|---|
| 1966 (a) | 24,000 | — | — | — | 22.00 | 28.00 |
| 1966 (a) Proof | 1,000 | Value: 85.00 | | | | |

**100 FRANCS** KM# M3 **Weight:** 37.0400 g. **Composition:** 0.9990 Silver 1.1896 oz. ASW **Subject:** 25th anniversary of reign

| Date | Mintage | F | VF | XF | Unc | BU |
|---|---|---|---|---|---|---|
| 1974 (a) Proof | 25,000 | Value: 50.00 | | | | |

**200 FRANCS** KM# M2 **Weight:** 32.0000 g. **Composition:** 0.9200 Gold .9466 oz. AGW **Subject:** 10th wedding anniversary

| Date | Mintage | F | VF | XF | Unc | BU |
|---|---|---|---|---|---|---|
| 1966 (a) | 5,000 | — | — | — | 450 | — |
| 1966 (a) Proof | 1,000 | Value: 650 | | | | |

**1000 FRANCS** KM# M4 **Composition:** 0.9970 Platinum APW **Subject:** 25th Anniversary of Reign

| Date | Mintage | F | VF | XF | Unc | BU |
|---|---|---|---|---|---|---|
| 1974 (a) Proof | 10,000 | Value: 325 | | | | |

**2000 FRANCS** KM# M5 **Composition:** 0.9970 Platinum APW **Subject:** 25th anniversary of reign

| Date | Mintage | F | VF | XF | Unc | BU |
|---|---|---|---|---|---|---|
| 1974 (a) Proof | 10,000 | Value: 650 | | | | |

**3000 FRANCS** KM# M6 **Composition:** 0.9990 Gold **Subject:** 25th Anniversary of Reign

| Date | Mintage | F | VF | XF | Unc | BU |
|---|---|---|---|---|---|---|
| 1974 (a) Proof | 5,000 | Value: 450 | | | | |

## ESSAIS

Standard metals unless otherwise noted

| KM# | Date | Mintage | Identification | Issue Price | Mkt Val |
|---|---|---|---|---|---|
| E1 | 1924 | — | 50 Centimes. Gold. KM#110 | — | 2,000 |
| E2 | 1924 | 12 | Franc. KM111 | — | 925 |

| KM# | Date | Mintage | Identification | Issue Price | Mkt Val |
|---|---|---|---|---|---|
| E3 | 1924 | — | Franc. Gold. KM111 | — | 3,000 |
| E4 | 1924 | 12 | 2 Francs. KM112 | — | 975 |

| KM# | Date | Mintage | Identification | Issue Price | Mkt Val |
|---|---|---|---|---|---|
| E5 | 1924 | — | 2 Francs. Gold. KM112 | — | 4,000 |
| E7 | (1943) (a) | 1,100 | Franc. Aluminum. KM120 | — | 25.00 |
| E8 | (1943) (a) | — | Franc. Aluminum-Bronze. KM120 | — | 25.00 |
| E9 | (1943) (a) | 250 | Franc. Silver. KM120 | — | 135 |

| KM# | Date | Mintage | Identification | Issue Price | Mkt Val |
|---|---|---|---|---|---|
| E10 | (1943) (a) | 250 | 2 Francs. 0.9000 Gold. | — | 725 |
| E11 | (1943) (a) | 1,100 | 2 Francs. Aluminum. KM121 | — | 35.00 |
| E12 | (1943) (a) | 1,100 | 2 Francs. Aluminum-Bronze. KM121 | — | 35.00 |

| KM# | Date | Mintage | Identification | Issue Price | Mkt Val |
|---|---|---|---|---|---|
| E6 | (1943) (a) | 250 | Franc. 0.9000 Gold. | — | 600 |
| E13 | (1943) (a) | 250 | 2 Francs. Silver. KM121 | — | 160 |

| KM# | Date | Mintage | Identification | Issue Price | Mkt Val |
|---|---|---|---|---|---|
| E14 | 1945 (a) | 250 | 5 Francs. 0.9000 Gold. | — | 800 |
| E15 | 1945 (a) | 1,100 | 5 Francs. Aluminum. KM122 | — | 50.00 |
| E16 | 1945 (a) | 150 | 5 Francs. Aluminum-Bronze. KM122 | — | 150 |
| E17 | 1945 (a) | 250 | 5 Francs. Silver. KM122 | — | 215 |
| E18 | 1945 (a) | 1,100 | 10 Francs. KM123 | — | 40.00 |
| E19 | 1945 (a) | 250 | 10 Francs. Silver. | — | 175 |

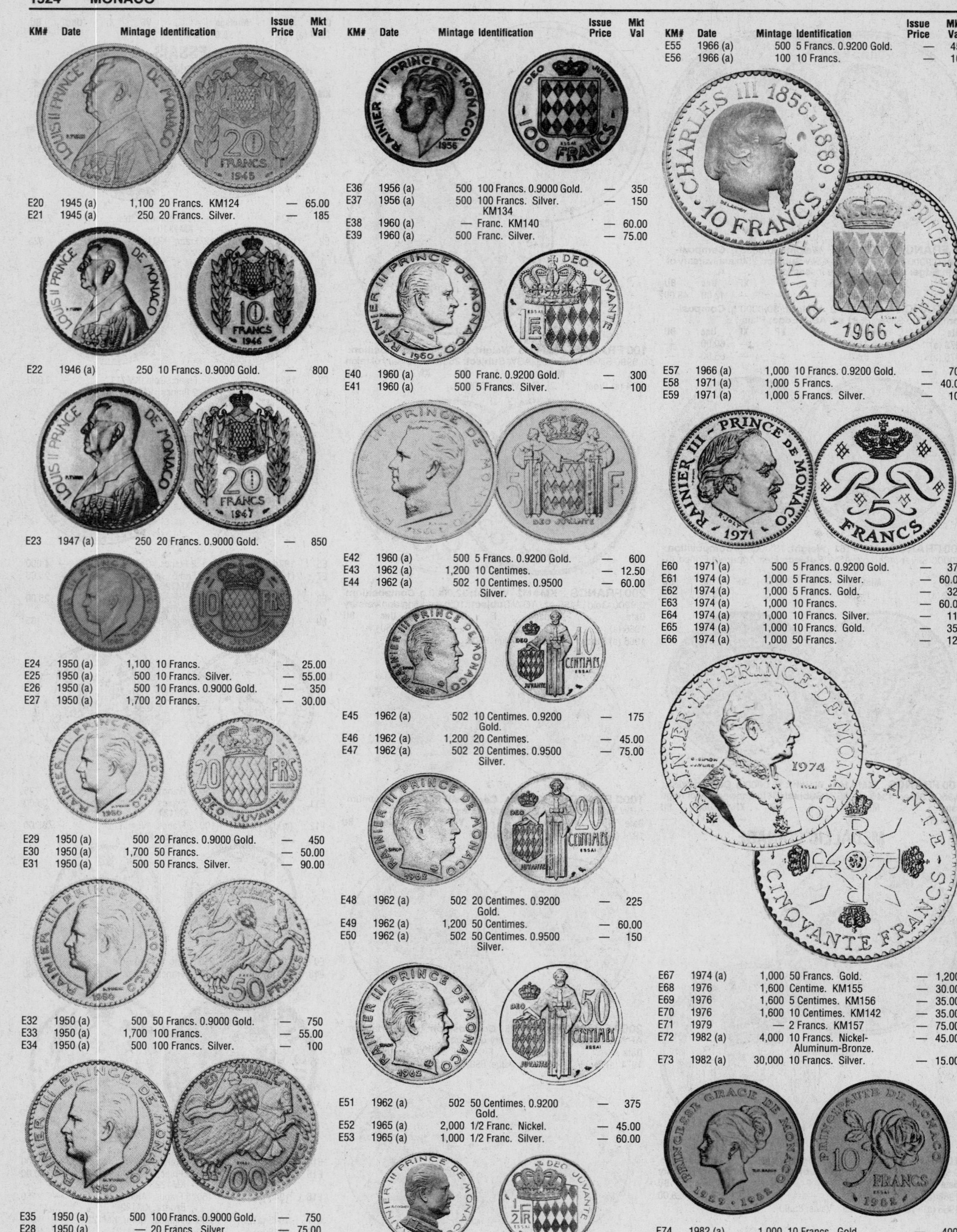

| KM# | Date | Mintage | Identification | Issue Price | Mkt Val |
|---|---|---|---|---|---|
| E20 | 1945 (a) | 1,100 | 20 Francs. KM124 | — | 65.00 |
| E21 | 1945 (a) | 250 | 20 Francs. Silver. | — | 185 |
| E22 | 1946 (a) | 250 | 10 Francs. 0.9000 Gold. | — | 800 |
| E23 | 1947 (a) | 250 | 20 Francs. 0.9000 Gold. | — | 850 |
| E24 | 1950 (a) | 1,100 | 10 Francs. | — | 25.00 |
| E25 | 1950 (a) | 500 | 10 Francs. Silver. | — | 55.00 |
| E26 | 1950 (a) | 500 | 10 Francs. 0.9000 Gold. | — | 350 |
| E27 | 1950 (a) | 1,700 | 20 Francs. | — | 30.00 |
| E29 | 1950 (a) | 500 | 20 Francs. 0.9000 Gold. | — | 450 |
| E30 | 1950 (a) | 1,700 | 50 Francs. | — | 50.00 |
| E31 | 1950 (a) | 500 | 50 Francs. Silver. | — | 90.00 |
| E32 | 1950 (a) | 500 | 50 Francs. 0.9000 Gold. | — | 750 |
| E33 | 1950 (a) | 1,700 | 100 Francs. | — | 55.00 |
| E34 | 1950 (a) | 500 | 100 Francs. Silver. | — | 100 |
| E35 | 1950 (a) | 500 | 100 Francs. 0.9000 Gold. | — | 750 |
| E28 | 1950 (a) | — | 20 Francs. Silver. | — | 75.00 |

| KM# | Date | Mintage | Identification | Issue Price | Mkt Val |
|---|---|---|---|---|---|
| E36 | 1956 (a) | 500 | 100 Francs. 0.9000 Gold. | — | 350 |
| E37 | 1956 (a) | 500 | 100 Francs. Silver. KM134 | — | 150 |
| E38 | 1960 (a) | — | Franc. KM140 | — | 60.00 |
| E39 | 1960 (a) | 500 | Franc. Silver. | — | 75.00 |
| E40 | 1960 (a) | 500 | Franc. 0.9200 Gold. | — | 300 |
| E41 | 1960 (a) | 500 | 5 Francs. Silver. | — | 100 |
| E42 | 1960 (a) | 500 | 5 Francs. 0.9200 Gold. | — | 600 |
| E43 | 1962 (a) | 1,200 | 10 Centimes. | — | 12.50 |
| E44 | 1962 (a) | 502 | 10 Centimes. 0.9500 Silver. | — | 60.00 |
| E45 | 1962 (a) | 502 | 10 Centimes. 0.9200 Gold. | — | 175 |
| E46 | 1962 (a) | 1,200 | 20 Centimes. | — | 45.00 |
| E47 | 1962 (a) | 502 | 20 Centimes. 0.9500 Silver. | — | 75.00 |
| E48 | 1962 (a) | 502 | 20 Centimes. 0.9200 Gold. | — | 225 |
| E49 | 1962 (a) | 1,200 | 50 Centimes. | — | 60.00 |
| E50 | 1962 (a) | 502 | 50 Centimes. 0.9500 Silver. | — | 150 |
| E51 | 1962 (a) | 502 | 50 Centimes. 0.9200 Gold. | — | 375 |
| E52 | 1965 (a) | 2,000 | 1/2 Franc. Nickel. | — | 45.00 |
| E53 | 1965 (a) | 1,000 | 1/2 Franc. Silver. | — | 60.00 |
| E54 | 1965 (a) | 1,000 | 1/2 Franc. 0.9200 Gold. | — | 200 |

| KM# | Date | Mintage | Identification | Issue Price | Mkt Val |
|---|---|---|---|---|---|
| E55 | 1966 (a) | 500 | 5 Francs. 0.9200 Gold. | — | 450 |
| E56 | 1966 (a) | 100 | 10 Francs. | — | 100 |
| E57 | 1966 (a) | 1,000 | 10 Francs. 0.9200 Gold. | — | 700 |
| E58 | 1971 (a) | 1,000 | 5 Francs. | — | 40.00 |
| E59 | 1971 (a) | 1,000 | 5 Francs. Silver. | — | 100 |
| E60 | 1971 (a) | 500 | 5 Francs. 0.9200 Gold. | — | 375 |
| E61 | 1974 (a) | 1,000 | 5 Francs. Silver. | — | 60.00 |
| E62 | 1974 (a) | 1,000 | 5 Francs. Gold. | — | 325 |
| E63 | 1974 (a) | 1,000 | 10 Francs. | — | 60.00 |
| E64 | 1974 (a) | 1,000 | 10 Francs. Silver. | — | 115 |
| E65 | 1974 (a) | 1,000 | 10 Francs. Gold. | — | 350 |
| E66 | 1974 (a) | 1,000 | 50 Francs. | — | 125 |
| E67 | 1974 (a) | 1,000 | 50 Francs. Gold. | — | 1,200 |
| E68 | 1976 | 1,600 | Centime. KM155 | — | 30.00 |
| E69 | 1976 | 1,600 | 5 Centimes. KM156 | — | 35.00 |
| E70 | 1976 | 1,600 | 10 Centimes. KM142 | — | 35.00 |
| E71 | 1979 | — | 2 Francs. KM157 | — | 75.00 |
| E72 | 1982 (a) | 4,000 | 10 Francs. Nickel-Aluminum-Bronze. | — | 45.00 |
| E73 | 1982 (a) | 30,000 | 10 Francs. Silver. | — | 15.00 |
| E74 | 1982 (a) | 1,000 | 10 Francs. Gold. | — | 400 |
| E75 | 1982 (a) | 1,000 | 100 Francs. 0.9000 Silver. KM161 | — | 65.00 |

| KM# | Date | Mintage | Identification | Issue Price | Mkt Val |
|---|---|---|---|---|---|

| KM# | Date | Mintage | Identification | Issue Price | Mkt Val |
|---|---|---|---|---|---|
| E76 | 1982 (a) | 1,000 | 100 Francs. Gold. | — | 400 |

## PATTERNS

Including off metal strikes

| KM# | Date | Mintage | Identification | Mkt Val |
|---|---|---|---|---|
| Pn15 | 1934A | 15 | 500 Francs. 0.9000 Gold. | 3,000 |

## PIEFORTS WITH ESSAI

Double thickness; Standard metals unless otherwise noted

| KM# | Date | Mintage | Identification | Issue Price | Mkt Val |
|---|---|---|---|---|---|
| PE1 | (1943) (a) | 15 | Franc. 0.9000 Gold. | — | 850 |
| PE2 | (1943) (a) | 15 | 2 Francs. 0.9000 Gold. | — | 950 |
| PE3 | 1945 (a) | 15 | 5 Francs. 0.9000 Gold. | — | 1,500 |

| KM# | Date | Mintage | Identification | Issue Price | Mkt Val |
|---|---|---|---|---|---|
| PE4 | 1946 (a) | 16 | 10 Francs. 0.9000 Gold. | — | 1,100 |
| PE5 | 1947 (a) | 16 | 20 Francs. 0.9000 Gold. | — | 1,350 |
| PE6a | 1950 (a) | 325 | 10 Francs. 0.9000 Gold. | — | 275 |
| PE6 | 1950 (a) | — | 10 Francs. Silver. | — | 75.00 |
| PE7 | 1950 (a) | — | 20 Francs. Silver. | — | 65.00 |
| PE7a | 1950 (a) | 325 | 20 Francs. 0.9000 Gold. | — | 300 |
| PE8 | 1950 (a) | — | 50 Francs. Silver. | — | 120 |
| PE8a | 1950 (a) | 325 | 50 Francs. 0.9000 Gold. | — | 425 |
| PE9 | 1950 (a) | — | 100 Francs. Silver. | — | 150 |
| PE9a | 1950 (a) | 325 | 100 Francs. 0.9000 Gold. | — | 550 |
| PE10 | 1956 (a) | 20 | 100 Francs. 0.9000 Gold. | — | 1,200 |
| PE11 | 1960 (a) | 25 | Franc. 0.9200 Gold. | — | 600 |
| PE12 | 1960 (a) | 25 | 5 Francs. 0.9200 Gold. | — | 1,200 |
| PE13 | 1962 (a) | 100 | 10 Centimes. 0.9500 Silver. | — | 125 |
| PE13a | 1962 (a) | 25 | 10 Centimes. 0.9200 Gold. | — | 700 |
| PE14 | 1962 (a) | 100 | 20 Centimes. 0.9500 Silver. | — | 150 |
| PE14a | 1962 (a) | 25 | 20 Centimes. 0.9200 Gold. | — | 800 |
| PE15 | 1962 (a) | 100 | 50 Centimes. 0.9500 Silver. | — | 200 |
| PE15a | 1962 (a) | 25 | 50 Centimes. 0.9200 Gold. | — | 900 |
| PE16 | 1966 (a) | 150 | 5 Francs. Nickel. | — | 60.00 |
| PE16a | 1971 (a) | 250 | 5 Francs. Silver. | — | 150 |
| PE16b | 1971 (a) | 250 | 5 Francs. 0.9200 Gold. | — | 600 |
| PE17 | 1974 (a) | 250 | 5 Francs. Silver. | — | 150 |

| KM# | Date | Mintage | Identification | Issue Price | Mkt Val |
|---|---|---|---|---|---|
| PE17a | 1974 (a) | 250 | 5 Francs. Gold. | — | 600 |
| PE18 | 1974 (a) | 250 | 10 Francs. Silver. | — | 200 |

| KM# | Date | Mintage | Identification | Issue Price | Mkt Val |
|---|---|---|---|---|---|
| PE18a | 1974 (a) | 250 | 10 Francs. Gold. | — | 500 |
| P18a | 1974 (a) | — | 10 Francs. Gold. Without Essai | — | 650 |
| PE19 | 1974 (a) | 250 | 50 Francs. Without Essai | — | 100 |

| KM# | Date | Mintage | Identification | Issue Price | Mkt Val |
|---|---|---|---|---|---|
| PE19a | 1974 (a) | 250 | 50 Francs. Gold. | — | 1,750 |
| P19a | 1974 (a) | 250 | 50 Francs. Gold. Without Essai | — | 1,500 |
| PE20 | 1982 (a) | 250 | 10 Francs. Silver. | — | 150 |
| PE20a | 1982 (a) | 250 | 10 Francs. Gold. | — | 500 |
| PE21 | 1982 (a) | 250 | 100 Francs. Silver. | — | 225 |
| PE21a | 1982 (a) | 250 | 100 Francs. Gold. | — | 700 |

## SPECIMEN SETS (SS)

| KM# | Date | Mintage | Identification | Issue Price | Mkt Val |
|---|---|---|---|---|---|
| SS1 | 1974 (7) | 7 | KM140, 142, 143, 145, 150, 151, 152.1. 3,000 sets not released. | 45.00 | 120 |
| SS2 | 1975 (7) | 8 | KM140, 142, 143, 145, 150, 152.2, 154 | — | 100 |
| SS3 | 1976 (9) | 6,000 | KM140, 142, 143, 145, 150, 152.2, 154-156 | — | 120 |
| SS6 | 1982 (11) | 10,000 | KM140, 142, 143, 145, 150, 154-157, 160, 161 | — | 150 |
| SS7 | 1995 (9) | — | KM140, 142, 143, 150, 155, 156, 163, 165, 166 | — | 120 |

# MONGOLIA

The State of Mongolia, (formerly the Mongolian Peoples Republic) a landlocked country in central Asia between Russia and the People's Republic of China, has an area of 604,250 sq. mi. (1,565,000 sq. km.) and a population of 2.26 million. Capital: Ulan Bator. Animal herds and flocks are the chief economic asset. Wool, cattle, butter, meat and hides are exported.

Mongolia (often referred to as Outer Mongolia), one of the world's oldest countries, attained its greatest power in the 13th century when Genghis Khan and his successors conquered all of China and extended their influence westward as far as Hungary and Poland. The empire dissolved in later centuries and in 1691 was brought under suzerainty of the Manchus, who had conquered China in 1644. After the Chinese republican movement led by Sun-Yat-sen overthrew the Manchus and set up the Chinese Republic in 1911. Mongolia, with the support of Russia, proclaimed their independence from China and, on March 13, 1921 a Provisional Peoples Government was established and later, on Nov. 26, 1924 the government proclaimed the Mongolian Peoples Republic.

Although nominally a dependency of China, Outer Mongolia voted at a plebiscite Oct. 20, 1945 to sever all ties with China and become an independent nation. Opposition to the communist party developed in late 1989 and after demonstrations and hunger strikes, the Politburo resigned on March 12, 1990 and the new State of Mongolia was organized.

On Feb. 12, 1992 it became the first to discard communism as the national political system by adopting a new constitution.

For earlier issues see Russia - Tannu Tuva.

**MONETARY SYSTEM**

100 Mongo = 1 Tugrik

## PEOPLE'S REPUBLIC

### DECIMAL COINAGE

**MONGO** KM# 1 **Composition:** Copper

| Date | Mintage | F | VF | XF | Unc | BU |
|---|---|---|---|---|---|---|
| AH15(1925) | — | 5.00 | 8.00 | 12.00 | 20.00 | — |

**MONGO** KM# 9 **Composition:** Aluminum-Bronze

| Date | Mintage | F | VF | XF | Unc | BU |
|---|---|---|---|---|---|---|
| AH27(1937) | — | 2.50 | 3.50 | 7.00 | 15.00 | — |

**MONGO** KM# 15 **Composition:** Aluminum-Bronze

| Date | Mintage | F | VF | XF | Unc | BU |
|---|---|---|---|---|---|---|
| AH35(1945) | — | 2.00 | 3.00 | 5.50 | 11.50 | — |

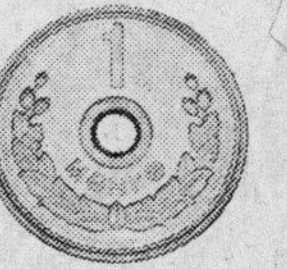

**MONGO** KM# 21 **Composition:** Aluminum

| Date | Mintage | F | VF | XF | Unc | BU |
|---|---|---|---|---|---|---|
| 1959 | 9,000,000 | 0.25 | 0.60 | 1.00 | 1.75 | — |

**MONGO KM# 27 Composition:** Aluminum

| Date | Mintage | F | VF | XF | Unc | BU |
|---|---|---|---|---|---|---|
| 1970 | — | 0.25 | 0.60 | 0.85 | 1.25 | — |
| 1977 | — | 0.25 | 0.60 | 0.85 | 1.25 | — |
| 1980 | — | 0.25 | 0.60 | 0.85 | 1.25 | — |
| 1981 | — | 0.25 | 0.60 | 0.85 | 1.25 | — |

**2 MONGO KM# 2 Composition:** Copper

| Date | Mintage | F | VF | XF | Unc | BU |
|---|---|---|---|---|---|---|
| AH15(1925) | — | 3.50 | 6.50 | 12.00 | 20.00 | — |

**2 MONGO KM# 10 Composition:** Aluminum-Bronze

| Date | Mintage | F | VF | XF | Unc | BU |
|---|---|---|---|---|---|---|
| AH27(1937) | — | 2.50 | 3.50 | 6.00 | 12.00 | — |

**2 MONGO KM# 16 Composition:** Aluminum-Bronze

| Date | Mintage | F | VF | XF | Unc | BU |
|---|---|---|---|---|---|---|
| AH35(1945) | — | 1.00 | 2.00 | 4.00 | 7.00 | — |

**2 MONGO KM# 22 Composition:** Aluminum

| Date | Mintage | F | VF | XF | Unc | BU |
|---|---|---|---|---|---|---|
| 1959 | 4,000,000 | 0.25 | 0.65 | 1.50 | 3.00 | — |

**2 MONGO KM# 28 Composition:** Aluminum

| Date | Mintage | F | VF | XF | Unc | BU |
|---|---|---|---|---|---|---|
| 1970 | — | 0.25 | 0.65 | 1.20 | 2.25 | — |
| 1977 | — | 0.25 | 0.65 | 1.20 | 2.25 | — |
| 1980 | — | 0.25 | 0.65 | 1.20 | 2.25 | — |
| 1981 | — | 0.25 | 0.65 | 1.20 | 2.25 | — |

**5 MONGO KM# 3 Composition:** Copper

| Date | Mintage | F | VF | XF | Unc | BU |
|---|---|---|---|---|---|---|
| AH15(1925) | — | 5.00 | 10.00 | 20.00 | 35.00 | — |

**Note:** Variety in obverse legend exists

**5 MONGO KM# 11 Composition:** Aluminum-Bronze

| Date | Mintage | F | VF | XF | Unc | BU |
|---|---|---|---|---|---|---|
| AH27(1937) | — | 2.75 | 3.50 | 6.00 | 12.00 | — |

**5 MONGO KM# 17 Composition:** Aluminum-Bronze

| Date | Mintage | F | VF | XF | Unc | BU |
|---|---|---|---|---|---|---|
| AH35(1945) | — | 1.75 | 2.50 | 5.00 | 10.00 | — |

**5 MONGO KM# 23 Composition:** Aluminum

| Date | Mintage | F | VF | XF | Unc | BU |
|---|---|---|---|---|---|---|
| 1959 | 2,400,000 | 0.25 | 1.00 | 2.00 | 3.00 | — |

**5 MONGO KM# 29 Composition:** Aluminum

| Date | Mintage | F | VF | XF | Unc | BU |
|---|---|---|---|---|---|---|
| 1970 | — | 0.25 | 0.85 | 1.75 | 2.75 | — |
| 1977 | — | 0.25 | 0.85 | 1.75 | 2.75 | — |
| 1980 | — | 0.25 | 0.85 | 1.75 | 2.75 | — |
| 1981 | — | 0.25 | 0.85 | 1.75 | 2.75 | — |

**10 MONGO KM# 4 Weight:** 1.7996 g. **Composition:** 0.5000 Silver .0289 oz. ASW

| Date | Mintage | VG | F | VF | XF | Unc |
|---|---|---|---|---|---|---|
| AH15(1925) | 1,500,000 | — | 3.00 | 5.00 | 9.00 | 17.50 |

**10 MONGO KM# 12 Composition:** Copper-Nickel

| Date | Mintage | F | VF | XF | Unc | BU |
|---|---|---|---|---|---|---|
| AH27(1937) | — | 2.00 | 3.50 | 7.00 | 14.00 | — |

 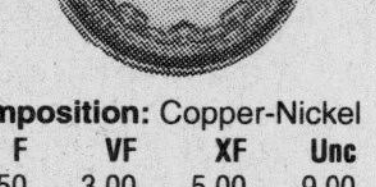

**10 MONGO KM# 18 Composition:** Copper-Nickel

| Date | Mintage | F | VF | XF | Unc | BU |
|---|---|---|---|---|---|---|
| AH35(1945) | — | 1.50 | 3.00 | 5.00 | 9.00 | — |

**10 MONGO KM# 24 Composition:** Aluminum

| Date | Mintage | F | VF | XF | Unc | BU |
|---|---|---|---|---|---|---|
| 1959 | 3,000,000 | 0.75 | 1.50 | 3.00 | 5.00 | — |

**10 MONGO KM# 30 Composition:** Copper-Nickel

| Date | Mintage | F | VF | XF | Unc | BU |
|---|---|---|---|---|---|---|
| 1970 | — | 0.35 | 0.85 | 1.75 | 2.75 | — |
| 1977 | — | 0.35 | 0.85 | 1.75 | 2.75 | — |
| 1980 | — | 0.35 | 0.85 | 1.75 | 2.75 | — |
| 1981 | — | 0.35 | 0.85 | 1.75 | 2.75 | — |

**15 MONGO KM# 5 Weight:** 2.6994 g. **Composition:** 0.5000 Silver .0433 oz. ASW

| Date | Mintage | VG | F | VF | XF | Unc |
|---|---|---|---|---|---|---|
| AH15(1925) | 417,000 | — | 3.50 | 6.00 | 12.00 | 20.00 |

**15 MONGO KM# 13 Composition:** Copper-Nickel

| Date | Mintage | F | VF | XF | Unc | BU |
|---|---|---|---|---|---|---|
| AH27(1937) | — | 2.00 | 3.00 | 6.00 | 12.00 | — |

**15 MONGO KM# 19 Composition:** Copper-Nickel

| Date | Mintage | F | VF | XF | Unc | BU |
|---|---|---|---|---|---|---|
| AH35(1945) | — | 1.50 | 2.25 | 4.00 | 8.00 | — |

**15 MONGO KM# 25 Composition:** Aluminum

| Date | Mintage | F | VF | XF | Unc | BU |
|---|---|---|---|---|---|---|
| 1959 | 4,600,000 | 0.35 | 0.85 | 1.75 | 3.50 | — |

**15 MONGO KM# 31 Composition:** Copper-Nickel

| Date | Mintage | F | VF | XF | Unc | BU |
|---|---|---|---|---|---|---|
| 1970 | — | 0.25 | 0.65 | 1.25 | 2.50 | — |
| 1977 | — | 0.25 | 0.65 | 1.25 | 2.50 | — |
| 1980 | — | 0.25 | 0.65 | 1.25 | 2.50 | — |
| 1981 | — | 0.25 | 0.65 | 1.25 | 2.50 | — |

**20 MONGO** **KM# 6** **Weight:** 3.5992 g. **Composition:** 0.5000 Silver .0578 oz. ASW

| Date | Mintage | VG | F | VF | XF | Unc |
|---|---|---|---|---|---|---|
| AH15(1925) | 1,625,000 | — | 4.00 | 7.50 | 14.00 | 25.00 |

**20 MONGO** **KM# 14** **Composition:** Copper-Nickel

| Date | Mintage | F | VF | XF | Unc | BU |
|---|---|---|---|---|---|---|
| AH27(1937) | — | 2.50 | 4.50 | 10.00 | 18.00 | — |

**20 MONGO** **KM# 20** **Composition:** Copper-Nickel

| Date | Mintage | F | VF | XF | Unc | BU |
|---|---|---|---|---|---|---|
| AH35(1945) | — | 1.50 | 2.50 | 5.00 | 10.00 | — |

**20 MONGO** **KM# 26** **Composition:** Aluminum

| Date | Mintage | F | VF | XF | Unc | BU |
|---|---|---|---|---|---|---|
| 1959 | 3,600,000 | 0.60 | 1.25 | 2.25 | 3.50 | — |

**20 MONGO** **KM# 32** **Composition:** Copper-Nickel

| Date | Mintage | F | VF | XF | Unc | BU |
|---|---|---|---|---|---|---|
| 1970 | — | 0.40 | 0.80 | 1.50 | 2.50 | — |
| 1977 | — | 0.40 | 0.80 | 1.50 | 2.50 | — |
| 1980 | — | 0.40 | 0.80 | 1.50 | 2.50 | — |
| 1981 | — | 0.40 | 0.80 | 1.50 | 2.50 | — |

**50 MONGO** **KM# 7** **Weight:** 9.9979 g. **Composition:** 0.9000 Silver .2893 oz. ASW

| Date | Mintage | VG | F | VF | XF | Unc |
|---|---|---|---|---|---|---|
| AH15(1925) | 920,000 | — | 7.50 | 12.00 | 18.50 | 30.00 |

**50 MONGO** **KM# 33** **Composition:** Copper-Nickel

| Date | Mintage | F | VF | XF | Unc | BU |
|---|---|---|---|---|---|---|
| 1970 | — | 0.50 | 1.00 | 1.75 | 3.00 | — |
| 1977 | — | 0.50 | 1.00 | 1.75 | 3.00 | — |
| 1980 | — | 0.50 | 1.00 | 1.75 | 3.00 | — |
| 1981 | — | 0.50 | 1.00 | 1.75 | 3.00 | — |

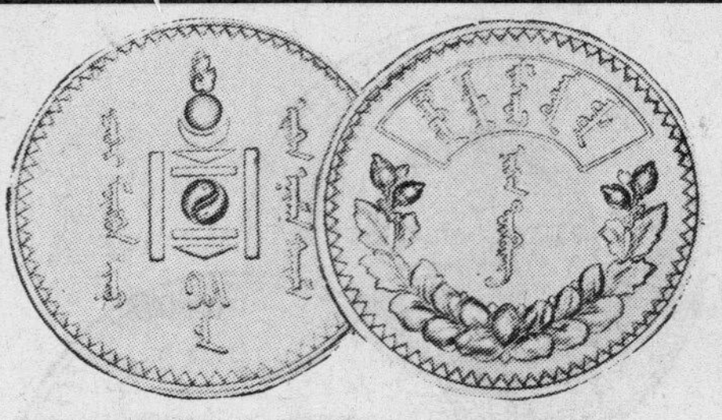

**TUGRIK** **KM# 8** **Weight:** 19.9957 g. **Composition:** 0.9000 Silver .5786 oz. ASW

| Date | Mintage | VG | F | VF | XF | Unc |
|---|---|---|---|---|---|---|
| AH15(1925) | 400,000 | — | 10.00 | 15.00 | 20.00 | 35.00 |

**TUGRIK** **KM# 34** **Composition:** Aluminum-Bronze **Subject:** 50th Anniversary of the Revolution **Note:** Date on edge.

| Date | Mintage | F | VF | XF | Unc | BU |
|---|---|---|---|---|---|---|
| 1971 | — | — | 4.00 | 6.00 | 10.00 | — |

**TUGRIK** **KM# 34a** **Composition:** Copper-Nickel

| Date | Mintage | F | VF | XF | Unc | BU |
|---|---|---|---|---|---|---|
| 1971 | — | 6.00 | 8.00 | 12.00 | 18.00 | — |

**TUGRIK** **KM# 34b** **Weight:** 18.4000 g. **Composition:** Silver

| Date | Mintage | F | VF | XF | Unc | BU |
|---|---|---|---|---|---|---|
| 1971 Proof | — | Value: 50.00 | | | | |

**TUGRIK** **KM# 34c** **Weight:** 30.0000 g. **Composition:** Gold **Subject:** 50th Anniversary of the Revolution **Note:** Mintage: 5-10.

| Date | Mintage | F | VF | XF | Unc | BU |
|---|---|---|---|---|---|---|
| 1971 Proof | — | Value: 2,500 | | | | |

**TUGRIK** **KM# 41** **Composition:** Aluminum-Bronze **Subject:** 60th Anniversary of the Revolution

| Date | Mintage | F | VF | XF | Unc | BU |
|---|---|---|---|---|---|---|
| 1981 | — | — | — | 4.00 | 7.50 | — |

**TUGRIK** **KM# 42** **Composition:** Aluminum-Bronze **Subject:** Soviet - Mongolian Space Flight

| Date | Mintage | F | VF | XF | Unc | BU |
|---|---|---|---|---|---|---|
| 1981 | — | — | — | 3.00 | 6.00 | — |

**TUGRIK** **KM# 43** **Composition:** Aluminum-Bronze **Subject:** 60th Anniversary of the State Bank

| Date | Mintage | F | VF | XF | Unc | BU |
|---|---|---|---|---|---|---|
| 1984 | — | — | — | 3.00 | 6.00 | — |

**Note:** Edge varieties exist

**TUGRIK** **KM# 44** **Composition:** Aluminum-Bronze **Subject:** 60th Anniversary of the People's Republic

| Date | Mintage | F | VF | XF | Unc | BU |
|---|---|---|---|---|---|---|
| 1984 | — | — | — | 3.00 | 5.50 | — |

**TUGRIK** **KM# 48** **Composition:** Aluminum-Bronze **Subject:** Year of Peace

| Date | Mintage | F | VF | XF | Unc | BU |
|---|---|---|---|---|---|---|
| 1986 | — | — | — | 3.00 | 5.50 | — |

**TUGRIK** **KM# 49** **Composition:** Aluminum-Bronze **Subject:** 65th Anniversary of the Revolution

| Date | Mintage | F | VF | XF | Unc | BU |
|---|---|---|---|---|---|---|
| 1986 | — | — | — | 3.00 | 5.50 | — |

**TUGRIK** **KM# 52** **Composition:** Aluminum-Bronze **Subject:** 170th Anniversary - Birth of Karl Marx

| Date | Mintage | F | VF | XF | Unc | BU |
|---|---|---|---|---|---|---|
| ND(1988) | — | — | — | 4.00 | 12.50 | — |
| ND(1988) | — | — | — | 4.00 | 12.50 | — |

**10 TUGRIK** KM# 35 **Composition:** Copper-Nickel **Subject:** 50th Anniversary of State Bank

| Date | Mintage | F | VF | XF | Unc | BU |
|---|---|---|---|---|---|---|
| ND(1974) | — | — | — | — | 9.00 | — |
| ND(1974) | — | — | — | — | 9.00 | — |

**25 TUGRIK** KM# 36 **Weight:** 28.2800 g. **Composition:** 0.9250 Silver .8411 oz. ASW **Subject:** Conservation **Reverse:** Arfali sheep

| Date | Mintage | F | VF | XF | Unc | BU |
|---|---|---|---|---|---|---|
| 1976 | 5,348 | — | — | — | 15.00 | — |
| 1976 Proof | 6,096 | Value: 20.00 | | | | |

**25 TUGRIK** KM# 39 **Weight:** 19.4400 g. **Composition:** 0.9250 Silver .5781 oz. ASW **Series:** International Year of the Child

| Date | Mintage | F | VF | XF | Unc | BU |
|---|---|---|---|---|---|---|
| 1980 Proof | 14,000 | Value: 22.50 | | | | |

**25 TUGRIK** KM# 47 **Weight:** 19.4400 g. **Composition:** 0.9250 Silver .5781 oz. ASW **Series:** Decade for Women

| Date | Mintage | F | VF | XF | Unc | BU |
|---|---|---|---|---|---|---|
| 1984 Proof | 1,249 | Value: 35.00 | | | | |

**25 TUGRIK** KM# 50 **Weight:** 28.2800 g. **Composition:** 0.9250 Silver .8411 oz. ASW **Series:** World Wildlife Fund **Reverse:** Snow leopard

| Date | Mintage | F | VF | XF | Unc | BU |
|---|---|---|---|---|---|---|
| 1987 Matte | 850 | — | — | — | 50.00 | — |
| 1987 Proof | 25,000 | Value: 30.00 | | | | |

**25 TUGRIK** KM# 54 **Weight:** 28.2800 g. **Composition:** 0.9250 Silver .8411 oz. ASW **Series:** Save the Children Fund

| Date | Mintage | F | VF | XF | Unc | BU |
|---|---|---|---|---|---|---|
| 1989 Proof | 20,000 | Value: 28.50 | | | | |

**50 TUGRIK** KM# 37 **Weight:** 35.0000 g. **Composition:** 0.9250 Silver 1.0409 oz. ASW **Subject:** Conservation **Obverse:** Siimilar to 25 Tugrik, KM#36 **Reverse:** Bactrian camel

| Date | Mintage | F | VF | XF | Unc | BU |
|---|---|---|---|---|---|---|
| 1976 | 5,328 | — | — | — | 20.00 | — |
| 1976 Proof | 5,900 | Value: 25.00 | | | | |

**50 TUGRIK** KM# 57 **Weight:** 31.1000 g. **Composition:** 0.9990 Silver 1.0000 oz. ASW **Subject:** Discovery of America **Reverse:** Columbus

| Date | Mintage | F | VF | XF | Unc | BU |
|---|---|---|---|---|---|---|
| 1992 Proof | 20,000 | Value: 32.50 | | | | |

**Note:** KM#57.2, previously listed here, has been correctly identified as belonging with coinage of The People's Republic.

**50 TUGRIK** KM# 170 **Weight:** 31.1000 g. **Composition:** 0.9990 Silver 1 oz. ASW **Subject:** Year of the Monkey **Obverse:** Similar to KM#57 **Reverse:** Similar to KM#86

| Date | Mintage | F | VF | XF | Unc | BU |
|---|---|---|---|---|---|---|
| 1992 | Est. 20,000 | — | — | — | 80.00 | — |

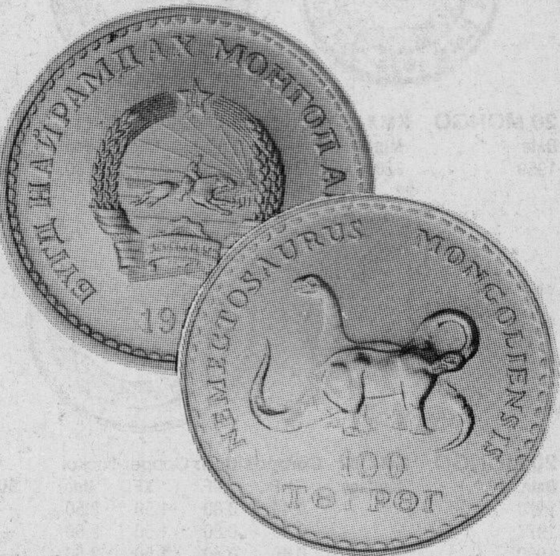

**100 TUGRIK** KM# 53 **Weight:** 28.0000 g. **Composition:** 0.9000 Silver .8102 oz. ASW **Subject:** Dinosaurs **Reverse:** Nemectosaurus

| Date | Mintage | F | VF | XF | Unc | BU |
|---|---|---|---|---|---|---|
| 1989 | 1,000 | — | — | — | 80.00 | — |

**100 TUGRIK** KM# 55 **Weight:** 28.0000 g. **Composition:** 0.9000 Silver .8102 oz. ASW **Subject:** Secret history of the Mongols **Obverse:** State emblem above denomination within English legend **Reverse:** Portrait of Genghis Khan in light clothing

| Date | Mintage | F | VF | XF | Unc | BU |
|---|---|---|---|---|---|---|
| 1990 | 4,000 | — | — | — | 50.00 | — |

**100 TUGRIK** KM# 58 **Weight:** 1.5600 g. **Composition:** 0.9990 Gold .0500 oz. AGW **Subject:** Discovery of America - Columbus **Obverse:** Similar to KM#53 **Reverse:** Portrait of Columbus and ship within circle and legend **Note:** Similar to 50 Tugrik, KM#57.

| Date | Mintage | F | VF | XF | Unc | BU |
|---|---|---|---|---|---|---|
| 1992 Proof | Est. 10,000 | Value: 45.00 | | | | |

**200 TUGRIK** KM# 59 **Weight:** 3.1100 g. **Composition:** 0.9990 Gold .1000 oz. AGW **Subject:** Discovery of America - Columbus **Obverse:** Similar to KM#53 **Reverse:** Portrait of Columbus and ship within circle and legend **Note:** Similar to 50 Tugrik, KM#57

| Date | Mintage | F | VF | XF | Unc | BU |
|---|---|---|---|---|---|---|
| 1992 Proof | Est. 10,000 | Value: 60.00 | | | | |

**250 TUGRIK** KM# 45 **Weight:** 7.1300 g. **Composition:** 0.9000 Gold .2026 oz. AGW **Series:** Decade for Women

| Date | Mintage | F | VF | XF | Unc | BU |
|---|---|---|---|---|---|---|
| 1984 Proof | 510 | Value: 150 | | | | |

**300 TUGRIK** KM# 72 **Weight:** 7.7700 g. **Composition:** 0.9990 Gold .25 oz. AGW **Subject:** Japanese royal wedding **Note:** Similar to 500 Tugrik, KM#73

| Date | Mintage | F | VF | XF | Unc | BU |
|---|---|---|---|---|---|---|
| 1993 Proof | Est. 500 | Value: 235 | | | | |

**750 TUGRIK KM# 38 Weight:** 33.4370 g. **Composition:** 0.9000 Gold .9676 oz. AGW **Subject:** Conservation **Reverse:** Przewalski horses

| Date | Mintage | F | VF | XF | Unc | BU |
|---|---|---|---|---|---|---|
| 1976 | 929 | — | — | — | 500 | — |
| 1976 Proof | 374 | Value: 750 | | | | |

**750 TUGRIK KM# 40 Weight:** 18.7900 g. **Composition:** 0.9000 Gold .5437 oz. AGW **Series:** International Year of the Child

| Date | Mintage | F | VF | XF | Unc | BU |
|---|---|---|---|---|---|---|
| 1980 Proof | 32,000 | Value: 225 | | | | |

**1000 TUGRIK KM# 56 Weight:** 20.7000 g. **Composition:** 0.9000 Gold .5990 oz. AGW **Subject:** Secret history of the Mongols **Obverse:** State emblem above denomination within English legend **Reverse:** Portrait of Genghis Khan in heavy clothing

| Date | Mintage | F | VF | XF | Unc | BU |
|---|---|---|---|---|---|---|
| 1990 | Est. 4,000 | — | — | — | 325 | — |

**1000 TUGRIK KM# 60 Weight:** 31.1000 g. **Composition:** 0.9990 Gold 1.0000 oz. AGW **Subject:** Discovery of America **Reverse:** Columbus

| Date | Mintage | F | VF | XF | Unc | BU |
|---|---|---|---|---|---|---|
| 1992 Proof | 2,000 | Value: 450 | | | | |

**1000 TUGRIK KM# 171 Subject:** Year of the Monkey **Obverse:** Similar to KM#60 **Reverse:** Similar to KM#91

| Date | Mintage | F | VF | XF | Unc | BU |
|---|---|---|---|---|---|---|
| 1992 | Est. 2,000 | — | — | — | 650 | — |

# STATE OF MONGOLIA

## DECIMAL COINAGE

**20 TUGRIK KM# 122 Composition:** Aluminum **Obverse:** National emblem **Reverse:** Denomination

| Date | Mintage | F | VF | XF | Unc | BU |
|---|---|---|---|---|---|---|
| 1994 | — | — | — | — | 1.50 | — |

**50 TUGRIK KM# 84 Weight:** 15.0000 g. **Composition:** 0.9990 Silver .4818 oz. ASW **Reverse:** Ugedei Khan, son of Genghis

| Date | Mintage | F | VF | XF | Unc | BU |
|---|---|---|---|---|---|---|
| 1992 Proof | Est. 1,000 | Value: 30.00 | | | | |

**50 TUGRIK KM# 86 Weight:** 31.1035 g. **Composition:** 0.9990 Silver 1.0000 oz. ASW **Subject:** Year of the Monkey

| Date | Mintage | F | VF | XF | Unc | BU |
|---|---|---|---|---|---|---|
| 1992 Proof | 20,000 | Value: 40.00 | | | | |

**50 TUGRIK KM# 166 Weight:** 31.1035 g. **Composition:** 0.9990 Silver 1 oz. ASW **Subject:** Discovery of America - Columbus **Obverse:** Similar to KM#86 **Reverse:** Similar to KM#57

| Date | Mintage | F | VF | XF | Unc | BU |
|---|---|---|---|---|---|---|
| 1992 Proof | — | Value: 42.50 | | | | |

**50 TUGRIK KM# 61 Weight:** 31.1035 g. **Composition:** 0.9990 Silver 1 oz. ASW **Subject:** Year of the Rooster

| Date | Mintage | F | VF | XF | Unc | BU |
|---|---|---|---|---|---|---|
| 1993 Proof | 20,000 | Value: 40.00 | | | | |

**50 TUGRIK KM# 69 Weight:** 31.1035 g. **Composition:** 0.9990 Silver 1 oz. ASW **Subject:** Japanese royal wedding

| Date | Mintage | F | VF | XF | Unc | BU |
|---|---|---|---|---|---|---|
| 1993 Proof | 1,962 | Value: 47.50 | | | | |

**50 TUGRIK KM# 75 Subject:** Year of the Dog

| Date | Mintage | F | VF | XF | Unc | BU |
|---|---|---|---|---|---|---|
| 1994 Proof | 4,000 | Value: 45.00 | | | | |

**50 TUGRIK KM# 123 Composition:** Aluminum **Obverse:** National emblem **Reverse:** Denomination

| Date | Mintage | F | VF | XF | Unc | BU |
|---|---|---|---|---|---|---|
| 1994 | — | — | — | — | 1.75 | — |

**50 TUGRIK KM# 94 Composition:** Copper-Nickel **Subject:** Year of the Pig **Obverse:** National emblem

| Date | Mintage | F | VF | XF | Unc | BU |
|---|---|---|---|---|---|---|
| 1995 Proof | 50,000 | Value: 15.00 | | | | |

**50 TUGRIK KM# 104 Composition:** Copper-Nickel **Subject:** Year of the Rat

| Date | Mintage | F | VF | XF | Unc | BU |
|---|---|---|---|---|---|---|
| 1996 Proof | 50,000 | Value: 15.00 | | | | |

**50 TUGRIK KM# 126 Composition:** Copper-Nickel **Subject:** Year of the Ox **Obverse:** National emblem

| Date | Mintage | F | VF | XF | Unc | BU |
|---|---|---|---|---|---|---|
| 1997 Proof | 25,000 | Value: 15.00 | | | | |

**50 TUGRIK KM# 172 Composition:** Copper-Nickel **Subject:** Year of the Tiger

| Date | Mintage | F | VF | XF | Unc | BU |
|---|---|---|---|---|---|---|
| 1998 | 25,000 | — | — | — | 12.50 | — |

**50 TUGRIK KM# 159 Composition:** Copper-Nickel **Subject:** Year of the Rabbit

| Date | Mintage | F | VF | XF | Unc | BU |
|---|---|---|---|---|---|---|
| 1999 | 25,000 | — | — | — | 12.50 | — |

**100 TUGRIK KM# 87 Weight:** 1.5600 g. **Composition:** 0.9990 Gold .0500 oz. AGW **Subject:** Year of the Monkey **Note:** Similar to 50 Tugrik, KM#86.

| Date | Mintage | F | VF | XF | Unc | BU |
|---|---|---|---|---|---|---|
| 1992 Proof | 10,000 | Value: 75.00 | | | | |

**100 TUGRIK KM# 167 Weight:** 1.5600 g. **Composition:** 0.9990 Gold .0500 oz. AGW **Subject:** Discovery of America - Columbus **Obverse:** Similar to KM#126 **Reverse:** Similar to KM#167

| Date | Mintage | F | VF | XF | Unc | BU |
|---|---|---|---|---|---|---|
| 1992 Proof | — | Value: 45.00 | | | | |

**100 TUGRIK KM# 62.1 Weight:** 1.5600 g. **Composition:** 0.9990 Gold .0500 oz. AGW **Subject:** Year of the Rooster **Note:** Similar to 50 Tugrik, KM#61.

| Date | Mintage | F | VF | XF | Unc | BU |
|---|---|---|---|---|---|---|
| 1993 Proof | 30,000 | Value: 50.00 | | | | |

**100 TUGRIK KM# 62.2 Weight:** 1.5600 g. **Composition:** 0.9990 Gold .0500 oz. AGW **Note:** Handstruck.

| Date | Mintage | F | VF | XF | Unc | BU |
|---|---|---|---|---|---|---|
| 1993 Proof | 500 | Value: 250 | | | | |

**Note:** Strikes tend to be crude and do not have ".999" on them.

**100 TUGRIK KM# 70 Weight:** 1.5600 g. **Composition:** 0.9990 Gold .0500 oz. AGW **Subject:** Japanese Royal Wedding **Note:** Similar to 50 Tugrik, KM#69.

| Date | Mintage | F | VF | XF | Unc | BU |
|---|---|---|---|---|---|---|
| 1993 Proof | Est. 3,000 | Value: 75.00 | | | | |

**100 TUGRIK** KM# 124 **Composition:** Copper-Nickel **Obverse:** National emblem **Reverse:** Denomination

| Date | Mintage | F | VF | XF | Unc | BU |
|---|---|---|---|---|---|---|
| 1994 | — | — | — | — | 3.50 | — |

**200 TUGRIK** KM# 168 **Weight:** 3.1100 g. **Composition:** 0.9990 Gold .1000 oz. AGW **Subject:** Discovery of America - Columbus **Obverse:** Similar to KM#86 **Reverse:** Similar to KM#59

| Date | Mintage | F | VF | XF | Unc | BU |
|---|---|---|---|---|---|---|
| 1992 Proof | — | Value: 60.00 | | | | |

**200 TUGRIK** KM# 63 **Weight:** 3.1100 g. **Composition:** 0.9990 Gold .1000 oz. AGW **Subject:** Year of the Rooster **Obverse:** National emblem above denomination at left, country name at right **Reverse:** Rooster **Note:** Similar to 50 Tigrik, KM#61

| Date | Mintage | F | VF | XF | Unc | BU |
|---|---|---|---|---|---|---|
| 1993 Proof | 500 | Value: 200 | | | | |

**200 TUGRIK** KM# 71 **Weight:** 3.1100 g. **Composition:** 0.9990 Gold .1000 oz. AGW **Subject:** Japanese Royal Wedding **Note:** Similar to 50 Tigrik, KM#69.

| Date | Mintage | F | VF | XF | Unc | BU |
|---|---|---|---|---|---|---|
| 1993 Proof | 100 | Value: 300 | | | | |

**200 TUGRIK** KM# 76 **Weight:** 3.1100 g. **Composition:** 0.9990 Gold .1000 oz. AGW **Subject:** Year of the Dog.

| Date | Mintage | F | VF | XF | Unc | BU |
|---|---|---|---|---|---|---|
| 1994 Proof | 500 | Value: 175 | | | | |

**200 TUGRIK** KM# 125 **Composition:** Copper-Nickel **Obverse:** Similar to 100 Tugrik KM#124

| Date | Mintage | F | VF | XF | Unc | BU |
|---|---|---|---|---|---|---|
| 1994 | — | — | — | — | 3.50 | — |

**250 TUGRIK** KM# 80 **Weight:** 31.4700 g. **Composition:** 0.9250 Silver .9359 oz. ASW **Subject:** Wildlife **Reverse:** Wolves

| Date | Mintage | F | VF | XF | Unc | BU |
|---|---|---|---|---|---|---|
| 1993 Proof | Est. 15,000 | Value: 35.00 | | | | |

**Note:** KM#89 previously listed here has been reported as never released.

| Date | Mintage | F | VF | XF | Unc | BU |
|---|---|---|---|---|---|---|
| 1993 Proof | 15,000 | Value: 35.00 | | | | |

**Note:** KM#89 previously listed here has been reported as never released

**250 TUGRIK** KM# 100 **Weight:** 31.4700 g. **Composition:** 0.9250 Silver .9359 oz. ASW **Subject:** Wildlife **Obverse:** National emblem **Reverse:** Przewalski's Horses

| Date | Mintage | F | VF | XF | Unc | BU |
|---|---|---|---|---|---|---|
| 1992 Proof | 20,000 | Value: 32.50 | | | | |

**250 TUGRIK** KM# 110 **Weight:** 31.4700 g. **Composition:** 0.9250 Silver .9359 oz. ASW **Series:** Endangered Wildlife **Reverse:** Saiga Antelope

| Date | Mintage | F | VF | XF | Unc | BU |
|---|---|---|---|---|---|---|
| 1993 Proof | Est. 10,000 | Value: 35.00 | | | | |

**250 TUGRIK** KM# 64 **Weight:** 155.5000 g. **Composition:** 0.9990 Silver 5.000 oz. ASW **Subject:** Year of the Rooster **Note:** Similar to 50 Tugrik, KM#61.

| Date | Mintage | F | VF | XF | Unc | BU |
|---|---|---|---|---|---|---|
| 1993 | 300 | Value: 145 | | | | |

**250 TUGRIK** KM# 77 **Weight:** 155.5000 g. **Composition:** 0.9990 Silver 5.0000 oz. ASW **Subject:** Year of the Dog **Size:** 65 mm. **Note:** Illustration reduced.

| Date | Mintage | F | VF | XF | Unc | BU |
|---|---|---|---|---|---|---|
| 1994 Proof | 200 | Value: 300 | | | | |

**250 TUGRIK** KM# 112 **Weight:** 31.4700 g. **Composition:** 0.9250 Silver .9359 oz. ASW **Series:** Olympics **Subject:** Archery

| Date | Mintage | F | VF | XF | Unc | BU |
|---|---|---|---|---|---|---|
| 1994 Proof | — | Value: 27.50 | | | | |
| 1995 Proof | Est. 40,000 | Value: 30.00 | | | | |

**250 TUGRIK** KM# 111 **Weight:** 31.4700 g. **Composition:** 0.9250 Silver .9359 oz. ASW **Series:** Olympics **Subject:** Boxing **Obverse:** National emblem

| Date | Mintage | F | VF | XF | Unc | BU |
|---|---|---|---|---|---|---|
| 1994 Proof | Est. 5,000 | Value: 50.00 | | | | |

**250 TUGRIK** KM# 186 **Weight:** 31.4000 g. **Composition:** 0.9250 Silver .9338 oz. ASW **Subject:** Sojus 39 and Saljut 6 **Obverse:** National arms **Reverse:** 2 space capsules **Edge:** Reeded **Size:** 38.4 mm.

| Date | Mintage | F | VF | XF | Unc | BU |
|---|---|---|---|---|---|---|
| 1994 Proof | — | Value: 65.00 | | | | |

**250 TUGRIK** KM# 103 **Weight:** 31.4700 g. **Composition:** 0.9250 Silver .9359 oz. ASW **Subject:** World Cup soccer

| Date | Mintage | F | VF | XF | Unc | BU |
|---|---|---|---|---|---|---|
| 1994 Proof | — | Value: 30.00 | | | | |

**500 TUGRIK** KM# 73 **Weight:** 15.5500 g. **Composition:** 0.9990 Gold .5000 oz. AGW **Subject:** Japanese Royal Wedding **Note:** Similar to 500 Tugrik, KM#73.

| Date | Mintage | F | VF | XF | Unc | BU |
|---|---|---|---|---|---|---|
| 1993 Proof | 160 | Value: 285 | | | | |

**500 TUGRIK** KM# 95 **Weight:** 31.1035 g. **Composition:** 0.9990 Silver 1.0000 oz. ASW **Subject:** Year of the Pig

| Date | Mintage | F | VF | XF | Unc | BU |
|---|---|---|---|---|---|---|
| 1995 Proof | 3,000 | Value: 45.00 | | | | |

**500 TUGRIK** KM# 101 **Weight:** 31.1035 g. **Composition:** 0.9990 Silver 1.0000 oz. ASW **Subject:** Moscow - Bejing Railroad

| Date | Mintage | F | VF | XF | Unc | BU |
|---|---|---|---|---|---|---|
| 1995 Proof | 20,000 | Value: 32.50 | | | | |

**500 TUGRIK** KM# 187 **Weight:** 31.6000 g. **Composition:** 0.9250 Silver .9398 oz. ASW **Series:** Endangered Wildlife **Obverse:** National emblem **Reverse:** Pelican

| Date | Mintage | F | VF | XF | Unc | BU |
|---|---|---|---|---|---|---|
| 1996 Proof | — | — | — | — | 30.00 | — |

**500 TUGRIK** KM# 105 **Weight:** 31.1035 g. **Composition:** 0.9990 Silver 1.0000 oz. ASW **Subject:** Year of the Rat **Note:** Similar to 50 Tugrik, KM#104, but with gold plated rat.

| Date | Mintage | F | VF | XF | Unc | BU |
|---|---|---|---|---|---|---|
| 1996 Proof | 500 | Value: 90.00 | | | | |

**500 TUGRIK** KM# 132 **Weight:** 25.0000 g. **Composition:** 0.9250 Silver .7435 oz. ASW **Subject:** Aquila Rapax **Obverse:** National emblem

| Date | Mintage | F | VF | XF | Unc | BU |
|---|---|---|---|---|---|---|
| 1996 Proof | 3,500 | Value: 35.00 | | | | |

**500 TUGRIK** KM# 133 **Weight:** 25.0000 g. **Composition:** 0.9250 Silver .7435 oz. ASW **Subject:** Equus Ferus **Obverse:** National emblem

| Date | Mintage | F | VF | XF | Unc | BU |
|---|---|---|---|---|---|---|
| 1996 Proof | 3,500 | Value: 35.00 | | | | |

**500 TUGRIK** KM# 134 **Weight:** 25.0000 g. **Composition:** 0.9250 Silver .7435 oz. ASW **Subject:** Cameleus Ferus **Obverse:** National emblem

| Date | Mintage | F | VF | XF | Unc | BU |
|---|---|---|---|---|---|---|
| 1996 Proof | 3,500 | Value: 35.00 | | | | |

**500 TUGRIK** KM# 135 **Weight:** 25.0000 g. **Composition:** 0.9250 Silver .7435 oz. ASW **Subject:** Panthera Tigris Altaica **Obverse:** National emblem

| Date | Mintage | F | VF | XF | Unc | BU |
|---|---|---|---|---|---|---|
| 1996 Proof | 3,500 | Value: 35.00 | | | | |

**500 TUGRIK** KM# 127 **Weight:** 31.1035 g. **Composition:** 0.9990 Silver With Partial Gold Plating .1000 oz. **Subject:** Year of the Ox **Note:** Similar to 50 Tugrik, KM#126.

| Date | Mintage | F | VF | XF | Unc | BU |
|---|---|---|---|---|---|---|
| 1997 Proof | 3,000 | Value: 50.00 | | | | |

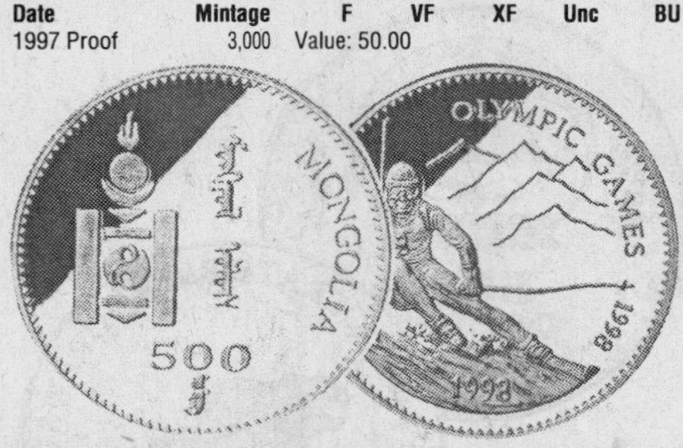

**500 TUGRIK** KM# 155 **Weight:** 15.0000 g. **Composition:** 0.9250 Silver .4461 oz. ASW **Series:** 1988 Olympics **Obverse:** National emblem **Reverse:** Skier

| Date | Mintage | F | VF | XF | Unc | BU |
|---|---|---|---|---|---|---|
| 1998 | — | Value: 30.00 | | | | |

**500 TUGRIK** KM# 156 **Weight:** 20.0000 g. **Composition:** 0.5000 Silver .3215 oz. ASW **Series:** 2000 Olympics **Obverse:** National emblem **Reverse:** 2 wrestlers

| Date | Mintage | VG | F | VF | XF | Unc |
|---|---|---|---|---|---|---|
| 1998 Proof | — | Value: 28.00 | | | | |

**500 TUGRIK** KM# 157 **Weight:** 31.4700 g. **Composition:** 0.9990 Silver 1.0108 oz. ASW **Subject:** Endangered wildlife **Obverse:** National emblem **Reverse:** Tiger and cubs

| Date | Mintage | F | VF | XF | Unc | BU |
|---|---|---|---|---|---|---|
| 1998 Proof | — | Value: 50.00 | | | | |

**500 TUGRIK** KM# 158 **Weight:** 1.2241 g. **Composition:** 0.9990 Gold .0400 oz. AGW **Subject:** Buddhist Diety Maitreya **Obverse:** National emblem

| Date | Mintage | F | VF | XF | Unc | BU |
|---|---|---|---|---|---|---|
| 1998 Proof | — | Value: 50.00 | | | | |

**500 TUGRIK** KM# 173 **Weight:** 31.1045 g. **Composition:** 0.9990 Silver 1.0000 oz. ASW **Subject:** Year of the Tiger

| Date | Mintage | F | VF | XF | Unc | BU |
|---|---|---|---|---|---|---|
| 1998 | 25,000 | — | — | — | 25.00 | — |

**500 TUGRIK** KM# 173a **Weight:** 31.1045 g. **Composition:** 0.9990 Silver 1.0000 oz. ASW **Subject:** Year of the Tiger **Note:** Gold plated tiger.

| Date | Mintage | F | VF | XF | Unc | BU |
|---|---|---|---|---|---|---|
| 1998 | 3,000 | — | — | — | 50.00 | — |

**500 TUGRIK** KM# 174 **Weight:** 1.2441 g. **Composition:** 0.9990 Gold .0400 oz. AGW **Subject:** Year of the TIger

| Date | Mintage | F | VF | XF | Unc | BU |
|---|---|---|---|---|---|---|
| 1998 | — | — | — | — | 40.00 | — |

**500 TUGRIK** KM# 178 **Weight:** 31.6100 g. **Composition:** 0.9250 Silver .9400 oz. ASW **Subject:** Millennium 2000 **Obverse:** National emblem **Reverse:** Rider and multicolored speckled hologram

| Date | Mintage | F | VF | XF | Unc | BU |
|---|---|---|---|---|---|---|
| 1998 Proof | Est. 10,000 | Value: 37.50 | | | | |

**500 TUGRIK** KM# 160 **Weight:** 31.1045 g. **Composition:** 0.9990 Silver 1.0000 oz. ASW **Subject:** Year of the Rabbit

| Date | Mintage | F | VF | XF | Unc | BU |
|---|---|---|---|---|---|---|
| 1999 | 3,000 | — | — | — | 30.00 | — |

**500 TUGRIK** KM# 160a **Weight:** 31.1045 g. **Composition:** 0.9990 Silver 1.0000 oz. ASW **Subject:** Year of the Rabbit **Note:** Gold plated rabbit.

| Date | Mintage | F | VF | XF | Unc | BU |
|---|---|---|---|---|---|---|
| 1999 | 3,000 | — | — | — | 50.00 | — |

**500 TUGRIK** KM# 161 **Weight:** 1.2441 g. **Composition:** 0.9990 Gold .0400 oz. AGW **Subject:** Year of the Rabbit

| Date | Mintage | F | VF | XF | Unc | BU |
|---|---|---|---|---|---|---|
| 1999 | 5,000 | — | — | — | 55.00 | — |

**500 TUGRIK** KM# 179 **Weight:** 25.2700 g. **Composition:** 0.9250 Silver .7515 oz. ASW **Subject:** Sita Tara **Obverse:** National emblem above denomination **Reverse:** Gold colored seated figure of Undur Geghen Zanabazar

| Date | Mintage | F | VF | XF | Unc | BU |
|---|---|---|---|---|---|---|
| 1999 Proof | 2,500 | Value: 42.50 | | | | |

**500 TUGRIK** KM# 180 **Ring Weight:** 25.0000 g. **Ring Composition:** 0.9250 Silver .7435 oz. ASW **Center Composition:** Goldine **Subject:** Genius of the Millennium - Gutenberg **Obverse:** National emblem **Reverse:** Open book, dates **Note:** Goldine center is square.

| Date | Mintage | F | VF | XF | Unc | BU |
|---|---|---|---|---|---|---|
| 1999 Proof | 2,500 | Value: 42.50 | | | | |

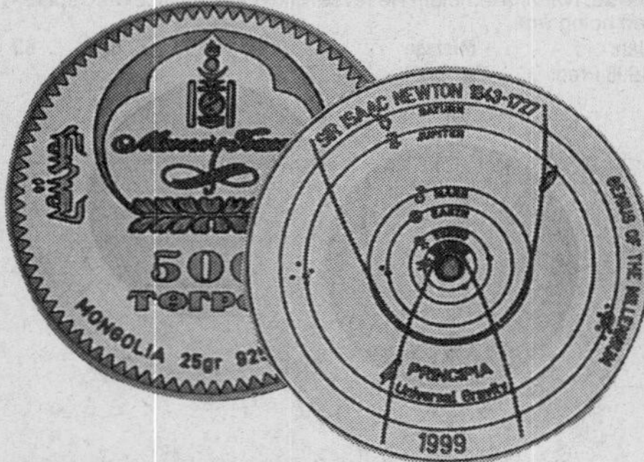


**500 TUGRIK** **KM# 181** **Ring Weight:** 25.0000 g. **Ring Composition:** 0.9250 Silver .7435 oz. ASW **Center Composition:** Goldine **Subject:** Genius of the Millennium - Da Vinci **Obverse:** National emblem **Reverse:** Male figure study **Note:** Goldine center is triangular.

| Date | Mintage | F | VF | XF | Unc | BU |
|---|---|---|---|---|---|---|
| 1999 Proof | 2,500 | Value: 42.50 | | | | |

**500 TUGRIK** **KM# 182** **Ring Weight:** 25.0000 g. **Ring Composition:** 0.9250 Silver .7435 oz. ASW **Center Composition:** Goldine **Subject:** Genius of the Millennium - Newton **Obverse:** National emblem **Reverse:** Solar system diagram **Note:** Goldine center is round.

| Date | Mintage | F | VF | XF | Unc | BU |
|---|---|---|---|---|---|---|
| 1999 Proof | 2,500 | Value: 42.50 | | | | |

**500 TUGRIK** **KM# 183** **Ring Weight:** 25.0000 g. **Ring Composition:** 0.9250 Silver .7435 oz. ASW **Subject:** Genius of the Millennium - von Goethe **Obverse:** National emblem **Reverse:** Goethe's portrait **Note:** Goldine center is round.

| Date | Mintage | F | VF | XF | Unc | BU |
|---|---|---|---|---|---|---|
| 1999 Proof | 2,500 | Value: 42.50 | | | | |

**500 TUGRIK** **KM# 184** **Ring Weight:** 25.0000 g. **Ring Composition:** 0.9250 Silver .7435 oz. ASW **Center Composition:** Goldine **Subject:** Genius of the Millennium - Edison **Obverse:** National emblem **Reverse:** Light bulb, telephone, record player **Note:** Goldine center is square.

| Date | Mintage | F | VF | XF | Unc | BU |
|---|---|---|---|---|---|---|
| 1999 Proof | 2,500 | Value: 42.50 | | | | |

**Note:** KM#90, previously listed here, has been reported as never released.

**500 TUGRIK** **KM# 189** **Weight:** 25.0000 g. **Composition:** 0.9250 Silver .7435 oz. ASW **Subject:** Protoceratops Andrewsi **Obverse:** National arms above denomination **Reverse:** Dinosaur **Edge:** Reeded **Size:** 38.7 mm.

| Date | Mintage | F | VF | XF | Unc | BU |
|---|---|---|---|---|---|---|
| 2001 Proof | 2,500 | — | — | — | 45.00 | — |

**500 TUGRIK** **KM# 191** **Weight:** 25.0000 g. **Composition:** 0.9250 Silver .7435 oz. ASW **Series:** Olympics **Obverse:** National arms above denomination **Reverse:** Speed skater

| Date | Mintage | F | VF | XF | Unc | BU |
|---|---|---|---|---|---|---|
| 2001 Proof | 15,000 | — | — | — | 35.00 | — |

**500 TUGRIK** **KM# 192** **Weight:** 25.0000 g. **Composition:** 0.9250 Silver .7435 oz. ASW **Series:** Olympics

**Obverse:** National arms above denomination **Reverse:** Three cross-country skiers

| Date | Mintage | F | VF | XF | Unc | BU |
|---|---|---|---|---|---|---|
| 2001 Proof | 20,000 | — | — | — | 35.00 | — |

**600 TUGRIK** **KM# 65** **Weight:** 373.2000 g. **Composition:** 0.9990 Silver 12.0000 oz. ASW **Subject:** Year of the Rooster **Note:** Similar to 50 Tugrik, KM#61

| Date | Mintage | F | VF | XF | Unc | BU |
|---|---|---|---|---|---|---|
| 1993 Proof | 200 | Value: 500 | | | | |

**1000 TUGRIK** **KM# 91** **Weight:** 31.1000 g. **Composition:** 0.9990 Gold 1.0000 oz. AGW **Subject:** Year of the Monkey **Note:** Similar to 50 Tugrik, KM#86.

| Date | Mintage | F | VF | XF | Unc | BU |
|---|---|---|---|---|---|---|
| 1992 Proof | 2,000 | Value: 475 | | | | |

**1000 TUGRIK** **KM# 85** **Weight:** 20.0000 g. **Composition:** 0.9000 Gold .5788 oz. AGW **Reverse:** Ugedei Khan, Son of Genghis

| Date | Mintage | F | VF | XF | Unc | BU |
|---|---|---|---|---|---|---|
| 1992 Proof | 500 | Value: 300 | | | | |

**1000 TUGRIK** **KM# 169** **Weight:** 20.0000 g. **Composition:** 0.9000 Gold .5788 oz. AGW **Subject:** Discovery of American - Columbus **Obverse:** Similar to KM#74 **Reverse:** Similar to KM#60

| Date | Mintage | F | VF | XF | Unc | BU |
|---|---|---|---|---|---|---|
| 1992 Proof | Est. 2,000 | Value: 450 | | | | |

**1000 TUGRIK** **KM# 66** **Weight:** 31.1000 g. **Composition:** 0.9990 Gold 1.0000 oz. AGW **Subject:** Year of the Rooster **Obverse:** National emblem above denomination at left, country name at right **Reverse:** Rooster **Note:** Similar to 50 Tugrik, KM#61.

| Date | Mintage | F | VF | XF | Unc | BU |
|---|---|---|---|---|---|---|
| 1993 Proof | 1,000 | Value: 650 | | | | |

**1000 TUGRIK** **KM# 74** **Weight:** 20.0000 g. **Composition:** 0.9000 Gold .5788 oz. AGW **Subject:** Japanese Royal Wedding

| Date | Mintage | F | VF | XF | Unc | BU |
|---|---|---|---|---|---|---|
| 1993 Proof | 145 | Value: 700 | | | | |

**1000 TUGRIK** **KM# 78** **Weight:** 31.1035 g. **Composition:** 0.9990 Gold 1.0000 oz. AGW **Subject:** Year of the Dog

| Date | Mintage | F | VF | XF | Unc | BU |
|---|---|---|---|---|---|---|
| 1994 Proof | 500 | Value: 525 | | | | |

**1000 TUGRIK** **KM# 96** **Weight:** 3.1100 g. **Composition:** 0.9990 Gold 1.0000 oz. AGW **Subject:** Year of the Pig **Obverse:** National emblem **Reverse:** Wild boar **Note:** Similar to 500 Tugrik, KM#95.

| Date | Mintage | F | VF | XF | Unc | BU |
|---|---|---|---|---|---|---|
| 1995 Proof | 500 | Value: 200 | | | | |

**1000 TUGRIK** **KM# 148** **Weight:** 4.4100 g. **Composition:** 0.9000 Gold .1276 oz. AGW **Subject:** Moscow - Ulaan Blaatar - Bejing Railroad **Obverse:** National emblem **Reverse:** Steam locomotive

| Date | Mintage | F | VF | XF | Unc | BU |
|---|---|---|---|---|---|---|
| 1995 Proof | — | Value: 100 | | | | |

**1000 TUGRIK** **KM# 106** **Weight:** 3.1100 g. **Composition:** 0.9990 Gold 1.0000 oz. AGW **Subject:** Year of the Rat **Note:** Similar to 50 Tugrik, KM#104.

| Date | Mintage | F | VF | XF | Unc | BU |
|---|---|---|---|---|---|---|
| 1996 Proof | 500 | Value: 150 | | | | |

**1000 TUGRIK** **KM# 115** **Weight:** 156.6100 g. **Composition:** 0.9990 Silver 5.0000 oz. ASW **Series:** Olympics **Reverse:** Ancient runners **Size:** 65.5 mm. **Note:** With gold inlay. Illustation reduced.

| Date | Mintage | F | VF | XF | Unc | BU |
|---|---|---|---|---|---|---|
| 1996 Matte | — | — | — | — | 225 | — |

**1000 TUGRIK** **KM# 128** **Weight:** 3.1100 g. **Composition:** 0.9990 Gold .1000 oz. AGW **Subject:** Year of the Ox **Note:** Similar to 50 Tugrik, KM#126.

| Date | Mintage | F | VF | XF | Unc | BU |
|---|---|---|---|---|---|---|
| 1997 Proof | 500 | Value: 100 | | | | |

**1000 TUGRIK** **KM# 185** **Weight:** 1.2441 g. **Composition:** 0.9999 Gold .0400 oz. AGW **Subject:** Genius of the Millennium - Da Vinci **Obverse:** National arms **Reverse:** Male figure study **Note:** Similar to 500 Tugrik, KM#181.

| Date | Mintage | F | VF | XF | Unc | BU |
|---|---|---|---|---|---|---|
| 1999 Proof | 25,000 | Value: 45.00 | | | | |

**1200 TUGRIK** **KM# 116** **Weight:** 7.7000 g. **Composition:** 0.9990 Silver .2496 oz. ASW **Subject:** Chinnggis Khan **Note:** Similar to 5,000 Tugrik, KM#118.

| Date | Mintage | F | VF | XF | Unc | BU |
|---|---|---|---|---|---|---|
| 1996 | Est. 10,000 | — | — | — | 10.00 | — |
| 1996 Proof | Est. 10,000 | Value: 15.00 | | | | |

**1200 TUGRIK** **KM# 149** **Weight:** 7.7000 g. **Composition:** 0.9990 Silver .2496 oz. ASW **Subject:** Ugedei Khan **Obverse:** National emblem **Reverse:** Portrait dates

| Date | Mintage | F | VF | XF | Unc | BU |
|---|---|---|---|---|---|---|
| 1997 Proof | Est. 10,000 | Value: 15.00 | | | | |

**2000 TUGRIK** **KM# 113** **Weight:** 7.7760 g. **Composition:** 0.5830 Gold .1458 oz. AGW **Series:** Endangered Wildlife **Reverse:** Snow leopard

| Date | Mintage | F | VF | XF | Unc | BU |
|---|---|---|---|---|---|---|
| 1994 Proof | Est. 5,000 | Value: 150 | | | | |

**2000 TUGRIK** **KM# 114** **Weight:** 7.7760 g. **Composition:** 0.5830 Gold .1458 oz. AGW **Series:** Olympics **Reverse:** Boxer

| Date | Mintage | F | VF | XF | Unc | BU |
|---|---|---|---|---|---|---|
| 1994 Proof | Est. 5,000 | Value: 150 | | | | |

**2000 TUGRIK** **KM# 175** **Weight:** 7.7760 g. **Composition:** 0.5830 Gold .1458 oz. AGW **Subject:** Year of the Tiger

| Date | Mintage | F | VF | XF | Unc | BU |
|---|---|---|---|---|---|---|
| 1998 | — | — | — | — | 65.00 | — |

**2500 TUGRIK** **KM# 97** **Weight:** 155.5150 g. **Composition:** 0.9990 Silver 5.0000 oz. ASW **Subject:** Year of the Pig **Size:** 65 mm. **Note:** Illustration reduced.

| Date | Mintage | F | VF | XF | Unc | BU |
|---|---|---|---|---|---|---|
| 1995 Proof | 300 | Value: 160 | | | | |

**2500 TUGRIK** **KM# 102** **Weight:** 155.5150 g. **Composition:** 0.9990 Silver 5.0000 oz. ASW **Subject:** Moscow - Bejing Railroad **Note:** Similar 500 Tugrik, KM#101

| Date | Mintage | F | VF | XF | Unc | BU |
|---|---|---|---|---|---|---|
| 1995 Proof | 5,000 | Value: 125 | | | | |

**2500 TUGRIK** **KM# 107** **Weight:** 155.5150 g. **Composition:** 0.9990 Silver 5.0000 oz. ASW **Subject:** Year of the Rat **Reverse:** Gold plated rat **Size:** 65 mm. **Note:** Illustration reduced.

| Date | Mintage | F | VF | XF | Unc | BU |
|---|---|---|---|---|---|---|
| 1996 Proof | 300 | Value: 250 | | | | |

**2500 TUGRIK** **KM# 117** **Weight:** 15.5500 g. **Composition:** 0.9990 Silver .4994 oz. ASW **Reverse:** Chinggis Khan **Note:** Similar to 5000 Tugrik, KM#118

| Date | Mintage | F | VF | XF | Unc | BU |
|---|---|---|---|---|---|---|
| 1996 | Est. 10,000 | — | — | — | 20.00 | — |
| 1996 Proof | Est. 10,000 | Value: 30.00 | | | | |

**2500 TUGRIK** KM# 129 **Weight:** 155.5150 g. **Composition:** 0.9990 Silver With Partial Gold Plating 5.0000 oz. **Subject:** Year of the Ox **Obverse:** National emblem

| Date | Mintage | F | VF | XF | Unc | BU |
|---|---|---|---|---|---|---|
| 1997 Proof | 300 | Value: 200 | | | | |

**2500 TUGRIK** KM# 150 **Weight:** 15.5517 g. **Composition:** 0.9990 Silver 5.0000 oz. ASW **Obverse:** National emblem **Reverse:** Ugedei Khan

| Date | Mintage | F | VF | XF | Unc | BU |
|---|---|---|---|---|---|---|
| 1997 Proof | Est. 10,000 | Value: 30.00 | | | | |

**4000 TUGRIK** KM# 81 **Weight:** 15.5940 g. **Composition:** 0.9999 Gold 5.0000 oz. AGW **Reverse:** Chinggis Khan on horse

| Date | Mintage | F | VF | XF | Unc | BU |
|---|---|---|---|---|---|---|
| 1992 Proof | Est. 9,000 | Value: 650 | | | | |

**5000 TUGRIK** KM# 67 **Weight:** 155.5000 g. **Composition:** 0.9990 Gold 5.0000 oz. AGW **Subject:** Year of the Rooster **Obverse:** National emblem above denomination at left, country name at right **Reverse:** Rooster **Note:** Similar to 50 Tugrik, KM#51.

| Date | Mintage | F | VF | XF | Unc | BU |
|---|---|---|---|---|---|---|
| 1993 Proof | 50 | Value: 3,750 | | | | |

**5000 TUGRIK** KM# 79 **Weight:** 155.5000 g. **Composition:** 0.9990 Gold 5.0000 oz. AGW **Subject:** Year of the dog

| Date | Mintage | F | VF | XF | Unc | BU |
|---|---|---|---|---|---|---|
| 1994 Proof | 25 | Value: 5,000 | | | | |

**5000 TUGRIK** KM# 118 **Weight:** 3.1000 g. **Composition:** 0.9990 Silver .9989 oz. ASW **Reverse:** Chinggis Khan

| Date | Mintage | F | VF | XF | Unc | BU |
|---|---|---|---|---|---|---|
| 1996 | Est. 10,000 | — | — | — | 30.00 | — |
| 1996 Proof | Est. 10,000 | Value: 50.00 | | | | |

**5000 TUGRIK** KM# 136 **Weight:** 155.5175 g. **Composition:** 0.9990 Silver 5.0000 oz. ASW **Subject:** Aquila Rapax **Note:** Similar to 500 Tugrik, KM#132.

| Date | Mintage | F | VF | XF | Unc | BU |
|---|---|---|---|---|---|---|
| 1997 Proof | 750 | Value: 225 | | | | |

**5000 TUGRIK** KM# 137 **Weight:** 155.5175 g. **Composition:** 0.9990 Silver 5.0000 oz. ASW **Subject:** Eguus Fergus **Note:** Similar to 500 Tugrik, KM#133.

| Date | Mintage | F | VF | XF | Unc | BU |
|---|---|---|---|---|---|---|
| 1997 Proof | 750 | Value: 225 | | | | |

**5000 TUGRIK** KM# 139 **Weight:** 155.5175 g. **Composition:** 0.9990 Silver 5.0000 oz. ASW **Subject:** Panthera Tigris Altaica **Note:** Similar to 500 Tugrik, KM#135.

| Date | Mintage | F | VF | XF | Unc | BU |
|---|---|---|---|---|---|---|
| 1997 Proof | 750 | Value: 225 | | | | |

**5000 TUGRIK** KM# 151 **Weight:** 31.1035 g. **Composition:** 0.9990 Silver 1.0000 oz. ASW **Obverse:** National emblem **Reverse:** Ugedei Khan

| Date | Mintage | F | VF | XF | Unc | BU |
|---|---|---|---|---|---|---|
| 1997 Proof | Est. 10,000 | Value: 50.00 | | | | |

**5000 TUGRIK** KM# 138 **Weight:** 155.5175 g. **Composition:** 0.9990 Silver 5 oz. ASW **Subject:** Camelus Ferus **Note:** Similar to 500 Tugrik, KM#134.

| Date | Mintage | F | VF | XF | Unc | BU |
|---|---|---|---|---|---|---|
| 1997 Proof | 750 | Value: 225 | | | | |

**8000 TUGRIK** KM# 82 **Weight:** 31.1620 g. **Composition:** 0.9999 Gold 1.0000 oz. AGW **Reverse:** Chinggis Khan

| Date | Mintage | F | VF | XF | Unc | BU |
|---|---|---|---|---|---|---|
| 1992 Proof | Est. 3,000 | Value: 1,200 | | | | |

**10000 TUGRIK** KM# 98 **Weight:** 31.1035 g. **Composition:** 0.9990 Gold 1.0000 oz. AGW **Subject:** Year of the Pig **Obverse:** National emblem **Reverse:** Wild boar **Note:** Similar to 500 Tugrik, KM#95.

| Date | Mintage | F | VF | XF | Unc | BU |
|---|---|---|---|---|---|---|
| 1995 Proof | 300 | Value: 600 | | | | |

**10000 TUGRIK** KM# 108 **Weight:** 31.1035 g. **Composition:** 0.9990 Gold 1.0000 oz. AGW **Subject:** Year of the Rat **Note:** Siimilar to 50 Tugrik, KM#104.

| Date | Mintage | F | VF | XF | Unc | BU |
|---|---|---|---|---|---|---|
| 1996 Proof | 300 | Value: 550 | | | | |

**10000 TUGRIK** KM# 140 **Weight:** 1000.1000 g. **Composition:** 0.9990 Silver 32.1575 oz. ASW **Subject:** Aquila Rapax **Note:** Similar to 500 Tugrik, KM#132.

| Date | Mintage | F | VF | XF | Unc | BU |
|---|---|---|---|---|---|---|
| 1996 Prooflike | 333 | — | — | — | — | — |

**10000 TUGRIK** KM# 143 **Weight:** 1000.1000 g. **Composition:** 0.9990 Silver 32.1575 oz. ASW **Subject:** Panthera Tigris Alaica **Note:** Siimilar to 500 Tugrik, KM#135.

| Date | Mintage | F | VF | XF | Unc | BU |
|---|---|---|---|---|---|---|
| 1996 Proof | 333 | — | — | — | — | — |

**10000 TUGRIK** KM# 141 **Weight:** 1000.1000 g. **Composition:** 0.9990 Silver 32.1575 oz. ASW **Subject:** Equus Ferus **Note:** Similar to 500 Tugrik, KM#133.

| Date | Mintage | F | VF | XF | Unc | BU |
|---|---|---|---|---|---|---|
| 1996 Prooflike | 333 | — | — | — | — | — |

**10000 TUGRIK** KM# 142 **Weight:** 1000.1000 g. **Composition:** 0.9990 Silver 32.1575 oz. ASW **Subject:** Camelus Ferus **Note:** Similar to 500 Tugrik, KM#134.

| Date | Mintage | F | VF | XF | Unc | BU |
|---|---|---|---|---|---|---|
| 1996 Prooflike | 333 | — | — | — | — | — |

**10000 TUGRIK** KM# 130 **Weight:** 31.1035 g. **Composition:** 0.9990 Gold 1.0000 oz. AGW **Subject:** Year of the Ox **Note:** Siimilar to 2,500 Tugrik, KM#129.

| Date | Mintage | F | VF | XF | Unc | BU |
|---|---|---|---|---|---|---|
| 1997 Proof | 300 | Value: 525 | | | | |

**10000 TUGRIK** KM# 176 **Weight:** 31.1035 g. **Composition:** 0.9990 Gold 1.0000 oz. AGW **Subject:** Year of the Tiger

| Date | Mintage | F | VF | XF | Unc | BU |
|---|---|---|---|---|---|---|
| 1998 | 250 | — | — | — | 525 | — |

**10000 TUGRIK** KM# 164 **Weight:** 31.1035 g. **Composition:** 0.9990 Gold 1 oz. AGW **Subject:** Year of the Rabbit

| Date | Mintage | F | VF | XF | Unc | BU |
|---|---|---|---|---|---|---|
| 1999 | 250 | — | — | — | 525 | — |

**12000 TUGRIK** KM# 68 **Weight:** 373.2000 g. **Composition:** 0.9990 Gold 12.0000 oz. AGW **Subject:** Year of the Rooster **Obverse:** National emblem above denomination at left, country name at right **Reverse:** Rooster **Note:** Similar to 50 Tugrik, KM#61.

| Date | Mintage | F | VF | XF | Unc | BU |
|---|---|---|---|---|---|---|
| 1993 Proof | 25 | Value: 6,000 | | | | |

**12000 TUGRIK** KM# 119 **Weight:** 7.7700 g. **Composition:** 0.9999 Gold .2498 oz. AGW **Subject:** Chinggis Khan **Note:** Similar to 50,000 Tugrik, KM#121.

| Date | Mintage | F | VF | XF | Unc | BU |
|---|---|---|---|---|---|---|
| 1996 Rare | 10 | — | — | — | — | — |
| 1996 Proof, rare | 10 | — | — | — | — | — |

**12000 TUGRIK** KM# 119a **Weight:** 7.7700 g. **Composition:** 0.9990 Gold .2495 oz. AGW **Subject:** Chinggis Khan

| Date | Mintage | F | VF | XF | Unc | BU |
|---|---|---|---|---|---|---|
| 1996 | Est. 10,000 | — | — | — | 150 | — |
| 1996 Proof | Est. 10,000 | Value: 175 | | | | |

**12000 TUGRIK** KM# 152 **Weight:** 7.7750 g. **Composition:** 0.9990 Gold .2500 oz. AGW **Obverse:** National emblem **Reverse:** Ugedei Khan

| Date | Mintage | F | VF | XF | Unc | BU |
|---|---|---|---|---|---|---|
| 1997 Proof | Est. 10,000 | Value: 300 | | | | |

**25000 TUGRIK** KM# 120 **Weight:** 15.5500 g. **Composition:** 0.9999 Gold .2495 oz. AGW **Subject:** Chinggis Khan **Note:** Similar to 50,000 Tugrik, KM#121.

| Date | Mintage | F | VF | XF | Unc | BU |
|---|---|---|---|---|---|---|
| 1996 Rare | 10 | — | — | — | — | — |
| 1996 Proof, rare | 10 | — | — | — | — | — |

**25000 TUGRIK** KM# 120a **Weight:** 15.5500 g. **Composition:** 0.9990 Gold .4994 oz. AGW

| Date | Mintage | F | VF | XF | Unc | BU |
|---|---|---|---|---|---|---|
| 1996 | Est. 10,000 | — | — | — | 250 | — |
| 1996 Proof | Est. 10,000 | Value: 350 | | | | |

**25000 TUGRIK** KM# 144 **Weight:** 15.5940 g. **Composition:** 0.9999 Gold .5000 oz. AGW **Subject:** Aquila Rapaz **Note:** Similar to 500 Tugrik, KM#132.

| Date | Mintage | F | VF | XF | Unc | BU |
|---|---|---|---|---|---|---|
| 1996 Proof | 300 | Value: 385 | | | | |

**25000 TUGRIK** KM# 145 **Weight:** 15.5940 g. **Composition:** 0.9999 Gold .5000 oz. AGW **Subject:** Equus Fergus **Note:** Similar to 500 Tugrik, KM#133.

| Date | Mintage | F | VF | XF | Unc | BU |
|---|---|---|---|---|---|---|
| 1996 Proof | 300 | Value: 385 | | | | |

**25000 TUGRIK** KM# 146 **Weight:** 15.5940 g. **Composition:** 0.9999 Gold .5000 oz. AGW **Subject:** Cameleus Ferus **Note:** Similar to 500 Tugrik, KM#134.

| Date | Mintage | F | VF | XF | Unc | BU |
|---|---|---|---|---|---|---|
| 1996 Proof | 300 | Value: 385 | | | | |

**25000 TUGRIK** KM# 147 **Weight:** 15.5940 g. **Composition:** 0.9999 Gold .5000 oz. AGW **Subject:** Panthera Tigris Altaica **Note:** Similar to 500 Tugrik, KM#135.

| Date | Mintage | F | VF | XF | Unc | BU |
|---|---|---|---|---|---|---|
| 1996 Proof | 300 | Value: 385 | | | | |

**25000 TUGRIK** KM# 153 **Weight:** 15.5517 g. **Composition:** 0.9990 Gold .5 oz. AGW **Subject:** Ugedei Khan **Obverse:** National arms

| Date | Mintage | F | VF | XF | Unc | BU |
|---|---|---|---|---|---|---|
| 1997 Proof | Est. 10,000 | Value: 600 | | | | |

**50000 TUGRIK** KM# 99 **Weight:** 155.5150 g. **Composition:** 0.9990 Gold 5.0000 oz. AGW **Subject:** Year of the Pig **Obverse:** National emblem **Reverse:** Pigs in field **Note:** Similar to 2500 Tigrik, KM#97

| Date | Mintage | F | VF | XF | Unc | BU |
|---|---|---|---|---|---|---|
| 1995 Proof | 25 | Value: 5,000 | | | | |

**50000 TUGRIK** KM# 109 **Weight:** 155.5150 g. **Composition:** 0.9990 Gold 5.0000 oz. AGW **Subject:** Year of the Rat **Note:** Similar to 50 Tugrik, KM#104.

| Date | Mintage | F | VF | XF | Unc | BU |
|---|---|---|---|---|---|---|
| 1996 Proof | 25 | Value: 4,250 | | | | |

**50000 TUGRIK** KM# 121 **Weight:** 31.1000 g. **Composition:** 0.9998 Gold .9998 oz. AGW **Reverse:** Chinggis Khan

| Date | Mintage | F | VF | XF | Unc | BU |
|---|---|---|---|---|---|---|
| 1996 Rare | 10 | — | — | — | — | — |
| 1996 Proof, rare | 10 | — | — | — | — | — |

**50000 TUGRIK** KM# 121a **Weight:** 31.1000 g. **Composition:** 0.9990 Gold .9998 oz. AGW **Subject:** Chinggis Khan

| Date | Mintage | F | VF | XF | Unc | BU |
|---|---|---|---|---|---|---|
| 1996 | Est. 10,000 | — | — | — | 600 | — |
| 1996 Proof | Est. 10,000 | Value: 800 | | | | |

**50000 TUGRIK** KM# 131 **Weight:** 155.5150 g. **Composition:** 0.9999 Gold 5.0000 oz. AGW **Subject:** Year of the Ox **Note:** Similar to 2,500 Tugrik, KM#129.

| Date | Mintage | F | VF | XF | Unc | BU |
|---|---|---|---|---|---|---|
| 1997 Proof | 25 | Value: 4,000 | | | | |

**50000 TUGRIK** KM# 154 **Weight:** 31.1035 g. **Composition:** 0.9990 Gold 1.0000 oz. AGW **Obverse:** National emblem **Reverse:** Ugedei Khan

| Date | Mintage | F | VF | XF | Unc | BU |
|---|---|---|---|---|---|---|
| 1997 Proof | Est. 10,000 | Value: 1,200 | | | | |

**50000 TUGRIK** KM# 177 **Weight:** 155.5150 g. **Composition:** 0.9999 Gold 5.0000 oz. AGW **Subject:** Year of the Tiger

| Date | Mintage | F | VF | XF | Unc | BU |
|---|---|---|---|---|---|---|
| 1998 | 99 | — | — | — | 3,500 | — |

**50000 TUGRIK** KM# 165 **Weight:** 155.5150 g. **Composition:** 0.9999 Gold 5.0000 oz. AGW **Subject:** Year of the Rabbit

| Date | Mintage | F | VF | XF | Unc | BU |
|---|---|---|---|---|---|---|
| 1999 | 99 | — | — | — | 3,500 | — |

**250000 TUGRIK** KM# 83 **Weight:** 1000.1000 g. **Composition:** 0.9999 Gold 32.1575 oz. AGW **Reverse:** Chinggis Khan **Size:** 85 mm. **Note:** Illustration reduced.

| Date | Mintage | F | VF | XF | Unc | BU |
|---|---|---|---|---|---|---|
| 1992 Proof | Est. 300 | Value: 25,000 | | | | |

## MEDALLIC COINAGE

**10 TUGRIK** KM# M1 **Composition:** Copper Nickel **Subject:** International games - Archery

| Date | Mintage | F | VF | XF | Unc | BU |
|---|---|---|---|---|---|---|
| 1984 Proof | — | Value: 13.50 | | | | |

**10 TUGRIK** KM# M2 **Composition:** Copper Nickel **Subject:** International games - Equestrian

| Date | Mintage | F | VF | XF | Unc | BU |
|---|---|---|---|---|---|---|
| 1984 Proof | — | Value: 15.00 | | | | |

## PIEFORTS

| KM# | Date | Mintage | Identification | Mkt Val |
|---|---|---|---|---|
| P1 | 1980 | 92 | 25 Tugrik. KM39. | 135 |
| P2 | 1980 | 550 | 750 Tugrik. KM40. | 750 |

## MINT SETS

| KM# | Date | Mintage | Identification | Issue Price | Mkt Val |
|---|---|---|---|---|---|
| MS1 | 1980 (8) | — | KM27-33, 41 | — | 25.00 |
| MS2 | 1996 (3) | 10,000 | KM116-118 | — | 40.00 |
| MS3 | 1996 (3) | 10 | KM119-121 | — | — |
| MS4 | 1996 (3) | 10,000 | KM119a-121a | — | 1,100 |

## PROOF SETS

| KM# | Date | Mintage | Identification | Mkt Val |
|---|---|---|---|---|
| PS1 | 1996 (3) | — | KM105, 106, 108 | 700 |
| PS2 | 1996 (3) | 10,000 | KM116-118. The *10,000 mintage limit is per denomination including proof and BU single coins as well as coins included in sets. | 70.00 |
| PS3 | 1996 (3) | 10 | KM119-121 | — |
| PS5 | 1996 (4) | 10 | KM116-118, 121 | — |
| PS6 | 1996 (4) | 10,000 | KM116-118, 121a. The *10,000 mintage limit is per denomination including proof and BU single coins as well as coins included in sets. | 975 |
| PS7 | 1996 (4) | 10 | KM118, 119-121 | — |
| PS8 | 1996 (4) | 10,000 | KM118, 119a-121a. The *10,000 mintage limit is per denomination including proof and BU single coins as well as coins included in sets. | 1,650 |
| PS4 | 1996 | 10,000 | KM119a-121a. The *10,000 mintage limit is per denomination including proof and BU single coins as well as coins included in sets. | 1,600 |
| PS10 | 1997 (3) | 10,000 | KM152-154 | 2,100 |
| PS9 | 1997 (3) | 10,000 | KM149-151 | 100 |

# MONTENEGRO

The former independent kingdom of Montenegro, now one of the nominally autonomous federated units of Yugoslavia, was located in southeastern Europe north of Albania. As a kingdom, it had an area of 5,333 sq. mi. (13,812 sq. km.) and a population of about 250,000. The capital city is Podgorica.

Montenegro became an independent state in 1355 following the break-up of the Serb empire. During the Turkish invasion of Albania and Herzegovina in the 15th century, the Montenegrins moved their capital to the remote mountain village of Cetinje where they maintained their independence through two centuries of intermittent attack, emerging as the only one of the Balkan states not subjugated by the Turks. When World War I began, Montenegro joined with Serbia and was subsequently invaded and occupied by the Austrians. Austria withdrew upon the defeat of the Central Powers, permitting the Serbians to move in and maintain the occupation. Montenegro then joined the kingdom of the Serbs, Croats and Slovenes, which later became Yugoslavia.

The coinage, issued under the autocratic rule of Prince Nicholas, is obsolete.

**RULERS**

Nicholas I as Prince 1860-1910
as King 1910-1918

**MINT MARKS**

- Paris, privy marks only

**MONETARY SYSTEM**

100 Para, @12SATA@05 = 1 Perper, @12SGTSGT

## KINGDOM

### STANDARD COINAGE

**PARA** KM# 1 **Composition:** Bronze **Ruler:** Nicholas I

| Date | Mintage | F | VF | XF | Unc | BU |
|---|---|---|---|---|---|---|
| 1906 | 200,000 | 8.00 | 16.00 | 35.00 | 75.00 | — |

**PARA** KM# 16 **Composition:** Bronze **Ruler:** Nicholas I

| Date | Mintage | F | VF | XF | Unc | BU |
|---|---|---|---|---|---|---|
| 1913 | 100,000 | 12.50 | 25.00 | 60.00 | 125 | — |
| 1914 | 200,000 | 6.00 | 12.00 | 25.00 | 70.00 | — |

**2 PARE** KM# 2 **Composition:** Bronze **Ruler:** Nicholas I

| Date | Mintage | F | VF | XF | Unc | BU |
|---|---|---|---|---|---|---|
| 1906 | 600,000 | 4.00 | 8.00 | 18.00 | 35.00 | — |
| 1908 | 250,000 | 8.00 | 18.00 | 32.00 | 70.00 | — |

**2 PARE** KM# 17 **Composition:** Bronze **Ruler:** Nicholas I

| Date | Mintage | F | VF | XF | Unc | BU |
|---|---|---|---|---|---|---|
| 1913 | 500,000 | 4.00 | 7.50 | 15.00 | 30.00 | — |
| 1914 | 400,000 | 4.50 | 9.00 | 18.00 | 45.00 | — |

**10 PARA** KM# 3 **Composition:** Nickel **Ruler:** Nicholas I

| Date | Mintage | F | VF | XF | Unc | BU |
|---|---|---|---|---|---|---|
| 1906 | 750,000 | 2.50 | 5.00 | 12.00 | 25.00 | — |
| 1908 | 250,000 | 3.00 | 6.50 | 16.00 | 32.00 | — |

**10 PARA** KM# 18 **Composition:** Nickel **Ruler:** Nicholas I

| Date | Mintage | F | VF | XF | Unc | BU |
|---|---|---|---|---|---|---|
| 1913 | 200,000 | 3.50 | 8.00 | 17.50 | 35.00 | — |
| 1914 | 800,000 | 2.50 | 5.00 | 12.00 | 25.00 | — |

**20 PARA** KM# 4 **Composition:** Nickel **Ruler:** Nicholas I

| Date | Mintage | F | VF | XF | Unc | BU |
|---|---|---|---|---|---|---|
| 1906 | 600,000 | 3.00 | 6.00 | 12.00 | 25.00 | — |
| 1908 | 400,000 | 3.00 | 7.00 | 15.00 | 30.00 | — |

**20 PARA** KM# 19 **Composition:** Nickel **Ruler:** Nicholas I

| Date | Mintage | F | VF | XF | Unc | BU |
|---|---|---|---|---|---|---|
| 1913 | 200,000 | 4.00 | 8.00 | 18.00 | 38.00 | — |
| 1914 | 800,000 | 3.00 | 6.00 | 12.00 | 25.00 | — |

**PERPER** KM# 5 **Weight:** 5.0000 g. **Composition:** 0.8350 Silver .1342 oz. ASW **Ruler:** Nicholas I **Note:** Approximately 30 percent melted.

| Date | Mintage | F | VF | XF | Unc | BU |
|---|---|---|---|---|---|---|
| 1909(a) | 500,000 | 10.00 | 20.00 | 40.00 | 95.00 | — |

**PERPER** KM# 14 **Weight:** 5.0000 g. **Composition:** 0.8350 Silver .1342 oz. ASW **Ruler:** Nicholas I

| Date | Mintage | F | VF | XF | Unc | BU |
|---|---|---|---|---|---|---|
| 1912 | 520,000 | 8.00 | 14.00 | 30.00 | 85.00 | — |
| 1914 | 500,000 | 9.00 | 18.00 | 35.00 | 90.00 | — |

**2 PERPERA** KM# 7 **Weight:** 10.0000 g. **Composition:** 0.8350 Silver .2685 oz. ASW **Ruler:** Nicholas I

| Date | Mintage | F | VF | XF | Unc | BU |
|---|---|---|---|---|---|---|
| 1910 | 300,000 | 15.00 | 30.00 | 65.00 | 165 | — |

**2 PERPERA** KM# 20 **Weight:** 10.0000 g. **Composition:** 0.8350 Silver .2685 oz. ASW **Ruler:** Nicholas I

| Date | Mintage | F | VF | XF | Unc | BU |
|---|---|---|---|---|---|---|
| 1914 | 200,000 | 15.00 | 35.00 | 75.00 | 175 | — |

**5 PERPERA** KM# 6 **Weight:** 24.0000 g. **Composition:** 0.9000 Silver .6944 oz. ASW **Ruler:** Nicholas I **Note:** Approximately 50 percent melted.

| Date | Mintage | F | VF | XF | Unc | BU |
|---|---|---|---|---|---|---|
| 1909(a) | 60,000 | 60.00 | 120 | 250 | 700 | — |

**5 PERPERA** KM# 15 **Weight:** 24.0000 g. **Composition:** 0.9000 Silver .6944 oz. ASW **Ruler:** Nicholas I

| Date | Mintage | F | VF | XF | Unc | BU |
|---|---|---|---|---|---|---|
| 1912 | 40,000 | 75.00 | 150 | 275 | 700 | — |
| 1914 | 20,000 | 85.00 | 160 | 300 | 950 | — |

**10 PERPERA** KM# 8 **Weight:** 3.3875 g. **Composition:** 0.9000 Gold .0980 oz. AGW **Ruler:** Nicholas I

| Date | Mintage | F | VF | XF | Unc | BU |
|---|---|---|---|---|---|---|
| 1910 | 40,000 | 100 | 200 | 300 | 450 | — |

**10 PERPERA** KM# 9 **Weight:** 3.3875 g. **Composition:** 0.9000 Gold .0980 oz. AGW **Ruler:** Nicholas I **Subject:** 50th year of reign

| Date | Mintage | F | VF | XF | Unc | BU |
|---|---|---|---|---|---|---|
| 1910 | 35,000 | 125 | 250 | 325 | 500 | — |

**20 PERPERA** KM# 10 **Weight:** 6.7751 g. **Composition:** 0.9000 Gold .1960 oz. AGW **Ruler:** Nicholas I

| Date | Mintage | F | VF | XF | Unc | BU |
|---|---|---|---|---|---|---|
| 1910 | 30,000 | 150 | 275 | 450 | 650 | — |

**20 PERPERA** KM# 11 **Weight:** 6.7751 g. **Composition:** 0.9000 Gold .1960 oz. AGW **Ruler:** Nicholas I **Subject:** 50th year of reign

| Date | Mintage | F | VF | XF | Unc | BU |
|---|---|---|---|---|---|---|
| 1910 | 30,000 | 150 | 275 | 450 | 650 | — |

**100 PERPERA** KM# 12 **Weight:** 33.8753 g. **Composition:** 0.9000 Gold .9802 oz. AGW **Ruler:** Nicholas I

| Date | Mintage | F | VF | XF | Unc | BU |
|---|---|---|---|---|---|---|
| 1910 | 300 | — | 4,500 | 6,500 | 10,000 | — |
| 1910 Proof | 25 | Value: 12,500 | | | | |

**100 PERPERA** KM# 13 **Weight:** 33.8753 g. **Composition:** 0.9000 Gold .9802 oz. AGW **Ruler:** Nicholas I **Subject:** 50th year of reign

| Date | Mintage | F | VF | XF | Unc | BU |
|---|---|---|---|---|---|---|
| 1910 | 500 | — | 4,500 | 6,500 | 10,000 | — |
| 1910 Proof | Inc. above | Value: 15,000 | | | | |

## PATTERNS

| KM# | Date | Mintage | Identification | Mkt Val |
|---|---|---|---|---|
| Pn1 | 1915 | — | Para. With ESSAI. Struck at Paris. | 1,200 |
| Pn2 | 1915 | — | 2 Pare. With ESSAI. Struck at Paris. | 1,200 |
| Pn3 | 1915 | — | 10 Para. With ESSAI. Struck at Paris. | — |
| Pn4 | 1915 | — | 20 Para. With ESSAI. Struck at Paris. | — |
| Pn5 | 1915 | — | Perper. With ESSAI. Struck at Paris. | 1,500 |
| Pn6 | 1915 | — | 2 Perpera. With ESSAI. Struck at Paris. | 2,000 |
| Pn7 | 1915 | — | 5 Perpera. With ESSAI. Struck at Paris. Bears the monogram EL for Edmond Lindauer, who copied the work of S. Schwarz of the Vienna Mint, where the regular issue coinage was struck. | 8,000 |

## TRIAL STRIKES

| KM# | Date | Mintage | Identification | Mkt Val |
|---|---|---|---|---|
| TS1 | (1910) | — | 100 Perpera. Hallmarked edge. Uniface. | 6,000 |
| TS2 | (1910) | — | 100 Perpera. TITRE ZZK ESSAI. | 5,000 |

Montserrat, a British crown colony located in the Lesser Antilles of the West Indies 27 miles (43 km.) southwest of Antigua, has an area of 38 sq. mi. (100 sq. krn.) and a population of 18,500. Capital: Plymouth. The island - actually a range of volcanic peaks rising from the Caribbean - exports cotton, limes and vegetables.

Columbus discovered Montserrat in 1493 and named it after Monserrado, a mountain in Spain. It was colonized by the English in 1632 and, except for brief periods of French occupancy in 1667 and 1782-83, has remained a British possession from that time. Currency of the British Caribbean Territories (Eastern Group) was used until later when the East Caribbean States coinage was introduced. Until becoming a separate colony in 1956, Montserrat was a presidency of the Leeward Islands.

The early 19th century countermarks of a crowned 3, 4,7, 9 or 18 over M as documented by Major Pridmore have been more correctly listed under St. Bartholomew.

**RULERS**
British

**MONETARY SYSTEM**
100 Cents = 1 Dollar

## CROWN COLONY

### MODERN COINAGE

**4 DOLLARS** KM# 30 **Composition:** Copper-Nickel **Series:** F.A.O.

| Date | Mintage | F | VF | XF | Unc | BU |
|---|---|---|---|---|---|---|
| 1970 | 13,000 | — | — | 7.50 | 14.50 | — |
| 1970 Proof | 2,000 | Value: 32.50 | | | | |

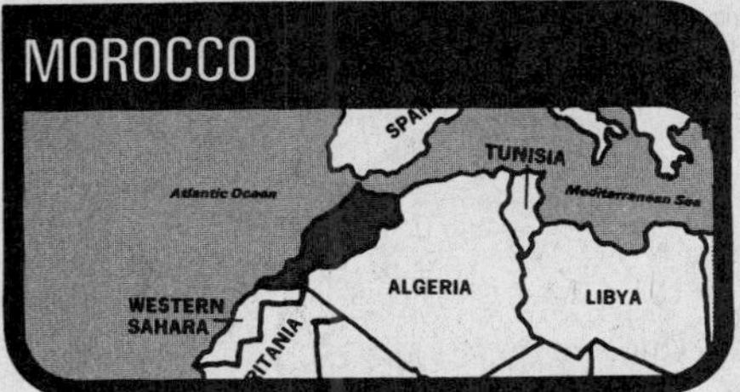


The Kingdom of Morocco, situated on the northwest corner of Africa, has an area of 275,117 sq. mi. (446,550 sq. km.) and a population of 22.5 million. Capital: Rabat. The economy is essentially agricultural. Phosphates, fresh and preserved vegetables, canned fish, and raw materials are exported.

Morocco's strategic position at the gateway to western Europe has been the principal determinant of its violent, frequently unfortunate history. Time and again the fertile plain between the rugged Atlas Mountains and the sea has echoed the battle's trumpet as Phoenicians, Romans, Vandals, Visigoths, Byzantine Greeks and Islamic Arabs successively conquered and occupied the land. Modern Morocco is a remnant of an early empire formed by the Arabs at the close of the 7th century which encompassed all of northwest Africa and most of the Iberian Peninsula. During the 17th and 18th centuries, while under the control of native dynasties, it was the headquarters of the famous Sale pirates. Morocco's strategic position involved it in the competition of 19th century European powers for political influence in Africa, and resulted in the division of Morocco into French and Spanish spheres of interest which were established as protectorates in 1912. Morocco became independent on March 2, 1956, after France agreed to end its protectorate. Spain signed similar agreements on April 7 of the same year.

**TITLES**

المغربية

Al-Maghribiya(t)

المملكة المغربية

Al-Mamlaka(t) al-Maghribiya(t)

المحمدية الشريفة

Al-Mohammediya(t) esh-Sherifiya(t)

**RULERS**
'Abd al-Aziz, AH1311-1326/1894-1908AD
al-Hafiz, AH1326-1330/1908-1912AD
**French Protectorate**, AH1330/1912AD
Yusuf, AH1330-1346/1912-1927AD
Mohammed V, AH1346-1375/1927-1955AD

**Kingdom**
Mohammed V, AH1376-1381/1956-1962AD
al-Hasan II, AH1381-1420/1962-1999AD
Sidi Mohammed, AH1420- /1999- AD

**MINTS**
(a) - Paris privy marks only

Bi - England (Birmingham) بانكلند

Ln = bi-England (London) بانكلند

Pa = bi-Bariz (Paris) بباريز

Fs = Fes (Fas, Fez) فاس

Py - Poissy Inscribed "Paris" but with thunderbolt privy mark.

**NOTE:** Some of the above forms of the mintnames are shown as they appear on the coins, not in regular Arabic script.

**NOTES:**

On the silver coins the denominations are written in words and each series has its own characteristic names:
**Y#9-13** (1313-1319) Denomination in 'Preferred" Dirhams.
**Y#18-22** (1320-1323) Denomination in fractions of a Rial, but on the 3 larger sizes, the equivalent is given in "Urti parts", 1 Rial 20 = Urti parts.
**Y#23-25** (1329) Denomination in Dirhams and in fraction of a Rial.
**Y#30-33** (1331-1336) Denomination in Yusuti or "Treasury" Dirhams.

On most of the larger denominations, the denomination is given in the form of a rhymed couplet.

## KINGDOM

### Alawi (Filali) Sharifs.

## Abd al-Aziz

### AH1311-1326 / 1894-1908AD

### REFORM COINAGE

50 Mazunas = 1 Dirham; 10 Dirhams = 1 Rial

Various copper and silver coins dated AH1297-1311 are believed to be patterns. Copper coins similar to Y#14-17, but without denomination on reverse, are patterns.

On the silver coins the denominations are written in words and each series has its own characteristic name: Y#4-8 (1299-1314) Denomination in Shar i Dirhams. Y#9-13 (1313-1319) Denomination in "Preferred" Dirhams. Y#18-22 (1320-1323) Denomination in fractions of a Rial, but on the 3 larger sizes, the equivalent is given in "Urti parts", 1 Rial 20 = Urti parts. Y#23-25 (1329) Denomination in Dirhams and in fraction of a Rial. Y#30-33 (1331-1336) Denomination in Yusuti or "Treasury Dirhams".

On most of the larger denominations, the denomination is given in the form of a rhymed couplet.

**MAZUNA** Y# 14 **Weight:** 29.1160 g. **Composition:** 0.9000 Silver .8425 oz. ASW **Note:** 5 million examples of 1320Pa were struck and melted, but at least one specimen is known to exist.

| Date | Mintage | F | VF | XF | Unc |
|---|---|---|---|---|---|
| AH1320Be Rare | 5 | — | — | — | — |
| AH1320Bi | 3,000,000 | 4.50 | 9.00 | 20.00 | 40.00 |
| AH1320Bi Proof | — | Value: 250 | | | |
| AH1320Fs | — | 20.00 | 40.00 | 80.00 | 150 |
| AH1321Bi | 900,000 | 6.50 | 13.50 | 32.50 | 60.00 |

**2 MAZUNAS** Y# 15.2 **Composition:** Bronze **Reverse:** Rim design reversed

| Date | Mintage | F | VF | XF | Unc |
|---|---|---|---|---|---|
| AH1320Fs | — | 30.00 | 75.00 | 150 | 275 |

**2 MAZUNAS** Y# 15.1 **Composition:** Bronze **Note:** Varieties exist.

| Date | Mintage | F | VF | XF | Unc |
|---|---|---|---|---|---|
| AH1320Be Rare | 5 | — | — | — | — |
| AH1320Bi | 1,500,000 | 8.50 | 18.50 | 35.00 | 75.00 |
| AH1320Bi Proof | — | Value: 250 | | | |
| AH1320Fs | — | 16.50 | 32.50 | 65.00 | 125 |
| AH1320Pa Proof | — | — | — | — | — |
| AH1321Bi | 450,000 | 12.50 | 25.00 | 50.00 | 90.00 |
| AH1321Pa | 6,500,000 | 2.00 | 5.00 | 10.00 | 25.00 |
| AH1322Fs | — | 30.00 | 75.00 | 150 | 275 |
| AH1323Fs | — | 20.00 | 42.50 | 80.00 | 150 |

**5 MAZUNAS** Y# 16 **Composition:** Bronze **Note:** Varieties exist.

| Date | Mintage | F | VF | XF | Unc |
|---|---|---|---|---|---|
| AH1320Be Proof | 5 | — | — | — | — |

**Note:** An additional 799,764 pieces are reported struck, but very few are known

| Date | Mintage | F | VF | XF | Unc |
|---|---|---|---|---|---|
| AH1320Bi | 2,400,000 | 1.00 | 3.00 | 7.00 | 25.00 |
| AH1320Bi Proof | — | Value: 325 | | | |
| AH1320Fs | — | 15.00 | 32.50 | 65.00 | 125 |
| AH1320Pa Proof | — | Value: 375 | | | |

| Date | Mintage | F | VF | XF | Unc |
|---|---|---|---|---|---|
| AH1321Bi | 720,000 | 2.00 | 4.00 | 8.00 | 32.00 |
| AH1321Pa | 7,950,000 | 5.00 | 10.00 | 20.00 | 37.50 |
| AH1322Fs | — | 25.00 | 60.00 | 125 | 200 |

**10 MAZUNAS** Y# 17 **Composition:** Bronze

| Date | Mintage | F | VF | XF | Unc |
|---|---|---|---|---|---|
| AH1320Be | 2,400,000 | 1.25 | 2.50 | 6.00 | 25.00 |
| AH1320Be Rare | 5 | — | — | — | — |
| Note: | | | | | |
| AH1320Bi | 1,200,000 | 1.50 | 4.00 | 6.50 | 25.00 |
| AH1320Bi Proof | — | Value: 400 | | | |
| AH1320Fs | — | 22.50 | 50.00 | 100 | 175 |
| AH1321Be | 2,600,000 | 1.25 | 3.00 | 6.00 | 25.00 |
| AH1321Bi | 360,000 | 1.00 | 2.00 | 3.25 | 25.00 |
| AH1321Fs | — | 15.00 | 35.00 | 85.00 | 150 |
| AH1323Fs Large 10 | — | 35.00 | 60.00 | 75.00 | 150 |
| AH1323Fs Small 10 | — | 50.00 | 100 | 250 | 450 |

**1/2 DIRHAM** Y# 9.2 **Weight:** 1.4558 g. **Composition:** 0.8350 Silver .0391 oz. ASW **Reverse:** Arrow heads point inward

| Date | Mintage | F | VF | XF | Unc |
|---|---|---|---|---|---|
| AH1319Pa | — | 8.50 | 17.50 | 32.50 | 60.00 |

**1/2 DIRHAM (1/20 Rial)** Y# 18 **Weight:** 1.2500 g. **Composition:** 0.8350 Silver .0336 oz. ASW

| Date | Mintage | F | VF | XF | Unc |
|---|---|---|---|---|---|
| AH1320Ln | 3,920,000 | 1.25 | 4.00 | 10.00 | 20.00 |
| AH1320Pa | 2,400,000 | 1.50 | 4.00 | 10.00 | 20.00 |
| AH1321Ln Mintage included with 1320Ln | — | 3.00 | 5.00 | 10.00 | 20.00 |

**1/10 RIAL** Y# 19 **Weight:** 2.5000 g. **Composition:** 0.8350 Silver .0671 oz. ASW

| Date | Mintage | F | VF | XF | Unc |
|---|---|---|---|---|---|
| AH1320Ln | 2,940,000 | 3.00 | 8.00 | 15.00 | 40.00 |
| AH1321Ln | 770,000 | 3.00 | 8.00 | 15.00 | 40.00 |

**1/4 RIAL** Y# 20 **Weight:** 6.2500 g. **Composition:** 0.8350 Silver .1678 oz. ASW

| Date | Mintage | F | VF | XF | Unc |
|---|---|---|---|---|---|
| AH1320Be | 380,000 | 4.00 | 12.50 | 20.00 | 50.00 |
| AH1320Ln | 3,056,000 | 4.00 | 10.00 | 12.50 | 40.00 |
| AH1320Pa | 640,000 | 4.00 | 11.00 | 17.50 | 45.00 |
| AH1321Be | 4,450,000 | 4.00 | 7.00 | 10.00 | 32.50 |
| AH1321Ln | 1,889,000 | 4.00 | 7.00 | 10.00 | 32.50 |
| AH1321Ln Proof | — | Value: 375 | | | |
| AH1321Pa | — | 40.00 | 60.00 | 125 | 275 |

**1/2 RIAL** Y# 21 **Weight:** 12.5000 g. **Composition:** 0.8350 Silver .3356 oz. ASW

| Date | Mintage | F | VF | XF | Unc |
|---|---|---|---|---|---|
| AH1320Be | 2,510,000 | 7.00 | 15.00 | 30.00 | 75.00 |
| AH1320Ln | 900,000 | 7.00 | 15.00 | 30.00 | 75.00 |
| AH1321Be Rare | — | — | — | — | — |
| AH1321Ln | 1,041,000 | 7.00 | 15.00 | 30.00 | 75.00 |
| AH1321Ln Proof | — | Value: 400 | | | |
| AH1321Pa | 1,800,000 | 7.00 | 17.50 | 35.00 | 85.00 |

| Date | Mintage | F | VF | XF | Unc |
|---|---|---|---|---|---|
| AH1322Pa | 540,000 | 7.00 | 20.00 | 40.00 | 100 |
| AH1323Pa | 1,090,000 | 7.00 | 20.00 | 40.00 | 100 |

**RIAL** Y# 22 **Weight:** 25.0000 g. **Composition:** 0.9000 Silver .7234 oz. ASW

| Date | Mintage | F | VF | XF | Unc |
|---|---|---|---|---|---|
| AH1320Ln | 330,000 | 17.50 | 25.00 | 40.00 | 120 |
| AH1320Ln Proof; Rare | — | — | — | — | — |
| AH1321Pa | 300,000 | 20.00 | 27.50 | 40.00 | 120 |

## al-Hafiz

### AH1326-1330 / 1908-1912AD

### REFORM COINAGE

50 Mazunas = 1 Dirham; 10 Dirhams = 1 Rial

Various copper and silver coins dated AH1297-1311 are believed to be patterns. Copper coins similar to Y#14-17, but without denomination on reverse, are patterns.

On the silver coins the denominations are written in words and each series has its own characteristic name: Y#4-8 (1299-1314) Denomination in Shar i Dirhams. Y#9-13 (1313-1319) Denomination in "Preferred" Dirhams. Y#18-22 (1320-1323) Denomination in fractions of a Rial, but on the 3 larger sizes, the equivalent is given in "Urti parts", 1 Rial 20 = Urti parts. Y#23-25 (1329) Denomination in Dirhams and in fraction of a Rial. Y#30-33 (1331-1336) Denomination in Yusuti or "Treasury Dirhams".

On most of the larger denominations, the denomination is given in the form of a rhymed couplet.

**1/4 RIAL** Y# 23 **Weight:** 6.2500 g. **Composition:** 0.8350 Silver .1678 oz. ASW

| Date | Mintage | F | VF | XF | Unc |
|---|---|---|---|---|---|
| AH1329Pa | 3,130,000 | 4.00 | 8.50 | 18.00 | 40.00 |

**1/2 RIAL** Y# 24 **Weight:** 12.5000 g. **Composition:** 0.8350 Silver .3356 oz. ASW

| Date | Mintage | F | VF | XF | Unc |
|---|---|---|---|---|---|
| AH1329Pa | 4,660,000 | 7.00 | 10.00 | 25.00 | 90.00 |

**RIAL** Y# 25 **Weight:** 25.0000 g. **Composition:** 0.9000 Silver .7234 oz. ASW

| Date | Mintage | F | VF | XF | Unc |
|---|---|---|---|---|---|
| AH1329Pa | 7,040,000 | 10.00 | 20.00 | 40.00 | 100 |

## PRIVATE TOKEN COINAGE

Enterprise Collet et Gouvernet

**FRANC** KM# Tn1 **Composition:** Aluminum **Issuer:** Entreprise Collet et Gouvernet

| Date | Mintage | F | VF | XF | Unc |
|---|---|---|---|---|---|
| ND | — | 18.00 | 30.00 | 50.00 | 100 |

**2 FRANCS** KM# Tn2 **Composition:** Aluminum

| Date | Mintage | F | VF | XF | Unc |
|---|---|---|---|---|---|
| ND | — | 20.00 | 35.00 | 60.00 | 100 |

**5 FRANCS** KM# Tn3 **Composition:** Aluminum

| Date | Mintage | F | VF | XF | Unc |
|---|---|---|---|---|---|
| ND | — | 30.00 | 50.00 | 80.00 | 150 |

**5 FRANCS** KM# Tn4 **Composition:** Aluminum

| Date | Mintage | F | VF | XF | Unc |
|---|---|---|---|---|---|
| ND | — | 35.00 | 60.00 | 100 | 175 |

# Yusuf

## AH1330-1346 / 1912-1927AD

### REFORM COINAGE

50 Mazunas = 1 Dirham; 10 Dirhams = 1 Rial

Various copper and silver coins dated AH1297-1311 are believed to be patterns. Copper coins similar to Y#14-17, but without denomination on reverse, are patterns.

On the silver coins the denominations are written in words and each series has its own characteristic name: Y#4-8 (1299-1314) Denomination in Shar i Dirhams. Y#9-13 (1313-1319) Denomination in "Preferred" Dirhams. Y#18-22 (1320-1323) Denomination in fractions of a Rial, but on the 3 larger sizes, the equivalent is given in "Urti parts", 1 Rial 20 = Urti parts. Y#23-25 (1329) Denomination in Dirhams and in fraction of a Rial. Y#30-33 (1331-1336) Denomination in Yusuti or "Treasury Dirhams".

On most of the larger denominations, the denomination is given in the form of a rhymed couplet.

**MAZUNA** Y# 26 **Composition:** Bronze

| Date | Mintage | F | VF | XF | Unc |
|---|---|---|---|---|---|
| AH1330Pa | 1,850,000 | 2.00 | 5.00 | 15.00 | 30.00 |

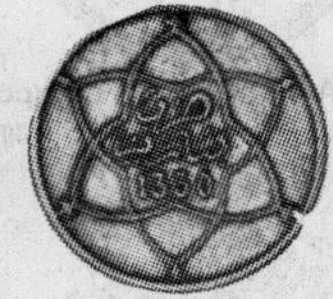

**2 MAZUNAS** Y# 27 **Composition:** Bronze

| Date | Mintage | F | VF | XF | Unc |
|---|---|---|---|---|---|
| AH1330Pa | 2,790,000 | 2.00 | 4.00 | 12.00 | 30.00 |

**Note:** Coins reportedly dated 1331Pa probably bore date AH1330

**5 MAZUNAS** Y# 28.1 **Composition:** Bronze

| Date | Mintage | F | VF | XF | Unc |
|---|---|---|---|---|---|
| AH1330Pa | 3,180,000 | 2.00 | 5.00 | 11.00 | 25.00 |
| AH1340Pa | — | 2.00 | 4.00 | 10.00 | 22.50 |

**5 MAZUNAS** Y# 28.2 **Composition:** Bronze **Reverse:** Privy marks

| Date | Mintage | F | VF | XF | Unc |
|---|---|---|---|---|---|
| AH1340Pa | 2,000,000 | 1.00 | 2.00 | 5.00 | 25.00 |
| AH1340Py | 2,010,000 | 2.00 | 5.00 | 8.00 | 27.50 |

**10 MAZUNAS** Y# 29.1 **Composition:** Bronze

| Date | Mintage | F | VF | XF | Unc |
|---|---|---|---|---|---|
| AH1330Pa | 1,500,000 | 0.75 | 2.50 | 10.00 | 30.00 |
| AH1340Pa | 1,000,000 | 0.75 | 1.50 | 7.50 | 25.00 |

**10 MAZUNAS** Y# 29.2 **Composition:** Bronze **Reverse:** Privy marks

| Date | Mintage | F | VF | XF | Unc |
|---|---|---|---|---|---|
| AH1340Py | 1,000,000 | 1.00 | 3.00 | 12.00 | 30.00 |

**1/10 RIAL (Dirham)** Y# 30 **Weight:** 2.5000 g. **Composition:** 0.8350 Silver .0671 oz. ASW

| Date | Mintage | F | VF | XF | Unc |
|---|---|---|---|---|---|
| AH1331Pa | 500,000 | 30.00 | 45.00 | 75.00 | 200 |
| AH1331Pa Proof | — | Value: 800 | | | |

**1/4 RIAL** Y# 31 **Weight:** 6.2500 g. **Composition:** 0.8350 Silver .1678 oz. ASW

| Date | Mintage | F | VF | XF | Unc |
|---|---|---|---|---|---|
| AH1331Pa | 2,500,000 | 30.00 | 45.00 | 90.00 | 225 |

**1/2 RIAL** Y# 32 **Composition:** 0.8350 Silver

| Date | Mintage | F | VF | XF | Unc |
|---|---|---|---|---|---|
| AH1331Pa | 1,500,000 | 7.00 | 16.00 | 25.00 | 60.00 |
| AH1336Pa | 11,500,000 | 6.00 | 11.00 | 20.00 | 50.00 |

**RIAL** Y# 33 **Weight:** 25.0000 g. **Composition:** 0.9000 Silver .7234 oz. ASW

| Date | Mintage | F | VF | XF | Unc |
|---|---|---|---|---|---|
| AH1331Pa | 7,000,000 | 9.00 | 20.00 | 35.00 | 70.00 |
| AH1336Pa | 2,600,000 | 9.00 | 17.50 | 25.00 | 55.00 |

# FRENCH PROTECTORATE

# Yusuf

## AH1330-1346 / 1912-1927AD

### STANDARD COINAGE

100 Centimes = 1 Franc

Note: Y#46-51 were struck for more than 20 years without change of date, until a new currency was introduced in 1974. Final mintage statistics not yet available.

**25 CENTIMES** Y# 34.1 **Composition:** Copper-Nickel **Obverse:** Without privy marks **Reverse:** Without privy marks

| Date | Mintage | F | VF | XF | Unc |
|---|---|---|---|---|---|
| ND(1921)Pa | 13,000,000 | 1.00 | 3.00 | 8.00 | 40.00 |

**25 CENTIMES** Y# 34.2 **Composition:** Copper-Nickel **Reverse:** Thunderbolt above CENTIMES

| Date | Mintage | F | VF | XF | Unc |
|---|---|---|---|---|---|
| ND(1924)Py | 6,020,000 | 1.00 | 3.00 | 8.00 | 40.00 |

**25 CENTIMES** Y# 34.3 **Composition:** Copper-Nickel **Reverse:** Thunderbolt and torch at left and right of CENTIMES

| Date | Mintage | F | VF | XF | Unc |
|---|---|---|---|---|---|
| ND(1924)Py | Inc. above | 1.00 | 3.00 | 8.00 | 40.00 |

**50 CENTIMES** Y# 35.1 **Composition:** Nickel **Obverse:** Without privy marks **Reverse:** Without privy marks

| Date | Mintage | F | VF | XF | Unc |
|---|---|---|---|---|---|
| ND(1921)Pa | 11,000,000 | 0.50 | 1.00 | 6.50 | 45.00 |

**50 CENTIMES** Y# 35.2 **Composition:** Nickel **Reverse:** Thunderbolt at bottom

| Date | Mintage | F | VF | XF | Unc |
|---|---|---|---|---|---|
| ND(1924)Py | 3,000,000 | 1.00 | 2.00 | 8.00 | 45.00 |

**FRANC** Y#36.2 **Composition:** Nickel **Reverse:** Thunderbolt below 1

| Date | Mintage | F | VF | XF | Unc |
|---|---|---|---|---|---|
| ND(1924)Py | 3,000,000 | 1.25 | 2.50 | 10.00 | 55.00 |

# Mohammed V
## AH1346-1381 / 1927-1962AD
## STANDARD COINAGE

100 Centimes = 1 Franc

Note: Y#46-51 were struck for more than 20 years without change of date, until a new currency was introduced in 1974. Final mintage statistics not yet available.

**50 CENTIMES** Y# 40 **Composition:** Aluminum-Bronze

| Date | Mintage | F | VF | XF | Unc |
|---|---|---|---|---|---|
| AH1364-1945(a) | — | — | 0.25 | 1.50 | 2.50 |

**FRANC** Y# 41 **Composition:** Aluminum-Bronze

| Date | Mintage | F | VF | XF | Unc |
|---|---|---|---|---|---|
| AH1364-1945(a) | 12,000,000 | — | 0.25 | 1.50 | 2.50 |

**FRANC** Y# 46 **Composition:** Aluminum

| Date | Mintage | F | VF | XF | Unc |
|---|---|---|---|---|---|
| AH1370-1950(a) | — | — | 0.15 | 0.35 | 1.25 |

**2 FRANCS** Y# 42 **Composition:** Aluminum-Bronze

| Date | Mintage | F | VF | XF | Unc |
|---|---|---|---|---|---|
| AH1364-1945(a) | 12,000,000 | — | 0.75 | 2.50 | 6.00 |

**2 FRANCS** Y# 47 **Composition:** Aluminum

| Date | Mintage | F | VF | XF | Unc |
|---|---|---|---|---|---|
| AH1370-1951(a) | — | — | 0.15 | 0.50 | 2.00 |

**5 FRANCS** Y# 37 **Weight:** 5.0000 g. **Composition:** 0.6800 Silver .1093 oz. ASW

| Date | Mintage | F | VF | XF | Unc |
|---|---|---|---|---|---|
| AH1347(a) | 4,000,000 | — | 2.50 | 7.00 | 32.00 |
| AH1352(a) | 5,000,000 | — | 1.50 | 4.00 | 18.00 |

**5 FRANCS** Y# 43 **Composition:** Aluminum-Bronze

| Date | Mintage | F | VF | XF | Unc |
|---|---|---|---|---|---|
| AH1365(a) | 20,000,000 | 0.25 | 0.50 | 0.75 | 2.00 |

**5 FRANCS** Y# 48 **Composition:** Aluminum

| Date | Mintage | F | VF | XF | Unc |
|---|---|---|---|---|---|
| AH1370(a) | — | 0.15 | 0.30 | 0.65 | 1.75 |

**10 FRANCS** Y# 38 **Weight:** 10.0000 g. **Composition:** 0.6800 Silver .2186 oz. ASW

| Date | Mintage | F | VF | XF | Unc |
|---|---|---|---|---|---|
| AH1347(a) | 1,600,000 | 4.00 | 10.00 | 22.00 | 80.00 |
| AH1352(a) | 2,900,000 | 2.25 | 3.00 | 8.00 | 27.50 |

**10 FRANCS** Y# 44 **Composition:** Copper-Nickel

| Date | Mintage | F | VF | XF | Unc |
|---|---|---|---|---|---|
| AH1366(a) | 20,000,000 | 0.50 | 1.00 | 1.50 | 2.50 |

**10 FRANCS** Y# 49 **Composition:** Aluminum-Bronze

| Date | Mintage | F | VF | XF | Unc |
|---|---|---|---|---|---|
| AH1371(a) | — | 0.15 | 0.40 | 0.85 | 2.00 |

**20 FRANCS** Y# 39 **Weight:** 20.0000 g. **Composition:** 0.6800 Silver .4372 oz. ASW

| Date | Mintage | F | VF | XF | Unc |
|---|---|---|---|---|---|
| AH1347(a) | — | 5.00 | 12.00 | 32.50 | 80.00 |
| AH1352(a) | 2,000,000 | 5.00 | 8.00 | 25.00 | 50.00 |

**20 FRANCS** Y# 45 **Composition:** Copper-Nickel

| Date | Mintage | F | VF | XF | Unc |
|---|---|---|---|---|---|
| AH1366(a) | 6,000,000 | 0.35 | 0.65 | 1.25 | 2.50 |
| AH1366(a) Proof | — | Value: 50.00 | | | |

**20 FRANCS** Y# 50 **Composition:** Aluminum-Bronze

| Date | Mintage | F | VF | XF | Unc |
|---|---|---|---|---|---|
| AH1371(a) | — | 0.25 | 0.50 | 1.00 | 2.00 |

**50 FRANCS** Y# 51 **Composition:** Aluminum-Bronze

| Date | Mintage | F | VF | XF | Unc |
|---|---|---|---|---|---|
| AH1371(a) | — | 0.35 | 0.65 | 1.25 | 2.25 |

**50 FRANCS** Y# 51a **Composition:** Gold

| Date | Mintage | F | VF | XF | Unc |
|---|---|---|---|---|---|
| AH1371(a) Rare | — | — | — | — | — |

**100 FRANCS** Y# A54 **Weight:** 2.5000 g. **Composition:** 0.7200 Silver .0579 oz. ASW

| Date | Mintage | F | VF | XF | Unc |
|---|---|---|---|---|---|
| AH1370(a) | 10,000,000 | — | — | — | 250 |

**Note:** Most were remelted

**100 FRANCS** **Y# 52** **Weight:** 2.5000 g. **Composition:** 0.7200 Silver .0579 oz. ASW

| Date | Mintage | F | VF | XF | Unc |
|---|---|---|---|---|---|
| AH1372(a) | 5,000,000 | — | 2.75 | 3.75 | 6.50 |

**200 FRANCS** **Y# 53** **Weight:** 8.0000 g. **Composition:** 0.7200 Silver .1851 oz. ASW

| Date | Mintage | F | VF | XF | Unc |
|---|---|---|---|---|---|
| AH1372(1952) (a) | 9,200,000 | — | 2.75 | 4.25 | 9.00 |

# KINGDOM

## Resumed.

## REFORM COINAGE

100 Francs = 1 Dirham

**250 DIRHAMS** **Y# 95** **Weight:** 25.0000 g. **Composition:** 0.9999 Gold .8037 oz. AGW **Subject:** World Children's Day **Obverse:** King's portrait **Reverse:** Two children on an open book and a world globe **Edge:** Reeded **Size:** 37 mm.

| Date | Mintage | F | VF | XF | Unc |
|---|---|---|---|---|---|
| AH1422(2001) Proof | 2,800 | Value: 500 | | | |

# Mohammed V

## AH1346-1381 / 1927-1962AD

## STANDARD COINAGE

100 Centimes = 1 Franc

Note: Y#46-51 were struck for more than 20 years without change of date, until a new currency was introduced in 1974. Final mintage statistics not yet available.

**500 FRANCS** **Y# 54** **Weight:** 22.5000 g. **Composition:** 0.9000 Silver .6511 oz. ASW

| Date | Mintage | F | VF | XF | Unc |
|---|---|---|---|---|---|
| AH1376-1956(a) | 2,000,000 | — | 8.00 | 10.00 | 20.00 |

## REFORM COINAGE

100 Francs = 1 Dirham

**DIRHAM** **Y# 55** **Weight:** 6.0000 g. **Composition:** 0.6000 Silver .1157 oz. ASW

| Date | Mintage | F | VF | XF | Unc |
|---|---|---|---|---|---|
| AH1380-1960(a) | 18,830,000 | — | 1.25 | 2.75 | 5.50 |

# al-Hasan II

## AH1381-1420 / 1962-1999AD

## REFORM COINAGE

100 Francs = 1 Dirham

**5 DIRHEMS** **Y# 57** **Weight:** 11.7500 g. **Composition:** 0.7200 Silver .2720 oz. ASW

| Date | Mintage | F | VF | XF | Unc |
|---|---|---|---|---|---|
| AH1384-1965(1965) (a) | 1,800 | — | 5.00 | 7.50 | 14.50 |
| AH1384-1965(1965) (a) Proof | 200 | Value: 60.00 | | | |

**DIRHAM** **Y# 56** **Composition:** Nickel

| Date | Mintage | F | VF | XF | Unc |
|---|---|---|---|---|---|
| AH1384-1965(a) | 22,190,000 | — | 0.50 | 0.75 | 1.00 |
| AH1388-1968(a) | 5,000,000 | — | 0.50 | 0.75 | 1.00 |
| AH1389-1969(a) | 10,000,000 | — | 0.50 | 0.75 | 1.00 |

## REFORM COINAGE

100 Santimat = 1 Dirham

**5 DIRHEMS** **Y# 64** **Composition:** Copper-Nickel **Series:** World Food Conference

| Date | Mintage | F | VF | XF | Unc |
|---|---|---|---|---|---|
| AH1395-1975 | 500,000 | — | — | 1.00 | 3.50 |
| AH1395-1975 Proof | 500 | Value: 9.00 | | | |

**5 DIRHEMS** **Y# 64a** **Weight:** 12.0000 g. **Composition:** 0.9250 Silver .3569 oz. ASW

| Date | Mintage | F | VF | XF | Unc |
|---|---|---|---|---|---|
| AH1395-1975 Proof | 200 | Value: 75.00 | | | |

**5 DIRHEMS** **Y# 64b** **Weight:** 23.6500 g. **Composition:** 0.9000 Gold .6844 oz. AGW **Series:** World Food Conference

| Date | Mintage | F | VF | XF | Unc |
|---|---|---|---|---|---|
| AH1395-1975 Proof | 20 | Value: 1,000 | | | |

**5 DIRHEMS** **Y# 72** **Composition:** Copper-Nickel

| Date | Mintage | F | VF | XF | Unc |
|---|---|---|---|---|---|
| AH1400-1980 | 10,000,000 | — | 1.50 | 4.00 | 6.50 |

**5 DIRHEMS** **Y# 82** **Ring Composition:** Stainless Steel **Center Composition:** Aluminum-Bronze

| Date | Mintage | F | VF | XF | Unc |
|---|---|---|---|---|---|
| AH1407-1987 | — | — | 2.00 | 4.50 | 7.50 |

**SANTIM** **Y# 58** **Composition:** Aluminum **Obverse:** Royal arms

| Date | Mintage | F | VF | XF | Unc |
|---|---|---|---|---|---|
| AH1394-1974 | 11,940,000 | — | — | 0.50 | 1.25 |
| AH1394-1974 Proof | 34,000 | Value: 1.00 | | | |
| AH1395-1975 | 1,700,000 | — | — | 0.10 | 1.00 |
| AH1395-1975 | 14,000 | Value: 2.50 | | | |

**SANTIM** **Y# 58a** **Composition:** 0.9170 Gold

| Date | Mintage | F | VF | XF | Unc |
|---|---|---|---|---|---|
| AH1394-1974 Proof | 30 | Value: 400 | | | |

**SANTIM** **Y# 93** **Composition:** Aluminum **Obverse:** Royal arms **Reverse:** Fish and denomination

| Date | Mintage | F | VF | XF | Unc |
|---|---|---|---|---|---|
| AH1407-1987 | — | — | — | — | 0.25 |

**5 SANTIMAT** **Y# 59** **Composition:** Brass **Series:** F.A.O.

| Date | Mintage | F | VF | XF | Unc |
|---|---|---|---|---|---|
| AH1394-1974 | 78,420,000 | — | — | 0.15 | 0.30 |
| AH1394-1974 Proof | 20,000 | Value: 1.25 | | | |
| AH1395-1975 | 11,000,000 | — | — | 0.10 | 0.25 |
| AH1398-1978 | 12,600,000 | — | — | 0.10 | 0.25 |

**5 SANTIMAT** **Y# 59a** **Composition:** 0.9170 Gold **Series:** F.A.O.

| Date | Mintage | F | VF | XF | Unc |
|---|---|---|---|---|---|
| AH1394-1974 Proof | 30 | Value: 475 | | | |

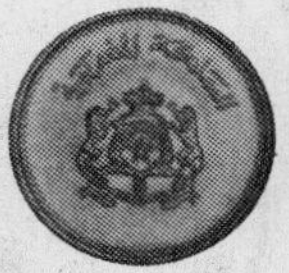

**5 SANTIMAT** **Y# 83** **Composition:** Brass **Series:** F.A.O.

| Date | Mintage | F | VF | XF | Unc |
|---|---|---|---|---|---|
| AH1407-1987 | — | — | — | — | 0.30 |

**10 SANTIMAT** Y# 60 **Composition:** Brass **Series:** F.A.O.

| Date | Mintage | F | VF | XF | Unc |
|---|---|---|---|---|---|
| AH1394-1974 | 79,850,000 | — | — | 0.15 | 0.30 |
| AH1394-1974 Proof | 20,000 | Value: 1.75 | | | |
| AH1395-1975 | 10,900,000 | — | — | 0.10 | 0.20 |
| AH1398-1978 | 1,000,000 | — | — | 0.10 | 0.30 |

**10 SANTIMAT** Y# 60a **Composition:** 0.9170 Gold **Series:** F.A.O.

| Date | Mintage | F | VF | XF | Unc |
|---|---|---|---|---|---|
| AH1394-1974 Proof | 30 | Value: 575 | | | |

**10 SANTIMAT** Y# 84 **Composition:** Brass **Series:** F.A.O.

| Date | Mintage | F | VF | XF | Unc |
|---|---|---|---|---|---|
| AH1407-1987 | — | — | — | — | 0.40 |

**20 SANTIMAT** Y# 61 **Composition:** Brass

| Date | Mintage | F | VF | XF | Unc |
|---|---|---|---|---|---|
| AH1394-1974 | 95,540,000 | — | 0.30 | 0.40 | 0.50 |
| AH1394-1974 Proof | — | Value: 2.50 | | | |
| AH1395-1975 | 10,700,000 | — | 0.10 | 0.15 | 0.35 |
| AH1397-1975 | 22,800,000 | — | 0.10 | 0.15 | 0.35 |
| AH1398-1978 | 2,200,000 | — | 0.10 | 0.15 | 0.35 |

**20 SANTIMAT** Y# 61a **Composition:** 0.9170 Gold

| Date | Mintage | F | VF | XF | Unc |
|---|---|---|---|---|---|
| AH1394-1974 Proof | 30 | Value: 575 | | | |

**20 SANTIMAT** Y# 85 **Composition:** Brass **Series:** F.A.O.

| Date | Mintage | F | VF | XF | Unc |
|---|---|---|---|---|---|
| AH1407-1987 | — | — | — | — | 0.50 |

**50 SANTIMAT** Y# 62 **Composition:** Copper-Nickel

| Date | Mintage | F | VF | XF | Unc |
|---|---|---|---|---|---|
| AH1394-1974 | 41,480,000 | — | 0.20 | 0.40 | 0.60 |
| AH1394-1974 Proof | 20,000 | Value: 3.00 | | | |
| AH1398-1978 | 1,100,000 | — | 0.25 | 0.50 | 0.75 |

**50 SANTIMAT** Y# 62a **Composition:** 0.9170 Gold

| Date | Mintage | F | VF | XF | Unc |
|---|---|---|---|---|---|
| AH1394-1974 Proof | 30 | Value: 575 | | | |

**1/2 DIRHAM** Y# 87 **Composition:** Copper-Nickel **Obverse:** Portrait of King **Reverse:** Arms above denomination

| Date | Mintage | F | VF | XF | Unc |
|---|---|---|---|---|---|
| AH1407-1987 | — | — | — | — | 1.25 |

**DIRHAM** Y# 63 **Composition:** Copper-Nickel

| Date | Mintage | F | VF | XF | Unc |
|---|---|---|---|---|---|
| AH1394(1974) | 37,850,000 | — | 0.30 | 0.50 | 0.75 |
| AH1394(1974) Proof | 37,850,000 | Value: 5.00 | | | |
| AH1398(1977) | 18,100,000 | — | 0.15 | 0.35 | 0.75 |

**DIRHAM** Y# 63a **Composition:** 0.9170 Gold

| Date | Mintage | F | VF | XF | Unc |
|---|---|---|---|---|---|
| AH1394(1974) Proof | 30 | Value: 675 | | | |

**DIRHAM** Y# 88 **Composition:** Copper-Nickel

| Date | Mintage | F | VF | XF | Unc |
|---|---|---|---|---|---|
| AH1407(1986) | — | — | — | — | 2.75 |

**10 DIRHAMS** Y# 92 **Ring Composition:** Brass **Center Composition:** Copper-Nickel **Obverse:** Hassan II **Reverse:** National arms

| Date | Mintage | F | VF | XF | Unc |
|---|---|---|---|---|---|
| AH1415-1995 | — | — | — | — | 8.00 |

**50 DIRHAMS** Y# 65 **Weight:** 35.0000 g. **Composition:** 0.9250 Silver 1.0409 oz. ASW **Subject:** 20th Anniversary of Independence

| Date | Mintage | F | VF | XF | Unc |
|---|---|---|---|---|---|
| AH1395-1975 | 6,000 | — | — | — | 21.50 |
| AH1395-1975 Proof | 4,400,000 | Value: 36.50 | | | |

**50 DIRHAMS** Y# 65a **Weight:** 60.1400 g. **Composition:** 0.9000 Gold 1.7404 oz. AGW **Subject:** 20th Anniversary of Independence

| Date | Mintage | F | VF | XF | Unc |
|---|---|---|---|---|---|
| AH1395-1975 Proof | 40 | Value: 1,200 | | | |

**50 DIRHAMS** Y# 67 **Weight:** 35.0000 g. **Composition:** 0.9250 Silver 1.0409 oz. ASW **Series:** International Women's Year **Obverse:** Similar to Y#65

| Date | Mintage | F | VF | XF | Unc |
|---|---|---|---|---|---|
| AH1395-1975 | 6,000 | — | — | — | 22.50 |
| AH1395-1975 Proof | 4,400,000 | Value: 37.50 | | | |

**50 DIRHAMS** Y# 67a **Weight:** 60.1400 g. **Composition:** 0.9000 Gold 1.7404 oz. AGW **Series:** International Women's Year **Obverse:** Similar to Y#65a

| Date | Mintage | F | VF | XF | Unc |
|---|---|---|---|---|---|
| AH1395-1975 Proof | 20 | Value: 1,500 | | | |

**50 DIRHAMS** Y# 68 **Weight:** 35.0000 g. **Composition:** 0.9250 Silver 1.0409 oz. ASW **Subject:** Anniversary - Green March **Obverse:** Similar to Y#65

| Date | Mintage | F | VF | XF | Unc |
|---|---|---|---|---|---|
| AH1396-1976 | 11,000 | — | — | — | 18.00 |
| AH1396-1976 Proof | 4,400 | Value: 36.50 | | | |
| AH1397-1977 | 3,500 | — | — | — | 0.35 |
| AH1397-1977 Proof | 200 | Value: 60.00 | | | |
| AH1398-1978 | 5,000 | — | — | — | 30.00 |
| AH1398-1978 Proof | 300 | Value: 55.00 | | | |
| AH1399-1979 | 3,000 | — | — | — | 35.00 |
| AH1399-1979 Proof | 300 | Value: 55.00 | | | |
| AH1400-1980 | 1,000 | — | — | — | 45.00 |
| AH1400-1980 Proof | 200 | Value: 60.00 | | | |

**50 DIRHAMS** Y# 68a **Weight:** 60.1400 g. **Composition:** 0.9000 Gold 1.7404 oz. AGW **Subject:** Anniversary - Green March **Obverse:** Similar to Y#65a

| Date | Mintage | F | VF | XF | Unc |
|---|---|---|---|---|---|
| AH1396-1976 Proof | 20 | Value: 1,750 | | | |
| AH1397-1977 Proof | 20 | Value: 1,700 | | | |
| AH1398-1978 Proof | 70 | Value: 1,200 | | | |
| AH1399-1979 Proof | 70 | Value: 1,200 | | | |
| AH1400-1980 Proof | 30 | Value: 1,450 | | | |

**50 DIRHAMS Y# 70 Weight:** 35.0000 g. **Composition:** 0.9250 Silver 1.0409 oz. ASW **Series:** International Year of the Child **Obverse:** Similar to Y#65

| Date | Mintage | F | VF | XF | Unc |
|---|---|---|---|---|---|
| AH1399-1979 | 5,000 | — | — | — | 30.00 |
| AH1399-1979 Proof | 500 | Value: 75.00 | | | |

**50 DIRHAMS Y# 76 Weight:** 35.0000 g. **Composition:** 0.9250 Silver 1.0409 oz. ASW **Subject:** 50th Birthday - King Hassan

| Date | Mintage | F | VF | XF | Unc |
|---|---|---|---|---|---|
| AH1399-1979 | 5,000 | — | — | — | 30.00 |
| AH1399-1979 Proof | 500 | Value: 65.00 | | | |

**50 DIRHAMS Y# 76a Weight:** 60.1400 g. **Composition:** 0.9000 Gold 1.7404 oz. AGW **Subject:** 50th Birthday - King Hassan **Obverse:** Similar to Y#65a

| Date | Mintage | F | VF | XF | Unc |
|---|---|---|---|---|---|
| AH1399-1979 Proof | 70 | Value: 1,400 | | | |

**50 DIRHAMS Y# 70a Weight:** 60.1400 g. **Composition:** 0.9000 Gold 1.7404 oz. AGW **Series:** International Year of the Child **Obverse:** Similar to 250 Dirhams, Y#66

| Date | Mintage | F | VF | XF | Unc |
|---|---|---|---|---|---|
| AH1399-1979 Proof | 70 | Value: 1,200 | | | |

**100 DIRHAMS Y# 75 Weight:** 25.0000 g. **Composition:** 0.9250 Silver .7436 oz. ASW **Subject:** 9th Mediterranean Games

| Date | Mintage | F | VF | XF | Unc |
|---|---|---|---|---|---|
| AH1403-1983 | 5,000 | — | — | — | 25.00 |
| AH1403-1983 Proof | 500 | Value: 75.00 | | | |

**100 DIRHAMS Y# 77 Weight:** 15.0000 g. **Composition:** 0.9250 Silver .4461 oz. ASW **Series:** 6th Panarab Sports Games - Olympics **Reverse:** Olympic rings above map

| Date | Mintage | F | VF | XF | Unc |
|---|---|---|---|---|---|
| AH1405-1985 | 2,300 | — | — | — | 30.00 |
| AH1405-1985 Proof | 300 | Value: 150 | | | |

**100 DIRHAMS Y# 78 Weight:** 15.0000 g. **Composition:** 0.9250 Silver .4461 oz. ASW **Subject:** 10th Anniversary of Green March

| Date | Mintage | F | VF | XF | Unc |
|---|---|---|---|---|---|
| AH1406-1985 | 1,200 | — | — | — | 35.00 |
| AH1406-1985 Proof | 200 | Value: 200 | | | |

**100 DIRHAMS Y# 79 Weight:** 15.0000 g. **Composition:** 0.9250 Silver .4461 oz. ASW **Subject:** 25th Year - Reign of King Hassan

| Date | Mintage | F | VF | XF | Unc |
|---|---|---|---|---|---|
| AH1406-1986 | — | — | — | — | 32.00 |

**100 DIRHAMS Y# 80 Weight:** 15.0000 g. **Composition:** 0.9250 Silver .4461 oz. ASW **Subject:** Visit of the Pope

| Date | Mintage | F | VF | XF | Unc |
|---|---|---|---|---|---|
| AH1406-1986 Proof | 2,000 | Value: 55.00 | | | |

**100 DIRHAMS Y# 86 Weight:** 15.0000 g. **Composition:** 0.9250 Silver .4461 oz. ASW **Subject:** Opening of the Rabat Mint

| Date | Mintage | F | VF | XF | Unc |
|---|---|---|---|---|---|
| AH1407-1987 | — | — | — | — | 25.00 |
| AH1407-1987 Proof | — | Value: 50.00 | | | |

**150 DIRHAMS Y# 74 Weight:** 35.0000 g. **Composition:** 0.9250 Silver 1.0409 oz. ASW **Subject:** 15th Hejira Calendar Century **Obverse:** Similar to Y#73

| Date | Mintage | F | VF | XF | Unc |
|---|---|---|---|---|---|
| AH1401-1980 | 3,000 | — | — | — | 35.00 |
| AH1401-1980 Proof | 300 | Value: 70.00 | | | |

**150 DIRHAMS Y# 74a Weight:** 60.1400 g. **Composition:** 0.9000 Gold 1.7404 oz. AGW **Subject:** 15th Hejira Calendar Century **Obverse:** Similar to Y#73a

| Date | Mintage | F | VF | XF | Unc |
|---|---|---|---|---|---|
| AH1401-1980 Proof | 30 | Value: 1,800 | | | |

**150 DIRHAMS Y# 73 Weight:** 35.0000 g. **Composition:** 0.9250 Silver 1.0409 oz. ASW **Subject:** 20th Anniversary - King Hassan's Coronation

| Date | Mintage | F | VF | XF | Unc |
|---|---|---|---|---|---|
| AH1401-1981 | 3,000 | — | — | — | 35.00 |
| AH1401-1981 Proof | 300 | Value: 70.00 | | | |

**150 DIRHAMS Y# 73a Weight:** 60.1400 g. **Composition:** 0.9000 Gold 1.7404 oz. AGW **Subject:** 20th Anniversary - King Hassan's Coronation

| Date | Mintage | F | VF | XF | Unc |
|---|---|---|---|---|---|
| AH1401-1981 Proof | 30 | Value: 1,700 | | | |

**200 DIRHAMS Y# 81 Weight:** 15.0000 g. **Composition:** 0.9250 Silver .4461 oz. ASW **Subject:** Moroccan - American Friendship Treaty

| Date | Mintage | F | VF | XF | Unc |
|---|---|---|---|---|---|
| AH1408-1987 Proof | Est. 5,000 | Value: 40.00 | | | |

**200 DIRHAMS** **Y# 91** **Weight:** 15.0000 g. **Composition:** 0.9250 Silver .4461 oz. ASW **Subject:** First Francophone Games

| Date | Mintage | F | VF | XF | Unc |
|---|---|---|---|---|---|
| AH1409-1989 | 5,000 | — | — | — | 30.00 |
| AH1409-1989 Proof | 500 | Value: 95.00 | | | |

**250 DIRHAMS** **Y# 66** **Weight:** 6.4500 g. **Composition:** 0.9000 Gold .1867 oz. AGW **Subject:** Birthday of King Hassan

| Date | Mintage | F | VF | XF | Unc |
|---|---|---|---|---|---|
| AH1395-1975 | 5,000 | — | — | — | 120 |
| AH1395-1975 Proof | 1,270 | Value: 150 | | | |
| AH1396-1976 | 3,200 | — | — | — | 120 |
| AH1396-1976 Proof | 450 | Value: 175 | | | |
| AH1397-1977 | 3,000 | — | — | — | 120 |
| AH1397-1977 Proof | 800 | Value: 125 | | | |
| AH1398-1978 | 2,000 | — | — | — | 120 |
| AH1398-1978 Proof | 150 | Value: 200 | | | |
| AH1399-1979 | 508 | — | — | — | 150 |
| AH1399-1979 Proof | 398 | Value: 175 | | | |

**500 DIRHAMS** **Y# 71** **Weight:** 12.9000 g. **Composition:** 0.9000 Gold .3733 oz. AGW **Subject:** Birthday of King Hassan

| Date | Mintage | F | VF | XF | Unc |
|---|---|---|---|---|---|
| AH1399-1979 | 3,000 | — | — | — | 210 |
| AH1399-1979 Proof | 300 | Value: 300 | | | |
| AH1400-1980 | 100 | — | — | — | 400 |
| AH1400-1980 Proof | 100 | Value: 500 | | | |
| AH1401-1981 | 100 | — | — | — | 400 |
| AH1401-1981 Proof | 100 | Value: 500 | | | |
| AH1402-1982 | 100 | — | — | — | 400 |
| AH1402-1982 Proof | 100 | Value: 500 | | | |
| AH1403-1983 | 2,500 | — | — | — | 210 |
| AH1403-1983 Proof | Inc. above | Value: 220 | | | |
| AH1404-1984 | 100 | — | — | — | 400 |
| AH1404-1984 Proof | 100 | Value: 500 | | | |
| AH1405-1985 | 275 | — | — | — | 250 |
| AH1405-1985 Proof | 125 | Value: 475 | | | |
| AH1406-1986 Proof | — | Value: 450 | | | |
| AH1407-1987 Proof | — | Value: 450 | | | |

## BULLION COINAGE

**500 DIRHAMS** **(Y250)** **Weight:** 33.9100 g. **Composition:** 0.9170 Gold 1.0000 oz. AGW **Issuer:** First Banking Corporation, Tangier **Obverse:** Hercules

| Date | Mintage | F | VF | XF | Unc |
|---|---|---|---|---|---|
| ND(1954) | — | — | — | 475 | 650 |

# Sidi Mohammed

### AH1420 / 1999AD

## REFORM COINAGE

100 Francs = 1 Dirham

**250 DIRHAMS** **Y# 94** **Weight:** 25.0000 g. **Composition:** 0.9250 Silver .7435 oz. ASW **Subject:** First Anniversary of Mohammed VI's Enthronement **Obverse:** King's portrait **Reverse:** National arms **Edge:** Reeded **Size:** 37 mm.

| Date | Mintage | F | VF | XF | Unc |
|---|---|---|---|---|---|
| AH1421 | — | — | — | — | 50.00 |

## STANDARD COINAGE

100 Centimes = 1 Franc

Note: Y#46-51 were struck for more than 20 years without change of date, until a new currency was introduced in 1974. Final mintage statistics not yet available.

## ESSAIS

| KM# | Date | Mintage | Identification | Mkt Val |
|---|---|---|---|---|
| E1 | 1329 | — | 5 Dirhams. Y24. | 375 |
| E2 | 1330 | — | Mazuna. Y26. | 90.00 |
| E3 | 1330 | — | 2 Mazunas. Y15. | 100 |
| E4 | 1330 | — | 5 Mazunas. Y16. | 95.00 |
| E5 | 1330 | — | 10 Mazunas. Y17. | 95.00 |
| E6 | 1331 | — | 5 Dirhams. Nickel. | 175 |
| E7 | 1331 | — | 5 Dirhams. Aluminum-Bronze. | 140 |
| E8 | 1331 | — | 5 Dirhams. Aluminum. Y32. | 140 |
| E8a | 1331 | — | 5 Dirhams. Nickel. Y32. | 160 |
| E10 | | — | 50 Centimes. | 130 |

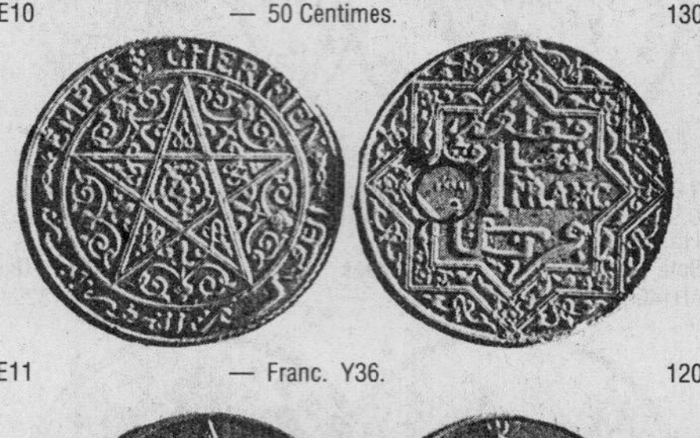

| KM# | Date | Mintage | Identification | Mkt Val |
|---|---|---|---|---|
| E11 | | — | Franc. Y36. | 120 |

| KM# | Date | Mintage | Identification | Mkt Val |
|---|---|---|---|---|
| E12 | 1340 | — | 5 Mazunas. Y28, | 85.00 |

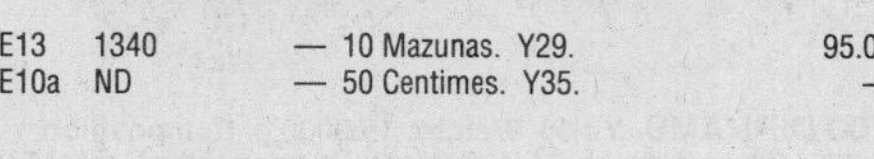

| KM# | Date | Mintage | Identification | Mkt Val |
|---|---|---|---|---|
| E13 | 1340 | — | 10 Mazunas. Y29. | 95.00 |
| E10a | ND | — | 50 Centimes. Y35. | — |

| KM# | Date | Mintage | Identification | Mkt Val |
|---|---|---|---|---|
| E9 | | — | 25 Centimes. Without hole or ESSAI, Y34. | 115 |

| KM# | Date | Mintage | Identification | Mkt Val |
|---|---|---|---|---|
| E9a | | — | 25 Centimes. With hole, Y34. | 125 |

| KM# | Date | Mintage | Identification | Mkt Val |
|---|---|---|---|---|
| E14 | 1346 | — | 10 Francs. Nickel. | 145 |
| E15 | 1346 | — | 10 Francs. Nickel. Without ESSAI. | 145 |
| E20 | 1347 | — | 5 Francs. Y37. | 150 |

| KM# | Date | Mintage | Identification | Mkt Val |
|---|---|---|---|---|
| E21 | 1347 | — | 10 Francs. Silver. | 225 |
| E22 | 1347 | — | 10 Francs. Silver. Without ESSAI. | 160 |
| E23 | 1347 | — | 10 Francs. Y38. | 145 |
| E24 | 1347 | — | 20 Francs. | 225 |
| E25 | 1347 | — | 20 Francs. Without ESSAI. | 220 |

| KM# | Date | Mintage | Identification | Mkt Val |
|---|---|---|---|---|
| E26 | 1347 | — | 20 Francs. Y39. | 235 |

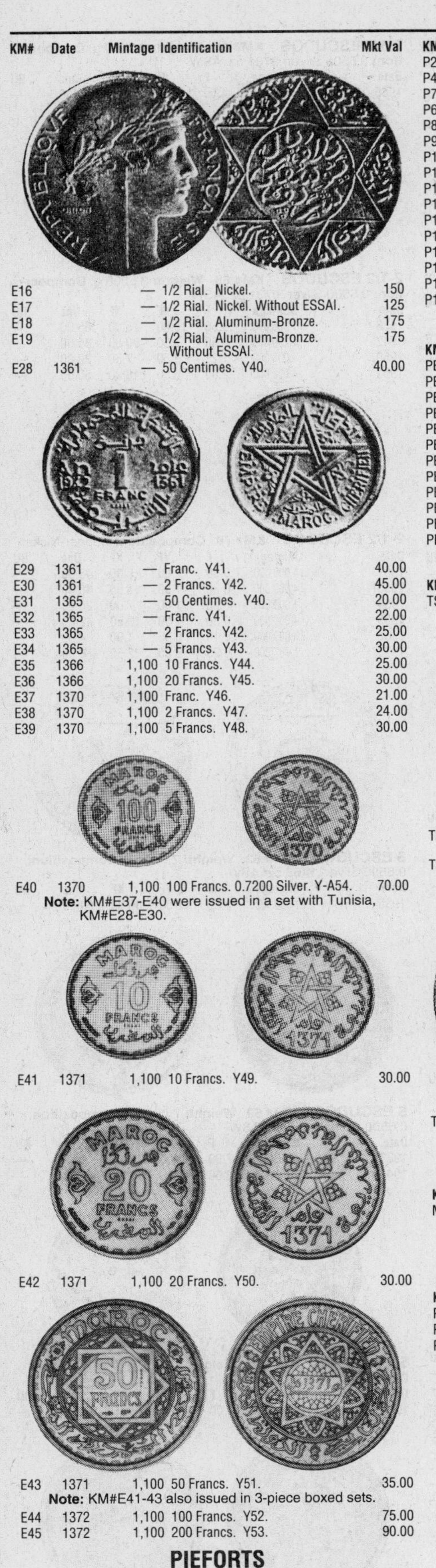

| KM# | Date | Mintage | Identification | Mkt Val |
|---|---|---|---|---|
| E16 | | — | 1/2 Rial. Nickel. | 150 |
| E17 | | — | 1/2 Rial. Nickel. Without ESSAI. | 125 |
| E18 | | — | 1/2 Rial. Aluminum-Bronze. | 175 |
| E19 | | — | 1/2 Rial. Aluminum-Bronze. Without ESSAI. | 175 |
| E28 | 1361 | — | 50 Centimes. Y40. | 40.00 |
| E29 | 1361 | — | Franc. Y41. | 40.00 |
| E30 | 1361 | — | 2 Francs. Y42. | 45.00 |
| E31 | 1365 | — | 50 Centimes. Y40. | 20.00 |
| E32 | 1365 | — | Franc. Y41. | 22.00 |
| E33 | 1365 | — | 2 Francs. Y42. | 25.00 |
| E34 | 1365 | — | 5 Francs. Y43. | 30.00 |
| E35 | 1366 | 1,100 | 10 Francs. Y44. | 25.00 |
| E36 | 1366 | 1,100 | 20 Francs. Y45. | 30.00 |
| E37 | 1370 | 1,100 | Franc. Y46. | 21.00 |
| E38 | 1370 | 1,100 | 2 Francs. Y47. | 24.00 |
| E39 | 1370 | 1,100 | 5 Francs. Y48. | 30.00 |
| E40 | 1370 | 1,100 | 100 Francs. 0.7200 Silver. Y-A54. | 70.00 |

**Note:** KM#E37-E40 were issued in a set with Tunisia, KM#E28-E30.

| KM# | Date | Mintage | Identification | Mkt Val |
|---|---|---|---|---|
| E41 | 1371 | 1,100 | 10 Francs. Y49. | 30.00 |
| E42 | 1371 | 1,100 | 20 Francs. Y50. | 30.00 |
| E43 | 1371 | 1,100 | 50 Francs. Y51. | 35.00 |

**Note:** KM#E41-43 also issued in 3-piece boxed sets.

| KM# | Date | Mintage | Identification | Mkt Val |
|---|---|---|---|---|
| E44 | 1372 | 1,100 | 100 Francs. Y52. | 75.00 |
| E45 | 1372 | 1,100 | 200 Francs. Y53. | 90.00 |

## PIEFORTS

Double thickness

| KM# | Date | Mintage | Identification | Mkt Val |
|---|---|---|---|---|
| P1 | 1395 | 10 | 5 Dirhams. Gold. Y64b | 700 |
| P3 | 1395 | 10 | 50 Dirhams. Gold. Y65a. | 2,100 |
| P5 | 1395 | 10 | 250 Dirhams. Gold. Y66 | 200 |
| P2 | 1395 | 40 | 50 Dirhams. Silver. Y65 | — |
| P4 | 1395 | 10 | 50 Dirhams. Gold. Y67a | 2,100 |
| P7 | 1396 | 10 | 250 Dirhams. Gold. Y66 | 200 |
| P6 | 1395 | 10 | 50 Dirhams. Gold. Y68a. | 2,100 |
| P8 | 1396 | 10 | 50 Dirhams. Gold. Y68a. | 2,100 |
| P9 | 1397 | 15 | 250 Dirhams. Gold. Y66. | — |
| P10 | 1397 | 15 | 250 Dirhams. Gold. Y68a. | — |
| P11 | 1398 | 20 | 250 Dirhams. Gold. Y66. | — |
| P16 | 1399 | 20 | 500 Dirhams. Gold. Y71. | — |
| P14 | 1399 | 20 | 50 Dirhams. 0.9250 Silver. Y76 | — |
| P12 | 1399 | 20 | 50 Dirhams. Gold. Y68a. | 2,000 |
| P13 | 1399 | 20 | 50 Dirhams. Silver. Y70. | 350 |
| P15 | 1399 | 20 | 50 Dirhams. Gold. Y76a. | 2,000 |
| P17 | 1400 | 10 | 50 Dirhams. Gold. Y68a. | 2,100 |
| P18 | 1400 | 10 | 150 Dirhams. 0.9000 Gold. Y74a. | 2,100 |
| P19 | 1401 | 10 | 150 Dirhams. 0.9000 Gold. Y73a. | 2,100 |

## PIEFORTS WITH ESSAI

| KM# | Date | Mintage | Identification | Mkt Val |
|---|---|---|---|---|
| PE-A1 | 1361 | — | 50 Centimes. Y40. | 90.00 |
| PE1 | 1361 | — | Franc. Y41. | 110 |
| PE2 | 1361 | — | 2 Francs. Y42. | 120 |
| PE3 | 1364 | 104 | 50 Centimes. Y40. | 70.00 |
| PE5 | 1364 | 104 | 2 Francs. Y42. | 90.00 |
| PE6 | 1365 | 104 | 5 Francs. Y43. | 100 |
| PE4 | 1364 | 104 | Franc. Y41 | 85.00 |
| PE7 | 1366 | 104 | 10 Francs. Y44. | 95.00 |
| PE8 | 1366 | 104 | 20 Francs. Y45. | 95.00 |
| PE9 | 1372 | 104 | 100 Francs. Y52. | 95.00 |
| PE10 | 1372 | 104 | 200 Francs. Y53. | 115 |
| PE11 | 1372 | — | 200 Francs. Gold. Y53. | 1,000 |

## TRIAL STRIKES

| KM# | Date | Mintage | Identification | Mkt Val |
|---|---|---|---|---|
| TS1 | 1347 | — | 10 Francs. Silvered Bronze. Silvered bronze | 300 |

| KM# | Date | Mintage | Identification | Mkt Val |
|---|---|---|---|---|
| TS2 | 1347 | — | 10 Francs. Silvered Bronze. Silvered bronze | 300 |
| TS3 | 1347 | — | 20 Francs. Silvered Bronze. Silvered bronze | 400 |

| KM# | Date | Mintage | Identification | Mkt Val |
|---|---|---|---|---|
| TS4 | 1347 | — | 20 Francs. Silvered Bronze. Silvered bronze | 400 |

## MINT SETS

| KM# | Date | Mintage | Identification | Issue Price | Mkt Val |
|---|---|---|---|---|---|
| MS1 | AH1370-84 (8) | — | Y46-48 (AH1370), 49-51 (AH1371), 56-57 (AH1384) | — | 17.50 |

## PROOF SETS

| KM# | Date | Mintage | Identification | Issue Price | Mkt Val |
|---|---|---|---|---|---|
| PS1 | AH1320 (4) | 5 | Y14, 15, 16, 17 | — | — |
| PS3 | 1974 (6) | 30 | Y58a-63a | — | 3,650 |
| PS2 | 1974-1975 (7) | 20,000 | Y#58-63 (1974), 64 (1975) | 20.00 | 25.00 |

# MOZAMBIQUE

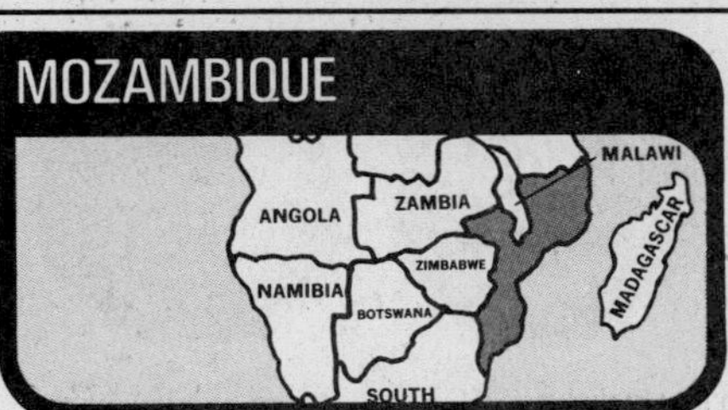


The Republic of Mozambique, a former overseas province of Portugal, stretches for 1,430 miles (2,301km.) along the southeast coast of Africa, has an area of 302,330 sq. mi. (801,590 sq. km.) and a population of 14.1 million, 99% of whom are native Africans of the Bantu tribes. Capital: Maputo. Agriculture is the chief industry. Cashew nuts, cotton, sugar, copra and tea are exported.

Vasco de Gama explored all the coast of Mozambique in 1498 and found Arab trading posts already established along the coast. Portuguese settlement dates from the establishment of the trading post of Mozambique in 1505.Within five years Portugal absorbed all the former Arab sultanates along the east African coast. The area was organized as a colony in 1907 and became an overseas province in 1952. In Sept. of 1974, after more than a decade of guerrilla warfare with the forces of the Mozambique Liberation Front, Portugal agreed to the independence of Mozambique, effective June 25, 1975.The Socialist party, led by President Joaquim Chissano was in power until the 2nd of November, 1990 when they became a republic.

Mozambique became a member of the Commonwealth of Nations in November 1995. The President is Head of State; the Prime Minister is Head of Government.

**RULERS**

Portuguese, until 1975

**MONETARY SYSTEM**

100 Centavos = 1 Escudo

# PORTUGUESE COLONY

## DECIMAL COINAGE

100 Centavos = 1 Escudo

**10 CENTAVOS** **KM# 63** **Composition:** Bronze

| Date | Mintage | F | VF | XF | Unc | BU |
|---|---|---|---|---|---|---|
| 1936 | 2,000,000 | 2.00 | 4.00 | 22.00 | 50.00 | — |

**10 CENTAVOS** **KM# 72** **Composition:** Bronze

| Date | Mintage | F | VF | XF | Unc | BU |
|---|---|---|---|---|---|---|
| 1942 | 2,000,000 | 1.00 | 2.50 | 7.50 | 20.00 | — |

**10 CENTAVOS** **KM# 83** **Composition:** Bronze

| Date | Mintage | F | VF | XF | Unc | BU |
|---|---|---|---|---|---|---|
| 1960 | 3,750,000 | — | 0.50 | 1.25 | 3.00 | — |
| 1961 | 10,300,000 | — | 0.25 | 1.00 | 2.50 | — |

**20 CENTAVOS** **KM# 64** **Composition:** Bronze

| Date | Mintage | F | VF | XF | Unc | BU |
|---|---|---|---|---|---|---|
| 1936 | 2,500,000 | 2.00 | 4.50 | 35.00 | 90.00 | — |

**20 CENTAVOS** KM# 71 **Composition:** Bronze

| Date | Mintage | F | VF | XF | Unc | BU |
|---|---|---|---|---|---|---|
| 1941 | 2,000,000 | 1.75 | 4.50 | 35.00 | 90.00 | — |

**20 CENTAVOS** KM# 75 **Composition:** Bronze

| Date | Mintage | F | VF | XF | Unc | BU |
|---|---|---|---|---|---|---|
| 1949 | 8,000,000 | 0.75 | 1.50 | 4.00 | 10.00 | — |
| 1950 | 12,500,000 | 0.75 | 1.50 | 3.00 | 8.50 | — |

**20 CENTAVOS** KM# 85 **Composition:** Bronze

| Date | Mintage | F | VF | XF | Unc | BU |
|---|---|---|---|---|---|---|
| 1961 | 12,500,000 | — | 0.25 | 1.00 | 2.50 | — |

**20 CENTAVOS** KM# 88 **Composition:** Bronze **Size:** 16 mm. **Note:** Reduced size.

| Date | Mintage | F | VF | XF | Unc | BU |
|---|---|---|---|---|---|---|
| 1973 | 1,798,000 | 1.00 | 2.00 | 3.00 | 7.50 | — |
| 1974 | 13,044,000 | 1.00 | 2.50 | 3.75 | 9.00 | — |

**50 CENTAVOS** KM# 65 **Composition:** Copper-Nickel

| Date | Mintage | F | VF | XF | Unc | BU |
|---|---|---|---|---|---|---|
| 1936 | 2,500,000 | 5.00 | 20.00 | 80.00 | 200 | — |

**50 CENTAVOS** KM# 73 **Composition:** Bronze

| Date | Mintage | F | VF | XF | Unc | BU |
|---|---|---|---|---|---|---|
| 1945 | 2,500,000 | 1.50 | 3.50 | 25.00 | 50.00 | — |

**50 CENTAVOS** KM# 76 **Composition:** Nickel-Bronze

| Date | Mintage | F | VF | XF | Unc | BU |
|---|---|---|---|---|---|---|
| 1950 | 20,000,000 | 1.00 | 3.00 | 7.00 | 20.00 | — |
| 1951 | 16,000,000 | 1.00 | 3.00 | 7.00 | 20.00 | — |

**50 CENTAVOS** KM# 81 **Composition:** Bronze

| Date | Mintage | F | VF | XF | Unc | BU |
|---|---|---|---|---|---|---|
| 1953 | 5,010,000 | 0.50 | 1.50 | 4.00 | 10.00 | — |
| 1957 | 24,990,000 | — | 0.50 | 1.25 | 4.50 | — |

**50 CENTAVOS** KM# 89 **Composition:** Bronze

| Date | Mintage | F | VF | XF | Unc | BU |
|---|---|---|---|---|---|---|
| 1973 | 6,841,000 | — | 0.50 | 1.00 | 3.00 | — |
| 1974 | 23,810,000 | — | 0.50 | 1.00 | 4.00 | — |

**ESCUDO** KM# 66 **Composition:** Copper-Nickel

| Date | Mintage | F | VF | XF | Unc | BU |
|---|---|---|---|---|---|---|
| 1936 | 2,000,000 | 4.00 | 14.00 | 65.00 | 200 | — |

**ESCUDO** KM# 74 **Composition:** Bronze

| Date | Mintage | F | VF | XF | Unc | BU |
|---|---|---|---|---|---|---|
| 1945 | 2,000,000 | 2.00 | 5.00 | 35.00 | 100 | — |

**ESCUDO** KM# 77 **Composition:** Nickel-Bronze

| Date | Mintage | F | VF | XF | Unc | BU |
|---|---|---|---|---|---|---|
| 1950 | 10,000,000 | 2.00 | 5.00 | 25.00 | 80.00 | — |
| 1951 | 10,000,000 | 1.50 | 3.00 | 12.50 | 30.00 | — |

**ESCUDO** KM# 82 **Composition:** Bronze

| Date | Mintage | F | VF | XF | Unc | BU |
|---|---|---|---|---|---|---|
| 1953 | 2,013,000 | 0.75 | 1.50 | 10.00 | 25.00 | — |
| 1957 | 2,987,000 | 0.75 | 1.50 | 12.50 | 35.00 | — |
| 1962 | 600,000 | 0.50 | 1.25 | 11.50 | 22.50 | — |
| 1963 | 3,258,000 | 0.50 | 0.75 | 4.00 | 12.50 | — |
| 1965 | 5,000,000 | — | 0.25 | 1.50 | 3.50 | — |
| 1968 | 4,500,000 | — | 0.25 | 1.50 | 3.50 | — |
| 1969 | 1,642,000 | — | 0.50 | 1.75 | 4.00 | — |
| 1973 | 501,000 | 0.20 | 0.50 | 2.00 | 6.50 | — |
| 1974 | 25,281,000 | — | 0.25 | 1.50 | 3.00 | — |

**2-1/2 ESCUDOS** KM# 61 **Weight:** 3.5000 g. **Composition:** 0.6500 Silver .0731 oz. ASW

| Date | Mintage | F | VF | XF | Unc | BU |
|---|---|---|---|---|---|---|
| 1935 | 1,200,000 | 4.50 | 12.50 | 40.00 | 100 | — |

**2-1/2 ESCUDOS** KM# 68 **Weight:** 3.5000 g. **Composition:** 0.6500 Silver .0731 oz. ASW

| Date | Mintage | F | VF | XF | Unc | BU |
|---|---|---|---|---|---|---|
| 1938 | 1,000,000 | 3.50 | 10.00 | 25.00 | 65.00 | — |
| 1942 | 1,200,000 | 2.50 | 7.50 | 20.00 | 55.00 | — |
| 1950 | 4,000,000 | 1.25 | 2.50 | 7.50 | 20.00 | — |
| 1951 | 4,000,000 | 2.00 | 6.50 | 18.00 | 50.00 | — |

**2-1/2 ESCUDOS** KM# 78 **Composition:** Copper-Nickel

| Date | Mintage | F | VF | XF | Unc | BU |
|---|---|---|---|---|---|---|
| 1952 | 4,000,000 | 0.50 | 2.00 | 15.00 | 45.00 | — |
| 1953 | 4,000,000 | 0.30 | 1.50 | 12.00 | 40.00 | — |
| 1954 | 4,000,000 | 0.25 | 1.00 | 7.00 | 20.00 | — |
| 1955 | 4,000,000 | 0.30 | 1.50 | 13.50 | 42.50 | — |
| 1965 | 8,000,000 | 0.10 | 0.25 | 1.00 | 4.00 | — |
| 1973 | 1,767,000 | 0.25 | 0.65 | 2.50 | 6.50 | — |

**5 ESCUDOS** KM# 62 **Weight:** 7.0000 g. **Composition:** 0.6500 Silver .1463 oz. ASW

| Date | Mintage | F | VF | XF | Unc | BU |
|---|---|---|---|---|---|---|
| 1935 | 1,000,000 | 5.50 | 12.50 | 35.00 | 90.00 | — |

**5 ESCUDOS** KM# 69 **Weight:** 7.0000 g. **Composition:** 0.6500 Silver .1463 oz. ASW

| Date | Mintage | F | VF | XF | Unc | BU |
|---|---|---|---|---|---|---|
| 1938 | 800,000 | 7.50 | 20.00 | 47.50 | 120 | — |
| 1949 | 8,000,000 | 2.00 | 5.50 | 17.50 | 45.00 | — |

**5 ESCUDOS** KM# 84 **Weight:** 4.0000 g. **Composition:** 0.6500 Silver .0835 oz. ASW

| Date | Mintage | F | VF | XF | Unc | BU |
|---|---|---|---|---|---|---|
| 1960 | 8,000,000 | 1.00 | 2.00 | 3.25 | 7.00 | — |

**5 ESCUDOS** KM# 86 **Composition:** Copper-Nickel

| Date | Mintage | F | VF | XF | Unc | BU |
|---|---|---|---|---|---|---|
| 1971 | 8,000,000 | 0.20 | 0.50 | 1.00 | 3.00 | — |
| 1973 | 3,352,000 | 0.20 | 0.50 | 1.75 | 4.50 | — |

**10 ESCUDOS** **KM# 67** **Weight:** 12.5000 g. **Composition:** 0.8350 Silver .3356 oz. ASW

| Date | Mintage | F | VF | XF | Unc | BU |
|---|---|---|---|---|---|---|
| 1936 | 497,000 | 10.00 | 20.00 | 47.50 | 120 | — |

**10 ESCUDOS** **KM# 70** **Weight:** 12.5000 g. **Composition:** 0.8350 Silver .3356 oz. ASW

| Date | Mintage | F | VF | XF | Unc | BU |
|---|---|---|---|---|---|---|
| 1938 | 530,000 | 20.00 | 35.00 | 55.00 | 150 | — |

**10 ESCUDOS** **KM# 79**

| Date | Mintage | VG | F | VF | XF | Unc |
|---|---|---|---|---|---|---|
| 1954 | 1,335,000 | — | 2.00 | 4.50 | 20.00 | 50.00 |
| 1955 | 1,162,000 | — | 2.00 | 4.50 | 15.00 | 35.00 |
| 1960 | 2,000,000 | — | 1.00 | 2.00 | 5.00 | 12.00 |

**10 ESCUDOS** **KM# 79a** **Weight:** 5.0000 g. **Composition:** 0.6800 Silver .1093 oz. ASW

| Date | Mintage | F | VF | XF | Unc | BU |
|---|---|---|---|---|---|---|
| 1966 | 500,000 | 1.00 | 2.00 | 5.50 | 12.50 | — |

**10 ESCUDOS** **KM# 79b** **Composition:** Copper-Nickel

| Date | Mintage | F | VF | XF | Unc | BU |
|---|---|---|---|---|---|---|
| 1968 | 5,000,000 | 0.30 | 0.70 | 2.50 | 5.00 | — |
| 1970 | 4,000,000 | 0.30 | 0.70 | 2.50 | 5.00 | — |
| 1974 | 3,366,000 | 0.40 | 1.00 | 3.00 | 6.50 | — |

**20 ESCUDOS** **KM# 80** **Weight:** 10.0000 g. **Composition:** 0.7200 Silver .2315 oz. ASW

| Date | Mintage | F | VF | XF | Unc | BU |
|---|---|---|---|---|---|---|
| 1952 | 1,004,000 | 1.50 | 3.00 | 10.00 | 25.00 | — |
| 1955 | 996,000 | 1.75 | 3.50 | 12.50 | 30.00 | — |
| 1960 | 2,000,000 | 1.25 | 2.50 | 5.00 | 11.50 | — |

**20 ESCUDOS** **KM# 80a** **Weight:** 10.0000 g. **Composition:** 0.6800 Silver .2186 oz. ASW

| Date | Mintage | F | VF | XF | Unc | BU |
|---|---|---|---|---|---|---|
| 1966 | 250,000 | 2.75 | 4.50 | 8.50 | 17.50 | — |

**20 ESCUDOS** **KM# 87** **Composition:** Nickel

| Date | Mintage | F | VF | XF | Unc | BU |
|---|---|---|---|---|---|---|
| 1971 | 2,000,000 | 0.35 | 0.75 | 1.75 | 5.00 | — |
| 1972 | 1,158,000 | 0.50 | 1.00 | 2.50 | 6.00 | — |

**5 METICAIS** **KM# 116** **Composition:** Brass Clad Steel

| Date | Mintage | F | VF | XF | Unc | BU |
|---|---|---|---|---|---|---|
| 1994 | — | — | — | — | 1.00 | — |

# PEOPLE'S REPUBLIC

## DECIMAL COINAGE

100 Centimos = 1 Metica

**CENTIMO** **KM# 90** **Composition:** Aluminum

| Date | Mintage | F | VF | XF | Unc | BU |
|---|---|---|---|---|---|---|
| 1975 | 15,050,000 | — | — | 125 | 225 | — |

**2 CENTIMOS** **KM# 91** **Composition:** Copper-Zinc

| Date | Mintage | F | VF | XF | Unc | BU |
|---|---|---|---|---|---|---|
| 1975 | 8,242,000 | — | — | 75.00 | 125 | — |

**5 CENTIMOS** **KM# 92** **Composition:** Copper-Zinc

| Date | Mintage | F | VF | XF | Unc | BU |
|---|---|---|---|---|---|---|
| 1975 | 14,898,000 | — | — | 60.00 | 110 | — |

**10 CENTIMOS** **KM# 93** **Composition:** Copper-Zinc

| Date | Mintage | F | VF | XF | Unc | BU |
|---|---|---|---|---|---|---|
| 1975 | 18,000,000 | — | — | 50.00 | 90.00 | — |

**20 CENTIMOS** **KM# 94** **Composition:** Copper-Nickel

| Date | Mintage | F | VF | XF | Unc | BU |
|---|---|---|---|---|---|---|
| 1975 | 8,050,000 | — | — | 125 | 225 | — |

**50 CENTIMOS** **KM# 95** **Composition:** Copper-Nickel

| Date | Mintage | F | VF | XF | Unc | BU |
|---|---|---|---|---|---|---|
| 1975 | 3,050,000 | — | — | 150 | 250 | — |

**METICA** **KM# 96** **Composition:** Copper-Nickel

| Date | Mintage | F | VF | XF | Unc | BU |
|---|---|---|---|---|---|---|
| 1975 | 2,550,000 | — | — | 50.00 | 85.00 | — |

**2-1/2 METICAS** **KM# 97** **Composition:** Copper-Nickel

| Date | Mintage | F | VF | XF | Unc | BU |
|---|---|---|---|---|---|---|
| 1975 | 1,500,000 | — | — | 125 | 200 | — |

## REFORM COINAGE

100 Centavos = 1 Metical

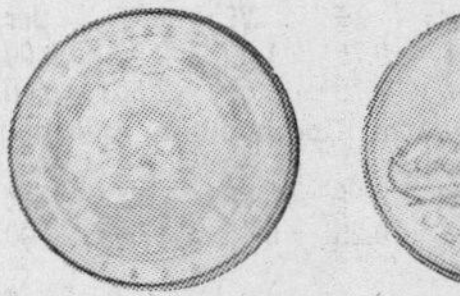

**50 CENTAVOS** **KM# 98** **Composition:** Aluminum **Reverse:** Musical instrument

| Date | Mintage | F | VF | XF | Unc | BU |
|---|---|---|---|---|---|---|
| 1980 | 5,160,000 | 0.15 | 0.30 | 0.60 | 1.25 | — |
| 1982 | — | 0.15 | 0.30 | 0.60 | 1.25 | — |

**2-1/2 METICAS** **KM# 100** **Composition:** Aluminum **Reverse:** Ship and crane in harbor **Note:** 1.80-2.00 grams.

| Date | Mintage | F | VF | XF | Unc | BU |
|---|---|---|---|---|---|---|
| 1980 | 1,088,000 | 0.25 | 0.50 | 1.00 | 1.75 | — |
| 1982 | — | 0.25 | 0.50 | 1.00 | 1.75 | — |
| 1986 | — | 0.25 | 0.50 | 1.00 | 1.75 | — |

**Note:** Edge varieties exist

**METICAL** **KM# 99** **Composition:** Brass **Reverse:** Female student

| Date | Mintage | F | VF | XF | Unc | BU |
|---|---|---|---|---|---|---|
| 1980 | 32,000 | 1.50 | 3.00 | 5.00 | 10.00 | — |
| 1982 | — | 1.50 | 3.00 | 5.00 | 10.00 | — |

**METICAL** **KM# 99a** **Composition:** Aluminum **Reverse:** Female student

| Date | Mintage | F | VF | XF | Unc | BU |
|---|---|---|---|---|---|---|
| 1986 | — | 0.20 | 0.40 | 0.60 | 1.00 | — |

**METICAL** **KM# 115** **Composition:** Brass Clad Steel

| Date | Mintage | F | VF | XF | Unc | BU |
|---|---|---|---|---|---|---|
| 1994 | — | — | — | — | 0.50 | — |

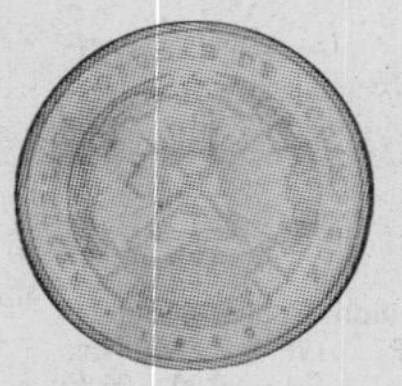

**5 METICAIS** **KM# 101** **Composition:** Aluminum **Reverse:** Tractor

| Date | Mintage | F | VF | XF | Unc | BU |
|---|---|---|---|---|---|---|
| 1980 | 7,736,000 | 0.35 | 0.75 | 1.25 | 2.00 | — |
| 1982 | — | 0.35 | 0.75 | 1.25 | 2.00 | — |
| 1986 | — | 0.35 | 0.75 | 1.25 | 2.00 | — |

**10 METICAIS** **KM# 102** **Composition:** Copper-Nickel **Reverse:** Industrial skyline

| Date | Mintage | F | VF | XF | Unc | BU |
|---|---|---|---|---|---|---|
| 1980 | 152,000 | 0.75 | 1.50 | 2.50 | 6.00 | — |
| 1981 | — | 0.75 | 1.50 | 2.50 | 6.00 | — |

**10 METICAIS** **KM# 102a** **Composition:** Aluminum **Reverse:** Industrial skyline

| Date | Mintage | F | VF | XF | Unc | BU |
|---|---|---|---|---|---|---|
| 1986 | — | 0.25 | 0.45 | 1.00 | 2.00 | — |

**10 METICAIS** **KM# 117** **Composition:** Brass Clad Steel **Reverse:** Cotton plant

| Date | Mintage | F | VF | XF | Unc | BU |
|---|---|---|---|---|---|---|
| 1994 | — | — | — | — | 1.25 | — |

**20 METICAIS** **KM# 103** **Composition:** Copper-Nickel **Reverse:** Panzer tank

| Date | Mintage | F | VF | XF | Unc | BU |
|---|---|---|---|---|---|---|
| 1980 | 78,000 | 1.00 | 2.00 | 4.00 | 9.00 | — |

**20 METICAIS** **KM# 103a** **Composition:** Aluminum

| Date | Mintage | F | VF | XF | Unc | BU |
|---|---|---|---|---|---|---|
| 1986 | — | 0.40 | 0.80 | 1.50 | 3.00 | — |

**20 METICAIS** **KM# 118** **Composition:** Brass Clad Steel **Reverse:** Pepper plant

| Date | Mintage | F | VF | XF | Unc | BU |
|---|---|---|---|---|---|---|
| 1994 | — | — | — | — | 1.50 | — |

**50 METICAIS** **KM# 106** **Composition:** Copper-Nickel **Subject:** World Fisheries Conference

| Date | Mintage | F | VF | XF | Unc | BU |
|---|---|---|---|---|---|---|
| 1983 | 130,000 | 2.50 | 5.00 | 8.00 | 12.50 | — |

**50 METICAIS** **KM# 106a** **Weight:** 22.0000 g. **Composition:** 0.9250 Silver .6543 oz. ASW **Subject:** World Fisheries Conference

| Date | Mintage | F | VF | XF | Unc | BU |
|---|---|---|---|---|---|---|
| 1983 Proof | 21,000 | Value: 50.00 | | | | |

**50 METICAIS** **KM# 106b** **Weight:** 22.0000 g. **Composition:** 0.9000 Gold .6366 oz. AGW **Subject:** World Fisheries Conference

| Date | Mintage | F | VF | XF | Unc | BU |
|---|---|---|---|---|---|---|
| 1983 Proof | 135 | Value: 1,000 | | | | |

**50 METICAIS** **KM# 112** **Composition:** Aluminum **Reverse:** Woman and soldier with provisions

| Date | Mintage | F | VF | XF | Unc | BU |
|---|---|---|---|---|---|---|
| 1986 | — | 0.75 | 1.50 | 2.50 | 5.50 | — |

**50 METICAIS** **KM# 119** **Composition:** Nickel Clad Steel **Reverse:** Leopard's head

| Date | Mintage | F | VF | XF | Unc | BU |
|---|---|---|---|---|---|---|
| 1994 | — | — | — | — | 2.75 | — |

**100 METICAIS** **KM# 120** **Composition:** Nickel Clad Steel **Reverse:** Lobster

| Date | Mintage | F | VF | XF | Unc | BU |
|---|---|---|---|---|---|---|
| 1994 | — | — | — | — | 3.50 | — |

**250 METICAIS** **KM# 107** **Weight:** 28.2800 g. **Composition:** 0.9250 Silver .8411 oz. ASW **Subject:** 10th Anniversary of Independence

| Date | Mintage | F | VF | XF | Unc | BU |
|---|---|---|---|---|---|---|
| 1985 Proof | 2,000 | Value: 42.50 | | | | |

**250 METICAIS** **KM# 107a** **Composition:** Copper-Nickel

| Date | Mintage | F | VF | XF | Unc | BU |
|---|---|---|---|---|---|---|
| 1985 | — | — | — | — | 10.00 | — |

**500 METICAIS** **KM# 104** **Weight:** 19.4000 g. **Composition:** 0.8000 Silver .4990 oz. ASW **Subject:** 5th Anniversary of Independence

| Date | Mintage | F | VF | XF | Unc | BU |
|---|---|---|---|---|---|---|
| 1980 Proof | 5,000 | Value: 35.00 | | | | |

**500 METICAIS** **KM# 110** **Weight:** 16.0000 g. **Composition:** 0.9990 Silver .5145 oz. ASW **Subject:** Defense of Nature **Reverse:** Lions

| Date | Mintage | F | VF | XF | Unc | BU |
|---|---|---|---|---|---|---|
| 1989 Proof | 2,500 | Value: 32.50 | | | | |

**500 METICAIS** **KM# 111** **Weight:** 16.0000 g. **Composition:** 0.9990 Silver .5145 oz. ASW **Subject:** Defense of Nature **Reverse:** Moorish Idol Fish

| Date | Mintage | F | VF | XF | Unc | BU |
|---|---|---|---|---|---|---|
| 1989 Proof | 2,000 | Value: 32.50 | | | | |

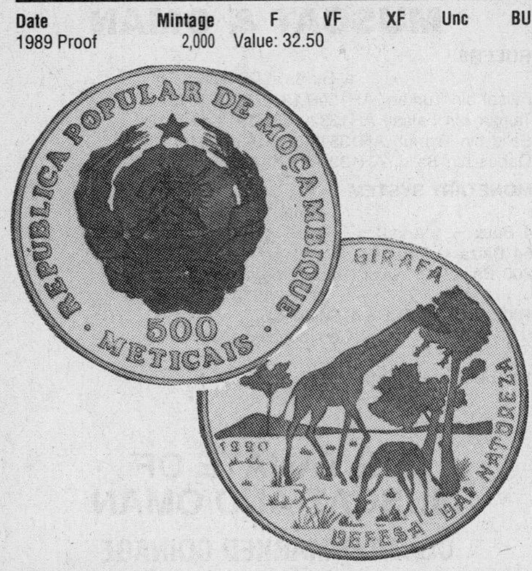


**500 METICAIS** **KM# 113** **Weight:** 16.0000 g. **Composition:** 0.9990 Silver .5145 oz. ASW **Subject:** Defense of Nature **Reverse:** Giraffes

| Date | Mintage | F | VF | XF | Unc | BU |
|---|---|---|---|---|---|---|
| 1990 Proof | 2,000 | Value: 35.00 | | | | |

**500 METICAIS** **KM# 121** **Composition:** Nickel Clad Steel

| Date | Mintage | F | VF | XF | Unc | BU |
|---|---|---|---|---|---|---|
| 1994 | — | — | — | — | 4.50 | — |

**500 METICAIS** **KM# 127** **Composition:** Nickel Clad Steel **Series:** 2000 Summer Olympics - Sydney

| Date | Mintage | F | VF | XF | Unc | BU |
|---|---|---|---|---|---|---|
| 1998 Proof | 10,000 | Value: 7.50 | | | | |

**1000 METICAIS** **KM# 109** **Composition:** Copper-Nickel **Subject:** Visit of Pope John Paul II

| Date | Mintage | F | VF | XF | Unc | BU |
|---|---|---|---|---|---|---|
| 1988 | Est. 80,000 | — | — | — | 8.00 | — |

**1000 METICAIS** **KM# 109a** **Weight:** 28.2800 g. **Composition:** 0.9250 Silver .8411 oz. ASW

| Date | Mintage | F | VF | XF | Unc | BU |
|---|---|---|---|---|---|---|
| 1988 Proof | Est. 3,500 | Value: 42.50 | | | | |

**1000 METICAIS** **KM# 122** **Composition:** Nickel Clad Steel

| Date | Mintage | F | VF | XF | Unc | BU |
|---|---|---|---|---|---|---|
| 1994 | — | — | — | — | 5.00 | — |

**1000 METICAIS** **KM# 128** **Weight:** 24.6200 g. **Composition:** 0.9250 Silver .7322 oz. ASW **Series:** 2000 Summer Olympics - Sydney

| Date | Mintage | F | VF | XF | Unc | BU |
|---|---|---|---|---|---|---|
| 1998 Proof | 10,000 | Value: 32.50 | | | | |

**2000 METICAIS** **KM# 108** **Weight:** 17.5000 g. **Composition:** 0.9170 Gold .5158 oz. AGW **Subject:** 10th Anniversary of Independence

| Date | Mintage | F | VF | XF | Unc | BU |
|---|---|---|---|---|---|---|
| 1985 Proof | 100 | Value: 650 | | | | |

**5000 METICAIS** **KM# 105** **Weight:** 17.2790 g. **Composition:** 0.9000 Gold .5000 oz. AGW **Subject:** 5th Anniversary of Independence **Obverse:** State emblem above denomination **Reverse:** Figure at left, corn plants in background, tractor above

| Date | Mintage | F | VF | XF | Unc | BU |
|---|---|---|---|---|---|---|
| 1980 Proof | 2,000 | Value: 325 | | | | |

**5000 METICAIS** **KM# 125** **Weight:** 411.4224 g. **Composition:** 0.9990 Silver 13.2143 oz. ASW **Obverse:** National arms **Reverse:** Rhinocerous right **Edge:** Reeded **Note:** Illustration reduced - actual size 90.7 millimeters.

| Date | Mintage | F | VF | XF | Unc | BU |
|---|---|---|---|---|---|---|
| 1997 Proof | 2,000 | Value: 300 | | | | |

**5000 METICAIS** **KM# 124** **Composition:** Nickel Clad Steel **Obverse:** State emblem **Reverse:** High power electric lines

| Date | Mintage | F | VF | XF | Unc | BU |
|---|---|---|---|---|---|---|
| 1998 | — | — | — | — | 5.00 | — |

**10000 METICAIS** **KM# 114.1** **Weight:** 20.0000 g. **Composition:** 0.9990 Silver .6430 oz. ASW **Subject:** World Cup Soccer

| Date | Mintage | F | VF | XF | Unc | BU |
|---|---|---|---|---|---|---|
| 1994 Proof | — | Value: 65.00 | | | | |

**10000 METICAIS** **KM# 114.2** **Weight:** 20.0000 g. **Composition:** 0.9990 Silver .6430 oz. ASW **Reverse:** Without 999

| Date | Mintage | F | VF | XF | Unc | BU |
|---|---|---|---|---|---|---|
| 1994 Proof | — | Value: 65.00 | | | | |

**10000 METICAIS** **KM# 123** **Weight:** 21.0600 g. **Composition:** 0.9990 Silver .6764 oz. ASW **Subject:** World Cup Soccer

| Date | Mintage | F | VF | XF | Unc | BU |
|---|---|---|---|---|---|---|
| 1994 Proof | — | Value: 65.00 | | | | |

**10000 METICAIS** **KM# 126** **Weight:** 822.8449 g. **Composition:** 0.9990 Silver 26.4286 oz. ASW **Obverse:** National arms **Reverse:** Elephant charging **Edge:** Reeded **Note:** Illustration reduced. Actual size: 100 millimeters.

| Date | Mintage | F | VF | XF | Unc | BU |
|---|---|---|---|---|---|---|
| 1997 Proof | 2,000 | Value: 500 | | | | |

**10000 METICAIS** **KM# 129** **Weight:** 822.8449 g. **Composition:** 0.9990 Silver 26.4286 oz. ASW **Series:** 2000 Summer Olympics - Sydney

| Date | Mintage | F | VF | XF | Unc | BU |
|---|---|---|---|---|---|---|
| 1998 Proof | 2,000 | Value: 365 | | | | |

## PATTERNS

Including off metal strikes

| KM# | Date | Mintage | Identification | Mkt Val |
|---|---|---|---|---|
| Pn1 | 1994 | — | 10000 Meticais. Copper-Nickel. KM#114.1. | — |
| Pn2 | 1994 | — | 10000 Meticais. Copper-Nickel. KM#123. | — |

## PIEFORTS

| KM# | Date | Mintage | Identification | Issue Price | Mkt Val |
|---|---|---|---|---|---|
| P1 | 1983 | 600 | 50 Meticais. 0.9250 Silver. | — | 70.00 |

## PROVAS

Standard Metals

| KM# | Date | Mintage | Identification | Issue Price | Mkt Val |
|---|---|---|---|---|---|
| Pr1 | 1935 | — | 2-1/2 Escudos. KM#61 | — | 125 |
| Pr2 | 1935 | — | 5 Escudos. KM62. | — | 145 |
| Pr3 | 1936 | — | 10 Centavos. KM63. | — | 60.00 |
| Pr4 | 1936 | — | 20 Centavos. KM64. | — | 60.00 |
| Pr5 | 1936 | — | 50 Centavos. KM65. | — | 90.00 |
| Pr6 | 1936 | — | Escudo. KM66 | — | 90.00 |
| Pr7 | 1936 | — | 10 Escudos. KM67. | — | 180 |
| Pr8 | 1938 | — | 2-1/2 Escudos. KM61. | — | 100 |
| Pr9 | 1938 | — | 5 Escudos. KM69. | — | 120 |
| Pr10 | 1938 | — | 10 Escudos. KM70. | — | 130 |
| Pr11 | 1941 | — | 10 Centavos. KM71. | — | 65.00 |
| Pr12 | 1942 | — | 10 Centavos. KM72. | — | 40.00 |
| Pr13 | 1942 | — | 2-1/2 Escudos. KM68. | — | 75.00 |
| Pr14 | 1945 | — | 50 Centavos. KM73. | — | 40.00 |
| Pr15 | 1945 | — | Escudo. KM74. | — | 40.00 |
| Pr16 | 1948 | — | 2-1/2 Escudos. | — | — |
| Pr17 | 1949 | — | 20 Centavos. KM75. | — | 40.00 |
| Pr18 | 1949 | — | 5 Escudos. KM69. | — | 75.00 |
| PrA19 | 1950 | — | 25 Centavos. KM75 | | |
| Pr19 | 1950 | — | 50 Centavos. KM76. | — | 45.00 |
| Pr20 | 1950 | — | Escudo. KM77. | — | 45.00 |
| Pr21 | 1950 | — | 2-1/2 Escudos. KM68. | — | 80.00 |
| Pr22 | 1951 | — | 50 Centavos. KM76. | — | 35.00 |
| Pr23 | 1951 | — | Escudo. KM77. | — | 35.00 |
| Pr24 | 1951 | — | 2-1/2 Escudos. KM68. | — | 65.00 |
| Pr25 | 1951 | — | 5 Escudos. | — | — |
| Pr27 | 1952 | — | 5 Escudos. | — | — |
| Pr26 | 1952 | — | 2-1/2 Escudos. KM78. | — | 65.00 |
| Pr28 | 1952 | — | 10 Escudos. KM79 | — | 65.00 |
| Pr29 | 1952 | — | 20 Escudos. KM80. | — | 75.00 |
| Pr30 | 1953 | — | 50 Centavos. KM81. | — | 35.00 |
| Pr31 | 1953 | — | Escudo. KM82. | — | 35.00 |
| Pr32 | 1953 | — | 2-1/2 Escudos. KM78. | — | 45.00 |
| Pr34 | 1954 | — | 10 Escudos. KM79. | — | 65.00 |
| Pr35 | 1955 | — | 2-1/2 Escudos. KM78. | — | 45.00 |
| Pr36 | 1955 | — | 10 Escudos. KM79. | | |
| Pr37 | 1955 | — | 20 Escudos. KM80. | — | 65.00 |
| Pr38 | 1957 | — | 50 Centavos. KM81. | — | 35.00 |
| Pr39 | 1957 | — | Escudo. KM82. | — | 35.00 |
| Pr40 | 1960 | — | 10 Centavos. KM83. | — | 35.00 |
| Pr41 | 1960 | — | 5 Escudos. KM84 | — | 65.00 |
| Pr42 | 1960 | — | 10 Escudos. KM79. | — | 65.00 |
| Pr43 | 1960 | — | 20 Escudos. KM80. | — | 65.00 |
| Pr44 | 1961 | — | 10 Centavos. KM83. | — | 35.00 |
| Pr45 | 1961 | — | 20 Centavos. KM85. | — | 35.00 |
| Pr46 | 1962 | — | Escudo. KM82. | — | 35.00 |
| Pr47 | 1963 | — | Escudo. KM82. | — | 35.00 |
| Pr48 | 1965 | — | Escudo. KM82. | — | 35.00 |
| Pr49 | 1965 | — | 2-1/2 Escudos. KM78. | — | 45.00 |
| Pr50 | 1966 | — | 10 Escudos. KM79a. | — | 65.00 |
| Pr51 | 1966 | — | 20 Escudos. KM80a | — | 75.00 |
| Pr52 | 1968 | — | Escudo. KM82. | — | 35.00 |
| Pr53 | 1968 | — | 10 Escudos. KM79b. | — | 45.00 |
| Pr54 | 1968 | — | 20 Escudos. | — | 45.00 |
| Pr55 | 1969 | — | Escudo. KM82. | — | 35.00 |
| Pr56 | 1969 | — | 20 Escudos. | — | 45.00 |
| Pr57 | 1970 | — | 10 Escudos. KM79b. | — | 45.00 |
| Pr58 | 1970 | — | 20 Escudos. | — | 45.00 |
| Pr59 | 1971 | — | 5 Escudos. KM86. | — | 45.00 |
| Pr60 | 1971 | — | 20 Escudos. KM87. | — | 45.00 |
| Pr61 | 1972 | — | 20 Escudos. KM87. | — | 85.00 |
| Pr62 | 1973 | — | 20 Centavos. KM88. | — | 65.00 |
| Pr63 | 1973 | — | 50 Centavos. KM89. | — | 85.00 |
| Pr64 | 1973 | — | Escudo. KM82. | — | 65.00 |
| Pr65 | 1973 | — | 2-1/2 Escudos. KM78. | — | 85.00 |
| Pr66 | 1973 | — | 5 Escudos. KM86. | — | 85.00 |
| Pr67 | 1973 | — | 20 Escudos. | — | 85.00 |
| Pr68 | 1974 | — | 20 Centavos. KM88. | — | 65.00 |
| Pr69 | 1974 | — | 50 Centavos. KM89. | — | 85.00 |
| Pr70 | 1974 | — | Escudo. KM82. | — | 65.00 |

## MINT SETS

| KM# | Date | Mintage | Identification | Issue Price | Mkt Val |
|---|---|---|---|---|---|
| MS1 | 1980 (6) | — | KM#98-103 | — | 30.00 |

## SPECIMEN SETS (SS)

| KM# | Date | Mintage | Identification | Issue Price | Mkt Val |
|---|---|---|---|---|---|
| SS1 | 1975 (8) | — | KM#90-97 | — | 2,250 |

# MUSCAT & OMAN

**RULERS**

al-Bu Sa'id Dynasty

Faisal bin Turkee, AH1306-1332/1888-1913AD
Taimur bin Faisal, AH1332-1351/1913-1932AD
Sa'id bin Taimur, AH1351-1390/1932-1970AD
Qabus bin Sa'id, AH1390-/1970-AD

**MONETARY SYSTEM**

Until 1970

4 Baiza = 1 Anna
64 Baiza = 1 Rupee
200 Baiza = 1 Saidi (Dasin Dog)/Dhofari Rial

1970-1972

1000 (new) Baisa = 1 Saidi Rial

Commencing 1972

1000 Baisa = 1 Omani Rial

## SULTANATE OF MUSCAT AND OMAN

### COUNTERMARKED COINAGE

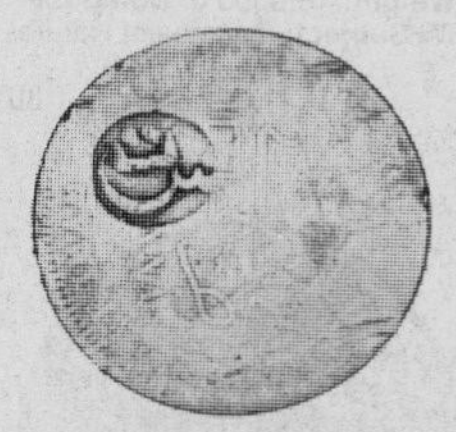

**1/4 ANNA** **C# 19.1** **Composition:** Copper **Countermark:** ST **Note:** Countermark in Arabic on 1/4 Anna, KM#3.

| CM Date | Host Date | Good | VG | F | VF | XF |
|---|---|---|---|---|---|---|
| AH | AH1315 | 15.00 | 25.00 | 40.00 | 60.00 | — |

**1/4 ANNA** **C# 19.2** **Composition:** Copper **Countermark:** ST **Note:** Countermark in Arabic on 1/4 Anna, KM#8. Countermark for Sultan Taimur or Sayyid Taimur.

| CM Date | Host Date | Good | VG | F | VF | XF |
|---|---|---|---|---|---|---|
| AH | AH1312 | 15.00 | 25.00 | 45.00 | 70.00 | — |

**1/4 ANNA** **C# 20.1** **Composition:** Copper **Countermark:** SS **Note:** Large 10mm countermark in Arabic on 1/4 Anna, KM#3.

| CM Date | Host Date | Good | VG | F | VF | XF |
|---|---|---|---|---|---|---|
| AH | AH1312 | 30.00 | 50.00 | 80.00 | 120 | — |
| AH | AH1315 | 30.00 | 50.00 | 80.00 | 120 | — |

**1/4 ANNA** **C# 20.2** **Composition:** Copper **Countermark:** SS **Note:** Large 10mm countermark in Arabic on 1/4 Anna, KM#8.

| CM Date | Host Date | Good | VG | F | VF | XF |
|---|---|---|---|---|---|---|
| AH | AH1312 | 30.00 | 50.00 | 80.00 | 120 | — |

**1/4 ANNA** **C# 21.1** **Composition:** Copper **Countermark:** SS **Note:** Small 8mm countermark in Arabic on 1/4 Anna, KM#3.

| CM Date | Host Date | Good | VG | F | VF | XF |
|---|---|---|---|---|---|---|
| AH | AH1312 | 30.00 | 50.00 | 80.00 | 120 | — |

**1/4 ANNA** **C# 21.2** **Composition:** Copper **Countermark:** SS **Note:** Small 8mm countermark in Arabic on 1/4 Anna, KM#8. Countermark for Sultan Sa'id or Sayyid Sa'id.

| CM Date | Host Date | Good | VG | F | VF | XF |
|---|---|---|---|---|---|---|
| AH | AH1312 | 30.00 | 50.00 | 80.00 | 120 | — |

### REFORM COINAGE

1000 (new) Baisa = 1 Saidi Rial

**2 BAISA (Baiza)** **KM# 25** **Composition:** Copper-Nickel **Ruler:** Sa'id bin Taimur

| Date | Mintage | F | VF | XF | Unc | BU |
|---|---|---|---|---|---|---|
| AH1365 | 1,500,000 | 0.50 | 0.75 | 1.00 | 2.00 | — |
| AH1365 Proof | — | Value: 4.00 | | | | |

**Note:** Coins of AH1365 have the monetary unit spelled Baiza; on all other coins it is spelled Baisa. Most of the proof issues of the AH1359 and 1365 dated coins of Muscat and Oman now on the market are probably later restrikes produced by the Bombay Mint

**2 BAISA (Baiza)** **KM# 36** **Composition:** Bronze **Ruler:** Sa'id bin Taimur

| Date | Mintage | F | VF | XF | Unc | BU |
|---|---|---|---|---|---|---|
| AH1390 | 4,000,000 | 0.10 | 0.15 | 0.25 | 0.50 | — |
| AH1390 Proof | — | Value: 2.50 | | | | |

**3 BAISA** **KM# 30** **Composition:** Bronze **Ruler:** Sa'id bin Taimur

| Date | Mintage | F | VF | XF | Unc | BU |
|---|---|---|---|---|---|---|
| AH1378 | 8,000,000 | 0.75 | 1.00 | 1.50 | 2.50 | — |
| AH1378 Proof | — | — | — | — | — | — |

**Note:** Struck for use in Dhofar province.

**3 BAISA** **KM# 32** **Composition:** Bronze **Ruler:** Sa'id bin Taimur

| Date | Mintage | F | VF | XF | Unc | BU |
|---|---|---|---|---|---|---|
| AH1380 | 10,000,000 | 0.35 | 0.50 | 0.60 | 1.25 | — |
| AH1380 Proof | Inc. above | — | — | — | — | — |

**Note:** Struck for use in Muscat province.

**5 BAISA (Baiza)** **KM# 26** **Composition:** Copper-Nickel **Ruler:** Sa'id bin Taimur

| Date | Mintage | F | VF | XF | Unc | BU |
|---|---|---|---|---|---|---|
| AH1365 | 3,849,000 | 1.00 | 1.25 | 1.50 | 2.50 | — |
| AH1365 Proof | — | Value: 5.00 | | | | |

**Note:** Coins of AH1365 have the monetary unit spelled Baiza. On all other coins it is spelled Baisa.

**5 BAISA (Baiza)** **KM# 33** **Composition:** Copper-Nickel **Ruler:** Sa'id bin Taimur

| Date | Mintage | F | VF | XF | Unc | BU |
|---|---|---|---|---|---|---|
| AH1381 | 5,000,000 | 0.40 | 0.60 | 1.00 | 2.00 | — |
| AH1381 Proof | Inc. above | — | — | — | — | — |

**Note:** Struck for use in Muscat province.

**5 BAISA (Baiza)** **KM# 37** **Composition:** Bronze **Ruler:** Sa'id bin Taimur

| Date | Mintage | F | VF | XF | Unc | BU |
|---|---|---|---|---|---|---|
| AH1390 | 3,400,000 | 0.10 | 0.15 | 0.25 | 0.50 | — |
| AH1390 Proof | — | Value: 2.00 | | | | |

**10 BAISA** **KM# 22** **Composition:** Copper-Nickel **Ruler:** Sa'id bin Taimur

| Date | Mintage | F | VF | XF | Unc | BU |
|---|---|---|---|---|---|---|
| AH1359 | 572,000 | 2.50 | 3.25 | 4.00 | 6.00 | — |
| AH1359 Proof | — | Value: 8.50 | | | | |

**Note:** Struck for use in Dhofar province.

**10 BAISA** **KM# 22a** **Composition:** Gold **Ruler:** Sa'id bin Taimur

| Date | Mintage | F | VF | XF | Unc | BU |
|---|---|---|---|---|---|---|
| AH1359 Proof | — | Value: 1,850 | | | | |

**10 BAISA** **KM# 38** **Composition:** Bronze **Ruler:** Sa'id bin Taimur

| Date | Mintage | F | VF | XF | Unc | BU |
|---|---|---|---|---|---|---|
| AH1390 | 4,500,000 | 0.10 | 0.15 | 0.25 | 0.50 | — |
| AH1390 Proof | — | Value: 2.50 | | | | |

**20 BAISA (Baiza)** **KM# 23** **Composition:** Copper-Nickel **Ruler:** Sa'id bin Taimur

| Date | Mintage | F | VF | XF | Unc | BU |
|---|---|---|---|---|---|---|
| AH1359 | 35,000 | 3.00 | 5.00 | 7.50 | 11.50 | — |
| AH1359 Proof | — | Value: 14.50 | | | | |

**Note:** Struck for use in Dhofar province.

**20 BAISA (Baiza)** **KM# 23a** **Composition:** Gold **Ruler:** Sa'id bin Taimur

| Date | Mintage | F | VF | XF | Unc | BU |
|---|---|---|---|---|---|---|
| AH1359 Proof | — | Value: 1,650 | | | | |

**20 BAISA (Baiza)** **KM# 27** **Composition:** Gold **Ruler:** Sa'id bin Taimur

| Date | Mintage | F | VF | XF | Unc | BU |
|---|---|---|---|---|---|---|
| AH1365 | 1,135,000 | 1.00 | 2.00 | 2.75 | 4.50 | — |
| AH1365 Proof | — | Value: 7.00 | | | | |

**20 BAISA (Baiza)** **KM# 28** **Composition:** Gold **Ruler:** Sa'id bin Taimur **Obverse:** KM#23 **Reverse:** KM#27 **Note:** Mule.

| Date | Mintage | F | VF | XF | Unc | BU |
|---|---|---|---|---|---|---|
| AH1359/1365 Restrike | — | — | — | — | 17.50 | — |

**25 BAISA** **KM# 39** **Composition:** Copper-Nickel **Ruler:** Sa'id bin Taimur

| Date | Mintage | F | VF | XF | Unc | BU |
|---|---|---|---|---|---|---|
| AH1390 | 2,000,000 | 0.15 | 0.20 | 0.35 | 0.75 | — |
| AH1390 Proof | — | Value: 2.75 | | | | |

**25 BAISA** **KM# 39a** **Weight:** 6.0100 g. **Composition:** 0.9160 Gold .1771 oz. AGW **Ruler:** Sa'id bin Taimur

| Date | Mintage | F | VF | XF | Unc | BU |
|---|---|---|---|---|---|---|
| AH1390 Proof | 350 | Value: 100 | | | | |

**50 BAISA** **KM# 24** **Composition:** Copper-Nickel **Ruler:** Sa'id bin Taimur

| Date | Mintage | F | VF | XF | Unc | BU |
|---|---|---|---|---|---|---|
| AH1359 | 65,000 | 0.20 | 6.50 | 8.50 | 12.50 | — |
| AH1359 Proof | — | Value: 16.50 | | | | |

**Note:** Struck for use in Dhofar province.

**50 BAISA** **KM# 24a** **Composition:** Gold **Ruler:** Sa'id bin Taimur

| Date | Mintage | F | VF | XF | Unc | BU |
|---|---|---|---|---|---|---|
| AH1359 Proof | — | Value: 1,750 | | | | |

**50 BAISA** **KM# 40** **Composition:** Gold **Ruler:** Sa'id bin Taimur

| Date | Mintage | F | VF | XF | Unc | BU |
|---|---|---|---|---|---|---|
| AH1390 | 1,600,000 | 0.20 | 0.35 | 0.60 | 1.25 | — |
| AH1390 Proof | — | Value: 3.50 | | | | |

**50 BAISA** **KM# 40a** **Weight:** 12.8100 g. **Composition:** 0.9160 Gold .3775 oz. AGW **Ruler:** Sa'id bin Taimur

| Date | Mintage | F | VF | XF | Unc | BU |
|---|---|---|---|---|---|---|
| AH1390 Proof | 350 | Value: 200 | | | | |

**100 BAISA** **KM# 41** **Composition:** Copper-Nickel **Ruler:** Sa'id bin Taimur

| Date | Mintage | F | VF | XF | Unc | BU |
|---|---|---|---|---|---|---|
| AH1390 | 1,000,000 | 0.30 | 0.45 | 0.70 | 1.50 | — |
| AH1390 Proof | — | Value: 5.00 | | | | |

**100 BAISA** **KM# 41a** **Weight:** 22.6300 g. **Composition:** 0.9160 Gold .6670 oz. AGW **Ruler:** Sa'id bin Taimur

| Date | Mintage | F | VF | XF | Unc | BU |
|---|---|---|---|---|---|---|
| AH1390 Proof | 350 | Value: 325 | | | | |

**1/2 DHOFARI RIAL** **KM# 29** **Weight:** 14.0300 g. **Composition:** 0.5000 Silver .2256 oz. ASW **Ruler:** Sa'id bin Taimur

| Date | Mintage | F | VF | XF | Unc | BU |
|---|---|---|---|---|---|---|
| AH1367 | 200,000 | 12.00 | 14.00 | 18.00 | 28.00 | — |
| AH1367 Proof | — | Value: 45.00 | | | | |

**Note:** Struck for use in Dhofar province.

**1/2 DHOFARI RIAL** **KM# 29a** **Weight:** 24.0300 g. **Composition:** 0.9170 Gold .6780 oz. AGW **Ruler:** Sa'id bin Taimur

| Date | Mintage | F | VF | XF | Unc | BU |
|---|---|---|---|---|---|---|
| AH1367 Proof | 2 | Value: 5,500 | | | | |

**Note:** Struck for presentation purposes.

**1/2 SAIDI RIAL** **KM# 34** **Weight:** 14.0300 g. **Composition:** 0.5000 Silver .2256 oz. ASW **Ruler:** Sa'id bin Taimur

| Date | Mintage | F | VF | XF | Unc | BU |
|---|---|---|---|---|---|---|
| AH1380 | 300,000 | 3.00 | 3.50 | 4.75 | 8.00 | — |
| AH1380 Proof | — | Value: 75.00 | | | | |
| AH1381 | 850,000 | 3.00 | 3.50 | 4.75 | 8.00 | — |

**1/2 SAIDI RIAL** **KM# 34a** **Weight:** 25.6000 g. **Composition:** 0.9160 Gold .7540 oz. AGW **Ruler:** Sa'id bin Taimur

| Date | Mintage | F | VF | XF | Unc | BU |
|---|---|---|---|---|---|---|
| AH1381 Proof | 150 | Value: 450 | | | | |
| AH1382 Proof | 100 | Value: 475 | | | | |
| AH1390 Proof | 350 | Value: 350 | | | | |

**Note:** Struck for presentation purposes

**SAIDI RIAL** **KM# 31** **Weight:** 28.0700 g. **Composition:** 0.8330 Silver .7518 oz. ASW **Ruler:** Sa'id bin Taimur

| Date | Mintage | F | VF | XF | Unc | BU |
|---|---|---|---|---|---|---|
| AH1378 | 1,000,000 | — | 12.00 | 15.00 | 20.00 | — |
| AH1378 Proof | 100 | Value: 650 | | | | |

**SAIDI RIAL** **KM# 31a** **Weight:** 28.0700 g. **Composition:** 0.5000 Silver .4512 oz. ASW **Ruler:** Sa'id bin Taimur

| Date | Mintage | F | VF | XF | Unc | BU |
|---|---|---|---|---|---|---|
| AH1378 | 400,000 | — | 10.00 | 12.50 | 15.00 | — |

**SAIDI RIAL** **KM# 31b** **Weight:** 46.6500 g. **Composition:** 0.9160 Gold 1.3740 oz. AGW **Ruler:** Sa'id bin Taimur **Size:** 33.7 mm.

| Date | Mintage | F | VF | XF | Unc | BU |
|---|---|---|---|---|---|---|
| AH1978 Proof | 100 | Value: 1,100 | | | | |
| AH1390 Proof | 350 | Value: 750 | | | | |

**Note:** Struck for presentation purposes.

**15 SAIDI RIALS** **KM# 35** **Weight:** 7.9900 g. **Composition:** 0.9160 Gold .2353 oz. AGW **Ruler:** Sa'id bin Taimur

| Date | Mintage | F | VF | XF | Unc | BU |
|---|---|---|---|---|---|---|
| AH1381 | 2,000 | — | — | — | 150 | — |
| AH1381 Proof | 100 | Value: 575 | | | | |

**Note:** Struck for presentation purposes

## MINT SETS

| KM# | Date | Mintage | Identification | Issue Price | Mkt Val |
|---|---|---|---|---|---|
| MS1 | AH1390 (1970) (6) | 5,500 | KM#36-41 | — | 4.50 |

## PROOF SETS

| KM# | Date | Mintage | Identification | Issue Price | Mkt Val |
|---|---|---|---|---|---|
| PS1 | AH1359, 65, 57 (1940, 45, 47) (6) | — | KM#22-26, 29 | — | 75.00 |
| PS2 | AH1359, 65, 57 (1940, 45, 47) (6) | — | KM#22, 24-27, 29 | — | 70.00 |
| PS4 | AH1390 (1970) (3) | 350 | KM#39a-41a | — | 625 |
| PS3 | AH1390 (1970) (6) | 2,102 | KM#36-41 | 11.00 | 16.50 |

# MYANMAR (Burma)

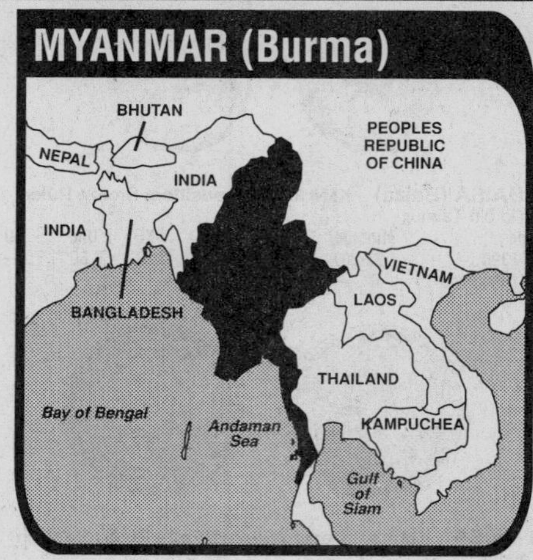


The Union of Myanmar, formerly Burma, a country of Southeast Asia fronting on the Bay of Bengal and the Andaman Sea, has an area of 261,218 sq. mi. (678,500 sq. km.) and a population of 38.8 million. Capital: Yangon (Rangoon). Myanmar is an agricultural country heavily dependent on its leading product (rice) which occupies two-thirds of the cultivated area and accounts for 40 % of the value of exports. Mineral resources are extensive, but production is low. Petroleum, lead, tin, silver, zinc, nickel cobalt, and precious stones are exported.

The first European to reach Burma, in about 1435, was Nicolo Di Conti, a Venetian merchant. During the beginning of the reign of Bodawpaya (1781-1819AD) the kingdom comprised most of the same area as it does today including Arakan which was taken over in 1784-85. The British East India Company, while unsuccessful in its1612 effort to establish posts along the Bay of Bengal, was enabled by the Anglo-Burmese Wars of 1824-86 to expand to the whole of Burma and to secure its annexation to British India. In 1937, Burma was separated from India, becoming a separate British colony with limited self-government. Burma became an independent nation outside the British Commonwealth on Jan. 4, 1948, the constitution of 1948 providing for a parliamentary democracy and the nationalization of certain industries. However, political and economic problems persisted, and on March 2, 1962, Gen. Ne Win took over the government, suspended the constitution, installed himself as chief of state, and pursued a socialistic program with nationalization of nearly all industry and trade. On Jan. 4, 1974, a new constitution adopted by referendum established Burma as a socialist republic under one-party rule. The country name was changed to Myanmar in 1989.

The coins issued by kings Mindon and Thibaw between1 852 and 1885 circulated in Upper Burma. Indian coins were current in Lower Burma, which was annexed in 1852. Burmese coins are frequently known by the equivalent Indian denominations, although their values are inscribed in Burmese units. Upper Burma was annexed in 1885 and the Burmese coinage remained in circulation until 1889,when Indian coins became current throughout Burma. Coins were again issued in the old Burmese denominations after independence in 1948, but these were replaced by decimal issues in 1952. The Chula-Sakarat (CS) dating is sometimes referred to as BE-Burmese Era and began in 638AD.

**RULERS**
British, 1886-1948

**MONETARY SYSTEM**
(Until 1952)
4 Pyas = 1 Pe
2 Pe = 1 Mu
2 Mu = 1 Mat
5 Mat = 1 Kyat
**NOTE:** Originally 10 light Mu = 1 Kyat, eventually 8 heavy Mu = 1 Kyat.

**Indian Equivalents**
1 Silver Kyat = 1 Rupee = 16 Annas
1 Gold Kyat = 1 Mohur = 16 Rupees

# UNION OF BURMA

## STANDARD COINAGE

**2 PYAS** **KM# 27** **Composition:** Copper-Nickel **Obverse:** Chinze

| Date | Mintage | F | VF | XF | Unc | BU |
|---|---|---|---|---|---|---|
| 1949 | 7,000,000 | 0.25 | 0.50 | 1.00 | 3.00 | — |
| 1949 Proof | 100 | Value: 100 | | | | |

 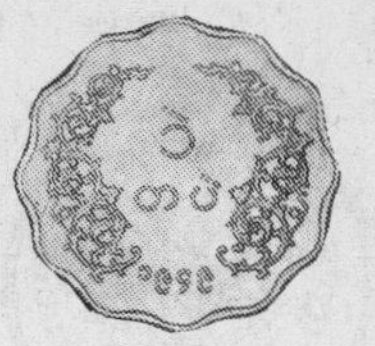

**PE** **KM# 28** **Composition:** Copper-Nickel **Obverse:** Chinze

| Date | Mintage | F | VF | XF | Unc | BU |
|---|---|---|---|---|---|---|
| 1949 | 8,000,000 | 0.35 | 0.75 | 1.50 | 4.00 | — |
| 1949 Proof | 100 | Value: 100 | | | | |
| 1950 | 9,500,000 | 0.35 | 0.75 | 1.50 | 4.00 | — |
| 1950 Proof | — | — | — | — | — | — |
| 1951 | 6,500,000 | 0.50 | 1.00 | 2.00 | 5.00 | — |
| 1951 Proof | — | — | — | — | — | — |

 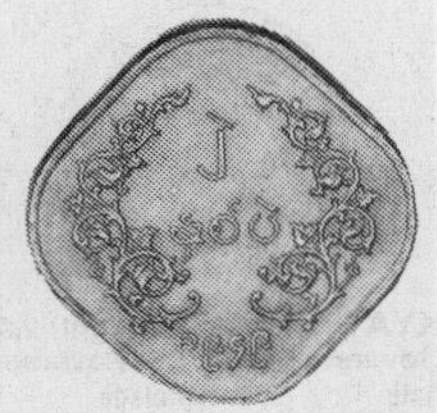

**¿ PE** **KM# 29** **Composition:** Copper-Nickel **Obverse:** Chinze

| Date | Mintage | F | VF | XF | Unc | BU |
|---|---|---|---|---|---|---|
| 1949 | 7,100,000 | 0.50 | 1.00 | 2.00 | 5.00 | — |
| 1949 Proof | 100 | Value: 100 | | | | |
| 1950 | 8,500,000 | 0.50 | 1.00 | 2.00 | 5.00 | — |
| 1950 Proof | — | — | — | — | — | — |
| 1951 | 7,480,000 | 0.50 | 1.00 | 2.00 | 5.00 | — |
| 1951 Proof | — | — | — | — | — | — |

**4 PE** **KM# 30** **Composition:** Nickel **Obverse:** Chinze

| Date | Mintage | F | VF | XF | Unc | BU |
|---|---|---|---|---|---|---|
| 1949 | 6,500,000 | 1.25 | 2.50 | 5.00 | 15.00 | — |
| 1949 Proof | 100 | Value: 100 | | | | |
| 1950 | 6,120,000 | 1.00 | 2.00 | 4.00 | 12.00 | — |

**8 PE** **KM# 31** **Composition:** Nickel **Obverse:** Chinze

| Date | Mintage | F | VF | XF | Unc | BU |
|---|---|---|---|---|---|---|
| 1949 | 3,270,000 | 1.50 | 3.00 | 6.00 | 25.00 | — |
| 1949 Proof | 100 | Value: 100 | | | | |
| 1950 | 3,900,000 | 1.25 | 2.50 | 5.00 | 20.00 | — |
| 1950 Proof | — | — | — | — | — | — |

 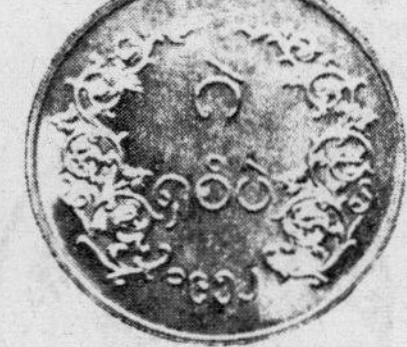

**8 PE** **KM# 31a** **Composition:** Copper-Nickel **Obverse:** Chinze

| Date | Mintage | VG | F | VF | XF | Unc |
|---|---|---|---|---|---|---|
| CS1314(1952) | 1,642,000 | — | 50.00 | 100 | 150 | 200 |
| CS1314(1952) Proof | — | Value: 400 | | | | |

## DECIMAL COINAGE

100 Pyas = 1 Kyat

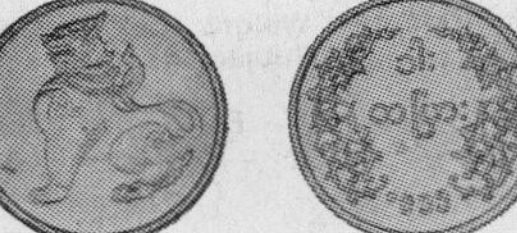

**PYA** **KM# 32** **Composition:** Bronze **Obverse:** Chinze

| Date | Mintage | VG | F | VF | XF | Unc |
|---|---|---|---|---|---|---|
| CS1314(1952) | 500,000 | — | 0.10 | 0.15 | 0.20 | 0.35 |
| CS1314(1952) Proof | 100 | Value: 60.00 | | | | |
| CS1315(1953) | 14,000,000 | — | 0.10 | 0.15 | 0.20 | 0.35 |
| CS1315(1953) Proof | — | — | — | — | — | — |
| CS1317(1955) | 30,000,000 | — | 0.10 | 0.15 | 0.20 | 0.35 |
| CS1317(1955) Proof | — | — | — | — | — | — |
| CS1318(1956) Proof | 100 | Value: 60.00 | | | | |
| CS1324(1962) Proof | 100 | Value: 60.00 | | | | |
| CS1327(1965) | 15,000,000 | — | 0.10 | 0.15 | 0.20 | 0.35 |
| CS1327(1965) Proof | — | — | — | — | — | — |

**PYA** **KM# 38** **Composition:** Aluminum **Subject:** Aung San

| Date | Mintage | VG | F | VF | XF | Unc |
|---|---|---|---|---|---|---|
| CS1328(1966) | 8,000,000 | — | 0.10 | 0.15 | 0.25 | 0.50 |

**5 PYAS** **KM# 33** **Composition:** Copper-Nickel **Obverse:** Chinze

| Date | Mintage | VG | F | VF | XF | Unc |
|---|---|---|---|---|---|---|
| CS1314(1952) | 20,000,000 | — | 0.10 | 0.15 | 0.35 | 0.75 |
| CS1314(1952) Proof | 100 | Value: 65.00 | | | | |
| CS1315(1953) | 59,700,000 | — | 0.10 | 0.15 | 0.35 | 0.75 |
| CS1315(1953) Proof | — | — | — | — | — | — |
| CS1317(1955) | 40,272,000 | — | 0.10 | 0.15 | 0.35 | 0.75 |
| CS1317(1955) Proof | — | — | — | — | — | — |
| CS1318(1956) | 20,000,000 | — | 0.10 | 0.15 | 0.35 | 0.75 |
| CS1318(1956) Proof | 100 | Value: 65.00 | | | | |
| CS1323(1961) | 12,000,000 | — | 0.10 | 0.15 | 0.35 | 0.75 |
| CS1323(1961) Proof | — | — | — | — | — | — |
| CS1324(1962) | 10,000,000 | — | 0.10 | 0.15 | 0.35 | 0.75 |
| CS1324(1962) Proof | 100 | Value: 65.00 | | | | |
| CS1325(1963) | 40,400,000 | — | 0.10 | 0.15 | 0.25 | 0.60 |
| CS1325(1963) Proof | — | — | — | — | — | — |
| CS1327(1965) | 43,600,000 | — | 0.10 | 0.15 | 0.20 | 0.40 |
| CS1327(1965) Proof | — | — | — | — | — | — |
| CS1328(1966) | 20,000,000 | — | 0.10 | 0.15 | 0.20 | 0.40 |
| CS1328(1966) Proof | — | — | — | — | — | — |

 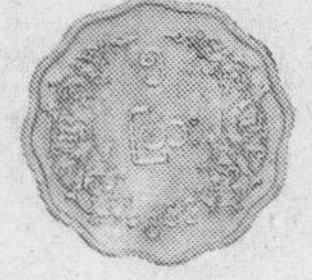

**5 PYAS** **KM# 39** **Composition:** Aluminum **Subject:** Aung San

| Date | Mintage | VG | F | VF | XF | Unc |
|---|---|---|---|---|---|---|
| CS1328(1966) | — | — | 0.10 | 0.20 | 0.35 | 0.60 |

**5 PYAS** **KM# 51** **Composition:** Aluminum-Bronze **Series:** F.A.O. **Obverse:** Rice plant

| Date | Mintage | F | VF | XF | Unc | BU |
|---|---|---|---|---|---|---|
| 1987 | — | 0.10 | 0.20 | 0.40 | 1.00 | — |

**10 PYAS** **KM# 34** **Composition:** Copper-Nickel **Obverse:** Chinze

| Date | Mintage | VG | F | VF | XF | Unc |
|---|---|---|---|---|---|---|
| CS1314(1952) | 20,000,000 | — | 0.10 | 0.20 | 0.40 | 1.00 |
| CS1314(1952) Proof | 100 | Value: 70.00 | | | | |
| CS1315(1953) | 37,250,000 | — | 0.10 | 0.20 | 0.40 | 1.00 |
| CS1315(1953) Proof | — | — | — | — | — | — |
| CS1317(1955) | 22,750,000 | — | 0.10 | 0.20 | 0.40 | 1.00 |
| CS1317(1955) Proof | — | — | — | — | — | — |
| CS1318(1956) | 35,000,000 | — | 0.10 | 0.15 | 0.40 | 1.00 |
| CS1318(1956) Proof | 100 | Value: 70.00 | | | | |
| CS1324(1962) | 6,000,000 | — | 0.10 | 0.20 | 0.40 | 1.00 |
| CS1324(1962) Proof | 100 | Value: 70.00 | | | | |
| CS1325(1963) | 10,750,000 | — | 0.10 | 0.20 | 0.40 | 1.00 |
| CS1325(1963) Proof | 10,750,000 | — | — | — | — | — |
| CS1327(1965) | 32,619,999 | — | 0.10 | 0.20 | 0.40 | 1.00 |
| CS1327(1965) Proof | — | — | — | — | — | — |

**10 PYAS** **KM# 40** **Composition:** Aluminum **Subject:** Aung San

| Date | Mintage | VG | F | VF | XF | Unc |
|---|---|---|---|---|---|---|
| CS1328(1966) | — | — | 0.15 | 0.30 | 0.60 | 1.00 |

**10 PYAS** **KM# 49** **Composition:** Brass **Series:** F.A.O. **Obverse:** Rice plant

| Date | Mintage | VG | F | VF | XF | Unc |
|---|---|---|---|---|---|---|
| 1983 | — | — | 0.15 | 0.30 | 0.60 | 1.00 |

**25 PYAS** **KM# 35** **Composition:** Copper-Nickel **Obverse:** Chinze

| Date | Mintage | VG | F | VF | XF | Unc |
|---|---|---|---|---|---|---|
| CS1314(1952) | 13,540,000 | — | 0.10 | 0.20 | 0.50 | 1.25 |
| CS1314(1952) Proof | 100 | Value: 75.00 | | | | |
| CS1316(1954) | 18,000,000 | — | 0.10 | 0.20 | 0.50 | 1.25 |
| CS1316(1954) Proof | — | — | — | — | — | — |
| CS1317(1955) Proof | — | Value: 75.00 | | | | |
| CS1318(1956) | 14,000,000 | — | 0.10 | 0.20 | 0.50 | 1.25 |
| CS1318(1956) Proof | 100 | Value: 75.00 | | | | |
| CS1321(1959) | 6,000,000 | — | 0.10 | 0.20 | 0.50 | 1.25 |
| CS1321(1959) Proof | — | — | — | — | — | — |
| CS1323(1961) | 4,000,000 | — | 0.10 | 0.20 | 0.50 | 1.25 |
| CS1323(1961) Proof | — | — | — | — | — | — |
| CS1324(1962) | 3,200,000 | — | 0.10 | 0.20 | 0.50 | 1.25 |
| CS1324(1962) Proof | 100 | Value: 75.00 | | | | |
| CS1325(1963) | 16,000,000 | — | 0.10 | 0.15 | 0.30 | 0.75 |
| CS1325(1963) Proof | — | — | — | — | — | — |
| CS1327(1965) | 26,000,000 | — | 0.10 | 0.15 | 0.30 | 0.75 |
| CS1327(1965) Proof | — | — | — | — | — | — |

**25 PYAS** **KM# 41** **Composition:** Aluminum **Subject:** Aung San

| Date | Mintage | VG | F | VF | XF | Unc |
|---|---|---|---|---|---|---|
| CS1328(1966) | — | — | 0.15 | 0.30 | 0.60 | 1.00 |

**25 PYAS** **KM# 48** **Composition:** Bronze **Series:** F.A.O. **Obverse:** Rice plant

| Date | Mintage | VG | F | VF | XF | Unc |
|---|---|---|---|---|---|---|
| 1980 | — | — | 0.15 | 0.30 | 0.60 | 1.00 |

**25 PYAS** **KM# 50** **Composition:** Bronze **Series:** F.A.O. **Obverse:** Rice plant

| Date | Mintage | VG | F | VF | XF | Unc |
|---|---|---|---|---|---|---|
| 1986 | — | — | 0.10 | 0.20 | 0.35 | 0.60 |

**50 PYAS** **KM# 36** **Composition:** Copper-Nickel **Obverse:** Chinze

| Date | Mintage | VG | F | VF | XF | Unc |
|---|---|---|---|---|---|---|
| CS1314(1952) | 2,500,000 | — | 0.20 | 0.50 | 0.75 | 1.75 |
| CS1314(1952) Proof | 100 | Value: 80.00 | | | | |
| CS1316(1954) | 12,000,000 | — | 0.20 | 0.50 | 0.75 | 1.75 |
| CS1316(1954) Proof | — | — | — | — | — | — |
| CS1318(1956) | 8,000,000 | — | 0.20 | 0.50 | 0.75 | 1.75 |
| CS1318(1956) Proof | 100 | Value: 80.00 | | | | |
| CS1323(1961) | 2,000,000 | — | 0.15 | 0.40 | 0.75 | 1.75 |
| CS1323(1961) Proof | — | — | — | — | — | — |
| CS1324(1962) | 600,000 | — | 0.25 | 0.75 | 1.25 | 2.25 |
| CS1324(1962) Proof | 100 | Value: 80.00 | | | | |
| CS1325(1963) | 4,800,000 | — | 0.15 | 0.25 | 0.65 | 1.25 |
| CS1325(1963) Proof | — | — | — | — | — | — |
| CS1327(1965) | 2,800,000 | — | 0.15 | 0.40 | 0.75 | 1.75 |
| CS1327(1965) Proof | — | — | — | — | — | — |
| CS1328(1966) | 3,400,000 | — | 0.10 | 0.30 | 0.75 | 1.75 |
| CS1328(1966) Proof | — | — | — | — | — | — |

**50 PYAS** **KM# 42** **Composition:** Aluminum **Subject:** Aung San

| Date | Mintage | VG | F | VF | XF | Unc |
|---|---|---|---|---|---|---|
| CS1328(1966) | — | — | 0.15 | 0.40 | 1.00 | 2.00 |

**50 PYAS** **KM# 46** **Composition:** Brass **Series:** F.A.O. **Obverse:** Rice plant

| Date | Mintage | VG | F | VF | XF | Unc |
|---|---|---|---|---|---|---|
| 1975 | — | — | 0.15 | 0.35 | 0.70 | 1.25 |
| 1976 | — | — | 0.15 | 0.35 | 0.70 | 1.25 |

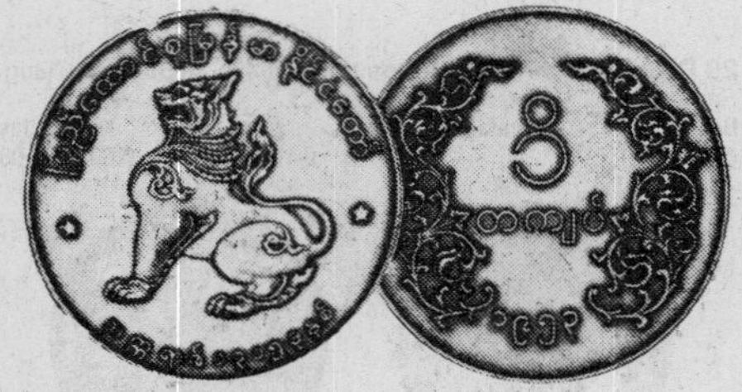

**KYAT** **KM# 37** **Composition:** Copper-Nickel

| Date | Mintage | VG | F | VF | XF | Unc |
|---|---|---|---|---|---|---|
| CS1314(1952) | 2,500,000 | — | 0.35 | 0.75 | 1.50 | 3.00 |
| CS1314(1952) Proof | 100 | Value: 85.00 | | | | |
| CS1315(1953) | 7,500,000 | — | 0.25 | 0.50 | 1.00 | 2.00 |
| CS1315(1953) Proof | — | — | — | — | — | — |
| CS1318(1956) | 3,500,000 | — | 0.35 | 0.75 | 1.50 | 3.00 |
| CS1318(1956) Proof | 100 | Value: 85.00 | | | | |
| CS1324(1962) Proof | 100 | Value: 85.00 | | | | |
| CS1327(1965) | 1,000,000 | — | 0.35 | 0.75 | 1.50 | 3.00 |
| CS1327(1965) Proof | — | — | — | — | — | — |

**KYAT** **KM# 47** **Composition:** Copper-Nickel **Series:** F.A.O. **Obverse:** Rice plant

| Date | Mintage | VG | F | VF | XF | Unc |
|---|---|---|---|---|---|---|
| 1975 | 20,000,000 | — | 0.25 | 0.50 | 1.00 | 2.00 |

## REVOLUTIONARY COINAGE

Patriotic Liberation Army

**MU** **KM# 43** **Weight:** 2.0000 g. **Composition:** 1.0000 Gold .0643 oz. AGW **Obverse:** UNION OF BURMA GOVERNMENT 1970-1971 around peacock **Reverse:** Legend: U NU in star SHWE MUZI below

| Date | Mintage | F | VF | XF | Unc | BU |
|---|---|---|---|---|---|---|
| 1970-71 | — | — | — | — | 125 | — |

**2 MU** **KM# 44** **Weight:** 4.0000 g. **Composition:** 1.0000 Gold .1286 oz. AGW

| Date | Mintage | F | VF | XF | Unc | BU |
|---|---|---|---|---|---|---|
| 1970-71 | — | — | — | — | 250 | — |
| 1970-71 | — | — | — | — | 250 | — |

**4 MU** **KM# 45** **Weight:** 8.0000 g. **Composition:** 1.0000 Gold .2572 oz. AGW

| Date | Mintage | F | VF | XF | Unc | BU |
|---|---|---|---|---|---|---|
| 1970-71 | — | — | — | — | 475 | — |

# UNION OF MYANMAR

## DECIMAL COINAGE

100 Pyas = 1 Kyat

**10 PYAS** **KM# 57** **Composition:** Brass **Obv. Legend:** Myanmar Central Bank **Note:** Similar to KM#49.

| Date | Mintage | VG | F | VF | XF | Unc |
|---|---|---|---|---|---|---|
| 1991 | — | — | 0.15 | 0.30 | 0.60 | 1.00 |

**25 PYAS** **KM# 58** **Composition:** Chrome Plated Steel **Obv. Legend:** Myanmar Central Bank **Note:** Similar to KM#50.

| Date | Mintage | VG | F | VF | XF | Unc |
|---|---|---|---|---|---|---|
| 1991 | — | — | 0.15 | 0.30 | 0.60 | 1.00 |

**50 PYAS** **KM# 59** **Composition:** Brass **Obv. Legend:** Myanmar Central Bank **Reverse:** Denomination **Edge:** Reeded **Size:** 24.6 mm. **Note:** Struck at Prome.

| Date | Mintage | VG | F | VF | XF | Unc |
|---|---|---|---|---|---|---|
| 1991 | — | — | 0.15 | 0.35 | 0.70 | 1.25 |

**KYAT** **KM# 60** **Weight:** 2.9500 g. **Composition:** Bronze **Obverse:** Seated lion **Reverse:** Denomination **Edge:** Plain

| Date | Mintage | F | VF | XF | Unc | BU |
|---|---|---|---|---|---|---|
| 1999 | — | — | — | — | 0.25 | — |

**5 KYATS** **KM# 61** **Weight:** 2.7300 g. **Composition:** Brass **Obverse:** Seated lion **Reverse:** Denomination **Edge:** Plain **Size:** 20 mm. **Note:** Similar to 50 Kyats, KM#63.

| Date | Mintage | F | VF | XF | Unc | BU |
|---|---|---|---|---|---|---|
| 1999 | — | — | — | — | 0.50 | — |

**10 KYATS** **KM# 62** **Composition:** Brass **Note:** Similar to 50 Kyats, KM#63.

| Date | Mintage | F | VF | XF | Unc | BU |
|---|---|---|---|---|---|---|
| 1999 | — | — | — | — | 0.75 | — |

**50 KYATS** **KM# 63** **Weight:** 5.0600 g. **Composition:** Copper-Nickel **Obverse:** Seated lion **Reverse:** Denomination **Edge:** Reeded **Size:** 23.85 mm.

| Date | Mintage | F | VF | XF | Unc | BU |
|---|---|---|---|---|---|---|
| 1999 | — | — | — | — | 1.75 | — |

**100 KYATS** **KM# 64** **Weight:** 7.5200 g. **Composition:** Copper-Nickel **Obverse:** Seated lion **Reverse:** Denomination **Edge:** Reeded **Size:** 26.8 mm. **Note:** Struck at Prome.

| Date | Mintage | F | VF | XF | Unc | BU |
|---|---|---|---|---|---|---|
| 1999 | — | — | — | — | 3.00 | — |

**300 KYAT** **KM# A51** **Weight:** 1.2441 g. **Composition:** 0.9990 Gold .04 oz. AGW **Subject:** Year of the Tiger **Obverse:** Lotus flower

| Date | Mintage | F | VF | XF | Unc | BU |
|---|---|---|---|---|---|---|
| 1998 | — | — | — | — | 35.00 | — |

**500 KYAT** **KM# 52** **Weight:** 20.0000 g. **Composition:** 0.9250 Silver .5948 oz. ASW **Subject:** Year of the Tiger **Obverse:** Lotus flower

| Date | Mintage | F | VF | XF | Unc | BU |
|---|---|---|---|---|---|---|
| 1987 Proof | Est. 15,000 | Value: 47.50 | | | | |

**500 KYAT** **KM# 53** **Weight:** 20.0000 g. **Composition:** 0.9250 Silver .5948 oz. ASW **Subject:** Year of the Tiger **Obverse:** Lotus flower

| Date | Mintage | F | VF | XF | Unc | BU |
|---|---|---|---|---|---|---|
| 1998 Proof | Est. 15,000 | Value: 50.00 | | | | |

**500 KYAT** **KM# 54** **Weight:** 20.0000 g. **Composition:** 0.9250 Silver .5948 oz. ASW **Subject:** Year of the Tiger **Obverse:** Lotus flower

| Date | Mintage | F | VF | XF | Unc | BU |
|---|---|---|---|---|---|---|
| 1998 Proof | 1,014,999 | Value: 37.50 | | | | |

**2000 KYAT** **KM# 55** **Weight:** 7.7759 g. **Composition:** 0.9999 Gold .2500 oz. AGW **Subject:** Year of the Tiger **Obverse:** Lotus flower

| Date | Mintage | F | VF | XF | Unc | BU |
|---|---|---|---|---|---|---|
| 1998 Proof | 1,998 | Value: 250 | | | | |

**Note:** In sets only.

**5000 KYAT** **KM# 56** **Weight:** 15.5518 g. **Composition:** 0.9999 Gold .5000 oz. AGW **Subject:** Year of the Tiger **Obverse:** Lotus flower

| Date | Mintage | F | VF | XF | Unc | BU |
|---|---|---|---|---|---|---|
| 1998 Proof | 5,798 | Value: 425 | | | | |

## PATTERNS

Including off metal strikes

| KM# | Date | Mintage | Identification | Mkt Val |
|---|---|---|---|---|
| Pn10 | 2602 | — | 4 Annas. Aluminum. 25 mm. | — |
| Pn11 | 2602 | — | 4 Annas. Aluminum. 19 mm. | — |
| Pn12 | 2602 | — | 4 Annas. Aluminum. 16 mm. | — |

## PROOF SETS

| KM# | Date | Mintage | Identification | Issue Price | Mkt Val |
|---|---|---|---|---|---|
| PS1 | 1949 (5) | 100 | KM#27-31 | — | 500 |
| PS2 | 1952 (6) | 100 | KM#32-37 | — | 435 |
| PS3 | 1956 (6) | 100 | KM#32-37 | — | 435 |
| PS4 | 1962 (6) | 100 | KM#32-37 | — | 435 |
| PS5 | 1998 (3) | 3,998 | KM#52-54 | — | 145 |
| PS6 | 1998 (2) | 1,998 | KM#55-56 | — | 675 |

# NAMIBIA

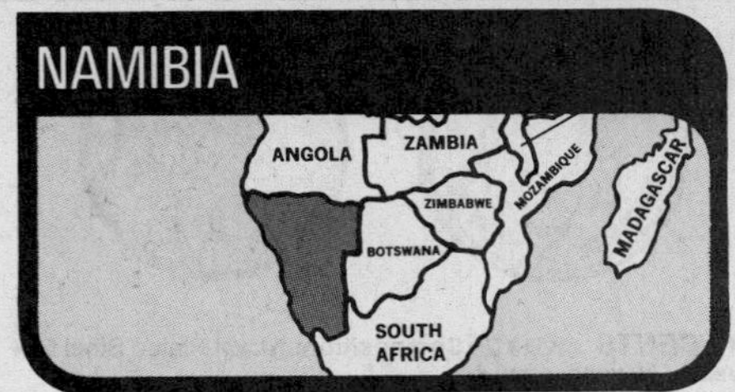


The Republic of Namibia, once the German colonial territory of German South West Africa, and later South West Africa, is situated on the Atlantic coast of southern Africa, bounded on the north by Angola, on the east by Botswana, and on the south by South Africa. It has an area of 318,261 sq. mi. (824,290 sq. km.) and a population of *1.4 million. Capital: Windhoek. Diamonds, copper, lead, zinc, and cattle are exported.

South Africa undertook the administration of South West Africa under the terms of a League of Nations mandate on Dec. 17, 1920. When the League of Nations was dissolved in 1946, its supervisory authority for South West Africa was inherited by the United Nations. In 1946 the UN denied South Africa's request to annex South West Africa. South Africa responded by refusing to place the territory under a UN trusteeship. In 1950 the International Court of Justice ruled that South Africa could not unilaterally modify the international status of South West Africa. A 1966 UN resolution declaring the mandate terminated was rejected by South Africa, and the status of the area remains in dispute. In June 1968 the UN General Assembly voted to rename the territory Namibia. In 1971 the International Court of Justice ruled that South Africa's presence in Namibia was illegal. In Dec. 1973 the UN appointed a UN Commissioner and a multi-racial Advisory Council was appointed. An interim government was formed in 1977 and independence was to be declared by Dec. 31, 1978. This resolution was rejected by major UN powers. In April 1978 South Africa accepted a plan for UN-supervised elections, which led to a political abstention by the South West Africa People's Organization (SWAPO) party leading to dissolving of the Minister's Council and National Assembly in Jan.1983. A Multi-Party Conference (MPC) was formed in May 1984, which held talks with SWAPO. The MPC petitioned South Africa for self-government and on June 17, 1985 the Transitional Government of National Unity was installed. Negotiations were held in 1988between Angola, Cuba, and South Africa reaching a peaceful settlement on Aug. 5, 1988. By April 1989 Cuban troops were to withdraw from Angola and South African troops from Namibia. The Transitional Government resigned on Feb. 28, 1988 for the upcoming elections of the constituent assembly in Nov. 1989.Independence was finally achieved on March 12, 1990 within the Commonwealth of Nations. The President is the Head of State; the Prime Minister is Head of Government.

**MONETARY SYSTEM**

100 Cents = 1 Namibia Dollar
1 Namibia Dollar = 1 South African Rand

# REPUBLIC OF NAMIBIA

## DECIMAL COINAGE

**5 CENTS** **KM# 1** **Composition:** Nickel Plated Steel **Obverse:** National arms

| Date | Mintage | F | VF | XF | Unc | BU |
|---|---|---|---|---|---|---|
| 1993(1993) | — | — | — | 0.20 | 0.50 | — |

**5 CENTS** **KM# 16** **Composition:** Stainless Steel **Obverse:** National arms **Reverse:** Horse mackerel fish, denomination

| Date | Mintage | F | VF | XF | Unc | BU |
|---|---|---|---|---|---|---|
| 2000 (1999) | — | — | — | — | 1.00 | — |

**10 CENTS** **KM# 2** **Composition:** Nickel Plated Steel **Obverse:** National arms

| Date | Mintage | F | VF | XF | Unc | BU |
|---|---|---|---|---|---|---|
| 1993 | — | — | — | 0.35 | 1.00 | — |
| 1996 | — | — | — | 0.35 | 1.00 | — |

**50 CENTS** **KM# 3** **Composition:** Nickel Plated Steel **Obverse:** National arms

| Date | Mintage | F | VF | XF | Unc | BU |
|---|---|---|---|---|---|---|
| 1993 | — | — | — | 0.75 | 1.75 | — |
| 1996 | — | — | — | 0.75 | 1.75 | — |

**DOLLAR** **KM# 4** **Composition:** Brass **Obverse:** National arms

| Date | Mintage | F | VF | XF | Unc | BU |
|---|---|---|---|---|---|---|
| 1993 | — | — | — | 1.25 | 3.50 | — |
| 1996 | — | — | — | 1.25 | 3.50 | — |

**DOLLAR** **KM# 6** **Composition:** Copper-Nickel **Subject:** 5th Year of Independence **Obverse:** National arms

| Date | Mintage | F | VF | XF | Unc | BU |
|---|---|---|---|---|---|---|
| 1995 | 50,000 | — | — | — | 10.00 | — |

**DOLLAR** **KM# 7** **Composition:** Copper-Nickel **Subject:** Miss Universe **Obverse:** National arms **Reverse:** Multi-colored gemsbok

| Date | Mintage | F | VF | XF | Unc | BU |
|---|---|---|---|---|---|---|
| 1995 | 50,000 | — | — | — | 10.00 | — |

**DOLLAR** **KM# 12** **Composition:** Copper-Nickel **Subject:** Marine Life Protection **Obverse:** National arms **Reverse:** Multi-color whale and calf

| Date | Mintage | F | VF | XF | Unc | BU |
|---|---|---|---|---|---|---|
| 1998 Proof | 7,500 | Value: 25.00 | | | | |

**5 DOLLARS** **KM# 5** **Composition:** Brass **Obverse:** National arms

| Date | Mintage | F | VF | XF | Unc | BU |
|---|---|---|---|---|---|---|
| 1993 | — | — | — | 3.00 | 6.50 | — |

**5 DOLLARS** **KM# 18** **Weight:** 1.2700 g. **Composition:** 0.9999 Gold .0408 oz. AGW **Subject:** 10 Years of Independence **Obverse:** National arms **Reverse:** 2 lions **Edge:** Reeded **Size:** 13.9 mm. **Note:** Struck at the Huguenin Mint.

| Date | Mintage | F | VF | XF | Unc | BU |
|---|---|---|---|---|---|---|
| 2000 Proof | 8,000 | Value: 35.00 | | | | |

**10 DOLLARS** **KM# 8** **Weight:** 25.0000 g. **Composition:** 0.9250 Silver .7435 oz. ASW **Subject:** 5th Year of Independence **Obverse:** National arms **Reverse:** Multi-colored desert view

| Date | Mintage | F | VF | XF | Unc | BU |
|---|---|---|---|---|---|---|
| 1995 Proof | 10,000 | Value: 35.00 | | | | |

**10 DOLLARS** **KM# 9** **Composition:** Copper-Nickel **Subject:** U.N. 50th Anniversary **Obverse:** National arms **Reverse:** Farm scene

| Date | Mintage | F | VF | XF | Unc | BU |
|---|---|---|---|---|---|---|
| 1995 | — | — | — | — | 12.50 | — |

**10 DOLLARS** **KM# 9a** **Weight:** 28.2800 g. **Composition:** 0.9250 Silver .8410 oz. ASW **Subject:** U.N. 50th Anniversary **Obverse:** National arms **Reverse:** Farm scene

| Date | Mintage | F | VF | XF | Unc | BU |
|---|---|---|---|---|---|---|
| 1995 Proof | — | Value: 50.00 | | | | |

**10 DOLLARS** **KM# 10** **Weight:** 25.0000 g. **Composition:** 0.9250 Silver .7435 oz. ASW **Subject:** Miss Universe **Obverse:** National arms **Reverse:** Multi-color leopard

| Date | Mintage | F | VF | XF | Unc | BU |
|---|---|---|---|---|---|---|
| 1995 Proof | 10,000 | Value: 37.50 | | | | |

**10 DOLLARS** **KM# 11** **Weight:** 25.0000 g. **Composition:** 0.9250 Silver .7435 oz. ASW **Series:** Olympic Games 1996 **Obverse:** National arms **Reverse:** Runner, Cheetah

| Date | Mintage | F | VF | XF | Unc | BU |
|---|---|---|---|---|---|---|
| 1996 Proof | — | Value: 35.00 | | | | |

**10 DOLLARS** **KM# 13** **Weight:** 25.0000 g. **Composition:** 0.9250 Silver .7435 oz. ASW **Subject:** Marine Life Protection **Obverse:** National arms **Reverse:** Multi-color whale and calf **Note:** Similar to 1 Dollar, KM#12.

| Date | Mintage | F | VF | XF | Unc | BU |
|---|---|---|---|---|---|---|
| 1998 Proof | — | Value: 75.00 | | | | |

**10 DOLLARS** **KM# 19** **Weight:** 25.0000 g. **Composition:** 0.9000 Silver .7234 oz. ASW **Subject:** 10 Years of Independence **Obverse:** National arms **Reverse:** 2 multi-color lions **Edge:** Reeded **Size:** 37.3 mm. **Note:** Struck at Huguenin.

| Date | Mintage | F | VF | XF | Unc | BU |
|---|---|---|---|---|---|---|
| 2000 Proof | 3,000 | Value: 40.00 | | | | |

**20 DOLLARS** **KM# 14** **Weight:** 155.5175 g. **Composition:** 0.9990 Silver 4.9950 oz. ASW **Obverse:** National arms **Reverse:** Multi-color whale and calf **Note:** Similar to 1 Dollar, KM#12.

| Date | Mintage | F | VF | XF | Unc | BU |
|---|---|---|---|---|---|---|
| 1998 Proof | — | Value: 350 | | | | |

**100 DOLLARS** **KM# 17** **Weight:** 31.1035 g. **Composition:** 0.9999 Gold 1.0000 oz. AGW **Series:** Olympic Games 1996 **Reverse:** Runner, Cheetah **Note:** Similar to 10 Dollar, KM#11.

| Date | Mintage | F | VF | XF | Unc | BU |
|---|---|---|---|---|---|---|
| 1996 Proof | 400 | Value: 750 | | | | |

**100 DOLLARS** **KM# 15** **Weight:** 31.1035 g. **Composition:** 0.9999 Gold 1.0000 oz. AGW **Subject:** Marine Life Protection **Obverse:** National arms **Reverse:** Multi-color whale and calf **Note:** Similar to 1 Dollar, KM#12.

| Date | Mintage | F | VF | XF | Unc | BU |
|---|---|---|---|---|---|---|
| 1998 Proof | 125 | Value: 800 | | | | |

## ESSAIS

| KM# | Date | Mintage | Identification | Mkt Val |
|---|---|---|---|---|
| E1 | 1996 | 30 | 10 Dollars. Copper-Nickel. Multi-color, KM#11. | 200 |
| E2 | 1996 | 30 | 100 Dollars. Copper-Nickel. Multi-color, KM#17. | 220 |

# NAURU ISLAND

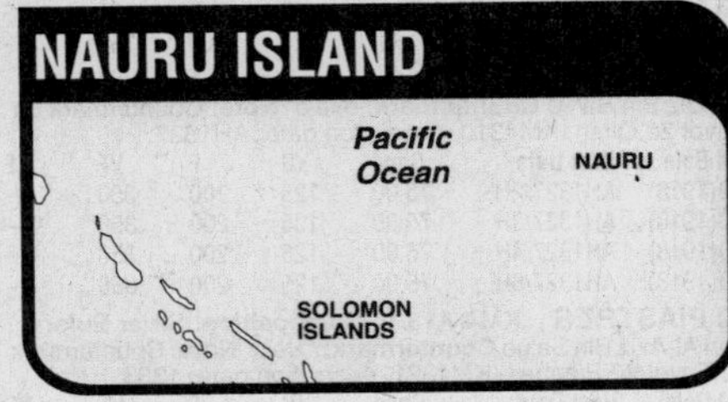


The Republic of Nauru, formerly Pleasant Island, is an island republic in the western Pacific Ocean west of the Gilbert Islands. It has an area of 8-1/2 sq. mi. and a population of 7,254. It is known for its phosphate deposits.

The island was discovered in 1798. It was annexed by Germany in 1888 and made a part of the Marshall Island protectorate. In 1914 the island was occupied by Australia and placed under mandate in 1919. During World War II it was seized by the Japanese in August, 1942.It became a joint Australian, British and New Zealand trust territory in 1947 and remained as such until it became an independent republic in 1968. Nauru has a unique relationship with the Commonwealth of Nations.

**RULERS**

British, until 1968

**MONETARY SYSTEM**

100 Cents = 1 (Australian) Dollar

## REPUBLIC OF NAURU

### DECIMAL COINAGE

**DOLLAR** **KM# 12** **Composition:** Copper-Nickel **Subject:** British Queen Mother **Obverse:** National arms **Reverse:** Queen Mother and Churchill **Edge:** Reeded **Size:** 38.6 mm. **Note:** Struck at the Royal Australian Mint.

| Date | Mintage | F | VF | XF | Unc | BU |
|---|---|---|---|---|---|---|
| 1996 | — | — | — | — | 10.00 | — |

**10 DOLLARS** **KM# 1** **Weight:** 38.7000 g. **Composition:** 0.9250 Silver 1.1508 oz. ASW **Subject:** Silver Jubilee of Independence

| Date | Mintage | F | VF | XF | Unc | BU |
|---|---|---|---|---|---|---|
| 1993 Proof | 1,000 | Value: 85.00 | | | | |

**10 DOLLARS** **KM# 2** **Weight:** 31.4700 g. **Composition:** 0.9250 Silver .9359 oz. ASW **Subject:** Noah's Ark

| Date | Mintage | F | VF | XF | Unc | BU |
|---|---|---|---|---|---|---|
| 1993 Proof | Est. 15,000 | Value: 65.00 | | | | |

**10 DOLLARS** **KM# 5** **Weight:** 31.4700 g. **Composition:** 0.9250 Silver .9359 oz. ASW **Series:** Endangered Wildlife **Reverse:** Songbirds

| Date | Mintage | F | VF | XF | Unc | BU |
|---|---|---|---|---|---|---|
| 1993 Proof | Est. 10,000 | Value: 50.00 | | | | |

**10 DOLLARS** **KM# 3** **Weight:** 31.4700 g. **Composition:** 0.9250 Silver .9359 oz. ASW **Subject:** World Cup Soccer

| Date | Mintage | F | VF | XF | Unc | BU |
|---|---|---|---|---|---|---|
| 1994 Proof | 30,000 | Value: 45.00 | | | | |

**10 DOLLARS** **KM# 6** **Weight:** 31.4700 g. **Composition:** 0.9250 Silver .9359 oz. ASW **Subject:** Queen Mother - Visits Bombed Palace

| Date | Mintage | F | VF | XF | Unc | BU |
|---|---|---|---|---|---|---|
| 1994 Proof | Est. 30,000 | Value: 45.00 | | | | |

**10 DOLLARS** **KM# 7** **Weight:** 31.4700 g. **Composition:** 0.9250 Silver .9359 oz. ASW **Subject:** John Fearn **Reverse:** Ship

| Date | Mintage | F | VF | XF | Unc | BU |
|---|---|---|---|---|---|---|
| 1994 Proof | Est. 15,000 | Value: 50.00 | | | | |

**10 DOLLARS** **KM# 8** **Weight:** 31.4700 g. **Composition:** 0.9250 Silver .9359 oz. ASW **Reverse:** Galileo Galilei -With Telescope

| Date | Mintage | F | VF | XF | Unc | BU |
|---|---|---|---|---|---|---|
| 1994 Proof | Est. 10,000 | Value: 52.50 | | | | |

**10 DOLLARS** **KM# 9** **Weight:** 31.4700 g. **Composition:** 0.9250 Silver .9359 oz. ASW **Series:** Olympics **Reverse:** Weight lifter

| Date | Mintage | F | VF | XF | Unc | BU |
|---|---|---|---|---|---|---|
| 1995 Proof | Est. 30,000 | Value: 45.00 | | | | |

**50 DOLLARS** **KM# 4** **Weight:** 8.0500 g. **Composition:** 0.9000 Gold .2329 oz. AGW **Series:** 1996 Olympics **Reverse:** Javelin throwing

| Date | Mintage | F | VF | XF | Unc | BU |
|---|---|---|---|---|---|---|
| 1994 Proof | 3,000 | Value: 165 | | | | |

**50 DOLLARS** **KM# 10** **Weight:** 7.7760 g. **Composition:** 0.5833 Gold .1458 oz. AGW **Subject:** The Ship Kaiser Wilhelm II **Reverse:** Ship and German eagle

| Date | Mintage | F | VF | XF | Unc | BU |
|---|---|---|---|---|---|---|
| 1994 Proof | Est. 3,000 | Value: 145 | | | | |

**50 DOLLARS** **KM# 11** **Weight:** 7.7760 g. **Composition:** 0.5833 Gold .1458 oz. AGW **Subject:** Endangered Wildlife **Reverse:** Dugong (Manatee-like creature)

| Date | Mintage | F | VF | XF | Unc | BU |
|---|---|---|---|---|---|---|
| 1995 Proof | Est. 2,000 | Value: 145 | | | | |

# NEJD

Nejd, a province of Saudi Arabia which may be described as an open steppe, occupies the core of the Arabian peninsula. The province became a nominal dependency of the Turkish empire in 1871 and a sultanate of King Abd Al-Aziz Bin Sa'ud in 1905.

**TITLES**

نجد

Nejd

**RULERS**

Abd Al-Aziz Bin Sa'ud, AH1322-1373/1905-1953AD

(Over all of Hejaz after 1925, and then in all Saudi Arabia after 1932).

**MONETARY SYSTEM**

40 Para = 1 Piastre (Ghirsh)
20 Piastres = 1 Riyal

## KINGDOM

### COUNTERMARKED COINAGE

Silver Coins

Following the defeat of the Ottomans in 1916, silver coins of various sizes were also countermarked "Nejd". The most common host coins include the Maria Theresa thalers of Austria, British India Rupees, and 5, 10, and 20 Kurush or Qirsh of Turkey and Egypt. The countermark occurs in various sizes and styles of script. These countermarks may have been applied by local silversmiths to discourage re-exportation of the badly needed hard currency and silver of known fineness.

Some crown-sized examples exist with both the "al-Hejaz" and "Nejd" countermarks. The authenticity of the silver countermarked coins has long been discussed, and it is likely that most were privatley produced. Other host coins are considered local or spurious.

**5 PIASTRES KM# 1 Composition:** Silver **Ruler:** Abd Al-Aziz Bin Sa'ud **Countermark:** "Nejd" **Note:** Accession date: AH1327. Countermark on Egypt 5 Piastres, KM#308.

| CM Date | Host Date | Good | VG | F | VF | XF |
|---|---|---|---|---|---|---|
| ND(1918) | AH1327/2H | 30.00 | 60.00 | 120 | 180 | — |
| ND(1918) | AH1327/3H | 25.00 | 50.00 | 100 | 150 | — |
| ND(1918) | AH1327/4H | 25.00 | 50.00 | 100 | 150 | — |
| ND(1918) | AH1327/6H | 25.00 | 50.00 | 100 | 150 | — |

**5 PIASTRES KM# 2.1 (KM2) Composition:** Silver **Countermark:** "Nejd" **Note:** Countermark on Egypt 5 Piastres, KM#318.1. Accession date: AH1335.

| CM Date | Host Date | Good | VG | F | VF | XF |
|---|---|---|---|---|---|---|
| ND(1918) | AH1335-1916 | 25.00 | 50.00 | 100 | 150 | — |
| ND(1918) | AH1335-1917 | 25.00 | 50.00 | 100 | 150 | — |

**5 PIASTRES KM# 2.2 Composition:** Silver **Ruler:** Abd Al-Aziz Bin Sa'ud **Countermark:** "Nejd" **Note:** Countermark on Egypt 5 Piastres, KM#318.2. Accession date: AH1333. Previous KM#2.

| CM Date | Host Date | Good | VG | F | VF | XF |
|---|---|---|---|---|---|---|
| ND(1918) | AH1335-1917H | 25.00 | 50.00 | 100 | 150 | — |

**5 PIASTRES KM# 3 Composition:** Silver **Ruler:** Abd Al-Aziz Bin Sa'ud **Countermark:** "Nejd" **Note:** Countermark on Turkey 5 Kurush, KM#750. Accession date: AH1327.

| CM Date | Host Date | Good | VG | F | VF | XF |
|---|---|---|---|---|---|---|
| ND(1918) | AH1327/1-7 | 25.00 | 50.00 | 100 | 150 | — |

**5 PIASTRES KM# 4 Composition:** Silver **Ruler:** Abd Al-Aziz Bin Sa'ud **Countermark:** "Nejd" **Note:** Countermark on Turkey 5 Kurush, KM#771. Accession date: AH1327.

| CM Date | Host Date | Good | VG | F | VF | XF |
|---|---|---|---|---|---|---|
| ND(1918) | AH1327/7-9 | 25.00 | 50.00 | 100 | 150 | — |

**RUPEE KM# 5 Composition:** Silver **Ruler:** Abd Al-Aziz Bin Sa'ud **Countermark:** "Nejd" **Note:** Countermark on India Rupee, KM#450.

| CM Date | Host Date | Good | VG | F | VF | XF |
|---|---|---|---|---|---|---|
| (1918) | 1835 | 25.00 | 50.00 | 100 | 150 | — |

**RUPEE KM# 6 Composition:** Silver **Ruler:** Abd Al-Aziz Bin Sa'ud **Countermark:** "Nejd" **Note:** Countermark on India Rupee, KM#457.

| CM Date | Host Date | Good | VG | F | VF | XF |
|---|---|---|---|---|---|---|
| (1918) | 1840 | 25.00 | 50.00 | 125 | 275 | — |

**RUPEE KM# 7 Composition:** Silver **Ruler:** Abd Al-Aziz Bin Sa'ud **Countermark:** "Nejd" **Note:** Countermark on India Rupee, KM#458.

| CM Date | Host Date | Good | VG | F | VF | XF |
|---|---|---|---|---|---|---|
| (1918) | 1840 | 25.00 | 50.00 | 125 | 225 | — |

**RUPEE KM# 8 Composition:** Silver **Ruler:** Abd Al-Aziz Bin Sa'ud **Countermark:** "Nejd" **Note:** Countermark on India Rupee, KM#473.

| CM Date | Host Date | Good | VG | F | VF | XF |
|---|---|---|---|---|---|---|
| (1918) | 1862-76 | 25.00 | 50.00 | 100 | 150 | — |

**RUPEE KM# A9 Composition:** Silver **Ruler:** Abd Al-Aziz Bin Sa'ud **Countermark:** "Nejd" **Note:** Countermark on India Rupee, KM#492.

| CM Date | Host Date | Good | VG | F | VF | XF |
|---|---|---|---|---|---|---|
| (1918) | 1877-1901 | 25.00 | 50.00 | 100 | 150 | — |

**10 PIASTRES Composition:** Silver **Countermark:** "Nejde" **Note:** Countermark on Egypt 10 Qirsh, KM#319 or KM#320.

| CM Date | Host Date | Good | VG | F | VF | XF |
|---|---|---|---|---|---|---|
| | 1916-17 | 50.00 | 80.00 | 125 | 200 | — |

**10 PIASTRES KM# 9 Composition:** Silver **Ruler:** Abd Al-Aziz Bin Sa'ud **Countermark:** "Nejd" **Note:** Countermark on Egypt 10 Qirsh, KM#295. Accession date: AH1293.

| CM Date | Host Date | Good | VG | F | VF | XF |
|---|---|---|---|---|---|---|
| ND(1918) | AH1293/27 w | 50.00 | 70.00 | 125 | 200 | — |
| ND(1918) | AH1293/29 w | 50.00 | 70.00 | 125 | 200 | — |
| ND(1918) | AH1293/29H | 50.00 | 70.00 | 125 | 200 | — |
| ND(1918) | AH1293/30H | 50.00 | 70.00 | 125 | 200 | — |
| ND(1918) | AH1293/31H | 60.00 | 90.00 | 150 | 250 | — |
| ND(1918) | AH1293/32H | 50.00 | 70.00 | 125 | 200 | — |
| ND(1918) | AH1293/33H | 50.00 | 70.00 | 125 | 200 | — |

**10 PIASTRES KM# 10 Composition:** Silver **Ruler:** Abd Al-Aziz Bin Sa'ud **Countermark:** "Nejd" **Note:** Countermark on Turkey 10 Kurush, KM#751. Accession date: AH1327.

| CM Date | Host Date | Good | VG | F | VF | XF |
|---|---|---|---|---|---|---|
| ND(1918) | AH1327/1-7 | 50.00 | 70.00 | 125 | 200 | — |

**10 PIASTRES KM# A11.1 Composition:** Silver **Ruler:** Abd Al-Aziz Bin Sa'ud **Countermark:** "Nejd" **Note:** Countermark on Egypt 10 Piastres, KM#319. Accession date: AH1333. Previous KM#A11.

| CM Date | Host Date | Good | VG | F | VF | XF |
|---|---|---|---|---|---|---|
| ND(1918) | AH1335-1916 | 50.00 | 85.00 | 125 | 200 | — |
| ND(1918) | AH1335-1917 | 50.00 | 85.00 | 125 | 200 | — |

**10 PIASTRES KM# A11.2 Composition:** Silver **Ruler:** Abd Al-Aziz Bin Sa'ud **Countermark:** "Nejd" **Note:** Countermark on Egypt 10 Piastres, KM#320. Accession date: AH1333. Previous KM#A11.

| CM Date | Host Date | Good | VG | F | VF | XF |
|---|---|---|---|---|---|---|
| ND(1918) | AH1335-1917H | 50.00 | 85.00 | 125 | 200 | — |

**10 PIASTRES KM# 11 Composition:** Silver **Ruler:** Abd Al-Aziz Bin Sa'ud **Countermark:** "Nejd" **Note:** Countermark on Turkey 10 Kurush, KM#772. Accession date: AH1327.

| CM Date | Host Date | Good | VG | F | VF | XF |
|---|---|---|---|---|---|---|
| ND(1918) | AH1327/7-10 | 50.00 | 70.00 | 125 | 200 | — |

**20 PIASTRES KM# B12.1 (KMB12) Composition:** Silver **Ruler:** Abd Al-Aziz Bin Sa'ud **Countermark:** "Nejd" **Note:** Countermark on Turkey 20 Kurush, KM#675. Accession date: AH1255.

| CM Date | Host Date | Good | VG | F | VF | XF |
|---|---|---|---|---|---|---|
| ND(1918) | AH1255/6-15 | 75.00 | 125 | 200 | 350 | — |

**20 PIASTRES KM# B12.2 Composition:** Silver **Ruler:** Abd Al-Aziz Bin Sa'ud **Countermark:** "Nejd" **Note:** Countermark on Turkey 20 Kurush, KM#676. Accession date: AH1255. Previous KM#B12.

| CM Date | Host Date | Good | VG | F | VF | XF |
|---|---|---|---|---|---|---|
| ND(1918) | AH1255/15-23 | 75.00 | 125 | 200 | 350 | — |

**20 PIASTRES KM# C12 Composition:** Silver **Ruler:** Abd Al-Aziz Bin Sa'ud **Countermark:** "Nejd" **Note:** Countermark on Turkey 20 Kurush, KM#693. Accession date: AH1277.

| CM Date | Host Date | Good | VG | F | VF | XF |
|---|---|---|---|---|---|---|
| ND(1918) | AH1277/1-15 | 75.00 | 125 | 200 | 350 | — |

**20 PIASTRES KM# A12 Composition:** Silver **Ruler:** Abd Al-Aziz Bin Sa'ud **Countermark:** "Nejd" **Note:** Countermark on Turkey 20 Kurush, KM#722. Accession date: AH1293.

| CM Date | Host Date | Good | VG | F | VF | XF |
|---|---|---|---|---|---|---|
| ND(1918) | AH1293/1-3 | 75.00 | 125 | 200 | 350 | — |

**20 PIASTRES KM# 12 Composition:** Silver **Ruler:** Abd Al-Aziz Bin Sa'ud **Countermark:** "Nejd" **Note:** Countermark on Egypt 20 Qirsh, KM#310. Accession date: AH1327.

| CM Date | Host Date | Good | VG | F | VF | XF |
|---|---|---|---|---|---|---|
| ND(1918) | AH1327/2H | 75.00 | 125 | 200 | 350 | — |
| ND(1918) | AH1327/3H | 75.00 | 125 | 200 | 350 | — |
| ND(1918) | AH1327/4H | 75.00 | 125 | 200 | 350 | — |
| ND(1918) | AH1327/6H | 75.00 | 125 | 200 | 350 | — |

**20 PIASTRES KM# A13.1 Composition:** Silver **Ruler:** Abd Al-Aziz Bin Sa'ud **Countermark:** "Nejd" **Note:** Countermark on Egypt 20 Piastres, KM#321. Accession date: 1333.

| CM Date | Host Date | Good | VG | F | VF | XF |
|---|---|---|---|---|---|---|
| ND(1918) | AH1335-1916 | 75.00 | 125 | 200 | 350 | — |
| ND(1918) | AH1335-1917 | 75.00 | 125 | 200 | 350 | — |

**20 PIASTRES KM# A13.2 Composition:** Silver **Ruler:** Abd Al-Aziz Bin Sa'ud **Countermark:** "Nejd" **Note:** Countermark on Egypt 20 Piastres, KM#322. Accession date: 1333.

| CM Date | Host Date | Good | VG | F | VF | XF |
|---|---|---|---|---|---|---|
| ND(1918) | AH1335-1917H | 90.00 | 150 | 250 | 425 | — |

**20 PIASTRES KM# 13 Composition:** Silver **Ruler:** Abd Al-Aziz Bin Sa'ud **Countermark:** "Nejd" **Note:** Countermark on Turkey 20 Kurush, KM#780. Accession date: AH1327.

| CM Date | Host Date | Good | VG | F | VF | XF |
|---|---|---|---|---|---|---|
| ND(1918) | AH1327/8-10 | 75.00 | 125 | 200 | 350 | — |

**20 PIASTRES KM# 14 Composition:** Silver **Ruler:** Abd Al-Aziz Bin Sa'ud **Countermark:** "Nejd" **Note:** Countermark on Austria Maria Theresa Thaler, KM#T1.

| CM Date | Host Date | Good | VG | F | VF | XF |
|---|---|---|---|---|---|---|
| (1918) | 1780 Restrike | 40.00 | 80.00 | 200 | 425 | — |

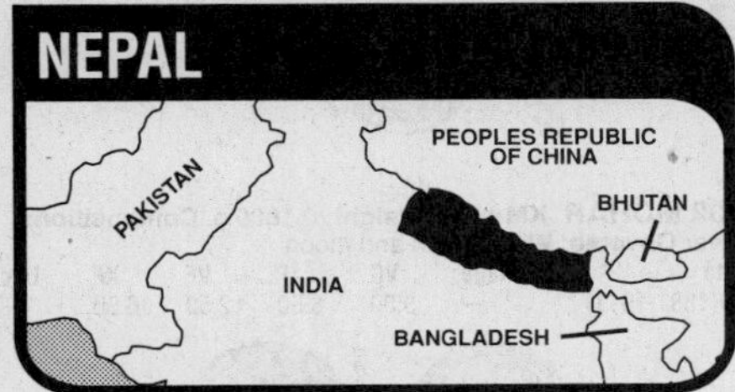


The Kingdom of Nepal, the world's only surviving Hindu kingdom, is a landlocked country occupying the southern slopes of the Himalayas. It has an area of 56,136 sq. mi. (140,800 sq. km.) and a population of 18 million. Capital: Kathmandu. Nepal has deposits of coal, copper, iron and cobalt, but they are largely unexploited. Agriculture is the principal economic activity. Rice, timber and jute are exported, with tourism being the other major foreign exchange earner.

Apart from a brief Muslim invasion in the 14th century, Nepal was able to avoid the mainstream of Northern Indian politics, due to its impregnable position in the mountains. It is therefore a unique survivor of the medieval Hindu and Buddhist culture of Northern India, which was largely destroyed by the successive waves of Muslim invasions.

Prior to the late 18th century, Nepal, as we know it today, was divided among a number of small states. Unless otherwise stated, the term *Nepal* applies to the small fertile valley, about 4,500 ft. above sea level, in which the three main cities of Kathmandu, Patan and Bhatgaon are situated.

During the reign of King Yaksha Malla (1428-1482AD), the Nepalese kingdom, with capital at Bhatgaon, was extended northwards into Tibet, and also controlled a considerable area to the south of the hills. After Yaksha Malla's death, the Kingdom was divided among his sons, so four kingdoms were established with capitals at Bhatgaon, Patan, Kathmandu and Banepa, all situated within the small valley, less than 20 miles square. Banepa was quickly absorbed within the territory of Bhatgaon, but the other three kingdoms remained until 1769. The internecine strife between the three kings effectively stopped Nepal from becoming a major military force during this period, although with its fertile land and strategic position, it was by far the wealthiest and most powerful of the Himalayan states.

Apart from agriculture, Nepal owed its prosperity to its position on one of the easiest trade routes between the great monasteries of central Tibet, and India. Nepal made full use of this, and a trading community was set up in Lhasa during the 16th century, and Nepalese coins became the accepted currency medium in Tibet.

The seeds of discord between Nepal and Tibet were sown during the first half of the 18th century, when the Nepalese debased the coinage, and the fate of the Malla kings of Nepal was sealed when Prithvi Narayan Shah, King of the small state of Gorkha, to the west of Kathmandu, was able to gain control of the trans-himalayan trade routes during the years after 1750.

Prithvi Narayan spent several years consolidating his position in hill areas before he finally succeeded in conquering the Kathmandu Valley in 1768, where he established the Shah dynasty, and moved his capital to Kathmandu.

After Prithvi Narayan's death a period of political instability ensued which lasted until the 1840's when the Rana family reduced the monarch to a figurehead and established the post of hereditary Prime Minister. A popular revolution in 1950 toppled the Rana family and reconstituted power in the throne. In 1959 King Mahendra declared Nepal a constitutional monarchy, and in 1962 a new constitution set up a system of *panchayat* (village council) democracy. In 1990, following political unrest, the king's powers were reduced. The country then adopted a system of parliamentary democracy.

On June 2, 2001 tragedy struck the royal family when Crown Prince Dipendra used an assault rifle to kill his father, mother and other members of the royal family as the result of a dispute over his current lady friend. He died 48 hours later, as King, from self inflicted gunshot wounds. Gyanendra began his second reign as King (his first was a short time as a toddler, 1950-51).

## DATING

### Saka Era (SE)

Up until 1888AD all coins of the Gorkha Dynasty were dated in the Saka era (SE). To convert from Saka to AD take Saka date and add 78 to arrive at the AD date. Coins dated with this era have SE before the date in the following listing.

### Bikram Samvat Era (VS)

From 1888AD most copper coins were dated in the Bikram Samvat (VS) era. To convert take VS date - 57 =AD date. Coins with this era have VS before the year in the listing. With the exception of a few gold coins struck in 1890 & 1892, silver and gold coins only changed to the VS era in 1911AD, but now this era is used for all coins struck in Nepal.

## RULERS

### SHAH DYNASTY

Prithvi Bira Bikrama

पृथ्वी वीर विक्रम

SE1803-1833/1881-1911AD, VS1938-1968/
Queen of Prithvi Bir Bikrama: Lakshmi Divyeswari

लक्ष्मी दिव्येश्वरी

Tribhuvana Bir Bikram

त्रिभुवनवीर विक्रम

VS1968-2007, 2007-2011/1911-1950, 1951-1955AD (first reign)
VS2058- / 2001- AD (second reign)
Gyanendra Bir Bikram

ज्ञानेन्द्वीर विक्रम

VS2007/1950-1951AD
Mahendra Bir Bikram

महेन्द्रवीर विक्रम

VS2012-2028/1955-1971AD
Queen of Mahendra Bir Bikrama: Ratna Rajya Lakshmi

रत्न राज लक्ष्मी

Virendra Bir Bikram

वीरेन्द्र वीर विक्रम

VS2028-2058 /1971-2001AD
Queen of Virendra Bir Bikram: Aishvarya Rajya Lakshmi

ऐश्वर्य राज्य लक्ष्मी देवी

VS2028-2058 /1971-2001AD

VS2058 / 2001AD (reign of 48 hours)
Dipendra Bir Bikram

## MONETARY SYSTEM

Many of the mohars circulated in Tibet as well as in Nepal, and on a number of occasions coins were struck from bullion supplied by the Tibetan authorities. The smaller denominations never circulated in Tibet, but some of the mohars were cut for use as small change in Tibet.

In these listings only major changes in design have been noted. There are numerous minor varieties of ornamentation or spelling.

With a few exceptions, most all coins were struck at Kathmandu.

### COPPER

Initially the copper paisa was not fixed in value relative to the silver coins, and generally fluctuated in value from1/32 mohar in 1865AD to around 1/50 mohar afterc1880AD, and was fixed at that value in 1903AD.

4 Dam = 1 Paisa
2 Paisa = 1 Dyak, Adhani

### COPPER and SILVER

Decimal Series

100 Paisa = 1 Rupee

Although the value of the copper paisa was fixed at 100 paisa to the rupee in 1903, it was not until 1932 that silver coins were struck in the decimal system.

### GOLD COINAGE

Nepalese gold coinage, until recently, did not carry any denominations and was traded for silver, etc. at the local bullion exchange rate. The three basic weight standards used in the following listing are distinguished for convenience, although all were known as Asarphi (gold coin) locally as follows:

### GOLD MOHAR

5.60 g multiples and fractions

### TOLA

12.48 g multiples and fractions

### GOLD RUPEE or ASHRAPI

11.66 g multiples and fractions
(Reduced to 10.00 g in 1966)

**NOTE:** In some instances the gold and silver issues were struck from the same dies.

## NUMERALS

Nepal has used more variations of numerals on theircoins than any other nation. The most common are illustrated in the numeral chart in the introduction. The chart below illustrates some variations encompassing the last four centuries.

| 1 | 2 | 3 | 4 | 5 | 6 | 7 | 8 | 9 | 0 |
|---|---|---|---|---|---|---|---|---|---|
| १ | २ | ३ | ४ | ५ | ६ | ७ | ८ | ९ | ० |

### NUMERICS

| | |
|---|---|
| Half | आधा |
| One | एक |
| Two | दुइ |
| Four | चार |
| Five | पाँच |
| Ten | दस |
| Twenty | विस |
| Twenty-five | पचीस |
| Fifty | पचास |
| Hundred | सय |

### DENOMINATIONS

| | |
|---|---|
| Paisa | पैसा |
| Dam | दाम |
| Mohar | मोहर |
| Rupee | रुपैयाँ |
| Ashrapi | अश्रफी |
| Asarfi | असर्फी |

### DIE VARIETIES

**DIE VARIETIES**

Although the same dies were usually used both for silver and gold minor denominations, the gold Mohar is easily recognized being less ornate. The following illustrations are of a silver Mohar, KM#602 and a gold Mohar KM#615 issued by Surendra Bikram Saha Deva in the period SE1769-1803/1847-1881AD. Note the similar reverse legend. The obverse usually will start with the character for the word Shri either in single or multiples, the latter as Shri Shri Shri or Shri 3.

### OBVERSE

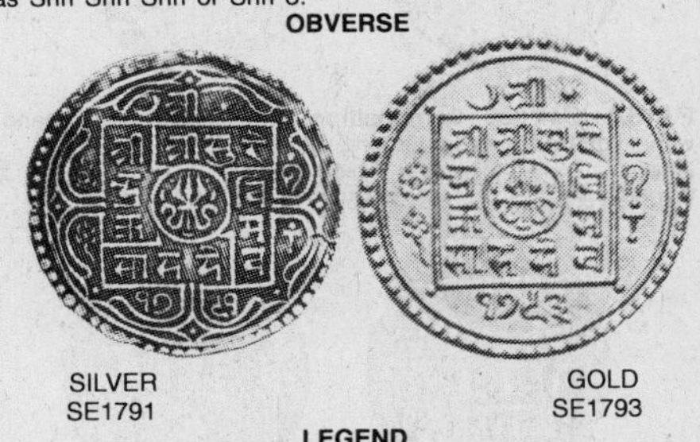

SILVER SE1791 GOLD SE1793

### LEGEND

श्री श्रीश्री सुरेन्द्र बिक्रम साहदेव

Shri Shri Shri Surendra Bikrama Saha Deva (date).

REVERSE

SILVER GOLD

**LEGEND**
(in center)

श्री ३ भवानी

**Shri 3 Bhavani**
(around outer circle)

श्री श्री श्री गोरखनाथ

Shri Shri Shri Gorakhanatha

## KINGDOM

### Shah Dynasty.

## Prithvi Bir Bikram

### VS1938-1968 / 1881-1911AD

### COPPER COINAGE

**1/2 PAISA** **KM# 622** **Composition:** Copper

| Date | Mintage | F | VF | XF | Unc |
|---|---|---|---|---|---|
| VS(19)64(1907) | — | 4.50 | 7.50 | 10.00 | 17.50 |
| VS(19)68(1911) | — | 4.50 | 7.50 | 10.00 | 17.50 |

**PAISA** **KM# 629** **Composition:** Copper **Obverse:** Legend within squares **Reverse:** Legend within squares

| Date | Mintage | Good | VG | F | VF | XF |
|---|---|---|---|---|---|---|
| VS1959(1902) | — | 1.00 | 1.50 | 2.50 | 4.00 | — |
| VS1962(1905) | — | 1.00 | 1.50 | 2.50 | 4.00 | — |
| VS1963(1906) | — | 1.00 | 1.50 | 2.50 | 4.00 | — |
| VS1964(1907) | — | 1.00 | 1.50 | 2.50 | 4.00 | — |
| VS1965(1908) | — | 1.00 | 1.50 | 2.50 | 4.00 | — |
| VS1966(1909) | — | 1.00 | 1.50 | 2.50 | 4.00 | — |
| VS1967(1910) | — | 1.00 | 1.50 | 2.50 | 4.00 | — |
| VS1968(1911) | — | 1.00 | 1.50 | 2.50 | 4.00 | — |

**PAISA** **KM# 630** **Composition:** Copper **Obverse:** Legend within square **Reverse:** Legend within circle

| Date | Mintage | Good | VG | F | VF | XF |
|---|---|---|---|---|---|---|
| VS1959(1902) | — | 7.50 | 12.50 | 20.00 | 33.50 | — |

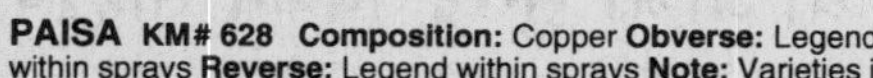

**PAISA** **KM# 628** **Composition:** Copper **Obverse:** Legend within sprays **Reverse:** Legend within sprays **Note:** Varieties in sprays exist. Coin and medal strikes exist. Coin and medal alignment varieties exist.

| Date | Mintage | Good | VG | F | VF | XF |
|---|---|---|---|---|---|---|
| VS1959(1902) | — | 1.00 | 1.50 | 3.00 | 5.00 | — |
| VS1960(1903) | — | 1.00 | 1.50 | 3.00 | 5.00 | — |
| VS1961(1904) | — | 1.00 | 1.50 | 3.00 | 5.00 | — |
| VS1962(1905) | — | 1.00 | 1.50 | 3.00 | 5.00 | — |
| VS1963(1906) | — | 1.00 | 1.50 | 3.00 | 5.00 | — |
| VS1964(1907) | — | 1.00 | 1.50 | 3.00 | 5.00 | — |

**PAISA** **KM# 631** **Composition:** Copper

| Date | Mintage | F | VF | XF | Unc |
|---|---|---|---|---|---|
| VS1964(1907) | — | 5.50 | 9.00 | 15.00 | 22.50 |
| VS1968(1911) | — | 8.50 | 13.50 | 20.00 | 30.00 |

**2 PAISA (Dak)** **KM# 633** **Composition:** Copper **Obverse:** Legend within square **Reverse:** Legend within circle

| Date | Mintage | Good | VG | F | VF | XF |
|---|---|---|---|---|---|---|
| VS1959(1902) | — | 12.50 | 17.50 | 25.00 | 50.00 | — |

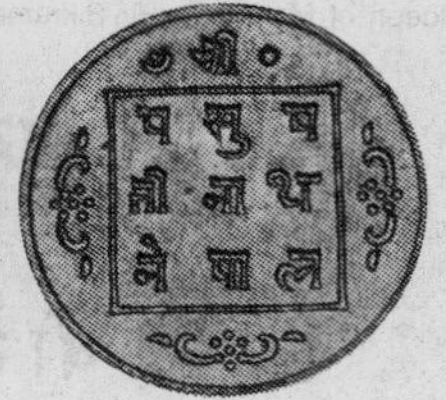

**2 PAISA (Dak)** **KM# 634** **Composition:** Copper

| Date | Mintage | F | VF | XF | Unc |
|---|---|---|---|---|---|
| VS1964(1907) | — | 8.50 | 13.50 | 20.00 | 30.00 |
| VS1968(1911) | — | 9.00 | 15.00 | 22.50 | 35.00 |

**DAM** **KM# 620.2** **Composition:** Copper

| Date | Mintage | F | VF | XF | Unc |
|---|---|---|---|---|---|
| VS(19)64(1907) | — | 7.50 | 12.00 | 15.00 | 20.00 |

**DAM** **KM# 621** **Composition:** Copper

| Date | Mintage | F | VF | XF | Unc |
|---|---|---|---|---|---|
| VS(19)68(1911) | — | 4.50 | 7.50 | 10.00 | 17.50 |

### SILVER COINAGE

**DAM** **KM# 636** **Weight:** 0.0400 g. **Composition:** Silver **Note:** Four characters around sword.

| Date | Mintage | VG | F | VF | XF | Unc |
|---|---|---|---|---|---|---|
| ND(1881-1911) | — | — | 15.00 | 25.00 | 30.00 | 40.00 |

**DAM** **KM# 635** **Weight:** 0.0400 g. **Composition:** Silver **Note:** Uniface. Five characters around sword.

| Date | Mintage | VG | F | VF | XF | Unc |
|---|---|---|---|---|---|---|
| ND(1881-1911) | — | — | 8.00 | 10.00 | 15.00 | 25.00 |

**1/32 MOHAR** **KM# 637** **Weight:** 0.1800 g. **Composition:** Silver **Obverse:** Sun and moon

| Date | Mintage | VG | F | VF | XF | Unc |
|---|---|---|---|---|---|---|
| ND(1881-1911) | — | 5.00 | 8.50 | 12.50 | 16.50 | — |

**1/32 MOHAR** **KM# 638** **Weight:** 0.1800 g. **Composition:** Silver **Obverse:** Without sun and moon

| Date | Mintage | VG | F | VF | XF | Unc |
|---|---|---|---|---|---|---|
| ND(1881-1911) | — | 5.00 | 8.50 | 12.50 | 16.50 | — |

**1/16 MOHAR** **KM# 639** **Weight:** 0.3500 g. **Composition:** Silver **Note:** Varieties exist.

| Date | Mintage | VG | F | VF | XF | Unc |
|---|---|---|---|---|---|---|
| ND(1881-1911) | — | — | 6.00 | 10.00 | 13.50 | 20.00 |

**1/8 MOHAR** **KM# 640** **Weight:** 0.7000 g. **Composition:** Silver **Note:** Varieties exist.

| Date | Mintage | VG | F | VF | XF | Unc |
|---|---|---|---|---|---|---|
| ND(1881-1911) | — | — | 7.50 | 12.50 | 18.50 | 27.50 |

**1/4 MOHAR** **KM# 643** **Weight:** 1.4000 g. **Composition:** Silver **Reverse:** Moon and dot for sun

| Date | Mintage | VG | F | VF | XF | Unc |
|---|---|---|---|---|---|---|
| SE1827(1905) | — | 1.75 | 3.00 | 5.00 | 7.00 | — |

**1/4 MOHAR** **KM# 644** **Weight:** 1.4000 g. **Composition:** Silver **Note:** Machine struck.

| Date | Mintage | VG | F | VF | XF | Unc |
|---|---|---|---|---|---|---|
| SE1833(1911) | — | 1.75 | 3.00 | 5.00 | 7.00 | — |
| SE1833 Proof | — | Value: 25.00 | | | | |

**1/2 MOHAR** **KM# 647** **Weight:** 2.7700 g. **Composition:** Silver **Edge:** Plain **Note:** Machine struck. Varieties exist.

| Date | Mintage | F | VF | XF | Unc |
|---|---|---|---|---|---|
| SE1824(1902) | — | 20.00 | 25.00 | 30.00 | 35.00 |

**1/2 MOHAR** **KM# 648** **Weight:** 2.7700 g. **Composition:** Silver

| Date | Mintage | F | VF | XF | Unc |
|---|---|---|---|---|---|
| SE1826(1904) | — | 3.00 | 5.00 | 7.00 | 10.00 |
| SE1827(1905) | — | 3.00 | 5.00 | 7.00 | 10.00 |
| SE1829(1907) | — | 3.50 | 5.50 | 8.50 | 11.50 |

**1/2 MOHAR** **KM# 649** **Weight:** 2.7700 g. **Composition:** Silver **Edge:** Milled **Note:** Machine struck.

| Date | Mintage | F | VF | XF | Unc |
|---|---|---|---|---|---|
| SE1832(1910) | — | 20.00 | 25.00 | 30.00 | 35.00 |
| SE1833(1911) | — | 2.25 | 3.50 | 5.00 | 7.00 |
| SE1833(1911) Proof | — | Value: 35.00 | | | |

**MOHAR** **KM# 651.1** **Weight:** 5.6000 g. **Composition:** Silver **Edge:** Plain **Note:** Machine struck.

| Date | Mintage | F | VF | XF | Unc |
|---|---|---|---|---|---|
| SE1823(1901) | — | 4.50 | 6.50 | 8.00 | 10.00 |
| SE1824(1902) | — | 4.50 | 6.50 | 8.00 | 10.00 |
| SE1825(1903) | — | 4.50 | 6.50 | 8.00 | 10.00 |
| SE1826(1904) | — | 4.50 | 6.50 | 8.00 | 10.00 |
| SE1827(1905) | — | 4.50 | 6.50 | 8.00 | 10.00 |

**MOHAR** **KM# 652** **Weight:** 5.6000 g. **Composition:** Silver **Reverse:** Gold die, in error

| Date | Mintage | F | VF | XF | Unc |
|---|---|---|---|---|---|
| SE1825(1903) | — | 10.00 | 15.00 | 25.00 | 32.50 |

**MOHAR** **KM# 651.2** **Weight:** 5.6000 g. **Composition:** Silver **Edge:** Milled **Note:** Machine struck.

| Date | Mintage | F | VF | XF | Unc |
|---|---|---|---|---|---|
| SE1826(1904) | — | 4.50 | 6.50 | 8.00 | 10.00 |
| SE1827(1905) | — | 4.50 | 6.50 | 8.00 | 10.00 |
| SE1828(1906) | — | 4.50 | 6.50 | 8.00 | 10.00 |
| SE1829(1907) | — | 4.50 | 6.50 | 8.00 | 10.00 |
| SE1830(1908) | — | 4.50 | 6.50 | 8.00 | 10.00 |
| SE1831(1909) | — | 4.50 | 6.50 | 8.00 | 10.00 |
| SE1832(1910) | — | 4.50 | 6.50 | 8.00 | 10.00 |
| SE1833(1911) | — | — | 25.00 | 35.00 | 50.00 |

**Note:** The date 1833 was only issued in presentation sets

**2 MOHARS** **KM# 655** **Weight:** 11.2000 g. **Composition:** Silver **Edge:** Milled **Note:** Machine struck.

| Date | Mintage | F | VF | XF | Unc |
|---|---|---|---|---|---|
| SE1829(1907) | — | 15.00 | 27.50 | 40.00 | 60.00 |
| SE1831(1909) | — | 6.00 | 9.00 | 12.50 | 20.00 |

**2 MOHARS** **KM# 656** **Composition:** Silver **Note:** Machine struck.

| Date | Mintage | F | VF | XF | Unc |
|---|---|---|---|---|---|
| SE1832(1910) | — | 7.00 | 9.00 | 11.50 | 18.50 |
| SE1833(1911) | — | 6.00 | 8.00 | 10.00 | 16.50 |

**4 MOHARS** **KM# 658** **Weight:** 22.4000 g. **Composition:** Silver **Edge:** Milled

| Date | Mintage | F | VF | XF | Unc |
|---|---|---|---|---|---|
| SE1833(1911) | — | 60.00 | 100 | 140 | 200 |

## GOLD COINAGE

**DAM** **KM# 661** **Weight:** 0.0400 g. **Composition:** Gold **Note:** Uniface. Circle around characters.

| Date | Mintage | VG | F | VF | XF | Unc |
|---|---|---|---|---|---|---|
| ND(1881-1911) | — | — | 10.00 | 14.00 | 20.00 | 27.50 |

**DAM** **KM# 659** **Weight:** 0.0400 g. **Composition:** Gold **Note:** Uniface. Five characters around sword. Similar to 1/64 Mohar, KM#664.

| Date | Mintage | VG | F | VF | XF | Unc |
|---|---|---|---|---|---|---|
| ND(1881-1911) | — | — | 10.00 | 14.00 | 20.00 | 27.50 |

**DAM** **KM# 660** **Weight:** 0.0400 g. **Composition:** Gold **Note:** Uniface. Four characters around sword. Similar to 1/64 Mohar, KM#663.

| Date | Mintage | VG | F | VF | XF | Unc |
|---|---|---|---|---|---|---|
| ND(1881-1911) | — | — | 10.00 | 14.00 | 20.00 | 27.50 |

**DAM** **KM# 662** **Weight:** 0.0400 g. **Composition:** Gold **Note:** Uniface. Two characters below sword.

| Date | Mintage | VG | F | VF | XF | Unc |
|---|---|---|---|---|---|---|
| ND(1881-1911) | — | — | 10.00 | 14.00 | 20.00 | 27.50 |

**1/64 MOHAR** **KM# 664** **Weight:** 0.0900 g. **Composition:** Gold **Note:** Uniface. Five characters around sword.

| Date | Mintage | VG | F | VF | XF | Unc |
|---|---|---|---|---|---|---|
| ND(1881-1911) | — | — | 12.50 | 17.50 | 22.50 | 30.00 |

**1/64 MOHAR** **KM# 663** **Weight:** 0.0900 g. **Composition:** Gold **Note:** Uniface. Four characters around sword.

| Date | Mintage | VG | F | VF | XF | Unc |
|---|---|---|---|---|---|---|
| ND(1881-1911) | — | — | 12.50 | 17.50 | 22.50 | 30.00 |

**1/32 MOHAR** **KM# 665** **Weight:** 0.1800 g. **Composition:** Gold **Note:** Uniface. Five characters around sword.

| Date | Mintage | VG | F | VF | XF | Unc |
|---|---|---|---|---|---|---|
| ND(1881-1911) | — | — | 20.00 | 40.00 | 75.00 | 100 |

**1/32 MOHAR** **KM# 666** **Weight:** 0.1800 g. **Composition:** Gold **Note:** Uniface. Four characters around sword.

| Date | Mintage | VG | F | VF | XF | Unc |
|---|---|---|---|---|---|---|
| ND(1881-1911) | — | — | 15.00 | 30.00 | 75.00 | 100 |

**1/16 MOHAR** **KM# 667** **Weight:** 0.3500 g. **Composition:** Gold

| Date | Mintage | VG | F | VF | XF | Unc |
|---|---|---|---|---|---|---|
| ND(1881-1911) | — | — | 15.00 | 40.00 | 75.00 | 100 |

**1/16 MOHAR** **KM# 668** **Weight:** 0.3500 g. **Composition:** Gold

| Date | Mintage | F | VF | XF | Unc |
|---|---|---|---|---|---|
| SE(18)33(1911) | — | 15.00 | 30.00 | 75.00 | 100 |

**1/8 MOHAR** **KM# 670** **Weight:** 0.7000 g. **Composition:** Gold

| Date | Mintage | F | VF | XF | Unc |
|---|---|---|---|---|---|
| SE(18)33(1911) | — | 22.50 | 40.00 | 75.00 | 100 |

**1/4 MOHAR** **KM# 671.1** **Weight:** 1.4000 g. **Composition:** Gold

| Date | Mintage | F | VF | XF | Unc |
|---|---|---|---|---|---|
| SE1823(1901) | — | 45.00 | 60.00 | 80.00 | 100 |
| SE1829(1907) | — | 40.00 | 50.00 | 60.00 | 80.00 |

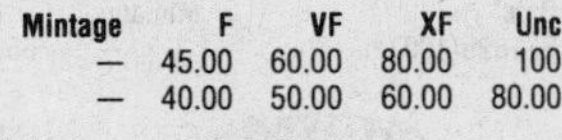

**1/4 MOHAR** **KM# 671.2** **Weight:** 1.4000 g. **Composition:** Gold

| Date | Mintage | F | VF | XF | Unc |
|---|---|---|---|---|---|
| SE1833(1911) | — | 40.00 | 50.00 | 60.00 | 80.00 |

**1/2 MOHAR** **KM# 672.3** **Weight:** 2.8000 g. **Composition:** Gold

| Date | Mintage | F | VF | XF | Unc |
|---|---|---|---|---|---|
| SE1823(1901) | — | 70.00 | 80.00 | 100 | 125 |

**1/2 MOHAR** **KM# 672.4** **Weight:** 2.8000 g. **Composition:** Gold

| Date | Mintage | F | VF | XF | Unc |
|---|---|---|---|---|---|
| SE1829(1907) | — | 65.00 | 75.00 | 85.00 | 100 |

**1/2 MOHAR** **KM# 672.5** **Weight:** 2.8000 g. **Composition:** Gold

| Date | Mintage | F | VF | XF | Unc |
|---|---|---|---|---|---|
| SE1833(1911) | — | 65.00 | 75.00 | 85.00 | 100 |

**MOHAR** **KM# 673.1** **Weight:** 5.6000 g. **Composition:** Gold

| Date | Mintage | F | VF | XF | Unc |
|---|---|---|---|---|---|
| SE1823(1901) | — | 115 | 125 | 150 | 200 |
| SE1825(1903) | — | 115 | 125 | 150 | 200 |
| SE1826(1904) | — | 115 | 125 | 150 | 200 |
| SE1827(1905) | — | 115 | 125 | 150 | 200 |

**MOHAR** **KM# 673.2** **Weight:** 5.6000 g. **Composition:** Gold **Edge:** Milled

| Date | Mintage | F | VF | XF | Unc |
|---|---|---|---|---|---|
| SE1828(1906) | — | 115 | 125 | 150 | 200 |
| SE1829(1907) | — | 115 | 125 | 150 | 200 |
| SE1831(1909) | — | 115 | 125 | 150 | 200 |
| SE1833(1911) | — | 115 | 125 | 150 | 200 |

**TOLA** KM# 674.3 **Weight:** 12.4800 g. **Composition:** Gold **Edge:** Plain

| Date | Mintage | F | VF | XF | Unc |
|---|---|---|---|---|---|
| SE1823(1901) | — | 235 | 255 | 275 | 300 |
| SE1824(1902) | — | 235 | 255 | 275 | 300 |
| SE1825(1903) | — | 235 | 255 | 275 | 300 |
| SE1826(1904) | — | 235 | 255 | 275 | 300 |

**TOLA** KM# 675.1 **Weight:** 12.4800 g. **Composition:** Gold **Edge:** Vertical milling

| Date | Mintage | F | VF | XF | Unc |
|---|---|---|---|---|---|
| SE1828(1906) | — | 235 | 255 | 275 | 300 |
| SE1829(1907) | — | 235 | 255 | 275 | 300 |
| SE1831(1909) | — | 235 | 255 | 275 | 300 |
| SE1832(1910) | — | 235 | 255 | 275 | 300 |
| SE1833(1911) | — | 235 | 255 | 275 | 300 |

**DUITOLA ASARPHI** KM# 679 **Weight:** 23.3200 g. **Composition:** Gold **Edge:** Milled

| Date | Mintage | F | VF | XF | Unc |
|---|---|---|---|---|---|
| SE1829(1907) | — | 550 | 600 | 700 | 800 |

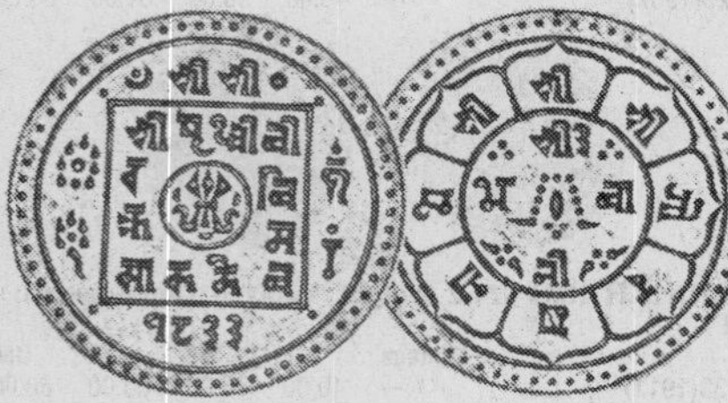

**DUITOLA ASARPHI** KM# 680 **Weight:** 23.3200 g. **Composition:** Gold **Edge:** Milled

| Date | Mintage | F | VF | XF | Unc |
|---|---|---|---|---|---|
| SE1833(1911) | — | 550 | 600 | 700 | 800 |

## TOKEN COINAGE

**12 PAISA** KM# Tn1 **Composition:** Iron

| Date | Mintage | VG | F | VF | XF | Unc |
|---|---|---|---|---|---|---|
| ND | — | 3.50 | 8.50 | 15.00 | 25.00 | — |

**14 PAISA** KM# Tn2 **Composition:** Iron

| Date | Mintage | VG | F | VF | XF | Unc |
|---|---|---|---|---|---|---|
| ND | — | 3.50 | 8.50 | 15.00 | 25.00 | — |

**16 PAISA** KM# Tn3 **Composition:** Brass

| Date | Mintage | VG | F | VF | XF | Unc |
|---|---|---|---|---|---|---|
| SE1824(1902) | — | 5.00 | 10.00 | 20.00 | 35.00 | — |

# Tribhuvan Bir Bikram

### VS1968-2007 / 1911-1950AD

## COPPER COINAGE

**1/2 PAISA** KM# 684 **Composition:** Copper **Note:** Struck only for presentation sets.

| Date | Mintage | F | VF | XF | Unc |
|---|---|---|---|---|---|
| VS1978(1921) | | | — | 50.00 | 75.00 |
| VS1985(1928) | — | — | — | 50.00 | 75.00 |

**PAISA** KM# 685.1 **Composition:** Copper **Note:** Machine struck.

| Date | Mintage | Good | VG | F | VF | XF |
|---|---|---|---|---|---|---|
| VS1968(1911) | — | 10.00 | 20.00 | 50.00 | 75.00 | — |

**PAISA** KM# 685.2 **Composition:** Copper **Note:** Hand struck.

| Date | Mintage | Good | VG | F | VF | XF |
|---|---|---|---|---|---|---|
| VS1969(1912) | — | 1.00 | 1.50 | 2.25 | 3.50 | — |
| VS1970(1913) | — | 1.00 | 1.50 | 2.25 | 3.50 | — |
| VS1971(1914) | — | 1.00 | 1.50 | 2.25 | 3.50 | — |
| VS1972(1915) | — | 1.00 | 1.50 | 2.25 | 3.50 | — |
| VS1973(1916) | — | 1.00 | 1.50 | 2.25 | 3.50 | — |
| VS1974(1917) | — | 1.00 | 1.50 | 2.25 | 3.50 | — |
| VS1975(1918) | — | 1.00 | 1.50 | 2.25 | 3.50 | — |
| VS1976(1919) | — | 1.00 | 1.50 | 2.25 | 3.50 | — |
| VS1977(1920) | — | 1.00 | 1.50 | 2.25 | 3.50 | — |

**PAISA** KM# 687.1 **Weight:** 3.7500 g. **Composition:** Copper **Note:** Machine struck. Varieties of the Khukris exist.

| Date | Mintage | F | VF | XF | Unc |
|---|---|---|---|---|---|
| VS1975(1918) | — | 1.25 | 1.75 | 3.00 | 6.00 |
| VS1976(1919) | — | 1.25 | 1.75 | 3.00 | 6.00 |
| VS1977(1920) | — | 1.25 | 1.75 | 3.00 | 6.00 |
| VS1977(1920) Inverted date | — | 3.00 | 4.50 | 7.50 | 15.00 |

**PAISA** KM# 686.1 **Composition:** Copper

| Date | Mintage | F | VF | XF | Unc |
|---|---|---|---|---|---|
| VS1975(1918) | — | — | — | 37.50 | 50.00 |

**PAISA** KM# 686.2 **Composition:** Copper

| Date | Mintage | Good | VG | F | VF | XF |
|---|---|---|---|---|---|---|
| VS1975(1918) | — | — | — | 60.00 | 90.00 | — |

**Note:** The above issues are believed to be patterns

**PAISA** KM# 687.2 **Weight:** 3.7500 g. **Composition:** Copper **Note:** Crude, hand struck. Varieties of the Khukris exist.

| Date | Mintage | Good | VG | F | VF | XF |
|---|---|---|---|---|---|---|
| VS1978(1921) | — | 2.00 | 3.00 | 4.50 | 7.50 | — |
| VS1979(1922) | — | 2.00 | 3.00 | 4.50 | 7.50 | — |
| VS1980(1923) | — | 4.00 | 5.00 | 7.50 | 12.50 | — |
| VS1981(1924) | — | 4.00 | 5.00 | 7.50 | 12.50 | — |
| VS1982(1925) | — | 4.00 | 5.00 | 7.50 | 12.50 | — |
| VS1983(1926) | — | 4.00 | 5.00 | 7.50 | 12.50 | — |

**PAISA** KM# 688 **Weight:** 2.8000 g. **Composition:** Copper **Note:** Machine struck.

| Date | Mintage | F | VF | XF | Unc |
|---|---|---|---|---|---|
| VS1978(1921) | — | 1.25 | 1.75 | 3.00 | 6.00 |
| VS1979(1922) | — | 1.25 | 1.75 | 3.00 | 6.00 |
| VS1980(1923) | — | 1.50 | 3.00 | 5.00 | 10.00 |
| VS1981(1924) | — | 1.50 | 3.00 | 5.00 | 10.00 |
| VS1982(1925) | — | 1.25 | 1.75 | 3.00 | 6.00 |
| VS1984(1927) | — | 1.25 | 1.75 | 3.00 | 6.00 |
| VS1985(1928) | — | 1.25 | 1.75 | 3.00 | 6.00 |
| VS1986(1929) | — | 1.25 | 1.75 | 3.00 | 6.00 |
| VS1987(1930) | — | 1.25 | 1.75 | 3.00 | 6.00 |

**2 PAISA** KM# 689.1 **Weight:** 7.5000 g. **Composition:** Copper **Note:** Machine struck. Varieties of the Khukris exist.

| Date | Mintage | VG | F | VF | XF | Unc |
|---|---|---|---|---|---|---|
| VS1976(1919) | — | 1.00 | 2.00 | 3.00 | 5.00 | — |
| VS1977(1920) | — | 1.00 | 2.00 | 3.00 | 5.00 | — |
| VS1977(1920) Inverted date | — | 3.50 | 5.00 | 8.50 | 13.50 | — |

**2 PAISA** KM# 689.2 **Weight:** 7.5000 g. **Composition:** Copper **Note:** Crude struck. Varieties of the Khukris exist.

| Date | Mintage | Good | VG | F | VF | XF |
|---|---|---|---|---|---|---|
| VS1978(1921) | — | 1.00 | 2.00 | 3.50 | 6.50 | — |
| VS1979(1922) | — | 1.00 | 2.00 | 3.50 | 6.50 | — |
| VS1980(1923) | — | 1.00 | 2.00 | 3.50 | 6.50 | — |
| VS1981(1924) | — | 1.00 | 2.00 | 3.50 | 6.50 | — |
| VS1982(1925) | — | 1.00 | 2.00 | 3.50 | 6.50 | — |
| VS1983(1926) | — | 1.00 | 2.00 | 3.50 | 6.50 | — |
| VS1984(1927) | — | 1.00 | 2.00 | 3.50 | 6.50 | — |
| VS1985(1928) | — | 1.00 | 2.00 | 3.50 | 6.50 | — |
| VS1986(1929) | — | 1.50 | 2.50 | 4.00 | 7.50 | — |
| VS1987(1930) | — | 1.50 | 2.50 | 4.00 | 7.50 | — |
| VS1988(1931) | — | 2.00 | 3.00 | 5.00 | 9.00 | — |

**2 PAISA** KM# 689.3 **Weight:** 5.0000 g. **Composition:** Copper **Note:** Machine struck.

| Date | Mintage | VG | F | VF | XF | Unc |
|---|---|---|---|---|---|---|
| VS1978(1921) | — | 1.00 | 2.00 | 3.00 | 4.50 | — |
| VS1979(1922) | — | 1.00 | 2.00 | 3.00 | 4.50 | — |
| VS1980(1923) | — | 1.00 | 2.00 | 3.00 | 4.50 | — |
| VS1981(1924) | — | 1.00 | 2.00 | 3.00 | 4.50 | — |
| VS1982(1925) | — | 1.00 | 2.00 | 3.00 | 4.50 | — |
| VS1983(1926) | — | 1.00 | 2.00 | 3.00 | 4.50 | — |
| VS1984(1927) | — | 1.00 | 2.00 | 3.00 | 4.50 | — |
| VS1991(1934) | — | 1.50 | 2.50 | 4.00 | 6.00 | — |

**5 PAISA** **KM# 690.1** **Weight:** 18.0000 g. **Composition:** Copper **Note:** Varieties of the Khukris exist.

| Date | Mintage | F | VF | XF | Unc |
|---|---|---|---|---|---|
| VS1976(1919) | — | 6.00 | 10.00 | 14.00 | 20.00 |
| VS1977(1920) | — | 1.25 | 2.25 | 3.50 | 6.00 |
| VS1977(1920) Inverted date | — | 3.00 | 5.00 | 8.50 | 12.50 |

**5 PAISA** **KM# 690.2** **Weight:** 18.0000 g. **Composition:** Copper **Note:** Crude struck. Varieties of the Khukris exist.

| Date | Mintage | F | VF | XF | Unc |
|---|---|---|---|---|---|
| VS1978(1921) | — | 1.75 | 3.00 | 5.00 | 8.00 |
| VS1979(1922) | — | 1.75 | 3.00 | 5.00 | 8.00 |
| VS1980(1923) | — | 1.75 | 3.00 | 5.00 | 8.00 |
| VS1981(1924) | — | 1.75 | 3.00 | 5.00 | 8.00 |
| VS1982(1925) | — | 1.75 | 3.00 | 5.00 | 8.00 |
| VS1983(1926) | — | 1.75 | 3.00 | 5.00 | 8.00 |
| VS1984(1927) | — | 1.75 | 3.00 | 5.00 | 8.00 |
| VS1985(1928) | — | 1.75 | 3.00 | 5.00 | 8.00 |
| VS1986(1929) | — | 1.75 | 3.00 | 5.00 | 8.00 |
| VS1987(1930) | — | 1.75 | 3.00 | 5.00 | 8.00 |
| VS1988(1931) | — | 6.00 | 10.00 | 14.00 | 20.00 |

**5 PAISA** **KM# 690.3** **Weight:** 14.0000 g. **Composition:** Copper **Note:** Machine struck, reduced weight. Varieties exist with both open and closed handles on Khukris.

| Date | Mintage | F | VF | XF | Unc |
|---|---|---|---|---|---|
| VS1978(1921) | — | 1.25 | 2.25 | 3.50 | 5.00 |
| VS1979(1922) | — | 1.25 | 2.25 | 3.50 | 5.00 |
| VS1980(1923) | — | 1.25 | 2.25 | 3.50 | 5.00 |
| VS1981(1924) | — | 1.25 | 2.25 | 3.50 | 5.00 |
| VS1982(1925) | — | 1.25 | 2.25 | 3.50 | 5.00 |
| VS1983(1926) | — | 1.25 | 2.25 | 3.50 | 5.00 |
| VS1984(1927) | — | 1.25 | 2.25 | 3.50 | 5.00 |
| VS1991(1934) | — | 15.00 | 20.00 | 25.00 | 30.00 |

## SILVER COINAGE

**DAM** **KM# 691** **Weight:** 0.0400 g. **Composition:** Silver **Note:** Uniface.

| Date | Mintage | F | VF | XF | Unc |
|---|---|---|---|---|---|
| ND(1911) | — | 15.00 | 25.00 | 30.00 | 50.00 |

**1/4 MOHAR** **KM# 692** **Weight:** 1.4000 g. **Composition:** Silver

| Date | Mintage | VG | F | VF | XF | Unc |
|---|---|---|---|---|---|---|
| VS1969(1912) | — | 1.75 | 3.00 | 5.00 | 7.00 | — |
| VS1970(1913) | — | 1.75 | 3.00 | 5.00 | 7.00 | — |

**1/2 MOHAR** **KM# 693** **Weight:** 2.8000 g. **Composition:** Silver

| Date | Mintage | F | VF | XF | Unc |
|---|---|---|---|---|---|
| VS1968(1911) | — | 2.25 | 3.50 | 5.00 | 7.00 |
| VS1970(1913) | — | 2.25 | 3.50 | 5.00 | 7.00 |
| VS1971(1914) | — | 2.25 | 3.50 | 5.00 | 7.00 |

**1/2 MOHAR** **KM# 681** **Weight:** 2.7700 g. **Composition:** Silver **Note:** In the name of "Queen Lakshmi Divyeswari - Regent for Tribhuvana Bir Bikram".

| Date | Mintage | F | VF | XF | Unc |
|---|---|---|---|---|---|
| VS1971(1914) | — | 4.00 | 6.00 | 9.00 | 11.50 |

**MOHAR** **KM# 694** **Weight:** 5.6000 g. **Composition:** Silver

| Date | Mintage | F | VF | XF | Unc |
|---|---|---|---|---|---|
| VS1968(1911) | — | 4.50 | 6.50 | 8.00 | 10.00 |
| VS1969(1912) | — | 4.50 | 6.50 | 8.00 | 10.00 |
| VS1971(1914) | — | 4.50 | 6.50 | 8.00 | 10.00 |

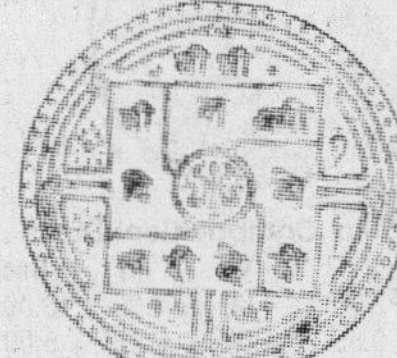
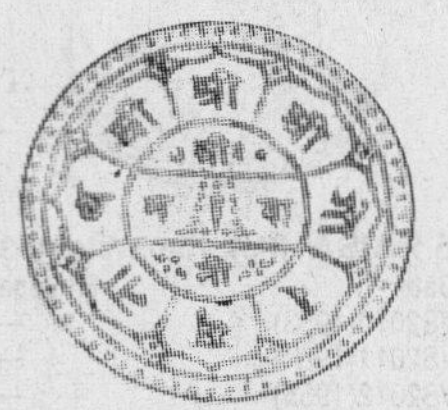

**MOHAR** **KM# 682** **Weight:** 5.6000 g. **Composition:** Silver **Note:** In the name of "Queen Lakshmi Divyeswari - Regent for Tribhuvana Bir Bikram".

| Date | Mintage | F | VF | XF | Unc |
|---|---|---|---|---|---|
| VS1971(1914) | — | 4.50 | 6.50 | 9.00 | 11.50 |

**2 MOHARS** **KM# 695** **Weight:** 11.2000 g. **Composition:** Silver **Note:** Varieties exist for this type.

| Date | Mintage | F | VF | XF | Unc |
|---|---|---|---|---|---|
| VS1968(1911) | — | BV | 7.50 | 10.00 | 16.50 |
| VS1969(1912) | — | BV | 7.50 | 10.00 | 16.50 |
| VS1970(1913) | — | BV | 7.50 | 10.00 | 16.50 |
| VS1971(1914) | — | BV | 7.50 | 10.00 | 16.50 |
| VS1972(1915) | — | BV | 7.50 | 10.00 | 16.50 |
| VS1973(1916) | — | BV | 7.50 | 10.00 | 16.50 |
| VS1974(1917) | — | BV | 7.50 | 10.00 | 16.50 |
| VS1975(1918) | — | BV | 7.50 | 10.00 | 16.50 |
| VS1976(1919) | — | BV | 7.50 | 10.00 | 16.50 |
| VS1977(1920) | — | BV | 7.50 | 10.00 | 16.50 |
| VS1978(1921) | — | BV | 7.50 | 10.00 | 16.50 |
| VS1979(1922) | — | BV | 7.50 | 10.00 | 16.50 |
| VS1980(1923) | — | BV | 7.50 | 10.00 | 16.50 |
| VS1982(1925) | — | BV | 7.50 | 10.00 | 16.50 |
| VS1983(1926) | — | BV | 7.50 | 10.00 | 16.50 |
| VS1984(1927) | — | BV | 7.50 | 10.00 | 16.50 |
| VS1985(1928) | — | BV | 7.50 | 10.00 | 16.50 |
| VS1986(1929) | — | BV | 7.50 | 10.00 | 16.50 |
| VS1987(1930) | — | BV | 7.50 | 10.00 | 16.50 |
| VS1988(1931) | — | BV | 7.50 | 10.00 | 16.50 |
| VS1989(1932) | — | BV | 7.50 | 10.00 | 16.50 |

**4 MOHARS** **KM# 696** **Weight:** 22.4000 g. **Composition:** Silver

| Date | Mintage | F | VF | XF | Unc |
|---|---|---|---|---|---|
| VS1971(1914) | — | 40.00 | 75.00 | 125 | 175 |

## GOLD COINAGE

**DAM** **KM# 697a** **Weight:** 0.0400 g. **Composition:** Gold **Note:** Uniface, machine struck.

| Date | Mintage | F | VF | XF | Unc |
|---|---|---|---|---|---|
| ND(1911-50)(1911) | — | 25.00 | 40.00 | 65.00 | 100 |

**DAM** **KM# 697** **Weight:** 0.0400 g. **Composition:** Gold **Note:** Uniface.

| Date | Mintage | F | VF | XF | Unc |
|---|---|---|---|---|---|
| ND(1911) | — | 25.00 | 40.00 | 75.00 | 100 |

**1/32 MOHAR** **KM# 698** **Weight:** 0.1800 g. **Composition:** Gold **Note:** Uniface.

| Date | Mintage | F | VF | XF | Unc |
|---|---|---|---|---|---|
| ND(1911) | — | 35.00 | 60.00 | 90.00 | 125 |

**1/16 MOHAR** **KM# 699** **Weight:** 0.3500 g. **Composition:** Gold

| Date | Mintage | F | VF | XF | Unc |
|---|---|---|---|---|---|
| VS(19)77(1920) | — | 50.00 | 90.00 | 120 | 150 |

**1/8 MOHAR** **KM# 700** **Weight:** 0.7000 g. **Composition:** Gold

| Date | Mintage | F | VF | XF | Unc |
|---|---|---|---|---|---|
| VS(19)76(1919) | — | 75.00 | 120 | 150 | 200 |

**1/2 MOHAR** **KM# 701** **Weight:** 2.8000 g. **Composition:** Gold

| Date | Mintage | F | VF | XF | Unc |
|---|---|---|---|---|---|
| VS1969(1912) | — | — | — | — | — |

**1/2 MOHAR** **KM# 717** **Weight:** 2.8000 g. **Composition:** Gold

| Date | Mintage | F | VF | XF | Unc |
|---|---|---|---|---|---|
| VS1995(1938) | — | — | — | — | — |

**MOHAR** **KM# 702** **Weight:** 5.6000 g. **Composition:** Gold

| Date | Mintage | F | VF | XF | Unc |
|---|---|---|---|---|---|
| VS1969(1912) | — | 100 | 125 | 150 | 200 |
| VS1975(1918) | — | 100 | 125 | 150 | 200 |
| VS1978(1921) | — | 100 | 125 | 150 | 200 |
| VS1979(1922) | — | 100 | 125 | 150 | 200 |
| VS1981(1924) | — | 100 | 125 | 150 | 200 |
| VS1983(1926) | — | 100 | 125 | 150 | 200 |
| VS1985(1928) | — | 100 | 125 | 150 | 200 |
| VS1986(1929) | — | 100 | 125 | 150 | 200 |
| VS1987(1930) | — | 100 | 125 | 150 | 200 |
| VS1989(1932) | — | 100 | 125 | 150 | 200 |
| VS1990(1933) | — | 100 | 125 | 150 | 200 |
| VS1991(1934) | — | 100 | 125 | 150 | 200 |
| VS1998(1941) | — | 100 | 125 | 150 | 200 |
| VS1999(1942) | — | 100 | 125 | 150 | 200 |
| VS2000(1943) | — | 100 | 125 | 150 | 200 |
| VS2003(1946) | — | 100 | 125 | 150 | 200 |
| VS2005(1948) | — | 100 | 125 | 150 | 200 |

**MOHAR** **KM# 683** **Weight:** 5.6000 g. **Composition:** Gold **Note:** In the name of "Queen Lakshmi Divyeswari - Regent for Tribhuvana Bir Bikram".

| Date | Mintage | F | VF | XF | Unc |
|---|---|---|---|---|---|
| VS1971(1914) | — | 100 | 125 | 145 | 175 |

**MOHAR** **KM# 722** **Weight:** 5.6000 g. **Composition:** Gold

| Date | Mintage | F | VF | XF | Unc |
|---|---|---|---|---|---|
| VS1993 | 376,000 | — | — | — | — |
| VS1994 | 283,000 | — | — | — | — |

**ASHRAPHI (Tola)** KM# 703.1 **Composition:** Gold

| Date | Mintage | F | VF | XF | Unc |
|---|---|---|---|---|---|
| VS1969(1912) | — | 225 | 245 | 275 | 300 |
| VS1974(1917) | — | 225 | 245 | 275 | 300 |
| VS1975(1918) | — | 225 | 245 | 275 | 300 |
| VS1976(1919) | — | 225 | 245 | 275 | 300 |
| VS1977(1920) | — | 225 | 245 | 275 | 300 |
| VS1978(1921) | — | 225 | 245 | 275 | 300 |
| VS1979(1922) | — | 225 | 245 | 275 | 300 |
| VS1980(1923) | — | 225 | 245 | 275 | 300 |
| VS1981(1924) | — | 225 | 245 | 275 | 300 |
| VS1982(1925) | — | 225 | 245 | 275 | 300 |
| VS1983(1926) | — | 225 | 245 | 275 | 300 |
| VS1984(1927) | — | 225 | 245 | 275 | 300 |
| VS1985(1928) | — | 225 | 245 | 275 | 300 |
| VS1986(1929) | — | 225 | 245 | 275 | 300 |
| VS1987(1930) | — | 225 | 245 | 275 | 300 |
| VS1988(1931) | — | 225 | 245 | 275 | 300 |
| VS1989(1932) | — | 225 | 245 | 275 | 300 |
| VS1990(1933) | — | 225 | 245 | 275 | 300 |
| VS1991(1934) | — | 225 | 245 | 275 | 300 |
| VS1998(1941) | — | 225 | 245 | 275 | 300 |
| VS1999(1942) | — | 225 | 245 | 275 | 300 |
| VS2000(1943) | — | 225 | 245 | 275 | 300 |
| VS2003(1946) | — | 225 | 245 | 275 | 300 |

**ASHRAPHI (Tola)** KM# 727 **Composition:** Gold **Obverse:** Trident in center

| Date | Mintage | F | VF | XF | Unc |
|---|---|---|---|---|---|
| VS1992(1935) | — | 235 | 250 | 285 | 350 |

**ASHRAPHI (Tola)** KM# 703.2 **Composition:** Gold

| Date | Mintage | F | VF | XF | Unc |
|---|---|---|---|---|---|
| VS2005(1948) | — | 225 | 245 | 275 | 300 |

**DUITOLA ASARPHI** KM# 728 **Composition:** Gold **Note:** Similar to 1 Tola, KM#703.

| Date | Mintage | F | VF | XF | Unc |
|---|---|---|---|---|---|
| VS2005(1948) | — | 450 | 500 | 550 | 650 |

## ANONYMOUS COINAGE

**PAISA** KM# 733 **Composition:** Brass

| Date | Mintage | F | VF | XF | Unc |
|---|---|---|---|---|---|
| VS2010(1953) | — | 8.00 | 15.00 | 20.00 | 25.00 |
| VS2011(1954) | — | 17.50 | 25.00 | 35.00 | 40.00 |
| VS2012(1955) Restrike | — | — | 1.00 | 1.50 | 2.00 |

**PAISA** KM# 734 **Composition:** Brass

| Date | Mintage | F | VF | XF | Unc |
|---|---|---|---|---|---|
| VS2012(1955) | — | 1.25 | 2.00 | 2.50 | 3.50 |

**2 PAISA** KM# 735 **Composition:** Brass

| Date | Mintage | F | VF | XF | Unc |
|---|---|---|---|---|---|
| VS2010(1953) | — | 12.50 | 20.00 | 37.50 | 60.00 |
| VS2011(1954) | — | 30.00 | 40.00 | 50.00 | 75.00 |
| VS2011(1954) Restrike | — | — | — | 1.50 | 2.50 |

**2 PAISA** KM# 749 **Composition:** Brass

| Date | Mintage | F | VF | XF | Unc |
|---|---|---|---|---|---|
| VS2012(1955) | — | 0.30 | 0.50 | 0.75 | 1.50 |
| VS2013(1956) | — | 0.30 | 0.50 | 0.75 | 1.50 |
| VS2014(1957) | — | 0.30 | 0.50 | 0.75 | 1.50 |

**4 PAISA** KM# 754 **Composition:** Brass

| Date | Mintage | F | VF | XF | Unc |
|---|---|---|---|---|---|
| VS2012(1955) | — | 1.00 | 1.75 | 3.00 | 5.00 |

**5 PAISA** KM# 736 **Weight:** 3.8900 g. **Composition:** Brass

| Date | Mintage | F | VF | XF | Unc |
|---|---|---|---|---|---|
| VS2010(1953) | — | 2.75 | 4.50 | 7.00 | 10.00 |
| VS2011(1954) | — | 0.65 | 1.00 | 2.75 | 5.00 |
| VS2012(1955) | — | 0.30 | 0.50 | 0.75 | 1.25 |
| VS2013(1956) | — | 0.30 | 0.50 | 0.75 | 1.25 |
| VS2014(1957) | — | 0.30 | 0.50 | 0.75 | 1.25 |

**5 PAISA** KM# 736a **Weight:** 4.0400 g. **Composition:** Copper-Nickel

| Date | Mintage | F | VF | XF | Unc |
|---|---|---|---|---|---|
| VS2014(1957) | — | — | — | — | — |

**10 PAISA** KM# 737 **Composition:** Bronze

| Date | Mintage | F | VF | XF | Unc |
|---|---|---|---|---|---|
| VS2010(1953) | — | 2.75 | 4.50 | 7.00 | 10.00 |
| VS2011(1954) | — | 0.15 | 0.25 | 0.50 | 1.00 |
| VS2011(1954) Restrike | — | — | — | 0.15 | 0.25 |
| VS2012(1955) | — | 0.15 | 0.25 | 0.50 | 1.00 |

**20 PAISA** KM# 738 **Composition:** Copper-Nickel

| Date | Mintage | F | VF | XF | Unc |
|---|---|---|---|---|---|
| VS2010(1953) | — | 12.50 | 20.00 | 30.00 | 40.00 |
| VS2010(1953) Restrike | — | — | — | 2.50 | 3.00 |
| VS2011(1954) | — | 32.50 | 40.00 | 50.00 | 60.00 |

**25 PAISA** KM# 739 **Composition:** Copper-Nickel

| Date | Mintage | F | VF | XF | Unc |
|---|---|---|---|---|---|
| VS2010(1953) | — | 2.00 | 3.50 | 4.50 | 6.00 |
| VS2011(1954) | — | 2.00 | 3.50 | 4.50 | 6.00 |
| VS2012(1955) | — | 1.25 | 2.00 | 2.50 | 3.50 |
| VS2014(1957) | — | 1.25 | 2.00 | 2.50 | 3.50 |

**1/5 ASARFI** KM# 768 **Weight:** 2.3300 g. **Composition:** Gold

| Date | Mintage | F | VF | XF | Unc |
|---|---|---|---|---|---|
| VS2010(1953) | — | — | 50.00 | 60.00 | 100 |

**Note:** Coins dated VS2010 are normally found as restrikes ca. 1968

| Date | Mintage | F | VF | XF | Unc |
|---|---|---|---|---|---|
| VS2012(1955) | — | — | — | — | — |

**1/4 ASARFI** KM# 774 **Weight:** 2.9000 g. **Composition:** Gold

| Date | Mintage | F | VF | XF | Unc |
|---|---|---|---|---|---|
| VS2010(1953) | — | 60.00 | 70.00 | 80.00 | 120 |

**Note:** Coins dated VS2010 are normally found as restrikes ca. 1968

| Date | Mintage | F | VF | XF | Unc |
|---|---|---|---|---|---|
| VS2012(1955) | — | — | — | — | — |

## DECIMAL COINAGE

100 Paisa = 1 Rupee

**1/2 PAISA** KM# 705 **Composition:** Copper

| Date | Mintage | F | VF | XF | Unc |
|---|---|---|---|---|---|
| VS2004(1947) | — | — | 25.00 | 30.00 | 40.00 |

**1/4 PAISA** KM# 704 **Composition:** Copper

| Date | Mintage | F | VF | XF | Unc |
|---|---|---|---|---|---|
| VS2000(1943) | — | 15.00 | 25.00 | 30.00 | 40.00 |
| VS2004(1947) | — | 15.00 | 25.00 | 30.00 | 40.00 |

**PAISA** KM# 706 **Composition:** Copper

| Date | Mintage | F | VF | XF | Unc |
|---|---|---|---|---|---|
| VS1990 | — | 0.75 | 1.50 | 3.00 | 5.00 |
| VS1991 | — | 0.75 | 1.50 | 3.00 | 5.00 |
| VS1992 | — | 0.75 | 1.50 | 3.00 | 5.00 |
| VS1993 | — | 0.75 | 1.50 | 3.00 | 5.00 |
| VS1994 | 456,000 | 0.75 | 1.50 | 3.00 | 5.00 |
| VS1995 | — | 0.75 | 1.50 | 3.00 | 5.00 |
| VS1996 | — | 0.75 | 1.50 | 3.00 | 5.00 |

**PAISA** KM# 707a **Composition:** Brass

| Date | Mintage | F | VF | XF | Unc |
|---|---|---|---|---|---|
| VS2001(1944) | — | 0.30 | 0.50 | 0.75 | 1.00 |
| VS2003(1946) | — | 0.30 | 0.50 | 0.75 | 1.00 |
| VS2004(1947) | — | 3.00 | 5.00 | 7.00 | 10.00 |
| VS2005(1948) | — | 0.30 | 0.50 | 0.75 | 1.00 |
| VS2006(1949) | — | 0.60 | 1.00 | 1.25 | 1.75 |

**PAISA** KM# 707 **Composition:** Copper

| Date | Mintage | F | VF | XF | Unc |
|---|---|---|---|---|---|
| VS2005(1948) | — | 0.75 | 1.25 | 1.75 | 2.50 |

**2 PAISA** **KM# 708** **Composition:** Copper

| Date | Mintage | VG | F | VF | XF | Unc |
|---|---|---|---|---|---|---|
| VS1992(1935) | — | 3.00 | 5.00 | 8.50 | 13.50 | — |

**2 PAISA** **KM# 709.2** **Composition:** Copper

| Date | Mintage | F | VF | XF | Unc |
|---|---|---|---|---|---|
| VS1992(1935) | — | 0.60 | 1.00 | 1.75 | 3.00 |
| VS1994(1937) | — | 0.50 | 0.75 | 1.50 | 2.50 |
| VS1995(1938) | — | 2.00 | 3.50 | 5.00 | 7.50 |
| VS1996(1939) | — | 0.30 | 0.50 | 1.00 | 1.50 |
| VS1997(1940) | — | 0.50 | 0.75 | 1.50 | 2.50 |
| VS1998(1941) | — | 0.50 | 0.75 | 1.50 | 2.50 |
| VS1999(1942) | — | 0.50 | 0.75 | 1.50 | 2.50 |

**2 PAISA** **KM# 709.1** **Composition:** Copper

| Date | Mintage | F | VF | XF | Unc |
|---|---|---|---|---|---|
| VS1993 | 473,000 | 1.00 | 2.00 | 3.00 | 5.00 |
| VS1994 | 1,133,000 | 1.00 | 2.00 | 3.00 | 5.00 |
| VS1995 | — | 1.00 | 2.00 | 3.00 | 5.00 |
| VS1996 | — | 1.00 | 2.00 | 3.00 | 5.00 |

**2 PAISA** **KM# 710** **Composition:** Copper

| Date | Mintage | F | VF | XF | Unc |
|---|---|---|---|---|---|
| VS1999(1942) | — | 0.30 | 0.50 | 1.00 | 2.00 |
| VS2000(1943) | — | 0.30 | 0.50 | 1.00 | 2.00 |
| VS2003(1946) | — | 0.30 | 0.50 | 1.00 | 2.00 |
| VS2005(1948) | — | 3.00 | 5.00 | 7.00 | 10.00 |

**2 PAISA** **KM# 710a** **Composition:** Brass

| Date | Mintage | F | VF | XF | Unc |
|---|---|---|---|---|---|
| VS1999(1942) | — | 0.30 | 0.50 | 1.00 | 2.00 |
| VS2000(1943) | — | 0.30 | 0.50 | 1.00 | 2.00 |
| VS2001(1944) | — | 0.30 | 0.50 | 1.00 | 2.00 |
| VS2005(1948) | — | 1.75 | 3.00 | 5.00 | 7.50 |
| VS2008(1951) | — | 0.30 | 0.50 | 1.00 | 2.00 |
| VS2009(1952) | — | 0.30 | 0.50 | 1.00 | 2.00 |
| VS2010(1953) | — | 0.30 | 0.50 | 1.00 | 2.00 |

**5 PAISA** **KM# 711** **Composition:** Copper

| Date | Mintage | F | VF | XF | Unc |
|---|---|---|---|---|---|
| VS1992 | — | 1.50 | 3.00 | 4.50 | 6.50 |
| VS1993 | 878,000 | 1.50 | 3.00 | 4.50 | 6.50 |
| VS1994 | 403,000 | 1.50 | 3.00 | 4.50 | 6.50 |
| VS1995 | — | 1.00 | 2.00 | 3.00 | 5.00 |
| VS1996 | — | 1.50 | 3.00 | 4.50 | 6.50 |
| VS1997 | — | 1.50 | 3.00 | 4.50 | 6.50 |
| VS1998 | — | — | — | — | — |

**5 PAISA** **KM# 712** **Composition:** Copper-Nickel-Zinc

| Date | Mintage | F | VF | XF | Unc |
|---|---|---|---|---|---|
| VS2000(1943) | — | 0.65 | 1.00 | 1.50 | 2.50 |
| VS2009(1952) | — | 1.75 | 3.00 | 5.00 | 8.50 |
| VS2010(1953) | — | 1.25 | 2.00 | 3.00 | 5.00 |

**5 PAISA** **KM# 712a** **Composition:** Copper-Nickel

| Date | Mintage | F | VF | XF | Unc |
|---|---|---|---|---|---|
| VS2010(1953) Restrike | — | 0.65 | 1.00 | 1.50 | 2.50 |

**20 PAISA** **KM# 714** **Weight:** 2.2161 g. **Composition:** 0.3330 Silver .0237 oz. ASW

| Date | Mintage | F | VF | XF | Unc |
|---|---|---|---|---|---|
| VS1989(1932) | — | 2.25 | 4.00 | 5.00 | 6.50 |
| VS1991(1934) | — | 1.75 | 3.50 | 4.50 | 6.00 |
| VS1992(1935) | — | 1.75 | 3.50 | 4.50 | 6.00 |
| VS1993(1936) | — | 1.75 | 3.50 | 4.50 | 6.00 |
| VS1994(1937) | — | 3.75 | 6.50 | 10.00 | 15.00 |
| VS1995(1938) | — | 1.75 | 3.50 | 4.50 | 6.00 |
| VS1996(1939) | — | 1.75 | 3.50 | 4.50 | 6.00 |
| VS1997(1940) | — | 1.75 | 3.50 | 4.50 | 6.00 |
| VS1998(1941) | — | 1.75 | 3.50 | 4.50 | 6.00 |
| VS1999(1942) | — | 1.75 | 3.50 | 4.50 | 6.00 |
| VS2000(1943) | — | 1.75 | 3.50 | 4.50 | 6.00 |
| VS2001(1944) | — | 1.75 | 3.50 | 4.50 | 6.00 |
| VS2003(1946) | — | 1.75 | 3.50 | 4.50 | 6.00 |
| VS2004(1947) | — | 1.75 | 3.50 | 4.50 | 6.00 |

**20 PAISA** **KM# 715** **Weight:** 2.2161 g. **Composition:** 0.3330 Silver .0237 oz. ASW

| Date | Mintage | F | VF | XF | Unc |
|---|---|---|---|---|---|
| VS1989(1932) | — | 2.25 | 4.00 | 6.00 | 8.50 |

**Note:** The date VS1989 is given in different style characters. Refer to 50 Paisa KM#719 and 1 Rupee, KM#724 for style

**20 PAISA** **KM# 716** **Weight:** 2.2161 g. **Composition:** 0.3330 Silver .0237 oz. ASW

| Date | Mintage | F | VF | XF | Unc |
|---|---|---|---|---|---|
| VS2006(1949) | — | 0.75 | 1.00 | 1.25 | 1.75 |
| VS2007(1950) | — | — | — | — | — |
| VS2009(1952) | — | 0.75 | 1.00 | 1.50 | 2.50 |
| VS2010(1953) | — | 0.75 | 1.00 | 1.50 | 2.50 |

**50 PAISA** **KM# 718** **Weight:** 5.5403 g. **Composition:** 0.8000 Silver .1425 oz. ASW

| Date | Mintage | F | VF | XF | Unc |
|---|---|---|---|---|---|
| VS1989(1932) | — | 5.50 | 6.50 | 8.00 | 10.00 |
| VS1991(1934) | — | 2.50 | 4.50 | 7.00 | 10.00 |
| VS1992(1935) | — | 2.50 | 4.50 | 7.00 | 10.00 |
| VS1993(1936) | — | 2.50 | 4.50 | 7.00 | 10.00 |
| VS1994(1937) | — | 2.50 | 4.50 | 7.00 | 10.00 |
| VS1995(1938) | — | 2.50 | 4.50 | 7.00 | 10.00 |
| VS1996(1939) | — | 2.50 | 4.50 | 7.00 | 10.00 |
| VS1997(1940) | — | 2.50 | 4.50 | 7.00 | 10.00 |
| VS1998(1941) | — | 2.50 | 4.50 | 7.00 | 10.00 |
| VS1999(1942) | — | 2.50 | 4.50 | 7.00 | 10.00 |
| VS2000(1943) | — | 2.50 | 4.50 | 7.00 | 10.00 |
| VS2001(1944) | — | 2.50 | 4.50 | 7.00 | 10.00 |
| VS2003(1946) | — | 2.50 | 4.50 | 7.00 | 10.00 |
| VS2004(1947) | — | 2.50 | 4.50 | 7.00 | 10.00 |
| VS2005(1948) | — | 2.50 | 4.50 | 7.00 | 10.00 |

**50 PAISA** **KM# 719** **Weight:** 5.5403 g. **Composition:** 0.8000 Silver .1425 oz. ASW

| Date | Mintage | F | VF | XF | Unc |
|---|---|---|---|---|---|
| VS1989(1932) | — | 2.50 | 4.50 | 7.00 | 9.00 |

**Note:** The date is given in different characters

**50 PAISA** **KM# 720** **Weight:** 5.5403 g. **Composition:** 0.3330 Silver .0593 oz. ASW **Obverse:** Four dots around trident

| Date | Mintage | F | VF | XF | Unc |
|---|---|---|---|---|---|
| VS2005(1948) | — | 45.00 | 65.00 | 90.00 | 125 |

**50 PAISA** **KM# 721** **Weight:** 5.5403 g. **Composition:** 0.3330 Silver .0593 oz. ASW **Obverse:** Without dots around trident

| Date | Mintage | F | VF | XF | Unc |
|---|---|---|---|---|---|
| VS2006(1949) | — | 1.50 | 2.00 | 2.75 | 4.50 |
| VS2007(1950) | — | 1.50 | 2.00 | 2.75 | 4.50 |
| VS2009/7(1952) | — | 1.50 | 2.25 | 3.00 | 5.00 |
| VS2009(1952) | — | 1.50 | 2.00 | 2.75 | 4.50 |
| VS2010(1953) | — | 1.50 | 2.00 | 2.75 | 4.50 |

**1/16 RUPEE** **KM# 713** **Composition:** Silver

| Date | Mintage | F | VF | XF | Unc |
|---|---|---|---|---|---|
| VS(19)96(1939) | — | 12.50 | 20.00 | 32.50 | 50.00 |

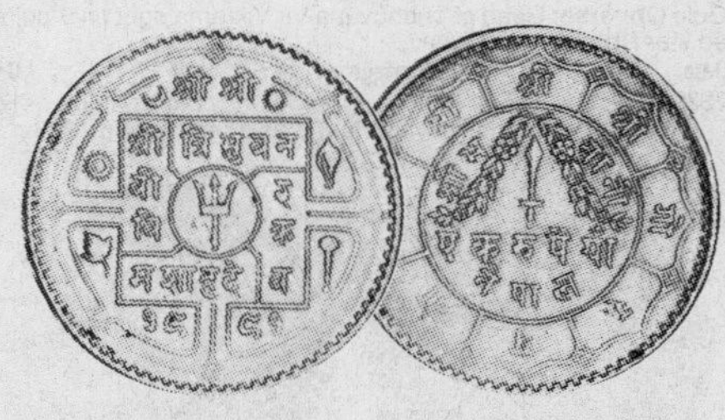

**RUPEE** **KM# 723** **Weight:** 11.0806 g. **Composition:** 0.8000 Silver .2850 oz. ASW

| Date | Mintage | F | VF | XF | Unc |
|---|---|---|---|---|---|
| VS1989 | — | 2.50 | 5.00 | 8.00 | 20.00 |
| VS1991 | — | 2.50 | 5.00 | 8.00 | 16.50 |
| VS1992 | — | 2.50 | 5.00 | 8.00 | 16.50 |
| VS1993 | 1,717,000 | 2.50 | 5.00 | 8.00 | 16.50 |
| VS1994 | 2,097,000 | 2.50 | 5.00 | 8.00 | 16.50 |
| VS1995 | — | 2.50 | 5.00 | 8.00 | 16.50 |
| VS1996 | — | 2.50 | 5.00 | 8.00 | 16.50 |
| VS1997 | — | 2.50 | 5.00 | 8.00 | 16.50 |
| VS1998 | — | 2.50 | 5.00 | 8.00 | 16.50 |
| VS1999 | — | 2.50 | 5.00 | 8.00 | 16.50 |
| VS2000 | — | 2.50 | 5.00 | 8.00 | 16.50 |
| VS2001 | — | 2.50 | 5.00 | 8.00 | 16.50 |

| Date | Mintage | F | VF | XF | Unc |
|---|---|---|---|---|---|
| VS2003 | — | 2.50 | 5.00 | 8.00 | 16.50 |
| VS2005 | — | 2.50 | 5.00 | 8.00 | 16.50 |

**RUPEE** **KM# 724** **Weight:** 11.0806 g. **Composition:** 0.8000 Silver .2850 oz. ASW

| Date | Mintage | F | VF | XF | Unc |
|---|---|---|---|---|---|
| VS1989(1932) | — | 7.50 | 10.00 | 12.50 | 15.00 |

**Note:** The date is given in different characters

**RUPEE** **KM# 725** **Weight:** 11.0806 g. **Composition:** 0.3330 Silver .1186 oz. ASW **Obverse:** Four dots around trident

| Date | Mintage | F | VF | XF | Unc |
|---|---|---|---|---|---|
| VS2005(1948) | — | 5.00 | 7.50 | 10.00 | 13.50 |

**RUPEE** **KM# 726** **Weight:** 11.0806 g. **Composition:** 0.3330 Silver .1186 oz. ASW **Obverse:** Without dots around trident

| Date | Mintage | F | VF | XF | Unc |
|---|---|---|---|---|---|
| VS2006(1949) | — | 2.50 | 3.50 | 5.00 | 7.50 |
| VS2007(1950) | — | 2.50 | 3.50 | 5.00 | 7.50 |
| VS2008(1951) | — | 2.50 | 3.50 | 5.00 | 7.50 |
| VS2009(1951) | — | 2.50 | 3.50 | 5.00 | 7.50 |
| VS2010(1952) | — | 2.50 | 3.50 | 5.00 | 7.50 |

**1/2 ASARPHI** **KM# 741** **Weight:** 5.8000 g. **Composition:** Gold **Obverse:** Head of Tribhuvana Vir Vikrama right on 5-pointed star **Note:** Portrait type.

| Date | Mintage | F | VF | XF | Unc |
|---|---|---|---|---|---|
| VS2010(1953) | — | — | 120 | 140 | 170 |

**Note:** KM#741 is normally found as a restrike ca. 1968

**ASARPHI** **KM# 744** **Weight:** 11.6600 g. **Composition:** Gold **Obverse:** Head of Tribhuvana Vir Vikrama right on 5-pointed star

| Date | Mintage | F | VF | XF | Unc |
|---|---|---|---|---|---|
| VS2010(1953) | — | — | 175 | 200 | 250 |

**Note:** KM#744 normally found as a restrike ca. 1968

## Gyanendra Bir Bikram
### VS2007 / 1950-51AD (first reign)

### DECIMAL COINAGE
100 Paisa = 1 Rupee

**50 PAISA** **KM# 729** **Weight:** 5.5403 g. **Composition:** 0.3330 Silver .0593 oz. ASW

| Date | Mintage | F | VF | XF | Unc |
|---|---|---|---|---|---|
| VS2007(1950) | 26 | — | 175 | 275 | 350 |

**MOHAR** **KM# 731** **Composition:** Gold

| Date | Mintage | F | VF | XF | Unc |
|---|---|---|---|---|---|
| VS2007(1950) Rare | — | — | — | — | — |

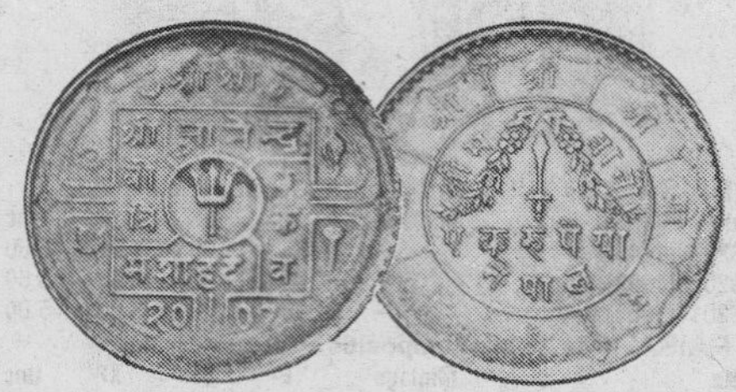

**RUPEE** **KM# 730** **Weight:** 11.0806 g. **Composition:** 0.3330 Silver .1186 oz. ASW

| Date | Mintage | F | VF | XF | Unc |
|---|---|---|---|---|---|
| VS2007(1950) | — | 4.50 | 6.50 | 9.00 | 12.50 |

**TOLA** **KM# 732** **Composition:** Gold

| Date | Mintage | F | VF | XF | Unc |
|---|---|---|---|---|---|
| VS2007(1950) Rare | — | — | — | — | — |

## Trivhuvan Bir Bikram
### VS2007-2011 / 1951-1955AD (second reign)

### DECIMAL COINAGE
100 Paisa = 1 Rupee

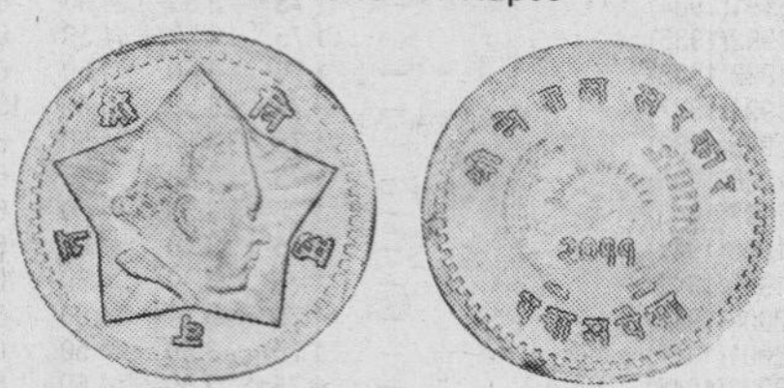

**50 PAISA** **KM# 740** **Composition:** Copper-Nickel **Obverse:** Head of Tribhuvana Vir Vikram right on 5-pointed star

| Date | Mintage | F | VF | XF | Unc |
|---|---|---|---|---|---|
| VS2010(1953) | — | 0.50 | 1.00 | 2.00 | 4.00 |
| VS2011(1954) | — | 0.35 | 0.75 | 1.50 | 3.00 |

**RUPEE** **KM# 742** **Composition:** Copper-Nickel **Obverse:** Head of Tribhuvana Vir Vikram right on 5-pointed star **Note:** Equal denticles at rim.

| Date | Mintage | F | VF | XF | Unc |
|---|---|---|---|---|---|
| VS2010(1953) | — | 0.75 | 1.25 | 2.25 | 4.50 |
| VS2011(1954) | — | 0.75 | 1.25 | 2.25 | 4.50 |

**RUPEE** **KM# 743** **Composition:** Copper-Nickel **Obverse:** Head of Tribhuvana Vir Vikram right on 5-pointed star **Note:** Unequal denticles at rim.

| Date | Mintage | F | VF | XF | Unc |
|---|---|---|---|---|---|
| VS2011(1954) | — | 0.75 | 1.25 | 2.25 | 4.50 |

## Mahendra Bir Bikram
### VS2012-2028 / 1955-1971AD

### DECIMAL COINAGE
100 Paisa = 1 Rupee

**PAISA** **KM# 745.1 (KM745)** **Composition:** Brass **Subject:** Mahendra Coronation

| Date | Mintage | F | VF | XF | Unc |
|---|---|---|---|---|---|
| VS2013(1956) Narrow rim | — | 0.30 | 0.50 | 0.75 | 1.00 |

**PAISA** **KM# 745.2** **Composition:** Brass **Subject:** Mahendra coronation

| Date | Mintage | F | VF | XF | Unc |
|---|---|---|---|---|---|
| VS2015(1956) Wide rim | — | 0.30 | 0.50 | 0.75 | 1.00 |

**PAISA** **KM# 746** **Composition:** Brass **Reverse:** Numerals with shading

| Date | Mintage | F | VF | XF | Unc |
|---|---|---|---|---|---|
| VS2014(1957) | — | 0.10 | 0.15 | 0.25 | 0.40 |
| VS2015(1958) | — | 0.10 | 0.15 | 0.25 | 0.40 |
| VS2018(1961) | — | 0.10 | 0.15 | 0.25 | 0.40 |
| VS2019(1962) | — | 0.10 | 0.15 | 0.25 | 0.40 |
| VS2020(1963) | — | 0.10 | 0.15 | 0.25 | 0.40 |

**PAISA** **KM# 747** **Composition:** Brass **Reverse:** Numerals without shading

| Date | Mintage | F | VF | XF | Unc |
|---|---|---|---|---|---|
| VS2021(1964) | — | 0.10 | 0.15 | 0.20 | 0.30 |
| VS2022(1965) | — | 0.10 | 0.15 | 0.25 | 0.40 |

**PAISA** **KM# 748** **Composition:** Aluminum **Reverse:** National flower

| Date | Mintage | F | VF | XF | Unc |
|---|---|---|---|---|---|
| VS2023(1966) | — | — | 0.10 | 0.15 | 0.25 |
| VS2025(1968) | — | — | 0.10 | 0.15 | 0.25 |
| VS2026(1969) | — | — | 0.10 | 0.15 | 0.25 |
| VS2027(1970) Proof | 2,187 | Value: 1.25 | | | |
| VS2028(1971) | — | — | 0.10 | 0.15 | 0.25 |
| VS2028(1971) Proof | 2,380 | Value: 1.25 | | | |

**2 PAISA** KM# 750.1 **Composition:** Brass **Subject:** Mahendra Coronation **Note:** Narrow rim.

| Date | Mintage | F | VF | XF | Unc |
|---|---|---|---|---|---|
| VS2013(1956) | — | 0.30 | 0.50 | 0.75 | 1.00 |

**2 PAISA** KM# 750.2 **Composition:** Brass **Note:** Wide rim.

| Date | Mintage | F | VF | XF | Unc |
|---|---|---|---|---|---|
| VS2013(1956) | — | 0.30 | 0.50 | 0.75 | 1.00 |

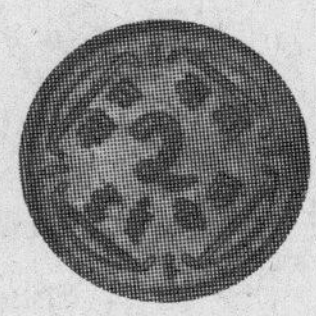

**2 PAISA** KM# 751 **Composition:** Brass **Reverse:** Numerals wtih shading

| Date | Mintage | F | VF | XF | Unc |
|---|---|---|---|---|---|
| VS2014(1957) | — | 0.10 | 0.15 | 0.25 | 0.40 |
| VS2015(1958) | — | 0.10 | 0.15 | 0.25 | 0.40 |
| VS2016(1959) | — | 0.10 | 0.15 | 0.25 | 0.40 |
| VS2018(1961) | — | 0.10 | 0.15 | 0.25 | 0.40 |
| VS2019(1962) | — | 0.10 | 0.15 | 0.25 | 0.40 |
| VS2020(1963) | — | 0.10 | 0.15 | 0.25 | 0.40 |

**2 PAISA** KM# 752 **Composition:** Brass **Reverse:** Numerals wtihout shading

| Date | Mintage | F | VF | XF | Unc |
|---|---|---|---|---|---|
| VS2021(1964) | — | 0.10 | 0.15 | 0.20 | 0.35 |
| VS2022(1965) | — | 0.10 | 0.15 | 0.25 | 0.50 |
| VS2023(1966) | — | 0.10 | 0.15 | 0.25 | 0.50 |

**2 PAISA** KM# 753 **Composition:** Aluminum **Reverse:** Himalayan Monal

| Date | Mintage | F | VF | XF | Unc |
|---|---|---|---|---|---|
| VS2023(1966) | — | — | 0.10 | 0.15 | 0.25 |
| VS2024(1967) | — | — | 0.10 | 0.15 | 0.25 |
| VS2025(1968) | — | — | 0.10 | 0.15 | 0.25 |
| VS2026(1969) | — | — | 0.10 | 0.15 | 0.25 |
| VS2027(1970) | — | — | 0.10 | 0.15 | 0.25 |
| VS2027(1970) Proof | 2,187 | Value: 1.50 | | | |
| VS2028(1971) | — | — | 0.10 | 0.15 | 0.25 |
| VS2028(1971) Proof | 2,380 | Value: 1.50 | | | |

**5 PAISA** KM# 756.2 **Composition:** Bronze **Note:** Narrow rim.

| Date | Mintage | F | VF | XF | Unc |
|---|---|---|---|---|---|
| VS2013(1956) Restrike | — | 0.35 | 0.60 | 1.00 | 1.50 |

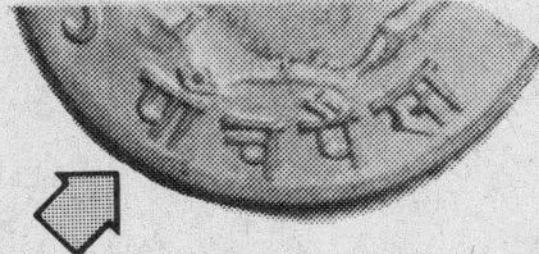

**5 PAISA** KM# 756.1 **Composition:** Bronze **Subject:** Mahendra Coronation **Note:** Wide rim with accent mark.

| Date | Mintage | F | VF | XF | Unc |
|---|---|---|---|---|---|
| VS2013(1956) | — | 10.00 | 20.00 | 30.00 | 40.00 |

**5 PAISA** KM# 756.3 **Composition:** Bronze **Note:** Without accent mark.

| Date | Mintage | F | VF | XF | Unc |
|---|---|---|---|---|---|
| VS2013(1956) | — | 1.00 | 2.00 | 3.00 | 5.00 |

**5 PAISA** KM# 757 **Composition:** Bronze **Reverse:** Numerals with shading

| Date | Mintage | F | VF | XF | Unc |
|---|---|---|---|---|---|
| VS2014(1957) | — | 0.10 | 0.20 | 0.30 | 0.75 |
| VS2015(1958) | — | 0.10 | 0.20 | 0.30 | 0.75 |
| VS2016(1959) | — | 0.10 | 0.30 | 0.50 | 1.00 |
| VS2017(1960) | — | 0.10 | 0.20 | 0.30 | 0.75 |
| VS2018(1961) | — | 0.10 | 0.20 | 0.30 | 0.75 |
| VS2019(1962) | — | 0.10 | 0.20 | 0.30 | 0.75 |
| VS2020(1963) | — | 0.10 | 0.20 | 0.30 | 0.75 |

**5 PAISA** KM# 758 **Composition:** Aluminum-Bronze **Reverse:** Numerals without shading

| Date | Mintage | F | VF | XF | Unc |
|---|---|---|---|---|---|
| VS2021(1964) | — | 0.50 | 1.00 | 1.50 | 2.50 |

**5 PAISA** KM# 758a **Composition:** Bronze

| Date | Mintage | F | VF | XF | Unc |
|---|---|---|---|---|---|
| VS2021(1964) | — | 0.10 | 0.15 | 0.25 | 0.50 |
| VS2022(1965) | — | 0.10 | 0.15 | 0.30 | 0.60 |
| VS2023(1966) | — | 0.10 | 0.15 | 0.30 | 0.60 |

**5 PAISA** KM# 759 **Composition:** Aluminum

| Date | Mintage | F | VF | XF | Unc |
|---|---|---|---|---|---|
| VS2023(1966) | — | — | 0.15 | 0.25 | 0.50 |
| VS2024(1967) | — | — | 0.10 | 0.20 | 0.35 |
| VS2025(1968) | — | — | 0.10 | 0.20 | 0.35 |
| VS2026(1969) | — | — | 0.10 | 0.20 | 0.25 |
| VS2027(1970) | — | — | 0.10 | 0.20 | 0.35 |
| VS2027(1970) Proof | 2,187 | Value: 1.75 | | | |
| VS2028(1971) | — | — | 0.10 | 0.20 | 0.35 |
| VS2028(1971) Proof | 2,038 | Value: 1.75 | | | |

**10 PAISA** KM# 761 **Composition:** Bronze **Subject:** Mahendra Coronation

| Date | Mintage | F | VF | XF | Unc |
|---|---|---|---|---|---|
| VS2013(1956) | — | 0.25 | 0.50 | 0.75 | 1.50 |

**10 PAISA** KM# 762 **Composition:** Bronze **Reverse:** Numerals with shading

| Date | Mintage | F | VF | XF | Unc |
|---|---|---|---|---|---|
| VS2014(1957) | — | 2.75 | 4.50 | 7.00 | 10.00 |
| VS2015(1958) | — | 0.15 | 0.25 | 0.50 | 0.75 |
| VS2016(1959) | — | 3.00 | 5.00 | 7.00 | 10.00 |
| VS2018(1961) | — | 0.15 | 0.25 | 0.50 | 0.75 |
| VS2019(1962) | — | 0.15 | 0.25 | 0.50 | 0.75 |
| VS2020(1963) | — | 0.15 | 0.25 | 0.50 | 0.75 |

**10 PAISA** KM# 763 **Composition:** Aluminum-Bronze **Reverse:** Numerals without shading

| Date | Mintage | F | VF | XF | Unc |
|---|---|---|---|---|---|
| VS2021(1964) | — | 0.75 | 1.25 | 2.00 | 3.00 |

**10 PAISA** KM# 764 **Composition:** Bronze **Note:** Modified design.

| Date | Mintage | F | VF | XF | Unc |
|---|---|---|---|---|---|
| VS2021(1964) | — | 0.10 | 0.15 | 0.25 | 0.50 |
| VS2022(1965) | — | 0.10 | 0.15 | 0.25 | 0.50 |
| VS2023(1966) | — | 0.10 | 0.15 | 0.25 | 0.50 |

**10 PAISA** KM# 765 **Composition:** Brass

| Date | Mintage | F | VF | XF | Unc |
|---|---|---|---|---|---|
| VS2023(1966) | — | — | 0.15 | 0.25 | 0.50 |
| VS2024(1967) | — | — | 0.15 | 0.25 | 0.50 |
| VS2025(1968) | — | — | 15.00 | 17.50 | 20.00 |
| VS2026(1969) | — | — | 0.10 | 0.20 | 0.35 |
| VS2027(1970) | — | — | 0.10 | 0.20 | 0.35 |
| VS2027(1970) Proof | 2,187 | Value: 2.00 | | | |
| VS2028(1971) | — | — | 0.10 | 0.20 | 0.35 |
| VS2028(1971) Proof | 2,380 | Value: 2.00 | | | |

**10 PAISA** KM# 766 **Composition:** Brass **Series:** F.A.O

| Date | Mintage | F | VF | XF | Unc |
|---|---|---|---|---|---|
| VS2028(1971) | 1,500,000 | — | 0.10 | 0.15 | 0.20 |

**25 PAISA** KM# 770 **Composition:** Brass **Subject:** Mahendra Coronation

| Date | Mintage | F | VF | XF | Unc |
|---|---|---|---|---|---|
| VS2013(1956) | — | 0.30 | 0.50 | 0.70 | 1.00 |

**25 PAISA** KM# 771 **Composition:** Brass **Obverse:** Four characters in line above trident **Reverse:** Small character at bottom (outer circle)

| Date | Mintage | F | VF | XF | Unc |
|---|---|---|---|---|---|
| VS2015(1958) | — | 1.50 | 2.50 | 4.00 | 6.00 |
| VS2018(1961) | — | 0.25 | 0.40 | 0.60 | 0.80 |
| VS2020(1963) | — | 0.25 | 0.40 | 0.60 | 0.80 |
| VS2022(1965) | — | 2.00 | 3.50 | 6.00 | 9.00 |

**25 PAISA** KM# 771a **Weight:** 2.9900 g. **Composition:** 840.0000 Silver .0913 oz. ASW

| Date | Mintage | F | VF | XF | Unc |
|---|---|---|---|---|---|
| VS2017/615(1960) | — | — | — | — | 100 |

**25 PAISA** **KM# 772** **Composition:** Copper-Nickel **Reverse:** Large different character at bottom **Note:** Two varieties of moon (obverse at upper left) exist as open crescent and almost closed circle.

| Date | Mintage | F | VF | XF | Unc |
|---|---|---|---|---|---|
| VS2021(1964) | — | 0.30 | 0.50 | 0.70 | 1.00 |
| VS2022(1965) | — | 0.30 | 0.50 | 0.70 | 1.00 |
| VS2023(1966) | — | 0.30 | 0.50 | 0.70 | 1.00 |

**25 PAISA** **KM# 773** **Composition:** Copper-Nickel **Obverse:** Five characters in line above trident

| Date | Mintage | F | VF | XF | Unc |
|---|---|---|---|---|---|
| VS2024(1967) | — | — | 0.35 | 0.50 | 0.75 |
| VS2025(1968) | — | — | 15.00 | 20.00 | 25.00 |
| VS2026(1969) | — | — | 0.35 | 0.50 | 0.75 |
| VS2027(1970) | — | — | 0.35 | 0.50 | 0.75 |
| VS2027(1970) Proof | 2,187 | Value: 2.50 | | | |
| VS2028(1971) | — | — | 0.35 | 0.50 | 0.75 |
| VS2028(1971) Proof | 2,380 | Value: 2.50 | | | |

**50 PAISA** **KM# 777** **Composition:** Copper-Nickel **Reverse:** Small character at bottom (outer circle)

| Date | Mintage | F | VF | XF | Unc |
|---|---|---|---|---|---|
| VS2011(1954) | — | 0.50 | 1.00 | 1.50 | 3.00 |
| VS2012(1955) | — | 0.25 | 0.50 | 0.75 | 1.00 |
| VS2013(1956) | — | 0.25 | 0.50 | 1.00 | 2.00 |
| VS2014(1957) | — | 0.25 | 0.50 | 1.00 | 2.00 |
| VS2015(1958) | — | 0.25 | 0.50 | 1.00 | 2.00 |
| VS2016(1959) | — | 0.25 | 0.50 | 1.00 | 2.00 |
| VS2017(1960) | — | 0.25 | 0.30 | 0.75 | 1.25 |
| VS2018(1961) | — | 0.25 | 0.50 | 1.00 | 2.00 |
| VS2020(1963) | — | 0.25 | 0.30 | 0.75 | 1.50 |

**50 PAISA** **KM# 795** **Composition:** Copper-Nickel **Note:** In the name of Queen Ratna Rajya Lakshmi.

| Date | Mintage | F | VF | XF | Unc |
|---|---|---|---|---|---|
| VS2012(1955) | — | 3,000 | 100 | 125 | 150 |

**50 PAISA** **KM# 776** **Composition:** Copper-Nickel **Subject:** Mahendra Coronation

| Date | Mintage | F | VF | XF | Unc |
|---|---|---|---|---|---|
| VS2013(1956) | — | 0.35 | 0.75 | 1.00 | 1.50 |

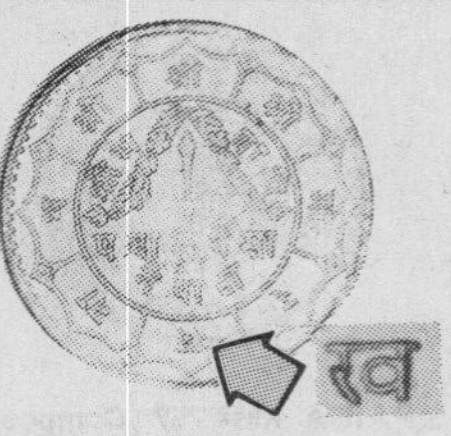

**50 PAISA** **KM# 778** **Composition:** Copper-Nickel **Reverse:** Large different character at bottom

| Date | Mintage | F | VF | XF | Unc |
|---|---|---|---|---|---|
| VS2021(1964) | — | 0.25 | 0.35 | 0.50 | 0.75 |
| VS2022(1965) | — | 0.25 | 0.50 | 0.75 | 1.50 |
| VS2023(1966) | — | 0.25 | 0.50 | 0.75 | 1.00 |

**50 PAISA** **KM# 779** **Composition:** Copper-Nickel **Obverse:** Four characters in line above trident **Note:** Reduced size.

| Date | Mintage | F | VF | XF | Unc |
|---|---|---|---|---|---|
| VS2023(1966) | — | 0.25 | 0.50 | 0.75 | 1.50 |

**50 PAISA** **KM# 780** **Composition:** Copper-Nickel **Obverse:** Five characters in line above trident

| Date | Mintage | F | VF | XF | Unc |
|---|---|---|---|---|---|
| VS2025(1968) | — | — | 0.30 | 0.50 | 1.00 |
| VS2026(1969) | — | — | 0.30 | 0.50 | 0.85 |
| VS2027(1970) Proof | 2,187 | Value: 3.00 | | | |
| VS2028(1971) Proof | 2,380 | Value: 3.00 | | | |

**RUPEE** **KM# 784** **Composition:** Copper-Nickel

| Date | Mintage | F | VF | XF | Unc |
|---|---|---|---|---|---|
| VS2011(1954) | — | 1.25 | 2.25 | 3.50 | 5.00 |
| VS2012(1955) | — | 1.00 | 1.75 | 2.50 | 4.00 |

**RUPEE** **KM# 785** **Composition:** Copper-Nickel **Reverse:** Small character at bottom (outer circle) **Note:** Reduced size.

| Date | Mintage | F | VF | XF | Unc |
|---|---|---|---|---|---|
| VS2012(1955) | — | 0.50 | 0.85 | 1.25 | 1.75 |
| VS2013(1956) | — | 0.50 | 0.85 | 1.25 | 1.75 |
| VS2014(1957) | — | 0.50 | 0.85 | 1.25 | 1.75 |
| VS2015(1958) | — | 0.50 | 0.85 | 1.25 | 1.75 |
| VS2016(1959) | — | 0.50 | 0.85 | 1.25 | 1.75 |
| VS2018(1961) | — | 0.50 | 0.85 | 1.25 | 1.75 |
| VS2020(1963) | — | 0.50 | 0.85 | 1.25 | 1.75 |

**RUPEE** **KM# 797** **Composition:** Copper-Nickel **Note:** In the name of Queen Ratna Rajya Lakshmi.

| Date | Mintage | F | VF | XF | Unc |
|---|---|---|---|---|---|
| VS2012(1955) | 2,000 | — | 100 | 150 | 175 |

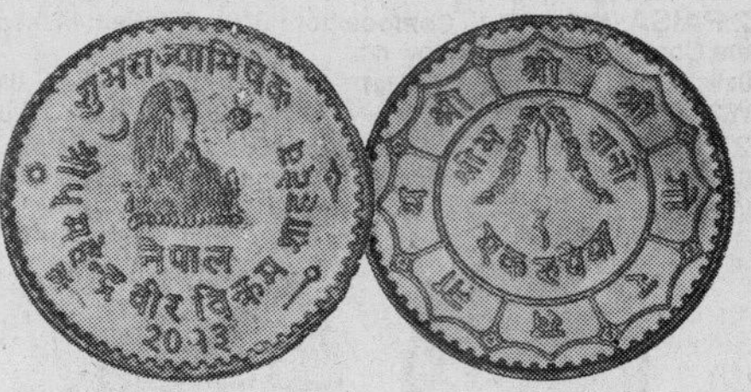

**RUPEE** **KM# 790** **Composition:** Copper-Nickel **Subject:** Mahendra Coronation

| Date | Mintage | F | VF | XF | Unc |
|---|---|---|---|---|---|
| VS2013(1956) | — | — | 1.25 | 1.75 | 2.50 |

**RUPEE** **KM# 786** **Composition:** Copper-Nickel **Reverse:** Large character at bottom

| Date | Mintage | F | VF | XF | Unc |
|---|---|---|---|---|---|
| VS2021(1964) | — | 0.50 | 0.75 | 1.00 | 1.50 |
| VS2022(1965) | — | 0.50 | 1.00 | 1.50 | 2.50 |
| VS2023(1966) | — | 4.50 | 7.50 | 10.00 | 15.00 |

**RUPEE** **KM# 787** **Composition:** Copper-Nickel **Obverse:** Four characters in line above trident **Note:** Reduced size.

| Date | Mintage | F | VF | XF | Unc |
|---|---|---|---|---|---|
| VS2023(1966) | — | 0.75 | 1.00 | 1.35 | 2.00 |

**RUPEE** **KM# 788** **Composition:** Copper-Nickel **Obverse:** Five characters in line above trident

| Date | Mintage | F | VF | XF | Unc |
|---|---|---|---|---|---|
| VS2025(1968) | — | — | 1.00 | 1.50 | 2.00 |
| VS2026(1969) | — | — | 1.00 | 1.40 | 2.00 |
| VS2027(1970) Proof | 2,187 | Value: 4.50 | | | |
| VS2028(1971) Proof | 2,380 | Value: 4.50 | | | |

**10 RUPEE** **KM# 794** **Weight:** 15.6000 g. **Composition:** 0.6000 Silver .3009 oz. ASW **Series:** F.A.O

| Date | Mintage | F | VF | XF | Unc |
|---|---|---|---|---|---|
| VS2025(1968) | 1,000,000 | — | 2.50 | 3.50 | 6.00 |

**1/2 ASARPHI** **KM# 796** **Composition:** Gold **Note:** In the name of Queen Ratna Rajya Lakshmi.

| Date | Mintage | F | VF | XF | Unc |
|---|---|---|---|---|---|
| VS2012(1955) | — | — | — | — | — |

**ASARPHI** **KM# 798** **Weight:** 11.6600 g. **Composition:** Gold **Note:** In the name of Queen Ratna Rajya Lakshmi.

| Date | Mintage | F | VF | XF | Unc |
|---|---|---|---|---|---|
| VS2012(1955) | — | — | — | — | — |

**1/6 ASARFI** **KM# 767** **Weight:** 1.9000 g. **Composition:** Gold **Subject:** Mahendra Coronation

| Date | Mintage | F | VF | XF | Unc |
|---|---|---|---|---|---|
| VS2013(1956) | — | — | 50.00 | 60.00 | 100 |

**1/4 ASARFI** **KM# 775** **Weight:** 2.5000 g. **Composition:** Gold **Note:** Reduced weight

| Date | Mintage | F | VF | XF | Unc |
|---|---|---|---|---|---|
| VS2026(1969) | — | — | — | 75.00 | 110 |

**1/2 ASARFI** **KM# 782** **Weight:** 5.8000 g. **Composition:** Gold

| Date | Mintage | F | VF | XF | Unc |
|---|---|---|---|---|---|
| VS2012(1955) | — | — | 120 | 135 | 165 |
| VS2019(1962) | — | — | 120 | 135 | 165 |

**1/2 ASARFI** **KM# 781** **Weight:** 5.8000 g. **Composition:** Gold **Subject:** Mahendra Coronation

| Date | Mintage | F | VF | XF | Unc |
|---|---|---|---|---|---|
| VS2013(1956) | — | — | 120 | 135 | 165 |

**1/2 ASARFI** **KM# 783** **Weight:** 5.0000 g. **Composition:** Gold **Subject:** Virendra Marriage

| Date | Mintage | F | VF | XF | Unc |
|---|---|---|---|---|---|
| VS2026(1969) | — | — | — | 150 | 180 |

**ASARFI** **KM# 789** **Composition:** Gold

| Date | Mintage | F | VF | XF | Unc |
|---|---|---|---|---|---|
| VS2012(1955) | — | — | 225 | 250 | 300 |
| VS2019(1962) | — | — | 225 | 250 | 300 |

**ASARFI** **KM# 791** **Composition:** Gold **Subject:** Mahendra Coronation

| Date | Mintage | F | VF | XF | Unc |
|---|---|---|---|---|---|
| VS2013(1956) | — | — | 225 | 250 | 300 |

**ASARFI** **KM# 792** **Weight:** 10.0000 g. **Composition:** Gold

| Date | Mintage | F | VF | XF | Unc |
|---|---|---|---|---|---|
| VS2026(1969) | — | — | 225 | 250 | 300 |

**2 ASARFI** **KM# 793** **Composition:** Gold

| Date | Mintage | F | VF | XF | Unc |
|---|---|---|---|---|---|
| VS2012(1955) | — | — | 500 | 550 | 625 |

## Birendra Bir Bikram
### VS2028-2058 / 1971-2001AD

### DECIMAL COINAGE
100 Paisa = 1 Rupee

**PAISA** **KM# 799** **Composition:** Aluminum **Reverse:** National flower

| Date | Mintage | F | VF | XF | Unc |
|---|---|---|---|---|---|
| VS2028(1971) | 10,000 | — | 0.20 | 0.30 | 0.40 |
| VS2029(1972) | 3,036,000 | — | 0.10 | 0.15 | 0.25 |
| VS2029(1972) Proof | 3,943 | Value: 0.60 | | | |
| VS2030(1973) | 1,279,000 | — | 0.10 | 0.15 | 0.25 |
| VS2030(1973) Proof | 8,891 | Value: 0.40 | | | |
| VS2031(1974) | 430,000 | — | 0.10 | 0.15 | 0.25 |
| VS2031(1974) Proof | 11,000 | Value: 0.40 | | | |
| VS2032(1975) | 324,000 | — | 0.10 | 0.15 | 0.25 |
| VS2033(1976) | 217,000 | — | — | 0.10 | 0.25 |
| VS2034(1977) | 1,040,000 | — | 0.10 | 0.15 | 0.25 |
| VS2035(1978) | 394,000 | — | 0.10 | 0.15 | 0.25 |
| VS2036(1979) | — | — | 0.10 | 0.15 | 0.25 |

**PAISA** **KM# 800** **Composition:** Aluminum **Subject:** Virendra Coronation

| Date | Mintage | F | VF | XF | Unc |
|---|---|---|---|---|---|
| VS2031(1974) | 75,000 | — | 0.10 | 0.15 | 0.25 |

**PAISA** **KM# 800a** **Composition:** Copper-Nickel

| Date | Mintage | F | VF | XF | Unc |
|---|---|---|---|---|---|
| VS2031(1974) Proof | 1,000 | Value: 2.50 | | | |

**PAISA** **KM# 1012** **Composition:** Aluminum

| Date | Mintage | F | VF | XF | Unc |
|---|---|---|---|---|---|
| VS2039(1982) | — | — | 4.00 | 6.00 | 8.00 |
| VS2040(1983) | 42,000 | — | — | — | — |

**2 PAISA** **KM# 801** **Composition:** Aluminum **Reverse:** Himalayan Monal

| Date | Mintage | F | VF | XF | Unc |
|---|---|---|---|---|---|
| VS2028(1971) | 8,319 | — | 0.20 | 0.30 | 0.50 |
| VS2029(1972) | 5,206,000 | — | 0.10 | 0.15 | 0.25 |
| VS2029(1972) Proof | 3,943 | Value: 0.70 | | | |
| VS2030(1973) | 2,563,000 | — | 0.10 | 0.15 | 0.25 |
| VS2030(1973) Proof | 8,891 | Value: 0.50 | | | |
| VS2031(1974) Proof | 11,000 | Value: 0.50 | | | |
| VS2033(1976) | 72,000 | — | 0.10 | 0.15 | 0.30 |
| VS2035(1978) | 26,000 | — | 0.10 | 0.15 | 0.30 |

**5 PAISA** **KM# 802** **Composition:** Aluminum

| Date | Mintage | F | VF | XF | Unc |
|---|---|---|---|---|---|
| VS2028(1971) | 3,700,000 | — | 0.10 | 0.20 | 0.50 |
| VS2029(1972) | 23,578,000 | — | 0.10 | 0.20 | 0.50 |
| VS2029(1972) Proof | 3,943 | Value: 0.85 | | | |
| VS2030(1973) | 12,320,000 | — | 0.10 | 0.20 | 0.50 |
| VS2030(1973) Proof | 8,891 | Value: 0.60 | | | |
| VS2031(1974) | 15,730,000 | — | 0.10 | 0.20 | 0.50 |
| VS2031(1974) Proof | 11,000 | Value: 0.60 | | | |
| VS2032(1975) | 19,747,000 | — | 0.10 | 0.20 | 0.50 |
| VS2033(1976) | 29,619,000 | — | 0.10 | 0.20 | 0.50 |
| VS2034(1977) | 27,222,000 | — | 0.10 | 0.20 | 0.50 |
| VS2035(1978) | 27,613,000 | — | 0.10 | 0.20 | 0.50 |
| VS2036(1979) | — | — | 0.10 | 0.20 | 0.50 |
| VS2037(1980) | 13,235,000 | — | 0.10 | 0.20 | 0.50 |
| VS2038(1981) | 15,137,000 | — | 0.10 | 0.20 | 0.50 |
| VS2039(1982) | 8,971,000 | — | 0.10 | 0.20 | 0.50 |

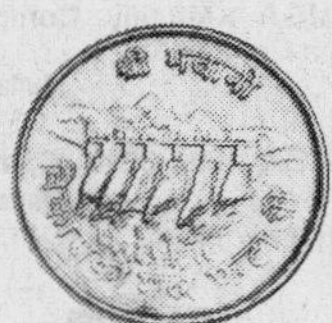

**5 PAISA** **KM# 803** **Composition:** Aluminum **Series:** F.A.O

| Date | Mintage | F | VF | XF | Unc |
|---|---|---|---|---|---|
| VS2031(1974) | 4,584,000 | — | 0.10 | 0.15 | 0.25 |

**5 PAISA** **KM# 804** **Composition:** Aluminum **Subject:** Virendra Coronation

| Date | Mintage | F | VF | XF | Unc |
|---|---|---|---|---|---|
| VS2031(1974) | 2,869,000 | — | 0.10 | 0.25 | 0.50 |

**5 PAISA** **KM# 804a** **Composition:** Copper-Nickel

| Date | Mintage | F | VF | XF | Unc |
|---|---|---|---|---|---|
| VS2031(1974) Proof | 1,000 | Value: 3.00 | | | |

**5 PAISA** **KM# 1013** **Composition:** Aluminum

| Date | Mintage | F | VF | XF | Unc |
|---|---|---|---|---|---|
| VS2039(1982) | 8,971,000 | — | 7.00 | 10.00 | 15.00 |
| VS2040(1983) | 6,430,000 | — | — | 0.10 | 0.25 |
| VS2041(1984) | 9,634,000 | — | — | 0.10 | 0.25 |
| VS2042(1985) | 58,000 | — | — | 0.10 | 0.25 |
| VS2043(1986) | 2,937,000 | — | — | 0.10 | 0.25 |
| VS2044(1987) | 3,126,000 | — | — | 0.10 | 0.25 |
| VS2045(1988) | 1,030,000 | — | — | 0.10 | 0.25 |
| VS2046(1989) | — | — | — | 0.10 | 0.25 |
| VS2047(1990) | — | — | — | 0.10 | 0.25 |

**10 PAISA** **KM# 806** **Composition:** Brass

| Date | Mintage | F | VF | XF | Unc |
|---|---|---|---|---|---|
| VS2028(1971) | 5,035,000 | — | 0.25 | 0.40 | 0.70 |

**10 PAISA** KM# 807 **Composition:** Brass

| Date | Mintage | F | VF | XF | Unc |
|---|---|---|---|---|---|
| VS2029(1972) | 3,297,000 | — | 0.15 | 0.25 | 0.40 |
| VS2029(1972) Proof | 3,943 | Value: 1.00 | | | |
| VS2030(1973) | 5,670,000 | — | 0.15 | 0.25 | 0.40 |
| VS2030(1973) Proof | 8,891 | Value: 0.70 | | | |
| VS2031(1974) Proof | 11,000 | Value: 0.70 | | | |

**10 PAISA** KM# 808 **Composition:** Aluminum **Subject:** Virendra Coronation

| Date | Mintage | F | VF | XF | Unc |
|---|---|---|---|---|---|
| VS2031(1974) | 192,000 | — | 0.10 | 0.20 | 0.35 |

**10 PAISA** KM# 808a **Composition:** Copper-Nickel

| Date | Mintage | F | VF | XF | Unc |
|---|---|---|---|---|---|
| VS2031(1974) Proof | 1,000 | Value: 3.50 | | | |

**10 PAISA** KM# 809 **Composition:** Brass **Series:** F.A.O. International Women's Year

| Date | Mintage | F | VF | XF | Unc |
|---|---|---|---|---|---|
| VS2032(1975) | 2,500,000 | — | 0.10 | 0.15 | 0.25 |

**10 PAISA** KM# 810 **Composition:** Brass **Subject:** Agricultural Developement

| Date | Mintage | F | VF | XF | Unc |
|---|---|---|---|---|---|
| VS2033(1976) | 10,000,000 | — | 0.10 | 0.15 | 0.25 |

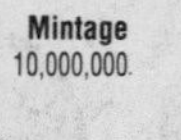

**10 PAISA** KM# 811 **Composition:** Aluminum **Series:** International Year of the Child

| Date | Mintage | F | VF | XF | Unc |
|---|---|---|---|---|---|
| VS2036(1979) | 213,000 | — | 0.10 | 0.15 | 0.25 |

**10 PAISA** KM# 812 **Composition:** Aluminum **Subject:** Education for Village Women

| Date | Mintage | F | VF | XF | Unc |
|---|---|---|---|---|---|
| VS2036(1979) | Inc. above | — | 0.10 | 0.15 | 0.50 |

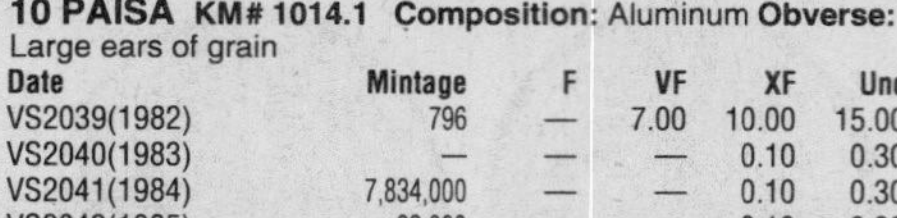

**10 PAISA** KM# 1014.1 **Composition:** Aluminum **Obverse:** Large ears of grain

| Date | Mintage | F | VF | XF | Unc |
|---|---|---|---|---|---|
| VS2039(1982) | 796 | — | 7.00 | 10.00 | 15.00 |
| VS2040(1983) | — | — | — | 0.10 | 0.30 |
| VS2041(1984) | 7,834,000 | — | — | 0.10 | 0.30 |
| VS2042(1985) | 99,000 | — | — | 0.10 | 0.30 |

**10 PAISA** KM# 1014.2 **Composition:** Aluminum **Reverse:** Small ears of grain

| Date | Mintage | F | VF | XF | Unc |
|---|---|---|---|---|---|
| VS2042(1985) | Inc. above | — | — | 0.10 | 0.30 |
| VS2043(1986) | 10,000 | — | — | 0.10 | 0.30 |
| VS2044(1987) | 30,172,000 | — | — | 0.10 | 0.30 |
| VS2045(1988) | 4,140,000 | — | — | 0.10 | 0.30 |
| VS2046(1989) | — | — | — | 0.10 | 0.30 |
| VS2047(1990) | — | — | — | 0.10 | 0.30 |
| VS2048(1991) | — | — | — | 0.10 | 0.30 |

**10 PAISA** KM# 1014.3 **Composition:** Aluminum **Note:** Reduced size.

| Date | Mintage | F | VF | XF | Unc |
|---|---|---|---|---|---|
| VS2051(1994) | — | — | — | 0.10 | 0.30 |
| VS2053(1996) | — | — | — | 0.10 | 0.30 |
| VS2054(1997) | — | — | — | 0.10 | 0.30 |
| VS2055(1998) | — | — | — | 0.10 | 0.30 |
| VS2056(1999) | — | — | — | 0.10 | 0.30 |
| VS2057(2000) | — | — | — | 0.10 | 0.30 |

**Note:**

**20 PAISA** KM# 813 **Composition:** Brass **Series:** F.A.O.

| Date | Mintage | F | VF | XF | Unc |
|---|---|---|---|---|---|
| VS2035(1978) | 234,000 | — | 0.35 | 0.75 | 1.00 |

**20 PAISA** KM# 814 **Composition:** Brass **Series:** International Year of the Child

| Date | Mintage | F | VF | XF | Unc |
|---|---|---|---|---|---|
| VS2036(1979) | 30,000 | — | 0.35 | 0.75 | 1.00 |

**25 PAISA** KM# 815 **Composition:** Copper-Nickel **Note:** Varieties exist.

| Date | Mintage | F | VF | XF | Unc |
|---|---|---|---|---|---|
| VS2028(1971) | 5,691 | — | 0.40 | 0.60 | 0.80 |
| VS2029(1972) Proof | 3,943 | Value: 1.25 | | | |
| VS2030(1973) | 8,676,000 | — | 0.30 | 0.40 | 0.50 |
| VS2030(1973) Proof | 8,891 | Value: 0.80 | | | |
| VS2031(1974) | 1,172,000 | — | 0.35 | 0.50 | 0.75 |
| VS2031(1974) Proof | 11,000 | Value: 0.80 | | | |
| VS2032(1975) | 4,584,000 | — | 0.30 | 0.40 | 0.50 |
| VS2033(1976) | 1,837,000 | — | 0.30 | 0.40 | 0.50 |
| VS2034(1977) | 3,808,000 | — | 0.30 | 0.40 | 0.50 |
| VS2035(1978) | 5,964,000 | — | 0.30 | 0.40 | 0.50 |
| VS2036(1979) | — | — | 0.30 | 0.40 | 0.50 |
| VS2037(1980) | 2,047,000 | — | 0.30 | 0.40 | 0.50 |
| VS2038(1981) | 1,580,000 | — | 0.30 | 0.40 | 0.50 |
| VS2039(1982) | 7,185,000 | — | 0.30 | 0.40 | 0.50 |

**25 PAISA** KM# 816.1 **Composition:** Copper-Nickel **Subject:** Virendra Coronation

| Date | Mintage | F | VF | XF | Unc |
|---|---|---|---|---|---|
| VS2031(1974) | 431,000 | — | 0.35 | 0.50 | 0.75 |

**25 PAISA** KM# 816.2 **Composition:** Copper-Nickel **Edge:** Reeded

| Date | Mintage | F | VF | XF | Unc |
|---|---|---|---|---|---|
| VS2031(1974) Proof | 1,000 | Value: 4.00 | | | |

**25 PAISA** KM# 817 **Composition:** Brass **Series:** World Food Day

| Date | Mintage | F | VF | XF | Unc |
|---|---|---|---|---|---|
| VS2038(1981) | 2,000,000 | — | — | 0.10 | 0.30 |

**25 PAISA** KM# 818 **Composition:** Brass **Series:** International Year of Disabled Persons

| Date | Mintage | F | VF | XF | Unc |
|---|---|---|---|---|---|
| VS2038(1981) | Inc. above | — | 0.10 | 0.25 | 0.50 |

**25 PAISA** KM# 1015.1 **Composition:** Aluminum **Obverse:** Royal crown

| Date | Mintage | F | VF | XF | Unc |
|---|---|---|---|---|---|
| VS2039(1982) | — | — | 4.00 | 6.00 | 8.00 |
| VS2040(1983) | 7,603,000 | — | 0.10 | 0.25 | 0.50 |
| VS2041(1984) | 15,534,000 | — | 0.10 | 0.25 | 0.50 |
| VS2042(1985) | 12,586,000 | — | 0.10 | 0.25 | 0.50 |
| VS2043(1986) | 54,000 | — | 0.10 | 0.25 | 0.50 |
| VS2044(1987) | 13,633,000 | — | 0.10 | 0.25 | 0.50 |
| VS2045(1988) | 13,046,000 | — | 0.10 | 0.25 | 0.50 |
| VS2046(1989) | — | — | 0.10 | 0.25 | 0.50 |
| VS2047(1990) | — | — | 0.10 | 0.25 | 0.50 |
| VS2048(1991) | — | — | 0.10 | 0.25 | 0.50 |
| VS2049(1992) | — | — | 0.10 | 0.25 | 0.50 |
| VS2050(1993) | — | — | 0.10 | 0.25 | 0.50 |

**25 PAISA** KM# 1015.2 **Composition:** Aluminum **Obverse:** Royal crown **Note:** Reduced size.

| Date | Mintage | F | VF | XF | Unc |
|---|---|---|---|---|---|
| VS2051(1994) | — | — | 0.10 | 0.25 | 0.50 |
| VS2053(1996) | — | — | 0.10 | 0.25 | 0.50 |
| VS2054(1997) | — | — | 0.10 | 0.25 | 0.50 |
| VS2055(1998) | — | — | 0.10 | 0.25 | 0.50 |
| VS2056(1999) | — | — | 0.10 | 0.25 | 0.50 |

**50 PAISA** **KM# 821** **Composition:** Copper-Nickel **Note:** Obverse die variations are known to exist.

| Date | Mintage | F | VF | XF | Unc |
|---|---|---|---|---|---|
| VS2028(1971) | 5,343 | — | 0.35 | 0.50 | 1.00 |
| VS2029(1972) | 347,000 | — | 0.35 | 0.50 | 0.90 |
| VS2029(1972) Proof | 3,943 | Value: 1.50 | | | |
| VS2030(1973) | 998,000 | — | 0.35 | 0.50 | 0.90 |
| VS2030(1973) Proof | 8,891 | Value: 1.00 | | | |
| VS2031(1974) | 16,000 | — | 0.35 | 0.50 | 1.00 |
| VS2031(1974) Proof | 11,000 | Value: 1.00 | | | |
| VS2032(1975) | 227,000 | — | 0.35 | 0.50 | 0.90 |
| VS2033(1976) | 3,446,000 | — | 0.35 | 0.50 | 0.75 |
| VS2034(1977) | 6,016,000 | — | 0.35 | 0.50 | 0.75 |
| VS2035(1978) | 2,355,000 | — | 0.35 | 0.50 | 0.75 |
| VS2036(1979) | — | — | 0.35 | 0.50 | 0.75 |
| VS2037(1980) | 4,861,000 | — | 0.35 | 0.50 | 0.75 |
| VS2038(1981) | 929,000 | — | 0.35 | 0.50 | 0.75 |
| VS2039(1982) | 2,954,000 | — | 0.35 | 0.50 | 0.75 |

**50 PAISA** **KM# 822.2** **Composition:** Copper-Nickel **Edge:** Reeded **Note:** 1.5mm thick.

| Date | Mintage | F | VF | XF | Unc |
|---|---|---|---|---|---|
| VS2031(1974) Proof | 1,000 | Value: 5.00 | | | |

**50 PAISA** **KM# 822.1** **Composition:** Copper-Nickel **Subject:** Virendra Coronation **Note:** 1mm thick.

| Date | Mintage | F | VF | XF | Unc |
|---|---|---|---|---|---|
| VS2031(1974) | 136,000 | — | 0.50 | 0.75 | 1.25 |

**50 PAISA** **KM# 846** **Composition:** Copper-Nickel **Note:** In the name of Queen Aishvarya Rajya Lakshmi

| Date | Mintage | F | VF | XF | Unc |
|---|---|---|---|---|---|
| VS2031(1974) | — | — | — | — | 100 |

**50 PAISA** **KM# 823** **Composition:** Copper-Nickel **Series:** World Food Day

| Date | Mintage | F | VF | XF | Unc |
|---|---|---|---|---|---|
| VS2038(1981) | 2,000,000 | — | 0.10 | 0.30 | 0.60 |

**50 PAISA** **KM# 824** **Composition:** Copper-Nickel **Series:** Internatinal Year of Disabled Persons

| Date | Mintage | F | VF | XF | Unc |
|---|---|---|---|---|---|
| VS2038(1981) | Inc. above | — | 0.50 | 0.75 | 1.25 |

**50 PAISA** **KM# 821a** **Composition:** Copper-Nickel

| Date | Mintage | F | VF | XF | Unc |
|---|---|---|---|---|---|
| VS2039(1982) | Inc. above | — | 0.10 | 0.25 | 0.50 |
| VS2040(1983) | 72,000 | — | 0.10 | 0.25 | 0.50 |
| VS2041(1984) | 5,917,000 | — | 0.10 | 0.25 | 0.50 |

**50 PAISA** **KM# 1016** **Composition:** Copper-Nickel **Subject:** Family Planning

| Date | Mintage | F | VF | XF | Unc |
|---|---|---|---|---|---|
| VS2041(1984) | — | — | 0.10 | 0.25 | 0.50 |

**50 PAISA** **KM# 1018.1** **Composition:** Stainless Steel **Obverse:** Smaller trident in center

| Date | Mintage | F | VF | XF | Unc |
|---|---|---|---|---|---|
| VS2044(1987) | 6,341,000 | — | 0.10 | 0.25 | 0.50 |
| VS2045(1988) | 7,350,000 | — | 0.10 | 0.25 | 0.50 |
| VS2046(1989) | — | — | 0.10 | 0.25 | 0.50 |

**50 PAISA** **KM# 1018.2** **Composition:** Stainless Steel **Obverse:** Larger trident in center

| Date | Mintage | F | VF | XF | Unc |
|---|---|---|---|---|---|
| VS2047(1990) | — | — | 0.10 | 0.25 | 0.50 |
| VS2048(1991) | — | — | 0.10 | 0.25 | 0.50 |
| VS2049(1992) | — | — | 0.10 | 0.25 | 0.50 |

**50 PAISA** **KM# 1072** **Composition:** Aluminum **Obverse:** Royal crown **Note:** Coins dated VS2051 exist in two minor varieties being struck at Kathmandu and Singapore.

| Date | Mintage | F | VF | XF | Unc |
|---|---|---|---|---|---|
| VS2051(1994) | — | — | 0.10 | 0.20 | 0.40 |
| VS2052(1995) | — | — | 0.10 | 0.20 | 0.40 |
| VS2053(1996) | — | — | 0.10 | 0.20 | 0.40 |
| VS2054(1997) | — | — | 0.10 | 0.20 | 0.40 |
| VS2055(1998) | — | — | 0.10 | 0.20 | 0.40 |
| VS2056(1999) | — | — | 0.10 | 0.20 | 0.40 |
| VS2057(2000) | — | — | 0.10 | 0.20 | 0.40 |

**RUPEE** **KM# 828** **Weight:** 10.2000 g. **Composition:** Copper-Nickel

| Date | Mintage | F | VF | XF | Unc |
|---|---|---|---|---|---|
| VS2028(1971) | 5,030 | — | 0.50 | 1.00 | 2.00 |
| VS2029(1972) | 22,000 | — | 0.50 | 1.00 | 1.50 |
| VS2029(1972) Proof | 3,943 | Value: 2.50 | | | |
| VS2030(1973) | 5,667 | — | 0.50 | 1.00 | 2.00 |
| VS2030(1973) Proof | 8,891 | Value: 2.00 | | | |
| VS2031(1974) Proof | 11,000 | Value: 1.50 | | | |

**RUPEE** **KM# 829.2** **Composition:** Copper-Nickel **Edge:** Reeded **Note:** 2.5mm thick.

| Date | Mintage | F | VF | XF | Unc |
|---|---|---|---|---|---|
| VS2031(1974) Proof | 1,000 | Value: 6.00 | | | |

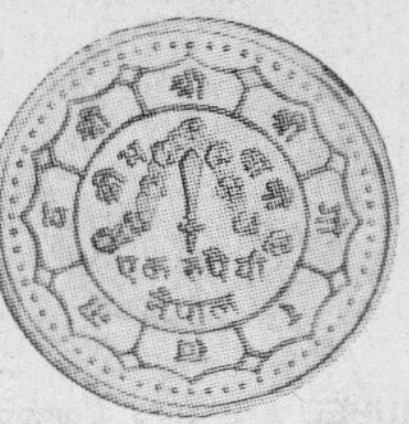

**RUPEE** **KM# 829.1** **Composition:** Copper-Nickel **Subject:** Virendra Coronation **Note:** 2mm thick.

| Date | Mintage | F | VF | XF | Unc |
|---|---|---|---|---|---|
| VS2031(1974) | — | — | 0.75 | 1.25 | 1.75 |

**RUPEE** **KM# 848** **Composition:** Copper-Nickel **Note:** In the name of Queen Aishvarya Rajya Lakshmi

| Date | Mintage | F | VF | XF | Unc |
|---|---|---|---|---|---|
| VS2031(1974) | — | — | — | — | 150 |

**RUPEE** **KM# 831** **Composition:** Copper-Nickel **Series:** F.A.O. International Women's Year

| Date | Mintage | F | VF | XF | Unc |
|---|---|---|---|---|---|
| VS2032(1975) | 1,500,000 | — | 0.25 | 0.50 | 1.25 |

**RUPEE** **KM# 828a** **Weight:** 7.5000 g. **Composition:** Copper-Nickel

| Date | Mintage | F | VF | XF | Unc |
|---|---|---|---|---|---|
| VS2033(1976) | 58,000 | — | 0.50 | 1.00 | 1.50 |
| VS2034(1977) | 30,000,000 | — | 0.25 | 0.50 | 1.00 |

**Note:** Coins dated VS2034 were struck at the Canberra Mint and have a very shiny surface

| Date | Mintage | F | VF | XF | Unc |
|---|---|---|---|---|---|
| VS2035(1978) | — | — | 0.25 | 0.50 | 1.00 |
| VS2036(1979) | — | — | 0.25 | 0.50 | 1.00 |
| VS2036(1979) | 30,000,000 | — | 0.25 | 0.50 | 1.00 |

**Note:** Coins dated VS2036 were struck at the Canberra Mint and have a very shiny surface

**RUPEE** **KM# 1019** **Composition:** Copper-Nickel **Subject:** Family Planning

| Date | Mintage | F | VF | XF | Unc |
|---|---|---|---|---|---|
| VS2041(1984) | 21,000 | — | — | — | 0.75 |

**RUPEE** **KM# 1061** **Composition:** Stainless Steel **Obverse:** Smaller trident in center

| Date | Mintage | F | VF | XF | Unc |
|---|---|---|---|---|---|
| VS2045(1988) Prooflike | — | — | 0.25 | 0.50 | 1.00 |
| VS2048(1991) Prooflike | — | — | 0.25 | 0.50 | 1.00 |
| VS2049(1992) Prooflike | — | — | 0.25 | 0.50 | 1.25 |

**RUPEE KM# 1073 Composition:** Brass Plated Steel **Reverse:** Large legends **Size:** 21 mm.

| Date | Mintage | F | VF | XF | Unc |
|---|---|---|---|---|---|
| VS2051(1994) | — | — | 0.25 | 0.50 | 1.00 |

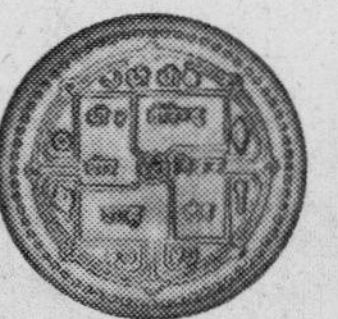

**RUPEE KM# 1073a Composition:** Brass **Obverse:** Traditional design. **Reverse:** Small legends **Size:** 20 mm.

| Date | Mintage | F | VF | XF | Unc |
|---|---|---|---|---|---|
| VS2052(1995) | — | — | — | — | 1.00 |
| VS2053(1996) | — | — | — | — | 1.00 |
| VS2054(1997) | — | — | — | — | 1.00 |
| VS2055(1998) | — | — | — | — | 1.00 |
| VS2056(1999) | — | — | — | — | 1.00 |
| VS2057(2000) | — | — | — | — | 1.00 |

**RUPEE KM# 1092.1 Composition:** Brass **Series:** U.N. 50th Anniversary

| Date | Mintage | F | VF | XF | Unc |
|---|---|---|---|---|---|
| VS2052(1995) | — | — | — | — | 1.75 |

**RUPEE Composition:** Brass **Obverse:** Similar to KM#1073

| Date | Mintage | F | VF | XF | Unc |
|---|---|---|---|---|---|
| VS2052(1995) | — | — | — | — | 1.75 |

**RUPEE KM# 1115 Composition:** Brass **Subject:** Visit Nepal '98 **Obverse:** Traditional design **Reverse:** Moon and sun flanking mountain top

| Date | Mintage | F | VF | XF | Unc |
|---|---|---|---|---|---|
| VS2054(1997) | — | — | — | — | 1.00 |

**RUPEE KM# 1139 Composition:** Brass **Subject:** Gorkhapatra Centenary **Reverse:** Inscription: "Gorkhapata 1958-VS2057" within wreath of 10 people reading newspapers

| Date | Mintage | F | VF | XF | Unc |
|---|---|---|---|---|---|
| VS2057(2000) | — | — | — | — | 1.00 |

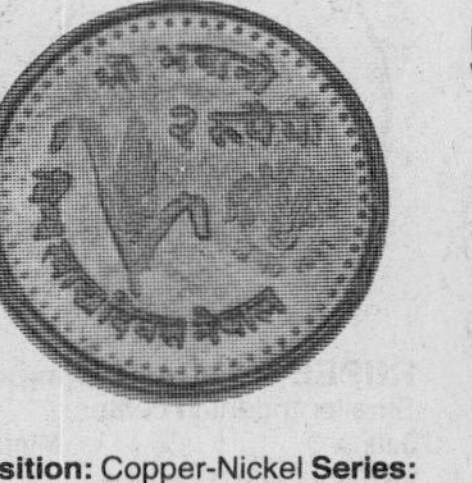

**2 RUPEES KM# 832 Composition:** Copper-Nickel **Series:** World Food Day

| Date | Mintage | F | VF | XF | Unc |
|---|---|---|---|---|---|
| VS2038(1981) | 1,000,000 | — | 0.50 | 0.75 | 1.50 |

**2 RUPEES KM# 1025 Composition:** Copper-Nickel **Series:** F.A.O. **Note:** Size of obverse square varies. Reverse varieties exist.

| Date | Mintage | F | VF | XF | Unc |
|---|---|---|---|---|---|
| VS2039(1982) | 366,000 | — | 0.50 | 0.75 | 1.50 |

**2 RUPEES KM# 1020 Composition:** Copper-Nickel **Subject:** Family Planning

| Date | Mintage | F | VF | XF | Unc |
|---|---|---|---|---|---|
| VS2041(1984) | 11,000 | — | 0.50 | 0.75 | 1.50 |

**2 RUPEES KM# 1074 Composition:** Brass Plated Steel

| Date | Mintage | F | VF | XF | Unc |
|---|---|---|---|---|---|
| VS2051(1994) | — | — | 0.35 | 0.60 | 1.25 |
| VS2053(1996) | — | — | 0.35 | 0.60 | 1.25 |

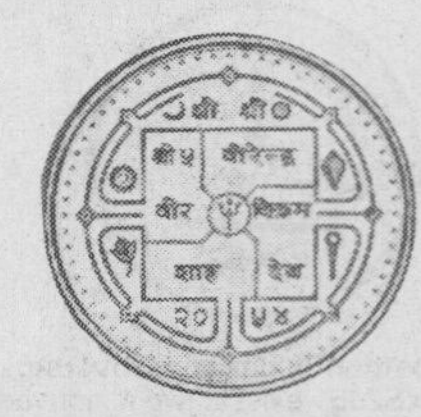

**2 RUPEES KM# 1116 Composition:** Brass Plated Steel **Subject:** Visit Nepal '98 **Obverse:** Traditional design **Reverse:** Moon and sun flanking mountain top

| Date | Mintage | F | VF | XF | Unc |
|---|---|---|---|---|---|
| VS2054(1997) | — | — | — | — | 1.25 |

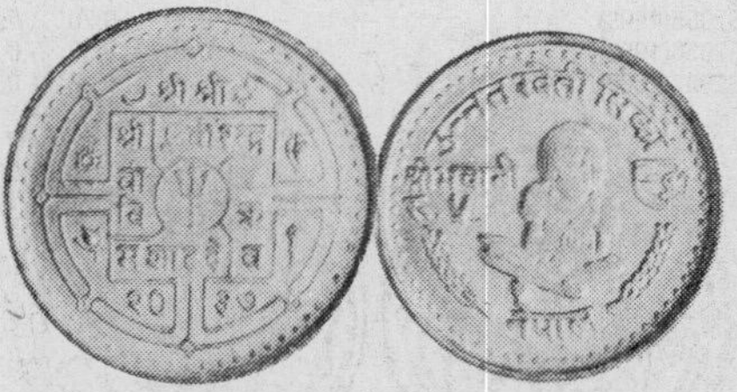

**5 RUPEE KM# 833 Composition:** Copper-Nickel **Subject:** Rural Women's Advancement

| Date | Mintage | F | VF | XF | Unc |
|---|---|---|---|---|---|
| VS2037(1980) | 50,000 | — | 0.75 | 1.50 | 3.00 |

**5 RUPEE KM# 834 Composition:** Copper-Nickel **Subject:** National Bank Silver Jubilee **Note:** Size varies 29-30 mm.

| Date | Mintage | F | VF | XF | Unc |
|---|---|---|---|---|---|
| VS2038(1981) | 64,000 | — | 0.75 | 1.50 | 3.00 |

**5 RUPEE KM# 1009 Composition:** Copper-Nickel **Note:** Circulation coinage

| Date | Mintage | F | VF | XF | Unc |
|---|---|---|---|---|---|
| VS2039(1982) | Inc. above | — | 0.50 | 1.00 | 2.00 |
| VS2040(1983) | 478,000 | — | 0.30 | 0.50 | 1.00 |

**5 RUPEE KM# 1017 Composition:** Copper-Nickel **Subject:** Family Planning

| Date | Mintage | F | VF | XF | Unc |
|---|---|---|---|---|---|
| VS2041(1984) | 458,000 | — | 0.50 | 1.00 | 2.00 |

**5 RUPEE KM# 1023 Composition:** Copper-Nickel **Subject:** Year of Youth

| Date | Mintage | F | VF | XF | Unc |
|---|---|---|---|---|---|
| VS2042(1985) | 1,124,000 | — | — | — | 2.50 |

**5 RUPEE KM# 1047 Composition:** Copper-Nickel **Subject:** Social Services

| Date | Mintage | F | VF | XF | Unc |
|---|---|---|---|---|---|
| VS2042(1985) | Inc. above | — | — | — | 3.50 |

**5 RUPEE KM# 1028 Composition:** Copper-Nickel **Series:** World Food Day

| Date | Mintage | F | VF | XF | Unc |
|---|---|---|---|---|---|
| VS2043(1986) | 99,000 | — | — | — | 3.50 |

**5 RUPEE KM# 1042 Composition:** Copper-Nickel **Subject:** 15th World Buddhist Conference **Note:** Varieties exist.

| Date | Mintage | F | VF | XF | Unc |
|---|---|---|---|---|---|
| VS2043(1986) | 135,000 | — | — | — | 3.50 |

**5 RUPEE KM# 1030 Composition:** Copper-Nickel **Subject:** 10th Year of National Social Security Administration

| Date | Mintage | F | VF | XF | Unc |
|---|---|---|---|---|---|
| VS2044(1987) | 104,000 | — | — | — | 3.50 |
| VS2045(1988) | — | — | — | — | 3.50 |

**5 RUPEE KM# 1043 Composition:** Copper **Subject:** 3rd SAARC Summit

| Date | Mintage | F | VF | XF | Unc |
|---|---|---|---|---|---|
| VS2044(1987) | 2,000 | — | — | — | 6.50 |

**5 RUPEE KM# 1053 Composition:** Copper-Nickel **Series:** World Food Day

| Date | Mintage | F | VF | XF | Unc |
|---|---|---|---|---|---|
| VS2047(1990) | — | — | — | — | 4.00 |

**5 RUPEE KM# 1063 Composition:** Copper-Nickel **Subject:** New Constitution

| Date | Mintage | F | VF | XF | Unc |
|---|---|---|---|---|---|
| VS2047(1990) | — | — | — | — | 3.25 |

**5 RUPEE KM# 1062 Composition:** Copper-Nickel **Subject:** Parliament Session

| Date | Mintage | F | VF | XF | Unc |
|---|---|---|---|---|---|
| VS2048(1991) | — | — | — | — | 3.00 |

**5 RUPEE KM# 1075.1 Composition:** Brass Plated Steel

| Date | Mintage | F | VF | XF | Unc |
|---|---|---|---|---|---|
| VS2051(1994) | — | — | — | — | 1.50 |

**5 RUPEE KM# 1075.2 Composition:** Brass Plated Steel

| Date | Mintage | F | VF | XF | Unc |
|---|---|---|---|---|---|
| VS2053(1996) | — | — | — | — | 1.50 |

**5 RUPEE KM# 1117 Composition:** Brass Plated Steel **Subject:** Visit Nepal '98 **Obverse:** Traditional design **Reverse:** Sun and moon flanking mountain top

| Date | Mintage | F | VF | XF | Unc |
|---|---|---|---|---|---|
| VS2054(1997) | — | — | — | — | 1.50 |

**10 RUPEE KM# 835 Weight:** 8.0000 g. **Composition:** 0.2500 Silver .0643 oz. ASW **Series:** F.A.O.

| Date | Mintage | F | VF | XF | Unc |
|---|---|---|---|---|---|
| VS2031(1974) | 39,000 | — | — | 4.00 | 6.00 |

**10 RUPEE KM# 1004 Composition:** Copper-Nickel **Subject:** 30th Anniversary - Ascent of Mt. Everest **Obverse:** Similar to 5 Rupee, KM#833

| Date | Mintage | F | VF | XF | Unc |
|---|---|---|---|---|---|
| VS2040(1983) | 2,000 | — | — | — | 12.50 |

**10 RUPEE KM# 1076 Composition:** Brass Plated Steel

| Date | Mintage | F | VF | XF | Unc |
|---|---|---|---|---|---|
| VS2051(1994) | — | — | — | — | 2.50 |

**10 RUPEE KM# 1083 Composition:** Copper-Nickel **Subject:** 75th Anniversary - International Labor Organization

| Date | Mintage | F | VF | XF | Unc |
|---|---|---|---|---|---|
| VS2051(1994) | — | — | — | — | 4.50 |

**10 RUPEE KM# 1089 Composition:** Copper-Nickel **Subject:** 50th Anniversary - F.A.O. Logo

| Date | Mintage | F | VF | XF | Unc |
|---|---|---|---|---|---|
| VS2052(1995) | — | — | — | — | 4.00 |

**10 RUPEE KM# 1118 Composition:** Copper-Nickel **Subject:** Visit Nepal '97 **Obverse:** Traditional design **Reverse:** Moon and sun flanking mountain top

| Date | Mintage | F | VF | XF | Unc |
|---|---|---|---|---|---|
| VS2054(1997) | — | — | — | — | 3.00 |

**20 RUPEE KM# 836 Weight:** 14.8500 g. **Composition:** 0.5000 Silver .2387 oz. ASW **Series:** F.A.O. International Women's Year

| Date | Mintage | F | VF | XF | Unc |
|---|---|---|---|---|---|
| VS2032(1975) | 50,000 | — | — | 3.50 | 7.50 |

**20 RUPEE KM# 837 Weight:** 14.8500 g. **Composition:** 0.5000 Silver .2387 oz. ASW **Series:** International Year of the Child

| Date | Mintage | F | VF | XF | Unc |
|---|---|---|---|---|---|
| VS2036(1979) | — | — | — | 2.50 | 5.00 |

**20 RUPEE KM# 837a Weight:** 15.0000 g. **Composition:** 0.9250 Silver .4461 oz. ASW

| Date | Mintage | F | VF | XF | Unc |
|---|---|---|---|---|---|
| VS2036(1979) Proof | 1,000 | Value: 27.50 | | | |

**25 RUPEE** **KM# 839** **Weight:** 25.6000 g. **Composition:** 0.5000 Silver .4115 oz. ASW **Series:** Conservation **Reverse:** Monal Pheasant

| Date | Mintage | F | VF | XF | Unc |
|---|---|---|---|---|---|
| VS2031(1974) | 11,000 | — | — | — | 12.50 |

**25 RUPEE** **KM# 839a** **Weight:** 28.2800 g. **Composition:** 0.9250 Silver .8411 oz. ASW **Reverse:** Monal Pheasant

| Date | Mintage | F | VF | XF | Unc |
|---|---|---|---|---|---|
| VS2031(1974) Proof | 11,000 | Value: 18.50 | | | |

**25 RUPEE** **KM# 838** **Weight:** 25.6000 g. **Composition:** 0.5000 Silver .4115 oz. ASW **Subject:** Virendra Coronation **Note:** 2mm thick.

| Date | Mintage | F | VF | XF | Unc |
|---|---|---|---|---|---|
| VS2031(1974) | 75,000 | — | — | 4.00 | 9.00 |

**25 RUPEE** **KM# 838a** **Weight:** 28.2800 g. **Composition:** 0.9250 Silver .8411 oz. ASW **Edge:** Reeded **Note:** 3mm thick.

| Date | Mintage | F | VF | XF | Unc |
|---|---|---|---|---|---|
| VS2031(1974) Proof | 2,000 | Value: 22.50 | | | |

**25 RUPEE** **KM# 1051** **Weight:** 12.0000 g. **Composition:** 0.2500 Silver .0965 oz. ASW

| Date | Mintage | F | VF | XF | Unc |
|---|---|---|---|---|---|
| VS2041(1984) | — | — | — | — | 15.00 |

**25 RUPEE** **KM# 1048** **Weight:** 12.0000 g. **Composition:** 0.2500 Silver .0965 oz. ASW **Subject:** 25th Anniversary of Panchayat

| Date | Mintage | F | VF | XF | Unc |
|---|---|---|---|---|---|
| VS2042(1985) | 9,962,000 | — | — | — | 10.00 |

**25 RUPEE** **KM# 1135** **Weight:** 8.5000 g. **Composition:** Copper Nickel **Subject:** Silver Jubilee of King's Accession **Obverse:** Traditional design. **Reverse:** Crown on radiant emblem. **Edge:** Plain. **Size:** 29 mm.

| Date | Mintage | F | VF | XF | Unc |
|---|---|---|---|---|---|
| VS2053(1996) | — | — | — | — | 3.50 |

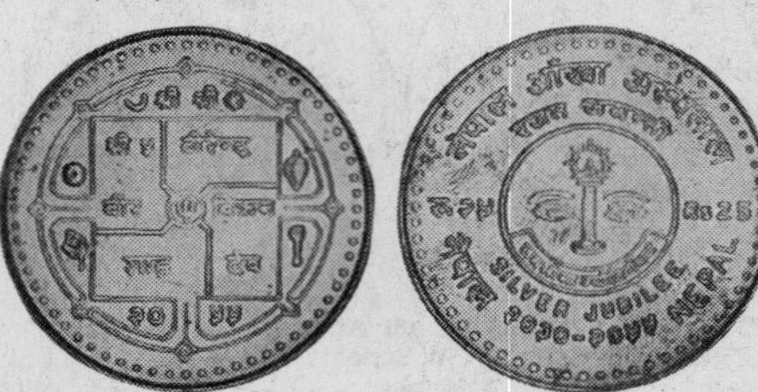

**25 RUPEE** **KM# 1126** **Composition:** Copper-Nickel **Subject:** Silver Jubilee **Obverse:** Traditional design **Reverse:** Stylized face design

| Date | Mintage | F | VF | XF | Unc |
|---|---|---|---|---|---|
| VS2055(1998) | — | — | — | — | 4.50 |

**50 RUPEE** **KM# 841** **Weight:** 31.8000 g. **Composition:** 0.5000 Silver .5112 oz. ASW **Series:** Conservation **Obverse:** Similar to 25 Rupee, KM#839 **Reverse:** Red panda

| Date | Mintage | F | VF | XF | Unc |
|---|---|---|---|---|---|
| VS2031(1974) | 11,000 | — | — | — | 16.50 |

**50 RUPEE** **KM# 841a** **Weight:** 35.0000 g. **Composition:** 0.9250 Silver 1.0409 oz. ASW

| Date | Mintage | F | VF | XF | Unc |
|---|---|---|---|---|---|
| VS2031(1974) Proof | 10,000 | Value: 22.50 | | | |

**50 RUPEE** **KM# 842** **Weight:** 25.0000 g. **Composition:** 0.5000 Silver .4018 oz. ASW **Subject:** Education for Village Women

| Date | Mintage | F | VF | XF | Unc |
|---|---|---|---|---|---|
| VS2036(1979) | 15,000 | — | — | — | 12.50 |

**50 RUPEE** **KM# 842a** **Weight:** 25.0000 g. **Composition:** 0.9250 Silver .7436 oz. ASW

| Date | Mintage | F | VF | XF | Unc |
|---|---|---|---|---|---|
| VS2036(1979) Proof | 1,000 | Value: 42.50 | | | |

**50 RUPEE** **KM# 843** **Weight:** 14.9000 g. **Composition:** 0.5000 Silver .2395 oz. ASW **Series:** International Year of Disabled Persons

| Date | Mintage | F | VF | XF | Unc |
|---|---|---|---|---|---|
| VS2038(1981) | 16,000 | — | — | — | 8.50 |

**50 RUPEE** **KM# A851** **Weight:** 15.0000 g. **Composition:** 0.4000 Silver .1929 oz. ASW **Series:** International Year of the Child **Note:** Similar to 100 Rupee, KM#851.

| Date | Mintage | F | VF | XF | Unc |
|---|---|---|---|---|---|
| VS2038(1981) | — | — | — | — | — |

**50 RUPEE** **KM# 1046** **Weight:** 15.0000 g. **Composition:** 0.5000 Silver .2406 oz. ASW **Subject:** 50th Anniversary of Kathmandu Mint

| Date | Mintage | F | VF | XF | Unc |
|---|---|---|---|---|---|
| VS2039(1982) | 8,765 | — | — | 13.50 | 17.50 |

**50 RUPEE** **KM# 1119** **Composition:** Bronze **Obverse:** Traditional square in circle design **Reverse:** Buddha's portrait and Ashoka pillar **Note:** Lord Buddha; Similar to 1500 Rupee, KM#1120.

| Date | Mintage | F | VF | XF | Unc |
|---|---|---|---|---|---|
| VS2055(1998) | 30,000 | — | — | — | 10.00 |

**50 RUPEE** **KM# 1136** **Composition:** Brass **Subject:** 50th Anniversary - Radio Nepal **Obverse:** Traditional design. **Reverse:** Stylized design. **Edge:** Plain. **Size:** 37.5 mm.

| Date | Mintage | F | VF | XF | Unc |
|---|---|---|---|---|---|
| VS2056(1999) | — | — | — | — | 10.00 |

**50 RUPEE** **KM# 1137** **Composition:** Brass **Subject:** St. Xavier's Golden Jubilee **Obverse:** Traditional design. **Reverse:** Coat of arms. **Edge:** Plain. **Size:** 37.5 mm.

| Date | Mintage | F | VF | XF | Unc |
|---|---|---|---|---|---|
| VS2057(2000) | — | — | — | — | 10.00 |

**50 RUPEE** **KM# 1127** **Composition:** Bronze **Subject:** Buddha **Obverse:** Traditional square design **Reverse:** Buddha and four figures **Edge:** Reeded **Size:** 38.7 mm.

| Date | Mintage | F | VF | XF | Unc |
|---|---|---|---|---|---|
| 2000(2000) | 30,000 | — | — | — | 10.00 |

**100 RUPEE** **KM# 850.1** **Weight:** 25.4900 g. **Composition:** 0.5000 Silver .4050 oz. ASW **Series:** World Food Day **Subject:** 50th Anniversary - Radio Nepal

| Date | Mintage | F | VF | XF | Unc |
|---|---|---|---|---|---|
| VS2038(1981) | 18,000 | — | — | — | 22.50 |

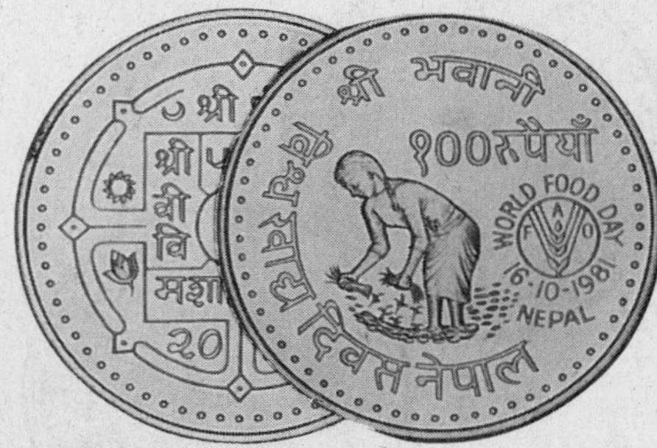

**100 RUPEE** **KM# 850.2** **Weight:** 25.4900 g. **Composition:** 0.9250 Silver .7580 oz. ASW

| Date | Mintage | F | VF | XF | Unc |
|---|---|---|---|---|---|
| VS2038(1981) | — | Value: 80.00 | | | |

**100 RUPEE** **KM# 851** **Weight:** 19.4400 g. **Composition:** 0.5000 Silver .3125 oz. ASW **Series:** International Year of the Child

| Date | Mintage | F | VF | XF | Unc |
|---|---|---|---|---|---|
| VS2038(1981) Proof | 9,270 | Value: 17.50 | | | |

**100 RUPEE** **KM# 1005** **Weight:** 31.1000 g. **Composition:** 0.9250 Silver .9250 oz. ASW **Subject:** 30th Anniversary Ascent of Mt. Everest **Obverse:** Similar to 5 Rupee, KM#833

| Date | Mintage | F | VF | XF | Unc |
|---|---|---|---|---|---|
| VS2040(1983) Proof | 1,500 | Value: 55.00 | | | |

**100 RUPEE** **KM# 1024** **Weight:** 15.0000 g. **Composition:** 0.5000 Silver .2411 oz. ASW **Subject:** Year of Youth

| Date | Mintage | F | VF | XF | Unc |
|---|---|---|---|---|---|
| VS2042(1985) | 8,199 | — | — | — | 12.00 |

**100 RUPEE** **KM# 1114** **Weight:** 12.0400 g. **Composition:** 0.6000 Silver .2323 oz. ASW **Series:** 50th Anniversary - F.A.O **Obverse:** Traditional design

| Date | Mintage | F | VF | XF | Unc |
|---|---|---|---|---|---|
| VS2052(1995) | — | — | — | — | 15.00 |

**100 RUPEE** **KM# 1102** **Composition:** Copper-Nickel **Series:** Nepal Wildlife **Obverse:** Traditional design **Reverse:** Multicolor tiger

| Date | Mintage | F | VF | XF | Unc |
|---|---|---|---|---|---|
| VS2054(1997) | 25,000 | — | — | — | 22.50 |

**100 RUPEE** **KM# 1103** **Composition:** Copper-Nickel **Series:** Nepal Wildlife **Obverse:** Traditional design **Reverse:** Multicolor rhino

| Date | Mintage | F | VF | XF | Unc |
|---|---|---|---|---|---|
| VS2054(1997) | 25,000 | — | — | — | 22.50 |

**200 RUPEE** **KM# 1031** **Weight:** 15.0000 g. **Composition:** 0.6000 Silver .2894 oz. ASW **Subject:** 10th Anniversary of National Social Security Administration

| Date | Mintage | F | VF | XF | Unc |
|---|---|---|---|---|---|
| VS2044(1987) | 4,145 | — | — | — | 25.00 |

**250 RUPEE** **KM# 1007** **Weight:** 28.2800 g. **Composition:** 0.9250 Silver .8411 oz. ASW **Subject:** 10th Anniversary of Reign

| Date | Mintage | F | VF | XF | Unc |
|---|---|---|---|---|---|
| VS2038(1981) Proof | 10,000 | Value: 90.00 | | | |

**250 RUPEE** **KM# 1010** **Weight:** 28.2800 g. **Composition:** 0.9250 Silver .8411 oz. ASW **Subject:** Year of the Scout

| Date | Mintage | F | VF | XF | Unc |
|---|---|---|---|---|---|
| VS2039(1982) | 10,000 | — | — | — | 45.00 |
| VS2039(1982) Proof | Inc. above | Value: 55.00 | | | |

**250 RUPEE** **KM# 1026** **Weight:** 19.4400 g. **Composition:** 0.9250 Silver .5782 oz. ASW **Series:** Wildlife Preservation **Reverse:** Deer

| Date | Mintage | F | VF | XF | Unc |
|---|---|---|---|---|---|
| VS2043(1986) Proof | 20,000 | Value: 22.50 | | | |

**250 RUPEE** **KM# 1049** **Weight:** 19.4400 g. **Composition:** 0.9250 Silver .5782 oz. ASW **Subject:** Silver Jubilee of Nepal Red Cross Society

| Date | Mintage | F | VF | XF | Unc |
|---|---|---|---|---|---|
| VS2045(1988) | 6,360 | — | — | — | 23.50 |

**250 RUPEE** **KM# 1052** **Weight:** 19.4400 g. **Composition:** 0.9250 Silver .5782 oz. ASW **Subject:** 25th Anniversary of Nepalese Power Company

| Date | Mintage | F | VF | XF | Unc |
|---|---|---|---|---|---|
| VS2046(1989) | — | — | — | — | 23.50 |

**250 RUPEE** **KM# 1055** **Weight:** 19.4400 g. **Composition:** 0.9250 Silver .5782 oz. ASW **Series:** Save the Children

| Date | Mintage | F | VF | XF | Unc |
|---|---|---|---|---|---|
| VS2047(1990) Proof | 20,000 | Value: 22.50 | | | |

**250 RUPEE** **KM# 1134** **Weight:** 19.4400 g. **Composition:** 0.9250 Silver .5782 oz. ASW **Subject:** Nepal Disabled Association

| Date | Mintage | F | VF | XF | Unc |
|---|---|---|---|---|---|
| VS2052(1995) | — | — | — | — | 27.50 |

**300 RUPEE** **KM# 1029** **Weight:** 25.2900 g. **Composition:** 0.5000 Silver .4066 oz. ASW **Subject:** First Scout Jamboree in Nepal

| Date | Mintage | F | VF | XF | Unc |
|---|---|---|---|---|---|
| VS2043(1986) | 6,967 | — | — | — | 27.50 |

**300 RUPEE** **KM# 1044** **Weight:** 25.0000 g. **Composition:** 0.9250 Silver .7436 oz. ASW **Subject:** 3rd SAARC Summit

| Date | Mintage | F | VF | XF | Unc |
|---|---|---|---|---|---|
| VS2044(1987) | 5,000 | — | — | — | 22.50 |

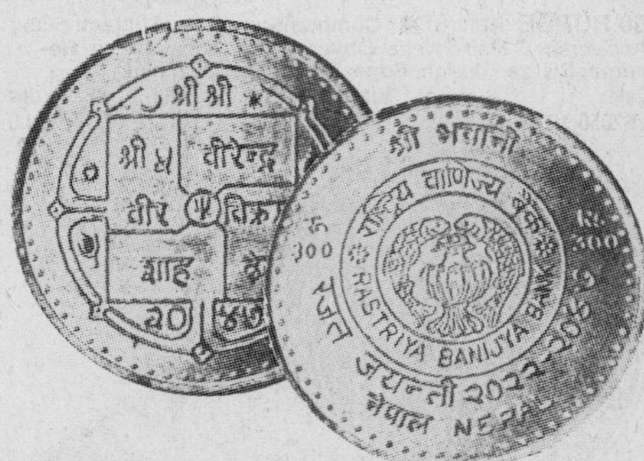


**300 RUPEE** **KM# 1057** **Weight:** 18.0500 g. **Composition:** 0.9250 Silver .5368 oz. ASW **Reverse:** Rastriya Banijya Bank

| Date | Mintage | F | VF | XF | Unc |
|---|---|---|---|---|---|
| VS2047(1990) | — | — | — | — | 22.50 |

**300 RUPEE** **KM# 1064** **Weight:** 18.3150 g. **Composition:** 0.9250 Silver .5447 oz. ASW **Subject:** New Constitution

| Date | Mintage | F | VF | XF | Unc |
|---|---|---|---|---|---|
| VS2047(1990) | — | — | — | — | 22.50 |

**300 RUPEE** **KM# 1065** **Weight:** 18.3150 g. **Composition:** 0.9250 Silver .5447 oz. ASW **Subject:** Parliament Session

| Date | Mintage | F | VF | XF | Unc |
|---|---|---|---|---|---|
| VS2048(1991) | — | — | — | — | 22.50 |

**300 RUPEE KM# 1068 Weight:** 17.8100 g. **Composition:** 0.9250 Silver .5297 oz. ASW **Reverse:** Agricultural Deveopment Bank

| Date | Mintage | F | VF | XF | Unc |
|---|---|---|---|---|---|
| VS2049(1992) | — | — | — | — | 22.50 |

**300 RUPEE KM# 1094 Weight:** 18.1300 g. **Composition:** 0.9250 Silver .5392 oz. ASW **Subject:** Rastriya Beema Sansthan Silver Jubilee

| Date | Mintage | F | VF | XF | Unc |
|---|---|---|---|---|---|
| VS2049(1992) | — | — | — | — | 22.50 |

**300 RUPEE KM# 1142 Weight:** 18.0000 g. **Composition:** 0.9250 Silver .5353 oz. ASW **Subject:** 75th Anniversary of I.L.O.

| Date | Mintage | F | VF | XF | Unc |
|---|---|---|---|---|---|
| VS2051(1994) | — | — | — | — | 22.50 |

**300 RUPEE KM# 1141 Weight:** 12.5000 g. **Composition:** 0.5000 Silver .200 oz. ASW **Subject:** International Year of Older Persons

| Date | Mintage | F | VF | XF | Unc |
|---|---|---|---|---|---|
| VS2056(1999) | — | — | — | — | 10.00 |

**350 RUPEE KM# 1032 Weight:** 23.3000 g. **Composition:** 0.5000 Silver .3746 oz. ASW **Subject:** Crown Prince, Sacred Thread Ceremony

| Date | Mintage | F | VF | XF | Unc |
|---|---|---|---|---|---|
| VS2044(1987) | 5,217 | — | — | — | 30.00 |

**500 RUPEE KM# 1035 Weight:** 35.0000 g. **Composition:** 0.5000 Silver .5627 oz. ASW **Subject:** 50th Anniversary of National Bank

| Date | Mintage | F | VF | XF | Unc |
|---|---|---|---|---|---|
| VS2044(1987) | 19,000 | — | — | — | 45.00 |

**500 RUPEE KM# 1058 Weight:** 31.4700 g. **Composition:** 0.9250 Silver .9359 oz. ASW **Series:** Olympics - Boxers

| Date | Mintage | F | VF | XF | Unc |
|---|---|---|---|---|---|
| VS2049(1992) | Est. 40,000 | — | — | — | 18.50 |

**500 RUPEE KM# 1069 Weight:** 31.4700 g. **Composition:** 0.9250 Silver .9359 oz. ASW **Reverse:** Soccer goal being scored

| Date | Mintage | F | VF | XF | Unc |
|---|---|---|---|---|---|
| VS2049(1992) Proof | 20,000 | Value: 28.50 | | | |

**500 RUPEE KM# 1071 Weight:** 31.8300 g. **Composition:** 0.9250 Silver .9466 oz. ASW **Series:** 1992 Olympics - Ski Jumping

| Date | Mintage | F | VF | XF | Unc |
|---|---|---|---|---|---|
| VS2049(1992) Proof | Est. 40,000 | Value: 18.50 | | | |

**500 RUPEE KM# 1090 Weight:** 31.4700 g. **Composition:** 0.9250 Silver .9359 oz. ASW **Series:** Endangered Wildlife **Reverse:** Red Panda

| Date | Mintage | F | VF | XF | Unc |
|---|---|---|---|---|---|
| VS2049(1992) Proof | Est. 15,000 | Value: 32.50 | | | |

**500 RUPEE KM# 1070 Weight:** 31.4700 g. **Composition:** 0.9250 Silver .9359 oz. ASW **Series:** Wildlife **Reverse:** Himalayan Black Bear

| Date | Mintage | F | VF | XF | Unc |
|---|---|---|---|---|---|
| VS2050(1993) Proof | 10,000 | Value: 37.50 | | | |

**500 RUPEE KM# 1066 Weight:** 31.7500 g. **Composition:** 0.9250 Silver .9443 oz. ASW **Series:** Olympics - Cross-country Skiing

| Date | Mintage | F | VF | XF | Unc |
|---|---|---|---|---|---|
| VS2050(1993) Proof | 40,000 | Value: 22.50 | | | |

**500 RUPEE KM# 1091 Weight:** 31.4700 g. **Composition:** 0.9250 Silver .9359 oz. ASW **Series:** Endangered Wildlife **Reverse:** Tiger

| Date | Mintage | F | VF | XF | Unc |
|---|---|---|---|---|---|
| VS2050(1993) Proof | Est. 15,000 | Value: 40.00 | | | |

**500 RUPEE KM# 1084 Weight:** 28.2800 g. **Composition:** 0.9250 Silver .8411 oz. ASW **Subject:** Conquest of Mt. Everest **Note:** Similar to 2500 Rupee, KM#1085.

| Date | Mintage | F | VF | XF | Unc |
|---|---|---|---|---|---|
| VS2050(1993) Proof | Est. 10,000 | Value: 32.50 | | | |

**500 RUPEE KM# 1133 Weight:** 31.1030 g. **Composition:** 0.9990 Silver 1.0000 oz. ASW **Subject:** International Monetary Fund

| Date | Mintage | F | VF | XF | Unc |
|---|---|---|---|---|---|
| VS2051(1994) | — | — | — | — | 45.00 |

**500 RUPEE KM# 1077 Weight:** 31.1035 g. **Composition:** 0.9250 Silver .9250 oz. ASW **Reverse:** Buddha

| Date | Mintage | F | VF | XF | Unc |
|---|---|---|---|---|---|
| VS2052(1995) Proof | 15,000 | Value: 37.50 | | | |

**500 RUPEE** **KM# 1125** **Weight:** 31.3500 g. **Composition:** 0.9990 Silver 1.0069 oz. ASW **Obverse:** Traditional square in circle design **Reverse:** Gold-plated lotus flowers

| Date | Mintage | F | VF | XF | Unc |
|---|---|---|---|---|---|
| VS2052(1995) Proof | Est. 7,000 | Value: 45.00 | | | |

**500 RUPEE** **KM# 1143** **Weight:** 25.2000 g. **Composition:** 0.9250 Silver .7494 oz. ASW **Subject:** 50th Anniversary of Universal Declaration of Human Rights

| Date | Mintage | F | VF | XF | Unc |
|---|---|---|---|---|---|
| VS2055(1998) | — | — | — | — | 22.50 |

**600 RUPEE** **KM# 1041** **Weight:** 31.1030 g. **Composition:** 0.9990 Silver 1.0000 oz. ASW **Subject:** 60th birthday - Queen Mother

| Date | Mintage | F | VF | XF | Unc |
|---|---|---|---|---|---|
| VS2045(1988) Proof | 5,000 | Value: 60.00 | | | |

**1000 RUPEE** **KM# 844** **Weight:** 33.4370 g. **Composition:** 0.9000 Gold .9676 oz. AGW **Series:** Conservation **Reverse:** Great Indian Rhinoceros **Note:** Very small quantity restruck in 1979.

| Date | Mintage | F | VF | XF | Unc |
|---|---|---|---|---|---|
| VS2031(1974) | 2,176 | — | — | — | 450 |
| VS2031(1974) Proof | 671 | Value: 650 | | | |

**1000 RUPEE** **KM# 1000** **Weight:** 33.4370 g. **Composition:** 0.9000 Gold .9676 oz. AGW **Subject:** Rural Women's Advancement

| Date | Mintage | F | VF | XF | Unc |
|---|---|---|---|---|---|
| VS2037(1980) Proof | 500 | Value: 150 | | | |

**1000 RUPEE** **KM# 1036** **Weight:** 155.5150 g. **Composition:** 0.9990 Silver 5.0000 oz. ASW **Reverse:** Snow Leopard **Note:** Illustration reduced.

| Date | Mintage | F | VF | XF | Unc |
|---|---|---|---|---|---|
| VS2045(1988) Proof | Est. 5,000 | Value: 170 | | | |

**1500 RUPEE** **KM# 1095** **Weight:** 31.1035 g. **Composition:** 0.9250 Silver .9250 oz. ASW **Subject:** Buddha's Birth **Obverse:** Traditional square in circle design

| Date | Mintage | F | VF | XF | Unc |
|---|---|---|---|---|---|
| VS2054(1997) Proof | — | Value: 37.50 | | | |

**1500 RUPEE** **KM# 1120** **Weight:** 20.0000 g. **Composition:** 0.9250 Silver .5948 oz. ASW **Obverse:** Tradional square in circle design **Reverse:** Portrait of Buddha, Ashoka pillar. Portrait halo glows under ultraviolet light **Note:** Lord Buddha

| Date | Mintage | F | VF | XF | Unc |
|---|---|---|---|---|---|
| VS2055(1998) Proof | 15,000 | Value: 50.00 | | | |

**1500 RUPEE** **KM# 1128** **Weight:** 20.0000 g. **Composition:** 0.9250 Silver .5948 oz. ASW **Subject:** Buddha **Obverse:** Traditional square design **Reverse:** Buddha with golden aura **Edge:** Reeded **Size:** 38.7 mm.

| Date | Mintage | F | VF | XF | Unc |
|---|---|---|---|---|---|
| 2000(2000) | — | — | — | — | 50.00 |

**2000 RUPEE** **KM# 1100** **Weight:** 31.2400 g. **Composition:** 0.9990 Silver 1.0034 oz. ASW **Subject:** Silver Jubilee of Kings' Accession **Obverse:** Traditional design **Reverse:** Multi-color crown

| Date | Mintage | F | VF | XF | Unc |
|---|---|---|---|---|---|
| VS2053(1996) Proof | Est. 5,000 | Value: 45.00 | | | |



**2000 RUPEE** **KM# 1104** **Weight:** 31.1700 g. **Composition:** 0.9990 Silver 1.011 oz. ASW **Series:** Nepal Wildlife **Obverse:** Traditional design **Reverse:** Multi-colored snow leopard

| Date | Mintage | F | VF | XF | Unc |
|---|---|---|---|---|---|
| VS2054(1997) Proof | 8,000 | Value: 42.50 | | | |

**2000 RUPEE** **KM# 1105** **Weight:** 31.1700 g. **Composition:** 0.9990 Silver 1.011 oz. ASW **Series:** Nepal Wildlife **Reverse:** Multi-colored elephants

| Date | Mintage | F | VF | XF | Unc |
|---|---|---|---|---|---|
| VS2054(1997) Proof | 8,000 | Value: 42.50 | | | |

**2000 RUPEE** **KM# 1121** **Weight:** 20.0000 g. **Composition:** 0.9250 Silver .5948 oz. ASW **Obverse:** Traditional square in circle design **Reverse:** Buddha's portrait with gold insert halo, Ashoka pillar at right **Note:** Lord Buudha; Similar to 1500 Rupee, KM#1120.

| Date | Mintage | F | VF | XF | Unc |
|---|---|---|---|---|---|
| VS2055(1998) Proof | 5,000 | Value: 75.00 | | | |

**2500 RUPEE** **KM# 1085** **Weight:** 155.5100 g. **Composition:** 0.9990 Silver 5.0000 oz. ASW **Subject:** Conquest of Mt. Everest **Note:** Illustration reduced.

| Date | Mintage | F | VF | XF | Unc |
|---|---|---|---|---|---|
| VS2050(1993) Proof | Est. 3,000 | Value: 145 | | | |

**2500 RUPEE** **KM# 1078** **Weight:** 155.5100 g. **Composition:** 0.9990 Silver 5.0000 oz. ASW **Reverse:** Buddha **Note:** Similar to 500 Rupee, KM#1077.

| Date | Mintage | F | VF | XF | Unc |
|---|---|---|---|---|---|
| VS2052(1995) Proof | 3,000 | Value: 200 | | | |

**5000 RUPEE** **KM# 1101** **Weight:** 155.5000 g. **Composition:** 0.9990 Silver 4.9944 oz. ASW **Subject:** Silver Jubilee of King's Accession **Obverse:** Traditional design **Reverse:** Multi-colored crown

| Date | Mintage | F | VF | XF | Unc |
|---|---|---|---|---|---|
| VS2053(1996) Proof | Est. 2,500 | Value: 200 | | | |

**5000 RUPEE** **KM# 1106** **Weight:** 155.5518 g. **Composition:** 0.9990 Silver 4.9961 oz. ASW **Series:** Nepal Wildlife **Reverse:** Multi-colored elephants **Note:** Similar to 2000 Rupee, KM#1105.

| Date | Mintage | F | VF | XF | Unc |
|---|---|---|---|---|---|
| VS2054(1997) Proof | 500 | Value: 250 | | | |

**0.3G ASARPHI** **KM# 1129** **Weight:** 0.3000 g. **Composition:** 0.9999 Gold .0096 oz. AGW **Subject:** Buddha **Obverse:** Traditional square design **Reverse:** Buddha with halo **Edge:** Reeded **Size:** 7 mm.

| Date | Mintage | F | VF | XF | Unc |
|---|---|---|---|---|---|
| VS2057(2000) | 25,000 | — | — | — | 10.00 |

**2.5G ASARPHI** **KM# 819** **Weight:** 7.7759 g. **Composition:** 0.9990 Gold .2500 oz. AGW

| Date | Mintage | F | VF | XF | Unc |
|---|---|---|---|---|---|
| VS2028(1971) | 4 | — | — | — | — |
| VS2030(1973) | — | — | — | — | 110 |
| VS2031(1974) | — | — | — | — | 110 |
| VS2036(1979) | — | — | — | — | 110 |
| VS2037(1980) | 48 | — | — | — | 110 |

**2.5G ASARPHI** **KM# 816a** **Weight:** 7.7759 g. **Composition:** 0.9990 Gold .2500 oz. AGW **Subject:** Virendra Coronation

| Date | Mintage | F | VF | XF | Unc |
|---|---|---|---|---|---|
| VS2031(1974) | 500 | — | — | — | 100 |

**2.5G ASARPHI** **KM# 1050** **Weight:** 2.5000 g. **Composition:** 0.9000 Gold .0724 oz. AGW

| Date | Mintage | F | VF | XF | Unc |
|---|---|---|---|---|---|
| VS2039(1982) | 11 | — | — | — | — |

**2.5G ASARPHI** **KM# 1038** **Weight:** 7.7700 g. **Composition:** 0.9990 Gold .2500 oz. AGW **Reverse:** Snow leopard **Note:** Similar to 1 Asarphi, KM#1040.

| Date | Mintage | F | VF | XF | Unc |
|---|---|---|---|---|---|
| VS2045(1988) | Est. 8,000 | — | — | — | 145 |
| VS2045(1988) Proof | Est. 2,000 | Value: 175 | | | |

**2.5G ASARPHI** **KM# 1059** **Weight:** 2.5000 g. **Composition:** 0.9990 Gold .0804 oz. AGW **Note:** Similar to 1 Asarphi, KM#1054.

| Date | Mintage | F | VF | XF | Unc |
|---|---|---|---|---|---|
| VS2047(1990) | — | — | — | — | 90.00 |

**2.5G ASARPHI** **KM# 1050a** **Weight:** 0.2500 g. **Composition:** Gold

| Date | Mintage | F | VF | XF | Unc |
|---|---|---|---|---|---|
| VS2051(1994) | — | — | — | — | 40.00 |
| VS2052(1995) | — | — | — | — | 40.00 |
| VS2053(1996) | — | — | — | — | 35.00 |
| VS2054(1997) | — | — | — | — | 35.00 |
| VS2055(1998) | — | — | — | — | 35.00 |
| VS2056(1999) | — | — | — | — | 35.00 |
| VS2057(2000) | — | — | — | — | 35.00 |

**2.5G ASARPHI** **KM# 1081** **Weight:** 7.7759 g. **Composition:** 0.9990 Gold .2500 oz. AGW **Reverse:** Buddha **Note:** Similar to 1 Asarphi, KM#1082.

| Date | Mintage | F | VF | XF | Unc |
|---|---|---|---|---|---|
| VS2052(1995) | 15,000 | — | — | — | 125 |

**2.5G ASARPHI** **KM# 1098** **Weight:** 7.7759 g. **Composition:** 0.9990 Gold .2500 oz. AGW **Subject:** Buddha's Birth **Note:** Similar to 1500 Rupees, KM#1095.

| Date | Mintage | F | VF | XF | Unc |
|---|---|---|---|---|---|
| VS2054(1997) | — | — | — | — | 125 |

**5.0G ASARPHI** **KM# 825** **Weight:** 5.0000 g. **Composition:** 0.9990 Gold .1607 oz. AGW

| Date | Mintage | F | VF | XF | Unc |
|---|---|---|---|---|---|
| VS2028(1971) | 4 | — | — | — | — |
| VS2030(1973) | — | — | — | — | 160 |
| VS2031(1974) | — | — | — | — | 160 |
| VS2036(1979) | 36 | — | — | — | 160 |
| VS2037(1980) | 45 | — | — | — | 160 |

**Note:** Reports indicate a mintage of 44 pieces struck in .960 gold in 1980

| Date | Mintage | F | VF | XF | Unc |
|---|---|---|---|---|---|
| VS2038(1981) | — | — | — | — | 160 |

**5.0G ASARPHI** **KM# 822a** **Weight:** 5.0000 g. **Composition:** 0.9990 Gold .1607 oz. AGW **Subject:** Virendra Coronation

| Date | Mintage | F | VF | XF | Unc |
|---|---|---|---|---|---|
| VS2031(1974) | 500 | — | — | — | 150 |

**5.0G ASARPHI** **KM# 1021** **Weight:** 5.0000 g. **Composition:** 0.9000 Gold .1447 oz. AGW

| Date | Mintage | F | VF | XF | Unc |
|---|---|---|---|---|---|
| VS2039(1982) | 23 | — | — | — | — |

**5.0G ASARPHI** **KM# 1021a** **Weight:** 0.5000 g. **Composition:** 0.9990 Gold .1607 oz. AGW

| Date | Mintage | F | VF | XF | Unc |
|---|---|---|---|---|---|
| VS2042(1985) | — | — | — | — | 100 |
| VS2043(1986) | — | — | — | — | 100 |
| VS2044(1987) | — | — | — | — | 100 |
| VS2045(1988) | — | — | — | — | 90.00 |
| VS2046(1989) | — | — | — | — | 90.00 |
| VS2048(1991) | — | — | — | — | 90.00 |
| VS2049(1992) | — | — | — | — | 90.00 |
| VS2050(1993) | — | — | — | — | 80.00 |
| VS2051(1994) | — | — | — | — | 80.00 |
| VS2052(1995) | — | — | — | — | 70.00 |
| VS2053(1996) | — | — | — | — | 70.00 |
| VS2054(1997) | — | — | — | — | 70.00 |
| VS2056(1999) | — | — | — | — | 70.00 |

**5.0G ASARPHI** **KM# 1033** **Weight:** 5.8300 g. **Composition:** 0.9600 Gold .1800 oz. AGW **Subject:** Crown Prince, Sacred Thread Ceremony

| Date | Mintage | F | VF | XF | Unc |
|---|---|---|---|---|---|
| VS2044(1987) | 2,774 | — | — | — | 110 |

**5.0G ASARPHI** **KM# 1060** **Weight:** 5.0000 g. **Composition:** 0.9990 Gold .1600 oz. AGW **Note:** Similar to 1 Asarphi, KM#1054.

| Date | Mintage | F | VF | XF | Unc |
|---|---|---|---|---|---|
| VS2047(1990) | — | — | — | — | 150 |

**5.0G ASARPHI** **KM# 1144** **Weight:** 0.5000 g. **Composition:** 0.9990 Gold .1606 oz. AGW **Subject:** New Parliament Session

| Date | Mintage | F | VF | XF | Unc |
|---|---|---|---|---|---|
| VS2048(1991) | — | — | — | — | 100 |

**10.0G ASARPHI** **KM# 827** **Weight:** 10.0000 g. **Composition:** 0.9990 Gold .3215 oz. AGW

| Date | Mintage | F | VF | XF | Unc |
|---|---|---|---|---|---|
| VS2028(1971) | Est. 4 | — | — | — | — |
| VS2030(1973) | 50 | — | — | — | 350 |
| VS2031(1974) | — | — | — | — | 350 |
| VS2033(1976) | — | — | — | — | 350 |
| VS2035(1978) | — | — | — | — | 3.50 |
| VS2036(1979) | 52 | — | — | — | 350 |
| VS2037(1980) | 30 | — | — | — | 350 |

**Note:** Reports indicate a mintage of 44 pieces struck in .960 gold in 1980

| Date | Mintage | F | VF | XF | Unc |
|---|---|---|---|---|---|
| VS2038(1981) | — | — | — | — | 3.50 |

**10.0G ASARPHI** **KM# 829a** **Weight:** 10.0000 g. **Composition:** 0.9990 Gold .3215 oz. AGW **Subject:** Virendra Coronation

| Date | Mintage | F | VF | XF | Unc |
|---|---|---|---|---|---|
| VS2031(1974) Proof | Est. 500 | Value: 285 | | | |

**10.0G ASARPHI** **KM# 829b** **Weight:** 10.0000 g. **Composition:** 0.5000 White Gold .1608 oz. AGW

| Date | Mintage | F | VF | XF | Unc |
|---|---|---|---|---|---|
| VS2031(1974) Proof | Est. 250 | Value: 350 | | | |

**Note:** Struck by Singapore Mint, sometimes referred to as 1000 Rupees

**10.0G ASARPHI** **KM# 852** **Weight:** 11.6600 g. **Composition:** 0.9000 Gold .3374 oz. AGW **Series:** International Year of the Child

| Date | Mintage | F | VF | XF | Unc |
|---|---|---|---|---|---|
| VS2038(1981) Proof | 4,055 | Value: 185 | | | |

**10.0G ASARPHI** **KM# 1022** **Weight:** 10.0000 g. **Composition:** 0.9000 Gold .2894 oz. AGW

| Date | Mintage | F | VF | XF | Unc |
|---|---|---|---|---|---|
| VS2039(1982) | 25 | — | — | — | — |

**10.0G ASARPHI** **KM# 1006** **Weight:** 10.0000 g. **Composition:** 0.5000 Gold .1608 oz. AGW **Subject:** 30th Anniversary Ascent of Mt. Everest **Obverse:** Similar to 5 Rupees, KM#833

| Date | Mintage | F | VF | XF | Unc |
|---|---|---|---|---|---|
| VS2040(1983) Proof | 350 | Value: 225 | | | |

**10.0G ASARPHI** **KM# 1022a** **Weight:** 10.0000 g. **Composition:** 0.9990 Gold .3212 oz. AGW

| Date | Mintage | F | VF | XF | Unc |
|---|---|---|---|---|---|
| VS2042(1985) | — | — | — | — | 180 |
| VS2046(1989) | — | — | — | — | 150 |
| VS2048(1991) | — | — | — | — | 150 |
| VS2049(1992) | — | — | — | — | 150 |
| VS2050(1993) | — | — | — | — | 130 |
| VS2052(1995) | — | — | — | — | 130 |
| VS2054(1997) | — | — | — | — | 130 |
| VS2056(1999) | — | — | — | — | 130 |

**10.0G ASARPHI** **KM# 1027** **Weight:** 10.0000 g. **Composition:** Gold **Series:** Wildlife Protection **Reverse:** Ganges River Dolphins

| Date | Mintage | F | VF | XF | Unc |
|---|---|---|---|---|---|
| VS2043(1986) Proof | 5,000 | Value: 185 | | | |

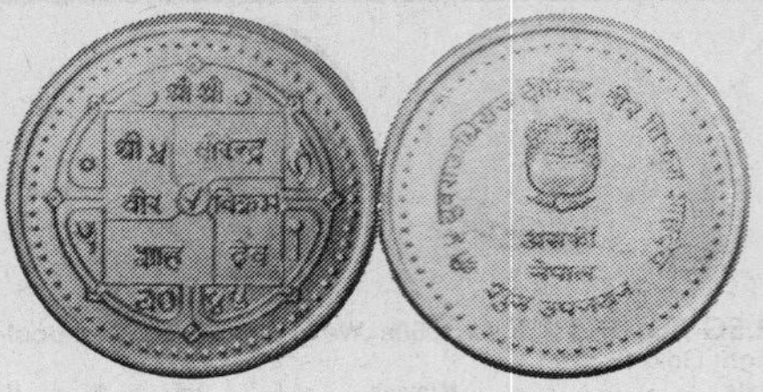

**10.0G ASARPHI** **KM# 1034** **Weight:** 10.0000 g. **Composition:** Gold **Subject:** Crown Prince, Sacred Thread Ceremony

| Date | Mintage | F | VF | XF | Unc |
|---|---|---|---|---|---|
| VS2044(1987) | 1,962 | — | — | — | 225 |

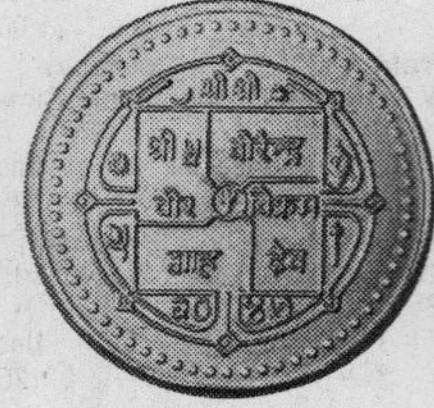

**10.0G ASARPHI** **KM# 1054** **Weight:** 10.0000 g. **Composition:** 0.9990 Gold .3215 oz. AGW **Subject:** The New Constitution

| Date | Mintage | F | VF | XF | Unc |
|---|---|---|---|---|---|
| VS2047(1990) | — | — | — | — | 240 |

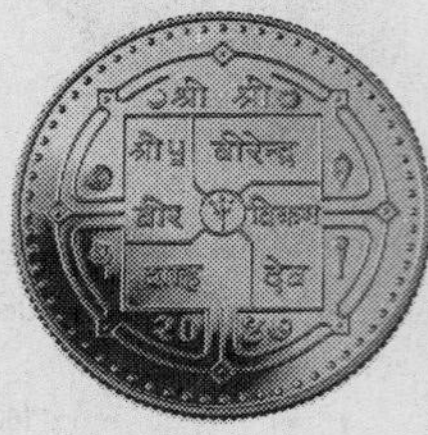

**10.0G ASARPHI** **KM# 1056** **Weight:** 11.6600 g. **Composition:** 0.9000 Gold .3374 oz. AGW **Series:** Save the Children

| Date | Mintage | F | VF | XF | Unc |
|---|---|---|---|---|---|
| VS2047(1990) Proof | 3,000 | Value: 240 | | | |

**10.0G ASARPHI** **KM# 1145** **Weight:** 10.0000 g. **Composition:** 0.9990 Gold .3212 oz. AGW **Subject:** 50th Anniversary International Monetary Fund

| Date | Mintage | F | VF | XF | Unc |
|---|---|---|---|---|---|
| VS2051(1994) | — | — | — | — | 150 |

**10.0G ASARPHI** **KM# 1146** **Weight:** 10.0000 g. **Composition:** 0.9990 Gold .3212 oz. AGW **Subject:** 50th Anniversary World Bank

| Date | Mintage | F | VF | XF | Unc |
|---|---|---|---|---|---|
| VS2051(1994) | — | — | — | — | 150 |

**10.0G ASARPHI** **KM# 1147** **Weight:** 10.0000 g. **Composition:** 0.9990 Gold .3212 oz. AGW **Subject:** Golden Anniversary

| Date | Mintage | F | VF | XF | Unc |
|---|---|---|---|---|---|
| VS2056(1999) | — | — | — | — | 150 |

**1/10-OZ. ASARFI** **KM# 1037** **Weight:** 3.1100 g. **Composition:** 0.9990 Gold .1000 oz. AGW **Reverse:** Snow leopard **Note:** Similar to 1 Asarphi, KM#1040.

| Date | Mintage | F | VF | XF | Unc |
|---|---|---|---|---|---|
| VS2045(1988) | Est. 10,000 | — | — | — | 50.00 |
| VS2045(1988) Proof | 2,000 | Value: 65.00 | | | |

**1/10-OZ. ASARFI** **KM# 1080** **Weight:** 3.1100 g. **Composition:** 0.9990 Gold .1000 oz. AGW **Reverse:** Buddha **Note:** Similar to 1 Asarphi, KM#1082.

| Date | Mintage | F | VF | XF | Unc |
|---|---|---|---|---|---|
| VS2052(1995) | 15,000 | — | — | — | 60.00 |

**1/10-OZ. ASARFI** **KM# 1097** **Weight:** 3.1100 g. **Composition:** 0.9990 Gold .1000 oz. AGW **Subject:** Buddha's Birth **Note:** Similar to 1500 Rupee, KM#1095.

| Date | Mintage | F | VF | XF | Unc |
|---|---|---|---|---|---|
| VS2054(1997) | — | — | — | — | 60.00 |

**1/10-OZ. ASARFI** **KM# 1131** **Weight:** 3.1100 g. **Composition:** 0.9990 Gold .1000 oz. AGW **Subject:** Buddha **Obverse:** Traditional square design **Reverse:** Buddha with halo **Edge:** Reeded **Size:** 18 mm.

| Date | Mintage | F | VF | XF | Unc |
|---|---|---|---|---|---|
| VS2057(2000) | 30,000 | — | — | — | 50.00 |

**1/20-OZ. ASARFI** **KM# 1079** **Weight:** 1.5532 g. **Composition:** 0.9990 Gold .0500 oz. AGW **Reverse:** Buddha **Note:** Similar to 1 Asarfi, KM#1082.

| Date | Mintage | F | VF | XF | Unc |
|---|---|---|---|---|---|
| VS2052(1995) | 15,000 | — | — | — | 35.00 |

**1/20-OZ. ASARFI** **KM# 1096** **Weight:** 1.5532 g. **Composition:** 0.9990 Gold .0500 oz. AGW **Subject:** Buddha's Birth **Note:** Similar to 1500 Rupee, KM#1095.

| Date | Mintage | F | VF | XF | Unc |
|---|---|---|---|---|---|
| VS2054(1997) | — | — | — | — | 35.00 |

**1/25-OZ. ASARFI** **KM# 1130** **Weight:** 1.2441 g. **Composition:** 0.9999 Gold .0400 oz. AGW **Subject:** Buddha **Obverse:** Traditional square design **Reverse:** Buddha with halo **Edge:** Reeded **Size:** 18 mm.

| Date | Mintage | F | VF | XF | Unc |
|---|---|---|---|---|---|
| VS2057(2000) | 30,000 | — | — | — | 30.00 |

**1/2-OZ. ASARFI** **Composition:** Gold

| Date | Mintage | F | VF | XF | Unc |
|---|---|---|---|---|---|
| VS2031(1974) | — | — | — | — | — |

**1/2-OZ. ASARFI** **KM# 1039** **Weight:** 15.5500 g. **Composition:** 0.9990 Gold .5000 oz. AGW **Reverse:** Snow leopard **Note:** Similar to 1 Asarphi, KM#1040.

| Date | Mintage | F | VF | XF | Unc |
|---|---|---|---|---|---|
| VS2045(1988) | Est. 8,000 | — | — | — | 220 |
| VS2045(1988) Proof | Est. 2,000 | Value: 265 | | | |

**1-OZ. ASARFI** **Composition:** Gold

| Date | Mintage | F | VF | XF | Unc |
|---|---|---|---|---|---|
| VS2031(1974) | — | — | — | — | — |

**Note:** The above coins were struck and sent to the Royal Palace. Few have emerged

**1-OZ. ASARFI** **KM# 1008** **Weight:** 15.9800 g. **Composition:** 0.9000 Gold .4624 oz. AGW **Subject:** 10th Anniversary of Reign

| Date | Mintage | F | VF | XF | Unc |
|---|---|---|---|---|---|
| VS2038(1981) | 27 | — | — | — | 450 |
| VS2038(1981) Proof | 5,092 | Value: 235 | | | |

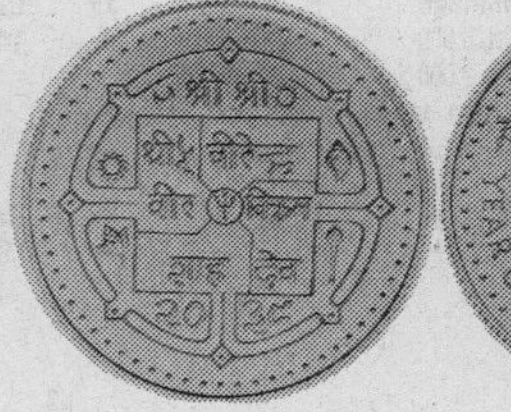

**1-OZ. ASARFI** KM# 1011 **Weight:** 15.9800 g. **Composition:** 0.9170 Gold .4712 oz. AGW **Series:** Year of the Scout

| Date | Mintage | F | VF | XF | Unc |
|---|---|---|---|---|---|
| VS2039(1982) | 2,000 | — | — | — | 400 |

**1-OZ. ASARFI** KM# 1045 **Weight:** 15.0000 g. **Composition:** 0.9000 Gold .4340 oz. AGW **Subject:** 3rd SAARC Summit **Note:** Similar to 300 Rupees, KM#1044.

| Date | Mintage | F | VF | XF | Unc |
|---|---|---|---|---|---|
| VS2044(1987) | 1,000 | — | — | — | 350 |

**1-OZ. ASARFI** KM# 1040 **Weight:** 31.1000 g. **Composition:** 0.9999 Gold 1.0000 oz. AGW **Reverse:** Snow leopard

| Date | Mintage | F | VF | XF | Unc |
|---|---|---|---|---|---|
| VS2045(1988) | Est. 10,000 | — | — | — | 425 |
| VS2045(1988) Proof | 2,000 | Value: 550 | | | |

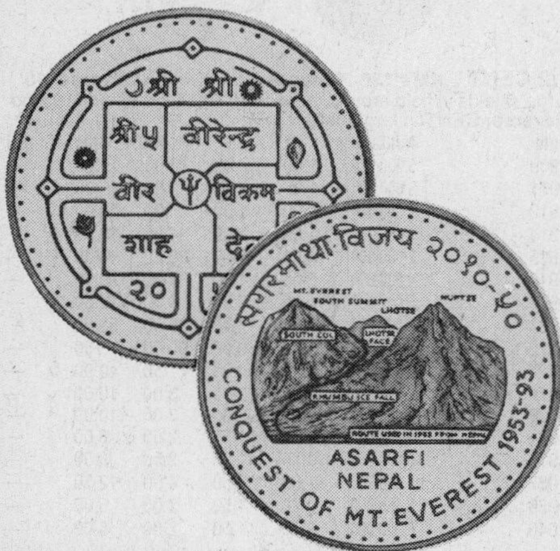


**1-OZ. ASARFI** KM# 1086 **Weight:** 44.6400 g. **Composition:** 0.9167 Gold 1.3156 oz. AGW **Subject:** Conquest of Mt. Everest

| Date | Mintage | F | VF | XF | Unc |
|---|---|---|---|---|---|
| VS2050(1993) Proof | Est. 100 | Value: 995 | | | |

**1-OZ. ASARFI** KM# 1082 **Weight:** 31.1035 g. **Composition:** 0.9999 Gold 1.0000 oz. AGW **Reverse:** Buddha

| Date | Mintage | F | VF | XF | Unc |
|---|---|---|---|---|---|
| VS2052(1995) Proof | 2,500 | Value: 600 | | | |

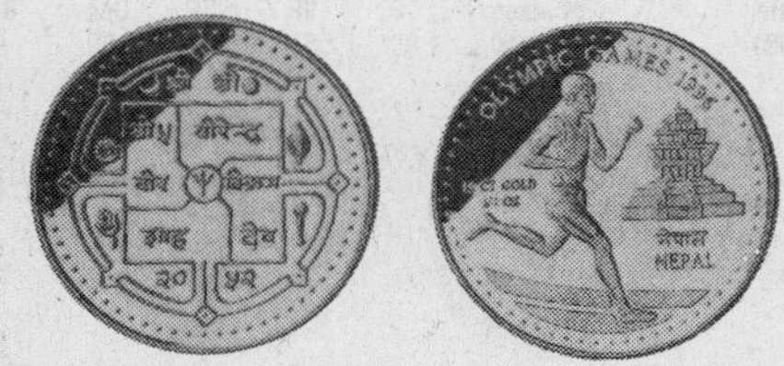


**1-OZ. ASARFI** KM# 1093 **Weight:** 7.7760 g. **Composition:** 0.5830 Gold .1457 oz. AGW **Series:** Olympics **Reverse:** Runner and temple

| Date | Mintage | F | VF | XF | Unc |
|---|---|---|---|---|---|
| VS2052(1995) | Est. 3,000 | — | — | — | 150 |

**1-OZ. ASARFI** KM# 1099 **Weight:** 31.1035 g. **Composition:** 0.9999 Gold 1.0000 oz. AGW **Subject:** Buddha's Birth **Obverse:** Traditional square in circle design **Reverse:** Woman holding onto a tree

| Date | Mintage | F | VF | XF | Unc |
|---|---|---|---|---|---|
| VS2054(1997) Proof | — | Value: 600 | | | |



**1-OZ. ASARFI** KM# 1124 **Weight:** 15.5518 g. **Composition:** 0.9999 Gold .5000 oz. AGW **Obverse:** Traditional square in circle design **Reverse:** Lord Buddha, Ashoka pillar

| Date | Mintage | F | VF | XF | Unc |
|---|---|---|---|---|---|
| VS2055(1998) Proof | 2,500 | Value: 285 | | | |

**1-OZ. ASARFI** KM# 1122 **Weight:** 1.2441 g. **Composition:** 0.9999 Gold .0400 oz. AGW **Obverse:** Traditional square in circle design **Reverse:** Buddha's portrait and Ashoka pillar **Note:** Lord Buddha; Similar to Asarfi KM#1124.

| Date | Mintage | F | VF | XF | Unc |
|---|---|---|---|---|---|
| VS2055(1998) Proof | 30,000 | Value: 35.00 | | | |

**1-OZ. ASARFI** KM# 1123 **Weight:** 3.1104 g. **Composition:** 0.9999 Gold .1000 oz. AGW **Obverse:** Traditional square in circle design **Reverse:** Buddha's portrait and Ashoka pillar **Note:** Lord Buddha; Similar to Asarfi KM#1124.

| Date | Mintage | F | VF | XF | Unc |
|---|---|---|---|---|---|
| VS2055(1998) Proof | 15,000 | Value: 65.00 | | | |

**1-OZ. ASARFI** KM# 1108 **Weight:** 1.5552 g. **Composition:** 0.9990 Gold .0500 oz. AGW **Series:** Nepal Wildlife **Reverse:** Multi-colored tiger **Note:** Similar to 100 Rupees, KM#1102.

| Date | Mintage | F | VF | XF | Unc |
|---|---|---|---|---|---|
| VS2054(1998) Proof | 15,000 | Value: 75.00 | | | |

**1-OZ. ASARFI** KM# 1111 **Weight:** 7.7759 g. **Composition:** 0.9990 Gold .2500 oz. AGW **Series:** Nepal Wildlife **Reverse:** Multi-colored tiger **Note:** Similar to 100 Rupees, KM#1102.

| Date | Mintage | F | VF | XF | Unc |
|---|---|---|---|---|---|
| VS2054(1998) Proof | 2,000 | Value: 175 | | | |

**1-OZ. ASARFI** KM# 1112 **Weight:** 7.7759 g. **Composition:** 0.9990 Gold .2500 oz. AGW **Series:** Nepal Wildlife **Reverse:** Multi-colored rhino **Note:** Similar to 100 Rupees, KM#1103.

| Date | Mintage | F | VF | XF | Unc |
|---|---|---|---|---|---|
| VS2054(1998) Proof | 2,000 | Value: 175 | | | |

**1-OZ. ASARFI** KM# 1113 **Weight:** 7.7759 g. **Composition:** 0.9990 Gold .2500 oz. AGW **Series:** Nepal Wildlife **Reverse:** Multi-colored snow leopard **Note:** Similar to 100 Rupees, KM#1104.

| Date | Mintage | F | VF | XF | Unc |
|---|---|---|---|---|---|
| VS2054(1998) Proof | 2,000 | Value: 175 | | | |

**1-OZ. ASARFI** KM# 1107 **Weight:** 1.5552 g. **Composition:** 0.9990 Gold .0500 oz. AGW **Series:** Nepal Wildlife **Reverse:** Multi-colored snow leopard **Note:** Similar to 2000 Rupees, KM#1104.

| Date | Mintage | F | VF | XF | Unc |
|---|---|---|---|---|---|
| VS2054(1998) Proof | 15,000 | Value: 75.00 | | | |

**1-OZ. ASARFI** KM# 1109 **Weight:** 3.1104 g. **Composition:** 0.9990 Gold .1000 oz. AGW **Series:** Nepal Wildlife **Reverse:** Multi-colored snow leopard **Note:** Similar to 2000 Rupees, KM#1104.

| Date | Mintage | F | VF | XF | Unc |
|---|---|---|---|---|---|
| VS2054(1998) Proof | 10,000 | Value: 100 | | | |

**1-OZ. ASARFI** KM# 1110 **Weight:** 7.7759 g. **Composition:** 0.9990 Gold .2500 oz. AGW **Series:** Nepal Wildlife **Reverse:** Multi-colored elephants **Note:** Similar to 2000 Rupees, KM#1105.

| Date | Mintage | F | VF | XF | Unc |
|---|---|---|---|---|---|
| VS2054(1998) Proof | 2,000 | Value: 175 | | | |

# Gyanendra Bir Bikram

## VS2058- / 2001- AD (second reign)

## DECIMAL COINAGE

100 Paisa = 1 Rupee

**25 PAISA** KM# 1148 **Composition:** Aluminum **Obverse:** Royal crown

| Date | Mintage | F | VF | XF | Unc |
|---|---|---|---|---|---|
| VS2058(2001) | — | — | — | — | 0.50 |

**50 PAISA** KM# 1149 **Composition:** Aluminum **Obverse:** Royal crown

| Date | Mintage | F | VF | XF | Unc |
|---|---|---|---|---|---|
| VS2058(2001) | — | — | — | — | 0.50 |

**RUPEE** KM# 1150 **Composition:** Brass

| Date | Mintage | F | VF | XF | Unc |
|---|---|---|---|---|---|
| VS2058(2001) | — | — | — | — | 1.00 |

**2 RUPEES** KM# 1151 **Composition:** Brass Plated Steel

| Date | Mintage | F | VF | XF | Unc |
|---|---|---|---|---|---|
| VS2058(2001) | — | — | — | — | 1.25 |

## PATTERNS

Including off metal strikes

| KM# | Date | Mintage | Identification | Mkt Val |
|---|---|---|---|---|
| Pn3 | 1975 | — | 5 Paisa. KM#690.1 | — |

## PIEFORTS

| KM# | Date | Mintage | Identification | Mkt Val |
|---|---|---|---|---|
| P1 | 2038 | 88 | 100 Rupee. KM#851. | 100 |
| P2 | 2039 | 48 | Asarphi. | 1,250 |

## MINT SETS

| KM# | Date | Mintage | Identification | Issue Price | Mkt Val |
|---|---|---|---|---|---|
| MS1 | 1932 (3) | — | | — | — |
| MS2 | 1949 (3) | — | KM#716, 718, 723 (restrikes) | — | 8.00 |
| MS3 | 1953 (8) | — | KM#733, 735-740, 742 | — | 160 |
| MS-A4 | 1996, 1995, 2011 (3) | — | KM#709.2 (1996); 711 (1995); 737 (2011) | — | 7.00 |
| MS4 | 1955 (3) | — | KM#712 (2000); 733; 749 (2012) | 0.85 | 5.00 |
| MS5 | 1956 (7) | — | KM#745, 750, 756.2, 761, 770, 776, 790 | — | 50.00 |
| MS6 | 1956 (7) | — | KM#745, 750, 756.3, 761, 770, 776, 790 (restrikes) | — | 13.50 |

| KM# | Date | Mintage | Identification | Issue Price | Mkt Val |
|---|---|---|---|---|---|
| MS7 | 1957 (4) | — | KM#740 (2011), 742, 738 (2010), 769 (2014) | 2.05 | 12.00 |
| MS8 | 1957 (6) | — | KM#709.1 (1996), 755 (2014), 760 (2011); 2 pieces each | 0.85 | 7.00 |
| MS9 | 1964 (7) | — | KM#747, 752, 758, 763, 772, 778, 785 | — | 10.00 |
| MS10 | 1964 (7) | — | KM#747, 752, 758a, 764, 772, 778, 785 | — | 50.00 |
| MS11 | 1965 (7) | — | KM#747, 752 (2022), 758, 763, 772, 778, 786 (2021) | 2.75 | 10.00 |
| MS12 | 1966 (7) | — | KM#748, 753, 759, 765, 772, 779, 787 | — | 7.00 |
| MS13 | 1967 (7) | — | KM#748, 753, 759, 765, 772, 779, 787 | — | 5.00 |
| MS14 | 1972 (7) | — | KM#799, 801, 802, 806, 815, 821, 828 | — | 5.00 |
| MS15 | 1974 (7) | — | KM#800, 804, 808, 816, 822, 829, 838 | — | 12.50 |
| MS16 | 1974 (2) | — | KM#829, 841 | 32.50 | 30.00 |
| MS17 | 1975 (5) | — | KM#808, 816, 822, 829, 838 | — | 13.00 |
| MS18 | 1975 (3) | — | KM#809, 831, 836 | — | 9.00 |
| MS19 | 1997 (3) | — | KM#1096-1098 | — | 225 |

## PROOF SETS

| KM# | Date | Mintage | Identification | Issue Price | Mkt Val |
|---|---|---|---|---|---|
| PS1 | 1911 | — | Copper, Silver | — | — |
| PS10 | 1988 (4) | 2,000 | KM#1037-1040 | — | 1,050 |
| PS11 | 1995-97 (2) | — | KM#1077, 1099 | — | 645 |
| PS2 | 1911 | — | Gold | — | — |
| PS3 | 1970 (7) | 2,187 | KM#748, 753, 759, 765, 733, 780, 788 | 10.00 | 15.00 |
| PS4 | 1971 (7) | 2,380 | KM#748, 753, 759, 765, 773, 780, 788 | 10.00 | 15.00 |
| PS5 | 1972 (7) | 3,943 | KM#799, 801, 802, 807, 815, 821, 828 | 10.00 | 8.50 |
| PS6 | 1973 (7) | 8,891 | KM#799, 801, 802, 807, 815, 821, 828 | 10.00 | 6.00 |
| PS7 | 1974 (7) | 10,543 | KM#799, 801, 802, 807, 815, 821, 828 | 10.00 | 5.50 |
| PS8 | 1974 (2) | 30,000 | KM#839a, 841a | 50.00 | 42.00 |
| PS9 | 1981 (7) | 1,000 | KM#800a, 804a, 808a, 816.2, 822.2, 829.2, 838a (dated 1974)Coins dated 2031 (1974) but this set was issued in 1981 to celebrate the 7th Anniversary of the Coronation. | 62.00 | 50.00 |

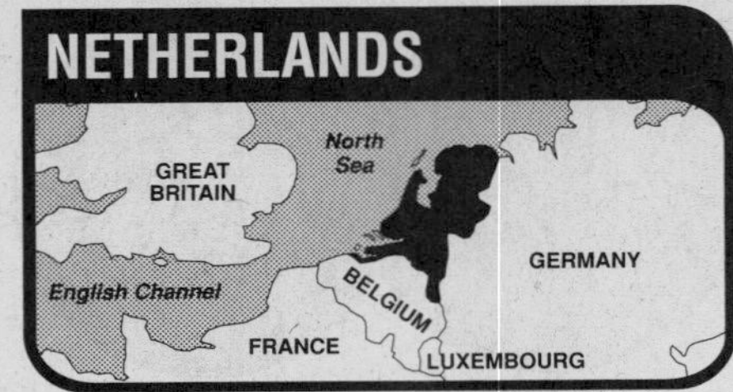


The Kingdom of the Netherlands, a country of western Europe fronting on the North Sea and bordered by Belgium and Germany, has an area of 15,770 sq. mi. (41,500 sq. km.) and a population of 15.7 million. Capital: Amsterdam, but the seat of government is at The Hague. The economy is based on dairy farming and a variety of industrial activities. Chemicals, yarns and fabrics, and meat products are exported.

After being a part of Charlemagne's empire in the 8th and 9th centuries, the Netherlands came under control of Burgundy and the Austrian Hapsburgs, and finally was subjected to Spanish dominion in the 16th century. Led by William of Orange, the Dutch revolted against Spain in 1568. The seven northern provinces formed the Union of Utrecht and declared their independence in 1581,becoming the Republic of the United Netherlands. In the following century, the *Golden Age* of Dutch history, the Netherlands became a great sea and colonial power, a patron of the arts and a refuge for the persecuted. The United Dutch Republic ended in 1795 when the French formed the Batavian Republic. Napoleon made his brother Louis, the King of Holland in 1806, however he abdicated in 1810 when Napoleon annexed Holland. The French were expelled in 1813, and all the provinces of Holland and Belgium were merged into the Kingdom of the United Netherlands under William I, in 1814. The Belgians withdrew in 1830 to form their own kingdom, the last substantial change in the configuration of European Netherlands. German forces invaded in 1940 as the royal family fled to England where a government-in-exile was formed. A German High Commissioner, Arthur Seyss-Inquart, was placed in command until 1945 when the arrival of Allied military forces ended the occupation.

**WORLD WAR II COINAGE**

Coinage of the Netherlands Homeland Types - KM#152, 153, 163, 164, 161.1 and 161.2 - were minted by U.S. mints in the name of the government in exile and its remaining Curacao and Surinam Colonies during the years 1941-45. The Curacao and Surinam strikes, distinguished by the presence of a palm tree in combination with a mint mark (P-Philadelphia; D-Denver; S-San Francisco) flanking the date, are incorporated under those titles in this volume. Pieces of this period struck in the name of the homeland bear an acorn and mint mark and are incorporated in the following tabulation.

**NOTE:** Excepting the World War II issues struck at U.S. mints, all of the modern coins were struck at the Utrecht Mint and bear the caduceus mint mark of that facility. They also bear the mintmasters marks.

**RULERS**

KINGDOM OF THE NETHERLANDS

Wilhelmina I, 1890-1948
Juliana, 1948-1980
Beatrix, 1980—

**MINT MARKS**

D - Denver, 1943-1945
P - Philadelphia, 1941-1945
S - San Francisco, 1944-1945

MINT PRIVY MARKS

Utrecht

| Date | Privy Mark |
|---|---|
| 1806-present | Caduceus |

**MINTMASTERS PRIVY MARKS**

**U. S. Mints**

| Date | Privy Mark |
|---|---|
| 1941-45 | Palm tree |

**Utrecht Mint**

| Date | Privy Mark |
|---|---|
| 1888-1909 | Halberd |
| 1909 | Halberd and star |
| 1909-1933 | Seahorse |
| 1933-42 | Grapes |
| 1943-1945 | No privy mark |
| 1945-69 | Fish |
| 1969-79 | Cock |
| 1980 | Cock and star (temporal) |
| 1980-88 | Anvil with hammer |
| 1989-99 | Bow and arrow |
| 2000- | Bow, arrow and star |

**NOTE:** A star adjoining the privy mark indicates that the piece was struck at the beginning of the term of office of a successor. (The star was used only if the successor had not chosen his own mark yet.)

**NOTE:** Since October, 1999, the Dutch Mint has taken the title of Royal Dutch Mint.

**MONETARY SYSTEM**

100 Cents = 1 Gulden

# KINGDOM OF THE NETHERLANDS

## DECIMAL COINAGE

**1/2 CENT** **KM# 109** **Composition:** Bronze **Obverse:** 17 samll shields in field **Obv. Legend:** KONINGRIJK. . .

| Date | Mintage | F | VF | XF | Unc | BU |
|---|---|---|---|---|---|---|
| 1901 | 6,000,000 | 1.50 | 3.00 | 6.00 | 17.50 | — |

**1/2 CENT** **KM# 133** **Composition:** Bronze **Obverse:** 17 samll shields in field **Obv. Legend:** KONINGRIJK. . .

| Date | Mintage | F | VF | XF | Unc | BU |
|---|---|---|---|---|---|---|
| 1903 | 10,000,000 | 1.00 | 2.00 | 3.00 | 10.00 | — |
| 1906 | 10,000,000 | 1.00 | 2.00 | 3.00 | 10.00 | — |

**1/2 CENT** **KM# 138** **Composition:** Bronze **Obverse:** 15 large shields in field around larger lion, smaller date and legend **Reverse:** CENT in larger letters

| Date | Mintage | F | VF | XF | Unc | BU |
|---|---|---|---|---|---|---|
| 1909 | 5,000,000 | 1.00 | 2.00 | 3.00 | 10.00 | — |
| 1911 | 5,000,000 | 1.00 | 2.00 | 3.00 | 10.00 | — |
| 1912 | 5,000,000 | 1.00 | 2.00 | 3.00 | 10.00 | — |
| 1914 | 5,000,000 | 1.00 | 2.00 | 4.00 | 12.50 | — |
| 1915 | 2,500,000 | 8.00 | 12.00 | 20.00 | 40.00 | — |
| 1916 | 4,000,000 | 2.00 | 4.00 | 9.00 | 20.00 | — |
| 1917 | 5,000,000 | 1.00 | 2.00 | 4.00 | 12.50 | — |
| 1921 | 1,500,000 | 7.00 | 15.00 | 25.00 | 50.00 | — |
| 1922/1 | — | 15.00 | 30.00 | 60.00 | 150 | — |
| 1922 | 2,500,000 | 5.00 | 10.00 | 17.50 | 40.00 | — |
| 1928 | 4,000,000 | 1.00 | 2.00 | 3.00 | 10.00 | — |
| 1930 | 6,000,000 | 1.00 | 2.00 | 3.00 | 10.00 | — |
| 1934 | 5,000,000 | 0.75 | 1.75 | 2.50 | 8.00 | — |
| 1936 | 5,000,000 | 0.75 | 1.75 | 2.50 | 8.00 | — |
| 1937 | 1,600,000 | 1.00 | 2.50 | 4.00 | 12.50 | — |
| 1938 | 8,400,000 | 0.70 | 1.50 | 2.00 | 5.00 | — |
| 1940 | 6,000,000 | 0.70 | 1.50 | 2.00 | 5.00 | — |

**CENT** **KM# 130** **Composition:** Bronze **Obverse:** 15 large shields in field **Obv. Legend:** KONINGRIJK

| Date | Mintage | F | VF | XF | Unc | BU |
|---|---|---|---|---|---|---|
| 1901 | 10,000,000 | 1.00 | 2.50 | 5.00 | 20.00 | — |

**CENT** **KM# 131** **Composition:** Bronze **Obverse:** 10 large shields in field **Obv. Legend:** KONINGRIJK

| Date | Mintage | F | VF | XF | Unc | BU |
|---|---|---|---|---|---|---|
| 1901 | 10,000,000 | 1.00 | 2.50 | 5.00 | 20.00 | — |

**CENT** **KM# 132.1** **Composition:** Bronze **Obverse:** 15 medium shields in field **Obv. Legend:** KONINGRIJK

| Date | Mintage | F | VF | XF | Unc | BU |
|---|---|---|---|---|---|---|
| 1902 | 10,000,000 | 1.00 | 2.00 | 3.00 | 15.00 | — |
| 1904 | 15,000,000 | 1.00 | 2.00 | 3.00 | 15.00 | — |
| 1905 | 10,000,000 | 1.00 | 2.00 | 3.00 | 15.00 | — |
| 1906 | 9,000,000 | 1.00 | 2.00 | 3.00 | 15.00 | — |
| 1907 | 6,000,000 | 5.00 | 10.00 | 20.00 | 40.00 | — |

**CENT** **KM# 132.2** **Composition:** Bronze **Obverse:** 15 medium shields in field **Obv. Legend:** KONINGRIJK **Edge:** Plain

| Date | Mintage | F | VF | XF | Unc | BU |
|---|---|---|---|---|---|---|
| 1906 Proof | — | Value: 875 | | | | |

**CENT** **KM# 152** **Composition:** Bronze

| Date | Mintage | F | VF | XF | Unc | BU |
|---|---|---|---|---|---|---|
| 1913 | 5,000,000 | 1.50 | 3.00 | 8.00 | 30.00 | — |
| 1914 | 9,000,000 | 1.00 | 2.00 | 3.00 | 15.00 | — |
| 1915 | 10,800,000 | 1.00 | 2.00 | 3.00 | 15.00 | — |
| 1916 | 21,700,000 | 0.75 | 1.00 | 2.00 | 10.00 | — |
| 1916 Proof | — | Value: 110 | | | | |
| 1917 | 20,000,000 | 0.75 | 1.00 | 2.00 | 10.00 | — |
| 1918 | 10,000,000 | 1.00 | 2.00 | 4.00 | 12.00 | — |
| 1919 | 6,000,000 | 1.75 | 2.50 | 5.00 | 15.00 | — |
| 1920 | 11,400,000 | 0.75 | 1.50 | 2.00 | 10.00 | — |
| 1921 | 12,600,000 | 0.75 | 1.50 | 2.00 | 10.00 | — |
| 1922 | 20,000,000 | 0.75 | 1.50 | 2.00 | 10.00 | — |
| 1924 | 1,400,000 | 15.00 | 25.00 | 35.00 | 70.00 | — |
| 1925 | 18,600,000 | 0.75 | 1.50 | 2.00 | 10.00 | — |
| 1926 | 10,000,000 | 0.75 | 1.50 | 2.00 | 10.00 | — |
| 1927 | 10,000,000 | 0.75 | 1.50 | 2.00 | 10.00 | — |
| 1928 | 10,000,000 | 0.75 | 1.50 | 2.00 | 10.00 | — |
| 1929 | 20,000,000 | 0.75 | 1.50 | 2.00 | 8.00 | — |
| 1930 | 10,000,000 | 0.75 | 1.50 | 2.00 | 8.00 | — |
| 1931 | 3,400,000 | 3.00 | 5.00 | 10.00 | 30.00 | — |
| 1937 | 10,000,000 | 0.75 | 1.50 | 2.00 | 7.50 | — |
| 1938 | 16,600,000 | 0.50 | 1.00 | 1.50 | 5.00 | — |
| 1939 | 22,000,000 | 0.50 | 1.00 | 1.50 | 5.00 | — |
| 1940 | 24,600,000 | 0.50 | 1.00 | 1.50 | 5.00 | — |
| 1941 | 66,600,000 | 0.25 | 0.60 | 1.00 | 2.50 | — |

**Note:** For similar coins dated 1942P see Curacao; 1943P, 1957-1960 see Surinam

**CENT** **KM# 170** **Composition:** Zinc

| Date | Mintage | F | VF | XF | Unc | BU |
|---|---|---|---|---|---|---|
| 1941 | 31,800,000 | 1.00 | 2.00 | 4.50 | 20.00 | — |
| 1942 | 241,000,000 | 0.25 | 0.50 | 1.50 | 5.00 | — |
| 1943 | 71,000,000 | 0.75 | 1.50 | 3.00 | 10.00 | — |
| 1944 | 29,600,000 | 1.00 | 2.00 | 4.50 | 20.00 | — |

**CENT** **KM# 175** **Composition:** Bronze

| Date | Mintage | F | VF | XF | Unc | BU |
|---|---|---|---|---|---|---|
| 1948 | 130,400,000 | — | 0.25 | 0.50 | 1.50 | 8.00 |
| 1948 Proof | — | Value: 40.00 | | | | |

**large date** **small date**

**CENT** **KM# 180** **Composition:** Bronze

| Date | Mintage | F | VF | XF | Unc | BU |
|---|---|---|---|---|---|---|
| 1950 | 91,000,000 | — | 0.10 | 0.25 | 0.75 | 4.00 |
| 1950 Proof | — | Value: 45.00 | | | | |
| 1951 | 45,800,000 | — | 0.10 | 0.25 | 0.75 | 4.00 |
| 1951 Proof | — | Value: 45.00 | | | | |
| 1952 | 68,000,000 | — | 0.10 | 0.25 | 0.75 | 4.00 |
| 1952 Proof | — | Value: 45.00 | | | | |
| 1953 | 54,000,000 | — | 0.10 | 0.25 | 0.75 | 4.00 |
| 1953 Proof | — | Value: 45.00 | | | | |
| 1954 | 54,000,000 | — | 0.10 | 0.25 | 0.75 | 4.00 |
| 1954 Proof | — | Value: 45.00 | | | | |
| 1955 | 52,000,000 | — | 0.10 | 0.25 | 0.75 | 4.00 |
| 1955 Proof | — | Value: 45.00 | | | | |
| 1956 | 34,800,000 | — | 0.10 | 0.25 | 0.75 | 4.00 |
| 1956 Proof | — | Value: 45.00 | | | | |
| 1957 | 48,000,000 | — | 0.10 | 0.25 | 0.75 | 4.00 |
| 1957 Proof | — | Value: 45.00 | | | | |
| 1958 | 34,000,000 | — | 0.10 | 0.25 | 0.75 | 4.00 |
| 1958 Proof | — | Value: 40.00 | | | | |
| 1959 | 36,000,000 | — | 0.10 | 0.25 | 0.75 | 4.00 |
| 1959 Proof | — | Value: 35.00 | | | | |
| 1960 | 40,000,000 | — | 0.10 | 0.25 | 0.75 | 3.00 |
| 1960 Proof | — | Value: 35.00 | | | | |
| 1961 | 52,000,000 | — | — | 0.10 | 0.35 | 2.00 |
| 1961 Proof | — | Value: 35.00 | | | | |
| 1962 | 57,000,000 | — | — | 0.10 | 0.35 | 2.00 |
| 1962 Proof | — | Value: 35.00 | | | | |
| 1963 | 70,000,000 | — | — | 0.10 | 0.35 | 2.00 |
| 1963 Proof | — | Value: 35.00 | | | | |
| 1964 | 73,000,000 | — | — | 0.10 | 0.35 | 2.00 |
| 1964 Proof | — | Value: 35.00 | | | | |
| 1965 | 91,000,000 | — | — | 0.10 | 0.35 | 2.00 |
| 1965 Proof | — | Value: 35.00 | | | | |
| 1966 large date | 104,000,000 | — | — | 0.10 | 0.25 | 1.00 |
| 1966 Proof, large date | — | Value: 35.00 | | | | |
| 1966 small date | Inc. above | — | — | 0.10 | 0.25 | 1.00 |
| 1966 Proof, small date | — | Value: 20.00 | | | | |
| 1967 | 140,000,000 | — | — | 0.10 | 0.25 | 1.00 |
| 1967 Proof | — | Value: 25.00 | | | | |
| 1968 | 28,000,000 | — | — | 0.10 | 0.25 | 1.00 |
| 1968 Proof | — | Value: 20.00 | | | | |
| 1969 fish privy mark | 50,000,000 | — | — | 0.10 | 0.25 | 1.00 |
| 1969 Proof, fish privy mark | — | Value: 20.00 | | | | |
| 1969 cock privy mark | 50,000,000 | — | — | 0.10 | 0.25 | 1.00 |
| 1969 Proof, cock privy mark | — | Value: 20.00 | | | | |
| 1970 | 100,000,000 | — | — | 0.10 | 0.15 | 1.00 |
| 1970 Proof | — | Value: 20.00 | | | | |
| 1971 | 70,000,000 | — | — | 0.10 | 0.15 | 1.00 |
| 1972 | 40,000,000 | — | — | — | 0.10 | 0.50 |
| 1973 | 34,000,000 | — | — | — | 0.10 | 0.50 |
| 1974 | 46,000,000 | — | — | — | 0.10 | 0.50 |
| 1975 | 25,000,000 | — | — | — | 0.10 | 0.50 |
| 1976 | 15,000,000 | — | — | — | 0.10 | 0.50 |
| 1977 | 15,000,000 | — | — | — | 0.10 | 0.50 |
| 1978 | 15,000,000 | — | — | — | 0.10 | 0.50 |
| 1979 | 15,000,000 | — | — | — | 0.10 | 0.50 |
| 1980 cock and star privy mark | 15,300,000 | — | — | — | 0.10 | 0.30 |

**2-1/2 CENT** **KM# 134** **Composition:** Bronze **Obverse:** 15 large shields in field **Obv. Legend:** KONINGRIJK.

| Date | Mintage | F | VF | XF | Unc | BU |
|---|---|---|---|---|---|---|
| 1903 | 4,000,000 | 2.00 | 3.50 | 6.50 | 25.00 | — |
| 1904 | 4,000,000 | 2.00 | 3.50 | 6.50 | 25.00 | — |
| 1905 | 4,000,000 | 2.00 | 3.50 | 6.50 | 25.00 | — |
| 1906 | 8,000,000 | 2.00 | 3.50 | 6.50 | 25.00 | — |

**2-1/2 CENT** **KM# 150** **Composition:** Bronze **Obverse:** 15 large shields in field **Obv. Legend:** KONINGRIJK.

| Date | Mintage | F | VF | XF | Unc | BU |
|---|---|---|---|---|---|---|
| 1912 | 2,000,000 | 5.00 | 10.00 | 20.00 | 45.00 | — |
| 1913 | 4,000,000 | 2.50 | 4.50 | 8.00 | 22.50 | — |
| 1914 | 2,000,000 | 5.00 | 10.00 | 20.00 | 45.00 | — |
| 1915 | 3,000,000 | 4.00 | 8.00 | 16.50 | 40.00 | — |
| 1916 | 8,000,000 | 2.00 | 3.50 | 6.00 | 20.00 | — |
| 1918 | 4,000,000 | 2.50 | 4.50 | 8.00 | 22.50 | — |
| 1919 | 2,000,000 | 3.00 | 6.00 | 15.00 | 35.00 | — |
| 1929 | 8,000,000 | 2.00 | 3.50 | 6.00 | 15.00 | — |
| 1941 | 19,800,000 | 1.25 | 2.00 | 3.00 | 6.50 | — |

**2-1/2 CENT** **KM# 171** **Composition:** Zinc

| Date | Mintage | F | VF | XF | Unc | BU |
|---|---|---|---|---|---|---|
| 1941 | 27,600,000 | 1.00 | 3.00 | 5.00 | 25.00 | — |
| 1942 | Est. 200,000 | 750 | 3,000 | 6,000 | 10,000 | — |

**Note:** Almost entire issue melted, about 30 pcs. known

**5 CENTS** **KM# 137** **Composition:** Copper-Nickel

| Date | Mintage | F | VF | XF | Unc | BU |
|---|---|---|---|---|---|---|
| 1907 | 6,000,000 | 3.00 | 6.00 | 10.00 | 30.00 | — |
| 1908 | 5,430,000 | 4.00 | 8.00 | 12.50 | 35.00 | — |
| 1909 | 2,570,000 | 20.00 | 30.00 | 45.00 | 100 | — |

**5 CENTS** **KM# 153** **Composition:** Copper-Nickel

| Date | Mintage | F | VF | XF | Unc | BU |
|---|---|---|---|---|---|---|
| 1913 | 6,000,000 | 1.50 | 3.00 | 5.00 | 20.00 | — |
| 1914 | 7,400,000 | 1.50 | 3.00 | 5.00 | 20.00 | — |
| 1923 | 10,000,000 | 1.50 | 3.00 | 5.00 | 20.00 | — |
| 1929 | 8,000,000 | 1.50 | 3.00 | 5.00 | 20.00 | — |
| 1932 | 2,000,000 | 4.50 | 9.00 | 15.00 | 40.00 | — |
| 1933 | 1,400,000 | 20.00 | 30.00 | 45.00 | 100 | — |
| 1934 | 2,600,000 | 4.00 | 6.00 | 10.00 | 25.00 | — |
| 1936 | 2,600,000 | 4.00 | 6.00 | 10.00 | 25.00 | — |
| 1938 | 4,200,000 | 2.00 | 3.50 | 4.50 | 15.00 | — |
| 1939 | 4,600,000 | 2.00 | 3.50 | 4.50 | 15.00 | — |
| 1940 | 7,200,000 | 2.00 | 3.50 | 4.50 | 15.00 | — |

**Note:** For a similar coin dated 1943, see Curacao

**5 CENTS** **KM# 172** **Composition:** Zinc

| Date | Mintage | F | VF | XF | Unc | BU |
|---|---|---|---|---|---|---|
| 1941 | 32,200,000 | 1.00 | 2.50 | 5.00 | 22.00 | — |
| 1942 | 11,800,000 | 2.50 | 3.50 | 6.00 | 32.00 | — |
| 1943 | 7,000,000 | 6.00 | 10.00 | 15.00 | 55.00 | — |

**5 CENTS** **KM# 176** **Composition:** Bronze

| Date | Mintage | F | VF | XF | Unc | BU |
|---|---|---|---|---|---|---|
| 1948 | 23,600,000 | — | 0.50 | 0.75 | 3.50 | 15.00 |
| 1948 Proof | — | Value: 80.00 | | | | |

**5 CENTS** **KM# 181** **Composition:** Bronze

| Date | Mintage | F | VF | XF | Unc | BU |
|---|---|---|---|---|---|---|
| 1950 | 20,000,000 | — | 0.10 | 0.25 | 1.50 | 5.00 |
| 1950 Proof | — | Value: 50.00 | | | | |
| 1951 | 16,200,000 | — | 0.10 | 0.25 | 1.50 | 5.00 |
| 1951 Proof | — | Value: 50.00 | | | | |
| 1952 | 14,400,000 | — | 0.10 | 0.25 | 1.50 | 5.00 |
| 1952 Proof | — | Value: 50.00 | | | | |
| 1953 | 12,000,000 | — | 0.10 | 0.25 | 1.50 | 5.00 |
| 1953 Proof | — | Value: 50.00 | | | | |
| 1954 | 14,000,000 | — | 0.10 | 0.25 | 1.50 | 5.00 |
| 1954 Proof | — | Value: 50.00 | | | | |
| 1955 | 11,400,000 | — | 0.10 | 0.25 | 1.50 | 5.00 |
| 1955 Proof | — | Value: 50.00 | | | | |
| 1956 | 7,400,000 | — | 0.15 | 0.35 | 2.50 | 8.00 |
| 1956 Proof | — | Value: 50.00 | | | | |
| 1957 | 16,000,000 | — | 0.10 | 0.25 | 1.50 | 5.00 |
| 1957 Proof | — | Value: 50.00 | | | | |
| 1958 | 9,000,000 | — | 0.10 | 0.25 | 1.50 | 5.00 |
| 1958 Proof | — | Value: 50.00 | | | | |
| 1960 | 11,000,000 | — | 0.10 | 0.25 | 1.00 | 3.00 |
| 1960 Proof | — | Value: 40.00 | | | | |
| 1961 | 12,000,000 | — | 0.10 | 0.25 | 0.75 | 2.00 |

| Date | Mintage | F | VF | XF | Unc | BU |
|---|---|---|---|---|---|---|
| 1961 Proof | — | Value: 40.00 | | | | |
| 1962 | 15,000,000 | — | 0.10 | 0.25 | 0.75 | 2.00 |
| 1962 Proof | — | Value: 40.00 | | | | |
| 1963 | 18,000,000 | — | 0.10 | 0.25 | 0.75 | 2.00 |
| 1963 Proof | — | Value: 40.00 | | | | |
| 1964 | 21,000,000 | — | 0.10 | 0.25 | 0.75 | 2.00 |
| 1964 Proof | — | Value: 40.00 | | | | |
| 1965 | 28,000,000 | — | 0.10 | 0.25 | 0.75 | 1.50 |
| 1965 Proof | — | Value: 40.00 | | | | |
| 1966 | 22,000,000 | — | 0.10 | 0.25 | 0.75 | 2.00 |
| 1966 Proof | — | Value: 40.00 | | | | |
| 1967 leaves far from rim | 32,000,000 | — | — | 0.20 | 0.50 | 1.50 |
| 1967 Proof, leaves far from rim | — | Value: 50.00 | | | | |
| 1967 leaves touching rim | Inc. above | — | 0.15 | 0.50 | 1.00 | 2.00 |
| 1967 Proof, leaves touching rim | — | Value: 40.00 | | | | |
| 1969 fish privy mark | 5,000,000 | — | 0.15 | 0.50 | 1.50 | 8.00 |
| 1969 Proof, fish privy mark | — | Value: 40.00 | | | | |
| 1969 cock privy mark | 11,000,000 | — | — | 0.10 | 0.25 | 4.00 |
| 1969 Proof, cock privy mark | — | Value: 40.00 | | | | |
| 1970 | 22,000,000 | — | — | 0.10 | 0.25 | 1.50 |
| 1970 Proof | — | Value: 25.00 | | | | |
| 1970 date close to rim | Inc. above | — | — | 0.10 | 0.25 | 1.00 |
| 1970 Proof, date close to rim | — | Value: 20.00 | | | | |
| 1971 | 25,000,000 | — | — | 0.10 | 0.25 | 1.00 |
| 1972 | 25,000,000 | — | — | 0.10 | 0.25 | 1.00 |
| 1973 | 22,000,000 | — | — | 0.10 | 0.25 | 1.00 |
| 1974 | 20,000,000 | — | — | — | 0.10 | 1.00 |
| 1975 | 46,000,000 | — | — | — | 0.10 | 0.75 |
| 1976 | 50,000,000 | — | — | — | 0.10 | 0.75 |
| 1977 | 50,000,000 | — | — | — | 0.10 | 0.75 |
| 1978 | 60,000,000 | — | — | — | 0.10 | 0.75 |
| 1979 | 80,000,000 | — | — | — | 0.10 | 0.75 |
| 1980 cock and star privy mark | 252,500,000 | — | — | — | 0.10 | 0.30 |

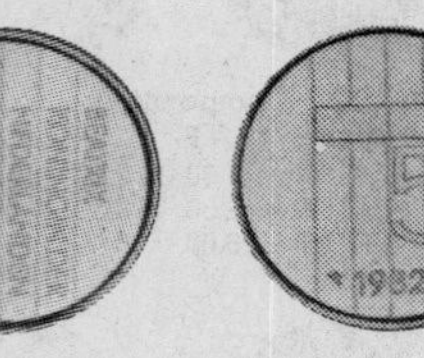

**5 CENTS** **KM# 202** **Composition:** Bronze

| Date | Mintage | F | VF | XF | Unc | BU |
|---|---|---|---|---|---|---|
| 1982 | 47,100,000 | — | — | — | 0.10 | 0.40 |
| 1982 Proof | 10,000 | Value: 10.00 | | | | |
| 1983 | 60,200,000 | — | — | — | 0.10 | 0.40 |
| 1983 Proof | 15,000 | Value: 7.50 | | | | |
| 1984 | 70,700,000 | — | — | — | 0.10 | 0.40 |
| 1984 Proof | 20,000 | Value: 4.00 | | | | |
| 1985 | 36,100,000 | — | — | — | 0.10 | 0.40 |
| 1985 Proof | 17,000 | Value: 4.00 | | | | |
| 1986 | 7,700,000 | — | — | — | 0.10 | 0.80 |
| 1986 Proof | 20,000 | Value: 4.00 | | | | |
| 1987 | 33,299,999 | — | — | — | — | 0.40 |
| 1987 Proof | 18,000 | Value: 4.00 | | | | |
| 1988 | 22,600,000 | — | — | — | — | 0.40 |
| 1988 Proof | 20,000 | Value: 4.00 | | | | |
| 1989 | 27,100,000 | — | — | — | — | 0.40 |
| 1989 Proof | 15,000 | Value: 4.00 | | | | |
| 1990 | 39,300,000 | — | — | — | — | 0.40 |
| 1990 Proof | 15,000 | Value: 4.00 | | | | |
| 1991 | 73,100,000 | — | — | — | — | 0.40 |
| 1991 Proof | 14,000 | Value: 4.00 | | | | |
| 1992 | 52,700,000 | — | — | — | — | 0.40 |
| 1992 Proof | 13,000 | Value: 4.00 | | | | |
| 1993 | 40,000,000 | — | — | — | — | 0.40 |
| 1993 Proof | 12,000 | Value: 4.00 | | | | |
| 1994 | 14,000,000 | — | — | — | — | 1.50 |
| 1994 Proof | 13,000 | Value: 4.00 | | | | |
| 1995 | 6,000,000 | — | — | — | — | 2.00 |
| 1995 Proof | 12,000 | Value: 4.00 | | | | |
| 1996 | 40,000,000 | — | — | — | — | 0.40 |
| 1996 Proof | 14,000 | Value: 4.00 | | | | |
| 1997 | 36,000,000 | — | — | — | — | 0.40 |
| 1997 Proof | 12,000 | Value: 4.00 | | | | |
| 1998 | 65,099,999 | — | — | — | — | 0.40 |
| 1998 Proof | 12,000 | Value: 4.00 | | | | |
| 1999 | 16,480,000 | — | — | — | — | 0.40 |
| 1999 Proof | 15,000 | Value: 4.00 | | | | |
| 2000 | 30,076,000 | — | — | — | — | 0.40 |
| 2000 Proof | 15,000 | Value: 4.00 | | | | |
| 2001 | — | — | — | — | — | 0.40 |
| 2001 Proof | — | Value: 4.00 | | | | |

**10 CENTS** **KM# 119** **Weight:** 1.4000 g. **Composition:** 0.6400 Silver .0288 oz. ASW **Obverse:** Small head, divided legend

| Date | Mintage | F | VF | XF | Unc | BU |
|---|---|---|---|---|---|---|
| 1901 | 2,000,000 | 10.00 | 25.00 | 40.00 | 120 | — |

**10 CENTS** **KM# 135** **Weight:** 1.4000 g. **Composition:** 0.6400 Silver .0288 oz. ASW **Obverse:** Large head

| Date | Mintage | F | VF | XF | Unc | BU |
|---|---|---|---|---|---|---|
| 1903 | 6,000,000 | 3.00 | 9.00 | 20.00 | 40.00 | — |

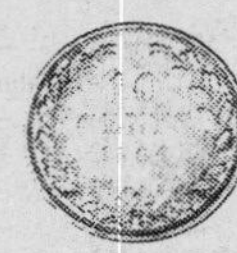

**10 CENTS** **KM# 136** **Weight:** 1.4000 g. **Composition:** 0.6400 Silver .0288 oz. ASW **Obverse:** Small head, continous legend

| Date | Mintage | F | VF | XF | Unc | BU |
|---|---|---|---|---|---|---|
| 1904 | 3,000,000 | 5.00 | 15.00 | 25.00 | 60.00 | — |
| 1905 | 2,000,000 | 7.00 | 20.00 | 30.00 | 80.00 | — |
| 1906 | 4,000,000 | 3.00 | 10.00 | 20.00 | 40.00 | — |

**10 CENTS** **KM# 145** **Weight:** 1.4000 g. **Composition:** 0.6400 Silver .0288 oz. ASW **Obverse:** Small head, continuous legend

| Date | Mintage | F | VF | XF | Unc | BU |
|---|---|---|---|---|---|---|
| 1910 | 2,250,000 | 8.00 | 20.00 | 30.00 | 100 | — |
| 1911 | 4,000,000 | 4.00 | 8.00 | 20.00 | 50.00 | — |
| 1912 | 4,000,000 | 4.00 | 8.00 | 20.00 | 50.00 | — |
| 1913 | 5,000,000 | 4.00 | 8.00 | 20.00 | 50.00 | — |
| 1914 | 9,000,000 | 1.50 | 4.00 | 8.00 | 20.00 | — |
| 1915 | 5,000,000 | 1.50 | 4.00 | 8.00 | 20.00 | — |
| 1916 | 5,000,000 | 1.50 | 4.00 | 8.00 | 20.00 | — |
| 1917 | 10,000,000 | 1.00 | 3.00 | 6.00 | 15.00 | — |
| 1918 | 20,000,000 | 0.75 | 2.00 | 4.00 | 12.50 | — |
| 1919 | 10,000,000 | 1.00 | 3.00 | 6.00 | 15.00 | — |
| 1921 | 5,000,000 | 1.50 | 5.00 | 8.00 | 20.00 | — |
| 1925 | 5,000,000 | 1.50 | 5.00 | 8.00 | 20.00 | — |

**10 CENTS** **KM# 163** **Weight:** 1.4000 g. **Composition:** 0.6400 Silver .0288 oz. ASW **Obverse:** Small head, continous legend

| Date | Mintage | F | VF | XF | Unc | BU |
|---|---|---|---|---|---|---|
| 1926 | 2,700,000 | 2.00 | 4.00 | 10.00 | 35.00 | — |
| 1927 | 2,300,000 | 2.00 | 4.00 | 10.00 | 35.00 | — |
| 1928 | 10,000,000 | 0.50 | 1.50 | 3.00 | 15.00 | — |
| 1930 | 5,000,000 | 0.75 | 2.50 | 4.00 | 20.00 | — |
| 1934 | 2,000,000 | 2.00 | 4.00 | 10.00 | 35.00 | — |
| 1935 | 8,000,000 | 0.50 | 1.00 | 2.00 | 8.00 | — |
| 1936 | 15,000,000 | 0.25 | 0.50 | 1.50 | 4.00 | — |
| 1937 | 18,600,000 | 0.25 | 0.50 | 1.50 | 4.00 | — |
| 1938 | 21,400,000 | 0.25 | 0.50 | 1.50 | 4.00 | — |
| 1939 | 20,000,000 | 0.25 | 0.50 | 1.50 | 4.00 | — |
| 1941 | 43,000,000 | 0.25 | 0.40 | 1.00 | 2.00 | — |
| 1943P Acorn privy mark | — | 0.50 | 1.00 | 2.00 | 7.00 | — |
| 1944P | 120,000,000 | 0.25 | 0.40 | 0.75 | 1.50 | — |
| 1944D | 25,400,000 | 1,000 | 2,000 | 2,800 | 4,500 | — |
| 1944S | 64,040,000 | 0.50 | 1.25 | 2.50 | 10.00 | — |
| 1945P | 90,560,000 | 150 | 300 | 500 | 800 | — |

**Note:** For similar coins dated 1941P-1943P with palm tree privy mark, see Curacao and Surinam

**10 CENTS** **KM# 173** **Composition:** Zinc

| Date | Mintage | F | VF | XF | Unc | BU |
|---|---|---|---|---|---|---|
| 1941 | 29,800,000 | 0.75 | 1.50 | 3.00 | 20.00 | — |
| 1942 | 95,600,000 | 0.25 | 0.50 | 1.50 | 15.00 | — |
| 1943 | 29,000,000 | 0.75 | 1.50 | 3.00 | 20.00 | — |

**10 CENTS** **KM# 177** **Composition:** Nickel

| Date | Mintage | F | VF | XF | Unc | BU |
|---|---|---|---|---|---|---|
| 1948 | 69,200,000 | — | 0.25 | 0.50 | 1.00 | 5.00 |
| 1948 Proof | — | Value: 90.00 | | | | |

**10 CENTS** **KM# 182** **Composition:** Nickel

| Date | Mintage | F | VF | XF | Unc | BU |
|---|---|---|---|---|---|---|
| 1950 | 56,600,000 | — | 0.10 | 0.35 | 0.75 | 3.00 |
| 1950 Proof | — | Value: 60.00 | | | | |
| 1951 | 54,200,000 | — | 0.10 | 0.35 | 0.75 | 3.00 |
| 1951 Proof | — | Value: 60.00 | | | | |
| 1954 | 8,200,000 | — | 0.20 | 0.50 | 1.00 | 4.00 |
| 1954 Proof | — | Value: 60.00 | | | | |
| 1955 | 18,200,000 | — | 0.10 | 0.35 | 0.75 | 3.00 |
| 1955 Proof | — | Value: 60.00 | | | | |
| 1956 | 12,000,000 | — | 0.10 | 0.35 | 0.75 | 3.00 |
| 1956 Proof | — | Value: 60.00 | | | | |
| 1957 | 18,600,000 | — | 0.10 | 0.35 | 0.75 | 3.00 |
| 1957 Proof | — | Value: 60.00 | | | | |
| 1958 | 34,000,000 | — | 0.10 | 0.35 | 0.75 | 2.00 |
| 1958 Proof | — | Value: 60.00 | | | | |
| 1959 | 44,000,000 | — | 0.10 | 0.35 | 0.75 | 2.00 |
| 1959 Proof | — | Value: 50.00 | | | | |
| 1960 | 12,000,000 | — | 0.10 | 0.35 | 0.75 | 2.00 |
| 1960 Proof | — | Value: 50.00 | | | | |
| 1961 | 25,000,000 | — | — | 0.10 | 0.25 | 1.50 |
| 1961 Proof | — | Value: 50.00 | | | | |
| 1962 | 30,000,000 | — | — | 0.10 | 0.25 | 1.50 |
| 1962 Proof | — | Value: 50.00 | | | | |
| 1963 | 35,000,000 | — | — | 0.10 | 0.25 | 1.50 |
| 1963 Proof | — | Value: 60.00 | | | | |
| 1964 | 41,000,000 | — | — | 0.10 | 0.25 | 1.50 |
| 1964 Proof | — | Value: 60.00 | | | | |
| 1965 | 59,000,000 | — | — | 0.10 | 0.25 | 1.50 |
| 1965 Proof | — | Value: 60.00 | | | | |
| 1966 | 44,000,000 | — | — | — | 0.10 | 1.00 |
| 1966 Proof | — | Value: 50.00 | | | | |
| 1967 | 39,000,000 | — | — | — | 0.10 | 1.00 |
| 1967 Proof | — | Value: 50.00 | | | | |
| 1968 | 42,000,000 | — | — | — | 0.10 | 1.00 |
| 1968 Proof | — | Value: 40.00 | | | | |
| 1969 fish privy mark | 29,100,000 | — | — | — | 0.10 | 1.50 |
| 1969 Proof, fish privy mark | — | Value: 40.00 | | | | |
| 1969 cock privy mark | 24,000,000 | — | — | — | 0.10 | 1.50 |
| 1969 Proof, cock privy mark | — | Value: 40.00 | | | | |
| 1970 | 50,000,000 | — | — | — | 0.10 | 1.00 |
| 1970 Proof | — | Value: 40.00 | | | | |
| 1971 | 55,000,000 | — | — | — | 0.10 | 1.00 |
| 1972 | 60,000,000 | — | — | — | 0.10 | 1.00 |
| 1973 | 90,000,000 | — | — | — | 0.10 | 1.00 |
| 1974 | 75,000,000 | — | — | — | 0.10 | 2.00 |
| 1975 | 110,000,000 | — | — | — | 0.10 | 1.00 |
| 1976 | 85,000,000 | — | — | — | 0.10 | 1.00 |
| 1977 | 100,000,000 | — | — | — | 0.10 | 1.00 |
| 1978 | 110,000,000 | — | — | — | 0.10 | 1.00 |
| 1979 | 120,000,000 | — | — | — | 0.10 | 1.00 |
| 1980 cock and star privy mark | 195,300,000 | — | — | — | 0.10 | 0.50 |

**10 CENTS** **KM# 203** **Composition:** Nickel

| Date | Mintage | F | VF | XF | Unc | BU |
|---|---|---|---|---|---|---|
| 1982 | 10,300,000 | — | — | — | 0.10 | 0.50 |
| 1982 Proof | 10,000 | Value: 10.00 | | | | |
| 1983 | 38,200,000 | — | — | — | — | 0.50 |
| 1983 Proof | 15,000 | Value: 8.00 | | | | |
| 1984 | 42,200,000 | — | — | — | 0.10 | 0.50 |
| 1984 Proof | 20,000 | Value: 4.00 | | | | |
| 1985 | 29,100,000 | — | — | — | 0.10 | 0.50 |
| 1985 Proof | 17,000 | Value: 4.00 | | | | |
| 1986 | 23,100,000 | — | — | — | 0.10 | 0.50 |
| 1986 Proof | 20,000 | Value: 4.00 | | | | |
| 1987 | 21,700,000 | — | — | — | 0.10 | 0.50 |
| 1987 Proof | 18,000 | Value: 4.00 | | | | |
| 1988 | 2,200,000 | — | — | — | 0.25 | 2.00 |
| 1988 Proof | 20,000 | Value: 6.00 | | | | |
| 1989 | 5,300,000 | — | — | — | — | 1.50 |
| 1989 Proof | 15,000 | Value: 5.00 | | | | |
| 1990 | 13,300,000 | — | — | — | — | 0.50 |
| 1990 Proof | 15,000 | Value: 4.00 | | | | |
| 1991 | 41,100,000 | — | — | — | — | 0.50 |
| 1991 Proof | 14,000 | Value: 4.00 | | | | |
| 1992 | 41,300,000 | — | — | — | — | 0.50 |
| 1992 Proof | 13,000 | Value: 4.00 | | | | |
| 1993 | 30,100,000 | — | — | — | — | 0.50 |
| 1993 Proof | 12,000 | Value: 4.00 | | | | |
| 1994 | 25,685,000 | — | — | — | — | 0.50 |
| 1994 Proof | 13,000 | Value: 4.00 | | | | |
| 1995 | 35,100,000 | — | — | — | — | 0.50 |
| 1995 Proof | 12,000 | Value: 4.00 | | | | |
| 1996 | 34,900,000 | — | — | — | — | 0.50 |
| 1996 Proof | 14,000 | Value: 4.00 | | | | |
| 1997 | 20,100,000 | — | — | — | — | 0.50 |
| 1997 Proof | 12,000 | Value: 4.00 | | | | |
| 1998 | 24,540,000 | — | — | — | — | 0.50 |
| 1998 Proof | 12,000 | Value: 4.00 | | | | |
| 1999 | 50,040,000 | — | — | — | — | 0.50 |
| 1999 Proof | 15,000 | Value: 4.00 | | | | |
| 2000 | 75,476,000 | — | — | — | — | 0.50 |
| 2000 Proof | 15,000 | Value: 4.00 | | | | |
| 2001 | — | — | — | — | — | 0.50 |
| 2001 Proof | — | Value: 4.00 | | | | |

**25 CENTS** **KM# 120.1** **Weight:** 3.5750 g. **Composition:** 0.6400 Silver .0736 oz. ASW **Obverse:** Bust with wide truncation

| Date | Mintage | F | VF | XF | Unc | BU |
|---|---|---|---|---|---|---|
| 1901 | 1,600,000 | 30.00 | 50.00 | 125 | 300 | — |

**25 CENTS** **KM# 120.2** **Weight:** 3.5750 g. **Composition:** 0.6400 Silver .0736 oz. ASW **Obverse:** Bust with narrow truncation

| Date | Mintage | F | VF | XF | Unc | BU |
|---|---|---|---|---|---|---|
| 1901 | Inc. above | 7.00 | 20.00 | 35.00 | 100 | — |
| 1901 Proof | 3 | Value: 1,500 | | | | |
| 1902 | 1,200,000 | 7.00 | 20.00 | 35.00 | 100 | — |
| 1903 | 1,200,000 | 7.00 | 20.00 | 35.00 | 100 | — |
| 1904 | 1,600,000 | 6.00 | 18.00 | 30.00 | 90.00 | — |
| 1905 | 1,200,000 | 7.00 | 20.00 | 35.00 | 100 | — |
| 1906 | 2,000,000 | 5.00 | 15.00 | 25.00 | 75.00 | — |

**25 CENTS** **KM# 146** **Weight:** 3.5750 g. **Composition:** 0.6400 Silver .0736 oz. ASW

| Date | Mintage | F | VF | XF | Unc | BU |
|---|---|---|---|---|---|---|
| 1910 | 880,000 | 15.00 | 25.00 | 50.00 | 150 | — |
| 1910 Proof | — | Value: 400 | | | | |
| 1911 | 1,600,000 | 6.00 | 15.00 | 25.00 | 175 | — |
| 1912 | 1,600,000 | 6.00 | 15.00 | 25.00 | 175 | — |
| 1913 | 1,200,000 | 8.00 | 20.00 | 40.00 | 100 | — |
| 1914 | 5,600,000 | 2.50 | 6.00 | 12.50 | 35.00 | — |
| 1915 | 2,000,000 | 3.00 | 8.00 | 15.00 | 40.00 | — |
| 1916 | 2,000,000 | 3.00 | 8.00 | 15.00 | 40.00 | — |
| 1917 | 4,000,000 | 2.50 | 6.00 | 12.50 | 35.00 | — |
| 1918 | 6,000,000 | 2.00 | 5.00 | 10.00 | 30.00 | — |
| 1919 | 4,000,000 | 2.50 | 6.00 | 12.50 | 35.00 | — |
| 1925 | 2,000,000 | 3.00 | 8.00 | 15.00 | 40.00 | — |

**25 CENTS** **KM# 164** **Weight:** 3.5750 g. **Composition:** 0.6400 Silver .0736 oz. ASW

| Date | Mintage | F | VF | XF | Unc | BU |
|---|---|---|---|---|---|---|
| 1926 | 2,000,000 | 5.00 | 10.00 | 20.00 | 50.00 | — |
| 1928 | 8,000,000 | 0.75 | 1.50 | 3.00 | 15.00 | — |
| 1939 | 4,000,000 | 0.75 | 1.50 | 3.00 | 8.00 | — |
| 1940 | 9,000,000 | 0.50 | 1.00 | 2.00 | 5.00 | — |
| 1941 | 40,000,000 | 0.35 | 0.60 | 1.50 | 2.50 | — |
| 1943P acorn privy mark | — | 0.50 | 1.25 | 3.50 | 10.00 | — |
| 1944P acorn privy mark | 40,000,000 | 0.35 | 0.60 | 1.50 | 2.50 | — |
| 1945 acorn privy mark | 92,000,000 | 40.00 | 100 | 200 | 350 | — |

**Note:** For similar coins dated 1941P and 1943P with palm tree privy mark, see Curacao.

**25 CENTS** **KM# 174** **Composition:** Zinc

| Date | Mintage | F | VF | XF | Unc | BU |
|---|---|---|---|---|---|---|
| 1941 | 34,600,000 | 0.50 | 1.00 | 2.00 | 25.00 | — |
| 1942 | 27,800,000 | 0.50 | 1.00 | 2.00 | 25.00 | — |
| 1943 | 13,600,000 | 2.00 | 5.00 | 8.00 | 50.00 | — |

**25 CENTS** **KM# 178** **Composition:** Nickel

| Date | Mintage | F | VF | XF | Unc | BU |
|---|---|---|---|---|---|---|
| 1948 | 27,400,000 | — | 0.25 | 0.50 | 1.50 | 6.00 |
| 1948 Proof | — | Value: 90.00 | | | | |

**25 CENTS** **KM# 183** **Composition:** Nickel

| Date | Mintage | F | VF | XF | Unc | BU |
|---|---|---|---|---|---|---|
| 1950 | 43,000,000 | — | 0.20 | 0.30 | 1.50 | 3.00 |
| 1950 Proof | — | Value: 65.00 | | | | |
| 1951 | 33,200,000 | — | 0.20 | 0.30 | 1.50 | 3.00 |
| 1951 Proof | — | Value: 65.00 | | | | |
| 1954 | 6,400,000 | — | 0.50 | 1.50 | 2.00 | 5.00 |
| 1954 Proof | — | Value: 65.00 | | | | |
| 1955 | 10,000,000 | — | 0.20 | 0.30 | 1.50 | 3.00 |
| 1955 Proof | — | Value: 65.00 | | | | |
| 1956 | 8,000,000 | — | 0.20 | 0.30 | 1.50 | 4.00 |
| 1956 Proof | — | Value: 65.00 | | | | |
| 1957 | 8,000,000 | — | 0.20 | 0.30 | 1.50 | 4.00 |
| 1957 Proof | — | Value: 65.00 | | | | |
| 1958 | 15,000,000 | — | 0.20 | 0.30 | 1.00 | 2.00 |
| 1958 Proof | — | Value: 65.00 | | | | |
| 1960 | 9,000,000 | — | 0.20 | 0.30 | 1.50 | 4.00 |
| 1960 Proof | — | Value: 60.00 | | | | |
| 1961 | 6,000,000 | — | 0.40 | 1.25 | 1.50 | 5.00 |
| 1961 Proof | — | Value: 50.00 | | | | |
| 1962 | 12,000,000 | — | 0.20 | 0.30 | 1.00 | 2.00 |
| 1962 Proof | — | Value: 50.00 | | | | |
| 1963 | 18,000,000 | — | 0.20 | 0.30 | 1.00 | 2.00 |
| 1963 Proof | — | Value: 50.00 | | | | |
| 1964 | 25,000,000 | — | 0.20 | 0.30 | 1.00 | 2.00 |
| 1964 Proof | — | Value: 50.00 | | | | |
| 1965 | 18,000,000 | — | 0.20 | 0.30 | 1.00 | 1.50 |
| 1965 Proof | — | Value: 50.00 | | | | |
| 1966 | 25,000,000 | — | — | 0.20 | 0.75 | 1.50 |
| 1966 Proof | — | Value: 50.00 | | | | |
| 1967 | 18,000,000 | — | — | 0.20 | 0.75 | 1.50 |
| 1967 Proof | — | Value: 60.00 | | | | |
| 1968 | 26,000,000 | — | — | 0.20 | 0.75 | 1.00 |
| 1968 Proof | — | Value: 60.00 | | | | |
| 1969 fish privy mark | 14,000,000 | — | — | 0.20 | 0.30 | 1.00 |
| 1969 Proof, fish privy mark | — | Value: 60.00 | | | | |
| 1969 cock privy mark | 21,000,000 | — | — | 0.20 | 0.75 | 1.00 |
| 1969 Proof, cock privy mark | — | Value: 60.00 | | | | |
| 1970 | 39,000,000 | — | — | 0.20 | 0.30 | 1.00 |
| 1970 Proof | — | Value: 60.00 | | | | |
| 1971 | 40,000,000 | — | — | 0.20 | 0.30 | 1.00 |
| 1972 | 50,000,000 | — | — | 0.20 | 0.30 | 1.00 |
| 1973 | 45,000,000 | — | — | 0.20 | 0.30 | 1.00 |
| 1974 | 10,000,000 | — | — | 0.20 | 0.50 | 1.50 |
| 1975 | 25,000,000 | — | — | 0.20 | 0.30 | 1.00 |
| 1976 | 64,000,000 | — | — | 0.20 | 0.30 | 1.00 |
| 1977 | 55,000,000 | — | — | 0.20 | 0.30 | 1.00 |
| 1978 | 35,000,000 | — | — | 0.20 | 0.30 | 1.00 |
| 1979 | 45,000,000 | — | — | 0.20 | 0.30 | 1.00 |
| 1980 cock and star privy mark | 159,300,000 | — | — | — | 0.20 | 0.50 |

**25 CENTS** **KM# 183a** **Composition:** Aluminum

| Date | Mintage | F | VF | XF | Unc | BU |
|---|---|---|---|---|---|---|
| 1980 | 15 | — | — | — | — | 500 |

**25 CENTS** **KM# 204** **Composition:** Nickel

| Date | Mintage | F | VF | XF | Unc | BU |
|---|---|---|---|---|---|---|
| 1982 | 18,300,000 | — | — | — | 0.20 | 0.60 |
| 1982 Proof | 10,000 | Value: 15.00 | | | | |
| 1983 | 18,200,000 | — | — | — | 0.20 | 0.60 |
| 1983 Proof | 15,000 | Value: 12.00 | | | | |
| 1984 | 19,200,000 | — | — | — | 0.20 | 0.60 |
| 1984 Proof | 20,000 | Value: 6.00 | | | | |
| 1985 | 29,100,000 | — | — | — | 0.20 | 0.60 |
| 1985 Proof | 17,000 | Value: 6.00 | | | | |
| 1986 | 20,300,000 | — | — | — | 0.20 | 0.60 |
| 1986 Proof | 20,000 | Value: 6.00 | | | | |
| 1987 | 30,100,000 | — | — | — | 0.20 | 0.60 |
| 1987 Proof | 18,000 | Value: 6.00 | | | | |
| 1988 | 17,400,000 | — | — | — | 0.20 | 0.60 |
| 1988 Proof | 20,000 | Value: 6.00 | | | | |
| 1989 | 30,500,000 | — | — | — | 0.20 | 0.60 |
| 1989 Proof | 15,000 | Value: 6.00 | | | | |
| 1990 | 23,100,000 | — | — | — | 0.20 | 0.60 |
| 1990 Proof | 15,000 | Value: 6.00 | | | | |
| 1991 | 25,100,000 | — | — | — | 0.20 | 0.60 |
| 1991 Proof | 14,000 | Value: 6.00 | | | | |
| 1992 | 41,600,000 | — | — | — | 0.20 | 0.60 |
| 1992 Proof | 13,000 | Value: 6.00 | | | | |
| 1993 | 15,100,000 | — | — | — | 0.25 | 1.00 |
| 1993 Proof | 12,000 | Value: 6.00 | | | | |
| 1994 | 1,700,000 | — | — | — | 1.00 | 3.00 |
| 1994 Proof | 13,000 | Value: 10.00 | | | | |
| 1995 | 30,300,000 | — | — | — | 0.50 | 1.25 |
| 1995 Proof | 12,000 | Value: 8.00 | | | | |
| 1996 | 24,900,000 | — | — | — | 0.20 | 0.60 |
| 1996 Proof | 14,000 | Value: 6.00 | | | | |
| 1997 | 29,900,000 | — | — | — | 0.20 | 0.60 |
| 1997 Proof | 12,000 | Value: 6.00 | | | | |
| 1998 | 69,660,000 | — | — | — | 0.20 | 0.60 |
| 1998 Proof | 12,000 | Value: 6.00 | | | | |
| 1999 | 107,000,000 | — | — | — | 0.20 | 0.80 |
| 1999 Proof | 15,000 | Value: 6.00 | | | | |
| 2000 | 31,176,000 | — | — | — | 0.20 | 0.60 |
| 2000 Proof | 15,000 | Value: 6.00 | | | | |
| 2001 | — | — | — | — | 0.20 | 0.60 |
| 2001 Proof | — | Value: 6.00 | | | | |

**1/2 GULDEN (50 Cents)** **KM# 121.2** **Weight:** 5.0000 g. **Composition:** 0.9450 Silver .1519 oz. ASW **Reverse:** Without 50 C. below shield

| Date | Mintage | F | VF | XF | Unc | BU |
|---|---|---|---|---|---|---|
| 1904 | 1,000,000 | 20.00 | 40.00 | 75.00 | 200 | — |
| 1905 | 4,000,000 | 6.00 | 12.50 | 30.00 | 75.00 | — |
| 1906 | 1,000,000 | 20.00 | 40.00 | 75.00 | 200 | — |
| 1907 | 3,300,000 | 6.00 | 12.50 | 30.00 | 75.00 | — |
| 1907 Proof | — | Value: 300 | | | | |
| 1908 | 4,000,000 | 6.00 | 12.50 | 30.00 | 75.00 | — |
| 1909 | 3,000,000 | 6.00 | 12.50 | 30.00 | 75.00 | — |

**1/2 GULDEN (50 Cents)** **KM# 147** **Weight:** 5.0000 g. **Composition:** 0.9450 Silver .1519 oz. ASW **Reverse:** Without 50 C. below shield

| Date | Mintage | F | VF | XF | Unc | BU |
|---|---|---|---|---|---|---|
| 1910 | 4,000,000 | 6.00 | 12.50 | 30.00 | 80.00 | — |
| 1912 | 4,000,000 | 6.00 | 12.50 | 30.00 | 80.00 | — |
| 1913 | 8,000,000 | 5.00 | 10.00 | 25.00 | 60.00 | — |
| 1919 | 8,000,000 | 5.00 | 10.00 | 25.00 | 60.00 | — |

**1/2 GULDEN (50 Cents)** **KM# 160** **Weight:** 5.0000 g. **Composition:** 0.7200 Silver .1157 oz. ASW **Reverse:** Without 50 C. below shield

| Date | Mintage | F | VF | XF | Unc | BU |
|---|---|---|---|---|---|---|
| 1921 | 5,000,000 | 1.00 | 2.00 | 3.00 | 20.00 | — |
| 1921 Proof | — | Value: 200 | | | | |
| 1922 | 11,240,000 | 0.75 | 1.50 | 2.50 | 15.00 | — |
| 1928 | 5,000,000 | 1.00 | 2.00 | 3.00 | 20.00 | — |
| 1929 | 9,500,000 | 0.75 | 1.50 | 2.50 | 12.50 | — |
| 1930 | 18,500,000 | 0.75 | 1.50 | 2.00 | 8.00 | — |

**GULDEN** **KM# 122.1** **Weight:** 10.0000 g. **Composition:** 0.9450 Silver .3038 oz. ASW

| Date | Mintage | F | VF | XF | Unc | BU |
|---|---|---|---|---|---|---|
| 1901 | 2,000,000 | 20.00 | 35.00 | 75.00 | 200 | — |
| 1901 Proof | — | Value: 500 | | | | |

**GULDEN** **KM# 122.2** **Weight:** 10.0000 g. **Composition:** 0.9450 Silver .3038 oz. ASW **Reverse:** Without 100 C. below shield

| Date | Mintage | F | VF | XF | Unc | BU |
|---|---|---|---|---|---|---|
| 1904 | 2,000,000 | 12.00 | 20.00 | 40.00 | 100 | — |
| 1905 | 1,000,000 | 20.00 | 35.00 | 75.00 | 200 | — |
| 1905 Proof | — | Value: 750 | | | | |
| 1906 | 500,000 | 80.00 | 150 | 300 | 550 | — |
| 1906 Proof | — | Value: 1,150 | | | | |
| 1907 | 5,100,000 | 8.00 | 20.00 | 35.00 | 90.00 | — |
| 1908 | 4,700,000 | 8.00 | 20.00 | 35.00 | 90.00 | — |
| 1908 Proof | — | Value: 450 | | | | |
| 1909 | 2,000,000 | 12.00 | 25.00 | 50.00 | 100 | — |

**GULDEN** **KM# 148** **Weight:** 10.0000 g. **Composition:** 0.9450 Silver .3038 oz. ASW **Obv. Legend:** Without 100 C. below shield

| Date | Mintage | F | VF | XF | Unc | BU |
|---|---|---|---|---|---|---|
| 1910 | 1,000,000 | 25.00 | 50.00 | 140 | 350 | — |
| 1910 | — | Value: 700 | | | | |
| 1911 | 2,000,000 | 20.00 | 40.00 | 100 | 250 | — |
| 1912 | 3,000,000 | 8.00 | 20.00 | 35.00 | 100 | — |
| 1913 | 8,000,000 | 6.00 | 18.00 | 30.00 | 75.00 | — |
| 1914 | 15,785,000 | 5.00 | 12.50 | 20.00 | 50.00 | — |
| 1915 | 14,215,000 | 5.00 | 15.00 | 25.00 | 55.00 | — |
| 1916 | 5,000,000 | 15.00 | 25.00 | 50.00 | 140 | — |
| 1917 | 2,300,000 | 20.00 | 30.00 | 60.00 | 150 | — |

**GULDEN** **KM# 161.1** **Weight:** 10.0000 g. **Composition:** 0.7200 Silver .2315 oz. ASW **Obv. Legend:** Ends below truncation

| Date | Mintage | F | VF | XF | Unc | BU |
|---|---|---|---|---|---|---|
| 1922 | 9,550,000 | 2.00 | 3.00 | 6.00 | 30.00 | — |
| 1922 Proof | — | Value: 400 | | | | |
| 1923 | 8,050,000 | 2.00 | 3.00 | 6.00 | 30.00 | — |
| 1924 | 8,000,000 | 2.00 | 4.00 | 10.00 | 40.00 | — |
| 1928 | 6,150,000 | BV | 2.00 | 5.00 | 25.00 | — |
| 1929 | 32,350,000 | BV | 2.00 | 3.00 | 12.00 | — |
| 1930 | 13,500,000 | BV | 2.00 | 4.00 | 15.00 | — |
| 1931 | 38,100,000 | BV | 2.00 | 3.00 | 10.00 | — |
| 1938 | 5,000,000 | 2.00 | 4.00 | 6.00 | 20.00 | — |
| 1939 | 14,200,000 | BV | BV | 2.50 | 6.00 | — |
| 1940 | 21,300,000 | BV | BV | 2.50 | 6.00 | — |
| 1940 Proof | — | Value: 200 | | | | |
| 1944P acorn privy mark | Inc. above | 50.00 | 125 | 200 | 200 | — |

**GULDEN** **KM# 161.2** **Weight:** 10.0000 g. **Composition:** 0.7200 Silver .2315 oz. ASW **Obv. Legend:** Ends at right of truncation

| Date | Mintage | F | VF | XF | Unc | BU |
|---|---|---|---|---|---|---|
| 1944P acorn privy mark | 105,125,000 | 7.00 | 12.50 | 20.00 | 45.00 | — |
| 1945P acorn privy mark | 25,375,000 | 200 | 450 | 650 | 1,300 | — |

**Note:** For similar coins dated 1943D with palm tree privy mark, see Netherlands East Indies

**GULDEN** **KM# 184** **Weight:** 6.5000 g. **Composition:** 0.7200 Silver .1504 oz. ASW

| Date | Mintage | F | VF | XF | Unc | BU |
|---|---|---|---|---|---|---|
| 1954 | 6,600,000 | — | — | BV | 3.00 | 6.00 |
| 1954 Proof | — | Value: 65.00 | | | | |
| 1955 | 37,500,000 | — | — | BV | 2.00 | 5.00 |
| 1955 Proof | — | Value: 65.00 | | | | |
| 1956 | 38,900,000 | — | — | BV | 2.00 | 5.00 |
| 1956 Proof | — | Value: 65.00 | | | | |
| 1957 | 27,000,000 | — | — | BV | 2.00 | 5.00 |
| 1957 Proof | — | Value: 65.00 | | | | |
| 1958 | 30,000,000 | — | — | BV | 2.50 | 6.50 |
| 1958 Proof | — | Value: 65.00 | | | | |
| 1963 | 5,000,000 | — | — | BV | 3.50 | 7.50 |
| 1963 Proof | — | Value: 80.00 | | | | |
| 1964 | 9,000,000 | — | — | BV | 2.00 | 5.00 |
| 1964 Proof | — | Value: 80.00 | | | | |
| 1965 | 21,000,000 | — | — | BV | 2.00 | 4.00 |
| 1965 Proof | — | Value: 80.00 | | | | |
| 1966 | 5,000,000 | — | — | BV | 2.00 | 5.00 |
| 1966 Proof | — | Value: 80.00 | | | | |
| 1967 | 7,000,000 | — | — | BV | 2.50 | 6.00 |
| 1967 Proof | — | Value: 110 | | | | |

**GULDEN** **KM# 184a** **Composition:** Nickel

| Date | Mintage | F | VF | XF | Unc | BU |
|---|---|---|---|---|---|---|
| 1967 | 31,000,000 | — | — | 0.75 | 2.00 | 5.00 |
| 1967 Proof | — | Value: 55.00 | | | | |
| 1968 | 61,000,000 | — | — | 0.75 | 2.00 | 5.00 |
| 1969 fish | 27,500,000 | — | — | — | 2.50 | 6.00 |
| 1969 Proof, fish | — | Value: 50.00 | | | | |
| 1969 cock | 15,500,000 | — | — | — | 2.50 | 6.00 |
| 1969 Proof, cock | — | Value: 50.00 | | | | |
| 1970 | 18,000,000 | — | — | 0.75 | 2.00 | 5.00 |
| 1970 Proof | — | Value: 50.00 | | | | |
| 1971 | 50,000,000 | — | — | — | 0.75 | 2.00 |
| 1972 | 60,000,000 | — | — | — | 0.75 | 2.00 |
| 1973 | 27,000,000 | — | — | — | 0.75 | 3.00 |
| 1975 | 9,000,000 | — | — | — | 2.00 | 5.00 |
| 1976 | 32,000,000 | — | — | — | 0.75 | 2.00 |
| 1977 | 38,000,000 | — | — | — | 0.75 | 2.00 |
| 1978 | 30,000,000 | — | — | — | 0.75 | 2.00 |
| 1979 | 25,000,000 | — | — | — | 0.75 | 2.00 |
| 1980 cock and star privy mark | 118,300,000 | — | — | — | 0.65 | 1.00 |

**GULDEN** **KM# 200** **Composition:** Nickel **Subject:** Investiture of New Queen

| Date | Mintage | F | VF | XF | Unc | BU |
|---|---|---|---|---|---|---|
| 1980 | 30,500,000 | — | — | — | 0.65 | 1.00 |

**GULDEN** **KM# 200a** **Composition:** Silver **Subject:** Investiture of New Queen

| Date | Mintage | F | VF | XF | Unc | BU |
|---|---|---|---|---|---|---|
| 1980 | 157 | — | — | — | — | 500 |

**GULDEN** **KM# 200b** **Composition:** Gold **Subject:** Investiture of New Queen

| Date | Mintage | F | VF | XF | Unc | BU |
|---|---|---|---|---|---|---|
| 1980 Rare | 7 | — | — | — | — | — |

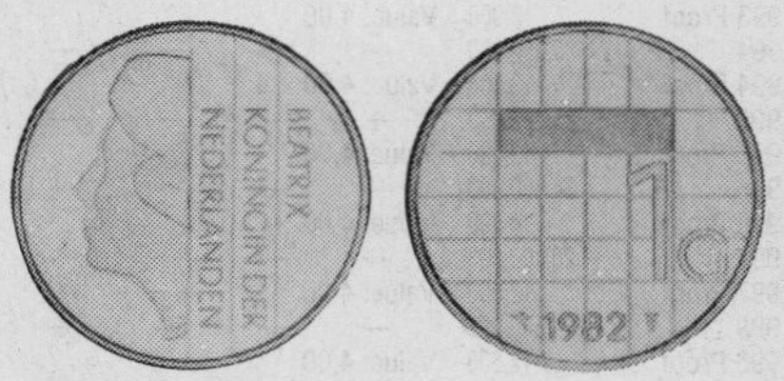

**GULDEN** **KM# 205** **Composition:** Nickel

| Date | Mintage | F | VF | XF | Unc | BU |
|---|---|---|---|---|---|---|
| 1982 | 31,300,000 | — | — | — | — | 1.25 |
| 1982 Proof | 10,000 | Value: 20.00 | | | | |
| 1983 | 5,200,000 | — | — | — | — | 1.50 |
| 1983 Proof | 15,000 | Value: 15.00 | | | | |
| 1984 | 4,200,000 | — | — | — | — | 1.50 |
| 1984 Proof | 20,000 | Value: 7.50 | | | | |
| 1985 | 3,100,000 | — | — | — | — | 1.75 |
| 1985 Proof | 17,000 | Value: 7.50 | | | | |
| 1986 | 12,100,000 | — | — | — | — | 1.75 |
| 1986 Proof | 18,000 | Value: 7.50 | | | | |
| 1987 | 20,100,000 | — | — | — | — | 1.75 |
| 1987 Proof | 20,000 | Value: 7.50 | | | | |
| 1988 | 13,600,000 | — | — | — | — | 1.75 |
| 1988 Proof | 20,000 | Value: 7.50 | | | | |
| 1989 | 1,100,000 | — | — | — | — | 2.00 |
| 1989 Proof | 15,000 | Value: 7.50 | | | | |
| 1990 | 1,100,000 | — | — | — | — | 2.00 |
| 1990 Proof | 15,000 | Value: 7.50 | | | | |
| 1991 | 500,000 | — | — | — | — | 4.00 |
| 1991 Proof | 14,000 | Value: 7.50 | | | | |
| 1992 | 10,100,000 | — | — | — | — | 1.50 |
| 1992 Proof | 13,000 | Value: 7.50 | | | | |
| 1993 | 15,100,000 | — | — | — | — | 1.50 |
| 1993 Proof | 12,000 | Value: 7.50 | | | | |
| 1994 | 16,600,000 | — | — | — | — | 1.50 |
| 1994 Proof | 13,000 | Value: 7.50 | | | | |
| 1995 | 12,600,000 | — | — | — | — | 1.50 |
| 1995 Proof | 12,000 | Value: 7.50 | | | | |
| 1996 | 6,660,000 | — | — | — | — | 1.50 |
| 1996 Proof | 14,000 | Value: 7.50 | | | | |
| 1997 | 12,800,000 | — | — | — | — | 1.50 |
| 1997 Proof | 12,000 | Value: 7.50 | | | | |
| 1998 | 15,100,000 | — | — | — | — | 1.75 |
| 1998 Proof | 12,000 | Value: 7.50 | | | | |
| 1999 | 8,080,000 | — | — | — | — | 1.25 |
| 1999 Proof | 15,000 | Value: 7.50 | | | | |
| 2000 | 37,680,000 | — | — | — | — | 1.25 |
| 2000 Proof | 15,000 | Value: 7.50 | | | | |
| 2001 | — | — | — | — | — | 1.25 |
| 2001 Proof | — | Value: 7.50 | | | | |

**GULDEN** **KM# 230** **Weight:** 11.0000 g. **Composition:** 0.7500 Gold .2652 oz. AGW **Reverse:** Small Tulip, "750" added **Note:** Similar to KM#205.

| Date | Mintage | F | VF | XF | Unc | BU |
|---|---|---|---|---|---|---|
| 1999 Proof | 1,000 | Value: 500 | | | | |

**Note:** Approximately 480 of the mintage were melted down.

**GULDEN** **KM# 205a** **Weight:** 13.2000 g. **Composition:** 0.9990 Gold .4243 oz. AGW

| Date | Mintage | F | VF | XF | Unc | BU |
|---|---|---|---|---|---|---|
| 2001 Proof like | 100,000 | — | — | — | 180 | |

**GULDEN** **KM# 233** **Weight:** 6.0400 g. **Composition:** Nickel **Obverse:** Queen's portrait. **Reverse:** Child art design. **Edge Lettering:** GOD ZIJ MET ONS. **Size:** 25 mm.

| Date | Mintage | F | VF | XF | Unc | BU |
|---|---|---|---|---|---|---|
| 2001 | — | — | — | — | 2.50 | — |

**GULDEN** **KM# 233a** **Weight:** 13.2000 g. **Composition:** 0.9250 Silver .3926 oz. ASW **Obverse:** Queen's portrait. **Reverse:** Child art design. **Edge Lettering:** GOD ZIJ MET ONS. **Size:** 25 mm.

| Date | Mintage | F | VF | XF | Unc | BU |
|---|---|---|---|---|---|---|
| 2001 | 200,000 | — | — | — | 17.50 | — |

**GULDEN** **KM# 233b** **Weight:** 13.2000 g. **Composition:** 0.9990 Gold .4240 oz. AGW **Obverse:** Queen's portrait. **Reverse:** Child art design. **Size:** 25 mm.

| Date | Mintage | F | VF | XF | Unc | BU |
|---|---|---|---|---|---|---|
| 2001 | 100,000 | — | — | — | 189 | — |

**2-1/2 GULDEN** **KM# 165** **Weight:** 25.0000 g. **Composition:** 0.7200 Silver .5787 oz. ASW

| Date | Mintage | F | VF | XF | Unc | BU |
|---|---|---|---|---|---|---|
| 1929 | 4,400,000 | 5.00 | 8.00 | 20.00 | 60.00 | — |
| 1930 | 11,600,000 | 4.00 | 7.50 | 15.00 | 30.00 | — |
| 1931 | 4,400,000 | 4.00 | 7.50 | 15.00 | 27.50 | — |
| 1932 | 6,320,000 | 4.00 | 7.50 | 15.00 | 30.00 | — |
| 1932 deep hair lines | Inc. above | 80.00 | 150 | 250 | 350 | — |
| 1933 | 3,560,000 | 6.00 | 10.00 | 20.00 | 50.00 | — |
| 1937 | 4,000,000 | 5.00 | 7.00 | 10.00 | 25.00 | — |
| 1938 | 2,000,000 | 6.00 | 10.00 | 18.00 | 40.00 | — |
| 1938 deep hair lines | Inc. above | 35.00 | 80.00 | 150 | 250 | — |
| 1939 | 3,760,000 | 4.00 | 7.00 | 10.00 | 25.00 | — |
| 1940 | 4,640,000 | 12.00 | 25.00 | 50.00 | 80.00 | — |

**Note:** For similar coins dated 1943D with palm tree privy mark, see Netherlands East Indies

**2-1/2 GULDEN** **KM# 185** **Weight:** 15.0000 g. **Composition:** 0.7200 Silver .3472 oz. ASW

| Date | Mintage | F | VF | XF | Unc | BU |
|---|---|---|---|---|---|---|
| 1959 | 7,200,000 | — | — | BV | 4.00 | 9.00 |
| 1959 Proof | — | Value: 175 | | | | |
| 1960 | 12,800,000 | — | — | BV | 4.00 | 9.00 |
| 1960 Proof | — | Value: 175 | | | | |
| 1961 | 10,000,000 | — | — | BV | 4.00 | 9.00 |
| 1961 Proof | — | Value: 175 | | | | |
| 1962 | 5,000,000 | — | — | BV | 4.00 | 10.00 |
| 1962 Proof | — | Value: 175 | | | | |
| 1963 | 4,000,000 | — | BV | 5.00 | 15.00 | 25.00 |
| 1963 Proof | — | Value: 175 | | | | |
| 1964 | 2,800,000 | — | 4.00 | 10.00 | 20.00 | 32.50 |
| 1964 Proof | — | Value: 175 | | | | |
| 1966 | 5,000,000 | — | — | BV | 4.00 | 9.00 |
| 1966 Proof | — | Value: 175 | | | | |

**2-1/2 GULDEN** **KM# 191** **Composition:** Nickel

| Date | Mintage | F | VF | XF | Unc | BU |
|---|---|---|---|---|---|---|
| 1969 fish privy mark | 1,200,000 | — | 1.50 | 3.50 | 6.00 | 10.00 |
| 1969 Proof, fish privy mark with front hair lock | — | Value: 70.00 | | | | |
| 1969 Proof, rare fish privy mark without front hair lock | — | — | — | — | — | — |
| 1969 cock privy mark | 15,600,000 | — | — | — | 2.00 | 5.00 |
| 1969 Proof, cocky privy mark | — | Value: 70.00 | | | | |
| 1970 | 22,000,000 | — | — | — | 2.00 | 5.00 |
| 1970 Proof | — | Value: 70.00 | | | | |
| 1971 | 8,000,000 | — | — | — | 2.00 | 5.00 |
| 1972 | 20,000,000 | — | — | — | 2.00 | 5.00 |
| 1978 | 5,000,000 | — | — | — | 2.00 | 4.00 |
| 1980 cock and star privy mark | 37,300,000 | — | — | — | 1.50 | 2.00 |

**2-1/2 GULDEN** **KM# 197** **Composition:** Nickel **Subject:** 400th Anniversary - The Union of Utrecht

| Date | Mintage | F | VF | XF | Unc | BU |
|---|---|---|---|---|---|---|
| 1979 | 25,000,000 | — | — | — | 1.50 | 2.00 |

**2-1/2 GULDEN** **KM# 201** **Composition:** Nickel **Subject:** Investiture of New Queen

| Date | Mintage | F | VF | XF | Unc | BU |
|---|---|---|---|---|---|---|
| 1980 | 30,500,000 | — | — | — | 1.50 | 2.00 |

**2-1/2 GULDEN** **KM# 201a** **Composition:** Silver **Subject:** Investiture of New Queen

| Date | Mintage | F | VF | XF | Unc | BU |
|---|---|---|---|---|---|---|
| 1980 | 157 | — | — | — | — | 500 |

**2-1/2 GULDEN** **KM# 201b** **Composition:** Gold **Subject:** Investiture of New Queen

| Date | Mintage | F | VF | XF | Unc | BU |
|---|---|---|---|---|---|---|
| 1980 Rare | 7 | — | — | — | — | — |

**2-1/2 GULDEN** **KM# 206** **Composition:** Nickel

| Date | Mintage | F | VF | XF | Unc | BU |
|---|---|---|---|---|---|---|
| 1982 | 14,300,000 | — | — | — | — | 2.00 |
| 1982 Proof | 10,000 | Value: 35.00 | | | | |
| 1983 | 3,800,000 | — | — | — | — | 2.50 |
| 1983 Proof | 15,000 | Value: 27.50 | | | | |
| 1984 | 5,200,000 | — | — | — | — | 2.50 |
| 1984 Proof | 20,000 | — | — | — | — | — |
| 1985 | 3,100,000 | — | — | — | — | 3.50 |
| 1985 Proof | 17,000 | Value: 16.00 | | | | |
| 1986 | 5,800,000 | — | — | — | — | 3.50 |
| 1986 Proof | 20,000 | Value: 16.00 | | | | |
| 1987 | 2,500,000 | — | — | — | — | 3.50 |
| 1987 Proof | 18,000 | Value: 16.00 | | | | |
| 1988 | 6,200,000 | — | — | — | — | 3.50 |
| 1988 Proof | 20,000 | Value: 16.00 | | | | |
| 1989 | 4,099,999 | — | — | — | — | 3.00 |
| 1989 Proof | 15,000 | Value: 16.00 | | | | |
| 1990 | 1,100,000 | — | — | — | — | 3.00 |
| 1990 Proof | 15,000 | Value: 16.00 | | | | |
| 1991 | 500,000 | — | — | — | — | 5.00 |
| 1991 Proof | 14,000 | Value: 16.00 | | | | |
| 1992 | 500,000 | — | — | — | — | 4.00 |
| 1992 Proof | 13,000 | Value: 16.00 | | | | |
| 1993 | 500,000 | — | — | — | — | 6.00 |
| 1993 Proof | 12,000 | Value: 16.00 | | | | |
| 1994 | 500,000 | — | — | — | — | 6.00 |
| 1994 Proof | 13,000 | Value: 16.00 | | | | |
| 1995 | 200,000 | — | — | — | — | 8.00 |
| 1995 Proof | 12,000 | Value: 16.00 | | | | |
| 1996 | 200,000 | — | — | — | — | 7.00 |
| 1996 Proof | 14,000 | Value: 16.00 | | | | |
| 1997 | 300,000 | — | — | — | — | 7.00 |
| 1997 Proof | 12,000 | Value: 16.00 | | | | |
| 1998 | 300,000 | — | — | — | — | 7.00 |
| 1998 Proof | 12,000 | Value: 16.00 | | | | |
| 1999 | 280,000 | — | — | — | — | 4.00 |
| 1999 Proof | 15,000 | Value: 16.00 | | | | |
| 2000 | 476,000 | — | — | — | — | 4.00 |
| 2000 Proof | 15,000 | Value: 16.00 | | | | |
| 2001 | — | — | — | — | — | 4.00 |
| 2001 Proof | — | Value: 16.00 | | | | |

**5 GULDEN** **KM# 151** **Weight:** 3.3645 g. **Composition:** 0.9000 Gold .0973 oz. AGW

| Date | Mintage | F | VF | XF | Unc | BU |
|---|---|---|---|---|---|---|
| 1912 | 1,000,000 | 40.00 | 60.00 | 90.00 | 150 | — |
| 1912 Matte Proof | 120 | Value: 800 | | | | |

**5 GULDEN** **KM# 210** **Composition:** Bronze Clad Nickel

| Date | Mintage | F | VF | XF | Unc | BU |
|---|---|---|---|---|---|---|
| 1987 Proof | 2 | — | — | — | — | — |
| 1988 | 73,700,000 | — | — | — | — | 4.50 |
| 1988 Proof | 20,000 | Value: 12.50 | | | | |
| 1989 | 69,100,000 | — | — | — | — | 4.50 |
| 1989 Proof | 15,000 | Value: 12.50 | | | | |
| 1990 | 47,300,000 | — | — | — | — | 4.50 |
| 1990 Proof | 15,000 | Value: 15.00 | | | | |
| 1991 | 17,100,000 | — | — | — | — | 4.00 |
| 1991 Proof | 14,000 | Value: 15.00 | | | | |
| 1992 | 500,000 | — | — | — | — | 4.00 |
| 1992 Proof | 13,000 | Value: 15.00 | | | | |
| 1993 | 5,500,000 | — | — | — | — | 4.00 |
| 1993 Proof | 12,000 | Value: 15.00 | | | | |
| 1994 | 500,000 | — | — | — | — | 6.00 |
| 1994 Proof | 13,000 | Value: 17.50 | | | | |
| 1995 | 500,000 | — | — | — | — | 6.00 |
| 1995 Proof | 12,000 | Value: 17.50 | | | | |
| 1996 | 200,000 | — | — | — | — | 6.00 |
| 1996 Proof | 14,000 | Value: 17.50 | | | | |
| 1997 | 300,000 | — | — | — | — | 6.00 |
| 1997 Proof | 12,000 | Value: 17.50 | | | | |
| 1998 | 200,000 | — | — | — | — | 8.00 |
| 1998 Proof | 12,000 | Value: 16.00 | | | | |
| 1999 | 260,000 | — | — | — | — | 6.50 |
| 1999 Proof | 15,000 | Value: 16.00 | | | | |
| 2000 | 376,000 | — | — | — | — | 3.50 |
| 2000 Proof | 15,000 | Value: 16.00 | | | | |
| 2001 | — | — | — | — | — | 3.50 |
| 2001 Proof | — | Value: 15.50 | | | | |

**5 GULDEN** **KM# 231** **Composition:** Brass Plated Nickel **Subject:** Soccer **Edge:** Reeded **Edge Lettering:** GOD * ZIJ * MET * ONS *

| Date | Mintage | F | VF | XF | Unc | BU |
|---|---|---|---|---|---|---|
| 2000 | 2,500,000 | — | — | — | 4.00 | 8.50 |
| 2000 Proof, small mm | Est. 1,000 | Value: 200 | | | | |
| 2000 Proof, large mm | — | Value: 12.50 | | | | |

**Note:** A joint issue proof set exists containing the Netherlands KM#231, Belgium KM#213-214 plus a medal

**10 GULDEN** **KM# 149** **Weight:** 6.7290 g. **Composition:** 0.9000 Gold .1947 oz. AGW

| Date | Mintage | F | VF | XF | Unc | BU |
|---|---|---|---|---|---|---|
| 1911 | 775,000 | — | BV | 62.00 | 85.00 | — |
| 1911 Proof | 8 | Value: 1,750 | | | | |
| 1912 | 3,000,000 | — | BV | 62.00 | 85.00 | — |
| 1912 Proof | 20 | Value: 1,500 | | | | |
| 1913 | 1,133,000 | — | BV | 62.00 | 85.00 | — |
| 1917 | 4,000,000 | — | BV | 62.00 | 85.00 | — |

**10 GULDEN** **KM# 162** **Weight:** 6.7290 g. **Composition:** 0.9000 Gold .1947 oz. AGW

| Date | Mintage | F | VF | XF | Unc | BU |
|---|---|---|---|---|---|---|
| 1925 | 2,000,000 | — | BV | 62.00 | 85.00 | — |
| 1925 Proof | 12 | Value: 1,500 | | | | |
| 1926 | 2,500,000 | — | BV | 62.00 | 85.00 | — |
| 1926 Proof | — | Value: 1,300 | | | | |
| 1927 | 1,000,000 | — | BV | 62.00 | 85.00 | — |
| 1932 | 4,324,000 | — | BV | 62.00 | 85.00 | — |
| 1933 | 2,462,000 | — | BV | 62.00 | 85.00 | — |

**10 GULDEN** **KM# 195** **Weight:** 25.0000 g. **Composition:** 0.7200 Silver .5787 oz. ASW **Subject:** 25th Anniversary of Liberation

| Date | Mintage | F | VF | XF | Unc | BU |
|---|---|---|---|---|---|---|
| ND(1970) | 6,000,000 | — | — | — | 8.00 | 10.00 |
| ND(1970) Proof like | 20,000 | — | — | — | — | 30.00 |
| ND(1970) Proof | 40 | Value: 700 | | | | |

**10 GULDEN** **KM# 196** **Weight:** 25.0000 g. **Composition:** 0.7200 Silver .5787 oz. ASW **Subject:** 25th Anniversary of Reign

| Date | Mintage | F | VF | XF | Unc | BU |
|---|---|---|---|---|---|---|
| 1973 | 4,500,000 | — | — | — | 8.00 | 10.00 |
| 1973 Proof | 106,000 | Value: 20.00 | | | | |

**10 GULDEN** **KM# 216** **Weight:** 15.0000 g. **Composition:** 0.7200 Silver .3473 oz. ASW **Subject:** BE-NE-LUX Treaty

| Date | Mintage | F | VF | XF | Unc | BU |
|---|---|---|---|---|---|---|
| 1994 | 2,000,000 | — | — | — | — | 12.50 |
| 1994 Proof | 67,000 | Value: 25.00 | | | | |

**Note:** 25,000 pieces issued in sets only

**10 GULDEN** **KM# 220** **Composition:** 0.8000 Silver **Subject:** 300th Anniversary - Death of Hugo de Groot

| Date | Mintage | F | VF | XF | Unc | BU |
|---|---|---|---|---|---|---|
| 1995 | 1,500,000 | — | — | — | — | 12.50 |
| 1995 Proof | 38,000 | Value: 22.50 | | | | |

**10 GULDEN** **KM# 223** **Composition:** 0.8000 Silver **Subject:** Artist Jan Steen - Mandolin Player

| Date | Mintage | F | VF | XF | Unc | BU |
|---|---|---|---|---|---|---|
| 1996 | 1,500,000 | — | — | — | — | 12.50 |
| 1996 Proof | 25,000 | Value: 22.50 | | | | |

**10 GULDEN** **KM# 224** **Weight:** 15.0000 g. **Composition:** 0.8000 Silver .3858 oz. ASW **Subject:** Marshall Plan **Obverse:** Head of Queen left

| Date | Mintage | F | VF | XF | Unc | BU |
|---|---|---|---|---|---|---|
| 1997 | 1,010,000 | — | — | — | — | 20.00 |
| 1997 Proof | 27,000 | Value: 28.00 | | | | |

**10 GULDEN** **KM# 228** **Weight:** 15.0000 g. **Composition:** 0.8000 Silver .3858 oz. ASW **Subject:** Millennium **Obverse:** Head of Queen above 12 concentric rings, 1999 **Reverse:** Head of Queen above 12 concentric rings, 2000 **Edge:** GOD ZIJ MET ONS

| Date | Mintage | F | VF | XF | Unc | BU |
|---|---|---|---|---|---|---|
| 1999 | 1,250,000 | — | — | — | — | 20.00 |
| 1999 Proof | 50,000 | Value: 28.00 | | | | |

**50 GULDEN** **KM# 207** **Weight:** 25.0000 g. **Composition:** 0.9250 Silver .7435 oz. ASW **Subject:** Dutch-American Friendship

| Date | Mintage | F | VF | XF | Unc | BU |
|---|---|---|---|---|---|---|
| ND(1982) | 190,000 | — | — | — | — | 22.50 |
| ND(1982) Proof | 50,000 | Value: 45.00 | | | | |

**50 GULDEN** **KM# 207a** **Composition:** Gold **Subject:** Dutch-American Friendship

| Date | Mintage | F | VF | XF | Unc | BU |
|---|---|---|---|---|---|---|
| ND(1982) Rare | 2 | — | — | — | — | — |

**50 GULDEN** **KM# 208** **Weight:** 25.0000 g. **Composition:** 0.9250 Silver .7435 oz. ASW **Subject:** 400th Anniversary - Death of William of Orange

| Date | Mintage | F | VF | XF | Unc | BU |
|---|---|---|---|---|---|---|
| 1984 | 905,000 | — | — | — | — | 20.00 |
| 1984 Proof like | 106,000 | — | — | — | — | 25.00 |
| 1984 Proof | 56,000 | Value: 40.00 | | | | |

**50 GULDEN** **KM# 209** **Weight:** 25.0000 g. **Composition:** 0.9250 Silver .7435 oz. ASW **Subject:** Golden Wedding Anniversary - Queen Mother and Prince Bernhard

| Date | Mintage | F | VF | XF | Unc | BU |
|---|---|---|---|---|---|---|
| 1987 | 1,035,000 | — | — | — | — | 20.00 |
| 1987 Proof like | 81,000 | — | — | — | — | 25.00 |
| 1987 Proof | 53,000 | Value: 40.00 | | | | |

**50 GULDEN** **KM# 212** **Weight:** 25.0000 g. **Composition:** 0.9250 Silver .7435 oz. ASW **Subject:** 300th Anniversary of William and Mary

| Date | Mintage | F | VF | XF | Unc | BU |
|---|---|---|---|---|---|---|
| 1988 | 710,000 | — | — | — | — | 20.00 |
| 1988 Proof like | 53,000 | — | — | — | — | 25.00 |
| 1988 Proof | 36,000 | Value: 42.50 | | | | |

**50 GULDEN** **KM# 212a** **Composition:** Gold **Subject:** 300th Anniversary of William and Mary

| Date | Mintage | F | VF | XF | Unc | BU |
|---|---|---|---|---|---|---|
| 1988 Rare | 4 | — | — | — | — | — |

**50 GULDEN** **KM# 214** **Weight:** 25.0000 g. **Composition:** 0.9250 Silver .7435 oz. ASW **Subject:** 100 Years of Queens

| Date | Mintage | F | VF | XF | Unc | BU |
|---|---|---|---|---|---|---|
| 1990 | 630,000 | — | — | — | — | 20.00 |
| 1990 Proof like | 50,000 | — | — | — | — | 30.00 |
| 1990 Proof | 35,000 | Value: 45.00 | | | | |

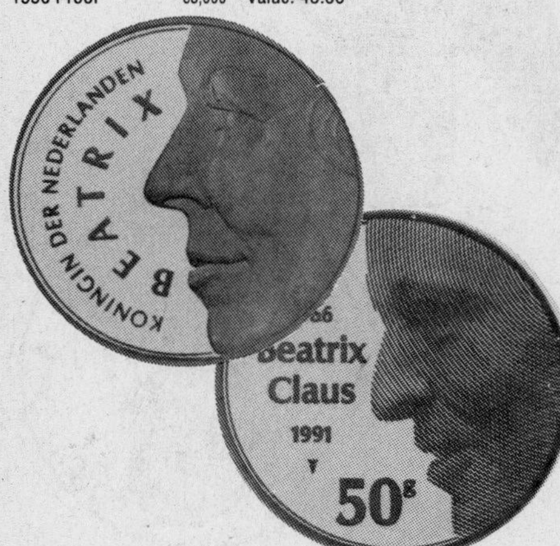


**50 GULDEN** **KM# 215** **Weight:** 25.0000 g. **Composition:** 0.9250 Silver .7435 oz. ASW **Subject:** Silver Wedding Anniversary

| Date | Mintage | F | VF | XF | Unc | BU |
|---|---|---|---|---|---|---|
| 1991 Coin | 575,000 | — | — | — | — | 20.00 |
| 1991 Medal | Inc. above | — | — | — | — | 20.00 |
| 1991 Proof like | 46,000 | — | — | — | — | 30.00 |
| 1991 Proof | 35,000 | Value: 45.00 | | | | |

**50 GULDEN** **KM# 217** **Weight:** 25.0000 g. **Composition:** 0.9250 Silver .7435 oz. ASW **Subject:** Maastricht Treaty

| Date | Mintage | F | VF | XF | Unc | BU |
|---|---|---|---|---|---|---|
| 1994 | 415,000 | — | — | — | — | 25.00 |
| 1994 Proof like | 28,000 | — | — | — | — | 40.00 |
| 1994 Proof | 25,000 | Value: 55.00 | | | | |

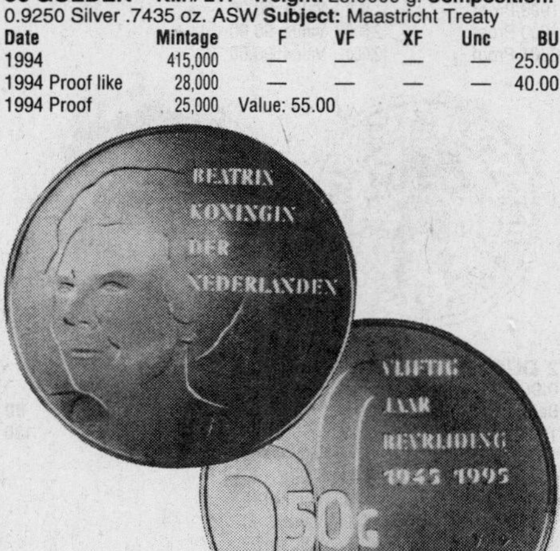


**50 GULDEN** **KM# 219** **Weight:** 25.0000 g. **Composition:** 0.9250 Silver .7435 oz. ASW **Subject:** 50th Anniversary of Liberation

| Date | Mintage | F | VF | XF | Unc | BU |
|---|---|---|---|---|---|---|
| ND(1995) | 475,000 | — | — | — | — | 25.00 |
| ND(1995) Proof like | 28,000 | — | — | — | — | 40.00 |
| ND(1995) Proof | 26,000 | Value: 55.00 | | | | |

**50 GULDEN** **KM# 227** **Weight:** 25.0000 g. **Composition:** 0.9250 Silver .7435 oz. ASW **Subject:** 350th Anniversary - Treaty of Munster **Obverse:** Head of Queen left **Reverse:** Mirror image of obverse **Edge Lettering:** GOD*'ZIJ*MET*ONS*

| Date | Mintage | F | VF | XF | Unc | BU |
|---|---|---|---|---|---|---|
| 1998 | 450,000 | — | — | — | — | 25.00 |

**Note:** 165,OOO were melted.

| Date | Mintage | F | VF | XF | Unc | BU |
|---|---|---|---|---|---|---|
| 1998 Proof like | 20,000 | — | — | — | — | 45.00 |
| 1998 Proof | 20,000 | Value: 55.00 | | | | |

## EURO COINAGE

European Economic Community Issues

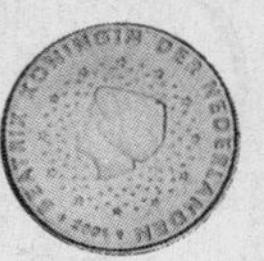

**EURO CENT** **KM# 234** **Weight:** 2.3100 g. **Composition:** Chrome Plated Steel **Obverse:** Queen's portrait **Reverse:** Denomination and globe **Edge:** Plain **Size:** 16.2 mm.

| Date | Mintage | F | VF | XF | Unc | BU |
|---|---|---|---|---|---|---|
| 1999 | 47,800,000 | — | — | — | — | — |
| 2000 | 276,800,000 | — | — | — | — | — |
| 2001 | 250,000,000 | — | — | — | 0.15 | — |
| 2002 | — | — | — | — | — | — |

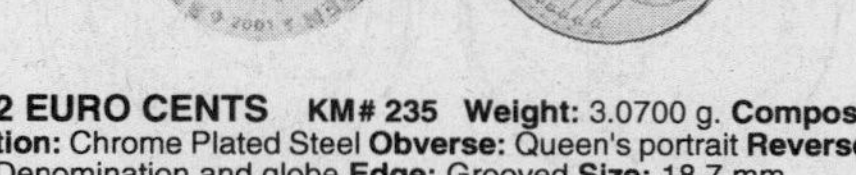

**2 EURO CENTS** **KM# 235** **Weight:** 3.0700 g. **Composition:** Chrome Plated Steel **Obverse:** Queen's portrait **Reverse:** Denomination and globe **Edge:** Grooved **Size:** 18.7 mm.

| Date | Mintage | F | VF | XF | Unc | BU |
|---|---|---|---|---|---|---|
| 1999 | 109,000,000 | — | — | — | — | — |
| 2000 | 122,000,000 | — | — | — | — | — |
| 2001 | 125,000,000 | — | — | — | 0.20 | — |
| 2002 | — | — | — | — | — | — |

**5 EURO CENTS** **KM# 236** **Weight:** 3.9000 g. **Composition:** Chrome Plated Steel **Obverse:** Queen's portrait **Reverse:** Denomination and globe **Edge:** Plain **Size:** 21.2 mm.

| Date | Mintage | F | VF | XF | Unc | BU |
|---|---|---|---|---|---|---|
| 1999 | 213,000,000 | — | — | — | — | — |
| 2000 | 184,200,000 | — | — | — | 0.25 | — |
| 2001 | 200,000,000 | — | — | — | — | — |
| 2002 | — | — | — | — | — | — |

**10 EURO CENTS** **KM# 237** **Weight:** 4.1000 g. **Composition:** Brass **Obverse:** Queen's portrait **Reverse:** Denomination and map **Size:** 19.7 mm.

| Date | Mintage | F | VF | XF | Unc | BU |
|---|---|---|---|---|---|---|
| 1999 | 149,700,000 | — | — | — | — | — |
| 2000 | 156,700,000 | — | — | — | — | — |
| 2001 | 150,000,000 | — | — | — | 0.35 | — |
| 2002 | — | — | — | — | — | — |

**20 EURO CENTS** **KM# 238** **Weight:** 5.7400 g. **Composition:** Brass **Obverse:** Queen's portrait **Reverse:** Denomination and map **Edge:** Notched **Size:** 22.2 mm.

| Date | Mintage | F | VF | XF | Unc | BU |
|---|---|---|---|---|---|---|
| 1999 | 86,500,000 | — | — | — | — | — |
| 2000 | 67,500,000 | — | — | — | — | — |
| 2001 | 75,000,000 | — | — | — | 0.40 | — |
| 2002 | — | — | — | — | — | — |

**50 EURO CENTS** **KM# 239** **Weight:** 7.8100 g. **Composition:** Brass **Obverse:** Queen's portrait **Reverse:** Denomination and map **Edge:** Notched **Size:** 24.2 mm.

| Date | Mintage | F | VF | XF | Unc | BU |
|---|---|---|---|---|---|---|
| 1999 | 99,600,000 | — | — | — | — | — |
| 2000 | 87,000,000 | — | — | — | 0.75 | — |
| 2001 | 75,000,000 | — | — | — | — | — |
| 2002 | — | — | — | — | — | — |

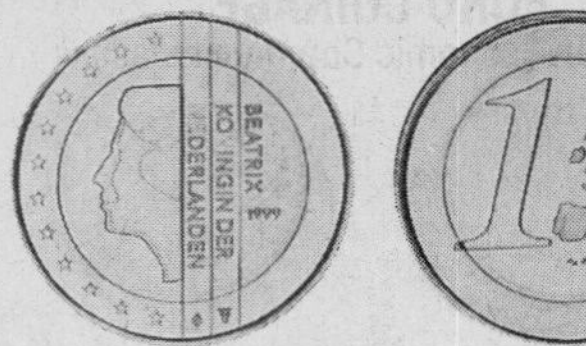

**EURO** **KM# 240** **Ring Weight:** 7.5300 g. **Ring Composition:** Brass **Center Composition:** Copper-Nickel **Obverse:** Queen's portrait **Reverse:** Denomination and map **Edge:** Plain and reeded sections **Size:** 23.2 mm.

| Date | Mintage | F | VF | XF | Unc | BU |
|---|---|---|---|---|---|---|
| 1999 | 63,500,000 | — | — | — | 1.50 | — |
| 2000 | 62,800,000 | — | — | — | — | — |
| 2001 | 67,500,000 | — | — | — | — | — |
| 2002 | — | — | — | — | — | — |

**2 EUROS** **KM# 241** **Ring Weight:** 8.4600 g. **Ring Composition:** Copper-Nickel **Center Composition:** Brass **Obverse:** Queen's portrait **Reverse:** Denomination and map **Edge:** Reeded **Edge Lettering:** "GOD*ZIJ*MET*ONS*" **Size:** 25.7 mm.

| Date | Mintage | F | VF | XF | Unc | BU |
|---|---|---|---|---|---|---|
| 1999 | 9,900,000 | — | — | — | — | — |
| 2000 | 24,500,000 | — | — | — | — | — |
| 2001 | 85,500,000 | — | — | — | 3.00 | — |
| 2002 | — | — | — | — | — | — |

## TRADE COINAGE

**DUCAT** **KM# 83.1** **Weight:** 3.5000 g. **Composition:** 0.9830 Gold .1106 oz. AGW

| Date | Mintage | F | VF | XF | Unc | BU |
|---|---|---|---|---|---|---|
| 1901 | 29,000 | 150 | 450 | 750 | 1,500 | — |
| 1903/1 | 91,000 | 300 | 600 | 1,000 | 2,000 | — |
| 1903 | Inc. above | 150 | 400 | 600 | 800 | — |
| 1905 | 88,000 | 150 | 400 | 600 | 800 | — |
| 1906 | 29,000 | 150 | 450 | 750 | 1,500 | — |
| 1908 | 91,000 | 125 | 250 | 400 | 600 | — |
| 1909 halberd with star privy mark | 106,000 | 125 | 400 | 600 | 800 | — |
| 1909 sea horse privy mark | 30,000 | 175 | 475 | 800 | 1,750 | — |
| 1910 | 421,000 | 150 | 275 | 400 | 550 | — |
| 1910 Proof | — | Value: 1,000 | | | | |
| 1912 | 148,000 | 150 | 275 | 400 | 650 | — |
| 1912 Proof | — | Value: 1,000 | | | | |
| 1913 | 205,000 | 150 | 275 | 400 | 650 | — |
| 1914 | 247,000 | 150 | 275 | 400 | 650 | — |
| 1916 | 117,000 | 150 | 275 | 400 | 650 | — |
| 1916 Proof | — | Value: 1,250 | | | | |
| 1917 | 217,000 | BV | 65.00 | 90.00 | 120 | — |
| 1920 | 293,000 | BV | 65.00 | 90.00 | 120 | — |
| 1920 Proof | — | Value: 800 | | | | |
| 1921 | 409,000 | BV | 60.00 | 70.00 | 100 | — |
| 1922 | 50,000 | 150 | 300 | 500 | 700 | — |
| 1923 | 107,000 | BV | 75.00 | 150 | 250 | — |
| 1924 | 84,000 | BV | 75.00 | 150 | 250 | — |
| 1925 | 573,000 | BV | 60.00 | 70.00 | 100 | — |
| 1925 Proof | Inc. above | Value: 450 | | | | |
| 1926 | 191,000 | BV | 60.00 | 80.00 | 120 | — |
| 1927 | 654,000 | — | BV | 40.00 | 55.00 | — |
| 1928 | 572,000 | — | BV | 40.00 | 55.00 | — |
| 1932 | 88,000 | 250 | 600 | 900 | 1,750 | — |
| 1937 | 117,000 | BV | 70.00 | 90.00 | 120 | — |

**DUCAT** **KM# 190.1** **Weight:** 3.5000 g. **Composition:** 0.9830 Gold .1106 oz. AGW **Obverse:** Knight with right leg bent, larger letters in legend

| Date | Mintage | F | VF | XF | Unc | BU |
|---|---|---|---|---|---|---|
| 1960 | 3,605 | 100 | 250 | 350 | 475 | — |
| 1972 Proof like | 29,000 | — | — | — | — | 70.00 |
| 1974 Proof like | 87,000 | — | — | — | — | 70.00 |
| 1974 medal struck | 2,000 | 100 | 250 | 350 | 475 | — |
| 1975 Proof like | 205,000 | — | — | — | — | 60.00 |
| 1976 Proof like | 38,000 | — | — | — | — | 90.00 |
| **Note:** Of 37,844 pieces struck, 32,000 were melted. | | | | | | |
| 1978 Proof like | 29,000 | — | — | — | — | 90.00 |
| 1985 Proofl like | 104,000 | — | — | — | — | 55.00 |

**DUCAT** **KM# 190.2** **Weight:** 3.5000 g. **Composition:** 0.9830 Gold .1106 oz. AGW **Obverse:** Knight with left leg bent, larger letters in legend

| Date | Mintage | F | VF | XF | Unc | BU |
|---|---|---|---|---|---|---|
| 1986 Proof like | 95,000 | — | — | — | — | 60.00 |
| 1989 Proof | 24,000 | Value: 80.00 | | | | |
| 1990 Proof | 18,000 | Value: 90.00 | | | | |
| 1991 Proof | 12,000 | Value: 85.00 | | | | |
| 1992 Proof | 14,000 | Value: 85.00 | | | | |
| 1993 Proof | 11,000 | Value: 95.00 | | | | |
| 1994 Proof | 12,000 | Value: 90.00 | | | | |
| 1995 Proof | 11,000 | Value: 90.00 | | | | |
| 1996 Proof | 12,000 | Value: 90.00 | | | | |
| 1997 Proof | 12,000 | Value: 90.00 | | | | |
| 1998 Proof | 12,000 | Value: 90.00 | | | | |
| 1999 Proof | 11,000 | Value: 90.00 | | | | |
| 2000 Proof | 12,000 | Value: 90.00 | | | | |
| 2001 Proof | 12,000 | Value: 90.00 | | | | |

**2 DUCAT** **KM# 211** **Weight:** 6.9880 g. **Composition:** 0.9830 Gold .2209 oz. AGW

| Date | Mintage | F | VF | XF | Unc | BU |
|---|---|---|---|---|---|---|
| 1988 Proof like | 24,000 | — | — | — | — | 130 |
| 1989 Proof | 18,000 | Value: 130 | | | | |
| 1991 Proof | 10,000 | Value: 140 | | | | |
| 1992 Proof | 12,000 | Value: 140 | | | | |
| 1996 Proof | 11,000 | Value: 140 | | | | |
| 1999 Proof | 9,300 | Value: 150 | | | | |
| 2000 Proof | 9,000 | Value: 140 | | | | |
| 2001 Proof | — | — | — | — | — | — |

## SILVER BULLION COINAGE

**SILVER DUCAT** **KM# 213** **Weight:** 28.2500 g. **Composition:** 0.8730 Silver .7948 oz. ASW

| Date | Mintage | F | VF | XF | Unc | BU |
|---|---|---|---|---|---|---|
| 1989 Proof | 36,000 | Value: 30.00 | | | | |
| 1992 Proof | 17,000 | Value: 45.00 | | | | |
| 1993 Proof | 13,000 | Value: 50.00 | | | | |

**SILVER DUCAT** **KM# 218** **Weight:** 28.2500 g. **Composition:** 0.8730 Silver .7948 oz. ASW **Subject:** Seven Provinces - Groningen

| Date | Mintage | F | VF | XF | Unc | BU |
|---|---|---|---|---|---|---|
| 1994 Proof | 11,000 | Value: 60.00 | | | | |

**SILVER DUCAT** **KM# 221** **Weight:** 28.2500 g. **Composition:** 0.8730 Silver .7948 oz. ASW **Subject:** Seven Provinces - Zeeland

| Date | Mintage | F | VF | XF | Unc | BU |
|---|---|---|---|---|---|---|
| 1995 Proof | 11,000 | Value: 50.00 | | | | |

**SILVER DUCAT** **KM# 222** **Weight:** 28.2500 g. **Composition:** 0.8730 Silver .7948 oz. ASW **Subject:** Seven Provinces - Holland

| Date | Mintage | F | VF | XF | Unc | BU |
|---|---|---|---|---|---|---|
| 1996 Proof | 13,000 | Value: 50.00 | | | | |

**SILVER DUCAT** **KM# 225** **Weight:** 28.2500 g. **Composition:** 0.8730 Silver .7948 oz. ASW **Subject:** Seven Provinces - Gelderland

| Date | Mintage | F | VF | XF | Unc | BU |
|---|---|---|---|---|---|---|
| 1997 Proof | 12,000 | Value: 50.00 | | | | |

**SILVER DUCAT** **KM# 226** **Weight:** 28.2500 g. **Composition:** 0.8730 Silver .7948 oz. ASW **Subject:** Seven Provinces - Friesland

| Date | Mintage | F | VF | XF | Unc | BU |
|---|---|---|---|---|---|---|
| 1998 Proof | 11,000 | Value: 50.00 | | | | |

**SILVER DUCAT** **KM# 229** **Weight:** 28.2500 g. **Composition:** 0.8730 Silver .7948 oz. ASW **Subject:** Seven Provinces - Utrecht

| Date | Mintage | F | VF | XF | Unc | BU |
|---|---|---|---|---|---|---|
| 1999 Proof | — | Value: 50.00 | | | | |

**SILVER DUCAT** **KM# 232** **Weight:** 28.2500 g. **Composition:** 0.8730 Silver .7948 oz. ASW **Obverse:** Crowned arms **Reverse:** Standing knight with the arms of Overijssel **Edge:** Reeded **Size:** 40 mm.

| Date | Mintage | F | VF | XF | Unc | BU |
|---|---|---|---|---|---|---|
| 2000 Proof | — | — | — | — | 47.50 | — |

## PATTERNS

Including off metal strikes

| KM# | Date | Mintage | Identification | Mkt Val |
|---|---|---|---|---|
| PnA101 | 190x | — | 5 Cents. Small 5. Reverse small 5. | — |
| Pn101 | 190x | — | 5 Cents. Bronze. Large 5. Reverse large 5. | — |
| Pn101a | 190x | — | 5 Cents. Silver. | — |
| PNA102 | 190x | — | 5 Cents. Bronze. 27 mm. | — |
| Pn102 | 190x | — | 5 Cents. Bronze. 29 mm. | — |
| Pn103 | 190x | — | 10 Cents. Nickel. | — |
| Pn95 | 190x | — | 5 Cents. Nickel. | — |
| PnA124 | 1928 | — | Gulden. Gold. 19 mm. | 550 |
| Pn96 | 1902 | — | Cent. Gold. KM132. | — |
| Pn97 | 1903 | — | 1/2 Cent. Gold. KM133. | — |
| Pn98 | 1903 | — | 2-1/2 Cent. Gold. KM134. | — |
| Pn99 | 1903 | — | 10 Cents. Gold. KM135. | — |
| Pn100 | 1903 | — | 25 Cents. Gold. KM120.2 | — |
| Pn104 | 1904 | — | Cent. Bronze-Nickel Plug. | — |
| Pn105 | 1904 | — | 5 Cents. Bronze. | — |
| Pn106 | 1904 | — | 5 Cents. Bronze. | — |
| Pn107 | 1904 | — | 5 Cents. Bronze. Holed. | — |
| Pn108 | 1904 | — | 5 Cents. Nickel. | — |
| Pn109 | 1904 | — | 5 Cents. Nickel. Holed. | — |
| PnA110 | 1904 | — | 5 Cents. 14-sided. | — |
| Pn110 | 1905 | — | 1/2 Gulden. Gold. KM121.2 | — |
| PnA111 | 1906 | — | 5 Cents. Silver. Plain edge. | 1,000 |
| Pn111 | 1906 | — | 5 Cents. Bronze. | — |
| Pn112 | 1906 | — | 5 Cents. Nickel. | — |
| Pn113 | 1906 | — | 5 Cents. Nickel. | — |
| Pn114 | 1906 | — | 5 Cents. Nickel. | — |
| Pn115 | 1906 | — | 5 Cents. Silver. | — |
| Pn116 | 1906 | — | 10 Cents. Nickel. | — |
| PnA117 | 1906 | — | 10 Cents. | — |
| Pn117 | 1907 | — | 5 Cents. Bronze. Crown. | — |
| Pn118 | 1907 | — | 5 Cents. Nickel. Small crown. | — |
| Pn119 | 1908 | — | Gulden. Bronze. KM122. | — |
| Pn120 | 1910 | — | 10 Cents. Gold. KM145. | — |
| PnA121 | 1911 | — | Gulden. Bronze. | 1,100 |
| PnB121 | 1912 | — | 5 Cents. Nickel. "Proof". | — |
| Pn121 | 1913 | — | 2-1/2 Gulden. Silver. KM148. | — |
| Pn122 | 1928 | — | Gulden. Silver. 28 mm. | 350 |
| Pn123 | 1928 | — | Gulden. Silver. 19 mm. | 250 |
| PnA123 | 1928 | — | Gulden. Gold. 28 mm. | 700 |
| Pn124 | 1929 | — | Gulden. Silver. | — |
| PnA125 | 1929 | — | 2-1/2 Gulden. Bronze. | 1,200 |
| Pn125 | 1929 | — | 2-1/2 Gulden. Silver. | 550 |
| PnA126 | 1929 | — | 2-1/2 Gulden. Gold. | 1,000 |
| Pn126 | 1934 | — | 10 Cents. Bronze. KM163. | — |
| PnA127 | 1935 | — | 5 Cents. Gold. | — |
| Pn127 | 1941 | — | Cent. Zinc. KM170 with center hole. | 550 |
| Pn128 | 1941 | — | 2-1/2 Cent. Zinc. KM171 with center hole. | 550 |
| Pn129 | 1941 | — | 10 Cents. Zinc. | 160 |
| PnB134 | 1969 | — | 25 Cents. Brass. | — |
| PnA134 | 1969 | — | 10 Cents. Nickel-Brass. | — |
| PnA130 | 1969 | — | Cent. Nickel. | — |
| Pn130 | 1969 | — | 5 Cents. Nickel. Plain edge. | — |
| Pn131 | 1969 | — | 5 Cents. Nickel. | — |
| Pn132 | 1969 | — | 5 Cents. Aluminum. 1.5000 g. | — |
| Pn133 | 1969 | — | 5 Cents. Aluminum. 1.2200 g. | — |
| PnC134 | 1970 | — | Cent. Aluminum. | — |
| Pn134 | 1973 | — | 10 Gulden. Silver. | — |
| Pn135 | 1979 | — | 10 Gulden. Nickel. | — |
| Pn136 | 1980 | — | 25 Cents. Aluminum. KM183a. | — |
| Pn140 | 1980 | — | 2-1/2 Gulden. Gold. KM201b. | — |
| Pn137 | 1980 | — | Gulden. Nickel. KM200b error, shield on both sides. | — |
| Pn138 | 1980 | — | Gulden. Gold. KM200b. | — |
| Pn141 | 1980 | — | 2-1/2 Gulden. Silver. KM201a. | 500 |
| Pn139 | 1980 | — | Gulden. Silver. KM200a. | 500 |
| Pn146 | 1982 | — | Gulden. Nickel. | — |
| Pn142 | 1982 | — | 5 Cents. Bronze. 17 mm. | — |
| Pn143 | 1982 | — | 5 Cents. Tombac. | — |
| Pn144 | 1982 | — | 5 Cents. Brass. | — |
| Pn145 | 1982 | — | 5 Cents. Copper Clad Steel. | — |
| Pn147 | 1982 | — | 50 Gulden. Gold. KM207. | — |
| Pn148 | 1984 | — | 5 Cents. Tombac. | 200 |
| Pn149 | 1984 | — | 10 Cents. Bronze. | 200 |
| Pn150 | 1985 | — | 5 Cents. Nickel. Plain edge. | 200 |
| Pn151 | 1986 | — | 25 Cents. Brass. KM204. | 300 |
| Pn152 | 1986 | — | 25 Cents. Aluminum. KM204. | 300 |
| Pn153 | 1986 | — | Ducat. Tombac. KM190.2. | 500 |
| Pn154 | 1987 | — | 5 Cents. Nickel. KM202. | — |
| Pn155 | 1988 | — | 5 Cents. Nickel Clad Steel. | — |
| Pn156 | 1988 | — | 5 Cents. Copper Clad Steel. | — |
| Pn157 | 1988 | — | 5 Cents. Brass Clad Steel. | — |
| Pn158 | 1988 | — | 50 Gulden. Gold. KM212. | — |
| PnA158 | 1988 | — | 50 Gulden. Tombac. | 750 |
| PnB158 | 1988 | — | 50 Gulden. Silver. | 850 |
| Pn159 | 1990 | — | 5 Cents. Aluminum. | — |
| Pn160 | 1991 | — | 5 Cents. Nickel. KM202. | — |
| Pn161 | 1991 | — | 50 Gulden. Silver. 1/4 Circle. Queen Beatrix and Prince Claus | — |
| Pn162 | 2001 | — | Gulden. Nickel. Medal rotation | — |

## PIEFORTS

| KM# | Date | Mintage | Identification | Mkt Val |
|---|---|---|---|---|
| P20 | 1905 | — | Gulden. Silver. KM122.2 | — |
| P19 | 1905 | — | 1/2 Gulden. Silver. KM121.2 | 900 |
| P21 | 1910 | — | 25 Cents. Bronze. KM146. | — |
| P22 | 1948 | — | Cent. Silver. KM175. | — |
| P23 | 1948 | — | 5 Cents. Silver. KM176. | — |
| P24 | 1948 | — | 10 Cents. Silver. KM177. | — |
| P25 | 1948 | — | 25 Cents. Silver. KM178. | — |
| PA26 | 1956 | — | Gulden. Silver. similar to KM#184 | — |
| P26 | 1958 | — | Gulden. Silver. KM184. | — |

## PROOF SETS

| KM# | Date | Mintage | Identification | Issue Price | Mkt Val |
|---|---|---|---|---|---|
| PSA1 | 1928-29 (3) | — | PN122-123, 125 | — | 1,150 |
| PSB1 | 1928-29 (3) | — | PnA123-A124, A126 | — | 2,250 |
| PS1 | 1948 (4) | 50 | KM175-178 with PROEF | — | 1,800 |
| PS2 | 1948 (4) | — | KM175-178 | — | 400 |
| PS3 | 1949 | — | KM180-183, head left, rare. | — | — |
| PS4 | 1950 (4) | — | KM180-183 with PROEF | — | 1,250 |
| PS5 | 1950 (4) | — | KM180-183 | — | 325 |
| PS6 | 1951 (4) | — | KM180-183 | — | 275 |
| PS7 | 1952 (2) | — | KM180-181 | — | 275 |
| PS8 | 1953 (2) | — | KM180-181 | — | 275 |
| PS9 | 1954 (5) | — | KM180-184 | — | 300 |
| PS10 | 1955 (5) | — | KM180-184 | — | 250 |
| PS11 | 1956 (5) | — | KM180-184 | — | 250 |
| PS12 | 1957 (5) | — | KM18-184 | — | 250 |
| PS13 | 1958 (5) | — | KM180-184 | — | 250 |
| PS14 | 1959 (3) | — | KM180, 182, 185 | — | 450 |
| PS15 | 1960 (5) | — | KM180-183, 185 | — | 450 |
| PS16 | 1961 (5) | — | KM180-183, 185 | — | 450 |
| PS17 | 1962 (5) | 40 | KM180-183, 185 | — | 450 |
| PS18 | 1963 (6) | 40 | KM180-185 | — | 475 |
| PS19 | 1964 (6) | 40 | KM180-185 | — | 475 |
| PS20 | 1965 (5) | — | KM180-184 | — | 250 |
| PS21 | 1966 (6) | — | KM180-185 | — | 450 |
| PS22 | 1967 (5) | — | KM180-183, 184a | — | 200 |
| PD23 | 1968 (3) | — | KM180, 182-183 | — | 175 |
| PS25 | 1969 (6) | — | KM180-183, 184a, 191. Fish. | — | 250 |
| PS24 | 1969 (6) | — | KM180-183, 184a, 191. Cock. | — | 250 |
| PS26 | 1970 (6) | — | KM180-183, 184a, 191 | — | 250 |
| PS27 | 1982 (5) | 10,000 | KM202-206 | 35.00 | 85.00 |
| PS28 | 1983 (5) | 15,000 | KM202-206 | 35.00 | 35.00 |
| PS29 | 1984 (5) | 20,406 | KM202-206 | 35.00 | 22.50 |
| PS30 | 1985 (5) | 17,100 | KM202-206 | 35.00 | 22.50 |
| PS31 | 1986 (5) | 19,500 | KM202-206 | 35.00 | 32.50 |
| PS32 | 1987 (5) | 18,100 | KM202-206, Utrecht medal | 35.00 | 32.50 |
| PS33 | 1988 (6) | 19,550 | KM202-206, 210, Groningen medal | 5.50 | 32.50 |
| PS34 | 1989 (6) | 15,300 | KM202-206,210, Flevoland medal | 50.00 | 45.00 |
| PS35 | 1989 (3) | 6,400 | LM190.2, 211, 213 | 260 | 200 |
| PS36 | 1990 (6) | 15,100 | KM202-206, 210, N. Brabant medal. Set also includes 1974 25 Cents. | 50.00 | 45.00 |
| PS37 | 1991 (6) | 14,240 | KM202-206, 210,Drenthe medal | 50.00 | 45.00 |
| PS38 | 1992 (6) | 12,600 | KM202-206, 210, Zeeland medal | 53.50 | 50.00 |
| PS39 | 1992 (3) | 6,300 | KM190.2, 211, 213 | 270 | 235 |
| PS40 | 1993 (6) | 12,000 | KM202-206, 210, Limburg medal | 53.50 | 55.00 |
| PS41 | 1994 (6) | 12,500 | KM202-206, 210, Friesland medal | 59.50 | 55.00 |
| PS42 | 1994 (3) | 25,000 | BE NE LUX, Belgium KM195, Netherlands KM216, Luxemburg KM68 | 65.00 | 55.00 |
| PS43 | 1995 (6) | 11,500 | KM202-206, 210, Zuid-Holland medal | 59.50 | 55.00 |
| PS44 | 1996 (6) | 13,500 | KM202-206, 210 Booklet, 5 cents, Stuiver | 60.00 | 75.00 |
| PS45 | 1996 (2) | 6,500 | KM190.2, 211 | 247 | 225 |
| PS46 | 1997 (6) | 12,000 | KM202-206, 210 Booklet, 10 Cents | 60.00 | 70.00 |
| PS47 | 1998 (6) | — | KM202-206, 210 Booklet, 25 Cents | 60.00 | 70.00 |
| PS48 | 1999 (6) | — | KM202-206, 210, Booklet, 1 Guilden | 50.00 | 50.00 |
| PS49 | 1999 (3) | 2,500 | KM190.2, 211, 229 | — | 280 |
| PS50 | 1999 (2) | 1,800 | KM190.2, 211 | — | 240 |

## SELECT SETS (FLEUR DE COIN)

| KM# | Date | Mintage | Identification | Issue Price | Mkt Val |
|---|---|---|---|---|---|
| SS1 | 1819 (9) | — | KM47-49, 51-56 | — | 47,500 |
| SS2 | 1971 (6) | 1,000 | KM180-183, 184a, 191 | — | 300 |
| SS3 | 1972 (1) | 2,000 | KM191 | — | 45.00 |
| SS4 | 1972 (5) | 2,000 | KM180-183, 184a | — | 150 |
| SS5 | 1973 (5) | 10,000 | KM180-183, 184a | — | 40.00 |
| SS6 | 1974 (3) | 10,000 | KM180-182 | 6.50 | 20.00 |
| SS7 | 1975 (6) | 12,000 | KM180-183, 184a | 6.50 | 40.00 |
| SS8 | 1976 (5) | 15,000 | KM180-183, 184a | 6.50 | 70.00 |
| SS9 | 1977 (5) | 17,000 | KM180-183, 184a | 6.50 | 60.00 |
| SS10 | 1978 (6) | 21,500 | KM180-183, 184a, 191 | 6.50 | 40.00 |
| SS11 | 1979 (6) | 50,000 | KM180-183, 184a, 197 | 6.50 | 11.50 |
| SS12 | 1980 (6) | 249,732 | KM180-183, 184a, 191 | 6.50 | 4.00 |
| SS13 | 1980 (2) | 504,000 | KM200-201 | 12.00 | 4.00 |
| SS14 | 1980 (2) | 157 | KM200-201 | — | 1,200 |
| SS15 | 1980 (2) | 7 | KM200b-201b. Gold. | — | — |
| SS16 | 1982 (5) | 242,701 | KM202-206 | 12.00 | 4.50 |
| SS17 | 1983 | 156,165 | KM202-206 | 12.00 | 5.50 |
| SS18 | 1984 (5) | 131,748 | KM202-206 | 12.00 | 5.50 |
| SS19 | 1985 (5) | 113,079 | KM202-206 | 12.00 | 12.50 |
| SS20 | 1986 (5) | 112,190 | KM202-206 | 12.00 | 15.00 |
| SS21 | 1987 (5) | 120,850 | KM202-206, Utrecht medal | 15.00 | 18.00 |
| SS22 | 1988 (6) | 132,957 | KM202-206, 210, Groningen medal | 15.00 | 20.00 |
| SS23 | 1988 (6) | 5,000 | KM202-206, 210, ERU medal | — | 300 |
| SS24 | 1989 (6) | 103,607 | KM202-206, 210, Flevoland medal | 15.00 | 16.00 |
| SS25 | 1990 (6) | 102,750 | KM202-206, 210, N-Brabant medal | 15.00 | 20.00 |
| SS26 | 1991 (6) | 100,000 | KM202-206, 210, Drenthe medal | 15.00 | 20.00 |
| SS27 | 1991 (6) | 4,000 | KM202-206, 210, RABO Bank medal | — | 100 |
| SS28 | 1992 (6) | 94,000 | KM202-206, 210, Zeeland medal | 15.00 | 20.00 |
| SS29 | 1992 (6) | 3,000 | KM202-206, 210, numismatic year medal | 17.50 | 35.00 |
| SS30 | 1993 (6) | 87,000 | KM202-206, 210, Limburg medal | 15.00 | 27.50 |
| SS31 | 1993 (6) | 2,900 | KM202-206, 210, V.O.C. medal | 17.50 | 37.50 |
| SS32 | 1994 (6) | 85,000 | KM202-206, 210, Friesland medal | 15.00 | 25.00 |
| SS33 | 1994 (6) | 3,000 | KM202-206, 210, millennium of mint | 17.50 | 30.00 |
| SS34 | 1995 (6) | 81,000 | KM202-206, 210, Zuid-Holland medal | 15.00 | 20.00 |
| SS35 | 1995 (6) | 2,500 | KM202-206, 210, Rijks mint medal | 17.50 | 40.00 |
| SS36 | 1995 (6) | 1,500 | KM202-206, 210, Ehrbecker mint medal | — | 25.00 |
| SS37 | 1995 (6) | 1,500 | KM202-206, 210, Utrecht medal | 14.50 | 950 |
| SS38 | 1995 (6) | 900 | KM202-206, 210, DeCampen medal, Lion Daalder from shipwreck | 200 | 225 |
| SS39 | 1996 (6) | 1,500 | KM202-206, 210, Utrecht: Town of the Mint medal | 17.50 | 35.00 |
| SS40 | 1996 (6) | 80,000 | KM202-206, 210, Overyssel medal | 15.00 | 17.50 |
| SS41 | 1996 (6) | 3,000 | KM202-206, 210, French Occupation (1795-1813) medal | 17.50 | 30.00 |
| SS42 | 1996 (6) | 2,100 | KM202-206, 210, Baby set | 17.50 | 35.00 |
| SS43 | 1996 (6) | 350 | KM202-206, 210, DeCampen medal, 1/2 Lion Daalder from shipwreck | 240 | 375 |
| SS44 | 1996 (6) | 1,300 | KM202-206, 210, Westpark I medal | — | 70.00 |
| SS45 | 1996 (6) | 1,000 | KM202-206, 210, Utrecht II medal | — | 1,000 |
| SS46 | 1997 (6) | 85,000 | KM202-206, 210, Gelderland medal | 15.00 | 17.50 |
| SS47 | 1997 (6) | 3,500 | KM202-206, 210, King Willem I medal | 17.50 | 35.00 |
| SS48 | 1997 (6) | — | KM202-206, 210, Baby set | 17.50 | 32.50 |
| SS49 | 1997 (6) | 1,430 | KM202-206, 210, Ice skating/11 cities medal | 45.00 | 45.00 |
| SS50 | 1997 (6) | 700 | KM202-206, 210, Westpark II medal | — | 100 |
| SS51 | 1997 (6) | 1,000 | KM202-206, 210, Den Besterd I medal | — | 60.00 |
| SS52 | 1997 (6) | 500 | KM202-206, 210, Den Besterd IImedal | — | 140 |
| SS53 | 1997 (6) | 1,000 | KM202-206, 210, Czar Peter medal | — | 110 |
| SS54 | 1997 (6) | 500 | KM202-206, 210, 't Vliegent heart medal, Ducaton from shipwreck | 240 | 325 |
| SS55 | 1997 (6) | 1,150 | KM202-206, 210, Royal Navy medal | — | 300 |
| SS56 | 1997 (6) | 700 | KM202-206, 210, BFBN medal | — | 195 |
| SS57 | 1997 (6) | 1,500 | KM202-206, 210, Maasdonk medal | 50.00 | 35.00 |
| SS58 | 1997 (6) | 1,000 | KM202-206, 210, BNN medal | 75.00 | 75.00 |
| SS59 | 1997 (6) | 1,000 | KM202-206, 210, Overyssel medal | — | 500 |
| SS60 | 1997 (6) | 1,000 | KM202-206, 210, van Rign I medal | 45.00 | 45.00 |
| SS61 | 1997 (6) | 1,000 | KM202-206, 210, van Gogh I medal | 45.00 | 45.00 |
| SS62 | 1997 (6) | 1,000 | KM202-206, 210, Stuurman medal | 75.00 | 70.00 |
| SS63 | 1998 (6) | 83,500 | KM202-206, 210, N. Holland medal | 15.00 | 16.00 |
| SS64 | 1998 (6) | 3,500 | KM202-206, 210, King Willem II medal | 17.50 | 30.00 |
| SS65 | 1998 (6) | 100 | KM202-206, 210, 't Vliegent heart medal, Ducaton from shipwreck | 1,000 | 1,250 |
| SS66 | 1998 (6) | 8,400 | KM202-206, 210, Baby set | 17.50 | 22.50 |
| SS67 | 1998 (6) | 1,000 | KM202-206, 210, van Rign II medal | 40.00 | 40.00 |
| SS68 | 1998 (6) | 1,000 | KM202-206, 210, van Gogh II medal | 40.00 | 40.00 |
| SS69 | 1998 (6) | 1,000 | KM202-206, 210, Frans Hals medal | 50.00 | 50.00 |
| SS70 | 1998 (6) | 1,000 | KM202-206, 210, Statenjacht medal | — | 35.00 |
| SS71 | 1998 (6) | 1,000 | KM202-206,210, Theo Peters medal | — | 75.00 |
| SS72 | 1998 (6) | 1,000 | KM202-206,210, Vermeer medal | — | 50.00 |
| SS73 | 1998 (6) | 1,000 | KM202-206, 210, Knippenberg medal | — | 45.00 |
| SS74 | 1998 (6) | 2,500 | KM202-206, 210, Holland medal | 40.00 | 40.00 |
| SS75 | 1998 (6) | 2,500 | KM202-206, 210, Zeeland medal | 40.00 | 40.00 |
| SS76 | 1999 (6) | 3,500 | KM202-206, 210, King Willem III medal | 17.50 | 30.00 |
| SS77 | 1999 (6) | 1,000 | KM202-206, 210, Statenjacht medal | 30.00 | 30.00 |
| SS78 | 1999 (6) | 2,500 | KM202-206, 210, Friesland medal | 40.00 | 40.00 |
| SS79 | 1999 (6) | 2,500 | KM202-206, 210, West Friesland medal | 40.00 | 40.00 |
| SS80 | 1999 (6) | — | KM202-206, 210, Baby set | 15.50 | 17.50 |
| SS81 | 2000 (6) | — | KM202-206, 210 | — | 18.00 |

The Netherlands Antilles, comprises two groups of islands in the West Indies: Aruba (until 1986), Bonaire and Curacao and their dependencies near the Venezuelan coast and St. Eustatius, Saba, and the southern part of St. Martin (*St. Maarten*) southeast of Puerto Rico. The island group has an area of 371 sq. mi. (960 sq. km.) and a population of 225,000. Capital: Willemstad. Chief industries are the refining of crude oil and tourism. Petroleum products and phosphates are exported.

On Dec. 15, 1954, the Netherlands Antilles were given complete domestic autonomy and granted equality within the Kingdom with Surinam and the Netherlands. On Jan. I, 1986, Aruba achieved *status aparte* as the fourth part of the Dutch realm that was a step towards total independence.

**RULERS**

Juliana, 1948-1980
Beatrix, 1980-

**MINT MARKS**

Utrecht - privy marks only
FM - Franklin Mint, U.S.A.

**NOTE:** See Kingdom of the Netherlands for more details.

**NOTE:** From 1975-1985 the Franklin Mint produced coinage in up to 3 different qualities. Qualities of issue are designated in ( ) after each date and are defined as follows:

**(M) MATTE** - Normal circulation strike or a dull finish produced by sandblasting special uncirculated (polish finish) or proof quality dies.

**(U) SPECIAL UNCIRCULATED** - Polished or proof-like in appearance without any frosted features.

**(P) PROOF** - The highest quality obtainable having mirror-like fields and frosted features.

**MONETARY SYSTEM**

100 Cents = 1 Gulden

## KINGDOM

### DECIMAL COINAGE

**CENT** **KM# 1** **Composition:** Bronze

| Date | Mintage | F | VF | XF | Unc | BU |
|---|---|---|---|---|---|---|
| 1952 | 1,000,000 | 1.50 | 3.00 | 6.00 | 12.50 | — |
| 1952 Proof | 100 | Value: 40.00 | | | | |
| 1954 | 1,000,000 | 1.00 | 2.00 | 4.00 | 8.00 | — |
| 1954 Proof | 200 | Value: 22.50 | | | | |
| 1957 | 1,000,000 | 0.50 | 1.00 | 2.00 | 4.00 | — |
| 1957 Proof | 250 | Value: 22.50 | | | | |
| 1959 | 1,000,000 | 0.25 | 0.50 | 1.25 | 2.50 | — |
| 1959 Proof | 250 | Value: 22.50 | | | | |
| 1960 Proof | 300 | Value: 22.50 | | | | |
| 1961 | 1,000,000 | 0.25 | 0.50 | 1.25 | 4.00 | — |
| 1961 Proof | — | Value: 22.50 | | | | |
| 1963 | 1,000,000 | 0.25 | 0.50 | 1.25 | 4.00 | — |
| 1963 Proof | — | Value: 22.50 | | | | |
| 1964 Proof | — | Value: 22.50 | | | | |
| 1965 | 1,200,000 | 0.25 | 0.50 | 1.25 | 4.00 | — |
| 1965 Proof | — | Value: 22.50 | | | | |
| 1967 | 850,000 | 0.50 | 1.00 | 2.00 | 4.00 | — |
| 1967 Proof | — | Value: 22.50 | | | | |
| 1968 fish | 900,000 | 0.50 | 1.00 | 2.00 | 4.00 | — |
| 1968 star and fish | 700,000 | 1.00 | 2.00 | 4.00 | 8.00 | — |
| 1970 | 200,000 | 0.75 | 1.50 | 3.00 | 6.00 | — |
| 1970 Proof | — | Value: 25.00 | | | | |

**CENT** **KM# 8** **Composition:** Bronze

| Date | Mintage | F | VF | XF | Unc | BU |
|---|---|---|---|---|---|---|
| 1970 | 1,200,000 | 0.10 | 0.15 | 0.30 | 1.00 | — |
| 1970 Proof | — | Value: 17.50 | | | | |
| 1971 | 3,000,000 | 0.10 | 0.15 | 0.30 | 1.00 | — |
| 1971 Proof | — | Value: 17.50 | | | | |
| 1972 | 1,000,000 | 0.10 | 0.15 | 0.30 | 1.00 | — |
| 1973 | 3,000,000 | 0.10 | 0.15 | 0.30 | 0.75 | — |
| 1973 Proof | — | Value: 17.50 | | | | |
| 1974 | 3,000,000 | 0.10 | 0.15 | 0.30 | 0.75 | — |
| 1974 Proof | — | Value: 17.50 | | | | |
| 1975 | 2,000,000 | 0.10 | 0.15 | 0.30 | 0.75 | — |
| 1975 Proof | — | Value: 17.50 | | | | |
| 1976 | 3,000,000 | — | 0.10 | 0.20 | 0.35 | — |
| 1977 | 4,000,000 | — | 0.10 | 0.20 | 0.35 | — |
| 1978 | 2,000,000 | — | 0.10 | 0.20 | 0.35 | — |

**Note:** 1969 date is now listed in the Patterns section.

**CENT** **KM# 8a** **Composition:** Aluminum

| Date | Mintage | F | VF | XF | Unc | BU |
|---|---|---|---|---|---|---|
| 1979 | 7,512,000 | — | 0.10 | 0.15 | 0.25 | — |
| 1979 Proof | — | Value: 7.50 | | | | |
| 1980 | 2,518,000 | — | 0.10 | 0.15 | 0.25 | — |
| 1981 | 2,423,000 | — | 0.10 | 0.15 | 0.25 | — |
| 1982 | 2,410,000 | — | 0.10 | 0.15 | 0.25 | — |
| 1983 | 2,925,000 | — | 0.10 | 0.15 | 0.25 | — |
| 1984 | 3,626,000 | — | 0.10 | 0.15 | 0.25 | — |
| 1985 | 3,024,000 | — | 0.10 | 0.15 | 0.25 | — |

**CENT** **KM# 32** **Composition:** Aluminum

| Date | Mintage | F | VF | XF | Unc | BU |
|---|---|---|---|---|---|---|
| 1989 | 1,365,000 | — | — | — | 0.20 | — |
| 1990 | 2,711,000 | — | — | — | 0.20 | — |
| 1991 | 4,016,000 | — | — | — | 0.20 | — |
| 1992 | 3,049,000 | — | — | — | 0.20 | — |
| 1993 | 3,997,000 | — | — | — | 0.20 | — |
| 1994 | 1,997,000 | — | — | — | 0.20 | — |
| 1995 | 997,000 | — | — | — | 0.20 | — |
| 1996 | 3,595,000 | — | — | — | 0.20 | — |
| 1997 | 4,107,000 | — | — | — | 0.20 | — |
| 1998 | 5,757,000 | — | — | — | 0.20 | — |
| 1999 | — | — | — | — | 0.20 | — |
| 2000 | — | — | — | — | 0.20 | — |

**2-1/2 CENTS** **KM# 5** **Composition:** Bronze

| Date | Mintage | F | VF | XF | Unc | BU |
|---|---|---|---|---|---|---|
| 1956 | 400,000 | 1.00 | 2.00 | 3.50 | 7.50 | — |
| 1956 Proof | 500 | Value: 30.00 | | | | |
| 1959 | 1,000,000 | 0.40 | 0.75 | 1.75 | 3.50 | — |
| 1959 Proof | 250 | Value: 30.00 | | | | |
| 1965 fish | 500,000 | 0.50 | 1.25 | 2.50 | 5.00 | — |
| 1965 Proof | — | Value: 25.00 | | | | |
| 1965 fish and star | 150,000 | 1.50 | 3.00 | 6.00 | 12.50 | — |

**2-1/2 CENTS** **KM# 9** **Composition:** Bronze

| Date | Mintage | F | VF | XF | Unc | BU |
|---|---|---|---|---|---|---|
| 1970 | 500,000 | 0.25 | 0.50 | 1.00 | 1.50 | — |
| 1970 Proof | — | Value: 20.00 | | | | |
| 1971 | 3,000,000 | 0.10 | 0.15 | 0.30 | 0.60 | — |
| 1971 Proof | — | Value: 20.00 | | | | |
| 1973 | 1,000,000 | 0.10 | 0.15 | 0.30 | 0.60 | — |
| 1973 Proof | — | Value: 20.00 | | | | |
| 1974 | 1,000,000 | 0.10 | 0.15 | 0.30 | 0.60 | — |
| 1974 Proof | — | Value: 20.00 | | | | |
| 1975 | 1,000,000 | 0.10 | 0.15 | 0.30 | 0.60 | — |
| 1976 | 1,000,000 | 0.10 | 0.15 | 0.30 | 0.60 | — |
| 1977 | 1,000,000 | 0.10 | 0.15 | 0.30 | 0.60 | — |
| 1978 | 1,500,000 | 0.10 | 0.15 | 0.30 | 0.60 | — |

**Note:** 1969 date is now found in the Patterns section.

**2-1/2 CENTS** **KM# 9a** **Composition:** Aluminum

| Date | Mintage | F | VF | XF | Unc | BU |
|---|---|---|---|---|---|---|
| 1979 | 2,012,000 | — | 0.10 | 0.20 | 0.40 | — |
| 1979 Proof | — | Value: 10.00 | | | | |
| 1980 | 2,018,000 | — | 0.10 | 0.20 | 0.40 | — |
| 1981 | 1,023,000 | — | 0.10 | 0.20 | 0.40 | — |
| 1982 | 1,010,000 | — | 0.10 | 0.20 | 0.40 | — |
| 1983 | 1,025,000 | — | 0.10 | 0.20 | 0.40 | — |
| 1984 | 1,026,000 | — | 0.10 | 0.20 | 0.40 | — |
| 1985 | 1,024,000 | — | 0.10 | 0.20 | 0.40 | — |

**5 CENTS** **KM# 6** **Composition:** Copper-Nickel

| Date | Mintage | F | VF | XF | Unc | BU |
|---|---|---|---|---|---|---|
| 1957 | 500,000 | 0.60 | 1.00 | 2.00 | 4.00 | — |
| 1957 Proof | 250 | Value: 35.00 | | | | |
| 1962 | 250,000 | 1.50 | 2.50 | 5.00 | 10.00 | — |
| 1962 Proof | 200 | Value: 30.00 | | | | |
| 1963 | 400,000 | 0.35 | 0.75 | 1.50 | 3.50 | — |
| 1963 Proof | — | Value: 30.00 | | | | |
| 1965 | 500,000 | 0.35 | 0.75 | 1.50 | 3.50 | — |
| 1965 Proof | — | Value: 30.00 | | | | |
| 1967 | 600,000 | 0.35 | 0.75 | 1.50 | 3.50 | — |
| 1967 Proof | — | Value: 30.00 | | | | |
| 1970 | 450,000 | 0.35 | 0.75 | 1.50 | 3.50 | — |
| 1970 Proof | — | Value: 30.00 | | | | |

**Note:** KM#A13, previously listed here, is now under Patterns.

**5 CENTS** **KM# 13** **Composition:** Copper-Nickel

| Date | Mintage | F | VF | XF | Unc | BU |
|---|---|---|---|---|---|---|
| 1971 | 2,000,000 | 0.10 | 0.20 | 0.40 | 0.75 | — |
| 1971 Proof | — | Value: 22.50 | | | | |
| 1974 | 500,000 | 0.35 | 0.75 | 1.50 | 3.00 | — |
| 1974 Proof | — | Value: 22.50 | | | | |
| 1975 | 2,000,000 | 0.10 | 0.20 | 0.40 | 0.75 | — |
| 1975 Proof | — | Value: 22.50 | | | | |
| 1976 | 1,500,000 | 0.10 | 0.20 | 0.40 | 0.75 | — |
| 1977 | 1,000,000 | 0.10 | 0.20 | 0.40 | 0.75 | — |
| 1978 | 1,500,000 | 0.10 | 0.20 | 0.40 | 0.75 | — |
| 1979 | 1,512,000 | 0.10 | 0.20 | 0.40 | 0.75 | — |
| 1980 | 1,518,000 | — | 0.10 | 0.25 | 0.50 | — |
| 1981 | 1,022,999 | — | 0.10 | 0.25 | 0.50 | — |
| 1982 | 1,010,000 | — | 0.10 | 0.25 | 0.50 | — |
| 1983 | 1,024,999 | — | 0.10 | 0.25 | 0.50 | — |
| 1984 | 1,526,000 | — | 0.10 | 0.25 | 0.50 | — |
| 1985 | 1,524,000 | — | 0.10 | 0.25 | 0.50 | — |

**5 CENTS** **KM# 33** **Composition:** Aluminum

| Date | Mintage | F | VF | XF | Unc | BU |
|---|---|---|---|---|---|---|
| 1989 | 915,000 | — | — | 0.25 | 0.50 | — |
| 1990 | 1,811,000 | — | — | 0.25 | 0.50 | — |
| 1991 | 2,513,000 | — | — | — | 0.50 | — |
| 1992 | 1,599,000 | — | — | — | 0.50 | — |
| 1993 | 2,497,000 | — | — | — | 0.50 | — |
| 1994 | 1,497,000 | — | — | — | 0.50 | — |
| 1995 | 997,000 | — | — | — | 0.50 | — |
| 1996 | 796,000 | — | — | — | 0.50 | — |
| 1997 | 2,207,000 | — | — | — | 0.50 | — |
| 1998 | 2,507,000 | — | — | — | 0.50 | — |
| 1999 | — | — | — | — | 0.50 | — |
| 2000 | — | — | — | — | 0.50 | — |

**1/10 GULDEN** **KM# 3** **Weight:** 1.4000 g. **Composition:** 0.6400 Silver .0288 oz. ASW

| Date | Mintage | F | VF | XF | Unc | BU |
|---|---|---|---|---|---|---|
| 1954 | 200,000 | 3.00 | 6.00 | 12.50 | 25.00 | — |
| 1954 Proof | 200 | Value: 40.00 | | | | |
| 1956 | 250,000 | 1.25 | 2.50 | 5.00 | 10.00 | — |
| 1956 Proof | 500 | Value: 35.00 | | | | |
| 1957 | 250,000 | 1.25 | 2.50 | 5.00 | 10.00 | — |
| 1957 Proof | 250 | Value: 35.00 | | | | |
| 1959 | 250,000 | 1.25 | 2.50 | 5.00 | 10.00 | — |
| 1959 Proof | 250 | Value: 35.00 | | | | |
| 1960 | 400,000 | 0.50 | 0.85 | 1.75 | 3.50 | — |
| 1960 Proof | 300 | Value: 45.00 | | | | |

| Date | Mintage | F | VF | XF | Unc | BU |
|---|---|---|---|---|---|---|
| 1962 | 400,000 | 0.50 | 0.85 | 1.75 | 3.50 | — |
| 1962 Proof | 200 | Value: 35.00 | | | | |
| 1963 | 900,000 | 0.50 | 0.85 | 1.75 | 3.50 | — |
| 1963 Proof | — | Value: 35.00 | | | | |
| 1966 fish | 1,000,000 | 0.50 | 0.85 | 1.75 | — | — |
| 1966 fish and star | 200,000 | 0.50 | 0.85 | 1.75 | 3.50 | — |
| 1970 | 300,000 | 0.50 | 0.85 | 1.75 | 3.50 | — |
| 1970 Proof | — | Value: 35.00 | | | | |

**10 CENTS** **KM# 10** **Composition:** Nickel

| Date | Mintage | F | VF | XF | Unc | BU |
|---|---|---|---|---|---|---|
| 1970 | 1,000,000 | — | 0.35 | 0.75 | 1.35 | — |
| 1970 Proof | — | Value: 25.00 | | | | |
| 1971 | 3,000,000 | — | 0.25 | 0.50 | 1.00 | — |
| 1971 Proof | — | Value: 25.00 | | | | |
| 1974 | 1,000,000 | — | 0.25 | 0.50 | 1.00 | — |
| 1974 Proof | — | Value: 25.00 | | | | |
| 1975 | 1,500,000 | — | 0.25 | 0.50 | 1.00 | — |
| 1975 Proof | — | Value: 25.00 | | | | |
| 1976 | 2,000,000 | — | 0.15 | 0.30 | 0.60 | — |
| 1977 | 1,000,000 | — | 0.15 | 0.30 | 0.60 | — |
| 1978 | 1,500,000 | — | 0.15 | 0.30 | 0.60 | — |
| 1979 | 1,512,000 | — | 0.15 | 0.30 | 0.60 | — |
| 1979 Proof | — | Value: 12.50 | | | | |
| 1980 | 1,518,000 | — | 0.10 | 0.25 | 0.50 | — |
| 1981 | 1,022,999 | — | 0.10 | 0.25 | 0.50 | — |
| 1982 | 1,010,000 | — | 0.10 | 0.25 | 0.50 | — |
| 1983 | 1,024,999 | — | 0.10 | 0.25 | 0.50 | — |
| 1984 | 1,026,000 | — | 0.10 | 0.25 | 0.50 | — |
| 1985 | 1,024,000 | — | 0.10 | 0.25 | 0.50 | — |

**Note:** 1969 date of this variety is now in the Patterns section

**10 CENTS** **KM# 34** **Composition:** Nickel Bonded Steel

| Date | Mintage | F | VF | XF | Unc | BU |
|---|---|---|---|---|---|---|
| 1989 | 915,000 | — | — | — | 0.60 | — |
| 1990 | 1,811,000 | — | — | — | 0.45 | — |
| 1991 | 2,513,000 | — | — | — | 0.45 | — |
| 1992 | 898,000 | — | — | — | 0.45 | — |
| 1993 | 1,996,000 | — | — | — | 0.45 | — |
| 1994 | 997,000 | — | — | — | 0.45 | — |
| 1995 | 97,000 | — | — | — | 0.45 | — |
| 1996 | 895,000 | — | — | — | 0.45 | — |
| 1997 | 1,607,000 | — | — | — | 0.45 | — |
| 1998 | 2,007,000 | — | — | — | 0.45 | — |
| 1999 | — | — | — | — | 0.45 | — |
| 2000 | — | — | — | — | 0.45 | — |

**1/4 GULDEN** **KM# 4** **Weight:** 3.5800 g. **Composition:** 0.6400 Silver .0736 oz. ASW

| Date | Mintage | F | VF | XF | Unc | BU |
|---|---|---|---|---|---|---|
| 1954 | 200,000 | 4.00 | 8.00 | 15.00 | 30.00 | — |
| 1954 Proof | 200 | Value: 45.00 | | | | |
| 1956 | 200,000 | 1.25 | 2.50 | 6.50 | 15.00 | — |
| 1956 Proof | 500 | Value: 40.00 | | | | |
| 1957 | 200,000 | 1.25 | 2.50 | 6.50 | 15.00 | — |
| 1957 Proof | 250 | Value: 45.00 | | | | |
| 1960 | 240,000 | 0.65 | 1.25 | 3.00 | 6.00 | — |
| 1960 Proof | 300 | Value: 45.00 | | | | |
| 1962 | 240,000 | 0.65 | 1.25 | 3.00 | 6.00 | — |
| 1962 Proof | 200 | Value: 45.00 | | | | |
| 1963 | 300,000 | 0.65 | 1.25 | 3.00 | 6.00 | — |
| 1963 Proof | — | Value: 45.00 | | | | |
| 1965 | 500,000 | 0.65 | 1.25 | 3.00 | 6.00 | — |
| 1965 Proof | — | Value: 45.00 | | | | |
| 1967 fish | 310,000 | 0.65 | 1.25 | 3.00 | 6.00 | — |
| 1967 Proof, fish | — | Value: 45.00 | | | | |
| 1967 fish and star | 200,000 | 0.75 | 1.50 | 3.00 | 6.00 | — |
| 1970 | 150,000 | 0.65 | 1.25 | 3.00 | 6.00 | — |
| 1970 Proof | — | Value: 35.00 | | | | |

**25 CENTS** **KM# 11** **Composition:** Nickel

| Date | Mintage | F | VF | XF | Unc | BU |
|---|---|---|---|---|---|---|
| 1970 | 750,000 | 0.30 | 0.60 | 1.25 | 2.50 | — |
| 1970 Proof | — | Value: 30.00 | | | | |
| 1971 | 3,000,000 | — | 0.25 | 0.50 | 1.00 | — |
| 1971 Proof | — | Value: 30.00 | | | | |
| 1975 | 1,000,000 | — | 0.25 | 0.50 | 1.00 | — |
| 1975 Proof | — | Value: 30.00 | | | | |
| 1976 | 1,000,000 | — | 0.20 | 0.40 | 0.75 | — |
| 1977 | 1,000,000 | — | 0.20 | 0.40 | 0.75 | — |
| 1978 | 1,000,000 | — | 0.20 | 0.40 | 0.75 | — |
| 1979 | 1,012,000 | — | 0.20 | 0.40 | 0.75 | — |
| 1979 Proof | — | Value: 17.50 | | | | |
| 1980 cock and star | 1,018,000 | — | 0.30 | 0.60 | 1.25 | — |
| 1981 | 1,022,999 | — | 0.15 | 0.30 | 0.60 | — |
| 1982 | 1,010,000 | — | 0.15 | 0.30 | 0.60 | — |
| 1983 | 1,024,999 | — | 0.15 | 0.30 | 0.60 | — |
| 1984 | 1,026,000 | — | 0.15 | 0.30 | 0.60 | — |
| 1985 | 774,000 | — | 0.15 | 0.30 | 0.60 | — |

**25 CENTS** **KM# 35** **Composition:** Nickel Bonded Steel **Obverse:** Orange blossom

| Date | Mintage | F | VF | XF | Unc | BU |
|---|---|---|---|---|---|---|
| 1989 | 915,000 | — | — | — | 0.50 | — |
| 1990 | 1,811,000 | — | — | — | 0.50 | — |
| 1991 | 2,013,000 | — | — | — | 0.50 | — |
| 1992 | 898,000 | — | — | — | 0.50 | — |
| 1993 | 997,000 | — | — | — | 0.50 | — |
| 1994 | 997,000 | — | — | — | 0.50 | — |
| 1995 | 297,000 | — | — | — | 0.50 | — |
| 1996 | 420,000 | — | — | — | 0.50 | — |
| 1997 | 1,297,000 | — | — | — | 0.50 | — |
| 1998 | 2,007,000 | — | — | — | 0.50 | — |
| 1999 | — | — | — | — | 0.50 | — |
| 2000 | — | — | — | — | 0.50 | — |

**50 CENTS** **KM# 36** **Composition:** Aureate Steel **Obverse:** Orange blossom

| Date | Mintage | F | VF | XF | Unc | BU |
|---|---|---|---|---|---|---|
| 1989 | 315,000 | — | — | — | 0.85 | — |
| 1990 | 611,000 | — | — | — | 0.85 | — |
| 1991 | 513,000 | — | — | — | 0.85 | — |
| 1992 | 48,000 | — | — | — | 0.85 | — |
| 1993 In sets only | 8,560 | — | — | — | 2.00 | — |
| 1994 In sets only | 9,000 | — | — | — | 1.50 | — |
| 1995 In sets only | 9,000 | — | — | — | 1.50 | — |
| 1996 In sets only | 7,500 | — | — | — | 1.50 | — |
| 1997 | 32,000 | — | — | — | 0.85 | — |
| 1998 | 132,000 | — | — | — | 0.85 | — |
| 1999 | — | — | — | — | 0.85 | — |
| 2000 | — | — | — | — | 0.85 | — |

**GULDEN** **KM# 2** **Weight:** 10.0000 g. **Composition:** 0.7200 Silver .2315 oz. ASW

| Date | Mintage | F | VF | XF | Unc | BU |
|---|---|---|---|---|---|---|
| 1952 | 1,000,000 | 1.25 | 2.50 | 5.00 | 10.00 | — |
| 1952 Proof | 100 | Value: 125 | | | | |
| 1963 | 100,000 | 2.00 | 4.00 | 8.00 | 16.00 | — |
| 1963 Proof | — | Value: 100 | | | | |
| 1964 fish | 300,000 | 1.50 | 3.00 | 6.00 | 12.00 | — |
| 1964 Proof | — | Value: 100 | | | | |
| 1964 fish and star | 200,000 | 2.00 | 3.75 | 7.50 | 15.00 | — |
| 1970 | 50,000 | 2.00 | 4.00 | 8.00 | 16.00 | — |
| 1970 Proof | — | Value: 100 | | | | |

**GULDEN** **KM# 12** **Composition:** Nickel **Obverse:** Bust of Queen Juliana

| Date | Mintage | F | VF | XF | Unc | BU |
|---|---|---|---|---|---|---|
| 1970 | 500,000 | 0.65 | 1.00 | 2.00 | 4.00 | — |
| 1970 Proof | — | Value: 50.00 | | | | |
| 1971 | 3,000,000 | — | 0.75 | 1.50 | 3.00 | — |
| 1971 Proof | — | Value: 50.00 | | | | |
| 1978 | 500,000 | — | 0.50 | 1.00 | 2.00 | — |
| 1979 | 512,000 | — | 0.50 | 1.00 | 2.00 | — |
| 1979 Proof | — | Value: 25.00 | | | | |
| 1980 cock and star | 518,000 | — | 0.50 | 1.00 | 2.00 | — |

**Note:** 1969 date is now listed in the Patterns section.

**GULDEN** **KM# 24** **Composition:** Nickel **Obverse:** Bust of Queen Beatrix

| Date | Mintage | F | VF | XF | Unc | BU |
|---|---|---|---|---|---|---|
| 1980 anvil | 223,000 | — | 0.40 | 0.80 | 1.60 | — |
| 1981 | 223,000 | — | 0.40 | 0.80 | 1.60 | — |
| 1982 | 510,000 | — | 0.40 | 0.80 | 1.60 | — |
| 1983 | 525,000 | — | 0.40 | 0.80 | 1.60 | — |
| 1984 | 526,000 | — | 0.40 | 0.80 | 1.60 | — |
| 1985 | 424,000 | — | 0.40 | 0.80 | 1.60 | — |

**GULDEN** **KM# 37** **Composition:** Aureate Steel

| Date | Mintage | F | VF | XF | Unc | BU |
|---|---|---|---|---|---|---|
| 1989 | 715,000 | — | — | 0.50 | 1.00 | — |
| 1990 | 1,411,000 | — | — | 0.50 | 1.00 | — |
| 1991 | 2,013,000 | — | — | 0.50 | 1.00 | — |
| 1992 | 1,198,000 | — | — | 0.50 | 1.00 | — |
| 1993 | 1,986,000 | — | — | 0.50 | 1.00 | — |
| 1994 | 997,000 | — | — | 0.50 | 1.00 | — |
| 1995 In sets only | 9,000 | — | — | — | 2.00 | — |
| 1996 In sets only | 7,500 | — | — | — | 2.00 | — |
| 1997 | 2,507,000 | — | — | 0.50 | 1.00 | — |
| 1998 | 12,507,000 | — | — | 0.50 | 1.00 | — |
| 1999 | — | — | — | 0.50 | 1.00 | — |
| 2000 | — | — | — | 0.50 | 1.00 | — |

**2-1/2 GULDEN** **KM# 7** **Weight:** 25.0000 g. **Composition:** 0.7200 Silver .5787 oz. ASW

| Date | Mintage | F | VF | XF | Unc | BU |
|---|---|---|---|---|---|---|
| 1964 | — | — | BV | 3.50 | 7.00 | — |
| 1964 Proof | — | Value: 200 | | | | |

**2-1/2 GULDEN** **KM# 19** **Composition:** Nickel **Obverse:** Bust of Queen Juliana

| Date | Mintage | F | VF | XF | Unc | BU |
|---|---|---|---|---|---|---|
| 1978 | 100,000 | — | — | 2.00 | 4.00 | — |
| 1979 | 212,000 | — | — | 2.00 | 4.00 | — |
| 1979 Proof | — | Value: 35.00 | | | | |
| 1980 cock and star | 200,000 | — | 1.50 | 3.00 | 6.00 | — |

**2-1/2 GULDEN** **KM# 25** **Composition:** Nickel **Obverse:** Bust of Queen Beatrix

| Date | Mintage | F | VF | XF | Unc | BU |
|---|---|---|---|---|---|---|
| 1980 anvil | 80,000 | — | — | 2.00 | 4.00 | — |
| 1981 | 30,000 | — | — | 2.00 | 4.00 | — |
| 1982 | 44,000 | — | — | 2.00 | 4.00 | — |
| 1984 | 30,000 | — | — | 2.00 | 4.00 | — |
| 1985 | 37,000 | — | — | 2.00 | 4.00 | — |

**2-1/2 GULDEN** **KM# 38** **Composition:** Aureate Steel

| Date | Mintage | F | VF | XF | Unc | BU |
|---|---|---|---|---|---|---|
| 1989 | 35,000 | — | — | — | 3.00 | — |
| 1990 | 60,000 | — | — | — | 3.00 | — |
| 1991 | 63,000 | — | — | — | 3.00 | — |
| 1992 | 23,000 | — | — | — | 3.50 | — |
| 1993 In sets only | 8,560 | — | — | — | 4.25 | — |
| 1994 In sets only | 9,000 | — | — | — | 3.50 | — |
| 1995 In sets only | 9,000 | — | — | — | 3.50 | — |
| 1996 In sets only | 7,500 | — | — | — | 3.50 | — |
| 1997 | 9,500 | — | — | — | 3.00 | — |
| 1998 | 20,000 | — | — | — | 3.00 | — |
| 1999 | — | — | — | — | 3.00 | — |
| 2000 | — | — | — | — | 3.00 | — |

**5 GULDEN** **KM# 26** **Weight:** 3.3600 g. **Composition:** 0.9000 Gold .0972 oz. AGW **Obverse:** Bust of Queen Beatrix left

| Date | Mintage | F | VF | XF | Unc | BU |
|---|---|---|---|---|---|---|
| 1980(1982) Proof, cock and star | 16,000 | Value: 55.00 | | | | |

**5 GULDEN** **KM# 43** **Composition:** Brass Plated Steel **Obverse:** Head of Queen Beatrix left **Reverse:** Crowned arms divide denomination **Edge Lettering:** GOD ZIJ MET ONS

| Date | Mintage | F | VF | XF | Unc | BU |
|---|---|---|---|---|---|---|
| 1998 | 607,000 | — | — | — | 5.50 | — |
| 1999 | — | — | — | — | 5.50 | — |
| 2000 | — | — | — | — | 5.50 | — |

**10 GULDEN** **KM# 20** **Weight:** 25.0000 g. **Composition:** 0.7200 Silver .5787 oz. ASW **Subject:** 150th Anniversary of Bank

| Date | Mintage | F | VF | XF | Unc | BU |
|---|---|---|---|---|---|---|
| 1978 | 35,000 | — | — | — | 7.00 | — |
| 1978 Proof | 15,000 | Value: 9.00 | | | | |

**10 GULDEN** **KM# 27** **Weight:** 6.7200 g. **Composition:** 0.9000 Gold .1945 oz. AGW **Obverse:** Head of Queen Beatrix left

| Date | Mintage | F | VF | XF | Unc | BU |
|---|---|---|---|---|---|---|
| 1980 Proof, cock and star | 6,000 | Value: 100 | | | | |

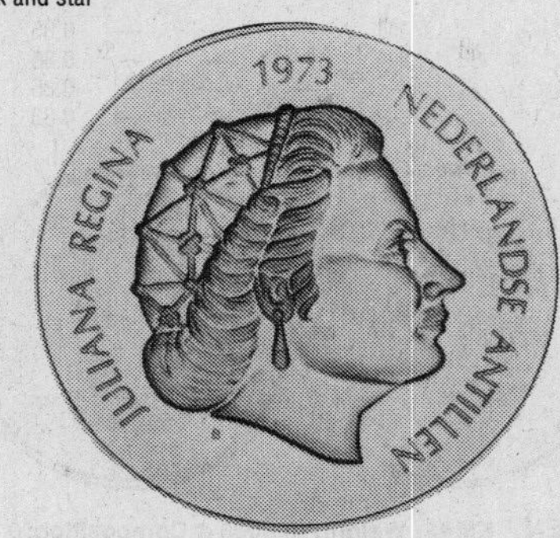

**25 GULDEN** **KM# 14** **Weight:** 41.7000 g. **Composition:** 0.9250 Silver 1.2401 oz. ASW **Subject:** 25th Anniversary of Reign

| Date | Mintage | F | VF | XF | Unc | BU |
|---|---|---|---|---|---|---|
| 1973 | 40,000 | — | — | — | 12.50 | — |
| 1973 Proof | 20,000 | Value: 15.00 | | | | |

**25 GULDEN** **KM# 15** **Weight:** 41.7000 g. **Composition:** 0.9250 Silver 1.2401 oz. ASW **Subject:** U.S. Bicentennial

| Date | Mintage | F | VF | XF | Unc | BU |
|---|---|---|---|---|---|---|
| 1976 FM(M) | 200 | — | — | — | 165 | — |
| 1976 FM(U) | 9,425 | — | — | — | 17.50 | — |
| 1976 FM(P) | 13,000 | Value: 25.00 | | | | |

**25 GULDEN** **KM# 17** **Weight:** 41.7000 g. **Composition:** 0.9250 Silver 1.2401 oz. ASW **Subject:** Peter Stuyvesant

| Date | Mintage | F | VF | XF | Unc | BU |
|---|---|---|---|---|---|---|
| 1977 | — | — | — | 80.00 | 160 | — |

**25 GULDEN** **KM# 22** **Weight:** 27.2200 g. **Composition:** 0.9250 Silver .8095 oz. ASW **Series:** International Year of the Child

| Date | Mintage | F | VF | XF | Unc | BU |
|---|---|---|---|---|---|---|
| 1979 | 1,000 | — | — | — | 75.00 | — |
| 1979 Proof like | 4,000 | — | — | — | — | 32.50 |
| 1979 Proof | 17,000 | Value: 22.50 | | | | |

**25 GULDEN** **KM# 39** **Weight:** 25.0000 g. **Composition:** 0.9250 Silver .7435 oz. ASW **Subject:** Visit of Pope John Paul II

| Date | Mintage | F | VF | XF | Unc | BU |
|---|---|---|---|---|---|---|
| 1990 | 10,000 | — | — | — | 35.00 | — |
| 1990 Proof | 6,500 | Value: 37.50 | | | | |

**25 GULDEN** **KM# 40** **Weight:** 25.0000 g. **Composition:** 0.9250 Silver .7435 oz. ASW **Subject:** First Amsterdam to Curacao Flight in 1934

| Date | Mintage | F | VF | XF | Unc | BU |
|---|---|---|---|---|---|---|
| 1994 Proof | — | Value: 35.00 | | | | |

**25 GULDEN** **KM# 41** **Weight:** 25.0000 g. **Composition:** 0.9250 Silver .7435 oz. ASW **Series:** Olympics **Obverse:** Crowned arms **Reverse:** Weight lifter, dates

| Date | Mintage | F | VF | XF | Unc | BU |
|---|---|---|---|---|---|---|
| 1995 Proof | — | Value: 25.00 | | | | |

**25 GULDEN** **KM# 42** **Weight:** 25.0000 g. **Composition:** 0.9250 Silver .7435 oz. ASW **Subject:** Fort Nassau 1797-1997 **Reverse:** Old sidewheeler and sail ship, dates

| Date | Mintage | F | VF | XF | Unc | BU |
|---|---|---|---|---|---|---|
| ND(1997) Proof | 25,000 | Value: 35.00 | | | | |

**25 GULDEN** **KM# 44** **Weight:** 25.0000 g. **Composition:** 0.9250 Silver .7435 oz. ASW **Series:** World Wildlife Fund **Obverse:** Crowned arms, denomination **Reverse:** Buck and doe, WWF logo

| Date | Mintage | F | VF | XF | Unc | BU |
|---|---|---|---|---|---|---|
| 1998 Proof like | 500 | — | — | — | — | 27.50 |
| 1998 Proof | — | Value: 35.00 | | | | |

**25 GULDEN** **KM# 45** **Weight:** 25.0000 g. **Composition:** 0.9250 Silver .7435 oz. ASW **Subject:** Von Bini Na Curacao **Obverse:** Crowned arms, date **Reverse:** 500-year-old sailing ship **Edge Lettering:** DIOS KU NOS **Note:** Edge inscription repeats 3x.

| Date | Mintage | F | VF | XF | Unc | BU |
|---|---|---|---|---|---|---|
| 1999 Proof | 9,500 | Value: 35.00 | | | | |

**50 GULDEN** **KM# 23** **Weight:** 3.3600 g. **Composition:** 0.9000 Gold .0972 oz. AGW **Subject:** 75th Anniversary of the Royal Convenant

| Date | Mintage | F | VF | XF | Unc | BU |
|---|---|---|---|---|---|---|
| 1979 | 11,000 | — | — | — | 40.00 | — |
| 1979 Proof | 64,000 | Value: 45.00 | | | | |

**50 GULDEN** **KM# 28** **Weight:** 24.0000 g. **Composition:** 0.5000 Silver .3859 oz. ASW

| Date | Mintage | F | VF | XF | Unc | BU |
|---|---|---|---|---|---|---|
| 1980 cock and star | 8,600 | — | — | — | 20.00 | — |
| 1980 Proof, cock and star | 16,000 | Value: 22.50 | | | | |

**50 GULDEN** **KM# 30** **Weight:** 25.0000 g. **Composition:** 0.9250 Silver .7435 oz. ASW **Subject:** Dutch American Friendship

| Date | Mintage | F | VF | XF | Unc | BU |
|---|---|---|---|---|---|---|
| 1982 Y Proof | 40,000 | Value: 22.50 | | | | |

**50 GULDEN** **KM# 31** **Weight:** 25.0000 g. **Composition:** 0.9250 Silver .7435 oz. ASW **Subject:** Mikve Israel Emanuel Synagogue

| Date | Mintage | F | VF | XF | Unc | BU |
|---|---|---|---|---|---|---|
| ND(1982) Proof | 10,000 | Value: 45.00 | | | | |

**75 GULDEN** **KM# 47** **Composition:** Bi-Metallic Gold And Silver **Subject:** Enkuentro Di Pueblonan **Reverse:** World above five heads

| Date | Mintage | F | VF | XF | Unc | BU |
|---|---|---|---|---|---|---|
| 1999 Proof | — | Value: 200 | | | | |

**100 GULDEN** **KM# 21** **Weight:** 6.7200 g. **Composition:** 0.9000 Gold .1944 oz. AGW **Subject:** 150th Anniersary of Bank

| Date | Mintage | F | VF | XF | Unc | BU |
|---|---|---|---|---|---|---|
| 1978 | 27,000 | — | — | — | 75.00 | — |
| 1978 Proof | 24,000 | Value: 80.00 | | | | |

**100 GULDEN** **KM# 46** **Weight:** 7.7700 g. **Composition:** 0.9990 Gold .2500 oz. AGW **Subject:** Yeggado Do Spanonan **Reverse:** 500 year-old sailing ship

| Date | Mintage | F | VF | XF | Unc | BU |
|---|---|---|---|---|---|---|
| 1999 Proof | — | Value: 175 | | | | |

**200 GULDEN** **KM# 16** **Weight:** 7.9500 g. **Composition:** 0.9000 Gold .2300 oz. AGW **Subject:** U.S. Bicentennial

| Date | Mintage | F | VF | XF | Unc | BU |
|---|---|---|---|---|---|---|
| 1976 FM(M) | 100 | — | — | — | 300 | — |
| 1976 FM(U) | 5,626 | — | — | — | 120 | — |
| 1976 FM(P) | 15,000 | Value: 100 | | | | |

**200 GULDEN** **KM# 18** **Weight:** 7.9500 g. **Composition:** 0.9000 Gold .2300 oz. AGW **Subject:** Peter Stuyvesant

| Date | Mintage | F | VF | XF | Unc | BU |
|---|---|---|---|---|---|---|
| 1977 FM(M) | 1,000 | — | — | — | 150 | — |
| 1977 FM(U) | 645 | — | — | — | 275 | — |
| 1977 FM(P) | 6,878 | Value: 125 | | | | |

**300 GULDEN** **KM# 29.1** **Weight:** 5.0400 g. **Composition:** 0.9000 Gold .1458 oz. AGW **Subject:** Abdication of Queen Juliana

| Date | Mintage | F | VF | XF | Unc | BU |
|---|---|---|---|---|---|---|
| 1980 (u) cock and star | — | — | — | — | 60.00 | — |
| 1980 (u) Proof, cock and star | 29,000 | Value: 65.00 | | | | |

**300 GULDEN** **KM# 29.2** **Weight:** 5.0400 g. **Composition:** 0.9000 Gold .1458 oz. AGW **Subject:** Abdication of Queen Juliana **Reverse:** Without mint mark

| Date | Mintage | F | VF | XF | Unc | BU |
|---|---|---|---|---|---|---|
| 1980 Proof | Inc. above | Value: 250 | | | | |

## PATTERNS

Including off metal strikes

| KM# | Date | Mintage | Identification | Mkt Val |
|---|---|---|---|---|
| Pn1 | 1969 | 200 | Cent. Nickel. (KM8). | 550 |
| Pn2 | 1969 | 200 | 2-1/2 Cents. Nickel. (KM9). | 550 |

| KM# | Date | Mintage | Identification | Mkt Val |
|---|---|---|---|---|
| Pn3 | 1969 | 200 | 5 Cents. Nickel. (KMA13). | 550 |
| Pn4 | 1969 | 200 | 10 Cents. Nickel. (KM10). | 550 |
| Pn5 | 1969 | 200 | 25 Cents. Nickel. (KM11). | 550 |
| Pn6 | 1969 | 200 | Gulden. Nickel. (KM12). | 550 |
| Pn7 | 1981 Y | — | 125 Gulden. Gilt Bronze. | 750 |
| Pn8 | 1981 Y | — | 125 Gulden. Gold. | 3,000 |
| Pn10 | 1981 Y | — | 250 Gulden. Gold. | 4,000 |

| KM# | Date | Mintage | Identification | Mkt Val |
|---|---|---|---|---|
| Pn9 | 1981 Y | — | 250 Gulden. Gilt Bronze. | 850 |
| Pn11 | 1981 Y | — | 500 Gulden. Gilt Bronze. | 950 |
| Pn12 | 1981 Y | — | 500 Gulden. Gold. | 5,000 |

## PIEFORT

| KM# | Date | Mintage | Identification | Mkt Val |
|---|---|---|---|---|
| P1 | 1979 | 7,162 | 25 Gulden. KM22. | 75.00 |

## MINT SETS

| KM# | Date | Mintage | Identification | Issue Price | Mkt Val |
|---|---|---|---|---|---|
| MS1 | 1971 (7) | — | KM8-13 and Curacao KM46 | — | 22.00 |
| MS2 | 1979 (7) | 12,000 | KM8a-9a, 10-13, 19 | — | 14.50 |
| MS3 | 1980 (7) | 18,000 | KM8a-9a, 10-13, 19 | — | 12.00 |
| MS4 | 1980 (2) | 23,000 | KM24-25 | — | 6.00 |
| MS5 | 1981 (7) | 23,000 | KM8a-9a, 10-12, 24, 25 | — | 12.00 |
| MS6 | 1982 (7) | 10,000 | KM8a-9a, 10-12, 24, 25 | — | 12.00 |
| MS7 | 1983 (6) | 25,000 | KM8a-9a, 10-12, 24 and medallion | 14.00 | 12.00 |
| MS8 | 1984 (7) | 26,000 | KM8a-9a, 10-12, 24, 25 | 14.50 | 12.00 |
| MS9 | 1985 (7) | 24,000 | KM8a-9a, 10-12, 24, 25 | — | 12.00 |
| MS10 | 1989 (7) | 15,000 | KM32-38 | — | 15.00 |
| MS11 | 1990 (7) | 10,000 | KM32-38 | 13.00 | 15.00 |
| MS12 | 1991 (7) | 12,500 | KM32-38 | 13.50 | 15.00 |
| MS13 | 1992 (7) | 10,500 | MS32-38 | — | 15.00 |
| MS14 | 1993 (7) | 8,560 | KM32-38 | — | 15.00 |
| MS15 | 1994 (7) | 9,000 | KM32-38 | 17.00 | 15.00 |
| MS16 | 1995 (7) | 9,000 | KM32-38 | 17.50 | 15.00 |
| MS17 | 1996 (7) | 7,500 | KM32-38 | 18.50 | 14.50 |
| MS18 | 1997 (7) | 7,000 | KM32-38 | — | 14.50 |
| MS19 | 1998 (8) | 7,000 | KM32-38, 43 | — | 14.50 |
| MS20 | 1999 (8) | — | KM32-38, 43 | — | 14.50 |
| MS21 | 2000 (8) | — | KM32-38, 43 | — | 14.50 |

## PROOF SETS

| KM# | Date | Mintage | Identification | Issue Price | Mkt Val |
|---|---|---|---|---|---|
| PS1 | 1952 (2) | 100 | KM1-2 | — | 180 |
| PS2 | 1954 (3) | 200 | KM1, 3-4 | — | 120 |
| PS3 | 1956 (3) | 500 | KM3-5 | — | 120 |
| PS4 | 1957 (4) | 250 | KM1, 3-4, 6 | — | 160 |
| PS5 | 1959 (3) | 250 | KM1, 3, 5 | — | 100 |
| PS6 | 1960 (3) | 300 | KM1, 3-4 | — | 110 |
| PS7 | 1962 (3) | 200 | KM3-4, 6 | — | 110 |
| PS8 | 1963 (5) | — | KM1-4, 6 | — | 235 |
| PS9 | 1964 (3) | — | KM1-2, 7 | — | 325 |
| PS10 | 1965 (4) | — | KM1, 4-6 | — | 125 |
| PS11 | 1967 (3) | — | KM1, 4, 6 | — | 100 |
| PS12 | 1969 (6) | 200 | KM8-12, A13, Pattern set | — | 650 |
| PS13 | 1970 (10) | — | KM1-4, 6, 8-12 | — | 350 |
| PS14 | 1971 (6) | — | KM8-13 | — | 165 |
| PS15 | 1973 (3) | — | KM8-9, 14 | — | 87.50 |
| PS16 | 1974 (4) | — | KM8-10, 13 | — | 85.00 |
| PS17 | 1975 (4) | — | KM8, 10-11, 13 | — | 240 |
| PS18 | 1976 (2) | 13,000 | KM15-16 | 187 | 325 |
| PS19 | 1979 (7) | — | KM8a-9a, 10-13, 19 | — | 120 |
| PS20 | 1999 (5) | — | KM45-47, with Aruba KM18-19 | — | 625 |

# NETHERLANDS EAST INDIES

Netherlands East Indies, (Kingdom of the Netherlands) is the world's largest archipelago extending for more than 3,000 mi. along the equator from the mainland of southeast Asia to Australia. At present time, since the late 1940's, it is known as Indonesia. The Dutch were in control until 1945 when Indonesia declared its independence from the Netherlands.

**RULERS**
Dutch, 1816-1942

## KINGDOM

### DECIMAL COINAGE

**1/2 CENT** **KM# 306** **Composition:** Copper

| Date | Mintage | F | VF | XF | Unc | BU |
|---|---|---|---|---|---|---|
| 1855(u) Proof | — | Value: 125 | | | | |
| 1856(u) | 10,800,000 | 12.50 | 20.00 | 35.00 | 60.00 | — |
| 1857(u) | 36,800,000 | 10.00 | 15.00 | 25.00 | 40.00 | — |
| 1858(u) | 53,588,000 | 3.50 | 6.00 | 12.50 | 25.00 | — |
| 1858(u) Proof | — | — | — | — | — | — |
| 1859(u) | 219,600,000 | 2.50 | 4.00 | 10.00 | 20.00 | — |
| 1860(u) | 107,124,000 | 2.50 | 4.00 | 10.00 | 20.00 | — |
| 1902(u) | 20,000,000 | 3.00 | 5.00 | 10.00 | 20.00 | — |
| 1902(u) Proof | — | Value: 13.00 | | | | |
| 1908(u) | 10,600,000 | 5.00 | 10.00 | 20.00 | 40.00 | — |
| 1908(u) Proof | — | Value: 50.00 | | | | |
| 1909(u) | 4,400,000 | 6.50 | 12.50 | 25.00 | 50.00 | — |

**1/2 CENT** **KM# 314.1** **Composition:** Bronze **Note:** Mintmasters mark: Sea horse

| Date | Mintage | F | VF | XF | Unc | BU |
|---|---|---|---|---|---|---|
| 1914(u) | 50,000,000 | 1.00 | 1.50 | 3.00 | 5.00 | — |
| 1916(u) | 10,000,000 | 1.60 | 3.25 | 6.50 | 13.50 | — |
| 1921(u) | 4,000,000 | 4.00 | 8.00 | 16.00 | 35.00 | — |
| 1932(u) | 10,000,000 | 1.60 | 3.25 | 6.50 | 13.50 | — |
| 1933(u) | 15,000,000 | 1.60 | 3.25 | 6.50 | 13.50 | — |

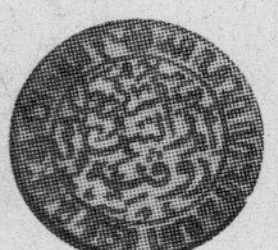

**1/2 CENT** **KM# 314.2** **Composition:** Bronze **Note:** Mintmasters mark: Grapes

| Date | Mintage | F | VF | XF | Unc | BU |
|---|---|---|---|---|---|---|
| 1933(u) | 5,000,000 | 18.00 | 35.00 | 70.00 | 120 | — |
| 1934(u) | 30,000,000 | 0.75 | 1.50 | 2.50 | 5.00 | — |
| 1935(u) | 14,000,000 | 1.50 | 2.50 | 5.00 | 9.00 | — |
| 1936(u) | 12,000,000 | 1.50 | 2.50 | 5.00 | 9.00 | — |
| 1936(u) Proof | — | Value: 35.00 | | | | |
| 1937(u) | 8,400,000 | 1.50 | 2.50 | 5.00 | 9.00 | — |
| 1937(u) Proof | — | Value: 35.00 | | | | |
| 1938(u) | 3,600,000 | 5.00 | 10.00 | 20.00 | 30.00 | — |
| 1939(u) | 2,000,000 | 6.00 | 12.00 | 25.00 | 45.00 | — |
| 1945P | 400,000,000 | 0.15 | 0.30 | 0.65 | 1.25 | — |

**CENT** **KM# 307.2** **Composition:** Copper **Obverse:** Legend begins and ends beside date

| Date | Mintage | F | VF | XF | Unc | BU |
|---|---|---|---|---|---|---|
| 1856(u) | Inc. above | 3.50 | 6.00 | 10.00 | 17.50 | — |
| 1856(u) Proof | — | Value: 50.00 | | | | |
| 1857(u) | 162,000,000 | 2.00 | 4.00 | 10.00 | 15.00 | — |
| 1858(u) | 119,431,000 | 2.00 | 4.00 | 10.00 | 15.00 | — |
| 1859(u) | 40,800,000 | 3.50 | 6.00 | 10.00 | 17.50 | — |
| 1860(u) | 14,455,000 | 4.00 | 8.00 | 15.00 | 30.00 | — |
| 1896(u) | 60,400,000 | 3.50 | 6.00 | 10.00 | 17.50 | — |
| 1896(u) Proof | — | Value: 65.00 | | | | |
| 1897(u) | 69,600,000 | 5.00 | 10.00 | 20.00 | 35.00 | — |
| 1897(u) Proof | — | Value: 100 | | | | |
| 1898(u) | 36,600,000 | 3.50 | 6.00 | 10.00 | 17.50 | — |
| 1899(u) | 18,400,000 | 6.00 | 12.50 | 25.00 | 60.00 | — |
| 1899(u) Proof | — | Value: 65.00 | | | | |
| 1901(u) | 15,000,000 | 5.00 | 10.00 | 20.00 | 35.00 | — |
| 1901(u) Proof | — | Value: 55.00 | | | | |
| 1902(u) | 10,000,000 | 5.00 | 10.00 | 20.00 | 35.00 | — |
| 1907(u) | 7,500,000 | 5.00 | 10.00 | 20.00 | 35.00 | — |
| 1907(u) Proof | — | Value: 100 | | | | |
| 1908(u) | 12,500,000 | 5.00 | 10.00 | 20.00 | 35.00 | — |
| 1908(u) Proof | — | Value: 55.00 | | | | |
| 1909(u) | 7,500,000 | 5.00 | 10.00 | 20.00 | 35.00 | — |
| 1912(u) | 25,000,000 | 2.00 | 4.25 | 8.75 | 17.50 | — |

**CENT** **KM# 315** **Composition:** Bronze

| Date | Mintage | F | VF | XF | Unc | BU |
|---|---|---|---|---|---|---|
| 1914(u) | 85,000,000 | 1.00 | 2.00 | 4.00 | 8.00 | — |
| 1914(u) Proof | — | Value: 30.00 | | | | |
| 1916(u) | 16,440,000 | 3.00 | 6.00 | 12.50 | 25.00 | — |
| 1919(u) | 20,000,000 | 3.00 | 6.00 | 12.50 | 25.00 | — |
| 1919(u) Proof | — | Value: 60.00 | | | | |
| 1920(u) | 120,000,000 | 1.00 | 2.00 | 4.00 | 8.00 | — |
| 1926(u) | 10,000,000 | 3.00 | 6.00 | 12.50 | 25.00 | — |
| 1929(u) | 50,000,000 | 1.00 | 2.00 | 4.00 | 8.00 | — |
| 1929(u) Proof | — | Value: 100 | | | | |

**CENT** **KM# 317** **Composition:** Bronze

| Date | Mintage | F | VF | XF | Unc | BU |
|---|---|---|---|---|---|---|
| 1936(u) | 52,000,000 | 0.50 | 1.00 | 2.00 | 4.00 | — |
| 1937(u) | 120,400,000 | 0.45 | 0.85 | 1.75 | 3.50 | — |
| 1937(u) Proof | — | Value: 40.00 | | | | |
| 1938(u) | 150,000,000 | 0.40 | 0.75 | 1.50 | 3.00 | — |
| 1939(u) | 81,400,000 | 0.45 | 0.75 | 1.75 | 3.50 | — |
| 1942P | 100,000,000 | 0.10 | 0.25 | 0.50 | 1.00 | — |
| 1945P | 335,000,000 | 0.10 | 0.25 | 0.50 | 1.00 | — |
| 1945D | 133,800,000 | 0.10 | 0.25 | 0.50 | 1.00 | — |
| 1945S | 102,568,000 | 0.10 | 0.25 | 0.50 | 1.00 | — |

**2-1/2 CENTS** **KM# 308** **Composition:** Copper

| Date | Mintage | F | VF | XF | Unc | BU |
|---|---|---|---|---|---|---|
| 1856 | 2,480,000 | 30.00 | 50.00 | 85.00 | 145 | — |
| 1856 Proof | — | Value: 135 | | | | |
| 1857 | 36,560,000 | 10.00 | 15.00 | 25.00 | 45.00 | — |
| 1857 Proof | — | Value: 135 | | | | |
| 1858 | 40,990,000 | 8.00 | 12.50 | 20.00 | 40.00 | — |
| 1896 | 1,120,000 | 25.00 | 40.00 | 65.00 | 120 | — |
| 1897 | 18,105,000 | 5.00 | 10.00 | 17.50 | 35.00 | — |
| 1898 | 7,600,000 | 8.00 | 12.50 | 20.00 | 40.00 | — |
| 1899 | 10,400,000 | 5.00 | 10.00 | 17.50 | 35.00 | — |
| 1902 | 6,000,000 | 5.00 | 10.00 | 20.00 | 40.00 | — |
| 1907 | 3,000,000 | 8.00 | 16.00 | 30.00 | 60.00 | — |
| 1908 | 5,940,000 | 5.00 | 10.00 | 20.00 | 40.00 | — |
| 1908 Proof | — | Value: 135 | | | | |
| 1909 | 3,060,000 | 8.00 | 12.50 | 25.00 | 50.00 | — |
| 1913 | 4,000,000 | 8.00 | 12.50 | 25.00 | 50.00 | — |
| 1913 Proof | — | Value: 135 | | | | |

**2-1/2 CENTS** **KM# 316** **Composition:** Bronze

| Date | Mintage | F | VF | XF | Unc | BU |
|---|---|---|---|---|---|---|
| 1914(u) | 22,000,000 | 2.50 | 5.00 | 10.00 | 20.00 | — |
| 1914(u) | — | Value: 165 | | | | |
| 1915(u) | 6,000,000 | 3.75 | 7.50 | 15.00 | 30.00 | — |
| 1920(u) | 48,000,000 | 2.00 | 4.00 | 7.50 | 15.00 | — |
| 1920(u) | — | Value: 165 | | | | |
| 1945P | 200,000,000 | 0.35 | 0.75 | 1.50 | 2.50 | — |

**5 CENTS** **KM# 313** **Composition:** Copper-Nickel

| Date | Mintage | F | VF | XF | Unc | BU |
|---|---|---|---|---|---|---|
| 1913(u) | 60,000,000 | 0.75 | 1.75 | 3.50 | 7.00 | — |
| 1913(u) Proof | — | Value: 90.00 | | | | |
| 1921(u) | 40,000,000 | 0.75 | 1.25 | 2.50 | 5.00 | — |
| 1921(u) Proof | — | Value: 220 | | | | |
| 1922(u) | 20,000,000 | 1.00 | 2.00 | 4.00 | 8.00 | — |

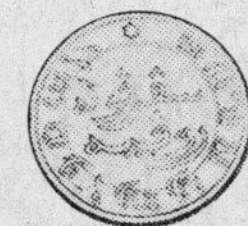

**1/10 GULDEN** **KM# 304** **Weight:** 1.2500 g. **Composition:** 0.7200 Silver .0289 oz. ASW

| Date | Mintage | F | VF | XF | Unc | BU |
|---|---|---|---|---|---|---|
| 1854(u) | 3,550,000 | 2.00 | 4.00 | 7.50 | 15.00 | — |
| 1854(u) Proof | — | Value: 75.00 | | | | |
| 1855(u) | 6,452,000 | 2.00 | 4.00 | 7.50 | 15.00 | — |
| 1855(u) Proof | — | — | — | — | — | — |

| Date | Mintage | F | VF | XF | Unc | BU |
|---|---|---|---|---|---|---|
| 1856(u) | 3,000,000 | 2.50 | 5.00 | 10.00 | 20.00 | — |
| 1857(u) | 11,000,000 | 1.50 | 3.00 | 6.00 | 10.00 | — |
| 1857(u) Proof | — | Value: 50.00 | | | | |
| 1858(u) | 14,000,000 | 1.50 | 3.00 | 6.00 | 10.00 | — |
| 1882(u) | 7,500,000 | 2.00 | 4.00 | 7.50 | 15.00 | — |
| 1884(u) | 3,550,000 | 2.00 | 4.00 | 7.50 | 15.00 | — |
| 1884(u) Proof | — | Value: 100 | | | | |
| 1885(u) | 825,000 | 10.00 | 20.00 | 40.00 | 75.00 | — |
| 1891(u) | 5,000,000 | 2.00 | 4.00 | 7.50 | 15.00 | — |
| 1891(u) Proof | — | Value: 85.00 | | | | |
| 1893(u) | 5,000,000 | 2.00 | 4.00 | 7.50 | 15.00 | — |
| 1893(u) Proof | — | Value: 85.00 | | | | |
| 1896(u) | 3,075,000 | 2.00 | 4.00 | 7.50 | 15.00 | — |
| 1896(u) Proof | — | Value: 100 | | | | |
| 1898(u) | 2,500,000 | 4.00 | 8.00 | 15.00 | 25.00 | — |
| 1898(u) Proof | — | Value: 120 | | | | |
| 1900(u) | 6,850,000 | 2.00 | 4.00 | 7.50 | 15.00 | — |
| 1901(u) | 5,000,000 | 2.00 | 4.00 | 7.50 | 15.00 | — |
| 1901(u) Proof | — | Value: 120 | | | | |

**1/10 GULDEN** **KM# 309** **Weight:** 1.2500 g. **Composition:** 0.7200 Silver .0289 oz. ASW

| Date | Mintage | F | VF | XF | Unc | BU |
|---|---|---|---|---|---|---|
| 1903(u) | 5,000,000 | 2.00 | 4.00 | 8.00 | 16.50 | — |
| 1903(u) Proof | — | Value: 110 | | | | |
| 1904(u) | 5,000,000 | 2.00 | 4.00 | 8.00 | 16.50 | — |
| 1905(u) | 5,000,000 | 2.00 | 4.00 | 8.00 | 16.50 | — |
| 1906(u) | 7,500,000 | 1.00 | 2.25 | 4.50 | 9.00 | — |
| 1907(u) | 14,000,000 | 1.00 | 2.25 | 4.50 | 9.00 | — |
| 1907(u) Proof | — | Value: 55.00 | | | | |
| 1908(u) | 3,000,000 | 2.00 | 4.00 | 8.00 | 16.50 | — |
| 1909(u) | 10,000,000 | 0.75 | 1.50 | 3.00 | 6.00 | — |
| 1909(u) Proof | — | Value: 110 | | | | |

**1/10 GULDEN** **KM# 311** **Weight:** 1.2500 g. **Composition:** 0.7200 Silver .0289 oz. ASW **Obverse:** Wide rims and small legend **Reverse:** Wide rims and small legend

| Date | Mintage | F | VF | XF | Unc | BU |
|---|---|---|---|---|---|---|
| 1910(u) | 15,000,000 | 0.75 | 1.50 | 3.00 | 6.00 | — |
| 1910(u) Proof | — | Value: 140 | | | | |
| 1911(u) | 10,000,000 | 0.75 | 1.50 | 3.00 | 6.00 | — |
| 1912(u) | 25,000,000 | 0.50 | 1.00 | 2.00 | 4.50 | — |
| 1913(u) | 15,000,000 | 0.75 | 1.50 | 3.00 | 6.00 | — |
| 1914(u) | 25,000,000 | 0.50 | 1.00 | 2.00 | 4.50 | — |
| 1915(u) | 15,000,000 | 0.75 | 1.50 | 3.00 | 6.00 | — |
| 1918(u) | 30,000,000 | 0.75 | 1.50 | 3.00 | 6.00 | — |
| 1919(u) | 20,000,000 | 0.75 | 1.50 | 3.00 | 6.00 | — |
| 1920(u) | 8,500,000 | 0.50 | 1.00 | 2.00 | 4.50 | — |
| 1928(u) | 30,000,000 | 0.50 | 1.00 | 2.00 | 4.50 | — |
| 1930(u) | 15,000,000 | 0.50 | 1.00 | 2.00 | 4.50 | — |

**1/10 GULDEN** **KM# 318** **Weight:** 1.2500 g. **Composition:** 0.7200 Silver .0289 oz. ASW **Obverse:** Narrow rims and large legend **Reverse:** Narrow rims and large legend

| Date | Mintage | F | VF | XF | Unc | BU |
|---|---|---|---|---|---|---|
| 1937(u) | 20,000,000 | 0.35 | 0.75 | 1.50 | 3.00 | — |
| 1937(u) Proof | — | Value: 130 | | | | |
| 1938(u) | 30,000,000 | 0.35 | 0.75 | 1.50 | 3.00 | — |
| 1939(u) | 5,400,000 | 0.75 | 1.50 | 3.00 | 6.00 | — |
| 1939(u) Proof | — | Value: 130 | | | | |
| 1940(u) | 10,000,000 | 0.40 | 0.85 | 1.75 | 3.50 | — |
| 1941P | 41,850,000 | 0.15 | 0.35 | 0.80 | 1.25 | — |
| 1941S | 58,150,000 | 0.15 | 0.35 | 0.80 | 1.25 | — |
| 1942S | 75,000,000 | 0.10 | 0.25 | 0.50 | 1.00 | — |
| 1945P | 100,720,000 | 0.10 | 0.25 | 0.50 | 1.00 | — |
| 1945S | 19,280,000 | 0.25 | 0.40 | 0.75 | 1.50 | — |

**1/4 GULDEN** **KM# 305** **Weight:** 3.1800 g. **Composition:** 0.7200 Silver .0736 oz. ASW

| Date | Mintage | F | VF | XF | Unc | BU |
|---|---|---|---|---|---|---|
| 1854(u) | 11,460,000 | 8.00 | 12.50 | 22.50 | 37.50 | — |
| 1854(u) Proof | — | Value: 85.00 | | | | |
| 1855(u) | 4,541,000 | 5.50 | 9.00 | 15.00 | 25.00 | — |
| 1855(u) Proof | — | Value: 85.00 | | | | |
| 1857(u) | 2,400,000 | 9.00 | 15.00 | 25.00 | 40.00 | — |
| 1858(u) | 4,800,000 | 5.50 | 9.00 | 15.00 | 25.00 | — |
| 1858(u) Proof | — | Value: 80.00 | | | | |
| 1882(u) | 2,200,000 | 10.00 | 20.00 | 37.50 | 55.00 | — |
| 1883(u) | 800,000 | 25.00 | 40.00 | 65.00 | 110 | — |
| 1883(u) Proof | — | Value: 175 | | | | |
| 1885(u) | 1,750,000 | 12.50 | 22.50 | 45.00 | 80.00 | — |
| 1890(u) | 1,140,000 | 12.50 | 22.50 | 45.00 | 80.00 | — |
| 1891(u) | 860,000 | 30.00 | 60.00 | 120 | 200 | — |
| 1893(u) | 2,000,000 | 10.00 | 20.00 | 37.50 | 55.00 | — |
| 1893(u) Proof | — | Value: 175 | | | | |
| 1896(u) | 1,230,000 | 11.50 | 21.50 | 40.00 | 65.00 | — |
| 1898(u) | 3,000,000 | 10.00 | 20.00 | 37.50 | 55.00 | — |
| 1898(u) Proof | — | Value: 120 | | | | |
| 1900(u) | 2,800,000 | 10.00 | 20.00 | 37.50 | 55.00 | — |
| 1901(u) | 2,000,000 | 10.00 | 20.00 | 37.50 | 55.00 | — |
| 1901(u) Proof | — | Value: 100 | | | | |

**1/4 GULDEN** **KM# 310** **Weight:** 3.1800 g. **Composition:** 0.7200 Silver .0736 oz. ASW

| Date | Mintage | F | VF | XF | Unc | BU |
|---|---|---|---|---|---|---|
| 1903(u) | 2,000,000 | 3.00 | 6.00 | 12.50 | 25.00 | — |
| 1903(u) Proof | — | Value: 100 | | | | |
| 1904(u) | 2,000,000 | 3.00 | 6.00 | 12.50 | 25.00 | — |
| 1904(u) Proof | — | Value: 100 | | | | |
| 1905(u) | 2,000,000 | 3.00 | 6.00 | 12.50 | 25.00 | — |
| 1905(u) Proof | — | Value: 170 | | | | |
| 1906(u) | 4,000,000 | 2.50 | 5.00 | 10.00 | 20.00 | — |
| 1907(u) | 4,400,000 | 2.50 | 5.00 | 10.00 | 20.00 | — |
| 1907(u) Proof | — | Value: 100 | | | | |
| 1908(u) | 2,000,000 | 3.00 | 6.00 | 12.50 | 25.00 | — |
| 1909(u) | 4,000,000 | 2.50 | 5.00 | 10.00 | 20.00 | — |
| 1909(u) Proof | — | Value: 80.00 | | | | |

**1/4 GULDEN** **KM# 312** **Weight:** 3.1800 g. **Composition:** 0.7200 Silver .0736 oz. ASW **Obverse:** Wide rims and small legend **Reverse:** Wide rims and small legend

| Date | Mintage | F | VF | XF | Unc | BU |
|---|---|---|---|---|---|---|
| 1910(u) | 6,000,000 | 3.75 | 7.50 | 15.00 | 30.00 | — |
| 1911(u) | 4,000,000 | 3.75 | 7.50 | 15.00 | 30.00 | — |
| 1911(u) Proof | — | Value: 80.00 | | | | |
| 1912(u) | 10,000,000 | 2.50 | 5.00 | 10.00 | 20.00 | — |
| 1913(u) | 6,000,000 | 2.50 | 5.00 | 10.00 | 20.00 | — |
| 1914(u) | 10,000,000 | 2.50 | 5.00 | 10.00 | 20.00 | — |
| 1915(u) | 6,000,000 | 2.50 | 5.00 | 10.00 | 20.00 | — |
| 1917(u) | 12,000,000 | 1.25 | 2.50 | 5.00 | 10.00 | — |
| 1919(u) | 6,000,000 | 2.50 | 5.00 | 10.00 | 20.00 | — |
| 1920(u) | 20,000,000 | 0.75 | 1.50 | 3.00 | 6.00 | — |
| 1921(u) | 24,000,000 | 0.75 | 1.50 | 3.00 | 6.00 | — |
| 1929(u) | 5,000,000 | 1.25 | 2.50 | 5.00 | 10.00 | — |
| 1930(u) | 7,000,000 | 1.25 | 2.50 | 5.00 | 10.00 | — |
| 1930(u) Proof | — | Value: 160 | | | | |

**1/4 GULDEN** **KM# 319** **Weight:** 3.1800 g. **Composition:** 0.7200 Silver .0736 oz. ASW **Obverse:** Narrow rims and large legend **Reverse:** Narrow rims and large legend

| Date | Mintage | F | VF | XF | Unc | BU |
|---|---|---|---|---|---|---|
| 1937(u) | 8,000,000 | 1.00 | 2.00 | 3.50 | 6.00 | — |
| 1938(u) | 12,000,000 | 1.00 | 2.00 | 3.50 | 6.00 | — |
| 1939(u) | 10,400,000 | 0.75 | 1.75 | 3.25 | 5.00 | — |
| 1939 Proof | — | Value: 65.00 | | | | |
| 1941P | 34,947,000 | 0.20 | 0.40 | 0.75 | 1.50 | — |
| 1941S | 5,053,000 | 0.50 | 1.00 | 2.00 | 4.00 | — |
| 1942S | 32,000,000 | 0.25 | 0.50 | 1.00 | 2.25 | — |
| 1945S | 56,000,000 | 0.25 | 0.50 | 1.00 | 2.25 | — |

**WORLD WAR II COINAGE**

Netherlands and Netherlands East Indies coins of the 1941-45 period were struck at U.S. Mints (P-Philadelphia, D-Denver, S-San Francisco) and bear the mint mark and a palm tree (acorn on Homeland issues) flanking the date. The following issues, KM#330 and KM#331, are of the usual Netherlands type, being distinguished from similar 1944-45 issues produced in the name of the Homeland by the presence of the palm tree, but were produced for release in the colony. See other related issues under Curacao and Suriname.

## TRADE COINAGE

These gold coins, intended primarily for circulation in the Netherlands East Indies, will be found listed as KM#83.1 in the Netherlands section.

**DUCAT** **KM# T1** **Composition:** 0.9860 Gold

| Date | Mintage | VG | F | VF | XF | Unc |
|---|---|---|---|---|---|---|
| (1901-37) | — | — | — | — | — | — |

## HOMELAND COINAGE

**GULDEN** **KM# 330** **Weight:** 10.0000 g. **Composition:** 0.7200 Silver .2315 oz. ASW

| Date | Mintage | F | VF | XF | Unc | BU |
|---|---|---|---|---|---|---|
| 1943D | 20,000,000 | 2.00 | 3.50 | 6.50 | 12.50 | — |

**2-1/2 GULDEN** **KM# 331** **Weight:** 25.0000 g. **Composition:** 0.7200 Silver .5787 oz. ASW

| Date | Mintage | F | VF | XF | Unc | BU |
|---|---|---|---|---|---|---|
| 1943D | 2,000,000 | 6.00 | 9.00 | 13.50 | 18.50 | — |

## OCCUPATION COINAGE

Japan

These coins were struck primarily for circulation in the East Indies. The Sen, 5 Sen and 10 Sen are inscribed DAI NIPON (Great Japan) and are found listed under Japan - Occupation issues as Y#22, Y#24 and Pn48.

**10 SEN** **KM# J1** **Composition:** Tin Alloy

| Date | Mintage | VG | F | VF | XF | Unc |
|---|---|---|---|---|---|---|
| ND(1943-45) | — | — | — | — | — | — |

## PATTERNS

| KM# | Date | Mintage | Identification | Mkt Val |
|---|---|---|---|---|
| Pn11 | ND1902(u) | — | 1/2 Cent. Silver. KM#306 | — |
| Pn12 | ND1902(u) | — | 1/2 Cent. Gold. KM#306 | — |
| Pn13 | ND1902(u) | — | Cent. Silver. KM#307 | — |
| Pn14 | ND1902(u) | — | Cent. Gold. KM#307 | — |
| Pn15 | ND1902(u) | — | 2-1/2 Cents. Silver. 13.5000 g. KM#308 | — |
| Pn16 | ND1902(u) | — | 2-1/2 Cents. Gold. KM#308 | — |
| Pn18 | ND1903(u) | — | 1/4 Gulden. Gold. KM#310 | — |
| Pn19 | ND1908 | — | 1/2 Cent. Silver. | — |
| Pn20 | ND1908 | — | 1/2 Cent. Gold. | — |
| Pn21 | ND1908 | — | Cent. Iron. | — |
| Pn22 | ND1908 | — | Cent. Silver. | — |
| Pn23 | ND1908 | — | Cent. Gold. | — |
| Pn24 | ND1908 | — | 2-1/2 Cents. Silver. KM#308 | — |
| Pn25 | ND1908 | — | 2-1/2 Cents. Gold. 22.1220 g. KM#308 | — |
| Pn17 | ND1908(u) | — | 1/10 Gulden. Gold. KM#309 | — |
| Pn27 | ND1914 | — | 10 Sen. Tin. | — |
| Pn28 | ND1914 | 5 | 5 Cents. Tin. | — |
| Pn29 | ND1914 | — | 5 Cents. Gold. | — |
| PnA30 | ND1934 | — | 1/4 Cent. Copper. | — |
| Pn30 | ND1934 | — | 1/4 Cent. Copper. Holed | — |
| Pn31 | ND1934 | — | 1/2 Cent. Copper. KM#314 | — |
| Pn32 | ND1934 | — | 1/4 Cent. Copper. KM#320 | — |
| Pn26 | ND1934(u) | — | 5 Cents. Copper-Nickel. KM#313 | — |
| Pn33 | ND1945 | — | 1/4 Gulden. Gold. KM#319 | 50.00 |

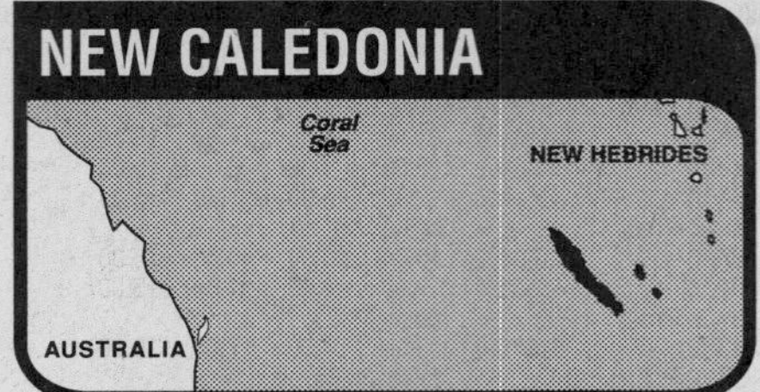


The French Overseas Territory of New Caledonia, are a group of about 25 islands in the South Pacific. It is situated about 750 miles (1,207 km.) east of Australia. The territory, which includes the dependencies of Ile des Pins, Loyalty Islands, Ile Huon, Isles Belep, Isles Chesterfield, and Ile Walpole, has a total land area of 7,358 sq. mi.(19,060 sq. km.) and a population of *156,000. Capital: Noumea. The islands are rich in minerals; New Caledonia has the world's largest known deposit of nickel. Nickel, nickel castings, coffee and copra are exported.

The first European to sight New Caledonia was the British navigator Capt. James Cook in 1774. The French took possession in 1853, and established a penal colony on the island in 1854. The European population of the colony remained disproportionately convict until 1894.New Caledonia became an overseas territory within the French Community in 1946, and in 1958 and 1972 chose to remain affiliated with France.

**MINT MARKS**

Paris, privy marks only

**MONETARY SYSTEM**

100 Centimes = 1 Franc

## FRENCH OVERSEAS TERRITORY

## DECIMAL COINAGE

**50 CENTIMES** **KM# 1** **Composition:** Aluminum **Reverse:** Kagu bird

| Date | Mintage | F | VF | XF | Unc | BU |
|---|---|---|---|---|---|---|
| 1949(a) | 1,000,000 | — | 0.50 | 1.00 | 3.50 | — |

**FRANC** **KM# 2** **Composition:** Aluminum **Reverse:** Kagu bird

| Date | Mintage | F | VF | XF | Unc | BU |
|---|---|---|---|---|---|---|
| 1949(a) | 4,000,000 | — | 0.25 | 0.75 | 3.00 | — |

**FRANC** **KM# 8** **Composition:** Aluminum **Reverse:** Kagu bird

| Date | Mintage | F | VF | XF | Unc | BU |
|---|---|---|---|---|---|---|
| 1971(a) | 1,000,000 | — | 0.25 | 0.75 | 2.00 | — |

**FRANC** **KM# 10** **Composition:** Aluminum **Obverse:** Legend added **Obv. Legend:** I. E. O. M. **Reverse:** Kagu bird

| Date | Mintage | F | VF | XF | Unc | BU |
|---|---|---|---|---|---|---|
| 1972(a) | 600,000 | — | 0.25 | 0.75 | 2.50 | — |
| 1973(a) | 1,000,000 | — | 0.15 | 0.25 | 1.00 | — |
| 1977(a) | 1,500,000 | — | 0.15 | 0.25 | 1.00 | — |
| 1979(a) | — | — | 0.10 | 0.20 | 0.65 | — |
| 1981(a) | 1,000,000 | — | 0.10 | 0.20 | 0.65 | — |
| 1982(a) | 1,000,000 | — | 0.10 | 0.20 | 0.65 | — |
| 1983(a) | 2,000,000 | — | 0.10 | 0.20 | 0.65 | — |
| 1984(a) | — | — | 0.10 | 0.20 | 0.65 | — |
| 1985(a) | 2,000,000 | — | 0.10 | 0.20 | 0.65 | — |
| 1988(a) | 2,000,000 | — | 0.10 | 0.20 | 0.65 | — |
| 1989(a) | 1,000,000 | — | 0.10 | 0.20 | 0.65 | — |
| 1990(a) | — | — | 0.10 | 0.20 | 0.65 | — |
| 1991(a) | — | — | 0.10 | 0.20 | 0.65 | — |
| 1994(a) | — | — | 0.10 | 0.20 | 0.65 | — |

**2 FRANCS** **KM# 3** **Composition:** Aluminum **Reverse:** Kagu bird

| Date | Mintage | F | VF | XF | Unc | BU |
|---|---|---|---|---|---|---|
| 1949(a) | 3,000,000 | — | 0.50 | 1.75 | 5.00 | — |

**2 FRANCS** **KM# 9** **Composition:** Aluminum **Reverse:** Kagu bird

| Date | Mintage | F | VF | XF | Unc | BU |
|---|---|---|---|---|---|---|
| 1971(a) | 1,000,000 | — | 0.35 | 1.25 | 3.00 | — |

**2 FRANCS** **KM# 14** **Composition:** Aluminum **Obverse:** Legend added **Obv. Legend:** I. E. O. M. **Reverse:** Kagu bird

| Date | Mintage | F | VF | XF | Unc | BU |
|---|---|---|---|---|---|---|
| 1973(a) | 400,000 | — | 0.20 | 0.75 | 2.50 | — |
| 1977(a) | 1,500,000 | — | 0.20 | 0.50 | 1.50 | — |
| 1979(a) | — | — | 0.20 | 0.40 | 0.75 | — |
| 1982(a) | 1,000,000 | — | 0.20 | 0.35 | 0.75 | — |
| 1983(a) | 2,000,000 | — | 0.20 | 0.35 | 0.75 | — |
| 1987(a) | 2,000,000 | — | 0.20 | 0.35 | 0.75 | — |
| 1989(a) | 1,200,000 | — | 0.20 | 0.35 | 0.75 | — |
| 1990(a) | — | — | 0.20 | 0.35 | 0.75 | — |
| 1991(a) | — | — | 0.20 | 0.35 | 0.75 | — |
| 1995(a) | — | — | 0.20 | 0.35 | 0.75 | — |
| 1996(a) | — | — | 0.20 | 0.35 | 0.75 | — |

**5 FRANCS** **KM# 4** **Composition:** Aluminum **Reverse:** Kagu bird

| Date | Mintage | F | VF | XF | Unc | BU |
|---|---|---|---|---|---|---|
| 1952(a) | 4,000,000 | — | 0.50 | 1.50 | 4.00 | — |

**5 FRANCS** **KM# 16** **Composition:** Aluminum **Obverse:** Legend added **Obv. Legend:** I. E. O. M. **Reverse:** Kagu bird

| Date | Mintage | F | VF | XF | Unc | BU |
|---|---|---|---|---|---|---|
| 1983(a) | 500,000 | — | 0.50 | 1.00 | 3.00 | — |
| 1986(a) | 1,000,000 | — | 0.50 | 1.00 | 3.00 | — |
| 1989(a) | 500,000 | — | 0.50 | 1.00 | 3.00 | — |
| 1990(a) | — | — | 0.50 | 1.00 | 3.00 | — |
| 1991(a) | — | — | 0.50 | 1.00 | 3.00 | — |
| 1992(a) | — | — | 0.50 | 1.00 | 3.00 | — |
| 1994(a) | — | — | 0.50 | 1.00 | 3.00 | — |

**10 FRANCS** KM# 5 **Composition:** Nickel

| Date | Mintage | F | VF | XF | Unc | BU |
|---|---|---|---|---|---|---|
| 1967(a) | 400,000 | — | 1.00 | 2.00 | 4.50 | — |
| 1970(a) | 1,000,000 | — | 0.50 | 0.75 | 2.50 | — |

**10 FRANCS** KM# 11 **Composition:** Nickel **Obverse:** Legend added **Obv. Legend:** I. E. O. M.

| Date | Mintage | F | VF | XF | Unc | BU |
|---|---|---|---|---|---|---|
| 1972(a) | 600,000 | — | 0.50 | 0.75 | 2.00 | — |
| 1973(a) | 400,000 | — | 0.50 | 0.75 | 2.00 | — |
| 1977(a) | 1,000,000 | — | 0.50 | 0.75 | 1.00 | — |
| 1979(a) | — | — | 0.35 | 0.50 | 1.00 | — |
| 1983(a) | 800,000 | — | 0.35 | 0.50 | 1.00 | — |
| 1986(a) | 1,000,000 | — | 0.35 | 0.50 | 1.00 | — |
| 1989(a) | 500,000 | — | 0.35 | 0.50 | 1.00 | — |
| 1990(a) | — | — | 0.35 | 0.50 | 1.00 | — |
| 1991(a) | — | — | 0.35 | 0.50 | 1.00 | — |
| 1995(a) | — | — | 0.35 | 0.50 | 1.00 | — |

**20 FRANCS** KM# 6 **Composition:** Nickel

| Date | Mintage | F | VF | XF | Unc | BU |
|---|---|---|---|---|---|---|
| 1967(a) | 300,000 | — | 1.25 | 2.50 | 5.00 | — |
| 1970(a) | 1,200,000 | — | 0.60 | 1.00 | 2.00 | — |

**20 FRANCS** KM# 12 **Composition:** Nickel **Obverse:** Legend added **Obv. Legend:** I. O. E. M.

| Date | Mintage | F | VF | XF | Unc | BU |
|---|---|---|---|---|---|---|
| 1972(a) | 700,000 | — | 0.75 | 1.00 | 2.00 | — |
| 1977(a) | 350,000 | — | 0.75 | 1.00 | 3.00 | — |
| 1979(a) | — | — | 0.50 | 0.85 | 1.50 | — |
| 1983(a) | 600,000 | — | 0.50 | 0.85 | 1.50 | — |
| 1986(a) | 800,000 | — | 0.50 | 0.85 | 1.50 | — |
| 1990(a) | — | — | 0.50 | 0.85 | 1.50 | — |
| 1991(a) | — | — | 0.50 | 0.85 | 1.50 | — |
| 1992(a) | — | — | 0.50 | 0.85 | 1.50 | — |

**50 FRANCS** KM# 7 **Composition:** Nickel

| Date | Mintage | F | VF | XF | Unc | BU |
|---|---|---|---|---|---|---|
| 1967(a) | 700,000 | — | 1.50 | 3.00 | 7.00 | — |

**50 FRANCS** KM# 13 **Composition:** Nickel **Obverse:** Legend added **Obv. Legend:** I. E. O. M.

| Date | Mintage | F | VF | XF | Unc | BU |
|---|---|---|---|---|---|---|
| 1972(a) | 300,000 | — | 1.50 | 2.00 | 5.00 | — |
| 1979(a) | — | — | 1.50 | 2.00 | 5.00 | — |
| 1983(a) | 300,000 | — | 1.50 | 2.00 | 5.00 | — |
| 1987(a) | 300,000 | — | 1.50 | 2.00 | 5.00 | — |
| 1991(a) | — | — | 1.50 | 2.00 | 5.00 | — |
| 1992(a) | — | — | 1.50 | 2.00 | 5.00 | — |

**100 FRANCS** KM# 15 **Composition:** Nickel-Bronze

| Date | Mintage | F | VF | XF | Unc | BU |
|---|---|---|---|---|---|---|
| 1976(a) | 2,000,000 | — | 1.50 | 2.50 | 6.00 | — |
| 1979(a) | — | — | 1.50 | 2.50 | 6.00 | — |
| 1984(a) | 600,000 | — | 1.50 | 2.50 | 6.00 | — |
| 1987(a) | 800,000 | — | 1.50 | 2.50 | 6.00 | — |
| 1988(a) | — | — | 1.50 | 2.50 | 6.00 | — |
| 1991(a) | — | — | 1.50 | 2.50 | 6.00 | — |
| 1994 | — | — | 1.50 | 2.50 | 6.00 | — |
| 1995(a) | — | — | 1.50 | 2.50 | 6.00 | — |
| 1997 | — | — | 1.50 | 2.50 | 6.00 | — |

## ESSAIS

| KM# | Date | Mintage | Identification | Issue Price | Mkt Val |
|---|---|---|---|---|---|
| E1 | 1948(a) | 1,100 | 50 Centimes. Nickel-Bronze. Incuse design, flat rim | — | 15.00 |
| E3 | 1948(a) | 1,100 | Franc. Nickel-Bronze. Incuse design, flat rim. | — | 17.50 |
| E5 | 1948(a) | 1,100 | 2 Francs. Nickel-Bronze. Incuse design, flat rim. | — | 20.00 |
| E5a | 1948(a) | — | 2 Francs. Aluminum. Incuse design, flat rim. | — | 40.00 |
| E3a | 1948(a) | — | Franc. Aluminum. Incuse design, flat rim. | — | 35.00 |
| E1a | 1948(a) | — | 50 Centimes. Aluminum. Incuse design, flat rim | — | 30.00 |
| E2 | 1948(a) | 1,100 | 50 Centimes. Nickel-Bronze. Incuse design, raised rim. | — | 15.00 |
| E4 | 1948(a) | 1,100 | Franc. Nickel-Bronze. Incuse design, raised rim. | — | 20.00 |
| E6 | 1948(a) | 1,100 | 2 Francs. Nickel-Bronze. Incuse design, raised rim. | — | 15.00 |
| E6a | 1948(a) | — | 2 Francs. Aluminum. Incuse design, raised rim. | — | 40.00 |
| E4a | 1948(a) | — | Franc. Aluminum. Incuse design, raised rim. | — | 35.00 |
| E2a | 1948(a) | — | 50 Centimes. Aluminum. Incuse design, raised rim. | — | 30.00 |
| E7 | 1949(a) | 2,000 | 50 Centimes. Copper Nickel. KM1. | — | 12.00 |
| E8 | 1949(a) | 2,000 | Franc. Copper Nickel. KM2. | — | 15.00 |
| E9 | 1949(a) | 2,000 | 2 Francs. Copper Nickel. KM3. | — | 18.00 |
| E10 | 1952(a) | 1,200 | 5 Francs. KM4. | — | 20.00 |
| E11 | 1967(a) | 1,700 | 10 Francs. KM5. | — | 10.00 |
| E12 | 1967(a) | 1,700 | 20 Francs. KM6. | — | 10.00 |
| E13 | 1967(a) | 1,700 | 50 Francs. KM7. | — | 12.50 |
| E14 | 1976(a) | 1,900 | 100 Francs. KM15. | — | 22.50 |

## PIEFORTS

Several gold pieforts were melted in 1983.

| KM# | Date | Mintage | Identification | Issue Price | Mkt Val |
|---|---|---|---|---|---|
| P9b | 1979(a) | 96 | 50 Francs. 0.9200 Gold. KM13. | — | 1,350 |
| P1 | 1967(a) | 500 | 10 Francs. KM5. | — | 25.00 |
| P2 | 1967(a) | 500 | 20 Francs. KM6. | — | 30.00 |
| P3 | 1967(a) | 500 | 50 Francs. KM7. | — | 35.00 |
| P3a | 1967(a) | 50 | 50 Francs. 0.9500 Silver. KM7. | — | 200 |
| P2a | 1967(a) | 50 | 20 Francs. 0.9500 Silver. KM6. | — | 175 |
| P1a | 1967(a) | 50 | 10 Francs. 0.9500 Silver. KM5. | — | 150 |
| P1b | 1967(a) | 20 | 10 Francs. 0.9200 Gold. KM5. | — | 800 |
| P2b | 1967(a) | 20 | 20 Francs. 0.9200 Gold. KM6. | — | 1,000 |
| P3b | 1967(a) | 20 | 50 Francs. 0.9200 Gold. KM7. | — | 1,350 |
| P4 | 1979(a) | 150 | Franc. KM10. | — | 10.00 |
| P5 | 1979(a) | 150 | 2 Francs. KM14. | — | 15.00 |
| P6 | 1979(a) | 150 | 5 Francs. KM4. | — | 25.00 |
| P7 | 1979(a) | 150 | 10 Francs. KM11. | — | 40.00 |
| P8 | 1979(a) | 150 | 20 Francs. KM12. | — | 40.00 |
| P10 | 1979(a) | 150 | 100 Francs. KM15. | — | 75.00 |
| P9 | 1979(a) | 150 | 50 Francs. KM13. | — | 50.00 |
| P9a | 1979(a) | 250 | 50 Francs. 0.9250 Silver. KM13. | — | 100 |
| P10a | 1979(a) | 350 | 100 Francs. 0.9250 Silver. KM15. | — | 125 |
| P8a | 1979(a) | 250 | 20 Francs. 0.9250 Silver. | — | 100 |
| P7a | 1979(a) | 250 | 10 Francs. 0.9250 Silver. KM11. | — | 100 |
| P6a | 1979(a) | 250 | 5 Francs. 0.9250 Silver. KM4. | — | 75.00 |
| P5a | 1979(a) | 250 | 2 Francs. 0.9250 Silver. KM14. | — | 50.00 |
| P4a | 1979(a) | 250 | Franc. 0.9250 Silver. KM10. | — | 25.00 |
| P4b | 1979(a) | 94 | Franc. 0.9200 Gold. KM10. | — | 550 |
| P5b | 1979(a) | 96 | 2 Francs. 0.9200 Gold. KM14. | — | 925 |
| P6b | 1979(a) | 94 | 5 Francs. 0.9200 Gold. KM4. | — | 1,300 |
| P7b | 1979(a) | 93 | 10 Francs. 0.9200 Gold. KM11. | — | 850 |
| P8b | 1979(a) | 95 | 20 Francs. 0.9200 Gold. | — | 1,200 |
| P10b | 1979(a) | 96 | 100 Francs. 0.9200 Gold. KM15. | — | 1,250 |

## PIEFORTS WITH ESSAI

Double thickness

| KM# | Date | Mintage | Identification | Issue Price | Mkt Val |
|---|---|---|---|---|---|
| PE2 | 1949(a) | 104 | Franc. Double thickness. KM2. | — | 70.00 |
| PE3 | 1949(a) | 104 | 2 Francs. Double thickness. KM3. | — | 80.00 |
| PE4 | 1952(a) | 104 | 5 Francs. Double thickness. KM4. | — | 90.00 |

## SPECIMEN SETS (SS)

| KM# | Date | Mintage | Identification | Issue Price | Mkt Val |
|---|---|---|---|---|---|
| SS1 | 1967 (3) | 2,200 | KM5-7. This set issued with New Hebrides and French Polynesia 1967 set. | 10.00 | 20.00 |

# NEWFOUNDLAND

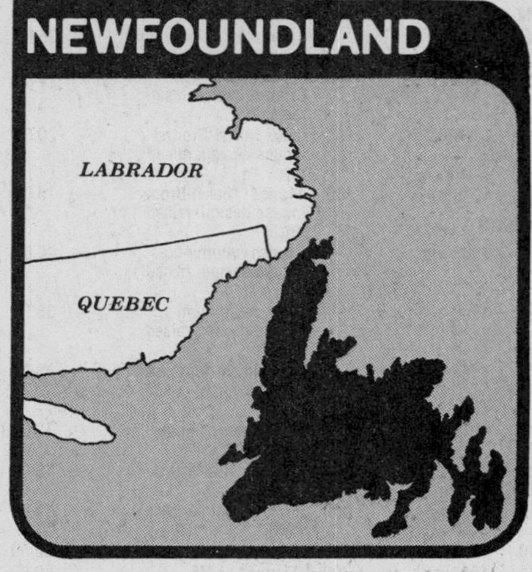


Canadian province discovered by John Cabot in 1497, formally occupied by Sir Humphrey Gilbert in 1583, on behalf of the British Crown. Attempts to colonize this area were unsuccessful until 1904, though British sovereignty was recognized by the Treaty of Utrecht in 1713. Newfoundland remained outside the Canadian Confederation in 1867 and continued to govern itself until 1934, when the British assumed responsibility for governing the colony and Labrador. This continued until the union with Canada in 1949. The province comprises an area of 143,501 sq. miles to the north and east of Quebec, with an estimated population of 564,000. The capital city is St. John.

## PROVINCE

### CIRCULATION COINAGE

**CENT (Large)** **Composition:** Bronze

| KM | Date | Mintage | VG-8 | F-12 | VF-20 | XF-40 | MS-60 | MS-63 | Proof |
|---|---|---|---|---|---|---|---|---|---|
| 9 | 1904H | 100,000 | 7.00 | 11.00 | 22.00 | 37.50 | 275 | 650 | — |
| | 1904H Proof | — | — | — | — | — | — | — | 4,000 |
| | 1907 | 200,000 | 1.50 | 2.50 | 4.00 | 12.00 | 110 | 375 | — |
| | 1909 | 200,000 | 1.50 | 2.50 | 4.00 | 10.50 | 90.00 | 150 | — |

**CENT (Large)** **Composition:** Bronze **Obverse:** George V bust facing left **Reverse:** Similar to KM#9

| KM | Date | Mintage | VG-8 | F-12 | VF-20 | XF-40 | MS-60 | MS-63 | Proof |
|---|---|---|---|---|---|---|---|---|---|
| 16 | 1913 | 400,000 | 0.75 | 1.50 | 2.00 | 4.00 | 40.00 | 75.00 | — |
| | 1917C | 702,350 | 0.75 | 1.50 | 2.00 | 4.00 | 65.00 | 185 | — |
| | 1917C Proof | — | — | — | — | — | — | — | 800 |
| | 1919C | 300,000 | 0.80 | 1.60 | 2.25 | 5.00 | 100 | 275 | — |
| | 1920C | 302,184 | 0.75 | 1.50 | 3.50 | 12.00 | 200 | 1,000 | — |
| | 1929C | 300,000 | 0.75 | 1.50 | 2.00 | 4.00 | 55.00 | 100 | — |
| | 1936 | 300,000 | 0.75 | 1.25 | 1.75 | 3.00 | 28.00 | 75.00 | — |

**CENT (Small)** **Composition:** Bronze

| KM | Date | Mintage | VG-8 | F-12 | VF-20 | XF-40 | MS-60 | MS-63 | Proof |
|---|---|---|---|---|---|---|---|---|---|
| 18 | 1938 | 500,000 | 0.50 | 0.75 | 1.50 | 2.50 | 16.00 | 40.00 | — |
| | 1940 | 300,000 | 1.25 | 2.00 | 3.00 | 7.00 | 35.00 | 175 | — |
| | 1940 re-engraved date | — | 16.00 | 27.50 | 40.00 | 70.00 | 185 | 500 | — |
| | 1940 Proof | — | — | — | — | — | — | — | 1,000 |
| | 1941C | 827,662 | 0.35 | 0.45 | 0.70 | 1.50 | 13.50 | 120 | — |
| | 1941C re-engraved date | — | 8.00 | 13.00 | 20.00 | 35.00 | 100 | 400 | — |
| | 1942 | 1,996,889 | 0.35 | 0.45 | 0.70 | 1.50 | 13.50 | 70.00 | — |
| | 1943C | 1,239,732 | 0.35 | 0.45 | 0.70 | 1.50 | 13.50 | 70.00 | — |
| | 1944C | 1,328,776 | 1.00 | 2.00 | 3.00 | 7.00 | 90.00 | 335 | — |
| | 1947C | 313,772 | 0.80 | 1.65 | 2.50 | 6.00 | 35.00 | 200 | — |
| | 1947C Proof | — | — | — | — | — | — | — | 2,000 |

**5 CENTS** **Weight:** 1.1782 g. **Composition:** 0.9250 Silver .0350 oz. ASW

| KM | Date | Mintage | VG-8 | F-12 | VF-20 | XF-40 | MS-60 | MS-63 | Proof |
|---|---|---|---|---|---|---|---|---|---|
| 7 | 1903 | 100,000 | 3.00 | 6.00 | 18.00 | 45.00 | 425 | 1,200 | — |
| | 1903 Proof | — | — | — | — | — | — | — | 2,000 |
| | 1904H Proof | — | — | — | — | — | — | — | 1,200 |
| | 1904H | 100,000 | 2.00 | 5.00 | 14.00 | 35.00 | 160 | 275 | — |
| | 1908 | 400,000 | 1.75 | 3.50 | 11.50 | 25.00 | 160 | 400 | — |

**5 CENTS** **Weight:** 1.1782 g. **Composition:** 0.9250 Silver .0350 oz. ASW **Obverse:** George V bust facing left **Reverse:** Similar to KM#7

| KM | Date | Mintage | VG-8 | F-12 | VF-20 | XF-40 | MS-60 | MS-63 | Proof |
|---|---|---|---|---|---|---|---|---|---|
| 13 | 1912 | 300,000 | 1.00 | 2.00 | 5.00 | 20.00 | 125 | 275 | — |
| | 1912 Proof | — | — | — | — | — | — | — | 2,000 |
| | 1917C Proof | — | — | — | — | — | — | — | 2,000 |
| | 1917C | 300,319 | 1.00 | 2.00 | 4.00 | 14.00 | 200 | 450 | — |
| | 1919C | 100,844 | 1.25 | 3.00 | 10.00 | 30.00 | 750 | 1,250 | — |
| | 1919C Proof | — | — | — | — | — | — | — | 2,000 |
| | 1929 | 300,000 | 1.00 | 1.75 | 3.25 | 12.00 | 165 | 350 | — |

**5 CENTS** **Weight:** 1.1782 g. **Composition:** 0.9250 Silver .0350 oz. ASW

| KM | Date | Mintage | VG-8 | F-12 | VF-20 | XF-40 | MS-60 | MS-63 | Proof |
|---|---|---|---|---|---|---|---|---|---|
| 19 | 1938 | 100,000 | 0.80 | 0.90 | 1.50 | 4.00 | 65.00 | 150 | — |
| | 1940C | 200,000 | 0.80 | 0.90 | 1.50 | 4.00 | 60.00 | 200 | — |
| | 1940C Proof | — | — | — | — | — | — | — | 2,000 |
| | 1941C | 621,641 | 0.60 | 0.90 | 1.50 | 2.50 | 15.00 | 30.00 | — |
| | 1942C | 298,348 | 0.85 | 0.90 | 2.00 | 2.50 | 15.00 | 30.00 | — |
| | 1943C | 351,666 | 0.55 | 0.85 | 1.25 | 2.50 | 15.00 | 27.50 | — |

Mintmark

**5 CENTS** **Weight:** 1.1664 g. **Composition:** 0.8000 Silver .0300 oz. ASW

| KM | Date | Mintage | VG-8 | F-12 | VF-20 | XF-40 | MS-60 | MS-63 | Proof |
|---|---|---|---|---|---|---|---|---|---|
| 19a | 1944C | 286,504 | 1.25 | 1.75 | 3.00 | 4.00 | 25.00 | 50.00 | — |
| | 1945C | 203,828 | 0.55 | 0.85 | 1.25 | 2.50 | 13.00 | 26.00 | — |
| | 1946C | 2,041 | 200 | 225 | 325 | 400 | 1,100 | 1,750 | — |
| | 1947C | 38,400 | 2.00 | 3.00 | 5.00 | 10.00 | 60.00 | 100 | — |

**10 CENTS** **Weight:** 2.3564 g. **Composition:** 0.9250 Silver .0701 oz. ASW

| KM | Date | Mintage | VG-8 | F-12 | VF-20 | XF-40 | MS-60 | MS-63 | Proof |
|---|---|---|---|---|---|---|---|---|---|
| 8 | 1903 | 100,000 | 5.00 | 10.00 | 35.00 | 110 | 850 | 2,000 | — |
| | 1903 Proof | — | — | — | — | — | — | — | 2,500 |
| | 1904H Proof | — | — | — | — | — | — | — | 1,500 |
| | 1904H | 100,000 | 2.50 | 6.50 | 20.00 | 55.00 | 175 | 250 | — |

**10 CENTS** **Weight:** 2.3564 g. **Composition:** 0.9250 Silver .0701 oz. ASW

| KM | Date | Mintage | VG-8 | F-12 | VF-20 | XF-40 | MS-60 | MS-63 | Proof |
|---|---|---|---|---|---|---|---|---|---|
| 20 | 1938 | 100,000 | 0.75 | 1.50 | 2.75 | 7.00 | 80.00 | 300 | — |
| | 1940 | 100,000 | 0.65 | 1.20 | 2.50 | 6.00 | 80.00 | 300 | — |
| | 1940 Proof | — | — | — | — | — | — | — | 2,500 |
| | 1941C | 483,630 | 0.60 | 1.40 | 2.20 | 3.50 | 27.00 | 125 | — |
| | 1942C | 293,736 | 0.60 | 1.50 | 2.20 | 3.50 | 30.00 | 130 | — |
| | 1943C | 104,706 | 0.60 | 1.50 | 2.40 | 3.50 | 60.00 | 200 | — |
| | 1944C | 151,471 | 2.00 | 3.00 | 4.00 | 7.00 | 90.00 | 250 | — |

**10 CENTS** **Weight:** 2.3328 g. **Composition:** 0.8000 Silver .0600 oz. ASW

| KM | Date | Mintage | VG-8 | F-12 | VF-20 | XF-40 | MS-60 | MS-63 | Proof |
|---|---|---|---|---|---|---|---|---|---|
| 20a | 1945C | 175,833 | 0.65 | 1.25 | 2.00 | 4.00 | 27.00 | 185 | — |
| | 1946C | 38,400 | 1.75 | 3.50 | 7.00 | 15.00 | 60.00 | 250 | — |
| | 1946C Proof | — | — | — | — | — | — | — | 700 |
| | 1947C | 61,988 | 1.50 | 3.00 | 4.50 | 9.00 | 45.00 | 245 | — |

**20 CENTS** **Weight:** 4.7127 g. **Composition:** 0.9250 Silver .1401 oz. ASW

| KM | Date | Mintage | VG-8 | F-12 | VF-20 | XF-40 | MS-60 | MS-63 | Proof |
|---|---|---|---|---|---|---|---|---|---|
| 10 | 1904H | 75,000 | 6.00 | 16.00 | 50.00 | 175 | 2,000 | 4,250 | — |

**20 CENTS** **Weight:** 4.7127 g. **Composition:** 0.9250 Silver .1401 oz. ASW **Obverse:** George V bust facing left **Reverse:** Similar to KM#10

| KM | Date | Mintage | VG-8 | F-12 | VF-20 | XF-40 | MS-60 | MS-63 | Proof |
|---|---|---|---|---|---|---|---|---|---|
| 15 | 1912 | 350,000 | 2.00 | 3.00 | 8.00 | 30.00 | 275 | 650 | — |
| | 1912 Proof | — | — | — | — | — | — | — | 2,500 |

Mintmark

**25 CENTS** **Weight:** 5.8319 g. **Composition:** 0.9250 Silver .1734 oz. ASW

| KM | Date | Mintage | VG-8 | F-12 | VF-20 | XF-40 | MS-60 | MS-63 | Proof |
|---|---|---|---|---|---|---|---|---|---|
| 17 | 1917C | 464,779 | 1.50 | 2.00 | 4.00 | 8.00 | 120 | 250 | — |
| | 1917C Proof | — | — | — | — | — | — | — | 2,500 |
| | 1919C Proof | — | — | — | — | — | — | — | 2,500 |
| | 1919C | 163,939 | 1.50 | 2.25 | 4.25 | 12.00 | 220 | 700 | — |

**50 CENTS** **Weight:** 11.7800 g. **Composition:** 0.9250 Silver .3504 oz. ASW

| KM | Date | Mintage | VG-8 | F-12 | VF-20 | XF-40 | MS-60 | MS-63 | Proof |
|---|---|---|---|---|---|---|---|---|---|
| 11 | 1904H | 140,000 | 3.25 | 5.00 | 13.00 | 35.00 | 225 | 650 | — |
| | 1904H Proof | — | — | — | — | — | — | — | 5,000 |
| | 1907 | 100,000 | 3.00 | 5.00 | 13.00 | 45.00 | 250 | 800 | — |
| | 1908 | 160,000 | 3.25 | 4.50 | 12.50 | 32.50 | 175 | 600 | — |
| | 1909 | 200,000 | 3.25 | 4.50 | 12.50 | 35.00 | 200 | 600 | — |

**50 CENTS** **Weight:** 11.7800 g. **Composition:** 0.9250 Silver .3504 oz. ASW

| KM | Date | Mintage | VG-8 | F-12 | VF-20 | XF-40 | MS-60 | MS-63 | Proof |
|---|---|---|---|---|---|---|---|---|---|
| 12 | 1911 | 200,000 | 2.75 | 3.25 | 6.00 | 20.00 | 175 | 450 | — |
| | 1917C | 375,560 | 2.75 | 3.25 | 6.00 | 16.50 | 125 | 285 | — |
| | 1917C Proof | — | — | — | — | — | — | — | 2,500 |
| | 1918C | 294,824 | 2.75 | 3.25 | 6.00 | 16.50 | 125 | 285 | — |
| | 1919C | 306,267 | 2.75 | 3.25 | 6.00 | 16.50 | 125 | 380 | — |
| | 1919C Proof | — | — | — | — | — | — | — | 2,500 |

## TRIAL STRIKES

| KM# | Date | Mintage | Identification | Mkt Val |
|---|---|---|---|---|
| TS3 | 1945 C | — | 10 Cents. Nickel. | — |

# NEW GUINEA

Spanish navigator Jorge de Menezes, who landed on the northwest shore in 1527, discovered New Guinea, the world's largest island after Greenland. European interests, attracted by exaggerated estimates of the resources of the area, resulted in the island being claimed in part by Spain, the Netherlands, Great Britain and Germany.

**RULERS**
British, 1910-1952

**MONETARY SYSTEM**
12 Pence = 1 Shilling
20 Shillings = 1 Pound

## BRITISH ADMINISTRATION
### 1910-1952

### STANDARD COINAGE

12 Pence = 1 Shilling; 20 Shillings = 1 Pound

**1/2 PENNY** KM# 1a **Composition:** Nickel

| Date | Mintage | F | VF | XF | Unc | BU |
|---|---|---|---|---|---|---|
| 1929 Proof | — | Value: 650 | | | | |

**1/2 PENNY** KM# 1 **Composition:** Copper-Nickel **Note:** Entire mintage returned to Melbourne Mint which later sold 400 pcs. in sets with KM#2. The balance of mintage was destroyed.

| Date | Mintage | F | VF | XF | Unc | BU |
|---|---|---|---|---|---|---|
| 1929 | 25,000 | — | — | 225 | 375 | — |
| 1929 Proof | — | Value: 450 | | | | |

**PENNY** KM# 2a **Composition:** Nickel

| Date | Mintage | F | VF | XF | Unc | BU |
|---|---|---|---|---|---|---|
| 1929 Proof | — | Value: 650 | | | | |

**PENNY** KM# 2 **Composition:** Copper-Nickel **Note:** Entire mintage returned to Melbourne Mint which later sold 400 pcs. in sets with KM#1. The balance of mintage was destroyed.

| Date | Mintage | F | VF | XF | Unc | BU |
|---|---|---|---|---|---|---|
| 1929 | 63,000 | — | — | 225 | 375 | — |
| 1929 Proof | — | Value: 450 | | | | |

**PENNY** KM# 6 **Composition:** Bronze

| Date | Mintage | F | VF | XF | Unc | BU |
|---|---|---|---|---|---|---|
| 1936 | 360,000 | 0.75 | 1.00 | 2.00 | 6.00 | — |
| 1936 Proof | — | Value: 275 | | | | |

**PENNY** KM# 7 **Composition:** Bronze

| Date | Mintage | F | VF | XF | Unc | BU |
|---|---|---|---|---|---|---|
| 1938 | 360,000 | 1.75 | 4.00 | 7.00 | 16.50 | — |
| 1944 | 240,000 | 1.00 | 2.00 | 4.00 | 9.00 | — |

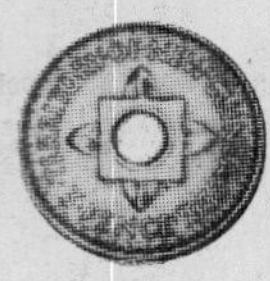

**3 PENCE** KM# 3 **Composition:** Copper-Nickel

| Date | Mintage | F | VF | XF | Unc | BU |
|---|---|---|---|---|---|---|
| 1935 | 1,200,000 | 3.00 | 6.00 | 10.00 | 32.00 | — |
| 1935 Proof | — | Value: 225 | | | | |

**3 PENCE** KM# 10 **Composition:** Copper-Nickel

| Date | Mintage | F | VF | XF | Unc | BU |
|---|---|---|---|---|---|---|
| 1944 | 500,000 | 2.00 | 4.00 | 8.50 | 30.00 | — |

**6 PENCE** KM# 4 **Composition:** Copper-Nickel

| Date | Mintage | F | VF | XF | Unc | BU |
|---|---|---|---|---|---|---|
| 1935 | 2,000,000 | 2.50 | 4.00 | 8.00 | 32.00 | — |
| 1935 Proof | — | Value: 225 | | | | |

**6 PENCE** KM# 9 **Composition:** Copper-Nickel

| Date | Mintage | F | VF | XF | Unc | BU |
|---|---|---|---|---|---|---|
| 1943 | 130,000 | 3.00 | 6.00 | 12.50 | 40.00 | — |

**SHILLING** KM# 5 **Weight:** 5.3800 g. **Composition:** 0.9250 Silver .16 oz. ASW

| Date | Mintage | F | VF | XF | Unc | BU |
|---|---|---|---|---|---|---|
| 1935 | 2,100,000 | BV | 2.00 | 3.00 | 7.50 | — |
| 1936 | 1,360,000 | BV | 2.00 | 3.00 | 7.50 | — |

**SHILLING** KM# 8 **Weight:** 5.3800 g. **Composition:** 0.9250 Silver .16 oz. ASW

| Date | Mintage | F | VF | XF | Unc | BU |
|---|---|---|---|---|---|---|
| 1938 | 3,400,000 | BV | 2.00 | 3.00 | 7.50 | — |
| 1945 | 2,000,000 | BV | 2.00 | 3.00 | 7.50 | — |

### PROOF SETS

| KM# | Date | Mintage | Identification | Issue Price | Mkt Val |
|---|---|---|---|---|---|
| PS1 | 1929 (2) | — | KM#1, 2 | — | 900 |
| PS2 | 1929 | 20 | KM#1a, 2a | — | 1,300 |

# NEW HEBRIDES

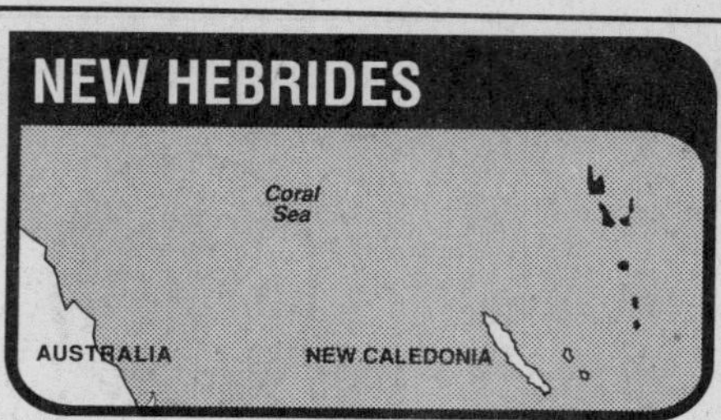


The New Hebrides were discovered by Portuguese navigator Pedro de Quiros in 1606, visited by French explorer Bougainville in 1768, and named by British navigator Capt. James Cook in 1774. Ships of all nations converged on the islands to trade for sandalwood, prompting France and Britain to relinquish their individual claims and declare the islands a neutral zone in 1878. The New Hebrides were placed under the control of a mixed Anglo-French commission of naval officers during the native uprisings of 1887, and established as a condominium under the joint sovereignty of France and Great Britain in 1906.

**MINT MARKS**
(a) - Paris, privy marks only

**MONETARY SYSTEM**
100 Centimes = 1 Franc

## FRENCH/BRITISH CONDOMINIUM
### (Jointly Governed Territory)

### STANDARD COINAGE

**FRANC** KM# 4.1 **Composition:** Nickel-Brass

| Date | Mintage | F | VF | XF | Unc | BU |
|---|---|---|---|---|---|---|
| 1970(a) | 435,000 | — | 0.25 | 0.50 | 0.85 | — |

**FRANC** KM# 4.2 **Composition:** Nickel-Brass **Obverse:** Legend added **Obv. Legend:** I.E.O.M.

| Date | Mintage | F | VF | XF | Unc | BU |
|---|---|---|---|---|---|---|
| 1975(a) | 350,000 | — | 0.20 | 0.40 | 0.75 | — |
| 1978(a) | 200,000 | — | 0.20 | 0.40 | 0.75 | — |
| 1979(a) | 350,000 | — | 0.20 | 0.40 | 0.75 | — |
| 1982(a) | — | — | 0.20 | 0.40 | 0.75 | — |

**2 FRANCS** KM# 5.1 **Composition:** Nickel-Brass

| Date | Mintage | F | VF | XF | Unc | BU |
|---|---|---|---|---|---|---|
| 1970(a) | 264,000 | — | 0.60 | 1.25 | 2.25 | — |

**2 FRANCS** KM# 5.2 **Composition:** Nickel-Brass **Obverse:** Legend added **Obv. Legend:** I.E.O.M.

| Date | Mintage | F | VF | XF | Unc | BU |
|---|---|---|---|---|---|---|
| 1973(a) | 200,000 | — | 0.20 | 0.40 | 0.75 | — |
| 1975(a) | 300,000 | — | 0.20 | 0.40 | 0.75 | — |
| 1978(a) | 150,000 | — | 0.20 | 0.40 | 0.75 | — |
| 1979(a) | 250,000 | — | 0.20 | 0.40 | 0.75 | — |
| 1982(a) | — | — | 0.20 | 0.40 | 0.75 | — |

**5 FRANCS** KM# 6.1 **Composition:** Nickel-Brass

| Date | Mintage | F | VF | XF | Unc | BU |
|---|---|---|---|---|---|---|
| 1970(a) | 375,000 | — | 0.50 | 0.75 | 1.65 | — |

**5 FRANCS** KM# 6.2 **Composition:** Nickel-Brass **Obverse:** Legend added **Obv. Legend:** I.E.O.M.

| Date | Mintage | F | VF | XF | Unc | BU |
|---|---|---|---|---|---|---|
| 1975(a) | 350,000 | — | 0.30 | 0.60 | 1.25 | — |
| 1979(a) | 250,000 | — | 0.30 | 0.60 | 1.25 | — |
| 1982(a) | — | — | 0.30 | 0.60 | 1.25 | — |

**10 FRANCS** KM# 2.1 **Composition:** Nickel

| Date | Mintage | F | VF | XF | Unc | BU |
|---|---|---|---|---|---|---|
| 1967(a) | 250,000 | — | 0.30 | 0.65 | 1.50 | — |
| 1970(a) | 400,000 | — | 0.30 | 0.65 | 1.50 | — |

**10 FRANCS** KM# 2.2 **Composition:** Nickel **Obverse:** Legend added **Obv. Legend:** I.E.O.M.

| Date | Mintage | F | VF | XF | Unc | BU |
|---|---|---|---|---|---|---|
| 1973(a) | 200,000 | — | 0.30 | 0.65 | 1.50 | — |
| 1975(a) | 300,000 | — | 0.30 | 0.65 | 1.50 | — |
| 1977(a) | 200,000 | — | 0.30 | 0.65 | 1.50 | — |
| 1979(a) | 400,000 | — | 0.30 | 0.65 | 1.50 | — |
| 1982(a) | — | — | 0.30 | 0.65 | 1.50 | — |

**20 FRANCS** KM# 3.1 **Composition:** Nickel

| Date | Mintage | F | VF | XF | Unc | BU |
|---|---|---|---|---|---|---|
| 1967(a) | 250,000 | — | 0.60 | 1.25 | 2.25 | — |
| 1970(a) | 300,000 | — | 0.60 | 1.25 | 2.25 | — |

**20 FRANCS** KM# 3.2 **Composition:** Nickel **Obverse:** Legend added **Obv. Legend:** I.E.O.M.

| Date | Mintage | F | VF | XF | Unc | BU |
|---|---|---|---|---|---|---|
| 1973(a) | 200,000 | — | 0.60 | 1.25 | 2.25 | — |
| 1975(a) | 150,000 | — | 0.60 | 1.25 | 2.25 | — |
| 1977(a) | 150,000 | — | 0.60 | 1.25 | 2.25 | — |
| 1979(a) | 300,000 | — | 0.60 | 1.25 | 2.25 | — |
| 1982(a) | — | — | 0.60 | 1.25 | 2.25 | — |

**50 FRANCS** KM# 7 **Composition:** Nickel

| Date | Mintage | F | VF | XF | Unc | BU |
|---|---|---|---|---|---|---|
| 1972(a) | 200,000 | — | 1.50 | 2.50 | 4.00 | — |

**100 FRANCS** KM# 1 **Weight:** 25.0000 g. **Composition:** 0.8350 Silver .6712 oz. ASW

| Date | Mintage | F | VF | XF | Unc | BU |
|---|---|---|---|---|---|---|
| 1966(a) | 200,000 | — | — | — | 15.00 | — |
| 1979(a) | — | — | — | — | 20.00 | — |

## ESSAIS

| KM# | Date | Mintage | Identification | Issue Price | Mkt Val |
|---|---|---|---|---|---|
| E1 | 1966(a) | 3,000 | 100 Francs. | — | 35.00 |
| E2 | 1967(a) | 1,700 | 10 Francs. | — | 15.00 |
| E3 | 1967(a) | 1,700 | 20 Francs. | — | 15.00 |
| E4 | 1970(a) | 1,700 | Franc. | — | 15.00 |
| E5 | 1970(a) | 1,700 | 2 Francs. | — | 15.00 |
| E6 | 1970(a) | 1,700 | 5 Francs. | — | 15.00 |
| E7 | 1972(a) | 1,300 | 50 Francs. | — | 17.50 |

## PATTERNS

Including off metal strikes

| KM# | Date | Mintage | Identification | Mkt Val |
|---|---|---|---|---|
| Pn1 | 1979 | 60 | 500 Francs. Copper-Nickel-Aluminum. | 300 |
| Pn2 | 1979 | 60 | 500 Francs. 0.9990 Silver. | 450 |
| Pn3 | 1979 | — | 500 Francs. 0.9990 Gold. 62.2000 g. | 5,000 |
| Pn4 | 1979 | 1 | 500 Francs. 0.9990 Platinum. 62.2000 g. | 9,000 |

## PIEFORTS WITH ESSAI

Double thickness

| KM# | Date | Mintage | Identification | Issue Price | Mkt Val |
|---|---|---|---|---|---|
| PE1 | 1966(a) | 500 | 100 Francs. | — | 140 |
| PE2 | 1966(a) | 50 | 100 Francs. 0.9200 Gold. | — | 3,500 |

| KM# | Date | Mintage | Identification | Issue Price | Mkt Val |
|---|---|---|---|---|---|
| PE3 | 1967(a) | 500 | 10 Francs. | — | 15.00 |
| PE4 | 1967(a) | 50 | 10 Francs. 0.9500 Silver. | — | 75.00 |
| PE5 | 1967(a) | 20 | 10 Francs. 0.9200 Gold. | — | 500 |
| PE6 | 1967(a) | 500 | 20 Francs. | — | 15.00 |

| KM# | Date | Mintage | Identification | Issue Price | Mkt Val |
|---|---|---|---|---|---|
| PE7 | 1967(a) | 50 | 20 Francs. 0.9500 Silver. | — | 125 |
| PE8 | 1967(a) | 20 | 20 Francs. 0.9200 Gold. | — | 1,000 |
| PE10 | 1974(a) | 500 | 100 Francs. 0.9250 Silver. | — | 100 |
| PE11 | 1974(a) | 119 | 100 Francs. 0.9200 Gold. | — | 2,850 |
| PE12 | 1979(a) | 150 | Franc. | — | 10.00 |
| PE13 | 1979 | 250 | Franc. 0.9250 Silver. | — | 20.00 |
| PE14 | 1979(a) | 123 | Franc. 0.9200 Gold. | — | 200 |
| PE15 | 1979(a) | 150 | 2 Francs. | — | 12.50 |
| PE16 | 1979(a) | 250 | 2 Francs. 0.9250 Silver. | — | 20.00 |
| PE17 | 1979(a) | 115 | 2 Francs. 0.9200 Gold. | — | 250 |
| PE18 | 1979(a) | 150 | 5 Francs. | — | 15.00 |
| PE19 | 1979(a) | 250 | 5 Francs. 0.9250 Silver. | — | 20.00 |
| PE20 | 1979(a) | 116 | 5 Francs. 0.9200 Gold. | — | 350 |
| PE21 | 1979(a) | 150 | 10 Francs. | — | 17.50 |
| PE22 | 1979(a) | 250 | 10 Francs. 0.9250 Silver. | — | 20.00 |
| PE23 | 1979(a) | 116 | 10 Francs. 0.9200 Gold. | — | 500 |
| PE24 | 1979(a) | 150 | 20 Francs. | — | 20.00 |
| PE25 | 1979(a) | 250 | 20 Francs. 0.9250 Silver. | — | 20.00 |
| PE26 | 1979(a) | 115 | 20 Francs. 0.9200 Gold. | — | 600 |
| PE27 | 1979(a) | 150 | 50 Francs. | — | 25.00 |
| PE28 | 1979(a) | 250 | 50 Francs. 0.9250 Silver. | — | 100 |
| PE29 | 1979(a) | 116 | 50 Francs. 0.9200 Gold. | — | 1,250 |

## "FDC" SETS

This fleur-de-coin set was issued with New Caledonia and French Polynesia 1967 sets.

| KM# | Date | Mintage | Identification | Issue Price | Mkt Val |
|---|---|---|---|---|---|
| SS1 | 1966-67 (3) | 2,200 | KM#1, 2.1, 3.1 | 10.00 | 10.00 |

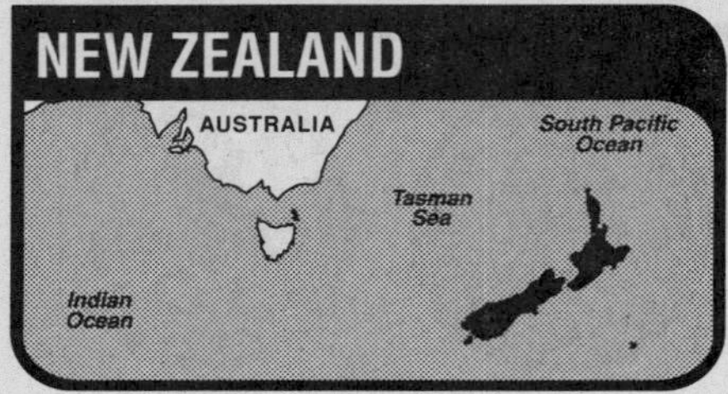


New Zealand, a parliamentary state located in the Southwest Pacific 1,250 miles (2,011 km.) east of Australia, has an area of 103,883 sq. mi. (268,680 sq. km.) and a population of *3.4 million. Capital: Wellington. Wool, meat, dairy products and some manufactured items are exported.

The first European to sight New Zealand was the Dutch navigator Abel Tasman in 1642. The islands were explored by British navigator Capt. James Cook who surveyed it in 1769 and annexed the land to Great Britain. The British government disavowed the annexation and for the next 70years the only white settlers to arrive were adventurers attracted by the prospects of lumbering, sealing and whaling. Great Britain annexed the land in 1840 by treaty with the native chiefs and made it a dependency of New South Wales. The colony was granted self-government in1852, a ministerial form of government in 1856, and full dominion status on Sept. 26, 1907. Full internal and external autonomy, which New Zealand had in effect possessed for many years, was formally extended in 1947.New Zealand is a member of the Commonwealth of Nations. The Queen of England is Head of State as Queen of New Zealand.

Prior to 1933 English coins were the official legal tender but Australian coins were accepted in small transactions. Currency fluctuations caused a distinctive New Zealand coinage to be introduced in 1933. The 1935 Waitangi crown and proof set were originally intended to mark the introduction but delays caused their date to be changed to 1935. The 1940 half crown marked the centennial of British rule, the 1949 and 1953 crowns commemorated Royal visits and the 1953 proof set marked the coronation of Queen Elizabeth.

Decimal Currency was introduced in 1967 with special sets commemorating the last issued of pound sterling (1965) and the first of the decimal issues. Since then dollars and set of coins have been issued nearly every year.

**RULERS**
British

**MONETARY SYSTEM**
12 Pence = 1 Shilling
2 Shillings = 1 Florin
2 Shillings & 6 Pence = Half Crown
5 Shillings = 1 Crown
20 Shillings = 1 Pound
2 Dollars = 1 Pound

# BRITISH PARLIAMENTARY STATE

## POUND STERLING COINAGE

**1/2 PENNY** KM# 12 **Composition:** Bronze **Subject:** Hei Tiki

| Date | Mintage | F | VF | XF | Unc | BU |
|---|---|---|---|---|---|---|
| 1940 | 3,432,000 | 0.25 | 0.65 | 2.00 | 15.00 | — |
| 1940 Proof; 5 known | — | Value: 800 | | | | |
| 1941 | 960,000 | 0.25 | 0.65 | 2.00 | 15.00 | — |
| 1941 | — | Value: 225 | | | | |
| 1942 | 1,960,000 | 0.35 | 0.75 | 6.00 | 30.00 | — |
| 1944 | 2,035,000 | 0.50 | 1.00 | 5.00 | 15.00 | — |
| 1945 | 1,516,000 | 0.50 | 1.00 | 3.50 | 15.00 | — |
| 1945 Proof | — | Value: 175 | | | | |
| 1946 | 3,120,000 | 0.50 | 1.00 | 3.50 | 15.00 | — |
| 1946 Proof | — | Value: 175 | | | | |
| 1947 | 2,726,000 | 0.25 | 0.50 | 1.50 | 12.50 | — |
| 1947 Proof | — | Value: 150 | | | | |

**1/2 PENNY** KM# 20 **Composition:** Bronze

| Date | Mintage | F | VF | XF | Unc | BU |
|---|---|---|---|---|---|---|
| 1949 | 1,766,000 | 0.10 | 0.25 | 3.50 | 15.00 | — |
| 1949 Proof | — | Value: 150 | | | | |
| 1950 | 1,426,000 | 0.10 | 0.25 | 2.50 | 12.50 | — |
| 1950 Proof | — | Value: 175 | | | | |
| 1951 | 2,342,000 | 0.10 | 0.25 | 1.50 | 7.50 | — |
| 1951 Proof | — | Value: 150 | | | | |
| 1952 | 2,400,000 | 0.10 | 0.20 | 1.50 | 6.00 | — |
| 1952 Proof | — | Value: 150 | | | | |

**1/2 PENNY** KM# 23.1 **Composition:** Bronze **Obverse:** Without shoulder strap

| Date | Mintage | F | VF | XF | Unc | BU |
|---|---|---|---|---|---|---|
| 1953 | 720,000 | 0.10 | 0.25 | 1.50 | 7.50 | — |
| 1953 Proof | 7,000 | Value: 5.00 | | | | |
| 1953 Matte proof | — | Value: 100 | | | | |
| 1954 | 240,000 | 0.75 | 1.25 | 7.00 | 27.50 | — |
| 1954 Proof | — | Value: 135 | | | | |
| 1955 | 240,000 | 0.75 | 1.25 | 7.00 | 27.50 | — |
| 1955 | — | Value: 135 | | | | |

**1/2 PENNY** KM# 23.2 **Composition:** Bronze **Obverse:** With shoulder strap

| Date | Mintage | F | VF | XF | Unc | BU |
|---|---|---|---|---|---|---|
| 1956 | 1,200,000 | 0.10 | 0.35 | 0.80 | 7.50 | — |
| 1956 Proof | — | Value: 135 | | | | |
| 1957 | 1,440,000 | 0.10 | 0.35 | 0.80 | 7.50 | — |
| 1957 Proof | — | Value: 135 | | | | |
| 1958 | 1,920,000 | 0.10 | 0.30 | 0.75 | 5.00 | — |
| 1958 Proof | — | Value: 135 | | | | |
| 1959 | 1,920,000 | 0.10 | 0.20 | 0.50 | 5.00 | — |
| 1959 Proof | — | Value: 135 | | | | |
| 1960 | 2,400,000 | 0.10 | 0.20 | 0.50 | 5.00 | — |
| 1960 Proof | — | Value: 135 | | | | |
| 1961 | 2,880,000 | 0.10 | 0.15 | 0.40 | 3.50 | — |
| 1961 Proof | — | Value: 135 | | | | |
| 1962 | 2,880,000 | 0.10 | 0.15 | 0.40 | 3.50 | — |
| 1962 Proof | — | Value: 135 | | | | |
| 1963 | 1,680,000 | 0.10 | 0.15 | 0.30 | 2.50 | — |
| 1963 Proof | — | Value: 135 | | | | |
| 1964 | 2,885,000 | 0.10 | 0.15 | 0.20 | 1.50 | — |
| 1964 Proof | — | Value: 135 | | | | |
| 1965 | 175,000 | 0.10 | 0.15 | 0.20 | 0.80 | — |
| 1965 Prooflike | 25,000 | — | — | — | — | 1.25 |
| 1965 Proof | Est. 10 | — | — | — | — | — |

**PENNY** KM# 13 **Composition:** Bronze **Subject:** Tui Bird

| Date | Mintage | F | VF | XF | Unc | BU |
|---|---|---|---|---|---|---|
| 1940 | 5,424,000 | 0.25 | 1.00 | 3.50 | 20.00 | — |
| 1940 Proof; 5 known | — | Value: 1,000 | | | | |
| 1941 | 1,200,000 | 0.25 | 1.00 | 6.00 | 28.50 | — |
| 1942 | 3,120,000 | 0.25 | 1.00 | 7.00 | 45.00 | — |
| 1942 Proof | — | Value: 275 | | | | |
| 1943 | 8,400,000 | 0.25 | 0.50 | 3.50 | 15.00 | — |
| 1943 Proof | — | Value: 225 | | | | |
| 1944 | 3,696,000 | 0.50 | 1.00 | 3.50 | 15.00 | — |
| 1944 Proof | — | Value: 225 | | | | |
| 1945 | 4,764,000 | 0.25 | 0.50 | 3.50 | 20.00 | — |
| 1945 Proof | — | Value: 225 | | | | |
| 1946 | 6,720,000 | 0.25 | 0.50 | 3.00 | 15.00 | — |
| 1946 Proof | — | Value: 225 | | | | |
| 1947 | 5,880,000 | 0.25 | 0.50 | 3.00 | 15.00 | — |
| 1947 Proof | — | Value: 225 | | | | |

**PENNY** KM# 13a **Composition:** Bronze **Note:** Burnished

| Date | Mintage | F | VF | XF | Unc | BU |
|---|---|---|---|---|---|---|
| 1945 | — | — | — | 80.00 | 250 | — |

**Note:** Struck in error by the Royal Mint on Great Britain blanks

**PENNY** KM# 21 **Composition:** Bronze

| Date | Mintage | F | VF | XF | Unc | BU |
|---|---|---|---|---|---|---|
| 1949 | 2,016,000 | 0.20 | 0.60 | 3.50 | 20.00 | — |
| 1949 Proof | — | Value: 225 | | | | |
| 1950 | 5,784,000 | 0.15 | 0.50 | 2.50 | 15.00 | — |
| 1950 Proof | — | Value: 175 | | | | |
| 1951 | 6,888,000 | 0.15 | 0.50 | 1.50 | 12.50 | — |
| 1951 Proof | — | Value: 175 | | | | |
| 1952 | 10,800,000 | 0.15 | 0.50 | 1.25 | 10.00 | — |
| 1952 Proof | — | Value: 150 | | | | |

**PENNY** KM# 24.1 **Composition:** Bronze **Obverse:** Without shoulder strap

| Date | Mintage | F | VF | XF | Unc | BU |
|---|---|---|---|---|---|---|
| 1953 | 2,400,000 | 0.10 | 0.25 | 2.50 | 10.00 | — |
| 1953 Proof | 7,000 | Value: 10.00 | | | | |
| 1953 Matte proof | — | Value: 100 | | | | |
| 1954 | 1,080,000 | 0.25 | 1.00 | 7.50 | 28.50 | — |
| 1954 Proof | — | Value: 175 | | | | |
| 1955 | 3,720,000 | 0.10 | 0.25 | 2.50 | 12.50 | — |
| 1955 Proof | — | Value: 150 | | | | |
| 1956 | | 25.00 | 40.00 | 125 | 425 | — |

**PENNY** KM# 24.2 **Composition:** Bronze **Obverse:** With shoulder strap

| Date | Mintage | F | VF | XF | Unc | BU |
|---|---|---|---|---|---|---|
| 1956 | 3,600,000 | 0.10 | 0.20 | 2.00 | 10.00 | — |
| 1956 Proof | — | Value: 150 | | | | |
| 1957 | 2,400,000 | 0.20 | 0.50 | 1.50 | 7.50 | — |
| 1957 Proof | — | Value: 150 | | | | |
| 1958 | 10,800,000 | 0.10 | 0.20 | 1.25 | 8.00 | — |
| 1958 Proof | — | Value: 150 | | | | |
| 1959 | 8,400,000 | 0.10 | 0.20 | 1.25 | 8.00 | — |
| 1959 Proof | — | Value: 150 | | | | |
| 1960 | 7,200,000 | 0.10 | 0.20 | 0.50 | 4.00 | — |
| 1960 Proof | — | Value: 135 | | | | |
| 1961 | 7,200,000 | 0.10 | 0.20 | 0.50 | 3.50 | — |
| 1961 Proof | — | Value: 135 | | | | |
| 1962 | 6,000,000 | — | 0.10 | 0.45 | 2.50 | — |
| 1962 Proof | — | Value: 135 | | | | |
| 1963 | 2,400,000 | — | 0.10 | 0.20 | 1.75 | — |
| 1963 Proof | — | Value: 135 | | | | |
| 1964 | 18,000,000 | — | 0.10 | 0.15 | 1.00 | — |
| 1964 Proof | — | Value: 135 | | | | |
| 1965 | 175,000 | — | 0.50 | 1.00 | 2.50 | — |
| 1965 Prooflike | 25,000 | — | — | — | — | 2.00 |
| 1965 Proof | Est. 10 | — | — | — | — | — |

**3 PENCE** KM# 1 **Composition:** Silver .0226 oz. ASW **Subject:** Crossed Patu

| Date | Mintage | F | VF | XF | Unc | BU |
|---|---|---|---|---|---|---|
| 1933 | 6,000,000 | 0.35 | 0.75 | 3.25 | 15.00 | — |
| 1933 Proof | Est. 20 | Value: 450 | | | | |

| Date | Mintage | F | VF | XF | Unc | BU |
|---|---|---|---|---|---|---|
| 1934 | 6,000,000 | 0.35 | 0.75 | 3.25 | 15.00 | — |
| 1934 Proof | Est. 20 | Value: 1,500 | | | | |
| 1935 | 40,000 | 40.00 | 100 | 175 | 625 | — |
| 1935 Proof | 364 | Value: 550 | | | | |
| 1936 | 2,760,000 | 0.35 | 0.75 | 3.50 | 20.00 | — |
| 1936 Proof | — | Value: 450 | | | | |

**3 PENCE** **KM# 7** **Composition:** Copper **Subject:** Crossed Patu

| Date | Mintage | F | VF | XF | Unc | BU |
|---|---|---|---|---|---|---|
| 1937 | 2,880,000 | 0.35 | 0.75 | 2.50 | 15.00 | — |
| 1937 Proof | Est. 200 | Value: 400 | | | | |
| 1939 | 3,000,000 | 0.35 | 0.60 | 2.25 | 15.00 | — |
| 1939 Proof | — | Value: 400 | | | | |
| 1940 | 2,000,000 | 0.35 | 1.00 | 3.50 | 25.00 | — |
| 1940 Proof | — | Value: 400 | | | | |
| 1941 | 1,760,000 | 0.40 | 1.50 | 12.50 | 75.00 | — |
| 1941 Proof | — | Value: 350 | | | | |
| 1942 | 3,120,000 | 0.30 | 0.60 | 2.00 | 12.50 | — |
| 1942 With 1 dot | Inc. above | 4.00 | 8.00 | 100 | 300 | — |
| 1943 | 4,400,000 | 0.30 | 0.50 | 1.25 | 10.00 | — |
| 1944 | 2,840,000 | 0.30 | 0.50 | 1.25 | 12.50 | — |
| 1944 Proof | — | Value: 350 | | | | |
| 1945 | 2,520,000 | 0.30 | 0.50 | 1.25 | 7.50 | — |
| 1945 Proof | — | Value: 350 | | | | |
| 1946 | 6,080,000 | 0.30 | 0.50 | 1.25 | 7.50 | — |
| 1946 Proof | — | Value: 350 | | | | |

**3 PENCE** **KM# 7a** **Composition:** Copper-Nickel

| Date | Mintage | F | VF | XF | Unc | BU |
|---|---|---|---|---|---|---|
| 1947 | 6,400,000 | 0.15 | 0.35 | 2.50 | 12.50 | — |
| 1947 Proof | Est. 20 | Value: 300 | | | | |

**3 PENCE** **KM# 15** **Composition:** Copper-Nickel

| Date | Mintage | F | VF | XF | Unc | BU |
|---|---|---|---|---|---|---|
| 1948 | 4,000,000 | 0.30 | 0.70 | 3.25 | 15.00 | — |
| 1948 Proof | — | Value: 175 | | | | |
| 1950 | 800,000 | 0.50 | 2.00 | 12.50 | 75.00 | — |
| 1950 Proof | — | Value: 225 | | | | |
| 1951 | 3,600,000 | 0.30 | 0.70 | 2.50 | 10.00 | — |
| 1951 Proof | — | Value: 175 | | | | |
| 1952 | 8,000,000 | 0.30 | 0.70 | 2.00 | 7.50 | — |
| 1952 Proof | — | Value: 175 | | | | |

**3 PENCE** **KM# 25.1** **Composition:** Copper-Nickel **Obverse:** Without shoulder strap

| Date | Mintage | F | VF | XF | Unc | BU |
|---|---|---|---|---|---|---|
| 1953 | 4,000,000 | 0.15 | 0.35 | 0.75 | 6.00 | — |
| 1953 Proof | 7,000 | Value: 7.00 | | | | |
| 1953 Matte proof | — | Value: 125 | | | | |
| 1954 | 4,000,000 | 0.15 | 0.35 | 1.00 | 8.00 | — |
| 1954 Proof | — | Value: 175 | | | | |
| 1955 | 4,000,000 | 0.15 | 0.35 | 1.00 | 8.00 | — |
| 1955 Proof | — | Value: 175 | | | | |
| 1956 | | 2.50 | 4.00 | 35.00 | 150 | — |
| 1956 Proof | — | Value: 250 | | | | |

**3 PENCE** **KM# 25.2** **Composition:** Copper-Nickel **Obverse:** With shoulder strap

| Date | Mintage | F | VF | XF | Unc | BU |
|---|---|---|---|---|---|---|
| 1956 | 4,800,000 | 0.10 | 0.20 | 0.50 | 4.00 | — |
| 1956 Proof | — | Value: 175 | | | | |
| 1957 | 8,000,000 | 0.10 | 0.20 | 0.30 | 3.50 | — |
| 1957 Proof | — | Value: 175 | | | | |
| 1958 | 4,800,000 | 0.10 | 0.20 | 0.30 | 2.50 | — |
| 1958 Proof | — | Value: 175 | | | | |
| 1959 | 4,000,000 | 0.10 | 0.20 | 0.30 | 2.50 | — |
| 1959 Proof | — | Value: 175 | | | | |
| 1960 | 4,000,000 | 0.10 | 0.20 | 0.30 | 2.50 | — |
| 1960 Proof | — | Value: 175 | | | | |
| 1961 | 4,800,000 | 0.10 | 0.15 | 0.30 | 1.25 | — |
| 1961 Proof | — | Value: 175 | | | | |
| 1962 | 6,000,000 | 0.10 | 0.15 | 0.30 | 1.50 | — |
| 1962 Proof | — | Value: 175 | | | | |
| 1963 | 4,000,000 | 0.10 | 0.15 | 0.25 | 0.50 | — |
| 1963 Proof | — | Value: 175 | | | | |
| 1964 | 6,400,000 | 0.10 | 0.15 | 0.25 | 0.50 | — |
| 1964 Proof | — | Value: 175 | | | | |
| 1965 | 175,000 | — | 0.10 | 0.15 | 0.50 | — |
| 1965 Prooflike | 25,000 | — | — | — | — | 0.75 |
| 1965 Proof | Est. 10 | — | — | — | — | — |

**6 PENCE** **KM# 2** **Weight:** 2.8300 g. **Composition:** 0.5000 Silver .0454 oz. ASW **Reverse:** Huia Bird

| Date | Mintage | F | VF | XF | Unc | BU |
|---|---|---|---|---|---|---|
| 1933 | 3,000,000 | 0.60 | 1.50 | 10.00 | 40.00 | — |
| 1933 Proof | 20 | Value: 450 | | | | |
| 1934 | 3,600,000 | 0.60 | 1.50 | 10.00 | 40.00 | — |
| 1934 Proof | 20 | Value: 1,500 | | | | |
| 1935 | 560,000 | 2.00 | 6.00 | 40.00 | 225 | — |
| 1935 Proof | 364 | Value: 275 | | | | |
| 1936 | 1,480,000 | 0.75 | 2.25 | 10.00 | 40.00 | — |
| 1936 Proof | — | — | — | — | — | — |

**6 PENCE** **KM# 8** **Weight:** 2.8300 g. **Composition:** 0.5000 Silver .0454 oz. ASW

| Date | Mintage | F | VF | XF | Unc | BU |
|---|---|---|---|---|---|---|
| 1937 | 1,280,000 | 0.50 | 1.50 | 7.00 | 50.00 | — |
| 1937 Proof | Est. 200 | Value: 350 | | | | |
| 1939 | 700,000 | 0.50 | 1.50 | 7.50 | 50.00 | — |
| 1939 Proof | — | Value: 350 | | | | |
| 1940 | 800,000 | 0.50 | 2.25 | 12.50 | 60.00 | — |
| 1940 Proof | — | Value: 350 | | | | |
| 1941 | 440,000 | 2.00 | 4.00 | 40.00 | 275 | — |
| 1941 Proof | — | Value: 550 | | | | |
| 1942 | 360,000 | 2.00 | 4.00 | 40.00 | 275 | — |
| 1943 | 1,800,000 | 0.50 | 1.00 | 7.00 | 30.00 | — |
| 1944 | 1,160,000 | 1.00 | 2.00 | 8.00 | 30.00 | — |
| 1944 Proof | — | Value: 300 | | | | |
| 1945 | 940,000 | 1.50 | 3.50 | 10.00 | 30.00 | — |
| 1945 Proof | — | Value: 300 | | | | |
| 1946 | 2,120,000 | 0.75 | 1.50 | 4.00 | 15.00 | — |
| 1946 | — | Value: 300 | | | | |

**6 PENCE** **KM# 8a** **Composition:** Copper-Nickel

| Date | Mintage | F | VF | XF | Unc | BU |
|---|---|---|---|---|---|---|
| 1947 | 3,200,000 | 1.00 | 2.00 | 7.50 | 40.00 | — |
| 1947 Proof | Est. 20 | Value: 300 | | | | |

**6 PENCE** **KM# 16** **Composition:** Copper-Nickel

| Date | Mintage | F | VF | XF | Unc | BU |
|---|---|---|---|---|---|---|
| 1948 | 2,000,000 | 1.00 | 2.00 | 4.00 | 35.00 | — |
| 1948 Proof | — | Value: 275 | | | | |
| 1950 | 800,000 | 1.00 | 3.50 | 16.00 | 100 | — |
| 1950 Proof | — | Value: 275 | | | | |
| 1951 | 1,800,000 | 0.40 | 0.75 | 1.50 | 4.00 | — |
| 1951 Proof | — | Value: 275 | | | | |
| 1952 | 3,200,000 | 0.40 | 0.75 | 2.00 | 15.00 | — |
| 1952 Proof | — | Value: 225 | | | | |

**6 PENCE** **KM# 26.1** **Composition:** Copper-Nickel **Obverse:** Without shoulder strap

| Date | Mintage | F | VF | XF | Unc | BU |
|---|---|---|---|---|---|---|
| 1953 | 1,200,000 | 0.15 | 0.30 | 2.50 | 7.50 | — |
| 1953 Proof | 14,000 | Value: 6.50 | | | | |
| 1953 Matte proof | — | — | — | — | 125 | — |
| 1954 | 1,200,000 | 0.15 | 0.30 | 2.50 | 14.00 | — |
| 1954 Proof | — | Value: 175 | | | | |
| 1955 | 1,600,000 | 0.15 | 0.30 | 2.50 | 15.00 | — |
| 1957 | | 1.50 | 3.50 | 60.00 | 175 | — |
| 1957 Proof | — | Value: 600 | | | | |

**6 PENCE** **KM# 26.2** **Composition:** Copper-Nickel **Obverse:** With shoulder strap

| Date | Mintage | F | VF | XF | Unc | BU |
|---|---|---|---|---|---|---|
| 1955 Proof | — | Value: 2,800 | | | | |
| 1956 | 2,000,000 | 0.20 | 0.50 | 1.50 | 4.00 | — |
| 1956 Proof | — | Value: 200 | | | | |
| 1957 | 2,400,000 | 0.20 | 0.50 | 0.75 | 4.00 | — |

| Date | Mintage | F | VF | XF | Unc | BU |
|---|---|---|---|---|---|---|
| 1957 Proof | — | Value: 200 | | | | |
| 1958 | 3,000,000 | 0.15 | 0.50 | 0.75 | 4.00 | — |
| 1958 Proof | — | Value: 200 | | | | |
| 1959 | 2,000,000 | 0.15 | 0.50 | 0.75 | 2.50 | — |
| 1959 Proof | — | Value: 200 | | | | |
| 1960 | 1,600,000 | 0.15 | 0.25 | 0.40 | 1.50 | — |
| 1960 Proof | — | Value: 200 | | | | |
| 1961 | 800,000 | 0.10 | 0.15 | 0.25 | 2.50 | — |
| 1961 Proof | — | Value: 200 | | | | |
| 1962 | 1,200,000 | 0.10 | 0.15 | 0.25 | 2.50 | — |
| 1962 Proof | — | Value: 200 | | | | |
| 1963 | 800,000 | 0.10 | 0.15 | 0.25 | 2.00 | — |
| 1963 Proof | — | Value: 200 | | | | |
| 1964 | 7,800,000 | — | 0.10 | 0.15 | 2.00 | — |
| 1964 Proof | — | Value: 175 | | | | |
| 1965 | 175,000 | — | — | 0.10 | 0.75 | — |
| 1965 Broken wing | Inc. above | — | 15.00 | 25.00 | 60.00 | — |
| 1965 Prooflike | 25,000 | — | — | — | — | 1.00 |
| 1965 Proof | Est. 10 | — | — | — | — | — |

**SHILLING** **KM# 3** **Weight:** 5.6500 g. **Composition:** 0.5000 Silver .0908 oz. ASW **Subject:** Maori Warrior

| Date | Mintage | F | VF | XF | Unc | BU |
|---|---|---|---|---|---|---|
| 1933 | 3,000,000 | 1.50 | 3.00 | 20.00 | 100 | — |
| 1933 Proof | Est. 20 | Value: 600 | | | | |
| 1934 | 3,600,000 | 1.50 | 3.50 | 15.00 | 75.00 | — |
| 1934 Proof | Est. 20 | Value: 1,800 | | | | |
| 1935 | 560,000 | 2.50 | 4.00 | 28.50 | 150 | — |
| 1935 Proof | 364 | Value: 275 | | | | |

**SHILLING** **KM# 9** **Weight:** 5.6500 g. **Composition:** 0.5000 Silver .0908 oz. ASW

| Date | Mintage | F | VF | XF | Unc | BU |
|---|---|---|---|---|---|---|
| 1937 | 890,000 | 1.25 | 3.00 | 12.50 | 70.00 | — |
| 1937 Proof | Est. 200 | Value: 550 | | | | |
| 1940 | 500,000 | 1.25 | 2.00 | 10.00 | 90.00 | — |
| 1940 Proof | — | Value: 550 | | | | |
| 1941 | 360,000 | 1.75 | 4.00 | 40.00 | 225 | — |
| 1941 Proof | — | Value: 550 | | | | |
| 1942 | 240,000 | 1.75 | 4.00 | 40.00 | 225 | — |
| 1943 | 900,000 | 2.00 | 4.00 | 12.50 | 55.00 | — |
| 1944 | 480,000 | 2.00 | 4.00 | 12.50 | 55.00 | — |
| 1944 Proof | — | Value: 550 | | | | |
| 1945 | 1,030,000 | 1.00 | 3.00 | 8.00 | 45.00 | — |
| 1945 Proof | — | Value: 550 | | | | |
| 1946 | 1,060,000 | 1.00 | 3.00 | 8.00 | 45.00 | — |
| 1946 Proof | — | Value: 550 | | | | |

**SHILLING** **KM# 9a** **Composition:** Copper-Nickel

| Date | Mintage | F | VF | XF | Unc | BU |
|---|---|---|---|---|---|---|
| 1947 | 2,800,000 | 1.50 | 3.00 | 25.00 | 75.00 | — |
| 1947 Proof | Est. 20 | Value: 350 | | | | |

**SHILLING** **KM# 17** **Composition:** Copper-Nickel

| Date | Mintage | F | VF | XF | Unc | BU |
|---|---|---|---|---|---|---|
| 1948 | 1,000,000 | 2.00 | 5.00 | 20.00 | 70.00 | — |
| 1948 Proof | — | Value: 350 | | | | |
| 1950 | 600,000 | 2.00 | 5.00 | 15.00 | 70.00 | — |
| 1950 Proof | — | Value: 350 | | | | |
| 1951 | 1,200,000 | 2.00 | 5.00 | 15.00 | 70.00 | — |
| 1951 Proof | — | Value: 350 | | | | |
| 1952 | 600,000 | 2.00 | 5.00 | 15.00 | 70.00 | — |
| 1952 Proof | — | Value: 350 | | | | |

**SHILLING** **KM# 27.1** **Composition:** Copper-Nickel **Obverse:** Without shoulder strap

| Date | Mintage | F | VF | XF | Unc | BU |
|---|---|---|---|---|---|---|
| 1953 | 200,000 | 0.60 | 1.00 | 4.00 | 12.00 | — |
| 1953 Proof | 14,000 | Value: 8.00 | | | | |
| 1953 Matte proof | — | Value: 125 | | | | |
| 1955 | 200,000 | 1.00 | 2.00 | 10.00 | 60.00 | — |
| 1955 Proof | — | Value: 350 | | | | |

**SHILLING** **KM# 27.2** **Composition:** Copper-Nickel **Obverse:** With shoulder strap

| Date | Mintage | F | VF | XF | Unc | BU |
|---|---|---|---|---|---|---|
| 1956 | 800,000 | 1.00 | 2.00 | 3.50 | 15.00 | — |
| 1956 Proof | — | Value: 350 | | | | |
| 1957 | 800,000 | 1.00 | 2.00 | 3.50 | 15.00 | — |
| 1957 Proof | — | Value: 350 | | | | |
| 1958 | 1,000,000 | 0.50 | 1.00 | 2.50 | 12.50 | — |
| 1958 Proof | — | Value: 350 | | | | |
| 1959 | 600,000 | 0.75 | 1.50 | 3.00 | 12.50 | — |
| 1959 Proof | — | Value: 350 | | | | |
| 1960 | 600,000 | 0.75 | 1.50 | 3.00 | 12.50 | — |
| 1960 Proof | — | Value: 350 | | | | |
| 1961 | 400,000 | 0.15 | 0.30 | 0.60 | 8.00 | — |
| 1961 Proof | — | Value: 350 | | | | |
| 1962 | 1,000,000 | 0.15 | 0.30 | 0.50 | 6.00 | — |
| 1962 Proof | — | Value: 350 | | | | |
| 1963 | 600,000 | 0.15 | 0.30 | 0.50 | 4.00 | — |
| 1963 Proof | — | Value: 350 | | | | |
| 1964 | 3,400,000 | 0.10 | 0.15 | 0.30 | 1.25 | — |
| 1964 Proof | — | Value: 350 | | | | |
| 1965 | 175,000 | 0.10 | 0.15 | 0.30 | 1.00 | — |
| 1965 Prooflike | 25,000 | — | — | — | — | 1.25 |
| 1965 Proof | Est. 10 | — | — | — | — | — |

**FLORIN** **KM# 4** **Weight:** 11.3100 g. **Composition:** 0.5000 Silver .1818 oz. ASW **Reverse:** Kiwi

| Date | Mintage | F | VF | XF | Unc | BU |
|---|---|---|---|---|---|---|
| 1933 | 2,100,000 | 1.50 | 3.00 | 25.00 | 120 | — |
| 1933 Proof | Est. 20 | Value: 600 | | | | |
| 1934 | 2,850,000 | 1.50 | 3.00 | 25.00 | 100 | — |
| 1934 Proof | Est. 20 | Value: 2,000 | | | | |
| 1935 | 755,000 | 2.00 | 5.00 | 40.00 | 150 | — |
| 1935 Proof | 364 | Value: 300 | | | | |
| 1936 | 150,000 | 6.00 | 12.50 | 85.00 | 775 | — |
| 1936 Proof | — | Value: 1,250 | | | | |

**FLORIN** **KM# 10.1** **Weight:** 11.3100 g. **Composition:** 0.5000 Silver .1818 oz. ASW

| Date | Mintage | F | VF | XF | Unc | BU |
|---|---|---|---|---|---|---|
| 1937 | 1,190,000 | 1.50 | 2.50 | 8.00 | 80.00 | — |
| 1937 Proof | Est. 200 | Value: 600 | | | | |
| 1940 | 500,000 | 3.00 | 10.00 | 80.00 | 600 | — |
| 1940 Proof | — | Value: 800 | | | | |
| 1941 | 820,000 | 1.50 | 3.00 | 8.00 | 70.00 | — |
| 1941 Proof | — | Value: 600 | | | | |
| 1942 | 150,000 | 1.50 | 4.00 | 25.00 | 90.00 | — |
| 1943 | 1,400,000 | 1.25 | 2.50 | 8.00 | 55.00 | — |
| 1944 | 140,000 | 3.00 | 10.00 | 35.00 | 160 | — |
| 1944 Proof | — | Value: 800 | | | | |
| 1945 | 515,000 | 2.00 | 4.00 | 8.00 | 55.00 | — |
| 1945 Proof | — | Value: 650 | | | | |
| 1946 | 1,200,000 | 2.00 | 5.00 | 10.00 | 70.00 | — |
| 1946 Proof | — | Value: 650 | | | | |

**FLORIN** **KM# 10.2** **Weight:** 11.3100 g. **Composition:** 0.5000 Silver .1818 oz. ASW **Reverse:** Flat back on Kiwi

| Date | Mintage | F | VF | XF | Unc | BU |
|---|---|---|---|---|---|---|
| 1946 | Inc. above | 6.00 | 15.00 | 125 | 450 | — |

**FLORIN** **KM# 10.2a** **Composition:** Copper-Nickel

| Date | Mintage | F | VF | XF | Unc | BU |
|---|---|---|---|---|---|---|
| 1947 | 2,500,000 | 1.00 | 2.00 | 30.00 | 125 | — |
| 1947 Proof | Est. 20 | Value: 450 | | | | |

**FLORIN** **KM# 18** **Composition:** Copper-Nickel

| Date | Mintage | F | VF | XF | Unc | BU |
|---|---|---|---|---|---|---|
| 1948 | 1,750,000 | 1.00 | 2.00 | 17.50 | 100 | — |
| 1948 Proof | — | Value: 400 | | | | |
| 1949 | 3,500,000 | 1.00 | 2.00 | 17.50 | 80.00 | — |
| 1949 Proof | — | Value: 400 | | | | |
| 1950 | 3,500,000 | 1.00 | 2.00 | 7.00 | 25.00 | — |
| 1950 Proof | — | Value: 400 | | | | |
| 1951 | 1,000,000 | 1.00 | 2.00 | 7.00 | 25.00 | — |
| 1951 Proof | — | Value: 400 | | | | |

**FLORIN** **KM# 28.1** **Composition:** Copper-Nickel **Obverse:** Without shoulder strap

| Date | Mintage | F | VF | XF | Unc | BU |
|---|---|---|---|---|---|---|
| 1953 | 250,000 | 1.00 | 1.50 | 2.50 | 10.00 | — |
| 1953 Proof | 7,000 | Value: 12.50 | | | | |
| 1953 Matte proof | — | Value: 180 | | | | |

**FLORIN** **KM# 28.2** **Composition:** Copper-Nickel **Obverse:** With shoulder strap

| Date | Mintage | F | VF | XF | Unc | BU |
|---|---|---|---|---|---|---|
| 1961 | 1,500,000 | 0.15 | 0.25 | 1.00 | 8.00 | — |
| 1961 Proof | — | Value: 375 | | | | |
| 1962 | 1,500,000 | 0.15 | 0.25 | 1.00 | 8.00 | — |
| 1962 Proof | — | Value: 375 | | | | |
| 1963 | 100,000 | 0.15 | 0.60 | 1.25 | 10.00 | — |
| 1963 Proof | — | Value: 375 | | | | |
| 1964 | 7,000,000 | 0.15 | 0.20 | 0.35 | 3.50 | — |
| 1964 Proof | — | Value: 375 | | | | |
| 1965 | 175,000 | 0.15 | 0.20 | 0.35 | 1.75 | — |
| 1965 Prooflike | 25,000 | — | — | — | — | 2.00 |
| 1965 Proof | Est. 10 | — | — | — | — | — |

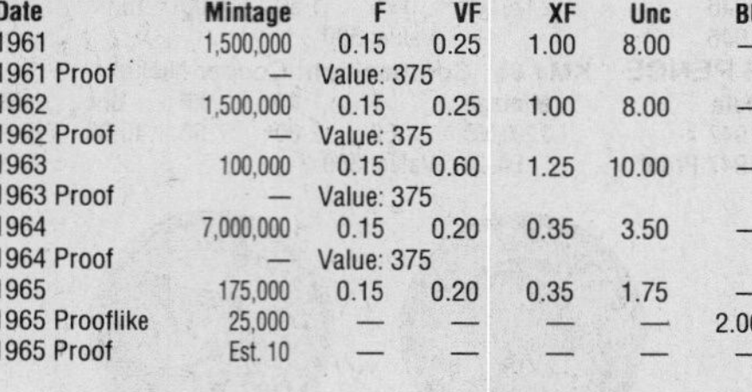

**1/2 CROWN** **KM# 5** **Weight:** 14.1400 g. **Composition:** 0.5000 Silver .2273 oz. ASW

| Date | Mintage | F | VF | XF | Unc | BU |
|---|---|---|---|---|---|---|
| 1933 | 2,000,000 | 2.50 | 8.00 | 25.00 | 125 | — |
| 1933 Proof | Est. 20 | Value: 650 | | | | |
| 1934 | 2,720,000 | 2.50 | 8.00 | 20.00 | 120 | — |
| 1934 Proof | Est. 20 | Value: 2,250 | | | | |
| 1935 | 612,000 | 3.50 | 10.00 | 45.00 | 275 | — |
| 1935 Proof | 364 | Value: 600 | | | | |

**1/2 CROWN** **KM# 11** **Weight:** 14.1400 g. **Composition:** 0.5000 Silver .2273 oz. ASW

| Date | Mintage | F | VF | XF | Unc | BU |
|---|---|---|---|---|---|---|
| 1937 | 672,000 | 2.25 | 5.00 | 17.50 | 100 | — |
| 1937 Proof | 200 | Value: 700 | | | | |
| 1941 | 776,000 | 2.25 | 6.00 | 17.50 | 100 | — |
| 1941 Proof | — | Value: 700 | | | | |
| 1942 | 240,000 | 2.25 | 6.00 | 20.00 | 100 | — |
| 1943 | 1,120,000 | 1.75 | 3.50 | 12.50 | 80.00 | — |
| 1944 | 180,000 | 5.00 | 10.00 | 60.00 | 350 | — |
| 1944 Proof | — | Value: 700 | | | | |
| 1945 | 420,000 | 3.00 | 6.00 | 17.50 | 120 | — |
| 1945 Proof | — | Value: 700 | | | | |
| 1946 | 960,000 | 3.00 | 6.00 | 17.50 | 120 | — |
| 1946 Proof | — | Value: 700 | | | | |

**1/2 CROWN** **KM# 14** **Weight:** 14.1400 g. **Composition:** 0.5000 Silver .2273 oz. ASW **Subject:** New Zealand Centennial **Reverse:** Maori Wahine

| Date | Mintage | F | VF | XF | Unc | BU |
|---|---|---|---|---|---|---|
| 1940 | 101,000 | 2.50 | 4.00 | 10.00 | 32.00 | — |
| 1940 Proof | — | Value: 5,000 | | | | |

**1/2 CROWN** **KM# 11a** **Composition:** Copper-Nickel

| Date | Mintage | F | VF | XF | Unc | BU |
|---|---|---|---|---|---|---|
| 1947 | 1,600,000 | 0.40 | 2.00 | 7.00 | 110 | — |
| 1947 Proof | Est. 20 | Value: 550 | | | | |

**1/2 CROWN** **KM# 19** **Composition:** Copper-Nickel

| Date | Mintage | F | VF | XF | Unc | BU |
|---|---|---|---|---|---|---|
| 1948 | 1,400,000 | 0.40 | 1.50 | 7.00 | 100 | |
| 1948 Proof | — | Value: 500 | | | | |
| 1949 | 2,800,000 | 0.40 | 1.50 | 7.00 | 90.00 | — |
| 1949 Proof | — | Value: 500 | | | | |
| 1950 K. G. close to dots | 3,600,000 | 0.40 | 1.00 | 2.00 | 20.00 | — |
| 1950 Proof | — | Value: 500 | | | | |
| 1950 K. G. close to rim | Inc. above | 0.40 | 1.00 | 2.00 | 20.00 | — |
| 1950 Proof | — | Value: 500 | | | | |
| 1951 | 1,200,000 | 0.40 | 1.00 | 2.00 | 20.00 | — |
| 1951 Proof | — | Value: 500 | | | | |

**1/2 CROWN** **KM# 29.1** **Composition:** Copper-Nickel **Reverse:** Without shoulder strap

| Date | Mintage | F | VF | XF | Unc | BU |
|---|---|---|---|---|---|---|
| 1953 | 120,000 | 1.00 | 2.50 | 4.00 | 15.00 | — |
| 1953 Proof | 7,000 | Value: 10.00 | | | | |
| 1953 Matte proof | — | Value: 245 | | | | |

**1/2 CROWN** KM# 29.2 **Composition:** Copper-Nickel **Obverse:** With shoulder strap

| Date | Mintage | F | VF | XF | Unc | BU |
|---|---|---|---|---|---|---|
| 1961 | 80,000 | 0.40 | 0.80 | 2.00 | 10.00 | — |
| 1961 Proof | — | Value: 450 | | | | |
| 1962 | 600,000 | 0.30 | 0.70 | 1.50 | 7.50 | — |
| 1962 Proof | — | Value: 450 | | | | |
| 1963 | 400,000 | 0.50 | 0.70 | 1.50 | 6.00 | — |
| 1963 Proof | — | Value: 450 | | | | |
| 1965 | 175,000 | 0.50 | 0.70 | 1.00 | 2.50 | — |
| 1965 Prooflike | 25,000 | — | — | — | — | 3.00 |
| 1965 Proof | 10 | — | — | — | — | — |

**CROWN** KM# 6 **Weight:** 28.2800 g. **Composition:** 0.5000 Silver .4546 oz. ASW **Subject:** Treaty of Waitangi in 1840. **Reverse:** Woka Nene and Governor Hobson

| Date | Mintage | F | VF | XF | Unc | BU |
|---|---|---|---|---|---|---|
| 1935 | 764 | 1,100 | 1,350 | 2,250 | 2,750 | — |
| 1935 Proof | 364 | Value: 2,500 | | | | |

**CROWN** KM# 22 **Weight:** 28.2800 g. **Composition:** 0.5000 Silver .4546 oz. ASW **Subject:** Proposed Royal visit **Reverse:** Silver Fern Leaf

| Date | Mintage | F | VF | XF | Unc | BU |
|---|---|---|---|---|---|---|
| 1949 | 200,000 | — | 2.50 | 4.00 | 12.00 | — |
| 1949 Proof | Est. 3 | Value: 4,250 | | | | |

**CROWN** KM# 30 **Composition:** Copper-Nickel **Subject:** Queen Elizabeth II Coronation

| Date | Mintage | F | VF | XF | Unc | BU |
|---|---|---|---|---|---|---|
| 1953 | 250,000 | — | — | 2.00 | 4.00 | — |
| 1953 Proof | 7,000 | Value: 20.00 | | | | |

## DECIMAL COINAGE

100 Cents = 1 Dollar

(c) Royal Australian Mint, Canberra
(l) Royal Mint, Llantrisant
(o) Royal Canadian Mint, Ottawa

**CENT** KM# 31 **Composition:** Bronze **Reverse:** Silver Fern Leaf

| Date | Mintage | F | VF | XF | Unc | BU |
|---|---|---|---|---|---|---|
| 1967 | 250,000 | — | — | 0.10 | 0.15 | — |
| 1967 Prooflike | 50,000 | — | — | — | — | 0.80 |
| 1967 Proof | 10 | — | — | — | — | — |
| 1968 | 35,000 | — | — | 0.15 | 1.00 | — |
| 1968 Prooflike | 40,000 | — | — | — | — | 1.25 |
| 1969 | 50,000 | — | — | 0.15 | 1.00 | — |
| 1969 Prooflike | 50,000 | — | — | — | — | 1.25 |
| 1970 | 30,000 | — | — | 0.15 | 0.60 | — |
| 1970 Prooflike | 20,010 | — | — | — | — | 1.00 |
| 1971(c) Serifs on date numerals | 10,000,000 | — | — | 0.20 | 4.00 | — |
| 1971(l) Without serifs | 15,000 | — | — | 0.15 | 2.75 | — |
| 1971(l) Proof | 5,000 | Value: 12.50 | | | | |
| 1972 | 10,055,000 | — | — | 0.15 | 2.75 | — |
| 1972 Proof | 8,045 | Value: 5.00 | | | | |
| 1973 | 15,055,000 | — | — | 0.10 | 2.50 | — |
| 1973 Proof | 8,000 | Value: 5.00 | | | | |
| 1974 | 35,035,000 | — | — | 0.10 | 2.00 | — |
| 1974 Proof | 8,000 | Value: 4.00 | | | | |
| 1975 | 60,015,000 | — | — | 0.10 | 1.00 | — |
| 1975 Proof | 10,000 | Value: 4.00 | | | | |
| 1976 | 20,016,000 | — | — | 0.10 | 0.60 | — |
| 1976 Proof | 11,000 | Value: 4.00 | | | | |
| 1977 | 20,000 | — | — | 0.20 | 6.00 | — |
| 1977 Proof | 12,000 | Value: 5.00 | | | | |
| 1978(o) | 15,023,000 | — | — | 0.10 | 1.25 | — |
| 1978(o) Proof | 15,000 | Value: 3.50 | | | | |
| 1979(o) | 35,025,000 | — | — | 0.10 | 0.60 | — |
| 1979(o) Proof | 16,000 | Value: 3.50 | | | | |
| 1980(l) Smooth shoulder folds in gown | 27,000 | — | — | 0.10 | 1.25 | — |
| 1980(l) Proof | 17,000 | Value: 3.50 | | | | |
| 1980(o) Incised shoulder folds in gown | 4,000,000 | — | — | 0.10 | 0.80 | — |
| 1981(o) Incised shoulder folds in gown. | 10,000,000 | — | — | 0.10 | 0.40 | — |
| 1981(l) Smooth shoulder folds in gown. | 25,000 | — | — | 0.10 | 1.00 | — |
| 1981(l) Proof; Smooth shoulder folds in gown | 18,000 | Value: 3.50 | | | | |
| 1982(o) Blunt tipped 2 | 10,000,000 | — | — | 0.10 | 0.40 | — |
| 1982(l) Round tipped 2 | 25,000 | — | — | 0.10 | 0.80 | — |
| 1982(l) Proof; Round tipped 2 | 18,000 | Value: 2.50 | | | | |
| 1983(o) Round top 3 | 40,000,000 | — | — | 0.10 | 0.40 | — |
| 1983(l) Flat top 3 | 25,000 | — | — | 0.10 | 0.80 | — |
| 1983(l) Proof; Flat top 3 | 18,000 | Value: 2.50 | | | | |
| 1984(o) Wiry hair, bushy eyebrow | 30,000,000 | — | — | 0.10 | 0.25 | — |
| 1984(l) Smooth shoulder folds | 25,000 | — | — | — | 0.80 | — |
| 1984(l) Proof; Smooth shoulder folds | 15,000 | Value: 1.50 | | | | |
| 1985(o) Wiry hair, bush eyebrow | 40,000,000 | — | — | — | 0.25 | — |
| 1985(c) Smooth shoulder folds | 20,000 | — | — | — | 1.25 | — |
| 1985(c) Proof | 12,000 | Value: 1.00 | | | | |

**CENT** KM# 58 **Composition:** Bronze **Obverse:** Similar to 1 Dollar, KM# 57

| Date | Mintage | F | VF | XF | Unc | BU |
|---|---|---|---|---|---|---|
| 1986(o) | 25,000,000 | — | — | — | 0.25 | — |
| 1986(l) | 18,000 | — | — | — | 1.25 | — |
| 1986(l) Proof | 10,000 | Value: 1.00 | | | | |
| 1987(o) | 27,500,000 | — | — | — | 0.25 | — |
| 1987(l) | 18,000 | — | — | — | 1.25 | — |
| 1987(l) Proof | 10,000 | Value: 1.00 | | | | |
| 1988(l) | 15,000 | — | — | — | 7.00 | — |
| 1988(l) Proof | 9,000 | Value: 2.00 | | | | |

**Note:** 1988 cent was struck for sets only.

**2 CENTS** KM# 32 **Composition:** Bronze **Reverse:** Kowhai Leaves

| Date | Mintage | F | VF | XF | Unc | BU |
|---|---|---|---|---|---|---|
| 1967 | 250,000 | — | — | 0.10 | 0.15 | — |
| 1967 Prooflike | 50,000 | — | — | — | — | 0.75 |
| 1967 Proof | 10 | — | — | — | — | — |
| 1968 | 35,000 | — | — | 0.15 | 0.75 | — |
| 1968 Prooflike | 40,000 | — | — | — | — | 1.25 |
| 1969 | 50,000 | — | — | 0.15 | 0.50 | — |
| 1969 Prooflike | 50,000 | — | — | — | — | 1.25 |
| 1970 | 30,000 | — | — | 0.15 | 2.75 | — |
| 1970 Prooflike | 20,010 | — | — | — | — | 1.25 |
| 1971(c) Serifs on date numerals | 15,050,000 | — | — | 0.20 | 3.50 | — |
| 1971(l) Without serifs | 15,000 | — | — | 0.20 | 3.50 | — |
| 1971(l) Proof | 5,000 | Value: 12.50 | | | | |
| 1972 | 17,525,000 | — | — | 0.15 | 2.50 | — |
| 1972 Proof | 8,045 | Value: 5.00 | | | | |
| 1973 | 38,565,000 | — | — | 0.10 | 2.25 | — |
| 1973 Proof | 8,000 | Value: 5.25 | | | | |
| 1974 | 50,015,000 | — | — | 0.10 | 2.25 | — |
| 1974 Proof | 8,000 | Value: 3.25 | | | | |
| 1975 | 20,015,000 | — | — | 0.10 | 1.00 | — |
| 1975 Proof | 10,000 | Value: 3.25 | | | | |
| 1976 | 15,016,000 | — | — | 0.10 | 0.60 | — |
| 1976 Proof | 11,000 | Value: 3.25 | | | | |
| 1977 | 20,000,000 | — | — | 0.10 | 0.75 | — |
| 1977 Proof | 12,000 | Value: 3.25 | | | | |
| 1978 | 23,000 | — | — | 0.10 | 6.00 | — |
| 1978 Proof | 15,000 | Value: 3.25 | | | | |
| 1979 | 25,000 | — | — | 0.10 | 4.00 | — |
| 1979 | 16,000 | Value: 3.25 | | | | |
| 1980(l) Smooth shoulder folds on gown | 27,000 | — | — | 0.10 | 0.80 | — |
| 1980(l) Proof | 17,000 | Value: 2.75 | | | | |
| 1980(o) Incised shoulder folds on gown | 10,000,000 | — | — | 0.10 | 1.00 | — |
| 1981(o) Incised shoulder folds on gown | 25,000,000 | — | — | 0.10 | 1.00 | — |
| 1981(l) Smooth shoulder folds on gown | 25,000 | — | — | 0.10 | 1.00 | — |
| 1981(l) Proof | 18,000 | Value: 2.75 | | | | |
| 1982(o) Blunt open 2 | 50,000,000 | — | — | 0.10 | 0.75 | — |
| 1982(l) Pointed tight 2 | 25,000 | — | — | 0.10 | 0.60 | — |
| 1982(l) Proof | 18,000 | Value: 2.75 | | | | |
| 1983(o) Round topped 3 | 15,000,000 | — | — | 0.10 | 0.75 | — |
| 1983(l) Flat topped 3 | 25,000 | — | — | 0.10 | 0.60 | — |
| 1983(l) Proof | 18,000 | Value: 2.75 | | | | |
| 1984(o) Wiry hair, bushy eyebrow | 10,000,000 | — | — | 0.10 | 0.60 | — |
| 1984(l) Smooth shoulder folds | 25,000 | — | — | 0.10 | 2.00 | — |
| 1984(l) Proof | 15,000 | Value: 1.75 | | | | |
| 1985(o) Wiry hair, bushy eyebrow | 22,500,000 | — | — | 0.10 | 0.60 | — |
| 1985(c) Smooth shoulder folds | 20,000 | — | — | 0.10 | 2.00 | — |
| 1985(c) Proof | 12,000 | Value: 1.25 | | | | |

**2 CENTS** KM# 33 **Composition:** Bronze **Obverse:** Bahamas 5 Cent, KM#3 **Reverse:** KM#32 **Note:** Mule.

| Date | Mintage | F | VF | XF | Unc | BU |
|---|---|---|---|---|---|---|
| ND(1967) | Est. 50,000 | — | 7.50 | 10.00 | 20.00 | — |

**2 CENTS** KM# 59 **Composition:** Bronze **Obverse:** Similar to 1 Dollar, KM#57

| Date | Mintage | F | VF | XF | Unc | BU |
|---|---|---|---|---|---|---|
| 1986(l) | 18,000 | — | — | — | 5.00 | — |
| 1986(l) Proof | 10,000 | Value: 1.25 | | | | |
| 1987(o) | 36,250,000 | — | — | — | 0.35 | — |
| 1987(l) | 18,000 | — | — | — | 1.50 | — |
| 1987(l) Proof | 10,000 | Value: 1.25 | | | | |
| 1988(l) | 15,000 | — | — | — | 5.00 | — |
| 1988(l) Proof | 9,000 | Value: 1.25 | | | | |

**5 CENTS** KM# 34 **Composition:** Copper-Nickel **Subject:** Tuatara

| Date | Mintage | F | VF | XF | Unc | BU |
|---|---|---|---|---|---|---|
| 1967 | 250,000 | — | — | 0.10 | 0.25 | — |
| 1967 Without sea line | Inc. above | — | 3.00 | 7.50 | 28.50 | — |
| 1967 Prooflike | 50,000 | — | — | — | — | 1.00 |
| 1967 Proof | 10 | — | — | — | — | — |
| 1968 | 35,000 | — | — | 0.15 | 1.25 | — |
| 1968 Prooflike | 40,000 | — | — | — | — | 1.50 |
| 1969 | 50,000 | — | — | 0.15 | 0.50 | — |
| 1969 Prooflike | 50,000 | — | — | — | — | — |
| 1970 | 30,000 | — | — | 0.15 | 0.50 | — |
| 1970 Prooflike | 20,010 | — | — | — | — | 1.50 |

| Date | Mintage | F | VF | XF | Unc | BU |
|---|---|---|---|---|---|---|
| 1971(c) Serifs on date numerals | 11,520,000 | — | — | 0.15 | 3.75 | — |
| 1971(l) Without serifs | 15,000 | — | — | 0.15 | 3.75 | — |
| 1971(l) Proof | 5,000 | Value: 15.00 | | | | |
| 1972 | 20,015,000 | — | — | 0.10 | 2.75 | — |
| 1972 Proof | 8,045 | Value: 5.00 | | | | |
| 1973 | 4,038,999 | — | — | 0.10 | 2.00 | — |
| 1973 Proof | 8,000 | Value: 4.50 | | | | |
| 1974 | 18,015,000 | — | — | 0.10 | 2.75 | — |
| 1974 Proof | 8,000 | Value: 4.00 | | | | |
| 1975 | 32,015,000 | — | — | 0.10 | 1.50 | — |
| 1975 Proof | 10,000 | Value: 4.50 | | | | |
| 1976 | 16,000 | — | — | 0.20 | 7.50 | — |
| 1976 Proof | 11,000 | Value: 4.00 | | | | |
| 1977 | 20,000 | — | — | 0.15 | 5.50 | — |
| 1977 Proof | 12,000 | Value: 4.00 | | | | |
| 1978 | 20,023,000 | — | — | 0.10 | 0.40 | — |
| 1978 Proof | 15,000 | Value: 4.00 | | | | |
| 1979 | 25,000 | — | — | 0.15 | 6.00 | — |
| 1979 Proof | 16,000 | Value: 4.00 | | | | |
| 1980(l) Smooth shoulder folds on gown | 27,000 | — | — | 0.10 | 1.00 | — |
| 1980(l) Proof | 17,000 | Value: 4.00 | | | | |
| 1980(o) Incised shoulder folds on gown | 12,000,000 | — | — | 0.10 | 0.75 | — |
| 1981(o) Incised shoulder folds on gown | 20,000,000 | — | — | 0.10 | 0.75 | — |
| 1981(l) Smooth shoulder folds on gown | 25,000 | — | — | 0.10 | 1.00 | — |
| 1981(l) Proof | 18,000 | Value: 3.00 | | | | |
| 1982(o) Blunt 2 | 50,000,000 | — | — | 0.10 | 0.75 | — |
| 1982(l) Pointed 2 | 25,000 | — | — | 0.10 | 1.00 | — |
| 1982(l) Proof | 18,000 | Value: 3.00 | | | | |
| 1983(l) | 25,000 | — | — | 0.10 | 3.00 | — |
| 1983(l) Proof | 18,000 | Value: 2.75 | | | | |
| 1984(l) | 25,000 | — | — | 0.10 | 4.00 | — |
| 1984(l) Proof | 15,000 | Value: 3.00 | | | | |
| 1985(o) Wiry hair, bushy eyebrow | 14,000,000 | — | — | 0.10 | 0.75 | — |
| 1985(c) | 20,000 | — | — | 0.10 | 2.00 | — |
| 1985(c) Proof | 12,000 | Value: 3.00 | | | | |

**5 CENTS KM# 64 Composition:** Copper-Nickel **Obverse:** KM#34 **Reverse:** Canada 10 Cent, KM#77 **Note:** Mule.

| Date | Mintage | F | VF | XF | Unc | BU |
|---|---|---|---|---|---|---|
| 1981(o) Rare; Serif on 1 | — | — | — | — | — | — |

**5 CENTS KM# 60 Composition:** Copper-Nickel

| Date | Mintage | F | VF | XF | Unc | BU |
|---|---|---|---|---|---|---|
| 1986(o) | 18,000,000 | — | — | 0.10 | 0.25 | — |
| 1986(l) | 18,000 | — | — | — | 1.50 | — |
| 1986(l) Proof | 10,000 | Value: 3.00 | | | | |
| 1987(o) | 60,000,000 | — | — | 0.10 | 0.25 | — |
| 1987(l) | 18,000 | — | — | — | 1.50 | — |
| 1987(l) Proof | 10,000 | Value: 3.00 | | | | |
| 1988(c) Round topped numerals | 8,000,000 | — | — | 0.10 | 0.50 | — |
| 1988(l) Flat topped numerals | 15,000 | — | — | — | 1.50 | — |
| 1988(l) Proof | 9,000 | Value: 3.00 | | | | |
| 1989(o) | 36,000,000 | — | — | — | 0.25 | — |
| 1989(c) | 15,000 | — | — | — | 1.50 | — |
| 1989(c) Proof | 8,500,000 | Value: 3.00 | | | | |
| 1990(l) | 18,000 | — | — | — | 0.75 | — |
| 1990(l) Proof | 10,000 | Value: 3.00 | | | | |
| 1991(c) | 20,000 | — | — | — | 1.50 | — |
| 1991(c) Proof | 9,000 | Value: 3.00 | | | | |
| 1992(l) | 15,000 | — | — | — | 2.75 | — |
| 1992(l) Proof | 9,000 | Value: 3.00 | | | | |
| 1993(l) | 15,000 | — | — | — | 1.50 | — |
| 1993(l) Proof | 10,000 | Value: 3.00 | | | | |
| 1994(l) | 20,000,000 | — | — | — | 0.25 | — |
| 1994(l) Proof | 10,000 | Value: 3.00 | | | | |
| 1995(l) | — | — | — | — | 0.25 | — |
| 1995(l) Proof | Est. 4,000 | Value: 3.00 | | | | |
| 1996(l) | — | — | — | — | 0.25 | — |
| 1997(l) | — | — | — | — | 0.25 | — |
| 1997(l) Proof | — | Value: 3.00 | | | | |
| 1998(l) | — | — | — | — | 0.25 | — |
| 1998(l) Proof | Est. 2,000 | Value: 3.00 | | | | |

**5 CENTS KM# 72 Composition:** Copper-Nickel **Subject:** 1990 Anniversary Celebrations

| Date | Mintage | F | VF | XF | Unc | BU |
|---|---|---|---|---|---|---|
| 1990 | 10,000 | — | — | — | 1.00 | — |

**5 CENTS KM# 72a Weight:** 3.2700 g. **Composition:** 0.9250 Silver .0973 oz. ASW

| Date | Mintage | F | VF | XF | Unc | BU |
|---|---|---|---|---|---|---|
| 1990 Proof | 7,000 | Value: 10.00 | | | | |

**5 CENTS KM# 116 Composition:** Copper-Nickel **Obverse:** Rank-Broadley portrait of Queen Elizabeth II **Reverse:** Similar to KM#60

| Date | Mintage | F | VF | XF | Unc | BU |
|---|---|---|---|---|---|---|
| 1999 | — | — | — | — | 0.25 | — |
| 1999 Proof | Est. 2,000 | Value: 3.00 | | | | |
| 2000 | — | — | — | — | 0.25 | — |
| 2000 Proof | — | Value: 3.00 | | | | |

**10 CENTS KM# 35 Composition:** Copper-Nickel **Reverse:** Maori Mask

| Date | Mintage | F | VF | XF | Unc | BU |
|---|---|---|---|---|---|---|
| 1967 | 250,000 | — | — | 0.10 | 0.25 | — |
| 1967 Prooflike | 50,000 | — | — | — | — | 1.25 |
| 1967 Proof | 10 | — | — | — | — | — |
| 1968 | 35,000 | — | — | 0.15 | 1.50 | — |
| 1968 Prooflike | 40,000 | — | — | — | — | 2.00 |
| 1969 | 3,050,000 | — | — | 0.15 | 0.75 | — |
| 1969 Proof | 50,000 | Value: 1.50 | | | | |

**10 CENTS KM# 41 Composition:** Copper-Nickel

| Date | Mintage | F | VF | XF | Unc | BU |
|---|---|---|---|---|---|---|
| 1970 | 30,000 | — | — | 0.15 | 0.75 | — |
| 1970 Prooflike | 20,010 | — | — | — | — | 1.50 |
| 1971(c) Serifs on date numerals | 2,800,000 | — | 1.00 | 3.50 | 25.00 | — |
| 1971(l) Without serifs | 15,000 | — | — | 0.15 | 4.00 | — |
| 1971(l) Proof | 5,000 | Value: 25.00 | | | | |
| 1972 | 2,039,000 | — | — | 0.15 | 2.00 | — |
| 1972 Proof | 8,000 | Value: 15.00 | | | | |
| 1973 | 3,525,000 | — | — | 0.10 | 2.00 | — |
| 1973 Proof | 8,000 | Value: 6.00 | | | | |
| 1974 | 4,619,000 | — | — | 0.10 | 2.00 | — |
| 1974 Proof | 8,000 | Value: 6.00 | | | | |
| 1975 | 7,015,000 | — | — | 0.10 | 2.00 | — |
| 1975 Proof | 10,000 | Value: 5.00 | | | | |
| 1976 | 5,016,000 | — | — | 0.10 | 1.50 | — |
| 1976 Proof | 11,000 | Value: 5.00 | | | | |
| 1977 | 5,000,000 | — | — | 0.10 | 1.00 | — |
| 1977 Proof | 12,000 | Value: 5.00 | | | | |
| 1978 | 16,023,000 | — | — | 0.10 | 2.00 | — |
| 1978 Proof | 15,000 | Value: 4.00 | | | | |
| 1979 | 6,000,000 | — | — | 0.10 | 0.60 | — |
| 1979 Proof | 16,000 | Value: 4.00 | | | | |
| 1980(l) Smooth shoulder folds on gown | 27,000 | — | — | 0.10 | 0.80 | — |
| 1980(l) Proof | 17,000 | Value: 4.00 | | | | |
| 1980(o) Incised shoulder folds on gown | 28,000,000 | — | — | 0.10 | 2.50 | — |
| 1981(o) Oval holes in 8 | 5,000,000 | — | — | 0.10 | 2.50 | — |
| 1981(l) Round holes in 8 | 25,000 | — | — | 0.10 | 1.00 | — |
| 1981(l) Proof | 18,000 | Value: 4.00 | | | | |

| Date | Mintage | F | VF | XF | Unc | BU |
|---|---|---|---|---|---|---|
| 1982(o) Blunt open 2 | 18,000,000 | — | — | 0.10 | 2.50 | — |
| 1982(l) Point tipped 2 | 25,000 | — | — | 0.10 | 1.75 | — |
| 1982(l) Proof | 18,000 | Value: 4.00 | | | | |
| 1983(l) | 25,000 | — | — | 0.10 | 3.00 | — |
| 1983(l) Proof | 18,000 | Value: 4.00 | | | | |
| 1984(l) | 25,000 | — | — | 0.10 | 3.00 | — |
| 1984(l) Proof | 15,000 | Value: 4.00 | | | | |
| 1985(o) Wiry hair, bushy eyebrow | 8,000,000 | — | — | 0.10 | 3.50 | — |
| 1985(c) Smooth shoulder folds on gown | 20,000 | — | — | 0.10 | 2.75 | — |
| 1985(c) Proof | 12,000 | Value: 3.50 | | | | |

**10 CENTS KM# 61 Composition:** Copper-Nickel

| Date | Mintage | F | VF | XF | Unc | BU |
|---|---|---|---|---|---|---|
| 1986(l) | 18,000 | — | — | 0.15 | 5.00 | — |
| 1986(l) Proof | 10,000 | Value: 3.50 | | | | |
| 1987(o) | 21,000,000 | — | — | 0.10 | 1.50 | — |
| 1987(l) | 18,000 | — | — | 0.10 | 1.50 | — |
| 1987(l) Proof | 10,000 | Value: 3.75 | | | | |
| 1988(c) | 12,000,000 | — | — | 0.10 | 0.25 | — |
| 1988(l) | 15,000 | — | — | 0.10 | 1.50 | — |
| 1988(l) Proof | 9,000 | Value: 3.75 | | | | |
| 1989(c) | 9,000,000 | — | — | — | 0.25 | — |
| 1989(c) Proof | 8,500 | Value: 3.75 | | | | |
| 1989(o) | 15,000 | — | — | — | 1.50 | — |
| 1990(c) | 18,000 | — | — | — | 1.25 | — |
| 1990(c) Proof | 10,000 | Value: 3.75 | | | | |
| 1991(c) | 20,000 | — | — | — | 1.50 | — |
| 1991(c) Proof | 15,000 | Value: 3.75 | | | | |
| 1992 | 15,000 | — | — | — | 1.50 | — |
| 1992 Proof | 9,000 | Value: 3.75 | | | | |
| 1993 | 15,000 | — | — | — | 0.80 | — |
| 1993 Proof | 10,000 | Value: 3.75 | | | | |
| 1994 | — | — | — | — | 0.80 | — |
| 1994 Proof | 10,000 | Value: 3.75 | | | | |
| 1995 | — | — | — | — | 0.80 | — |
| 1995 Proof | Est. 4,000 | Value: 3.75 | | | | |
| 1996 | — | — | — | — | 0.80 | — |
| 1997 | — | — | — | — | 0.80 | — |
| 1997 Proof | — | Value: 3.75 | | | | |
| 1998 | — | — | — | — | 0.80 | — |
| 1998 Proof | Est. 2,000 | Value: 3.75 | | | | |

**10 CENTS KM# 73 Composition:** Copper-Nickel **Subject:** 1990 Anniversary Celebrations **Obverse:** Similar to 1 Dollar, KM#76

| Date | Mintage | F | VF | XF | Unc | BU |
|---|---|---|---|---|---|---|
| 1990 | 10,000 | — | — | — | 1.50 | — |

**10 CENTS KM# 73a Weight:** 6.5300 g. **Composition:** 0.9250 Silver .1942 oz. ASW

| Date | Mintage | F | VF | XF | Unc | BU |
|---|---|---|---|---|---|---|
| 1990 Proof | 7,000 | Value: 10.00 | | | | |

**10 CENTS KM# 117 Composition:** Copper-Nickel **Obverse:** Rank-Broadley portrait of Queen Elizabeth II **Reverse:** Similar to KM#61

| Date | Mintage | F | VF | XF | Unc | BU |
|---|---|---|---|---|---|---|
| 1999 | — | — | — | — | 0.50 | — |
| 1999 Proof | Est. 2,000 | Value: 4.00 | | | | |
| 2000 | — | — | — | — | 0.50 | — |
| 2000 Proof | — | Value: 4.00 | | | | |

**20 CENTS** **KM# 36** **Composition:** Copper-Nickel **Subject:** Kiwi

| Date | Mintage | F | VF | XF | Unc | BU |
|---|---|---|---|---|---|---|
| 1967 | 250,000 | — | — | 0.20 | 0.40 | — |
| 1967 Prooflike | 50,000 | — | — | — | — | 1.25 |
| 1967 Proof | 10 | — | — | — | — | — |
| 1968 | 35,000 | — | — | 0.20 | 1.50 | — |
| 1968 Prooflike | 40,000 | — | — | — | — | 2.50 |
| 1969 | 50,000 | — | — | 0.20 | 0.60 | — |
| 1969 Prooflike | 50,000 | — | — | — | — | 2.00 |
| 1970 | 30,000 | — | — | 0.25 | 4.00 | — |
| 1970 Prooflike | 20,010 | — | — | — | — | 2.50 |
| 1971(c) Serifs on date numerals | 1,600,000 | — | 1.00 | 4.00 | 20.00 | — |
| 1971(l) Without serifs | 15,000 | — | — | 0.25 | 4.00 | — |
| 1971(l) Proof | 5,000 | Value: 40.00 | | | | |
| 1972 | 1,531,000 | — | — | 0.15 | 2.00 | — |
| 1972 Proof | 8,000 | Value: 12.50 | | | | |
| 1973 | 3,043,000 | — | — | 0.15 | 2.00 | — |
| 1973 Proof | 8,000 | Value: 7.00 | | | | |
| 1974 | 4,527,000 | — | — | 0.15 | 4.00 | — |
| 1974 Proof | 8,000 | Value: 8.00 | | | | |
| 1975 | 5,015,000 | — | — | 0.15 | 2.00 | — |
| 1975 Proof | 12,000 | Value: 6.50 | | | | |
| 1976 | 7,516,000 | — | — | 0.15 | 2.00 | — |
| 1976 Proof | 11,000 | Value: 6.00 | | | | |
| 1977 | 7,500,000 | — | — | 0.15 | 2.00 | — |
| 1977 Proof | 12,000 | Value: 6.50 | | | | |
| 1978 | 2,523,000 | — | — | 0.15 | 2.00 | — |
| 1978 Proof | 15,000 | Value: 5.00 | | | | |
| 1979 | 8,000,000 | — | — | 0.15 | 1.00 | — |
| 1979 Proof | 16,000 | Value: 5.00 | | | | |
| 1980(l) Smooth shoulder folds on gown | 27,000 | — | — | 0.15 | 1.00 | — |
| 1980(l) Proof | 17,000 | Value: 5.00 | | | | |
| 1980(o) Incised shoulder folds on gown | 9,000,000 | — | — | 0.15 | 5.00 | — |
| 1981(o) Incised shoulder folds on gown | 7,500,000 | — | — | 0.15 | 5.00 | — |
| 1981(l) Smooth shoulder folds on gown | 25,000 | — | — | 0.15 | 1.00 | — |
| 1981(l) Proof | 18,000 | Value: 4.00 | | | | |
| 1982(o) Blunt 2 | 17,500,000 | — | — | 0.15 | 5.00 | — |
| 1982(l) Pointed 2 | 25,000 | — | — | 0.15 | 1.00 | — |
| 1982(l) Proof | 18,000 | Value: 5.00 | | | | |
| 1983(o) Round topped 3 | 2,500,000 | — | — | 0.15 | 5.00 | — |
| 1983(l) Flat topped 3 | 25,000 | — | — | 0.15 | 1.00 | — |
| 1983(l) Proof | 18,000 | Value: 4.00 | | | | |
| 1984(o) Wiry hair, bushy eyebrows | 1,500,000 | — | — | 0.15 | 5.00 | — |
| 1984(l) Smooth shoulder folds on gown | 25,000 | — | — | 0.15 | 0.60 | — |
| 1984(l) Proof | 18,000 | Value: 4.00 | | | | |
| 1985(o) Pointed tip 5 | 6,000,000 | — | — | 0.15 | 7.00 | — |
| 1985(c) Round tip 5 | 20,000 | — | — | 0.15 | 1.50 | — |
| 1985(c) Proof | 12,000 | Value: 4.00 | | | | |

**20 CENTS** **KM# 62** **Composition:** Copper-Nickel **Obverse:** Similar to 1 Dollar, KM#57

| Date | Mintage | F | VF | XF | Unc | BU |
|---|---|---|---|---|---|---|
| 1986(o) | 12,500,000 | — | — | 0.15 | 0.50 | — |
| 1986(l) | 18,000 | — | — | 0.25 | 1.50 | — |
| 1986(l) Proof | 10,000 | Value: 4.00 | | | | |
| 1987(o) | 14,000,000 | — | — | 0.15 | 0.40 | — |
| 1987(l) | 18,000 | — | — | 0.25 | 1.50 | — |
| 1987(l) Proof | 10,000 | Value: 4.00 | | | | |
| 1988(c) | 6,500,000 | — | — | 0.15 | 0.40 | — |
| 1988(l) | 15,000 | — | — | 0.25 | 1.50 | — |
| 1988(l) Proof | 9,000 | Value: 4.00 | | | | |
| 1989(o) | 2,000,000 | — | — | — | 0.40 | — |
| 1989(o) Proof | 8,500 | Value: 4.00 | | | | |
| 1989(c) | 15,000 | — | — | — | 1.50 | — |

**20 CENTS** **KM# 74** **Composition:** Copper-Nickel **Subject:** 1990 Anniversary Celebrations

| Date | Mintage | F | VF | XF | Unc | BU |
|---|---|---|---|---|---|---|
| 1990(c) | 10,000 | — | — | — | 1.75 | — |

**20 CENTS** **KM# 74a** **Weight:** 13.0700 g. **Composition:** 0.9250 Silver .3887 oz. ASW

| Date | Mintage | F | VF | XF | Unc | BU |
|---|---|---|---|---|---|---|
| 1990(c) Proof | 7,000 | Value: 10.00 | | | | |

**20 CENTS** **KM# 81** **Composition:** Copper-Nickel

| Date | Mintage | F | VF | XF | Unc | BU |
|---|---|---|---|---|---|---|
| 1990(l) | 5,000,000 | — | — | — | 0.40 | — |
| 1990(c) | 18,000 | — | — | — | 1.50 | — |
| 1990(c) Proof | 10,000 | Value: 4.00 | | | | |
| 1991(c) | 20,000 | — | — | — | 1.50 | — |
| 1991(c) Proof | 15,000 | Value: 4.00 | | | | |
| 1992(l) | 15,000 | — | — | — | 1.50 | — |
| 1992(l) Proof | 9,000 | Value: 4.00 | | | | |
| 1993(l) | 15,000 | — | — | — | 1.50 | — |
| 1993(l) Proof | 10,000 | Value: 4.00 | | | | |
| 1994(l) | — | — | — | — | 1.50 | — |
| 1994(l) Proof | 10,000 | Value: 4.00 | | | | |
| 1995(l) | — | — | — | — | 1.50 | — |
| 1995(l) Proof | Est. 4,000 | Value: 4.00 | | | | |
| 1996(l) | — | — | — | — | 1.50 | — |
| 1997(l) | — | — | — | — | 1.50 | — |
| 1997(l) Proof | — | Value: 4.00 | | | | |
| 1998(l) | — | — | — | — | 1.50 | — |
| 1998(l) Proof | Est. 2,000 | Value: 4.00 | | | | |

**20 CENTS** **KM# 81a** **Weight:** 13.0700 g. **Composition:** 0.9250 Silver .3887 oz. ASW

| Date | Mintage | F | VF | XF | Unc | BU |
|---|---|---|---|---|---|---|
| 1995 Proof | Est. 2,500 | Value: 12.50 | | | | |

**20 CENTS** **KM# 118** **Composition:** Copper-Nickel **Obverse:** Rank-Broadley portrait of Queen Elizabeth II **Reverse:** Similar to KM#81

| Date | Mintage | F | VF | XF | Unc | BU |
|---|---|---|---|---|---|---|
| 1999 | — | — | — | — | 0.75 | — |
| 1999 Proof | Est. 2,000 | Value: 4.00 | | | | |
| 2000 | — | — | — | — | 0.75 | — |
| 2000 Proof | — | Value: 4.00 | | | | |

**50 CENTS** **KM# 37** **Composition:** Copper-Nickel **Subject:** H.M.B. Endeavour

| Date | Mintage | F | VF | XF | Unc | BU |
|---|---|---|---|---|---|---|
| 1967 | 250,000 | — | — | 0.40 | 0.60 | — |
| 1967 Dot above 1 | Inc. above | — | 2.50 | 5.00 | 25.00 | — |
| 1967 Prooflike | 50,000 | — | — | — | — | 1.50 |
| 1967 | 10 | — | — | — | — | — |
| 1968 | 35,000 | — | — | 0.45 | 2.00 | — |
| 1968 Prooflike | 40,000 | — | — | — | — | 3.00 |
| 1970 | 30,000 | — | — | 0.45 | 3.50 | — |
| 1970 Prooflike | 20,010 | — | — | — | — | 3.50 |
| 1971(c) Serifs on date numerals | 1,123,000 | — | 1.00 | 4.50 | 30.00 | — |
| 1971(l) Without serifs | 15,000 | — | — | 0.35 | 3.50 | — |
| 1971(l) Proof | 5,000 | Value: 40.00 | | | | |
| 1972 | 1,423,000 | — | — | 0.35 | 4.00 | — |
| 1972 Proof | 8,045 | Value: 15.00 | | | | |
| 1973 | 2,523,000 | — | — | 0.35 | 3.50 | — |
| 1973 Proof | 8,000 | Value: 10.00 | | | | |
| 1974 | 1,215,000 | — | — | 0.35 | 3.50 | — |
| 1974 Proof | 8,000 | Value: 10.00 | | | | |
| 1975 | 3,815,000 | — | — | 0.35 | 3.50 | — |
| 1975 Proof | 10,000 | Value: 7.50 | | | | |
| 1976 | 2,016,000 | — | — | 0.35 | 3.50 | — |
| 1976 Proof | 11,000 | Value: 7.50 | | | | |
| 1977 | 2,000,000 | — | — | 0.35 | 2.00 | — |
| 1977 Proof | 12,000 | Value: 7.50 | | | | |
| 1978 | 2,023,000 | — | — | 0.35 | 2.00 | — |
| 1978 Proof | 15,000 | Value: 6.00 | | | | |
| 1979 | 2,400,000 | — | — | 0.35 | 2.00 | — |
| 1979 Proof | 16,000 | Value: 6.00 | | | | |
| 1980(l) Smooth back line to hair | 27,000 | — | — | 0.35 | 2.00 | — |
| 1980(l) Proof | 17,000 | Value: 6.00 | | | | |
| 1980(o) Strong back line to hair | 8,000,000 | — | — | 0.50 | 10.00 | — |
| 1981(o) Blunt end on 9 | 4,000,000 | — | — | 0.50 | 10.00 | — |
| 1981(l) Pointed end on 9 | 25,000 | — | — | 0.35 | 1.25 | — |
| 1981(l) Proof | 18,000 | Value: 6.00 | | | | |
| 1982(o) Blunt end on 2 | 6,000,000 | — | — | 0.50 | 10.00 | — |
| 1982(l) Pointed end on 2 | 25,000 | — | — | 0.35 | 3.00 | — |
| 1982(l) Proof | 18,000 | Value: 6.00 | | | | |
| 1983(l) | 25,000 | — | — | 0.35 | 3.00 | — |
| 1983(l) Proof | 18,000 | Value: 6.00 | | | | |
| 1984(o) Wiry hair, bushy eyebrows | 2,000,000 | — | — | 0.50 | 10.00 | — |
| 1984(l) Incised shoulder folds on gown | 25,000 | — | — | 0.35 | 3.00 | — |
| 1984(l) Proof | 15,000 | Value: 5.00 | | | | |
| 1985(o) Wiry hair, bushy eyebrows | 2,000,000 | — | — | 0.50 | 10.00 | — |
| 1985(c) | 20,000 | — | — | 0.35 | 3.00 | — |
| 1985(c) Proof | 12,000 | Value: 5.00 | | | | |

**50 CENTS** **KM# 39** **Composition:** Copper-Nickel **Subject:** 200th Anniversary - Captain Cook's Voyage **Edge Lettering:** Cook Bi-Centenary 1769-1969 **Note:** Similar to KM#37.

| Date | Mintage | F | VF | XF | Unc | BU |
|---|---|---|---|---|---|---|
| 1969 | 50,000 | — | — | 0.75 | 3.00 | — |
| 1969 Prooflike | 50,000 | — | — | — | — | 3.50 |

**50 CENTS** **KM# 95** **Composition:** Nickel **Obverse:** KM#37 **Reverse:** Canada 1 Dollar KM#120 **Note:** Mule.

| Date | Mintage | F | VF | XF | Unc | BU |
|---|---|---|---|---|---|---|
| 1985 6 known | — | — | 1,200 | 1,900 | — | — |

**50 CENTS** **KM# 63** **Composition:** Copper-Nickel

| Date | Mintage | F | VF | XF | Unc | BU |
|---|---|---|---|---|---|---|
| 1986(o) | 5,200,000 | — | — | 0.35 | 0.75 | — |
| 1986(l) | 18,000 | — | — | 0.50 | 1.00 | — |
| 1986(l) Proof | 10,000 | Value: 5.00 | | | | |
| 1987(o) | 3,600,000 | — | — | 0.35 | 0.75 | — |
| 1987(l) | 18,000 | — | — | 0.50 | 1.00 | — |
| 1987(l) Proof | 10,000 | Value: 5.00 | | | | |
| 1988(c) | 4,400,000 | — | — | 0.35 | 0.75 | — |
| 1988(l) | 15,000 | — | — | 0.50 | 1.50 | — |
| 1988(l) Proof | 9,000 | Value: 5.00 | | | | |
| 1989(c) | 15,000 | — | — | — | 1.00 | — |
| 1989(c) Proof | 8,500 | Value: 5.00 | | | | |
| 1990(l) | 18,000 | — | — | — | 1.00 | — |
| 1990(l) Proof | 10,000 | Value: 5.00 | | | | |
| 1991(c) | 200,000 | — | — | — | 1.00 | — |
| 1991(c) Proof | 15,000 | Value: 5.00 | | | | |
| 1992(l) | 15,000 | — | — | — | 1.00 | — |
| 1992(l) Proof | 9,000 | Value: 5.00 | | | | |
| 1993(l) | 15,000 | — | — | — | 1.00 | — |
| 1993(l) Proof | 10,000 | Value: 5.00 | | | | |
| 1995(l) | — | — | — | — | 1.00 | — |
| 1995(l) Proof | Est. 4,000 | Value: 5.00 | | | | |
| 1996(l) | — | — | — | — | 1.00 | — |
| 1997(l) | — | — | — | — | 1.00 | — |

| Date | Mintage | F | VF | XF | Unc | BU |
|---|---|---|---|---|---|---|
| 1997(I) Proof | — | Value: 5.00 | | | | |
| 1998(I) | — | — | — | — | 1.00 | — |
| 1998(I) Proof | Est. 2,000 | Value: 5.00 | | | | |

**50 CENTS** **KM# 75** **Composition:** Nickel **Subject:** 1990 Anniversary Celebrations

| Date | Mintage | F | VF | XF | Unc | BU |
|---|---|---|---|---|---|---|
| 1990(c) | 10,000 | — | — | — | 5.00 | — |

**50 CENTS** **KM# 75a** **Weight:** 15.7400 g. **Composition:** 0.9250 Silver .4682 oz. ASW

| Date | Mintage | F | VF | XF | Unc | BU |
|---|---|---|---|---|---|---|
| 1990(c) Proof | 7,000 | Value: 20.00 | | | | |

**50 CENTS** **KM# 90** **Ring Composition:** Copper-Nickel **Center Composition:** Aluminum-Bronze **Subject:** H.M.B. Endeavour

| Date | Mintage | F | VF | XF | Unc | BU |
|---|---|---|---|---|---|---|
| 1994 | 53,000 | — | — | — | 20.00 | — |

**50 CENTS** **KM# 90a** **Ring Composition:** 0.9250 Silver **Center Composition:** Aluminum-Bronze

| Date | Mintage | F | VF | XF | Unc | BU |
|---|---|---|---|---|---|---|
| 1994 Proof | 10,000 | Value: 25.00 | | | | |

**50 CENTS** **KM# 90b** **Ring Composition:** 0.3750 Gold **Center Composition:** 0.9160 Gold **Subject:** H.M.B. Endeavour

| Date | Mintage | F | VF | XF | Unc | BU |
|---|---|---|---|---|---|---|
| 1994 Proof | 500 | Value: 400 | | | | |

**50 CENTS** **KM# 119** **Composition:** Copper-Nickel **Obverse:** Rank-Broadley portrait of Queen Elizabeth II **Reverse:** Similar to KM#81

| Date | Mintage | F | VF | XF | Unc | BU |
|---|---|---|---|---|---|---|
| 1999 | — | — | — | — | 1.00 | — |
| 1999 Proof | Est. 2,000 | Value: 5.00 | | | | |
| 2000 | — | — | — | — | 1.00 | — |
| 2000 Proof | — | Value: 5.00 | | | | |

**DOLLAR** **KM# 38.1** **Composition:** Copper-Nickel **Subject:** Decimalization Commemorative **Edge:** Lettered

| Date | Mintage | F | VF | XF | Unc | BU |
|---|---|---|---|---|---|---|
| 1967 | 250,000 | — | — | 0.75 | 1.00 | — |
| 1967 Prooflike | 50,000 | — | — | — | — | 2.50 |
| 1967 Proof | 10 | — | — | — | — | — |

**DOLLAR** **KM# 40.1** **Composition:** Copper-Nickel **Subject:** 200th Anniversary - Captain Cook's Voyage

| Date | Mintage | F | VF | XF | Unc | BU |
|---|---|---|---|---|---|---|
| 1969 | 400,000 | — | — | 0.75 | 1.25 | — |
| 1969 Prooflike | 50,000 | — | — | — | — | 3.00 |

**DOLLAR** **KM# 40.2** **Composition:** Copper-Nickel **Edge:** No hyphen in edge inscription

| Date | Mintage | F | VF | XF | Unc | BU |
|---|---|---|---|---|---|---|
| 1969 | — | — | — | — | 7.50 | — |

**DOLLAR** **KM# 42** **Composition:** Copper-Nickel **Subject:** Royal Visit **Reverse:** Mount Cook

| Date | Mintage | F | VF | XF | Unc | BU |
|---|---|---|---|---|---|---|
| 1970 | 285,000 | — | — | 0.75 | 1.00 | — |
| 1970 Prooflike | 20,000 | — | — | — | — | 4.00 |

**DOLLAR** **KM# 43** **Composition:** Copper-Nickel **Subject:** Cook Islands

| Date | Mintage | F | VF | XF | Unc | BU |
|---|---|---|---|---|---|---|
| 1970 | 25,000 | — | — | 4.00 | 9.00 | — |
| 1970 Proof | 5,030 | Value: 22.50 | | | | |

**DOLLAR** **KM# 38.2** **Composition:** Copper-Nickel **Subject:** Regular Issue **Edge:** Reeded

| Date | Mintage | F | VF | XF | Unc | BU |
|---|---|---|---|---|---|---|
| 1971 | 45,000 | — | — | 2.00 | 3.00 | — |
| 1971 Proof | 5,000 | Value: 25.00 | | | | |
| 1972 | 42,000 | — | — | 2.00 | 3.00 | — |
| 1972 Proof | 8,045 | Value: 12.50 | | | | |
| 1972 RAM case; Proof | 3,000 | Value: 27.50 | | | | |
| 1973 | 37,000 | — | — | 2.00 | 3.00 | — |
| 1973 Proof | 16,000 | Value: 5.00 | | | | |
| 1975 | 30,000 | — | — | 2.00 | 3.00 | — |
| 1975 Proof | 20,000 | Value: 5.00 | | | | |
| 1976 | 36,000 | — | — | 2.00 | 3.00 | — |
| 1976 Proof | 22,000 | Value: 5.00 | | | | |

**DOLLAR** **KM# 44** **Composition:** Copper-Nickel **Subject:** Commonwealth Games

| Date | Mintage | F | VF | XF | Unc | BU |
|---|---|---|---|---|---|---|
| 1974 | 515,000 | — | — | 1.00 | 1.75 | — |

**DOLLAR** **KM# 44a** **Weight:** 27.2160 g. **Composition:** 0.9250 Silver .8095 oz. ASW

| Date | Mintage | F | VF | XF | Unc | BU |
|---|---|---|---|---|---|---|
| 1974 Proof | 18,000 | Value: 15.00 | | | | |

**DOLLAR** **KM# 45** **Composition:** Copper-Nickel **Subject:** New Zealand Day **Reverse:** Great Egret

| Date | Mintage | F | VF | XF | Unc | BU |
|---|---|---|---|---|---|---|
| 1974 | 50,000 | — | — | 3.00 | 8.00 | — |
| 1974 Proof | 5,000 | Value: 65.00 | | | | |

**DOLLAR** **KM# 46** **Composition:** Copper-Nickel **Subject:** Waitangi Day **Reverse:** Treaty House

| Date | Mintage | F | VF | XF | Unc | BU |
|---|---|---|---|---|---|---|
| 1977 | 90,000 | — | — | 1.50 | 3.00 | — |

**DOLLAR** **KM# 46a** **Weight:** 27.2160 g. **Composition:** 0.9250 Silver .8095 oz. ASW

| Date | Mintage | F | VF | XF | Unc | BU |
|---|---|---|---|---|---|---|
| 1977 Proof | 27,000 | Value: 10.00 | | | | |

**DOLLAR** **KM# 47** **Composition:** Copper-Nickel **Subject:** 25th Anniversary of Coronation **Reverse:** Parliament

| Date | Mintage | F | VF | XF | Unc | BU |
|---|---|---|---|---|---|---|
| 1978 | 123,000 | — | — | 0.75 | 1.75 | — |

**DOLLAR** **KM# 47a** **Weight:** 27.2160 g. **Composition:** 0.9250 Silver .8095 oz. ASW

| Date | Mintage | F | VF | XF | Unc | BU |
|---|---|---|---|---|---|---|
| 1978 Proof | 33,000 | Value: 7.50 | | | | |

**DOLLAR** **KM# 48** **Composition:** Copper-Nickel

| Date | Mintage | F | VF | XF | Unc | BU |
|---|---|---|---|---|---|---|
| 1979 | 110,000 | — | — | 0.75 | 1.75 | — |

**DOLLAR** **KM# 48a** **Weight:** 27.2160 g. **Composition:** 0.9250 Silver .8095 oz. ASW

| Date | Mintage | F | VF | XF | Unc | BU |
|---|---|---|---|---|---|---|
| 1979 Proof | 35,000 | Value: 10.00 | | | | |

**DOLLAR** **KM# 49** **Composition:** Copper-Nickel **Reverse:** Fantail

| Date | Mintage | F | VF | XF | Unc | BU |
|---|---|---|---|---|---|---|
| 1980 | 112,000 | — | — | 1.25 | 5.00 | — |

**DOLLAR** **KM# 49a** **Weight:** 27.2160 g. **Composition:** 0.9250 Silver .8095 oz. ASW

| Date | Mintage | F | VF | XF | Unc | BU |
|---|---|---|---|---|---|---|
| 1980 Proof | 37,000 | Value: 14.00 | | | | |

**DOLLAR** **KM# 50** **Composition:** Copper-Nickel **Subject:** Royal Visit **Reverse:** English Oak and N.Z. Kauri

| Date | Mintage | F | VF | XF | Unc | BU |
|---|---|---|---|---|---|---|
| 1981 | 100,000 | — | — | 0.75 | 2.00 | — |

**DOLLAR** **KM# 50a** **Weight:** 27.2160 g. **Composition:** 0.9250 Silver .8095 oz. ASW

| Date | Mintage | F | VF | XF | Unc | BU |
|---|---|---|---|---|---|---|
| 1981 Proof | 38,000 | Value: 8.50 | | | | |

**DOLLAR** **KM# 51** **Composition:** Copper-Nickel **Reverse:** Takahe

| Date | Mintage | F | VF | XF | Unc | BU |
|---|---|---|---|---|---|---|
| 1982 | 65,000 | — | — | 1.50 | 6.00 | — |

**DOLLAR** **KM# 51a** **Weight:** 27.2160 g. **Composition:** 0.9250 Silver .8095 oz. ASW

| Date | Mintage | F | VF | XF | Unc | BU |
|---|---|---|---|---|---|---|
| 1982 Proof | 35,000 | Value: 15.00 | | | | |

**DOLLAR** **KM# 52** **Composition:** Copper-Nickel **Subject:** Royal Visit

| Date | Mintage | F | VF | XF | Unc | BU |
|---|---|---|---|---|---|---|
| 1983 | 40,000 | — | — | 0.75 | 2.00 | — |

**DOLLAR** **KM# 52a** **Weight:** 27.2160 g. **Composition:** 0.9250 Silver .8095 oz. ASW

| Date | Mintage | F | VF | XF | Unc | BU |
|---|---|---|---|---|---|---|
| 1983 Proof | 17,000 | Value: 16.00 | | | | |

**DOLLAR** **KM# 53** **Composition:** Copper-Nickel **Subject:** 50 Years of New Zealand Coinage

| Date | Mintage | F | VF | XF | Unc | BU |
|---|---|---|---|---|---|---|
| 1983 | 65,000 | — | — | 1.25 | 4.00 | — |

**DOLLAR** **KM# 53a** **Weight:** 27.2160 g. **Composition:** 0.9250 Silver .8095 oz. ASW

| Date | Mintage | F | VF | XF | Unc | BU |
|---|---|---|---|---|---|---|
| 1983 Proof | 35,000 | Value: 10.00 | | | | |

**DOLLAR** **KM# 54** **Composition:** Copper-Nickel **Subject:** Chatham Island Black Robin

| Date | Mintage | F | VF | XF | Unc | BU |
|---|---|---|---|---|---|---|
| 1984 | 65,000 | — | — | 2.00 | 7.50 | — |

**DOLLAR** **KM# 54a** **Weight:** 27.2160 g. **Composition:** 0.9250 Silver .8095 oz. ASW

| Date | Mintage | F | VF | XF | Unc | BU |
|---|---|---|---|---|---|---|
| 1984 Proof | 30,000 | Value: 15.00 | | | | |

**DOLLAR** **KM# 55** **Composition:** Copper-Nickel **Subject:** Black Stilt **Obverse:** Similar to KM#38.1

| Date | Mintage | F | VF | XF | Unc | BU |
|---|---|---|---|---|---|---|
| 1985 | 60,000 | — | — | 1.00 | 2.50 | — |

**DOLLAR** **KM# 55a** **Weight:** 27.2160 g. **Composition:** 0.9250 Silver .8095 oz. ASW

| Date | Mintage | F | VF | XF | Unc | BU |
|---|---|---|---|---|---|---|
| 1985 Proof | 25,000 | Value: 13.50 | | | | |

**DOLLAR** **KM# 56** **Composition:** Copper-Nickel **Subject:** Royal Visit

| Date | Mintage | F | VF | XF | Unc | BU |
|---|---|---|---|---|---|---|
| 1986 | 40,000 | — | — | 1.00 | 2.50 | — |

**DOLLAR** **KM# 56a** **Weight:** 27.2160 g. **Composition:** 0.9250 Silver .8095 oz. ASW

| Date | Mintage | F | VF | XF | Unc | BU |
|---|---|---|---|---|---|---|
| 1986 Proof | 13,000 | Value: 12.50 | | | | |

**DOLLAR** **KM# 57** **Composition:** Copper-Nickel **Reverse:** Kakapo

| Date | Mintage | F | VF | XF | Unc | BU |
|---|---|---|---|---|---|---|
| 1986 | 53,000 | — | — | 1.25 | 5.00 | — |

**DOLLAR** **KM# 57a** **Weight:** 27.2160 g. **Composition:** 0.9250 Silver .8095 oz. ASW

| Date | Mintage | F | VF | XF | Unc | BU |
|---|---|---|---|---|---|---|
| 1986 Proof | 21,000 | Value: 15.50 | | | | |

**DOLLAR** **KM# 65** **Composition:** Copper-Nickel **Subject:** National Parks Centennial

| Date | Mintage | F | VF | XF | Unc | BU |
|---|---|---|---|---|---|---|
| 1987 | 53,000 | — | — | 1.00 | 2.50 | — |

**DOLLAR** **KM# 65a** **Weight:** 27.2160 g. **Composition:** 0.9250 Silver .8095 oz. ASW

| Date | Mintage | F | VF | XF | Unc | BU |
|---|---|---|---|---|---|---|
| 1987 Proof | 21,000 | Value: 12.50 | | | | |

**DOLLAR** **KM# 66** **Composition:** Copper-Nickel **Reverse:** Yellow-eyed Penguin

| Date | Mintage | F | VF | XF | Unc | BU |
|---|---|---|---|---|---|---|
| 1988 | Est. 45,000 | — | — | 2.50 | 7.50 | — |

**DOLLAR** **KM# 66a** **Weight:** 27.2160 g. **Composition:** 0.9250 Silver .8095 oz. ASW

| Date | Mintage | F | VF | XF | Unc | BU |
|---|---|---|---|---|---|---|
| 1988 Proof | Est. 19,000 | Value: 37.50 | | | | |

**DOLLAR** **KM# 67** **Composition:** Copper-Nickel **Subject:** XIV Commonwealth Games **Obverse:** Similar to KM#66 **Reverse:** Runner

| Date | Mintage | F | VF | XF | Unc | BU |
|---|---|---|---|---|---|---|
| 1989 | 140,000 | — | — | 1.25 | 3.00 | — |

**DOLLAR** **KM# 67a** **Weight:** 27.2160 g. **Composition:** 0.9250 Silver .8095 oz. ASW

| Date | Mintage | F | VF | XF | Unc | BU |
|---|---|---|---|---|---|---|
| 1989 Proof | 80,000 | Value: 15.00 | | | | |

**DOLLAR** **KM# 68** **Composition:** Copper-Nickel **Subject:** XIV Commonwealth Games **Obverse:** Similar to KM#66 **Reverse:** Gymnast

| Date | Mintage | F | VF | XF | Unc | BU |
|---|---|---|---|---|---|---|
| 1989 | 140,000 | — | — | 1.25 | 3.00 | — |

**DOLLAR** **KM# 68a** **Weight:** 27.2160 g. **Composition:** 0.9250 Silver .8095 oz. ASW

| Date | Mintage | F | VF | XF | Unc | BU |
|---|---|---|---|---|---|---|
| 1989 Proof | 80,000 | Value: 15.00 | | | | |

**DOLLAR** **KM# 69** **Composition:** Copper-Nickel **Subject:** XIV Commonwealth Games **Obverse:** Similar to KM#66 **Reverse:** Swimmer

| Date | Mintage | F | VF | XF | Unc | BU |
|---|---|---|---|---|---|---|
| 1989 | 140,000 | — | — | 1.25 | 3.00 | — |

**DOLLAR** **KM# 69a** **Weight:** 27.2160 g. **Composition:** 0.9250 Silver .8095 oz. ASW

| Date | Mintage | F | VF | XF | Unc | BU |
|---|---|---|---|---|---|---|
| 1989 Proof | 80,000 | Value: 15.00 | | | | |

**DOLLAR** **KM# 70** **Composition:** Copper-Nickel **Subject:** XIV Commonwealth Games **Obverse:** Similar to KM#66 **Reverse:** Weightlifter

| Date | Mintage | F | VF | XF | Unc | BU |
|---|---|---|---|---|---|---|
| 1989 | 140,000 | — | — | 1.25 | 3.00 | — |

**DOLLAR** **KM# 70a** **Weight:** 27.2160 g. **Composition:** 0.9250 Silver .8095 oz. ASW

| Date | Mintage | F | VF | XF | Unc | BU |
|---|---|---|---|---|---|---|
| 1989 Proof | 80,000 | Value: 15.00 | | | | |

**DOLLAR** **KM# 76** **Composition:** Copper-Nickel **Subject:** 1990 Anniversary Celebrations - Treaty of Waitangi

| Date | Mintage | F | VF | XF | Unc | BU |
|---|---|---|---|---|---|---|
| 1990 | 50,000 | — | — | 1.25 | 3.00 | — |

**DOLLAR** **KM# 76a** **Weight:** 27.2160 g. **Composition:** 0.9250 Silver .8095 oz. ASW

| Date | Mintage | F | VF | XF | Unc | BU |
|---|---|---|---|---|---|---|
| 1990 Proof | 14,000 | Value: 22.50 | | | | |

**DOLLAR** **KM# 78** **Composition:** Aluminum-Bronze **Reverse:** Kiwi Bird

| Date | Mintage | F | VF | XF | Unc | BU |
|---|---|---|---|---|---|---|
| 1990(l) | 40,000,000 | — | — | — | 1.00 | — |
| 1990(l) Proof | 18,000 | Value: 2.25 | | | | |
| 1990(c) | 10,000 | — | — | — | 4.00 | — |
| 1991(l) | 10,000,000 | — | — | — | 1.00 | — |
| 1991(c) | 20,000 | — | — | — | 2.25 | — |
| 1991(c) Proof | 15,000 | Value: 4.00 | | | | |
| 1992(l) | 15,000 | — | — | — | 2.25 | — |
| 1992(l) Proof | 9,000 | Value: 4.00 | | | | |
| 1993(l) | 15,000 | — | — | — | 2.25 | — |
| 1993(l) Proof | 10,000 | Value: 4.00 | | | | |
| 1994(l) | 16,000 | — | — | — | 2.50 | — |
| 1994(l) Proof | 10,000 | Value: 4.00 | | | | |
| 1995(l) | 10,000 | — | — | — | 2.50 | — |
| 1995(l) Proof | Est. 4,000 | Value: 4.00 | | | | |
| 1996(l) | — | — | — | — | 1.50 | — |
| 1997(l) | — | — | — | — | 1.50 | — |
| 1997(l) Proof | — | Value: 4.00 | | | | |
| 1998(l) | — | — | — | — | 1.50 | — |
| 1998(l) Proof | Est. 2,000 | Value: 4.00 | | | | |

**DOLLAR** **KM# 78a** **Weight:** 8.0000 g. **Composition:** 0.9250 Silver .2380 oz. ASW

| Date | Mintage | F | VF | XF | Unc | BU |
|---|---|---|---|---|---|---|
| 1990 Proof | 10,000 | Value: 20.00 | | | | |

**DOLLAR** **KM# 120** **Composition:** Aluminum-Bronze **Obverse:** Rank-Broadley portrait of Queen Elizabeth II **Reverse:** Similar to KM#78

| Date | Mintage | F | VF | XF | Unc | BU |
|---|---|---|---|---|---|---|
| 1999 | — | — | — | — | 1.75 | — |
| 1999 Proof | Est. 2,000 | Value: 5.00 | | | | |
| 2000 | — | — | — | — | 1.75 | — |
| 2000 Proof | — | Value: 5.00 | | | | |

**2 DOLLARS** **KM# 79** **Composition:** Aluminum-Bronze **Reverse:** Great Egret

| Date | Mintage | F | VF | XF | Unc | BU |
|---|---|---|---|---|---|---|
| 1990(l) | 30,000,000 | — | — | — | 2.00 | — |
| 1990(c) | 18,000 | — | — | — | 2.50 | — |
| 1990(l) Proof | 10,000 | Value: 4.00 | | | | |
| 1991(l) | 10,000,000 | — | — | — | 2.00 | — |
| 1991(c) | 20,000 | — | — | — | 2.50 | — |
| 1991(c) Proof | 15,000 | Value: 6.00 | | | | |
| 1992(l) | 15,000 | — | — | — | 2.50 | — |
| 1992(l) Proof | 9,000 | Value: 7.50 | | | | |
| 1994(l) | 16,000 | — | — | — | 2.50 | — |
| 1994(l) Proof | 10,000 | Value: 7.50 | | | | |
| 1995(l) | 10,000 | — | — | — | 3.00 | — |
| 1995(l) Proof | Est. 4,000 | Value: 7.00 | | | | |
| 1996(l) | — | — | — | — | 2.50 | — |
| 1997(l) Proof | — | Value: 7.00 | | | | |
| 1998(l) | — | — | — | — | 2.50 | — |
| 1998(l) Proof | Est. 2,000 | Value: 7.00 | | | | |

**2 DOLLARS** **KM# 79a** **Weight:** 10.0000 g. **Composition:** 0.9250 Silver .2974 oz. ASW

| Date | Mintage | F | VF | XF | Unc | BU |
|---|---|---|---|---|---|---|
| 1990 Proof | 10,000 | Value: 20.00 | | | | |

**2 DOLLARS** **KM# 87** **Composition:** Copper-Aluminum-Nickel **Reverse:** Sacred Kingfisher

| Date | Mintage | F | VF | XF | Unc | BU |
|---|---|---|---|---|---|---|
| 1993 | 40,000 | — | — | — | 6.50 | — |

**2 DOLLARS** **KM# 87a** **Weight:** 10.0000 g. **Composition:** 0.9250 Silver .2974 oz. ASW

| Date | Mintage | F | VF | XF | Unc | BU |
|---|---|---|---|---|---|---|
| 1993 Proof | 10,000 | Value: 15.00 | | | | |

**2 DOLLARS** **KM# 121** **Composition:** Aluminum-Bronze **Obverse:** Rank-Broadley portrait of Queen Elizabeth II **Reverse:** Similar to KM#79

| Date | Mintage | F | VF | XF | Unc | BU |
|---|---|---|---|---|---|---|
| 1999 | — | — | — | — | 2.50 | — |
| 1999 Proof | Est. 2,000 | Value: 7.50 | | | | |
| 2000 | — | — | — | — | 2.50 | — |
| 2000 Proof | — | Value: 7.50 | | | | |

**5 DOLLARS** **KM# 71** **Composition:** Aluminum-Bronze **Reverse:** ANZAC Memorial

| Date | Mintage | F | VF | XF | Unc | BU |
|---|---|---|---|---|---|---|
| 1990 Proof | 60,000 | Value: 27.50 | | | | |

**5 DOLLARS** **KM# 80** **Composition:** Copper-Nickel **Subject:** Rugby World Cup

| Date | Mintage | F | VF | XF | Unc | BU |
|---|---|---|---|---|---|---|
| 1991 | 120,000 | — | — | — | 3.50 | — |

**5 DOLLARS** **KM# 80a** **Weight:** 27.6000 g. **Composition:** 0.9250 Silver .8208 oz. ASW

| Date | Mintage | F | VF | XF | Unc | BU |
|---|---|---|---|---|---|---|
| 1991 Proof | Est. 15,000 | Value: 15.00 | | | | |

**5 DOLLARS** **KM# 82** **Composition:** Copper-Nickel **Subject:** 25th Anniversary of Decimal Currency

| Date | Mintage | F | VF | XF | Unc | BU |
|---|---|---|---|---|---|---|
| 1992 | 19,000 | — | — | — | 6.50 | — |

**5 DOLLARS** **KM# 82a** **Weight:** 27.2200 g. **Composition:** 0.9250 Silver .8096 oz. ASW

| Date | Mintage | F | VF | XF | Unc | BU |
|---|---|---|---|---|---|---|
| 1992 Proof | 8,000 | Value: 15.00 | | | | |

**5 DOLLARS** **KM# 83** **Composition:** Copper-Nickel **Subject:** Mythological Maori Hero - Kupe

| Date | Mintage | F | VF | XF | Unc | BU |
|---|---|---|---|---|---|---|
| 1992 | 40,000 | — | — | — | 3.50 | — |

**5 DOLLARS** **KM# 84** **Composition:** Copper-Nickel **Subject:** Abel Tasman

| Date | Mintage | F | VF | XF | Unc | BU |
|---|---|---|---|---|---|---|
| 1992 | 40,000 | — | — | — | 3.50 | — |

**5 DOLLARS** **KM# 85** **Composition:** Copper-Nickel **Subject:** Captain James Cook

| Date | Mintage | F | VF | XF | Unc | BU |
|---|---|---|---|---|---|---|
| 1992 | 40,000 | — | — | — | 3.50 | — |

**5 DOLLARS** **KM# 86** **Composition:** Copper-Nickel **Subject:** Christopher Columbus

| Date | Mintage | F | VF | XF | Unc | BU |
|---|---|---|---|---|---|---|
| 1992 | 40,000 | — | — | — | 3.50 | — |

**5 DOLLARS** **KM# 88** **Composition:** Copper-Nickel **Subject:** 40th Anniversary of Coronation

| Date | Mintage | F | VF | XF | Unc | BU |
|---|---|---|---|---|---|---|
| 1993 | 15,000 | — | — | — | 5.00 | — |

**5 DOLLARS** **KM# 88a** **Weight:** 27.2200 g. **Composition:** 0.9250 Silver .8095 oz. ASW

| Date | Mintage | F | VF | XF | Unc | BU |
|---|---|---|---|---|---|---|
| 1993 Proof | Est. 15,000 | Value: 20.00 | | | | |

**5 DOLLARS** **KM# 88b** **Weight:** 47.5250 g. **Composition:** 0.9170 Gold 1.4010 oz. AGW **Subject:** 40th Anniversary of Coronation

| Date | Mintage | F | VF | XF | Unc | BU |
|---|---|---|---|---|---|---|
| 1993 Proof | Est. 500 | Value: 775 | | | | |

**5 DOLLARS** **KM# 89** **Weight:** 31.4700 g. **Composition:** 0.9250 Silver .9357 oz. ASW **Reverse:** Hooker Sea Lion **Size:** Endangered Wildlife mm.

| Date | Mintage | F | VF | XF | Unc | BU |
|---|---|---|---|---|---|---|
| 1993 Proof | 18,000 | Value: 38.00 | | | | |

**5 DOLLARS** **KM# 91** **Weight:** 27.2200 g. **Composition:** 0.9250 Silver .8096 oz. ASW **Reverse:** Queen Mother and Infant Elizabeth

| Date | Mintage | F | VF | XF | Unc | BU |
|---|---|---|---|---|---|---|
| 1994 Proof | Est. 35,000 | Value: 25.00 | | | | |

**5 DOLLARS** **KM# 96** **Weight:** 27.2200 g. **Composition:** 0.9250 Silver **Series:** Winter Olympics - 1994 **Obverse:** Queen's portrait **Reverse:** Downhill skier

| Date | Mintage | F | VF | XF | Unc | BU |
|---|---|---|---|---|---|---|
| 1994 Proof | — | Value: 20.00 | | | | |

**5 DOLLARS** **KM# 92** **Weight:** 27.2200 g. **Composition:** 0.9250 Silver **Subject:** Antarctica **Reverse:** James Clark Ross

| Date | Mintage | F | VF | XF | Unc | BU |
|---|---|---|---|---|---|---|
| 1995 Proof | Est. 12,000 | Value: 28.50 | | | | |

**5 DOLLARS** **KM# 93** **Composition:** Copper-Nickel **Reverse:** Bird - Tui

| Date | Mintage | F | VF | XF | Unc | BU |
|---|---|---|---|---|---|---|
| 1995 | Est. 11,000 | — | — | — | 7.50 | — |

**5 DOLLARS** **KM# 93a** **Weight:** 28.2800 g. **Composition:** 0.9250 Silver .8411 oz. ASW

| Date | Mintage | F | VF | XF | Unc | BU |
|---|---|---|---|---|---|---|
| 1995 Proof | Est. 7,000 | Value: 25.00 | | | | |

**5 DOLLARS** **KM# 97** **Composition:** Copper-Nickel **Reverse:** Kaka (Bush Parrot)

| Date | Mintage | F | VF | XF | Unc | BU |
|---|---|---|---|---|---|---|
| 1996 | — | — | — | — | 12.50 | — |

**5 DOLLARS** **KM# 97a** **Weight:** 28.2800 g. **Composition:** 0.9250 Silver .8410 oz. ASW

| Date | Mintage | F | VF | XF | Unc | BU |
|---|---|---|---|---|---|---|
| 1996 Proof | — | Value: 40.00 | | | | |

**5 DOLLARS** **KM# 99** **Composition:** Copper-Nickel **Subject:** Auckland City of Sails **Reverse:** Bridge, Boats

| Date | Mintage | F | VF | XF | Unc | BU |
|---|---|---|---|---|---|---|
| 1996 | Est. 6,000 | — | — | — | 12.50 | — |

**5 DOLLARS** **KM# 99a** **Weight:** 28.2800 g. **Composition:** 0.9250 Silver .8410 oz. ASW

| Date | Mintage | F | VF | XF | Unc | BU |
|---|---|---|---|---|---|---|
| 1996 Proof | Est. 3,000 | Value: 32.50 | | | | |

**5 DOLLARS** KM# 101 **Weight:** 28.4500 g. **Composition:** 0.9250 Silver .8461 oz. ASW **Obverse:** Queen Elizabeth II

| Date | Mintage | F | VF | XF | Unc | BU |
|---|---|---|---|---|---|---|
| 1996 | Est. 3,000 | — | — | — | 50.00 | — |

**Note:** In sets only with $20 commemorative banknote.

**5 DOLLARS** KM# 102 **Weight:** 25.2200 g. **Composition:** 0.9250 Silver .8096 oz. ASW **Subject:** De Heemskerck **Obverse:** Queen Elizabeth II **Reverse:** Sail ship on globe with map

| Date | Mintage | F | VF | XF | Unc | BU |
|---|---|---|---|---|---|---|
| 1996 Proof | Est. 18,000 | Value: 45.00 | | | | |

**5 DOLLARS** KM# 103 **Composition:** Copper-Nickel **Subject:** WWF Conserving Nature **Obverse:** Queen Elizabeth II **Reverse:** Saddleback

| Date | Mintage | F | VF | XF | Unc | BU |
|---|---|---|---|---|---|---|
| 1997 | — | — | — | — | 8.00 | — |

**5 DOLLARS** KM# 103a **Weight:** 28.2800 g. **Composition:** 0.9250 Silver .8411 oz. ASW

| Date | Mintage | F | VF | XF | Unc | BU |
|---|---|---|---|---|---|---|
| 1997 Proof | — | Value: 22.50 | | | | |

**5 DOLLARS** KM# 105 **Composition:** Copper-Nickel **Subject:** Queen's Golden Wedding Anniversary **Obverse:** Queen Elizabeth II

| Date | Mintage | F | VF | XF | Unc | BU |
|---|---|---|---|---|---|---|
| 1997 | — | — | — | — | 10.00 | — |

**5 DOLLARS** KM# 106 **Subject:** City of Christchurch **Obverse:** Queen Elizabeth II **Reverse:** Cathedral

| Date | Mintage | F | VF | XF | Unc | BU |
|---|---|---|---|---|---|---|
| 1997 | Est. 5,000 | — | — | — | 10.00 | — |

**5 DOLLARS** **Weight:** 28.2800 g. **Composition:** 0.9250 Silver .8410 oz. ASW

| Date | Mintage | F | VF | XF | Unc | BU |
|---|---|---|---|---|---|---|
| 1997 | 3,000 | Value: 45.00 | | | | |

**5 DOLLARS** KM# 106a **Weight:** 28.2800 g. **Composition:** 0.9250 Silver .8410 oz. ASW

| Date | Mintage | F | VF | XF | Unc | BU |
|---|---|---|---|---|---|---|
| 1997 | Est. 3,000 | Value: 45.00 | | | | |

**5 DOLLARS** KM# 107 **Composition:** Copper-Nickel **Obverse:** Queen Elizabeth II **Reverse:** Royal Albatross

| Date | Mintage | F | VF | XF | Unc | BU |
|---|---|---|---|---|---|---|
| 1998 | Est. 6,500 | — | — | — | 10.00 | — |

**5 DOLLARS** KM# 107a **Weight:** 29.2000 g. **Composition:** 0.9250 Silver .8684 oz. ASW

| Date | Mintage | F | VF | XF | Unc | BU |
|---|---|---|---|---|---|---|
| 1998 Proof | Est. 4,000 | Value: 65.00 | | | | |

**5 DOLLARS** KM# 109 **Composition:** Copper-Nickel **Subject:** Pride in New Zealand **Obverse:** Queen Elizabeth II **Reverse:** Four stars

| Date | Mintage | F | VF | XF | Unc | BU |
|---|---|---|---|---|---|---|
| 1998 In mint sets only | 2,000 | — | — | — | 10.00 | — |

**5 DOLLARS** KM# 109a **Weight:** 6.0000 g. **Composition:** 0.9990 Silver .1927 oz. ASW

| Date | Mintage | F | VF | XF | Unc | BU |
|---|---|---|---|---|---|---|
| 1998 In proof sets only | 1,200 | — | — | — | 15.00 | — |

**5 DOLLARS** KM# 110 **Composition:** Copper-Nickel **Subject:** Pride in New Zealand **Obverse:** Queen Elizabeth II **Reverse:** Fleece

| Date | Mintage | F | VF | XF | Unc | BU |
|---|---|---|---|---|---|---|
| 1998 In mint sets only | 2,000 | — | — | — | 10.00 | — |

**5 DOLLARS** KM# 110a **Weight:** 6.0000 g. **Composition:** 0.9990 Silver .1927 oz. ASW

| Date | Mintage | F | VF | XF | Unc | BU |
|---|---|---|---|---|---|---|
| 1998 In proof sets only | 1,200 | — | — | — | 15.00 | — |

**5 DOLLARS** KM# 111 **Composition:** Copper-Nickel **Subject:** Pride in New Zealand **Obverse:** Queen Elizabeth II **Reverse:** Wheat sheaf

| Date | Mintage | F | VF | XF | Unc | BU |
|---|---|---|---|---|---|---|
| 1998 In mint sets only | 2,000 | — | — | — | 10.00 | — |

**5 DOLLARS** KM# 111a **Weight:** 6.0000 g. **Composition:** 0.9990 Silver .1927 oz. ASW

| Date | Mintage | F | VF | XF | Unc | BU |
|---|---|---|---|---|---|---|
| 1998 In proof sets only | 1,200 | — | — | — | 15.00 | — |

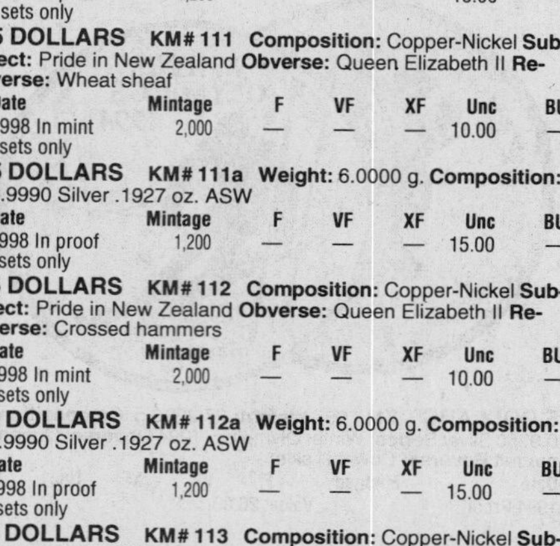

**5 DOLLARS** KM# 112 **Composition:** Copper-Nickel **Subject:** Pride in New Zealand **Obverse:** Queen Elizabeth II **Reverse:** Crossed hammers

| Date | Mintage | F | VF | XF | Unc | BU |
|---|---|---|---|---|---|---|
| 1998 In mint sets only | 2,000 | — | — | — | 10.00 | — |

**5 DOLLARS** KM# 112a **Weight:** 6.0000 g. **Composition:** 0.9990 Silver .1927 oz. ASW

| Date | Mintage | F | VF | XF | Unc | BU |
|---|---|---|---|---|---|---|
| 1998 In proof sets only | 1,200 | — | — | — | 15.00 | — |

**5 DOLLARS** KM# 113 **Composition:** Copper-Nickel **Subject:** Dunedin **Obverse:** Queen Elizabeth II **Reverse:** Larnach Castle

| Date | Mintage | F | VF | XF | Unc | BU |
|---|---|---|---|---|---|---|
| 1998 | 4,000 | — | — | — | 10.00 | — |

**5 DOLLARS** KM# 113a **Weight:** 28.2800 g. **Composition:** 0.9250 Silver .8684 oz. ASW

| Date | Mintage | F | VF | XF | Unc | BU |
|---|---|---|---|---|---|---|
| 1998 Proof | 2,500 | Value: 30.00 | | | | |

**5 DOLLARS** KM# 115 **Composition:** Copper-Nickel **Obverse:** Rank-Broadley portrait of Queen Elizabeth II **Reverse:** Morepork owl

| Date | Mintage | F | VF | XF | Unc | BU |
|---|---|---|---|---|---|---|
| 1999 | Est. 7,500 | — | — | — | 10.00 | — |

**5 DOLLARS** KM# 115a **Weight:** 28.2800 g. **Composition:** 0.9990 Silver .9083 oz. ASW

| Date | Mintage | F | VF | XF | Unc | BU |
|---|---|---|---|---|---|---|
| 1999 Proof | Est. 7,000 | Value: 35.00 | | | | |

**5 DOLLARS** KM# 123 **Weight:** 31.0500 g. **Composition:** 0.9250 Silver .9234 oz. ASW **Subject:** Wellington Harbour Capital **Obverse:** Queen's head right **Reverse:** City view with ship **Edge:** Reeded **Size:** 38.7 mm.

| Date | Mintage | F | VF | XF | Unc | BU |
|---|---|---|---|---|---|---|
| 1999 Proof | — | Value: 30.00 | | | | |

**5 DOLLARS** KM# 125a **Weight:** 31.1300 g. **Composition:** 0.9990 Silver .9998 oz. ASW **Note:** Heavier than the official weight of 28.28 grams.

| Date | Mintage | F | VF | XF | Unc | BU |
|---|---|---|---|---|---|---|
| 2000 Proof | 5,000 | Value: 35.00 | | | | |

**5 DOLLARS** KM# 125 **Weight:** 32.2000 g. **Composition:** Copper-Nickel **Obverse:** Queen's head right **Reverse:** Perching cormorant **Edge:** Reeded **Size:** 38.6 mm. **Note:** Struck at Valcombi.

| Date | Mintage | F | VF | XF | Unc | BU |
|---|---|---|---|---|---|---|
| 2000 Frosted finish | 5,500 | — | — | — | 10.00 | — |

**5 DOLLARS** **KM# 128** **Weight:** 28.2800 g. **Composition:** Copper-Nickel **Subject:** Kereru Bird **Obverse:** Queen's portrait **Reverse:** Pigeon on branch **Edge:** Reeded **Size:** 38.6 mm.

| Date | Mintage | F | VF | XF | Unc | BU |
|---|---|---|---|---|---|---|
| 2001 | 7,500 | — | — | — | 12.50 | — |

**5 DOLLARS** **KM# 128a** **Weight:** 28.2800 g. **Composition:** 0.9990 Silver .9083 oz. ASW

| Date | Mintage | F | VF | XF | Unc | BU |
|---|---|---|---|---|---|---|
| 2001 Proof | 4,500 | Value: 35.00 | | | | |

**10 DOLLARS** **KM# 94** **Composition:** Aluminum-Bronze **Reverse:** Gold Prospector

| Date | Mintage | F | VF | XF | Unc | BU |
|---|---|---|---|---|---|---|
| 1995 | 5,400 | — | — | — | 15.00 | — |

**10 DOLLARS** **KM# 94a** **Composition:** Gold .5000 oz. AGW

| Date | Mintage | F | VF | XF | Unc | BU |
|---|---|---|---|---|---|---|
| 1995 Proof | 600 | Value: 325 | | | | |

**10 DOLLARS** **KM# 98** **Subject:** Sinking of General Grant

| Date | Mintage | F | VF | XF | Unc | BU |
|---|---|---|---|---|---|---|
| 1996 Prooflike | 6,000 | — | — | — | — | 15.00 |

**10 DOLLARS** **KM# 98a** **Composition:** Gold .5000 oz. AGW

| Date | Mintage | F | VF | XF | Unc | BU |
|---|---|---|---|---|---|---|
| 1996 Proof | 650 | Value: 350 | | | | |

**10 DOLLARS** **KM# 104** **Composition:** Aluminum-Bronze **Subject:** Gabriel's Gully **Obverse:** Queen Elizabeth II **Reverse:** Prospector

| Date | Mintage | F | VF | XF | Unc | BU |
|---|---|---|---|---|---|---|
| 1997 | Est. 3,000 | — | — | — | 17.50 | — |

**10 DOLLARS** **KM# 104a** **Composition:** Gold .5000 oz. AGW

| Date | Mintage | F | VF | XF | Unc | BU |
|---|---|---|---|---|---|---|
| 1997 Proof | — | Value: 325 | | | | |

**10 DOLLARS** **KM# 114** **Composition:** Aluminum-Bronze **Subject:** Century of Motoring **Obverse:** Queen Elizabeth II **Reverse:** Karl Benz driving his automobile

| Date | Mintage | F | VF | XF | Unc | BU |
|---|---|---|---|---|---|---|
| 1998 | 2,000 | — | — | — | 15.00 | — |

**10 DOLLARS** **KM# 114a** **Composition:** Gold Plated Aluminum-Bronze

| Date | Mintage | F | VF | XF | Unc | BU |
|---|---|---|---|---|---|---|
| 1998 Proof | 1,500 | Value: 45.00 | | | | |

**10 DOLLARS** **KM# 124** **Weight:** 15.4500 g. **Composition:** 0.9990 Silver .4962 oz. ASW **Obverse:** Queen's head right **Reverse:** Kiwi bird **Edge:** Reeded **Size:** 29.9 mm.

| Date | Mintage | F | VF | XF | Unc | BU |
|---|---|---|---|---|---|---|
| 1998 | — | — | — | — | 15.00 | — |

**10 DOLLARS** **KM# 122** **Weight:** 28.3700 g. **Composition:** 0.9250 Silver .8437 oz. ASW **Subject:** New Zealand - First to the Future **Obverse:** Rank-Broadley portrait of Queen Elizabeth II **Reverse:** Gold plated map of New Zealand, gold printed radiant sun **Edge:** Gold plated, reeded

| Date | Mintage | F | VF | XF | Unc | BU |
|---|---|---|---|---|---|---|
| 2000(1999) Proof | Est. 33,000 | Value: 40.00 | | | | |

**10 DOLLARS** **KM# 129** **Weight:** 3.8879 g. **Composition:** 0.9990 Gold .1250 oz. AGW **Subject:** The Salvage Ship Claymore **Obverse:** Queen's portrait **Reverse:** Ship above denomination and name **Edge:** Reeded **Size:** 18 mm.

| Date | Mintage | F | VF | XF | Unc | BU |
|---|---|---|---|---|---|---|
| 2001 Proof | 600 | Value: 102 | | | | |

**10 DOLLARS** **KM# 130** **Weight:** 7.7759 g. **Composition:** 0.9990 Gold .2500 oz. AGW **Subject:** Royal Mail Steam Ship Niagra **Obverse:** Queen's portrait **Reverse:** Ship above denomination and name **Edge:** Reeded **Size:** 22 mm.

| Date | Mintage | F | VF | XF | Unc | BU |
|---|---|---|---|---|---|---|
| 2001 Proof | 600 | Value: 205 | | | | |

**20 DOLLARS** **KM# 100** **Weight:** 31.1030 g. **Composition:** 0.9250 Silver .9250 oz. ASW **Subject:** Salute to Bravery **Obverse:** Queen Elizabeth II **Reverse:** Charles H Upham

| Date | Mintage | F | VF | XF | Unc | BU |
|---|---|---|---|---|---|---|
| 1995 Proof | 3,500 | Value: 40.00 | | | | |

**20 DOLLARS** **KM# 108** **Weight:** 28.2800 g. **Composition:** 0.9250 Silver .8410 oz. ASW **Subject:** Queen's Golden Wedding Anniversary **Note:** Similar to 5 Dollars, KM#105.

| Date | Mintage | F | VF | XF | Unc | BU |
|---|---|---|---|---|---|---|
| 1997 Proof | Est. 2,000 | Value: 40.00 | | | | |

**150 DOLLARS** **KM# 77** **Weight:** 16.9500 g. **Composition:** 0.9170 Gold .4996 oz. AGW **Reverse:** Kiwi

| Date | Mintage | F | VF | XF | Unc | BU |
|---|---|---|---|---|---|---|
| 1990 Proof | 10,000 | Value: 250 | | | | |

**150 DOLLARS** **KM# 126** **Weight:** 15.6000 g. **Composition:** 0.9950 Platinum .4990 oz. APW **Obverse:** Queen's portrait. **Reverse:** Two Kiwi and fern. **Edge:** Reeded. **Size:** 30 mm.

| Date | Mintage | F | VF | XF | Unc | BU |
|---|---|---|---|---|---|---|
| 1998 Proof | — | Value: 400 | | | | |

## PATTERNS

Including off metal strikes

| KM# | Date | Mintage | Identification | Mkt Val |
|---|---|---|---|---|
| pn2 | 1933 | — | 3 Pence. Silver. | — |
| pn3 | 1933 | — | Shilling. Silver. | 20,000 |
| pn4 | 1935 | — | Crown. Silver. | 50,000 |

## PIEFORTS

| KM# | Date | Mintage | Identification | Mkt Val |
|---|---|---|---|---|
| p1 | 1992 | 3,300 | Dollar. 0.9250 Silver. KM78. | 100 |
| p2 | 1995 | 2,500 | 20 Cents. Silver. KM81 | 95.00 |

## MINT SETS

| KM# | Date | Mintage | Identification | Issue Price | Mkt Val |
|---|---|---|---|---|---|
| MS50 | 2001 (7) | 5,000 | KM#116-121, 128 | 18.50 | 20.00 |
| MS1 | 1965 (7) | 100,000 | KM23.2-29.2, pink label, flat pack | 2.00 | 3.00 |
| MSA1 | 1965 (7) | 75,000 | KM23.2-29.2, green label, flat pack | 2.50 | 10.00 |
| MS2 | 1967 (7) | 250,000 | KM31-32, 34-37, 38.1 | 4.50 | 2.00 |
| MS4 | 1968 (6) | 35,000 | KM31-32, 34-37 | 2.15 | 3.00 |
| MS5 | 1969 (7) | 50,000 | KM31-32, 34-36, 39-40 | 3.25 | 5.00 |
| MS7 | 1970 (7) | 30,000 | KM31-32, 34, 36-37, 41-42 | 3.50 | 5.00 |
| MS10 | 1971 (7) | 15,000 | KM31-32, 36-37, 38.2, 41 | 3.50 | 10.00 |
| MS12 | 1972 (7) | 15,000 | KM31-32, 34, 36-37, 38.2, 41 | 3.50 | 5.00 |
| MS14 | 1973 (7) | 15,000 | KM31-32, 34, 36-37, 38.2, 41 | 3.50 | 7.00 |
| MS17 | 1974 (7) | 15,000 | KM31-32, 34, 36-37, 41, 44 | 4.35 | 8.00 |
| MS20 | 1975 (7) | 15,000 | KM31-32, 34, 36-37, 38.2, 41 | 4.50 | 5.00 |
| MS22 | 1976 (7) | 16,000 | KM31-32, 34, 36-37, 38.2, 41 | 4.75 | 7.50 |
| MS23 | 1977 (7) | 20,000 | KM31-32, 34, 36-37, 41, 46 | 4.75 | 7.00 |
| MS24 | 1978 (7) | 23,000 | KM31-32, 34, 36-37, 41, 47 | 5.25 | 4.00 |
| MS25 | 1979 (7) | 25,000 | KM31-32, 34, 36-37, 41, 48 | 5.50 | 4.00 |
| MS26 | 1980 (7) | 27,000 | KM31-32, 34, 36-37, 41, 49 | 5.75 | 6.00 |
| MS27 | 1981 (7) | 25,000 | KM31-32, 34, 36-37, 41, 50 | 5.75 | 4.00 |
| MS28 | 1982 (7) | 25,000 | KM31-32, 34, 36-37, 41, 51 | 6.00 | 4.00 |
| MS29 | 1983 (7) | 25,000 | KM31-32, 34, 36-37, 41, 53 | 6.25 | 4.00 |
| MS30 | 1984 (7) | 25,000 | KM31-32, 34, 36-37, 41, 54 | 4.75 | 6.50 |
| MS31 | 1985 (7) | 20,000 | KM31-32, 34, 36-37, 41, 55 | 4.00 | 8.00 |
| MS32 | 1986 | 18,000 | KM57-63 | 5.00 | 7.00 |
| MS33 | 1987 (7) | 18,000 | KM58-63, 65 | 7.50 | 7.00 |
| MS34 | 1988 (7) | 15,000 | KM58-63, 66 | 8.00 | 15.00 |
| MS35 | 1989 (5) | 10 | KM60-63, 67 | 14,600 | 11.00 |
| MS37 | 1990 (5) | 10,000 | KM72-76 | 11.00 | 25.00 |
| MS36 | 1990 (6) | 18,000 | KM60-61, 63, 78-79, 81 | 13.00 | 12.50 |
| MS38 | 1991 (7) | 20,000 | KM60-61, 63, 78-81 | 16.00 | 12.50 |
| MS39 | 1992 (4) | 15,000 | KM60-61, 63, 78-79, 81-82 | 15.00 | 12.50 |
| MS40 | 1992 (4) | 24,000 | KM83-86 | — | 12.50 |
| MS41 | 1993 (6) | 15,000 | KM60-61, 63, 78, 81, 87 | — | 10.00 |
| MS42 | 1994 (6) | 16,000 | KM60-61, 78-79,81,90 | 20.00 | 10.00 |
| MS43 | 1995 (7) | 6,000 | KM60-61, 63, 78-79, 81, 93 | 17.00 | 12.50 |
| MS44 | 1996 (7) | — | KM60-61, 63, 78-79, 81, 97 | 17.00 | 16.00 |
| MS45 | 1997 (7) | — | KM60-63, 78-79, 81, 103 | — | 15.00 |
| MS46 | 1998 | 4,000 | KM60-61, 63, 78-79, 81, 107 | 15.00 | 18.00 |
| MS47 | 1998 (4) | 2,000 | KM109-112 | — | 50.00 |
| MS48 | 1999 (7) | 5,000 | KM115-121 | 20.00 | 18.00 |
| MS49 | 2000 (7) | 3,000 | KM116-121, 127 | 18.00 | 18.00 |

## PROOF SETS

| KM# | Date | Mintage | Identification | Issue Price | Mkt Val |
|---|---|---|---|---|---|
| PS45 | 2001 (7) | 2,000 | KM#116-121, 128 | 49.25 | 60.00 |
| PS46 | 2001 (2) | 600 | KM#129-130 | 307 | — |
| PS8 | 1954 (4) | — | KM23-26 | — | 750 |
| PS9 | 1964 (6) | — | KM23-28 | — | 1,350 |
| PS1 | 1933 (5) | 20 | KM1-5 | — | 2,850 |
| PS2 | 1934 (5) | 20 | KM1-5 | — | 9,000 |
| PS3 | 1935 (6) | 364 | KM1-6 | — | 4,650 |
| PS4 | 1937 (5) | 200 | KM7-11 | — | 2,700 |

| KM# | Date | Mintage | Identification | Issue Price | Mkt Val |
|---|---|---|---|---|---|
| PS5 | 1947 (5) | 20 | KM7a-11a | — | 2,150 |
| PSA6 | 1950 (7) | — | KM15-21 | — | 2,100 |
| PS6 | 1953 (8) | 7,000 | KM23-30 | — | 75.00 |
| PS7 | 1953 (8) | — | KM23-30, Matte Proof | — | 1,350 |
| PS10 | 1965 (7) | 10 | KM23.2-29.2 | — | — |
| PS11 | 1967 (7) | 10 | KM31-32,34-38 | — | — |
| PS12 | 1971 (7) | 5,000 | KM31-32, 34, 36-37, 38.2, 41 | 15.00 | 70.00 |
| PS13 | 1972 (7) | 8,000 | KM31-32, 34, 36-37, 38.2, 41 | 16.00 | 15.00 |
| PS14 | 1973 (7) | 8,000 | KM31-32, 34, 36-37, 38.2, 41 | 16.00 | 12.50 |
| PS15 | 1974 (7) | 8,000 | KM31-32, 34, 36-37, 41, 44a | 14.00 | 20.00 |
| PS16 | 1975 (7) | 10,000 | KM31-32, 34, 36-37, 38.2, 41 | 18.50 | 7.00 |
| PS17 | 1976 (7) | 11,000 | KM31-32, 34, 36-37, 38.2, 41 | 19.00 | 7.00 |
| PS18 | 1977 (7) | 12,000 | KM31-32, 34, 36-37, 41, 46a | 19.50 | 12.50 |
| PS19 | 1977 (7) | 10 | KM31-32, 34, 36-37, 41, 46a, Official card | — | — |
| PS20 | 1978 (7) | 15,000 | KM31-32, 34, 36-37, 41, 47a | 23.50 | 12.50 |
| PS21 | 1979 (7) | 16,000 | KM31-32, 34, 36-37, 41, 48a | 25.50 | 10.00 |
| PS22 | 1980 (7) | 17,000 | KM31-32, 34, 36-37, 41, 49a | 42.00 | 12.50 |
| PS23 | 1981 (7) | 18,000 | KM31-32, 34, 36-37, 41, 50a | 37.00 | 10.00 |
| PS24 | 1982 (7) | 18,000 | KM31-32, 34, 36-37, 41, 51a | 33.00 | 12.50 |
| PS25 | 1983 (7) | 18,000 | KM31-32, 34, 36-37, 41, 53a | 40.00 | 14.00 |
| PS26 | 1984 (7) | 15,000 | KM31-32, 34, 36-37, 41, 54a | 28.00 | 15.00 |
| PS27 | 1985 (7) | 11,500 | KM31-32, 34, 36-37, 41, 55a | 27.00 | 15.00 |
| PS28 | 1986 (7) | 10,000 | KM57a, 58-63 | 30.00 | 20.00 |
| PS29 | 1987 (7) | 10,000 | KM58-63, 65a | 38.00 | 20.00 |
| PS30 | 1988 (7) | 9,000 | KM58-63, 66a | 43.00 | 35.00 |
| PS31 | 1989 (5) | 8,500 | KM60-63, 67a | 44.50 | 30.00 |
| PS32 | 1989 (4) | 8,600 | KM67a-70a | 132 | 55.00 |
| PS33 | 1990 (6) | 10,000 | KM60-61, 63, 78a-79a, 81 | 52.00 | 60.00 |
| PS34 | 1990 (5) | 7,000 | KM72a-76a | 110 | 80.00 |
| PS35 | 1991 (7) | 12,000 | KM60-61, 63, 78-79, 80a, 81 | 61.00 | 30.00 |
| PS36 | 1992 (7) | 9,000 | KM60-61, 63, 78-79, 81, 82a | 58.00 | 37.50 |
| PS37 | 1993 (6) | 10,000 | KM60-61, 63, 78, 81, 87a | 75.00 | 37.50 |
| PS38 | 1994 (6) | 10,000 | KM60-61, 78-79, 81, 90a | 45.00 | 30.00 |
| PS39 | 1995 (7) | 4,000 | KM60-61, 63, 78-79, 81, 93a | 57.50 | 35.00 |
| PS40 | 1997 (7) | — | KM60-63, 78-79, 81, 103a | — | 35.00 |
| PS41 | 1998 (7) | 2,000 | KM60-61, 63, 78-79, 81, 107a | 55.00 | 85.00 |
| PS42 | 1998 (4) | 1,200 | KM109a-112a | — | 75.00 |
| PS43 | 1999 (7) | 2,000 | KM115a, 116-121 | 59.00 | 70.00 |
| PS44 | 2000 (7) | 1,500 | KM116-121, 125a | 54.00 | 55.00 |

## PROOF-LIKE SETS (PL)

| KM# | Date | Mintage | Identification | Issue Price | Mkt Val |
|---|---|---|---|---|---|
| PLS1 | 1965 (7) | 25,000 | KM23.2-29.2 flat pack | — | 7.00 |
| PLS2 | 1965 (7) | 400 | KM23.2-29.2 red plush case; reported, not confirmed | — | — |
| PLS3 | 1967 (7) | 49,500 | KM31-32, 34-38 flat pack | 10.00 | 3.00 |
| PLS4 | 1967 | 500 | KM31-32, 34-38 blue plush case | — | 110 |
| PLS5 | 1967 (7) | 10 | KM31-32, 34-38 | — | — |
| PLS6 | 1968 (6) | 40,000 | KM31-32, 34-37 flat pack | 7.00 | 2.50 |
| PLS7 | 1968 (6) | I.A. | KM31-32, 34-37 blue plush case | — | 7.50 |
| PLS8 | 1969 (7) | 50,000 | KM31-32, 34-36, 39-40 flat packet | 7.00 | 4.00 |
| PLS9 | 1969 (7) | I.A. | KM31-32, 34-36, 39-40 blue plush case | — | 10.00 |
| PLS10 | 1970 (7) | 20,000 | KM31-32, 34, 36-37, 41-42, flat pack | 7.00 | 7.00 |
| PLS11 | 1970 (7) | I.A. | KM31-32, 34, 36-37, 41-42, blue plush case | — | 12.50 |
| PLS12 | 1970 (7) | 10 | KM31-32, 34, 36-37, 41-42, official card, red plush case | — | — |

# NICARAGUA

The Republic of Nicaragua, situated in Central America between Honduras and Costa Rica, has an area of 50,193 sq. mi. (129,494 sq. km.) and a population of *3.7 million. Capital: Managua. Agriculture, mining (gold and silver) and hardwood logging are the principal industries. Cotton, meat, coffee and sugar are exported.

Columbus sighted the coast of Nicaragua on Sept. 12,1502 during the course of his last voyage of discovery. It was first visited in 1522 by conquistadors from Panama, under the command of Gil Gonzalez. Francisco Hernandez de Cordoba established the first settlements in 1524 at Granada and Leon. Nicaragua was incorporated, for administrative purpose, in the Captaincy General of Guatemala, which included every Central American state but Panama. On September 15, 1821 the Captaincy General of Guatemala declared itself and all the Central American provinces independent of Spain. The next year Nicaragua united with the Mexican Empire of Augustin de Iturbide, only to join in 1823 the federation of the Central American Republic. Within Nicaragua rival cities or juntas such as Leon, Granada and El Viejo vied for power, wealth and influence, often attacking each other at will. To further prove their legitimacy as well as provide an acceptable circulating coinage in those turbulent times (1821-1825), provisional mints functioned intermittently at Granada, Leon and ElViejo. The early coinage reflected traditional but crude Spanish colonial cob-style designs. Nicaragua's first governor was Pedro Arias Davila, appointed on June 1, 1827. When the federation was dissolved, Nicaragua declared itself an independent republic on April 30, 1838.

Dissension between the Liberals and Conservatives of the contending cities kept Nicaragua in turmoil, which made it possible for William Walker to make himself President in 1855. The two major political parties finally united to drive him out and in 1857 he was expelled. A relative peace followed, but by1912, Nicaragua had requested the U.S. Marines to restore order, which began a U.S. involvement that lasted until the Good Neighbor Policy was adopted in 1933. Anastasio Somoza Garcia assumed the Presidency in 1936. This family dynasty dominated Nicaragua until its overthrow in 1979. Formal elections in 1990 renewed a democratic government in power.

**MINT MARKS**

H - Heaton, Birmingham
HF - Huguenin Freres, Le Locle, Switzerland
Mo - Mexico City
-Philadelphia, Pa.
-Sherritt Mint, Canada
-Waterbury, Ct.

**MONETARY SYSTEM**

100 Centavos = 1 Peso

# REPUBLIC

## DECIMAL COINAGE

### 1/2 CENTAVO KM# 10 Composition: Bronze

| Date | Mintage | F | VF | XF | Unc | BU |
|---|---|---|---|---|---|---|
| 1912H | 900,000 | 1.00 | 2.50 | 15.00 | 40.00 | — |
| 1912H Proof | — | Value: 275 | | | | |
| 1915H | 320,000 | 1.50 | 4.00 | 30.00 | 100 | — |
| 1916H | 720,000 | 1.50 | 4.00 | 30.00 | 100 | — |
| 1917 | 720,000 | 1.50 | 4.00 | 12.00 | 65.00 | — |
| 1922 | 400,000 | 2.00 | 5.00 | 20.00 | 80.00 | — |
| 1924 | 400,000 | 1.00 | 3.00 | 12.00 | 70.00 | — |
| 1934 | 500,000 | 1.00 | 3.00 | 10.00 | 45.00 | — |
| 1936 | 600,000 | 0.50 | 0.75 | 5.00 | 20.00 | — |
| 1937 | 1,000,000 | 0.40 | 0.60 | 4.00 | 15.00 | — |

### CENTAVO KM# 11 Composition: Bronze

| Date | Mintage | F | VF | XF | Unc | BU |
|---|---|---|---|---|---|---|
| 1912H | 450,000 | 1.00 | 3.00 | 10.00 | 45.00 | — |
| 1912H Proof | — | Value: 275 | | | | |
| 1914H | 300,000 | 3.00 | 6.00 | 18.00 | 85.00 | — |
| 1915H | 500,000 | 2.00 | 5.00 | 15.00 | 100 | — |
| 1916H | 450,000 | 2.00 | 5.00 | 15.00 | 100 | — |
| 1917 | 450,000 | 2.00 | 5.00 | 15.00 | 65.00 | — |
| 1919 | 750,000 | 1.00 | 4.00 | 12.50 | 45.00 | — |
| 1920 | 700,000 | 1.00 | 4.00 | 12.50 | 40.00 | — |
| 1922 | 500,000 | 1.00 | 4.00 | 12.50 | 45.00 | — |
| 1924 | 300,000 | 1.00 | 5.00 | 15.00 | 50.00 | — |
| 1927 | 250,000 | 1.50 | 7.50 | 18.00 | 65.00 | — |
| 1928 | 500,000 | 1.00 | 4.00 | 12.00 | 35.00 | — |
| 1929 | 500,000 | 1.00 | 4.00 | 12.00 | 30.00 | — |
| 1930 | 250,000 | 1.50 | 7.50 | 18.00 | 60.00 | — |
| 1934 | 500,000 | 1.00 | 3.00 | 6.00 | 25.00 | — |
| 1935 | 500,000 | 0.50 | 2.00 | 4.00 | 20.00 | — |
| 1936 | 500,000 | 0.50 | 2.00 | 4.00 | 20.00 | — |
| 1937 | 1,000,000 | 0.10 | 0.50 | 3.00 | 12.50 | — |
| 1938 | 2,000,000 | 0.10 | 0.50 | 3.00 | 10.00 | — |
| 1940 | 2,000,000 | 0.10 | 0.50 | 3.00 | 10.00 | — |

### CENTAVO KM# 20 Composition: Brass

| Date | Mintage | F | VF | XF | Unc | BU |
|---|---|---|---|---|---|---|
| 1943 | 1,000,000 | 0.50 | 1.50 | 4.50 | 18.00 | — |

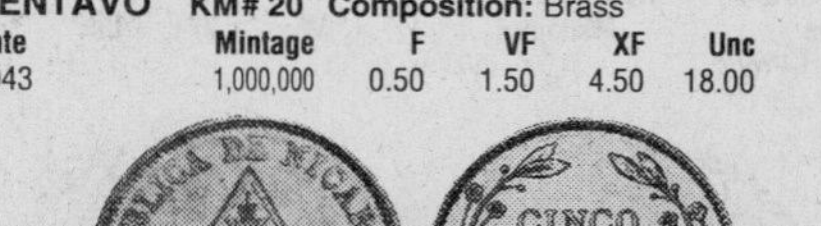

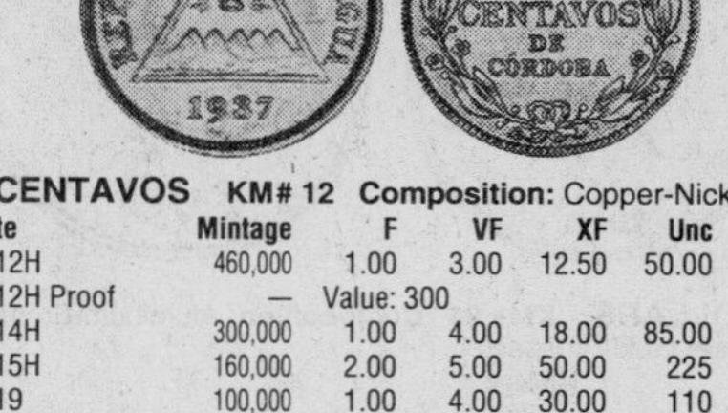

### 5 CENTAVOS KM# 12 Composition: Copper-Nickel

| Date | Mintage | F | VF | XF | Unc | BU |
|---|---|---|---|---|---|---|
| 1912H | 460,000 | 1.00 | 3.00 | 12.50 | 50.00 | — |
| 1912H Proof | — | Value: 300 | | | | |
| 1914H | 300,000 | 1.00 | 4.00 | 18.00 | 85.00 | — |
| 1915H | 160,000 | 2.00 | 5.00 | 50.00 | 225 | — |
| 1919 | 100,000 | 1.00 | 4.00 | 30.00 | 110 | — |
| 1920 | 150,000 | 1.00 | 3.00 | 25.00 | 90.00 | — |
| 1927 | 100,000 | 2.00 | 5.00 | 25.00 | 80.00 | — |
| 1928 | 100,000 | 1.00 | 3.00 | 18.00 | 50.00 | — |
| 1929 | 100,000 | 1.00 | 3.00 | 15.00 | 45.00 | — |
| 1930 | 100,000 | 1.00 | 3.00 | 15.00 | 45.00 | — |
| 1934 | 200,000 | 1.00 | 3.00 | 12.50 | 40.00 | — |
| 1935 | 200,000 | 1.00 | 3.00 | 12.50 | 35.00 | — |
| 1936 | 300,000 | 0.50 | 1.00 | 5.00 | 18.00 | — |
| 1937 | 300,000 | 0.50 | 1.00 | 8.00 | 25.00 | — |
| 1938 | 800,000 | 0.50 | 1.00 | 5.00 | 15.00 | — |
| 1940 | 800,000 | 0.50 | 1.00 | 5.00 | 12.50 | — |

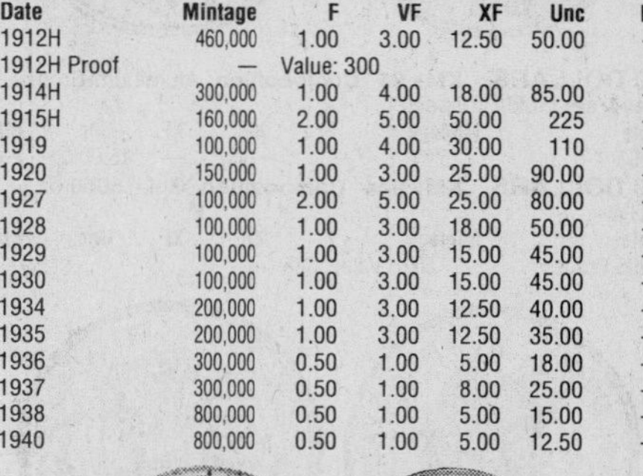

### 5 CENTAVOS KM# 21 Composition: Brass Edge: Plain

| Date | Mintage | F | VF | XF | Unc | BU |
|---|---|---|---|---|---|---|
| 1943 | 2,000,000 | 0.75 | 2.50 | 10.00 | 60.00 | — |

### 5 CENTAVOS KM# 24.1 Composition: Copper-Nickel

**Edge Lettering:** B. N. N **Note:** Reduced size.

| Date | Mintage | F | VF | XF | Unc | BU |
|---|---|---|---|---|---|---|
| 1946 | 4,000,000 | 0.10 | 0.25 | 2.50 | 18.00 | — |
| 1946 Proof | — | Value: 200 | | | | |
| 1950 | — | 0.10 | 0.25 | 2.50 | 18.00 | — |
| 1952 | 4,000,000 | 0.10 | 0.25 | 3.50 | 25.00 | — |
| 1952 Proof | — | Value: 250 | | | | |
| 1954 | 4,000,000 | 0.10 | 0.15 | 0.25 | 5.00 | — |
| 1954 Proof | — | Value: 250 | | | | |
| 1956 | 5,000,000 | 0.10 | 0.15 | 0.50 | 5.00 | — |
| 1956 Proof | — | Value: 250 | | | | |

### 5 CENTAVOS KM# 24.2 Composition: Copper-Nickel

**Edge Lettering:** B. C. N

| Date | Mintage | F | VF | XF | Unc | BU |
|---|---|---|---|---|---|---|
| 1962 | 3,000,000 | — | 0.10 | 0.15 | 2.00 | — |
| 1962 Proof | — | Value: 150 | | | | |
| 1964 | 4,000,000 | — | 0.10 | 0.15 | 2.00 | — |
| 1965 | 10,000,000 | — | 0.10 | 0.15 | 2.00 | — |

**5 CENTAVOS** **KM# 24.3** **Composition:** Copper-Nickel **Edge:** Reeded

| Date | Mintage | F | VF | XF | Unc | BU |
|---|---|---|---|---|---|---|
| 1972 Proof | 20,000 | Value: 2.50 | | | | |

**5 CENTAVOS** **KM# 24.2a (KM24.3a)** **Composition:** Nickel Clad Steel **Edge Lettering:** B.C.N.

| Date | Mintage | F | VF | XF | Unc | BU |
|---|---|---|---|---|---|---|
| 1972 | 10,020,000 | — | — | 0.10 | 0.50 | — |

**5 CENTAVOS** **KM# 27** **Composition:** Aluminum **Series:** F.A.O.

| Date | Mintage | F | VF | XF | Unc | BU |
|---|---|---|---|---|---|---|
| 1974 | 2,000,000 | — | — | 0.40 | 2.00 | — |

**5 CENTAVOS** **KM# 28** **Composition:** Aluminum **Series:** F.A.O.

| Date | Mintage | F | VF | XF | Unc | BU |
|---|---|---|---|---|---|---|
| 1974 | 16,200,000 | — | — | 0.10 | 0.50 | — |

**5 CENTAVOS** **KM# 49** **Composition:** Aluminum **Series:** F.A.O.

| Date | Mintage | F | VF | XF | Unc | BU |
|---|---|---|---|---|---|---|
| 1981 | — | — | — | 0.40 | 1.50 | — |

**5 CENTAVOS** **KM# 55** **Composition:** Aluminum **Series:** F.A.O.

| Date | Mintage | F | VF | XF | Unc | BU |
|---|---|---|---|---|---|---|
| 1987 | — | — | — | 0.40 | 1.00 | — |

**5 CENTAVOS** **KM# 80** **Composition:** Chromium Plated Steel

| Date | Mintage | F | VF | XF | Unc | BU |
|---|---|---|---|---|---|---|
| 1994 | 1,000,000 | — | — | — | 0.50 | — |

**10 CENTAVOS** **KM# 13** **Weight:** 2.5000 g. **Composition:** 0.8000 Silver .0643 oz. ASW **Note:** All dates struck with medal rotation except 1935, which appears only in coin rotation.

| Date | Mintage | F | VF | XF | Unc | BU |
|---|---|---|---|---|---|---|
| 1912H | 230,000 | 1.50 | 3.50 | 20.00 | 80.00 | — |
| 1912H Proof | — | Value: 250 | | | | |
| 1914H | 220,000 | 2.50 | 7.50 | 35.00 | 115 | — |
| 1914H Proof | — | Value: 375 | | | | |
| 1927 | 500,000 | 1.00 | 2.00 | 10.00 | 75.00 | — |
| 1928 | 1,000,000 | 0.50 | 1.50 | 10.00 | 50.00 | — |
| 1930 | 150,000 | 1.50 | 3.00 | 30.00 | 95.00 | — |
| 1935 | 250,000 | 1.00 | 2.00 | 7.50 | 45.00 | — |
| 1936 | 250,000 | 1.00 | 2.00 | 7.50 | 30.00 | — |

**10 CENTAVOS** **KM# 17.1** **Composition:** Copper-Nickel **Edge Lettering:** B.N.N

| Date | Mintage | F | VF | XF | Unc | BU |
|---|---|---|---|---|---|---|
| 1939 | 2,500,000 | 0.50 | 1.00 | 4.00 | 20.00 | — |
| 1939 Proof | — | Value: 150 | | | | |
| 1946 | 2,000,000 | 0.25 | 0.50 | 2.00 | 22.00 | — |
| 1946 Proof | — | Value: 200 | | | | |
| 1950 | 2,000,000 | 0.25 | 0.50 | 3.00 | 20.00 | — |
| 1950 Proof | — | Value: 200 | | | | |
| 1952 | 1,500,000 | 0.25 | 0.50 | 3.00 | 25.00 | — |
| 1952 Proof | — | Value: 200 | | | | |
| 1954 | 3,000,000 | 0.10 | 0.25 | 1.50 | 10.00 | — |
| 1954 Proof | — | Value: 200 | | | | |
| 1956 | 5,000,000 | 0.10 | 0.20 | 1.00 | 6.00 | — |
| 1956 Proof | — | Value: 200 | | | | |

**10 CENTAVOS** **KM# 22** **Composition:** Brass **Edge:** Reeded

| Date | Mintage | F | VF | XF | Unc | BU |
|---|---|---|---|---|---|---|
| 1943 | 2,000,000 | 0.50 | 1.00 | 5.00 | 40.00 | — |

**10 CENTAVOS** **KM# 17.2** **Composition:** Copper-Nickel **Edge Lettering:** B.C.N

| Date | Mintage | F | VF | XF | Unc | BU |
|---|---|---|---|---|---|---|
| 1962 | 4,000,000 | — | 0.10 | 0.15 | 5.00 | — |
| 1962 Proof | — | Value: 225 | | | | |
| 1964 | 4,000,000 | — | 0.10 | 0.15 | 5.00 | — |
| 1965 | 12,000,000 | — | 0.10 | 0.15 | 1.00 | — |

**10 CENTAVOS** **KM# 17.3** **Composition:** Copper-Nickel **Edge:** Reeded

| Date | Mintage | F | VF | XF | Unc | BU |
|---|---|---|---|---|---|---|
| 1972 Proof | 20,000 | Value: 2.50 | | | | |

**10 CENTAVOS** **KM# 17.2a (KM17.3a)** **Composition:** Nickel Clad Steel **Edge Lettering:** B.C.N.

| Date | Mintage | F | VF | XF | Unc | BU |
|---|---|---|---|---|---|---|
| 1972 | 10,020,000 | — | 0.10 | 0.15 | 0.30 | — |

**10 CENTAVOS** **KM# 29** **Composition:** Aluminum **Series:** F.A.O

| Date | Mintage | F | VF | XF | Unc | BU |
|---|---|---|---|---|---|---|
| 1974 | 2,000,000 | — | — | 0.10 | 1.00 | — |

**10 CENTAVOS** **KM# 30** **Composition:** Aluminum

| Date | Mintage | F | VF | XF | Unc | BU |
|---|---|---|---|---|---|---|
| 1974 | 20,000,000 | — | — | 0.10 | 0.20 | — |

**10 CENTAVOS** **KM# 31** **Composition:** Copper-Nickel

| Date | Mintage | F | VF | XF | Unc | BU |
|---|---|---|---|---|---|---|
| 1975 | 2,000,000 | — | — | — | — | — |
| 1978 | — | — | — | 0.40 | 2.00 | — |

**10 CENTAVOS** **KM# 50** **Composition:** Aluminum

| Date | Mintage | F | VF | XF | Unc | BU |
|---|---|---|---|---|---|---|
| 1981 | — | — | — | 0.15 | 1.00 | — |

**10 CENTAVOS** **KM# 56** **Composition:** Aluminum

| Date | Mintage | F | VF | XF | Unc | BU |
|---|---|---|---|---|---|---|
| 1987 | — | — | — | 0.15 | 0.40 | — |

**10 CENTAVOS** **KM# 81** **Composition:** Chromium Plated Steel

| Date | Mintage | F | VF | XF | Unc | BU |
|---|---|---|---|---|---|---|
| 1994 | 1,500,000 | — | — | — | 0.75 | — |

**25 CENTAVOS** **KM# 14** **Weight:** 6.2500 g. **Composition:** 0.8000 Silver .1607 oz. ASW

| Date | Mintage | F | VF | XF | Unc | BU |
|---|---|---|---|---|---|---|
| 1912H | 320,000 | 2.00 | 5.00 | 35.00 | 90.00 | — |
| 1912H Proof | — | Value: 350 | | | | |
| 1914H | 100,000 | 4.00 | 6.00 | 50.00 | 170 | — |
| 1928 | 200,000 | 2.00 | 5.00 | 30.00 | 60.00 | — |
| 1929 | 20,000 | 6.00 | 20.00 | 60.00 | 275 | — |
| 1930 | 20,000 | 6.00 | 20.00 | 60.00 | 250 | — |
| 1936 | 100,000 | 1.50 | 3.00 | 15.00 | 50.00 | — |

**25 CENTAVOS** **KM# 18.1** **Composition:** Copper-Nickel **Edge Lettering:** B. N. N

| Date | Mintage | F | VF | XF | Unc | BU |
|---|---|---|---|---|---|---|
| 1939 | 1,000,000 | 0.50 | 1.50 | 6.50 | 30.00 | — |
| 1939 Proof | — | Value: 250 | | | | |
| 1946 | 1,000,000 | 0.25 | 0.50 | 1.50 | 20.00 | — |
| 1946 Proof | — | Value: 280 | | | | |
| 1950 | 1,000,000 | 0.25 | 0.50 | 1.50 | 20.00 | — |
| 1950 Proof | — | Value: 300 | | | | |
| 1952 | 1,000,000 | 0.25 | 0.50 | 1.50 | 15.00 | — |
| 1952 Proof | — | Value: 280 | | | | |
| 1954 | 2,000,000 | 0.10 | 0.20 | 0.50 | 6.00 | — |
| 1954 Proof | — | Value: 280 | | | | |
| 1956 | 3,000,000 | 0.10 | 0.20 | 0.50 | 5.00 | — |
| 1956 Proof | — | Value: 280 | | | | |

**25 CENTAVOS** **KM# 23** **Composition:** Brass **Edge:** Reeded

| Date | Mintage | F | VF | XF | Unc | BU |
|---|---|---|---|---|---|---|
| 1943 | 1,000,000 | 0.50 | 1.50 | 8.50 | 50.00 | — |

**25 CENTAVOS** **KM# 18.2** **Composition:** Copper-Nickel **Edge Lettering:** B. C. N

| Date | Mintage | F | VF | XF | Unc | BU |
|---|---|---|---|---|---|---|
| 1964 | 3,000,000 | 0.10 | 0.20 | 0.40 | 4.00 | — |
| 1965 | 4,400,000 | 0.10 | 0.20 | 0.30 | 4.00 | — |

**25 CENTAVOS** **KM# 18.3** **Composition:** Copper-Nickel **Edge:** Reeded

| Date | Mintage | F | VF | XF | Unc | BU |
|---|---|---|---|---|---|---|
| 1972 | 4,000,000 | — | 0.10 | 0.15 | 2.00 | — |
| 1972 Proof | 20,000 | Value: 2.50 | | | | |
| 1974 | 6,000,000 | — | 0.10 | 0.15 | 2.00 | — |

**25 CENTAVOS** **KM# 51** **Composition:** Nickel Clad Steel **Note:** Struck at Sherritt Mint.

| Date | Mintage | F | VF | XF | Unc | BU |
|---|---|---|---|---|---|---|
| 1981 | — | — | — | 0.25 | 1.50 | — |
| 1985 | — | 5.00 | 10.00 | 20.00 | 30.00 | — |

**25 CENTAVOS** **KM# 57** **Composition:** Aluminum

| Date | Mintage | F | VF | XF | Unc | BU |
|---|---|---|---|---|---|---|
| 1987 | — | — | — | 0.25 | 2.00 | — |

**25 CENTAVOS** **KM# 82** **Composition:** Chromium Plated Steel

| Date | Mintage | F | VF | XF | Unc | BU |
|---|---|---|---|---|---|---|
| 1994 | 2,500,000 | — | — | — | 1.00 | — |

**50 CENTAVOS** **KM# 15** **Weight:** 12.5000 g. **Composition:** 0.8000 Silver .3215 oz. ASW

| Date | Mintage | F | VF | XF | Unc | BU |
|---|---|---|---|---|---|---|
| 1912H | 260,000 | 3.00 | 10.00 | 35.00 | 175 | — |
| 1912H Proof | — | Value: 500 | | | | |
| 1929 | 20,000 | 5.00 | 15.00 | 50.00 | 275 | — |

**50 CENTAVOS** **KM# 19.1** **Composition:** Copper-Nickel **Edge Lettering:** B. N. N

| Date | Mintage | F | VF | XF | Unc | BU |
|---|---|---|---|---|---|---|
| 1939 | 1,000,000 | 0.50 | 2.00 | 10.00 | 50.00 | — |
| 1939 Proof | — | Value: 250 | | | | |
| 1946 | 500,000 | 0.50 | 1.00 | 8.00 | 45.00 | — |
| 1946 Proof | — | Value: 300 | | | | |
| 1950 | 500,000 | 0.50 | 1.50 | 10.00 | 50.00 | — |
| 1950 Proof | — | Value: 300 | | | | |
| 1952 | 1,000,000 | 0.25 | 1.00 | 5.00 | 30.00 | — |
| 1952 Proof | — | Value: 300 | | | | |
| 1954 | 2,000,000 | 0.15 | 0.50 | 2.00 | 5.00 | — |
| 1954 Proof | — | Value: 300 | | | | |
| 1956 | 2,000,000 | 0.15 | 0.25 | 1.00 | 8.00 | — |
| 1956 Proof | — | Value: 300 | | | | |

**50 CENTAVOS** **KM# 19.2** **Composition:** Copper-Nickel **Edge Lettering:** B. C. N

| Date | Mintage | F | VF | XF | Unc | BU |
|---|---|---|---|---|---|---|
| 1965 | 600,000 | 0.50 | 1.25 | 3.50 | 8.00 | — |
| 1965 Proof | — | Value: 150 | | | | |

**50 CENTAVOS** **KM# 19.3** **Composition:** Copper-Nickel **Edge:** Reeded

| Date | Mintage | F | VF | XF | Unc | BU |
|---|---|---|---|---|---|---|
| 1972 | — | — | — | — | — | — |
| 1972 Proof | 20,000 | Value: 2.50 | | | | |
| 1974 | 2,000,000 | 0.10 | 0.25 | 0.50 | 3.50 | — |

**50 CENTAVOS** **KM# 42** **Composition:** Copper-Nickel

| Date | Mintage | F | VF | XF | Unc | BU |
|---|---|---|---|---|---|---|
| 1980Mo | 5,000,000 | 0.10 | 0.25 | 0.50 | 1.75 | — |
| 1981Mo | — | 0.10 | 0.25 | 0.50 | 1.75 | — |

**50 CENTAVOS** **KM# 42a** **Composition:** Nickel Clad Steel

| Date | Mintage | F | VF | XF | Unc | BU |
|---|---|---|---|---|---|---|
| 1983 | — | — | — | 0.40 | 2.50 | — |
| 1985 | — | 3.50 | 7.50 | 15.00 | 25.00 | — |

**50 CENTAVOS** **KM# 58** **Composition:** Aluminum-Bronze

| Date | Mintage | F | VF | XF | Unc | BU |
|---|---|---|---|---|---|---|
| 1987 | — | — | — | 0.40 | 2.50 | — |

**50 CENTAVOS** **KM# 83** **Composition:** Chromium Plated Steel

| Date | Mintage | F | VF | XF | Unc | BU |
|---|---|---|---|---|---|---|
| 1994 | 6,000,000 | — | — | — | 1.25 | — |

**50 CENTAVOS** **KM# 88** **Composition:** Nickel Clad Steel **Obverse:** National emblem **Reverse:** Denomination

| Date | Mintage | F | VF | XF | Unc | BU |
|---|---|---|---|---|---|---|
| 1997 | 20,000,000 | — | — | — | 1.25 | — |

**CORDOBA** **KM# 16** **Weight:** 25.0000 g. **Composition:** 0.9000 Silver .7234 oz. ASW

| Date | Mintage | F | VF | XF | Unc | BU |
|---|---|---|---|---|---|---|
| 1912H | 35,000 | 30.00 | 75.00 | 285 | 1,900 | — |
| 1912H Proof | — | Value: 2,850 | | | | |

**CORDOBA** **KM# 26** **Composition:** Copper-Nickel **Edge:** Reeded

| Date | Mintage | F | VF | XF | Unc | BU |
|---|---|---|---|---|---|---|
| 1972 | 20,000,000 | 0.10 | 0.20 | 2.00 | 4.00 | — |
| 1972 Proof | 20,000 | Value: 5.00 | | | | |

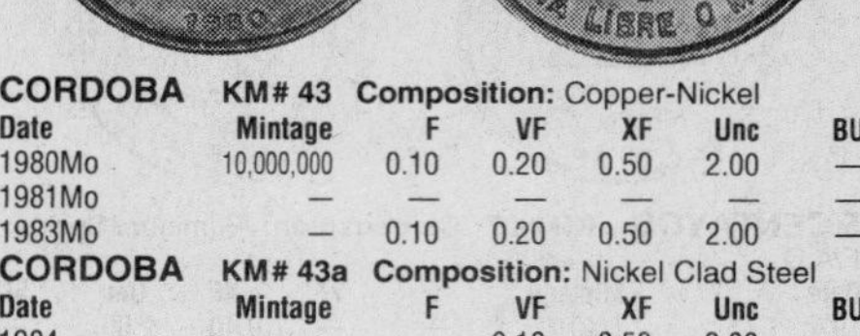

**CORDOBA** **KM# 43** **Composition:** Copper-Nickel

| Date | Mintage | F | VF | XF | Unc | BU |
|---|---|---|---|---|---|---|
| 1980Mo | 10,000,000 | 0.10 | 0.20 | 0.50 | 2.00 | — |
| 1981Mo | — | — | — | — | — | — |
| 1983Mo | — | 0.10 | 0.20 | 0.50 | 2.00 | — |

**CORDOBA** **KM# 43a** **Composition:** Nickel Clad Steel

| Date | Mintage | F | VF | XF | Unc | BU |
|---|---|---|---|---|---|---|
| 1984 | — | — | 0.10 | 0.50 | 2.00 | — |
| 1985 | — | 1.00 | 2.00 | 7.00 | 35.00 | — |

**CORDOBA** **KM# 59** **Composition:** Aluminum-Bronze

| Date | Mintage | F | VF | XF | Unc | BU |
|---|---|---|---|---|---|---|
| 1987 | — | — | 0.75 | 1.00 | 3.75 | — |

**CORDOBA** **KM# 77** **Weight:** 27.0000 g. **Composition:** 0.9250 Silver .8029 oz. ASW **Subject:** Ibero - American Series **Reverse:** 2 figures

| Date | Mintage | F | VF | XF | Unc | BU |
|---|---|---|---|---|---|---|
| 1991 Proof | 50,000 | Value: 60.00 | | | | |

**CORDOBA** **KM# 84** **Weight:** 13.8200 g. **Composition:** 0.9250 Silver .4110 oz. ASW **Subject:** National Ruben Dario Theater

| Date | Mintage | F | VF | XF | Unc | BU |
|---|---|---|---|---|---|---|
| 1994 Proof | 2,000 | Value: 40.00 | | | | |

**CORDOBA** **KM# 85** **Weight:** 14.1700 g. **Composition:** 0.9250 Silver .4214 oz. ASW **Subject:** 100th Anniversary - City of Boaco

| Date | Mintage | F | VF | XF | Unc | BU |
|---|---|---|---|---|---|---|
| 1995 Proof | 1,000 | Value: 45.00 | | | | |

**CORDOBA** **KM# 87** **Weight:** 13.9600 g. **Composition:** 0.8250 Silver .3703 oz. ASW **Subject:** 50th Anniversary - F.A.O **Obverse:** National emblem **Reverse:** F.A.O. logo

| Date | Mintage | F | VF | XF | Unc | BU |
|---|---|---|---|---|---|---|
| 1995 Proof | 30,000 | Value: 37.50 | | | | |

**CORDOBA** **KM# 89** **Composition:** Nickel Clad Steel **Obverse:** National emblem **Reverse:** Denomination

| Date | Mintage | F | VF | XF | Unc | BU |
|---|---|---|---|---|---|---|
| 1997 | 32,000,000 | — | — | — | 2.50 | — |

**5 CORDOBAS** **KM# 44** **Composition:** Copper-Nickel

| Date | Mintage | F | VF | XF | Unc | BU |
|---|---|---|---|---|---|---|
| 1980 | 10,000,000 | 0.15 | 0.25 | 1.00 | 3.00 | — |

**5 CORDOBAS** **KM# 44a** **Composition:** Nickel Clad Steel

| Date | Mintage | F | VF | XF | Unc | BU |
|---|---|---|---|---|---|---|
| 1984 | — | — | 0.25 | 1.00 | 3.50 | — |

**5 CORDOBAS** **KM# 60** **Composition:** Aluminum-Bronze

| Date | Mintage | F | VF | XF | Unc | BU |
|---|---|---|---|---|---|---|
| 1987 | — | — | 1.00 | 2.50 | 4.00 | — |



**5 CORDOBAS** **KM# 86** **Weight:** 27.0000 g. **Composition:** 0.9250 Silver .8030 oz. ASW **Subject:** Environmental Protection **Obverse:** Howler Monkey

| Date | Mintage | F | VF | XF | Unc | BU |
|---|---|---|---|---|---|---|
| 1994 Proof | 20,000 | Value: 45.00 | | | | |

**5 CORDOBAS** **KM# 90** **Composition:** Nickel Clad Steel **Obverse:** National emblem **Reverse:** Denomination

| Date | Mintage | F | VF | XF | Unc | BU |
|---|---|---|---|---|---|---|
| 1997 | 50,000,000 | — | — | — | 4.00 | — |

**10 CORDOBAS** **KM# 76** **Weight:** 25.7000 g. **Composition:** 0.9990 Silver .8263 oz. ASW **Subject:** Soccer

| Date | Mintage | F | VF | XF | Unc | BU |
|---|---|---|---|---|---|---|
| 1991 Proof | 10,000 | Value: 65.00 | | | | |

**10 CORDOBAS** **KM# 78** **Weight:** 19.9500 g. **Composition:** 0.9990 Silver .6408 oz. ASW **Subject:** Spanish Royal Visit

| Date | Mintage | F | VF | XF | Unc | BU |
|---|---|---|---|---|---|---|
| 1991 Proof | — | Value: 55.00 | | | | |

**20 CORDOBAS** **KM# 32** **Weight:** 5.0300 g. **Composition:** 0.9250 Silver .1496 oz. ASW **Subject:** Earthquake Relief Issue

| Date | Mintage | F | VF | XF | Unc | BU |
|---|---|---|---|---|---|---|
| 1975 | 2,491 | — | — | — | 14.50 | — |
| 1975 Proof | 1,750 | Value: 20.00 | | | | |

**50 CORDOBAS** **KM# 25** **Weight:** 35.6000 g. **Composition:** 0.9000 Gold 1.0300 oz. AGW **Subject:** 100th Anniversary - Birth of Ruben Dario

| Date | Mintage | F | VF | XF | Unc | BU |
|---|---|---|---|---|---|---|
| 1967HF Prooflike | Est. 17,000 | — | — | — | — | 450 |

**Note:** Originally 500 pieces were issued in blue boxes with certificates. An additional 1600 pieces were struck later on. Boxed originals demand a premium

**50 CORDOBAS** **KM# 33** **Weight:** 12.5700 g. **Composition:** 0.9250 Silver .3738 oz. ASW **Subject:** U.S. Bicentennial **Note:** Mintages are included with KM#34.

| Date | Mintage | F | VF | XF | Unc | BU |
|---|---|---|---|---|---|---|
| 1975 | — | — | — | — | 21.50 | — |
| 1975 Proof | — | Value: 30.00 | | | | |

**50 CORDOBAS** **KM# 34** **Weight:** 12.5700 g. **Composition:** 0.9250 Silver .3738 oz. ASW **Subject:** Earthquake Relief Issue

| Date | Mintage | F | VF | XF | Unc | BU |
|---|---|---|---|---|---|---|
| 1975 | 4,482 | — | — | — | 18.00 | — |
| 1975 Proof | 3,500 | Value: 27.50 | | | | |

**50 CORDOBAS** **KM# 61** **Weight:** 16.6000 g. **Composition:** 0.8250 Silver .4403 oz. ASW **Series:** Winter Olympics **Reverse:** Skier

| Date | Mintage | F | VF | XF | Unc | BU |
|---|---|---|---|---|---|---|
| 1988 Proof | 10,000 | Value: 22.50 | | | | |



**50 CORDOBAS** **KM# 62** **Weight:** 16.6000 g. **Composition:** 0.8250 Silver .4403 oz. ASW **Series:** Olympics **Reverse:** Sailboat

| Date | Mintage | F | VF | XF | Unc | BU |
|---|---|---|---|---|---|---|
| 1988 Proof | 10,000 | Value: 22.50 | | | | |

**100 CORDOBAS** **KM# 35** **Weight:** 25.1400 g. **Composition:** 0.9250 Silver .6668 oz. ASW **Subject:** U.S. Bicentennial **Note:** Mintages included with KM#36.

| Date | Mintage | F | VF | XF | Unc | BU |
|---|---|---|---|---|---|---|
| 1975 | — | — | — | — | 35.00 | — |
| 1975 | — | Value: 45.00 | | | | |

**100 CORDOBAS** **KM# 36** **Weight:** 25.1400 g. **Composition:** 0.9250 Silver .6668 oz. ASW **Subject:** Earthquake Relief Issue

| Date | Mintage | F | VF | XF | Unc | BU |
|---|---|---|---|---|---|---|
| 1975 | 4,682 | — | — | — | 35.00 | — |
| 1975 Proof | 3,500 | Value: 45.00 | | | | |

**200 CORDOBAS** **KM# 37** **Weight:** 2.1000 g. **Composition:** 0.9000 Gold .0608 oz. AGW **Subject:** Pieta

| Date | Mintage | F | VF | XF | Unc | BU |
|---|---|---|---|---|---|---|
| 1975 | 1,200 | — | — | — | 55.00 | — |
| 1975 Proof | 1,650 | Value: 70.00 | | | | |

**250 CORDOBAS** **KM# 79** **Weight:** 171.0700 g. **Composition:** 0.9990 Silver 5.4946 oz. ASW **Subject:** Spanish Royal Visit **Obverse:** Similar to KM#78

| Date | Mintage | F | VF | XF | Unc | BU |
|---|---|---|---|---|---|---|
| 1992 Proof | — | Value: 125 | | | | |

**500 CORDOBAS** **KM# 38** **Weight:** 5.4000 g. **Composition:** 0.9000 Gold .1563 oz. AGW **Subject:** Colonial Church

| Date | Mintage | F | VF | XF | Unc | BU |
|---|---|---|---|---|---|---|
| 1975 | 200 | — | — | — | 300 | — |
| 1975 Proof | 100 | Value: 600 | | | | |

**500 CORDOBAS** **KM# 39** **Weight:** 5.4000 g. **Composition:** 0.9000 Gold .1563 oz. AGW **Subject:** Earthquake Relief Issue

| Date | Mintage | F | VF | XF | Unc | BU |
|---|---|---|---|---|---|---|
| 1975 | 1,750 | — | — | — | 135 | — |
| 1975 Proof | 1,120 | Value: 190 | | | | |

**500 CORDOBAS** **KM# 45** **Weight:** 14.0000 g. **Composition:** 0.9250 Silver .4164 oz. ASW **Subject:** A. C. Standino

| Date | Mintage | F | VF | XF | Unc | BU |
|---|---|---|---|---|---|---|
| 1980Mo Proof | 21,000 | Value: 35.00 | | | | |

**500 CORDOBAS** **KM# 46** **Weight:** 14.0000 g. **Composition:** 0.9250 Silver .4164 oz. ASW **Subject:** Dobas Carlos Fonseca

| Date | Mintage | F | VF | XF | Unc | BU |
|---|---|---|---|---|---|---|
| 1980Mo Proof | 21,000 | Value: 35.00 | | | | |

**500 CORDOBAS** **KM# 47** **Weight:** 14.0000 g. **Composition:** 0.9250 Silver .4164 oz. ASW **Subject:** Rigoberto Lopez Perez

| Date | Mintage | F | VF | XF | Unc | BU |
|---|---|---|---|---|---|---|
| 1980Mo Proof | 21,000 | Value: 35.00 | | | | |

**500 CORDOBAS** **KM# 69** **Weight:** 14.0000 g. **Composition:** 0.9990 Silver .4502 oz. ASW **Subject:** Birthplace of Augusto Cesar Sandino

| Date | Mintage | F | VF | XF | Unc | BU |
|---|---|---|---|---|---|---|
| ND(1984) Proof | — | Value: 45.00 | | | | |

**500 CORDOBAS** **KM# 70** **Weight:** 14.0000 g. **Composition:** 0.9990 Silver .4502 oz. ASW **Subject:** Generals Sandino, Estrada and Umanzor

| Date | Mintage | F | VF | XF | Unc | BU |
|---|---|---|---|---|---|---|
| ND(1984) Proof | — | Value: 45.00 | | | | |

**500 CORDOBAS** **KM# 73** **Weight:** 14.0000 g. **Composition:** 0.9990 Silver .4502 oz. ASW **Subject:** 50th Anniversary - The murder of General Augusto Cesar Sandino

| Date | Mintage | F | VF | XF | Unc | BU |
|---|---|---|---|---|---|---|
| ND(1984) Proof | — | Value: 45.00 | | | | |

**500 CORDOBAS** **KM# 63** **Composition:** Aluminum

| Date | Mintage | F | VF | XF | Unc | BU |
|---|---|---|---|---|---|---|
| 1987 | — | — | — | 2.50 | 6.50 | — |

**1000 CORDOBAS** **KM# 40** **Weight:** 9.5000 g. **Composition:** 0.9000 Gold .2749 oz. AGW **Subject:** U.S. Bicentennial

| Date | Mintage | F | VF | XF | Unc | BU |
|---|---|---|---|---|---|---|
| 1975 | 3,380 | — | — | — | 165 | — |
| 1975 Proof | 2,270 | Value: 220 | | | | |

**1000 CORDOBAS** **KM# 48** **Weight:** 20.0000 g. **Composition:** 0.9000 Gold .5788 oz. AGW **Subject:** 1st Aniversary of Revolution

| Date | Mintage | F | VF | XF | Unc | BU |
|---|---|---|---|---|---|---|
| 1980Mo Proof | 6,000 | Value: 450 | | | | |

**1000 CORDOBAS** **KM# 52** **Weight:** 20.0000 g. **Composition:** 0.9170 Gold .5896 oz. AGW **Subject:** 50th Anniversary - The murder of General Augusto Cesar Sandino

| Date | Mintage | F | VF | XF | Unc | BU |
|---|---|---|---|---|---|---|
| 1984 Proof | 1,000 | Value: 500 | | | | |

**1000 CORDOBAS** **KM# 53** **Weight:** 20.0000 g. **Composition:** 0.9170 Gold .5896 oz. AGW **Reverse:** Birthplace of Augusto Cesar Sandino

| Date | Mintage | F | VF | XF | Unc | BU |
|---|---|---|---|---|---|---|
| 1984 Proof | 1,000 | Value: 500 | | | | |

**1000 CORDOBAS** **KM# 54** **Weight:** 20.0000 g. **Composition:** 0.9170 Gold .5896 oz. AGW **Reverse:** Generals Sandino, Estrada and Umanzor

| Date | Mintage | F | VF | XF | Unc | BU |
|---|---|---|---|---|---|---|
| 1984 Proof | 1,000 | Value: 500 | | | | |

**2000 CORDOBAS** **KM# 41** **Weight:** 19.2000 g. **Composition:** 0.9000 Gold .5556 oz. AGW **Subject:** U.S. Bicentennial

| Date | Mintage | F | VF | XF | Unc | BU |
|---|---|---|---|---|---|---|
| 1975 | 320 | — | — | — | 500 | — |
| 1975 Proof | 100 | Value: 825 | | | | |

**2000 CORDOBAS** **KM# 65** **Weight:** 16.6000 g. **Composition:** 0.8250 Silver .4404 oz. ASW **Subject:** Soccer - 1 player

| Date | Mintage | F | VF | XF | Unc | BU |
|---|---|---|---|---|---|---|
| 1988 Proof | 10,000 | Value: 40.00 | | | | |

**10000 CORDOBAS** KM# 64 **Weight:** 20.0000 g. **Composition:** 0.9990 Silver .6431 oz. ASW **Subject:** Discovery of Nicaragua by Columbus

| Date | Mintage | F | VF | XF | Unc | BU |
|---|---|---|---|---|---|---|
| 1989 Proof | Est. 10,000 | Value: 45.00 | | | | |

**10000 CORDOBAS** KM# 66 **Weight:** 26.4000 g. **Composition:** 0.9990 Silver .8480 oz. ASW **Subject:** Soccer **Reverse:** 2 soccer players

| Date | Mintage | F | VF | XF | Unc | BU |
|---|---|---|---|---|---|---|
| 1990 Proof | 10,000 | Value: 45.00 | | | | |

**10000 CORDOBAS** KM# 67 **Weight:** 26.0000 g. **Composition:** 0.9990 Silver .8352 oz. ASW **Subject:** Discovery of America **Reverse:** Sailing ship

| Date | Mintage | F | VF | XF | Unc | BU |
|---|---|---|---|---|---|---|
| 1990 Proof | — | Value: 47.50 | | | | |

**10000 CORDOBAS** KM# 68 **Weight:** 26.0000 g. **Composition:** 0.9990 Silver .8352 oz. ASW **Series:** 1992 Summer Olympics **Reverse:** Bicyclist

| Date | Mintage | F | VF | XF | Unc | BU |
|---|---|---|---|---|---|---|
| 1990 Proof | 10,000 | Value: 42.50 | | | | |

**10000 CORDOBAS** KM# 71 **Weight:** 26.0000 g. **Composition:** 0.9990 Silver .8352 oz. ASW **Subject:** Wildlife **Reverse:** Ocelot

| Date | Mintage | F | VF | XF | Unc | BU |
|---|---|---|---|---|---|---|
| 1990 Proof | — | Value: 42.50 | | | | |

**10000 CORDOBAS** KM# 72.1 **Weight:** 20.4000 g. **Composition:** 0.9990 Silver .6553 oz. ASW **Series:** 1992 Summer Olympics **Reverse:** Equestrian

| Date | Mintage | F | VF | XF | Unc | BU |
|---|---|---|---|---|---|---|
| 1990 Proof | 10,000 | Value: 60.00 | | | | |

**10000 CORDOBAS** KM# 72.2 **Weight:** 20.0000 g. **Composition:** 0.9990 Silver .6431 oz. ASW **Reverse:** "999" added at 4 o'clock

| Date | Mintage | F | VF | XF | Unc | BU |
|---|---|---|---|---|---|---|
| 1990 Proof | Inc. above | Value: 45.00 | | | | |

**10000 CORDOBAS** KM# 74 **Weight:** 25.9000 g. **Composition:** 0.9990 Silver .8320 oz. ASW **Series:** 1992 Summer Olympics **Reverse:** Tennis player proclaiming victory

| Date | Mintage | F | VF | XF | Unc | BU |
|---|---|---|---|---|---|---|
| 1990 Proof | 10,000 | Value: 50.00 | | | | |

**10000 CORDOBAS** KM# 75 **Weight:** 20.0000 g. **Composition:** 0.9990 Silver .6431 oz. ASW **Series:** 1992 Winter Olympics **Reverse:** Figure skater

| Date | Mintage | F | VF | XF | Unc | BU |
|---|---|---|---|---|---|---|
| 1990 Proof | 10,000 | Value: 47.50 | | | | |

## REVOLUTIONARY TOKEN COINAGE

**10 PESOS** KM# Tn1 **Weight:** 18.0000 g. **Composition:** Lead **Issuer:** General Augusto Cesar Sandino, 1925-1934

| Date | Mintage | VG | F | VF | XF | Unc |
|---|---|---|---|---|---|---|
| ND(1927) | — | 400 | 700 | 1,200 | 2,500 | — |

## PATTERNS

Including off metal strikes.

| KM# | Date | Mintage | Identification | Mkt Val |
|---|---|---|---|---|
| Pn10 | ND1912H | 2 | 1/2 Centavo. Silver. KM10; 2 known. | — |
| Pn11 | ND1912H | 1 | 1/2 Centavo. Gold. KM10; unique. | — |
| Pn13 | ND1912H | 1 | Centavo. Gold. KM#11. | — |
| Pn14 | ND1912H | 2 | 5 Centavos. Silver. KM12. | — |
| Pn15 | ND1912H | 1 | 5 Centavos. Gold. KM12. | — |
| Pn16 | ND1912H | 1 | 10 Centavos. Gold. KM13. | — |
| Pn17 | ND1912H | 1 | 25 Centavos. Gold. KM14. | — |
| Pn19 | ND1912H | 1 | Cordoba. Gold. KM16. | — |
| Pn18 | ND1912H | 1 | 50 Centavos. Gold. KM#15. | — |
| Pn12 | ND1912H | 2 | Centavo. Silver. KM11; 2 known. | 4,000 |
| Pn20 | ND1975 | — | 20 Cordobas. KM32 with 4.65 gram Plata Fino, LEY 925 below date. | — |
| Pn21 | ND1975 | — | 50 Cordobas. KM34 with 11.63 gram. Plata Fino, LEY 925 below date. | — |
| Pn22 | ND1975 | — | 100 Cordobas. KM36 with 23.25 gram. Plata Fino, LEY 925 below date. | — |

## TRIAL STRIKES

| KM# | Date | Mintage | Identification | Mkt Val |
|---|---|---|---|---|
| TS7 | ND(1912) | — | Cordoba. 18.0000 Aluminum. Obverse. | — |
| TS8 | ND(1912) | — | Cordoba. 18.0000 Aluminum. Reverse. | — |
| TS1 | ND(1912) | — | 10 Centavos. Aluminum. Obverse. | 350 |

| KM# | Date | Mintage | Identification | Mkt Val |
|---|---|---|---|---|
| TS2 | ND(1912) | — | 10 Centavos. Aluminum. Reverse, | 350 |
| TS3 | ND(1912) | — | 25 Centavos. Aluminum. Obverse. | 360 |
| TS4 | ND(1912) | — | 25 Centavos. Aluminum. Reverse. | 360 |

| KM# | Date | Mintage | Identification | Mkt Val |
|---|---|---|---|---|
| TS5 | ND(1912) | — | 50 Centavos. Aluminum. Obverse. | 375 |

| KM# | Date | Mintage | Identification | Mkt Val |
|---|---|---|---|---|
| TS6 | ND(1912) | — | 50 Centavos. Aluminum. | 375 |
| TS9 | ND1965 | — | 5 Centavos. Nickel. Raised "Trial" left of bust on obverse, above rays on reverse. KM24.2. | — |
| TS10 | ND1965 | — | 10 Centavos. Nickel. Raised "Trial" left of bust on obverse, above rays on reverse. KM17.2. | — |

## MINT SETS

| KM# | Date | Mintage | Identification | Issue Price | Mkt Val |
|---|---|---|---|---|---|
| MS1 | 1975 (5) | — | KM37-41 | — | 1,150 |
| MS2 | 1975 (5) | 2,250 | KM#32-36 | — | 110 |

## PROOF SETS

| KM# | Date | Mintage | Identification | Issue Price | Mkt Val |
|---|---|---|---|---|---|
| PS1 | 1912 (7) | 10 | KM10-16 | — | 4,500 |
| PS2 | 1912 (3) | 2 | Pn10, Pn12, Pn14 | — | 4,500 |
| PS3 | 1912 (7) | 1 | Pn11, Pn13, Pn15-19 | — | — |
| PS4 | 1972 (5) | 20,000 | KM17.3-19.3, 24.3, 26 | 8.00 | 15.00 |
| PS5 | 1975 (7) | — | KM32, 33, 35, 37, 38, 40, 41 | — | 1,750 |
| PS6 | 1975 (5) | 2,000 | KM32-36 | — | 160 |
| PS7 | 1975 (3) | — | KM32, 33, 35 | 115 | 90.00 |
| PS8 | 1975 (3) | — | KM34, 36, 39 | — | 255 |
| PS9 | 1975 (2) | — | KM37, 39 | — | 255 |

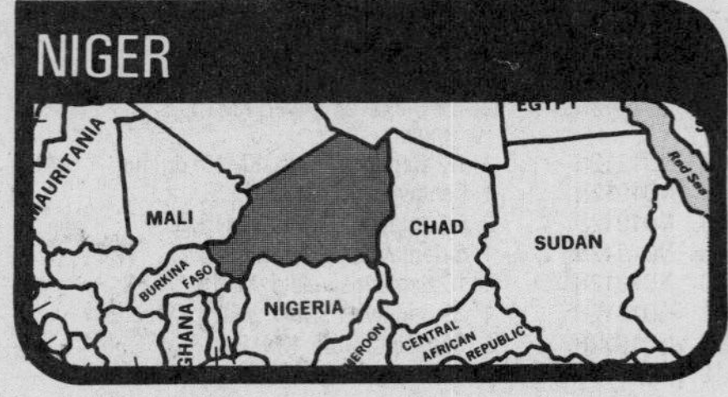


The Republic of Niger, located in West Africa's Sahara region 1,000 miles (1,609 km.) from the Mediterranean shore, has an area of 489,191 sq. mi. (1,267,000 sq. km.) and a population of *7.4 million. Capital: Niamey. The economy is based on subsistence agriculture and raising livestock.. Peanuts, peanut oil, and livestock are exported.

Although four-fifths of Niger is arid desert, it was, some 6,000 years ago inhabited and an important economic crossroads. Its modern history began in the 19th century with the beginning of contacts with British and German explorers searching for the mouth of the Niger River. Niger was incorporated into French West Africa in 1896, but it was 1922 before all native resistance was quelled and Niger became a French colony. In 1958 the voters approved the new French Constitution and elected to become an autonomous republic within the French Community. On Aug. 3, 1960, Niger withdrew from the Community and proclaimed its independence.

# REPUBLIC

## DECIMAL COINAGE

**10 FRANCS** KM# 1 **Weight:** 4.2000 g. **Composition:** 0.9000 Gold .1215 oz. AGW **Subject:** Independence Commemorataive

| Date | Mintage | F | VF | XF | Unc | BU |
|---|---|---|---|---|---|---|
| ND(1960) Proof | 1,000 | Value: 85.00 | | | | |

**10 FRANCS** KM# 7 **Weight:** 3.2000 g. **Composition:** 0.9000 Gold .0926 oz. AGW **Obverse:** Ostriches

| Date | Mintage | F | VF | XF | Unc | BU |
|---|---|---|---|---|---|---|
| 1968 Proof | 1,000 | Value: 120 | | | | |

**10 FRANCS** KM# 8.1 **Weight:** 20.0000 g. **Composition:** 0.9000 Silver .5845 oz. ASW **Note:** Sharp details, raised rim.

| Date | Mintage | F | VF | XF | Unc | BU |
|---|---|---|---|---|---|---|
| 1968 Proof | 1,000 | Value: 65.00 | | | | |

**10 FRANCS** KM# 8.2 **Weight:** 24.5400 g. **Composition:** 0.9000 Silver .7100 oz. ASW **Obverse:** Exists with and without accent marks above first E in REPUBLIQUE **Note:** Dull details, machined-down rim

| Date | Mintage | F | VF | XF | Unc | BU |
|---|---|---|---|---|---|---|
| 1968 Proof | — | — | — | — | 40.00 | — |

**25 FRANCS** KM# 2 **Weight:** 8.0000 g. **Composition:** 0.9000 Gold .2315 oz. AGW **Subject:** Independence Commemorative

| Date | Mintage | F | VF | XF | Unc | BU |
|---|---|---|---|---|---|---|
| ND(1960) Proof | 1,000 | Value: 135 | | | | |

**25 FRANCS** KM# 9 **Weight:** 8.0000 g. **Composition:** 0.9000 Gold .2315 oz. AGW **Obverse:** Barbary sheep

| Date | Mintage | F | VF | XF | Unc | BU |
|---|---|---|---|---|---|---|
| 1968 Proof | 1,000 | Value: 175 | | | | |

**50 FRANCS** KM# 3 **Weight:** 16.0000 g. **Composition:** 0.9000 Gold .4630 oz. AGW **Subject:** Independence Commemorative

| Date | Mintage | F | VF | XF | Unc | BU |
|---|---|---|---|---|---|---|
| ND(1960) Proof | 1,000 | Value: 250 | | | | |

**50 FRANCS** KM# 10 **Weight:** 16.0000 g. **Composition:** 0.9000 Gold .4630 oz. AGW **Subject:** Independence Commemorative

| Date | Mintage | F | VF | XF | Unc | BU |
|---|---|---|---|---|---|---|
| 1968 Proof | 1,000 | Value: 400 | | | | |

**100 FRANCS** KM# 4 **Weight:** 32.0000 g. **Composition:** 0.9000 Gold .9260 oz. AGW **Subject:** Independence Commemorative

| Date | Mintage | F | VF | XF | Unc | BU |
|---|---|---|---|---|---|---|
| ND(1960) Proof | 1,000 | Value: 400 | | | | |

**100 FRANCS** KM# 11 **Weight:** 32.0000 g. **Composition:** 0.9000 Gold .9260 oz. AGW **Subject:** Independence Commemorative

| Date | Mintage | F | VF | XF | Unc | BU |
|---|---|---|---|---|---|---|
| 1968 Proof | 1,000 | Value: 550 | | | | |

**500 FRANCS** KM# 5 **Weight:** 10.0000 g. **Composition:** 0.9000 Silver .2893 oz. ASW **Subject:** Independence Commemorative

| Date | Mintage | F | VF | XF | Unc | BU |
|---|---|---|---|---|---|---|
| ND(1960) Proof | — | Value: 35.00 | | | | |

**1000 FRANCS** KM# 6 **Weight:** 20.0000 g. **Composition:** 0.9000 Silver .5787 oz. ASW **Subject:** Independence Commemorative

| Date | Mintage | F | VF | XF | Unc | BU |
|---|---|---|---|---|---|---|
| ND(1960) Proof | — | Value: 55.00 | | | | |

## ESSAIS

| KM# | Date | Mintage | Identification | Issue Price | Mkt Val |
|---|---|---|---|---|---|
| E1 | ND1960 | — | 10 Francs. | — | 110 |
| E2 | ND1960 | — | 25 Francs. | — | 200 |
| E3 | ND1960 | — | 50 Francs. | — | 325 |
| E4 | ND1960 | — | 100 Francs. | — | 650 |
| E5 | ND1960 | 1,000 | 500 Francs. KM5. | — | 35.00 |
| E6 | ND(1960) | 1,000 | 1000 Francs. KM5. | — | 55.00 |

| KM# | Date | Mintage | Identification | Issue Price | Mkt Val |
|---|---|---|---|---|---|
| E7 | ND1968 | — | 10 Francs. Gold. 31.7800 g. KM8. | — | 1,600 |
| E8 | ND1968 | — | 10 Francs. Silver. | — | 95.00 |
| E9 | ND1968 | — | 25 Francs. Silver. | — | 30.00 |
| E10 | ND1968 | — | 50 Francs. Silver. | — | 35.00 |
| E11 | ND1968 | — | 100 Francs. Silver. | — | 45.00 |

## PATTERNS

Including off metal strikes

| KM# | Date | Mintage | Identification | Mkt Val |
|---|---|---|---|---|
| Pn1 | ND1968 | — | 10 Francs. Copper. 18.8200 g. Reeded edge. KM8.1. | 200 |

## PROOF SETS

| KM# | Date | Mintage | Identification | Issue Price | Mkt Val |
|---|---|---|---|---|---|
| PS1 | 1960 (4) | 1,000 | KM1-4 | — | 870 |
| PS2 | 1968 (4) | — | KM7, 9-11 | — | 1,250 |

## NIGERIA

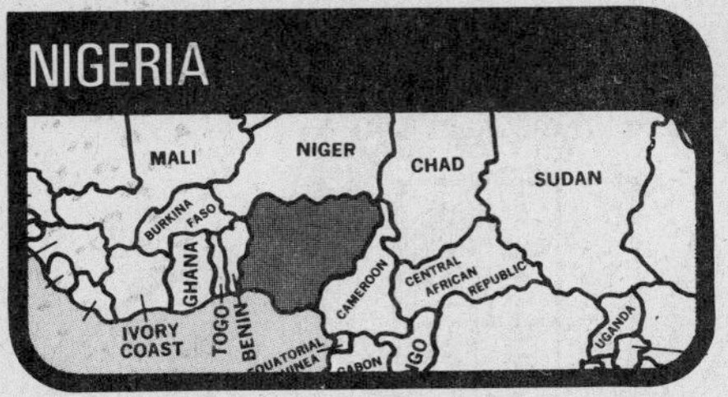


The Federal Republic of Nigeria, situated on the Atlantic coast of West Africa has an area of 356,669 sq. mi. (923,770 sq. km.) and a population of *115.2 million. Capital: Abuja. The economy is based on petroleum and agriculture. Crude oil, cocoa, natural gas, tobacco and tin are exported.

Following the Napoleonic Wars, the British expanded their trade with the interior of Nigeria. The Berlin Conference of 1885 recognized British claims to a sphere of influence in that area, and in the following year the Royal Niger Company was chartered. Direct British control of the territory was initiated in 1900, and in 1914 the amalgamation of Northern and Southern Nigeria into the Colony and Protectorate of Nigeria was effected. In 1960, following a number of territorial and constitutional changes, Nigeria was granted independence within the British Commonwealth as a federation of the Northern, Western and Eastern regions. Nigeria altered its political relationship with Great Britain on Oct. 1, 1963, by proclaiming itself a republic. It did, however, elect to remain a member of the Commonwealth of Nations.

On May 30, 1967, the Eastern Region of the republic -an area occupied principally by the proud and resourceful Ibo tribe - seceded from Nigeria and proclaimed itself the independent Republic of Biafra with Odumegwu Ojukwu as Chief of State. Civil war erupted and raged for 31 months. Casualties, including civilian, were about two million, the majority succumbing to malnutrition and disease. Biafra surrendered to the federal government on January 15, 1970.

As of November 1995, Nigeria has been suspended from the Commonwealth. Presidential democratic elections continue to be held.

For earlier coinage refer to British West Africa.

**RULERS**
Elizabeth II, 1952-1963

**MONETARY SYSTEM**
12 Pence = 1 Shilling
20 Shillings = 1 Pound

# BRITISH PROTECTORATE OF NIGERIA

## POUND STERLING COINAGE

**1/2 PENNY** **KM# 1** **Composition:** Bronze

| Date | Mintage | F | VF | XF | Unc | BU |
|---|---|---|---|---|---|---|
| 1959 | 52,800,000 | — | 0.15 | 0.25 | 0.75 | — |
| 1959 Proof | 6,031 | Value: 2.50 | | | | |

**PENNY** **KM# 2** **Composition:** Bronze

| Date | Mintage | F | VF | XF | Unc | BU |
|---|---|---|---|---|---|---|
| 1959 | 93,368,000 | — | 0.15 | 0.25 | 1.25 | — |
| 1959 Proof | 6,031 | Value: 2.50 | | | | |

**3 PENCE** **KM# 3** **Composition:** Nickel-Brass

| Date | Mintage | F | VF | XF | Unc | BU |
|---|---|---|---|---|---|---|
| 1959 | 52,000,000 | — | 0.20 | 0.40 | 1.50 | — |
| 1959 Proof | 6,031 | Value: 3.50 | | | | |

**6 PENCE** **KM# 4** **Composition:** Copper-Nickel

| Date | Mintage | F | VF | XF | Unc | BU |
|---|---|---|---|---|---|---|
| 1959 | 35,000,000 | — | 0.40 | 0.80 | 2.50 | — |
| 1959 Proof | 6,031 | Value: 5.00 | | | | |

**SHILLING** **KM# 5** **Composition:** Copper-Nickel

| Date | Mintage | F | VF | XF | Unc | BU |
|---|---|---|---|---|---|---|
| 1959 | 18,000,000 | — | 0.65 | 1.45 | 3.50 | — |
| 1959 Proof | 6,031 | Value: 6.50 | | | | |
| 1961 | 48,584,000 | — | 0.65 | 1.45 | 3.50 | — |
| 1961 Reported, not confirmed | — | — | — | — | — | — |
| 1962 | 39,416,000 | — | 0.65 | 1.45 | 3.50 | — |

**2 SHILLING** **KM# 6.1** **Composition:** Copper-Nickel **Edge:** Security

| Date | Mintage | F | VF | XF | Unc | BU |
|---|---|---|---|---|---|---|
| 1959 | 15,000,000 | — | 1.25 | 2.50 | 6.00 | — |
| 1959 Proof | 6,031 | Value: 9.00 | | | | |

**2 SHILLING** **KM# 6.2** **Composition:** Copper-Nickel **Edge:** Reeded

| Date | Mintage | F | VF | XF | Unc | BU |
|---|---|---|---|---|---|---|
| 1959 | Inc. above | — | 1.25 | 2.50 | 6.00 | — |

# REPUBLIC

## DECIMAL COINAGE

**1/2 KOBO** **KM# 7** **Composition:** Bronze

| Date | Mintage | F | VF | XF | Unc | BU |
|---|---|---|---|---|---|---|
| 1973 | 166,618,000 | — | 0.45 | 1.00 | 3.50 | — |
| 1973 Proof | 10,000 | Value: 3.50 | | | | |

**KOBO** **KM# 8.1** **Composition:** Bronze **Obverse:** Arms **Obv. Legend:** Unity and faith

| Date | Mintage | F | VF | XF | Unc | BU |
|---|---|---|---|---|---|---|
| 1973 | 586,944,000 | — | 0.25 | 0.50 | 2.00 | — |
| 1973 Proof | 10,000 | Value: 3.50 | | | | |
| 1974 | 14,500,000 | — | 0.25 | 0.50 | 3.00 | — |

**KOBO** **KM# 8.2** **Composition:** Bronze **Obverse:** Arms **Obv. Legend:** Unity and faith, peace and progress

| Date | Mintage | F | VF | XF | Unc | BU |
|---|---|---|---|---|---|---|
| 1987 | — | — | 0.50 | 1.50 | 6.00 | — |
| 1988 | — | — | 0.50 | 1.50 | 6.00 | — |

**KOBO** **KM# 8.2a** **Composition:** Copper Plated Steel

| Date | Mintage | F | VF | XF | Unc | BU |
|---|---|---|---|---|---|---|
| 1991 | — | — | — | — | 0.25 | — |

**5 KOBO** **KM# 9.1** **Composition:** Copper-Nickel **Obverse:** Arms **Obv. Legend:** Unity and faith

| Date | Mintage | F | VF | XF | Unc | BU |
|---|---|---|---|---|---|---|
| 1973 | 96,920,000 | — | 0.35 | 0.75 | 2.75 | — |
| 1973 Proof | 10,000 | Value: 4.00 | | | | |
| 1974 | — | — | 0.45 | 0.85 | 3.00 | — |
| 1976 | 9,800,000 | — | 0.45 | 0.85 | 3.00 | — |
| 1986 | — | — | 0.45 | 0.85 | 3.00 | — |

**5 KOBO** **KM# 9.2** **Composition:** Copper-Nickel **Obverse:** Arms **Obv. Legend:** Unity and faith, peace and progress

| Date | Mintage | F | VF | XF | Unc | BU |
|---|---|---|---|---|---|---|
| 1987 | — | — | 1.00 | 2.50 | 7.00 | — |
| 1988 | — | — | 1.00 | 2.50 | 7.00 | — |
| 1989 | — | — | 1.00 | 2.50 | 7.00 | — |

**10 KOBO** **KM# 10.1** **Composition:** Copper-Nickel **Obverse:** Arms **Obv. Legend:** Unity and faith

| Date | Mintage | F | VF | XF | Unc | BU |
|---|---|---|---|---|---|---|
| 1973 | 340,870,000 | — | 0.50 | 1.00 | 3.50 | — |
| 1973 Proof | 10,000 | Value: 5.00 | | | | |
| 1974 | — | — | 0.60 | 1.20 | 3.75 | — |
| 1976 | 7,000,000 | — | 0.60 | 1.20 | 3.75 | — |

**10 KOBO** **KM# 10.2** **Composition:** Copper-Nickel **Obverse:** Arms **Obv. Legend:** Unity and faith, peace and progress

| Date | Mintage | F | VF | XF | Unc | BU |
|---|---|---|---|---|---|---|
| 1987 | — | — | 1.25 | 3.50 | 9.00 | — |
| 1988 | — | — | 1.25 | 3.50 | 9.00 | — |
| 1989 | — | — | 1.25 | 3.50 | 9.00 | — |
| 1990 | — | — | 1.25 | 3.50 | 9.00 | — |

**10 KOBO** **KM# 12** **Composition:** Copper Plated Steel

| Date | Mintage | F | VF | XF | Unc | BU |
|---|---|---|---|---|---|---|
| 1991 | — | — | — | — | 0.45 | — |

**25 KOBO** **KM# 11** **Composition:** Copper-Nickel

| Date | Mintage | F | VF | XF | Unc | BU |
|---|---|---|---|---|---|---|
| 1973 | 4,616,000 | — | 1.00 | 2.50 | 7.50 | — |
| 1973 Proof | 10,000 | Value: 8.50 | | | | |
| 1975 | — | — | 1.00 | 2.50 | 7.50 | — |

**25 KOBO** **KM# 11a** **Composition:** Copper Plated Steel

| Date | Mintage | F | VF | XF | Unc | BU |
|---|---|---|---|---|---|---|
| 1991 | — | — | — | — | 0.65 | — |

**50 KOBO** **KM# 13** **Composition:** Nickel Plated Steel

| Date | Mintage | F | VF | XF | Unc | BU |
|---|---|---|---|---|---|---|
| 1991 | — | — | — | — | 1.25 | — |
| 1993 | — | — | — | — | 1.25 | — |

**NAIRA** **KM# 14** **Composition:** Nickel Plated Steel

| Date | Mintage | F | VF | XF | Unc | BU |
|---|---|---|---|---|---|---|
| 1991 | — | — | — | — | 1.75 | — |
| 1993 | — | — | — | — | 1.75 | — |

**100 NAIRA** **KM# 15** **Weight:** 28.2800 g. **Composition:** 0.9250 Silver .8410 oz. ASW **Subject:** 100 Years - Baning in Nigeria **Obverse:** National arms **Reverse:** Bank building **Edge:** Reeded

| Date | Mintage | F | VF | XF | Unc | BU |
|---|---|---|---|---|---|---|
| 1994 Proof | 5,000 | Value: 600 | | | | |

**Note:** Issue price at Bank in Lagos approximately $1,400.

**1000 NAIRA** **KM# 16** **Weight:** 47.5400 g. **Composition:** 0.9166 Gold 1.4010 oz. AGW **Subject:** 100 Years - Banking in Nigeria **Obverse:** National arms **Reverse:** Bank building **Edge:** Reeded

| Date | Mintage | F | VF | XF | Unc | BU |
|---|---|---|---|---|---|---|
| 1994 Proof | 100 | Value: 2,250 | | | | |

## PATTERNS

Including off metal strikes

| KM# | Date | Mintage | Identification | Mkt Val |
|---|---|---|---|---|
| Pn1 | 1962 | — | Shilling. Bronze. KM5. | 200 |
| Pn2 | 1973 | — | 10 Kobo. Bronze. KM10. | 175 |

## TRIAL STRIKES

| KM# | Date | Mintage | Identification | Mkt Val |
|---|---|---|---|---|
| TS1 | 1962 | — | Shilling. Copper-Nickel. "TRIAL" in field on obverse and reverse. | 80.00 |

## PROOF SETS

| KM# | Date | Mintage | Identification | Issue Price | Mkt Val |
|---|---|---|---|---|---|
| PS1 | 1959 (6) | 1,031 | KM1-5, 6.1, red case, originals | — | 30.00 |
| PS2 | 1959 (6) | 5,000 | KM1-5, 6.1, blue case, restirkes | — | 16.50 |
| PS3 | 1973 (5) | 102,000 | KM7, 8.1-10.1,11 | 14.70 | 25.00 |

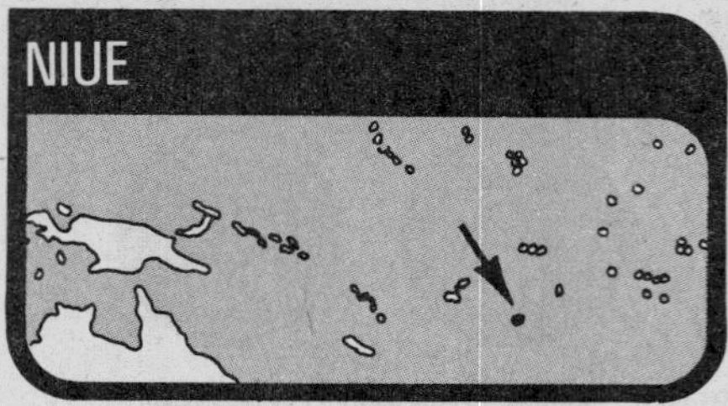


Niue, or Savage Island, a dependent state of New Zealand is located in the Pacific Ocean east of Tonga and southeast of Samoa. The size is 100 sq. mi. (260 sq. km.) with a population of *2,000. Chief village and port is Alofi. Bananas and copra are exported.

Discovered by Captain Cook in 1774, it was originally part of the Cook Islands administration but has been separate since 1922.

**MINT MARKS**

PM - Pobjoy Mint

# NEW ZEALAND DEPENDENT STATE

## DECIMAL COINAGE

**DOLLAR** **KM# 122** **Weight:** 10.0000 g. **Composition:** 0.5000 Silver .1608 oz. ASW **Series:** Protect Our World **Obverse:** National arms **Reverse:** Oak tree **Edge:** Reeded **Size:** 30 mm.

| Date | Mintage | F | VF | XF | Unc | BU |
|---|---|---|---|---|---|---|
| 1996 Proof | — | — | — | — | 15.00 | — |

**DOLLAR** **KM# 85** **Weight:** 10.0200 g. **Composition:** 0.5000 Silver .1608 oz. ASW **Obverse:** National arms **Reverse:** The Bounty

| Date | Mintage | F | VF | XF | Unc | BU |
|---|---|---|---|---|---|---|
| 1996 Proof | — | Value: 20.00 | | | | |

**DOLLAR** **KM# 113** **Weight:** 10.0200 g. **Composition:** 0.5000 Silver .1608 oz. ASW **Series:** Endangered Wildlife **Obverse:** Arms **Reverse:** Jaguar on tree limb

| Date | Mintage | F | VF | XF | Unc | BU |
|---|---|---|---|---|---|---|
| 1996 Proof | — | Value: 20.00 | | | | |

**DOLLAR** **KM# 87** **Composition:** Copper-Nickel **Obverse:** Arms **Reverse:** Diana **Rev. Legend:** . . . The People's Princess

| Date | Mintage | F | VF | XF | Unc | BU |
|---|---|---|---|---|---|---|
| 1997 | — | — | — | — | 10.00 | — |

**DOLLAR** **KM# 88** **Composition:** Copper-Nickel **Obverse:** Arms **Reverse:** Diana **Rev. Legend:** . . . Princess of Wales **Note:** Similar to 10 Dollars, KM#91.

| Date | Mintage | F | VF | XF | Unc | BU |
|---|---|---|---|---|---|---|
| 1997 | — | — | — | — | 10.00 | — |

**DOLLAR** **KM# 89** **Composition:** Copper-Nickel **Obverse:** Arms **Reverse:** Diana, sprays below bust **Rev. Legend:** . . . Princess of Wales **Note:** Similar to 10 Dollars, KM#92.

| Date | Mintage | F | VF | XF | Unc | BU |
|---|---|---|---|---|---|---|
| 1997 | — | — | — | — | 10.00 | — |

**DOLLAR** **KM# 102** **Composition:** Copper-Nickel **Obverse:** Queen Elizabethh II **Reverse:** Diana **Rev. Legend:** . . . In Memoriam **Note:** Similar to 10 Dollars, KM#104.

| Date | Mintage | F | VF | XF | Unc | BU |
|---|---|---|---|---|---|---|
| 1998 | — | — | — | — | 10.00 | — |

**DOLLAR** **KM# 103** **Composition:** Copper-Nickel **Obverse:** Queen Elizabethh II **Reverse:** Diana **Rev. Legend:** . . . Princess of Wales **Note:** Similar to 10 Dollars, KM#105.

| Date | Mintage | F | VF | XF | Unc | BU |
|---|---|---|---|---|---|---|
| 1998 | — | — | — | — | 10.00 | — |

**DOLLAR** **KM# 115** **Composition:** Copper-Nickel **Subject:** 50th Anniversary of Peanuts **Obverse:** Queen's portrait **Reverse:** Snoopy and Woodstock **Note:** Similar to 10 Dollars, KM#116.

| Date | Mintage | F | VF | XF | Unc | BU |
|---|---|---|---|---|---|---|
| 2000 | Est. 100,000 | — | — | — | 12.00 | — |

**DOLLAR** **KM# 123** **Weight:** 28.2800 g. **Composition:** Copper-Nickel **Subject:** Snoopy as an Ace **Obverse:** Queen's portrait **Reverse:** Snoopy flying his dog house **Edge:** Reeded **Size:** 38.6 mm.

| Date | Mintage | F | VF | XF | Unc | BU |
|---|---|---|---|---|---|---|
| 2001 | 100,000 | — | — | — | 10.00 | — |

**DOLLAR** **KM# 128** **Weight:** 28.2800 g. **Composition:** Copper-Nickel **Series:** Pokeman **Obverse:** National arms **Reverse:** "Bulbasaur" **Edge:** Reeded **Size:** 38.6 mm.

| Date | Mintage | F | VF | XF | Unc | BU |
|---|---|---|---|---|---|---|
| 2001 | 100,000 | — | — | — | 10.00 | — |

**DOLLAR** **KM# 129** **Weight:** 7.7700 g. **Composition:** 0.9990 Silver .2496 oz. ASW **Series:** Pokeman **Obverse:** National arms **Reverse:** "Bulbasaur" **Edge:** Reeded **Size:** 22 mm.

| Date | Mintage | F | VF | XF | Unc | BU |
|---|---|---|---|---|---|---|
| 2001 Proof | 20,000 | Value: 13.50 | | | | |

**DOLLAR** **KM# 131** **Weight:** 28.2800 g. **Composition:** Copper-Nickel **Series:** Pokeman **Obverse:** National arms **Reverse:** "Charmander" **Edge:** Reeded **Size:** 38.6 mm.

| Date | Mintage | F | VF | XF | Unc | BU |
|---|---|---|---|---|---|---|
| 2001 | 100,000 | — | — | — | 10.00 | — |

**DOLLAR** **KM# 132** **Weight:** 7.7700 g. **Composition:** 0.9990 Silver .2496 oz. ASW **Series:** Pokeman **Obverse:** National arms **Reverse:** "Charmander" **Edge:** Reeded **Size:** 22 mm.

| Date | Mintage | F | VF | XF | Unc | BU |
|---|---|---|---|---|---|---|
| 2001 Proof | 20,000 | Value: 13.50 | | | | |

**DOLLAR** **KM# 134** **Weight:** 28.2800 g. **Composition:** Copper-Nickel **Series:** Pokeman **Obverse:** National arms **Reverse:** "Meowth" **Edge:** Reeded **Size:** 38.6 mm.

| Date | Mintage | F | VF | XF | Unc | BU |
|---|---|---|---|---|---|---|
| 2001 | 100,000 | — | — | — | 10.00 | — |

**DOLLAR** **KM# 135** **Weight:** 7.7700 g. **Composition:** 0.9990 Silver .2496 oz. ASW **Series:** Pokeman **Obverse:** National arms **Reverse:** "Meowth" **Edge:** Reeded **Size:** 22 mm.

| Date | Mintage | F | VF | XF | Unc | BU |
|---|---|---|---|---|---|---|
| 2001 Proof | 20,000 | Value: 13.50 | | | | |

**DOLLAR** **KM# 137** **Weight:** 28.2800 g. **Composition:** Copper-Nickel **Series:** Pokeman **Obverse:** National arms **Reverse:** "Pikachu" **Edge:** Reeded **Size:** 38.6 mm.

| Date | Mintage | F | VF | XF | Unc | BU |
|---|---|---|---|---|---|---|
| 2001 | 100,000 | — | — | — | 10.00 | — |

**DOLLAR** **KM# 138** **Weight:** 7.7700 g. **Composition:** 0.9990 Silver .2496 oz. ASW **Series:** Pokeman **Obverse:** National arms **Reverse:** "Pikachu" **Edge:** Reeded **Size:** 22 mm.

| Date | Mintage | F | VF | XF | Unc | BU |
|---|---|---|---|---|---|---|
| 2001 Proof | 20,000 | Value: 13.50 | | | | |

**DOLLAR** **KM# 140** **Weight:** 28.2800 g. **Composition:** Copper-Nickel **Series:** Pokeman **Obverse:** National arms **Reverse:** "Squirtle" **Edge:** Reeded **Size:** 38.6 mm.

| Date | Mintage | F | VF | XF | Unc | BU |
|---|---|---|---|---|---|---|
| 2001 | 100,000 | — | — | — | 10.00 | — |

**DOLLAR** **KM# 141** **Weight:** 7.7700 g. **Composition:** 0.9990 Silver .2496 oz. ASW **Series:** Pokeman **Obverse:** National arms **Reverse:** "Squirtle" **Edge:** Reeded **Size:** 22 mm.

| Date | Mintage | F | VF | XF | Unc | BU |
|---|---|---|---|---|---|---|
| 2001 Proof | 20,000 | Value: 13.50 | | | | |

**5 DOLLARS** **KM# 1** **Composition:** Copper-Nickel **Series:** Olympics **Subject:** Tennis **Obverse:** Arms **Reverse:** Boris Becker

| Date | Mintage | F | VF | XF | Unc | BU |
|---|---|---|---|---|---|---|
| 1987 | 80,000 | — | — | — | 5.50 | — |

**5 DOLLARS** **KM# 5** **Composition:** Copper-Nickel **Series:** Olympics **Subject:** Tennis **Obverse:** Arms **Reverse:** Steffi Graf

| Date | Mintage | F | VF | XF | Unc | BU |
|---|---|---|---|---|---|---|
| 1987 | 50,000 | — | — | — | 5.50 | — |

**5 DOLLARS** **KM# 11** **Composition:** Copper-Nickel **Series:** Olympics **Subject:** Tennis **Obverse:** Arms **Reverse:** Steffi Graf

| Date | Mintage | F | VF | XF | Unc | BU |
|---|---|---|---|---|---|---|
| 1988 | 80,000 | — | — | — | 5.50 | — |

**5 DOLLARS** **KM# 12** **Composition:** Copper-Nickel **Series:** Olympics **Subject:** Soccer **Obverse:** Arms **Reverse:** Franz Beckenbauer

| Date | Mintage | F | VF | XF | Unc | BU |
|---|---|---|---|---|---|---|
| 1988 | 50,000 | — | — | — | 5.50 | — |

**5 DOLLARS** **KM# 15** **Composition:** Copper-Nickel **Series:** Olympics **Subject:** Tennis **Obverse:** Arms **Reverse:** Navratilova, Graf and Evert

| Date | Mintage | F | VF | XF | Unc | BU |
|---|---|---|---|---|---|---|
| 1988 | 80,000 | — | — | — | 5.50 | — |

**5 DOLLARS** **KM# 17** **Composition:** Copper-Nickel **Obverse:** Arms **Reverse:** President John F. Kennedy

| Date | Mintage | F | VF | XF | Unc | BU |
|---|---|---|---|---|---|---|
| 1988 | 80,000 | — | — | — | 6.50 | — |

**5 DOLLARS KM# 22 Composition:** Copper-Nickel **Obverse:** Arms **Reverse:** General Douglas MacArthur

| Date | Mintage | F | VF | XF | Unc | BU |
|---|---|---|---|---|---|---|
| 1989 | — | — | — | — | 7.00 | — |

**5 DOLLARS KM# 24 Composition:** Copper-Nickel **Obverse:** Arms **Reverse:** Davis Cup Tennis

| Date | Mintage | F | VF | XF | Unc | BU |
|---|---|---|---|---|---|---|
| 1989 | Est. 50,000 | — | — | — | 6.00 | — |

**5 DOLLARS KM# 67 Composition:** Copper-Nickel **Series:** Olympics **Subject:** Tennis **Obverse:** Arms **Reverse:** Steffi Graf

| Date | Mintage | F | VF | XF | Unc | BU |
|---|---|---|---|---|---|---|
| 1989 | — | — | — | — | 6.50 | — |

**5 DOLLARS KM# 29 Composition:** Copper-Nickel **Obverse:** Arms **Reverse:** General Dwight D. Eisenhower

| Date | Mintage | F | VF | XF | Unc | BU |
|---|---|---|---|---|---|---|
| 1990 | — | — | — | — | 6.00 | — |

**5 DOLLARS KM# 31 Composition:** Copper-Nickel **Obverse:** Arms **Reverse:** General George S. Patton

| Date | Mintage | F | VF | XF | Unc | BU |
|---|---|---|---|---|---|---|
| 1990 | — | — | — | — | 6.00 | — |

**5 DOLLARS KM# 33 Composition:** Copper-Nickel **Obverse:** Arms **Reverse:** Admiral William Halsey

| Date | Mintage | F | VF | XF | Unc | BU |
|---|---|---|---|---|---|---|
| 1990 | — | — | — | — | 6.00 | — |

**5 DOLLARS KM# 35 Composition:** Copper-Nickel **Obverse:** Arms **Reverse:** President Franklin D. Roosevelt

| Date | Mintage | F | VF | XF | Unc | BU |
|---|---|---|---|---|---|---|
| 1990 | — | — | — | — | 6.00 | — |

**5 DOLLARS KM# 37 Composition:** Copper-Nickel **Obverse:** Arms **Reverse:** Sir Winston Churchill

| Date | Mintage | F | VF | XF | Unc | BU |
|---|---|---|---|---|---|---|
| 1990 | — | — | — | — | 6.00 | — |

**5 DOLLARS KM# 58 Weight:** 9.9300 g. **Composition:** 0.5000 Silver .1596 oz. ASW **Series:** World Cup Soccer **Obverse:** Arms **Reverse:** Player and Statue of Liberty

| Date | Mintage | F | VF | XF | Unc | BU |
|---|---|---|---|---|---|---|
| 1991 | 150,000 | — | — | — | 15.00 | — |

**5 DOLLARS KM# 55 Weight:** 10.0000 g. **Composition:** 0.5000 Silver .1608 oz. ASW **Obverse:** Arms **Reverse:** The HMS Bounty

| Date | Mintage | F | VF | XF | Unc | BU |
|---|---|---|---|---|---|---|
| 1992 | Est. 150,000 | — | — | — | 17.50 | — |

**5 DOLLARS KM# 60 Weight:** 10.0000 g. **Composition:** 0.5000 Silver .1608 oz. ASW **Series:** Endangered Wildlife **Obverse:** Arms **Reverse:** Jaguar

| Date | Mintage | F | VF | XF | Unc | BU |
|---|---|---|---|---|---|---|
| 1992 Proof | Est. 25,000 | Value: 17.50 | | | | |

**5 DOLLARS KM# 61 Weight:** 10.0000 g. **Composition:** 0.5000 Silver .1608 oz. ASW **Series:** Olympics 1996 **Obverse:** Arms **Reverse:** Sprinter

| Date | Mintage | F | VF | XF | Unc | BU |
|---|---|---|---|---|---|---|
| 1992 Proof | 100,000 | Value: 16.50 | | | | |

**5 DOLLARS KM# 68 Weight:** 9.8500 g. **Composition:** 0.5000 Silver .1584 oz. ASW **Subject:** First Moon Landing **Obverse:** Arms

| Date | Mintage | F | VF | XF | Unc | BU |
|---|---|---|---|---|---|---|
| 1992 Proof | — | Value: 16.50 | | | | |

**5 DOLLARS KM# 76 Weight:** 10.0000 g. **Composition:** 0.9250 Silver .1607 oz. ASW **Obverse:** Arms **Reverse:** Kennedy, Brandenburg Gate

| Date | Mintage | F | VF | XF | Unc | BU |
|---|---|---|---|---|---|---|
| 1992 Proof | Est. 50,000 | Value: 16.50 | | | | |

**5 DOLLARS KM# 80 Weight:** 9.9500 g. **Composition:** 0.5000 Silver .1599 oz. ASW **Series:** Endangered Wildlife **Obverse:** Arms **Reverse:** Commerson's dolphins

| Date | Mintage | F | VF | XF | Unc | BU |
|---|---|---|---|---|---|---|
| 1992 Proof | — | Value: 17.50 | | | | |

**5 DOLLARS** **KM# 62** **Weight:** 9.9500 g. **Composition:** 0.5000 Silver .1599 oz. ASW **Series:** Protect Our World **Obverse:** Arms **Reverse:** Oak tree

| Date | Mintage | F | VF | XF | Unc | BU |
|---|---|---|---|---|---|---|
| 1993 Proof | — | Value: 16.00 | | | | |

**5 DOLLARS** **KM# 114** **Weight:** 31.5000 g. **Composition:** 0.9250 Silver .9368 oz. ASW **Subject:** The Resolution **Obverse:** Crowned arms **Reverse:** Sail ship above denomination

| Date | Mintage | F | VF | XF | Unc | BU |
|---|---|---|---|---|---|---|
| 1996 Proof | — | Value: 45.00 | | | | |

**5 DOLLARS** **KM# 120** **Weight:** 31.4200 g. **Composition:** 0.9250 Silver .9344 oz. ASW **Subject:** Pterois Radiata **Obverse:** Queen's head right **Reverse:** Gold colored Clearfin lion fish **Edge:** Plain **Note:** 7-sided.

| Date | Mintage | F | VF | XF | Unc | BU |
|---|---|---|---|---|---|---|
| 1999 Proof | — | Value: 50.00 | | | | |

**5 DOLLARS** **KM# 121** **Weight:** 31.4200 g. **Composition:** 0.9250 Silver .9344 oz. ASW **Subject:** Fourcipiger Longirostris **Obverse:** Queen's head right **Reverse:** Gold colored big long nosed Butterfly fish **Edge:** Plain **Note:** 7-sided.

| Date | Mintage | F | VF | XF | Unc | BU |
|---|---|---|---|---|---|---|
| 1999 Proof | — | Value: 50.00 | | | | |

**10 DOLLARS** **KM# 46** **Weight:** 10.0000 g. **Composition:** 0.9250 Silver .2974 oz. ASW **Series:** Summer Olympics **Obverse:** Crowned arms **Reverse:** Runners

| Date | Mintage | F | VF | XF | Unc | BU |
|---|---|---|---|---|---|---|
| 1991 | 150,000 | — | — | — | 17.50 | — |

**10 DOLLARS** **KM# 56** **Weight:** 10.0000 g. **Composition:** 0.9250 Silver .2974 oz. ASW **Series:** Summer Olympics **Obverse:** Crowned arms **Reverse:** Discus Thrower

| Date | Mintage | F | VF | XF | Unc | BU |
|---|---|---|---|---|---|---|
| 1991 Proof | 50,000 | Value: 12.50 | | | | |

**10 DOLLARS** **KM# 59** **Weight:** 31.5300 g. **Composition:** 0.9999 Silver 1.0128 oz. ASW **Series:** World Cup Soccer **Obverse:** Crowned arms **Reverse:** Handshake

| Date | Mintage | F | VF | XF | Unc | BU |
|---|---|---|---|---|---|---|
| 1991 Proof | 20,000 | Value: 17.50 | | | | |

**10 DOLLARS** **KM# 69** **Weight:** 31.4300 g. **Composition:** 0.9999 Silver 1.0106 oz. ASW **Subject:** Cook's Pacific Voyage **Obverse:** Crowned arms

| Date | Mintage | F | VF | XF | Unc | BU |
|---|---|---|---|---|---|---|
| 1992 Proof | — | Value: 30.00 | | | | |

**10 DOLLARS** **KM# 70** **Weight:** 31.4300 g. **Composition:** 0.9999 Silver 1.0106 oz. ASW **Subject:** Moon Landing **Obverse:** Crowned arms **Reverse:** Luna 9

| Date | Mintage | F | VF | XF | Unc | BU |
|---|---|---|---|---|---|---|
| 1992 Proof | Est. 15,000 | Value: 35.00 | | | | |

**10 DOLLARS** **KM# 74** **Weight:** 31.4700 g. **Composition:** 0.9250 Silver .9359 oz. ASW **Series:** Endangered Wildlife **Obverse:** Crowned arms **Reverse:** Whales

| Date | Mintage | F | VF | XF | Unc | BU |
|---|---|---|---|---|---|---|
| 1992 Proof | 25,000 | Value: 30.00 | | | | |

**10 DOLLARS** **KM# 78** **Weight:** 31.4700 g. **Composition:** 0.9250 Silver .9359 oz. ASW **Subject:** The Resolution **Obverse:** Crowned arms **Reverse:** 3 masted ship

| Date | Mintage | F | VF | XF | Unc | BU |
|---|---|---|---|---|---|---|
| 1992 Proof | Est. 15,000 | Value: 37.50 | | | | |

**10 DOLLARS** **KM# 86** **Weight:** 31.0400 g. **Composition:** 0.9250 Silver .9231 oz. ASW **Obverse:** Crowned arms **Reverse:** Dr. Wernher von Braun, rocket launch

| Date | Mintage | F | VF | XF | Unc | BU |
|---|---|---|---|---|---|---|
| 1992 Proof | — | Value: 35.00 | | | | |

**10 DOLLARS** **KM# 81** **Weight:** 1.2440 g. **Composition:** 0.9990 Gold .0400 oz. AGW **Subject:** Liberty Gold Bullion **Obverse:** Head of Queen Elizabeth II right **Reverse:** Statue of Liberty

| Date | Mintage | F | VF | XF | Unc | BU |
|---|---|---|---|---|---|---|
| 1997 | — | — | — | — | 30.00 | — |

**10 DOLLARS** **KM# 90** **Weight:** 28.2800 g. **Composition:** 0.9250 Silver .8411 oz. ASW **Obverse:** Crowned arms **Reverse:** Diana **Rev. Legend:** . . . The People's Princess

| Date | Mintage | F | VF | XF | Unc | BU |
|---|---|---|---|---|---|---|
| 1997 Proof | Est. 10,000 | Value: 47.50 | | | | |

**10 DOLLARS** **KM# 91** **Weight:** 28.2800 g. **Composition:** 0.9250 Silver .8411 oz. ASW **Obverse:** Crowned arms **Reverse:** Diana **Rev. Legend:** . . . Princess of Wales

| Date | Mintage | F | VF | XF | Unc | BU |
|---|---|---|---|---|---|---|
| 1997 Proof | Est. 10,000 | Value: 47.50 | | | | |

**10 DOLLARS** **KM# 92** **Weight:** 28.2800 g. **Composition:** 0.9250 Silver .8411 oz. ASW **Obverse:** Crowned arms **Reverse:** Diana, sprays below bust **Rev. Legend:** . . . Princess of Wales

| Date | Mintage | F | VF | XF | Unc | BU |
|---|---|---|---|---|---|---|
| 1997 Proof | Est. 10,000 | Value: 47.50 | | | | |

**10 DOLLARS** **KM# 104** **Weight:** 28.2800 g. **Composition:** 0.9250 Silver .8411 oz. ASW **Obverse:** Head of Queen Elizabeth II right **Reverse:** Diana **Rev. Legend:** . . . In Memoriam

| Date | Mintage | F | VF | XF | Unc | BU |
|---|---|---|---|---|---|---|
| 1998 Proof | Est. 10,000 | Value: 47.50 | | | | |

**10 DOLLARS** **KM# 105** **Weight:** 28.2800 g. **Composition:** 0.9250 Silver .8411 oz. ASW **Obverse:** Head of Queen Elizabeth II right **Reverse:** Diana **Rev. Legend:** . . . Princess of Wales

| Date | Mintage | F | VF | XF | Unc | BU |
|---|---|---|---|---|---|---|
| 1998 Proof | Est. 10,000 | Value: 47.50 | | | | |

**10 DOLLARS** **KM# 116** **Weight:** 28.2800 g. **Composition:** 0.9250 Silver .8411 oz. ASW **Subject:** 50th Anniversary of Peanuts **Obverse:** Head of Queen Elizabeth II right **Reverse:** Snoopy and Woodstock

| Date | Mintage | F | VF | XF | Unc | BU |
|---|---|---|---|---|---|---|
| 2000 Proof | Est. 10,000 | Value: 50.00 | | | | |

**10 DOLLARS** **KM# 124** **Weight:** 28.2800 g. **Composition:** 0.9250 Silver .8410 oz. ASW **Subject:** Snoopy as an Ace **Obverse:** Queen's portrait **Reverse:** Snoopy flying his dog house **Edge:** Reeded **Size:** 38.6 mm.

| Date | Mintage | F | VF | XF | Unc | BU |
|---|---|---|---|---|---|---|
| 2001 Proof | 10,000 | Value: 47.50 | | | | |

**10 DOLLARS** **KM# 130** **Weight:** 28.2800 g. **Composition:** 0.9250 Silver .8410 oz. ASW **Series:** Pokeman **Obverse:** National arms **Reverse:** "Bulbasaur" **Edge:** Reeded **Size:** 38.6 mm.

| Date | Mintage | F | VF | XF | Unc | BU |
|---|---|---|---|---|---|---|
| 2001 Proof | 10,000 | Value: 47.50 | | | | |

**10 DOLLARS** **KM# 133** **Weight:** 28.2800 g. **Composition:** 0.9250 Silver .8410 oz. ASW **Series:** Pokeman **Obverse:** National arms **Reverse:** "Charmander" **Edge:** Reeded **Size:** 38.6 mm.

| Date | Mintage | F | VF | XF | Unc | BU |
|---|---|---|---|---|---|---|
| 2001 Proof | 10,000 | Value: 47.50 | | | | |

**10 DOLLARS** **KM# 136** **Weight:** 28.2800 g. **Composition:** 0.9250 Silver .8410 oz. ASW **Series:** Pokeman **Obverse:** National arms **Reverse:** "Meowth" **Edge:** Reeded **Size:** 38.6 mm.

| Date | Mintage | F | VF | XF | Unc | BU |
|---|---|---|---|---|---|---|
| 2001 Proof | 10,000 | Value: 47.50 | | | | |

**10 DOLLARS** **KM# 139** **Weight:** 28.2800 g. **Composition:** 0.9250 Silver .8410 oz. ASW **Series:** Pokeman **Obverse:** National arms **Reverse:** "Pikachu" **Edge:** Reeded **Size:** 38.6 mm.

| Date | Mintage | F | VF | XF | Unc | BU |
|---|---|---|---|---|---|---|
| 2001 Proof | 10,000 | Value: 47.50 | | | | |

**10 DOLLARS** **KM# 142** **Weight:** 28.2800 g. **Composition:** 0.9250 Silver .8410 oz. ASW **Series:** Pokeman **Obverse:** National arms **Reverse:** "Squirtle" **Edge:** Reeded **Size:** 38.6 mm.

| Date | Mintage | F | VF | XF | Unc | BU |
|---|---|---|---|---|---|---|
| 2001 Proof | 10,000 | Value: 47.50 | | | | |

**20 DOLLARS** **KM# 57** **Weight:** 31.4700 g. **Composition:** 0.9250 Silver .9359 oz. ASW **Subject:** 40th Anniversary of Coronation **Obverse:** Head of Queen Elizabeth II right

| Date | Mintage | F | VF | XF | Unc | BU |
|---|---|---|---|---|---|---|
| 1993 Proof | Est. 10,000 | Value: 55.00 | | | | |

**20 DOLLARS** **KM# 63** **Weight:** 31.4700 g. **Composition:** 0.9250 Silver .9359 oz. ASW **Series:** Protect Our World **Obverse:** Crowned arms **Reverse:** Hand ho;lding seedling

| Date | Mintage | F | VF | XF | Unc | BU |
|---|---|---|---|---|---|---|
| 1993 Proof | Est. 10,000 | Value: 30.00 | | | | |

**20 DOLLARS** **KM# 64** **Weight:** 31.4700 g. **Composition:** 0.9250 Silver .9359 oz. ASW **Obverse:** Crowned arms **Reverse:** Kennedy and Statue of Liberty

| Date | Mintage | F | VF | XF | Unc | BU |
|---|---|---|---|---|---|---|
| 1993 Proof | — | Value: 37.50 | | | | |

**20 DOLLARS** **KM# 93** **Weight:** 1.2440 g. **Composition:** 0.9990 Gold .0400 oz. AGW **Obverse:** Crowned arms **Reverse:** Diana **Rev. Legend:** . . . The people's Princess

| Date | Mintage | F | VF | XF | Unc | BU |
|---|---|---|---|---|---|---|
| 1997 Proof | Est. 10,000 | Value: 40.00 | | | | |

**20 DOLLARS** **KM# 94** **Weight:** 1.2440 g. **Composition:** 0.9990 Gold .0400 oz. AGW **Obverse:** Crowned arms **Reverse:** Diana **Rev. Legend:** . . . Princess of Wales

| Date | Mintage | F | VF | XF | Unc | BU |
|---|---|---|---|---|---|---|
| 1997 Proof | Est. 10,000 | Value: 45.00 | | | | |

**20 DOLLARS** **KM# 95** **Weight:** 1.2440 g. **Composition:** 0.9990 Gold .0400 oz. AGW **Obverse:** Crowned arms **Reverse:** Diana, sprays below bust **Rev. Legend:** . . . Princess of Wales

| Date | Mintage | F | VF | XF | Unc | BU |
|---|---|---|---|---|---|---|
| 1997 Proof | Est. 10,000 | Value: 45.00 | | | | |

**20 DOLLARS** **KM# 106** **Weight:** 1.2440 g. **Composition:** 0.9990 Gold .0400 oz. AGW **Obverse:** Head of Queen Elizabeth II right **Reverse:** Diana **Rev. Legend:** . . . In Memoriam

| Date | Mintage | F | VF | XF | Unc | BU |
|---|---|---|---|---|---|---|
| 1998 Proof | Est. 10,000 | Value: 45.00 | | | | |

**20 DOLLARS** **KM# 107** **Weight:** 1.2440 g. **Composition:** 0.9990 Gold .0400 oz. AGW **Obverse:** Head of Queen Elizabeth II right **Reverse:** Diana **Rev. Legend:** . . . Princess of Wales

| Date | Mintage | F | VF | XF | Unc | BU |
|---|---|---|---|---|---|---|
| 1998 Proof | Est. 10,000 | Value: 45.00 | | | | |

**20 DOLLARS** **KM# 117** **Weight:** 1.2400 g. **Composition:** 0.9990 Gold .0395 oz. AGW **Subject:** 50th Anniversary of Peanuts **Obverse:** Head of Queen Elizabeth II right **Reverse:** Snoopy and Woodstock

| Date | Mintage | F | VF | XF | Unc | BU |
|---|---|---|---|---|---|---|
| 2000 Proof | Est. 10,000 | Value: 50.00 | | | | |

**20 DOLLARS** **KM# 125** **Weight:** 1.2400 g. **Composition:** 0.9999 Gold .0399 oz. AGW **Subject:** Snoopy as an Ace **Obverse:** Queen's portrait **Reverse:** Snoopy flying his dog house **Edge:** Reeded **Size:** 13.9 mm.

| Date | Mintage | F | VF | XF | Unc | BU |
|---|---|---|---|---|---|---|
| 2001 Proof | 10,000 | Value: 58.00 | | | | |

**25 DOLLARS** **KM# 79** **Weight:** 1.2441 g. **Composition:** 0.9990 Gold .0400 oz. AGW **Obverse:** Crowned arms **Reverse:** Kennedy taking oath

| Date | Mintage | F | VF | XF | Unc | BU |
|---|---|---|---|---|---|---|
| 1994 Proof | Est. 25,000 | Value: 50.00 | | | | |

**25 DOLLARS** **KM# 82** **Weight:** 3.1000 g. **Composition:** 0.9990 Gold .1000 oz. AGW **Series:** Liberty Gold Bullion **Obverse:** Head of Queen Elizabeth II right **Reverse:** Statue of Liberty

| Date | Mintage | F | VF | XF | Unc | BU |
|---|---|---|---|---|---|---|
| 1997 | — | — | — | — | 65.00 | — |

**25 DOLLARS** **KM# 96** **Weight:** 3.1000 g. **Composition:** 0.9990 Gold .1000 oz. AGW **Obverse:** Crowned arms **Reverse:** Diana **Rev. Legend:** . . . The People's Princess

| Date | Mintage | F | VF | XF | Unc | BU |
|---|---|---|---|---|---|---|
| 1997 Proof | Est. 7,500 | Value: 95.00 | | | | |

**25 DOLLARS** **KM# 97** **Weight:** 3.1000 g. **Composition:** 0.9990 Gold .1000 oz. AGW **Obverse:** Crowned arms **Reverse:** Diana **Rev. Legend:** . . . Princess of Wales

| Date | Mintage | F | VF | XF | Unc | BU |
|---|---|---|---|---|---|---|
| 1997 Proof | Est. 7,500 | Value: 95.00 | | | | |

**25 DOLLARS** **KM# 98** **Weight:** 3.1000 g. **Composition:** 0.9990 Gold .1000 oz. AGW **Obverse:** Crowned arms **Reverse:** , sprays below bust **Rev. Legend:** . . . Princess of Wales

| Date | Mintage | F | VF | XF | Unc | BU |
|---|---|---|---|---|---|---|
| 1997 Proof | Est. 7,500 | Value: 95.00 | | | | |

**50 DOLLARS** **KM# 2** **Weight:** 27.1000 g. **Composition:** 0.6250 Silver .5446 oz. ASW **Series:** Olympics **Subject:** Tennis **Obverse:** Crowned arms **Reverse:** Boris Becker

| Date | Mintage | F | VF | XF | Unc | BU |
|---|---|---|---|---|---|---|
| 1987 Proof | 20,000 | Value: 18.50 | | | | |

**50 DOLLARS** **KM# 6** **Weight:** 27.1000 g. **Composition:** 0.6250 Silver .5446 oz. ASW **Series:** Olympics **Subject:** Tennis **Obverse:** Crowned arms **Reverse:** Steffi Graf

| Date | Mintage | F | VF | XF | Unc | BU |
|---|---|---|---|---|---|---|
| 1987 Proof | 20,000 | Value: 18.50 | | | | |

**50 DOLLARS** **KM# 13** **Weight:** 27.1000 g. **Composition:** 0.6250 Silver .5446 oz. ASW **Series:** Olympics **Subject:** Tennis **Obverse:** Crowned arms **Reverse:** Steffi Graf **Note:** Similar to 5 Dollars, KM#11.

| Date | Mintage | F | VF | XF | Unc | BU |
|---|---|---|---|---|---|---|
| 1988 Proof | Est. 20,000 | Value: 35.00 | | | | |

**50 DOLLARS** **KM# 14** **Weight:** 27.1000 g. **Composition:** 0.6250 Silver .5446 oz. ASW **Series:** Olympics **Subject:** Soccer **Obverse:** Crowned arms **Reverse:** Franz Beckenbauer

| Date | Mintage | F | VF | XF | Unc | BU |
|---|---|---|---|---|---|---|
| 1988 Proof | Est. 20,000 | Value: 25.00 | | | | |

**50 DOLLARS** **KM# 16** **Weight:** 27.1000 g. **Composition:** 0.6250 Silver .5446 oz. ASW **Series:** Olympics **Subject:** Tennis **Obverse:** Crowned arms **Reverse:** Navratilova, Graf and Evert

| Date | Mintage | F | VF | XF | Unc | BU |
|---|---|---|---|---|---|---|
| 1988 Proof | Est. 20,000 | Value: 35.00 | | | | |

**50 DOLLARS** **KM# 18** **Weight:** 28.2800 g. **Composition:** 0.9250 Silver .8411 oz. ASW **Obverse:** Crowned arms **Reverse:** President John F. Kennedy

| Date | Mintage | F | VF | XF | Unc | BU |
|---|---|---|---|---|---|---|
| 1988 Proof | 20,000 | Value: 32.50 | | | | |

**50 DOLLARS** **KM# 43** **Weight:** 28.2800 g. **Composition:** 0.9250 Silver .8411 oz. ASW **Subject:** Soccer **Obverse:** Crowned arms **Reverse:** 2 players

| Date | Mintage | F | VF | XF | Unc | BU |
|---|---|---|---|---|---|---|
| 1988 Proof | — | Value: 25.00 | | | | |

**50 DOLLARS** **KM# 23** **Weight:** 31.1030 g. **Composition:** 0.9990 Silver 1.0000 oz. ASW **Obverse:** Crowned arms **Reverse:** General Douglas MacArthur

| Date | Mintage | F | VF | XF | Unc | BU |
|---|---|---|---|---|---|---|
| 1989 Proof | Est. 50,000 | Value: 35.00 | | | | |

**50 DOLLARS** **KM# 25** **Weight:** 28.2800 g. **Composition:** 0.9250 Silver .8411 oz. ASW **Series:** Davis Cup Tennis **Obverse:** Crowned arms **Reverse:** 4 players

| Date | Mintage | F | VF | XF | Unc | BU |
|---|---|---|---|---|---|---|
| 1989 Proof | Est. 20,000 | Value: 35.00 | | | | |

**50 DOLLARS** **KM# 27** **Weight:** 28.2800 g. **Composition:** 0.9250 Silver .8411 oz. ASW **Series:** 1992 Olympics **Subject:** Rowing **Obverse:** Crowned arms **Reverse:** 2 men rowing

| Date | Mintage | F | VF | XF | Unc | BU |
|---|---|---|---|---|---|---|
| 1989 Proof | Est. 30,000 | Value: 27.50 | | | | |

**50 DOLLARS** **KM# 44** **Weight:** 28.2800 g. **Composition:** 0.9250 Silver .8411 oz. ASW **Series:** Olympics **Subject:** Tennis **Obverse:** Crowned arms **Reverse:** Steffi Graf

| Date | Mintage | F | VF | XF | Unc | BU |
|---|---|---|---|---|---|---|
| 1989 Proof | 20,000 | Value: 25.00 | | | | |

**50 DOLLARS** **KM# 30** **Weight:** 31.1030 g. **Composition:** 0.9990 Silver 1.000 oz. ASW **Obverse:** Crowned arms **Reverse:** General Dwight D. Eisenhower

| Date | Mintage | F | VF | XF | Unc | BU |
|---|---|---|---|---|---|---|
| 1990 Proof | Est. 50,000 | Value: 25.00 | | | | |

**50 DOLLARS** **KM# 32** **Weight:** 31.1030 g. **Composition:** 0.9990 Silver 1.000 oz. ASW **Obverse:** Crowned arms **Reverse:** General George S. Patton

| Date | Mintage | F | VF | XF | Unc | BU |
|---|---|---|---|---|---|---|
| 1990 Proof | Est. 50,000 | Value: 25.00 | | | | |

**50 DOLLARS** **KM# 34** **Weight:** 31.1030 g. **Composition:** 0.9990 Silver 1.000 oz. ASW **Obverse:** Crowned arms **Reverse:** Admiral William Halsey

| Date | Mintage | F | VF | XF | Unc | BU |
|---|---|---|---|---|---|---|
| 1990 Proof | Est. 50,000 | Value: 30.00 | | | | |

**50 DOLLARS** KM# 36 **Weight:** 31.1030 g. **Composition:** 0.9990 Silver 1.000 oz. ASW **Obverse:** Crowned arms **Reverse:** President Franklin D. Roosevelt

| Date | Mintage | F | VF | XF | Unc | BU |
|---|---|---|---|---|---|---|
| 1990 Proof | Est. 50,000 | Value: 25.00 | | | | |

**50 DOLLARS** KM# 38 **Weight:** 31.1030 g. **Composition:** 0.9990 Silver 1.000 oz. ASW **Obverse:** Crowned arms **Reverse:** Sir Winston Churchill

| Date | Mintage | F | VF | XF | Unc | BU |
|---|---|---|---|---|---|---|
| 1990 Proof | Est. 50,000 | Value: 25.00 | | | | |

**50 DOLLARS** KM# 47 **Weight:** 38.2000 g. **Composition:** 0.9250 Silver 1.1361 oz. ASW **Subject:** Soccer **Obverse:** Crowned arms **Reverse:** Player kicking ball

| Date | Mintage | F | VF | XF | Unc | BU |
|---|---|---|---|---|---|---|
| 1990 Proof | 20,000 | Value: 22.50 | | | | |

**50 DOLLARS** KM# 75 **Weight:** 28.5600 g. **Composition:** 0.9250 Silver .8984 oz. ASW **Subject:** Soccer **Obverse:** Crowned arms **Reverse:** 2 players

| Date | Mintage | F | VF | XF | Unc | BU |
|---|---|---|---|---|---|---|
| 1990 Proof | 20,000 | Value: 25.00 | | | | |

**50 DOLLARS** KM# 71 **Weight:** 7.7000 g. **Composition:** 0.5830 Gold .1444 oz. AGW **Series:** Olympics **Obverse:** Crowned arms **Reverse:** Discus thrower

| Date | Mintage | F | VF | XF | Unc | BU |
|---|---|---|---|---|---|---|
| 1992 Proof | 6,000 | Value: 125 | | | | |

**50 DOLLARS** KM# 65 **Weight:** 155.5175 g. **Composition:** 0.9990 Silver 5.000 oz. ASW **Obverse:** Crowned arms **Reverse:** Bust of President Kennedy left, Apollo rocket

| Date | Mintage | F | VF | XF | Unc | BU |
|---|---|---|---|---|---|---|
| 1993 Proof | — | Value: 200 | | | | |

**50 DOLLARS** KM# 66 **Weight:** 7.7760 g. **Composition:** 0.5830 Gold .1458 oz. AGW **Obverse:** Crowned arms **Reverse:** Bust of President John F. Kennedy left, Apollo rocket

| Date | Mintage | F | VF | XF | Unc | BU |
|---|---|---|---|---|---|---|
| 1993 Proof | — | Value: 110 | | | | |

**50 DOLLARS** KM# 72 **Weight:** 156.1700 g. **Composition:** 0.9990 Silver 5.0247 oz. ASW **Series:** World Cup Soccer **Obverse:** Crowned arms **Size:** 65 mm. **Note:** Illustration reduced.

| Date | Mintage | F | VF | XF | Unc | BU |
|---|---|---|---|---|---|---|
| 1994 Proof | Est. 3,000 | Value: 175 | | | | |

**50 DOLLARS** KM# 83 **Weight:** 6.2200 g. **Composition:** 0.9990 Gold .2000 oz. AGW **Series:** Liberty Gold Bullion **Obverse:** Bust of Queen Elizabeth II right **Reverse:** Statue of Liberty

| Date | Mintage | F | VF | XF | Unc | BU |
|---|---|---|---|---|---|---|
| 1997 | — | — | — | — | 110 | — |

**50 DOLLARS** KM# 108 **Weight:** 3.1100 g. **Composition:** 0.9999 Gold .1000 oz. AGW **Obverse:** Bust of Queen Elizabeth II right **Reverse:** Diana **Rev. Legend:** . . . In Memoriam

| Date | Mintage | F | VF | XF | Unc | BU |
|---|---|---|---|---|---|---|
| 1998 Proof | Est. 7,500 | Value: 95.00 | | | | |

**50 DOLLARS** KM# 109 **Weight:** 3.1100 g. **Composition:** 0.9999 Gold .1000 oz. AGW **Obverse:** Bust of Queen Elizabeth II right **Reverse:** Diana **Rev. Legend:** . . . Princess of Wales

| Date | Mintage | F | VF | XF | Unc | BU |
|---|---|---|---|---|---|---|
| 1998 Proof | Est. 7,500 | Value: 95.00 | | | | |

**50 DOLLARS** KM# 118 **Weight:** 3.1103 g. **Composition:** 0.9990 Gold .1000 oz. AGW **Subject:** 50th Anniversary of Peanuts **Obverse:** Head of Queen Elizabeth II right **Reverse:** Snoopy and Woodstock

| Date | Mintage | F | VF | XF | Unc | BU |
|---|---|---|---|---|---|---|
| 2000 Proof | Est. 7,500 | Value: 100 | | | | |

**50 DOLLARS** KM# 126 **Weight:** 3.1100 g. **Composition:** 0.9999 Gold .1000 oz. AGW **Subject:** Snoopy as an Ace **Obverse:** Queen's portrait **Reverse:** Snoopy flying his dog house **Edge:** Reeded **Size:** 17.9 mm.

| Date | Mintage | F | VF | XF | Unc | BU |
|---|---|---|---|---|---|---|
| 2001 Proof | 7,500 | Value: 95.00 | | | | |

**100 DOLLARS** KM# 7 **Weight:** 155.5175 g. **Composition:** 0.9990 Silver 5.0000 oz. ASW **Series:** Olympics **Subject:** Tennis **Obverse:** Crowned arms **Reverse:** Steffi Graf

| Date | Mintage | F | VF | XF | Unc | BU |
|---|---|---|---|---|---|---|
| 1987 | Est. 5,000 | Value: 100 | | | | |

**100 DOLLARS** KM# 3 **Weight:** 155.5175 g. **Composition:** 0.9990 Silver 5.0000 oz. ASW **Series:** Olympics **Subject:** Tennis **Obverse:** Crowned arms **Reverse:** Boris Becker **Size:** 65 mm. **Note:** Illustration reduced.

| Date | Mintage | F | VF | XF | Unc | BU |
|---|---|---|---|---|---|---|
| 1987 Proof | Est. 5,000 | Value: 80.00 | | | | |

**100 DOLLARS** KM# 19 **Weight:** 155.5175 g. **Composition:** 0.9990 Silver 5.0000 oz. ASW **Obverse:** Crowned arms **Reverse:** Head of President John F. Kennedy left

| Date | Mintage | F | VF | XF | Unc | BU |
|---|---|---|---|---|---|---|
| 1988 Proof | 3,000 | Value: 85.00 | | | | |

**100 DOLLARS** KM# 21 **Weight:** 155.5175 g. **Composition:** 0.9990 Silver 5.0000 oz. ASW **Subject:** Soccer **Obverse:** Crowned arms **Reverse:** Franz Beckenbauer

| Date | Mintage | F | VF | XF | Unc | BU |
|---|---|---|---|---|---|---|
| 1988 Proof | 3,000 | Value: 125 | | | | |

**100 DOLLARS** KM# 40 **Weight:** 155.5175 g. **Composition:** 0.9990 Silver 5.0000 oz. ASW **Series:** Olympics **Subject:** Tennis **Obverse:** Crowned arms **Reverse:** Navratilova, Graf and Evert

| Date | Mintage | F | VF | XF | Unc | BU |
|---|---|---|---|---|---|---|
| 1988 Proof | Est. 3,000 | Value: 120 | | | | |

**100 DOLLARS** KM# 28 **Weight:** 155.5175 g. **Composition:** 0.9990 Silver 5.0000 oz. ASW **Series:** Olympics **Subject:** Tennis **Obverse:** Crowned arms **Reverse:** Steffi Graf **Size:** 65 mm. **Note:** Illustration reduced.

| Date | Mintage | F | VF | XF | Unc | BU |
|---|---|---|---|---|---|---|
| 1989 Proof | 3,000 | Value: 120 | | | | |

**100 DOLLARS** KM# 73 **Weight:** 154.8500 g. **Composition:** 0.9990 Silver 4.9791 oz. ASW **Subject:** Tennis **Obverse:** Crowned arms **Reverse:** 1990 World Champion Italian soccer team **Size:** 65 mm. **Note:** Illustration reduced.

| Date | Mintage | F | VF | XF | Unc | BU |
|---|---|---|---|---|---|---|
| 1990 Proof | Est. 3,000 | Value: 175 | | | | |

**100 DOLLARS** KM# 84 **Weight:** 15.5517 g. **Composition:** 0.9990 Gold .5000 oz. AGW **Series:** Liberty Gold Bullion **Obverse:** Head of Queen Elizabeth II right **Reverse:** Statue of Liberty

| Date | Mintage | F | VF | XF | Unc | BU |
|---|---|---|---|---|---|---|
| 1997 | — | — | — | — | 225 | — |

**100 DOLLARS** KM# 99 **Weight:** 6.2200 g. **Composition:** 0.9990 Gold .2000 oz. AGW **Obverse:** Crowned arms **Reverse:** Diana **Rev. Legend:** . . . The People's Princess

| Date | Mintage | F | VF | XF | Unc | BU |
|---|---|---|---|---|---|---|
| 1997 Proof | Est. 5,000 | Value: 150 | | | | |

**100 DOLLARS** KM# 100 **Weight:** 6.2200 g. **Composition:** 0.9990 Gold .2000 oz. AGW **Obverse:** Crowned arms **Reverse:** Diana **Rev. Legend:** . . . Princess of Wales

| Date | Mintage | F | VF | XF | Unc | BU |
|---|---|---|---|---|---|---|
| 1997 Proof | Est. 5,000 | Value: 150 | | | | |

**100 DOLLARS** KM# 101 **Weight:** 6.2200 g. **Composition:** 0.9990 Gold .2000 oz. AGW **Obverse:** Crowned arms **Reverse:** Diana, sprays below bust **Rev. Legend:** . . . Princess of Wales

| Date | Mintage | F | VF | XF | Unc | BU |
|---|---|---|---|---|---|---|
| 1997 Proof | Est. 5,000 | Value: 150 | | | | |

**100 DOLLARS** KM# 110 **Weight:** 6.2200 g. **Composition:** 0.9990 Gold .2000 oz. AGW **Obverse:** Bust of Queen Elizabeth II right **Reverse:** Diana **Rev. Legend:** . . . In Memoriam

| Date | Mintage | F | VF | XF | Unc | BU |
|---|---|---|---|---|---|---|
| 1998 Proof | Est. 5,000 | Value: 150 | | | | |

**100 DOLLARS** KM# 111 **Weight:** 6.2200 g. **Composition:** 0.9990 Gold .2000 oz. AGW **Obverse:** Bust of Queen Elizabeth II right **Reverse:** Diana **Rev. Legend:** . . . Princess of Wales

| Date | Mintage | F | VF | XF | Unc | BU |
|---|---|---|---|---|---|---|
| 1998 Proof | Est. 5,000 | Value: 150 | | | | |

**100 DOLLARS** KM# 119 **Weight:** 6.2200 g. **Composition:** 0.9990 Gold .2000 oz. AGW **Subject:** 50th Anniversary of Peanuts **Obverse:** Bust of Queen Elizabeth II right **Reverse:** Snoopy and Woodstock

| Date | Mintage | F | VF | XF | Unc | BU |
|---|---|---|---|---|---|---|
| 2000 Proof | Est. 5,000 | Value: 175 | | | | |

**100 DOLLARS** KM# 127 **Weight:** 6.2200 g. **Composition:** 0.9999 Gold .2000 oz. AGW **Subject:** Snoopy as an Ace **Obverse:** Queen's portrait **Reverse:** Snoopy flying his dog house **Edge:** Reeded **Size:** 22 mm.

| Date | Mintage | F | VF | XF | Unc | BU |
|---|---|---|---|---|---|---|
| 2001 Proof | 5,000 | Value: 205 | | | | |

**200 DOLLARS** KM# 4 **Weight:** 311.0350 g. **Composition:** 0.9990 Silver 10.000 oz. ASW **Series:** Olympics **Subject:** Tennis **Obverse:** Crowned arms **Reverse:** Boris Becker

| Date | Mintage | F | VF | XF | Unc | BU |
|---|---|---|---|---|---|---|
| 1987 Proof | Est. 3,000 | Value: 165 | | | | |

**200 DOLLARS** KM# 8 **Weight:** 311.0350 g. **Composition:** 0.9990 Silver 10.000 oz. ASW **Series:** Olympics **Subject:** Tennis **Obverse:** Crowned arms **Reverse:** Steffi Graf

| Date | Mintage | F | VF | XF | Unc | BU |
|---|---|---|---|---|---|---|
| 1987 Proof | Est. 3,000 | Value: 165 | | | | |

**200 DOLLARS** KM# 42 **Weight:** 6.9117 g. **Composition:** 0.9000 Gold .2000 oz. AGW **Obverse:** Crowned arms **Reverse:** General Douglas MacArthur

| Date | Mintage | F | VF | XF | Unc | BU |
|---|---|---|---|---|---|---|
| 1989 Proof | Est. 2,500 | Value: 150 | | | | |

**200 DOLLARS** KM# 50 **Weight:** 6.9117 g. **Composition:** 0.9000 Gold .2000 oz. AGW **Obverse:** Crowned arms **Reverse:** General George S. Patton

| Date | Mintage | F | VF | XF | Unc | BU |
|---|---|---|---|---|---|---|
| 1989 Proof | — | Value: 150 | | | | |

**200 DOLLARS** KM# 45 **Weight:** 6.9117 g. **Composition:** 0.9000 Gold .2000 oz. AGW **Obverse:** Crowned arms **Reverse:** General Dwight D. Eisenhower

| Date | Mintage | F | VF | XF | Unc | BU |
|---|---|---|---|---|---|---|
| 1990 Proof | 2,500 | Value: 150 | | | | |

**200 DOLLARS** KM# 51 **Weight:** 6.9117 g. **Composition:** 0.9000 Gold .2000 oz. AGW **Obverse:** Crowned arms **Reverse:** Admiral William Halsey

| Date | Mintage | F | VF | XF | Unc | BU |
|---|---|---|---|---|---|---|
| 1990 Proof | — | Value: 150 | | | | |

**200 DOLLARS** KM# 52 **Weight:** 6.9117 g. **Composition:** 0.9000 Gold .2000 oz. AGW **Obverse:** Crowned arms **Reverse:** President Franklin D. Roosevelt

| Date | Mintage | F | VF | XF | Unc | BU |
|---|---|---|---|---|---|---|
| 1990 Proof | — | Value: 150 | | | | |

**200 DOLLARS** KM# 53 **Weight:** 6.9117 g. **Composition:** 0.9000 Gold .2000 oz. AGW **Obverse:** Crowned arms **Reverse:** Sir Winston Churchill

| Date | Mintage | F | VF | XF | Unc | BU |
|---|---|---|---|---|---|---|
| 1990 Proof | — | Value: 150 | | | | |

**250 DOLLARS** KM# 9 **Weight:** 8.4830 g. **Composition:** 0.9170 Gold .2500 oz. AGW **Series:** Olympics **Subject:** Tennis **Obverse:** Crowned arms **Reverse:** Boris Becker

| Date | Mintage | F | VF | XF | Unc | BU |
|---|---|---|---|---|---|---|
| 1987 Proof | 1,000 | Value: 200 | | | | |

**250 DOLLARS** KM# 10 **Weight:** 8.4830 g. **Composition:** 0.9170 Gold .2500 oz. AGW **Series:** Olympics **Subject:** Tennis **Obverse:** Crowned arms **Reverse:** Steffi Graf

| Date | Mintage | F | VF | XF | Unc | BU |
|---|---|---|---|---|---|---|
| 1987 Proof | 1,000 | Value: 275 | | | | |

**250 DOLLARS** KM# 20 **Weight:** 10.0000 g. **Composition:** 0.9170 Gold .2948 oz. AGW **Obverse:** Crowned arms **Reverse:** Head of President John F. Kennedy left

| Date | Mintage | F | VF | XF | Unc | BU |
|---|---|---|---|---|---|---|
| 1988 Proof | 5,000 | Value: 175 | | | | |

**250 DOLLARS** KM# 39 **Weight:** 10.0000 g. **Composition:** 0.9170 Gold .2948 oz. AGW **Subject:** Soccer **Obverse:** Crowned arms **Reverse:** Beckenbauer

| Date | Mintage | F | VF | XF | Unc | BU |
|---|---|---|---|---|---|---|
| 1988 Proof | Est. 5,000 | Value: 150 | | | | |

**250 DOLLARS** KM# 41 **Weight:** 10.0000 g. **Composition:** 0.9170 Gold .2948 oz. AGW **Series:** Olympics **Subject:** Tennis **Obverse:** Crowned arms **Reverse:** Navratilova, Graf and Evert

| Date | Mintage | F | VF | XF | Unc | BU |
|---|---|---|---|---|---|---|
| 1988 Proof | Est. 5,000 | Value: 200 | | | | |

**250 DOLLARS** KM# 48 **Weight:** 10.0000 g. **Composition:** 0.9170 Gold .2948 oz. AGW **Series:** Olympics **Subject:** Tennis **Obverse:** Crowned arms **Reverse:** Steffi Graf

| Date | Mintage | F | VF | XF | Unc | BU |
|---|---|---|---|---|---|---|
| 1988 Proof | 5,000 | Value: 190 | | | | |

**250 DOLLARS** KM# 26 **Weight:** 10.0000 g. **Composition:** 0.9170 Gold .2948 oz. AGW **Series:** Davis Cup Tennis **Obverse:** Crowned arms

| Date | Mintage | F | VF | XF | Unc | BU |
|---|---|---|---|---|---|---|
| 1989 Proof | 500 | Value: 245 | | | | |

**250 DOLLARS** KM# 49 **Weight:** 10.0000 g. **Composition:** 0.9170 Gold .2948 oz. AGW **Series:** Olympics **Subject:** Tennis **Obverse:** Crowned arms **Reverse:** Steffi Graf

| Date | Mintage | F | VF | XF | Unc | BU |
|---|---|---|---|---|---|---|
| 1989 Proof | 3,000 | Value: 225 | | | | |

**250 DOLLARS** KM# 54 **Weight:** 10.0000 g. **Composition:** 0.9170 Gold .2948 oz. AGW **Subject:** Soccer - Italian **Obverse:** Crowned arms

| Date | Mintage | F | VF | XF | Unc | BU |
|---|---|---|---|---|---|---|
| 1990 Proof | Est. 2,500 | Value: 225 | | | | |

**250 DOLLARS** KM# 112 **Weight:** 15.5500 g. **Composition:** 0.9999 Gold .5000 oz. AGW **Obverse:** Head of Queenf Elizabeth II right **Reverse:** Diana **Rev. Legend:** . . . In Memoriam

| Date | Mintage | F | VF | XF | Unc | BU |
|---|---|---|---|---|---|---|
| 1998 Proof | Est. 3,000 | Value: 340 | | | | |

**250 DOLLARS** **Weight:** 15.5500 g. **Composition:** 0.9999 Gold .5000 oz. AGW **Obverse:** Head of Queenf Elizabeth II right **Reverse:** Diana **Rev. Legend:** . . . Princess of Wales

| Date | Mintage | F | VF | XF | Unc | BU |
|---|---|---|---|---|---|---|
| 1998 Proof | 3,000 | Value: 340 | | | | |

**250 DOLLARS** KM# A113 **Weight:** 15.5500 g. **Composition:** 0.9999 Gold .5 oz. AGW **Obverse:** Head of Queen Elizabeth II right **Reverse:** Diana **Rev. Legend:** ... Princess of Wales

| Date | Mintage | F | VF | XF | Unc | BU |
|---|---|---|---|---|---|---|
| 1998 Proof | 3,000 | Value: 340 | | | | |

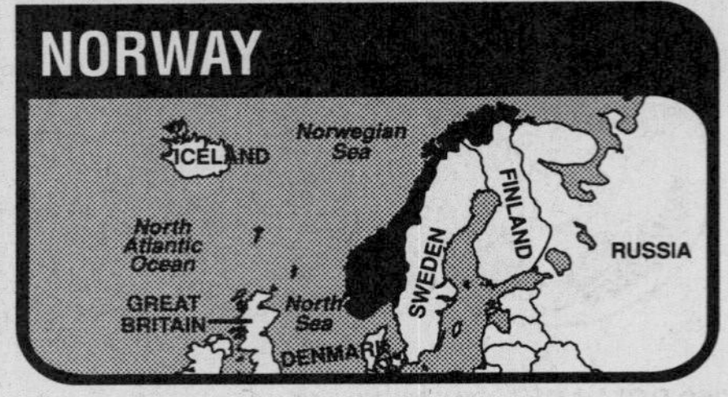


The Kingdom of Norway (*Norge, Noreg*), a constitutional monarchy located in northwestern Europe, has an area of 150,000sq. mi. (324,220 sq. km.), including the island territories of Spitzbergen (Svalbard) and Jan Mayen, and a population of *4.2 million. Capital: Oslo (Christiana). The diversified economic base of Norway includes shipping, fishing, forestry, agriculture, and manufacturing. Nonferrous metals, paper and paperboard, paper pulp, iron, steel and oil are exported.

A united Norwegian kingdom was established in the 9th century, the era of the indomitable Norse Vikings who ranged far and wide, visiting the coasts of northwestern Europe, the Mediterranean, Greenland and North America. In the 13th century the Norse kingdom was united briefly with Sweden, then passed through inheritance in 1380 to the rule of Denmark which was maintained until 1814. In 1814 Norway fell again under the rule of Sweden. The union lasted until 1905 when the Norwegian Parliament arranged a peaceful separation and invited a Danish prince (King Haakon VII) to ascend the throne of an independent Kingdom of Norway.

**RULERS**

Swedish, 1814-1905
Haakon VII, 1905-1957
Olav V, 1957-1991
Harald V, 1991-

**MINT MARKS**

(h) - Crossed hammers – Kongsberg

**MINT OFFICIALS INITIALS**

| Letter | Date | Name |
|---|---|---|
| AB, B | 1961-1980 | Arne Jon Bakken |
| AB* | 1980 | Ole R. Kolberg |
| I, IT | 1880-1918 | Ivar Trondsen, engraver |
| IAR | - | Angrid Austlid Rise, engraver |
| K | 1981 | Ole R. Kolberg |
| OH | 1959 | Oivind Hansen, engraver |

**MONETARY SYSTEM**

100 Ore = 1 Krone (30 Skilling)

# KINGDOM

## DECIMAL COINAGE

**ORE KM# 352 Composition:** Bronze **Note:** Varieties exist.

| Date | Mintage | VG | F | VF | XF | BU |
|---|---|---|---|---|---|---|
| 1902 | 4,500,000 | — | 2.00 | 4.00 | 10.00 | 35.00 |

**ORE KM# 361 Composition:** Bronze

| Date | Mintage | VG | F | VF | XF | BU |
|---|---|---|---|---|---|---|
| 1906 | 3,000,000 | — | 2.00 | 3.00 | 8.00 | 20.00 |
| 1907 | 2,550,000 | — | 2.00 | 3.00 | 8.00 | 20.00 |

**ORE KM# 367 Composition:** Bronze

| Date | Mintage | VG | F | VF | XF | BU |
|---|---|---|---|---|---|---|
| 1908 | 1,450,000 | — | 10.00 | 16.00 | 40.00 | 125 |
| 1910 | 2,480,000 | — | 1.00 | 2.50 | 10.00 | 30.00 |
| 1911 | 3,270,000 | — | 1.00 | 2.50 | 10.00 | 40.00 |
| 1912 | 2,850,000 | — | 3.00 | 7.00 | 30.00 | 150 |
| 1913 | 2,840,000 | — | 1.00 | 2.50 | 5.00 | 25.00 |
| 1914 | 5,020,000 | — | 1.00 | 2.50 | 5.00 | 30.00 |
| 1915 | 1,540,000 | — | 10.00 | 22.00 | 50.00 | 225 |
| 1921 | 3,805,000 | — | 20.00 | 40.00 | 80.00 | 225 |
| 1922 | Inc. above | — | 0.50 | 2.00 | 12.00 | 45.00 |
| 1923 | 770,000 | — | 6.00 | 14.00 | 30.00 | 125 |
| 1925 | 3,000,000 | — | 0.50 | 1.50 | 12.00 | 45.00 |
| 1926 | 2,200,000 | — | 0.50 | 1.50 | 12.00 | 45.00 |
| 1927 | 800,000 | — | 3.00 | 10.00 | 25.00 | 125 |
| 1928 | 3,000,000 | — | 0.25 | 0.75 | 4.00 | 20.00 |
| 1929 | 4,990,000 | — | 0.25 | 0.75 | 4.00 | 16.50 |
| 1930 large date | 2,009,999 | — | 0.50 | 1.00 | 5.00 | 22.00 |
| 1930 small date | Inc. above | — | 0.50 | 1.00 | 5.00 | 22.00 |
| 1931 | 2,000,000 | — | 0.50 | 1.00 | 5.00 | 20.00 |
| 1932 | 2,500,000 | — | 0.50 | 1.00 | 5.00 | 20.00 |
| 1933 | 2,000,000 | — | 0.50 | 1.00 | 5.00 | 16.50 |
| 1934 | 2,000,000 | — | 0.50 | 1.00 | 5.00 | 20.00 |
| 1935 | 5,495,000 | — | 0.25 | 0.75 | 2.00 | 10.00 |
| 1936 | 6,855,000 | — | 0.25 | 0.75 | 2.00 | 10.00 |
| 1937 | 6,020,000 | — | 0.20 | 0.50 | 1.25 | 6.00 |
| 1938 | 4,920,000 | — | 0.20 | 0.50 | 1.25 | 6.00 |
| 1939 | 2,500,000 | — | 0.20 | 0.50 | 1.25 | 10.00 |
| 1940 | 5,010,000 | — | 0.20 | 0.50 | 1.25 | 6.00 |
| 1941 | 12,260,000 | — | 0.10 | 0.25 | 1.25 | 6.00 |
| 1946 | 2,200,000 | — | 0.10 | 0.25 | 1.25 | 10.00 |
| 1947 | 4,870,000 | — | 0.10 | 0.25 | 0.75 | 5.00 |
| 1948 | 9,405,000 | — | 0.10 | 0.25 | 0.75 | 4.00 |
| 1949 | 2,785,000 | — | 0.10 | 0.25 | 0.75 | 6.00 |
| 1950 | 5,730,000 | — | 0.10 | 0.25 | 0.75 | 4.00 |
| 1951 | 16,670,000 | — | 0.10 | 0.25 | 0.75 | 4.00 |
| 1952 | Inc. above | — | 0.10 | 0.25 | 0.75 | 3.00 |

**ORE KM# 367a Composition:** Iron

| Date | Mintage | VG | F | VF | XF | BU |
|---|---|---|---|---|---|---|
| 1918 | 6,000,000 | — | 5.00 | 8.00 | 15.00 | 50.00 |
| 1919 | 12,930,000 | — | 1.50 | 3.50 | 10.00 | 22.50 |
| 1920 | 4,445,000 | — | 6.00 | 10.00 | 20.00 | 115 |
| 1921 | 2,270,000 | — | 30.00 | 35.00 | 55.00 | 150 |

**ORE KM# 387 Composition:** Iron **Subject:** World War II German occupation

| Date | Mintage | VG | F | VF | XF | BU |
|---|---|---|---|---|---|---|
| 1941 | 13,410,000 | — | 0.15 | 0.50 | 1.50 | 10.00 |
| 1942 | 37,710,000 | — | 0.15 | 0.50 | 1.50 | 4.50 |
| 1943 | 33,030,000 | — | 0.15 | 0.50 | 1.50 | 4.50 |
| 1944 | 8,820,000 | — | 0.25 | 0.75 | 2.00 | 5.00 |
| 1945 | 1,740,000 | — | 4.00 | 8.00 | 12.50 | 25.00 |

**ORE KM# 398 Composition:** Bronze

| Date | Mintage | VG | F | VF | XF | BU |
|---|---|---|---|---|---|---|
| 1952 | — | — | — | 0.10 | 0.80 | 5.00 |

**Note:** Mintage included with KM#367.

| Date | Mintage | VG | F | VF | XF | BU |
|---|---|---|---|---|---|---|
| 1953 | 7,440,000 | — | — | 0.10 | 0.80 | 3.50 |
| 1954 | 7,650,000 | — | — | 0.10 | 0.80 | 3.50 |
| 1955 | 8,635,000 | — | — | 0.10 | 0.80 | 3.50 |
| 1956 | 11,705,000 | — | — | 0.10 | 0.80 | 3.50 |
| 1957 | 15,750,000 | — | — | 0.10 | 0.60 | 2.50 |

**ORE KM# 403 Composition:** Bronze **Note:** Varieties exist.

| Date | Mintage | VG | F | VF | XF | BU |
|---|---|---|---|---|---|---|
| 1958 | 2,820,000 | — | 0.25 | 0.50 | 2.00 | 7.00 |
| 1959 | 9,120,000 | — | 0.10 | 0.20 | 0.75 | 6.00 |
| 1960 | 7,890,000 | — | — | 0.10 | 0.25 | 2.50 |
| 1961 | 5,671,000 | — | — | 0.10 | 0.25 | 2.50 |
| 1962 | 12,180,000 | — | — | 0.10 | 0.20 | 1.25 |
| 1963 | 8,010,000 | — | — | 0.10 | 0.25 | 2.50 |
| 1964 | 11,020,000 | — | — | — | 0.10 | 0.75 |
| 1965 | 8,081,000 | — | — | — | 0.10 | 1.50 |
| 1966 | 12,431,000 | — | — | — | 0.10 | 1.00 |
| 1967 | 13,026,000 | — | — | — | 0.10 | 0.75 |
| 1968 | 126,000 | — | 0.50 | 1.00 | 2.00 | 9.00 |
| 1969 | 6,291,000 | — | — | — | 0.10 | 0.50 |
| 1970 | 6,608,000 | — | — | — | 0.10 | 0.50 |
| 1971 | 18,966,000 | — | — | — | 0.10 | 0.50 |
| 1972 | 21,103,000 | — | — | — | 0.10 | 0.50 |

**2 ORE KM# 353 Composition:** Bronze

| Date | Mintage | VG | F | VF | XF | BU |
|---|---|---|---|---|---|---|
| 1902 | 1,005,000 | — | 1.50 | 4.00 | 10.00 | 90.00 |

**2 ORE KM# 362 Composition:** Bronze

| Date | Mintage | VG | F | VF | XF | BU |
|---|---|---|---|---|---|---|
| 1906 | 500,000 | — | 5.00 | 10.00 | 35.00 | 200 |
| 1907 | 980,000 | — | 3.00 | 4.00 | 15.00 | 90.00 |

**2 ORE KM# 371 Composition:** Bronze

| Date | Mintage | VG | F | VF | XF | BU |
|---|---|---|---|---|---|---|
| 1909 | 520,000 | — | 6.00 | 10.00 | 40.00 | 185 |
| 1910 | 500,000 | — | 6.00 | 10.00 | 40.00 | 350 |
| 1911 | 195,000 | — | 6.00 | 10.00 | 40.00 | 200 |
| 1912 | 805,000 | — | 6.00 | 10.00 | 40.00 | 200 |
| 1913 | 2,010,000 | — | 0.75 | 2.00 | 10.00 | 75.00 |
| 1914 | 2,990,000 | — | 0.75 | 2.00 | 10.00 | 75.00 |
| 1915 | Inc. above | — | 5.00 | 10.00 | 60.00 | 320 |
| 1921 | 2,028,000 | — | 0.50 | 1.00 | 10.00 | 55.00 |
| 1922 | 2,288,000 | — | 0.50 | 1.00 | 10.00 | 55.00 |
| 1923 | 745,000 | — | 1.00 | 2.00 | 25.00 | 110 |
| 1928 | 2,250,000 | — | 0.50 | 1.00 | 5.00 | 50.00 |
| 1929 | 750,000 | — | 1.00 | 2.00 | 15.00 | 75.00 |
| 1931 | 1,570,000 | — | 0.50 | 1.00 | 5.00 | 50.00 |
| 1932 | 630,000 | — | 3.50 | 6.00 | 28.00 | 160 |
| 1933 | 750,000 | — | 0.50 | 1.50 | 6.00 | 50.00 |
| 1934 | 500,000 | — | 0.50 | 1.50 | 6.00 | 50.00 |
| 1935 | 2,223,000 | — | 0.25 | 1.00 | 4.00 | 35.00 |
| 1936 | 4,533,000 | — | 0.25 | 1.00 | 4.00 | 35.00 |
| 1937 | 3,790,000 | — | 0.20 | 0.50 | 2.25 | 15.00 |
| 1938 | 3,765,000 | — | 0.20 | 0.50 | 2.25 | 15.00 |
| 1939 | 4,420,000 | — | 0.20 | 0.50 | 2.25 | 15.00 |
| 1940 | 2,655,000 | — | 0.20 | 0.50 | 2.25 | 15.00 |
| 1946 | 1,575,000 | — | 0.20 | 0.50 | 3.00 | 15.00 |
| 1947 | 4,679,000 | — | 0.10 | 0.25 | 1.00 | 10.00 |
| 1948 | 1,002,999 | — | 1.00 | 3.00 | 4.00 | 10.00 |
| 1949 | 1,455,000 | — | 0.10 | 0.25 | 1.00 | 7.00 |
| 1950 | 5,790,000 | — | 0.10 | 0.25 | 1.00 | 6.00 |
| 1951 | 10,540,000 | — | 0.10 | 0.25 | 1.00 | 6.00 |
| 1952 | Inc. above | — | 0.10 | 0.25 | 1.00 | 6.00 |

**2 ORE KM# 371a Composition:** Iron

| Date | Mintage | VG | F | VF | XF | BU |
|---|---|---|---|---|---|---|
| 1917 | 720,000 | — | 75.00 | 120 | 200 | 325 |
| 1918 | 1,280,000 | — | 25.00 | 45.00 | 75.00 | 175 |
| 1919 | 3,365,000 | — | 10.00 | 15.00 | 35.00 | 125 |
| 1920 | 2,635,000 | — | 10.00 | 15.00 | 45.00 | 200 |

**2 ORE KM# 394 Composition:** Iron **Note:** World War II German occupation issue.

| Date | Mintage | VG | F | VF | XF | BU |
|---|---|---|---|---|---|---|
| 1943 | 6,575,000 | — | 0.50 | 0.75 | 1.50 | 7.00 |
| 1944 | 9,805,000 | — | 0.50 | 0.75 | 1.50 | 7.00 |
| 1945 | 2,520,000 | — | 1.50 | 3.00 | 5.00 | 15.00 |

**2 ORE KM# 399 Composition:** Bronze

| Date | Mintage | VG | F | VF | XF | BU |
|---|---|---|---|---|---|---|
| 1952 | Inc. above | — | — | 0.10 | 0.80 | 6.50 |
| 1953 | 6,705,000 | — | — | 0.10 | 0.80 | 5.50 |
| 1954 | 2,805,000 | — | — | 0.10 | 0.80 | 5.50 |
| 1955 | 3,600,000 | — | — | 0.10 | 0.80 | 5.50 |
| 1956 | 6,780,000 | — | — | 0.10 | 0.80 | 5.50 |
| 1957 | 6,090,000 | — | — | 0.10 | 0.80 | 5.50 |

**2 ORE KM# 404 Composition:** Bronze **Reverse:** Small lettering

| Date | Mintage | VG | F | VF | XF | BU |
|---|---|---|---|---|---|---|
| 1958 | 2,700,000 | — | 0.20 | 0.50 | 1.50 | 8.00 |

**2 ORE** KM# 410 **Composition:** Bronze **Reverse:** Large lettering

| Date | Mintage | VG | F | VF | XF | BU |
|---|---|---|---|---|---|---|
| 1959 | 4,125,000 | — | 0.10 | 0.20 | 1.00 | 6.00 |
| 1960 | 3,735,000 | — | — | 0.10 | 0.75 | 10.00 |
| 1961 | 4,477,000 | — | — | 0.10 | 0.30 | 2.00 |
| 1962 | 6,205,000 | — | — | 0.10 | 0.30 | 2.00 |
| 1963 | 4,840,000 | — | — | 0.10 | 0.30 | 2.00 |
| 1964 | 7,250,000 | — | — | 0.10 | 0.15 | 1.25 |
| 1965 | 6,241,000 | — | — | 0.10 | 0.25 | 2.50 |
| 1966 | 10,485,000 | — | — | — | 0.10 | 2.00 |
| 1967 | 11,993,000 | — | — | — | 0.10 | 1.25 |
| 1968 | 3,467 | — | — | — | — | 700 |
| **Note:** In mint sets only | | | | | | |
| 1969 | 316,000 | — | 0.50 | 1.00 | 1.50 | 4.50 |
| 1970 | 6,794,000 | — | — | — | 0.10 | 0.80 |
| 1971 | 15,462,000 | — | — | — | 0.10 | 0.60 |
| 1972 | 15,898,000 | — | — | — | 0.10 | 0.50 |

**5 ORE** KM# 349 **Composition:** Bronze

| Date | Mintage | VG | F | VF | XF | BU |
|---|---|---|---|---|---|---|
| 1902 | 705,000 | — | 2.50 | 6.00 | 35.00 | 225 |

**5 ORE** KM# 364 **Composition:** Bronze

| Date | Mintage | VG | F | VF | XF | BU |
|---|---|---|---|---|---|---|
| 1907 | 200,000 | — | 3.50 | 9.00 | 45.00 | 225 |

**5 ORE** KM# 368 **Composition:** Bronze

| Date | Mintage | VG | F | VF | XF | BU |
|---|---|---|---|---|---|---|
| 1908 | 600,000 | — | 20.00 | 40.00 | 90.00 | 400 |
| 1911 | 480,000 | — | 2.00 | 10.00 | 40.00 | 200 |
| 1912 | 520,000 | — | 4.00 | 25.00 | 75.00 | 500 |
| 1913 | 1,000,000 | — | 1.25 | 2.50 | 20.00 | 110 |
| 1914 | 1,000,000 | — | 1.25 | 2.50 | 20.00 | 110 |
| 1915 | Inc. above | — | 8.00 | 30.00 | 90.00 | 550 |
| 1916 | 300,000 | — | 6.00 | 12.50 | 30.00 | 225 |
| 1921 | 683,000 | — | 1.50 | 6.00 | 45.00 | 220 |
| 1922 | 2,296,000 | — | 1.25 | 5.00 | 25.00 | 125 |
| 1923 | 456,000 | — | 2.50 | 7.50 | 45.00 | 200 |
| 1928 | 848,000 | — | 0.60 | 3.00 | 15.00 | 90.00 |
| 1929 | 452,000 | — | 3.00 | 9.00 | 45.00 | 220 |
| 1930 | 1,292,000 | — | 0.60 | 2.50 | 20.00 | 100 |
| 1931 | 808,000 | — | 0.60 | 2.50 | 20.00 | 100 |
| 1932 | 500,000 | — | 3.00 | 10.00 | 30.00 | 150 |
| 1933 | 300,000 | — | 3.00 | 10.00 | 45.00 | 225 |
| 1935 | 496,000 | — | 1.50 | 5.00 | 15.00 | 125 |
| 1936 | 760,000 | — | 1.00 | 2.50 | 12.50 | 75.00 |
| 1937 | 1,552,000 | — | 0.50 | 1.50 | 10.00 | 40.00 |
| 1938 | 1,332,000 | — | 0.50 | 1.50 | 10.00 | 40.00 |
| 1939 | 1,370,000 | — | 0.50 | 1.50 | 8.00 | 40.00 |
| 1940 | 2,554,000 | — | 0.30 | 1.00 | 6.00 | 25.00 |
| 1941 | 3,576,000 | — | 0.30 | 1.00 | 5.00 | 20.00 |
| 1951 | 8,128,000 | — | 0.25 | 0.50 | 2.00 | 15.00 |
| 1952 | Inc. above | — | 1.50 | 3.50 | 8.00 | 40.00 |

**5 ORE** KM# 368a **Composition:** Iron

| Date | Mintage | VG | F | VF | XF | BU |
|---|---|---|---|---|---|---|
| 1917 | 1,700,000 | — | 20.00 | 35.00 | 50.00 | 100 |
| 1918/7 | 432,000 | — | 120 | 175 | 325 | 700 |
| 1918 | Inc. above | — | 110 | 165 | 300 | 700 |
| 1919 | 3,464,000 | — | 8.00 | 25.00 | 50.00 | 150 |
| 1920 | 1,629,000 | — | 25.00 | 50.00 | 90.00 | 250 |

**5 ORE** KM# 388 **Composition:** Iron **Note:** World War II German occupation issue.

| Date | Mintage | VG | F | VF | XF | BU |
|---|---|---|---|---|---|---|
| 1941 | 6,608,000 | — | 0.50 | 1.50 | 4.50 | 30.00 |
| 1942 | 10,312,000 | — | 0.50 | 1.50 | 4.00 | 15.00 |
| 1943 | 6,184,000 | — | 0.75 | 2.00 | 6.00 | 25.00 |
| 1944 | 4,256,000 | — | 1.25 | 3.00 | 8.00 | 25.00 |
| 1945 | 408,000 | — | 135 | 150 | 225 | 400 |

**5 ORE** KM# 400 **Composition:** Bronze

| Date | Mintage | VG | F | VF | XF | BU |
|---|---|---|---|---|---|---|
| 1952 | — | — | 0.10 | 1.00 | 2.00 | 25.00 |
| **Note:** Mintage included with KM#368. | | | | | | |
| 1953 | 6,216,000 | — | 0.10 | 1.00 | 2.00 | 15.00 |
| 1954 | 4,536,000 | — | 0.10 | 1.00 | 2.00 | 15.00 |
| 1955 | 6,570,000 | — | 0.10 | 1.00 | 2.00 | 15.00 |
| 1956 | 2,959,000 | — | 0.10 | 1.00 | 2.00 | 20.00 |
| 1957 | 5,624,000 | — | 0.10 | 1.00 | 2.00 | 10.00 |

**5 ORE** KM# 405 **Composition:** Bronze

| Date | Mintage | VG | F | VF | XF | BU |
|---|---|---|---|---|---|---|
| 1958 | 2,205,000 | — | 1.00 | 2.00 | 5.00 | 30.00 |
| 1959 | 3,208,000 | — | 0.10 | 0.50 | 2.00 | 15.00 |
| 1960 | 5,519,000 | — | 0.10 | 0.20 | 1.00 | 10.00 |
| 1961 | 4,554,000 | — | 0.10 | 0.20 | 1.00 | 10.00 |
| 1962 | 7,764,000 | — | 0.10 | 0.15 | 0.75 | 5.00 |
| 1963 | 3,204,000 | — | 0.10 | 0.15 | 0.75 | 5.00 |
| 1964 | 6,108,000 | — | — | 0.10 | 0.50 | 2.50 |
| 1965 | 6,841,000 | — | — | 0.10 | 0.50 | 2.50 |
| 1966 | 8,415,000 | — | — | 0.10 | 0.50 | 2.50 |
| 1967 | 9,071,000 | — | — | 0.10 | 0.50 | 2.50 |
| 1968 | 4,286,000 | — | — | 0.10 | 0.80 | 3.50 |
| 1969 | 4,328,000 | — | — | 0.10 | 0.30 | 1.00 |
| 1970 | 7,351,000 | — | — | 0.10 | 0.30 | 1.00 |
| 1971 | 13,450,000 | — | — | 0.10 | 0.30 | 1.00 |
| 1972 | 19,002,000 | — | — | — | 0.10 | 0.75 |
| 1973 | 9,584,000 | — | — | — | 0.10 | 0.75 |

**5 ORE** KM# 415 **Composition:** Bronze **Note:** Varieties exist.

| Date | Mintage | VG | F | VF | XF | BU |
|---|---|---|---|---|---|---|
| 1973 | 52,886,000 | — | — | — | 0.10 | 0.35 |
| 1974 | 37,150,000 | — | — | — | 0.10 | 0.35 |
| 1975 | 32,479,000 | — | — | — | 0.10 | 0.35 |
| 1976 | 24,233,000 | — | — | — | 0.10 | 0.25 |
| 1977 | 29,646,000 | — | — | — | 0.10 | 0.25 |
| 1978 | 13,838,000 | — | — | — | 0.10 | 0.25 |
| 1979 | 25,255,000 | — | — | — | 0.10 | 0.25 |
| 1980 | 12,315,000 | — | — | — | 0.10 | 0.25 |
| 1980 Without star | 27,515,000 | — | — | — | 0.10 | 0.25 |
| 1981 | 24,529,000 | — | — | — | 0.10 | 0.25 |
| 1982 | 16,849,000 | — | — | — | 0.10 | 0.25 |

**10 ORE (3 Skilling)** KM# 350 **Weight:** 1.5000 g. **Composition:** 0.4000 Silver .0192 oz. ASW

| Date | Mintage | VG | F | VF | XF | BU |
|---|---|---|---|---|---|---|
| 1901 | 2,021,000 | — | 5.00 | 10.00 | 20.00 | 45.00 |
| 1903 | 1,501,000 | — | 5.00 | 10.00 | 20.00 | 45.00 |

**10 ORE (3 Skilling)** KM# 372 **Weight:** 1.5000 g. **Composition:** 0.4000 Silver .0192 oz. ASW

| Date | Mintage | VG | F | VF | XF | BU |
|---|---|---|---|---|---|---|
| 1909 | 2,000,000 | — | 4.00 | 7.50 | 17.50 | 50.00 |
| 1911 | 1,650,000 | — | 5.00 | 10.00 | 25.00 | 135 |
| 1912 | 2,350,000 | — | 4.00 | 6.00 | 15.00 | 50.00 |
| 1913 | 2,000,000 | — | 4.00 | 6.00 | 15.00 | 40.00 |
| 1914 | 1,180,000 | — | 7.00 | 15.00 | 25.00 | 90.00 |
| 1915 | 2,820,000 | — | 1.50 | 3.00 | 6.00 | 40.00 |
| 1916 | 1,500,000 | — | 6.00 | 9.00 | 25.00 | 75.00 |
| 1917 | 5,950,000 | — | 1.00 | 2.00 | 4.00 | 8.00 |
| 1918/7 | 1,650,000 | — | 15.00 | 35.00 | 75.00 | — |
| 1918 | Inc. above | — | 1.50 | 2.50 | 7.50 | 20.00 |
| 1919/7 | 7,800,000 | — | 1.00 | 2.00 | 4.00 | 8.00 |
| 1919/7 | 7,800,000 | — | 15.00 | 35.00 | 75.00 | — |
| 1919 | Inc. above | — | 1.00 | 2.00 | 4.00 | 8.00 |

**10 ORE (3 Skilling)** KM# 378 **Composition:** Copper-Nickel

| Date | Mintage | VG | F | VF | XF | BU |
|---|---|---|---|---|---|---|
| 1920 | 2,535,000 | — | 10.00 | 15.00 | 20.00 | 45.00 |
| 1921 | 6,465,000 | — | 5.00 | 10.00 | 15.00 | 40.00 |
| 1922 | 3,965,000 | — | 5.00 | 10.00 | 15.00 | 40.00 |
| 1923 | 7,135,000 | — | 10.00 | 15.00 | 20.00 | 45.00 |

**10 ORE (3 Skilling)** KM# 383 **Composition:** Copper-Nickel

| Date | Mintage | VG | F | VF | XF | BU |
|---|---|---|---|---|---|---|
| 1924 | 12,079,000 | — | 0.30 | 0.75 | 7.50 | 30.00 |
| 1925 | 7,051,000 | — | 0.30 | 0.75 | 7.50 | 45.00 |
| 1926 | 11,764,000 | — | 0.30 | 0.75 | 7.50 | 30.00 |
| 1927 | 527,000 | — | 5.00 | 15.00 | 100 | 475 |
| 1937 | 5,000,000 | — | 0.30 | 0.75 | 4.00 | 22.00 |
| 1938 | 3,413,000 | — | 0.30 | 0.75 | 4.00 | 20.00 |
| 1939 | 1,538,000 | — | 1.00 | 2.50 | 8.00 | 40.00 |
| 1940 | 4,800,000 | — | 0.30 | 0.75 | 1.50 | 10.00 |
| 1941 | 10,150,000 | — | 0.30 | 0.75 | 1.50 | 8.00 |
| 1945 | 1,719,000 | — | 0.10 | 0.25 | 1.50 | 10.00 |
| 1946 | 3,723,000 | — | 0.10 | 0.25 | 1.50 | 7.00 |
| 1947 | 7,257,000 | — | 0.10 | 0.25 | 1.50 | 5.00 |
| 1948 | 3,105,000 | — | 0.10 | 0.25 | 2.00 | 5.50 |
| 1949 | 11,546,000 | — | 0.10 | 0.25 | 1.50 | 5.50 |
| 1951 | 5,150,000 | — | 0.10 | 0.25 | 1.50 | 5.50 |

**10 ORE (3 Skilling)** KM# 389 **Composition:** Zinc **Note:** World War II German occupation issue.

| Date | Mintage | VG | F | VF | XF | BU |
|---|---|---|---|---|---|---|
| 1941 | 15,310,000 | — | 0.75 | 2.00 | 5.00 | 25.00 |
| 1942 | 50,388,000 | — | 0.35 | 1.00 | 3.00 | 10.00 |
| 1943 | 13,378,000 | — | 0.75 | 2.00 | 4.50 | 20.00 |
| 1944 | 3,549,000 | — | 7.50 | 12.50 | 25.00 | 90.00 |
| 1945 | 5,646,000 | — | 4.00 | 8.00 | 15.00 | 40.00 |

**10 ORE (3 Skilling)** KM# 391 **Composition:** Nickel-Brass **Note:** World War II government in exile issue.

| Date | Mintage | VG | F | VF | XF | BU |
|---|---|---|---|---|---|---|
| 1942 | 6,000,000 | — | — | — | 100 | 225 |
| **Note:** All except 9,667 were melted | | | | | | |

**10 ORE (3 Skilling)** KM# 396 **Composition:** Copper-Nickel

| Date | Mintage | VG | F | VF | XF | BU |
|---|---|---|---|---|---|---|
| 1951 | 17,400,000 | — | 0.10 | 0.30 | 2.00 | 40.00 |
| 1952 | Inc. above | — | 0.10 | 0.20 | 1.25 | 15.00 |
| 1953 | 7,700,000 | — | 0.10 | 0.20 | 1.25 | 15.00 |
| 1954 | 10,105,000 | — | 0.10 | 0.20 | 1.25 | 15.00 |
| 1955 | 9,830,000 | — | 0.10 | 0.20 | 1.25 | 30.00 |
| 1956 | 10,066,000 | — | 0.10 | 0.20 | 1.25 | 15.00 |
| 1957 | 22,900,000 | — | 0.10 | 0.20 | 1.25 | 10.00 |

**10 ORE (3 Skilling)** **KM# 406** **Composition:** Copper-Nickel **Reverse:** Small lettering

| Date | Mintage | VG | F | VF | XF | BU |
|---|---|---|---|---|---|---|
| 1958 | 1,425,000 | — | 0.50 | 1.50 | 2.50 | 15.00 |

**10 ORE (3 Skilling)** **KM# 411** **Composition:** Copper-Nickel **Reverse:** Large lettering

| Date | Mintage | VG | F | VF | XF | BU |
|---|---|---|---|---|---|---|
| 1959 | 2,500,000 | — | — | 0.75 | 2.50 | 15.00 |
| 1960 | 12,490,000 | — | — | 0.10 | 0.50 | 5.00 |
| 1961 | 10,386,000 | — | — | 0.10 | 0.50 | 15.00 |
| 1962 | 16,210,000 | — | — | 0.10 | 0.50 | 3.00 |
| 1963 | 17,560,000 | — | — | 0.10 | 0.50 | 3.00 |
| 1964 | 9,781,000 | — | — | 0.10 | 0.25 | 1.25 |
| 1965 | 10,561,000 | — | — | 0.10 | 0.50 | 6.00 |
| 1966 | 16,610,000 | — | — | 0.10 | 0.50 | 2.25 |
| 1967 | 18,243,000 | — | — | 0.10 | 0.30 | 2.25 |
| 1968 | 24,698,000 | — | — | 0.10 | 0.30 | 2.25 |
| 1969 | 27,157,000 | — | — | 0.10 | 0.20 | 2.00 |
| 1970 | 639,000 | — | 0.50 | 1.00 | 2.00 | 3.00 |
| 1971 | 8,904,000 | — | — | 0.10 | 0.15 | 1.25 |
| 1972 | 24,834,000 | — | — | — | 0.10 | 0.75 |
| 1973 | 22,301,000 | — | — | — | 0.10 | 0.75 |

**10 ORE (3 Skilling)** **KM# 416** **Composition:** Copper-Nickel **Note:** Varieties exist in monogram.

| Date | Mintage | VG | F | VF | XF | BU |
|---|---|---|---|---|---|---|
| 1974 | 30,995,000 | — | — | — | 0.10 | 0.50 |
| 1975 | 21,845,000 | — | — | — | 0.10 | 0.50 |
| 1976 | 42,403,000 | — | — | — | 0.10 | 0.35 |
| 1977 | 43,304,000 | — | — | — | 0.10 | 0.35 |
| 1978 | 37,395,000 | — | — | — | 0.10 | 0.35 |
| 1979 | 25,808,000 | — | — | — | 0.10 | 0.35 |
| 1980 | 28,620,000 | — | — | — | 0.10 | 0.35 |
| 1980 Without star | 14,050,000 | — | — | — | 0.10 | 0.35 |
| 1981 | 43,083,000 | — | — | — | 0.10 | 0.35 |
| 1982 | 40,974,000 | — | — | — | 0.10 | 0.35 |
| 1983 | 45,637,000 | — | — | — | 0.10 | 0.35 |
| 1984 | 100,066,000 | — | — | — | 0.10 | 0.30 |
| 1985 | 103,108,000 | — | — | — | 0.10 | 0.30 |
| 1986 | 146,392,000 | — | — | — | 0.10 | 0.30 |
| 1987 | 166,040,000 | — | — | — | 0.10 | 0.30 |
| 1988 | 94,677,000 | — | — | — | 0.10 | 0.30 |
| 1989 | 97,274,000 | — | — | — | 0.10 | 0.30 |
| 1990 | 150,290,000 | — | — | — | 0.10 | 0.30 |
| 1991 | — | — | — | — | 0.10 | 0.30 |

**25 ORE** **KM# 360** **Weight:** 2.4000 g. **Composition:** 0.6000 Silver .0463 oz. ASW

| Date | Mintage | VG | F | VF | XF | BU |
|---|---|---|---|---|---|---|
| 1901 | 607,000 | — | 10.00 | 20.00 | 35.00 | 85.00 |
| 1902 | 612,000 | — | 10.00 | 20.00 | 35.00 | 85.00 |
| 1904 | 600,000 | — | 10.00 | 20.00 | 35.00 | 85.00 |

**25 ORE** **KM# 373** **Weight:** 2.4000 g. **Composition:** 0.6000 Silver .0463 oz. ASW

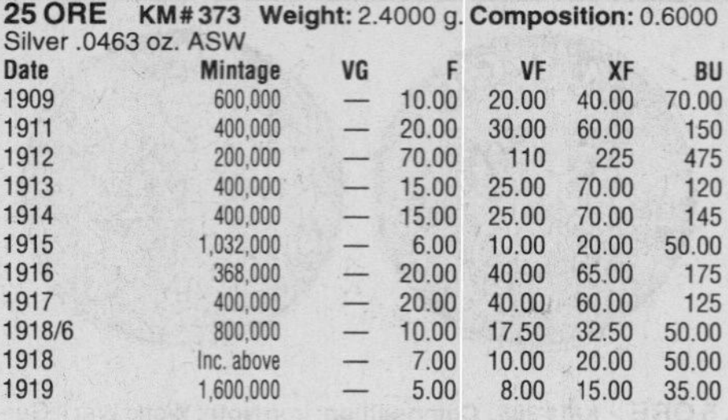

| Date | Mintage | VG | F | VF | XF | BU |
|---|---|---|---|---|---|---|
| 1909 | 600,000 | — | 10.00 | 20.00 | 40.00 | 70.00 |
| 1911 | 400,000 | — | 20.00 | 30.00 | 60.00 | 150 |
| 1912 | 200,000 | — | 70.00 | 110 | 225 | 475 |
| 1913 | 400,000 | — | 15.00 | 25.00 | 70.00 | 120 |
| 1914 | 400,000 | — | 15.00 | 25.00 | 70.00 | 145 |
| 1915 | 1,032,000 | — | 6.00 | 10.00 | 20.00 | 50.00 |
| 1916 | 368,000 | — | 20.00 | 40.00 | 65.00 | 175 |
| 1917 | 400,000 | — | 20.00 | 40.00 | 60.00 | 125 |
| 1918/6 | 800,000 | — | 10.00 | 17.50 | 32.50 | 50.00 |
| 1918 | Inc. above | — | 7.00 | 10.00 | 20.00 | 50.00 |
| 1919 | 1,600,000 | — | 5.00 | 8.00 | 15.00 | 35.00 |

**25 ORE** **KM# 381** **Composition:** Copper-Nickel

| Date | Mintage | VG | F | VF | XF | BU |
|---|---|---|---|---|---|---|
| 1921 | 4,800,000 | — | 7.50 | 10.00 | 15.00 | 30.00 |
| 1922 | 14,200,000 | — | 7.50 | 10.00 | 15.00 | 30.00 |
| 1923 | 5,200,000 | — | 15.00 | 20.00 | 27.50 | 40.00 |

**25 ORE** **KM# 382** **Composition:** Copper-Nickel

| Date | Mintage | VG | F | VF | XF | BU |
|---|---|---|---|---|---|---|
| 1921 | — | — | 3.00 | 5.00 | 40.00 | 400 |
| 1922 | — | — | 3.00 | 4.00 | 30.00 | 250 |
| 1923 | — | — | 1.50 | 3.00 | 20.00 | 150 |

**Note:** Respective mintages included with KM#381.

**25 ORE** **KM# 384** **Composition:** Copper-Nickel

| Date | Mintage | VG | F | VF | XF | BU |
|---|---|---|---|---|---|---|
| 1924 | 4,000,000 | — | 0.50 | 2.00 | 6.00 | 50.00 |
| 1927 | 6,200,000 | — | 0.50 | 1.50 | 6.00 | 50.00 |
| 1929 | 800,000 | — | 1.50 | 6.00 | 35.00 | 200 |
| 1939 | 1,220,000 | — | 0.25 | 0.75 | 3.00 | 40.00 |
| 1940 | 1,160,000 | — | 0.25 | 0.75 | 3.00 | 40.00 |
| 1946 | 1,850,000 | — | 0.20 | 0.50 | 1.50 | 15.00 |
| 1947 | 2,592,000 | — | 0.20 | 0.50 | 1.50 | 10.00 |
| 1949 | 2,602,000 | — | 0.20 | 0.50 | 1.50 | 10.00 |
| 1950 | 2,800,000 | — | 0.20 | 0.50 | 1.50 | 10.00 |

**25 ORE** **KM# 392** **Composition:** Nickel-Brass **Note:** World War II government in exile issue.

| Date | Mintage | VG | F | VF | XF | BU |
|---|---|---|---|---|---|---|
| 1942 | 2,400,000 | — | — | — | 100 | 200 |

**Note:** All but 10,300 were melted

**25 ORE** **KM# 395** **Composition:** Zinc **Note:** World War II German occupation

| Date | Mintage | VG | F | VF | XF | BU |
|---|---|---|---|---|---|---|
| 1943 | 14,105,000 | — | 1.00 | 1.50 | 3.50 | 20.00 |
| 1944 | 3,031,000 | — | 4.00 | 7.50 | 17.50 | 40.00 |
| 1945 | 3,010,000 | — | 6.00 | 10.00 | 20.00 | 50.00 |

**25 ORE** **KM# 401** **Composition:** Copper-Nickel **Note:** Mint marks exist with mint mark on square or without square.

| Date | Mintage | VG | F | VF | XF | BU |
|---|---|---|---|---|---|---|
| 1952 | 4,060,000 | — | 0.10 | 0.25 | 1.00 | 20.00 |
| 1953 | 3,320,000 | — | 0.10 | 0.25 | 1.00 | 25.00 |
| 1954 | 3,140,000 | — | 0.10 | 0.25 | 1.00 | 20.00 |
| 1955 | 2,000,000 | — | 0.10 | 0.25 | 1.00 | 50.00 |
| 1956 | 3,980,000 | — | 0.10 | 0.25 | 1.00 | 15.00 |
| 1957 | 7,660,000 | — | 0.10 | 0.25 | 1.00 | 15.00 |

**25 ORE** **KM# 407** **Composition:** Copper-Nickel

| Date | Mintage | VG | F | VF | XF | BU |
|---|---|---|---|---|---|---|
| 1958 | 1,316,000 | — | 0.50 | 1.00 | 2.50 | 25.00 |
| 1959 | 1,184,000 | — | 0.50 | 1.00 | 2.50 | 20.00 |
| 1960 | 3,964,000 | — | — | 0.10 | 1.00 | 10.00 |
| 1961 | 4,656,000 | — | — | 0.10 | 0.90 | 5.00 |
| 1962 | 6,304,000 | — | — | 0.10 | 0.90 | 5.00 |
| 1963 | 3,640,000 | — | — | 0.10 | 0.90 | 5.00 |
| 1964 | 4,953,000 | — | — | 0.10 | 0.40 | 2.00 |
| 1965 | 2,798,000 | — | — | 0.10 | 0.60 | 25.00 |
| 1966 | 6,075,000 | — | — | 0.10 | 0.60 | 2.50 |
| 1967 | 6,641,000 | — | — | 0.10 | 0.60 | 2.50 |
| 1968 | 4,963,000 | — | — | 0.10 | 0.40 | 2.00 |
| 1969 | 12,427,000 | — | — | 0.10 | 0.15 | 1.50 |
| 1970 | 1,545,000 | — | — | 0.10 | 0.60 | 5.00 |
| 1971 | 5,247,000 | — | — | — | 0.10 | 1.00 |
| 1972 | 7,929,000 | — | — | — | 0.10 | 1.00 |
| 1973 | 8,516,000 | — | — | — | 0.10 | 1.00 |

**25 ORE** **KM# 417** **Composition:** Copper-Nickel

| Date | Mintage | VG | F | VF | XF | BU |
|---|---|---|---|---|---|---|
| 1974 | 8,048,000 | — | — | — | 0.10 | 0.50 |
| 1975 | 15,595,000 | — | — | — | 0.10 | 0.50 |
| 1976 | 24,721,000 | — | — | — | 0.10 | 0.40 |
| 1977 | 20,150,000 | — | — | — | 0.10 | 0.40 |
| 1978 | 11,259,000 | — | — | — | 0.10 | 0.40 |
| 1979 | 16,666,000 | — | — | — | 0.10 | 0.40 |
| 1980 | 6,289,000 | — | — | — | 0.10 | 0.40 |
| 1980 Without star | 8,176,000 | — | — | — | 0.10 | 0.40 |
| 1981 | 17,971,000 | — | — | — | 0.10 | 0.40 |
| 1982 | 16,863,000 | — | — | — | 0.10 | 0.40 |

**50 ORE (15 Skilling)** **KM# 356** **Weight:** 5.0000 g. **Composition:** 0.6000 Silver .0964 oz. ASW **Reverse:** Without 15 SK

| Date | Mintage | VG | F | VF | XF | BU |
|---|---|---|---|---|---|---|
| 1901 | 404,000 | — | 7.50 | 22.00 | 55.00 | 145 |
| 1902 | 301,000 | — | 7.50 | 22.00 | 55.00 | 145 |
| 1904 | 101,000 | — | 65.00 | 115 | 220 | 350 |

**50 ORE (15 Skilling)** **KM# 374** **Weight:** 5.0000 g. **Composition:** 0.6000 Silver .0964 oz. ASW

| Date | Mintage | VG | F | VF | XF | BU |
|---|---|---|---|---|---|---|
| 1909 | 200,000 | — | 15.00 | 30.00 | 55.00 | 125 |
| 1911 | 200,000 | — | 25.00 | 40.00 | 75.00 | 175 |
| 1912 | 200,000 | — | 40.00 | 60.00 | 100 | 250 |
| 1913 | 200,000 | — | 25.00 | 40.00 | 75.00 | 175 |
| 1914 | 800,000 | — | 5.00 | 9.00 | 17.50 | 75.00 |
| 1915 | 300,000 | — | 17.50 | 25.00 | 50.00 | 150 |
| 1916 | 700,000 | — | 6.00 | 10.00 | 20.00 | 75.00 |
| 1918 | 3,090,000 | — | 2.00 | 4.00 | 10.00 | 60.00 |
| 1919 | 1,219,000 | — | 2.50 | 4.50 | 10.00 | 30.00 |

**50 ORE (15 Skilling)** **KM# 379** **Composition:** Copper Nickel

| Date | Mintage | VG | F | VF | XF | BU |
|---|---|---|---|---|---|---|
| 1920 | 1,236,000 | — | 25.00 | 35.00 | 50.00 | 75.00 |
| 1921 | 7,345,000 | — | 8.00 | 10.00 | 20.00 | 40.00 |

| Date | Mintage | VG | F | VF | XF | BU |
|---|---|---|---|---|---|---|
| 1922 | 3,000,000 | — | 8.00 | 10.00 | 20.00 | 40.00 |
| 1923 | 4,540,000 | — | 45.00 | 65.00 | 85.00 | 145 |

**50 ORE (15 Skilling)** **KM# 380** **Composition:** Copper Nickel **Note:** Respective mintages are included with KM#379.

| Date | Mintage | VG | F | VF | XF | BU |
|---|---|---|---|---|---|---|
| 1920 | — | — | 30.00 | 60.00 | 150 | 850 |
| 1921 | — | — | 3.00 | 8.00 | 80.00 | 500 |
| 1922 | — | — | 2.50 | 6.00 | 50.00 | 350 |
| 1923 | — | — | 2.50 | 6.00 | 35.00 | 250 |

**50 ORE (15 Skilling)** **KM# 386** **Composition:** Copper Nickel

| Date | Mintage | VG | F | VF | XF | BU |
|---|---|---|---|---|---|---|
| 1926 | 2,000,000 | — | 0.35 | 1.50 | 12.50 | 75.00 |
| 1927 | 2,502,000 | — | 0.35 | 1.50 | 10.00 | 60.00 |
| 1928/7 | 1,458,000 | — | 0.50 | 2.50 | 12.00 | 60.00 |
| 1928 | Inc. above | — | 0.35 | 1.50 | 12.50 | 75.00 |
| 1929 | 600,000 | — | 1.50 | 6.00 | 60.00 | 400 |
| 1939 | 900,000 | — | 0.25 | 0.60 | 4.00 | 100 |
| 1940 | 2,193,000 | — | 0.20 | 0.50 | 3.00 | 20.00 |
| 1941 | 2,373,000 | — | 0.20 | 0.50 | 3.00 | 15.00 |
| 1945 | 1,354,000 | — | 0.20 | 0.50 | 2.00 | 25.00 |
| 1946 | 1,533,000 | — | 0.20 | 0.50 | 3.00 | 15.00 |
| 1947 | 2,465,000 | — | 0.20 | 0.50 | 3.00 | 10.00 |
| 1948 | 5,911,000 | — | 0.20 | 0.40 | 1.50 | 10.00 |
| 1949 | 1,030,000 | — | 0.25 | 1.00 | 4.00 | 20.00 |

**50 ORE (15 Skilling)** **KM# 390** **Composition:** Zinc **Note:** World War II German occupation issue.

| Date | Mintage | VG | F | VF | XF | BU |
|---|---|---|---|---|---|---|
| 1941 | 7,761,000 | — | 1.25 | 3.00 | 10.00 | 75.00 |
| 1942 | 7,606,000 | — | 1.00 | 2.50 | 6.00 | 30.00 |
| 1943 | 3,349,000 | — | 15.00 | 20.00 | 50.00 | 150 |
| 1944 | 1,542,000 | — | 10.00 | 15.00 | 30.00 | 50.00 |
| 1945 | 226,000 | — | 175 | 275 | 385 | 650 |

**50 ORE (15 Skilling)** **KM# 393** **Composition:** Nickel-Brass **Note:** World War II government in exile issue.

| Date | Mintage | VG | F | VF | XF | BU |
|---|---|---|---|---|---|---|
| 1942 | 1,600,000 | — | — | — | 110 | 200 |

**Note:** All but 9,238 were melted

**50 ORE (15 Skilling)** **KM# 402** **Composition:** Copper-Nickel

| Date | Mintage | VG | F | VF | XF | BU |
|---|---|---|---|---|---|---|
| 1953 | 2,370,000 | — | 0.20 | 0.60 | 1.50 | 25.00 |
| 1954 | 230,000 | — | 3.50 | 9.00 | 60.00 | 350 |
| 1955 | 1,930,000 | — | 0.10 | 0.40 | 2.00 | 50.00 |
| 1956 | 1,630,000 | — | 0.10 | 0.40 | 2.00 | 50.00 |
| 1957 | 1,800,000 | — | 0.10 | 0.40 | 2.00 | 25.00 |

**50 ORE (15 Skilling)** **KM# 408** **Composition:** Copper-Nickel

| Date | Mintage | VG | F | VF | XF | BU |
|---|---|---|---|---|---|---|
| 1958 | 1,560,000 | — | 0.25 | 0.75 | 2.50 | 50.00 |
| 1959 | 340,000 | — | 1.00 | 2.00 | 10.00 | 50.00 |
| 1960 | 1,584,000 | — | — | 0.10 | 1.50 | 15.00 |
| 1961 | 2,425,000 | — | — | 0.10 | 0.75 | 10.00 |
| 1962 | 3,064,000 | — | — | 0.10 | 0.75 | 10.00 |
| 1963 | 2,168,000 | — | — | 0.10 | 0.75 | 10.00 |
| 1964 | 2,692,000 | — | — | 0.10 | 0.50 | 5.00 |
| 1965 | 1,248,000 | — | 0.25 | 0.75 | 2.50 | 30.00 |
| 1966 | 4,262,000 | — | — | 0.10 | 0.25 | 5.00 |
| 1967 | 4,001,000 | — | — | 0.10 | 0.25 | 5.00 |
| 1968 | 5,431,000 | — | — | 0.10 | 0.25 | 7.00 |
| 1969 | 7,591,000 | — | — | 0.10 | 0.25 | 2.00 |
| 1970 | 481,000 | — | 0.25 | 0.75 | 2.00 | 5.00 |
| 1971 | 2,489,000 | — | — | 0.10 | 0.15 | 2.00 |
| 1972 | 4,453,000 | — | — | 0.10 | 0.15 | 2.00 |
| 1973 | 3,317,000 | — | — | 0.10 | 0.15 | 2.00 |

**50 ORE (15 Skilling)** **KM# 418** **Composition:** Copper-Nickel **Note:** Varieties in shield exist.

| Date | Mintage | VG | F | VF | XF | BU |
|---|---|---|---|---|---|---|
| 1974 | 8,494,000 | — | — | 0.10 | 0.15 | 0.60 |
| 1975 | 10,123,000 | — | — | 0.10 | 0.15 | 0.60 |
| 1976 | 15,177,000 | — | — | 0.10 | 0.15 | 0.50 |
| 1977 | 19,412,000 | — | — | 0.10 | 0.15 | 0.40 |
| 1978 | 15,305,000 | — | — | 0.10 | 0.15 | 0.40 |
| 1979 | 10,152,000 | — | — | 0.10 | 0.15 | 0.40 |
| 1980 | 7,082,000 | — | — | 0.10 | 0.15 | 0.40 |
| 1980 Without star | 7,066,000 | — | — | 0.10 | 0.15 | 0.40 |
| 1981 | 3,402,000 | — | — | 0.10 | 0.15 | 0.40 |
| 1982 | 11,157,000 | — | — | 0.10 | 0.15 | 0.40 |
| 1983 | 15,762,000 | — | — | 0.10 | 0.15 | 0.40 |
| 1984 | 8,615,000 | — | — | 0.10 | 0.15 | 0.40 |
| 1985 | 4,444,000 | — | — | 0.10 | 0.15 | 0.40 |
| 1986 | 4,178,000 | — | — | 0.10 | 0.15 | 0.40 |
| 1987 | 5,167,000 | — | — | 0.10 | 0.15 | 0.40 |
| 1988 | 9,610,000 | — | — | 0.10 | 0.15 | 0.40 |
| 1989 | 5,785,000 | — | — | 0.10 | 0.15 | 0.40 |
| 1990 | 1,729,000 | — | — | 0.10 | 0.15 | 0.40 |
| 1991 | 2,924,000 | — | — | 0.10 | 0.15 | 0.40 |
| 1992 | — | — | — | 0.10 | 0.15 | 0.40 |
| 1992 Proof | 20,000 | Value: 10.00 | | | | |
| 1993 | — | — | — | 0.10 | 0.15 | 0.40 |
| 1994 | — | — | — | 0.10 | 0.15 | 0.40 |
| 1994 Proof | 12,000 | Value: 10.00 | | | | |
| 1995 | — | — | — | — | — | 0.40 |
| 1995 Proof | — | Value: 10.00 | | | | |
| 1996 | 86,456,000 | — | — | — | — | 0.40 |
| 1996 Proof | — | Value: 10.00 | | | | |

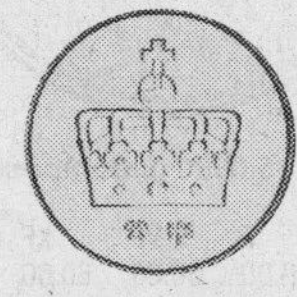

**50 ORE (15 Skilling)** **KM# 460** **Composition:** Bronze **Obverse:** Crown **Reverse:** Stylized animal, denomination

| Date | Mintage | VG | F | VF | XF | BU |
|---|---|---|---|---|---|---|
| 1997 | 25,469,000 | — | — | — | — | 0.50 |
| 1997 Proof | — | Value: 10.00 | | | | |
| 1998 | — | — | — | — | — | — |
| 1998 Proof | — | Value: 10.00 | | | | |
| 1999 | — | — | — | — | — | — |
| 1999 Proof | — | Value: 10.00 | | | | |
| 2000 | — | — | — | — | — | 0.50 |
| 2000 Proof | — | Value: 10.00 | | | | |
| 2001 | — | — | — | — | — | 0.50 |
| 2001 Proof | — | — | — | — | — | — |

**KRONE (30 Skilling)** **KM# 357** **Weight:** 7.5000 g. **Composition:** 0.8000 Silver .1929 oz. ASW **Note:** Without 30 SK

| Date | Mintage | VG | F | VF | XF | BU |
|---|---|---|---|---|---|---|
| 1901 | 152,000 | — | 20.00 | 45.00 | 100 | 325 |
| 1904 | 100,000 | — | 55.00 | 90.00 | 175 | 400 |

**KRONE (30 Skilling)** **KM# 369** **Weight:** 7.5000 g. **Composition:** 0.8000 Silver .1929 oz. ASW

| Date | Mintage | VG | F | VF | XF | BU |
|---|---|---|---|---|---|---|
| 1908 Crossed hammers on shield | 180,000 | — | 35.00 | 50.00 | 100 | 200 |
| 1908 Crossed hammers without shield | 170,000 | — | 20.00 | 40.00 | 75.00 | 150 |
| 1910 | 100,000 | — | 55.00 | 100 | 200 | 400 |
| 1912 | 200,000 | — | 35.00 | 60.00 | 100 | 225 |
| 1913 | 230,000 | — | 25.00 | 50.00 | 100 | 225 |
| 1914 | 602,000 | — | 10.00 | 20.00 | 40.00 | 90.00 |
| 1915 | 498,000 | — | 12.50 | 22.50 | 45.00 | 100 |
| 1916 | 400,000 | — | 15.00 | 25.00 | 50.00 | 200 |
| 1917 | 600,000 | — | 10.00 | 17.50 | 25.00 | 75.00 |

**KRONE (30 Skilling)** **KM# 385** **Composition:** Copper-Nickel

| Date | Mintage | VG | F | VF | XF | BU |
|---|---|---|---|---|---|---|
| 1925 | 8,686,000 | — | 0.30 | 3.00 | 15.00 | 110 |
| 1926 | 1,984,000 | — | 0.50 | 4.00 | 20.00 | 185 |
| 1927 | 1,000,000 | — | 1.00 | 5.00 | 45.00 | 375 |
| 1936 | 700,000 | — | 1.25 | 5.50 | 50.00 | 375 |
| 1937 | 1,000,000 | — | 1.00 | 4.00 | 25.00 | 225 |
| 1938 | 926,000 | — | 0.60 | 2.50 | 15.00 | 100 |
| 1939 | 2,253,000 | — | 0.60 | 1.50 | 7.50 | 70.00 |
| 1940 | 3,890,000 | — | 0.30 | 1.00 | 5.00 | 50.00 |
| 1946 | 5,499,000 | — | 0.25 | 0.50 | 2.50 | 16.00 |
| 1947 | 802,000 | — | 1.00 | 2.00 | 10.00 | 50.00 |
| 1949 | 7,846,000 | — | 0.20 | 0.50 | 2.50 | 12.00 |
| 1950 | 9,942,000 | — | 0.20 | 0.50 | 2.50 | 12.00 |
| 1951 | 4,761,000 | — | 0.20 | 0.50 | 2.50 | 12.00 |

**KRONE (30 Skilling)** **KM# 397** **Composition:** Copper-Nickel

| Date | Mintage | VG | F | VF | XF | BU |
|---|---|---|---|---|---|---|
| 1951 | 3,819,000 | — | 0.20 | 0.50 | 2.00 | 25.00 |
| 1953 | 1,465,000 | — | 0.20 | 0.50 | 2.00 | 50.00 |
| 1954 | 3,045,000 | — | 0.20 | 0.50 | 2.00 | 50.00 |
| 1955 | 1,970,000 | — | 0.20 | 0.50 | 2.00 | 75.00 |
| 1956 | 4,300,000 | — | 0.20 | 0.50 | 2.00 | 45.00 |
| 1957 | 7,630,000 | — | 0.20 | 0.50 | 2.00 | 25.00 |

**KRONE (30 Skilling)** **KM# 409** **Composition:** Copper-Nickel

| Date | Mintage | VG | F | VF | XF | BU |
|---|---|---|---|---|---|---|
| 1958 | 540,000 | — | 3.00 | 7.00 | 30.00 | 275 |
| 1959 | 4,450,000 | — | — | 0.20 | 2.00 | 30.00 |
| 1960 | 1,790,000 | — | — | 0.20 | 2.00 | 25.00 |
| 1961 | 3,934,000 | — | — | 0.20 | 0.75 | 12.00 |
| 1962 | 6,015,000 | — | — | 0.20 | 0.75 | 12.00 |
| 1963 | 4,677,000 | — | — | 0.20 | 0.75 | 12.00 |
| 1964 | 3,469,000 | — | — | 0.20 | 0.50 | 6.00 |
| 1965 | 3,222,000 | — | — | 0.20 | 1.00 | 50.00 |
| 1966 | 3,084,000 | — | — | 0.20 | 0.75 | 15.00 |
| 1967 | 6,680,000 | — | — | 0.20 | 0.75 | 15.00 |
| 1968 | 6,149,000 | — | — | 0.20 | 0.75 | 40.00 |
| 1969 | 5,186,000 | — | — | 0.20 | 0.35 | 3.00 |

| Date | Mintage | VG | F | VF | XF | BU |
|---|---|---|---|---|---|---|
| 1970 | 8,637,000 | — | — | 0.20 | 0.40 | 10.00 |
| 1971 | 10,258,000 | — | — | 0.20 | 0.35 | 3.00 |
| 1972 | 13,179,000 | — | — | 0.20 | 0.35 | 3.00 |
| 1973 | 9,140,000 | — | — | 0.20 | 0.35 | 3.00 |

**KRONE (30 Skilling)** **KM# 419** **Composition:** Copper-Nickel **Note:** Varieties with and without star mint mark exist.

| Date | Mintage | VG | F | VF | XF | BU |
|---|---|---|---|---|---|---|
| 1974 | 16,537,000 | — | — | 0.20 | 0.35 | 1.00 |
| 1975 | 26,044,000 | — | — | 0.20 | 0.35 | 1.00 |
| 1976 | 35,927,000 | — | — | 0.20 | 0.35 | 0.75 |
| 1977 | 26,264,000 | — | — | 0.20 | 0.35 | 0.75 |
| 1978 | 23,360,000 | — | — | 0.20 | 0.35 | 0.75 |
| 1979 | 15,897,000 | — | — | 0.20 | 0.35 | 0.75 |
| 1980 | 5,918,000 | — | — | 0.20 | 0.35 | 2.25 |
| 1981 | 16,308,000 | — | — | 0.20 | 0.35 | 0.75 |
| 1982 | 29,187,000 | — | — | 0.20 | 0.35 | 0.75 |
| 1983 | 34,293,000 | — | — | 0.20 | 0.35 | 0.75 |
| 1984 | 3,677,000 | — | — | 0.20 | 0.35 | 1.25 |
| 1985 | 10,985,000 | — | — | 0.20 | 0.35 | 0.75 |
| 1986 | 5,612,000 | — | — | 0.20 | 0.35 | 0.75 |
| 1987 | 11,015,000 | — | — | 0.20 | 0.35 | 0.75 |
| 1988 | 14,880,000 | — | — | 0.20 | 0.35 | 0.75 |
| 1989 | 5,605,000 | — | — | 0.20 | 0.35 | 0.75 |
| 1990 | 8,804,000 | — | — | 0.20 | 0.35 | 0.75 |
| 1990 Proof | 15,000 | Value: 85.00 | | | | |
| 1991 | 15,080,000 | — | — | 0.20 | 0.35 | 0.75 |

**KRONE (30 Skilling)** **KM# 436** **Composition:** Copper-Nickel

| Date | Mintage | VG | F | VF | XF | BU |
|---|---|---|---|---|---|---|
| 1992 | 7,426,000 | — | — | 0.20 | 0.35 | 0.75 |
| 1992 Proof | 20,000 | Value: 10.00 | | | | |
| 1993 | 12,295,000 | — | — | 0.20 | 0.35 | 0.75 |
| 1994 | 25,951,000 | — | — | 0.20 | 0.35 | 0.75 |
| 1994 Proof | 12,000 | Value: 10.00 | | | | |
| 1995 | 12,883,000 | — | — | 0.20 | 0.35 | 0.75 |
| 1995 Proof | — | Value: 10.00 | | | | |
| 1996 | — | — | — | 0.20 | 0.35 | 0.75 |
| 1996 Proof | — | Value: 10.00 | | | | |

**KRONE (30 Skilling)** **KM# 462** **Composition:** Copper-Nickel **Obverse:** Monogram cross **Reverse:** Bird on vine above date and denomination

| Date | Mintage | VG | F | VF | XF | BU |
|---|---|---|---|---|---|---|
| 1997 | — | — | — | — | — | 0.75 |
| 1997 Proof | — | Value: 10.00 | | | | |
| 1998 | — | — | — | — | — | 0.75 |
| 1998 Proof | — | Value: 10.00 | | | | |
| 1999 | — | — | — | — | — | 0.75 |
| 1999 Proof | — | Value: 10.00 | | | | |
| 2000 | — | — | — | — | — | 0.75 |
| 2000 Proof | — | Value: 10.00 | | | | |
| 2001 | — | — | — | — | — | 0.75 |
| 2001 Proof | — | — | — | — | — | — |

**2 KRONER** **KM# 359** **Weight:** 15.0000 g. **Composition:** 0.8000 Silver .3858 oz. ASW **Note:** Restrikes are made by the Royal Mint, Norway, in gold, silver and bronze.

| Date | Mintage | VG | F | VF | XF | BU |
|---|---|---|---|---|---|---|
| 1902 | 153,000 | — | 30.00 | 55.00 | 120 | 375 |
| 1904 | 76,000 | — | 45.00 | 85.00 | 175 | 400 |

**2 KRONER** **KM# 363** **Weight:** 15.0000 g. **Composition:** 0.8000 Silver .3858 oz. ASW **Subject:** Norway independence **Obverse:** Large shield

| Date | Mintage | VG | F | VF | XF | BU |
|---|---|---|---|---|---|---|
| 1906 | 100,000 | — | 10.00 | 15.00 | 25.00 | 60.00 |

**2 KRONER** **KM# 365** **Weight:** 15.0000 g. **Composition:** 0.8000 Silver .3858 oz. ASW **Obverse:** Smaller shield

| Date | Mintage | VG | F | VF | XF | BU |
|---|---|---|---|---|---|---|
| 1907 | 55,000 | — | 20.00 | 30.00 | 50.00 | 95.00 |

**2 KRONER** **KM# 366** **Weight:** 15.0000 g. **Composition:** 0.8000 Silver .3858 oz. ASW **Subject:** Border watch

| Date | Mintage | VG | F | VF | XF | BU |
|---|---|---|---|---|---|---|
| 1907 | 28,000 | — | 60.00 | 125 | 225 | 500 |

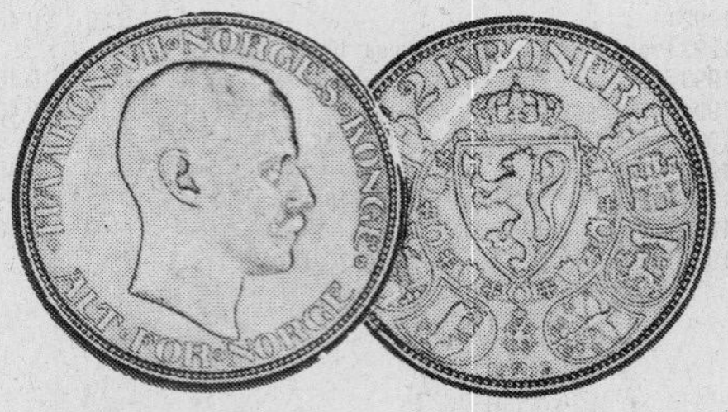


**2 KRONER** **KM# 370** **Weight:** 15.0000 g. **Composition:** 0.8000 Silver .3858 oz. ASW

| Date | Mintage | VG | F | VF | XF | BU |
|---|---|---|---|---|---|---|
| 1908 | 200,000 | — | 20.00 | 30.00 | 60.00 | 150 |
| 1910 | 150,000 | — | 35.00 | 60.00 | 100 | 300 |
| 1912 | 150,000 | — | 30.00 | 55.00 | 100 | 300 |
| 1913 | 270,000 | — | 15.00 | 25.00 | 50.00 | 125 |
| 1914 | 255,000 | — | 17.50 | 30.00 | 60.00 | 150 |
| 1915 | 225,000 | — | 17.50 | 30.00 | 60.00 | 150 |
| 1916 | 250,000 | — | 30.00 | 45.00 | 80.00 | 200 |
| 1917 | 378,000 | — | 10.00 | 15.00 | 30.00 | 100 |

**2 KRONER** **KM# 377** **Weight:** 15.0000 g. **Composition:** 0.8000 Silver .3858 oz. ASW **Subject:** Constitution centennial

| Date | Mintage | VG | F | VF | XF | BU |
|---|---|---|---|---|---|---|
| 1914 | 226,000 | — | 6.00 | 10.00 | 17.50 | 75.00 |

**5 KRONER** **KM# 412** **Composition:** Copper-Nickel

| Date | Mintage | VG | F | VF | XF | BU |
|---|---|---|---|---|---|---|
| 1963 | 7,074,000 | — | — | 1.00 | 3.00 | 20.00 |
| 1964 | 7,346,000 | — | — | 1.00 | 2.00 | 10.00 |
| 1965 | 2,233,000 | — | — | 1.00 | 2.50 | 80.00 |
| 1966 | 2,502,000 | — | — | 1.00 | 2.50 | 40.00 |
| 1967 | 583,000 | — | 1.00 | 1.75 | 5.00 | 40.00 |
| 1968 | 1,813,000 | — | — | 1.00 | 2.00 | 30.00 |
| 1969 | 2,404,000 | — | — | 1.00 | 2.00 | 10.00 |
| 1970 | 202,000 | — | 1.50 | 2.50 | 5.00 | 15.00 |
| 1971 | 178,000 | — | 1.50 | 2.50 | 6.00 | 20.00 |
| 1972 | 2,281,000 | — | — | — | 1.00 | 2.75 |
| 1973 | 2,778,000 | — | — | — | 1.00 | 6.00 |

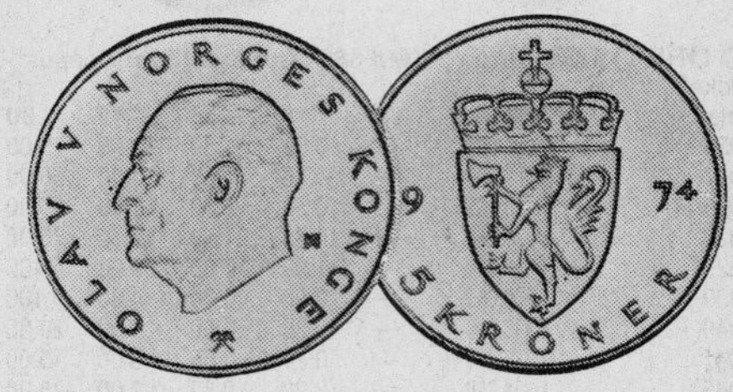


**5 KRONER** **KM# 420** **Composition:** Copper-Nickel **Note:** Varieties exist with large and small shields.

| Date | Mintage | VG | F | VF | XF | BU |
|---|---|---|---|---|---|---|
| 1974 | 1,983,000 | — | — | — | 1.00 | 6.00 |
| 1975 | 2,946,000 | — | — | — | 1.00 | 3.00 |
| 1976 | 9,056,000 | — | — | — | 1.00 | 1.75 |
| 1977 | 4,630,000 | — | — | — | 1.00 | 1.50 |
| 1978 | 5,853,000 | — | — | — | 1.00 | 1.50 |
| 1979 | 6,818,000 | — | — | — | 1.00 | 1.50 |
| 1980 | 1,578,000 | — | — | — | 1.00 | 2.25 |
| 1981 | 1,105,000 | — | — | — | 1.00 | 1.75 |
| 1982 | 3,920,000 | — | — | — | 1.00 | 1.50 |
| 1983 | 2,932,000 | — | — | — | 1.00 | 1.50 |
| 1984 | 1,233,000 | — | — | — | 1.00 | 1.75 |
| 1985 | 1,441,000 | — | — | — | 1.00 | 1.50 |
| 1987 | 900,000 | — | — | — | 1.00 | 2.25 |
| 1988 | 865,000 | — | — | — | 1.00 | 2.25 |

**5 KRONER** **KM# 421** **Composition:** Copper-Nickel **Subject:** 100th anniversary of krone system

| Date | Mintage | VG | F | VF | XF | BU |
|---|---|---|---|---|---|---|
| ND(1975) | 1,192,000 | — | — | 1.00 | 1.50 | 3.00 |

**5 KRONER** **KM# 422** **Composition:** Copper-Nickel **Subject:** 150th anniversary - immigration to America

| Date | Mintage | VG | F | VF | XF | BU |
|---|---|---|---|---|---|---|
| ND(1975) | 1,223,000 | — | — | 1.00 | 1.50 | 3.00 |

**5 KRONER** **KM# 423** **Composition:** Copper-Nickel **Subject:** 350th anniversary of Norwegian army

| Date | Mintage | VG | F | VF | XF | BU |
|---|---|---|---|---|---|---|
| ND(1978) | 2,990,000 | — | — | 1.00 | 1.50 | 2.50 |

**5 KRONER** **KM# 458** **Composition:** Copper-Nickel **Subject:** 50th anniversary - United Nations

| Date | Mintage | VG | F | VF | XF | BU |
|---|---|---|---|---|---|---|
| ND(1995) | 498,000 | — | — | — | — | 3.00 |

**5 KRONER** **KM# 428** **Composition:** Copper-Nickel **Subject:** 300th anniversary of the mint

| Date | Mintage | VG | F | VF | XF | BU |
|---|---|---|---|---|---|---|
| 1986 | 2,345,000 | — | — | 1.00 | 1.50 | 2.50 |
| 1986 Prooflike | 5,000 | — | — | — | — | — |

**5 KRONER** **KM# 459** **Composition:** Copper-Nickel **Subject:** Centennial - Nasen's return from the Arctic

| Date | Mintage | VG | F | VF | XF | BU |
|---|---|---|---|---|---|---|
| 1996 | 1,382,000 | — | — | — | — | 3.00 |
| 1996 Proof | 12,000 | Value: 20.00 | | | | |

**5 KRONER** **KM# 430** **Composition:** Copper-Nickel **Subject:** 175th anniversary of the national bank

| Date | Mintage | VG | F | VF | XF | BU |
|---|---|---|---|---|---|---|
| 1991 | 544,000 | — | — | — | — | 7.00 |

**5 KRONER** **KM# 461** **Composition:** Copper-Nickel **Subject:** 350th anniversary - Norwegian postal service

| Date | Mintage | VG | F | VF | XF | BU |
|---|---|---|---|---|---|---|
| ND(1997) | 3,636,000 | — | — | — | — | 3.00 |
| ND(1997) Proof | 15,000 | Value: 10.00 | | | | |

**5 KRONER** **KM# 437** **Composition:** Copper-Nickel **Obverse:** Harald V

| Date | Mintage | VG | F | VF | XF | BU |
|---|---|---|---|---|---|---|
| 1992 | 550,000 | — | — | — | — | 2.00 |

**Note:** 100,000 are in mint sets.

| Date | Mintage | VG | F | VF | XF | BU |
|---|---|---|---|---|---|---|
| 1992 Proof | 20,000 | Value: 10.00 | | | | |
| 1993 | 510,000 | — | — | — | — | 2.50 |
| 1994 | 2,112,000 | — | — | — | — | 2.00 |
| 1994 Proof | 12,000 | Value: 10.00 | | | | |

**5 KRONER** **KM# 456** **Composition:** Copper-Nickel **Obverse:** 1,000 years of Norwegian coinage

| Date | Mintage | VG | F | VF | XF | BU |
|---|---|---|---|---|---|---|
| 1995 | 511,000 | — | — | — | — | 3.00 |
| 1995 Proof | — | Value: 20.00 | | | | |

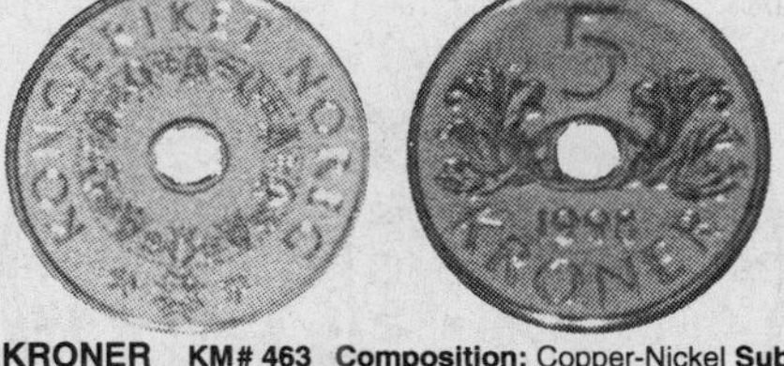


**5 KRONER** **KM# 463** **Composition:** Copper-Nickel **Subject:** Order of St. Olaf **Reverse:** Denomination and date

| Date | Mintage | VG | F | VF | XF | BU |
|---|---|---|---|---|---|---|
| 1997 | — | — | — | — | — | 2.00 |
| 1997 Proof | — | Value: 10.00 | | | | |
| 1998 | 45,808,000 | — | — | — | — | 2.00 |
| 1998 Proof | — | Value: 10.00 | | | | |
| 1999 | 21,754,000 | — | — | — | — | 2.00 |
| 1999 Proof | — | Value: 10.00 | | | | |
| 2000 | — | — | — | — | — | 2.00 |
| 2000 Proof | — | Value: 10.00 | | | | |
| 2001 | — | — | — | — | — | 2.00 |
| 2001 Proof | — | — | — | — | — | — |

**10 KRONER (2-1/2 Speciedaler)** **KM# 358** **Weight:** 4.4803 g. **Composition:** 0.9000 Gold .1296 oz. AGW

| Date | Mintage | F | VF | XF | Unc | BU |
|---|---|---|---|---|---|---|
| 1902 | 25,000 | 100 | 200 | 350 | 550 | — |

**10 KRONER (2-1/2 Speciedaler)** **KM# 375** **Weight:** 4.4803 g. **Composition:** 0.9000 Gold .1296 oz. AGW

| Date | Mintage | F | VF | XF | Unc | BU |
|---|---|---|---|---|---|---|
| 1910 | 53,000 | 80.00 | 165 | 250 | 400 | — |

**10 KRONER (2-1/2 Speciedaler)** **KM# 413** **Weight:** 20.0000 g. **Composition:** 0.9000 Silver .5707 oz. ASW **Subject:** Constitution sesquicentennial **Note:** Edge lettering varieties exist.

| Date | Mintage | VG | F | VF | XF | BU |
|---|---|---|---|---|---|---|
| ND(1964) | 1,408,000 | — | — | — | 3.00 | 7.00 |

**10 KRONER (2-1/2 Speciedaler)** **KM# 427** **Composition:** Copper-Zinc-Nickel

| Date | Mintage | VG | F | VF | XF | BU |
|---|---|---|---|---|---|---|
| 1983 | 20,193,000 | — | — | — | 2.00 | 5.00 |
| 1984 | 11,074,000 | — | — | — | 1.75 | 3.00 |
| 1985 | 22,458,000 | — | — | — | 1.75 | 3.00 |
| 1986 | 29,060,000 | — | — | — | 1.75 | 3.00 |
| 1987 | 8,809,000 | — | — | — | 1.75 | 3.00 |
| 1988 | 2,630,000 | — | — | — | 1.75 | 3.00 |
| 1989 | 3,259,000 | — | — | — | 1.75 | 3.00 |
| 1990 | 3,004,000 | — | — | — | 1.75 | 3.00 |
| 1991 | 5,068,000 | — | — | — | 1.75 | 3.00 |

**10 KRONER (2-1/2 Speciedaler)** **KM# 457** **Composition:** Copper-Zinc-Nickel **Reverse:** Church rooftop

| Date | Mintage | VG | F | VF | XF | BU |
|---|---|---|---|---|---|---|
| 1995 | 60,740,000 | — | — | — | — | 4.00 |
| 1995 Proof | — | Value: 10.00 | | | | |
| 1996 | 36,372,000 | — | — | — | — | 4.00 |
| 1996 Proof | — | Value: 10.00 | | | | |
| 1997 | 1,230,000 | — | — | — | — | 4.00 |
| 1997 Proof | — | Value: 10.00 | | | | |
| 1998 | 1,058,000 | — | — | — | — | 4.00 |
| 1998 Proof | — | Value: 10.00 | | | | |
| 1999 | 1,059,000 | — | — | — | — | 4.00 |
| 1999 Proof | — | Value: 10.00 | | | | |
| 2000 | — | — | — | — | — | 4.00 |
| 2000 Proof | — | Value: 10.00 | | | | |
| 2001 | — | — | — | — | — | 4.00 |
| 2001 Proof | — | — | — | — | — | — |

**20 KRONER (5 Speciedaler)** **KM# 355** **Weight:** 8.9606 g. **Composition:** 0.9000 Gold .2593 oz. AGW

| Date | Mintage | F | VF | XF | Unc | BU |
|---|---|---|---|---|---|---|
| 1902 | 50,000 | 80.00 | 120 | 175 | 300 | — |

**20 KRONER (5 Speciedaler)** **KM# 376** **Weight:** 8.9606 g. **Composition:** 0.9000 Gold .2593 oz. AGW

| Date | Mintage | F | VF | XF | Unc | BU |
|---|---|---|---|---|---|---|
| 1910 | 250,000 | 125 | 165 | 250 | 400 | — |

**20 KRONER (5 Speciedaler)** **KM# 453** **Composition:** Nickel-Bronze

| Date | Mintage | F | VF | XF | Unc | BU |
|---|---|---|---|---|---|---|
| 1994 | 18,598,000 | — | — | — | 6.50 | — |
| 1994 Proof | 12,000 | Value: 25.00 | | | | |
| 1995 | 21,760,000 | — | — | — | 6.50 | — |
| 1995 Proof | — | Value: 25.00 | | | | |
| 1996 | 1,520,000 | — | — | — | 6.50 | — |
| 1996 Proof | — | Value: 25.00 | | | | |
| 1997 | 1,050,000 | — | — | — | 6.50 | — |
| 1997 Proof | — | Value: 25.00 | | | | |
| 1998 | 5,008,000 | — | — | — | 6.50 | — |
| 1998 Proof | — | Value: 25.00 | | | | |
| 1999 | 6,171,000 | — | — | — | 6.50 | — |
| 1999 Proof | — | Value: 25.00 | | | | |
| 2000 | — | — | — | — | 6.50 | — |
| 2000 Proof | — | Value: 10.00 | | | | |
| 2001 | — | — | — | — | — | 6.50 |
| 2001 Proof | — | — | — | — | — | — |

**20 KRONER (5 Speciedaler)** **KM# 464** **Composition:** Copper-Zinc-Nickel **Subject:** 700th anniversary - Akershus Fortress **Obverse:** Seal of King Hakon V **Reverse:** Fortress

| Date | Mintage | F | VF | XF | Unc | BU |
|---|---|---|---|---|---|---|
| 1999 | 10,000 | — | — | — | 15.00 | — |

**20 KRONER (5 Speciedaler)** **KM# 465** **Composition:** Nickel-Bronze **Subject:** Vinland **Obverse:** King's portrait **Reverse:** Viking ship hull

| Date | Mintage | F | VF | XF | Unc | BU |
|---|---|---|---|---|---|---|
| 1999 | — | — | — | — | 10.00 | — |
| 1999 Proof | 2,500 | Value: 30.00 | | | | |

**Note:** In sets only.

**25 KRONER** **KM# 414** **Weight:** 29.0000 g. **Composition:** 0.8750 Silver .8159 oz. ASW **Subject:** 25th anniversary of liberation

| Date | Mintage | VG | F | VF | XF | BU |
|---|---|---|---|---|---|---|
| 1970 | 1,204,000 | — | — | — | — | 7.00 |

**50 KRONER** **KM# 424** **Weight:** 27.0000 g. **Composition:** 0.9250 Silver .8030 oz. ASW **Subject:** 75th birthday of King Olav V

| Date | Mintage | VG | F | VF | XF | BU |
|---|---|---|---|---|---|---|
| 1978 | 800,000 | — | — | — | — | 10.00 |

**50 KRONER** **KM# 431** **Weight:** 16.8100 g. **Composition:** 0.9250 Silver .5000 oz. ASW **Subject:** 1994 Olympics **Reverse:** Skiers

| Date | Mintage | VG | F | VF | XF | BU |
|---|---|---|---|---|---|---|
| 1991 | 95,000 | — | — | — | — | 35.00 |

**50 KRONER** **KM# 432** **Weight:** 16.8100 g. **Composition:** 0.9250 Silver .5000 oz. ASW **Subject:** 1994 Olympics **Reverse:** Child skiing

| Date | Mintage | VG | F | VF | XF | BU |
|---|---|---|---|---|---|---|
| 1991 | 120,000 | — | — | — | — | 35.00 |

**50 KRONER** **KM# 438** **Weight:** 16.8100 g. **Composition:** 0.9250 Silver .5000 oz. ASW **Subject:** 1994 Olympics **Reverse:** Grandfather and child

| Date | Mintage | VG | F | VF | XF | BU |
|---|---|---|---|---|---|---|
| 1992 | 74,000 | — | — | — | — | 35.00 |

**50 KRONER** **KM# 439** **Weight:** 16.8100 g. **Composition:** 0.9250 Silver .5000 oz. ASW **Subject:** 1994 Olympics **Reverse:** 2 children on sled

| Date | Mintage | VG | F | VF | XF | BU |
|---|---|---|---|---|---|---|
| 1992 | 88,000 | — | — | — | — | 35.00 |

**50 KRONER** **KM# 447** **Weight:** 16.8100 g. **Composition:** 0.9250 Silver .5000 oz. ASW **Subject:** 1994 Olympics **Reverse:** Cross-country skiers

| Date | Mintage | VG | F | VF | XF | BU |
|---|---|---|---|---|---|---|
| 1993 | 65,000 | — | — | — | — | 35.00 |

**50 KRONER** **KM# 448** **Weight:** 16.8100 g. **Composition:** 0.9250 Silver .5000 oz. ASW **Subject:** 1994 Olympics **Reverse:** Children ice skating

| Date | Mintage | VG | F | VF | XF | BU |
|---|---|---|---|---|---|---|
| 1993 | 77,000 | — | — | — | — | 35.00 |

**50 KRONER** **KM# 454** **Weight:** 16.8100 g. **Composition:** 0.9250 Silver .5000 oz. ASW **Subject:** 50th anniversary - United Nations

| Date | Mintage | VG | F | VF | XF | BU |
|---|---|---|---|---|---|---|
| ND(1995) Proof | 200,000 | Value: 40.00 | | | | |

**50 KRONER** **KM# 455** **Weight:** 16.8100 g. **Composition:** 0.9250 Silver .5000 oz. ASW **Subject:** 50th anniversary - end of World War II

| Date | Mintage | VG | F | VF | XF | BU |
|---|---|---|---|---|---|---|
| ND(1995) Proof | 50,000 | Value: 45.00 | | | | |

**100 KRONER** **KM# 426** **Weight:** 24.7300 g. **Composition:** 0.9250 Silver .7355 oz. ASW **Subject:** 25th anniversary of King Olaf's reign

| Date | Mintage | VG | F | VF | XF | BU |
|---|---|---|---|---|---|---|
| 1982 | 800,000 | — | — | — | — | 21.50 |

**100 KRONER** **KM# 433** **Weight:** 33.6200 g. **Composition:** 0.9250 Silver 1 oz. ASW **Subject:** 1994 Olympics **Obverse:** Similar to 50 Kroner, KM#431 **Reverse:** Cross-country skier

| Date | Mintage | VG | F | VF | XF | BU |
|---|---|---|---|---|---|---|
| 1991 | 88,000 | — | — | — | — | 60.00 |

**100 KRONER** **KM# 434** **Weight:** 33.6200 g. **Composition:** 0.9250 Silver 1 oz. ASW **Subject:** 1994 Olympics **Reverse:** 2 speed skaters

| Date | Mintage | VG | F | VF | XF | BU |
|---|---|---|---|---|---|---|
| 1991 | 116,000 | — | — | — | — | 60.00 |

**100 KRONER** **KM# 440** **Weight:** 33.6200 g. **Composition:** 0.9250 Silver 1 oz. ASW **Subject:** 1994 Olympics **Reverse:** Ski jumper

| Date | Mintage | VG | F | VF | XF | BU |
|---|---|---|---|---|---|---|
| 1992 | 85,000 | — | — | — | — | 60.00 |

**100 KRONER** **KM# 441** **Weight:** 33.6200 g. **Composition:** 0.9250 Silver 1 oz. ASW **Subject:** 1994 Olympics **Reverse:** Hockey players

| Date | Mintage | VG | F | VF | XF | BU |
|---|---|---|---|---|---|---|
| 1992 | 81,000 | — | — | — | — | 60.00 |

**100 KRONER** **KM# 443** **Weight:** 33.6200 g. **Composition:** 0.9250 Silver 1 oz. ASW **Subject:** World Cycling Championships **Reverse:** Cyclist

| Date | Mintage | VG | F | VF | XF | BU |
|---|---|---|---|---|---|---|
| 1993 | 9,288 | — | — | — | — | 70.00 |

**100 KRONER** **KM# 444** **Weight:** 33.6200 g. **Composition:** 0.9250 Silver 1 oz. ASW **Subject:** World Cycling Championships **Reverse:** 7 cyclists

| Date | Mintage | VG | F | VF | XF | BU |
|---|---|---|---|---|---|---|
| 1993 | 9,288 | — | — | — | — | 70.00 |

**100 KRONER** **KM# 449** **Weight:** 33.6200 g. **Composition:** 0.9250 Silver 1 oz. ASW **Subject:** 1984 Olympics **Reverse:** Figure skater

| Date | Mintage | VG | F | VF | XF | BU |
|---|---|---|---|---|---|---|
| 1993 | 96,000 | — | — | — | — | 60.00 |

**100 KRONER** **KM# 450** **Weight:** 33.6200 g. **Composition:** 0.9250 Silver 1 oz. ASW **Subject:** 1984 Olympics **Reverse:** Alpine skier

| Date | Mintage | VG | F | VF | XF | BU |
|---|---|---|---|---|---|---|
| 1993 | 85,000 | — | — | — | — | 60.00 |

**100 KRONER** **KM# 466** **Weight:** 33.8000 g. **Composition:** 0.9250 Silver 1.0052 oz. ASW **Subject:** Year 2000 **Obverse:** National arms **Reverse:** Cut tree trunk exposing rings

| Date | Mintage | F | VF | XF | Unc | BU |
|---|---|---|---|---|---|---|
| 1999 Proof | 50,000 | Value: 62.50 | | | | |

**100 KRONER** **KM# 469** **Weight:** 33.6000 g. **Composition:** 0.9250 Silver .9992 oz. ASW **Subject:** Nobel Peace Prize Centennial **Obverse:** National arms **Reverse:** Nobel's portrait **Edge:** Plain **Size:** 39 mm.

| Date | Mintage | F | VF | XF | Unc | BU |
|---|---|---|---|---|---|---|
| 2001 Proof | Est. 50,000 | — | — | — | 50.00 | — |

**175 KRONER** **KM# 429** **Weight:** 26.5000 g. **Composition:** 0.9250 Silver .7882 oz. ASW **Subject:** 175th anniversary of constitution

| Date | Mintage | VG | F | VF | XF | BU |
|---|---|---|---|---|---|---|
| ND(1989) | 85,000 | — | — | — | — | 70.00 |
| ND(1989) Proof | 15,000 | — | — | — | — | 275 |

**200 KRONER** **KM# 425** **Weight:** 26.8000 g. **Composition:** 0.6250 Silver .5385 oz. ASW **Subject:** 35th anniversary of liberation

| Date | Mintage | VG | F | VF | XF | BU |
|---|---|---|---|---|---|---|
| 1980 | 298,000 | — | — | — | — | 40.00 |

**1500 KRONER** **KM# 435** **Weight:** 17.0000 g. **Composition:** 0.9170 Gold .5 oz. AGW **Subject:** 1994 Olympics **Obverse:** Head of King Olav V right **Reverse:** Ancient Norwegian skier

| Date | Mintage | VG | F | VF | XF | BU |
|---|---|---|---|---|---|---|
| 1991 Proof | 30,000 | Value: 375 | | | | |

**1500 KRONER** **KM# 442** **Weight:** 17.0000 g. **Composition:** 0.9170 Gold .5 oz. AGW **Subject:** 1994 Olympics **Reverse:** Birkebeiners

| Date | Mintage | VG | F | VF | XF | BU |
|---|---|---|---|---|---|---|
| 1992 Proof | 30,000 | Value: 375 | | | | |

**1500 KRONER** **KM# 445** **Weight:** 17.0000 g. **Composition:** 0.9170 Gold .5 oz. AGW **Subject:** World Cycling Championships **Reverse:** 2 19th century cyclists

| Date | Mintage | VG | F | VF | XF | BU |
|---|---|---|---|---|---|---|
| 1993 Proof | 6,390 | Value: 475 | | | | |

**1500 KRONER** **KM# 446** **Weight:** 17.0000 g. **Composition:** 0.9170 Gold .5 oz. AGW **Subject:** Edvard Grieg

| Date | Mintage | VG | F | VF | XF | BU |
|---|---|---|---|---|---|---|
| 1993 Proof | 5,139 | Value: 525 | | | | |

**1500 KRONER** **KM# 451** **Weight:** 17.0000 g. **Composition:** 0.9170 Gold .5 oz. AGW **Subject:** 1994 Olympics **Reverse:** Telemark skier

| Date | Mintage | VG | F | VF | XF | BU |
|---|---|---|---|---|---|---|
| 1993 Proof | 30,000 | Value: 375 | | | | |

**1500 KRONER** **KM# 452** **Weight:** 17.0000 g. **Composition:** 0.9170 Gold .5 oz. AGW **Subject:** Roald Amundsen

| Date | Mintage | VG | F | VF | XF | BU |
|---|---|---|---|---|---|---|
| 1993 Proof | 22,000 | Value: 425 | | | | |

**1500 KRONER** **KM# 467** **Weight:** 16.9600 g. **Composition:** 0.9170 Gold .4994 oz. AGW **Subject:** Year 2000 **Obverse:** King Harald V right **Reverse:** Tree and roots

| Date | Mintage | VG | F | VF | XF | BU |
|---|---|---|---|---|---|---|
| 2000 Proof | 7,500 | Value: 400 | | | | |

**1500 KRONER** **KM# 470** **Weight:** 16.9600 g. **Composition:** 0.9170 Gold .5000 oz. AGW **Ruler:** Harald V **Subject:** Nobel Peace Prize Centennial **Obverse:** King's portrait **Reverse:** Reverse design of the prize medal **Edge:** Plain **Size:** 27 mm.

| Date | Mintage | VG | F | VF | XF | BU |
|---|---|---|---|---|---|---|
| ND(2001) Matte Proof | 7,500 | Value: 375 | | | | |

## PATTERNS

Including off metal strikes

| KM# | Date | Mintage | Identification | Mkt Val |
|---|---|---|---|---|
| Pn40 | ND1958 | 6 | Ore. | — |

## MINT SETS

| KM# | Date | Mintage | Identification | Issue Price | Mkt Val |
|---|---|---|---|---|---|
| MS1 | 1960 (7) | 200 | KM403, 405, 407-411 | — | — |
| MS2 | 1961 (7) | 475 | KM403, 405, 407-411 | — | — |
| MS3 | 1962 (7) | 570 | KM403, 405, 407-411 | — | — |
| MS4 | 1963 (8) | 430 | KM403, 405, 407-412 | — | — |
| MS6 | 1964 (8) | 1,200 | KM403, 405, 407-412 | — | — |
| MS7 | 1965 (8) | 1,800 | KM403, 405, 407-412. Plastic. | — | 180 |
| MS8 | 1966 (8) | 1,400 | KM403, 405, 407-412. Plastic. | — | 150 |
| MS9 | 1967 (8) | 2,490 | KM403, 405, 407-412. Soft plastic. | — | 140 |
| MS11 | 1968 (8) | 1,167 | KM403, 405, 407-412. Soft plastic. | — | 850 |
| MS12 | 1968 (8) | 2,300 | KM403, 405, 407-412. Sandhill. | — | 875 |
| MS13 | 1969 (8) | 3,140 | KM403, 405, 407-412 | — | 25.00 |
| MS14 | 1969 (8) | 7,450 | KM403, 405, 407-412. Sandhill. | — | 55.00 |
| MS15 | 1970 (8) | 2,005 | KM403, 405, 407-412. Soft plastic. | — | 50.00 |
| MS16 | 1970 (8) | 7,311 | KM403, 405, 407-412. Sandhill. | — | 90.00 |

| KM# | Date | Mintage | Identification | Issue Price | Mkt Val |
|---|---|---|---|---|---|
| MS17 | 1971 (8) | 2,010 | KM403, 405, 407-412. Soft plastic. | — | 50.00 |
| MS18 | 1971 (8) | 4,055 | KM403, 405, 407-412. Sandhill. | — | 110 |
| MS19 | 1972 (8) | 6,549 | KM403, 405, 407-412. Soft plastic. | — | 15.00 |
| MS20 | 1972 (8) | 6,435 | KM403, 405, 407-412. Sandhill. | — | 50.00 |
| MS21 | 1973 (7) | 7,085 | KM405, 407-409, 411-412, 415. Soft plastic. | — | 14.00 |
| MS22 | 1973 (7) | 13,090 | KM405, 407-409, 411-412, 415. Sandhill. | — | 35.00 |
| MS23 | 1974 (6) | 10,275 | KM415-420. Soft plastic. | — | 8.00 |
| MS24 | 1974 (6) | 29,695 | KM415-420. Sandhill. | — | 12.00 |
| MS25 | 1975 (8) | 30,207 | KM415-422. Sandhill. | 5.00 | 32.50 |
| MS26 | 1975 (7) | 5,287 | KM415-421. Soft plastic. | 5.00 | 20.00 |
| MS27 | 1976 (6) | 5,000 | KM415-420. Soft plastic. | 3.00 | 7.00 |
| MS28 | 1976 (6) | 25,000 | KM415-420. Sandhill. | 3.00 | 10.00 |
| MS29 | 1977 (6) | 5,000 | KM415-420. Soft plastic. | 3.40 | 12.00 |
| MS30 | 1977 (6) | 25,000 | KM415-420. Sandhill. | 3.40 | 25.00 |
| MS31 | 1978 (6) | 5,000 | KM415-420. Soft plastic. | 3.40 | 14.00 |
| MS32 | 1978 (6) | 30,000 | KM415-420. Sandhill. | 3.40 | 25.00 |
| MS33 | 1979 (6) | 8,000 | KM415-420. Soft plastic. | 3.40 | 6.00 |
| MS34 | 1979 (6) | 50,000 | KM415-420. Sandhill. | 3.40 | 9.00 |
| MS35 | 1980 (6) | 10,000 | KM415-420. Soft plastic. | 3.40 | 7.00 |
| MS36 | 1980 (6) | 70,000 | KM415-420. Sandhill. | 3.40 | 15.00 |
| MS37 | 1981 (6) | 100,000 | KM415-420. Hard plastic. | 4.25 | 8.00 |
| MS38 | 1982 (6) | 102,650 | KM415-420 | 4.50 | 10.00 |
| MS39 | 1983 (4) | 102,300 | KM416, 418-420 | 5.00 | 8.00 |
| MS40 | 1984 (5) | 101,000 | KM416, 418-420, 427 | 5.00 | 8.00 |
| MS41 | 1985 (5) | 110,000 | KM416, 418-420, 427 | 5.00 | 8.00 |
| MS42 | 1986 (5) | 100,000 | KM416, 418-419, 427-428 | 7.00 | 12.00 |
| MS43 | 1987 (5) | 85,000 | KM416, 418-420, 427 | 7.00 | 12.00 |
| MS44 | 1988 (4) | 102,000 | KM416, 418, 420, 427 | 7.00 | 10.00 |
| MS45 | 1989 (4) | 101,000 | KM416, 418-419, 427 | 8.00 | 12.00 |
| MS46 | 1990 (4) | 103,000 | KM416, 418-419, 427 | 8.00 | 12.00 |
| MS47 | 1991/1992 (5) | 100,000 | KM416, 418, 427, 436-437 | — | 8.50 |
| MS48 | 1991/1993 (5) | 100,000 | KM416, 418, 427, 436-437 | — | 18.00 |
| MS49 | 1994 (5) | 100,000 | KM418, 427, 436-437, 453 | — | 16.00 |
| MS50 | 1995 (5) | 100,000 | KM418, 436, 453, 456, 457 | — | 18.00 |
| MS51 | 1996 (5) | 90,000 | KM418, 436, 453, 457, 459 | — | 20.00 |
| MS52 | 1997 (5) | 90,000 | KM453, 457, 460, 461, 462 | — | 20.00 |
| MS53 | 1998 (5) | 90,000 | KM453, 457, 460, 462, 463 | — | 20.00 |
| MS54 | 1999 (5) | — | KM453, 457, 460, 462, 463 | — | 20.00 |
| MS55 | 1999 (5) | 50,000 | KM457, 460 462-464. Souvenir folder. | 13.00 | 15.00 |
| MS56 | 1999 (5) | 35,000 | KM457, 460, 462-464. Baby coin set. | 14.30 | 15.00 |
| MS57 | 1999 (5) | — | KM457, 460, 462-464 plus medal. | 26.00 | 26.00 |
| MS58 | 2000 (5) | — | KM453, 457, 460, 462, 463. Hard case. | — | 22.00 |
| MS59 | 2001 (5) | 55,000 | KM453, 457, 460, 462, 463. Folder. | 20.00 | 20.00 |
| MS60 | 2001 (5) | 30,000 | KM453, 457, 460, 462, 463. Baby gift set. | 18.00 | 20.00 |
| MS61 | 2001 (5) | 2,000 | KM453, 457, 460, 462, 463 plus medal. | 27.00 | 27.00 |
| MS62 | 2001 (5) | — | KM453, 457, 460, 462, 463. Sandhill. | — | 20.00 |

## PROOF SETS

| KM# | Date | Mintage | Identification | Issue Price | Mkt Val |
|---|---|---|---|---|---|
| PS1 | 1992 (3) | 20,000 | KM418, 436-437 | — | 30.00 |
| PS2 | 1993 (3) | 12,000 | KM443-445 | — | 650 |
| PS3 | 1994 (4) | 15,000 | KM418, 436-437, 453 | — | 56.00 |
| PS4 | 1995 (5) | 15,000 | KM418, 436, 453, 456, 457 | — | 75.00 |
| PS5 | 1996 (5) | 12,000 | KM418, 436, 453, 457, 459 | — | 75.00 |
| PS6 | 1997 (5) | 15,000 | KM453, 457, 460, 461, 462. Norwegian Heritage Set. | — | 65.00 |
| PS7 | 1997 (5) | — | KM453, 457, 460, 461, 462 | — | 65.00 |
| PS8 | 1998 (5) | 14,097 | KM453, 457, 460, 462, 463. Norwegian Heritage Set. | — | 65.00 |
| PS9 | 1998 (5) | — | KM453, 457, 460, 462, 463 | — | 65.00 |
| PS10 | 1999 (5) | 15,000 | KM453, 457, 460, 462, 463 | 60.00 | 70.00 |
| PS11 | 1999 (5) | 2,500 | KM457, 460, 462-463, 465 | — | — |
| PS12 | 2000 (5) | — | KM453, 457, 460, 462, 463 | — | 50.00 |

# OMAN

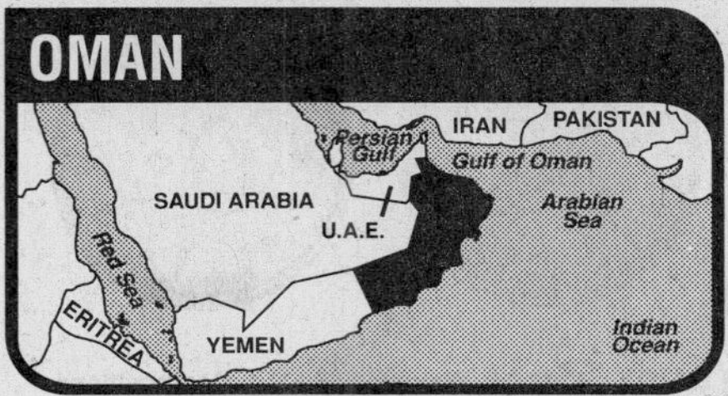


The Sultanate of Oman (formerly Muscat and Oman), an independent monarchy located in the southeastern part of the Arabian Peninsula, has an area of 82,030 sq. mi. (212,460 sq. km.) and a population of *1.3 million. Capital: Muscat. The economy is based on agriculture, herding and petroleum. Petroleum products, dates, fish and hides are exported.

The Portuguese who captured Muscat, the capital and chief port, in 1508, made the first European contact with Muscat and Oman. They occupied the city, utilizing it as a naval base and factory and holding it against land and sea attacks by Arabs and Persians until finally ejected by local Arabs in 1650. It was next occupied by the Persians who maintained control until 1741,when it was taken by Ahmed ibn Sa'id of the present ruling family. Muscat and Oman was the most powerful state in Arabia during the first half of the 19th century, until weakened by the persistent attack of interior nomadic tribes. British influence, initiated by the signing of a treaty of friendship with the Sultanate in 1798,remains a dominant fact of the civil and military phases of the government, although Britain recognizes the Sultanate as a sovereign state.

Sultan Sa'id bin Taimur was overthrown by his son, Qabus bin Sa'id, on July 23, 1970. The new sultan changed the nation's name to Sultanate of Oman.

**TITLES**

Muscat مسقط

Oman عمان

## SULTANATE

### DECIMAL COINAGE

1000 (new) Baisa = 1 Saidi Rial

**1/2 SAIDI RIAL** **KM# 42** **Weight:** 25.6000 g. **Composition:** 0.9170 Gold .7548 oz. AGW

| Date | Mintage | F | VF | XF | Unc | BU |
|---|---|---|---|---|---|---|
| AH1391(1971) Proof | 100 | Value: 650 | | | | |

**Note:** Struck for presentation purposes

**SAIDI RIAL** **KM# 44** **Weight:** 46.6500 g. **Composition:** 0.9170 Gold 1.3755 oz. AGW

| Date | Mintage | F | VF | XF | Unc | BU |
|---|---|---|---|---|---|---|
| AH1391(1971) Proof | 100 | Value: 750 | | | | |
| AH1394(1974) Proof | 250 | Value: 750 | | | | |

**Note:** Struck for presentation purposes

**15 SAIDI RIALS** **KM# 43** **Weight:** 5.8100 g. **Composition:** 0.9170 Gold .1713 oz. AGW

| Date | Mintage | F | VF | XF | Unc | BU |
|---|---|---|---|---|---|---|
| AH1391(1971) Proof | 112 | Value: 650 | | | | |

**Note:** Struck for presentation purposes

**15 SAIDI RIALS** **KM# 53** **Weight:** 7.9800 g. **Composition:** 0.9170 Gold .2353 oz. AGW

| Date | Mintage | F | VF | XF | Unc | BU |
|---|---|---|---|---|---|---|
| AH1391(1971) Proof | 224 | Value: 550 | | | | |

**Note:** Struck for presentation purposes

## REFORM COINAGE

1000 Baisa = 1 Omani Rial

**5 BAISA** **KM# 50** **Composition:** Bronze

| Date | Mintage | F | VF | XF | Unc | BU |
|---|---|---|---|---|---|---|
| AH1395(1975) | 6,000,000 | — | 0.10 | 0.20 | 0.45 | — |
| AH1400(1979) | 3,000,000 | — | 0.10 | 0.20 | 0.45 | — |
| AH1406(1985) | 2,000,000 | — | 0.10 | 0.20 | 0.45 | — |
| AH1410(1989) | 5,000,000 | — | 0.10 | 0.20 | 0.45 | — |

**5 BAISA** **KM# 76** **Composition:** Bronze **Subject:** 20th National Day - Sultan Qaboos **Obverse:** National emblem **Reverse:** Sports Complex

| Date | Mintage | F | VF | XF | Unc | BU |
|---|---|---|---|---|---|---|
| AH1411(1990) Proof | 3,200 | Value: 5.00 | | | | |

**10 BAISA** **KM# 51** **Composition:** Bronze **Series:** F.A.O.

| Date | Mintage | F | VF | XF | Unc | BU |
|---|---|---|---|---|---|---|
| AH1395(1975) | 1,000,000 | — | 0.15 | 0.30 | 0.65 | — |

**10 BAISA** **KM# 52.1** **Composition:** Bronze **Series:** F.A.O.

| Date | Mintage | F | VF | XF | Unc | BU |
|---|---|---|---|---|---|---|
| AH1395(1975) | 6,000,000 | — | 0.15 | 0.30 | 0.65 | — |
| AH1400(1979) | 5,250,000 | — | 0.15 | 0.30 | 0.65 | — |
| AH1406(1985) | 3,000,000 | — | 0.15 | 0.30 | 0.65 | — |
| AH1410(1989) | 6,000,000 | — | 0.15 | 0.30 | 0.65 | — |

**10 BAISA** **KM# 77** **Composition:** Bronze Clad Steel **Subject:** 20th National Day - Central Bank of Oman **Obverse:** National emblem

| Date | Mintage | F | VF | XF | Unc | BU |
|---|---|---|---|---|---|---|
| AH1411(1990) Proof | 3,200 | Value: 5.00 | | | | |

**10 BAISA** **KM# 94** **Composition:** Bronze Clad Steel **Series:** F.A.O. **Subject:** 50 Years

| Date | Mintage | F | VF | XF | Unc | BU |
|---|---|---|---|---|---|---|
| ND(1995) | — | — | — | — | 1.25 | — |
| ND(1995) | 224 | — | — | — | 1.25 | — |

**10 BAISA** **KM# 52.2** **Composition:** Bronze Clad Steel

| Date | Mintage | F | VF | XF | Unc | BU |
|---|---|---|---|---|---|---|
| AH1420(1999) | — | — | 0.15 | 0.30 | 0.65 | — |

**15 BAISA** **KM# 75** **Weight:** 20.0000 g. **Composition:** 0.9250 Silver .5949 oz. ASW **Subject:** 15th Anniversary - Reign of Sultan

| Date | Mintage | F | VF | XF | Unc | BU |
|---|---|---|---|---|---|---|
| AH1406(1985) Proof | 2,000 | Value: 160 | | | | |

**25 BAISA** **KM# 45** **Weight:** 5.9600 g. **Composition:** 0.9170 Gold .1757 oz. AGW

| Date | Mintage | F | VF | XF | Unc | BU |
|---|---|---|---|---|---|---|
| AH1392(1972) | 100 | — | — | — | 100 | — |
| AH1392(1972) Proof | 50 | Value: 150 | | | | |
| AH1394(1974) Proof | 250 | Value: 100 | | | | |
| AH1395(1975) Proof | 250 | Value: 100 | | | | |

**Note:** Struck for presentation purposes

**25 BAISA** **KM# 45a** **Composition:** Copper-Nickel

| Date | Mintage | F | VF | XF | Unc | BU |
|---|---|---|---|---|---|---|
| AH1395(1975) | 4,500,000 | — | 0.20 | 0.40 | 0.85 | — |
| AH1400(1979) | 5,250,000 | — | 0.20 | 0.40 | 0.85 | — |
| AH1406(1985) | 4,000,000 | — | 0.20 | 0.40 | 0.85 | — |
| AH1410(1989) | 7,000,000 | — | 0.20 | 0.40 | 0.85 | — |

**25 BAISA** **KM# 78** **Composition:** Copper-Nickel **Subject:** 20th National Day - Royal Hospital **Obverse:** National emblem

| Date | Mintage | F | VF | XF | Unc | BU |
|---|---|---|---|---|---|---|
| AH1411(1990) Proof | 3,200 | Value: 7.00 | | | | |

**50 BAISA** **KM# 46** **Weight:** 12.8900 g. **Composition:** 0.9170 Gold .3801 oz. AGW

| Date | Mintage | F | VF | XF | Unc | BU |
|---|---|---|---|---|---|---|
| AH1392(1972) | 200 | — | — | — | 200 | — |
| AH1392(1972) Proof | 50 | Value: 250 | | | | |
| AH1394(1974) Proof | 250 | Value: 200 | | | | |
| AH1395(1975) Proof | 250 | Value: 200 | | | | |

**Note:** Struck for presentation purposes

**50 BAISA** **KM# 46a** **Composition:** Copper-Nickel

| Date | Mintage | F | VF | XF | Unc | BU |
|---|---|---|---|---|---|---|
| AH1395(1975) | 2,500,000 | — | 0.30 | 0.60 | 1.50 | — |
| AH1400(1979) | 2,750,000 | — | 0.30 | 0.60 | 1.50 | — |
| AH1406(1985) | 4,000,000 | — | 0.30 | 0.60 | 1.50 | — |
| AH1410(1989) | 4,000,000 | — | 0.30 | 0.60 | 1.50 | — |

**50 BAISA** **KM# 79** **Composition:** Copper-Nickel **Subject:** 20th National Day - Irrigation Canal **Obverse:** National emblem

| Date | Mintage | F | VF | XF | Unc | BU |
|---|---|---|---|---|---|---|
| AH1411(1990) Proof | 3,200 | Value: 8.00 | | | | |

**50 BAISA** **KM# 95** **Composition:** Copper-Nickel **Subject:** U.N. - 50 Years

| Date | Mintage | F | VF | XF | Unc | BU |
|---|---|---|---|---|---|---|
| ND(1995) | — | — | — | — | 3.00 | — |

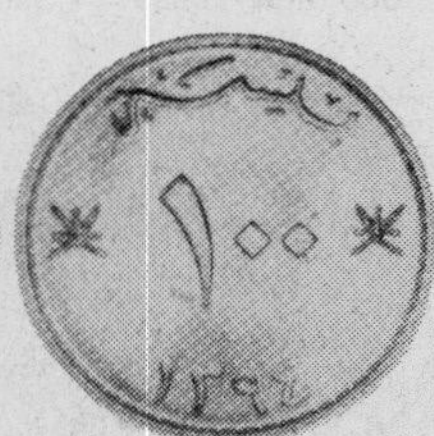

**100 BAISA** **KM# 47** **Weight:** 22.7400 g. **Composition:** 0.9170 Gold .6705 oz. AGW

| Date | Mintage | F | VF | XF | Unc | BU |
|---|---|---|---|---|---|---|
| AH1392(1972) | 200 | — | — | — | 320 | — |
| AH1392(1972) Proof | 50 | Value: 375 | | | | |
| AH1394(1974) Proof | 250 | Value: 320 | | | | |
| AH1395(1975) Proof | 250 | Value: 320 | | | | |

**Note:** Struck for presentation purposes

**100 BAISA** **KM# 68** **Composition:** Copper-Nickel

| Date | Mintage | F | VF | XF | Unc | BU |
|---|---|---|---|---|---|---|
| AH1404(1983) | 4,000,000 | — | 0.40 | 0.80 | 2.25 | — |

**100 BAISA** **KM# 80** **Composition:** Copper-Nickel **Subject:** 20th National Day - Sultan Qaboos University **Obverse:** National emblem

| Date | Mintage | F | VF | XF | Unc | BU |
|---|---|---|---|---|---|---|
| AH1411(1990) Proof | 3,200 | Value: 10.00 | | | | |

**100 BAISA** **KM# 82** **Ring Composition:** Copper-Nickel **Center Composition:** Aluminum-Bronze

| Date | Mintage | F | VF | XF | Unc | BU |
|---|---|---|---|---|---|---|
| AH1411(1990) | — | — | — | — | 5.00 | — |
| AH1411(1990) Proof | 1,000 | Value: 20.00 | | | | |

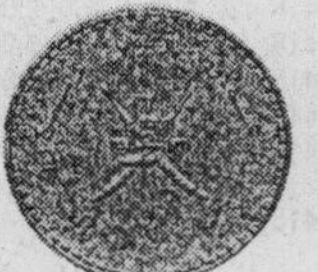

**1/4 OMANI RIAL** **KM# 57** **Weight:** 12.8900 g. **Composition:** 0.9170 Gold .3799 oz. AGW **Subject:** Fort al Hazam **Obverse:** Similar to 1/2 Omani Rial, KM#58 **Reverse:** Fort

| Date | Mintage | F | VF | XF | Unc | BU |
|---|---|---|---|---|---|---|
| AH1397(1976) Proof | 1,000 | Value: 250 | | | | |
| AH1408(1987) Proof | 250 | Value: 400 | | | | |

**1/4 OMANI RIAL** **KM# 66** **Composition:** Aluminum-Bronze

| Date | Mintage | F | VF | XF | Unc | BU |
|---|---|---|---|---|---|---|
| AH1400(1979) | 4,000,000 | — | 0.75 | 1.00 | 2.00 | — |

**1/2 OMANI RIAL** **KM# 48** **Weight:** 25.6000 g. **Composition:** 0.9170 Gold .7548 oz. AGW

| Date | Mintage | F | VF | XF | Unc | BU |
|---|---|---|---|---|---|---|
| AH1392(1972) Proof | 124 | Value: 650 | | | | |
| AH1394(1974) | 250 | — | — | — | 650 | — |
| AH1395(1975) | 250 | — | — | — | 600 | — |

**Note:** Struck for presentation purposes

**1/2 OMANI RIAL** **KM# 58** **Weight:** 19.6700 g. **Composition:** 0.9170 Gold .5797 oz. AGW **Subject:** Fort Mirbat

| Date | Mintage | F | VF | XF | Unc | BU |
|---|---|---|---|---|---|---|
| AH1397(1976) Proof | 1,000 | Value: 350 | | | | |
| AH1408(1987) Proof | 250 | Value: 500 | | | | |

**1/2 OMANI RIAL** **KM# 64** **Composition:** Copper-Nickel **Series:** F.A.O.

| Date | Mintage | F | VF | XF | Unc | BU |
|---|---|---|---|---|---|---|
| AH1398(1977) | 15,000 | — | 2.75 | 3.50 | 5.00 | — |

**1/2 OMANI RIAL** **KM# 67** **Composition:** Aluminum-Bronze

| Date | Mintage | F | VF | XF | Unc | BU |
|---|---|---|---|---|---|---|
| AH1400(1979) | 2,000,000 | — | 2.75 | 3.50 | 5.00 | — |

**1/2 OMANI RIAL** **KM# 69** **Weight:** 19.6700 g. **Composition:** 0.9170 Gold .5800 oz. AGW **Subject:** 10th National Day

| Date | Mintage | F | VF | XF | Unc | BU |
|---|---|---|---|---|---|---|
| AH1400(1979) Proof | 600 | Value: 450 | | | | |

**Note:** Struck for presentation purposes

**1/2 OMANI RIAL** **KM# 87** **Weight:** 10.0000 g. **Composition:** 0.9170 Gold .2947 oz. AGW **Subject:** Youth Year

| Date | Mintage | F | VF | XF | Unc | BU |
|---|---|---|---|---|---|---|
| AH1403(1982) Proof | 1,000 | Value: 225 | | | | |

**1/2 OMANI RIAL** **KM# 85** **Weight:** 28.2800 g. **Composition:** 0.9250 Silver .8411 oz. ASW **Subject:** Year of Agriculture

| Date | Mintage | F | VF | XF | Unc | BU |
|---|---|---|---|---|---|---|
| AH1409(1988) Proof | 300 | Value: 135 | | | | |

**1/2 OMANI RIAL** **KM# 86** **Weight:** 28.2800 g. **Composition:** 0.9250 Silver .8411 oz. ASW **Subject:** Year of Industry

| Date | Mintage | F | VF | XF | Unc | BU |
|---|---|---|---|---|---|---|
| AH1411(1990) Proof | 810 | Value: 110 | | | | |

**1/2 OMANI RIAL** **KM# 134** **Weight:** 15.0000 g. **Composition:** 0.9250 Silver .4461 oz. ASW **Subject:** Youth Year **Obverse:** Crown above crossed swords **Reverse:** Radiant design. Similar to KM#91

| Date | Mintage | F | VF | XF | Unc | BU |
|---|---|---|---|---|---|---|
| AH1413(1992) Proof; Rare | 310 | — | — | — | — | — |

**1/2 OMANI RIAL** **KM# 91** **Weight:** 15.0000 g. **Composition:** 0.9250 Silver .4461 oz. ASW **Subject:** Youth Year **Reverse:** Radiant design

| Date | Mintage | F | VF | XF | Unc | BU |
|---|---|---|---|---|---|---|
| AH1413(1992) Proof | 600 | Value: 85.00 | | | | |

**1/2 OMANI RIAL** **KM# 92** **Weight:** 28.2800 g. **Composition:** 0.9250 Silver .8411 oz. ASW **Subject:** Heritage Year **Reverse:** Radiant design

| Date | Mintage | F | VF | XF | Unc | BU |
|---|---|---|---|---|---|---|
| AH1414(1993) Proof | 840 | Value: 100 | | | | |

**1/2 OMANI RIAL** **KM# 111** **Weight:** 28.2800 g. **Composition:** 0.9250 Silver .8411 oz. ASW **Subject:** 250th Anniversary - Al Bu Sa'id Dynasty

| Date | Mintage | F | VF | XF | Unc | BU |
|---|---|---|---|---|---|---|
| AH1414(1993) Proof | 500 | Value: 110 | | | | |

**OMANI RIAL** **KM# 54** **Weight:** 46.6500 g. **Composition:** 0.9170 Gold 1.3755 oz. AGW

| Date | Mintage | F | VF | XF | Unc | BU |
|---|---|---|---|---|---|---|
| AH1392(1972) Proof | 124 | Value: 750 | | | | |
| AH1394(1974) Proof | 250 | Value: 750 | | | | |
| AH1395(1975) Proof | 250 | Value: 750 | | | | |

**Note:** Struck for presentation purposes

**OMANI RIAL** **KM# 59** **Weight:** 25.6000 g. **Composition:** 0.9170 Gold .7545 oz. AGW **Subject:** Fort Buraimi

| Date | Mintage | F | VF | XF | Unc | BU |
|---|---|---|---|---|---|---|
| AH1397(1976) Proof | 1,000 | Value: 450 | | | | |
| AH1408(1987) Proof | 250 | Value: 600 | | | | |

**OMANI RIAL** **KM# 65** **Weight:** 15.0000 g. **Composition:** 0.5000 Silver .2412 oz. ASW **Series:** F.A.O.

| Date | Mintage | F | VF | XF | Unc | BU |
|---|---|---|---|---|---|---|
| AH1398(1978) | 15,000 | — | — | 7.50 | 11.50 | — |

**OMANI RIAL** **KM# 70** **Weight:** 25.6000 g. **Composition:** 0.9170 Gold .7548 oz. AGW **Subject:** 10th National Day

| Date | Mintage | F | VF | XF | Unc | BU |
|---|---|---|---|---|---|---|
| AH1400(1979) Proof | 300 | Value: 600 | | | | |

**Note:** Struck for presentation purposes

**OMANI RIAL** **KM# 84** **Weight:** 14.8400 g. **Composition:** 0.9250 Silver .4413 oz. ASW **Subject:** Youth Year

| Date | Mintage | F | VF | XF | Unc | BU |
|---|---|---|---|---|---|---|
| AH1403(1982) Proof | 1,200 | Value: 75.00 | | | | |

**OMANI RIAL** **KM# 84a** **Weight:** 20.0000 g. **Composition:** 0.9170 Gold .5894 oz. AGW **Subject:** Youth Year **Size:** 30 mm.

| Date | Mintage | F | VF | XF | Unc | BU |
|---|---|---|---|---|---|---|
| AH1403(1982) Proof | 900 | Value: 350 | | | | |

**OMANI RIAL** **KM# 135** **Weight:** 20.0000 g. **Composition:** 0.9170 Gold .5894 oz. AGW **Subject:** Youth Year **Obverse:** Crown above crossed swords **Note:** Similar to 1/2 Omani Rial, KM#91.

| Date | Mintage | F | VF | XF | Unc | BU |
|---|---|---|---|---|---|---|
| AH1413(1992) Proof; Rare | 110 | — | — | — | — | — |

**OMANI RIAL** **KM# 112** **Weight:** 20.0000 g. **Composition:** 0.9170 Gold .5894 oz. AGW **Subject:** Youth Year **Obverse:** Without crown above crossed swords **Note:** Similar to 1/2 Omani Rial, KM#91.

| Date | Mintage | F | VF | XF | Unc | BU |
|---|---|---|---|---|---|---|
| AH1413(1992) Proof | 900 | Value: 400 | | | | |

**OMANI RIAL** **KM# 93** **Weight:** 39.9400 g. **Composition:** 0.9167 Gold 1.1771 oz. AGW **Subject:** Heritage Year **Note:** Similar to 1/2 Omani Rial, KM#92.

| Date | Mintage | F | VF | XF | Unc | BU |
|---|---|---|---|---|---|---|
| AH1414(1993) Proof | 1,000 | Value: 900 | | | | |

**OMANI RIAL** **KM# 146** **Weight:** 39.9400 g. **Composition:** 0.9167 Gold 1.1771 oz. AGW **Subject:** 250th Anniversary - Al Bu Sa'id Dynasty **Note:** Similar to 1/2 Omani Rial, KM#111.

| Date | Mintage | F | VF | XF | Unc | BU |
|---|---|---|---|---|---|---|
| AH1414(1993) Proof | 500 | Value: 975 | | | | |

**OMANI RIAL** **KM# 96** **Weight:** 10.0000 g. **Composition:** 0.9250 Silver .2974 oz. ASW **Subject:** F.A.O. - 50 Years **Size:** 30 mm.

| Date | Mintage | F | VF | XF | Unc | BU |
|---|---|---|---|---|---|---|
| ND(1995) Proof | — | Value: 30.00 | | | | |

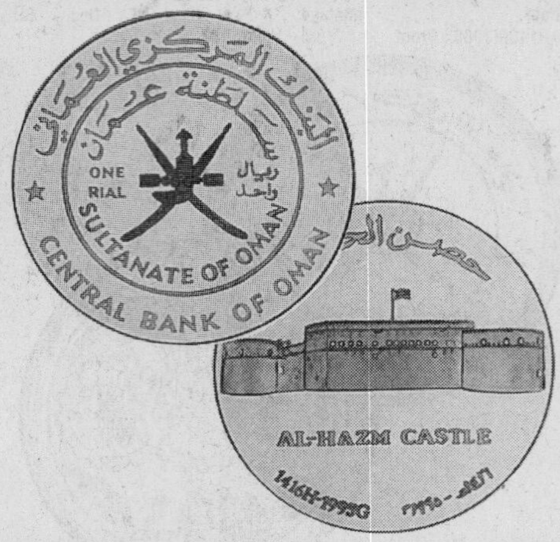


**OMANI RIAL** **KM# 114** **Weight:** 28.2800 g. **Composition:** 0.9250 Silver .8410 oz. ASW **Subject:** Al-Hazm Castle **Obverse:** National arms **Reverse:** Al-Hazm castle

| Date | Mintage | F | VF | XF | Unc | BU |
|---|---|---|---|---|---|---|
| AH1416(1995) Proof | — | Value: 37.50 | | | | |

**OMANI RIAL** **KM# 115** **Weight:** 28.2800 g. **Composition:** 0.9250 Silver .8410 oz. ASW **Subject:** Al-Jalali Fort **Obverse:** National arms **Reverse:** Al-Jalali fort

| Date | Mintage | F | VF | XF | Unc | BU |
|---|---|---|---|---|---|---|
| AH1416(1995) Proof | — | Value: 37.50 | | | | |

**OMANI RIAL** **KM# 116** **Weight:** 28.2800 g. **Composition:** 0.9250 Silver .8410 oz. ASW **Subject:** Al-Mirani Fort **Obverse:** National arms **Reverse:** Al-Mirani fort

| Date | Mintage | F | VF | XF | Unc | BU |
|---|---|---|---|---|---|---|
| AH1416(1995) Proof | — | Value: 37.50 | | | | |

**OMANI RIAL** **KM# 117** **Weight:** 28.2800 g. **Composition:** 0.9250 Silver .8410 oz. ASW **Subject:** Al-Rustaq Fort **Obverse:** National arms **Reverse:** Al-Rustaq fort

| Date | Mintage | F | VF | XF | Unc | BU |
|---|---|---|---|---|---|---|
| AH1416(1995) Proof | — | Value: 37.50 | | | | |

**OMANI RIAL** **KM# 118** **Weight:** 28.2800 g. **Composition:** 0.9250 Silver .8410 oz. ASW **Subject:** Al-Wafi Castle **Obverse:** National arms **Reverse:** Al-Wafi castle

| Date | Mintage | F | VF | XF | Unc | BU |
|---|---|---|---|---|---|---|
| AH1416(1995) Proof | — | Value: 37.50 | | | | |

**OMANI RIAL** **KM# 119** **Weight:** 28.2800 g. **Composition:** 0.9250 Silver .8410 oz. ASW **Subject:** Bait Al-Falaj Fort **Obverse:** National arms **Reverse:** Bait Al-Falaj fort

| Date | Mintage | F | VF | XF | Unc | BU |
|---|---|---|---|---|---|---|
| AH1416(1995) Proof | — | Value: 37.50 | | | | |

**OMANI RIAL** **KM# 120** **Weight:** 28.2800 g. **Composition:** 0.9250 Silver .8410 oz. ASW **Subject:** Bait Al-Na'Aman Castle **Obverse:** National arms **Reverse:** Bait Al-Na'Aman castle

| Date | Mintage | F | VF | XF | Unc | BU |
|---|---|---|---|---|---|---|
| AH1416(1995) Proof | — | Value: 37.50 | | | | |

**OMANI RIAL** **KM# 121** **Weight:** 28.2800 g. **Composition:** 0.9250 Silver .8410 oz. ASW **Subject:** Bahla Fort **Obverse:** National arms **Reverse:** Bahla fort

| Date | Mintage | F | VF | XF | Unc | BU |
|---|---|---|---|---|---|---|
| AH1416(1995) Proof | — | Value: 37.50 | | | | |

**OMANI RIAL** **KM# 122** **Weight:** 28.2800 g. **Composition:** 0.9250 Silver .8410 oz. ASW **Subject:** Barka Fort **Obverse:** National arms **Reverse:** Barka fort

| Date | Mintage | F | VF | XF | Unc | BU |
|---|---|---|---|---|---|---|
| AH1416(1995) Proof | — | Value: 37.50 | | | | |

**OMANI RIAL** **KM# 123** **Weight:** 28.2800 g. **Composition:** 0.9250 Silver .8410 oz. ASW **Subject:** Barkat-Al-Mauz Castle **Obverse:** National arms **Reverse:** Barkat-Al-Mauz castle

| Date | Mintage | F | VF | XF | Unc | BU |
|---|---|---|---|---|---|---|
| AH1416(1995) Proof | — | Value: 37.50 | | | | |

**OMANI RIAL** **KM# 124** **Weight:** 28.2800 g. **Composition:** 0.9250 Silver .8410 oz. ASW **Subject:** Buraimi Fort **Obverse:** National arms **Reverse:** Buraimi fort

| Date | Mintage | F | VF | XF | Unc | BU |
|---|---|---|---|---|---|---|
| AH1416(1995) Proof | — | Value: 37.50 | | | | |

**OMANI RIAL** **KM# 125** **Weight:** 28.2800 g. **Composition:** 0.9250 Silver .8410 oz. ASW **Subject:** Ja'Alan Bani Bu Hassan Castle **Obverse:** National arms **Reverse:** Ja'Alan Bani Bu Hassan castle

| Date | Mintage | F | VF | XF | Unc | BU |
|---|---|---|---|---|---|---|
| AH1416(1995) Proof | — | Value: 37.50 | | | | |

**OMANI RIAL** **KM# 126** **Weight:** 28.2800 g. **Composition:** 0.9250 Silver .8410 oz. ASW **Subject:** Jabrin Castle **Obverse:** National arms **Reverse:** Jabrin castle

| Date | Mintage | F | VF | XF | Unc | BU |
|---|---|---|---|---|---|---|
| AH1416(1995) Proof | — | Value: 37.50 | | | | |

**OMANI RIAL** **KM# 127** **Weight:** 28.2800 g. **Composition:** 0.9250 Silver .8410 oz. ASW **Subject:** Khasab Fort **Obverse:** National arms **Reverse:** Khasab fort

| Date | Mintage | F | VF | XF | Unc | BU |
|---|---|---|---|---|---|---|
| AH1416(1995) Proof | — | Value: 37.50 | | | | |

**OMANI RIAL** **KM# 128** **Weight:** 28.2800 g. **Composition:** 0.9250 Silver .8410 pz. ASW **Subject:** Matrah Fort **Obverse:** National arms **Reverse:** Matrah fort

| Date | Mintage | F | VF | XF | Unc | BU |
|---|---|---|---|---|---|---|
| AH1416(1995) Proof | — | Value: 37.50 | | | | |

**OMANI RIAL** **KM# 129** **Weight:** 28.2800 g. **Composition:** 0.9250 Silver .8410 oz. ASW **Subject:** Mirbat Castle **Obverse:** National arms **Reverse:** Mirbat castle

| Date | Mintage | F | VF | XF | Unc | BU |
|---|---|---|---|---|---|---|
| AH1416(1995) Proof | — | Value: 37.50 | | | | |

**OMANI RIAL** **KM# 130** **Weight:** 28.2800 g. **Composition:** 0.9250 Silver .8410 oz. ASW **Subject:** Nakhl Fort **Obverse:** National arms **Reverse:** Nakhl fort

| Date | Mintage | F | VF | XF | Unc | BU |
|---|---|---|---|---|---|---|
| AH1416(1995) Proof | — | Value: 37.50 | | | | |

**OMANI RIAL** **KM# 131** **Weight:** 28.2800 g. **Composition:** 0.9250 Silver .8410 oz. ASW **Subject:** Nizwa Fort **Obverse:** National arms **Reverse:** Nizwa fort

| Date | Mintage | F | VF | XF | Unc | BU |
|---|---|---|---|---|---|---|
| AH1416(1995) Proof | — | Value: 37.50 | | | | |

**OMANI RIAL** **KM# 132** **Weight:** 28.2800 g. **Composition:** 0.9250 Silver .8410 oz. ASW **Subject:** Sohar Fort **Obverse:** National arms **Reverse:** Sohar fort

| Date | Mintage | F | VF | XF | Unc | BU |
|---|---|---|---|---|---|---|
| AH1416(1995) Proof | — | Value: 37.50 | | | | |

**OMANI RIAL** **KM# 133** **Weight:** 28.2800 g. **Composition:** 0.9250 Silver .8410 oz. ASW **Subject:** Sur Castle **Obverse:** National arms **Reverse:** Sur castle

| Date | Mintage | F | VF | XF | Unc | BU |
|---|---|---|---|---|---|---|
| AH1416(1995) Proof | — | Value: 37.50 | | | | |

**OMANI RIAL** **KM# 140** **Weight:** 13.9000 g. **Composition:** 0.9250 Silver .4134 oz. ASW **Subject:** 25th National Day Anniversary - Burj Al Nahda

| Date | Mintage | F | VF | XF | Unc | BU |
|---|---|---|---|---|---|---|
| 1995 Proof | — | Value: 65.00 | | | | |

**OMANI RIAL** **KM# 140a** **Weight:** 22.8000 g. **Composition:** 0.9160 Gold .6715 oz. AGW

| Date | Mintage | F | VF | XF | Unc | BU |
|---|---|---|---|---|---|---|
| 1995 Proof | — | Value: 450 | | | | |

**OMANI RIAL** **KM# 145** **Weight:** 28.2800 g. **Composition:** 0.9250 Silver .8410 oz. ASW **Subject:** U.N. - 50 Years **Size:** 30 mm.

| Date | Mintage | F | VF | XF | Unc | BU |
|---|---|---|---|---|---|---|
| ND(1995) Proof | 25,000 | Value: 40.00 | | | | |

**OMANI RIAL** **KM# 101** **Weight:** 31.4700 g. **Composition:** 0.9250 Silver .9359 oz. ASW **Subject:** 26th National Day Anniversary - Sultanah **Obverse:** Omani arms

| Date | Mintage | F | VF | XF | Unc | BU |
|---|---|---|---|---|---|---|
| 1996 Proof | — | Value: 45.00 | | | | |

**OMANI RIAL** **KM# 102** **Weight:** 37.8000 g. **Composition:** 0.9160 Gold 1.1132 oz. AGW **Subject:** 26th National Day Anniversary - Sultanah **Obverse:** Omani arms

| Date | Mintage | F | VF | XF | Unc | BU |
|---|---|---|---|---|---|---|
| 1996 Proof | — | Value: 625 | | | | |

**OMANI RIAL** **KM# 103** **Weight:** 28.2800 g. **Composition:** 0.9250 Silver .8411 oz. ASW **Subject:** 26th National Day Anniversary - Al Battil **Obverse:** Omani arms

| Date | Mintage | F | VF | XF | Unc | BU |
|---|---|---|---|---|---|---|
| 1996 Proof | — | Value: 35.00 | | | | |

**OMANI RIAL** **KM# 104** **Weight:** 28.2800 g. **Composition:** 0.9250 Silver .8411 oz. ASW **Subject:** 26th National Day Anniversary - Al Badan **Obverse:** Omani arms

| Date | Mintage | F | VF | XF | Unc | BU |
|---|---|---|---|---|---|---|
| 1996 Proof | — | Value: 35.00 | | | | |

**OMANI RIAL** **KM# 105** **Weight:** 28.2800 g. **Composition:** 0.9250 Silver .8411 oz. ASW **Subject:** 26th National Day Anniversary - Al Baglah **Obverse:** Omani arms

| Date | Mintage | F | VF | XF | Unc | BU |
|---|---|---|---|---|---|---|
| 1996 Proof | — | Value: 35.00 | | | | |

**OMANI RIAL** **KM# 106** **Weight:** 28.2800 g. **Composition:** 0.9250 Silver .8411 oz. ASW **Subject:** 26th National Day Anniversary - Al Boum **Obverse:** Omani arms

| Date | Mintage | F | VF | XF | Unc | BU |
|---|---|---|---|---|---|---|
| 1996 Proof | — | Value: 35.00 | | | | |

**OMANI RIAL** **KM# 107** **Weight:** 28.2800 g. **Composition:** 0.9250 Silver .8411 oz. ASW **Subject:** 26th National Day Anniversary - Al Jalbout **Obverse:** Omani arms

| Date | Mintage | F | VF | XF | Unc | BU |
|---|---|---|---|---|---|---|
| 1996 Proof | — | Value: 35.00 | | | | |

**OMANI RIAL** **KM# 108** **Weight:** 28.2800 g. **Composition:** 0.9250 Silver .8411 oz. ASW **Subject:** 26th National Day Anniversary - Al Sanbuq **Obverse:** Omani arms

| Date | Mintage | F | VF | XF | Unc | BU |
|---|---|---|---|---|---|---|
| 1996 Proof | — | Value: 35.00 | | | | |

**OMANI RIAL** **KM# 109** **Weight:** 28.2800 g. **Composition:** 0.9250 Silver .8411 oz. ASW **Subject:** 26th National Day Anniversary - Al Ghanjah **Obverse:** Omani arms

| Date | Mintage | F | VF | XF | Unc | BU |
|---|---|---|---|---|---|---|
| 1996 Proof | — | Value: 35.00 | | | | |

**OMANI RIAL** **KM# 110** **Weight:** 28.2800 g. **Composition:** 0.9250 Silver .8411 oz. ASW **Subject:** 26th National Day Anniversary - Al Lateen **Obverse:** Omani arms

| Date | Mintage | F | VF | XF | Unc | BU |
|---|---|---|---|---|---|---|
| 1996 Proof | — | Value: 35.00 | | | | |

**OMANI RIAL** **KM# 136** **Weight:** 28.2800 g. **Composition:** 0.9250 Silver .8411 oz. ASW **Subject:** 27th National Day Anniversary - Al Nahdha **Reverse:** Al Nahdha Tower, coconut tree and Frankincense tree from the Dhofar Region. **Size:** 38.6 mm. **Note:** Struck by Royal Mint - London.

| Date | Mintage | F | VF | XF | Unc | BU |
|---|---|---|---|---|---|---|
| AH1417(1996) Proof | — | Value: 45.00 | | | | |

**OMANI RIAL** **KM# 136a** **Weight:** 37.8000 g. **Composition:** 0.9167 Gold 1.1141 oz. AGW **Subject:** 27th National Day Anniversary - Al Nahdha **Reverse:** Al Nahdha Tower, coconut tree and Frankincense tree from the Dhofar Region. **Size:** 38.6 mm. **Note:** Struck by Royal Mint - London.

| Date | Mintage | F | VF | XF | Unc | BU |
|---|---|---|---|---|---|---|
| AH1417(1996) Proof | — | Value: 650 | | | | |

**OMANI RIAL** KM# 138 **Weight:** 28.2800 g. **Composition:** 0.9250 Silver .8411 oz. ASW **Series:** World Wildlife Fund **Reverse:** Leopard

| Date | Mintage | F | VF | XF | Unc | BU |
|---|---|---|---|---|---|---|
| 1997 Proof | 15,000 | Value: 40.00 | | | | |

**OMANI RIAL** KM# 113 **Weight:** 28.2800 g. **Composition:** 0.9250 Silver .8411 oz. ASW **Series:** World Wildlife Fund **Obverse:** National emblem **Reverse:** Mountain gazelle **Size:** 38.6 mm. **Note:** Struck at Royal Norwegian Mint.

| Date | Mintage | F | VF | XF | Unc | BU |
|---|---|---|---|---|---|---|
| 1997 Proof | 15,000 | Value: 40.00 | | | | |

**OMANI RIAL** KM# 139 **Weight:** 28.2800 g. **Composition:** 0.9250 Silver .8411 oz. ASW **Subject:** 28th National Day Anniversary - Private Sector Year **Size:** 38.6 mm.

| Date | Mintage | F | VF | XF | Unc | BU |
|---|---|---|---|---|---|---|
| AH1418(1997) Proof | — | Value: 45.00 | | | | |

**OMANI RIAL** KM# 139a **Weight:** 37.8000 g. **Composition:** 0.9167 Gold 1.1141 oz. AGW **Subject:** 28th National Day Anniversary - Private Sector Year **Size:** 38.6 mm.

| Date | Mintage | F | VF | XF | Unc | BU |
|---|---|---|---|---|---|---|
| AH1418(1997) | — | — | — | — | 650 | — |

**OMANI RIAL** KM# 149 **Weight:** 28.2800 g. **Composition:** 0.9250 Silver .8410 oz. ASW **Subject:** 29th National Day Anniversary - 1420/1999 **Obverse:** National arms. **Reverse:** Palm tree (Khalas) and camels caravan. **Size:** 38.61 mm. **Note:** Struck by Royal Mint - London.

| Date | Mintage | F | VF | XF | Unc | BU |
|---|---|---|---|---|---|---|
| ND(1999) | — | — | — | — | — | — |

**OMANI RIAL** KM# 149a **Weight:** 37.8000 g. **Composition:** 0.9167 Gold 1.1141 oz. AGW **Subject:** 29th National Day Anniversary - 1420/1999 **Obverse:** National arms. **Reverse:** Palm tree (Khalas) and camels caravan. **Size:** 38.61 mm. **Note:** Struck by Royal Mint - London.

| Date | Mintage | F | VF | XF | Unc | BU |
|---|---|---|---|---|---|---|
| ND(1999) | — | — | — | — | — | — |

**OMANI RIAL** KM# 148 **Weight:** 27.8700 g. **Composition:** 0.9250 Silver .8288 oz. ASW **Subject:** Central Bank's 25th Anniversary **Obverse:** National arms **Reverse:** Central Bank of Oman **Size:** 38.6 mm.

| Date | Mintage | F | VF | XF | Unc | BU |
|---|---|---|---|---|---|---|
| ND(2000) Proof | 500 | — | — | — | 100 | — |

**OMANI RIAL** KM# 147 **Weight:** 27.8700 g. **Composition:** 0.9250 Silver .8288 oz. ASW **Subject:** 30th National Day **Obverse:** National arms **Reverse:** Factory and various items **Edge:** Reeded **Size:** 38.61 mm. **Note:** Struck by Huguenin & Kramer - Switzerland.

| Date | Mintage | F | VF | XF | Unc | BU |
|---|---|---|---|---|---|---|
| 2000 Proof | 300 | — | — | — | 100 | — |

**OMANI RIAL** KM# 147a **Weight:** 37.8000 g. **Composition:** 0.9160 Gold 1.1141 oz. AGW **Subject:** 30th National Day **Obverse:** National arms. **Reverse:** Factory and various items. **Edge:** Reeded. **Size:** 38.61 mm. **Note:** Struck by Huguenin & Kramer - Switzerland.

| Date | Mintage | F | VF | XF | Unc | BU |
|---|---|---|---|---|---|---|
| 2000 | — | — | — | — | — | — |

**2 OMANI RIALS** KM# 81 **Weight:** 20.0000 g. **Composition:** 0.9250 Silver .5948 oz. ASW **Subject:** 20th National Day - Sultan Sa'id

| Date | Mintage | F | VF | XF | Unc | BU |
|---|---|---|---|---|---|---|
| AH1411(1990) Proof | 3,200 | Value: 50.00 | | | | |

**2-1/2 OMANI RIALS** KM# 60 **Weight:** 28.2800 g. **Composition:** 0.9250 Silver .8411 oz. ASW **Subject:** Conservation **Reverse:** Caracal Lynx

| Date | Mintage | F | VF | XF | Unc | BU |
|---|---|---|---|---|---|---|
| AH1397(1976) | 4,539 | — | — | — | 25.00 | — |
| AH1397(1976) Proof | 4,407 | Value: 30.00 | | | | |

**2-1/2 OMANI RIALS** KM# 71 **Weight:** 28.2800 g. **Composition:** 0.9250 Silver .8411 oz. ASW **Obverse:** Crown above crossed swords **Reverse:** Verreaux's eagle

| Date | Mintage | F | VF | XF | Unc | BU |
|---|---|---|---|---|---|---|
| AH1407(1986) Proof; Rare | — | — | — | — | — | — |

**Note:** Struck for presentation purposes

**2-1/2 OMANI RIALS** KM# 73 **Weight:** 28.2800 g. **Composition:** 0.9250 Silver .8411 oz. ASW **Series:** World Wildlife Fund **Reverse:** Verreaux's eagle

| Date | Mintage | F | VF | XF | Unc | BU |
|---|---|---|---|---|---|---|
| AH1407(1987) Proof | 25,000 | Value: 30.00 | | | | |

**2-1/2 OMANI RIALS** KM# 83 **Weight:** 28.2800 g. **Composition:** 0.9250 Silver .8411 oz. ASW **Series:** Save the Children

| Date | Mintage | F | VF | XF | Unc | BU |
|---|---|---|---|---|---|---|
| AH1411(1990) Proof | Est. 20,000 | Value: 37.50 | | | | |

**2-1/2 OMANI RIALS** **KM# 97** **Weight:** 28.2800 g. **Composition:** 0.9250 Silver .8411 oz. ASW **Obverse:** Similar to KM#71 **Reverse:** KM#83

| Date | Mintage | F | VF | XF | Unc | BU |
|---|---|---|---|---|---|---|
| AH1411(1990) Proof; Rare | — | — | — | — | — | — |

**Note:** Struck for presentation purposes

**5 OMANI RIALS** **KM# 61** **Weight:** 35.0000 g. **Composition:** 0.9250 Silver 1.0409 oz. ASW **Subject:** Conservation **Reverse:** Arabian White Oryx

| Date | Mintage | F | VF | XF | Unc | BU |
|---|---|---|---|---|---|---|
| AH1397(1976) | 4,359 | — | — | — | 27.50 | — |
| AH1397(1976) Proof | 4,401 | Value: 35.00 | | | | |

**5 OMANI RIALS** **KM# 62** **Weight:** 45.6500 g. **Composition:** 0.9170 Gold 1.3454 oz. AGW **Subject:** 7th Anniversary - Reign of Sultan Qabus bin Sa'id

| Date | Mintage | F | VF | XF | Unc | BU |
|---|---|---|---|---|---|---|
| AH1397(1976) Proof | 1,000 | Value: 850 | | | | |
| AH1408(1987) Proof | 250 | Value: 950 | | | | |

**5 OMANI RIALS** **KM# 89** **Weight:** 20.0000 g. **Composition:** 0.9170 Gold .5894 oz. AGW **Subject:** Agricultural Year **Note:** Similar to 1/2 Omani Rial, KM#85.

| Date | Mintage | F | VF | XF | Unc | BU |
|---|---|---|---|---|---|---|
| AH1409(1988) Proof | 200 | Value: 350 | | | | |

**5 OMANI RIALS** **KM# 90** **Weight:** 20.0000 g. **Composition:** 0.9170 Gold .5894 oz. AGW **Subject:** Industry Year **Note:** Similar to 1/2 Omani Rial, KM#86.

| Date | Mintage | F | VF | XF | Unc | BU |
|---|---|---|---|---|---|---|
| AH1411(1990) Proof | 410 | Value: 350 | | | | |

**5 OMANI RIALS** **KM# 141** **Weight:** 18.8000 g. **Composition:** 0.9250 Silver .5591 oz. ASW **Subject:** 25th National Day Anniversary - Burj Al Sahwa

| Date | Mintage | F | VF | XF | Unc | BU |
|---|---|---|---|---|---|---|
| 1995 Proof | — | Value: 75.00 | | | | |

**5 OMANI RIALS** **KM# 141a** **Weight:** 31.0000 g. **Composition:** 0.9160 Gold .9130 oz. AGW

| Date | Mintage | F | VF | XF | Unc | BU |
|---|---|---|---|---|---|---|
| 1995 Proof | — | Value: 550 | | | | |

**10 OMANI RIALS** **KM# 142** **Weight:** 23.2000 g. **Composition:** 0.9250 Silver .6900 oz. ASW **Subject:** 25th National Day Anniversary - Central Bank

| Date | Mintage | F | VF | XF | Unc | BU |
|---|---|---|---|---|---|---|
| 1995 Proof | — | Value: 85.00 | | | | |

**10 OMANI RIALS** **KM# 142a** **Weight:** 36.4000 g. **Composition:** 0.9160 Gold 1.0720 oz. AGW

| Date | Mintage | F | VF | XF | Unc | BU |
|---|---|---|---|---|---|---|
| 1995 Proof | — | Value: 650 | | | | |

**15 OMANI RIALS** **KM# 49** **Weight:** 7.9900 g. **Composition:** 0.9170 Gold .2355 oz. AGW

| Date | Mintage | F | VF | XF | Unc | BU |
|---|---|---|---|---|---|---|
| AH1392(1972) Proof | 124 | Value: 350 | | | | |
| AH1394(1974) | 300 | — | — | — | 200 | — |

**Note:** Struck for presentation purposes

**15 OMANI RIALS** **KM# 55** **Weight:** 7.9900 g. **Composition:** 0.9170 Gold .2355 oz. AGW **Subject:** 10th National Day

| Date | Mintage | F | VF | XF | Unc | BU |
|---|---|---|---|---|---|---|
| AH1400(1979) Proof | 1,000 | Value: 400 | | | | |

**Note:** Struck for presentation purposes

**15 OMANI RIALS** **KM# 56** **Weight:** 20.0000 g. **Composition:** 0.9170 Gold .5897 oz. AGW **Subject:** 15th Anniversary - Reign of Sultan

| Date | Mintage | F | VF | XF | Unc | BU |
|---|---|---|---|---|---|---|
| AH1406(1985) Proof | 2,000 | Value: 350 | | | | |

**15 OMANI RIALS** **KM# 56a** **Weight:** 31.0100 g. **Composition:** 0.9170 Gold .9144 oz. AGW

| Date | Mintage | F | VF | XF | Unc | BU |
|---|---|---|---|---|---|---|
| AH1406(1985) Proof | 200 | Value: 800 | | | | |

**20 OMANI RIALS** **KM# 98** **Weight:** 20.0000 g. **Composition:** 0.9170 Gold .5897 oz. AGW **Subject:** 20th National Day - Sultan Sa'id **Note:** Similar to 2 Omani Rials, KM#81.

| Date | Mintage | F | VF | XF | Unc | BU |
|---|---|---|---|---|---|---|
| AH1411(1990) Proof | 1,200 | Value: 375 | | | | |

**20 OMANI RIALS** **KM# 137** **Weight:** 65.3700 g. **Composition:** 0.9170 Gold 1.9273 oz. AGW **Subject:** 20th Anniversary of Sultan's Reign

| Date | Mintage | F | VF | XF | Unc | BU |
|---|---|---|---|---|---|---|
| ND(AH1411) (1990) Proof | — | — | — | — | — | — |

**20 OMANI RIALS** **KM# 143** **Weight:** 27.4000 g. **Composition:** 0.9250 Silver .8149 oz. ASW **Subject:** 25th National Day Anniversary **Reverse:** Emblem

| Date | Mintage | F | VF | XF | Unc | BU |
|---|---|---|---|---|---|---|
| 1995 Proof | — | Value: 95.00 | | | | |

**20 OMANI RIALS** **KM# 143a** **Weight:** 41.2000 g. **Composition:** 0.9160 Gold 1.2133 oz. AGW

| Date | Mintage | F | VF | XF | Unc | BU |
|---|---|---|---|---|---|---|
| 1995 Proof | — | Value: 750 | | | | |

**25 OMANI RIALS** **KM# 74** **Weight:** 10.0000 g. **Composition:** 0.9170 Gold .2947 oz. AGW **Series:** World Wildlife Fund **Reverse:** Masked Booby

| Date | Mintage | F | VF | XF | Unc | BU |
|---|---|---|---|---|---|---|
| AH1407(1986) Proof | 5,000 | Value: 165 | | | | |

**25 OMANI RIALS** KM# 99 **Weight:** 10.0000 g. **Composition:** 0.9170 Gold .2947 oz. AGW **Obverse:** Crown above crossed swords

| Date | Mintage | F | VF | XF | Unc | BU |
|---|---|---|---|---|---|---|
| AH1407(1986) Proof; Rare | — | — | — | — | — | — |

**Note:** Struck for presentation purposes

**25 OMANI RIALS** KM# 88 **Weight:** 10.0000 g. **Composition:** 0.9170 Gold .2947 oz. AGW **Series:** Save the Children **Reverse:** School Master, Pupils

| Date | Mintage | F | VF | XF | Unc | BU |
|---|---|---|---|---|---|---|
| AH1411(1990) Proof | Est. 3,000 | Value: 200 | | | | |

**25 OMANI RIALS** KM# 100 **Weight:** 10.0000 g. **Composition:** 0.9170 Gold .2947 oz. AGW **Obverse:** Crown above crossed swords

| Date | Mintage | F | VF | XF | Unc | BU |
|---|---|---|---|---|---|---|
| AH1411(1990) Proof; Rare | — | — | — | — | — | — |

**Note:** Struck for presentation purposes

**25 OMANI RIALS** KM# 144 **Weight:** 31.7000 g. **Composition:** 0.9250 Silver .9427 oz. ASW **Subject:** 25th National Day Anniversary - Sultan Qaboos bin Said **Reverse:** Multicolor portrait

| Date | Mintage | F | VF | XF | Unc | BU |
|---|---|---|---|---|---|---|
| 1995 Proof | — | Value: 100 | | | | |

**25 OMANI RIALS** KM# 144a **Weight:** 50.2000 g. **Composition:** 0.9160 Gold 1.4784 oz. AGW

| Date | Mintage | F | VF | XF | Unc | BU |
|---|---|---|---|---|---|---|
| 1995 Proof | — | Value: 900 | | | | |

**75 OMANI RIALS** KM# 63 **Weight:** 33.4370 g. **Composition:** 0.9000 Gold .9676 oz. AGW **Subject:** Conservation **Reverse:** Arabian Tahr

| Date | Mintage | F | VF | XF | Unc | BU |
|---|---|---|---|---|---|---|
| AH1397(1976) | 825 | — | — | — | 475 | — |
| AH1397(1976) Proof | 325 | Value: 700 | | | | |

## MEDALLIC COINAGE

Government in Exile

A series of 3 silver and 4 gold medallic coins were produced in AH1391/1971AD and are inscribed STATE OF OMAN (Dawlat Uman). These were issued by the exile government of Imam Ghalib Ibn Ali in Dammam, Saudi Arabia, and distributed from a post box in Amman, Jordan. The Imamate had enjoyed effective autonomy in the interior of Oman from 1920-54, at which time the Sultan resumed direct control. Imamist forces in Oman were finally driven out in 1959. The Imam has been in exile since 1955.

**5 RYALS** KM# M1 **Weight:** 4.0000 g. **Composition:** 0.9250 Silver .1190 oz. ASW **Obverse:** Star and crescent above crossed flags and 2 swords **Reverse:** Flower between English and Arabic denominations

| Date | Mintage | F | VF | XF | Unc | BU |
|---|---|---|---|---|---|---|
| AH1391(1971) | 4,000 | — | — | — | 25.00 | — |

**10 RYALS** KM# M2 **Weight:** 8.0000 g. **Composition:** 0.9250 Silver .2379 oz. ASW **Obverse:** Star and crescent above crossed flags and 2 swords **Reverse:** Secretary bird with snake in claws

| Date | Mintage | F | VF | XF | Unc | BU |
|---|---|---|---|---|---|---|
| AH1391(1971) | 4,000 | — | — | — | 35.00 | — |

**20 RYALS** KM# M3 **Weight:** 16.0000 g. **Composition:** 0.9250 Silver .4759 oz. ASW **Obverse:** Star and crescent above crossed flags and 2 swords **Reverse:** Mosque

| Date | Mintage | F | VF | XF | Unc | BU |
|---|---|---|---|---|---|---|
| AH1391(1971) | 4,000 | — | — | — | 50.00 | — |

**50 RYALS** KM# M4 **Weight:** 4.0000 g. **Composition:** 0.9170 Gold .1179 oz. AGW **Obverse:** Star and crescent above crossed flags and 2 swords **Reverse:** Sailboat and rocky coast

| Date | Mintage | F | VF | XF | Unc | BU |
|---|---|---|---|---|---|---|
| AH1391(1971) | 4,000 | — | — | — | 175 | — |

**100 RYALS** KM# M5 **Weight:** 8.0000 g. **Composition:** 0.9170 Gold .2359 oz. AGW **Obverse:** Star and crescent above crossed flags and 2 swords **Reverse:** Flower

| Date | Mintage | F | VF | XF | Unc | BU |
|---|---|---|---|---|---|---|
| AH1391(1971) | 4,000 | — | — | — | 225 | — |

**200 RYALS** KM# M6 **Weight:** 16.0000 g. **Composition:** 0.9170 Gold .4718 oz. AGW **Obverse:** Star and crescent above crossed flags and 2 swords **Reverse:** Secretary bird

| Date | Mintage | F | VF | XF | Unc | BU |
|---|---|---|---|---|---|---|
| AH1391(1971) | 4,000 | — | — | — | 350 | — |

**500 RYALS** KM# M7 **Weight:** 40.0000 g. **Composition:** 0.9170 Gold 1.1794 oz. AGW **Obverse:** Star and crescent above crossed flags and 2 swords **Reverse:** Mosque

| Date | Mintage | F | VF | XF | Unc | BU |
|---|---|---|---|---|---|---|
| AH1391(1971) | 4,000 | — | — | — | 850 | — |

## PROOF SETS

| KM# | Date | Mintage | Identification | Issue Price | Mkt Val |
|---|---|---|---|---|---|
| PS1 | AH1394 (3) | 250 | KM#45-47 | — | 620 |
| PS2 | AH1395 (3) | 250 | KM#45-47 | — | 620 |
| PS3 | AH1397 (3) | — | KM#60, 61, 63 | 780 | 765 |
| PS4 | AH1397 (2) | — | KM#60, 61 | 60.00 | 65.00 |
| PS5 | AH1411 (6) | 3,200 | KM#76-81 | 84.50 | 95.00 |
| PS6 | AH1416 (20) | — | KM#114-133 | — | 750 |
| PSA6 | 1996 (2) | — | KM#101-102 | 640 | 670 |
| PS7 | 1996 (4) | — | KM#103-106 | 125 | 140 |
| PS9 | 1996 (8) | — | KM#103-110 | 247 | 280 |
| PS8 | 1996 (4) | — | KM#107-110 | 125 | 140 |

The Islamic Republic of Pakistan, located on the Indian subcontinent between India and Afghanistan, has an area of 310,404 sq. mi. (803,940 sq. km.) and a population of130 million. Capital: Islamabad. Pakistan is mainly an agricultural land although the industrial base is expanding rapidly. Yarn, textiles, cotton, rice, medical instruments, sports equipment and leather are exported.

Afghan and Turkish intrusions into northern India between the 11th and 18th centuries resulted in large numbers of Indians being converted to Islam. The idea of a separate Moslem state independent of Hindu India developed in the 1930's and was agreed to by Britain in1946. The Islamic majority areas of India, consisting of the separate geographic entities known as East and West Pakistan, achieved self-government as Pakistan, with dominion status in the British Commonwealth, when the British withdrew from India on Aug. 14, 1947. Pakistan became a republic in 1956. When a basic constitutional crisis initiated by the election of Dec. 1, 1970 - the first direct general election in Pakistani history - could not be resolved by the leaders of East and West Pakistan, the East Pakistanis seceded from the Islamic Republic of Pakistan (March 26, 1971) and formed the independent People's Republic of Bangladesh. After many years of vacillation between civilian and military regimes, the people of Pakistan held a free national election in November, 1988 and installed the first of a series of democratic governments under a parliamentary system.

**TITLE**

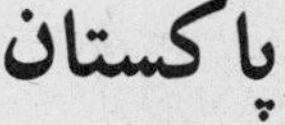


Pakistan

**MONETARY SYSTEM**
3 Pies = 1 Pice
4 Pice = 1 Anna
16 Annas = 1 Rupee

## ISLAMIC REPUBLIC

### STANDARD COINAGE

3 Pies = 1 Pice; 4 Pice = 1 Anna;
16 Annas = 1 Rupee

**PIE** KM# 11 **Composition:** Bronze

| Date | Mintage | F | VF | XF | Unc | BU |
|---|---|---|---|---|---|---|
| 1951 | 2,950,000 | 0.25 | 0.50 | 1.00 | 2.50 | — |
| 1951 Proof | — | Value: 4.00 | | | | |
| 1953 | 110,000 | 0.25 | 0.75 | 1.50 | 3.00 | — |
| 1953 Proof | — | Value: 5.00 | | | | |
| 1955 | 211,000 | 0.25 | 0.75 | 1.50 | 3.00 | — |
| 1955 Proof | — | Value: 15.00 | | | | |
| 1956 | 3,390,000 | 0.25 | 0.50 | 1.00 | 2.50 | — |
| 1957 | — | 0.25 | 0.50 | 1.00 | 2.50 | — |

**PICE** KM# 1 **Composition:** Bronze **Note:** Varieties exist.

| Date | Mintage | F | VF | XF | Unc | BU |
|---|---|---|---|---|---|---|
| 1948 | 101,070,000 | 0.20 | 0.40 | 0.75 | 1.50 | — |
| 1948 Proof | — | Value: 2.00 | | | | |
| 1949 | 25,740,000 | 0.20 | 0.40 | 0.75 | 1.50 | — |
| 1949 Proof | — | Value: 2.00 | | | | |
| 1951 | 14,050,000 | 0.20 | 0.45 | 0.85 | 1.75 | — |
| 1952 | 41,680,000 | 0.20 | 0.40 | 0.75 | 1.50 | — |

**PICE** KM# 12 **Composition:** Nickel-Brass

| Date | Mintage | F | VF | XF | Unc | BU |
|---|---|---|---|---|---|---|
| 1953 | 47,540,000 | 0.15 | 0.30 | 0.50 | 1.00 | — |
| 1953 Proof | — | Value: 1.50 | | | | |
| 1955 | 31,280,000 | 0.15 | 0.30 | 0.50 | 1.00 | — |
| 1956 | 9,710,000 | 0.20 | 0.35 | 0.60 | 1.15 | — |
| 1957 | 57,790,000 | 0.15 | 0.30 | 0.50 | 1.00 | — |
| 1958 | 52,470,000 | 0.15 | 0.30 | 0.50 | 1.00 | — |
| 1959 | 41,620,000 | 0.15 | 0.30 | 0.50 | 1.00 | — |

**1/2 ANNA** KM# 2 **Composition:** Copper-Nickel

| Date | Mintage | F | VF | XF | Unc | BU |
|---|---|---|---|---|---|---|
| 1948 | 73,920,000 | 0.15 | 0.30 | 0.50 | 1.00 | — |
| 1948 Proof | — | Value: 1.50 | | | | |
| 1949 Dot after date | 16,940,000 | 0.20 | 0.35 | 0.60 | 1.15 | — |
| 1951 | 75,360,000 | 0.15 | 0.30 | 0.50 | 1.00 | — |

**1/2 ANNA** KM# 13 **Composition:** Nickel-Brass

| Date | Mintage | F | VF | XF | Unc | BU |
|---|---|---|---|---|---|---|
| 1953 | 8,350,000 | 0.20 | 0.35 | 0.60 | 1.15 | — |
| 1953 Proof | — | Value: 1.50 | | | | |
| 1955 | 17,310,000 | 0.15 | 0.30 | 0.50 | 1.00 | — |
| 1958 | 38,250,000 | 0.15 | 0.30 | 0.50 | 1.00 | — |

**ANNA** KM# 3 **Composition:** Copper-Nickel

| Date | Mintage | F | VF | XF | Unc | BU |
|---|---|---|---|---|---|---|
| 1948 | 73,460,000 | 0.15 | 0.30 | 0.50 | 1.00 | — |
| 1948 Proof | — | Value: 1.50 | | | | |
| 1949 | 11,140,000 | 0.20 | 0.35 | 0.60 | 1.15 | — |
| 1949 Dot after date | — | 0.15 | 0.30 | 0.50 | 1.00 | — |

**Note:** Mintage included with KM#8.

| Date | Mintage | F | VF | XF | Unc | BU |
|---|---|---|---|---|---|---|
| 1951 | 40,800,000 | 0.15 | 0.30 | 0.50 | 1.00 | — |
| 1952 | 15,430,000 | 0.20 | 0.35 | 0.60 | 1.15 | — |

**ANNA** KM# 8 **Composition:** Copper-Nickel

| Date | Mintage | F | VF | XF | Unc | BU |
|---|---|---|---|---|---|---|
| 1950 | 94,830,000 | 3.00 | 4.50 | 6.50 | 10.00 | — |
| 1950 Proof | — | Value: 15.00 | | | | |

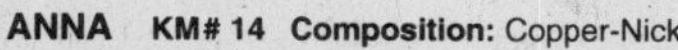

**ANNA** KM# 14 **Composition:** Copper-Nickel

| Date | Mintage | F | VF | XF | Unc | BU |
|---|---|---|---|---|---|---|
| 1953 | 9,350,000 | 0.15 | 0.30 | 0.50 | 1.00 | — |
| 1953 Proof | — | Value: 1.50 | | | | |
| 1954 | 35,360,000 | 0.15 | 0.30 | 0.50 | 1.00 | — |
| 1955 | 6,230,000 | 0.20 | 0.35 | 0.60 | 1.15 | — |
| 1956 | 4,580,000 | 0.20 | 0.35 | 0.60 | 1.15 | — |
| 1957 | 12,500,000 | 0.15 | 0.30 | 0.50 | 1.00 | — |
| 1958 | 44,320,000 | 0.15 | 0.30 | 0.50 | 1.00 | — |

**2 ANNAS** KM# 4 **Composition:** Copper-Nickel

| Date | Mintage | F | VF | XF | Unc | BU |
|---|---|---|---|---|---|---|
| 1948 | 55,930,000 | 0.15 | 0.30 | 0.50 | 1.00 | — |
| 1948 Proof | — | Value: 1.50 | | | | |
| 1949 | 19,720,000 | 0.15 | 0.30 | 0.50 | 1.00 | — |
| 1949 Dot after date | — | 0.20 | 0.35 | 0.60 | 1.15 | — |

**Note:** Mintage included with KM#9.

| Date | Mintage | F | VF | XF | Unc | BU |
|---|---|---|---|---|---|---|
| 1951 | 33,130,000 | 0.15 | 0.30 | 0.50 | 1.00 | — |

**2 ANNAS** KM# 9 **Composition:** Copper-Nickel

| Date | Mintage | F | VF | XF | Unc | BU |
|---|---|---|---|---|---|---|
| 1950 | 21,190,000 | 3.50 | 5.00 | 7.50 | 12.50 | — |
| 1950 Proof | — | Value: 20.00 | | | | |

**2 ANNAS** KM# 15 **Composition:** Copper-Nickel

| Date | Mintage | F | VF | XF | Unc | BU |
|---|---|---|---|---|---|---|
| 1953 | 7,910,000 | 0.15 | 0.30 | 0.50 | 1.00 | — |
| 1953 Proof | — | Value: 1.50 | | | | |
| 1954 | 5,740,000 | 0.15 | 0.30 | 0.50 | 1.00 | — |
| 1955 | 6,230,000 | 0.15 | 0.30 | 0.50 | 1.00 | — |
| 1956 | 1,370,000 | 0.20 | 0.35 | 0.60 | 1.15 | — |
| 1957 | 2,570,000 | 0.20 | 0.35 | 0.60 | 1.15 | — |
| 1958 | 6,200,000 | 0.15 | 0.30 | 0.50 | 1.00 | — |
| 1959 | 8,010,000 | 0.15 | 0.30 | 0.50 | 1.00 | — |

**1/4 RUPEE** KM# 5 **Composition:** Nickel

| Date | Mintage | F | VF | XF | Unc | BU |
|---|---|---|---|---|---|---|
| 1948 | 52,680,000 | 0.20 | 0.30 | 0.50 | 1.00 | — |
| 1948 Proof | — | Value: 2.25 | | | | |
| 1949 | 46,000,000 | 0.20 | 0.30 | 0.50 | 1.00 | — |
| 1951 | 19,120,000 | 0.20 | 0.35 | 0.60 | 1.15 | — |

**1/4 RUPEE** KM# 10 **Composition:** Nickel

| Date | Mintage | F | VF | XF | Unc | BU |
|---|---|---|---|---|---|---|
| 1950 | 19,400,000 | 5.00 | 7.50 | 12.00 | 20.00 | — |
| 1950 Proof | — | Value: 25.00 | | | | |

**1/2 RUPEE** KM# 6 **Composition:** Nickel

| Date | Mintage | F | VF | XF | Unc | BU |
|---|---|---|---|---|---|---|
| 1948 | 33,260,000 | 0.40 | 0.60 | 0.75 | 1.50 | — |
| 1948 Proof | — | Value: 2.00 | | | | |
| 1949 | 20,300,000 | 0.40 | 0.60 | 0.75 | 1.50 | — |
| 1951 | 11,430,000 | 0.40 | 0.65 | 0.90 | 1.75 | — |

**RUPEE** KM# 7 **Composition:** Nickel **Note:** Varieties exist.

| Date | Mintage | F | VF | XF | Unc | BU |
|---|---|---|---|---|---|---|
| 1948 | 46,200,000 | 0.75 | 1.25 | 2.00 | 3.50 | — |
| 1948 Proof | — | Value: 5.00 | | | | |
| 1949 | 37,100,000 | 0.75 | 1.25 | 2.00 | 3.50 | — |

## DECIMAL COINAGE

100 Paisa (Pice) = 1 Rupee

**PICE** KM# 16 **Composition:** Bronze

| Date | Mintage | F | VF | XF | Unc | BU |
|---|---|---|---|---|---|---|
| 1961 | 74,910,000 | 0.15 | 0.30 | 0.50 | 1.00 | — |

**PAISA** KM# 17 **Composition:** Bronze

| Date | Mintage | F | VF | XF | Unc | BU |
|---|---|---|---|---|---|---|
| 1961 | 134,650,000 | 0.15 | 0.25 | 0.40 | 0.80 | — |
| 1961 Proof | — | Value: 1.50 | | | | |
| 1962 | 149,380,000 | 0.15 | 0.25 | 0.40 | 0.80 | — |
| 1963 | 127,810,000 | 0.15 | 0.25 | 0.40 | 0.80 | — |

**PAISA** KM# 24 **Composition:** Bronze

| Date | Mintage | F | VF | XF | Unc | BU |
|---|---|---|---|---|---|---|
| 1964 | 39,890,000 | 0.20 | 0.35 | 0.50 | 1.00 | — |
| 1964 Proof | — | Value: 1.50 | | | | |
| 1965 | 69,660,000 | 0.20 | 0.35 | 0.50 | 1.00 | — |

**PAISA** KM# 24a **Composition:** Nickel-Brass

| Date | Mintage | F | VF | XF | Unc | BU |
|---|---|---|---|---|---|---|
| 1965 | 32,950,000 | 0.20 | 0.35 | 0.50 | 1.00 | — |
| 1966 | 179,370,000 | 0.15 | 0.25 | 0.40 | 0.80 | — |

**PAISA** KM# 29 **Composition:** Aluminum

| Date | Mintage | F | VF | XF | Unc | BU |
|---|---|---|---|---|---|---|
| 1967 | 170,070,000 | — | 0.10 | 0.15 | 0.30 | — |
| 1968 | — | — | 0.10 | 0.15 | 0.30 | — |
| 1969 | — | — | 0.10 | 0.15 | 0.30 | — |
| 1970 | 204,606,000 | — | 0.10 | 0.15 | 0.30 | — |
| 1971 | 191,880,000 | — | 0.10 | 0.15 | 0.30 | — |
| 1972 | 108,510,000 | — | 0.10 | 0.15 | 0.30 | — |
| 1973 | Inc. above | — | 0.10 | 0.15 | 0.30 | — |

**PAISA** **KM# 33** **Composition:** Aluminum **Series:** F.A.O. **Reverse:** Abstract cotton plant

| Date | Mintage | F | VF | XF | Unc | BU |
|---|---|---|---|---|---|---|
| 1974 | 14,230,000 | — | 0.10 | 0.15 | 0.30 | — |
| 1975 | 43,000,000 | — | 0.10 | 0.15 | 0.30 | — |
| 1976 | 49,180,000 | — | 0.10 | 0.15 | 0.30 | — |
| 1977 | 62,750,000 | — | 0.10 | 0.15 | 0.30 | — |
| 1978 | 20,380,000 | — | 0.10 | 0.15 | 0.30 | — |
| 1979 | 5,630,000 | — | 0.10 | 0.15 | 0.30 | — |

**2 PAISA** **KM# 25** **Composition:** Bronze

| Date | Mintage | F | VF | XF | Unc | BU |
|---|---|---|---|---|---|---|
| 1964 | 67,660,000 | 0.15 | 0.25 | 0.35 | 0.70 | — |
| 1964 Proof | — | Value: 1.50 | | | | |
| 1965 | 27,880,000 | 0.15 | 0.25 | 0.35 | 0.70 | — |
| 1966 | 50,590,000 | 0.15 | 0.25 | 0.35 | 0.70 | — |

**2 PAISA** **KM# 28** **Composition:** Aluminum

| Date | Mintage | F | VF | XF | Unc | BU |
|---|---|---|---|---|---|---|
| 1966 | 11,940,000 | — | 0.10 | 0.15 | 0.30 | — |
| 1967 | 73,970,000 | — | 0.10 | 0.15 | 0.30 | — |
| 1968 | — | — | 0.10 | 0.15 | 0.30 | — |

**2 PAISA** **KM# 25a** **Composition:** Aluminum

| Date | Mintage | F | VF | XF | Unc | BU |
|---|---|---|---|---|---|---|
| 1968 | — | — | 0.10 | 0.15 | 0.30 | — |
| 1969 | — | — | 0.10 | 0.15 | 0.30 | — |
| 1970 | 24,401,000 | — | 0.10 | 0.15 | 0.30 | — |
| 1971 | 10,140,000 | — | 0.10 | 0.15 | 0.30 | — |
| 1972 | 4,040,000 | 0.10 | 0.15 | 0.20 | 0.40 | — |

**2 PAISA** **KM# 34** **Composition:** Aluminum **Series:** F.A.O. **Reverse:** Rice plant

| Date | Mintage | F | VF | XF | Unc | BU |
|---|---|---|---|---|---|---|
| 1974 | 3,600,000 | 0.10 | 0.15 | 0.20 | 0.40 | — |
| 1975 | 4,020,000 | 0.10 | 0.15 | 0.20 | 0.40 | — |
| 1976 | 5,750,000 | 0.10 | 0.15 | 0.20 | 0.40 | — |

**5 PICE** **KM# 18** **Composition:** Nickel-Brass

| Date | Mintage | F | VF | XF | Unc | BU |
|---|---|---|---|---|---|---|
| 1961 | 40,050,000 | 0.20 | 0.30 | 0.40 | 0.80 | — |

**5 PAISA** **KM# 19** **Composition:** Nickel-Brass

| Date | Mintage | F | VF | XF | Unc | BU |
|---|---|---|---|---|---|---|
| 1961 | 40,790,000 | 0.15 | 0.25 | 0.35 | 0.70 | — |
| 1961 Proof | — | Value: 1.50 | | | | |
| 1962 | 48,200,000 | 0.15 | 0.25 | 0.35 | 0.70 | — |
| 1963 | 45,020,000 | 0.15 | 0.25 | 0.35 | 0.70 | — |

**5 PAISA** **KM# 26** **Composition:** Nickel-Brass

| Date | Mintage | F | VF | XF | Unc | BU |
|---|---|---|---|---|---|---|
| 1964 | 82,730,000 | 0.15 | 0.25 | 0.35 | 0.70 | — |
| 1965 | 72,570,000 | 0.15 | 0.25 | 0.35 | 0.70 | — |
| 1966 | 32,900,000 | 0.15 | 0.25 | 0.35 | 0.70 | — |
| 1967 | 24,470,000 | 0.15 | 0.25 | 0.35 | 0.70 | — |
| 1968 | — | 0.15 | 0.25 | 0.35 | 0.70 | — |
| 1969 | 5,690,000 | 0.20 | 0.30 | 0.40 | 0.80 | — |
| 1970 | 24,655,000 | 0.15 | 0.25 | 0.35 | 0.70 | — |
| 1971 | 23,860,000 | 0.15 | 0.25 | 0.35 | 0.70 | — |
| 1972 | 40,345,000 | 0.15 | 0.25 | 0.35 | 0.70 | — |
| 1973 | Inc. above | 0.15 | 0.25 | 0.35 | 0.70 | — |
| 1974 | 7,695,000 | 0.20 | 0.30 | 0.40 | 0.80 | — |

**5 PAISA** **KM# 35** **Composition:** Aluminum **Series:** F.A.O. **Reverse:** Sugar cane

| Date | Mintage | F | VF | XF | Unc | BU |
|---|---|---|---|---|---|---|
| 1974 | 23,395,000 | — | 0.10 | 0.15 | 0.30 | — |
| 1975 | 50,030,000 | — | 0.10 | 0.15 | 0.30 | — |
| 1976 | 58,255,000 | — | 0.10 | 0.15 | 0.30 | — |
| 1977 | 32,840,000 | — | 0.10 | 0.15 | 0.30 | — |
| 1978 | 61,940,000 | — | 0.10 | 0.15 | 0.30 | — |
| 1979 | 65,485,000 | — | 0.10 | 0.15 | 0.30 | — |
| 1980 | 55,940,000 | — | 0.10 | 0.15 | 0.30 | — |
| 1981 | 18,290,000 | — | 0.10 | 0.15 | 0.30 | — |

**5 PAISA** **KM# 52** **Composition:** Aluminum

| Date | Mintage | F | VF | XF | Unc | BU |
|---|---|---|---|---|---|---|
| 1981 | 16,730,000 | — | 0.10 | 0.15 | 0.30 | — |
| 1982 | 51,210,000 | — | 0.10 | 0.15 | 0.30 | — |
| 1983 | 42,915,000 | — | 0.10 | 0.15 | 0.30 | — |
| 1984 | 45,105,000 | — | 0.10 | 0.15 | 0.30 | — |
| 1985 | 46,555,000 | — | 0.10 | 0.15 | 0.30 | — |
| 1986 | 20,065,000 | — | — | 0.10 | 0.20 | — |
| 1987 | 37,710,000 | — | — | 0.10 | 0.20 | — |
| 1988 | 40,150,000 | — | — | 0.10 | 0.20 | — |
| 1989 | — | — | — | 0.10 | 0.20 | — |
| 1990 | — | — | — | 0.10 | 0.20 | — |
| 1991 | — | — | — | 0.10 | 0.20 | — |
| 1992 | — | — | — | 0.10 | 0.20 | — |
| 1993 | — | — | — | 0.10 | 0.20 | — |
| 1994 | — | — | — | 0.10 | 0.20 | — |
| 1996 | — | — | — | 0.10 | 0.20 | — |

**10 PICE** **KM# 20** **Composition:** Copper-Nickel

| Date | Mintage | F | VF | XF | Unc | BU |
|---|---|---|---|---|---|---|
| 1961 | 22,230,000 | 0.20 | 0.30 | 0.50 | 1.00 | — |

**10 PAISA** **KM# 21** **Composition:** Copper-Nickel

| Date | Mintage | F | VF | XF | Unc | BU |
|---|---|---|---|---|---|---|
| 1961 | 31,090,000 | 0.15 | 0.25 | 0.35 | 0.70 | — |
| 1961 Proof | — | Value: 2.00 | | | | |
| 1962 | 29,440,000 | 0.15 | 0.25 | 0.35 | 0.70 | — |
| 1963 | 19,760,000 | 0.15 | 0.25 | 0.35 | 0.70 | — |

**10 PAISA** **KM# 27** **Composition:** Copper-Nickel

| Date | Mintage | F | VF | XF | Unc | BU |
|---|---|---|---|---|---|---|
| 1964 | 52,580,000 | 0.15 | 0.25 | 0.35 | 0.70 | — |
| 1965 | 51,540,000 | 0.15 | 0.25 | 0.35 | 0.70 | — |
| 1966 | — | 0.15 | 0.25 | 0.35 | 0.70 | — |
| 1967 | 16,430,000 | 0.15 | 0.25 | 0.35 | 0.70 | — |
| 1968 | — | 0.15 | 0.25 | 0.35 | 0.70 | — |

**10 PAISA** **KM# 31** **Composition:** Copper-Nickel **Note:** Reduced size.

| Date | Mintage | F | VF | XF | Unc | BU |
|---|---|---|---|---|---|---|
| 1969 | — | 0.15 | 0.25 | 0.35 | 0.70 | — |
| 1970 | 30,250,000 | 0.15 | 0.25 | 0.35 | 0.70 | — |
| 1971 | 26,270,000 | 0.15 | 0.25 | 0.35 | 0.70 | — |
| 1972 | 24,845,000 | 0.15 | 0.25 | 0.35 | 0.70 | — |
| 1973 | Inc. above | 0.15 | 0.25 | 0.35 | 0.70 | — |
| 1974 | 4,780,000 | 0.20 | 0.30 | 0.40 | 0.80 | — |

**10 PAISA** **KM# 36** **Composition:** Aluminum **Series:** F.A.O. **Reverse:** Wheat ears

| Date | Mintage | F | VF | XF | Unc | BU |
|---|---|---|---|---|---|---|
| 1974 | 18,640,000 | — | 0.10 | 0.15 | 0.30 | — |
| 1975 | 28,875,000 | — | 0.10 | 0.15 | 0.30 | — |
| 1976 | 43,755,000 | — | 0.10 | 0.15 | 0.30 | — |
| 1977 | 29,045,000 | — | 0.10 | 0.15 | 0.30 | — |
| 1978 | 55,185,000 | — | 0.10 | 0.15 | 0.30 | — |
| 1979 | 56,100,000 | — | 0.10 | 0.15 | 0.30 | — |
| 1980 | 40,985,000 | — | 0.10 | 0.15 | 0.30 | — |
| 1981 | 15,500,000 | — | 0.10 | 0.15 | 0.30 | — |

**10 PAISA** **KM# 53** **Composition:** Aluminum

| Date | Mintage | F | VF | XF | Unc | BU |
|---|---|---|---|---|---|---|
| 1981 | 7,995,000 | 0.10 | 0.15 | 0.20 | 0.40 | — |
| 1982 | 39,770,000 | — | 0.10 | 0.15 | 0.30 | — |
| 1983 | 44,705,000 | — | 0.10 | 0.15 | 0.30 | — |
| 1984 | 35,255,000 | — | 0.10 | 0.15 | 0.30 | — |
| 1985 | 41,545,000 | — | 0.10 | 0.15 | 0.30 | — |
| 1986 | 43,280,000 | — | — | 0.10 | 0.20 | — |
| 1987 | 39,090,000 | — | — | 0.10 | 0.20 | — |
| 1988 | 42,510,000 | — | — | 0.10 | 0.20 | — |
| 1989 | — | — | — | 0.10 | 0.20 | — |

| Date | Mintage | F | VF | XF | Unc | BU |
|---|---|---|---|---|---|---|
| 1990 | — | — | — | 0.10 | 0.20 | — |
| 1991 | — | — | — | 0.10 | 0.20 | — |
| 1992 | — | — | — | 0.10 | 0.20 | — |
| 1993 | — | — | — | 0.10 | 0.20 | — |
| 1994 | — | — | — | 0.10 | 0.20 | — |
| 1995 | — | — | — | 0.10 | 0.20 | — |

**25 PAISA** **KM# 22** **Composition:** Nickel

| Date | Mintage | F | VF | XF | Unc | BU |
|---|---|---|---|---|---|---|
| 1963 | 16,900,000 | 0.15 | 0.25 | 0.35 | 0.70 | — |
| 1964 | 7,990,000 | 0.15 | 0.25 | 0.35 | 0.70 | — |
| 1965 | 9,290,000 | 0.15 | 0.25 | 0.35 | 0.70 | — |
| 1966 | 6,650,000 | 0.15 | 0.25 | 0.35 | 0.70 | — |
| 1967 | 3,740,000 | 0.20 | 0.30 | 0.40 | 0.80 | — |

**25 PAISA** **KM# 30** **Composition:** Copper-Nickel

| Date | Mintage | F | VF | XF | Unc | BU |
|---|---|---|---|---|---|---|
| 1967 | 5,500,000 | 0.10 | 0.15 | 0.25 | 0.50 | — |
| **Note:** Mintage unconfirmed. | | | | | | |
| 1968 | 5,500,000 | 0.10 | 0.15 | 0.25 | 0.50 | — |
| **Note:** Mintage unconfirmed. | | | | | | |
| 1969 | — | 0.10 | 0.15 | 0.25 | 0.50 | — |
| 1970 | 30,392,000 | 0.10 | 0.15 | 0.25 | 0.50 | — |
| 1971 | 12,664,000 | 0.10 | 0.15 | 0.25 | 0.50 | — |
| 1972 | 10,824,000 | 0.10 | 0.15 | 0.25 | 0.50 | — |
| 1973 | — | 0.10 | 0.15 | 0.25 | 0.50 | — |
| 1974 | 9,756,000 | 0.10 | 0.20 | 0.30 | 0.55 | — |

**25 PAISA** **KM# 37** **Composition:** Copper-Nickel

| Date | Mintage | F | VF | XF | Unc | BU |
|---|---|---|---|---|---|---|
| 1975 | 14,264,000 | 0.10 | 0.15 | 0.20 | 0.40 | — |
| 1976 | 20,440,000 | 0.10 | 0.15 | 0.20 | 0.40 | — |
| 1977 | 22,092,000 | 0.10 | 0.15 | 0.20 | 0.40 | — |
| 1978 | 33,544,000 | 0.10 | 0.15 | 0.20 | 0.40 | — |
| 1979 | 29,648,000 | 0.10 | 0.15 | 0.20 | 0.40 | — |
| 1980 | 49,556,000 | 0.10 | 0.15 | 0.20 | 0.40 | — |
| 1981 | 33,952,000 | 0.10 | 0.15 | 0.20 | 0.40 | — |

**25 PAISA** **KM# 58** **Composition:** Copper-Nickel **Note:** Varieties in date and crescent size exist.

| Date | Mintage | F | VF | XF | Unc | BU |
|---|---|---|---|---|---|---|
| 1981 | 5,648,000 | — | 0.10 | 0.15 | 0.35 | — |
| 1982 | 28,940,000 | — | 0.10 | 0.15 | 0.35 | — |
| 1983 | 40,844,000 | — | 0.10 | 0.15 | 0.35 | — |
| 1984 | 50,988,000 | — | 0.10 | 0.15 | 0.35 | — |
| 1985 | 53,748,000 | — | 0.10 | 0.15 | 0.35 | — |
| 1986 | 75,764,000 | — | 0.10 | 0.15 | 0.35 | — |
| 1987 | 53,560,000 | — | 0.10 | 0.15 | 0.35 | — |
| 1988 | 58,900,000 | — | 0.10 | 0.15 | 0.35 | — |
| 1989 | — | — | 0.10 | 0.15 | 0.35 | — |
| 1990 | — | — | 0.10 | 0.15 | 0.35 | — |
| 1991 | — | — | 0.10 | 0.15 | 0.35 | — |
| 1992 | — | — | 0.10 | 0.15 | 0.35 | — |
| 1993 | — | — | 0.10 | 0.15 | 0.35 | — |
| 1994 | — | — | 0.10 | 0.15 | 0.35 | — |
| 1995 | — | — | 0.10 | 0.15 | 0.35 | — |
| 1996 | — | — | 0.10 | 0.15 | 0.35 | — |

**50 PAISA** **KM# 23** **Composition:** Nickel

| Date | Mintage | F | VF | XF | Unc | BU |
|---|---|---|---|---|---|---|
| 1963 | 8,110,000 | 0.15 | 0.25 | 0.40 | 0.80 | — |
| 1964 | 4,580,000 | 0.20 | 0.30 | 0.50 | 1.00 | — |
| 1965 | 8,980,000 | 0.15 | 0.25 | 0.40 | 0.80 | — |
| 1966 | 2,860,000 | 0.20 | 0.30 | 0.50 | 1.00 | — |
| 1968 | — | 0.15 | 0.25 | 0.40 | 0.80 | — |
| 1969 | — | 0.15 | 0.25 | 0.40 | 0.80 | — |

**50 PAISA** **KM# 32** **Composition:** Copper-Nickel

| Date | Mintage | F | VF | XF | Unc | BU |
|---|---|---|---|---|---|---|
| 1970 | 9,240,000 | 0.15 | 0.25 | 0.35 | 0.70 | — |
| 1971 | 4,670,000 | 0.15 | 0.25 | 0.35 | 0.70 | — |
| 1972 | 4,900,000 | 0.15 | 0.25 | 0.35 | 0.70 | — |
| 1974 | 1,128,000 | 0.20 | 0.30 | 0.40 | 0.80 | — |

**50 PAISA** **KM# 38** **Composition:** Copper-Nickel **Note:** Varieties in date size exist.

| Date | Mintage | F | VF | XF | Unc | BU |
|---|---|---|---|---|---|---|
| 1975 | 9,180,000 | 0.15 | 0.20 | 0.30 | 0.60 | — |
| 1976 | — | 0.15 | 0.20 | 0.30 | 0.60 | — |
| 1977 | 5,548,000 | 0.15 | 0.20 | 0.30 | 0.60 | — |
| 1978 | 18,252,000 | 0.15 | 0.20 | 0.30 | 0.60 | — |
| 1979 | 14,596,000 | 0.15 | 0.20 | 0.30 | 0.60 | — |
| 1980 | 22,332,000 | 0.15 | 0.20 | 0.30 | 0.60 | — |
| 1981 | 13,552,000 | 0.15 | 0.20 | 0.30 | 0.60 | — |

**50 PAISA** **KM# 39** **Composition:** Copper-Nickel **Subject:** 100th anniversary - birth of Mohammad Ali Jinnah

| Date | Mintage | F | VF | XF | Unc | BU |
|---|---|---|---|---|---|---|
| 1976 | 5,600,000 | 0.15 | 0.25 | 0.50 | 1.00 | — |

**50 PAISA** **KM# 54** **Composition:** Copper-Nickel

| Date | Mintage | F | VF | XF | Unc | BU |
|---|---|---|---|---|---|---|
| 1981 | 4,612,000 | 0.10 | 0.15 | 0.25 | 0.55 | — |
| 1982 | 15,844,000 | 0.10 | 0.15 | 0.25 | 0.55 | — |
| 1983 | 9,608,000 | 0.10 | 0.15 | 0.25 | 0.55 | — |
| 1984 | 17,520,000 | 0.10 | 0.15 | 0.25 | 0.55 | — |
| 1985 | 20,144,000 | 0.10 | 0.15 | 0.25 | 0.55 | — |
| 1986 | 14,116,000 | — | 0.10 | 0.15 | 0.50 | — |
| 1987 | 23,044,000 | — | 0.10 | 0.15 | 0.50 | — |
| 1988 | 37,140,000 | — | 0.10 | 0.15 | 0.50 | — |
| 1989 | — | — | 0.10 | 0.15 | 0.50 | — |
| 1990 | — | — | 0.10 | 0.15 | 0.50 | — |
| 1991 | — | — | 0.10 | 0.15 | 0.50 | — |
| 1992 | — | — | 0.10 | 0.15 | 0.50 | — |
| 1993 | — | — | 0.10 | 0.15 | 0.50 | — |
| 1994 | — | — | 0.10 | 0.15 | 0.50 | — |
| 1995 | — | — | 0.10 | 0.15 | 0.50 | — |

**50 PAISA** **KM# 51** **Composition:** Copper-Nickel **Subject:** 1,400th Hejira anniversary

| Date | Mintage | F | VF | XF | Unc | BU |
|---|---|---|---|---|---|---|
| AH1401(1981) | — | — | 0.25 | 0.50 | 1.00 | — |

**RUPEE** **KM# 45** **Composition:** Copper-Nickel **Subject:** Islamic Summit Conference

| Date | Mintage | F | VF | XF | Unc | BU |
|---|---|---|---|---|---|---|
| 1977 | 5,074,000 | 0.25 | 0.50 | 1.00 | 2.00 | — |

**RUPEE** **KM# 46** **Composition:** Copper-Nickel **Subject:** 100th anniversary - birth of Allama Mohammad Iqbal

| Date | Mintage | F | VF | XF | Unc | BU |
|---|---|---|---|---|---|---|
| 1977 | 5,000,000 | 0.25 | 0.50 | 1.00 | 2.00 | — |

**RUPEE** **KM# 57.1** **Composition:** Copper-Nickel **Size:** 26.5 mm.

| Date | Mintage | F | VF | XF | Unc | BU |
|---|---|---|---|---|---|---|
| 1979 | — | 0.30 | 0.40 | 0.55 | 1.15 | — |
| 1980 | 14,522,000 | 0.30 | 0.40 | 0.55 | 1.15 | — |
| 1981 | 12,038,000 | 0.30 | 0.40 | 0.55 | 1.15 | — |

**RUPEE** **KM# 57.2** **Composition:** Copper-Nickel **Size:** 25 mm.

| Date | Mintage | F | VF | XF | Unc | BU |
|---|---|---|---|---|---|---|
| 1981 | 4,084,000 | 0.25 | 0.40 | 0.55 | 1.00 | — |
| 1982 | 27,878,000 | 0.20 | 0.35 | 0.50 | 1.00 | — |
| 1983 | 18,746,000 | 0.20 | 0.35 | 0.50 | 1.00 | — |
| 1984 | 14,562,000 | 0.20 | 0.35 | 0.50 | 1.00 | — |
| 1985 | 4,934,000 | 0.25 | 0.40 | 0.55 | 1.00 | — |
| 1986 | 11,840,000 | 0.15 | 0.25 | 0.40 | 0.80 | — |
| 1987 | 50,416,000 | 0.15 | 0.25 | 0.40 | 0.80 | — |
| 1988 | 10,644,000 | 0.15 | 0.25 | 0.40 | 0.80 | — |
| 1990 | — | 0.15 | 0.25 | 0.40 | 0.80 | — |

**RUPEE** **KM# 55** **Composition:** Copper-Nickel **Subject:** 1,400th Hejira anniversary

| Date | Mintage | F | VF | XF | Unc | BU |
|---|---|---|---|---|---|---|
| AH1401(1981) | 45,000 | — | 0.60 | 1.25 | 2.50 | — |

**RUPEE** **KM# 56** **Composition:** Copper-Nickel **Series:** World Food Day

| Date | Mintage | F | VF | XF | Unc | BU |
|---|---|---|---|---|---|---|
| 1981 | 45,000 | 0.35 | 0.75 | 1.50 | 3.00 | — |

**RUPEE** **KM# 62** **Composition:** Bronze **Obverse:** Portrait of Mohammad Ali Jinnah **Reverse:** Mosque and denomination

| Date | Mintage | F | VF | XF | Unc | BU |
|---|---|---|---|---|---|---|
| 1998 | — | 0.15 | 0.25 | 0.35 | 0.65 | — |
| 1999 | — | 0.15 | 0.25 | 0.35 | 0.65 | — |
| 2000 | — | 0.15 | 0.25 | 0.35 | 0.65 | — |

**2 RUPEES** **KM# 63** **Composition:** Nickel-Brass **Obverse:** National emblem **Reverse:** Mosque

| Date | Mintage | F | VF | XF | Unc | BU |
|---|---|---|---|---|---|---|
| 1998 | — | 0.20 | 0.30 | 0.45 | 0.85 | — |

**2 RUPEES** **KM# 64** **Weight:** 5.0000 g. **Composition:** Nickel-Brass **Obverse:** National emblem **Reverse:** Clouds above mosque **Edge:** Reeded **Size:** 22.75 mm.

| Date | Mintage | F | VF | XF | Unc | BU |
|---|---|---|---|---|---|---|
| 1999 | — | 0.20 | 0.30 | 45.00 | 0.85 | — |
| 2000 | — | 0.20 | 0.30 | 0.45 | 0.85 | — |

**5 RUPEES** **KM# 59** **Composition:** Copper **Subject:** United Nations 50th year **Reverse:** 50, UN logo **Note:** Four die varieties are reported to exist.

| Date | Mintage | F | VF | XF | Unc | BU |
|---|---|---|---|---|---|---|
| 1995 | 500,000 | — | — | — | 5.50 | — |

**10 RUPEES** **KM# 61** **Composition:** Copper-Nickel **Subject:** 25th anniversary - Pakistan's senate **Obverse:** Star and crescent

| Date | Mintage | F | VF | XF | Unc | BU |
|---|---|---|---|---|---|---|
| 1998 | 100,000 | — | — | — | 6.50 | — |

**50 RUPEES** **KM# 60** **Composition:** Copper-Nickel **Subject:** 50th anniversary - national independence **Obverse:** Star and crescent

| Date | Mintage | F | VF | XF | Unc | BU |
|---|---|---|---|---|---|---|
| 1997 | 500,000 | — | — | — | 7.50 | — |

**100 RUPEES** **KM# 40** **Weight:** 28.2800 g. **Composition:** 0.9250 Silver .8411 oz. ASW **Series:** Conservation **Reverse:** Tropogan pheasant

| Date | Mintage | F | VF | XF | Unc | BU |
|---|---|---|---|---|---|---|
| 1976 | 5,120 | — | — | — | 30.00 | — |
| 1976 Proof | 5,837 | Value: 35.00 | | | | |

**100 RUPEES** **KM# 41** **Weight:** 20.4400 g. **Composition:** 0.9250 Silver .6079 oz. ASW **Subject:** 100th anniversary - birth of Mohammad Ali Jinnah

| Date | Mintage | F | VF | XF | Unc | BU |
|---|---|---|---|---|---|---|
| ND(1976) | 1,300 | — | — | — | 30.00 | — |
| ND(1976) Proof | 2,800 | Value: 35.00 | | | | |

**100 RUPEES** **KM# 47** **Weight:** 20.4400 g. **Composition:** 0.9250 Silver .6079 oz. ASW **Subject:** Islamic Summit Conference

| Date | Mintage | F | VF | XF | Unc | BU |
|---|---|---|---|---|---|---|
| 1977 | 1,500 | — | — | — | 30.00 | — |
| 1977 Proof | 2,500 | Value: 35.00 | | | | |

**100 RUPEES** **KM# 48** **Weight:** 20.4400 g. **Composition:** 0.9250 Silver .6079 oz. ASW **Subject:** 100th anniversary - birth of Allama Mohammad Iqbal **Obverse:** Iqbal bust leaning on hand

| Date | Mintage | F | VF | XF | Unc | BU |
|---|---|---|---|---|---|---|
| 1977 | 3,000 | — | — | — | 30.00 | — |
| 1977 Proof | 300 | Value: 50.00 | | | | |

**150 RUPEES** **KM# 42** **Weight:** 35.0000 g. **Composition:** 0.9250 Silver 1.0409 oz. ASW **Series:** Conservation **Obverse:** Similar to 100 Rupees, KM#40 **Reverse:** Gavial crocodile

| Date | Mintage | F | VF | XF | Unc | BU |
|---|---|---|---|---|---|---|
| 1976 | 5,119 | — | — | — | 37.50 | — |
| 1976 Proof | 5,637 | Value: 42.50 | | | | |

**500 RUPEES** KM# 43 **Weight:** 4.5000 g. **Composition:** 0.9170 Gold .1325 oz. AGW **Subject:** 100th anniversary - birth of Mohammad Ali Jinnah

| Date | Mintage | F | VF | XF | Unc | BU |
|---|---|---|---|---|---|---|
| ND(1976) | 500 | — | — | — | 125 | — |
| ND(1976) Proof | 500 | Value: 150 | | | | |

**500 RUPEES** KM# 49 **Weight:** 3.6400 g. **Composition:** 0.9170 Gold .1073 oz. AGW **Subject:** 100th anniversary - birth of Allama Mohammad Iqbal

| Date | Mintage | F | VF | XF | Unc | BU |
|---|---|---|---|---|---|---|
| 1977 | 500 | — | — | — | 125 | — |
| 1977 Proof | 200 | Value: 150 | | | | |

**1000 RUPEES** KM# 50 **Weight:** 9.0000 g. **Composition:** 0.9170 Gold .2650 oz. AGW **Subject:** Islamic Summit Conference

| Date | Mintage | F | VF | XF | Unc | BU |
|---|---|---|---|---|---|---|
| 1977 | 400 | — | — | — | 200 | — |
| 1977 Proof | 400 | Value: 275 | | | | |

**3000 RUPEES** KM# 44 **Weight:** 33.4370 g. **Composition:** 0.9000 Gold .9676 oz. AGW **Reverse:** Astor Markhor

| Date | Mintage | F | VF | XF | Unc | BU |
|---|---|---|---|---|---|---|
| 1976 | 902 | — | — | — | 475 | — |
| 1976 Proof | 273 | Value: 750 | | | | |

## MINT SETS

| KM# | Date | Mintage | Identification | Issue Price | Mkt Val |
|---|---|---|---|---|---|
| MS1 | 1948 (7) | — | KM1-7 | — | 10.00 |
| MS2 | 1948, 1951, 1953 (8) | — | KM5-7 (1948), 11 (1951), 12-15 (1953). Restrikes have been issued. | 4.00 | 12.50 |
| MS3 | 1948, 1961 (6) | — | KM5-7 (1948), 17, 19, 21 (1961). Restrikes have been issued. | 2.00 | 6.50 |
| MS4 | 1948, 1964 (7) | — | KM7 (1948), 22-27 (1964). Restrikes have been issued. | 2.00 | 6.50 |
| MS5 | 1948, 1975 (7) | — | KM7 (1948), 33-38 (1975). Restrikes have been issued. | — | 5.00 |
| MS6 | 1951, 1953 (5) | — | KM11 (1951), 12-15 (1953). Restrikes have been issued. | — | 8.00 |
| MS7 | 1961 (3) | — | KM17, 19, 21 | — | 3.50 |
| MS8 | 1976 (2) | — | KM41, 43 | 63.00 | 155 |
| MS9 | 1976 (2) | — | KM40, 42 | — | 68.00 |
| MS10 | 1977 (2) | — | KM47, 50 | — | 225 |

## PROOF SETS

| KM# | Date | Mintage | Identification | Issue Price | Mkt Val |
|---|---|---|---|---|---|
| PS1 | 1948 (7) | 5,000 | KM1-7 | 4.00 | 15.50 |
| PS3 | 1950 (3) | — | KM8-10 | — | 60.00 |
| PS4 | 1953 (5) | — | KM11-15 | 2.00 | 11.50 |
| PS5 | 1961 (3) | — | KM17, 19, 21 | 1.00 | 5.00 |
| PS6 | 1976 (2) | — | KM41, 43 | 90.50 | 185 |
| PS7 | 1976 (2) | — | KM40, 42 | — | 78.00 |
| PS8 | 1977 (2) | — | KM47, 50 | — | 300 |

# PALAU

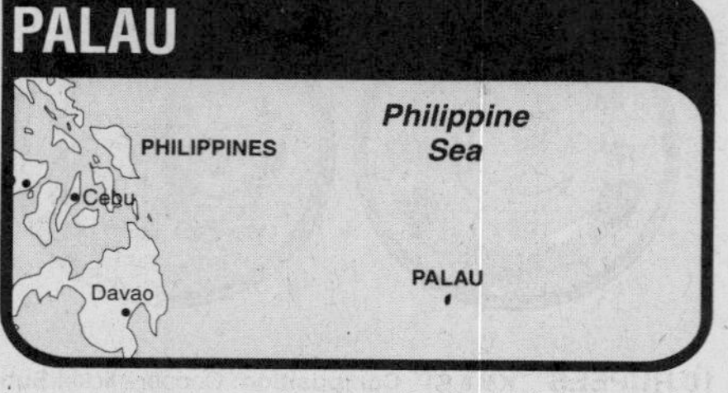


The Republic of Palau, a group of about 100 islands and islets, is generally considered a part of the Caroline Islands. It is located about 1,000 miles southeast of Manila and about the same distance southwest of Saipan and has an area of 179 sq. mi. and a population of 12,116. Capital: Koror.

The islands were administered as part of the Caroline Islands under the Spanish regime until they were sold to Germany in 1899. Seized by Japan in 1914, it was mandated to them in 1919 and Koror was made the administrative headquarters of all the Japanese mandated islands in 1921. During World War II the islands were taken by the Allies, in 1944, with the heaviest fighting taking place on Peleliu. They became part of the U.S. Trust Territory of the Pacific Islands in 1947. In 1980 they became internally self-governing and independent. Control over foreign policy, except defense, was approved in 1986. Palau became an independent nation in 1995.

## REPUBLIC

### COLLECTOR COINAGE

**DOLLAR** KM# 1 **Composition:** Copper-Nickel **Subject:** Year of Marine - life protection **Reverse:** Multicolor

| Date | Mintage | F | VF | XF | Unc | BU |
|---|---|---|---|---|---|---|
| 1992 Proof | Est. 50,000 | Value: 40.00 | | | | |

**DOLLAR** KM# 3 **Composition:** Copper-Nickel **Series:** Marine Life Protection **Reverse:** Multicolor

| Date | Mintage | F | VF | XF | Unc | BU |
|---|---|---|---|---|---|---|
| 1993 Proof | 50,000 | Value: 22.50 | | | | |

**DOLLAR** KM# 5 **Composition:** Copper-Nickel **Series:** Marine Life Protection **Reverse:** Multicolor

| Date | Mintage | F | VF | XF | Unc | BU |
|---|---|---|---|---|---|---|
| 1994 Proof | — | Value: 22.50 | | | | |

**DOLLAR** KM# 8 **Composition:** Copper-Nickel **Subject:** Independence **Obverse:** Neptune and mermaid **Reverse:** Multicolor

| Date | Mintage | F | VF | XF | Unc | BU |
|---|---|---|---|---|---|---|
| 1994 Proof | — | Value: 25.00 | | | | |

**DOLLAR** KM# 11 **Composition:** Copper-Nickel **Subject:** Marine Life Protection **Reverse:** Multicolor sea horse and lion fish

| Date | Mintage | F | VF | XF | Unc | BU |
|---|---|---|---|---|---|---|
| 1995 Proof | 50,000 | Value: 32.00 | | | | |

**DOLLAR** KM# 14 **Composition:** Copper-Nickel **Subject:** United Nations 50th Anniversary

| Date | Mintage | F | VF | XF | Unc | BU |
|---|---|---|---|---|---|---|
| 1995 Proof | 30,000 | Value: 27.50 | | | | |

**DOLLAR** KM# 25 **Composition:** Copper-Nickel **Series:** Marine Life Protection **Obverse:** 2 mermaids **Reverse:** Multicolored high-relief dolphin

| Date | Mintage | F | VF | XF | Unc | BU |
|---|---|---|---|---|---|---|
| 1998 Proof | 13,000 | Value: 27.50 | | | | |

**DOLLAR** KM# 26 **Weight:** 1.2441 g. **Composition:** 0.9999 Gold .0400 oz. AGW **Series:** Marine Life Protection **Obverse:** 2 mermaids **Reverse:** Multicolored high-relief dolphin

| Date | Mintage | F | VF | XF | Unc | BU |
|---|---|---|---|---|---|---|
| 1998 Proof | 10,000 | Value: 50.00 | | | | |

**DOLLAR** **KM# 30** **Composition:** Copper-Nickel **Series:** Marine Life Protection **Obverse:** Mermaid with cockatoo **Reverse:** Multicolored high-relief turtle

| Date | Mintage | F | VF | XF | Unc | BU |
|---|---|---|---|---|---|---|
| 1998 Proof | — | Value: 27.50 | | | | |

**DOLLAR** **KM# 31** **Weight:** 1.2441 g. **Composition:** 0.9999 Gold .0400 oz. AGW **Series:** Marine Life Protection **Obverse:** Mermaid with cockatoo **Reverse:** Multicolored high-relief turtle

| Date | Mintage | F | VF | XF | Unc | BU |
|---|---|---|---|---|---|---|
| 1998 Proof | — | Value: 50.00 | | | | |

**DOLLAR** **KM# 35** **Composition:** Copper-Nickel **Series:** Marine Life Protection **Obverse:** Mermaid and dolphin **Reverse:** Multicolored high-relief manta ray

| Date | Mintage | F | VF | XF | Unc | BU |
|---|---|---|---|---|---|---|
| 1999 Proof | — | Value: 25.00 | | | | |

**DOLLAR** **KM# 36** **Weight:** 1.2441 g. **Composition:** 0.9999 Gold .0400 oz. AGW **Series:** Marine Life Protection **Obverse:** Mermaid and dolphin **Reverse:** Multicolored high-relief manta ray

| Date | Mintage | F | VF | XF | Unc | BU |
|---|---|---|---|---|---|---|
| 1999 Proof | — | Value: 50.00 | | | | |

**DOLLAR** **KM# 40** **Composition:** Copper-Nickel **Series:** Marine Life Protection **Obverse:** Mermaid and dolphin **Reverse:** Multicolored shark

| Date | Mintage | F | VF | XF | Unc | BU |
|---|---|---|---|---|---|---|
| 1999 Proof | — | Value: 27.50 | | | | |

**DOLLAR** **KM# 43** **Weight:** 26.6500 g. **Composition:** Copper-Nickel **Series:** Marine Life Protection **Obverse:** Mermaid and ship **Reverse:** Multicolored fish and coral

| Date | Mintage | F | VF | XF | Unc | BU |
|---|---|---|---|---|---|---|
| 2000 Proof | — | Value: 30.00 | | | | |

**DOLLAR** **KM# 52** **Weight:** 26.8600 g. **Composition:** Copper Nickel **Subject:** Marine Life Protection **Obverse:** Mermaid figurehead. **Reverse:** Multicolor jellyfish. **Edge:** Reeded. **Size:** 37.3 mm.

| Date | Mintage | F | VF | XF | Unc | BU |
|---|---|---|---|---|---|---|
| 2001 | — | — | — | — | 35.00 | — |

**5 DOLLARS** **KM# 2** **Weight:** 25.0000 g. **Composition:** 0.9000 Silver .7234 oz. ASW **Series:** Marine Life Protection **Reverse:** Multicolor

| Date | Mintage | F | VF | XF | Unc | BU |
|---|---|---|---|---|---|---|
| 1992 Proof | Est. 6,000 | Value: 80.00 | | | | |

**5 DOLLARS** **KM# 4** **Weight:** 25.0000 g. **Composition:** 0.9000 Silver .7234 oz. ASW **Series:** Marine Life Protection **Obverse:** Neptune in shell **Reverse:** Similar to Dollar, KM#3

| Date | Mintage | F | VF | XF | Unc | BU |
|---|---|---|---|---|---|---|
| 1993 Proof | 6,000 | Value: 75.00 | | | | |

**5 DOLLARS** **KM# 6** **Weight:** 25.0000 g. **Composition:** 0.9000 Silver .7234 oz. ASW **Series:** Marine Life Protection **Obverse:** Neptune and sea scape

| Date | Mintage | F | VF | XF | Unc | BU |
|---|---|---|---|---|---|---|
| 1994 Proof | 6,000 | Value: 55.00 | | | | |

**5 DOLLARS** **KM# 9** **Weight:** 25.0000 g. **Composition:** 0.9000 Silver .7234 oz. ASW **Series:** Independence **Obverse:** Mermaid and Neptune **Reverse:** Nautilus and sea scape

| Date | Mintage | F | VF | XF | Unc | BU |
|---|---|---|---|---|---|---|
| 1994 Proof | — | Value: 55.00 | | | | |

**5 DOLLARS** **KM# 12** **Weight:** 25.0000 g. **Composition:** 0.9000 Silver .7234 oz. ASW **Series:** Marine Life Protection **Reverse:** Seahorse and lion fish

| Date | Mintage | F | VF | XF | Unc | BU |
|---|---|---|---|---|---|---|
| 1995 Proof | 7,500 | Value: 50.00 | | | | |

**5 DOLLARS** **KM#15** **Weight:** 25.0000 g. **Composition:** 0.9000 Silver .7234 oz. ASW **Subject:** United Nations 50th Anniversary

| Date | Mintage | F | VF | XF | Unc | BU |
|---|---|---|---|---|---|---|
| 1995 Proof | — | Value: 50.00 | | | | |

**5 DOLLARS** **KM# 46** **Weight:** 24.6400 g. **Composition:** 0.9000 Silver .7130 oz. ASW **Series:** Marine Life Protection **Obverse:** Mermaid and sailboat **Reverse:** Multicolored shark

| Date | Mintage | F | VF | XF | Unc | BU |
|---|---|---|---|---|---|---|
| 1998 Proof | — | Value: 70.00 | | | | |
| 1999 Proof | — | Value: 70.00 | | | | |

**5 DOLLARS** **KM# 27** **Weight:** 25.0000 g. **Composition:** 0.9000 Silver .7234 oz. ASW **Series:** Marine Life Protection **Obverse:** 2 mermaids **Reverse:** Multicolored high-relief dolphin **Note:** Similar to Dollar, KM#25.

| Date | Mintage | F | VF | XF | Unc | BU |
|---|---|---|---|---|---|---|
| 1998 Proof | 5,000 | Value: 70.00 | | | | |

**5 DOLLARS** **KM# 32** **Weight:** 25.0000 g. **Composition:** 0.9000 Silver .7234 oz. ASW **Series:** Marine Life Protection **Obverse:** Mermaid holding cockatoo **Reverse:** Multicolored high-relief turtle **Note:** Similar to Dollar, KM#30.

| Date | Mintage | F | VF | XF | Unc | BU |
|---|---|---|---|---|---|---|
| 1998 Proof | — | Value: 70.00 | | | | |

**5 DOLLARS** **KM# 44** **Weight:** 24.6400 g. **Composition:** 0.9000 Silver .7130 oz. ASW **Series:** Marine Life Protection **Obverse:** Neptune and ship **Reverse:** Multicolored dolphin jumping **Edge:** Reeded

| Date | Mintage | F | VF | XF | Unc | BU |
|---|---|---|---|---|---|---|
| 1998 Proof | — | Value: 70.00 | | | | |

**5 DOLLARS** **KM# 45** **Weight:** 24.6400 g. **Composition:** 0.9000 Silver .7130 oz. ASW **Series:** Marine Life Protection **Obverse:** Neptune and 2 dolphins **Reverse:** Multicolored sea turtle

| Date | Mintage | F | VF | XF | Unc | BU |
|---|---|---|---|---|---|---|
| 1998 Proof | — | Value: 70.00 | | | | |

**5 DOLLARS** **KM# 37** **Weight:** 25.0000 g. **Composition:** 0.9000 Silver .7234 oz. ASW **Subject:** Marine Life Protection **Obverse:** Mermaid and dolphin **Reverse:** Multicolor high relief manta ray **Edge:** Reeded **Size:** 37 mm.

| Date | Mintage | F | VF | XF | Unc | BU |
|---|---|---|---|---|---|---|
| 1999 Proof | — | Value: 70.00 | | | | |

**5 DOLLARS** **KM# 23** **Weight:** 25.0000 g. **Composition:** 0.9250 Silver .7435 oz. ASW **Series:** International Coins **Subject:** German South West Africa **Obverse:** Whilhelm II portrait from Prussian 5 Mark coin of 1913-1914 **Reverse:** Colonial arms and trooper on camel

| Date | Mintage | F | VF | XF | Unc | BU |
|---|---|---|---|---|---|---|
| 1999 Proof | — | Value: 45.00 | | | | |

**5 DOLLARS** **KM# 47** **Weight:** 24.6400 g. **Composition:** 0.9000 Silver .7130 oz. ASW **Series:** Marine Life Protection **Obverse:** Mermaid in profile, sailboat **Reverse:** Multicolored manta ray

| Date | Mintage | F | VF | XF | Unc | BU |
|---|---|---|---|---|---|---|
| 1999 Proof | — | Value: 75.00 | | | | |

**5 DOLLARS** **KM# 16** **Weight:** 25.0000 g. **Composition:** 0.9250 Silver .7435 oz. ASW **Series:** International Coins **Subject:** Spanish 5 Peseta - 1896-1899 **Obverse:** Spanish arms **Reverse:** Portrait of Alfonso XIII

| Date | Mintage | F | VF | XF | Unc | BU |
|---|---|---|---|---|---|---|
| 1999 Proof | — | Value: 37.50 | | | | |

**5 DOLLARS** **KM# 17** **Weight:** 25.0000 g. **Composition:** 0.9250 Silver .7435 oz. ASW **Series:** International Coins **Subject:** Prussian 5 Mark - 1891-1908 **Obverse:** German heraldic eagle **Reverse:** Portrait of Wilhelm II

| Date | Mintage | F | VF | XF | Unc | BU |
|---|---|---|---|---|---|---|
| 1999 Proof | — | Value: 40.00 | | | | |

**5 DOLLARS** **KM# 18** **Weight:** 25.0000 g. **Composition:** 0.9250 Silver .7435 oz. ASW **Series:** International Coins **Subject:** German East Africa **Obverse:** Elephant based on G.E.A. 15 Rupien of 1916 **Reverse:** Portrait of V. Lettow-Vorbeck, colonial arms

| Date | Mintage | F | VF | XF | Unc | BU |
|---|---|---|---|---|---|---|
| 1999 Proof | — | Value: 45.00 | | | | |

**5 DOLLARS** **KM# 19** **Weight:** 25.0000 g. **Composition:** 0.9250 Silver .7435 oz. ASW **Series:** International Coins **Subject:** German Cameroon **Obverse:** Portrait of Wilhelm I **Reverse:** Germania and colonial arms

| Date | Mintage | F | VF | XF | Unc | BU |
|---|---|---|---|---|---|---|
| 1999 Proof | — | Value: 37.50 | | | | |

**5 DOLLARS** **KM# 20** **Weight:** 25.0000 g. **Composition:** 0.9250 Silver .7435 oz. ASW **Series:** International Coins **Subject:** Kiau Chau **Obverse:** Ships in harbor **Reverse:** Emblem based on 1909 coinage

| Date | Mintage | F | VF | XF | Unc | BU |
|---|---|---|---|---|---|---|
| 1999 Proof | — | Value: 42.50 | | | | |

**5 DOLLARS** **KM# 21** **Weight:** 25.0000 g. **Composition:** 0.9250 Silver .7435 oz. ASW **Series:** International Coins **Subject:** German New Guinea **Obverse:** Large ship **Reverse:** Colonial arms

| Date | Mintage | F | VF | XF | Unc | BU |
|---|---|---|---|---|---|---|
| 1999 Proof | — | Value: 42.50 | | | | |

**5 DOLLARS** **KM# 22** **Weight:** 25.0000 g. **Composition:** 0.9250 Silver .7435 oz. ASW **Series:** International Coins **Subject:** German Samoa **Obverse:** Whilhelm II portrait from German East African coinage **Reverse:** Colonial arms

| Date | Mintage | F | VF | XF | Unc | BU |
|---|---|---|---|---|---|---|
| 1999 Proof | — | Value: 37.50 | | | | |

**5 DOLLARS** **KM# 24** **Weight:** 25.0000 g. **Composition:** 0.9250 Silver .7435 oz. ASW **Series:** International Coins **Subject:** German Togo **Obverse:** Seated Germania from the German 100 Mark notes of 1908-1910 **Reverse:** Colonial arms

| Date | Mintage | F | VF | XF | Unc | BU |
|---|---|---|---|---|---|---|
| 1999 Proof | — | Value: 37.50 | | | | |

**5 DOLLARS** **KM# 48** **Weight:** 24.6400 g. **Composition:** 0.9000 Silver .7130 oz. ASW **Series:** Marine Life Protection **Obverse:** Neptune seated **Reverse:** Multicolored 3 fish and coral

| Date | Mintage | F | VF | XF | Unc | BU |
|---|---|---|---|---|---|---|
| 2000 Proof | — | Value: 75.00 | | | | |

**5 DOLLARS** KM# 51 **Weight:** 24.9400 g. **Composition:** 0.9000 Silver .7217 oz. ASW **Subject:** Our world - our future **Obverse:** Dancer **Reverse:** Multicolored world map **Edge:** Reeded **Size:** 38.6 mm.

| Date | Mintage | F | VF | XF | Unc | BU |
|---|---|---|---|---|---|---|
| 2000 Proof | — | Value: 47.50 | | | | |

**5 DOLLARS** KM# 53 **Weight:** 25.0000 g. **Composition:** 0.9000 Silver .7234 oz. ASW **Series:** Marine Life Protection **Obverse:** Neptune. **Reverse:** Multicolored manta ray. **Edge:** Reeded. **Size:** 37.2 mm.

| Date | Mintage | F | VF | XF | Unc | BU |
|---|---|---|---|---|---|---|
| 2001 | — | — | — | — | 90.00 | — |

**20 DOLLARS** KM# 7 **Weight:** 155.5175 g. **Composition:** 0.9990 Silver 5.0000 oz. ASW **Series:** Marine Life Protection **Subject:** Marine to outer space **Size:** 63.9 mm. **Note:** Illustration reduced.

| Date | Mintage | F | VF | XF | Unc | BU |
|---|---|---|---|---|---|---|
| 1994 Proof | 3,000 | Value: 165 | | | | |

**20 DOLLARS** KM# 42 **Weight:** 155.5175 g. **Composition:** 0.9990 Silver 5.0000 oz. ASW **Subject:** Independence - October 1994 **Obverse:** Similar to 200 Dollars, KM#10 **Reverse:** Multicolored sea scape with rautilus **Size:** 63.9 mm. **Note:** Illustration reduced.

| Date | Mintage | F | VF | XF | Unc | BU |
|---|---|---|---|---|---|---|
| ND(1994) Proof | — | Value: 185 | | | | |

**20 DOLLARS** KM# 13 **Weight:** 155.5175 g. **Composition:** 0.9990 Silver 5.0000 oz. ASW **Series:** Marine Life Protection **Reverse:** Seahorse and lion fish **Note:** Similar to Dollar, KM#11.

| Date | Mintage | F | VF | XF | Unc | BU |
|---|---|---|---|---|---|---|
| 1995 Proof | 3,000 | Value: 165 | | | | |

**20 DOLLARS** KM# 41 **Weight:** 15.6500 g. **Composition:** 0.9990 Silver 4.9993 oz. ASW **Series:** 50th Anniversary - United Nations Member **Obverse:** Mermaid driving quadrigia **Reverse:** Multicolored sea scape, globe of earth below **Size:** 64.5 mm. **Note:** Illustration reduced.

| Date | Mintage | F | VF | XF | Unc | BU |
|---|---|---|---|---|---|---|
| 1995 Proof | — | Value: 165 | | | | |

**20 DOLLARS** KM# 28 **Weight:** 155.5175 g. **Composition:** 0.9990 Silver 4.9950 oz. ASW **Series:** Marine Life Protection **Obverse:** 2 mermaids **Reverse:** Multicolored high-relief dolphin **Note:** Similar to Dollar, KM#25.

| Date | Mintage | F | VF | XF | Unc | BU |
|---|---|---|---|---|---|---|
| 1998 Proof | 700 | Value: 210 | | | | |

**20 DOLLARS** KM# 33 **Weight:** 155.5175 g. **Composition:** 0.9990 Silver 4.9950 oz. ASW **Series:** Marine Life Protection **Obverse:** Mermaid with cockatoo **Reverse:** Multicolored high-relief turtle **Note:** Similar to Dollar, KM#30.

| Date | Mintage | F | VF | XF | Unc | BU |
|---|---|---|---|---|---|---|
| 1998 Proof | 500 | Value: 210 | | | | |

**20 DOLLARS** KM# 38 **Weight:** 155.5175 g. **Composition:** 0.9990 Silver 4.9950 oz. ASW **Series:** Marine Life Protection **Obverse:** Mermaid with dolphin **Reverse:** Multicolored high-relief manta ray **Note:** Similar to Dollar, KM#35.

| Date | Mintage | F | VF | XF | Unc | BU |
|---|---|---|---|---|---|---|
| 1999 Proof | 500 | Value: 210 | | | | |

**20 DOLLARS** KM# 49 **Weight:** 153.9400 g. **Composition:** 0.9990 Silver 4.9443 oz. ASW **Series:** Marine Life Protection **Obverse:** Seated mermaid and sailboat **Reverse:** Multicolored shark **Edge:** Reeded

| Date | Mintage | F | VF | XF | Unc | BU |
|---|---|---|---|---|---|---|
| 1999 Proof | 500 | Value: 210 | | | | |

**20 DOLLARS** KM# 50 **Weight:** 153.9400 g. **Composition:** 0.9990 Silver 4.9443 oz. ASW **Series:** Marine Life Protection **Obverse:** Mermaid and ship **Reverse:** Multicolored 3 fish and coral

| Date | Mintage | F | VF | XF | Unc | BU |
|---|---|---|---|---|---|---|
| 2000 Proof | 500 | Value: 210 | | | | |

**200 DOLLARS** KM# 10 **Weight:** 31.1035 g. **Composition:** 0.9990 Gold 1.0000 oz. AGW **Subject:** Independence **Obverse:** Mermaid and Neptune **Reverse:** Nautilus and sea scape, similar to Dollar, KM#8

| Date | Mintage | F | VF | XF | Unc | BU |
|---|---|---|---|---|---|---|
| 1994 Proof | — | Value: 775 | | | | |

**200 DOLLARS** KM# 29 **Weight:** 31.1035 g. **Composition:** 0.9990 Gold 1.0000 oz. AGW **Series:** Marine Life Protection **Obverse:** 2 mermaids **Reverse:** Multicolored high-relief dolphin **Note:** Similar to Dollar, KM#25.

| Date | Mintage | F | VF | XF | Unc | BU |
|---|---|---|---|---|---|---|
| 1998 Proof | 200 | Value: 775 | | | | |

**200 DOLLARS** KM# 34 **Weight:** 31.1035 g. **Composition:** 0.9990 Gold 1.0000 oz. AGW **Series:** Marine Life Protection **Obverse:** Mermaid with cockatoo **Reverse:** Multicolored high-relief turtle **Note:** Similar to Dollar, KM#30.

| Date | Mintage | F | VF | XF | Unc | BU |
|---|---|---|---|---|---|---|
| 1998 Proof | — | Value: 775 | | | | |

**200 DOLLARS** KM# 39 **Weight:** 31.1035 g. **Composition:** 0.9990 Gold 1.0000 oz. AGW **Series:** Marine Life Protection **Obverse:** Mermaid with dolphin **Reverse:** Multicolored high-relief manta ray **Note:** Similar to Dollar, KM#35.

| Date | Mintage | F | VF | XF | Unc | BU |
|---|---|---|---|---|---|---|
| 1999 Proof | — | Value: 775 | | | | |

## ESSAIS

Standard metals unless otherwise noted

| KM# | Date | Mintage | Identification | Issue Price | Mkt Val |
|---|---|---|---|---|---|
| E1 | 1992 | — | Dollar. 0.9990 Gold. 25.9600 g. Seated mermaid and sailboat. Multicolor sea life. KM1. | — | 1,500 |

| KM# | Date | Mintage | Identification | Issue Price | Mkt Val |
|---|---|---|---|---|---|
| E2 | 1992 | — | 5 Dollars. 0.9990 Gold. 25.9700 g. Seated Neptune and ship. Multicolor sea life. Reeded edge. KM2. | — | 1,500 |
| E3 | 1995 | 30 | Dollar. Silver. KM41. | — | 125 |
| E4 | 1995 | 30 | 5 Dollars. Copper-Nickel. KM41. | — | 100 |
| E5 | 1995 | 30 | 200 Dollars. Copper-Nickel. KM41. | — | 120 |
| E6 | 1995 | 30 | 200 Dollars. Silver. KM41. | — | 185 |
| E7 | 1998 | 20 | Dollar. Silver. KM25. | — | 145 |
| E8 | 1998 | 20 | 5 Dollars. Copper-Nickel. KM25. | — | 145 |
| E9 | 1998 | 20 | 200 Dollars. Silver. KM25. | — | 145 |

## PROOF SETS

| KM# | Date | Mintage | Identification | Issue Price | Mkt Val |
|---|---|---|---|---|---|
| PS1 | 1992 | — | KME1, E2 | — | 3,000 |
| PS2 | 1995 (4) | 20 | KME3, E4, E5, E6 | — | 600 |
| PS3 | 1998 (3) | 20 | KME7, E8, E9 | — | 450 |

# PANAMA

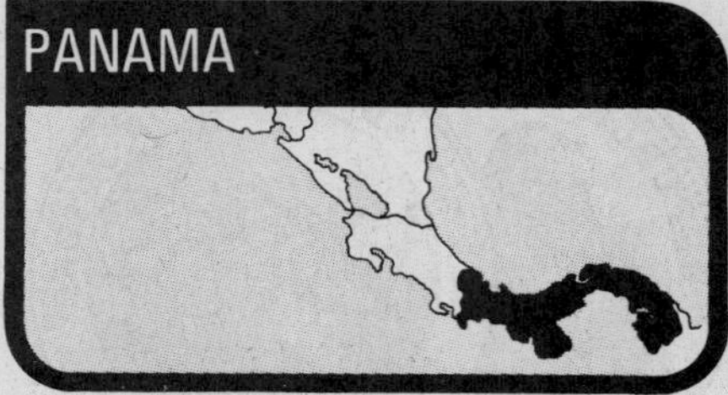

The Republic of Panama, a Central American Country situated between Costa Rica and Colombia, has an area of 29,762 sq. mi. (78,200 sq. km.) and a population of *2.4 million. Capital: Panama City. The Panama Canal is the country's biggest asset; servicing world related transit trade and international commerce. Bananas, refined petroleum, sugar and shrimp are exported.

Discovered in 1501 by the Spanish conquistador Rodrigo Galvan de Bastidas, the land of Panama was soon explored and after a few attempts at settlement was successfully colonized by the Spanish. It was in Panama in 1513 that Vasco Nunez de Balboa became the first European to see the Pacific Ocean. The first Pacific-coast settlement, founded in 1519 on the site of a village the natives called Panama, was named *Nuestra Senora de la Asuncion de Panama* (Our Lady of the Assumption of Panama). The settlement soon became a city and eventually, albeit briefly, an Audiencia (judicial tribunal).

In 1578 the city of Panama, being a primary transshipment center for treasure and supplies to and from Spain's South Pacific-coast colonies, was chosen for a new mint, and minting had begun there by 1580. By late 1582 or 1583 production was halted, possibly due to the fact that there were no nearby silver mines to sustain it. In it's brief operation, the Panama Mint must not have made many coins, as the corpus of surviving specimens known today from this colonial mint is less than 40.

The city of Panama, known today as the Old City of Panama, was sacked and burned in 1671 by the famous Henry Morgan in one of the greatest pirate victories against the Spanish Main.

Panama declared its independence in 1821 and joined the Confederation of Greater Colombia. In 1903, after Colombia rejected a treaty enabling the United States to build a canal across the Isthmus, Panama with the support of the United States proclaimed its independence from Colombia and became a sovereign republic.

The 1904 2-1/2 centesimos known as the 'Panama Pill' or 'Panama Pearl' is one of the world's smaller silver coins and a favorite with collectors.

**MINT MARKS**

FM - Franklin Mint, U.S.A.*

CHI in circle - Valcambi Mint, Balerna, Switzerland

***NOTE:** From 1975-1985 the Franklin Mint produced coinage in up to 3 different qualities. Qualities of issue are designated in ( ) after each date and are defined as follows:

**(M) MATTE** - Normal circulation strike or a dull finish produced by sandblasting special uncirculated (polish finish) or proof quality dies.

**(U) SPECIAL UNCIRCULATED** - Polished or proof-like in appearance without any frosted features.

**(P) PROOF** - The highest quality obtainable having mirror-like fields and frosted features.

**MONETARY SYSTEM**

100 Centesimos = 1 Balboa

# REPUBLIC

## DECIMAL COINAGE

**1/2 CENTESIMO** **KM# 6** **Composition:** Copper-Nickel
**Note:** Previously listed re-engraved overdates were struck from very common doubled dies. The plain date in unc. is scarcer.

| Date | Mintage | F | VF | XF | Unc | BU |
|---|---|---|---|---|---|---|
| 1907 | 1,000,000 | 1.00 | 2.00 | 3.00 | 10.00 | — |
| 1907 Proof | — | Value: 200 | | | | |

**CENTESIMO** **KM# 14** **Composition:** Bronze **Subject:** Uracca

| Date | Mintage | F | VF | XF | Unc | BU |
|---|---|---|---|---|---|---|
| 1935 | 200,000 | 2.00 | 5.00 | 15.00 | 50.00 | — |
| 1937 | 200,000 | 1.50 | 3.50 | 10.00 | 45.00 | — |

**CENTESIMO** **KM# 17** **Composition:** Bronze **Subject:** 50th Anniversary of the Republic

| Date | Mintage | F | VF | XF | Unc | BU |
|---|---|---|---|---|---|---|
| 1953 | 1,500,000 | 0.10 | 0.25 | 0.75 | 3.00 | — |

**CENTESIMO** **KM# 22** **Composition:** Bronze **Note:** Varieties exist.

| Date | Mintage | F | VF | XF | Unc | BU |
|---|---|---|---|---|---|---|
| 1961 | 2,500,000 | — | 0.15 | 0.25 | 2.00 | — |
| 1962 | 2,000,000 | — | 0.15 | 0.25 | 2.00 | — |
| 1962 Proof | Est. 50 | Value: 160 | | | | |
| 1966 | 3,000,000 | — | 0.15 | 0.25 | 1.25 | — |
| 1966 Proof | 13,000 | Value: 1.00 | | | | |
| 1967 | 7,600,000 | — | 0.15 | 0.25 | 1.00 | — |
| 1967 Proof | 20,000 | Value: 1.00 | | | | |
| 1968 | 25,000,000 | — | 0.10 | 0.15 | 0.85 | — |
| 1968 Proof | 23,000 | Value: 1.00 | | | | |
| 1969 Proof | 14,000 | Value: 1.00 | | | | |
| 1970 Proof | 9,528 | Value: 1.00 | | | | |
| 1971 Proof | 11,000 | Value: 1.00 | | | | |
| 1972 Proof | 13,000 | Value: 1.00 | | | | |
| 1973 Proof | 17,000 | Value: 1.00 | | | | |
| 1974 | Est. 10,000,000 | — | 0.10 | 0.15 | 0.75 | — |

**Note:** The 1974 circulation coins were stuck at West Point, NY.

| Date | Mintage | F | VF | XF | Unc | BU |
|---|---|---|---|---|---|---|
| 1974 Proof | Est. 18,000 | Value: 1.00 | | | | |

**Note:** The 1974 proof coins were struck at San Francisco

| Date | Mintage | F | VF | XF | Unc | BU |
|---|---|---|---|---|---|---|
| 1975 | 10,000,000 | — | 0.10 | 0.15 | 0.85 | — |
| 1977 | 10,000,000 | — | 0.10 | 0.15 | 0.75 | — |
| 1978 | 10,000,000 | — | 0.10 | 0.15 | 0.75 | — |
| 1979 | 10,000,000 | — | 0.10 | 0.15 | 0.75 | — |
| 1980 | 20,500,000 | — | 0.10 | 0.15 | 0.75 | — |
| 1982 | 20,000,000 | — | 0.10 | 0.15 | 0.75 | — |
| 1983FM (P) | — | Value: 2.00 | | | | |
| 1983 | 5,000,000 | — | 0.15 | 0.25 | 1.00 | — |
| 1984FM (P) | — | Value: 2.00 | | | | |
| 1986 | 20,000,000 | — | 0.10 | 0.15 | 0.75 | — |
| 1987 | 20,000,000 | — | — | — | 0.75 | — |

**CENTESIMO** **KM# 33.1** **Composition:** Copper Coated Zinc

| Date | Mintage | F | VF | XF | Unc | BU |
|---|---|---|---|---|---|---|
| 1975 (RCM) | 500,000 | — | 0.10 | 0.20 | 0.75 | — |
| 1975FM (M) | 125,000 | — | 0.10 | 0.25 | 1.00 | — |
| 1975FM (U) | 1,410 | — | — | — | 3.00 | — |
| 1975FM (P) | 41,000 | Value: 1.00 | | | | |
| 1976 (RCM) | 50,000 | — | 0.10 | 0.20 | 1.00 | — |
| 1976FM (M) | 63,000 | — | 0.10 | 0.20 | 1.00 | — |
| 1976FM (P) | 12,000 | Value: 1.00 | | | | |
| 1977FM (U) | 63,000 | — | 0.10 | 0.20 | 1.00 | — |
| 1977FM (P) | 9,548 | Value: 1.00 | | | | |
| 1979FM (U) | 20,000 | — | 0.10 | 0.20 | 1.00 | — |
| 1979FM (P) | 5,949 | Value: 1.00 | | | | |
| 1980FM (U) | 40,000 | — | 0.10 | 0.20 | 1.00 | — |
| 1981FM (P) | 1,973 | Value: 1.00 | | | | |
| 1982FM (U) | 5,000 | — | 0.75 | 1.50 | 3.50 | — |
| 1982FM (P) | 1,480 | Value: 1.00 | | | | |

**CENTESIMO** **KM# 45** **Composition:** Copper Coated Zinc **Subject:** 75th Anniversary of Independence

| Date | Mintage | F | VF | XF | Unc | BU |
|---|---|---|---|---|---|---|
| 1978FM (U) | 50,000 | — | 0.10 | 0.20 | 1.00 | — |
| 1978FM (P) | 11,000 | Value: 1.25 | | | | |

**CENTESIMO** **KM# 33.2** **Composition:** Copper Coated Zinc **Edge Lettering:** 1830 BOLIVAR 1980

| Date | Mintage | F | VF | XF | Unc | BU |
|---|---|---|---|---|---|---|
| 1980FM (P) | 2,629 | Value: 1.00 | | | | |

**CENTESIMO** **KM# 22a** **Composition:** Copper Coated Zinc

| Date | Mintage | F | VF | XF | Unc | BU |
|---|---|---|---|---|---|---|
| 1983 | 45,000,000 | — | 0.10 | 0.15 | 0.50 | — |

**CENTESIMO** **KM# 124** **Composition:** Copper Plated Zinc

| Date | Mintage | F | VF | XF | Unc | BU |
|---|---|---|---|---|---|---|
| 1991 | — | — | — | — | 0.50 | — |
| 1993 | 30,000,000 | — | — | — | 0.50 | — |

**CENTESIMO** **KM# 125** **Composition:** Copper Plated Zinc

| Date | Mintage | F | VF | XF | Unc | BU |
|---|---|---|---|---|---|---|
| 1996 | 180,000,000 | — | — | — | 0.25 | — |

**CENTESIMO** **KM# 132** **Weight:** 1.6400 g. **Composition:** Aluminum **Series:** F.A.O **Subject:** 132nd Anniversary of the Peseta **Obverse:** National arms **Reverse:** Ship in canal **Edge:** Plain **Size:** 22.8 mm.

| Date | Mintage | F | VF | XF | Unc | BU |
|---|---|---|---|---|---|---|
| 2000 | — | — | — | — | 1.00 | — |

**1-1/4 CENTESIMOS** **KM# 15** **Composition:** Bronze

| Date | Mintage | F | VF | XF | Unc | BU |
|---|---|---|---|---|---|---|
| 1940 | 1,600,000 | 0.50 | 1.00 | 2.50 | 12.00 | — |

**2-1/2 CENTESIMOS** **KM# 1** **Weight:** 1.2500 g. **Composition:** 0.9000 Silver .0362 oz. ASW **Note:** This coin is popularly referred to as the "Panama Pill."

| Date | Mintage | F | VF | XF | Unc | BU |
|---|---|---|---|---|---|---|
| 1904 | 400,000 | 6.00 | 9.00 | 12.50 | 30.00 | — |

**2-1/2 CENTESIMOS** **KM# 7.1** **Composition:** Copper-Nickel **Rev. Legend:** DOS Y MEDIOS

| Date | Mintage | F | VF | XF | Unc | BU |
|---|---|---|---|---|---|---|
| 1907 | 800,000 | 1.25 | 4.00 | 12.50 | 50.00 | — |

**2-1/2 CENTESIMOS** **KM# 7.2** **Composition:** Copper-Nickel **Rev. Legend:** DOS Y MEDIO

| Date | Mintage | F | VF | XF | Unc | BU |
|---|---|---|---|---|---|---|
| 1916 | 800,000 | 1.25 | 5.00 | 20.00 | 100 | — |
| 1918 7 Known | — | — | 1,600 | 2,400 | — | — |

**Note:** Unauthorized issue, 1 million pieces melted June 1918.

**2-1/2 CENTESIMOS** **KM# 8** **Composition:** Copper-Nickel

| Date | Mintage | F | VF | XF | Unc | BU |
|---|---|---|---|---|---|---|
| 1929 | 1,000,000 | 1.00 | 4.00 | 20.00 | 120 | — |
| 1929 Proof | — | — | — | — | — | — |

**2-1/2 CENTESIMOS** **KM# 16** **Composition:** Copper-Nickel

| Date | Mintage | F | VF | XF | Unc | BU |
|---|---|---|---|---|---|---|
| 1940 | 1,200,000 | 0.50 | 1.00 | 3.50 | 12.00 | — |

**2-1/2 CENTESIMOS** **KM# 32** **Composition:** Copper-Nickel Clad Copper **Series:** F.A.O.

| Date | Mintage | F | VF | XF | Unc | BU |
|---|---|---|---|---|---|---|
| 1973 | 2,000,000 | — | — | 0.10 | 0.35 | — |
| 1975 | 1,000,000 | — | — | 0.10 | 0.50 | — |

**2-1/2 CENTESIMOS** **KM# 34.1** **Composition:** Copper-Nickel Clad Copper **Subject:** Victoriano Lorenzo

| Date | Mintage | F | VF | XF | Unc | BU |
|---|---|---|---|---|---|---|
| 1975 (RCM) | 40,000 | — | 0.50 | 0.75 | 1.50 | — |
| 1975FM (M) | 50,000 | — | 0.50 | 0.75 | 1.50 | — |
| 1975FM (U) | 1,410 | — | 1.00 | 2.00 | 3.00 | — |
| 1975FM (P) | 41,000 | Value: 1.00 | | | | |
| 1976 (RCM) | 20,000 | — | 0.50 | 0.75 | 2.25 | — |
| 1976FM (M) | 25,000 | — | 0.50 | 0.75 | 2.00 | — |
| 1976FM (P) | 24,000 | Value: 1.00 | | | | |
| 1977FM (U) | 25,000 | — | 0.50 | 0.75 | 2.00 | — |
| 1977FM (P) | 9,548 | Value: 1.00 | | | | |
| 1979FM (U) | 12,000 | — | 0.50 | 0.75 | 2.50 | — |
| 1979FM (P) | 5,949 | Value: 1.00 | | | | |
| 1980FM (U) | 40,000 | — | 0.50 | 0.75 | 1.50 | — |
| 1981FM (P) | 1,973 | Value: 2.50 | | | | |
| 1982FM (U) | 2,000 | — | 1.00 | 2.00 | 3.50 | — |
| 1982FM (P) | 1,480 | Value: 3.00 | | | | |

**2-1/2 CENTESIMOS** **KM# 46** **Composition:** Copper-Nickel Clad Copper **Subject:** 75th Anniversary of Independence

| Date | Mintage | F | VF | XF | Unc | BU |
|---|---|---|---|---|---|---|
| 1978FM (U) | 40,000 | — | 0.25 | 0.50 | 2.00 | — |
| 1978FM (P) | 11,000 | Value: 1.50 | | | | |

**2-1/2 CENTESIMOS** **KM# 34.2** **Composition:** Copper-Nickel Clad Copper **Edge Lettering:** 1830 BOLIVAR 1980

| Date | Mintage | F | VF | XF | Unc | BU |
|---|---|---|---|---|---|---|
| 1980FM (P) | 2,629 | Value: 2.00 | | | | |

**2-1/2 CENTESIMOS** **KM# 85** **Composition:** Copper-Nickel Clad Copper

| Date | Mintage | F | VF | XF | Unc | BU |
|---|---|---|---|---|---|---|
| 1983FM (P) | — | Value: 3.00 | | | | |
| 1984FM (P) | — | Value: 3.00 | | | | |

**5 CENTESIMOS** **KM# 2** **Weight:** 2.5000 g. **Composition:** 0.9000 Silver .0723 oz. ASW

| Date | Mintage | F | VF | XF | Unc | BU |
|---|---|---|---|---|---|---|
| 1904 | 1,500,000 | 2.50 | 4.00 | 12.50 | 50.00 | — |
| 1904 Proof | 12 | Value: 1,250 | | | | |
| 1916 | 100,000 | 40.00 | 70.00 | 130 | 300 | — |

**5 CENTESIMOS** **KM# 9** **Composition:** Copper-Nickel

| Date | Mintage | F | VF | XF | Unc | BU |
|---|---|---|---|---|---|---|
| 1929 | 500,000 | 2.50 | 4.50 | 12.00 | 75.00 | — |
| 1932 | 332,000 | 3.00 | 5.00 | 13.50 | 80.00 | — |

**5 CENTESIMOS** **KM# 23.1** **Composition:** Copper-Nickel

| Date | Mintage | F | VF | XF | Unc | BU |
|---|---|---|---|---|---|---|
| 1961 | 1,000,000 | — | 0.50 | 1.00 | 2.50 | — |

**5 CENTESIMOS** **KM# 23.2** **Composition:** Copper-Nickel **Note:** The 1962 & 1966 Royal Mint strikes are normally sharper in detail. The stars on the reverse above the eagle are flat while previous dates are raised. Varieties exist.

| Date | Mintage | F | VF | XF | Unc | BU |
|---|---|---|---|---|---|---|
| 1962 | 2,600,000 | — | 0.25 | 0.50 | 2.00 | — |
| 1962 Proof | Est. 25 | Value: 350 | | | | |
| 1966 | 4,900,000 | — | 0.10 | 0.20 | 1.00 | — |
| 1966 Proof | 13,000 | Value: 1.00 | | | | |
| 1967 | 2,600,000 | — | 0.10 | 0.20 | 1.00 | — |
| 1967 Proof | 20,000 | Value: 1.00 | | | | |
| 1968 | 6,000,000 | — | 0.10 | 0.20 | 1.00 | — |
| 1968 Proof | 23,000 | Value: 1.00 | | | | |
| 1969 Proof | 14,000 | Value: 1.00 | | | | |
| 1970 | 5,000,000 | — | 0.10 | 0.20 | 1.00 | — |
| 1970 Proof | 9,528 | Value: 1.00 | | | | |
| 1971 Proof | 11,000 | Value: 1.00 | | | | |
| 1972 Proof | 13,000 | Value: 1.00 | | | | |
| 1973 | 5,000,000 | — | 0.10 | 0.20 | 1.50 | — |
| 1973 Proof | 17,000 | Value: 1.00 | | | | |
| 1974 Proof | 19,000 | Value: 1.00 | | | | |
| 1975 | 5,000,000 | — | 0.10 | 0.15 | 1.50 | — |
| 1982 | 8,000,000 | — | 0.10 | 0.15 | 1.00 | — |
| 1983 | 7,500,000 | — | 0.10 | 0.15 | 1.00 | — |
| 1993 | 6,000,000 | — | 0.10 | 0.15 | 1.00 | — |
| 1993 Proof | — | Value: 250 | | | | |

**Note:** The 1993 proof strike was not authorized by the Panamanian government

**5 CENTESIMOS** **KM# 35.1** **Composition:** Copper-Nickel Clad Copper **Subject:** Carlos J. Finlay

| Date | Mintage | F | VF | XF | Unc | BU |
|---|---|---|---|---|---|---|
| 1975 (RCM) | 80,000 | — | 0.25 | 0.50 | 1.00 | — |
| 1975FM (M) | 15,000 | — | 0.25 | 0.50 | 1.00 | — |
| 1975FM (U) | 1,410 | — | — | — | 2.50 | — |
| 1975FM (P) | 41,000 | Value: 1.00 | | | | |
| 1976 (RCM) | 20,000 | — | 0.25 | 0.50 | 1.25 | — |
| 1976FM (M) | 13,000 | — | 0.25 | 0.50 | 1.50 | — |
| 1976FM (P) | 12,000 | Value: 1.00 | | | | |
| 1977FM (U) | 13,000 | — | 0.25 | 0.50 | 1.50 | — |
| 1977FM (P) | 9,548 | Value: 1.00 | | | | |
| 1979FM (U) | 12,000 | — | 0.25 | 0.50 | 2.00 | — |
| 1979FM (P) | 5,949 | Value: 1.00 | | | | |
| 1980FM (U) | 43,000 | — | 0.25 | 0.50 | 1.50 | — |
| 1981FM (P) | 1,973 | Value: 1.50 | | | | |
| 1982FM (U) | 3,000 | — | 2.00 | 4.00 | 8.50 | — |
| 1982FM (P) | 1,480 | Value: 1.50 | | | | |

**5 CENTESIMOS** **KM# 47** **Composition:** Copper-Nickel Clad Copper **Subject:** 75th Anniversary of Independence

| Date | Mintage | F | VF | XF | Unc | BU |
|---|---|---|---|---|---|---|
| 1978FM (U) | 30,000 | — | — | — | 1.00 | — |
| 1978FM (P) | 11,000 | Value: 1.00 | | | | |

**5 CENTESIMOS** **KM# 35.2** **Composition:** Copper-Nickel Clad Copper **Edge Lettering:** 1830 BOLIVAR 1980

| Date | Mintage | F | VF | XF | Unc | BU |
|---|---|---|---|---|---|---|
| 1980FM (P) | 2,629 | Value: 1.50 | | | | |

**5 CENTESIMOS** **KM# 86** **Composition:** Copper-Nickel Clad Copper

| Date | Mintage | F | VF | XF | Unc | BU |
|---|---|---|---|---|---|---|
| 1983FM (P) | — | Value: 2.50 | | | | |
| 1984FM (P) | — | Value: 2.50 | | | | |

**5 CENTESIMOS** **KM# 126** **Composition:** Copper-Nickel **Obverse:** National arms **Rev. Legend:** Denomination

| Date | Mintage | F | VF | XF | Unc | BU |
|---|---|---|---|---|---|---|
| 1996 | 4,000,000 | — | — | — | 0.40 | — |

**10 CENTESIMOS** **KM# 3** **Weight:** 5.0000 g. **Composition:** 0.9000 Silver .1447 oz. ASW

| Date | Mintage | F | VF | XF | Unc | BU |
|---|---|---|---|---|---|---|
| 1904 | 1,100,000 | 3.50 | 8.00 | 25.00 | 150 | — |
| 1904 Proof | 12 | Value: 1,250 | | | | |

**10 CENTESIMOS** **KM# 36.1** **Composition:** Copper-Nickel Clad Copper **Subject:** Manuel E. Amador

| Date | Mintage | F | VF | XF | Unc | BU |
|---|---|---|---|---|---|---|
| 1975 (RCM) | 50,000 | — | 0.20 | 0.50 | 1.00 | — |
| 1975 FM (M) | 13,000 | — | 0.20 | 0.50 | 1.50 | — |
| 1975 FM (U) | 1,410 | — | — | — | 2.50 | — |
| 1975 FM (P) | 41,000 | Value: 1.00 | | | | |
| 1976 (RCM) | 20,000 | — | 0.20 | 1.00 | 1.50 | — |
| 1976 FM (M) | 6,250 | — | 0.50 | 1.25 | 2.50 | — |
| 1976 FM (P) | 12,000 | Value: 1.50 | | | | |
| 1977 FM (U) | 6,250 | — | 0.50 | 1.25 | 2.50 | — |
| 1977 FM (P) | 9,548 | Value: 1.50 | | | | |
| 1979 FM (U) | 10,000 | — | 0.50 | 1.00 | 2.00 | — |
| 1979 FM (P) | 5,949 | Value: 2.00 | | | | |
| 1980 FM (U) | 40,000 | — | 0.50 | 1.00 | 2.00 | — |
| 1981 FM (P) | 1,973 | Value: 1.50 | | | | |
| 1982 FM (U) | 2,500 | — | 0.75 | 1.50 | 3.00 | — |
| 1982 Proof | 1,480 | Value: 2.50 | | | | |

**10 CENTESIMOS** **KM# 48** **Composition:** Copper-Nickel Clad Copper **Subject:** 75th Anniversary of Independence

| Date | Mintage | F | VF | XF | Unc | BU |
|---|---|---|---|---|---|---|
| 1978 FM (U) | 20,000 | — | 0.20 | 0.50 | 1.50 | — |
| 1978 FM (P) | 11,000 | Value: 1.50 | | | | |

**10 CENTESIMOS** **KM# 36.2** **Composition:** Copper-Nickel Clad Copper **Edge Lettering:** 1830 BOLIVAR 1980

| Date | Mintage | F | VF | XF | Unc | BU |
|---|---|---|---|---|---|---|
| 1980 FM (P) | 2,629 | Value: 2.50 | | | | |

**1/10 BALBOA** **KM# 10.1** **Weight:** 2.5000 g. **Composition:** 0.9000 Silver .0723 oz. ASW **Note:** High relief.

| Date | Mintage | F | VF | XF | Unc | BU |
|---|---|---|---|---|---|---|
| 1930 | 500,000 | 2.00 | 4.00 | 8.00 | 40.00 | — |
| 1930 Matte proof | 20 | — | — | — | 1,000 | — |
| 1931 | 200,000 | 2.50 | 5.00 | 17.50 | 100 | — |
| 1932 | 150,000 | 3.00 | 6.00 | 18.00 | 120 | — |
| 1933 | 100,000 | 6.50 | 12.50 | 30.00 | 175 | — |
| 1934 | 75,000 | 8.00 | 16.00 | 40.00 | 200 | — |
| 1947 | 1,000,000 | 0.75 | 1.50 | 5.00 | 17.50 | — |

**1/10 BALBOA** **KM# 18** **Weight:** 2.5000 g. **Composition:** 0.9000 Silver .0723 oz. ASW **Subject:** 50th Anniversary of rhe Republic

| Date | Mintage | F | VF | XF | Unc | BU |
|---|---|---|---|---|---|---|
| 1953 | 3,300,000 | BV | 0.75 | 1.50 | 4.00 | — |

**1/10 BALBOA** **KM# 24** **Weight:** 2.5000 g. **Composition:** 0.9000 Silver .0723 oz. ASW

| Date | Mintage | F | VF | XF | Unc | BU |
|---|---|---|---|---|---|---|
| 1961 | 2,500,000 | BV | 0.65 | 1.25 | 3.00 | — |

**1/10 BALBOA** **KM# 10.2** **Weight:** 2.5000 g. **Composition:** 0.9000 Silver .0723 oz. ASW **Note:** Low relief.

| Date | Mintage | F | VF | XF | Unc | BU |
|---|---|---|---|---|---|---|
| 1962 | 5,000,000 | BV | — | 1.00 | 3.00 | — |
| 1962 Proof | Est. 25 | Value: 500 | | | | |

**1/10 BALBOA** **KM# 10a** **Composition:** Copper-Nickel Clad Copper

| Date | Mintage | F | VF | XF | Unc | BU |
|---|---|---|---|---|---|---|
| 1966 Type 1 | 6,955,000 | — | 0.50 | 0.85 | 3.00 | — |

**Note:** The Type I is similar to the 1962 strike on a thick flan (London) with diamonds on both sides of DE

| Date | Mintage | F | VF | XF | Unc | BU |
|---|---|---|---|---|---|---|
| 1966 Type 2 | 1,000,000 | — | 0.75 | 2.00 | 10.00 | — |

**Note:** The Type II strike similar to the 1947 strikes on a thin flan (U.S.) with elongated diamonds on both sides of DE

| Date | Mintage | F | VF | XF | Unc | BU |
|---|---|---|---|---|---|---|
| 1966 | 6,955,000 | — | 0.50 | 0.85 | 3.00 | — |

**Note:** The type 1 variety is similar to the 1962 strike (London) on a thick flan with diamonds on both sides of DE

| Date | Mintage | F | VF | XF | Unc | BU |
|---|---|---|---|---|---|---|
| 1966 | 1,000,000 | — | 0.75 | 2.00 | 10.00 | — |

**Note:** The type 2 variety is similar to the 1947 strike (U.S.) on a thin flan with elongated diamonds on both sides of DE

| Date | Mintage | F | VF | XF | Unc | BU |
|---|---|---|---|---|---|---|
| 1966 Proof | 13,000 | Value: 1.00 | | | | |
| 1967 Proof | 20,000 | Value: 1.00 | | | | |
| 1968 | 5,000,000 | — | 0.20 | 0.30 | 1.50 | — |
| 1968 Proof | 23,000 | Value: 1.00 | | | | |
| 1969 Proof | 14,000 | Value: 1.00 | | | | |
| 1970 | 7,500,000 | — | 0.15 | 0.25 | 1.00 | — |
| 1970 Proof | 9,528 | Value: 1.00 | | | | |
| 1971 Proof | 11,000 | Value: 1.00 | | | | |
| 1972 Proof | 13,000 | Value: 1.00 | | | | |
| 1973 | 10,000,000 | — | 0.15 | 0.20 | 1.50 | — |
| 1973 Proof | 17,000 | Value: 1.00 | | | | |
| 1974 Proof | 18,000 | Value: 1.00 | | | | |
| 1975 | 500,000 | — | 0.25 | 0.50 | 2.00 | — |
| 1980 | 5,000,000 | — | 0.20 | 0.30 | 1.25 | — |
| 1982 | 7,740,000 | — | 0.15 | 0.25 | 1.25 | — |
| 1983 (RCM) | 7,750,000 | — | 0.15 | 0.25 | 1.00 | — |
| 1986 (RCM) | 1,000,000 | — | 0.15 | 0.25 | 1.50 | — |

| Date | Mintage | F | VF | XF | Unc | BU |
|---|---|---|---|---|---|---|
| 1993 | 7,000,000 | — | 0.15 | 0.25 | 1.00 | — |
| 1993 Proof | — | Value: 300 | | | | |

**Note:** Unorthorized striking.

**1/10 BALBOA** **KM# 87** **Composition:** Copper-Nickel Clad Copper

| Date | Mintage | F | VF | XF | Unc | BU |
|---|---|---|---|---|---|---|
| 1983 FM (P) | — | Value: 3.00 | | | | |
| 1984 FM (P) | — | Value: 3.00 | | | | |

**1/10 BALBOA** **KM# 127** **Composition:** Copper-Nickel Clad Copper **Obverse:** National arms **Reverse:** Balboa's portrait

| Date | Mintage | F | VF | XF | Unc | BU |
|---|---|---|---|---|---|---|
| 1996 | 21,000,000 | — | — | — | 0.50 | — |

**25 CENTESIMOS** **KM# 4** **Weight:** 12.5000 g. **Composition:** 0.9000 Silver .3617 oz. ASW

| Date | Mintage | F | VF | XF | Unc | BU |
|---|---|---|---|---|---|---|
| 1904 | 16,000,000 | 5.00 | 10.00 | 35.00 | 125 | — |
| 1904 Proof | 12 | Value: 2,000 | | | | |

**25 CENTESIMOS** **KM# 37.1** **Composition:** Copper-Nickel Clad Copper

| Date | Mintage | F | VF | XF | Unc | BU |
|---|---|---|---|---|---|---|
| 1975 (RCM) | 40,000 | — | 0.35 | 0.50 | 1.00 | — |
| 1975 FM (M) | 5,000 | — | 1.00 | 1.75 | 3.00 | — |
| 1975 FM (U) | 1,410 | — | — | — | 4.00 | — |
| 1975 FM (P) | 41,000 | Value: 1.50 | | | | |
| 1976 (RCM) | 12,000 | — | 0.45 | 0.60 | 1.50 | — |
| 1976 FM (M) | 2,500 | — | 0.75 | 1.50 | 3.00 | — |
| 1976 FM (P) | 12,000 | Value: 1.50 | | | | |
| 1977 FM (U) | 2,500 | — | 0.75 | 1.50 | 2.50 | — |
| 1977 FM (P) | 9,548 | Value: 1.50 | | | | |
| 1979 FM (U) | 4,000 | — | 1.00 | 1.50 | 3.50 | — |
| 1979 FM (P) | 5,949 | Value: 1.50 | | | | |
| 1980 FM (U) | 4,000 | — | 1.00 | 1.50 | 3.50 | — |
| 1981 FM (P) | 1,973 | Value: 2.00 | | | | |
| 1982 FM (U) | 2,000 | — | 1.50 | 2.50 | 4.50 | — |
| 1982 Proof | 1,480 | Value: 2.00 | | | | |

**25 CENTESIMOS** **KM# 49** **Composition:** Copper-Nickel Clad Copper **Subject:** 75th Anniversary of Independence

| Date | Mintage | F | VF | XF | Unc | BU |
|---|---|---|---|---|---|---|
| 1978 FM (U) | 8,000 | — | 0.75 | 1.25 | 2.50 | — |
| 1978 FM (P) | 11,000 | Value: 2.00 | | | | |
| 1978 FM (P) | 11,000 | Value: 2.00 | | | | |

**25 CENTESIMOS** **KM# 37.2** **Composition:** Copper-Nickel Clad Copper **Edge Lettering:** 1830 BOLIVAR 1980

| Date | Mintage | F | VF | XF | Unc | BU |
|---|---|---|---|---|---|---|
| 1980 FM (P) | 2,629 | Value: 2.00 | | | | |

**1/4 BALBOA** **KM# 11.1** **Weight:** 6.2500 g. **Composition:** 0.9000 Silver .1809 oz. ASW

| Date | Mintage | F | VF | XF | Unc | BU |
|---|---|---|---|---|---|---|
| 1930 | 400,000 | 2.00 | 3.00 | 25.00 | 65.00 | — |
| 1930 Matte proof | 20 | — | — | — | 2,000 | — |
| 1931 | 48,000 | 15.00 | 30.00 | 250 | 1,500 | — |
| 1932 | 126,000 | 3.00 | 7.00 | 85.00 | 400 | — |
| 1933 | 120,000 | 3.00 | 6.00 | 30.00 | 185 | — |
| 1934 | 90,000 | 3.00 | 6.00 | 20.00 | 150 | — |
| 1947 | 700,000 | 1.00 | 2.00 | 5.00 | 25.00 | — |

**1/4 BALBOA** **KM# 19** **Weight:** 6.2500 g. **Composition:** 0.9000 Silver .1809 oz. ASW

| Date | Mintage | F | VF | XF | Unc | BU |
|---|---|---|---|---|---|---|
| 1953 | 1,200,000 | BV | 1.50 | 4.00 | 18.50 | — |
| 1953 Proof | Est. 5 | Value: 1,350 | | | | |

**1/4 BALBOA** **KM# 25** **Weight:** 6.2500 g. **Composition:** 0.9000 Silver .1809 oz. ASW

| Date | Mintage | F | VF | XF | Unc | BU |
|---|---|---|---|---|---|---|
| 1961 | 2,000,000 | BV | 1.25 | 1.75 | 3.75 | — |

**1/4 BALBOA** **KM# 11.2** **Weight:** 6.2500 g. **Composition:** 0.9000 Silver .1809 oz. ASW **Note:** Low relief.

| Date | Mintage | F | VF | XF | Unc | BU |
|---|---|---|---|---|---|---|
| 1962 | 4,000,000 | BV | 1.00 | 2.00 | 4.00 | — |
| 1962 Proof | 25 | Value: 500 | | | | |

**1/4 BALBOA** **KM# 11a** **Composition:** Copper-Nickel Clad Copper **Note:** Varieties exist.

| Date | Mintage | F | VF | XF | Unc | BU |
|---|---|---|---|---|---|---|
| 1966 (RCM) | 7,400,000 | — | 35.00 | 50.00 | 1.00 | — |
| 1966 (RCM) Proof | 13,000 | Value: 2.00 | | | | |
| 1967 Proof | 20,000 | Value: 1.50 | | | | |
| 1968 | 1,200,000 | — | 0.35 | 0.60 | 1.50 | — |
| 1968 Proof | 23,000 | Value: 1.50 | | | | |
| 1969 Proof | 14,000 | Value: 1.50 | | | | |
| 1970 | 2,000,000 | — | 0.35 | 0.60 | 2.00 | — |
| 1970 Proof | 9,528 | Value: 2.00 | | | | |
| 1971 Proof | 11,000 | Value: 2.00 | | | | |
| 1972 Proof | 13,000 | Value: 2.00 | | | | |
| 1973 | 800,000 | — | 0.40 | 1.00 | 2.00 | — |
| 1973 Proof | 17,000 | Value: 2.00 | | | | |
| 1974 Proof | 18,000 | Value: 2.00 | | | | |
| 1975 | 1,500,000 | — | 0.35 | 0.50 | 2.00 | — |
| 1979 | 2,000,000 | — | 0.25 | 0.45 | 1.50 | — |

| Date | Mintage | F | VF | XF | Unc | BU |
|---|---|---|---|---|---|---|
| 1980 | 2,000,000 | — | 0.25 | 0.45 | 2.00 | — |
| 1982 | 3,000,000 | — | 0.25 | 0.45 | 2.00 | — |
| 1983 (RCM) | 6,000,000 | — | 0.25 | 0.45 | 1.50 | — |
| 1986 (RCM) | 3,000,000 | — | 0.25 | 0.50 | 1.50 | — |
| 1993 | 4,000,000 | — | 0.25 | 0.45 | 1.00 | — |
| 1993 Proof | — | Value: 350 | | | | |

**Note:** The 1993 Proof strikes were not authorized by the Panamanian government

**1/4 BALBOA** **KM# 88** **Composition:** Copper-Nickel Clad Copper

| Date | Mintage | F | VF | XF | Unc | BU |
|---|---|---|---|---|---|---|
| 1983 FM (P) | — | Value: 4.00 | | | | |
| 1984 FM (P) | — | Value: 4.00 | | | | |

**1/4 BALBOA** **KM# 128** **Composition:** Copper-Nickel Clad Copper **Obverse:** National arms **Reverse:** Balboa's portrait

| Date | Mintage | F | VF | XF | Unc | BU |
|---|---|---|---|---|---|---|
| 1996 | 7,200,000 | — | — | — | 0.75 | — |

**50 CENTESIMOS** **KM# 5** **Weight:** 25.0000 g. **Composition:** 0.9000 Silver .7235 oz. ASW

| Date | Mintage | F | VF | XF | Unc | BU |
|---|---|---|---|---|---|---|
| 1904 | 1,000,000 | 15.00 | 30.00 | 60.00 | 225 | — |
| 1904 Proof | 12 | Value: 2,500 | | | | |
| 1905 | 1,800,000 | 25.00 | 50.00 | 135 | 500 | — |

**Note:** 51,000,000 of both 1904 and 1905 dates were melted in 1931 for the metal to issue 1 Balboa coin at San Francisco Mint

**50 CENTESIMOS** **KM# 38.1** **Composition:** Copper-Nickel Clad Copper **Subject:** Fernando de Lesseps

| Date | Mintage | F | VF | XF | Unc | BU |
|---|---|---|---|---|---|---|
| 1975 (RCM) | 20,000 | — | 1.00 | 1.50 | 2.00 | — |
| 1975FM (M) | 2,000 | — | 1.50 | 3.00 | 5.00 | — |
| 1975FM (U) | 1,410 | — | — | — | 6.50 | — |
| 1975FM (P) Proof | 41,000 | Value: 2.00 | | | | |
| 1976 (RCM) | 12,000 | — | 1.25 | 1.75 | 3.00 | — |
| 1976FM (M) | 1,250 | — | 1.00 | 2.25 | 8.00 | — |
| 1976FM (P) Proof | 12,000 | Value: 2.50 | | | | |
| 1977FM (U) | 1,250 | — | 1.00 | 2.25 | 8.00 | — |
| 1977FM (P) Proof | 9,548 | Value: 2.50 | | | | |
| 1979FM (U) | 2,000 | — | 2.00 | 3.50 | 9.00 | — |

| Date | Mintage | F | VF | XF | Unc | BU |
|---|---|---|---|---|---|---|
| 1979FM (P) Proof | 5,949 | Value: 2.50 | | | | |
| 1980FM (U) | 2,000 | — | 2.00 | 3.50 | 9.00 | — |
| 1981FM (P) Proof | 1,973 | Value: 5.00 | | | | |
| 1982FM (U) | 1,000 | — | 3.00 | 5.00 | 11.50 | — |
| 1982FM (P) Proof | 1,480 | Value: 5.00 | | | | |

**Note:** (Error) Without edge lettering

**50 CENTESIMOS** **KM# 50** **Composition:** Copper-Nickel Clad Copper **Subject:** 75th Anniversary of Independence

| Date | Mintage | F | VF | XF | Unc | BU |
|---|---|---|---|---|---|---|
| 1978FM (U) | 8,000 | — | 1.50 | 3.00 | 5.00 | — |
| 1978FM (P) | 11,000 | Value: 5.00 | | | | |

**50 CENTESIMOS** **KM# 38.2** **Composition:** Copper-Nickel Clad Copper **Edge Lettering:** 1830 BOLIVAR 1980

| Date | Mintage | F | VF | XF | Unc | BU |
|---|---|---|---|---|---|---|
| 1980 FM (P) | 2,629 | Value: 5.00 | | | | |
| 1980 Proof | Inc. above | Value: 125 | | | | |

**Note:** (error) without edge lettering

**1/2 BALBOA** **KM# 12.1** **Weight:** 12.5000 g. **Composition:** 0.9000 Silver .3617 oz. ASW **Note:** High relief.

| Date | Mintage | F | VF | XF | Unc | BU |
|---|---|---|---|---|---|---|
| 1930 | 300,000 | 3.50 | 8.00 | 30.00 | 95.00 | — |
| 1930 Matte proof | 20 | Value: 2,200 | | | | |
| 1932 | 63,000 | 5.00 | 10.00 | 125 | 650 | — |
| 1933 | 120,000 | 4.00 | 6.00 | 40.00 | 325 | — |
| 1934 | 90,000 | 4.00 | 6.00 | 40.00 | 275 | — |
| 1947 | 450,000 | BV | 3.50 | 10.00 | 35.00 | — |

**1/2 BALBOA** **KM# 20** **Weight:** 12.5000 g. **Composition:** 0.9000 Silver .3617 oz. ASW

| Date | Mintage | F | VF | XF | Unc | BU |
|---|---|---|---|---|---|---|
| 1953 | 600,000 | — | BV | 3.50 | 6.50 | — |
| 1953 Proof | Est. 5 | Value: 1,850 | | | | |

**1/2 BALBOA** **KM# 26** **Weight:** 12.5000 g. **Composition:** 0.9000 Silver .3617 oz. ASW

| Date | Mintage | F | VF | XF | Unc | BU |
|---|---|---|---|---|---|---|
| 1961 | 350,000 | — | BV | 4.00 | 8.00 | — |

**1/2 BALBOA** **KM# 12.2** **Weight:** 12.5000 g. **Composition:** 0.9000 Silver .3617 oz. ASW **Note:** Low relief.

| Date | Mintage | F | VF | XF | Unc | BU |
|---|---|---|---|---|---|---|
| 1962 | 700,000 | — | BV | 3.00 | 6.50 | — |
| 1962 Proof | 25 | Value: 750 | | | | |

**1/2 BALBOA** **KM# 12a.2** **Weight:** 12.5000 g. **Composition:** 0.4000 Silver Clad .1608 oz. ASW **Note:** Error: Type II helmet rim incomplete.

| Date | Mintage | F | VF | XF | Unc | BU |
|---|---|---|---|---|---|---|
| 1966 | Inc. above | — | 3.50 | 7.50 | 20.00 | — |

**1/2 BALBOA** **KM# 12a.1** **Weight:** 12.5000 g. **Composition:** 0.4000 Silver Clad .1608 oz. ASW **Obverse:** Normal helmet **Note:** Varieties exist.

| Date | Mintage | F | VF | XF | Unc | BU |
|---|---|---|---|---|---|---|
| 1966 (RCM) | 1,000,000 | — | 1.50 | 2.00 | 5.00 | — |
| 1966 (RCM) Proof | 13,000 | Value: 3.00 | | | | |
| 1967 | 300,000 | — | 1.50 | 2.00 | 5.00 | — |
| 1967 Proof | 20,000 | Value: 3.00 | | | | |
| 1968 | 1,000,000 | — | 1.50 | 2.00 | 4.00 | — |
| 1968 Proof | 23,000 | Value: 3.00 | | | | |
| 1969 Proof | 14,000 | Value: 3.00 | | | | |
| 1970 | 610,000 | — | 1.50 | 2.00 | 5.00 | — |
| 1970 Proof | 9,528 | Value: 4.00 | | | | |
| 1971 Proof | 11,000 | Value: 3.00 | | | | |
| 1972 Proof | 13,000 | Value: 3.00 | | | | |
| 1993 Proof | — | Value: 450 | | | | |

**Note:** The 1993 Proof strike was not authorized by the Panamanian government

**1/2 BALBOA** **KM# 12b** **Composition:** Copper-Nickel Clad Copper **Note:** Varieties exist.

| Date | Mintage | F | VF | XF | Unc | BU |
|---|---|---|---|---|---|---|
| 1973 | 1,000,000 | — | 1.00 | 1.25 | 2.00 | — |
| 1973 Proof | 17,000 | Value: 2.00 | | | | |
| 1974 Proof | 18,000 | Value: 2.00 | | | | |
| 1975 | 1,200,000 | — | 0.75 | 1.25 | 1.75 | — |
| 1979 | 1,000,000 | — | — | 0.75 | 1.50 | — |
| 1980 | 400,000 | — | — | 0.75 | 2.00 | — |
| 1982 | 400,000 | — | — | 0.75 | 2.00 | — |
| 1983 (RCM) | 1,850,000 | — | — | 0.75 | 1.50 | — |
| 1986 (RCM) | 200,000 | — | 0.75 | 1.50 | 5.00 | — |
| 1993 | 600,000 | — | 0.75 | 1.25 | 2.00 | — |

**1/2 BALBOA** **KM# 89** **Composition:** Copper-Nickel Clad Copper

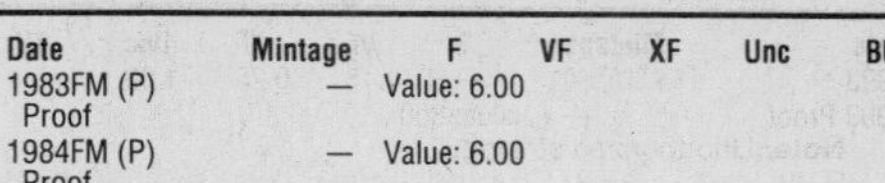

| Date | Mintage | F | VF | XF | Unc | BU |
|---|---|---|---|---|---|---|
| 1983FM (P) Proof | — | Value: 6.00 | | | | |
| 1984FM (P) Proof | — | Value: 6.00 | | | | |

**1/2 BALBOA** **KM# 129** **Composition:** Copper-Nickel Clad Copper **Obverse:** National arms **Reverse:** Balboa's Portrait

| Date | Mintage | F | VF | XF | Unc | BU |
|---|---|---|---|---|---|---|
| 1996 | 200,000 | — | 0.75 | 1.00 | 3.00 | — |

**BALBOA** **KM# 13** **Weight:** 26.7300 g. **Composition:** 0.9000 Silver .7735 oz. ASW **Subject:** Vasco Nunez de Balboa

| Date | Mintage | F | VF | XF | Unc | BU |
|---|---|---|---|---|---|---|
| 1931 | 200,000 | 6.00 | 8.00 | 20.00 | 75.00 | — |
| 1931 Proof | 20 | Value: 3,000 | | | | |
| 1934 | 225,000 | 6.00 | 7.50 | 17.50 | 70.00 | — |
| 1947 | 500,000 | BV | 4.50 | 6.00 | 20.00 | — |

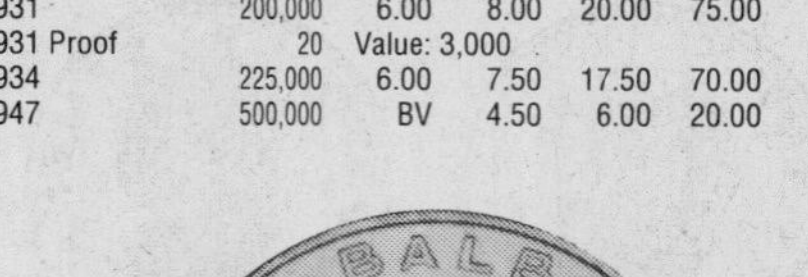

**BALBOA** **KM# 21** **Weight:** 26.7300 g. **Composition:** 0.9000 Silver .7735 oz. ASW **Subject:** 50th Anniversary of the Republic **Obverse:** Similar to KM#13

| Date | Mintage | F | VF | XF | Unc | BU |
|---|---|---|---|---|---|---|
| 1953 | 50,000 | 6.50 | 8.00 | 12.00 | 32.00 | — |

**BALBOA** **KM# 27** **Weight:** 26.7300 g. **Composition:** 0.9000 Silver .7735 oz. ASW **Note:** More than 200,000 of 1966 dates were melted down in 1971 for silver for the 20 Balboas. Varieties exist.

| Date | Mintage | F | VF | XF | Unc | BU |
|---|---|---|---|---|---|---|
| 1966 (RCM) | 300,000 | — | — | — | 10.00 | — |
| 1966 (RCM) Proof | 13,000 | Value: 15.00 | | | | |
| 1967 Proof | 20,000 | Value: 12.00 | | | | |
| 1968 | 23,000 | Value: 12.00 | | | | |
| 1969 Proof | 14,000 | Value: 15.00 | | | | |
| 1970 Proof | 13,000 | Value: 15.00 | | | | |
| 1971 Proof | 18,000 | Value: 13.50 | | | | |
| 1972 Proof | 23,000 | Value: 12.00 | | | | |
| 1973 Proof | 30,000 | Value: 12.00 | | | | |
| 1974 Proof | 30,000 | Value: 12.00 | | | | |

**BALBOA** **KM# 39.1** **Composition:** Copper-Nickel Clad Copper

| Date | Mintage | F | VF | XF | Unc | BU |
|---|---|---|---|---|---|---|
| 1975FM (M) | 4,035 | — | — | — | 18.00 | — |
| 1975FM (U) | 1,410 | — | — | — | 35.00 | — |
| 1976FM (M) | 625 | — | — | — | 75.00 | — |
| 1977FM (U) | 625 | — | — | — | 75.00 | — |
| 1979FM (U) | 1,000 | — | — | — | 50.00 | — |
| 1980FM (U) | 1,000 | — | — | — | 50.00 | — |
| 1982FM (U) | 500 | — | — | — | 65.00 | — |

**BALBOA** **KM# 39.1a** **Weight:** 26.7300 g. **Composition:** 0.9250 Silver .7950 oz. ASW

| Date | Mintage | F | VF | XF | Unc | BU |
|---|---|---|---|---|---|---|
| 1975FM (P) | 45,000 | Value: 10.00 | | | | |
| 1976FM (P) | 14,000 | Value: 12.00 | | | | |
| 1977FM (P) | 11,000 | Value: 12.00 | | | | |
| 1979FM (P) | 7,160 | Value: 20.00 | | | | |

**BALBOA** **KM# 39.2** **Composition:** Copper-Nickel Clad Copper **Obverse:** Erroneous silver content (LEY .925) below arms

| Date | Mintage | F | VF | XF | Unc | BU |
|---|---|---|---|---|---|---|
| 1975 (RCM) | 10,000 | — | — | — | 8.00 | — |
| 1976 (RCM) | 12,000 | — | — | — | 8.00 | — |

**BALBOA** **KM# 51** **Composition:** Copper-Nickel Clad Copper **Subject:** 75th Anniversary of Independence

| Date | Mintage | F | VF | XF | Unc | BU |
|---|---|---|---|---|---|---|
| 1978FM (U) | 4,000 | — | — | — | 12.50 | — |

**BALBOA** **KM# 51a** **Composition:** 0.9250 Silver

| Date | Mintage | F | VF | XF | Unc | BU |
|---|---|---|---|---|---|---|
| 1978FM (P) | 13,000 | Value: 20.00 | | | | |

**BALBOA** **KM# 39.3** **Weight:** 2.7400 g. **Composition:** 0.5000 Silver .3334 oz. ASW **Edge Lettering:** 1830 BALBOA 1980

| Date | Mintage | F | VF | XF | Unc | BU |
|---|---|---|---|---|---|---|
| 1980FM (P) | 2,629 | Value: 20.00 | | | | |

**BALBOA** **KM# 39.1b** **Weight:** 20.7400 g. **Composition:** 0.5000 Silver .3334 oz. ASW

| Date | Mintage | F | VF | XF | Unc | BU |
|---|---|---|---|---|---|---|
| 1981FM (P) | 2,633 | Value: 20.00 | | | | |
| 1982FM (P) | 1,837 | Value: 22.00 | | | | |

**BALBOA** **KM# 39.4** **Composition:** Copper-Nickel Clad Copper **Obverse:** Erroneous silver content (LEY .500) below arms

| Date | Mintage | F | VF | XF | Unc | BU |
|---|---|---|---|---|---|---|
| 1982FM (U) | 11 | — | — | — | 600 | — |

**BALBOA** **KM# 76** **Composition:** Copper Nickel **Subject:** Death of General Omar Torrijos

| Date | Mintage | F | VF | XF | Unc | BU |
|---|---|---|---|---|---|---|
| 1982 | 200,000 | — | — | 1.50 | 4.00 | — |
| 1982 Frosted obverse and reverse. Proof | 200 | Value: 125 | | | | |
| 1982 Frosted obverse. Proof | 50 | Value: 200 | | | | |
| 1983 | 200,000 | — | — | 1.50 | 4.00 | — |
| 1984 | 200,000 | — | — | 1.50 | 4.00 | — |

**BALBOA** **KM# 90** **Weight:** 20.7400 g. **Composition:** 0.5000 Silver .3334 oz. ASW

| Date | Mintage | F | VF | XF | Unc | BU |
|---|---|---|---|---|---|---|
| 1983FM (P) | 1,602 | Value: 27.50 | | | | |
| 1984FM (P) | 1,044 | Value: 30.00 | | | | |
| 1985FM (P) | 954 | Value: 50.00 | | | | |

**5 BALBOAS** **KM# 28** **Weight:** 35.7000 g. **Composition:** 0.9250 Silver 1.0617 oz. ASW **Subject:** 11th Central American and Caribbean Games

| Date | Mintage | F | VF | XF | Unc | BU |
|---|---|---|---|---|---|---|
| 1970FM | 1,647,000 | — | — | — | 8.00 | — |
| 1970FM (U) | 603,000 | — | — | — | — | — |
| 1970FM (P) | 59,000 | Value: 10.00 | | | | |

**5 BALBOAS** **KM# 30** **Weight:** 35.0000 g. **Composition:** 0.9000 Silver 1.0128 oz. ASW **Subject:** F.A.O. **Obverse:** Similar to KM#28

| Date | Mintage | F | VF | XF | Unc | BU |
|---|---|---|---|---|---|---|
| 1972 | 70,000 | — | — | — | 9.00 | — |
| 1972 Proof | 10,000 | Value: 20.00 | | | | |

**5 BALBOAS** **KM# 40.1** **Composition:** Copper-Nickel Clad Copper **Subject:** Belisario Porras **Obverse:** Similar to KM#28

| Date | Mintage | F | VF | XF | Unc | BU |
|---|---|---|---|---|---|---|
| 1975FM (M) | 5,125 | — | — | — | 10.00 | — |
| 1975FM (U) | 1,410 | — | — | — | 20.00 | — |
| 1976FM (M) | 125 | — | — | — | 175 | — |
| 1977FM (U) | 125 | — | — | — | 175 | — |
| 1979FM (U) | 1,000 | — | — | — | 25.00 | — |
| 1980FM (U) | 1,000 | — | — | — | 25.00 | — |
| 1982FM (U) | 1,200 | — | — | — | 22.50 | — |

**5 BALBOAS** **KM# 40.1a** **Weight:** 35.1200 g. **Composition:** 0.9250 Silver 1.0446 oz. ASW

| Date | Mintage | F | VF | XF | Unc | BU |
|---|---|---|---|---|---|---|
| 1975FM (P) | 41,000 | Value: 15.00 | | | | |
| 1976FM (P) | 12,000 | Value: 20.00 | | | | |
| 1977FM (P) | 9,548 | Value: 20.00 | | | | |
| 1979FM (P) | 5,949 | Value: 30.00 | | | | |

**5 BALBOAS** **KM# 40.2** **Composition:** Copper-Nickel Clad Copper **Obverse:** Erroneous silver content (LEY .925) below arms

| Date | Mintage | F | VF | XF | Unc | BU |
|---|---|---|---|---|---|---|
| 1975 | 4,000 | — | — | — | 8.50 | — |
| 1976 | 5,000 | — | — | — | 8.50 | — |

**5 BALBOAS** **KM# 52** **Composition:** Copper-Nickel Clad Copper 500 oz. **Subject:** 75th Anniversary of Independence

| Date | Mintage | F | VF | XF | Unc | BU |
|---|---|---|---|---|---|---|
| 1978FM (U) | 2,000 | — | — | — | 20.00 | — |

**5 BALBOAS** **KM# 52a** **Weight:** 35.1200 g. **Composition:** 0.9250 Silver 1.0466 oz. ASW

| Date | Mintage | F | VF | XF | Unc | BU |
|---|---|---|---|---|---|---|
| 1978FM (P) | 11,000 | Value: 22.50 | | | | |

**5 BALBOAS** **KM# 58** **Weight:** 35.1200 g. **Composition:** 0.9250 Silver 1.0466 oz. ASW **Subject:** Panama Canal Treaty Implementation

| Date | Mintage | F | VF | XF | Unc | BU |
|---|---|---|---|---|---|---|
| 1979FM (P) | 6,854 | Value: 30.00 | | | | |

**5 BALBOAS** **KM# 63** **Weight:** 24.1100 g. **Composition:** 0.5000 Silver .3875 oz. ASW **Subject:** Champions of Boxing

| Date | Mintage | F | VF | XF | Unc | BU |
|---|---|---|---|---|---|---|
| 1980 Proof | 1,261 | Value: 45.00 | | | | |

**5 BALBOAS** **KM# 40.3** **Weight:** 23.3300 g. **Composition:** 0.5000 Silver .3751 oz. ASW **Edge Lettering:** 1830 BALBOA 1980

| Date | Mintage | F | VF | XF | Unc | BU |
|---|---|---|---|---|---|---|
| 1980FM (P) | 2,629 | Value: 20.00 | | | | |

**5 BALBOAS** **KM# 40.1b** **Weight:** 23.3300 g. **Composition:** 0.5000 Silver .3751 oz. ASW

| Date | Mintage | F | VF | XF | Unc | BU |
|---|---|---|---|---|---|---|
| 1981FM (P) | 1,973 | Value: 30.00 | | | | |
| 1982FM (P) | 1,480 | Value: 30.00 | | | | |

**5 BALBOAS** **KM# 40.4** **Weight:** 23.3300 g. **Composition:** 0.5000 Silver .3751 oz. ASW **Obverse:** Erroneous silver content (LEY .925) below arms

| Date | Mintage | F | VF | XF | Unc | BU |
|---|---|---|---|---|---|---|
| 1982FM (P) | — | Value: 65.00 | | | | |

**5 BALBOAS** **KM# 40.5** **Composition:** Copper-Nickel Clad Copper 500 oz. **Obverse:** Erroneous silver content (LEY .500) below arms

| Date | Mintage | F | VF | XF | Unc | BU |
|---|---|---|---|---|---|---|
| 1982FM (U) | 200 | — | — | — | 135 | — |

**5 BALBOAS** **KM# 77** **Weight:** 24.1600 g. **Composition:** 0.9250 Silver .7186 oz. ASW **Subject:** Chanpions of Soccer

| Date | Mintage | F | VF | XF | Unc | BU |
|---|---|---|---|---|---|---|
| 1982 Proof | 9,446 | Value: 40.00 | | | | |

**5 BALBOAS** **KM# 91** **Weight:** 23.3300 g. **Composition:** 0.5000 Silver .3751 oz. ASW

| Date | Mintage | F | VF | XF | Unc | BU |
|---|---|---|---|---|---|---|
| 1983FM (P) | 1,776 | Value: 47.50 | | | | |
| 1984FM (P) | 889 | Value: 50.00 | | | | |

**5 BALBOAS** **KM# 104** **Weight:** 23.3300 g. **Composition:** 0.5000 Silver .3751 oz. ASW **Subject:** Discovery of the Pacific Ocean

| Date | Mintage | F | VF | XF | Unc | BU |
|---|---|---|---|---|---|---|
| 1985FM (P) | 765 | Value: 115 | | | | |

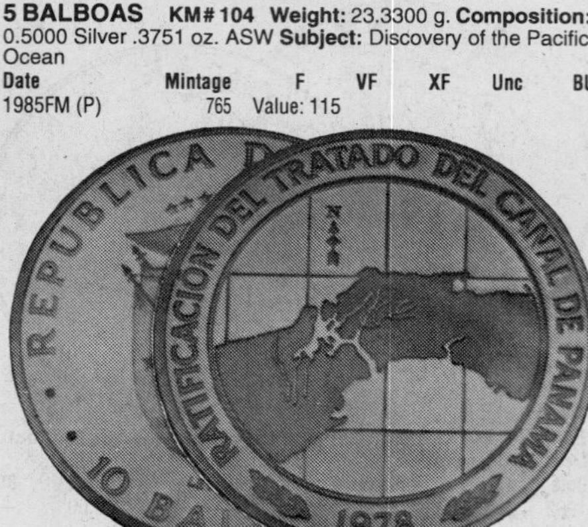


**10 BALBOAS** **KM# 53** **Weight:** 42.4800 g. **Composition:** 0.9250 Silver 1.2635 oz. ASW **Subject:** Panama Canal Treaty Ratification

| Date | Mintage | F | VF | XF | Unc | BU |
|---|---|---|---|---|---|---|
| 1978FM (P) | 12,000 | Value: 37.50 | | | | |

**10 BALBOAS** **KM# 53a** **Composition:** Nickel

| Date | Mintage | F | VF | XF | Unc | BU |
|---|---|---|---|---|---|---|
| 1978 | 300,000 | — | — | 10.00 | 18.50 | — |

**10 BALBOAS** **KM# 59** **Weight:** 42.4800 g. **Composition:** 0.9250 Silver 1.2635 oz. ASW **Subject:** Panama Canal Treaty Implementation

| Date | Mintage | F | VF | XF | Unc | BU |
|---|---|---|---|---|---|---|
| 1979FM (P) | 7,229 | Value: 47.50 | | | | |

**10 BALBOAS** **KM# 64** **Weight:** 26.5000 g. **Composition:** 0.5000 Silver .4260 oz. ASW **Subject:** Balseria Game

| Date | Mintage | F | VF | XF | Unc | BU |
|---|---|---|---|---|---|---|
| 1980 Proof | 1,267 | Value: 50.00 | | | | |

**10 BALBOAS** **KM# 78** **Weight:** 26.5000 g. **Composition:** 0.5000 Silver .4260 oz. ASW **Subject:** Champions of Soccer

| Date | Mintage | F | VF | XF | Unc | BU |
|---|---|---|---|---|---|---|
| 1982 Proof | 9,076 | Value: 47.50 | | | | |

**10 BALBOAS** **KM# 79** **Weight:** 26.5000 g. **Composition:** 0.5000 Silver .4260 oz. ASW **Subject:** International Year of the Child

| Date | Mintage | F | VF | XF | Unc | BU |
|---|---|---|---|---|---|---|
| 1982 Proof | 8,460 | Value: 35.00 | | | | |

**10 BALBOAS** **KM# 130** **Weight:** 31.0000 g. **Composition:** 0.9250 Silver .9219 oz. ASW **Subject:** Panama Canal Transfer **Obverse:** President's portrait **Reverse:** Ship in canal under Panamanian flag

| Date | Mintage | F | VF | XF | Unc | BU |
|---|---|---|---|---|---|---|
| 1999 Proof | 4,500 | Value: 50.00 | | | | |

**20 BALBOAS** **KM# 29** **Weight:** 129.5900 g. **Composition:** 0.9250 Silver 3.8544 oz. ASW **Subject:** 150th Anniversary of Central American Independence **Obverse:** Similar to 5 Balboas, KM#28 **Size:** 61 mm. **Note:** Illustration reduced.

| Date | Mintage | F | VF | XF | Unc | BU |
|---|---|---|---|---|---|---|
| 1971FM (M) | 69,000 | — | — | — | 32.50 | — |
| 1971FM (U) | — | — | — | — | 37.50 | — |
| 1971FM (P) | 40,000 | Value: 40.00 | | | | |

**20 BALBOAS** **KM# 31** **Weight:** 129.5900 g. **Composition:** 0.9250 Silver 3.8544 oz. ASW **Subject:** Regular Issue: Simon Bolivar **Obverse:** Similar to 5 Balboas, KM#28 **Size:** 61 mm. **Note:** Illustration reduced.

| Date | Mintage | F | VF | XF | Unc | BU |
|---|---|---|---|---|---|---|
| 1972FM (M) | 37,000 | — | — | — | 35.00 | — |
| 1972FM (P) | 48,000 | Value: 40.00 | | | | |
| 1973FM (M) | 94,000 | — | — | — | 35.00 | — |
| 1973FM (P) | 74,000 | Value: 40.00 | | | | |
| 1974FM (M) | 99,000 | — | — | — | 35.00 | — |
| 1974FM (P) | 161,000 | Value: 40.00 | | | | |
| 1975FM (M) | 2,500 | — | — | — | 60.00 | — |
| 1975FM (P) | 62,000 | Value: 35.00 | | | | |
| 1975FM (U) | — | — | — | — | 100 | — |
| 1976FM (M) | 2,500 | — | — | 35.00 | 70.00 | — |
| 1976FM (P) | 22,000 | Value: 40.00 | | | | |

**20 BALBOAS** **KM# 44** **Weight:** 129.5900 g. **Composition:** 0.9250 Silver 3.8544 oz. ASW **Subject:** Vasco Nunez de Balboa **Obverse:** Similar to 5 Balboas, KM#28 **Size:** 61 mm. **Note:** Illustration reduced.

| Date | Mintage | F | VF | XF | Unc | BU |
|---|---|---|---|---|---|---|
| 1977FM (U) | 2,879 | — | — | — | 75.00 | — |
| 1977FM (P) | 24,000 | Value: 45.00 | | | | |
| 1979FM (U) | 2,500 | — | — | — | 75.00 | — |
| 1979FM (P) | 13,000 | Value: 50.00 | | | | |

**20 BALBOAS** **KM# 54** **Weight:** 129.5900 g. **Composition:** 0.9250 Silver 3.8544 oz. ASW **Subject:** 75th Anniversary of Independence **Reverse:** Similar to KM#44

| Date | Mintage | F | VF | XF | Unc | BU |
|---|---|---|---|---|---|---|
| 1978FM (U) | 2,500 | — | — | — | 65.00 | — |
| 1978FM (P) | 23,000 | Value: 45.00 | | | | |



**20 BALBOAS** **KM# 65** **Weight:** 119.8800 g. **Composition:** 0.5000 Silver 1.9273 oz. ASW **Subject:** Sesquicentenarium - Death of Simon Bolivar **Obverse:** Similar to 5 Balboas KM$28

| Date | Mintage | F | VF | XF | Unc | BU |
|---|---|---|---|---|---|---|
| 1980FM (U) | 1,000 | — | — | — | 120 | — |
| 1980FM (P) | 3,714 | Value: 95.00 | | | | |

**20 BALBOAS** **KM# 71** **Weight:** 118.5700 g. **Composition:** 0.5000 Silver 1.9060 oz. ASW **Subject:** Simon Bolivar, El Libertador

| Date | Mintage | F | VF | XF | Unc | BU |
|---|---|---|---|---|---|---|
| 1981FM (U) | 500 | — | — | — | 140 | — |
| 1981FM (P) | 3,528 | Value: 95.00 | | | | |

**20 BALBOAS** **KM# 72** **Weight:** 2.1400 g. **Composition:** 0.5000 Gold .0344 oz. AGW **Subject:** Figure of eight butterfly

| Date | Mintage | F | VF | XF | Unc | BU |
|---|---|---|---|---|---|---|
| 1981FM (U) | 205 | — | — | — | 175 | — |
| 1981FM (P) | 4,445 | Value: 65.00 | | | | |

**20 BALBOAS** **KM# 80** **Weight:** 119.8800 g. **Composition:** 0.5000 Silver 1.9273 oz. ASW **Subject:** Balboa discoverer of the Pacific

| Date | Mintage | F | VF | XF | Unc | BU |
|---|---|---|---|---|---|---|
| 1982FM (P) | 2,352 | Value: 110 | | | | |

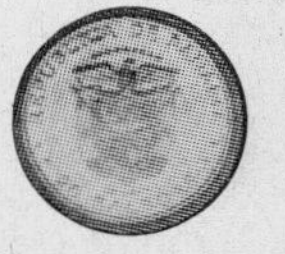

**20 BALBOAS** **KM# 81** **Weight:** 2.1400 g. **Composition:** 0.5000 Gold .0344 oz. AGW **Subject:** Hummingbird

| Date | Mintage | F | VF | XF | Unc | BU |
|---|---|---|---|---|---|---|
| 1982FM (U) | 140 | — | — | — | 215 | — |
| 1982FM (P) | 3,445 | Value: 55.00 | | | | |

**20 BALBOAS** **KM# 92** **Weight:** 2.1400 g. **Composition:** 0.5000 Gold .0344 oz. AGW **Subject:** Banded Butterfly Fish

| Date | Mintage | F | VF | XF | Unc | BU |
|---|---|---|---|---|---|---|
| 1983FM (U) | — | — | — | — | 175 | — |
| 1983FM (P) | 1,671 | Value: 70.00 | | | | |

**20 BALBOAS** **KM# 93** **Weight:** 18.5700 g. **Composition:** 0.5000 Silver 1.9060 oz. ASW **Subject:** 200th Anniversary - Birth of Bolivar **Obverse:** Similar to 5 Balboas, KM#77

| Date | Mintage | F | VF | XF | Unc | BU |
|---|---|---|---|---|---|---|
| 1983FM (U) | 500 | — | — | — | 135 | — |
| 1983FM (P) | 3,186 | Value: 75.00 | | | | |

**20 BALBOAS** **KM# 97** **Weight:** 2.1400 g. **Composition:** 0.5000 Gold .0344 oz. AGW **Subject:** Puma

| Date | Mintage | F | VF | XF | Unc | BU |
|---|---|---|---|---|---|---|
| 1984FM (U) | 100 | — | — | — | 275 | — |
| 1984FM (P) | 357 | Value: 180 | | | | |

**20 BALBOAS** KM# 98 **Weight:** 119.8800 g. **Composition:** 0.5000 Silver 1.9273 oz. ASW **Subject:** Balboa and Indian guide

| Date | Mintage | F | VF | XF | Unc | BU |
|---|---|---|---|---|---|---|
| 1984FM (P) | 1,760 | Value: 150 | | | | |

**20 BALBOAS** KM# 102 **Weight:** 2.1400 g. **Composition:** 0.5000 Gold .0344 oz. AGW **Subject:** Harpy Eagle

| Date | Mintage | F | VF | XF | Unc | BU |
|---|---|---|---|---|---|---|
| 1985FM (P) | 817 | Value: 120 | | | | |

**20 BALBOAS** KM# 105 **Weight:** 119.8800 g. **Composition:** 0.5000 Silver 1.9273 oz. ASW **Subject:** Discovery of the Pacific Ocean

| Date | Mintage | F | VF | XF | Unc | BU |
|---|---|---|---|---|---|---|
| 1985FM (P) | 1,402 | Value: 135 | | | | |

**50 BALBOAS** KM# 73 **Weight:** 5.3700 g. **Composition:** 0.5000 Gold .0861 oz. AGW **Subject:** Christmas 1981

| Date | Mintage | F | VF | XF | Unc | BU |
|---|---|---|---|---|---|---|
| 1981FM (U) | 154 | — | — | — | 200 | — |
| 1981FM (P) | 1,940 | Value: 75.00 | | | | |

**50 BALBOAS** KM# 82 **Weight:** 5.3700 g. **Composition:** 0.5000 Gold .0861 oz. AGW **Subject:** Christmas 1982

| Date | Mintage | F | VF | XF | Unc | BU |
|---|---|---|---|---|---|---|
| 1982FM (U) | 60 | — | — | — | 350 | — |
| 1982FM (P) | 1,361 | Value: 80.00 | | | | |

**50 BALBOAS** KM# 94 **Weight:** 5.3700 g. **Composition:** 0.5000 Gold .0861 oz. AGW **Subject:** Christmas 1983

| Date | Mintage | F | VF | XF | Unc | BU |
|---|---|---|---|---|---|---|
| 1983FM (U) | — | — | — | — | 175 | — |
| 1983FM (P) | 1,283 | Value: 80.00 | | | | |

**50 BALBOAS** KM# 99 **Weight:** 5.3700 g. **Composition:** 0.5000 Gold .0861 oz. AGW **Subject:** Peace at Christmas

| Date | Mintage | F | VF | XF | Unc | BU |
|---|---|---|---|---|---|---|
| 1984FM (P) | — | Value: 250 | | | | |

**75 BALBOAS** KM# 55 **Weight:** 10.6000 g. **Composition:** 0.5000 Gold .1704 oz. AGW **Subject:** 75th Anniversary of Independence

| Date | Mintage | F | VF | XF | Unc | BU |
|---|---|---|---|---|---|---|
| ND1978FM (U) | 410 | — | — | — | 150 | — |
| ND1978FM (P) | 9,161 | Value: 82.50 | | | | |

**100 BALBOAS** KM# 41 **Weight:** 8.1600 g. **Composition:** 0.9000 Gold .2361 oz. AGW **Subject:** 500th Anniversary - Birth of Balboa

| Date | Mintage | F | VF | XF | Unc | BU |
|---|---|---|---|---|---|---|
| 1975FM (U) | 44,000 | — | — | — | 95.00 | — |
| 1975FM (P) | 75,000 | Value: 100 | | | | |
| 1976FM (M) | 50 | — | — | — | 450 | — |
| 1976FM (U) | 3,013 | — | — | — | 115 | — |
| 1976FM (P) | 11,000 | Value: 110 | | | | |
| 1977FM (M) | 50 | — | — | — | 350 | — |
| 1977FM (U) | 324 | — | — | — | 200 | — |
| 1977FM (P) | 5,092 | Value: 125 | | | | |

**100 BALBOAS** KM# 56 **Weight:** 8.1600 g. **Composition:** 0.9000 Gold .2361 oz. AGW **Subject:** Peace and progress

| Date | Mintage | F | VF | XF | Unc | BU |
|---|---|---|---|---|---|---|
| 1978FM (M) | 50 | — | — | — | 350 | — |
| 1978FM (U) | 300 | — | — | — | 220 | — |
| 1978FM (P) | 6,086 | Value: 125 | | | | |

**100 BALBOAS** KM# 60 **Weight:** 8.1600 g. **Composition:** 0.9000 Gold .2361 oz. AGW **Subject:** Pre-Columbian Art - Golden Turtle

| Date | Mintage | F | VF | XF | Unc | BU |
|---|---|---|---|---|---|---|
| 1979FM (M) | 50 | — | — | — | 350 | — |
| 1979FM (U) | 240 | — | — | — | 250 | — |
| 1979FM (P) | 4,829 | Value: 150 | | | | |

**100 BALBOAS** KM# 66 **Weight:** 8.1600 g. **Composition:** 0.9000 Gold .2361 oz. AGW **Subject:** Pre-Columbian Art - Golden Condor

| Date | Mintage | F | VF | XF | Unc | BU |
|---|---|---|---|---|---|---|
| 1980FM (U) | 209 | — | — | — | 275 | — |
| 1980FM (P) | 2,411 | Value: 165 | | | | |

**100 BALBOAS** KM# 67 **Weight:** 7.1300 g. **Composition:** 0.5000 Gold .1146 oz. AGW **Subject:** Panama Canal Centennial

| Date | Mintage | F | VF | XF | Unc | BU |
|---|---|---|---|---|---|---|
| ND (1980)FM (U) | 77 | — | — | — | 475 | — |
| ND (1980)FM (P) | 2,468 | Value: 125 | | | | |

**100 BALBOAS** KM# 74 **Weight:** 7.1300 g. **Composition:** 0.5000 Gold .1146 oz. AGW **Subject:** Pre-Columbian Art **Reverse:** Cocle Peoples Ceremonial Mask

| Date | Mintage | F | VF | XF | Unc | BU |
|---|---|---|---|---|---|---|
| 1981FM (U) | 174 | — | — | — | 300 | — |
| 1981FM (P) | 1,841 | Value: 150 | | | | |

**100 BALBOAS** KM# 83 **Weight:** 7.1300 g. **Composition:** 0.5000 Gold .1146 oz. AGW **Subject:** Pre-Columbian Art **Reverse:** Native design

| Date | Mintage | F | VF | XF | Unc | BU |
|---|---|---|---|---|---|---|
| 1982FM (U) | 26 | — | — | — | 600 | — |
| 1982FM (P) | 578 | Value: 185 | | | | |

**100 BALBOAS** KM# 95 **Weight:** 7.1300 g. **Composition:** 0.5000 Gold .1146 oz. AGW **Subject:** Pre-Columbian Art **Reverse:** Cocle style birds

| Date | Mintage | F | VF | XF | Unc | BU |
|---|---|---|---|---|---|---|
| 1983FM (U) | — | — | — | — | 300 | — |
| 1983FM (P) | 1,308 | Value: 150 | | | | |

**100 BALBOAS** KM# 100 **Weight:** 7.1300 g. **Composition:** 0.5000 Gold .1146 oz. AGW **Subject:** Pre-Columbian Art **Reverse:** Native art

| Date | Mintage | F | VF | XF | Unc | BU |
|---|---|---|---|---|---|---|
| 1984FM (U) | — | — | — | — | 300 | — |
| 1984FM (P) | — | Value: 150 | | | | |

**100 BALBOAS** **KM# 131** **Weight:** 8.3000 g. **Composition:** 0.9000 Gold .2402 oz. AGW **Subject:** Panama Canal Transfer **Obverse:** Presidents; portrait **Reverse:** Ship in canal under Panamanian flag

| Date | Mintage | F | VF | XF | Unc | BU |
|---|---|---|---|---|---|---|
| 1999 Proof | 1,000 | Value: 300 | | | | |

**150 BALBOAS** **KM# 43** **Weight:** 9.3000 g. **Composition:** 0.9990 Platinum .2987 oz. APW **Subject:** 150th Anniversary - Panamanian Congress

| Date | Mintage | F | VF | XF | Unc | BU |
|---|---|---|---|---|---|---|
| ND (1976)FM (M) | 30 | — | — | — | 850 | — |
| ND (1976)FM (U) | 510 | — | — | — | 250 | — |
| ND (1976)FM (P) | 13,000 | Value: 220 | | | | |

**150 BALBOAS** **KM# 68** **Weight:** 7.6700 g. **Composition:** 0.5000 Gold .1233 oz. AGW **Subject:** Sesquicentenarium - Death of Simon Bolivar

| Date | Mintage | F | VF | XF | Unc | BU |
|---|---|---|---|---|---|---|
| ND (1980)FM (U) | 169 | — | — | — | 350 | — |
| ND (1980)FM (P) | 1,837 | Value: 180 | | | | |

**200 BALBOAS** **KM# 61** **Weight:** 9.5000 g. **Composition:** 0.9800 Platinum .2994 oz. APW **Subject:** Panai Canal Treaty Implementation

| Date | Mintage | F | VF | XF | Unc | BU |
|---|---|---|---|---|---|---|
| 1979FM (P) | 2,178 | Value: 285 | | | | |

**200 BALBOAS** **KM# 69** **Weight:** 9.9300 g. **Composition:** 0.9800 Platinum .2940 oz. APW **Subject:** Champions of Boxing

| Date | Mintage | F | VF | XF | Unc | BU |
|---|---|---|---|---|---|---|
| 1980 Proof | 219 | Value: 500 | | | | |

**500 BALBOAS** **KM# 42** **Weight:** 41.7000 g. **Composition:** 0.9000 Gold 1.2067 oz. AGW **Subject:** 500th Anniversary - Birth of Balboa

| Date | Mintage | F | VF | XF | Unc | BU |
|---|---|---|---|---|---|---|
| 1975FM (M) | 10 | — | — | — | 2,000 | — |
| 1975FM (U) | 1,496 | — | — | — | 525 | — |
| 1975FM (P) | 9,824 | Value: 485 | | | | |
| 1976FM (M) | 10 | — | — | — | 1,900 | — |
| 1976FM (U) | 160 | — | — | — | 800 | — |
| 1976FM (P) | 2,669 | Value: 525 | | | | |
| 1977FM (M) | 10 | — | — | — | 1,800 | — |
| 1977FM (U) | 59 | — | — | — | 1,250 | — |
| 1977FM (P) | 1,980 | Value: 575 | | | | |

**500 BALBOAS** **KM# 57** **Weight:** 41.7000 g. **Composition:** 0.9000 Gold 1.2067 oz. AGW **Subject:** 30th Anniversary - Organization of American States **Obverse:** Similar to KM#42

| Date | Mintage | F | VF | XF | Unc | BU |
|---|---|---|---|---|---|---|
| NDFM (M) | 10 | — | — | — | 1,800 | — |
| NDFM (U) | 106 | — | — | — | 900 | — |
| NDFM (P) | 2,009 | Value: 575 | | | | |

**500 BALBOAS** **KM# 62** **Weight:** 41.7000 g. **Composition:** 0.9000 Gold 1.2067 oz. AGW **Subject:** Golden Jaguar **Obverse:** Similar to KM#42

| Date | Mintage | F | VF | XF | Unc | BU |
|---|---|---|---|---|---|---|
| 1979FM (U) | 130 | — | — | — | 875 | — |
| 1979FM (P) | 1,657 | Value: 600 | | | | |

**500 BALBOAS** **KM# 70** **Weight:** 37.1800 g. **Composition:** 0.5000 Gold .5977 oz. AGW **Subject:** Great Egrets **Obverse:** Similar to KM#42

| Date | Mintage | F | VF | XF | Unc | BU |
|---|---|---|---|---|---|---|
| 1980FM (U) | 54 | — | — | — | 1,350 | — |
| 1980FM (P) | 612 | Value: 675 | | | | |

**500 BALBOAS** **KM# 75** **Weight:** 37.1800 g. **Composition:** 0.5000 Gold .5977 oz. AGW **Subject:** Sailfish **Obverse:** Similar to KM#42

| Date | Mintage | F | VF | XF | Unc | BU |
|---|---|---|---|---|---|---|
| 1981FM (U) | 41 | — | — | — | 1,500 | — |
| 1981FM (P) | 487 | Value: 745 | | | | |

**500 BALBOAS** **KM# 84** **Weight:** 37.1800 g. **Composition:** 0.5000 Gold .5977 oz. AGW **Subject:** Death of General Omar Torrijos **Obverse:** Similar to KM#42

| Date | Mintage | F | VF | XF | Unc | BU |
|---|---|---|---|---|---|---|
| 1982FM (U) | 97 | — | — | — | 950 | — |
| 1982FM (P) | 398 | Value: 775 | | | | |

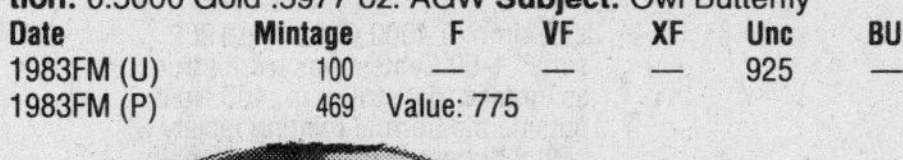

**500 BALBOAS** **KM# 96** **Weight:** 37.1800 g. **Composition:** 0.5000 Gold .5977 oz. AGW **Subject:** Owl Butterfly

| Date | Mintage | F | VF | XF | Unc | BU |
|---|---|---|---|---|---|---|
| 1983FM (U) | 100 | — | — | — | 925 | — |
| 1983FM (P) | 469 | Value: 775 | | | | |

**500 BALBOAS** **KM# 101** **Weight:** 37.1200 g. **Composition:** 0.5000 Gold .5968 oz. AGW **Subject:** Golden Eagle

| Date | Mintage | F | VF | XF | Unc | BU |
|---|---|---|---|---|---|---|
| 1984FM (U) | 10 | — | — | — | 4,000 | — |
| 1984FM (P) | 156 | Value: 1,450 | | | | |

**500 BALBOAS** KM# 103 **Weight:** 37.1800 g. **Composition:** 0.5000 Gold .5977 oz. AGW **Subject:** National Eagle

| Date | Mintage | F | VF | XF | Unc | BU |
|---|---|---|---|---|---|---|
| 1985FM (P) | 184 | Value: 1,400 | | | | |

## PATTERNS

Including off metal strikes.

| KM# | Date | Mintage | Identification | Mkt Val |
|---|---|---|---|---|
| Pn1 | 1904 | — | 2-1/2 Centesimos. Silver. | 1,500 |
| | | — | 2-1/2 Centesimos. Silver. | 1,500 |
| PnA3 | 1907 | — | 1/2 Centesimo. Bronze. KM6. | — |
| Pn2 | 1907 | — | Half Cent. | 3,500 |
| Pn3 | 1907 | — | 2-1/2 Centesimos. Silver. | — |
| PnD4 | 1953 | — | 1/10 Balboa. Silver. | 18.00 |
| PnF4 | 1953 | — | 1/4 Balboa. Silver. | 19.00 |
| PnH4 | 1953 | — | 1/2 Balboa. Silver. | 20.00 |
| PnB4 | 1953 | — | Centesimo. Silver. 17a | — |
| PnC4 | 1953 | — | Centesimo. 0.9000 Gold. 17b | — |
| PnE4 | 1953 | — | 1/10 Balboa. 0.9000 Gold. 18a | — |
| PnG4 | 1953 | — | 1/4 Balboa. 0.9000 Gold. 19a | — |
| PnI4 | 1953 | — | 1/2 Balboa. 0.9000 Gold. 20a | — |
| Pn4 | 1986 | 10 | Balboa. Copper-Nickel. Type 1 | 3,000 |
| Pn5 | 1986 | 10 | Balboa. Copper Nickel. Type II. | 3,000 |
| Pn6 | 1987 | 10 | 1/10 Balboa. Copper-Nickel Clad Copper. Similar to KM10a. | 1,000 |
| Pn7 | 1987 | 10 | 1/4 Balboa. Copper-Nickel Clad Copper. Similar to KM11a. | 1,500 |
| Pn8 | 1987 | 10 | 1/2 Balboa. Copper-Nickel Clad Copper. Similar to KM12. | 2,000 |
| Pn10 | 1988 | 10 | 1/4 Balboa. Copper-Nickel. KM25. | 1,500 |
| Pn11 | 1988 | 10 | 1/2 Balboa. Copper-Nickel. KM26. | 2,000 |
| Pn9 | 1988 | 10 | 1/10 Balboa. Copper-Nickel. KM24. | — |

## PIEFORTS

| KM# | Date | Mintage | Identification | Mkt Val |
|---|---|---|---|---|
| P1 | 1982 | — | Centesimo. 0.4000 Gold. The 1982 series of 1-50 Centesimos were struck as piefort in .400 Gold outside the normal minting facility without consent from the National Bank of Panama. | 275 |
| P2 | 1982 | — | 5 Centesimos. 0.4000 Gold. | 325 |
| P3 | 1982 | — | 1/10 Balboa. 0.4000 Gold. | 400 |
| P4 | 1982 | — | 1/4 Balboa. 0.4000 Gold. | 550 |
| P5 | 1982 | — | 50 Centesimos. 0.4000 Gold. | 600 |

## TRIAL STRIKES

| KM# | Date | Mintage | Identification | Mkt Val |
|---|---|---|---|---|
| TS1 | 1982 | — | Centesimo. 0.4000 Gold. The 1982 series 1-50 Centesimos were struck as uniface trial strikes in .400 Gold outside the normal minting facility without consent from the National Bank or authorization from the Government of Panama. Reverse piefort. | 250 |
| | | — | Centesimo. 0.4000 Gold. The 1982 series 1-50 Centesimos were struck as uniface trial strikes in .400 Gold outside the normal minting facility without consent from the National Bank or authorization from the Government of Panama. Reverse piefort. | 250 |
| TS2 | 1982 | — | Centesimo. 0.4000 Gold. Obverse piefort. | 250 |
| TS3 | | Est 15 | 5 Centisimos, 0.4000 Gold. Reverse piefort | — |
| TS4 | 1982 | — | 5 Centesimos. 0.4000 Gold. Obverse piefort | 30,000 |
| | | — | 5 Centesimos. 0.4000 Gold. Obverse piefort | 300 |
| TS5 | 1982 | — | 1/10 Balboa. 0.4000 Gold. Reverse piefort | 375 |
| | | — | 1/10 Balboa. 0.4000 Gold. Reverse piefort | 375 |
| TS6 | 1982 | — | 1/10 Balboa. 0.4000 Gold. Obverse piefort | 375 |
| | | — | 1/10 Balboa. 0.4000 Gold. Obverse piefort | 375 |
| TS7 | 1982 | — | 1/4 Balboa. 0.4000 Gold. Reverse piefort | 500 |
| | | — | 1/4 Balboa. 0.4000 Gold. Reverse piefort | 500 |
| TS8 | 1982 | — | 1/4 Balboa. 0.4000 Gold. Obverse piefort | 500 |
| | | — | 1/4 Balboa. 0.4000 Gold. Obverse piefort | 500 |
| TS9 | 1982 | — | 50 Centesimos. 0.4000 Gold. Reverse piefort | 500 |
| TS10 | 1982 | — | 50 Centesimos. 0.4000 Gold. Obverse piefort | 500 |

## MINT SETS

| KM# | Date | Mintage | Identification | Issue Price | Mkt Val |
|---|---|---|---|---|---|
| MS1 | 1975 (8) | 1,410 | KM33.1-40.1 | 25.00 | 85.00 |

## PROOF SETS

| KM# | Date | Mintage | Identification | Issue Price | Mkt Val |
|---|---|---|---|---|---|
| PS1 | 1904 (4) | 12 | KM2-5 | — | 9,500 |
| PS2 | 1930 (3) | 20 | KM10.1-12.1 | — | 4,800 |
| PS3 | 1962 (5) | 25 | KM10.2-12.2, 22, 23.2 | — | 2,750 |
| PS4 | 1966 (6) | 12,701 | KM10a-11a, 12a.1, 22, 23.2, 27 | 15.25 | 21.50 |
| PS5 | 1967 (6) | 19,983 | KM10a-11a, 12a.1, 22, 23.2, 27 | 15.25 | 18.00 |
| PS6 | 1968 (6) | 23,210 | KM10a-11a, 12a.1, 22, 23.2, 27 | 15.25 | 18.00 |
| PS7 | 1969 (6) | 14,000 | KM10a-11a, 12a.1, 22, 23.2, 27 | 15.25 | 18.00 |
| PS8 | 1970 (6) | 9,528 | KM10a-11a, 12a.1, 22, 23.2, 27 | 15.25 | 21.50 |
| PS9 | 1971 (6) | 10,696 | KM10a-11a, 12a.1, 22, 23.2, 27 | 15.25 | 20.00 |
| PS10 | 1972 (6) | 13,322 | KM10a-11a, 12a.1, 22, 23.2, 27 | 15.25 | 20.00 |
| PS11 | 1973 (6) | 16,946 | KM10a-11a, 12b, 22, 23.2, 27 | 17.50 | 25.00 |
| PS12 | 1974 (6) | 17,521 | KM10a-11a, 12b, 22, 23.2, 27 | 17.50 | 25.00 |
| PS13 | 1975 (9) | 37,041 | KM31, 33.1-38.1, 39.1a-40.1a | 130 | 75.00 |
| PS14 | 1975 (8) | 4,057 | KM31, 34.1-38.1, 39.1a-40.1a | 50.00 | 35.00 |
| PS15 | 1976 (9) | 10,610 | KM31, 33.1-38.1, 39.1a-40.1a | 102 | 90.00 |
| PS16 | 1976 (8) | 1,792 | KM33.1-38.1, 39.1a-40.1a | 50.00 | 40.00 |
| PS17 | 1976 (2) | 11,479 | KM31, 34.1 | 51.00 | 40.00 |
| PS18 | 1977 (9) | 8,093 | KM33.1-38.1, 39.1a-40.1a, 44 | 100 | 90.00 |
| PS19 | 1977 (8) | 1,455 | KM33.1-38.1, 39.1a-40.1a | 50.00 | 40.00 |
| PS20 | 1978 (9) | 9,667 | KM45-50, 51a, 52a, 54 | 110 | 120 |
| PS21 | 1978 (8) | 1,122 | KM45-50, 51a, 52a | — | 40.00 |
| PS22 | 1979 (9) | 4,974 | KM33.1-38.1, 39.1a-40.1a, 44 | 132 | 100 |
| PS23 | 1979 (8) | 975 | KM33.1-38.1, 39.1a-40.1a | 60.00 | 40.00 |
| PS24 | 1979 (2) | 1,775 | KM58-59 | 125 | 65.00 |
| PS25 | 1980 (9) | 1,686 | KM33.2-38.2, 39.3-40.3, 65 | 287 | 150 |
| PS26 | 1980 (8) | 943 | KM33.2-38.2, 39.3-40.3 | 87.00 | 50.00 |
| PS27 | 1981 (9) | 1,279 | KM33.1-38.1, 39.1b-40.1b, 71 | 212 | 170 |
| PS28 | 1981 (8) | 694 | KM33.1-38.1, 39.1b-40.1b | 87.00 | 65.00 |
| PS29 | 1982 (9) | 746 | KM33.1-38.1, 39.1b-40.1b, 80 | 212 | 200 |
| PS30 | 1982 (9) | — | Error set; KM33-38, 39.1b, 40.4, 80 | 212 | 250 |
| PS31 | 1982 (8) | 734 | KM33-38, 39.1b-40.1b | 87.00 | 75.00 |
| PS32 | 1982 (8) | — | Error set; KM33-38, 39.1b, 40.4 | — | 150 |
| PS33 | 1983 (9) | — | KM22, 85-89, 90a, 91, 93 | 87.00 | 150 |
| PS34 | 1983 (8) | — | KM22, 85-89, 90a, 91 | — | 80.00 |
| PS35 | 1984 (9) | — | KM22, 85-89, 90a, 91, 98 | — | 200 |
| PS36 | 1984 (8) | — | KM22, 85-89, 90a, 91 | 72.00 | 80.00 |
| PS37 | 1985 (8) | 765 | KM22, 85-89, 90a, 104 | 72.00 | 180 |
| PS39 | 1993 (4) | — | KM10a-11a, 12a.1, 23.2 | — | 1,350 |

# PALO SECO

Palo Seco Leper Colony was established in Balboa, Canal Zone in 1907. It is known today as Palo Seco Hospital. The original issue of tokens totaled $1,800.00 of which $1,492.75 was destroyed on November 28, 1955. The issue was backed by United States Currency and was replaced by United States circulation coinage.

## COLONY

## LEPROSARIUM TOKEN COINAGE

**CENT** KM# Tn1 **Composition:** Copper

| Date | Mintage | VG | F | VF | XF | Unc |
|---|---|---|---|---|---|---|
| ND(1919) | — | 35.00 | 65.00 | 125 | — | — |

**5 CENTS** KM# Tn2 **Composition:** Brass

| Date | Mintage | VG | F | VF | XF | Unc |
|---|---|---|---|---|---|---|
| ND(1919) | — | 50.00 | 75.00 | 150 | — | — |

**10 CENTS** KM# Tn3 **Composition:** Aluminum

| Date | Mintage | VG | F | VF | XF | Unc |
|---|---|---|---|---|---|---|
| ND(1919) | — | 75.00 | 100 | 200 | — | — |

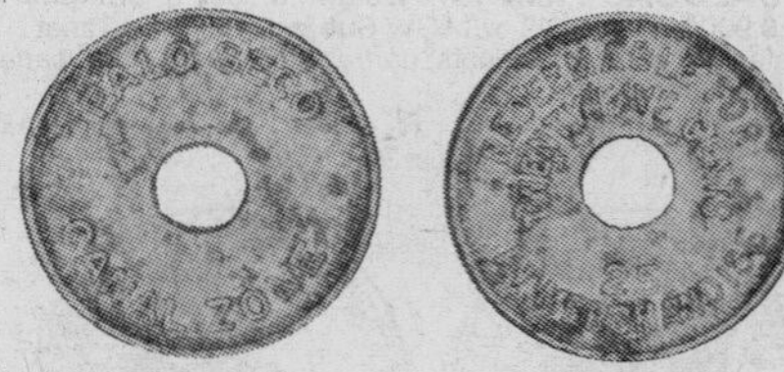

**25 CENTS** KM# Tn4 **Composition:** Aluminum

| Date | Mintage | VG | F | VF | XF | Unc |
|---|---|---|---|---|---|---|
| ND(1919) | — | 100 | 200 | 300 | — | — |

**50 CENTS** KM# Tn5 **Composition:** Aluminum

| Date | Mintage | VG | F | VF | XF | Unc |
|---|---|---|---|---|---|---|
| ND(1919) | — | 150 | 250 | 400 | — | — |

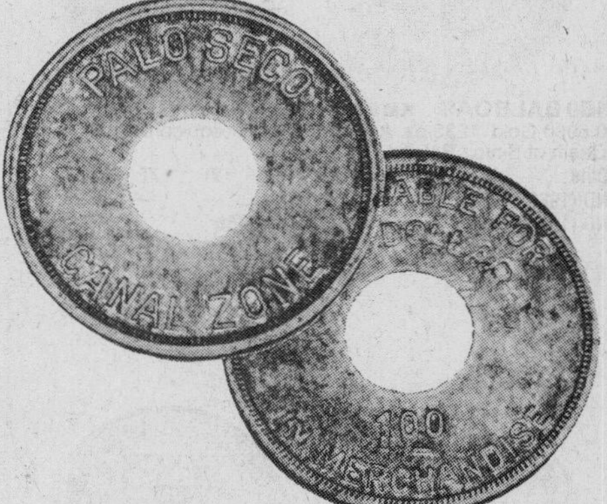


**DOLLAR** KM# Tn6 **Composition:** Aluminum

| Date | Mintage | VG | F | VF | XF | Unc |
|---|---|---|---|---|---|---|
| ND(1919) | — | 200 | 300 | 500 | — | — |

# PAPUA NEW GUINEA

Papua New Guinea, an independent member of the British Commonwealth, occupies the eastern half of the island of New Guinea. It lies north of Australia near the equator and borders on West Irian. The country, which includes nearby Bismark archipelago, Buka and Bougainville, has an area of 178,260 sq. mi. (461,690 sq. km.) and a population of *3.7 million who are divided into more than 1,000 separate tribes speaking more than 700 mutually unintelligible languages. Capital: Port Moresby. The economy is agricultural, and exports copra, rubber, cocoa, coffee, tea, gold and copper

Australian troops occupied German New Guinea in Aug. 1914, shortly after Great Britain declared war on Germany. It was mandated to Australia by the League of Nations in 1920, known as the Territory of New Guinea. The territory was invaded and most of it was occupied by Japan in 1942. Following the Japanese surrender, it came under U.N. trusteeship, Dec. 13, 1946, with Australia as the administering power.

The Papua and New Guinea act, 1949, provided for the government of Papua and New Guinea as one administrative unit. On Dec. 1, 1973, Papua New Guinea became self-governing with Australia retaining responsibility for defense and foreign affairs. Full independence was achieved on Sept. 16, 1975. Papua New Guinea is a member of the Commonwealth of Nations. Elizabeth II is Head of State, as Queen of Papua New Guinea.

**MINT MARKS**

FM - Franklin Mint, U.S.A.*

***NOTE:** From 1975-1985 the Franklin Mint produced coinage in up to 3 different qualities. Qualities of issue are designated in ( ) after each date and are defined as follows:

**(M) MATTE** - Normal circulation strike or a dull finish produced by sandblasting special uncirculated (polish finish) or proof quality dies.

**(U) SPECIAL UNCIRCULATED** - Polished or proof-like in appearance without any frosted features.

**(P) PROOF** - The highest quality obtainable having mirror-like fields and frosted features.

**MONETARY SYSTEM**

100 Toea = 1 Kina

## BRITISH ADMINISTRATION

### STANDARD COINAGE

100 Toea = 1 Kina

**TOEA** **KM# 1** **Composition:** Bronze **Obverse:** Paradise bird **Reverse:** Wing butterfly

| Date | Mintage | F | VF | XF | Unc | BU |
|---|---|---|---|---|---|---|
| 1975 | 14,400,000 | — | — | 0.15 | 0.25 | — |
| 1975FM (M) | 83,000 | — | — | — | 0.30 | — |
| 1975FM (U) | 4,134 | — | — | — | 1.00 | — |
| 1975FM (P) | 67,000 | Value: 1.00 | | | | |
| 1976 | 25,175,000 | — | — | — | 0.20 | — |
| 1976FM (M) | 84,000 | — | — | — | 0.20 | — |
| 1976FM (U) | 976 | — | — | — | 1.00 | — |
| 1976FM (P) | 16,000 | Value: 1.00 | | | | |
| 1977FM (M) | 84,000 | — | — | — | 0.20 | — |
| 1977FM (U) | 603 | — | — | — | 1.50 | — |
| 1977FM (P) | 7,721 | Value: 1.50 | | | | |
| 1978 | — | — | — | — | 0.25 | — |
| 1978FM (M) | 83,000 | — | — | — | 0.20 | — |
| 1978FM (U) | 777 | — | — | — | 1.00 | — |
| 1978FM (P) | 5,540 | Value: 1.50 | | | | |
| 1979FM (M) | 84,000 | — | — | — | 0.20 | — |
| 1979FM (U) | 1,366 | — | — | — | 1.00 | — |
| 1979FM (P) | 2,728 | Value: 1.50 | | | | |
| 1980FM (U) | 1,160 | — | — | — | 1.00 | — |
| 1980FM (P) | 2,125 | Value: 1.50 | | | | |
| 1981 | — | — | — | — | 1.00 | — |
| 1981FM (P) | 10,000 | Value: 2.25 | | | | |
| 1981FM (M) | — | — | — | — | 0.20 | — |
| 1982FM (M) | — | — | — | — | 1.00 | — |
| 1982FM (P) | — | Value: 2.25 | | | | |
| 1983 | — | — | — | — | 0.25 | — |
| 1983FM (U) | 360 | — | — | — | 0.30 | — |
| 1983FM (P) | — | Value: 2.25 | | | | |
| 1984 | — | — | — | — | 0.25 | — |
| 1984FM (P) | — | Value: 2.25 | | | | |

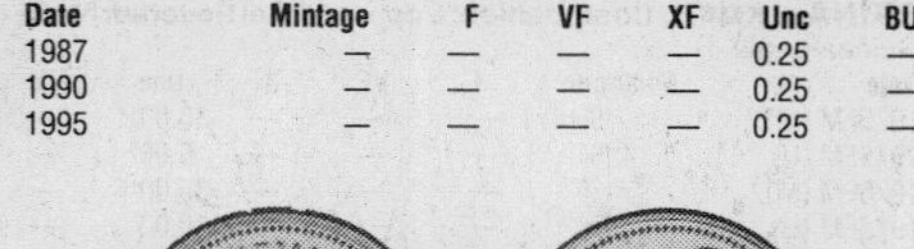

| Date | Mintage | F | VF | XF | Unc | BU |
|---|---|---|---|---|---|---|
| 1987 | — | — | — | — | 0.25 | — |
| 1990 | — | — | — | — | 0.25 | — |
| 1995 | — | — | — | — | 0.25 | — |

**2 TOEA** **KM# 2** **Composition:** Bronze **Obverse:** Ornate butterfly **Reverse:** Cod

| Date | Mintage | F | VF | XF | Unc | BU |
|---|---|---|---|---|---|---|
| 1975 | 11,400,000 | — | — | 0.10 | 0.30 | — |
| 1975FM (M) | 42,000 | — | — | — | 0.35 | — |
| 1975FM (U) | 4,134 | — | — | — | 1.00 | — |
| 1975FM (P) | 67,000 | Value: 1.00 | | | | |
| 1976 | 15,175,000 | — | — | 0.10 | 0.25 | — |
| 1976FM (M) | 42,000 | — | — | — | 0.25 | — |
| 1976FM (U) | 976 | — | — | — | 1.00 | — |
| 1976FM (P) | 16,000 | Value: 1.00 | | | | |
| 1977FM (M) | 42,000 | — | — | — | 0.25 | — |
| 1977FM (U) | 603 | — | — | — | 1.50 | — |
| 1977FM (P) | 7,721 | Value: 1.75 | | | | |
| 1978 | — | — | — | — | 0.30 | — |
| 1978FM (M) | 42,000 | — | — | — | 0.25 | — |
| 1978FM (U) | 777 | — | — | — | 1.00 | — |
| 1978FM (P) | 5,540 | Value: 1.75 | | | | |
| 1979FM (M) | 42,000 | — | — | — | 0.25 | — |
| 1979FM (U) | 1,366 | — | — | — | 1.00 | — |
| 1979FM (P) | 2,728 | Value: 1.75 | | | | |
| 1980FM (U) | 1,160 | — | — | — | 1.00 | — |
| 1980FM (P) | 2,125 | Value: 1.75 | | | | |
| 1981 | — | — | — | — | 0.25 | — |
| 1981FM (P) | 10,000 | Value: 2.50 | | | | |
| 1982FM (M) | — | — | — | — | 1.00 | — |
| 1982FM (P) | — | Value: 2.50 | | | | |
| 1983 | — | — | — | — | 0.25 | — |
| 1983FM (U) | 360 | — | — | — | 1.50 | — |
| 1983FM (P) | — | Value: 2.50 | | | | |
| 1984 | — | — | — | — | 0.25 | — |
| 1984 Proof | — | Value: 2.50 | | | | |
| 1987 | — | — | — | — | 0.25 | — |
| 1990 | — | — | — | — | 0.25 | — |
| 1995 | — | — | — | — | 0.25 | — |

**5 TOEA** **KM# 3** **Composition:** Copper-Nickel **Reverse:** Plateless turtle

| Date | Mintage | F | VF | XF | Unc | BU |
|---|---|---|---|---|---|---|
| 1975 | 11,000,000 | — | 0.15 | 0.25 | 0.75 | — |
| 1975FM (M) | 17,000 | — | — | — | 0.75 | — |
| 1975FM (U) | 4,134 | — | — | — | 1.25 | — |
| 1975FM (P) | 67,000 | Value: 1.75 | | | | |
| 1976 | 24,000,000 | — | 0.15 | 0.25 | 0.75 | — |
| 1976FM (M) | 17,000 | — | — | — | 0.75 | — |
| 1976FM (U) | 976 | — | — | — | 1.25 | — |
| 1976FM (P) | 16,000 | Value: 1.75 | | | | |
| 1977FM (M) | 17,000 | — | — | — | 0.75 | — |
| 1977FM (U) | 603 | — | — | — | 1.75 | — |
| 1977FM (P) | 7,721 | Value: 2.25 | | | | |
| 1978 | 2,000 | — | — | — | 2.50 | — |
| 1978FM (M) | 17,000 | — | — | — | 0.75 | — |
| 1978FM (U) | 777 | — | — | — | 1.25 | — |
| 1978FM (P) | 5,540 | Value: 2.25 | | | | |
| 1979 | — | — | — | — | 0.75 | — |
| 1979FM (M) | 17,000 | — | — | — | 0.75 | — |
| 1979FM (U) | 1,366 | — | — | — | 1.25 | — |
| 1979FM (P) | 2,728 | Value: 2.25 | | | | |
| 1980FM (U) | 1,160 | — | — | — | 1.25 | — |
| 1980FM (P) | 2,125 | Value: 2.25 | | | | |
| 1981FM (P) | 10,000 | Value: 3.50 | | | | |
| 1982 | — | — | — | — | 0.75 | — |
| 1982FM (M) | — | — | — | — | 1.25 | — |
| 1982FM (P) | — | Value: 3.50 | | | | |
| 1983FM (U) | 360 | — | — | — | 2.25 | — |
| 1983FM (P) | — | Value: 3.50 | | | | |
| 1984 | — | — | — | — | 0.75 | — |
| 1984FM (P) | — | Value: 3.50 | | | | |
| 1987 | — | — | — | — | 0.75 | — |
| 1990 | — | — | — | — | 0.75 | — |
| 1995 | — | — | — | — | 0.75 | — |

**10 TOEA** **KM# 4** **Composition:** Copper-Nickel **Reverse:** Cuscus

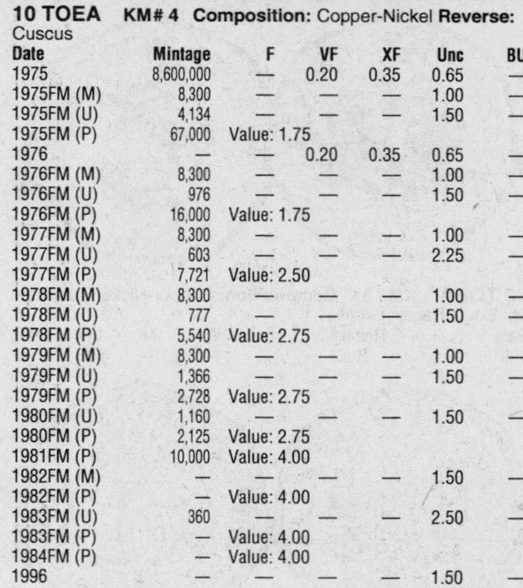

| Date | Mintage | F | VF | XF | Unc | BU |
|---|---|---|---|---|---|---|
| 1975 | 8,600,000 | — | 0.20 | 0.35 | 0.65 | — |
| 1975FM (M) | 8,300 | — | — | — | 1.00 | — |
| 1975FM (U) | 4,134 | — | — | — | 1.50 | — |
| 1975FM (P) | 67,000 | Value: 1.75 | | | | |
| 1976 | — | — | 0.20 | 0.35 | 0.65 | — |
| 1976FM (M) | 8,300 | — | — | — | 1.00 | — |
| 1976FM (U) | 976 | — | — | — | 1.50 | — |
| 1976FM (P) | 16,000 | Value: 1.75 | | | | |
| 1977FM (M) | 8,300 | — | — | — | 1.00 | — |
| 1977FM (U) | 603 | — | — | — | 2.25 | — |
| 1977FM (P) | 7,721 | Value: 2.50 | | | | |
| 1978FM (M) | 8,300 | — | — | — | 1.00 | — |
| 1978FM (U) | 777 | — | — | — | 1.50 | — |
| 1978FM (P) | 5,540 | Value: 2.75 | | | | |
| 1979FM (M) | 8,300 | — | — | — | 1.00 | — |
| 1979FM (U) | 1,366 | — | — | — | 1.50 | — |
| 1979FM (P) | 2,728 | Value: 2.75 | | | | |
| 1980FM (U) | 1,160 | — | — | — | 1.50 | — |
| 1980FM (P) | 2,125 | Value: 2.75 | | | | |
| 1981FM (P) | 10,000 | Value: 4.00 | | | | |
| 1982FM (M) | — | — | — | — | 1.50 | — |
| 1982FM (P) | — | Value: 4.00 | | | | |
| 1983FM (U) | 360 | — | — | — | 2.50 | — |
| 1983FM (P) | — | Value: 4.00 | | | | |
| 1984FM (P) | — | Value: 4.00 | | | | |
| 1996 | — | — | — | — | 1.50 | — |

**20 TOEA** **KM# 5** **Composition:** Copper-Nickel **Reverse:** Bennett's Cassowary

| Date | Mintage | F | VF | XF | Unc | BU |
|---|---|---|---|---|---|---|
| 1975 | 15,500,000 | — | 0.30 | 0.65 | 1.25 | — |
| 1975FM (M) | 4,150 | — | — | — | 2.00 | — |
| 1975FM (U) | 4,134 | — | — | — | 2.00 | — |
| 1975FM (P) | 67,000 | Value: 2.50 | | | | |
| 1976FM (M) | 4,150 | — | — | — | 2.00 | — |
| 1976FM (U) | 976 | — | — | — | 2.00 | — |
| 1976FM (P) | 16,000 | Value: 2.50 | | | | |
| 1977FM (M) | 4,150 | — | — | — | 2.00 | — |
| 1977FM (U) | 603 | — | — | — | 2.50 | — |
| 1977FM (P) | 7,721 | Value: 3.50 | | | | |
| 1978 | 2,500,000 | — | 0.45 | 0.75 | 1.25 | — |
| 1978FM (M) | 4,150 | — | — | — | 2.00 | — |
| 1978FM (U) | 777 | — | — | — | 2.00 | — |
| 1978FM (P) | 5,540 | Value: 3.50 | | | | |
| 1979FM (M) | 4,150 | — | — | — | 2.00 | — |
| 1979FM (U) | 1,366 | — | — | — | 2.00 | — |
| 1979FM (P) | 2,728 | Value: 3.50 | | | | |
| 1980FM (U) | 1,160 | — | — | — | 2.00 | — |
| 1980FM (P) | 2,125 | Value: 3.50 | | | | |
| 1981 | — | — | 0.25 | 0.50 | 1.00 | — |
| 1981FM (P) | 10,000 | Value: 5.00 | | | | |
| 1982FM (M) | — | — | — | — | 2.00 | — |
| 1982FM (P) | — | Value: 5.00 | | | | |
| 1983FM (U) | 360 | — | — | — | 3.00 | — |
| 1983FM (P) | — | Value: 5.00 | | | | |
| 1984 | — | — | 0.25 | 0.50 | 1.00 | — |
| 1984FM (P) | — | Value: 5.00 | | | | |
| 1987 | — | — | 0.25 | 0.50 | 1.00 | — |
| 1990 | — | — | 0.25 | 0.50 | 1.00 | — |
| 1995 | — | — | 0.25 | 0.50 | 1.00 | — |

**50 TOEA** **KM# 15** **Composition:** Copper-Nickel **Subject:** South Pacific Festival of Arts

| Date | Mintage | F | VF | XF | Unc | BU |
|---|---|---|---|---|---|---|
| 1980 | — | — | 0.75 | 1.25 | 2.75 | — |
| 1980FM (U) | 1,160 | — | — | — | 12.50 | — |
| 1980FM (P) | 2,125 | Value: 8.50 | | | | |

**50 TOEA** **KM# 31** **Composition:** Copper-Nickel **Subject:** 9th South Pacific Games

| Date | Mintage | F | VF | XF | Unc | BU |
|---|---|---|---|---|---|---|
| 1991 | 25,000 | — | — | — | 5.00 | — |

**50 TOEA** **KM# 41** **Weight:** 13.6300 g. **Composition:** Copper Nickel **Subject:** Silver Jubilee of Bank **Obverse:** National emblem. **Reverse:** Symbolic design. **Edge:** Reeded. **Shape:** Seven sided. **Size:** 30 mm.

| Date | Mintage | F | VF | XF | Unc | BU |
|---|---|---|---|---|---|---|
| 1998 | — | — | — | — | 5.50 | — |

**KINA** **KM# 6** **Composition:** Copper-Nickel **Reverse:** Sea and river crocodiles

| Date | Mintage | F | VF | XF | Unc | BU |
|---|---|---|---|---|---|---|
| 1975 | 2,000,000 | — | 1.35 | 2.00 | 3.25 | — |
| 1975FM (M) | 829 | — | — | — | 8.50 | — |
| 1975FM (U) | 4,134 | — | — | — | 3.25 | — |
| 1975FM (P) | 67,000 | Value: 3.25 | | | | |
| 1976FM (M) | 829 | — | — | — | 8.50 | — |
| 1976FM (U) | 976 | — | — | — | 3.25 | — |
| 1976FM (P) | 16,000 | Value: 3.50 | | | | |
| 1977FM (M) | 829 | — | — | — | 8.50 | — |
| 1977FM (U) | 603 | — | — | — | 12.50 | — |
| 1977FM (P) | 7,721 | Value: 4.50 | | | | |
| 1978FM (M) | 829 | — | — | — | 8.50 | — |
| 1978FM (U) | 777 | — | — | — | 3.00 | — |
| 1978FM (P) | 5,540 | Value: 4.00 | | | | |
| 1979FM (M) | 829 | — | — | — | 8.50 | — |
| 1979FM (U) | 1,366 | — | — | — | 3.25 | — |
| 1979FM (P) | 2,728 | Value: 6.00 | | | | |
| 1980FM (U) | 1,160 | — | — | — | 3.25 | — |
| 1980FM (P) | 2,125 | Value: 6.00 | | | | |
| 1981FM (P) | 10,000 | Value: 3.25 | | | | |
| 1982FM (M) | — | — | — | — | 3.25 | — |
| 1982FM (P) | — | Value: 7.50 | | | | |
| 1983FM (U) | 360 | — | — | — | 14.50 | — |
| 1983FM (P) | — | Value: 7.00 | | | | |
| 1984FM (P) | — | Value: 7.00 | | | | |
| 1996 | — | — | — | — | 3.25 | — |

**5 KINA** **KM#7** **Composition:** Copper-Nickel **Reverse:** New Guinea eagle

| Date | Mintage | F | VF | XF | Unc | BU |
|---|---|---|---|---|---|---|
| 1975FM (M) | 166 | — | — | — | 35.00 | — |
| 1975FM (U) | 4,134 | — | — | — | 6.00 | — |
| 1976FM (M) | 166 | — | — | — | 35.00 | — |
| 1976FM (U) | 976 | — | — | — | 10.00 | — |
| 1977FM (M) | 166 | — | — | — | 35.00 | — |
| 1977FM (U) | 603 | — | — | — | 20.00 | — |
| 1978FM (M) | 166 | — | — | — | 35.00 | — |
| 1978FM (U) | 777 | — | — | — | 10.00 | — |
| 1979FM (M) | 166 | — | — | — | 35.00 | — |
| 1979FM (U) | 1,366 | — | — | — | 7.50 | — |
| 1980FM (U) | 1,160 | — | — | — | 7.50 | — |

**5 KINA** **KM# 7a** **Weight:** 27.6000 g. **Composition:** 0.5000 Silver .4436 oz. ASW **Reverse:** New Guinea eagle

| Date | Mintage | F | VF | XF | Unc | BU |
|---|---|---|---|---|---|---|
| 1975FM (P) | 67,000 | Value: 5.00 | | | | |
| 1976FM (P) | 16,000 | Value: 7.00 | | | | |
| 1977FM (P) | 7,721 | Value: 7.50 | | | | |
| 1978FM (P) | 5,540 | Value: 7.50 | | | | |
| 1979FM (P) | 2,728 | Value: 10.00 | | | | |
| 1980FM (P) | 2,125 | Value: 10.00 | | | | |

**5 KINA** **KM# 18** **Weight:** 28.2800 g. **Composition:** 0.5000 Silver .4656 oz. ASW **Series:** International Year of the Child

| Date | Mintage | F | VF | XF | Unc | BU |
|---|---|---|---|---|---|---|
| 1981 | 8,775 | — | — | — | 10.00 | — |

**5 KINA** **KM# 20** **Composition:** Copper-Nickel **Subject:** Defense of the Kokoda Trail **Obverse:** Similar to 20 Toea, KM#5

| Date | Mintage | F | VF | XF | Unc | BU |
|---|---|---|---|---|---|---|
| 1982FM (M) | — | — | — | — | 7.50 | — |

**5 KINA** **KM# 20a** **Weight:** 28.2800 g. **Composition:** 0.9250 Silver .8411 oz. ASW **Subject:** Defense of the Kokoda Trail **Obverse:** Similar to 20 Toea, KM#5

| Date | Mintage | F | VF | XF | Unc | BU |
|---|---|---|---|---|---|---|
| 1982FM (P) | 1,795 | Value: 25.00 | | | | |

**5 KINA** **KM# 23** **Composition:** Copper-Nickel **Subject:** 10th anniversary - Bank of Papua New Guinea **Obverse:** Similar to 20 Toea, KM#5

| Date | Mintage | F | VF | XF | Unc | BU |
|---|---|---|---|---|---|---|
| 1983FM (U) | 360 | — | — | — | 7.50 | — |

**5 KINA** **KM# 23a** **Weight:** 28.2800 g. **Composition:** 0.9250 Silver .8411 oz. ASW **Subject:** 10th anniversary - Bank of Papua New Guinea **Obverse:** Similar to 20 Toea, KM#5

| Date | Mintage | F | VF | XF | Unc | BU |
|---|---|---|---|---|---|---|
| 1983FM (P) | 673 | Value: 32.50 | | | | |

**5 KINA** **KM# 25 (KM25a)** **Weight:** 28.2800 g. **Composition:** 0.9250 Silver .8411 oz. ASW **Subject:** New Parliament building

| Date | Mintage | F | VF | XF | Unc | BU |
|---|---|---|---|---|---|---|
| 1984FM (P) Proof | — | Value: 32.50 | | | | |

**5 KINA** **KM# 28** **Weight:** 28.2800 g. **Composition:** 0.9250 Silver .8411 oz. ASW **Series:** Decade for Women

| Date | Mintage | F | VF | XF | Unc | BU |
|---|---|---|---|---|---|---|
| 1984FM Proof | 1,050 | Value: 28.00 | | | | |

**5 KINA** **KM# 34** **Weight:** 23.3300 g. **Composition:** 0.9250 Silver .6938 oz. ASW **Reverse:** Queen Alexandra butterfly

| Date | Mintage | F | VF | XF | Unc | BU |
|---|---|---|---|---|---|---|
| 1992FM | 500 | — | — | — | 85.00 | — |
| 1992FM (P) | — | — | — | — | — | — |

**5 KINA** **KM# 37** **Weight:** 27.7800 g. **Composition:** 0.9000 Silver .8038 oz. ASW **Subject:** Centennial of first coinage **Reverse:** Bird of paradise

| Date | Mintage | F | VF | XF | Unc | BU |
|---|---|---|---|---|---|---|
| ND(1994) Proof | 7,500 | Value: 40.00 | | | | |

**5 KINA** **KM# 39** **Weight:** 31.4700 g. **Composition:** 0.9250 Silver .9359 oz. ASW **Series:** Endangered wildlife **Obverse:** National emblem **Reverse:** 2 ribbon sweetlips fish

| Date | Mintage | F | VF | XF | Unc | BU |
|---|---|---|---|---|---|---|
| 1997 Proof | 10,000 | Value: 28.00 | | | | |

**5 KINA** **KM# 43** **Weight:** 31.5000 g. **Composition:** 0.9250 Silver .9368 oz. ASW **Series:** Olympic Games 2000 **Subject:** La Recherche **Obverse:** National emblem **Reverse:** Ship and native sculpture **Edge:** Reeded **Size:** 38.6 mm.

| Date | Mintage | F | VF | XF | Unc | BU |
|---|---|---|---|---|---|---|
| 1997 Proof | — | Value: 30.00 | | | | |

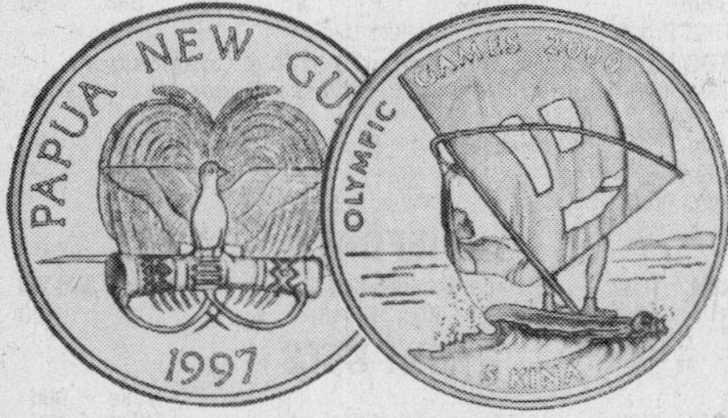


**5 KINA** **KM# 40** **Weight:** 20.0000 g. **Composition:** 0.9000 Silver .5787 oz. ASW **Series:** Olympic Games 2000 **Obverse:** National emblem **Reverse:** Sailboarder

| Date | Mintage | F | VF | XF | Unc | BU |
|---|---|---|---|---|---|---|
| 1997 Proof | — | Value: 25.00 | | | | |

**5 KINA** **KM# 44** **Weight:** 31.4300 g. **Composition:** 0.9250 Silver .9347 oz. ASW **Subject:** Green Tree Python **Obverse:** National arms **Reverse:** Snake in tree **Edge:** Reeded **Size:** 38.6 mm.

| Date | Mintage | F | VF | XF | Unc | BU |
|---|---|---|---|---|---|---|
| 1998 Proof | — | Value: 45.00 | | | | |

**10 KINA** **KM# 8** **Composition:** Copper-Nickel **Reverse:** Bird of paradise

| Date | Mintage | F | VF | XF | Unc | BU |
|---|---|---|---|---|---|---|
| 1975FM (M) | 82 | — | — | — | 65.00 | — |
| 1975FM (U) | 4,134 | — | — | — | 7.50 | — |
| 1976FM (M) | 82 | — | — | — | 65.00 | — |
| 1976FM (U) | 976 | — | — | — | 7.50 | — |
| 1978FM (M) | 168 | — | — | — | 55.00 | — |
| 1978FM (U) | 777 | — | — | — | 15.00 | — |
| 1979FM (M) | 82 | — | — | — | 65.00 | — |
| 1979FM (U) | 1,366 | — | — | — | 10.00 | — |
| 1980FM (U) | 776 | — | — | — | 12.50 | — |
| 1983FM (U) | 360 | — | — | — | 15.00 | — |

**10 KINA** **KM# 8a** **Weight:** 41.6000 g. **Composition:** 0.9250 Silver 1.2371 oz. ASW **Reverse:** Bird of paradise

| Date | Mintage | F | VF | XF | Unc | BU |
|---|---|---|---|---|---|---|
| 1975FM (P) | 79,000 | Value: 7.00 | | | | |
| 1976FM (P) | 21,000 | Value: 8.50 | | | | |
| 1978FM (P) | 7,352 | Value: 10.00 | | | | |
| 1979FM (P) | 4,147 | Value: 12.50 | | | | |
| 1980FM (P) | 2,752 | Value: 20.00 | | | | |
| 1983FM (P) | 1,025 | Value: 22.50 | | | | |

**10 KINA** **KM# 11** **Composition:** Copper-Nickel **Subject:** Silver jubilee of Queen Elizabeth II

| Date | Mintage | F | VF | XF | Unc | BU |
|---|---|---|---|---|---|---|
| 1977FM (M) | 82 | — | — | — | 70.00 | — |
| 1977FM (U) | 603 | — | — | — | 25.00 | — |

**10 KINA** **KM# 11a** **Weight:** 40.0000 g. **Composition:** 0.9250 Silver 1.2046 oz. ASW **Subject:** Silver jubilee of Queen Elizabeth II

| Date | Mintage | F | VF | XF | Unc | BU |
|---|---|---|---|---|---|---|
| 1977FM (P) | 14,000 | Value: 10.00 | | | | |

**10 KINA** **KM# 21** **Composition:** Copper-Nickel **Subject:** Royal visit **Obverse:** Similar to 5 Kina, KM#7

| Date | Mintage | F | VF | XF | Unc | BU |
|---|---|---|---|---|---|---|
| 1982FM (M) | — | — | — | — | 12.50 | — |

**10 KINA** **KM# 21a** **Weight:** 40.5000 g. **Composition:** 0.9250 Silver 1.2046 oz. ASW **Subject:** Royal visit **Obverse:** Similar to 5 Kina, KM#7

| Date | Mintage | F | VF | XF | Unc | BU |
|---|---|---|---|---|---|---|
| 1982FM (P) | 1,185 | Value: 32.50 | | | | |

**10 KINA** **KM# 26 (KM26a)** **Weight:** 35.6000 g. **Composition:** 0.9250 Silver 1.0587 oz. ASW **Subject:** Papal visit **Obverse:** Similar to 5 Kina, KM#7

| Date | Mintage | F | VF | XF | Unc | BU |
|---|---|---|---|---|---|---|
| 1984FM (P) | 597 | Value: 40.00 | | | | |

**10 KINA** **KM# 30** **Weight:** 42.1200 g. **Composition:** 0.9250 Silver 1.2528 oz. ASW **Subject:** 9th South Pacific Games

| Date | Mintage | F | VF | XF | Unc | BU |
|---|---|---|---|---|---|---|
| 1991 Proof | 1,971 | Value: 27.50 | | | | |

**10 KINA** **KM# 33** **Weight:** 1.5710 g. **Composition:** 0.9990 Gold .0504 oz. AGW **Reverse:** Butterfly

| Date | Mintage | F | VF | XF | Unc | BU |
|---|---|---|---|---|---|---|
| 1992 Proof | — | Value: 60.00 | | | | |

**10 KINA** **KM# 33a** **Weight:** 1.5710 g. **Composition:** 0.9950 Platinum .0502 oz. APW **Reverse:** Butterfly

| Date | Mintage | F | VF | XF | Unc | BU |
|---|---|---|---|---|---|---|
| 1992 Proof | — | Value: 70.00 | | | | |

**25 KINA** **KM# 36** **Weight:** 136.0000 g. **Composition:** 0.9250 Silver And Enamel 4.0445 oz. **Reverse:** Bird of paradise **Size:** 63 mm. **Note:** Illustration reduced.

| Date | Mintage | F | VF | XF | Unc | BU |
|---|---|---|---|---|---|---|
| ND(1994) Proof | 1,000 | Value: 300 | | | | |

**50 KINA** **KM# 42** **Weight:** 6.2200 g. **Composition:** 0.9000 Gold .18 oz. AGW **Obverse:** Queen's head right **Reverse:** Golden butterfly and denomination **Edge:** Reeded **Size:** 21.9 mm.

| Date | Mintage |
|---|---|
| 1993 Proof | — Value: 110 |

**50 KINA** **KM# 38** **Weight:** 7.9700 g. **Composition:** 0.9000 Gold .2306 oz. AGW **Subject:** Centennial of first coinage **Note:** Similar to 5 Kina, KM#37.

| Date | Mintage | F | VF | XF | Unc | BU |
|---|---|---|---|---|---|---|
| 1994 Proof | 1,500 | Value: 200 | | | | |

**100 KINA** **KM# 9** **Weight:** 9.5700 g. **Composition:** 0.9000 Gold .2769 oz. AGW **Subject:** Independence

| Date | Mintage | F | VF | XF | Unc | BU |
|---|---|---|---|---|---|---|
| 1975FM (M) | 100 | — | — | — | 225 | — |
| 1975FM (U) | 8,081 | — | — | — | 100 | — |
| 1975FM (P) | 18,000 | Value: 100 | | | | |

**100 KINA** **KM# 10** **Weight:** 9.5700 g. **Composition:** 0.9000 Gold .2769 oz. AGW **Subject:** 1st anniversary of independence

| Date | Mintage | F | VF | XF | Unc | BU |
|---|---|---|---|---|---|---|
| 1976FM (M) | 100 | — | — | — | 225 | — |
| 1976FM (U) | 250 | — | — | — | 150 | — |
| 1976FM (P) | 8,020 | Value: 120 | | | | |

**100 KINA** **KM# 12** **Weight:** 9.5700 g. **Composition:** 0.9000 Gold .2769 oz. AGW **Reverse:** Papuan hornbill

| Date | Mintage | F | VF | XF | Unc | BU |
|---|---|---|---|---|---|---|
| 1977FM (M) | 100 | — | — | — | 200 | — |
| 1977FM (U) | 362 | — | — | — | 145 | — |
| 1977FM (P) | 3,460 | Value: 125 | | | | |

**100 KINA** **KM# 13** **Weight:** 9.5700 g. **Composition:** 0.9000 Gold .2769 oz. AGW **Reverse:** Bird wing butterfly

| Date | Mintage | F | VF | XF | Unc | BU |
|---|---|---|---|---|---|---|
| 1978FM (U) | 400 | — | — | — | 225 | — |
| 1978FM (P) | 4,751 | Value: 175 | | | | |

**100 KINA** **KM# 14** **Weight:** 9.5700 g. **Composition:** 0.9000 Gold .2769 oz. AGW **Subject:** 4 faces of the nation

| Date | Mintage | F | VF | XF | Unc | BU |
|---|---|---|---|---|---|---|
| 1979FM (M) | 102 | — | — | — | 180 | — |
| 1979FM (U) | 286 | — | — | — | 160 | — |
| 1979FM (P) | 3,492 | Value: 125 | | | | |

**100 KINA** **KM# 16** **Weight:** 7.8300 g. **Composition:** 0.5000 Gold .1258 oz. AGW **Subject:** South Pacific Festival of Arts

| Date | Mintage | F | VF | XF | Unc | BU |
|---|---|---|---|---|---|---|
| 1980 Proof | 7,500 | Value: 110 | | | | |

**100 KINA** **KM# 17** **Weight:** 9.5700 g. **Composition:** 0.9000 Gold .2769 oz. AGW **Subject:** 5th anniversary of independence

| Date | Mintage | F | VF | XF | Unc | BU |
|---|---|---|---|---|---|---|
| 1980FM (M) | 30 | — | — | — | 350 | — |
| 1980FM (P) | 1,118 | Value: 175 | | | | |

**100 KINA** **KM# 19** **Weight:** 9.5700 g. **Composition:** 0.9000 Gold .2769 oz. AGW **Obverse:** Prime Minister Sir Julius Chan bust facing left

| Date | Mintage | F | VF | XF | Unc | BU |
|---|---|---|---|---|---|---|
| 1981FM (P) | 685 | Value: 175 | | | | |

**100 KINA** **KM# 22** **Weight:** 9.5700 g. **Composition:** 0.9000 Gold .2769 oz. AGW **Subject:** Royal Visit

| Date | Mintage | F | VF | XF | Unc | BU |
|---|---|---|---|---|---|---|
| 1982FM (P) | 484 | Value: 225 | | | | |

**100 KINA** **KM# 24** **Weight:** 9.5700 g. **Composition:** 0.9000 Gold .2769 oz. AGW **Subject:** 10th anniversary - Bank of Papua New Guinea

| Date | Mintage | F | VF | XF | Unc | BU |
|---|---|---|---|---|---|---|
| 1983FM (P) | 378 | Value: 260 | | | | |

**100 KINA** **KM# 27** **Weight:** 9.5700 g. **Composition:** 0.9000 Gold .2769 oz. AGW **Subject:** 100th anniversary - founding of British and German protectorates

| Date | Mintage | F | VF | XF | Unc | BU |
|---|---|---|---|---|---|---|
| 1984FM (P) | 274 | Value: 250 | | | | |

**100 KINA** **KM# 29** **Weight:** 9.5700 g. **Composition:** 0.9000 Gold .2769 oz. AGW **Reverse:** Queen Alexandra butterfly

| Date | Mintage | F | VF | XF | Unc | BU |
|---|---|---|---|---|---|---|
| 1990 | 500 | — | — | — | 225 | — |
| 1990 Proof | Est. 5,000 | Value: 300 | | | | |
| 1992 Proof | Est. 5,000 | Value: 325 | | | | |

**100 KINA** **KM# 35** **Weight:** 9.5700 g. **Composition:** 0.9000 Gold .2769 oz. AGW **Subject:** 9th South Pacific Games

| Date | Mintage | F | VF | XF | Unc | BU |
|---|---|---|---|---|---|---|
| 1991 Proof | 5,000 | Value: 150 | | | | |

**100 KINA** **KM# 29a** **Weight:** 9.5700 g. **Composition:** 0.9950 Platinum .3061 oz. APW **Reverse:** Queen Alexandra butterfly

| Date | Mintage | F | VF | XF | Unc | BU |
|---|---|---|---|---|---|---|
| 1992 | 500 | — | — | — | 235 | — |
| 1992 Proof | Est. 5,000 | Value: 285 | | | | |

## PIEFORTS

| KM# | Date | Mintage | Identification | Mkt Val |
|---|---|---|---|---|
| P1 | 1982 | 39 | 5 Kina. KM18. | 100 |

## MINT SETS

| KM# | Date | Mintage | Identification | Issue Price | Mkt Val |
|---|---|---|---|---|---|
| MS1 | 1975FM (8) | 4,134 | KM1-8 | 30.00 | 22.50 |
| MS2 | 1976FM (8) | 976 | KM1-8 | 30.00 | 35.00 |
| MS3 | 1977FM (8) | 603 | KM1-7, 11 | 30.00 | 55.00 |
| MS4 | 1978FM (8) | 777 | | 30.00 | 35.00 |
| MS5 | 1979FM (8) | 1,366 | KM1-8 | 31.00 | 30.00 |
| MS6 | 1980FM (9) | — | KM1-8, 15 | 35.00 | 30.00 |
| MS7 | 1982FM (8) | — | KM1-6, 20, 21 | 36.00 | 30.00 |
| MS8 | 1983FM (8) | 360 | KM1-6, 8, 23 | 36.00 | 30.00 |

## PROOF SETS

| KM# | Date | Mintage | Identification | Issue Price | Mkt Val |
|---|---|---|---|---|---|
| PS1 | 1975FM (8) | 42,340 | KM1-6, 7a, 8a | 60.00 | 27.50 |
| PS2 | 1976FM (8) | 16,323 | KM1-6, 7a, 8a | 60.00 | 27.50 |
| PS3 | 1977FM (8) | 7,721 | KM1-6, 7a, 11a | 60.00 | 35.00 |
| PS4 | 1978FM (8) | 5,540 | KM1-6, 7a, 8a | 70.00 | 40.00 |
| PS5 | 1979FM (8) | 2,728 | KM1-6, 7a, 8a | 72.00 | 45.00 |
| PS6 | 1980FM (9) | — | KM1-6, 7a, 8a, 15 | 130 | 60.00 |
| PS7 | 1981FM (6) | 10,000 | KM1-6 | 29.00 | 10.00 |
| PS8 | 1982FM (8) | — | KM1-6, 20a, 21a | 92.00 | 90.00 |
| PS9 | 1983FM (8) | — | KM1-6, 8a, 23a | 132 | 100 |
| PS10 | 1984FM (8) | — | KM1-6, 25, 26 | 133 | 100 |
| PS11 | 1992 (4) | — | KM29a, 33, 33a, 34 | — | 525 |

The Republic of Paraguay, a landlocked country in the heart of South America surrounded by Argentina, Bolivia and Brazil, has an area of 157,048 sq. mi. (406,750 sq. km.) and a population of *4.5 million, 95 percent of whom are of mixed Spanish and Indian descent. Capital: Asuncion. The country is predominantly agrarian, with no important mineral deposits or oil reserves. Meat, timber, hides, oilseeds, tobacco and cotton account for 70 percent of Paraguay's export revenue.

Paraguay was first visited by a ship-wrecked Spaniard named Alejo Garcia, in 1524. The interior was explored by Sebastian Cabot in 1527 and 1528, when he sailed up the Parana and Paraguay rivers. Asuncion, which would become the center of a Spanish colonial province embracing much of southern South America, was established by the Spanish explorer Juan de Salazar on Aug. 15,1537. For 150 years the history of Paraguay was largely the history of the agricultural colonies established by the Jesuits in the south and east to Christianize the Indians. In 1811, following the outbreak of the South American wars of independence, Paraguayan patriots over-threw the local Spanish authorities and proclaimed their country's independence.

During the Triple Alliance War (1864-1870) in which Paraguay faced Argentina, Brazil and Uruguay, Asuncion's ladies gathered in an Assembly on Feb. 24, 1867 and decided to give up their jewelry in order to help the national defense. The President of the Republic, Francisco Solano Lopez accepted the offering and ordered one twentieth of it be used to mint the first Paraguayan gold coins according to the Decree of the 11th of Sept.,1867.

Two dies were made, one by Bouvet, and another by an American, Leonard Charles, while only the die made by Bouvet was eventually used.

**MONETARY SYSTEM**

100 Centavos (Centesimos) = 1 Peso

# REPUBLIC

## DECIMAL COINAGE

100 Centavos (Centesimos) = Peso

**5 CENTAVOS** KM# 6 **Composition:** Copper-Nickel

| Date | Mintage | F | VF | XF | Unc | BU |
|---|---|---|---|---|---|---|
| 1903 | 600,000 | 1.00 | 2.00 | 6.50 | 50.00 | — |

**5 CENTAVOS** KM# 9 **Composition:** Copper-Nickel

| Date | Mintage | F | VF | XF | Unc | BU |
|---|---|---|---|---|---|---|
| 1908 | 400,000 | 1.50 | 5.00 | 30.00 | 75.00 | — |

**10 CENTAVOS** KM# 7 **Composition:** Copper-Nickel

| Date | Mintage | F | VF | XF | Unc | BU |
|---|---|---|---|---|---|---|
| 1903 | 1,200,000 | 1.00 | 2.00 | 6.50 | 25.00 | — |

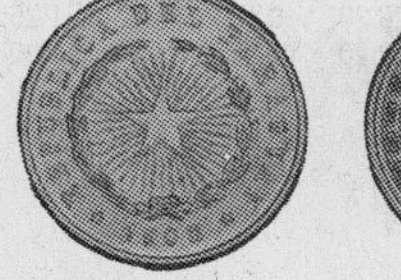
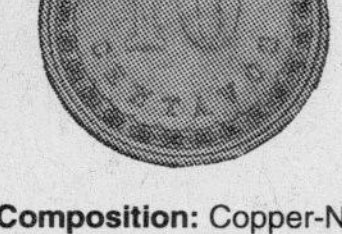

**10 CENTAVOS** KM# 10 **Composition:** Copper-Nickel

| Date | Mintage | F | VF | XF | Unc | BU |
|---|---|---|---|---|---|---|
| 1908 | 800,000 | 2.50 | 5.00 | 25.00 | 70.00 | — |

**20 CENTAVOS** KM# 8 **Composition:** Copper-Nickel

| Date | Mintage | F | VF | XF | Unc | BU |
|---|---|---|---|---|---|---|
| 1903 | 750,000 | 1.00 | 2.00 | 7.50 | 45.00 | — |

**20 CENTAVOS** KM# 11 **Composition:** Copper-Nickel

| Date | Mintage | F | VF | XF | Unc | BU |
|---|---|---|---|---|---|---|
| 1908 | 1,000,000 | 2.50 | 5.00 | 25.00 | 70.00 | — |

**50 CENTAVOS** KM# 12 **Composition:** Copper-Nickel

| Date | Mintage | F | VF | XF | Unc | BU |
|---|---|---|---|---|---|---|
| 1925 | 4,000,000 | 0.50 | 1.50 | 5.00 | 10.00 | — |

**50 CENTAVOS** KM# 15 **Composition:** Aluminum

| Date | Mintage | F | VF | XF | Unc | BU |
|---|---|---|---|---|---|---|
| 1938 | 400,000 | 0.50 | 1.00 | 3.50 | 7.50 | — |

**PESO** KM# 13 **Composition:** Copper-Nickel

| Date | Mintage | F | VF | XF | Unc | BU |
|---|---|---|---|---|---|---|
| 1925 | 3,500,000 | 0.50 | 1.00 | 5.00 | 8.00 | — |

**PESO** KM# 16 **Composition:** Aluminum

| Date | Mintage | F | VF | XF | Unc | BU |
|---|---|---|---|---|---|---|
| 1938 | — | 0.50 | 1.50 | 3.00 | 6.50 | — |

**2 PESOS** KM# 14 **Composition:** Copper-Nickel

| Date | Mintage | F | VF | XF | Unc | BU |
|---|---|---|---|---|---|---|
| 1925 | 2,500,000 | 0.50 | 1.00 | 6.00 | 9.00 | — |

**2 PESOS** KM# 17 **Composition:** Aluminum

| Date | Mintage | F | VF | XF | Unc | BU |
|---|---|---|---|---|---|---|
| 1938 | — | 0.50 | 1.50 | 3.00 | 6.50 | — |

**5 PESOS** KM# 18 **Composition:** Copper-Nickel

| Date | Mintage | F | VF | XF | Unc | BU |
|---|---|---|---|---|---|---|
| 1939 | 4,000,000 | 1.00 | 2.50 | 7.50 | 15.00 | — |

**10 PESOS** KM# 19 **Composition:** Copper-Nickel

| Date | Mintage | F | VF | XF | Unc | BU |
|---|---|---|---|---|---|---|
| 1939 | 4,000,000 | 1.00 | 2.00 | 7.00 | 14.00 | — |

## REFORM COINAGE

100 Centimos = 1 Guarani

**CENTIMO** KM# 20 **Composition:** Aluminum-Bronze **Obverse:** Flower

| Date | Mintage | F | VF | XF | Unc | BU |
|---|---|---|---|---|---|---|
| 1944 | 3,500,000 | 0.10 | 0.50 | 1.00 | 2.00 | — |
| 1948HF | 2,000,000 | 0.10 | 0.50 | 1.00 | 2.00 | — |
| 1950HF | 1,096,000 | 0.10 | 0.25 | 0.75 | 1.50 | — |

**5 CENTIMOS** KM# 21 **Composition:** Aluminum-Bronze **Obverse:** Passion flower

| Date | Mintage | F | VF | XF | Unc | BU |
|---|---|---|---|---|---|---|
| 1944 | 2,195,000 | 0.10 | 0.50 | 1.00 | 2.50 | — |
| 1947HF | 13,111,000 | 0.10 | 0.20 | 0.50 | 1.00 | — |

**10 CENTIMOS** KM# 22 **Composition:** Aluminum-Bronze **Obverse:** Orchid

| Date | Mintage | F | VF | XF | Unc | BU |
|---|---|---|---|---|---|---|
| 1944 | 975,000 | 0.25 | 0.75 | 2.50 | 5.00 | — |
| 1947 | 6,656,000 | 0.10 | 0.25 | 0.50 | 1.00 | — |
| 1947HF | — | 0.10 | 0.25 | 0.50 | 1.00 | — |

**10 CENTIMOS** KM# 25 **Composition:** Aluminum-Bronze **Obverse:** Orchid

| Date | Mintage | F | VF | XF | Unc | BU |
|---|---|---|---|---|---|---|
| 1953 | 5,000,000 | 0.10 | 0.15 | 0.30 | 0.60 | — |
| 1953 Proof; 1 known | — | Value: 350 | | | | |

**Note:** Medal die rotation

**15 CENTIMOS** **KM# 26** **Composition:** Aluminum-Bronze

| Date | Mintage | F | VF | XF | Unc | BU |
|---|---|---|---|---|---|---|
| 1953 | 5,000,000 | 0.10 | 0.20 | 0.35 | 0.75 | — |
| 1953 Proof; 1 known | — | Value: 350 | | | | |

**Note:** Medal die rotation

**25 CENTIMOS** **KM# 23** **Composition:** Aluminum-Bronze **Obverse:** Orchid

| Date | Mintage | F | VF | XF | Unc | BU |
|---|---|---|---|---|---|---|
| 1944 | 700,000 | 0.25 | 1.00 | 3.00 | 10.00 | — |
| 1948HF | 600,000 | 0.25 | 0.75 | 2.50 | 7.00 | — |
| 1951HF | 1,000,000 | 0.25 | 0.75 | 1.25 | 2.50 | — |

**25 CENTIMOS** **KM# 27** **Composition:** Aluminum-Bronze

| Date | Mintage | F | VF | XF | Unc | BU |
|---|---|---|---|---|---|---|
| 1953 | 2,000,000 | 0.10 | 0.15 | 0.30 | 0.75 | — |
| 1953 Proof; 1 known | — | Value: 400 | | | | |

**Note:** Medal die rotation

**50 CENTIMOS** **KM# 24** **Composition:** Aluminum-Bronze

| Date | Mintage | F | VF | XF | Unc | BU |
|---|---|---|---|---|---|---|
| 1944 | 2,485,000 | 0.25 | 1.00 | 2.00 | 5.00 | — |
| 1951 | 2,893,000 | 0.25 | 0.50 | 1.25 | 2.00 | — |

**50 CENTIMOS** **KM# 28** **Composition:** Aluminum-Bronze

| Date | Mintage | F | VF | XF | Unc | BU |
|---|---|---|---|---|---|---|
| 1953 | 2,000,000 | 0.10 | 0.15 | 0.30 | 0.75 | — |
| 1953 Proof; 1 known | — | Value: 400 | | | | |

**Note:** Medal die rotation

**GUARANI** **KM# 151** **Composition:** Stainless Steel

| Date | Mintage | F | VF | XF | Unc | BU |
|---|---|---|---|---|---|---|
| 1975 | 10,000,000 | — | — | 0.15 | 0.50 | — |
| 1975 Proof | 1,000 | Value: 6.00 | | | | |
| 1976 | 12,000,000 | — | — | 0.10 | 0.40 | — |
| 1976 Proof | 1,000 | Value: 8.00 | | | | |

**GUARANI** **KM# 165** **Composition:** Stainless Steel **Series:** F.A.O **Note:** Varieties exist.

| Date | Mintage | F | VF | XF | Unc | BU |
|---|---|---|---|---|---|---|
| 1978 | 15,000,000 | — | — | 0.15 | 0.50 | — |
| 1980 | 13,000,000 | — | — | 0.15 | 0.50 | — |
| 1980 Proof | 1,000 | Value: 6.00 | | | | |
| 1984 | 15,000,000 | — | — | 0.10 | 0.30 | — |
| 1986 | 15,000,000 | — | — | 0.10 | 0.30 | — |
| 1988 | 15,000,000 | — | — | 0.10 | 0.30 | — |

**GUARANI** **KM# 192** **Composition:** Brass Plated Steel **Series:** F.A.O.

| Date | Mintage | F | VF | XF | Unc | BU |
|---|---|---|---|---|---|---|
| 1993 | 5,000,000 | — | — | 0.15 | 0.50 | — |

**GUARANI** **KM# 193** **Weight:** 27.0000 g. **Composition:** 0.9250 Silver .8030 oz. ASW **Subject:** Encuentro De Dos Mundos **Obverse:** Paraguayan arms in circle of arms **Reverse:** Dancer

| Date | Mintage | F | VF | XF | Unc | BU |
|---|---|---|---|---|---|---|
| 1997 Proof | — | Value: 45.00 | | | | |

**5 GUARANIES** **KM# 152** **Composition:** Stainless Steel

| Date | Mintage | F | VF | XF | Unc | BU |
|---|---|---|---|---|---|---|
| 1975 | 7,500,000 | — | — | 0.15 | 0.50 | — |
| 1975 Proof | 1,000 | Value: 6.00 | | | | |

**5 GUARANIES** **KM# 166** **Composition:** Stainless Steel **Series:** F.A.O. **Note:** Varieties exist.

| Date | Mintage | F | VF | XF | Unc | BU |
|---|---|---|---|---|---|---|
| 1978 | 10,000,000 | — | — | 0.15 | 0.60 | — |
| 1980 | 12,000,000 | — | — | 0.15 | 0.60 | — |
| 1980 Proof | 1,000 | Value: 6.00 | | | | |
| 1984 | 15,000,000 | — | — | 0.10 | 0.40 | — |
| 1986 | 15,000,000 | — | — | 0.10 | 0.40 | — |

**5 GUARANIES** **KM# 166a** **Composition:** Nickel-Bronze **Series:** F.A.O.

| Date | Mintage | F | VF | XF | Unc | BU |
|---|---|---|---|---|---|---|
| 1992 | 15,000,000 | — | — | 0.10 | 0.30 | — |

**10 GUARANIES** **KM# 153** **Composition:** Stainless Steel

| Date | Mintage | F | VF | XF | Unc | BU |
|---|---|---|---|---|---|---|
| 1975 | 10,000,000 | — | 0.10 | 0.20 | 0.75 | — |
| 1975 Proof | 1,000 | Value: 8.00 | | | | |
| 1976 | 10,000,000 | — | 0.10 | 0.20 | 0.75 | — |
| 1976 Proof | 1,000 | Value: 10.00 | | | | |

**10 GUARANIES** **KM# 167** **Composition:** Stainless Steel **Series:** F.A.O. **Note:** Varieties exist.

| Date | Mintage | F | VF | XF | Unc | BU |
|---|---|---|---|---|---|---|
| 1978 | 15,000,000 | — | 0.10 | 0.20 | 0.75 | — |
| 1980 | 15,000,000 | — | 0.10 | 0.20 | 0.75 | — |
| 1980 Proof | 1,000 | Value: 8.00 | | | | |
| 1984 | 20,000,000 | — | 0.10 | 0.15 | 0.50 | — |
| 1986 | 35,000,000 | — | 0.10 | 0.15 | 0.50 | — |
| 1988 | 40,000,000 | — | 0.10 | 0.15 | 0.50 | — |

**10 GUARANIES** **KM# 178** **Composition:** Nickel-Bronze **Series:** F.A.O. **Reverse:** Cow

| Date | Mintage | F | VF | XF | Unc | BU |
|---|---|---|---|---|---|---|
| 1990 | 40,000,000 | — | — | 0.10 | 0.40 | — |
| 1996 | — | — | — | 0.10 | 0.40 | — |

**50 GUARANIES** **KM# 154** **Composition:** Stainless Steel

| Date | Mintage | F | VF | XF | Unc | BU |
|---|---|---|---|---|---|---|
| 1975 | 9,500,000 | 0.20 | 0.40 | 0.60 | 1.25 | — |
| 1975 Proof | 1,000 | Value: 10.00 | | | | |

**50 GUARANIES** **KM# 169** **Composition:** Stainless Steel **Obverse:** General Estigarribia **Reverse:** Acaray River Dam **Note:** Varieties exist.

| Date | Mintage | F | VF | XF | Unc | BU |
|---|---|---|---|---|---|---|
| 1980 | 10,700,000 | 0.20 | 0.40 | 0.60 | 1.25 | — |
| 1980 Proof | 1,000 | Value: 10.00 | | | | |
| 1986 | 15,000,000 | 0.20 | 0.40 | 0.60 | 1.25 | — |
| 1988 | 25,000,000 | 0.20 | 0.30 | 0.50 | 1.00 | — |

**50 GUARANIES** **KM# 191** **Composition:** Copper-Zinc-Nickel **Obverse:** General Estigarribia **Reverse:** Acaray River Dam

| Date | Mintage | F | VF | XF | Unc | BU |
|---|---|---|---|---|---|---|
| 1992 | 35,000,000 | — | — | — | 0.75 | — |
| 1995 | 35,000,000 | — | — | — | 0.75 | — |

**100 GUARANIES** **KM# 177** **Composition:** Copper-Zinc-Nickel

| Date | Mintage | F | VF | XF | Unc | BU |
|---|---|---|---|---|---|---|
| 1990 | 35,000,000 | — | — | — | 2.25 | — |

**100 GUARANIES** **KM# 177a** **Composition:** Brass Plated Steel

| Date | Mintage | F | VF | XF | Unc | BU |
|---|---|---|---|---|---|---|
| 1993 | 35,000,000 | — | — | — | 1.50 | — |
| 1995 | 35,000,000 | — | — | — | 1.50 | — |
| 1996 | — | — | — | — | 1.50 | — |

**150 GUARANIES** **KM# 31** **Weight:** 25.0000 g. **Composition:** 0.9990 Silver .8030 oz. ASW **Obverse:** Arms **Reverse:** Bust of General A. Stroessner facing

| Date | Mintage | F | VF | XF | Unc | BU |
|---|---|---|---|---|---|---|
| 1972 Proof | Est. 10,000 | Value: 60.00 | | | | |

**150 GUARANIES** **KM# 32** **Weight:** 25.0000 g. **Composition:** 0.9990 Silver .8030 oz. ASW **Subject:** Munich Olympics **Obverse:** Arms **Reverse:** Runner

| Date | Mintage | F | VF | XF | Unc | BU |
|---|---|---|---|---|---|---|
| 1972 | Est. 10,000 | Value: 70.00 | | | | |

**150 GUARANIES** **KM# 33** **Weight:** 25.0000 g. **Composition:** 0.9990 Silver .8030 oz. ASW **Subject:** Munich Olympics **Obverse:** Arms **Reverse:** Broad jumper

| Date | Mintage | F | VF | XF | Unc | BU |
|---|---|---|---|---|---|---|
| 1972 | Est. 10,000 | Value: 70.00 | | | | |

**150 GUARANIES** **KM# 34** **Weight:** 25.0000 g. **Composition:** 0.9990 Silver .8030 oz. ASW **Subject:** Munich Olympics **Obverse:** Arms **Reverse:** Soccer

| Date | Mintage | F | VF | XF | Unc | BU |
|---|---|---|---|---|---|---|
| 1972 | Est. 10,000 | Value: 70.00 | | | | |

**150 GUARANIES** **KM# 35** **Weight:** 25.0000 g. **Composition:** 0.9990 Silver .8030 oz. ASW **Subject:** Munich Olympics **Obverse:** Arms **Reverse:** Hurdler

| Date | Mintage | F | VF | XF | Unc | BU |
|---|---|---|---|---|---|---|
| 1972 | Est. 10,000 | Value: 70.00 | | | | |

**150 GUARANIES** **KM# 36** **Weight:** 25.0000 g. **Composition:** 0.9990 Silver .8030 oz. ASW **Subject:** Munich Olympics **Obverse:** Arms **Reverse:** High jumper

| Date | Mintage | F | VF | XF | Unc | BU |
|---|---|---|---|---|---|---|
| 1972 | Est. 10,000 | Value: 70.00 | | | | |

**150 GUARANIES** **KM# 37** **Weight:** 25.0000 g. **Composition:** 0.9990 Silver .8030 oz. ASW **Subject:** Munich Olympics **Obverse:** Arms **Reverse:** Boxer

| Date | Mintage | F | VF | XF | Unc | BU |
|---|---|---|---|---|---|---|
| 1973 | Est. 10,000 | Value: 70.00 | | | | |

**150 GUARANIES** **KM# 59** **Weight:** 25.0000 g. **Composition:** 0.9990 Silver .8030 oz. ASW **Obverse:** Arms **Reverse:** Bust of Mariscal Jose F. Estigarribia facing

| Date | Mintage | F | VF | XF | Unc | BU |
|---|---|---|---|---|---|---|
| 1973 | Est. 10,000 | Value: 55.00 | | | | |

**150 GUARANIES** **KM# 60** **Weight:** 25.0000 g. **Composition:** 0.9990 Silver .8030 oz. ASW **Obverse:** Arms **Reverse:** Bust of Mariscal Francisco Solano Lopez facing

| Date | Mintage | F | VF | XF | Unc | BU |
|---|---|---|---|---|---|---|
| 1973 | Est. 10,000 | Value: 55.00 | | | | |

**150 GUARANIES** **KM# 61** **Weight:** 25.0000 g. **Composition:** 0.9990 Silver .8030 oz. ASW **Obverse:** Arms **Reverse:** Bust of General Jose E. Diaz facing

| Date | Mintage | F | VF | XF | Unc | BU |
|---|---|---|---|---|---|---|
| 1973 | Est. 10,000 | Value: 52.50 | | | | |

**150 GUARANIES** **KM# 62** **Weight:** 25.0000 g. **Composition:** 0.9990 Silver .8030 oz. ASW **Obverse:** Arms **Reverse:** Bust of General Bernardino Caballero facing

| Date | Mintage | F | VF | XF | Unc | BU |
|---|---|---|---|---|---|---|
| 1973 | Est. 10,000 | Value: 52.50 | | | | |

**150 GUARANIES** **KM# 63** **Weight:** 25.0000 g. **Composition:** 0.9990 Silver .8030 oz. ASW **Obverse:** Arms **Reverse:** Teotihucana Culture sculpture

| Date | Mintage | F | VF | XF | Unc | BU |
|---|---|---|---|---|---|---|
| 1973 | Est. 10,000 | Value: 52.50 | | | | |

**150 GUARANIES** **KM# 64** **Weight:** 25.0000 g. **Composition:** 0.9990 Silver .8030 oz. ASW **Obverse:** Arms **Reverse:** Huasteca Culture sculpture

| Date | Mintage | F | VF | XF | Unc | BU |
|---|---|---|---|---|---|---|
| 1973 | Est. 10,000 | Value: 52.50 | | | | |

**150 GUARANIES** **KM# 65** **Weight:** 25.0000 g. **Composition:** 0.9990 Silver .8030 oz. ASW **Obverse:** Arms **Reverse:** Mixteca Culture animal sculpture

| Date | Mintage | F | VF | XF | Unc | BU |
|---|---|---|---|---|---|---|
| 1973 | Est. 10,000 | Value: 52.50 | | | | |

**150 GUARANIES** **KM# 66** **Weight:** 25.0000 g. **Composition:** 0.9990 Silver .8030 oz. ASW **Obverse:** Arms **Reverse:** Veracruz Ceramica Vase

| Date | Mintage | F | VF | XF | Unc | BU |
|---|---|---|---|---|---|---|
| 1973 | Est. 10,000 | Value: 52.50 | | | | |

**150 GUARANIES** **KM# 67** **Weight:** 25.0000 g. **Composition:** 0.9990 Silver .8030 oz. ASW **Obverse:** Arms **Reverse:** Veracruz Culture sculpture

| Date | Mintage | F | VF | XF | Unc | BU |
|---|---|---|---|---|---|---|
| 1973 | Est. 10,000 | Value: 52.50 | | | | |

**150 GUARANIES** **KM# 68** **Weight:** 25.0000 g. **Composition:** 0.9990 Silver .8030 oz. ASW **Obverse:** Arms **Reverse:** Bust of Albrecht Durer facing

| Date | Mintage | F | VF | XF | Unc | BU |
|---|---|---|---|---|---|---|
| 1973 | Est. 10,000 | Value: 65.00 | | | | |

**150 GUARANIES** **KM# 69** **Weight:** 25.0000 g. **Composition:** 0.9990 Silver .8030 oz. ASW **Obverse:** Arms **Reverse:** Bust of Johann Wolfgang Goethe facing

| Date | Mintage | F | VF | XF | Unc | BU |
|---|---|---|---|---|---|---|
| 1973 | Est. 10,000 | Value: 65.00 | | | | |

**150 GUARANIES** **KM# 107** **Weight:** 25.0000 g. **Composition:** 0.9990 Silver .8030 oz. ASW **Obverse:** Arms **Reverse:** Bust of President Abraham Lincoln left

| Date | Mintage | F | VF | XF | Unc | BU |
|---|---|---|---|---|---|---|
| 1974 | Est. 10,000 | Value: 75.00 | | | | |

**150 GUARANIES** **KM# 108** **Weight:** 25.0000 g. **Composition:** 0.9990 Silver .8030 oz. ASW **Obverse:** Arms **Reverse:** Bust of Ludwig van Beethoven half left

| Date | Mintage | F | VF | XF | Unc | BU |
|---|---|---|---|---|---|---|
| 1974 | Est. 10,000 | Value: 75.00 | | | | |

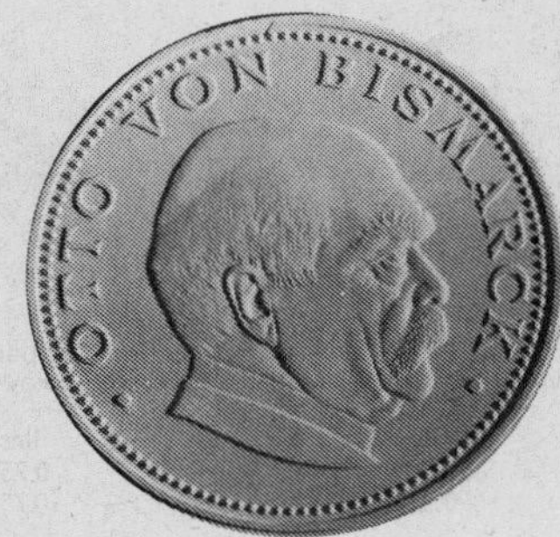


**150 GUARANIES** **KM# 109** **Weight:** 25.0000 g. **Composition:** 0.9990 Silver .8030 oz. ASW **Obverse:** Arms **Reverse:** Bust of Otto von Bismarck right

| Date | Mintage | F | VF | XF | Unc | BU |
|---|---|---|---|---|---|---|
| 1974 | Est. 10,000 | Value: 75.00 | | | | |

**150 GUARANIES** **KM# 110** **Weight:** 25.0000 g. **Composition:** 0.9990 Silver .8030 oz. ASW **Obverse:** Arms **Reverse:** Bust of Albert Einstein left

| Date | Mintage | F | VF | XF | Unc | BU |
|---|---|---|---|---|---|---|
| 1974 | Est. 10,000 | Value: 85.00 | | | | |

**150 GUARANIES** **KM# 111** **Weight:** 25.0000 g. **Composition:** 0.9990 Silver .8030 oz. ASW **Obverse:** Arms **Reverse:** Bust of Giuseppe Garibaldi facing

| Date | Mintage | F | VF | XF | Unc | BU |
|---|---|---|---|---|---|---|
| 1974 | Est. 10,000 | Value: 65.00 | | | | |

**150 GUARANIES** **KM# 112** **Weight:** 25.0000 g. **Composition:** 0.9990 Silver .8030 oz. ASW **Obverse:** Arms **Reverse:** Bust of Alessandro Manzoni facing

| Date | Mintage | F | VF | XF | Unc | BU |
|---|---|---|---|---|---|---|
| 1974 | Est. 10,000 | Value: 57.50 | | | | |

**150 GUARANIES** **KM# 113** **Weight:** 25.0000 g. **Composition:** 0.9990 Silver .8030 oz. ASW **Obverse:** Arms **Reverse:** William Tell and son standing facing

| Date | Mintage | F | VF | XF | Unc | BU |
|---|---|---|---|---|---|---|
| 1974 | Est. 10,000 | Value: 57.50 | | | | |

**150 GUARANIES** **KM# 114** **Weight:** 25.0000 g. **Composition:** 0.9990 Silver .8030 oz. ASW **Obverse:** Arms **Reverse:** Bust of President John F. Kennedy left

| Date | Mintage | F | VF | XF | Unc | BU |
|---|---|---|---|---|---|---|
| 1974 | Est. 10,000 | Value: 55.00 | | | | |

**150 GUARANIES** **KM# 115** **Weight:** 25.0000 g. **Composition:** 0.9990 Silver .8030 oz. ASW **Obverse:** Arms **Reverse:** Bust of Konrad Adenauer left

| Date | Mintage | F | VF | XF | Unc | BU |
|---|---|---|---|---|---|---|
| 1974 | Est. 10,000 | Value: 65.00 | | | | |

**150 GUARANIES** **KM# 116** **Weight:** 25.0000 g. **Composition:** 0.9990 Silver .8030 oz. ASW **Obverse:** Arms **Reverse:** Bust of Winston Churchill left

| Date | Mintage | F | VF | XF | Unc | BU |
|---|---|---|---|---|---|---|
| 1974 | Est. 10,000 | Value: 55.00 | | | | |

**150 GUARANIES** **KM# 117** **Weight:** 25.0000 g. **Composition:** 0.9990 Silver .8030 oz. ASW **Obverse:** Arms **Reverse:** Bust of Pope John XXIII left

| Date | Mintage | F | VF | XF | Unc | BU |
|---|---|---|---|---|---|---|
| 1974 | Est. 10,000 | Value: 65.00 | | | | |

**150 GUARANIES** **KM# 118** **Weight:** 25.0000 g. **Composition:** 0.9990 Silver .8030 oz. ASW **Obverse:** Arms **Reverse:** Bust of Pope Paul VI left

| Date | Mintage | F | VF | XF | Unc | BU |
|---|---|---|---|---|---|---|
| 1974 | Est. 10,000 | Value: 65.00 | | | | |

**150 GUARANIES** **KM# 155** **Weight:** 25.0000 g. **Composition:** 0.9990 Silver .8030 oz. ASW **Obverse:** Arms **Reverse:** Parliament building of Paraguay

| Date | Mintage | F | VF | XF | Unc | BU |
|---|---|---|---|---|---|---|
| 1975 | Est. 10,000 | Value: 55.00 | | | | |

**150 GUARANIES** **KM# 156** **Weight:** 25.0000 g. **Composition:** 0.9990 Silver .8030 oz. ASW **Subject:** Apollo 11 Mission **Obverse:** Arms **Reverse:** Eagle landing on moon with earth at left

| Date | Mintage | F | VF | XF | Unc | BU |
|---|---|---|---|---|---|---|
| 1975 | Est. 10,000 | Value: 65.00 | | | | |

**150 GUARANIES** **KM# 157** **Weight:** 25.0000 g. **Composition:** 0.9990 Silver .8030 oz. ASW **Subject:** Apollo 15 Mission **Obverse:** Arms

| Date | Mintage | F | VF | XF | Unc | BU |
|---|---|---|---|---|---|---|
| 1975 | Est. 10,000 | Value: 65.00 | | | | |

**150 GUARANIES** **KM# 158** **Weight:** 25.0000 g. **Composition:** 0.9990 Silver .8030 oz. ASW **Obverse:** Arms **Reverse:** Friendship Bridge

| Date | Mintage | F | VF | XF | Unc | BU |
|---|---|---|---|---|---|---|
| 1975 | Est. 10,000 | Value: 57.50 | | | | |

**150 GUARANIES** **KM# 159** **Weight:** 25.0000 g. **Composition:** 0.9990 Silver .8030 oz. ASW **Obverse:** Arms **Reverse:** Holy Trinity Church

| Date | Mintage | F | VF | XF | Unc | BU |
|---|---|---|---|---|---|---|
| 1975 | Est. 10,000 | Value: 57.50 | | | | |

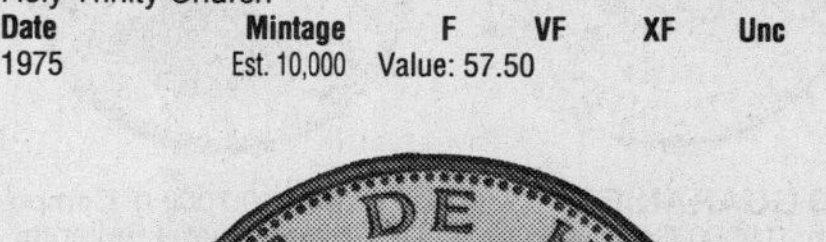

**150 GUARANIES** **KM# 160** **Weight:** 25.0000 g. **Composition:** 0.9990 Silver .8030 oz. ASW **Obverse:** Arms **Reverse:** Ruins of Humaita

| Date | Mintage | F | VF | XF | Unc | BU |
|---|---|---|---|---|---|---|
| 1975 | Est. 10,000 | Value: 57.50 | | | | |

**300 GUARANIES** **KM# 29** **Weight:** 26.6000 g. **Composition:** 0.7200 Silver .6157 oz. ASW **Subject:** 4th Term of President Stroessner **Obverse:** Lion arms **Reverse:** Bust of President A. Stroessner left

| Date | Mintage | F | VF | XF | Unc | BU |
|---|---|---|---|---|---|---|
| 1968 | 250,000 | — | — | 6.00 | 9.00 | — |

**500 GUARANIES** **KM# 194** **Composition:** Brass **Obverse:** Bust of General Bernardino Caballero facing **Reverse:** Central Bank of Paraguay

| Date | Mintage | F | VF | XF | Unc | BU |
|---|---|---|---|---|---|---|
| 1997 | — | — | — | — | 2.50 | — |

**500 GUARANIES** **KM# 195** **Composition:** Brass **Obverse:** Bust of General Bernardino Caballero facing **Reverse:** Central Bank of Paraguay above denomination

| Date | Mintage | F | VF | XF | Unc | BU |
|---|---|---|---|---|---|---|
| 1998 | 15,000 | — | — | — | 2.50 | — |

**1500 GUARANIES** **KM# 38** **Weight:** 10.7000 g. **Composition:** 0.9000 Gold .3096 oz. AGW **Obverse:** Arms **Reverse:** Bust of General A. Stroessner facing

| Date | Mintage | F | VF | XF | Unc | BU |
|---|---|---|---|---|---|---|
| 1972 | Est. 1,500 | Value: 300 | | | | |

**1500 GUARANIES** **KM# 39** **Weight:** 10.7000 g. **Composition:** 0.9000 Gold .3096 oz. AGW **Subject:** Munich Olympics **Obverse:** Arms **Reverse:** Runner

| Date | Mintage | F | VF | XF | Unc | BU |
|---|---|---|---|---|---|---|
| 1972 | Est. 1,500 | Value: 750 | | | | |

**1500 GUARANIES** **KM# 40** **Weight:** 10.7000 g. **Composition:** 0.9000 Gold .3096 oz. AGW **Subject:** Munich Olympics **Obverse:** Arms **Reverse:** Broad jumper

| Date | Mintage | F | VF | XF | Unc | BU |
|---|---|---|---|---|---|---|
| 1972 | Est. 1,500 | Value: 750 | | | | |

**1500 GUARANIES** **KM# 41** **Weight:** 10.7000 g. **Composition:** 0.9000 Gold .3096 oz. AGW **Subject:** Munich Olympics **Obverse:** Arms **Reverse:** Soccer

| Date | Mintage | F | VF | XF | Unc | BU |
|---|---|---|---|---|---|---|
| 1972 | Est. 1,500 | Value: 750 | | | | |

**1500 GUARANIES** **KM# 42** **Weight:** 10.7000 g. **Composition:** 0.9000 Gold .3096 oz. AGW **Subject:** Munich Olympics **Obverse:** Arms **Reverse:** Hurdler

| Date | Mintage | F | VF | XF | Unc | BU |
|---|---|---|---|---|---|---|
| 1972 | Est. 1,500 | Value: 750 | | | | |

**1500 GUARANIES** **KM# 43** **Weight:** 10.7000 g. **Composition:** 0.9000 Gold .3096 oz. AGW **Subject:** Munich Olympics **Obverse:** Arms **Reverse:** High Jumper

| Date | Mintage | F | VF | XF | Unc | BU |
|---|---|---|---|---|---|---|
| 1973 | 1,500 | Value: 750 | | | | |

**1500 GUARANIES** **KM# 44** **Weight:** 10.7000 g. **Composition:** 0.9000 Gold .3096 oz. AGW **Subject:** Munich Olympics **Obverse:** Arms **Reverse:** Boxer

| Date | Mintage | F | VF | XF | Unc | BU |
|---|---|---|---|---|---|---|
| 1973 | Est. 1,500 | Value: 750 | | | | |

**1500 GUARANIES** **KM# 70** **Weight:** 10.7000 g. **Composition:** 0.9000 Gold .3096 oz. AGW **Obverse:** Arms **Reverse:** Bust of Jose F. Estigarribia facing

| Date | Mintage | F | VF | XF | Unc | BU |
|---|---|---|---|---|---|---|
| 1973 | Est. 1,500 | Value: 400 | | | | |

**1500 GUARANIES** **KM# 71** **Weight:** 10.7000 g. **Composition:** 0.9000 Gold .3096 oz. AGW **Obverse:** Arms **Reverse:** Bust of Mariscal Francisco Solano Lopez facing

| Date | Mintage | F | VF | XF | Unc | BU |
|---|---|---|---|---|---|---|
| 1973 | Est. 1,500 | Value: 400 | | | | |

**1500 GUARANIES** **KM# 72** **Weight:** 10.7000 g. **Composition:** 0.9000 Gold .3096 oz. AGW **Obverse:** Arms **Reverse:** Bust of General Jose E. Diaz facing

| Date | Mintage | F | VF | XF | Unc | BU |
|---|---|---|---|---|---|---|
| 1973 | Est. 1,500 | Value: 400 | | | | |

**1500 GUARANIES** **KM# 73** **Weight:** 10.7000 g. **Composition:** 0.9000 Gold .3096 oz. AGW **Obverse:** Arms **Reverse:** Busty of General Bernardino Caballero facing

| Date | Mintage | F | VF | XF | Unc | BU |
|---|---|---|---|---|---|---|
| 1973 | Est. 1,500 | Value: 400 | | | | |

**1500 GUARANIES** **KM# 74** **Weight:** 10.7000 g. **Composition:** 0.9000 Gold .3096 oz. AGW **Obverse:** Arms **Reverse:** Teotihucana Culture sculpture

| Date | Mintage | F | VF | XF | Unc | BU |
|---|---|---|---|---|---|---|
| 1973 | Est. 1,500 | Value: 400 | | | | |

**1500 GUARANIES** **KM# 75** **Weight:** 10.7000 g. **Composition:** 0.9000 Gold .3096 oz. AGW **Obverse:** Arms **Reverse:** Huasteca Culture sculpture

| Date | Mintage | F | VF | XF | Unc | BU |
|---|---|---|---|---|---|---|
| 1973 | Est. 1,500 | Value: 400 | | | | |

**1500 GUARANIES** **KM# 76** **Weight:** 10.7000 g. **Composition:** 0.9000 Gold .3096 oz. AGW **Obverse:** Arms **Reverse:** Mixteca Culture sculpture

| Date | Mintage | F | VF | XF | Unc | BU |
|---|---|---|---|---|---|---|
| 1973 | Est. 1,500 | Value: 400 | | | | |

**1500 GUARANIES** **KM# 77** **Weight:** 10.7000 g. **Composition:** 0.9000 Gold .3096 oz. AGW **Obverse:** Arms **Reverse:** Veracruz Ceramica vase

| Date | Mintage | F | VF | XF | Unc | BU |
|---|---|---|---|---|---|---|
| 1973 | Est. 1,500 | Value: 400 | | | | |

**1500 GUARANIES** **KM# 78** **Weight:** 10.7000 g. **Composition:** 0.9000 Gold .3096 oz. AGW **Obverse:** Arms **Reverse:** Veracruz Culture sculpture

| Date | Mintage | F | VF | XF | Unc | BU |
|---|---|---|---|---|---|---|
| 1973 | Est. 1,500 | Value: 400 | | | | |

**1500 GUARANIES** **KM# 79** **Weight:** 10.7000 g. **Composition:** 0.9000 Gold .3096 oz. AGW **Obverse:** Arms **Reverse:** Bust of Albrecht Durer facing

| Date | Mintage | F | VF | XF | Unc | BU |
|---|---|---|---|---|---|---|
| 1973 | Est. 1,500 | Value: 400 | | | | |

**1500 GUARANIES** **KM# 80** **Weight:** 10.7000 g. **Composition:** 0.9000 Gold .3096 oz. AGW **Obverse:** Arms **Reverse:** Bust of Johann Wolfgang Goethe facing

| Date | Mintage | F | VF | XF | Unc | BU |
|---|---|---|---|---|---|---|
| 1973 | Est. 1,500 | Value: 400 | | | | |

**1500 GUARANIES** **KM# 119** **Weight:** 10.7000 g. **Composition:** 0.9000 Gold .3096 oz. AGW **Obverse:** Arms **Reverse:** Bust of President Abraham Lincoln left

| Date | Mintage | F | VF | XF | Unc | BU |
|---|---|---|---|---|---|---|
| 1974 | Est. 1,500 | Value: 400 | | | | |

**1500 GUARANIES** **KM# 120** **Weight:** 10.7000 g. **Composition:** 0.9000 Gold .3096 oz. AGW **Obverse:** Arms **Reverse:** Bust of Ludwig van Beethoven half left

| Date | Mintage | F | VF | XF | Unc | BU |
|---|---|---|---|---|---|---|
| 1974 | Est. 1,500 | Value: 750 | | | | |

**1500 GUARANIES** **KM# 121** **Weight:** 10.7000 g. **Composition:** 0.9000 Gold .3096 oz. AGW **Obverse:** Arms **Reverse:** Bust of Otto von Bismarck right

| Date | Mintage | F | VF | XF | Unc | BU |
|---|---|---|---|---|---|---|
| 1974 | Est. 1,500 | Value: 400 | | | | |

**1500 GUARANIES** **KM# 122** **Weight:** 10.7000 g. **Composition:** 0.9000 Gold .3096 oz. AGW **Obverse:** Arms **Reverse:** Bust of Albert Einstein left

| Date | Mintage | F | VF | XF | Unc | BU |
|---|---|---|---|---|---|---|
| 1974 | Est. 1,500 | Value: 400 | | | | |

**1500 GUARANIES** **KM# 123** **Weight:** 10.7000 g. **Composition:** 0.9000 Gold .3096 oz. AGW **Obverse:** Arms **Reverse:** Bust of Giuseppe Garibaldi facing

| Date | Mintage | F | VF | XF | Unc | BU |
|---|---|---|---|---|---|---|
| 1974 | Est. 1,500 | Value: 400 | | | | |

**1500 GUARANIES** **KM# 124** **Weight:** 10.7000 g. **Composition:** 0.9000 Gold .3096 oz. AGW **Obverse:** Arms **Reverse:** Bust of Alessandro Manzoni facing

| Date | Mintage | F | VF | XF | Unc | BU |
|---|---|---|---|---|---|---|
| 1974 | Est. 1,500 | Value: 400 | | | | |

**1500 GUARANIES** **KM# 125** **Weight:** 10.7000 g. **Composition:** 0.9000 Gold .3096 oz. AGW **Obverse:** Arms **Reverse:** William Tell and son standing facing

| Date | Mintage | F | VF | XF | Unc | BU |
|---|---|---|---|---|---|---|
| 1974 | Est. 1,500 | Value: 400 | | | | |

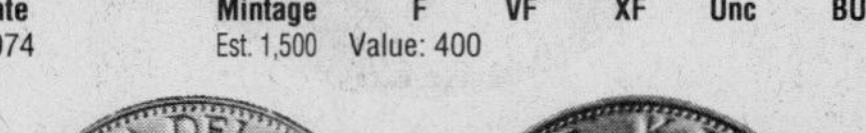

**1500 GUARANIES** **KM# 126** **Weight:** 10.7000 g. **Composition:** 0.9000 Gold .3096 oz. AGW **Obverse:** Arms **Reverse:** Bust of President John F. Kennedy left

| Date | Mintage | F | VF | XF | Unc | BU |
|---|---|---|---|---|---|---|
| 1974 | Est. 1,500 | Value: 400 | | | | |

**1500 GUARANIES** **KM# 127** **Weight:** 10.7000 g. **Composition:** 0.9000 Gold .3096 oz. AGW **Obverse:** Arms **Reverse:** Bust of Konrad Adenauer left

| Date | Mintage | F | VF | XF | Unc | BU |
|---|---|---|---|---|---|---|
| 1974 | Est. 1,500 | Value: 400 | | | | |

**1500 GUARANIES** **KM# 128** **Weight:** 10.7000 g. **Composition:** 0.9000 Gold .3096 oz. AGW **Obverse:** Arms **Reverse:** Bust of Winston Churchill left

| Date | Mintage | F | VF | XF | Unc | BU |
|---|---|---|---|---|---|---|
| 1974 | Est. 1,500 | Value: 400 | | | | |

**1500 GUARANIES** **KM# 129** **Weight:** 10.7000 g. **Composition:** 0.9000 Gold .3096 oz. AGW **Obverse:** Arms **Reverse:** Bust of Pope John XXIII left

| Date | Mintage | F | VF | XF | Unc | BU |
|---|---|---|---|---|---|---|
| 1974 | Est. 1,500 | Value: 400 | | | | |

**1500 GUARANIES** **KM# 130** **Weight:** 10.7000 g. **Composition:** 0.9000 Gold .3096 oz. AGW **Obverse:** Arms **Reverse:** Bust of Pope Paul VI left

| Date | Mintage | F | VF | XF | Unc | BU |
|---|---|---|---|---|---|---|
| 1974 | Est. 1,500 | Value: 400 | | | | |

**1500 GUARANIES** **KM# 179** **Weight:** 10.7000 g. **Composition:** 0.9000 Gold .3096 oz. AGW **Obverse:** Arms **Reverse:** Parliament building of Paraguay

| Date | Mintage | F | VF | XF | Unc | BU |
|---|---|---|---|---|---|---|
| 1975 | 1,500 | Value: 400 | | | | |

**1500 GUARANIES** **KM# 180** **Weight:** 10.7000 g. **Composition:** 0.9000 Gold **Subject:** Apollo 11 Mission **Obverse:** Arms **Reverse:** Eagle landing on moon with earth at left

| Date | Mintage | F | VF | XF | Unc | BU |
|---|---|---|---|---|---|---|
| 1975 | 1,500 | Value: 500 | | | | |

**1500 GUARANIES** **KM# 181** **Weight:** 10.7000 g. **Composition:** 0.9000 Gold **Subject:** Apollo 15 Mission **Obverse:** Arms

| Date | Mintage | F | VF | XF | Unc | BU |
|---|---|---|---|---|---|---|
| 1975 | 1,500 | Value: 500 | | | | |

**1500 GUARANIES** **KM# 182** **Weight:** 10.7000 g. **Composition:** 0.9000 Gold **Obverse:** Arms **Reverse:** Friendship Bridge

| Date | Mintage | F | VF | XF | Unc | BU |
|---|---|---|---|---|---|---|
| 1975 | 1,500 | Value: 400 | | | | |

**1500 GUARANIES** **KM# 183** **Weight:** 10.7000 g. **Composition:** 0.9000 Gold **Obverse:** Arms **Reverse:** Holy Trinity Chruch

| Date | Mintage | F | VF | XF | Unc | BU |
|---|---|---|---|---|---|---|
| 1975 | 1,500 | Value: 400 | | | | |

**1500 GUARANIES** **KM# 184** **Weight:** 10.7000 g. **Composition:** 0.9000 Gold **Obverse:** Arms **Reverse:** Ruins of Humaita

| Date | Mintage | F | VF | XF | Unc | BU |
|---|---|---|---|---|---|---|
| 1975 | Est. 1,500 | Value: 400 | | | | |

**3000 GUARANIES** **KM# 45** **Weight:** 21.3000 g. **Composition:** 0.9000 Gold .6164 oz. AGW **Obverse:** Arms **Reverse:** Bust of General A. Stroessner facing

| Date | Mintage | F | VF | XF | Unc | BU |
|---|---|---|---|---|---|---|
| 1972 | Est. 1,500 | Value: 450 | | | | |

**3000 GUARANIES** **KM# 46** **Weight:** 21.3000 g. **Composition:** 0.9000 Gold .6164 oz. AGW **Subject:** Munich Olympics **Obverse:** Arms **Reverse:** Runner

| Date | Mintage | F | VF | XF | Unc | BU |
|---|---|---|---|---|---|---|
| 1972 | Est. 1,500 | Value: 1,500 | | | | |

**3000 GUARANIES** **KM# 47** **Weight:** 21.3000 g. **Composition:** 0.9000 Gold .6164 oz. AGW **Subject:** Munich Olympics **Obverse:** Arms **Reverse:** Broad Jumper

| Date | Mintage | F | VF | XF | Unc | BU |
|---|---|---|---|---|---|---|
| 1972 | Est. 1,500 | Value: 1,500 | | | | |

**3000 GUARANIES** **KM# 48** **Weight:** 21.3000 g. **Composition:** 0.9000 Gold .6164 oz. AGW **Subject:** Munich Olympics **Obverse:** Arms **Reverse:** Soccer

| Date | Mintage | F | VF | XF | Unc | BU |
|---|---|---|---|---|---|---|
| 1972 | Est. 1,500 | Value: 1,500 | | | | |

**3000 GUARANIES** **KM# 49** **Weight:** 21.3000 g. **Composition:** 0.9000 Gold .6164 oz. AGW **Subject:** Munich Olympics **Obverse:** Arms **Reverse:** Hurdler

| Date | Mintage | F | VF | XF | Unc | BU |
|---|---|---|---|---|---|---|
| 1972 | Est. 1,500 | Value: 1,500 | | | | |

**3000 GUARANIES** **KM# 50** **Weight:** 21.3000 g. **Composition:** 0.9000 Gold .6164 oz. AGW **Subject:** Munich Olympics **Obverse:** Arms **Reverse:** High jumper

| Date | Mintage | F | VF | XF | Unc | BU |
|---|---|---|---|---|---|---|
| 1972 | Est. 1,500 | Value: 1,500 | | | | |

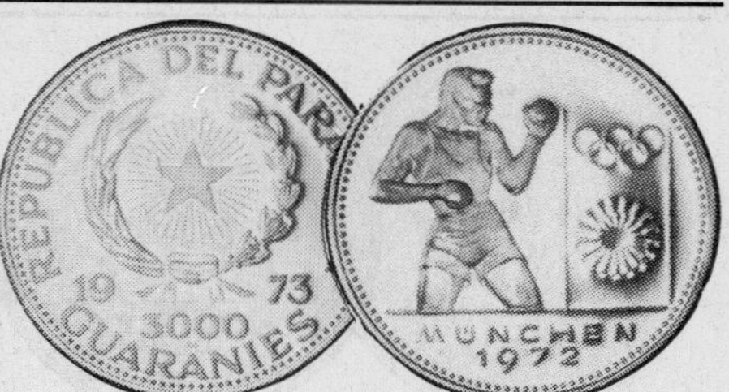


**3000 GUARANIES** **KM# 51** **Weight:** 21.3000 g. **Composition:** 0.9000 Gold .6164 oz. AGW **Subject:** Munich Olympics **Obverse:** Arms **Reverse:** Boxer

| Date | Mintage | F | VF | XF | Unc | BU |
|---|---|---|---|---|---|---|
| 1973 | Est. 1,500 | Value: 1,500 | | | | |

**3000 GUARANIES** **KM# 81** **Weight:** 21.3000 g. **Composition:** 0.9000 Gold .6164 oz. AGW **Obverse:** Arms **Reverse:** Bust of Jose F. Estigarribia facing

| Date | Mintage | F | VF | XF | Unc | BU |
|---|---|---|---|---|---|---|
| 1973 | Est. 1,500 | Value: 700 | | | | |

**3000 GUARANIES** **KM# 82** **Weight:** 21.3000 g. **Composition:** 0.9000 Gold .6164 oz. AGW **Obverse:** Arms **Reverse:** Bust of Mariscal Francisco Solano Lopez facing

| Date | Mintage | F | VF | XF | Unc | BU |
|---|---|---|---|---|---|---|
| 1973 | Est. 1,500 | Value: 700 | | | | |

**3000 GUARANIES** **KM# 83** **Weight:** 21.3000 g. **Composition:** 0.9000 Gold .6164 oz. AGW **Obverse:** Arms **Reverse:** Bust of General Jose E. Diaz facing

| Date | Mintage | F | VF | XF | Unc | BU |
|---|---|---|---|---|---|---|
| 1973 | Est. 1,500 | Value: 700 | | | | |

**3000 GUARANIES** **KM# 84** **Weight:** 21.3000 g. **Composition:** 0.9000 Gold .6164 oz. AGW **Obverse:** Arms **Reverse:** Bust of General Bernardino Caballero facing

| Date | Mintage | F | VF | XF | Unc | BU |
|---|---|---|---|---|---|---|
| 1973 | Est. 1,500 | Value: 700 | | | | |

**3000 GUARANIES** **KM# 85** **Weight:** 21.3000 g. **Composition:** 0.9000 Gold .6164 oz. AGW **Obverse:** Arms **Reverse:** Teotihucana Culture sculpture

| Date | Mintage | F | VF | XF | Unc | BU |
|---|---|---|---|---|---|---|
| 1973 | Est. 1,500 | Value: 700 | | | | |

**3000 GUARANIES** **KM# 86** **Weight:** 21.3000 g. **Composition:** 0.9000 Gold .6164 oz. AGW **Obverse:** Arms **Reverse:** Huasteca Culture sculpture

| Date | Mintage | F | VF | XF | Unc | BU |
|---|---|---|---|---|---|---|
| 1973 | Est. 1,500 | Value: 700 | | | | |

**3000 GUARANIES** **KM# 87** **Weight:** 21.3000 g. **Composition:** 0.9000 Gold .6164 oz. AGW **Obverse:** Arms **Reverse:** Mixteca Culture sculpture

| Date | Mintage | F | VF | XF | Unc | BU |
|---|---|---|---|---|---|---|
| 1973 | Est. 1,500 | Value: 700 | | | | |

**3000 GUARANIES** **KM# 88** **Weight:** 21.3000 g. **Composition:** 0.9000 Gold .6164 oz. AGW **Obverse:** Arms **Reverse:** Veracruz Ceramica vase

| Date | Mintage | F | VF | XF | Unc | BU |
|---|---|---|---|---|---|---|
| 1973 | Est. 1,500 | Value: 700 | | | | |

**3000 GUARANIES** **KM# 89** **Weight:** 21.3000 g. **Composition:** 0.9000 Gold .6164 oz. AGW **Obverse:** Arms **Reverse:** Veracruz Culture sculpture

| Date | Mintage | F | VF | XF | Unc | BU |
|---|---|---|---|---|---|---|
| 1973 | Est. 1,500 | Value: 700 | | | | |

**3000 GUARANIES** **KM# 90** **Weight:** 21.3000 g. **Composition:** 0.9000 Gold .6164 oz. AGW **Obverse:** Arms **Reverse:** Bust of Albrecht Durer facing

| Date | Mintage | F | VF | XF | Unc | BU |
|---|---|---|---|---|---|---|
| 1973 | Est. 1,500 | Value: 700 | | | | |

**3000 GUARANIES** **KM# 91** **Weight:** 21.3000 g. **Composition:** 0.9000 Gold .6164 oz. AGW **Obverse:** Arms **Reverse:** Bust of Johann Wolfgang von Goethe facing

| Date | Mintage | F | VF | XF | Unc | BU |
|---|---|---|---|---|---|---|
| 1973 | Est. 1,500 | Value: 700 | | | | |

**3000 GUARANIES** **KM# 131** **Weight:** 21.3000 g. **Composition:** 0.9000 Gold .6164 oz. AGW **Obverse:** Arms **Reverse:** Bust of President Abraham Lincoln left

| Date | Mintage | F | VF | XF | Unc | BU |
|---|---|---|---|---|---|---|
| 1974 | Est. 1,500 | Value: 700 | | | | |

**3000 GUARANIES** **KM# 132** **Weight:** 21.3000 g. **Composition:** 0.9000 Gold .6164 oz. AGW **Obverse:** Arms **Reverse:** Bust of Ludwig van Beethoven facing half left

| Date | Mintage | F | VF | XF | Unc | BU |
|---|---|---|---|---|---|---|
| 1974 | Est. 1,500 | Value: 1,350 | | | | |

**3000 GUARANIES** **KM# 133** **Weight:** 21.3000 g. **Composition:** 0.9000 Gold .6164 oz. AGW **Obverse:** Arms **Reverse:** Bust of Otto von Bismarck right

| Date | Mintage | F | VF | XF | Unc | BU |
|---|---|---|---|---|---|---|
| 1974 | Est. 1,500 | Value: 700 | | | | |

**3000 GUARANIES** **KM# 134** **Weight:** 21.3000 g. **Composition:** 0.9000 Gold .6164 oz. AGW **Obverse:** Arms **Reverse:** Bust of Albert Einstein left

| Date | Mintage | F | VF | XF | Unc | BU |
|---|---|---|---|---|---|---|
| 1974 | Est. 1,500 | Value: 700 | | | | |

**3000 GUARANIES** **KM# 135** **Weight:** 21.3000 g. **Composition:** 0.9000 Gold .6164 oz. AGW **Obverse:** Arms **Reverse:** Bust of Giuseppe Garibaldi facing

| Date | Mintage | F | VF | XF | Unc | BU |
|---|---|---|---|---|---|---|
| 1974 | Est. 1,500 | Value: 700 | | | | |

**3000 GUARANIES** **KM# 136** **Weight:** 21.3000 g. **Composition:** 0.9000 Gold .6164 oz. AGW **Obverse:** Arms **Reverse:** Bust of Alessandro Manzoni facing

| Date | Mintage | F | VF | XF | Unc | BU |
|---|---|---|---|---|---|---|
| 1974 | Est. 1,500 | Value: 700 | | | | |

**3000 GUARANIES** **KM# 137** **Weight:** 21.3000 g. **Composition:** 0.9000 Gold .6164 oz. AGW **Obverse:** Arms **Reverse:** William Tell and son standing facing

| Date | Mintage | F | VF | XF | Unc | BU |
|---|---|---|---|---|---|---|
| 1974 | Est. 1,500 | Value: 700 | | | | |

**3000 GUARANIES** **KM# 138** **Weight:** 21.3000 g. **Composition:** 0.9000 Gold .6164 oz. AGW **Obverse:** Arms **Reverse:** Bust of President John F. Kennedy left

| Date | Mintage | F | VF | XF | Unc | BU |
|---|---|---|---|---|---|---|
| 1974 | Est. 1,500 | Value: 700 | | | | |

**3000 GUARANIES** **KM# 139** **Weight:** 21.3000 g. **Composition:** 0.9000 Gold .6164 oz. AGW **Obverse:** Arms **Reverse:** Bust of Konrad Adenauer left

| Date | Mintage | F | VF | XF | Unc | BU |
|---|---|---|---|---|---|---|
| 1974 | Est. 1,500 | Value: 700 | | | | |

**3000 GUARANIES** **KM# 140** **Weight:** 21.3000 g. **Composition:** 0.9000 Gold .6164 oz. AGW **Obverse:** Arms **Reverse:** Bust of Sir Winston Churchill left

| Date | Mintage | F | VF | XF | Unc | BU |
|---|---|---|---|---|---|---|
| 1974 | Est. 1,500 | Value: 700 | | | | |

**3000 GUARANIES** **KM# 141** **Weight:** 21.3000 g. **Composition:** 0.9000 Gold .6164 oz. AGW **Obverse:** Arms **Reverse:** Bust of Pope John XXIII left

| Date | Mintage | F | VF | XF | Unc | BU |
|---|---|---|---|---|---|---|
| 1974 | Est. 1,500 | Value: 700 | | | | |

**3000 GUARANIES** **KM# 142** **Weight:** 21.3000 g. **Composition:** 0.9000 Gold .6164 oz. AGW **Obverse:** Arms **Reverse:** Bust of Pope Paul VI left

| Date | Mintage | F | VF | XF | Unc | BU |
|---|---|---|---|---|---|---|
| 1974 | Est. 1,500 | Value: 700 | | | | |

**3000 GUARANIES** **KM# 161** **Weight:** 21.3000 g. **Composition:** 0.9000 Gold .6164 oz. AGW **Obverse:** Arms **Reverse:** Holy Trinity Chruch

| Date | Mintage | F | VF | XF | Unc | BU |
|---|---|---|---|---|---|---|
| 1975 | — | Value: 650 | | | | |

**3000 GUARANIES** **KM# 162** **Weight:** 21.3000 g. **Composition:** 0.9000 Gold .6164 oz. AGW **Obverse:** Arms **Reverse:** Parliament building of Paraguay

| Date | Mintage | F | VF | XF | Unc | BU |
|---|---|---|---|---|---|---|
| 1975 | — | Value: 650 | | | | |

**3000 GUARANIES** **KM# 163** **Weight:** 21.3000 g. **Composition:** 0.9000 Gold .6164 oz. AGW **Obverse:** Arms **Reverse:** Friendship bridge

| Date | Mintage | F | VF | XF | Unc | BU |
|---|---|---|---|---|---|---|
| 1975 | — | Value: 650 | | | | |

**3000 GUARANIES** **KM# 164** **Weight:** 21.3000 g. **Composition:** 0.9000 Gold .6164 oz. AGW **Obverse:** Arms **Reverse:** Humaita ruins

| Date | Mintage | F | VF | XF | Unc | BU |
|---|---|---|---|---|---|---|
| 1975 | — | Value: 650 | | | | |

**3000 GUARANIES** **KM# 175** **Weight:** 21.3000 g. **Composition:** 0.9000 Gold .6164 oz. AGW **Subject:** Apollo 11 Mission **Obverse:** Arms **Reverse:** Eagle landing on moon with earth at upper left

| Date | Mintage | F | VF | XF | Unc | BU |
|---|---|---|---|---|---|---|
| 1975 | — | Value: 1,000 | | | | |

**3000 GUARANIES** **KM# 176** **Weight:** 21.3000 g. **Composition:** 0.9000 Gold .6164 oz. AGW **Subject:** Apollo 15 Mission **Obverse:** Arms

| Date | Mintage | F | VF | XF | Unc | BU |
|---|---|---|---|---|---|---|
| 1975 | — | Value: 1,000 | | | | |

**4500 GUARANIES** **KM# 52** **Weight:** 31.9000 g. **Composition:** 0.9000 Gold .9231 oz. AGW **Obverse:** Arms **Reverse:** Bust of General A. Stroessner facing

| Date | Mintage | F | VF | XF | Unc | BU |
|---|---|---|---|---|---|---|
| 1972 | Est. 1,500 | Value: 750 | | | | |

**4500 GUARANIES** **KM# 53** **Weight:** 31.9000 g. **Composition:** 0.9000 Gold .9231 oz. AGW **Subject:** Munich Olympics **Obverse:** Arms **Reverse:** Runner

| Date | Mintage | F | VF | XF | Unc | BU |
|---|---|---|---|---|---|---|
| 1972 | Est. 1,500 | Value: 2,700 | | | | |

**4500 GUARANIES** **KM# 54** **Weight:** 31.9000 g. **Composition:** 0.9000 Gold .9231 oz. AGW **Subject:** Munich Olympics **Obverse:** Arms **Reverse:** Broad jumper

| Date | Mintage | F | VF | XF | Unc | BU |
|---|---|---|---|---|---|---|
| 1972 | Est. 1,500 | Value: 2,700 | | | | |

**4500 GUARANIES** **KM# 55** **Weight:** 31.9000 g. **Composition:** 0.9000 Gold .9231 oz. AGW **Subject:** Munich Olympics **Obverse:** Arms **Reverse:** Soccer

| Date | Mintage | F | VF | XF | Unc | BU |
|---|---|---|---|---|---|---|
| 1972 | Est. 1,500 | Value: 2,700 | | | | |

**4500 GUARANIES** **KM# 56** **Weight:** 31.9000 g. **Composition:** 0.9000 Gold .9231 oz. AGW **Subject:** Munich Olympics **Obverse:** Arms **Reverse:** Hurdler

| Date | Mintage | F | VF | XF | Unc | BU |
|---|---|---|---|---|---|---|
| 1972 | Est. 1,500 | Value: 2,700 | | | | |

**4500 GUARANIES** **KM# 57** **Weight:** 31.9000 g. **Composition:** 0.9000 Gold .9231 oz. AGW **Subject:** Munich Olympics **Obverse:** Arms **Reverse:** High jumper

| Date | Mintage | F | VF | XF | Unc | BU |
|---|---|---|---|---|---|---|
| 1972 | Est. 1,500 | Value: 2,700 | | | | |

**4500 GUARANIES** **KM# 58** **Weight:** 31.9000 g. **Composition:** 0.9000 Gold .9231 oz. AGW **Subject:** Munich Olympics **Obverse:** Arms **Reverse:** Boxer

| Date | Mintage | F | VF | XF | Unc | BU |
|---|---|---|---|---|---|---|
| 1973 | Est. 1,500 | Value: 2,700 | | | | |

**4500 GUARANIES** **KM# 92** **Weight:** 31.9000 g. **Composition:** 0.9000 Gold .9231 oz. AGW **Obverse:** Arms **Reverse:** Bust of Mariscal Jose F. Estigarribia facing

| Date | Mintage | F | VF | XF | Unc | BU |
|---|---|---|---|---|---|---|
| 1973 | Est. 1,500 | Value: 1,200 | | | | |

**4500 GUARANIES** **KM# 93** **Weight:** 31.9000 g. **Composition:** 0.9000 Gold .9231 oz. AGW **Obverse:** Arms **Reverse:** Bust of Mariscal Francisco Solano Lopez facing

| Date | Mintage | F | VF | XF | Unc | BU |
|---|---|---|---|---|---|---|
| 1973 | Est. 1,500 | Value: 1,200 | | | | |

**4500 GUARANIES** **KM# 94** **Weight:** 31.9000 g. **Composition:** 0.9000 Gold .9231 oz. AGW **Obverse:** Arms **Reverse:** Bust of General Jose E. Diaz facing

| Date | Mintage | F | VF | XF | Unc | BU |
|---|---|---|---|---|---|---|
| 1973 | Est. 1,500 | Value: 1,200 | | | | |

**4500 GUARANIES** **KM# 95** **Weight:** 31.9000 g. **Composition:** 0.9000 Gold .9231 oz. AGW **Obverse:** Arms **Reverse:** Bust of General Bernardino Caballero facing

| Date | Mintage | F | VF | XF | Unc | BU |
|---|---|---|---|---|---|---|
| 1973 | Est. 1,500 | Value: 1,200 | | | | |

**4500 GUARANIES** **KM# 96** **Weight:** 31.9000 g. **Composition:** 0.9000 Gold .9231 oz. AGW **Obverse:** Arms **Reverse:** Teotihucana Culture sculpture

| Date | Mintage | F | VF | XF | Unc | BU |
|---|---|---|---|---|---|---|
| 1973 | Est. 1,500 | Value: 1,200 | | | | |

**4500 GUARANIES** **KM# 97** **Weight:** 31.9000 g. **Composition:** 0.9000 Gold .9231 oz. AGW **Obverse:** Arms **Reverse:** Huasteca Culture sculpture

| Date | Mintage | F | VF | XF | Unc | BU |
|---|---|---|---|---|---|---|
| 1973 | Est. 1,500 | Value: 1,200 | | | | |

**4500 GUARANIES** **KM# 98** **Weight:** 31.9000 g. **Composition:** 0.9000 Gold .9231 oz. AGW **Obverse:** Arms **Reverse:** Mixteca Culture sculpture

| Date | Mintage | F | VF | XF | Unc | BU |
|---|---|---|---|---|---|---|
| 1973 | Est. 1,500 | Value: 1,200 | | | | |

**4500 GUARANIES** **KM# 99** **Weight:** 31.9000 g. **Composition:** 0.9000 Gold .9231 oz. AGW **Obverse:** Arms **Reverse:** Veracruz Ceramica sculpture

| Date | Mintage | F | VF | XF | Unc | BU |
|---|---|---|---|---|---|---|
| 1973 | Est. 1,500 | Value: 1,200 | | | | |

**4500 GUARANIES** **KM# 100** **Weight:** 31.9000 g. **Composition:** 0.9000 Gold .9231 oz. AGW **Obverse:** Arms **Reverse:** Veracruz Culture bust

| Date | Mintage | F | VF | XF | Unc | BU |
|---|---|---|---|---|---|---|
| 1973 | Est. 1,500 | Value: 1,200 | | | | |

**4500 GUARANIES** **KM# 101** **Weight:** 31.9000 g. **Composition:** 0.9000 Gold .9231 oz. AGW **Obverse:** Arms **Reverse:** Bust of Albrecht Durer facing

| Date | Mintage | F | VF | XF | Unc | BU |
|---|---|---|---|---|---|---|
| 1973 | Est. 1,500 | Value: 1,200 | | | | |

**4500 GUARANIES** **KM# 102** **Weight:** 31.9000 g. **Composition:** 0.9000 Gold .9231 oz. AGW **Obverse:** Arms **Reverse:** Bust of Johann Wolfgang von Goethe facing

| Date | Mintage | F | VF | XF | Unc | BU |
|---|---|---|---|---|---|---|
| 1973 | Est. 1,500 | Value: 1,200 | | | | |

**4500 GUARANIES** **KM# 103** **Weight:** 31.9000 g. **Composition:** 0.9000 Gold .9231 oz. AGW **Obverse:** Arms **Reverse:** Bust of Ludwig van Beethoven half left

| Date | Mintage | F | VF | XF | Unc | BU |
|---|---|---|---|---|---|---|
| 1974 | Est. 1,500 | Value: 2,100 | | | | |

**4500 GUARANIES** **KM# 104** **Weight:** 31.9000 g. **Composition:** 0.9000 Gold .9231 oz. AGW **Obverse:** Arms **Reverse:** Bust of Otto von Bismarck right

| Date | Mintage | F | VF | XF | Unc | BU |
|---|---|---|---|---|---|---|
| 1974 | Est. 1,500 | Value: 1,200 | | | | |

**4500 GUARANIES** **KM# 105** **Weight:** 31.9000 g. **Composition:** 0.9000 Gold .9231 oz. AGW **Obverse:** Arms **Reverse:** Bust of Giuseppe Garibaldi facing

| Date | Mintage | F | VF | XF | Unc | BU |
|---|---|---|---|---|---|---|
| 1974 | Est. 1,500 | Value: 1,200 | | | | |

**4500 GUARANIES** KM# 106 **Weight:** 31.9000 g. **Composition:** 0.9000 Gold .9231 oz. AGW **Obverse:** Arms **Reverse:** Bust of Alessandro Manzoni facing

| Date | Mintage | F | VF | XF | Unc | BU |
|---|---|---|---|---|---|---|
| 1974 | Est. 1,500 | Value: 1,200 | | | | |

**4500 GUARANIES** KM# 143 **Weight:** 31.9000 g. **Composition:** 0.9000 Gold .9231 oz. AGW **Obverse:** Arms **Reverse:** Bust of President Abraham Lincoln left

| Date | Mintage | F | VF | XF | Unc | BU |
|---|---|---|---|---|---|---|
| 1974 | Est. 1,500 | Value: 1,200 | | | | |

**4500 GUARANIES** KM# 144 **Weight:** 31.9000 g. **Composition:** 0.9000 Gold .9231 oz. AGW **Obverse:** Arms **Reverse:** Bust of Albert Einstein left

| Date | Mintage | F | VF | XF | Unc | BU |
|---|---|---|---|---|---|---|
| 1974 | Est. 1,500 | Value: 1,200 | | | | |

**4500 GUARANIES** KM# 145 **Weight:** 31.9000 g. **Composition:** 0.9000 Gold .9231 oz. AGW **Obverse:** Arms **Reverse:** William Tell and son standing facing

| Date | Mintage | F | VF | XF | Unc | BU |
|---|---|---|---|---|---|---|
| 1974 | Est. 1,500 | Value: 1,200 | | | | |

**4500 GUARANIES** KM# 146 **Weight:** 31.9000 g. **Composition:** 0.9000 Gold .9231 oz. AGW **Obverse:** Arms **Reverse:** Bust of President John F. Kennedy left

| Date | Mintage | F | VF | XF | Unc | BU |
|---|---|---|---|---|---|---|
| 1974 | Est. 1,500 | Value: 1,200 | | | | |

**4500 GUARANIES** KM# 147 **Weight:** 31.9000 g. **Composition:** 0.9000 Gold .9231 oz. AGW **Obverse:** Arms **Reverse:** Bust of Konrad Adenauer left

| Date | Mintage | F | VF | XF | Unc | BU |
|---|---|---|---|---|---|---|
| 1974 | Est. 1,500 | Value: 1,200 | | | | |

**4500 GUARANIES** KM# 148 **Weight:** 31.9000 g. **Composition:** 0.9000 Gold .9231 oz. AGW **Obverse:** Arms **Reverse:** Bust of Winston Churchill left

| Date | Mintage | F | VF | XF | Unc | BU |
|---|---|---|---|---|---|---|
| 1974 | Est. 1,500 | Value: 1,200 | | | | |

**4500 GUARANIES** KM# 149 **Weight:** 31.9000 g. **Composition:** 0.9000 Gold .9231 oz. AGW **Obverse:** Arms **Reverse:** Bust of Pope John XXIII left

| Date | Mintage | F | VF | XF | Unc | BU |
|---|---|---|---|---|---|---|
| 1974 | Est. 1,500 | Value: 1,200 | | | | |

**4500 GUARANIES** KM# 150 **Weight:** 31.9000 g. **Composition:** 0.9000 Gold .9231 oz. AGW **Obverse:** Arms **Reverse:** Bust of Pope Paul VI left

| Date | Mintage | F | VF | XF | Unc | BU |
|---|---|---|---|---|---|---|
| 1974 | Est. 1,500 | Value: 1,200 | | | | |

**4500 GUARANIES** KM# 185 **Weight:** 31.9000 g. **Composition:** 0.9000 Gold .9231 oz. AGW **Obverse:** Arms **Reverse:** Parliament building of Paraguay

| Date | Mintage | F | VF | XF | Unc | BU |
|---|---|---|---|---|---|---|
| 1975 | Est. 1,500 | Value: 1,200 | | | | |

**4500 GUARANIES** KM# 186 **Weight:** 31.9000 g. **Composition:** 0.9000 Gold .9231 oz. AGW **Subject:** Apollo 11 Mission **Obverse:** Arms **Reverse:** Eagle landing on moon with earth at upper left

| Date | Mintage | F | VF | XF | Unc | BU |
|---|---|---|---|---|---|---|
| 1975 | Est. 1,500 | Value: 1,200 | | | | |

**4500 GUARANIES** KM# 187 **Weight:** 31.9000 g. **Composition:** 0.9000 Gold .9231 oz. AGW **Subject:** Apollo 15 Mission **Obverse:** Arms

| Date | Mintage | F | VF | XF | Unc | BU |
|---|---|---|---|---|---|---|
| 1975 | Est. 1,500 | Value: 1,200 | | | | |

**4500 GUARANIES** KM# 188 **Weight:** 31.9000 g. **Composition:** 0.9000 Gold .9231 oz. AGW **Obverse:** Arms **Reverse:** Friendship bridge

| Date | Mintage | F | VF | XF | Unc | BU |
|---|---|---|---|---|---|---|
| 1975 | Est. 1,500 | Value: 1,200 | | | | |

**4500 GUARANIES** KM# 189 **Weight:** 31.9000 g. **Composition:** 0.9000 Gold .9231 oz. AGW **Obverse:** Arms **Reverse:** Holy Trinity Church

| Date | Mintage | F | VF | XF | Unc | BU |
|---|---|---|---|---|---|---|
| 1975 | Est. 1,500 | Value: 1,200 | | | | |

**4500 GUARANIES** KM# 190 **Weight:** 31.9000 g. **Composition:** 0.9000 Gold .9231 oz. AGW **Obverse:** Arms **Reverse:** Ruins of Humaita

| Date | Mintage | F | VF | XF | Unc | BU |
|---|---|---|---|---|---|---|
| 1975 | Est. 1,500 | Value: 1,200 | | | | |

**10000 GUARANIES** KM# 30 **Weight:** 46.0100 g. **Composition:** 0.9000 Gold 1.3315 oz. AGW **Subject:** 4th Term of President Stroessner **Obverse:** Lion arms **Reverse:** Bust of General A. Stroessner facing **Note:** Similar to 300 Guaranies KM#29.

| Date | Mintage | F | VF | XF | Unc | BU |
|---|---|---|---|---|---|---|
| 1968 | Est. 50 | Value: 4,500 | | | | |

**Note:** KM#30 struck for presentation

**10000 GUARANIES** KM# 171 **Weight:** 28.7000 g. **Composition:** 0.9990 Silver .9219 oz. ASW **Obverse:** Central Bank building of Paraguay **Reverse:** Conjoined busts of Caballero and Stroessner left

| Date | Mintage | F | VF | XF | Unc | BU |
|---|---|---|---|---|---|---|
| ND(1987) Proof | 1,000 | Value: 40.00 | | | | |

**10000 GUARANIES** KM# 173 **Weight:** 28.7000 g. **Composition:** 0.9990 Silver .9219 oz. ASW **Subject:** 8th Term of President A. Stroessner **Obverse:** Lion arms **Reverse:** Bust of President A. Stroessner left

| Date | Mintage | F | VF | XF | Unc | BU |
|---|---|---|---|---|---|---|
| ND(1988) Proof | 1,000 | Value: 40.00 | | | | |

**70000 GUARANIES** KM# 168 **Weight:** 46.0000 g. **Composition:** 0.9000 Gold 1.3310 oz. AGW **Subject:** 6th Term of President A. Stroessner **Obverse:** Lion arms **Reverse:** Bust of President A. Stroessner left

| Date | Mintage | F | VF | XF | Unc | BU |
|---|---|---|---|---|---|---|
| ND(1978) Proof | 300 | Value: 750 | | | | |

**100000 GUARANIES** KM# 170 **Weight:** 46.0000 g. **Composition:** 0.9000 Gold 1.3310 oz. AGW **Subject:** 7th Term of President A. Stroessner **Obverse:** Lion arms **Reverse:** Bust of President A. Stroessner left

| Date | Mintage | F | VF | XF | Unc | BU |
|---|---|---|---|---|---|---|
| ND(1983) Proof | 300 | Value: 750 | | | | |

**250000 GUARANIES** KM# 172 **Weight:** 46.0000 g. **Composition:** 0.9170 Gold 1.3561 oz. AGW **Obverse:** Central Bank building of Paraguay **Reverse:** Conjoined busts of Caballero - Stroessner left

| Date | Mintage | F | VF | XF | Unc | BU |
|---|---|---|---|---|---|---|
| ND(1987) Proof | Est. 500 | Value: 750 | | | | |

**Note:** 250 pieces remelted

**300000 GUARANIES** KM# 174 **Weight:** 46.0000 g. **Composition:** 0.9170 Gold 1.3561 oz. AGW **Subject:** 8th Term of President A. Stroessner **Obverse:** Lion arms **Reverse:** Bust of President A. Stroessner left

| Date | Mintage | F | VF | XF | Unc | BU |
|---|---|---|---|---|---|---|
| ND(1988) Proof | Est. 500 | Value: 750 | | | | |

**Note:** 250 pieces remelted

## PATTERNS

Including off metal strikes

| KM# | Date | Mintage | Identification | Mkt Val |
|---|---|---|---|---|
| Pn40 | ND1925 | — | 2 Pesos. Aluminum. Narrow flan, KM14. | 100 |
| Pn41 | ND1925 | — | 2 Pesos. Aluminum. Broad flan, KM14. | 125 |
| Pn42 | ND1939 | — | 5 Pesos. Brass. KM#8. | 175 |
| Pn43 | ND1939 | — | 5 Pesos. Copper. KM18. | 175 |
| Pn44 | ND1976 | 10 | Guarani. Gold. | 400 |
| Pn45 | ND1976 | 10 | 10 Guaranies. Gold. | 700 |
| Pn46 | ND1978 | 10 | Guarani. Gold. | 400 |
| Pn47 | ND1978 | 10 | 5 Guaranies. Gold. | 500 |
| Pn48 | ND1978 | 10 | 10 Guaranies. Gold. | 700 |
| Pn49 | ND1980 | 10 | Guarani. Gold. | 400 |
| Pn50 | ND1980 | 10 | 5 Guaranies. Gold. | 500 |
| Pn51 | ND1980 | 10 | 10 Guaranies. Gold. | 700 |
| Pn52 | ND1980 | 10 | 50 Guaranies. Gold. | 1,000 |

## PROOF SETS

| KM# | Date | Mintage | Identification | Issue Price | Mkt Val |
|---|---|---|---|---|---|
| PS1 | 1953(4) (4) | 1 | KM25-28 | — | 1,500 |
| PS2 | 1972 (24) | — | KM31-36, 38-43, 45-50, 52-57 | — | — |
| PS3 | 1973 (48) | — | KM37, 44, 51, 58-102 | — | — |
| PS4 | 1974 (48) | — | KM103-150 | — | — |
| PS5 | 1975 (24) | — | KM155-164, 175-176, 179-190 | — | — |
| PS6 | 1975 (4) | 1,000 | KM151-154 | — | 30.00 |
| PS7 | 1976 (2) | 1,000 | KM151, 153 | — | 20.00 |
| PS8 | 1980 (4) | 1,000 | KM165-167, 169 | — | 30.00 |

The Republic of Peru, located on the Pacific coast of South America, has an area of 496,225 sq. mi. (1,285,220sq. km.) and a population of *21.4 million. Capital: Lima. The diversified economy includes mining, fishing and agriculture. Fish meal, copper, sugar, zinc and iron ore are exported.

Once part of the great Inca Empire that reached from northern Ecuador to central Chile, the conquest of Peru by Francisco Pizarro began in 1531. Desirable as the richest of the Spanish viceroyalties, it was torn by warfare between avaricious Spaniards until the arrival in 1569 of Francisco de Toledo, who initiated 2-1/2 centuries of efficient colonial rule, which made Lima the most aristocratic colonial capital and the stronghold of Spain's American possessions. Jose de San Martin of Argentina proclaimed Peru's independence on July 28, 1821;Simon Bolivar of Venezuela cleared it in December, 1824 when he defeated the last Spanish army in South America. After several futile attempts to re-establish its South American empire, Spain recognized Peru's independence in 1879.

Andres de Santa Cruz, whose mother was a high-ranking Inca, was the best of Bolivia's early presidents, and temporarily united Peru and Bolivia 1836-39, thus realizing his dream of a Peruvian/Bolivian confederation. This prompted the separate coinages of North and South Peru. Peruvian resistance and Chilean intervention finally broke up the confederation, sending Santa Cruz into exile. A succession of military strongman presidents ruled Peru until Marshall Castilla revitalized Peruvian politics in themid-19th century and repulsed Spain's attempt to reclaim its one-time colony. Subsequent loss of southern territory to Chile in the War of the Pacific, 1879-81, and gradually increasing rejection of foreign economic domination, combined with recent serious inflation, affected the country numismatically.

As a result of the discovery of silver at Potosi in 1545, a mint was eventually authorized in 1565with the first coinage taking place in 1568. The mint had an uneven life span during the Spanish Colonial period from 1568-72. It was closed from 1573-76, reopened from 1577-88. It remained closed until 1659-1660 when an unauthorized coinage in both silver and gold were struck. After being closed in 1660, it remained closed until 1684 when it struck cob style coins until 1752.

**MINT MARKS**

AREQUIPA, AREQ = Arequipa
AYACUCHO = Ayacucho
(B) = Brussels
CUZCO (monogram), Cuzco, Co. Cuzco
L, LIMAE (monogram), Lima
(monogram), LIMA = Lima
(L) = London
PASCO (monogram), Pasco, Paz, Po= Pasco
P, (P) = Philadelphia
S = San Francisco
(W) = Waterbury, CT, USA

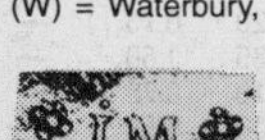  

**NOTE:** The LIMAE monogram appears in three forms. The early LM monogram form looks like a dotted L with M. The later LIMAE monogram has all the letters of LIMAE more readily distinguishable. The third form appears as an M monogram during early Republican issues.

**MINT ASSAYERS INITIALS**

The letter(s) following the dates of Peruvian coins are the assayer's initials appearing on the coins. They generally appear at the 11 o'clock position on the Colonial coinage and at the 5 o'clock position along the rim on the obverse or reverse on the Republican coinage.

**DATING**

Peruvian 5, 10 and 20 centavos, issued from 1918-1944, bear the dates written in Spanish. The following table translates those written dates into numerals:

1918 - UN MIL NOVECIENTOS DIECIOCHO
1919 - UN MIL NOVECIENTOS DIECINUEVE
1920 - UN MIL NOVECIENTOS VEINTE
1921 - UN MIL NOVECIENTOS VEINTIUNO
1923 - UN MIL NOVECIENTOS VEINTITRES
1926 - UN MIL NOVECIENTOS VEINTISEIS
1934 - UN MIL NOVECIENTOS TREINTICUATRO
1935 - UN MIL NOVECIENTOS TREINTICINCO
1937 - UN MIL NOVECIENTOS TREINTISIETE
1939 - UN MIL NOVECIENTOS TREINTINUEVE
1940 - UN MIL NOVECIENTOS CUARENTA
1941 - UN MIL NOVECIENTOS CUARENTIUNO

**U.S. Mints**

1942 - MIL NOVECIENTOS CUARENTA Y DOS

**Lima Mint**

1942 - UN MIL NOVECIENTOS CUARENTIDOS

**U.S. Mints**

1943 - MIL NOVECIENTOS CUARENTA Y TRES
1944 - MIL NOVECIENTOS CUARENTA Y CUATRO

**Lima Mint**

1944 - MIL NOVECIENTOS CUARENTICUATRO

**MONETARY SYSTEM**

100 Centavos (10 Dineros) = 1 Sol
10 Soles = 1 Libra

# REPUBLIC

## Republic of Peru

## DECIMAL COINAGE

100 Centavos (10 Dineros) = 1 Sol; 10 Soles = 1 Libra

**CENTAVO** KM# 208.1 **Composition:** Bronze **Obverse:** Small date at bottom and legend **Reverse:** Straight centavo **Note:** Thick planchet.

| Date | Mintage | F | VF | XF | Unc | BU |
|---|---|---|---|---|---|---|
| 1901 | 600,000 | 1.00 | 2.50 | 4.00 | 15.00 | — |
| 1904 | 1,000,000 | 4.50 | 8.00 | 14.00 | 45.00 | — |

**CENTAVO** KM# 211 **Composition:** Bronze **Obverse:** Large date and legend **Reverse:** Curved centavo **Note:** Thick planchet.

| Date | Mintage | F | VF | XF | Unc | BU |
|---|---|---|---|---|---|---|
| 1909 | 252,000 | 7.50 | 15.00 | 20.00 | 50.00 | — |
| 1909/999 R | Inc. above | 7.50 | 15.00 | 20.00 | 50.00 | — |
| 1909 R | Inc. above | 7.50 | 15.00 | 20.00 | 50.00 | — |
| 1915 | 250,000 | 3.00 | 6.00 | 10.00 | 25.00 | — |
| 1916 | 360,000 | 1.00 | 2.00 | 4.50 | 14.00 | — |
| 1916 R | Inc. above | 1.00 | 2.00 | 4.50 | 14.00 | — |
| 1917 | 830,000 | 1.00 | 2.00 | 4.00 | 14.00 | — |
| 1917 R | Inc. above | 1.00 | 2.00 | 4.00 | 14.00 | — |
| 1918 | 1,060,000 | 1.00 | 2.00 | 4.00 | 12.00 | — |
| 1918 R | Inc. above | 1.00 | 2.00 | 4.00 | 12.00 | — |
| 1920 | 360,000 | 1.00 | 2.50 | 4.50 | 15.00 | — |
| 1920 R | Inc. above | 1.00 | 2.50 | 4.50 | 15.00 | — |
| 1933 R Inc. KM208.2 | — | 1.00 | 2.50 | 4.50 | 15.00 | — |
| 1934 Inc. KM208.2 | — | 4.50 | 8.00 | 14.00 | 45.00 | — |
| 1935 R Inc. KM208.2 | — | 4.00 | 7.00 | 12.00 | 40.00 | — |
| 1936 R Inc. KM208.2 | — | 1.50 | 3.50 | 6.00 | 15.00 | — |
| 1937 | — | — | — | — | — | — |
| 1937 R Inc. KM208.2 | — | 1.50 | 3.50 | 6.00 | 15.00 | — |
| 1939 R Inc. KM208.2 | — | 4.50 | 8.00 | 14.00 | 45.00 | — |

**Note:** Engravers initial R appears below ribbon on most or all new dies, but often became weak or filled. Most coins show at least a faint trace of R. Date varieties also exist

**CENTAVO** KM# 187.2 **Composition:** Bronze **Obverse:** Date at top **Reverse:** Straight centavo **Note:** Sharper diework.

| Date | Mintage | F | VF | XF | Unc | BU |
|---|---|---|---|---|---|---|
| 1919 (P) | 4,000,000 | 0.50 | 1.00 | 2.50 | 10.00 | — |

**CENTAVO** KM# 208.2 **Composition:** Bronze **Obverse:** Large date and legend **Reverse:** Straight centavo **Note:** Thick planchet; Varieties exist.

| Date | Mintage | F | VF | XF | Unc | BU |
|---|---|---|---|---|---|---|
| 1933 | 275,000 | 1.50 | 3.00 | 5.50 | 16.00 | — |
| 1934 | 1,185,000 | 0.75 | 1.50 | 2.50 | 10.00 | — |
| 1935 | 1,105,000 | 0.75 | 1.50 | 2.50 | 10.00 | — |
| 1936 | 565,000 | 1.50 | 3.00 | 5.50 | 16.00 | — |
| 1937/6 | 735,000 | 1.00 | 2.00 | 4.00 | 12.00 | — |
| 1937 | Inc. above | 0.75 | 1.50 | 2.50 | 10.00 | — |
| 1938 | 340,000 | 0.75 | 1.50 | 2.50 | 10.00 | — |
| 1939 | 1,225,000 | 1.50 | 3.00 | 5.50 | 15.00 | — |
| 1940 | 1,250,000 | 1.50 | 3.00 | 5.50 | 15.00 | — |
| 1941 | 2,593,000 | 0.40 | 0.75 | 1.50 | 8.00 | — |

**CENTAVO** KM# 211a **Composition:** Bronze **Obverse:** Large date and legend **Reverse:** Curved centavo **Note:** Thin plancet; Many varieties exist.

| Date | Mintage | F | VF | XF | Unc | BU |
|---|---|---|---|---|---|---|
| 1941 Inc. KM208.2 | — | 1.00 | 2.00 | 3.50 | 12.50 | — |
| 1942 Inc. KM208a | — | 0.50 | 1.00 | 1.75 | 7.50 | — |
| 1943 | — | 2.50 | 5.00 | 12.50 | 30.00 | — |
| 1944 | 2,490,000 | 0.15 | 0.40 | 0.75 | 2.50 | — |
| 1945 | 2,157,000 | 0.15 | 0.40 | 0.75 | 2.50 | — |
| 1946 | 3,198,000 | 0.15 | 0.40 | 0.75 | 2.00 | — |
| 1947 | 2,976,000 | 0.15 | 0.40 | 0.75 | 2.50 | — |
| 1948 | 3,195,000 | 0.15 | 0.40 | 0.75 | 2.00 | — |
| 1949 | 1,104,000 | 0.25 | 0.65 | 1.25 | 3.50 | — |

**CENTAVO** KM# 208a **Composition:** Bronze **Obverse:** Large date and legend **Reverse:** Straight centavo **Note:** Thin planchet.

| Date | Mintage | F | VF | XF | Unc | BU |
|---|---|---|---|---|---|---|
| 1941 Inc. KM208.2 | — | 0.40 | 0.75 | 1.50 | 6.00 | — |
| 1942 | 2,865,000 | 0.50 | 1.00 | 1.75 | 7.50 | — |
| 1944 | — | 4.00 | 9.00 | 16.00 | 50.00 | — |

**CENTAVO** KM# 227 **Composition:** Zinc **Note:** Varieties exist.

| Date | Mintage | F | VF | XF | Unc | BU |
|---|---|---|---|---|---|---|
| 1950 | 3,196,000 | 0.35 | 0.75 | 1.25 | 4.00 | — |
| 1951 | 3,289,000 | 0.25 | 0.40 | 0.65 | 2.00 | — |
| **Note:** Copper plated examples of type dated 1951 are known | | | | | | |
| 1952 | 3,050,000 | 0.25 | 0.40 | 0.65 | 2.00 | — |
| 1953 | 3,260,000 | 0.35 | 0.60 | 1.00 | 3.00 | — |
| 1954 | 3,215,000 | 0.75 | 1.50 | 2.50 | 8.00 | — |
| 1955 | 3,400,000 | 0.25 | 0.40 | 0.65 | 2.00 | — |
| 1956 Pointed 6 | 2,500,000 | 0.25 | 0.40 | 0.65 | 2.00 | — |
| 1956 Knobbed 6 | Inc. above | 0.25 | 0.40 | 0.65 | 2.00 | — |
| 1957 | 4,400,000 | 0.40 | 0.85 | 1.50 | 5.00 | — |
| 1958/7 | — | 0.35 | 0.60 | 1.00 | 3.00 | — |
| 1958 | 2,600,000 | 0.35 | 0.60 | 1.00 | 3.00 | — |
| 1958/8 | 3,200,000 | 0.50 | 1.00 | 2.00 | 5.00 | — |
| 1959 | Inc. above | 0.25 | 0.40 | 0.65 | 2.00 | — |
| 1960/50 | 3,060,000 | 0.35 | 0.60 | 1.00 | 3.00 | — |
| 1960 | Inc. above | 0.75 | 1.50 | 3.00 | 6.00 | — |
| 1961/51 | 2,600,000 | 0.25 | 0.40 | 0.65 | 2.00 | — |
| 1961 | Inc. above | 0.25 | 0.40 | 0.65 | 2.00 | — |
| 1962/52 | 2,600,000 | 0.25 | 0.40 | 0.65 | 2.00 | — |
| 1962 | Inc. above | 0.25 | 0.40 | 0.65 | 2.00 | — |
| 1963/53 | 2,400,000 | 0.25 | 0.40 | 0.65 | 2.00 | — |
| 1963 | Inc. above | 0.25 | 0.40 | 0.65 | 2.00 | — |
| 1965 | 360,000 | 0.75 | 1.50 | 2.50 | 8.00 | — |

**2 CENTAVOS** KM# 212.1 **Composition:** Copper Or Bronze **Obverse:** Date at bottom **Note:** Thick planchet.

| Date | Mintage | F | VF | XF | Unc | BU |
|---|---|---|---|---|---|---|
| 1917 C | 73,000 | 4.00 | 6.50 | 12.50 | 30.00 | — |
| 1918/17 | 580,000 | 3.50 | 6.00 | 9.00 | 22.50 | — |
| 1918 | Inc. above | 3.50 | 6.00 | 12.00 | 30.00 | — |
| 1918 C | Inc. above | 3.50 | 6.00 | 12.00 | 30.00 | — |
| 1918/17 C | Inc. above | 4.00 | 7.00 | 15.00 | 40.00 | — |
| 1920/7 C | 328,000 | 2.00 | 4.00 | 8.00 | 20.00 | — |
| 1920 | Inc. above | 1.00 | 1.75 | 3.00 | 10.00 | — |
| 1920 C | Inc. above | 1.00 | 1.75 | 3.00 | 10.00 | — |
| 1933 | 285,000 | 1.00 | 1.75 | 3.00 | 10.00 | — |
| 1933 C | Inc. above | 1.00 | 1.75 | 3.00 | 10.00 | — |
| 1934 | 973,000 | 0.75 | 1.50 | 2.50 | 10.00 | — |
| 1934 C | Inc. above | 0.75 | 1.50 | 2.50 | 10.00 | — |
| 1935 | 950,000 | 0.75 | 1.50 | 2.50 | 10.00 | — |
| 1935 C | Inc. above | 0.75 | 1.50 | 2.50 | 10.00 | — |
| 1936 | 763,000 | 0.75 | 1.50 | 2.50 | 10.00 | — |
| 1936/5 C | Inc. above | 1.50 | 2.50 | 5.00 | 15.00 | — |
| 1936 C | Inc. above | 0.75 | 1.25 | 2.25 | 9.00 | — |
| 1937 | 963,000 | 0.75 | 1.50 | 2.50 | 10.00 | — |
| 1937 C | Inc. above | 0.75 | 1.50 | 2.50 | 10.00 | — |
| 1938 C | 428,000 | 1.00 | 1.75 | 3.00 | 10.00 | — |
| 1939/8 C Reported, not confirmed | — | — | — | — | — | — |
| 1939/8 | — | 1.50 | 2.50 | 5.00 | 15.00 | — |
| 1939 C Inverted A for V in CENTAVOS | 783,000 | 0.75 | 1.50 | 2.50 | 10.00 | — |
| 1940 | — | — | — | — | — | — |
| 1940 C | 565,000 | 1.00 | 1.75 | 3.00 | 10.00 | — |
| 1941/0 | Inc. above | — | — | — | — | — |
| 1941/0 C | Inc. above | — | — | — | — | — |
| 1941/22 | Inc. above | — | — | — | — | — |
| 1941 | Inc. above | — | — | — | — | — |
| 1941 C | Inc. above | 2.00 | 5.00 | 10.00 | 15.00 | — |

**Note:** Engravers initial C appeared below ribbon on most or all new dies, but often became weak or filled. Most coins show at least a faint trace of C. Other varieties also exist

**2 CENTAVOS** **KM# A212** **Composition:** Copper Or Bronze **Note:** Sharper diework.

| Date | Mintage | F | VF | XF | Unc | BU |
|---|---|---|---|---|---|---|
| 1919 (P) | 3,000,000 | 0.35 | 0.75 | 2.00 | 9.00 | — |

**2 CENTAVOS** **KM# 212.2** **Composition:** Copper Or Bronze **Obverse:** Date at bottom **Note:** Thin planchet; Varieties exist.

| Date | Mintage | F | VF | XF | Unc | BU |
|---|---|---|---|---|---|---|
| 1941/32 | 870,000 | — | — | — | — | — |
| 1941/33 C | Inc. above | 1.00 | 2.00 | 3.50 | 10.00 | — |
| 1941/33 | Inc. above | — | — | — | — | — |
| 1941/38 | Inc. above | — | — | — | — | — |
| 1941/38 C | Inc. above | 1.00 | 2.00 | 3.50 | 10.00 | — |
| 1941/39 C | Inc. above | 1.00 | 2.00 | 3.50 | 10.00 | — |
| 1941/0 | Inc. above | 1.00 | 2.00 | 3.50 | 10.00 | — |
| 1941 | Inc. above | 0.35 | 0.75 | 1.25 | 4.00 | — |
| 1942/22 | 4,418,000 | — | — | — | — | — |
| 1942/32 | 4,418,000 | — | — | — | — | — |
| 1942 | Inc. above | 0.25 | 0.50 | 1.00 | 3.00 | — |
| 1943/2 | 1,829,000 | 0.50 | 1.00 | 2.00 | 7.00 | — |
| 1943 | Inc. above | 0.50 | 1.00 | 2.00 | 7.00 | — |
| 1944 | 2,068,000 | 0.75 | 1.50 | 3.00 | 9.00 | — |
| 1945 | 2,288,000 | 0.75 | 1.50 | 3.00 | 9.00 | — |
| 1946 | 2,121,000 | 0.25 | 0.50 | 0.75 | 2.50 | — |
| 1947 | 1,280,000 | 0.25 | 0.50 | 0.75 | 2.50 | — |
| 1948 | 1,518,000 | 0.25 | 0.50 | 0.75 | 3.00 | — |
| 1949/8 | 938,000 | 0.25 | 0.60 | 3.50 | 5.00 | — |
| 1949 | Inc. above | — | — | — | — | — |

**2 CENTAVOS** **KM# 228** **Composition:** Zinc

| Date | Mintage | F | VF | XF | Unc | BU |
|---|---|---|---|---|---|---|
| 1950 | 1,702,000 | 0.35 | 0.75 | 1.25 | 3.00 | — |
| 1951 | 3,289,000 | 0.35 | 0.75 | 1.25 | 3.00 | — |

**Note:** Copper plated examples of type dated 1951 exist

| Date | Mintage | F | VF | XF | Unc | BU |
|---|---|---|---|---|---|---|
| 1952 | 1,155,000 | 0.35 | 0.75 | 1.25 | 3.00 | — |
| 1953 | 1,150,000 | 0.40 | 0.85 | 1.50 | 4.00 | — |
| 1954 | — | 2.00 | 4.00 | 8.00 | 22.00 | — |
| 1955 | 1,185,000 | 0.35 | 0.75 | 1.25 | 3.00 | — |
| 1956 | 400,000 | 0.50 | 1.00 | 2.00 | 5.00 | — |
| 1957 | 520,000 | 1.50 | 3.00 | 6.00 | 15.00 | — |
| 1958 | 200,000 | 1.25 | 2.50 | 4.50 | 13.50 | — |

**1/2 DINERO** **KM# 206.2** **Weight:** 1.2500 g. **Composition:** 0.9000 Silver .0362 oz. ASW **Obverse:** Without JR on stems **Reverse:** Denomination in straight line

| Date | Mintage | F | VF | XF | Unc | BU |
|---|---|---|---|---|---|---|
| 1901/801 JF | 500,000 | 0.60 | 1.25 | 2.50 | 6.00 | — |
| 1901/801/701 JF | Inc. above | 0.60 | 1.25 | 2.50 | 6.00 | — |
| 1901/891/791 | Inc. above | 0.60 | 1.25 | 2.00 | 5.00 | — |
| 1901/891 JF | Inc. above | 0.60 | 1.25 | 2.00 | 5.00 | — |
| 1901 JF | Inc. above | 0.75 | 1.50 | 3.50 | 10.00 | — |
| 1902/802 JF | 616,000 | 0.60 | 1.25 | 2.00 | 5.00 | — |
| 1902/892 JF | Inc. above | 0.60 | 1.25 | 2.00 | 5.00 | — |
| 1902/92 | Inc. above | 0.60 | 1.25 | 2.00 | 5.00 | — |
| 1902 JF | Inc. above | 0.75 | 1.50 | 3.50 | 10.00 | — |
| 1903/803 JF | 1,798,000 | 0.50 | 1.50 | 3.00 | 9.00 | — |
| 1903/893 JF | Inc. above | 0.50 | 1.50 | 3.00 | 9.00 | — |
| 1903/897 JF | Inc. above | 0.50 | 1.00 | 2.50 | 7.00 | — |
| 1903 JF | Inc. above | 0.75 | 1.50 | 3.00 | 10.00 | — |
| 1904/804 JF | 723,000 | 0.60 | 1.25 | 2.00 | 5.00 | — |
| 1904/804 JF FFLIZ, error | Inc. above | 3.00 | 6.00 | 12.00 | 25.00 | — |
| 1904/884 JF | Inc. above | 0.60 | 1.25 | 2.00 | 6.00 | — |
| 1904/891 JF | Inc. above | 0.60 | 1.25 | 2.00 | 6.00 | — |
| 1904/893 JF | Inc. above | 0.60 | 1.25 | 2.00 | 5.00 | — |
| 1904/894 JF | Inc. above | 0.60 | 1.25 | 2.00 | 5.00 | — |
| 1904/894 JF FFLIZ, error | Inc. above | 2.00 | 4.50 | 8.00 | 12.00 | — |
| 1904 JF | Inc. above | 0.75 | 1.50 | 3.50 | 10.00 | — |
| 1904 JF FFLIZ, error | Inc. above | 2.00 | 4.50 | 8.00 | 12.00 | — |
| 1905/805 JF | 1,400,000 | 0.75 | 1.50 | 3.50 | 8.00 | — |
| 1905/891 JF | Inc. above | 1.00 | 2.00 | 4.50 | 12.00 | — |
| 1905/893 JF | Inc. above | 1.00 | 2.00 | 4.50 | 12.00 | — |
| 1905/894 | Inc. above | 1.00 | 2.00 | 4.50 | 12.00 | — |
| 1905/895 JF | Inc. above | 0.50 | 1.25 | 2.00 | 5.00 | — |
| 1905/3 JF | Inc. above | 1.00 | 2.00 | 4.50 | 12.00 | — |
| 1905 JF | Inc. above | 0.75 | 1.50 | 3.50 | 10.00 | — |
| 1906/806 JF | 900,000 | 0.75 | 1.50 | 3.50 | 8.00 | — |
| 1906/886 JF | Inc. above | 0.75 | 1.50 | 3.50 | 8.00 | — |
| 1906/895 JF | Inc. above | 0.75 | 1.50 | 3.50 | 8.00 | — |
| 1906/896 JF | Inc. above | 0.50 | 1.25 | 2.00 | 5.00 | — |
| 1906 JF | Inc. above | 0.75 | 1.50 | 3.00 | 10.00 | — |
| 1907 FG | 600,000 | 0.75 | 1.50 | 3.00 | 10.00 | — |
| 1908/7 FG | 200,000 | 1.50 | 3.00 | 6.00 | 15.00 | — |
| 1908 FG | Inc. above | 0.75 | 1.50 | 3.50 | 10.00 | — |
| 1909/7 FG | — | 3.00 | 6.00 | 12.50 | 27.50 | — |
| 1909 FG | — | 0.75 | 1.50 | 3.50 | 8.00 | — |
| 1910 FG | 640,000 | 0.50 | 1.00 | 2.00 | 5.00 | — |
| 1911 FG | 460,000 | 0.50 | 1.25 | 2.00 | 5.00 | — |
| 1912 FG | 120,000 | 0.60 | 1.25 | 2.50 | 6.00 | — |
| 1913 FG | 480,000 | 0.50 | 1.00 | 2.00 | 5.00 | — |
| 1914/3 FG | — | 0.75 | 1.50 | 3.50 | 8.00 | — |
| 1914/03 FG | — | 1.00 | 2.50 | 5.50 | 15.00 | — |
| 1914/04 FG | — | 1.00 | 2.50 | 5.50 | 15.00 | — |
| 1914 FG | — | 0.50 | 1.00 | 2.00 | 5.00 | — |
| 1916/3 FG | 860,000 | 0.50 | 1.00 | 2.00 | 5.00 | — |
| 1916/3 FG FERUANA, error | — | 1.00 | 2.00 | 4.50 | 12.00 | — |
| 1916 FG | Inc. above | 0.35 | 0.75 | 1.75 | 4.50 | — |
| 1916/5 FG PERUANA, error | Inc. above | 1.00 | 2.00 | 4.50 | 12.00 | — |
| 1916/5 FG FERUANA, error | Inc. above | 1.00 | 2.00 | 4.50 | 12.00 | — |
| 1916/5 Without FERUANA | Inc. above | 1.00 | 2.00 | 4.50 | 12.00 | — |
| 1916 FG FERUANA, error | Inc. above | 1.00 | 2.00 | 4.50 | 12.00 | — |
| 1916 Matte | — | — | — | — | — | — |
| 1917/87 FG | 140,000 | 0.50 | 1.00 | 2.00 | 5.00 | — |
| 1917 FG | Inc. above | 0.50 | 1.00 | 2.00 | 5.00 | — |

**Note:** Most coins 1900-06 show faint to strong traces of 9/8 or 90/89 in date. Non-overdates without such traces are scarce. Most coins of 1907-17 have engravers initial R at left of shield tip on reverse. Many other varieties exist

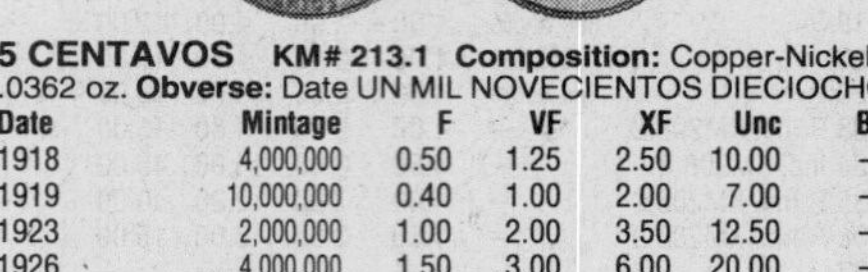

**5 CENTAVOS** **KM# 213.1** **Composition:** Copper-Nickel .0362 oz. **Obverse:** Date UN MIL NOVECIENTOS DIECIOCHO

| Date | Mintage | F | VF | XF | Unc | BU |
|---|---|---|---|---|---|---|
| 1918 | 4,000,000 | 0.50 | 1.25 | 2.50 | 10.00 | — |
| 1919 | 10,000,000 | 0.40 | 1.00 | 2.00 | 7.00 | — |
| 1923 | 2,000,000 | 1.00 | 2.00 | 3.50 | 12.50 | — |
| 1926 | 4,000,000 | 1.50 | 3.00 | 6.00 | 20.00 | — |

**5 CENTAVOS** **KM# 213.2** **Composition:** Copper-Nickel .0362 oz. **Obverse:** Date UN MIL NOVECIENTOS DIECIOCHO

| Date | Mintage | F | VF | XF | Unc | BU |
|---|---|---|---|---|---|---|
| 1934 | 4,000,000 | 0.75 | 2.00 | 3.00 | 8.50 | — |
| 1934 Proof | — | Value: 175 | | | | |
| 1935 | 4,000,000 | 0.50 | 1.25 | 2.00 | 6.00 | — |
| 1935 Proof | — | — | — | — | — | — |
| 1937 | 2,000,000 | 0.75 | 2.00 | 3.00 | 8.50 | — |
| 1937 Proof | — | — | — | — | — | — |
| 1939 | 2,000,000 | 0.50 | 1.25 | 2.00 | 6.00 | — |
| 1939 Proof | — | — | — | — | — | — |
| 1940 | 2,000,000 | 0.50 | 1.25 | 2.00 | 6.00 | — |
| 1940 Proof | — | — | — | — | — | — |
| 1941 | 2,000,000 | 0.50 | 1.25 | 2.00 | 6.00 | — |
| 1941 Proof | — | — | — | — | — | — |

**5 CENTAVOS** **KM# 213.2a.1** **Composition:** Brass .0362 oz. **Obverse:** Date MIL NOVECIENTOS CUARENTA Y DOS

| Date | Mintage | F | VF | XF | Unc | BU |
|---|---|---|---|---|---|---|
| 1942 | 4,000,000 | 1.00 | 3.00 | 5.00 | 12.00 | — |
| 1943 | 4,000,000 | 1.00 | 3.00 | 5.00 | 12.00 | — |
| 1944 | 4,000,000 | 1.00 | 2.75 | 4.50 | 10.00 | — |

**5 CENTAVOS** **KM# 213.2a.2** **Composition:** Brass .0362 oz. **Obverse:** Date MIL NOVECIENTOS CUARENTA Y DOS

| Date | Mintage | F | VF | XF | Unc | BU |
|---|---|---|---|---|---|---|
| 1942S | 4,000,000 | 2.50 | 4.50 | 9.00 | 25.00 | — |
| 1943S | 4,000,000 | 2.50 | 4.50 | 8.00 | 20.00 | — |

**5 CENTAVOS** **KM# 213.2a.3** **Composition:** Brass .0362 oz. **Obverse:** Date MIL NOVECIENTOS CUARENTICUATRO

| Date | Mintage | F | VF | XF | Unc | BU |
|---|---|---|---|---|---|---|
| 1944 | 1,106,000 | 1.50 | 3.50 | 6.00 | 15.00 | — |

**5 CENTAVOS** **KM# 223.1** **Composition:** Brass .0362 oz. **Obverse:** Short Legend **Note:** Thick planchet.

| Date | Mintage | F | VF | XF | Unc | BU |
|---|---|---|---|---|---|---|
| 1945 | 2,768,000 | 0.35 | 0.75 | 1.50 | 4.00 | — |
| 1946/5 | 4,270,000 | 1.00 | 2.50 | 5.00 | 14.00 | — |
| 1946 | Inc. above | 0.25 | 0.50 | 1.00 | 3.50 | — |

**5 CENTAVOS** **KM# 223.3** **Composition:** Brass .0362 oz. **Obverse:** Long legend **Note:** Thick planchet.

| Date | Mintage | F | VF | XF | Unc | BU |
|---|---|---|---|---|---|---|
| 1947 | 7,683,000 | 0.25 | 0.50 | 1.00 | 3.00 | — |
| 1948 | 6,711,000 | 0.25 | 0.50 | 1.00 | 3.00 | — |
| 1949/8 | 5,550,000 | 1.00 | 2.00 | 4.00 | 10.00 | — |

**5 CENTAVOS** **KM# 223.4** **Composition:** Brass .0362 oz. **Obverse:** Different legend style **Note:** Thick planchet.

| Date | Mintage | F | VF | XF | Unc | BU |
|---|---|---|---|---|---|---|
| 1949 | Inc. above | 1.00 | 2.00 | 4.00 | 10.00 | — |
| 1950 | 7,933,000 | 0.25 | 0.50 | 1.00 | 3.00 | — |
| 195.1 | 8,064,000 | 0.25 | 0.50 | 1.00 | 3.00 | — |
| 1951 | Inc. above | 1.00 | 2.00 | 4.00 | 20.00 | — |

**5 CENTAVOS** **KM# 223.2** **Composition:** Brass **Note:** Thin planchet; Varieties exist.

| Date | Mintage | F | VF | XF | Unc | BU |
|---|---|---|---|---|---|---|
| 1951 | Inc. above | 0.10 | 0.25 | 0.50 | 2.50 | — |
| 1952 | 7,840,000 | 0.10 | 0.25 | 0.50 | 2.50 | — |
| 1953 | 6,976,000 | 0.10 | 0.25 | 0.50 | 2.50 | — |
| 1953 AFP | — | — | — | — | — | — |
| 1954 | 6,244,000 | 0.10 | 0.20 | 0.40 | 1.00 | — |
| 1955 | 8,064,000 | 0.10 | 0.20 | 0.40 | 2.00 | — |
| 1956 | 16,200,000 | — | 0.10 | 0.35 | 1.50 | — |
| 1957 Small date | 16,000,000 | — | 0.10 | 0.25 | 0.75 | — |
| 1957 Large date | Inc. above | — | 0.10 | 0.25 | 0.75 | — |
| 1958 | 4,600,000 | — | 0.10 | 0.25 | 1.00 | — |
| 1959 | 8,300,000 | — | 0.10 | 0.25 | 1.00 | — |
| 1960/50 | 9,900,000 | — | 0.10 | 0.25 | 0.75 | — |
| 1960 Large date | Inc. above | — | 0.10 | 0.25 | 0.75 | — |
| 1960 Small date | Inc. above | — | 0.10 | 0.25 | 0.75 | — |
| 1961 | 10,200,000 | — | 0.10 | 0.20 | 0.75 | — |
| 1962 Curved 9 | 11,064,000 | — | 0.10 | 0.20 | 0.75 | — |
| 1962 Straight 9 | Inc. above | — | 0.10 | 0.20 | 0.75 | — |
| 1963 | 12,012,000 | — | 0.10 | 0.20 | 0.75 | — |
| 1964/3 | 12,304,000 | — | 0.10 | 0.35 | 1.50 | — |
| 1964 | Inc. above | — | — | 0.10 | 0.75 | — |
| 1965 Small date | 12,500,000 | — | — | 0.10 | 0.50 | — |
| 1965 Large date | Inc. above | — | 0.10 | 0.20 | 1.00 | — |
| 1965 Proof | — | Value: 20.00 | | | | |

**5 CENTAVOS** **KM# 232** **Composition:** Brass **Obverse:** President Castilla

| Date | Mintage | F | VF | XF | Unc | BU |
|---|---|---|---|---|---|---|
| 1954 | 2,080,000 | 1.00 | 2.00 | 4.00 | 8.00 | — |

**5 CENTAVOS** **KM# 290** **Composition:** Brass **Subject:** 400th Anniversary of Lima Mint **Obverse:** President Castilla

| Date | Mintage | F | VF | XF | Unc | BU |
|---|---|---|---|---|---|---|
| 1965 | 712,000 | — | — | 0.25 | 0.50 | — |
| 1965 Proof | — | Value: 100 | | | | |

**5 CENTAVOS** **KM# 244.1** **Composition:** Brass **Obverse:** Large arms

| Date | Mintage | F | VF | XF | Unc | BU |
|---|---|---|---|---|---|---|
| 1966 | 14,620,000 | — | — | 0.10 | 0.20 | — |

**Note:** PAREJA in field at lower left of arms

| Date | Mintage | F | VF | XF | Unc | BU |
|---|---|---|---|---|---|---|
| 1966 Proof | 1,000 | Value: 2.50 | | | | |
| 1967 | 14,088,000 | — | — | 0.10 | 0.20 | — |
| 1968 | 17,880,000 | — | — | 0.10 | 0.20 | — |

**5 CENTAVOS** **KM# 244.1a** **Composition:** Silver Plated Brass

| Date | Mintage | F | VF | XF | Unc | BU |
|---|---|---|---|---|---|---|
| 1967 | — | — | — | — | — | — |

**5 CENTAVOS** **KM# 244.1b** **Composition:** Silver

| Date | Mintage | F | VF | XF | Unc | BU |
|---|---|---|---|---|---|---|
| 1967 | — | — | — | — | — | — |

**5 CENTAVOS** **KM# 244.2** **Composition:** Brass **Edge:** Plain

| Date | Mintage | F | VF | XF | Unc | BU |
|---|---|---|---|---|---|---|
| 1969 | 17,880,000 | — | — | — | 0.10 | — |
| 1970 | — | — | — | — | 0.10 | — |
| 1971 | 24,320,000 | — | — | — | 0.10 | — |
| 1972 | 24,342,000 | — | — | — | 0.10 | — |
| 1973 | 25,074,000 | — | — | — | 0.10 | — |

**5 CENTAVOS** **KM# 244.3** **Composition:** Brass **Obverse:** Small arms **Edge:** Plain

| Date | Mintage | F | VF | XF | Unc | BU |
|---|---|---|---|---|---|---|
| 1973 | Inc. above | — | — | — | 0.10 | — |
| 1974 | — | — | — | — | 0.10 | — |
| 1975 | — | — | — | — | 0.10 | — |

**DINERO** **KM# 204.2** **Weight:** 2.5000 g. **Composition:** 0.9000 Silver .0723 oz. ASW **Obverse:** Large wreath **Reverse:** Denomination in curved line **Note:** Varieties exist.

| Date | Mintage | F | VF | XF | Unc | BU |
|---|---|---|---|---|---|---|
| 1902/1 JF | 375,000 | 1.00 | 2.00 | 3.50 | 10.00 | — |
| 1902/891 JF | Inc. above | 1.00 | 2.00 | 3.50 | 10.00 | — |
| 1902/892 JF | Inc. above | 1.00 | 2.00 | 3.50 | 10.00 | — |
| 1902/897 JF | Inc. above | 1.00 | 2.00 | 3.50 | 10.00 | — |
| 1902 JF | Inc. above | 1.00 | 2.00 | 4.00 | 12.00 | — |
| 1903/803 JF | 887,000 | 1.00 | 2.00 | 3.50 | 10.00 | — |
| 1903/807 JF | Inc. above | 1.00 | 2.00 | 3.50 | 10.00 | — |
| 1903/892 JF | Inc. above | 0.75 | 2.00 | 3.50 | 8.00 | — |
| 1903/893 JF | Inc. above | 0.75 | 2.00 | 3.50 | 8.00 | — |
| 1903/92 JF | Inc. above | 0.75 | 2.00 | 3.50 | 8.00 | — |
| 1903 JF | Inc. above | 0.75 | 2.00 | 3.50 | 10.00 | — |
| 1904 JF | 380,000 | 1.00 | 2.50 | 4.00 | 12.50 | — |
| 1905/1 JF | 700,000 | 1.00 | 2.50 | 4.00 | 10.00 | — |
| 1905/3 JF | Inc. above | 1.00 | 2.50 | 4.00 | 10.00 | — |
| 1905 JF | Inc. above | 0.75 | 2.00 | 3.50 | 10.00 | — |
| 1906 JF | 826,000 | 0.75 | 2.00 | 3.50 | 8.00 | — |
| 1907 JF Rare | 500,000 | — | — | — | — | — |
| 1907 FG/JF | Inc. above | 1.25 | 2.50 | 4.50 | 10.00 | — |
| 1907 FG | Inc. above | 1.00 | 1.75 | 3.00 | 8.00 | — |
| 1908/6 FG/JF | Inc. above | 1.00 | 2.25 | 4.00 | 10.00 | — |
| 1908 FG/JF | 200,000 | 1.00 | 2.25 | 4.00 | 10.00 | — |
| 1908 FG/GF | Inc. above | 1.00 | 2.25 | 4.00 | 10.00 | — |
| 1908 FG | Inc. above | 1.00 | 1.75 | 3.00 | 8.00 | — |
| 1909 FG | — | 2.00 | 4.00 | 8.00 | 15.00 | — |
| 1909 FG/FO | — | 2.00 | 4.00 | 8.00 | 15.00 | — |
| 1909 FG/FF | — | 2.00 | 4.00 | 8.00 | 15.00 | — |
| 1910 FG | 210,000 | 0.60 | 1.25 | 3.00 | 10.00 | — |
| 1910 FG/JF | Inc. above | 1.00 | 2.25 | 4.00 | 12.50 | — |
| 1910 FG/JG | Inc. above | 1.00 | 2.25 | 4.00 | 12.50 | — |
| 1911 FG | 200,000 | 0.75 | 1.50 | 3.00 | 10.00 | — |
| 1911 FG/JF | Inc. above | 1.00 | 2.25 | 4.00 | 12.50 | — |
| 1911 FG/JG | Inc. above | 1.00 | 2.25 | 4.00 | 12.50 | — |
| 1912 FG | 400,000 | 0.60 | 1.25 | 3.00 | 10.00 | — |
| 1912/02 FG/JF | Inc. above | 1.00 | 2.25 | 4.00 | 12.50 | — |
| 1912 FG/JF | Inc. above | 1.00 | 2.25 | 4.00 | 12.50 | — |
| 1912 FG/JG | Inc. above | 1.00 | 2.25 | 4.00 | 12.50 | — |
| 1913/1 FG/JF | Inc. above | 1.00 | 2.25 | 4.00 | 12.50 | — |
| 1913/2 FG | 360,000 | 1.00 | 2.25 | 4.00 | 12.50 | — |
| 1913/7 FG/G | Inc. above | 1.00 | 2.25 | 4.00 | 12.50 | — |
| 1913 FG | Inc. above | 0.60 | 1.25 | 3.00 | 10.00 | — |
| 1913 FG/G | Inc. above | 0.60 | 1.25 | 2.50 | 8.00 | — |
| 1913 FG/JB | Inc. above | 1.50 | 3.00 | 5.50 | 12.50 | — |
| 1916 FG Large date | 430,000 | 1.25 | 2.50 | 4.50 | 10.00 | — |
| 1916 FG Small date | Inc. above | 0.60 | 1.25 | 2.00 | 6.00 | — |
| 1916 FG/JG | Inc. above | 2.00 | 5.00 | 7.50 | 15.00 | — |
| 1916 FG/FF | Inc. above | 2.00 | 5.00 | 7.50 | 15.00 | — |

**10 CENTAVOS** **KM# 214.1** **Composition:** Copper-Nickel **Obv. Legend:** UN MIL NOVECIENTOS DIECIOCHO

| Date | Mintage | F | VF | XF | Unc | BU |
|---|---|---|---|---|---|---|
| 1918 | 3,000,000 | 0.40 | 1.00 | 2.00 | 7.00 | — |
| 1919 | 2,500,000 | 0.40 | 1.00 | 2.00 | 7.00 | — |
| 1920 | 3,080,000 | 0.35 | 0.75 | 1.50 | 6.00 | — |
| 1921 | 6,920,000 | 0.35 | 0.75 | 1.50 | 6.00 | — |
| 1926 | 3,000,000 | 2.50 | 5.00 | 8.50 | 22.50 | — |

**10 CENTAVOS** **KM# 214.2** **Composition:** Copper-Nickel

| Date | Mintage | F | VF | XF | Unc | BU |
|---|---|---|---|---|---|---|
| 1935 | 1,000,000 | 0.75 | 1.50 | 3.00 | 12.00 | — |
| 1935 Proof | — | Value: 150 | | | | |
| 1937 | 1,000,000 | 0.40 | 1.00 | 2.00 | 7.00 | — |
| 1937 Proof | — | — | — | — | — | — |
| 1939 | 2,000,000 | 0.35 | 0.75 | 1.25 | 5.00 | — |
| 1939 Proof | — | — | — | — | — | — |
| 1940 | 2,000,000 | 0.35 | 0.75 | 1.25 | 5.00 | — |
| 1940 Proof | — | Value: 125 | | | | |
| 1941 | 2,000,000 | 0.35 | 0.75 | 1.25 | 5.00 | — |
| 1941 Proof | — | — | — | — | — | — |

**10 CENTAVOS** **KM# 214a.1** **Composition:** Brass **Obverse:** Date begins MIL..., spelled out without "Y"

| Date | Mintage | F | VF | XF | Unc | BU |
|---|---|---|---|---|---|---|
| 1942 | 2,000,000 | 1.50 | 3.00 | 6.00 | 16.00 | — |
| 1943 | 2,000,000 | 1.50 | 3.00 | 6.00 | 16.00 | — |
| 1944 | 2,000,000 | 1.50 | 3.50 | 7.00 | 20.00 | — |

**10 CENTAVOS** **KM# 214a.2** **Composition:** Brass **Edge:** Plain

| Date | Mintage | F | VF | XF | Unc | BU |
|---|---|---|---|---|---|---|
| 1942S | 2,000,000 | 6.00 | 12.00 | 20.00 | 45.00 | — |
| 1943S | 2,000,000 | 1.50 | 3.00 | 6.00 | 16.00 | — |

**10 CENTAVOS** **KM# 214a.3** **Composition:** Brass **Obverse:** Date begins MIL..., spelled out with an "I"

| Date | Mintage | F | VF | XF | Unc | BU |
|---|---|---|---|---|---|---|
| 1942 | — | 5.00 | 9.00 | 15.00 | 35.00 | — |

**10 CENTAVOS** **KM# 214a.4** **Composition:** Brass **Obverse:** Date begins MIL..., spelled out with an "I" **Note:** Varieties exist.

| Date | Mintage | F | VF | XF | Unc | BU |
|---|---|---|---|---|---|---|
| 1944 | — | 3.50 | 7.00 | 12.00 | 30.00 | — |

**10 CENTAVOS** **KM# 224.1** **Composition:** Brass **Obverse:** Short legend **Note:** Thick planchet.

| Date | Mintage | F | VF | XF | Unc | BU |
|---|---|---|---|---|---|---|
| 1945 | 2,810,000 | 0.25 | 0.50 | 1.50 | 4.00 | — |
| 1946/5 | 4,863,000 | 0.50 | 1.00 | 2.50 | 8.00 | — |
| 1946 | Inc. above | 0.35 | 0.75 | 2.00 | 7.00 | — |

**10 CENTAVOS** **KM# 226.1** **Composition:** Brass **Obverse:** Long legend **Note:** Thick planchet

| Date | Mintage | F | VF | XF | Unc | BU |
|---|---|---|---|---|---|---|
| 1947 | 6,806,000 | 0.25 | 0.50 | 1.00 | 3.00 | — |

| Date | Mintage | F | VF | XF | Unc | BU |
|---|---|---|---|---|---|---|
| 1948 | 5,771,000 | 0.25 | 0.50 | 1.25 | 4.00 | — |
| 1949/8 | 4,730,000 | 0.50 | 1.00 | 1.50 | 7.50 | — |

**10 CENTAVOS** **KM# 226.2** **Composition:** Brass **Obverse:** Different legend style

| Date | Mintage | F | VF | XF | Unc | BU |
|---|---|---|---|---|---|---|
| 1949 | Inc. above | 0.25 | 0.50 | 1.25 | 4.00 | — |
| 1950 | 5,298,000 | 0.25 | 0.50 | 1.00 | 3.00 | — |
| 1950 AFP | Inc. above | 0.20 | 0.40 | 0.80 | 2.00 | — |
| 1951 | 7,324,000 | 6.00 | 10.00 | 15.00 | 35.00 | — |
| 1951/0 AFP | — | 0.25 | 0.50 | 1.00 | 3.00 | — |
| 1951 AFP | — | 0.20 | 0.40 | 0.80 | 2.00 | — |

**10 CENTAVOS** **KM# 224.2** **Composition:** Brass **Obverse:** Long legend **Note:** Thin planchet -1.3mm; Date varieties exist.

| Date | Mintage | F | VF | XF | Unc | BU |
|---|---|---|---|---|---|---|
| 1951 | Inc. above | 0.10 | 0.20 | 0.40 | 2.00 | — |
| 1951 AFP | — | 0.10 | 0.20 | 0.40 | 2.00 | — |
| 1952 | 6,694,000 | 0.10 | 0.20 | 0.40 | 3.00 | — |
| 1952 AFP | — | 0.10 | 0.20 | 0.40 | 3.00 | — |
| 1953 | 5,668,000 | 0.10 | 0.20 | 0.40 | 2.00 | — |
| 1953 AFP | — | 0.10 | 0.20 | 0.40 | 2.00 | — |
| 1954 | 7,786,000 | — | 0.10 | 0.35 | 1.50 | — |
| 1954 AFP | — | — | 0.10 | 0.35 | 1.50 | — |
| 1955 | 6,690,000 | — | 0.10 | 0.35 | 1.50 | — |
| 1955 AFP | — | — | 0.10 | 0.35 | 1.50 | — |
| 1956/5 | 8,410,000 | 0.10 | 0.35 | 0.75 | 3.50 | — |
| 1956 | Inc. above | — | 0.10 | 0.25 | 1.00 | — |
| 1956 AFP | — | — | 0.20 | 0.40 | 2.00 | — |
| 1957 | 8,420,000 | — | 0.10 | 0.25 | 0.75 | — |
| 1957 AFP | — | — | 0.10 | 0.25 | 1.00 | — |
| 1958 | 10,380,000 | — | 0.10 | 0.25 | 1.00 | — |
| 1958 AFP | — | — | — | — | — | — |
| 1959 | 8,300,000 | — | 0.10 | 0.25 | 0.75 | — |
| 1959 AFP | — | — | — | — | — | — |
| 1960 | 12,600,000 | — | 0.10 | 0.25 | 0.50 | — |
| 1961 | 12,700,000 | — | 0.10 | 0.15 | 0.60 | — |
| 1962 | 14,598,000 | — | 0.10 | 0.15 | 0.50 | — |
| 1963 | 16,100,000 | — | 0.10 | 0.15 | 0.50 | — |
| 1964 | 16,504,000 | — | 0.10 | 0.15 | 0.60 | — |
| 1965 | 17,808,000 | — | 0.10 | 0.15 | 0.50 | — |
| 1965 Proof | — | Value: 25.00 | | | | |

**10 CENTAVOS** **KM# 233** **Composition:** Brass **Obverse:** President Castilla

| Date | Mintage | F | VF | XF | Unc | BU |
|---|---|---|---|---|---|---|
| 1954 | 1,818,000 | 1.00 | 2.00 | 4.50 | 10.00 | — |

**10 CENTAVOS** **KM# 237** **Composition:** Brass **Subject:** 400th Anversary of Lima Mint

| Date | Mintage | F | VF | XF | Unc | BU |
|---|---|---|---|---|---|---|
| 1965 | 572,000 | — | — | 0.35 | 0.75 | — |
| 1965 Proof | — | Value: 150 | | | | |

**10 CENTAVOS** **KM# 245.1** **Composition:** Brass **Obverse:** Large arms **Edge:** Reeded **Note:** Date varieties exist.

| Date | Mintage | F | VF | XF | Unc | BU |
|---|---|---|---|---|---|---|
| 1966 | 14,930,000 | — | — | 0.10 | 0.25 | — |

**Note:** PAREJA in field at lower left of arms

| Date | Mintage | F | VF | XF | Unc | BU |
|---|---|---|---|---|---|---|
| 1966 Proof | 1,000 | Value: 2.50 | | | | |

| Date | Mintage | F | VF | XF | Unc | BU |
|---|---|---|---|---|---|---|
| 1967 | 19,330,000 | — | — | 0.10 | 0.25 | — |
| 1968 | 24,390,000 | — | — | 0.10 | 0.25 | — |

**10 CENTAVOS** **KM# 245.2** **Composition:** Brass **Obverse:** Vicuna arms **Edge:** Plain **Note:** Date varieties exist.

| Date | Mintage | F | VF | XF | Unc | BU |
|---|---|---|---|---|---|---|
| 1967 | — | — | — | 0.10 | 0.25 | — |
| 1969 | 24,390,000 | — | — | 0.10 | 0.25 | — |
| 1970 | 29,110,000 | — | — | 0.10 | 0.20 | — |
| 1971 | 30,590,000 | — | — | 0.10 | 0.20 | — |
| 1972 | 34,442,000 | — | — | 0.10 | 0.20 | — |
| 1973 | 33,864,000 | — | — | 0.10 | 0.20 | — |

**10 CENTAVOS** **KM# 245.1a** **Composition:** Silver Plated Brass

| Date | Mintage | F | VF | XF | Unc | BU |
|---|---|---|---|---|---|---|
| 1967 | — | — | — | — | — | — |

**10 CENTAVOS** **KM# 245.3** **Composition:** Brass **Obverse:** Small arms **Edge:** Plain

| Date | Mintage | F | VF | XF | Unc | BU |
|---|---|---|---|---|---|---|
| 1973 | Inc. above | — | — | 0.10 | 0.15 | — |
| 1974 | — | — | — | 0.10 | 0.15 | — |
| 1975 | 10,430,000 | — | — | 0.10 | 0.15 | — |

**10 CENTAVOS** **KM# 263** **Composition:** Brass

| Date | Mintage | F | VF | XF | Unc | BU |
|---|---|---|---|---|---|---|
| 1975 | — | — | — | 0.10 | 0.15 | — |

**1/5 SOL** **KM# 205.2** **Weight:** 5.0000 g. **Composition:** 0.9000 Silver .1447 oz. ASW **Reverse:** Libertad incuse **Edge:** Plain **Note:** Die varieties exist.

| Date | Mintage | F | VF | XF | Unc | BU |
|---|---|---|---|---|---|---|
| 1901 JF | 638,000 | 1.50 | 3.00 | 5.50 | 12.00 | — |
| 1903/1 JF | 702,000 | 2.00 | 4.00 | 7.00 | 17.50 | — |
| 1903/13 JF | Inc. above | 1.75 | 3.50 | 6.00 | 15.00 | — |
| 1903 JF | Inc. above | 1.50 | 3.00 | 5.50 | 12.00 | — |
| 1906 JF | 660,000 | 1.50 | 3.00 | 5.50 | 12.00 | — |
| 1907 JF | 1,370,000 | 1.25 | 2.00 | 4.00 | 10.00 | — |
| 1907 FG | Inc. above | 1.50 | 3.00 | 5.50 | 12.00 | — |
| 1908/7 FG | 560,000 | 1.75 | 3.50 | 6.00 | 15.00 | — |
| 1908 FG | Inc. above | 1.50 | 3.00 | 5.50 | 12.00 | — |
| 1909 FG | 42,000 | 2.00 | 4.00 | 9.00 | 27.50 | — |
| 1910/00 FG | 165,000 | 3.00 | 7.00 | 12.00 | 25.00 | — |
| 1910 FG | Inc. above | 3.00 | 7.00 | 12.00 | 25.00 | — |
| 1911 FG | 250,000 | 1.50 | 3.00 | 5.50 | 9.00 | — |
| 1911 FG-R | Inc. above | 1.50 | 3.00 | 5.50 | 9.00 | — |
| 1912 FG | 300,000 | 1.25 | 2.00 | 4.00 | 8.00 | — |
| 1912 FG-R | Inc. above | 1.50 | 3.00 | 5.50 | 9.00 | — |
| 1913 FG | 223,000 | 1.75 | 3.50 | 6.00 | 15.00 | — |
| 1913 FG-R | Inc. above | 1.75 | 3.50 | 6.00 | 15.00 | — |
| 1914 FG | 10,000 | 5.00 | 10.00 | 20.00 | 45.00 | — |
| 1915 FG | — | 25.00 | 35.00 | 60.00 | 100 | — |
| 1916 FG | 425,000 | 2.00 | 5.00 | 10.00 | 25.00 | — |
| 1916 FG-R | Inc. above | 1.50 | 3.00 | 5.00 | 9.00 | — |
| 1917 FG-R | 20,000 | 8.00 | 15.00 | 30.00 | 60.00 | — |

**Note:** Some coins 1893-1900 have engravers initials JR left of shield tip on reverse and some 1911-17 have R in same location.

**20 CENTAVOS** **KM# 215.1** **Composition:** Copper-Nickel **Obverse:** Date UN NOVECIENTOS DIECIOCHO

| Date | Mintage | F | VF | XF | Unc | BU |
|---|---|---|---|---|---|---|
| 1918 | 2,500,000 | 0.40 | 1.00 | 2.50 | 13.50 | — |
| 1919 | 1,250,000 | 0.50 | 1.25 | 3.00 | 15.00 | — |
| 1920 | 1,464,000 | 0.50 | 1.25 | 3.00 | 12.50 | — |
| 1921 | 8,536,000 | 0.35 | 0.85 | 2.00 | 10.00 | — |
| 1926 | 2,500,000 | 0.75 | 2.50 | 6.00 | 25.00 | — |

**20 CENTAVOS** **KM# 215.2** **Composition:** Copper-Nickel

| Date | Mintage | F | VF | XF | Unc | BU |
|---|---|---|---|---|---|---|
| 1940 | 1,000,000 | 0.25 | 0.75 | 1.75 | 5.50 | — |
| 1940 Proof | — | Value: 150 | | | | |
| 1941 | 1,000,000 | 0.35 | 1.00 | 2.50 | 7.50 | — |
| 1941 Proof | — | Value: 125 | | | | |

**20 CENTAVOS** **KM# 215a.1** **Composition:** Copper-Nickel **Obverse:** Date MIL NOVECIENTOS CUARENTA Y TRES

| Date | Mintage | F | VF | XF | Unc | BU |
|---|---|---|---|---|---|---|
| 1942 | 500,000 | 3.00 | 6.00 | 13.50 | 50.00 | — |
| 1943 | 500,000 | 3.00 | 6.00 | 13.50 | 50.00 | — |
| 1944 | 500,000 | 4.00 | 7.50 | 16.50 | 55.00 | — |

**20 CENTAVOS** **KM# 215a.2** **Composition:** Copper-Nickel

| Date | Mintage | F | VF | XF | Unc | BU |
|---|---|---|---|---|---|---|
| 1942S | 500,000 | 6.00 | 12.00 | 25.00 | 90.00 | — |
| 1943S | 500,000 | 3.00 | 6.00 | 12.50 | 60.00 | — |

**20 CENTAVOS** **KM# 221.1** **Composition:** Copper-Nickel **Obverse:** Divided legend **Note:** Thick planchet

| Date | Mintage | F | VF | XF | Unc | BU |
|---|---|---|---|---|---|---|
| 1942 | 300,000 | 1.00 | 2.50 | 5.00 | 12.50 | — |
| 1943 | 1,900,000 | 0.75 | 1.50 | 2.50 | 7.50 | — |
| 1944 | 2,963,000 | 0.60 | 1.25 | 2.00 | 6.00 | — |

**20 CENTAVOS** **KM# 221.3** **Composition:** Copper-Nickel **Obverse:** Continuous legend

| Date | Mintage | F | VF | XF | Unc | BU |
|---|---|---|---|---|---|---|
| 1945 | 3,043,000 | 0.25 | 0.50 | 0.75 | 1.50 | — |
| 1946/5 | Inc. above | 0.25 | 0.65 | 1.00 | 2.00 | — |
| 1946 | Inc. above | 0.25 | 0.50 | 0.75 | 1.50 | — |

**20 CENTAVOS** **KM# 221.2** **Composition:** Copper-Nickel **Obverse:** AFP on truncation continuous legend

| Date | Mintage | F | VF | XF | Unc | BU |
|---|---|---|---|---|---|---|
| 1946 | 3,410,000 | 0.25 | 0.50 | 0.85 | 3.00 | — |
| 1947 | 4,307,000 | 0.25 | 0.50 | 0.85 | 3.00 | — |
| 1948 | 3,578,000 | 0.25 | 0.50 | 0.85 | 3.00 | — |
| 1949/8 | 2,709,000 | 0.75 | 1.50 | 2.50 | 6.50 | — |

**20 CENTAVOS** **KM# 221.2a** **Composition:** Copper

| Date | Mintage | F | VF | XF | Unc | BU |
|---|---|---|---|---|---|---|
| 1947 | 300 | — | — | — | 100 | — |

**20 CENTAVOS** **KM# 221.4** **Composition:** Copper-Nickel **Obverse:** Different legend style

| Date | Mintage | F | VF | XF | Unc | BU |
|---|---|---|---|---|---|---|
| 1949 | Inc. above | 0.50 | 1.00 | 1.75 | 4.50 | — |
| 1950 | 2,427,000 | 1.00 | 1.75 | 3.00 | 8.00 | — |
| 1951 | 2,941,000 | 3.00 | 7.50 | 12.50 | 30.00 | — |

**20 CENTAVOS** **KM# 221.2b** **Composition:** Brass **Note:** Thin planchet. 1.3mm AFP; Date varieties exist.

| Date | Mintage | F | VF | XF | Unc | BU |
|---|---|---|---|---|---|---|
| 1951 | Inc. above | 0.20 | 0.40 | 0.75 | 2.00 | — |
| 1951 Without AFP | — | — | — | — | — | — |
| 1952 | 4,410,000 | 0.20 | 0.40 | 0.75 | 2.50 | — |
| 1952 Without AFP | Inc. above | — | — | — | — | — |
| 1953 | 2,615,000 | 0.20 | 0.40 | 0.75 | 2.00 | — |
| 1954 | 1,816,000 | 1.50 | 2.50 | 4.00 | 9.00 | — |
| 1955 Large date | 4,050,000 | 0.10 | 0.15 | 0.30 | 1.50 | — |
| 1955 Small date | Inc. above | 0.15 | 0.25 | 0.50 | 2.00 | — |
| 1956 | 3,760,000 | 0.10 | 0.15 | 0.30 | 1.50 | — |
| 1957 | 3,680,000 | 0.10 | 0.15 | 0.30 | 1.00 | — |
| 1958 | 3,100,000 | 0.10 | 0.15 | 0.30 | 1.00 | — |
| 1959 | 5,450,000 | — | 0.10 | 0.20 | 0.75 | — |
| 1959 Without AFP | — | — | — | — | — | — |
| 1960/90 Without AFP | — | — | — | — | — | — |
| 1960 | 6,750,000 | — | 0.10 | 0.20 | 0.75 | — |
| 1960 Without AFP | — | 0.25 | 0.75 | 1.50 | 4.00 | — |
| 1961 | 6,800,000 | — | 0.10 | 0.20 | 0.75 | — |
| 1961 Without AFP | — | — | — | — | — | — |
| 1962 | 7,357,000 | — | 0.10 | 0.20 | 0.75 | — |
| 1963/2 | 8,843,000 | 0.15 | 0.25 | 0.50 | 2.00 | — |
| 1963 | Inc. above | — | 0.10 | 0.20 | 1.00 | — |
| 1964 | 9,550,000 | — | 0.10 | 0.20 | 0.75 | — |
| 1965 With inverted V for A in AFP | — | — | 0.10 | 0.20 | 0.75 | — |
| 1965 Without AFP | — | — | — | — | — | — |

**20 CENTAVOS** **KM# 234** **Composition:** Copper-Nickel **Subject:** President Castilla **Edge:** Reeded **Note:** Thin planchet. 1.3mm AFP

| Date | Mintage | F | VF | XF | Unc | BU |
|---|---|---|---|---|---|---|
| 1954 | 799,000 | 2.00 | 4.00 | 8.00 | 15.00 | — |

**20 CENTAVOS** **KM# 221.2c** **Composition:** Copper-Nickel **Edge:** Reeded **Note:** Thin planchet. 1.3mm AFP

| Date | Mintage | F | VF | XF | Unc | BU |
|---|---|---|---|---|---|---|
| 1958 | — | — | — | — | 150 | — |
| 1965 Proof | — | Value: 30.00 | | | | |

**20 CENTAVOS** **KM# 264** **Composition:** Copper-Nickel

| Date | Mintage | F | VF | XF | Unc | BU |
|---|---|---|---|---|---|---|
| 1975 | — | 0.10 | 0.20 | 0.50 | 1.00 | — |

**25 CENTAVOS** **KM# 238** **Composition:** Brass **Subject:** 400th Anniversary of Lima Mint

| Date | Mintage | F | VF | XF | Unc | BU |
|---|---|---|---|---|---|---|
| 1965 | 1,113,000 | — | 0.25 | 0.35 | 0.75 | — |
| 1965 Proof | — | Value: 200 | | | | |

**25 CENTAVOS** **KM# 246.1** **Composition:** Brass **Obverse:** Large arms **Edge:** Reeded

| Date | Mintage | F | VF | XF | Unc | BU |
|---|---|---|---|---|---|---|
| 1966 PAREJA in field at lower left of arms | 9,300,000 | — | 0.15 | 0.25 | 0.50 | — |
| 1966 Proof | 1,000 | Value: 2.50 | | | | |

| Date | Mintage | F | VF | XF | Unc | BU |
|---|---|---|---|---|---|---|
| 1967 | 8,150,000 | — | 0.15 | 0.25 | 0.50 | — |
| 1968 | 7,440,000 | — | 0.15 | 0.25 | 0.50 | — |

**25 CENTAVOS** **KM# 246.1a** **Composition:** Silver Plated Brass

| Date | Mintage | F | VF | XF | Unc | BU |
|---|---|---|---|---|---|---|
| 1967 | Inc. above | — | — | — | — | — |

**25 CENTAVOS** **KM# 246.2** **Composition:** Brass **Edge:** Plain

| Date | Mintage | F | VF | XF | Unc | BU |
|---|---|---|---|---|---|---|
| 1968 AP | Inc. above | — | 0.15 | 0.25 | 0.50 | — |
| 1969 AP on reverse | 7,440,000 | — | 0.20 | 0.40 | 1.00 | — |
| 1969 With inverted V for A in A | Inc. above | — | 0.20 | 0.40 | 1.00 | — |
| 1969 Wihout AP | Inc. above | — | 0.15 | 0.25 | 0.50 | — |
| 1970 | 6,341,000 | — | 0.20 | 0.40 | 1.00 | — |
| 1971 | 3,196,000 | — | 0.20 | 0.40 | 1.00 | — |
| 1972 | 5,523,000 | — | 0.20 | 0.40 | 1.00 | — |
| 1973 | 7,492,000 | — | 0.15 | 0.25 | 0.50 | — |

**25 CENTAVOS** **KM# 259** **Composition:** Brass **Obverse:** Small arms

| Date | Mintage | F | VF | XF | Unc | BU |
|---|---|---|---|---|---|---|
| 1973 | Inc. above | — | 0.10 | 0.15 | 0.25 | — |
| 1974 | — | — | 0.10 | 0.15 | 0.25 | — |
| 1975 | — | — | 0.10 | 0.15 | 0.25 | — |

**1/2 SOL** **KM# 203** **Weight:** 12.5000 g. **Composition:** 0.9000 Silver .3617 oz. ASW **Obverse:** Large wreath **Reverse:** Denomination in straight line **Note:** Mint mark: LIMA; Date varieties exist.

| Date | Mintage | F | VF | XF | Unc | BU |
|---|---|---|---|---|---|---|
| 1907LIMA FG-JR | 1,000,000 | BV | 4.00 | 10.00 | 20.00 | — |
| 1908/7LIMA FG-JR | 30,000 | 15.00 | 30.00 | 60.00 | 250 | — |
| 1908LIMA FG-JR | Inc. above | 12.00 | 25.00 | 50.00 | 150 | — |
| 1914LIMA FG-JR | 173,000 | BV | 4.50 | 15.00 | 35.00 | — |
| 1915LIMA FG-JR | 570,000 | BV | 3.50 | 6.50 | 15.00 | — |
| 1916LIMA FG | 384,000 | BV | 3.50 | 6.50 | 15.00 | — |
| 1916LIMA FG-JR | — | BV | 3.50 | 6.50 | 15.00 | — |
| 1917LIMA FG-JR | 178,000 | BV | 4.00 | 10.00 | 20.00 | — |

**Note:** Most coins have engravers initials JR left of shield tip on reverse

**1/2 SOL** **KM# 216** **Weight:** 12.5000 g. **Composition:** 0.5000 Silver .2009 oz. ASW **Note:** Date varieties exist.

| Date | Mintage | F | VF | XF | Unc | BU |
|---|---|---|---|---|---|---|
| 1922LIMA LIBERTAD incuse, J.R. on rev | 465,000 | BV | 4.50 | 18.50 | 50.00 | — |
| 1922LIMA LIBERTAD in relief | Inc. above | BV | 4.50 | 18.50 | 50.00 | — |
| 1923LIMA LIBER/TAD GM round top 3 | 2,520,000 | BV | 2.50 | 6.00 | 20.00 | — |
| 1923/2LIMA Flat top 3 | Inc. above | BV | 2.50 | 5.50 | 20.00 | — |
| 1923LIMA Flat top 3 | Inc. above | BV | 2.50 | 5.50 | 20.00 | — |
| 1924LIMA GM | 238,000 | 3.00 | 6.00 | 20.00 | 50.00 | — |
| 1926LIMA GM | 694,000 | BV | 3.50 | 7.50 | 25.00 | — |
| 1927LIMA GM | 2,640,000 | BV | 2.50 | 5.50 | 15.00 | — |
| 1928/7LIMA GM | 3,028,000 | — | — | — | — | — |
| 1928LIMA GM | Inc. above | BV | 2.50 | 5.50 | 15.00 | — |
| 1929LIMA GM | 3,068,000 | BV | 2.50 | 5.50 | 15.00 | — |
| 1935LIMA AP | 2,653,000 | BV | 2.50 | 5.00 | 14.00 | — |
| 1935LIMA | — | — | — | — | — | — |

**Note:** Engravers initials appear on stems of obverse wreath

**1/2 SOL** **KM# 220.1** **Composition:** Brass **Obverse:** 5 palm leaves point to llama on shield

| Date | Mintage | F | VF | XF | Unc | BU |
|---|---|---|---|---|---|---|
| 1935 | 10,000,000 | 0.50 | 1.25 | 2.25 | 7.00 | — |
| 1935 Proof | — | Value: 200 | | | | |
| 1941 | 4,000,000 | 0.50 | 1.25 | 2.25 | 7.00 | — |

**1/2 SOL** **KM# 220.4** **Composition:** Brass **Obverse:** 3 palm leaf points to llama on shield

| Date | Mintage | F | VF | XF | Unc | BU |
|---|---|---|---|---|---|---|
| 1941 | 2,000,000 | 3.00 | 6.50 | 12.50 | 35.00 | — |
| 1942 | Inc. above | 1.50 | 3.00 | 5.00 | 15.00 | — |
| 1942 AP | — | — | — | — | — | — |
| 1943 | 2,000,000 | 0.50 | 1.00 | 2.00 | 8.00 | — |
| 1944/2 | 4,000,000 | — | — | — | — | — |
| 1944 | Inc. above | 0.40 | 0.85 | 1.75 | 7.00 | — |
| 1944 AP | Inc. above | — | — | — | — | — |
| 1945 | 4,000,000 | 0.75 | 1.50 | 3.00 | 10.00 | — |

**Note:** Dates 1941-44 have thick flat-top 4 w/o serifs. 1945 has narrow 4 like KM#220.5

**1/2 SOL** **KM# 220.5** **Composition:** Brass **Obverse:** 3 palm leaf point to llama on shield

| Date | Mintage | F | VF | XF | Unc | BU |
|---|---|---|---|---|---|---|
| 1942 Long-top 2 | Inc. above | 1.50 | 3.00 | 5.00 | 15.00 | — |
| 1944 | Inc. above | 0.75 | 1.50 | 3.00 | 10.00 | — |
| 1944 AP | Inc. above | 0.50 | 1.00 | 2.00 | 7.00 | — |
| 1945 | Inc. above | 0.75 | 1.50 | 3.00 | 10.00 | — |
| 1945 AP | Inc. above | 0.75 | 1.50 | 3.00 | 10.00 | — |
| 1946/5 AP | 3,744,000 | 2.00 | 3.50 | 6.50 | 17.50 | — |
| 1946 AP | Inc. above | 0.40 | 0.75 | 1.25 | 4.00 | — |
| 1947 AP | 6,066,000 | 0.40 | 0.75 | 1.25 | 5.00 | — |
| 1947 | Inc. above | 0.40 | 0.75 | 1.25 | 5.00 | — |
| 1948 | 3,324,000 | 0.40 | 0.75 | 1.25 | 4.00 | — |
| 1949/8 | 420,000 | 1.00 | 2.00 | 4.00 | 12.00 | — |
| 1949 | Inc. above | 1.50 | 3.00 | 6.00 | 18.00 | — |
| 1950 | 91,000 | 1.25 | 2.25 | 4.50 | 15.00 | — |
| 1951/8 | 930,000 | 0.50 | 1.00 | 2.00 | 7.00 | — |
| 1951 | Inc. above | 0.50 | 1.00 | 2.00 | 7.00 | — |
| 1952 | 935,000 | 0.75 | 1.50 | 3.00 | 10.00 | — |
| 1953 | 817,000 | 0.50 | 1.00 | 2.00 | 7.00 | — |
| 1954 | 637,000 | 0.75 | 1.50 | 3.00 | 10.00 | — |
| 1955 | 1,383,000 | 0.15 | 0.35 | 0.75 | 4.00 | — |
| 1956 | 2,309,000 | 0.10 | 0.25 | 0.40 | 1.50 | — |
| 1957 | 2,700,000 | 0.10 | 0.25 | 0.50 | 2.00 | — |
| 1958 | 2,691,000 | 0.10 | 0.25 | 0.40 | 1.50 | — |
| 1959 | 3,609,000 | 0.10 | 0.25 | 0.40 | 1.50 | — |
| 1960 | 5,600,000 | 0.10 | 0.20 | 0.35 | 0.75 | — |
| 1961 | 4,400,000 | 0.10 | 0.20 | 0.35 | 0.75 | — |
| 1962 | 3,540,000 | 0.10 | 0.20 | 0.35 | 1.00 | — |
| 1963 | 4,345,000 | 0.10 | 0.20 | 0.35 | 0.75 | — |
| 1964 | 5,315,000 | 0.10 | 0.20 | 0.35 | 1.50 | — |
| 1965 | 7,090,000 | 0.10 | 0.20 | 0.35 | 1.75 | — |
| 1965 Proof | — | Value: 50.00 | | | | |

**Note:** 1942, 1944 AP and all 1945-49 have narrow 4 w/o serif on crossbar. 1944 w/o AP has flat-top 4 like KM#220.4. Engravers initials AP appear on wreath stems of some 1944-45, all 1946 and some 1947 coins. Varie- ties exist, including narrow and wide dates for 1956 and 1961 issues

**1/2 SOL** **KM# 220.2** **Composition:** Brass

| Date | Mintage | F | VF | XF | Unc | BU |
|---|---|---|---|---|---|---|
| 1942 | 4,000,000 | 1.50 | 3.00 | 5.00 | 15.00 | — |
| 1943 | 4,000,000 | 3.00 | 6.50 | 12.50 | 35.00 | — |
| 1944 | Inc. above | 1.50 | 3.00 | 5.00 | 15.00 | — |

**1/2 SOL** **KM# 220.3** **Composition:** Brass

| Date | Mintage | F | VF | XF | Unc | BU |
|---|---|---|---|---|---|---|
| 1942S | 1,668,000 | 1.50 | 3.00 | 5.00 | 15.00 | — |
| 1943S | 6,332,000 | 1.50 | 3.00 | 5.00 | 15.00 | — |

**Note:** The coins struck in Philadelphia and San Francisco have a serif on the "4" of the date; the Lima and London coins do not

**1/2 SOL** **KM# 239** **Composition:** Brass **Subject:** 400th Anniversary of Lima Mint

| Date | Mintage | F | VF | XF | Unc | BU |
|---|---|---|---|---|---|---|
| ND(1965) | 10,971,000 | — | 0.10 | 0.15 | 0.35 | — |
| ND(1965) Proof | — | Value: 400 | | | | |

**1/2 SOL** **KM# 247** **Composition:** Brass **Obverse:** Large arms **Reverse:** Vicuna

| Date | Mintage | F | VF | XF | Unc | BU |
|---|---|---|---|---|---|---|
| 1966 | 13,720,000 | — | 0.10 | 0.20 | 0.50 | — |
| 1966 Proof | 1,000 | Value: 4.00 | | | | |
| 1967 | 15,500,000 | — | 0.10 | 0.20 | 0.50 | — |
| 1967 PAREJA on .obv. and rev | — | 3.00 | 7.00 | 15.00 | 30.00 | — |
| 1968 | 13,890,000 | — | 0.10 | 0.20 | 0.50 | — |
| 1968 JAS | — | — | 0.10 | 0.20 | 0.50 | — |
| 1969 | 13,890,000 | — | 0.10 | 0.20 | 0.50 | — |
| 1970 | 11,901,000 | — | 0.10 | 0.20 | 0.50 | — |
| 1971 | 7,524,000 | — | 0.15 | 0.20 | 0.50 | — |
| 1972 | 19,441,000 | — | 0.10 | 0.20 | 0.50 | — |
| 1973 | 14,951,000 | — | 0.10 | 0.20 | 0.50 | — |

**Note:** Date varieties exist for 1970

**1/2 SOL** **KM# 247a** **Composition:** Silver Plated Brass

| Date | Mintage | F | VF | XF | Unc | BU |
|---|---|---|---|---|---|---|
| 1967 | — | — | — | — | — | — |

**1/2 SOL** **KM# 247b** **Composition:** Silver

| Date | Mintage | F | VF | XF | Unc | BU |
|---|---|---|---|---|---|---|
| 1967 | — | — | — | — | — | — |

**1/2 SOL** **KM# 260** **Composition:** Silver Plated Brass **Obverse:** Small arms

| Date | Mintage | F | VF | XF | Unc | BU |
|---|---|---|---|---|---|---|
| 1973 | Inc. above | — | 0.10 | 0.20 | 0.50 | — |
| 1974/1 | — | — | 0.10 | 0.20 | 0.50 | — |
| 1974 | 14,518,000 | — | 0.10 | 0.20 | 0.50 | — |
| 1975 | 14,039,000 | — | 0.10 | 0.20 | 0.50 | — |

**1/2 SOL** **KM# 265** **Composition:** Silver **Note:** Without mint mark.

| Date | Mintage | F | VF | XF | Unc | BU |
|---|---|---|---|---|---|---|
| 1975 | 62,682,000 | — | 0.10 | 0.20 | 0.30 | — |
| 1976 | 369,828,000 | — | 0.10 | 0.20 | 0.30 | — |
| 1977 | 18,943,000 | — | 0.10 | 0.20 | 0.30 | — |

**1/2 SOL** **KM# 268** **Weight:** 9.3500 g. **Composition:** 0.9000 Silver .2706 oz. ASW **Subject:** 150th Anniversary - Battle of Ayacucho

| Date | Mintage | F | VF | XF | Unc | BU |
|---|---|---|---|---|---|---|
| 1976 | 10,000 | — | — | — | 150 | — |

**SOL** **KM# 196.26** **Weight:** 250000.0000 g. **Composition:** 0.9000 Silver .7234 oz. ASW **Reverse:** Libertad incuse **Note:** Type XII. Legends have smaller lettering; Varieties exist.

| Date | Mintage | F | VF | XF | Unc | BU |
|---|---|---|---|---|---|---|
| 1914 FG | 620,000 | 6.00 | 7.00 | 9.00 | 22.00 | — |
| 1915 FG | Inc. above | 6.00 | 7.00 | 9.00 | 20.00 | — |

**SOL** KM# 196.27 **Weight:** 250000.0000 g. **Composition:** 0.9000 Silver .7234 oz. ASW **Reverse:** Libertad incuse

| Date | Mintage | F | VF | XF | Unc | BU |
|---|---|---|---|---|---|---|
| 1916 FG | 1,927,000 | 6.00 | 7.00 | 8.00 | 20.00 | — |

**SOL** KM# 196.28 **Weight:** 250000.0000 g. **Composition:** 0.9000 Silver .7234 oz. ASW **Reverse:** Libertad in relief **Note:** Type III.

| Date | Mintage | F | VF | XF | Unc | BU |
|---|---|---|---|---|---|---|
| 1916 FG | Inc. above | 6.00 | 7.00 | 8.00 | 20.00 | — |

**SOL** KM# 217.1 **Weight:** 250000.0000 g. **Composition:** 0.5000 Silver .4019 oz. ASW **Obv. Legend:** Fineness omitted **Reverse:** Libertad in relief

| Date | Mintage | F | VF | XF | Unc | BU |
|---|---|---|---|---|---|---|
| 1922 Rare | — | — | — | — | — | — |
| 1923 | 3,600 | 15.00 | 30.00 | 70.00 | 275 | — |

**SOL** KM# 217.2 **Weight:** 250000.0000 g. **Composition:** 0.5000 Silver .4019 oz. ASW **Reverse:** LIBERTAD incuse

| Date | Mintage | F | VF | XF | Unc | BU |
|---|---|---|---|---|---|---|
| 1923 | 1,400 | 35.00 | 75.00 | 165 | 475 | — |

**SOL** KM# 218.1 **Weight:** 250000.0000 g. **Composition:** 0.5000 Silver .4019 oz. ASW **Note:** Small letters. The Philadelphia and Lima strikings may be distinguished by the fact that the letters in the legends are smaller on those pieces produced at Philadelphia. All bear the name of the Lima Mint.

| Date | Mintage | F | VF | XF | Unc | BU |
|---|---|---|---|---|---|---|
| 1923 | Est. 2,369,000 | BV | 5.50 | 8.50 | 15.00 | — |
| 1924/824 | Est. 3,113,000 | 5.50 | 10.00 | 20.00 | 40.00 | — |
| 1924 | Inc. above | BV | 5.50 | 8.50 | 15.00 | — |
| 1925 | 1,291,000 | BV | 5.50 | 10.00 | 20.00 | — |
| 1926 | 2,157,000 | BV | 5.50 | 8.50 | 15.00 | — |

**SOL** KM# 218.2 **Weight:** 25.0000 g. **Composition:** 0.5000 Silver .4019 oz. ASW **Obverse:** Engraver's initials GM on stems flanking date **Note:** Large letters.

| Date | Mintage | F | VF | XF | Unc | BU |
|---|---|---|---|---|---|---|
| 1924 | 96,000 | 5.50 | 9.00 | 20.00 | 65.00 | — |
| 1925 | 1,004,999 | BV | 5.50 | 8.50 | 15.00 | — |
| 1930 | 76,000 | BV | 5.50 | 10.00 | 20.00 | — |
| 1931 | 24,000 | BV | 5.50 | 10.00 | 22.00 | — |
| 1933 | 5,000 | 6.00 | 12.00 | 20.00 | 40.00 | — |
| 1934/3 | 2,855,000 | BV | 5.50 | 10.00 | 20.00 | — |
| 1934 | Inc. above | BV | 5.50 | 7.00 | 12.50 | — |
| 1935 | 695,000 | BV | 5.50 | 10.00 | 20.00 | — |

**SOL** KM# 222 **Composition:** Brass **Note:** Date varieties exist.

| Date | Mintage | F | VF | XF | Unc | BU |
|---|---|---|---|---|---|---|
| 1943 | 10,000,000 | 0.35 | 1.25 | 3.00 | 8.00 | — |
| 1944 | Inc. above | 0.35 | 1.25 | 3.00 | 7.00 | — |
| 1945 | — | 0.50 | 1.50 | 3.50 | 9.00 | — |
| 1946 | 1,752,000 | 0.50 | 1.50 | 3.00 | 8.00 | — |
| 1947 | 3,302,000 | 0.35 | 1.00 | 2.00 | 6.00 | — |
| 1948 | 1,992,000 | 0.35 | 1.00 | 2.00 | 6.00 | — |
| 1949/8 | 751,000 | 2.00 | 4.00 | 7.00 | 20.00 | — |
| 1949 | Inc. above | 3.50 | 7.50 | 12.00 | 25.00 | — |
| 1950 | 1,249,000 | 7.00 | 10.00 | 15.00 | 25.00 | — |
| 1951/0 | 2,093,999 | 0.25 | 0.50 | 1.50 | 6.00 | — |
| 1951 | Inc. above | 0.25 | 0.50 | 1.50 | 6.00 | — |
| 1952 | 2,037,000 | 0.25 | 0.50 | 1.50 | 6.00 | — |
| 1953 | 1,243,000 | 3.00 | 6.00 | 10.00 | 25.00 | — |
| 1954 | 1,220,000 | 0.35 | 0.75 | 1.75 | 6.00 | — |
| 1955 | 1,323,000 | 0.35 | 0.75 | 1.75 | 6.00 | — |
| 1956 | 3,450,000 | 0.15 | 0.35 | 0.75 | 3.00 | — |
| 1957 | 3,086,000 | 0.15 | 0.35 | 1.00 | 5.00 | — |
| 1958 | 3,390,000 | 0.15 | 0.35 | 0.75 | 3.00 | — |
| 1959 | 4,975,000 | 0.15 | 0.35 | 1.00 | 5.00 | — |
| 1960 | 5,800,000 | 0.15 | 0.35 | 0.75 | 1.50 | — |
| 1961 | 5,200,000 | 0.15 | 0.35 | 0.75 | 2.00 | — |
| 1962 | 5,102,000 | 0.15 | 0.35 | 0.75 | 1.50 | — |
| 1963 | 5,499,000 | 0.15 | 0.35 | 0.75 | 2.00 | — |
| 1964 | 5,888,000 | 0.15 | 0.35 | 0.75 | 2.00 | — |
| 1965 | 5,504,000 | 0.15 | 0.35 | 0.75 | 2.00 | — |
| 1965 Proof | — | Value: 75.00 | | | | |

**SOL** KM# 240 **Composition:** Brass **Subject:** 400th Anniversary of Lima Mint

| Date | Mintage | F | VF | XF | Unc | BU |
|---|---|---|---|---|---|---|
| ND(1965) | 3,103,000 | — | 0.35 | 0.75 | 1.50 | — |
| ND(1965) Proof | — | Value: 500 | | | | |

**SOL** KM# 248 **Composition:** Brass

| Date | Mintage | F | VF | XF | Unc | BU |
|---|---|---|---|---|---|---|
| 1966 | 16,410,000 | — | 0.10 | 0.25 | 0.60 | — |
| 1966 Proof | 1,000 | Value: 5.00 | | | | |
| 1967 | 13,920,000 | — | 0.10 | 0.25 | 0.60 | — |
| 1968 | 12,260,000 | — | 0.10 | 0.25 | 0.60 | — |
| 1969 | 12,260,000 | — | 0.10 | 0.25 | 0.60 | — |
| 1970 | 12,336,000 | — | 0.10 | 0.25 | 0.60 | — |
| 1971 | 11,927,000 | — | 0.10 | 0.25 | 0.60 | — |
| 1972 | 3,945,000 | — | 0.10 | 0.25 | 0.60 | — |
| 1973 | 12,856,000 | — | 0.10 | 0.25 | 0.60 | — |
| 1974 | 14,966,000 | — | 0.10 | 0.25 | 0.60 | — |
| 1975 | — | — | 0.10 | 0.25 | 0.60 | — |

**SOL** KM# 248a **Composition:** Silver Plated Brass

| Date | Mintage | F | VF | XF | Unc | BU |
|---|---|---|---|---|---|---|
| 1967 | — | — | — | — | — | — |

**SOL** KM# 248b **Composition:** Silver

| Date | Mintage | F | VF | XF | Unc | BU |
|---|---|---|---|---|---|---|
| 1967 | — | — | — | — | — | — |

**SOL** KM# 266.1 **Composition:** Brass

| Date | Mintage | F | VF | XF | Unc | BU |
|---|---|---|---|---|---|---|
| 1975 | 354,485,000 | — | — | 0.10 | 0.25 | — |
| 1976 | 114,660,000 | — | — | 0.10 | 0.25 | — |

**SOL** KM# 269 **Weight:** 23.4000 g. **Composition:** 0.9000 Gold .6772 oz. AGW **Subject:** 150th Anniversary - Battle of Ayacucho **Note:** Mint mark in monogram.

| Date | Mintage | F | VF | XF | Unc | BU |
|---|---|---|---|---|---|---|
| 1976 LIMA | 10,000 | — | — | — | 450 | — |

**SOL** KM# 266.2 **Composition:** Brass **Note:** Mint mark in monogram.

| Date | Mintage | F | VF | XF | Unc | BU |
|---|---|---|---|---|---|---|
| 1978 LIMA | 9,000,000 | — | — | 0.15 | 0.35 | — |
| 1979 LIMA | 4,842,000 | — | — | 0.15 | 0.35 | — |
| 1980 LIMA | 28,826,000 | — | — | 0.15 | 0.35 | — |
| 1981 LIMA | 51,630,000 | — | — | 0.15 | 0.35 | — |
| 1982 LIMA | 4,155,000 | — | — | 0.15 | 0.35 | — |

**5 SOLES** KM# 235 **Weight:** 2.3404 g. **Composition:** 0.9000 Gold .0677 oz. AGW

| Date | Mintage | F | VF | XF | Unc | BU |
|---|---|---|---|---|---|---|
| 1956 | 4,510 | — | — | — | 50.00 | — |
| 1957 | 2,146 | — | — | — | 50.00 | — |
| 1959 | 1,536 | — | — | — | 60.00 | — |
| 1960 | 8,133 | — | — | — | 50.00 | — |
| 1961 | 1,154 | — | — | — | 60.00 | — |
| 1962 | 1,550 | — | — | — | 60.00 | — |
| 1963 | 3,945 | — | — | — | 50.00 | — |
| 1964 | 2,063 | — | — | — | 55.00 | — |
| 1965 | 14,000 | — | — | — | 50.00 | — |
| 1966 | 4,738 | — | — | — | 50.00 | — |
| 1967 | 3,651 | — | — | — | 50.00 | — |
| 1969 | 127 | — | — | — | 175 | — |

**5 SOLES** KM# 252 **Weight:** 2.3404 g. **Composition:** 0.9000 Copper Nickel .0677 oz.

| Date | Mintage | F | VF | XF | Unc | BU |
|---|---|---|---|---|---|---|
| 1969 | 10,000,000 | 0.20 | 0.40 | 0.60 | 1.50 | — |

**5 SOLES** **KM# 254** **Composition:** Copper-Nickel **Subject:** 150th Anniversary of Independence **Note:** Mint mark: LIMA monogram.

| Date | Mintage | F | VF | XF | Unc | BU |
|---|---|---|---|---|---|---|
| 1971LIMA | 3,480,000 | 0.20 | 0.40 | 0.80 | 2.00 | — |

**5 SOLES** **KM# 257** **Composition:** Copper-Nickel **Note:** Regular issue.

| Date | Mintage | F | VF | XF | Unc | BU |
|---|---|---|---|---|---|---|
| 1972LIMA | 2,068,000 | — | 0.10 | 0.35 | 1.00 | — |
| 1973LIMA | 475,000 | — | 0.10 | 0.35 | 1.00 | — |
| 1974LIMA | — | — | 0.10 | 0.35 | 1.50 | — |
| 1975LIMA | — | — | 0.10 | 0.35 | 1.50 | — |

**5 SOLES** **KM# 267** **Composition:** Copper-Nickel

| Date | Mintage | F | VF | XF | Unc | BU |
|---|---|---|---|---|---|---|
| 1975 | — | — | 0.10 | 0.35 | 1.00 | — |
| 1976 | 17,016,000 | — | 0.10 | 0.35 | 1.00 | — |
| 1977 | 94,272,000 | — | 0.10 | 0.35 | 1.00 | — |

**5 SOLES** **KM# 271** **Composition:** Brass

| Date | Mintage | F | VF | XF | Unc | BU |
|---|---|---|---|---|---|---|
| 1978 | 38,016,000 | — | 0.10 | 0.20 | 0.60 | — |
| 1979 | 64,524,000 | — | 0.10 | 0.20 | 0.60 | — |
| 1980 | 76,964,000 | — | 0.10 | 0.20 | 0.60 | — |
| 1981 | 31,632,000 | — | 0.10 | 0.20 | 0.60 | — |
| 1982 | 23,262,000 | — | 0.10 | 0.20 | 0.60 | — |
| 1983 | 650 | 20.00 | 30.00 | 40.00 | 60.00 | — |

**10 SOLES** **KM# 236** **Weight:** 4.6070 g. **Composition:** 0.9000 Gold .1354 oz. AGW

| Date | Mintage | F | VF | XF | Unc | BU |
|---|---|---|---|---|---|---|
| 1956 | 5,410 | — | — | BV | 75.00 | — |
| 1957 | 1,300 | — | — | BV | 85.00 | — |
| 1959 | 1,103 | — | — | BV | 85.00 | — |
| 1960 | 7,178 | — | — | BV | 75.00 | — |
| 1961 | 1,634 | — | — | BV | 85.00 | — |
| 1962 | 1,676 | — | — | BV | 85.00 | — |
| 1963 | 3,372 | — | — | BV | 75.00 | — |
| 1964 | 1,554 | — | — | BV | 85.00 | — |
| 1965 | 14,000 | — | — | BV | 70.00 | — |
| 1966 | 2,601 | — | — | BV | 75.00 | — |
| 1967 | 3,002 | — | — | BV | 75.00 | — |
| 1968 | 100 | — | BV | 100 | 200 | — |
| 1969 | 100 | — | BV | 100 | 200 | — |

**10 SOLES** **KM# 253** **Composition:** Copper-Nickel

| Date | Mintage | F | VF | XF | Unc | BU |
|---|---|---|---|---|---|---|
| 1969 | 15,000,000 | 0.25 | 0.50 | 0.75 | 1.75 | — |

**10 SOLES** **KM# 255** **Composition:** Copper-Nickel **Note:** Mint mark in monogram.

| Date | Mintage | F | VF | XF | Unc | BU |
|---|---|---|---|---|---|---|
| 1971 LIMA | 2,460,000 | 0.25 | 0.50 | 1.00 | 2.50 | — |

**10 SOLES** **KM# 258** **Composition:** Copper-Nickel

| Date | Mintage | F | VF | XF | Unc | BU |
|---|---|---|---|---|---|---|
| 1972 LIMA | 2,235 | — | 0.10 | 0.40 | 1.25 | — |
| 1973 LIMA | 1,765 | — | 0.10 | 0.40 | 1.25 | — |
| 1974 LIMA | — | — | 0.10 | 0.40 | 1.25 | — |
| 1975 LIMA | — | — | 0.10 | 0.40 | 1.25 | — |

**10 SOLES** **KM# 272.1** **Composition:** Brass **Obverse:** Large arms, small letters. Inner circle 18.1mm **Edge:** Plain

| Date | Mintage | F | VF | XF | Unc | BU |
|---|---|---|---|---|---|---|
| 1978 | 46,970,000 | — | 0.10 | 0.40 | 0.85 | — |

**10 SOLES** **KM# 272.2** **Composition:** Brass **Obverse:** Small arms, small letters. Inner circle 17.2mm

| Date | Mintage | F | VF | XF | Unc | BU |
|---|---|---|---|---|---|---|
| 1978 | — | — | 0.10 | 0.40 | 0.85 | — |
| 1979 | 82,220,000 | — | 0.10 | 0.40 | 0.85 | — |
| 1980 | 99,595,000 | — | 0.10 | 0.40 | 0.85 | — |
| 1981 | 25,660,000 | — | 0.10 | 0.40 | 0.85 | — |
| 1982 | 61,035,000 | — | 0.10 | 0.40 | 0.85 | — |
| 1983 | 15,820,000 | — | 0.10 | 0.40 | 0.85 | — |

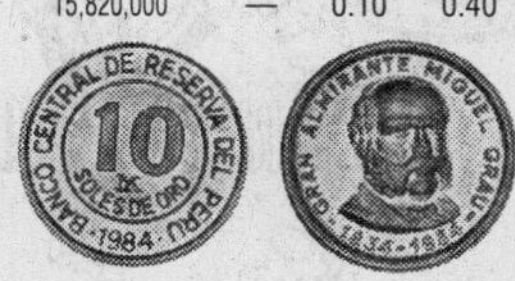

**10 SOLES** **KM# 287** **Composition:** Brass **Subject:** 150th Anniversary - Birth of Admiral Grau

| Date | Mintage | F | VF | XF | Unc | BU |
|---|---|---|---|---|---|---|
| 1984 | 30,000,000 | — | — | 0.20 | 0.50 | — |

**20 SOLES** **KM# 229** **Weight:** 9.3614 g. **Composition:** 0.9000 Gold .2709 oz. AGW **Subject:** 150th Anniversary - Birth of Admiral Grau

| Date | Mintage | F | VF | XF | Unc | BU |
|---|---|---|---|---|---|---|
| 1950 | 1,800 | — | — | BV | 200 | — |
| 1951 | 9,264 | — | — | BV | 150 | — |
| 1952 | 424 | — | — | BV | 225 | — |
| 1953 | 1,435 | — | — | BV | 200 | — |
| 1954 | 1,732 | — | — | BV | 200 | — |
| 1955 | 1,971 | — | — | BV | 200 | — |
| 1956 | 1,201 | — | — | BV | 200 | — |
| 1957 | 11,000 | — | — | BV | 150 | — |
| 1958 | 11,000 | — | — | BV | 150 | — |
| 1959 | 12,000 | — | — | BV | 150 | — |
| 1960 | 7,753 | — | — | BV | 150 | — |
| 1961 | 1,825 | — | — | BV | 200 | — |
| 1962 | 2,282 | — | — | BV | 175 | — |
| 1963 | 3,892 | — | — | BV | 165 | — |
| 1964 | 1,302 | — | — | BV | 200 | — |
| 1965 | 12,000 | — | — | BV | 150 | — |
| 1966 | 4,001 | — | — | BV | 150 | — |
| 1967 | 5,003 | — | — | BV | 150 | — |
| 1968 | 640 | — | — | BV | 200 | — |
| 1969 | 640 | — | — | BV | 200 | — |

**20 SOLES** **KM# 241** **Weight:** 8.0000 g. **Composition:** 0.9000 Silver .2315 oz. ASW **Subject:** 400th Anniversary of Lima Mint

| Date | Mintage | F | VF | XF | Unc | BU |
|---|---|---|---|---|---|---|
| ND(1965) | 150,000 | — | — | — | 7.00 | — |

**20 SOLES** **KM# 249** **Weight:** 7.9700 g. **Composition:** 0.9000 Silver .2306 oz. ASW **Subject:** 100th Anniversary of Peru - Spain Naval Battle

| Date | Mintage | F | VF | XF | Unc | BU |
|---|---|---|---|---|---|---|
| ND(1966) | 4,001 | — | — | — | 16.50 | — |

**50 SOLES** **KM# 219** **Weight:** 33.4363 g. **Composition:** 0.9000 Gold .9675 oz. AGW

| Date | Mintage | F | VF | XF | Unc | BU |
|---|---|---|---|---|---|---|
| 1930 | 5,584 | 475 | 625 | 950 | 1,600 | — |
| 1931 | 5,538 | 475 | 625 | 950 | 1,500 | — |
| 1967 | 10,000 | — | — | — | 500 | — |
| 1968 | 300 | — | — | — | 650 | — |
| 1969 | 403 | — | — | — | 650 | — |

**50 SOLES** **KM# 230** **Weight:** 23.4056 g. **Composition:** 0.9000 Gold .6772 oz. AGW

| Date | Mintage | F | VF | XF | Unc | BU |
|---|---|---|---|---|---|---|
| 1950 | 1,927 | — | — | BV | 350 | — |
| 1951 | 5,292 | — | — | BV | 350 | — |
| 1952 | 1,201 | — | — | BV | 450 | — |
| 1953 | 1,464 | — | — | BV | 400 | — |
| 1954 | 1,839 | — | — | BV | 375 | — |
| 1955 | 1,898 | — | — | BV | 375 | — |
| 1956 | 11,000 | — | — | BV | 325 | — |
| 1957 | 11,000 | — | — | BV | 325 | — |
| 1958 | 11,000 | — | — | BV | 325 | — |
| 1959 | 5,734 | — | — | BV | 325 | — |
| 1960 | 2,139 | — | — | BV | 365 | — |
| 1961 | 1,110 | — | — | BV | 450 | — |
| 1962 | 3,319 | — | — | BV | 350 | — |
| 1963 | 3,089 | — | — | BV | 350 | — |
| 1964/3 | 2,425 | — | — | BV | 350 | — |
| 1964 | Inc. above | — | — | BV | 360 | — |
| 1965 | 23,000 | — | — | BV | 325 | — |
| 1966 | 3,409 | — | — | BV | 350 | — |
| 1967 | 5,805 | — | — | BV | 350 | — |
| 1968 | 443 | — | — | BV | 450 | — |
| 1969 | 443 | — | — | BV | 450 | — |
| 1970 | 553 | — | — | BV | 450 | — |

**50 SOLES** **KM# 242** **Weight:** 23.4056 g. **Composition:** 0.9000 Gold .6772 oz. AGW **Subject:** 400th Anniversary of Lima Mint

| Date | Mintage | F | VF | XF | Unc | BU |
|---|---|---|---|---|---|---|
| ND(1965) | 17,000 | — | — | — | 350 | — |

**50 SOLES** **KM# 250** **Weight:** 23.4056 g. **Composition:** 0.9000 Gold .6772 oz. AGW **Subject:** 100th Anniversary of Peru - Spain Naval Battle

| Date | Mintage | F | VF | XF | Unc | BU |
|---|---|---|---|---|---|---|
| ND(1966) | 6,409 | — | — | — | 550 | — |

**50 SOLES** **KM# 256** **Weight:** 21.4500 g. **Composition:** 0.8000 Silver .5517 oz. ASW **Subject:** 150th Anniversary of Independence **Note:** Struck at Lima. Mint mark in monogram.

| Date | Mintage | F | VF | XF | Unc | BU |
|---|---|---|---|---|---|---|
| 1971LIMA | 100,000 | — | — | — | 7.00 | — |

**50 SOLES** **KM# 273** **Composition:** Aluminum-Bronze

| Date | Mintage | F | VF | XF | Unc | BU |
|---|---|---|---|---|---|---|
| 1979 | 1,323,000 | — | 0.15 | 0.35 | 1.00 | — |
| 1980 | 42,573,000 | — | 0.10 | 0.20 | 0.50 | — |
| 1981 | 19,923,000 | — | 0.10 | 0.20 | 0.50 | — |
| 1982 LIMA | 18,471,000 | — | 0.10 | 0.20 | 0.50 | — |
| 1982 Without Lima | Inc. above | — | 0.15 | 0.35 | 1.00 | — |
| 1983 | 8,175,000 | — | 0.10 | 0.20 | 0.50 | — |

**50 SOLES** **KM# 297** **Composition:** Brass **Subject:** 150th Anniversary - Birth of Admiral Grau

| Date | Mintage | F | VF | XF | Unc | BU |
|---|---|---|---|---|---|---|
| 1984 | 11,475,000 | — | — | 0.20 | 0.50 | — |
| 1985 | 8,525,000 | — | — | 0.20 | 0.50 | — |

**100 SOLES** **KM# 231** **Weight:** 46.8071 g. **Composition:** 0.9000 Gold 1.3544 oz. AGW

| Date | Mintage | F | VF | XF | Unc | BU |
|---|---|---|---|---|---|---|
| 1950 | 1,176 | — | — | BV | 700 | — |
| 1951 | 8,241 | — | — | BV | 650 | — |
| 1952 | 126 | — | — | 2,000 | 3,000 | — |
| 1953 | 498 | — | — | BV | 750 | — |
| 1954 | 1,808 | — | — | BV | 650 | — |
| 1955 | 901 | — | — | BV | 750 | — |
| 1956 | 1,159 | — | — | BV | 650 | — |
| 1957 | 550 | — | — | BV | 750 | — |
| 1958 | 101 | — | — | 3,000 | 4,000 | — |
| 1959 | 4,710 | — | — | BV | 625 | — |
| 1960 | 2,207 | — | — | BV | 625 | — |
| 1961 | 6,982 | — | — | BV | 600 | — |
| 1962 | 9,678 | — | — | BV | 600 | — |
| 1963 | 7,342 | — | — | BV | 600 | — |
| 1964 | 11,000 | — | — | BV | 600 | — |
| 1965 | 23,000 | — | — | BV | 600 | — |
| 1966 | 3,409 | — | — | BV | 625 | — |
| 1967 | 6,431 | — | — | BV | 625 | — |
| 1968 | 540 | — | — | BV | 750 | — |
| 1969 | 540 | — | — | BV | 750 | — |
| 1970 | 425 | — | — | BV | 750 | — |

**100 SOLES** **KM# 243** **Weight:** 46.8071 g. **Composition:** 0.9000 Gold 1.3544 oz. AGW **Subject:** 400th Anniversary of Lima Mint

| Date | Mintage | F | VF | XF | Unc | BU |
|---|---|---|---|---|---|---|
| ND(1965) | 27,000 | — | — | — | 650 | — |

**100 SOLES** **KM# 251** **Weight:** 46.8071 g. **Composition:** 0.9000 Gold 1.3544 oz. AGW **Subject:** 100th Anniversary of Peru - Spain Naval Battle

| Date | Mintage | F | VF | XF | Unc | BU |
|---|---|---|---|---|---|---|
| ND(1966) | 6,253 | — | — | — | 825 | — |

**100 SOLES** **KM# 261** **Weight:** 22.4500 g. **Composition:** 0.8000 Silver .5774 oz. ASW **Subject:** Centennial Peru - Japan trade relations **Note:** Mint mark in monogram.

| Date | Mintage | F | VF | XF | Unc | BU |
|---|---|---|---|---|---|---|
| 1973 LIMA | 375,000 | — | — | — | 12.50 | — |

**100 SOLES** **KM# 283** **Composition:** Copper-Nickel **Note:** Without mint mark.

| Date | Mintage | F | VF | XF | Unc | BU |
|---|---|---|---|---|---|---|
| 1980 | 100,000,000 | — | 0.20 | 0.40 | 1.50 | — |
| 1982 | — | — | 0.20 | 0.40 | 1.50 | — |

**100 SOLES** **KM# 288** **Composition:** Brass **Subject:** 150th Anniversary - Birth of Admiral Grau **Note:** Mint mark in monogram.

| Date | Mintage | F | VF | XF | Unc | BU |
|---|---|---|---|---|---|---|
| 1984LIMA | 20,000,000 | — | 0.15 | 0.35 | 1.00 | — |

**200 SOLES** **KM# 262** **Weight:** 22.0000 g. **Composition:** 0.8000 Silver .5659 oz. ASW **Subject:** Aviation heroes - Chavez and Guinones

| Date | Mintage | F | VF | XF | Unc | BU |
|---|---|---|---|---|---|---|
| 1974 | 25,000 | — | — | — | 15.00 | — |
| 1975 | 90,000 | — | — | — | 10.00 | — |
| 1976 | 25,000 | — | — | — | 20.00 | — |
| 1977 | 3,000 | — | — | — | 30.00 | — |
| 1978 | 3,000 | — | — | — | 30.00 | — |

**400 SOLES** **KM# 270** **Weight:** 28.1000 g. **Composition:** 0.9000 Silver .8131 oz. ASW **Subject:** 150th Anniversary - Battle of Ayacucho **Obverse:** Similar to 200 Soled, KM#262 **Note:** Mint mark in monogram.

| Date | Mintage | F | VF | XF | Unc | BU |
|---|---|---|---|---|---|---|
| 1976LIMA | 350,000 | — | — | — | 15.00 | — |

**500 SOLES** **KM# 289** **Composition:** Brass **Subject:** 150th Anniversary - Birth of Admiral Grau **Note:** Mint mark in monogram.

| Date | Mintage | F | VF | XF | Unc | BU |
|---|---|---|---|---|---|---|
| 1984LIMA | 16,962,000 | — | 0.20 | 0.50 | 2.00 | — |

**500 SOLES** **KM# 310** **Composition:** Brass **Note:** Admiral Grau without date. Mint mark in monogram.

| Date | Mintage | F | VF | XF | Unc | BU |
|---|---|---|---|---|---|---|
| 1985 LIMA | 13,038,000 | — | 0.20 | 0.50 | 2.50 | — |

**1000 SOLES** **KM# 275** **Weight:** 15.5500 g. **Composition:** 0.5000 Silver .2500 oz. ASW **Subject:** National Congress **Edge:** Smooth with incuse stars **Note:** Mint mark in monogram.

| Date | Mintage | F | VF | XF | Unc | BU |
|---|---|---|---|---|---|---|
| 1979LIMA | 200,000 | — | — | — | 5.00 | — |

**5000 SOLES** **KM# 276** **Weight:** 31.1077 g. **Composition:** 0.9250 Silver .9251 oz. ASW **Subject:** 100th Anniversary - Battle of Iquique **Note:** Mint mark in monogram.

| Date | Mintage | F | VF | XF | Unc | BU |
|---|---|---|---|---|---|---|
| 1979LIMA | 100,000 | — | — | 12.50 | 20.00 | — |

**5000 SOLES** **KM# 284** **Weight:** 23.3700 g. **Composition:** 0.9250 Silver .6951 oz. ASW **Subject:** Champions of Soccer **Note:** Mint mark in monogram.

| Date | Mintage | F | VF | XF | Unc | BU |
|---|---|---|---|---|---|---|
| 1982 LIMA Proof | 8,250 | Value: 26.50 | | | | |

**5000 SOLES** **KM# 285** **Composition:** Silver **Subject:** Champions of Soccer **Note:** Mint mark in monogram.

| Date | Mintage | F | VF | XF | Unc | BU |
|---|---|---|---|---|---|---|
| 1982 LIMA Proof | 8,300 | Value: 26.50 | | | | |

**10000 SOLES** **KM# 286** **Weight:** 16.8000 g. **Composition:** 0.9250 Silver .4997 oz. ASW **Subject:** Battle of La Brena and **Reverse:** General Caceras **Note:** Mint mark in monogram.

| Date | Mintage | F | VF | XF | Unc | BU |
|---|---|---|---|---|---|---|
| 1982 LIMA | 100,000 | — | — | — | 12.50 | — |

**50000 SOLES** **KM# 277** **Weight:** 16.8600 g. **Composition:** 0.9170 Gold .5004 oz. AGW **Reverse:** Alfonso Urgarte **Note:** Mint mark in monogram.

| Date | Mintage | F | VF | XF | Unc | BU |
|---|---|---|---|---|---|---|
| 1979 LIMA | 10,000 | — | — | — | 285 | — |

**50000 SOLES** **KM# 278** **Weight:** 16.8600 g. **Composition:** 0.9170 Gold .5004 oz. AGW **Reverse:** Elias Aguirre **Note:** Mint mark in monogram.

| Date | Mintage | F | VF | XF | Unc | BU |
|---|---|---|---|---|---|---|
| 1979 LIMA | 10,000 | — | — | — | 285 | — |

**50000 SOLES** **KM# 279** **Weight:** 16.8600 g. **Composition:** 0.9170 Gold .5004 oz. AGW **Reverse:** Garcia Calderon **Note:** Mint mark in monogram.

| Date | Mintage | F | VF | XF | Unc | BU |
|---|---|---|---|---|---|---|
| 1979 LIMA | 10,000 | — | — | — | 285 | — |

**100000 SOLES** **KM# 280** **Weight:** 33.9000 g. **Composition:** 0.9170 Gold .9995 oz. AGW **Reverse:** Francisco Bolognese **Note:** Mint mark in monogram.

| Date | Mintage | F | VF | XF | Unc | BU |
|---|---|---|---|---|---|---|
| 1979 LIMA | 10,000 | — | — | — | 500 | — |

**100000 SOLES** **KM# 281** **Weight:** 33.9000 g. **Composition:** 0.9170 Gold .9995 oz. AGW **Reverse:** Andres A. Caceres **Note:** Mint mark in monogram.

| Date | Mintage | F | VF | XF | Unc | BU |
|---|---|---|---|---|---|---|
| 1979 LIMA | 10,000 | — | — | — | 500 | — |

**100000 SOLES** **KM# 282** **Weight:** 33.9000 g. **Composition:** 0.9170 Gold .9995 oz. AGW **Reverse:** Miguel Grau **Note:** Mint mark in monogram.

| Date | Mintage | F | VF | XF | Unc | BU |
|---|---|---|---|---|---|---|
| 1979 LIMA | 10,000 | — | — | — | 500 | — |

**2 NUEVOS SOLES** **KM# 313** **Ring Composition:** Steel **Center Composition:** Brass .2306 oz. **Subject:** Centennial of Japanese Immigration **Obverse:** National arms **Reverse:** Radiant sun above maps

| Date | Mintage | F | VF | XF | Unc | BU |
|---|---|---|---|---|---|---|
| 1994 | — | — | — | — | 4.50 | — |
| 1995 | — | — | — | — | 4.50 | — |

**5 NUEVOS SOLES** **KM# 316** **Ring Composition:** Steel **Center Composition:** Brass .2306 oz. **Subject:** Centennial of Japanese Immigration **Obverse:** National arms **Reverse:** Radiant sun above maps **Note:** Mint mark in monogram.

| Date | Mintage | F | VF | XF | Unc | BU |
|---|---|---|---|---|---|---|
| 1994 LIMA | — | — | — | — | 6.50 | — |
| 1995 LIMA | — | — | — | — | 6.50 | — |

## REFORM COINAGE

1000 Soles de Oro = 1 Inti

**CENTIMO** **KM# 291** **Composition:** Brass **Note:** Mint mark in monogram.

| Date | Mintage | F | VF | XF | Unc | BU |
|---|---|---|---|---|---|---|
| 1985 LIMA | 4,179,999 | — | — | — | 0.25 | — |
| 1986 LIMA | 20,000 | — | — | — | 0.35 | — |
| 1987 LIMA | — | — | — | — | 0.35 | — |
| 1988 LIMA | — | — | — | — | 0.35 | — |

**5 CENTIMOS** KM# 292 **Composition:** Brass **Note:** Mint mark in monogram.

| Date | Mintage | F | VF | XF | Unc | BU |
|---|---|---|---|---|---|---|
| 1985 LIMA | 20,000,000 | — | — | — | 0.35 | — |
| 1986 LIMA | — | — | — | — | 0.45 | — |
| 1987 LIMA | — | — | — | — | 0.45 | — |
| 1988 | — | — | — | — | 0.45 | — |

**10 CENTIMOS** KM# 293 **Composition:** Brass **Note:** Mint mark in monogram.

| Date | Mintage | F | VF | XF | Unc | BU |
|---|---|---|---|---|---|---|
| 1985 LIMA | 143,900,000 | — | — | — | 1.00 | — |
| 1986 LIMA | 48,730,000 | — | — | — | 0.65 | — |
| 1987 LIMA | 42,370,000 | — | — | — | 0.65 | — |
| 1988 LIMA | — | — | — | — | 0.65 | — |

**20 CENTIMOS** KM# 294 **Composition:** Brass **Note:** Mint mark in monogram.

| Date | Mintage | F | VF | XF | Unc | BU |
|---|---|---|---|---|---|---|
| 1985 LIMA | 4,739,000 | — | — | — | 1.25 | — |
| 1986 LIMA | 96,699,000 | — | — | — | 1.00 | — |
| 1987 LIMA | 59,668,000 | — | — | — | 1.00 | — |
| 1988 LIMA | — | — | — | — | 1.00 | — |

**50 CENTIMOS** KM# 295 **Composition:** Brass **Note:** Mint mark in monogram.

| Date | Mintage | F | VF | XF | Unc | BU |
|---|---|---|---|---|---|---|
| 1985 LIMA | 43,320,000 | — | — | — | 1.25 | — |
| 1986 LIMA | 72,802,000 | — | — | — | 1.25 | — |
| 1987 LIMA | 63,878,000 | — | — | — | 1.25 | — |
| 1988 LIMA | 80,000,000 | — | — | — | 1.25 | — |

**1/2 INTI** KM# 301a **Composition:** Copper-Nickel

| Date | Mintage | F | VF | XF | Unc | BU |
|---|---|---|---|---|---|---|
| 1989 | — | — | — | — | — | — |

**1/2 INTI** KM# 301 **Weight:** 16.8000 g. **Composition:** 0.9250 Silver .4997 oz. ASW **Subject:** Pachacutec **Note:** Mint mark in monogram.

| Date | Mintage | F | VF | XF | Unc | BU |
|---|---|---|---|---|---|---|
| 1989 LIMA | — | — | — | — | 20.00 | — |

**INTI** KM# 296 **Composition:** Copper-Nickel **Note:** Mint mark in monogram.

| Date | Mintage | F | VF | XF | Unc | BU |
|---|---|---|---|---|---|---|
| 1985 LIMA | 15,760,000 | — | — | — | 1.75 | — |
| 1986 LIMA | 87,240,000 | — | — | — | 1.25 | — |
| 1987 LIMA | 120,000,000 | — | — | — | 1.00 | — |
| 1988 LIMA | 17,304,000 | — | — | — | 1.75 | — |

**5 INTIS** KM# 300 **Composition:** Copper-Nickel **Reverse:** Admiral Grau **Note:** Mint mark in monogram.

| Date | Mintage | F | VF | XF | Unc | BU |
|---|---|---|---|---|---|---|
| 1985 LIMA | 3,972 | — | — | — | — | — |
| 1986 LIMA | 28,000 | — | — | — | 3.50 | — |
| 1987 LIMA | 20,106,000 | — | — | — | 2.50 | — |
| 1988 LIMA | 34,084,000 | — | — | — | 2.50 | — |

**100 INTIS** KM# 298 **Weight:** 11.1100 g. **Composition:** 0.9250 Silver .3271 oz. ASW **Subject:** 150th Anniversary - Birth of Marshal Caceres **Note:** Mint mark in monogram.

| Date | Mintage | F | VF | XF | Unc | BU |
|---|---|---|---|---|---|---|
| ND(1986) LIMA | 10,000 | — | — | — | 17.50 | — |

**200 INTIS** KM# 299 **Weight:** 22.0400 g. **Composition:** 0.9250 Silver .6543 oz. ASW **Subject:** 150th Anniversary - Birth of Marshal Caceres **Note:** Mint mark in monogram.

| Date | Mintage | F | VF | XF | Unc | BU |
|---|---|---|---|---|---|---|
| ND(1986) LIMA | — | — | — | — | 32.50 | — |

## REFORM COINAGE

1/M Intis = 1 Nuevo Sol; 100 (New) Centimos = 1 Nuevo Sol

**CENTIMO** KM# 303 **Composition:** Brass **Note:** Mint mark in monogram; Varieties exist.

| Date | Mintage | F | VF | XF | Unc | BU |
|---|---|---|---|---|---|---|
| 1991 LIMA Chavez | — | — | — | — | 0.35 | — |
| 1992 LIMA Chavez | — | — | — | — | 0.45 | — |
| 1993 LIMA | — | — | — | — | 0.35 | — |

**5 CENTIMOS** KM# 304 **Composition:** Brass **Note:** Mint mark in monogram; Varieties exist.

| Date | Mintage | F | VF | XF | Unc | BU |
|---|---|---|---|---|---|---|
| 1991 LIMA Chavez | — | — | — | — | 0.45 | — |
| 1992 LIMA Chavez | — | — | — | — | 0.50 | — |
| 1993 LIMA | — | — | — | — | 0.45 | — |
| 1993 LIMA Chavez | — | — | — | — | 0.45 | — |
| 1994 LIMA | — | — | — | — | 0.45 | — |
| 1996 LIMA | — | — | — | — | 0.45 | — |

**10 CENTIMOS** KM# 305 **Composition:** Brass **Note:** Mint mark in monogram; Varieties exist.

| Date | Mintage | F | VF | XF | Unc | BU |
|---|---|---|---|---|---|---|
| 1991 LIMA | — | — | — | — | 0.65 | — |
| 1992 LIMA | — | — | — | — | 0.70 | — |
| 1993 LIMA | — | — | — | — | 0.65 | — |
| 1993 LIMA Chavez | — | — | — | — | 0.65 | — |
| 1994 LIMA | — | — | — | — | 0.65 | — |
| 1995 LIMA | — | — | — | — | 0.65 | — |
| 1997 LIMA | — | — | — | — | 0.65 | — |

**20 CENTIMOS** KM# 306 **Composition:** Brass **Note:** Mint mark in monogram.

| Date | Mintage | F | VF | XF | Unc | BU |
|---|---|---|---|---|---|---|
| 1991 LIMA Chavez | — | — | — | — | 0.85 | — |
| 1992 LIMA | — | — | — | — | 0.85 | — |
| 1993 LIMA | — | — | — | — | 0.85 | — |
| 1994 LIMA | — | — | — | — | 0.85 | — |

**50 CENTIMOS** KM# 307 **Composition:** Copper-Nickel **Note:** Mint mark in monogram; Varieties exist.

| Date | Mintage | F | VF | XF | Unc | BU |
|---|---|---|---|---|---|---|
| 1991 LIMA | — | — | — | — | 1.50 | — |
| 1992 LIMA | — | — | — | — | 1.75 | — |
| 1993 LIMA | — | — | — | — | 1.50 | — |
| 1994 LIMA | — | — | — | — | 1.50 | — |

**NUEVO SOL** KM# 302 **Weight:** 27.0000 g. **Composition:** 0.9250 Silver .8029 oz. ASW **Subject:** Ibero - American Series

| Date | Mintage | F | VF | XF | Unc | BU |
|---|---|---|---|---|---|---|
| 1991 | 60,000 | Value: 45.00 | | | | |

**NUEVO SOL** KM# 308.1 **Composition:** Copper-Nickel **Note:** Mint mark in monogram.

| Date | Mintage | F | VF | XF | Unc | BU |
|---|---|---|---|---|---|---|
| 1991 LIMA | — | — | — | — | 5.00 | — |
| 1992 LIMA | — | — | — | — | 5.00 | — |
| 1993 LIMA | — | — | — | — | 5.00 | — |
| 1994 LIMA | — | — | — | — | 4.00 | — |
| 1995 LIMA | — | — | — | — | 4.00 | — |

**NUEVO SOL KM# 308.2 Composition:** Copper Nickel **Reverse:** With F. DIAZ below wreath **Note:** Mint mark in monogram.

| Date | Mintage | F | VF | XF | Unc | BU |
|---|---|---|---|---|---|---|
| 1991 LIMA | — | — | — | — | — | — |

**NUEVO SOL KM# 311 Weight:** 33.6250 g. **Composition:** 0.9170 Gold 1.0000 oz. AGW **Subject:** Pre-Inca Moche Cultural Artifacts **Reverse:** With F. DIAZ below wreath **Note:** Mint mark in monogram.

| Date | Mintage | F | VF | XF | Unc | BU |
|---|---|---|---|---|---|---|
| 1994 LIMA | 3,300 | — | — | — | — | — |
| 1994 LIMA Proof | 2,000 | Value: 47.50 | | | | |

**NUEVO SOL KM# 312 Weight:** 17.0250 g. **Composition:** 0.9170 Gold .5000 oz. AGW **Note:** Similar to KM#311. Mint mark in monogram.

| Date | Mintage | F | VF | XF | Unc | BU |
|---|---|---|---|---|---|---|
| 1994 LIMA | 899 | — | — | — | — | — |
| 1994 LIMA Proof | 100 | Value: 350 | | | | |

**NUEVO SOL KM# 314 Weight:** 20.0000 g. **Composition:** 0.9990 Silver .6430 oz. ASW **Subject:** Enviromental Protection - 2 Young Vicunas **Note:** Mint mark in monogram.

| Date | Mintage | F | VF | XF | Unc | BU |
|---|---|---|---|---|---|---|
| 1994 LIMA Proof | 30,000 | Value: 45.00 | | | | |

**NUEVO SOL KM# 317 Weight:** 27.0000 g. **Composition:** 0.9250 Silver .8030 oz. ASW **Subject:** Enviromental Protection **Reverse:** Vicuna, yellow-tailed wooly monkey and American crocodile

| Date | Mintage | F | VF | XF | Unc | BU |
|---|---|---|---|---|---|---|
| 1994 Proof | 20,000 | Value: 47.50 | | | | |

**NUEVO SOL KM# 318 Weight:** 33.6250 g. **Composition:** 0.9250 Silver 1.000 oz. ASW **Subject:** Centennial of Victor Raul Haya de la Torre

| Date | Mintage | F | VF | XF | Unc | BU |
|---|---|---|---|---|---|---|
| 1995 | 883 | — | — | — | 75.00 | — |

**NUEVO SOL KM# 319 Weight:** 33.6250 g. **Composition:** 0.9250 Silver 1.000 oz. ASW **Subject:** National Mineral and Petroleum Society Centennial **Reverse:** Miner, oil derrick and cart

| Date | Mintage | F | VF | XF | Unc | BU |
|---|---|---|---|---|---|---|
| 1996 | — | — | — | — | 40.00 | — |

**NUEVO SOL KM# 323 Weight:** 33.4700 g. **Composition:** 0.9250 Silver .9954 oz. ASW **Subject:** Centennial of Chorrillos Military School **Obverse:** National arms. **Reverse:** Monument and building. **Edge:** Reeded. **Size:** 37.1 mm.

| Date | Mintage | F | VF | XF | Unc | BU |
|---|---|---|---|---|---|---|
| 1998 Proof | — | Value: 45.00 | | | | |

**NUEVO SOL KM# 322 Weight:** 33.6250 g. **Composition:** 0.9250 Silver 1.000 oz. ASW **Subject:** Centennial of Japanese Immigration **Obverse:** National arms **Reverse:** Radiant sun above maps

| Date | Mintage | F | VF | XF | Unc | BU |
|---|---|---|---|---|---|---|
| 1999 Proof | — | Value: 45.00 | | | | |

**20 NUEVO SOLES KM# 309 Weight:** 33.6250 g. **Composition:** 0.9250 Silver 1.000 oz. ASW **Subject:** Rio De Janeiro Protocal

| Date | Mintage | F | VF | XF | Unc | BU |
|---|---|---|---|---|---|---|
| 1992 | 50,000 | — | — | — | 22.50 | — |

**20 NUEVO SOLES KM# 315 Weight:** 33.6250 g. **Composition:** 0.9250 Silver 1.000 oz. ASW **Subject:** Rio De Janeiro Protocal **Reverse:** Cesar Vallejo

| Date | Mintage | F | VF | XF | Unc | BU |
|---|---|---|---|---|---|---|
| 1992 Proof | — | Value: 22.50 | | | | |

**50 NUEVOS SOLES** KM# 320 **Weight:** 33.6250 g. **Composition:** 0.9250 Silver 1.000 oz. ASW **Subject:** Peru-Japan Commercial Exchange **Obverse:** Peruvian arms **Reverse:** Stylized bird design

| Date | Mintage | F | VF | XF | Unc | BU |
|---|---|---|---|---|---|---|
| 1993 | — | — | — | — | 40.00 | — |

## TRADE COINAGE

**1/5 LIBRA (Pound)** KM# 210 **Weight:** 1.5976 g. **Composition:** 0.9170 Gold .0471 oz. AGW

| Date | Mintage | F | VF | XF | Unc | BU |
|---|---|---|---|---|---|---|
| 1906 GOZF | 106,000 | — | BV | 25.00 | 35.00 | — |
| 1907 GOZF | 31,000 | — | BV | 25.00 | 35.00 | — |
| 1907 GOZG | — | — | BV | 25.00 | 35.00 | — |
| 1909 GOZG | — | — | BV | 25.00 | 35.00 | — |
| 1910 GOZG | — | — | BV | 25.00 | 35.00 | — |
| 1911 GOZF | 62,000 | — | BV | 25.00 | 35.00 | — |
| 1912 GOZG | — | — | BV | 25.00 | 35.00 | — |
| 1912 POZG | — | — | BV | 25.00 | 35.00 | — |
| 1913 POZG | 60,000 | — | BV | 25.00 | 35.00 | — |
| 1914 POZG | 25,000 | — | BV | 25.00 | 35.00 | — |
| 1914 PBLG Reported, not confirmed | Inc. above | — | — | — | — | — |
| 1915 | 10,000 | — | BV | 25.00 | 35.00 | — |
| 1916 Reported, not confirmed | 13,000 | — | — | — | — | — |
| 1917 | 3,896 | — | BV | 25.00 | 35.00 | — |
| 1918 | 16,000 | — | BV | 25.00 | 35.00 | — |
| 1919 | 10,000 | — | BV | 25.00 | 35.00 | — |
| 1920 | 72,000 | — | BV | 25.00 | 35.00 | — |
| 1922 | 8,110 | — | BV | 25.00 | 35.00 | — |
| 1923 | 27,000 | — | BV | 25.00 | 35.00 | — |
| 1924 | — | — | BV | 25.00 | 35.00 | — |
| 1925 | 20,000 | — | BV | 25.00 | 35.00 | — |
| 1926 | 11,000 | — | BV | 25.00 | 35.00 | — |
| 1927 | 14,000 | — | BV | 25.00 | 35.00 | — |
| 1928 | 9,322 | — | BV | 25.00 | 35.00 | — |
| 1929 | 8,971 | — | BV | 25.00 | 35.00 | — |
| 1930 | 9,991 | — | BV | 35.00 | 50.00 | — |
| 1953 BBR | 9,821 | — | — | — | 40.00 | — |
| 1955 ZBR | 10,000 | — | — | — | 40.00 | — |
| 1958 ZBR | 5,098 | — | — | — | 32.50 | — |
| 1959 ZBR | 6,308 | — | — | — | 32.50 | — |
| 1960 ZBR | 6,083 | — | — | — | 32.50 | — |
| 1961 ZBR | 12,000 | — | — | — | 32.50 | — |
| 1962 ZBR | 5,431 | — | — | — | 32.50 | — |
| 1963 ZBR | 11,000 | — | — | — | 32.50 | — |
| 1964 ZBR | 25,000 | — | — | — | 32.50 | — |
| 1965 ZBR | 19,000 | — | — | — | 32.50 | — |
| 1966 ZBR | 60,000 | — | — | — | 32.50 | — |
| 1967 BBR | 9,914 | — | — | — | 32.50 | — |
| 1968 BBB | 4,781 | — | — | — | 32.50 | — |
| 1969 BBB | 15,000 | — | — | — | 32.50 | — |

**1/2 LIBRA (Pound)** KM# 209 **Weight:** 3.9940 g. **Composition:** 0.9170 Gold .1177 oz. AGW

| Date | Mintage | F | VF | XF | Unc | BU |
|---|---|---|---|---|---|---|
| 1902 ROZF | 7,800 | — | BV | 50.00 | 75.00 | — |
| 1903 ROZF | 7,245 | — | BV | 50.00 | 75.00 | — |
| 1904 ROZF | 8,360 | — | BV | 50.00 | 75.00 | — |
| 1905 ROZF | 8,010 | — | BV | 50.00 | 75.00 | — |
| 1905 GOZF | Inc. above | — | BV | 50.00 | 75.00 | — |
| 1906 GOZF | 9,176 | — | BV | 50.00 | 75.00 | — |
| 1907 GOZG | — | — | BV | 50.00 | 75.00 | — |
| 1908 GOZG | 8,180 | — | BV | 50.00 | 75.00 | — |
| 1953 BBR | 9,210 | — | BV | 50.00 | 75.00 | — |
| 1955 ZBR | 14,000 | — | BV | 50.00 | 70.00 | — |
| 1961 ZBR | 752 | — | — | BV | 100 | — |
| 1962 ZBR | 4,286 | — | — | BV | 75.00 | — |
| 1963 ZBR | 908 | — | — | BV | 100 | — |
| 1964 ZBR | 10,000 | — | — | BV | 65.00 | — |
| 1965 ZBR | 5,490 | — | — | BV | 75.00 | — |
| 1966 ZBR | 44,000 | — | — | BV | 65.00 | — |
| 1967 BBR | — | — | — | BV | 65.00 | — |
| 1968 BBB | Inc. above | — | — | BV | 65.00 | — |
| 1969 BBB | 4,400 | — | — | BV | 75.00 | — |

**LIBRA (Pound)** KM# 207 **Weight:** 7.9881 g. **Composition:** 0.9170 Gold .2354 oz. AGW

| Date | Mintage | F | VF | XF | Unc | BU |
|---|---|---|---|---|---|---|
| 1898 ROZF | — | — | BV | 100 | 165 | — |
| 1899 ROZF | — | — | BV | 100 | 165 | — |
| 1900 ROZF | 64,000 | — | BV | 100 | 15.00 | — |
| 1901 ROZF | 81,000 | — | BV | 100 | 145 | — |
| 1902 ROZF | 89,000 | — | BV | 100 | 145 | — |
| 1903 ROZF | 100,000 | — | BV | 100 | 145 | — |
| 1904 ROZF | 33,000 | — | BV | 100 | 145 | — |
| 1905 ROZF | 141,000 | — | BV | 100 | 160 | — |
| 1905 GOZF | — | — | BV | 100 | 135 | — |
| 1906 GOZF | 201,000 | — | BV | 100 | 135 | — |
| 1907 GOZG | Inc. above | — | BV | 100 | 135 | — |
| 1908 GOZG | 36,000 | — | BV | 100 | 160 | — |
| 1909 GOZG | 52,000 | — | BV | 100 | 160 | — |
| 1910 GOZG | 47,000 | — | BV | 100 | 160 | — |
| 1911 GOZG | 42,000 | — | BV | 100 | 160 | — |
| 1912 GOZG | 54,000 | — | BV | 100 | 160 | — |
| 1912 POZG | Inc. above | — | BV | 100 | 175 | — |
| 1913 POZG | — | — | BV | 100 | 160 | — |
| 1914 POZG | — | — | BV | 100 | 175 | — |
| 1914 PBLG | 119,000 | — | BV | 100 | 160 | — |
| 1915 PVG | 91,000 | — | BV | 100 | 170 | — |
| 1915 PMGG | Inc. above | — | BV | 115 | 200 | — |
| 1915 | Inc. above | — | BV | 100 | 150 | — |
| 1916 | 582,000 | — | BV | 100 | 135 | — |
| 1917 | 1,928,000 | — | BV | 100 | 135 | — |
| 1918 | 600,000 | — | BV | 100 | 135 | — |
| 1919 | Inc. above | — | BV | 100 | 145 | — |
| 1920 | 152,000 | — | BV | 100 | 160 | — |
| 1921 | Inc. above | — | BV | 100 | 165 | — |
| 1922 | 13,000 | — | BV | 110 | 175 | — |
| 1923 | 15,000 | — | BV | 110 | 175 | — |
| 1924 | 8,113 | — | BV | 110 | 175 | — |
| 1925 | 9,068 | — | BV | 100 | 165 | — |
| 1926 | 4,596 | — | BV | 100 | 160 | — |
| 1927 | 8,360 | — | BV | 100 | 160 | — |
| 1928 | 2,184 | — | BV | 100 | 160 | — |
| 1929 | 3,119 | — | BV | 100 | 160 | — |
| 1930 | 1,050 | — | BV | 100 | 145 | — |
| 1959 ZBR | 605 | — | BV | 120 | 240 | — |
| 1961 ZBR | 402 | — | BV | 120 | 240 | — |
| 1962 ZBR | 6,203 | — | BV | 110 | 165 | — |
| 1963 ZBR | 302 | — | BV | 120 | 250 | — |
| 1964 ZBR | 13,000 | — | BV | 110 | 165 | — |
| 1965 ZBR | 9,917 | — | BV | 110 | 165 | — |
| 1966 ZBR | 39,000 | — | BV | 110 | 165 | — |
| 1967 BBR | 2,002 | — | BV | 110 | 165 | — |
| 1968 BBR | 7,307 | — | BV | 115 | 175 | — |
| 1969 BBR | 7,307 | — | BV | 115 | 175 | — |

## TOKEN COINAGE

**50 CENTAVOS** KM# Tn3 **Composition:** Silver **Subject:** National Defense

| Date | Mintage | F | VF | XF | Unc | BU |
|---|---|---|---|---|---|---|
| 1932 | — | 7.00 | 12.50 | 20.00 | 32.50 | — |

**SOL** KM# Tn1 **Composition:** 0.9000 Silver **Subject:** efense

| Date | Mintage | F | VF | XF | Unc | BU |
|---|---|---|---|---|---|---|
| 1910 | — | 8.50 | 12.50 | 18.50 | 30.00 | — |

**SOL** KM# Tn4 **Composition:** Silver **Subject:** National Defense

| Date | Mintage | F | VF | XF | Unc | BU |
|---|---|---|---|---|---|---|
| 1932 | — | 5.00 | 11.50 | 16.50 | 28.50 | — |

**5 SOLES** KM# Tn2 **Weight:** 2.3404 g. **Composition:** 0.9000 Gold .0677 oz. AGW

| Date | Mintage | F | VF | XF | Unc | BU |
|---|---|---|---|---|---|---|
| 1910 | — | 60.00 | 80.00 | 110 | 150 | — |

**5 SOLES** KM# Tn5 **Composition:** Silver **Subject:** National Defense

| Date | Mintage | F | VF | XF | Unc | BU |
|---|---|---|---|---|---|---|
| 1932 | — | 12.00 | 17.50 | 28.50 | 42.50 | — |

**10 SOLES** KM# Tn6 **Composition:** Gold Plated Silver **Subject:** National Defense

| Date | Mintage | F | VF | XF | Unc | BU |
|---|---|---|---|---|---|---|
| 1932 | — | 15.00 | 20.00 | 38.50 | 55.00 | — |

## TRIAL STRIKES

| KM# | Date | Mintage | Identification | Mkt Val |
|---|---|---|---|---|
| TS4 | 1935 | — | Sol. KM218.2. Alloy percentage, N. 3/25 PLT/ 0 NKL1- ZNC/55 CRE. | — |
| TS5 | 1935 | — | Sol. KM218.2. Alloy percentage, N. 4/20, PLT/15 NKL/10 ZNC/55 CRE. | — |

## PATTERNS

including off metal strikes

| KM# | Date | Mintage | Identification | Mkt Val |
|---|---|---|---|---|
| PnF26 | 1930 | 3 | 50 Soles. Native inscription. | — |
| Pn26 | 1932 | — | Sol. | — |
| PnG26 | 1932 | — | 50 Centavos. | — |
| Pn27 | 1932 | — | 5 Soles. | — |
| PnA28 | 1932 | — | 10 Soles. | — |
| Pn28 | 1947 | — | 100 Soles. Gilt Bronze. | — |
| Pn29 | 1948 | — | Sol. Aluminum. | — |
| PnA30 | 1949 | — | Centavo. Zinc. KM211. | 75.00 |
| PnB30 | 1949 | — | 2 Centavos. Zinc. KM212.2. | 50.00 |
| Pn30 | 1952 | — | 1 Sol De Oro. Brass. | — |
| Pn31 | 1958 | — | 50 Soles. Silver. With PRUEBA. | 900 |
| PnA31 | 1958 | — | 20 Centavos. Copper Nickel. | 50.00 |
| Pn32 | 1964 | — | 50 Soles. Silver. With PRUEBA. | 900 |
| Pn33 | 1965 | — | 50 Soles. Silver. With PRUEBA. | 900 |
| PnA33 | 1965 | — | 5 Centavos. Copper-Nickel-Zinc. KM290 | 900 |
| Pn34 | 1966 | 200 | Sol. Silver. With PAREJA. With PAREJA. | — |
| Pn35 | 1967 | — | 1/2 Sol. With PAREJA. With PAREJA. | — |
| Pn36 | 1967 | 7 | 50 Soles. Silver. | — |
| Pn37 | 1988 | — | Inti. Brass. KM296. | — |
| Pn38 | 198x | — | 5 Intis. Copper-Nickel-Zinc. KM300. | — |
| Pn39 | 1988 | — | 10 Intis. Brass. | — |

# PHILIPPINES

The Republic of the Philippines, an archipelago in the western Pacific 500 miles (805 km.) from the southeast coast of Asia, has an area of 115,830 sq. mi. (300,000 sq. km.) and a population of *64.9 million. Capital: Manila. The economy of the 7,000-island group is based on agriculture, forestry and fishing. Timber, coconut products, sugar and hemp are exported.

Migration to the Philippines began about 30,000 years ago when land bridges connected the islands with Borneo and Sumatra. Ferdinand Magellan claimed the islands for Spain in 1521. The first permanent settlement was established by Miguel de Legazpi at Cebu April, 1565. Manila was established in 1572. A British expedition captured Manila and occupied the Spanish colony in October 1762, but returned it to Spain by the treaty of Paris, 1763. Spain held the Philippines despite growing Filipino nationalism until 1898 when they were ceded to the United States at the end of the Spanish-American War. The Philippines became a self-governing commonwealth under the United States in 1935, and attained independence as the Republic of the Philippines on July 4, 1946.

**MINT MARKS**

(b) Brussels, privy marks only
BSP - Bangko Sentral Pilipinas
D - Denver, 1944-1945
(Lt) - Llantrisant
M, MA - Manila
PM - Pobjoy Mint
S - San Francisco, 1903-1947
SGV - Madrid
(Sh) - Sherritt
(US) - United States
FM - Franklin Mint, U.S.A.*
(VDM) - Vereinigte Deutsche Metall Werks; Altona, Germany
Star - Manila (Spanish) = Manila

***NOTE:** From 1975-1977 the Franklin Mint produced coinage in up to 3 different qualities. Beginning in 1978only (U) and (P) were struck. Qualities of issue are designated in ( ) after each date and are defined as follows:

**(M) MATTE** - Normal circulation strike or a dull finish produced by sandblasting special uncirculated (polish-finish) or proof quality dies.

**(U) SPECIAL UNCIRCULATED** - Polished or proof-like in appearance without any frosted features.

**(P) PROOF** - The highest quality obtainable having mirror-like fields and frosted features.

**MONETARY SYSTEM**

8 Octavos = 4 Quartos = 1 Real
8 Reales = 1 Peso

## UNITED STATES ADMINISTRATION

### 100 Centavos = 1 Peso

### DECIMAL COINAGE

**1/2 CENTAVO** **KM# 162** **Composition:** Bronze

| Date | Mintage | F | VF | XF | Unc | BU |
|---|---|---|---|---|---|---|
| 1903 | 12,084,000 | 0.50 | 1.00 | 2.00 | 15.00 | — |
| 1903 Proof | 2,558 | Value: 45.00 | | | | |
| 1904 | 5,654,000 | 0.50 | 1.25 | 2.50 | 20.00 | — |
| 1904 Proof | 1,355 | Value: 50.00 | | | | |
| 1905 Proof | 471 | Value: 120 | | | | |
| 1906 Proof | 500 | Value: 100 | | | | |
| 1908 Proof | 500 | Value: 100 | | | | |

**CENTAVO** **KM# 163** **Composition:** Bronze

| Date | Mintage | F | VF | XF | Unc | BU |
|---|---|---|---|---|---|---|
| 1903 | 10,790,000 | 0.50 | 1.00 | 2.50 | 20.00 | — |
| 1903 Proof | 2,558 | Value: 45.00 | | | | |
| 1904 | 17,040,000 | 0.50 | 1.00 | 2.50 | 18.00 | — |
| 1904 Proof | 1,355 | Value: 50.00 | | | | |
| 1905 | 10,000,000 | 0.50 | 1.00 | 3.50 | 25.00 | — |
| 1905 Proof | 471 | Value: 125 | | | | |
| 1906 Proof | 500 | Value: 100 | | | | |
| 1908 Proof | 500 | Value: 100 | | | | |
| 1908S | 2,187,000 | 2.50 | 5.50 | 10.00 | 60.00 | — |
| 1909S | 1,738,000 | 6.00 | 14.00 | 22.00 | 100 | — |
| 1910S | 2,700,000 | 2.00 | 4.50 | 8.50 | 45.00 | — |
| 1911S | 4,803,000 | 1.00 | 3.00 | 7.00 | 40.00 | — |
| 1912S | 3,000,000 | 2.50 | 5.50 | 10.00 | 65.00 | — |
| 1913S | 5,000,000 | 1.00 | 2.50 | 6.00 | 55.00 | — |
| 1914S | 5,000,000 | 1.00 | 2.50 | 6.00 | 40.00 | — |
| 1914S Large S | Inc. above | — | — | — | — | — |
| 1915S | 2,500,000 | 15.00 | 40.00 | 90.00 | 425 | — |
| 1916S | 4,330,000 | 5.00 | 10.00 | 25.00 | 125 | — |
| 1917/6S | 7,070,000 | 12.50 | 25.00 | 50.00 | 175 | — |
| 1917S | Inc. above | 1.50 | 4.00 | 10.00 | 45.00 | — |
| 1918S | 11,660,000 | 1.50 | 3.50 | 5.00 | 45.00 | — |
| 1918S Large S | Inc. above | 90.00 | 145 | 225 | 750 | — |
| 1919S | 4,540,000 | 0.75 | 2.00 | 6.00 | 45.00 | — |
| 1920S | 2,500,000 | 6.00 | 12.00 | 18.00 | 125 | — |
| 1920 | 3,552,000 | 1.00 | 2.00 | 10.00 | 45.00 | — |
| 1921 | 7,283,000 | 1.00 | 2.00 | 7.00 | 45.00 | — |
| 1922 | 3,519,000 | 0.50 | 1.50 | 6.00 | 45.00 | — |
| 1925M | 9,332,000 | 0.50 | 1.50 | 4.00 | 35.00 | — |
| 1926M | 9,000,000 | 0.50 | 1.50 | 4.00 | 40.00 | — |
| 1927M | 9,270,000 | 0.25 | 1.00 | 3.50 | 35.00 | — |
| 1928M | 9,150,000 | 0.25 | 1.00 | 4.00 | 35.00 | — |
| 1929M | 5,657,000 | 1.00 | 3.00 | 7.50 | 50.00 | — |
| 1930M | 5,577,000 | 0.25 | 1.50 | 3.00 | 25.00 | — |
| 1931M | 5,659,000 | 0.25 | 1.50 | 4.00 | 30.00 | — |
| 1932M | 4,000,000 | 0.75 | 2.50 | 6.00 | 40.00 | — |
| 1933M | 8,393,000 | 0.25 | 1.75 | 3.00 | 25.00 | — |
| 1934M | 3,179,000 | 0.50 | 2.00 | 4.00 | 30.00 | — |
| 1936M | 17,455,000 | 0.25 | 1.00 | 3.00 | 30.00 | — |

**5 CENTAVOS** **KM# 164** **Composition:** Copper-Nickel

| Date | Mintage | F | VF | XF | Unc | BU |
|---|---|---|---|---|---|---|
| 1903 | 8,910,000 | 0.50 | 1.00 | 3.00 | 22.00 | — |
| 1903 Proof | 2,558 | Value: 55.00 | | | | |
| 1904 | 1,075,000 | 0.75 | 1.75 | 4.00 | 27.00 | — |
| 1904 Proof | 1,355 | Value: 65.00 | | | | |
| 1905 Proof | 471 | Value: 135 | | | | |
| 1906 Proof | 500 | Value: 120 | | | | |
| 1908 Proof | 500 | Value: 120 | | | | |
| 1916S | 300,000 | 25.00 | 60.00 | 85.00 | 500 | — |
| 1917S | 2,300,000 | 2.00 | 4.00 | 12.00 | 110 | — |
| 1918S | 2,780,000 | 1.50 | 3.00 | 10.00 | 100 | — |
| 1919S | 1,220,000 | 2.00 | 6.00 | 12.00 | 130 | — |
| 1920 | 1,421,000 | 2.50 | 7.50 | 15.00 | 150 | — |
| 1921 | 2,132,000 | 2.50 | 6.00 | 15.00 | 120 | — |
| 1925M | 1,000,000 | 5.00 | 20.00 | 30.00 | 175 | — |
| 1926M | 1,200,000 | 3.00 | 10.00 | 20.00 | 90.00 | — |
| 1927M | 1,000,000 | 2.00 | 5.00 | 12.00 | 85.00 | — |
| 1928M | 1,000,000 | 3.00 | 8.00 | 15.00 | 85.00 | — |

**5 CENTAVOS** **KM# 173** **Composition:** Copper-Nickel **Obverse:** KM#164 **Reverse:** 20 Centavos, KM#170 **Note:** Mule.

| Date | Mintage | F | VF | XF | Unc | BU |
|---|---|---|---|---|---|---|
| 1918S | — | 100 | 200 | 500 | 2,150 | — |

**5 CENTAVOS** **KM# 175** **Composition:** Copper-Nickel

| Date | Mintage | F | VF | XF | Unc | BU |
|---|---|---|---|---|---|---|
| 1930M | 2,905,000 | 1.00 | 2.00 | 5.00 | 60.00 | — |
| 1931M | 3,477,000 | 1.00 | 2.00 | 6.00 | 60.00 | — |
| 1932M | 3,956,000 | 1.00 | 2.00 | 5.00 | 50.00 | — |
| 1934M | 2,154,000 | 1.00 | 3.00 | 8.00 | 90.00 | — |
| 1935M | 2,754,000 | 1.00 | 2.00 | 6.00 | 75.00 | — |

**10 CENTAVOS** **KM# 165** **Weight:** 2.6924 g. **Composition:** 0.9000 Silver .0779 oz. ASW

| Date | Mintage | F | VF | XF | Unc | BU |
|---|---|---|---|---|---|---|
| 1903 | 5,103,000 | 1.50 | 2.50 | 5.00 | 35.00 | — |
| 1903 Proof | 2,558 | Value: 60.00 | | | | |
| 1903S | 1,200,000 | 7.50 | 15.00 | 30.00 | 350 | — |
| 1904 | 11,000 | 10.00 | 18.00 | 30.00 | 100 | — |
| 1904 Proof | 1,355 | Value: 95.00 | | | | |
| 1904S | 5,040,000 | 1.50 | 2.50 | 4.00 | 45.00 | — |
| 1905 Proof | 471 | Value: 145 | | | | |
| 1906 Proof | 500 | Value: 125 | | | | |

**10 CENTAVOS** **KM# 169** **Weight:** 2.0000 g. **Composition:** 0.7500 Silver .0482 oz. ASW

| Date | Mintage | F | VF | XF | Unc | BU |
|---|---|---|---|---|---|---|
| 1907 | 1,501,000 | 1.50 | 3.00 | 5.00 | 45.00 | — |
| 1907S | 4,930,000 | 1.00 | 2.50 | 3.50 | 40.00 | — |
| 1908 Proof | 500 | Value: 125 | | | | |
| 1908S | 3,364,000 | 1.00 | 2.00 | 4.00 | 45.00 | — |
| 1909S | 312,000 | 15.00 | 25.00 | 50.00 | 350 | — |
| 1910S | — | — | — | — | — | — |

**Note:** Unknown in any collection. Counterfeits of the 1910S are commonly encountered.

| Date | Mintage | F | VF | XF | Unc | BU |
|---|---|---|---|---|---|---|
| 1911S | 1,101,000 | 1.50 | 4.00 | 8.00 | 60.00 | — |
| 1912S | 1,010,000 | 2.00 | 5.00 | 9.00 | 65.00 | — |
| 1913S | 1,361,000 | 1.50 | 4.00 | 9.00 | 65.00 | — |
| 1914S | 1,180,000 | 3.00 | 6.50 | 12.50 | 150 | — |
| 1915S | 450,000 | 10.00 | 16.00 | 35.00 | 275 | — |
| 1917S | 5,991,000 | 1.00 | 2.00 | 3.00 | 30.00 | — |
| 1918S | 8,420,000 | 0.75 | 1.75 | 2.50 | 25.00 | — |
| 1919S | 1,630,000 | 1.00 | 2.00 | 3.50 | 40.00 | — |
| 1920 | 520,000 | 4.00 | 6.00 | 12.00 | 75.00 | — |
| 1921 | 3,863,000 | 0.75 | 1.50 | 2.50 | 25.00 | — |
| 1929M | 1,000,000 | 0.75 | 1.50 | 2.50 | 20.00 | — |
| 1935M | 1,280,000 | 0.75 | 1.50 | 2.50 | 20.00 | — |

**20 CENTAVOS** **KM# 166** **Weight:** 5.3849 g. **Composition:** 0.9000 Silver .1558 oz. ASW

| Date | Mintage | F | VF | XF | Unc | BU |
|---|---|---|---|---|---|---|
| 1903 | 5,353,000 | 2.50 | 3.50 | 6.00 | 40.00 | — |
| 1903 Proof | 2,558 | Value: 85.00 | | | | |
| 1903S | 150,000 | 12.50 | 25.00 | 60.00 | 325 | — |
| 1904 | 11,000 | 15.00 | 30.00 | 45.00 | 120 | — |
| 1904 Proof | 1,355 | Value: 100 | | | | |
| 1904S | 2,060,000 | 2.50 | 4.00 | 7.50 | 60.00 | — |
| 1905 Proof | 471 | Value: 200 | | | | |
| 1905S | 420,000 | 7.50 | 12.50 | 20.00 | 150 | — |
| 1906 Proof | 500 | Value: 175 | | | | |

**20 CENTAVOS** **KM# 170** **Weight:** 4.0000 g. **Composition:** 0.7500 Silver .0965 oz. ASW

| Date | Mintage | F | VF | XF | Unc | BU |
|---|---|---|---|---|---|---|
| 1907 | 1,251,000 | 2.00 | 4.00 | 10.00 | 85.00 | — |
| 1907S | 3,165,000 | 2.00 | 3.00 | 7.50 | 60.00 | — |
| 1908 Proof | 500 | Value: 175 | | | | |
| 1908S | 1,535,000 | 2.00 | 3.00 | 6.00 | 50.00 | — |
| 1909S | 450,000 | 8.00 | 15.00 | 50.00 | 350 | — |
| 1910S | 500,000 | 8.00 | 15.00 | 50.00 | 425 | — |
| 1911S | 505,000 | 6.00 | 12.00 | 30.00 | 300 | — |
| 1912S | 750,000 | 5.00 | 8.00 | 20.00 | 175 | — |
| 1913S/S | 949,000 | 12.50 | 22.50 | 40.00 | 225 | — |
| 1913S | Inc. above | 3.00 | 6.00 | 12.00 | 175 | — |
| 1914S | 795,000 | 2.50 | 4.00 | 15.00 | 100 | — |
| 1915S | 655,000 | 4.50 | 12.00 | 40.00 | 275 | — |
| 1916S | 1,435,000 | 3.00 | 6.00 | 15.00 | 100 | — |
| 1917S | 3,151,000 | 1.25 | 3.00 | 5.00 | 55.00 | — |
| 1918S | 5,560,000 | 1.00 | 2.50 | 4.00 | 50.00 | — |
| 1919S | 850,000 | 1.50 | 4.00 | 6.00 | 60.00 | — |
| 1920 | 1,046,000 | 1.50 | 4.00 | 10.00 | 110 | — |
| 1921 | 1,843,000 | 1.00 | 2.00 | 4.00 | 40.00 | — |
| 1929M | 1,970,000 | 1.00 | 2.00 | 4.00 | 30.00 | — |

**20 CENTAVOS** KM# 174 **Weight:** 4.0000 g. **Composition:** 0.7500 Silver .0965 oz. ASW **Obverse:** KM#170 **Reverse:** 5 Centavos, KM#164 **Note:** Mule.

| Date | Mintage | F | VF | XF | Unc | BU |
|---|---|---|---|---|---|---|
| 1928/7M | 100,000 | 3.00 | 10.00 | 35.00 | 350 | — |

**50 CENTAVOS** KM# 167 **Weight:** 13.4784 g. **Composition:** 0.9000 Silver .3900 oz. ASW

| Date | Mintage | F | VF | XF | Unc | BU |
|---|---|---|---|---|---|---|
| 1903 | 3,102,000 | 5.00 | 8.00 | 12.00 | 70.00 | — |
| 1903 Proof | 2,558 | Value: 135 | | | | |
| 1903S | — | — | — | 22,000 | — | — |
| 1904 | 11,000 | 25.00 | 32.00 | 45.00 | 125 | — |
| 1904 Proof | 1,355 | Value: 150 | | | | |
| 1904S | 2,160,000 | 5.00 | 10.00 | 17.50 | 150 | — |
| 1905 Proof | 471 | Value: 350 | | | | |
| 1905S | 852,000 | 8.00 | 15.00 | 35.00 | 250 | — |
| 1906 Proof | 500 | Value: 300 | | | | |

**50 CENTAVOS** KM# 171 **Weight:** 10.0000 g. **Composition:** 0.7500 Silver .2411 oz. ASW

| Date | Mintage | F | VF | XF | Unc | BU |
|---|---|---|---|---|---|---|
| 1907 | 1,201,000 | 4.00 | 9.00 | 20.00 | 90.00 | — |
| 1907S | 2,112,000 | 2.50 | 5.00 | 12.50 | 80.00 | — |
| 1908 Proof | 500 | Value: 300 | | | | |
| 1908S | 1,601,000 | 2.50 | 5.00 | 12.50 | 70.00 | — |
| 1909S | 528,000 | 5.00 | 10.00 | 30.00 | 225 | — |
| 1917S | 674,000 | 4.00 | 9.00 | 20.00 | 150 | — |
| 1918S | 2,202,000 | 3.00 | 5.00 | 8.00 | 65.00 | — |
| 1919S | 1,200,000 | 3.50 | 5.50 | 9.00 | 90.00 | — |
| 1920 | 420,000 | 3.00 | 5.00 | 8.00 | 35.00 | — |
| 1921 | 2,317,000 | 2.50 | 4.00 | 6.50 | 30.00 | — |

**PESO** KM# 168 **Weight:** 26.9568 g. **Composition:** 0.9000 Silver .7800 oz. ASW

| Date | Mintage | F | VF | XF | Unc | BU |
|---|---|---|---|---|---|---|
| 1903 | 2,791,000 | 12.00 | 16.00 | 35.00 | 190 | — |
| 1903 Proof | 2,558 | Value: 250 | | | | |
| 1903S | 11,361,000 | 9.00 | 14.00 | 25.00 | 130 | — |
| 1904 | 11,000 | 35.00 | 65.00 | 120 | 250 | — |
| 1904 Proof | 1,355 | Value: 300 | | | | |
| 1904S | 6,600,000 | 10.00 | 15.00 | 30.00 | 135 | — |
| 1905 Proof | 471 | Value: 850 | | | | |
| 1905S straight serif on 1 | — | 20.00 | 30.00 | 60.00 | 350 | — |
| 1905S curved serif on 1 | 6,056,000 | 12.00 | 20.00 | 40.00 | 250 | — |
| 1906 Proof | 500 | Value: 575 | | | | |
| 1906S | 201,000 | 700 | 1,200 | 2,500 | 10,500 | — |

**Note:** Counterfeits of the 1906S exist

**PESO** KM# 172 **Weight:** 20.0000 g. **Composition:** 0.8000 Silver .5144 oz. ASW

| Date | Mintage | F | VF | XF | Unc | BU |
|---|---|---|---|---|---|---|
| 1907S Proof | — | — | — | — | — | — |

**Note:** 2 pieces known.

| Date | Mintage | F | VF | XF | Unc | BU |
|---|---|---|---|---|---|---|
| 1907 | 10,276,000 | BV | 5.50 | 10.00 | 75.00 | — |
| 1908 Proof | 500 | Value: 575 | | | | |
| 1908S | 20,955,000 | BV | 5.50 | 10.00 | 70.00 | — |
| 1909S | 7,578,000 | BV | 5.50 | 12.00 | 80.00 | — |
| 1910S | 3,154,000 | BV | 7.50 | 20.00 | 150 | — |
| 1911S | 463,000 | 11.00 | 20.00 | 60.00 | 550 | — |
| 1912S | 680,000 | 11.00 | 20.00 | 60.00 | 650 | — |

# UNITED STATES ADMINISTRATION

## Commonwealth

## DECIMAL COINAGE

**CENTAVO** KM# 179 **Composition:** Bronze

| Date | Mintage | F | VF | XF | Unc | BU |
|---|---|---|---|---|---|---|
| 1937M | 15,790,000 | — | 1.00 | 2.00 | 12.00 | 17.00 |
| 1938M | 10,000,000 | — | 0.75 | 2.00 | 10.00 | 16.00 |
| 1939M | 6,500,000 | — | 1.00 | 2.00 | 15.00 | 20.00 |
| 1940M | 4,000,000 | — | 0.75 | 1.50 | 10.00 | 15.00 |
| 1941M | 5,000,000 | — | 1.00 | 2.00 | 15.00 | 25.00 |
| 1944S | 58,000,000 | — | 0.15 | 0.20 | 0.75 | 1.50 |

**5 CENTAVOS** KM# 180 **Composition:** Copper-Nickel

| Date | Mintage | F | VF | XF | Unc | BU |
|---|---|---|---|---|---|---|
| 1937M | 2,494,000 | — | 2.00 | 5.00 | 25.00 | 40.00 |
| 1938M | 4,000,000 | — | 1.25 | 2.50 | 12.00 | 20.00 |
| 1941M | 2,750,000 | — | 3.00 | 10.00 | 25.00 | 40.00 |

**5 CENTAVOS** KM# 180a **Composition:** Copper-Nickel-Zinc

| Date | Mintage | F | VF | XF | Unc | BU |
|---|---|---|---|---|---|---|
| 1944 | 21,198,000 | — | 0.15 | 0.50 | 1.25 | 2.00 |
| 1944S | 14,040,000 | — | 0.15 | 0.25 | 0.75 | 1.25 |
| 1945S | 72,796,000 | — | 0.15 | 0.20 | 0.50 | 1.00 |

**10 CENTAVOS** KM# 181 **Weight:** 2.0000 g. **Composition:** 0.7500 Silver .0482 oz. ASW

| Date | Mintage | F | VF | XF | Unc | BU |
|---|---|---|---|---|---|---|
| 1937M | 3,500,000 | — | 1.50 | 3.00 | 15.00 | 20.00 |
| 1938M | 3,750,000 | — | 0.75 | 2.00 | 10.00 | 15.00 |
| 1941M | 2,500,000 | — | 1.00 | 2.50 | 12.50 | 18.00 |
| 1944D | 31,592,000 | — | BV | 0.50 | 1.00 | 1.50 |
| 1945D | 137,208,000 | — | BV | 0.35 | 0.75 | 1.25 |

**Note:** 1937, 1938, and 1941 dated strikes have inverted Ws for Ms

**20 CENTAVOS** KM# 182 **Weight:** 4.0000 g. **Composition:** 0.7500 Silver .0965 oz. ASW

| Date | Mintage | F | VF | XF | Unc | BU |
|---|---|---|---|---|---|---|
| 1937M | 2,665,000 | — | 2.00 | 4.00 | 15.00 | 30.00 |
| 1938M | 3,000,000 | — | 1.25 | 2.50 | 6.00 | 10.00 |
| 1941M | 1,500,000 | — | 2.00 | 3.00 | 8.00 | 15.00 |
| 1944D | 28,596,000 | — | BV | 0.75 | 1.25 | 2.00 |
| 1944D/S | — | — | | 25.00 | 60.00 | 85.00 |
| 1945D | 82,804,000 | — | BV | 0.50 | 1.00 | 1.50 |

**50 CENTAVOS** KM# 176 **Weight:** 10.0000 g. **Composition:** 0.7500 Silver .2411 oz. ASW **Subject:** Establishment of the Commonwealth

| Date | Mintage | F | VF | XF | Unc | BU |
|---|---|---|---|---|---|---|
| 1936 | 20,000 | — | 25.00 | 45.00 | 65.00 | 85.00 |

**50 CENTAVOS** KM# 183 **Weight:** 10.0000 g. **Composition:** 0.7500 Silver .2411 oz. ASW

| Date | Mintage | F | VF | XF | Unc | BU |
|---|---|---|---|---|---|---|
| 1944S | 19,187,000 | — | BV | 1.50 | 3.50 | 4.50 |
| 1945S | 18,120,000 | — | BV | 1.50 | 3.50 | 4.50 |

**PESO** KM# 177 **Weight:** 20.0000 g. **Composition:** 0.9000 Silver .5787 oz. ASW **Subject:** Establishment of the Commonwealth **Obverse:** Busts of Presidents Roosevelt and Quezon facing left

| Date | Mintage | F | VF | XF | Unc | BU |
|---|---|---|---|---|---|---|
| 1936 | 10,000 | — | 50.00 | 65.00 | 125 | 150 |

**PESO** KM# 178 **Weight:** 20.0000 g. **Composition:** 0.9000 Silver .5787 oz. ASW **Subject:** Establishment of the Commonwealth **Obverse:** Busts of Governor General Murphy and President Quezon facing left **Reverse:** Similar to KM#177

| Date | Mintage | F | VF | XF | Unc | BU |
|---|---|---|---|---|---|---|
| 1936 | 10,000 | — | 50.00 | 65.00 | 125 | 150 |

# REPUBLIC

## DECIMAL COINAGE

**CENTAVO** **KM# 186** **Composition:** Bronze

| Date | Mintage | F | VF | XF | Unc | BU |
|---|---|---|---|---|---|---|
| 1958 | 20,000,000 | — | — | 0.10 | 0.25 | 0.50 |
| 1960 | 40,000,000 | — | — | 0.10 | 0.15 | 0.35 |
| 1962 | 30,000,000 | — | — | 0.10 | 0.15 | 0.35 |
| 1963 | 130,000,000 | — | — | 0.10 | 0.15 | 0.35 |

**5 CENTAVOS** **KM# 187** **Composition:** Brass

| Date | Mintage | F | VF | XF | Unc | BU |
|---|---|---|---|---|---|---|
| 1958 | 10,000,000 | — | — | 0.10 | 0.25 | 0.50 |
| 1959 | 10,000,000 | — | — | 0.10 | 0.20 | 0.50 |
| 1960 | 40,000,000 | — | — | 0.10 | 0.15 | 0.40 |
| 1962 | 40,000,000 | — | — | 0.10 | 0.15 | 0.40 |
| 1963 | 50,000,000 | — | — | 0.10 | 0.15 | 0.40 |
| 1964 | 100,000,000 | — | — | — | 0.10 | 0.40 |
| 1966 | 10,000,000 | — | — | 0.10 | 0.20 | 0.50 |

**10 CENTAVOS** **KM# 188** **Composition:** Nickel-Brass

| Date | Mintage | F | VF | XF | Unc | BU |
|---|---|---|---|---|---|---|
| 1958 | 10,000,000 | — | — | 0.15 | 0.25 | 0.50 |
| 1960 | 70,000,000 | — | — | 0.15 | 0.20 | 0.40 |
| 1962 | 50,000,000 | — | — | 0.15 | 0.20 | 0.40 |
| 1963 | 50,000,000 | — | — | 0.15 | 0.20 | 0.40 |
| 1964 | 100,000,000 | — | — | 0.10 | 0.20 | 0.40 |
| 1966 | 110,000,000 | — | — | 0.10 | 0.20 | 0.45 |

**25 CENTAVOS** **KM# 189.1** **Composition:** Nickel-Brass **Obverse:** Eight smoke rings from volcano

| Date | Mintage | F | VF | XF | Unc | BU |
|---|---|---|---|---|---|---|
| 1958 | 10,000,000 | — | — | 0.25 | 0.50 | 0.75 |
| 1960 | 10,000,000 | — | — | 0.30 | 0.50 | 0.75 |
| 1962 | 40,000,000 | — | — | 0.25 | 0.50 | 0.75 |
| 1964 | 49,800,000 | — | — | 0.20 | 0.35 | 0.75 |
| 1966 | 50,000,000 | — | 0.25 | 0.50 | 1.00 | 1.25 |

**25 CENTAVOS** **KM# 189.2** **Composition:** Nickel-Brass **Obverse:** Six smoke rings from volcano

| Date | Mintage | F | VF | XF | Unc | BU |
|---|---|---|---|---|---|---|
| 1966 | 40,000,000 | — | — | 0.20 | 0.40 | 0.75 |
| 1966 Matte finish | Inc. above | — | — | — | — | — |

**50 CENTAVOS** **KM# 184** **Weight:** 10.0000 g. **Composition:** 0.7500 Silver .2411 oz. ASW **Note:** General Douglas MacArthur

| Date | Mintage | F | VF | XF | Unc | BU |
|---|---|---|---|---|---|---|
| 1947S | 200,000 | — | BV | 2.50 | 6.00 | 7.00 |

**50 CENTAVOS** **KM# 190** **Composition:** Nickel-Brass

| Date | Mintage | F | VF | XF | Unc | BU |
|---|---|---|---|---|---|---|
| 1958 | 5,000,000 | — | 0.30 | 0.45 | 1.00 | 1.25 |
| 1964 | 25,000,000 | — | 0.20 | 0.30 | 0.60 | 1.00 |

**1/2 PESO** **KM# 191** **Weight:** 12.5000 g. **Composition:** 0.9000 Silver .3617 oz. ASW **Subject:** 100th Anniversary Birth of Dr. Jose Rizal

| Date | Mintage | F | VF | XF | Unc | BU |
|---|---|---|---|---|---|---|
| ND1961 | 100,000 | — | — | 3.00 | 4.00 | 5.00 |
| ND(1961) | 100,000 | — | — | 3.00 | 4.00 | 5.00 |

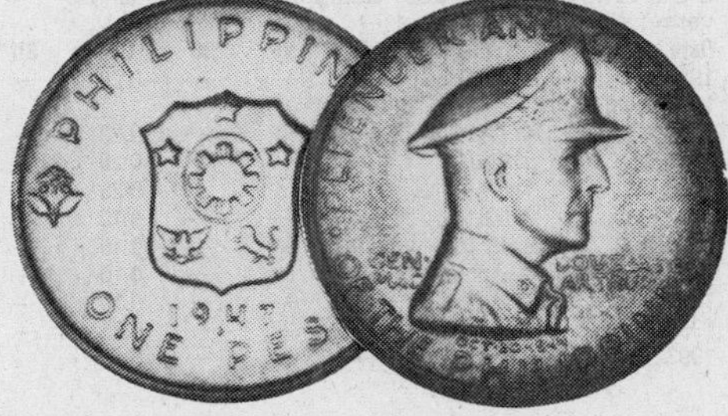


**PESO** **KM# 185** **Weight:** 20.0000 g. **Composition:** 0.9000 Silver .5787 oz. ASW **Obverse:** Bust of General Douglas MacArthur facing right

| Date | Mintage | F | VF | XF | Unc | BU |
|---|---|---|---|---|---|---|
| 1947S | 100,000 | — | BV | 6.00 | 12.50 | 16.50 |

**PESO** **KM# 192** **Weight:** 26.0000 g. **Composition:** 0.9000 Silver .7697 oz. ASW **Subject:** 100th Anniversary Birth of Dr. Jose Rizal

| Date | Mintage | F | VF | XF | Unc | BU |
|---|---|---|---|---|---|---|
| ND(1961) | 100,000 | — | — | 4.50 | 7.50 | 9.00 |

**PESO** **KM# 193** **Weight:** 26.0000 g. **Composition:** 0.9000 Silver .7697 oz. ASW **Subject:** 100th Anniversary Birth of Andres Bonifacio

| Date | Mintage | F | VF | XF | Unc | BU |
|---|---|---|---|---|---|---|
| ND(1963) | 100,000 | — | — | 4.50 | 7.50 | 9.00 |

**PESO** **KM# 194** **Weight:** 26.0000 g. **Composition:** 0.9000 Silver .7697 oz. ASW **Subject:** 100th Anniversary Birth of Apolinario Mabini

| Date | Mintage | F | VF | XF | Unc | BU |
|---|---|---|---|---|---|---|
| ND(1964) | 100,000 | — | — | 4.50 | 7.50 | 9.00 |

**PESO** **KM# 195** **Weight:** 26.0000 g. **Composition:** 0.9000 Silver .7697 oz. ASW **Subject:** 25th Anniversary of Bataan Day

| Date | Mintage | F | VF | XF | Unc | BU |
|---|---|---|---|---|---|---|
| ND(1967) | 100,000 | — | — | 4.50 | 7.50 | 9.00 |

**Note:** KM#195 is a proof-like issue.

## REFORM COINAGE

100 Sentimos = 1 Piso

**SENTIMO** **KM# 196** **Composition:** Aluminum **Obverse:** Bust of King Lapu-Lapu facing left

| Date | Mintage | F | VF | XF | Unc | BU |
|---|---|---|---|---|---|---|
| 1967 | 10,000,000 | — | — | — | 0.25 | — |
| 1968 | 27,940,000 | — | — | — | 0.10 | — |
| 1969/6 | 12,060,000 | — | — | — | 0.20 | — |
| 1970 | 130,000,000 | — | — | — | 0.10 | — |
| 1974 0 | 165,000,000 | — | — | — | 0.10 | — |
| 1974 1 Proof | 10,000 | Value: 3.50 | | | | |

**SENTIMO** **KM# 205** **Composition:** Aluminum

| Date | Mintage | F | VF | XF | Unc | BU |
|---|---|---|---|---|---|---|
| 1975FM (M) | 108,000 | — | — | — | 0.50 | — |
| 1975FM (U) | 5,875 | — | — | — | 2.00 | — |
| 1975FM (P) | 37,000 | Value: 1.50 | | | | |
| 1975(Lt) | 10,000,000 | — | — | — | 0.10 | — |
| 1975(US) | 60,190,000 | — | — | — | 0.10 | — |
| 1976FM (M) | 10,000 | — | — | — | 0.75 | — |
| 1976FM (U) | 1,826 | — | — | 1.00 | 2.50 | — |
| 1976FM (P) | 9,901 | Value: 2.00 | | | | |
| 1976(US) | 60,000,000 | — | — | — | 0.10 | — |
| 1977 | 4,808,000 | — | — | — | 0.25 | — |
| 1977FM (M) | 10,000 | — | — | — | 1.00 | — |
| 1977FM (U) | 354 | — | — | — | 4.00 | — |
| 1977FM (P) | 4,822 | Value: 2.00 | | | | |
| 1978 | 24,813,000 | — | — | — | 0.10 | — |
| 1978FM (U) | 10,000 | — | — | — | 1.00 | — |
| 1978FM (P) | 4,792 | Value: 2.00 | | | | |

**SENTIMO** **KM# 224** **Composition:** Aluminum **Reverse:** Redesigned seal **Note:** Varieties exist in date.

| Date | Mintage | F | VF | XF | Unc | BU |
|---|---|---|---|---|---|---|
| 1979BSP | — | — | — | — | 0.25 | — |
| 1979FM (U) | 10,000 | — | — | — | 1.00 | — |
| 1979FM (P) | 3,645 | Value: 2.00 | | | | |
| 1980BSP | 12,601,000 | — | — | — | 0.25 | — |
| 1980FM (U) | 10,000 | — | — | — | 1.00 | — |
| 1980FM (P) | 3,133 | Value: 2.00 | | | | |
| 1981BSP | 33,391,000 | — | — | — | 0.20 | — |
| 1981FM (U) | — | — | — | — | 1.00 | — |
| 1981FM (P) | 1,795 | Value: 2.00 | | | | |
| 1982BSP | 51,730,000 | — | — | — | 0.10 | — |
| 1982FM (P) | — | Value: 2.00 | | | | |

**SENTIMO** **KM# 238** **Composition:** Aluminum **Obverse:** King Lapu-Lapu bust facing left **Reverse:** Sea shell

| Date | Mintage | F | VF | XF | Unc | BU |
|---|---|---|---|---|---|---|
| 1983 | 62,090,000 | — | — | — | 0.35 | — |
| 1983 Proof | — | Value: 2.00 | | | | |
| 1984 | 320,000 | — | — | — | 0.75 | — |
| 1985 | 16,000 | — | — | — | 1.00 | — |
| 1986 | 80,000 | — | — | — | 1.00 | — |
| 1987 | 13,570,000 | — | — | — | 0.35 | — |
| 1988 | 26,861,000 | — | — | — | 0.35 | — |
| 1989 | — | — | — | — | 0.35 | — |
| 1990 | — | — | — | — | 0.35 | — |
| 1991 | — | — | — | — | 0.35 | — |
| 1992 | — | — | — | — | 0.35 | — |
| 1993 | — | — | 0.35 | 1.50 | 9.00 | — |

**SENTIMO** **KM# 273** **Composition:** Copper Plated Steel **Obverse:** Denomination **Reverse:** Central bank seal

| Date | Mintage | F | VF | XF | Unc | BU |
|---|---|---|---|---|---|---|
| 1995 | — | — | — | — | 0.35 | — |
| 1996 | — | — | — | — | 0.35 | — |
| 1997 | — | — | — | — | 0.35 | — |
| 1998 | — | — | — | — | 0.35 | — |
| 1999 | — | — | — | — | 0.35 | — |
| 2000 | — | — | — | — | 0.35 | — |

**5 SENTIMOS** **KM# 197** **Composition:** Brass **Reverse:** Bust of Melchora Aquino facing right

| Date | Mintage | F | VF | XF | Unc | BU |
|---|---|---|---|---|---|---|
| 1967 | 40,000,000 | — | — | — | 0.30 | — |
| 1968 | 50,000,000 | — | — | — | 0.30 | — |
| 1970 | 5,000,000 | — | — | 1.00 | 3.50 | — |
| 1972 | 71,744,000 | — | — | — | 0.30 | — |
| 1974 | 90,025,000 | — | — | — | 0.30 | — |
| 1974 Proof | 10,000 | Value: 4.00 | | | | |

**5 SENTIMOS** **KM# 206** **Composition:** Brass

| Date | Mintage | F | VF | XF | Unc | BU |
|---|---|---|---|---|---|---|
| 1975FM (M) | 104,000 | — | — | — | 0.50 | — |
| 1975FM (U) | 5,875 | — | — | — | 2.50 | — |
| 1975FM (P) | 37,000 | Value: 2.00 | | | | |
| 1975(US) | 98,928,000 | — | — | — | 0.10 | — |
| 1975(Lt) | 10,000,000 | — | — | — | 0.10 | — |
| 1976FM (M) | 10,000 | — | — | — | 1.50 | — |
| 1976FM (U) | 1,826 | — | — | — | 4.00 | — |
| 1976FM (P) | 9,901 | Value: 2.50 | | | | |
| 1976(US) | 98,000,000 | — | — | — | 0.20 | — |
| 1977 | 19,367,000 | — | — | — | 0.35 | — |
| 1977FM (M) | 10,000 | — | — | — | 1.50 | — |
| 1977FM (U) | 354 | — | — | — | 4.00 | — |
| 1977FM (P) | 4,822 | Value: 2.50 | | | | |
| 1978 | 61,838,000 | — | — | — | 0.20 | — |
| 1978FM (U) | 10,000 | — | — | — | 1.50 | — |
| 1978FM (P) | 4,792 | Value: 2.50 | | | | |

**5 SENTIMOS** **KM# 225** **Composition:** Brass **Reverse:** Redesigned seal

| Date | Mintage | F | VF | XF | Unc | BU |
|---|---|---|---|---|---|---|
| 1979BSP | 12,805,000 | — | — | — | 0.30 | — |
| 1979FM (U) | 10,000 | — | — | — | 1.00 | — |
| 1979FM (P) | 3,645 | Value: 2.50 | | | | |
| 1980BSP | 111,339,000 | — | — | — | 0.10 | — |
| 1980FM (U) | — | — | — | — | 1.00 | — |
| 1980FM (P) | 3,133 | Value: 2.50 | | | | |
| 1981BSP | — | — | — | — | 0.10 | — |
| 1981FM (U) | — | — | — | — | 1.00 | — |
| 1981FM (P) | 1,795 | Value: 3.00 | | | | |
| 1982BSP | — | — | — | — | 0.10 | — |
| 1982FM (P) | — | Value: 3.00 | | | | |

**5 SENTIMOS** **KM# 239** **Composition:** Aluminum **Reverse:** Waling-Waling orchid

| Date | Mintage | F | VF | XF | Unc | BU |
|---|---|---|---|---|---|---|
| 1983 | 100,016,000 | — | — | — | 0.20 | — |
| 1983 Proof | — | Value: 2.00 | | | | |
| 1984 | 141,744,000 | — | — | — | 0.20 | — |
| 1985 | 50,416,000 | — | — | — | 0.20 | — |
| 1986 | 11,664,000 | — | — | — | 0.25 | — |
| 1987 | 79,008,000 | — | — | — | 0.10 | — |
| 1988 | 90,487,000 | — | — | — | 0.10 | — |
| 1989 | — | — | — | — | 0.10 | — |
| 1990 | — | — | — | — | 0.10 | — |
| 1991 | — | — | — | — | 0.25 | — |
| 1992 | — | — | — | — | 0.10 | — |

**5 SENTIMOS** **KM# 268** **Composition:** Copper Plated Steel **Rev. Legend:** 1993 BANGKO CENTRAL NG PILIPINAS **Note:** Hole punched out of center.

| Date | Mintage | F | VF | XF | Unc | BU |
|---|---|---|---|---|---|---|
| 1995 | — | — | — | — | 0.25 | — |
| 1996 | — | — | — | — | 0.25 | — |
| 1997 | — | — | — | — | 0.25 | — |
| 1998 | — | — | — | — | 0.25 | — |
| 1999 | — | — | — | — | 0.25 | — |
| 2000 | — | — | — | — | 0.25 | — |

**10 SENTIMOS** **KM# 198** **Composition:** Copper-Nickel **Reverse:** Bust of Francisco Baltasar facing left

| Date | Mintage | F | VF | XF | Unc | BU |
|---|---|---|---|---|---|---|
| 1967 | 50,000,000 | — | — | — | 0.35 | — |
| 1968 | 60,000,000 | — | — | — | 0.35 | — |
| 1969 | 40,000,000 | — | — | — | 0.35 | — |
| 1970 | 50,000,000 | — | — | — | 0.35 | — |
| 1971 | 80,000,000 | — | — | — | 0.35 | — |
| 1972 | 121,390,000 | — | — | — | 0.35 | — |
| 1974 | 60,208,000 | — | — | — | 0.35 | — |
| 1974 Proof | 10,000 | Value: 4.00 | | | | |

**10 SENTIMOS** **KM# 207** **Composition:** Copper-Nickel

| Date | Mintage | F | VF | XF | Unc | BU |
|---|---|---|---|---|---|---|
| 1975FM (M) | 104,000 | — | — | — | 0.50 | — |
| 1975FM (U) | 5,875 | — | — | — | 2.50 | — |
| 1975FM (P) | 37,000 | Value: 2.00 | | | | |
| 1975(VDM) | 10,000,000 | — | — | — | 0.25 | — |
| 1975(US) | 50,000,000 | — | — | — | 0.10 | — |
| 1976FM (M) | 10,000 | — | — | — | 0.50 | — |
| 1976FM (U) | 1,826 | — | — | — | 5.00 | — |
| 1976FM (P) | 9,901 | Value: 3.00 | | | | |
| 1976(US) | 50,000,000 | — | — | — | 0.10 | — |
| 1977 | 29,314,000 | — | — | — | 0.10 | — |
| 1977FM (M) | 10,000 | — | — | — | 1.50 | — |
| 1977FM (U) | 354 | — | — | — | 6.50 | — |
| 1977FM (P) | 4,822 | Value: 3.00 | | | | |
| 1978 | 60,042,000 | — | — | — | 0.10 | — |
| 1978FM (U) | 10,000 | — | — | — | 2.00 | — |
| 1978FM (P) | 4,792 | Value: 3.00 | | | | |

**10 SENTIMOS** **KM# 226** **Composition:** Copper-Nickel **Reverse:** Redesigned seal **Note:** Varieties with thick and thin legends exist for coins with BSP mint mark.

| Date | Mintage | F | VF | XF | Unc | BU |
|---|---|---|---|---|---|---|
| 1979BSP | 6,446,000 | — | — | — | 0.30 | — |
| 1979FM (U) | 10,000 | — | — | — | 1.00 | — |
| 1979FM (P) | 3,645 | Value: 3.00 | | | | |
| 1980BSP | — | — | — | — | 0.10 | — |
| 1980FM (U) | 10,000 | — | — | — | 1.50 | — |
| 1980FM (P) | 3,133 | Value: 3.25 | | | | |
| 1981BSP | — | — | — | — | 0.10 | — |
| 1981FM (U) | — | — | — | — | 1.00 | — |
| 1981FM (P) | 1,795 | Value: 3.50 | | | | |
| 1982BSP | — | — | — | — | 0.10 | — |
| 1982FM (P) | — | Value: 3.50 | | | | |

**10 SENTIMOS** **Composition:** Copper-Nickel **Reverse:** Redesigned seal **Note:** Varieties with thick and thin legends exist for coins with BSP mint markl

| Date | Mintage | F | VF | XF | Unc | BU |
|---|---|---|---|---|---|---|
| 1979BSP | 6,446,000 | — | — | — | — | — |
| 1979FM (U) | 10,000 | — | — | — | — | — |

**10 SENTIMOS** **KM# 240.1** **Composition:** Aluminum **Series:** F.A.O **Subject:** World Conference on Fisheries **Reverse:** Fish's name in error: PANDAKA PYGMEA

| Date | Mintage | F | VF | XF | Unc | BU |
|---|---|---|---|---|---|---|
| 1983 | 95,640,000 | — | — | — | 1.25 | — |
| 1983 Proof | — | Value: 3.00 | | | | |
| 1987 | | — | — | — | 0.35 | — |

**10 SENTIMOS** **KM# 240.2** **Composition:** Aluminum **Series:** F.A.O **Subject:** World Conference on Fisheries **Reverse:** Fish's name: PANDAKA PYGMAEA

| Date | Mintage | F | VF | XF | Unc | BU |
|---|---|---|---|---|---|---|
| 1983 | — | — | — | — | 0.25 | — |
| 1984 | 235,900,000 | — | — | — | 0.25 | — |
| 1985 | 90,169,000 | — | — | — | 0.25 | — |
| 1986 | 4,270,000 | — | — | — | 0.50 | — |
| 1987 | 99,520,000 | — | — | — | 0.25 | — |
| 1988 | 117,166,000 | — | — | — | 0.25 | — |
| 1989 | — | — | — | — | 0.25 | — |
| 1990 | — | — | — | — | 0.25 | — |
| 1991 | — | — | — | — | 0.25 | — |
| 1992 | — | — | — | — | 0.25 | — |
| 1993 | — | — | — | — | 0.50 | — |
| 1994 | — | — | — | — | 0.50 | — |

**10 SENTIMOS** **KM# 270** **Composition:** Bronze Plated Steel **Reverse:** Central Bank seal

| Date | Mintage | F | VF | XF | Unc | BU |
|---|---|---|---|---|---|---|
| 1995 | — | — | — | — | 0.40 | — |
| 1996 | — | — | — | — | 0.40 | — |
| 1997 | — | — | — | — | 0.20 | — |
| 1998 | — | — | — | — | 0.20 | — |
| 1999 | — | — | — | — | 0.20 | — |

**25 SENTIMOS** **KM# 199** **Composition:** Copper-Nickel **Reverse:** Bust of Juan Luna facing left

| Date | Mintage | F | VF | XF | Unc | BU |
|---|---|---|---|---|---|---|
| 1967 | 40,000,000 | — | — | 0.10 | 0.40 | — |
| 1968 | 10,000,000 | — | — | 0.10 | 0.40 | — |
| 1969 | 10,000,000 | — | — | 0.10 | 0.40 | — |
| 1970 | 40,000,000 | — | — | 0.10 | 0.40 | — |
| 1971 | 60,000,000 | — | — | 0.10 | 0.40 | — |
| 1972 | 90,000,000 | — | — | 0.10 | 0.40 | — |
| 1974 | 10,000,000 | — | — | 0.10 | 0.50 | — |
| 1974 Proof | 10,000 | Value: 10.00 | | | | |

**25 SENTIMOS** **KM# 208** **Composition:** Copper-Nickel

| Date | Mintage | F | VF | XF | Unc | BU |
|---|---|---|---|---|---|---|
| 1975FM (M) | 104,000 | — | — | — | 0.80 | — |
| 1975FM (U) | 5,875 | — | — | — | 4.25 | — |
| 1975FM (P) | 37,000 | Value: 3.00 | | | | |
| 1975(US) | 10,000,000 | — | — | 0.10 | 0.30 | — |
| 1975(VDM) | 10,000,000 | — | — | 0.10 | 0.30 | — |
| 1976FM (M) | 10,000 | — | — | 0.10 | 1.00 | — |
| 1976FM (U) | 1,826 | — | — | — | 6.50 | — |
| 1976FM (P) | 9,901 | Value: 3.50 | | | | |
| 1976(US) | 10,000,000 | — | — | 0.10 | 0.25 | — |
| 1977 | 24,654,000 | — | — | 0.10 | 0.25 | — |
| 1977FM (M) | 10,000 | — | — | — | 1.50 | — |
| 1977FM (U) | 354 | — | — | — | 8.00 | — |
| 1977FM (P) | 4,822 | Value: 4.50 | | | | |
| 1978 | 40,466,000 | — | — | 0.10 | 0.25 | — |
| 1978FM (U) | 10,000 | — | — | — | 2.50 | — |
| 1978FM (P) | 4,792 | Value: 4.00 | | | | |

**25 SENTIMOS** **KM# 227** **Composition:** Copper-Nickel **Reverse:** Redesigned seal

| Date | Mintage | F | VF | XF | Unc | BU |
|---|---|---|---|---|---|---|
| 1979BSP | 20,725,000 | — | — | 0.10 | 0.50 | — |
| 1979FM (U) | 10,000 | — | — | — | 1.50 | — |
| 1979FM (P) | 3,645 | Value: 4.50 | | | | |
| 1980BSP | — | — | — | 0.10 | 0.75 | — |
| 1980FM (U) | 10,000 | — | — | — | 2.00 | — |
| 1980FM (P) | 3,133 | Value: 4.50 | | | | |
| 1981BSP | — | — | — | 0.10 | 0.75 | — |
| 1981FM (U) | — | — | — | — | 1.50 | — |
| 1981FM (P) | 1,795 | Value: 5.00 | | | | |
| 1982BSP | — | — | — | 0.10 | 0.50 | — |
| 1982FM (P) | — | Value: 5.00 | | | | |

**25 SENTIMOS** **KM# 241.1** **Composition:** Brass **Reverse:** Butterfly

| Date | Mintage | F | VF | XF | Unc | BU |
|---|---|---|---|---|---|---|
| 1983 | 92,944,000 | — | — | 0.15 | 0.50 | — |
| 1983 Proof | — | Value: 3.00 | | | | |
| 1984 | 254,324,000 | — | — | 0.15 | 0.50 | — |
| 1985 | 84,922,000 | — | — | 0.15 | 0.50 | — |
| 1986 | 65,284,000 | — | — | 0.15 | 0.50 | — |
| 1987 | 1,680,000 | — | — | 0.50 | 1.75 | — |
| 1988 | 51,062,000 | — | — | — | 0.50 | — |
| 1989 | — | — | — | — | 0.50 | — |
| 1990 | — | — | — | — | 0.50 | — |

**25 SENTIMOS** **KM# 241.2** **Composition:** Brass **Note:** Reduced size.

| Date | Mintage | F | VF | XF | Unc | BU |
|---|---|---|---|---|---|---|
| 1991 | — | — | — | — | 0.50 | — |
| 1992 | — | — | — | — | 0.50 | — |
| 1993 | — | — | — | — | 1.00 | — |
| 1994 | — | — | — | — | 1.00 | — |

**25 SENTIMOS** **KM# 271** **Composition:** Brass **Reverse:** Central Bank seal

| Date | Mintage | F | VF | XF | Unc | BU |
|---|---|---|---|---|---|---|
| 1995 | — | — | — | — | 0.75 | — |
| 1996 | — | — | — | — | 0.75 | — |
| 1997 | — | — | — | — | 0.75 | — |
| 1998 | — | — | — | — | 0.75 | — |
| 1999 | — | — | — | — | 0.75 | — |
| 2000 | — | — | — | — | 0.75 | — |

**50 SENTIMOS** **KM# 200** **Composition:** Copper-Nickel-Zinc **Reverse:** Bust of Marcelo H. del Pilar facing right

| Date | Mintage | F | VF | XF | Unc | BU |
|---|---|---|---|---|---|---|
| 1967 | 20,000,000 | — | 0.10 | 0.25 | 0.75 | |
| 1971 | 10,000,000 | — | 0.10 | 0.50 | 1.00 | |
| 1972 Serif on 2 | 30,000,000 | — | 0.10 | 1.25 | 2.00 | |
| 1972 Plain 2 | 20,517,000 | — | 0.10 | 1.00 | 1.50 | |
| 1974 | 5,004,000 | — | 0.10 | 0.75 | 1.25 | |
| 1974 Proof | 10,000 | Value: 18.00 | | | | |
| 1975 | 5,714,000 | — | 0.10 | 0.20 | 1.00 | — |

**50 SENTIMOS** **KM# 242.1** **Composition:** Copper-Nickel **Reverse:** Monkey-eating eagle **Note:** Eagle's name: PITHECOPHAGA

| Date | Mintage | F | VF | XF | Unc | BU |
|---|---|---|---|---|---|---|
| 1983 | 27,644,000 | — | 0.10 | 0.50 | 1.25 | — |
| 1983 Proof | — | Value: 5.00 | | | | |
| 1984 | 121,408,000 | — | 0.10 | 0.20 | 0.75 | — |
| 1985 | 107,048,000 | — | 0.10 | 0.20 | 0.75 | — |
| 1986 | 120,000,000 | — | 0.10 | 0.20 | 0.75 | — |
| 1987 | 1,078,000 | — | 0.10 | 1.00 | 1.50 | — |
| 1988 | 24,008,000 | — | 0.10 | 0.20 | 0.75 | — |
| 1989 | — | — | 0.10 | 0.20 | 0.75 | — |
| 1990 | — | — | 0.10 | 0.20 | 0.75 | — |

**50 SENTIMOS** **KM# 242.2** **Composition:** Copper-Nickel **Reverse:** Monkey-eating eagle **Note:** Error eagle's name: PITHECOBHAGA

| Date | Mintage | F | VF | XF | Unc | BU |
|---|---|---|---|---|---|---|
| 1983 | Inc. above | — | 3.00 | 5.00 | 10.00 | — |

**50 SENTIMOS** **KM# 242.3** **Composition:** Brass **Note:** Reduced size.

| Date | Mintage | F | VF | XF | Unc | BU |
|---|---|---|---|---|---|---|
| 1991 | — | — | — | 0.25 | 1.00 | — |
| 1992 | — | — | — | 0.25 | 1.00 | — |
| 1993 | — | — | — | 0.25 | 1.50 | — |
| 1994 | — | — | — | 0.25 | 1.50 | — |

**PISO** **KM# 201** **Weight:** 26.4500 g. **Composition:** 0.9000 Silver .7653 oz. ASW **Subject:** Centennial - Birth of Aquinaldo

| Date | Mintage | F | VF | XF | Unc | BU |
|---|---|---|---|---|---|---|
| 1969 | 100,000 | — | — | 5.00 | 8.00 | 9.00 |

**Note:** These coins are "prooflike" issues

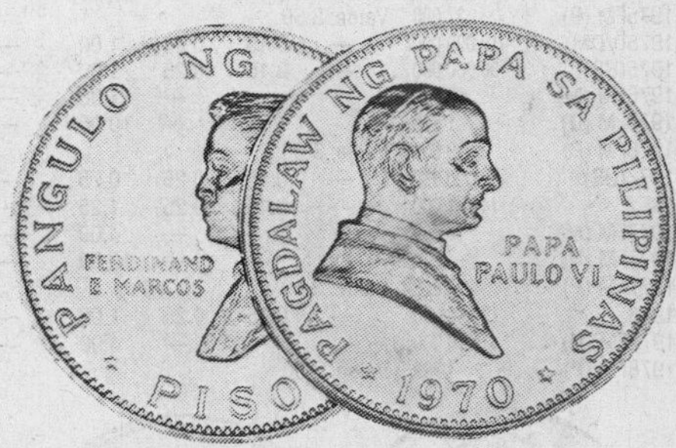


**PISO** **KM# 202** **Composition:** Nickel **Subject:** Pope Paul VI visit

| Date | Mintage | F | VF | XF | Unc | BU |
|---|---|---|---|---|---|---|
| 1970 | 70,000 | — | — | 1.00 | 2.50 | 3.50 |

**PISO** **KM# 202a** **Weight:** 26.4500 g. **Composition:** 0.9000 Silver .7653 oz. ASW

| Date | Mintage | F | VF | XF | Unc | BU |
|---|---|---|---|---|---|---|
| 1970 | 30,000 | — | — | 7.00 | 10.00 | 12.00 |

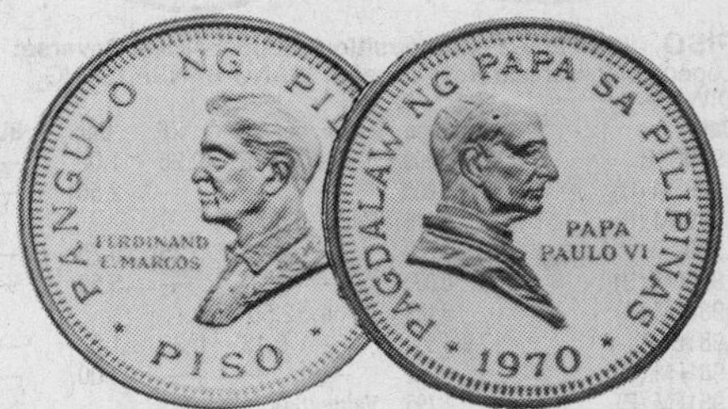


**PISO** **KM# 202b** **Weight:** 19.3000 g. **Composition:** 0.9170 Gold .5691 oz. AGW **Subject:** Pope Paul VI visit

| Date | Mintage | F | VF | XF | Unc | BU |
|---|---|---|---|---|---|---|
| 1970 | 1,000 | — | — | — | — | 475 |

**PISO KM# 203 Composition:** Copper-Nickel **Reverse:** Bust of Jose Rizal facing left

| Date | Mintage | F | VF | XF | Unc | BU |
|---|---|---|---|---|---|---|
| 1972 | 121,821,000 | — | 0.25 | 0.50 | 1.50 | — |
| 1974 | 45,631,000 | — | 0.25 | 0.50 | 1.50 | — |
| 1974 Proof | 10,000 | Value: 30.00 | | | | |

**PISO KM# 209.1 Composition:** Copper-Nickel

| Date | Mintage | F | VF | XF | Unc | BU |
|---|---|---|---|---|---|---|
| 1975FM (M) | 104,000 | — | — | — | 2.00 | — |
| 1975FM (U) | 5,877 | — | — | — | 5.50 | — |
| 1975FM (P) | 37,000 | Value: 3.50 | | | | |
| 1975(VDM) | 10,000,000 | — | 0.15 | 0.25 | 1.00 | — |
| 1975(US) | 30,000,000 | — | 0.15 | 0.25 | 1.00 | — |
| 1976FM (M) | 10,000 | — | — | — | 1.00 | — |
| 1976FM (U) | 1,826 | — | — | — | 10.00 | — |
| 1976FM (P) | 9,901 | Value: 3.00 | | | | |
| 1976(US) | 30,000,000 | — | 0.15 | 0.25 | 0.75 | — |
| 1977 | 14,771,000 | — | 0.15 | 0.25 | 1.25 | — |
| 1977FM (M) | 12,000 | — | — | — | 4.00 | — |
| 1977FM (U) | 354 | — | — | — | 10.00 | — |
| 1977FM (P) | 4,822 | Value: 3.50 | | | | |
| 1978 | 19,408,000 | — | 0.15 | 0.25 | 1.00 | — |
| 1978FM (U) | 10,000 | — | — | — | 4.00 | — |
| 1978FM (P) | 4,792 | Value: 6.50 | | | | |

**PISO KM# 209.2 Composition:** Copper-Nickel **Reverse:** Legend below shield **Rev. Legend:** ISANG BANSA ISANG DIWA

| Date | Mintage | F | VF | XF | Unc | BU |
|---|---|---|---|---|---|---|
| 1979BSP | 321,000 | — | 0.15 | 0.25 | 1.00 | — |
| 1979FM (U) | 10,000 | — | — | — | 2.50 | — |
| 1979FM (P) | 3,645 | Value: 3.50 | | | | |
| 1980BSP | 19,693,000 | — | 0.15 | 0.25 | 0.75 | — |
| 1980FM (U) | 10,000 | — | — | — | 5.50 | — |
| 1980FM (P) | 3,133 | Value: 12.50 | | | | |
| 1981BSP | 7,944,000 | — | 0.15 | 0.25 | 1.00 | — |
| 1981FM (U) | — | — | — | — | 3.00 | — |
| 1981FM (P) | 1,795 | Value: 6.00 | | | | |
| 1982FM (P) | — | Value: 6.00 | | | | |
| 1982BSP Large date | 52,110,000 | — | 0.15 | 0.25 | 0.75 | — |
| 1982BSP Small date | Inc. above | — | 0.15 | 0.25 | 0.75 | — |

**PISO KM# 243.1 Composition:** Copper-Nickel **Reverse:** Tamara bull **Note:** Large legends and design elements.

| Date | Mintage | F | VF | XF | Unc | BU |
|---|---|---|---|---|---|---|
| 1983 | 55,869,000 | — | — | 0.30 | 1.25 | — |
| 1983 Proof | — | Value: 6.50 | | | | |
| 1984 | 4,997,000 | — | — | 1.00 | 2.50 | — |
| 1985 | 182,592,000 | — | — | 0.30 | 1.25 | — |
| 1986 | 19,072,000 | — | — | 0.30 | 1.25 | — |
| 1987 | 1,391,000 | — | — | 1.00 | 2.00 | — |
| 1988 | 54,636,000 | — | — | 0.30 | 1.25 | — |

**PISO KM# 243.3 Composition:** Copper-Nickel **Note:** Smaller legends and design elements.

| Date | Mintage | F | VF | XF | Unc | BU |
|---|---|---|---|---|---|---|
| 1989 | — | — | — | 0.30 | 1.25 | — |
| 1990 | — | — | — | 0.30 | 1.25 | — |

**PISO KM# 251 Composition:** Copper-Nickel **Subject:** Philippine Cultures Decade

| Date | Mintage | F | VF | XF | Unc | BU |
|---|---|---|---|---|---|---|
| 1989 | — | — | — | — | 2.50 | — |

**PISO KM# 257 Composition:** Copper-Nickel **Note:** Waterfall, ship, and flower.

| Date | Mintage | F | VF | XF | Unc | BU |
|---|---|---|---|---|---|---|
| 1991 | — | — | — | — | 2.00 | — |

**PISO KM# 243.2 Composition:** Stainless Steel **Note:** Reduced size.

| Date | Mintage | F | VF | XF | Unc | BU |
|---|---|---|---|---|---|---|
| 1991 | — | — | — | 0.50 | 1.00 | — |
| 1992 | — | — | — | 0.50 | 1.00 | — |
| 1993 | — | — | — | 0.75 | 2.00 | — |
| 1994 | — | — | — | 0.75 | 2.00 | — |

**PISO KM# 260 Composition:** Nickel Clad Steel **Subject:** 50th Anniversary - Battle of Kagitingan

| Date | Mintage | F | VF | XF | Unc | BU |
|---|---|---|---|---|---|---|
| ND(1992) | — | — | — | — | 2.50 | — |

**PISO KM# 269 Composition:** Copper-Nickel **Obverse:** Jose Rizal **Reverse:** Bank seal, date 1993

| Date | Mintage | F | VF | XF | Unc | BU |
|---|---|---|---|---|---|---|
| 1995 | — | — | — | — | 2.00 | — |
| 1996 | — | — | — | — | 1.00 | — |
| 1997 | — | — | — | — | 1.00 | — |
| 1998 | — | — | — | — | 1.00 | — |
| 1999 | — | — | — | — | 1.00 | — |
| 2000 | — | — | — | — | 1.00 | — |

**2 PISO KM# 244 Composition:** Copper-Nickel **Obverse:** Bust of Andres Bonifacio facing left

| Date | Mintage | F | VF | XF | Unc | BU |
|---|---|---|---|---|---|---|
| 1983 | 15,640,000 | — | — | 0.35 | 4.00 | — |
| 1983 Proof | — | Value: 10.00 | | | | |
| 1984 | 121,111,000 | — | — | 0.35 | 1.25 | — |
| 1985 | 115,211,000 | — | — | 0.35 | 1.25 | — |
| 1986 | 25,260,000 | — | — | 0.35 | 1.25 | — |
| 1987 | 2,196,000 | — | — | 0.35 | 2.25 | — |
| 1988 | 16,094,000 | — | — | — | 1.25 | — |
| 1989 | — | — | — | — | 1.25 | — |
| 1990 | — | — | — | — | 1.25 | — |

**2 PISO KM# 253 Composition:** Copper-Nickel **Reverse:** Bust of Elpidio Quirino facing right

| Date | Mintage | F | VF | XF | Unc | BU |
|---|---|---|---|---|---|---|
| ND(1991) | 10,000,000 | — | — | — | 3.00 | — |

**2 PISO KM# 258 Composition:** Stainless Steel **Obverse:** Bust of Andres Bonifacio facing left

| Date | Mintage | F | VF | XF | Unc | BU |
|---|---|---|---|---|---|---|
| 1991 | — | — | — | — | 2.50 | — |
| 1992 | — | — | — | — | 2.50 | — |
| 1993 | — | — | — | — | 2.50 | — |
| 1994 | — | — | — | — | 2.50 | — |

**2 PISO KM# 261 Composition:** Nickel Clad Steel **Reverse:** Bust of Manuel A. Roxas facing right

| Date | Mintage | F | VF | XF | Unc | BU |
|---|---|---|---|---|---|---|
| ND(1992) | — | — | — | — | 3.50 | — |

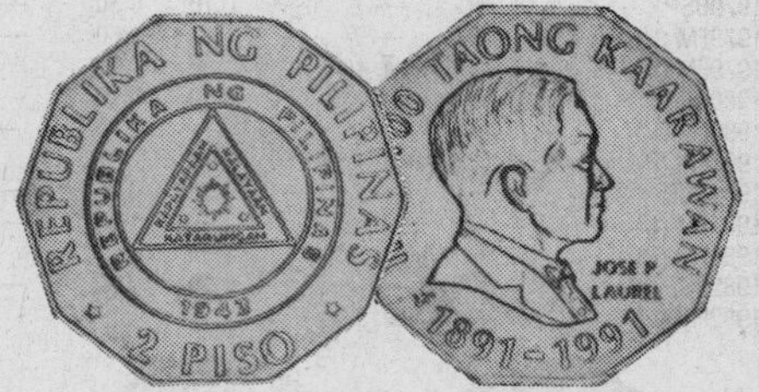

**2 PISO KM# 256 Composition:** Copper-Nickel **Reverse:** Bust of Jose Laurel facing right

| Date | Mintage | F | VF | XF | Unc | BU |
|---|---|---|---|---|---|---|
| ND(1992) | — | — | — | 1.75 | 3.50 | — |

**5 PISO** **KM# 210.1** **Composition:** Nickel **Reverse:** Bust of Ferdinand E. Marcos facing left

| Date | Mintage | F | VF | XF | Unc | BU |
|---|---|---|---|---|---|---|
| 1975FM (M) | 3,850 | — | — | — | 10.00 | — |
| 1975FM (U) | 7,875 | — | — | — | 8.00 | — |
| 1975FM (P) | 39,000 | Value: 5.00 | | | | |
| 1975(Sh) | 20,000,000 | — | 0.50 | 1.00 | 2.00 | — |
| 1976FM (M) | 10,000 | — | — | — | 5.00 | — |
| 1976FM (U) | 1,826 | — | — | — | 15.00 | — |
| 1976FM (P) | 9,901 | Value: 6.00 | | | | |
| 1977FM (M) | 10,000 | — | — | — | 5.00 | — |
| 1977FM (U) | 354 | — | — | — | 15.00 | — |
| 1977FM (P) | 4,822 | Value: 7.50 | | | | |
| 1978FM (U) | 10,000 | — | — | — | 5.00 | — |
| 1978FM (P) | 4,792 | Value: 7.50 | | | | |
| 1982 | — | — | 0.50 | 0.75 | 1.50 | — |

**5 PISO** **KM# 210.2** **Composition:** Nickel **Obverse:** Legend below shield **Obv. Legend:** ISANG BANSA ISANG DIWA

| Date | Mintage | F | VF | XF | Unc | BU |
|---|---|---|---|---|---|---|
| 1979FM (U) | 10,000 | — | — | — | 4.50 | — |
| 1979FM (P) | 3,645 | Value: 8.00 | | | | |
| 1980FM (U) | 10,000 | — | — | — | 4.50 | — |
| 1980FM (P) | 3,133 | Value: 10.00 | | | | |
| 1981FM (U) | 11,000 | — | — | — | 4.50 | — |
| 1981FM (P) | 1,795 | Value: 10.00 | | | | |
| 1982FM (P) | — | Value: 10.00 | | | | |

**5 PISO** **KM# 259** **Composition:** Nickel-Brass **Obverse:** Bust of Emilio Aguinaldo facing right; Pterocarpus Indicus flower

| Date | Mintage | F | VF | XF | Unc | BU |
|---|---|---|---|---|---|---|
| 1991 | — | — | — | — | 4.00 | — |
| 1992 | — | — | — | — | 3.50 | — |
| 1993 | — | — | — | — | 5.00 | — |
| 1994 | — | — | — | — | 5.00 | — |

**5 PISO** **KM# 262** **Composition:** Nickel-Brass **Subject:** 30th Chess Olympiad **Note:** Varieties exist.

| Date | Mintage | F | VF | XF | Unc | BU |
|---|---|---|---|---|---|---|
| 1992 | — | — | — | — | 10.00 | — |

**5 PISO** **KM# 263** **Composition:** Nickel-Brass **Subject:** Leyte Gulf Landings

| Date | Mintage | F | VF | XF | Unc | BU |
|---|---|---|---|---|---|---|
| ND(1994) | 7,800 | — | — | — | 7.50 | — |

**5 PISO** **KM# 272** **Composition:** Nickel-Brass **Obverse:** Aguinaldo **Reverse:** Central Bank seal

| Date | Mintage | F | VF | XF | Unc | BU |
|---|---|---|---|---|---|---|
| 1995 | — | — | — | — | 2.50 | — |
| 1996 | — | — | — | — | 1.50 | — |
| 1997 | — | — | — | — | 1.50 | — |
| 1997BSP | — | — | — | — | 1.50 | — |
| 1998 | — | — | — | — | 1.50 | — |

**10 PISO** **KM# 250** **Composition:** Nickel **Subject:** People Power Revolution

| Date | Mintage | F | VF | XF | Unc | BU |
|---|---|---|---|---|---|---|
| 1988 | — | — | — | — | 5.00 | — |

**10 PISO** **KM# 278** **Ring Weight:** 8.7000 g. **Ring Composition:** Copper-Nickel **Center Composition:** Brass **Obverse:** Mobini and Bonifacio's portraits **Reverse:** Bank seal **Edge:** Plain and reeded sections **Size:** 26.5 mm.

| Date | Mintage | F | VF | XF | Unc | BU |
|---|---|---|---|---|---|---|
| 2000 | — | — | — | — | 3.50 | — |
| 2001 | — | — | — | — | 3.00 | — |

**25 PISO** **KM# 204** **Weight:** 26.4000 g. **Composition:** 0.9000 Silver .7639 oz. ASW **Subject:** 25th Anniversary of Bank

| Date | Mintage | F | VF | XF | Unc | BU |
|---|---|---|---|---|---|---|
| ND(1974) | 90,000 | — | — | — | 7.00 | — |

**25 PISO** **KM# 204a** **Weight:** 26.4000 g. **Composition:** 0.9000 Silver .7639 oz. ASW

| Date | Mintage | F | VF | XF | Unc | BU |
|---|---|---|---|---|---|---|
| ND(1974) Proof | 10,000 | Value: 13.50 | | | | |

**25 PISO** **KM# 211** **Weight:** 25.0000 g. **Composition:** 0.5000 Silver .4018 oz. ASW **Obverse:** Bust of Emilio Aguinaldo facing right

| Date | Mintage | F | VF | XF | Unc | BU |
|---|---|---|---|---|---|---|
| 1975FM (M) | 10,000 | — | — | — | 10.00 | — |
| 1975FM (U) | 5,875 | — | — | — | 15.00 | — |
| 1975FM (P) | 37,000 | Value: 10.00 | | | | |

**25 PISO** **KM# 214** **Weight:** 25.0000 g. **Composition:** 0.5000 Silver .4018 oz. ASW **Series:** F.A.O

| Date | Mintage | F | VF | XF | Unc | BU |
|---|---|---|---|---|---|---|
| 1976FM (M) | 22,000 | — | — | — | 15.00 | — |
| 1976FM (U) | 1,826 | — | — | — | 22.50 | — |
| 1976FM (P) | 9,901 | Value: 18.50 | | | | |

**25 PISO** **KM# 217** **Weight:** 25.0000 g. **Composition:** 0.5000 Silver .4018 oz. ASW **Subject:** Banaue Rice Terraces

| Date | Mintage | F | VF | XF | Unc | BU |
|---|---|---|---|---|---|---|
| 1977FM (M) | 10,000 | — | — | — | 15.00 | — |
| 1977FM (U) | 354 | — | — | — | 35.00 | — |
| 1977FM (P) | 4,822 | Value: 22.50 | | | | |

**25 PISO** **KM# 221** **Weight:** 25.0000 g. **Composition:** 0.5000 Silver .4018 oz. ASW **Subject:** 100th Anniversary - Birth of Quezon

| Date | Mintage | F | VF | XF | Unc | BU |
|---|---|---|---|---|---|---|
| ND(1978)FM (U) | 10,000 | — | — | — | 13.50 | — |
| ND(1978)FM (P) | 9,930 | Value: 15.00 | | | | |

**25 PISO** **KM# 228** **Weight:** 25.0000 g. **Composition:** 0.5000 Silver .4018 oz. ASW **Subject:** UN Conference on Trade and Development

| Date | Mintage | F | VF | XF | Unc | BU |
|---|---|---|---|---|---|---|
| 1979FM (U) | 10,000 | — | — | — | 15.00 | — |
| 1979FM (P) | 7,093 | Value: 18.50 | | | | |

**25 PISO** **KM# 230** **Weight:** 25.0000 g. **Composition:** 0.5000 Silver .4018 oz. ASW **Subject:** 100th Anniversary - Birth of Gen. Douglas MacArthur **Reverse:** Bust of Gen. Douglas MacArthur turned left

| Date | Mintage | F | VF | XF | Unc | BU |
|---|---|---|---|---|---|---|
| ND(1980)FM (U) | 9,800 | — | — | — | 20.00 | — |
| ND(1980)FM (P) | 6,318 | Value: 40.00 | | | | |

**25 PISO** **KM# 232** **Weight:** 25.0000 g. **Composition:** 0.5000 Silver .4018 oz. ASW **Subject:** World Food Day

| Date | Mintage | F | VF | XF | Unc | BU |
|---|---|---|---|---|---|---|
| 1981FM (U) | 10,000 | — | — | — | 20.00 | — |
| 1981FM (P) | 3,033 | Value: 25.00 | | | | |

**25 PISO** **KM# 235** **Weight:** 25.0000 g. **Composition:** 0.5000 Silver .4018 oz. ASW **Reverse:** Presidents Marcos and Reagan profiles

| Date | Mintage | F | VF | XF | Unc | BU |
|---|---|---|---|---|---|---|
| 1982 | 8,000 | — | — | — | 30.00 | — |
| 1982 Proof | 250 | Value: 475 | | | | |

**25 PISO** **KM# 246** **Weight:** 18.4100 g. **Composition:** 0.9250 Silver .5475 oz. ASW **Subject:** President Aquino's visit in Washington

| Date | Mintage | F | VF | XF | Unc | BU |
|---|---|---|---|---|---|---|
| 1986 Proof | Est. 1,000 | Value: 110 | | | | |

**50 PISO** **KM# 212** **Weight:** 27.4000 g. **Composition:** 0.9250 Silver .8148 oz. ASW **Subject:** 3rd Anniversary of the New Society

| Date | Mintage | F | VF | XF | Unc | BU |
|---|---|---|---|---|---|---|
| 1975FM (M) | 10,000 | — | — | — | 10.00 | — |
| 1975FM (U) | 7,875 | — | — | — | 15.00 | — |
| 1975FM (P) | 54,000 | Value: 10.00 | | | | |

**50 PISO** **KM# 215** **Weight:** 27.4000 g. **Composition:** 0.9250 Silver .8148 oz. ASW **Subject:** I.M.F. Meeting

| Date | Mintage | F | VF | XF | Unc | BU |
|---|---|---|---|---|---|---|
| 1976 Proof | 5,477 | Value: 20.00 | | | | |
| 1976FM (M) | 10,000 | — | — | — | 12.50 | — |
| 1976FM (U) | 1,826 | — | — | — | 40.00 | — |
| 1976FM (P) | 15,000 | Value: 17.50 | | | | |

**50 PISO** **KM# 218** **Weight:** 27.4000 g. **Composition:** 0.9250 Silver .8148 oz. ASW **Subject:** Inauguration of new mint facilities

| Date | Mintage | F | VF | XF | Unc | BU |
|---|---|---|---|---|---|---|
| 1977FM (M) | 10,000 | — | — | — | 15.00 | — |
| 1977FM (U) | 354 | — | — | — | 50.00 | — |
| 1977FM (P) | 6,704 | Value: 18.50 | | | | |

**50 PISO** **KM# 222** **Weight:** 27.4000 g. **Composition:** 0.9250 Silver .8148 oz. ASW **Subject:** 100th Anniversary - Birth of Quezon

| Date | Mintage | F | VF | XF | Unc | BU |
|---|---|---|---|---|---|---|
| ND(1978)FM (U) | 10,000 | — | — | — | 12.50 | — |
| ND(1978)FM (P) | 9,969 | Value: 18.50 | | | | |

**50 PISO** **KM# 229** **Weight:** 27.4000 g. **Composition:** 0.9250 Silver .8148 oz. ASW **Subject:** International Year of the Child

| Date | Mintage | F | VF | XF | Unc | BU |
|---|---|---|---|---|---|---|
| 1979FM (U) | 10,000 | — | — | — | 12.50 | — |
| 1979FM (P) | 27,000 | Value: 12.50 | | | | |

**50 PISO** **KM# 233** **Weight:** 27.4000 g. **Composition:** 0.9250 Silver .8148 oz. ASW **Subject:** Pope John Paul II visit

| Date | Mintage | F | VF | XF | Unc | BU |
|---|---|---|---|---|---|---|
| 1981FM (U) | 10,000 | — | — | — | 40.00 | — |
| 1981FM (P) | 3,353 | Value: 65.00 | | | | |

**50 PISO** **KM# 236** **Weight:** 27.4000 g. **Composition:** 0.9250 Silver .8148 oz. ASW **Subject:** 40th Anniversary of Bataan-Corregidor

| Date | Mintage | F | VF | XF | Unc | BU |
|---|---|---|---|---|---|---|
| ND(1982)FM (U) | 13,000 | — | — | — | 20.00 | — |
| ND(1982)FM (P) | 4,626 | Value: 50.00 | | | | |

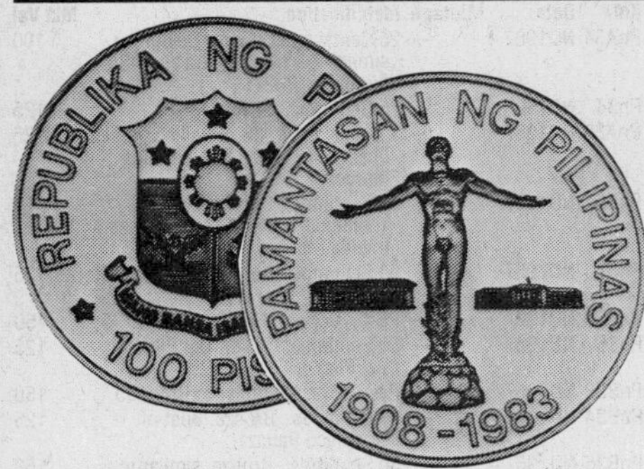

**100 PISO** **KM# 245** **Weight:** 25.0000 g. **Composition:** 0.5000 Silver .4019 oz. ASW **Subject:** 75th Anniversary - University of the Philippines

| Date | Mintage | F | VF | XF | Unc | BU |
|---|---|---|---|---|---|---|
| ND(1983) | 15,000 | — | — | — | 15.00 | — |
| ND(1983) Proof | 2,000 | Value: 36.50 | | | | |

**100 PISO** **KM# 264** **Weight:** 10.0000 g. **Composition:** 0.9250 Silver .2974 oz. ASW **Subject:** Papal Visit 1995

| Date | Mintage | F | VF | XF | Unc | BU |
|---|---|---|---|---|---|---|
| ND(1994) Proof | 1,000 | Value: 80.00 | | | | |

**100 PISO** **KM# 279** **Weight:** 16.7300 g. **Composition:** 0.8000 Silver .4303 oz. ASW **Subject:** Leyte Gulf Landing

| Date | Mintage | F | VF | XF | Unc | BU |
|---|---|---|---|---|---|---|
| ND(1994) Proof | 1,000 | Value: 75.00 | | | | |

**150 PISO** **KM# 254** **Weight:** 16.8200 g. **Composition:** 0.9250 Silver .5002 oz. ASW **Subject:** Southeast Asian Games **Reverse:** Official logo

| Date | Mintage | F | VF | XF | Unc | BU |
|---|---|---|---|---|---|---|
| 1991 Proof | 5,000 | Value: 55.00 | | | | |

**200 PISO** **KM# 248** **Weight:** 25.0000 g. **Composition:** 0.9250 Silver .7436 oz. ASW **Subject:** World Wildlife Fund **Reverse:** Mindoro Buffalo

| Date | Mintage | F | VF | XF | Unc | BU |
|---|---|---|---|---|---|---|
| 1987 Proof | 25,000 | Value: 45.00 | | | | |

**200 PISO** **KM# 252** **Weight:** 25.0000 g. **Composition:** 0.9250 Silver .7436 oz. ASW **Subject:** Save the Children fund

| Date | Mintage | F | VF | XF | Unc | BU |
|---|---|---|---|---|---|---|
| 1990 Proof | Est. 20,000 | Value: 50.00 | | | | |

**200 PISO** **KM# 265** **Weight:** 15.5600 g. **Composition:** 0.9990 Silver .4998 oz. ASW **Subject:** Papal Visit 1995 **Note:** Similar to 100 Piso, KM#264.

| Date | Mintage | F | VF | XF | Unc | BU |
|---|---|---|---|---|---|---|
| ND(1994) Proof | 1,000 | Value: 110 | | | | |

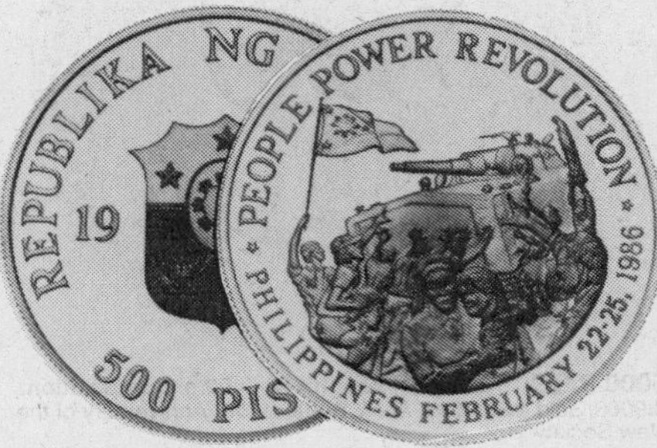

**500 PISO** **KM# 249** **Weight:** 28.0000 g. **Composition:** 0.9250 Silver .8328 oz. ASW **Subject:** People Power Revolution

| Date | Mintage | F | VF | XF | Unc | BU |
|---|---|---|---|---|---|---|
| 1988 Proof | Est. 7,500 | Value: 50.00 | | | | |

**500 PISO** **KM# 280** **Weight:** 23.1000 g. **Composition:** 0.9250 Silver .6870 oz. ASW **Subject:** Leyte Gulf Landing

| Date | Mintage | F | VF | XF | Unc | BU |
|---|---|---|---|---|---|---|
| ND(1994) Proof | 1,000 | Value: 150 | | | | |

**500 PISO** **KM# 276** **Weight:** 28.2800 g. **Composition:** 0.9250 Silver .8410 oz. ASW **Subject:** Centennial - Andres Bonifacio 1897-1997

| Date | Mintage | F | VF | XF | Unc | BU |
|---|---|---|---|---|---|---|
| ND(1997) Proof | — | Value: 75.00 | | | | |

**500 PISO** **KM# 274** **Weight:** 28.2800 g. **Composition:** 0.9250 Silver .8410 oz. ASW **Subject:** Carlos P. Romulo Centennial **Obverse:** National arms above denomination **Reverse:** Portrait, dates

| Date | Mintage | F | VF | XF | Unc | BU |
|---|---|---|---|---|---|---|
| ND(1998) Proof | Est. 2,100 | Value: 75.00 | | | | |

**500 PISO** **KM# 277** **Weight:** 28.2800 g. **Composition:** 0.9250 Silver .8410 oz. ASW **Subject:** Centennial - Emilio F. Aguinaldo 1898-1998

| Date | Mintage | F | VF | XF | Unc | BU |
|---|---|---|---|---|---|---|
| ND(1998) Proof | 2,100 | Value: 75.00 | | | | |

**500 PISO** **KM# 275** **Weight:** 28.2800 g. **Composition:** 0.9250 Silver .8410 oz. ASW **Subject:** 50th Anniversary - Central Bank **Obverse:** Old and new bank buildings **Reverse:** Old and new bank seals

| Date | Mintage | F | VF | XF | Unc | BU |
|---|---|---|---|---|---|---|
| ND(1999) Proof | Est. 5,000 | Value: 50.00 | | | | |

**1000 PISO** **KM# 213** **Weight:** 9.9500 g. **Composition:** 0.9000 Gold .2879 oz. AGW **Subject:** 3rd Anniversary of the New Society

| Date | Mintage | F | VF | XF | Unc | BU |
|---|---|---|---|---|---|---|
| 1975 | 23,000 | — | — | — | 135 | — |
| 1975 Proof | 13,000 | Value: 150 | | | | |

**1000 PISO** **KM# 281** **Weight:** 31.1000 g. **Composition:** 0.9990 Silver .9989 oz. ASW **Subject:** Leyte Gulf Landing

| Date | Mintage | F | VF | XF | Unc | BU |
|---|---|---|---|---|---|---|
| ND(1994) Proof | 1,000 | Value: 225 | | | | |

**1500 PISO** **KM# 216** **Weight:** 20.5500 g. **Composition:** 0.9000 Gold .5947 oz. AGW **Subject:** I.M.F. Meeting

| Date | Mintage | F | VF | XF | Unc | BU |
|---|---|---|---|---|---|---|
| 1976 | 5,500 | — | — | — | 250 | — |
| 1976 Proof | 6,500 | Value: 275 | | | | |

**1500 PISO** **KM# 219** **Weight:** 20.5500 g. **Composition:** 0.9000 Gold .5947 oz. AGW **Subject:** 5th Anniversary of the New Society

| Date | Mintage | F | VF | XF | Unc | BU |
|---|---|---|---|---|---|---|
| ND(1977) | 4,000 | — | — | — | 250 | — |
| ND(1977) Proof | 6,000 | Value: 275 | | | | |

**1500 PISO** KM# 223 **Weight:** 20.5500 g. **Composition:** 0.9000 Gold .5947 oz. AGW **Subject:** Inauguration of new mint facilities

| Date | Mintage | F | VF | XF | Unc | BU |
|---|---|---|---|---|---|---|
| 1978 | 3,000 | — | — | — | 275 | — |
| 1978 Proof | 3,000 | Value: 300 | | | | |

**1500 PISO** KM# 234 **Weight:** 9.9500 g. **Composition:** 0.9000 Gold .2879 oz. AGW **Subject:** Pope John Paul II visit

| Date | Mintage | F | VF | XF | Unc | BU |
|---|---|---|---|---|---|---|
| 1981 Proof | 1,000 | Value: 475 | | | | |
| 1982 Proof | — | — | — | — | — | — |

**1500 PISO** KM# 237 **Weight:** 9.7800 g. **Composition:** 0.9000 Gold .2830 oz. AGW **Subject:** 40th Anniversary of Bataan-Corregidor

| Date | Mintage | F | VF | XF | Unc | BU |
|---|---|---|---|---|---|---|
| ND(1982)FM (U) | 1,000 | — | — | — | 300 | — |
| ND(1982)FM (P) | 445 | Value: 450 | | | | |

**2500 PISO** KM# 231 **Weight:** 14.5700 g. **Composition:** 0.5000 Gold .2342 oz. AGW **Subject:** 100th Anniversary - Birth of Gen. Douglas MacArthur

| Date | Mintage | F | VF | XF | Unc | BU |
|---|---|---|---|---|---|---|
| ND(1980)FM (P) | 3,073 | Value: 275 | | | | |

**2500 PISO** KM# 247 **Weight:** 15.0000 g. **Composition:** 0.5000 Gold .2414 oz. AGW **Subject:** President Aquino's visit in Washington

| Date | Mintage | F | VF | XF | Unc | BU |
|---|---|---|---|---|---|---|
| 1986 Proof | Est. 250 | Value: 500 | | | | |

**2500 PISO** KM# 266 **Weight:** 7.9800 g. **Composition:** 0.9167 Gold .2352 oz. AGW **Subject:** Papal Visit 1995 **Note:** Similar to 100 Piso, KM#264.

| Date | Mintage | F | VF | XF | Unc | BU |
|---|---|---|---|---|---|---|
| ND(1994) Proof | — | Value: 400 | | | | |

**5000 PISO** KM# 220 **Weight:** 68.7400 g. **Composition:** 0.9000 Gold 1.9893 oz. AGW **Subject:** 5th Anniversary of the New Society

| Date | Mintage | F | VF | XF | Unc | BU |
|---|---|---|---|---|---|---|
| ND(1977)FM (U) | 100 | — | — | — | 1,600 | — |
| ND(1977)FM (P) | 3,832 | Value: 975 | | | | |

**5000 PISO** KM# 267 **Weight:** 16.8100 g. **Composition:** 0.9250 Gold .4999 oz. AGW **Subject:** Papal visit 1995 **Note:** Similar to 100 Piso, KM#264.

| Date | Mintage | F | VF | XF | Unc | BU |
|---|---|---|---|---|---|---|
| ND(1994) Proof | — | Value: 700 | | | | |

**10000 PESOS** KM# 255 **Weight:** 33.5500 g. **Composition:** 0.9250 Gold 1 oz. AGW **Subject:** People Power

| Date | Mintage | F | VF | XF | Unc | BU |
|---|---|---|---|---|---|---|
| ND(1992) Proof | 1,600 | Value: 650 | | | | |

## PATTERNS

Including off metal strikes

| KM# | Date | Mintage | Identification | Mkt Val |
|---|---|---|---|---|
| Pn20 | ND1922 | — | Centavo. Silver. KM#163. | — |
| Pn21 | ND | — | Peso. Silver. Marcos | — |
| Pn30 | ND1966 | — | Peso. Silver. Ferd and Imelda Marcos | — |
| Pn22 | ND1966 | — | Centavo. Copper. Central Bank | 100 |
| Pn23 | ND1966 | — | Brass. | 100 |
| Pn24 | ND1966 | — | Copper. | 100 |
| Pn25 | ND1966 | — | Silver. | 125 |
| Pn26 | ND1966 | — | Copper. | 100 |
| Pn27 | ND1966 | — | Brass. | 100 |
| PnA28 | ND1966 | — | Copper. Similar to Pn28. Conjoined busts of Ferdinand and Imelda Marcos. | 125 |
| PnB28 | ND1966 | — | Copper. As Pn28 | 125 |
| Pn28 | ND1966 | — | Silver. | 200 |
| Pn29 | ND1966 | — | Piso. Silver. | 200 |
| PnA31 | ND1966 | — | Piso. Copper. Similar to Pn28. As Pn38. | 150 |
| PnB31 | ND1966 | — | Piso. Brass. Similar to Pn38 wtihout eagle and lion on arms | 150 |
| Pn31 | ND1967 | — | Copper. | 100 |
| Pn32 | ND1967 | — | | 125 |
| Pn33 | ND1967 | — | Copper. Similar to Pn32. Similar to Pn27. | 125 |
| PnA34 | ND1967 | — | 25 Centavos. Copper. Design similar to Pn28, legend as Pn34. Similar to Pn27. | 100 |
| Pn34 | ND1967 | — | 25 Sentimos. Silver. | 125 |
| PnA35 | ND1967 | — | Copper. As Pn 36. Small conjoined busts of Ferdinand and Imelda Marcos. | 125 |
| Pn35 | ND1967 | — | 50 Sentimos. Copper. Large conjoined busts of Ferdinand and Imelda Marcos. | 150 |
| Pn37 | ND1967 | — | 50 Sentimos. Copper. Del Pilar left. Del Pilar | 125 |
| PnA38 | ND1967 | — | Peso. Copper. Similar to KM#195 | 150 |
| Pn36 | ND1967 | — | 50 Sentimos. Silver. Del Pilar left. Del Pilar | 125 |
| PnB38 | ND1967 | — | Peso. Brass. Similar to KM#195 | 150 |
| PnB34 | ND1967 | — | 10 Centavos. Bronze. Bust of Francisco Baltazar. | 125 |
| PnB35 | ND1967 | — | 50 Sentimos. Bronze. similar to Pn28. Bust of Juan Luna. | 150 |
| Pn38 | ND1968 | — | Peso. Silver. Sower walking left. | 225 |
| Pn39 | ND1968 | — | Piso. Silver. Sower walking right. | 225 |
| PnA40 | ND1969 | — | Peso. Copper. Similar to KM#195. As Pn40. | 150 |
| Pn40 | ND1969 | — | Piso. Silver. Dated 1966. Aquinaldo | 225 |
| Pn41 | NDND | — | Peso. Copper. Similar to KM#195. Conjoined busts of Marcos and Pope Paul VI left. | 150 |
| Pn42 | ND1970 | — | Peso. Copper. Similar to KM#195. Bust of Pope Paul VI 3/4 right. | 150 |

## PIEFORTS

All standard metals unless otherwise indicated

| KM# | Date | Mintage | Identification | Mkt Val |
|---|---|---|---|---|
| P1 | ND1999 | — | 50 Pisa. KM#229 | — |

## TRIAL STRIKES

| KM# | Date | Mintage | Identification | Mkt Val |
|---|---|---|---|---|
| TS8 | ND1967 | — | Peso. Brass. KM#195. Bataan Day | 75.00 |

## MINT SETS

| KM# | Date | Mintage | Identification | Issue Price | Mkt Val |
|---|---|---|---|---|---|
| MS10 | 1977 (8) | 10,000 | KM#205-210, 217-218 | — | 30.00 |
| MS15 | 1982 (5) | — | KM#209.2, 224-227 | — | 2.50 |
| MS5 | 1975 (8) | 5,877 | KM#205-208, 209.1, 210-212. Enclosed in Franklin Mint folder | 33.50 | 30.00 |
| MS6 | 1975 (8) | 3,850 | KM#205-208, 209.1, 210-212 | — | 45.00 |
| MS7 | 1976 (8) | 1,826 | KM#205-210, 214-215. Enclosed in Franklin Mint folder | — | 150 |
| MS8 | 1976 (8) | 10,000 | KM#205-210, 214-215 | — | 30.00 |
| MS9 | 1977 (8) | 354 | KM#205-210, 217-218; Enclosed in Franklin Mint folder. | — | 175 |
| MS1 | 1936 (3) | — | KM#176-178 | — | 325 |
| MS2 | 1947 (2) | — | KM#184-185 | — | 20.00 |
| MS3 | 1958 (5) | — | KM#186-190 | — | 2.50 |
| MS4 | 1970 (2) | — | KM#202-202a | — | 15.00 |
| MS11 | 1978 (8) | 10,000 | KM#205-210, 221-222 | — | 30.00 |
| MS12 | 1979 (8) | 10,000 | KM#209.2-210.2, 224-229 | — | 30.00 |
| MS13 | 1980 (7) | 9,800 | KM#209.2-210.2, 224-227, 230 | — | 25.00 |
| MS14 | 1981 (8) | 10,000 | KM#209.2-210.2, 224-227, 232-233 | — | 45.00 |
| MS16 | 1983 (8) | — | KM#238-239, 240.2, 241, 242.1, 243-245BRM | — | 16.00 |
| MS18 | 1983 (7) | — | KM#238-239, 240.2, 241.1, 242.1, 243-244 | — | 5.00 |
| MS17 | 1983 (7) | — | KM#238-239, 240.1, 241, 242.1, 243-244 | — | 5.00 |
| MS19 | 1985 (7) | — | KM#238-239, 240.2, 241.1, 242.1, 243-244 | — | 5.00 |
| MS20 | 1986 (7) | — | KM#238-239, 240.2, 241.1, 243-244 | — | 5.00 |
| MS21 | 1987 (7) | — | KM#238-239, 240.2, 241.1, 242.1, 243-244 | — | 5.00 |
| MS22 | 1988 (7) | — | KM#238-239, 240.2, 241.1, 242.1, 243-244 | — | 5.00 |
| MS23 | 1989 (7) | — | KM#238-239, 240.2, 241.1, 242.1, 243-244 | — | 5.00 |

| KM# | Date | Mintage | Identification | Issue Price | Mkt Val |
|---|---|---|---|---|---|
| MS24 | 1989 (7) | — | KM#238-239, 240.2, 241, 242.1, 243-244 | — | 5.00 |
| MS25 | 1990 (7) | — | KM#238-239, 240.2, 241.1, 242.1, 243-244 | — | 5.00 |
| MS26 | 1990 (7) | — | KM#238-239, 240.2, 241.1, 242.1, 243-244 | — | 5.00 |
| MS27 | 1991 (8) | — | KM#238-239, 240.2, 241.2, 242.3, 243.2, 258-259 | — | 10.00 |
| MS28 | 1992 (8) | — | KM#238-239, 240.2, 241.2, 242.3, 243.2, 258-259 | — | 10.00 |
| MS29 | 1995 (6) | — | KM#268-273 | — | 10.00 |
| MS30 | 1996 (6) | — | KM#268-273 | — | 10.00 |
| MS31 | 1997 (6) | — | KM#268-273 | — | 20.00 |
| MS32 | 1998 (5) | — | KM#268-269, 271-273 | — | 20.00 |
| MS33 | 1999 (5) | — | KM#268-269, 271-273 | — | 20.00 |
| MS34 | 2000 (5) | — | KM#268-269, 271, 273, 278 | — | — |

## PROOF SETS

| KM# | Date | Mintage | Identification | Issue Price | Mkt Val |
|---|---|---|---|---|---|
| PS1 | 1903 (7) | 2,558 | KM#162-168 | — | 700 |
| PS1i | 1903 (7) | I.A. | KM#162-168 (impaired) | — | 300 |
| PS2 | 1904 (7) | 1,355 | KM#162-168 | — | 800 |
| PS2i | 1904 (7) | I.A. | KM#162-168 (impaired) | — | 425 |
| PS3 | 1905 (7) | 471 | KM#162-168 | — | 2,500 |
| PS3i | 1905 (7) | I.A. | KM#162-168 (impaired) | — | 950 |
| PS4 | 1906 (7) | 500 | KM#162-168 | — | 1,600 |
| PS4i | 1906 (7) | I.A. | KM#162-168 (impaired) | — | 750 |
| PS5 | 1908 (7) | 500 | KM#162-164, 169-172 | — | 1,600 |
| PS5i | 1908 (7) | I.A. | KM#162-164, 169-172 (impaired) | — | 700 |
| PS6 | 1958 (5) | — | KM#186-190 | — | — |
| PS7 | 1974 (6) | 10,000 | KM#196-200, 203; Not released to the general public | — | 65.00 |
| PS8 | 1975 (8) | 36,516 | KM#205-208, 209.1-210.1, 211-212 | 67.00 | 25.00 |
| PS9 | 1975 (6) | — | KM#205-208, 209.1-210.1 | — | — |
| PS10 | 1976 (8) | 9,901 | KM#205-208, 209.1-210.1, 214-215 | 67.00 | 35.00 |
| PS12 | 1978 (8) | 4,792 | KM#205-208, 209.1-210.1, 220-221 | 70.00 | 50.00 |
| PS11 | 1977 (8) | 4,822 | KM#205-208, 209.1-210.1, 217-218 | 70.00 | 45.00 |
| PS13 | 1978 (2) | 3,911 | KM#221-222 | 46.00 | 30.00 |
| PS14 | 1979 (8) | 3,645 | KM#209.2-210.2, 224-229 | 68.00 | 50.00 |
| PS15 | 1979 (2) | 2,448 | KM#228-229 | 47.50 | 30.00 |
| PS16 | 1980 (7) | 3,133 | KM#209.2-210.2, 224-227, 230 | 65.00 | 50.00 |
| PS17 | 1981 (8) | 1,795 | KM#209.2-210.2, 224-227, 232-233 | — | 115 |
| PS18 | 1982 (7) | — | KM#209.2-210.2, 224-227, 236 | 52.00 | 60.00 |
| PS19 | 1983 (8) | — | KM#238-239, 240.1, 241, 242.1, 243-245 | 50.00 | 75.00 |
| PS20 | 1986 (2) | — | KM#246-247 | — | 610 |

## CULION ISLAND

The Culion Leper Colony was established around 1903 on the island of Culion about 150 miles southeast of Manila by the Commission of Public Health. The first issue of coins valid only in the colony was produced by a private firm, Frank & Company. Later issues were struck at the Manila Mint.

**MINT MARKS**
PM = Philippine Mint at Manila

**MONETARY SYSTEM**
100 Centavos = 1 Peso

# CULION LEPER COLONY

### Philippine Commission of Public Health

## LEPROSARIUM COINAGE

The Culion Leper Colony was established around 1903 on the island of Culion about 150 miles southeast of Manila by the Commission of Public Health. The first issue of coins valid only in the colony was produced by a private firm, Frank & Company. Later issues were struck at the Manila Mint.

**1/2 CENTAVO** **KM# 1** **Composition:** Aluminum

| Date | Mintage | F | VF | XF | Unc | BU |
|---|---|---|---|---|---|---|
| 1913 | 17,000 | 1.00 | 2.00 | 5.00 | 9.00 | 12.00 |

**Note:** Some authorities doubt that this coin circulated

**CENTAVO** **KM# 2** **Composition:** Aluminum

| Date | Mintage | Good | VG | F | VF | XF |
|---|---|---|---|---|---|---|
| 1913 | 33,000 | 70.00 | 150 | 375 | 650 | — |

**Note:** This coin exists with thick and thin planchets

**CENTAVO** **KM# 3** **Composition:** Copper-Nickel **Note:** Similar to KM#4 but first die, better strike.

| Date | Mintage | Good | VG | F | VF | XF |
|---|---|---|---|---|---|---|
| 1927PM | 30,000 | 10.00 | 15.00 | 25.00 | 50.00 | — |

**CENTAVO** **KM# 4** **Composition:** Copper-Nickel **Note:** Second die, poor strike.

| Date | Mintage | Good | VG | F | VF | XF |
|---|---|---|---|---|---|---|
| 1927PM | Inc. above | 12.00 | 17.50 | 30.00 | 60.00 | — |

**Note:** This coin exists with thick and thin planchets

**CENTAVO** **KM# 5** **Composition:** Copper-Nickel **Obverse:** Bust of Rizal in circle **Reverse:** PHILIPPINE HEALTH SERVICE/LEPER COIN ONE CENTAVO

| Date | Mintage | Good | VG | F | VF | XF |
|---|---|---|---|---|---|---|
| 1930 | — | — | — | — | — | — |

**Note:** Reported, not confirmed

**5 CENTAVOS** **KM# 6** **Composition:** Aluminum

| Date | Mintage | Good | VG | F | VF | XF |
|---|---|---|---|---|---|---|
| 1913 | 6,600 | 35.00 | 65.00 | 225 | 400 | — |

**5 CENTAVOS** **KM# 7** **Composition:** Copper-Nickel

| Date | Mintage | Good | VG | F | VF | XF |
|---|---|---|---|---|---|---|
| 1927 | 16,000 | 3.00 | 6.00 | 10.00 | 18.00 | — |

**10 CENTAVOS** **KM# 8** **Composition:** Aluminum **Note:** Similar to 1/2 Centavo, KM#1.

| Date | Mintage | Good | VG | F | VF | XF |
|---|---|---|---|---|---|---|
| 1913 | 6,600 | 12.00 | 20.00 | 35.00 | 100 | — |

**10 CENTAVOS** **KM# 9** **Composition:** Aluminum **Note:** Similar to 1 Peso, KM#14.

| Date | Mintage | Good | VG | F | VF | XF |
|---|---|---|---|---|---|---|
| 1920 | 20,000 | 4.00 | 10.00 | 22.50 | 50.00 | — |

**10 CENTAVOS** **KM# 10** **Composition:** Copper-Nickel

| Date | Mintage | VG | F | VF | XF | Unc |
|---|---|---|---|---|---|---|
| 1930 | 17,000 | 2.00 | 4.00 | 7.50 | 15.00 | 25.00 |

**Note:** One pattern in copper, has been authenticated by ANACS

**20 CENTAVOS** **KM# 11** **Composition:** Aluminum **Note:** Similar to 1/2 Centavo, KM#1.

| Date | Mintage | Good | VG | F | VF | XF |
|---|---|---|---|---|---|---|
| 1913 | 10,000 | 30.00 | 50.00 | 85.00 | 150 | — |

**20 CENTAVOS** **KM# 12** **Composition:** Aluminum

| Date | Mintage | Good | VG | F | VF | XF |
|---|---|---|---|---|---|---|
| 1920 | 10,000 | 5.00 | 10.00 | 20.00 | 45.00 | — |

**20 CENTAVOS** **KM# 13** **Composition:** Copper-Nickel

| Date | Mintage | Good | VG | F | VF | Unc |
|---|---|---|---|---|---|---|
| 1922PM | 10,000 | 5.00 | 10.00 | 17.50 | 30.00 | — |

**Note:** This coin exists with thick and thin planchets

**PESO** **KM# 14** **Composition:** Aluminum

| Date | Mintage | VG | F | VF | XF | Unc |
|---|---|---|---|---|---|---|
| 1913 | 8,600 | 5.00 | 10.00 | 17.50 | 35.00 | — |

**Note:** This coin exists with thick and thin planchets

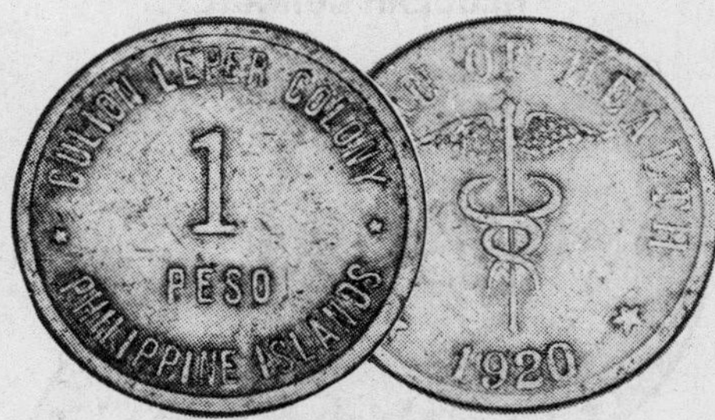


**PESO** **KM# 15** **Composition:** Aluminum

| Date | Mintage | VG | F | VF | XF | Unc |
|---|---|---|---|---|---|---|
| 1920 | 4,000 | 6.00 | 12.50 | 20.00 | 40.00 | — |

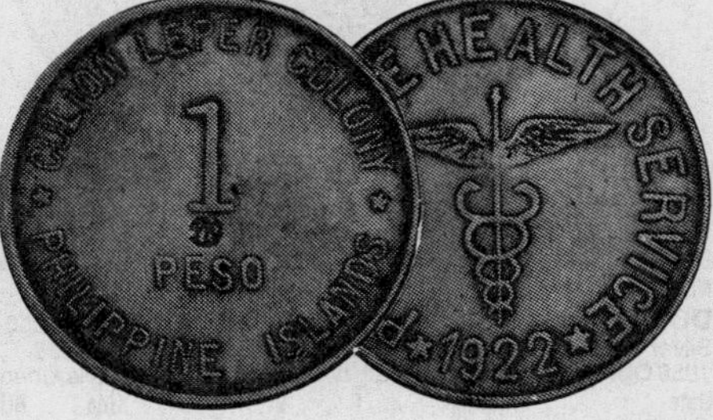


**PESO** **KM# 16** **Composition:** Copper-Nickel **Note:** Varieties exist.

| Date | Mintage | VG | F | VF | XF | Unc |
|---|---|---|---|---|---|---|
| 1922 | 8,280 | 5.00 | 10.00 | 15.00 | 25.00 | — |

**PESO** **KM# 17** **Composition:** Copper-Nickel **Note:** Similar to KM#16, but caduceus has curved wings.

| Date | Mintage | VG | F | VF | XF | Unc |
|---|---|---|---|---|---|---|
| 1922PM | Inc. above | 35.00 | 60.00 | 90.00 | 175 | — |

**PESO** **KM# 18** **Composition:** Copper-Nickel

| Date | Mintage | VG | F | VF | XF | Unc |
|---|---|---|---|---|---|---|
| 1925 | 20,000 | 2.00 | 5.00 | 10.00 | 25.00 | — |

A small volcanic island, along with the uninhabited islands of Oeno, Henderson, and Ducie, constitute the British Colony of Pitcairn Islands. The main island has an area of about 2 sq. mi. (5 sq. km.) and a population of *68. It is located 1350 miles southeast of Tahiti. The islanders subsist on fishing, garden produce and crops. The sale of postage stamps and carved curios to passing ships brings cash income.

Discovered in 1767 by a British naval officer, Pitcairn was not occupied until 1790 when Fletcher Christian and nine mutineers from the British ship, *HMS Bounty*, along with some Tahitian men and women went ashore, and survived in obscurity until discovered by American whalers in 1808.

Adamstown is the chief settlement, located on the north coast, one of the few places that island-made longboats can land. The primary religion is Seventh-day Adventist and a public school provides basic education. In 1898 the settlement was placed under the jurisdiction of the Commissioner for the Western Pacific. Since 1970 this British settlement has been governed through a locally elected council under a governor.

New Zealand currency has been used since July 10, 1967.

# BRITISH COLONY

## REGULAR COINAGE

**DOLLAR** KM# 3 **Composition:** Copper Nickel **Subject:** Drafting of constitution, 1838-1988 **Obverse:** Queen Elizabeth II **Reverse:** Ship with sails furled

| Date | Mintage | F | VF | XF | Unc | BU |
|---|---|---|---|---|---|---|
| ND(1988) | — | — | — | — | 8.00 | — |

**DOLLAR** KM# 3a **Weight:** 28.2800 g. **Composition:** 0.9250 Silver .8411 oz. ASW **Subject:** Drafting of constitution, 1838-1988 **Obverse:** Queen Elizabeth II **Reverse:** Ship with sails furled

| Date | Mintage | F | VF | XF | Unc | BU |
|---|---|---|---|---|---|---|
| ND(1988) Proof | — | Value: 40.00 | | | | |

**DOLLAR** KM# 4 **Composition:** Copper Nickel **Subject:** HMAV Bounty, 1789-1989 **Obverse:** Queen Elizabeth II

| Date | Mintage | F | VF | XF | Unc | BU |
|---|---|---|---|---|---|---|
| ND(1989) | 50,000 | — | — | — | 8.00 | — |

**DOLLAR** KM# 4a **Weight:** 28.2800 g. **Composition:** 0.9250 Silver .8411 oz. ASW **Subject:** HMAV Bounty, 1789-1989 **Obverse:** Queen Elizabeth II

| Date | Mintage | F | VF | XF | Unc | BU |
|---|---|---|---|---|---|---|
| ND(1989) Proof | 20,000 | Value: 40.00 | | | | |

**DOLLAR** KM# 7 **Composition:** Copper Nickel **Subject:** Establishment of settlement, 1790-1990 **Obverse:** Queen Elizabeth II **Reverse:** Ship in flames

| Date | Mintage | F | VF | XF | Unc | BU |
|---|---|---|---|---|---|---|
| ND(1990) | — | — | — | — | 8.00 | — |

**DOLLAR** KM# 7a **Weight:** 28.2800 g. **Composition:** 0.9250 Silver .8411 oz. ASW **Subject:** Establishment of settlement, 1790-1990 **Obverse:** Queen Elizabeth II **Reverse:** Ship in flames

| Date | Mintage | F | VF | XF | Unc | BU |
|---|---|---|---|---|---|---|
| ND(1990) Proof | 10,000 | Value: 45.00 | | | | |

**DOLLAR** KM# 10 **Composition:** Copper-Nickel **Subject:** British Queen Mother **Obverse:** Queen's head right **Reverse:** Queen Mother and the Order of the Garter **Size:** 38.5 mm. **Note:** Struck at the British Royal Mint.

| Date | Mintage | F | VF | XF | Unc | BU |
|---|---|---|---|---|---|---|
| 1997 | — | — | — | — | 10.00 | — |

**50 DOLLARS** KM# 1 **Weight:** 155.6000 g. **Composition:** 0.9990 Silver 5 oz. ASW **Subject:** Drafting of constitution, 1838-1988 **Obverse:** Queen Elizabeth II **Reverse:** Ship with sails furled **Size:** 65 mm. **Note:** Illustration reduced.

| Date | Mintage | F | VF | XF | Unc | BU |
|---|---|---|---|---|---|---|
| ND(1988) Proof | 10,000 | Value: 125 | | | | |

**50 DOLLARS** KM# 5 **Weight:** 155.6000 g. **Composition:** 0.9990 Silver 5 oz. ASW **Subject:** HMAV Bounty, 1789-1989 **Note:** Similar to 250 Dollars, KM#2.

| Date | Mintage | F | VF | XF | Unc | BU |
|---|---|---|---|---|---|---|
| ND(1989) Proof | 10,000 | Value: 135 | | | | |

**50 DOLLARS** KM# 8 **Weight:** 155.6000 g. **Composition:** 0.9990 Silver 5 oz. ASW **Subject:** Establishment of settlement, 1790-1990 **Note:** Similar to 250 Dollars, KM#9.

| Date | Mintage | F | VF | XF | Unc | BU |
|---|---|---|---|---|---|---|
| ND(1990) Proof | 2,500 | Value: 165 | | | | |

**250 DOLLARS** KM# 2 **Weight:** 15.9800 g. **Composition:** 0.9170 Gold .4708 oz. AGW **Subject:** Drafting of Constitution, 1838-1988 **Obverse:** Queen Elizabeth II **Reverse:** Ship with sails furled

| Date | Mintage | F | VF | XF | Unc | BU |
|---|---|---|---|---|---|---|
| ND(1988) Proof | 2,500 | Value: 300 | | | | |

**250 DOLLARS** KM# 6 **Weight:** 15.9800 g. **Composition:** 0.9170 Gold .4708 oz. AGW **Subject:** HMAV Bounty, 1789-1989 **Obverse:** Queen Elizabeth II

| Date | Mintage | F | VF | XF | Unc | BU |
|---|---|---|---|---|---|---|
| ND(1989) Proof | 2,500 | Value: 300 | | | | |

**250 DOLLARS** KM# 9 **Weight:** 15.9800 g. **Composition:** 0.9170 Gold .4708 oz. AGW **Subject:** Establishment of settlement, 1790-1990 **Obverse:** Queen Elizabeth II

| Date | Mintage | F | VF | XF | Unc | BU |
|---|---|---|---|---|---|---|
| ND(1990) Proof | 500 | Value: 350 | | | | |

**Obverse:** Rifle Corps symbol below eagle **Reverse:** Jozef Pilsudski

| Date | Mintage | F | VF | XF | Unc | BU |
|---|---|---|---|---|---|---|
| 1934(w) | 300,000 | 5.00 | 8.00 | 16.50 | 40.00 | — |

**5 ZLOTYCH** **Y# 28** **Weight:** 11.0000 g. **Composition:** 0.7500 Silver .2652 oz. ASW **Obverse:** Jozef Pilsudski

| Date | Mintage | F | VF | XF | Unc | BU |
|---|---|---|---|---|---|---|
| 1934(w) | 6,510,000 | 2.50 | 4.00 | 9.00 | 22.00 | — |
| 1935(w) | 1,800,000 | 3.00 | 4.50 | 10.00 | 25.00 | — |
| 1936(w) | 1,800,000 | 3.00 | 4.50 | 10.00 | 25.00 | — |
| 1938(w) | 289,000 | 5.00 | 7.50 | 15.00 | 30.00 | — |

**5 ZLOTYCH** **Y# 31** **Weight:** 11.0000 g. **Composition:** 0.7500 Silver .2652 oz. ASW **Subject:** 15th Anniversary of Gdynia Seaport

| Date | Mintage | F | VF | XF | Unc | BU |
|---|---|---|---|---|---|---|
| 1936(w) | 1,000,000 | 7.00 | 12.00 | 25.00 | 50.00 | — |

**10 ZLOTYCH** **Y# 32** **Weight:** 3.2258 g. **Composition:** 0.9000 Gold .0933 oz. AGW **Reverse:** Boleslaw I **Note:** Never released into circulation.

| Date | Mintage | F | VF | XF | Unc | BU |
|---|---|---|---|---|---|---|
| ND(1925)(w) | 50,000 | — | 50.00 | 65.00 | 100 | — |

**10 ZLOTYCH** **Y# 22** **Weight:** 22.0000 g. **Composition:** 0.7500 Silver .5305 oz. ASW

| Date | Mintage | F | VF | XF | Unc | BU |
|---|---|---|---|---|---|---|
| 1932(w) | 3,100,000 | 5.00 | 8.00 | 12.50 | 32.50 | — |
| 1932 (London) without mint mark | 6,000,000 | 5.00 | 8.00 | 12.50 | 32.50 | — |
| 1932(w) Proof | 100 | — | — | — | — | — |
| 1933(w) | 2,800,000 | 5.00 | 8.00 | 12.50 | 32.50 | — |
| 1933(w) Proof | 100 | — | — | — | — | — |

**10 ZLOTYCH** **Y# 23** **Weight:** 22.0000 g. **Composition:** 0.7500 Silver .5305 oz. ASW **Subject:** Jan III Sobieski's Victory Over the Turks **Obverse:** Similar to Y#22

| Date | Mintage | F | VF | XF | Unc | BU |
|---|---|---|---|---|---|---|
| ND(1933)(w) | 300,000 | 8.00 | 16.00 | 25.00 | 55.00 | — |
| ND(1933)(w) Proof | 100 | — | — | — | — | — |

**10 ZLOTYCH** **Y# 24** **Weight:** 22.0000 g. **Composition:** 0.7500 Silver .5305 oz. ASW **Subject:** 70th Anniversary of 1863 Insurrection **Obverse:** Similar to Y#23

| Date | Mintage | F | VF | XF | Unc | BU |
|---|---|---|---|---|---|---|
| ND(1933)(w) | 300,000 | 10.00 | 20.00 | 35.00 | 60.00 | — |
| ND(1933)(w) Proof | 100 | — | — | — | — | — |

**10 ZLOTYCH** **Y# 26** **Weight:** 22.0000 g. **Composition:** 0.7500 Silver .5305 oz. ASW **Subject:** Rifle Corps August 6, 1914 **Obverse:** Rifle Corps symbol below eagle **Reverse:** Jozef Pilsudski

| Date | Mintage | F | VF | XF | Unc | BU |
|---|---|---|---|---|---|---|
| 1934(w) | 300,000 | 9.00 | 17.50 | 25.00 | 50.00 | — |

**10 ZLOTYCH** **Y# 29** **Weight:** 22.0000 g. **Composition:** 0.7500 Silver .5305 oz. ASW **Obverse:** Jozef Pilsudski

| Date | Mintage | F | VF | XF | Unc | BU |
|---|---|---|---|---|---|---|
| 1934(w) | 200,000 | 12.00 | 18.00 | 25.00 | 55.00 | — |
| 1935(w) | 1,670,000 | 4.00 | 7.00 | 14.00 | 35.00 | — |
| 1936(w) | 2,130,000 | 4.00 | 7.00 | 14.00 | 35.00 | — |
| 1937(w) | 908,000 | 4.00 | 7.00 | 16.00 | 40.00 | — |
| 1938(w) | 234,000 | 6.00 | 9.00 | 20.00 | 50.00 | — |
| 1939(w) | — | 4.00 | 7.00 | 16.00 | 40.00 | — |

**20 ZLOTYCH** **Y# 33** **Weight:** 6.4516 g. **Composition:** 0.9000 Gold .1867 oz. AGW **Reverse:** Boleslaw I **Note:** Never released into circulation.

| Date | Mintage | F | VF | XF | Unc | BU |
|---|---|---|---|---|---|---|
| ND(1925)(w) | 27,000 | — | 90.00 | 100 | 185 | — |

## MEDALLIC COINAGE

**GROSZ** **KM# M10** **Weight:** 1.5000 g. **Composition:** Bronze **Subject:** Mint Dedication **Reverse:** 21.V below GROSZ

| Date | Mintage | F | VF | XF | Unc | BU |
|---|---|---|---|---|---|---|
| 1925(w) | 1,000 | 1.75 | 3.50 | 6.00 | 10.00 | — |

**2 GROSZE** **KM# M11** **Weight:** 2.0000 g. **Composition:** Bronze **Subject:** Visit of President I Moscickiego **Reverse:** 27/x IM26 below GROSZE

| Date | Mintage | F | VF | XF | Unc | BU |
|---|---|---|---|---|---|---|
| 1926(w) | 600 | 5.00 | 8.00 | 13.50 | 22.50 | — |

**5 GROSZY** **KM# M12** **Weight:** 3.5000 g. **Composition:** Brass **Subject:** Visit of President St. Wojciechowski **Reverse:** 12/IV SW 24 below GROSZY

| Date | Mintage | F | VF | XF | Unc | BU |
|---|---|---|---|---|---|---|
| 1923 | 500 | 3.00 | 6.00 | 10.00 | 20.00 | — |

**5 GROSZY** **KM# M13** **Composition:** Brass **Subject:** 2nd Polish Numismatic and Medallographic Society Meeting at Posen on June 3, 1929

| Date | Mintage | F | VF | XF | Unc | BU |
|---|---|---|---|---|---|---|
| 1929(w) | 45 | 50.00 | 75.00 | 100 | 150 | — |

**5 ZLOTYCH** **KM# M14** **Weight:** 25.0000 g. **Composition:** Silver **Obverse:** SW and WG monograms and 3/V **Reverse:** 100 pears in circle

| Date | Mintage | F | VF | XF | Unc | BU |
|---|---|---|---|---|---|---|
| 1925 | 100 | 250 | 450 | 800 | 1,250 | — |

**5 ZLOTYCH** **KM# M14a** **Composition:** Gold

| Date | Mintage | F | VF | XF | Unc | BU |
|---|---|---|---|---|---|---|
| 1925 Rare | 2 | — | — | — | — | — |

# WWII GERMAN OCCUPATION

## OCCUPATION COINAGE

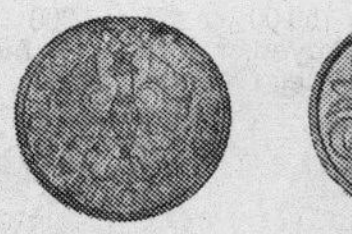

**GROSZ** **Y# 34** **Composition:** Zinc

| Date | Mintage | F | VF | XF | Unc | BU |
|---|---|---|---|---|---|---|
| 1939(w) | 33,909,000 | 0.50 | 1.00 | 1.75 | 3.50 | — |

**5 GROSZY** **Y# 35** **Composition:** Zinc

| Date | Mintage | F | VF | XF | Unc | BU |
|---|---|---|---|---|---|---|
| 1939(w) | 15,324,000 | 0.50 | 1.50 | 2.00 | 5.00 | — |

**10 GROSZY** **Y# 36** **Composition:** Zinc

| Date | Mintage | F | VF | XF | Unc | BU |
|---|---|---|---|---|---|---|
| 1923(w) | 42,175,000 | 0.10 | 0.20 | 0.40 | 2.00 | — |

**Note:** Actually struck in 1941-44

**20 GROSZY** **Y# 37** **Composition:** Zinc

| Date | Mintage | F | VF | XF | Unc | BU |
|---|---|---|---|---|---|---|
| 1923(w) | 40,025,000 | 0.15 | 0.25 | 0.50 | 2.00 | — |

**Note:** Actually struck in 1941-44

**50 GROSZY** Y# 38 **Composition:** Nickel Plated Iron

| Date | Mintage | F | VF | XF | Unc | BU |
|---|---|---|---|---|---|---|
| 1938(w) | 32,000,000 | 1.00 | 2.00 | 4.00 | 8.50 | — |

**50 GROSZY** Y# 38a **Composition:** Iron

| Date | Mintage | F | VF | XF | Unc | BU |
|---|---|---|---|---|---|---|
| 1938(w) | — | 1.25 | 2.50 | 5.00 | 10.00 | — |

**Note:** Varities exist

## TOKEN COINAGE

### Lodz Ghetto, 1942-1944

A major industrial city in western Poland before World War II and site of the first wartime ghetto under German occupation (May 1940). It was also the last ghetto to close during the war (August 1944). Token coinage was struck in 1942 and 1943. This series has seen very little circulation, but is commonly found in conditions from slightly to badly corroded. The badly corroded specimens have the appearance of zinc.

**10 PFENNIG** KM# Tn1 **Composition:** Aluminum-Magnesium

| Date | Mintage | VG | F | VF | XF | Unc |
|---|---|---|---|---|---|---|
| 1942 | Est. 100,000 | 60.00 | 125 | 200 | — | — |

**Note:** Most were destroyed or remelted as the design was too similar to regular German coinage

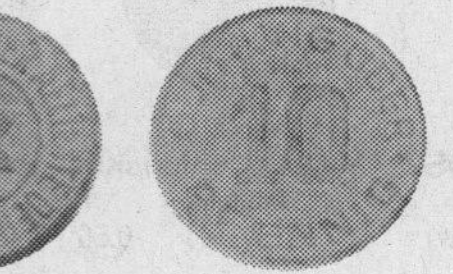

**10 PFENNIG** KM# Tn5 **Composition:** Aluminum-Magnesium

| Date | Mintage | VG | F | VF | XF | Unc |
|---|---|---|---|---|---|---|
| 1942 | 100,000 | 35.00 | 50.00 | 65.00 | 125 | — |

**5 MARK** KM# Tn2 **Composition:** Aluminum

| Date | Mintage | VG | F | VF | XF | Unc |
|---|---|---|---|---|---|---|
| 1943 | 600,000 | 5.00 | 10.00 | 25.00 | 45.00 | — |

**5 MARK** KM# Tn2a **Composition:** Aluminum-Magnesium

| Date | Mintage | VG | F | VF | XF | Unc |
|---|---|---|---|---|---|---|
| 1943 | Inc. above | 20.00 | 40.00 | 75.00 | — | — |

**10 MARK** KM# Tn3 **Composition:** Aluminum **Note:** Thick and thin planchets exist.

| Date | Mintage | VG | F | VF | XF | Unc |
|---|---|---|---|---|---|---|
| 1943 | 100,000 | 5.00 | 10.00 | 25.00 | 45.00 | — |

**10 MARK** KM# Tn3a **Composition:** Aluminum-Magnesium

| Date | Mintage | VG | F | VF | XF | Unc |
|---|---|---|---|---|---|---|
| 1943 | Inc. above | 25.00 | 45.00 | 85.00 | — | — |

**20 MARK** KM# Tn4 **Composition:** Aluminum **Note:** Beware of numerous counterfeits.

| Date | Mintage | VG | F | VF | XF | Unc |
|---|---|---|---|---|---|---|
| 1943 | — | 75.00 | 110 | 150 | 250 | — |

## REPUBLIC

### Post War

## STANDARD COINAGE

**GROSZ** Y# 39 **Composition:** Aluminum **Note:** 116,000 were struck at Warsaw, the remainder at Budapest.

| Date | Mintage | F | VF | XF | Unc | BU |
|---|---|---|---|---|---|---|
| 1949 | 400,116,000 | 0.10 | 0.20 | 0.30 | 0.75 | — |

**2 GROSZE** Y# 40 **Composition:** Aluminum **Note:** 106,000 were struck at Warsaw, the remainder at Budapest.

| Date | Mintage | F | VF | XF | Unc | BU |
|---|---|---|---|---|---|---|
| 1949 | 300,106,000 | 0.10 | 0.25 | 0.50 | 1.00 | — |

**5 GROSZY** Y# 41 **Composition:** Bronze **Note:** Struck at Basel.

| Date | Mintage | F | VF | XF | Unc | BU |
|---|---|---|---|---|---|---|
| 1949 | 300,000,000 | 0.10 | 0.25 | 0.50 | 1.00 | — |

**5 GROSZY** Y# 41a **Composition:** Aluminum **Note:** Struck at Kremnica.

| Date | Mintage | F | VF | XF | Unc | BU |
|---|---|---|---|---|---|---|
| 1949 | 200,000,000 | 0.10 | 0.25 | 0.75 | 1.50 | — |

**10 GROSZY** Y# 42 **Composition:** Copper-Nickel **Note:** Struck at Kremnica.

| Date | Mintage | F | VF | XF | Unc | BU |
|---|---|---|---|---|---|---|
| 1949 | 200,000,000 | 0.20 | 0.40 | 0.60 | 1.50 | — |

**10 GROSZY** Y# 42a **Composition:** Aluminum **Note:** Struck at Warsaw.

| Date | Mintage | F | VF | XF | Unc | BU |
|---|---|---|---|---|---|---|
| 1949 | 31,047,000 | 0.10 | 0.25 | 0.75 | 2.50 | — |

**20 GROSZY** Y# 43 **Composition:** Copper-Nickel **Note:** Struck at Kremnica.

| Date | Mintage | F | VF | XF | Unc | BU |
|---|---|---|---|---|---|---|
| 1949 | 133,383,000 | 0.25 | 0.45 | 0.75 | 2.00 | — |

**20 GROSZY** Y# 43a **Composition:** Aluminum

| Date | Mintage | F | VF | XF | Unc | BU |
|---|---|---|---|---|---|---|
| 1949 | 197,472,000 | 0.10 | 0.25 | 0.75 | 2.50 | — |

**50 GROSZY** Y# 44 **Composition:** Copper-Nickel **Note:** Struck at Kremnica.

| Date | Mintage | F | VF | XF | Unc | BU |
|---|---|---|---|---|---|---|
| 1949 | 109,000,000 | 0.35 | 0.65 | 1.00 | 2.50 | — |

**50 GROSZY** Y# 44a **Composition:** Aluminum **Note:** Struck at Warsaw.

| Date | Mintage | F | VF | XF | Unc | BU |
|---|---|---|---|---|---|---|
| 1949 | 59,393,000 | 0.10 | 0.25 | 1.50 | 5.00 | — |

**ZLOTY** Y# 45 **Composition:** Copper-Nickel **Note:** Struck at Kremnica.

| Date | Mintage | F | VF | XF | Unc | BU |
|---|---|---|---|---|---|---|
| 1949 | 87,053,000 | 1.00 | 1.50 | 2.25 | 4.00 | — |

**ZLOTY** Y# 45a **Composition:** Aluminum **Note:** Struck at Warsaw.

| Date | Mintage | F | VF | XF | Unc | BU |
|---|---|---|---|---|---|---|
| 1949 | 43,000,000 | 0.10 | 0.25 | 2.50 | 6.00 | — |

## PEOPLES REPUBLIC

## STANDARD COINAGE

**5 GROSZY** Y# A46 **Composition:** Aluminum

| Date | Mintage | F | VF | XF | Unc | BU |
|---|---|---|---|---|---|---|
| 1958 | 53,521,000 | — | — | 0.10 | 0.20 | — |
| 1959 | 28,564,000 | — | — | 0.10 | 0.15 | — |
| 1960 | 12,246,000 | — | 0.50 | 1.50 | 2.75 | — |
| 1961 | 29,502,000 | — | — | 0.10 | 0.20 | — |
| 1962 | 90,257,000 | — | — | 0.10 | 0.15 | — |
| 1963 | 20,878,000 | — | — | 0.10 | 0.15 | — |
| 1965MW | 5,050,000 | — | 0.75 | 2.00 | 4.00 | — |
| 1967MW | 10,056,000 | — | 0.75 | 2.00 | 4.00 | — |
| 1968MW | 10,196,000 | — | 0.75 | 2.00 | 4.00 | — |
| 1970MW | 20,095,000 | — | — | 0.10 | 0.20 | — |
| 1971MW | 20,000,000 | — | — | 0.10 | 0.20 | — |
| 1972MW | 10,000,000 | — | — | 0.10 | 0.20 | — |

**10 GROSZY** Y# AA47 **Composition:** Aluminum **Note:** Varieties in date size exist.

| Date | Mintage | F | VF | XF | Unc | BU |
|---|---|---|---|---|---|---|
| 1961 | 73,400,000 | — | 0.75 | 2.50 | 4.00 | — |
| 1962 | 25,362,000 | — | 1.75 | 5.00 | 20.00 | — |
| 1963 | 40,434,000 | — | — | 0.50 | 1.50 | — |
| 1965MW | 50,521,000 | — | 0.25 | 1.00 | 2.00 | — |
| 1966MW | 70,749,000 | — | — | 0.50 | 1.50 | — |
| 1967MW | 62,059,000 | — | — | 0.50 | 1.50 | — |
| 1968MW | 62,204,000 | — | — | 0.50 | 1.50 | — |
| 1969MW | 71,566,000 | — | — | 0.50 | 1.00 | — |
| 1970MW | 38,844,000 | — | — | 0.10 | 0.50 | — |
| 1971MW | 50,000,000 | — | — | 0.10 | 0.50 | — |
| 1972MW | 60,000,000 | — | — | 0.10 | 0.50 | — |
| 1973MW | 80,000,000 | — | — | 0.10 | 0.25 | — |
| 1973 Rare | — | — | — | — | — | — |
| 1974 Kremnica Mint | 50,000,000 | — | — | — | — | — |
| 1975MW | 50,000,000 | — | — | 0.10 | 0.15 | — |
| 1976MW | 100,000,000 | — | — | — | 0.10 | — |
| 1977MW | 100,000,000 | — | — | — | 0.10 | — |
| 1978MW | 71,204,000 | — | — | — | 0.10 | — |
| 1979MW | 73,191,000 | — | — | — | 0.10 | — |
| 1980MW | 60,623,000 | — | — | — | 0.10 | — |
| 1981MW | 70,000,000 | — | — | — | 0.10 | — |

| Date | Mintage | F | VF | XF | Unc | BU |
|---|---|---|---|---|---|---|
| 1983MW | 9,600,000 | — | — | — | 0.10 | — |
| 1985MW | 9,957,000 | — | — | — | 0.10 | — |

**20 GROSZY** Y# A47 **Composition:** Aluminum **Note:** Date varieties exist.

| Date | Mintage | F | VF | XF | Unc | BU |
|---|---|---|---|---|---|---|
| 1957 | 3,940,000 | — | 5.00 | 17.00 | 40.00 | — |
| 1961 | 53,108,000 | — | 1.75 | 3.75 | 8.00 | — |
| 1962 | 19,140,000 | — | 2.00 | 5.00 | 12.50 | — |
| 1963 | 41,217,000 | — | — | 0.50 | 2.00 | — |
| 1965MW | 32,022,000 | — | — | 0.50 | 2.00 | — |
| 1966MW | 23,860,000 | — | — | 0.50 | 2.00 | — |
| 1967MW | 29,099,000 | — | — | 1.00 | 5.00 | — |
| 1968MW | 29,191,000 | — | — | 1.00 | 5.00 | — |
| 1969MW | 40,227,000 | — | — | 0.50 | 1.50 | — |
| 1970MW | 20,028,000 | — | — | 0.10 | 1.00 | — |
| 1971MW | 20,000,000 | — | — | 0.10 | 1.00 | — |
| 1972MW | 60,000,000 | — | — | 0.10 | 1.00 | — |
| 1973 Kremnica Mint | 50,000,000 | — | — | 0.10 | 0.50 | — |
| **Note:** 1973 dated types were struck at Kremnica | | | | | | |
| 1973MW | 65,000,000 | — | — | 0.10 | 0.50 | — |
| **Note:** 1973 dated types were struck at Kremnica | | | | | | |
| 1975MW | 50,000,000 | — | — | 0.10 | 0.50 | — |
| 1976MW Large date | 100,000,000 | — | — | 0.10 | 0.50 | — |
| 1976MW Small date | Inc. above | — | — | 0.10 | 0.50 | — |
| 1977MW | 80,730,000 | — | — | 0.10 | 0.20 | — |
| 1978MW | 50,730,000 | — | — | 0.10 | 0.20 | — |
| 1979MW | 45,252,000 | — | — | 0.10 | 0.20 | — |
| 1980MW | 30,020,000 | — | — | 0.10 | 0.20 | — |
| 1981MW | 60,082,000 | — | — | 0.10 | 0.20 | — |
| 1983MW | — | — | — | 0.10 | 0.20 | — |
| 1985MW | 16,227,000 | — | — | 0.10 | 0.20 | — |

**50 GROSZY** Y# 48.1 **Composition:** Aluminum

| Date | Mintage | F | VF | XF | Unc | BU |
|---|---|---|---|---|---|---|
| 1957 | 91,316,000 | — | 0.75 | 2.00 | 5.00 | — |
| 1965MW | 22,090,000 | — | 0.25 | 1.50 | 4.00 | — |
| 1967MW | 2,027,000 | — | 1.25 | 4.00 | 15.00 | — |
| 1968MW | 2,065,000 | — | 1.25 | 4.00 | 15.00 | — |
| 1970MW | 3,273,000 | — | 0.15 | 0.30 | 2.00 | — |
| 1971MW | 7,000,000 | — | 0.10 | 0.25 | 1.00 | — |
| 1972MW | 10,000,000 | — | 0.10 | 0.25 | 0.50 | — |
| 1973MW | 39,000 | — | 0.10 | 0.20 | 0.50 | — |
| 1974MW | 33,000,000 | — | 0.10 | 0.20 | 0.50 | — |
| 1975 Kremnica Mint | 25,000,000 | — | 0.10 | 0.20 | 0.50 | — |
| 1976 Kremnica Mint | 25,000,000 | — | 0.10 | 0.20 | 0.40 | — |
| 1977MW | 50,000,000 | — | 0.10 | 0.20 | 0.40 | — |
| 1978 Kremnica Mint | 18,600,000 | — | 0.10 | 0.20 | 0.40 | — |
| 1978MW | 50,020,000 | — | 0.10 | 0.20 | 0.40 | — |
| 1982MW | 16,067,000 | — | 0.10 | 0.20 | 0.40 | — |
| 1983MW | 39,667,000 | — | 0.10 | 0.20 | 0.40 | — |
| 1984MW | 44,217,000 | — | 0.10 | 0.20 | 0.40 | — |
| 1985MW | 49,052,000 | — | 0.10 | 0.20 | 0.40 | — |

**50 GROSZY** Y# 48.2 **Composition:** Aluminum **Obverse:** Redesigned eagle

| Date | Mintage | F | VF | XF | Unc | BU |
|---|---|---|---|---|---|---|
| 1986MW | 45,796,000 | — | 0.10 | 0.20 | 0.40 | — |
| 1986MW Proof | 5,000 | Value: 3.50 | | | | |
| 1987MW | 21,257,000 | — | 0.10 | 0.20 | 0.40 | — |
| 1987MW Proof | 5,000 | Value: 3.50 | | | | |

**ZLOTY** Y# 49.1 **Composition:** Aluminum

| Date | Mintage | F | VF | XF | Unc | BU |
|---|---|---|---|---|---|---|
| 1957 | 58,631,000 | — | 1.00 | 3.50 | 20.00 | — |
| 1965MW | 15,015,000 | — | 0.50 | 1.00 | 3.00 | — |
| 1966MW | 18,185,000 | — | 0.75 | 2.00 | 4.00 | — |
| 1967MW | 1,002,000 | — | 2.25 | 6.00 | 15.00 | — |
| 1968MW | 1,176,000 | — | 2.25 | 6.00 | 15.00 | — |
| 1969MW | 3,024,000 | — | 1.25 | 3.00 | 6.00 | — |
| 1970MW | 6,016,000 | — | 0.15 | 0.50 | 1.50 | — |
| 1971MW | 6,000,000 | — | 0.15 | 0.50 | 1.00 | — |
| 1972MW | 7,000,000 | — | 0.15 | 0.50 | 1.00 | — |
| 1973MW | 15,000,000 | — | 0.10 | 0.50 | 1.00 | — |
| 1974MW | 42,000,000 | — | 0.10 | 0.15 | 0.50 | — |
| 1975 Kremnica Mint | 22,000,000 | — | 0.10 | 0.15 | 0.50 | — |
| 1975MW | 33,000,000 | — | 0.10 | 0.15 | 0.50 | — |
| 1976 Kremnica Mint | 22,000,000 | — | 0.10 | 0.50 | 1.00 | — |
| 1977MW | 65,000,000 | — | 0.10 | 0.50 | 1.00 | — |
| 1978 Kremnica Mint | 16,399,999 | — | 0.10 | 0.50 | 1.50 | — |
| 1978MW | 80,000,000 | — | 0.10 | 0.50 | 1.00 | — |
| 1980MW | 100,002,000 | — | 0.10 | 0.15 | 0.50 | — |
| 1981MW | 4,082,000 | — | 0.10 | 0.15 | 1.00 | — |
| 1982MW | 59,643,000 | — | 0.10 | 0.15 | 0.30 | — |
| 1983MW | 49,636,000 | — | 0.10 | 0.15 | 0.25 | — |
| 1984MW | 61,036,000 | — | 0.10 | 0.15 | 0.25 | — |
| 1985MW | 167,939,000 | — | 0.10 | 0.15 | 0.25 | — |

**ZLOTY** Y# 49.2 **Composition:** Aluminum **Obverse:** Redesigned eagle

| Date | Mintage | F | VF | XF | Unc | BU |
|---|---|---|---|---|---|---|
| 1986MW | 130,697,000 | — | 0.10 | 0.15 | 0.25 | — |
| 1986MW Proof | 5,000 | Value: 3.50 | | | | |
| 1987MW | 100,081,000 | — | 0.10 | 0.15 | 0.25 | — |
| 1987MW Proof | 5,000 | Value: 3.50 | | | | |
| 1988MW | 96,400,000 | — | 0.10 | 0.15 | 0.25 | — |
| 1988MW Proof | 5,000 | Value: 3.50 | | | | |

**ZLOTY** Y# 49.3 **Composition:** Aluminum

| Date | Mintage | F | VF | XF | Unc | BU |
|---|---|---|---|---|---|---|
| 1989MW | 49,410,000 | — | 0.10 | 0.15 | 0.25 | — |
| 1989MW Proof | 5,000 | Value: 3.50 | | | | |
| 1990MW | 30,667,000 | — | 0.10 | 0.15 | 0.25 | — |
| 1990MW Proof | 5,000 | Value: 3.50 | | | | |

**2 ZLOTE** Y# 46 **Composition:** Aluminum

| Date | Mintage | F | VF | XF | Unc | BU |
|---|---|---|---|---|---|---|
| 1958 | 83,640,000 | — | 0.20 | 1.50 | 6.00 | — |
| 1959 | 7,170,000 | — | 0.50 | 4.00 | 20.00 | — |
| 1960 | 36,131,000 | — | 0.20 | 0.50 | 3.00 | — |
| 1970MW | 2,013,999 | — | 0.30 | 1.00 | 4.00 | — |
| 1971MW | 3,000,000 | — | 0.20 | 1.00 | 4.00 | — |
| 1972MW | 3,000,000 | — | 0.20 | 1.00 | 4.00 | — |
| 1973MW | 10,000,000 | — | 0.15 | 0.50 | 1.50 | — |
| 1974MW | 46,000,000 | — | 0.15 | 0.30 | 1.00 | — |

**2 ZLOTE** Y# 80.1 **Composition:** Brass

| Date | Mintage | F | VF | XF | Unc | BU |
|---|---|---|---|---|---|---|
| 1975 Leningrade Mint | 25,000,000 | — | 0.15 | 0.25 | 0.50 | — |
| 1976 Leningrade Mint | 60,000,000 | — | 0.15 | 0.25 | 0.50 | — |
| 1977 Leningrade Mint | 50,000,000 | — | 0.15 | 0.25 | 0.50 | — |
| 1978 Leningrade Mint | 2,600,000 | — | 0.15 | 0.25 | 1.75 | — |
| 1978MW | 2,382,000 | — | 0.15 | 0.25 | 1.75 | — |
| 1979MW | 85,752,000 | — | 0.15 | 0.25 | 0.50 | — |
| 1980MW | 66,610,000 | — | 0.15 | 0.25 | 0.50 | — |
| 1981MW | 40,306,000 | — | 0.15 | 0.25 | 0.50 | — |
| 1982MW | 43,318,000 | — | 0.15 | 0.25 | 0.50 | — |
| 1983MW | 35,244,000 | — | 0.15 | 0.25 | 0.50 | — |
| 1984MW | 59,999,000 | — | 0.15 | 0.25 | 0.50 | — |
| 1985MW | 100,300,000 | — | 0.15 | 0.25 | 0.50 | — |

**2 ZLOTE** Y# 80.2 **Composition:** Brass **Obverse:** Redesigned eagle

| Date | Mintage | F | VF | XF | Unc | BU |
|---|---|---|---|---|---|---|
| 1986MW | 60,718,000 | — | 0.15 | 0.25 | 0.50 | — |
| 1986MW Proof | 5,000 | Value: 3.50 | | | | |
| 1987MW | 44,673,000 | — | 0.15 | 0.25 | 0.50 | — |
| 1987MW Proof | 5,000 | Value: 3.50 | | | | |
| 1988MW | 94,651,000 | — | 0.15 | 0.25 | 0.50 | — |
| 1988MW Proof | 5,000 | Value: 3.50 | | | | |

**2 ZLOTE** Y# 80.3 **Composition:** Aluminum **Size:** 17.9 mm.

| Date | Mintage | F | VF | XF | Unc | BU |
|---|---|---|---|---|---|---|
| 1989MW | 91,494,000 | — | 0.10 | 0.20 | 0.40 | — |
| 1989MW Proof | 5,000 | Value: 3.50 | | | | |
| 1990MW | 40,723,000 | — | 0.10 | 0.20 | 0.40 | — |
| 1990MW Proof | 5,000 | Value: 3.50 | | | | |

**5 ZLOTYCH** Y# 47 **Composition:** Aluminum

| Date | Mintage | F | VF | XF | Unc | BU |
|---|---|---|---|---|---|---|
| 1958 | 1,328,000 | — | 7.50 | 12.50 | 20.00 | — |
| **Note:** Two date varieties exist for strikes dated 1958 | | | | | | |
| 1959 | 56,811,000 | — | 0.75 | 2.50 | 7.00 | — |
| 1960 | 16,300,999 | — | 0.25 | 1.50 | 5.00 | — |
| 1971MW | 1,000,000 | — | 7.50 | 12.50 | 20.00 | — |
| 1973MW | 5,000,000 | — | 0.20 | 1.00 | 4.00 | — |
| 1974MW | 46,000,000 | — | 0.20 | 0.50 | 2.50 | — |

**5 ZLOTYCH** Y# 81.1 **Composition:** Brass **Note:** Variety of size of letters exist.

| Date | Mintage | F | VF | XF | Unc | BU |
|---|---|---|---|---|---|---|
| 1975 Leningrade Mint | 25,000,000 | — | 0.20 | 0.40 | 0.85 | — |
| 1976 Leningrade Mint | 60,000,000 | — | 0.20 | 0.40 | 0.85 | — |
| 1977 Leningrade Mint | 50,000,000 | — | 0.20 | 0.40 | 0.85 | — |
| 1978MW Rare | — | — | — | — | — | — |
| 1979MW | 5,098,000 | — | 0.20 | 0.40 | 1.50 | — |

| Date | Mintage | F | VF | XF | Unc | BU |
|---|---|---|---|---|---|---|
| 1980MW | 10,100,000 | — | 0.20 | 0.40 | 0.85 | — |
| 1981MW | 4,008,000 | — | 0.20 | 0.40 | 1.75 | — |
| 1982MW | 25,379,000 | — | 0.20 | 0.40 | 0.85 | — |
| 1983MW | 30,531,000 | — | 0.20 | 0.40 | 0.85 | — |
| 1984MW | 85,598,000 | — | 0.20 | 0.40 | 0.85 | — |
| 1985MW | 20,501,000 | — | 0.20 | 0.40 | 0.85 | — |

**5 ZLOTYCH** **Y# 81.2** **Composition:** Brass **Obverse:** Redesigned eagle **Size:** 24 mm.

| Date | Mintage | F | VF | XF | Unc | BU |
|---|---|---|---|---|---|---|
| 1986MW | 57,108,000 | — | 0.20 | 0.40 | 0.85 | — |
| 1986MW Proof | 5,000 | Value: 3.50 | | | | |
| 1987MW | 58,843,000 | — | 0.20 | 0.40 | 0.85 | — |
| 1987MW Proof | 5,000 | Value: 3.50 | | | | |
| 1988MW | 18,668,000 | — | 0.20 | 0.40 | 0.85 | — |
| 1988MW Proof | 5,000 | Value: 3.50 | | | | |

**5 ZLOTYCH** **Y# 81.3** **Composition:** Aluminum **Size:** 20 mm.

| Date | Mintage | F | VF | XF | Unc | BU |
|---|---|---|---|---|---|---|
| 1989MW | 30,253,000 | — | 0.15 | 0.30 | 0.65 | — |
| 1989MW Proof | 5,000 | Value: 3.50 | | | | |
| 1990MW | 38,248,000 | — | 0.15 | 0.30 | 0.65 | — |
| 1990MW Proof | 5,000 | Value: 3.50 | | | | |

**10 ZLOTYCH** **Y# 50** **Composition:** Copper-Nickel **Reverse:** Tadeusz Kosciuszko **Size:** 31 mm.

| Date | Mintage | F | VF | XF | Unc | BU |
|---|---|---|---|---|---|---|
| 1959 | 13,107,000 | — | 0.60 | 2.00 | 6.50 | — |
| 1960 | 27,551,000 | — | 0.60 | 2.00 | 6.50 | — |
| 1966MW | 4,157,000 | — | 1.00 | 8.00 | 18.00 | — |

**10 ZLOTYCH** **Y# 51** **Composition:** Copper-Nickel **Reverse:** Mikolaj Kopernik

| Date | Mintage | F | VF | XF | Unc | BU |
|---|---|---|---|---|---|---|
| 1959 | 12,559,000 | — | 0.75 | 1.25 | 2.50 | — |
| 1965MW | 3,000,000 | — | 1.00 | 5.00 | 15.00 | — |

**10 ZLOTYCH** **Y# 52** **Composition:** Copper-Nickel **Subject:** 600th Anniversary of Jagiello University **Note:** Legends raised.

| Date | Mintage | F | VF | XF | Unc | BU |
|---|---|---|---|---|---|---|
| ND(1964) | 2,610,000 | — | 0.50 | 1.50 | 3.50 | — |

**10 ZLOTYCH** **Y# 52a** **Composition:** Copper-Nickel **Note:** Legends incuse.

| Date | Mintage | F | VF | XF | Unc | BU |
|---|---|---|---|---|---|---|
| ND(1964) | 2,612,000 | — | 0.50 | 1.50 | 3.50 | — |

**10 ZLOTYCH** **Y# 54** **Composition:** Copper-Nickel **Subject:** 700th Anniversary of Warsaw

| Date | Mintage | F | VF | XF | Unc | BU |
|---|---|---|---|---|---|---|
| 1965MW | 3,492,000 | — | 0.75 | 2.00 | 4.50 | — |

**10 ZLOTYCH** **Y# 55** **Composition:** Copper-Nickel **Subject:** 700th Anniversary of Warsaw

| Date | Mintage | F | VF | XF | Unc | BU |
|---|---|---|---|---|---|---|
| 1965MW | 2,000,000 | — | 0.75 | 2.00 | 4.50 | — |

**10 ZLOTYCH** **Y# 56** **Composition:** Copper-Nickel **Subject:** 200th Anniversary of Warsaw Mint

| Date | Mintage | F | VF | XF | Unc | BU |
|---|---|---|---|---|---|---|
| 1966MW | 102,000 | — | 2.00 | 6.00 | 20.00 | — |

**10 ZLOTYCH** **Y# 51a** **Composition:** Copper-Nickel **Note:** Reduced size.

| Date | Mintage | F | VF | XF | Unc | BU |
|---|---|---|---|---|---|---|
| 1967MW | 2,128,000 | — | 0.75 | 2.00 | 7.50 | — |
| 1968MW | 9,389,000 | — | 0.75 | 1.25 | 2.50 | — |
| 1969MW | 8,612,000 | — | 0.75 | 1.25 | 2.75 | — |

**10 ZLOTYCH** **Y# 58** **Composition:** Copper-Nickel **Subject:** 20th Anniversary - Death of General Swierczewski

| Date | Mintage | F | VF | XF | Unc | BU |
|---|---|---|---|---|---|---|
| 1967MW | 2,000,000 | — | 0.50 | 1.00 | 2.25 | — |

**10 ZLOTYCH** **Y# 59** **Composition:** Copper-Nickel **Subject:** Centennial - Birth of Marie Sklodowska Curie

| Date | Mintage | F | VF | XF | Unc | BU |
|---|---|---|---|---|---|---|
| 1967MW | 2,000,000 | — | 0.50 | 1.00 | 2.25 | — |

**10 ZLOTYCH** **Y# 60** **Composition:** Copper-Nickel **Subject:** 25th Anniversary - Peoples Army

| Date | Mintage | F | VF | XF | Unc | BU |
|---|---|---|---|---|---|---|
| 1968MW | 2,000,000 | — | 0.50 | 1.00 | 2.25 | — |

**10 ZLOTYCH** **Y# 50a** **Composition:** Copper-Nickel **Size:** 28 mm. **Note:** Reduced size.

| Date | Mintage | F | VF | XF | Unc | BU |
|---|---|---|---|---|---|---|
| 1969MW | 5,428,000 | — | 0.50 | 1.75 | 5.00 | — |
| 1970MW | 13,783,000 | — | 0.50 | 1.00 | 2.00 | — |
| 1971MW | 12,000,000 | — | 0.50 | 1.00 | 2.00 | — |
| 1972MW | 10,000,000 | — | 0.50 | 1.00 | 2.00 | — |
| 1973MW | 3,900,000 | — | 0.50 | 2.00 | 8.00 | — |

**10 ZLOTYCH** **Y# 61** **Composition:** Copper-Nickel **Subject:** 25th Anniversary - Peoples Republic

| Date | Mintage | F | VF | XF | Unc | BU |
|---|---|---|---|---|---|---|
| 1969MW | 2,000,000 | — | 0.50 | 1.00 | 2.25 | — |

**10 ZLOTYCH** Y# 62 **Composition:** Copper-Nickel **Subject:** 25th Anniversary - Provincial Annexations

| Date | Mintage | F | VF | XF | Unc | BU |
|---|---|---|---|---|---|---|
| 1970MW | 2,000,000 | — | 0.50 | 1.00 | 2.25 | — |

**10 ZLOTYCH** Y# 63 **Composition:** Copper-Nickel **Series:** F.A.O.

| Date | Mintage | F | VF | XF | Unc | BU |
|---|---|---|---|---|---|---|
| 1971MW | 2,000,000 | — | 0.75 | 1.50 | 4.50 | — |

**10 ZLOTYCH** Y# 64 **Composition:** Copper-Nickel **Subject:** 50th Anniversary - Battle of Upper Silesia

| Date | Mintage | F | VF | XF | Unc | BU |
|---|---|---|---|---|---|---|
| 1971MW | 2,000,000 | — | 0.50 | 1.00 | 2.25 | — |

**10 ZLOTYCH** Y# 65 **Composition:** Copper-Nickel **Subject:** 50th Anniversary - Gdynia Seaport

| Date | Mintage | F | VF | XF | Unc | BU |
|---|---|---|---|---|---|---|
| 1972MW | 2,000,000 | — | 0.50 | 1.00 | 2.25 | — |

**10 ZLOTYCH** Y# 73 **Composition:** Copper-Nickel **Reverse:** Boleslaw Prus

| Date | Mintage | F | VF | XF | Unc | BU |
|---|---|---|---|---|---|---|
| 1975MW | 35,000,000 | — | 0.25 | 0.65 | 1.25 | — |
| 1976MW | 20,000,000 | — | 0.25 | 0.65 | 1.25 | — |
| 1977MW | 25,000,000 | — | 0.25 | 0.65 | 1.25 | — |
| 1978MW | 4,006,999 | — | 0.25 | 0.75 | 2.25 | — |
| 1981MW | 2,655,000 | — | 0.25 | 1.00 | 3.75 | — |
| 1982MW | 16,341,000 | — | 0.25 | 0.65 | 1.25 | — |
| 1983MW | 14,248,000 | — | 0.25 | 0.65 | 1.25 | — |
| 1984MW | 19,064,000 | — | 0.25 | 0.65 | 1.25 | — |

**10 ZLOTYCH** Y# 74 **Composition:** Copper-Nickel **Reverse:** Adam Mickiewicz

| Date | Mintage | F | VF | XF | Unc | BU |
|---|---|---|---|---|---|---|
| 1975MW | 35,000,000 | — | 0.25 | 0.65 | 1.25 | — |
| 1976MW | 20,000,000 | — | 0.25 | 0.65 | 1.25 | — |

**10 ZLOTYCH** Y# 152.1 **Composition:** Copper-Nickel **Size:** 25 mm.

| Date | Mintage | F | VF | XF | Unc | BU |
|---|---|---|---|---|---|---|
| 1984MW | 15,756,000 | — | 0.20 | 0.50 | 1.00 | — |
| 1985MW | 5,282,000 | — | 0.20 | 0.50 | 1.00 | — |
| 1986MW | 31,043,000 | — | 0.20 | 0.50 | 1.00 | — |
| 1986MW Proof | 5,000 | Value: 4.00 | | | | |
| 1987MW | 69,636,000 | — | 0.20 | 0.50 | 1.00 | — |
| 1987MW Proof | 5,000 | Value: 4.00 | | | | |
| 1988MW | 102,493,000 | — | 0.20 | 0.50 | 1.00 | — |
| 1988MW Proof | 5,000 | Value: 4.00 | | | | |

**10 ZLOTYCH** Y# 152.2 **Composition:** Brass **Size:** 21.8 mm.

| Date | Mintage | F | VF | XF | Unc | BU |
|---|---|---|---|---|---|---|
| 1989MW | 80,800,000 | — | 0.20 | 0.40 | 0.80 | — |
| 1989MW Proof | 5,000 | Value: 4.00 | | | | |
| 1990MW | 106,892,000 | — | 0.20 | 0.40 | 0.80 | — |
| 1990MW Proof | 5,000 | Value: 4.00 | | | | |

**20 ZLOTYCH** Y# 67 **Composition:** Copper-Nickel

| Date | Mintage | F | VF | XF | Unc | BU |
|---|---|---|---|---|---|---|
| 1973 Kremnica Mint | 25,000,000 | — | 0.25 | 1.00 | 2.50 | — |
| 1974 Kremnica Mint | 12,000,000 | — | 0.25 | 0.75 | 1.50 | — |
| 1976 Warsaw Mint | 20,000,000 | — | 0.25 | 0.75 | 1.50 | — |

**20 ZLOTYCH** Y# 69 **Composition:** Copper-Nickel **Reverse:** Marceli Nowotko

| Date | Mintage | F | VF | XF | Unc | BU |
|---|---|---|---|---|---|---|
| 1974MW | 10,000,000 | — | 0.25 | 1.00 | 2.50 | — |
| 1975 Kremnica Mint | 10,000,000 | — | 0.25 | 1.00 | 2.00 | — |
| 1976 Kremnica Mint | 20,000,000 | — | 0.25 | 0.75 | 1.50 | — |
| 1976MW | 30,000,000 | — | 0.25 | 0.75 | 1.50 | — |
| 1977MW | 16,000,000 | — | 0.25 | 1.00 | 2.00 | — |
| 1983MW | 152,000 | — | 0.25 | 5.00 | 12.50 | — |

**20 ZLOTYCH** Y# 70 **Composition:** Copper-Nickel **Subject:** 25th Anniversary of the Comcon

| Date | Mintage | F | VF | XF | Unc | BU |
|---|---|---|---|---|---|---|
| 1974MW | 2,000,000 | — | 0.75 | 1.25 | 2.50 | — |

**20 ZLOTYCH** Y# 75 **Composition:** Copper-Nickel **Subject:** International Women's Year

| Date | Mintage | F | VF | XF | Unc | BU |
|---|---|---|---|---|---|---|
| 1975MW | 2,000,000 | — | 0.75 | 1.25 | 2.50 | — |

**20 ZLOTYCH** Y# 95 **Composition:** Copper-Nickel **Reverse:** Maria Konopnicka

| Date | Mintage | F | VF | XF | Unc | BU |
|---|---|---|---|---|---|---|
| 1978MW | 2,010,000 | — | 0.75 | 1.25 | 2.75 | — |

**20 ZLOTYCH** Y# 97 **Composition:** Copper-Nickel **Subject:** First Polish Cosmonaut

| Date | Mintage | F | VF | XF | Unc | BU |
|---|---|---|---|---|---|---|
| 1978MW | 2,009,000 | — | 0.75 | 1.25 | 2.75 | — |

**20 ZLOTYCH** Y# 99 **Composition:** Copper-Nickel **Series:** International Year of the Child

| Date | Mintage | F | VF | XF | Unc | BU |
|---|---|---|---|---|---|---|
| 1979MW | 2,007,000 | — | 1.00 | 1.50 | 3.00 | — |

**20 ZLOTYCH** **Y# 108** **Composition:** Copper-Nickel **Series:** 1980 Olympics **Reverse:** Runner

| Date | Mintage | F | VF | XF | Unc | BU |
|---|---|---|---|---|---|---|
| 1980MW | 2,012,000 | — | 1.00 | 1.75 | 5.00 | — |
| 1980MW Proof | 100 | Value: 30.00 | | | | |

**20 ZLOTYCH** **Y# 112** **Composition:** Copper-Nickel **Subject:** 50th Anniversary - Training Ship Daru Pomorza

| Date | Mintage | F | VF | XF | Unc | BU |
|---|---|---|---|---|---|---|
| 1980MW | 2,007,000 | — | 1.00 | 1.75 | 3.50 | — |

**20 ZLOTYCH** **Y# 153.1** **Composition:** Copper-Nickel **Note:** Circulation coinage.

| Date | Mintage | F | VF | XF | Unc | BU |
|---|---|---|---|---|---|---|
| 1984MW | 12,703,000 | — | 0.25 | 0.60 | 1.25 | — |
| 1985MW | 15,514,000 | — | 0.25 | 0.60 | 1.25 | — |
| 1986MW | 37,959,000 | — | 0.25 | 0.60 | 1.25 | — |
| 1986MW Proof | 5,000 | Value: 4.00 | | | | |
| 1987MW | 22,213,000 | — | 0.25 | 0.60 | 1.25 | — |
| 1987MW Proof | 5,000 | Value: 4.00 | | | | |
| 1988MW | 14,994,000 | — | 0.25 | 0.60 | 1.25 | — |
| 1988MW Proof | 5,000 | Value: 4.00 | | | | |

**20 ZLOTYCH** **Y# 153.2** **Composition:** Copper-Nickel **Size:** 23.9 mm. **Note:** Reduced size.

| Date | Mintage | F | VF | XF | Unc | BU |
|---|---|---|---|---|---|---|
| 1989MW | 95,974,000 | — | 0.25 | 0.35 | 0.75 | — |
| 1989MW Proof | 5,000 | Value: 4.00 | | | | |
| 1990MW | 104,712,000 | — | 0.25 | 0.35 | 0.75 | — |
| 1990MW Proof | 5,000 | Value: 4.00 | | | | |

**50 ZLOTYCH** **Y# 66** **Weight:** 12.6400 g. **Composition:** 0.7500 Silver .3048 oz. ASW **Reverse:** Fryderyk Chopin

| Date | Mintage | F | VF | XF | Unc | BU |
|---|---|---|---|---|---|---|
| 1972MW Proof | 50,000 | Value: 11.50 | | | | |
| 1974MW Proof | 10,000 | Value: 16.50 | | | | |

**50 ZLOTYCH** **Y# 100** **Composition:** Copper-Nickel **Reverse:** Duke Mieszko I

| Date | Mintage | F | VF | XF | Unc | BU |
|---|---|---|---|---|---|---|
| 1979MW | 2,640,000 | — | 1.00 | 2.00 | 5.00 | — |

**50 ZLOTYCH** **Y# 114** **Composition:** Copper-Nickel **Reverse:** King Boleslaw I Chrobry

| Date | Mintage | F | VF | XF | Unc | BU |
|---|---|---|---|---|---|---|
| 1980MW | 2,564,000 | — | 1.00 | 2.00 | 5.00 | — |

**50 ZLOTYCH** **Y# 117** **Composition:** Copper-Nickel **Reverse:** Duke Kazimierz I Odnowiciel

| Date | Mintage | F | VF | XF | Unc | BU |
|---|---|---|---|---|---|---|
| 1980MW | 2,504,000 | — | 1.00 | 2.00 | 5.00 | — |

**50 ZLOTYCH** **Y# 122** **Composition:** Copper-Nickel **Reverse:** General Broni Wladyslaw Sikorski

| Date | Mintage | F | VF | XF | Unc | BU |
|---|---|---|---|---|---|---|
| 1981MW | 2,505,000 | — | 1.00 | 2.00 | 5.00 | — |

**50 ZLOTYCH** **Y# 124** **Composition:** Copper-Nickel **Reverse:** King Koleslaw II Smialy

| Date | Mintage | F | VF | XF | Unc | BU |
|---|---|---|---|---|---|---|
| 1981MW | 2,538,000 | — | 1.00 | 2.00 | 4.50 | — |

**50 ZLOTYCH** **Y# 127** **Composition:** Copper-Nickel **Series:** F.A.O. - World Food Day

| Date | Mintage | F | VF | XF | Unc | BU |
|---|---|---|---|---|---|---|
| 1981MW | 2,524,000 | — | 1.00 | 2.00 | 4.50 | — |

**50 ZLOTYCH** **Y# 128** **Composition:** Copper-Nickel **Reverse:** King Wladyslaw I Herman

| Date | Mintage | F | VF | XF | Unc | BU |
|---|---|---|---|---|---|---|
| 1981MW | 2,500,000 | — | 1.00 | 2.00 | 4.50 | — |

**50 ZLOTYCH** **Y# 133** **Composition:** Copper-Nickel **Reverse:** King Boleslaw III Krzywousty

| Date | Mintage | F | VF | XF | Unc | BU |
|---|---|---|---|---|---|---|
| 1982MW | 2,616,000 | — | 1.00 | 2.00 | 4.50 | — |

**50 ZLOTYCH** **Y# 142** **Composition:** Copper-Nickel **Subject:** 150th Anniversary of Great Theater

| Date | Mintage | F | VF | XF | Unc | BU |
|---|---|---|---|---|---|---|
| 1983MW | 615,000 | — | 1.00 | 4.00 | 8.00 | — |

**50 ZLOTYCH** **Y# 145** **Composition:** Copper-Nickel **Reverse:** King Jan III Sobieski

| Date | Mintage | F | VF | XF | Unc | BU |
|---|---|---|---|---|---|---|
| 1983MW | 2,576,000 | — | 1.00 | 2.00 | 4.50 | — |

**50 ZLOTYCH** **Y# 146** **Composition:** Copper-Nickel **Reverse:** Ignacy Lukasiewicz

| Date | Mintage | F | VF | XF | Unc | BU |
|---|---|---|---|---|---|---|
| 1983MW | 612,000 | — | 1.00 | 4.00 | 8.00 | — |

**100 ZLOTYCH** **Y# 57** **Weight:** 20.0000 g. **Composition:** 0.9000 Silver .5787 oz. ASW **Subject:** Polish Millennium

| Date | Mintage | F | VF | XF | Unc | BU |
|---|---|---|---|---|---|---|
| 1966MW | 198,000 | — | — | 6.00 | 11.50 | — |

**100 ZLOTYCH** **Y# 68** **Weight:** 16.5000 g. **Composition:** 0.6250 Silver .3316 oz. ASW **Subject:** 500th Anniversary - Birth of Mikolaj Kopernik

| Date | Mintage | F | VF | XF | Unc | BU |
|---|---|---|---|---|---|---|
| 1973MW Proof | 51,000 | Value: 9.00 | | | | |
| 1974MW Proof | 50,000 | Value: 9.00 | | | | |

**100 ZLOTYCH** **Y# 71** **Weight:** 16.5000 g. **Composition:** 0.6250 Silver .3316 oz. ASW **Subject:** 40th Anniversary - Death of Maria Sklodowska Curie

| Date | Mintage | F | VF | XF | Unc | BU |
|---|---|---|---|---|---|---|
| 1974MW Proof | 50,000 | Value: 9.00 | | | | |

**100 ZLOTYCH** **Y# 76** **Weight:** 16.5000 g. **Composition:** 0.6250 Silver .3316 oz. ASW **Reverse:** Royal Castle in Warsaw

| Date | Mintage | F | VF | XF | Unc | BU |
|---|---|---|---|---|---|---|
| 1975MW Proof | 50,000 | Value: 9.00 | | | | |

**100 ZLOTYCH** **Y# 77** **Weight:** 16.5000 g. **Composition:** 0.6250 Silver .3316 oz. ASW **Reverse:** Ignacy Jan Paderewski

| Date | Mintage | F | VF | XF | Unc | BU |
|---|---|---|---|---|---|---|
| 1975MW Proof | 60,000 | Value: 6.50 | | | | |

**100 ZLOTYCH** **Y# 78** **Weight:** 16.5000 g. **Composition:** 0.6250 Silver .3316 oz. ASW **Reverse:** Helena Modrzejewska

| Date | Mintage | F | VF | XF | Unc | BU |
|---|---|---|---|---|---|---|
| 1975MW Proof | 60,000 | Value: 6.50 | | | | |

**100 ZLOTYCH** **Y# 82** **Weight:** 16.5000 g. **Composition:** 0.6250 Silver .3316 oz. ASW **Reverse:** Tadeusz Kosciuszko

| Date | Mintage | F | VF | XF | Unc | BU |
|---|---|---|---|---|---|---|
| 1976MW Proof | 100,000 | Value: 6.50 | | | | |

**100 ZLOTYCH** **Y# 84** **Weight:** 16.5000 g. **Composition:** 0.6250 Silver .3316 oz. ASW **Reverse:** Kazimierz Pulaski

| Date | Mintage | F | VF | XF | Unc | BU |
|---|---|---|---|---|---|---|
| 1976MW Proof | 100,000 | Value: 7.00 | | | | |

**100 ZLOTYCH** **Y# 87** **Weight:** 16.5000 g. **Composition:** 0.6250 Silver .3316 oz. ASW **Series:** Environment Protection **Reverse:** Aurchs

| Date | Mintage | F | VF | XF | Unc | BU |
|---|---|---|---|---|---|---|
| 1977MW Proof | 30,000 | Value: 20.00 | | | | |

**100 ZLOTYCH** **Y# 88** **Weight:** 16.5000 g. **Composition:** 0.6250 Silver .3316 oz. ASW **Reverse:** Henryk Sienkiewicz

| Date | Mintage | F | VF | XF | Unc | BU |
|---|---|---|---|---|---|---|
| 1977MW Proof | 20,000 | Value: 8.50 | | | | |

**100 ZLOTYCH** **Y# 89** **Weight:** 16.5000 g. **Composition:** 0.6250 Silver .3316 oz. ASW **Reverse:** Wladyslaw Reymont

| Date | Mintage | F | VF | XF | Unc | BU |
|---|---|---|---|---|---|---|
| 1977MW Proof | 20,000 | Value: 8.50 | | | | |

**100 ZLOTYCH** **Y# 91** **Weight:** 16.5000 g. **Composition:** 0.6250 Silver .3316 oz. ASW **Reverse:** Wawel Castle in Krakow

| Date | Mintage | F | VF | XF | Unc | BU |
|---|---|---|---|---|---|---|
| 1977MW Proof | 30,000 | Value: 11.50 | | | | |

**100 ZLOTYCH** **Y# 92** **Weight:** 16.5000 g. **Composition:** 0.6250 Silver .3316 oz. ASW **Reverse:** Adam Mickiewicz

| Date | Mintage | F | VF | XF | Unc | BU |
|---|---|---|---|---|---|---|
| 1978MW Proof | 30,000 | Value: 12.50 | | | | |

**100 ZLOTYCH** **Y# 93** **Weight:** 16.5000 g. **Composition:** 0.6250 Silver .3316 oz. ASW **Series:** Environment Protection **Reverse:** Moose

| Date | Mintage | F | VF | XF | Unc | BU |
|---|---|---|---|---|---|---|
| 1978MW Proof | 30,000 | Value: 20.00 | | | | |

**100 ZLOTYCH** **Y# 94** **Weight:** 16.5000 g. **Composition:** 0.6250 Silver .3316 oz. ASW **Subject:** 100th Anniversary - Birth of Janusz Korczak

| Date | Mintage | F | VF | XF | Unc | BU |
|---|---|---|---|---|---|---|
| 1978MW Proof | 30,000 | Value: 9.00 | | | | |

**100 ZLOTYCH** **Y# 96** **Weight:** 16.5000 g. **Composition:** 0.6250 Silver .3316 oz. ASW **Series:** Environment Protection **Reverse:** Beaver

| Date | Mintage | F | VF | XF | Unc | BU |
|---|---|---|---|---|---|---|
| 1978MW Proof | 30,000 | Value: 20.00 | | | | |

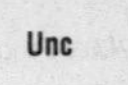

**100 ZLOTYCH** **Y# 98** **Weight:** 16.5000 g. **Composition:** 0.6250 Silver .3316 oz. ASW **Reverse:** Henryk Wieniawski

| Date | Mintage | F | VF | XF | Unc | BU |
|---|---|---|---|---|---|---|
| 1979MW Proof | 30,000 | Value: 9.00 | | | | |

**100 ZLOTYCH** **Y# 103** **Weight:** 16.5000 g. **Composition:** 0.6250 Silver .3316 oz. ASW **Reverse:** Ludwik Zamenhof

| Date | Mintage | F | VF | XF | Unc | BU |
|---|---|---|---|---|---|---|
| 1979MW Proof | 30,000 | Value: 9.00 | | | | |

**100 ZLOTYCH** **Y# 104** **Weight:** 16.5000 g. **Composition:** 0.6250 Silver .3316 oz. ASW **Series:** Environment Protection **Reverse:** Lynx

| Date | Mintage | F | VF | XF | Unc | BU |
|---|---|---|---|---|---|---|
| 1979MW Proof | 20,000 | Value: 21.50 | | | | |

**100 ZLOTYCH** **Y# 105** **Weight:** 16.5000 g. **Composition:** 0.6250 Silver .3316 oz. ASW **Series:** Environment Protection **Reverse:** Chamois

| Date | Mintage | F | VF | XF | Unc | BU |
|---|---|---|---|---|---|---|
| 1979MW Proof | 20,000 | Value: 21.50 | | | | |

**100 ZLOTYCH** **Y# 120** **Weight:** 16.5000 g. **Composition:** 0.6250 Silver .3316 oz. ASW **Subject:** 450th Anniversary - Birth of Jan Kochanowski

| Date | Mintage | F | VF | XF | Unc | BU |
|---|---|---|---|---|---|---|
| 1980MW Proof | 10,000 | Value: 17.50 | | | | |

**100 ZLOTYCH** **Y# 109** **Weight:** 16.5000 g. **Composition:** 0.6250 Silver .3316 oz. ASW **Series:** 1980 Olympics **Reverse:** Olympic rings and runner

| Date | Mintage | F | VF | XF | Unc | BU |
|---|---|---|---|---|---|---|
| 1980MW Proof | 10,000 | Value: 32.50 | | | | |

**100 ZLOTYCH** **Y# 121** **Weight:** 16.5000 g. **Composition:** 0.6250 Silver .3316 oz. ASW **Series:** Environment Protection **Reverse:** Cappercaillie

| Date | Mintage | F | VF | XF | Unc | BU |
|---|---|---|---|---|---|---|
| 1980MW Proof | 18,000 | Value: 17.50 | | | | |

**100 ZLOTYCH** **Y# 123** **Weight:** 16.5000 g. **Composition:** 0.6250 Silver .3316 oz. ASW **Reverse:** General Broni Wladyslaw Sikorski

| Date | Mintage | F | VF | XF | Unc | BU |
|---|---|---|---|---|---|---|
| 1981MW Proof | 12,000 | Value: 16.00 | | | | |

**100 ZLOTYCH** **Y# 126** **Weight:** 16.5000 g. **Composition:** 0.6250 Silver .3316 oz. ASW **Series:** Environment Protection **Reverse:** Horse

| Date | Mintage | F | VF | XF | Unc | BU |
|---|---|---|---|---|---|---|
| 1981MW Proof | 12,000 | Value: 25.00 | | | | |

**100 ZLOTYCH** **Y# 136** **Weight:** 14.1500 g. **Composition:** 0.7500 Silver .3412 oz. ASW **Subject:** Visit of Pope John Paul II

| Date | Mintage | F | VF | XF | Unc | BU |
|---|---|---|---|---|---|---|
| 1982CHI | 8,700 | — | — | — | 45.00 | — |
| 1982CHI Proof | 3,750 | Value: 80.00 | | | | |
| 1985CHI | 1 | — | — | — | — | — |
| 1985CHI Proof | 5 | — | — | — | — | — |
| 1986CHI | 80 | — | — | — | 400 | — |
| 1986CHI Proof | 128 | Value: 450 | | | | |

**100 ZLOTYCH** **Y# 141** **Weight:** 16.5000 g. **Composition:** 0.6250 Silver .3316 oz. ASW **Series:** Environment Protection **Reverse:** Stork

| Date | Mintage | F | VF | XF | Unc | BU |
|---|---|---|---|---|---|---|
| 1982MW Proof | 12,000 | Value: 25.00 | | | | |

**100 ZLOTYCH** **Y# 147** **Weight:** 16.5000 g. **Composition:** 0.6250 Silver .3316 oz. ASW **Series:** Environment Protection **Reverse:** Bear

| Date | Mintage | F | VF | XF | Unc | BU |
|---|---|---|---|---|---|---|
| 1983MW Proof | 8,000 | Value: 30.00 | | | | |

**100 ZLOTYCH** **Y# 148** **Composition:** Copper-Nickel **Reverse:** Wincenty Witos

| Date | Mintage | F | VF | XF | Unc | BU |
|---|---|---|---|---|---|---|
| 1984MW | 1,530,000 | — | — | — | 3.00 | — |

**100 ZLOTYCH** **Y# 151** **Composition:** Copper-Nickel **Subject:** 40th Anniversary of Peoples Republic

| Date | Mintage | F | VF | XF | Unc | BU |
|---|---|---|---|---|---|---|
| 1984MW | 2,595,000 | — | — | — | 3.00 | — |

**100 ZLOTYCH Y# 155 Composition:** Copper-Nickel **Reverse:** King Przemyslaw II

| Date | Mintage | F | VF | XF | Unc | BU |
|---|---|---|---|---|---|---|
| 1985MW | 2,924,000 | — | — | — | 3.00 | — |

**100 ZLOTYCH Y# 157 Composition:** Nickel Plated Steel **Reverse:** Woman and Child - Polish Women's Memorial Hospital Center

| Date | Mintage | F | VF | XF | Unc | BU |
|---|---|---|---|---|---|---|
| 1985MW | 1,927,000 | — | — | — | 3.00 | — |

**100 ZLOTYCH Y# 160 Composition:** Copper-Nickel **Reverse:** King Wladyslaw I Lokietek

| Date | Mintage | F | VF | XF | Unc | BU |
|---|---|---|---|---|---|---|
| 1986MW | 2,540,000 | — | — | — | 3.00 | — |
| 1986MW Proof | 5,000 | Value: 12.00 | | | | |

**100 ZLOTYCH Y# 167 Composition:** Copper-Nickel **Reverse:** King Kazimierz III

| Date | Mintage | F | VF | XF | Unc | BU |
|---|---|---|---|---|---|---|
| 1987MW | 2,479,000 | — | — | — | 4.00 | — |
| 1987MW Proof | 5,000 | Value: 12.00 | | | | |

**100 ZLOTYCH Y# 182 Composition:** Copper-Nickel **Subject:** 70th Anniversary - Wielkopolskiego Insurrection

| Date | Mintage | F | VF | XF | Unc | BU |
|---|---|---|---|---|---|---|
| 1988MW | 2,513,000 | — | — | — | 3.00 | — |
| 1988MW Proof | 5,000 | Value: 12.00 | | | | |

**100 ZLOTYCH Y# 183 Composition:** Copper-Nickel **Reverse:** Queen Jadwiga 1384-1399

| Date | Mintage | F | VF | XF | Unc | BU |
|---|---|---|---|---|---|---|
| 1988MW | 2,469,000 | — | — | — | 3.00 | — |
| 1988MW Proof | 5,000 | Value: 12.00 | | | | |

**200 ZLOTYCH Y# 72 Weight:** 14.4700 g. **Composition:** 0.6250 Silver .2907 oz. ASW **Subject:** 30th Anniversary - Polish Peoples Republic

| Date | Mintage | F | VF | XF | Unc | BU |
|---|---|---|---|---|---|---|
| 1974MW | 13,062,000 | — | — | — | 3.50 | — |
| 1974MW Proof | 6,000 | Value: 22.50 | | | | |

**200 ZLOTYCH Y# 79 Weight:** 14.4700 g. **Composition:** 0.7500 Silver .3490 oz. ASW **Subject:** 30th Anniversary - Victory Over Fascism

| Date | Mintage | F | VF | XF | Unc | BU |
|---|---|---|---|---|---|---|
| 1975MW | 1,826,000 | — | — | — | 4.50 | — |
| 1975MW Proof | 2,600 | Value: 25.00 | | | | |

**200 ZLOTYCH Y# 86 Weight:** 14.4700 g. **Composition:** 0.6250 Silver .2907 oz. ASW **Series:** XXI Olympics **Reverse:** Rings and torch

| Date | Mintage | F | VF | XF | Unc | BU |
|---|---|---|---|---|---|---|
| 1976MW | 2,072,000 | — | — | — | 8.50 | — |
| 1976MW Proof | 11,000 | Value: 22.50 | | | | |

**200 ZLOTYCH Y# 101 Weight:** 17.6000 g. **Composition:** 0.7500 Silver .4244 oz. ASW **Reverse:** Duke Mieszko I

| Date | Mintage | F | VF | XF | Unc | BU |
|---|---|---|---|---|---|---|
| 1979MW Proof | 12,000 | Value: 25.00 | | | | |

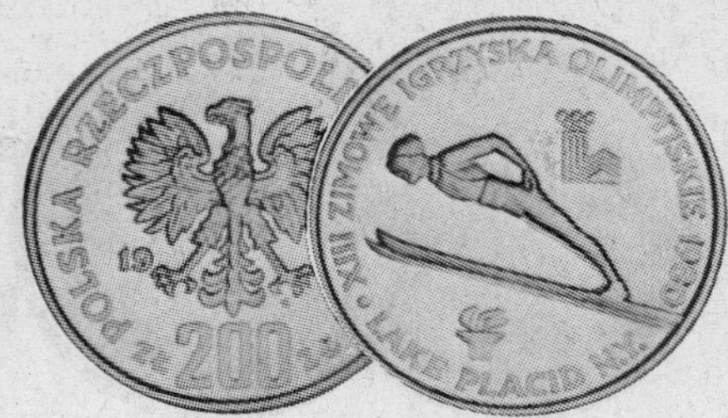

**200 ZLOTYCH Y# 110 Weight:** 17.6000 g. **Composition:** 0.7500 Silver .4244 oz. ASW **Series:** Winter Olympics **Reverse:** Torch below ski jumper

| Date | Mintage | F | VF | XF | Unc | BU |
|---|---|---|---|---|---|---|
| 1980MW Proof | 32,000 | Value: 20.00 | | | | |

**200 ZLOTYCH Y# 110a Weight:** 17.6000 g. **Composition:** 0.7500 Silver .4244 oz. ASW **Reverse:** Without torch below ski jumper

| Date | Mintage | F | VF | XF | Unc | BU |
|---|---|---|---|---|---|---|
| 1980MW Proof | 28,000 | Value: 10.00 | | | | |

**200 ZLOTYCH Y# 115 Weight:** 17.6000 g. **Composition:** 0.7500 Silver .4244 oz. ASW **Reverse:** King Boleslaw I Chrobry

| Date | Mintage | F | VF | XF | Unc | BU |
|---|---|---|---|---|---|---|
| 1980MW Proof | 12,000 | Value: 25.00 | | | | |

**200 ZLOTYCH Y# 118 Weight:** 17.6000 g. **Composition:** 0.7500 Silver .4244 oz. ASW **Reverse:** Duke Kazimierz I

| Date | Mintage | F | VF | XF | Unc | BU |
|---|---|---|---|---|---|---|
| 1980MW Proof | 12,000 | Value: 15.00 | | | | |

**200 ZLOTYCH Y# 125 Weight:** 17.6000 g. **Composition:** 0.7500 Silver .4244 oz. ASW **Reverse:** King Bolaslaw II Smialy

| Date | Mintage | F | VF | XF | Unc | BU |
|---|---|---|---|---|---|---|
| 1981MW Proof | 12,000 | Value: 18.50 | | | | |

**200 ZLOTYCH** **Y# 129** **Weight:** 17.6000 g. **Composition:** 0.7500 Silver .4244 oz. ASW **Reverse:** King Wladyslaw I Herman

| Date | Mintage | F | VF | XF | Unc | BU |
|---|---|---|---|---|---|---|
| 1981MW Proof | 12,000 | Value: 20.00 | | | | |

**200 ZLOTYCH** **Y# 130** **Weight:** 17.6000 g. **Composition:** 0.7500 Silver .4244 oz. ASW **Subject:** World Soccer Championship Games in Spain

| Date | Mintage | F | VF | XF | Unc | BU |
|---|---|---|---|---|---|---|
| 1982MW Proof | 21,000 | Value: 16.50 | | | | |

**200 ZLOTYCH** **Y# 132** **Weight:** 17.6000 g. **Composition:** 0.7500 Silver .4244 oz. ASW **Reverse:** King Koleslaw III Krzywousty

| Date | Mintage | F | VF | XF | Unc | BU |
|---|---|---|---|---|---|---|
| 1982MW Proof | 12,000 | Value: 20.00 | | | | |

**200 ZLOTYCH** **Y# 137** **Weight:** 28.3000 g. **Composition:** 0.7500 Silver .6825 oz. ASW **Subject:** Visit of Pope John Paul II **Obverse:** Similar to Y#132

| Date | Mintage | F | VF | XF | Unc | BU |
|---|---|---|---|---|---|---|
| 1982CHI | 3,000 | — | — | — | 100 | — |
| 1982CHI Proof | 3,650 | Value: 125 | | | | |
| 1985CHI | 1 | — | — | — | — | — |
| 1985CHI Proof | 5 | — | — | — | — | — |
| 1986CHI | 32 | — | — | — | 700 | — |
| 1986CHI Proof | 75 | Value: 750 | | | | |

**200 ZLOTYCH** **Y# 143** **Weight:** 17.6000 g. **Composition:** 0.7500 Silver .4244 oz. ASW **Reverse:** King Jan III Sobieski

| Date | Mintage | F | VF | XF | Unc | BU |
|---|---|---|---|---|---|---|
| 1983MW Proof | 11,000 | Value: 25.00 | | | | |

**200 ZLOTYCH** **Y# 149** **Weight:** 17.6000 g. **Composition:** 0.7500 Silver .4244 oz. ASW **Series:** Winter Olympics **Reverse:** Ice Skater

| Date | Mintage | F | VF | XF | Unc | BU |
|---|---|---|---|---|---|---|
| 1984MW Proof | 15,000 | Value: 22.50 | | | | |

**200 ZLOTYCH** **Y# 150** **Weight:** 17.6000 g. **Composition:** 0.7500 Silver .4244 oz. ASW **Series:** Summer Olympics **Reverse:** Hurdler

| Date | Mintage | F | VF | XF | Unc | BU |
|---|---|---|---|---|---|---|
| 1984MW Proof | 16,000 | Value: 20.00 | | | | |

**500 ZLOTYCH** **Y# 83** **Weight:** 30.0000 g. **Composition:** 0.9000 Gold .8681 oz. AGW **Reverse:** Tadeusz Kosciuszko

| Date | Mintage | F | VF | XF | Unc | BU |
|---|---|---|---|---|---|---|
| 1976MW | 2,318 | — | — | — | 425 | — |

**500 ZLOTYCH** **Y# 85** **Weight:** 30.0000 g. **Composition:** 0.9000 Gold .8681 oz. AGW **Reverse:** Kazimierz Pulaski

| Date | Mintage | F | VF | XF | Unc | BU |
|---|---|---|---|---|---|---|
| 1976MW | 2,315 | — | — | — | 425 | — |

**500 ZLOTYCH** **Y# 154** **Weight:** 16.5000 g. **Composition:** 0.6250 Silver .3283 oz. ASW **Series:** Environment Protection **Reverse:** Mute Swan

| Date | Mintage | F | VF | XF | Unc | BU |
|---|---|---|---|---|---|---|
| 1984MW Proof | 10,000 | Value: 30.00 | | | | |

**500 ZLOTYCH** **Y# 156** **Weight:** 16.5000 g. **Composition:** 0.7500 Silver .3979 oz. ASW **Reverse:** King Przemyslaw II

| Date | Mintage | F | VF | XF | Unc | BU |
|---|---|---|---|---|---|---|
| 1985MW Proof | 8,000 | Value: 25.00 | | | | |

**500 ZLOTYCH** **Y# 158** **Weight:** 16.5000 g. **Composition:** 0.7500 Silver .3979 oz. ASW **Subject:** 40th Anniversary of United Nations

| Date | Mintage | F | VF | XF | Unc | BU |
|---|---|---|---|---|---|---|
| 1985MW Proof | 10,000 | Value: 22.50 | | | | |

**500 ZLOTYCH** **Y# 159** **Weight:** 16.5000 g. **Composition:** 0.7500 Silver .3979 oz. ASW **Series:** Environmental Protection **Reverse:** Red Squirrel

| Date | Mintage | F | VF | XF | Unc | BU |
|---|---|---|---|---|---|---|
| 1985MW Proof | 8,000 | Value: 27.50 | | | | |

**500 ZLOTYCH** **Y# 161** **Weight:** 16.5000 g. **Composition:** 0.7500 Silver .3979 oz. ASW **Reverse:** King Wladyslaw I Lokietek

| Date | Mintage | F | VF | XF | Unc | BU |
|---|---|---|---|---|---|---|
| 1986MW Proof | 8,000 | Value: 22.00 | | | | |

**500 ZLOTYCH** Y# 162 **Weight:** 16.5000 g. **Composition:** 0.7500 Silver .3979 oz. ASW **Series:** Environment Protection **Reverse:** Eagle Owl

| Date | Mintage | F | VF | XF | Unc | BU |
|---|---|---|---|---|---|---|
| 1986MW Proof | 12,000 | Value: 27.50 | | | | |

**500 ZLOTYCH** Y# 225 **Weight:** 16.5000 g. **Composition:** 0.7500 Silver .3979 oz. ASW **Reverse:** Soccer - Ball in net

| Date | Mintage | F | VF | XF | Unc | BU |
|---|---|---|---|---|---|---|
| 1986MW Proof | 16,000 | Value: 30.00 | | | | |

**500 ZLOTYCH** Y# 165 **Weight:** 16.5000 g. **Composition:** 0.7500 Silver .3979 oz. ASW **Series:** Olympics **Reverse:** Equestrian

| Date | Mintage | F | VF | XF | Unc | BU |
|---|---|---|---|---|---|---|
| 1987MW Proof | 15,000 | Value: 25.00 | | | | |

**500 ZLOTYCH** Y# 166 **Weight:** 16.5000 g. **Composition:** 0.7500 Silver .3979 oz. ASW **Subject:** European Championship Soccer Games

| Date | Mintage | F | VF | XF | Unc | BU |
|---|---|---|---|---|---|---|
| 1987MW Proof | 12,000 | Value: 30.00 | | | | |

**500 ZLOTYCH** Y# 172 **Weight:** 16.5000 g. **Composition:** 0.7500 Silver .3979 oz. ASW **Series:** Winter Olympics **Reverse:** Ice Hockey Goalie

| Date | Mintage | F | VF | XF | Unc | BU |
|---|---|---|---|---|---|---|
| 1987MW Proof | 15,000 | Value: 20.00 | | | | |

**500 ZLOTYCH** Y# 173 **Weight:** 16.5000 g. **Composition:** 0.7500 Silver .3979 oz. ASW **Reverse:** King Kazimierz III

| Date | Mintage | F | VF | XF | Unc | BU |
|---|---|---|---|---|---|---|
| 1987MW Proof | 8,000 | Value: 25.00 | | | | |

**500 ZLOTYCH** Y# 181 **Weight:** 16.5000 g. **Composition:** 0.7500 Silver .3979 oz. ASW **Reverse:** Queen Jadwiga 1384-1399

| Date | Mintage | F | VF | XF | Unc | BU |
|---|---|---|---|---|---|---|
| 1988MW Proof | 8,000 | Value: 22.50 | | | | |

**500 ZLOTYCH** Y# 184 **Weight:** 16.5000 g. **Composition:** 0.7500 Silver .3979 oz. ASW **Reverse:** Colosseum in Rome - Soccer 1990

| Date | Mintage | F | VF | XF | Unc | BU |
|---|---|---|---|---|---|---|
| 1988MW Proof | 15,000 | Value: 22.50 | | | | |

**500 ZLOTYCH** Y# 185 **Composition:** Copper-Nickel **Subject:** 50th Anniversary - Beginning of WWII

| Date | Mintage | F | VF | XF | Unc | BU |
|---|---|---|---|---|---|---|
| 1989MW | 10,135,000 | — | — | — | 2.50 | — |
| 1989MW Proof | 5,000 | Value: 10.00 | | | | |

**500 ZLOTYCH** Y# 194 **Composition:** Copper-Nickel **Reverse:** King Wladyslaw II 1386-1434

| Date | Mintage | F | VF | XF | Unc | BU |
|---|---|---|---|---|---|---|
| 1989MW | 2,544,000 | — | — | — | 3.00 | — |
| 1989MW Proof | 5,000 | Value: 10.00 | | | | |

**1000 ZLOTYCH** Y# 138 **Weight:** 3.4000 g. **Composition:** 0.9000 Gold .0984 oz. AGW **Subject:** Visit of Pope John Paul II

| Date | Mintage | F | VF | XF | Unc | BU |
|---|---|---|---|---|---|---|
| 1982CHI | 900 | — | — | — | 125 | — |
| 1982CHI Proof | 1,700 | Value: 150 | | | | |
| 1985CHI | 1 | — | — | — | 650 | — |
| 1985CHI Proof | 2 | Value: 850 | | | | |
| 1986CHI | 83 | — | — | — | 300 | — |
| 1986CHI Proof | 53 | Value: 350 | | | | |

**1000 ZLOTYCH** Y# 144 **Weight:** 14.5000 g. **Composition:** 0.7500 Silver .3497 oz. ASW **Subject:** Visit of Pope John Paul II

| Date | Mintage | F | VF | XF | Unc | BU |
|---|---|---|---|---|---|---|
| 1982MW | 803,000 | — | — | — | 12.50 | — |
| 1983MW | 1,530,000 | — | — | — | 9.00 | — |
| 1983MW Proof | 10,000 | Value: 27.50 | | | | |

**1000 ZLOTYCH** Y# 168 **Weight:** 3.1100 g. **Composition:** 0.9990 Gold .1000 oz. AGW **Subject:** Papal Visit in America

| Date | Mintage | F | VF | XF | Unc | BU |
|---|---|---|---|---|---|---|
| 1987MW Proof | 201 | Value: 250 | | | | |

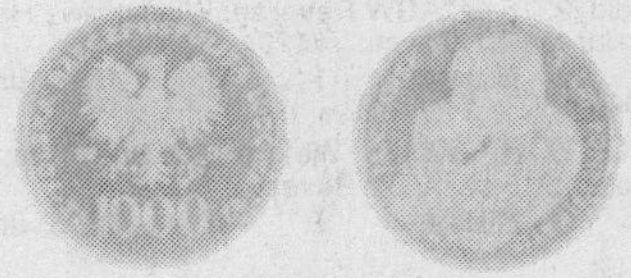

**1000 ZLOTYCH** Y# 174 **Weight:** 3.1100 g. **Composition:** 0.9990 Gold .1000 oz. AGW **Subject:** 10th Anniversary of Pope John Paul II

| Date | Mintage | F | VF | XF | Unc | BU |
|---|---|---|---|---|---|---|
| 1988MW Proof | 1,000 | Value: 125 | | | | |

**1000 ZLOTYCH** Y# 186 **Weight:** 3.1100 g. **Composition:** 0.9990 Gold .1000 oz. AGW **Subject:** Pope John Paul II **Obverse:** Similar to Y#174 **Reverse:** Similar to 200,000 Zlotych, Y#190

| Date | Mintage | F | VF | XF | Unc | BU |
|---|---|---|---|---|---|---|
| 1989MW In sets only | Est. 1,000 | — | — | — | 125 | — |

**2000 ZLOTYCH** Y# 90 **Weight:** 8.0000 g. **Composition:** 0.9000 Gold .2315 oz. AGW **Reverse:** Fryderyk Chopin

| Date | Mintage | F | VF | XF | Unc | BU |
|---|---|---|---|---|---|---|
| 1977MW Proof | 4,000 | Value: 135 | | | | |

**2000 ZLOTYCH** Y# 102 **Weight:** 8.0000 g. **Composition:** 0.9000 Gold .2315 oz. AGW **Reverse:** Duke Mieszko I

| Date | Mintage | F | VF | XF | Unc | BU |
|---|---|---|---|---|---|---|
| 1979MW Proof | 3,000 | Value: 135 | | | | |

**2000 ZLOTYCH** **Y# 106** **Weight:** 8.0000 g. **Composition:** 0.9000 Gold .2315 oz. AGW **Reverse:** Mikolaj Kopernik

| Date | Mintage | F | VF | XF | Unc | BU |
|---|---|---|---|---|---|---|
| 1979MW Proof | 5,000 | Value: 135 | | | | |

**2000 ZLOTYCH** **Y# 107** **Weight:** 8.0000 g. **Composition:** 0.9000 Gold .2315 oz. AGW **Reverse:** Maria Sklodowska Curie

| Date | Mintage | F | VF | XF | Unc | BU |
|---|---|---|---|---|---|---|
| 1979MW Proof | 5,000 | Value: 135 | | | | |

**2000 ZLOTYCH** **Y# 111** **Weight:** 8.0000 g. **Composition:** 0.9000 Gold .2315 oz. AGW **Series:** Winter Olympics **Obverse:** Similar to Y#107 **Reverse:** Ski Jumper

| Date | Mintage | F | VF | XF | Unc | BU |
|---|---|---|---|---|---|---|
| 1980MW Proof | 5,250 | Value: 135 | | | | |

**2000 ZLOTYCH** **Y# 116** **Weight:** 8.0000 g. **Composition:** 0.9000 Gold .2315 oz. AGW **Reverse:** King Koleslaw I Chrobry

| Date | Mintage | F | VF | XF | Unc | BU |
|---|---|---|---|---|---|---|
| 1980MW Proof | 2,500 | Value: 150 | | | | |

**2000 ZLOTYCH** **Y# 119** **Weight:** 8.0000 g. **Composition:** 0.9000 Gold .2315 oz. AGW **Reverse:** Kazimierz I

| Date | Mintage | F | VF | XF | Unc | BU |
|---|---|---|---|---|---|---|
| 1980MW Proof | 2,500 | Value: 150 | | | | |

**2000 ZLOTYCH** **Y# 131** **Weight:** 8.0000 g. **Composition:** 0.9000 Gold .2315 oz. AGW **Reverse:** Wladyslaw I Herman **Note:** Similar to 200 Zlotych, Y#129.

| Date | Mintage | F | VF | XF | Unc | BU |
|---|---|---|---|---|---|---|
| 1981MW Proof | 3,113 | Value: 150 | | | | |

**2000 ZLOTYCH** **Y# 135** **Weight:** 8.0000 g. **Composition:** 0.9000 Gold .2315 oz. AGW **Reverse:** Boleslaw II

| Date | Mintage | F | VF | XF | Unc | BU |
|---|---|---|---|---|---|---|
| 1981MW | — | — | — | — | — | — |

**2000 ZLOTYCH** **Y# 139** **Weight:** 6.8000 g. **Composition:** 0.9000 Gold .1968 oz. AGW **Subject:** Visit of Pope John Paul II

| Date | Mintage | F | VF | XF | Unc | BU |
|---|---|---|---|---|---|---|
| 1982CHI | 500 | — | — | — | 250 | — |
| 1982CHI Proof | 1,250 | Value: 300 | | | | |
| 1985CHI | 1 | — | — | — | 900 | — |
| 1985CHI Proof | Est. 2 | Value: 1,100 | | | | |
| 1986CHI | Est. 54 | — | — | — | 450 | — |
| 1986CHI Proof | Est. 79 | Value: 500 | | | | |

**2000 ZLOTYCH** **Y# 169** **Weight:** 7.7700 g. **Composition:** 0.9990 Gold .2500 oz. AGW **Subject:** Papal Visit in America

| Date | Mintage | F | VF | XF | Unc | BU |
|---|---|---|---|---|---|---|
| 1987MW Proof | 201 | Value: 350 | | | | |

**2000 ZLOTYCH** **Y# 175** **Weight:** 7.7700 g. **Composition:** 0.9990 Gold .2500 oz. AGW **Subject:** 10th Anniversary of Pope John Paul II

| Date | Mintage | F | VF | XF | Unc | BU |
|---|---|---|---|---|---|---|
| 1988 Proof | 1,000 | Value: 200 | | | | |

**2000 ZLOTYCH** **Y# 187** **Weight:** 7.7700 g. **Composition:** 0.9990 Gold .2500 oz. AGW **Obverse:** Similar to Y#175 **Reverse:** Similar to 200,000 Zlotych, Y#190 **Note:** Pope John Paul II.

| Date | Mintage | F | VF | XF | Unc | BU |
|---|---|---|---|---|---|---|
| 1989MW In sets only | Est. 1,000 | — | — | — | 200 | — |

**5000 ZLOTYCH** **Y# 170** **Weight:** 15.5500 g. **Composition:** 0.9990 Gold .5000 oz. AGW **Subject:** Papal Visit in America

| Date | Mintage | F | VF | XF | Unc | BU |
|---|---|---|---|---|---|---|
| 1987MW Proof | 201 | Value: 550 | | | | |

**5000 ZLOTYCH** **Y# 176** **Weight:** 15.5500 g. **Composition:** 0.9990 Gold .5000 oz. AGW **Subject:** 10th Anniversary of Pope John Paul II

| Date | Mintage | F | VF | XF | Unc | BU |
|---|---|---|---|---|---|---|
| 1988MW Proof | 1,000 | Value: 300 | | | | |

**5000 ZLOTYCH** **Y# 188** **Weight:** 15.5500 g. **Composition:** 0.9990 Gold .5000 oz. AGW **Obverse:** Similar to Y#176 **Reverse:** Similar to 200,000 Zlotych, Y#190 **Note:** Pope John Paul II.

| Date | Mintage | F | VF | XF | Unc | BU |
|---|---|---|---|---|---|---|
| 1989MW In sets only | Est. 1,000,000 | — | — | — | 300 | — |

**5000 ZLOTYCH** **Y# 191** **Weight:** 16.5000 g. **Composition:** 0.7500 Silver .3978 oz. ASW **Reverse:** Torun - Kopernik

| Date | Mintage | F | VF | XF | Unc | BU |
|---|---|---|---|---|---|---|
| 1989MW Proof | 20,000 | Value: 30.00 | | | | |

**5000 ZLOTYCH** **Y# 192** **Weight:** 16.5000 g. **Composition:** 0.7500 Silver .3978 oz. ASW **Reverse:** Torunia Town Hall

| Date | Mintage | F | VF | XF | Unc | BU |
|---|---|---|---|---|---|---|
| 1989MW Proof | 20,000 | Value: 30.00 | | | | |

**5000 ZLOTYCH** **Y# 193** **Weight:** 16.5000 g. **Composition:** 0.7500 Silver .3978 oz. ASW **Reverse:** Henryk Sucharski

| Date | Mintage | F | VF | XF | Unc | BU |
|---|---|---|---|---|---|---|
| 1989MW Proof | 25,000 | Value: 27.50 | | | | |

**5000 ZLOTYCH** **Y# 197** **Weight:** 16.5000 g. **Composition:** 0.7500 Silver .3978 oz. ASW **Reverse:** King Wladyslaw II - Bust

| Date | Mintage | F | VF | XF | Unc | BU |
|---|---|---|---|---|---|---|
| 1989MW Proof | 8,000 | Value: 35.00 | | | | |

**5000 ZLOTYCH** **Y# 198** **Weight:** 16.5000 g. **Composition:** 0.7500 Silver .3978 oz. ASW **Reverse:** King Wladyslaw II - Half Length

| Date | Mintage | F | VF | XF | Unc | BU |
|---|---|---|---|---|---|---|
| 1989MW Proof | 2,500 | Value: 45.00 | | | | |

**10000 ZLOTYCH** **Y# 140** **Weight:** 34.5000 g. **Composition:** 0.9000 Gold .9984 oz. AGW **Subject:** Visit of Pope John Paul II

| Date | Mintage | F | VF | XF | Unc | BU |
|---|---|---|---|---|---|---|
| 1982CHI | 200 | — | — | — | 1,250 | — |
| 1982CHI Proof | 700 | Value: 1,500 | | | | |
| 1985CHI Proof | 1 | — | — | — | — | — |
| 1986CHI | Est. 6 | — | — | — | 1,750 | — |
| 1986CHI Proof | Est. 13 | Value: 1,850 | | | | |

**10000 ZLOTYCH** **Y# 399** **Weight:** 28.3100 g. **Composition:** 0.9000 Silver .8192 oz. ASW **Subject:** Pope John Paul II **Obverse:** Eagle **Reverse:** Bust of Pope John Paul II left **Edge:** Plain **Size:** 40.2 mm. **Note:** Pope John Paul II.

| Date | Mintage | F | VF | XF | Unc | BU |
|---|---|---|---|---|---|---|
| 1986 Proof | — | Value: 800 | | | | |

**10000 ZLOTYCH** **Y# 164** **Weight:** 19.0600 g. **Composition:** 0.7500 Silver .4582 oz. ASW **Subject:** Papal Visit

| Date | Mintage | F | VF | XF | Unc | BU |
|---|---|---|---|---|---|---|
| 1987MW | 908,000 | — | — | — | 25.00 | — |
| 1987MW Proof | 15,000 | Value: 42.50 | | | | |

**10000 ZLOTYCH** **Y# 171** **Weight:** 31.1030 g. **Composition:** 0.9990 Gold 1.0000 oz. AGW **Subject:** Papal Visit in America

| Date | Mintage | F | VF | XF | Unc | BU |
|---|---|---|---|---|---|---|
| 1987MW Proof | 201 | Value: 1,150 | | | | |

**10000 ZLOTYCH** **Y# 177** **Weight:** 31.1030 g. **Composition:** 0.9990 Gold 1.0000 oz. AGW **Subject:** 10th Anniversary of Pope John Paul II

| Date | Mintage | F | VF | XF | Unc | BU |
|---|---|---|---|---|---|---|
| 1988MW | 1,000 | — | — | — | 550 | — |
| 1988MW Proof | 1,000 | Value: 600 | | | | |

**10000 ZLOTYCH** **Y# 177a** **Weight:** 31.1030 g. **Composition:** 0.9990 Silver 1.0000 oz. ASW

| Date | Mintage | F | VF | XF | Unc | BU |
|---|---|---|---|---|---|---|
| 1988MW | 5,000 | — | — | — | 40.00 | — |
| 1988MW Proof | — | Value: 50.00 | | | | |

**10000 ZLOTYCH** **Y# 179** **Weight:** 31.1030 g. **Composition:** 0.9990 Silver 1.0000 oz. ASW **Subject:** Pope John Paul - Christmas

| Date | Mintage | F | VF | XF | Unc | BU |
|---|---|---|---|---|---|---|
| 1988MW Proof | 5,000 | Value: 37.50 | | | | |

**10000 ZLOTYCH** **Y# 189** **Weight:** 31.1030 g. **Composition:** 0.9990 Gold 1.0000 oz. AGW **Reverse:** Pope John Paul II

| Date | Mintage | F | VF | XF | Unc | BU |
|---|---|---|---|---|---|---|
| 1989MW Proof | Est. 2,000 | Value: 575 | | | | |

**10000 ZLOTYCH** **Y# 189a** **Weight:** 31.1000 g. **Composition:** 0.9990 Silver 1.0000 oz. ASW

| Date | Mintage | F | VF | XF | Unc | BU |
|---|---|---|---|---|---|---|
| 1989MW | — | — | — | — | 40.00 | — |
| 1989MW Proof | 5,000 | Value: 50.00 | | | | |

**10000 ZLOTYCH** **Y# 237** **Weight:** 31.1000 g. **Composition:** 0.9990 Silver 1.0000 oz. ASW **Reverse:** Pope John Paul II

| Date | Mintage | F | VF | XF | Unc | BU |
|---|---|---|---|---|---|---|
| 1989MW Proof | — | Value: 40.00 | | | | |

**20000 ZLOTYCH** **Y# 223** **Weight:** 19.0000 g. **Composition:** 0.7500 Silver .4558 oz. ASW **Reverse:** Soccer - Ball, Map and Globe

| Date | Mintage | F | VF | XF | Unc | BU |
|---|---|---|---|---|---|---|
| 1989 Proof | 25,000 | Value: 35.00 | | | | |

**20000 ZLOTYCH** **Y# 224** **Weight:** 19.0000 g. **Composition:** 0.7500 Silver .4558 oz. ASW **Reverse:** Soccer - Player behind vertical lines

| Date | Mintage | F | VF | XF | Unc | BU |
|---|---|---|---|---|---|---|
| 1989 Proof | 25,000 | Value: 35.00 | | | | |

**50000 ZLOTYCH** **Y# 180** **Weight:** 19.3000 g. **Composition:** 0.7500 Silver .4654 oz. ASW **Subject:** 70 Years of Polish Independence

| Date | Mintage | F | VF | XF | Unc | BU |
|---|---|---|---|---|---|---|
| 1988 | 1,000,000 | — | — | — | 10.00 | — |
| 1988 Proof | 20,000 | Value: 45.00 | | | | |

**200000 ZLOTYCH** **Y# 163** **Weight:** 373.2420 g. **Composition:** 0.9990 Gold 12.0000 oz. AGW **Subject:** Papal Visit in America **Size:** 70 mm. **Note:** Illustration reduced.

| Date | Mintage | F | VF | XF | Unc | BU |
|---|---|---|---|---|---|---|
| 1987 Proof | 101 | Value: 6,500 | | | | |

**200000 ZLOTYCH** **Y# 178** **Weight:** 373.2420 g. **Composition:** 0.9990 Gold 12.0000 oz. AGW **Subject:** 10th Anniversary of Pope John Paul II **Size:** 70 mm. **Note:** Illustration reduced.

| Date | Mintage | F | VF | XF | Unc | BU |
|---|---|---|---|---|---|---|
| 1988MW Proof | 300 | Value: 5,500 | | | | |

**200000 ZLOTYCH** **Y# 190** **Weight:** 373.2420 g. **Composition:** 0.9990 Gold 12.0000 oz. AGW **Obverse:** Similar to 10,000 Zlotych, Y#179 **Reverse:** Pope John Paul II **Note:** Illustration reduced.

| Date | Mintage | F | VF | XF | Unc | BU |
|---|---|---|---|---|---|---|
| 1989MW Proof | Est. 200 | Value: 6,000 | | | | |

## REPUBLIC
### Democratic
### STANDARD COINAGE

**50 ZLOTYCH** **Y# 216**

| Date | Mintage | F | VF | XF | Unc | BU |
|---|---|---|---|---|---|---|
| 1990MW | 28,707,000 | — | — | — | 1.25 | — |
| 1990MW Proof | 5,000 | Value: 12.00 | | | | |

**100 ZLOTYCH** **Y# 214**

| Date | Mintage | F | VF | XF | Unc | BU |
|---|---|---|---|---|---|---|
| 1990MW | 37,341,000 | — | — | — | 2.00 | — |
| 1990MW Proof | 5,000 | Value: 15.00 | | | | |

**10000 ZLOTYCH** **Y# 195** **Composition:** Copper-Nickel **Subject:** 10th Anniversary of Solidarity

| Date | Mintage | F | VF | XF | Unc | BU |
|---|---|---|---|---|---|---|
| 1990MW | 15,164,000 | — | — | — | 4.50 | — |
| 1990MW Proof | 5,000 | Value: 16.50 | | | | |

**10000 ZLOTYCH** **Y# 217** **Composition:** Nickel Plated Steel **Subject:** 200th Anniversary of Polish Constitution

| Date | Mintage | F | VF | XF | Unc | BU |
|---|---|---|---|---|---|---|
| 1991MW | 2,605,000 | — | — | — | 6.00 | — |

**10000 ZLOTYCH** **Y# 246** **Composition:** Copper-Nickel **Reverse:** Wladyslaw III

| Date | Mintage | F | VF | XF | Unc | BU |
|---|---|---|---|---|---|---|
| 1992MW | 2,500,000 | — | — | — | 3.50 | — |

**20000 ZLOTYCH** **Y# 219** **Weight:** 3.1100 g. **Composition:** 0.9990 Gold .1 oz. AGW **Subject:** 10th Anniversary of Solidarity **Note:** SImilar to 10000 Zlotych, Y#195.

| Date | Mintage | F | VF | XF | Unc | BU |
|---|---|---|---|---|---|---|
| 1990 Proof | 1,004 | Value: 120 | | | | |

**20000 ZLOTYCH** **Y# 215** **Ring Composition:** Brass **Center Composition:** Copper-Nickel **Subject:** 225th Anniversary of Warsaw Mint

| Date | Mintage | F | VF | XF | Unc | BU |
|---|---|---|---|---|---|---|
| 1991MW | 100,000 | — | — | — | 18.00 | — |

**20000 ZLOTYCH** **Y# 243** **Composition:** Copper-Nickel **Reverse:** Barn Swallows

| Date | Mintage | F | VF | XF | Unc | BU |
|---|---|---|---|---|---|---|
| 1993MW | 500,000 | — | — | — | 5.00 | — |

**20000 ZLOTYCH** **Y# 244** **Composition:** Copper-Nickel **Reverse:** Lancut Castle

| Date | Mintage | F | VF | XF | Unc | BU |
|---|---|---|---|---|---|---|
| 1993MW | 500,000 | — | — | — | 4.50 | — |

**20000 ZLOTYCH** **Y# 256** **Composition:** Copper-Nickel **Reverse:** Kazimierz IV

| Date | Mintage | F | VF | XF | Unc | BU |
|---|---|---|---|---|---|---|
| 1993 | 1,500,000 | — | — | — | 4.50 | — |

**20000 ZLOTYCH** **Y# 261** **Composition:** Copper-Nickel **Series:** Olympics **Reverse:** Slalom Skier

| Date | Mintage | F | VF | XF | Unc | BU |
|---|---|---|---|---|---|---|
| 1993 | 988,000 | — | — | — | 7.50 | — |

**20000 ZLOTYCH** **Y# 265** **Composition:** Copper-Nickel **Subject:** 75th Anniversary - Disabled Association

| Date | Mintage | F | VF | XF | Unc | BU |
|---|---|---|---|---|---|---|
| 1994 | 75,000 | — | — | — | 4.50 | — |

**20000 ZLOTYCH** **Y# 270** **Composition:** Copper-Nickel **Reverse:** New Mint Building

| Date | Mintage | F | VF | XF | Unc | BU |
|---|---|---|---|---|---|---|
| 1994 | 252,000 | — | — | — | 4.50 | — |

**20000 ZLOTYCH** **Y# 271** **Composition:** Copper-Nickel **Subject:** 200th Anniversary - Kosciuszko Insurrection

| Date | Mintage | F | VF | XF | Unc | BU |
|---|---|---|---|---|---|---|
| 1994 | 100,000 | — | — | — | 5.00 | — |

**20000 ZLOTYCH** **Y# 272** **Composition:** Copper-Nickel **Reverse:** Zygmunt I, 1506-1548

| Date | Mintage | F | VF | XF | Unc | BU |
|---|---|---|---|---|---|---|
| 1994 | 1,500,000 | — | — | — | 4.50 | — |

**50000 ZLOTYCH** **Y# 220** **Weight:** 13.1000 g. **Composition:** 0.9990 Gold .4212 oz. AGW **Subject:** 10th Anniversary of Solidarity **Note:** Similar to 10000 Zlotych, Y#195.

| Date | Mintage | F | VF | XF | Unc | BU |
|---|---|---|---|---|---|---|
| 1990 Proof | 1,001 | Value: 265 | | | | |

**50000 ZLOTYCH** **Y# 229** **Composition:** Copper-Nickel **Subject:** 200th Anniversary of Order Virtuti Militari

| Date | Mintage | F | VF | XF | Unc | BU |
|---|---|---|---|---|---|---|
| 1992 Proof | 100,000 | Value: 12.50 | | | | |

**100000 ZLOTYCH** **Y# 196.1** **Weight:** 31.1000 g. **Composition:** 0.9990 Silver 1.0000 oz. ASW **Subject:** 10th Anniversary of Solidarity

| Date | Mintage | F | VF | XF | Unc | BU |
|---|---|---|---|---|---|---|
| 1990 | 500,000 | — | — | — | 18.00 | — |
| 1990 Proof | — | Value: 90.00 | | | | |

**100000 ZLOTYCH** **Y# 196.2** **Weight:** 31.1000 g. **Composition:** 0.9990 Silver 1.0000 oz. ASW **Size:** 31.9 mm. **Note:** Reduced size.

| Date | Mintage | F | VF | XF | Unc | BU |
|---|---|---|---|---|---|---|
| 1990 Proof | — | Value: 60.00 | | | | |

**100000 ZLOTYCH** **Y# 199** **Weight:** 31.1000 g. **Composition:** 0.9990 Silver 1.0000 oz. ASW **Reverse:** Fryderyk Chopin

| Date | Mintage | F | VF | XF | Unc | BU |
|---|---|---|---|---|---|---|
| 1990 Proof | 10,000 | Value: 25.00 | | | | |

**100000 ZLOTYCH** **Y# 200** **Weight:** 31.1000 g. **Composition:** 0.9990 Silver 1.0000 oz. ASW **Reverse:** Tadeusz Kosciuszko

| Date | Mintage | F | VF | XF | Unc | BU |
|---|---|---|---|---|---|---|
| 1990 Proof | 10,000 | Value: 25.00 | | | | |

**100000 ZLOTYCH** **Y# 201** **Weight:** 31.1000 g. **Composition:** 0.9990 Silver 1.0000 oz. ASW **Reverse:** Marszalek Pilsudski

| Date | Mintage | F | VF | XF | Unc | BU |
|---|---|---|---|---|---|---|
| 1990 Proof | 10,000 | Value: 25.00 | | | | |

**100000 ZLOTYCH** **Y# 221** **Weight:** 15.5500 g. **Composition:** 0.9990 Gold .5000 oz. AGW **Subject:** 10th Anniversary of Solidarity **Note:** Similar to 10000 Zlotych, Y#195.

| Date | Mintage | F | VF | XF | Unc | BU |
|---|---|---|---|---|---|---|
| 1990 Proof | Est. 1,000 | Value: 280 | | | | |

**100000 ZLOTYCH** **Y# 235** **Weight:** 16.5000 g. **Composition:** 0.7500 Silver .3979 oz. ASW **Series:** WWII **Reverse:** Major Henrik Dobrzanski - Hubal - Cavalry

| Date | Mintage | F | VF | XF | Unc | BU |
|---|---|---|---|---|---|---|
| 1991 Proof | 12,000 | Value: 27.50 | | | | |

**100000 ZLOTYCH** **Y# 236** **Weight:** 16.5000 g. **Composition:** 0.7500 Silver .3979 oz. ASW **Series:** WWII **Reverse:** Defense of Narvik - Polish Troops

| Date | Mintage | F | VF | XF | Unc | BU |
|---|---|---|---|---|---|---|
| 1991 Proof | 12,000 | Value: 27.50 | | | | |

**100000 ZLOTYCH** **Y# 238** **Weight:** 16.5000 g. **Composition:** 0.7500 Silver .3979 oz. ASW **Series:** WWII **Reverse:** Polish Troops at Battle of Tabruk

| Date | Mintage | F | VF | XF | Unc | BU |
|---|---|---|---|---|---|---|
| 1991 Proof | 12,000 | Value: 27.50 | | | | |

**100000 ZLOTYCH** **Y# 239** **Weight:** 16.5000 g. **Composition:** 0.7500 Silver .3979 oz. ASW **Series:** WWII **Reverse:** Polish Pilots in Battle of Britain

| Date | Mintage | F | VF | XF | Unc | BU |
|---|---|---|---|---|---|---|
| 1991 Proof | 12,000 | Value: 27.50 | | | | |

**100000 ZLOTYCH** **Y# 227** **Weight:** 16.5000 g. **Composition:** 0.7500 Silver .3979 oz. ASW **Subject:** Unification of Upper Silesia and Poland

| Date | Mintage | F | VF | XF | Unc | BU |
|---|---|---|---|---|---|---|
| 1992 Proof | 30,000 | Value: 27.50 | | | | |

**100000 ZLOTYCH** **Y# 268** **Weight:** 16.5000 g. **Composition:** 0.9000 Silver .4775 oz. ASW **Subject:** Warsaw Uprising

| Date | Mintage | F | VF | XF | Unc | BU |
|---|---|---|---|---|---|---|
| 1994 | 150,000 | — | — | — | 32.50 | — |

**200000 ZLOTYCH** **Y# 240** **Weight:** 19.0600 g. **Composition:** 0.9990 Silver .6122 oz. ASW **Reverse:** General Dyw. Stefan Rowecki "Grot"

| Date | Mintage | F | VF | XF | Unc | BU |
|---|---|---|---|---|---|---|
| 1990 Proof | 25,000 | Value: 45.00 | | | | |
| 1991 Proof | — | Value: 45.00 | | | | |

**200000 ZLOTYCH Y# 202 Weight:** 155.5000 g. **Composition:** 0.9990 Silver 5.0000 oz. ASW **Reverse:** Fryderyk Chopin **Note:** Similar to 100,000 Zlotych, Y#199.

| Date | Mintage | F | VF | XF | Unc | BU |
|---|---|---|---|---|---|---|
| 1990 Proof | 10,000 | Value: 90.00 | | | | |

**200000 ZLOTYCH Y# 203 Weight:** 155.5000 g. **Composition:** 0.9990 Silver 5.0000 oz. ASW **Reverse:** Tadeusz Kosciuszko **Note:** Similar to 100,000 Zlotych, Y#200.

| Date | Mintage | F | VF | XF | Unc | BU |
|---|---|---|---|---|---|---|
| 1990 Proof | 10,000 | Value: 90.00 | | | | |

**200000 ZLOTYCH Y# 204 Weight:** 155.5000 g. **Composition:** 0.9990 Silver 5.0000 oz. ASW **Reverse:** Marszalck Pilsudski **Note:** Similar to 100,000 Zlotych, Y#201.

| Date | Mintage | F | VF | XF | Unc | BU |
|---|---|---|---|---|---|---|
| 1990 Proof | 10,000 | Value: 90.00 | | | | |

**200000 ZLOTYCH Y# 205 Weight:** 31.1000 g. **Composition:** 0.9990 Gold 1.0000 oz. AGW **Reverse:** Fryderyk Chopin

| Date | Mintage | F | VF | XF | Unc | BU |
|---|---|---|---|---|---|---|
| 1990 Proof | 10,000 | Value: 475 | | | | |

**200000 ZLOTYCH Y# 206 Weight:** 31.1000 g. **Composition:** 0.9990 Gold 1.0000 oz. AGW **Reverse:** Tadeusz Kosciuszko

| Date | Mintage | F | VF | XF | Unc | BU |
|---|---|---|---|---|---|---|
| 1990 Proof | 10,000 | Value: 475 | | | | |

**200000 ZLOTYCH Y# 207 Weight:** 31.1000 g. **Composition:** 0.9990 Gold 1.0000 oz. AGW **Reverse:** Marszalck Pilsudski

| Date | Mintage | F | VF | XF | Unc | BU |
|---|---|---|---|---|---|---|
| 1990 Proof | 10,000 | Value: 475 | | | | |

**200000 ZLOTYCH Y# 222 Weight:** 31.1000 g. **Composition:** 0.9990 Gold 1.0000 oz. AGW **Subject:** Solidarity **Reverse:** Solidarity monument with city view background

| Date | Mintage | F | VF | XF | Unc | BU |
|---|---|---|---|---|---|---|
| 1990 Proof | Est. 1,000 | Value: 600 | | | | |

**200000 ZLOTYCH Y# 250 Weight:** 19.2650 g. **Composition:** 0.9990 Silver .6188 oz. ASW **Reverse:** General Komorowski

| Date | Mintage | F | VF | XF | Unc | BU |
|---|---|---|---|---|---|---|
| 1990 Proof | 25,000 | Value: 27.50 | | | | |

**200000 ZLOTYCH Y# 218 Weight:** 38.9000 g. **Composition:** 0.9990 Silver 1.2496 oz. ASW **Subject:** 200th Anniversary of Polish Constitution

| Date | Mintage | F | VF | XF | Unc | BU |
|---|---|---|---|---|---|---|
| 1991 | 100,000 | — | — | — | 20.00 | — |

**200000 ZLOTYCH Y# 226 Weight:** 31.1000 g. **Composition:** 0.9250 Silver .9250 oz. ASW **Series:** Albertville Olympics **Reverse:** Slalom SKier

| Date | Mintage | F | VF | XF | Unc | BU |
|---|---|---|---|---|---|---|
| 1991 Proof | 20,000 | Value: 27.50 | | | | |

**200000 ZLOTYCH Y# 228 Weight:** 31.1000 g. **Composition:** 0.9250 Silver .9250 oz. ASW **Series:** Barcelona Olympics **Reverse:** Weightlifter

| Date | Mintage | F | VF | XF | Unc | BU |
|---|---|---|---|---|---|---|
| 1991 Proof | 20,000 | Value: 27.50 | | | | |

**200000 ZLOTYCH Y# 241 Weight:** 31.1600 g. **Composition:** 0.9250 Silver .9267 oz. ASW **Series:** Barcelona Olympics **Reverse:** 2 sailboats

| Date | Mintage | F | VF | XF | Unc | BU |
|---|---|---|---|---|---|---|
| 1991 Proof | 20,000 | Value: 37.50 | | | | |

**200000 ZLOTYCH Y# 242 Weight:** 19.3300 g. **Composition:** 0.7500 Silver .4661 oz. ASW **Subject:** 70th Anniversary of Poznan Fair

| Date | Mintage | F | VF | XF | Unc | BU |
|---|---|---|---|---|---|---|
| 1991 Proof | 20,000 | Value: 27.50 | | | | |

**200000 ZLOTYCH Y# 251 Weight:** 19.3300 g. **Composition:** 0.7500 Silver .4661 oz. ASW **Reverse:** General Okulicki

| Date | Mintage | F | VF | XF | Unc | BU |
|---|---|---|---|---|---|---|
| 1991 Proof | 25,000 | Value: 27.50 | | | | |

**200000 ZLOTYCH Y# 252 Weight:** 19.3300 g. **Composition:** 0.7500 Silver .4661 oz. ASW **Reverse:** General Tokarzewski - Karaszewicz

| Date | Mintage | F | VF | XF | Unc | BU |
|---|---|---|---|---|---|---|
| 1991 Proof | 25,000 | Value: 27.50 | | | | |

**200000 ZLOTYCH Y# 230 Weight:** 31.1000 g. **Composition:** 0.9990 Silver 1.0000 oz. ASW **Reverse:** Discovery of America - Portrait and Ship

| Date | Mintage | F | VF | XF | Unc | BU |
|---|---|---|---|---|---|---|
| 1992 Proof | 20,000 | Value: 40.00 | | | | |

**200000 ZLOTYCH Y# 231 Weight:** 31.1000 g. **Composition:** 0.9990 Silver 1.0000 oz. ASW **Reverse:** Seville Expo '92

| Date | Mintage | F | VF | XF | Unc | BU |
|---|---|---|---|---|---|---|
| 1992 Proof | 45,000 | Value: 25.00 | | | | |

**200000 ZLOTYCH Y# 232 Weight:** 16.5000 g. **Composition:** 0.7500 Silver .3979 oz. ASW **Series:** WWII **Reverse:** Polish Protection of WWII Sea Convoys

| Date | Mintage | F | VF | XF | Unc | BU |
|---|---|---|---|---|---|---|
| 1992 Proof | 15,000 | Value: 27.50 | | | | |

**200000 ZLOTYCH** Y# 233 **Weight:** 16.5000 g. **Composition:** 0.7500 Silver .3979 oz. ASW **Reverse:** Stanislaw Staszic

| Date | Mintage | F | VF | XF | Unc | BU |
|---|---|---|---|---|---|---|
| 1992 Proof | 20,000 | Value: 27.50 | | | | |

**200000 ZLOTYCH** Y# 253 **Weight:** 16.5000 g. **Composition:** 0.7500 Silver .3979 oz. ASW **Reverse:** Full bust Wladyslaw III

| Date | Mintage | F | VF | XF | Unc | BU |
|---|---|---|---|---|---|---|
| 1992 Proof | 15,000 | Value: 27.50 | | | | |

**200000 ZLOTYCH** Y# 254 **Weight:** 16.5000 g. **Composition:** 0.7500 Silver .3979 oz. ASW **Reverse:** Half bust Wladyslaw III

| Date | Mintage | F | VF | XF | Unc | BU |
|---|---|---|---|---|---|---|
| 1992 Proof | 5,000 | Value: 30.00 | | | | |

**200000 ZLOTYCH** Y# 255 **Weight:** 16.5000 g. **Composition:** 0.7500 Silver .3979 oz. ASW **Subject:** 750th Anniversary - City of Stettin

| Date | Mintage | F | VF | XF | Unc | BU |
|---|---|---|---|---|---|---|
| 1993 Proof | 20,000 | Value: 25.00 | | | | |

**200000 ZLOTYCH** Y# 257 **Weight:** 16.5000 g. **Composition:** 0.7500 Silver .3979 oz. ASW **Reverse:** Kazimierz IV

| Date | Mintage | F | VF | XF | Unc | BU |
|---|---|---|---|---|---|---|
| 1993 Proof | 15,000 | Value: 25.00 | | | | |

**200000 ZLOTYCH** Y# 258 **Weight:** 16.5000 g. **Composition:** 0.7500 Silver .3979 oz. ASW **Reverse:** Kazimierz IV - Enthroned

| Date | Mintage | F | VF | XF | Unc | BU |
|---|---|---|---|---|---|---|
| 1993 Proof | 5,000 | Value: 32.50 | | | | |

**200000 ZLOTYCH** Y# 259 **Weight:** 16.5000 g. **Composition:** 0.7500 Silver .3979 oz. ASW **Series:** WWII **Reverse:** Polish Partisans Sabotaging Railways - WWII

| Date | Mintage | F | VF | XF | Unc | BU |
|---|---|---|---|---|---|---|
| 1993 Proof | 10,000 | Value: 27.50 | | | | |

**200000 ZLOTYCH** Y# 262 **Weight:** 16.5000 g. **Composition:** 0.7500 Silver .3979 oz. ASW **Series:** WWII **Reverse:** Battle of Monte Cassino

| Date | Mintage | F | VF | XF | Unc | BU |
|---|---|---|---|---|---|---|
| 1994 Proof | 15,000 | Value: 37.50 | | | | |

**200000 ZLOTYCH** Y# 266 **Weight:** 16.5000 g. **Composition:** 0.7500 Silver .3979 oz. ASW **Subject:** 75th Anniversary - Disabled Association

| Date | Mintage | F | VF | XF | Unc | BU |
|---|---|---|---|---|---|---|
| 1994 Proof | 15,000 | Value: 27.50 | | | | |

**200000 ZLOTYCH** Y# 273 **Weight:** 16.5000 g. **Composition:** 0.7500 Silver .3979 oz. ASW **Reverse:** Sigismund I, 1506-1548

| Date | Mintage | F | VF | XF | Unc | BU |
|---|---|---|---|---|---|---|
| 1994 Proof | 15,000 | Value: 27.50 | | | | |

**200000 ZLOTYCH** Y# 274 **Weight:** 16.5000 g. **Composition:** 0.7500 Silver .3979 oz. ASW **Reverse:** Sigismund I - Half-length portrait

| Date | Mintage | F | VF | XF | Unc | BU |
|---|---|---|---|---|---|---|
| 1994 Proof | 5,000 | Value: 32.50 | | | | |

**200000 ZLOTYCH** Y# 275 **Weight:** 16.5000 g. **Composition:** 0.7500 Silver .3979 oz. ASW **Subject:** 200th Anniversary - Kosciuszko Insurrection

| Date | Mintage | F | VF | XF | Unc | BU |
|---|---|---|---|---|---|---|
| 1994 Proof | 15,000 | Value: 32.50 | | | | |

**300000 ZLOTYCH** Y# 245 **Weight:** 31.1600 g. **Composition:** 0.9250 Silver .9267 oz. ASW **Subject:** 50th Anniversary of Warsaw Ghetto Uprising

| Date | Mintage | F | VF | XF | Unc | BU |
|---|---|---|---|---|---|---|
| 1993 Proof | 30,000 | Value: 37.50 | | | | |

**300000 ZLOTYCH** Y# 247 **Weight:** 31.1600 g. **Composition:** 0.9250 Silver .9267 oz. ASW **Series:** 1994 Olympics **Reverse:** Lillehammer

| Date | Mintage | F | VF | XF | Unc | BU |
|---|---|---|---|---|---|---|
| 1993 Proof | 20,000 | Value: 27.50 | | | | |

**300000 ZLOTYCH** Y# 248 **Weight:** 31.1450 g. **Composition:** 0.9990 Silver 1.0004 oz. ASW **Reverse:** Barn Swallows

| Date | Mintage | F | VF | XF | Unc | BU |
|---|---|---|---|---|---|---|
| 1993 Proof | 20,000 | Value: 42.50 | | | | |

**300000 ZLOTYCH** **Y# 249** **Weight:** 31.1450 g. **Composition:** 0.9990 Silver 1.0004 oz. ASW **Reverse:** Lancut Castle

| Date | Mintage | F | VF | XF | Unc | BU |
|---|---|---|---|---|---|---|
| 1993 Proof | 20,000 | Value: 37.50 | | | | |

**300000 ZLOTYCH** **Y# 260** **Weight:** 31.1000 g. **Composition:** 0.9990 Silver .9990 oz. ASW **Reverse:** Aerial View of Zamosc

| Date | Mintage | F | VF | XF | Unc | BU |
|---|---|---|---|---|---|---|
| 1993 Proof | 20,000 | Value: 32.50 | | | | |

**300000 ZLOTYCH** **Y# 263** **Weight:** 31.1600 g. **Composition:** 0.9250 Silver .9267 oz. ASW **Reverse:** St. Maksymilian Kolbe

| Date | Mintage | F | VF | XF | Unc | BU |
|---|---|---|---|---|---|---|
| 1994 Proof | 15,000 | Value: 37.50 | | | | |

**300000 ZLOTYCH** **Y# 264** **Weight:** 31.1000 g. **Composition:** 0.9250 Silver .9250 oz. ASW **Subject:** 70th Anniversary - Polish National Bank

| Date | Mintage | F | VF | XF | Unc | BU |
|---|---|---|---|---|---|---|
| 1994 Proof | 20,000 | Value: 45.00 | | | | |

**300000 ZLOTYCH** **Y# 269** **Weight:** 31.1035 g. **Composition:** 0.9990 Silver 1.0000 oz. ASW **Subject:** Warsaw Uprising

| Date | Mintage | F | VF | XF | Unc | BU |
|---|---|---|---|---|---|---|
| 1994 Proof | 30,000 | Value: 37.50 | | | | |

**500000 ZLOTYCH** **Y# 208** **Weight:** 62.2000 g. **Composition:** 0.9990 Gold 2.0000 oz. AGW **Reverse:** Fryderyk Chopin **Note:** Similar to 100,000 Zlotych, Y#199.

| Date | Mintage | F | VF | XF | Unc | BU |
|---|---|---|---|---|---|---|
| 1990 Proof | 2,000 | Value: 900 | | | | |

**500000 ZLOTYCH** **Y# 209** **Weight:** 62.2000 g. **Composition:** 0.9990 Gold 2.0000 oz. AGW **Reverse:** Tadeusz Kosciuszko **Note:** Similar to 100,000 Zlotych, Y#200.

| Date | Mintage | F | VF | XF | Unc | BU |
|---|---|---|---|---|---|---|
| 1990 Proof | 2,000 | Value: 900 | | | | |

**500000 ZLOTYCH** **Y# 210** **Weight:** 62.2000 g. **Composition:** 0.9990 Gold 2.0000 oz. AGW **Reverse:** Marszalek Pilsudski **Note:** Similar to 100,000 Zlotych, Y#201.

| Date | Mintage | F | VF | XF | Unc | BU |
|---|---|---|---|---|---|---|
| 1990 Proof | 2,000 | Value: 900 | | | | |

**1000000 ZLOTYCH** **Y# 211** **Weight:** 373.2000 g. **Composition:** 0.9990 Gold 12.0000 oz. AGW **Reverse:** Fryderyk Chopin **Note:** Similar to 100,000 Zlotych, Y#199.

| Date | Mintage | F | VF | XF | Unc | BU |
|---|---|---|---|---|---|---|
| 1990 Proof | 250 | Value: 6,250 | | | | |

**1000000 ZLOTYCH** **Y# 212** **Weight:** 373.2000 g. **Composition:** 0.9990 Gold 12.0000 oz. AGW **Reverse:** Tadeusz Kosciuszko **Note:** Similar to 100,000 Zlotych, Y#200.

| Date | Mintage | F | VF | XF | Unc | BU |
|---|---|---|---|---|---|---|
| 1990 Proof | 250 | Value: 6,250 | | | | |

**1000000 ZLOTYCH** **Y# 213** **Weight:** 373.2000 g. **Composition:** 0.9990 Gold 12.0000 oz. AGW **Reverse:** Marszalek Pilsudski **Note:** Similar to 100,000 Zlotych, Y#201.

| Date | Mintage | F | VF | XF | Unc | BU |
|---|---|---|---|---|---|---|
| 1990 Proof | 250 | Value: 6,250 | | | | |

## REFORM COINAGE

100 Old Zlotych = 1 Grosz;
10,000 Old Zlotych = 1 Zloty

As far back as 1990, production was initiated for the new 1 Grosz - 1 Zlotych coins for a forthcoming monetary reform. It wasn't announced until the Act of July 7, 1994 and was enacted on January 1, 1995.

**GROSZ** **Y# 276** **Composition:** Brass

| Date | Mintage | F | VF | XF | Unc | BU |
|---|---|---|---|---|---|---|
| 1990 | — | — | — | — | 0.10 | — |
| 1991 | — | — | — | — | 0.10 | — |
| 1992 | — | — | — | — | 0.10 | — |
| 1993 | — | — | — | — | 0.10 | — |
| 1995 | — | — | — | — | 0.10 | — |
| 1997 | — | — | — | — | 0.10 | — |
| 1998 | — | — | — | — | 0.10 | — |
| 1999 | — | — | — | — | 0.10 | — |

**2 GROSZE** **Y# 277** **Composition:** Brass

| Date | Mintage | F | VF | XF | Unc | BU |
|---|---|---|---|---|---|---|
| 1990 | — | — | — | — | 0.15 | — |
| 1991 | — | — | — | — | 0.15 | — |
| 1992 | — | — | — | — | 0.15 | — |
| 1997 | — | — | — | — | 0.15 | — |
| 1998 | — | — | — | — | 0.15 | — |
| 1999 | — | — | — | — | 0.15 | — |

**5 GROSZY** **Y# 278** **Composition:** Brass

| Date | Mintage | F | VF | XF | Unc | BU |
|---|---|---|---|---|---|---|
| 1990 | — | — | — | — | 0.25 | — |
| 1991 | — | — | — | — | 0.25 | — |
| 1992 | — | — | — | — | 0.25 | — |
| 1993 | — | — | — | — | 0.25 | — |
| 1998 | — | — | — | — | 0.25 | — |
| 1999 | — | — | — | — | 0.25 | — |

**10 GROSZY** **Y# 279** **Composition:** Copper-Nickel

| Date | Mintage | F | VF | XF | Unc | BU |
|---|---|---|---|---|---|---|
| 1990 | — | — | — | — | 0.40 | — |
| 1991 | — | — | — | — | 0.40 | — |
| 1992 | — | — | — | — | 0.40 | — |
| 1993 | — | — | — | — | 0.40 | — |
| 1998 | — | — | — | — | 0.40 | — |
| 1999 | — | — | — | — | 0.40 | — |
| 2000 | — | — | — | — | 0.40 | — |

**20 GROSZY** **Y# 280** **Composition:** Copper-Nickel

| Date | Mintage | F | VF | XF | Unc | BU |
|---|---|---|---|---|---|---|
| 1990 | — | — | — | — | 0.65 | — |
| 1991 | — | — | — | — | 0.65 | — |
| 1992 | — | — | — | — | 0.65 | — |
| 1996 | — | — | — | — | 0.65 | — |
| 1997 | — | — | — | — | 0.65 | — |
| 1998 | — | — | — | — | 0.65 | — |
| 1999 | — | — | — | — | 0.65 | — |

**50 GROSZY** **Y# 281** **Composition:** Copper-Nickel

| Date | Mintage | F | VF | XF | Unc | BU |
|---|---|---|---|---|---|---|
| 1990 | — | — | — | — | 1.00 | — |
| 1991 | — | — | — | — | 1.00 | — |
| 1992 | — | — | — | — | 1.00 | — |
| 1995 | — | — | — | — | 1.00 | — |
| 1996 | — | — | — | — | 1.00 | — |
| 1997 | — | — | — | — | 1.00 | — |
| 1998 | — | — | — | — | 1.00 | — |

**ZLOTY** **Y# 282** **Composition:** Copper-Nickel

| Date | Mintage | F | VF | XF | Unc | BU |
|---|---|---|---|---|---|---|
| 1990 | — | — | — | — | 1.75 | — |
| 1991 | — | — | — | — | 1.75 | — |
| 1992 | — | — | — | — | 1.75 | — |
| 1993 | — | — | — | — | 1.75 | — |
| 1994 | — | — | — | — | 1.75 | — |
| 1995 | — | — | — | — | 1.75 | — |

**2 ZLOTE** **Y# 283** **Ring Composition:** Brass **Center Composition:** Copper-Nickel

| Date | Mintage | F | VF | XF | Unc | BU |
|---|---|---|---|---|---|---|
| 1994 | — | — | — | — | 4.00 | — |
| 1995 | — | — | — | — | 4.00 | — |
| 1998 | — | — | — | — | 4.00 | — |

**2 ZLOTE** **Y# 285** **Composition:** Copper-Nickel **Subject:** 55th Anniversary - Katyn Forest Massacre

| Date | Mintage | F | VF | XF | Unc | BU |
|---|---|---|---|---|---|---|
| 1995 | 300,000 | — | — | — | 3.50 | — |

**2 ZLOTE** **Y# 289** **Composition:** Copper-Nickel **Reverse:** European Catfish

| Date | Mintage | F | VF | XF | Unc | BU |
|---|---|---|---|---|---|---|
| 1995 | 300,000 | — | — | — | 4.00 | — |

**2 ZLOTE** **Y# 297** **Composition:** Copper-Nickel **Subject:** 75th Anniversary - Battle of Warsaw

| Date | Mintage | F | VF | XF | Unc | BU |
|---|---|---|---|---|---|---|
| 1995 | 300,000 | — | — | — | 3.50 | — |

**2 ZLOTE** **Y# 300** **Composition:** Copper-Nickel **Series:** 1996 Olympics Games **Reverse:** Centennial

| Date | Mintage | F | VF | XF | Unc | BU |
|---|---|---|---|---|---|---|
| 1995 | — | — | — | — | 3.50 | — |

**2 ZLOTE** **Y# 303** **Composition:** Copper-Nickel **Series:** 1996 Olympics - Atlanta **Reverse:** Wrestling

| Date | Mintage | F | VF | XF | Unc | BU |
|---|---|---|---|---|---|---|
| 1995 | — | — | — | — | 3.50 | — |

**2 ZLOTE** **Y# 310** **Composition:** Copper-Nickel **Series:** 1996 Olympics - Atlanta **Reverse:** Lazienki Royal Palace

| Date | Mintage | F | VF | XF | Unc | BU |
|---|---|---|---|---|---|---|
| 1995 | 287,000 | — | — | — | 3.75 | — |

**2 ZLOTE** **Y# 306** **Composition:** Brass **Reverse:** Bust of Zygmunt II

| Date | Mintage | F | VF | XF | Unc | BU |
|---|---|---|---|---|---|---|
| 1996 | 200,000 | — | — | — | 4.00 | — |

**2 ZLOTE** **Y# 311** **Composition:** Copper-Zinc-Tin **Reverse:** Hedgehog with Young

| Date | Mintage | F | VF | XF | Unc | BU |
|---|---|---|---|---|---|---|
| 1996 | Est. 500 | — | — | — | 6.00 | — |

**2 ZLOTE** **Y# 313** **Composition:** Copper-Aluminum-Zinc-Tin **Reverse:** Ligzbark Warminski Castle, with Bishop's arms

| Date | Mintage | F | VF | XF | Unc | BU |
|---|---|---|---|---|---|---|
| 1996 | Est. 500,000 | — | — | — | 3.00 | — |

**2 ZLOTE** **Y# 315** **Composition:** Copper-Aluminum-Zinc-Tin **Reverse:** Henryk Sienkiewicz

| Date | Mintage | F | VF | XF | Unc | BU |
|---|---|---|---|---|---|---|
| 1996 | Est. 500,000 | — | — | — | 3.00 | — |

**2 ZLOTE** **Y# 325** **Composition:** Brass **Obverse:** Polish eagle **Reverse:** Stefan Batory

| Date | Mintage | F | VF | XF | Unc | BU |
|---|---|---|---|---|---|---|
| 1997 | — | — | — | — | 3.50 | — |

**2 ZLOTE** **Y# 329** **Composition:** Brass **Obverse:** Polish eagle **Reverse:** Stag beetle **Note:** Jelenek Rogacz - Lucanus cervus.

| Date | Mintage | F | VF | XF | Unc | BU |
|---|---|---|---|---|---|---|
| 1997 | — | — | — | — | 4.00 | — |

**2 ZLOTE** **Y# 331** **Composition:** Brass **Obverse:** Polish eagle **Reverse:** Zamek W Pieskowej Skale

| Date | Mintage | F | VF | XF | Unc | BU |
|---|---|---|---|---|---|---|
| 1997 | — | — | — | — | 3.00 | — |

**2 ZLOTE** **Y# 333** **Composition:** Copper-Aluminum-Zinc-Tin **Obverse:** Polish eagle **Reverse:** Pawel Edmund Strzelecki

| Date | Mintage | F | VF | XF | Unc | BU |
|---|---|---|---|---|---|---|
| 1997 | Est. 500 | — | — | — | 5.00 | — |

**2 ZLOTE** **Y# 335** **Composition:** Brass **Series:** Nagano Olympics **Obverse:** Polish eagle **Reverse:** Snow boarder

| Date | Mintage | F | VF | XF | Unc | BU |
|---|---|---|---|---|---|---|
| 1998 | 400,000 | — | — | — | 3.00 | — |

**2 ZLOTE** **Y# 336** **Composition:** Brass **Obverse:** Polish eagle **Reverse:** Sigismund III (1587-1632)

| Date | Mintage | F | VF | XF | Unc | BU |
|---|---|---|---|---|---|---|
| 1998 | 400,000 | — | — | — | 3.00 | — |

**2 ZLOTE** **Y# 340** **Composition:** Brass **Obverse:** Polish eagle **Reverse:** Popucha Paskowka - Toad

| Date | Mintage | F | VF | XF | Unc | BU |
|---|---|---|---|---|---|---|
| 1998 | — | — | — | — | 3.50 | — |

**2 ZLOTE** **Y# 344** **Composition:** Brass **Obverse:** Polish eagle **Reverse:** Discovery of Radium and Polomium

| Date | Mintage | F | VF | XF | Unc | BU |
|---|---|---|---|---|---|---|
| 1998 | — | — | — | — | 3.00 | — |

**2 ZLOTE** **Y# 347** **Composition:** Brass **Obverse:** Polish eagle **Reverse:** Zamek W. Korniku - Palace

| Date | Mintage | F | VF | XF | Unc | BU |
|---|---|---|---|---|---|---|
| 1998 | 400,000 | — | — | — | 3.50 | — |

**2 ZLOTE** **Y# 349** **Composition:** Brass **Subject:** 80th Anniversary - Polish Independence **Obverse:** Polish eagle **Reverse:** 1918 on flaming map

| Date | Mintage | F | VF | XF | Unc | BU |
|---|---|---|---|---|---|---|
| 1998 | 400,000 | — | — | — | 3.00 | — |

**2 ZLOTE** **Y# 352** **Composition:** Brass **Subject:** 200th Birthday - Adam Mickiewicz **Obverse:** Polish eagle **Reverse:** Portrait, dates

| Date | Mintage | F | VF | XF | Unc | BU |
|---|---|---|---|---|---|---|
| 1998 | 400,000 | — | — | — | 3.00 | — |

**2 ZLOTE** **Y# 355** **Composition:** Brass **Obverse:** Polish eagle **Reverse:** Parent gray wolves and cubs **Edge Lettering:** POLSKI NARODOWY BANK

| Date | Mintage | F | VF | XF | Unc | BU |
|---|---|---|---|---|---|---|
| 1999 | — | — | — | — | 3.50 | — |

**2 ZLOTE** **Y# 356** **Composition:** Brass **Obverse:** Polish eagle **Reverse:** Portrait Juliusz Slowacki, dates

| Date | Mintage | F | VF | XF | Unc | BU |
|---|---|---|---|---|---|---|
| 1999 | — | — | — | — | 3.00 | — |

**2 ZLOTE** **Y# 357** **Composition:** Brass **Obverse:** Polish eagle **Reverse:** NATO globe, soldiers repelling from helicopter **Edge Lettering:** NARODOWY BANK POLSKI

| Date | Mintage | F | VF | XF | Unc | BU |
|---|---|---|---|---|---|---|
| 1999 | 450,000 | — | — | — | 3.00 | — |

**2 ZLOTE** **Y# 358** **Composition:** Brass **Obverse:** Polish eagle **Reverse:** Portrait of Ernest Malinowsky above slanted text

| Date | Mintage | F | VF | XF | Unc | BU |
|---|---|---|---|---|---|---|
| 1999 | — | — | — | — | 3.00 | — |

**2 ZLOTE** **Y# 363** **Composition:** Brass **Obverse:** Polish eagle **Reverse:** Portraits of Laski and Erasmus **Edge Lettering:** NARODOWY BANK POLSKI

| Date | Mintage | F | VF | XF | Unc | BU |
|---|---|---|---|---|---|---|
| 1999 | 450,000 | — | — | — | 3.00 | — |

**2 ZLOTE** **Y# 365** **Composition:** Brass **Obverse:** Polish eagle **Reverse:** Fryderyk Chopin with stylized piano and music score

| Date | Mintage | F | VF | XF | Unc | BU |
|---|---|---|---|---|---|---|
| 1999 | 420,000 | — | — | — | 3.00 | — |

**2 ZLOTE** **Y# 368** **Composition:** Brass **Obverse:** Polish eagle **Reverse:** Portrait of Wladyslaw IV **Edge Lettering:** NARODOWY BANK POLSKI

| Date | Mintage | F | VF | XF | Unc | BU |
|---|---|---|---|---|---|---|
| 1999 | 500,000 | — | — | — | 3.00 | — |

**2 ZLOTE** **Y# 372** **Composition:** Brass **Obverse:** Polish eagle **Reverse:** Radzyn Podlaski Palace behind sculpted arms

| Date | Mintage | F | VF | XF | Unc | BU |
|---|---|---|---|---|---|---|
| 1999 | 450,000 | — | — | — | 3.50 | — |

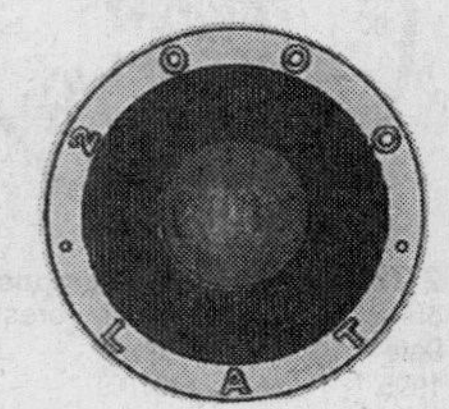

**2 ZLOTE** **Y# 374** **Ring Composition:** Brass **Center Weight:** 8.3100 g. **Center Composition:** Copper-Nickel **Obverse:** Crowned eagle in center **Reverse:** Latent image dates in center **Edge Lettering:** NARODOWY BANK POLSKI **Note:** Millennium.

| Date | Mintage | F | VF | XF | Unc | BU |
|---|---|---|---|---|---|---|
| 2000 | 2,000 | — | — | — | 3.00 | — |

**2 ZLOTE** **Y# 376** **Weight:** 8.1500 g. **Composition:** Brass **Obverse:** Polish eagle **Reverse:** Cross with holy symbolic animals **Note:** Holy Year.

| Date | Mintage | F | VF | XF | Unc | BU |
|---|---|---|---|---|---|---|
| 2000 | 1,500 | — | — | — | 5.00 | — |

**2 ZLOTE** **Y# 377** **Weight:** 8.1500 g. **Composition:** Brass **Subject:** 1000th Anniversary - Gniezno Convention **Reverse:** Denar coin design of Boleslaw Chrobry

| Date | Mintage | F | VF | XF | Unc | BU |
|---|---|---|---|---|---|---|
| 2000 | 450,000 | — | — | — | 5.00 | — |

**2 ZLOTE** **Y# 388** **Weight:** 8.1400 g. **Composition:** Brass **Subject:** "Dudek-Upupa epops" **Obverse:** Polish eagle **Reverse:** Long billed Hoopoe **Edge Lettering:** NARODOWY BANK POLSKI **Size:** 26.8 mm. **Note:** Dudek - Upupa epops - Hoopoe.

| Date | Mintage | F | VF | XF | Unc | BU |
|---|---|---|---|---|---|---|
| 2000 | — | — | — | — | 3.00 | — |

**2 ZLOTE** **Y# 389** **Weight:** 8.1400 g. **Composition:** Brass **Subject:** 1000th Anniversary - Wroclawia (Breslau) **Obverse:** Polish eagle **Reverse:** Jesus with city view in background

| Date | Mintage | F | VF | XF | Unc | BU |
|---|---|---|---|---|---|---|
| 2000 | — | — | — | — | 3.00 | — |

**2 ZLOTE** **Y# 390** **Weight:** 8.1400 g. **Composition:** Brass **Reverse:** Wilanowie Palace

| Date | Mintage | F | VF | XF | Unc | BU |
|---|---|---|---|---|---|---|
| 2000 | — | — | — | — | 3.00 | — |

**2 ZLOTE** **Y# 394** **Weight:** 8.2200 g. **Composition:** Brass **Subject:** Solidarity **Reverse:** Solidarity logo, map, children **Edge Lettering:** NARODOWY BANK POLSKI

| Date | Mintage | F | VF | XF | Unc | BU |
|---|---|---|---|---|---|---|
| 2000 | — | — | — | — | 3.00 | — |

**2 ZLOTE** **Y# 398** **Weight:** 8.2200 g. **Composition:** Brass **Obverse:** Crowned eagle **Reverse:** Bust Jan II Kazimierz facing **Edge Lettering:** POLSKA NARODOWY BANK **Note:** Jan II Kazimierz - 1648-68.

| Date | Mintage | F | VF | XF | Unc | BU |
|---|---|---|---|---|---|---|
| 2000 | — | — | — | — | 3.00 | — |

**2 ZLOTE** **Y# 421** **Weight:** 8.1000 g. **Composition:** Brass **Issuer:** Michal Siedlecki **Obverse:** Eagle **Reverse:** Portrait and art work **Edge:** "NBP" eight times **Size:** 26.8 mm.

| Date | Mintage | F | VF | XF | Unc | BU |
|---|---|---|---|---|---|---|
| 2001 | — | — | — | — | 3.00 | — |

**2 ZLOTE** **Y# 422** **Composition:** Brass **Subject:** Koledicy **Obverse:** Eagle **Reverse:** Christmas celebration scene

| Date | Mintage | F | VF | XF | Unc | BU |
|---|---|---|---|---|---|---|
| 2001 | — | — | — | — | 3.00 | — |

**2 ZLOTY** **Y# 404** **Weight:** 8.1500 g. **Composition:** Brass **Subject:** Grudnia 1970 **Obverse:** Crowned eagle **Reverse:** Fist **Edge:** NBP repeatedly **Size:** 26.7 mm.

| Date | Mintage | F | VF | XF | Unc | BU |
|---|---|---|---|---|---|---|
| 2000 | 750,000 | — | — | — | 3.00 | — |

**2 ZLOTY** **Y# 408** **Weight:** 8.1500 g. **Composition:** Brass **Subject:** Wieliczka Salt Mine **Obverse:** Crowned eagle **Reverse:** Ancient salt miners

| Date | Mintage | F | VF | XF | Unc | BU |
|---|---|---|---|---|---|---|
| 2001 | 500,000 | — | — | — | 3.00 | — |

**2 ZLOTY** **Y# 410** **Weight:** 8.1500 g. **Composition:** Brass **Subject:** Amber Route **Obverse:** Crowned eagle **Reverse:** Ancient Roman coin and man with route marked in stars

| Date | Mintage | F | VF | XF | Unc | BU |
|---|---|---|---|---|---|---|
| 2001 | 500,000 | — | — | — | 3.00 | — |

**2 ZLOTY** **Y# 412** **Weight:** 8.1500 g. **Composition:** Brass **Subject:** 15th Constitutional Congress **Obverse:** Crowned eagle **Reverse:** Crowned eagle head and scale **Edge:** "*NBP*" eight times **Size:** 27 mm.

| Date | Mintage | F | VF | XF | Unc | BU |
|---|---|---|---|---|---|---|
| 2001 | 500,000 | — | — | — | 3.00 | — |

**2 ZLOTY** **Y# 414** **Weight:** 8.1500 g. **Composition:** Brass **Subject:** Swallowtail Butterfly **Obverse:** Crowned eagle **Reverse:** Flying butterfly **Edge:** "*NBP*" eight times **Size:** 27 mm.

| Date | Mintage | F | VF | XF | Unc | BU |
|---|---|---|---|---|---|---|
| 2001 | 600,000 | — | — | — | 3.00 | — |

**2 ZLOTY** **Y# 418** **Weight:** 8.1500 g. **Composition:** Brass **Subject:** Cardinal Stefan Wyszynski **Obverse:** Polish eagle **Reverse:** Portrait wearing mitre **Edge:** "NBP" eight times **Size:** 27 mm.

| Date | Mintage | F | VF | XF | Unc | BU |
|---|---|---|---|---|---|---|
| 2001 | 1,200 | — | — | — | 3.00 | — |

**5 ZLOTYCH** **Y# 284** **Ring Composition:** Copper-Nickel **Center Composition:** Brass

| Date | Mintage | F | VF | XF | Unc | BU |
|---|---|---|---|---|---|---|
| 1994 | — | — | — | — | 7.00 | — |
| 1996 | — | — | — | — | 7.00 | — |

**10 ZLOTYCH** **Y# 287** **Weight:** 16.5500 g. **Composition:** 0.7500 Silver .3979 oz. ASW **Reverse:** Capture of Berlin

| Date | Mintage | F | VF | XF | Unc | BU |
|---|---|---|---|---|---|---|
| 1995 Proof | 12,000 | Value: 22.50 | | | | |

**10 ZLOTYCH** **Y# 301** **Weight:** 16.4400 g. **Composition:** 0.9250 Silver .4889 oz. ASW **Series:** 1996 Olympics **Reverse:** Centennial - Atlanta

| Date | Mintage | F | VF | XF | Unc | BU |
|---|---|---|---|---|---|---|
| 1995 Proof | 20,000 | Value: 20.00 | | | | |

**10 ZLOTYCH** **Y# 305** **Weight:** 16.5000 g. **Composition:** 0.9250 Silver .4907 oz. ASW **Subject:** Centennial of Organized Peasant Movement **Reverse:** Wincenty Witos

| Date | Mintage | F | VF | XF | Unc | BU |
|---|---|---|---|---|---|---|
| 1995 Proof | 20,000 | Value: 25.00 | | | | |

**10 ZLOTYCH** **Y# 307** **Weight:** 16.5000 g. **Composition:** 0.9250 Silver .4907 oz. ASW **Reverse:** Zygmunt II August - Bust, monogram

| Date | Mintage | F | VF | XF | Unc | BU |
|---|---|---|---|---|---|---|
| 1996 Proof | 15,000 | Value: 25.00 | | | | |

**10 ZLOTYCH** **Y# 308** **Weight:** 16.5000 g. **Composition:** 0.9250 Silver .4907 oz. ASW **Reverse:** Zygmunt II August - 1/2 length figure

| Date | Mintage | F | VF | XF | Unc | BU |
|---|---|---|---|---|---|---|
| 1996 Proof | 5,000 | Value: 28.00 | | | | |

**10 ZLOTYCH** **Y# 317** **Weight:** 16.5000 g. **Composition:** 0.9250 Silver .4907 oz. ASW **Reverse:** Stanislaw Mikolajczyk

| Date | Mintage | F | VF | XF | Unc | BU |
|---|---|---|---|---|---|---|
| 1996 Proof | 15,000 | Value: 25.00 | | | | |

**10 ZLOTYCH** **Y# 318** **Weight:** 16.5000 g. **Composition:** 0.9250 Silver .4907 oz. ASW **Reverse:** Mazurka of Dabrowski

| Date | Mintage | F | VF | XF | Unc | BU |
|---|---|---|---|---|---|---|
| 1996 Proof | 15,000 | Value: 25.00 | | | | |

**10 ZLOTYCH** **Y# 324** **Weight:** 16.5000 g. **Composition:** 0.9250 Silver .4907 oz. ASW **Subject:** 40th Anniversary - Poznan Workers Protest **Obverse:** Polish eagle

| Date | Mintage | F | VF | XF | Unc | BU |
|---|---|---|---|---|---|---|
| 1996 Proof | — | Value: 25.00 | | | | |

**10 ZLOTYCH** **Y# 321** **Weight:** 14.1400 g. **Composition:** 0.9250 Silver .4205 oz. ASW **Subject:** St. Adalbert's Martyrdom **Obverse:** Polish eagle **Reverse:** Birth and funeral scenes

| Date | Mintage | F | VF | XF | Unc | BU |
|---|---|---|---|---|---|---|
| 1997 Proof | 25,000 | Value: 25.00 | | | | |

**10 ZLOTYCH** **Y# 322** **Weight:** 14.1400 g. **Composition:** 0.9250 Silver .4205 oz. ASW **Subject:** 46th Eucharistic Congress **Obverse:** Polish eagle in design **Reverse:** Pope

| Date | Mintage | F | VF | XF | Unc | BU |
|---|---|---|---|---|---|---|
| 1997 Proof | Est. 50,000 | Value: 28.00 | | | | |

**10 ZLOTYCH** **Y# 326** **Weight:** 14.1400 g. **Composition:** 0.9250 Silver .4205 oz. ASW **Obverse:** Polish eagle **Reverse:** Stefan Batory

| Date | Mintage | F | VF | XF | Unc | BU |
|---|---|---|---|---|---|---|
| 1997 Proof | 5,000 | Value: 32.50 | | | | |

**10 ZLOTYCH** **Y# 327** **Weight:** 14.1400 g. **Composition:** 0.9250 Silver .4205 oz. ASW **Obverse:** Polish eagle **Reverse:** Stefan Batory

| Date | Mintage | F | VF | XF | Unc | BU |
|---|---|---|---|---|---|---|
| 1997 Proof | 15,000 | Value: 25.00 | | | | |

**10 ZLOTYCH** **Y# 334** **Weight:** 14.1400 g. **Composition:** 0.9250 Silver .4205 oz. ASW **Obverse:** Polish eagle **Reverse:** Pawel Edmund Strzelecki **Edge Lettering:** 200 LECIE URODZIN

| Date | Mintage | F | VF | XF | Unc | BU |
|---|---|---|---|---|---|---|
| 1997 Proof | 20,000 | Value: 25.00 | | | | |

**10 ZLOTYCH** **Y# 337** **Weight:** 14.1400 g. **Composition:** 0.9250 Silver .4205 oz. ASW **Obverse:** Polish eagle **Reverse:** Sigismund III (1587-1632)

| Date | Mintage | F | VF | XF | Unc | BU |
|---|---|---|---|---|---|---|
| 1998 Proof | 22,000 | Value: 25.00 | | | | |

**10 ZLOTYCH** **Y# 338** **Weight:** 14.1400 g. **Composition:** 0.9250 Silver .4205 oz. ASW **Obverse:** Polish eagle **Reverse:** Sigismund III (1587-1632)

| Date | Mintage | F | VF | XF | Unc | BU |
|---|---|---|---|---|---|---|
| 1998 Proof | 14,000 | Value: 27.50 | | | | |

**10 ZLOTYCH** **Y# 341** **Weight:** 14.1400 g. **Composition:** 0.9250 Silver .4205 oz. ASW **Series:** 1998 Winter Olympics **Obverse:** Polish eagle **Reverse:** Snow boarder

| Date | Mintage | F | VF | XF | Unc | BU |
|---|---|---|---|---|---|---|
| 1998 Proof | 30,000 | Value: 20.00 | | | | |

**10 ZLOTYCH** **Y# 342** **Weight:** 14.1400 g. **Composition:** 0.9250 Silver .4205 oz. ASW **Obverse:** Polish eagle **Reverse:** Brigadier General August Emil Fieldorf

| Date | Mintage | F | VF | XF | Unc | BU |
|---|---|---|---|---|---|---|
| 1998 Proof | — | Value: 32.50 | | | | |

**10 ZLOTYCH** **Y# 345** **Weight:** 14.1400 g. **Composition:** 0.9250 Silver .4205 oz. ASW **Obverse:** Denomination and eagles in cross design **Reverse:** Pope John Paul II

| Date | Mintage | F | VF | XF | Unc | BU |
|---|---|---|---|---|---|---|
| 1998 Proof | 65,000 | Value: 35.00 | | | | |

**10 ZLOTYCH** **Y# 350** **Weight:** 14.1400 g. **Composition:** 0.9250 Silver .4205 oz. ASW **Subject:** 80th Anniversary - Polish Independence **Obverse:** Polish eagle on stylized flames **Reverse:** Anniversary dates

| Date | Mintage | F | VF | XF | Unc | BU |
|---|---|---|---|---|---|---|
| 1998 Proof | 20,000 | Value: 27.50 | | | | |

**10 ZLOTYCH** **Y# 351** **Weight:** 14.1400 g. **Composition:** 0.9250 Silver .4205 oz. ASW **Subject:** Universal Declaration of Human Rights **Obverse:** Polish eagle **Reverse:** Human figure between two hands **Edge Lettering:** 50 ROCZNICA UCHWALENIA (3 times)

| Date | Mintage | F | VF | XF | Unc | BU |
|---|---|---|---|---|---|---|
| 1998 Proof | 14,000 | Value: 27.50 | | | | |

**10 ZLOTYCH** **Y# 359** **Weight:** 14.1400 g. **Composition:** 0.9250 Silver .4205 oz. ASW **Subject:** NATO **Obverse:** Polish eagle **Reverse:** NATO globe, soldiers repelling from helicopter

| Date | Mintage | F | VF | XF | Unc | BU |
|---|---|---|---|---|---|---|
| 1999 Proof | 22,000 | Value: 20.00 | | | | |

**10 ZLOTYCH** **Y# 360** **Weight:** 14.1400 g. **Composition:** 0.9250 Silver .4205 oz. ASW **Obverse:** Crucifix designs and Polish eagle **Reverse:** Portrait of Pope John Paul II and dove

| Date | Mintage | F | VF | XF | Unc | BU |
|---|---|---|---|---|---|---|
| 1999 Proof | 70,000 | Value: 30.00 | | | | |

**10 ZLOTYCH** **Y# 362** **Weight:** 14.1400 g. **Composition:** 0.9250 Silver .4205 oz. ASW **Obverse:** Polish eagle **Reverse:** Queen Jadwiga and coat of arms **Edge Lettering:** 1400-2000. (5x) **Note:** Cracow University.

| Date | Mintage | F | VF | XF | Unc | BU |
|---|---|---|---|---|---|---|
| 1999 Proof | 22,000 | Value: 21.50 | | | | |

**10 ZLOTYCH** **Y# 364** **Weight:** 14.1400 g. **Composition:** 0.9250 Silver .4205 oz. ASW **Obverse:** Polish eagle above windowed brick wall **Reverse:** Portrait of Laski with Erasmus in background **Note:** Jan Laski 1490-1560.

| Date | Mintage | F | VF | XF | Unc | BU |
|---|---|---|---|---|---|---|
| 1999 Proof | 20,000 | Value: 21.50 | | | | |

**10 ZLOTYCH** **Y# 366** **Weight:** 14.1400 g. **Composition:** 0.9250 Silver .4205 oz. ASW **Obverse:** Polish eagle over twisted chords **Reverse:** Portrait of Fryderyk Chopin with stylized design

| Date | Mintage | F | VF | XF | Unc | BU |
|---|---|---|---|---|---|---|
| 1999 Proof | 27,000 | Value: 21.50 | | | | |

**10 ZLOTYCH** **Y# 369** **Weight:** 14.1400 g. **Composition:** 0.9250 Silver .4205 oz. ASW **Obverse:** Polish eagle **Reverse:** Portrait of Wladyslaw IV, dates

| Date | Mintage | F | VF | XF | Unc | BU |
|---|---|---|---|---|---|---|
| 1999 Proof | 20,000 | Value: 21.50 | | | | |

**10 ZLOTYCH** **Y# 370** **Weight:** 14.1400 g. **Composition:** 0.9250 Silver .4205 oz. ASW **Obverse:** Polish eagle **Reverse:** Framed 1/2 length portrait of Wladyslaw IV

| Date | Mintage | F | VF | XF | Unc | BU |
|---|---|---|---|---|---|---|
| 1999 Proof | 13,000 | Value: 25.00 | | | | |

**10 ZLOTYCH** **Y# 378** **Weight:** 14.1400 g. **Composition:** 0.9250 Silver .4205 oz. ASW **Obverse:** World glove and Polish eagle **Reverse:** Bust Ernest Malinowski facing, train in background **Edge Lettering:** 100-LECIE SMIERCI twice

| Date | Mintage | F | VF | XF | Unc | BU |
|---|---|---|---|---|---|---|
| 1999 Proof | — | Value: 32.50 | | | | |

**10 ZLOTYCH** **Y# 379** **Weight:** 14.1400 g. **Composition:** 0.9250 Silver .4205 oz. ASW **Obverse:** Inscription and Polish eagle **Reverse:** Bust Juliusz Slowacki half right **Edge:** Plain

| Date | Mintage | F | VF | XF | Unc | BU |
|---|---|---|---|---|---|---|
| 1999 Proof | — | Value: 27.50 | | | | |

**10 ZLOTYCH** **Y# 380** **Weight:** 14.1400 g. **Composition:** 0.9250 Silver .4205 oz. ASW **Subject:** Holy Year **Obverse:** Polish eagle in frame **Reverse:** Cross with holy symbolis animals **Edge Lettering:** WIELKI JUBILEUSZ ROKU 2000

| Date | Mintage | F | VF | XF | Unc | BU |
|---|---|---|---|---|---|---|
| 2000 Proof | 60,000 | Value: 32.50 | | | | |

**10 ZLOTYCH** **Y# 381** **Weight:** 14.1400 g. **Composition:** 0.9250 Silver .4205 oz. ASW **Subject:** 1000th Anniversary - Gniezno Convention **Obverse:** Old coin designs in oxidized center **Reverse:** Seated figures of Boleslaw Chrobry and Otto III in oxidized center **Edge:** Plain

| Date | Mintage | F | VF | XF | Unc | BU |
|---|---|---|---|---|---|---|
| 2000 Proof | 32,000 | Value: 32.50 | | | | |

**10 ZLOTYCH** **Y# 392** **Weight:** 14.2000 g. **Composition:** 0.9250 Silver .4223 oz. ASW **Subject:** 1000 Years Wroclaw (Breslau) **Obverse:** Polish eagle in front of city view **Reverse:** City arms in arch **Edge:** Plain

| Date | Mintage | F | VF | XF | Unc | BU |
|---|---|---|---|---|---|---|
| 2000 Proof | — | Value: 25.00 | | | | |

**10 ZLOTYCH** **Y# 395** **Weight:** 14.2200 g. **Composition:** 0.9250 Silver .4229 oz. ASW **Obverse:** Polish eagle **Reverse:** Solidarity logo and 2 children **Edge:** Plain **Size:** 32 mm. **Note:** Solidarity.

| Date | Mintage | F | VF | XF | Unc | BU |
|---|---|---|---|---|---|---|
| 2000 Proof | — | Value: 27.50 | | | | |

**10 ZLOTYCH** **Y# 400** **Subject:** Jan Kazimierz II (1648-68) **Obverse:** Crowned eagle **Reverse:** Half-length portrait with crown **Edge:** Plain **Size:** 32 mm.

| Date | Mintage | F | VF | XF | Unc | BU |
|---|---|---|---|---|---|---|
| 2000 Proof | 14,000 | — | — | — | 27.50 | — |

**10 ZLOTYCH** **Y# 401** **Weight:** 14.1400 g. **Composition:** 0.9250 Silver .4205 oz. ASW **Subject:** Jan Kazimierz II (1648-68) **Obverse:** Crowned eagle **Reverse:** Portrait

| Date | Mintage | F | VF | XF | Unc | BU |
|---|---|---|---|---|---|---|
| 2000 Proof | 20,000 | — | — | — | 27.50 | — |

**10 ZLOTYCH** **Y# 403** **Weight:** 14.1400 g. **Composition:** 0.9250 Silver .4205 oz. ASW **Subject:** Rapperswil Polish Museum **Obverse:** Crowned eagle and denomination between two buildings **Reverse:** Eagle-topped column

| Date | Mintage | F | VF | XF | Unc | BU |
|---|---|---|---|---|---|---|
| 2000 Proof | 25,000 | — | — | — | 27.50 | — |

**10 ZLOTYCH** **Y# 405** **Weight:** 14.1400 g. **Composition:** 0.9250 Silver .4205 oz. ASW **Subject:** Grudnia 1970 **Obverse:** Two crowned eagles **Reverse:** Shadow figures on pavement

| Date | Mintage | F | VF | XF | Unc | BU |
|---|---|---|---|---|---|---|
| 2000 Proof | 37,000 | — | — | — | 27.50 | — |

**Note:** Antiqued finish

**10 ZLOTYCH** **Y# 406** **Weight:** 14.1400 g. **Composition:** 0.9250 Silver .4205 oz. ASW **Subject:** Year 2001 **Obverse:** Crowned eagle **Reverse:** Printed circuit board

| Date | Mintage | F | VF | XF | Unc | BU |
|---|---|---|---|---|---|---|
| 2001 Proof | 35,000 | — | — | — | 27.50 | — |

**10 ZLOTYCH** **Y# 413** **Weight:** 14.1400 g. **Composition:** 0.9250 Silver .4205 oz. ASW **Subject:** 15th Constitutional Tribunal **Obverse:** Crowned eagle suspended from a judge's neck chain **Reverse:** Crowned eagle head and balance scale **Edge Lettering:** "TRYBUNAL KONSTYTUCYJNY W SLUZBIE PANSTWA PRAWA" **Size:** 32 mm.

| Date | Mintage | F | VF | XF | Unc | BU |
|---|---|---|---|---|---|---|
| 2001 Proof | 25,000 | — | — | — | 22.50 | — |

**10 ZLOTYCH** **Y# 419** **Weight:** 14.1400 g. **Composition:** 0.9250 Silver .4205 oz. ASW **Subject:** Cardinal Stefan Wyszynski **Obverse:** Polish eagle above ribbon **Reverse:** Portrait with raised handle **Edge Lettering:** "100.ROCZNIA URODZIN" **Size:** 32 mm.

| Date | Mintage | F | VF | XF | Unc | BU |
|---|---|---|---|---|---|---|
| 2001 Proof | 60,000 | Value: 27.50 | | | | |

**20 ZLOTYCH** **Y# 286** **Weight:** 31.1100 g. **Composition:** 0.9990 Silver .9990 oz. ASW **Subject:** Katyn Forest Massacre

| Date | Mintage | F | VF | XF | Unc | BU |
|---|---|---|---|---|---|---|
| 1995 Proof | 30,000 | Value: 30.00 | | | | |

**20 ZLOTYCH** **Y# 288** **Weight:** 31.1100 g. **Composition:** 0.9990 Silver .9990 oz. ASW **Subject:** 500th Anniversary - Plock Province

| Date | Mintage | F | VF | XF | Unc | BU |
|---|---|---|---|---|---|---|
| 1995 Proof | 15,000 | Value: 35.00 | | | | |

**20 ZLOTYCH** **Y# 290** **Weight:** 31.1100 g. **Composition:** 0.9990 Silver .9990 oz. ASW **Reverse:** European Catfish

| Date | Mintage | F | VF | XF | Unc | BU |
|---|---|---|---|---|---|---|
| 1995 Proof | 20,000 | Value: 32.50 | | | | |

**20 ZLOTYCH** **Y# 291** **Weight:** 31.1100 g. **Composition:** 0.9990 Silver .9990 oz. ASW **Subject:** 50th Anniversary - United Nations

| Date | Mintage | F | VF | XF | Unc | BU |
|---|---|---|---|---|---|---|
| 1995 Proof | 20,000 | Value: 32.50 | | | | |

**20 ZLOTYCH** **Y# 296** **Weight:** 31.1700 g. **Composition:** 0.9990 Silver 1.0011 oz. ASW **Reverse:** Lazienki Royal Palace

| Date | Mintage | F | VF | XF | Unc | BU |
|---|---|---|---|---|---|---|
| 1995 Prof | 20,000 | Value: 35.00 | | | | |

**20 ZLOTYCH** **Y# 298** **Weight:** 30.9200 g. **Composition:** 0.9250 Silver .9195 oz. ASW **Subject:** 75th Anniversary - Battle of Warsaw

| Date | Mintage | F | VF | XF | Unc | BU |
|---|---|---|---|---|---|---|
| 1995 Proof | 20,000 | Value: 32.50 | | | | |

**20 ZLOTYCH** **Y# 302** **Weight:** 31.0500 g. **Composition:** 0.9250 Silver .9234 oz. ASW **Reverse:** Copernicus and Ecu

| Date | Mintage | F | VF | XF | Unc | BU |
|---|---|---|---|---|---|---|
| 1995 Proof | 15,000 | Value: 37.50 | | | | |

**20 ZLOTYCH** **Y# 304** **Weight:** 31.1000 g. **Composition:** 0.9250 Silver .9240 oz. ASW **Series:** 1996 Olympics - Atlanta **Reverse:** Wrestlers

| Date | Mintage | F | VF | XF | Unc | BU |
|---|---|---|---|---|---|---|
| 1995 Proof | — | Value: 37.50 | | | | |

**20 ZLOTYCH** **Y# 309** **Weight:** 31.1000 g. **Composition:** 0.9250 Silver .9240 oz. ASW **Subject:** 400th Anniversary - Warsaw as Capital City

| Date | Mintage | F | VF | XF | Unc | BU |
|---|---|---|---|---|---|---|
| 1996 Proof | Est. 20,000 | Value: 30.00 | | | | |

**20 ZLOTYCH** **Y# 312** **Weight:** 31.1000 g. **Composition:** 0.9250 Silver .9240 oz. ASW **Subject:** Hedgehog with Young

| Date | Mintage | F | VF | XF | Unc | BU |
|---|---|---|---|---|---|---|
| 1996 Proof | Est. 20,000 | Value: 37.50 | | | | |

**20 ZLOTYCH** **Y# 314** **Weight:** 31.1000 g. **Composition:** 0.9250 Silver .9240 oz. ASW **Reverse:** Bishop's arms and Lidzibark Warminski castle

| Date | Mintage | F | VF | XF | Unc | BU |
|---|---|---|---|---|---|---|
| 1996 Proof | Est. 20,000 | Value: 28.00 | | | | |

**20 ZLOTYCH** **Y# 319** **Weight:** 31.1000 g. **Composition:** 0.9250 Silver .9240 oz. ASW **Subject:** Millennium of Gdansk (Danzig) **Edge Lettering:** MONUMENTUM MILLENNII CIVITATIS GEDANENSIS

| Date | Mintage | F | VF | XF | Unc | BU |
|---|---|---|---|---|---|---|
| 1996 Proof | 20,000 | Value: 37.50 | | | | |

**20 ZLOTYCH** **Y# 330** **Weight:** 28.5200 g. **Composition:** 0.9250 Silver .8482 oz. ASW **Obverse:** Polish eagle **Reverse:** Stag beetle **Note:** Jelonek Rogacz - Lucanus Cervus.

| Date | Mintage | F | VF | XF | Unc | BU |
|---|---|---|---|---|---|---|
| 1997 Proof | — | Value: 32.50 | | | | |

**20 ZLOTYCH** **Y# 332** **Weight:** 28.5200 g. **Composition:** 0.9250 Silver .8482 oz. ASW **Obverse:** Polish eagle **Reverse:** Zemek W Pieskowej Skale

| Date | Mintage | F | VF | XF | Unc | BU |
|---|---|---|---|---|---|---|
| 1997 | — | — | — | — | 3.00 | — |

**20 ZLOTYCH** **Y# 343** **Weight:** 28.4700 g. **Composition:** 0.9250 Silver .8467 oz. ASW **Obverse:** Polish eagle **Reverse:** Ropucha Paskowka - Natterjack Toad

| Date | Mintage | F | VF | XF | Unc | BU |
|---|---|---|---|---|---|---|
| 1998 Proof | — | Value: 37.50 | | | | |

**20 ZLOTYCH** **Y# 348** **Weight:** 28.2800 g. **Composition:** 0.9250 Silver .8410 oz. ASW **Obverse:** Polish eagle **Reverse:** Zamek W. Koniku - Palace

| Date | Mintage | F | VF | XF | Unc | BU |
|---|---|---|---|---|---|---|
| 1998 Proof | 20,000 | Value: 37.50 | | | | |

**20 ZLOTYCH** **Y# 354** **Weight:** 28.1500 g. **Composition:** 0.9250 Silver .8372 oz. ASW **Subject:** Discovery of Radium and Polonium **Obverse:** Atom **Reverse:** Madame and Monsieur Curie and formulas

| Date | Mintage | F | VF | XF | Unc | BU |
|---|---|---|---|---|---|---|
| 1998 Proof | — | Value: 35.00 | | | | |

**20 ZLOTYCH** **Y# 373** **Weight:** 28.2800 g. **Composition:** 0.9250 Silver .8410 oz. ASW **Obverse:** Polish eagle within inner circle **Reverse:** Radzyn Podlaski Palace behind sculpted arms

| Date | Mintage | F | VF | XF | Unc | BU |
|---|---|---|---|---|---|---|
| 1999 Proof | 15,000 | Value: 35.00 | | | | |

**20 ZLOTYCH** **Y# 382** **Weight:** 28.3000 g. **Composition:** 0.9250 Silver .8416 oz. ASW **Reverse:** Wolf family

| Date | Mintage | F | VF | XF | Unc | BU |
|---|---|---|---|---|---|---|
| 1999 Proof | — | Value: 37.50 | | | | |

**20 ZLOTYCH** **Y# 387** **Weight:** 28.3700 g. **Composition:** 0.9250 Silver .8437 oz. ASW **Reverse:** Dudek - Upupa epops - Eurasian Hoopoe

| Date | Mintage | F | VF | XF | Unc | BU |
|---|---|---|---|---|---|---|
| 2000 Proof | — | Value: 32.50 | | | | |

**20 ZLOTYCH** **Y# 391** **Weight:** 28.2400 g. **Composition:** 0.9250 Silver .8398 oz. ASW **Obverse:** Polish eagle **Reverse:** View of Wilanowie Palace thru front gate **Edge:** Plain **Size:** 38.5 mm.

| Date | Mintage | F | VF | XF | Unc | BU |
|---|---|---|---|---|---|---|
| 2000 Proof | — | Value: 37.50 | | | | |

**20 ZLOTYCH** **Y# 409** **Weight:** 28.2800 g. **Composition:** 0.9250 Silver .8410 oz. ASW **Subject:** Wieliezce Salt Mine **Obverse:** Crowned eagle and rock **Reverse:** Ancient salt miners **Edge:** Plain **Size:** 38.6 mm.

| Date | Mintage | F | VF | XF | Unc | BU |
|---|---|---|---|---|---|---|
| 2001 Proof | 25,000 | — | — | — | 40.00 | — |

**20 ZLOTYCH** **Y# 411** **Weight:** 28.2800 g. **Composition:** 0.9250 Silver .8410 oz. ASW **Subject:** Amber Route **Obverse:** Crowned eagle and two ancient Roman silver cups **Reverse:** Piece of amber mounted above an ancient Roman coin design and map with the route marked with stars **Edge:** Plain **Size:** 38.6 mm.

| Date | Mintage | F | VF | XF | Unc | BU |
|---|---|---|---|---|---|---|
| 2001 | 30,000 | — | — | — | 50.00 | — |

**Note:** Antiqued finish

**20 ZLOTYCH** **Y# 415** **Weight:** 28.2800 g. **Composition:** 0.9250 Silver .8410 oz. ASW **Subject:** Swallowtail Butterfly **Obverse:** Crowned eagle between two flags **Reverse:** Flying butterfly **Edge:** Plain **Size:** 38.6 mm.

| Date | Mintage | F | VF | XF | Unc | BU |
|---|---|---|---|---|---|---|
| 2001 Proof | 27,000 | — | — | — | 40.00 | — |

**50 ZLOTYCH** **Y# 292** **Weight:** 3.1000 g. **Composition:** 0.9999 Gold .1000 oz. AGW **Reverse:** Golden eagle

| Date | Mintage | F | VF | XF | Unc | BU |
|---|---|---|---|---|---|---|
| 1995 | 2,000 | — | — | — | 140 | — |

**100 ZLOTYCH** **Y# 293** **Weight:** 7.7800 g. **Composition:** 0.9999 Gold .2500 oz. AGW **Reverse:** Golden eagle

| Date | Mintage | F | VF | XF | Unc | BU |
|---|---|---|---|---|---|---|
| 1995 | 1,500 | — | — | — | 245 | — |

**100 ZLOTYCH** **Y# 328** **Weight:** 8.0000 g. **Composition:** 0.9000 Gold .2315 oz. AGW **Obverse:** Polish eagle **Reverse:** Stefan Batory

| Date | Mintage | F | VF | XF | Unc | BU |
|---|---|---|---|---|---|---|
| 1997 Proof | 2,000 | Value: 220 | | | | |

**100 ZLOTYCH** **Y# 339** **Weight:** 8.0000 g. **Composition:** 0.9000 Gold .2315 oz. AGW **Obverse:** Polish eagle **Reverse:** Sigismund III

| Date | Mintage | F | VF | XF | Unc | BU |
|---|---|---|---|---|---|---|
| 1998 Proof | 2,500 | Value: 220 | | | | |

**100 ZLOTYCH** **Y# 361** **Weight:** 8.0000 g. **Composition:** 0.9000 Gold .2315 oz. AGW **Obverse:** Polish eagle in inner circle **Reverse:** Pope John Paul II and crucifix

| Date | Mintage | F | VF | XF | Unc | BU |
|---|---|---|---|---|---|---|
| 1999 Proof | 7,000 | Value: 190 | | | | |

**100 ZLOTYCH** **Y# 371** **Weight:** 8.0000 g. **Composition:** 0.9000 Gold .2315 oz. AGW **Obverse:** Polish eagle **Reverse:** Framed portrait of Wladyslaw IV

| Date | Mintage | F | VF | XF | Unc | BU |
|---|---|---|---|---|---|---|
| 1999 Proof | 2,300 | Value: 220 | | | | |

**100 ZLOTYCH** **Y# 383** **Weight:** 8.0000 g. **Composition:** 0.9000 Gold .2315 oz. AGW **Obverse:** Polish eagle **Reverse:** Bust King Zygmunt II left

| Date | Mintage | F | VF | XF | Unc | BU |
|---|---|---|---|---|---|---|
| 1999 Proof | 2,000 | Value: 140 | | | | |

**100 ZLOTYCH** **Y# 384** **Weight:** 8.0000 g. **Composition:** 0.9000 Gold .2315 oz. AGW **Subject:** 100th Anniversary - Gniezno Convention **Obverse:** Old coin designs **Reverse:** Seated figures of Boleslaw Chrobry and Otto III

| Date | Mintage | F | VF | XF | Unc | BU |
|---|---|---|---|---|---|---|
| 2000 Proof | 2,200 | Value: 140 | | | | |

**100 ZLOTYCH** **Y# 396** **Weight:** 8.0000 g. **Composition:** 0.9000 Gold .2315 oz. AGW **Obverse:** Polish eagle **Reverse:** 1/2 length bust of Queen Jadwiga facing **Edge:** Plain

| Date | Mintage | F | VF | XF | Unc | BU |
|---|---|---|---|---|---|---|
| 2000 Proof | 2,000 | Value: 220 | | | | |

**100 ZLOTYCH** **Y# 402** **Weight:** 8.0000 g. **Composition:** 0.9000 Gold .2315 oz. AGW **Subject:** Jan Kazimierz II (1648-68) **Obverse:** Crowned eagle **Reverse:** Portrait with name and dates **Edge:** Plain **Size:** 21 mm.

| Date | Mintage | F | VF | XF | Unc | BU |
|---|---|---|---|---|---|---|
| 2000 Proof | 2,000 | Value: 225 | | | | |

**100 ZLOTYCH** **Y# 416** **Weight:** 8.0000 g. **Composition:** 0.9000 Gold .2315 oz. AGW **Subject:** Wladyslaw I (1320-33) **Obverse:** Crowned eagle **Reverse:** Crowned portrait **Edge:** Plain **Size:** 21 mm.

| Date | Mintage | F | VF | XF | Unc | BU |
|---|---|---|---|---|---|---|
| 2001 Proof | 2,000 | Value: 225 | | | | |

**100 ZLOTYCH** **Y# 417** **Weight:** 8.0000 g. **Composition:** 0.9000 Gold .2315 oz. AGW **Subject:** Boleslaw III (1102-1138) **Obverse:** Polish eagle **Reverse:** Portrait **Edge:** Plain **Size:** 21 mm.

| Date | Mintage | F | VF | XF | Unc | BU |
|---|---|---|---|---|---|---|
| 2001 Proof | 2,000 | Value: 220 | | | | |

**200 ZLOTYCH** **Y# 294** **Weight:** 15.5000 g. **Composition:** 0.9000 Gold .4485 oz. AGW **Reverse:** Golden eagle

| Date | Mintage | F | VF | XF | Unc | BU |
|---|---|---|---|---|---|---|
| 1995 | 1,000 | — | — | — | 485 | — |

**200 ZLOTYCH** **Y# 299** **Weight:** 15.5000 g. **Composition:** 0.9000 Gold .4485 oz. AGW **Subject:** XII Chopin Piano Competition **Edge:** Lettered

| Date | Mintage | F | VF | XF | Unc | BU |
|---|---|---|---|---|---|---|
| 1995 Proof | 500 | Value: 420 | | | | |

**200 ZLOTYCH** **Y# 316** **Weight:** 15.5000 g. **Composition:** 0.9000 Gold .4485 oz. AGW **Reverse:** Henryk Sienkiewicz

| Date | Mintage | F | VF | XF | Unc | BU |
|---|---|---|---|---|---|---|
| 1996 Proof | Est. 1,000 | Value: 385 | | | | |

**200 ZLOTYCH** **Y# 320** **Weight:** 15.5000 g. **Composition:** 0.9000 Gold .4485 oz. AGW **Subject:** Millenium of Gdansk (Danzig) **Reverse:** City arms in old coin style

| Date | Mintage | F | VF | XF | Unc | BU |
|---|---|---|---|---|---|---|
| 1996 | 2,000 | — | — | — | 340 | — |

**200 ZLOTYCH** **Y# 323** **Weight:** 15.5000 g. **Composition:** 0.9000 Gold .4485 oz. AGW **Subject:** St. Adalbert's Martyrdom **Obverse:** Police eagle

| Date | Mintage | F | VF | XF | Unc | BU |
|---|---|---|---|---|---|---|
| 1997 Proof | 2,000 | Value: 340 | | | | |

**200 ZLOTYCH** **Y# 346** **Weight:** 15.5000 g. **Composition:** 0.9000 Gold .4485 oz. AGW **Obverse:** Polish eagle **Reverse:** Pope John Paul II

| Date | Mintage | F | VF | XF | Unc | BU |
|---|---|---|---|---|---|---|
| 1998 Proof | 5,000 | Value: 350 | | | | |

**200 ZLOTYCH** **Y# 353** **Weight:** 15.5000 g. **Composition:** 0.9000 Gold .4485 oz. AGW **Subject:** 200th Birthday - Adam Mickiewicz **Obverse:** Smal Polish eagle, quote **Reverse:** Portrait with silhouette

| Date | Mintage | F | VF | XF | Unc | BU |
|---|---|---|---|---|---|---|
| 1998 Proof | 3,000 | Value: 340 | | | | |

**200 ZLOTYCH** **Y# 367** **Weight:** 15.5000 g. **Composition:** 0.9000 Gold .4485 oz. AGW **Obverse:** Polish eagle on sash, music **Reverse:** Portrait of Fryderyk Chopin with music background

| Date | Mintage | F | VF | XF | Unc | BU |
|---|---|---|---|---|---|---|
| 1999 Proof | 2,200 | Value: 340 | | | | |

**200 ZLOTYCH** **Y# 385** **Weight:** 15.5000 g. **Composition:** 0.9000 Gold .4485 oz. AGW **Obverse:** Polish eagle **Reverse:** Head Juliusz Slowacki left

| Date | Mintage | F | VF | XF | Unc | BU |
|---|---|---|---|---|---|---|
| 1999 Proof | 1,900 | Value: 325 | | | | |

**200 ZLOTYCH** **Y# 386** **Weight:** 15.5000 g. **Composition:** 0.9000 Gold .4485 oz. AGW **Subject:** 1000th Anniversary - Gniezno Convention **Obverse:** Old coin designs **Reverse:** Seated figures of Boleslaw Chrobry and Otto III

| Date | Mintage | F | VF | XF | Unc | BU |
|---|---|---|---|---|---|---|
| 2000 Proof | 1,250 | Value: 340 | | | | |

**200 ZLOTYCH** **Y# 393** **Weight:** 15.5000 g. **Composition:** 0.9000 Gold .4485 oz. AGW **Subject:** 1000 Years - Wroclzaw (Breslau) **Obverse:** Polish eagle **Reverse:** Bust of Jesus holding city arms **Edge:** Plain **Size:** 27 mm.

| Date | Mintage | F | VF | XF | Unc | BU |
|---|---|---|---|---|---|---|
| 2000 Proof | 2,500 | Value: 340 | | | | |

**200 ZLOTYCH** **Y# 397** **Weight:** 23.3200 g. **Composition:** 0.9000 Gold .6748 oz. AGW **Subject:** Solidarity **Obverse:** Polish eagle **Reverse:** Multicolor Soldiarity logo, map and 2 children **Edge:** Plain

| Date | Mintage | F | VF | XF | Unc | BU |
|---|---|---|---|---|---|---|
| 2000 Proof | 2,500 | Value: 485 | | | | |

**200 ZLOTYCH** **Y# 375** **Ring Weight:** 0.9250 g. **Ring Composition:** 0.9000 Silver **Center Weight:** 13.6000 g. **Center Composition:** 0.9000 Gold **Subject:** Millennium **Obverse:** Crowned eagle and world globe **Reverse:** Various computer, DNA and atomic symbols **Note:** 13.6000 g, .900 Gold center in .925 Silver inner ring in a .900 Gold outer ring.

| Date | Mintage | F | VF | XF | Unc | BU |
|---|---|---|---|---|---|---|
| 2000 Proof | 6,000 | Value: 150 | | | | |

**200 ZLOTYCH** **Y# 407** **Ring Composition:** 0.9000 Gold With Silver **Center Composition:** 0.9000 Gold With Palladium .4398 oz. **Subject:** Year 2001 **Obverse:** Crowned eagle in a swirl **Reverse:** Couple looking into the future **Edge:** Plain **Size:** 27 mm.

| Date | Mintage | F | VF | XF | Unc | BU |
|---|---|---|---|---|---|---|
| 2001 Proof | 4,000 | Value: 150 | | | | |

**200 ZLOTYCH** **Y# 420** **Weight:** 15.5000 g. **Composition:** 0.9000 Gold .4485 oz. AGW **Subject:** Cardinal Stefan Wyszynski **Obverse:** Pillar divides arms and eagle **Reverse:** Cardinal's portrait **Edge Lettering:** "100 ROCZNIA URODZIN" **Size:** 27 mm.

| Date | Mintage | F | VF | XF | Unc | BU |
|---|---|---|---|---|---|---|
| 2001 Proof | 4,500 | Value: 340 | | | | |

**500 ZLOTYCH** **Y# 295** **Weight:** 31.1035 g. **Composition:** 0.9999 Gold 1.0000 oz. AGW

| Date | Mintage | F | VF | XF | Unc | BU |
|---|---|---|---|---|---|---|
| 1995 | 500 | — | — | — | 775 | — |

**1000 ZLOTYCH** **Y# 267** **Weight:** 27.9500 g. **Composition:** 0.9250 Silver .8313 oz. ASW **Reverse:** World Cup Soccer - Stadium

| Date | Mintage | F | VF | XF | Unc | BU |
|---|---|---|---|---|---|---|
| 1994MW Proof | 10,000 | Value: 25.00 | | | | |

## PATTERNS

Including off metal strikes

| KM# | Date | Mintage | Identification | Mkt Val |
|---|---|---|---|---|
| Pn232 | 1919 | — | 50 Groszy. Nickel. 7.5600 g. Small eagle. | — |
| Pn233 | 1919 | — | 50 Groszy. Nickel. Large eagle. | — |
| Pn234 | 1922 | 60 | 100 Marek. Copper. 8.8400 g. | 175 |
| Pn235 | 1922 | 100 | 100 Marek. Bronze. 8.8400 g. | 80.00 |
| Pn236 | 1922 | 10 | 100 Marek. Brass. 8.8400 g. | — |
| Pn237 | 1922 | 4 | 100 Marek. Tin. 4.5700 g. | — |
| Pn238 | 1922 | 50 | 100 Marek. Silver. 8.8000 g. | 175 |
| Pn239 | 1922 | 3 | 100 Marek. Gold. | — |
| Pn240 | 1923 | 120 | 50 Marek. Bronze. 5.1300 g. | 80.00 |
| Pn241 | 1923 | 12 | 50 Marek. Silver. 5.2500 g. | — |
| Pn242 | 1923 | 1 | 50 Marek. Gold. | — |
| Pn243 | 1923 | 30 | Grosz. Bronze. 1.5000 g. | 150 |
| Pn244 | 1923 | 125 | 2 Grosze. Bronze. 1.5600 g. | 160 |
| Pn245 | 1923 | — | 2 Grosze. Gold. | — |
| Pn246 | 1923 | 10 | 5 Groszy. Brass. 3.0000 g. | — |
| Pn247 | 1923 | 100 | 5 Groszy. Silver. 3.2900 g. | 80.00 |
| Pn248 | 1923 | 3 | 5 Groszy. Brass. 3.0000 g. | 125 |
| Pn249 | 1923 | 30 | 20 Groszy. Brass. 4.5200 g. | 60.00 |
| Pn250 | 1923 | 30 | 50 Groszy. Brass. 4.5200 g. | — |
| Pn251 | 1923 | — | 50 Groszy. Nickel. HUGUENIN in 0 of 50. | — |
| Pn265 | 1924 | 105 | 50 Zlotych. Copper. 10.4200 g. | 100 |
| Pn252 | 1924 | 10 | 20 Groszy. Nickel. 3.0000 g. | — |
| Pn253 | 1924 | 15 | Zloty. Silver. 5.0000 g. ESSAI. | — |
| Pn254 | 1924 | 40 | Zloty. Silver. With torch. | 400 |
| Pn255 | 1924 H | 8 | Zloty. Silver. | — |
| Pn256 | 1924 | 40 | 2 Zlote. Brass. 9.6500 g. | 175 |
| Pn257 | 1924 | 100 | 2 Zlote. Brass. 10.0000 g. Rotated dies. | 150 |
| Pn258 | 1924 | 15 | 2 Zlote. Silver. 10.0000 g. ESSAI. Paris Mint. | — |
| Pn259 | 1924 H | 60 | 2 Zlote. Silver. 10.0000 g. | 400 |
| Pn260 | 1924 | 10 | 2 Zlote. Silver. 10.0000 g. | — |
| Pn261 | 1924 | 3 | 2 Zlote. Silver. 10.0000 g. Larger eagle. | — |
| Pn262 | 1924 | 120 | 20 Zlotych. Bronze. 3.3500 g. | 100 |
| Pn263 | 1924 | 10 | 20 Zlotych. Silver. 5.6900 g. | 225 |
| Pn264 | 1924 | 10 | 20 Zlotych. Gold. | — |
| Pn266 | 1924 | 2 | 50 Zlotych. Lead. 7.8000 g. | — |
| Pn267 | 1924 | 2 | 50 Zlotych. Aluminum. 2.8000 g. | — |
| Pn268 | 1924 | 1 | 50 Zlotych. Gold. | — |
| Pn269 | 1925 | 15 | 5 Groszy. Brass. 3.0000 g. | — |
| Pn272 | 1925 | 100 | 10 Zlotych. Bronze. 3.3100 g. | 100 |
| Pn273 | 1925 | 50 | 10 Zlotych. Silver. 4.3700 g. | 125 |
| Pn274 | 1925 | 1 | 10 Zlotych. Gold. | — |
| Pn275 | 1925 | 105 | 20 Zlotych. Bronze. 5.3900 g. | 100 |
| Pn276 | 1925 | 10 | 20 Zlotych. Copper. 5.3900 g. | 150 |
| Pn277 | 1925 | 12 | 20 Zlotych. Silver. 4.3200 g. | 200 |
| Pn278 | 1925 | 5 | 20 Zlotych. Gold. | — |
| Pn279 | 1925 | 35 | 20 Zlotych. Brass. 3.2700 g. Boleslaus I, Y#33. | — |
| Pn280 | 1925 | 20 | 20 Zlotych. Nickel. 3.5000 g. Boleslaus I, Y#33. | — |
| Pn281 | 1925 | 2 | 100 Zlotych. Silver. 24.2000 g. Plain edge. | — |
| Pn282 | 1925 | 100 | 100 Zlotych. Silver. 24.5300 g. Edge lettering: SALUS REIPUBLICAE SUPREMA LEX. | — |
| Pn283 | 1925 | 100 | 100 Zlotych. Bronze. 3.5000 g. Kopernik Commemorative. | 90.00 |
| Pn284 | 1925 | 50 | 100 Zlotych. Silver. 4.1500 g. | 175 |
| Pn285 | 1925 | 1 | 100 Zlotych. Gold. | — |
| Pn286 | 1926 | 20 | 2 Grosze. Nickel. 2.4700 g. | — |
| Pn287 | 1926 | 100 | 2 Grosze. Silver. 2.2900 g. | 80.00 |
| Pn288 | 1927 | 100 | Grosz. Silver. 5.2500 g. | — |
| Pn289 | 1927 | 6 | Grosz. Gold. | — |
| Pn290 | 1927 | 100 | 2 Zlote. 10.0000 g. | 65.00 |
| Pn291 | 1927 | 10 | 2 Zlote. Bronze. 9.8600 g. With PROBA. | — |
| Pn292 | 1927 | 100 | 2 Zlote. Silver. 10.0000 g. Warsau Mint. | 65.00 |
| Pn293 | 1927 | 81 | 5 Zlotych. Silver. 18.4000 g. With MM, PROBA. | 225 |
| Pn294 | 1927 | 20 | 5 Zlotych. Silver. 18.4000 g. Without MM, without PROBA. | — |
| Pn295 | 1927 | 100 | 5 Zlotych. Silver. 16.0000 g. Without MM, with PROBA. | — |
| Pn296 | 1928 | 2 | Zloty. Copper. 7.9000 g. | — |
| Pn297 | 1928 | 2 | Zloty. Tombac. 6.0000 g. | — |
| Pn298 | 1928 | 25 | Zloty. Nickel. 6.8400 g. | — |
| Pn300 | 1928 | 35 | Zloty. Nickel. 7.0000 g. Mint mark. | — |
| Pn299 | 1928 | 110 | Zloty. Nickel. 7.0000 g. | 50.00 |
| Pn301 | 1928 | 35 | Zloty. Bronze. 7.0000 g. | — |
| Pn302 | 1928 | 15 | Zloty. Nickel. 7.0700 g. | — |
| Pn303 | 1928 | 8 | Zloty. Tombac. 6.0000 g. | — |
| Pn304 | 1928 | 2 | Zloty. Copper. 6.9800 g. | — |
| Pn305 | 1928 | 125 | Zloty. Bronze. 6.0000 g. | 200 |
| Pn306 | 1928 | — | Zloty. Nickel. Madonna. | — |
| Pn307 | 1928 | — | 2 Zlotych. Aluminum. Madonna. | — |
| Pn308 | 1928 | — | 2 Zlotych. Copper. Madonna. | — |
| Pn309 | 1928 | — | 2 Zlotych. Silver. Madonna. | — |
| Pn310 | 1928 | — | 2 Zlotych. Gold. Madonna. | 525 |
| Pn311 | 1928 | — | 2 Zlotych. Platinum. Madonna. | 700 |
| Pn312 | 1928 | — | 5 Zlotych. Aluminum. Madonna. | — |
| Pn313 | 1928 | — | 5 Zlotych. Copper. Madonna. | — |
| Pn314 | 1928 | — | 5 Zlotych. Nickel. Madonna. | — |
| Pn315 | 1928 | — | 5 Zlotych. Silver. Madonna. | 175 |
| Pn316 | 1928 | — | 5 Zlotych. Gold. Madonna. | 1,200 |
| Pn317 | 1928 | — | 5 Zlotych. Platinum. Madonna. | 1,485 |
| Pn318 | 1928 | 20 | 5 Zlotych. Silver. 18.4000 g. Nike. | — |
| Pn319 | 1928 | — | 5 Zlotych. Tombac. ESSAI/30. | 275 |
| Pn320 | 1928 | 20 | 5 Zlotych. Tombac. Denticals instead of dots. | 450 |
| Pn321 | 1929 | 10 | Zloty. Aluminum. 2.2800 g. | — |
| Pn322 | 1929 | 12 | Zloty. Bronze. 4.8700 g. | — |
| Pn323 | 1929 | 115 | Zloty. Nickel. 6.8400 g. Without PROBA. | 55.00 |
| Pn324 | 1930 | 20 | 5 Zlotych. Bronze. 16.0000 g. PROBA. | 150 |
| Pn325 | 1930 | 200 | 5 Zlotych. Bronze. Without PROBA. | — |
| Pn326 | 1932 | 100 | Zloty. Bronze. 2.0500 g. | 60.00 |
| Pn327 | 1932 | 120 | Zloty. Silver. 2.0200 g. | 75.00 |
| Pn328 | 1932 | 100 | 2 Zlote. Bronze. 3.8700 g. | 65.00 |
| Pn329 | 1932 | 110 | 2 Zlote. Silver. 4.4000 g. | 60.00 |
| Pn330 | 1932 | 100 | 10 Zlotych. Silver. 22.0000 g. | 165 |
| Pn331 | 1932 | 10 | 10 Zlotych. Bronze. 19.2200 g. | — |
| Pn332 | 1932 | 100 | 10 Zlotych. Bronze. 19.7000 g. | 125 |
| PnA333 | 1933 | — | 2 Zlote. Silver. PROBA. | — |
| Pn333 | 1933 | 100 | 5 Zlotych. Bronze. 10.0700 g. | 85.00 |
| Pn334 | 1933 | 100 | 5 Zlotych. Silver. 11.0000 g. | 100 |
| Pn335 | 1933 | 100 | 10 Zlotych. Silver. 22.0000 g. | 450 |
| Pn336 | 1933 | 100 | 10 Zlotych. Silver. 22.0000 g. PROBA. | 450 |
| Pn337 | 1933 | 100 | 10 Zlotych. Silver. 30.0000 g. Klippe. | 300 |
| Pn338 | 1933 | 100 | 10 Zlotych. Silver. 30.0000 g. Klippe. | 450 |
| Pn339 | 1934 | 100 | 5 Zlotych. Bronze. 9.4700 g. PROBA. | 85.00 |
| Pn340 | 1934 | 100 | 5 Zlotych. Silver. 11.0000 g. PROBA. | 100 |
| Pn341 | 1934 | 100 | 5 Zlotych. Silver. 11.0000 g. Without PROBA. | — |
| PnA342 | 1934 | — | 10 Zlotych. Silver. | — |
| Pn342 | 1934 | 2 | 10 Zlotych. Aluminum. | 250 |
| Pn343 | 1934 | 130 | 10 Zlotych. Iron-Plated Nickel. 4.9700 g. | 125 |
| Pn344 | 1934 | 3 | 10 Zlotych. Tombac. 10.3000 g. | 350 |
| Pn345 | 1934 | 100 | 10 Zlotych. Silver. 22.0000 g. PROBA. | 400 |
| Pn346 | 1934 | 100 | 10 Zlotych. Silver. 22.0000 g. Without PROBA. | — |
| Pn347 | 1934 | 100 | 10 Zlotych. Bronze. 19.4000 g. PROBA. | — |
| Pn348 | 1934 | 3 | 10 Zlotych. Silver. 15.0000 g. | 425 |
| Pn349 | 1934 | 300 | 10 Zlotych. Silver. 42.0000 g. Klippe. | 650 |
| Pn351 | 1936 | 110 | 5 Zlotych. 11.0000 g. | 150 |
| Pn350 | 1936 | 100 | 2 Zlote. Silver. 4.4000 g. With PROBA. | 90.00 |
| PnA351 | 1936 | 100 | 2 Zlote. Silver. 4.4000 g. Without PROBA. | — |
| Pn352 | 1936 | 200 | 5 Zlotych. Bronze. 17.4600 g. Klippe. | 300 |
| Pn353 | 1936 | 200 | 5 Zlotych. Silver. 20.0000 g. Klippe. | 600 |
| PnA356 | 1938 | 100 | 20 Groszy. Nickeled Iron. Without PROBA. | — |
| Pn354 | 1938 | 100 | 10 Groszy. Bronze. 4.9000 g. | 90.00 |
| Pn355 | 1938 | 100 | 20 Groszy. Nickeled Iron. 3.4900 g. With PROBA. | 60.00 |
| Pn356 | 1938 | 120 | 50 Groszy. Iron. | 50.00 |
| Pn357 | 1938 | 10 | 50 Groszy. Aluminum. | — |
| Pn358 | 1938 | 100 | 50 Groszy. Iron. 4.5000 g. | 50.00 |
| Pn359 | 1938 | 1 | 50 Groszy. Bronze. 3.4000 g. | — |
| Pn360 | 1938 | 3 | 50 Groszy. Aluminum. | — |
| Pn361 | 1938 | 200 | 50 Groszy. Iron-Plated Nickel. | 35.00 |
| Pn362 | 1939 | 200 | Grosz. Zinc. 14.7000 g. | 35.00 |
| Pn363 | 1939 | 200 | 2 Grosze. Zinc. 1.7500 g. | 35.00 |
| Pn364 | 1939 | 200 | 5 Groszy. Zinc. 1.7200 g. 2/hole. | 35.00 |
| Pn365 | 1981MW | 3,000 | 2000 Zlotych. Gold. 8.0000 g. Boleslaw II. | — |

## PIEFORTS

| KM# | Date | Mintage | Identification | Mkt Val |
|---|---|---|---|---|
| P1 | 1989 | — | 10000 Zlotych. Y#189. | — |
| P2 | 1989 | — | 10000 Zlotych. Y#237. | — |

## PROBAS

Standard metals unless otherwise stated

In Poland, rejected coin designs are often minted in large numbers for sale to collectors. These coins have the word PROBA on them, usually stamped incuse. The coins struck in nickel are not available to the general public. Of the 500 pieces struck, 250 pieces are distributed among the members of the Polish Numismatic Society and the other 250 pieces are distributed between various banks and museums.

| KM# | Date | Mintage | Identification | Mkt Val |
|---|---|---|---|---|
| PrA1 | 1929 | — | Zloty. Nickel. | — |
| Pr1 | 1949 | — | Grosz. Aluminum. | — |
| Pr12 | 1949 | 500 | 10 Groszy. Nickel. Y#42. | 45.00 |
| Pr18 | 1949 | 500 | 50 Groszy. Nickel. Y#44. | 45.00 |

| KM# | Date | Mintage | Identification | Mkt Val |
|---|---|---|---|---|
| Pr2 | 1949 | 100 | Grosz. Brass. Y#39. | 65.00 |
| Pr3 | 1949 | 500 | Grosz. Nickel. Y#39. | 40.00 |
| Pr4 | 1949 | 100 | 2 Grosze. Brass. Y#40. | 65.00 |
| Pr5 | 1949 | 500 | 2 Grosze. Nickel. Y#40. | 45.00 |
| Pr6 | 1949 | — | 2 Grosze. Aluminum. | — |
| Pr7 | 1949 | 100 | 5 Groszy. Brass. Y#41. | 75.00 |
| PrA7 | 1949 | 500 | 5 Groszy. Nickel. Y#41. | 45.00 |
| Pr8 | 1949 | 100 | 5 Groszy. Brass. | — |
| Pr9 | 1949 | — | 5 Groszy. Aluminum. | — |
| Pr10 | 1949 | — | 10 Groszy. Aluminum. | — |
| Pr11 | 1949 | 100 | 10 Groszy. Brass. Y#42. | 65.00 |
| Pr13 | 1949 | 100 | 20 Groszy. Brass. Y#43. | 65.00 |
| Pr14 | 1949 | 500 | 20 Groszy. Nickel. Y#43. | 45.00 |
| Pr15 | 1949 | — | 20 Groszy. Aluminum. | — |
| Pr16 | 1949 | 100 | 50 Groszy. Brass. Y#44. | 65.00 |
| Pr17 | 1949 | 20 | 50 Groszy. Tombac. Y#44. | — |
| Pr19 | 1949 | — | 50 Groszy. Aluminum. | — |
| Pr20 | 1949 | 100 | Zloty. Brass. Y#45. | 80.00 |
| Pr21 | 1949 | — | Zloty. Aluminum. | — |

| KM# | Date | Mintage | Identification | Mkt Val |
|---|---|---|---|---|
| Pr22 | 1949 | 500 | Zloty. Nickel. Y#45. | 45.00 |
| Pr23 | 1957 | 100 | 20 Groszy. Brass. Y#A47. | 80.00 |
| Pr24 | 1957 | 100 | 50 Groszy. Brass. Y#48.1. | 80.00 |
| Pr25 | 1957 | 500 | 50 Groszy. Nickel. Y#48.1. | 45.00 |
| Pr26 | 1957 | 100 | Zloty. Brass. Y#49.1. | 80.00 |
| Pr27 | 1957 | 500 | Zloty. Nickel. Y#49.1. | 45.00 |
| Pr28 | 1957 | 5 | Zloty. Copper-Nickel-Zinc. Y#49.1 without PROBA. | — |
| Pr29 | 1958 | 100 | 5 Groszy. Brass. Y#A46. | — |
| Pr30 | 1958 | 245 | 50 Groszy. Aluminum. Crossed hammers. | 35.00 |
| Pr31 | 1958 | 500 | 50 Groszy. Nickel. Crossed hammers. | 35.00 |
| Pr32 | 1958 | 198 | 50 Groszy. Aluminum. Antenna below denomination. | 35.00 |
| Pr33 | 1958 | 500 | 50 Groszy. Nickel. Antenna below denomination. | 35.00 |
| Pr34 | 1958 | 212 | 50 Groszy. Aluminum. 50 above spears of grain. | 35.00 |
| Pr35 | 1958 | 500 | 50 Groszy. Nickel. 50 above spears of grain. | 35.00 |
| Pr36 | 1958 | 234 | Zloty. Aluminum. 1 between spears of grain. | 30.00 |
| Pr37 | 1958 | 500 | Zloty. Nickel. 1 between spears of grain. | 35.00 |

| KM# | Date | Mintage | Identification | Mkt Val |
|---|---|---|---|---|
| Pr38 | 1958 | 235 | Zloty. Aluminum. 1 within circle. | 35.00 |
| Pr39 | 1958 | 500 | Zloty. Nickel. 1 within circle. | 35.00 |
| Pr40 | 1958 | 211 | Zloty. Aluminum. Acorns and oak leaves. | 30.00 |
| Pr41 | 1958 | 500 | Zloty. Nickel. Acorns and oak leaves. | 35.00 |
| Pr42 | 1958 | 210 | Zloty. Aluminum. 1 between doves, low relief. | 30.00 |
| Pr43 | 1958 | 53 | Zloty. Aluminum. 1 between doves, high relief. | 125 |
| Pr44 | 1958 | 500 | Zloty. Nickel. 1 between birds. | 35.00 |
| Pr45 | 1958 | 100 | 2 Zlote. Brass. Y#46. | 55.00 |
| Pr46 | 1958 | 5 | 5 Zlotych. Aluminum. Hammer and shovel without PROBA. | — |
| Pr47 | 1958 | 5 | 5 Zlotych. Brass. Ship. | — |
| Pr48 | 1958 | 20 | 5 Zlotych. Aluminum. Ship, without PROBA. | 150 |

| KM# | Date | Mintage | Identification | Mkt Val |
|---|---|---|---|---|
| Pr49 | 1958 | 500 | 5 Zlotych. Nickel. Ship. | 35.00 |
| Pr50 | 1958 | 10 | 5 Zlotych. Aluminum. Without PROBA, reverse of Pr49. | — |
| Pr51 | 1958 | 5 | 10 Zlotych. Aluminum. Caliper and gear, without PROBA. | 100 |
| Pr52 | 1958 | 10 | 10 Zlotych. Aluminum. Kosciuszko with ornaments, without PROBA. | — |
| Pr53 | 1958 | 10 | 10 Zlotych. Copper-Nickel. Kosciuszko with ornaments, without PROBA. | — |
| Pr54 | 1958 | 5 | 10 Zlotych. Aluminum. With ornaments and PROBA. | 100 |
| Pr55 | 1958 | 5 | 10 Zlotych. Brass. Kosciuszko with ornaments without PROBA. | — |
| Pr56 | 1958 | 5 | 10 Zlotych. Copper-Nickel. Kosciuszko with ornaments and PROBA. | — |
| Pr57 | 1958 | 10 | 10 Zlotych. Aluminum. | — |
| Pr58 | 1958 | 5 | 10 Zlotych. Copper-Nickel. Without ornaments and PROBA, high relief. | — |
| Pr59 | 1959 | 500 | 2 Zlote. Nickel. Y#46. | 30.00 |

| KM# | Date | Mintage | Identification | Mkt Val |
|---|---|---|---|---|
| Pr60 | 1959 | 100 | 5 Zlotych. Brass. Y#47. | 65.00 |
| Pr61 | 1959 | 500 | 5 Zlotych. Nickel. Y#47. | 30.00 |
| Pr62 | 1959 | 500 | 5 Zlotych. Nickel. Industrial collage. | 30.00 |
| Pr63 | 1959 | 500 | 5 Zlotych. Nickel. Hammer and shove. | 30.00 |
| Pr64 | 1959 | 10 | 10 Zlotych. Aluminum. Y#51. | — |
| Pr65 | 1959 | 500 | 10 Zlotych. Nickel. Y#51. | 30.00 |
| Pr71 | 1960 | 10 | 100 Zlotych. Nickel. Y#57, with crosshatched field. | — |
| Pr66 | 1960 | 196 | 5 Zlotych. Aluminum. Ship. | — |
| Pr67 | 1960 | 500 | 5 Zlotych. Nickel. Ship. | 32.50 |

| KM# | Date | Mintage | Identification | Mkt Val |
|---|---|---|---|---|
| Pr68 | 1960 | 500 | 10 Zlotych. Nickel. Caliper and gear. | 30.00 |
| Pr69 | 1960 | 500 | 10 Zlotych. Nickel. Kosciuszko with ornaments and PROBA. | 30.00 |
| Pr70 | 1960 | 500 | 10 Zlotych. Nickel. Kosciuszko with PROBA in front of neck. | 30.00 |
| Pr72 | 1960 | 500 | 100 Zlotych. Nickel. Y#57, with crosshatched field. | 35.00 |
| Pr73 | 1960 | 50 | 100 Zlotych. 0.5000 Silver. Without PROBA, Y#57 with crosshatched field. | 40.00 |
| Pr74 | 1960 | 20 | 100 Zlotych. 0.7500 Silver. Y#57, with crosshatched field. | 40.00 |
| Pr75 | 1960 | 500 | 100 Zlotych. Nickel. Y#57. | 35.00 |
| Pr76 | 1960 | 12 | 100 Zlotych. 0.7500 Silver. | 100 |
| Pr77 | 1960 | 14 | 100 Zlotych. 0.7500 Silver. | 100 |
| Pr78 | 1960 | 4 | 100 Zlotych. 0.7000 Silver. High relief. | — |
| Pr79 | 1960 | 9 | 100 Zlotych. 0.7000 Silver. Flat relief. | — |
| Pr80 | 1960 | 20 | 100 Zlotych. 0.5000 Silver. | 100 |
| Pr81 | 1960 | 13 | 100 Zlotych. 0.7500 Silver. | 100 |
| Pr82 | 1960 | 500 | 100 Zlotych. Nickel. | 30.00 |
| Pr83 | 1960 | 5 | 100 Zlotych. 0.7500 Silver. | 120 |

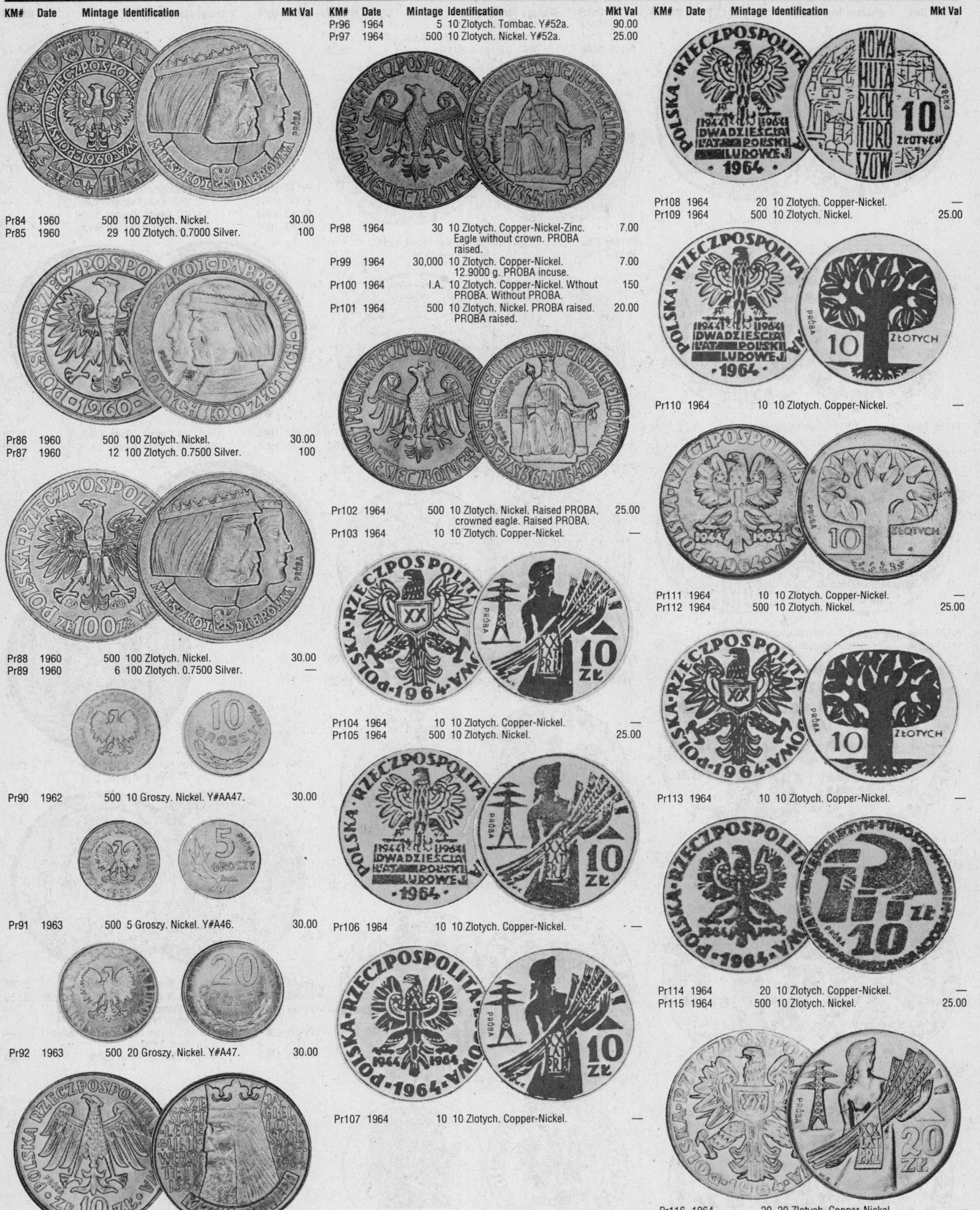

| KM# | Date | Mintage | Identification | Mkt Val |
|---|---|---|---|---|
| Pr84 | 1960 | 500 | 100 Zlotych. Nickel. | 30.00 |
| Pr85 | 1960 | 29 | 100 Zlotych. 0.7000 Silver. | 100 |
| Pr86 | 1960 | 500 | 100 Zlotych. Nickel. | 30.00 |
| Pr87 | 1960 | 12 | 100 Zlotych. 0.7500 Silver. | 100 |
| Pr88 | 1960 | 500 | 100 Zlotych. Nickel. | 30.00 |
| Pr89 | 1960 | 6 | 100 Zlotych. 0.7500 Silver. | — |
| Pr90 | 1962 | 500 | 10 Groszy. Nickel. Y#AA47. | 30.00 |
| Pr91 | 1963 | 500 | 5 Groszy. Nickel. Y#A46. | 30.00 |
| Pr92 | 1963 | 500 | 20 Groszy. Nickel. Y#A47. | 30.00 |
| Pr93 | 1964 | 125 | 10 Zlotych. Copper-Nickel. Raised legend, Y#52. | 50.00 |
| Pr94 | 1964 | 500 | 10 Zlotych. Nickel. Y#52a. | 25.00 |
| Pr95 | 1964 | 125 | 10 Zlotych. Copper-Nickel. Incuse legend, Y#52a. | 50.00 |

| KM# | Date | Mintage | Identification | Mkt Val |
|---|---|---|---|---|
| Pr96 | 1964 | 5 | 10 Zlotych. Tombac. Y#52a. | 90.00 |
| Pr97 | 1964 | 500 | 10 Zlotych. Nickel. Y#52a. | 25.00 |
| Pr98 | 1964 | 30 | 10 Zlotych. Copper-Nickel-Zinc. Eagle without crown. PROBA raised. | 7.00 |
| Pr99 | 1964 | 30,000 | 10 Zlotych. Copper-Nickel. 12.9000 g. PROBA incuse. | 7.00 |
| Pr100 | 1964 | I.A. | 10 Zlotych. Copper-Nickel. Wthout PROBA. Without PROBA. | 150 |
| Pr101 | 1964 | 500 | 10 Zlotych. Nickel. PROBA raised. PROBA raised. | 20.00 |
| Pr102 | 1964 | 500 | 10 Zlotych. Nickel. Raised PROBA, crowned eagle. Raised PROBA. | 25.00 |
| Pr103 | 1964 | 10 | 10 Zlotych. Copper-Nickel. | — |
| Pr104 | 1964 | 10 | 10 Zlotych. Copper-Nickel. | — |
| Pr105 | 1964 | 500 | 10 Zlotych. Nickel. | 25.00 |
| Pr106 | 1964 | 10 | 10 Zlotych. Copper-Nickel. | — |
| Pr107 | 1964 | 10 | 10 Zlotych. Copper-Nickel. | — |

| KM# | Date | Mintage | Identification | Mkt Val |
|---|---|---|---|---|
| Pr108 | 1964 | 20 | 10 Zlotych. Copper-Nickel. | — |
| Pr109 | 1964 | 500 | 10 Zlotych. Nickel. | 25.00 |
| Pr110 | 1964 | 10 | 10 Zlotych. Copper-Nickel. | — |
| Pr111 | 1964 | 10 | 10 Zlotych. Copper-Nickel. | — |
| Pr112 | 1964 | 500 | 10 Zlotych. Nickel. | 25.00 |
| Pr113 | 1964 | 10 | 10 Zlotych. Copper-Nickel. | — |
| Pr114 | 1964 | 20 | 10 Zlotych. Copper-Nickel. | — |
| Pr115 | 1964 | 500 | 10 Zlotych. Nickel. | 25.00 |
| Pr116 | 1964 | 20 | 20 Zlotych. Copper-Nickel. | — |
| Pr117 | 1964 | 500 | 20 Zlotych. Nickel. | 25.00 |

| KM# | Date | Mintage | Identification | Mkt Val |
|---|---|---|---|---|
| Pr118 | 1964 | 20 | 20 Zlotych. Copper-Nickel. | — |
| Pr119 | 1964 | 10 | 20 Zlotych. Copper-Nickel. | — |
| Pr120 | 1964 | 20 | 20 Zlotych. Copper-Nickel. | — |
| Pr121 | 1964 | 500 | 20 Zlotych. Nickel. | 25.00 |
| Pr122 | 1964 | 20 | 20 Zlotych. Copper-Nickel. | — |
| Pr123 | 1964 | 500 | 20 Zlotych. Nickel. | 25.00 |
| Pr124 | 1964 | 20 | 20 Zlotych. Copper-Nickel. | — |
| Pr125 | 1964 | 20 | 20 Zlotych. Copper-Nickel. | — |
| Pr126 | 1964 | 500 | 20 Zlotych. Nickel. | 25.00 |
| Pr127 | 1965 | 20 | 10 Zlotych. Copper-Nickel. | — |
| Pr128 | 1965 | 500 | 10 Zlotych. Nickel. | 25.00 |
| Pr129 | 1965 | 20 | 10 Zlotych. Copper-Nickel. Y#54. | — |
| Pr130 | 1965 | 500 | 10 Zlotych. Nickel. Y#54. | 35.00 |
| Pr131 | 1965 | 30,000 | 10 Zlotych. Copper-Nickel. 12.9000 g. | 10.00 |
| Pr132 | 1965 | 500 | 10 Zlotych. Nickel. | 25.00 |
| Pr133 | 1965 | 30,000 | 10 Zlotych. Copper-Nickel. 12.9000 g. | 10.00 |
| Pr134 | 1965 | 500 | 10 Zlotych. Nickel. | 25.00 |
| Pr135 | 1965 | 20 | 10 Zlotych. Copper-Nickel. | — |
| Pr136 | 1965 | 500 | 10 Zlotych. Nickel. | 25.00 |
| Pr137 | 1965 | 5 | 10 Zlotych. Aluminum. Kopernik. | — |
| Pr138 | 1966 | 25 | 10 Zlotych. Copper-Nickel. | — |
| Pr139 | 1966 | 500 | 10 Zlotych. Nickel. | 25.00 |
| Pr140 | 1966 | 500 | 10 Zlotych. Nickel. | 25.00 |
| Pr141 | 1966 | 10 | 10 Zlotych. Copper-Nickel. | — |
| Pr142 | 1966 | 10 | 100 Zlotych. Copper-Nickel. | — |
| Pr143 | 1966 | 10 | 100 Zlotych. 0.7500 Silver. | — |
| Pr144 | 1966 | 500 | 100 Zlotych. Nickel. Y#57. | 25.00 |
| Pr145 | 1966 | 500 | 100 Zlotych. Nickel. | 25.00 |
| Pr146 | 1966 | 31,000 | 100 Zlotych. 0.9000 Silver. 20.0000 g. 2 busts. | 22.50 |
| Pr147 | 1966 | 500 | 100 Zlotych. Nickel. 2 heads. | 25.00 |
| Pr148 | 1966 | 30,000 | 100 Zlotych. 0.9000 Silver. 2 heads. | 22.50 |
| Pr149 | 1967 | 10 | 10 Zlotych. Copper-Nickel. Plain edge. Y#59. | — |
| Pr150 | 1967 | 16 | 10 Zlotych. Copper-Nickel. Milled edge. Y#59. | — |
| Pr151 | 1967 | 500 | 10 Zlotych. Nickel. Y#59. | 25.00 |
| Pr152 | 1967 | 20 | 10 Zlotych. Copper-Nickel. | — |
| Pr153 | 1967 | 500 | 10 Zlotych. Nickel. | 25.00 |

| KM# | Date | Mintage | Identification | Mkt Val |
|---|---|---|---|---|
| Pr154 | 1967 | 16 | 10 Zlotych. Copper-Nickel. | — |
| Pr155 | 1967 | 10 | 10 Zlotych. Plain edge. | — |
| Pr156 | 1967 | 500 | 10 Zlotych. Nickel. | 25.00 |
| Pr157 | 1967 | 25 | 10 Zlotych. Copper-Nickel. | — |
| Pr158 | 1967 | 500 | 10 Zlotych. Nickel. | 12.50 |
| Pr159 | 1967 | 40 | 10 Zlotych. Copper-Nickel. | — |
| Pr160 | 1967 | 500 | 10 Zlotych. Nickel. | 12.50 |
| Pr161 | 1967 | 17 | 10 Zlotych. Aluminum. Kopernik. | — |
| Pr162 | 1967 | 1 | 10 Zlotych. Copper-Nickel. Kopernik. | — |
| Pr163 | 1967 | 10 | 10 Zlotych. Aluminum. Kopernik. | — |
| Pr164 | 1968 | 20 | 10 Zlotych. Copper-Nickel. | — |
| Pr165 | 1968 | 500 | 10 Zlotych. Nickel. | 25.00 |
| Pr166 | 1969 | 20 | 10 Zlotych. Copper-Nickel. PROBA at lower right. | — |
| Pr167 | 1969 | 500 | 10 Zlotych. Nickel. PROBA at lower right. | — |
| Pr168 | 1969 | 5 | 10 Zlotych. Gold. PROBA at lower right. | — |
| Pr169 | 1969 | 20 | 10 Zlotych. Copper-Nickel. PROBA at right. | — |
| Pr170 | 1969 | 500 | 10 Zlotych. Nickel. PROBA at right. | — |
| Pr171 | 1969 | 500 | 10 Zlotych. Nickel. Wthout PROBA. | 25.00 |

| KM# | Date | Mintage | Identification | Mkt Val |
|---|---|---|---|---|
| Pr172 | 1969 | 20 | 10 Zlotych. Copper-Nickel. | — |
| Pr173 | 1969 | 500 | 10 Zlotych. Nickel. | 25.00 |
| Pr174 | 1969 | 20 | 10 Zlotych. Copper-Nickel. | — |
| Pr175 | 1969 | 500 | 10 Zlotych. Nickel. | 25.00 |
| Pr176 | 1970 | 20 | 10 Zlotych. Copper-Nickel. 25th Anniversary of Provincial Annexation. | — |
| Pr177 | 1970 | 500 | 10 Zlotych. Nickel. 25th Anniversary of Provincial Annexation. | 20.00 |
| Pr178 | 1970 | 10 | 10 Zlotych. Copper-Nickel. Without PROBA. | — |
| Pr179 | 1970 | 20 | 10 Zlotych. Copper-Nickel. Y#62. | — |
| Pr180 | 1970 | 500 | 10 Zlotych. Nickel. Y#62. | 20.00 |
| Pr181 | 1970 | 300 | 10 Zlotych. Silver. Y#62. | 35.00 |
| Pr182 | 1970 | 5 | 10 Zlotych. Aluminum. Kopernik. | — |
| Pr183 | 1971 | 20 | 10 Zlotych. Copper-Nickel. Y#63. | — |
| Pr184 | 1971 | 500 | 10 Zlotych. Nickel. Y#63. | 20.00 |
| Pr185 | 1971 | 51,000 | 10 Zlotych. Copper-Nickel. FAO, baby nursing. | 12.50 |
| Pr186 | 1971 | 500 | 10 Zlotych. Nickel. FAO, baby nursing. | 20.00 |
| Pr187 | 1971 | 52,000 | 10 Zlotych. Copper-Nickel. 9.5000 g. FAO, wheat. | 12.50 |
| Pr188 | 1971 | 500 | 10 Zlotych. Nickel. FAO, wheat. | 20.00 |
| Pr189 | 1971 | 20 | 10 Zlotych. Copper-Nickel. Y#64. | — |

| KM# | Date | Mintage | Identification | Mkt Val |
|---|---|---|---|---|
| Pr190 | 1971 | 500 | 10 Zlotych. Nickel. Y#64. | 20.00 |
| Pr191 | 1971 | 20 | 10 Zlotych. Copper-Nickel. Medal. | — |
| Pr192 | 1971 | 500 | 10 Zlotych. Nickel. Medal. | 20.00 |
| Pr193 | 1972 | 20 | 10 Zlotych. Copper-Nickel. Y#65 but date inside legend. | 20.00 |
| Pr194 | 1972 | 500 | 10 Zlotych. Nickel. Y#65 but date inside legend. | — |
| Pr195 | 1972 | 20 | 10 Zlotych. Copper-Nickel. Y#65. | — |
| Pr196 | 1972 | 500 | 10 Zlotych. Nickel. Y#65. | 20.00 |
| Pr197 | 1972 | — | 50 Zlotych. Copper-Nickel. | — |
| Pr198 | 1972 | 20 | 50 Zlotych. 0.7500 Silver. Y#66, Chopin. | — |
| Pr199 | 1972 | 500 | 50 Zlotych. Nickel. Y#66. | 18.00 |
| Pr200 | 1972 | — | 50 Zlotych. Bronze. Chopin, without PROBA. | — |
| Pr201 | 1972 | 20 | 50 Zlotych. 0.7500 Silver. Chopin, without PROBA. | — |
| Pr202 | 1972 | 15,000 | 50 Zlotych. 0.7500 Silver. Chopin. | 12.50 |
| Pr203 | 1972 | 500 | 50 Zlotych. Nickel. Chopin. | 20.00 |
| Pr204 | 1973 | 20 | 10 Zlotych. Copper-Nickel. | — |
| Pr205 | 1973 | 500 | 10 Zlotych. Nickel. | 20.00 |
| Pr206 | 1973 | 20 | 10 Zlotych. Copper-Nickel. | — |
| Pr207 | 1973 | 500 | 10 Zlotych. Nickel. | 20.00 |
| Pr208 | 1973 | 10 | 10 Zlotych. Copper-Nickel. Kopernik. | — |
| Pr209 | 1973 | 500 | 10 Zlotych. Nickel. Kopernik. | — |

| KM# | Date | Mintage | Identification | Mkt Val |
|---|---|---|---|---|
| Pr210 | 1973 | 20 | 20 Zlotych. Copper-Nickel. Plain edge. Without PROBA, Y#67. | — |
| Pr211 | 1973 | 20 | 20 Zlotych. Copper-Nickel. Ornamented edge. | 20.00 |
| Pr212 | 1973 | 13,000 | 20 Zlotych. Copper-Nickel. 10.1500 g. Milled edge. Y#67. | — |
| Pr213 | 1973 | 500 | 20 Zlotych. Nickel. Y#67. | 20.00 |
| Pr214 | 1973 | 16,000 | 20 Zlotych. Copper-Nickel. 10.1500 g. Tree. | — |
| Pr215 | 1973 | 500 | 20 Zlotych. Nickel. Tree. | 20.00 |
| Pr216 | 1973 | — | 100 Zlotych. Copper. Kopernik. | — |
| Pr217 | 1973 | 20 | 100 Zlotych. 0.6250 Silver. Kopernik. | — |
| Pr218 | 1973 | 500 | 100 Zlotych. Nickel. Kopernik. | 20.00 |
| Pr219 | 1973 | 500 | 100 Zlotych. Nickel. Y#68 | 15.00 |
| Pr220 | 1973 | 5,000 | 100 Zlotych. 0.6250 Silver. Y#68. | 12.50 |
| Pr221 | 1973 | 1,222 | 100 Zlotych. 0.6250 Silver. Kopernik. | 25.00 |
| Pr222 | 1973 | 500 | 100 Zlotych. Nickel. Kopernik. | 20.00 |
| Pr223 | 1974 | 40 | 10 Zlotych. Copper-Nickel. Sienkiewicz. | — |
| Pr224 | 1974 | 500 | 10 Zlotych. Nickel. Sienkiewicz. | 20.00 |
| Pr225 | 1974 | 40 | 10 Zlotych. Copper-Nickel. Y#74. | — |
| Pr226 | 1974 | 500 | 10 Zlotych. Nickel. Y#74. | 20.00 |
| Pr227 | 1974 | 10,000 | 20 Zlotych. Copper-Nickel. Y#69. | — |
| Pr228 | 1974 | 500 | 20 Zlotych. Nickel. Y#69. | 20.00 |
| Pr229 | 1974 | 20 | 20 Zlotych. Copper-Nickel. 4 laborers. | — |
| Pr230 | 1974 | 500 | 20 Zlotych. Nickel. 4 laborers. | 20.00 |
| Pr231 | 1974 | 20 | 20 Zlotych. Copper-Nickel. | — |
| Pr232 | 1974 | 500 | 20 Zlotych. Nickel. | — |
| Pr233 | 1974 | 20 | 20 Zlotych. Copper-Nickel. XXX LAT PRL. | — |
| Pr234 | 1974 | 500 | 20 Zlotych. Nickel. XXX LAT PRL. | 20.00 |
| Pr235 | 1974 | 20 | 20 Zlotych. Copper-Nickel. Y#70. | — |
| Pr236 | 1974 | 500 | 20 Zlotych. Nickel. Y#70. | — |
| Pr237 | 1974 | 20 | 20 Zlotych. Copper-Nickel. | — |
| Pr238 | 1974 | 500 | 20 Zlotych. Nickel. | 20.00 |
| Pr239 | 1974 | 500 | 100 Zlotych. Nickel. Curie left. | 20.00 |
| Pr240 | 1974 | 10,000 | 100 Zlotych. 0.6250 Silver. Curie left. | 7.50 |
| Pr241 | 1974 | 500 | 100 Zlotych. Nickel. Y#71. | 30.00 |
| Pr242 | 1974 | 10 | 100 Zlotych. 0.6250 Silver. Y#71. | 10.00 |
| Pr243 | 1974 | 500 | 100 Zlotych. Nickel. Curie right. | 12.50 |
| Pr244 | 1974 | 10,000 | 100 Zlotych. 0.6250 Silver. Curie right. | 12.50 |
| Pr245 | 1974 | 500 | 100 Zlotych. Nickel. Royal Castle in Warsaw. | — |
| Pr246 | 1974 | 20 | 100 Zlotych. 0.6250 Silver. Royal Castle in Warsaw. | — |
| Pr247 | 1974 | 500 | 200 Zlotych. Nickel. | 20.00 |
| Pr248 | 1974 | 20 | 200 Zlotych. 0.6250 Silver. | — |
| Pr249 | 1975 | — | 10 Zlotych. Aluminum. Boleslaw Prus. | — |
| Pr250 | 1975 | 40 | 10 Zlotych. Copper-Nickel. Boleslaw Prus. | — |
| Pr251 | 1975 | 500 | 10 Zlotych. Nickel. Boleslaw Prus. | 20.00 |
| Pr252 | 1975 | 20 | 20 Zlotych. Copper-Nickel. Year of the Woman. | — |
| Pr253 | 1975 | 500 | 20 Zlotych. Nickel. Year of the Woman. | 20.00 |

| KM# | Date | Mintage | Identification | Mkt Val |
|---|---|---|---|---|
| Pr254 | 1975 | 20 | 20 Zlotych. Copper-Nickel. Globe. | — |
| Pr255 | 1975 | 500 | 20 Zlotych. Nickel. Globe. | 12.50 |
| Pr256 | 1975 | 5,000 | 100 Zlotych. 0.6250 Silver. Y#76. | 7.50 |
| Pr257 | 1975 | 500 | 100 Zlotych. Nickel. Y#78. | 20.00 |
| Pr258 | 1975 | 20 | 100 Zlotych. 0.6250 Silver. Y#78. | — |
| Pr259 | 1975 | 500 | 100 Zlotych. Nickel. Modrzeiewska. | 20.00 |
| Pr260 | 1975 | 20 | 100 Zlotych. 0.6250 Silver. Modrzeiewska. | — |
| Pr261 | 1975 | 500 | 100 Zlotych. Nickel. Y#77. | 20.00 |
| Pr262 | 1975 | 20 | 100 Zlotych. 0.6250 Silver. Y#77. | — |
| Pr263 | 1975 | 500 | 100 Zlotych. Nickel. Paderewski. | 12.50 |
| Pr264 | 1975 | 20 | 100 Zlotych. 0.6250 Silver. Paderewski. | — |
| Pr265 | 1975 | 500 | 200 Zlotych. Nickel. | 20.00 |
| Pr266 | 1975 | 10,000 | 200 Zlotych. 0.7500 Silver. | 17.50 |
| Pr267 | 1975 | 500 | 200 Zlotych. Nickel. | 20.00 |
| Pr268 | 1975 | 10,000 | 200 Zlotych. 0.7500 Silver. | 10.00 |
| Pr269 | 1975 | 500 | 200 Zlotych. Nickel. Y#79. | 20.00 |
| Pr270 | 1975 | 2,600 | 200 Zlotych. 0.7500 Silver. Y#79. | — |
| Pr271 | 1976 | 20 | 20 Zlotych. Copper-Nickel. 30 Years of Budget Bill. | — |
| Pr272 | 1976 | 500 | 20 Zlotych. Nickel. 30 Years of Budget Bill. | — |
| Pr273 | 1976 | 20 | 20 Zlotych. Copper-Nickel. 30 Years of Budget Bill - PRL. | — |
| Pr274 | 1976 | 500 | 20 Zlotych. Nickel. PRL. | — |
| Pr275 | 1976 | 500 | 100 Zlotych. Nickel. Y#82. | 20.00 |
| Pr276 | 1976 | 20 | 100 Zlotych. 0.6250 Silver. Y#82. | — |
| Pr277 | 1976 | 3,000 | 100 Zlotych. 0.6250 Silver. Kosciuszko. | 30.00 |
| Pr278 | 1976 | 500 | 100 Zlotych. Nickel. Kosciuszko. | 20.00 |
| Pr279 | 1976 | 20 | 100 Zlotych. | — |
| Pr280 | 1976 | 500 | 100 Zlotych. Nickel. Pulaski. | 20.00 |
| Pr281 | 1976 | 3,000 | 100 Zlotych. 0.6250 Silver. Pulaski. | 27.00 |
| Pr282 | 1976 | 20 | 200 Zlotych. 0.6250 Silver. Olympics. | — |
| Pr283 | 1976 | — | 200 Zlotych. Nickel. Olympic rings and torch. | — |
| Pr284 | 1976 | 500 | 200 Zlotych. Nickel. Y#86. | 30.00 |
| Pr285 | 1976 | 6,048 | 200 Zlotych. 0.7500 Silver. Y#86. | 13.50 |
| Pr286 | 1976 | 500 | 200 Zlotych. Nickel. | 25.00 |
| Pr287 | 1976 | 6,050 | 200 Zlotych. 0.6250 Silver. | 20.00 |
| Pr288 | 1976 | 500 | 500 Zlotych. Nickel. Y#83. | 20.00 |
| Pr289 | 1976 | 300 | 500 Zlotych. 0.9000 Gold. Y#83. | 550 |
| Pr290 | 1976 | 500 | 500 Zlotych. Nickel. Kosciuszko. | 20.00 |
| Pr291 | 1976 | 500 | 500 Zlotych. Nickel. Y#85. | 20.00 |
| Pr292 | 1976 | 300 | 500 Zlotych. 0.9000 Gold. Y#85. | 550 |
| Pr293 | 1976 | 500 | 500 Zlotych. Nickel. Pulaski facing. | 20.00 |
| Pr294 | 1977 | 100 | 20 Zlotych. Copper-Nickel. Y#96. | — |
| Pr295 | 1977 | 200 | 20 Zlotych. Nickel. Y#96. | — |
| Pr296 | 1977 | 500 | 100 Zlotych. Nickel. Y#88. | — |
| Pr297 | 1977 | 3,000 | 100 Zlotych. 0.6250 Silver. Y#88. | 7.50 |

| KM# | Date | Mintage | Identification | Mkt Val |
|---|---|---|---|---|
| Pr298 | 1977 | 500 | 100 Zlotych. Nickel. Sienkiewicz facing. | 12.50 |
| Pr299 | 1977 | 3,000 | 100 Zlotych. 0.6250 Silver. Sienkiewicz facing. | 22.50 |
| Pr300 | 1977 | 500 | 100 Zlotych. Nickel. Y#89. | — |
| Pr301 | 1977 | 3,100 | 100 Zlotych. 0.6250 Silver. Y#89. | 7.50 |
| Pr302 | 1977 | 500 | 100 Zlotych. Nickel. Reymont profile left. | — |
| Pr303 | 1977 | 3,100 | 100 Zlotych. 0.6250 Silver. Reymont profile left. | 17.50 |
| Pr304 | 1977 | 500 | 100 Zlotych. Nickel. Fish. | 25.00 |
| Pr305 | 1977 | 5,100 | 100 Zlotych. 0.6250 Silver. Fish. | 15.00 |
| Pr306 | 1977 | 500 | 100 Zlotych. Nickel. Y#91. | 25.00 |
| Pr307 | 1977 | 100 | 100 Zlotych. 0.6250 Silver. Y#91. | — |
| Pr308 | 1977 | 500 | 100 Zlotych. Nickel. Distant Krakow castle. | — |
| Pr309 | 1977 | 3,100 | 100 Zlotych. 0.6250 Silver. Distant Krakow castle. | 32.50 |

| KM# | Date | Mintage | Identification | Mkt Val |
|---|---|---|---|---|
| Pr310 | 1977 | 500 | 100 Zlotych. Nickel. Bison. | 35.00 |
| Pr311 | 1977 | 5,400 | 100 Zlotych. 0.6250 Silver. Bison. | 20.00 |
| Pr312 | 1977 | 6 | 2000 Zlotych. Gold. Chopin. | — |
| Pr313 | 1977 | 500 | 2000 Zlotych. Nickel. Chopin. | — |
| Pr314 | 1978 | 100 | 20 Zlotych. Copper-Nickel. Y#97. | — |
| Pr315 | 1978 | 500 | 20 Zlotych. Nickel. Y#97. | — |
| Pr316 | 1978 | 100 | 20 Zlotych. Copper-Nickel. Y#96. | — |
| Pr317 | 1978 | 500 | 20 Zlotych. Nickel. Y#96. | — |
| Pr318 | 1978 | 100 | 100 Zlotych. 0.6250 Silver. Y#92. | — |
| Pr319 | 1978 | 500 | 100 Zlotych. Nickel. Y#92. | — |
| Pr320 | 1978 | 100 | 100 Zlotych. 0.6250 Silver. Similar to KM#PrM255 but with lock of hair at left of face. | — |
| Pr321 | 1978 | 500 | 100 Zlotych. Nickel. Similar to KM#PrK255. | — |
| Pr322 | 1978 | 500 | 100 Zlotych. Nickel. Mickiewicz profile. | — |
| Pr323 | 1978 | 3,100 | 100 Zlotych. 0.6250 Silver. Mickiewicz profile. | 28.50 |
| Pr324 | 1978 | 100 | 100 Zlotych. 0.6250 Silver. Y#93. | — |
| Pr325 | 1978 | 500 | 100 Zlotych. Nickel. Y#93. | — |
| Pr326 | 1978 | 500 | 100 Zlotych. Nickel. Elk head. | — |
| Pr327 | 1978 | 3,100 | 100 Zlotych. 0.6250 Silver. Moose head. | 30.00 |
| Pr328 | 1978 | 500 | 100 Zlotych. Nickel. Beaver on wood. | — |
| Pr329 | 1978 | 3,100 | 100 Zlotych. 0.6250 Silver. Beaver on wood. | — |

| KM# | Date | Mintage | Identification | Mkt Val |
|---|---|---|---|---|
| Pr330 | 1978 | 500 | 100 Zlotych. Nickel. Beaver on grass. | — |
| Pr331 | 1978 | 3,100 | 100 Zlotych. 0.6250 Silver. Beaver on grass. | 35.00 |
| Pr332 | 1978 | 100 | 100 Zlotych. 0.6250 Silver. Y#94. | — |
| Pr333 | 1978 | 500 | 100 Zlotych. Nickel. Y#94. | — |
| Pr334 | 1978 | 500 | 100 Zlotych. Nickel. Korczak. | — |
| Pr335 | 1978 | 3,100 | 100 Zlotych. 0.6250 Silver. Korczak. | 15.00 |
| Pr336 | 1978 | 500 | 100 Zlotych. Nickel. Globe in legend. | — |
| Pr337 | 1978 | 3,100 | 100 Zlotych. 0.6250 Silver. Globe in legend. | 28.50 |
| Pr338 | 1979 | 500 | 2 Zlotych. Nickel. | — |
| Pr339 | 1979 | 500 | 5 Zlotych. Nickel. | — |
| Pr340 | 1979 | 500 | 20 Zlotych. Nickel. I.Y.C., dancers. | — |
| Pr341 | 1979 | 4,100 | 20 Zlotych. 0.6250 Silver. I.Y.C. | 22.00 |
| Pr342 | 1979 | 500 | 20 Zlotych. Nickel. I.Y.C. Health Center. | — |
| Pr343 | 1979 | 30,000 | 20 Zlotych. Copper-Nickel. I.Y.C. Health Center. | 5.00 |
| Pr344 | 1979 | 100 | 50 Zlotych. Copper-Nickel. Mieszko I. | — |
| Pr345 | 1979 | 500 | 50 Zlotych. Nickel. Mieszko I. | — |
| Pr346 | 1979 | 100 | 100 Zlotych. 0.6250 Silver. Y#98. | — |
| Pr347 | 1979 | 500 | 100 Zlotych. Nickel. Y#98. | — |
| Pr348 | 1979 | 500 | 100 Zlotych. Nickel. Wieniawski profile. | — |

| KM# | Date | Mintage | Identification | Mkt Val |
|---|---|---|---|---|
| Pr349 | 1979 | 3,100 | 100 Zlotych. 0.6250 Silver. Wieniawski profile. | 10.00 |
| Pr350 | 1979 | 100 | 100 Zlotych. 0.6250 Silver. Y#104. | — |
| Pr351 | 1979 | 500 | 100 Zlotych. Nickel. Y#104. | — |
| Pr352 | 1979 | 500 | 100 Zlotych. Nickel. Lynx. | 35.00 |
| Pr353 | 1979 | 4,100 | 100 Zlotych. 0.6250 Silver. Lynx. | 22.50 |
| Pr354 | 1979 | 100 | 100 Zlotych. 0.6250 Silver. Y#105. | — |
| Pr355 | 1979 | 500 | 100 Zlotych. Nickel. Y#105. | — |
| Pr356 | 1979 | 500 | 100 Zlotych. Nickel. Mountain goat on rock. | 30.00 |
| Pr357 | 1979 | 4,100 | 100 Zlotych. 0.6250 Silver. Mountain goat on rock. | 25.00 |
| Pr358 | 1979 | 100 | 100 Zlotych. 0.6250 Silver. Y#103. | — |
| Pr359 | 1979 | 500 | 100 Zlotych. Nickel. Y#103. | — |
| Pr360 | 1979 | 500 | 100 Zlotych. Nickel. Zamenhof facing. | — |
| Pr361 | 1979 | 3,100 | 100 Zlotych. 0.6250 Silver. Zamenhof facing. | 25.00 |
| Pr362 | 1979 | 100 | 200 Zlotych. 0.7500 Silver. Y#101. | — |
| Pr363 | 1979 | 500 | 200 Zlotych. Nickel. Y#101. | — |
| Pr364 | 1979 | 500 | 200 Zlotych. Nickel. Mieszko. | — |
| Pr365 | 1979 | 4,100 | 200 Zlotych. 0.7500 Silver. Mieszko I. | 12.50 |
| Pr366 | 1979 | 5 | 2000 Zlotych. 0.9000 Gold. Y#106. | — |
| Pr367 | 1979 | 500 | 2000 Zlotych. Nickel. Y#106. | — |
| Pr368 | 1979 | 6 | 2000 Zlotych. 0.9000 Gold. Y#107. | — |
| Pr369 | 1979 | 500 | 2000 Zlotych. Nickel. Y#107. | — |
| Pr370 | 1979 | 4 | 2000 Zlotych. 0.9000 Gold. Y#102. | — |
| Pr371 | 1979 | — | 2000 Zlotych. Bronze. Y#102. | — |
| Pr372 | 1979 | 500 | 2000 Zlotych. Nickel. Y#102. | — |
| Pr373 | 1979 | 4 | 2000 Zlotych. 0.9000 Gold. Mieszko I, PrG266. | — |
| Pr374 | 1979 | — | 2000 Zlotych. Bronze. PrG266. | — |
| Pr375 | 1979 | 500 | 2000 Zlotych. Nickel. PrG266. | — |
| Pr396 | 1980 | 20 | 100 Zlotych. 0.6250 Silver. Y#121. | — |
| Pr376 | 1980 | 100 | 20 Zlotych. 0.6250 Silver. Y#108. | — |
| Pr377 | 1980 | 500 | 20 Zlotych. Nickel. Y#108. | 70.00 |

| KM# | Date | Mintage | Identification | Mkt Val |
|---|---|---|---|---|
| PrA378 | 1980 | 100 | 20 Zlotych. Nickel. | 80.00 |
| Pr378 | 1980 | 100 | 20 Zlotych. Copper-Nickel. Y#112. | — |
| Pr379 | 1980 | 500 | 20 Zlotych. Nickel. Y#112. | — |
| Pr380 | 1980 | 20 | 20 Zlotych. Copper-Nickel. Ship. | — |
| Pr381 | 1980 | 500 | 20 Zlotych. Nickel. Ship. | — |
| Pr382 | 1980 | 500 | 20 Zlotych. Nickel. 1905-Lodz. | — |
| Pr383 | 1980 | 10,000 | 20 Zlotych. Copper-Nickel. 1905-Lodz. | — |
| Pr384 | 1980 | 20 | 20 Zlotych. Copper-Nickel. 75th Anniversary of Lodz riots. | — |
| Pr385 | 1980 | 500 | 20 Zlotych. Nickel. 75th Anniversary of Lodz riots. | — |
| Pr386 | 1980 | 20 | 50 Zlotych. Copper-Nickel. Y#114. | — |
| Pr387 | 1980 | 500 | 50 Zlotych. Nickel. Y#114. | — |
| Pr388 | 1980 | 20 | 50 Zlotych. Copper-Nickel. Boleslaw I inscription below. | — |
| Pr389 | 1980 | 500 | 50 Zlotych. Nickel. Boleslaw I, inscription below. | — |
| Pr390 | 1980 | 20 | 50 Zlotych. Copper-Nickel. Y#117. | — |
| Pr391 | 1980 | 500 | 100 Zlotych. Nickel. Ship. | — |
| Pr392 | 1980 | 4,000 | 100 Zlotych. 0.6250 Silver. Ship. | 27.50 |
| Pr393 | 1980 | 100 | 100 Zlotych. Copper-Nickel. Olympic flame and rings. | — |
| Pr394 | 1980 | 500 | 100 Zlotych. Nickel. Olympic flame and rings. | 85.00 |
| Pr395 | 1980 | 4,100 | 100 Zlotych. 0.6250 Silver. Olympic flame and rings. | 32.50 |
| PrA396 | 1980 | 500 | 100 Zlotych. Nickel. Y#109. | 85.00 |
| Pr397 | 1980 | 500 | 100 Zlotych. Nickel. Y#121. | — |

| KM# | Date | Mintage | Identification | Mkt Val |
|---|---|---|---|---|
| Pr398 | 1980 | 500 | 100 Zlotych. Nickel. Birds. | 35.00 |
| Pr399 | 1980 | 4,018 | 100 Zlotych. 0.6250 Silver. Birds. | 22.50 |
| Pr400 | 1980 | 100 | 100 Zlotych. 0.6250 Silver. Y#120. | — |
| Pr401 | 1980 | 500 | 100 Zlotych. Nickel. | — |
| Pr402 | 1980 | 500 | 100 Zlotych. Nickel. Larger head of Kochanowski. | — |
| Pr403 | 1980 | 4,100 | 100 Zlotych. 0.6250 Silver. Larger head of Kochanowski. | 12.50 |
| Pr404 | 1980 | 100 | 200 Zlotych. 0.7500 Silver. Y#110. | — |
| Pr405 | 1980 | 500 | 200 Zlotych. Nickel. Y#110. | 85.00 |
| Pr406 | 1980 | 100 | 200 Zlotych. 0.7500 Silver. Y#110a. | — |
| Pr407 | 1980 | 500 | 200 Zlotych. Nickel. Y#110a. | 85.00 |
| Pr408 | 1980 | 500 | 200 Zlotych. Nickel. Olympic skier with torch mm. | 100 |
| Pr409 | 1980 | 3,620 | 200 Zlotych. 0.7500 Silver. Olympic skier with torch mm. | 20.00 |
| Pr410 | 1980 | 500 | 200 Zlotych. Nickel. Olympic skier without mm. | 100 |
| Pr411 | 1980 | 3,620 | 200 Zlotych. 0.7500 Silver. Olympic skier without mm. | 20.00 |
| Pr412 | 1980 | 20 | 200 Zlotych. 0.7500 Silver. Y#115. | — |
| Pr413 | 1980 | 500 | 200 Zlotych. Nickel. Y#115. | — |
| Pr414 | 1980 | 500 | 200 Zlotych. Nickel. Boleslaw I torso. | — |
| Pr417 | 1980 | 500 | 200 Zlotych. Nickel. Y#118. | — |
| Pr415 | 1980 | 4,020 | 200 Zlotych. 0.7500 Silver. Boleslaw I torso. | 25.00 |
| Pr416 | 1980 | 20 | 200 Zlotych. 0.7500 Silver. Y#118. | — |
| Pr418 | 1980 | 500 | 200 Zlotych. Nickel. Kazimierz I torso. | — |
| Pr419 | 1980 | 4,020 | 200 Zlotych. 0.7500 Silver. Kazimierz I torso. | 25.00 |
| Pr420 | 1980 | 3 | 2000 Zlotych. 0.9000 Gold. Y#111. | — |
| Pr421 | 1980 | — | 2000 Zlotych. Bronze. Y#111. | — |
| Pr422 | 1980 | 500 | 2000 Zlotych. Nickel. Y#111. | — |
| Pr423 | 1980 | 6 | 2000 Zlotych. 0.9000 Gold. Y#116. | — |
| Pr424 | 1980 | 500 | 2000 Zlotych. Nickel. Y#116. | — |
| Pr425 | 1980 | 6 | 2000 Zlotych. 0.9000 Gold. Odnowiciel. | — |
| Pr426 | 1980 | 500 | 2000 Zlotych. Nickel. Odnowiciel. | — |
| Pr427 | 1980 | 500 | 2000 Zlotych. Nickel. Olympic skier without torch mm. | — |

| KM# | Date | Mintage | Identification | Mkt Val |
|---|---|---|---|---|
| Pr428 | 1980 | 1,500 | 2000 Zlotych. 0.9000 Gold. Olympic skier without torch mm. | 200 |
| Pr429 | 1981 | 500 | 20 Zlotych. Nickel. Restoration of Krakow. | — |
| Pr430 | 1981 | 30,000 | 20 Zlotych. Copper-Nickel. Restoration of Krakow. | 6.00 |
| Pr431 | 1981 | 20 | 50 Zlotych. Copper-Nickel. Y#122. | — |
| Pr432 | 1981 | 500 | 50 Zlotych. Nickel. Y#122. | — |
| Pr433 | 1981 | 20 | 50 Zlotych. Copper-Nickel. Y#124. | — |
| Pr434 | 1981 | 500 | 50 Zlotych. Nickel. Y#124. | — |
| Pr435 | 1981 | 20 | 50 Zlotych. Copper-Nickel. Y#128. | — |
| Pr436 | 1981 | 500 | 50 Zlotych. Nickel. Y#128. | — |
| Pr437 | 1981 | 20 | 50 Zlotych. Copper-Nickel. Y#127. | — |
| Pr438 | 1981 | 500 | 50 Zlotych. Nickel. Y#127. | — |
| Pr439 | 1981 | 120 | 100 Zlotych. 0.6250 Silver. Y#123. | — |
| Pr440 | 1981 | 500 | 100 Zlotych. Nickel. Y#123. | — |
| Pr441 | 1981 | 500 | 100 Zlotych. Nickel. Sikorski. | — |
| Pr442 | 1981 | 5,020 | 100 Zlotych. 0.6250 Silver. Sikorski. | 20.00 |
| Pr443 | 1981 | 500 | 100 Zlotych. Nickel. St. Mary's Church. | — |
| Pr444 | 1981 | 4,020 | 100 Zlotych. 0.6250 Silver. St. Mary's Church. | 28.50 |
| Pr445 | 1981 | 20 | 100 Zlotych. 0.6250 Silver. Y#126. | — |
| Pr446 | 1981 | 500 | 100 Zlotych. Nickel. Y#126. | — |
| Pr447 | 1981 | 500 | 100 Zlotych. Nickel. | 40.00 |
| Pr448 | 1981 | 4,020 | 100 Zlotych. 0.6250 Silver. Horses. | 30.00 |
| Pr449 | 1981 | 20 | 100 Zlotych. 0.7500 Silver. Y#125. | — |
| Pr450 | 1981 | 500 | 200 Zlotych. Nickel. Y#125. | — |
| Pr451 | 1981 | 500 | 200 Zlotych. Nickel. Boleslaw II. | — |
| Pr452 | 1981 | 4,020 | 200 Zlotych. 0.7500 Silver. Boleslaw II. | 25.00 |
| Pr453 | 1981 | 20 | 200 Zlotych. 0.7500 Silver. Y#129. | — |
| Pr454 | 1981 | 500 | 200 Zlotych. Nickel. Y#129. | — |
| Pr455 | 1981 | 500 | 200 Zlotych. Nickel. Wladyslaw I Herman. | — |
| Pr456 | 1981 | 4,020 | 200 Zlotych. 0.7500 Silver. | — |
| Pr457 | 1981 | — | 200 Zlotych. 0.7500 Silver. Wladyslaw I. | — |
| Pr458 | 1981 | 4 | 2000 Zlotych. 0.9000 Gold. Y#126. | — |
| Pr459 | 1981 | 500 | 2000 Zlotych. Nickel. Y#126. | — |
| Pr460 | 1981 | 4 | 2000 Zlotych. 0.9000 Gold. Y#131. | — |
| Pr461 | 1981 | 500 | 2000 Zlotych. 0.9000 Gold. Y#131. | — |
| Pr462 | 1982 | 20 | 50 Zlotych. Copper-Nickel. Y#133. | — |
| Pr463 | 1982 | 500 | 50 Zlotych. Nickel. Y#133. | — |
| Pr464 | 1982 | 500 | 100 Zlotych. Nickel. Y#141. | — |
| Pr465 | 1982 | 500 | 100 Zlotych. Nickel. Storks. | 40.00 |
| Pr466 | 1982 | 4,000 | 100 Zlotych. 0.6250 Silver. Storks. | 30.00 |
| Pr467 | 1982 | 20 | 200 Zlotych. 0.7500 Silver. Y#132. | — |
| Pr468 | 1982 | 500 | 200 Zlotych. Nickel. Y#132. | — |
| Pr469 | 1982 | 500 | 200 Zlotych. Nickel. | — |
| Pr470 | 1982 | 3,000 | 200 Zlotych. 0.7500 Silver. | 20.00 |
| Pr471 | 1982 | 6,000 | 200 Zlotych. 0.7500 Silver. Soccer player leaning right. | 27.50 |
| Pr472 | 1982 | 6,002 | 200 Zlotych. 0.7500 Silver. Soccer player leaning left. | 27.50 |
| Pr473 | 1982 | 500 | 200 Zlotych. Nickel. Soccer player leaning right. | — |
| Pr474 | 1982 | 500 | 200 Zlotych. Nickel. Without Espana 82, Y#130. | — |
| Pr475 | 1982 | 500 | 200 Zlotych. Nickel. Soccer player leaning left. | — |
| Pr476 | 1982 | 500 | 500 Zlotych. Nickel. Ship. | — |
| Pr477 | 1982 | 25,000 | 500 Zlotych. 0.6250 Silver. Ship. | 22.50 |
| Pr478 | 1982 | 10,000 | 1000 Zlotych. 0.7500 Silver. Pope John Paul II. | 25.00 |
| Pr479 | 1982 | 500 | 1000 Zlotych. Nickel. Y#144. | — |
| Pr480 | 1982 | 500 | 1000 Zlotych. Nickel. | — |
| Pr481 | 1983 | 20 | 50 Zlotych. Copper-Nickel. Y#142. | — |
| Pr482 | 1983 | 500 | 50 Zlotych. Nickel. Y#142. | — |
| Pr483 | 1983 | 20 | 50 Zlotych. Copper-Nickel. Y#145. | — |
| Pr484 | 1983 | 500 | 50 Zlotych. Nickel. Y#145. | — |
| Pr485 | 1983 | 20 | 50 Zlotych. Copper-Nickel. Y#146. | — |
| Pr486 | 1983 | 500 | 50 Zlotych. Nickel. Y#146. | — |
| Pr487 | 1983 | 500 | 100 Zlotych. Nickel. Y#147. | — |
| Pr488 | 1983 | 500 | 100 Zlotych. Nickel. | — |
| Pr489 | 1983 | 3,000 | 100 Zlotych. 0.6250 Silver. Bears. | 35.00 |
| Pr490 | 1983 | 500 | 200 Zlotych. Nickel. Y#143. | — |
| Pr491 | 1983 | 500 | 200 Zlotych. Nickel. | — |
| Pr492 | 1983 | 4,000 | 200 Zlotych. 0.7500 Silver. Jan III Sobieski. | 35.00 |
| Pr494 | 1983 | 7,000 | 500 Zlotych. 0.7500 Silver. Gymnast. | 32.50 |

| KM# | Date | Mintage | Identification | Mkt Val |
|---|---|---|---|---|
| Pr495 | 1983 | 500 | 500 Zlotych. Nickel. | — |
| Pr496 | 1983 | 6,000 | 500 Zlotych. 0.7500 Silver. Speed skater. | 32.50 |
| Pr493 | 1983 | 500 | 500 Zlotych. Nickel. | — |
| Pr497 | 1984 | 500 | 10 Zlotych. Nickel. Y#152.1. | — |
| Pr498 | 1984 | 500 | 20 Zlotych. Nickel. Y#153.1. | — |
| Pr499 | 1984 | 500 | 100 Zlotych. Nickel. Y#148. | — |
| Pr500 | 1984 | 500 | 100 Zlotych. Nickel. Y#151. | — |
| Pr501 | 1984 | 500 | 200 Zlotych. Nickel. Y#149. | — |
| Pr502 | 1984 | 500 | 200 Zlotych. Nickel. Y#150. | — |
| Pr503 | 1984 | 500 | 500 Zlotych. Nickel. Y#154. | — |
| Pr504 | 1984 | 500 | 1000 Zlotych. Nickel. Wincenty Witos. | — |
| Pr505 | 1984 | 3,000 | 1000 Zlotych. 0.6250 Silver. Wincenty Witos. | 30.00 |
| Pr506 | 1984 | 500 | 1000 Zlotych. Nickel. PRL. | — |
| Pr507 | 1984 | 2,004 | 1000 Zlotych. 0.6250 Silver. 40th Anniversary of Peoples Republic. | 30.00 |
| Pr508 | 1984 | 500 | 1000 Zlotych. Nickel. Swans. | — |
| Pr509 | 1984 | 5,700 | 1000 Zlotych. 0.6250 Silver. Environment. | 25.00 |
| Pr510 | 1985 | 500 | 100 Zlotych. Nickel. Y#155. | — |
| Pr511 | 1985 | 500 | 100 Zlotych. Nickel. Y#157. | — |
| Pr512 | 1985 | 500 | 200 Zlotych. Nickel. | — |
| Pr513 | 1985 | 15,000 | 200 Zlotych. Copper-Nickel. | 7.50 |
| Pr514 | 1985 | 500 | 200 Zlotych. Nickel. Hospital Center. | — |
| Pr515 | 1985 | 37,300 | 200 Zlotych. Nickel Plated Iron. Hospital Center, soccer. | 12.50 |
| Pr516 | 1985 | 500 | 500 Zlotych. Nickel. Y#156. | — |
| Pr517 | 1985 | 500 | 500 Zlotych. Nickel. Y#158. | — |
| Pr518 | 1985 | 500 | 500 Zlotych. Nickel. Y#159. | — |
| Pr519 | 1985 | 500 | 1000 Zlotych. Nickel. Przemyslaw II. | — |
| Pr520 | 1985 | 2,500 | 1000 Zlotych. 0.7500 Silver. Przemyslaw II. | 10.00 |
| Pr521 | 1985 | 500 | 1000 Zlotych. Nickel. Hospital Center. | — |
| Pr522 | 1985 | 2,500 | 1000 Zlotych. 0.7500 Silver. Hospital Center. | 40.00 |
| Pr523 | 1985 | 500 | 1000 Zlotych. Nickel. U.N. | — |
| Pr524 | 1985 | 2,500 | 1000 Zlotych. 0.7500 Silver. U.N. | 40.00 |
| Pr525 | 1985 | 500 | 1000 Zlotych. Nickel. Squirrel. | — |
| Pr526 | 1985 | 2,500 | 1000 Zlotych. 0.7500 Silver. Squirrel. | 30.00 |
| Pr531 | 1986 | 500 | 100 Zlotych. Nickel. Y#160. | — |
| Pr527 | 1986 | 500 | 50 Groszy. Nickel. Y#48.2. | — |
| Pr528 | 1986 | 500 | Zloty. Nickel. Y#49.2. | — |
| Pr529 | 1986 | 500 | 2 Zlote. Nickel. Y#80.2. | — |
| Pr530 | 1986 | 500 | 5 Zlotych. Nickel. Y#81.2. | — |
| Pr532 | 1986 | 500 | 200 Zlotych. Nickel. Y#162. | 40.00 |
| Pr533 | 1986 | 6,000 | 200 Zlotych. Copper-Nickel. Y#162. | 30.00 |
| Pr534 | 1986 | 500 | 200 Zlotych. Nickel. Wladyslaw. | — |
| Pr535 | 1986 | 10,000 | 200 Zlotych. Copper-Nickel. Wladyslaw. | 15.00 |
| Pr536 | 1986 | 500 | 500 Zlotych. Nickel. Y#161. | — |
| Pr537 | 1986 | 500 | 500 Zlotych. Nickel. Y#162. | — |
| Pr538 | 1986 | 500 | 500 Zlotych. Nickel. Y#166. | — |
| Pr539 | 1986 | — | 500 Zlotych. Nickel. Y#225. | — |
| Pr540 | 1986 | 500 | 1000 Zlotych. Nickel. Soccer. | — |
| Pr541 | 1986 | 9,000 | 1000 Zlotych. 0.7500 Silver. Soccer. | — |
| Pr542 | 1986 | 500 | 1000 Zlotych. Nickel. Education. | — |
| Pr543 | 1986 | 25,400 | 1000 Zlotych. 0.6250 Silver. Education. | — |
| Pr544 | 1986 | 22,000 | 1000 Zlotych. 0.7500 Silver. Hospital Center. | — |
| Pr545 | 1986 | 500 | 1000 Zlotych. Nickel. Wladyslaw I. | — |
| Pr546 | 1986 | 2,500 | 1000 Zlotych. 0.7500 Silver. Wladyslaw I. | 26.00 |
| Pr547 | 1986 | 500 | 1000 Zlotych. Nickel. Owl. | 45.00 |
| Pr548 | 1986 | 6,000 | 1000 Zlotych. 0.7500 Silver. Owl. | 40.00 |
| Pr549 | 1986 | — | 1000 Zlotych. Nickel. | — |

| KM# | Date | Mintage | Identification | Mkt Val |
|---|---|---|---|---|
| Pr550 | 1986 | — | 1000 Zlotych. 0.6250 Silver. School aid. | — |
| Pr551 | 1987 | 500 | 100 Zlotych. Nickel. Y#167. | — |
| Pr552 | 1987 | 500 | 200 Zlotych. Nickel. Europe soccer. | — |
| Pr553 | 1987 | 15,000 | 200 Zlotych. Copper-Nickel. Europe soccer. | 12.00 |
| Pr554 | 1987 | 500 | 200 Zlotych. Nickel. Olympics - Tennis. | — |
| Pr555 | 1987 | 10,000 | 200 Zlotych. Copper-Nickel. Olympics - Tennis. | 17.00 |
| Pr556 | 1987 | 500 | 500 Zlotych. Nickel. Y#165. | — |
| Pr557 | 1987 | 500 | 500 Zlotych. Nickel. Y#166. | — |
| Pr558 | 1987 | 500 | 500 Zlotych. Nickel. Y#172. | — |
| Pr559 | 1987 | 500 | 500 Zlotych. Nickel. Y#173. | — |
| Pr560 | 1987 | 500 | 1000 Zlotych. Nickel. Wratislavia. | — |
| Pr561 | 1987 | 24,000 | 1000 Zlotych. 0.7500 Silver. Wratislavia. | 22.50 |
| Pr562 | 1987 | 500 | 1000 Zlotych. Nickel. Slaskie Museum. | — |
| Pr563 | 1987 | 11,500 | 1000 Zlotych. 0.7500 Silver. Slaskie Museum. | 27.50 |
| Pr564 | 1987 | 500 | 1000 Zlotych. Nickel. Olympic cross country skier. | — |
| Pr565 | 1987 | 10,000 | 1000 Zlotych. 0.7500 Silver. Olympic cross country skier. | 16.50 |
| Pr566 | 1987 | 500 | 1000 Zlotych. Nickel. Olympic archery. | — |
| Pr567 | 1987 | 10,000 | 1000 Zlotych. 0.7500 Silver. Olympic archery. | 37.50 |
| Pr568 | 1987 | 500 | 1000 Zlotych. Nickel. Kazimierz III. | — |
| Pr569 | 1987 | 2,500 | 1000 Zlotych. 0.7500 Silver. Kazimierz III. | 47.50 |
| Pr570 | 1987 | 9 | 1000 Zlotych. Gold. Y#168. | — |
| Pr571 | 1987 | 9 | 2000 Zlotych. Gold. Y#169. | — |
| Pr572 | 1987 | 9 | 5000 Zlotych. Gold. Y#170. | — |
| Pr573 | 1987 | 9 | 10000 Zlotych. Gold. Y#171. | — |
| Pr574 | 1987 | 5 | 200000 Zlotych. Gold. Y#163. | — |
| Pr575 | 1988 | 500 | 200 Zlotych. Nickel. Soccer 1990. | — |
| Pr576 | 1988 | 10,000 | 200 Zlotych. Copper-Nickel. Soccer 1990. | 15.00 |
| Pr577 | 1988 | 7,000 | 500 Zlotych. Soccer 1990, Y#184. | — |
| Pr578 | 1988 | 500 | 1000 Zlotych. Nickel. Queen Jadwiga. | — |
| Pr579 | 1988 | 2,500 | 1000 Zlotych. 0.7500 Silver. Queen Jadwiga. | 37.50 |
| Pr580 | 1988 | 500 | 1000 Zlotych. Nickel. Soccer 1990. | — |
| Pr581 | 1988 | 7,000 | 1000 Zlotych. 0.7500 Silver. Soccer 1990. | 27.50 |
| Pr582 | 1991 | 300 | 20000 Zlotych. 0.9990 Gold. Pope John Paul II right. | 200 |

| KM# | Date | Mintage | Identification | Mkt Val |
|---|---|---|---|---|

| Pr583 | 1991 | — | 50000 Zlotych. 0.9990 Gold. Pope John Paul II right. | 300 |
|---|---|---|---|---|

| Pr584 | 1991 | — | 100000 Zlotych. 0.9990 Gold. Pope John Paul II right. | 400 |
|---|---|---|---|---|

| Pr585 | 1991 | — | 200000 Zlotych. 0.9990 Gold. Pope John Paul II right. | 500 |
|---|---|---|---|---|

| Pr586 | 1994 | — | 1000 Zlotych. Copper-Nickel. Y#267. | — |
|---|---|---|---|---|

## TRIAL STRIKES

| KM# | Date | Mintage | Identification | Mkt Val |
|---|---|---|---|---|
| TS1 | 1923 | — | Grosz. Copper. Uniface. | 75.00 |
| TS2 | 1923 | — | Grosz. Copper. Uniface. | 75.00 |

## MINT SETS

| KM# | Date | Mintage | Identification | Issue Price | Mkt Val |
|---|---|---|---|---|---|
| MSA1 | 1964 (3) | — | Y#52, 52A, Pr100 | — | 160 |
| MS1 | 1979 (6) | 5,000 | Y#AA47, A47, 80.1-81.1, 99, 100 | — | 32.50 |
| MS2 | 1980 (5) | 5,000 | Y#AA47, A47, 49.1, 80.1-81.1 | — | 20.00 |
| MS3 | 1980 (4) | 5,000 | Y#108, 112, 114, 117 | — | 20.00 |
| MS4 | 1981 (6) | 5,000 | Y#AA47, A47, 49.1, 73, 80.1-81.1 | — | 20.00 |
| MS5 | 1981 (4) | 5,000 | Y#122, 124, 127-128 | — | 20.00 |
| MS6 | 1982 (6) | 5,000 | Y#48.1-49.1, 73, 80.1-81.1, 133 | — | 20.00 |

## PROOF SETS

| KM# | Date | Mintage | Identification | Issue Price | Mkt Val |
|---|---|---|---|---|---|
| PS1 | 1986 (7) | 5,000 | Y#48.2, 49.2, 80.2, 81.2, 152.1, 153.1, 160 | — | 85.00 |
| PS3 | 1987 (5) | 6 | Y#163, 168-171 | — | — |
| PS4 | 1987 | 300 | Y#168-171 | — | — |
| PS5 | 1987 (4) | 201 | Y#168-171 | — | — |
| PS2 | 1987 (7) | 500 | Y#48.2, 49.2, 80.2, 81.2, 152.1, 153.1, 167 | — | 85.00 |
| PS7 | 1988 (4) | 1,000 | Y#174-177 | — | 1,125 |
| PS6 | 1988 (7) | 5,000 | Y#49.2, 80.2, 81.2, 152.1, 153.1, 182, 183 Mint medal | — | 85.00 |
| PS9 | 1989 (4) | 1,000 | Y#186-189 | 1,595 | 1,100 |
| PS8 | 1989 (7) | 5,000 | Y#49.3, 80.3, 81.3, 152.2, 153.2, 185, 194 | — | 85.00 |
| PS10 | 1990 (4) | 1,000 | Y#219-222 | 1,495 | 1,300 |
| PS11 | 1990 (8) | 5,000 | Y#49.3, 80.3, 81.3, 152.2, 153.2, 195, 214, 216 | — | 65.00 |

# DANZIG

Danzig is an important seaport on the northern coast of Poland with access to the Baltic Sea. It has at different times belonged to the Teutonic Knights, Pomerania, Russia, and Prussia. It was part of the Polish Kingdom from 1587-1772.

Danzig (Gdansk) was a free city from 1919 to 1939 during which most of its modern coinage was made.

**FREE CITY MONETARY SYSTEM**

Until 1923
100 Pfennig = 1 Mark
Commencing 1923
100 Pfennig = 1 Gulden

## FREE CITY

### STANDARD COINAGE

**PFENNIG** **KM# 140** **Composition:** Bronze

| Date | Mintage | F | VF | XF | Unc | BU |
|---|---|---|---|---|---|---|
| 1923 | 4,000,000 | 1.00 | 3.00 | 5.00 | 10.00 | — |
| 1923 Proof | — | Value: 50.00 | | | | |
| 1926 | 1,500,000 | 1.50 | 4.00 | 8.00 | 16.00 | — |
| 1929 | 1,000,000 | 2.50 | 7.50 | 12.00 | 20.00 | — |
| 1930 | 2,000,000 | 1.25 | 3.50 | 6.50 | 12.00 | — |
| 1937 | 3,000,000 | 1.25 | 3.50 | 6.50 | 12.00 | — |

**2 PFENNIG** **KM# 141** **Composition:** Bronze

| Date | Mintage | F | VF | XF | Unc | BU |
|---|---|---|---|---|---|---|
| 1923 | 1,000,000 | 1.75 | 4.50 | 7.50 | 15.00 | — |
| 1923 Proof | — | Value: 65.00 | | | | |
| 1926 | 1,750,000 | 1.75 | 4.50 | 7.50 | 15.00 | — |
| 1937 | 500,000 | 2.75 | 6.50 | 11.00 | 18.50 | — |

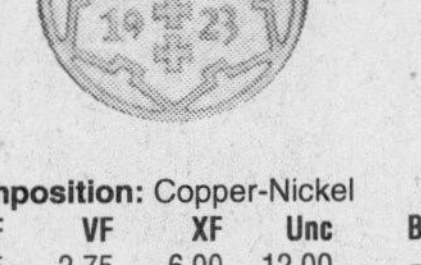

**5 PFENNIG** **KM# 142** **Composition:** Copper-Nickel

| Date | Mintage | F | VF | XF | Unc | BU |
|---|---|---|---|---|---|---|
| 1923 | 3,000,000 | 1.25 | 2.75 | 6.00 | 12.00 | — |
| 1923 Proof | — | Value: 100 | | | | |
| 1928 | 1,000,000 | 3.50 | 8.25 | 14.00 | 27.50 | — |
| 1928 Proof | — | Value: 175 | | | | |

**5 PFENNIG** **KM# 151** **Composition:** Aluminum-Bronze

| Date | Mintage | F | VF | XF | Unc | BU |
|---|---|---|---|---|---|---|
| 1932 | 4,000,000 | 1.25 | 2.25 | 6.00 | 16.00 | — |

**10 PFENNIG** **KM# 143** **Composition:** Copper-Nickel

| Date | Mintage | F | VF | XF | Unc | BU |
|---|---|---|---|---|---|---|
| 1923 | 5,000,000 | 2.00 | 3.00 | 8.00 | 18.00 | — |
| 1923 Proof | — | Value: 115 | | | | |

**10 PFENNIG** **KM# 152** **Composition:** Aluminum-Bronze

| Date | Mintage | F | VF | XF | Unc | BU |
|---|---|---|---|---|---|---|
| 1932 | 5,000,000 | 1.50 | 2.50 | 7.00 | 17.00 | — |

**1/2 GULDEN** **KM# 144** **Weight:** 2.5000 g. **Composition:** 0.7500 Silver .0603 oz. ASW

| Date | Mintage | F | VF | XF | Unc | BU |
|---|---|---|---|---|---|---|
| 1923 | 1,000,000 | 7.50 | 20.00 | 35.00 | 75.00 | — |
| 1923 Proof | — | Value: 150 | | | | |
| 1927 | 400,000 | 17.50 | 35.00 | 70.00 | 125 | — |
| 1927 Proof | — | Value: 250 | | | | |

**1/2 GULDEN** **KM# 153** **Composition:** Nickel

| Date | Mintage | F | VF | XF | Unc | BU |
|---|---|---|---|---|---|---|
| 1932 | 1,400,000 | 8.00 | 25.00 | 37.50 | 70.00 | — |

**GULDEN** **KM# 145** **Weight:** 5.0000 g. **Composition:** 0.7500 Silver .1206 oz. ASW

| Date | Mintage | F | VF | XF | Unc | BU |
|---|---|---|---|---|---|---|
| 1923 | 2,500,000 | 11.00 | 27.50 | 40.00 | 95.00 | — |
| 1923 Proof | — | Value: 200 | | | | |

**GULDEN** **KM# 154** **Composition:** Nickel

| Date | Mintage | F | VF | XF | Unc | BU |
|---|---|---|---|---|---|---|
| 1932 | 2,500,000 | 8.00 | 25.00 | 35.00 | 60.00 | — |

**2 GULDEN** **KM# 146** **Weight:** 10.0000 g. **Composition:** 0.7500 Silver .2411 oz. ASW

| Date | Mintage | F | VF | XF | Unc | BU |
|---|---|---|---|---|---|---|
| 1923 | 1,250,000 | 25.00 | 65.00 | 120 | 225 | — |
| 1923 Proof | — | Value: 300 | | | | |

**2 GULDEN** KM# 155 **Weight:** 10.0000 g. **Composition:** 0.5000 Silver .1608 oz. ASW

| Date | Mintage | F | VF | XF | Unc | BU |
|---|---|---|---|---|---|---|
| 1932 | 1,250,000 | — | 150 | 200 | 375 | — |

**5 GULDEN** KM# 147 **Weight:** 25.0000 g. **Composition:** 0.7500 Silver .6028 oz. ASW

| Date | Mintage | F | VF | XF | Unc | BU |
|---|---|---|---|---|---|---|
| 1923 | 700,000 | 65.00 | 135 | 220 | 450 | — |
| 1923 Proof | — | Value: 550 | | | | |
| 1927 | 160,000 | 150 | 250 | 375 | 650 | — |
| 1927 Proof | — | Value: 1,000 | | | | |

**5 GULDEN** KM# 156 **Weight:** 14.8200 g. **Composition:** 0.5000 Silver .2382 oz. ASW

| Date | Mintage | F | VF | XF | Unc | BU |
|---|---|---|---|---|---|---|
| 1932 | 430,000 | 125 | 225 | 350 | 950 | — |

**5 GULDEN** KM# 157 **Weight:** 14.8200 g. **Composition:** 0.5000 Silver .2382 oz. ASW

| Date | Mintage | F | VF | XF | Unc | BU |
|---|---|---|---|---|---|---|
| 1932 | 430,000 | 150 | 350 | 850 | 1,500 | — |

**5 GULDEN** KM# 158 **Composition:** Nickel

| Date | Mintage | F | VF | XF | Unc | BU |
|---|---|---|---|---|---|---|
| 1935 | 800,000 | 100 | 160 | 235 | 475 | — |

**10 GULDEN** KM# 159 **Composition:** Nickel

| Date | Mintage | F | VF | XF | Unc | BU |
|---|---|---|---|---|---|---|
| 1935 | 380,000 | 300 | 500 | 700 | 1,350 | — |

**25 GULDEN** KM# 148 **Weight:** 7.9881 g. **Composition:** 0.9170 Gold .2354 oz. AGW **Note:** Presented to senate members.

| Date | Mintage | F | VF | XF | Unc | BU |
|---|---|---|---|---|---|---|
| 1923 | 800 | — | 1,500 | 1,850 | 2,700 | — |
| 1923 Proof | 200 | Value: 3,500 | | | | |

**25 GULDEN** KM# 150 **Weight:** 7.9881 g. **Composition:** 0.9170 Gold .2354 oz. AGW **Note:** Not released for circulation. A few were given Sept. 1, 1939, in VIP presentation cases.

| Date | Mintage | F | VF | XF | Unc | BU |
|---|---|---|---|---|---|---|
| 1930 | Est. 4,000 | — | — | 6,500 | 9,500 | — |

## TOKEN COINAGE

**10 PFENNIG** KM# Tn1 **Composition:** Zinc

| Date | Mintage | F | VF | XF | Unc | BU |
|---|---|---|---|---|---|---|
| 1920 | 876,000 | 10.00 | 15.00 | 30.00 | 65.00 | — |

**10 PFENNIG** KM# Tn2 **Composition:** Zinc

| Date | Mintage | F | VF | XF | Unc | BU |
|---|---|---|---|---|---|---|
| 1920 | 124,000 | 100 | 150 | 225 | 350 | — |

## PATTERNS

Including off metal strikes

| KM# | Date | Mintage | Identification | Mkt Val |
|---|---|---|---|---|
| Pn43 | 1920 | 30 | 10 Pfennig. Silver. | 3,250 |
| Pn44 | 1920 | 30 | 10 Pfennig. Silver. Large 10. | 3,250 |
| Pn45 | 1923 | — | 5 Pfennig. Brass. | 165 |
| Pn46 | 1923 | — | 10 Pfennig. Brass. | 170 |
| Pn47 | 1923 | 10 | Gulden. Gold. KM145. | 7,500 |
| Pn48 | 1927 | — | 2 Pfennig. Brass. | — |
| Pn49 | 1935 | — | 5 Gulden. Nickel. PROBE. | — |
| Pn50 | 1935 | — | 10 Gulden. Nickel. PROBE. | — |
| Pn51 | 1935 | — | 10 Gulden. Tin. | 110 |

## PROOF SETS

| KM# | Date | Mintage | Identification | Issue Price | Mkt Val |
|---|---|---|---|---|---|
| PS1 | 1923 (8) | — | KM140-147 | — | 1,475 |

# PORTUGAL

The Portuguese Republic, located in the western part of the Iberian Peninsula in southwestern Europe, has an area of 35,553 sq. mi. (92,080 sq. km.) and a population of *10.5 million. Capital: Lisbon. Portugal's economy is based on agriculture, tourism, minerals, fisheries and a rapidly expanding industrial sector. Textiles account for 33% of the exports and Portuguese wine is world famous. Portugal has become Europe's number one producer of copper and the world's largest producer of cork.

After centuries of domination by Romans, Visigoths and Moors, Portugal emerged in the 12th century as an independent kingdom financially and philosophically prepared for the great period of exploration that would soon follow. Attuned to the inspiration of Prince Henry the Navigator (1394-1460), Portugal's daring explorers of the15th and 16th centuries roamed the world's oceans from Brazil to Japan in an unprecedented burst of energy and endeavor that culminated in 1494 with Portugal laying claim to half the transoceanic world. Unfortunately for the fortunes of the tiny kingdom, the Portuguese population was too small to colonize this vast territory. Less than a century after Portugal laid claim to half the world, English, French and Dutch trading companies had seized the lion's share of the world's colonies and commerce, and Portugal's place as an imperial power was lost forever. The monarchy was overthrown in 1910 and a republic was established.

On April 25, 1974, the government of Portugal was seized by a military junta which reached agreements providing for independence for the Portuguese overseas provinces of Portuguese Guinea (*Guinea-Bissau*), Mozambique, Cape Verde Islands, Angola, and St. Thomas and Prince Islands (*Sao Tome and Principe*).

On January 1, 1986, Portugal became the eleventh member of the European Economic Community and in the first half of 1992 held its first EEC Presidency.

**RULERS**

Carlos I, 1889-1908
Manuel II, 1908-1910
Republic, 1910 to date

**MONETARY SYSTEM**

Beginning in 1836 all coins were expressed in terms of Reis and arranged in a decimal sequence (until 1910).

Commencing 1910

100 Centavos = 1 Escudo

# KINGDOM

## DECIMAL COINAGE

**5 REIS** KM# 530 **Composition:** Bronze **Obverse:** Bust of Carlos I right

| Date | Mintage | F | VF | XF | Unc | BU |
|---|---|---|---|---|---|---|
| 1901 | 1,070,000 | 2.50 | 12.50 | 40.00 | 90.00 | — |
| 1904 | 720,000 | 0.75 | 1.75 | 12.50 | 30.00 | — |
| 1905 | 1,340,000 | 0.50 | 1.00 | 4.50 | 12.50 | — |
| 1906/0 | 1,260 | 0.30 | 1.00 | 2.50 | 8.00 | — |
| 1906/9 | Inc. above | 0.25 | 0.75 | 2.00 | 7.00 | — |
| 1906 | Inc. above | 0.30 | 1.00 | 2.50 | 8.00 | — |

**5 REIS** KM# 555 **Composition:** Bronze **Obverse:** Bust of Emanuel II left

| Date | Mintage | F | VF | XF | Unc | BU |
|---|---|---|---|---|---|---|
| 1910 | 1,000,000 | 0.30 | 1.00 | 2.50 | 7.00 | — |

**100 REIS** KM# 548 **Weight:** 2.5000 g. **Composition:** 0.8350 Silver .0671 oz. ASW **Obverse:** Bust of Emanuel II left

| Date | Mintage | F | VF | XF | Unc | BU |
|---|---|---|---|---|---|---|
| 1909 | 6,363,000 | 1.50 | 3.50 | 6.50 | 22.00 | — |
| 1910 | Inc. above | 1.00 | 2.00 | 3.50 | 9.00 | — |

**200 REIS** **KM# 534** **Weight:** 5.0000 g. **Composition:** 0.9170 Silver .1474 oz. ASW **Obverse:** Bust right **Obv. Legend:** CARLOS I..

| Date | Mintage | VG | F | VF | XF | Unc |
|---|---|---|---|---|---|---|
| 1901 | 205,000 | 30.00 | 75.00 | 125 | 300 | — |
| 1903 | 200,000 | 12.50 | 35.00 | 165 | 115 | — |

**200 REIS** **KM# 549** **Weight:** 5.0000 g. **Composition:** 0.8350 Silver .1342 oz. ASW **Obverse:** Bust left **Obv. Legend:** EMANVEL II..

| Date | Mintage | VG | F | VF | XF | Unc |
|---|---|---|---|---|---|---|
| 1909 | 7,656,000 | 1.50 | 2.50 | 4.50 | 9.00 | — |

**500 REIS** **KM# 535** **Weight:** 12.5000 g. **Composition:** 0.9170 Silver .3684 oz. ASW **Obverse:** Head right **Obv. Legend:** CARLOS I..

| Date | Mintage | VG | F | VF | XF | Unc |
|---|---|---|---|---|---|---|
| 1901 | 1,050,000 | 6.50 | 22.50 | 40.00 | 75.00 | — |
| 1903 | 680,000 | 4.00 | 9.00 | 15.00 | 30.00 | — |
| 1906/3 | 240,000 | 15.00 | 35.00 | 70.00 | 100 | — |
| 1906 | Inc. above | 12.00 | 30.00 | 60.00 | 90.00 | — |
| 1907 | 384,000 | 4.00 | 6.00 | 10.00 | 18.00 | — |
| 1908 | 1,840,000 | 4.00 | 6.00 | 10.00 | 16.00 | — |

**500 REIS** **KM# 547** **Weight:** 12.5000 g. **Composition:** 0.9170 Silver .3684 oz. ASW **Obverse:** Bust left **Obv. Legend:** EMANVEL II..

| Date | Mintage | VG | F | VF | XF | Unc |
|---|---|---|---|---|---|---|
| 1908 | 2,500,000 | 3.50 | 6.00 | 10.00 | 18.00 | — |
| 1909/8 | 1,513,000 | 8.00 | 25.00 | 45.00 | 85.00 | — |
| 1909 | Inc. above | 8.00 | 25.00 | 45.00 | 85.00 | — |

**500 REIS** **KM# 556** **Weight:** 12.5000 g. **Composition:** 0.9170 Silver .3684 oz. ASW **Subject:** Peninsular War Centennial **Obv. Legend:** EMANVEL II..

| Date | Mintage | VG | F | VF | XF | Unc |
|---|---|---|---|---|---|---|
| 1910 | 200,000 | 12.50 | 35.00 | 55.00 | 90.00 | — |

**500 REIS** **KM# 557** **Weight:** 12.5000 g. **Composition:** 0.9170 Silver .3684 oz. ASW **Subject:** Marquis De Pombal **Obv. Legend:** EMANVEL II..

| Date | Mintage | VG | F | VF | XF | Unc |
|---|---|---|---|---|---|---|
| 1910 | 400,000 | 6.50 | 13.50 | 22.50 | 38.00 | — |
| 1910 Proof | — | Value: 600 | | | | |

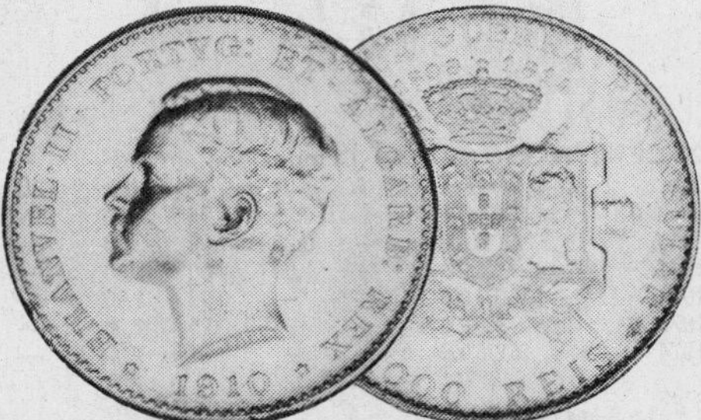

**1000 REIS** **KM# 558** **Weight:** 25.0000 g. **Composition:** 0.9170 Silver .7368 oz. ASW **Subject:** Peninsular War Centennial **Obv. Legend:** EMANVEL II..

| Date | Mintage | VG | F | VF | XF | Unc |
|---|---|---|---|---|---|---|
| 1910 | 200,000 | 15.00 | 40.00 | 65.00 | 100 | — |
| 1910 Proof | — | Value: 900 | | | | |

# REPUBLIC

## DECIMAL COINAGE

**CENTAVO** **KM# 565** **Composition:** Bronze

| Date | Mintage | F | VF | XF | Unc | BU |
|---|---|---|---|---|---|---|
| 1917 | 2,250,000 | 0.25 | 0.50 | 1.00 | 3.50 | — |
| 1918 | 22,996,000 | 0.25 | 0.50 | 1.00 | 3.50 | — |
| 1920 | 12,535,000 | 0.50 | 1.00 | 2.50 | 7.50 | — |
| 1921 | 4,492,000 | 10.00 | 20.00 | 35.00 | 70.00 | — |
| 1922 Rare | Inc. above | — | — | — | — | — |

**2 CENTAVOS** **KM# 567** **Composition:** Iron

| Date | Mintage | F | VF | XF | Unc | BU |
|---|---|---|---|---|---|---|
| 1918 | 170,000 | 65.00 | 125 | 300 | 700 | — |

**2 CENTAVOS** **KM# 568** **Composition:** Bronze

| Date | Mintage | F | VF | XF | Unc | BU |
|---|---|---|---|---|---|---|
| 1918 | 4,295,000 | 0.25 | 0.50 | 1.50 | 4.00 | — |
| 1920 | 10,109,000 | 0.50 | 1.50 | 3.00 | 6.50 | — |
| 1921 | 679,000 | 25.00 | 45.00 | 80.00 | 150 | — |

**4 CENTAVOS** **KM# 566** **Composition:** Copper Nickel

| Date | Mintage | F | VF | XF | Unc | BU |
|---|---|---|---|---|---|---|
| 1917 | 4,961,000 | 0.25 | 0.50 | 1.50 | 4.00 | — |
| 1919 | 10,067,000 | 0.50 | 1.00 | 2.00 | 5.00 | — |

**5 CENTAVOS** **KM# 569** **Center Composition:** Bronze

| Date | Mintage | F | VF | XF | Unc | BU |
|---|---|---|---|---|---|---|
| 1920 | 114,000 | 35.00 | 70.00 | 120 | 200 | — |
| 1921 | 5,916,000 | 0.50 | 1.50 | 3.50 | 7.00 | — |
| 1922 | Inc. above | 125 | 250 | 400 | 700 | — |

**5 CENTAVOS** **KM# 572** **Composition:** Bronze

| Date | Mintage | F | VF | XF | Unc | BU |
|---|---|---|---|---|---|---|
| 1924 | 6,480,000 | 0.50 | 1.50 | 6.00 | 14.00 | — |
| 1925 | 7,260,000 | 3.50 | 7.50 | 22.00 | 40.00 | — |
| 1927 | 26,320,000 | 0.25 | 0.75 | 2.00 | 5.00 | — |

**10 CENTAVOS** **KM# 563** **Weight:** 2.5000 g. **Composition:** 0.8350 Silver .0671 oz. ASW

| Date | Mintage | F | VF | XF | Unc | BU |
|---|---|---|---|---|---|---|
| 1915 | 3,418,000 | 1.00 | 2.00 | 3.00 | 8.00 | — |

**10 CENTAVOS** **KM# 570** **Composition:** Copper Nickel

| Date | Mintage | F | VF | XF | Unc | BU |
|---|---|---|---|---|---|---|
| 1920 | 1,120,000 | 3.00 | 6.00 | 12.00 | 20.00 | — |
| 1921 | 1,285,000 | 3.00 | 6.00 | 12.00 | 20.00 | — |

**10 CENTAVOS** **KM# 573** **Composition:** Bronze

| Date | Mintage | F | VF | XF | Unc | BU |
|---|---|---|---|---|---|---|
| 1924 | 1,210,000 | 3.00 | 12.50 | 45.00 | 100 | — |
| 1925 | 9,090,000 | 0.50 | 1.00 | 12.50 | 30.00 | — |
| 1926 | 26,250,000 | 0.75 | 1.50 | 14.50 | 35.00 | — |
| 1930 | 1,730,000 | 55.00 | 125 | 250 | 650 | — |
| 1938 | 2,000,000 | 5.00 | 15.00 | 50.00 | 100 | — |
| 1940 | 3,384,000 | 1.50 | 4.00 | 12.50 | 30.00 | — |

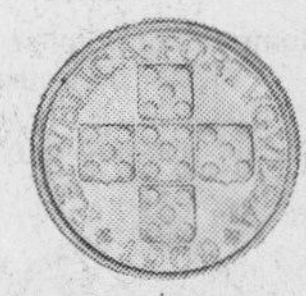

**10 CENTAVOS** **KM# 583** **Composition:** Bronze

| Date | Mintage | F | VF | XF | Unc | BU |
|---|---|---|---|---|---|---|
| 1942 | 1,035,000 | 2.00 | 6.00 | 22.50 | 45.00 | — |
| 1943 | 18,765,000 | 1.50 | 5.00 | 20.00 | 40.00 | — |
| 1944 | 5,090,000 | 1.50 | 3.50 | 15.00 | 30.00 | — |
| 1945 | 6,090,000 | 1.50 | 4.00 | 17.50 | 35.00 | — |
| 1946 | 7,740,000 | 1.00 | 2.50 | 12.50 | 25.00 | — |
| 1947 | 9,283,000 | 1.00 | 2.00 | 7.50 | 15.00 | — |
| 1948 | 5,900,000 | 10.00 | 30.00 | 100 | 275 | — |
| 1949 | 15,240,000 | 0.25 | 1.00 | 5.00 | 10.00 | — |
| 1950 | 8,860,000 | 1.50 | 3.00 | 35.00 | 100 | — |
| 1951 | 5,040,000 | 1.50 | 3.00 | 35.00 | 100 | — |
| 1952 | 4,960,000 | 2.50 | 12.00 | 90.00 | 225 | — |
| 1953 | 7,548,000 | 0.75 | 1.50 | 20.00 | 55.00 | — |
| 1954 | 2,452,000 | 1.50 | 4.00 | 17.50 | 35.00 | — |
| 1955 | 10,000,000 | 0.10 | 0.50 | 2.50 | 6.00 | — |

| Date | Mintage | F | VF | XF | Unc | BU |
|---|---|---|---|---|---|---|
| 1956 | 3,336,000 | 0.10 | 0.50 | 2.00 | 5.00 | — |
| 1957 | 6,654,000 | 0.10 | 0.25 | 2.00 | 5.00 | — |
| 1958 | 7,320,000 | 0.10 | 0.25 | 2.00 | 5.00 | — |
| 1959 | 7,140,000 | 0.10 | 0.25 | 2.00 | 5.00 | — |
| 1960 | 15,055,000 | 0.10 | 0.25 | 2.00 | 5.00 | — |
| 1961 | 5,020,000 | — | 0.10 | 1.50 | 4.00 | — |
| 1962 | 14,980,000 | — | 0.10 | 0.50 | 1.00 | — |
| 1963 | 5,393,000 | — | 0.10 | 1.25 | 3.50 | — |
| 1964 | 10,257,000 | — | 0.10 | 0.75 | 1.50 | — |
| 1965 | 15,550,000 | — | 0.10 | 1.00 | 2.50 | — |
| 1966 | 10,200,000 | — | 0.10 | 0.50 | 1.00 | — |
| 1967 | 18,592,000 | — | 0.10 | 0.50 | 1.00 | — |
| 1968 | 22,515,000 | — | 0.10 | 0.50 | 1.00 | — |
| 1969 | 3,871,000 | 0.10 | 0.25 | 1.25 | 2.50 | — |

**10 CENTAVOS** **KM# 594** **Composition:** Aluminum

| Date | Mintage | F | VF | XF | Unc | BU |
|---|---|---|---|---|---|---|
| 1969 | — | — | 400 | 600 | 900 | — |
| 1970 Rare | — | — | — | — | — | — |
| 1971 | 25,673,000 | — | — | 0.50 | 1.00 | — |
| 1972 | 10,558,000 | — | — | 0.50 | 1.00 | — |
| 1973 | 3,149,000 | — | — | 1.25 | 3.50 | — |
| 1974 | 17,043,000 | — | — | 0.50 | 1.00 | — |
| 1975 | 22,410,000 | — | — | 0.50 | 1.00 | — |
| 1976 | 19,907,000 | — | — | 0.50 | 1.00 | — |
| 1977 | 8,431,000 | — | — | 0.50 | 1.00 | — |
| 1978 | 2,205,000 | — | — | 0.50 | 1.00 | — |
| 1979 | 9,083,000 | — | — | 1.00 | 2.50 | — |

**20 CENTAVOS** **KM# 562** **Weight:** 5.0000 g. **Composition:** 0.8350 Silver .1342 oz. ASW

| Date | Mintage | F | VF | XF | Unc | BU |
|---|---|---|---|---|---|---|
| 1913 | 540,000 | 5.00 | 20.00 | 40.00 | 175 | — |
| 1916 | 706,000 | 3.00 | 15.00 | 30.00 | 100 | — |

**20 CENTAVOS** **KM# 571** **Composition:** Copper Nickel

| Date | Mintage | F | VF | XF | Unc | BU |
|---|---|---|---|---|---|---|
| 1920 | 1,568,000 | 3.50 | 7.00 | 12.00 | 20.00 | — |
| 1921 | 3,030,000 | 4.00 | 8.00 | 14.00 | 22.50 | — |
| 1922 | 580,000 | 500 | 900 | 1,500 | 3,000 | — |

**20 CENTAVOS** **KM# 574** **Composition:** Bronze

| Date | Mintage | F | VF | XF | Unc | BU |
|---|---|---|---|---|---|---|
| 1924 | 6,220,000 | 0.75 | 3.00 | 20.00 | 45.00 | — |
| 1925 | 10,580,000 | 0.75 | 3.00 | 20.00 | 45.00 | — |

**20 CENTAVOS** **KM# 584** **Composition:** Bronze

| Date | Mintage | F | VF | XF | Unc | BU |
|---|---|---|---|---|---|---|
| 1942 | 10,170,000 | 1.50 | 3.50 | 25.00 | 60.00 | — |
| 1943 | Inc. above | 1.00 | 2.00 | 25.00 | 60.00 | — |
| 1944 | 7,290,000 | 1.00 | 2.00 | 25.00 | 60.00 | — |
| 1945 | 7,552,000 | 1.00 | 2.00 | 25.00 | 60.00 | — |
| 1948 | 2,750,000 | 2.50 | 12.00 | 50.00 | 135 | — |
| 1949 | 12,250,000 | 0.10 | 0.50 | 6.00 | 12.50 | — |
| 1951 | 3,185,000 | 0.50 | 2.00 | 60.00 | 160 | — |
| 1952 | 1,815,000 | 2.00 | 12.00 | 100 | 250 | — |
| 1953 | 9,426,000 | — | 0.50 | 3.50 | 8.00 | — |
| 1955 | 5,574,000 | — | 0.50 | 3.50 | 8.00 | — |
| 1956 | 6,450,000 | — | 0.50 | 3.50 | 8.00 | — |
| 1958 | 7,470,000 | — | 0.50 | 3.50 | 8.00 | — |
| 1959 | 4,780,000 | — | 0.50 | 3.50 | 8.00 | — |
| 1960 | 4,790,000 | — | 0.50 | 3.50 | 8.00 | — |
| 1961 | 5,180,000 | — | 0.50 | 3.50 | 8.00 | — |
| 1962 | 2,500,000 | 0.25 | 1.50 | 15.00 | 35.00 | — |
| 1963 | 7,990,000 | — | 0.25 | 2.00 | 5.00 | — |
| 1964 | 7,010,000 | — | 0.25 | 1.50 | 4.00 | — |
| 1965 | 7,365,000 | — | 0.25 | 1.00 | 2.50 | — |
| 1966 | 8,074,999 | — | 0.25 | 0.50 | 2.00 | — |
| 1967 | 9,220,000 | — | 0.25 | 0.50 | 2.00 | — |
| 1968 | 10,372,000 | — | 0.25 | 0.50 | 2.00 | — |
| 1969 | 8,657,000 | — | 0.25 | 1.00 | 3.00 | — |

**20 CENTAVOS** **KM# 595** **Composition:** Bronze

| Date | Mintage | F | VF | XF | Unc | BU |
|---|---|---|---|---|---|---|
| 1969 | 10,891,000 | — | 0.25 | 0.75 | 2.50 | — |
| 1970 | 16,120,000 | — | 0.25 | 1.00 | 3.00 | — |
| 1971 | 1,933,000 | — | 1.00 | 2.50 | 7.50 | — |
| 1972 | 16,354,000 | — | — | 0.25 | 1.00 | — |
| 1973 | 4,900,000 | — | — | 0.25 | 1.00 | — |
| 1974 | 26,975,000 | — | — | 0.25 | 1.00 | — |

**50 CENTAVOS** **KM# 561** **Weight:** 12.5000 g. **Composition:** 0.8350 Silver .3356 oz. ASW

| Date | Mintage | F | VF | XF | Unc | BU |
|---|---|---|---|---|---|---|
| 1912 | 1,695,000 | 4.00 | 8.00 | 15.00 | 30.00 | — |
| 1913 | 4,443,000 | 3.00 | 5.00 | 9.00 | 20.00 | — |
| 1914 | 4,992,000 | 4.00 | 8.00 | 15.00 | 30.00 | — |
| 1916 | 5,080,000 | 3.00 | 5.00 | 9.00 | 20.00 | — |

**50 CENTAVOS** **KM# 575** **Composition:** Aluminum-Bronze

| Date | Mintage | F | VF | XF | Unc | BU |
|---|---|---|---|---|---|---|
| 1924 | 810,000 | 65.00 | 125 | 250 | 475 | — |
| 1925 | — | 1,000 | 2,000 | 4,500 | 8,500 | — |
| 1926 | 4,340,000 | 2.00 | 6.00 | 18.00 | 40.00 | — |

**50 CENTAVOS** **KM# 577** **Composition:** Copper Nickel

| Date | Mintage | F | VF | XF | Unc | BU |
|---|---|---|---|---|---|---|
| 1927 | 2,330,000 | 2.50 | 12.50 | 75.00 | 165 | — |
| 1928 | 6,823,000 | 2.50 | 12.50 | 100 | 220 | — |
| 1929 | 9,779,000 | 2.50 | 12.50 | 75.00 | 165 | — |
| 1930 | 1,116,000 | 2.50 | 20.00 | 200 | 550 | — |
| 1931 | 7,127,000 | 4.00 | 20.00 | 200 | 550 | — |
| 1935 For exclusive use in Azores | 902,000 | 8.50 | 35.00 | 300 | 875 | — |
| 1938 | 923,000 | 8.00 | 37.00 | 375 | 950 | — |
| 1940 | 2,000,000 | 1.00 | 5.00 | 50.00 | 125 | — |
| 1944 | 2,974,000 | 0.25 | 1.00 | 9.00 | 25.00 | — |
| 1945 | 5,700,000 | 0.25 | 1.00 | 8.00 | 25.00 | — |
| 1946 | 4,334,000 | — | 2.00 | 20.00 | 50.00 | — |
| 1947 | 6,998,000 | 0.10 | 1.00 | 9.00 | 25.00 | — |
| 1951 | 4,610,000 | — | 0.50 | 4.00 | 15.00 | — |
| 1952 | 2,421,000 | 0.10 | 1.00 | 12.00 | 30.00 | — |
| 1953 | 2,369,000 | 0.10 | 1.00 | 12.50 | 32.00 | — |
| 1955 | 3,057,000 | 0.10 | 0.50 | 3.00 | 9.00 | — |
| 1956 | 3,003,000 | — | 0.50 | 3.00 | 9.00 | — |
| 1957 | 3,940,000 | — | 0.50 | 3.00 | 9.00 | — |
| 1958 | 2,687,000 | — | 0.50 | 4.00 | 12.00 | — |
| 1959 | 4,027,000 | — | 0.50 | 3.00 | 9.00 | — |
| 1960 | 2,592,000 | — | 0.50 | 3.00 | 9.00 | — |
| 1961 | 3,324,000 | — | 0.25 | 1.50 | 4.00 | — |
| 1962 | 6,678,000 | — | 0.25 | 1.00 | 2.50 | — |
| 1963 | 2,346,000 | — | 0.25 | 3.00 | 9.00 | — |
| 1964 | 7,654,000 | — | 0.25 | 1.00 | 2.50 | — |
| 1965 | 3,366,000 | — | 0.25 | 1.00 | 2.50 | — |
| 1966 | 6,085,000 | — | 0.25 | 1.00 | 2.50 | — |
| 1967 | 19,391,000 | — | 0.25 | 1.00 | 2.50 | — |
| 1968 | 11,448,000 | — | 0.25 | 1.00 | 2.50 | — |

**50 CENTAVOS** **KM# 596** **Composition:** Bronze

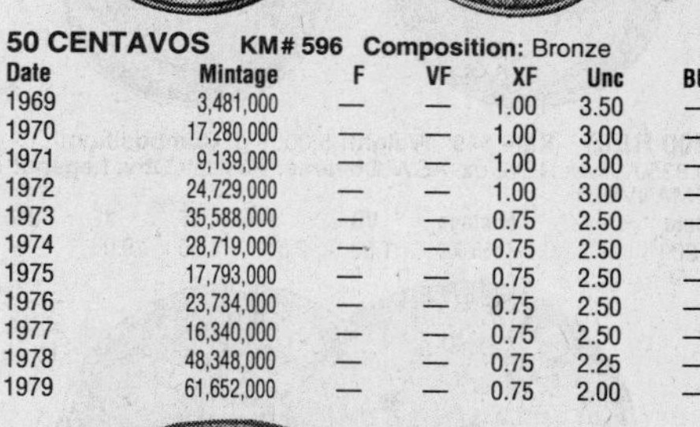

| Date | Mintage | F | VF | XF | Unc | BU |
|---|---|---|---|---|---|---|
| 1969 | 3,481,000 | — | — | 1.00 | 3.50 | — |
| 1970 | 17,280,000 | — | — | 1.00 | 3.00 | — |
| 1971 | 9,139,000 | — | — | 1.00 | 3.00 | — |
| 1972 | 24,729,000 | — | — | 1.00 | 3.00 | — |
| 1973 | 35,588,000 | — | — | 0.75 | 2.50 | — |
| 1974 | 28,719,000 | — | — | 0.75 | 2.50 | — |
| 1975 | 17,793,000 | — | — | 0.75 | 2.50 | — |
| 1976 | 23,734,000 | — | — | 0.75 | 2.50 | — |
| 1977 | 16,340,000 | — | — | 0.75 | 2.50 | — |
| 1978 | 48,348,000 | — | — | 0.75 | 2.25 | — |
| 1979 | 61,652,000 | — | — | 0.75 | 2.00 | — |

**ESCUDO** **KM# 560** **Weight:** 25.0000 g. **Composition:** 0.8350 Silver .6711 oz. ASW **Subject:** October 5, 1910, Birth of the Republic

| Date | Mintage | F | VF | XF | Unc | BU |
|---|---|---|---|---|---|---|
| 1910 | Est. 1,000 | 25.00 | 50.00 | 85.00 | 150 | — |

**Note:** Struck in 1914

**ESCUDO** **KM# 564** **Weight:** 25.0000 g. **Composition:** 0.8350 Silver .6711 oz. ASW

| Date | Mintage | F | VF | XF | Unc | BU |
|---|---|---|---|---|---|---|
| 1915 | 1,818,000 | 10.00 | 20.00 | 30.00 | 60.00 | — |
| 1916 | 1,405,000 | 12.00 | 22.00 | 35.00 | 70.00 | — |

**ESCUDO** **KM# 576** **Composition:** Aluminum-Bronze

| Date | Mintage | F | VF | XF | Unc | BU |
|---|---|---|---|---|---|---|
| 1924 | 2,709,000 | 5.00 | 10.00 | 25.00 | 60.00 | — |
| 1926 | 2,346,000 | 85.00 | 175 | 300 | 700 | — |

**ESCUDO** **KM# 578** **Composition:** Copper Nickel

| Date | Mintage | F | VF | XF | Unc | BU |
|---|---|---|---|---|---|---|
| 1927 | 1,917,000 | 2.00 | 15.00 | 85.00 | 200 | — |
| 1928 | 7,462,000 | 1.00 | 15.00 | 100 | 225 | — |
| 1929 | 1,617,000 | 1.00 | 15.00 | 110 | 300 | — |
| 1930 | 1,911,000 | 6.00 | 25.00 | 350 | 1,000 | — |
| 1931 | 2,039,000 | 7.50 | 25.00 | 350 | 1,000 | — |
| 1935 For exclusive use in Azores | — | 125 | 325 | 2,750 | 6,000 | — |
| 1939 | 304,000 | 10.00 | 30.00 | 250 | 700 | — |
| 1940 | 1,259,000 | 1.00 | 15.00 | 65.00 | 150 | — |
| 1944 | 993,000 | 10.00 | 30.00 | 200 | 400 | — |
| 1945 | Inc. above | 0.50 | 1.50 | 22.00 | 50.00 | — |
| 1946 | 2,507,000 | 0.50 | 1.50 | 20.00 | 50.00 | — |
| 1951 | 2,500,000 | 0.25 | 0.50 | 6.00 | 12.00 | — |
| 1952 | 2,500,000 | 0.75 | 2.50 | 40.00 | 90.00 | — |
| 1957 | 1,656,000 | 0.10 | 0.50 | 7.00 | 15.00 | — |
| 1958 | 1,447,000 | 0.10 | 0.50 | 7.00 | 15.00 | — |
| 1959 | 1,908,000 | 0.10 | 0.50 | 7.00 | 15.00 | — |
| 1961 | 2,505,000 | 0.10 | 0.25 | 2.50 | 6.50 | — |
| 1962 | 2,757,000 | 0.10 | 0.25 | 2.00 | 5.00 | — |
| 1964 | 1,611,000 | 0.10 | 0.25 | 2.00 | 5.00 | — |
| 1965 | 1,683,000 | 0.10 | 0.25 | 1.50 | 4.00 | — |
| 1966 | 2,607,000 | 0.10 | 0.20 | 1.50 | 4.00 | — |
| 1968 | 4,099,000 | 0.10 | 0.20 | 1.50 | 3.50 | — |

**ESCUDO** **KM# 597** **Composition:** Bronze

| Date | Mintage | F | VF | XF | Unc | BU |
|---|---|---|---|---|---|---|
| 1969 | 3,020,000 | — | 0.10 | 1.50 | 5.00 | — |
| 1970 | 6,009,000 | — | 0.10 | 1.50 | 4.00 | — |
| 1971 | 7,860,000 | — | 0.10 | 1.50 | 4.00 | — |
| 1972 | 3,815,000 | — | 0.10 | 1.50 | 4.50 | — |
| 1973 | 20,467,000 | — | 0.10 | 1.00 | 3.00 | — |
| 1974 | 11,444,000 | — | 0.10 | 1.00 | 3.00 | — |
| 1975 | 8,473,000 | — | 0.10 | 1.00 | 3.00 | — |
| 1976 | 7,353,000 | — | 0.10 | 0.50 | 2.00 | — |
| 1977 | 6,218,000 | — | 0.10 | 0.50 | 2.00 | — |
| 1978 | 7,061,000 | — | 0.10 | 0.50 | 2.00 | — |
| 1979 | 14,241,000 | — | 0.10 | 0.25 | 1.50 | — |

**ESCUDO** **KM# 614** **Composition:** Nickel-Brass **Note:** (Previously KM 611)

| Date | Mintage | F | VF | XF | Unc | BU |
|---|---|---|---|---|---|---|
| 1981 | 30,165,000 | — | — | 0.10 | 0.50 | — |
| 1982 | 53,018,000 | — | — | 0.10 | 0.50 | — |
| 1983 | 53,165,000 | — | — | 0.10 | 0.50 | — |
| 1984 | 59,463,000 | — | — | 0.10 | 0.50 | — |
| 1985 | 46,832,000 | — | — | 0.10 | 0.50 | — |
| 1986 | 8,029,999 | — | — | 0.10 | 2.00 | — |

**ESCUDO** **KM# 612** **Composition:** Nickel-Brass **Subject:** World Roller Hockey Championship Games

| Date | Mintage | F | VF | XF | Unc | BU |
|---|---|---|---|---|---|---|
| ND(1983) | 1,990,000 | — | 0.10 | 0.25 | 0.75 | — |

**ESCUDO** **KM# 631** **Composition:** Nickel-Brass

| Date | Mintage | F | VF | XF | Unc | BU |
|---|---|---|---|---|---|---|
| 1986 | 14,882,000 | — | — | 0.10 | 0.35 | — |
| 1987 | 21,922,000 | — | — | 0.10 | 0.35 | — |
| 1988 | 17,168,000 | — | — | 0.10 | 0.35 | — |
| 1989 | 17,194,000 | — | — | 0.10 | 0.35 | — |
| 1990 | 19,008,000 | — | — | 0.10 | 0.35 | — |
| 1991 | 21,500,000 | — | — | — | 0.35 | — |
| 1992 | 22,000,000 | — | — | — | 0.35 | — |
| 1993 | 10,505,000 | — | — | — | 0.35 | — |
| 1994 | — | — | — | — | 0.35 | — |
| 1995 In Mint sets only | — | — | — | — | 0.50 | — |
| 1996 | — | — | — | — | 0.35 | — |
| 1996 Proof | 7,000 | Value: 0.50 | | | | |
| 1997 | — | — | — | — | 0.35 | — |
| 1997 Proof | — | Value: 0.50 | | | | |
| 1998 | — | — | — | — | 0.35 | — |
| 1998 Proof | — | Value: 2.00 | | | | |
| 1999 | — | — | — | — | 0.35 | — |

**2-1/2 ESCUDOS** **KM# 580** **Weight:** 3.5000 g. **Composition:** 0.6500 Silver .0731 oz. ASW

| Date | Mintage | F | VF | XF | Unc | BU |
|---|---|---|---|---|---|---|
| 1932 | 2,592,000 | 5.00 | 20.00 | 50.00 | 120 | — |
| 1933 | 2,457,000 | 20.00 | 50.00 | 100 | 200 | — |
| 1937 | 1,000,000 | 150 | 350 | 650 | 1,250 | — |
| 1940 | 2,763,000 | 3.00 | 12.00 | 30.00 | 70.00 | — |
| 1942 | 3,847,000 | BV | 3.00 | 9.00 | 20.00 | — |
| 1943 | 8,302,000 | BV | 1.75 | 4.00 | 10.00 | — |
| 1944 | 9,134,000 | BV | 1.50 | 2.50 | 7.00 | — |
| 1945 | 6,316,000 | BV | 3.50 | 12.00 | 28.00 | — |
| 1946 | 3,208,000 | BV | 3.00 | 10.00 | 22.00 | — |
| 1947 | 2,610,000 | BV | 3.00 | 10.00 | 22.00 | — |
| 1948 | 1,814,000 | 10.00 | 20.00 | 40.00 | 110 | — |
| 1951 | 4,000,000 | BV | 1.25 | 2.00 | 5.00 | — |

**2-1/2 ESCUDOS** **KM# 590** **Composition:** Copper-Nickel

| Date | Mintage | F | VF | XF | Unc | BU |
|---|---|---|---|---|---|---|
| 1963 | 12,711,000 | — | 0.50 | 20.00 | 45.00 | — |
| 1964 | 17,948,000 | — | 0.50 | 20.00 | 45.00 | — |
| 1965 | 19,512,000 | — | 0.25 | 5.00 | 15.00 | — |
| 1966 | 3,828,000 | — | 2.00 | 35.00 | 85.00 | — |
| 1967 | 5,545,000 | — | 0.25 | 7.00 | 18.00 | — |
| 1968 | 6,087,000 | — | 0.25 | 2.75 | 6.00 | — |
| 1969 | 9,969,000 | — | 0.25 | 1.75 | 5.00 | — |
| 1970 | 2,400,000 | — | 0.25 | 2.25 | 6.00 | — |
| 1971 | 6,791,000 | — | 0.25 | 1.50 | 4.50 | — |
| 1972 | 6,713,000 | — | 0.25 | 1.75 | 5.00 | — |
| 1973 | 9,104,000 | — | 0.25 | 1.00 | 3.00 | — |
| 1974 | 22,743,000 | — | 0.10 | 0.75 | 2.50 | — |
| 1975 | 16,623,999 | — | 0.10 | 0.50 | 1.50 | — |
| 1976 | 21,516,000 | — | 0.10 | 0.50 | 1.50 | — |
| 1977 | 45,726,000 | — | 0.10 | 0.50 | 1.50 | — |
| 1978 | 27,375,000 | — | 0.10 | 0.25 | 1.00 | — |
| 1979 | 44,804,000 | — | 0.10 | 0.25 | 1.00 | — |
| 1980 | 22,319,000 | — | 0.10 | 0.25 | 1.00 | — |
| 1981 | 25,420,000 | — | 0.10 | 0.20 | 1.00 | — |
| 1982 | 45,910,000 | — | 0.10 | 0.20 | 1.00 | — |
| 1983 | 62,946,000 | — | 0.10 | 0.20 | 1.00 | — |
| 1984 | 58,210,000 | — | 0.10 | 0.20 | 1.00 | — |
| 1985 | 60,142,000 | — | 0.10 | 0.20 | 1.00 | — |

**2-1/2 ESCUDOS** **KM# 605** **Composition:** Copper-Nickel **Subject:** 100th Anniversary - Death of Alexandre Herculano

| Date | Mintage | F | VF | XF | Unc | BU |
|---|---|---|---|---|---|---|
| ND(1977) | 5,990,000 | — | 0.20 | 0.75 | 2.00 | — |
| ND(1977) Proof | 13,000 | Value: 3.50 | | | | |

**2-1/2 ESCUDOS** **KM# 613** **Composition:** Copper-Nickel **Subject:** World Rolller Hockey Championship Games

| Date | Mintage | F | VF | XF | Unc | BU |
|---|---|---|---|---|---|---|
| ND(1983) | 1,990,000 | — | 0.10 | 0.25 | 1.00 | — |

**2-1/2 ESCUDOS** **KM# 617** **Composition:** Copper-Nickel **Series:** F.A.O.

| Date | Mintage | F | VF | XF | Unc | BU |
|---|---|---|---|---|---|---|
| 1983 | 995,000 | — | 0.10 | 0.35 | 1.25 | — |

**5 ESCUDOS** **KM# 581** **Weight:** 7.0000 g. **Composition:** 0.6500 Silver .1463 oz. ASW

| Date | Mintage | F | VF | XF | Unc | BU |
|---|---|---|---|---|---|---|
| 1932 | 800,000 | 10.00 | 65.00 | 200 | 450 | — |
| 1933 | 6,717,000 | 2.00 | 7.00 | 25.00 | 70.00 | — |
| 1934 | 1,012,000 | 4.00 | 15.00 | 30.00 | 120 | — |
| 1937 | 1,500,000 | 20.00 | 80.00 | 250 | 500 | — |
| 1940 | 1,500,000 | 4.00 | 15.00 | 50.00 | 120 | — |
| 1942 | 2,051,000 | 2.00 | 4.00 | 8.00 | 20.00 | — |
| 1943 | 1,354,000 | 6.00 | 20.00 | 60.00 | 140 | — |
| 1946 | 404,000 | 4.00 | 12.50 | 28.00 | 60.00 | — |
| 1947 | 2,420,000 | 2.00 | 3.00 | 5.00 | 12.00 | — |
| 1948 | 2,017,999 | 1.75 | 3.00 | 5.00 | 12.00 | — |
| 1951 | 966,000 | 1.50 | 2.50 | 4.00 | 10.00 | — |

**5 ESCUDOS** **KM# 587** **Weight:** 7.0000 g. **Composition:** 0.6500 Silver .1463 oz. ASW **Subject:** 500th Anniversary - Death of Prince Henry the Navigator

| Date | Mintage | F | VF | XF | Unc | BU |
|---|---|---|---|---|---|---|
| 1960 | 800,000 | — | 2.00 | 3.00 | 6.00 | — |
| 1960 Matte | — | — | — | — | 20.00 | — |

**Note:** A small quantity of these coins were given a matte finish by the Lisbon Mint on private contract

**5 ESCUDOS** **KM# 591** **Composition:** Copper-Nickel

| Date | Mintage | F | VF | XF | Unc | BU |
|---|---|---|---|---|---|---|
| 1963 | 2,200,000 | — | 0.50 | 15.00 | 40.00 | — |
| 1964 | 4,268,000 | — | 0.50 | 12.50 | 35.00 | — |
| 1965 | 7,294,000 | — | 0.35 | 12.50 | 35.00 | — |
| 1966 | 8,119,999 | — | 0.35 | 10.00 | 30.00 | — |
| 1967 | 8,128,000 | — | 0.25 | 7.00 | 20.00 | — |
| 1968 | 5,023,000 | — | 0.25 | 3.00 | 10.00 | — |

| Date | Mintage | F | VF | XF | Unc | BU |
|---|---|---|---|---|---|---|
| 1969 | 3,571,000 | — | 0.10 | 2.00 | 6.00 | — |
| 1970 | 1,200,000 | — | 0.10 | 2.50 | 7.00 | — |
| 1971 | 2,721,000 | — | 0.10 | 2.00 | 6.00 | — |
| 1972 | 1,880,000 | — | 0.10 | 2.00 | 6.00 | — |
| 1973 | 2,836,000 | — | 0.10 | 1.25 | 4.00 | — |
| 1974 | 3,984,000 | — | 0.10 | 1.00 | 3.50 | — |
| 1975 | 7,496,000 | — | 0.10 | 1.00 | 3.50 | — |
| 1976 | 11,379,000 | — | 0.10 | 1.00 | 3.50 | — |
| 1977 | 29,058,000 | — | 0.10 | 0.50 | 1.50 | — |
| 1978 | 672,000 | — | 2.00 | 8.00 | 20.00 | — |
| 1979 | 19,546,000 | — | 0.10 | 0.50 | 1.50 | — |
| 1980 | 46,244,000 | — | 0.10 | 0.50 | 1.50 | — |
| 1981 | 15,267,000 | — | 0.10 | 0.50 | 1.50 | — |
| 1982 | 31,318,000 | — | 0.10 | 0.50 | 1.50 | — |
| 1983 | 51,056,000 | — | 0.10 | 0.50 | 1.50 | — |
| 1984 | 46,794,000 | — | 0.10 | 0.50 | 1.50 | — |
| 1985 | 45,441,000 | — | 0.10 | 0.50 | 1.50 | — |
| 1986 | 18,753,000 | — | 0.10 | 0.50 | 1.50 | — |

**5 ESCUDOS** KM# 606 **Composition:** Copper-Nickel **Subject:** 100th Anniversary - Death of Alexandre Herculano

| Date | Mintage | F | VF | XF | Unc | BU |
|---|---|---|---|---|---|---|
| ND(1977) | 9,176,000 | — | 0.35 | 1.00 | 3.00 | — |
| ND(1977) Proof | 10,000 | Value: 4.00 | | | | |

**5 ESCUDOS** KM# 615 **Composition:** Copper-Nickel **Subject:** World Roller Hockey Championship Games

| Date | Mintage | F | VF | XF | Unc | BU |
|---|---|---|---|---|---|---|
| ND(1983) | 1,990,000 | — | 0.25 | 0.50 | 1.50 | — |

**5 ESCUDOS** KM# 618 **Composition:** Copper-Nickel **Series:** F.A.O.

| Date | Mintage | F | VF | XF | Unc | BU |
|---|---|---|---|---|---|---|
| ND(1983) | 995,000 | — | 0.30 | 0.75 | 2.00 | — |

**5 ESCUDOS** KM# 632 **Composition:** Nickel-Brass

| Date | Mintage | F | VF | XF | Unc | BU |
|---|---|---|---|---|---|---|
| 1986 | 21,426,000 | — | 0.10 | 0.25 | 0.50 | — |
| 1987 | 40,548,000 | — | 0.10 | 0.25 | 0.50 | — |
| 1988 | 19,382,000 | — | 0.10 | 0.25 | 0.50 | — |
| 1989 | 27,641,000 | — | 0.10 | 0.25 | 0.50 | — |
| 1990 | 77,977,000 | — | 0.10 | 0.25 | 0.50 | — |
| 1991 | 32,000,000 | — | — | — | 0.50 | — |
| 1992 | 16,000,000 | — | — | — | 0.50 | — |
| 1993 | 8,300,000 | — | — | — | 0.50 | — |
| 1994 | — | — | — | — | 0.50 | — |
| 1995 | — | — | — | — | 0.50 | — |
| 1996 | — | — | — | — | 0.50 | — |
| 1996 Proof | 7,000 | Value: 0.75 | | | | |
| 1997 | — | — | — | — | 0.50 | — |
| 1997 Proof | — | Value: 0.75 | | | | |
| 1998 | — | — | — | — | 0.50 | — |
| 1998 Proof | — | Value: 0.75 | | | | |
| 1999 | — | — | — | — | 0.50 | — |

**10 ESCUDOS** KM# 579 **Weight:** 12.5000 g. **Composition:** 0.8350 Silver .3356 oz. ASW

| Date | Mintage | F | VF | XF | Unc | BU |
|---|---|---|---|---|---|---|
| 1928 | 200,000 | 6.00 | 15.00 | 25.00 | 55.00 | — |

**10 ESCUDOS** KM# 582 **Weight:** 12.5000 g. **Composition:** 0.8350 Silver .3356 oz. ASW

| Date | Mintage | F | VF | XF | Unc | BU |
|---|---|---|---|---|---|---|
| 1932 | 3,220,000 | 4.00 | 10.00 | 22.00 | 58.00 | — |
| 1933 | 1,780,000 | 30.00 | 70.00 | 200 | 600 | — |
| 1934 | 400,000 | 15.00 | 30.00 | 70.00 | 150 | — |
| 1937 | 500,000 | 60.00 | 120 | 225 | 650 | — |
| 1940 | 1,200,000 | 7.00 | 16.00 | 30.00 | 60.00 | — |
| 1942 | 186,000 | 200 | 300 | 550 | 1,150 | — |
| 1948 | 507,000 | 30.00 | 60.00 | 100 | 220 | — |

**10 ESCUDOS** KM# 586 **Weight:** 12.5000 g. **Composition:** 0.6800 Silver .2732 oz. ASW

| Date | Mintage | F | VF | XF | Unc | BU |
|---|---|---|---|---|---|---|
| 1954 | 5,764,000 | 2.00 | 3.00 | 5.00 | 8.00 | — |
| 1955 | 4,056,000 | 2.00 | 3.00 | 5.00 | 8.00 | — |

**10 ESCUDOS** KM# 588 **Weight:** 12.5000 g. **Composition:** 0.6800 Silver .2732 oz. ASW **Subject:** 500th Anniversary - Death of Prince Henry the Navigator

| Date | Mintage | F | VF | XF | Unc | BU |
|---|---|---|---|---|---|---|
| 1960 | 200,000 | — | 10.00 | 18.00 | 30.00 | — |
| 1960 Matte | — | — | — | — | 35.00 | — |

**Note:** A small quantity of these coins were given a matte finish by the Lisbon Mint on private contract

**10 ESCUDOS** KM# 600 **Composition:** Copper-Nickel Clad Nickel

| Date | Mintage | F | VF | XF | Unc | BU |
|---|---|---|---|---|---|---|
| 1971 | 3,876,000 | — | 0.25 | 0.75 | 2.50 | — |
| 1972 | 2,694,000 | — | 0.25 | 1.00 | 3.00 | — |
| 1973 | 5,418,000 | — | 0.25 | 0.75 | 2.50 | — |
| 1974 | 4,043,000 | — | 0.25 | 0.75 | 2.50 | — |

**10 ESCUDOS** KM# 633 **Composition:** Nickel-Brass

| Date | Mintage | F | VF | XF | Unc | BU |
|---|---|---|---|---|---|---|
| 1986 | 12,818,000 | — | 0.20 | 0.40 | 1.00 | — |
| 1987 | 32,814,999 | — | 0.20 | 0.40 | 1.00 | — |
| 1988 | 32,579,000 | — | 0.20 | 0.40 | 1.00 | — |
| 1989 | 12,788,000 | — | 0.20 | 0.40 | 1.00 | — |
| 1990 | 26,500,000 | — | 0.20 | 0.40 | 1.00 | — |
| 1991 | 9,500,000 | — | — | — | 1.00 | — |
| 1992 | 5,600,000 | — | — | — | 1.00 | — |
| 1993 In Mint sets only | 20,000 | — | — | — | 10.00 | — |
| 1994 In Mint sets only | 20,000 | — | — | — | 10.00 | — |
| 1995 In Mint sets only | — | — | — | — | 10.00 | — |
| 1996 | — | — | — | — | 1.00 | — |
| 1996 Proof | 7,000 | Value: 2.50 | | | | |
| 1997 | — | — | — | — | 1.00 | — |
| 1997 Proof | — | Value: 2.50 | | | | |
| 1998 | — | — | — | — | 1.00 | — |
| 1998 Proof | — | Value: 3.00 | | | | |
| 1999 | — | — | — | — | 1.00 | — |

**10 ESCUDOS** KM# 638 **Composition:** Nickel-Brass **Subject:** Rural World

| Date | Mintage | F | VF | XF | Unc | BU |
|---|---|---|---|---|---|---|
| 1987 | 2,000,000 | — | 0.40 | 0.60 | 1.50 | — |

**20 ESCUDOS** KM# 585 **Weight:** 21.0000 g. **Composition:** 0.8000 Silver .5401 oz. ASW **Subject:** 25th Anniversary of Financial Reform

| Date | Mintage | F | VF | XF | Unc | BU |
|---|---|---|---|---|---|---|
| 1953 | 1,000,000 | — | 4.00 | 6.00 | 9.00 | — |
| 1953 Matte | — | — | — | — | — | — |

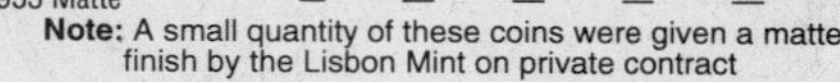

**Note:** A small quantity of these coins were given a matte finish by the Lisbon Mint on private contract

**20 ESCUDOS** KM# 589 **Weight:** 21.0000 g. **Composition:** 0.8000 Silver .5401 oz. ASW **Subject:** 500th Anniversary - Death of Prince Henry the Navigator

| Date | Mintage | F | VF | XF | Unc | BU |
|---|---|---|---|---|---|---|
| 1960 | 200,000 | — | 12.00 | 18.00 | 30.00 | — |
| 1960 Matte | — | — | — | — | 55.00 | — |

**Note:** A small quantity of these coins were given a matte finish by the Lisbon Mint on private contract

**20 ESCUDOS** **KM# 592** **Weight:** 10.0000 g. **Composition:** 0.6500 Silver .2090 oz. ASW **Subject:** Opening of Salazar Bridge

| Date | Mintage | F | VF | XF | Unc | BU |
|---|---|---|---|---|---|---|
| 1966 | 2,000,000 | — | 2.00 | 3.00 | 5.00 | — |
| 1966 Matte | 200 | — | — | — | 35.00 | — |

**Note:** A small quantity of these coins were given a matte finish by the Lisbon Mint on private contract

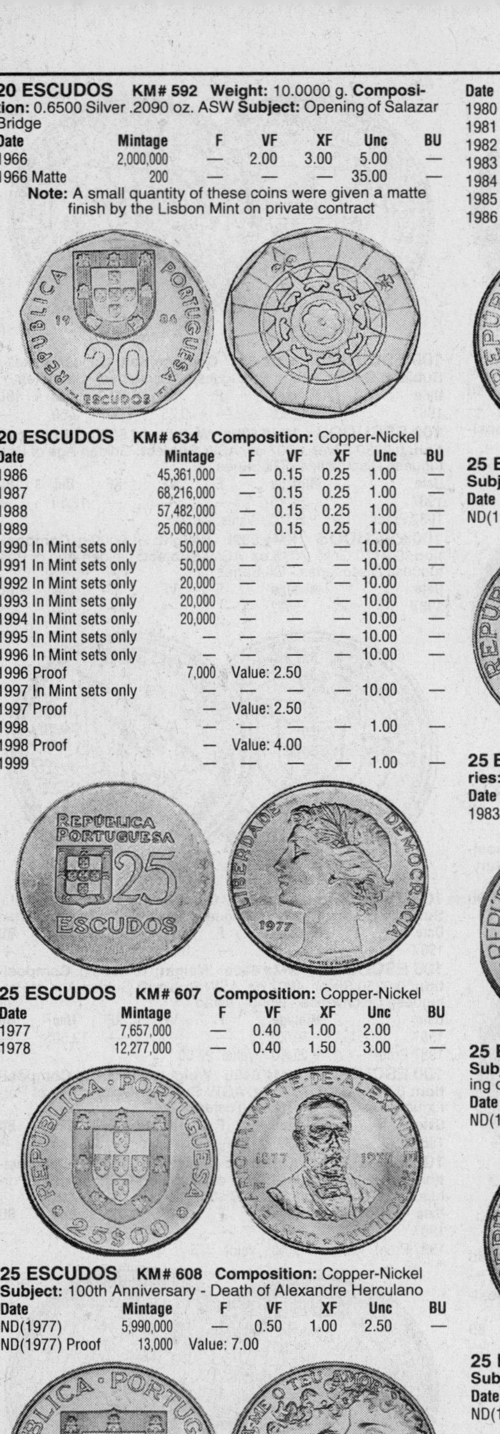

**20 ESCUDOS** **KM# 634** **Composition:** Copper-Nickel

| Date | Mintage | F | VF | XF | Unc | BU |
|---|---|---|---|---|---|---|
| 1986 | 45,361,000 | — | 0.15 | 0.25 | 1.00 | — |
| 1987 | 68,216,000 | — | 0.15 | 0.25 | 1.00 | — |
| 1988 | 57,482,000 | — | 0.15 | 0.25 | 1.00 | — |
| 1989 | 25,060,000 | — | 0.15 | 0.25 | 1.00 | — |
| 1990 In Mint sets only | 50,000 | — | — | — | 10.00 | — |
| 1991 In Mint sets only | 50,000 | — | — | — | 10.00 | — |
| 1992 In Mint sets only | 20,000 | — | — | — | 10.00 | — |
| 1993 In Mint sets only | 20,000 | — | — | — | 10.00 | — |
| 1994 In Mint sets only | 20,000 | — | — | — | 10.00 | — |
| 1995 In Mint sets only | — | — | — | — | 10.00 | — |
| 1996 In Mint sets only | — | — | — | — | 10.00 | — |
| 1996 Proof | 7,000 | Value: 2.50 | | | | |
| 1997 In Mint sets only | — | — | — | — | 10.00 | — |
| 1997 Proof | — | Value: 2.50 | | | | |
| 1998 | — | — | — | — | 1.00 | — |
| 1998 Proof | — | Value: 4.00 | | | | |
| 1999 | — | — | — | — | 1.00 | — |

**25 ESCUDOS** **KM# 607** **Composition:** Copper-Nickel

| Date | Mintage | F | VF | XF | Unc | BU |
|---|---|---|---|---|---|---|
| 1977 | 7,657,000 | — | 0.40 | 1.00 | 2.00 | — |
| 1978 | 12,277,000 | — | 0.40 | 1.50 | 3.00 | — |

**25 ESCUDOS** **KM# 608** **Composition:** Copper-Nickel **Subject:** 100th Anniversary - Death of Alexandre Herculano

| Date | Mintage | F | VF | XF | Unc | BU |
|---|---|---|---|---|---|---|
| ND(1977) | 5,990,000 | — | 0.50 | 1.00 | 2.50 | — |
| ND(1977) Proof | 13,000 | Value: 7.00 | | | | |

**25 ESCUDOS** **KM# 609** **Composition:** Copper-Nickel **Subject:** International Year of the Child

| Date | Mintage | F | VF | XF | Unc | BU |
|---|---|---|---|---|---|---|
| 1979 | 990,000 | — | 0.50 | 1.00 | 2.50 | — |
| 1979 Prooflike | 10,000 | — | — | — | 8.00 | — |

**25 ESCUDOS** **KM# 610** **Composition:** Copper-Nickel **Size:** 28.5 mm. **Note:** Increased size.

| Date | Mintage | F | VF | XF | Unc | BU |
|---|---|---|---|---|---|---|
| 1980 | 750,000 | — | 0.40 | 0.80 | 1.50 | — |
| 1981 | 19,924,000 | — | 0.40 | 0.80 | 1.50 | — |
| 1982 | 12,158,000 | — | 0.40 | 0.80 | 1.50 | — |
| 1983 | 5,622,000 | — | 0.40 | 0.80 | 1.50 | — |
| 1984 | 3,453,000 | — | 0.40 | 0.80 | 1.50 | — |
| 1985 | 25,027,000 | — | 0.40 | 0.80 | 1.50 | — |
| 1986 | — | — | 0.40 | 0.80 | 1.50 | — |

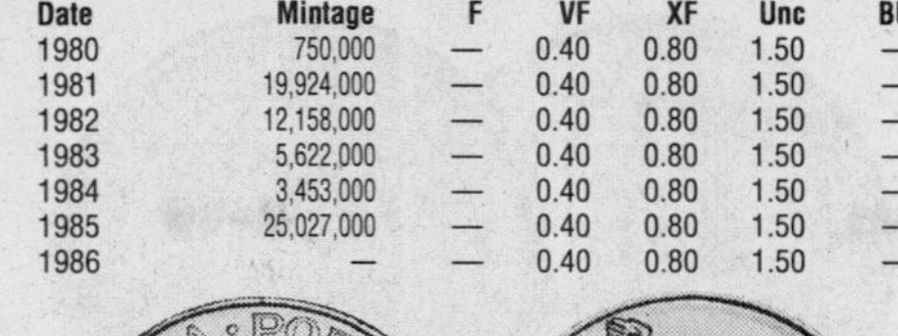

**25 ESCUDOS** **KM# 616** **Composition:** Copper-Nickel **Subject:** World Roller Hockey Championship Games

| Date | Mintage | F | VF | XF | Unc | BU |
|---|---|---|---|---|---|---|
| ND(1983) | 1,990,000 | — | 0.50 | 1.00 | 2.25 | — |

**25 ESCUDOS** **KM# 619** **Composition:** Copper-Nickel **Series:** F.A.O

| Date | Mintage | F | VF | XF | Unc | BU |
|---|---|---|---|---|---|---|
| 1983 | 995,000 | — | 0.60 | 1.25 | 2.85 | — |

**25 ESCUDOS** **KM# 623** **Composition:** Copper-Nickel **Subject:** 10th Anniversary of Revolution **Obverse:** Waves breaking over arms **Reverse:** Stylized 25

| Date | Mintage | F | VF | XF | Unc | BU |
|---|---|---|---|---|---|---|
| ND(1984) | 1,980,000 | — | 0.40 | 1.00 | 2.00 | — |

**25 ESCUDOS** **KM# 624** **Composition:** Copper-Nickel **Subject:** International Year of Disabled Persons

| Date | Mintage | F | VF | XF | Unc | BU |
|---|---|---|---|---|---|---|
| ND(1984) | 1,990,000 | — | 0.40 | 1.00 | 2.00 | — |

**25 ESCUDOS** **KM# 627** **Composition:** Copper-Nickel **Subject:** 600th Anniversary - Battle of Aljubarrota

| Date | Mintage | F | VF | XF | Unc | BU |
|---|---|---|---|---|---|---|
| ND(1985) | 500,000 | — | 0.50 | 1.00 | 2.75 | — |

**25 ESCUDOS** **KM# 627a** **Weight:** 10.8300 g. **Composition:** 0.9250 Silver .3270 oz. ASW

| Date | Mintage | F | VF | XF | Unc | BU |
|---|---|---|---|---|---|---|
| ND(1985) In Mint sets only. | 20,000 | — | — | — | 15.00 | — |
| ND(1985) In Proof sets only | 5,000 | Value: 40.00 | | | | |

**25 ESCUDOS** **KM# 635** **Composition:** Copper-Nickel **Subject:** Admission to European Common Market

| Date | Mintage | F | VF | XF | Unc | BU |
|---|---|---|---|---|---|---|
| 1986 | 4,990,000 | — | 0.40 | 1.00 | 2.00 | — |

**25 ESCUDOS** **KM# 635a** **Weight:** 11.0000 g. **Composition:** 0.9250 Silver .3272 oz. ASW

| Date | Mintage | F | VF | XF | Unc | BU |
|---|---|---|---|---|---|---|
| 1986 Proof | 5,000 | Value: 85.00 | | | | |

**50 ESCUDOS** **KM# 593** **Weight:** 18.0000 g. **Composition:** 0.6500 Silver .3761 oz. ASW **Subject:** 500th Anniversary - Birth of Pedro Alvares Cabral

| Date | Mintage | F | VF | XF | Unc | BU |
|---|---|---|---|---|---|---|
| 1968 | 1,000,000 | — | — | — | 6.00 | — |
| 1968 Matte | 400 | — | — | — | 32.50 | — |

**Note:** A small quantity of these coins were given a matte finish by the Lisbon Mint on private contract

**50 ESCUDOS** **KM# 598** **Weight:** 18.0000 g. **Composition:** 0.6500 Silver .3761 oz. ASW **Subject:** 500th Anniversary - Birth of Vasco Da Gama

| Date | Mintage | F | VF | XF | Unc | BU |
|---|---|---|---|---|---|---|
| ND(1969) | 1,000,000 | — | — | — | 6.50 | — |
| ND(1969) Matte | 400 | — | — | — | 32.50 | — |

**Note:** A small quantity of these coins were given a matte finish by the Lisbon Mint on private contract

**50 ESCUDOS** **KM# 599** **Weight:** 18.0000 g. **Composition:** 0.6500 Silver .3761 oz. ASW **Subject:** 100th Anniversary - Birth of Marechal Carmona

| Date | Mintage | F | VF | XF | Unc | BU |
|---|---|---|---|---|---|---|
| ND(1969) | 500,000 | — | — | — | 7.50 | — |
| ND(1969) Matte | 400 | — | — | — | 32.50 | — |

**Note:** A small quantity of these coins were given a matte finish by the Lisbon Mint on private contract

**50 ESCUDOS** **KM# 601** **Weight:** 18.0000 g. **Composition:** 0.6500 Silver .3761 oz. ASW **Subject:** 125th Anniversary - Bank of Portugal

| Date | Mintage | F | VF | XF | Unc | BU |
|---|---|---|---|---|---|---|
| ND(1971) | 500,000 | — | — | — | 8.50 | — |
| ND(1971) Matte | — | — | — | — | 32.50 | — |

**Note:** A small quantity of these coins were given a matte finish by the Lisbon Mint on private contract

**50 ESCUDOS** **KM# 602** **Weight:** 18.0000 g. **Composition:** 0.6500 Silver .3761 oz. ASW **Subject:** 400th Anniversary of Heroic Epic 'Os Lusiadas'

| Date | Mintage | F | VF | XF | Unc | BU |
|---|---|---|---|---|---|---|
| ND(1972) | 1,000,000 | — | — | — | 6.50 | — |
| ND(1972) Matte | — | — | — | — | 32.50 | — |

**Note:** A small quantity of these coins were given a matte finish by the Lisbon Mint on private contract

**50 ESCUDOS** **KM# 636** **Composition:** Copper-Nickel

| Date | Mintage | F | VF | XF | Unc | BU |
|---|---|---|---|---|---|---|
| 1986 | 51,110,000 | — | — | — | 2.25 | — |
| 1987 | 28,248,000 | — | — | — | 2.25 | — |
| 1988 | 41,905,000 | — | — | — | 2.25 | — |
| 1989 | 18,327,000 | — | — | — | 2.25 | — |
| 1990 In Mint sets only | 50,000 | — | — | — | 15.00 | — |
| 1991 | 2,000,000 | — | — | — | 3.00 | — |
| 1992 In Mint sets only | 20,000 | — | — | — | 15.00 | — |
| 1993 In Mint sets only | 20,000 | — | — | — | 15.00 | — |
| 1994 In Mint sets only | 20,000 | — | — | — | 15.00 | — |
| 1995 In Mint sets only | 20,000 | — | — | — | 15.00 | — |
| 1996 In Mint sets only | — | — | — | — | 8.00 | — |
| 1996 Proof | 7,000 | Value: 5.00 | | | | |
| 1997 In Mint sets only | — | — | — | — | 8.00 | — |
| 1997 Proof | — | Value: 5.00 | | | | |
| 1998 In Mint sets only | — | — | — | — | 8.00 | — |
| 1998 Proof | — | Value: 6.00 | | | | |
| 1999 | — | — | — | — | 3.00 | — |

**100 ESCUDOS** **KM# 603** **Weight:** 18.0000 g. **Composition:** 0.6500 Silver .3762 oz. ASW **Subject:** 1974 Revolution

| Date | Mintage | F | VF | XF | Unc | BU |
|---|---|---|---|---|---|---|
| ND(1976) | 950,000 | — | 3.00 | 5.00 | 9.00 | — |
| ND(1976) Proof | 10,000 | Value: 15.00 | | | | |

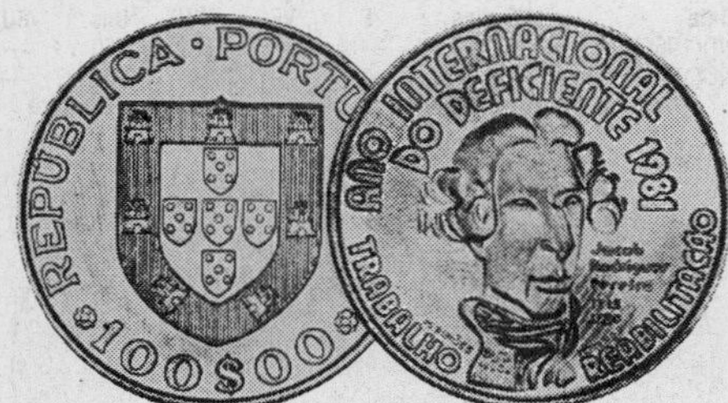


**100 ESCUDOS** **KM# 625** **Composition:** Copper-Nickel **Subject:** International Year of Disabled Persons

| Date | Mintage | F | VF | XF | Unc | BU |
|---|---|---|---|---|---|---|
| ND(1984) | 990,000 | — | 0.75 | 1.50 | 3.00 | — |

**100 ESCUDOS** **KM# 628** **Composition:** Copper-Nickel **Subject:** 50th Anniversary - Death of Fernando Pessoa - Poet

| Date | Mintage | F | VF | XF | Unc | BU |
|---|---|---|---|---|---|---|
| 1985 | 480,000 | — | 0.75 | 2.00 | 4.00 | — |

**100 ESCUDOS** **KM# 628a** **Weight:** 16.5000 g. **Composition:** 0.9250 Silver .4907 oz. ASW

| Date | Mintage | F | VF | XF | Unc | BU |
|---|---|---|---|---|---|---|
| 1985 Proof | 5,000 | Value: 200 | | | | |

**100 ESCUDOS** **KM# 629** **Composition:** Copper-Nickel **Subject:** 800th Anniversary - Death of King Alfonso Henriques

| Date | Mintage | F | VF | XF | Unc | BU |
|---|---|---|---|---|---|---|
| 1985 | 500,000 | — | 0.75 | 2.00 | 4.00 | — |

**100 ESCUDOS** **KM# 629a** **Weight:** 16.5000 g. **Composition:** 0.9250 Silver .4907 oz. ASW **Subject:** 800th Anniversary - Death of King Alfonso Henriques

| Date | Mintage | F | VF | XF | Unc | BU |
|---|---|---|---|---|---|---|
| 1985 | 20,000 | — | — | — | 27.00 | — |
| 1985 Proof | 5,000 | Value: 110 | | | | |

**100 ESCUDOS** **KM# 630** **Composition:** Copper-Nickel **Subject:** 600th Anniversary - Battle of Aljubarrota

| Date | Mintage | F | VF | XF | Unc | BU |
|---|---|---|---|---|---|---|
| ND(1985) | 500,000 | — | 0.75 | 2.00 | 4.00 | — |

**100 ESCUDOS** **KM# 630a** **Weight:** 16.5000 g. **Composition:** 0.9250 Silver .4907 oz. ASW

| Date | Mintage | F | VF | XF | Unc | BU |
|---|---|---|---|---|---|---|
| ND(1985) | 20,000 | — | — | — | 22.00 | — |
| ND(1985) Proof | 5,000 | Value: 80.00 | | | | |

**100 ESCUDOS** **KM# 637** **Composition:** Copper-Nickel **Subject:** World Cup Soccer - Mexico

| Date | Mintage | F | VF | XF | Unc | BU |
|---|---|---|---|---|---|---|
| 1986 | 500,000 | — | 0.75 | 2.00 | 4.00 | — |

**100 ESCUDOS** **KM# 637a** **Weight:** 16.5000 g. **Composition:** 0.9250 Silver .4907 oz. ASW **Subject:** World Cup Soccer - Mexico

| Date | Mintage | F | VF | XF | Unc | BU |
|---|---|---|---|---|---|---|
| 1986 | 50,000 | — | — | — | 12.50 | — |
| 1986 Proof | 20,000 | Value: 27.50 | | | | |

**100 ESCUDOS** **KM# 639** **Composition:** Copper Nickel **Subject:** Golden Age of Portuguese Discoveries - Gil Eanes

| Date | Mintage | F | VF | XF | Unc | BU |
|---|---|---|---|---|---|---|
| 1987 | 1,000,000 | — | 0.75 | 1.00 | 2.50 | — |

**100 ESCUDOS** **KM# 639a** **Weight:** 16.5000 g. **Composition:** 0.9250 Silver .4907 oz. ASW **Subject:** Golden Age of Portuguese Discoveries - Gil Eanes

| Date | Mintage | F | VF | XF | Unc | BU |
|---|---|---|---|---|---|---|
| 1987 | 50,000 | — | — | — | 12.50 | — |
| 1987 Proof | 22,000 | Value: 22.50 | | | | |

**100 ESCUDOS** **KM# 639b** **Weight:** 24.0000 g. **Composition:** 0.9170 Gold .7075 oz. AGW **Subject:** Golden Age of Portuguese Discoveries - Gil Eanes

| Date | Mintage | F | VF | XF | Unc | BU |
|---|---|---|---|---|---|---|
| 1987 | 5,772 | — | — | — | 500 | — |

**100 ESCUDOS** **KM# 640** **Composition:** Copper-Nickel **Subject:** Golden Age of Portuguese Discoveries - Nuno Tristao

| Date | Mintage | F | VF | XF | Unc | BU |
|---|---|---|---|---|---|---|
| 1987 | 1,000,000 | — | 0.75 | 1.00 | 2.50 | — |

**100 ESCUDOS** **KM# 640a** **Weight:** 16.5000 g. **Composition:** 0.9250 Silver .4907 oz. ASW **Subject:** Golden Age of Portuguese Discoveries - Nuno Tristao

| Date | Mintage | F | VF | XF | Unc | BU |
|---|---|---|---|---|---|---|
| 1987 | 50,000 | — | — | — | 12.50 | — |
| 1987 Proof | 20,000 | Value: 22.50 | | | | |

**100 ESCUDOS** **KM# 640b** **Weight:** 24.0000 g. **Composition:** 0.9170 Gold .7075 oz. AGW **Subject:** Golden Age of Portuguese Discoveries - Nuno Tristao

| Date | Mintage | F | VF | XF | Unc | BU |
|---|---|---|---|---|---|---|
| 1987 | 5,497 | — | — | — | 500 | — |

**100 ESCUDOS** **KM# 640c** **Weight:** 31.1190 g. **Composition:** 0.9990 Palladium 1.0000 oz. **Subject:** Golden Age of Portuguese Discoveries - Nuno Tristao

| Date | Mintage | F | VF | XF | Unc | BU |
|---|---|---|---|---|---|---|
| 1987 | 323 | — | — | — | 765 | — |
| 1987 Proof | 2,000 | Value: 775 | | | | |

**100 ESCUDOS** **KM# 641** **Composition:** Copper-Nickel **Subject:** Golden Age of Portuguese Discoveries - Diogo Cao

| Date | Mintage | F | VF | XF | Unc | BU |
|---|---|---|---|---|---|---|
| 1987 | 1,000,000 | — | 0.75 | 1.00 | 2.50 | — |

**100 ESCUDOS** **KM# 641a** **Weight:** 16.5000 g. **Composition:** 0.9250 Silver .4907 oz. ASW **Subject:** Golden Age of Portuguese Discoveries - Diogo Cao

| Date | Mintage | F | VF | XF | Unc | BU |
|---|---|---|---|---|---|---|
| 1987 | 50,000 | — | — | — | 12.50 | — |
| 1987 Proof | 20,000 | Value: 22.50 | | | | |

**100 ESCUDOS** **KM# 641b** **Weight:** 24.0000 g. **Composition:** 0.9170 Gold .7075 oz. AGW **Subject:** Golden Age of Portuguese Discoveries - Diogo Cao

| Date | Mintage | F | VF | XF | Unc | BU |
|---|---|---|---|---|---|---|
| 1987 | 5,256 | — | — | — | 450 | — |
| 1987 Proof | 5,387 | Value: 500 | | | | |

**100 ESCUDOS** **KM# 644** **Composition:** Copper-Nickel **Subject:** Amadeo De Souza Cardoso

| Date | Mintage | F | VF | XF | Unc | BU |
|---|---|---|---|---|---|---|
| 1987 | 800,000 | — | 0.75 | 1.25 | 3.00 | — |

**100 ESCUDOS** **KM# 644a** **Weight:** 21.0000 g. **Composition:** 0.9250 Silver .6246 oz. ASW **Subject:** Amadeo De Souza Cardoso

| Date | Mintage | F | VF | XF | Unc | BU |
|---|---|---|---|---|---|---|
| 1987 | 30,000 | — | — | — | 18.50 | — |
| 1987 Proof | 15,000 | Value: 30.00 | | | | |

**100 ESCUDOS** **KM# 642** **Composition:** Copper-Nickel **Subject:** Golden Age of Portuguese Discoveries - Bartolomeu Dias

| Date | Mintage | F | VF | XF | Unc | BU |
|---|---|---|---|---|---|---|
| ND(1988) | 1,000,000 | — | 0.75 | 1.00 | 2.50 | — |

**100 ESCUDOS** **KM# 642a** **Weight:** 16.5000 g. **Composition:** 0.9250 Silver .4907 oz. ASW **Subject:** Golden Age of Portuguese Discoveries - Bartolomeu Dias

| Date | Mintage | F | VF | XF | Unc | BU |
|---|---|---|---|---|---|---|
| ND(1988) | 50,000 | — | — | — | 12.50 | — |
| ND(1988) Proof | 20,000 | Value: 22.50 | | | | |

**100 ESCUDOS** **KM# 642b** **Weight:** 24.0000 g. **Composition:** 0.9170 Gold .7077 oz. AGW **Subject:** Golden Age of Portuguese Discoveries - Bartolomeu Dias

| Date | Mintage | F | VF | XF | Unc | BU |
|---|---|---|---|---|---|---|
| ND(1988) | 5,503 | — | — | — | 450 | — |

**100 ESCUDOS** **KM# 642c** **Weight:** 31.1190 g. **Composition:** 0.9990 Platinum 1.0000 oz. APW **Subject:** Golden Age of Portuguese Discoveries - Bartolomeu Dias

| Date | Mintage | F | VF | XF | Unc | BU |
|---|---|---|---|---|---|---|
| ND(1988) | 907 | — | — | — | 750 | — |
| ND(1988) Proof | 2,000 | Value: 1,450 | | | | |

**100 ESCUDOS** **KM# 645.1** **Ring Composition:** Copper-Nickel **Center Composition:** Aluminum-Bronze **Reverse:** Pedro Nunes **Edge:** 5 reeded and 5 plain sections

| Date | Mintage | F | VF | XF | Unc | BU |
|---|---|---|---|---|---|---|
| 1989 | 20,000,000 | — | — | 1.00 | 2.50 | — |
| 1990 | 52,000,000 | — | — | 1.00 | 2.50 | — |
| 1991 | 45,500,000 | — | — | 1.00 | 2.50 | — |
| 1992 | 14,500,000 | — | — | 1.00 | 2.50 | — |
| 1993 In Mint sets only | 20,000 | — | — | — | 15.00 | — |
| 1994 In Mint sets only | 20,000 | — | — | — | 15.00 | — |
| 1996 In Mint sets only | — | — | — | — | 15.00 | — |
| 1996 Proof | 7,000 | Value: 10.00 | | | | |
| 1997 | — | — | — | — | 2.50 | — |
| 1997 Proof | — | Value: 2.50 | | | | |
| 1998 | — | — | — | — | 2.50 | — |
| 1998 Proof | — | Value: 10.00 | | | | |
| 1999 | — | — | — | — | 2.50 | — |

**100 ESCUDOS** **KM# 645.2** **Ring Composition:** Copper-Nickel **Center Composition:** Aluminum-Bronze **Reverse:** Pedro Nunes **Edge:** 6 reeded and 6 plain sections

| Date | Mintage | F | VF | XF | Unc | BU |
|---|---|---|---|---|---|---|
| 1989 | 20 | — | — | 1.00 | 2.50 | — |
| 1990 | Inc. above | — | — | 1.50 | 2.50 | — |
| 1991 | Inc. above | — | — | 1.00 | 3.00 | — |

**100 ESCUDOS** **KM# 646** **Composition:** Copper-Nickel **Subject:** Discovery of the Canary Islands

| Date | Mintage | F | VF | XF | Unc | BU |
|---|---|---|---|---|---|---|
| 1989 | 2,000,000 | — | — | 1.00 | 2.50 | — |

**100 ESCUDOS** **KM# 646a** **Weight:** 21.0000 g. **Composition:** 0.9250 Silver .6246 oz. ASW **Subject:** Discovery of the Canary Islands

| Date | Mintage | F | VF | XF | Unc | BU |
|---|---|---|---|---|---|---|
| 1989 | 50,000 | — | — | — | 12.50 | — |
| 1989 Proof | 23,000 | Value: 22.50 | | | | |

**100 ESCUDOS** **KM# 646b** **Weight:** 24.0000 g. **Composition:** 0.9170 Gold .7077 oz. AGW **Subject:** Discovery of the Canary Islands

| Date | Mintage | F | VF | XF | Unc | BU |
|---|---|---|---|---|---|---|
| 1989 Proof | 2,981 | Value: 550 | | | | |

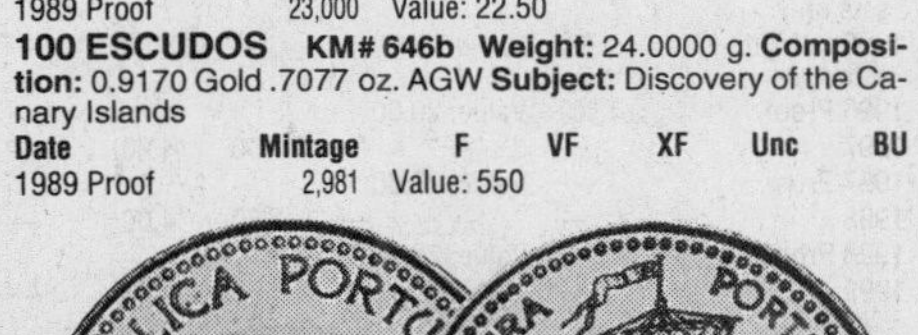

**100 ESCUDOS** **KM# 647** **Composition:** Copper-Nickel **Subject:** Discovery of Madeira

| Date | Mintage | F | VF | XF | Unc | BU |
|---|---|---|---|---|---|---|
| 1989 | 2,000,000 | — | — | 1.00 | 2.50 | — |

**100 ESCUDOS** **KM# 647a** **Weight:** 21.0000 g. **Composition:** 0.9250 Silver .6246 oz. ASW **Subject:** Discovery of Madeira

| Date | Mintage | F | VF | XF | Unc | BU |
|---|---|---|---|---|---|---|
| 1989 | 50,000 | — | — | — | 12.50 | — |
| 1989 Proof | 20,000 | Value: 22.50 | | | | |

**100 ESCUDOS** **KM# 647b** **Weight:** 24.0000 g. **Composition:** 0.9170 Gold .7077 oz. AGW **Subject:** Discovery of Madeira

| Date | Mintage | F | VF | XF | Unc | BU |
|---|---|---|---|---|---|---|
| 1989 Proof | 2,996 | Value: 550 | | | | |

**100 ESCUDOS** **KM# 647c** **Weight:** 31.1190 g. **Composition:** 0.9990 Palladium 1.0000 oz. **Subject:** Discovery of Madeira

| Date | Mintage | F | VF | XF | Unc | BU |
|---|---|---|---|---|---|---|
| 1989 Proof | 2,500 | Value: 775 | | | | |

**100 ESCUDOS** **KM# 648** **Composition:** Copper-Nickel **Subject:** Discovery of the Azores

| Date | Mintage | F | VF | XF | Unc | BU |
|---|---|---|---|---|---|---|
| ND(1989) | 2,000,000 | — | — | 1.00 | 2.50 | — |

**100 ESCUDOS** **KM# 648a** **Weight:** 21.0000 g. **Composition:** 0.9250 Silver .6246 oz. ASW **Subject:** Discovery of the Azores

| Date | Mintage | F | VF | XF | Unc | BU |
|---|---|---|---|---|---|---|
| ND(1989) | 50,000 | — | — | — | 12.50 | — |
| ND(1989) Proof | 20,000 | Value: 22.50 | | | | |

**100 ESCUDOS** **KM# 648b** **Weight:** 24.0000 g. **Composition:** 0.9170 Gold .7077 oz. AGW **Subject:** Discovery of the Avores

| Date | Mintage | F | VF | XF | Unc | BU |
|---|---|---|---|---|---|---|
| ND(1989) Proof | 5,495 | Value: 500 | | | | |

**100 ESCUDOS** **KM# 649** **Composition:** Copper-Nickel **Subject:** Celestial Navigation

| Date | Mintage | F | VF | XF | Unc | BU |
|---|---|---|---|---|---|---|
| 1990 | 2,000,000 | — | — | 1.00 | 2.50 | — |

**100 ESCUDOS** **KM# 649a** **Weight:** 21.0000 g. **Composition:** 0.9250 Silver .6246 oz. ASW **Subject:** Celestial Navigation

| Date | Mintage | F | VF | XF | Unc | BU |
|---|---|---|---|---|---|---|
| 1990 | 50,000 | — | — | — | 12.50 | — |
| 1990 Proof | 20,000 | Value: 22.50 | | | | |

**100 ESCUDOS** **KM# 649b** **Weight:** 24.0000 g. **Composition:** 0.9170 Gold .7077 oz. AGW **Subject:** Celestial Navigation

| Date | Mintage | F | VF | XF | Unc | BU |
|---|---|---|---|---|---|---|
| 1990 Proof | 2,958 | Value: 550 | | | | |

**100 ESCUDOS** **KM# 649c** **Weight:** 31.1190 g. **Composition:** 0.9990 Platinum 1.0000 oz. APW **Subject:** Celestial Navigation

| Date | Mintage | F | VF | XF | Unc | BU |
|---|---|---|---|---|---|---|
| 1990 Proof | 2,500 | Value: 1,500 | | | | |

**100 ESCUDOS** **KM# 651** **Composition:** Copper-Nickel **Subject:** 350th Anniversary - Restoration of Portuguese Independence

| Date | Mintage | F | VF | XF | Unc | BU |
|---|---|---|---|---|---|---|
| ND(1990) | 1,000,000 | — | — | 1.00 | 2.50 | — |

**100 ESCUDOS** **KM# 651a** **Weight:** 18.5000 g. **Composition:** 0.9250 Silver .5502 oz. ASW **Subject:** 350th Anniversary - Restoration of Portuguese

| Date | Mintage | F | VF | XF | Unc | BU |
|---|---|---|---|---|---|---|
| ND(1990) | 25,000 | — | — | — | 20.00 | — |
| ND(1990) Proof | 10,000 | Value: 40.00 | | | | |

**100 ESCUDOS** **KM# 656** **Composition:** Copper-Nickel **Reverse:** Camilo Castelo Branco

| Date | Mintage | F | VF | XF | Unc | BU |
|---|---|---|---|---|---|---|
| 1990 | 1,000,000 | — | — | 1.00 | 2.50 | — |

**100 ESCUDOS** **KM# 656a** **Weight:** 18.5000 g. **Composition:** 0.9250 Silver .5502 oz. ASW **Reverse:** Camilo Castelo Branco

| Date | Mintage | F | VF | XF | Unc | BU |
|---|---|---|---|---|---|---|
| 1990 | 25,000 | — | — | — | 18.50 | — |
| 1990 Proof | 10,000 | Value: 42.00 | | | | |

**100 ESCUDOS** **KM# 678** **Ring Composition:** Copper-Nickel **Center Composition:** Aluminum-Bronze **Subject:** 50TH Anniversary - F.A.O

| Date | Mintage | F | VF | XF | Unc | BU |
|---|---|---|---|---|---|---|
| 1995 | 500,000 | — | — | 1.50 | 4.00 | — |
| 1995 In Proof sets only | 17,000 | Value: 15.00 | | | | |

**100 ESCUDOS** **KM# 680** **Composition:** Copper-Nickel **Subject:** 400th Anniversary - Antonio Prior de Crato

| Date | Mintage | F | VF | XF | Unc | BU |
|---|---|---|---|---|---|---|
| ND(1995) | — | — | — | 1.00 | 2.50 | — |

**100 ESCUDOS** **KM# 680a** **Weight:** 18.5000 g. **Composition:** 0.9250 Silver .5502 oz. ASW **Subject:** 400th Anniversary - Antonio Prior de Crato

| Date | Mintage | F | VF | XF | Unc | BU |
|---|---|---|---|---|---|---|
| ND(1995) | 5,000 | — | — | — | 30.00 | — |
| ND(1995) Proof | 10,000 | Value: 35.00 | | | | |

**100 ESCUDOS** **KM# 693** **Ring Composition:** Copper-Nickel **Center Composition:** Aluminum-Bronze **Subject:** Lisbon World Expo '98 **Obverse:** National arms and denomination **Reverse:** Sea Lion

| Date | Mintage | F | VF | XF | Unc | BU |
|---|---|---|---|---|---|---|
| 1997 | — | — | — | 1.50 | 4.00 | — |
| 1997 In Mint sets only | 7,000 | — | — | — | 15.00 | — |

**100 ESCUDOS** **KM# 722.1** **Ring Composition:** Copper Nickel **Center Weight:** 8.3200 g. **Center Composition:** Brass **Obverse:** National arms, denomination and country name. **Reverse:** UNICEF logo. **Edge:** Reeded and plain sections. **Size:** 25 mm.

| Date | Mintage | F | VF | XF | Unc | BU |
|---|---|---|---|---|---|---|
| 1999 | — | — | — | — | 5.00 | — |

**100 ESCUDOS** **KM# 722.2** **Ring Composition:** Copper Nickel **Center Weight:** 8.3200 g. **Center Composition:** Brass **Obverse:** Country name as "PORTUGUSA." **Reverse:** UNICEF logo. **Edge:** Reeded and plain sections. **Size:** 25 mm.

| Date | Mintage | F | VF | XF | Unc | BU |
|---|---|---|---|---|---|---|
| 1999 | — | — | — | — | 6.00 | — |

**200 ESCUDOS** **KM# 659** **Composition:** Copper-Nickel **Subject:** Westward Navigation **Reverse:** Stylized Ship

| Date | Mintage | F | VF | XF | Unc | BU |
|---|---|---|---|---|---|---|
| 1991 | 1,500,000 | — | — | 1.50 | 4.50 | — |

**200 ESCUDOS** **KM# 659a** **Weight:** 26.5000 g. **Composition:** 0.9250 Silver .7880 oz. ASW **Subject:** Westward Navigation **Reverse:** Stylized ship.

| Date | Mintage | F | VF | XF | Unc | BU |
|---|---|---|---|---|---|---|
| 1991 | 10,000 | — | — | — | 15.00 | — |
| 1991 Proof | 15,000 | Value: 25.00 | | | | |

**200 ESCUDOS** **KM# 659b** **Weight:** 27.2000 g. **Composition:** 0.9170 Gold .8000 oz. AGW **Subject:** Westward Navigation **Reverse:** Stylized Ship

| Date | Mintage | F | VF | XF | Unc | BU |
|---|---|---|---|---|---|---|
| 1991 Proof | 3,500 | Value: 550 | | | | |

**200 ESCUDOS** **KM# 659c** **Weight:** 31.1190 g. **Composition:** 0.9990 Platinum 1.0000 oz. APW **Subject:** Westward Navigation **Reverse:** Stylized ship.

| Date | Mintage | F | VF | XF | Unc | BU |
|---|---|---|---|---|---|---|
| 1991 Proof | 2,500 | Value: 750 | | | | |

**200 ESCUDOS** **KM# 659d** **Weight:** 31.1190 g. **Composition:** 0.9990 Palladium 1.0000 oz. **Subject:** Westward Navigation **Reverse:** Stylized ship.

| Date | Mintage | F | VF | XF | Unc | BU |
|---|---|---|---|---|---|---|
| 1991 Proof | 2,500 | Value: 775 | | | | |

**200 ESCUDOS** **KM# 655** **Ring Composition:** Aluminum-Bronze **Center Composition:** Copper-Nickel **Reverse:** Garcia De Orta

| Date | Mintage | F | VF | XF | Unc | BU |
|---|---|---|---|---|---|---|
| 1991 | 33,000,000 | — | — | 1.25 | 3.00 | — |
| 1992 | 11,000,000 | — | — | 1.50 | 4.00 | — |
| 1993 In Mint sets only | 20,000 | — | — | — | 18.00 | — |
| 1996 In Mint sets only | — | — | — | — | 18.00 | — |
| 1996 Proof | 7,000 | Value: 20.00 | | | | |
| 1997 | — | — | — | 1.50 | 4.00 | — |
| 1997 Proof | — | Value: 20.00 | | | | |
| 1998 | — | — | — | 1.50 | 4.00 | — |
| 1998 Proof | — | Value: 20.00 | | | | |
| 1999 | — | — | — | 1.50 | 4.00 | — |

**200 ESCUDOS** **KM# 658** **Composition:** Copper-Nickel **Subject:** Columbus and Portugal

| Date | Mintage | F | VF | XF | Unc | BU |
|---|---|---|---|---|---|---|
| 1991 | 1,500,000 | — | — | 1.50 | 4.50 | — |

**200 ESCUDOS** **KM# 658a** **Weight:** 26.5000 g. **Composition:** 0.9250 Silver .788 oz. ASW **Subject:** Columbus and Portugal

| Date | Mintage | F | VF | XF | Unc | BU |
|---|---|---|---|---|---|---|
| 1991 | 10,000 | — | — | — | 15.00 | — |
| 1991 Proof | 15,000 | Value: 30.00 | | | | |

**200 ESCUDOS** **KM# 658b** **Weight:** 27.2000 g. **Composition:** 0.9170 Gold .8000 oz. AGW **Subject:** Columbus and Portugal

| Date | Mintage | F | VF | XF | Unc | BU |
|---|---|---|---|---|---|---|
| 1991 Proof | 3,500 | Value: 550 | | | | |

**200 ESCUDOS** **KM# 658c** **Weight:** 31.1190 g. **Composition:** 0.9990 Platinum 1.000 oz. APW **Subject:** Columbus and Portugal

| Date | Mintage | F | VF | XF | Unc | BU |
|---|---|---|---|---|---|---|
| 1991 Proof | 2,500 | Value: 750 | | | | |

**200 ESCUDOS** **KM# 658d** **Weight:** 31.1190 g. **Composition:** 0.9990 Palladium 1.0000 oz. **Subject:** Columbus and Portugal.

| Date | Mintage | F | VF | XF | Unc | BU |
|---|---|---|---|---|---|---|
| 1991 Proof | 2,500 | Value: 775 | | | | |

**200 ESCUDOS** **KM# 660** **Composition:** Copper-Nickel **Subject:** New World - America **Reverse:** Columbus and Ships

| Date | Mintage | F | VF | XF | Unc | BU |
|---|---|---|---|---|---|---|
| ND(1992) | 1,300,000 | — | — | 1.50 | 4.50 | — |

**200 ESCUDOS** **KM# 660a** **Weight:** 26.5000 g. **Composition:** 0.9250 Silver .7880 oz. ASW **Subject:** New World - America **Reverse:** Columbus and ships.

| Date | Mintage | F | VF | XF | Unc | BU |
|---|---|---|---|---|---|---|
| ND(1992) | 10,000 | — | — | — | 15.00 | — |
| ND(1992) Proof | 15,000 | Value: 25.00 | | | | |

**200 ESCUDOS** **KM# 660b** **Weight:** 27.2000 g. **Composition:** 0.9170 Gold .8000 oz. AGW **Subject:** New World - America **Reverse:** Columbus and Ships

| Date | Mintage | F | VF | XF | Unc | BU |
|---|---|---|---|---|---|---|
| ND(1992) Proof | 6,000 | Value: 550 | | | | |

**200 ESCUDOS** **KM# 660c** **Weight:** 31.1190 g. **Composition:** 0.9990 Platinum 1.0000 oz. APW **Subject:** New World - America **Reverse:** Columbus and ships.

| Date | Mintage | F | VF | XF | Unc | BU |
|---|---|---|---|---|---|---|
| ND(1992) Proof | 2,500 | Value: 750 | | | | |

**200 ESCUDOS** **KM# 660d** **Weight:** 31.1190 g. **Composition:** 0.9990 Palladium 1.0000 oz. **Subject:** New World - America **Reverse:** Columbus and ships.

| Date | Mintage | F | VF | XF | Unc | BU |
|---|---|---|---|---|---|---|
| ND(1992) Proof | 2,500 | Value: 775 | | | | |

**200 ESCUDOS** **KM# 661** **Composition:** Copper-Nickel **Reverse:** Joao Rodrigues Cabrilho - Map

| Date | Mintage | F | VF | XF | Unc | BU |
|---|---|---|---|---|---|---|
| ND(1992) | 1,300,000 | — | — | 1.50 | 4.50 | — |

**200 ESCUDOS** **KM# 661a** **Weight:** 26.5000 g. **Composition:** 0.9250 Silver .7880 oz. ASW **Reverse:** Joao Rodrigues Cabrilho - Map.

| Date | Mintage | F | VF | XF | Unc | BU |
|---|---|---|---|---|---|---|
| ND(1992) | 10,000 | — | — | — | 15.00 | — |
| ND(1992) Proof | 15,000 | Value: 25.00 | | | | |

**200 ESCUDOS** **KM# 661b** **Weight:** 27.2000 g. **Composition:** 0.9170 Gold .8000 oz. AGW **Reverse:** Joao Rodrigues Cabrilho - Map

| Date | Mintage | F | VF | XF | Unc | BU |
|---|---|---|---|---|---|---|
| ND(1992) Proof | 3,500 | Value: 550 | | | | |

**200 ESCUDOS** **KM# 661c** **Weight:** 31.1190 g. **Composition:** 0.9990 Platinum 1.0000 oz. APW **Reverse:** Joao Rodrigues Cabrilho - Map.

| Date | Mintage | F | VF | XF | Unc | BU |
|---|---|---|---|---|---|---|
| ND(1992) Proof | 2,500 | Value: 750 | | | | |

**200 ESCUDOS** **KM# 661d** **Weight:** 31.1190 g. **Composition:** 0.9990 Palladium 1.0000 oz. **Reverse:** Joao Rodrigues Cabrilho - Map.

| Date | Mintage | F | VF | XF | Unc | BU |
|---|---|---|---|---|---|---|
| ND(1992) Proof | 2,500 | Value: 775 | | | | |

**200 ESCUDOS** **KM# 662** **Composition:** Copper-Nickel **Subject:** Olympics **Reverse:** Stylized Runner

| Date | Mintage | F | VF | XF | Unc | BU |
|---|---|---|---|---|---|---|
| 1992 | 1,000,000 | — | — | 1.50 | 4.50 | — |

**200 ESCUDOS** **KM# 662a** **Weight:** 26.5000 g. **Composition:** 0.9250 Silver .7881 oz. ASW **Subject:** Olympics **Reverse:** Stylized runner.

| Date | Mintage | F | VF | XF | Unc | BU |
|---|---|---|---|---|---|---|
| 1992 | 20,000 | — | — | — | 17.50 | — |
| 1992 Proof | 30,000 | Value: 32.50 | | | | |

**200 ESCUDOS** **KM# 663** **Composition:** Copper-Nickel **Subject:** Portugal's Presidency of the European Community

| Date | Mintage | F | VF | XF | Unc | BU |
|---|---|---|---|---|---|---|
| 1992 | 1,000,000 | — | — | 1.50 | 4.50 | — |

**200 ESCUDOS** **KM# 663a** **Weight:** 26.5000 g. **Composition:** 0.9250 Silver .7881 oz. ASW **Subject:** Portugal's Presidency of the European Community

| Date | Mintage | F | VF | XF | Unc | BU |
|---|---|---|---|---|---|---|
| 1992 | 20,000 | — | — | — | 20.00 | — |
| 1992 Proof | 30,000 | Value: 35.00 | | | | |

**200 ESCUDOS** **KM# 665** **Composition:** Copper-Nickel **Subject:** Tanegashima - Site 1st Portuguese Landing in Japan

| Date | Mintage | F | VF | XF | Unc | BU |
|---|---|---|---|---|---|---|
| ND(1993) | 1,000,000 | — | — | 1.50 | 4.50 | — |

**200 ESCUDOS** **KM# 665a** **Weight:** 26.5000 g. **Composition:** 0.9250 Silver .7881 oz. ASW **Subject:** Tanegashima - Site 1st Portuguese Landing in Japan

| Date | Mintage | F | VF | XF | Unc | BU |
|---|---|---|---|---|---|---|
| ND(1993) | 30,000 | — | — | — | 18.50 | — |
| ND(1993) Proof | 22,000 | Value: 35.00 | | | | |

**200 ESCUDOS** **KM# 665b** **Weight:** 27.2000 g. **Composition:** 0.9170 Gold .8020 oz. AGW **Subject:** Tanegashima - 1st Portuguese Ship to Japan

| Date | Mintage | F | VF | XF | Unc | BU |
|---|---|---|---|---|---|---|
| ND(1993) Proof | 7,000 | Value: 600 | | | | |

**200 ESCUDOS** **KM# 666** **Composition:** Copper-Nickel **Subject:** Espingarda **Reverse:** Musket

| Date | Mintage | F | VF | XF | Unc | BU |
|---|---|---|---|---|---|---|
| 1993 | 1,000,000 | — | — | 1.50 | 4.50 | — |

**200 ESCUDOS** **KM# 666a** **Weight:** 26.5000 g. **Composition:** 0.9250 Silver .7881 oz. ASW **Subject:** Espingarda **Reverse:** Musket.

| Date | Mintage | F | VF | XF | Unc | BU |
|---|---|---|---|---|---|---|
| 1993 | 30,000 | — | — | — | 18.50 | — |
| 1993 Proof | 20,000 | Value: 35.00 | | | | |

**200 ESCUDOS** **KM# 666b** **Weight:** 27.2000 g. **Composition:** 0.9170 Gold .8020 oz. AGW **Subject:** Espingarda **Reverse:** Musket

| Date | Mintage | F | VF | XF | Unc | BU |
|---|---|---|---|---|---|---|
| 1993 Proof | 7,000 | Value: 600 | | | | |

**200 ESCUDOS** **KM# 666c** **Weight:** 31.1190 g. **Composition:** 0.9990 Palladium 1.0000 oz. **Subject:** Espingarda **Reverse:** Musket.

| Date | Mintage | F | VF | XF | Unc | BU |
|---|---|---|---|---|---|---|
| 1993 Proof | 2,000 | Value: 775 | | | | |

**200 ESCUDOS** **KM# 667** **Composition:** Copper-Nickel **Reverse:** Enviados Daimos Kiushu

| Date | Mintage | F | VF | XF | Unc | BU |
|---|---|---|---|---|---|---|
| 1993 | 1,000,000 | — | — | 1.50 | 4.50 | — |

**200 ESCUDOS** **KM# 667a** **Weight:** 26.5000 g. **Composition:** 0.9250 Silver .7881 oz. ASW **Reverse:** Enviados Daimos Kiushu.

| Date | Mintage | F | VF | XF | Unc | BU |
|---|---|---|---|---|---|---|
| 1993 | 30,000 | — | — | — | 18.50 | — |
| 1993 Proof | 20,000 | Value: 35.00 | | | | |

**200 ESCUDOS** **KM# 667b** **Weight:** 27.2000 g. **Composition:** 0.9170 Gold .8020 oz. AGW **Reverse:** Enviados Daimos Kiushu.

| Date | Mintage | F | VF | XF | Unc | BU |
|---|---|---|---|---|---|---|
| 1993 Proof | 7,000 | Value: 600 | | | | |

**200 ESCUDOS** **KM# 668** **Composition:** Copper-Nickel **Reverse:** Arte Namban

| Date | Mintage | F | VF | XF | Unc | BU |
|---|---|---|---|---|---|---|
| 1993 | 1,000,000 | — | — | 1.50 | 4.50 | — |

**200 ESCUDOS** **KM# 668a** **Weight:** 26.5000 g. **Composition:** 0.9250 Silver .7881 oz. ASW **Reverse:** Arte Namban.

| Date | Mintage | F | VF | XF | Unc | BU |
|---|---|---|---|---|---|---|
| 1993 | 30,000 | — | — | — | 18.50 | — |
| 1993 Proof | 22,000 | Value: 35.00 | | | | |

**200 ESCUDOS** **KM# 668b** **Weight:** 27.2000 g. **Composition:** 0.9170 Gold .8020 oz. AGW **Reverse:** Arte Namban

| Date | Mintage | F | VF | XF | Unc | BU |
|---|---|---|---|---|---|---|
| 1993 Proof | 7,000 | Value: 600 | | | | |

**200 ESCUDOS** **KM# 668c** **Weight:** 31.1190 g. **Composition:** 0.9990 Platinum 1.000 oz. APW **Reverse:** Arte Namban.

| Date | Mintage | F | VF | XF | Unc | BU |
|---|---|---|---|---|---|---|
| 1993 Proof | 2,000 | Value: 750 | | | | |

**200 ESCUDOS** **KM# 669** **Ring Composition:** Aluminum-Bronze **Center Composition:** Copper-Nickel **Subject:** Lisbon - European Cultural Capital

| Date | Mintage | F | VF | XF | Unc | BU |
|---|---|---|---|---|---|---|
| 1994 | 1,000,000 | — | — | — | 4.50 | — |
| 1994 Proof Sets | 7,000 | — | — | — | 20.00 | — |

**200 ESCUDOS** **KM# 670** **Composition:** Copper-Nickel **Reverse:** Prince Henry the Navigator.

| Date | Mintage | F | VF | XF | Unc | BU |
|---|---|---|---|---|---|---|
| ND(1994) | 750,000 | — | — | — | 5.50 | — |

**200 ESCUDOS** **KM# 670a** **Weight:** 26.5000 g. **Composition:** 0.9250 Silver .7881 oz. ASW **Reverse:** Prince Henry the Navigator.

| Date | Mintage | F | VF | XF | Unc | BU |
|---|---|---|---|---|---|---|
| ND(1994) | 20,000 | — | — | — | 17.50 | — |
| ND(1994) Proof | 13,000 | Value: 27.50 | | | | |

**200 ESCUDOS** **KM# 670b** **Weight:** 27.2000 g. **Composition:** 0.9170 Gold .8020 oz. AGW **Reverse:** Prince Henry the Navigator

| Date | Mintage | F | VF | XF | Unc | BU |
|---|---|---|---|---|---|---|
| ND(1994) Proof | 2,000 | Value: 600 | | | | |

**200 ESCUDOS** **KM# 671** **Composition:** Copper-Nickel **Subject:** Treaty of Tordesilhas

| Date | Mintage | F | VF | XF | Unc | BU |
|---|---|---|---|---|---|---|
| ND(1994) | 750,000 | — | — | — | 5.50 | — |

**200 ESCUDOS** **KM# 671a** **Weight:** 26.5000 g. **Composition:** 0.9250 Silver .7881 oz. ASW **Subject:** Treaty of Tordesilhas.

| Date | Mintage | F | VF | XF | Unc | BU |
|---|---|---|---|---|---|---|
| ND(1994) | 20,000 | — | — | — | 17.50 | — |
| ND(1994) Proof | 13,000 | Value: 27.50 | | | | |

**200 ESCUDOS** **KM# 671b** **Weight:** 27.2000 g. **Composition:** 0.9170 Gold .8020 oz. AGW **Subject:** Treaty of Tordesilhas

| Date | Mintage | F | VF | XF | Unc | BU |
|---|---|---|---|---|---|---|
| ND(1994) Proof | 2,000 | Value: 600 | | | | |

**200 ESCUDOS** **KM# 671c** **Weight:** 31.1190 g. **Composition:** 0.9990 Palladium 1.0000 oz. **Subject:** Treaty of Tordesilhas.

| Date | Mintage | F | VF | XF | Unc | BU |
|---|---|---|---|---|---|---|
| ND(1994) Proof | 1,000 | Value: 800 | | | | |

**200 ESCUDOS** **KM# 672** **Composition:** Copper-Nickel **Subject:** Dividing Up The World

| Date | Mintage | F | VF | XF | Unc | BU |
|---|---|---|---|---|---|---|
| 1994 | 750,000 | — | — | — | 5.50 | — |

**200 ESCUDOS** **KM# 672a** **Weight:** 26.5000 g. **Composition:** 0.9250 Silver .7881 oz. ASW **Subject:** Dividing up the World.

| Date | Mintage | F | VF | XF | Unc | BU |
|---|---|---|---|---|---|---|
| 1994 | 20,000 | — | — | — | 17.50 | — |
| 1994 Proof | 12,000 | Value: 27.50 | | | | |

**200 ESCUDOS** **KM# 672b** **Weight:** 27.2000 g. **Composition:** 0.9170 Gold .8020 oz. AGW **Subject:** Dividing Up The World

| Date | Mintage | F | VF | XF | Unc | BU |
|---|---|---|---|---|---|---|
| 1994 Proof | 3,000 | Value: 600 | | | | |

**200 ESCUDOS** **KM# 673** **Composition:** Copper-Nickel **Reverse:** King John II

| Date | Mintage | F | VF | XF | Unc | BU |
|---|---|---|---|---|---|---|
| ND(1994) | 750,000 | — | — | — | 5.50 | — |

**200 ESCUDOS** **KM# 673a** **Weight:** 26.5000 g. **Composition:** 0.9250 Silver .7881 oz. ASW **Reverse:** King John II.

| Date | Mintage | F | VF | XF | Unc | BU |
|---|---|---|---|---|---|---|
| ND(1994) | 20,000 | — | — | — | 18.50 | — |
| ND(1994) Proof | 13,000 | Value: 37.50 | | | | |

**200 ESCUDOS** **KM# 673b** **Weight:** 27.2000 g. **Composition:** 0.9170 Gold .8020 oz. AGW **Reverse:** King John II

| Date | Mintage | F | VF | XF | Unc | BU |
|---|---|---|---|---|---|---|
| ND(1994) Proof | 2,000 | Value: 600 | | | | |

**200 ESCUDOS** **KM# 673c** **Weight:** 31.1190 g. **Composition:** 0.9990 Platinum 1.0000 oz. APW **Reverse:** King John II.

| Date | Mintage | F | VF | XF | Unc | BU |
|---|---|---|---|---|---|---|
| ND(1994) Proof | 1,000 | Value: 750 | | | | |

**200 ESCUDOS** **KM# 679** **Ring Composition:** Aluminum-Bronze **Center Composition:** Copper Nickel **Subject:** 50th Anniversary - United Nations

| Date | Mintage | F | VF | XF | Unc | BU |
|---|---|---|---|---|---|---|
| 1995 | 500,000 | — | — | — | 5.50 | — |
| 1995 In proof sets only | 17,000 | Value: 20.00 | | | | |

**200 ESCUDOS** KM# 681 **Composition:** Copper-Nickel **Reverse:** Afonso de Albuquerque

| Date | Mintage | F | VF | XF | Unc | BU |
|---|---|---|---|---|---|---|
| 1995 | 750,000 | — | — | — | 5.00 | — |

**200 ESCUDOS** KM# 681a **Weight:** 26.5000 g. **Composition:** 0.9250 Silver .7881 oz. ASW **Reverse:** Afonso de Albuquerque

| Date | Mintage | F | VF | XF | Unc | BU |
|---|---|---|---|---|---|---|
| 1995 | 20,000 | — | — | — | 18.50 | — |
| 1995 Proof | 13,000 | Value: 32.50 | | | | |

**200 ESCUDOS** KM# 681b **Weight:** 27.2000 g. **Composition:** 0.9170 Gold .8016 oz. AGW **Reverse:** Afonso de Albuquerque

| Date | Mintage | F | VF | XF | Unc | BU |
|---|---|---|---|---|---|---|
| 1995 Proof | 4,000 | Value: 500 | | | | |

**200 ESCUDOS** KM# 682 **Composition:** Copper-Nickel **Reverse:** Moluca Islands

| Date | Mintage | F | VF | XF | Unc | BU |
|---|---|---|---|---|---|---|
| 1995 | 750,000 | — | — | — | 5.00 | — |

**200 ESCUDOS** KM# 682a **Weight:** 26.5000 g. **Composition:** 0.9250 Silver .7881 oz. ASW **Reverse:** Moluca Islands.

| Date | Mintage | F | VF | XF | Unc | BU |
|---|---|---|---|---|---|---|
| 1995 | 20,000 | — | — | — | 18.50 | — |
| 1995 Proof | 13,000 | Value: 35.00 | | | | |

**200 ESCUDOS** KM# 682b **Weight:** 27.2000 g. **Composition:** 0.9170 Gold .8016 oz. AGW **Reverse:** Moluca Islands

| Date | Mintage | F | VF | XF | Unc | BU |
|---|---|---|---|---|---|---|
| 1995 Proof | 4,000 | Value: 500 | | | | |

**200 ESCUDOS** KM# 682c **Weight:** 31.1190 g. **Composition:** 0.9995 Palladium 1.0000 oz. **Reverse:** Moluca Islands.

| Date | Mintage | F | VF | XF | Unc | BU |
|---|---|---|---|---|---|---|
| 1995 In proof sets only | 1,000 | Value: 800 | | | | |

**200 ESCUDOS** KM# 683 **Composition:** Copper-Nickel **Reverse:** Solor & Timor Islands

| Date | Mintage | F | VF | XF | Unc | BU |
|---|---|---|---|---|---|---|
| 1995 | 750,000 | — | — | — | 5.00 | — |

**200 ESCUDOS** KM# 683a **Weight:** 26.5000 g. **Composition:** 0.9250 Silver .7881 oz. ASW **Reverse:** Solor & Timor Islands.

| Date | Mintage | F | VF | XF | Unc | BU |
|---|---|---|---|---|---|---|
| 1995 | 20,000 | — | — | — | 18.50 | — |
| 1995 Proof | 13,000 | Value: 35.00 | | | | |

**200 ESCUDOS** KM# 683b **Weight:** 27.2000 g. **Composition:** 0.9170 Gold .8016 oz. AGW **Reverse:** Solar & Timor Islands

| Date | Mintage | F | VF | XF | Unc | BU |
|---|---|---|---|---|---|---|
| 1995 Proof | 4,000 | Value: 500 | | | | |

**200 ESCUDOS** KM# 684 **Composition:** Copper-Nickel **Reverse:** Australia

| Date | Mintage | F | VF | XF | Unc | BU |
|---|---|---|---|---|---|---|
| 1995 | 750,000 | — | — | — | 5.00 | — |

**200 ESCUDOS** KM# 684a **Weight:** 26.5000 g. **Composition:** 0.9250 Silver .7881 oz. ASW **Reverse:** Australia.

| Date | Mintage | F | VF | XF | Unc | BU |
|---|---|---|---|---|---|---|
| 1995 | 20,000 | — | — | — | 18.50 | — |
| 1995 Proof | 13,000 | Value: 35.00 | | | | |

**200 ESCUDOS** KM# 684b **Weight:** 27.2000 g. **Composition:** 0.9170 Gold .8016 oz. AGW **Reverse:** Australia

| Date | Mintage | F | VF | XF | Unc | BU |
|---|---|---|---|---|---|---|
| 1995 Proof | 4,000 | Value: 500 | | | | |

**200 ESCUDOS** KM# 684c **Weight:** 31.1190 g. **Composition:** 0.9995 Platinum 1.0000 oz. APW **Reverse:** Australia.

| Date | Mintage | F | VF | XF | Unc | BU |
|---|---|---|---|---|---|---|
| 1995 In proof sets only | 1,000 | Value: 750 | | | | |

**200 ESCUDOS** KM# 687 **Ring Composition:** Brass **Center Composition:** Copper-Nickel **Subject:** Olympics **Reverse:** High jumper.

| Date | Mintage | F | VF | XF | Unc | BU |
|---|---|---|---|---|---|---|
| 1996 | 7,000 | — | — | — | 5.00 | — |
| 1996 Proof | — | Value: 20.00 | | | | |

**200 ESCUDOS** KM# 687a **Weight:** 26.4500 g. **Composition:** 0.9250 Silver .7866 oz. ASW **Subject:** Olympics **Reverse:** High jumper.

| Date | Mintage | F | VF | XF | Unc | BU |
|---|---|---|---|---|---|---|
| 1996 Proof | 20,000 | Value: 50.00 | | | | |

**200 ESCUDOS** KM# 689 **Composition:** Copper-Nickel **Subject:** 1512 Portugal - Siam Alliance **Reverse:** Portuguese and Siamese arms

| Date | Mintage | F | VF | XF | Unc | BU |
|---|---|---|---|---|---|---|
| 1996 | — | — | — | — | 5.00 | — |

**200 ESCUDOS** KM# 689a **Weight:** 26.5000 g. **Composition:** 0.9250 Silver .7881 oz. ASW **Subject:** 1512 Portugal - Siam Alliance **Reverse:** Portuguese and Siamese arms.

| Date | Mintage | F | VF | XF | Unc | BU |
|---|---|---|---|---|---|---|
| 1996 | 20,000 | — | — | — | 18.50 | — |
| 1996 Proof | 11,000 | Value: 35.00 | | | | |

**200 ESCUDOS** KM# 689b **Weight:** 27.0000 g. **Composition:** 0.9166 Gold .8015 oz. AGW **Subject:** 1512 Portugal - Siam Alliance **Reverse:** Portuguese and Siamese arms.

| Date | Mintage | F | VF | XF | Unc | BU |
|---|---|---|---|---|---|---|
| 1996 Proof | 3,000 | Value: 500 | | | | |

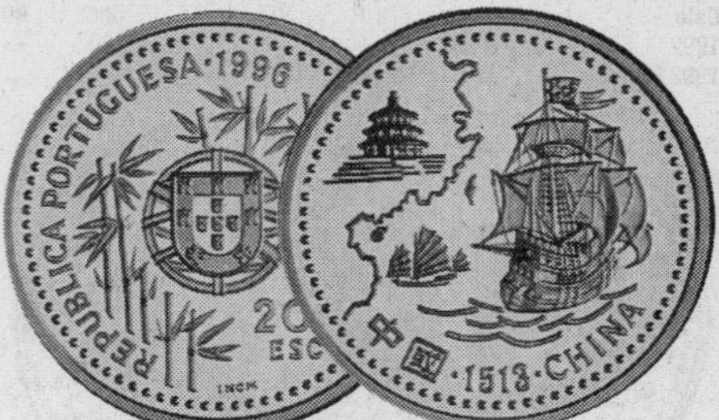


**200 ESCUDOS** KM# 690 **Composition:** Copper-Nickel **Subject:** 1513 Portuguese Arrival in China

| Date | Mintage | F | VF | XF | Unc | BU |
|---|---|---|---|---|---|---|
| 1996 | — | — | — | — | 6.00 | — |

**200 ESCUDOS** KM# 690a **Weight:** 26.5000 g. **Composition:** 0.9250 Silver .7881 oz. ASW **Subject:** 1513 Portuguese Arrival in China

| Date | Mintage | F | VF | XF | Unc | BU |
|---|---|---|---|---|---|---|
| 1996 | 20,000 | — | — | — | 22.50 | — |
| 1996 Proof | 10,000 | Value: 40.00 | | | | |

**200 ESCUDOS** KM# 690b **Weight:** 27.2000 g. **Composition:** 0.9166 Gold .8015 oz. AGW **Subject:** 1513 Portuguese Arrival in China

| Date | Mintage | F | VF | XF | Unc | BU |
|---|---|---|---|---|---|---|
| 1996 Proof | 3,000 | Value: 500 | | | | |

**200 ESCUDOS** KM# 690c **Weight:** 31.1190 g. **Composition:** 0.9995 Palladium 1.0000 oz. **Subject:** 1513 Portuguese Arrival in China

| Date | Mintage | F | VF | XF | Unc | BU |
|---|---|---|---|---|---|---|
| 1996 Proof | 1,000 | Value: 800 | | | | |

**200 ESCUDOS** KM# 691 **Composition:** Copper-Nickel **Subject:** 1557 Portuguese Establishment in Macau

| Date | Mintage | F | VF | XF | Unc | BU |
|---|---|---|---|---|---|---|
| 1996 | — | — | — | — | 5.00 | — |

**200 ESCUDOS** KM# 691a **Weight:** 26.5000 g. **Composition:** 0.9250 Silver .7881 oz. ASW **Subject:** 1557 Portuguese Establishment in Macau

| Date | Mintage | F | VF | XF | Unc | BU |
|---|---|---|---|---|---|---|
| 1996 | 20,000 | — | — | — | 17.50 | — |
| 1996 Proof | 10,000 | Value: 32.50 | | | | |

**200 ESCUDOS** KM# 691b **Weight:** 27.2000 g. **Composition:** 0.9166 Gold .8015 oz. AGW **Subject:** 1557 Portuguese Establishment in Macau

| Date | Mintage | F | VF | XF | Unc | BU |
|---|---|---|---|---|---|---|
| 1996 Proof | 4,000 | Value: 500 | | | | |

**200 ESCUDOS** KM# 692 **Composition:** Copper-Nickel **Subject:** 1582 Portuguese Discovery of Taiwan

| Date | Mintage | F | VF | XF | Unc | BU |
|---|---|---|---|---|---|---|
| 1996 | — | — | — | — | 5.00 | — |

**200 ESCUDOS** KM# 692a **Weight:** 26.5000 g. **Composition:** 0.9250 Silver .7881 oz. ASW **Subject:** 1582 Portuguese Discovery of Taiwan

| Date | Mintage | F | VF | XF | Unc | BU |
|---|---|---|---|---|---|---|
| 1996 | 20,000 | — | — | — | 17.50 | — |
| 1996 Proof | 10,000 | Value: 32.50 | | | | |

**200 ESCUDOS** KM# 692b **Weight:** 27.2000 g. **Composition:** 0.9166 Gold .8015 oz. AGW **Subject:** 1582 Portuguese Discovery of Taiwan

| Date | Mintage | F | VF | XF | Unc | BU |
|---|---|---|---|---|---|---|
| 1996 Proof | 3,000 | Value: 500 | | | | |

**200 ESCUDOS** KM# 692c **Weight:** 31.1190 g. **Composition:** 0.9995 Platinum 1.0000 oz. APW **Subject:** 1582 Portuguese Discovery of Taiwan

| Date | Mintage | F | VF | XF | Unc | BU |
|---|---|---|---|---|---|---|
| 1996 Proof | 1,000 | Value: 750 | | | | |

**200 ESCUDOS** **KM# 694** **Ring Composition:** Copper-Aluminum **Center Composition:** Copper-Nickel **Subject:** Lisbon World Expo '98 **Obverse:** National arms and denomination **Reverse:** Dolphins

| Date | Mintage | F | VF | XF | Unc | BU |
|---|---|---|---|---|---|---|
| 1997 | — | — | — | — | 5.00 | — |
| 1997 In proof sets only | 7,000 | Value: 20.00 | | | | |

**200 ESCUDOS** **KM# 697** **Composition:** Copper-Nickel **Obverse:** National arms **Reverse:** S. Francisco Xavier

| Date | Mintage | F | VF | XF | Unc | BU |
|---|---|---|---|---|---|---|
| 1997 | — | — | — | — | 5.00 | — |

**200 ESCUDOS** **KM# 697a** **Weight:** 26.5000 g. **Composition:** 0.9250 Silver .7881 oz. ASW **Obverse:** National arms. **Reverse:** S. Francisco Xavier.

| Date | Mintage | F | VF | XF | Unc | BU |
|---|---|---|---|---|---|---|
| 1997 | 25,000 | — | — | — | 20.00 | — |
| 1997 Proof | 25,000 | Value: 35.00 | | | | |

**200 ESCUDOS** **KM# 697b** **Weight:** 27.2000 g. **Composition:** 0.9167 Gold .8017 oz. AGW **Obverse:** National arms. **Reverse:** S Francisco Xavier

| Date | Mintage | F | VF | XF | Unc | BU |
|---|---|---|---|---|---|---|
| 1997 Proof | 4,000 | Value: 500 | | | | |

**200 ESCUDOS** **KM# 698** **Composition:** Copper-Nickel **Obverse:** National arms **Reverse:** Pe. Luis Frois - Japanese Man

| Date | Mintage | F | VF | XF | Unc | BU |
|---|---|---|---|---|---|---|
| 1997 | — | — | — | — | 5.00 | — |

**200 ESCUDOS** **KM# 698a** **Weight:** 26.5000 g. **Composition:** 0.9250 Silver .7881 oz. ASW **Obverse:** National arms. **Reverse:** Pe. Luis Frois - Japanese Man.

| Date | Mintage | F | VF | XF | Unc | BU |
|---|---|---|---|---|---|---|
| 1997 | 25,000 | — | — | — | 20.00 | — |
| 1997 Proof | 24,000 | Value: 35.00 | | | | |

**200 ESCUDOS** **KM# 698b** **Weight:** 27.2000 g. **Composition:** 0.9167 Gold .8017 oz. AGW **Obverse:** National arms. **Reverse:** Pe. Luis Frois - Japanese Man.

| Date | Mintage | F | VF | XF | Unc | BU |
|---|---|---|---|---|---|---|
| 1997 Proof | 5,000 | Value: 500 | | | | |

**200 ESCUDOS** **KM# 699** **Composition:** Copper-Nickel **Obverse:** National arms and map of South America **Reverse:** Bto. Jose de Anchieta

| Date | Mintage | F | VF | XF | Unc | BU |
|---|---|---|---|---|---|---|
| 1997 | — | — | — | — | 5.00 | — |

**200 ESCUDOS** **KM# 699a** **Weight:** 26.5000 g. **Composition:** 0.9250 Silver .7881 oz. ASW **Obverse:** National arms and map of South America. **Reverse:** Bto. Jose de Anchieta.

| Date | Mintage | F | VF | XF | Unc | BU |
|---|---|---|---|---|---|---|
| 1997 | 25,000 | — | — | — | 20.00 | — |
| 1997 Proof | 24,000 | Value: 35.00 | | | | |

**200 ESCUDOS** **KM# 699b** **Weight:** 27.2000 g. **Composition:** 0.9167 Gold .8017 oz. AGW **Obverse:** National arms and map of South America. **Reverse:** Bto. Jose de Anchieta.

| Date | Mintage | F | VF | XF | Unc | BU |
|---|---|---|---|---|---|---|
| 1997 Proof | 4,000 | Value: 500 | | | | |

**200 ESCUDOS** **KM# 699c** **Weight:** 31.1190 g. **Composition:** 0.9995 Palladium 1.0000 oz. **Obverse:** National arms and map of South America. **Reverse:** Bt. Jose de Anchieta.

| Date | Mintage | F | VF | XF | Unc | BU |
|---|---|---|---|---|---|---|
| 1997 Proof | 1,000 | Value: 800 | | | | |

**200 ESCUDOS** **KM# 700** **Composition:** Copper-Nickel **Obverse:** National cross and arms **Reverse:** Irmao Bento de Gois - Map of China's Coast

| Date | Mintage | F | VF | XF | Unc | BU |
|---|---|---|---|---|---|---|
| 1997 | — | — | — | — | 5.00 | — |

**200 ESCUDOS** **KM# 700a** **Weight:** 26.5000 g. **Composition:** 0.9250 Silver .7881 oz. ASW **Obverse:** National cross and arms. **Reverse:** Irmao Bento de Gois - Map of China's Coast.

| Date | Mintage | F | VF | XF | Unc | BU |
|---|---|---|---|---|---|---|
| 1997 | 25,000 | — | — | — | 20.00 | — |
| 1997 Proof | 24,000 | Value: 35.00 | | | | |

**200 ESCUDOS** **KM# 700b** **Weight:** 27.2000 g. **Composition:** 0.9160 Gold .8017 oz. AGW **Obverse:** National cross and arms. **Reverse:** Irmao Bento de Gois - Map of China's Coast

| Date | Mintage | F | VF | XF | Unc | BU |
|---|---|---|---|---|---|---|
| 1997 Proof | 4,000 | Value: 500 | | | | |

**200 ESCUDOS** **KM# 700c** **Weight:** 31.1190 g. **Composition:** 0.9995 Platinum 1.0000 oz. APW **Obverse:** National cross and arms. **Reverse:** Irmao Bento de Gois - Map of China's Coast.

| Date | Mintage | F | VF | XF | Unc | BU |
|---|---|---|---|---|---|---|
| 1997 Proof | 1,000 | Value: 900 | | | | |

**200 ESCUDOS** **KM# 706** **Ring Composition:** Aluminum-Bronze **Center Composition:** Copper-Nickel **Subject:** International Year of the Oceans Expo **Obverse:** Arms above denominations

| Date | Mintage | F | VF | XF | Unc | BU |
|---|---|---|---|---|---|---|
| 1998 | Est. 50,000 | — | — | — | 4.00 | — |
| 1998 In proof sets only | Est. 20,000 | Value: 12.00 | | | | |

**200 ESCUDOS** **KM# 709** **Composition:** Copper-Nickel **Obverse:** 3 ships, arms and denomination **Reverse:** Portrait of Vasco Da Gama, dates

| Date | Mintage | F | VF | XF | Unc | BU |
|---|---|---|---|---|---|---|
| 1998 | — | — | — | — | 5.00 | — |

**200 ESCUDOS** **KM# 709a** **Weight:** 26.5000 g. **Composition:** 0.9250 Silver .7881 oz. ASW **Obverse:** 3 ships, arms and denomination. **Reverse:** Bust of Vasco da Gama left, dates.

| Date | Mintage | F | VF | XF | Unc | BU |
|---|---|---|---|---|---|---|
| 1998 Proof | 25,000 | Value: 35.00 | | | | |

**200 ESCUDOS** **KM# 709b** **Weight:** 27.2000 g. **Composition:** 0.9167 Gold .8017 oz. AGW **Obverse:** 3 ships, arms and denomination. **Reverse:** Bust of Vasco Da Gama left, dates.

| Date | Mintage | F | VF | XF | Unc | BU |
|---|---|---|---|---|---|---|
| 1998 Proof | 5,000 | Value: 500 | | | | |

**200 ESCUDOS** **KM# 709c** **Weight:** 31.1190 g. **Composition:** 0.9995 Platinum 1.0000 oz. APW **Obverse:** 3 ships, arms and denomination. **Reverse:** Bust of Vasco da Gama, dates.

| Date | Mintage | F | VF | XF | Unc | BU |
|---|---|---|---|---|---|---|
| 1998 Proof | 1,000 | Value: 900 | | | | |

**200 ESCUDOS** **KM# 710** **Composition:** Copper-Nickel **Subject:** Discovery of Africa **Obverse:** Arms, ship and palm tree. **Reverse:** Ship, map, and hunter

| Date | Mintage | F | VF | XF | Unc | BU |
|---|---|---|---|---|---|---|
| 1998 | — | — | — | — | 5.00 | — |

**200 ESCUDOS** **KM# 710a** **Weight:** 26.5000 g. **Composition:** 0.9250 Silver .7881 oz. ASW **Subject:** Discovery of Africa **Obverse:** Arms, ship and palm tree. **Reverse:** Ship, map, and hunter.

| Date | Mintage | F | VF | XF | Unc | BU |
|---|---|---|---|---|---|---|
| 1998 | 25,000 | — | — | — | 18.50 | — |
| 1998 Proof | 26,000 | Value: 32.50 | | | | |

**200 ESCUDOS** **KM# 710b** **Weight:** 27.2000 g. **Composition:** 0.9167 Gold .8017 oz. AGW **Subject:** Discovery of Africa **Obverse:** Arms, ship and palm tree. **Reverse:** Ship, map, and hunter.

| Date | Mintage | F | VF | XF | Unc | BU |
|---|---|---|---|---|---|---|
| 1998 Proof | 5,000 | Value: 500 | | | | |

**200 ESCUDOS** **KM# 711** **Composition:** Copper-Nickel **Subject:** Mozambique **Obverse:** Arms above mermaid **Reverse:** 2 ships and island map

| Date | Mintage | F | VF | XF | Unc | BU |
|---|---|---|---|---|---|---|
| 1998 | — | — | — | — | 5.00 | — |

**200 ESCUDOS** **KM# 711a** **Weight:** 26.5000 g. **Composition:** 0.9250 Silver .7881 oz. ASW **Subject:** Mozambique **Obverse:** Arms above mermaid. **Reverse:** 2 ships and island map.

| Date | Mintage | F | VF | XF | Unc | BU |
|---|---|---|---|---|---|---|
| 1998 | 25,000 | — | — | — | 20.00 | — |
| 1998 Proof | 25,000 | Value: 35.00 | | | | |

**200 ESCUDOS** **KM# 711b** **Weight:** 27.2000 g. **Composition:** 0.9167 Gold .8017 oz. AGW **Subject:** Mozambique **Obverse:** Arms above mermaid. **Reverse:** 2 ships and island map.

| Date | Mintage | F | VF | XF | Unc | BU |
|---|---|---|---|---|---|---|
| 1998 Proof | 6,000 | Value: 500 | | | | |

**200 ESCUDOS** **KM# 712** **Composition:** Copper-Nickel **Subject:** India 1498 **Obverse:** Arms and sailing ship. **Reverse:** Ship and coastal map of India

| Date | Mintage | F | VF | XF | Unc | BU |
|---|---|---|---|---|---|---|
| 1998 | — | — | — | — | 5.00 | — |

**200 ESCUDOS** **KM# 712a** **Weight:** 26.5000 g. **Composition:** 0.9250 Silver .7881 oz. ASW **Subject:** India 1498 **Obverse:** Arms and sailboat. **Reverse:** Ship and coastal map of India.

| Date | Mintage | F | VF | XF | Unc | BU |
|---|---|---|---|---|---|---|
| 1998 | 25,000 | — | — | — | 20.00 | — |
| 1998 Proof | 25,000 | Value: 35.00 | | | | |

**200 ESCUDOS** **KM# 712b** **Weight:** 27.2000 g. **Composition:** 0.9167 Gold .8017 oz. AGW **Subject:** India 1498 **Obverse:** Arms and sailing ship. **Reverse:** Ship and coastal map of India.

| Date | Mintage | F | VF | XF | Unc | BU |
|---|---|---|---|---|---|---|
| 1998 Proof | 5,000 | Value: 500 | | | | |

**200 ESCUDOS** **KM# 712c** **Weight:** 31.1190 g. **Composition:** 0.9995 Palladium 1.0000 oz. **Subject:** India 1498 **Obverse:** Arms and sailing ship. **Reverse:** Ship and coastal map of India.

| Date | Mintage | F | VF | XF | Unc | BU |
|---|---|---|---|---|---|---|
| 1998 Proof | 1,000 | Value: 800 | | | | |

**200 ESCUDOS** **KM# 716** **Composition:** Copper-Nickel 1.0000 oz. **Subject:** Death on the Sea **Obverse:** National arms and ropes **Reverse:** Stylized sinking ship **Edge:** Reeded

| Date | Mintage | F | VF | XF | Unc | BU |
|---|---|---|---|---|---|---|
| 1999 | — | — | — | — | 4.00 | — |

**200 ESCUDOS** **KM# 716a** **Weight:** 26.5000 g. **Composition:** 0.9250 Silver .7881 oz. ASW **Subject:** Death on the Sea **Obverse:** National arms and ropes **Reverse:** Stylized sinking ship **Edge:** Reeded **Size:** 36 mm.

| Date | Mintage | F | VF | XF | Unc | BU |
|---|---|---|---|---|---|---|
| 1999 | 10,000 | — | — | — | 20.00 | — |
| 1999 Proof | 10,000 | Value: 35.00 | | | | |

**200 ESCUDOS** **KM# 716b** **Weight:** 27.2000 g. **Composition:** 0.9167 Gold .8017 oz. AGW **Subject:** Death on the Sea **Obverse:** National arms and ropes. **Reverse:** Stylized sinking ship. **Edge:** Reeded. **Size:** 36 mm.

| Date | Mintage | F | VF | XF | Unc | BU |
|---|---|---|---|---|---|---|
| 1999 Proof | 1,000 | Value: 450 | | | | |

**200 ESCUDOS** **KM# 717** **Composition:** Copper-Nickel **Subject:** Brasil 1500. **Obverse:** Fleet of sailing ships. **Reverse:** Head of Pedro Alvares Cabral right.

| Date | Mintage | F | VF | XF | Unc | BU |
|---|---|---|---|---|---|---|
| 1999 | — | — | — | — | 4.00 | — |

**200 ESCUDOS** **KM# 717a** **Weight:** 26.5000 g. **Composition:** 0.9250 Silver .7881 oz. ASW **Subject:** Brasil 1500. **Obverse:** Fleet of sailing ships. **Reverse:** Head of Pedro Alvares Cabral right.

| Date | Mintage | F | VF | XF | Unc | BU |
|---|---|---|---|---|---|---|
| 1999 | 1,000 | — | — | — | 20.00 | — |
| 1999 Proof | 1,000 | Value: 35.00 | | | | |

**200 ESCUDOS** **KM# 717b** **Weight:** 27.2000 g. **Composition:** 0.9167 Gold .8017 oz. AGW **Subject:** Brasil 1500. **Obverse:** Fleet of sailing ships. **Reverse:** Head of Pedro alvares Cabral.

| Date | Mintage | F | VF | XF | Unc | BU |
|---|---|---|---|---|---|---|
| 1999 Proof | 1,000 | Value: 450 | | | | |

**200 ESCUDOS** **KM# 718** **Composition:** Copper-Nickel **Subject:** Brasil **Obverse:** Natives, palm trees. **Reverse:** Ship, native and map.

| Date | Mintage | F | VF | XF | Unc | BU |
|---|---|---|---|---|---|---|
| 1999 | — | — | — | — | 4.00 | — |

**200 ESCUDOS** **KM# 718a** **Weight:** 26.5000 g. **Composition:** 0.9250 Silver .7881 oz. ASW **Subject:** Brasil. **Obverse:** Natives, palm trees. **Reverse:** Ship, native and map.

| Date | Mintage | F | VF | XF | Unc | BU |
|---|---|---|---|---|---|---|
| 1999 | Est. 10,000 | — | — | — | 20.00 | — |
| 1999 Proof | Est. 10,000 | Value: 35.00 | | | | |

**200 ESCUDOS** **KM# 718b** **Weight:** 27.2000 g. **Composition:** 0.9167 Gold .8017 oz. AGW **Subject:** Brasil. **Obverse:** Natives and palm trees. **Reverse:** Ship, native and map.

| Date | Mintage | F | VF | XF | Unc | BU |
|---|---|---|---|---|---|---|
| 1999 Proof | 1,000 | Value: 450 | | | | |

**200 ESCUDOS** **KM# 719** **Composition:** Copper-Nickel **Subject:** Duarte Pacheco Pereira **Reverse:** Armored 1/2 -length bust of Duarte Pacheco Pereira facing

| Date | Mintage | F | VF | XF | Unc | BU |
|---|---|---|---|---|---|---|
| 1999 | — | — | — | — | 4.00 | — |

**200 ESCUDOS** **KM# 719a** **Weight:** 26.5000 g. **Composition:** 0.9250 Silver .7881 oz. ASW **Subject:** Duarte Pacheco Pereira **Reverse:** Armored 1/2-length bust of Duarte Pacheco Pereira facing.

| Date | Mintage | F | VF | XF | Unc | BU |
|---|---|---|---|---|---|---|
| 1999 | 1,000 | — | — | — | 20.00 | — |
| 1999 Proof | 1,000 | Value: 35.00 | | | | |

**200 ESCUDOS** **KM# 719b** **Weight:** 27.2000 g. **Composition:** 0.9167 Gold .8017 oz. AGW **Subject:** Duarte Pacheco Pereira **Reverse:** Armored 1/2-length bust of Duarte Pacheco Pereira facing.

| Date | Mintage | F | VF | XF | Unc | BU |
|---|---|---|---|---|---|---|
| 1999 Proof | 1,000 | Value: 450 | | | | |

**200 ESCUDOS** **KM# 720** **Ring Composition:** Brass **Center Composition:** Copper-Nickel **Obverse:** National arms above denominations **Reverse:** Push toy and logo **Edge:** Reeded and plain sections

| Date | Mintage | F | VF | XF | Unc | BU |
|---|---|---|---|---|---|---|
| 1999 | — | — | — | — | 3.50 | — |

**200 ESCUDOS** **KM# 726** **Ring Composition:** Nickel-Brass **Center Composition:** Copper-Nickel **Obverse:** Torch, arms and denomination **Reverse:** Olympic logo **Edge:** Reeded and plain sections

| Date | Mintage | F | VF | XF | Unc | BU |
|---|---|---|---|---|---|---|
| 2000 | 10,000 | — | — | — | 4.00 | — |
| 2000 Proof | 5,000 | Value: 7.50 | | | | |

**200 ESCUDOS** **KM# 728** **Weight:** 21.1000 g. **Composition:** Copper-Nickel **Subject:** Terra Do Lavrado **Obverse:** National arms, compass, etc. **Reverse:** Labrador coast and ship **Edge:** Reeded **Size:** 36 mm.

| Date | Mintage | F | VF | XF | Unc | BU |
|---|---|---|---|---|---|---|
| 2000 | — | — | — | — | 4.00 | — |

**200 ESCUDOS** **KM# 728a** **Weight:** 26.5000 g. **Composition:** 0.9250 Silver .7881 oz. ASW **Subject:** Terra do Lavrado **Obverse:** National arms, compass, etc. **Obv. Legend:** Labrador coast and ship. **Edge:** Reeded. **Size:** 36 mm.

| Date | Mintage | F | VF | XF | Unc | BU |
|---|---|---|---|---|---|---|
| 2000 | Est. 10,000 | — | — | — | 25.00 | — |
| 2000 Proof | Est. 10,000 | Value: 37.50 | | | | |

**200 ESCUDOS** **KM# 728b** **Weight:** 27.2000 g. **Composition:** 0.9166 Gold .8016 oz. AGW **Subject:** Terra Do Lavrado **Obverse:** National arms, compass, etc. **Reverse:** Labrador coast and ship. **Edge:** Reeded. **Size:** 36 mm.

| Date | Mintage | F | VF | XF | Unc | BU |
|---|---|---|---|---|---|---|
| 2000 Proof | Est. 1,375 | Value: 500 | | | | |

**200 ESCUDOS** **KM# 729** **Weight:** 21.1400 g. **Composition:** Copper-Nickel **Subject:** Terra Dos Corte-Real **Obverse:** Cross above national arms **Reverse:** Ship above 1501-1502 **Edge:** Reeded **Size:** 36 mm.

| Date | Mintage | F | VF | XF | Unc | BU |
|---|---|---|---|---|---|---|
| 2000 | — | — | — | — | 4.00 | — |

**200 ESCUDOS** **KM# 729a** **Weight:** 26.5000 g. **Composition:** 0.9250 Silver .7881 oz. ASW **Subject:** Terra Dos Corte-Real **Obverse:** Cross above national arms. **Reverse:** Ship above 1501-1502. **Edge:** Reeded. **Size:** 36 mm.

| Date | Mintage | F | VF | XF | Unc | BU |
|---|---|---|---|---|---|---|
| 2000 | Est. 10,000 | — | — | — | 25.00 | — |
| 2000 Proof | Est. 10,000 | Value: 37.50 | | | | |

**200 ESCUDOS** **KM# 729b** **Weight:** 27.2000 g. **Composition:** 0.9166 Gold .8016 oz. AGW **Subject:** Terra Dos Corte-Real **Obverse:** Cross above national arms. **Reverse:** Ship above 1501-1502.

| Date | Mintage | F | VF | XF | Unc | BU |
|---|---|---|---|---|---|---|
| 2000 Proof | Est. 1,375 | Value: 500 | | | | |

**200 ESCUDOS** **KM# 729c** **Weight:** 31.1190 g. **Composition:** 0.9995 Palladium 1.0000 oz. **Subject:** Terra Dos Corte-Real **Obverse:** Cross above national arms. **Reverse:** Ship above 1501-1502. **Edge:** Reeded.

| Date | Mintage | F | VF | XF | Unc | BU |
|---|---|---|---|---|---|---|
| 2000 Proof | Est. 250 | Value: 900 | | | | |

**200 ESCUDOS** **KM# 730** **Weight:** 21.1400 g. **Composition:** Copper-Nickel **Subject:** Terra Florida **Obverse:** National arms above compass **Reverse:** Ship and Florida coast **Edge:** Reeded **Size:** 36 mm.

| Date | Mintage | F | VF | XF | Unc | BU |
|---|---|---|---|---|---|---|
| 2000 | — | — | — | — | 4.00 | — |

**200 ESCUDOS** **KM# 730a** **Weight:** 26.5000 g. **Composition:** 0.9250 Silver .7881 oz. ASW **Subject:** Terra Florida **Obverse:** National arms above compass. **Reverse:** Ship and Florida coast. **Edge:** Reeded.

| Date | Mintage | F | VF | XF | Unc | BU |
|---|---|---|---|---|---|---|
| 2000 | Est. 10,000 | — | — | — | 25.00 | — |
| 2000 Proof | Est. 10,000 | Value: 37.50 | | | | |

**200 ESCUDOS** **KM# 730b** **Weight:** 27.2000 g. **Composition:** 0.9166 Gold .8016 oz. AGW **Obverse:** National arms above compass. **Reverse:** Ship and Florida coast. **Edge:** Reeded. **Edge Lettering:** Terra Florida.

| Date | Mintage | F | VF | XF | Unc | BU |
|---|---|---|---|---|---|---|
| 2000 Proof | Est. 1,375 | Value: 500 | | | | |

**200 ESCUDOS** **KM# 731** **Weight:** 21.1400 g. **Composition:** Copper-Nickel **Subject:** Fernao De Magalhaes **Obverse:** National arms, ship, and denomination **Reverse:** Bearded portrait **Edge:** Reeded **Size:** 36 mm.

| Date | Mintage | F | VF | XF | Unc | BU |
|---|---|---|---|---|---|---|
| 2000 | — | — | — | — | 4.00 | — |

**200 ESCUDOS** **KM# 731a** **Weight:** 26.5000 g. **Composition:** 0.9250 Silver .7881 oz. ASW **Subject:** Fernao de Magalhaes **Obverse:** National arms, ship, and denomination. **Reverse:** Bearded portrait. **Edge:** Reeded.

| Date | Mintage | F | VF | XF | Unc | BU |
|---|---|---|---|---|---|---|
| 2000 | Est. 10,000 | — | — | — | 25.00 | — |

**200 ESCUDOS** **KM# 731b** **Weight:** 27.2000 g. **Composition:** 0.9166 Gold .8016 oz. AGW **Subject:** Fernao de Magalhaes **Obverse:** National arms, ship, and denomination. **Reverse:** Bearded portrait. **Edge:** Reeded.

| Date | Mintage | F | VF | XF | Unc | BU |
|---|---|---|---|---|---|---|
| 2000 Proof | Est. 1,375 | Value: 500 | | | | |

**200 ESCUDOS** **KM# 731c** **Weight:** 31.1190 g. **Composition:** 0.9995 Platinum 1.0000 oz. APW **Subject:** Fernao de Magalhaes **Obverse:** National arms, ship, and denomination. **Reverse:** Bearded portrait. **Edge:** Reeded.

| Date | Mintage | F | VF | XF | Unc | BU |
|---|---|---|---|---|---|---|
| 2000 Proof | Est. 250 | Value: 1,000 | | | | |

**250 ESCUDOS** **KM# 604** **Weight:** 25.0000 g. **Composition:** 0.6800 Silver .5466 oz. ASW **Subject:** 1974 Revolution

| Date | Mintage | F | VF | XF | Unc | BU |
|---|---|---|---|---|---|---|
| ND(1976) | 950,000 | — | — | 6.00 | 10.00 | — |
| ND(1976) Proof | 10,000 | Value: 18.50 | | | | |

**250 ESCUDOS** **KM# 626** **Composition:** Copper-Nickel **Subject:** World Fisheries Conference

| Date | Mintage | F | VF | XF | Unc | BU |
|---|---|---|---|---|---|---|
| ND(1984) | 24,000 | — | — | 30.00 | 65.00 | — |

**250 ESCUDOS** **KM# 626a** **Weight:** 23.0000 g. **Composition:** 0.9250 Silver .6841 oz. ASW **Edge Lettering:** World Fisheries Conference.

| Date | Mintage | F | VF | XF | Unc | BU |
|---|---|---|---|---|---|---|
| ND(1984) Proof | 8,000 | Value: 120 | | | | |

**250 ESCUDOS** **KM# 643** **Composition:** Copper-Nickel **Subject:** Seoul Olympics **Reverse:** Runners

| Date | Mintage | F | VF | XF | Unc | BU |
|---|---|---|---|---|---|---|
| 1988 | 850,000 | — | — | 2.50 | 5.00 | — |

**250 ESCUDOS** **KM# 643a** **Weight:** 28.0000 g. **Composition:** 0.9250 Silver .8327 oz. ASW **Subject:** Seoul Olympics **Obv. Legend:** Runners.

| Date | Mintage | F | VF | XF | Unc | BU |
|---|---|---|---|---|---|---|
| 1988 | 70,000 | — | — | — | 16.00 | — |
| 1988 Proof | 30,000 | Value: 28.50 | | | | |

**250 ESCUDOS** **KM# 650** **Composition:** Copper-Nickel **Subject:** 850th Anniversary - Founding of Portugal

| Date | Mintage | F | VF | XF | Unc | BU |
|---|---|---|---|---|---|---|
| 1989 | 750,000 | — | — | 2.50 | 5.00 | — |

**250 ESCUDOS** **KM# 650a** **Weight:** 28.0000 g. **Composition:** 0.9250 Silver .8327 oz. ASW **Subject:** 850th Anniversary - Founding of Portugal.

| Date | Mintage | F | VF | XF | Unc | BU |
|---|---|---|---|---|---|---|
| 1989 | 15,000 | — | — | — | 22.50 | — |
| 1989 Proof | 30,000 | Value: 40.00 | | | | |

**500 ESCUDOS** **KM# 620** **Weight:** 7.0000 g. **Composition:** 0.8350 Silver .1879 oz. ASW **Subject:** XVII European Art Exhibition

| Date | Mintage | F | VF | XF | Unc | BU |
|---|---|---|---|---|---|---|
| 1983 | 200,000 | — | — | 6.00 | 12.00 | — |
| 1983 Proof | 8,500 | Value: 30.00 | | | | |

**500 ESCUDOS** **KM# 686a** **Weight:** 7.0000 g. **Composition:** 0.8350 Silver .1879 oz. ASW **Subject:** 800th Anniversary - Birth of Saint Anthony

| Date | Mintage | F | VF | XF | Unc | BU |
|---|---|---|---|---|---|---|
| 1995 | — | — | — | — | 8.50 | — |

**500 ESCUDOS** **KM# 686b** **Weight:** 14.0000 g. **Composition:** 0.9250 Silver .4163 oz. ASW **Subject:** 800th Anniversary - Birth of Saint Anthony

| Date | Mintage | F | VF | XF | Unc | BU |
|---|---|---|---|---|---|---|
| 1995 Proof | 10,000 | Value: 45.00 | | | | |

**500 ESCUDOS** **KM# 686c** **Weight:** 17.5000 g. **Composition:** 0.9177 Gold .5159 oz. AGW **Subject:** 800th Anniversary - Birth of Saint Anthony

| Date | Mintage | F | VF | XF | Unc | BU |
|---|---|---|---|---|---|---|
| 1995 Proof | 5,000 | Value: 325 | | | | |

**500 ESCUDOS** **KM# 702** **Weight:** 13.8700 g. **Composition:** 0.5000 Silver .2230 oz. ASW **Obverse:** National arms **Reverse:** Bank seal - Banco de Portugal

| Date | Mintage | F | VF | XF | Unc | BU |
|---|---|---|---|---|---|---|
| ND(1996) | — | — | — | — | 8.50 | — |

**500 ESCUDOS** **KM# 701** **Composition:** Copper-Nickel **Obverse:** National arms superimposed on radiant sun **Reverse:** Head of Padre Antonio Vieira facing.

| Date | Mintage | F | VF | XF | Unc | BU |
|---|---|---|---|---|---|---|
| ND(1997) | — | — | — | — | 5.50 | — |

**500 ESCUDOS** **KM# 701a** **Weight:** 14.0000 g. **Composition:** 0.9250 Silver .4051 oz. ASW **Obverse:** National arms superimposed on radiant sun. **Reverse:** Head of Padre Antonio Vieira facing.

| Date | Mintage | F | VF | XF | Unc | BU |
|---|---|---|---|---|---|---|
| ND(1997) Proof | — | Value: 37.50 | | | | |

**500 ESCUDOS** **KM# 701b** **Composition:** Silver And Gold **Obverse:** National arms superimposed on radiant sun. **Reverse:** Head of Padre Antonio Vieira facing. **Note:** 14.0000 gram, .925 Silver, .4051 ounce with 3.1000 gram .9167 gold, .0914 ounce lamination on reverse.

| Date | Mintage | F | VF | XF | Unc | BU |
|---|---|---|---|---|---|---|
| ND(1997) Proof | 15,000 | Value: 125 | | | | |

**500 ESCUDOS** **KM# 705** **Weight:** 14.0000 g. **Composition:** 0.9250 Silver .4164 oz. ASW **Obverse:** Arms and denomination **Reverse:** Vasco Da Gama Bridge

| Date | Mintage | F | VF | XF | Unc | BU |
|---|---|---|---|---|---|---|
| 1998 | — | — | — | — | 6.50 | — |
| 1998 Proof | 30,000 | Value: 42.50 | | | | |

**500 ESCUDOS** **KM# 705a** **Ring Composition:** Silver **Center Composition:** Gold **Obverse:** Arms and denomination **Reverse:** Vasco Da Gama Bridge **Note:** 14.000 gram, .925 Silver, .4164 ounce with 3.1000 gram .9167 gold, .0914 ounce lamination on reverse.

| Date | Mintage | F | VF | XF | Unc | BU |
|---|---|---|---|---|---|---|
| 1998 Proof | 15,000 | Value: 125 | | | | |

**500 ESCUDOS** **KM# 723** **Weight:** 14.0000 g. **Composition:** 0.5000 Silver .2236 oz. ASW **Subject:** Macao's Return to China **Obverse:** Partial bridge above arms **Reverse:** Bridge above monument **Edge:** Reeded

| Date | Mintage | F | VF | XF | Unc | BU |
|---|---|---|---|---|---|---|
| 1999 | — | — | — | — | 5.50 | — |

**500 ESCUDOS** **KM# 725** **Weight:** 14.0000 g. **Composition:** 0.0925 Silver .4164 oz. ASW **Subject:** Eca de Queiroz **Obverse:** National arms and denomination **Reverse:** Stylized portrait of Eca de Gueiroz **Edge:** Reeded

| Date | Mintage | F | VF | XF | Unc | BU |
|---|---|---|---|---|---|---|
| ND(2000) | 450,000 | — | — | — | 8.50 | — |
| ND(2000) Proof | 10,000 | Value: 45.00 | | | | |

**500 ESCUDOS** **KM# 725a** **Weight:** 14.0000 g. **Composition:** 0.9250 Silver .4164 oz. ASW **Subject:** Eca de Queiroz **Obverse:** National arms above denomination **Reverse:** Stylized portrait of Eca de Queiroz **Edge:** Reeded **Note:** 14.000 gram, .925 Silver, .4164 ounce with 3.1000 gram .9167 gold, .1000 ounce lamination on reverse.

| Date | Mintage | F | VF | XF | Unc | BU |
|---|---|---|---|---|---|---|
| ND(2000) Proof | 10,000 | Value: 125 | | | | |

**500 ESCUDOS** **KM# 733** **Weight:** 13.9600 g. **Composition:** 0.5000 Silver .2244 oz. ASW **Subject:** European Culture Capital **Obverse:** National arms and denomination **Reverse:** Stylized design **Edge:** Reeded **Size:** 30.1 mm.

| Date | Mintage | F | VF | XF | Unc | BU |
|---|---|---|---|---|---|---|
| 2001 | — | — | — | — | 6.50 | — |

**750 ESCUDOS** **KM# 621** **Weight:** 12.5000 g. **Composition:** 0.8350 Silver .3356 oz. ASW **Subject:** XVII European Art Exhibition

| Date | Mintage | F | VF | XF | Unc | BU |
|---|---|---|---|---|---|---|
| 1983 | 200,000 | — | — | 6.50 | 13.50 | — |
| 1983 Proof | 8,500 | Value: 35.00 | | | | |

**1000 ESCUDOS** **KM# 622** **Weight:** 21.0000 g. **Composition:** 0.8350 Silver .5638 oz. ASW **Subject:** XVII European Art Exhibition

| Date | Mintage | F | VF | XF | Unc | BU |
|---|---|---|---|---|---|---|
| 1983 | 200,000 | — | — | 7.50 | 16.50 | — |
| 1983 Proof | 8,500 | Value: 40.00 | | | | |

**1000 ESCUDOS** **KM# 611** **Weight:** 17.0000 g. **Composition:** 0.9250 Silver .5056 oz. ASW **Subject:** 400th Anniversary - Death of Louis de Camoes

| Date | Mintage | F | VF | XF | Unc | BU |
|---|---|---|---|---|---|---|
| ND(1983) | 150,000 | — | — | — | 16.50 | — |
| ND(1983) Proof | 10,000 | Value: 42.50 | | | | |

**1000 ESCUDOS** **KM# 657** **Weight:** 27.0000 g. **Composition:** 0.5000 Silver .4340 oz. ASW **Subject:** Ibero - American Series

| Date | Mintage | F | VF | XF | Unc | BU |
|---|---|---|---|---|---|---|
| ND(1992) | 326,000 | — | — | — | 17.50 | — |

**1000 ESCUDOS** **KM# 657a** **Weight:** 27.0000 g. **Composition:** 0.9250 Silver .8029 oz. ASW **Subject:** Ibero - American Series

| Date | Mintage | F | VF | XF | Unc | BU |
|---|---|---|---|---|---|---|
| ND(1992) Proof | 30,000 | Value: 50.00 | | | | |

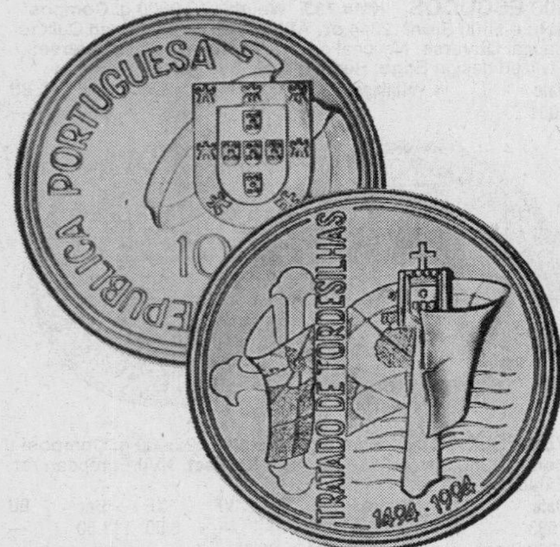


**1000 ESCUDOS** **KM# 675** **Weight:** 28.0000 g. **Composition:** 0.5000 Silver .4501 oz. ASW **Subject:** Treaty of Tordesilhas

| Date | Mintage | F | VF | XF | Unc | BU |
|---|---|---|---|---|---|---|
| ND(1994) | — | — | — | — | 14.50 | — |

**1000 ESCUDOS** **KM# 675a** **Weight:** 28.0000 g. **Composition:** 0.9250 Silver .8327 oz. ASW **Subject:** Treaty of Tordesilhas

| Date | Mintage | F | VF | XF | Unc | BU |
|---|---|---|---|---|---|---|
| ND(1994) Proof | 10,000 | Value: 45.00 | | | | |

**1000 ESCUDOS** **KM# 676** **Weight:** 28.0000 g. **Composition:** 0.5000 Silver .4501 oz. ASW **Subject:** Endangered Wildlife **Reverse:** Gray wolves

| Date | Mintage | F | VF | XF | Unc | BU |
|---|---|---|---|---|---|---|
| 1994 | 70,000 | — | — | — | 125 | — |

**1000 ESCUDOS** **KM# 676a** **Weight:** 28.0000 g. **Composition:** 0.9250 Silver .8327 oz. ASW **Subject:** Endangered Wildlife

| Date | Mintage | F | VF | XF | Unc | BU |
|---|---|---|---|---|---|---|
| 1994 Proof | 30,000 | Value: 150 | | | | |

**1000 ESCUDOS** **KM# 685** **Weight:** 28.0000 g. **Composition:** 0.5000 Silver .4501 oz. ASW **Subject:** 500th Anniversary - Death of John II

| Date | Mintage | F | VF | XF | Unc | BU |
|---|---|---|---|---|---|---|
| ND(1995) | 650,000 | — | — | — | 13.50 | — |

**1000 ESCUDOS** **KM# 685a** **Weight:** 28.0000 g. **Composition:** 0.9250 Silver .8327 oz. ASW **Subject:** 500th Anniversary - Death of John II

| Date | Mintage | F | VF | XF | Unc | BU |
|---|---|---|---|---|---|---|
| ND(1995) Proof | 15,000 | Value: 40.00 | | | | |

**1000 ESCUDOS** **KM# 688** **Weight:** 28.0000 g. **Composition:** 0.5000 Silver .4501 oz. ASW **Subject:** Restoration of the Frigate Ferdinand II and Gloria **Obverse:** Arms, figure head, ship's hull

| Date | Mintage | F | VF | XF | Unc | BU |
|---|---|---|---|---|---|---|
| ND(1996) | — | — | — | — | 15.00 | — |

**1000 ESCUDOS** **KM# 688a** **Weight:** 28.0000 g. **Composition:** 0.9250 Silver .8327 oz. ASW **Subject:** Restoration of the Frigate Ferdinand II and Gloria **Obverse:** Arms, figure head, ship's hull

| Date | Mintage | F | VF | XF | Unc | BU |
|---|---|---|---|---|---|---|
| ND(1996) Proof | 15,000 | Value: 45.00 | | | | |

**1000 ESCUDOS** **KM# 696** **Weight:** 28.0000 g. **Composition:** 0.5000 Silver .4501 oz. ASW **Subject:** N. S. Da Conceicao Padroeira de Portugal **Obverse:** National arms **Reverse:** Madonna and child

| Date | Mintage | F | VF | XF | Unc | BU |
|---|---|---|---|---|---|---|
| ND(1996) | — | — | — | — | 15.00 | — |

**1000 ESCUDOS** **KM# 696a** **Weight:** 28.0000 g. **Composition:** 0.9250 Silver .8327 oz. ASW **Subject:** N. S. Da Conceicao Padroeira de Portugal **Obverse:** National arms. **Reverse:** Madonna and child.

| Date | Mintage | F | VF | XF | Unc | BU |
|---|---|---|---|---|---|---|
| ND(1996) Proof | — | Value: 45.00 | | | | |

**1000 ESCUDOS** **KM# 695** **Weight:** 28.0000 g. **Composition:** 0.5000 Silver .4501 oz. ASW **Subject:** 100th Anniversary - Portuguese Oceanic Expedition **Obverse:** National arms and fish

| Date | Mintage | F | VF | XF | Unc | BU |
|---|---|---|---|---|---|---|
| 1997 | — | — | — | — | 15.00 | — |

**1000 ESCUDOS** **KM# 695a** **Weight:** 28.0000 g. **Composition:** 0.9250 Silver .8327 oz. ASW **Subject:** 100th Anniversary - Portuguese Oceanic Expedition **Obverse:** National arms and fish

| Date | Mintage | F | VF | XF | Unc | BU |
|---|---|---|---|---|---|---|
| 1997 Proof | Est. 15,000 | Value: 45.00 | | | | |

**1000 ESCUDOS** **KM# 703** **Weight:** 28.0000 g. **Composition:** 0.5000 Silver .4501 oz. ASW **Subject:** Credito Publico **Obverse:** National arms and hexagonal design

| Date | Mintage | F | VF | XF | Unc | BU |
|---|---|---|---|---|---|---|
| 1997 | Est. 335,000 | — | — | — | 13.50 | — |

**1000 ESCUDOS** **KM# 703a** **Weight:** 28.0000 g. **Composition:** 0.9250 Silver .8327 oz. ASW **Subject:** Credito Publico **Obverse:** National arms and hexagonal design

| Date | Mintage | F | VF | XF | Unc | BU |
|---|---|---|---|---|---|---|
| 1997 Proof | Est. 15,000 | Value: 50.00 | | | | |

**1000 ESCUDOS** **KM# 704** **Weight:** 27.0000 g. **Composition:** 0.5000 Silver .4340 oz. ASW **Subject:** Pauliteiros Dancers **Obverse:** Natioanl arms within circle of arms

| Date | Mintage | F | VF | XF | Unc | BU |
|---|---|---|---|---|---|---|
| 1997 | — | — | — | — | 13.50 | — |

**1000 ESCUDOS** **KM# 704a** **Weight:** 27.0000 g. **Composition:** 0.9250 Silver .8327 oz. ASW **Subject:** Pauliteiros Dancers **Obverse:** Natioanl arms within circle of arms

| Date | Mintage | F | VF | XF | Unc | BU |
|---|---|---|---|---|---|---|
| 1997 Proof | — | Value: 45.00 | | | | |

**1000 ESCUDOS** **KM# 707** **Weight:** 27.0000 g. **Composition:** 0.5000 Silver .4340 oz. ASW **Subject:** International Year of the Oceans Expo **Obverse:** National arms and logo

| Date | Mintage | F | VF | XF | Unc | BU |
|---|---|---|---|---|---|---|
| 1998 | — | — | — | — | 13.50 | — |

**1000 ESCUDOS** **KM# 707a** **Weight:** 27.0000 g. **Composition:** 0.9250 Silver .8030 oz. ASW **Subject:** International Year of the Oceans Expo **Obverse:** National arms and logo

| Date | Mintage | F | VF | XF | Unc | BU |
|---|---|---|---|---|---|---|
| 1998 Proof | Est. 20,000 | Value: 45.00 | | | | |

**1000 ESCUDOS** **KM# 708** **Weight:** 27.0000 g. **Composition:** 0.5000 Silver .4340 oz. ASW **Subject:** 500th Anniversary - Misericordia Church **Obverse:** Basket design

| Date | Mintage | F | VF | XF | Unc | BU |
|---|---|---|---|---|---|---|
| ND(1998) | — | — | — | — | 13.50 | — |

**1000 ESCUDOS** **KM# 708a** **Weight:** 27.0000 g. **Composition:** 0.9250 Silver .8030 oz. ASW **Subject:** 500th Anniversary - Misericordia Church **Obverse:** Basket design

| Date | Mintage | F | VF | XF | Unc | BU |
|---|---|---|---|---|---|---|
| ND(1998) Proof | — | Value: 45.00 | | | | |

**1000 ESCUDOS** **KM# 713** **Weight:** 27.0000 g. **Composition:** 0.5000 Silver .4340 oz. ASW **Obverse:** 2 ships, crowned arms, armillary sphere **Reverse:** King Dom Manuel I with sword seated at throne

| Date | Mintage | F | VF | XF | Unc | BU |
|---|---|---|---|---|---|---|
| 1998 | — | — | — | — | 13.50 | — |

**1000 ESCUDOS** **KM# 713a** **Weight:** 27.0000 g. **Composition:** 0.9250 Silver .8030 oz. ASW **Obverse:** 2 ships, crowned arms, armillary sphere **Reverse:** King Dom Manuel I with sword seated at throne

| Date | Mintage | F | VF | XF | Unc | BU |
|---|---|---|---|---|---|---|
| 1998 Proof | Est. 15,000 | Value: 45.00 | | | | |

**1000 ESCUDOS** **KM# 714** **Weight:** 27.0000 g. **Composition:** 0.5000 Silver .4340 oz. ASW **Subject:** 75th Anniversary - League of Combatants **Obverse:** Stylized arms **Reverse:** Sword and laurel branch

| Date | Mintage | F | VF | XF | Unc | BU |
|---|---|---|---|---|---|---|
| 1998 | — | — | — | — | 13.50 | — |

**1000 ESCUDOS** **KM# 714a** **Weight:** 27.0000 g. **Composition:** 0.9250 Silver .8030 oz. ASW **Subject:** 75th Anniversary - League of Combatants **Obverse:** Stylized arms **Reverse:** Sword and laurel branch

| Date | Mintage | F | VF | XF | Unc | BU |
|---|---|---|---|---|---|---|
| 1998 Proof | — | Value: 45.00 | | | | |

**1000 ESCUDOS** **KM# 715** **Weight:** 27.0000 g. **Composition:** 0.5000 Silver .4340 oz. ASW **Subject:** 25th Anniversary - Revolution of April 25 **Obverse:** National arms and denomination **Reverse:** Date and anniversary number

| Date | Mintage | F | VF | XF | Unc | BU |
|---|---|---|---|---|---|---|
| 1999 | — | — | — | — | 13.50 | — |

**1000 ESCUDOS** **KM# 715a** **Weight:** 27.0000 g. **Composition:** 0.9250 Silver .8030 oz. ASW **Subject:** 25th Anniversary - Revolution of April 25 **Obverse:** National arms and denomination **Reverse:** Date and anniversary number

| Date | Mintage | F | VF | XF | Unc | BU |
|---|---|---|---|---|---|---|
| 1999 Proof | Est. 15,000 | Value: 45.00 | | | | |

**1000 ESCUDOS** **KM# 721** **Weight:** 27.2000 g. **Composition:** 0.5000 Silver .4372 oz. ASW **Subject:** Millennium of Atlantic Sailing **Obverse:** National arms above logo **Reverse:** Ship on stormy waves **Edge:** Reeded

| Date | Mintage | F | VF | XF | Unc | BU |
|---|---|---|---|---|---|---|
| 1999 | — | — | — | — | 18.50 | — |

**1000 ESCUDOS** **KM# 721a** **Weight:** 27.0000 g. **Composition:** 0.9250 Silver .8030 oz. ASW **Subject:** Millennium of Atlantic Sailing **Obverse:** National arms above logo **Reverse:** Ship on stormy waves **Edge:** Reeded

| Date | Mintage | F | VF | XF | Unc | BU |
|---|---|---|---|---|---|---|
| 1999 Proof | 15,000 | Value: 45.00 | | | | |

**1000 ESCUDOS** **KM# 727** **Weight:** 27.0000 g. **Composition:** 0.5000 Silver .4340 oz. ASW **Series:** Ibero-America **Ob-**

**verse:** Portuguese arms within circle of foreign arms **Reverse:** Lusitano horses and rider **Edge:** Reeded **Size:** 40 mm.

| Date | Mintage | F | VF | XF | Unc | BU |
|---|---|---|---|---|---|---|
| 2000 | Est. 450,000 | — | — | — | 20.00 | — |

**1000 ESCUDOS** **KM# 727a** **Weight:** 27.0000 g. **Composition:** 0.9250 Silver .8030 oz. ASW **Subject:** Ibero-America **Obverse:** Portuguese arms within circle of foreign arms **Reverse:** Lusitano horses and rider **Edge:** Reeded **Size:** 40 mm.

| Date | Mintage | F | VF | XF | Unc | BU |
|---|---|---|---|---|---|---|
| 2000 Proof | Est. 20,000 | — | — | — | 100 | — |

**1000 ESCUDOS** **KM# 732** **Weight:** 27.0000 g. **Composition:** 0.5000 Silver .4340 oz. ASW **Subject:** D. Joso De Castro **Obverse:** Portuguese arms above denomination **Reverse:** Bearded portrait

| Date | Mintage | F | VF | XF | Unc | BU |
|---|---|---|---|---|---|---|
| 2000 | — | — | — | — | 20.00 | — |

**1000 ESCUDOS** **KM# 724** **Weight:** 27.0000 g. **Composition:** 0.5000 Silver .4340 oz. ASW **Subject:** Presidency of the European Union **Obverse:** National arms and cave drawings **Reverse:** Stylized design **Edge:** Reeded **Size:** 40.2 mm.

| Date | Mintage | F | VF | XF | Unc | BU |
|---|---|---|---|---|---|---|
| 2000 | — | — | — | — | 13.50 | — |

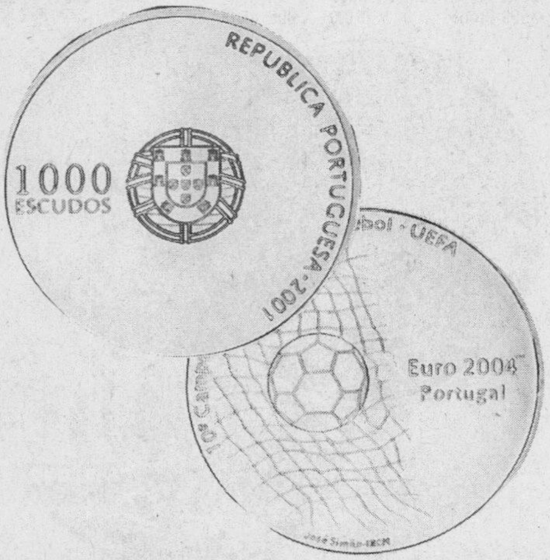

**1000 ESCUDOS** **KM# 734** **Weight:** 26.9500 g. **Composition:** 0.5000 Silver .4332 oz. ASW **Obverse:** National arms and denomination **Reverse:** Soccer ball **Edge:** Reeded **Size:** 40 mm.

| Date | Mintage | F | VF | XF | Unc | BU |
|---|---|---|---|---|---|---|
| 2001 | — | — | — | — | 13.50 | — |

## TRIAL STRIKES

| KM# | Date | Mintage | Identification | Mkt Val |
|---|---|---|---|---|
| TS33 | 1910 | — | 1000 Reis. Nickel Alloy. KM558; ALP | 400 |
| TS34 | 1915 | — | Escudo. Nickel Alloy. KM564; ALP. | 400 |
| TS38 | | — | 2 Escudos. Brass. Uniface, KM#591. | 25.00 |

## ESSAIS

| KM# | Date | Mintage | Identification | Mkt Val |
|---|---|---|---|---|
| E1 | 1986 | 30 | 100 Escudos. Copper Nickel. KM637 | — |
| E2 | 1998 | — | 100 Escudos. Silver. "ENSAIO" on obverse and reverse. | — |
| E3 | 1998 | — | 100 Escudos. Silver. "ENSAIO" on reverse only. | — |

## PROVAS

Stamped

| KM# | Date | Mintage | Identification | Mkt Val |
|---|---|---|---|---|
| TS35 | 1927 | — | 5 Centavos. Bronze. Reverse. | — |
| TS36 | | — | 20 Centavos. Brass. Reverse, Roman numeral. | — |
| TS37 | | — | 50 Centavos. Brass. Reverse. | — |
| PrB7 | 1942 | — | 20 Centavos. Bronze. KM584. | 55.00 |
| PrA7 | 1942 | — | 10 Centavos. Bronze. KM583. | — |
| Pr7 | 1943 | — | 5 Escudos. Silver. KM581. | 35.00 |
| Pr8 | 1943 | — | 10 Centavos. Bronze. KM583. | 20.00 |
| Pr9 | 1943 | — | 20 Centavos. Bronze. KM584. | 20.00 |
| Pr10 | 1960 | — | 5 Escudos. Silver. KM587. | 15.00 |
| Pr11 | 1960 | — | 10 Escudos. Silver. KM588. | 20.00 |
| Pr12 | 1960 | — | 20 Escudos. | 30.00 |
| PrA13 | 1962 | — | 10 Centavos. Bronze. KM583. | — |
| PrB13 | 1962 | — | 20 Centavos. Bronze. KM584. | — |
| PrC13 | 1962 | — | 50 Centavos. Copper Nickel. KM577. | — |
| PrD13 | 1962 | — | Escudo. Copper Nickel. KM578. | — |
| Pr13 | 1964 | — | Escudo. KM578. | — |
| Pr14 | 1964 | — | 2-1/2 Escudos. KM590. | — |
| Pr15 | 1966 | — | 20 Centavos. KM584. | — |
| Pr16 | 1966 | — | Escudo. KM578. | — |
| Pr18 | 1966 | — | 5 Escudos. KM591. | 15.00 |
| Pr17 | 1966 | — | 2-1/2 Escudos. KM590. | 17.50 |
| Pr19 | 1966 | — | 20 Escudos. Silver. Salazar Bridge, KM592. | 25.00 |
| Pr20 | 1966 | — | 20 Escudos. Gold. Salazar Bridge, KM592. | 2,500 |
| Pr21 | 1968 | — | 50 Escudos. KM593. | 30.00 |
| Pr23 | 1969 | — | 50 Escudos. KM598, 'Prova' in relef. | 35.00 |
| Pr24 | 1969 | — | 50 Escudos. KM599. | 30.00 |
| Pr22 | 1969 | — | 50 Escudos. KM598, 'Prova' incuse. | 30.00 |
| Pr25 | 1971 | — | 50 Escudos. KM601. | 30.00 |
| Pr26 | 1972 | — | 50 Escudos. KM602. | 30.00 |
| Pr27 | (1984) | 100 | 25 Escudos. KM623, Revolution. | 15.00 |
| Pr28 | 1985 | 5,000 | 100 Escudos. KM629, Henrique. | — |

## PATTERNS

Including off metal strikes

| KM# | Date | Mintage | Identification | Mkt Val |
|---|---|---|---|---|
| Pn200 | 1903 | — | 2 Reis. Nickel. Plain royal arms. | — |
| Pn201 | 1903 | — | 20 Reis. Nickel. Royal arms with wreath. | 350 |
| Pn202 | 1903 | — | 20 Reis. Nickel. Plain edge. Without wreath. | 350 |
| Pn203 | 1903 | — | 20 Reis. Nickel. Reeded edge. Value on reeded edge. | 275 |
| Pn204 | 1903 | — | 20 Reis. Nickel. Plain edge. Value on plain edge. | 275 |
| Pn205 | 1903 | — | 100 Reis. Silver. Crowned value. | 1,500 |
| Pn206 | 1903 | — | 200 Reis. Silver. Crowned value. | 2,200 |
| Pn207 | | — | 20 Centavos. Silver. Two reverses. | 600 |
| Pn208 | 1912 | — | 50 Centavos. Copper. Plain edge. Type as adopted. | 750 |
| Pn209 | 1912 | — | 50 Centavos. Silver. Reeded edge. Type as adopted. | 1,000 |
| Pn210 | 1912 | — | Escudo. Gold. 'October 5, 1910'. | 550 |
| Pn211 | 1912 | — | Escudo. Gold. Obverse variety. | 550 |
| Pn212 | 1912 | — | Escudo. Gold. | 550 |
| Pn213 | 1919 | — | 4 Centavos. Copper Nickel. Plain edge. Wide border. | — |
| Pn214 | 1919 | — | 4 Centavos. Copper Nickel. Reeded edge. Wide border. | — |
| Pn215 | 1919 | — | 4 Centavos. Copper Nickel. Plain edge. Semi-wide border. | — |
| Pn216 | 1919 | — | 4 Centavos. Copper Nickel. Alternate edge. Narrow border. | — |
| Pn218 | 1920 | — | 10 Centavos. Brass. Plain edge. Larger type. | — |
| Pn217 | 1920 | — | 10 Centavos. Copper Nickel. Plain edge. Larger type. | 1,500 |
| Pn219 | 1920 | — | 5 Escudos. Copper. 'Abundance Through Labor' | 1,000 |
| Pn220 | 1920 | — | 5 Escudos. Copper Nickel. 'Abundance Through Labor' | 1,000 |
| Pn221 | 1920 | — | 5 Escudos. Gold. 'Abundance Through Labor' | — |
| Pn222 | 1921 | — | 10 Centavos. Bronze. Reeded edge. 19mm | 500 |
| Pn224 | 1927 | — | 50 Centavos. Silver. Obverse 1924 type. | 500 |
| Pn225 | 1927 | — | Escudo. Silver. Reverse 1924 type. | — |
| Pn223 | 1927 | — | 50 Centavos. Silver. Reeded edge. Large type. | 500 |
| Pn226 | 1928 | — | Escudo. Brass. | 650 |
| Pn227 | 1928 | — | 10 Escudos. Copper. 'Battle of Orique'. | 750 |
| Pn228 | 1929 | — | 10 Escudos. Brass. 'Battle of Orique'. | — |
| Pn230 | 1932 | — | 10 Escudos. Copper. | 225 |
| Pn231 | 1932 | — | 10 Escudos. Copper Nickel. Type adopted. | 225 |
| Pn229 | 1932 | — | 5 Escudos. Copper Nickel. Type adopted. | — |
| Pn232 | 1940 | — | 10 Escudos. Copper Nickel. Large type. | 225 |
| Pn233 | 1953 | — | 20 Escudos. Copper. 'National Revival'. | 650 |
| Pn235 | 1953 | — | 20 Escudos. Silver. Variety of type adopted. | 1,250 |
| Pn234 | 1953 | — | 20 Escudos. Gold. 'National Revival'. | — |
| Pn236 | 1961 | — | 2-1/2 Escudos. Nickel. Reeded edge. | — |
| Pn237 | 1961 | — | 2-1/2 Escudos. Nickel. Reeded edge. | — |
| Pn238 | 1961 | — | 2-1/2 Escudos. Copper Nickel. | — |
| Pn241 | 1961 | — | 10 Escudos. Silver. | — |
| Pn242 | 1961 | — | 10 Escudos. Copper Nickel. Legend in relief. | — |
| Pn243 | | — | 10 Centavos. Aluminum. | — |
| Pn246 | | — | 10 Escudos. Nickel. Reeded edge. Type adopted. | — |
| Pn247 | | — | 10 Escudos. Nickel. Plain edge. Type adopted. | — |
| Pn248 | | — | 10 Centavos. Bronze-Aluminum. Plain edge. | — |
| Pn239 | 1961 | — | 10 Escudos. Silver. Legend incuse. | 600 |
| Pn240 | 1961 | — | 10 Escudos. Copper Nickel. | 350 |
| Pn244 | | — | 20 Centavos. Brass. | 225 |
| Pn245 | | — | 5 Escudos. Brass. Type adopted. | 225 |
| Pn249 | 1966 | — | Escudo. Bronze-Aluminum. | 200 |
| Pn250 | 1966 | — | Escudo. Bronze-Aluminum. Reeded edge. | 200 |
| Pn251 | 1966 | — | 20 Escudos. Nickel. Reeded edge. | 350 |
| Pn252 | 1968 | — | 10 Centavos. Aluminum. Similar to 1942 type. | 225 |
| Pn253 | 1969 | — | 10 Centavos. Aluminum. Large type as adopted. | — |
| Pn254 | 1970 | — | Escudo. Nickel. Type adopted. | 100 |
| Pn255 | 1970 | — | 20 Escudos. Nickel. Reeded edge. | 200 |
| Pn256 | 1970 | — | 20 Escudos. Nickel. Plain edge. | 200 |
| Pn257 | 1970 | — | 20 Escudos. Nickel. Reeded edge. | 200 |
| Pn258 | 1970 | — | 20 Escudos. Nickel. Plain edge. | 200 |
| Pn259 | 1979 | — | 50 Escudos. Reeded edge. | 125 |
| Pn260 | 1979 | — | Escudo. Reeded edge. | 125 |
| Pn261 | 1979 | — | 5 Escudos. Aluminum. | 150 |
| Pn262 | | — | 250 Escudos. Copper Nickel. Decade of Women, United Nations. | — |
| Pn263 | 1989 | — | 100 Escudos. | 1,650 |

## MINT SETS

| KM# | Date | Mintage | Identification | Issue Price | Mkt Val |
|---|---|---|---|---|---|
| MS31 | 2000 | 10,000 | KM#728a-731a | 65.00 | 95.00 |
| MS1 | 1960 (3) | — | KM587-589 | — | 50.00 |
| MS2 | 1982 (4) | 10,000 | KM612-613, 615-616 | 3.00 | 7.00 |
| MS3 | 1983 (3) | 50,000 | KM620-622 | 30.00 | 30.00 |
| MS4 | 1983 (3) | 5,000 | KM617-619 | 4.00 | 25.00 |
| MS5 | 1984 (2) | 10,000 | KM624-625 | 3.00 | 25.00 |
| MS6 | 1985 (2) | 20,000 | KM627a, 630a | 20.00 | 37.50 |
| MSA6 | 1985 (2) | — | KM627, 630 | — | 10.00 |
| MS7 | 1986 (5) | 50,000 | KM631-634, 636 | 6.00 | 30.00 |
| MS10 | 1987 (6) | 5,000 | KM631-634, 636, 638 | 10.00 | 30.00 |
| MS8 | 1987/8 (4) | 40,000 | KM639a-642a | 78.00 | 70.00 |
| MS9 | 1987/8 (4) | 5,000 | KM639b-642b | 2,080 | 2,200 |
| MS11 | 1988 (5) | 30,000 | KM631-634, 636 | 10.00 | 200 |
| MS12 | 1989 (6) | 50,000 | KM631-634, 636, 645.1 | 12.00 | 20.00 |
| MS14 | 1989/90 (4) | 30,000 | KM646a-649a | 79.50 | 80.00 |
| MSA14 | 1989/90 (4) | — | KM646-649 | — | 15.00 |
| MS13 | 1990 (6) | 50,000 | KM631-634, 636, 645.1 | 15.00 | 17.50 |
| MS15 | 1991 (7) | — | KM631-634, 636, 645.1, 655 | 17.50 | 17.50 |
| MS16 | 1992 (7) | — | KM631-634, 636, 645.1, 655 | — | 32.50 |
| MS17 | 1993 (7) | — | KM631-634, 636, 645.1, 655 | — | 25.00 |

| KM# | Date | Mintage | Identification | Issue Price | Mkt Val |
|---|---|---|---|---|---|
| MS18 | 1993 (4) | 30,000 | KM665a-668a | 79.50 | 75.00 |
| MS19 | 1994 (7) | — | KM631-634, 636, 645.1, 669 | — | 32.50 |
| MS20 | 1994 (4) | — | KM670a-673a | — | 90.00 |
| MS21 | 1995 (7) | — | KM631-634, 636, 678-679 | — | 20.00 |
| MS23 | 1995 (2) | 5,000 | KM678-679 | — | 60.00 |
| MS22 | 1995 (4) | 20,000 | KM681a-684a | 77.50 | 70.00 |
| MS24 | 1996 (8) | — | KM631-634, 636, 645.1, 655, 687 | — | 35.00 |
| MS25 | 1996 (4) | 10,000 | KM689a, 690a, 691a, 692a | 105 | 70.00 |
| MS26 | 1997 (9) | 20,000 | KM631-634, 636, 645.1, 655, 693-694 | 32.50 | 30.00 |
| MS27 | 1998 (8) | 50,000 | KM631-634, 636, 645.1, 655, 706 | 32.50 | 30.00 |
| MS28 | 1998 (4) | 25,000 | KM709a-712a | 95.00 | 95.00 |
| MS29 | 1999 (9) | — | KM631-634, 636, 645.1, 655, 720, 722 | — | 30.00 |
| MS30 | 1999 (4) | 10,000 | KM716a-719a | 95.00 | 95.00 |

## PROOF SETS

| KM# | Date | Mintage | Identification | Issue Price | Mkt Val |
|---|---|---|---|---|---|
| PS1 | 1960 (3) | — | KM587-589; matte finish | — | — |
| PS2 | 1974 (2) | 10,000 | KM603-604 | 6.00 | 35.00 |
| PS3 | 1977 (3) | 10,000 | KM605-606, 608 | 2.50 | 25.00 |
| PS4 | 1983 (3) | 8,500 | KM620-622 | 60.00 | 100 |
| PS5 | 1985 (2) | 5,000 | KM627a, 630a | 40.00 | 150 |
| PS6 | 1985 (2) | 5,000 | KM628, 628a | 35.00 | 300 |
| PS7 | 1987 (4) | 20,000 | KM639a-642a | 128 | 150 |
| PS8 | 1987/88 (4) | 2,000 | KM639a, 640c, 641b, 642c; Prestige | 2,200 | 2,750 |
| PS10 | 1989/90 (4) | 5,000 | KM646b-649b | 2,425 | 2,450 |
| PS11 | 1989/90 (4) | 2,500 | KM646a, 647c, 648b, 649c; Prestige | 2,650 | 2,800 |
| PS9 | 1989/90 (4) | 20,000 | KM646a-649a | 137 | 150 |
| PS12 | 1991/92 (4) | 15,000 | KM658a-661a | 150 | 150 |
| PS13 | 1991/92 (4) | 3,500 | KM658b-661b | 2,350 | 2,350 |
| PS14 | 1991/92 (4) | 2,500 | KM658c-661c; Prestige | 2,400 | 3,000 |
| PS15 | 1993 (7) | — | KM631-634, 636, 645.1, 655 | — | 100 |
| PS16 | 1993 (4) | 22,000 | KM665a-668a | 150 | 150 |
| PS17 | 1993 (4) | 5,000 | KM665b-668b | 1,980 | 2,500 |
| PS18 | 1993 (4) | 2,000 | KM665a, 666c, 667b, 668c; Prestige | 2,300 | 2,150 |
| PS19 | 1994 (7) | — | KM631-634, 636, 645.1, 669 | — | 50.00 |
| PS20 | 1994 (4) | 10,000 | KM670a-673a | — | 150 |
| PS21 | 1994 (4) | — | KM670b-673b | — | 2,400 |
| PS22 | 1994 (4) | 1,000 | KM670a, 671c, 672b, 673c; Prestige | — | 2,175 |
| PS23 | 1995 (7) | 7,000 | KM631-634, 636, 678, 679 | 47.50 | 50.00 |
| PS27 | 1995 (2) | 10,000 | KM678, 679 | — | 35.00 |
| PS24 | 1995 (4) | 13,000 | KM681a-684a | 150 | 150 |
| PS26 | 1995 (4) | 1,000 | KM681a, 682c, 683b, 684c | 1,800 | 2,100 |
| PS25 | 1995 (4) | 2,000 | KM681b-684b | 1,980 | 2,000 |
| PS28 | 1996 (8) | 7,000 | KM631-634, 636, 645.1, 655, 687 | — | 50.00 |
| PS29 | 1996 (4) | 10,000 | KM689a, 690a, 691a, 692a | 160 | 150 |
| PS30 | 1996 (4) | 2,000 | KM689b, 690b, 691b, 692b | — | 2,000 |
| PS31 | 1996 (4) | 1,000 | KM689a, 690c, 691b, 692c | — | 2,100 |
| PS32 | 1997 (9) | 7,000 | KM631-634, 636, 645.1, 655, 693-694 | 55.00 | 50.00 |
| PS33 | 1997 (4) | 24,000 | KM697a-700a | 145 | 150 |
| PS35 | 1997 (4) | 1,000 | KM697a, 698b, 699c, 700c | 2,000 | 2,250 |
| PS34 | 1997 (4) | 4,000 | KM697b-700b | 1,980 | 2,000 |
| PS36 | 1998 (8) | 20,000 | KM631-634, 636, 645.1, 655, 706 | 52.50 | 50.00 |
| PS37 | 1998 (4) | 25,000 | KM709a-712a | 150 | 150 |
| PS38 | 1998 (4) | 5,000 | KM709b-712b | 1,980 | 1,980 |
| PS39 | 1998 (4) | 1,000 | KM709c, 710a, 711b, 712c | 2,000 | 2,250 |
| PS40 | 1999 (4) | 10,000 | KM716a-719a | 150 | 150 |
| PS41 | 1999 (4) | 1,000 | KM716b-719b | 1,800 | 1,800 |

# QATAR

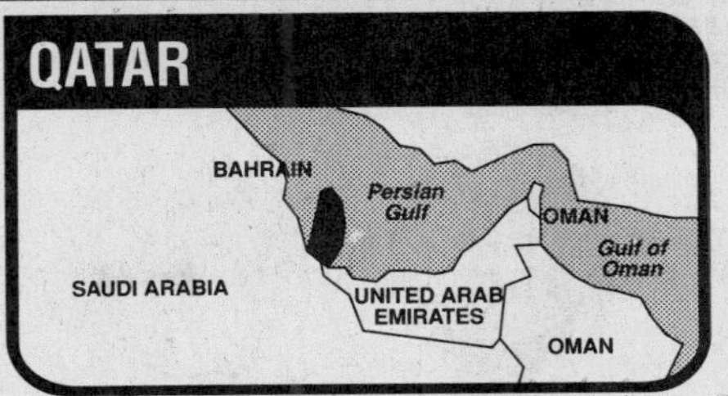


The State of Qatar, an emirate in the Persian Gulf between Bahrain and Trucial Oman, has an area of 4,247sq. mi. (11,000 sq. km.) and a population of *469,000. Capital: Doha. Oil is the chief industry and export.

Qatar was under Turkish control from 1872 until the beginning of World War I when the Ottoman Turks evacuated the Qatar Peninsula. In 1916 Sheikh Abdullah placed Qatar under the protection of Great Britain and gave Britain responsibility for its defense and foreign relations. Qatar joined with Dubai in a Monetary Union and issued coins and paper money in 1966 and 1969. When Britain announced in 1968 that it would end treaty relationships with the Persian Gulf sheikhdoms in 1971, this union was dissolved; Qatar joined Bahrain and the seven trucial sheikhdoms (called the United Arab Emirates) in an effort to form a union of Arab Emirates. However the nine sheikhdoms were unable to agree on terms of union, and Qatar declared its independence as the State of Qatar on Sept. 3, 1971.

**TITLES**

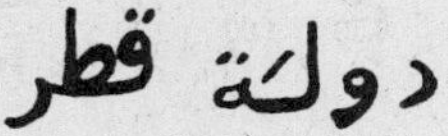

Daulat Qatar

**RULERS**

**Al-Thani Dynasty**

Qasim Bin Muhammad, 1876-1913
Abdullah Bin Qasim, 1913-1948
Ali Bin Abdullah, 1948-1960
Ahmad Bin Ali, 1960-1972
Khalifah bin Hamad, 1972-1995
Hamad bin Khalifah, 1995-

**MONETARY SYSTEM**

100 Dirhem = 1 Riyal

## REPUBLIC

### STANDARD COINAGE

**DIRHEM KM# 2 Composition:** Bronze **Ruler:** Khalifah Bin Hamad

| Date | Mintage | F | VF | XF | Unc | BU |
|---|---|---|---|---|---|---|
| AH1393(1973) | 500,000 | — | 0.10 | 0.25 | 0.60 | — |

**5 DIRHEMS KM# 3 Composition:** Bronze **Ruler:** Khalifah Bin Hamad

| Date | Mintage | F | VF | XF | Unc | BU |
|---|---|---|---|---|---|---|
| AH1393(1973) | 1,000,000 | — | 0.10 | 0.25 | 0.75 | — |
| AH1398(1978) | 1,000,000 | — | 0.10 | 0.25 | 0.75 | — |

**10 DIRHEMS KM# 1 Composition:** Bronze **Ruler:** Khalifah Bin Hamad

| Date | Mintage | F | VF | XF | Unc | BU |
|---|---|---|---|---|---|---|
| AH1392(1972) | 1,500,000 | — | 0.50 | 1.00 | 2.50 | — |
| AH1393(1973) | 1,500,000 | — | 0.20 | 0.50 | 1.50 | — |

**25 DIRHEMS KM# 4 Composition:** Copper-Nickel **Ruler:** Khalifah Bin Hamad

| Date | Mintage | F | VF | XF | Unc | BU |
|---|---|---|---|---|---|---|
| AH1393(1973) | 1,500,000 | — | 0.25 | 0.65 | 1.50 | — |
| AH1396(1976) | 2,000,000 | — | 0.25 | 0.65 | 1.75 | — |
| AH1398(1978) | — | — | 0.25 | 0.65 | 1.75 | — |
| AH1401(1981) | — | — | 0.25 | 0.65 | 1.75 | — |
| AH1407(1987) | — | — | 0.25 | 0.65 | 1.75 | — |
| AH1410(1990) | — | — | 0.25 | 0.65 | 1.75 | — |
| AH1414(1993) | — | — | 0.25 | 0.65 | 1.75 | — |

**50 DIRHEMS KM# 5 Composition:** Copper-Nickel **Ruler:** Khalifah Bin Hamad

| Date | Mintage | F | VF | XF | Unc | BU |
|---|---|---|---|---|---|---|
| AH1393(1973) | 1,500,000 | — | 0.40 | 0.85 | 2.00 | — |
| AH1398(1978) | 2,000,000 | — | 0.40 | 0.85 | 2.25 | — |
| AH1401(1981) | — | — | 0.40 | 0.85 | 2.25 | — |
| AH1407(1987) | — | — | 0.40 | 0.85 | 2.25 | — |
| AH1410(1990) | — | — | 0.40 | 0.85 | 2.25 | — |
| AH1414(1993) | — | — | 0.40 | 0.85 | 2.25 | — |

**100 RIYALS KM# 6 Weight:** 22.2000 g. **Composition:** 0.9250 Silver .6602 oz. ASW **Ruler:** Hamad bin Khalifah **Subject:** Central Bank **Obverse:** National arms **Reverse:** Bank building **Edge:** Reeded **Size:** 37 mm.

| Date | Mintage | F | VF | XF | Unc | BU |
|---|---|---|---|---|---|---|
| ND(1998) Proof | 400 | Value: 250 | | | | |

**500 RIYALS KM# 7 Weight:** 17.0000 g. **Composition:** 0.9170 Gold .5012 oz. AGW **Ruler:** Hamad bin Khalifah **Subject:** Central Bank **Obverse:** National arms **Reverse:** Bank building **Edge:** Reeded **Size:** 31 mm.

| Date | Mintage | F | VF | XF | Unc | BU |
|---|---|---|---|---|---|---|
| ND(1998) Proof | 100 | Value: 600 | | | | |

# QATAR & DUBAI

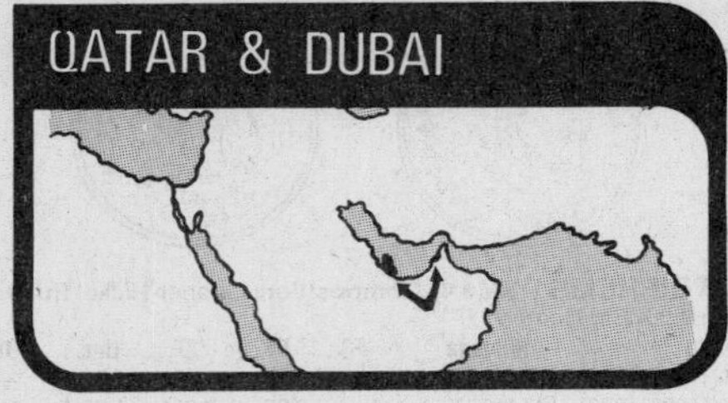

The State of Qatar, which occupies the Qatar Peninsula jutting into the Persian Gulf from eastern Saudi Arabia, has an area of 4,247 sq. mi. (11,000 sq. km.) and a population of *469,000. Capital: Doha. The traditional occupations of pearling, fishing, and herding have been replaced in economics by petroleum-related industries. Crude oil, petroleum products, and tomatoes are exported.

Dubai is one of the seven sheikhdoms comprising the United Arab Emirates (formerly Trucial States) located along the southern shore of the Persian Gulf. It has a population of about 60,000. Capital (of the United Arab Emirates): Abu Dhabi.

Qatar, which initiated protective treaty relations with Great Britain in 1916, achieved independence on Sept. 3,1971, upon withdrawal of the British military presence from the Persian Gulf, and replaced its special treaty arrangement with Britain with a treaty of general friendship. Dubai attained independence on Dec. 1, 1971, upon termination of Britain's protective treaty with the trucial Sheikhdoms, and on Dec. 2, 1971, entered into the union of the United Arab Emirates.

Despite the fact that the Emirate of Qatar and the Sheikhdom of Dubai were merged under a monetary union, the two territories were governed independently from each other. Qatar now uses its own currency while Dubai uses the United Arab Emirates currency and coins.

**TITLES**

Qatar Wa Dubai

**RULERS**

Ahmad II, 1960-1972

**MONETARY SYSTEM**

100 Dirhem = 1 Riyal

## BRITISH PROTECTORATES

### STANDARD COINAGE

**DIRHEM** **KM# 1** **Composition:** Bronze **Ruler:** Ahmad II **Obverse:** Denomination **Reverse:** Goitered gazelle

| Date | Mintage | F | VF | XF | Unc | BU |
|---|---|---|---|---|---|---|
| AH1386(1966) | 1,000,000 | — | 0.10 | 0.30 | 0.70 | — |

**5 DIRHEMS** **KM# 2** **Composition:** Bronze **Ruler:** Ahmad II **Obverse:** Denomination **Reverse:** Goitered gazelle

| Date | Mintage | F | VF | XF | Unc | BU |
|---|---|---|---|---|---|---|
| AH1386(1966) | 2,000,000 | — | 0.10 | 0.30 | 0.85 | — |
| AH1389(1969) | 2,000,000 | — | 0.10 | 0.30 | 0.85 | — |

**10 DIRHEMS** **KM# 3** **Composition:** Bronze **Ruler:** Ahmad II **Obverse:** Denomination **Reverse:** Goitered gazelle

| Date | Mintage | F | VF | XF | Unc | BU |
|---|---|---|---|---|---|---|
| AH1386(1966) | 2,000,000 | — | 0.20 | 0.60 | 1.50 | — |
| AH1391(1971) | 1,500 | — | — | — | 15.00 | — |

**Note:** Official mintage figure reported for Qatar by British Royal Mint.

**25 DIRHEMS** **KM# 4** **Composition:** Copper-Nickel **Ruler:** Ahmad II **Obverse:** Denomination **Reverse:** Goitered gazelle

| Date | Mintage | F | VF | XF | Unc | BU |
|---|---|---|---|---|---|---|
| AH1386(1966) | 2,000,000 | — | 0.30 | 0.75 | 2.00 | — |
| AH1389(1969) | 2,000,000 | — | 0.30 | 0.75 | 2.00 | — |

**50 DIRHEMS** **KM# 5** **Composition:** Copper-Nickel **Ruler:** Ahmad II **Obverse:** Denomination **Reverse:** Goitered gazelle

| Date | Mintage | F | VF | XF | Unc | BU |
|---|---|---|---|---|---|---|
| AH1386(1966) | 2,000,000 | — | 0.50 | 1.00 | 2.50 | — |

# QUAITI STATE OF HADHRAMAUT

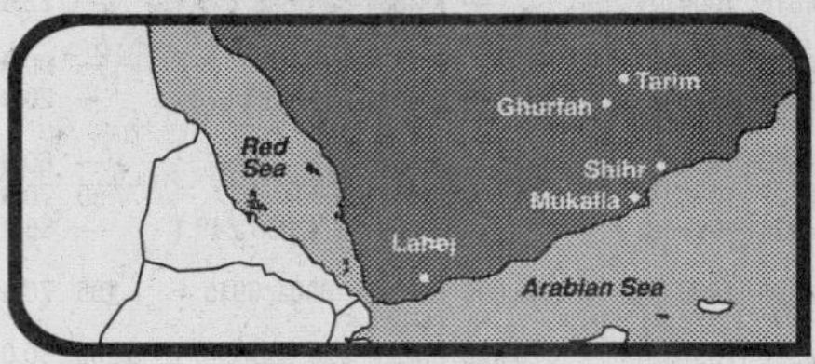


### GHUAFAH

A city sultanate of Eastern Aden Protectorate was an oasis settlement located in the Hadhramaut Wadi region of southern Arabia.

**TITLES**

al-Ghurfa(t)

**RULERS**

Saleh 'Ubayd bin Abdat, AH1339-1358/1920-1939AD
Ubayd bin Saleh bin Abdat, AH1358-1365/1939-1945AD

**NOTE:** The Arabic *129* in the obv. leg. is an anagram for Saleh.

## EAST ADEN PROTECTORATE

Between 1200 B.C. and the 6th century A.D., what is now the People's Democratic Republic of Yemen was part of the Minaean Kingdom. In subsequent years it was controlled by Persians, Egyptians and Turks. Aden, one of the cities mentioned in the Bible, had been a port for trade between the East and West for 2,000 years. British rule began in 1839 when the British East India Co. seized control to put an end to the piracy threatening trade with India. To protect their foothold in Aden, the British found it necessary to extend their control into the area known historically as the Hadhramaut, and to sign protection treaties with the shaiks of the hinterland.

### STANDARD COINAGE

**4 KHUMSI** **KM# 1** **Weight:** 0.6500 g. **Composition:** 0.9000 Silver .0188 oz. ASW **Ruler:** Saleh 'Ubayd bin Abdat AH1339-1358/1920-1939AD

| Date | Mintage | F | VF | XF | Unc | BU |
|---|---|---|---|---|---|---|
| AH1344 | 5,000 | 30.00 | 45.00 | 65.00 | 100 | — |

**8 KHUMSI** **KM# 2** **Weight:** 1.1000 g. **Composition:** 0.9000 Silver .0318 oz. ASW **Ruler:** Saleh 'Ubayd bin Abdat AH1339-1358/1920-1939AD

| Date | Mintage | F | VF | XF | Unc | BU |
|---|---|---|---|---|---|---|
| AH1344 | 5,000 | 27.50 | 37.50 | 55.00 | 85.00 | — |

**15 KHUMSI** **KM# 3** **Weight:** 2.0000 g. **Composition:** 0.9000 Silver .0578 oz. ASW **Ruler:** Saleh 'Ubayd bin Abdat AH1339-1358/1920-1939AD

| Date | Mintage | F | VF | XF | Unc | BU |
|---|---|---|---|---|---|---|
| AH1344 | 10,000 | 10.00 | 15.00 | 22.50 | 35.00 | — |

**30 KHUMSI** **KM# 4** **Weight:** 3.9500 g. **Composition:** 0.9000 Silver .1142 oz. ASW **Ruler:** Saleh 'Ubayd bin Abdat AH1339-1358/1920-1939AD

| Date | Mintage | F | VF | XF | Unc | BU |
|---|---|---|---|---|---|---|
| AH1344 | 10,000 | 15.00 | 22.50 | 32.50 | 50.00 | — |

**45 KHUMSI** KM# 5 **Weight:** 5.9000 g. **Composition:** 0.9000 Silver .1707 oz. ASW **Ruler:** Saleh 'Ubayd bin Abdat AH1339-1358/1920-1939AD

| Date | Mintage | F | VF | XF | Unc | BU |
|---|---|---|---|---|---|---|
| AH1344 | 10,000 | 175 | 275 | 425 | 600 | — |

**60 KHUMSI** KM# 6 **Weight:** 7.8000 g. **Composition:** 0.9000 Silver .2257 oz. ASW **Ruler:** Saleh 'Ubayd bin Abdat AH1339-1358/1920-1939AD

| Date | Mintage | F | VF | XF | Unc | BU |
|---|---|---|---|---|---|---|
| AH1344 | 10,000 | 37.50 | 55.00 | 80.00 | 125 | — |

# RAS AL-KHAIMAH

Ras al-Khaimah is only one of the coin issuing emirates that was not one of the original members of the United Arab Emirates. It was a part of Sharjah. It has an estimated area of 650 sq. mi. (1700 sq. km.) and a population of 30,000. Ras al Khaimah is the only member of the United Arab Emirates that has agriculture as its principal industry.

**TITLES**

راس الخيمة

Ras al-Khaimah(t)

**RULERS**

Sultan bin Salim al-Qasimi,/1921-1948
Saqr Bin Muhammad al-Qasimi,/1948—

**MONETARY SYSTEM**

100 Dirhams = 1 Rial

## UNITED ARAB EMIRAT

### NON-CIRCULATING LEGAL TENDER COINAGE

**50 DIRHAMS** KM# 28 **Composition:** Copper-Nickel **Ruler:** Saqr bin Muhammad al Qasimi **Reverse:** Barbary Falcon

| Date | Mintage | F | VF | XF | Unc | BU |
|---|---|---|---|---|---|---|
| AH1390(1970) | — | — | — | — | 18.00 | — |

**RIAL** KM# 1 **Weight:** 3.9500 g. **Composition:** 0.6400 Silver .0812 oz. ASW **Ruler:** Saqr bin Muhammad al Qasimi

| Date | Mintage | F | VF | XF | Unc | BU |
|---|---|---|---|---|---|---|
| AH1389(1969) | — | — | — | — | 12.50 | — |
| AH1389(1969) Proof | 1,500 | Value: 25.00 | | | | |

**2 RIALS** KM# 2 **Weight:** 6.4500 g. **Composition:** 0.8350 Silver .1731 oz. ASW **Ruler:** Saqr bin Muhammad al Qasimi

| Date | Mintage | F | VF | XF | Unc | BU |
|---|---|---|---|---|---|---|
| AH1389(1969) | — | — | — | — | 17.50 | — |
| AH1389(1969) Proof | 1,500 | Value: 35.00 | | | | |

**2-1/2 RIALS** KM# 29 **Weight:** 7.5000 g. **Composition:** 0.9250 Silver .2231 oz. ASW **Ruler:** Saqr bin Muhammad al Qasimi **Reverse:** Barbary Falcon

| Date | Mintage | F | VF | XF | Unc | BU |
|---|---|---|---|---|---|---|
| AH1390(1970) | — | — | — | — | 22.50 | — |

**5 RIALS** KM# 3 **Weight:** 15.0000 g. **Composition:** 0.8350 Silver .4027 oz. ASW **Ruler:** Saqr bin Muhammad al Qasimi

| Date | Mintage | F | VF | XF | Unc | BU |
|---|---|---|---|---|---|---|
| AH1389(1969) | — | — | — | — | 25.00 | — |
| AH1389(1969) Proof | 1,500 | Value: 45.00 | | | | |

**7-1/2 RIYALS** KM# 17 **Weight:** 22.5000 g. **Composition:** 0.9250 Silver .6692 oz. ASW **Ruler:** Saqr bin Muhammad al Qasimi **Subject:** Centennial of Rome **Reverse:** Man plowing

| Date | Mintage | F | VF | XF | Unc | BU |
|---|---|---|---|---|---|---|
| 1970 Proof | Est. 2,000 | Value: 120 | | | | |

**7-1/2 RIYALS** KM# 32 **Weight:** 22.5000 g. **Composition:** 0.9250 Silver .6692 oz. ASW **Ruler:** Saqr bin Muhammad al Qasimi **Subject:** World Championship Football **Reverse:** Jules Rimet Cup

| Date | Mintage | F | VF | XF | Unc | BU |
|---|---|---|---|---|---|---|
| 1970 Proof | Est. 2,000 | Value: 235 | | | | |

**7-1/2 RIYALS** KM# 30 **Weight:** 22.5000 g. **Composition:** 0.9250 Silver .6692 oz. ASW **Ruler:** Saqr bin Muhammad al Qasimi **Reverse:** Barbary Falcon

| Date | Mintage | F | VF | XF | Unc | BU |
|---|---|---|---|---|---|---|
| AH1390(1970) | — | — | — | — | 65.00 | — |

**7-1/2 RIYALS** **KM# 5** **Weight:** 22.5000 g. **Composition:** 0.9250 Silver .6692 oz. ASW **Ruler:** Saqr bin Muhammad al Qasimi **Reverse:** Giacomo Agostini

| Date | Mintage | F | VF | XF | Unc | BU |
|---|---|---|---|---|---|---|
| ND(1970) Proof | Est. 2,000 | Value: 425 | | | | |

**10 RIYALS** **KM# 31** **Weight:** 30.0000 g. **Composition:** 0.9250 Silver .8921 oz. ASW **Ruler:** Saqr bin Muhammad al Qasimi **Subject:** 1st Anniversary - Death of Dwight Eisenhower

| Date | Mintage | F | VF | XF | Unc | BU |
|---|---|---|---|---|---|---|
| 1970 | 4,500 | — | — | — | 15.00 | — |
| 1970 Proof | 1,400 | Value: 30.00 | | | | |

**10 RIYALS** **KM# 6** **Weight:** 30.0000 g. **Composition:** 0.9250 Silver .8921 oz. ASW **Ruler:** Saqr bin Muhammad al Qasimi **Subject:** World Championship Football **Obverse:** Similar to KM#18 **Reverse:** Jules Rimet Cup

| Date | Mintage | F | VF | XF | Unc | BU |
|---|---|---|---|---|---|---|
| 1970 Proof | Est. 2,000 | Value: 350 | | | | |

**10 RIYALS** **KM# 18** **Weight:** 30.0000 g. **Composition:** 0.9250 Silver .8921 oz. ASW **Ruler:** Saqr bin Muhammad al Qasimi **Subject:** Centennial of Rome **Reverse:** Emperor Standing With Charging Horses

| Date | Mintage | F | VF | XF | Unc | BU |
|---|---|---|---|---|---|---|
| 1970 Proof | Est. 2,000 | Value: 175 | | | | |

**10 RIYALS** **KM# 7** **Weight:** 30.0000 g. **Composition:** 0.9250 Silver .8921 oz. ASW **Ruler:** Saqr bin Muhammad al Qasimi **Subject:** Felice Gimondi **Obverse:** Similar to KM#18

| Date | Mintage | F | VF | XF | Unc | BU |
|---|---|---|---|---|---|---|
| ND(1970) Proof | Est. 2,000 | Value: 500 | | | | |

**15 RIYALS** **KM# 8** **Weight:** 45.0000 g. **Composition:** 0.9250 Silver 1.3384 oz. ASW **Ruler:** Saqr bin Muhammad al Qasimi **Subject:** Champions of Sport **Obverse:** Denomination

| Date | Mintage | F | VF | XF | Unc | BU |
|---|---|---|---|---|---|---|
| ND(1970) Proof | Est. 2,000 | Value: 675 | | | | |

**15 RIYALS** **KM# 19** **Weight:** 45.0000 g. **Composition:** 0.9250 Silver 1.3384 oz. ASW **Ruler:** Saqr bin Muhammad al Qasimi **Subject:** Centennial of Rome **Reverse:** Founders - 3 heads facing right

| Date | Mintage | F | VF | XF | Unc | BU |
|---|---|---|---|---|---|---|
| 1970 Proof | Est. 2,000 | Value: 220 | | | | |

**15 RIYALS** **KM# 33** **Weight:** 45.0000 g. **Composition:** 0.9250 Silver 1.3384 oz. ASW **Ruler:** Saqr bin Muhammad al Qasimi **Subject:** World Championship Football - Jules Rimet Cup

| Date | Mintage | F | VF | XF | Unc | BU |
|---|---|---|---|---|---|---|
| 1970 Proof | — | Value: 525 | | | | |

**50 RIYALS** **KM# 21** **Weight:** 10.3500 g. **Composition:** 0.9000 Gold .2995 oz. AGW **Ruler:** Saqr bin Muhammad al Qasimi **Subject:** Centennial of Rome **Reverse:** Vittorio Emanuele II head left

| Date | Mintage | F | VF | XF | Unc | BU |
|---|---|---|---|---|---|---|
| 1970 Proof | Est. 2,000 | Value: 325 | | | | |

**50 RIYALS** **KM# 10** **Weight:** 10.3500 g. **Composition:** 0.9000 Gold .2995 oz. AGW **Ruler:** Saqr bin Muhammad al Qasimi **Subject:** Gigi Riva

| Date | Mintage | F | VF | XF | Unc | BU |
|---|---|---|---|---|---|---|
| ND(1970) Proof | Est. 2,000 | Value: 350 | | | | |

**75 RIYALS** **KM# 22** **Weight:** 15.5300 g. **Composition:** 0.9000 Gold .4494 oz. AGW **Ruler:** Saqr bin Muhammad al Qasimi **Subject:** Centennial of Rome Capitol

| Date | Mintage | F | VF | XF | Unc | BU |
|---|---|---|---|---|---|---|
| 1970 Proof | Est. 2,000 | Value: 450 | | | | |

**75 RIYALS** KM# 11 **Weight:** 15.5300 g. **Composition:** 0.9000 Gold .4494 oz. AGW **Ruler:** Saqr bin Muhammad al Qasimi **Subject:** Gianni Rivera

| Date | Mintage | F | VF | XF | Unc | BU |
|---|---|---|---|---|---|---|
| ND(1970) Proof | Est. 2,000 | Value: 425 | | | | |

**100 RIYALS** KM# 12 **Weight:** 20.7000 g. **Composition:** 0.9000 Gold .5990 oz. AGW **Ruler:** Saqr bin Muhammad al Qasimi **Subject:** World Chmapionship Football - Jules Rimet Cup

| Date | Mintage | F | VF | XF | Unc | BU |
|---|---|---|---|---|---|---|
| 1970 Proof | Est. 2,000 | Value: 625 | | | | |

**100 RIYALS** KM# 23 **Weight:** 20.7000 g. **Composition:** 0.9000 Gold .5990 oz. AGW **Ruler:** Saqr bin Muhammad al Qasimi **Subject:** Centennial of Rome - WWI Victory

| Date | Mintage | F | VF | XF | Unc | BU |
|---|---|---|---|---|---|---|
| 1970 Proof | Est. 2,000 | Value: 525 | | | | |

**100 RIYALS** KM# 24 **Weight:** 31.0500 g. **Composition:** 0.9000 Gold .8985 oz. AGW **Ruler:** Saqr bin Muhammad al Qasimi **Subject:** Centennial of Rome **Reverse:** Standing Liberty

| Date | Mintage | F | VF | XF | Unc | BU |
|---|---|---|---|---|---|---|
| 1970 Proof | Est. 2,000 | Value: 950 | | | | |

**150 RIYALS** KM# 13 **Weight:** 31.0500 g. **Composition:** 0.9000 Gold .8985 oz. AGW **Ruler:** Saqr bin Muhammad al Qasimi **Series:** 1972 Munich Olympics

| Date | Mintage | F | VF | XF | Unc | BU |
|---|---|---|---|---|---|---|
| ND(1970) Proof | 3,060 | Value: 1,800 | | | | |

**200 RIYALS** KM# 25 **Weight:** 41.4000 g. **Composition:** 0.9000 Gold 1.1980 oz. AGW **Ruler:** Saqr bin Muhammad al Qasimi **Subject:** Centennial of Rome - Romulus and Remus

| Date | Mintage | F | VF | XF | Unc | BU |
|---|---|---|---|---|---|---|
| 1970 Proof | Est. 2,000 | Value: 1,200 | | | | |

**200 RIYALS** KM# 14 **Weight:** 41.4000 g. **Composition:** 0.9000 Gold 1.1980 oz. AGW **Ruler:** Saqr bin Muhammad al Qasimi **Subject:** Champions of Sport

| Date | Mintage | F | VF | XF | Unc | BU |
|---|---|---|---|---|---|---|
| ND(1970) Proof | Est. 2,000 | Value: 1,350 | | | | |

## ESSAIS

| KM# | Date | Mintage | Identification | Issue Price | Mkt Val |
|---|---|---|---|---|---|
| E1 | ND1969 | — | Riyal. With ASSAY. | — | 15.00 |
| E2 | ND1969 | — | 2 Riyals. With ASSAY. | — | 22.50 |
| E3 | ND1969 | — | 5 Riyals. With ASSAY. | — | 37.50 |
| E4 | ND1970 | — | 10 Riyals. With ASSAY. | — | 45.00 |

## MINT SETS

| KM# | Date | Mintage | Identification | Issue Price | Mkt Val |
|---|---|---|---|---|---|
| MS1 | 1969 (3) | — | KM#1-3 | — | 55.00 |

## PROOF SETS

| KM# | Date | Mintage | Identification | Issue Price | Mkt Val |
|---|---|---|---|---|---|
| PS1 | 1969 (3) | 1,500 | KM#1-3 | 10.80 | 100 |
| PS2 | (1970) (9) | — | KM#5-8, 10-14 | — | 6,500 |
| PS3 | 1970 (8) | — | KM#17-19, 21-25 | — | 4,000 |
| PS4 | (1970) (5) | — | KM#10-14 | — | 4,550 |
| PS5 | 1970 (5) | — | KM#21-25 | — | 3,450 |
| PS6 | (1970) (4) | — | KM#5-8 | 41.50 | 1,950 |
| PS7 | 1970 (3) | — | KM#17-19 | — | 500 |
| PS8 | 1970 (4) | — | KM#6, 10-12 | — | 1,750 |

# REUNION

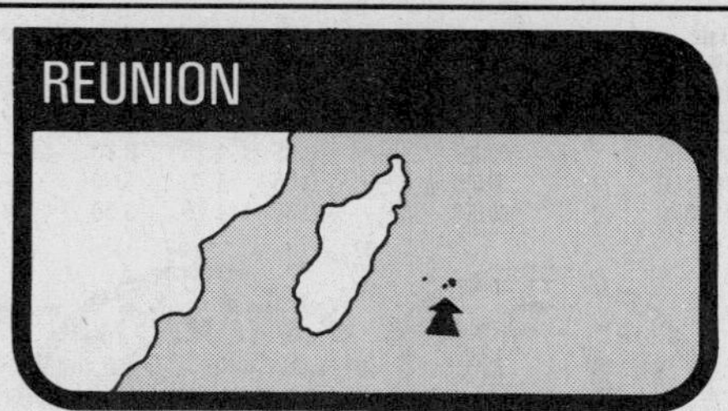

The Department of Reunion, an overseas department of France located in the Indian Ocean 400 miles (640 km.) east of Madagascar, has an area of 969 sq. mi. (2,510 sq. km.) and a population of *566,000. Capital: Saint-Denis. The island's volcanic soil is extremely fertile. Sugar, vanilla, coffee and rum are exported.

Although first visited by Portuguese navigators in the 16th century, Reunion was uninhabited when claimed for France by Capt. Goubert in 1638. The French first colonized the Isle de Bourbon in 1662 as a layover station for ships rounding the Cape of Good Hope to India. It was renamed Reunion in 1793. The island remained in French possession except for the period of 1810-15, when the British occupied it. Reunion became an overseas department of France in 1946, and in 1958 voted to continue that status within the new French Union.

During the first half of the 19th century, Reunion was officially known as Isle de Bonaparte (1801-14) and Isle de Bourbon (1814-48). Reunion coinage of those periods is so designated.

**Mint Marks**

(a) – Paris, privy marks only

**MONETARY SYSTEM**

100 Centimes = 1 Franc

## FRENCH DEPARTMENT

### STANDARD COINAGE

**FRANC** KM# 6.1 **Composition:** Aluminum

| Date | Mintage | F | VF | XF | Unc | BU |
|---|---|---|---|---|---|---|
| 1948(a) | 3,000,000 | — | 0.35 | 0.60 | 2.00 | — |
| 1964(a) | 1,000,000 | — | 0.35 | 0.60 | 2.50 | — |
| 1968(a) | 450,000 | — | 0.60 | 1.25 | 4.00 | — |
| 1969(a) | 500,000 | — | 0.60 | 0.85 | 3.00 | — |
| 1971(a) | 800,000 | — | 0.60 | 0.85 | 2.50 | — |
| 1973(a) | 500,000 | — | 0.60 | 0.85 | 3.00 | — |

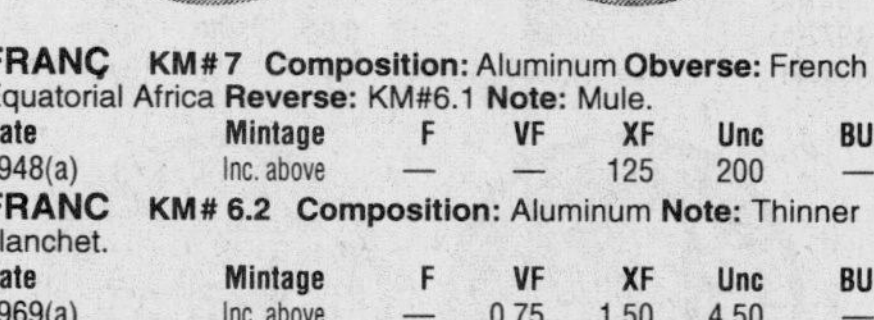

**FRANÇ** KM# 7 **Composition:** Aluminum **Obverse:** French Equatorial Africa **Reverse:** KM#6.1 **Note:** Mule.

| Date | Mintage | F | VF | XF | Unc | BU |
|---|---|---|---|---|---|---|
| 1948(a) | Inc. above | — | — | 125 | 200 | — |

**FRANC** KM# 6.2 **Composition:** Aluminum **Note:** Thinner planchet.

| Date | Mintage | F | VF | XF | Unc | BU |
|---|---|---|---|---|---|---|
| 1969(a) | Inc. above | — | 0.75 | 1.50 | 4.50 | — |

**2 FRANCS** KM# 8 **Composition:** Aluminum

| Date | Mintage | F | VF | XF | Unc | BU |
|---|---|---|---|---|---|---|
| 1948(a) | 2,000,000 | — | 0.35 | 0.85 | 3.00 | — |
| 1968(a) | 100,000 | — | 3.00 | 5.00 | 10.00 | — |
| 1969(a) | 150,000 | — | 1.75 | 3.50 | 6.50 | — |
| 1970(a) | 300,000 | — | 0.85 | 1.75 | 3.50 | — |
| 1971(a) | 300,000 | — | 0.85 | 1.75 | 3.50 | — |
| 1973(a) | 500,000 | — | 0.85 | 1.75 | 3.50 | — |

**5 FRANCS** KM# 9 **Composition:** Aluminum

| Date | Mintage | F | VF | XF | Unc | BU |
|---|---|---|---|---|---|---|
| 1955(a) | 3,000,000 | — | 0.60 | 1.00 | 2.50 | — |
| 1969(a) | 100,000 | — | 2.50 | 5.00 | 9.00 | — |
| 1970(a) | 200,000 | — | 1.75 | 3.50 | 6.50 | — |
| 1971(a) | 100,000 | — | 1.75 | 3.50 | 6.50 | — |
| 1972(a) | 300,000 | — | 0.85 | 1.75 | 3.00 | — |
| 1973(a) | 250,000 | — | 0.85 | 1.75 | 3.00 | — |

**10 FRANCS** KM# 10 **Composition:** Aluminum-Bronze

| Date | Mintage | F | VF | XF | Unc | BU |
|---|---|---|---|---|---|---|
| 1955(a) | 1,500,000 | — | 0.45 | 0.75 | 2.50 | — |
| 1962(a) | 700,000 | — | 1.75 | 3.50 | 6.50 | — |
| 1964(a) | 1,000,000 | — | 0.45 | 0.75 | 2.50 | — |

**10 FRANCS** KM# 10a **Composition:** Aluminum-Nickel-Bronze

| Date | Mintage | VG | F | VF | XF | Unc |
|---|---|---|---|---|---|---|
| 1964(a) | Inc. above | — | — | 0.45 | 0.75 | 2.50 |
| 1969(a) | 300,000 | — | — | 1.25 | 2.50 | 5.50 |
| 1970(a) | 300,000 | — | — | 1.25 | 2.50 | 4.50 |
| 1971(a) | 200,000 | — | — | 1.75 | 3.75 | 7.50 |
| 1972(a) | 400,000 | — | — | 1.25 | 2.50 | 5.50 |
| 1973(a) | 700,000 | — | — | 0.85 | 1.75 | 3.00 |

**20 FRANCS** KM# 11 **Composition:** Aluminum-Bronze

| Date | Mintage | F | VF | XF | Unc | BU |
|---|---|---|---|---|---|---|
| 1955(a) | 1,250,000 | — | 0.75 | 1.50 | 3.50 | — |
| 1960(a) | 100,000 | — | 3.00 | 6.00 | 12.00 | — |
| 1961(a) | 300,000 | — | 2.50 | 4.75 | 8.00 | — |
| 1962(a) | 190,000 | — | 2.75 | 5.50 | 9.00 | — |
| 1964(a) | 750,000 | — | 0.75 | 1.50 | 3.00 | — |

**20 FRANCS** KM# 11a **Composition:** Aluminum-Nickel-Bronze

| Date | Mintage | F | VF | XF | Unc | BU |
|---|---|---|---|---|---|---|
| 1969(a) | 200,000 | — | 2.75 | 5.50 | 9.00 | — |
| 1970(a) | 200,000 | — | 2.75 | 5.50 | 9.00 | — |
| 1971(a) | 200,000 | — | 2.75 | 5.50 | 9.00 | — |
| 1972(a) | 300,000 | — | 2.00 | 3.50 | 6.50 | — |
| 1973(a) | 550,000 | — | 0.75 | 1.50 | 3.00 | — |

**50 FRANCS** KM# 12 **Composition:** Nickel

| Date | Mintage | F | VF | XF | Unc | BU |
|---|---|---|---|---|---|---|
| 1962(a) | 1,000,000 | — | 1.50 | 2.50 | 4.50 | — |
| 1964(a) | 500,000 | — | 2.00 | 3.00 | 5.50 | — |
| 1969(a) | 100,000 | — | 2.75 | 5.00 | 8.50 | — |
| 1970(a) | 100,000 | — | 2.75 | 5.00 | 8.50 | — |
| 1973(a) | 350,000 | — | 2.00 | 3.50 | 6.00 | — |

**100 FRANCS** KM# 13 **Composition:** Nickel

| Date | Mintage | F | VF | XF | Unc | BU |
|---|---|---|---|---|---|---|
| 1964(a) | 2,000,000 | — | 1.00 | 2.00 | 3.50 | — |
| 1969(a) | 200,000 | — | 2.25 | 4.50 | 7.00 | — |
| 1970(a) | 150,000 | — | 2.25 | 5.00 | 8.50 | — |
| 1971(a) | 100,000 | — | 2.75 | 6.00 | 12.50 | — |
| 1972(a) | 400,000 | — | 2.00 | 3.50 | 5.50 | — |
| 1973(a) | 200,000 | — | 2.25 | 4.50 | 7.00 | — |

## TOKEN COINAGE

**5 CENTIMES** KM# Tn1 **Composition:** Aluminum **Note:** Bank token. Demonetized 1941.

| Date | Mintage | F | VF | XF | Unc | BU |
|---|---|---|---|---|---|---|
| 1920 | — | 30.00 | 65.00 | 200 | 500 | — |

**10 CENTIMES** KM# Tn2 **Composition:** Aluminum **Note:** Bank token. Demonetized 1941.

| Date | Mintage | F | VF | XF | Unc | BU |
|---|---|---|---|---|---|---|
| 1920 | — | 35.00 | 75.00 | 200 | 500 | — |

**25 CENTIMES** KM# Tn3 **Composition:** Aluminum **Note:** Bank token. Demonetized 1941.

| Date | Mintage | F | VF | XF | Unc | BU |
|---|---|---|---|---|---|---|
| 1920 | — | 50.00 | 100 | 275 | 775 | — |

## ESSAIS

Standard metals unless otherwise noted

| KM# | Date | Mintage | Identification | Mkt Val |
|---|---|---|---|---|
| E3 | 1948(a) | 2,000 | Franc. Copper-Nickel. KM6.1. | 25.00 |
| E4 | 1948(a) | 2,000 | 2 Francs. Copper-Nickel. KM8. | 27.50 |
| E5 | 1955(a) | 1,200 | 5 Francs. KM9. | 20.00 |
| E6 | 1955(a) | 1,200 | 10 Francs. KM10. | 20.00 |
| E7 | 1955(a) | 1,200 | 20 Francs. KM11. | 20.00 |
| E8 | 1962(a) | 1,200 | 50 Francs. KM12. | 22.50 |
| E9 | 1964(a) | 2,000 | 50 Francs. KM12. | 30.00 |
| E10 | 1964(a) | 2,000 | 100 Francs. KM13. | 40.00 |

## PIEFORTS WITH ESSAI

Double thickness; standard metals unless otherwise noted

| KM# | Date | Mintage | Identification | Mkt Val |
|---|---|---|---|---|
| PE3 | 1948(a) | 104 | Franc. KM6.1. | 75.00 |
| PE4 | 1948(a) | 104 | 2 Francs. KM8. | 90.00 |

## "FDC" SETS

| KM# | Date | Mintage | Identification | Issue Price | Mkt Val |
|---|---|---|---|---|---|
| SS1 | 1964 (5) | — | KM6.1, 10-13. Issued with Comoros set. | — | 20.00 |

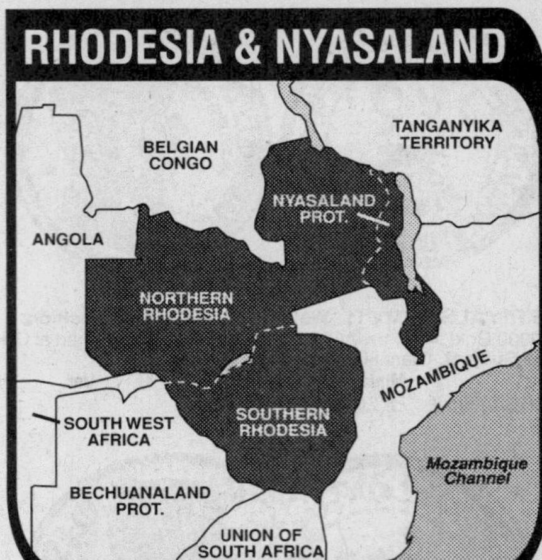


The Federation of Rhodesia and Nyasaland was located in the east-central part of southern Africa. The multiracial federation has an area of about 487,000 sq. mi. (1,261,330 sq. km.) and a population of 6.8 million. Capital: Salisbury, in Southern Rhodesia.

The geographical unity of the three British possessions suggested the desirability of political and economic union as early as 1924. Despite objections by the African constituency of Northern Rhodesia and Nyasaland, who feared that African self-determination would be retarded by the dominant influence of prosperous and self-governing Southern Rhodesia. The Central African Federation was established in Sept. of 1953. As feared by the European constituency, Southern Rhodesia despite the fact that the three component countries largely retained their pre-federation political structure effectively and profitably dominated the Federation. It was dissolved at the end of 1963, largely because of the effective opposition of the Nyasaland African Congress. Northern Rhodesia and Nyasaland became the independent states of Zambia and Malawi in 1964. Southern Rhodesia unilaterally declared its independence the following year, which was not recognized by the British Government.

For earlier coinage refer to Southern Rhodesia. For later coinage refer to Malawi, Zambia, Rhodesia and Zimbabwe.

**RULERS**

Elizabeth II, 1952-1964

**MONETARY SYSTEM**

12 Pence = 1 Shilling
5 Shillings = 1 Crown
20 Shillings = 1 Pound

# FEDERATION

## STANDARD COINAGE

**1/2 PENNY** KM# 1 **Composition:** Bronze **Ruler:** Elizabeth II **Obverse:** Giraffes

| Date | Mintage | F | VF | XF | Unc | BU |
|---|---|---|---|---|---|---|
| 1955 | 720,000 | 0.15 | 0.25 | 0.50 | 2.50 | — |
| 1955 Proof | 2,010 | Value: 5.00 | | | | |
| 1956 | 480,000 | 0.20 | 0.50 | 1.00 | 3.00 | — |
| 1956 Proof | — | Value: 400 | | | | |
| 1957 | 1,920,000 | 0.10 | 0.15 | 0.25 | 2.50 | — |
| 1957 Proof | — | Value: 400 | | | | |
| 1958 | 2,400,000 | 0.10 | 0.15 | 0.25 | 2.50 | — |
| 1958 Proof | — | Value: 400 | | | | |
| 1964 | 1,440,000 | 0.10 | 0.15 | 0.25 | 2.50 | — |

**PENNY** KM# 2 **Composition:** Bronze **Ruler:** Elizabeth II **Obverse:** Elephants

| Date | Mintage | F | VF | XF | Unc | BU |
|---|---|---|---|---|---|---|
| 1955 | 2,040,000 | 0.15 | 0.25 | 0.75 | 3.00 | — |
| 1955 Proof | 2,010 | Value: 5.00 | | | | |
| 1956 | 4,800,000 | 0.15 | 0.25 | 0.50 | 2.50 | — |
| 1956 Proof | — | Value: 400 | | | | |

| Date | Mintage | F | VF | XF | Unc | BU |
|---|---|---|---|---|---|---|
| 1957 | 7,200,000 | 0.10 | 0.15 | 0.25 | 2.00 | — |
| 1957 Proof | — | — | — | — | — | — |
| 1958 | 2,880,000 | 0.10 | 0.15 | 0.25 | 2.00 | — |
| 1958 Proof | — | Value: 400 | | | | |
| 1961 | 4,800,000 | 0.10 | 0.15 | 0.25 | 1.50 | — |
| 1961 Proof | — | — | — | — | — | — |
| 1962 | 6,000,000 | 0.10 | 0.15 | 0.25 | 1.50 | — |
| 1963 | 6,000,000 | 0.10 | 0.15 | 0.25 | 1.50 | — |
| 1963 Proof | — | Value: 400 | | | | |

**3 PENCE** **KM# 3** **Composition:** Copper-Nickel **Ruler:** Elizabeth II **Obverse:** Flame lily

| Date | Mintage | F | VF | XF | Unc | BU |
|---|---|---|---|---|---|---|
| 1955 | 1,200,000 | 0.20 | 0.50 | 1.00 | 4.00 | — |
| 1955 Proof | 10 | Value: 400 | | | | |
| 1956 | 3,200,000 | 0.50 | 1.00 | 2.50 | 20.00 | — |
| 1956 Proof | — | Value: 600 | | | | |
| 1957 | 6,000,000 | 0.20 | 0.50 | 0.75 | 3.00 | — |
| 1957 Proof | — | Value: 600 | | | | |
| 1962 | 4,000,000 | 0.20 | 0.50 | 0.75 | 3.00 | — |
| 1962 Proof | — | — | — | — | — | — |
| 1963 | 2,000,000 | 0.20 | 0.50 | 0.75 | 3.00 | — |
| 1963 Proof | — | — | — | — | — | — |
| 1964 | 3,600,000 | 0.15 | 0.25 | 0.50 | 1.50 | — |

**3 PENCE** **KM# 3a** **Weight:** 1.4100 g. **Composition:** 0.5000 Silver .0226 oz. ASW **Ruler:** Elizabeth II **Obverse:** Flame lily

| Date | Mintage | F | VF | XF | Unc | BU |
|---|---|---|---|---|---|---|
| 1955 Proof | 2,000 | Value: 7.50 | | | | |

**6 PENCE** **KM# 4** **Composition:** Copper-Nickel **Ruler:** Elizabeth II **Reverse:** Lion

| Date | Mintage | F | VF | XF | Unc | BU |
|---|---|---|---|---|---|---|
| 1955 | 400,000 | 0.50 | 1.00 | 2.50 | 7.50 | — |
| 1955 Proof | 10 | Value: 400 | | | | |
| 1956 | 800,000 | 0.75 | 2.00 | 7.00 | 40.00 | — |
| 1956 Proof | — | — | — | — | — | — |
| 1957 | 4,000,000 | 0.20 | 0.50 | 1.00 | 4.00 | — |
| 1957 Proof | — | — | — | — | — | — |
| 1962 | 2,800,000 | 0.20 | 0.50 | 1.00 | 4.00 | — |
| 1962 Proof | — | — | — | — | — | — |
| 1963 | 800,000 | 5.00 | 10.00 | 20.00 | 45.00 | — |
| 1963 Proof | — | — | — | — | — | — |

**6 PENCE** **KM# 4a** **Weight:** 2.8300 g. **Composition:** 0.5000 Silver .0454 oz. ASW **Ruler:** Elizabeth II **Reverse:** Lion

| Date | Mintage | F | VF | XF | Unc | BU |
|---|---|---|---|---|---|---|
| 1955 Proof | 2,000 | Value: 10.00 | | | | |

**SHILLING** **KM# 5** **Composition:** Copper-Nickel **Ruler:** Elizabeth II **Reverse:** Antelope

| Date | Mintage | F | VF | XF | Unc | BU |
|---|---|---|---|---|---|---|
| 1955 | 200,000 | 1.50 | 2.50 | 7.00 | 18.00 | — |
| 1955 Proof | 10 | Value: 400 | | | | |
| 1956 | 1,700,000 | 0.75 | 1.50 | 3.50 | 30.00 | — |
| 1956 Proof | — | — | — | — | — | — |
| 1957 | 3,500,000 | 0.50 | 1.00 | 2.50 | 8.00 | — |
| 1957 Proof | — | — | — | — | — | — |

**SHILLING** **KM# 5a** **Weight:** 5.6600 g. **Composition:** 0.5000 Silver .0909 oz. ASW **Ruler:** Elizabeth II **Reverse:** Antelope

| Date | Mintage | F | VF | XF | Unc | BU |
|---|---|---|---|---|---|---|
| 1955 Proof | 2,000 | Value: 25.00 | | | | |

**2 SHILLINGS** **KM# 6** **Composition:** Copper-Nickel **Ruler:** Elizabeth II **Reverse:** African fish eagle

| Date | Mintage | F | VF | XF | Unc | BU |
|---|---|---|---|---|---|---|
| 1955 | 1,750,000 | 1.25 | 2.50 | 5.00 | 12.50 | — |
| 1955 Proof | 10 | Value: 400 | | | | |
| 1956 | 1,850,000 | 1.25 | 2.50 | 4.50 | 12.00 | — |
| 1956 Proof | — | — | — | — | — | — |
| 1957 | 1,500,000 | 1.25 | 2.50 | 4.50 | 12.00 | — |
| 1957 Proof | — | — | — | — | — | — |

**2 SHILLINGS** **KM# 6a** **Weight:** 11.3100 g. **Composition:** 0.5000 Silver .1818 oz. ASW **Ruler:** Elizabeth II **Reverse:** African fish eagle

| Date | Mintage | F | VF | XF | Unc | BU |
|---|---|---|---|---|---|---|
| 1955 Proof | 2,000 | Value: 30.00 | | | | |

**1/2 CROWN** **KM# 7** **Composition:** Copper-Nickel **Ruler:** Elizabeth II

| Date | Mintage | F | VF | XF | Unc | BU |
|---|---|---|---|---|---|---|
| 1955 | 1,600,000 | 1.50 | 3.00 | 6.00 | 15.00 | — |
| 1955 Proof | 10 | Value: 550 | | | | |
| 1956 | 160,000 | 7.50 | 15.00 | 35.00 | 250 | — |
| 1956 Proof | — | — | — | — | — | — |
| 1957 | 2,400,000 | 7.50 | 15.00 | 35.00 | 75.00 | — |
| 1957 Proof | — | — | — | — | — | — |

**1/2 CROWN** **KM# 7a** **Weight:** 14.1400 g. **Composition:** 0.5000 Silver .2273 oz. ASW **Ruler:** Elizabeth II

| Date | Mintage | F | VF | XF | Unc | BU |
|---|---|---|---|---|---|---|
| 1955 Proof | 2,000 | Value: 35.00 | | | | |

## PROOF SETS

| KM# | Date | Mintage | Identification | Issue Price | Mkt Val |
|---|---|---|---|---|---|
| PS1 | 1955 (7) | 10 | KM1-7 | — | 2,200 |
| PS2 | 1955 (7) | 2,000 | KM1-2, 3a-7a | — | 110 |

# RHODESIA

**RULERS**
British, until 1966

**MONETARY SYSTEM**
12 Pence = 1 Shilling = 10 Cents
10 Shillings = 1 Dollar
20 Shillings = 1 Pound

## BRITISH PROTECTORATE

### POUND COINAGE

**3 PENCE = 2-1/2 CENTS** **KM# 8** **Composition:** Copper-Nickel

| Date | Mintage | F | VF | XF | Unc | BU |
|---|---|---|---|---|---|---|
| 1968 | 2,400,000 | 0.25 | 0.50 | 0.75 | 2.00 | — |
| 1968 Proof | 10 | Value: 1,000 | | | | |

**6 PENCE = 5 CENTS** **KM# 1** **Composition:** Copper-Nickel **Reverse:** Flame lily

| Date | Mintage | F | VF | XF | Unc | BU |
|---|---|---|---|---|---|---|
| 1964 | 13,500,000 | 0.15 | 0.25 | 0.40 | 1.25 | — |
| 1964 Proof | 2,060 | Value: 10.00 | | | | |

**SHILLING = 10 CENTS** **KM# 2** **Composition:** Copper-Nickel

| Date | Mintage | F | VF | XF | Unc | BU |
|---|---|---|---|---|---|---|
| 1964 | 15,500,000 | 0.15 | 0.25 | 0.65 | 1.50 | — |
| 1964 Proof | 2,060 | Value: 10.00 | | | | |

**2 SHILLINGS = 20 CENTS** **KM# 3** **Composition:** Copper-Nickel **Reverse:** Bird sculpture

| Date | Mintage | F | VF | XF | Unc | BU |
|---|---|---|---|---|---|---|
| 1964 | 10,500,000 | 0.25 | 0.50 | 1.25 | 3.00 | — |
| 1964 Proof | 2,060 | Value: 12.50 | | | | |

**2-1/2 SHILLINGS = 25 CENTS** **KM# 4** **Composition:** Copper-Nickel **Reverse:** Sable antelope

| Date | Mintage | F | VF | XF | Unc | BU |
|---|---|---|---|---|---|---|
| 1964 | 11,500,000 | 0.50 | 1.00 | 2.00 | 4.00 | — |
| 1964 Proof | 2,060 | Value: 17.50 | | | | |

**10 SHILLINGS** KM# 5 **Weight:** 3.9940 g. **Composition:** 0.9160 Gold .1177 oz. AGW

| Date | Mintage | F | VF | XF | Unc | BU |
|---|---|---|---|---|---|---|
| 1966 Proof | 6,000 | Value: 100 | | | | |

**POUND** KM# 6 **Weight:** 7.9881 g. **Composition:** 0.9160 Gold .2354 oz. AGW

| Date | Mintage | F | VF | XF | Unc | BU |
|---|---|---|---|---|---|---|
| 1966 Proof | 5,000 | Value: 175 | | | | |

**5 POUNDS** KM# 7 **Weight:** 39.9403 g. **Composition:** 0.9160 Gold 1.1772 oz. AGW

| Date | Mintage | F | VF | XF | Unc | BU |
|---|---|---|---|---|---|---|
| 1966 Proof | 3,000 | Value: 550 | | | | |

## REPUBLIC

### DECIMAL COINAGE

**1/2 CENT** KM# 9 **Composition:** Bronze

| Date | Mintage | F | VF | XF | Unc | BU |
|---|---|---|---|---|---|---|
| 1970 | 10,000,000 | — | 0.10 | 0.20 | 0.50 | — |
| 1970 Proof | 12 | Value: 750 | | | | |
| 1971 | 2,000,000 | — | 0.10 | 0.25 | 1.00 | — |
| 1972 | 2,000,000 | — | 0.10 | 0.25 | 1.00 | — |
| 1972 Proof | 12 | Value: 750 | | | | |
| 1975 | 10,001,000 | — | 0.10 | 0.20 | 0.50 | — |
| 1975 Proof | 10 | Value: 750 | | | | |
| 1977 | — | — | — | 800 | 1,500 | — |

**Note:** Circulation mintage melted, less than 10 surviving specimens known

| Date | Mintage | F | VF | XF | Unc | BU |
|---|---|---|---|---|---|---|
| 1977 Proof | 10 | Value: 1,500 | | | | |

**CENT** KM# 10 **Composition:** Bronze

| Date | Mintage | F | VF | XF | Unc | BU |
|---|---|---|---|---|---|---|
| 1970 | 25,000,000 | — | 0.10 | 0.20 | 0.50 | — |
| 1970 Proof | 12 | Value: 750 | | | | |
| 1971 | 15,000,000 | — | 0.10 | 0.20 | 0.50 | — |
| 1972 | 10,000,000 | — | 0.10 | 0.20 | 0.50 | — |
| 1972 Proof | 12 | Value: 750 | | | | |
| 1973 | 5,000,000 | — | 0.10 | 0.20 | 0.75 | — |
| 1973 Proof | 10 | Value: 750 | | | | |
| 1974 | — | — | 0.10 | 0.20 | 0.50 | — |
| 1975 | 10,000,000 | — | 0.10 | 0.20 | 0.50 | — |
| 1975 Proof | 10 | Value: 750 | | | | |
| 1976 | 20,000,000 | — | 0.10 | 0.20 | 0.50 | — |
| 1976 Proof | 10 | Value: 750 | | | | |
| 1977 | 10,000,000 | — | 0.10 | 0.20 | 0.50 | — |

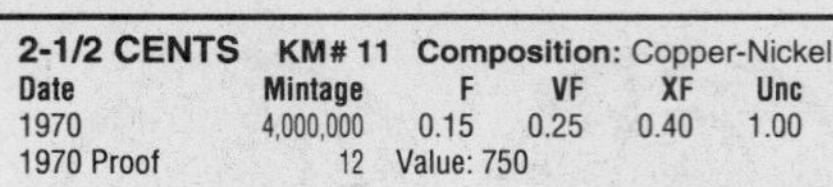

**2-1/2 CENTS** KM# 11 **Composition:** Copper-Nickel

| Date | Mintage | F | VF | XF | Unc | BU |
|---|---|---|---|---|---|---|
| 1970 | 4,000,000 | 0.15 | 0.25 | 0.40 | 1.00 | — |
| 1970 Proof | 12 | Value: 750 | | | | |

**5 CENTS** KM# 12 **Composition:** Copper-Nickel

| Date | Mintage | F | VF | XF | Unc | BU |
|---|---|---|---|---|---|---|
| 1973 | — | 0.25 | 0.75 | 1.50 | 3.00 | — |
| 1973 Proof | 10 | Value: 750 | | | | |

**5 CENTS** KM# 13 **Composition:** Copper-Nickel

| Date | Mintage | F | VF | XF | Unc | BU |
|---|---|---|---|---|---|---|
| 1975 | 3,500,000 | 0.15 | 0.25 | 0.40 | 0.75 | — |
| 1975 Proof | 10 | Value: 750 | | | | |
| 1976 | 8,038,000 | 0.15 | 0.25 | 0.40 | 0.75 | — |
| 1977 | 3,015,000 | 0.25 | 0.75 | 1.50 | 3.00 | — |

**10 CENTS** KM# 14 **Composition:** Copper-Nickel

| Date | Mintage | F | VF | XF | Unc | BU |
|---|---|---|---|---|---|---|
| 1975 | 2,003,000 | 0.15 | 0.30 | 0.60 | 1.50 | — |
| 1975 Proof | 10 | Value: 750 | | | | |

**20 CENTS** KM# 15 **Composition:** Copper-Nickel

| Date | Mintage | F | VF | XF | Unc | BU |
|---|---|---|---|---|---|---|
| 1975 | 1,937,000 | 0.50 | 0.75 | 1.00 | 3.00 | — |
| 1975 Proof | 10 | Value: 750 | | | | |
| 1977 | — | 0.50 | 0.75 | 1.50 | 3.50 | — |

**25 CENTS** KM# 16 **Composition:** Copper-Nickel

| Date | Mintage | F | VF | XF | Unc | BU |
|---|---|---|---|---|---|---|
| 1975 | 1,011,000 | 0.50 | 1.00 | 2.00 | 4.00 | — |
| 1975 Proof | 10 | Value: 750 | | | | |

## PROOF SETS

| KM# | Date | Mintage | Identification | Issue Price | Mkt Val |
|---|---|---|---|---|---|
| PS1 | 1964 (8) | 10 | KM#1-4 Double set | — | 250 |
| PS2 | 1964 (4) | 2,060 | KM#1-4 | — | 50.00 |
| PS3 | 1966 (3) | 2,000 | KM#5-7 | 280 | 825 |
| PS4 | 1968 (2) | 3 | KM#8 Double set | — | 2,250 |
| PS5 | 1970 (6) | 3 | KM#9-11 Double set | — | 4,500 |
| PS6 | 1973 (2) | 2 | KM#12 Double set | — | 1,500 |
| PS7 | 1975 (8) | 1 | KM#13-16 Double set | — | 7,000 |
| PS8 | 1975 (6) | 4 | KM#9, 10, 13-16 | — | 5,000 |
| PS9 | 1975 (4) | 4 | KM#13-16 | — | 3,500 |

# ROMANIA

Romania (formerly the Socialist Republic of Romania), a country in southeast Europe, has an area of 91,699 sq. mi. (237,500 sq. km.) and a population of 23.2 million. Capital: Bucharest. Machinery, foodstuffs, raw minerals and petroleum products are exported. Heavy industry and oil have become increasingly important to the economy since 1959.

In 1526, Hungary came under Turkish rule. With defeat in 1526, Hungary came under Turkish rule. Transylvania became a separate principality under the protection of the Sultan (1541).

In 1881, Carol I became king. In 1888, Romania became a constitutional monarchy with a bicameral legislature. Neutral during the First Balkan War (1912), Romania joined Serbia and Greece in the Second Balkan War (1913) against Bulgaria The intervention and deployment of Romanian troops into Bulgaria resulted in the acquisition of southern Dobruja.

When WW I began, the kingdom was neutral until 1916, when the Romanian army invaded Transylvania, but Austro-German, Turkish and Bulgarian forces occupied the south of the country. The Romanians, with the triumph of the Allies, persisted in keeping Moldavia. In March 1918, the Bessarabian legislature voted in favor of reunification with Romania. With the triumph of the Allies, the Romanian army liberated their southern region and reoccupied Transylvania. Bukovina (Oct. 28, 1918) and Transylvania (Dec. 1) proclaimed their reunification with Romania. In 1919, the Romanian army shattered the Bolshevik forces, which were installed in Hungary.

A new constitution was adopted in 1923. During this period in history, the Romanian government struggled with domestic problems, agrarian reform and economic reconstruction.

In the background of WW II, in 1940, after the defeat of France, following the Soviet-Nazi agreement of August1939, the Red army occupied Bessarabia and northern Bukovina (June). Later, northern Transylvania was annexed by Hungary (August) and southern Dobruja was returned to Bulgaria (September). In this context, King Carol II abdicated in favor of his son Mihai.

The government was reorganized along Fascist lines between September 14, 1940 & January 23, 1941. A military dictatorship followed when the German's Antonescu installed himself as chief of state. When the Germans invaded the Soviet Union, Romania also became involved in recovering the regions of Bessarabia and northern Bukovina annexed by Stalin in 1940.

On August 23, 1944, King Mihai I proclaimed an armistice with the Allied Forces. The Romanian army drove out the Germans and Hungarians in northern Transylvania, but the country was subsequently occupied by the Soviet army. That monarchy was abolished on December 30, 1947,and Romania became a "People's Republic" based on the Soviet regime. The process of sovietization included Soviet regime. The anti-Communist combative resistance movement developed frequent purges of dissidents: mainly political but also clerical, cultural and peasants. Romanian elite disappeared into the concentration camps. The anti-Communist combative resistance movement developed in spite of the Soviet army presence until 1956. The partisans remained in the mountains until 1964. With the accession of N. Ceausescu to power, Romania began to exercise a considerable degree of independence, refusing to participate in the invasion of Czechoslovakia (August 1968). In 1965, it was proclaimed a "Socialist Republic". After 1977, an oppressed and impoverished domestic scene worsened.

On December 17, 1989, an anti-Communist revolt in Timisoara. On December 22, 1989 the Communist government was overthrown. Ceausescu and his wife were arrested and later executed. The new government established a republic, the constitutional name being Romania.

**RULERS**

Carol I (as Prince), 1866-81 (as King), 1881-1914
Ferdinand I, 1914-1927
Mihai I, 1927-1930
Carol II, 1930-1940
Mihai I, 1940-1947

**MINT MARKS**

(a) - Paris, privy marks only
(b) - Brussels, privy marks only
angel head (1872-1876),
no marks (1894-1924)
B - Bucharest (1870-1900)
B - Hamburg, Germany
C - Candescu, chief engineer of the Bucharest Mint (1870- )
FM - Franklin Mint, USA
H - Heaton, Birmingham, England
HF - Huguenin Freres & Co., Le Locle, Switzerland
J - Hamburg
KN - Kings Norton, Birmingham, England
(p) - Thunderbolt - Poissy, France
zig zag (1924)
V - Vienna, Austria
W - Watt (James Watt & Co.)
Huguenin - Le Locle, Switzerland
( ) - no marks, 1930 (10, 20 Lei),
1932 (100 Lei), Royal Mint – London

**MONETARY SYSTEM**

100 Bani = 1 Leu

# KINGDOM

## STANDARD COINAGE

**5 BANI** **KM# 31** **Composition:** Copper-Nickel **Ruler:** Carol I as King = Rege

| Date | Mintage | F | VF | XF | Unc | BU |
|---|---|---|---|---|---|---|
| 1905 | 2,000,000 | 0.50 | 1.00 | 3.50 | 12.00 | — |
| 1905 Proof | — | Value: 40.00 | | | | |
| 1906 | 48,000,000 | 0.25 | 0.50 | 2.00 | 9.00 | — |
| 1906J | 24,000,000 | 0.25 | 0.50 | 1.50 | 6.00 | — |

**10 BANI** **KM# 32** **Composition:** Copper-Nickel **Ruler:** Carol I as King = Rege

| Date | Mintage | F | VF | XF | Unc | BU |
|---|---|---|---|---|---|---|
| 1905 | 10,820,000 | 0.50 | 1.00 | 4.00 | 16.00 | — |
| 1906 | 24,180,000 | 0.25 | 0.75 | 2.50 | 10.00 | — |
| 1906J | 17,000,000 | 0.25 | 0.75 | 1.50 | 6.00 | — |

**20 BANI** **KM# 33** **Composition:** Copper-Nickel **Ruler:** Carol I as King = Rege

| Date | Mintage | F | VF | XF | Unc | BU |
|---|---|---|---|---|---|---|
| 1905 | 2,500,000 | 2.00 | 6.00 | 15.00 | 48.00 | — |
| 1906 | 3,000,000 | 2.00 | 4.00 | 12.00 | 36.00 | — |
| 1906J | 2,500,000 | 2.00 | 4.00 | 12.00 | 35.00 | — |

**25 BANI** **KM# 44** **Composition:** Aluminum **Ruler:** Ferdinand I **Note:** Center hole sizes vary from 4 to 4.5 millimeters. No engraver name.

| Date | Mintage | F | VF | XF | Unc | BU |
|---|---|---|---|---|---|---|
| 1921HF | 20,000,000 | 0.50 | 1.00 | 2.50 | 7.50 | — |

**50 BANI** **KM# 23** **Weight:** 2.5000 g. **Composition:** 0.8350 Silver .0671 oz. ASW **Ruler:** Carol I as King = Rege **Reverse:** Small letters

| Date | Mintage | F | VF | XF | Unc | BU |
|---|---|---|---|---|---|---|
| 1901 | 205,000 | 6.00 | 16.00 | 50.00 | 200 | — |

**50 BANI** **KM# 41** **Weight:** 2.5000 g. **Composition:** 0.8350 Silver .0671 oz. ASW **Ruler:** Carol I as King = Rege

| Date | Mintage | F | VF | XF | Unc | BU |
|---|---|---|---|---|---|---|
| 1910 | 3,600,000 | 1.50 | 3.00 | 8.00 | 17.00 | — |
| **Note:** Edge varieties (round or flat) exist. | | | | | | |
| 1910 Proof | — | Value: 150 | | | | |
| 1911 | 3,000,000 | 2.00 | 4.00 | 10.00 | 20.00 | — |
| 1912 | 1,800,000 | 1.50 | 3.00 | 8.00 | 18.00 | — |
| 1914 | 1,600,000 | 1.25 | 2.00 | 4.50 | 12.00 | — |
| **Note:** Edge varieties (round or flat) exist. | | | | | | |
| 1914 Proof | — | Value: 90.00 | | | | |

**50 BANI** **KM# 45** **Composition:** Aluminum **Ruler:** Ferdinand I **Note:** Center hole size varies from 4 to 4.5 millimeters.

| Date | Mintage | F | VF | XF | Unc | BU |
|---|---|---|---|---|---|---|
| 1921HF | 30,000,000 | 0.50 | 1.00 | 3.50 | 9.00 | — |

**LEU** **KM# 24** **Weight:** 5.0000 g. **Composition:** 0.8350 Silver .1342 oz. ASW **Ruler:** Carol I as King = Rege

| Date | Mintage | F | VF | XF | Unc | BU |
|---|---|---|---|---|---|---|
| 1901 | 370,000 | 4.00 | 10.00 | 32.00 | 125 | — |
| 1901 Proof | — | Value: 250 | | | | |

**LEU** **KM# 34 (KM34.1)** **Weight:** 5.0000 g. **Composition:** 0.8350 Silver .1342 oz. ASW **Ruler:** Carol I as King = Rege **Subject:** 40th anniversary - reign of Carol I **Reverse:** A.MICHAUX below truncation

| Date | Mintage | F | VF | XF | Unc | BU |
|---|---|---|---|---|---|---|
| ND(1906) | 2,500,000 | 5.00 | 12.00 | 25.00 | 56.00 | — |
| ND(1906) Proof | — | Value: 200 | | | | |

**LEU** **KM# 42** **Weight:** 5.0000 g. **Composition:** 0.8350 Silver .1342 oz. ASW **Ruler:** Carol I as King = Rege

| Date | Mintage | F | VF | XF | Unc | BU |
|---|---|---|---|---|---|---|
| 1910 | 4,600,000 | 3.00 | 6.00 | 9.00 | 25.00 | — |
| **Note:** Edge varieties (round or flat) exist. | | | | | | |
| 1910 Proof | — | Value: 350 | | | | |
| 1911 | 2,573,000 | 4.00 | 8.00 | 12.00 | 30.00 | — |
| 1912 | 3,540,000 | 3.00 | 5.00 | 8.00 | 19.00 | — |
| 1914 | 4,283,000 | 2.00 | 3.00 | 6.00 | 15.00 | — |
| **Note:** Edge varieties (round or flat) exist. | | | | | | |
| 1914 Proof | — | Value: 100 | | | | |

**LEU** **KM# 46** **Composition:** Copper-Nickel **Ruler:** Ferdinand I **Edge:** reeded

| Date | Mintage | F | VF | XF | Unc | BU |
|---|---|---|---|---|---|---|
| 1924(b) Thin | 100,000,000 | 0.50 | 1.50 | 3.50 | 9.00 | — |
| 1924(p) Thick | 100,006,000 | 0.50 | 1.50 | 4.00 | 10.00 | — |

**LEU** **KM# 56 (KM56.1)** **Composition:** Nickel-Brass **Edge:** plain **Note:** Without mint mark.

| Date | Mintage | F | VF | XF | Unc | BU |
|---|---|---|---|---|---|---|
| 1938 | 27,900,000 | 0.20 | 0.60 | 1.60 | 4.50 | — |
| 1939 | 72,200,000 | 0.20 | 0.50 | 1.50 | 3.00 | — |
| 1940 | Inc. above | 0.20 | 0.50 | 1.00 | 2.50 | — |
| 1941 | Inc. above | 0.20 | 0.50 | 1.50 | 3.50 | — |

**2 LEI** **KM# 25** **Weight:** 10.0000 g. **Composition:** 0.8350 Silver .2684 oz. ASW **Edge:** reeded

| Date | Mintage | F | VF | XF | Unc | BU |
|---|---|---|---|---|---|---|
| 1901 | 12,000 | 350 | 520 | 860 | 1,950 | — |

**2 LEI** **KM# 43** **Weight:** 10.0000 g. **Composition:** 0.8350 Silver .2684 oz. ASW **Ruler:** Carol I as King = Rege

| Date | Mintage | F | VF | XF | Unc | BU |
|---|---|---|---|---|---|---|
| 1910 | 1,800,000 | 4.00 | 8.00 | 15.00 | 36.00 | — |
| **Note:** Edge varieties (round and flat) exist. | | | | | | |
| 1910 Proof | — | Value: 200 | | | | |
| 1911 | 1,000,000 | 6.00 | 12.00 | 25.00 | 50.00 | — |
| 1912 | 1,500,000 | 4.00 | 7.00 | 12.00 | 30.00 | — |
| 1914 | 2,452,000 | 3.00 | 5.00 | 9.00 | 20.00 | — |
| **Note:** Edge varieties (round and flat) exist. | | | | | | |
| 1914 Proof | — | Value: 120 | | | | |

**2 LEI** **KM# 47** **Composition:** Copper-Nickel **Ruler:** Ferdinand I **Edge:** reeded

| Date | Mintage | F | VF | XF | Unc | BU |
|---|---|---|---|---|---|---|
| 1924(b) | 50,000,000 | 1.00 | 1.75 | 4.00 | 11.00 | — |
| 1924(p) | 50,008,000 | 1.00 | 1.75 | 4.50 | 12.00 | — |

**2 LEI** **KM# 58** **Composition:** Zinc **Ruler:** Mihai II

| Date | Mintage | F | VF | XF | Unc | BU |
|---|---|---|---|---|---|---|
| 1941 | 101,778,000 | 0.50 | 1.50 | 3.00 | 9.50 | — |

**5 LEI** **KM# 17.2** **Weight:** 25.0000 g. **Composition:** 0.9000 Silver .7234 oz. ASW **Ruler:** Carol I as King = Rege **Edge:** Reeded

| Date | Mintage | F | VF | XF | Unc | BU |
|---|---|---|---|---|---|---|
| 1901B | 460,000 | 45.00 | 70.00 | 160 | 350 | — |
| 1901B Proof | — | Value: 950 | | | | |

**5 LEI** **KM# 35** **Weight:** 25.0000 g. **Composition:** 0.9000 Silver .7234 oz. ASW **Ruler:** Carol I as King = Rege **Subject:** 40th anniversary - reign of Carol I

| Date | Mintage | F | VF | XF | Unc | BU |
|---|---|---|---|---|---|---|
| ND(1906) | 200,000 | 40.00 | 70.00 | 160 | 320 | — |
| ND(1906) Proof | — | Value: 950 | | | | |

**5 LEI** **KM# 48** **Composition:** Nickel-Brass **Ruler:** Mihai I **Obverse:** Bust of King Mihai I **Edge:** reeded

| Date | Mintage | F | VF | XF | Unc | BU |
|---|---|---|---|---|---|---|
| 1930H | 15,000,000 | 1.50 | 2.50 | 6.50 | 19.00 | — |
| 1930KN | 15,000,000 | 1.50 | 3.50 | 8.00 | 22.00 | — |
| 1930(a) | 30,000,000 | 1.00 | 2.50 | 5.50 | 16.00 | — |

**5 LEI** **KM# 61** **Composition:** Zinc **Ruler:** Mihai II

| Date | Mintage | F | VF | XF | Unc | BU |
|---|---|---|---|---|---|---|
| 1942 | 140,000,000 | 0.50 | 1.25 | 2.75 | 7.50 | — |

**10 LEI** **KM# 49** **Composition:** Nickel-Brass **Ruler:** Carol II **Obverse:** Bust of King Carol II **Edge:** reeded

| Date | Mintage | F | VF | XF | Unc | BU |
|---|---|---|---|---|---|---|
| 1930 | 15,000,000 | 1.00 | 3.00 | 8.00 | 24.00 | — |
| 1930 Proof | — | — | — | — | — | — |
| 1930(a) | 30,000,000 | 1.00 | 3.00 | 7.50 | 22.00 | — |
| 1930H | 7,500,000 | 2.50 | 4.50 | 10.00 | 28.00 | — |
| 1930KN | 7,500,000 | 3.00 | 7.00 | 15.00 | 36.00 | — |
| 1930(a) Proof | — | Value: 175 | | | | |

**12-1/2 LEI** **KM# 36** **Weight:** 4.0323 g. **Composition:** 0.9000 Gold .1167 oz. AGW **Ruler:** Carol I as King = Rege **Subject:** 40th anniversary - reign of Carol I

| Date | Mintage | F | VF | XF | Unc | BU |
|---|---|---|---|---|---|---|
| 1906 | 32,000 | 70.00 | 95.00 | 130 | 260 | — |

**20 LEI** **KM# 37** **Weight:** 6.4516 g. **Composition:** 0.9000 Gold .1867 oz. AGW **Ruler:** Carol I as King = Rege **Subject:** 40th anniversary - reign of Carol I

| Date | Mintage | F | VF | XF | Unc | BU |
|---|---|---|---|---|---|---|
| ND(1906)(b) | 15,000 | 115 | 145 | 190 | 320 | — |

**20 LEI** **KM# 50** **Composition:** Nickel-Brass **Ruler:** Mihai I **Obverse:** Bust of King Mihai I **Edge:** reeded

| Date | Mintage | F | VF | XF | Unc | BU |
|---|---|---|---|---|---|---|
| 1930 London | 40,000,000 | 2.00 | 6.50 | 18.00 | 38.00 | — |
| 1930 Proof | — | — | — | — | — | — |
| 1930H | 5,000,000 | 3.00 | 8.00 | 25.00 | 50.00 | — |
| 1930KN | 5,000,000 | 3.00 | 10.00 | 30.00 | 70.00 | — |

**20 LEI** **KM# 51** **Composition:** Nickel-Brass **Ruler:** Carol II **Obverse:** Bust of King Carol II **Edge:** reeded

| Date | Mintage | F | VF | XF | Unc | BU |
|---|---|---|---|---|---|---|
| 1930 | 6,750,000 | 1.50 | 3.00 | 12.00 | 23.00 | — |
| 1930 Proof | — | — | — | — | — | — |
| 1930(a) | 17,500,000 | 1.00 | 2.00 | 10.00 | 22.00 | — |
| 1930H | 7,750,000 | 2.00 | 4.00 | 16.00 | 37.50 | — |
| 1930KN | 7,750,000 | 2.50 | 6.00 | 25.00 | 55.00 | — |
| 1930(a) Proof | — | Value: 185 | | | | |

**20 LEI** **KM# 62** **Composition:** Zinc **Ruler:** Mihai II **Edge:** reeded

| Date | Mintage | F | VF | XF | Unc | BU |
|---|---|---|---|---|---|---|
| 1942 | 44,000,000 | 0.75 | 1.50 | 3.00 | 8.00 | — |
| 1943 | 25,783,000 | 1.00 | 2.25 | 4.00 | 9.00 | — |
| 1944 | 5,034,000 | 1.50 | 3.00 | 5.00 | 12.00 | — |

**25 LEI** **KM# 38** **Weight:** 8.0645 g. **Composition:** 0.9000 Gold .2333 oz. AGW **Ruler:** Carol I as King = Rege **Subject:** 40th anniversary - reign of Carol I

| Date | Mintage | F | VF | XF | Unc | BU |
|---|---|---|---|---|---|---|
| ND(1906)(b) | 24,000 | 145 | 185 | 300 | 460 | — |

**50 LEI** **KM# 39** **Weight:** 16.1290 g. **Composition:** 0.9000 Gold .4667 oz. AGW **Ruler:** Carol I as King = Rege **Subject:** 40th anniversary - reign of Carol I

| Date | Mintage | F | VF | XF | Unc | BU |
|---|---|---|---|---|---|---|
| ND(1906)(b) | 28,000 | 240 | 360 | 520 | 920 | — |

**50 LEI** **KM# 55** **Composition:** Nickel **Ruler:** Carol II **Edge:** reeded **Note:** 16,731 melted.

| Date | Mintage | F | VF | XF | Unc | BU |
|---|---|---|---|---|---|---|
| 1937 | 12,000,000 | 1.25 | 2.50 | 4.50 | 11.00 | — |
| 1938 | 8,000,000 | 3.00 | 6.00 | 14.00 | 35.00 | — |

**100 LEI** **KM# 40** **Weight:** 32.2580 g. **Composition:** 0.9000 Gold .9335 oz. AGW **Ruler:** Carol I as King = Rege **Subject:** 40th anniversary - reign of Carol I

| Date | Mintage | F | VF | XF | Unc | BU |
|---|---|---|---|---|---|---|
| ND(1906)(b) | 3,000 | 460 | 760 | 1,200 | 2,200 | — |

**100 LEI** **KM# 52** **Weight:** 14.0000 g. **Composition:** 0.5000 Silver .1929 oz. ASW **Ruler:** Carol II **Edge:** reeded

| Date | Mintage | F | VF | XF | Unc | BU |
|---|---|---|---|---|---|---|
| 1932(a) | 2,000,000 | 10.00 | 20.00 | 45.00 | 145 | — |
| 1932 | 16,400,000 | 5.00 | 10.00 | 20.00 | 90.00 | — |
| 1932 Proof | — | Value: 250 | | | | |

**100 LEI** **KM# 54** **Composition:** Nickel **Ruler:** Carol II **Edge:** reeded **Note:** 17,030 melted.

| Date | Mintage | F | VF | XF | Unc | BU |
|---|---|---|---|---|---|---|
| 1936 | 20,230,000 | 2.00 | 4.00 | 8.00 | 15.00 | — |
| 1938 | 3,250,000 | 3.00 | 7.00 | 12.50 | 40.00 | — |

**100 LEI** **KM# 64** **Composition:** Nickel Clad Steel **Ruler:** Mihai II **Edge:** incuse lettering **Edge Lettering:** NIHIL SINE DEO

| Date | Mintage | F | VF | XF | Unc | BU |
|---|---|---|---|---|---|---|
| 1943 | 40,590,000 | 0.25 | 0.50 | 1.20 | 4.00 | — |
| **Note:** Portrait varieties exist. | | | | | | |
| 1944 | 21,289,000 | 0.25 | 0.50 | 1.40 | 5.00 | — |

**200 LEI** **KM# 63** **Weight:** 6.0000 g. **Composition:** 0.8350 Silver .1611 oz. ASW **Ruler:** Mihai II **Edge:** incuse lettering **Edge Lettering:** NIHIL SINE DEO

| Date | Mintage | F | VF | XF | Unc | BU |
|---|---|---|---|---|---|---|
| 1942 | 30,025,000 | 1.50 | 2.50 | 6.00 | 15.00 | — |

**200 LEI** **KM# 66** **Composition:** Brass **Ruler:** Mihai II **Note:** Many were silver plated privately.

| Date | Mintage | F | VF | XF | Unc | BU |
|---|---|---|---|---|---|---|
| 1945 | 1,399,000 | 1.00 | 2.00 | 5.00 | 13.00 | — |

**250 LEI** **KM# 53** **Weight:** 13.5000 g. **Composition:** 0.7500 Silver .3255 oz. ASW **Ruler:** Carol II

| Date | Mintage | F | VF | XF | Unc | BU |
|---|---|---|---|---|---|---|
| 1935 | 4,500,000 | 12.00 | 24.00 | 60.00 | 160 | — |

**250 LEI** **KM# 57** **Weight:** 12.0000 g. **Composition:** 0.8350 Silver .3222 oz. ASW **Ruler:** Carol II **Edge:** incuse lettering, line interrupted by 2 rhombs **Edge Lettering:** MUNCA CREDINTA REGE NATIUNE

| Date | Mintage | F | VF | XF | Unc | BU |
|---|---|---|---|---|---|---|
| 1939 | 10,000,000 | 6.00 | 12.00 | 30.00 | 75.00 | — |
| 1940 | 8,000,000 | 10.00 | 18.00 | 42.00 | 125 | — |

**250 LEI** **KM# 59.1** **Weight:** 12.0000 g. **Composition:** 0.8350 Silver .3222 oz. ASW **Ruler:** Carol II **Reverse:** Date divided by portcullis **Edge:** incuse lettering **Edge Lettering:** TOTUL PENTRU TARA **Note:** Mintage unissued and reportedly melted.

| Date | Mintage | F | VF | XF | Unc | BU |
|---|---|---|---|---|---|---|
| 1940 | — | — | — | — | 3,500 | — |

**250 LEI** **KM# 59.2** **Weight:** 12.0000 g. **Composition:** 0.8350 Silver .3222 oz. ASW **Ruler:** Mihai II **Reverse:** Date not divided **Edge:** incuse lettering **Edge Lettering:** TOTUL PENTRU TARA

| Date | Mintage | F | VF | XF | Unc | BU |
|---|---|---|---|---|---|---|
| 1941 | 2,250,000 | 9.00 | 15.00 | 32.00 | 68.00 | — |

**250 LEI** **KM# 59.3** **Weight:** 12.0000 g. **Composition:** 0.8350 Silver .3222 oz. ASW **Ruler:** Mihai II **Edge:** Lettered **Edge Lettering:** NIHIL SINE DEO

| Date | Mintage | F | VF | XF | Unc | BU |
|---|---|---|---|---|---|---|
| 1941B | 13,750,000 | 6.00 | 9.00 | 15.00 | 28.00 | — |

**500 LEI** **KM# 60** **Weight:** 25.0000 g. **Composition:** 0.8350 Silver .6711 oz. ASW **Ruler:** Mihai II **Subject:** Basarabia Reunion **Reverse:** On bended knee, King Stephen presents Putna Monastery to the Lord **Edge:** incuse lettering **Edge Lettering:** PRIN STATORNICIE LA IZBANADA +

| Date | Mintage | F | VF | XF | Unc | BU |
|---|---|---|---|---|---|---|
| 1941 | 775,000 | 8.00 | 12.00 | 18.00 | 34.00 | — |

**500 LEI** **KM# 65** **Weight:** 12.0000 g. **Composition:** 0.7000 Silver .2701 oz. ASW **Ruler:** Mihai II **Edge:** incuse lettering **Edge Lettering:** NIHIL SINE DEO

| Date | Mintage | F | VF | XF | Unc | BU |
|---|---|---|---|---|---|---|
| 1944 | 9,731,000 | 2.50 | 3.50 | 5.00 | 10.00 | — |

**500 LEI** **KM# 67** **Composition:** Brass **Ruler:** Mihai II **Edge:** reeded **Note:** Many were silver plated privately.

| Date | Mintage | F | VF | XF | Unc | BU |
|---|---|---|---|---|---|---|
| 1945 | 3,422,000 | 1.00 | 2.00 | 4.00 | 8.00 | — |

**500 LEI** **KM# 68** **Composition:** Aluminum **Ruler:** Mihai II **Edge:** reeded **Note:** Without designer's name, the result of a filled die.

| Date | Mintage | F | VF | XF | Unc | BU |
|---|---|---|---|---|---|---|
| 1946 | 5,823,000 | 0.50 | 1.00 | 3.00 | 7.00 | — |

**2000 LEI** **KM# 69** **Composition:** Brass **Ruler:** Mihai II **Edge:** incuse lettering **Edge Lettering:** NIHIL SINE DEO **Note:** Many were silver plated privately.

| Date | Mintage | F | VF | XF | Unc | BU |
|---|---|---|---|---|---|---|
| 1946 | 24,619,000 | 0.50 | 1.00 | 3.00 | 7.50 | — |

**10000 LEI** **KM# 76** **Composition:** Brass **Ruler:** Mihai II **Edge:** incuse lettering **Edge Lettering:** NIHIL SINE DEO **Note:** Many were silver plated privately.

| Date | Mintage | F | VF | XF | Unc | BU |
|---|---|---|---|---|---|---|
| 1947 | 11,850,000 | 1.00 | 2.00 | 4.00 | 8.50 | — |

**25000 LEI** **KM# 70** **Weight:** 12.5000 g. **Composition:** 0.7000 Silver .2813 oz. ASW **Ruler:** Mihai II **Edge:** incuse lettering **Edge Lettering:** NIHIL SINE DEO

| Date | Mintage | F | VF | XF | Unc | BU |
|---|---|---|---|---|---|---|
| 1946 | 2,372,000 | 2.00 | 3.00 | 6.00 | 12.00 | — |

**100000 LEI** **KM# 71** **Weight:** 25.0000 g. **Composition:** 0.7000 Silver .5626 oz. ASW **Ruler:** Mihai II **Edge:** incuse lettering **Edge Lettering:** NIHIL SINE DEO

| Date | Mintage | F | VF | XF | Unc | BU |
|---|---|---|---|---|---|---|
| 1946 | 2,002,000 | 5.00 | 7.00 | 10.00 | 19.00 | — |

## REFORM COINAGE

Aug. 15, 1947; 100 Bani = 1 Leu

**50 BANI** **KM# 72** **Composition:** Brass **Ruler:** Mihai II **Edge:** plain

| Date | Mintage | F | VF | XF | Unc | BU |
|---|---|---|---|---|---|---|
| 1947 | 13,266,000 | 1.00 | 2.00 | 3.00 | 9.50 | — |

**LEU** **KM# 73** **Composition:** Brass **Ruler:** Mihai II **Edge:** plain

| Date | Mintage | F | VF | XF | Unc | BU |
|---|---|---|---|---|---|---|
| 1947 | 88,341,000 | 1.00 | 2.25 | 4.00 | 10.00 | — |

**2 LEI** **KM# 74** **Composition:** Bronze **Ruler:** Mihai II **Edge:** plain

| Date | Mintage | F | VF | XF | Unc | BU |
|---|---|---|---|---|---|---|
| 1947 | 40,000,000 | 1.00 | 2.50 | 5.00 | 14.00 | — |

**5 LEI** **KM# 75** **Composition:** Aluminum **Ruler:** Mihai II

| Date | Mintage | F | VF | XF | Unc | BU |
|---|---|---|---|---|---|---|
| 1947 | 56,026,000 | 1.50 | 2.50 | 6.50 | 18.00 | — |

## MEDALLIC COINAGE

**20 LEI** **KM# M1** **Weight:** 6.4516 g. **Composition:** 0.9000 Gold .1867 oz. AGW **Ruler:** Ferdinand I **Subject:** Ferdinand I coronation

| Date | Mintage | F | VF | XF | Unc | BU |
|---|---|---|---|---|---|---|
| 1922 | 300,000 | 150 | 275 | 400 | 500 | — |

**20 LEI** **KM# M2** **Weight:** 6.4516 g. **Composition:** 0.9000 Gold .1867 oz. AGW **Ruler:** Carol II **Subject:** Centennial - birth of Carol I

| Date | Mintage | F | VF | XF | Unc | BU |
|---|---|---|---|---|---|---|
| 1939 C | — | 125 | 200 | 550 | 750 | — |

**20 LEI** **KM# M3** **Weight:** 6.4516 g. **Composition:** 0.9000 Gold .1867 oz. AGW **Ruler:** Carol II

| Date | Mintage | F | VF | XF | Unc | BU |
|---|---|---|---|---|---|---|
| 1939 C | — | 125 | 200 | 550 | 750 | — |

**20 LEI** **KM# M4** **Weight:** 6.4516 g. **Composition:** 0.9000 Gold .1867 oz. AGW **Ruler:** Carol II **Subject:** Carol II 10th anniversary

| Date | Mintage | F | VF | XF | Unc | BU |
|---|---|---|---|---|---|---|
| 1940 C | — | 125 | 200 | 550 | 750 | — |

**20 LEI** **KM# M5** **Weight:** 6.4516 g. **Composition:** 0.9000 Gold .1867 oz. AGW **Ruler:** Carol II

| Date | Mintage | F | VF | XF | Unc | BU |
|---|---|---|---|---|---|---|
| 1940 C | — | 125 | 225 | 550 | 750 | — |

**20 LEI** **KM# M6** **Weight:** 6.5500 g. **Composition:** 0.9000 Gold .1895 oz. AGW **Ruler:** Mihai II **Subject:** Romanian kings

| Date | Mintage | F | VF | XF | Unc | BU |
|---|---|---|---|---|---|---|
| 1944 | 1,000,000 | — | BV | 85.00 | 125 | — |

**25 LEI** **KM# M7** **Weight:** 8.0645 g. **Composition:** 0.9000 Gold .2333 oz. AGW **Ruler:** Ferdinand I **Subject:** Ferdinand I coronation

| Date | Mintage | F | VF | XF | Unc | BU |
|---|---|---|---|---|---|---|
| 1922 | 150,000 | 250 | 400 | 500 | 700 | — |

**50 LEI** **KM# M8** **Weight:** 16.1290 g. **Composition:** 0.9000 Gold .4667 oz. AGW **Ruler:** Ferdinand I **Subject:** Ferdinand I coronation

| Date | Mintage | F | VF | XF | Unc | BU |
|---|---|---|---|---|---|---|
| 1922 | 105,000 | 350 | 500 | 850 | 1,250 | — |

**100 LEI** **KM# M9** **Weight:** 32.2580 g. **Composition:** 0.9000 Gold .9335 oz. AGW **Ruler:** Ferdinand I **Subject:** Ferdinand I coronation

| Date | Mintage | F | VF | XF | Unc | BU |
|---|---|---|---|---|---|---|
| 1922 | 30,000 | 600 | 1,000 | 1,650 | 2,350 | — |

**100 LEI** **KM# M10** **Weight:** 32.5000 g. **Composition:** 0.9000 Gold .9404 oz. AGW **Ruler:** Carol II **Subject:** Centennial - birth of Carol I

| Date | Mintage | F | VF | XF | Unc | BU |
|---|---|---|---|---|---|---|
| 1939 C | — | 1,500 | 2,500 | 3,750 | 5,000 | — |

**100 LEI** **KM# M11** **Weight:** 32.5000 g. **Composition:** 0.9000 Gold .9404 oz. AGW **Ruler:** Carol II

| Date | Mintage | F | VF | XF | Unc | BU |
|---|---|---|---|---|---|---|
| 1939 C | — | 1,500 | 2,500 | 3,750 | 5,000 | — |

**100 LEI** **KM# M12** **Weight:** 32.5000 g. **Composition:** 0.9000 Gold .9404 oz. AGW **Ruler:** Carol II **Subject:** Carol II 10th anniversary

| Date | Mintage | F | VF | XF | Unc | BU |
|---|---|---|---|---|---|---|
| ND(1940) C | — | 1,250 | 2,000 | 3,000 | 4,000 | — |

**100 LEI** **KM# M14** **Weight:** 32.5000 g. **Composition:** 0.9000 Gold .9404 oz. AGW **Ruler:** Carol II

| Date | Mintage | F | VF | XF | Unc | BU |
|---|---|---|---|---|---|---|
| ND(1940) C | — | 1,250 | 2,000 | 3,000 | 4,000 | — |

## GALBENI MEDALLIC ISSUES

These medals were issued with the commemorative gold coins listed earlier in this section. Gilt-brass paterns exist for M15-M18.

**100 LEI** KM# M15 **Weight:** 42.0000 g. **Composition:** 0.9000 Gold 1.2153 oz. AGW **Ruler:** Carol II

| Date | Mintage | F | VF | XF | Unc | BU |
|---|---|---|---|---|---|---|
| 1939 | — | — | — | 1,000 | 1,600 | — |

**100 LEI** KM# M16 **Weight:** 42.0000 g. **Composition:** 0.9000 Gold 1.2153 oz. AGW **Ruler:** Carol II

| Date | Mintage | F | VF | XF | Unc | BU |
|---|---|---|---|---|---|---|
| 1939 | — | — | — | 1,000 | 1,600 | — |

**100 LEI** KM# M17 **Weight:** 42.0000 g. **Composition:** 0.9000 Gold 1.2153 oz. AGW **Ruler:** Carol II **Subject:** Carol II 10th anniversary **Note:** Similar to KM#M16.

| Date | Mintage | F | VF | XF | Unc | BU |
|---|---|---|---|---|---|---|
| ND(1940) | — | — | — | 1,500 | 2,700 | — |

**100 LEI** KM# M18 **Weight:** 42.0000 g. **Composition:** 0.9000 Gold 1.2153 oz. AGW **Ruler:** Carol II **Reverse:** Mounted horse facing right

| Date | Mintage | F | VF | XF | Unc | BU |
|---|---|---|---|---|---|---|
| ND(1940) | — | — | — | 2,900 | 4,000 | — |

# PEOPLE'S REPUBLIC

## STANDARD COINAGE

**LEU** KM# 78 **Composition:** Copper-Nickel-Zinc **Edge:** plain

| Date | Mintage | F | VF | XF | Unc | BU |
|---|---|---|---|---|---|---|
| 1949 | — | 0.75 | 1.50 | 3.00 | 8.50 | — |
| 1950 | — | 0.75 | 1.50 | 3.25 | 8.00 | — |
| 1951 | — | 1.00 | 2.00 | 4.50 | 10.00 | — |

**LEU** KM# 78a **Composition:** Aluminum

| Date | Mintage | F | VF | XF | Unc | BU |
|---|---|---|---|---|---|---|
| 1951 | — | 1.00 | 2.00 | 5.00 | 11.50 | — |
| 1952 | — | 6.00 | 12.00 | 22.00 | 60.00 | — |

**2 LEI** KM# 79 **Composition:** Copper-Nickel-Zinc **Edge:** plain

| Date | Mintage | F | VF | XF | Unc | BU |
|---|---|---|---|---|---|---|
| 1950 | — | 1.00 | 2.50 | 5.00 | 10.00 | — |
| 1951 | — | 2.00 | 5.00 | 10.00 | 22.00 | — |

**2 LEI** KM# 79a **Composition:** Aluminum

| Date | Mintage | F | VF | XF | Unc | BU |
|---|---|---|---|---|---|---|
| 1951 | — | 0.75 | 2.00 | 4.00 | 10.00 | — |
| 1952 | — | 6.00 | 12.50 | 26.00 | 65.00 | — |

**5 LEI** KM# 77 **Composition:** Aluminum **Edge:** plain

| Date | Mintage | F | VF | XF | Unc | BU |
|---|---|---|---|---|---|---|
| 1948 | — | 1.50 | 2.50 | 4.50 | 18.00 | — |
| 1949 | — | 1.25 | 2.00 | 3.50 | 10.00 | — |
| 1950 | — | 1.25 | 2.00 | 3.50 | 10.00 | — |
| 1951 | — | 1.25 | 2.00 | 4.00 | 14.00 | — |

**20 LEI** KM# 80 **Composition:** Aluminum **Edge:** plain

| Date | Mintage | F | VF | XF | Unc | BU |
|---|---|---|---|---|---|---|
| 1951 | — | 2.00 | 6.00 | 16.00 | 45.00 | — |

## REFORM COINAGE

Jan. 26, 1952; 100 Bani = 1 Leu

**BAN** KM# 81.1 **Composition:** Copper-Nickel-Zinc **Obverse:** Without star at top of arms **Edge:** reeded

| Date | Mintage | F | VF | XF | Unc | BU |
|---|---|---|---|---|---|---|
| 1952 | — | 0.20 | 0.50 | 1.00 | 2.00 | — |

**BAN** KM# 81.2 **Composition:** Copper-Nickel-Zinc **Obverse:** Star at top of arms

| Date | Mintage | F | VF | XF | Unc | BU |
|---|---|---|---|---|---|---|
| 1953 | — | 1.00 | 2.00 | 6.00 | 15.00 | — |
| 1954 | — | 2.00 | 4.00 | 8.00 | 30.00 | — |

**3 BANI** KM# 82.1 **Composition:** Copper-Nickel-Zinc **Obverse:** Without star at top of arms **Edge:** reeded

| Date | Mintage | F | VF | XF | Unc | BU |
|---|---|---|---|---|---|---|
| 1952 | — | 1.00 | 2.00 | 4.00 | 10.00 | — |

**3 BANI** KM# 82.2 **Composition:** Copper-Nickel-Zinc **Obverse:** Star at top of arms

| Date | Mintage | F | VF | XF | Unc | BU |
|---|---|---|---|---|---|---|
| 1953 | — | 0.50 | 1.00 | 2.00 | 7.00 | — |
| 1954 | — | 3.00 | 6.50 | 17.00 | 46.00 | — |

**5 BANI** KM# 83.1 **Composition:** Copper-Nickel-Zinc **Obverse:** Without star at top of arms **Edge:** reeded

| Date | Mintage | F | VF | XF | Unc | BU |
|---|---|---|---|---|---|---|
| 1952 | — | 0.50 | 1.00 | 2.50 | 7.00 | — |

**5 BANI** KM# 83.2 **Composition:** Copper-Nickel-Zinc **Obverse:** Star at top of arms

| Date | Mintage | F | VF | XF | Unc | BU |
|---|---|---|---|---|---|---|
| 1953 | — | 0.25 | 0.50 | 1.50 | 5.00 | — |
| 1954 | — | 0.25 | 0.50 | 1.50 | 4.00 | — |
| 1955 | — | 0.25 | 0.50 | 1.50 | 4.00 | — |
| 1956 | — | 0.25 | 0.50 | 1.25 | 3.50 | — |
| 1957 | — | 0.25 | 0.50 | 1.75 | 5.00 | — |

**5 BANI** KM# 89 **Composition:** Nickel Clad Steel **Obverse:** RPR on ribbon in arms **Edge:** plain

| Date | Mintage | F | VF | XF | Unc | BU |
|---|---|---|---|---|---|---|
| 1963 | — | 0.20 | 0.50 | 1.00 | 2.00 | — |

**10 BANI** **KM# 84.1** **Composition:** Copper-Nickel **Obverse:** Without star at top of arms **Edge:** reeded

| Date | Mintage | F | VF | XF | Unc | BU |
|---|---|---|---|---|---|---|
| 1952 | — | 1.50 | 2.50 | 7.50 | 18.00 | — |

**10 BANI** **KM# 84.2** **Composition:** Copper-Nickel **Obverse:** Star at top of arms **Obv. Legend:** ROMANA

| Date | Mintage | F | VF | XF | Unc | BU |
|---|---|---|---|---|---|---|
| 1954 | — | 0.30 | 1.50 | 3.00 | 7.00 | — |

**10 BANI** **KM# 84.3** **Composition:** Copper-Nickel **Obv. Legend:** ROMINA

| Date | Mintage | F | VF | XF | Unc | BU |
|---|---|---|---|---|---|---|
| 1955 | — | 0.10 | 0.20 | 0.75 | 3.00 | — |
| 1956 | — | 0.10 | 0.20 | 0.75 | 3.00 | — |

**15 BANI** **KM# 87** **Composition:** Nickel Clad Steel **Edge:** plain

| Date | Mintage | F | VF | XF | Unc | BU |
|---|---|---|---|---|---|---|
| 1960 | — | 0.10 | 0.25 | 0.60 | 2.00 | — |

**25 BANI** **KM# 85.1** **Composition:** Copper-Nickel **Obverse:** Without star at top of arms **Edge:** reeded

| Date | Mintage | F | VF | XF | Unc | BU |
|---|---|---|---|---|---|---|
| 1952 | — | 1.50 | 3.50 | 10.00 | 25.00 | — |

**25 BANI** **KM# 85.2** **Composition:** Copper-Nickel **Obverse:** Star at top of arms **Obv. Legend:** ROMANA

| Date | Mintage | F | VF | XF | Unc | BU |
|---|---|---|---|---|---|---|
| 1953 | — | 0.20 | 0.75 | 2.00 | 5.00 | — |
| 1954 | — | 0.20 | 0.60 | 1.50 | 4.00 | — |

**25 BANI** **KM# 85.3** **Composition:** Copper-Nickel **Obv. Legend:** ROMINA

| Date | Mintage | F | VF | XF | Unc | BU |
|---|---|---|---|---|---|---|
| 1955 | — | 0.15 | 0.35 | 0.80 | 3.00 | — |

**25 BANI** **KM# 88** **Composition:** Nickel Clad Steel **Edge:** plain

| Date | Mintage | F | VF | XF | Unc | BU |
|---|---|---|---|---|---|---|
| 1960 | — | 0.15 | 0.30 | 0.60 | 2.00 | — |

**50 BANI** **KM# 86** **Composition:** Copper-Nickel **Edge:** reeded

| Date | Mintage | F | VF | XF | Unc | BU |
|---|---|---|---|---|---|---|
| 1955 | — | 1.00 | 2.00 | 3.50 | 12.00 | — |
| 1956 | — | 0.50 | 1.00 | 2.00 | 10.00 | — |

**LEU** **KM# 90** **Composition:** Nickel Clad Steel **Edge:** plain

| Date | Mintage | F | VF | XF | Unc | BU |
|---|---|---|---|---|---|---|
| 1963 | — | 0.25 | 0.50 | 0.75 | 2.00 | — |

**3 LEI** **KM# 91** **Composition:** Nickel Clad Steel **Edge:** plain

| Date | Mintage | F | VF | XF | Unc | BU |
|---|---|---|---|---|---|---|
| 1963 | — | 0.25 | 0.50 | 1.20 | 3.00 | — |

# SOCIALIST REPUBLIC

## STANDARD COINAGE

**5 BANI** **KM# 92** **Composition:** Nickel Clad Steel **Obverse:** ROMANIA on ribbon in arms **Edge:** plain

| Date | Mintage | F | VF | XF | Unc | BU |
|---|---|---|---|---|---|---|
| 1966 | — | 0.10 | 0.20 | 0.60 | 1.50 | — |

**5 BANI** **KM# 92a** **Composition:** Aluminum **Edge:** plain

| Date | Mintage | F | VF | XF | Unc | BU |
|---|---|---|---|---|---|---|
| 1975 | — | — | 0.10 | 0.20 | 0.50 | — |

**15 BANI** **KM# 93** **Composition:** Nickel Clad Steel **Edge:** plain

| Date | Mintage | F | VF | XF | Unc | BU |
|---|---|---|---|---|---|---|
| 1966 | — | — | 0.15 | 0.35 | 1.20 | — |

**15 BANI** **KM# 93a** **Composition:** Aluminum **Edge:** plain

| Date | Mintage | F | VF | XF | Unc | BU |
|---|---|---|---|---|---|---|
| 1975 | — | — | 0.10 | 0.25 | 0.75 | — |

**25 BANI** **KM# 94** **Composition:** Nickel Clad Steel **Edge:** plain

| Date | Mintage | F | VF | XF | Unc | BU |
|---|---|---|---|---|---|---|
| 1966 | — | — | 0.20 | 0.55 | 2.00 | — |

**25 BANI** **KM# 94a** **Composition:** Aluminum **Edge:** plain

| Date | Mintage | F | VF | XF | Unc | BU |
|---|---|---|---|---|---|---|
| 1982 | — | — | 0.50 | 1.00 | 3.00 | — |

**LEU** **KM# 95** **Composition:** Nickel Clad Steel

| Date | Mintage | F | VF | XF | Unc | BU |
|---|---|---|---|---|---|---|
| 1966 | — | 0.10 | 0.25 | 0.60 | 2.20 | — |

**3 LEI** **KM# 96** **Composition:** Nickel Clad Steel **Edge:** plain

| Date | Mintage | F | VF | XF | Unc | BU |
|---|---|---|---|---|---|---|
| 1966 | — | 0.25 | 0.50 | 1.20 | 3.00 | — |

**5 LEI** **KM# 97** **Composition:** Aluminum **Reverse:** Large and small dot varieties exist **Edge:** security

| Date | Mintage | F | VF | XF | Unc | BU |
|---|---|---|---|---|---|---|
| 1978 | — | — | 0.50 | 1.00 | 3.50 | — |

**50 LEI** **KM# 100** **Weight:** 13.8800 g. **Composition:** 0.9250 Silver .4128 oz. ASW **Subject:** 2,050th anniversary of first independent state **Obverse:** Similar to 100 Lei, KM#98

| Date | Mintage | F | VF | XF | Unc | BU |
|---|---|---|---|---|---|---|
| 1983FM Proof | 7,000 | Value: 75.00 | | | | |
| 1983FM Proof | 1,000 | Value: 220 | | | | |

**Note:** Serially numbered on edge

**100 LEI** **KM# 98** **Weight:** 27.7500 g. **Composition:** 0.9250 Silver .8253 oz. ASW **Subject:** 2,050th anniversary of first independent state

| Date | Mintage | F | VF | XF | Unc | BU |
|---|---|---|---|---|---|---|
| 1982FM Proof | 7,500 | Value: 90.00 | | | | |
| 1983FM Proof | 7,000 | Value: 95.00 | | | | |
| 1983FM Proof | 1,000 | Value: 320 | | | | |

**Note:** Serially numbered on edge

**500 LEI** **KM# 99** **Weight:** 7.2000 g. **Composition:** 0.9000 Gold .2038 oz. AGW **Subject:** 2,050th anniversary of first independent state

| Date | Mintage | F | VF | XF | Unc | BU |
|---|---|---|---|---|---|---|
| 1982FM Proof | 7,500 | Value: 360 | | | | |
| 1983FM Proof | 7,000 | Value: 380 | | | | |
| 1983FM Proof | 1,000 | Value: 520 | | | | |

**Note:** Serially numbered on edge

**1000 LEI** **KM# 101** **Weight:** 14.4000 g. **Composition:** 0.9000 Gold .4167 oz. AGW **Subject:** 2,050th anniversary of first independent state **Obverse:** Similar to 500 Lei, KM#99

| Date | Mintage | F | VF | XF | Unc | BU |
|---|---|---|---|---|---|---|
| 1983FM Proof | 7,000 | Value: 560 | | | | |
| 1983FM Proof | 1,000 | Value: 900 | | | | |

**Note:** Serially numbered on edge

## REPUBLIC

### STANDARD COINAGE

**LEU** **KM# 113** **Composition:** Copper Clad Steel **Subject:** National Bank of Romania **Edge:** plain

| Date | Mintage | F | VF | XF | Unc | BU |
|---|---|---|---|---|---|---|
| 1992 | Est. 60,000,000 | 0.10 | 0.40 | 0.80 | 3.00 | — |

**LEU** **KM# 115** **Composition:** Copper Clad Steel **Reverse:** Coat of arms

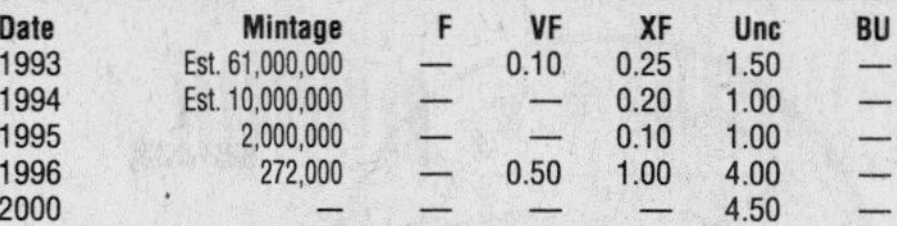

| Date | Mintage | F | VF | XF | Unc | BU |
|---|---|---|---|---|---|---|
| 1993 | Est. 61,000,000 | — | 0.10 | 0.25 | 1.50 | — |
| 1994 | Est. 10,000,000 | — | — | 0.20 | 1.00 | — |
| 1995 | 2,000,000 | — | — | 0.10 | 1.00 | — |
| 1996 | 272,000 | — | 0.50 | 1.00 | 4.00 | — |
| 2000 | — | — | — | — | 4.50 | — |

**Note:** 2000-dated strikes in sets only.

**5 LEI** **KM# 112** **Composition:** Aluminum **Subject:** Prince Mahai Viteazul **Note:** Similar to 100 Lei, KM#111. Not released for circulation; majority were melted.

| Date | Mintage | F | VF | XF | Unc | BU |
|---|---|---|---|---|---|---|
| 1991 | — | — | — | — | 95.00 | — |

**5 LEI** **KM# 114** **Composition:** Nickel Plated Steel **Edge:** plain

| Date | Mintage | F | VF | XF | Unc | BU |
|---|---|---|---|---|---|---|
| 1992 CD VG | Est. 30,000,000 | — | 0.25 | 0.60 | 3.00 | — |
| 1993 CD | Est. 70,000,000 | — | — | 0.30 | 2.00 | — |
| 1994 | Est. 10,000,000 | — | — | 0.20 | 1.00 | — |
| 1995 | 25,000,000 | — | — | 0.20 | 1.00 | — |
| 2000 Proof | — | — | — | — | 4.50 | — |

**Note:** 2000-dated strikes in sets only.

**10 LEI** **KM# 108** **Composition:** Nickel-Clad Steel **Subject:** Revolution anniversary **Note:** Rotated die varieties exist.

| Date | Mintage | F | VF | XF | Unc | BU |
|---|---|---|---|---|---|---|
| 1990 | 30,000,000 | — | 0.50 | 1.00 | 3.00 | — |
| 1991 | 31,303,000 | — | 0.25 | 0.60 | 2.00 | — |
| 1992 | 60,000,000 | — | 0.25 | 0.50 | 1.00 | — |

**10 LEI** **KM# 116** **Composition:** Nickel-Clad Steel

| Date | Mintage | F | VF | XF | Unc | BU |
|---|---|---|---|---|---|---|
| 1993 | Est. 6,000,000 | — | 0.75 | 1.50 | 3.50 | — |
| 1994 | Est. 7,000,000 | — | 0.50 | 1.00 | 3.00 | — |
| 1995 | 30,000,000 | — | — | 0.30 | 1.00 | — |
| 1996 | 5,000 | — | — | — | — | — |
| 2000 Proof | — | — | — | — | 4.50 | — |

**Note:** 2000-dated strikes in sets only.

**10 LEI** **KM# 117.1** **Composition:** Nickel Plated Steel **Series:** F.A.O. **Subject:** 50 years - F.A.O. **Edge:** plain

| Date | Mintage | F | VF | XF | Unc | BU |
|---|---|---|---|---|---|---|
| 1995 | 200,000 | — | — | 2.00 | 5.00 | — |

**10 LEI** **KM# 117.2** **Composition:** Nickel Plated Steel **Series:** F.A.O. **Subject:** 50 years - F.A.O. **Obverse:** N in diamond at right for Numismatists

| Date | Mintage | F | VF | XF | Unc | BU |
|---|---|---|---|---|---|---|
| 1995 | 30,000 | — | — | 3.00 | 7.50 | — |

**10 LEI** **KM# 120** **Composition:** Nickel Plated Steel **Series:** 1996 Olympics Games - U.S.A. **Reverse:** Swimmer

| Date | Mintage | F | VF | XF | Unc | BU |
|---|---|---|---|---|---|---|
| 1996 | 10,000 | — | — | — | 7.00 | — |

**10 LEI** **KM# 121** **Composition:** Nickel Plated Steel **Series:** 1996 Olympics Games - U.S.A. **Reverse:** 4 Olympic scenes

| Date | Mintage | F | VF | XF | Unc | BU |
|---|---|---|---|---|---|---|
| 1996 | 10,000 | — | — | — | 7.00 | — |

**10 LEI** **KM# 122** **Composition:** Nickel Plated Steel **Series:** 1996 Olympics Games - U.S.A. **Reverse:** Windsurfer

| Date | Mintage | F | VF | XF | Unc | BU |
|---|---|---|---|---|---|---|
| 1996 | 10,000 | — | — | — | 7.00 | — |

**10 LEI** **KM# 123** **Composition:** Nickel Plated Steel **Series:** 1996 Olympics Games - U.S.A. **Reverse:** Sailboat with 2 racers

| Date | Mintage | F | VF | XF | Unc | BU |
|---|---|---|---|---|---|---|
| 1996 | 10,000 | — | — | — | 7.00 | — |

**10 LEI** **KM# 124** **Composition:** Nickel Plated Steel **Series:** 1996 Olympics Games - U.S.A. **Reverse:** Canoe with 2 racers

| Date | Mintage | F | VF | XF | Unc | BU |
|---|---|---|---|---|---|---|
| 1996 | 10,000 | — | — | — | 7.00 | — |

**10 LEI** **KM# 125** **Composition:** Nickel Plated Steel **Series:** 1996 Olympics Games - U.S.A. **Reverse:** Scullcraft with racers

| Date | Mintage | F | VF | XF | Unc | BU |
|---|---|---|---|---|---|---|
| 1996 | 10,000 | — | — | — | 7.00 | — |

**10 LEI** **KM# 126** **Composition:** Nickel Plated Steel **Subject:** World Food Summit - Rome

| Date | Mintage | F | VF | XF | Unc | BU |
|---|---|---|---|---|---|---|
| 1996 | 50,000 | — | — | — | 5.00 | — |

**10 LEI** **KM# 134** **Composition:** Nickel Plated Steel **Subject:** Euro soccer **Reverse:** Players

| Date | Mintage | F | VF | XF | Unc | BU |
|---|---|---|---|---|---|---|
| 1996 | 50,000 | — | — | — | 5.50 | — |

**20 LEI** **KM# 109** **Composition:** Brass Clad Steel **Obverse:** Bust of King Stefan Cel Mare **Edge:** plain **Note:** Date varieties exist.

| Date | Mintage | F | VF | XF | Unc | BU |
|---|---|---|---|---|---|---|
| 1991 | Est. 43,200,000 | — | — | 1.00 | 2.50 | — |
| 1992 | Est. 48,000,000 | — | — | 0.60 | 2.50 | — |
| 1993 | Est. 33,800,000 | — | — | 0.50 | 2.25 | — |
| 1994 | Est. 5,000,000 | — | — | 1.25 | 3.00 | — |
| 1995 | 8,000,000 | — | — | 0.75 | 3.00 | — |
| 1996 | 500,000 | — | 0.75 | 1.50 | 6.00 | — |
| 2000 Proof | — | — | — | — | 6.00 | — |

**Note:** 2000-dated strikes available in sets only.

**50 LEI** **KM# 110** **Composition:** Brass Clad Steel **Obverse:** Bust of Prince Alexandru Ioan Cuza **Edge:** plain

| Date | Mintage | F | VF | XF | Unc | BU |
|---|---|---|---|---|---|---|
| 1991 | Est. 29,600,000 | — | — | 1.50 | 3.00 | — |
| 1992 | Est. 70,800,000 | — | — | 1.00 | 1.85 | — |

**Note:** 1992 date varieties exist.

| Date | Mintage | F | VF | XF | Unc | BU |
|---|---|---|---|---|---|---|
| 1993 | Est. 34,600,000 | — | — | 1.00 | 1.85 | — |
| 1994 | Est. 30,000,000 | — | — | 1.00 | 2.00 | — |
| 1995 | 20,000,000 | — | — | 1.00 | 2.00 | — |
| 1996 | 4,900,000 | — | — | 1.00 | 3.50 | — |
| 2000 Proof | — | — | — | — | 7.00 | — |

**Note:** 2000-dated strikes available in sets only.

**100 LEI** **KM# 111** **Composition:** Nickel Plated Steel **Obverse:** Bust of Prince Mahai Viteazul **Edge Lettering:** ROMANIA

| Date | Mintage | F | VF | XF | Unc | BU |
|---|---|---|---|---|---|---|
| 1991 | Est. 12,600,000 | — | — | 2.50 | 6.00 | — |
| 1992 | Est. 70,500,000 | — | — | 1.50 | 3.00 | — |

**Note:** Reported edge varieties for 1992 with TOTUL PENTRU TARA; without ROMANIA are presumed mint errors.

| Date | Mintage | F | VF | XF | Unc | BU |
|---|---|---|---|---|---|---|
| 1993 | Est. 78,000,000 | — | — | 1.50 | 3.00 | — |
| 1994 | Est. 125,000,000 | — | — | 1.50 | 2.50 | — |
| 1995 | 30,000,000 | — | — | 1.50 | 3.00 | — |
| 1996 | 11,000,000 | — | — | 2.50 | 8.00 | — |
| 2000 | — | — | — | — | 8.50 | — |

**Note:** 2000-dated strikes available in sets only.

**100 LEI** **KM# 118** **Weight:** 27.5000 g. **Composition:** 0.9250 Silver .8178 oz. ASW **Series:** F.A.O. **Subject:** 50 years - F.A.O.

| Date | Mintage | F | VF | XF | Unc | BU |
|---|---|---|---|---|---|---|
| 1995 | 30,000 | — | — | — | 22.50 | — |

**100 LEI** **KM# 119** **Weight:** 27.0000 g. **Composition:** 0.9250 Silver .8030 oz. ASW **Subject:** Euro soccer **Reverse:** Players

| Date | Mintage | F | VF | XF | Unc | BU |
|---|---|---|---|---|---|---|
| 1996 Proof | 12,000 | Value: 25.00 | | | | |

**100 LEI** **KM# 127** **Weight:** 27.0000 g. **Composition:** 0.9250 Silver .8030 oz. ASW **Series:** 1996 Olympic Games - U.S.A. **Reverse:** Swimmer

| Date | Mintage | F | VF | XF | Unc | BU |
|---|---|---|---|---|---|---|
| 1996 Proof | 10,000 | Value: 25.00 | | | | |

**100 LEI** **KM# 128** **Weight:** 27.0000 g. **Composition:** 0.9250 Silver .8030 oz. ASW **Series:** 1996 Olympic Games - U.S.A. **Reverse:** 4 Olympic scenes

| Date | Mintage | F | VF | XF | Unc | BU |
|---|---|---|---|---|---|---|
| 1996 Proof | 10,000 | Value: 27.50 | | | | |

**100 LEI** **KM# 129** **Weight:** 27.0000 g. **Composition:** 0.9250 Silver .8030 oz. ASW **Series:** 1996 Olympic Games - U.S.A. **Reverse:** Windsurfer

| Date | Mintage | F | VF | XF | Unc | BU |
|---|---|---|---|---|---|---|
| 1996 Proof | 10,000 | Value: 26.50 | | | | |

**100 LEI** **KM# 130** **Weight:** 27.0000 g. **Composition:** 0.9250 Silver .8030 oz. ASW **Series:** 1996 Olympic Games - U.S.A. **Reverse:** Sailboat with 3 crewmen

| Date | Mintage | F | VF | XF | Unc | BU |
|---|---|---|---|---|---|---|
| 1996 Proof | 10,000 | Value: 26.50 | | | | |

**100 LEI** **KM# 131** **Weight:** 27.0000 g. **Composition:** 0.9250 Silver .8030 oz. ASW **Series:** 1996 Olympic Games - U.S.A. **Reverse:** Canoe with 2 canoeists

| Date | Mintage | F | VF | XF | Unc | BU |
|---|---|---|---|---|---|---|
| 1996 Proof | 10,000 | Value: 27.50 | | | | |

**100 LEI** **KM# 132** **Weight:** 27.0000 g. **Composition:** 0.9250 Silver .8030 oz. ASW **Series:** 1996 Olympic Games - U.S.A. **Reverse:** Scullcraft with rowers

| Date | Mintage | F | VF | XF | Unc | BU |
|---|---|---|---|---|---|---|
| 1996 Proof | 10,000 | Value: 27.50 | | | | |

**100 LEI** **KM# 133** **Weight:** 27.5000 g. **Composition:** 0.9250 Silver .8178 oz. ASW **Subject:** World Food Summit - Rome

| Date | Mintage | F | VF | XF | Unc | BU |
|---|---|---|---|---|---|---|
| 1996 Proof | 5,000 | Value: 32.50 | | | | |

**100 LEI** **KM# 135** **Weight:** 27.0000 g. **Composition:** 0.9250 Silver .8030 oz. ASW **Subject:** 50th anniversary - UNICEF

| Date | Mintage | F | VF | XF | Unc | BU |
|---|---|---|---|---|---|---|
| 1996 Proof | 5,000 | Value: 32.50 | | | | |

**100 LEI** **KM# 138** **Weight:** 27.0000 g. **Composition:** 0.9250 Silver .8030 oz. ASW **Subject:** 120th anniversary of independence **Obverse:** National arms above denomination **Reverse:** 3 soldiers, flag and cannon

| Date | Mintage | F | VF | XF | Unc | BU |
|---|---|---|---|---|---|---|
| 1998 Proof | Est. 5,000 | Value: 37.50 | | | | |

**100 LEI** **KM# 139** **Weight:** 27.0000 g. **Composition:** 0.9250 Silver .8030 oz. ASW **Subject:** Andrei Saguna **Obverse:** National arms divide denomination **Reverse:** Portrait, church towers, and date

| Date | Mintage | F | VF | XF | Unc | BU |
|---|---|---|---|---|---|---|
| 1998 Proof | 2,000 | Value: 45.00 | | | | |

**100 LEI** **KM# 140** **Weight:** 27.0000 g. **Composition:** 0.9250 Silver .8030 oz. ASW **Series:** Olympic Games - Nagano 1998 **Reverse:** Bobsled

| Date | Mintage | F | VF | XF | Unc | BU |
|---|---|---|---|---|---|---|
| 1998 Proof | 2,000 | Value: 42.50 | | | | |

**100 LEI** **KM# 141** **Weight:** 27.0000 g. **Composition:** 0.9250 Silver .8030 oz. ASW **Series:** Olympic Games - Nagano 1998 **Reverse:** Figure skater

| Date | Mintage | F | VF | XF | Unc | BU |
|---|---|---|---|---|---|---|
| 1998 Proof | 2,000 | Value: 42.50 | | | | |

**100 LEI** **KM# 142** **Weight:** 27.0000 g. **Composition:** 0.9250 Silver .8030 oz. ASW **Series:** Olympic Games - Nagano 1998 **Reverse:** Slalom

| Date | Mintage | F | VF | XF | Unc | BU |
|---|---|---|---|---|---|---|
| 1998 Proof | 2,000 | Value: 42.50 | | | | |

**100 LEI** **KM# 143** **Weight:** 27.0000 g. **Composition:** 0.9250 Silver .8030 oz. ASW **Subject:** World Cup soccer - France 1998 **Reverse:** Eiffel Tower

| Date | Mintage | F | VF | XF | Unc | BU |
|---|---|---|---|---|---|---|
| 1998 Proof | 5,000 | Value: 37.50 | | | | |

**100 LEI** **KM# 149** **Weight:** 27.0000 g. **Composition:** 0.9250 Silver .8030 oz. ASW **Subject:** Visit of Pope John Paul II **Obverse:** National arms **Reverse:** Portraits of pope and Patriarch Theoctist

| Date | Mintage | F | VF | XF | Unc | BU |
|---|---|---|---|---|---|---|
| 1999 Proof | 2,000 | Value: 47.50 | | | | |

**100 LEI** **KM# 150** **Weight:** 27.0000 g. **Composition:** 0.9250 Silver .8030 oz. ASW **Subject:** 100th anniversary - Belgica Expedition **Obverse:** National arms **Reverse:** Silhouette of Belgica ship, bust of scientist Emil Racovita

| Date | Mintage | F | VF | XF | Unc | BU |
|---|---|---|---|---|---|---|
| 1999 Proof | 20,000 | Value: 32.50 | | | | |

**500 LEI** **KM# 136** **Weight:** 8.6400 g. **Composition:** 0.9000 Gold .25 oz. AGW **Subject:** Revolution of 1848

| Date | Mintage | F | VF | XF | Unc | BU |
|---|---|---|---|---|---|---|
| 1998 Proof | Est. 2,000 | Value: 275 | | | | |

**500 LEI** **KM# 145** **Composition:** Aluminum **Obverse:** Denomination **Reverse:** National arms **Edge:** Lettered **Edge Lettering:** ROMANIA (3x)

| Date | Mintage | F | VF | XF | Unc | BU |
|---|---|---|---|---|---|---|
| 1998 | — | — | — | — | — | — |
| 1999 | — | — | — | 0.50 | 1.50 | — |
| 2000 | — | — | — | 0.50 | 1.50 | — |
| 2000 Proof | — | — | — | — | 6.00 | — |

**Note:** Available in sets only.

**500 LEI** **KM# 146** **Composition:** Aluminum **Subject:** Solar eclipse **Obverse:** National arms **Reverse:** Solar eclipse **Edge:** Lettered **Edge Lettering:** ROMANIA (3x)

| Date | Mintage | VG | F | VF | XF | Unc |
|---|---|---|---|---|---|---|
| 1999 Proof | 3,000 | Value: 15.00 | | | | |

**500 LEI** **KM# 147** **Composition:** Aluminum **Subject:** Solar eclipse **Obverse:** National arms, eclipse and observatory **Reverse:** Solar eclipse **Edge:** Lettered **Edge Lettering:** ROMANIA (3x) **Note:** This design never gained broad release and is considered to be a pattern by several authorities

| Date | Mintage | VG | F | VF | XF | Unc |
|---|---|---|---|---|---|---|
| 1999 | 4,000,000 | — | — | — | — | 3.00 |

**500 LEI** **KM# 154** **Weight:** 27.0000 g. **Composition:** 0.9990 Silver .8030 oz. ASW **Subject:** Alexander the Good of Moldavia **Obverse:** Old seal design and denomination **Reverse:** Crowned portrait **Edge:** Plain **Size:** 37 mm.

| Date | Mintage | F | VF | XF | Unc | BU |
|---|---|---|---|---|---|---|
| 2000 Proof | Est. 1,000 | Value: 60.00 | | | | |

**1000 LEI** **KM# 137** **Weight:** 31.1035 g. **Composition:** 0.9990 Gold 1 oz. AGW **Subject:** Revolution of 1848

| Date | Mintage | F | VF | XF | Unc | BU |
|---|---|---|---|---|---|---|
| 1998 Proof | Est. 1,000 | Value: 675 | | | | |

**1000 LEI** **KM# 144** **Weight:** 31.1035 g. **Composition:** 0.9990 Gold 1 oz. AGW **Subject:** 80th anniversary - Union of Transylvania **Obverse:** Arms of Wallachia, Moldova and Transylvania

| Date | Mintage | F | VF | XF | Unc | BU |
|---|---|---|---|---|---|---|
| 1998 Proof | 2,000 | Value: 650 | | | | |

**1000 LEI** **KM# 151** **Weight:** 31.1035 g. **Composition:** 0.9990 Gold 1 oz. AGW **Subject:** Visit of Pope John Paul II **Obverse:** National arms **Reverse:** Portraits of pope and Patriarch Theoctist

| Date | Mintage | F | VF | XF | Unc | BU |
|---|---|---|---|---|---|---|
| 1999 Proof | 1,000 | Value: 700 | | | | |

**1000 LEI** **KM# 153** **Weight:** 2.0000 g. **Composition:** Aluminum **Subject:** Constantin Brancoveanu **Obverse:** Denomination above arms **Reverse:** Portrait **Edge:** Reeded and plain sections **Size:** 22.2 mm.

| Date | Mintage | VG | F | VF | XF | Unc |
|---|---|---|---|---|---|---|
| 2000 | — | — | — | — | — | 3.00 |
| 2000 Proof | — | Value: 10.00 | | | | |
| **Note:** In sets only. | | | | | | |
| 2001 | — | — | — | — | — | 2.50 |

**1000 LEI** **KM# 156** **Weight:** 15.5510 g. **Composition:** 0.9990 Gold .4995 oz. AGW **Subject:** 1900th Anniversary of the First Roman-Dacian War **Obverse:** Trojan's column. **Reverse:** Monument and cameo portraits of Trajan and King Decebal. **Edge:** Plain. **Size:** 27 mm.

| Date | Mintage | VG | F | VF | XF | Unc |
|---|---|---|---|---|---|---|
| 2001 Proof | 500 | Value: 400 | | | | |

**2000 LEI** **KM# 157** **Weight:** 31.1030 g. **Composition:** 0.9990 Gold .9990 oz. AGW **Subject:** Mihai Eminescu **Obverse:** National arms and quill. **Reverse:** Portrait. **Edge:** Plain. **Size:** 35 mm.

| Date | Mintage | VG | F | VF | XF | Unc |
|---|---|---|---|---|---|---|
| 2000 Proof | 1,500 | Value: 675 | | | | |

**5000 LEI** **KM# 155** **Weight:** 31.1030 g. **Composition:** 0.9990 Gold .9990 oz. AGW **Subject:** Michael the Brave's Unification of Romania in 1600 **Obverse:** National arms and old seal **Reverse:** Bearded portrait **Edge:** Plain **Size:** 35 mm.

| Date | Mintage | F | VF | XF | Unc | BU |
|---|---|---|---|---|---|---|
| 2000 Proof | Est. 1,500 | Value: 725 | | | | |

## ESSAIS

| KM# | Date | Mintage | Identification | Mkt Val |
|---|---|---|---|---|
| E1 | 1905 | — | 10 Bani. Copper-Nickel. KM29. With center hole. | 200 |
| E2 | 1910 | — | 50 Bani. Silver. | 300 |
| E3 | 1910 | — | Leu. Silver. | 300 |
| E4 | 1910 | — | 2 Lei. Silver. | 300 |
| E5 | 1914 | — | 50 Bani. Silver. | 200 |
| E7 | 1914 | — | Leu. Silver. | 250 |
| E9 | 1914 | — | 2 Lei. Silver. | 275 |
| E8 | 1914 | — | Leu. Silver. KM42. | — |
| E10 | 1914 | — | 2 Lei. Silver. KM43. | — |
| E6 | 1914 | — | 50 Bani. Silver. KM41 | 150 |
| E11 | 1924 | — | 2 Lei. Silver. | 125 |

## PATTERNS

Including off metal strikes

| KM# | Date | Mintage | Identification | Mkt Val |
|---|---|---|---|---|
| Pn49 | 1905 | — | 5 Bani. White Metal. KM28. | 100 |
| Pn50 | 1905 | — | 5 Bani. Pewter. KM28. | — |
| Pn51 | 1905 | — | 5 Bani. Aluminum. KM28. | — |
| Pn52 | 1905 | — | 5 Bani. Zinc. KM28. | — |
| Pn53 | 1905 | — | 5 Bani. Bronze. KM28. | — |
| Pn54 | 1905 | — | 5 Bani. Brass. KM28. | 125 |
| Pn55 | 1905 | — | 5 Bani. Copper. KM28. With center hole. | 125 |
| Pn56 | 1905 | — | 5 Bani. Copper. KM28. | 500 |
| Pn57 | 1905 | — | 5 Bani. Gilt Copper. KM28. | — |
| Pn58 | 1905 | — | 5 Bani. Silver. KM31. Without center hole. | 250 |
| Pn59 | 1905 | — | 5 Bani. Bronze. KM31. Without center hole. | — |
| Pn60 | 1905 | — | 5 Bani. Pewter. KM31. Without center hole. | 100 |
| Pn61 | 1905 | — | 5 Bani. Aluminum. KM31. Without center hole. | — |
| Pn62 | 1905 | — | 5 Bani. Zinc. KM31. Without center hole. | — |
| Pn63 | 1905 | — | 5 Bani. Copper-Nickel. KM31. Without center hole. | — |
| Pn64 | 1905 | — | 5 Bani. Gold. Without center hole. | 1,500 |
| Pn65 | 1905 | — | 5 Bani. Gold. Without center hole. | 1,200 |
| PnA66 | 1905 | — | 10 Bani. White Metal. With center hole. | — |
| PnB66 | 1905 | — | 10 Bani. White Metal. Without center hole. | — |
| Pn66 | 1905 | — | 10 Bani. Pewter. KM29. With center hole. | 125 |
| Pn67 | 1905 | — | 10 Bani. Brass. KM29. With center hole. | 125 |
| Pn68 | 1905 | — | 10 Bani. Aluminum. KM29. With center hole. | 75.00 |
| PnA69 | 1905 | — | 10 Bani. Bronze. KM29. Red. With center hole. | — |
| Pn69 | 1905 | — | 10 Bani. Bronze. KM29. Red. Without center hole. | 100 |
| Pn70 | 1905 | — | 10 Bani. Bronze. KM29. Green. Without center hole. | 100 |
| Pn71 | 1905 | — | 10 Bani. Zinc. KM29. | 160 |
| PnA72 | 1905 | — | 10 Bani. Gilt Bronze. KM29. With center hole. | — |
| Pn72 | 1905 | — | 10 Bani. Gilt Bronze. KM29. Without center hole. | 100 |
| Pn73 | 1905 | — | 10 Bani. Copper-Nickel-Zinc. With center hole. | 150 |
| Pn74 | 1905 | — | 10 Bani. Nickel. KM29. With center hole. | — |
| Pn75 | 1905 | — | 10 Bani. Silver. KM29. Without center hole. | 350 |
| Pn76 | 1905 | — | 10 Bani. Silver. KM29. With center hole. | 250 |
| PnA77 | 1905 | — | 10 Bani. Gilt Copper. With branches and small date. Without center hole. | — |
| Pn77 | 1905 | — | 10 Bani. Copper. KM29. Without center hole. | 100 |
| Pn78 | 1905 | — | 10 Bani. Gold. Without branches. KM29. Without center hole. | 1,650 |
| Pn79 | 1905 | — | 10 Bani. Gold. KM29. With center hole. | 1,400 |
| Pn80 | 1905 | — | 10 Bani. Pewter. KM32. Without center hole. | 150 |
| Pn81 | 1905 | — | 10 Bani. Brass. KM32. Without center hole. | 150 |

| KM# | Date | Mintage | Identification | Mkt Val |
|---|---|---|---|---|
| Pn82 | 1905 | — | 10 Bani. Aluminum. KM32. Without center hole. | 100 |
| Pn83 | 1905 | — | 10 Bani. Bronze. KM32. Without center hole. | 125 |
| Pn84 | 1905 | — | 10 Bani. Gold. KM32. Without center hole. | 1,250 |
| Pn85 | 1905 | — | 20 Bani. Lead. KM30. | 100 |
| Pn86 | 1905 | — | 20 Bani. Brass. KM30. | 150 |
| Pn87 | 1905 | — | 20 Bani. Copper. KM30. | 125 |
| Pn88 | 1905 | — | 20 Bani. Aluminum. KM30. | 100 |
| Pn89 | 1905 | — | 20 Bani. White Metal. KM30. | 100 |
| Pn90 | 1905 | — | 20 Bani. Zinc. KM30. | — |
| Pn91 | 1905 | — | 20 Bani. Pewter. KM30. | — |
| Pn92 | 1905 | — | 20 Bani. Gilt Bronze. KM30. | 125 |
| PnA93 | 1905 | — | 20 Bani. Bronze. KM30. | — |
| Pn93 | 1905 | — | 20 Bani. Silver. KM30. | 250 |
| Pn94 | 1905 | — | 20 Bani. Gold. Without center hole. | 1,750 |
| Pn95 | 1905 | — | 20 Bani. Gold. With center hole. | 1,500 |
| Pn96 | 1905 | — | 20 Bani. Brass. KM33. Without center hole. | — |
| Pn97 | 1905 | — | 20 Bani. Copper. KM33. Without center hole. | 200 |
| Pn98 | 1905 | — | 20 Bani. Aluminum. KM33. Without center hole. | — |
| Pn99 | 1905 | — | 20 Bani. Pewter. KM33. Without center hole. | 200 |
| Pn100 | 1905 | — | 20 Bani. Silver. KM33. Without center hole. | 400 |
| Pn101 | 1906 | — | Leu. White Metal. | 125 |
| Pn102 | 1906 | — | Leu. Brass. | 150 |
| Pn103 | 1906 | — | Leu. Aluminum. | 100 |
| Pn104 | 1906 | — | Leu. Copper. | 125 |
| Pn105 | 1906 | — | Leu. Gilt Bronze. | 125 |
| Pn106 | 1906 | — | Leu. Copper-Nickel. | — |
| Pn107 | 1906 | — | Leu. Gilt Bronze. | 125 |
| Pn108 | 1906 | — | Leu. Silver. | 250 |
| Pn109 | 1906 | — | Leu. Gold. | — |
| Pn110 | 1906 | — | 5 Lei. Silver. | 4,500 |
| Pn111 | 1906 | — | 12-1/2 Lei. Lead. | 250 |
| Pn112 | 1906 | — | 12-1/2 Lei. White Metal. | 250 |
| Pn113 | 1906 | — | 12-1/2 Lei. Brass. | 250 |
| Pn114 | 1906 | — | 12-1/2 Lei. Pewter. | — |
| Pn115 | 1906 | — | 12-1/2 Lei. Gilt Bronze. | 250 |
| PnA116 | 1906 | — | 12-1/2 Lei. Bronze. Plain edge. | 250 |
| Pn116 | 1906 | — | 12-1/2 Lei. Aluminum. | 250 |
| Pn117 | 1906 | — | 12-1/2 Lei. Aluminum. Gilt. | 250 |
| Pn118 | 1906 | — | 12-1/2 Lei. Copper. | 350 |
| Pn119 | 1906 | — | 12-1/2 Lei. Copper-Nickel. | — |
| Pn120 | 1906 | — | 12-1/2 Lei. Silver. | 550 |
| Pn121 | 1906 | — | 12-1/2 Lei. Gold. | 1,200 |
| Pn122 | 1906 | — | 12-1/2 Lei. Gold. Pale. | 2,150 |
| Pn123 | 1906 | — | 20 Lei. Copper. | 350 |
| Pn124 | 1906 | — | 20 Lei. Bronze. | 200 |
| Pn125 | 1906 | — | 20 Lei. White Metal. | — |
| Pn126 | 1906 | — | 20 Lei. White Metal. Gilt. | — |
| Pn127 | 1906 | — | 20 Lei. Gold. | 1,200 |
| Pn128 | 1906 | — | 20 Lei. Gold. Pale. | 2,150 |
| Pn129 | 1906 | — | 25 Lei. Pewter. | 250 |
| Pn130 | 1906 | — | 25 Lei. Zinc. | 400 |
| Pn131 | 1906 | — | 25 Lei. Lead. | 200 |
| Pn132 | 1906 | — | 25 Lei. Copper. | 175 |
| Pn133 | 1906 | — | 25 Lei. Gilt Copper. | — |
| Pn134 | 1906 | — | 25 Lei. Aluminum. | 175 |
| Pn135 | 1906 | — | 25 Lei. Brass. | 175 |
| Pn136 | 1906 | — | 25 Lei. Bronze. Antique. | 175 |
| Pn137 | 1906 | — | 25 Lei. Gilt Bronze. | 175 |
| Pn138 | 1906 | — | 25 Lei. Silver. | 800 |
| Pn139 | 1906 | — | 25 Lei. Gold. | 2,400 |
| Pn140 | 1906 | — | 25 Lei. Gold. Pale. | 4,000 |
| Pn141 | 1906 | — | 50 Lei. Aluminum. | 350 |
| Pn142 | 1906 | — | 50 Lei. Bronze. | 400 |
| Pn143 | 1906 | — | 50 Lei. White Metal. | — |
| Pn144 | 1906 | — | 50 Lei. Pewter. | 425 |
| Pn145 | 1906 | — | 50 Lei. Brass. | 400 |
| Pn146 | 1906 | — | 50 Lei. Silver. | 850 |
| Pn147 | 1906 | 12 | 50 Lei. Gold. | 12,500 |
| Pn148 | 1906 | — | 100 Lei. Copper. | 650 |
| Pn149 | 1906 | — | 100 Lei. Bronze. | 650 |
| Pn150 | 1906 | — | 100 Lei. Silver. | — |
| Pn151 | 1906 | — | 100 Lei. Gold. | 5,000 |
| PnA152 | 1910 | — | 10 Bani. Zinc. | — |
| Pn152 | 1910 | — | 10 Bani. Copper. | — |
| Pn153 | 1910 | — | 50 Bani. Lead. | — |
| Pn154 | 1910 | — | 50 Bani. Tin. | — |
| PnA155 | 1910 | — | 50 Bani. Pewter. Plain edge. | — |
| Pn155 | 1910 | — | 50 Bani. Pewter. Milled edge. | 100 |
| Pn156 | 1910 | — | 50 Bani. White Metal. | 75.00 |
| Pn157 | 1910 | — | 50 Bani. Aluminum. | 60.00 |
| Pn158 | 1910 | — | 50 Bani. Zinc. | — |
| Pn159 | 1910 | — | 50 Bani. Copper. | — |
| Pn160 | 1910 | — | 50 Bani. Copper-Nickel. | — |
| Pn161 | 1910 | — | 50 Bani. Brass. | 75.00 |
| PnA162 | 1910 | — | 50 Bani. Bronze. Plain edge. Thin planchet. | — |
| PnB162 | 1910 | — | 50 Bani. Bronze. Plain edge. Thick planchet. | — |
| PnC162 | 1910 | — | 50 Bani. Bronze. Milled edge. Thin planchet. | — |
| PnD162 | 1910 | — | 50 Bani. Bronze. Milled edge. Thick planchet. | — |
| Pn162 | 1910 | — | 50 Bani. Nickel. | 100 |
| Pn163 | 1910 | — | Leu. Lead. | 100 |
| Pn164 | 1910 | — | Leu. Aluminum. | 100 |
| Pn165 | 1910 | — | Leu. Bronze. | 85.00 |

| KM# | Date | Mintage | Identification | Mkt Val |
|---|---|---|---|---|
| Pn166 | 1910 | — | Leu. Gilt Bronze. | 85.00 |
| Pn167 | 1910 | — | Leu. Pewter. | 125 |
| Pn168 | 1910 | — | Leu. Zinc. | — |
| PnA169 | 1910 | — | Leu. Gilt Copper. | — |
| Pn169 | 1910 | — | Leu. Copper. | — |
| Pn170 | 1910 | — | Leu. Copper-Nickel. | — |
| Pn171 | 1910 | — | 2 Lei. Lead. | 100 |
| Pn172 | 1910 | — | 2 Lei. Tin. | 150 |
| Pn173 | 1910 | — | 2 Lei. Pewter. | 150 |
| Pn174 | 1910 | — | 2 Lei. Aluminum. | 100 |
| Pn175 | 1910 | — | 2 Lei. Brass. | 100 |
| PnA176 | 1910 | — | 2 Lei. Gilt Copper. | — |
| Pn176 | 1910 | — | 2 Lei. Copper. | — |
| Pn177 | 1910 | — | 2 Lei. Gilt Bronze. | 100 |
| PnA178 | 1910 | — | 2 Lei. Bronze. | — |
| Pn178 | 1910 | — | 2 Lei. Nickel. | — |
| PnA179 | 1910 | — | 2 Lei. Silver. | — |
| Pn179 | 1921 | — | 25 Bani. Aluminum. HF at left of date. | 125 |
| PnA180 | 1921 | — | 25 Bani. Bronze. HF at left of date. | 200 |
| PnB180 | 1921 | — | 25 Bani. Copper-Nickel. | 185 |
| PnC180 | 1921 | — | 25 Bani. Bronze. Without hole. | 185 |
| PnD180 | 1921 | — | 25 Bani. Nickel. | 200 |
| Pn180 | 1921 | — | 50 Bani. Nickel. | 200 |
| PnA181 | 1921 | — | 50 Bani. Bronze. | 200 |
| Pn181 | 1921 | — | 1.25 Leu. Nickel. | 325 |
| PnA182 | 1921 | — | 5 Lei. Billon. Arms, cornucopia. Hand numbered 1-15. Struck at Paris. | — |
| Pn182 | 1921 | — | 5 Lei. Copper-Nickel. | 450 |
| Pn183 | 1921 | — | 5 Lei. Nickel. | — |
| Pn184 | 1922 | — | 25 Bani. Aluminum. | — |
| Pn185 | 1922 | — | 50 Bani. Aluminum. | 175 |
| Pn186 | 1922 | — | Leu. Bronze. | 220 |
| Pn187 | 1922 | — | Leu. Nickel. | 250 |
| Pn188 | 1922 | — | Leu. Copper-Nickel. | 210 |
| Pn189 | 1922 | — | 2 Lei. Bronze. | 250 |
| Pn190 | 1922 | — | 2 Lei. Nickel. | 250 |
| Pn191 | 1922 | — | 2 Lei. Brass. | 150 |
| Pn192 | 1922 | — | 5 Lei. Bronze. | 285 |
| Pn193 | 1922 | — | 5 Lei. Copper-Nickel. | 285 |
| Pn194 | 1922 | — | 5 Lei. Nickel. | 265 |
| Pn195 | 1922 | — | 5 Lei. Brass. | 265 |
| Pn196 | 1922 | — | 5 Lei. Copper-Nickel. | 265 |
| Pn197 | 1922 | — | 20 Lei. Gold. | 2,000 |
| Pn198 | 1922 | — | 25 Lei. Gold. | 2,500 |
| Pn199 | 1922 | — | 50 Lei. Gold. | 4,000 |
| Pn200 | 1922 | — | 100 Lei. Gold. | 5,500 |
| PnA201 | 1923 | — | Leu. Nickel. | 275 |
| Pn201 | 1924 | — | Leu. Nickel. | 65.00 |
| Pn202 | 1924 | — | Leu. Aluminum. | 45.00 |
| Pn203 | 1924 | — | Leu. Tin. | 45.00 |
| Pn204 | 1924 | — | Leu. Zinc. | — |
| Pn205 | 1924 | — | Leu. Copper. | — |
| Pn206 | 1924 | — | Leu. Brass. | 110 |
| Pn207 | 1924 | — | Leu. Bronze. | 60.00 |
| Pn208 | 1924 | — | Leu. Gilt Bronze. | 50.00 |
| Pn209 | 1924 | — | Leu. Silver. Plain edge. | 125 |
| Pn210 | 1924 | — | Leu. Silver. Reeded edge. | 125 |
| Pn211 | 1924 | — | 2 Lei. Zinc. | 75.00 |
| Pn212 | 1924 | — | 2 Lei. Aluminum. | 50.00 |
| Pn213 | 1924 | — | 2 Lei. Tin. | — |
| Pn214 | 1924 | — | 2 Lei. Bronze. | 240 |
| Pn215 | 1924 | — | 2 Lei. Brass. | 100 |
| Pn216 | 1924 | — | 2 Lei. Copper. | 65.00 |
| Pn217 | 1924 | — | 2 Lei. Nickel. | 75.00 |
| PnA217 | 1924 | — | 2 Lei. Copper-Nickel. | — |
| Pn218 | 1924 | — | 2 Lei. Silver. Plain edge. Thick planchet. | 200 |
| PnA219 | 1930 | — | 10 Lei. Copper-Nickel. KM49. | 100 |
| Pn219 | 1930 | — | 20 Lei. Gold. Plain. | — |
| Pn220 | 1930 | — | 20 Lei. Gold. Ornamented. | — |
| Pn221 | 1930 | — | 100 Lei. Gold. Plain. | — |
| Pn222 | 1930 | — | 100 Lei. Gold. Ornamented. | — |
| Pn223 | 1931 | — | 20 Lei. Gold. Plain. | — |
| Pn224 | 1931 | — | 20 Lei. Gold. Ornamented. | — |
| Pn225 | 1931 | — | 100 Lei. Gold. Plain. | — |
| Pn226 | 1931 | — | 100 Lei. Gold. Ornamented. | — |
| Pn227 | 1932 | — | 20 Lei. Gold. Plain. | — |
| Pn228 | 1932 | — | 20 Lei. Gold. Ornamented. | — |
| Pn229 | 1932 | — | 100 Lei. Silver. Y62. | 75.00 |
| Pn230 | 1932 | — | 100 Lei. Gold. Plain. | — |
| Pn231 | 1932 | — | 100 Lei. Gold. Ornamented. | — |
| Pn232 | 1933 | — | 20 Lei. Gold. Plain. | — |
| Pn233 | 1933 | — | 20 Lei. Gold. Ornamented. | — |
| Pn234 | 1933 | — | 100 Lei. Gold. Plain. | — |
| Pn235 | 1933 | — | 100 Lei. Gold. Ornamented. | — |
| Pn236 | 1934 | — | 20 Lei. Gold. Plain. | — |
| Pn237 | 1934 | — | 20 Lei. Gold. Ornamented. | — |
| Pn238 | 1934 | — | 100 Lei. Gold. Plain. | — |
| Pn239 | 1934 | — | 100 Lei. Gold. Ornamented. | — |
| Pn240 | 1935 | — | 20 Lei. Gold. Plain. | — |
| Pn241 | 1935 | — | 20 Lei. Gold. Ornamented. | — |
| Pn242 | 1935 | — | 50 Lei. Silver. | — |
| Pn243 | 1935 | — | 100 Lei. Gold. Plain. | — |
| Pn244 | 1935 | — | 100 Lei. Gold. Ornamented. | — |
| Pn245 | 1935 | — | 200 Lei. Silver. | 450 |
| PnA245 | 1935 | — | 250 Lei. Nickel. | — |
| PnB245 | 1935 | — | 250 Lei. Brass. | — |
| Pn246 | 1936 | — | 20 Lei. Gold. Plain. | — |
| Pn247 | 1936 | — | 20 Lei. Gold. Ornamented. | — |
| Pn248 | 1936 | — | 50 Lei. Nickel. | — |

| KM# | Date | Mintage | Identification | Mkt Val |
|---|---|---|---|---|
| Pn249 | 1936 | — | 100 Lei. Gold. Plain. | — |
| Pn250 | 1936 | — | 100 Lei. Gold. Ornamented. | — |
| PnA251 | 1937 | — | 50 Lei. Nickel. KM55. | 12.00 |
| Pn251 | 1937 | — | Leu. Copper-Nickel-Zinc. | — |
| Pn252 | | — | Leu. Copper-Nickel-Zinc. | — |
| Pn253 | 1937 | — | 2 Lei. Copper-Nickel-Zinc. | — |
| Pn254 | 1937 | — | 20 Lei. Gold. Plain. | — |
| Pn255 | 1937 | — | 20 Lei. Gold. Ornamented. | — |
| Pn256 | 1937 | — | 50 Lei. Copper-Nickel-Zinc. | 240 |
| Pn257 | 1937 | — | 100 Lei. Gold. Plain. | — |
| Pn258 | 1937 | — | 100 Lei. Gold. Ornamented. | — |
| Pn259 | 1938 | — | Leu. Copper-Nickel-Zinc. | — |
| Pn260 | 1938 | — | 20 Lei. Gold. Plain. | — |
| Pn261 | 1938 | — | 20 Lei. Gold. Ornamented. | — |
| Pn262 | 1938 | — | 100 Lei. Gold. Plain. | — |
| Pn263 | 1938 | — | 100 Lei. Gold. Ornamented. | — |
| Pn264 | 1939 | — | 20 Lei. Gold. Plain. | — |
| Pn265 | 1939 | — | 20 Lei. Gold. Ornamented. | — |
| Pn266 | 1939 | — | 20 Lei. Gold. Arms. | — |
| Pn267 | 1939 | — | 20 Lei. Gold. Eagle. | — |
| Pn268 | 1939 | — | 100 Lei. Gold. Plain. | — |
| Pn269 | 1939 | — | 100 Lei. Gold. Ornamented. | — |
| Pn270 | 1939 | — | 100 Lei. Gold. Bust. | — |
| Pn271 | 1940 | — | 20 Lei. Gold. Plain. | — |
| Pn272 | 1940 | — | 20 Lei. Gold. Ornamented. | — |
| Pn273 | 1940 | — | 100 Lei. Gold. Plain. | — |
| Pn274 | 1940 | — | 100 Lei. Gold. Ornamented. | — |
| Pn275 | 1940 | — | 250 Lei. 0.7500 Silver. Iron guard emblem. | 9,000 |
| Pn276 | 1941 | — | Leu. Zinc. | — |
| Pn277 | 1941 | — | Leu. Copper-Nickel-Zinc. | — |
| Pn278 | 1944 | — | 20 Lei. Copper-Nickel-Zinc. | — |
| PnA279 | 1944 | — | 500 Lei. Silver. Plain edge. | 180 |
| Pn279 | 1944 | — | 500 Lei. Aluminum. | 115 |
| Pn280 | 1945 | — | 100 Lei. Nickel Clad Steel. | 125 |
| PnA280 | 1945 | — | 200 Lei. Aluminum. | — |
| Pn281 | 1945 | — | 500 Lei. Brass. Nickel plated. | 125 |
| Pn282 | 1945 | — | 2000 Lei. Brass. Nickel plated. | — |
| PnA283 | 1946 | — | 1000 Lei. Aluminum. | — |
| PnB283 | 1946 | — | 500 Lei. Aluminum. | — |
| Pn283 | 1946 | — | 25000 Lei. Silver. | 800 |
| PnA284 | 1952 | — | 10 Bani. Copper-Nickel. With cogged wheel instead of wreath. | — |
| PnB284 | 1956 | — | 10 Bani. Aluminum. | 100 |
| PnC284 | 1956 | — | 50 Bani. Aluminum. | 150 |
| Pn284 | 1958 | — | 5 Bani. Copper-Nickel-Zinc. | 100 |
| PnD284 | | — | 5 Bani. Aluminum-Bronze. | — |
| Pn285 | 1960 | — | 10 Bani. Nickel. 20 teeth to wheel. | 100 |
| PnA285 | 1960 | — | 10 Bani. Nickel. 12 teeth to wheel. | — |
| PnB285 | 1966 | — | 5 Bani. Aluminum. | — |
| PnC285 | 1966 | — | 15 Bani. Aluminum. | — |
| PnD285 | 1966 | — | 15 Bani. Brass. | — |
| PnE285 | 1966 | — | 15 Bani. Copper. | — |
| PnF285 | 1966 | — | 3 Lei. Silver. | — |
| PnG285 | 1966 | — | 5 Lei. Copper. Factory. | — |
| PnH285 | 1966 | — | 5 Lei. Copper. | — |
| PnI285 | 1966 | — | 5 Lei. Brass. | — |
| PnJ285 | 1984 | — | 100 Lei. Silver. | — |
| PnK285 | (1984) | — | 100 Lei. | — |
| PnL285 | 1987 | — | 2 Lei. Nickel Plated Steel. | 180 |
| Pn286 | 1987 | — | 10 Lei. Nickel. Steel plated. | 75.00 |
| Pn287 | 1987 | — | 10 Lei. Aluminum. | 70.00 |
| Pn288 | 1987 | — | 10 Lei. Aluminum. | 70.00 |
| Pn289 | 1987 | — | 10 Lei. Bronze. | 80.00 |
| Pn290 | 1987 | — | 10 Lei. Nickel. Steel plated. | 75.00 |
| PnA290 | 1987 | — | 10 Lei. Nickel Plated Steel. | — |
| PnB290 | 1987 | — | 10 Lei. Aluminum. | — |
| PnC290 | 1987 | — | 10 Lei. Brass. | — |
| Pn291 | 1988 | — | 10 Lei. Aluminum. | 75.00 |
| Pn292 | 1988 | — | 10 Lei. Aluminum. | 75.00 |
| PnA293 | 1990 | — | 10 Lei. Aluminum. | 100 |
| PnB293 | 1991 | — | Leu. Copper-Nickel. 3 oak leaves. | 60.00 |
| Pn293 | 1991 | — | 5 Lei. Iron. Nickel clad. Similar to 100 Lei, KM#111. | 70.00 |
| Pn294 | 1991 | — | 5 Lei. Brass. Similar to 100 Lei, KM#111. | 70.00 |
| PnA296 | 1991 | — | 20 Lei. Aluminum. | 70.00 |
| PnB296 | 1991 | — | 20 Lei. Nickel Plated Steel. Similar to 100 Lei, KM#111. | 95.00 |
| PnC296 | 1991 | — | 50 Lei. Aluminum. | 60.00 |
| PnD296 | 1991 | — | 50 Lei. Copper-Nickel. | 60.00 |
| Pn296 | 1991 | — | 50 Lei. Silver. KM110. | 150 |
| PnA297 | 1991 | — | 100 Lei. Brass. King Stephen. | 300 |
| PnB297 | 1991 | — | 100 Lei. Brass. Prince M. Viteazul. | 200 |
| PnC297 | 1991 | — | 100 Lei. Aluminum. Prince M. Viteazul. | 150 |
| PnD297 | 1991 | — | 100 Lei. Nickel Plated Steel. Lettered edge. | — |
| PnE297 | 1991 | — | 100 Lei. Nickel Plated Steel. Sinus line edge. | 90.00 |
| PnF297 | 1991 | — | 100 Lei. Nickel Plated Steel. Lettered edge. | 90.00 |
| PnG297 | 1991 | — | 100 Lei. Nickel Plated Steel. Lettered edge. | 90.00 |
| PnH297 | (1992) | — | Leu. Nickel. | — |
| Pn297 | 1992 | — | Leu. Silver. | 100 |
| Pn298 | (1992) | — | Leu. Nickel. | 80.00 |
| PnA299 | 1992 | — | Leu. Silver. | — |
| PnB299 | 1992 | — | 5 Lei. Brass. | 70.00 |
| PnC299 | 1992 | — | 5 Lei. Copper-Nickel. | 70.00 |
| PnD299 | 1992 | — | 5 Lei. Nickel Plated Steel. | 70.00 |
| Pn299 | 1992 | — | 5 Lei. Aluminum. | 50.00 |
| PnA300 | 1993 | — | Leu. Copper. Like KM#113. | 80.00 |

| KM# | Date | Mintage | Identification | Mkt Val |
|---|---|---|---|---|
| pnB300 | 1995 | — | 100 Lei. Aluminum. KM#118. | 40.00 |
| PnA315.1 | 1996 | 125 | 100 Lei. Aluminum. National arms. Gymnast on balance beam. Plain with denomination edge. Piefort version. | 35.00 |
| PnA326 | 1996 | 125 | 100 Lei. Aluminum. 37 mm. National arms. Shooter and target. | 30.00 |
| PnA326a | 1996 | 125 | 100 Lei. Aluminum. Piefort version. | 35.00 |
| PnB326 | 1996 | 125 | 100 Lei. Bronze. | 30.00 |
| PnB326a | 1996 | 125 | 100 Lei. Bronze. Piefort version. | 35.00 |
| PnC326 | 1996 | 125 | 100 Lei. Copper. | 30.00 |
| PnC326a | 1996 | 125 | 100 Lei. Copper. Piefort version. | 35.00 |
| PnD326 | 1996 | 125 | 100 Lei. Bi-Metallic. | 35.00 |
| PnD326a | 1996 | 125 | 100 Lei. Bi-Metallic. Piefort version. | 40.00 |
| PnE326 | 1996 | 125 | 100 Lei. 0.9250 Silver. 27.2500 g. | 75.00 |
| PnE326a | 1996 | 126 | 100 Lei. 0.9250 Silver. 27.2500 g. Piefort version. | 90.00 |
| PnB315.1 | 1996 | 125 | 100 Lei. Aluminum. 37 mm. National arms. Horse and rider. Plain with denomination edge. Piefort version. | 35.00 |
| PnB315A | 1996 | 125 | 100 Lei. Brass. 37 mm. National arms. Horse and rider. Plain with denomination edge. | 30.00 |
| PnB315A1 | 1996 | 125 | 100 Lei. Brass. 37 mm. National arms. Horse and rider. Plain with denomination edge. Piefort version. | 35.00 |
| PnB315B | 1996 | 125 | 100 Lei. Copper. 37 mm. National arms. Horse and rider. Plain with denomination edge. | 30.00 |
| PnB315B1 | 1996 | 125 | 100 Lei. Copper. 37 mm. National arms. Horse and rider. Plain with denomination edge. Piefort version. | 35.00 |
| PnB315C | 1996 | 125 | 100 Lei. Brass center. Copper-Nickel ring. 37 mm. National arms. Horse and rider. Plain with denomination edge. | 35.00 |
| PnB315C1 | 1996 | 125 | 100 Lei. Brass center. Copper-Nickel ring. 37 mm. National arms. Horse and rider. Plain with denomination edge. Piefort version. | 40.00 |
| PnB315E | 1996 | 125 | 100 Lei. 0.9250 Silver. 27.2500 g. 37 mm. National arms. Horse and rider. Plain with denomination edge. | 75.00 |
| PnB315E1 | 1996 | 125 | 100 Lei. 0.9250 Silver. 27.2500 g. 37 mm. National arms. Horse and rider. Plain with denomination edge. Piefort version. | 90.00 |
| PnA315a | 1996 | 125 | 100 Lei. Brass. 37 mm. National arms. Gymnast on balance beam. Plain with denomination edge. | 30.00 |
| PnC315.1 | 1996 | 125 | 100 Lei. Aluminum. 37 mm. National arms. Two basketbal players. Plain with denomination edge. Piefort version. | 35.00 |
| PnC315A | 1996 | 125 | 100 Lei. Brass. 37 mm. National arms. Two basketball players. Plain with denomination edge. | 30.00 |
| PnC315A1 | 1996 | 125 | 100 Lei. Brass. 37 mm. National arms. Two basketball players. Plain with denomination edge. Piefort version. | 35.00 |
| PnC315B | 1996 | 125 | 100 Lei. Copper. 37 mm. National arms. Two basketball players. Plain with denomination edge. | 30.00 |
| PnC315B1 | 1996 | 125 | 100 Lei. Copper. 37 mm. National arms. Two basketball players. Plain with denomination edge. Piefort version. | 35.00 |
| PnC315C | 1996 | 125 | 100 Lei. Brass center. Copper-Nickel ring. 37 mm. National arms. Two basketball players. Plain with denomination edge. | 35.00 |
| PnC315C1 | 1996 | 125 | 100 Lei. Brass center. Copper-Nickel ring. 37 mm. National arms. Two basketball players. Plain with denomination edge. Piefort version. | 40.00 |
| PnC315D | 1996 | 125 | 100 Lei. 0.9250 Silver. 27.2500 g. 37 mm. National arms. Two basketball players. Plain with denomination edge. | 75.00 |
| PnC315D1 | 1996 | 125 | 100 Lei. 0.9250 Silver. 27.2500 g. 37 mm. National arms. Two basketball players. Plain with denomination edge. Piefort version. | 90.00 |
| PnD315.1 | 1996 | 125 | 100 Lei. Aluminum. 37 mm. National arms. Tennis player. Plain with denomination edge. Piefort version. | 35.00 |
| | 1996 | 125 | 100 Lei. Brass. 37 mm. National arms. Tennis player. Plain with denomination edge. | 30.00 |
| PnD315A1 | 1996 | 125 | 100 Lei. Brass. 37 mm. National arms. Tennis player. Plain with denomination edge. Piefort version. | 35.00 |
| PnD315B | 1996 | 125 | 100 Lei. Copper. 37 mm. National arms. Tennis player. Plain with denomination edge. | 30.00 |
| PnD315B1 | 1996 | 125 | 100 Lei. Copper. 37 mm. National arms. Tennis player. Plain with denomination edge. Piefort version. | 35.00 |
| PnD315C | 1996 | 125 | 100 Lei. Brass center. Copper-Nickel ring. 37 mm. National arms. Tennis player. Plain with denomination edge. | 35.00 |
| PnD315C1 | 1996 | 125 | 100 Lei. Brass center. Copper-Nickel ring. 37 mm. National arms. Tennis player. Plain with denomination edge. Piefort version. | 40.00 |
| PnD315D | 1996 | 125 | 100 Lei. 0.9250 Silver. 27.2500 g. 37 mm. National arms. Tennis player. Plain with denomination edge. | 75.00 |

| KM# | Date | Mintage | Identification | Mkt Val |
|---|---|---|---|---|
| PnD315D1 | 1996 | 125 | 100 Lei. 0.9250 Silver. 27.2500 g. 37 mm. National arms. Tennis player. Plain with denomination edge. Piefort version. | 90.00 |
| Pn351.1 | 1996 | 125 | 100 Lei. Aluminum. 37 mm. National arms. Skier. Plain with denomination edge. Piefort version. | 35.00 |
| Pn351A1 | 1996 | 125 | 100 Lei. Aluminum. 37 mm. National arms. Skier. Plain with denomination edge. Piefort version. | 35.00 |
| Pn351B | 1996 | 125 | 100 Lei. Copper. 37 mm. National arms. Skier. Plain with denomination edge. | 30.00 |
| Pn351B1 | 1996 | 125 | 100 Lei. Copper. 37 mm. National arms. Skier. Plain with denomination edge. Piefort version. | 35.00 |
| Pn351C | 1996 | 125 | 100 Lei. Brass center. Copper-Nickel ring. 37 mm. National arms. Skier. Plain with denomination edge. | 35.00 |
| Pn351c1 | 1996 | 125 | 100 Lei. Brass center. Copper-Nickel ring. 37 mm. National arms. Skier. Plain with denomination edge. Piefort version. | 40.00 |
| Pn351D | 1996 | 125 | 100 Lei. 0.9250 Silver. 27.2500 g. 37 mm. National arms. Skier. Plain with denomination edge. | 75.00 |
| Pn351D1 | 1996 | 125 | 100 Lei. 0.9250 Silver. 27.2500 g. 37 mm. National arms. Skier. Plain with denomination edge. Piefort version. | 90.00 |
| PnD315A | 1996 | 125 | 100 Lei. Brass. 37 mm. National arms. Tennis player. Plain with denomination edge. | 30.00 |
| PnA315D1 | 1996 | 125 | 100 Lei. 0.9250 Silver. 27.2500 g. 37 mm. Nationl arms. Gymnast on balance beam. Plain with denomination edge. Piefort version. | 90.00 |
| PnA315B | 1996 | 125 | 100 Lei. Copper. 37 mm. National arms. Gymnast on balance beam. Plain with denomination edge. | 30.00 |
| PnA315B1 | 1996 | 125 | 100 Lei. Copper. 37 mm. National arms. Gymnast on balance beam. Plain with denomination edge. Piefort version. | 35.00 |
| PnA315C | 1996 | 125 | 100 Lei. Brass center. Copper-Nickel ring. 37 mm. National arms. Gymnast on balance beam. Plain with denomination edge. | 35.00 |
| | 1996 | 125 | 100 Lei. Brass center. Copper-Nickel ring. Piefort. | 40.00 |
| PnA315D | 1996 | 125 | 100 Lei. 0.9250 Silver. 27.2500 g. 37 mm. National arms. Gymnast on balance beam. Plain with denomination edge. | 75.00 |
| Pn300 | 1996 | — | 10 Lei. Nickel Plated Steel. Similar to KM#117. KM#134. | 35.00 |
| Pn301 | 1996 | — | 100 Lei. Aluminum. KM#119. | 45.00 |
| Pn302 | 1996 | — | 100 Lei. Brass. KM#119. | 50.00 |
| Pn303 | 1996 | — | 100 Lei. Copper-Nickel. KM#127. Brass plated. | 45.00 |
| Pn304 | 1996 | — | 100 Lei. Aluminum. KM#127. | 40.00 |
| Pn305 | 1996 | — | 100 Lei. Copper-Nickel. KM#128. Brass plated. | 45.00 |
| Pn306 | 1996 | — | 100 Lei. Aluminum. KM#128. | 40.00 |
| Pn307 | 1996 | — | 100 Lei. Copper-Nickel. KM#129. Brass plated. | 45.00 |
| Pn351A | 1996 | — | 100 Lei. Brass. 37 mm. National arms. Skier. Plain with denomination edge. | 30.00 |
| Pn308 | 1996 | — | 100 Lei. Aluminum. KM#129. | 40.00 |
| Pn309 | 1996 | — | 100 Lei. Copper-Nickel. KM#130. Brass plated. | 45.00 |
| Pn310 | 1996 | — | 100 Lei. Aluminum. KM#130. | 40.00 |
| Pn311 | 1996 | — | 100 Lei. Copper-Nickel. KM#131. Brass plated. | 45.00 |
| Pn312 | 1996 | — | 100 Lei. Aluminum. KM#131. | 40.00 |
| Pn313 | 1996 | — | 100 Lei. Copper-Nickel. KM#132. Brass plated. | 45.00 |
| | 1996 | 125 | 100 Lei. 0.9250 Silver. 27.2500 g. Lettered edge. Piefort. Balance beam. | 90.00 |
| | 1996 | 125 | 100 Lei. Brass. Lettered edge. Balance beam. | 35.00 |
| Pn314 | 1996 | — | 100 Lei. Aluminum. KM#132. | 40.00 |
| | 1996 | 125 | 100 Lei. Brass. Lettered edge. Piefort. Balance beam. | 50.00 |
| PnA315 | 1996 | 125 | 100 Lei. Aluminum. 37 mm. National arms. Gymnast on balance beam. Plain with denomination edge. | 30.00 |
| | 1996 | 125 | 100 Lei. Aluminum. Lettered edge. Balance beam. | 30.00 |
| PnB315 | 1996 | 125 | 100 Lei. Aluminum. 37 mm. National arms. Horse and rider. Plain with denomination edge. | 30.00 |
| PnC315 | 1996 | 125 | 100 Lei. Aluminum. 37 mm. National arms. Two basketball players. Plain with denomination edge. | 30.00 |
| PnD315 | 1996 | 125 | 100 Lei. Aluminum. 37 mm. National arms. Tennis player. Plain with denomination edge. | 30.00 |
| PnA315A1 | 1996 | — | 100 Lei. Brass. 37 mm. National arms. Gymnast on balance beam. Plain with denomination edge. Piefort version. | 35.00 |
| PnE315 | 1996 | 125 | 100 Lei. Aluminum. Lettered edge. Piefort. Balance beam. | 35.00 |
| Pn316 | 1996 | — | 100 Lei. Aluminum. KM#133. | 45.00 |
| Pn317 | 1996 | — | 100 Lei. Brass. KM#135. | 50.00 |
| Pn318 | 1996 | — | 500 Lei. Brass. KM#147. Arms without outline. | — |
| Pn319 | 1996 | — | 500 Lei. Aluminum. KM#147. Arms without outline. | — |
| Pn320 | 1996 | — | 500 Lei. Nickel. KM#147. Arms without outline. | — |
| Pn351 | 1996 | 125 | 100 Lei. Aluminum. 37 mm. National arms. Skier. Plain with denomination edge. | 30.00 |
| Pn321 | 1996 | — | 500 Lei. KM#147. Arms without outline. Bimetal. | — |
| Pn322 | 1996 | — | 3000 Lei. Copper. 1 ECU. Dracula. | — |
| Pn323 | 1996 | — | 3000 Lei. 1 ECU. Dracula. Golden brass. | — |
| Pn324 | 1996 | — | 3000 Lei. Silver. 1 ECU. Dracula. | — |
| Pn325 | 1996 | — | 3000 Lei. Aluminum. 1 ECU. Dracula. | — |
| Pn350.1 | 1998 | 125 | 100 Lei. Aluminum. 37 mm. National arms. Two hockey players. Plain with denomination edge. Piefort version. | 35.00 |
| Pn350A1 | 1998 | 125 | 100 Lei. Brass. 37 mm. National arms. Two hockey players. Plain with denomination edge. Piefort version. | 35.00 |
| Pn350B | 1998 | 125 | 100 Lei. Copper. 37 mm. National arms. Two hockey players. Plain with denomination edge. | 30.00 |
| Pn350B1 | 1998 | 125 | 100 Lei. Copper. 37 mm. National arms. Two hockey players. Plain with denomination edge. Piefort version. | 35.00 |
| Pn350C | 1998 | 125 | 100 Lei. Brass center. Copper-Nickel ring. 37 mm. National arms. Two hockey players. Plain with denomination edge. | 35.00 |
| Pn350C1 | 1998 | 125 | 100 Lei. Brass center. Copper-Nickel ring. 37 mm. National arms. Two hockey players. Plain with denomination edge. Piefort version. | 40.00 |
| Pn350D | 1998 | 125 | 100 Lei. 0.9250 Silver. 27.2500 g. 37 mm. National arms. Two hockey players. Plain with denomination edge. | 75.00 |
| Pn350D1 | 1998 | 125 | 100 Lei. 0.9250 Silver. 27.2500 g. 37 mm. National arms. Two hockey players. Plain with denomination edge. Piefort version. | 90.00 |
| Pn353.1 | 1998 | 125 | 100 Lei. Aluminum. 37 mm. National arms. Two ice dancers. Plain with denomination edge. Piefort version. | 35.00 |
| Pn353A1 | 1998 | 125 | 100 Lei. Brass. 37 mm. National arms. Two ice dancers. Plain with denomination edge. Piefort version. | 35.00 |
| Pn353B | 1998 | 125 | 100 Lei. Copper. 37 mm. National arms. Two ice dancers. Plain with denomination edge. | 30.00 |
| Pn353B1 | 1998 | 125 | 100 Lei. Copper. 37 mm. National arms. Two ice dancers. Plain with denomination edge. Piefort version. | 35.00 |
| Pn353C | 1998 | 125 | 100 Lei. Brass center. Copper-Nickel ring. 37 mm. National arms. Two ice dancers. Plain with denomination edge. | 35.00 |
| Pn353C1 | 1998 | 125 | 100 Lei. Brass center. Copper-Nickel ring. 37 mm. National arms. Two ice dancers. Plain with denomination edge. Piefort version. | 40.00 |
| Pn353D | 1998 | 125 | 100 Lei. 0.9250 Silver. 27.2500 g. 37 mm. National arms. Two ice dancers. Plain with denomination edge. | 75.00 |
| Pn353D1 | 1998 | 125 | 100 Lei. 0.9250 Silver. 27.2500 g. 37 mm. National arms. Two ice dancers. Plain with denomination edge. Piefort version. | 90.00 |
| Pn326 | 1998 | — | 100 Lei. KM#119. Eiffel Tower. Golden brass. | — |
| Pn327 | 1998 | — | 100 Lei. Aluminum. KM#119. Eiffel Tower. | — |
| Pn328 | 1998 | — | 100 Lei. Brass. One player. | — |
| Pn329 | 1998 | — | 100 Lei. One player. Bimetal. | — |
| Pn330 | 1998 | — | 100 Lei. Brass. Two players. | — |
| Pn331 | 1998 | — | 100 Lei. Two players. Bimetal. | — |
| Pn332 | 1998 | — | 100 Lei. Bimetal. Gaelic cock. | — |
| Pn350a | 1998 | — | 100 Lei. Brass. Hockey. | 35.00 |
| Pn333 | 1998 | — | 500 Lei. Silver. | — |
| Pn334 | 1998 | — | 500 Lei. Golden brass. | — |
| Pn335 | 1998 | — | 500 Lei. Brass. KM#136. | 25.00 |
| Pn353A | 1998 | — | 100 Lei. Brass. Ice dancing. | 35.00 |
| Pn336 | 1998 | — | 1000 Lei. Silver. Arms at 6. | — |
| Pn337 | 1998 | — | 1000 Lei. Brass. Arms at 6. | 45.00 |
| Pn338 | 1998 | — | 1000 Lei. Arms at 9. Golden brass. | 50.00 |
| Pn339 | 1998 | — | 500 Lei. Brass. KM#147. Arms without outline. | 35.00 |
| Pn340 | 1998 | — | 500 Lei. Nickel. KM#147. Arms without outline. | 40.00 |
| Pn341 | 1998 | — | 500 Lei. Aluminum. KM#147. Arms without outline. | 30.00 |
| Pn342 | 1998 | — | 500 Lei. KM#147. Arms without outline. Bimetal. | 45.00 |
| Pn343 | 1998 | — | 100 Lei. Brass. | — |
| Pn344 | 1998 | — | 100 Lei. KM#138. Bimetal. | — |
| Pn345 | 1998 | — | 100 Lei. Aluminum. KM#138. | — |
| Pn346 | 1998 | — | 100 Lei. Brass. | — |
| Pn347 | 1998 | — | 100 Lei. Silver. | — |
| Pn348 | 1998 | — | 100 Lei. Bimetal. | — |
| Pn349 | 1998 | — | 100 Lei. Aluminum. | — |
| Pn350 | 1998 | 125 | 100 Lei. Aluminum. 37 mm. National arms. Two hockey players. Plain with denomination edge. | 30.00 |
| Pn352 | 1998 | — | 100 Lei. Brass. Women single. | 35.00 |
| Pn353 | 1998 | 125 | 100 Lei. Aluminum. 37 mm. National arms. Two ice dancers. Plain with denomination edge. | 30.00 |
| Pn354 | 1998 | — | 100 Lei. Brass. Ice dancing, without inscription. | 35.00 |
| Pn355 | 1998 | — | 100 Lei. Brass. Bobsled, without inscription. | 40.00 |
| Pn356 | 1998 | — | 100 Lei. Brass. Slalom, without inscription. | 40.00 |
| Pn357 | 1998 | — | 1000 Lei. Brass. Large. | — |
| Pn358 | 1998 | — | 1000 Lei. Brass. Thin. | — |
| Pn359 | 1998 | — | 1000 Lei. Golden brass. | — |
| Pn360 | 1999 | — | 100 Lei. Brass. Young. | — |
| Pn361 | 1999 | — | 100 Lei. Brass. Old. | — |
| Pn362 | 1999 | — | 100 Lei. Brass. | — |
| Pn363 | 1999 | — | 100 Lei. Brass. | — |
| Pn364 | 1999 | — | 100 Lei. Aluminum. Plain edge. KM146. | 100 |
| Pn365 | 1999 | — | 100 Lei. Aluminum. Plain edge. KM147. | 100 |

## PIEFORTS

| KM# | Date | Mintage | Identification | Mkt Val |
|---|---|---|---|---|
| P3 | 1905 | — | 20 Bani. Aluminum-Bronze. | 200 |
| P4 | 1905 | — | 20 Bani. Bronze. | 200 |
| P5 | 1906 | — | 12-1/2 Lei. Gold. | — |
| P6 | 1906 | — | 25 Lei. Gold. | — |
| P7 | 1906 | — | 50 Lei. Lead. | 325 |
| P8 | 1906 | — | 50 Lei. Copper. | 325 |
| P9 | 1906 | — | 50 Lei. Silver. | 1,200 |
| P10 | 1906 | — | 50 Lei. Gold. | — |

## TRIAL COINAGE

| KM# | Date | Mintage | Identification | Mkt Val |
|---|---|---|---|---|
| TS1 | 1906 | — | 5 Lei. Silver. | 4,500 |
| TS2 | 1906 | — | 100 Lei. Silver. | 400 |
| TS3 | 1910 | — | Leu. Pewter. Milled edge. Thin planchet. | — |
| TS4 | 1910 | — | Leu. Pewter. Milled edge. Thick planchet. | — |
| TS5 | 1996 | — | 10 Lei. Nickel Plated Steel. KM#134. | 100 |


## TRIAL COINAGE

| KM# | Date | Mintage | Identification | Mkt Val |
|---|---|---|---|---|
| TS1 | 1906 | — | 5 Lei. Silver. | 4,500 |
| TS2 | 1906 | — | 100 Lei. Silver. | 400 |
| TS3 | 1910 | — | Leu. Pewter. Milled edge. Thin planchet. | — |
| TS4 | 1910 | — | Leu. Pewter. Milled edge. Thick planchet. | — |
| TS5 | 1996 | — | 10 Lei. Nickel Plated Steel. KM#134. | 100 |


## PROOF SETS

| KM# | Date | Mintage | Identification | Issue Price | Mkt Val |
|---|---|---|---|---|---|
| PS1 | 1982 (2) | 7,000 | KM98-99 | 429 | 420 |
| PS2 | 1983 (4) | 1,000 | KM98, 99, 101, 110 edge numbering | 850 | 1,900 |
| PS3 | 2000 (8) | — | KM109-111, 114-116, 145, 153 | — | 45.00 |

# RUSSIA (U.S.S.R.)

Russia, formerly the central power of the Union of Soviet Socialist Republics and now of the Commonwealth of Independent States occupies the northern part of Asia and the eastern part of Europe, has an area of 17,075,400 sq. km. and a population of *146.2 million. Capital: Moscow. Exports include iron and steel, crude oil, timber, and nonferrous metals.

The first Russian dynasty was founded in Novgorod by the Viking Rurik in 862 A.D. under Yaroslav the Wise (1019-54). The subsequent Kievan state became one of the great commercial and cultural centers of Europe before falling to the Mongols of the Batu Khan, 13th century, who were suzerains of Russia until late in the 15th century when Ivan III threw off the Mongol yoke. The Russian Empire was enlarged, solidified and Westernized during the reigns of Ivan the Terrible, Peter the Great and Catherine the Great, and by 1881 extended to the Pacific and into Central Asia. Contemporary Russian history began in March of 1917 when Tsar Nicholas II abdicated under pressure and was replaced by a provisional government composed of both radical and conservative elements. This government rapidly lost ground to the Bolshevik wing of the Socialist Democratic Labor Party which attained power following the Bolshevik Revolution which began on Nov. 7, 1917. After the Russian Civil War, the regional governments, national states and armies became federal republics of the Russian Socialist Federal Soviet Republic. These autonomous republics united to form the Union of Soviet Socialist Republics that was established as a federation under the premiership of Lenin on Dec. 30, 1922.

In the fall of 1991, events moved swiftly in the Soviet Union. Estonia, Latvia and Lithuania won their independence and were recognized by Moscow, Sept. 6. The Commonwealth of Independent States was formed Dec. 8, 1991 in Mensk by Belarus, Russia and Ukraine. It was expanded at a summit Dec. 21, 1991 to include 11 of the 12 remaining republics (excluding Georgia) of the old U.S.S.R.

## EMPIRE

**RULERS**

Nicholas II, 1894-1917

**MINT MARKS**

Л – Leningrad, 1991
М – Moscow, 1990
СП – St. Petersburg, 1999
СПБ – St. Petersburg, 1724-1914
СПМД – St. Petersburg, 1999

(sp) (l) – LMD (ЛМД) monogram in oval, (Leningrad), (St. Petersburg) 1977-1997

(m) – MMD (ММД) monogram in oval, Moscow, 1977-

**MINT OFFICIAL'S INITIALS**

**Leningrad Mint**

| Initials | Years | Mint Official |
|---|---|---|
| АГ | 1921-22 | A.F. Hartman |
| ПЛ | 1922-27 | P.V. Latishev |

**London Mint**

| Initials | Years | Mint Official |
|---|---|---|
| T.P. | 1924 | Thomas Ross |
| ФР | 1924 | Thomas Ross |

**St. Petersburg Mint**

| Initials | Years | Mint Official |
|---|---|---|
| ФЗ | 1899-1901 | Felix Zaleman |
| АР | 1901-05 | Alexander Redko |
| ЭБ | 1906-13 | Elikum Babayantz |
| ВС | 1913-17 | Victor Smirnov |

**NOTE**: St. Petersburg Mint became Petrograd in 1914 and Leningrad in 1924. It was renamed St. Petersburg in 1991.

**MONETARY SYSTEM**

1/4 Kopek = Polushka ПОЛУШКА
1/2 Kopek = Denga, Denezhka ДЕНГА, ДЕНЕЖКА
Kopek = КОПѢЙКА
(2, 3 & 4) Kopeks КОПѢЙКИ
(5 and up) Kopeks КОПѢЕКЪ
(1924 – 5 and up) Kopeks КОПЕЕК
50 Kopeks = Poltina, Poltinnik ПОЛТИНА,...ПОЛРУБЛЪ
100 Kopeks = Rouble, Ruble РУБЛЪ
10 Roubles = Imperial ИМПЕРІАЛЪ
10 Roubles = Chervonetz ЧЕРВОНЕЦ

**NOTE:** Mintage figures for years after 1885 are for fiscal years and may or may not reflect actual rarity, the commemorative and 1917 silver figures being exceptions.

## STANDARD COINAGE

**POLUSHKA (1/4 Kopek)** **Y# 47.1** **Weight:** 3.0000 g. **Composition:** Copper

| Date | Mintage | F | VF | XF | Unc | BU |
|---|---|---|---|---|---|---|
| 1909 | 2,000,000 | 1.00 | 2.00 | 4.00 | 12.00 | — |
| 1910 | 8,000,000 | 4.00 | 8.00 | 15.00 | 30.00 | — |
| 1909-1910 Proof | — | Value: 125 | | | | |

**POLUSHKA (1/4 Kopek)** **Y# 47.2** **Weight:** 3.0000 g. **Composition:** Copper

| Date | Mintage | F | VF | XF | Unc | BU |
|---|---|---|---|---|---|---|
| 1915 | 500,000 | 2.00 | 5.00 | 10.00 | 20.00 | — |
| 1916 | 1,200,000 | 40.00 | 80.00 | 150 | 300 | — |

**1/2 KOPEK** **Y# 48.1** **Weight:** 4.0000 g. **Composition:** Copper

| Date | Mintage | F | VF | XF | Unc | BU |
|---|---|---|---|---|---|---|
| Common date Proof | — | Value: 125 | | | | |
| 1908СПБ | 8,000,000 | 0.25 | 0.50 | 1.00 | 5.00 | — |
| 1909СПБ | 49,500,000 | 0.25 | 0.50 | 1.00 | 4.00 | — |
| 1910СПБ | 24,000,000 | 0.25 | 0.50 | 1.00 | 5.00 | — |
| 1911СПБ | 35,800,000 | 0.25 | 0.50 | 1.00 | 5.00 | — |
| 1912СПБ | 28,000,000 | 0.25 | 0.50 | 1.00 | 5.00 | — |
| 1913СПБ | 50,000,000 | 0.25 | 0.50 | 1.00 | 5.00 | — |
| 1914СПБ | 14,000,000 | 0.25 | 0.50 | 1.00 | 5.00 | — |
| 1908-14 Proof | — | Value: 125 | | | | |

**Note:** Above value for common date proof

**1/2 KOPEK** **Y# 48.2** **Weight:** 4.0000 g. **Composition:** Copper **Note:** Struck at Petrograd without mint mark.

| Date | Mintage | F | VF | XF | Unc | BU |
|---|---|---|---|---|---|---|
| 1915 | 12,000,000 | 0.25 | 0.50 | 1.00 | 5.00 | — |
| 1916 | 9,400,000 | 0.25 | 0.50 | 1.00 | 5.00 | — |

**KOPEK** **Y# 9.2** **Weight:** 4.0000 g. **Composition:** Copper

| Date | Mintage | F | VF | XF | Unc | BU |
|---|---|---|---|---|---|---|
| 1897СПБ | 30,000,000 | 0.25 | 0.50 | 1.50 | 8.00 | — |
| 1901СПБ | 30,000,000 | 0.25 | 0.50 | 1.50 | 8.00 | — |
| 1902СПБ | 20,000,000 | 2.50 | 5.00 | 10.00 | 20.00 | — |
| 1903СПБ | 74,400,000 | 0.25 | 0.50 | 1.50 | 8.00 | — |
| 1904СПБ | 30,600,000 | 0.25 | 0.50 | 1.50 | 8.00 | — |
| 1905СПБ | 23,000 | 0.25 | 0.50 | 1.50 | 8.00 | — |
| 1906СПБ | 20,000,000 | 0.25 | 0.50 | 1.50 | 8.00 | — |
| 1907СПБ | 20,000,000 | 0.25 | 0.50 | 1.50 | 8.00 | — |
| 1908СПБ | 40,000,000 | 0.25 | 0.50 | 1.50 | 8.00 | — |
| 1909СПБ | 27,500,000 | 0.25 | 0.50 | 1.50 | 8.00 | — |
| 1910СПБ | 36,500,000 | 0.25 | 0.50 | 1.50 | 8.00 | — |
| 1911СПБ | 38,150,000 | 0.25 | 0.50 | 1.50 | 8.00 | — |
| 1912СПБ | 31,850,000 | 0.25 | 0.50 | 1.50 | 8.00 | — |
| 1913СПБ | 61,500,000 | 0.25 | 0.50 | 1.50 | 8.00 | — |
| 1914СПБ | 32,500,000 | 0.25 | 0.50 | 1.50 | 8.00 | — |
| 1901-14 Proof | — | Value: 150 | | | | |

**Note:** Above value for common date proof

**KOPEK** **Y# 9.3** **Weight:** 4.0000 g. **Composition:** Copper **Note:** Struck at Petrograd without mint mark.

| Date | Mintage | F | VF | XF | Unc | BU |
|---|---|---|---|---|---|---|
| 1915 | 58,000,000 | 0.25 | 0.50 | 1.50 | 8.00 | — |
| 1916 | 46,500,000 | 0.25 | 0.50 | 1.50 | 8.00 | — |
| 1917 Unique | — | — | — | — | — | — |

**2 KOPEKS** **Y# 10.2** **Composition:** Copper

| Date | Mintage | F | VF | XF | Unc | BU |
|---|---|---|---|---|---|---|
| 1901СПБ | 20,000,000 | 0.50 | 1.00 | 2.00 | 8.00 | — |
| 1902СПБ | 10,000,000 | 0.50 | 1.00 | 2.00 | 8.00 | — |
| 1903СПБ | 29,200,000 | 0.50 | 1.00 | 2.00 | 8.00 | — |
| 1904СПБ | 13,300,000 | 0.50 | 1.00 | 2.00 | 8.00 | — |
| 1905СПБ | 15,000,000 | 0.50 | 1.00 | 2.00 | 8.00 | — |
| 1906СПБ | 6,250,000 | 0.50 | 1.00 | 2.00 | 8.00 | — |
| 1907СПБ | 7,500,000 | 0.50 | 1.00 | 2.00 | 8.00 | — |
| 1908СПБ | 19,000,000 | 0.50 | 1.00 | 2.00 | 8.00 | — |
| 1909СПБ | 16,250,000 | 0.50 | 1.00 | 2.00 | 8.00 | — |
| 1910СПБ | 12,000,000 | 0.50 | 1.00 | 2.00 | 8.00 | — |
| 1911СПБ | 17,200,000 | 0.50 | 1.00 | 2.00 | 8.00 | — |
| 1912СПБ | 17,050,000 | 0.50 | 1.00 | 2.00 | 8.00 | — |
| 1913СПБ | 26,000,000 | 0.50 | 1.00 | 2.00 | 8.00 | — |
| 1914СПБ | 20,000,000 | 0.50 | 1.00 | 2.00 | 8.00 | — |
| 1901-14СПБ Proof | — | Value: 165 | | | | |

**Note:** Above value for common date proof

**2 KOPEKS** **Y# 10.3** **Composition:** Copper **Note:** Struck at Petrograd without mint mark.

| Date | Mintage | F | VF | XF | Unc | BU |
|---|---|---|---|---|---|---|
| 1915 | 33,750,000 | 0.50 | 1.00 | 2.00 | 5.00 | — |
| 1916 | 31,500,000 | 0.50 | 1.00 | 2.00 | 5.00 | — |

**3 KOPEKS** Y# 11.2 **Composition:** Copper

| Date | Mintage | F | VF | XF | Unc | BU |
|---|---|---|---|---|---|---|
| 1901СПБ | 10,000,000 | 0.75 | 1.50 | 3.00 | 15.00 | — |
| 1902СПБ | 3,333,000 | 0.75 | 1.50 | 3.00 | 15.00 | — |
| 1903СПБ | 11,400,000 | 0.75 | 1.50 | 3.00 | 15.00 | — |
| 1904СПБ | 6,934,000 | 0.75 | 1.50 | 3.00 | 15.00 | — |
| 1905СПБ | 3,333,000 | 0.75 | 1.50 | 3.00 | 15.00 | — |
| 1906СПБ | 5,667,000 | 0.75 | 1.50 | 3.00 | 15.00 | — |
| 1907СПБ | 2,500,000 | 0.75 | 1.50 | 3.00 | 15.00 | — |
| 1908СПБ | 12,667,000 | 0.75 | 1.50 | 3.00 | 15.00 | — |
| 1909СПБ | 6,733,000 | 0.75 | 1.50 | 3.00 | 15.00 | — |
| 1910СПБ | 6,667,000 | 0.75 | 1.50 | 3.00 | 15.00 | — |
| 1911СПБ | 9,467,000 | 0.75 | 1.50 | 3.00 | 15.00 | — |
| 1912СПБ | 8,533,000 | 0.75 | 1.50 | 3.00 | 15.00 | — |
| 1913СПБ | 15,333,000 | 0.75 | 1.50 | 3.00 | 15.00 | — |
| 1914СПБ | 8,167,000 | 0.75 | 1.50 | 3.00 | 15.00 | — |
| 1901-14СПБ Proof | — | Value: 175 | | | | |

**Note:** Above value for common date proof

**3 KOPEKS** Y# 11.3 **Composition:** Copper **Note:** Struck at Petrograd without mint mark.

| Date | Mintage | F | VF | XF | Unc | BU |
|---|---|---|---|---|---|---|
| 1915 | 19,833,000 | 0.75 | 1.50 | 3.00 | 16.00 | — |
| 1916 | 25,667,000 | 0.75 | 1.50 | 3.00 | 16.00 | — |
| 1917 Rare | — | — | — | — | — | — |

**5 KOPEKS** Y# 19a.1 **Weight:** 0.8998 g. **Composition:** 0.5000 Silver .0144 oz. ASW **Obverse:** Eagle **Edge:** Reeded

| Date | Mintage | F | VF | XF | Unc | BU |
|---|---|---|---|---|---|---|
| 1901СПБ ФЗ | 5,790,000 | 1.00 | 2.00 | 4.00 | 15.00 | — |
| 1901СПБ АР | Inc. above | 1.00 | 2.00 | 4.00 | 15.00 | — |
| 1902СПБ АР | 6,000,000 | 1.00 | 2.00 | 4.00 | 15.00 | — |
| 1903СПБ АР | 9,000,000 | 1.00 | 2.00 | 4.00 | 15.00 | — |
| 1904СПБ АР Rare | 9 | — | — | — | — | — |
| 1905СПБ АР | 10,000,000 | 1.00 | 2.00 | 4.00 | 15.00 | — |
| 1906СПБ ЭБ | 4,000,000 | 1.00 | 2.00 | 4.00 | 15.00 | — |
| 1908СПБ ЭБ | 400,000 | 1.00 | 2.00 | 4.00 | 15.00 | — |
| 1909СПБ ЭБ | 3,100,000 | 1.00 | 2.00 | 4.00 | 15.00 | — |
| 1910СПБ ЭБ | 2,500,000 | 1.00 | 2.00 | 4.00 | 15.00 | — |
| 1911СПБ ЭБ | 2,700,000 | 1.00 | 2.00 | 4.00 | 15.00 | — |
| 1912СПБ ЭБ | 3,000,000 | 1.00 | 2.00 | 4.00 | 15.00 | — |
| 1913СПБ ЭБ Proof | | Value: 150 | | | | |
| 1913СПБ ВС | 1,300,000 | 1.00 | 2.00 | 4.00 | 15.00 | — |
| 1914СПБ ВС | 4,200,000 | 1.00 | 2.00 | 4.00 | 15.00 | — |
| 1901-14 Proof | — | Value: 150 | | | | |

**Note:** Above value for common date proof

**5 KOPEKS** Y# 12.2 **Composition:** Copper

| Date | Mintage | F | VF | XF | Unc | BU |
|---|---|---|---|---|---|---|
| 1911СПБ | 3,800,000 | 6.00 | 12.50 | 25.00 | 50.00 | — |
| 1912СПБ | 2,700,000 | 10.00 | 17.50 | 35.00 | 70.00 | — |

**5 KOPEKS** Y# 19a.2 **Weight:** 0.8998 g. **Composition:** 0.5000 Silver .0144 oz. ASW **Note:** Struck at Petrograd without mint mark.

| Date | Mintage | F | VF | XF | Unc | BU |
|---|---|---|---|---|---|---|
| 1915 ВС | 3,000,000 | 1.00 | 2.00 | 4.00 | 15.00 | — |

**5 KOPEKS** Y# 12.3 **Composition:** Copper **Note:** Struck at Petrograd without mint mark.

| Date | Mintage | F | VF | XF | Unc | BU |
|---|---|---|---|---|---|---|
| 1916 | 8,000,000 | 40.00 | 80.00 | 150 | 250 | — |
| 1917 Rare | — | — | — | — | — | — |

**10 KOPEKS** Y# 20a.2 **Weight:** 1.7996 g. **Composition:** 0.5000 Silver .0289 oz. ASW **Edge:** Reeded

| Date | Mintage | F | VF | XF | Unc | BU |
|---|---|---|---|---|---|---|
| 1867СПБ HI | 6,445,000 | 0.50 | 1.00 | 3.00 | 25.00 | — |
| 1868СПБ HI | 4,740,000 | 0.50 | 1.00 | 3.00 | 25.00 | — |
| 1869СПБ HI | 3,710,000 | 0.50 | 1.00 | 3.00 | 25.00 | — |
| 1870СПБ HI | 3,310,000 | 0.50 | 1.00 | 3.00 | 25.00 | — |
| 1871СПБ HI | 4,195,000 | 0.50 | 1.00 | 3.00 | 25.00 | — |
| 1872СПБ HI | 2,130,000 | 0.50 | 1.00 | 3.00 | 25.00 | — |
| 1873СПБ HI | 2,620,000 | 0.50 | 1.00 | 3.00 | 25.00 | — |
| 1901СПБ ФЗ | 15,000,000 | 0.50 | 1.00 | 2.00 | 15.00 | — |
| 1901СПБ АР | Inc. above | 0.50 | 1.00 | 2.00 | 15.00 | — |
| 1902СПБ АР | 17,000,000 | 0.50 | 1.00 | 2.00 | 15.00 | — |
| 1903СПБ АР | 28,500,000 | 0.50 | 1.00 | 2.00 | 15.00 | — |
| 1904СПБ АР | 20,000,000 | 0.50 | 1.00 | 2.00 | 15.00 | — |
| 1905СПБ АР | 25,000,000 | 0.50 | 1.00 | 2.00 | 15.00 | — |
| 1906СПБ ЭБ | 17,500,000 | 0.50 | 1.00 | 2.00 | 15.00 | — |
| 1908СПБ ЭБ | 8,210,000 | 0.50 | 1.00 | 2.00 | 15.00 | — |
| 1909СПБ ЭБ | 25,290,000 | 0.50 | 1.00 | 2.00 | 15.00 | — |
| 1910СПБ ЭБ | 20,000,000 | 0.50 | 1.00 | 2.00 | 15.00 | — |
| 1911СПБ ЭБ | 19,180,000 | 0.50 | 1.00 | 2.00 | 15.00 | — |
| 1912СПБ ЭБ | 20,000,000 | 0.50 | 1.00 | 2.00 | 15.00 | — |
| 1913СПБ ЭБ Proof | | Value: 265 | | | | |
| 1913СПБ ВС | 7,250,000 | 0.50 | 1.00 | 2.00 | 15.00 | — |
| 1914СПБ ВС | 51,250,000 | 0.50 | 1.00 | 2.00 | 15.00 | — |
| 1901-14 Proof | — | Value: 265 | | | | |

**Note:** Above value for common date proof

**10 KOPEKS** Y# 20a.3 **Weight:** 1.7996 g. **Composition:** 0.5000 Silver .0289 oz. ASW **Note:** Struck at Petrograd without mint mark.

| Date | Mintage | F | VF | XF | Unc | BU |
|---|---|---|---|---|---|---|
| 1915 ВС | 82,500,000 | 0.50 | 0.75 | 1.00 | 6.00 | — |
| 1916 ВС | 121,500,000 | 0.50 | 0.75 | 1.00 | 6.00 | — |
| 1917 ВС | 17,600,000 | — | 20.00 | 30.00 | 80.00 | — |

**10 KOPEKS** Y# 20a.1 **Weight:** 1.7996 g. **Composition:** 0.5000 Silver .0289 oz. ASW **Note:** Struck at Osaka, Japan without mint mark.

| Date | Mintage | F | VF | XF | Unc | BU |
|---|---|---|---|---|---|---|
| 1916 | 70,001,000 | BV | 1.00 | 2.00 | 10.00 | — |

**15 KOPEKS** Y# 21a.2 **Weight:** 2.6994 g. **Composition:** 0.5000 Silver .0434 oz. ASW **Edge:** Reticulated

| Date | Mintage | F | VF | XF | Unc | BU |
|---|---|---|---|---|---|---|
| 1901СПБ ФЗ | 6,670,000 | 0.75 | 1.00 | 2.00 | 10.00 | — |
| 1901СПБ АР | Inc. above | 0.75 | 1.00 | 2.00 | 10.00 | — |
| 1902СПБ АР | 28,667,000 | 0.75 | 1.00 | 2.00 | 10.00 | — |
| 1903СПБ АР | 16,667,000 | 0.75 | 1.00 | 2.00 | 10.00 | — |
| 1904СПБ АР | 15,600,000 | 0.75 | 1.00 | 2.00 | 10.00 | — |
| 1905СПБ АР | 24,000,000 | 0.75 | 1.00 | 2.00 | 10.00 | — |
| 1906СПБ ЭБ | 23,333,000 | 0.75 | 1.00 | 2.00 | 10.00 | — |
| 1907СПБ ЭБ | 30,000,000 | 0.75 | 1.00 | 2.00 | 10.00 | — |
| 1908СПБ ЭБ | 29,000,000 | 0.75 | 1.00 | 2.00 | 10.00 | — |
| 1909СПБ ЭБ | 21,667,000 | 0.75 | 1.00 | 2.00 | 10.00 | — |
| 1911СПБ ЭБ | 6,313,000 | 0.75 | 1.00 | 2.00 | 10.00 | — |
| 1912СПБ ЭБ | 13,333,000 | 0.75 | 1.00 | 2.00 | 10.00 | — |
| 1912СПБ ВС | Inc. above | 2.00 | 5.00 | 12.50 | 40.00 | — |
| 1913СПБ ЭБ Proof | | Value: 265 | | | | |
| 1913СПБ ВС | 5,300,000 | 0.75 | 1.00 | 2.00 | 10.00 | — |
| 1914СПБ ВС | 43,367,000 | 0.75 | 1.00 | 2.00 | 10.00 | — |
| 1901-14 Proof | — | Value: 265 | | | | |

**Note:** Above value for common date proof

**15 KOPEKS** Y# 21a.3 **Weight:** 2.6994 g. **Composition:** 0.5000 Silver .0434 oz. ASW **Note:** Struck at Petrograd without mint mark.

| Date | Mintage | F | VF | XF | Unc | BU |
|---|---|---|---|---|---|---|
| 1915 ВС | 59,333,000 | 0.75 | 1.50 | 2.00 | 10.00 | — |
| 1916 ВС | 96,773,000 | 0.75 | 1.50 | 2.00 | 10.00 | — |
| 1917 ВС | 14,320,000 | — | 20.00 | 30.00 | 80.00 | — |

**15 KOPEKS** Y# 21a.1 **Weight:** 2.6994 g. **Composition:** 0.5000 Silver .0434 oz. ASW **Edge:** Reeded **Note:** Struck at Osaka, Japan without mint mark.

| Date | Mintage | F | VF | XF | Unc | BU |
|---|---|---|---|---|---|---|
| 1916 | 96,666,000 | BV | 1.00 | 2.00 | 10.00 | — |

**20 KOPEKS** Y# 22a.1 **Weight:** 3.5992 g. **Composition:** 0.5000 Silver .0579 oz. ASW

| Date | Mintage | F | VF | XF | Unc | BU |
|---|---|---|---|---|---|---|
| 1901СПБ ФЗ | 7,750,000 | 0.75 | 1.00 | 2.00 | 12.50 | — |
| 1901СПБ АР | Inc. above | 0.75 | 1.00 | 2.00 | 12.50 | — |
| 1902СПБ АР | 10,000,000 | 0.75 | 1.00 | 2.00 | 12.50 | — |
| 1903СПБ АР | Inc. above | 0.75 | 1.00 | 2.00 | 12.50 | — |
| 1904СПБ АР | 13,000,000 | 0.75 | 1.00 | 2.00 | 12.50 | — |
| 1905СПБ АР | 11,000,000 | 0.75 | 1.00 | 2.00 | 12.50 | — |
| 1906СПБ ЭБ | 15,000,000 | 0.75 | 1.00 | 2.00 | 12.50 | — |
| 1907СПБ ЭБ | 20,000,000 | 0.75 | 1.00 | 2.00 | 12.50 | — |
| 1908СПБ ЭБ | 5,000,000 | 0.75 | 1.00 | 2.00 | 12.50 | — |
| 1909СПБ ЭБ | 18,875,000 | 0.75 | 1.00 | 2.00 | 12.50 | — |
| 1910СПБ ЭБ | 11,000,000 | 0.75 | 1.00 | 2.00 | 12.50 | — |
| 1911СПБ ЭБ | 7,100,000 | 0.75 | 1.00 | 2.00 | 12.50 | — |
| 1912СПБ ЭБ | 15,000,000 | 0.75 | 1.00 | 2.00 | 12.50 | — |
| 1912СПБ ВС | Inc. above | 5.00 | 10.00 | 20.00 | 60.00 | — |
| 1913СПБ ЭБ Proof | | Value: 265 | | | | |
| 1913СПБ ВС | 4,250,000 | 0.75 | 1.00 | 2.00 | 12.50 | — |
| 1914СПБ ВС | 52,750,000 | 0.75 | 1.00 | 2.00 | 12.50 | — |
| 1901-14 Proof | — | Value: 265 | | | | |

**Note:** Above value for common date proofs

**20 KOPEKS** Y# 22a.2 **Weight:** 3.5992 g. **Composition:** 0.5000 Silver .0579 oz. ASW **Note:** Struck at Petrograd without mint mark.

| Date | Mintage | F | VF | XF | Unc | BU |
|---|---|---|---|---|---|---|
| 1915 ВС | 105,500,000 | BV | 1.00 | 2.00 | 10.00 | — |
| 1916 ВС | 131,670,000 | BV | 1.00 | 2.00 | 10.00 | — |
| 1917 ВС | 3,500,000 | — | 25.00 | 35.00 | 100 | — |
| 1915-17 Proof | — | Value: 265 | | | | |

**Note:** Above value for common date proof

**25 KOPEKS** Y# 57 **Weight:** 4.9990 g. **Composition:** 0.9000 Silver .1446 oz. ASW **Note:** Struck at St. Petersburg without mint mark.

| Date | Mintage | F | VF | XF | Unc | BU |
|---|---|---|---|---|---|---|
| 1901 Proof | Est. 150 | Value: 1,250 | | | | |

**50 KOPEKS** Y# 58.2 **Weight:** 9.9980 g. **Composition:** 0.9000 Silver .2893 oz. ASW **Note:** Struck at St. Petersburg without mint mark.

| Date | Mintage | F | VF | XF | Unc | BU |
|---|---|---|---|---|---|---|
| 1901 АР | 412,000 | 5.00 | 12.50 | 35.00 | 80.00 | — |
| 1901 ФЗ | Inc. above | 5.00 | 12.50 | 35.00 | 80.00 | — |
| 1902 АР | 36,000 | 10.00 | 20.00 | 40.00 | 175 | — |
| 1903 АР Proof | — | Value: 2,000 | | | | |
| 1904 АР | 4,010,000 | 100 | 200 | 400 | 1,200 | — |
| 1906 ЭБ | — | 25.00 | 50.00 | 100 | 300 | — |
| 1907 ЭБ | 200,000 | 10.00 | 20.00 | 40.00 | 175 | — |
| 1908 ЭБ | 40,000 | 10.00 | 20.00 | 40.00 | 175 | — |
| 1909 ЭБ | 50,000 | 10.00 | 20.00 | 40.00 | 175 | — |
| 1910 ЭБ | 150,000 | 10.00 | 20.00 | 40.00 | 175 | — |
| 1911 ЭБ | 800,000 | 10.00 | 20.00 | 40.00 | 80.00 | — |
| 1912 ЭБ | 7,085,000 | 50.00 | 8.00 | 150 | 45.00 | — |
| 1913 ЭБ | 6,420,000 | 7.50 | 15.00 | 35.00 | 70.00 | — |
| 1913 ВС | Inc. above | 5.00 | 10.00 | 20.00 | 45.00 | — |
| 1914 ВС | 1,200,000 | 5.00 | 10.00 | 20.00 | 45.00 | — |
| 1901-14 Proof | — | Value: 500 | | | | |

**Note:** Above value for common date proof

**ROUBLE** Y# 59.3 **Weight:** 19.9960 g. **Composition:** 0.9000 Silver .5786 oz. ASW **Note:** Struck at St. Petersburg without mint mark.

| Date | Mintage | F | VF | XF | Unc | BU |
|---|---|---|---|---|---|---|
| 1901 ФЗ | 2,608,000 | 9.00 | 16.00 | 45.00 | 200 | — |
| 1901 АР | Inc. above | 40.00 | 80.00 | 125 | 450 | — |
| 1902 АН | 140,000 | 20.00 | 30.00 | 60.00 | 400 | — |
| 1903 АР | 56,000 | 40.00 | 80.00 | 180 | 750 | — |
| 1904 АР | 12,000 | 75.00 | 150 | 300 | 900 | — |
| 1905 АР | 21,000 | 40.00 | 80.00 | 180 | 750 | — |
| 1906 ЭБ | 46,000 | 40.00 | 80.00 | 180 | 750 | — |
| 1907 ЭБ | 400,000 | 20.00 | 30.00 | 60.00 | 400 | — |
| 1908 ЭБ | 130,000 | 75.00 | 150 | 300 | 900 | — |
| 1909 ЭБ | 51,000 | 40.00 | 80.00 | 180 | 600 | — |
| 1910 ЭБ | 75,000 | 25.00 | 40.00 | 80.00 | 450 | — |
| 1911 ЭБ | 129,000 | 25.00 | 40.00 | 80.00 | 400 | — |
| 1912 ЭБ | 2,111,000 | 9.00 | 15.00 | 40.00 | 180 | — |
| 1913 ЭБ | 22,000 | 50.00 | 100 | 200 | 700 | — |
| 1913 ВС | Inc. above | 50.00 | 100 | 200 | 700 | — |
| 1914 ВС | 536,000 | 25.00 | 35.00 | 90.00 | 550 | — |
| 1915 ВС | 5,000 | 30.00 | 60.00 | 125 | 350 | — |

**Note:** Varieties exist with plain edge; these are mint errors and rare

| Date | Mintage | F | VF | XF | Unc | BU |
|---|---|---|---|---|---|---|
| 1901-15 Proof | — | Value: 900 | | | | |

**Note:** Above value for common date proof

**ROUBLE** Y# 68 **Weight:** 19.9960 g. **Composition:** 0.9000 Silver .5786 oz. ASW **Subject:** Centennial - Napolean's Defeat

| Date | Mintage | F | VF | XF | Unc | BU |
|---|---|---|---|---|---|---|
| 1912 ЭБ | 46,000 | 60.00 | 110 | 225 | 400 | — |
| 1912 ЭБ Proof | — | Value: 2,000 | | | | |

**ROUBLE** Y# 69 **Weight:** 19.9960 g. **Composition:** 0.9000 Silver .5786 oz. ASW **Note:** Alexander III Memorial

| Date | Mintage | F | VF | XF | Unc | BU |
|---|---|---|---|---|---|---|
| 1912 ЭБ | 2,100 | 200 | 400 | 1,000 | 1,600 | — |
| 1912 ЭБ Proof | — | Value: 2,250 | | | | |

**ROUBLE** Y# 70 **Weight:** 19.9960 g. **Composition:** 0.9000 Silver .5786 oz. ASW **Subject:** 300th Anniversary - Romanov Dynasty **Note:** Struck at St. Petersburg without mint mark.

| Date | Mintage | F | VF | XF | Unc | BU |
|---|---|---|---|---|---|---|
| 1913 BC | 1,472,000 | 12.00 | 22.00 | 32.00 | 100 | — |

**ROUBLE** Y# 71 **Weight:** 19.9960 g. **Composition:** 0.9000 Silver .5786 oz. ASW **Subject:** 200th Anniversary - Battle of Gangut

| Date | Mintage | F | VF | XF | Unc | BU |
|---|---|---|---|---|---|---|
| 1914 BC | Est. 30,000 | 400 | 600 | 1,700 | 3,000 | — |

**Note:** Only 317 pieces were issued through 1917, but an unknown number of restrikes were made in the 1920's

**5 ROUBLES** Y# 62 **Weight:** 6.4516 g. **Composition:** 0.9000 Gold .1244 oz. AGW **Note:** Struck at St. Petersburg without mint mark.

| Date | Mintage | F | VF | XF | Unc | BU |
|---|---|---|---|---|---|---|
| 1901 ФЗ | 7,500,000 | — | BV | 55.00 | 75.00 | — |
| 1901 AP | Inc. above | — | BV | 70.00 | 100 | — |
| 1902 AP | 6,240,000 | — | BV | 55.00 | 75.00 | — |
| 1903 AP | 5,148,000 | — | BV | 55.00 | 75.00 | — |
| 1904 AP | 2,016,000 | — | BV | 55.00 | 75.00 | — |
| 1906 ЭБ | 10 | — | — | 7,000 | 10,000 | — |
| 1907 ЭБ | 109 | — | — | 4,000 | 7,500 | — |
| 1909 ЭБ | — | BV | 60.00 | 75.00 | 90.00 | — |
| 1910 ЭБ | 200,000 | BV | 60.00 | 75.00 | 100 | — |
| 1911 ЭБ | 100,000 | BV | 60.00 | 150 | 250 | — |
| 1901-11 Proof | — | Value: 1,500 | | | | |

**Note:** Above value for common date proof

**10 ROUBLES** Y# 64 **Weight:** 8.6026 g. **Composition:** 0.9000 Gold .2489 oz. AGW **Note:** Struck at St. Petersburg without mint mark.

| Date | Mintage | F | VF | XF | Unc | BU |
|---|---|---|---|---|---|---|
| 1901 ФЗ | 2,377,000 | — | BV | 100 | 150 | — |
| 1901 AP | Inc. above | — | BV | 110 | 165 | — |
| 1902 AP | 2,019,000 | — | BV | 100 | 150 | — |
| 1903 AP | 2,817,000 | — | BV | 100 | 145 | — |
| 1904 AP | 1,025,000 | — | BV | 100 | 145 | — |
| 1906 ЭБ Proof | 10 | Value: 8,500 | | | | |
| 1909 ЭБ | 50,000 | BV | 110 | 125 | 200 | — |
| 1910 ЭБ | 100,000 | BV | 110 | 125 | 200 | — |
| 1911 ЭБ | 50,000 | BV | 110 | 125 | 200 | — |
| 1901-11 Proof | — | Value: 2,500 | | | | |

**Note:** Above value for common date proof

**25 ROUBLES** Y# A65 **Weight:** 32.2500 g. **Composition:** 0.9000 Gold .9332 oz. AGW **Rev. Legend:** 2-1/2 ИМПЕРІАЛА (IMPERIALS) **Note:** Struck at St. Petersburg without mint mark.

| Date | Mintage | F | VF | XF | Unc | BU |
|---|---|---|---|---|---|---|
| 1908 | 150 | — | 7,500 | 9,500 | 20,000 | — |
| 1908 Proof | 25 | Value: 23,000 | | | | |

**37 ROUBLES 50 KOPEKS** Y# B65a **Composition:** Copper-Nickel **Reverse:** Letter "P" after "1902 G" **Edge:** Plain

| Date | Mintage | F | VF | XF | Unc | BU |
|---|---|---|---|---|---|---|
| 1902 G P Restrike | — | — | — | — | 12.50 | — |

**37 ROUBLES 50 KOPEKS** Y# B65 **Weight:** 32.2500 g. **Composition:** 0.9000 Gold .9335 oz. AGW **Rev. Legend:** 100 ФРАНКОВЪ **Note:** Struck at St. Petersburg without mint mark.

| Date | Mintage | F | VF | XF | Unc | BU |
|---|---|---|---|---|---|---|
| 1902 | 225 | — | 7,500 | 15,000 | 25,000 | — |
| 1902 Proof | — | Value: 25,000 | | | | |

## GOLD MINE INGOTS

During the late 19th and early 20th century, Russian law provided that gold mine owners who supplied gold to the mints should receive back whatever silver was recovered during refining of the gold. The silver was returned in the form of circular ingots of various weights which resembled coins. These pieces have often been erroneously described as Russian trade coins for use in Mongolia, China, and Turkestan.

Note: Both the Doyla and the Zolotnik are weights, not denominations.

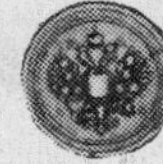

**24 DOLYA** KM# 1 **Weight:** 1.0664 g. **Composition:** 0.9900 Silver .0343 oz. ASW **Ruler:** Nicholas II

| Date | Mintage | F | VF | XF | Unc | BU |
|---|---|---|---|---|---|---|
| ND(1901) | — | — | 350 | 450 | 650 | — |

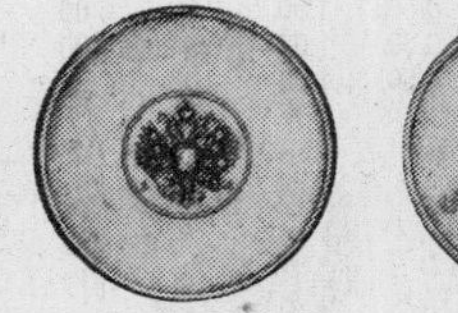

**ZOLOTNIK** KM# 2 **Weight:** 4.2656 g. **Composition:** 0.9900 Silver .1371 oz. ASW **Ruler:** Nicholas II

| Date | Mintage | F | VF | XF | Unc | BU |
|---|---|---|---|---|---|---|
| ND(1901) | — | — | 225 | 325 | 475 | — |

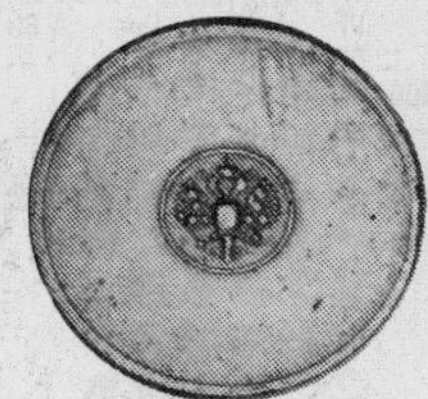

**3 ZOLOTNIKS** KM# 3 **Weight:** 12.7969 g. **Composition:** 0.9900 Silver .4114 oz. ASW **Ruler:** Nicholas II

| Date | Mintage | F | VF | XF | Unc | BU |
|---|---|---|---|---|---|---|
| ND(1901) | — | — | 1,000 | 1,500 | 2,000 | — |

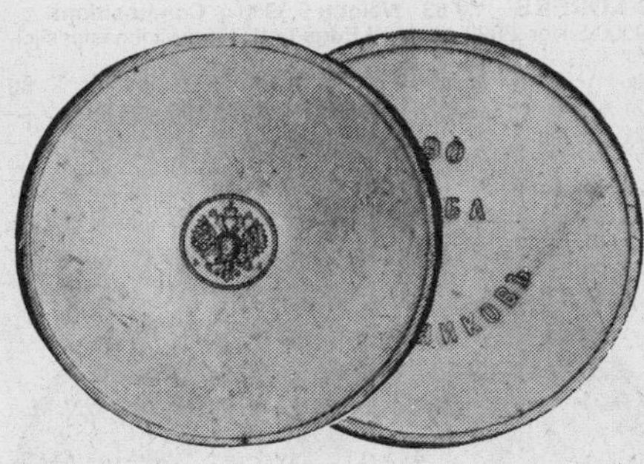

**10 ZOLOTNIKS** KM# 4 **Weight:** 42.6563 g. **Composition:** 0.9900 Silver 1.3714 oz. ASW **Ruler:** Nicholas II

| Date | Mintage | F | VF | XF | Unc | BU |
|---|---|---|---|---|---|---|
| ND(1901) | — | — | 250 | 450 | 700 | — |

## РСФСР (R.S.F.S.R.)
## (Russian Soviet Federated Socialist Republic)

## STANDARD COINAGE

**10 KOPEKS** Y# 80 **Weight:** 1.8000 g. **Composition:** 0.5000 Silver .0289 oz. ASW

| Date | Mintage | F | VF | XF | Unc | BU |
|---|---|---|---|---|---|---|
| 1921 | 950,000 | 5.00 | 10.00 | 25.00 | 50.00 | — |
| 1921 Proof | — | Value: 250 | | | | |
| 1922 | 18,640,000 | 1.00 | 2.00 | 4.50 | 12.00 | — |
| 1922 Proof | — | Value: 115 | | | | |
| 1923 | 33,424,000 | 1.00 | 2.00 | 4.00 | 10.00 | — |
| 1923 Proof | — | Value: 60.00 | | | | |

**15 KOPEKS** Y# 81 **Weight:** 2.7000 g. **Composition:** 0.5000 Silver .0434 oz. ASW

| Date | Mintage | F | VF | XF | Unc | BU |
|---|---|---|---|---|---|---|
| 1921 | 933,000 | 6.00 | 12.00 | 30.00 | 60.00 | — |
| 1921 Proof | — | Value: 275 | | | | |
| 1922 | 13,633,000 | 2.00 | 3.00 | 6.00 | 16.00 | — |
| 1922 Proof | — | Value: 140 | | | | |
| 1923 | 28,504,000 | 1.50 | 2.50 | 4.50 | 12.00 | — |
| 1923 Proof | — | Value: 80.00 | | | | |

**20 KOPEKS** Y# 82 **Weight:** 3.6000 g. **Composition:** 0.5000 Silver .0578 oz. ASW **Note:** Varieties exist.

| Date | Mintage | F | VF | XF | Unc | BU |
|---|---|---|---|---|---|---|
| 1921 | 825,000 | 6.00 | 12.00 | 30.00 | 60.00 | — |
| 1921 Proof | — | Value: 300 | | | | |
| 1922 | 14,220,000 | 2.00 | 4.00 | 8.00 | 20.00 | — |
| 1922 Proof | — | Value: 165 | | | | |
| 1923 | 27,580,000 | 2.00 | 3.50 | 7.00 | 15.00 | — |
| 1923 Proof | — | Value: 100 | | | | |

**50 KOPEKS** **Y# 83** **Weight:** 9.9980 g. **Composition:** 0.9000 Silver .2893 oz. ASW **Edge Lettering:** Mintmaster's initials

| Date | Mintage | F | VF | XF | Unc | BU |
|---|---|---|---|---|---|---|
| 1921 АГ | 1,400,000 | 5.00 | 7.00 | 10.00 | 25.00 | — |
| 1921 АГ Proof | — | Value: 325 | | | | |
| 1922 АГ | 8,224,000 | 5.00 | 7.00 | 10.00 | 25.00 | — |
| 1922 АГ Proof | — | Value: 350 | | | | |
| 1922 ПЛ | Inc. above | 5.00 | 7.00 | 10.00 | 25.00 | — |
| 1922 ПЛ Proof | — | Value: 250 | | | | |

**ROUBLE** **Y# 84** **Weight:** 19.9960 g. **Composition:** 0.9000 Silver .5786 oz. ASW **Edge Lettering:** Mintmasters initials **Note:** Varieties exist.

| Date | Mintage | F | VF | XF | Unc | BU |
|---|---|---|---|---|---|---|
| 1921 АГ | 1,000,000 | 8.50 | 13.50 | 25.00 | 65.00 | 90.00 |
| 1921 АГ Proof | — | Value: 425 | | | | |
| 1922 АГ | 2,050,000 | 10.00 | 18.00 | 35.00 | 85.00 | 110 |
| 1922 АГ Proof | — | Value: 600 | | | | |
| 1922 ПЛ | Inc. above | 10.00 | 18.00 | 35.00 | 85.00 | 110 |
| 1922 ПЛ Proof | — | Value: 450 | | | | |

## TRADE COINAGE

**CHERVONETZ (10 Roubles)** **Y# 85** **Weight:** 8.6026 g. **Composition:** 0.9000 Gold .2489 oz. AGW **Obverse:** РСФСР below arms **Edge Lettering:** Mintmasters initials

| Date | Mintage | F | VF | XF | Unc | BU |
|---|---|---|---|---|---|---|
| 1923 ПЛ | 2,751,000 | 130 | 160 | 200 | 250 | — |
| 1923 ПЛ Proof | — | Value: 1,350 | | | | |
| 1975 | 250,000 | — | — | — | BV+10% | — |
| 1976 ЛМД | 1,000,000 | — | — | — | BV+10% | — |
| 1977 ММД | 1,000,000 | — | — | — | BV+10% | — |
| 1977 ЛМД | 1,000,000 | — | — | — | BV+10% | — |
| 1978 ММД | 350,000 | — | — | — | BV+10% | — |
| 1979 ММД | 1,000,000 | — | — | — | BV+10% | — |
| 1980 ММД | 900,000 | — | — | — | BV+10% | — |
| 1980 ММД Proof | 100,000 | Value: 150 | | | | |
| 1981 | 1,000,000 | — | — | — | BV+10% | — |
| 1982 | 65,000 | — | — | — | BV+10% | — |

**CHERVONETZ (10 Roubles)** **Y# A86** **Weight:** 8.6026 g. **Composition:** 0.9000 Gold .2489 oz. AGW **Obverse:** CCCP below arms

| Date | Mintage | F | VF | XF | Unc | BU |
|---|---|---|---|---|---|---|
| 1925 Unique | 600,000 | — | — | — | — | — |

**Note:** Chervonetz were first struck in 1923 under the R.S.F.S.R. government; in 1925 the U.S.S.R. government attempted a new issue of these coins, of which only one remaining coin is known; from 1975 to 1982 the U.S.S.R. government continued striking the original type with new dates

# CCCP (U.S.S.R.)
# (Union of Soviet Socialist Republics)

## STANDARD COINAGE

**1/2 KOPEK** **Y# 75** **Composition:** Copper

| Date | Mintage | F | VF | XF | Unc | BU |
|---|---|---|---|---|---|---|
| 1925 | 45,380,000 | 3.50 | 7.50 | 14.50 | 30.00 | — |
| 1927 | 45,380,000 | 3.50 | 7.50 | 14.50 | 30.00 | — |
| 1927 Proof | — | Value: 100 | | | | |
| 1928 | — | 4.50 | 8.00 | 16.50 | 35.00 | — |

**KOPEK** **Y# 76** **Composition:** Bronze

| Date | Mintage | F | VF | XF | Unc | BU |
|---|---|---|---|---|---|---|
| 1924 Reeded edge | 34,705,000 | 5.00 | 10.00 | 20.00 | 45.00 | — |
| 1924 Reeded edge; Proof | — | Value: 125 | | | | |
| 1924 Plain edge | Inc. above | 30.00 | 60.00 | 120 | 250 | — |
| 1925 | 141,806,000 | 45.00 | 90.00 | 160 | 275 | — |

**KOPEK** **Y# 91** **Composition:** Aluminum-Bronze **Note:** Varieties exist.

| Date | Mintage | F | VF | XF | Unc | BU |
|---|---|---|---|---|---|---|
| 1926 | 87,915,000 | 0.50 | 1.00 | 1.50 | 5.50 | — |
| 1926 Proof | — | Value: 60.00 | | | | |
| 1927 | — | 0.50 | 1.00 | 1.50 | 5.00 | — |
| 1928 | — | 0.50 | 1.00 | 1.50 | 5.00 | — |
| 1929 | 95,950,000 | 0.50 | 1.00 | 1.50 | 5.00 | — |
| 1930 | 85,351,000 | 0.50 | 1.00 | 1.50 | 5.00 | — |
| 1931 | 106,100,000 | 0.50 | 1.00 | 1.50 | 5.00 | — |
| 1932 | 56,900,000 | 0.50 | 1.00 | 1.50 | 5.00 | — |
| 1933 | 111,257,000 | 0.50 | 1.00 | 1.50 | 5.00 | — |
| 1934 | 100,245 | 0.50 | 1.00 | 1.50 | 5.00 | — |
| 1935 | 66,405,000 | 0.50 | 1.00 | 2.00 | 6.00 | — |

**KOPEK** **Y# 98** **Composition:** Aluminum-Bronze

| Date | Mintage | F | VF | XF | Unc | BU |
|---|---|---|---|---|---|---|
| 1935 Mintage inc.Y91 | — | 0.50 | 1.00 | 2.50 | 9.00 | — |
| 1936 | 132,204,000 | 0.50 | 1.00 | 2.00 | 7.50 | — |

**KOPEK** **Y# 105** **Composition:** Aluminum-Bronze **Note:** Varieties exist.

| Date | Mintage | F | VF | XF | Unc | BU |
|---|---|---|---|---|---|---|
| 1937 | — | 0.25 | 0.65 | 1.00 | 4.00 | — |
| 1938 | — | 0.25 | 0.65 | 1.00 | 4.00 | — |
| 1939 | — | 0.25 | 0.65 | 1.00 | 4.00 | — |
| 1940 | — | 0.25 | 0.65 | 1.00 | 4.00 | — |
| 1941 | — | 0.50 | 1.00 | 2.00 | 6.00 | — |
| 1945 | — | 0.50 | 1.00 | 2.00 | 6.00 | — |
| 1946 | — | 0.50 | 1.00 | 2.00 | 6.00 | — |

**KOPEK** **Y# 112** **Composition:** Aluminum-Bronze **Obverse:** Eight and seven ribbons on wreath **Note:** Varieties exist.

| Date | Mintage | F | VF | XF | Unc | BU |
|---|---|---|---|---|---|---|
| 1948 | — | 0.50 | 1.00 | 2.00 | 5.00 | — |
| 1949 | — | 0.50 | 1.00 | 2.00 | 5.00 | — |
| 1950 | — | 0.50 | 1.00 | 2.50 | 8.00 | — |
| 1951 | — | 0.50 | 1.00 | 2.50 | 8.00 | — |
| 1952 | — | 0.30 | 0.75 | 1.50 | 3.00 | — |
| 1953 | — | 0.30 | 0.75 | 1.50 | 3.00 | — |
| 1954 | — | 0.30 | 0.75 | 1.50 | 3.00 | — |
| 1955 | — | 0.30 | 0.75 | 1.50 | 3.00 | — |
| 1956 | — | 0.30 | 0.75 | 1.50 | 3.00 | — |

**KOPEK** **Y# 119** **Composition:** Aluminum-Bronze **Obverse:** Seven and seven ribbons on wreath

| Date | Mintage | F | VF | XF | Unc | BU |
|---|---|---|---|---|---|---|
| 1957 | — | 1.00 | 2.00 | 4.00 | 12.00 | — |

**KOPEK** **Y# 126** **Composition:** Copper-Nickel

| Date | Mintage | F | VF | XF | Unc | BU |
|---|---|---|---|---|---|---|
| 1958 | 30,265,000 | — | — | — | 250 | — |

**Note:** Never officially released for circulation; majority of mintage remelted

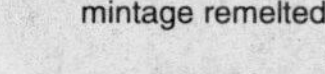

**KOPEK** **Y# 126a** **Composition:** Brass **Note:** Varieties exist.

| Date | Mintage | F | VF | XF | Unc | BU |
|---|---|---|---|---|---|---|
| 1961 | — | 0.10 | 0.15 | 0.25 | 1.00 | — |
| 1962 | — | 0.10 | 0.15 | 0.25 | 0.50 | — |
| 1963 | — | 0.10 | 0.15 | 0.25 | 0.50 | — |
| 1964 | — | 0.20 | 0.30 | 0.50 | 2.00 | — |
| 1965 | — | 0.10 | 0.15 | 0.25 | 0.50 | — |
| 1966 | — | 0.10 | 0.15 | 0.25 | 0.50 | — |
| 1967 | — | 0.10 | 0.15 | 0.25 | 0.50 | — |
| 1968 | — | 0.10 | 0.15 | 0.25 | 0.50 | — |
| 1969 | — | 0.10 | 0.15 | 0.25 | 0.50 | — |
| 1970 | — | 0.10 | 0.15 | 0.25 | 0.50 | — |
| 1971 | — | 0.10 | 0.15 | 0.25 | 0.50 | — |
| 1972 | — | 0.10 | 0.15 | 0.25 | 0.50 | — |
| 1973 | — | 0.10 | 0.15 | 0.25 | 0.50 | — |
| 1974 | — | 0.10 | 0.15 | 0.25 | 0.50 | — |
| 1975 | — | 0.10 | 0.15 | 0.25 | 0.50 | — |
| 1976 | — | 0.10 | 0.15 | 0.25 | 0.50 | — |
| 1977 | — | 0.10 | 0.15 | 0.25 | 0.50 | — |
| 1978 | — | 0.10 | 0.15 | 0.25 | 0.50 | — |
| 1979 | — | 0.10 | 0.15 | 0.25 | 0.50 | — |
| 1980 | — | 0.10 | 0.15 | 0.25 | 0.50 | — |
| 1981 | — | 0.10 | 0.15 | 0.25 | 0.50 | — |
| 1982 | — | 0.10 | 0.15 | 0.25 | 0.50 | — |
| 1983 | — | 0.10 | 0.15 | 0.25 | 0.50 | — |
| 1984 | — | 0.10 | 0.15 | 0.25 | 0.50 | — |
| 1985 | — | 0.10 | 0.15 | 0.25 | 0.50 | — |
| 1986 | — | 0.10 | 0.15 | 0.25 | 0.50 | — |
| 1987 | — | 0.10 | 0.15 | 0.25 | 0.50 | — |
| 1988 | — | 0.10 | 0.15 | 0.25 | 0.50 | — |
| 1989 | — | 0.10 | 0.15 | 0.20 | 0.30 | — |
| 1990 | — | 0.10 | 0.15 | 0.20 | 0.30 | — |
| 1991 (M) | — | 0.10 | 0.15 | 0.20 | 0.30 | — |
| 1991 (l) | — | 0.10 | 0.15 | 0.20 | 0.30 | — |

**2 KOPEKS** **Y# 77** **Composition:** Bronze **Note:** Varieties exist.

| Date | Mintage | F | VF | XF | Unc | BU |
|---|---|---|---|---|---|---|
| 1924 Reeded edge | 119,996,000 | 5.00 | 12.00 | 22.00 | 50.00 | — |
| 1924 Plain edge | Inc. above | 30.00 | 60.00 | 120 | 250 | — |
| 1925 Rare | Inc. above | — | — | — | — | — |

**2 KOPEKS** Y# 92 **Composition:** Aluminum-Bronze **Note:** Varieties exist.

| Date | Mintage | F | VF | XF | Unc | BU |
|---|---|---|---|---|---|---|
| 1926 | 105,053,000 | 0.25 | 0.50 | 1.00 | 4.00 | — |
| 1926 Proof | — | Value: 65.00 | | | | |
| 1927 Rare | — | — | — | — | — | — |
| 1928 | — | 0.25 | 0.50 | 1.00 | 4.00 | — |
| 1929 | 80,000,000 | 0.25 | 0.50 | 1.00 | 5.00 | — |
| 1930 | 134,186,000 | 0.25 | 0.50 | 1.00 | 4.00 | — |
| 1931 | 99,523,000 | 0.25 | 0.50 | 1.00 | 4.00 | — |
| 1932 | 39,573,000 | 0.35 | 0.65 | 1.25 | 4.50 | — |
| 1933 | 54,874,000 | 0.50 | 1.00 | 2.00 | 7.00 | — |
| 1934 | 61,574,000 | 0.35 | 0.65 | 1.25 | 4.50 | — |
| 1935 | 81,121,000 | 0.35 | 0.65 | 1.50 | 5.00 | — |

**2 KOPEKS** Y# 99 **Composition:** Aluminum-Bronze **Note:** Varieties exist.

| Date | Mintage | F | VF | XF | Unc | BU |
|---|---|---|---|---|---|---|
| 1935 | — | 0.50 | 1.00 | 2.50 | 9.00 | — |
| 1936 | 94,354,000 | 0.25 | 0.50 | 2.00 | 7.00 | — |

**2 KOPEKS** Y# 106 **Composition:** Aluminum-Bronze

| Date | Mintage | F | VF | XF | Unc | BU |
|---|---|---|---|---|---|---|
| 1937 | — | 0.25 | 0.65 | 1.00 | 3.00 | — |
| 1938 | — | 0.25 | 0.65 | 1.00 | 3.00 | — |
| 1939 | — | 0.25 | 0.65 | 1.00 | 3.00 | — |
| 1940 | — | 0.25 | 0.65 | 1.00 | 3.00 | — |
| 1941 | — | 0.25 | 0.65 | 1.00 | 3.00 | — |
| 1945 | — | 0.50 | 1.00 | 2.00 | 5.00 | — |
| 1946 | — | 0.25 | 0.65 | 1.00 | 4.00 | — |
| 1948 | — | 40.00 | 70.00 | 130 | 225 | — |

**2 KOPEKS** Y# 113 **Composition:** Aluminum-Bronze **Obverse:** Eight and seven ribbons on wreath **Note:** Varieties exist.

| Date | Mintage | F | VF | XF | Unc | BU |
|---|---|---|---|---|---|---|
| 1948 | — | 0.25 | 0.50 | 1.00 | 2.50 | — |
| 1949 | — | 0.25 | 0.50 | 1.00 | 2.50 | — |
| 1950 | — | 0.25 | 0.50 | 1.00 | 2.50 | — |
| 1951 | — | 0.50 | 1.00 | 2.00 | 6.00 | — |
| 1952 | — | 0.25 | 0.50 | 0.50 | 3.00 | — |
| 1953 | — | 0.20 | 0.50 | 0.50 | 2.00 | — |
| 1954 | — | 0.20 | 0.50 | 0.50 | 2.00 | — |
| 1955 | — | 0.20 | 0.50 | 0.50 | 2.00 | — |
| 1956 | — | 0.20 | 0.50 | 0.50 | 2.00 | — |

**2 KOPEKS** Y# 120 **Composition:** Aluminum-Bronze **Obverse:** Seven and seven ribbons on wreath

| Date | Mintage | F | VF | XF | Unc | BU |
|---|---|---|---|---|---|---|
| 1957 | — | 0.50 | 1.00 | 2.50 | 9.00 | — |

**2 KOPEKS** Y# 127 **Composition:** Copper-Nickel

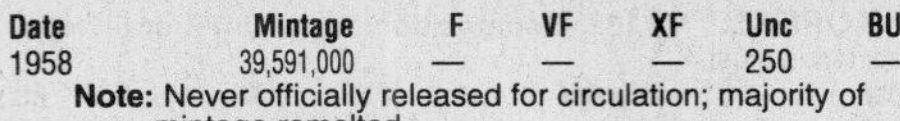

| Date | Mintage | F | VF | XF | Unc | BU |
|---|---|---|---|---|---|---|
| 1958 | 39,591,000 | — | — | — | 250 | — |

**Note:** Never officially released for circulation; majority of mintage remelted

**2 KOPEKS** Y# 127a **Composition:** Brass **Note:** Varieties exist.

| Date | Mintage | F | VF | XF | Unc | BU |
|---|---|---|---|---|---|---|
| 1961 | — | 0.10 | 0.15 | 0.25 | 0.50 | — |
| 1962 | — | 0.10 | 0.15 | 0.25 | 0.50 | — |
| 1963 | — | 0.10 | 0.15 | 0.25 | 0.50 | — |
| 1964 | — | 0.15 | 0.25 | 0.50 | 1.00 | — |
| 1965 | — | 0.10 | 0.15 | 0.25 | 0.50 | — |
| 1966 | — | 0.10 | 0.15 | 0.25 | 0.50 | — |
| 1967 | — | 0.10 | 0.15 | 0.25 | 0.50 | — |
| 1968 | — | 0.10 | 0.15 | 0.25 | 0.50 | — |
| 1969 | — | 0.10 | 0.15 | 0.25 | 0.50 | — |
| 1970 | — | 0.10 | 0.15 | 0.25 | 0.50 | — |
| 1971 | — | 0.10 | 0.15 | 0.25 | 0.50 | — |
| 1972 | — | 0.10 | 0.15 | 0.25 | 0.50 | — |
| 1973 | — | 0.10 | 0.15 | 0.25 | 0.50 | — |
| 1974 | — | 0.10 | 0.15 | 0.25 | 0.50 | — |
| 1975 | — | 0.10 | 0.15 | 0.25 | 0.50 | — |
| 1976 | — | 0.10 | 0.15 | 0.25 | 0.50 | — |
| 1977 | — | 0.10 | 0.15 | 0.25 | 0.50 | — |
| 1978 | — | 0.10 | 0.15 | 0.25 | 0.50 | — |
| 1979 | — | 0.10 | 0.15 | 0.25 | 0.50 | — |
| 1980 | — | 0.10 | 0.15 | 0.25 | 0.50 | — |
| 1981 | — | 0.10 | 0.15 | 0.25 | 0.50 | — |
| 1982 | — | 0.10 | 0.15 | 0.25 | 0.50 | — |
| 1983 | — | 0.10 | 0.15 | 0.25 | 0.50 | — |
| 1984 | — | 0.10 | 0.15 | 0.25 | 0.50 | — |
| 1985 | — | 0.10 | 0.15 | 0.25 | 0.50 | — |
| 1986 | — | 0.10 | 0.15 | 0.25 | 0.50 | — |
| 1987 | — | 0.10 | 0.15 | 0.25 | 0.50 | — |
| 1988 | — | 0.10 | 0.15 | 0.25 | 0.50 | — |
| 1989 | — | 0.10 | 0.15 | 0.20 | 0.35 | — |
| 1990 | — | 0.10 | 0.15 | 0.20 | 0.35 | — |
| 1991 (M) | — | 0.10 | 0.15 | 0.20 | 0.35 | — |
| 1991 (l) | — | 0.10 | 0.15 | 0.20 | 0.35 | — |

**3 KOPEKS** Y# 78 **Composition:** Bronze **Note:** Varieties exist.

| Date | Mintage | F | VF | XF | Unc | BU |
|---|---|---|---|---|---|---|
| 1924 Reeded edge | 101,283,000 | 50.00 | 100 | 175 | 275 | — |
| 1924 Plain edge | Inc. above | 6.00 | 12.50 | 25.00 | 65.00 | — |

**3 KOPEKS** Y# 93 **Composition:** Aluminum-Bronze **Note:** Varieties exist.

| Date | Mintage | F | VF | XF | Unc | BU |
|---|---|---|---|---|---|---|
| 1926 | 19,940,000 | 1.25 | 2.00 | 4.00 | 7.00 | — |
| 1926 Proof | — | Value: 75.00 | | | | |
| 1926 Obverse of Y#100; rare | — | — | — | — | — | — |
| 1927 | — | 5.00 | 10.00 | 20.00 | 40.00 | — |
| 1928 | — | 1.00 | 2.00 | 4.00 | 7.00 | — |
| 1929 | 50,150,000 | 1.00 | 2.00 | 4.00 | 8.00 | — |
| 1930 | 74,159,000 | 0.50 | 0.75 | 1.50 | 5.00 | — |
| 1931 | 121,168,000 | 0.50 | 0.75 | 1.50 | 5.00 | — |
| 1931 Without CCCP obverse; rare | — | — | — | — | — | — |
| 1932 | 37,718,000 | 0.50 | 0.75 | 1.50 | 5.00 | — |
| 1933 | 44,764,000 | 0.50 | 0.75 | 2.00 | 6.00 | — |
| 1934 | 44,529,000 | 0.50 | 0.75 | 2.00 | 6.00 | — |
| 1935 | 58,303,000 | 0.50 | 0.75 | 2.50 | 7.00 | — |

**3 KOPEKS** Y# 100 **Composition:** Aluminum-Bronze **Note:** Varieties exist.

| Date | Mintage | F | VF | XF | Unc | BU |
|---|---|---|---|---|---|---|
| 1935 | — | 0.50 | 2.00 | 5.00 | 14.00 | — |
| 1936 | 62,757,000 | 0.25 | 1.00 | 4.00 | 10.00 | — |

**3 KOPEKS** Y# 107 **Composition:** Aluminum-Bronze **Note:** Varieties exist.

| Date | Mintage | F | VF | XF | Unc | BU |
|---|---|---|---|---|---|---|
| 1937 | — | 0.25 | 0.50 | 1.00 | 4.00 | — |
| 1938 | — | 0.25 | 0.50 | 1.00 | 4.00 | — |
| 1939 | — | 0.25 | 0.50 | 1.00 | 4.00 | — |
| 1940 | — | 0.25 | 0.50 | 1.00 | 3.00 | — |
| 1941 | — | 0.25 | 0.50 | 1.00 | 4.00 | — |
| 1943 | — | 0.25 | 0.50 | 1.00 | 5.00 | — |
| 1945 | — | 0.50 | 1.00 | 3.00 | 9.00 | — |
| 1946 | — | 0.25 | 0.50 | 1.00 | 5.00 | — |
| 1948 | — | 40.00 | 70.00 | 130 | 225 | — |

**3 KOPEKS** Y# 114 **Composition:** Aluminum-Bronze **Obverse:** Eight and seven ribbons on wreath **Note:** Varieties exist.

| Date | Mintage | F | VF | XF | Unc | BU |
|---|---|---|---|---|---|---|
| 1948 | — | 0.25 | 0.50 | 1.00 | 5.00 | — |
| 1949 | — | 0.25 | 0.50 | 1.00 | 4.00 | — |
| 1950 | — | 0.25 | 0.50 | 1.00 | 4.00 | — |
| 1951 | — | 0.50 | 1.00 | 2.00 | 7.00 | — |
| 1952 | — | 0.25 | 0.50 | 1.00 | 4.00 | — |
| 1953 | — | 0.25 | 0.50 | 1.00 | 3.00 | — |
| 1954 | — | 0.25 | 0.50 | 1.00 | 3.00 | — |
| 1955 | — | 0.25 | 0.50 | 1.00 | 3.00 | — |
| 1956 | — | 0.25 | 0.50 | 1.00 | 3.00 | — |
| 1957 | — | 2.50 | 0.50 | 10.00 | 30.00 | — |

**3 KOPEKS** Y# 121 **Composition:** Aluminum-Bronze **Obverse:** Seven and seven ribbons on wreath

| Date | Mintage | F | VF | XF | Unc | BU |
|---|---|---|---|---|---|---|
| 1957 | — | 0.50 | 1.00 | 2.50 | 9.00 | — |

**3 KOPEKS** Y# 128 **Composition:** Copper-Zinc

| Date | Mintage | F | VF | XF | Unc | BU |
|---|---|---|---|---|---|---|
| 1958 | 26,676,000 | — | — | — | 250 | — |

**Note:** Never officially released for circulation; majority of mintage remelted

**3 KOPEKS** Y# 128a **Composition:** Aluminum-Bronze **Note:** Varieties exist.

| Date | Mintage | F | VF | XF | Unc | BU |
|---|---|---|---|---|---|---|
| 1961 | — | 0.10 | 0.15 | 0.25 | 0.60 | — |
| 1962 | — | 0.10 | 0.15 | 0.25 | 0.60 | — |
| 1965 | — | 0.10 | 0.15 | 0.25 | 0.60 | — |
| 1966 | — | 0.10 | 0.15 | 0.25 | 0.60 | — |
| 1967 | — | 0.10 | 0.15 | 0.25 | 0.60 | — |
| 1968 | — | 0.10 | 0.15 | 0.25 | 0.60 | — |
| 1969 | — | 0.10 | 0.15 | 0.25 | 0.60 | — |
| 1970 | — | 0.10 | 0.15 | 0.25 | 0.60 | — |
| 1971 | — | 0.10 | 0.15 | 0.25 | 0.60 | — |
| 1972 | — | 0.10 | 0.15 | 0.25 | 0.60 | — |
| 1973 | — | 0.10 | 0.15 | 0.25 | 0.60 | — |
| 1974 | — | 0.10 | 0.15 | 0.25 | 0.60 | — |
| 1975 | — | 0.10 | 0.15 | 0.25 | 0.60 | — |
| 1976 | — | 0.10 | 0.15 | 0.25 | 0.60 | — |
| 1977 | — | 0.10 | 0.15 | 0.25 | 0.60 | — |
| 1978 | — | 0.10 | 0.15 | 0.25 | 0.60 | — |
| 1979 | — | 0.10 | 0.15 | 0.25 | 0.60 | — |
| 1980 | — | 0.10 | 0.15 | 0.25 | 0.60 | — |
| 1981 | — | 0.10 | 0.15 | 0.25 | 0.60 | — |
| 1982 | — | 0.10 | 0.15 | 0.25 | 0.60 | — |
| 1983 | — | 0.10 | 0.15 | 0.25 | 0.60 | — |
| 1984 | — | 0.10 | 0.15 | 0.25 | 0.60 | — |
| 1985 | — | 0.10 | 0.15 | 0.25 | 0.60 | — |
| 1986 | — | 0.10 | 0.15 | 0.25 | 0.60 | — |
| 1987 | — | 0.10 | 0.15 | 0.25 | 0.60 | — |
| 1988 | — | 0.10 | 0.15 | 0.25 | 0.60 | — |
| 1989 | — | 0.10 | 0.15 | 0.20 | 0.40 | — |
| 1990 | — | 0.10 | 0.15 | 0.20 | 0.40 | — |
| 1991 (M) | — | 0.10 | 0.15 | 0.20 | 0.40 | — |
| 1991 (l) | — | 0.10 | 0.15 | 0.20 | 0.40 | — |

**5 KOPEKS** Y# 79 **Composition:** Bronze **Note:** Varieties exist.

| Date | Mintage | F | VF | XF | Unc | BU |
|---|---|---|---|---|---|---|
| 1924 Reeded edge | 88,510,000 | 50.00 | 100 | 175 | 275 | — |
| 1924 Plain edge | Inc. above | 7.00 | 15.00 | 30.00 | 75.00 | — |

**5 KOPEKS** Y# 94 **Composition:** Aluminum-Bronze **Note:** Varieties exist.

| Date | Mintage | F | VF | XF | Unc | BU |
|---|---|---|---|---|---|---|
| 1926 | 14,697,000 | 1.00 | 2.00 | 6.00 | 10.00 | — |
| 1926 Proof | — | Value: 85.00 | | | | |
| 1927 | — | 5.00 | 10.00 | 20.00 | 40.00 | — |
| 1928 | — | 0.75 | 1.25 | 3.00 | 7.00 | — |
| 1929 | 20,220,000 | 0.75 | 1.25 | 3.00 | 7.00 | — |
| 1930 | 44,490,000 | 0.75 | 1.25 | 2.00 | 6.00 | — |
| 1931 | 89,540,000 | 0.75 | 1.25 | 2.00 | 6.00 | — |
| 1932 | 65,100,000 | 0.75 | 1.25 | 2.00 | 6.00 | — |
| 1932 | 18,135,000 | 15.00 | 30.00 | 75.00 | 250 | — |
| 1934 | 5,354,000 | 2.00 | 4.00 | 12.00 | 30.00 | — |
| 1935 | 11,735,000 | 3.00 | 6.00 | 15.00 | 50.00 | — |

**5 KOPEKS** Y# 101 **Composition:** Aluminum-Bronze **Note:** Varieties exist.

| Date | Mintage | F | VF | XF | Unc | BU |
|---|---|---|---|---|---|---|
| 1935 | — | 2.00 | 4.00 | 9.00 | 26.00 | — |
| 1936 | 5,242,000 | 2.00 | 4.00 | 9.00 | 28.00 | — |

**5 KOPEKS** Y# 108 **Composition:** Aluminum-Bronze **Note:** Varieties exist.

| Date | Mintage | F | VF | XF | Unc | BU |
|---|---|---|---|---|---|---|
| 1937 | — | 2.00 | 4.00 | 9.00 | 28.00 | — |
| 1938 | — | 0.25 | 0.50 | 1.00 | 4.50 | — |
| 1939 | — | 0.25 | 0.50 | 1.00 | 4.50 | — |
| 1940 | — | 0.25 | 0.50 | 1.00 | 4.00 | — |
| 1941 | — | 0.25 | 0.50 | 1.00 | 4.50 | — |
| 1943 | — | 0.25 | 0.50 | 1.00 | 4.50 | — |
| 1945 | — | 1.00 | 2.00 | 5.00 | 12.00 | — |
| 1946 | — | 0.25 | 0.50 | 1.00 | 6.00 | — |

**5 KOPEKS** Y# 115 **Composition:** Aluminum-Bronze **Obverse:** Eight and seven ribbons on wreath **Note:** Varieties exist.

| Date | Mintage | F | VF | XF | Unc | BU |
|---|---|---|---|---|---|---|
| 1948 | — | 0.25 | 0.50 | 1.50 | 5.00 | — |
| 1949 | — | 0.25 | 0.50 | 1.00 | 4.00 | — |
| 1950 | — | 0.25 | 0.50 | 1.00 | 4.00 | — |
| 1951 | — | 0.50 | 1.00 | 2.00 | 5.00 | — |
| 1952 | — | 0.25 | 0.50 | 1.00 | 4.00 | — |
| 1953 | — | 0.25 | 0.50 | 1.00 | 4.00 | — |
| 1954 | — | 0.25 | 0.50 | 1.00 | 4.00 | — |
| 1955 | — | 0.25 | 0.50 | 1.00 | 4.00 | — |
| 1956 | — | 0.25 | 0.50 | 1.00 | 4.00 | — |

**5 KOPEKS** Y# 122 **Composition:** Aluminum-Bronze **Obverse:** Seven and seven ribbons on wreath **Note:** Varieties exist.

| Date | Mintage | F | VF | XF | Unc | BU |
|---|---|---|---|---|---|---|
| 1957 | — | 1.00 | 2.00 | 3.00 | 9.00 | — |

**5 KOPEKS** Y# 129 **Composition:** Copper-Zinc

| Date | Mintage | F | VF | XF | Unc | BU |
|---|---|---|---|---|---|---|
| 1958 | 61,119,000 | — | — | — | 375 | — |

**Note:** Never officially released for circulation; majority of mintage remelted

**5 KOPEKS** Y# 129a **Composition:** Aluminum-Bronze **Note:** Varieties exist.

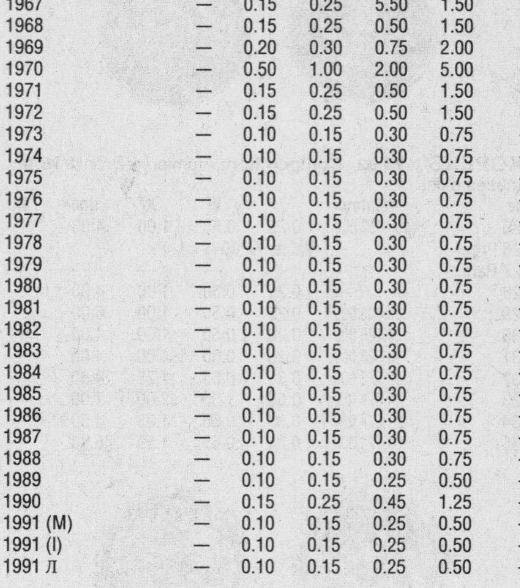

| Date | Mintage | F | VF | XF | Unc | BU |
|---|---|---|---|---|---|---|
| 1961 | — | 0.10 | 0.15 | 0.30 | 0.75 | — |
| 1962 | — | 0.10 | 0.15 | 0.30 | 0.75 | — |
| 1965 | — | 0.25 | 0.50 | 1.00 | 3.00 | — |
| 1966 | — | 0.20 | 0.30 | 0.70 | 2.00 | — |
| 1967 | — | 0.15 | 0.25 | 5.50 | 1.50 | — |
| 1968 | — | 0.15 | 0.25 | 0.50 | 1.50 | — |
| 1969 | — | 0.20 | 0.30 | 0.75 | 2.00 | — |
| 1970 | — | 0.50 | 1.00 | 2.00 | 5.00 | — |
| 1971 | — | 0.15 | 0.25 | 0.50 | 1.50 | — |
| 1972 | — | 0.15 | 0.25 | 0.50 | 1.50 | — |
| 1973 | — | 0.10 | 0.15 | 0.30 | 0.75 | — |
| 1974 | — | 0.10 | 0.15 | 0.30 | 0.75 | — |
| 1975 | — | 0.10 | 0.15 | 0.30 | 0.75 | — |
| 1976 | — | 0.10 | 0.15 | 0.30 | 0.75 | — |
| 1977 | — | 0.10 | 0.15 | 0.30 | 0.75 | — |
| 1978 | — | 0.10 | 0.15 | 0.30 | 0.75 | — |
| 1979 | — | 0.10 | 0.15 | 0.30 | 0.75 | — |
| 1980 | — | 0.10 | 0.15 | 0.30 | 0.75 | — |
| 1981 | — | 0.10 | 0.15 | 0.30 | 0.75 | — |
| 1982 | — | 0.10 | 0.15 | 0.30 | 0.70 | — |
| 1983 | — | 0.10 | 0.15 | 0.30 | 0.75 | — |
| 1984 | — | 0.10 | 0.15 | 0.30 | 0.75 | — |
| 1985 | — | 0.10 | 0.15 | 0.30 | 0.75 | — |
| 1986 | — | 0.10 | 0.15 | 0.30 | 0.75 | — |
| 1987 | — | 0.10 | 0.15 | 0.30 | 0.75 | — |
| 1988 | — | 0.10 | 0.15 | 0.30 | 0.75 | — |
| 1989 | — | 0.10 | 0.15 | 0.25 | 0.50 | — |
| 1990 | — | 0.15 | 0.25 | 0.45 | 1.25 | — |
| 1991 (M) | — | 0.10 | 0.15 | 0.25 | 0.50 | — |
| 1991 (l) | — | 0.10 | 0.15 | 0.25 | 0.50 | — |
| 1991 Л | — | 0.10 | 0.15 | 0.25 | 0.50 | — |

**10 KOPEKS** Y# 86 **Weight:** 1.8000 g. **Composition:** 0.5000 Silver .0289 oz. ASW **Note:** Varieties exist.

| Date | Mintage | F | VF | XF | Unc | BU |
|---|---|---|---|---|---|---|
| 1924 | 67,351,000 | 0.50 | 1.00 | 3.00 | 9.00 | — |
| 1924 Proof | — | Value: 200 | | | | |
| 1925 | 101,013,000 | 0.50 | 1.00 | 2.50 | 8.00 | — |
| 1925 Proof | — | Value: 75.00 | | | | |
| 1927 | — | 0.50 | 1.00 | 3.00 | 9.00 | — |
| 1927 Proof | — | Value: 75.00 | | | | |
| 1928 | — | 0.50 | 1.00 | 2.50 | 8.00 | — |
| 1929 | 64,900,000 | 0.50 | 1.00 | 3.00 | 9.00 | — |
| 1930 | 163,424,000 | 0.50 | 1.00 | 2.50 | 8.00 | — |
| 1931 Rare | 8,791,000 | — | — | — | — | — |

**10 KOPEKS** Y# 95 **Composition:** Copper-Nickel **Note:** Varieties exist.

| Date | Mintage | F | VF | XF | Unc | BU |
|---|---|---|---|---|---|---|
| 1931 | 122,511,000 | 1.00 | 2.00 | 4.00 | 8.00 | — |
| 1932 | 171,641,000 | 0.25 | 0.50 | 1.00 | 4.00 | — |
| 1933 | 163,125,000 | 0.25 | 0.50 | 1.00 | 4.00 | — |
| 1934 | 104,059,000 | 0.25 | 0.50 | 1.00 | 5.00 | — |

**10 KOPEKS** Y# 102 **Composition:** Copper-Nickel

| Date | Mintage | F | VF | XF | Unc | BU |
|---|---|---|---|---|---|---|
| 1935 | 79,628,000 | 0.25 | 0.50 | 1.00 | 5.00 | — |
| 1936 | 122,260,000 | 0.25 | 0.50 | 1.00 | 4.00 | — |

**10 KOPEKS** Y# 109 **Composition:** Copper-Nickel **Note:** Varieties exist.

| Date | Mintage | F | VF | XF | Unc | BU |
|---|---|---|---|---|---|---|
| 1937 | — | 0.50 | 1.00 | 2.50 | 6.00 | — |
| 1938 | — | 0.30 | 0.75 | 1.25 | 2.50 | — |
| 1939 | — | 0.30 | 0.60 | 1.00 | 2.00 | — |
| 1940 | — | 0.30 | 0.60 | 1.00 | 2.00 | — |
| 1941 | — | 0.30 | 0.60 | 1.00 | 3.00 | — |
| 1942 | — | 7.50 | 15.00 | 40.00 | 75.00 | — |
| 1943 | — | 0.30 | 0.60 | 1.00 | 2.00 | — |
| 1944 | — | 0.50 | 1.00 | 2.00 | 5.00 | — |

| Date | Mintage | F | VF | XF | Unc | BU |
|---|---|---|---|---|---|---|
| 1945 | — | 0.30 | 0.75 | 1.25 | 3.00 | — |
| 1946 | — | 0.30 | 0.75 | 1.25 | 3.00 | — |

**10 KOPEKS** **Y# A110** **Composition:** Copper-Nickel **Obverse:** Y#102. **Reverse:** Y#109. **Note:** Mule.

| Date | Mintage | F | VF | XF | Unc | BU |
|---|---|---|---|---|---|---|
| 1946 Rare | — | — | — | — | — | — |

**10 KOPEKS** **Y# 116** **Composition:** Copper-Nickel **Obverse:** Eight and seven ribbons on wreath **Note:** Varieties exist.

| Date | Mintage | F | VF | XF | Unc | BU |
|---|---|---|---|---|---|---|
| 1948 | — | 0.25 | 0.50 | 2.00 | 5.00 | — |
| 1949 | — | 0.25 | 0.50 | 1.00 | 3.00 | — |
| 1950 | — | 0.25 | 0.50 | 1.00 | 2.00 | — |
| 1951 | — | 0.25 | 0.50 | 1.00 | 5.00 | — |
| 1952 | — | 0.25 | 0.50 | 1.00 | 4.00 | — |
| 1953 | — | 0.25 | 0.50 | 1.00 | 2.00 | — |
| 1954 | — | 0.25 | 0.50 | 1.00 | 2.00 | — |
| 1955 | — | 0.25 | 0.50 | 1.00 | 2.00 | — |
| 1956 | — | 0.25 | 0.50 | 1.00 | 2.00 | — |
| 1956 Reverse of Y#123 | — | 50.00 | 75.00 | 150 | 250 | — |

**10 KOPEKS** **Y# 123** **Composition:** Copper-Nickel **Obverse:** Seven and seven ribbons on wreath

| Date | Mintage | F | VF | XF | Unc | BU |
|---|---|---|---|---|---|---|
| 1957 Reverse of Y#116 | — | 50.00 | 75.00 | 150 | 250 | — |
| 1957 | — | 0.25 | 0.50 | 2.00 | 6.00 | — |

**10 KOPEKS** **Y# A130** **Composition:** Copper-Nickel

| Date | Mintage | F | VF | XF | Unc | BU |
|---|---|---|---|---|---|---|
| 1958 | 108,023,000 | — | — | — | 350 | — |

**Note:** Never officially released for circulation; majority of mintage remelted

**10 KOPEKS** **Y# 130** **Composition:** Copper-Nickel-Zinc

| Date | Mintage | F | VF | XF | Unc | BU |
|---|---|---|---|---|---|---|
| 1961 | — | 0.10 | 0.20 | 0.35 | 0.75 | — |
| 1962 | — | 0.10 | 0.20 | 0.35 | 0.75 | — |
| 1965 | — | 0.10 | 0.20 | 0.35 | 0.75 | — |
| 1966 | — | 0.10 | 0.20 | 0.35 | 0.75 | — |
| 1967 | — | 0.10 | 0.20 | 0.35 | 0.75 | — |
| 1968 | — | 0.10 | 0.20 | 0.35 | 0.75 | — |
| 1969 | — | 0.10 | 0.20 | 0.35 | 0.75 | — |
| 1970 | — | 0.10 | 0.20 | 0.35 | 0.75 | — |
| 1971 | — | 0.10 | 0.20 | 0.35 | 0.75 | — |
| 1972 | — | 0.10 | 0.20 | 0.35 | 0.75 | — |
| 1973 | — | 0.10 | 0.20 | 0.35 | 0.75 | — |
| 1974 | — | 0.10 | 0.20 | 0.35 | 0.75 | — |
| 1975 | — | 0.10 | 0.20 | 0.35 | 0.75 | — |
| 1976 | — | 0.10 | 0.20 | 0.35 | 0.75 | — |
| 1977 | — | 0.10 | 0.20 | 0.35 | 0.75 | — |
| 1978 | — | 0.10 | 0.20 | 0.35 | 0.75 | — |
| 1979 | — | 0.10 | 0.20 | 0.35 | 0.75 | — |
| 1980 | — | 0.10 | 0.20 | 0.35 | 0.75 | — |
| 1981 | — | 0.10 | 0.20 | 0.35 | 0.75 | — |
| 1982 | — | 0.10 | 0.20 | 0.35 | 0.75 | — |
| 1983 | — | 0.10 | 0.20 | 0.35 | 0.75 | — |
| 1984 | — | 0.10 | 0.20 | 0.35 | 0.75 | — |
| 1985 | — | 0.10 | 0.20 | 0.35 | 0.75 | — |
| 1986 | — | 0.10 | 0.20 | 0.35 | 0.75 | — |
| 1987 | — | 0.10 | 0.20 | 0.35 | 0.75 | — |
| 1988 | — | 0.10 | 0.20 | 0.35 | 0.75 | — |
| 1989 | — | 0.10 | 0.20 | 0.30 | 0.50 | — |
| 1990 | — | 0.25 | 0.50 | 1.00 | 2.50 | — |
| 1990 Л | — | 0.10 | 0.20 | 0.30 | 0.50 | — |
| 1991 | — | 0.15 | 0.25 | 0.50 | 1.25 | — |
| 1991 Л | — | 0.10 | 0.20 | 0.30 | 0.50 | — |

| Date | Mintage | F | VF | XF | Unc | BU |
|---|---|---|---|---|---|---|
| 1991 M | — | 0.10 | 0.20 | 0.30 | 0.50 | — |
| 1991 (l) | — | 0.10 | 0.20 | 0.30 | 0.50 | — |
| 1991 (m) | — | 0.10 | 0.20 | 0.30 | 0.50 | — |

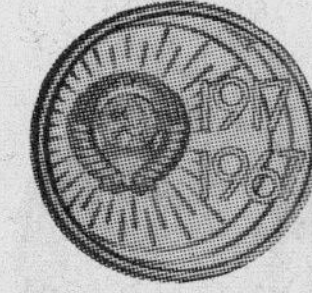

**10 KOPEKS** **Y# 136** **Composition:** Copper-Nickel-Zinc **Subject:** 50th Anniversary of Revolution

| Date | Mintage | F | VF | XF | Unc | BU |
|---|---|---|---|---|---|---|
| 1967 | 49,789,000 | — | 0.20 | 0.30 | 1.00 | — |
| 1967 Prooflike | 211,000 | — | — | — | — | — |

**15 KOPEKS** **Y# 87** **Weight:** 2.7000 g. **Composition:** 0.5000 Silver .0434 oz. ASW **Note:** Varieties exist.

| Date | Mintage | F | VF | XF | Unc | BU |
|---|---|---|---|---|---|---|
| 1924 | 72,426,000 | 0.75 | 1.25 | 3.50 | 10.00 | — |
| 1924 Proof | — | Value: 200 | | | | |
| 1925 | 112,709,000 | 0.75 | 1.25 | 2.50 | 8.00 | — |
| 1925 Proof | — | Value: 75.00 | | | | |
| 1927 | — | 0.75 | 1.25 | 2.50 | 8.00 | — |
| 1927 Proof | — | Value: 75.00 | | | | |
| 1928 | — | 0.75 | 1.25 | 2.50 | 8.00 | — |
| 1929 | 46,400,000 | 0.75 | 1.25 | 2.50 | 8.00 | — |
| 1930 | 79,868,000 | 0.75 | 1.25 | 2.50 | 8.00 | — |
| 1931 Rare | 5,099,000 | — | — | — | — | — |

**Note:**

**15 KOPEKS** **Y# 96** **Composition:** Copper-Nickel **Note:** Varieties exist.

| Date | Mintage | F | VF | XF | Unc | BU |
|---|---|---|---|---|---|---|
| 1931 | 75,859,000 | 0.50 | 1.00 | 1.75 | 4.50 | — |
| 1932 | 136,046,000 | 0.50 | 1.00 | 1.75 | 4.00 | — |
| 1933 | 127,591,000 | 0.50 | 1.00 | 1.75 | 4.00 | — |
| 1934 | 58,367,000 | 0.50 | 1.00 | 2.00 | 5.50 | — |

**15 KOPEKS** **Y# 103** **Composition:** Copper-Nickel

| Date | Mintage | F | VF | XF | Unc | BU |
|---|---|---|---|---|---|---|
| 1935 | 51,308,000 | 0.50 | 1.00 | 1.75 | 4.50 | — |
| 1936 | 52,183,000 | 0.35 | 0.75 | 1.50 | 4.00 | — |

**15 KOPEKS** **Y# 110** **Composition:** Copper-Nickel **Note:** Varieties exist.

| Date | Mintage | F | VF | XF | Unc | BU |
|---|---|---|---|---|---|---|
| 1937 | — | 0.35 | 0.75 | 1.50 | 3.00 | — |
| 1938 | — | 0.30 | 0.50 | 1.00 | 2.00 | — |
| 1939 | — | 0.30 | 0.50 | 1.00 | 2.00 | — |
| 1940 | — | 0.30 | 0.50 | 1.00 | 2.00 | — |
| 1941 | — | 0.30 | 0.50 | 1.00 | 2.00 | — |
| 1942 | — | 7.50 | 15.00 | 40.00 | 75.00 | — |
| 1943 | — | 0.35 | 0.75 | 1.25 | 2.50 | — |
| 1944 | — | 1.00 | 1.00 | 5.00 | 10.00 | — |
| 1945 | — | 0.50 | 1.25 | 2.50 | 5.00 | — |
| 1946 | — | 0.35 | 0.75 | 2.00 | 4.00 | — |

**15 KOPEKS** **Y# 117** **Composition:** Copper-Nickel **Obverse:** Eight and seven ribbons on wreath **Note:** Varieties exist.

| Date | Mintage | F | VF | XF | Unc | BU |
|---|---|---|---|---|---|---|
| 1948 | — | 0.35 | 0.75 | 2.00 | 4.00 | — |
| 1949 | — | 0.35 | 0.75 | 1.50 | 3.50 | — |
| 1950 | — | 0.30 | 0.50 | 1.00 | 2.00 | — |
| 1951 | — | 0.50 | 1.00 | 2.50 | 8.00 | — |
| 1952 | — | 0.30 | 0.50 | 1.00 | 2.00 | — |
| 1953 | — | 0.30 | 0.50 | 1.00 | 2.00 | — |
| 1954 | — | 0.30 | 0.50 | 1.00 | 2.00 | — |
| 1955 | — | 0.30 | 0.50 | 1.00 | 2.00 | — |
| 1956 | — | 0.30 | 0.50 | 1.00 | 2.00 | — |

**15 KOPEKS** **Y# 124** **Composition:** Copper-Nickel **Obverse:** Seven and seven ribbons on wreath

| Date | Mintage | F | VF | XF | Unc | BU |
|---|---|---|---|---|---|---|
| 1957 | — | 0.30 | 0.50 | 1.00 | 5.00 | — |

**15 KOPEKS** **Y# A131** **Composition:** Copper-Nickel

| Date | Mintage | F | VF | XF | Unc | BU |
|---|---|---|---|---|---|---|
| 1958 | 80,052,000 | — | — | — | 450 | — |

**Note:** Never officially released for circulation; majority of mintage remelted

**15 KOPEKS** **Y# 131** **Composition:** Copper-Nickel-Zinc

| Date | Mintage | F | VF | XF | Unc | BU |
|---|---|---|---|---|---|---|
| 1961 | — | 0.10 | 0.20 | 0.40 | 0.75 | — |
| 1962 | — | 0.10 | 0.20 | 0.40 | 1.00 | — |
| 1965 | — | 0.10 | 0.20 | 0.40 | 0.75 | — |
| 1966 | — | 0.10 | 0.20 | 0.40 | 0.75 | — |
| 1967 | — | 0.10 | 0.20 | 0.40 | 0.75 | — |
| 1968 | — | 0.10 | 0.20 | 0.40 | 0.75 | — |
| 1969 | — | 0.10 | 0.20 | 0.40 | 0.75 | — |
| 1970 | — | 0.10 | 0.20 | 0.40 | 0.75 | — |
| 1971 | — | 0.10 | 0.20 | 0.40 | 0.75 | — |
| 1972 | — | 0.10 | 0.20 | 0.40 | 0.75 | — |
| 1973 | — | 0.10 | 0.20 | 0.40 | 0.75 | — |
| 1974 | — | 0.10 | 0.20 | 0.40 | 0.75 | — |
| 1975 | — | 0.10 | 0.20 | 0.40 | 0.75 | — |
| 1976 | — | 0.10 | 0.20 | 0.40 | 0.75 | — |
| 1977 | — | 0.10 | 0.20 | 0.40 | 0.75 | — |
| 1978 | — | 0.10 | 0.20 | 0.40 | 0.75 | — |
| 1979 | — | 0.10 | 0.20 | 0.40 | 0.75 | — |
| 1980 | — | 0.10 | 0.20 | 0.40 | 0.75 | — |
| 1981 | — | 0.10 | 0.20 | 0.40 | 0.75 | — |
| 1982 | — | 0.10 | 0.20 | 0.40 | 0.75 | — |
| 1983 | — | 0.10 | 0.20 | 0.40 | 0.75 | — |

**Note:**

| Date | Mintage | F | VF | XF | Unc | BU |
|---|---|---|---|---|---|---|
| 1984 | — | 0.10 | 0.20 | 0.40 | 0.75 | — |
| 1985 | — | 0.10 | 0.20 | 0.40 | 0.75 | — |
| 1986 | — | 0.10 | 0.20 | 0.40 | 0.75 | — |
| 1987 | — | 0.10 | 0.20 | 0.40 | 0.75 | — |
| 1988 | — | 0.10 | 0.20 | 0.40 | 0.75 | — |
| 1989 | — | 0.10 | 0.20 | 0.30 | 0.50 | — |
| 1990 | — | 0.10 | 0.20 | 0.30 | 0.50 | — |
| 1991 (l) | — | 0.10 | 0.20 | 0.30 | 0.50 | — |
| 1991 (m) | — | 0.10 | 0.20 | 0.30 | 0.50 | — |

**15 KOPEKS** **Y# 137** **Composition:** Copper-Nickel-Zinc **Subject:** 50th Anniversary of Revolution

| Date | Mintage | F | VF | XF | Unc | BU |
|---|---|---|---|---|---|---|
| 1967 | 49,789,000 | 0.15 | 0.30 | 0.50 | 1.50 | — |
| 1967 Prooflike | 211,000 | — | — | — | — | — |

**20 KOPEKS** **Y# 88** **Weight:** 3.6000 g. **Composition:** 0.5000 Silver .0578 oz. ASW

| Date | Mintage | F | VF | XF | Unc | BU |
|---|---|---|---|---|---|---|
| 1924 | 93,810,000 | 1.00 | 1.75 | 3.50 | 10.00 | — |
| 1924 Proof | — | Value: 225 | | | | |
| 1925 | 135,188,000 | 1.00 | 1.75 | 3.00 | 9.00 | — |
| 1925 Proof | — | Value: 75.00 | | | | |
| 1927 | — | 1.00 | 2.00 | 4.00 | 12.00 | — |
| 1928 | — | 1.00 | 1.75 | 3.00 | 9.00 | — |
| 1929 | 67,250,000 | 1.00 | 1.75 | 3.00 | 9.00 | — |
| 1930 | 125,658,000 | 1.00 | 1.75 | 3.00 | 9.00 | — |
| 1931 Rare | 9,530,000 | — | — | — | — | — |

**20 KOPEKS** **Y# 97** **Composition:** Copper-Nickel **Note:** Varieties exist.

| Date | Mintage | F | VF | XF | Unc | BU |
|---|---|---|---|---|---|---|
| 1931 | 82,200,000 | 0.50 | 1.00 | 2.00 | 5.00 | — |
| 1932 | 175,350,000 | 0.50 | 1.00 | 2.00 | 5.00 | — |
| 1933 | 143,927,000 | 0.50 | 1.00 | 2.00 | 5.00 | — |
| 1934 | 70,425,000 | — | — | — | — | — |

**20 KOPEKS** **Y# 104** **Composition:** Copper-Nickel **Note:** Varieties exist.

| Date | Mintage | F | VF | XF | Unc | BU |
|---|---|---|---|---|---|---|
| 1935 | 125,165,000 | 0.50 | 1.00 | 2.00 | 4.50 | — |
| 1936 | 52,968,000 | 0.50 | 1.00 | 2.00 | 5.00 | — |

**20 KOPEKS** **Y# 111** **Composition:** Copper-Nickel **Note:** Varieties exist.

| Date | Mintage | F | VF | XF | Unc | BU |
|---|---|---|---|---|---|---|
| 1937 | — | 0.40 | 0.60 | 1.00 | 3.00 | — |
| 1938 | — | 0.40 | 0.60 | 1.00 | 3.00 | — |
| 1939 | — | 0.40 | 0.60 | 1.00 | 3.00 | — |
| 1940 | — | 0.40 | 0.60 | 1.00 | 3.00 | — |
| 1941 | — | 0.40 | 0.60 | 1.00 | 3.00 | — |
| 1942 | — | 0.50 | 0.75 | 1.50 | 4.00 | — |
| 1943 | — | 0.40 | 0.60 | 1.00 | 3.00 | — |
| 1944 | — | 0.60 | 1.25 | 2.50 | 6.00 | — |
| 1945 | — | 0.40 | 0.60 | 1.50 | 4.00 | — |
| 1946 | — | 0.45 | 0.75 | 2.50 | 5.00 | — |

**20 KOPEKS** **Y# 118** **Composition:** Copper-Nickel **Obverse:** Eight and seven ribbons on wreath **Note:** Varieties exist.

| Date | Mintage | F | VF | XF | Unc | BU |
|---|---|---|---|---|---|---|
| 1948 | — | 0.45 | 0.75 | 1.50 | 4.00 | — |
| 1949 | — | 0.45 | 0.75 | 1.50 | 4.00 | — |
| 1950 | — | 1.00 | 2.00 | 5.00 | 10.00 | — |
| 1951 | — | 0.50 | 1.00 | 2.50 | 7.00 | — |
| 1952 | — | 0.40 | 0.60 | 1.00 | 2.00 | — |
| 1953 | — | 0.40 | 0.60 | 1.00 | 2.00 | — |
| 1954 | — | 0.40 | 0.60 | 1.00 | 2.00 | — |
| 1955 | — | 0.40 | 0.60 | 1.00 | 2.00 | — |
| 1956 | — | 0.40 | 0.60 | 1.00 | 2.00 | — |

**20 KOPEKS** **Y# 125** **Composition:** Copper-Nickel **Obverse:** Seven and seven ribbons on wreath

| Date | Mintage | F | VF | XF | Unc | BU |
|---|---|---|---|---|---|---|
| 1957 | — | 0.40 | 0.60 | 1.00 | 4.00 | — |

**20 KOPEKS** **Y# A132** **Composition:** Copper-Nickel

| Date | Mintage | F | VF | XF | Unc | BU |
|---|---|---|---|---|---|---|
| 1958 | 175,355,000 | — | — | — | 450 | — |

**Note:** Never officially released for circulation; majority of mintage remelted

**20 KOPEKS** **Y# 132** **Composition:** Copper-Nickel-Zinc **Note:** Varieties exist.

| Date | Mintage | F | VF | XF | Unc | BU |
|---|---|---|---|---|---|---|
| 1961 | — | 0.15 | 0.30 | 0.50 | 1.00 | — |
| 1962 | — | 0.15 | 0.35 | 0.75 | 1.50 | — |
| 1965 | — | 0.15 | 0.30 | 0.50 | 1.00 | — |
| 1966 | — | 0.15 | 0.30 | 0.50 | 1.00 | — |
| 1967 | — | 0.15 | 0.30 | 0.50 | 1.00 | — |
| 1968 | — | 0.15 | 0.30 | 0.50 | 1.00 | — |
| 1969 | — | 0.15 | 0.30 | 0.50 | 1.00 | — |
| 1970 | — | 0.15 | 0.30 | 0.50 | 1.00 | — |
| 1971 | — | 0.15 | 0.30 | 0.50 | 1.00 | — |
| 1972 | — | 0.15 | 0.30 | 0.50 | 1.00 | — |
| 1973 | — | 0.15 | 0.30 | 0.50 | 1.00 | — |
| 1974 | — | 0.15 | 0.30 | 0.50 | 1.00 | — |
| 1975 | — | 0.10 | 0.30 | 0.50 | 1.00 | — |
| 1976 | — | 2.00 | 2.00 | 4.00 | 7.50 | — |
| 1977 | — | 0.15 | 0.30 | 0.50 | 1.00 | — |
| 1978 | — | 0.15 | 0.30 | 0.50 | 1.00 | — |
| 1979 | — | 0.15 | 0.30 | 0.50 | 1.00 | — |
| 1980 | — | 0.15 | 0.30 | 0.50 | 1.00 | — |
| 1981 | — | 0.15 | 0.30 | 0.50 | 1.00 | — |
| 1982 | — | 0.15 | 0.30 | 0.50 | 1.00 | — |
| 1983 | — | 0.15 | 0.30 | 0.50 | 1.00 | — |
| 1984 | — | 0.15 | 0.30 | 0.50 | 1.00 | — |
| 1985 | — | 0.15 | 0.30 | 0.50 | 1.00 | — |
| 1986 | — | 0.15 | 0.30 | 0.50 | 1.00 | — |
| 1987 | — | 0.15 | 0.30 | 0.50 | 1.00 | — |
| 1988 | — | 0.15 | 0.30 | 0.50 | 1.00 | — |
| 1989 | — | 0.10 | 0.20 | 0.30 | 0.75 | — |
| 1990 | — | 0.10 | 0.20 | 0.30 | 0.75 | — |
| 1991 | — | 0.20 | 0.40 | 0.65 | 1.50 | — |
| 1991 Л | — | 0.10 | 0.20 | 0.30 | 0.50 | — |
| 1991 М | — | 0.10 | 0.20 | 0.30 | 0.50 | — |
| 1991 (l) | — | 0.10 | 0.20 | 0.30 | 0.75 | — |
| 1991 (m) | — | 0.10 | 0.20 | 0.30 | 0.75 | — |

**20 KOPEKS** **Y# 138** **Composition:** Copper-Nickel-Zinc **Subject:** 50th Anniversary of Revolution

| Date | Mintage | F | VF | XF | Unc | BU |
|---|---|---|---|---|---|---|
| 1967 | 49,789,000 | 0.40 | 0.60 | 0.75 | 2.00 | — |
| 1967 Prooflike | 211,000 | — | — | — | — | — |

**50 KOPEKS** **Y# 89.1** **Weight:** 9.9980 g. **Composition:** 0.9000 Silver .2893 oz. ASW **Edge Lettering:** Weight shown in old Russian units

| Date | Mintage | F | VF | XF | Unc | BU |
|---|---|---|---|---|---|---|
| 1924 ПЛ | 26,559,000 | 5.00 | 7.00 | 11.50 | 25.00 | — |
| 1924 ПЛ Proof | — | Value: 250 | | | | |
| 1924 ТР | 40,000,000 | 5.00 | 7.00 | 11.50 | 25.00 | — |

**50 KOPEKS** **Y# 89.2** **Weight:** 9.9980 g. **Composition:** 0.9000 Silver .2893 oz. ASW **Edge Lettering:** Weight shown in Грамм (grams) only **Note:** Varieties exist.

| Date | Mintage | F | VF | XF | Unc | BU |
|---|---|---|---|---|---|---|
| 1925 ПЛ | 43,558,000 | 5.00 | 7.00 | 11.50 | 25.00 | — |
| 1925 ПЛ Proof | — | Value: 125 | | | | |
| 1926 ПЛ | 24,374,000 | 5.00 | 7.00 | 11.50 | 25.00 | — |
| 1926 ПЛ Proof | — | Value: 125 | | | | |
| 1927 ПЛ | — | 5.00 | 8.00 | 15.00 | 35.00 | — |
| 1927 ПЛ Proof | — | Value: 165 | | | | |

**50 KOPEKS** **Y# 133** **Composition:** Copper-Nickel

| Date | Mintage | F | VF | XF | Unc | BU |
|---|---|---|---|---|---|---|
| 1958 | 40,600,000 | — | — | — | — | — |

**Note:** Never officially released for circulation; majority of mintage remelted

**50 KOPEKS** **Y# 133a.1** **Composition:** Copper-Nickel-Zinc **Edge:** Plain **Note:** Varieties exist.

| Date | Mintage | F | VF | XF | Unc | BU |
|---|---|---|---|---|---|---|
| 1961 | — | 1.00 | 2.00 | 5.00 | 12.00 | — |

**50 KOPEKS** **Y# 133a.2** **Composition:** Copper-Nickel-Zinc **Edge:** Lettered with date

| Date | Mintage | F | VF | XF | Unc | BU |
|---|---|---|---|---|---|---|
| 1964 | — | 0.20 | 0.40 | 0.75 | 1.50 | — |
| 1965 | — | 0.20 | 0.40 | 0.75 | 1.50 | — |
| 1966 | — | 0.20 | 0.40 | 0.75 | 1.50 | — |
| 1967 | — | 0.20 | 0.40 | 0.75 | 1.50 | — |
| 1968 | — | 0.20 | 0.40 | 0.75 | 1.50 | — |
| 1969 | — | 0.20 | 0.40 | 0.75 | 1.50 | — |
| 1970 | — | 0.20 | 0.40 | 0.75 | 1.50 | — |
| 1971 | — | 0.20 | 0.40 | 0.75 | 1.50 | — |
| 1972 | — | 0.20 | 0.40 | 0.75 | 1.50 | — |
| 1973 | — | 0.20 | 0.40 | 0.75 | 1.50 | — |
| 1974 | — | 0.20 | 0.40 | 0.75 | 1.50 | — |
| 1975 | — | 0.20 | 0.40 | 0.75 | 1.50 | — |
| 1976 | — | 0.20 | 0.40 | 0.75 | 1.50 | — |
| 1977 | — | 0.20 | 0.40 | 0.75 | 1.50 | — |
| 1978 | — | 0.20 | 0.40 | 0.75 | 1.50 | — |
| 1979 | — | 0.20 | 0.40 | 0.75 | 1.50 | — |
| 1980 | — | 0.20 | 0.40 | 0.75 | 1.50 | — |
| 1981 | — | 0.20 | 0.40 | 0.75 | 1.50 | — |
| 1982 | — | 0.20 | 0.40 | 0.75 | 1.50 | — |
| 1983 | — | 0.20 | 0.40 | 0.75 | 1.50 | — |
| 1984 | — | 0.20 | 0.40 | 0.75 | 1.50 | — |
| 1985 | — | 0.20 | 0.40 | 0.75 | 1.50 | — |
| 1986 With 1985 edge | — | 1.00 | 2.00 | 4.00 | 10.00 | — |
| 1986 | — | 0.20 | 0.40 | 0.75 | 1.50 | — |

| Date | Mintage | F | VF | XF | Unc | BU |
|---|---|---|---|---|---|---|
| 1987 | — | 0.20 | 0.40 | 0.75 | 1.50 | — |
| 1988 With 1987 edge | — | 1.00 | 2.00 | 4.00 | 10.00 | — |
| 1988 | — | 0.20 | 0.40 | 0.75 | 1.50 | — |
| 1989 | — | 0.15 | 0.25 | 0.50 | 1.00 | — |
| 1990 With 1989 edge | — | 2.50 | 5.00 | 10.00 | 25.00 | — |
| 1990 | — | 0.15 | 0.25 | 0.50 | 1.00 | — |
| 1991 M | — | 0.15 | 0.25 | 0.50 | 1.00 | — |
| 1991 L | — | 0.15 | 0.25 | 0.50 | 1.00 | — |

**50 KOPEKS** **Y# 139** **Composition:** Copper-Nickel-Zinc **Subject:** 50th Anniversary of Revolution

| Date | Mintage | F | VF | XF | Unc | BU |
|---|---|---|---|---|---|---|
| ND(1967) | 49,789,000 | — | 1.00 | 1.50 | 2.50 | — |
| ND(1967) Prooflike | — | — | — | — | 3.00 | — |

**ROUBLE** **Y# 90.2** **Weight:** 19.9960 g. **Composition:** 0.9000 Silver .5786 oz. ASW **Edge:** 4 Zolotniks 21 Dolyas

| Date | Mintage | F | VF | XF | Unc | BU |
|---|---|---|---|---|---|---|
| 1924 Rare | — | — | — | — | — | — |

**ROUBLE** **Y# 90.1** **Weight:** 19.9960 g. **Composition:** 0.9000 Silver .5786 oz. ASW **Edge Lettering:** 18 Грамм (grams) (43.21d) **Note:** Varieties exist.

| Date | Mintage | F | VF | XF | Unc | BU |
|---|---|---|---|---|---|---|
| 1924 ПЛ | 12,998,000 | 7.50 | 12.50 | 22.50 | 50.00 | 75.00 |
| 1924 ПЛ Proof | — | Value: 750 | | | | |

**ROUBLE** **Y# 134** **Composition:** Copper-Nickel

| Date | Mintage | F | VF | XF | Unc | BU |
|---|---|---|---|---|---|---|
| 1958 | 30,700,000 | — | — | — | — | — |

**Note:** Never officially released for circulation; majority of mintage remelted

**ROUBLE** **Y# 134a.1** **Composition:** Copper-Nickel-Zinc **Edge:** Plain

| Date | Mintage | F | VF | XF | Unc | BU |
|---|---|---|---|---|---|---|
| 1961 | — | 2.00 | 3.50 | 6.00 | 15.00 | — |

**ROUBLE** **Y# 134a.2** **Composition:** Copper-Nickel-Zinc **Edge:** Lettered with date

| Date | Mintage | F | VF | XF | Unc | BU |
|---|---|---|---|---|---|---|
| 1964 | — | 0.40 | 0.75 | 1.50 | 2.50 | — |
| 1965 | — | 0.40 | 0.75 | 1.50 | 2.50 | — |
| 1966 | — | 0.40 | 0.75 | 1.50 | 2.50 | — |
| 1967 With 1966 edge | — | 3.00 | 6.00 | 12.00 | 30.00 | — |
| 1967 | — | 0.40 | 0.75 | 1.50 | 2.50 | — |
| 1968 | — | 0.40 | 0.75 | 1.50 | 2.50 | — |
| 1969 | — | 0.40 | 0.75 | 1.50 | 2.50 | — |
| 1970 | — | 0.40 | 0.75 | 1.50 | 2.50 | — |
| 1971 | — | 0.40 | 0.75 | 1.50 | 2.50 | — |
| 1972 | — | 0.40 | 0.75 | 1.50 | 2.50 | — |
| 1973 | — | 0.40 | 0.75 | 1.50 | 2.50 | — |
| 1974 | — | 0.40 | 0.75 | 1.50 | 2.50 | — |
| 1975 | — | 0.40 | 0.75 | 1.50 | 2.50 | — |
| 1976 | — | 0.40 | 0.75 | 1.50 | 2.50 | — |
| 1977 | — | 0.40 | 0.75 | 1.50 | 2.50 | — |
| 1978 | — | 0.40 | 0.75 | 1.50 | 2.50 | — |
| 1979 | — | 0.40 | 0.75 | 1.50 | 2.50 | — |
| 1980 | — | 0.40 | 0.75 | 1.50 | 2.50 | — |
| 1981 | — | 0.40 | 0.75 | 1.50 | 2.50 | — |
| 1982 | — | 0.40 | 0.75 | 1.50 | 2.50 | — |
| 1983 | — | 0.40 | 0.75 | 1.50 | 2.50 | — |
| 1984 | — | 0.40 | 0.75 | 1.50 | 2.50 | — |
| 1985 | — | 0.40 | 0.75 | 1.50 | 2.50 | — |
| 1986 | — | 0.40 | 0.75 | 1.50 | 2.50 | — |
| 1987 | — | 0.40 | 0.75 | 1.50 | 2.50 | — |
| 1988 | — | 0.40 | 0.75 | 1.50 | 2.50 | — |
| 1989 | — | 0.25 | 0.50 | 1.00 | 2.50 | — |
| 1990 With 1989 edge | — | 1.50 | 3.00 | 6.00 | 15.00 | — |
| 1990 | — | 0.25 | 0.50 | 1.00 | 2.50 | — |
| 1991 (m) | — | 0.25 | 0.50 | 1.00 | 2.50 | — |
| 1991 (l) | — | 0.25 | 0.50 | 1.00 | 2.50 | — |

**ROUBLE** **Y# 135.1** **Composition:** Copper-Nickel-Zinc **Subject:** 20th Anniversary of World War II Victory

| Date | Mintage | F | VF | XF | Unc | BU |
|---|---|---|---|---|---|---|
| 1965 | 59,989,000 | — | 0.50 | 1.00 | 2.50 | — |
| 1965 Prooflike | — | — | — | — | 3.00 | — |
| 1965 Proof | — | Value: 30.00 | | | | |

**ROUBLE** **Y# 135.2** **Composition:** Copper-Nickel-Zinc **Edge Lettering:** 1988.N.

| Date | Mintage | F | VF | XF | Unc | BU |
|---|---|---|---|---|---|---|
| 1965 Proof; restrike | 55,000 | Value: 3.50 | | | | |

**ROUBLE** **Y# 140.1** **Composition:** Copper-Nickel-Zinc **Subject:** 50th Anniversary of Revolution **Edge:** Lettered, with date

| Date | Mintage | F | VF | XF | Unc | BU |
|---|---|---|---|---|---|---|
| 1967 | 52,289,000 | — | 0.50 | 1.00 | 2.50 | — |
| 1967 Prooflike | — | — | — | — | 3.00 | — |
| 1967 Proof | — | Value: 30.00 | | | | |

**ROUBLE** **Y# 140.2** **Composition:** Copper-Nickel-Zinc **Edge Lettering:** 1988.N.

| Date | Mintage | F | VF | XF | Unc | BU |
|---|---|---|---|---|---|---|
| 1967 Proof; restrike | 55,000 | Value: 4.00 | | | | |

**ROUBLE** **Y# 141** **Composition:** Copper-Nickel-Zinc **Subject:** Centennial of Lenin's Birth

| Date | Mintage | F | VF | XF | Unc | BU |
|---|---|---|---|---|---|---|
| ND(1970) | 99,889,000 | — | 0.50 | 1.00 | 2.50 | — |
| ND(1970) Prooflike | — | — | — | — | 3.00 | — |
| ND(1970) Proof | — | Value: 50.00 | | | | |

**ROUBLE** **Y# 142.2** **Composition:** Copper-Nickel-Zinc **Edge Lettering:** 1988.N.

| Date | Mintage | F | VF | XF | Unc | BU |
|---|---|---|---|---|---|---|
| ND(1975) Proof; restrike | 55,000 | Value: 3.50 | | | | |

**ROUBLE** **Y# 142.1** **Composition:** Copper-Nickel-Zinc **Subject:** 30th Anniversary of World War II Victory **Edge:** Date **Note:** Varieties exist.

| Date | Mintage | F | VF | XF | Unc | BU |
|---|---|---|---|---|---|---|
| ND(1975) | 14,989,000 | — | 0.50 | 1.00 | 2.50 | — |
| ND(1975) Prooflike | — | — | — | — | 3.00 | — |
| ND(1975) Proof | — | Value: 25.00 | | | | |

**ROUBLE** **Y# A144** **Composition:** Copper-Nickel-Zinc **Obverse:** KM#143.1 **Reverse:** KM#144 **Note:** Mule

| Date | Mintage | F | VF | XF | Unc | BU |
|---|---|---|---|---|---|---|
| 1977 Rare | — | — | — | — | — | — |

**ROUBLE** **Y# 143.1** **Composition:** Copper-Nickel-Zinc **Subject:** 60th Anniversary of Bolshevik Revolution

| Date | Mintage | F | VF | XF | Unc | BU |
|---|---|---|---|---|---|---|
| ND(1977) | 4,987,000 | — | 0.50 | 1.00 | 2.50 | — |
| ND(1977) Prooflike | — | — | — | — | 3.00 | — |
| ND(1977) Proof | — | Value: 25.00 | | | | |

**ROUBLE** **Y# 143.2** **Composition:** Copper-Nickel-Zinc **Edge Lettering:** 1988.N.

| Date | Mintage | F | VF | XF | Unc | BU |
|---|---|---|---|---|---|---|
| ND(1977) Proof; restrike | 55,000 | Value: 3.50 | | | | |

**ROUBLE** **Y# 144** **Composition:** Copper-Nickel-Zinc **Series:** 1980 Olympics **Reverse:** Emblem

| Date | Mintage | F | VF | XF | Unc | BU |
|---|---|---|---|---|---|---|
| 1977 | 8,665,000 | — | 0.50 | 1.00 | 2.50 | — |
| 1977 Prooflike | — | — | — | — | 3.00 | — |
| 1977 Proof | — | Value: 25.00 | | | | |

**ROUBLE** **Y# 153.1** **Composition:** Copper-Nickel-Zinc **Series:** 1980 Olympics **Reverse:** Moscow Kremlin

| Date | Mintage | F | VF | XF | Unc | BU |
|---|---|---|---|---|---|---|
| 1978 | 6,490,000 | — | 0.50 | 1.00 | 2.50 | — |
| 1978 Prooflike | — | — | — | — | 3.00 | — |
| 1978 Proof | — | Value: 50.00 | | | | |

**ROUBLE** **Y# 153.2** **Composition:** Copper-Nickel-Zinc **Reverse:** Clock on tower shows Roman 6 instead 4

| Date | Mintage | F | VF | XF | Unc | BU |
|---|---|---|---|---|---|---|
| 1978 | Inc. above | — | 8.00 | 16.00 | 25.00 | — |

**ROUBLE** **Y# 165** **Composition:** Copper-Nickel-Zinc **Series:** 1980 Olympics **Reverse:** Monument, Sputnik, and Sojuz

| Date | Mintage | F | VF | XF | Unc | BU |
|---|---|---|---|---|---|---|
| 1979 | 4,665,000 | — | 0.50 | 1.00 | 2.50 | — |
| 1979 Prooflike | — | — | — | — | 3.00 | — |
| 1979 Proof | — | Value: 25.00 | | | | |

**ROUBLE** **Y# 164** **Composition:** Copper-Nickel-Zinc **Series:** 1980 Olympics **Reverse:** Moscow University **Note:** Varieties in window arrangements exist.

| Date | Mintage | F | VF | XF | Unc | BU |
|---|---|---|---|---|---|---|
| 1979 | 4,665,000 | — | 0.50 | 1.00 | 2.50 | — |
| 1979 Prooflike | — | — | — | — | 3.00 | — |
| 1979 Proof | — | Value: 25.00 | | | | |

**ROUBLE** **Y# 177** **Composition:** Copper-Nickel **Series:** 1980 Olympics **Reverse:** Dolgorukij Monument

| Date | Mintage | F | VF | XF | Unc | BU |
|---|---|---|---|---|---|---|
| 1980 | 4,490,000 | — | 0.50 | 1.00 | 2.50 | — |
| 1980 Prooflike | — | — | — | — | 3.00 | — |
| 1980 Proof | — | Value: 25.00 | | | | |

**ROUBLE** **Y# 178** **Composition:** Copper-Nickel **Series:** 1980 Olympics **Reverse:** Torch

| Date | Mintage | F | VF | XF | Unc | BU |
|---|---|---|---|---|---|---|
| 1980 | 4,490,000 | — | 0.50 | 1.00 | 2.50 | — |
| 1980 Prooflike | — | — | — | — | 3.00 | — |
| 1980 Proof | — | Value: 25.00 | | | | |

**ROUBLE** **Y# 188.1** **Composition:** Copper-Nickel **Subject:** 20th Anniversary of Manned Space Flights **Reverse:** Yuri Gagarin

| Date | Mintage | F | VF | XF | Unc | BU |
|---|---|---|---|---|---|---|
| ND(1981) | 3,962,000 | — | 0.50 | 1.00 | 3.00 | — |
| ND(1981) Proof | — | Value: 7.50 | | | | |

**ROUBLE** **Y# 188.2** **Composition:** Copper-Nickel **Edge Lettering:** 1988.N.

| Date | Mintage | F | VF | XF | Unc | BU |
|---|---|---|---|---|---|---|
| ND(1981) Proof; restrike | 55,000 | Value: 3.50 | | | | |

**ROUBLE** **Y# 189.1** **Composition:** Copper-Nickel **Subject:** Russian-Bulgarian Friendship

| Date | Mintage | F | VF | XF | Unc | BU |
|---|---|---|---|---|---|---|
| 1981 | 1,984,000 | — | 0.50 | 1.00 | 3.00 | — |
| 1981 | 16,000 | Value: 20.00 | | | | |

**ROUBLE** **Y# 189.2** **Composition:** Copper-Nickel **Edge Lettering:** 1988.N.

| Date | Mintage | F | VF | XF | Unc | BU |
|---|---|---|---|---|---|---|
| 1981 Proof; restrike | 55,000 | Value: 3.50 | | | | |

**Note:** The same reverse die was used for both Russia 1 Rouble KM#189 and Bulgaria 1 Lev KM#119

**ROUBLE** **Y# 190.1** **Composition:** Copper-Nickel **Subject:** 60th Anniversary of the Soviet Union

| Date | Mintage | F | VF | XF | Unc | BU |
|---|---|---|---|---|---|---|
| ND(1982) | 1,921,000 | — | 0.50 | 1.50 | 3.50 | — |
| ND(1982) Proof | 79,000 | Value: 6.00 | | | | |

**ROUBLE** **Y# 190.2** **Composition:** Copper-Nickel **Edge Lettering:** 1988.N.

| Date | Mintage | F | VF | XF | Unc | BU |
|---|---|---|---|---|---|---|
| ND(1982) Proof; restrike | 55,000 | Value: 4.50 | | | | |

**ROUBLE** **Y# 191.1** **Composition:** Copper-Nickel **Subject:** Death of Karl Marx Centennial

| Date | Mintage | F | VF | XF | Unc | BU |
|---|---|---|---|---|---|---|
| 1983 | 1,921,000 | — | 0.50 | 1.50 | 3.50 | — |
| 1983 Proof | 79,000 | Value: 6.00 | | | | |

**ROUBLE** **Y# 191.2** **Composition:** Copper-Nickel **Edge Lettering:** 1988.N.

| Date | Mintage | F | VF | XF | Unc | BU |
|---|---|---|---|---|---|---|
| 1983 Proof; restrike | 55,000 | Value: 4.50 | | | | |

**ROUBLE** **Y# 192.1** **Composition:** Copper-Nickel **Subject:** 20th Anniversary of First Woman in Space **Reverse:** Valentina Tereshkova

| Date | Mintage | F | VF | XF | Unc | BU |
|---|---|---|---|---|---|---|
| 1983 | 1,945,000 | — | 0.50 | 1.00 | 3.00 | — |
| 1983 Proof | 55,000 | Value: 6.00 | | | | |

**ROUBLE** **Y# 192.2** **Composition:** Copper-Nickel **Edge Lettering:** 1988.N.

| Date | Mintage | F | VF | XF | Unc | BU |
|---|---|---|---|---|---|---|
| 1983 Proof; restrike | 55,000 | Value: 3.50 | | | | |

**ROUBLE** **Y# 193.1** **Composition:** Copper-Nickel **Subject:** First Russian Printer **Reverse:** Ivan Fedorov

| Date | Mintage | F | VF | XF | Unc | BU |
|---|---|---|---|---|---|---|
| 1983 | 1,965,000 | — | 0.50 | 1.00 | 3.00 | — |
| 1983 Proof | 35,000 | Value: 5.00 | | | | |

**Note:**

**ROUBLE** **Y# 193.2** **Composition:** Copper-Nickel **Edge Lettering:** 1988.N.

| Date | Mintage | F | VF | XF | Unc | BU |
|---|---|---|---|---|---|---|
| 1983 Proof; restrike | 55,000 | Value: 3.50 | | | | |

**ROUBLE** **Y# 200.2** **Composition:** Copper-Nickel **Edge Lettering:** 1988.N.

| Date | Mintage | F | VF | XF | Unc | BU |
|---|---|---|---|---|---|---|
| 1983 Error | — | — | — | — | — | — |
| 1983 Proof; restrike | — | Value: 4.50 | | | | |
| 1985 Proof; restrike | 55,000 | Value: 4.50 | | | | |

**ROUBLE** **Y# 202.2** **Composition:** Copper-Nickel **Edge Lettering:** 1988.N.

| Date | Mintage | F | VF | XF | Unc | BU |
|---|---|---|---|---|---|---|
| 1984 Error | — | — | — | — | — | — |
| 1986 Proof; restrike | 55,000 | Value: 3.50 | | | | |

**ROUBLE** **Y# 194.1** **Composition:** Copper-Nickel **Subject:** 150th Anniversary - Birth of Dmitri Ivanovich Mendeleyev

| Date | Mintage | F | VF | XF | Unc | BU |
|---|---|---|---|---|---|---|
| 1984 | 1,965,000 | — | 0.50 | 1.00 | 3.00 | — |
| 1984 Proof | 35,000 | Value: 5.00 | | | | |

**ROUBLE** **Y# 194.2** **Composition:** Copper-Nickel **Edge Lettering:** 1988.N.

| Date | Mintage | F | VF | XF | Unc | BU |
|---|---|---|---|---|---|---|
| 1984 Proof; restrike | 55,000 | Value: 3.50 | | | | |

**ROUBLE** **Y# 195.1** **Composition:** Copper-Nickel **Subject:** 125th Anniversary - Birth of Alexander Popov

| Date | Mintage | F | VF | XF | Unc | BU |
|---|---|---|---|---|---|---|
| 1984 | 1,965,000 | — | 0.50 | 1.00 | 3.00 | — |
| 1984 Proof | 35,000 | Value: 5.00 | | | | |

**ROUBLE** **Y# 195.2** **Composition:** Copper-Nickel **Edge Lettering:** 1988.N.

| Date | Mintage | F | VF | XF | Unc | BU |
|---|---|---|---|---|---|---|
| 1984 Proof; restrike | 55,000 | Value: 3.50 | | | | |

**ROUBLE Y# 196.1 Composition:** Copper-Nickel **Subject:** 185th Anniversary - Birth of Alexander Sergeevich Pushkin

| Date | Mintage | F | VF | XF | Unc | BU |
|---|---|---|---|---|---|---|
| 1984 | 1,965,000 | — | 0.50 | 1.00 | 3.00 | — |
| 1984 Proof | 35,000 | Value: 5.00 | | | | |

**ROUBLE Y# 196.2 Composition:** Copper-Nickel **Edge Lettering:** 1988.N.

| Date | Mintage | F | VF | XF | Unc | BU |
|---|---|---|---|---|---|---|
| 1984 Proof; restrike | 55,000 | Value: 3.50 | | | | |
| 1985 Error | — | — | — | — | — | — |
| 1985 Proof; restrike | — | Value: 4.50 | | | | |

**ROUBLE Y# 197.1 Composition:** Copper-Nickel **Subject:** 115th Anniversary - Birth of Vladimir Lenin

| Date | Mintage | F | VF | XF | Unc | BU |
|---|---|---|---|---|---|---|
| 1985 | 1,960,000 | — | 0.50 | 1.50 | 3.50 | — |
| 1985 Proof | 40,000 | Value: 6.00 | | | | |

**ROUBLE Y# 197.2 Composition:** Copper-Nickel **Edge Lettering:** 1988.N.

| Date | Mintage | F | VF | XF | Unc | BU |
|---|---|---|---|---|---|---|
| 1985 Proof; restrike | 55,000 | Value: 4.50 | | | | |
| 1988 Error | — | — | — | — | — | — |

**ROUBLE Y# 198.1 Composition:** Copper-Nickel **Subject:** 40th Anniversary - World War II Victory

| Date | Mintage | F | VF | XF | Unc | BU |
|---|---|---|---|---|---|---|
| 1985 | 5,960,000 | — | 0.50 | 1.00 | 3.00 | — |
| 1985 Proof | 40,000 | Value: 6.00 | | | | |

**ROUBLE Y# 198.2 Composition:** Copper-Nickel **Edge Lettering:** 1988.N.

| Date | Mintage | F | VF | XF | Unc | BU |
|---|---|---|---|---|---|---|
| 1985 Proof; restrike | 55,000 | Value: 3.50 | | | | |

**ROUBLE Y# 199.1 Composition:** Copper-Nickel **Subject:** 12th World Youth Festival in Moscow

| Date | Mintage | F | VF | XF | Unc | BU |
|---|---|---|---|---|---|---|
| 1985 | 5,960,000 | — | 0.50 | 1.00 | 3.00 | — |
| 1985 Proof | 40,000 | Value: 6.00 | | | | |

**ROUBLE Y# 199.2 Composition:** Copper-Nickel **Edge Lettering:** 1988.N.

| Date | Mintage | F | VF | XF | Unc | BU |
|---|---|---|---|---|---|---|
| 1985 Proof; restrike | 55,000 | Value: 3.50 | | | | |

**ROUBLE Y# 200.1 Composition:** Copper-Nickel **Subject:** 165th Anniversary - Birth of Friedrich Engels

| Date | Mintage | F | VF | XF | Unc | BU |
|---|---|---|---|---|---|---|
| 1985 | 1,960,000 | — | 0.50 | 1.50 | 3.50 | — |
| 1985 Proof | — | Value: 6.00 | | | | |

**ROUBLE Y# 201.3 Composition:** Copper-Nickel **Note:** Rouble written РУБЛЬ.

| Date | Mintage | F | VF | XF | Unc | BU |
|---|---|---|---|---|---|---|
| 1986 | 3,955,000 | — | 0.50 | 1.00 | 3.00 | — |
| 1986 Proof | 45,000 | Value: 5.00 | | | | |

**ROUBLE Y# 201.1 Composition:** Copper-Nickel **Subject:** International Year of Peace **Note:** Rouble written with inverted "V" for Л.

| Date | Mintage | F | VF | XF | Unc | BU |
|---|---|---|---|---|---|---|
| 1986 | 3,955,000 | — | 0.50 | 1.00 | 3.00 | — |
| 1986 Proof | 45,000 | Value: 5.00 | | | | |

**ROUBLE Y# 201.2 Composition:** Copper-Nickel **Edge Lettering:** 1988.N.

| Date | Mintage | F | VF | XF | Unc | BU |
|---|---|---|---|---|---|---|
| 1986 Proof; restrike | 55,000 | Value: 3.50 | | | | |

**ROUBLE Y# 201.4 Composition:** Copper-Nickel **Edge Lettering:** 1988.N.

| Date | Mintage | F | VF | XF | Unc | BU |
|---|---|---|---|---|---|---|
| 1986 | — | — | — | — | — | — |

**ROUBLE Y# 202.1 Composition:** Copper-Nickel **Subject:** 275th Anniversary - Birth of Mikhail Lomonosov

| Date | Mintage | F | VF | XF | Unc | BU |
|---|---|---|---|---|---|---|
| 1986 | 1,965,000 | — | 0.50 | 1.00 | 3.00 | — |
| 1986 Proof | 35,000 | Value: 5.00 | | | | |

**ROUBLE Y# 205 Composition:** Copper-Nickel **Subject:** 130th Anniversary - Birth of Constantin Tsiolkovsky

| Date | Mintage | F | VF | XF | Unc | BU |
|---|---|---|---|---|---|---|
| 1987 | 3,830,000 | — | 0.50 | 1.00 | 3.00 | — |
| 1987 Proof | 170,000 | Value: 5.00 | | | | |

**ROUBLE Y# 203 Composition:** Copper-Nickel **Subject:** 175th Anniversary - Battle of Borodino - Soldiers **Note:** Varieties with wheat in coat of arms.

| Date | Mintage | F | VF | XF | Unc | BU |
|---|---|---|---|---|---|---|
| 1987 | 3,780,000 | — | 0.50 | 1.00 | 3.00 | — |
| 1987 Proof | 220,000 | Value: 5.00 | | | | |

**ROUBLE Y# 204 Composition:** Copper-Nickel **Subject:** 175th Anniversary - Battle of Borodino - Kutuzov Monument **Note:** Varieties with wheat in coat of arms.

| Date | Mintage | F | VF | XF | Unc | BU |
|---|---|---|---|---|---|---|
| 1987 | 3,780,000 | — | 0.50 | 1.00 | 3.00 | — |
| 1987 Proof | 220,000 | Value: 5.00 | | | | |

**ROUBLE Y# 206 Composition:** Copper-Nickel **Subject:** 70th Anniversary of Bolshevik Revolution **Note:** Varieties with wheat in coat of arms.

| Date | Mintage | F | VF | XF | Unc | BU |
|---|---|---|---|---|---|---|
| 1987 | 3,800,000 | — | 0.50 | 1.00 | 3.00 | — |
| 1987 Proof | 200,000 | Value: 6.00 | | | | |

**ROUBLE Y# 216 Composition:** Copper-Nickel **Subject:** 160th Anniversary - Birth of Leo Tolstoi

| Date | Mintage | F | VF | XF | Unc | BU |
|---|---|---|---|---|---|---|
| 1987 Error | — | — | — | — | — | — |
| 1988 | 3,775,000 | — | 0.50 | 1.00 | 3.00 | — |
| 1988 Proof | 225,000 | Value: 5.00 | | | | |

**ROUBLE Y# 209 Composition:** Copper-Nickel **Subject:** 120th Anniversary - Birth of Maxin Gorky

| Date | Mintage | F | VF | XF | Unc | BU |
|---|---|---|---|---|---|---|
| 1988 | 3,775,000 | — | 0.50 | 1.00 | 3.00 | — |
| 1988 Proof | 225,000 | Value: 6.00 | | | | |

**ROUBLE** **Y# 220** **Composition:** Copper-Nickel **Subject:** 150th anniversary - Birth of Musorgsky

| Date | Mintage | F | VF | XF | Unc | BU |
|---|---|---|---|---|---|---|
| 1989 | 2,700,000 | — | 0.50 | 1.00 | 3.00 | — |
| 1989 Proof | 300,000 | Value: 5.50 | | | | |

**ROUBLE** **Y# 228** **Composition:** Copper-Nickel **Subject:** 175th Anniversary - Birth of M.Y. Lermontov

| Date | Mintage | F | VF | XF | Unc | BU |
|---|---|---|---|---|---|---|
| 1989 | 2,700,000 | — | 0.50 | 1.00 | 3.00 | — |
| 1989 Proof | 300,000 | Value: 6.00 | | | | |

**ROUBLE** **Y# 232** **Composition:** Copper-Nickel **Subject:** 100th Anniversary - Birth of Hamza Hakim-zade Niyazi

| Date | Mintage | F | VF | XF | Unc | BU |
|---|---|---|---|---|---|---|
| 1989 | 1,800,000 | — | 0.50 | 1.00 | 3.00 | — |
| 1989 Proof | 200,000 | Value: 6.00 | | | | |

**ROUBLE** **Y# 233** **Composition:** Copper-Nickel **Subject:** 100th Anniversary - Death of Mihai Eminescu

| Date | Mintage | F | VF | XF | Unc | BU |
|---|---|---|---|---|---|---|
| 1989 | 1,800,000 | — | 0.50 | 1.00 | 3.00 | — |
| 1989 Proof | 200,000 | Value: 6.00 | | | | |

**ROUBLE** **Y# 235** **Composition:** Copper-Nickel **Subject:** 175th Anniversary - Birth of T.G. Shevchenko

| Date | Mintage | F | VF | XF | Unc | BU |
|---|---|---|---|---|---|---|
| 1989 | 2,700,000 | — | 0.50 | 1.00 | 3.00 | — |
| 1989 Proof | 300,000 | Value: 5.50 | | | | |

**ROUBLE** **Y# 236** **Composition:** Copper-Nickel **Subject:** 100th Anniversary - Birth of Tschaikovsky - Composer

| Date | Mintage | F | VF | XF | Unc | BU |
|---|---|---|---|---|---|---|
| 1990 | 2,600,000 | — | — | — | 3.00 | — |
| 1990 Proof | 400,000 | Value: 6.50 | | | | |

**ROUBLE** **Y# 237** **Composition:** Copper-Nickel **Subject:** Anniversary - Marshal Zhukov

| Date | Mintage | F | VF | XF | Unc | BU |
|---|---|---|---|---|---|---|
| 1990 | 1,600,000 | — | — | — | 3.00 | — |
| 1990 Proof | 400,000 | Value: 6.50 | | | | |

**ROUBLE** **Y# 240** **Composition:** Copper-Nickel **Subject:** 130th Anniversary - Birth of Anton Chekhov

| Date | Mintage | F | VF | XF | Unc | BU |
|---|---|---|---|---|---|---|
| 1990 | 2,600,000 | — | — | — | 3.00 | — |
| 1990 Proof | 400,000 | Value: 6.50 | | | | |

**ROUBLE** **Y# 257** **Composition:** Copper-Nickel **Subject:** 125th Anniversary - Birth of Janis Rainis

| Date | Mintage | F | VF | XF | Unc | BU |
|---|---|---|---|---|---|---|
| 1990 | 2,600,000 | — | — | — | 3.00 | — |
| 1990 Proof | 400,000 | Value: 6.50 | | | | |

**ROUBLE** **Y# 258** **Composition:** Copper-Nickel **Subject:** 500th Anniversary - Birth of Francisk Scorina

| Date | Mintage | F | VF | XF | Unc | BU |
|---|---|---|---|---|---|---|
| 1990 | 2,600,000 | — | — | — | 3.00 | — |
| 1990 Proof | 400,000 | Value: 6.50 | | | | |

Note:

**ROUBLE** **Y# 260** **Composition:** Copper-Nickel **Subject:** 550th Anniversary - Birth of Alisher Navoi

| Date | Mintage | F | VF | XF | Unc | BU |
|---|---|---|---|---|---|---|
| 1990 Error | — | — | — | — | — | — |
| 1991 | 2,150,000 | — | — | — | 3.00 | — |
| 1991 Proof | 350,000 | Value: 5.50 | | | | |

**ROUBLE** **Y# 261** **Composition:** Copper-Nickel **Subject:** 125th Anniversary - Birth of P. N. Lebedev

| Date | Mintage | F | VF | XF | Unc | BU |
|---|---|---|---|---|---|---|
| 1991 | 2,150,000 | — | — | — | 3.00 | — |
| 1991 Proof | 350,000 | Value: 5.50 | | | | |

**ROUBLE** **Y# 263** **Composition:** Copper-Nickel **Subject:** 100th Birthday of Sergey Prokofiev

| Date | Mintage | F | VF | XF | Unc | BU |
|---|---|---|---|---|---|---|
| 1991 | 2,150,000 | — | — | — | 3.00 | — |
| 1991 Proof | 350,000 | Value: 5.50 | | | | |

**ROUBLE** **Y#282** **Composition:** Copper-Nickel **Subject:** K. V. Ivanon **Reverse:** K.T. Ivanov.

| Date | Mintage | F | VF | XF | Unc | BU |
|---|---|---|---|---|---|---|
| 1991 | 3,150,000 | — | — | — | 3.00 | — |
| 1991 Proof | 350,000 | Value: 5.50 | | | | |

**ROUBLE** **Y# 283** **Composition:** Copper-Nickel **Reverse:** Turkman Poet Makhtumkuli.

| Date | Mintage | F | VF | XF | Unc | BU |
|---|---|---|---|---|---|---|
| 1991 | 2,150,000 | — | — | — | 3.00 | — |
| 1991 Proof | 350,000 | Value: 5.50 | | | | |

**ROUBLE** **Y# 284** **Composition:** Copper-Nickel **Subject:** 850th Anniversary - Birth of Nizami Gyanzhevi - Poet

| Date | Mintage | F | VF | XF | Unc | BU |
|---|---|---|---|---|---|---|
| 1991 | 2,200,000 | — | — | — | 3.00 | — |
| 1991 Proof | 300,000 | Value: 5.50 | | | | |

**ROUBLE** **Y# 289** **Composition:** Copper-Nickel **Series:** Olympics **Reverse:** Wrestlers.

| Date | Mintage | F | VF | XF | Unc | BU |
|---|---|---|---|---|---|---|
| 1991 Proof | 250,000 | Value: 5.50 | | | | |

**ROUBLE** **Y# 290** **Composition:** Copper-Nickel **Series:** Olympics **Reverse:** Javelin thrower.

| Date | Mintage | F | VF | XF | Unc | BU |
|---|---|---|---|---|---|---|
| 1991 Proof | 250,000 | Value: 5.50 | | | | |

**ROUBLE** **Y# 291** **Composition:** Copper-Nickel **Series:** Olympics **Reverse:** Cyclist and charioteer.

| Date | Mintage | F | VF | XF | Unc | BU |
|---|---|---|---|---|---|---|
| 1991 Proof | 250,000 | Value: 5.50 | | | | |

**ROUBLE** **Y# 299** **Composition:** Copper-Nickel **Series:** Olympics **Reverse:** Weight lifters.

| Date | Mintage | F | VF | XF | Unc | BU |
|---|---|---|---|---|---|---|
| 1991 Proof | 250,000 | Value: 5.50 | | | | |

**ROUBLE** **Y# 300** **Composition:** Copper-Nickel **Series:** Olympics **Reverse:** Broad jumpers.

| Date | Mintage | F | VF | XF | Unc | BU |
|---|---|---|---|---|---|---|
| 1991 Proof | 250,000 | Value: 5.50 | | | | |

**ROUBLE** **Y# 302** **Composition:** Copper-Nickel **Series:** Olympics **Reverse:** Runners.

| Date | Mintage | F | VF | XF | Unc | BU |
|---|---|---|---|---|---|---|
| 1991 Proof | 250,000 | Value: 5.50 | | | | |

**2 ROUBLES** **Y# A134** **Composition:** Copper-Nickel

| Date | Mintage | F | VF | XF | Unc | BU |
|---|---|---|---|---|---|---|
| 1958 | 20,976,000 | — | — | — | 250 | — |

**Note:** Never officially released for circulation; majority of mintage remelted

**3 ROUBLES** **Y# B134** **Composition:** Copper-Nickel

| Date | Mintage | F | VF | XF | Unc | BU |
|---|---|---|---|---|---|---|
| 1958 | 4,050,000 | — | — | — | — | — |

**Note:** Never officially released for circulation; majority of mintage remelted

**3 ROUBLES** **Y# 207** **Composition:** Copper-Nickel **Subject:** 70th Anniversary - Bolshevik Revolution

| Date | Mintage | F | VF | XF | Unc | BU |
|---|---|---|---|---|---|---|
| 1987 | 2,300,000 | — | — | — | 5.00 | — |
| 1987 Proof | 200,000 | Value: 7.50 | | | | |

**3 ROUBLES** **Y# 210** **Weight:** 34.5600 g. **Composition:** 0.9000 Silver 1.0000 oz. ASW **Subject:** 1000th Anniversary of Russian Architecture **Reverse:** Cathedral of St. Sophie in Kiev.

| Date | Mintage | F | VF | XF | Unc | BU |
|---|---|---|---|---|---|---|
| 1988 (m) Proof | Est. 35,000 | Value: 45.00 | | | | |

**3 ROUBLES** **Y# 211** **Weight:** 34.5600 g. **Composition:** 0.9000 Silver 1.0000 oz. ASW **Subject:** 1000th Anniversary of Minting in Russian **Reverse:** Coin design of St. Vladimir, 977-1015.

| Date | Mintage | F | VF | XF | Unc | BU |
|---|---|---|---|---|---|---|
| 1988 (l) Proof | Est. 35,000 | Value: 42.50 | | | | |

**3 ROUBLES** **Y# 222** **Weight:** 34.5600 g. **Composition:** 0.9000 Silver 1.0000 oz. ASW **Subject:** 500th Anniversary United Russia **Obverse:** State emblem and denomination **Reverse:** Kremlin.

| Date | Mintage | F | VF | XF | Unc | BU |
|---|---|---|---|---|---|---|
| 1989 (l) Proof | Est. 40,000 | Value: 32.50 | | | | |

**3 ROUBLES** **Y# 223** **Weight:** 34.5600 g. **Composition:** 0.9000 Silver 1.0000 oz. ASW **Subject:** 500th Anniversary of the First All-Russian Coinage

| Date | Mintage | F | VF | XF | Unc | BU |
|---|---|---|---|---|---|---|
| 1989 (l) Proof | Est. 40,000 | Value: 37.50 | | | | |

**3 ROUBLES** **Y# 234** **Composition:** Copper-Nickel **Subject:** Armenian Earthquake Relief

| Date | Mintage | F | VF | XF | Unc | BU |
|---|---|---|---|---|---|---|
| 1989 | 2,700,000 | — | — | — | 4.00 | — |
| 1989 Proof | 300,000 | Value: 6.50 | | | | |

**3 ROUBLES** **Y# 242** **Weight:** 34.5600 g. **Composition:** 0.9000 Silver 1.0000 oz. ASW **Reverse:** Capt. Cook on Unalaska Island.

| Date | Mintage | F | VF | XF | Unc | BU |
|---|---|---|---|---|---|---|
| 1990 (l) Proof | 25,000 | Value: 47.50 | | | | |

**3 ROUBLES** **Y# 247** **Weight:** 34.5600 g. **Composition:** 0.9000 Silver 1.0000 oz. ASW **Subject:** World Summit for Children

| Date | Mintage | F | VF | XF | Unc | BU |
|---|---|---|---|---|---|---|
| 1990 (l) Proof | 20,000 | Value: 40.00 | | | | |

**3 ROUBLES** **Y# 248** **Weight:** 34.5600 g. **Composition:** 0.9000 Silver 1.0000 oz. ASW **Reverse:** Peter the Great's fleet

| Date | Mintage | F | VF | XF | Unc | BU |
|---|---|---|---|---|---|---|
| 1990 (m) Proof | 40,000 | Value: 30.00 | | | | |

**3 ROUBLES** **Y# 249** **Weight:** 34.5600 g. **Composition:** 0.9000 Silver 1.0000 oz. ASW **Reverse:** St. Peter and Paul Fortress in Leningrad

| Date | Mintage | F | VF | XF | Unc | BU |
|---|---|---|---|---|---|---|
| 1990 (l) Proof | 40,000 | Value: 30.00 | | | | |

**3 ROUBLES** **Y# 262** **Weight:** 34.5600 g. **Composition:** 0.9000 Silver 1.0000 oz. ASW **Reverse:** Yuri Gagarin Monument

| Date | Mintage | F | VF | XF | Unc | BU |
|---|---|---|---|---|---|---|
| 1991 (l) Proof | 35,000 | Value: 32.50 | | | | |

**3 ROUBLES** **Y# 264** **Weight:** 34.5600 g. **Composition:** 0.9000 Silver 1.0000 oz. ASW **Reverse:** Fort Ross in California

| Date | Mintage | F | VF | XF | Unc | BU |
|---|---|---|---|---|---|---|
| 1991 (l) Proof | Est. 25,000 | Value: 40.00 | | | | |

**3 ROUBLES** **Y# 274** **Weight:** 34.5600 g. **Composition:** 0.9000 Silver 1.0000 oz. ASW **Reverse:** Bolshoi Theater

| Date | Mintage | F | VF | XF | Unc | BU |
|---|---|---|---|---|---|---|
| 1991 (l) Proof | 40,000 | Value: 22.50 | | | | |

**3 ROUBLES** **Y# 275** **Weight:** 34.5600 g. **Composition:** 0.9000 Silver 1.0000 oz. ASW **Reverse:** Moscow's Arch of Triumph

| Date | Mintage | F | VF | XF | Unc | BU |
|---|---|---|---|---|---|---|
| 1991 (m) Proof | 40,000 | Value: 22.50 | | | | |

**3 ROUBLES** **Y# 301** **Composition:** Copper-Nickel **Subject:** 50th Anniversary - Defense of Moscow

| Date | Mintage | F | VF | XF | Unc | BU |
|---|---|---|---|---|---|---|
| 1991 | 2,150,000 | — | — | — | 4.50 | — |
| 1991 Proof | — | Value: 6.50 | | | | |

**5 ROUBLES** **Y# C134** **Composition:** Copper-Nickel

| Date | Mintage | F | VF | XF | Unc | BU |
|---|---|---|---|---|---|---|
| 1958 | 5,150,000 | — | — | — | 300 | — |

**Note:** Never officially released for circulation; majority of mintage remelted

**5 ROUBLES** **Y# 145** **Weight:** 16.6700 g. **Composition:** 0.9000 Silver .4824 oz. ASW **Series:** 1980 Olympics **Reverse:** Scenes of Kiev

| Date | Mintage | F | VF | XF | Unc | BU |
|---|---|---|---|---|---|---|
| 1977 (l) | 250,000 | — | — | — | 4.50 | — |
| 1977 (l) Frosted unc. | Inc. above | — | — | — | — | — |
| 1977 (l) Proof | 121,000 | Value: 6.00 | | | | |
| 1977 (m) Proof | — | Value: 6.00 | | | | |

**5 ROUBLES** **Y# 146** **Weight:** 16.6700 g. **Composition:** 0.9000 Silver .4824 oz. ASW **Series:** 1980 Olympics **Reverse:** Scenes of Leningrad

| Date | Mintage | F | VF | XF | Unc | BU |
|---|---|---|---|---|---|---|
| 1977 (l) | 250,000 | — | — | — | 4.50 | — |
| 1977 (l) Frosted unc. | Inc. above | — | — | — | — | — |
| 1977 (l) Proof | 121,000 | Value: 6.00 | | | | |
| 1977 (m) | Inc. above | — | — | — | 4.50 | — |
| 1977 (m) Proof | Inc. above | Value: 6.00 | | | | |

**5 ROUBLES** **Y# 147** **Weight:** 16.6700 g. **Composition:** 0.9000 Silver .4824 oz. ASW **Series:** 1980 Olympics **Reverse:** Scenes of Minsk

| Date | Mintage | F | VF | XF | Unc | BU |
|---|---|---|---|---|---|---|
| 1977(l) | 250,000 | — | — | — | 4.50 | — |
| 1977(l) Proof | 121,000 | Value: 6.00 | | | | |
| 1977(m) Proof | Inc. above | Value: 6.00 | | | | |

**5 ROUBLES** **Y# 148** **Weight:** 16.6700 g. **Composition:** 0.9000 Silver .4824 oz. ASW **Series:** 1980 Olympics **Reverse:** Scenes of Tallinn

| Date | Mintage | F | VF | XF | Unc | BU |
|---|---|---|---|---|---|---|
| 1977(l) | 252,000 | — | — | — | 4.50 | — |
| 1977(l) Frosted | Inc. above | — | — | — | — | — |
| 1977(l) Proof | 122,000 | Value: 6.00 | | | | |
| 1977(m) | Inc. above | — | — | — | 4.50 | — |
| 1977(m) Proof | Inc. above | Value: 6.00 | | | | |

**5 ROUBLES** **Y# 154** **Weight:** 16.6700 g. **Composition:** 0.9000 Silver .4824 oz. ASW **Series:** 1980 Olympics **Reverse:** Runner in front of stadium.

| Date | Mintage | F | VF | XF | Unc | BU |
|---|---|---|---|---|---|---|
| 1978(l) | 227,000 | — | — | — | 4.50 | — |
| 1978(m) Proof | 118,000 | Value: 6.00 | | | | |
| 1978(l) Matte proof | — | Value: 25.00 | | | | |

**5 ROUBLES** **Y# 155** **Weight:** 16.6700 g. **Composition:** 0.9000 Silver .4824 oz. ASW **Series:** 1980 Olympics **Subject:** Swimming

| Date | Mintage | F | VF | XF | Unc | BU |
|---|---|---|---|---|---|---|
| 1978(l) | 227,000 | — | — | — | 4.50 | — |
| 1978(l) Proof | 118,000 | Value: 6.00 | | | | |
| 1978(l) Frosted | Inc. above | — | — | — | — | — |
| 1978(l) Matte proof | — | Value: 25.00 | | | | |

**5 ROUBLES** **Y# 156** **Weight:** 16.6700 g. **Composition:** 0.9000 Silver .4824 oz. ASW **Series:** 1980 Olympics **Subject:** High jumping

| Date | Mintage | F | VF | XF | Unc | BU |
|---|---|---|---|---|---|---|
| 1978(l) | 221,000 | — | — | — | 4.50 | — |
| 1978(l) Proof | 119,000 | Value: 6.00 | | | | |
| 1978(m) | Inc. above | — | — | — | 4.50 | — |
| 1978(m) Proof | Inc. above | Value: 6.00 | | | | |

**5 ROUBLES** **Y# 157** **Weight:** 16.6700 g. **Composition:** 0.9000 Silver .4824 oz. ASW **Series:** 1980 Olympics **Subject:** Equestrian show jumping

| Date | Mintage | F | VF | XF | Unc | BU |
|---|---|---|---|---|---|---|
| 1978(l) | 221,000 | — | — | — | 4.50 | — |
| 1978(l) Proof | 119,000 | Value: 6.00 | | | | |
| 1978(m) | Inc. above | — | — | — | 4.50 | — |
| 1978(m) Proof | Inc. above | Value: 6.00 | | | | |

**5 ROUBLES** **Y# 166** **Weight:** 16.6700 g. **Composition:** 0.9000 Silver 0.4824 oz. ASW **Series:** 1980 Olympics **Subject:** Weightlifting

| Date | Mintage | F | VF | XF | Unc | BU |
|---|---|---|---|---|---|---|
| 1979(l) | 207,000 | — | — | — | 4.50 | — |
| 1979(l) Proof | 108,000 | Value: 6.00 | | | | |
| 1979(m) | Inc. above | — | — | — | 4.50 | — |
| 1979(m) Proof | Inc. above | Value: 6.00 | | | | |

**5 ROUBLES** **Y# 167** **Weight:** 16.6700 g. **Composition:** 0.9000 Silver .4824 oz. ASW **Series:** 1980 Olympics **Subject:** Hammer throw

| Date | Mintage | F | VF | XF | Unc | BU |
|---|---|---|---|---|---|---|
| 1979(l) | 207,000 | — | — | — | 4.50 | — |
| 1979(l) Proof | 119,000 | Value: 6.00 | | | | |
| 1979(m) | Inc. above | — | — | — | 4.50 | — |
| 1979(m) Proof | Inc. above | Value: 6.00 | | | | |

**5 ROUBLES** **Y# 179** **Weight:** 16.6700 g. **Composition:** 0.9000 Silver **Series:** 1980 Olympics **Subject:** Archery

| Date | Mintage | F | VF | XF | Unc | BU |
|---|---|---|---|---|---|---|
| 1980(l) | 126,000 | — | — | — | 5.00 | — |
| 1980(l) Proof | 95,000 | Value: 7.00 | | | | |
| 1980(m) | Inc. above | — | — | — | 5.00 | — |
| 1980(m) Proof | Inc. above | Value: 7.00 | | | | |

**5 ROUBLES** **Y# 180** **Weight:** 16.6700 g. **Composition:** 0.9000 Silver **Series:** 1980 Olympics **Subject:** Gymnastics

| Date | Mintage | F | VF | XF | Unc | BU |
|---|---|---|---|---|---|---|
| 1980(l) | 126,000 | — | — | — | 5.00 | — |
| 1980(l) Proof | 95,000 | Value: 7.00 | | | | |
| 1980(m) | Inc. above | — | — | — | 5.00 | — |
| 1980(m) Proof | Inc. above | Value: 7.00 | | | | |

**5 ROUBLES** **Y# 181** **Weight:** 16.6700 g. **Composition:** 0.9000 Silver **Series:** 1980 Olympics **Subject:** Equestrian - Isindi

| Date | Mintage | F | VF | XF | Unc | BU |
|---|---|---|---|---|---|---|
| 1980(l) | 126,000 | — | — | — | 5.00 | — |
| 1980(l) Proof | 96,000 | Value: 7.00 | | | | |

**5 ROUBLES** **Y# 182** **Weight:** 16.6700 g. **Composition:** 0.9000 Silver **Series:** 1980 Olympics **Subject:** Gorodki - Stick Throwing

| Date | Mintage | F | VF | XF | Unc | BU |
|---|---|---|---|---|---|---|
| 1980(l) | 126,000 | — | — | — | 5.00 | — |
| 1980(l) Proof | 96,000 | Value: 7.00 | | | | |

**5 ROUBLES** **Y# 208** **Composition:** Copper-Nickel **Subject:** 70th Anniversary - Bolshevik Revolution

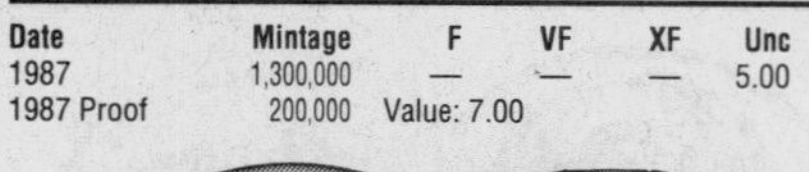

| Date | Mintage | F | VF | XF | Unc | BU |
|---|---|---|---|---|---|---|
| 1987 | 1,300,000 | — | — | — | 5.00 | — |
| 1987 Proof | 200,000 | Value: 7.00 | | | | |

**5 ROUBLES** **Y# 217** **Composition:** Copper-Nickel **Reverse:** Peter the Great mounted on horse in Leningrad.

| Date | Mintage | F | VF | XF | Unc | BU |
|---|---|---|---|---|---|---|
| 1988 | 1,675,000 | — | — | — | 5.00 | — |
| 1988 Proof | 325,000 | Value: 7.00 | | | | |

**5 ROUBLES** **Y# 218** **Composition:** Copper-Nickel **Reverse:** Novgorod Monument to the Russian millennium

| Date | Mintage | F | VF | XF | Unc | BU |
|---|---|---|---|---|---|---|
| 1988 | 1,675,000 | — | — | — | 5.00 | — |
| 1988 Proof | 325,000 | Value: 7.00 | | | | |

**5 ROUBLES** **Y# 219** **Composition:** Copper-Nickel **Reverse:** St. Sophia Cathedral in Kiev

| Date | Mintage | F | VF | XF | Unc | BU |
|---|---|---|---|---|---|---|
| 1988 | 1,675,000 | — | — | — | 5.00 | — |
| 1988 Proof | 325,000 | Value: 7.00 | | | | |

**5 ROUBLES** **Y# 221** **Composition:** Copper-Nickel **Reverse:** Pokrowsky Cathedral in Moscow

| Date | Mintage | F | VF | XF | Unc | BU |
|---|---|---|---|---|---|---|
| 1989 | 1,700,000 | — | — | — | 5.00 | — |
| 1989 Proof | 300,000 | Value: 7.00 | | | | |

**5 ROUBLES** **Y# 229** **Composition:** Copper-Nickel **Reverse:** Samarkand

| Date | Mintage | F | VF | XF | Unc | BU |
|---|---|---|---|---|---|---|
| 1989 | 1,700,000 | — | — | — | 5.00 | — |
| 1989 Proof | 300,000 | Value: 7.00 | | | | |

**5 ROUBLES** **Y# 230** **Composition:** Copper-Nickel **Reverse:** Cathedral of the Annunciation in Moscow

| Date | Mintage | F | VF | XF | Unc | BU |
|---|---|---|---|---|---|---|
| 1989 | 1,700,000 | — | — | — | 5.00 | — |
| 1989 Proof | 300,000 | Value: 7.00 | | | | |

**5 ROUBLES** **Y# 241** **Composition:** Copper-Nickel **Reverse:** Petergoff Palace

| Date | Mintage | F | VF | XF | Unc | BU |
|---|---|---|---|---|---|---|
| 1990 | 2,600,000 | — | — | — | 5.00 | — |
| 1990 Proof | 400,000 | Value: 7.00 | | | | |

**5 ROUBLES** **Y# 246** **Composition:** Copper-Nickel **Reverse:** Uspenski Cathedral

| Date | Mintage | F | VF | XF | Unc | BU |
|---|---|---|---|---|---|---|
| 1990 | 2,600,000 | — | — | — | 5.00 | — |
| 1990 Proof | 400,000 | Value: 7.00 | | | | |

**5 ROUBLES** **Y# 259** **Composition:** Copper-Nickel **Reverse:** Matenadarin Depository of Ancient Armenian Manuscripts

| Date | Mintage | F | VF | XF | Unc | BU |
|---|---|---|---|---|---|---|
| 1990 | 2,600,000 | — | — | — | 5.00 | — |
| 1990 Proof | 350,000 | Value: 7.00 | | | | |

**5 ROUBLES** **Y# 268** **Weight:** 7.7758 g. **Composition:** 0.9990 Palladium .2500 oz. **Series:** Ballet

| Date | Mintage | F | VF | XF | Unc | BU |
|---|---|---|---|---|---|---|
| 1991 | 9,000 | — | — | — | 275 | — |

**5 ROUBLES** **Y# 271** **Composition:** Copper-Nickel **Reverse:** Cathedral of the Archangel Michael in Moscow

| Date | Mintage | F | VF | XF | Unc | BU |
|---|---|---|---|---|---|---|
| 1991 | 2,150,000 | — | — | — | 5.00 | — |
| 1991 Proof | 350,000 | Value: 7.00 | | | | |

**5 ROUBLES** **Y# 272** **Composition:** Copper-Nickel **Reverse:** State bank building in Moscow

| Date | Mintage | F | VF | XF | Unc | BU |
|---|---|---|---|---|---|---|
| 1991 | 2,600,000 | — | — | — | 5.00 | — |
| 1991 Proof | 400,000 | Value: 7.00 | | | | |

**5 ROUBLES** **Y# 273** **Composition:** Copper-Nickel **Reverse:** David Sasunsky Monument

| Date | Mintage | F | VF | XF | Unc | BU |
|---|---|---|---|---|---|---|
| 1991 | 2,150,000 | — | — | — | 5.00 | — |
| 1991 Proof | 350,000 | Value: 7.00 | | | | |

**10 ROUBLES** **Y# 149** **Weight:** 33.3000 g. **Composition:** 0.9000 Silver .9636 oz. ASW **Series:** 1980 Olympics **Reverse:** Scenes of Moscow

| Date | Mintage | F | VF | XF | Unc | BU |
|---|---|---|---|---|---|---|
| 1977(l) | 250,000 | — | — | — | 10.00 | — |
| 1977(l) Proof | 121,000 | Value: 12.00 | | | | |
| 1977(m) | Inc. above | — | — | — | 10.00 | — |
| 1977(m) Proof | Inc. above | Value: 12.00 | | | | |

**10 ROUBLES** **Y# 150** **Weight:** 33.3000 g. **Composition:** 0.9000 Silver .9636 oz. ASW **Series:** 1980 Olympics **Obverse:** Similar to Y#149 **Reverse:** Map of U.S.S.R.

| Date | Mintage | F | VF | XF | Unc | BU |
|---|---|---|---|---|---|---|
| 1977(l) | 250,000 | — | — | — | 10.00 | — |
| 1977(l) Proof | 121,000 | Value: 12.00 | | | | |

**10 ROUBLES** **Y# 158.1** **Weight:** 33.3000 g. **Composition:** 0.9000 Silver .9636 oz. ASW **Series:** 1980 Olympics **Subject:** Cycling **Obverse:** Similar to Y#149

| Date | Mintage | F | VF | XF | Unc | BU |
|---|---|---|---|---|---|---|
| 1978(l) | 227,000 | — | — | — | 10.00 | — |
| 1978(l) Proof | 118,000 | Value: 12.00 | | | | |

**10 ROUBLES** **Y# 159** **Weight:** 33.3000 g. **Composition:** 0.9000 Silver .9636 oz. ASW **Series:** 1980 Olympics **Subject:** Canoeing **Obverse:** Similar to Y#149

| Date | Mintage | F | VF | XF | Unc | BU |
|---|---|---|---|---|---|---|
| 1978(l) | 34,000 | — | — | — | 25.00 | — |
| 1978(m) | 192,000 | — | — | — | 10.00 | — |
| 1978(m) Proof | 118,000 | Value: 12.00 | | | | |

**10 ROUBLES** **Y# 160** **Weight:** 33.3000 g. **Composition:** 0.9000 Silver .9636 oz. ASW **Series:** 1980 Olympics **Subject:** Equestrian Sport **Obverse:** Similar to Y#149

| Date | Mintage | F | VF | XF | Unc | BU |
|---|---|---|---|---|---|---|
| 1978(l) | 34,000 | — | — | — | 25.00 | — |
| 1978(m) | 192,000 | — | — | — | 10.00 | — |
| 1978(m) Proof | 118,000 | Value: 12.00 | | | | |

**10 ROUBLES** **Y# 161** **Weight:** 33.3000 g. **Composition:** 0.9000 Silver .9636 oz. ASW **Series:** 1980 Olympics **Subject:** Pole vaulting **Obverse:** Similar to Y#149

| Date | Mintage | F | VF | XF | Unc | BU |
|---|---|---|---|---|---|---|
| 1978(l) | 221,000 | — | — | — | 10.00 | — |
| 1978(l) Proof | 119,000 | Value: 12.00 | | | | |
| 1978(m) | Inc. above | — | — | — | 10.00 | — |
| 1978(m) Proof | Inc. above | Value: 12.00 | | | | |

**10 ROUBLES** **Y# 158.2** **Weight:** 33.3000 g. **Composition:** 0.9000 Silver .9636 oz. ASW **Series:** 1980 Olympics **Reverse:** Without mint mark **Note:** Struck at Leningrad without mint mark.

| Date | Mintage | F | VF | XF | Unc | BU |
|---|---|---|---|---|---|---|
| 1978 | — | — | — | — | — | — |
| 1978 Proof | 100 | Value: 120 | | | | |

**10 ROUBLES** **Y# 168** **Weight:** 33.3000 g. **Composition:** 0.9000 Silver .9636 oz. ASW **Series:** 1980 Olympics **Subject:** Basketball **Obverse:** Similar to Y#149

| Date | Mintage | F | VF | XF | Unc | BU |
|---|---|---|---|---|---|---|
| 1979(l) | 221,000 | — | — | — | 10.00 | — |
| 1979(l) Proof | 119,000 | Value: 12.00 | | | | |
| 1979 | — | — | — | — | 120 | — |

**10 ROUBLES** **Y# 169** **Weight:** 33.3000 g. **Composition:** 0.9000 Silver .9636 oz. ASW **Series:** 1980 Olympics **Subject:** Volleyball **Obverse:** Similar to Y#149

| Date | Mintage | F | VF | XF | Unc | BU |
|---|---|---|---|---|---|---|
| 1979(l) | 221,000 | — | — | — | 10.00 | — |
| 1979(l) Proof | 119,000 | Value: 12.00 | | | | |

**10 ROUBLES** **Y# 170** **Weight:** 33.3000 g. **Composition:** 0.9000 Silver .9636 oz. ASW **Series:** 1980 Olympics **Subject:** Boxing **Obverse:** Similar to Y#149

| Date | Mintage | F | VF | XF | Unc | BU |
|---|---|---|---|---|---|---|
| 1979(l) | 207,000 | — | — | — | 12.00 | — |
| 1979(l) Proof | 108,000 | Value: 15.00 | | | | |

**10 ROUBLES** **Y# 171** **Weight:** 33.3000 g. **Composition:** 0.9000 Silver .9636 oz. ASW **Series:** 1980 Olympics **Subject:** Judo **Obverse:** Similar to Y#149

| Date | Mintage | F | VF | XF | Unc | BU |
|---|---|---|---|---|---|---|
| 1979(l) | 207,000 | — | — | — | 12.00 | — |
| 1979(l) Proof | 108,000 | Value: 15.00 | | | | |
| 1979(m) | Inc. above | — | — | — | 12.00 | — |
| 1979(m) Proof | Inc. above | Value: 15.00 | | | | |

**10 ROUBLES** **Y# 172** **Weight:** 33.3000 g. **Composition:** 0.9000 Silver .9636 oz. ASW **Series:** 1980 Olympics **Subject:** Lifting of the Weight **Obverse:** Similar to Y#149

| Date | Mintage | F | VF | XF | Unc | BU |
|---|---|---|---|---|---|---|
| 1979(l) | 207,000 | — | — | — | 12.00 | — |
| 1979(l) Proof | 108,000 | Value: 15.00 | | | | |

**10 ROUBLES** **Y# 183** **Weight:** 33.3000 g. **Composition:** 0.9000 Silver .9636 oz. ASW **Series:** 1980 Olympics **Subject:** Wrestling **Obverse:** Similar to Y#149

| Date | Mintage | F | VF | XF | Unc | BU |
|---|---|---|---|---|---|---|
| 1980(l) | 126,000 | — | — | — | 12.00 | — |
| 1980(l) Proof | 95,000 | Value: 15.00 | | | | |
| 1980(m) | Inc. above | — | — | — | 12.00 | — |
| 1980(m) Proof | Inc. above | Value: 15.00 | | | | |

**10 ROUBLES** **Y# 184** **Weight:** 33.3000 g. **Composition:** 0.9000 Silver .9636 oz. ASW **Series:** 1980 Olympics **Subject:** Tug of War **Obverse:** Similar to Y#149

| Date | Mintage | F | VF | XF | Unc | BU |
|---|---|---|---|---|---|---|
| 1980(l) | 126,000 | — | — | — | 12.00 | — |
| 1980(l) Proof | 95,000 | Value: 15.00 | | | | |

**10 ROUBLES** Y# 185 **Weight:** 33.3000 g. **Composition:** 0.9000 Silver .9636 oz. ASW **Series:** 1980 Olympics **Subject:** Reindeer racing **Obverse:** Similar to Y#149

| Date | Mintage | F | VF | XF | Unc | BU |
|---|---|---|---|---|---|---|
| 1980(l) | 126,000 | — | — | — | 12.00 | — |
| 1980(l) Proof | 95,000 | Value: 15.00 | | | | |

**10 ROUBLES** Y# 238 **Weight:** 15.5500 g. **Composition:** 0.9990 Palladium .5000 oz. **Subject:** Ballet. **Obverse:** Similar to Y#269 **Reverse:** Ballerina.

| Date | Mintage | F | VF | XF | Unc | BU |
|---|---|---|---|---|---|---|
| 1990 | Est. 15,000 | — | — | — | 350 | — |

**10 ROUBLES** Y# 269 **Weight:** 15.5500 g. **Composition:** 0.9990 Palladium .5000 oz. **Subject:** Ballet. **Reverse:** Ballerina.

| Date | Mintage | F | VF | XF | Unc | BU |
|---|---|---|---|---|---|---|
| 1991 | 15,000 | — | — | — | 350 | — |

**10 ROUBLES** Y# 285 **Weight:** 2.6600 g. **Composition:** 0.5850 Gold .0500 oz. AGW **Subject:** Bolshoi Ballet. **Obverse:** Similar to 50 Roubles, Y#287 **Reverse:** Ballerina.

| Date | Mintage | F | VF | XF | Unc | BU |
|---|---|---|---|---|---|---|
| 1991 | 6,000 | — | — | — | 50.00 | — |

**25 ROUBLES** Y# 212 **Weight:** 31.1000 g. **Composition:** 0.9990 Palladium 1.0000 oz. **Reverse:** Monument to Vladimir, Graand Duke of Kiev and to the Millennium of Christianity in Russia.

| Date | Mintage | F | VF | XF | Unc | BU |
|---|---|---|---|---|---|---|
| 1988(l) | 7,000 | — | — | — | 750 | — |

**25 ROUBLES** Y# 224 **Weight:** 31.1000 g. **Composition:** 0.9990 Palladium 1.0000 oz. **Subject:** 500th Anniversary of Russian State **Reverse:** Ivan III

| Date | Mintage | F | VF | XF | Unc | BU |
|---|---|---|---|---|---|---|
| 1989(l) Proof | Est. 12,000 | Value: 775 | | | | |

**25 ROUBLES** Y# 231 **Weight:** 31.1000 g. **Composition:** 0.9990 Palladium 1.0000 oz. **Subject:** Ballet. **Reverse:** Ballerina.

| Date | Mintage | F | VF | XF | Unc | BU |
|---|---|---|---|---|---|---|
| 1989 | 27,000 | — | — | — | 750 | — |
| 1989 Matte proof | — | Value: 775 | | | | |
| 1989 Proof | 3,000 | Value: 775 | | | | |

**25 ROUBLES** Y# 239 **Weight:** 31.1000 g. **Composition:** 0.9990 Palladium 1.0000 oz. **Subject:** Ballet. **Reverse:** Ballerina.

| Date | Mintage | F | VF | XF | Unc | BU |
|---|---|---|---|---|---|---|
| 1990 | 27,000 | — | — | — | 750 | — |
| 1990 Proof | 3,000 | Value: 775 | | | | |

**25 ROUBLES** Y# 243 **Weight:** 31.1000 g. **Composition:** 0.9990 Palladium 1.0000 oz. **Subject:** 250th Anniversary - Discovery of Russian America - Ship - St. Peter

| Date | Mintage | F | VF | XF | Unc | BU |
|---|---|---|---|---|---|---|
| 1990(l) Proof | 6,500 | Value: 775 | | | | |

**25 ROUBLES** Y# 244 **Weight:** 31.1000 g. **Composition:** 0.9990 Palladium 1.0000 oz. **Subject:** 250th Anniversary - Discovery of Russian America - Ship - St. Paul

| Date | Mintage | F | VF | XF | Unc | BU |
|---|---|---|---|---|---|---|
| 1990(l) Proof | 6,500 | Value: 775 | | | | |

**25 ROUBLES** Y# 250 **Weight:** 31.1000 g. **Composition:** 0.9990 Palladium 1.0000 oz. **Subject:** 500th Anniversary of Russian State - Peter the Great

| Date | Mintage | F | VF | XF | Unc | BU |
|---|---|---|---|---|---|---|
| 1990(l) Proof | 12,000 | Value: 775 | | | | |

**25 ROUBLES** Y# 270 **Weight:** 31.1000 g. **Composition:** 0.9990 Palladium 1.0000 oz. **Subject:** Ballet. **Reverse:** Ballerina.

| Date | Mintage | F | VF | XF | Unc | BU |
|---|---|---|---|---|---|---|
| 1991 | 30,000 | — | — | — | 750 | — |
| 1991 Proof | 30,000 | Value: 775 | | | | |

**25 ROUBLES** Y# 276 **Weight:** 31.1000 g. **Composition:** 0.9990 Palladium 1.0000 oz. **Subject:** 500th Anniversary of Russian State - Abolition of Serfdom in Russia **Obverse:** State emblem

| Date | Mintage | F | VF | XF | Unc | BU |
|---|---|---|---|---|---|---|
| 1991(l) Proof | Est. 12,000 | Value: 775 | | | | |

**25 ROUBLES** Y# 286 **Weight:** 5.3200 g. **Composition:** 0.5850 Gold 1.0000 oz. AGW **Subject:** Bolshoi Ballet

| Date | Mintage | F | VF | XF | Unc | BU |
|---|---|---|---|---|---|---|
| 1991 | 5,000 | — | — | — | 100 | — |

**25 ROUBLES** Y# 286a **Weight:** 3.1100 g. **Composition:** 0.9990 Gold 1.0000 oz. AGW

| Date | Mintage | F | VF | XF | Unc | BU |
|---|---|---|---|---|---|---|
| 1991 Proof | 1,500 | Value: 250 | | | | |

**25 ROUBLES** Y# 266 **Weight:** 31.1000 g. **Composition:** 0.9990 Palladium 1.0000 oz. **Note:** Novo Archangelsk 1799 - three-masted ship

| Date | Mintage | F | VF | XF | Unc | BU |
|---|---|---|---|---|---|---|
| 1991(l) Proof | Est. 6,500 | Value: 775 | | | | |

**25 ROUBLES** Y# 265 **Weight:** 31.1000 g. **Composition:** 0.9990 Palladium 1.0000 oz. **Note:** Three Saints Harbor - Russian settlement in America

| Date | Mintage | F | VF | XF | Unc | BU |
|---|---|---|---|---|---|---|
| 1991 Proof | Est. 6,500 | Value: 775 | | | | |

**50 ROUBLES** **Y# 213** **Weight:** 8.6397 g. **Composition:** 0.9000 Gold .2500 oz. AGW **Subject:** 1000th Anniversary of Russian Architecture **Obverse:** Similar to 100 Roubles, Y#A163 **Reverse:** Cathedral of St. Sophia in Novgorod

| Date | Mintage | F | VF | XF | Unc | BU |
|---|---|---|---|---|---|---|
| 1988(m) | 25,000 | — | — | — | 125 | — |

**50 ROUBLES** **Y# 225** **Weight:** 8.6397 g. **Composition:** 0.9000 Gold .2500 oz. AGW **Subject:** 500th Anniversary of Russian State **Obverse:** State emblem and denomination **Reverse:** Cathedral of the Ascension

| Date | Mintage | F | VF | XF | Unc | BU |
|---|---|---|---|---|---|---|
| 1989(m) Proof | Est. 25,000 | Value: 140 | | | | |

**50 ROUBLES** **Y# 251** **Weight:** 8.6397 g. **Composition:** 0.9000 Gold .2500 oz. AGW **Subject:** 500th Anniversary of Russian State **Reverse:** Moscow Church of the Archangel

| Date | Mintage | F | VF | XF | Unc | BU |
|---|---|---|---|---|---|---|
| 1990(m) Proof | 25,000 | Value: 140 | | | | |

**50 ROUBLES** **Y# 277** **Weight:** 8.6440 g. **Composition:** 0.9000 Gold .2500 oz. AGW **Subject:** 500th Anniversary of Russian State **Reverse:** St. Isaac Cathedral in St. Petersburg

| Date | Mintage | F | VF | XF | Unc | BU |
|---|---|---|---|---|---|---|
| 1991(m) Proof | 25,000 | Value: 140 | | | | |

**50 ROUBLES** **Y# 287** **Weight:** 13.3000 g. **Composition:** 0.5850 Gold .2500 oz. AGW **Subject:** Bolshoi Ballet. **Reverse:** Ballerina.

| Date | Mintage | F | VF | XF | Unc | BU |
|---|---|---|---|---|---|---|
| 1991 | 2,400 | — | — | — | 250 | — |

**50 ROUBLES** **Y# 287a** **Weight:** 7.7800 g. **Composition:** 0.9990 Gold .2500 oz. AGW **Reverse:** Ballerina. **Edge Lettering:** Bolshoi Ballet.

| Date | Mintage | F | VF | XF | Unc | BU |
|---|---|---|---|---|---|---|
| 1991 Proof | 1,500 | Value: 450 | | | | |

**100 ROUBLES** **Y# A163** **Weight:** 17.2800 g. **Composition:** 0.9000 Gold .5000 oz. AGW **Series:** 1980 Olympics **Reverse:** Symbols

| Date | Mintage | F | VF | XF | Unc | BU |
|---|---|---|---|---|---|---|
| 1977(l) | 44,000 | — | — | — | 175 | — |
| 1977(l) Proof | 38,000 | Value: 200 | | | | |
| 1977(m) | Inc. above | — | — | — | 175 | — |
| 1977(m) Proof | Inc. above | Value: 200 | | | | |

**100 ROUBLES** **Y# 151** **Weight:** 17.2800 g. **Composition:** 0.9000 Gold .5000 oz. AGW **Series:** 1980 Olympics **Reverse:** Lenin Stadium

| Date | Mintage | F | VF | XF | Unc | BU |
|---|---|---|---|---|---|---|
| 1978(l) | 62,000 | — | — | — | 175 | — |
| 1978(l) Proof | 45,000 | Value: 200 | | | | |
| 1978(m) | Inc. above | — | — | — | 175 | — |
| 1978(m) Proof | Inc. above | Value: 200 | | | | |

**100 ROUBLES** **Y# 162** **Weight:** 17.2800 g. **Composition:** 0.9000 Gold .5000 oz. AGW **Series:** 1980 Olympics **Reverse:** Waterside grandstand

| Date | Mintage | F | VF | XF | Unc | BU |
|---|---|---|---|---|---|---|
| 1978(l) | 57,000 | — | — | — | 175 | — |
| 1978 Matte | 30,000 | — | — | — | — | — |
| 1978(l) Proof | 43,000 | Value: 200 | | | | |
| 1978(m) | Inc. above | — | — | — | 175 | — |
| 1978(m) Proof | Inc. above | Value: 200 | | | | |

**100 ROUBLES** **Y# 173** **Weight:** 17.2800 g. **Composition:** 0.9000 Gold .5000 oz. AGW **Series:** 1980 Olympics **Reverse:** Velodrome building

| Date | Mintage | F | VF | XF | Unc | BU |
|---|---|---|---|---|---|---|
| 1979(l) | 55,000 | — | — | — | 175 | — |
| 1979(l) Proof | 42,000 | Value: 200 | | | | |
| 1979(m) | Inc. above | — | — | — | 175 | — |
| 1979(m) Proof | Inc. above | Value: 200 | | | | |

**100 ROUBLES** **Y# 174** **Weight:** 17.2800 g. **Composition:** 0.9000 Gold .5000 oz. AGW **Series:** 1980 Olympics **Reverse:** Druzhba Sports Hall

| Date | Mintage | F | VF | XF | Unc | BU |
|---|---|---|---|---|---|---|
| 1979(m) | 54,000 | — | — | — | 175 | — |
| 1979(l) Proof | 38,000 | Value: 200 | | | | |

**100 ROUBLES** **Y# 186** **Weight:** 17.2800 g. **Composition:** 0.9000 Gold .5000 oz. AGW **Series:** 1980 Olympics **Reverse:** Torch

| Date | Mintage | F | VF | XF | Unc | BU |
|---|---|---|---|---|---|---|
| 1980(m) | 25,000 | — | — | — | 175 | — |
| 1980(l) Proof | 28,000 | Value: 200 | | | | |

**100 ROUBLES** **Y# 214** **Weight:** 17.2800 g. **Composition:** 0.9000 Gold .5000 oz. AGW **Series:** 1980 Olympics **Subject:** 1000th Anniversary of Minting in Russia - Coin design of St. Vladimir, 977-1015 **Obverse:** Similar to Y#186

| Date | Mintage | F | VF | XF | Unc | BU |
|---|---|---|---|---|---|---|
| 1988(m) | 14,000 | — | — | — | 250 | — |

**100 ROUBLES** **Y# 226** **Weight:** 17.2800 g. **Composition:** 0.9000 Gold .5000 oz. AGW **Series:** 1980 Olympics **Subject:** 500th Anniversary of Russian State **Obverse:** State emblem and denomination **Reverse:** Seal of Ivan III

| Date | Mintage | F | VF | XF | Unc | BU |
|---|---|---|---|---|---|---|
| 1989(m) Proof | Est. 14,000 | Value: 265 | | | | |

**100 ROUBLES** **Y# 252** **Weight:** 17.2800 g. **Composition:** 0.9000 Gold .5000 oz. AGW **Series:** 1980 Olympics **Subject:** 500th Anniversary of Russian State **Reverse:** Peter the Great Monument

| Date | Mintage | F | VF | XF | Unc | BU |
|---|---|---|---|---|---|---|
| 1990(m) Proof | 14,000 | Value: 250 | | | | |

**100 ROUBLES** **Y# 278** **Weight:** 17.2800 g. **Composition:** 0.9000 Gold .5000 oz. AGW **Series:** 1980 Olympics **Subject:** 500th Anniversary of Russian State **Reverse:** Tolstoi Monument

| Date | Mintage | F | VF | XF | Unc | BU |
|---|---|---|---|---|---|---|
| 1991(m) Proof | 14,000 | Value: 250 | | | | |

**100 ROUBLES** **Y# 288** **Weight:** 26.5900 g. **Composition:** 0.5850 Gold .5000 oz. AGW **Subject:** Bolshoi Ballet. **Reverse:** Ballerina.

| Date | Mintage | F | VF | XF | Unc | BU |
|---|---|---|---|---|---|---|
| 1991 | 1,200 | — | — | — | 500 | — |

**100 ROUBLES** **Y# 288a** **Weight:** 15.5500 g. **Composition:** 0.9990 Gold .5000 oz. AGW **Subject:** Bolshoi Ballet. **Reverse:** Ballerina.

| Date | Mintage | F | VF | XF | Unc | BU |
|---|---|---|---|---|---|---|
| 1991 Proof | 1,500 | Value: 750 | | | | |

**150 ROUBLES** **Y# 152** **Weight:** 15.5400 g. **Composition:** 0.9990 Platinum .4991 oz. APW **Series:** 1980 Olympics **Reverse:** Symbols over logo.

| Date | Mintage | F | VF | XF | Unc | BU |
|---|---|---|---|---|---|---|
| 1977(l) | 9,910 | — | — | — | 320 | — |
| 1977(m) Proof | 24,000 | Value: 350 | | | | |

**150 ROUBLES** **Y# 163** **Weight:** 15.5400 g. **Composition:** 0.9990 Platinum .4991 oz. APW **Series:** 1980 Olympics **Reverse:** Throwing discus

| Date | Mintage | F | VF | XF | Unc | BU |
|---|---|---|---|---|---|---|
| 1978(l) | 13,000 | — | — | — | 320 | — |
| 1978(l) Proof | 20,000 | Value: 350 | | | | |

**150 ROUBLES** **Y# 175** **Weight:** 15.5400 g. **Composition:** 0.9990 Platinum .4991 oz. APW **Series:** 1980 Olympics **Reverse:** Greek wrestlers

| Date | Mintage | F | VF | XF | Unc | BU |
|---|---|---|---|---|---|---|
| 1979(l) | 14,000 | — | — | — | 320 | — |
| 1979(l) | 19,000 | — | — | — | 350 | — |

**150 ROUBLES** **Y# 176** **Weight:** 15.5400 g. **Composition:** 0.9990 Platinum .4991 oz. APW **Series:** 1980 Olympics **Reverse:** Roman chariot race

| Date | Mintage | F | VF | XF | Unc | BU |
|---|---|---|---|---|---|---|
| 1979(l) | 9,728 | — | — | — | 320 | — |
| 1979(l) Proof | 17,000 | Value: 350 | | | | |

**150 ROUBLES** **Y# 187** **Weight:** 15.5400 g. **Composition:** 0.9990 Platinum .4991 oz. APW **Series:** 1980 Olympics **Reverse:** Ancient Greek runners

| Date | Mintage | F | VF | XF | Unc | BU |
|---|---|---|---|---|---|---|
| 1980(l) | 7,820 | — | — | — | 320 | — |
| 1980(l) Proof | 13,000 | Value: 350 | | | | |

**150 ROUBLES** **Y# 215** **Weight:** 15.5500 g. **Composition:** 0.9990 Platinum .5000 oz. APW **Subject:** 1000th Anniversary of Russian Literature **Obverse:** Similar to Y#187 **Reverse:** Chronill-er writing epic about Grand Duke Igor.

| Date | Mintage | F | VF | XF | Unc | BU |
|---|---|---|---|---|---|---|
| 1988(l) | 16,000 | — | — | — | 325 | — |

**150 ROUBLES** **Y# 227** **Weight:** 15.5500 g. **Composition:** 0.9990 Platinum .5000 oz. APW **Subject:** 500th Anniversary of Russian State **Obverse:** State emblem and denomination **Reverse:** Ugra River encounter.

| Date | Mintage | F | VF | XF | Unc | BU |
|---|---|---|---|---|---|---|
| 1989(l) Proof | Est. 16,000 | Value: 325 | | | | |

**150 ROUBLES** **Y# 245** **Weight:** 15.5500 g. **Composition:** 0.9990 Platinum .5000 oz. APW **Subject:** 250th Anniversary - Discovery of Russian America - Ship - St. Gavriil **Obverse:** Similar to Y#187

| Date | Mintage | F | VF | XF | Unc | BU |
|---|---|---|---|---|---|---|
| 1990(l) Proof | 6,500 | Value: 365 | | | | |

**150 ROUBLES** **Y# 253** **Weight:** 15.5500 g. **Composition:** 0.9990 Platinum .5000 oz. APW **Subject:** 500th Anniversary of Russian State **Reverse:** Battle of Poltava River.

| Date | Mintage | F | VF | XF | Unc | BU |
|---|---|---|---|---|---|---|
| 1990(l) Proof | 16,000 | Value: 325 | | | | |

**150 ROUBLES** **Y# 267** **Weight:** 15.5500 g. **Composition:** 0.9990 Platinum .5000 oz. APW **Subject:** 250th Anniversary - Discovery of Russian America **Reverse:** Bishop Veniaminov.

| Date | Mintage | F | VF | XF | Unc | BU |
|---|---|---|---|---|---|---|
| 1991(l) Proof | Est. 6,500 | Value: 365 | | | | |

**150 ROUBLES** **Y# 279** **Weight:** 17.5000 g. **Composition:** 0.9990 Platinum .5000 oz. APW **Subject:** 500th Anniversary of Russian State - War of liberation Against Napoleon

| Date | Mintage | F | VF | XF | Unc | BU |
|---|---|---|---|---|---|---|
| 1991(l) Proof | 16,000 | Value: 345 | | | | |

## GOVERNMENT BANK ISSUES

1991-1992

**10 KOPEKS** **Y# 296** **Composition:** Copper Clad Steel **Obverse:** Kremlin tower and dome

| Date | Mintage | F | VF | XF | Unc | BU |
|---|---|---|---|---|---|---|
| 1991 M | — | 0.10 | 0.15 | 0.25 | 0.35 | — |

**50 KOPEKS** **Y# 292** **Composition:** Copper-Nickel

| Date | Mintage | F | VF | XF | Unc | BU |
|---|---|---|---|---|---|---|
| 1991Л | — | 0.15 | 0.25 | 0.35 | 0.50 | — |

**ROUBLE** **Y# 293**

| Date | Mintage | F | VF | XF | Unc | BU |
|---|---|---|---|---|---|---|
| 1991(l) | — | — | — | — | 0.75 | — |
| 1991(m) | — | — | — | — | 1.25 | — |

**5 ROUBLES** **Y# 280** **Ring Composition:** Copper-Nickel **Center Composition:** Brass **Series:** Wildlife **Reverse:** Owl

| Date | Mintage | F | VF | XF | Unc | BU |
|---|---|---|---|---|---|---|
| 1991(l) | 500,000 | — | — | — | 1.50 | — |

**5 ROUBLES** **Y# 281** **Ring Composition:** Copper-Nickel **Center Composition:** Brass **Series:** Wildlife **Reverse:** Mountain Goat

| Date | Mintage | F | VF | XF | Unc | BU |
|---|---|---|---|---|---|---|
| 1991(l) | 500,000 | — | — | — | 1.50 | — |

**5 ROUBLES** Y# 294 **Composition:** Copper-Nickel

| Date | Mintage | F | VF | XF | Unc | BU |
|---|---|---|---|---|---|---|
| 1991(l) | — | — | — | — | 2.50 | — |
| 1991(m) | — | — | — | — | 5.00 | — |

**10 ROUBLES** Y# 295 **Center Composition:** Aluminum-Bronze

| Date | Mintage | F | VF | XF | Unc | BU |
|---|---|---|---|---|---|---|
| 1991(l) | — | 0.25 | 0.50 | 1.00 | 3.00 | — |
| 1991(m) | — | 4.50 | 3.00 | 5.00 | 10.00 | — |
| 1992(l) Error | — | — | 30.00 | 50.00 | 80.00 | — |

# COMMONWEALTH OF INDEPENDENT STATES

## Issued by БАНК РОССИИ (Bank Russia)

## STANDARD COINAGE

**KOPEK** Y# 600 **Composition:** Nickel Clad Steel **Obverse:** St. George **Reverse:** Denomination

| Date | Mintage | F | VF | XF | Unc | BU |
|---|---|---|---|---|---|---|
| 1997 M | — | — | — | — | 0.25 | — |
| 1997 SP | — | — | — | — | 0.25 | — |
| 1998 M | — | — | — | — | 0.25 | — |
| 1998 SP | — | — | — | — | 0.25 | — |
| 1999 M | — | — | — | — | 0.25 | — |
| 1999 SP | — | — | — | — | 0.25 | — |
| 2000 M | — | — | — | — | 0.25 | — |
| 2000 SP | — | — | — | — | 0.25 | — |
| 2001 M | — | — | — | — | 0.25 | — |
| 2001 SP | — | — | — | — | 0.25 | — |

**5 KOPEKS** Y# 601 **Composition:** Nickel Clad Steel **Obverse:** St. George **Reverse:** Denomination

| Date | Mintage | F | VF | XF | Unc | BU |
|---|---|---|---|---|---|---|
| 1997 M | — | — | — | — | 0.35 | — |
| 1997 SP | — | — | — | — | 0.35 | — |
| 1998 M | — | — | — | — | 0.35 | — |
| 1998 SP | — | — | — | — | 0.35 | — |
| 1999 M | — | — | — | — | 0.35 | — |
| 1999 SP | — | — | — | — | 0.35 | — |
| 2000 M | — | — | — | — | 0.35 | — |
| 2000 SP | — | — | — | — | 0.35 | — |
| 2001 M | — | — | — | — | 0.35 | — |
| 2001 SP | — | — | — | — | 0.35 | — |

**10 KOPEKS** Y# 602 **Composition:** Brass **Obverse:** St. George **Reverse:** Denomination

| Date | Mintage | F | VF | XF | Unc | BU |
|---|---|---|---|---|---|---|
| 1997 M | — | — | — | — | 0.50 | — |
| 1997 SP | — | — | — | — | 0.50 | — |
| 1998 M | — | — | — | — | 0.50 | — |
| 1998 SP | — | — | — | — | 0.50 | — |
| 1999 M | — | — | — | — | 0.50 | — |
| 1999 SP | — | — | — | — | 0.50 | — |
| 2000 M | — | — | — | — | 0.50 | — |
| 2000 SP | — | — | — | — | 0.50 | — |
| 2001 M | — | — | — | — | 0.50 | — |
| 2001 SP | — | — | — | — | 0.50 | — |

**50 KOPEKS** Y# 603 **Composition:** Brass **Obverse:** Stanislavski **Reverse:** Denomination

| Date | Mintage | F | VF | XF | Unc | BU |
|---|---|---|---|---|---|---|
| 1997 M | — | — | — | — | 0.75 | — |
| 1997 SP | — | — | — | — | 0.75 | — |
| 1998 | — | — | — | — | 0.75 | — |

**ROUBLE** Y# 303 **Composition:** Copper-Nickel **Subject:** Rebirth of Russian Sovereignty and Democracy

| Date | Mintage | F | VF | XF | Unc | BU |
|---|---|---|---|---|---|---|
| 1992(l) | 700,000 | — | — | — | 2.50 | — |
| 1992(l) Proof | 300,000 | Value: 5.00 | | | | |

**ROUBLE** Y# 305 **Composition:** Copper-Nickel **Subject:** 110th Anniversary - Birth of Jacob Kolas

| Date | Mintage | F | VF | XF | Unc | BU |
|---|---|---|---|---|---|---|
| 1992(l) | — | — | — | — | 2.50 | — |
| 1992(l) Proof | — | Value: 5.00 | | | | |

**ROUBLE** Y# 306 **Composition:** Copper-Nickel **Subject:** 190th Anniversary - Birth of Admiral Nakhimov

| Date | Mintage | F | VF | XF | Unc | BU |
|---|---|---|---|---|---|---|
| 1992(l) | — | — | — | — | 2.50 | — |
| 1992(l) Proof | — | Value: 5.00 | | | | |

**ROUBLE** Y# 311 **Composition:** Brass Clad Steel **Obverse:** Double-headed eagle

| Date | Mintage | F | VF | XF | Unc | BU |
|---|---|---|---|---|---|---|
| 1992 | — | 2.00 | 5.00 | 10.00 | 20.00 | — |
| 1992Л | — | — | — | — | 1.25 | — |
| 1992M | — | — | — | — | 1.00 | — |
| 1992(m) | — | — | — | — | 2.00 | — |
| 1992(l) | — | — | — | — | 2.50 | — |

**ROUBLE** Y# 320 **Composition:** Copper-Nickel **Reverse:** Yanka Kupala

| Date | Mintage | F | VF | XF | Unc | BU |
|---|---|---|---|---|---|---|
| 1992(l) | 1,000,000 | — | — | — | 2.50 | — |
| 1992(l) Prooflike | 200,000 | — | — | — | — | — |
| 1992(l) Proof | 350,000 | Value: 5.00 | | | | |

**ROUBLE** Y# 321 **Composition:** Copper-Nickel **Obverse:** Double-headed eagle **Reverse:** N. I. Lobachevsky

| Date | Mintage | F | VF | XF | Unc | BU |
|---|---|---|---|---|---|---|
| 1992(m) | 1,000,000 | — | — | — | 2.50 | — |
| 1992(m) Prooflike | 500,000 | — | — | — | — | — |
| 1992(m) Proof | — | Value: 5.00 | | | | |

**ROUBLE** Y# 319.1 **Composition:** Copper-Nickel **Obverse:** Double-headed eagle **Reverse:** Vladimir Ivanovich Vernadsky

| Date | Mintage | F | VF | XF | Unc | BU |
|---|---|---|---|---|---|---|
| 1993(l) | 450,000 | — | — | — | 2.50 | — |
| 1993(l) Prooflike | 15,000 | — | — | — | — | — |
| 1993(l) Proof | 35,000 | Value: 5.50 | | | | |

**ROUBLE** Y# 319.2 **Composition:** Copper-Nickel **Obverse:** Double-headed eagle, without mintmark below eagle's claw **Reverse:** Vladimir Ivanovich Vernadsky

| Date | Mintage | F | VF | XF | Unc | BU |
|---|---|---|---|---|---|---|
| 1993 | — | — | — | — | 2.50 | — |
| 1993 Proof | — | — | — | — | 5.00 | — |

**ROUBLE** Y# 325 **Composition:** Copper-Nickel **Obverse:** Double-headed eagle **Reverse:** Gavrilla Romanovich Derzhavin

| Date | Mintage | F | VF | XF | Unc | BU |
|---|---|---|---|---|---|---|
| 1993(l) | — | — | — | — | 2.50 | — |
| 1993(l) Proof | — | Value: 5.00 | | | | |

**ROUBLE** **Y# 326** **Composition:** Copper-Nickel **Obverse:** Double-headed eagle **Reverse:** K. A. Timiryazev

| Date | Mintage | F | VF | XF | Unc | BU |
|---|---|---|---|---|---|---|
| 1993(m) | — | — | — | — | 2.50 | — |
| 1993(m) Proof | — | Value: 5.00 | | | | |

**ROUBLE** **Y# 327** **Composition:** Copper-Nickel **Reverse:** V. Maikovski

| Date | Mintage | F | VF | XF | Unc | BU |
|---|---|---|---|---|---|---|
| 1993(m) | — | — | — | — | 2.50 | — |
| 1993(m) Proof | — | Value: 5.00 | | | | |

**ROUBLE** **Y# 335** **Weight:** 15.5500 g. **Composition:** 0.9000 Silver .4500 oz. ASW **Series:** Red Book Wildlife **Reverse:** Tiger

| Date | Mintage | F | VF | XF | Unc | BU |
|---|---|---|---|---|---|---|
| 1993 Proof | — | Value: 20.00 | | | | |

**ROUBLE** **Y# 336** **Weight:** 15.5500 g. **Composition:** 0.9000 Silver .4500 oz. ASW **Series:** Red Book Wildlife **Reverse:** Blackiston's Fish Owl

| Date | Mintage | F | VF | XF | Unc | BU |
|---|---|---|---|---|---|---|
| 1993 Proof | — | Value: 20.00 | | | | |

**ROUBLE** **Y# 337** **Weight:** 15.5500 g. **Composition:** 0.9000 Silver .4500 oz. ASW **Series:** Red Book Wildlife **Reverse:** Mountain goat (Markhor)

| Date | Mintage | F | VF | XF | Unc | BU |
|---|---|---|---|---|---|---|
| 1993 Proof | — | Value: 15.00 | | | | |

**ROUBLE** **Y# 347** **Composition:** Copper-Nickel **Reverse:** A. P. Borodin

| Date | Mintage | F | VF | XF | Unc | BU |
|---|---|---|---|---|---|---|
| 1993(m) | — | — | — | — | 2.50 | — |
| 1993(m) Proof | — | Value: 5.00 | | | | |

**ROUBLE** **Y# 348** **Composition:** Copper-Nickel **Reverse:** I. S. Turgenev

| Date | Mintage | F | VF | XF | Unc | BU |
|---|---|---|---|---|---|---|
| 1993(l) | — | — | — | — | 2.50 | — |
| 1993(l) Proof | — | Value: 5.00 | | | | |

**ROUBLE** **Y# 372** **Weight:** 15.5500 g. **Composition:** 0.9000 Silver .4500 oz. ASW **Series:** Wildlife **Reverse:** Red-breasted Kazarka

| Date | Mintage | F | VF | XF | Unc | BU |
|---|---|---|---|---|---|---|
| 1994 Proof | 50,000 | Value: 18.50 | | | | |

**ROUBLE** **Y# 373** **Weight:** 15.5500 g. **Composition:** 0.9000 Silver .4500 oz. ASW **Series:** Wildlife **Obverse:** Similar to KM#372 **Reverse:** Asiatic Cobra

| Date | Mintage | F | VF | XF | Unc | BU |
|---|---|---|---|---|---|---|
| 1994 Proof | 50,000 | Value: 18.50 | | | | |

**ROUBLE** **Y# 374** **Weight:** 15.5500 g. **Composition:** 0.9000 Silver .4500 oz. ASW **Series:** Wildlife **Obverse:** Similar to KM#372 **Reverse:** Asiatic Bear

| Date | Mintage | F | VF | XF | Unc | BU |
|---|---|---|---|---|---|---|
| 1994 Proof | 50,000 | Value: 20.00 | | | | |

**ROUBLE** **Y# 399** **Composition:** Aluminum-Bronze **Subject:** WWII Victory **Reverse:** Mother Russia calling for volunteers

| Date | Mintage | F | VF | XF | Unc | BU |
|---|---|---|---|---|---|---|
| 1995 | 200,000 | — | — | — | 1.50 | — |

**Note:** In mint sets only

**ROUBLE** **Y# 446** **Weight:** 17.4600 g. **Composition:** 0.9000 Silver .5052 oz. ASW **Series:** Wildlife **Reverse:** Oriental White Stork

| Date | Mintage | F | VF | XF | Unc | BU |
|---|---|---|---|---|---|---|
| 1995 Proof | 20,000 | Value: 18.50 | | | | |

**ROUBLE** **Y# 447** **Weight:** 17.4600 g. **Composition:** 0.9000 Silver .5052 oz. ASW **Series:** Wildlife **Reverse:** Caucasian Black Grouse

| Date | Mintage | F | VF | XF | Unc | BU |
|---|---|---|---|---|---|---|
| 1995 Proof | 20,000 | Value: 18.50 | | | | |

**ROUBLE** **Y# 448** **Weight:** 17.4600 g. **Composition:** 0.9000 Silver .5052 oz. ASW **Series:** Wildlife **Reverse:** Black Sea Porpoise

| Date | Mintage | F | VF | XF | Unc | BU |
|---|---|---|---|---|---|---|
| 1995 Proof | 20,000 | Value: 18.50 | | | | |

**ROUBLE** **Y# 492** **Weight:** 17.4600 g. **Composition:** 0.9000 Silver .5052 oz. ASW **Series:** Wildlife **Reverse:** Peregrine Falcon

| Date | Mintage | F | VF | XF | Unc | BU |
|---|---|---|---|---|---|---|
| 1996 Proof | 50,000 | Value: 20.00 | | | | |

**ROUBLE** Y# 493 **Weight:** 17.4600 g. **Composition:** 0.9000 Silver .5052 oz. ASW **Series:** Wildlife **Reverse:** Turkmenian Gecko

| Date | Mintage | F | VF | XF | Unc | BU |
|---|---|---|---|---|---|---|
| 1996 Proof | 50,000 | Value: 20.00 | | | | |

**ROUBLE** Y# 494 **Weight:** 17.4600 g. **Composition:** 0.9000 Silver .5052 oz. ASW **Series:** Wildlife **Reverse:** Ukrainian Blind Mole Rat

| Date | Mintage | F | VF | XF | Unc | BU |
|---|---|---|---|---|---|---|
| 1996 Proof | 50,000 | Value: 20.00 | | | | |

**ROUBLE** Y# 504 **Composition:** Brass **Subject:** 300th Anniversary - Russian Fleet

| Date | Mintage | F | VF | XF | Unc | BU |
|---|---|---|---|---|---|---|
| 1996 | 100,000 | — | — | — | 1.50 | — |

**Note:** In sets only

**ROUBLE** Y# 561 **Weight:** 8.4150 g. **Composition:** 0.9250 Silver .2502 oz. ASW **Subject:** 850th Anniversary - Moscow **Obverse:** Double-headed eagle

| Date | Mintage | F | VF | XF | Unc | BU |
|---|---|---|---|---|---|---|
| 1997 Proof | 25,000 | Value: 14.50 | | | | |

**ROUBLE** Y# 562 **Weight:** 8.4150 g. **Composition:** 0.9250 Silver .2502 oz. ASW **Subject:** 850th Anniversary - Moscow **Obverse:** Double-headed eagle **Reverse:** Cathedral of the Kazan Icon of the Holy Virgin

| Date | Mintage | F | VF | XF | Unc | BU |
|---|---|---|---|---|---|---|
| 1997 Proof | 25,000 | Value: 14.50 | | | | |

**ROUBLE** Y# 563 **Weight:** 8.4150 g. **Composition:** 0.9250 Silver .2502 oz. ASW **Subject:** 850th Anniversary - Moscow **Obverse:** Double-headed eagle **Reverse:** State University

| Date | Mintage | F | VF | XF | Unc | BU |
|---|---|---|---|---|---|---|
| 1997 Proof | 25,000 | Value: 14.50 | | | | |

**ROUBLE** Y# 564 **Weight:** 8.4150 g. **Composition:** 0.9250 Silver .2502 oz. ASW **Subject:** 850th Anniversary - Moscow **Obverse:** Double-headed eagle **Reverse:** Bolshoi Theatre

| Date | Mintage | F | VF | XF | Unc | BU |
|---|---|---|---|---|---|---|
| 1997 Proof | 25,000 | Value: 14.50 | | | | |

**ROUBLE** Y# 565 **Weight:** 8.4150 g. **Composition:** 0.9250 Silver .2502 oz. ASW **Subject:** 850th Anniversary - Moscow **Obverse:** Double-headed eagle **Reverse:** Resurrection Gate on Red Square

| Date | Mintage | F | VF | XF | Unc | BU |
|---|---|---|---|---|---|---|
| 1997 Proof | 25,000 | Value: 14.50 | | | | |

**ROUBLE** Y# 566 **Weight:** 8.4150 g. **Composition:** 0.9250 Silver .2502 oz. ASW **Subject:** 850th Anniversary - Moscow **Obverse:** Double-headed eagle **Reverse:** Temple of Christ the Savior

| Date | Mintage | F | VF | XF | Unc | BU |
|---|---|---|---|---|---|---|
| 1997 Proof | 25,000 | Value: 14.50 | | | | |

**ROUBLE** Y# 576 **Weight:** 8.4150 g. **Composition:** 0.9250 Silver .2502 oz. ASW **Series:** World Soccer Championship **Subject:** Paris 1998 - Soccer players, Eiffel Tower, globe

| Date | Mintage | F | VF | XF | Unc | BU |
|---|---|---|---|---|---|---|
| 1997(l) Proof | 20,000 | Value: 17.50 | | | | |

**ROUBLE** Y# 577 **Weight:** 8.4150 g. **Composition:** 0.9250 Silver .2502 oz. ASW **Series:** 1998 Winter Olympics **Subject:** Ice hockey

| Date | Mintage | F | VF | XF | Unc | BU |
|---|---|---|---|---|---|---|
| 1997(m) Proof | 20,000 | Value: 17.50 | | | | |

**ROUBLE** Y# 578 **Weight:** 8.4150 g. **Composition:** 0.9250 Silver .2502 oz. ASW **Series:** 1998 Winter Olympics **Subject:** Biathalon

| Date | Mintage | F | VF | XF | Unc | BU |
|---|---|---|---|---|---|---|
| 1997(m) Proof | 20,000 | Value: 17.50 | | | | |

**ROUBLE** Y# 579 **Weight:** 8.4150 g. **Composition:** 0.9250 Silver .2502 oz. ASW **Subject:** 1897 Soccer **Reverse:** Three soccer players

| Date | Mintage | F | VF | XF | Unc | BU |
|---|---|---|---|---|---|---|
| 1997(l) Proof | 25,000 | Value: 17.50 | | | | |

**ROUBLE** Y# 580 **Weight:** 8.4150 g. **Composition:** 0.9250 Silver .2502 oz. ASW **Subject:** 1945 Soccer **Reverse:** Goalie

| Date | Mintage | F | VF | XF | Unc | BU |
|---|---|---|---|---|---|---|
| 1997(l) Proof | 25,000 | Value: 17.50 | | | | |

**ROUBLE** Y# 581 **Weight:** 8.4150 g. **Composition:** 0.9250 Silver .2502 oz. ASW **Subject:** 1956 Soccer **Reverse:** Players and kangaroo

| Date | Mintage | F | VF | XF | Unc | BU |
|---|---|---|---|---|---|---|
| 1997(l) Proof | 25,000 | Value: 17.50 | | | | |

**ROUBLE** Y# 582 **Weight:** 8.4150 g. **Composition:** 0.9250 Silver .2502 oz. ASW **Subject:** 1960 Soccer **Reverse:** Players, Eiffel Tower

| Date | Mintage | F | VF | XF | Unc | BU |
|---|---|---|---|---|---|---|
| 1997(l) Proof | 25,000 | Value: 17.50 | | | | |

**ROUBLE** Y# 583 **Weight:** 8.4150 g. **Composition:** 0.9250 Silver .2502 oz. ASW **Subject:** 1988 Soccer **Reverse:** Three players

| Date | Mintage | F | VF | XF | Unc | BU |
|---|---|---|---|---|---|---|
| 1997(l) Proof | 25,000 | Value: 17.50 | | | | |

**ROUBLE** **Y# 611** **Weight:** 17.5500 g. **Composition:** 0.9000 Silver .5078 oz. ASW **Series:** Wildlife **Reverse:** Two flamingos

| Date | Mintage | F | VF | XF | Unc | BU |
|---|---|---|---|---|---|---|
| 1997 Proof | 15,000 | Value: 22.50 | | | | |

**ROUBLE** **Y# 612** **Weight:** 17.5500 g. **Composition:** 0.9000 Silver .5078 oz. ASW **Series:** Wildlife **Reverse:** Goitered Gazelle

| Date | Mintage | F | VF | XF | Unc | BU |
|---|---|---|---|---|---|---|
| 1997 Proof | 15,000 | Value: 22.50 | | | | |

**ROUBLE** **Y# 613** **Weight:** 17.5500 g. **Composition:** 0.9000 Silver .5078 oz. ASW **Series:** Wildlife **Reverse:** European Bison

| Date | Mintage | F | VF | XF | Unc | BU |
|---|---|---|---|---|---|---|
| 1997 Proof | 15,000 | Value: 20.00 | | | | |

**ROUBLE** **Y# 604** **Composition:** Copper-Nickel-Zinc **Reverse:** Denomination

| Date | Mintage | F | VF | XF | Unc | BU |
|---|---|---|---|---|---|---|
| 1997(m) | — | — | — | — | 1.00 | — |
| 1997(sp) | — | — | — | — | 1.00 | — |
| 1998 M | — | — | — | — | 1.00 | — |

**ROUBLE** **Y# 614** **Weight:** 8.5300 g. **Composition:** 0.9250 Silver .2357 oz. ASW **Series:** World Youth Games **Reverse:** Female tennis player

| Date | Mintage | F | VF | XF | Unc | BU |
|---|---|---|---|---|---|---|
| 1998 Proof | 25,000 | Value: 13.50 | | | | |

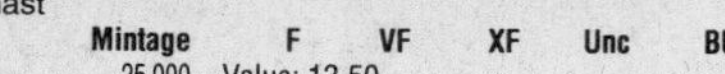

**ROUBLE** **Y# 615** **Weight:** 8.5300 g. **Composition:** 0.9250 Silver .2357 oz. ASW **Series:** World Youth Games **Reverse:** Female gymnast

| Date | Mintage | F | VF | XF | Unc | BU |
|---|---|---|---|---|---|---|
| 1998 Proof | 25,000 | Value: 13.50 | | | | |

**ROUBLE** **Y# 616** **Weight:** 8.5300 g. **Composition:** 0.9250 Silver .2357 oz. ASW **Series:** World Youth Games **Reverse:** Fencer

| Date | Mintage | F | VF | XF | Unc | BU |
|---|---|---|---|---|---|---|
| 1998 Proof | 25,000 | — | — | — | — | — |

**ROUBLE** **Y# 617** **Weight:** 8.5300 g. **Composition:** 0.9250 Silver .2357 oz. ASW **Series:** World Youth Games **Reverse:** Hammer thrower

| Date | Mintage | F | VF | XF | Unc | BU |
|---|---|---|---|---|---|---|
| 1998 Proof | 25,000 | Value: 13.50 | | | | |

**ROUBLE** **Y# 618** **Weight:** 8.5300 g. **Composition:** 0.9250 Silver .2357 oz. ASW **Series:** World Youth Games **Reverse:** Female gymnast

| Date | Mintage | F | VF | XF | Unc | BU |
|---|---|---|---|---|---|---|
| 1998 Proof | 25,000 | Value: 13.50 | | | | |

**ROUBLE** **Y# 619** **Weight:** 8.5300 g. **Composition:** 0.9250 Silver .2357 oz. ASW **Series:** World Youth Games **Reverse:** Volleyball player

| Date | Mintage | F | VF | XF | Unc | BU |
|---|---|---|---|---|---|---|
| 1998 Proof | 25,000 | Value: 13.50 | | | | |

**ROUBLE** **Y# 628** **Weight:** 17.5500 g. **Composition:** 0.9000 Silver .5078 oz. ASW **Series:** Wildlife **Reverse:** Far Eastern Skink

| Date | Mintage | F | VF | XF | Unc | BU |
|---|---|---|---|---|---|---|
| 1998 Proof | 15,000 | Value: 27.50 | | | | |

**ROUBLE** **Y# 629** **Weight:** 17.5500 g. **Composition:** 0.9000 Silver .5078 oz. ASW **Series:** Wildlife **Reverse:** Lavtev Walrus

| Date | Mintage | F | VF | XF | Unc | BU |
|---|---|---|---|---|---|---|
| 1998 Proof | 15,000 | Value: 27.50 | | | | |

**ROUBLE** **Y# 630** **Weight:** 17.5500 g. **Composition:** 0.9000 Silver .5078 oz. ASW **Series:** Wildlife **Reverse:** White-neck Goose

| Date | Mintage | F | VF | XF | Unc | BU |
|---|---|---|---|---|---|---|
| 1998 Proof | 15,000 | Value: 22.50 | | | | |

**ROUBLE** **Y# 640** **Composition:** Copper-Nickel-Zinc **Obverse:** Double-headed eagle **Reverse:** Alexander Pushkin portrait

| Date | Mintage | F | VF | XF | Unc | BU |
|---|---|---|---|---|---|---|
| 1999(m) | 5,000,000 | — | — | — | 0.75 | — |
| 1999СП | 5,000,000 | — | — | — | 0.75 | — |

**ROUBLE** **Y# 641** **Weight:** 17.4400 g. **Composition:** 0.9000 Silver .5046 oz. ASW **Series:** Wildlife **Obverse:** Double-headed eagle **Reverse:** Hedgehogs

| Date | Mintage | F | VF | XF | Unc | BU |
|---|---|---|---|---|---|---|
| 1999 Proof | 15,000 | Value: 25.00 | | | | |

**ROUBLE** **Y# 642** **Weight:** 17.4400 g. **Composition:** 0.9000 Silver .5046 oz. ASW **Series:** Wildlife **Obverse:** Double-headed eagle **Reverse:** Amur viper

| Date | Mintage | F | VF | XF | Unc | BU |
|---|---|---|---|---|---|---|
| 1999 Proof | 15,000 | Value: 25.00 | | | | |

**ROUBLE** **Y# 643** **Weight:** 17.4400 g. **Composition:** 0.9000 Silver .5046 oz. ASW **Series:** Wildlife **Obverse:** Double-headed eagle **Reverse:** Gull standing on shore

| Date | Mintage | F | VF | XF | Unc | BU |
|---|---|---|---|---|---|---|
| 1999 Proof | 15,000 | Value: 25.00 | | | | |

**ROUBLE** **Y# 719** **Weight:** 17.4400 g. **Composition:** 0.9000 Silver .5046 oz. ASW **Subject:** Queen Mother's 100th Birthday **Obverse:** Two headed eagle **Reverse:** Two black cranes **Edge:** Reeded **Size:** 33 mm.

| Date | Mintage | F | VF | XF | Unc | BU |
|---|---|---|---|---|---|---|
| 2000 (SP) Proof | 3,000 | Value: 25.00 | | | | |

**ROUBLE** **Y# 720** **Weight:** 17.4400 g. **Composition:** 0.9000 Silver .5046 oz. ASW **Obverse:** Two headed eagle **Reverse:** Leopard Runner snake

| Date | Mintage | F | VF | XF | Unc | BU |
|---|---|---|---|---|---|---|
| 2000 (SP) Proof | 3,000 | Value: 25.00 | | | | |

**ROUBLE** **Y# 721** **Weight:** 17.4400 g. **Composition:** 0.9000 Silver .5046 oz. ASW **Obverse:** Two headed eagle **Reverse:** Muskrat

| Date | Mintage | F | VF | XF | Unc | BU |
|---|---|---|---|---|---|---|
| 2000 (SP) Proof | 3,000 | Value: 25.00 | | | | |

**ROUBLE** **Y# 731** **Weight:** 3.2100 g. **Composition:** Copper-Nickel **Obverse:** Two headed eagle **Reverse:** Stylized design above hologram **Edge:** Reeded **Size:** 20.7 mm.

| Date | Mintage | F | VF | XF | Unc | BU |
|---|---|---|---|---|---|---|
| 2001 | — | — | — | — | 1.50 | — |

**2 ROUBLES** **Y# 342** **Weight:** 15.8700 g. **Composition:** 0.5000 Silver .2552 oz. ASW **Obverse:** Double-headed eagle **Reverse:** Pavel Bazhov - author of Ural Tales

| Date | Mintage | F | VF | XF | Unc | BU |
|---|---|---|---|---|---|---|
| 1994 Proof | 250,000 | Value: 12.50 | | | | |

**2 ROUBLES** **Y# 343** **Weight:** 15.8700 g. **Composition:** 0.5000 Silver .2552 oz. ASW **Obverse:** Double-headed eagle **Reverse:** Ivan Krylov - author of Fables

| Date | Mintage | F | VF | XF | Unc | BU |
|---|---|---|---|---|---|---|
| 1994 Proof | 250,000 | Value: 12.50 | | | | |

**2 ROUBLES** **Y# 344** **Weight:** 15.8700 g. **Composition:** 0.5000 Silver .2552 oz. ASW **Obverse:** Double-headed eagle **Reverse:** Nickolai Gogol - writer

| Date | Mintage | F | VF | XF | Unc | BU |
|---|---|---|---|---|---|---|
| 1994 Proof | 250,000 | Value: 12.50 | | | | |

**2 ROUBLES** **Y# 363** **Weight:** 15.8700 g. **Composition:** 0.5000 Silver .2552 oz. ASW **Obverse:** Double-headed eagle **Reverse:** Admiral Ushakov

| Date | Mintage | F | VF | XF | Unc | BU |
|---|---|---|---|---|---|---|
| 1994 Proof | 250,000 | Value: 12.50 | | | | |

**2 ROUBLES** **Y# 364** **Weight:** 15.8700 g. **Composition:** 0.5000 Silver .2552 oz. ASW **Obverse:** Double-headed eagle **Reverse:** Ilya Repin - painter

| Date | Mintage | F | VF | XF | Unc | BU |
|---|---|---|---|---|---|---|
| 1994 Proof | 250,000 | Value: 12.50 | | | | |

**2 ROUBLES** **Y# 377** **Weight:** 15.8700 g. **Composition:** 0.5000 Silver .2552 oz. ASW **Obverse:** Double-headed eagle **Reverse:** A. S. Griboyedov

| Date | Mintage | F | VF | XF | Unc | BU |
|---|---|---|---|---|---|---|
| 1995 Proof | 200,000 | Value: 14.50 | | | | |

**2 ROUBLES** **Y# 391** **Weight:** 15.8700 g. **Composition:** 0.5000 Silver .2552 oz. ASW **Series:** WWII Victory **Subject:** Victory parade **Obverse:** Kremlin

| Date | Mintage | F | VF | XF | Unc | BU |
|---|---|---|---|---|---|---|
| 1995 Proof | 200,000 | Value: 16.50 | | | | |

**2 ROUBLES** **Y# 392** **Weight:** 15.8700 g. **Composition:** 0.5000 Silver .2552 oz. ASW **Series:** WWII **Obverse:** Kremlin **Reverse:** Marshal Zhukov on horseback

| Date | Mintage | F | VF | XF | Unc | BU |
|---|---|---|---|---|---|---|
| 1995 Proof | 200,000 | Value: 16.50 | | | | |

**2 ROUBLES** **Y# 393** **Weight:** 15.8700 g. **Composition:** 0.5000 Silver .2552 oz. ASW **Series:** WWII **Obverse:** Kremlin **Reverse:** Nuremberg trial

| Date | Mintage | F | VF | XF | Unc | BU |
|---|---|---|---|---|---|---|
| 1995 Proof | 200,000 | Value: 16.50 | | | | |

**2 ROUBLES** **Y# 414** **Weight:** 15.8700 g. **Composition:** 0.5000 Silver .2552 oz. ASW **Obverse:** Double-headed eagle **Reverse:** Sergei Esenin

| Date | Mintage | F | VF | XF | Unc | BU |
|---|---|---|---|---|---|---|
| 1995 Proof | 200,000 | Value: 14.50 | | | | |

**2 ROUBLES** **Y# 415** **Weight:** 15.8700 g. **Composition:** 0.5000 Silver .2552 oz. ASW **Obverse:** Double-headed eagle **Reverse:** Field Marshal Kutozov

| Date | Mintage | F | VF | XF | Unc | BU |
|---|---|---|---|---|---|---|
| 1995 Proof | 200,000 | Value: 13.50 | | | | |

**2 ROUBLES** **Y# 449** **Weight:** 15.8700 g. **Composition:** 0.5000 Silver .2552 oz. ASW **Obverse:** Double-headed eagle **Reverse:** Ivan Bunin

| Date | Mintage | F | VF | XF | Unc | BU |
|---|---|---|---|---|---|---|
| 1995 Proof | 200,000 | Value: 14.50 | | | | |

**2 ROUBLES** **Y# 514** **Weight:** 15.8700 g. **Composition:** 0.5000 Silver .2552 oz. ASW **Obverse:** Double-headed eagle **Reverse:** Nikolai Nekrasov

| Date | Mintage | F | VF | XF | Unc | BU |
|---|---|---|---|---|---|---|
| 1996 Proof | 50,000 | Value: 13.50 | | | | |

**2 ROUBLES** **Y# 515** **Weight:** 15.8700 g. **Composition:** 0.5000 Silver .2552 oz. ASW **Obverse:** Double-headed eagle **Reverse:** Fyodor Dostoevsky

| Date | Mintage | F | VF | XF | Unc | BU |
|---|---|---|---|---|---|---|
| 1996 Proof | 50,000 | Value: 17.50 | | | | |

**2 ROUBLES** **Y# 549** **Weight:** 15.8700 g. **Composition:** 0.5000 Silver .2552 oz. ASW **Obverse:** Double-headed eagle **Reverse:** N. E. Zhukovsky

| Date | Mintage | F | VF | XF | Unc | BU |
|---|---|---|---|---|---|---|
| 1997 Proof | 50,000 | Value: 17.50 | | | | |

**2 ROUBLES** **Y# 550** **Weight:** 15.8700 g. **Composition:** 0.5000 Silver .2552 oz. ASW **Obverse:** Double-headed eagle **Reverse:** A. N. Skryabin - musician

| Date | Mintage | F | VF | XF | Unc | BU |
|---|---|---|---|---|---|---|
| 1997 Proof | 50,000 | Value: 18.50 | | | | |

**2 ROUBLES** **Y# 551** **Weight:** 15.8700 g. **Composition:** 0.5000 Silver .2552 oz. ASW **Obverse:** Double-headed eagle **Reverse:** A. L. Chizhevsky

| Date | Mintage | F | VF | XF | Unc | BU |
|---|---|---|---|---|---|---|
| 1997 Proof | 10,000 | Value: 20.00 | | | | |

**2 ROUBLES** **Y# 558** **Weight:** 15.8700 g. **Composition:** 0.5000 Silver .2552 oz. ASW **Obverse:** Double-headed eagle **Reverse:** Afanasi Nikitin - sailing ship

| Date | Mintage | F | VF | XF | Unc | BU |
|---|---|---|---|---|---|---|
| 1997 Proof | 15,000 | Value: 20.00 | | | | |

**2 ROUBLES** **Y# 559** **Weight:** 15.8700 g. **Composition:** 0.5000 Silver .2552 oz. ASW **Obverse:** Double-headed eagle **Reverse:** Afanasi Nikitin - indian scene

| Date | Mintage | F | VF | XF | Unc | BU |
|---|---|---|---|---|---|---|
| 1997 Proof | 7,500 | Value: 20.00 | | | | |

**2 ROUBLES** **Y# 584** **Weight:** 15.8700 g. **Composition:** 0.5000 Silver .2552 oz. ASW **Obverse:** Double-headed eagle **Reverse:** A. K. Savrasov - church, trees

| Date | Mintage | F | VF | XF | Unc | BU |
|---|---|---|---|---|---|---|
| 1997 Proof | 7,500 | Value: 20.00 | | | | |

**2 ROUBLES** **Y# 605** **Composition:** Copper-Nickel-Zinc **Reverse:** Denomination

| Date | Mintage | F | VF | XF | Unc | BU |
|---|---|---|---|---|---|---|
| 1997(m) | — | — | — | — | 1.65 | — |
| 1997(sp) | — | — | — | — | 1.65 | — |

**2 ROUBLES** **Y# 607** **Weight:** 16.8108 g. **Composition:** 0.9250 Silver .4999 oz. ASW **Subject:** 100th Anniversary - Sergei Eisenstein **Obverse:** Double-headed eagle

| Date | Mintage | F | VF | XF | Unc | BU |
|---|---|---|---|---|---|---|
| 1998 | 15,000 | — | — | — | 16.50 | — |

**2 ROUBLES** **Y# 608** **Weight:** 16.8108 g. **Composition:** 0.9250 Silver .4999 oz. ASW **Subject:** 100th Anniversary - Sergei Eisenstein **Obverse:** Double-headed eagle

| Date | Mintage | F | VF | XF | Unc | BU |
|---|---|---|---|---|---|---|
| 1998 | 15,000 | — | — | — | 17.50 | — |

**2 ROUBLES** **Y# 609** **Weight:** 16.8108 g. **Composition:** 0.9250 Silver .4999 oz. ASW **Obverse:** Double-headed eagle **Reverse:** K. S. Stanslavski

| Date | Mintage | F | VF | XF | Unc | BU |
|---|---|---|---|---|---|---|
| 1998 | 15,000 | — | — | — | 17.50 | — |

**2 ROUBLES** **Y# 610** **Weight:** 16.8108 g. **Composition:** 0.9250 Silver .4999 oz. ASW **Obverse:** Double-headed eagle **Reverse:** Maxim Gorky play - Stanislavsky method

| Date | Mintage | F | VF | XF | Unc | BU |
|---|---|---|---|---|---|---|
| 1998 | 15,000 | — | — | — | 17.50 | — |

**2 ROUBLES** **Y# 620** **Weight:** 17.0000 g. **Composition:** 0.9250 Silver .5056 oz. ASW **Obverse:** Double-headed eagle **Reverse:** Victor Mikhailovich Vasnetsov - three ancient warriors

| Date | Mintage | F | VF | XF | Unc | BU |
|---|---|---|---|---|---|---|
| 1998 | 15,000 | — | — | — | 17.50 | — |

**2 ROUBLES** **Y# 621** **Weight:** 17.0000 g. **Composition:** 0.9250 Silver .5056 oz. ASW **Obverse:** Double-headed eagle **Reverse:** Victor Mikhailovich Vasnetsov - three seated figures

| Date | Mintage | F | VF | XF | Unc | BU |
|---|---|---|---|---|---|---|
| 1998 | 15,000 | — | — | — | 17.50 | — |

**2 ROUBLES** **Y# 649** **Weight:** 17.0000 g. **Composition:** 0.9250 Silver .5056 oz. ASW **Subject:** K. L. Khetagurov 1859-1906 **Obverse:** Double-headed eagle **Reverse:** Portrait with mountain tops and buildings

| Date | Mintage | F | VF | XF | Unc | BU |
|---|---|---|---|---|---|---|
| 1999 Proof | 3,000 | Value: 22.50 | | | | |

**2 ROUBLES** **Y# 650** **Weight:** 17.0000 g. **Composition:** 0.9250 Silver .5056 oz. ASW **Subject:** N. K. Rerikh 1874-1947 **Obverse:** Double-headed eagle **Reverse:** Painter with mountains in the background

| Date | Mintage | F | VF | XF | Unc | BU |
|---|---|---|---|---|---|---|
| 1999 Proof | 15,000 | Value: 17.50 | | | | |

**2 ROUBLES** **Y# 651** **Weight:** 17.0000 g. **Composition:** 0.9250 Silver .5056 oz. ASW **Subject:** The Human Acts by Rerikh. **Obverse:** Double-headed eagle **Reverse:** Detail from painting, artist's portrait above

| Date | Mintage | F | VF | XF | Unc | BU |
|---|---|---|---|---|---|---|
| 1999 Proof | 15,000 | Value: 17.50 | | | | |

**2 ROUBLES** **Y# 652** **Weight:** 17.0000 g. **Composition:** 0.9250 Silver .5056 oz. ASW **Subject:** K. P. Bryulbv 1799-1852 **Obverse:** Double-headed eagle **Reverse:** Portrait of painter

| Date | Mintage | F | VF | XF | Unc | BU |
|---|---|---|---|---|---|---|
| 1999 Proof | 15,000 | Value: 22.50 | | | | |

**2 ROUBLES** **Y# 653** **Weight:** 17.0000 g. **Composition:** 0.9250 Silver .5056 oz. ASW **Subject:** The Last Day of Pompei **Obverse:** Double-headed eagle **Reverse:** Detail from painting, portrait in exergue

| Date | Mintage | F | VF | XF | Unc | BU |
|---|---|---|---|---|---|---|
| 1999 Proof | 15,000 | Value: 17.50 | | | | |

**2 ROUBLES** **Y# 654** **Weight:** 17.0000 g. **Composition:** 0.9250 Silver .5056 oz. ASW **Obverse:** Double-headed eagle **Reverse:** 1/2 bust of I.P. Pavlov, dog, books, cap, and gown.

| Date | Mintage | F | VF | XF | Unc | BU |
|---|---|---|---|---|---|---|
| 1999 Proof | 15,000 | Value: 17.50 | | | | |

**2 ROUBLES** **Y# 655** **Weight:** 17.0000 g. **Composition:** 0.9250 Silver .5056 oz. ASW **Obverse:** Double-headed eagle **Reverse:** Portrait and silence tower

| Date | Mintage | F | VF | XF | Unc | BU |
|---|---|---|---|---|---|---|
| 1999 Proof | 15,000 | Value: 17.50 | | | | |

**2 ROUBLES** **Y# 659** **Weight:** 17.0000 g. **Composition:** 0.9250 Silver .5056 oz. ASW **Subject:** Eugeny Abramovich Baratynsky **Reverse:** Bust of Baratynsky at right, scenery at left. **Edge:** Reeded

| Date | Mintage | F | VF | XF | Unc | BU |
|---|---|---|---|---|---|---|
| 2000 Proof | 5,000 | Value: 22.50 | | | | |

**2 ROUBLES** **Y# 660** **Weight:** 17.0000 g. **Composition:** 0.9250 Silver .5056 oz. ASW **Subject:** F. A. Vassiliyev **Reverse:** Cameo bust of Vassiliyev left, dates below, scenery at left

| Date | Mintage | F | VF | XF | Unc | BU |
|---|---|---|---|---|---|---|
| 2000 Proof | 5,000 | Value: 22.50 | | | | |

**2 ROUBLES** **Y# 662** **Weight:** 17.0000 g. **Composition:** 0.9250 Silver .5056 oz. ASW **Subject:** S. V. Kovaleuskaya **Reverse:** Cameo bust of Kovaleuskaya right at left, academic items at right

| Date | Mintage | F | VF | XF | Unc | BU |
|---|---|---|---|---|---|---|
| 2000 Proof | 5,000 | Value: 22.50 | | | | |

**2 ROUBLES** **Y# 663** **Weight:** 5.1000 g. **Composition:** Copper-Nickel-Zinc **Series:** World War II **Obverse:** Denomination **Reverse:** Infantry assault at Stalingrad **Edge:** Reeded and plain sections.

| Date | Mintage | F | VF | XF | Unc | BU |
|---|---|---|---|---|---|---|
| 2000 (SP) | 10,000,000 | — | — | — | 1.25 | — |

**2 ROUBLES** **Y# 664** **Composition:** Copper-Nickel-Zinc **Reverse:** Cannon manufacturing scene in Tula

| Date | Mintage | F | VF | XF | Unc | BU |
|---|---|---|---|---|---|---|
| 2000 (M) | 10,000,000 | — | — | — | 1.25 | — |

**2 ROUBLES** **Y# 665** **Composition:** Copper-Nickel-Zinc **Reverse:** Truck-mounted rocket launchers in Smolensk

| Date | Mintage | F | VF | XF | Unc | BU |
|---|---|---|---|---|---|---|
| 2000 (M) | 10,000,000 | — | — | — | 1.25 | — |

**2 ROUBLES** **Y# 666** **Composition:** Copper-Nickel-Zinc **Reverse:** Murmansk ship convoy

| Date | Mintage | F | VF | XF | Unc | BU |
|---|---|---|---|---|---|---|
| 2000 (M) | 10,000,000 | — | — | — | 1.25 | — |

**2 ROUBLES** **Y# 667** **Composition:** Copper-Nickel-Zinc **Reverse:** Defense of Moscow scene

| Date | Mintage | F | VF | XF | Unc | BU |
|---|---|---|---|---|---|---|
| 2000 (M) | 10,000,000 | — | — | — | 1.25 | — |

**2 ROUBLES** **Y# 668** **Composition:** Copper-Nickel-Zinc **Reverse:** Marine landing scene in Novorusiisk

| Date | Mintage | F | VF | XF | Unc | BU |
|---|---|---|---|---|---|---|
| 2000 (SP) | 10,000,000 | — | — | — | 1.25 | — |

**2 ROUBLES** **Y# 669** **Composition:** Copper-Nickel-Zinc **Reverse:** Siege of Leningrad truck convoy scene

| Date | Mintage | F | VF | XF | Unc | BU |
|---|---|---|---|---|---|---|
| 2000 (SP) | 10,000,000 | — | — | — | 1.25 | — |

**2 ROUBLES** **Y# 704** **Weight:** 17.4400 g. **Composition:** 0.9250 Silver .5056 oz. ASW **Subject:** M.I. Chigorin **Obverse:** Two headed eagle **Reverse:** Cameo portrait and chess pieces **Edge:** Reeded **Size:** 33 mm.

| Date | Mintage | F | VF | XF | Unc | BU |
|---|---|---|---|---|---|---|
| 2000 (SP) Proof | 5,000 | Value: 25.00 | | | | |

**2 ROUBLES** **Y# 730** **Weight:** 17.0000 g. **Composition:** 0.9250 Silver .5056 oz. ASW **Subject:** V.I. Dal **Obverse:** Two headed eagle **Reverse:** Portrait, book, signature, figures **Edge:** Reeded **Size:** 33 mm.

| Date | Mintage | F | VF | XF | Unc | BU |
|---|---|---|---|---|---|---|
| 2001(m) Proof | 7,500 | Value: 22.50 | | | | |

**2 ROUBLES** **Y# 675** **Weight:** 5.2000 g. **Composition:** Copper-Nickel **Subject:** Yuri Gagarin **Obverse:** Denomination and date **Reverse:** Uniformed portrait **Edge:** Segmented reeding **Size:** 23 mm.

| Date | Mintage | F | VF | XF | Unc | BU |
|---|---|---|---|---|---|---|
| 2001 | — | — | — | — | 2.00 | — |

**3 ROUBLES** **Y# 297** **Composition:** Copper-Nickel **Subject:** International Space Year

| Date | Mintage | F | VF | XF | Unc | BU |
|---|---|---|---|---|---|---|
| 1992(m) | 600,000 | — | — | — | 3.50 | — |
| 1992(m) Proof | 400,000 | Value: 5.50 | | | | |

**3 ROUBLES** **Y# 298** **Composition:** Copper-Nickel **Subject:** Battle of Chudskoye Lake

| Date | Mintage | F | VF | XF | Unc | BU |
|---|---|---|---|---|---|---|
| 1992(l) | 600,000 | — | — | — | 3.50 | — |
| 1992(l) Proof | 400,000 | Value: 5.50 | | | | |

**3 ROUBLES** **Y# 317** **Composition:** Copper-Nickel **Subject:** 1st Anniversary - Defeat of Communist attempted coup

| Date | Mintage | F | VF | XF | Unc | BU |
|---|---|---|---|---|---|---|
| 1992(m) | — | — | — | — | 3.50 | — |
| 1992(m) Prooflike | — | — | — | — | 4.00 | — |
| 1992(m) Proof | — | Value: 5.50 | | | | |

**3 ROUBLES** **Y# 349** **Weight:** 34.5600 g. **Composition:** 0.9000 Silver 1.0000 oz. ASW **Reverse:** St. Petersburg Trinity Cathedral

| Date | Mintage | F | VF | XF | Unc | BU |
|---|---|---|---|---|---|---|
| 1992 Proof | 40,000 | Value: 18.50 | | | | |

**3 ROUBLES** **Y# 350** **Weight:** 34.5600 g. **Composition:** 0.9000 Silver 1.0000 oz. ASW **Reverse:** St. Petersburg Academy of Science

| Date | Mintage | F | VF | XF | Unc | BU |
|---|---|---|---|---|---|---|
| 1992 Proof | 40,000 | Value: 21.50 | | | | |

**3 ROUBLES** **Y# 304** **Composition:** Copper-Nickel **Series:** WWII **Note:** Allied supply convoys to Murmansk.

| Date | Mintage | F | VF | XF | Unc | BU |
|---|---|---|---|---|---|---|
| 1992(l) Proof | 400,000 | Value: 5.50 | | | | |

**3 ROUBLES** **Y# 323** **Weight:** 34.5600 g. **Composition:** 0.9000 Silver 1.0000 oz. ASW **Subject:** Bolshoi Ballet. **Reverse:** Ballet couple. **Note:** Struck at Moscow without mint mark.

| Date | Mintage | F | VF | XF | Unc | BU |
|---|---|---|---|---|---|---|
| 1993 | 125,000 | — | — | — | 12.00 | — |
| 1993 Proof | 40,000 | Value: 16.50 | | | | |

**3 ROUBLES** **Y# 318** **Composition:** Copper-Nickel **Subject:** Battle of Stalingrad

| Date | Mintage | F | VF | XF | Unc | BU |
|---|---|---|---|---|---|---|
| 1993(m) | 150,000 | — | — | — | 3.50 | — |
| 1993(m) Prooflike | — | — | — | — | 4.00 | — |
| 1993(m) Proof | 350,000 | Value: 5.50 | | | | |

**3 ROUBLES** **Y# 328** **Composition:** Copper-Nickel **Subject:** 50th Anniversary - Battle of Kursk **Reverse:** Kremlin

| Date | Mintage | F | VF | XF | Unc | BU |
|---|---|---|---|---|---|---|
| 1993(l) | — | — | — | — | 3.50 | — |
| 1993(l) Proof | — | Value: 5.50 | | | | |

**3 ROUBLES** **Y# 340** **Composition:** Copper-Nickel **Subject:** 50th Anniversary - Kiev's Liberation from German fascists **Reverse:** Kremlin

| Date | Mintage | F | VF | XF | Unc | BU |
|---|---|---|---|---|---|---|
| 1993(m) | — | — | — | — | 3.50 | — |
| 1993(m) Proof | — | Value: 5.50 | | | | |

**3 ROUBLES** **Y# 351** **Weight:** 34.5600 g. **Composition:** 0.9000 Silver 1.0000 oz. ASW **Series:** Olympics **Subject:** Soccer **Obverse:** Double-headed eagle

| Date | Mintage | F | VF | XF | Unc | BU |
|---|---|---|---|---|---|---|
| 1993 Proof | 40,000 | Value: 27.50 | | | | |

**3 ROUBLES** **Y# 409** **Weight:** 34.5600 g. **Composition:** 0.9000 Silver 1.0000 oz. ASW **Series:** Wildlife **Obverse:** Similar to KM#323 **Reverse:** Bear

| Date | Mintage | F | VF | XF | Unc | BU |
|---|---|---|---|---|---|---|
| 1993 Proof | 5,000 | Value: 65.00 | | | | |

**3 ROUBLES** **Y# 450** **Weight:** 34.5600 g. **Composition:** 0.9000 Silver 1.0000 oz. ASW **Subject:** Ballet. **Reverse:** Ballerina - Anna Pavlova.

| Date | Mintage | F | VF | XF | Unc | BU |
|---|---|---|---|---|---|---|
| 1993 Proof | 45,000 | Value: 27.50 | | | | |

**3 ROUBLES** **Y# 451** **Weight:** 34.5600 g. **Composition:** 0.9000 Silver 1.0000 oz. ASW **Reverse:** Fedor Schalyapin

| Date | Mintage | F | VF | XF | Unc | BU |
|---|---|---|---|---|---|---|
| 1993 Proof | 45,000 | Value: 25.00 | | | | |

**3 ROUBLES** **Y# 456** **Weight:** 34.5600 g. **Composition:** 0.9000 Silver 1.0000 oz. ASW **Reverse:** Vasilyblazheny Cathedral, Moscow

| Date | Mintage | F | VF | XF | Unc | BU |
|---|---|---|---|---|---|---|
| 1993 Proof | 30,000 | Value: 22.50 | | | | |

**3 ROUBLES** **Y# 457** **Weight:** 34.5600 g. **Composition:** 0.9000 Silver 1.0000 oz. ASW **Reverse:** Ivan the Great Cathedral, Moscow

| Date | Mintage | F | VF | XF | Unc | BU |
|---|---|---|---|---|---|---|
| 1993 Proof | 30,000 | Value: 22.50 | | | | |

**3 ROUBLES** **Y# 464** **Weight:** 34.5600 g. **Composition:** 0.9000 Silver 1.0000 oz. ASW **Reverse:** Sailing ships "Nadezhda" and "Neva" on world voyage

| Date | Mintage | F | VF | XF | Unc | BU |
|---|---|---|---|---|---|---|
| 1993 Proof | — | Value: 32.50 | | | | |

**3 ROUBLES** **Y# 465** **Weight:** 34.5600 g. **Composition:** 0.9000 Silver 1.0000 oz. ASW **Subject:** Russ-French space flight

| Date | Mintage | F | VF | XF | Unc | BU |
|---|---|---|---|---|---|---|
| 1993 Proof | 40,000 | Value: 35.00 | | | | |

**3 ROUBLES** **Y# 341** **Composition:** Copper-Nickel **Subject:** 50th Anniversary - Battle of Leningrad **Reverse:** Kremlin

| Date | Mintage | F | VF | XF | Unc | BU |
|---|---|---|---|---|---|---|
| 1994(l) Proof | 250,000 | Value: 5.50 | | | | |

**3 ROUBLES** **Y# 345** **Weight:** 34.5600 g. **Composition:** 0.9000 Silver 1.0000 oz. ASW **Obverse:** Double-headed eagle **Reverse:** Cathedral of the Nativity of the Mother of God

| Date | Mintage | F | VF | XF | Unc | BU |
|---|---|---|---|---|---|---|
| 1994 Proof | 30,000 | Value: 30.00 | | | | |

**3 ROUBLES** **Y# 346** **Composition:** Copper-Nickel **Subject:** 50th Anniversary - Liberation of Sevastopol from German fascists **Reverse:** Kremlin

| Date | Mintage | F | VF | XF | Unc | BU |
|---|---|---|---|---|---|---|
| 1994(l) Proof | 250,000 | Value: 5.50 | | | | |

**3 ROUBLES** **Y# 362** **Composition:** Copper-Nickel **Subject:** Normandy invasion **Reverse:** Kremlin

| Date | Mintage | F | VF | XF | Unc | BU |
|---|---|---|---|---|---|---|
| 1994(m) Proof | 250,000 | Value: 5.50 | | | | |

**3 ROUBLES** **Y# 365** **Composition:** Copper-Nickel **Series:** WWII **Subject:** Partisans activities **Reverse:** Kremlin

| Date | Mintage | F | VF | XF | Unc | BU |
|---|---|---|---|---|---|---|
| 1994(m) Proof | 250,000 | Value: 5.50 | | | | |

**3 ROUBLES** **Y# 366** **Composition:** Copper-Nickel **Series:** WWII **Subject:** Liberation of Belgrade **Reverse:** Kremlin

| Date | Mintage | F | VF | XF | Unc | BU |
|---|---|---|---|---|---|---|
| 1994(m) Proof | 250,000 | Value: 5.50 | | | | |

**3 ROUBLES** **Y# 389 (Y398)** **Weight:** 34.8800 g. **Composition:** 0.9000 Silver 1.0093 oz. ASW **Subject:** Trans-Siberian railway **Obverse:** Double-headed eagle

| Date | Mintage | F | VF | XF | Unc | BU |
|---|---|---|---|---|---|---|
| 1994 Proof | 25,000 | Value: 35.00 | | | | |

**3 ROUBLES** **Y# 405** **Weight:** 34.5600 g. **Composition:** 0.9000 Silver 1.0000 oz. ASW **Subject:** Ballet **Reverse:** Ballet couple.

| Date | Mintage | F | VF | XF | Unc | BU |
|---|---|---|---|---|---|---|
| 1994 Proof | 40,000 | Value: 22.50 | | | | |

**3 ROUBLES** **Y# 458** **Weight:** 34.5600 g. **Composition:** 0.9000 Silver 1.0000 oz. ASW **Reverse:** Pocrov Church on the Nerl

| Date | Mintage | F | VF | XF | Unc | BU |
|---|---|---|---|---|---|---|
| 1994 Proof | 30,000 | Value: 20.00 | | | | |

**3 ROUBLES** **Y# 460** **Weight:** 34.5600 g. **Composition:** 0.9000 Silver 1.0000 oz. ASW **Series:** Wildlife **Reverse:** Sable

| Date | Mintage | F | VF | XF | Unc | BU |
|---|---|---|---|---|---|---|
| 1994 Proof | 10,000 | Value: 35.00 | | | | |

**3 ROUBLES** **Y# 466** **Weight:** 34.5600 g. **Composition:** 0.9000 Silver 1.0000 oz. ASW **Subject:** Discovery of Antarctica **Reverse:** Sailing ships Vostok and Mirny

| Date | Mintage | F | VF | XF | Unc | BU |
|---|---|---|---|---|---|---|
| 1994 Proof | 25,000 | Value: 30.00 | | | | |

**3 ROUBLES** **Y# 513** **Weight:** 34.6800 g. **Composition:** 0.9000 Silver 1.0034 oz. ASW **Reverse:** Building and churches

| Date | Mintage | F | VF | XF | Unc | BU |
|---|---|---|---|---|---|---|
| 1994 Proof | 30,000 | Value: 20.00 | | | | |

**3 ROUBLES** **Y# 520** **Weight:** 34.6800 g. **Composition:** 0.9000 Silver 1.0034 oz. ASW **Obverse:** Double-headed eagle **Reverse:** Ryazan Kremlin - city view

| Date | Mintage | F | VF | XF | Unc | BU |
|---|---|---|---|---|---|---|
| 1994 Proof | 30,000 | Value: 22.50 | | | | |

**3 ROUBLES** **Y# 528** **Weight:** 34.6800 g. **Composition:** 0.9000 Silver 1.0034 oz. ASW **Obverse:** Double-headed eagle **Reverse:** Vassili Ivanovich Surikov; Siberian sled scene

| Date | Mintage | F | VF | XF | Unc | BU |
|---|---|---|---|---|---|---|
| 1994 Proof | 40,000 | Value: 20.00 | | | | |

**3 ROUBLES** **Y# 529** **Weight:** 34.6800 g. **Composition:** 0.9000 Silver 1.0034 oz. ASW **Obverse:** Double-headed eagle **Reverse:** Alexander Andreyevich Ivannov

| Date | Mintage | F | VF | XF | Unc | BU |
|---|---|---|---|---|---|---|
| 1994 Proof | 40,000 | Value: 20.00 | | | | |

**3 ROUBLES** **Y# 378** **Composition:** Copper-Nickel **Subject:** Liberation of Warsaw **Obverse:** Kremlin

| Date | Mintage | F | VF | XF | Unc | BU |
|---|---|---|---|---|---|---|
| 1995(l) Proof | 200,000 | Value: 6.00 | | | | |

**3 ROUBLES** **Y# 379** **Composition:** Copper-Nickel **Subject:** Liberation of Budapest **Obverse:** Kremlin

| Date | Mintage | F | VF | XF | Unc | BU |
|---|---|---|---|---|---|---|
| 1995(m) Proof | 200,000 | Value: 6.00 | | | | |

**3 ROUBLES** **Y# 380** **Composition:** Copper-Nickel **Series:** WWII **Subject:** Capture of Konigsberg

| Date | Mintage | F | VF | XF | Unc | BU |
|---|---|---|---|---|---|---|
| 1995(m) Proof | 200,000 | Value: 6.00 | | | | |

**3 ROUBLES** **Y# 381** **Composition:** Copper-Nickel **Series:** WWII **Subject:** Capture of Vienna

| Date | Mintage | F | VF | XF | Unc | BU |
|---|---|---|---|---|---|---|
| 1995(l) Proof | 200,000 | Value: 6.00 | | | | |

**3 ROUBLES** **Y# 383** **Composition:** Copper-Nickel **Series:** WWII **Subject:** Capture of Berlin

| Date | Mintage | F | VF | XF | Unc | BU |
|---|---|---|---|---|---|---|
| 1995(l) Proof | 200,000 | Value: 6.00 | | | | |

**3 ROUBLES** **Y# 384** **Composition:** Copper-Nickel **Series:** WWII **Subject:** German surrender

| Date | Mintage | F | VF | XF | Unc | BU |
|---|---|---|---|---|---|---|
| 1995(l) Proof | 200,000 | Value: 6.00 | | | | |

**3 ROUBLES** **Y# 385** **Composition:** Copper-Nickel **Series:** WWII **Subject:** Liberation of Prague

| Date | Mintage | F | VF | XF | Unc | BU |
|---|---|---|---|---|---|---|
| 1995(m) Proof | 200,000 | Value: 6.00 | | | | |

**3 ROUBLES** **Y# 386** **Composition:** Copper-Nickel **Series:** WWII **Subject:** Surrender of Japanese army in Kwantung.

| Date | Mintage | F | VF | XF | Unc | BU |
|---|---|---|---|---|---|---|
| 1995(m) Proof | 200,000 | Value: 6.00 | | | | |

**3 ROUBLES** **Y# 387** **Composition:** Copper-Nickel **Series:** WWII **Subject:** Japanese formal surrender on battleship U.S.S. Missouri.

| Date | Mintage | F | VF | XF | Unc | BU |
|---|---|---|---|---|---|---|
| 1995 Proof | 200,000 | Value: 6.00 | | | | |

**3 ROUBLES** **Y# 388** **Weight:** 34.5600 g. **Composition:** 0.9000 Silver 1.0000 oz. ASW **Obverse:** Double-headed eagle **Reverse:** Vladimir's Golden Gate

| Date | Mintage | F | VF | XF | Unc | BU |
|---|---|---|---|---|---|---|
| 1995 Proof | 30,000 | Value: 32.50 | | | | |

**3 ROUBLES** **Y# 394** **Weight:** 34.5600 g. **Composition:** 0.9000 Silver 1.0000 oz. ASW **Subject:** Ballet - Sleeping Beauty.

| Date | Mintage | F | VF | XF | Unc | BU |
|---|---|---|---|---|---|---|
| 1995 Proof | 40,000 | Value: 25.00 | | | | |

**3 ROUBLES** **Y# 407** **Weight:** 34.5600 g. **Composition:** 0.9000 Silver 1.0000 oz. ASW **Subject:** 50th Anniversary - United Nations

| Date | Mintage | F | VF | XF | Unc | BU |
|---|---|---|---|---|---|---|
| 1995 Proof | 20,000 | Value: 35.00 | | | | |

**3 ROUBLES** **Y# 445** **Weight:** 34.5600 g. **Composition:** 0.9000 Silver 1.0000 oz. ASW **Reverse:** Smolensk Kremlin

| Date | Mintage | F | VF | XF | Unc | BU |
|---|---|---|---|---|---|---|
| 1995 Proof | 30,000 | Value: 30.00 | | | | |

**3 ROUBLES** **Y# 459** **Weight:** 34.5600 g. **Composition:** 0.9000 Silver 1.0000 oz. ASW **Reverse:** Kizhi Church on Onega Lake

| Date | Mintage | F | VF | XF | Unc | BU |
|---|---|---|---|---|---|---|
| 1995 Proof | 30,000 | Value: 30.00 | | | | |

**3 ROUBLES** **Y# 462** **Weight:** 34.5600 g. **Composition:** 0.9000 Silver 1.0000 oz. ASW **Reverse:** Ronald Amundsen - arctic explorer

| Date | Mintage | F | VF | XF | Unc | BU |
|---|---|---|---|---|---|---|
| 1995 Proof | 25,000 | Value: 32.50 | | | | |

**3 ROUBLES** **Y# 463** **Weight:** 34.5600 g. **Composition:** 0.9000 Silver 1.0000 oz. ASW **Subject:** 200th Anniversary - Russian National Library

| Date | Mintage | F | VF | XF | Unc | BU |
|---|---|---|---|---|---|---|
| 1995 Proof | 15,000 | Value: 32.50 | | | | |

**3 ROUBLES** **Y# 467** **Weight:** 34.5600 g. **Composition:** 0.9000 Silver 1.0000 oz. ASW **Subject:** Russian Millennium of Belgorod

| Date | Mintage | F | VF | XF | Unc | BU |
|---|---|---|---|---|---|---|
| 1995 Proof | 30,000 | Value: 25.00 | | | | |

**3 ROUBLES** **Y# 468** **Weight:** 34.5600 g. **Composition:** 0.9000 Silver 1.0000 oz. ASW **Subject:** Russian Millennium **Reverse:** Novgorod Kremlin.

| Date | Mintage | F | VF | XF | Unc | BU |
|---|---|---|---|---|---|---|
| 1995 Proof | — | Value: 25.00 | | | | |

**3 ROUBLES** **Y# 469** **Weight:** 34.5600 g. **Composition:** 0.9000 Silver 1.0000 oz. ASW **Subject:** Russian Millennium **Reverse:** Spaso - Preobrazhensky Cathedral

| Date | Mintage | F | VF | XF | Unc | BU |
|---|---|---|---|---|---|---|
| 1995 Proof | 40,000 | Value: 22.50 | | | | |

**3 ROUBLES** **Y# 473** **Weight:** 34.5600 g. **Composition:** 0.9000 Silver 1.0000 oz. ASW **Series:** Wildlife **Reverse:** Sable on branch

| Date | Mintage | F | VF | XF | Unc | BU |
|---|---|---|---|---|---|---|
| 1995(l) Matte | 500,000 | — | — | — | 27.50 | — |
| 1995(m) Matte | 500,000 | — | — | — | 27.50 | — |

**3 ROUBLES** **Y# 474** **Weight:** 34.5600 g. **Composition:** 0.9000 Silver 1.0000 oz. ASW **Series:** Wildlife **Reverse:** Lynx

| Date | Mintage | F | VF | XF | Unc | BU |
|---|---|---|---|---|---|---|
| 1995(l) | 25,000 | — | — | — | 35.00 | — |

**3 ROUBLES** **Y# 382** **Composition:** Copper-Nickel **Series:** WWII **Reverse:** American and Russian soldiers in front of their country's respective flag. **Note:** 50-star U.S.A. flag.

| Date | Mintage | F | VF | XF | Unc | BU |
|---|---|---|---|---|---|---|
| 1995(m) Proof | 200,000 | Value: 6.00 | | | | |

**3 ROUBLES** **Y# 461** **Weight:** 34.5600 g. **Composition:** 0.9000 Silver 1.0000 oz. ASW **Note:** Arctic Explorers 1733-43

| Date | Mintage | F | VF | XF | Unc | BU |
|---|---|---|---|---|---|---|
| 1995 Proof | 25,000 | Value: 32.50 | | | | |

**3 ROUBLES** **Y# 470** **Weight:** 34.5600 g. **Composition:** 0.9000 Silver 1.0000 oz. ASW **Reverse:** Ilya the Prophet's Church in Yaroslavl

| Date | Mintage | F | VF | XF | Unc | BU |
|---|---|---|---|---|---|---|
| 1996 Proof | 30,000 | Value: 27.50 | | | | |

**3 ROUBLES** **Y# 477** **Weight:** 34.5600 g. **Composition:** 0.9000 Silver 1.0000 oz. ASW **Subject:** Combat between Peresvet and Chelubey

| Date | Mintage | F | VF | XF | Unc | BU |
|---|---|---|---|---|---|---|
| 1996 Proof | 40,000 | Value: 25.00 | | | | |

**3 ROUBLES** **Y# 478** **Weight:** 34.5600 g. **Composition:** 0.9000 Silver 1.0000 oz. ASW **Reverse:** Old Testament Trinity icon.

| Date | Mintage | F | VF | XF | Unc | BU |
|---|---|---|---|---|---|---|
| 1996 Proof | 40,000 | Value: 28.00 | | | | |

**3 ROUBLES** **Y# 482** **Weight:** 34.5600 g. **Composition:** 0.9000 Silver 1.0000 oz. ASW **Subject:** Nutcracker ballet

| Date | Mintage | F | VF | XF | Unc | BU |
|---|---|---|---|---|---|---|
| 1996 Proof | 25,000 | Value: 30.00 | | | | |

**3 ROUBLES** **Y# 483** **Weight:** 34.5600 g. **Composition:** 0.9000 Silver 1.0000 oz. ASW **Subject:** Nutcracker ballet - duel with mouse king

| Date | Mintage | F | VF | XF | Unc | BU |
|---|---|---|---|---|---|---|
| 1996 Proof | 25,000 | Value: 30.00 | | | | |

**3 ROUBLES** **Y# 490** **Weight:** 34.5600 g. **Composition:** 0.9000 Silver 1.0000 oz. ASW **Reverse:** Kremlin of Kazan

| Date | Mintage | F | VF | XF | Unc | BU |
|---|---|---|---|---|---|---|
| 1996 Proof | 20,000 | Value: 32.50 | | | | |

**3 ROUBLES** **Y# 491** **Weight:** 34.5600 g. **Composition:** 0.9000 Silver 1.0000 oz. ASW **Reverse:** Kremlin of Tobolsk - city view

| Date | Mintage | F | VF | XF | Unc | BU |
|---|---|---|---|---|---|---|
| 1996 Proof | 50,000 | Value: 30.00 | | | | |

**3 ROUBLES** **Y# 510** **Weight:** 34.5600 g. **Composition:** 0.9000 Silver 1.0000 oz. ASW **Reverse:** Alexander Column and Hermitage

| Date | Mintage | F | VF | XF | Unc | BU |
|---|---|---|---|---|---|---|
| 1996 Proof | 20,000 | Value: 32.50 | | | | |

**3 ROUBLES** **Y# 511** **Weight:** 34.5600 g. **Composition:** 0.9000 Silver 1.0000 oz. ASW **Subject:** 300th Anniversary - Russian Navy **Reverse:** Icebreaker

| Date | Mintage | F | VF | XF | Unc | BU |
|---|---|---|---|---|---|---|
| 1996 Proof | 10,000 | Value: 35.00 | | | | |

**3 ROUBLES** **Y# 512** **Weight:** 34.5600 g. **Composition:** 0.9000 Silver 1.0000 oz. ASW **Subject:** 300th Anniversary - Russian Navy **Reverse:** Carrier ship

| Date | Mintage | F | VF | XF | Unc | BU |
|---|---|---|---|---|---|---|
| 1996 Proof | 10,000 | Value: 27.50 | | | | |

**3 ROUBLES** **Y# 535** **Weight:** 34.5600 g. **Composition:** 0.9000 Silver 1.0000 oz. ASW **Series:** Wildlife **Reverse:** Amur tiger

| Date | Mintage | F | VF | XF | Unc | BU |
|---|---|---|---|---|---|---|
| 1996 Proof | 10,000 | Value: 30.00 | | | | |

**3 ROUBLES** **Y# 552** **Weight:** 34.5600 g. **Composition:** 0.9000 Silver 1.0000 oz. ASW **Subject:** 850th Anniversary - Moscow **Reverse:** Workers rebuilding original Moscow, modern skyline behind

| Date | Mintage | F | VF | XF | Unc | BU |
|---|---|---|---|---|---|---|
| 1997 Proof | 40,000 | Value: 30.00 | | | | |

**3 ROUBLES** **Y# 553** **Weight:** 34.5600 g. **Composition:** 0.9000 Silver 1.0000 oz. ASW **Subject:** 850th Anniversary - Moscow **Reverse:** Riverside city view

| Date | Mintage | F | VF | XF | Unc | BU |
|---|---|---|---|---|---|---|
| 1997 Proof | 40,000 | Value: 30.00 | | | | |

**3 ROUBLES** **Y# 560** **Weight:** 34.5600 g. **Composition:** 0.9000 Silver 1.0000 oz. ASW **Reverse:** Monastery of the Saint Virgin in Yaroslavl

| Date | Mintage | F | VF | XF | Unc | BU |
|---|---|---|---|---|---|---|
| 1997 Proof | 15,000 | Value: 37.50 | | | | |

**3 ROUBLES** **Y# 567** **Weight:** 34.5600 g. **Composition:** 0.9000 Silver 1.0000 oz. ASW **Subject:** Ballet - Swan Lake **Reverse:** Four ballerinas

| Date | Mintage | F | VF | XF | Unc | BU |
|---|---|---|---|---|---|---|
| 1997 Proof | 10,000 | Value: 35.00 | | | | |

**3 ROUBLES** **Y# 568** **Weight:** 34.5600 g. **Composition:** 0.9000 Silver 1.0000 oz. ASW **Subject:** Ballet - Swan Lake **Reverse:** Between Rothbart and Prince Siegfried

| Date | Mintage | F | VF | XF | Unc | BU |
|---|---|---|---|---|---|---|
| 1997 Proof | 10,000 | Value: 35.00 | | | | |

**3 ROUBLES** **Y# 575** **Weight:** 34.5600 g. **Composition:** 0.9000 Silver 1.0000 oz. ASW **Subject:** First Anniversary - Russian-Belarus Treaty **Reverse:** Two city views

| Date | Mintage | F | VF | XF | Unc | BU |
|---|---|---|---|---|---|---|
| 1997 Proof | 10,000 | Value: 35.00 | | | | |

**3 ROUBLES** **Y# 585** **Weight:** 34.5600 g. **Composition:** 0.9000 Silver 1.0000 oz. ASW **Subject:** Underroot Nativity of the Virgin Hermitage Monastery of Kursk. **Reverse:** Painting above monastery

| Date | Mintage | F | VF | XF | Unc | BU |
|---|---|---|---|---|---|---|
| 1997 Proof | 15,000 | Value: 37.50 | | | | |

**3 ROUBLES** **Y# 586** **Weight:** 34.5600 g. **Composition:** 0.9000 Silver 1.0000 oz. ASW **Reverse:** Sergy Julievich Witte

| Date | Mintage | F | VF | XF | Unc | BU |
|---|---|---|---|---|---|---|
| 1997 Proof | 10,000 | Value: 32.50 | | | | |

**3 ROUBLES** **Y# 587** **Weight:** 34.5600 g. **Composition:** 0.9000 Silver 1.0000 oz. ASW **Subject:** Year of Reconciliation

| Date | Mintage | F | VF | XF | Unc | BU |
|---|---|---|---|---|---|---|
| 1997 Proof | 7,500 | Value: 38.50 | | | | |

**3 ROUBLES** **Y# 591** **Weight:** 34.5600 g. **Composition:** 0.9000 Silver 1.0000 oz. ASW **Reverse:** Solovetski Monastery

| Date | Mintage | F | VF | XF | Unc | BU |
|---|---|---|---|---|---|---|
| 1997 Proof | 15,000 | Value: 37.50 | | | | |

**3 ROUBLES** **Y# 593** **Weight:** 34.5600 g. **Composition:** 0.9000 Silver 1.0000 oz. ASW **Series:** Wildlife **Reverse:** Polar bear watching walrus

| Date | Mintage | F | VF | XF | Unc | BU |
|---|---|---|---|---|---|---|
| 1997 Proof | 10,000 | Value: 37.50 | | | | |

**3 ROUBLES** **Y# 624** **Weight:** 34.5600 g. **Composition:** 0.9000 Silver 1.0000 oz. ASW **Reverse:** Officer Davydov

| Date | Mintage | F | VF | XF | Unc | BU |
|---|---|---|---|---|---|---|
| 1998 Proof | 15,000 | Value: 25.00 | | | | |

**3 ROUBLES** **Y# 625** **Weight:** 34.5600 g. **Composition:** 0.9000 Silver 1.0000 oz. ASW **Reverse:** "Russian Sosaveta" sculpture

| Date | Mintage | F | VF | XF | Unc | BU |
|---|---|---|---|---|---|---|
| 1998 Proof | 15,000 | Value: 25.00 | | | | |

**3 ROUBLES** **Y# 626** **Weight:** 34.5600 g. **Composition:** 0.9000 Silver 1.0000 oz. ASW **Reverse:** Archangel's head

| Date | Mintage | F | VF | XF | Unc | BU |
|---|---|---|---|---|---|---|
| 1998 Proof | 15,000 | Value: 25.00 | | | | |

**3 ROUBLES** **Y# 627** **Weight:** 34.5600 g. **Composition:** 0.9000 Silver 1.0000 oz. ASW **Reverse:** "Merchant Woman Drinking Tea"

| Date | Mintage | F | VF | XF | Unc | BU |
|---|---|---|---|---|---|---|
| 1998 Proof | 15,000 | Value: 25.00 | | | | |

**3 ROUBLES** **Y# 631** **Weight:** 34.5600 g. **Composition:** 0.9000 Silver 1.0000 oz. ASW **Subject:** Nilo-Stikibebsjaya Hermitage **Reverse:** Saint.

| Date | Mintage | F | VF | XF | Unc | BU |
|---|---|---|---|---|---|---|
| 1998 Proof | 15,000 | Value: 37.50 | | | | |

**3 ROUBLES** **Y# 632** **Weight:** 34.5600 g. **Composition:** 0.9000 Silver 1.0000 oz. ASW **Reverse:** Church, view from bell tower

| Date | Mintage | F | VF | XF | Unc | BU |
|---|---|---|---|---|---|---|
| 1998 Proof | 5,000 | Value: 35.00 | | | | |

**3 ROUBLES** **Y# 633** **Weight:** 34.8800 g. **Composition:** 0.9000 Silver 1.0093 oz. ASW **Subject:** Russian Human Rights Year **Reverse:** Document, people, and map **Edge:** Reeded

| Date | Mintage | F | VF | XF | Unc | BU |
|---|---|---|---|---|---|---|
| 1998 Proof | 15,000 | Value: 37.50 | | | | |

**3 ROUBLES** **Y# 634** **Weight:** 34.7700 g. **Composition:** 0.9000 Silver 1.0061 oz. ASW **Subject:** 275th Anniversary - St. Petersburg University **Obverse:** Double-headed eagle **Reverse:** Four portraits and building

| Date | Mintage | F | VF | XF | Unc | BU |
|---|---|---|---|---|---|---|
| 1999 Proof | 15,000 | Value: 40.00 | | | | |

**3 ROUBLES** **Y# 635** **Weight:** 34.7300 g. **Composition:** 0.9000 Silver 1.0049 oz. ASW **Obverse:** Double-headed eagle **Reverse:** Mardjany Mosque in Kazan

| Date | Mintage | F | VF | XF | Unc | BU |
|---|---|---|---|---|---|---|
| 1999 Proof | 15,000 | Value: 40.00 | | | | |

**3 ROUBLES** **Y# 636** **Weight:** 34.7300 g. **Composition:** 0.9000 Silver 1.0049 oz. ASW **Subject:** 200th Birthday - A. S. Pushkin **Obverse:** Double-headed eagle **Reverse:** Pushkin at his desk

| Date | Mintage | F | VF | XF | Unc | BU |
|---|---|---|---|---|---|---|
| 1999 Proof | 15,000 | Value: 35.00 | | | | |

**3 ROUBLES** **Y# 637** **Weight:** 34.7300 g. **Composition:** 0.9000 Silver 1.0049 oz. ASW **Subject:** 200th Birthday - A. S. Pushkin **Obverse:** Double-headed eagle **Reverse:** Pushkin standing

| Date | Mintage | F | VF | XF | Unc | BU |
|---|---|---|---|---|---|---|
| 1999 Proof | 15,000 | Value: 35.00 | | | | |

**3 ROUBLES** **Y# 638** **Weight:** 34.7300 g. **Composition:** 0.9000 Silver 1.0049 oz. ASW **Subject:** First Tibet Exhibition 1879-1880 **Obverse:** Double-headed eagle **Reverse:** Men on horseback

| Date | Mintage | F | VF | XF | Unc | BU |
|---|---|---|---|---|---|---|
| 1999 Proof | 15,000 | Value: 30.00 | | | | |

**3 ROUBLES** **Y# 639** **Weight:** 34.7300 g. **Composition:** 0.9000 Silver 1.0049 oz. ASW **Subject:** Second Tibet Exhibition 1883-1885 **Obverse:** Double-headed eagle **Reverse:** Camp scene

| Date | Mintage | F | VF | XF | Unc | BU |
|---|---|---|---|---|---|---|
| 1999 Proof | 15,000 | Value: 30.00 | | | | |

**3 ROUBLES** **Y# 644** **Weight:** 34.7100 g. **Composition:** 0.9000 Silver 1.0044 oz. ASW **Subject:** Science Academy. **Obverse:** Double-headed eagle **Reverse:** Allegorical figure, building, portraits, imperial double eagle

| Date | Mintage | F | VF | XF | Unc | BU |
|---|---|---|---|---|---|---|
| 1999 Proof | 5,000 | Value: 40.00 | | | | |

**3 ROUBLES** **Y# 645** **Weight:** 34.7100 g. **Composition:** 0.9000 Silver 1.0044 oz. ASW **Subject:** Estada Kuskovo palace. **Obverse:** Double-headed eagle **Reverse:** Palace from three perspectives

| Date | Mintage | F | VF | XF | Unc | BU |
|---|---|---|---|---|---|---|
| 1999 Proof | 15,000 | Value: 37.50 | | | | |

**3 ROUBLES** **Y# 646** **Weight:** 34.7100 g. **Composition:** 0.9000 Silver 1.0044 oz. ASW **Subject:** Juryev Monastery, Movgorod. **Obverse:** Double-headed eagle **Reverse:** Building view and detail from interior

| Date | Mintage | F | VF | XF | Unc | BU |
|---|---|---|---|---|---|---|
| 1999 Proof | 15,000 | Value: 37.50 | | | | |

**3 ROUBLES** **Y# 647** **Weight:** 34.8800 g. **Composition:** 0.9000 Silver 1.0093 oz. ASW **Subject:** 50th Anniversary - Diplomacy wtih China **Obverse:** Double-headed eagle **Reverse:** Moscow Kremlin and Tiananmen gate

| Date | Mintage | F | VF | XF | Unc | BU |
|---|---|---|---|---|---|---|
| 1999 Proof | 3,000 | Value: 250 | | | | |

**3 ROUBLES** **Y# 657** **Weight:** 34.7300 g. **Composition:** 0.9000 Silver 1.0049 oz. ASW **Subject:** Ballet **Obverse:** Double-headed eagle **Reverse:** Sword fight

| Date | Mintage | F | VF | XF | Unc | BU |
|---|---|---|---|---|---|---|
| 1999 Proof | 10,000 | Value: 45.00 | | | | |

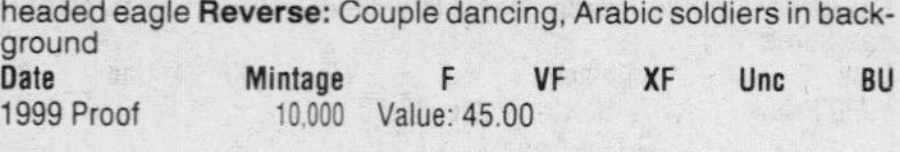

**3 ROUBLES** **Y# 658** **Weight:** 34.7300 g. **Composition:** 0.9000 Silver 1.0049 oz. ASW **Subject:** Ballet **Obverse:** Double-headed eagle **Reverse:** Couple dancing, Arabic soldiers in background

| Date | Mintage | F | VF | XF | Unc | BU |
|---|---|---|---|---|---|---|
| 1999 Proof | 10,000 | Value: 45.00 | | | | |

**3 ROUBLES** **Y# 690** **Weight:** 34.7300 g. **Composition:** 0.9000 Silver 1.0049 oz. ASW **Subject:** Ufa Friendship Monument **Obverse:** Russian eagle **Reverse:** Five people and monument **Edge:** Reeded **Size:** 38.8 mm.

| Date | Mintage | F | VF | XF | Unc | BU |
|---|---|---|---|---|---|---|
| 1999 Proof | 3,000 | Value: 40.00 | | | | |

**3 ROUBLES** **Y# 661** **Weight:** 34.8800 g. **Composition:** 0.9000 Silver 1.0093 oz. ASW **Subject:** World Ice Hockey Championship **Reverse:** Two hockey players **Edge:** Reeded

| Date | Mintage | F | VF | XF | Unc | BU |
|---|---|---|---|---|---|---|
| 2000 Proof | 3,000 | Value: 40.00 | | | | |

**3 ROUBLES** **Y# 671** **Weight:** 34.7600 g. **Composition:** 0.9000 Silver 1.0058 oz. ASW **Series:** Olympics **Reverse:** 2000 Olympic design **Edge:** Reeded

| Date | Mintage | F | VF | XF | Unc | BU |
|---|---|---|---|---|---|---|
| 2000 Proof | 5,000 | Value: 45.00 | | | | |

**3 ROUBLES** **Y# 673** **Weight:** 34.6700 g. **Composition:** 0.9990 Silver 1.1135 oz. ASW **Subject:** Soccer **Obverse:** Double eagle **Reverse:** Two soccer players, map, and net **Edge:** Reeded

| Date | Mintage | F | VF | XF | Unc | BU |
|---|---|---|---|---|---|---|
| 2000 Proof | 3,000 | Value: 40.00 | | | | |

**3 ROUBLES** **Y# 674** **Weight:** 34.9400 g. **Composition:** 0.9000 Silver 1.0110 oz. ASW **Series:** WWII **Subject:** 55th Anniversary - WWII **Obverse:** Seated soldier **Reverse:** Soviet Order of Glory **Edge:** Lettered **Edge Lettering:** BANK of RUSSIA THREE ROUBLES 2000

| Date | Mintage | F | VF | XF | Unc | BU |
|---|---|---|---|---|---|---|
| 2000 Proof | 5,000 | Value: 45.00 | | | | |

**3 ROUBLES** **Y# 705** **Weight:** 34.8800 g. **Composition:** 0.9000 Silver 1.0093 oz. ASW **Subject:** St. Nicholas Monastery **Obverse:** Two headed eagle **Reverse:** Saint and buildings **Edge:** Reeded **Size:** 39 mm.

| Date | Mintage | F | VF | XF | Unc | BU |
|---|---|---|---|---|---|---|
| 2000(m) Proof | 5,000 | Value: 45.00 | | | | |

**3 ROUBLES** **Y# 706** **Weight:** 34.8800 g. **Composition:** 0.9000 Silver 1.0093 oz. ASW **Subject:** Novgorod Kremlin **Obverse:** Two headed eagle **Reverse:** Buildings

| Date | Mintage | F | VF | XF | Unc | BU |
|---|---|---|---|---|---|---|
| 2000(m) Proof | 5,000 | Value: 45.00 | | | | |

**3 ROUBLES** **Y# 707** **Weight:** 34.8800 g. **Composition:** 0.9000 Silver 1.0093 oz. ASW **Subject:** City of Pushkin **Obverse:** Two headed eagle **Reverse:** Park and city view

| Date | Mintage | F | VF | XF | Unc | BU |
|---|---|---|---|---|---|---|
| 2000(m) Proof | 5,000 | Value: 45.00 | | | | |

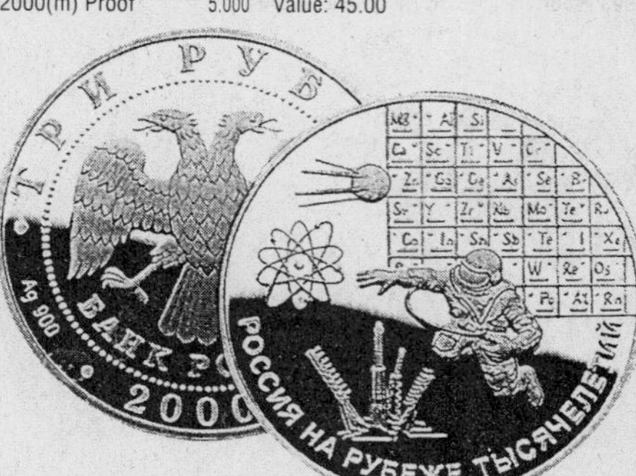


**3 ROUBLES** **Y# 708** **Weight:** 34.8800 g. **Composition:** 0.9000 Silver 1.0093 oz. ASW **Series:** Third Mellennium **Subject:** Science **Obverse:** Two headed eagle **Reverse:** Astronaut, atomic elements chart etc **Edge:** Reeded **Size:** 39 mm.

| Date | Mintage | F | VF | XF | Unc | BU |
|---|---|---|---|---|---|---|
| 2000(m) Proof | 5,000 | Value: 45.00 | | | | |

**3 ROUBLES** **Y# 709** **Weight:** 34.8800 g. **Composition:** 0.9000 Silver 1.0093 oz. ASW **Series:** Third Millennium **Subject:** Human Role **Obverse:** Two headed eagle. **Reverse:** People between cog wheel and computer.

| Date | Mintage | F | VF | XF | Unc | BU |
|---|---|---|---|---|---|---|
| 2000(m) Proof | 5,000 | Value: 45.00 | | | | |

**3 ROUBLES** **Y# 714** **Weight:** 34.8800 g. **Composition:** 0.9000 Silver 1.0093 oz. ASW **Subject:** 140th Anniversary - State Bank of Russia **Obverse:** Two headed eagle **Reverse:** Seated allegorical woman.

| Date | Mintage | F | VF | XF | Unc | BU |
|---|---|---|---|---|---|---|
| 2000(m) Proof | 3,000 | Value: 45.00 | | | | |

**3 ROUBLES** **Y# 716** **Weight:** 34.8800 g. **Composition:** 1.0093 Silver **Subject:** Field Marshal Suvorov in Switzerland **Obverse:** Two headed eagle **Reverse:** Battle scene

| Date | Mintage | F | VF | XF | Unc | BU |
|---|---|---|---|---|---|---|
| 2000(sp) Proof | 5,000 | Value: 45.00 | | | | |

**3 ROUBLES** **Y# 722** **Weight:** 34.8800 g. **Composition:** 0.9000 Silver 1.0093 oz. ASW **Subject:** Snow Leopard **Obverse:** Two headed eagle **Reverse:** Leopard on log

| Date | Mintage | F | VF | XF | Unc | BU |
|---|---|---|---|---|---|---|
| 2000(m) Proof | 5,000 | Value: 45.00 | | | | |

**3 ROUBLES** **Y# 677** **Weight:** 34.8800 g. **Composition:** 0.9000 Silver 1.0093 oz. ASW **Subject:** 225 Years - Bolshoi Theater **Obverse:** Two headed eagle. **Reverse:** Five men, one with pole ax. **Edge:** Reeded. **Size:** 39 mm.

| Date | Mintage | F | VF | XF | Unc | BU |
|---|---|---|---|---|---|---|
| 2001 Proof | 7,500 | Value: 35.00 | | | | |

**3 ROUBLES** **Y# 680** **Weight:** 34.8800 g. **Composition:** 0.9000 Silver 1.0093 oz. ASW **Subject:** Yuri Gagarin **Obverse:** Two headed eagle. **Reverse:** Uniformed portrait holding dove. **Edge:** Reeded. **Size:** 39 mm.

| Date | Mintage | F | VF | XF | Unc | BU |
|---|---|---|---|---|---|---|
| 2001 Proof | 7,500 | Value: 35.00 | | | | |

**3 ROUBLES** **Y# 682** **Weight:** 34.8800 g. **Composition:** 0.9000 Silver 1.0093 oz. ASW **Subject:** Siberian Exploration **Obverse:** Two headed eagle. **Reverse:** Men riding horses, deer and sleds. **Edge:** Reeded. **Size:** 39 mm.

| Date | Mintage | F | VF | XF | Unc | BU |
|---|---|---|---|---|---|---|
| 2001 Proof | 5,000 | Value: 35.00 | | | | |

**5 ROUBLES** **Y# 312** **Composition:** Brass Clad Steel **Obverse:** Double-headed eagle

| Date | Mintage | F | VF | XF | Unc | BU |
|---|---|---|---|---|---|---|
| 1992Л | — | — | — | — | 1.75 | — |
| 1992M | — | — | — | — | 1.50 | — |
| 1992(m) | — | — | — | — | 2.00 | — |
| 1992(l) | — | — | — | — | 2.50 | — |

**5 ROUBLES** **Y# 322** **Composition:** Brass Clad Steel **Subject:** Kazakhstan

| Date | Mintage | F | VF | XF | Unc | BU |
|---|---|---|---|---|---|---|
| 1992(l) Proof | 200,000 | Value: 10.00 | | | | |

**5 ROUBLES** **Y# 324** **Composition:** Brass Clad Steel **Subject:** Troitsk - Sergievsk Monastery

| Date | Mintage | F | VF | XF | Unc | BU |
|---|---|---|---|---|---|---|
| 1993(l) | — | — | — | — | 6.00 | — |
| 1993(l) Proof | — | Value: 9.00 | | | | |

**5 ROUBLES** **Y# 339** **Composition:** Copper-Nickel **Subject:** 2500 Years of Merv Minaret, Turkmenistan

| Date | Mintage | F | VF | XF | Unc | BU |
|---|---|---|---|---|---|---|
| 1993(l) | — | — | — | — | 4.00 | — |
| 1993(l) Proof | 6 | Value: 6.50 | | | | |

**5 ROUBLES** **Y# 420** **Weight:** 7.7758 g. **Composition:** 0.9990 Palladium .2500 oz. **Subject:** Ballet **Reverse:** Ballerina.

| Date | Mintage | F | VF | XF | Unc | BU |
|---|---|---|---|---|---|---|
| 1993 | 6,000 | — | — | — | 200 | — |
| 1993 Proof | — | Value: 250 | | | | |

**5 ROUBLES** **Y# 431** **Weight:** 7.7758 g. **Composition:** 0.9990 Palladium .2500 oz. **Subject:** Ballet - Sleeping Beauty **Reverse:** Ballerina.

| Date | Mintage | F | VF | XF | Unc | BU |
|---|---|---|---|---|---|---|
| 1994 | 4,000 | — | — | — | 275 | — |
| 1994 Proof | 5,000 | Value: 300 | | | | |

**5 ROUBLES** **Y# 400** **Composition:** Aluminum-Bronze **Series:** WWII **Reverse:** Infantry officer leading attack

| Date | Mintage | F | VF | XF | Unc | BU |
|---|---|---|---|---|---|---|
| 1995 | 200,000 | — | — | — | 1.50 | — |

**Note:** In mint sets only

**5 ROUBLES** **Y# 435** **Weight:** 7.7758 g. **Composition:** 0.9990 Palladium .2500 oz. **Reverse:** Infantry officer leading attack.

| Date | Mintage | F | VF | XF | Unc | BU |
|---|---|---|---|---|---|---|
| 1995 Proof | 4,000 | Value: 225 | | | | |

**5 ROUBLES** **Y# 505** **Composition:** Brass **Subject:** 300th Anniversary - Russian Fleet

| Date | Mintage | F | VF | XF | Unc | BU |
|---|---|---|---|---|---|---|
| 1996 | 100,000 | — | — | — | 2.50 | — |

**Note:** In mint sets only

**5 ROUBLES** **Y# 606.1** **Composition:** Copper-Nickel Clad Copper **Reverse:** Denomination **Edge:** Reeded and plain sections

| Date | Mintage | F | VF | XF | Unc | BU |
|---|---|---|---|---|---|---|
| 1997(m) | — | — | — | — | 2.00 | — |
| 1997(sp) | — | — | — | — | 2.00 | — |

**5 ROUBLES** **Y# 606.2** **Composition:** Copper-Nickel Clad Copper **Edge:** Plain

| Date | Mintage | F | VF | XF | Unc | BU |
|---|---|---|---|---|---|---|
| 1997(m) | — | — | — | — | 2.00 | — |
| 1997(sp) Reported, not confirmed | — | — | — | — | — | — |

**10 ROUBLES** **Y# 307** **Ring Composition:** Copper-Nickel **Center Composition:** Aluminum-Bronze **Series:** Wildlife **Reverse:** Red-breasted Kazarka

| Date | Mintage | F | VF | XF | Unc | BU |
|---|---|---|---|---|---|---|
| 1992(l) | 300,000 | — | — | — | 2.00 | — |

**10 ROUBLES** **Y# 308** **Center Composition:** Aluminum-Bronze **Series:** Wildlife **Reverse:** Tiger

| Date | Mintage | F | VF | XF | Unc | BU |
|---|---|---|---|---|---|---|
| 1992(l) | 300,000 | — | — | — | 2.50 | — |

**10 ROUBLES** **Y# 309** **Center Composition:** Aluminum-Bronze **Series:** Wildlife **Reverse:** Cobra

| Date | Mintage | F | VF | XF | Unc | BU |
|---|---|---|---|---|---|---|
| 1992(l) | 300,000 | — | — | — | 2.50 | — |

**10 ROUBLES** **Y# 313** **Composition:** Copper-Nickel **Obverse:** Double-headed eagle **Reverse:** Denomination **Edge:** Reeded **Note:** St. Petersburg minted coins have a round top 3 in date. Moscow minted coins have a flat top 3 in date.

| Date | Mintage | F | VF | XF | Unc | BU |
|---|---|---|---|---|---|---|
| 1992(l) | — | — | — | — | 1.50 | — |
| 1992(m) | — | — | — | — | 2.00 | — |
| 1993(l) | — | — | — | — | 1.50 | — |
| 1993(m) | — | — | — | — | 10.00 | — |

**10 ROUBLES** **Y# 313a** **Composition:** Copper-Nickel Clad Steel **Edge:** Plain **Note:** St. Petersburg minted coins have a round top 3 in date. Moscow minted coins have a flat top 3 in date.

| Date | Mintage | F | VF | XF | Unc | BU |
|---|---|---|---|---|---|---|
| 1992(m) | — | — | — | — | 10.00 | — |
| 1993(l) | — | — | — | — | 1.50 | — |
| 1993(m) | — | — | — | — | 1.50 | — |

**10 ROUBLES** **Y# 352** **Weight:** 15.5517 g. **Composition:** 0.9990 Palladium .5000 oz. **Series:** Olympics **Reverse:** Cubertin and Butovsky

| Date | Mintage | F | VF | XF | Unc | BU |
|---|---|---|---|---|---|---|
| 1993 Proof | 7,500 | Value: 550 | | | | |

**10 ROUBLES** **Y# 416** **Weight:** 1.5552 g. **Composition:** 0.9990 Gold .0500 oz. AGW **Subject:** Ballet **Reverse:** Ballerina

| Date | Mintage | F | VF | XF | Unc | BU |
|---|---|---|---|---|---|---|
| 1993 | 57,000 | — | — | — | 45.00 | — |
| 1993 Proof | — | Value: 60.00 | | | | |

**10 ROUBLES** **Y# 421** **Weight:** 15.5500 g. **Composition:** 0.9990 Palladium .5000 oz.

| Date | Mintage | F | VF | XF | Unc | BU |
|---|---|---|---|---|---|---|
| 1993 | 4,000 | — | — | — | 350 | — |
| 1993 Proof | 2,000 | Value: 400 | | | | |

**10 ROUBLES** **Y# 424** **Weight:** 1.5552 g. **Composition:** 0.9990 Gold .0500 oz. AGW

| Date | Mintage | F | VF | XF | Unc | BU |
|---|---|---|---|---|---|---|
| 1994 Proof | 7,000 | Value: 60.00 | | | | |

**10 ROUBLES** **Y# 432** **Weight:** 15.5500 g. **Composition:** 0.9990 Palladium .5000 oz.

| Date | Mintage | F | VF | XF | Unc | BU |
|---|---|---|---|---|---|---|
| 1994 | 3,000 | — | — | — | 350 | — |
| 1994 Proof | 1,500 | Value: 400 | | | | |

**10 ROUBLES** **Y# 401** **Composition:** Copper-Nickel **Series:** WWII **Reverse:** Munitions workers.

| Date | Mintage | F | VF | XF | Unc | BU |
|---|---|---|---|---|---|---|
| 1995 | 200,000 | — | — | — | 2.00 | — |

**Note:** In mint sets only

**10 ROUBLES** **Y# 436** **Weight:** 15.5500 g. **Composition:** 0.9990 Palladium .5000 oz. **Subject:** Ballet - Sleeping Beauty **Reverse:** Ballerina

| Date | Mintage | F | VF | XF | Unc | BU |
|---|---|---|---|---|---|---|
| 1995 Proof | 1,500 | Value: 400 | | | | |

**10 ROUBLES** **Y# 438** **Weight:** 1.5552 g. **Composition:** 0.9990 Gold .0500 oz. AGW

| Date | Mintage | F | VF | XF | Unc | BU |
|---|---|---|---|---|---|---|
| 1995 Proof | 7,000 | Value: 60.00 | | | | |

**10 ROUBLES** **Y# 484** **Weight:** 1.5552 g. **Composition:** 0.9990 Gold .0500 oz. AGW **Subject:** Ballet **Reverse:** Nutcracker doll

| Date | Mintage | F | VF | XF | Unc | BU |
|---|---|---|---|---|---|---|
| 1996 Proof | 7,500 | Value: 60.00 | | | | |

**10 ROUBLES** **Y# 506** **Composition:** Copper-Nickel **Subject:** 300th Anniversary - Russian fleet **Reverse:** Cargo ship

| Date | Mintage | F | VF | XF | Unc | BU |
|---|---|---|---|---|---|---|
| 1996 | 100,000 | — | — | — | 3.00 | — |

**Note:** In mint sets only

**10 ROUBLES** **Y# 569** **Weight:** 1.5500 g. **Composition:** 0.9990 Gold .0498 oz. AGW **Subject:** Ballet - Swan Lake

| Date | Mintage | F | VF | XF | Unc | BU |
|---|---|---|---|---|---|---|
| 1997 Proof | 2,500 | Value: 65.00 | | | | |

**10 ROUBLES** **Y# 695** **Weight:** 1.5500 g. **Composition:** 0.9990 Gold .0499 oz. AGW **Subject:** Russian Ballet **Obverse:** Two headed eagle **Reverse:** Standing knight Jean de Brienne **Edge:** Reeded **Size:** 12 mm.

| Date | Mintage | F | VF | XF | Unc | BU |
|---|---|---|---|---|---|---|
| 1999(m) Proof | 2,500 | Value: 65.00 | | | | |

**10 ROUBLES** **Y# 670** **Ring Composition:** Brass **Center Weight:** 8.2600 g. **Center Composition:** Copper-Nickel **Series:** WWII **Subject:** 55th Anniversary - Victorious Conclusion of WWII **Obverse:** Denomination **Reverse:** Infantry officer leading an assault **Edge:** Reeded and lettered **Note:** Struck at St. Petersburg Mint.

| Date | Mintage | F | VF | XF | Unc | BU |
|---|---|---|---|---|---|---|
| 2000(sp) | 10,000,000 | — | — | — | 3.00 | — |
| 2000(m) | 10,000,000 | — | — | — | 3.00 | — |

**10 ROUBLES** **Y# 676** **Ring Weight:** 8.2200 g. **Ring Composition:** Brass **Center Composition:** Copper-Nickel **Subject:** Yuri Gagarin **Obverse:** Denomination with latent image in zero, and date **Reverse:** Helmeted portrait **Edge:** Reeding over denomination **Size:** 27 mm.

| Date | Mintage | F | VF | XF | Unc | BU |
|---|---|---|---|---|---|---|
| 2001 | — | — | — | — | 3.00 | — |

**10 ROUBLES** **Y# 686** **Weight:** 1.6100 g. **Composition:** 0.9990 Gold .0517 oz. AGW **Subject:** Bolshoi Theater 225 Years **Obverse:** Two headed eagle. **Reverse:** Building above number 225. **Edge:** Reeded. **Size:** 12 mm.

| Date | Mintage | F | VF | XF | Unc | BU |
|---|---|---|---|---|---|---|
| 2001 Proof | 3,000 | Value: 50.00 | | | | |

**20 ROUBLES** **Y# 314** **Composition:** Copper-Nickel **Obverse:** Double-headed eagle **Reverse:** Denomination **Edge:** Reeded and plain sections

| Date | Mintage | F | VF | XF | Unc | BU |
|---|---|---|---|---|---|---|
| 1992(l) | — | — | — | — | 2.00 | — |
| 1992(m) | — | — | — | — | 2.50 | — |
| 1993(m) | — | — | — | — | 20.00 | — |

**20 ROUBLES** **Y#314a** **Composition:** Copper-Nickel Clad Steel **Edge:** Plain

| Date | Mintage | F | VF | XF | Unc | BU |
|---|---|---|---|---|---|---|
| 1993(l) | — | — | — | — | 2.50 | — |
| 1993(m) | — | — | — | — | 2.50 | — |

**20 ROUBLES** **Y# 402** **Composition:** Copper-Nickel **Series:** WWII **Reverse:** Soldiers and tanks

| Date | Mintage | F | VF | XF | Unc | BU |
|---|---|---|---|---|---|---|
| 1995 | 200,000 | — | — | — | 3.00 | — |

**Note:** In mint sets only

**20 ROUBLES** **Y# 507** **Composition:** Copper-Nickel **Subject:** 300th Anniversary - Russian Fleet **Reverse:** Scientific research ship

| Date | Mintage | F | VF | XF | Unc | BU |
|---|---|---|---|---|---|---|
| 1996 | 100,000 | — | — | — | 4.50 | — |

**Note:** In mint sets only

**25 ROUBLES** **Y# 353** **Weight:** 31.1035 g. **Composition:** 0.9990 Palladium 1.0000 oz. **Reverse:** Catherine the Great

| Date | Mintage | F | VF | XF | Unc | BU |
|---|---|---|---|---|---|---|
| 1992 Proof | 5,500 | Value: 775 | | | | |

**25 ROUBLES** **Y# 395** **Weight:** 3.1104 g. **Composition:** 0.9990 Platinum .1000 oz. APW **Subject:** Ballet **Reverse:** Ballerina

| Date | Mintage | F | VF | XF | Unc | BU |
|---|---|---|---|---|---|---|
| 1993 | 750 | — | — | — | 125 | — |

**Note:** Proof sets only

**25 ROUBLES** **Y# 410** **Weight:** 3.1100 g. **Composition:** 0.9990 Gold .1000 oz. AGW **Series:** Wildlife **Reverse:** Bear

| Date | Mintage | F | VF | XF | Unc | BU |
|---|---|---|---|---|---|---|
| 1993 Proof | 2,000 | Value: 120 | | | | |

**25 ROUBLES** **Y# 417** **Weight:** 3.1100 g. **Composition:** 0.9990 Gold .1000 oz. AGW **Subject:** Ballet

| Date | Mintage | F | VF | XF | Unc | BU |
|---|---|---|---|---|---|---|
| 1993 | 12,500 | — | — | — | 100 | — |
| 1993 Proof | 6,000 | Value: 120 | | | | |

**25 ROUBLES** **Y# 422** **Weight:** 31.1035 g. **Composition:** 0.9990 Palladium 1.0000 oz.

| Date | Mintage | F | VF | XF | Unc | BU |
|---|---|---|---|---|---|---|
| 1993 | 3,000 | — | — | — | 750 | — |
| 1993 Proof | 2,000 | Value: 775 | | | | |

**25 ROUBLES** **Y# 452** **Weight:** 31.1035 g. **Composition:** 0.9990 Palladium 1.0000 oz. **Reverse:** M. P. Musorgsky

| Date | Mintage | F | VF | XF | Unc | BU |
|---|---|---|---|---|---|---|
| 1993 Proof | 5,500 | Value: 775 | | | | |

**25 ROUBLES** **Y# 517** **Weight:** 31.1035 g. **Composition:** 0.9990 Palladium 1.0000 oz. **Subject:** First Russian Global Circumnavigation **Reverse:** Sloop "Nadyezhda"

| Date | Mintage | F | VF | XF | Unc | BU |
|---|---|---|---|---|---|---|
| 1993 Proof | 25,000 | Value: 775 | | | | |

**25 ROUBLES** **Y# 518** **Weight:** 31.1035 g. **Composition:** 0.9990 Palladium 1.0000 oz. **Reverse:** Sloop "Neva"

| Date | Mintage | F | VF | XF | Unc | BU |
|---|---|---|---|---|---|---|
| 1993 Proof | 25,000 | Value: 775 | | | | |

**25 ROUBLES** **Y# 406** **Weight:** 156.0400 g. **Composition:** 0.9990 Silver 5.0118 oz. ASW **Subject:** Ballet **Note:** Illustration reduced.

| Date | Mintage | F | VF | XF | Unc | BU |
|---|---|---|---|---|---|---|
| 1993 Proof | 10,000 | Value: 85.00 | | | | |

**25 ROUBLES** **Y# 390** **Weight:** 172.8300 g. **Composition:** 0.9000 Silver 5.0009 oz. ASW **Reverse:** Trans-Siberian railroad. Similar to Y#398.

| Date | Mintage | F | VF | XF | Unc | BU |
|---|---|---|---|---|---|---|
| 1994 Proof | 3,000 | Value: 175 | | | | |

**25 ROUBLES** **Y# 423** **Weight:** 172.8300 g. **Composition:** 0.9000 Silver 5.0009 oz. ASW **Subject:** Ballet

| Date | Mintage | F | VF | XF | Unc | BU |
|---|---|---|---|---|---|---|
| 1994 Proof | 7,500 | Value: 150 | | | | |

**25 ROUBLES** **Y# 425** **Weight:** 3.1100 g. **Composition:** 0.9990 Gold .1000 oz. AGW

| Date | Mintage | F | VF | XF | Unc | BU |
|---|---|---|---|---|---|---|
| 1994 Proof | 5,000 | Value: 110 | | | | |

**25 ROUBLES** **Y# 428** **Weight:** 3.1104 g. **Composition:** 0.9990 Platinum .1000 oz. APW

| Date | Mintage | F | VF | XF | Unc | BU |
|---|---|---|---|---|---|---|
| 1994 Proof | 900 | Value: 150 | | | | |

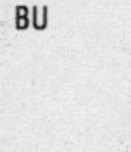

**25 ROUBLES** **Y# 433** **Weight:** 31.1035 g. **Composition:** 0.9990 Palladium 1.0000 oz.

| Date | Mintage | F | VF | XF | Unc | BU |
|---|---|---|---|---|---|---|
| 1994 | 2,000 | — | — | — | 750 | — |
| 1994 Proof | 1,500 | Value: 775 | | | | |

**25 ROUBLES** **Y# 521** **Weight:** 31.1035 g. **Composition:** 0.9990 Palladium 1.0000 oz. **Reverse:** Sloop "Mirny"

| Date | Mintage | F | VF | XF | Unc | BU |
|---|---|---|---|---|---|---|
| 1994 Proof | 4,000 | Value: 775 | | | | |

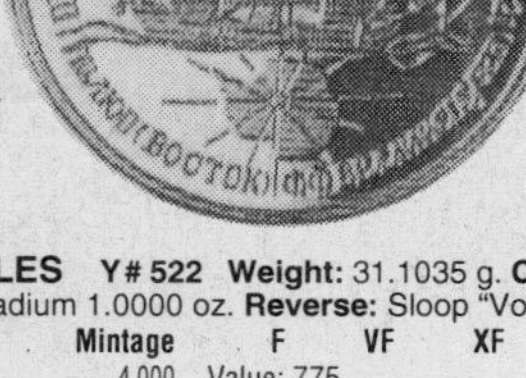

**25 ROUBLES** **Y# 522** **Weight:** 31.1035 g. **Composition:** 0.9990 Palladium 1.0000 oz. **Reverse:** Sloop "Vostok"

| Date | Mintage | F | VF | XF | Unc | BU |
|---|---|---|---|---|---|---|
| 1994 Proof | 4,000 | Value: 775 | | | | |

**25 ROUBLES** **Y# 524** **Weight:** 3.1103 g. **Composition:** 0.9990 Gold .1000 oz. AGW **Series:** Wildlife **Reverse:** Sable's head

| Date | Mintage | F | VF | XF | Unc | BU |
|---|---|---|---|---|---|---|
| 1994 Proof | 4,000 | Value: 100 | | | | |

**25 ROUBLES** **Y# 530** **Weight:** 31.1035 g. **Composition:** 0.9990 Palladium 1.0000 oz. **Reverse:** Andrei Ruble

| Date | Mintage | F | VF | XF | Unc | BU |
|---|---|---|---|---|---|---|
| 1994 Proof | 6,000 | Value: 775 | | | | |

**25 ROUBLES** **Y# 534** **Weight:** 4.3198 g. **Composition:** 0.9000 Gold .1245 oz. AGW **Reverse:** Baikal railroad tunnel.

| Date | Mintage | F | VF | XF | Unc | BU |
|---|---|---|---|---|---|---|
| 1994 Proof | 3,000 | Value: 115 | | | | |

**25 ROUBLES** **Y# 437** **Weight:** 31.1035 g. **Composition:** 0.9990 Palladium 1.0000 oz.

| Date | Mintage | F | VF | XF | Unc | BU |
|---|---|---|---|---|---|---|
| 1995 Proof | 1,500 | Value: 775 | | | | |

**25 ROUBLES** **Y# 439** **Weight:** 3.1100 g. **Composition:** 0.9990 Gold .1000 oz. AGW

| Date | Mintage | F | VF | XF | Unc | BU |
|---|---|---|---|---|---|---|
| 1995 Proof | 5,000 | Value: 120 | | | | |

**25 ROUBLES** **Y# 442** **Weight:** 3.1104 g. **Composition:** 0.9990 Platinum .1000 oz. APW

| Date | Mintage | F | VF | XF | Unc | BU |
|---|---|---|---|---|---|---|
| 1995 Proof | 900 | Value: 150 | | | | |

**25 ROUBLES** **Y# 472** **Weight:** 155.5000 g. **Composition:** 0.9000 Silver 4.4995 oz. ASW **Subject:** First Station at North Pole **Reverse:** Men, ship, and airplane

| Date | Mintage | F | VF | XF | Unc | BU |
|---|---|---|---|---|---|---|
| 1995 Proof | 5,000 | Value: 175 | | | | |

**25 ROUBLES** **Y# 475** **Weight:** 31.1035 g. **Composition:** 0.9990 Palladium 1.0000 oz. **Reverse:** Alexander Nevski

| Date | Mintage | F | VF | XF | Unc | BU |
|---|---|---|---|---|---|---|
| 1995 Proof | 5,425 | Value: 775 | | | | |

**25 ROUBLES** **Y# 471** **Weight:** 155.5000 g. **Composition:** 0.9000 Silver 4.4995 oz. ASW **Series:** Wildlife **Reverse:** Lynx on log **Note:** Illustration reduced.

| Date | Mintage | F | VF | XF | Unc | BU |
|---|---|---|---|---|---|---|
| 1995 Proof | 5,000 | Value: 115 | | | | |

**25 ROUBLES** **Y# 485** **Weight:** 155.5175 g. **Composition:** 0.9990 Silver 5.0000 oz. ASW **Subject:** Ballet - Nutcracker **Reverse:** Children dancing around tree **Note:** Illustration reduced.

| Date | Mintage | F | VF | XF | Unc | BU |
|---|---|---|---|---|---|---|
| 1996 Proof | 5,000 | Value: 175 | | | | |

**25 ROUBLES** **Y# 536** **Weight:** 172.7972 g. **Composition:** 0.9000 Silver 5.0000 oz. ASW **Series:** Wildlife **Reverse:** Amur tiger **Note:** Illustration reduced.

| Date | Mintage | F | VF | XF | Unc | BU |
|---|---|---|---|---|---|---|
| 1996 Proof | — | Value: 125 | | | | |

**25 ROUBLES** **Y# 542** **Weight:** 172.7972 g. **Composition:** 0.9000 Silver 5.0000 oz. ASW **Subject:** Battle of Gangut, 1714 **Note:** Illustration reduced.

| Date | Mintage | F | VF | XF | Unc | BU |
|---|---|---|---|---|---|---|
| 1996 Proof | 3,000 | Value: 175 | | | | |

**25 ROUBLES** **Y# 543** **Weight:** 172.7972 g. **Composition:** 0.9000 Silver 5.0000 oz. ASW **Subject:** Battle of Chesme, 1770 **Note:** Illustration reduced.

| Date | Mintage | F | VF | XF | Unc | BU |
|---|---|---|---|---|---|---|
| 1996 Proof | 3,000 | Value: 175 | | | | |

**25 ROUBLES** **Y# 544** **Weight:** 172.7972 g. **Composition:** 0.9000 Silver 5.0000 oz. ASW **Subject:** Battle of Corfu, 1779 **Note:** Illustration reduced.

| Date | Mintage | F | VF | XF | Unc | BU |
|---|---|---|---|---|---|---|
| 1996 Proof | 3,000 | Value: 175 | | | | |

**25 ROUBLES** **Y# 545** **Weight:** 172.7972 g. **Composition:** 0.9000 Silver 5.0000 oz. ASW **Subject:** Battle of Sinop, 1853 **Note:** Illustration reduced.

| Date | Mintage | F | VF | XF | Unc | BU |
|---|---|---|---|---|---|---|
| 1996 Proof | 3,000 | Value: 175 | | | | |

**25 ROUBLES** **Y# 486** **Weight:** 3.1103 g. **Composition:** 0.9990 Gold .1000 oz. AGW **Subject:** Ballet - Nutcracker **Reverse:** Marsha with nutcracker doll

| Date | Mintage | F | VF | XF | Unc | BU |
|---|---|---|---|---|---|---|
| 1996 Proof | 5,000 | Value: 125 | | | | |

**25 ROUBLES** **Y# 479** **Weight:** 155.5000 g. **Composition:** 0.9000 Silver 4.4995 oz. ASW **Subject:** Battle of Kulikova Plains

| Date | Mintage | F | VF | XF | Unc | BU |
|---|---|---|---|---|---|---|
| 1996 Proof | 5,000 | Value: 175 | | | | |

**25 ROUBLES** **Y# 554** **Weight:** 172.7972 g. **Composition:** 0.9000 Silver 5.0000 oz. ASW **Subject:** 850th Anniversary - Moscow **Reverse:** Monument

| Date | Mintage | F | VF | XF | Unc | BU |
|---|---|---|---|---|---|---|
| 1997 Proof | 5,000 | Value: 155 | | | | |

**25 ROUBLES** **Y# 571** **Weight:** 3.1103 g. **Composition:** 0.9990 Gold .1000 oz. AGW **Subject:** Ballet - Swan Lake **Reverse:** Winged figure of Rothbart and swan

| Date | Mintage | F | VF | XF | Unc | BU |
|---|---|---|---|---|---|---|
| 1997 Proof | 2,000 | Value: 175 | | | | |

**25 ROUBLES** **Y# 594** **Weight:** 172.7972 g. **Composition:** 0.9000 Silver 5.0000 oz. ASW **Series:** Wildlife **Reverse:** Polar bear, caribou, seal

| Date | Mintage | F | VF | XF | Unc | BU |
|---|---|---|---|---|---|---|
| 1997 Proof | 3,000 | Value: 175 | | | | |

**25 ROUBLES** Y#622 **Weight:** 173.2900 g. **Composition:** 0.9000 Silver 5.0143 oz. ASW **Series:** Wildlife **Reverse:** Sable

| Date | Mintage | F | VF | XF | Unc | BU |
|---|---|---|---|---|---|---|
| 1997 Proof | 1,000 | Value: 185 | | | | |

**25 ROUBLES** Y#570 **Weight:** 172.7972 g. **Composition:** 0.9000 Silver 5.0000 oz. ASW **Subject:** Ballet - Swan Lake **Reverse:** Prince Siegfried dancing with Odile **Note:** Illustration reduced.

| Date | Mintage | F | VF | XF | Unc | BU |
|---|---|---|---|---|---|---|
| 1997 Proof | 3,000 | Value: 175 | | | | |

**25 ROUBLES** Y#592 **Weight:** 172.7972 g. **Composition:** 0.9000 Silver 5.0000 oz. ASW **Series:** Wildlife **Reverse:** Bear with cub **Note:** Illustration reduced.

| Date | Mintage | F | VF | XF | Unc | BU |
|---|---|---|---|---|---|---|
| 1997 Proof | 1,000 | Value: 175 | | | | |

**25 ROUBLES** Y#691 **Weight:** 173.2900 g. **Composition:** 0.9000 Silver 5.0143 oz. ASW **Subject:** Alexander Pushkin **Obverse:** Two headed eagle **Reverse:** Walking figure with hat and cane **Edge:** Reeded **Size:** 60 mm. **Note:** Illustration reduced. Actual size: 60mm.

| Date | Mintage | F | VF | XF | Unc | BU |
|---|---|---|---|---|---|---|
| 1999(m) Proof | 3,000 | Value: 175 | | | | |

**25 ROUBLES** Y#696 **Weight:** 173.2900 g. **Composition:** 0.9000 Silver 5.0143 oz. ASW **Subject:** Russian Ballet **Obverse:** Two headed eagle **Reverse:** Raymonda and the knight dance scene **Edge:** Reeded **Size:** 60 mm. **Note:** Illustration reduced. Actual size: 60mm.

| Date | Mintage | F | VF | XF | Unc | BU |
|---|---|---|---|---|---|---|
| 1999(m) Proof | 3,000 | Value: 175 | | | | |

**25 ROUBLES** Y#701 **Weight:** 173.2900 g. **Composition:** 0.9000 Silver 5.0143 oz. ASW **Subject:** Russian Exploers: N.M. Przhevalsky **Obverse:** Two headed eagle **Reverse:** Caravan in Central Asia **Edge:** Reeded **Size:** 60 mm. **Note:** Illustration reduced. Actual size: 60mm.

| Date | Mintage | F | VF | XF | Unc | BU |
|---|---|---|---|---|---|---|
| 1999(sp) Proof | 3,000 | Value: 175 | | | | |

**25 ROUBLES** Y#697 **Weight:** 3.2000 g. **Composition:** 0.9990 Gold .1028 oz. AGW **Subject:** Russian Ballet **Obverse:** Two headed eagle **Reverse:** Dancing Saracen **Edge:** Reeded **Size:** 16 mm.

| Date | Mintage | F | VF | XF | Unc | BU |
|---|---|---|---|---|---|---|
| 1999(sp) Proof | 2,000 | Value: 150 | | | | |

**25 ROUBLES** Y#717 **Weight:** 173.2900 g. **Composition:** 0.9000 Silver 5.0143 oz. ASW **Subject:** Field Marshal Suvorov **Obverse:** Two headed eagle **Reverse:** Suvorov with maps and battle scene **Edge:** Reeded **Size:** 60 mm.

| Date | Mintage | F | VF | XF | Unc | BU |
|---|---|---|---|---|---|---|
| 2000(m) Proof | 1,000 | Value: 185 | | | | |

**25 ROUBLES** Y#710 **Weight:** 173.2900 g. **Composition:** 0.9000 Silver 5.0143 oz. ASW **Series:** Third Millennium **Subject:** Education **Obverse:** Two headed eagle **Reverse:** Ancient monk and modern student **Edge:** Reeded **Size:** 60 mm. **Note:** Illustration reduced. Actual size: 60mm.

| Date | Mintage | F | VF | XF | Unc | BU |
|---|---|---|---|---|---|---|
| 2000(m) Proof | 1,000 | Value: 185 | | | | |

**25 ROUBLES** Y#715 **Weight:** 173.2900 g. **Composition:** 0.9000 Silver 5.0143 oz. ASW **Subject:** State Bank of Russia 140th Anniversary **Obverse:** Two headed eagle **Reverse:** Document, portrait and building **Edge:** Reeded **Size:** 60 mm. **Note:** Illustration reduced. Actual size: 60mm.

| Date | Mintage | F | VF | XF | Unc | BU |
|---|---|---|---|---|---|---|
| 2000(m) Proof | 1,000 | Value: 185 | | | | |

**25 ROUBLES Y# 723 Weight:** 173.2900 g. **Composition:** 0.9000 Silver 5.0143 oz. ASW **Subject:** Snow Leopard **Obverse:** Two headed eagle **Reverse:** Leopard on branch **Edge:** Reeded **Size:** 60 mm. **Note:** Illustration reduced. Actual size: 60mm.

| Date | Mintage | F | VF | XF | Unc | BU |
|---|---|---|---|---|---|---|
| 2000(m) Proof | 1,000 | Value: 185 | | | | |

**25 ROUBLES Y# 678 Weight:** 173.2900 g. **Composition:** 0.9000 Silver 5.0143 oz. ASW **Subject:** Bolshoi Theater 225 Years **Obverse:** Two headed eagle. **Reverse:** Dancing couple scene. **Edge:** Reeded. **Size:** 60 mm. **Note:** Illustration reduced. Actual size: 60mm.

| Date | Mintage | F | VF | XF | Unc | BU |
|---|---|---|---|---|---|---|
| 2001 Proof | 2,000 | Value: 100 | | | | |

**25 ROUBLES Y# 683 Weight:** 173.2900 g. **Composition:** 0.9000 Silver 5.0143 oz. ASW **Subject:** Siberian Exploration **Obverse:** Two headed eagle. **Reverse:** Standing king and river boats. **Edge:** Reeded. **Size:** 60 mm. **Note:** Illustration reduced. Actual size: 60mm.

| Date | Mintage | F | VF | XF | Unc | BU |
|---|---|---|---|---|---|---|
| 2001 Proof | 1,000 | Value: 125 | | | | |

**25 ROUBLES Y# 687 Weight:** 3.2000 g. **Composition:** 0.9990 Gold .1028 oz. AGW **Subject:** Bolshoi Theater 225 Years **Obverse:** Two headed eagle. **Reverse:** Ballerina. **Edge:** Reeded. **Size:** 16 mm.

| Date | Mintage | F | VF | XF | Unc | BU |
|---|---|---|---|---|---|---|
| 2001 Proof | 2,500 | Value: 125 | | | | |

**50 ROUBLES Y# 315 Ring Composition:** Copper-Nickel **Center Composition:** Aluminum-Bronze **Obverse:** Double-headed eagle **Reverse:** Denomination

| Date | Mintage | F | VF | XF | Unc | BU |
|---|---|---|---|---|---|---|
| 1992(l) | — | 0.50 | 0.75 | 1.00 | 2.50 | — |
| 1992(m) | — | 0.75 | 1.00 | 1.50 | 3.50 | — |

**50 ROUBLES Y# 354 Weight:** 8.6397 g. **Composition:** 0.9000 Gold .2500 oz. AGW **Obverse:** Double-headed eagle **Reverse:** Moscow's Pashkov Palace

| Date | Mintage | F | VF | XF | Unc | BU |
|---|---|---|---|---|---|---|
| 1992 Proof | 7,500 | Value: 150 | | | | |

**50 ROUBLES Y# 516 Weight:** 8.6397 g. **Composition:** 0.9000 Gold .2500 oz. AGW **Obverse:** Double-headed eagle **Reverse:** Chubuku (snow ram) on map **Note:** Yukutia

| Date | Mintage | F | VF | XF | Unc | BU |
|---|---|---|---|---|---|---|
| 1992 Proof | 25,000 | Value: 200 | | | | |

**50 ROUBLES Y# 329.1 Composition:** Aluminum-Bronze **Edge:** Reeded and plain sections

| Date | Mintage | F | VF | XF | Unc | BU |
|---|---|---|---|---|---|---|
| 1993(l) | — | — | — | — | 2.50 | — |
| 1993(m) | — | — | — | — | 2.50 | — |

**50 ROUBLES Y# 329.2 Composition:** Brass Clad Steel **Edge:** Plain

| Date | Mintage | F | VF | XF | Unc | BU |
|---|---|---|---|---|---|---|
| 1993(l) Reported, not confirmed | — | — | — | — | — | — |
| 1993(m) | — | — | — | — | 2.50 | — |

**50 ROUBLES Y# 330 Ring Composition:** Copper-Nickel **Center Composition:** Aluminum-Bronze **Series:** Wildlife **Reverse:** Bear

| Date | Mintage | F | VF | XF | Unc | BU |
|---|---|---|---|---|---|---|
| 1993(l) | 300,000 | — | — | — | 2.00 | — |

**50 ROUBLES Y# 331 Ring Composition:** Copper-Nickel **Center Composition:** Aluminum-Bronze **Series:** Wildlife **Reverse:** Gecko

| Date | Mintage | F | VF | XF | Unc | BU |
|---|---|---|---|---|---|---|
| 1993(l) | 300,000 | — | — | — | 2.50 | — |

**50 ROUBLES Y# 332 Ring Composition:** Copper-Nickel **Center Composition:** Aluminum-Bronze **Series:** Wildlife **Reverse:** Caucasian grouse

| Date | Mintage | F | VF | XF | Unc | BU |
|---|---|---|---|---|---|---|
| 1993(l) | 300,000 | — | — | — | 2.00 | — |

**50 ROUBLES Y# 333 Ring Composition:** Copper-Nickel **Center Composition:** Aluminum-Bronze **Series:** Wildlife **Reverse:** Far Eastern stork

| Date | Mintage | F | VF | XF | Unc | BU |
|---|---|---|---|---|---|---|
| 1993(l) | 300,000 | — | — | — | 2.00 | — |

**50 ROUBLES Y# 334 Ring Composition:** Copper-Nickel **Center Composition:** Aluminum-Bronze **Series:** Wildlife **Reverse:** Black sea porpoise

| Date | Mintage | F | VF | XF | Unc | BU |
|---|---|---|---|---|---|---|
| 1993(l) | 300,000 | — | — | — | 2.00 | — |

**50 ROUBLES Y# 355 Weight:** 8.6397 g. **Composition:** 0.9000 Gold .2500 oz. AGW **Series:** Olympics **Reverse:** Figure skater

| Date | Mintage | F | VF | XF | Unc | BU |
|---|---|---|---|---|---|---|
| 1993 Proof | 7,500 | Value: 160 | | | | |

**50 ROUBLES Y# 356 Weight:** 7.7758 g. **Composition:** 0.9990 Platinum .2498 oz. APW **Series:** Olympics **Subject:** Formal riding

| Date | Mintage | F | VF | XF | Unc | BU |
|---|---|---|---|---|---|---|
| 1993 Proof | 7,500 | Value: 235 | | | | |

**50 ROUBLES Y# 396 Weight:** 7.7758 g. **Composition:** 0.9990 Platinum .2498 oz. APW **Subject:** Bolshoi Ballet **Reverse:** Ballerina.

| Date | Mintage | F | VF | XF | Unc | BU |
|---|---|---|---|---|---|---|
| 1993 | 750 | — | — | — | 250 | — |

**Note:** Proof sets only

**50 ROUBLES** **Y# 411** **Weight:** 7.7800 g. **Composition:** 0.9990 Gold .2500 oz. AGW **Series:** Wildlife **Reverse:** Bear

| Date | Mintage | F | VF | XF | Unc | BU |
|---|---|---|---|---|---|---|
| 1993 Proof | 1,480 | Value: 200 | | | | |

**50 ROUBLES** **Y# 418** **Weight:** 7.7800 g. **Composition:** 0.9990 Gold .2500 oz. AGW **Subject:** Bolshoi Ballet **Reverse:** Ballerina.

| Date | Mintage | F | VF | XF | Unc | BU |
|---|---|---|---|---|---|---|
| 1993 | 4,700 | — | — | — | 300 | — |
| 1993 Proof | 1,500 | Value: 350 | | | | |

**Note:**

**50 ROUBLES** **Y# 453** **Weight:** 7.7800 g. **Composition:** 0.9990 Gold .2500 oz. AGW **Reverse:** Sergei Rachmaninov

| Date | Mintage | F | VF | XF | Unc | BU |
|---|---|---|---|---|---|---|
| 1993 Proof | 7,500 | Value: 175 | | | | |

**50 ROUBLES** **Y# 367** **Ring Composition:** Copper-Nickel **Center Composition:** Aluminum-Bronze **Series:** Wildlife **Reverse:** Spalax

| Date | Mintage | F | VF | XF | Unc | BU |
|---|---|---|---|---|---|---|
| 1994(I) | 300,000 | — | — | — | 2.50 | — |

**50 ROUBLES** **Y# 368** **Ring Composition:** Copper-Nickel **Center Composition:** Aluminum-Bronze **Series:** Wildlife **Reverse:** Bison

| Date | Mintage | F | VF | XF | Unc | BU |
|---|---|---|---|---|---|---|
| 1994(I) | 300,000 | — | — | — | 2.50 | — |

**50 ROUBLES** **Y# 369** **Ring Composition:** Copper-Nickel **Center Composition:** Aluminum-Bronze **Series:** Wildlife **Reverse:** Gazelle

| Date | Mintage | F | VF | XF | Unc | BU |
|---|---|---|---|---|---|---|
| 1994(I) | 300,000 | — | — | — | 2.50 | — |

**50 ROUBLES** **Y# 370** **Ring Composition:** Copper-Nickel **Center Composition:** Aluminum-Bronze **Series:** Wildlife **Reverse:** Peregrine falcon

| Date | Mintage | F | VF | XF | Unc | BU |
|---|---|---|---|---|---|---|
| 1994(I) | 300,000 | — | — | — | 2.50 | — |

**50 ROUBLES** **Y# 371** **Ring Composition:** Copper-Nickel **Center Composition:** Aluminum-Bronze **Series:** Wildlife **Reverse:** Two flamingos

| Date | Mintage | F | VF | XF | Unc | BU |
|---|---|---|---|---|---|---|
| 1994(I) | 300,000 | — | — | — | 2.50 | — |

**50 ROUBLES** **Y# 426** **Weight:** 7.7759 g. **Composition:** 0.9990 Gold .2500 oz. AGW **Subject:** Bolshoi Ballet **Reverse:** Ballerina.

| Date | Mintage | F | VF | XF | Unc | BU |
|---|---|---|---|---|---|---|
| 1994 Proof | 2,500 | Value: 250 | | | | |

**50 ROUBLES** **Y# 429** **Weight:** 7.7759 g. **Composition:** 0.9990 Platinum .2500 oz. APW **Subject:** Bolshoi Ballet **Reverse:** Ballerina.

| Date | Mintage | F | VF | XF | Unc | BU |
|---|---|---|---|---|---|---|
| 1994 Proof | 900 | Value: 400 | | | | |

**50 ROUBLES** **Y# 525** **Weight:** 7.7759 g. **Composition:** 0.9990 Gold .2500 oz. AGW **Series:** Wildlife **Reverse:** Sable

| Date | Mintage | F | VF | XF | Unc | BU |
|---|---|---|---|---|---|---|
| 1994 Proof | 2,500 | Value: 185 | | | | |

**50 ROUBLES** **Y# 531** **Weight:** 7.7759 g. **Composition:** 0.9990 Gold .2500 oz. AGW **Reverse:** Dimitri Grigorievich Levitsky

| Date | Mintage | F | VF | XF | Unc | BU |
|---|---|---|---|---|---|---|
| 1994 Proof | 8,000 | Value: 225 | | | | |

**50 ROUBLES** **Y# 403** **Composition:** Aluminum-Bronze **Series:** WWII **Reverse:** Two sailors, ship, and plane

| Date | Mintage | F | VF | XF | Unc | BU |
|---|---|---|---|---|---|---|
| 1995 | 200,000 | — | — | — | 4.00 | — |

**Note:** In mint sets only

**50 ROUBLES** **Y# 440** **Weight:** 7.7800 g. **Composition:** 0.9990 Gold .2499 oz. AGW **Subject:** Bolshoi Ballet - Sleeping Beauty **Reverse:** Ballerina.

| Date | Mintage | F | VF | XF | Unc | BU |
|---|---|---|---|---|---|---|
| 1995 Proof | 2,500 | Value: 350 | | | | |

**50 ROUBLES** **Y# 443** **Weight:** 7.7759 g. **Composition:** 0.9990 Platinum .2500 oz. APW **Subject:** Bolshoi Ballet - Sleeping Beauty **Reverse:** Ballerina.

| Date | Mintage | F | VF | XF | Unc | BU |
|---|---|---|---|---|---|---|
| 1995 Proof | 900 | Value: 400 | | | | |

**50 ROUBLES** **Y# A475** **Weight:** 7.7800 g. **Composition:** 0.9990 Gold .2499 oz. AGW **Series:** Wildlife **Reverse:** Lynx

| Date | Mintage | F | VF | XF | Unc | BU |
|---|---|---|---|---|---|---|
| 1995 Proof | 5,000 | Value: 185 | | | | |

**50 ROUBLES** **Y# 408** **Weight:** 7.7800 g. **Composition:** 0.9990 Gold .2499 oz. AGW **Subject:** 50th Anniversary - United Nations **Note:** Similar to 3 Roubles, Y#407.

| Date | Mintage | F | VF | XF | Unc | BU |
|---|---|---|---|---|---|---|
| 1995 Proof | 5,000 | Value: 200 | | | | |

**50 ROUBLES** **Y# 496** **Weight:** 8.6397 g. **Composition:** 0.9000 Gold .2500 oz. AGW **Subject:** F. Nansen and the "Fram".

| Date | Mintage | F | VF | XF | Unc | BU |
|---|---|---|---|---|---|---|
| 1995 Proof | 5,000 | Value: 175 | | | | |

**50 ROUBLES** **Y# 501** **Weight:** 8.6397 g. **Composition:** 0.9000 Gold .2500 oz. AGW **Reverse:** Church of the Savior on the Nereditza River

| Date | Mintage | F | VF | XF | Unc | BU |
|---|---|---|---|---|---|---|
| 1996 Proof | 10,000 | Value: 175 | | | | |

**50 ROUBLES** **Y# 508** **Weight:** 8.6397 g. **Composition:** 0.9000 Gold .2500 oz. AGW **Subject:** 300th Anniversary - Russian Fleet **Reverse:** Submarine

| Date | Mintage | F | VF | XF | Unc | BU |
|---|---|---|---|---|---|---|
| 1996 | 100,000 | — | — | — | 6.00 | — |

**Note:** In mint sets only

**50 ROUBLES** **Y# 537** **Weight:** 7.7759 g. **Composition:** 0.9990 Gold .2500 oz. AGW **Series:** Wildlife **Reverse:** Amur tiger

| Date | Mintage | F | VF | XF | Unc | BU |
|---|---|---|---|---|---|---|
| 1996 Proof | 1,500 | Value: 185 | | | | |

**50 ROUBLES** **Y# 546** **Weight:** 8.6397 g. **Composition:** 0.9000 Gold .2500 oz. AGW **Reverse:** Cruiser Varyag 1904

| Date | Mintage | F | VF | XF | Unc | BU |
|---|---|---|---|---|---|---|
| 1996 Proof | 1,500 | Value: 250 | | | | |

**50 ROUBLES** **Y# 480** **Weight:** 7.7800 g. **Composition:** 0.9990 Gold .2499 oz. AGW **Reverse:** Dmitri Donskoy Monument

| Date | Mintage | F | VF | XF | Unc | BU |
|---|---|---|---|---|---|---|
| 1996 Proof | 10,000 | Value: 200 | | | | |

**50 ROUBLES** **Y# 487** **Weight:** 7.7800 g. **Composition:** 0.9990 Gold .2499 oz. AGW **Subject:** Ballet - Nutcracker **Reverse:** Marsha and Drosselmeyer with broken doll

| Date | Mintage | F | VF | XF | Unc | BU |
|---|---|---|---|---|---|---|
| 1996 Proof | 2,500 | Value: 250 | | | | |

**50 ROUBLES** **Y# 555** **Weight:** 8.6397 g. **Composition:** 0.9000 Gold .2500 oz. AGW **Subject:** 850th Anniversary - Moscow

| Date | Mintage | F | VF | XF | Unc | BU |
|---|---|---|---|---|---|---|
| 1997 Proof | 10,000 | Value: 200 | | | | |

**50 ROUBLES** **Y# 572** **Weight:** 7.7759 g. **Composition:** 0.9990 Gold .2500 oz. AGW **Subject:** Ballet - Swan Lake **Reverse:** Prince Siegfried with crossbow and swan

| Date | Mintage | F | VF | XF | Unc | BU |
|---|---|---|---|---|---|---|
| 1997 Proof | 1,500 | Value: 225 | | | | |

**50 ROUBLES** **Y# 595** **Weight:** 7.7759 g. **Composition:** 0.9990 Gold .2500 oz. AGW **Series:** Wildlife **Reverse:** Polar bear

| Date | Mintage | F | VF | XF | Unc | BU |
|---|---|---|---|---|---|---|
| 1997 Proof | 1,500 | Value: 200 | | | | |

**50 ROUBLES** **Y# 648** **Weight:** 8.7500 g. **Composition:** 0.9000 Gold .2532 oz. AGW **Subject:** 50th Anniversary - Diplomacy with China **Obverse:** Double-headed eagle **Reverse:** Moscow Kremllin and Tiananmen gate

| Date | Mintage | F | VF | XF | Unc | BU |
|---|---|---|---|---|---|---|
| 1999 Proof | 1,000 | Value: 265 | | | | |

**50 ROUBLES** **Y# 692** **Weight:** 8.7500 g. **Composition:** 0.9000 Gold .2532 oz. AGW **Subject:** Alexander Pushkin **Obverse:** Two headed eagle **Reverse:** Portrait above quill and signature **Edge:** Reeded **Size:** 22.6 mm.

| Date | Mintage | F | VF | XF | Unc | BU |
|---|---|---|---|---|---|---|
| 1999(m) Proof | 1,500 | Value: 225 | | | | |

**50 ROUBLES** **Y# 698** **Weight:** 8.7500 g. **Composition:** 0.9990 Gold .2534 oz. AGW **Subject:** Russian Ballet **Obverse:** Two headed eagle **Reverse:** Raymonda and Saracen dancing **Edge:** Reeded **Size:** 22.6 mm.

| Date | Mintage | F | VF | XF | Unc | BU |
|---|---|---|---|---|---|---|
| 1999(m) Proof | 1,500 | Value: 225 | | | | |

**50 ROUBLES** **Y# 702** **Weight:** 8.7500 g. **Composition:** 0.9000 Gold .2532 oz. AGW **Subject:** Russian Explorer N.M. Przhevalsky **Obverse:** Two headed eagle **Reverse:** Portrait **Edge:** Reeded **Size:** 22.6 mm.

| Date | Mintage | F | VF | XF | Unc | BU |
|---|---|---|---|---|---|---|
| 1999(sp) Proof | 1,500 | Value: 225 | | | | |

**50 ROUBLES** **Y# 718** **Weight:** 8.7500 g. **Composition:** 0.9000 Gold .2532 oz. AGW **Subject:** Field Marshal Suvorov **Obverse:** Two headed eagle **Reverse:** Portrait above cannons **Edge:** Reeded **Size:** 22.6 mm.

| Date | Mintage | F | VF | XF | Unc | BU |
|---|---|---|---|---|---|---|
| 2000(sp) Proof | 500 | Value: 265 | | | | |

**50 ROUBLES** **Y# 725** **Weight:** 7.8900 g. **Composition:** 0.9990 Gold .2534 oz. AGW **Subject:** Snow Leopard **Obverse:** Two headed eagle **Reverse:** Leopard head **Edge:** Reeded **Size:** 22.6 mm.

| Date | Mintage | F | VF | XF | Unc | BU |
|---|---|---|---|---|---|---|
| 2000(sp) Proof | 1,000 | Value: 250 | | | | |

**50 ROUBLES** **Y# 672** **Weight:** 8.7100 g. **Composition:** 0.9000 Gold .2520 oz. AGW **Series:** Olympics **Obverse:** Double-headed eagle **Reverse:** Torch runner on map

| Date | Mintage | F | VF | XF | Unc | BU |
|---|---|---|---|---|---|---|
| 2000 Proof | 1,000 | Value: 265 | | | | |

**50 ROUBLES** **Y# 679** **Weight:** 8.7500 g. **Composition:** 0.9990 Gold .2532 oz. AGW **Subject:** Bolshoi Theater 225 Years **Obverse:** Two headed eagle. **Reverse:** Dueling figures. **Edge:** Reeded. **Size:** 22.6 mm.

| Date | Mintage | F | VF | XF | Unc | BU |
|---|---|---|---|---|---|---|
| 2001 Proof | 2,000 | Value: 150 | | | | |

**50 ROUBLES** **Y# 684** **Weight:** 8.7500 g. **Composition:** 0.9990 Gold .2532 oz. AGW **Subject:** Siberian Exploration **Obverse:** Two headed eagle. **Reverse:** Portrait and boat. **Edge:** Reeded. **Size:** 22.6 mm.

| Date | Mintage | F | VF | XF | Unc | BU |
|---|---|---|---|---|---|---|
| 2001 Proof | 1,500 | Value: 150 | | | | |

**100 ROUBLES** **Y# 316** **Ring Composition:** Aluminum-Bronze **Center Composition:** Copper-Nickel **Obverse:** Double-headed eagle **Reverse:** Denomination

| Date | Mintage | F | VF | XF | Unc | BU |
|---|---|---|---|---|---|---|
| 1992(l) | — | 0.50 | 0.75 | 1.00 | 3.00 | — |
| 1992(m) | — | 0.75 | 1.00 | 1.50 | 4.50 | — |

**100 ROUBLES** **Y# 357** **Weight:** 17.5000 g. **Composition:** 0.9000 Gold .5000 oz. AGW **Obverse:** Double-headed eagle **Reverse:** Michael Lomonosov

| Date | Mintage | F | VF | XF | Unc | BU |
|---|---|---|---|---|---|---|
| 1992 Proof | 5,700 | Value: 275 | | | | |

**100 ROUBLES** **Y# 375** **Weight:** 17.5000 g. **Composition:** 0.9000 Gold .5000 oz. AGW **Obverse:** Double-headed eagle **Reverse:** Wooly Mammoth **Note:** Yakutia

| Date | Mintage | F | VF | XF | Unc | BU |
|---|---|---|---|---|---|---|
| 1992 | 14,000 | — | — | — | 300 | — |

**100 ROUBLES** **Y# 338** **Composition:** Copper-Nickel-Zinc

| Date | Mintage | F | VF | XF | Unc | BU |
|---|---|---|---|---|---|---|
| 1993(l) | — | 0.25 | 0.50 | 1.00 | 3.00 | — |
| 1993(m) | — | 0.25 | 0.50 | 1.00 | 3.00 | — |

**100 ROUBLES** **Y# 412** **Weight:** 15.5500 g. **Composition:** 0.9990 Gold .5000 oz. AGW **Series:** Wildlife **Reverse:** Bear

| Date | Mintage | F | VF | XF | Unc | BU |
|---|---|---|---|---|---|---|
| 1993 Proof | 1,400 | Value: 325 | | | | |

**100 ROUBLES** **Y# 419** **Weight:** 15.5500 g. **Composition:** 0.9990 Gold .5000 oz. AGW **Subject:** Bolshoi Ballet **Reverse:** Ballerina.

| Date | Mintage | F | VF | XF | Unc | BU |
|---|---|---|---|---|---|---|
| 1993 | 2,700 | — | — | — | 500 | — |
| 1993 Proof | 1,500 | Value: 700 | | | | |

**100 ROUBLES** **Y# 454** **Weight:** 17.5000 g. **Composition:** 0.9000 Gold .5000 oz. AGW **Reverse:** Peter Tchaikovsky

| Date | Mintage | F | VF | XF | Unc | BU |
|---|---|---|---|---|---|---|
| 1993 Proof | 5,700 | Value: 275 | | | | |

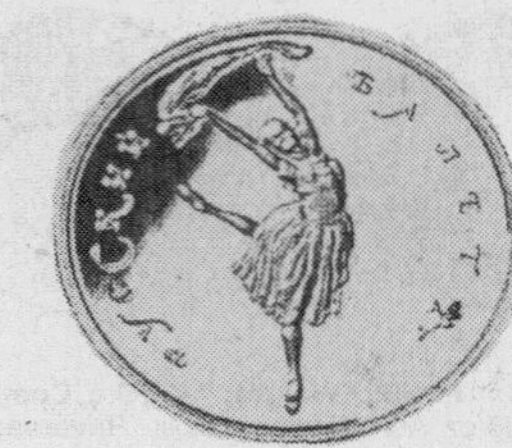

**100 ROUBLES** **Y# 427** **Weight:** 15.5500 g. **Composition:** 0.9990 Gold .5000 oz. AGW **Subject:** Bolshoi Ballet **Reverse:** Ballerina.

| Date | Mintage | F | VF | XF | Unc | BU |
|---|---|---|---|---|---|---|
| 1994 Proof | 2,500 | Value: 695 | | | | |

**100 ROUBLES** **Y# 526** **Weight:** 15.5500 g. **Composition:** 0.9990 Gold .5000 oz. AGW **Series:** Wildlife **Reverse:** Sable

| Date | Mintage | F | VF | XF | Unc | BU |
|---|---|---|---|---|---|---|
| 1994 Proof | 2,500 | Value: 400 | | | | |

**100 ROUBLES** **Y# 532** **Weight:** 15.5500 g. **Composition:** 0.9990 Gold .5000 oz. AGW **Note:** Vassili Vassilievich Kandinsky - The Blue Horse

| Date | Mintage | F | VF | XF | Unc | BU |
|---|---|---|---|---|---|---|
| 1994 Proof | 6,000 | Value: 275 | | | | |

**100 ROUBLES** **Y# A387** **Weight:** 1000.2108 g. **Composition:** 0.9000 Silver 28.9417 oz. ASW **Series:** WWII **Subject:** WWII Victory **Reverse:** Allied commanders **Note:** Illustration reduced. Actual size: 103mm.

| Date | Mintage | F | VF | XF | Unc | BU |
|---|---|---|---|---|---|---|
| 1995 Proof | 1,500 | Value: 750 | | | | |

**100 ROUBLES** **Y# 502** **Weight:** 17.5000 g. **Composition:** 0.9000 Gold .5000 oz. AGW **Note:** Order of Alexander Nevsky

| Date | Mintage | F | VF | XF | Unc | BU |
|---|---|---|---|---|---|---|
| 1995 Proof | 5,000 | Value: 275 | | | | |

**100 ROUBLES** **Y# 376** **Weight:** 1111.0861 g. **Composition:** 0.9000 Silver 32.1500 oz. ASW **Series:** Wildlife **Reverse:** Mother bear with cubs **Note:** Illustration reduced. Actual size" 100mm.

| Date | Mintage | F | VF | XF | Unc | BU |
|---|---|---|---|---|---|---|
| 1995 Proof | 500 | Value: 950 | | | | |

**100 ROUBLES** **Y# 434** **Weight:** 912.3693 g. **Composition:** 0.9000 Silver 26.4000 oz. ASW **Subject:** Ballet - Sleeping Beauty **Note:** Illustration reduced. Actual size: 100mm.

| Date | Mintage | F | VF | XF | Unc | BU |
|---|---|---|---|---|---|---|
| 1995 Proof | 1,000 | Value: 600 | | | | |

**100 ROUBLES** **Y# 441** **Weight:** 15.5500 g. **Composition:** 0.9990 Gold .5000 oz. AGW **Subject:** Ballet - Sleeping Beauty **Obv. Legend:** Ballerina.

| Date | Mintage | F | VF | XF | Unc | BU |
|---|---|---|---|---|---|---|
| 1995 Proof | 2,500 | Value: 695 | | | | |

**100 ROUBLES** **Y# 404** **Composition:** Copper-Nickel **Series:** WWII **Reverse:** Berlin Soldier Monument

| Date | Mintage | F | VF | XF | Unc | BU |
|---|---|---|---|---|---|---|
| 1995 | 200,000 | — | — | — | 5.00 | — |

**Note:** In mint sets only

**100 ROUBLES** **Y# 497** **Weight:** 17.5000 g. **Composition:** 0.9000 Gold .5000 oz. AGW **Reverse:** Icebreaker "Krassin"

| Date | Mintage | F | VF | XF | Unc | BU |
|---|---|---|---|---|---|---|
| 1995 Proof | 2,500 | Value: 300 | | | | |

**100 ROUBLES** **Y# 498** **Weight:** 912.3693 g. **Composition:** 0.9000 Silver 26.4000 oz. ASW **Series:** Wildlife **Reverse:** Lynx with two kits

| Date | Mintage | F | VF | XF | Unc | BU |
|---|---|---|---|---|---|---|
| 1995 Proof | 500 | Value: 1,100 | | | | |

**100 ROUBLES** **Y# 499** **Weight:** 17.5000 g. **Composition:** 0.9000 Gold .5000 oz. AGW **Series:** Wildlife **Reverse:** Lynx

| Date | Mintage | F | VF | XF | Unc | BU |
|---|---|---|---|---|---|---|
| 1995 Proof | 3,500 | Value: 275 | | | | |

**100 ROUBLES** **Y# 481** **Weight:** 17.5000 g. **Composition:** 0.9000 Gold .5000 oz. AGW **Obverse:** Double-headed eagle **Reverse:** All Saints Church in Kulishki

| Date | Mintage | F | VF | XF | Unc | BU |
|---|---|---|---|---|---|---|
| 1996 Proof | 5,000 | Value: 275 | | | | |

**100 ROUBLES** **Y# 489** **Weight:** 15.5517 g. **Composition:** 0.9990 Gold .5000 oz. AGW **Subject:** Ballet - Nutcracker **Reverse:** Dancing prince

| Date | Mintage | F | VF | XF | Unc | BU |
|---|---|---|---|---|---|---|
| 1996 Proof | 2,500 | Value: 400 | | | | |

**100 ROUBLES** **Y# 495** **Weight:** 912.3693 g. **Composition:** 0.9000 Silver 26.4000 oz. ASW **Obverse:** Double-headed eagle **Reverse:** Sables around walled city

| Date | Mintage | F | VF | XF | Unc | BU |
|---|---|---|---|---|---|---|
| 1996 Proof | 500 | Value: 1,500 | | | | |

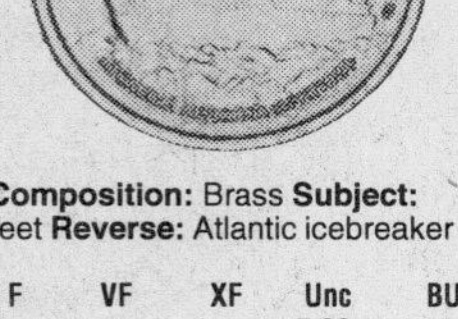

**100 ROUBLES** **Y# 509** **Composition:** Brass **Subject:** 300th Anniversary - Russian Fleet **Reverse:** Atlantic icebreaker "Arctic"

| Date | Mintage | F | VF | XF | Unc | BU |
|---|---|---|---|---|---|---|
| 1996 | 100,000 | — | — | — | 7.00 | — |

**Note:** In mint sets only

**100 ROUBLES** **Y# 539** **Weight:** 15.5517 g. **Composition:** 0.9990 Gold .5000 oz. AGW **Series:** Wildlife **Reverse:** Amur tiger

| Date | Mintage | F | VF | XF | Unc | BU |
|---|---|---|---|---|---|---|
| 1996 Proof | 1,000 | Value: 300 | | | | |

**100 ROUBLES** **Y# 548** **Weight:** 17.5000 g. **Composition:** 0.9000 Gold .5000 oz. AGW **Series:** WWII **Subject:** Battleships of WWII **Reverse:** Destroyers "Gremyshiy" and "Soobrazitelny"

| Date | Mintage | F | VF | XF | Unc | BU |
|---|---|---|---|---|---|---|
| 1996 Proof | 1,000 | Value: 450 | | | | |

**100 ROUBLES** **Y# 488** **Weight:** 1111.0861 g. **Composition:** 0.9990 Silver 32.1500 oz. ASW **Subject:** Ballet - Nutcracker **Reverse:** Marsha cradling nutcracker doll **Note:** Illustration reduced.

| Date | Mintage | F | VF | XF | Unc | BU |
|---|---|---|---|---|---|---|
| 1996 Proof | 1,000 | Value: 750 | | | | |

**100 ROUBLES** **Y# 538** **Weight:** 1111.0861 g. **Composition:** 0.9000 Silver 32.1500 oz. ASW **Series:** Wildlife **Reverse:** Amur tiger **Note:** Illustration reduced.

| Date | Mintage | F | VF | XF | Unc | BU |
|---|---|---|---|---|---|---|
| 1996 Proof | 1,000 | Value: 750 | | | | |

**100 ROUBLES** **Y# 547** **Weight:** 912.3693 g. **Composition:** 0.9000 Silver 26.4000 oz. ASW **Reverse:** War ship - Poltava, 1712 **Note:** Illustration reduced.

| Date | Mintage | F | VF | XF | Unc | BU |
|---|---|---|---|---|---|---|
| 1996 Proof | 1,000 | Value: 750 | | | | |

**100 ROUBLES** **Y# 556** **Weight:** 1111.0861 g. **Composition:** 0.9000 Silver 32.1500 oz. ASW **Subject:** 850th Anniversary - Moscow **Reverse:** Kuzma Minin and Dmitri Pozharsky monument **Note:** Illustration reduced.

| Date | Mintage | F | VF | XF | Unc | BU |
|---|---|---|---|---|---|---|
| 1997 Proof | 1,000 | Value: 750 | | | | |

**100 ROUBLES** **Y# 573** **Weight:** 1111.0861 g. **Composition:** 0.9000 Silver 32.1500 oz. ASW **Subject:** Ballet - Swan Lake **Reverse:** Prince Siegfried dancing with Odette **Note:** Illustration reduced.

| Date | Mintage | F | VF | XF | Unc | BU |
|---|---|---|---|---|---|---|
| 1997 Proof | 1,000 | Value: 750 | | | | |

**100 ROUBLES** **Y# 588** **Weight:** 1111.0861 g. **Composition:** 0.9000 Silver 32.1500 oz. ASW **Reverse:** The Bark "Krusenstern" 4-masted ship **Note:** Illustration reduced.

| Date | Mintage | F | VF | XF | Unc | BU |
|---|---|---|---|---|---|---|
| 1997 Proof | 500 | Value: 775 | | | | |

**100 ROUBLES** **Y# 557** **Weight:** 17.2890 g. **Composition:** 0.9000 Gold .5000 oz. AGW **Subject:** 850th Anniversary - Moscow **Reverse:** Yuri Dolgoruky monument

| Date | Mintage | F | VF | XF | Unc | BU |
|---|---|---|---|---|---|---|
| 1997 Proof | 5,000 | Value: 325 | | | | |

**100 ROUBLES** **Y# 574** **Weight:** 15.5517 g. **Composition:** 0.9990 Gold .5000 oz. AGW **Subject:** Ballet - Swan Lake **Reverse:** Prince Siegfried and Odette's duet

| Date | Mintage | F | VF | XF | Unc | BU |
|---|---|---|---|---|---|---|
| 1997 Proof | 1,500 | Value: 400 | | | | |

**100 ROUBLES** **Y# 596** **Weight:** 15.5517 g. **Composition:** 0.9990 Gold .5000 oz. AGW **Series:** Wildlife **Reverse:** Polar bear on ice floe

| Date | Mintage | F | VF | XF | Unc | BU |
|---|---|---|---|---|---|---|
| 1997 Proof | 1,000 | Value: 425 | | | | |

**Note:** Notice the face on the bear's hind quarter

**100 ROUBLES** **Y# 597** **Weight:** 1111.0861 g. **Composition:** 0.9000 Silver 32.1500 oz. ASW **Series:** Wildlife **Reverse:** Two polar bears

| Date | Mintage | F | VF | XF | Unc | BU |
|---|---|---|---|---|---|---|
| 1997 Proof | 1,000 | Value: 750 | | | | |

**100 ROUBLES** **Y# 623** **Weight:** 15.7200 g. **Composition:** 0.9990 Gold .5049 oz. AGW

| Date | Mintage | F | VF | XF | Unc | BU |
|---|---|---|---|---|---|---|
| 1997 Proof | 1,000 | Value: 400 | | | | |

**100 ROUBLES** **Y# 694** **Weight:** 17.4500 g. **Composition:** 0.9000 Gold .5049 oz. AGW **Subject:** Alexander Pushkin **Obverse:** Two headed eagle **Reverse:** Portrait and scenes **Edge:** Reeded **Size:** 30 mm.

| Date | Mintage | F | VF | XF | Unc | BU |
|---|---|---|---|---|---|---|
| 1999 Proof | 1,000 | Value: 400 | | | | |

**100 ROUBLES** **Y# 700** **Weight:** 15.7200 g. **Composition:** 0.9990 Gold .5049 oz. AGW **Subject:** Russian Ballet **Obverse:** Two headed eagle **Reverse:** Raymonda dancing alone **Edge:** Reeded **Size:** 30 mm.

| Date | Mintage | F | VF | XF | Unc | BU |
|---|---|---|---|---|---|---|
| 1999(sp) Proof | 1,500 | Value: 400 | | | | |

**100 ROUBLES** **Y# 703** **Weight:** 17.4500 g. **Composition:** 0.9000 Gold .5049 oz. AGW **Subject:** Russian Explorer N.M. Przhevalsky **Obverse:** Two headed eagle **Reverse:** Two men viewing lake **Edge:** Reeded **Size:** 30 mm.

| Date | Mintage | F | VF | XF | Unc | BU |
|---|---|---|---|---|---|---|
| 1999(sp) Proof | 1,000 | Value: 400 | | | | |

**100 ROUBLES** **Y# 693** **Weight:** 1111.1200 g. **Composition:** 0.9000 Silver 32.1510 oz. ASW **Subject:** Alexander Pushkin **Obverse:** Two headed eagle **Reverse:** Statue, monuments and buildings **Edge:** Reeded **Size:** 100 mm. **Note:** Illustration reduced. Actual size: 100mm.

| Date | Mintage | F | VF | XF | Unc | BU |
|---|---|---|---|---|---|---|
| 1999(m) Proof | 1,000 | Value: 775 | | | | |

**100 ROUBLES** **Y# 711** **Weight:** 1111.1200 g. **Composition:** 0.9000 Silver 32.1510 oz. ASW **Subject:** Russian State **Obverse:** Two headed eagle **Reverse:** Mother Russia, mythological bird and map **Edge:** Reeded **Size:** 100 mm. **Note:** Illustration reduced. Actual size: 100mm.

| Date | Mintage | F | VF | XF | Unc | BU |
|---|---|---|---|---|---|---|
| 2000(m) Proof | 500 | Value: 775 | | | | |

**100 ROUBLES** **Y# 724** **Weight:** 1111.1200 g. **Composition:** 0.9000 Silver 32.1510 oz. ASW **Subject:** Snow Leopard **Obverse:** Two headed eagle **Reverse:** Two leopards **Edge:** Reeded **Size:** 100 mm. **Note:** Illustration reduced. Actual size: 100mm.

| Date | Mintage | F | VF | XF | Unc | BU |
|---|---|---|---|---|---|---|
| 2000(sp) Proof | 500 | Value: 775 | | | | |

**100 ROUBLES** **Y# 729** **Weight:** 1111.1200 g. **Composition:** 0.9000 Silver 32.1510 oz. ASW **Subject:** WWII Victory 55th Anniversary **Obverse:** Russian soldier writing on Reichstag buildin pillar **Reverse:** Conference scene **Edge:** Reeded **Size:** 100 mm. **Note:** Illustration reduced. Actual size: 100mm.

| Date | Mintage | F | VF | XF | Unc | BU |
|---|---|---|---|---|---|---|
| 2000(sp) Proof | 500 | Value: 775 | | | | |

**100 ROUBLES** **Y# 713** **Weight:** 17.4500 g. **Composition:** 0.9000 Gold .5049 oz. AGW **Subject:** Department of Mining 300 Years **Obverse:** Two headed eagle **Reverse:** Miner and equipment **Edge:** Reeded **Size:** 30 mm.

| Date | Mintage | F | VF | XF | Unc | BU |
|---|---|---|---|---|---|---|
| 2000(m) Proof | 1,000 | Value: 325 | | | | |

**100 ROUBLES** **Y# 726** **Weight:** 15.7200 g. **Composition:** 0.9990 Gold .5049 oz. AGW **Subject:** Snow Leopard **Obverse:** Two headed eagle **Reverse:** Leopard on branch **Edge:** Reeded **Size:** 30 mm.

| Date | Mintage | F | VF | XF | Unc | BU |
|---|---|---|---|---|---|---|
| 2000(sp) Proof | 1,000 | Value: 400 | | | | |

**100 ROUBLES** **Y# 685** **Weight:** 17.4500 g. **Composition:** 0.9000 Gold .5049 oz. AGW **Subject:** Siberian Exploration **Obverse:** Two headed eagle. **Reverse:** Two portraits and sail boat. **Edge:** Reeded. **Size:** 30 mm.

| Date | Mintage | F | VF | XF | Unc | BU |
|---|---|---|---|---|---|---|
| 2001 Proof | 1,000 | Value: 275 | | | | |

**100 ROUBLES** **Y# 688** **Weight:** 15.7200 g. **Composition:** 0.9990 Gold .5049 oz. AGW **Subject:** Bolshoi Theater 225 Years **Obverse:** Two headed eagle. **Reverse:** Three dancers with swords. **Edge:** Reeded. **Size:** 30 mm.

| Date | Mintage | F | VF | XF | Unc | BU |
|---|---|---|---|---|---|---|
| 2001 Proof | 1,500 | Value: 275 | | | | |

**100 ROUBLES** **Y# 681** **Weight:** 1111.1000 g. **Composition:** 0.9000 Silver 32.1504 oz. ASW **Subject:** Yuri Gagarin **Obverse:** Two headed eagle. **Reverse:** Astronaut and rocket in space. **Edge:** Reeded. **Size:** 100 mm. **Note:** Illustration reduced. Actual size: 100mm.

| Date | Mintage | F | VF | XF | Unc | BU |
|---|---|---|---|---|---|---|
| 2001 Proof | 750 | Value: 800 | | | | |

**100 ROUBLES** **Y# 689** **Weight:** 1111.1000 g. **Composition:** 0.9000 Silver 32.1504 oz. ASW **Subject:** Bolshoi Theater 225 Years **Obverse:** Two headed eagle. **Reverse:** Casino gambling scene. **Edge:** Reeded. **Size:** 100 mm. **Note:** Illustration reduced. Actual size: 100mm.

| Date | Mintage | F | VF | XF | Unc | BU |
|---|---|---|---|---|---|---|
| 2001 Proof | 500 | Value: 1,000 | | | | |

**150 ROUBLES** **Y# 358** **Weight:** 15.5517 g. **Composition:** 0.9990 Platinum .5000 oz. APW **Note:** Naval battle of Cesme

| Date | Mintage | F | VF | XF | Unc | BU |
|---|---|---|---|---|---|---|
| 1992 Proof | 3,000 | Value: 475 | | | | |

**150 ROUBLES** **Y# 397** **Weight:** 15.5517 g. **Composition:** 0.9990 Platinum .5000 oz. APW **Subject:** Ballet **Reverse:** Ballerina

| Date | Mintage | F | VF | XF | Unc | BU |
|---|---|---|---|---|---|---|
| 1993 | 750 | — | — | — | 500 | — |

**Note:** Proof sets only

**150 ROUBLES** **Y# 455** **Weight:** 15.5517 g. **Composition:** 0.9990 Platinum .5000 oz. APW **Reverse:** Igor Stravinsky

| Date | Mintage | F | VF | XF | Unc | BU |
|---|---|---|---|---|---|---|
| 1993 Proof | 3,000 | Value: 475 | | | | |

**150 ROUBLES** **Y# 519** **Weight:** 15.5517 g. **Composition:** 0.9990 Platinum .5000 oz. APW **Subject:** First Global Circumnavigation **Reverse:** Sloops - "Nadyezdha" and "Neva"

| Date | Mintage | F | VF | XF | Unc | BU |
|---|---|---|---|---|---|---|
| 1993 Proof | 25,000 | Value: 475 | | | | |

**150 ROUBLES** **Y# 430** **Weight:** 15.5517 g. **Composition:** 0.9990 Platinum .5000 oz. APW **Subject:** Bolshoi Ballet **Reverse:** Ballerina.

| Date | Mintage | F | VF | XF | Unc | BU |
|---|---|---|---|---|---|---|
| 1994 Proof | 900 | Value: 800 | | | | |

**150 ROUBLES** **Y# 523** **Weight:** 15.5517 g. **Composition:** 0.9990 Platinum .5000 oz. APW **Subject:** First Global Circumnavigation **Reverse:** Sloops - "Mirny" and "Vostok"

| Date | Mintage | F | VF | XF | Unc | BU |
|---|---|---|---|---|---|---|
| 1994 Proof | 4,000 | Value: 475 | | | | |

**150 ROUBLES** **Y# 533** **Weight:** 15.5517 g. **Composition:** 0.9990 Platinum .5000 oz. APW **Subject:** Michail Alexandrowich Vrubel - The Demon.

| Date | Mintage | F | VF | XF | Unc | BU |
|---|---|---|---|---|---|---|
| 1994 Proof | 3,000 | Value: 475 | | | | |

**150 ROUBLES** **Y# 444** **Weight:** 15.5517 g. **Composition:** 0.9990 Platinum .5000 oz. APW **Subject:** Ballet - Sleeping Beauty **Reverse:** Male dancer.

| Date | Mintage | F | VF | XF | Unc | BU |
|---|---|---|---|---|---|---|
| 1995 Proof | 900 | Value: 795 | | | | |

**150 ROUBLES** **Y# 503** **Weight:** 15.5517 g. **Composition:** 0.9990 Platinum .5000 oz. APW **Subject:** Battle of the Neve River in 1240

| Date | Mintage | F | VF | XF | Unc | BU |
|---|---|---|---|---|---|---|
| 1995 Proof | 3,000 | Value: 475 | | | | |

**200 ROUBLES** **Y# 413** **Weight:** 31.1035 g. **Composition:** 0.9990 Gold 1.0000 oz. AGW **Series:** Wildlife **Reverse:** Bear

| Date | Mintage | F | VF | XF | Unc | BU |
|---|---|---|---|---|---|---|
| 1993 Proof | 1,000 | Value: 600 | | | | |

**200 ROUBLES** **Y# 527** **Weight:** 31.1035 g. **Composition:** 0.9990 Gold 1.0000 oz. AGW **Series:** Wildlife **Reverse:** Two sables

| Date | Mintage | F | VF | XF | Unc | BU |
|---|---|---|---|---|---|---|
| 1994 Proof | 2,000 | Value: 500 | | | | |

**200 ROUBLES** **Y# 500** **Weight:** 31.1035 g. **Composition:** 0.9990 Gold 1.0000 oz. AGW **Series:** Wildlife **Reverse:** Seated lynx

| Date | Mintage | F | VF | XF | Unc | BU |
|---|---|---|---|---|---|---|
| 1995 Proof | 1,750 | Value: 500 | | | | |

**200 ROUBLES** **Y# 540** **Weight:** 31.1035 g. **Composition:** 0.9990 Gold 1.0000 oz. AGW **Series:** Wildlife **Reverse:** Amur tiger

| Date | Mintage | F | VF | XF | Unc | BU |
|---|---|---|---|---|---|---|
| 1996 Proof | 1,000 | Value: 550 | | | | |

**200 ROUBLES** **Y# 598** **Weight:** 31.1035 g. **Composition:** 0.9990 Gold 1.0000 oz. AGW **Series:** Wildlife **Reverse:** Seated polar bear

| Date | Mintage | F | VF | XF | Unc | BU |
|---|---|---|---|---|---|---|
| 1997 Proof | 1,000 | Value: 750 | | | | |

**200 ROUBLES** **Y# 656** **Weight:** 3342.3899 g. **Composition:** 0.9000 Silver 96.7142 oz. ASW **Subject:** 25th Anniversary - St. Petersburg Mint **Obverse:** Double-headed eagle **Reverse:** Peter the Great, mint view, coin designs, and medal of the Imperial Order **Note:** Illustration reduced.

| Date | Mintage | F | VF | XF | Unc | BU |
|---|---|---|---|---|---|---|
| 1999 Proof | 150 | — | — | — | — | — |

**200 ROUBLES** **Y# 727** **Weight:** 31.3700 g. **Composition:** 0.9990 Gold 1.0076 oz. AGW **Subject:** Snow Leopard **Obverse:** Two headed eagle **Reverse:** Leopard on branch **Edge:** Reeded **Size:** 33 mm.

| Date | Mintage | F | VF | XF | Unc | BU |
|---|---|---|---|---|---|---|
| 2000(sp) Proof | 500 | Value: 600 | | | | |

**1000 ROUBLES** **Y# 589** **Weight:** 155.5000 g. **Composition:** 0.9990 Gold 4.9944 oz. AGW **Reverse:** The Bark "Krusenstern" - 4-masted ship

| Date | Mintage | F | VF | XF | Unc | BU |
|---|---|---|---|---|---|---|
| 1997 Proof | 250 | Value: 3,250 | | | | |

**10000 ROUBLES** **Y# 541** **Weight:** 1111.0861 g. **Composition:** 0.9990 Gold 35.6865 oz. AGW **Series:** Wildlife **Obverse:** Double-headed eagle **Reverse:** Amur tiger with two cubs **Note:** Illustration reduced.

| Date | Mintage | F | VF | XF | Unc | BU |
|---|---|---|---|---|---|---|
| 1996 Prooflike | 100 | — | — | — | — | — |

**10000 ROUBLES** **Y# 599** **Weight:** 1111.0861 g. **Composition:** 0.9990 Gold 35.6865 oz. AGW **Series:** Wildlife **Obverse:** Double-headed eagle **Reverse:** Polar bear with two cubs

| Date | Mintage | F | VF | XF | Unc | BU |
|---|---|---|---|---|---|---|
| 1997 Proof | 100 | Value: 16,500 | | | | |

**10000 ROUBLES** **Y# 728** **Weight:** 822.8449 g. **Composition:** 0.9990 Gold 26.4551 oz. AGW **Subject:** Snow Leopard **Obverse:** Two headed eagle **Reverse:** Leopard with two cubs **Edge:** Reeded **Size:** 100 mm.

| Date | Mintage | F | VF | XF | Unc | BU |
|---|---|---|---|---|---|---|
| 2000(m) Proof | 100 | Value: 16,500 | | | | |

## PATTERNS

Including off metal strikes

| KM# | Date | Mintage | Identification | Mkt Val |
|---|---|---|---|---|
| Pn160 | 1911 | — | 5 Kopeks. Nickel. | — |
| Pn161 | 1911 | — | 10 Kopeks. Nickel. | — |
| Pn162 | 1911 | — | 20 Kopeks. Nickel. | — |
| Pn163 | 1911 | — | 20 Kopeks. Nickel. | — |
| Pn164 | 1911 | — | 25 Kopeks. Nickel. Eagle, date below. 25 in circle. | — |
| Pn165 | 1916 | — | Kopek. Copper. Dotted background in circle, date. | — |
| Pn166 | 1916 | — | Kopek. Copper. Plain background. | — |
| Pn167 | 1916 | — | Kopek. Copper. Value, date below. | — |
| Pn168 | 1916 | — | 2 Kopeks. Copper. Eagle in circle. 2 in circle, value, date below. | — |

| KM# | Date | Mintage | Identification | Mkt Val |
|---|---|---|---|---|
| Pn169 | 1916 | — | 3 Kopeks. Copper. Eagle in circle. 3 in circle, value, date below. | — |
| Pn170 | 1916 | — | 5 Kopeks. Copper. | — |
| Pn171 | 1916 | — | 5 Roubles. Unknown Metal. | 2,000 |
| Pn172 | 1917 | — | 3 Kopeks. Copper. 8.2500 g. Plain edge. 1/2milimeter larger than 1916. | 2,000 |
| Pn173 | 1922 | — | 20 Kopeks. Bronze. Y#82 | — |
| Pn174 | 1922 | — | 50 Kopeks. Silver. Plain edge. Y#89 | — |
| Pn175 | 1923 | — | 20 Kopeks. Bronze. Y#82 | 150 |
| Pn176 | 1923 | — | 20 Kopeks. Copper. Y#82 | 150 |
| Pn202 | 1924 | — | 50 Kopeks. Copper-Nickel. Plain edge. Y#89; London Mint. | 650 |
| Pn203 | 1924 | — | 50 Kopeks. Copper-Nickel. Plain edge. Y#89 | 1,000 |
| Pn177 | 1924 | — | Kopek. Copper-Aluminum. Y#76 | — |
| Pn178 | 1924 | — | Kopek. Bronze. Y#76 | — |
| Pn179 | 1924 | — | Kopek. Aluminum. Y#76 | — |
| Pn180 | 1924 | — | Kopek. Copper-Nickel. Y#76 | — |
| Pn181 | 1924 | — | Kopek. Copper-Zinc. Y#76 | — |
| | | | **Note:** Additional metals exist | |
| Pn182 | 1924 | — | 2 Kopeks. Copper-Aluminum. Y#77 | — |
| Pn183 | 1924 | — | 2 Kopeks. Bronze. Y#77 | — |
| Pn184 | 1924 | — | 2 Kopeks. Aluminum. Y#77 | — |
| Pn185 | 1924 | — | 2 Kopeks. Copper-Nickel. Y#77 | — |
| Pn186 | 1924 | — | 2 Kopeks. Copper-Zinc. Y#77 | — |
| | | | **Note:** Additional metals exist | |
| Pn187 | 1924 | — | 3 Kopeks. Copper-Aluminum. Y#78 | — |
| Pn188 | 1924 | — | 3 Kopeks. Bronze. Y#78 | — |
| Pn189 | 1924 | — | 3 Kopeks. Aluminum. Y#78 | — |
| Pn190 | 1924 | — | 3 Kopeks. Copper-Nickel. Y#78 | — |
| Pn191 | 1924 | — | 3 Kopeks. Copper-Zinc. Y#78 | — |
| | | | **Note:** Additional metals exist | |
| Pn192 | 1924 | — | 5 Kopeks. Unknown Metal. | — |
| Pn193 | 1924 | — | 5 Kopeks. Copper-Zinc. 12.0000 g. Y#79 | — |
| Pn194 | 1924 | — | 5 Kopeks. Copper-Zinc. 18.0000 g. Y#79 | — |
| Pn195 | 1924 | — | 5 Kopeks. Copper-Zinc. 20.0000 g. Y#79 | — |
| Pn196 | 1924 | — | 10 Kopeks. Bronze. Y#86 | — |
| Pn197 | 1924 | — | 15 Kopeks. Bronze. Y#87 | — |
| Pn198 | 1924 | — | 15 Kopeks. Copper. Y#87 | — |
| Pn199 | 1924 | — | 20 Kopeks. Bronze. Y#88 | — |
| Pn200 | 1924 | — | 50 Kopeks. Bronze. Y#89 | — |
| Pn201 | 1924 | — | 50 Kopeks. Unknown Metal. Y#89 | — |
| Pn204 | 1924 | — | Ruble. Aluminum. Y#90 | — |
| | | | **Note:** There are additional 1924 patterns but information is sketchy at present | |
| Pn205 | 1925 | — | 1/2 Kopek. Copper-Aluminum. Y#75 | — |
| Pn206 | 1925 | — | 1/2 Kopek. Aluminum. Y#75 | — |
| Pn207 | 1925 | — | 1/2 Kopek. Copper-Nickel. Y#75 | — |
| Pn208 | 1925 | — | 1/2 Kopek. Bronze. Y#75 | — |
| Pn209 | 1925 | — | 1/2 Kopek. Copper-Zinc. Y#75 | — |
| | | | **Note:** Additional metals exist | |
| Pn210 | 1925 | — | 10 Kopeks. Nickel. Y#86 | — |
| Pn211 | 1925 | — | 10 Kopeks. Aluminum-Bronze. Y#86 | — |
| Pn212 | 1925 | — | 15 Kopeks. Nickel. Y#87 | — |
| Pn213 | 1925 | — | 15 Kopeks. Copper. Y#87 | — |
| Pn214 | 1925 | — | 15 Kopeks. Aluminum-Bronze. Y#87 | — |
| Pn215 | 1925 | — | 20 Kopeks. Nickel. Y#88 | — |
| Pn216 | 1925 | — | 20 Kopeks. Copper. Y#88 | — |
| Pn217 | 1925 | — | 20 Kopeks. Aluminum-Bronze. Y#88 | — |
| Pn218 | 1925 | — | 50 Kopeks. Silver. Plain edge. Y#89.2 | — |
| Pn219 | 1925 | — | 50 Kopeks. Bronze. Y#89.2 | — |
| Pn221 | 1925 | — | Chervonetz. Copper. Y#85 | — |
| Pn220 | 1925 | — | 50 Kopeks. Lead. Y#89.2 | 175 |
| Pn222 | 1926 | — | 3 Kopeks. Aluminum. | — |
| Pn223 | 1926 | — | 3 Kopeks. Aluminum. | — |
| Pn224 | 1926 | — | 3 Kopeks. Unknown Metal. Y#100 | — |
| Pn225 | 1929 | — | 10 Kopeks. Nickel. | — |
| Pn226 | 1929 | — | 15 Kopeks. 35% Silver; Y#87 | — |
| Pn227 | 1929 | — | 50 Kopeks. Unknown Metal. | — |
| Pn228 | 1931 | — | 2 Kopeks. Copper. Y#92 | — |
| Pn229 | 1931 | — | 3 Kopeks. Copper. Y#93 | — |
| Pn230 | 1931 | — | 10 Kopeks. Unknown Metal. Y#93 | — |
| Pn231 | 1931 | — | 20 Kopeks. Bronze. Y#97 | — |
| Pn232 | 1932 | — | 3 Kopeks. Copper. KM#93 | — |
| | | | **Note:** Additional metals exist | |
| Pn233 | 1932 | — | 15 Kopeks. Unknown Metal. Y#96 | — |
| Pn234 | 1933 | — | 10 Kopeks. Unknown Metal. Similar to Y#95 | — |
| Pn235 | 1934 | — | 2 Kopeks. Copper. Y#92 | — |
| Pn236 | 1934 | — | 3 Kopeks. Copper. Y#93 | — |
| Pn237 | 1936 | — | 20 Kopeks. Aluminum. Y#104 | — |
| Pn238 | 1937 | — | 20 Kopeks. Aluminum. Y#111 | — |
| Pn239 | 1938 | — | 5 Kopeks. Unknown Metal. Y#101 | — |
| Pn240 | 1938 | — | 15 Kopeks. Aluminum. Plain edge. Y#110 | — |
| Pn241 | 1941 | — | 3 Kopeks. Unknown Metal. Y#107 | — |
| Pn242 | 1941 | — | 50 Kopeks. Unknown Metal. Similar to Y#109 | — |
| Pn243 | 1943 | — | Rouble. Unknown Metal. Portrait Stalin. | — |
| Pn244 | 1946 | — | 10 Kopeks. Unknown Metal. Y#102 | — |
| Pn245 | 1946 | — | 20 Kopeks. Unknown Metal. Y#111 | — |
| Pn246 | 1947 | — | Kopek. Aluminum-Bronze. Similar to Y#112; 16 bands on wreath. | — |
| Pn247 | 1947 | — | 2 Kopeks. Aluminum-Bronze. Similar to Y#113; 16 bands on wreath. | — |
| Pn248 | 1947 | — | 3 Kopeks. Unknown Metal. Similar to Y#114; 16 bands on wreath. | — |
| Pn249 | 1947 | — | 5 Kopeks. Aluminum-Bronze. Similar to Y#115; 16 bands on wreath. | — |
| Pn250 | 1947 | — | 10 Kopeks. Nickel. Similar to Y#116; 16 bands on wreath. | — |
| Pn251 | 1947 | — | 15 Kopeks. Unknown Metal. Similar to Y#117; 16 bands on wreath. | — |
| Pn252 | 1947 | — | 20 Kopeks. Nickel. Similar to Y#118; 16 bands on wreath. | — |
| Pn253 | 1949 | — | Chervonetz. Copper. | — |
| Pn255 | 1953 | — | Kopek. Aluminum. | — |
| Pn256 | 1953 | — | Kopek. Nickel. | — |
| | | | **Note:** Additional metals exist | |
| Pn257 | 1953 | — | Kopek. Copper-Nickel. With legend. Hammer and sickle, value above, date below. | — |
| Pn258 | 1953 | — | Kopek. Aluminum. | — |
| Pn259 | 1953 | — | Kopek. Nickel. | — |
| | | | **Note:** Additonal metals exist | |
| Pn261 | 1953 | — | 2 Kopeks. Aluminum. | — |
| Pn262 | 1953 | — | 2 Kopeks. Nickel. | — |
| | | | **Note:** Additional metals exist | |
| Pn264 | 1953 | — | 2 Kopeks. Aluminum. | — |
| Pn265 | 1953 | — | 2 Kopeks. Nickel. | — |
| | | | **Note:** Additional metals exist | |
| Pn267 | 1953 | — | 3 Kopeks. Aluminum. | — |
| Pn268 | 1953 | — | 3 Kopeks. Nickel. | — |
| | | | **Note:** Additional metals exist | |
| Pn270 | 1953 | — | 3 Kopeks. Aluminum. | — |
| Pn271 | 1953 | — | 3 Kopeks. Nickel. | — |
| | | | **Note:** Additional metals exist | |
| Pn272 | 1953 | — | 5 Kopeks. Aluminum. With legend. | — |
| Pn273 | 1953 | — | 5 Kopeks. Nickel. | — |
| | | | **Note:** Additional metals exist | |
| Pn274 | 1953 | — | 5 Kopeks. Aluminum. Without legend. | — |
| Pn275 | 1953 | — | 5 Kopeks. Nickel. | — |
| | | | **Note:** Additional metals exist | |
| Pn276 | 1953 | — | 10 Kopeks. Aluminum. With legend. Value and date within wreath. | — |
| Pn277 | 1953 | — | 10 Kopeks. Aluminum. Value, star above, date below. | — |
| Pn278 | 1953 | — | 10 Kopeks. Aluminum. Value, date below. | — |
| Pn279 | 1953 | — | 10 Kopeks. Aluminum. Value in wreath, star above date. | — |
| Pn280 | 1953 | — | 10 Kopeks. Aluminum. Value in wreath, date incircle at bottom. | — |
| Pn281 | 1953 | — | 10 Kopeks. Aluminum. Value in wreath in pellet border, date in circle at bottom. | — |
| Pn282 | 1953 | — | 10 Kopeks. Aluminum. Oak leaves behind value. | — |
| Pn283 | 1953 | — | 10 Kopeks. Aluminum. Without legend. Similar to KM#Pn276. | — |
| Pn284 | 1953 | — | 10 Kopeks. Aluminum. Similar to KM#Pn277. | — |
| Pn285 | 1953 | — | 10 Kopeks. Aluminum. Similar to KM#Pn278. | — |
| Pn286 | 1953 | — | 10 Kopeks. Aluminum. Similar to KM#Pn279. | — |
| Pn287 | 1953 | — | 10 Kopeks. Aluminum. Similar to KM#Pn280. | — |
| Pn288 | 1953 | — | 10 Kopeks. Aluminum. Similar to KM#Pn281. | — |
| Pn289 | 1953 | — | 10 Kopeks. Aluminum. Similar to KM#Pn282. | — |
| | | | **Note:** For Pn276-Pn289 at least four other base metal strikings exist of each | |
| Pn290 | 1953 | — | 15 Kopeks. Aluminum. With legend. Value and date within wreath. | — |
| Pn291 | 1953 | — | 15 Kopeks. Aluminum. Value, star above, date below. | — |
| Pn292 | 1953 | — | 15 Kopeks. Aluminum. Value, date below. | — |
| Pn293 | 1953 | — | 15 Kopeks. Aluminum. Value in wreath, star above date in circle at bottom. | — |
| Pn294 | 1953 | — | 15 Kopeks. Aluminum. Value in wreath, date in circle at bottom. | — |
| Pn295 | 1953 | — | 15 Kopeks. Aluminum. Value in wreath, pellet border, date in circle at bottom. | — |
| Pn296 | 1953 | — | 15 Kopeks. Aluminum. Oak leaves behind value, date below. | — |
| Pn297 | 1953 | — | 15 Kopeks. Aluminum. Legend. Similar to KM#Pn290. | — |
| Pn298 | 1953 | — | 15 Kopeks. Aluminum. Similar to KM#Pn291. | — |
| Pn299 | 1953 | — | 15 Kopeks. Aluminum. Similar to KM#Pn292. | — |
| Pn300 | 1953 | — | 15 Kopeks. Aluminum. Similar to KM#Pn293. | — |
| Pn301 | 1953 | — | 15 Kopeks. Aluminum. Similar to KM#Pn294. | — |
| Pn302 | 1953 | — | 15 Kopeks. Aluminum. Similar to KM#Pn295. | — |
| Pn303 | 1953 | — | 15 Kopeks. Aluminum. Similar to KM#Pn296. | — |
| | | | **Note:** For Pn290-Pn303 at least four other base metal strikings exist of each | |
| Pn304 | 1953 | — | 20 Kopeks. Aluminum. With legend. Value and date within wreath. | — |
| Pn305 | 1953 | — | 20 Kopeks. Aluminum. Value, star above, date below. | — |
| Pn306 | 1953 | — | 20 Kopeks. Aluminum. Value, date below. | — |
| Pn307 | 1953 | — | 20 Kopeks. Aluminum. Value in wreath, star above date in circle at bottom. | — |
| Pn308 | 1953 | — | 20 Kopeks. Aluminum. Value in wreath, date in circle at bottom. | — |
| Pn309 | 1953 | — | 20 Kopeks. Aluminum. Value in wreath, pellet border, date in circle at bottom. | — |
| Pn310 | 1953 | — | 20 Kopeks. Aluminum. Oak leaves behind value, date below. | — |
| Pn311 | 1953 | — | 20 Kopeks. Aluminum. Without legend. Similar to KM#Pn304. | — |
| Pn312 | 1953 | — | 20 Kopeks. Aluminum. Similar to KM#Pn305. | — |
| Pn313 | 1953 | — | 20 Kopeks. Aluminum. Similar to KM#Pn306. | — |
| Pn314 | 1953 | — | 20 Kopeks. Aluminum. Similar to KM#Pn307. | — |
| Pn315 | 1953 | — | 20 Kopeks. Aluminum. Similar to KM#Pn308. | — |
| Pn316 | 1953 | — | 20 Kopeks. Aluminum. Similar to KM#Pn309. | — |
| Pn317 | 1953 | — | 20 Kopeks. Aluminum. Similar to KM#Pn310. | — |
| | | | **Note:** Pn304-Pn317 exist in at least four additional metals | |
| Pn318 | 1953 | — | 50 Kopeks. Bronze. | — |
| Pn319 | 1953 | — | 50 Kopeks. Aluminum. | — |
| Pn320 | 1953 | — | 50 Kopeks. Bronze. | — |
| Pn321 | 1953 | — | 50 Kopeks. Aluminum. | — |
| Pn322 | 1953 | — | 50 Kopeks. Bronze. | — |
| Pn323 | 1953 | — | 50 Kopeks. Aluminum. | — |
| Pn324 | 1953 | — | 50 Kopeks. Bronze. | — |
| Pn325 | 1953 | — | 50 Kopeks. Aluminum. | — |
| | | | **Note:** Pn318-Pn325 exist in at least one other metal | |
| Pn254 | 1953 | — | Kopek. Copper-Nickel. With legend. Hammer and sickle, value above, date below. | 350 |
| Pn260 | 1953 | — | 2 Kopeks. Copper-Nickel. With legend. | 350 |
| Pn263 | 1953 | — | 2 Kopeks. Copper-Nickel. Without legend. | 350 |
| Pn266 | 1953 | — | 3 Kopeks. Copper-Nickel. With legend. | 350 |
| Pn269 | 1953 | — | 3 Kopeks. Copper-Nickel. Without legend. | 350 |
| Pn326 | 1955 | — | 25 Kopeks. Probably copper-nickel | — |
| Pn327 | 1956 | — | 10 Kopeks. Nickel. | — |
| Pn328 | 1956 | — | 10 Kopeks. Brass. | — |
| Pn329 | 1956 | — | 10 Kopeks. Copper. | — |
| Pn330 | 1956 | — | 10 Kopeks. Aluminum. | — |
| Pn331 | 1956 | — | 15 Kopeks. Nickel. | — |
| Pn332 | 1956 | — | 15 Kopeks. Brass. | — |
| Pn333 | 1956 | — | 15 Kopeks. Copper. | — |
| Pn334 | 1956 | — | 15 Kopeks. Aluminum. | — |
| Pn335 | 1956 | — | 20 Kopeks. Nickel. | — |
| Pn336 | 1956 | — | 20 Kopeks. Brass. | — |
| Pn337 | 1956 | — | 20 Kopeks. Copper. | — |
| Pn338 | 1956 | — | 20 Kopeks. Aluminum. | — |
| Pn339 | 1956 | — | 50 Kopeks. Nickel. | — |
| Pn340 | 1956 | — | 50 Kopeks. Brass. | — |
| Pn341 | 1956 | — | 50 Kopeks. Copper. | — |
| Pn342 | 1956 | — | 50 Kopeks. Aluminum. | — |
| Pn343 | 1956 | — | Rouble. Nickel. | — |
| Pn344 | 1956 | — | Rouble. Brass. | — |
| Pn345 | 1956 | — | Rouble. Copper. | — |
| Pn346 | 1956 | — | Rouble. Aluminum. | — |
| Pn347 | 1956 | — | 2 Roubles. Nickel. | — |
| Pn348 | 1956 | — | 2 Roubles. Brass. | — |
| Pn349 | 1956 | — | 2 Roubles. Copper. | — |
| Pn350 | 1956 | — | 2 Roubles. Aluminum. | — |
| Pn351 | 1956 | — | 3 Roubles. Nickel. | — |
| Pn352 | 1956 | — | 3 Roubles. Brass. | — |
| Pn353 | 1956 | — | 3 Roubles. Copper. | — |
| Pn354 | 1956 | — | 3 Roubles. Aluminum. | — |
| Pn355 | 1956 | — | 5 Roubles. Nickel. | — |
| Pn356 | 1956 | — | 5 Roubles. Brass. | — |
| Pn357 | 1956 | — | 5 Roubles. Copper. | — |
| Pn358 | 1956 | — | 5 Roubles. Aluminum. | — |
| Pn359 | 1957 | — | 10 Kopeks. Copper-Nickel. Y#123 | — |
| Pn360 | 1957 | — | 10 Kopeks. Aluminum. Y#123 | — |
| Pn361 | 1957 | — | 20 Kopeks. Copper-Nickel. Y#125 | — |
| Pn362 | 1958 | — | Kopek. Aluminum. Y#126 | — |
| Pn363 | 1958 | — | 2 Kopeks. Aluminum. Y#127 | — |
| Pn364 | 1958 | — | 3 Kopeks. Aluminum. Y#128 | — |
| Pn365 | 1958 | — | 5 Kopeks. Aluminum. Y#129 | — |
| Pn366 | 1958 | — | 10 Kopeks. Aluminum. Y#A130 | — |
| Pn367 | 1958 | — | 15 Kopeks. Aluminum. Y#A131 | — |
| Pn368 | 1958 | — | 20 Kopeks. Aluminum. Y#A132 | — |
| Pn369 | 1958 | — | 50 Kopeks. Aluminum. Y#133 | — |
| Pn370 | 1958 | — | Rouble. Aluminum. Y#134 | — |
| Pn371 | 1958 | — | 2 Roubles. Aluminum. Y#A134 | — |
| Pn372 | 1958 | — | 3 Roubles. Aluminum. Y#B134 | — |
| Pn373 | 1958 | — | 5 Roubles. Aluminum. Y#C134 | — |
| Pn374 | 1959 | — | 10 Kopeks. Copper-Nickel. | — |
| Pn375 | 1959 | — | 15 Kopeks. Copper-Nickel. | — |
| Pn376 | 1959 | — | 20 Kopek. Copper-Nickel. | — |
| Pn377 | 1961 | — | 1/2 Kopek. Copper. | — |
| Pn378 | 1961 | — | Kopek. Copper. Y#126 | — |
| Pn379 | 1961 | — | 2 Kopeks. Copper. Y#127 | — |
| Pn380 | 1961 | — | 3 Kopeks. Copper. Y#128 | — |
| Pn381 | 1961 | — | 5 Kopeks. Copper. Y#129 | — |
| Pn382 | 1961 | — | 10 Kopeks. Copper. Y#130 | — |
| Pn383 | 1961 | — | 15 Kopeks. Copper. Y#131 | — |
| Pn384 | 1961 | — | 20 Kopeks. Copper. Y#132 | — |
| Pn385 | 1962 | — | 50 Kopeks. Copper-Nickel. Y#133.1 | — |
| Pn386 | 1962 | — | 50 Kopeks. Copper-Nickel. | — |
| Pn387 | 1962 | — | Rouble. Copper-Nickel. Y#134.1 | — |
| Pn388 | 1962 | — | Rouble. Copper-Nickel. | — |
| Pn389 | 1963 | — | 50 Kopeks. Copper-Nickel. | — |
| Pn390 | 1963 | — | Rouble. Copper-Nickel. | — |
| Pn393 | 1967 | — | 15 Kopeks. Unknown Metal. Uncertain 1917-67 commemorative disign | — |
| Pn395 | 1967 | — | 50 Kopeks. Unknown Metal. Uncertain 1917-67 commemorative disign | — |
| Pn391 | 1967 | — | 10 Kopeks. Copper-Nickel-Zinc. Arms. Ship. | 150 |
| Pn392 | 1967 | — | 10 Kopeks. Copper-Nickel-Zinc. Arms. Worker and soldier. | 150 |
| Pn396 | | — | 100 Roubles. 0.9000 Gold. Y#162 | — |
| | | | **Note:** Pn390-Pn396 minor varieties exist | |

## TRIAL STRIKES

| KM# | Date | Mintage | Identification | Mkt Val |
|---|---|---|---|---|
| TS1 | 1924 | — | 5 Kopeks. Copper. Y#79. | 300 |
| TS2 | 1924 | — | 5 Kopeks. Copper. Y#79. | 300 |

## MINT SETS

| KM# | Date | Mintage | Identification | Issue Price | Mkt Val |
|---|---|---|---|---|---|
| MS10 | 1969 (9) | — | Y#126-132, 133a.2, 134a.2 | 7.00 | 8.00 |
| MS11 | 1970 (9) | — | Y#126-132, 133a.2, 134a.2 | 11.00 | 15.00 |

| KM# | Date | Mintage | Identification | Issue Price | Mkt Val |
|---|---|---|---|---|---|
| MS12 | 1971 (9) | — | Y#126-132, 133a.2, 134a.2 | 6.00 | 10.00 |
| MS13 | 1972 (9) | 10,000 | Y#126-132, 133a.2, 134a.2 | 7.00 | 8.00 |
| MS14 | 1973 (9) | 800 | Y#126-132, 133a.2, 134a.2 | 11.00 | 8.00 |
| MS15 | 1974 (9) | 27,500 | Y#126-132, 133a.2, 134a.2, square mint token | 11.00 | 8.00 |
| MS16 | 1975 (9) | 27,000 | Y#126-132, 133a.2, 134a.2 | 11.00 | 8.00 |
| MS17 | 1976 (9) | 55,000 | Y#126-132, 133a.2, 134a.2 | 11.00 | 10.00 |
| MS18 | 1977 (9) | 58,750 | Y#126-132, 133a.2, 134a.2 | 11.00 | 8.00 |
| MS19 | 1978 (9) | 62,500 | Y#126-132, 133a.2, 134a.2 | 11.00 | 8.00 |
| MS2 | 1961 (9) | — | Y#126-132, 133a.1, 134a.1 | 4.50 | 32.00 |
| MS20 | 1979 (9) | 75,000 | Y#126-132, 133a.2, 134a.2 | 19.00 | 8.00 |
| MS21 | 1980 (9) | — | Y#126-132, 133a.2, 134a.2 | 19.00 | 8.00 |
| MS22 | 1981 (9) | — | Y#126-132, 133a.2, 134a.2 | — | 8.00 |
| MS23 | 1982 (9) | — | Y#126-132, 133a.2, 134a.2 | — | 8.00 |
| MS24 | 1983 (9) | — | Y#126-132, 133a.2, 134a.2 | — | 8.00 |
| MS25 | 1984 (9) | — | Y#126-132, 133a.2, 134a.2 | — | 8.00 |
| MS26 | 1985 (9) | — | Y#126-132, 133a.2, 134a.2 | — | 8.00 |
| MS27 | Mixed dates (9) | — | Y#135, 140-143, 188-189 | — | 25.00 |
| MS28 | Mixed dates (8) | — | Y#135, 140-143, 188-189 | — | 25.00 |
| MS29 | 1987 (9) | — | Y#126-132, 133a.2-134a.2 | — | 10.00 |
| MS3 | 1962 (7) | — | Y#126-132 | 2.25 | 4.50 |
| MS30 | 1988 (9) | — | Y#126-133, 134a.2 | — | 8.00 |
| MS31 | 1989 (9) | — | Y#126-133, 134a.2 | — | 8.00 |
| MS34 | 1992 (6) | — | Y#311-316 | 15.00 | 10.00 |
| MS4 | 1964 (4) | — | Y#126, 127, 133a.2, 134a.2 | 2.55 | 4.00 |
| MS5 | 1965 (9) | — | Y#126-132, 133a.2, 134a.2 | 4.50 | 8.00 |
| MS6 | 1966 (9) | — | Y#126-132, 133a.2, 134a.2 | 4.50 | 14.00 |
| MS7 | 1967 (9) | — | Y#126-132, 133a.2, 134a.2 | 4.50 | 8.00 |
| MS9 | 1968 (9) | — | Y#126-132, 133a.2, 134a.2 and mint token | 6.00 | 10.00 |
| MS1 | 1957 (4) | — | Y#122-125 | 2.25 | 35.00 |
| MS8 | 1967 (5) | 211,250 | Y#136-140 | 6.00 | 8.00 |
| MSA27 | 1986 (9) | — | Y#126a-129a, 130-132, 133a.2, 134a.2 | — | 14.00 |
| MS32 | 1990 (9) | — | Y#126a-129a, 130-132, 133a.2, 134a.2 | — | 12.00 |
| MSA32 | 1990 (9) | — | Y#126a-129a, 130-132, 133a.2, 134a.2 | — | 12.00 |
| MS33 | 1991 (3) | — | Y#268-270 | 245 | 1,950 |
| MSA33 | 1991 (9) | — | Y#126a-129a, 130-132, 133a.2, 134a.2 | — | 10.00 |
| MS35 | 1993 (4) | 2,700 | Y#416-419 | — | 960 |
| MS36 | 1993 (3) | 3,000 | Y#420-422 | — | 1,950 |
| MS37 | 1994 (3) | 2,000 | Y#431-433 | — | 1,950 |
| MS38 | 1995 (6) | 200,000 | Y#399-404 and medal | — | 17.00 |
| MS39 | 1996 (6) | 100,000 | Y#504-509 and medal | — | 25.00 |
| MS40 | 1997(SP) (7) | — | Y#600-606 | — | 12.50 |

## PROOF SETS

| KM# | Date | Mintage | Identification | Issue Price | Mkt Val |
|---|---|---|---|---|---|
| PS1 | Mixed dates (5) | — | Y#152, 163, 175-176, 187 | — | 1,500 |
| PS2 | 1987 (3) | — | Y#206-208 | — | 37.50 |
| PS3 | 1990 (9) | — | Y#126a-129a, 130-132, 133a.2, 134a.2 | — | 15.00 |
| PS5 | 1991 (3) | 1,500 | Y#286a-288a | — | 1,450 |
| PS4 | 1991(L) (9) | — | Y#126a-129a, 130-132, 133a.2, 134a.2 | — | 15.00 |
| PS7 | 1993 (3) | 750 | Y#395-397 | — | 725 |
| PS9 | 1993 (2) | 10,000 | Y#323, 406 | — | 150 |
| PS6 | 1993 (4) | 1,500 | Y#416-419 | — | 1,230 |
| PS8 | 1993 (3) | 2,000 | Y#420-422 | — | 2,050 |
| PS10 | 1994 (4) | 2,500 | Y#424-427 | — | 1,255 |
| PS11 | 1994 (3) | 900 | Y#428-430 | — | 1,360 |
| PS13 | 1994 (2) | 7,500 | Y#405, 423 | — | 180 |
| PS12 | 1994 (3) | 1,500 | Y#431-433 | — | 2,050 |
| PS14 | 1995 (4) | 2,500 | Y#438-441 | 1,250 | 1,250 |
| PS15 | 1995 (3) | 1,500 | Y#435-437 | 875 | 875 |
| PS16 | 1995 (3) | 900 | Y#442-444 | 1,350 | 1,350 |

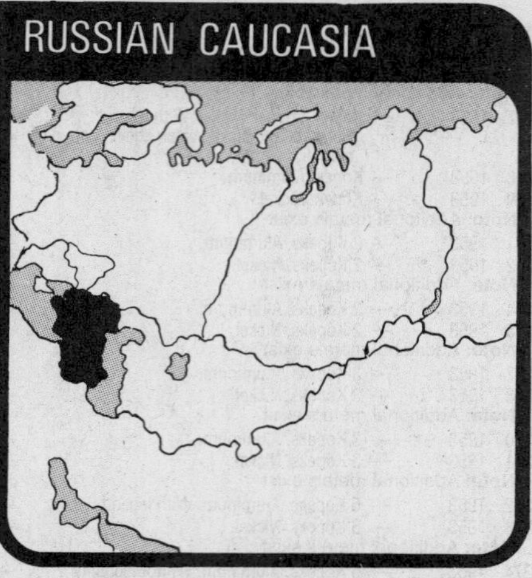


Russian Caucasia, a natural area in Russia located between the Black and Caspian Seas, was a region of mystery and myth to the Ancient Greeks. It was there that Prometheus was bound for the eagle's torment and the Argonauts sought the Golden Fleece. For more than a thousand years Caucasia was the refuge for wave after wave of migrating peoples. Greeks, Romans, Persians, Turks, Huns, Mongols and finally the Russians invaded the treeless steppes and wooded highlands of this range-flanked granite bridge between Europe and Asia. Russian aggression, heroically resisted by the independent mountain races, began early in the 18th century and continued until the last opposition was stifled. The several states of Caucasia made a futile attempt to establish an independent federated republic during the Russian February Revolution of 1917, but were quickly reconquered after the triumph of Bolshevism over the Kerensky administration.

The following areas of Russian Caucasia were coin-issuing entities of interest to numismatists.

## ARMAVIR

Armavir is a city located in Krasnodar Territory, Southern Russia north of the Caucasus.

**LOCAL CURRENCY UNDER THE WHITE RUSSIANS**

## CITY

### LOCAL COINAGE

Under the White Russians

**ROUBLE** **KM# 1** **Composition:** Copper **Obverse:** Monogram below tail **Edge:** Reeded **Note:** Thin planchet.

| Date | Mintage | VG | F | VF | XF | Unc |
|---|---|---|---|---|---|---|
| 1918 | — | 75.00 | 150 | 250 | 400 | — |

**3 ROUBLES** **KM# 2.2** **Composition:** Copper **Note:** Monogram below claw.

| Date | Mintage | VG | F | VF | XF | Unc |
|---|---|---|---|---|---|---|
| 1918 | — | 50.00 | 100 | 175 | 275 | — |

**3 ROUBLES** **KM# 2.1** **Composition:** Copper **Obverse:** Monogram below tail **Edge:** Reeded **Note:** Varieties exist.

| Date | Mintage | VG | F | VF | XF | Unc |
|---|---|---|---|---|---|---|
| 1918 | — | 40.00 | 80.00 | 150 | 250 | — |

**5 ROUBLES** **KM# 3** **Composition:** Copper

| Date | Mintage | VG | F | VF | XF | Unc |
|---|---|---|---|---|---|---|
| 1918 | — | 150 | 225 | 400 | 550 | — |

### PATTERNS

Including off metal strikes

| KM# | Date | Mintage | Identification | Mkt Val |
|---|---|---|---|---|
| Pn1 | 1918 | — | Rouble. Copper. 28 mm. Reeded edge. Thin planchet. Y1. | — |
| Pn6 | 1918 | — | 5 Roubles. Aluminum. Y3. | — |

| KM# | Date | Mintage | Identification | Mkt Val |
|---|---|---|---|---|
| Pn4 | 1918 | — | 3 Roubles. Copper. 31 mm. Monogram under tail. Y2.1. | 350 |
| Pn2 | 1918 | — | Rouble. Copper. 28 mm. Plain edge. Thin planchet. Y1. | — |
| Pn3 | 1918 | — | Rouble. Copper. 28 mm. Plain edge. Thick planchet. Y1. | — |
| Pn3a | 1918 | — | Rouble. Brass. | — |
| Pn5 | 1918 | — | 3 Roubles. Silver. Y2.1. | 650 |

## DAGHISTAN

Dagestan

Daghistan is a mountainous republic bounded on the north by Chechno-Ingush, on the south by Azerbaijan, on the east by the Caspian Sea, and on the west by Georgia. It was annexed from Persia in 1723. In 1806 Derbend was captured and their autonomy, albeit under Persian domination, ended. The republic was created in 1921 from the former province of Daghistan, after a civil war 1917-1920. It is now part of the CIS.

**RULERS**

Emir Uzun-Hayir (Uzun-Kheir), AH1338-1339/1919-1920AD

**MINTNAME**

داغستان

Daghistan

**2-1/2 TOMAN**

A 2-1/2 Toman coin dated AH1338 was reportedly struck, but no specimens are known.

## PROVINCE

### STANDARD COINAGE

**10 TOMAN** **KM# 3** **Composition:** Brass **Ruler:** Emir Uzun-Hayir (Uzun-Kheir) 1919-1920 **Obverse:** Balance scale, crescent below **Reverse:** Arabic inscription **Note:** Possibly a pattern.

| Date | Mintage | F | VF | XF | Unc | BU |
|---|---|---|---|---|---|---|
| AH1338(1919) | — | — | — | — | — | — |

**10 TOMAN** **KM# 4** **Composition:** Copper **Ruler:** Emir Uzun-Hayir (Uzun-Kheir) 1919-1920 **Obverse:** Balance scale, crescent below **Reverse:** Russian legend around Arabic inscription, date **Note:** Struck over Russia 2 Kopek, Y#10. Possibly a pattern.

| Date | Mintage | F | VF | XF | Unc | BU |
|---|---|---|---|---|---|---|
| AH1338(1919) | — | — | — | — | — | — |

# RWANDA

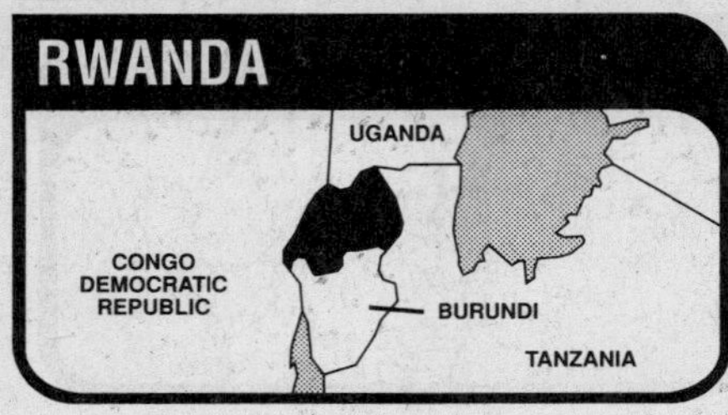


The Republic of Rwanda, located in central Africa between the Republic of the Congo and Tanzania, has an area of 10,169 sq. mi. (26,340 sq. km.) and a population of 7.3 million. Capital: Kigali. The economy is based on agriculture and mining. Coffee and tin are exported.

German Lieutenant Count von Goetzen was the first European to visit Rwanda, 1894. Four years later the court of the Mwami (the Tutsi king of Rwanda) willingly permitted the kingdom to become a protectorate of Germany. In 1916, during the African campaigns of World War I, Belgian troops from Congo occupied Rwanda. After the war it, together with Burundi, became a Belgian League of Nations mandate under the name of the Territory of Ruanda-Urundi. Following World War II, Ruanda-Urundi became a Belgian administered U.N. trust territory. The Tutsi monarchy was deposed by the U.N. supervised election of 1961, after which Belgium granted Rwanda internal autonomy. On July 1, 1962, the U.N. terminated the Belgian trusteeship and granted full independence to both Rwanda and Burundi.

For earlier coinage see Belgian Congo, and Rwanda and Burundi.

**MINT MARKS**

(a) - Paris, privy marks only
(b) - Brussels, privy marks only

**MONETARY SYSTEM**

100 Centimes = 1 Franc

## REPUBLIC

### STANDARD COINAGE

**1/2 FRANC** **KM# 9** **Composition:** Aluminum

| Date | Mintage | F | VF | XF | Unc | BU |
|---|---|---|---|---|---|---|
| 1970 | 5,000,000 | — | 0.50 | 0.85 | 1.75 | — |

**FRANC** **KM# 5** **Composition:** Copper-Nickel

| Date | Mintage | F | VF | XF | Unc | BU |
|---|---|---|---|---|---|---|
| 1964(b) | 3,000,000 | — | 5.00 | 10.00 | 20.00 | — |
| 1965(b) | 4,500,000 | — | 0.50 | 0.85 | 1.75 | — |

**FRANC** **KM# 8** **Composition:** Aluminum

| Date | Mintage | F | VF | XF | Unc | BU |
|---|---|---|---|---|---|---|
| 1969 | 5,000,000 | — | 0.50 | 1.50 | 3.50 | — |

**FRANC** **KM# 12** **Composition:** Aluminum

| Date | Mintage | F | VF | XF | Unc | BU |
|---|---|---|---|---|---|---|
| 1974 | 13,000,000 | — | 0.20 | 0.50 | 1.00 | — |
| 1977 | 15,000,000 | — | 0.15 | 0.25 | 0.75 | — |
| 1985 | — | — | 0.10 | 0.15 | 0.65 | — |

**2 FRANCS** **KM# 10** **Composition:** Aluminum **Series:** F.A.O.

| Date | Mintage | F | VF | XF | Unc | BU |
|---|---|---|---|---|---|---|
| 1970 | 5,000,000 | — | 0.10 | 0.20 | 0.50 | — |

**5 FRANCS** **KM# 6** **Composition:** Bronze

| Date | Mintage | F | VF | XF | Unc | BU |
|---|---|---|---|---|---|---|
| 1964(b) | 4,000,000 | — | 0.25 | 0.50 | 1.75 | — |
| 1965(b) | 3,000,000 | — | 5.00 | 10.00 | 20.00 | — |

**5 FRANCS** **KM# 13** **Composition:** Bronze

| Date | Mintage | F | VF | XF | Unc | BU |
|---|---|---|---|---|---|---|
| 1974 | 7,000,000 | — | 1.00 | 3.00 | 6.00 | — |
| 1977 | 7,002,000 | — | 1.00 | 2.00 | 4.00 | — |
| 1987 | — | — | 0.25 | 0.50 | 1.85 | — |

**10 FRANCS** **KM# 7** **Composition:** Copper-Nickel

| Date | Mintage | F | VF | XF | Unc | BU |
|---|---|---|---|---|---|---|
| 1964(b) | 6,000,000 | — | 1.00 | 2.00 | 4.50 | — |

**10 FRANCS** **KM# 1** **Weight:** 3.0000 g. **Composition:** 0.9000 Gold .1085 oz. AGW

| Date | Mintage | VG | F | VF | XF | Unc |
|---|---|---|---|---|---|---|
| 1965 | 10,000 | — | — | — | — | 60.00 |
| 1965 Proof | — | Value: 65.00 | | | | |

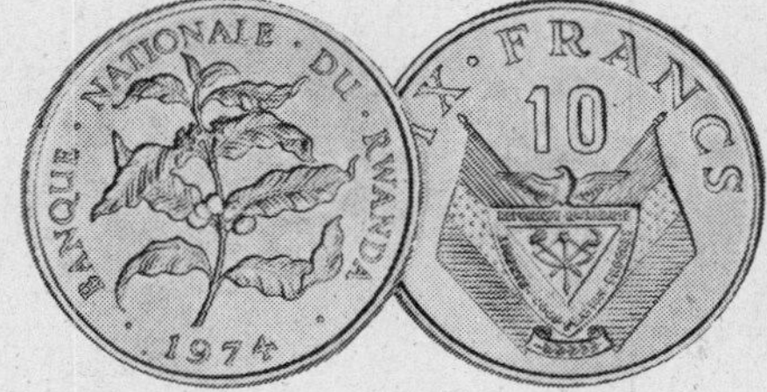

**10 FRANCS** **KM# 14.1** **Composition:** Copper-Nickel

| Date | Mintage | F | VF | XF | Unc | BU |
|---|---|---|---|---|---|---|
| 1974 | 6,000,000 | — | 3.00 | 5.00 | 10.00 | — |

**10 FRANCS** **KM# 14.2** **Composition:** Copper-Nickel **Note:** Reduced size.

| Date | Mintage | F | VF | XF | Unc | BU |
|---|---|---|---|---|---|---|
| 1985 | — | — | 0.50 | 0.85 | 1.85 | — |

**20 FRANCS** **KM# 15** **Composition:** Brass

| Date | Mintage | F | VF | XF | Unc | BU |
|---|---|---|---|---|---|---|
| 1977(a) | 22,000,000 | — | 1.00 | 2.00 | 4.00 | — |

**25 FRANCS** **KM# 2** **Weight:** 7.5000 g. **Composition:** 0.9000 Gold .2170 oz. AGW **Note:** Similar to 10 Francs, KM#1.

| Date | Mintage | F | VF | XF | Unc | BU |
|---|---|---|---|---|---|---|
| 1965 Proof | 4,000 | Value: 100 | | | | |

**50 FRANCS** **KM# 3** **Weight:** 15.0000 g. **Composition:** 0.9000 Gold .4340 oz. AGW **Note:** Similar to 10 Francs, KM#1.

| Date | Mintage | F | VF | XF | Unc | BU |
|---|---|---|---|---|---|---|
| 1965 Proof | 3,000 | Value: 175 | | | | |

**50 FRANCS** **KM# 16** **Composition:** Brass

| Date | Mintage | F | VF | XF | Unc | BU |
|---|---|---|---|---|---|---|
| 1977(a) | 9,000,000 | — | 2.50 | 3.50 | 7.00 | — |

**100 FRANCS** **KM# 4** **Weight:** 30.0000 g. **Composition:** 0.9000 Gold .8681 oz. AGW

| Date | Mintage | F | VF | XF | Unc | BU |
|---|---|---|---|---|---|---|
| 1965 Proof | 3,000 | Value: 360 | | | | |

**100 FRANCS** KM# 18 **Weight:** 31.2300 g. **Composition:** 0.9990 Silver 1.0041 oz. ASW **Subject:** Nelson Mandela

| Date | Mintage | F | VF | XF | Unc | BU |
|---|---|---|---|---|---|---|
| 1990 | — | — | — | — | 30.00 | — |
| 1990 Proof | Est. 50,000 | Value: 40.00 | | | | |

**100 FRANCS** KM# 21 **Weight:** 31.1035 g. **Composition:** 0.9990 Silver 1 oz. ASW **Subject:** Environmental protection **Reverse:** Gorilla

| Date | Mintage | F | VF | XF | Unc | BU |
|---|---|---|---|---|---|---|
| 1993 Proof | Est. 20,000 | Value: 45.00 | | | | |

**200 FRANCS** KM# 11 **Weight:** 18.0000 g. **Composition:** 0.8000 Silver .4630 oz. ASW **Series:** F.A.O. **Subject:** 10th anniversray of independence and F.A.O. issue

| Date | Mintage | F | VF | XF | Unc | BU |
|---|---|---|---|---|---|---|
| 1972 | 30,000 | — | — | 6.00 | 11.50 | — |

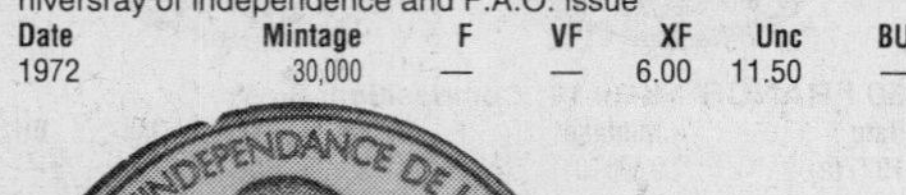

**1000 FRANCS** KM# 17 **Weight:** 31.6400 g. **Composition:** 0.9990 Silver 1.0173 oz. ASW **Subject:** 25th anniversary of national bank

| Date | Mintage | F | VF | XF | Unc | BU |
|---|---|---|---|---|---|---|
| 1989 | — | — | — | — | 45.00 | — |

**2000 FRANCS** KM# 19 **Weight:** 7.8000 g. **Composition:** 0.9990 Gold .25 oz. AGW **Subject:** Nelson Mandela **Note:** Similar to 5,000 Francs, KM#20.

| Date | Mintage | F | VF | XF | Unc | BU |
|---|---|---|---|---|---|---|
| 1990 Proof | Est. 50,000 | Value: 200 | | | | |

**5000 FRANCS** KM# 20 **Weight:** 15.5300 g. **Composition:** 0.9990 Gold .5 oz. AGW **Subject:** Nelson Mandela

| Date | Mintage | F | VF | XF | Unc | BU |
|---|---|---|---|---|---|---|
| 1990 Proof | 3,000 | Value: 400 | | | | |

## ESSAIS

| KM# | Date | Mintage | Identification | Issue Price | Mkt Val |
|---|---|---|---|---|---|
| E1 | 1964(b) | — | Franc. Aluminum. | — | 35.00 |

| KM# | Date | Mintage | Identification | Issue Price | Mkt Val |
|---|---|---|---|---|---|
| E2 | 1964(b) | — | 5 Francs. Bronze. | — | 55.00 |
| E3 | 1964(b) | — | 10 Francs. Copper-Nickel. | — | 70.00 |
| E4 | 1977(a) | — | Franc. Aluminum. | — | 22.00 |
| E5 | 1977(a) | — | 5 Francs. Bronze. | — | 25.00 |
| E6 | 1977(a) | — | 20 Francs. Brass. | — | 25.00 |
| E7 | 1977(a) | — | 50 Francs. Brass. | — | 28.00 |

## PROOF SETS

| KM# | Date | Mintage | Identification | Issue Price | Mkt Val |
|---|---|---|---|---|---|
| PS1 | 1965(a) (4) | 3,000 | KM1-4 | — | 700 |

Rwanda-Burundi, a Belgian League of Nations mandate and United Nations trust territory comprising the provinces of Ruanda-Urundi of the former colony of German East Africa, was located in central Africa between the present Democratic Republic of the Congo, Uganda and mainland Tanzania. The mandate-trust territory had an area of 20,916 sq. mi. (54,272 sq. km.) and a population of 4.3 million.

For specific statistics and history of Ruanda and of Urundi see individual entries.

When Rwanda and Burundi were formed into a mandate for administration by Belgium, their names were combined as Ruanda-Urundi and they were organized as an integral part of the Belgian Congo. During the mandate-trust territory period, they utilized the coinage of the Belgian Congo, which from 1954 through 1960carried the appropriate dual identification. After the Belgian Congo acquired independence as the Democratic Republic of the Congo, the provinces of Ruanda and Urundi reverted to their former names of Rwanda and Burundi and utilized a common currency issued by a Central Bank (B.E.R.B.) established for that purpose until the time when, as independent republics, each issued its own national coinage.

For earlier coinage see Belgian Congo.

**MONETARY SYSTEM**

100 Centimes = 1 Franc

# PROVINCES

## STANDARD COINAGE

**FRANC** KM# 1 **Composition:** Brass

| Date | Mintage | F | VF | XF | Unc | BU |
|---|---|---|---|---|---|---|
| 1960 | 2,000,000 | — | 3.50 | 7.50 | 17.50 | — |
| 1961 | 16,000,000 | — | 0.50 | 1.00 | 3.00 | — |
| 1964 | 3,000,000 | — | 3.00 | 6.50 | 15.00 | — |

**FRANC** KM# 2 **Composition:** Copper-Nickel **Obverse:** Rwanda-Burundi KM#1 **Reverse:** Belgium Franc, KM#142 or KM#143 **Note:** Mule.

| Date | Mintage | F | VF | XF | Unc | BU |
|---|---|---|---|---|---|---|
| 1961 Rare | 50 | — | — | — | — | — |

## ESSAIS

| KM# | Date | Mintage | Identification | Issue Price | Mkt Val |
|---|---|---|---|---|---|
| E1 | 1960 | — | Franc. Bronze. | — | 150 |

| KM# | Date | Mintage | Identification | Issue Price | Mkt Val |
|---|---|---|---|---|---|
| E2 | 1960 | — | Franc. Brass. KM1. | — | 75.00 |
| E3 | 1960 | — | Franc. Silver. KM1. | — | 145 |

# SAARLAND

The Saar, the 10th state of the German Federal Republic, is located in the coal-rich Saar basin on the Franco-German frontier, and has an area of 991 sq. mi. and a population of 1.2 million. Capital: Saarbrucken. It is an important center of mining and heavy industry.

From the late 14th century until the fall of Napoleon, the city of Saarbrucken was ruled by the counts of Nassau-Saarbrucken, but the surrounding territory was subject to the political and cultural domination of France. At the close of the Napoleonic era, the Saarland came under the control of Prussia. France was awarded the Saar coal mines following World War I, and the Saarland was made an autonomous territory of the League of Nations, its future political affiliation to be determined by referendum. The plebiscite, 1935, chose re-incorporation into Germany. France reoccupied the Saarland, 1945, establishing strong economic ties and assuming the obligation of defense and foreign affairs. After sustained agitation by West Germany, France agreed, 1955, to the return of the Saar to Germany by Jan. 1957.

**MINT MARKS**

(a) - Paris - privy marks only

## GERMAN REPUBLIC STATE

### STANDARD COINAGE

**10 FRANKEN** **KM# 1** **Composition:** Aluminum-Bronze

| Date | Mintage | F | VF | XF | Unc | BU |
|---|---|---|---|---|---|---|
| 1954(a) | 11,000,000 | 0.75 | 1.50 | 3.00 | 7.00 | — |

**20 FRANKEN** **KM# 2** **Composition:** Aluminum-Bronze

| Date | Mintage | F | VF | XF | Unc | BU |
|---|---|---|---|---|---|---|
| 1954(a) | 12,950,000 | 0.75 | 1.50 | 3.50 | 9.00 | — |

**50 FRANKEN** **KM# 3** **Composition:** Aluminum-Bronze

| Date | Mintage | F | VF | XF | Unc | BU |
|---|---|---|---|---|---|---|
| 1954(a) | 5,300,000 | 3.00 | 6.00 | 12.00 | 25.00 | — |

**100 FRANKEN** **KM# 4** **Composition:** Copper-Nickel

| Date | Mintage | F | VF | XF | Unc | BU |
|---|---|---|---|---|---|---|
| 1955(a) | 11,000,000 | 2.00 | 4.00 | 8.00 | 18.00 | — |

## ESSAIS

Standard metals unless otherwise noted

| KM# | Date | Mintage | Identification | Issue Price | Mkt Val |
|---|---|---|---|---|---|
| E1 | 1954(a) | 1,100 | 10 Franken. KM1. | — | 30.00 |
| E3 | 1954(a) | 1,100 | 20 Franken. KM2. | — | 40.00 |
| E4 | 1954(a) | 50 | 20 Franken. Gold. KM2. | — | 1,850 |
| E5 | 1954(a) | 1,100 | 50 Franken. KM3. | — | 50.00 |

| KM# | Date | Mintage | Identification | Issue Price | Mkt Val |
|---|---|---|---|---|---|
| E7 | 1955(a) | 50 | 100 Franken. Gold. KM4. | — | 2,250 |

# SAHARAWI ARAB D.R.

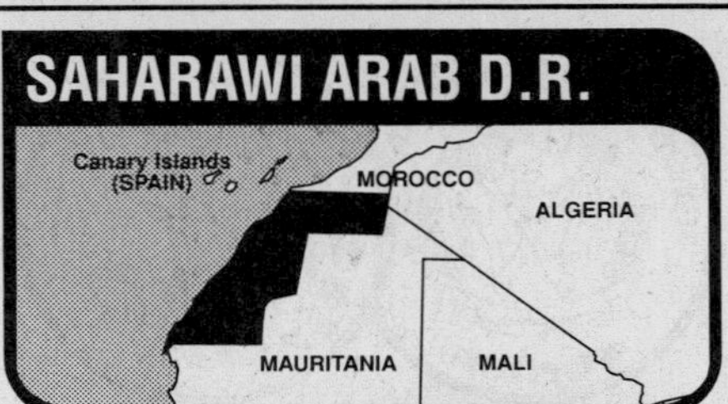


The Saharawi Arab Democratic Republic, located in northwest Africa has an area of 102,703 sq. mi. and a population (census taken 1974) of 76,425. Formerly known as Spanish Sahara, the area is bounded on the north by Morocco, on the east and southeast by Mauritania, on the northeast by Algeria, and on the west by the Atlantic Ocean. Capital: El Aaium. Agriculture, fishing and mining are the two main industries. Exports are barley, livestock and phosphates.

A Spanish trading post was established in 1476 but was abandoned in 1524. A Spanish protectorate for the region was proclaimed in 1884. The status of the Spanish Sahara changed from a colony to an overseas province in 1958. Spain relinquished its holdings in 1975 and it was divided between Mauritania, which gave up its claim in August 1979 and Morocco, which subsequently occupied the entire territory. The official languages are Spanish and an Arab dialect: The Hassaniya.

## DEMOCRATIC REPUBLIC

### NON-CIRCULATING COLLECTOR COINAGE

**PESETA** **KM# 14** **Composition:** Copper-Nickel **Reverse:** Arab and camel

| Date | Mintage | F | VF | XF | Unc | BU |
|---|---|---|---|---|---|---|
| 1992 | — | — | — | — | 0.75 | — |

**2 PESETAS** **KM# 15** **Composition:** Copper-Nickel **Reverse:** Arab and camel

| Date | Mintage | F | VF | XF | Unc | BU |
|---|---|---|---|---|---|---|
| 1992 | — | — | — | — | 1.25 | — |

**5 PESETAS** **KM# 16** **Composition:** Copper-Nickel **Reverse:** Arab and camel

| Date | Mintage | F | VF | XF | Unc | BU |
|---|---|---|---|---|---|---|
| 1992 | — | — | — | — | 2.00 | — |

**50 PESETAS** **KM# 1** **Composition:** Copper-Nickel **Reverse:** Arab and camel

| Date | Mintage | F | VF | XF | Unc | BU |
|---|---|---|---|---|---|---|
| 1990 | — | — | — | — | 6.00 | — |

**100 PESETAS** **KM# 18** **Composition:** Copper-Nickel **Reverse:** Arab and sailing ship

| Date | Mintage | F | VF | XF | Unc | BU |
|---|---|---|---|---|---|---|
| 1990 | — | — | — | — | 10.00 | — |

**100 PESETAS** **KM# 20** **Composition:** Copper-Nickel **Reverse:** Arab and camel

| Date | Mintage | F | VF | XF | Unc | BU |
|---|---|---|---|---|---|---|
| 1990 | — | — | — | — | 9.50 | — |

**100 PESETAS** **KM# 25** **Composition:** Copper-Nickel **Reverse:** Arab and sail boat

| Date | Mintage | F | VF | XF | Unc | BU |
|---|---|---|---|---|---|---|
| 1990 | — | — | — | — | 8.00 | — |

**100 PESETAS** **KM# 39** **Composition:** Copper-Nickel **Obverse:** National emblem **Reverse:** Antique sailing ship

| Date | Mintage | F | VF | XF | Unc | BU |
|---|---|---|---|---|---|---|
| 1990 Proof | 87 | Value: 60.00 | | | | |

**100 PESETAS** **KM# 7** **Composition:** Nickel Plated Steel **Series:** Olympics **Subject:** Equestrian event

| Date | Mintage | F | VF | XF | Unc | BU |
|---|---|---|---|---|---|---|
| 1991 | 5,000 | — | — | — | 10.00 | — |

**100 PESETAS** **KM# 26** **Composition:** Nickel Plated Steel **Reverse:** Ship above Canary Islands map

| Date | Mintage | F | VF | XF | Unc | BU |
|---|---|---|---|---|---|---|
| 1992 | — | — | — | — | 12.00 | — |

**100 PESETAS** **KM# 40** **Composition:** Copper **Subject:** Columbus' ship - Santa Maria **Obverse:** National emblem

| Date | Mintage | F | VF | XF | Unc | BU |
|---|---|---|---|---|---|---|
| 1992 Proof | 78 | Value: 60.00 | | | | |

**100 PESETAS** **KM# 13** **Composition:** Copper-Nickel **Series:** Prehistoric Animals **Subject:** Brontosaurus

| Date | Mintage | F | VF | XF | Unc | BU |
|---|---|---|---|---|---|---|
| 1992 | — | — | — | — | 22.50 | — |

**100 PESETAS** **KM# 19** **Composition:** Copper **Series:** Prehistoric Animals **Subject:** Tarbosaurus Bataar

| Date | Mintage | F | VF | XF | Unc | BU |
|---|---|---|---|---|---|---|
| 1993 | — | — | — | — | 22.50 | — |

**100 PESETAS** **KM# 17** **Composition:** Nickel Clad Steel **Series:** Prehistoric Animals **Subject:** Triceratops

| Date | Mintage | F | VF | XF | Unc | BU |
|---|---|---|---|---|---|---|
| 1994 | — | — | — | — | 22.50 | — |

**100 PESETAS** **KM# 41** **Composition:** Nickel Clad Steel **Series:** Prehistoric Animals **Subject:** Camaarasaurus **Obverse:** National emblem

| Date | Mintage | F | VF | XF | Unc | BU |
|---|---|---|---|---|---|---|
| 1994 Proof | 100 | Value: 60.00 | | | | |

**100 PESETAS** **KM# 23** **Composition:** Nickel Clad Steel And Enamel **Reverse:** WWII British Spitfire MK II

| Date | Mintage | F | VF | XF | Unc | BU |
|---|---|---|---|---|---|---|
| 1995 | — | — | — | — | 20.00 | — |

**100 PESETAS** **KM# 22** **Composition:** Copper **Series:** Olympics **Reverse:** Wrestlers

| Date | Mintage | F | VF | XF | Unc | BU |
|---|---|---|---|---|---|---|
| 1996 | — | — | — | — | 8.00 | — |

**200 PESETAS** **KM# 31** **Composition:** Copper **Subject:** 20th Anniversary - Proclamation of Republic **Obverse:** Republic emblem

| Date | Mintage | F | VF | XF | Unc | BU |
|---|---|---|---|---|---|---|
| 1996 Proof | — | Value: 7.50 | | | | |

**500 PESETAS** **KM# 2** **Weight:** 16.0000 g. **Composition:** 0.9990 Silver .5145 oz. ASW **Series:** Transportation **Reverse:** Arab walking camel

| Date | Mintage | F | VF | XF | Unc | BU |
|---|---|---|---|---|---|---|
| 1990 | — | — | — | — | 27.50 | — |

**500 PESETAS** **KM# 3** **Weight:** 16.0000 g. **Composition:** 0.9990 Silver .5145 oz. ASW **Reverse:** Arab and sailing ship

| Date | Mintage | F | VF | XF | Unc | BU |
|---|---|---|---|---|---|---|
| 1990 | — | — | — | — | 30.00 | — |

**500 PESETAS** **KM# 42** **Composition:** Copper **Obverse:** National arms **Reverse:** Antique sailing ship

| Date | Mintage | F | VF | XF | Unc | BU |
|---|---|---|---|---|---|---|
| 1990 Proof | 13 | Value: 1,450 | | | | |

**500 PESETAS** **KM# 4** **Weight:** 6.0000 g. **Composition:** 0.9990 Silver .1929 oz. ASW **Series:** Olympics **Reverse:** Tennis player - skier

| Date | Mintage | F | VF | XF | Unc | BU |
|---|---|---|---|---|---|---|
| 1991 | — | — | — | — | 22.50 | — |

**500 PESETAS** **KM# 5** **Weight:** 12.0000 g. **Composition:** 0.9990 Silver .3858 oz. ASW **Subject:** Soccer **Reverse:** Player kicking ball

| Date | Mintage | F | VF | XF | Unc | BU |
|---|---|---|---|---|---|---|
| 1991 | — | — | — | — | 32.50 | — |

**500 PESETAS** **KM# 8** **Weight:** 15.8400 g. **Composition:** 0.9990 Silver .5093 oz. ASW **Subject:** Soccer **Reverse:** Ball divided by inscription

| Date | Mintage | F | VF | XF | Unc | BU |
|---|---|---|---|---|---|---|
| 1991 | 15,000 | — | — | — | 35.00 | — |

**500 PESETAS** **KM# 9.1a** **Composition:** Copper

| Date | Mintage | F | VF | XF | Unc | BU |
|---|---|---|---|---|---|---|
| 1992 Proof | 22 | Value: 1,250 | | | | |
| 1992 Proof | — | Value: 32.50 | | | | |

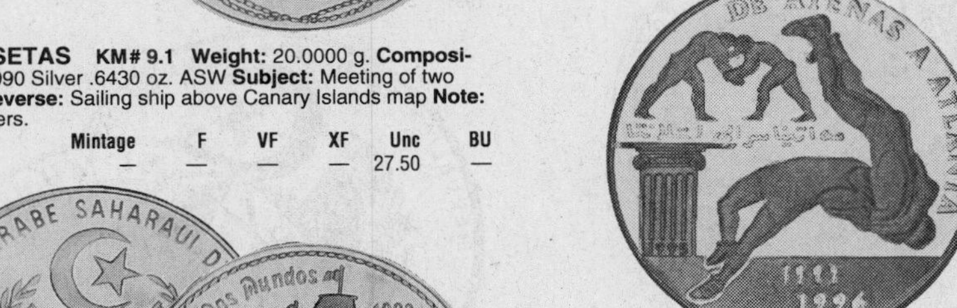

**500 PESETAS** **KM# 9.1** **Weight:** 20.0000 g. **Composition:** 0.9990 Silver .6430 oz. ASW **Subject:** Meeting of two worlds **Reverse:** Sailing ship above Canary Islands map **Note:** Thick letters.

| Date | Mintage | F | VF | XF | Unc | BU |
|---|---|---|---|---|---|---|
| 1992 | — | — | — | — | 27.50 | — |

**500 PESETAS** **KM# 9.2** **Composition:** Copper **Note:** Thin letters.

| Date | Mintage | F | VF | XF | Unc | BU |
|---|---|---|---|---|---|---|
| 1992 Proof | — | Value: 35.00 | | | | |

**500 PESETAS** **KM# 11** **Composition:** Copper **Subject:** Defense of Nature **Reverse:** Elephant

| Date | Mintage | F | VF | XF | Unc | BU |
|---|---|---|---|---|---|---|
| 1993 | — | — | — | — | 35.00 | — |

**500 PESETAS** **KM# 12** **Weight:** 16.0000 g. **Composition:** 0.9990 Silver .5140 oz. ASW **Series:** Prehistoric Animals **Subject:** Tarbosaurus Bataar

| Date | Mintage | F | VF | XF | Unc | BU |
|---|---|---|---|---|---|---|
| 1993 | — | — | — | — | 32.50 | — |

**500 PESETAS** **KM# 27** **Weight:** 16.0000 g. **Composition:** 0.9990 Silver .5140 oz. ASW **Series:** Prehistoric Animals **Subject:** Camarasaurus

| Date | Mintage | F | VF | XF | Unc | BU |
|---|---|---|---|---|---|---|
| 1994 | — | — | — | — | 30.00 | — |

**500 PESETAS** **KM# 21** **Weight:** 20.0000 g. **Composition:** 0.9990 Silver .6430 oz. ASW **Series:** 1996 Olympics **Reverse:** Wrestlers

| Date | Mintage | F | VF | XF | Unc | BU |
|---|---|---|---|---|---|---|
| 1995 Proof | 15,000 | — | — | — | 22.50 | — |

**500 PESETAS** **KM#24** **Weight:** 20.0000 g. **Composition:** 0.9990 Silver .6430 oz. ASW **Reverse:** WWII British Spitfire MK II

| Date | Mintage | F | VF | XF | Unc | BU |
|---|---|---|---|---|---|---|
| 1995 Proof | 15,000 | Value: 32.50 | | | | |

**500 PESETAS** **KM#28** **Weight:** 16.0000 g. **Composition:** 0.9990 Silver .5140 oz. ASW **Series:** Prehistoric Animals **Subject:** Plateosaurus

| Date | Mintage | F | VF | XF | Unc | BU |
|---|---|---|---|---|---|---|
| 1995 Proof | — | Value: 37.50 | | | | |

**500 PESETAS** **KM#32** **Weight:** 20.0000 g. **Composition:** 0.9990 Silver .6430 oz. ASW **Subject:** XVI Copa Mundial - Francia 1998 - Soccer **Reverse:** Player kicking ball

| Date | Mintage | F | VF | XF | Unc | BU |
|---|---|---|---|---|---|---|
| 1996 Proof | — | Value: 50.00 | | | | |

**500 PESETAS** **KM#29** **Weight:** 20.0000 g. **Composition:** 0.9990 Silver .6424 oz. ASW **Reverse:** Leopard **Note:** Added enamel.

| Date | Mintage | F | VF | XF | Unc | BU |
|---|---|---|---|---|---|---|
| 1996 Proof | — | Value: 50.00 | | | | |

**500 PESETAS** **KM#33** **Weight:** 20.0000 g. **Composition:** 0.9990 Silver .6430 oz. ASW **Subject:** XVI Copa Mundial - Francia 1998 - Soccer **Reverse:** Player kicking ball **Note:** With multi-colored applique

| Date | Mintage | F | VF | XF | Unc | BU |
|---|---|---|---|---|---|---|
| 1996 Proof | — | Value: 50.00 | | | | |

**500 PESETAS** **KM#34** **Weight:** 20.0000 g. **Composition:** 0.9990 Silver .6430 oz. ASW **Series:** XXVII Olympiada - Sydney 2000 **Reverse:** Kayaker **Note:** With multi-colored applique

| Date | Mintage | F | VF | XF | Unc | BU |
|---|---|---|---|---|---|---|
| 1996 Proof | — | Value: 35.00 | | | | |

**500 PESETAS** **KM#30** **Weight:** 16.0000 g. **Composition:** 0.9990 Silver .6424 oz. ASW **Series:** Sydney Olympics **Reverse:** Weight lifter **Note:** With added enamel.

| Date | Mintage | F | VF | XF | Unc | BU |
|---|---|---|---|---|---|---|
| 1997 Proof | — | Value: 32.50 | | | | |

**1000 PESETAS** **KM#6** **Weight:** 3.1000 g. **Composition:** 0.9990 Gold .1000 oz. AGW **Series:** Transportation **Reverse:** Arab walking with camel **Note:** Similar to 500 Pesetas, KM#2.

| Date | Mintage | F | VF | XF | Unc | BU |
|---|---|---|---|---|---|---|
| 1991 | 508 | — | — | — | 125 | — |

**1000 PESETAS** **KM#44** **Weight:** 30.5000 g. **Composition:** 0.9990 Silver .9796 oz. ASW **Subject:** Thor Heyerdahl **Obverse:** National arms **Reverse:** Multi-colored reed boats **Edge:** Plain

| Date | Mintage | F | VF | XF | Unc | BU |
|---|---|---|---|---|---|---|
| 1996 | — | Value: 32.50 | | | | |

**1000 PESETAS** **KM#45** **Weight:** 30.5000 g. **Composition:** 0.9990 Silver .9796 oz. ASW **Subject:** Horudsch Chaireddin **Obverse:** National arms **Reverse:** Multi-colored pirates sailing vessels in background

| Date | Mintage | F | VF | XF | Unc | BU |
|---|---|---|---|---|---|---|
| 1996 Proof | — | Value: 32.50 | | | | |

**1000 PESETAS** **KM#37** **Weight:** 31.5000 g. **Composition:** 0.9990 Silver 1.0117 oz. ASW **Subject:** 15th Anniversary - Diplomacy between Venezuela and Arabic Sahara **Obverse:** Pillar between national emblems **Reverse:** Bolivar and El Vali standing by canon

| Date | Mintage | F | VF | XF | Unc | BU |
|---|---|---|---|---|---|---|
| 1997 | 200 | — | — | — | 65.00 | — |
| 1997 Proof | 800 | Value: 55.00 | | | | |

**1000 PESETAS** **KM#43** **Composition:** Silver **Obverse:** National emblem **Reverse:** Viking ship

| Date | Mintage | F | VF | XF | Unc | BU |
|---|---|---|---|---|---|---|
| 1998 Proof | 100 | Value: 110 | | | | |

**1000 PESETAS - 10 ECU** **KM#10** **Weight:** 31.0000 g. **Composition:** 0.9990 Silver .9957 oz. ASW **Subject:** European Community

| Date | Mintage | F | VF | XF | Unc | BU |
|---|---|---|---|---|---|---|
| ND(1992) Proof | 15,000 | Value: 40.00 | | | | |

**5000 PESETAS** KM# 35 **Weight:** 33.5400 g. **Composition:** 0.9200 Silver .9975 oz. ASW **Subject:** 20th Anniversary - Proclamation of Republic **Obverse:** Republican emblem **Reverse:** Female guerilla with rifle

| Date | Mintage | F | VF | XF | Unc | BU |
|---|---|---|---|---|---|---|
| 1996 Proof | — | Value: 65.00 | | | | |

**5000 PESETAS** KM# 36 **Weight:** 33.5400 g. **Composition:** 0.9200 Silver .9975 oz. ASW **Subject:** 20th Anniversary - Proclamation of Republic **Reverse:** Land Rover with armed guerillas

| Date | Mintage | F | VF | XF | Unc | BU |
|---|---|---|---|---|---|---|
| 1996 Proof | — | Value: 65.00 | | | | |

**40000 PESETAS** KM# 38 **Weight:** 15.5200 g. **Composition:** 0.9000 Gold .4491 oz. AGW **Subject:** 20th Anniversary - Diplomacy between Venezuela and Saharawi Arab Democratic Republic **Reverse:** Bolivar and El Vali

| Date | Mintage | F | VF | XF | Unc | BU |
|---|---|---|---|---|---|---|
| 1997 Proof | 90 | Value: 1,000 | | | | |

**40000 PESETAS** KM# 38a **Weight:** 15.5000 g. **Composition:** 0.9990 Gold .4978 oz. AGW

| Date | Mintage | F | VF | XF | Unc | BU |
|---|---|---|---|---|---|---|
| 1997 Proof, rare | 10 | — | — | — | — | — |

## ESSAIS

| KM# | Date | Mintage | Identification | Mkt Val |
|---|---|---|---|---|
| E1 | 1997 | 8 | 1000 Pesetas. Copper. KM#37. | 3,000 |

## PATTERNS

| KM# | Date | Mintage | Identification | Mkt Val |
|---|---|---|---|---|
| Pn2 | 1997 | 8 | 40000 Pesetas. Copper. KM#38. | 3,000 |
| Pn3 | 1997 | 8 | 40000 Pesetas. Silver. KM#38. | 3,000 |

## PIEFORTS

| KM# | Date | Mintage | Identification | Mkt Val |
|---|---|---|---|---|
| P1 | 1990 | 110 | 500 Pesetas. KM#3. | 80.00 |
| P2 | 1997 | 8 | 40000 Pesetas. KM#38. | 6,000 |

# SAINT HELENA & ASCENSION

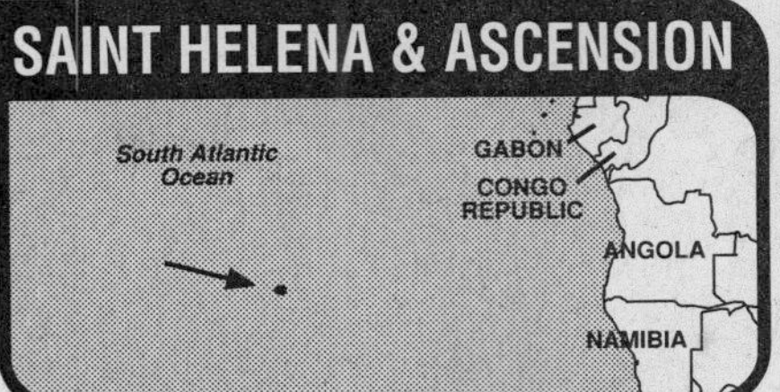


Saint Helena, a British colony located about 1,150 miles (1,850 km.) from the west coast of Africa, has an area of 47 sq. mi. (410 sq. km.) and a population of *7,000. Capital: Jamestown. Flax, lace, and rope are produced for export. Ascension and Tristan da Cunha are dependencies of Saint Helena.

The island was discovered and named by the Portuguese navigator Joao de Nova Castella in 1502. The Portuguese imported livestock, fruit trees, and vegetables but established no permanent settlement. The Dutch occupied the island temporarily, 1645-51. The original European settlement was founded by representatives of the British East India Company sent to annex the island after the departure of the Dutch. The Dutch returned and captured Saint Helena from the British on New Year's Day, 1673, but were in turn ejected by a British force under Sir Richard Munden. Thereafter Saint Helena was the undisputed possession of Great Britain. The island served as the place of exile for Napoleon, several Zulu chiefs, and an ex-sultan of Zanzibar.

**RULERS**
British

**MINT MARKS**
PM - Pobjoy Mint

**MONETARY SYSTEM**
12 Pence = 1 Shilling
100 Pence = 1 Pound

## SAINT HELENA
### Under British Administration
## STANDARD COINAGE

100 Pence = 1 Pound

**25 PENCE (Crown)** KM# 5 **Composition:** Copper-Nickel **Subject:** St. Helena tercentenary

| Date | Mintage | F | VF | XF | Unc | BU |
|---|---|---|---|---|---|---|
| ND(1973) | 100,000 | — | — | — | 4.00 | — |

**25 PENCE (Crown)** KM# 5a **Weight:** 28.2800 g. **Composition:** 0.9250 Silver .8411 oz. ASW **Subject:** St. Helena tercentenary

| Date | Mintage | F | VF | XF | Unc | BU |
|---|---|---|---|---|---|---|
| ND(1973) Proof | 10,000 | Value: 20.00 | | | | |

**25 PENCE (Crown)** KM# 6 **Composition:** Copper-Nickel **Subject:** Queen Elizabeth II silver jubilee

| Date | Mintage | F | VF | XF | Unc | BU |
|---|---|---|---|---|---|---|
| ND(1977) | 50,000 | — | — | — | 6.00 | — |

**25 PENCE (Crown)** KM# 6a **Weight:** 28.2800 g. **Composition:** 0.9250 Silver .8411 oz. ASW **Subject:** Queen Elizabeth II silver jubilee

| Date | Mintage | F | VF | XF | Unc | BU |
|---|---|---|---|---|---|---|
| ND(1977) Proof | 25,000 | Value: 13.50 | | | | |

**25 PENCE (Crown)** KM# 7 **Composition:** Copper-Nickel **Subject:** 25th anniversary of coronation

| Date | Mintage | F | VF | XF | Unc | BU |
|---|---|---|---|---|---|---|
| 1978PM | — | — | — | — | 3.50 | — |

**25 PENCE (Crown)** KM# 7a **Weight:** 28.2800 g. **Composition:** 0.9250 Silver .8411 oz. ASW **Subject:** 25th anniversary of coronation

| Date | Mintage | F | VF | XF | Unc | BU |
|---|---|---|---|---|---|---|
| 1978PM | 70,000 | — | — | — | 11.50 | — |
| 1978 Proof | 25,000 | Value: 16.50 | | | | |

**25 PENCE (Crown)** KM# 8 **Composition:** Copper-Nickel **Subject:** 80th birthday of Queen Mother

| Date | Mintage | F | VF | XF | Unc | BU |
|---|---|---|---|---|---|---|
| 1980 | 100,000 | — | — | — | 3.50 | — |

**25 PENCE (Crown)** KM# 8a **Weight:** 28.2800 g. **Composition:** 0.9250 Silver .8411 oz. ASW **Subject:** 80th birthday of Queen Mother

| Date | Mintage | F | VF | XF | Unc | BU |
|---|---|---|---|---|---|---|
| 1980 Proof | 25,000 | Value: 13.50 | | | | |

**25 PENCE (Crown)** KM# 9 **Composition:** Copper-Nickel **Subject:** Wedding of Prince Charles and Lady Diana

| Date | Mintage | F | VF | XF | Unc | BU |
|---|---|---|---|---|---|---|
| ND(1981) | 50,000 | — | — | — | 3.50 | — |

**25 PENCE (Crown)** KM# 9a **Weight:** 28.2800 g. **Composition:** 0.9250 Silver .8411 oz. ASW **Subject:** Wedding of Prince Charles and Lady Diana

| Date | Mintage | F | VF | XF | Unc | BU |
|---|---|---|---|---|---|---|
| ND(1981) Proof | 30,000 | Value: 20.00 | | | | |

**25 PENCE (Crown)** **KM# 10** **Weight:** 28.2800 g. **Composition:** 0.9250 Silver .8411 oz. ASW **Series:** International Year of the Scout **Obverse:** Queen Elizabeth II

| Date | Mintage | F | VF | XF | Unc | BU |
|---|---|---|---|---|---|---|
| ND(1983) | 10,000 | — | — | — | 30.00 | — |
| ND(1983) Proof | 10,000 | Value: 40.00 | | | | |

**50 PENCE** **KM# 12** **Composition:** Copper-Nickel **Subject:** 150th anniversary - colony of Saint Helena

| Date | Mintage | F | VF | XF | Unc | BU |
|---|---|---|---|---|---|---|
| ND(1984) | 10,000 | — | — | — | 4.00 | — |

**50 PENCE** **KM# 12a** **Weight:** 28.2800 g. **Composition:** 0.9250 Silver .8411 oz. ASW **Subject:** 150th anniversary - colony of Saint Helena

| Date | Mintage | F | VF | XF | Unc | BU |
|---|---|---|---|---|---|---|
| ND(1984) Proof | 5,000 | Value: 28.00 | | | | |

**50 PENCE** **KM# 12b** **Weight:** 47.5400 g. **Composition:** 0.9170 Gold 1.4017 oz. AGW **Subject:** 150th anniversary - colony of Saint Helena

| Date | Mintage | F | VF | XF | Unc | BU |
|---|---|---|---|---|---|---|
| ND(1984) Proof | 150 | Value: 825 | | | | |

**50 PENCE** **KM# 13** **Composition:** Copper-Nickel **Subject:** Royal visit of Prince Andrew

| Date | Mintage | F | VF | XF | Unc | BU |
|---|---|---|---|---|---|---|
| 1984 | 125,000 | — | — | — | 3.00 | — |

**50 PENCE** **KM# 13a** **Weight:** 28.2800 g. **Composition:** 0.9250 Silver .8411 oz. ASW **Subject:** Royal visit of Prince Andrew

| Date | Mintage | F | VF | XF | Unc | BU |
|---|---|---|---|---|---|---|
| 1984 Proof | 5,000 | Value: 30.00 | | | | |

**50 PENCE** **KM# 14** **Composition:** Copper-Nickel **Reverse:** Queen Mother

| Date | Mintage | F | VF | XF | Unc | BU |
|---|---|---|---|---|---|---|
| 1995 | — | — | — | — | 6.00 | — |

**50 PENCE** **KM# 14a** **Weight:** 28.2800 g. **Composition:** 0.9250 Silver .8411 oz. ASW **Reverse:** Queen Mother

| Date | Mintage | F | VF | XF | Unc | BU |
|---|---|---|---|---|---|---|
| 1995 Proof | 10,000 | Value: 50.00 | | | | |

**50 PENCE** **KM# 14b** **Weight:** 47.5400 g. **Composition:** 0.9160 Gold 1.4011 oz. AGW **Reverse:** Queen Mother

| Date | Mintage | F | VF | XF | Unc | BU |
|---|---|---|---|---|---|---|
| 1995 Proof | 150 | Value: 950 | | | | |

**50 PENCE** **KM# 15** **Composition:** Copper-Nickel **Subject:** 70th birthday - Queen Elizabeth II **Reverse:** Mounted guardsman

| Date | Mintage | F | VF | XF | Unc | BU |
|---|---|---|---|---|---|---|
| 1996 | — | — | — | — | 6.00 | — |

**50 PENCE** **KM# 15a** **Weight:** 28.2800 g. **Composition:** 0.9250 Silver .8411 oz. ASW **Subject:** 70th birthday - Queen Elizabeth II **Reverse:** Mounted guardsman

| Date | Mintage | F | VF | XF | Unc | BU |
|---|---|---|---|---|---|---|
| 1996 Proof | 5,000 | Value: 50.00 | | | | |

**50 PENCE** **KM# 18** **Composition:** Copper-Nickel **Subject:** Elizabeth and Philip **Obverse:** Queen's portrait **Reverse:** Royal couple reviewing troops

| Date | Mintage | F | VF | XF | Unc | BU |
|---|---|---|---|---|---|---|
| ND(1997) | — | — | — | — | 6.50 | — |

**50 PENCE** **KM# 16** **Composition:** Copper-Nickel **Subject:** World Wildlife Fund - conserving nature **Reverse:** 3 blue whales

| Date | Mintage | F | VF | XF | Unc | BU |
|---|---|---|---|---|---|---|
| 1998 | — | — | — | — | 8.00 | — |

**50 PENCE** **KM# 17** **Composition:** Copper-Nickel **Subject:** World Wildlife Fund - conserving nature **Obverse:** Queen's portrait **Reverse:** Rain piper bird, shoreline, lily

| Date | Mintage | F | VF | XF | Unc | BU |
|---|---|---|---|---|---|---|
| 1998 | — | — | — | — | 7.00 | — |

**2 POUNDS** **KM# 11** **Weight:** 15.9800 g. **Composition:** 0.9170 Gold .4712 oz. AGW **Series:** International Year of the Scout

| Date | Mintage | F | VF | XF | Unc | BU |
|---|---|---|---|---|---|---|
| ND(1983) | 2,000 | — | — | — | 450 | — |
| ND(1983) Proof | 2,000 | Value: 500 | | | | |

# SAINT HELENA-ASCENSION

## STANDARD COINAGE

100 Pence = 1 Pound

**PENNY** **KM# 20** **Composition:** Bronze **Reverse:** Tuna

| Date | Mintage | F | VF | XF | Unc | BU |
|---|---|---|---|---|---|---|
| 1984 | — | — | — | 0.15 | 0.35 | — |
| 1984 Proof | 10,000 | Value: 1.25 | | | | |

**PENNY** **KM# 33** **Composition:** Bronze **Obverse:** Queen's portrait by dePedery-Hunt

| Date | Mintage | F | VF | XF | Unc | BU |
|---|---|---|---|---|---|---|
| 1991 | — | — | — | 0.15 | 0.35 | — |

**PENNY** **KM# 22** **Composition:** Chrome Plated Steel

| Date | Mintage | F | VF | XF | Unc | BU |
|---|---|---|---|---|---|---|
| 1997 | — | — | — | 0.15 | 0.35 | — |

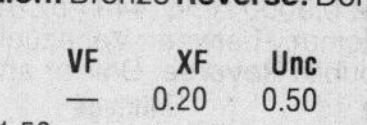

**2 PENCE** **KM# 23** **Composition:** Bronze **Reverse:** Donkey with Fire Wood

| Date | Mintage | F | VF | XF | Unc | BU |
|---|---|---|---|---|---|---|
| 1984 | — | — | — | 0.20 | 0.50 | — |
| 1984 Proof | 10,000 | Value: 1.50 | | | | |

**2 PENCE** **KM# 34** **Composition:** Bronze **Obverse:** Queen's portrait by dePedery-Hunt

| Date | Mintage | F | VF | XF | Unc | BU |
|---|---|---|---|---|---|---|
| 1991 | — | — | — | 0.20 | 0.50 | — |

**5 PENCE** **KM# 24** **Composition:** Copper-Nickel **Reverse:** Rain Piper

| Date | Mintage | F | VF | XF | Unc | BU |
|---|---|---|---|---|---|---|
| 1984 | — | — | — | 0.20 | 0.50 | — |
| 1984 Proof | — | Value: 1.75 | | | | |

**5 PENCE** **KM# 35** **Composition:** Copper-Nickel **Obverse:** Queen's portrait by dePedery-Hunt

| Date | Mintage | F | VF | XF | Unc | BU |
|---|---|---|---|---|---|---|
| 1991 | — | — | — | 0.20 | 0.50 | — |

**5 PENCE** **KM# 42** **Composition:** Copper-Nickel **Subject:** The Giant Tortoise **Obverse:** Queen's portrait **Reverse:** Giant tortoise

| Date | Mintage | F | VF | XF | Unc | BU |
|---|---|---|---|---|---|---|
| 1998 | — | — | — | — | 0.75 | — |

**10 PENCE** **KM# 25** **Composition:** Copper-Nickel **Reverse:** Arum Lily

| Date | Mintage | F | VF | XF | Unc | BU |
|---|---|---|---|---|---|---|
| 1984 | — | — | — | 0.30 | 1.00 | — |
| 1984 Proof | — | Value: 2.00 | | | | |

**10 PENCE** **KM# 36** **Composition:** Copper-Nickel **Obverse:** Queen's portrait by dePedery-Hunt

| Date | Mintage | F | VF | XF | Unc | BU |
|---|---|---|---|---|---|---|
| 1991 | — | — | — | 0.30 | 1.00 | — |

**10 PENCE** **KM# 43** **Composition:** Copper-Nickel **Obverse:** Queen's portrait **Reverse:** Dolphins

| Date | Mintage | F | VF | XF | Unc | BU |
|---|---|---|---|---|---|---|
| 1998 | — | — | — | — | 1.00 | — |

**20 PENCE** **KM# 44** **Composition:** Copper-Nickel **Obverse:** Queen's portrait **Reverse:** Flower

| Date | Mintage | F | VF | XF | Unc | BU |
|---|---|---|---|---|---|---|
| 1998 | — | — | — | — | 1.25 | — |

**50 PENCE** **KM# 26** **Composition:** Copper-Nickel **Reverse:** Sea Turtle

| Date | Mintage | F | VF | XF | Unc | BU |
|---|---|---|---|---|---|---|
| 1984 | — | — | — | 1.50 | 3.50 | — |
| 1984 Proof | — | Value: 4.00 | | | | |

**50 PENCE** **KM# 28** **Composition:** Copper-Nickel **Subject:** Wedding of Prince Andrew and Sarah Ferguson

| Date | Mintage | F | VF | XF | Unc | BU |
|---|---|---|---|---|---|---|
| ND(1986) | 13,000 | — | — | — | 4.00 | — |

**50 PENCE** **KM# 28a** **Weight:** 28.2800 g. **Composition:** 0.9250 Silver .8411 oz. ASW

| Date | Mintage | F | VF | XF | Unc | BU |
|---|---|---|---|---|---|---|
| ND(1986) Proof | 2,500 | Value: 27.50 | | | | |

**50 PENCE** **KM# 28b** **Weight:** 47.5400 g. **Composition:** 0.9170 Gold 1.4017 oz. AGW **Subject:** Wedding of Prince Andrew and Sarah Ferguson

| Date | Mintage | F | VF | XF | Unc | BU |
|---|---|---|---|---|---|---|
| ND(1986) Proof | 50 | Value: 1,150 | | | | |

**50 PENCE** **KM# 29** **Composition:** Copper-Nickel **Subject:** 165th Anniversary of Napoleon's Death

| Date | Mintage | F | VF | XF | Unc | BU |
|---|---|---|---|---|---|---|
| 1986 | 50,000 | — | — | — | 5.00 | — |

**50 PENCE** **KM# 37** **Composition:** Copper-Nickel **Obverse:** Similar to 2 Pence, KM#12

| Date | Mintage | F | VF | XF | Unc | BU |
|---|---|---|---|---|---|---|
| 1991 | — | — | — | — | 5.00 | — |

**50 PENCE** **KM# 40** **Composition:** Copper-Nickel **Subject:** Normandy Invasion

| Date | Mintage | F | VF | XF | Unc | BU |
|---|---|---|---|---|---|---|
| ND(1994) | — | — | — | — | 6.00 | — |

**50 PENCE** **KM# 40a** **Weight:** 28.2800 g. **Composition:** 0.9250 Silver .8411 oz. ASW

| Date | Mintage | F | VF | XF | Unc | BU |
|---|---|---|---|---|---|---|
| ND(1994) Proof | 5,000 | Value: 40.00 | | | | |

**POUND** **KM# 27** **Composition:** Nickel-Brass **Reverse:** Sooty Terns

| Date | Mintage | F | VF | XF | Unc | BU |
|---|---|---|---|---|---|---|
| 1984 | — | — | — | 2.25 | 5.00 | — |
| 1984 Proof | — | Value: 5.00 | | | | |

**POUND** **KM# 27a** **Weight:** 9.5000 g. **Composition:** 0.9250 Silver .2826 oz. ASW

| Date | Mintage | F | VF | XF | Unc | BU |
|---|---|---|---|---|---|---|
| 1984 Proof | 10,000 | Value: 18.00 | | | | |

**POUND** **KM# 38** **Composition:** Nickel-Brass **Obverse:** Similar to 2 Pence, KM#12

| Date | Mintage | F | VF | XF | Unc | BU |
|---|---|---|---|---|---|---|
| 1991 | — | — | — | 2.25 | 5.00 | — |

**2 POUNDS** **KM# 32** **Composition:** Copper-Nickel **Subject:** Queen Mother

| Date | Mintage | F | VF | XF | Unc | BU |
|---|---|---|---|---|---|---|
| ND(1990) | — | — | — | — | 12.00 | — |

**2 POUNDS** **KM# 32a** **Weight:** 28.2800 g. **Composition:** 0.9250 Silver .8411 oz. ASW

| Date | Mintage | F | VF | XF | Unc | BU |
|---|---|---|---|---|---|---|
| ND(1990) Proof | 50,000 | Value: 50.00 | | | | |

**2 POUNDS** **KM# 39** **Weight:** 28.2800 g. **Composition:** 0.9250 Silver .8411 oz. ASW **Subject:** 40th Anniversary - Coronation of Elizabeth II

| Date | Mintage | F | VF | XF | Unc | BU |
|---|---|---|---|---|---|---|
| ND(1993) Proof | 10,000 | Value: 55.00 | | | | |

**25 POUNDS** KM# 30 **Weight:** 155.0000 g. **Composition:** 0.9990 Silver 4.9839 oz. ASW **Subject:** 165th Anniversary of Napoleon's Death **Obverse:** Similar to 50 Pence, KM#7 **Note:** Illustration reduced.

| Date | Mintage | F | VF | XF | Unc | BU |
|---|---|---|---|---|---|---|
| 1986 Proof | 15,000 | Value: 115 | | | | |

**25 POUNDS** KM# 41 **Weight:** 155.5175 g. **Composition:** 0.9990 Silver 5.0000 oz. ASW **Subject:** 70th Birthday - Queen Elizabeth II **Reverse:** Mounted drummer **Note:** Illustration reduced.

| Date | Mintage | F | VF | XF | Unc | BU |
|---|---|---|---|---|---|---|
| 1996 Proof | 1,000 | Value: 200 | | | | |

**50 POUNDS** KM# 31 **Weight:** 32.2600 g. **Composition:** 0.9990 Platinum 1.0051 oz. APW **Subject:** 165th Anniversary of Napoleon's Death

| Date | Mintage | F | VF | XF | Unc | BU |
|---|---|---|---|---|---|---|
| 1986 Proof | 5,000 | Value: 650 | | | | |

## PIEFORTS

| KM# | Date | Mintage | Identification | Issue Price | Mkt Val |
|---|---|---|---|---|---|
| P1 | 1984 | 500 | 50 Pence. Silver. KM13a. | — | 50.00 |
| P3 | 1984 | 2,500 | Pound. KM#6a. | 49.75 | 28.00 |
| P4 | 1986 | 250 | 50 Pence. KM#7a. | 74.00 | 75.00 |
| P5 | 1994 | 500 | 50 Pence. KM#19. | — | 65.00 |
| P2 | 1995 | 500 | 50 Pence. Silver. KM14a. | — | 90.00 |

## MINT SETS

| KM# | Date | Mintage | Identification | Issue Price | Mkt Val |
|---|---|---|---|---|---|
| MS1 | 1984 (6) | — | KM#20, 23-27 | — | 5.50 |

## PROOF SETS

| KM# | Date | Mintage | Identification | Issue Price | Mkt Val |
|---|---|---|---|---|---|
| PS1 | 1984 (6) | — | KM#20, 23-27 | — | 25.00 |

# SAINT KITTS & NEVIS

Saint Kitts (Saint Christopher), a West Indian island located in the Leeward Islands southeast of Puerto Rico, is the principal component of a British associated state com-posed of the islands of Saint Kitts, Nevis, and Anguilla. The associated state has an area of 104 sq. mi. (360 sq. km.) and a population of *40,000. Capital: Basseterre, on Saint Kitts. The islands export sugar, molasses, rum, cotton, and coconuts.

Saint Kitts was discovered by Columbus in 1493 and was settled by Thomas Warner, an Englishman, in 1623. The island was ceded to the British by the Treaty of Utrecht, 1713. France protested British occupancy, and on three occasions between 1616 and 1782 seized the island and held it for short periods. Saint Kitts used the coins and currency of the British Caribbean Territories (Eastern Group).

In early 1967 Saint Kitts was united politically with Nevis and Anguilla to form a self-governing British associated state. In June 1967 Anguilla declared its independence of the federated state, and in Feb. 1969 unilaterally severed all ties with Britain and established the Republic of Anguilla. Britain refused to accept the unilateral movement and installed a commissioner to govern Anguilla, which would remain a nominal part of the associated state. Currently, Elizabeth II is Head of State, as Queen of Saint Christopher & Nevis.

From approximately 1750-1830, billon 2 sous of the French colony of Cayenne were countermarked SK' and used on Saint Kitts. They were valued at 1-1/3 Pence.

**RULERS**
British

**MONETARY SYSTEM**
100 Cents = 1 Dollar

**NOTE:** The grades shown describe the condition of the raised countermarks, not the host coin itself, which is typically well worn.

## BRITISH ASSOCIATED STATE

### STANDARD COINAGE

100 Cents = 1 Dollar

**4 DOLLARS** KM# 1 **Composition:** Copper-Nickel **Series:** F.A.O

| Date | Mintage | F | VF | XF | Unc | BU |
|---|---|---|---|---|---|---|
| 1970 | 13,000 | — | 3.50 | 7.00 | 12.50 | — |
| 1970 Proof | 2,000 | Value: 22.50 | | | | |

**10 DOLLARS** KM# 3 **Composition:** Copper-Nickel **Subject:** Royal Visit

| Date | Mintage | F | VF | XF | Unc | BU |
|---|---|---|---|---|---|---|
| 1985 | 100,000 | — | — | — | 8.00 | — |

**10 DOLLARS** KM# 3a **Weight:** 28.2800 g. **Composition:** 0.9250 Silver .8411 oz. ASW

| Date | Mintage | F | VF | XF | Unc | BU |
|---|---|---|---|---|---|---|
| 1985 Proof | 5,000 | Value: 40.00 | | | | |

**10 DOLLARS** KM# 3b **Weight:** 47.5400 g. **Composition:** 0.9170 Gold 1.4013 oz. AGW **Subject:** Royal Visit

| Date | Mintage | F | VF | XF | Unc | BU |
|---|---|---|---|---|---|---|
| 1985 Proof | 250 | Value: 1,100 | | | | |

**20 DOLLARS** KM# 4 **Composition:** Copper-Nickel **Subject:** 200th Anniversary - Battle of the Saints

| Date | Mintage | F | VF | XF | Unc | BU |
|---|---|---|---|---|---|---|
| ND(1982) | — | — | — | — | 12.50 | — |

**20 DOLLARS** KM# 4a **Weight:** 28.2800 g. **Composition:** 0.9250 Silver .8411 oz. ASW

| Date | Mintage | F | VF | XF | Unc | BU |
|---|---|---|---|---|---|---|
| ND(1982) Proof | 2,500 | Value: 42.50 | | | | |

**20 DOLLARS** KM# 2 **Composition:** Copper-Nickel **Subject:** Attainment of Independence

| Date | Mintage | F | VF | XF | Unc | BU |
|---|---|---|---|---|---|---|
| 1983 | — | — | — | — | 15.00 | — |

**20 DOLLARS** KM# 2a **Weight:** 28.2800 g. **Composition:** 0.9250 Silver .8411 oz. ASW

| Date | Mintage | F | VF | XF | Unc | BU |
|---|---|---|---|---|---|---|
| 1983 Proof | 5,000 | Value: 40.00 | | | | |

**100 DOLLARS** KM# 5 **Weight:** 7.9900 g. **Composition:** 0.9170 Gold .2356 oz. AGW **Subject:** 200th Anniversary - Seige of Brimstone Hill

| Date | Mintage | F | VF | XF | Unc | BU |
|---|---|---|---|---|---|---|
| ND(1982) | 250 | — | — | — | 200 | — |
| ND(1982) Proof | 15 | Value: 675 | | | | |

**100 DOLLARS** KM# 6 **Weight:** 129.5900 g. **Composition:** 0.9250 Silver 3.8543 oz. ASW **Subject:** Tropical birds **Reverse:** Green-throated Carib Hummingbird **Size:** 63 mm. **Note:** Illustration reduced.

| Date | Mintage | F | VF | XF | Unc | BU |
|---|---|---|---|---|---|---|
| 1988 Proof | Est. 10,000 | Value: 125 | | | | |

# SAINT LUCIA

Saint Lucia, an independent island nation located in the Windward Islands of the West Indies between Saint Vincent and Martinique, has an area of 238 sq. mi. (620 sq. km.) and a population of *150,000. Capital: Castries. The economy is agricultural. Bananas, copra, cocoa, sugar and logwood are exported.

Columbus discovered Saint Lucia in 1502. The first attempts at settlement undertaken by the British in1605 and 1638 were frustrated by sickness and the determined hostility of the fierce Carib inhabitants. The French settled it in 1650 and made a treaty with the natives. Until 1814, when the island became a definite British possession, it was the scene of a continuous conflict between the British and French, which saw the island change, hands on at least 14 occasions. In 1967,under the West Indies Act, Saint Lucia was established as a British associated state, self-governing in internal affairs. Complete independence was attained on February 22,1979. Saint Lucia is a member of the Commonwealth of Nations. Elizabeth II is Head of State as Queen of Saint Lucia.

Prior to 1950, the island used sterling, which was superseded by the currency of the British Caribbean Territories (Eastern Group) and the East Caribbean State.

**RULERS**
British

**MONETARY SYSTEM**
100 Cents = 1 Dollar

## BRITISH ASSOCIATED STATE

### MODERN COINAGE

100 Cents = 1 Dollar

**4 DOLLARS** KM# 11 **Composition:** Copper-Nickel **Series:** F.A.O

| Date | Mintage | F | VF | XF | Unc | BU |
|---|---|---|---|---|---|---|
| 1970 | 13,000 | — | 3.50 | 7.00 | 12.50 | — |
| 1970 Proof | 2,000 | Value: 22.50 | | | | |

**5 DOLLARS** KM# 14 **Composition:** Copper-Nickel **Subject:** Papal Visit **Obverse:** Similar to 10 Dollars, KM#12

| Date | Mintage | F | VF | XF | Unc | BU |
|---|---|---|---|---|---|---|
| 1986 | — | — | — | — | 8.50 | — |

**5 DOLLARS** KM# 14a **Weight:** 28.2800 g. **Composition:** 0.9250 Silver .8411 oz. ASW

| Date | Mintage | F | VF | XF | Unc | BU |
|---|---|---|---|---|---|---|
| 1986 Proof | 2,120 | Value: 42.50 | | | | |

**10 DOLLARS** KM# 12 **Composition:** Copper-Nickel **Subject:** 200th Anniversary - Battle of the Saints

| Date | Mintage | F | VF | XF | Unc | BU |
|---|---|---|---|---|---|---|
| 1982 | — | — | — | — | 12.50 | — |

**10 DOLLARS** KM# 12a **Weight:** 28.2800 g. **Composition:** 0.9250 Silver .8411 oz. ASW

| Date | Mintage | F | VF | XF | Unc | BU |
|---|---|---|---|---|---|---|
| 1982 Proof | 2,500 | Value: 42.50 | | | | |

**10 DOLLARS** KM# 13 **Composition:** Copper-Nickel **Subject:** Royal Visit - Queen Elizabeth II

| Date | Mintage | F | VF | XF | Unc | BU |
|---|---|---|---|---|---|---|
| 1985 | 100,000 | — | — | — | 8.50 | — |

**10 DOLLARS** KM# 13a **Weight:** 28.2800 g. **Composition:** 0.9250 Silver .8411 oz. ASW

| Date | Mintage | F | VF | XF | Unc | BU |
|---|---|---|---|---|---|---|
| 1985 Proof | 5,000 | Value: 40.00 | | | | |

**10 DOLLARS** KM# 13b **Weight:** 47.5400 g. **Composition:** 0.9170 Gold 1.4013 oz. AGW **Subject:** Royal Visit

| Date | Mintage | F | VF | XF | Unc | BU |
|---|---|---|---|---|---|---|
| 1985 Proof | 250 | Value: 1,100 | | | | |

**10 DOLLARS** KM# 16 **Weight:** 28.2800 g. **Composition:** 0.9250 Silver .8411 oz. ASW **Subject:** Commonwealth Finance Ministers Meeting

| Date | Mintage | F | VF | XF | Unc | BU |
|---|---|---|---|---|---|---|
| 1986 Proof | 1,000 | Value: 55.00 | | | | |

**100 DOLLARS** KM# 17 **Weight:** 129.5900 g. **Composition:** 0.9250 Silver 3.8543 oz. ASW **Subject:** Tropical Birds **Reverse:** Two St. Lucia Amazon Parrots **Size:** 63 mm. **Note:** Illustration reduced.

| Date | Mintage | F | VF | XF | Unc | BU |
|---|---|---|---|---|---|---|
| 1988 Proof | Est. 10,000 | Value: 125 | | | | |

**500 DOLLARS** KM# 15 **Weight:** 15.9800 g. **Composition:** 0.9170 Gold .4709 oz. AGW **Subject:** Papal Visit

| Date | Mintage | F | VF | XF | Unc | BU |
|---|---|---|---|---|---|---|
| 1986 Proof | 100 | Value: 850 | | | | |

# SAINT PIERRE & MIQUELON

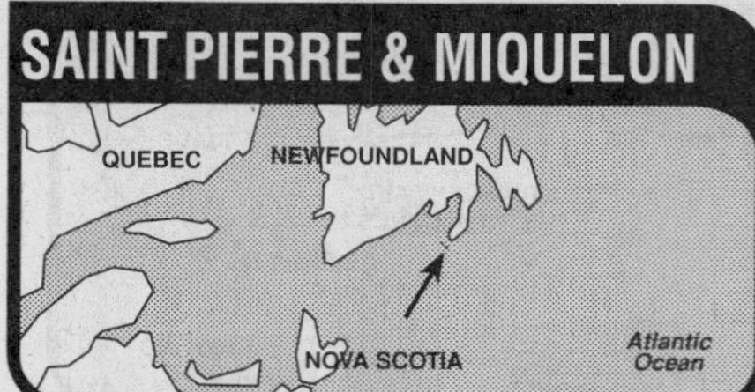


The Territorial Collectivity of Saint Pierre and Miquelon, a French overseas territory located 10 miles (16 km.) off the south coast of Newfoundland, has an area of 93 sq. mi. (242 sq. km.) and a population of *6,000. Capital: Saint Pierre. The economy of the barren archipelago is based on cod fishing and fur farming. Fish and fish products, and mink and silver fox pelts are exported.

The islands were occupied by the French in 1604, then were captured by the British in 1702 and held until 1763, at which time they were returned to the possession of France and employed as a fishing station. They passed between France and England on six more occasions between 1778 and 1814 when the Treaty of Paris awarded them permanently to France. The rugged, soil-poor granite islands, which will support only evergreen shrubs, are all that remain of France's extensive North American colonies. In 1958 Saint Pierre and Miquelon voted in favor of the new constitution of the Fifth Republic of France, thereby choosing to remain within the new French Community.

**RULERS**
French

**MINT MARKS**
(a) - Paris, privy marks only

**MONETARY SYSTEM**
100 Centimes = 1 Franc

## FRENCH REPUBLIC

### STANDARD COINAGE

100 Centimes = 1 Franc

**FRANC** KM# 1 **Composition:** Aluminum

| Date | Mintage | F | VF | XF | Unc | BU |
|---|---|---|---|---|---|---|
| 1948(a) | 600,000 | 0.50 | 0.75 | 1.50 | 5.50 | — |

**2 FRANCS** KM# 2 **Composition:** Aluminum

| Date | Mintage | F | VF | XF | Unc | BU |
|---|---|---|---|---|---|---|
| 1948(a) | 300,000 | 0.75 | 1.00 | 2.00 | 6.50 | — |

### ESSAIS

Standard metals unless otherwise noted

| KM# | Date | Mintage | Identification | Issue Price | Mkt Val |
|---|---|---|---|---|---|
| E1a | 1948(a) | 2,000 | Franc. Copper-Nickel. | — | 40.00 |
| E2a | 1948(a) | 2,000 | 2 Francs. Copper-Nickel. | — | 45.00 |

### PIEFORTS WITH ESSAIS

Double thickness, standard metals unless otherwise noted

| KM# | Date | Mintage | Identification | Issue Price | Mkt Val |
|---|---|---|---|---|---|
| PE1 | 1948(a) | 104 | Franc. | — | 120 |
| PE2 | 1948(a) | 104 | 2 Francs. | — | 150 |

# SAINT THOMAS & PRINCE

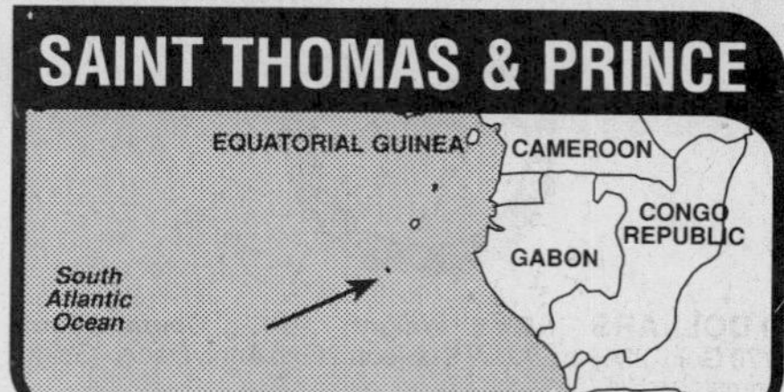


The Democratic Republic of Sao Tome and Principe (formerly the Portuguese overseas province of Saint Thomas and Prince Islands) is located in the Gulf of Guinea 150 miles (241 km.) off the western coast of Africa. It has an area of 372 sq. mi. (960 sq. km.) and a population of *121,000. Capital: Sao Tome. The economy of the islands is based on cocoa, copra and coffee.

Saint Thomas and Saint Prince were uninhabited when discovered by Portuguese navigators Joao de Santarem and Pedro de Escobar in 1470. After the failure of their initial settlement of 1485, the Portuguese successfully colonized St. Thomas with a colony of prisoners and exiled Jews in 1493. An initial prosperity based on the sugar trade gave way to a time of misfortune, 1567-1709, that saw the colony attacked and occupied or plundered by the French and Dutch, ravaged by the slave revolt of 1595; and finally rendered destitute by the transfer of the world sugar trade to Brazil. In the late 1800s, the colony turned from the production of sugar to cocoa, the basis of its present economy

The islands were designated a Portuguese overseas province in 1951. On April 25, 1974, the government of Portugal was seized by a military junta, which reached agreements providing for independence for the Portuguese overseas provinces of Portuguese Guinea (Guinea-Bissau), Mozambique, Cape Verde Islands, Angola, and Saint Thomas and Prince Islands. The Democratic Republic of Sao Tome and Principe was declared on July 12, 1975.

**RULERS**
Portuguese, until 1975

**MINT MARKS**
R – Rio

**MONETARY SYSTEM**
100 Centavos = 1 Escudo

## COLONIAL

### REFORM COINAGE

100 Centavos = 1 Escudo

**10 CENTAVOS** KM# 2 **Composition:** Nickel-Bronze

| Date | Mintage | F | VF | XF | Unc | BU |
|---|---|---|---|---|---|---|
| 1929 | 500,000 | 1.50 | 5.50 | 20.00 | 50.00 | — |

**10 CENTAVOS** KM# 15 **Composition:** Bronze

| Date | Mintage | F | VF | XF | Unc | BU |
|---|---|---|---|---|---|---|
| 1962 | 500,000 | 0.50 | 1.25 | 4.50 | 12.00 | — |

**10 CENTAVOS** KM# 15a **Composition:** Aluminum

| Date | Mintage | F | VF | XF | Unc | BU |
|---|---|---|---|---|---|---|
| 1971 | 1,000,000 | 0.35 | 0.65 | 1.25 | 3.50 | — |

**20 CENTAVOS** KM# 3 **Composition:** Nickel-Bronze

| Date | Mintage | F | VF | XF | Unc | BU |
|---|---|---|---|---|---|---|
| 1929 | 250,000 | 1.50 | 5.50 | 20.00 | 50.00 | — |

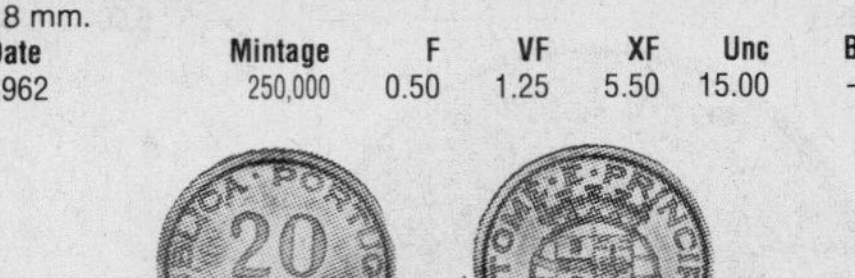

**20 CENTAVOS** **KM# 16.1** **Composition:** Bronze **Size:** 18 mm.

| Date | Mintage | F | VF | XF | Unc | BU |
|---|---|---|---|---|---|---|
| 1962 | 250,000 | 0.50 | 1.25 | 5.50 | 15.00 | — |

**20 CENTAVOS** **KM# 16.2** **Composition:** Bronze **Size:** 16 mm.

| Date | Mintage | F | VF | XF | Unc | BU |
|---|---|---|---|---|---|---|
| 1971 | 750,000 | 0.35 | 0.75 | 1.50 | 4.00 | — |

**50 CENTAVOS** **KM# 1** **Composition:** Nickel-Bronze

| Date | Mintage | F | VF | XF | Unc | BU |
|---|---|---|---|---|---|---|
| 1928 | — | 30.00 | 90.00 | 350 | 900 | — |
| 1929 | 400,000 | 3.50 | 12.00 | 50.00 | 150 | — |

**50 CENTAVOS** **KM# 8** **Composition:** Nickel-Bronze

| Date | Mintage | F | VF | XF | Unc | BU |
|---|---|---|---|---|---|---|
| 1948 | 80,000 | 10.00 | 30.00 | 100 | 265 | — |

**50 CENTAVOS** **KM# 10** **Composition:** Copper-Nickel

| Date | Mintage | F | VF | XF | Unc | BU |
|---|---|---|---|---|---|---|
| 1951 | 48,000 | 1.75 | 3.50 | 25.00 | 70.00 | — |

**50 CENTAVOS** **KM# 17.1** **Composition:** Bronze **Size:** 20 mm.

| Date | Mintage | F | VF | XF | Unc | BU |
|---|---|---|---|---|---|---|
| 1962 | 480,000 | 0.25 | 0.50 | 2.50 | 5.00 | — |

**50 CENTAVOS** **KM# 17.2** **Composition:** Bronze **Size:** 22 mm.

| Date | Mintage | F | VF | XF | Unc | BU |
|---|---|---|---|---|---|---|
| 1971 | 600,000 | 0.20 | 0.35 | 1.50 | 3.00 | — |

**ESCUDO** **KM# 4** **Composition:** Copper-Nickel

| Date | Mintage | F | VF | XF | Unc | BU |
|---|---|---|---|---|---|---|
| 1939 | 100,000 | 9.00 | 25.00 | 100 | 285 | — |

**ESCUDO** **KM# 9** **Composition:** Nickel-Bronze

| Date | Mintage | F | VF | XF | Unc | BU |
|---|---|---|---|---|---|---|
| 1948 | 60,000 | 12.50 | 40.00 | 120 | 300 | — |

**ESCUDO** **KM# 11** **Composition:** Copper-Nickel

| Date | Mintage | F | VF | XF | Unc | BU |
|---|---|---|---|---|---|---|
| 1951 | 18,000 | 3.50 | 12.00 | 60.00 | 175 | — |

**ESCUDO** **KM# 18** **Composition:** Bronze

| Date | Mintage | F | VF | XF | Unc | BU |
|---|---|---|---|---|---|---|
| 1962 | 160,000 | 0.75 | 2.50 | 15.00 | 35.00 | — |
| 1971 | 350,000 | 0.35 | 0.75 | 1.50 | 3.50 | — |

**2-1/2 ESCUDOS** **KM# 5** **Weight:** 3.5000 g. **Composition:** 0.6500 Silver .0732 oz. ASW

| Date | Mintage | F | VF | XF | Unc | BU |
|---|---|---|---|---|---|---|
| 1939 | 80,000 | 10.00 | 30.00 | 100 | 300 | — |
| 1948 | 120,000 | 15.00 | 35.00 | 100 | 300 | — |

**2-1/2 ESCUDOS** **KM# 12** **Weight:** 3.5000 g. **Composition:** 0.6500 Silver .0732 oz. ASW

| Date | Mintage | F | VF | XF | Unc | BU |
|---|---|---|---|---|---|---|
| 1951 | 64,000 | 2.50 | 6.00 | 30.00 | 100 | — |

**2-1/2 ESCUDOS** **KM# 19** **Composition:** Copper-Nickel

| Date | Mintage | F | VF | XF | Unc | BU |
|---|---|---|---|---|---|---|
| 1962 | 140,000 | 0.75 | 1.50 | 5.00 | 15.00 | — |
| 1971 | 250,000 | 0.50 | 1.00 | 2.50 | 7.00 | — |

**5 ESCUDOS** **KM# 6** **Weight:** 7.0000 g. **Composition:** 0.6500 Silver .1462 oz. ASW

| Date | Mintage | F | VF | XF | Unc | BU |
|---|---|---|---|---|---|---|
| 1939 | 60,000 | 12.50 | 35.00 | 100 | 300 | — |
| 1948 | 100,000 | 18.00 | 45.00 | 110 | 300 | — |

**5 ESCUDOS** **KM# 13** **Weight:** 7.0000 g. **Composition:** 0.6500 Silver .1462 oz. ASW **Size:** 25 mm.

| Date | Mintage | F | VF | XF | Unc | BU |
|---|---|---|---|---|---|---|
| 1951 | 72,000 | 2.50 | 6.00 | 20.00 | 45.00 | — |

**5 ESCUDOS** **KM# 20** **Weight:** 4.0000 g. **Composition:** 0.6000 Silver .0771 oz. ASW **Size:** 22 mm.

| Date | Mintage | F | VF | XF | Unc | BU |
|---|---|---|---|---|---|---|
| 1962 | 88,000 | 1.00 | 2.00 | 5.50 | 12.00 | — |

**5 ESCUDOS** **KM# 22** **Composition:** Copper-Nickel

| Date | Mintage | F | VF | XF | Unc | BU |
|---|---|---|---|---|---|---|
| 1971 | 100,000 | 0.75 | 1.50 | 3.50 | 8.00 | — |

**10 ESCUDOS** **KM# 7** **Weight:** 12.5000 g. **Composition:** 0.8350 Silver .3356 oz. ASW

| Date | Mintage | F | VF | XF | Unc | BU |
|---|---|---|---|---|---|---|
| 1939 | 40,000 | 12.00 | 25.00 | 65.00 | 250 | — |

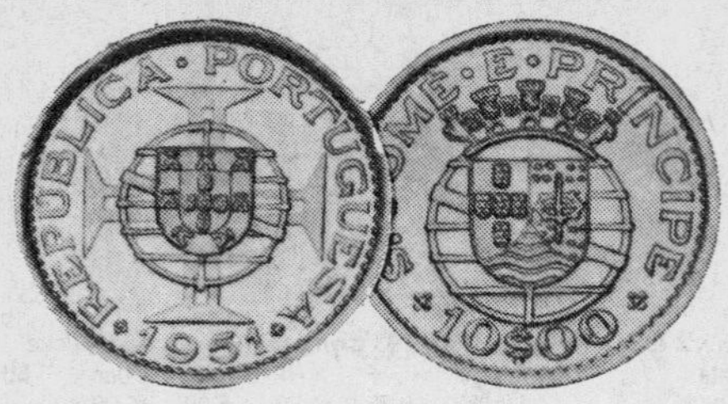

**10 ESCUDOS** KM# 14 **Weight:** 12.5000 g. **Composition:** 0.7200 Silver .2894 oz. ASW

| Date | Mintage | F | VF | XF | Unc | BU |
|---|---|---|---|---|---|---|
| 1951 | 40,000 | 3.00 | 7.00 | 15.00 | 35.00 | — |

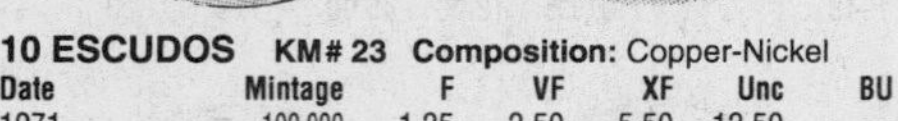

**10 ESCUDOS** KM# 23 **Composition:** Copper-Nickel

| Date | Mintage | F | VF | XF | Unc | BU |
|---|---|---|---|---|---|---|
| 1971 | 100,000 | 1.25 | 2.50 | 5.50 | 12.50 | — |

**20 ESCUDOS** KM# 24 **Composition:** Nickel

| Date | Mintage | F | VF | XF | Unc | BU |
|---|---|---|---|---|---|---|
| 1971 | 75,000 | 1.50 | 3.00 | 6.00 | 13.50 | — |

**50 ESCUDOS** KM# 21 **Weight:** 18.0000 g. **Composition:** 0.6500 Silver .3762 oz. ASW **Subject:** 500th anniversary of discovery

| Date | Mintage | F | VF | XF | Unc | BU |
|---|---|---|---|---|---|---|
| 1970 | 150,000 | — | — | — | 8.00 | — |
| 1970 Matte proof | Est. 200 | — | — | — | — | — |

**Note:** Produced at the Lisbon Mint on private contract.

## REPUBLIC

### STANDARD COINAGE

100 Centimos = 1 Dobra

**50 CENTIMOS** KM# 25 **Composition:** Brass **Series:** F.A.O.

| Date | Mintage | F | VF | XF | Unc | BU |
|---|---|---|---|---|---|---|
| 1977 | 2,000,000 | — | 0.10 | 0.20 | 0.75 | — |
| 1977 Proof | 2,500 | Value: 3.00 | | | | |

**DOBRA** KM# 26 **Composition:** Brass **Series:** F.A.O.

| Date | Mintage | F | VF | XF | Unc | BU |
|---|---|---|---|---|---|---|
| 1977 | 1,500,000 | — | 0.15 | 0.25 | 1.00 | — |
| 1977 Proof | 2,500 | Value: 3.00 | | | | |

**2 DOBRAS** KM# 27 **Composition:** Copper-Nickel **Series:** F.A.O.

| Date | Mintage | F | VF | XF | Unc | BU |
|---|---|---|---|---|---|---|
| 1977 | 1,000,000 | — | 0.25 | 0.40 | 1.50 | — |
| 1977 Proof | 2,500 | Value: 3.50 | | | | |

**5 DOBRAS** KM# 28 **Composition:** Copper-Nickel **Series:** F.A.O.

| Date | Mintage | F | VF | XF | Unc | BU |
|---|---|---|---|---|---|---|
| 1977 | 750,000 | — | 0.35 | 0.65 | 2.00 | — |
| 1977 Proof | 2,500 | Value: 5.00 | | | | |

**10 DOBRAS** KM# 29 **Composition:** Copper-Nickel **Series:** F.A.O.

| Date | Mintage | F | VF | XF | Unc | BU |
|---|---|---|---|---|---|---|
| 1977 | 300,000 | — | 0.60 | 1.25 | 4.00 | — |
| 1977 Proof | 2,500 | Value: 7.00 | | | | |

**10 DOBRAS** KM# 29a **Composition:** Copper-Nickel Clad Steel **Series:** F.A.O.

| Date | Mintage | F | VF | XF | Unc | BU |
|---|---|---|---|---|---|---|
| 1990 | — | — | 0.60 | 1.25 | 4.00 | — |

**20 DOBRAS** KM# 30 **Composition:** Copper-Nickel Clad Steel **Series:** F.A.O.

| Date | Mintage | F | VF | XF | Unc | BU |
|---|---|---|---|---|---|---|
| 1977 | 500,000 | — | 1.00 | 2.00 | 6.00 | — |
| 1977 Proof | 2,500 | Value: 10.00 | | | | |

**50 DOBRAS** KM# 52 **Composition:** Copper-Nickel Clad Steel **Series:** F.A.O.

| Date | Mintage | F | VF | XF | Unc | BU |
|---|---|---|---|---|---|---|
| 1990 | — | — | — | — | 6.00 | — |

**100 DOBRAS** KM# 41 **Composition:** Copper-Nickel **Subject:** World Fisheries Conference

| Date | Mintage | F | VF | XF | Unc | BU |
|---|---|---|---|---|---|---|
| ND(1984) | 1,000,000 | — | — | — | 9.00 | — |

**100 DOBRAS** KM# 41a **Weight:** 28.2800 g. **Composition:** 0.9250 Silver .8411 oz. ASW **Subject:** World Fisheries Conference

| Date | Mintage | F | VF | XF | Unc | BU |
|---|---|---|---|---|---|---|
| ND(1984) Proof | 20,000 | Value: 37.50 | | | | |

**100 DOBRAS** KM# 41b **Weight:** 47.5400 g. **Composition:** 0.9170 Gold 1.4017 oz. AGW **Subject:** World Fisheries Conference

| Date | Mintage | F | VF | XF | Unc | BU |
|---|---|---|---|---|---|---|
| ND(1984) Proof | 100 | Value: 1,250 | | | | |

**100 DOBRAS** KM# 42 **Composition:** Copper-Nickel **Subject:** 10th anniversary of independence

| Date | Mintage | F | VF | XF | Unc | BU |
|---|---|---|---|---|---|---|
| ND(1985) | — | — | — | — | 6.50 | — |

**100 DOBRAS** KM# 42a **Weight:** 28.2800 g. **Composition:** 0.9250 Silver .8411 oz. ASW **Subject:** 10th anniversary of independence

| Date | Mintage | F | VF | XF | Unc | BU |
|---|---|---|---|---|---|---|
| ND(1985) Proof | 1,000 | Value: 40.00 | | | | |

**100 DOBRAS** KM# 42b **Weight:** 47.5400 g. **Composition:** 0.9170 Gold 1.4017 oz. AGW **Subject:** 10th anniversary of independence

| Date | Mintage | F | VF | XF | Unc | BU |
|---|---|---|---|---|---|---|
| ND(1985) Proof | 50 | Value: 1,400 | | | | |

**100 DOBRAS** KM# 87 **Composition:** Chrome Clad Steel **Obverse:** National arms **Reverse:** Denomination below bird

| Date | Mintage | F | VF | XF | Unc | BU |
|---|---|---|---|---|---|---|
| 1997 | — | — | — | — | 1.25 | — |

**250 DOBRAS** **KM# 31** **Weight:** 17.4000 g. **Composition:** 0.9250 Silver .5175 oz. ASW **Obverse:** Independence - world population

| Date | Mintage | F | VF | XF | Unc | BU |
|---|---|---|---|---|---|---|
| 1977 | 450 | — | — | — | 42.50 | — |
| 1977 Proof | 750 | Value: 40.00 | | | | |

**250 DOBRAS** **KM# 32** **Weight:** 17.4000 g. **Composition:** 0.9250 Silver .5175 oz. ASW **Obverse:** Independence - world friendship

| Date | Mintage | F | VF | XF | Unc | BU |
|---|---|---|---|---|---|---|
| 1977 | 450 | — | — | — | 42.50 | — |
| 1977 Proof | 800 | Value: 40.00 | | | | |

**250 DOBRAS** **KM# 33** **Weight:** 17.4000 g. **Composition:** 0.9250 Silver .5175 oz. ASW **Obverse:** Independence - folklore

| Date | Mintage | F | VF | XF | Unc | BU |
|---|---|---|---|---|---|---|
| 1977 | 300 | — | — | — | 42.50 | — |
| 1977 Proof | 600 | Value: 40.00 | | | | |

**250 DOBRAS** **KM# 34** **Weight:** 17.4000 g. **Composition:** 0.9250 Silver .5175 oz. ASW **Obverse:** Independence - world unity

| Date | Mintage | F | VF | XF | Unc | BU |
|---|---|---|---|---|---|---|
| 1977 | 400 | — | — | — | 42.50 | — |
| 1977 Proof | 700 | Value: 40.00 | | | | |

**250 DOBRAS** **KM# 35** **Weight:** 17.4000 g. **Composition:** 0.9250 Silver .5175 oz. ASW **Obverse:** Independence - mother and child

| Date | Mintage | F | VF | XF | Unc | BU |
|---|---|---|---|---|---|---|
| 1977 | 350 | — | — | — | 42.50 | — |
| 1977 Proof | 700 | Value: 40.00 | | | | |

**250 DOBRAS** **KM# 88** **Composition:** Chrome Clad Steel **Obverse:** National arms **Reverse:** Denomination above bird

| Date | Mintage | F | VF | XF | Unc | BU |
|---|---|---|---|---|---|---|
| 1997 | — | — | — | — | 1.50 | — |

**500 DOBRAS** **KM# 70** **Composition:** Copper-Nickel **Reverse:** Elvis Presley

| Date | Mintage | F | VF | XF | Unc | BU |
|---|---|---|---|---|---|---|
| 1993 | — | — | — | — | 12.50 | — |

**500 DOBRAS** **KM# 89** **Composition:** Chrome Clad Steel **Reverse:** Monkey

| Date | Mintage | F | VF | XF | Unc | BU |
|---|---|---|---|---|---|---|
| 1997 | — | — | — | — | 2.00 | — |

**1000 DOBRAS** **KM# 44** **Weight:** 23.3300 g. **Composition:** 0.9250 Silver .6938 oz. ASW **Subject:** Soccer **Reverse:** 2 players

| Date | Mintage | F | VF | XF | Unc | BU |
|---|---|---|---|---|---|---|
| 1990 Proof | 15,000 | Value: 30.00 | | | | |

**1000 DOBRAS** **KM# 45** **Weight:** 23.3300 g. **Composition:** 0.9250 Silver .6938 oz. ASW **Subject:** Soccer **Reverse:** 2 players running

| Date | Mintage | F | VF | XF | Unc | BU |
|---|---|---|---|---|---|---|
| 1990 Proof | 15,000 | Value: 30.00 | | | | |

**1000 DOBRAS** **KM# 47** **Weight:** 25.9600 g. **Composition:** 0.9990 Silver .8347 oz. ASW **Subject:** Soccer **Obverse:** Similar to KM#45 **Reverse:** 1 player

| Date | Mintage | F | VF | XF | Unc | BU |
|---|---|---|---|---|---|---|
| 1990 Proof | — | Value: 45.00 | | | | |

**1000 DOBRAS** **KM# 48** **Weight:** 25.9600 g. **Composition:** 0.9990 Silver .8347 oz. ASW **Subject:** Soccer **Reverse:** 2 players and ball

| Date | Mintage | F | VF | XF | Unc | BU |
|---|---|---|---|---|---|---|
| 1990 Proof | — | Value: 45.00 | | | | |

**1000 DOBRAS** **KM# 49** **Weight:** 20.0000 g. **Composition:** 0.9990 Silver .6431 oz. ASW **Subject:** National independence

| Date | Mintage | F | VF | XF | Unc | BU |
|---|---|---|---|---|---|---|
| 1990 Proof | — | Value: 37.50 | | | | |

**1000 DOBRAS** **KM# 50** **Weight:** 20.0000 g. **Composition:** 0.9990 Silver .6431 oz. ASW **Subject:** Vasco de Gama

| Date | Mintage | F | VF | XF | Unc | BU |
|---|---|---|---|---|---|---|
| 1990 Proof | — | Value: 40.00 | | | | |

**1000 DOBRAS** **KM# 53** **Weight:** 20.0000 g. **Composition:** 0.9990 Silver .6431 oz. ASW **Subject:** Olympics and discovery of America

| Date | Mintage | F | VF | XF | Unc | BU |
|---|---|---|---|---|---|---|
| 1990 Proof | — | Value: 37.50 | | | | |

**1000 DOBRAS** **KM# 73** **Weight:** 23.7400 g. **Composition:** 0.9250 Silver .7060 oz. ASW **Series:** 1992 Olympics **Reverse:** Flame

| Date | Mintage | F | VF | XF | Unc | BU |
|---|---|---|---|---|---|---|
| 1990 Proof | 10,000 | Value: 32.50 | | | | |

**1000 DOBRAS** **KM# 74** **Weight:** 23.7400 g. **Composition:** 0.9250 Silver .7060 oz. ASW **Series:** 1992 Olympics **Reverse:** Diver

| Date | Mintage | F | VF | XF | Unc | BU |
|---|---|---|---|---|---|---|
| 1990 Proof | 10,000 | Value: 30.00 | | | | |

**1000 DOBRAS** **KM# 54** **Composition:** Copper-Nickel **Series:** Atlanta Olympics **Reverse:** Wrestling

| Date | Mintage | F | VF | XF | Unc | BU |
|---|---|---|---|---|---|---|
| ND(1993) Proof | — | Value: 30.00 | | | | |

**1000 DOBRAS** **KM# 63** **Composition:** Copper-Nickel **Series:** Atlanta Olympics **Reverse:** Swimmers

| Date | Mintage | F | VF | XF | Unc | BU |
|---|---|---|---|---|---|---|
| ND(1993) Proof | — | Value: 30.00 | | | | |

**1000 DOBRAS** **KM# 55** **Composition:** Copper-Nickel **Series:** Atlanta Olympics **Reverse:** Soccer players

| Date | Mintage | F | VF | XF | Unc | BU |
|---|---|---|---|---|---|---|
| ND(1993) Proof | — | Value: 30.00 | | | | |

**1000 DOBRAS** **KM# 56** **Composition:** Copper-Nickel **Series:** Atlanta Olympics **Reverse:** Boxer

| Date | Mintage | F | VF | XF | Unc | BU |
|---|---|---|---|---|---|---|
| ND(1993) Proof | — | Value: 30.00 | | | | |

**1000 DOBRAS** **KM# 57** **Composition:** Copper-Nickel **Series:** Atlanta Olympics **Reverse:** Bicyclist

| Date | Mintage | F | VF | XF | Unc | BU |
|---|---|---|---|---|---|---|
| ND(1993) Proof | — | Value: 30.00 | | | | |

**1000 DOBRAS** **KM# 58** **Composition:** Copper-Nickel **Series:** Atlanta Olympics **Reverse:** Karate competition

| Date | Mintage | F | VF | XF | Unc | BU |
|---|---|---|---|---|---|---|
| ND(1993) Proof | — | Value: 30.00 | | | | |

**1000 DOBRAS** **KM# 59** **Composition:** Copper-Nickel **Series:** Atlanta Olympics **Reverse:** Runner

| Date | Mintage | F | VF | XF | Unc | BU |
|---|---|---|---|---|---|---|
| ND(1993) Proof | — | Value: 30.00 | | | | |

**1000 DOBRAS** **KM# 60** **Composition:** Copper-Nickel **Series:** Atlanta Olympics **Reverse:** Field hockey players

| Date | Mintage | F | VF | XF | Unc | BU |
|---|---|---|---|---|---|---|
| ND(1993) Proof | — | Value: 30.00 | | | | |

**1000 DOBRAS** **KM# 61** **Composition:** Copper-Nickel **Series:** Atlanta Olympics **Reverse:** 4 track and field events

| Date | Mintage | F | VF | XF | Unc | BU |
|---|---|---|---|---|---|---|
| ND(1993) Proof | — | Value: 30.00 | | | | |

**1000 DOBRAS** KM# 62 **Composition:** Copper-Nickel **Series:** Atlanta Olympics **Reverse:** Surfer

| Date | Mintage | F | VF | XF | Unc | BU |
|---|---|---|---|---|---|---|
| ND(1993) Proof | — | Value: 30.00 | | | | |

**1000 DOBRAS** KM# 64 **Composition:** Copper-Nickel **Series:** Atlanta Olympics **Reverse:** 3 gymnastic events

| Date | Mintage | F | VF | XF | Unc | BU |
|---|---|---|---|---|---|---|
| ND(1993) Proof | — | Value: 30.00 | | | | |

**1000 DOBRAS** KM# 65 **Composition:** Copper-Nickel **Series:** Atlanta Olympics **Reverse:** Tennis players

| Date | Mintage | F | VF | XF | Unc | BU |
|---|---|---|---|---|---|---|
| ND(1993) Proof | — | Value: 30.00 | | | | |

**1000 DOBRAS** KM# 71 **Weight:** 25.0000 g. **Composition:** 0.9250 Silver .7242 oz. ASW **Reverse:** Elvis Presley

| Date | Mintage | F | VF | XF | Unc | BU |
|---|---|---|---|---|---|---|
| 1993 Proof | — | Value: 30.00 | | | | |

**1000 DOBRAS** KM# 76 **Weight:** 25.0000 g. **Composition:** 0.9250 Silver .7242 oz. ASW **Reverse:** Arms & falcon **Note:** Enamel.

| Date | Mintage | F | VF | XF | Unc | BU |
|---|---|---|---|---|---|---|
| 1995 Proof | 15,000 | Value: 35.00 | | | | |

**1000 DOBRAS** KM# 77 **Weight:** 25.0000 g. **Composition:** 0.9250 Silver .7242 oz. ASW **Reverse:** Porcelain rose **Note:** Enamel.

| Date | Mintage | F | VF | XF | Unc | BU |
|---|---|---|---|---|---|---|
| 1995 Proof | 15,000 | Value: 35.00 | | | | |

**1000 DOBRAS** KM# 78 **Weight:** 25.0000 g. **Composition:** 0.9250 Silver .7242 oz. ASW **Reverse:** Seahorse and crab **Note:** Enamel.

| Date | Mintage | F | VF | XF | Unc | BU |
|---|---|---|---|---|---|---|
| 1995 Proof | 15,000 | Value: 35.00 | | | | |

**1000 DOBRAS** KM# 85.1 **Weight:** 31.1035 g. **Composition:** 0.9990 Silver 1 oz. ASW **Subject:** Diana - Queen of the Hearts

| Date | Mintage | F | VF | XF | Unc | BU |
|---|---|---|---|---|---|---|
| 1997 Proof | 5,000 | Value: 35.00 | | | | |

**1000 DOBRAS** KM# 85.2 **Weight:** 1.2500 g. **Composition:** 0.9990 Gold .0402 oz. AGW **Subject:** Diana - Queen of the Hearts **Obverse:** National arms **Reverse:** Profile of Lady Diana, crowds

| Date | Mintage | F | VF | XF | Unc | BU |
|---|---|---|---|---|---|---|
| 1997 Proof | 3,000 | Value: 60.00 | | | | |

**1000 DOBRAS** KM# 90 **Composition:** Chrome Clad Steel **Reverse:** Flowers and denomination

| Date | Mintage | F | VF | XF | Unc | BU |
|---|---|---|---|---|---|---|
| 1997 | — | — | — | — | 2.75 | — |

**1000 DOBRAS** KM# 92 **Composition:** Copper-Nickel **Reverse:** Heidiland - girl with goats

| Date | Mintage | F | VF | XF | Unc | BU |
|---|---|---|---|---|---|---|
| 1998 | 15,000 | — | — | — | 10.00 | — |

**1000 DOBRAS** KM# 93 **Weight:** 25.0000 g. **Composition:** 0.9250 Silver .7435 oz. ASW **Reverse:** Heidiland

| Date | Mintage | F | VF | XF | Unc | BU |
|---|---|---|---|---|---|---|
| 1998 Proof | 10,000 | Value: 35.00 | | | | |

**1000 DOBRAS** KM# 79 **Weight:** 31.1035 g. **Composition:** 0.9990 Silver 1 oz. ASW **Reverse:** Peacock hologram

| Date | Mintage | F | VF | XF | Unc | BU |
|---|---|---|---|---|---|---|
| 1998(1997) Prooflike | 10,000 | — | — | — | 42.50 | — |

**1000 DOBRAS** KM# 80 **Weight:** 31.1035 g. **Composition:** 0.9990 Silver 1 oz. ASW **Reverse:** Hummingbird hologram

| Date | Mintage | F | VF | XF | Unc | BU |
|---|---|---|---|---|---|---|
| 1998(1997) Prooflike | 10,000 | — | — | — | 42.50 | — |

**1000 DOBRAS** KM# 94 **Weight:** 25.1400 g. **Composition:** 0.9250 Silver .7476 oz. ASW **Subject:** World Cup soccer - France 1998

| Date | Mintage | F | VF | XF | Unc | BU |
|---|---|---|---|---|---|---|
| 1998 Proof | 10,000 | Value: 35.00 | | | | |

**1000 DOBRAS** KM# 82 **Weight:** 31.1035 g. **Composition:** 0.9990 Silver 1 oz. ASW **Reverse:** Butterfly hologram

| Date | Mintage | F | VF | XF | Unc | BU |
|---|---|---|---|---|---|---|
| 1998(1997) Prooflike | 10,000 | — | — | — | 42.50 | — |

**1000 DOBRAS** KM# 81 **Weight:** 31.1035 g. **Composition:** 0.9990 Silver 1 oz. ASW **Reverse:** Fish hologram

| Date | Mintage | F | VF | XF | Unc | BU |
|---|---|---|---|---|---|---|
| 1998(1997) Prooflike | 10,000 | — | — | — | 42.50 | — |

**1000 DOBRAS** KM# 99 **Weight:** 36.5500 g. **Subject:** Millennium **Obverse:** National arms **Reverse:** Perforated gold insert exposing digital clock **Edge:** Reeded **Size:** 34.9 mm. **Note:** Silver shell with gold insert encased digital clock. 8.1 millimeters thick.

| Date | Mintage | F | VF | XF | Unc | BU |
|---|---|---|---|---|---|---|
| 1999 Proof | — | Value: 37.50 | | | | |

**2000 DOBRAS** KM# 91 **Composition:** Chrome Clad Steel **Reverse:** Tropical food plants

| Date | Mintage | F | VF | XF | Unc | BU |
|---|---|---|---|---|---|---|
| 1997 | — | — | — | — | 3.75 | — |

**2000 DOBRAS** KM# 86 **Weight:** 25.0000 g. **Composition:** 0.9250 Silver .7435 oz. ASW **Subject:** Third Christian millennium **Reverse:** Year 2000 CE calendar

| Date | Mintage | F | VF | XF | Unc | BU |
|---|---|---|---|---|---|---|
| 1998 Proof | 5,000 | Value: 28.00 | | | | |

**2000 DOBRAS** KM# 86a **Composition:** Copper-Nickel **Subject:** Third Christian millennium **Reverse:** Year 2000 CE calendar

| Date | Mintage | F | VF | XF | Unc | BU |
|---|---|---|---|---|---|---|
| 1998 Prooflike | — | — | — | — | 10.00 | — |

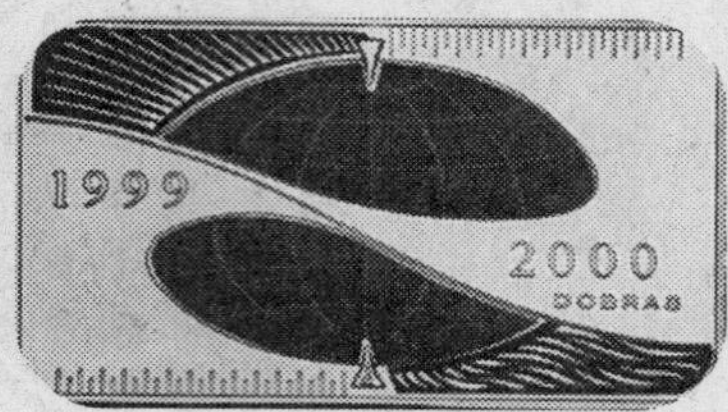


**2000 DOBRAS** KM# 98 **Weight:** 31.1600 g. **Composition:** 0.9990 Silver 1 oz. ASW **Subject:** Pseudo - millennium **Obverse:** National arms **Reverse:** Multicolored world and year split **Edge:** Plain **Note:** 27.1 x 47.2 millimeters.

| Date | Mintage | VG | F | VF | XF | Unc |
|---|---|---|---|---|---|---|
| 1998 Proof | — | Value: 47.50 | | | | |

**2500 DOBRAS** KM# 36 **Weight:** 6.4800 g. **Composition:** 0.9000 Gold .1875 oz. AGW **Subject:** Independence - world friendship

| Date | Mintage | F | VF | XF | Unc | BU |
|---|---|---|---|---|---|---|
| 1977 | 100 | — | — | — | 240 | — |
| 1977 Proof | 170 | Value: 190 | | | | |

**2500 DOBRAS** KM# 37 **Weight:** 6.4800 g. **Composition:** 0.9000 Gold .1875 oz. AGW **Subject:** Independence - world population

| Date | Mintage | F | VF | XF | Unc | BU |
|---|---|---|---|---|---|---|
| 1977 | 100 | — | — | — | 240 | — |
| 1977 Proof | 170 | Value: 190 | | | | |

**2500 DOBRAS** KM# 38 **Weight:** 6.4800 g. **Composition:** 0.9000 Gold .1875 oz. AGW **Subject:** Independence - folklore

| Date | Mintage | F | VF | XF | Unc | BU |
|---|---|---|---|---|---|---|
| 1977 | 100 | — | — | — | 240 | — |
| 1977 Proof | 170 | Value: 190 | | | | |

**2500 DOBRAS** KM# 39 **Weight:** 6.4800 g. **Composition:** 0.9000 Gold .1875 oz. AGW **Subject:** Independence - world unity

| Date | Mintage | F | VF | XF | Unc | BU |
|---|---|---|---|---|---|---|
| 1977 | 100 | — | — | — | 240 | — |
| 1977 Proof | 170 | Value: 190 | | | | |

**2500 DOBRAS** KM# 40 **Weight:** 6.4800 g. **Composition:** 0.9000 Gold .1875 oz. AGW **Subject:** Independence - mother and child

| Date | Mintage | F | VF | XF | Unc | BU |
|---|---|---|---|---|---|---|
| 1977 | 100 | — | — | — | 240 | — |
| 1977 Proof | 170 | Value: 190 | | | | |

**2500 DOBRAS** KM# 83 **Weight:** 6.2207 g. **Composition:** 0.9999 Gold .2000 oz. AGW **Reverse:** Hummingbird hologram **Note:** Similar to 1,000 Dobras, KM#80.

| Date | Mintage | F | VF | XF | Unc | BU |
|---|---|---|---|---|---|---|
| 1998(1997) Proof | 2,500 | Value: 250 | | | | |

**2500 DOBRAS** **KM# 84** **Weight:** 6.2207 g. **Composition:** 0.9999 Gold .2000 oz. AGW **Reverse:** Butterfly hologram **Note:** Similar to 1,000 Dobras, KM#82.

| Date | Mintage | F | VF | XF | Unc | BU |
|---|---|---|---|---|---|---|
| 1998(1997) Proof | 2,500 | Value: 250 | | | | |

**3500 DOBRAS** **KM# 46** **Weight:** 136.0800 g. **Composition:** 0.9250 Silver 4.3755 oz. ASW **Subject:** Wildlife protection **Reverse:** Sea turtle **Size:** 63 mm. **Note:** Illustration reduced.

| Date | Mintage | F | VF | XF | Unc | BU |
|---|---|---|---|---|---|---|
| 1990 Proof | 750 | Value: 125 | | | | |

**5000 DOBRAS** **KM# 100** **Weight:** 168.5600 g. **Subject:** Millennium **Obverse:** National arms **Reverse:** Perforated silver insert exposing digital clock **Edge:** Reeded **Note:** Silver shell with encased digital clock. 9 millimeters thick.

| Date | Mintage | F | VF | XF | Unc | BU |
|---|---|---|---|---|---|---|
| 1999 Proof | — | Value: 80.00 | | | | |

**10000 DOBRAS** **KM# 51** **Weight:** 7.7750 g. **Composition:** 0.9000 Gold .2250 oz. AGW **Reverse:** Sea turtle

| Date | Mintage | F | VF | XF | Unc | BU |
|---|---|---|---|---|---|---|
| 1992 Proof | 500 | Value: 300 | | | | |

**25000 DOBRAS** **KM# 72** **Weight:** 15.5500 g. **Composition:** 0.9990 Gold .5 oz. AGW **Obverse:** National emblem **Reverse:** Elvis Presley

| Date | Mintage | F | VF | XF | Unc | BU |
|---|---|---|---|---|---|---|
| 1993 Proof | — | Value: 550 | | | | |

## DUALLY DENOMINATED COINAGE

**500 DOBRAS - 1 ECU** **KM# 67** **Composition:** Copper-Nickel **Subject:** 15th anniversary of association with European Common Market

| Date | Mintage | F | VF | XF | Unc | BU |
|---|---|---|---|---|---|---|
| 1993 | 20,000 | — | — | — | 11.50 | — |

**2500 DOBRAS - 5 ECU** **KM# 68** **Weight:** 25.0000 g. **Composition:** 0.9250 Silver .7434 oz. ASW **Subject:** 15th anniversary of association with European Common Market

| Date | Mintage | F | VF | XF | Unc | BU |
|---|---|---|---|---|---|---|
| 1993 Proof | 12,000 | Value: 32.50 | | | | |

**25000 DOBRAS - 50 ECU** **KM# 69** **Weight:** 6.7200 g. **Composition:** 0.9000 Gold .1944 oz. AGW **Subject:** 15th anniversary of association with European Common Market **Obverse:** National arms **Reverse:** Old harbor scene **Note:** Similar to 2500 Dobras, 5 Ecu, KM#68.

| Date | Mintage | F | VF | XF | Unc | BU |
|---|---|---|---|---|---|---|
| 1993 Proof | 1,000 | Value: 200 | | | | |

**2000 DOBRAS - 1 EURO** **KM# 95** **Composition:** Copper-Nickel **Obverse:** National arms **Reverse:** Helvetia portrait and multicolored Swiss flag in circle of stars applique, denomination

| Date | Mintage | F | VF | XF | Unc | BU |
|---|---|---|---|---|---|---|
| 1997 Proof | 5,000 | Value: 12.50 | | | | |

**10000 DOBRAS - 5 EURO** **KM# 96** **Weight:** 25.0000 g. **Composition:** 0.9250 Silver .7435 oz. ASW **Obverse:** National arms **Reverse:** Helvetia portrait and Swiss flag in star circle, denomination

| Date | Mintage | F | VF | XF | Unc | BU |
|---|---|---|---|---|---|---|
| 1998 Proof | 5,000 | Value: 37.50 | | | | |

## MEDALLIC COINAGE

**20 DOBRAS** **KM# M1** **Composition:** Silver **Subject:** International Games **Reverse:** Gymnast

| Date | Mintage | F | VF | XF | Unc | BU |
|---|---|---|---|---|---|---|
| 1984 Proof | — | Value: 15.00 | | | | |

## PATTERNS

| KM# | Date | Mintage | Identification | Mkt Val |
|---|---|---|---|---|
| Pn1 | (1994) | — | 1000 Dobras. Copper-Nickel. 1 player. | 55.00 |
| Pn2 | (1994) | — | 1000 Dobras. Copper-Nickel. With denticles. | 55.00 |
| Pn3 | (1994) | — | 1000 Dobras. 0.9990 Silver. 19.7100 g. With 999 CuNi in error. | 65.00 |
| Pn4 | (1994) | — | 1000 Dobras. Copper-Nickel. 2 soccer players and E.P. 999. | 55.00 |
| Pn5 | (1994) | — | 1000 Dobras. 0.9990 Silver. 21.0000 g. E.P. 999. | 65.00 |

## PIEFORTS

| KM# | Date | Mintage | Identification | Mkt Val |
|---|---|---|---|---|
| P1 | 1984 | 500 | 100 Dobras. Silver. | 65.00 |

## PROVAS

Standard metals; stamped "PROVA" in field

| KM# | Date | Mintage | Identification | Mkt Val |
|---|---|---|---|---|
| Pr1 | 1928 | — | 50 Centavos. KM1. | 200 |
| Pr2 | 1929 | — | 10 Centavos. KM2. | 50.00 |
| Pr3 | 1929 | — | 20 Centavos. KM3. | 50.00 |
| Pr4 | 1929 | — | 50 Centavos. KM1. | 125 |
| Pr5 | 1939 | — | Escudo. KM5. | 200 |
| Pr6 | 1939 | — | 2-1/2 Escudos. KM5. | 150 |
| Pr7 | 1939 | — | 5 Escudos. KM6. | 150 |
| Pr8 | 1939 | — | 10 Escudos. KM7. | 300 |
| Pr9 | 1948 | — | 50 Centavos. KM8. | 65.00 |
| Pr10 | 1948 | — | Escudo. KM9. | 65.00 |
| Pr11 | 1948 | — | 2-1/2 Escudos. KM5. | 65.00 |
| Pr12 | 1948 | — | 5 Escudos. KM6. | 70.00 |
| Pr13 | 1951 | — | 50 Centavos. KM10. | 85.00 |
| Pr14 | 1951 | — | Escudo. KM11. | 125 |
| Pr15 | 1951 | — | 2-1/2 Escudos. KM12. | 40.00 |
| Pr16 | 1951 | — | 5 Escudos. KM13. | 60.00 |
| Pr17 | 1951 | — | 10 Escudos. KM14. | 100 |
| Pr18 | 1962 | — | 10 Centavos. KM15. | 20.00 |
| Pr19 | 1962 | — | 20 Centavos. KM16. | 22.50 |
| Pr20 | 1962 | — | 50 Centavos. KM17. | 22.50 |
| Pr21 | 1962 | — | Escudo. KM18. | 25.00 |
| Pr22 | 1962 | — | 2-1/2 Escudos. KM19. | 27.50 |
| Pr23 | 1962 | — | 5 Escudos. KM20. | 40.00 |
| Pr24 | 1970 | — | 50 Escudos. KM21. | 65.00 |
| Pr25 | 1971 | — | 10 Centavos. KM15a. | 20.00 |
| Pr26 | 1971 | — | 20 Centavos. KM16.2. | 20.00 |
| Pr27 | 1971 | — | 50 Centavos. KM17.2. | 20.00 |
| Pr28 | 1971 | — | Escudo. KM18. | 20.00 |
| Pr29 | 1971 | — | 2-1/2 Escudos. KM19. | 22.50 |
| Pr30 | 1971 | — | 5 Escudos. KM22. | 25.00 |
| Pr31 | 1971 | — | 10 Escudos. KM23. | 27.50 |
| Pr32 | 1971 | — | 20 Escudos. KM24. | 30.00 |

## MINT SETS

| KM# | Date | Mintage | Identification | Issue Price | Mkt Val |
|---|---|---|---|---|---|
| MS1 | 1977 (5) | — | KM31-35 | 71.00 | 215 |
| MS2 | 1977 (5) | 100 | KM36-40 | 655 | 1,200 |

## PROOF SETS

| KM# | Date | Mintage | Identification | Issue Price | Mkt Val |
|---|---|---|---|---|---|
| PS1 | 1977 (5) | — | KM31-35 | 93.50 | 200 |
| PS2 | 1977 (5) | 170 | KM36-40 | 805 | 950 |

# SAINT VINCENT

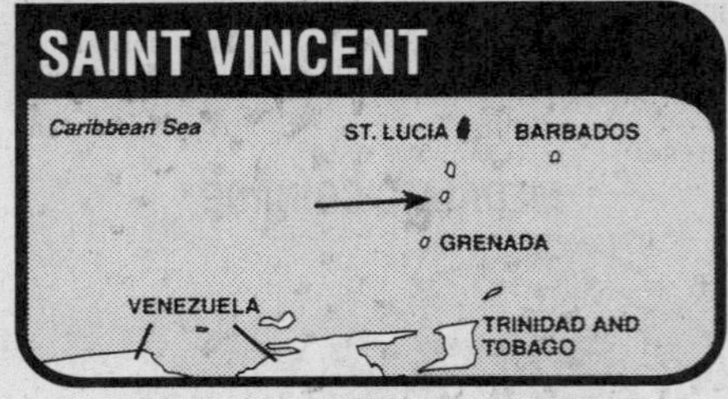


Saint Vincent and the Grenadines, consisting of the island of Saint Vincent and the northern Grenadines (a string of islets stretching southward from Saint Vincent), is located in the Windward Islands of the West Indies, West of Barbados and south of Saint Lucia. The tiny nation has an area of 150sq. mi. (340 sq. km.) and a population of *105,000. Capital: Kingstown. Arrowroot, cotton, sugar, molasses, rum and cocoa are exported. Tourism is a principal industry.

Saint Vincent was discovered by Columbus on Jan. 22,1498, but was left undisturbed for more than a century. The British began colonization early in the 18th century against bitter and prolonged Carib resistance. The island was taken by the French in 1779, but was restored to the British in 1783, at the end of the American Revolution. Saint Vincent and the northern Grenadines became a British associated state in Oct. 1969. Independence under the name of Saint Vincent and the Grenadines was attained at midnight of Oct. 26, 1979. The new nation chose to become a member of the Commonwealth of Nations with Elizabeth II as Head of State and Queen of Saint Vincent.

A local coinage was introduced in 1797, with the gold withdrawn in 1818 and the silver in 1823. This was replaced by sterling. From the mid-1950's, Saint Vincent used the currency of the British Caribbean Territories (Eastern Group), than that of the East Caribbean States.

**RULERS**
British

**MONETARY SYSTEM**
Commencing 1979
100 Cents = 1 Dollar

## BRITISH ADMINISTRATION

### MODERN COINAGE

**4 DOLLARS** KM# 13 **Composition:** Copper-Nickel **Series:** F.A.O

| Date | Mintage | F | VF | XF | Unc | BU |
|---|---|---|---|---|---|---|
| 1970 | 13,000 | — | 3.50 | 7.00 | 12.50 | — |
| 1970 Proof | 2,000 | Value: 22.50 | | | | |

**10 DOLLARS** KM# 14 **Composition:** Copper-Nickel **Subject:** Royal Visit

| Date | Mintage | F | VF | XF | Unc | BU |
|---|---|---|---|---|---|---|
| 1985 | 100,000 | — | — | — | 10.00 | — |

**10 DOLLARS** KM# 14a **Weight:** 28.2800 g. **Composition:** 0.9250 Silver .8411 oz. ASW

| Date | Mintage | F | VF | XF | Unc | BU |
|---|---|---|---|---|---|---|
| 1985 Proof | 5,000 | Value: 55.00 | | | | |

**10 DOLLARS** KM# 14b **Weight:** 47.5400 g. **Composition:** 0.9170 Gold 1.4013 oz. AGW **Subject:** Royal Visit

| Date | Mintage | F | VF | XF | Unc | BU |
|---|---|---|---|---|---|---|
| 1985 Proof | 250 | Value: 875 | | | | |

**100 DOLLARS** KM# 15 **Weight:** 129.5900 g. **Composition:** 0.9250 Silver 3.8543 oz. ASW **Subject:** Tropical Birds - Pelican **Obverse:** Coat of arms **Size:** 63 mm. **Note:** Illustration reduced.

| Date | Mintage | F | VF | XF | Unc | BU |
|---|---|---|---|---|---|---|
| 1988 Proof | Est. 10,000 | Value: 125 | | | | |

# SAN MARINO

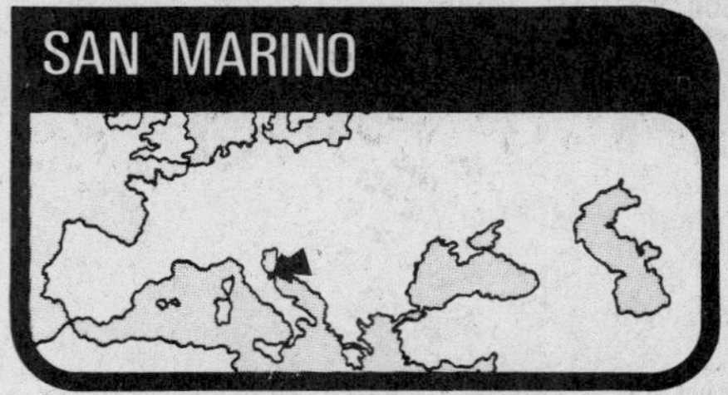

The Republic of San Marino, the oldest and smallest republic in the world is located in north central Italy entirely surrounded by the Province of Emilia-Romagna. It has an area of 24 sq. mi. (60 sq. km.) and a population of *23,000. Capital: San Marino. The principal economic activities are farming, livestock raising, cheese making, tourism and light manufacturing. Building stone, lime, wheat, hides and baked goods are exported. The government derives most of its revenue from the sale of postage stamps for philatelic purposes.

According to tradition, San Marino was founded about350AD by a Christian stonecutter as a refuge against religious persecution. While gradually acquiring the institutions of an independent state, it avoided the factional fights of the Middle Ages and, except for a brief period in fief to Cesare Borgia, retained its freedom despite attacks on its sovereignty by the Papacy, the Lords of Rimini, Napoleon and Mussolini. In 1862 San Marino established a customs union with, and put itself under the protection of, Italy. A Communist-Socialist coalition controlled the Government for 12 years after World War II. The Christian Democratic Party has been the core of government since1957. In 1978 a Communist-Socialist coalition again came into power and remained in control until 1991.

San Marino has its own coinage, but Italian and Vatican City coins and currency are also in circulation.

**MINT MARKS**
M - Milan
R – Rome

**MONETARY SYSTEM**
100 Centesimi = 1 Lira

## REPUBLIC

### STANDARD COINAGE

100 Centesimi = 1 Lira

**5 CENTESIMI** KM# 12 **Composition:** Bronze

| Date | Mintage | F | VF | XF | Unc | BU |
|---|---|---|---|---|---|---|
| 1935R | 400,000 | 1.25 | 2.00 | 3.00 | 5.50 | — |
| 1936R | 400,000 | 1.25 | 2.00 | 3.00 | 5.50 | — |
| 1937R | 400,000 | 1.25 | 2.00 | 3.00 | 5.50 | — |
| 1938R | 200,000 | 1.50 | 2.25 | 3.50 | 6.50 | — |

**10 CENTESIMI** KM# 13 **Composition:** Bronze

| Date | Mintage | F | VF | XF | Unc | BU |
|---|---|---|---|---|---|---|
| 1935R | 300,000 | 1.50 | 2.25 | 3.50 | 7.00 | — |
| 1936R | 300,000 | 1.50 | 2.25 | 3.50 | 7.00 | — |
| 1937R | 300,000 | 1.50 | 2.25 | 3.50 | 7.00 | — |
| 1938R | 400,000 | 1.50 | 2.25 | 3.50 | 7.00 | — |

**LIRA** KM# 4 **Weight:** 5.0000 g. **Composition:** 0.8350 Silver .1342 oz. ASW

| Date | Mintage | F | VF | XF | Unc | BU |
|---|---|---|---|---|---|---|
| 1906R | 30,000 | 15.00 | 22.50 | 40.00 | 75.00 | — |

**LIRA** KM# 14 **Composition:** Aluminum

| Date | Mintage | F | VF | XF | Unc | BU |
|---|---|---|---|---|---|---|
| 1972 | 291,000 | — | — | 0.10 | 0.20 | — |

**LIRA** **KM# 22** **Composition:** Aluminum

| Date | Mintage | F | VF | XF | Unc | BU |
|---|---|---|---|---|---|---|
| 1973 | 291,000 | — | — | 0.10 | 0.20 | — |

**LIRA** **KM# 30** **Composition:** Aluminum

| Date | Mintage | F | VF | XF | Unc | BU |
|---|---|---|---|---|---|---|
| 1974 | 276,000 | — | — | 0.20 | 1.00 | — |

**LIRA** **KM# 40** **Composition:** Aluminum

| Date | Mintage | F | VF | XF | Unc | BU |
|---|---|---|---|---|---|---|
| 1975 | 291,000 | — | — | 0.20 | 1.00 | — |

**LIRA** **KM# 51** **Composition:** Aluminum

| Date | Mintage | F | VF | XF | Unc | BU |
|---|---|---|---|---|---|---|
| 1976 | 195,000 | — | — | 0.10 | 0.20 | — |

**LIRA** **KM# 63** **Composition:** Aluminum **Series:** F.A.O.

| Date | Mintage | F | VF | XF | Unc | BU |
|---|---|---|---|---|---|---|
| 1977 | 1,180,000 | — | — | 0.10 | 0.20 | — |

**LIRA** **KM# 76** **Composition:** Aluminum

| Date | Mintage | F | VF | XF | Unc | BU |
|---|---|---|---|---|---|---|
| 1978 | 130,000 | — | — | 0.15 | 0.30 | — |

**LIRA** **KM# 89** **Composition:** Aluminum

| Date | Mintage | F | VF | XF | Unc | BU |
|---|---|---|---|---|---|---|
| 1979 | 125,000 | — | — | 0.15 | 0.30 | — |

**LIRA** **KM# 102** **Composition:** Aluminum **Series:** 1980 Olympics

| Date | Mintage | F | VF | XF | Unc | BU |
|---|---|---|---|---|---|---|
| 1980 | 125,000 | — | — | 0.15 | 0.30 | — |

**LIRA** **KM# 116** **Composition:** Aluminum

| Date | Mintage | F | VF | XF | Unc | BU |
|---|---|---|---|---|---|---|
| 1981 | 100,000 | — | — | 0.15 | 0.30 | — |

**LIRA** **KM# 131** **Composition:** Aluminum **Subject:** Social conquest

| Date | Mintage | F | VF | XF | Unc | BU |
|---|---|---|---|---|---|---|
| 1982R | 78,000 | — | — | 0.15 | 0.30 | — |

**LIRA** **KM# 145** **Composition:** Aluminum **Subject:** Nuclear war threat **Reverse:** Beast of war

| Date | Mintage | F | VF | XF | Unc | BU |
|---|---|---|---|---|---|---|
| 1983R | 72,000 | — | — | 0.20 | 0.40 | — |

**LIRA** **KM# 159** **Composition:** Aluminum **Reverse:** Hippocrates

| Date | Mintage | F | VF | XF | Unc | BU |
|---|---|---|---|---|---|---|
| 1984R | 65,000 | — | — | 0.20 | 0.40 | — |

**LIRA** **KM# 173** **Composition:** Aluminum **Subject:** War on drugs **Reverse:** Male figure

| Date | Mintage | F | VF | XF | Unc | BU |
|---|---|---|---|---|---|---|
| 1985R | 60,000 | — | — | 0.10 | 0.25 | — |

**LIRA** **KM# 187** **Composition:** Aluminum **Subject:** Revolution of technology

| Date | Mintage | F | VF | XF | Unc | BU |
|---|---|---|---|---|---|---|
| 1986R | 50,000 | — | — | 0.10 | 0.25 | — |

**LIRA** **KM# 201** **Composition:** Aluminum **Subject:** 15th anniversary - resumption of coinage

| Date | Mintage | F | VF | XF | Unc | BU |
|---|---|---|---|---|---|---|
| 1987R | 83,000 | — | — | 0.10 | 0.25 | — |

**LIRA** **KM# 218** **Composition:** Aluminum **Subject:** Fortifications **Reverse:** Corner Tower

| Date | Mintage | F | VF | XF | Unc | BU |
|---|---|---|---|---|---|---|
| 1988R | 38,000 | — | — | 0.10 | 0.25 | — |

**LIRA** **KM# 231** **Composition:** Aluminum **Subject:** History **Reverse:** Stone Age tool

| Date | Mintage | F | VF | XF | Unc | BU |
|---|---|---|---|---|---|---|
| 1989R | 37,000 | — | — | 0.10 | 0.25 | — |

**LIRA** **KM# 248** **Composition:** Aluminum **Subject:** 1,600 years of history **Reverse:** Saint

| Date | Mintage | F | VF | XF | Unc | BU |
|---|---|---|---|---|---|---|
| 1990R | 36,000 | — | — | 0.10 | 0.25 | — |

**LIRA** **KM# 261** **Composition:** Aluminum **Reverse:** Hands holding hammer and chisel

| Date | Mintage | F | VF | XF | Unc | BU |
|---|---|---|---|---|---|---|
| 1991R | — | — | — | 0.10 | 0.25 | — |

**LIRA** **KM# 278** **Composition:** Aluminum **Subject:** Columbus **Reverse:** Potato plant and potatoes

| Date | Mintage | F | VF | XF | Unc | BU |
|---|---|---|---|---|---|---|
| ND(1992)R | — | — | — | 0.10 | 0.25 | — |

**LIRA** **KM# 293** **Composition:** Aluminum **Reverse:** Seedling

| Date | Mintage | F | VF | XF | Unc | BU |
|---|---|---|---|---|---|---|
| 1993R | — | — | — | 0.10 | 0.25 | — |

**LIRA** **KM# 306** **Composition:** Aluminum **Reverse:** Mother and child

| Date | Mintage | F | VF | XF | Unc | BU |
|---|---|---|---|---|---|---|
| 1994R | 40,000 | — | — | 0.10 | 0.25 | — |

**LIRA** **KM# 322** **Composition:** Aluminum **Reverse:** Child on broken sword

| Date | Mintage | F | VF | XF | Unc | BU |
|---|---|---|---|---|---|---|
| 1995R | — | — | — | 0.10 | 0.25 | — |

**LIRA** **KM# 349** **Composition:** Aluminum **Subject:** Talete - Child of the Universe

| Date | Mintage | F | VF | XF | Unc | BU |
|---|---|---|---|---|---|---|
| 1996 | 32,000 | — | — | 0.10 | 0.25 | — |

**LIRA** **KM# 359** **Composition:** Aluminum **Subject:** The arts - prehistoric

| Date | Mintage | F | VF | XF | Unc | BU |
|---|---|---|---|---|---|---|
| 1997 | 28,000 | — | — | 0.10 | 0.25 | — |

**2 LIRE** **KM# 5** **Weight:** 10.0000 g. **Composition:** 0.8350 Silver .2684 oz. ASW

| Date | Mintage | F | VF | XF | Unc | BU |
|---|---|---|---|---|---|---|
| 1906R | 15,000 | 25.00 | 40.00 | 80.00 | 165 | — |

**2 LIRE** **KM# 15** **Composition:** Aluminum

| Date | Mintage | F | VF | XF | Unc | BU |
|---|---|---|---|---|---|---|
| 1972 | 291,000 | — | — | 0.10 | 0.30 | — |

**2 LIRE** **KM# 23** **Composition:** Aluminum

| Date | Mintage | F | VF | XF | Unc | BU |
|---|---|---|---|---|---|---|
| 1973 | 291,000 | — | — | 0.15 | 0.75 | — |

**2 LIRE** **KM# 31** **Composition:** Aluminum

| Date | Mintage | F | VF | XF | Unc | BU |
|---|---|---|---|---|---|---|
| 1974 | 276,000 | — | — | 0.20 | 1.00 | — |

**2 LIRE** **KM# 41** **Composition:** Aluminum

| Date | Mintage | F | VF | XF | Unc | BU |
|---|---|---|---|---|---|---|
| 1975 | 291,000 | — | — | 0.20 | 1.00 | — |

**2 LIRE** **KM# 52** **Composition:** Aluminum

| Date | Mintage | F | VF | XF | Unc | BU |
|---|---|---|---|---|---|---|
| 1976 | 195,000 | — | — | 0.10 | 0.30 | — |

**2 LIRE** **KM# 64** **Composition:** Aluminum

| Date | Mintage | F | VF | XF | Unc | BU |
|---|---|---|---|---|---|---|
| 1977 | 180,000 | — | — | 0.10 | 0.30 | — |

**2 LIRE** **KM# 77** **Composition:** Aluminum

| Date | Mintage | F | VF | XF | Unc | BU |
|---|---|---|---|---|---|---|
| 1978 | 130,000 | — | — | 0.10 | 0.30 | — |

**2 LIRE** **KM# 90** **Composition:** Aluminum

| Date | Mintage | F | VF | XF | Unc | BU |
|---|---|---|---|---|---|---|
| 1979 | 125,000 | — | — | 0.10 | 0.30 | — |

**2 LIRE** **KM# 103** **Composition:** Aluminum **Series:** 1980 Olympics **Reverse:** Soccer player

| Date | Mintage | F | VF | XF | Unc | BU |
|---|---|---|---|---|---|---|
| 1980 | 125,000 | — | — | 0.25 | 0.75 | — |

**2 LIRE** **KM# 117** **Composition:** Aluminum

| Date | Mintage | F | VF | XF | Unc | BU |
|---|---|---|---|---|---|---|
| 1981 | 100,000 | — | — | 0.10 | 0.30 | — |

**2 LIRE** **KM# 132** **Composition:** Aluminum **Subject:** Social conquests

| Date | Mintage | F | VF | XF | Unc | BU |
|---|---|---|---|---|---|---|
| 1982R | 78,000 | — | — | 0.10 | 0.30 | — |

**2 LIRE** **KM# 146** **Composition:** Aluminum **Subject:** Nuclear war threat **Reverse:** 2 arms

| Date | Mintage | F | VF | XF | Unc | BU |
|---|---|---|---|---|---|---|
| 1983R | 72,000 | — | — | 0.20 | 0.40 | — |

**2 LIRE** **KM# 160** **Composition:** Aluminum **Reverse:** Leonardo da Vinci

| Date | Mintage | F | VF | XF | Unc | BU |
|---|---|---|---|---|---|---|
| 1984R | 65,000 | — | — | 0.20 | 0.40 | — |

**2 LIRE** **KM# 174** **Composition:** Aluminum **Subject:** War on drugs **Reverse:** Clenched fist

| Date | Mintage | F | VF | XF | Unc | BU |
|---|---|---|---|---|---|---|
| 1985R | 60,000 | — | — | 0.10 | 0.25 | — |

**2 LIRE** **KM# 188** **Composition:** Aluminum **Subject:** Revolution of technology

| Date | Mintage | F | VF | XF | Unc | BU |
|---|---|---|---|---|---|---|
| 1986R | 50,000 | — | — | 0.10 | 0.25 | — |

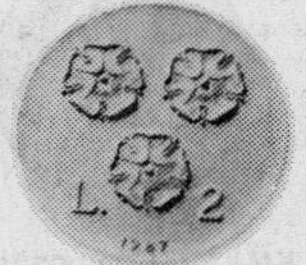

**2 LIRE** **KM# 202** **Composition:** Aluminum **Subject:** 15th anniversary - resumption of coinage

| Date | Mintage | F | VF | XF | Unc | BU |
|---|---|---|---|---|---|---|
| 1987R | 83,000 | — | — | 0.10 | 0.25 | — |

**2 LIRE** **KM# 219** **Composition:** Aluminum **Subject:** Fortifications **Reverse:** Fortified archway

| Date | Mintage | F | VF | XF | Unc | BU |
|---|---|---|---|---|---|---|
| 1988R | 38,000 | — | — | 0.10 | 0.25 | — |

**2 LIRE** **KM# 232** **Composition:** Aluminum **Subject:** History **Reverse:** Wheat stalk and olive branch

| Date | Mintage | F | VF | XF | Unc | BU |
|---|---|---|---|---|---|---|
| 1989R | 37,000 | — | — | 0.10 | 0.25 | — |

**2 LIRE** **KM# 249** **Composition:** Aluminum **Subject:** 1,600 years of history **Reverse:** Figure with spear

| Date | Mintage | F | VF | XF | Unc | BU |
|---|---|---|---|---|---|---|
| 1990R | 36,000 | — | — | 0.10 | 0.25 | — |

**2 LIRE** **KM# 262** **Composition:** Aluminum **Reverse:** Hands with interlocked fingers

| Date | Mintage | F | VF | XF | Unc | BU |
|---|---|---|---|---|---|---|
| 1991R | — | — | — | 0.10 | 0.25 | — |

**2 LIRE** **KM# 279** **Composition:** Aluminum **Subject:** Columbus **Reverse:** Ear of corn

| Date | Mintage | F | VF | XF | Unc | BU |
|---|---|---|---|---|---|---|
| ND(1992)R | — | — | — | 0.10 | 0.25 | — |

**2 LIRE** **KM# 294** **Composition:** Aluminum **Reverse:** Rose

| Date | Mintage | F | VF | XF | Unc | BU |
|---|---|---|---|---|---|---|
| 1993R | — | — | — | 0.10 | 0.25 | — |

**2 LIRE** **KM# 307** **Composition:** Aluminum **Reverse:** Stonecutter at work

| Date | Mintage | F | VF | XF | Unc | BU |
|---|---|---|---|---|---|---|
| 1994R | 40,000 | — | — | 0.10 | 0.25 | — |

**2 LIRE** **KM# 323** **Composition:** Aluminum **Reverse:** Child with toy castle

| Date | Mintage | F | VF | XF | Unc | BU |
|---|---|---|---|---|---|---|
| 1995R | — | — | — | 0.10 | 0.25 | — |

**2 LIRE** **KM# 350** **Composition:** Aluminum **Reverse:** Socrates

| Date | Mintage | F | VF | XF | Unc | BU |
|---|---|---|---|---|---|---|
| 1996 | 32,000 | — | — | 0.10 | 0.25 | — |

**2 LIRE** **KM# 360** **Composition:** Aluminum **Subject:** The arts - literature **Reverse:** Dante holding Divine Comedy

| Date | Mintage | F | VF | XF | Unc | BU |
|---|---|---|---|---|---|---|
| 1997 | 28,000 | — | — | 0.10 | 0.25 | — |

**5 LIRE** **KM# 9** **Weight:** 5.0000 g. **Composition:** 0.8350 Silver .1342 oz. ASW

| Date | Mintage | F | VF | XF | Unc | BU |
|---|---|---|---|---|---|---|
| 1931R | 50,000 | 3.50 | 5.50 | 10.00 | 25.00 | — |
| 1932R | 50,000 | 3.50 | 5.50 | 10.00 | 25.00 | — |
| 1933R | 50,000 | 3.50 | 5.50 | 8.50 | 20.00 | — |
| 1935R | 200,000 | 3.50 | 5.50 | 8.50 | 20.00 | — |
| 1936R | Inc. above | 3.50 | 5.50 | 8.50 | 20.00 | — |
| 1937R | 100,000 | 3.50 | 5.50 | 8.50 | 20.00 | — |
| 1938R | 120,000 | 3.50 | 5.50 | 8.50 | 20.00 | — |

**5 LIRE** **KM# 16** **Composition:** Aluminum

| Date | Mintage | F | VF | XF | Unc | BU |
|---|---|---|---|---|---|---|
| 1972 | 291,000 | — | — | 0.10 | 0.35 | — |

**5 LIRE** **KM# 24** **Composition:** Aluminum

| Date | Mintage | F | VF | XF | Unc | BU |
|---|---|---|---|---|---|---|
| 1973 | 291,000 | — | — | 0.10 | 0.35 | — |

**5 LIRE** **KM# 32** **Composition:** Aluminum

| Date | Mintage | F | VF | XF | Unc | BU |
|---|---|---|---|---|---|---|
| 1974 | 276,000 | — | — | 0.20 | 1.00 | — |

**5 LIRE** **KM# 42** **Composition:** Aluminum

| Date | Mintage | F | VF | XF | Unc | BU |
|---|---|---|---|---|---|---|
| 1975 | 291,000 | — | — | 0.20 | 0.75 | — |

**5 LIRE** **KM# 53** **Composition:** Aluminum **Series:** F.A.O.

| Date | Mintage | F | VF | XF | Unc | BU |
|---|---|---|---|---|---|---|
| 1976 | 695,000 | — | — | 0.10 | 0.25 | — |

**5 LIRE** **KM# 65** **Composition:** Aluminum

| Date | Mintage | F | VF | XF | Unc | BU |
|---|---|---|---|---|---|---|
| 1977 | 180,000 | — | — | 0.10 | 0.35 | — |

**5 LIRE** **KM# 78** **Composition:** Aluminum

| Date | Mintage | F | VF | XF | Unc | BU |
|---|---|---|---|---|---|---|
| 1978 | 130,000 | — | — | 0.10 | 0.35 | — |

**5 LIRE** **KM# 91** **Composition:** Aluminum

| Date | Mintage | F | VF | XF | Unc | BU |
|---|---|---|---|---|---|---|
| 1979 | 125,000 | — | — | 0.10 | 0.35 | — |

**5 LIRE** **KM# 104** **Composition:** Aluminum **Series:** 1980 Olympics

| Date | Mintage | F | VF | XF | Unc | BU |
|---|---|---|---|---|---|---|
| 1980 | 125,000 | — | — | 0.25 | 0.75 | — |

**5 LIRE** **KM# 118** **Composition:** Aluminum

| Date | Mintage | F | VF | XF | Unc | BU |
|---|---|---|---|---|---|---|
| 1981 | 100,000 | — | — | 0.25 | 0.75 | — |

**5 LIRE** **KM# 133** **Composition:** Aluminum **Subject:** Social conquests

| Date | Mintage | F | VF | XF | Unc | BU |
|---|---|---|---|---|---|---|
| 1982R | 78,000 | — | — | 0.10 | 0.30 | — |

**5 LIRE** **KM# 147** **Composition:** Aluminum **Subject:** Nuclear war threat **Reverse:** Arm in window

| Date | Mintage | F | VF | XF | Unc | BU |
|---|---|---|---|---|---|---|
| 1983R | 72,000 | — | — | 0.20 | 0.40 | — |

**5 LIRE** **KM# 161** **Composition:** Aluminum **Reverse:** Galileo

| Date | Mintage | F | VF | XF | Unc | BU |
|---|---|---|---|---|---|---|
| 1984R | 65,000 | — | — | 0.20 | 0.40 | — |

**5 LIRE** **KM# 175** **Composition:** Aluminum **Subject:** War on drugs **Reverse:** Face of addict

| Date | Mintage | F | VF | XF | Unc | BU |
|---|---|---|---|---|---|---|
| 1985R | 60,000 | — | — | 0.10 | 0.30 | — |

**5 LIRE** **KM# 189** **Composition:** Aluminum **Subject:** Revolution of technology

| Date | Mintage | F | VF | XF | Unc | BU |
|---|---|---|---|---|---|---|
| 1986R | 50,000 | — | — | 0.10 | 0.30 | — |

**5 LIRE** **KM# 203** **Composition:** Aluminum **Subject:** 15th anniversary - resumption of coinage

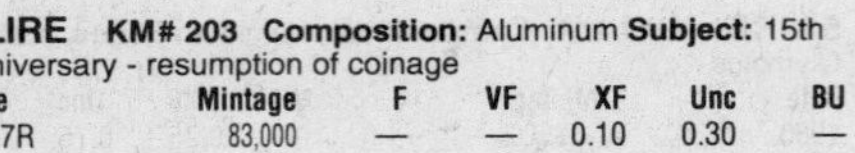

| Date | Mintage | F | VF | XF | Unc | BU |
|---|---|---|---|---|---|---|
| 1987R | 83,000 | — | — | 0.10 | 0.30 | — |

**5 LIRE** **KM# 220** **Composition:** Aluminum **Subject:** Fortification **Reverse:** Round corner tower

| Date | Mintage | F | VF | XF | Unc | BU |
|---|---|---|---|---|---|---|
| 1988R | 38,000 | — | — | 0.10 | 0.30 | — |

**5 LIRE** **KM# 233** **Composition:** Aluminum **Subject:** History **Reverse:** Bunch of grapes

| Date | Mintage | F | VF | XF | Unc | BU |
|---|---|---|---|---|---|---|
| 1989R | 37,000 | — | — | 0.10 | 0.30 | — |

**5 LIRE** **KM# 250** **Composition:** Aluminum **Subject:** 1,600 years of history **Reverse:** 2 facing figures

| Date | Mintage | F | VF | XF | Unc | BU |
|---|---|---|---|---|---|---|
| 1990R | 36,000 | — | — | 0.10 | 0.30 | — |

**5 LIRE** **KM# 263** **Composition:** Aluminum **Reverse:** Hand holding quill

| Date | Mintage | F | VF | XF | Unc | BU |
|---|---|---|---|---|---|---|
| 1991R | — | — | — | 0.10 | 0.30 | — |

**5 LIRE** **KM# 280** **Composition:** Aluminum **Subject:** Columbus **Reverse:** Cotton plants

| Date | Mintage | F | VF | XF | Unc | BU |
|---|---|---|---|---|---|---|
| ND(1992)R | — | — | — | 0.10 | 0.30 | — |

**5 LIRE** **KM# 295** **Composition:** Aluminum **Reverse:** Spade and hoe

| Date | Mintage | F | VF | XF | Unc | BU |
|---|---|---|---|---|---|---|
| 1993R | — | — | — | 0.10 | 0.30 | — |

**5 LIRE** **KM# 308** **Composition:** Aluminum **Reverse:** Marino and Leo with tools

| Date | Mintage | F | VF | XF | Unc | BU |
|---|---|---|---|---|---|---|
| 1994R | 40,000 | — | — | 0.10 | 0.30 | — |

**5 LIRE** **KM# 324** **Composition:** Aluminum **Reverse:** Child with 2 deer

| Date | Mintage | F | VF | XF | Unc | BU |
|---|---|---|---|---|---|---|
| 1995R | — | — | — | 0.10 | 0.30 | — |

**5 LIRE** **KM# 351** **Composition:** Aluminum **Reverse:** Plato

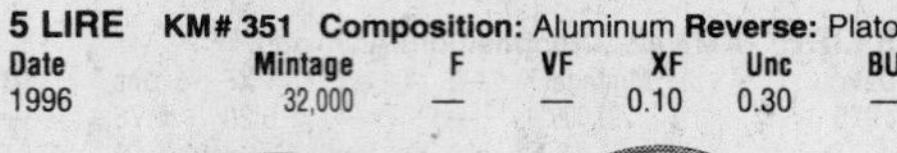

| Date | Mintage | F | VF | XF | Unc | BU |
|---|---|---|---|---|---|---|
| 1996 | 32,000 | — | — | 0.10 | 0.30 | — |

**5 LIRE** **KM# 361** **Composition:** Aluminum **Subject:** The arts - theater **Reverse:** Hamlet, skull

| Date | Mintage | F | VF | XF | Unc | BU |
|---|---|---|---|---|---|---|
| 1997 | 28,000 | — | — | 0.10 | 0.30 | — |

**10 LIRE** **KM# 7** **Weight:** 3.2258 g. **Composition:** 0.9000 Gold .0933 oz. AGW **Note:** 16,000 coins melted at the mint.

| Date | Mintage | F | VF | XF | Unc | BU |
|---|---|---|---|---|---|---|
| 1925R | 20,000 | 175 | 325 | 450 | 750 | — |

**10 LIRE** **KM# 10** **Weight:** 10.0000 g. **Composition:** 0.8350 Silver .2684 oz. ASW

| Date | Mintage | F | VF | XF | Unc | BU |
|---|---|---|---|---|---|---|
| 1931R | 25,000 | 8.50 | 15.00 | 35.00 | 75.00 | — |
| 1932R | 25,000 | 8.50 | 15.00 | 35.00 | 75.00 | — |
| 1933R | 25,000 | 8.50 | 15.00 | 35.00 | 75.00 | — |
| 1935R | 30,000 | 6.50 | 10.00 | 25.00 | 60.00 | — |
| 1936R | Inc. above | 10.00 | 18.00 | 40.00 | 85.00 | — |
| 1937R | 15,000 | 6.50 | 10.00 | 25.00 | 60.00 | — |
| 1938R | 10,000 | 12.00 | 20.00 | 50.00 | 100 | — |

**10 LIRE** **KM# 17** **Composition:** Aluminum

| Date | Mintage | F | VF | XF | Unc | BU |
|---|---|---|---|---|---|---|
| 1972 | 291,000 | — | 0.10 | 0.20 | 0.50 | — |

**10 LIRE** **KM# 25** **Composition:** Aluminum

| Date | Mintage | F | VF | XF | Unc | BU |
|---|---|---|---|---|---|---|
| 1973 | 291,000 | — | 0.10 | 0.15 | 0.40 | — |

**10 LIRE** **KM# 33** **Composition:** Aluminum **Series:** F.A.O.

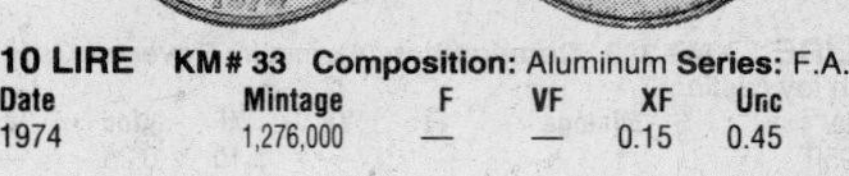

| Date | Mintage | F | VF | XF | Unc | BU |
|---|---|---|---|---|---|---|
| 1974 | 1,276,000 | — | — | 0.15 | 0.45 | — |

**10 LIRE** **KM# 43** **Composition:** Aluminum

| Date | Mintage | F | VF | XF | Unc | BU |
|---|---|---|---|---|---|---|
| 1975 | 291,000 | — | 0.10 | 0.25 | 1.00 | — |

**10 LIRE** **KM# 54** **Composition:** Aluminum

| Date | Mintage | F | VF | XF | Unc | BU |
|---|---|---|---|---|---|---|
| 1976 | 195,000 | — | 0.10 | 0.15 | 0.40 | — |

**10 LIRE** **KM# 66** **Composition:** Aluminum

| Date | Mintage | F | VF | XF | Unc | BU |
|---|---|---|---|---|---|---|
| 1977 | 180,000 | — | 0.10 | 0.15 | 0.40 | — |

**10 LIRE** **KM# 79** **Composition:** Aluminum

| Date | Mintage | F | VF | XF | Unc | BU |
|---|---|---|---|---|---|---|
| 1978 | 130,000 | — | 0.10 | 0.15 | 0.40 | — |

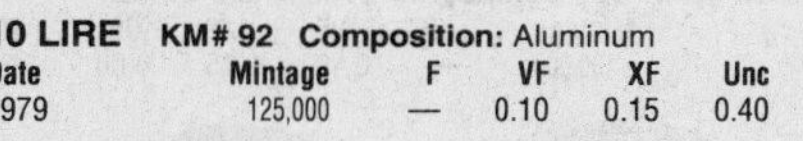

**10 LIRE** **KM# 92** **Composition:** Aluminum

| Date | Mintage | F | VF | XF | Unc | BU |
|---|---|---|---|---|---|---|
| 1979 | 125,000 | — | 0.10 | 0.15 | 0.40 | — |

**10 LIRE** **KM# 105** **Composition:** Aluminum **Series:** 1980 Olympics

| Date | Mintage | F | VF | XF | Unc | BU |
|---|---|---|---|---|---|---|
| 1980 | 125,000 | — | 0.25 | 0.50 | 0.80 | — |

**10 LIRE** **KM# 119** **Composition:** Aluminum

| Date | Mintage | F | VF | XF | Unc | BU |
|---|---|---|---|---|---|---|
| 1981 | 100,000 | — | 0.10 | 0.20 | 0.50 | — |

**10 LIRE** **KM# 134** **Composition:** Aluminum **Subject:** Social conquests

| Date | Mintage | F | VF | XF | Unc | BU |
|---|---|---|---|---|---|---|
| 1982R | 78,000 | — | 0.10 | 0.20 | 0.50 | — |

**10 LIRE** **KM# 148** **Composition:** Aluminum **Subject:** Nuclear war threat **Reverse:** 2 arms in frame

| Date | Mintage | F | VF | XF | Unc | BU |
|---|---|---|---|---|---|---|
| 1983R | 72,000 | — | 0.10 | 0.25 | 0.75 | — |

**10 LIRE** **KM# 162** **Composition:** Aluminum **Reverse:** Alessandro Volta

| Date | Mintage | F | VF | XF | Unc | BU |
|---|---|---|---|---|---|---|
| 1984R | 65,000 | — | 0.10 | 0.25 | 0.75 | — |

**10 LIRE** **KM# 176** **Composition:** Aluminum **Subject:** War on drugs **Reverse:** Mother lecturing son

| Date | Mintage | F | VF | XF | Unc | BU |
|---|---|---|---|---|---|---|
| 1985R | 60,000 | — | — | 0.10 | 0.35 | — |

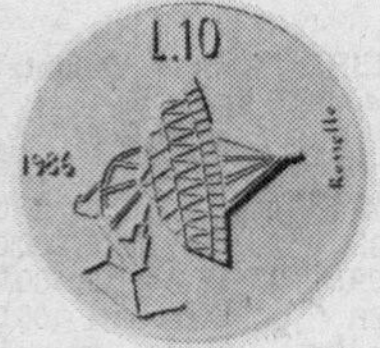

**10 LIRE** **KM# 190** **Composition:** Aluminum **Subject:** Revolution of technology

| Date | Mintage | F | VF | XF | Unc | BU |
|---|---|---|---|---|---|---|
| 1986R | 50,000 | — | — | 0.10 | 0.35 | — |

**10 LIRE** **KM# 204** **Composition:** Aluminum **Subject:** 15th anniversary - resumption of coinage

| Date | Mintage | F | VF | XF | Unc | BU |
|---|---|---|---|---|---|---|
| 1987R | 83,000 | — | — | 0.10 | 0.35 | — |

**10 LIRE** **KM# 221** **Composition:** Aluminum **Subject:** Fortifications **Reverse:** Sloping fortress wall

| Date | Mintage | F | VF | XF | Unc | BU |
|---|---|---|---|---|---|---|
| 1988R | 38,000 | — | — | 0.10 | 0.35 | — |

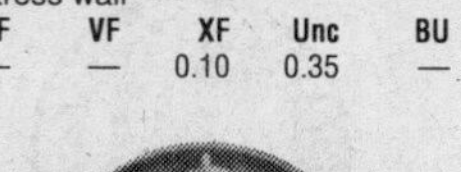

**10 LIRE** **KM# 234** **Composition:** Aluminum **Subject:** History **Reverse:** Ancient pottery

| Date | Mintage | F | VF | XF | Unc | BU |
|---|---|---|---|---|---|---|
| 1989R | 37,000 | — | — | 0.10 | 0.35 | — |

**10 LIRE** **KM# 251** **Composition:** Aluminum **Subject:** 1,600 years of history **Reverse:** Soldier

| Date | Mintage | F | VF | XF | Unc | BU |
|---|---|---|---|---|---|---|
| 1990R | 36,000 | — | — | 0.10 | 0.35 | — |

**10 LIRE** **KM# 264** **Composition:** Aluminum **Reverse:** Hand holding castle tower

| Date | Mintage | F | VF | XF | Unc | BU |
|---|---|---|---|---|---|---|
| 1991R | — | — | — | 0.10 | 0.35 | — |

**10 LIRE** **KM# 281** **Composition:** Aluminum **Subject:** Columbus **Reverse:** Dolphin and ship

| Date | Mintage | F | VF | XF | Unc | BU |
|---|---|---|---|---|---|---|
| ND(1992)R | — | — | — | 0.20 | 0.75 | — |

**10 LIRE** **KM# 296** **Composition:** Aluminum **Reverse:** Corinthian column

| Date | Mintage | F | VF | XF | Unc | BU |
|---|---|---|---|---|---|---|
| 1993R | — | — | — | 0.10 | 0.35 | — |

**10 LIRE** **KM# 309** **Composition:** Aluminum **Reverse:** Marino and Leo working

| Date | Mintage | F | VF | XF | Unc | BU |
|---|---|---|---|---|---|---|
| 1994R | 40,000 | — | — | 0.10 | 0.35 | — |

**10 LIRE** **KM# 325** **Composition:** Aluminum **Reverse:** Child with 2 urns

| Date | Mintage | F | VF | XF | Unc | BU |
|---|---|---|---|---|---|---|
| 1995R | — | — | — | 0.10 | 0.35 | — |

**10 LIRE** **KM# 352** **Composition:** Aluminum **Reverse:** Aristotle

| Date | Mintage | F | VF | XF | Unc | BU |
|---|---|---|---|---|---|---|
| 1996 | 28,000 | — | — | 0.10 | 0.35 | — |

**10 LIRE** KM# 362 **Composition:** Aluminum **Subject:** The arts - architecture

| Date | Mintage | F | VF | XF | Unc | BU |
|---|---|---|---|---|---|---|
| 1997 | 28,000 | — | — | 0.10 | 0.35 | — |

**10 LIRE** KM# 378 **Composition:** Aluminum **Subject:** Mathematics **Reverse:** Hand and geometric shape

| Date | Mintage | F | VF | XF | Unc | BU |
|---|---|---|---|---|---|---|
| 1998 | — | — | — | 0.10 | 0.35 | — |

**10 LIRE** KM# 389 **Composition:** Aluminum **Subject:** Exploration **Obverse:** Crowned arms **Reverse:** Earth flat, as once envisioned

| Date | Mintage | F | VF | XF | Unc | BU |
|---|---|---|---|---|---|---|
| 1999 | — | — | — | 0.10 | 0.35 | — |

**10 LIRE** KM# 399 **Weight:** 1.6000 g. **Composition:** Aluminum **Subject:** Love **Obverse:** Child of the Universe **Reverse:** Child on flower on star **Edge:** Plain **Size:** 23.3 mm. **Note:** Struck at Rome.

| Date | Mintage | F | VF | XF | Unc | BU |
|---|---|---|---|---|---|---|
| 2000 | — | — | — | — | 0.35 | — |

**10 LIRE** KM# 424 **Weight:** 1.6000 g. **Composition:** Aluminum **Obverse:** Three towers. **Reverse:** Wheat stalks. **Edge:** Plain. **Size:** 23.3 mm.

| Date | Mintage | F | VF | XF | Unc | BU |
|---|---|---|---|---|---|---|
| 2001 | — | — | — | — | 0.35 | — |

**20 LIRE** KM# 8 **Weight:** 6.4516 g. **Composition:** 0.9000 Gold .1867 oz. AGW **Note:** 7,334 coins were melted at the mint.

| Date | Mintage | F | VF | XF | Unc | BU |
|---|---|---|---|---|---|---|
| 1925R | 9,334 | 400 | 700 | 1,150 | 2,200 | — |

**20 LIRE** KM# 11 **Weight:** 15.0000 g. **Composition:** 0.8000 Silver .3858 oz. ASW

| Date | Mintage | F | VF | XF | Unc | BU |
|---|---|---|---|---|---|---|
| 1931R | 10,000 | 25.00 | 45.00 | 90.00 | 185 | — |
| 1932R | 10,000 | 35.00 | 60.00 | 110 | 220 | — |
| 1933R | 10,000 | 30.00 | 50.00 | 100 | 200 | — |
| 1935R | 10,000 | 30.00 | 50.00 | 100 | 200 | — |
| 1936R | Inc. above | 60.00 | 125 | 200 | 400 | — |

**20 LIRE** KM# 11a **Weight:** 20.0000 g. **Composition:** 0.8000 Silver .5145 oz. ASW

| Date | Mintage | F | VF | XF | Unc | BU |
|---|---|---|---|---|---|---|
| 1935R Rare | — | — | — | — | — | — |
| 1937R | 5,100 | 100 | 200 | 400 | 725 | — |
| 1938R | 2,500 | 200 | 400 | 800 | 1,250 | — |

**20 LIRE** KM# 18 **Composition:** Aluminum-Bronze

| Date | Mintage | F | VF | XF | Unc | BU |
|---|---|---|---|---|---|---|
| 1972 | 291,000 | — | 0.10 | 0.25 | 0.60 | — |

**20 LIRE** KM# 26 **Composition:** Aluminum-Bronze

| Date | Mintage | F | VF | XF | Unc | BU |
|---|---|---|---|---|---|---|
| 1973 | 291,000 | — | 0.10 | 0.25 | 0.60 | — |

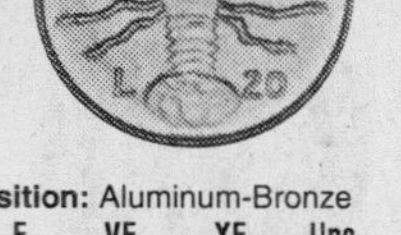

**20 LIRE** KM# 34 **Composition:** Aluminum-Bronze

| Date | Mintage | F | VF | XF | Unc | BU |
|---|---|---|---|---|---|---|
| 1974 | 276,000 | — | 0.10 | 0.30 | 1.00 | — |

**20 LIRE** KM# 44 **Composition:** Aluminum-Bronze **Series:** F.A.O.

| Date | Mintage | F | VF | XF | Unc | BU |
|---|---|---|---|---|---|---|
| 1975 | 291,000 | — | 0.10 | 0.30 | 0.75 | — |

**20 LIRE** KM# 55 **Composition:** Aluminum-Bronze

| Date | Mintage | F | VF | XF | Unc | BU |
|---|---|---|---|---|---|---|
| 1976 | 195,000 | — | 0.10 | 0.25 | 0.60 | — |

**20 LIRE** KM# 67 **Composition:** Aluminum-Bronze

| Date | Mintage | F | VF | XF | Unc | BU |
|---|---|---|---|---|---|---|
| 1977 | 180,000 | — | 0.10 | 0.25 | 0.60 | — |

**20 LIRE** KM# 80 **Composition:** Aluminum-Bronze

| Date | Mintage | F | VF | XF | Unc | BU |
|---|---|---|---|---|---|---|
| 1978 | 130,000 | — | 0.10 | 0.25 | 0.60 | — |

**20 LIRE** KM# 93 **Composition:** Aluminum-Bronze

| Date | Mintage | F | VF | XF | Unc | BU |
|---|---|---|---|---|---|---|
| 1979 | 125,000 | — | 0.10 | 0.30 | 0.60 | — |

**20 LIRE** KM# 106 **Composition:** Aluminum-Bronze **Series:** 1980 Olympics

| Date | Mintage | F | VF | XF | Unc | BU |
|---|---|---|---|---|---|---|
| 1980 | 125,000 | — | 0.25 | 0.50 | 1.00 | — |

**20 LIRE** KM# 120 **Composition:** Aluminum-Bronze

| Date | Mintage | F | VF | XF | Unc | BU |
|---|---|---|---|---|---|---|
| 1981 | 100,000 | — | 0.10 | 0.30 | 0.65 | — |

**20 LIRE** KM# 135 **Composition:** Aluminum-Bronze **Subject:** Social conquests

| Date | Mintage | F | VF | XF | Unc | BU |
|---|---|---|---|---|---|---|
| 1982R | 78,000 | — | 0.10 | 0.25 | 0.60 | — |

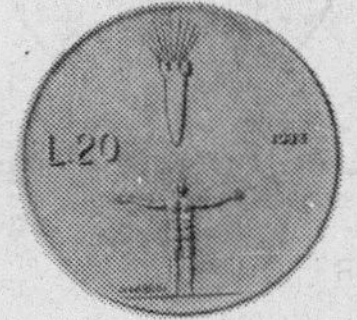

**20 LIRE** KM# 149 **Composition:** Aluminum-Bronze **Subject:** Nuclear war threat **Reverse:** Torch above man

| Date | Mintage | F | VF | XF | Unc | BU |
|---|---|---|---|---|---|---|
| 1983R | 72,000 | — | 0.10 | 0.30 | 0.75 | — |

**20 LIRE** **KM# 163** **Composition:** Aluminum-Bronze **Reverse:** Louis Pasteur

| Date | Mintage | F | VF | XF | Unc | BU |
|---|---|---|---|---|---|---|
| 1984R | 65,000 | — | 0.10 | 0.30 | 0.75 | — |

**20 LIRE** **KM# 177** **Composition:** Aluminum-Bronze **Subject:** War on drugs **Reverse:** Open hand

| Date | Mintage | F | VF | XF | Unc | BU |
|---|---|---|---|---|---|---|
| 1985R | 60,000 | — | — | 0.15 | 0.55 | — |

**20 LIRE** **KM# 191** **Composition:** Aluminum-Bronze **Subject:** Revolution of technology

| Date | Mintage | F | VF | XF | Unc | BU |
|---|---|---|---|---|---|---|
| 1986R | 50,000 | — | — | 0.15 | 0.55 | — |

**20 LIRE** **KM# 205** **Composition:** Aluminum-Bronze **Subject:** 15th anniversary - resumption of coinage

| Date | Mintage | F | VF | XF | Unc | BU |
|---|---|---|---|---|---|---|
| 1987R | 83,000 | — | — | 0.15 | 0.55 | — |

**20 LIRE** **KM# 222** **Composition:** Aluminum-Bronze **Subject:** Fortifications **Reverse:** Small fortified gate

| Date | Mintage | F | VF | XF | Unc | BU |
|---|---|---|---|---|---|---|
| 1988R | 38,000 | — | — | 0.15 | 0.55 | — |

**20 LIRE** **KM# 235** **Composition:** Aluminum-Bronze **Subject:** History **Reverse:** Sword and flag

| Date | Mintage | F | VF | XF | Unc | BU |
|---|---|---|---|---|---|---|
| 1989R | 37,000 | — | — | 0.15 | 0.55 | — |

**20 LIRE** **KM# 252** **Composition:** Aluminum-Bronze **Subject:** 1,600 years of history **Reverse:** Figure straddling denomination

| Date | Mintage | F | VF | XF | Unc | BU |
|---|---|---|---|---|---|---|
| 1990R | 96,000 | — | — | 0.15 | 0.55 | — |

**20 LIRE** **KM# 265** **Composition:** Aluminum-Bronze **Reverse:** Gloved hand rejecting cardinal ring

| Date | Mintage | F | VF | XF | Unc | BU |
|---|---|---|---|---|---|---|
| 1991R | — | — | — | 0.15 | 0.55 | — |

**20 LIRE** **KM# 282** **Composition:** Aluminum-Bronze **Reverse:** Columbus landing on Hispaniola

| Date | Mintage | F | VF | XF | Unc | BU |
|---|---|---|---|---|---|---|
| 1992R | — | — | — | 0.10 | 0.55 | — |

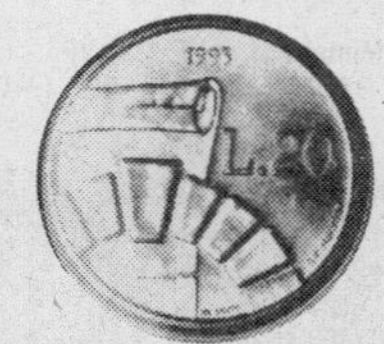

**20 LIRE** **KM# 297** **Composition:** Aluminum-Bronze **Reverse:** Scroll and arch

| Date | Mintage | F | VF | XF | Unc | BU |
|---|---|---|---|---|---|---|
| 1993R | — | — | — | 0.10 | 0.55 | — |

**20 LIRE** **KM# 310** **Composition:** Aluminum-Bronze **Reverse:** Workers pulling stone

| Date | Mintage | F | VF | XF | Unc | BU |
|---|---|---|---|---|---|---|
| 1994R | 40,000 | — | — | 0.10 | 0.55 | — |

**20 LIRE** **KM# 326** **Composition:** Aluminum-Bronze **Reverse:** Child straddling cornucopia

| Date | Mintage | F | VF | XF | Unc | BU |
|---|---|---|---|---|---|---|
| 1995R | — | — | — | 0.10 | 0.55 | — |

**20 LIRE** **KM# 353** **Composition:** Aluminum-Bronze **Obverse:** St. Thomas

| Date | Mintage | F | VF | XF | Unc | BU |
|---|---|---|---|---|---|---|
| 1996 | 32,000 | — | — | 0.10 | 0.55 | — |

**20 LIRE** **KM# 363** **Composition:** Aluminum-Bronze **Subject:** The arts - cinema **Reverse:** Film strips

| Date | Mintage | F | VF | XF | Unc | BU |
|---|---|---|---|---|---|---|
| 1997 | 28,000 | — | — | 0.10 | 0.55 | — |

**20 LIRE** **KM# 379** **Composition:** Aluminum-Bronze **Subject:** Communications **Reverse:** Two profiles in silhouette

| Date | Mintage | F | VF | XF | Unc | BU |
|---|---|---|---|---|---|---|
| 1998 | — | — | — | 0.10 | 0.55 | — |

**20 LIRE** **KM# 390** **Composition:** Aluminum-Bronze **Subject:** Exploration **Obverse:** Crowned arms **Reverse:** Earth as known today

| Date | Mintage | F | VF | XF | Unc | BU |
|---|---|---|---|---|---|---|
| 1999 | — | — | — | 0.10 | 0.55 | — |

**20 LIRE** **KM# 400** **Weight:** 3.6000 g. **Composition:** Aluminum-Bronze **Subject:** Solidarity **Obverse:** Child of the Universe **Reverse:** 2 hands about to grasp **Edge:** Plain **Size:** 21.8 mm. **Note:** Struck at Rome.

| Date | Mintage | F | VF | XF | Unc | BU |
|---|---|---|---|---|---|---|
| 2000 | — | — | — | 0.10 | 0.55 | — |

**20 LIRE** **KM# 425** **Weight:** 3.6000 g. **Composition:** Aluminum-Bronze **Obverse:** Three towers. **Reverse:** Two dolphins. **Edge:** Plain. **Size:** 21.8 mm.

| Date | Mintage | F | VF | XF | Unc | BU |
|---|---|---|---|---|---|---|
| 2001 | — | — | — | — | 0.35 | — |

**50 LIRE** **KM# 19** **Composition:** Steel

| Date | Mintage | F | VF | XF | Unc | BU |
|---|---|---|---|---|---|---|
| 1972 | 291,000 | 0.15 | 0.25 | 0.50 | 1.00 | — |

**50 LIRE** **KM# 27** **Composition:** Steel

| Date | Mintage | F | VF | XF | Unc | BU |
|---|---|---|---|---|---|---|
| 1973 | 291,000 | 0.15 | 0.25 | 0.50 | 1.00 | — |

**50 LIRE** **KM# 35** **Composition:** Steel

| Date | Mintage | F | VF | XF | Unc | BU |
|---|---|---|---|---|---|---|
| 1974 | 276,000 | 0.15 | 0.25 | 0.60 | 1.25 | — |

**50 LIRE** **KM# 45** **Composition:** Steel

| Date | Mintage | F | VF | XF | Unc | BU |
|---|---|---|---|---|---|---|
| 1975 | 831,000 | 0.15 | 0.25 | 0.60 | 1.25 | — |

**50 LIRE** **KM# 56** **Composition:** Steel

| Date | Mintage | F | VF | XF | Unc | BU |
|---|---|---|---|---|---|---|
| 1976 | 195,000 | 0.15 | 0.25 | 0.50 | 1.00 | — |

**50 LIRE** **KM# 68** **Composition:** Steel

| Date | Mintage | F | VF | XF | Unc | BU |
|---|---|---|---|---|---|---|
| 1977 | 180,000 | 0.15 | 0.25 | 0.50 | 1.00 | — |

**50 LIRE** **KM# 81** **Composition:** Steel

| Date | Mintage | F | VF | XF | Unc | BU |
|---|---|---|---|---|---|---|
| 1978 | 130,000 | 0.15 | 0.25 | 0.50 | 1.00 | — |

**50 LIRE** **KM# 94** **Composition:** Steel

| Date | Mintage | F | VF | XF | Unc | BU |
|---|---|---|---|---|---|---|
| 1979 | 125,000 | 0.15 | 0.25 | 0.50 | 1.00 | — |

**50 LIRE** **KM# 107** **Composition:** Steel **Series:** 1980 Olympics **Reverse:** Downhill skier

| Date | Mintage | F | VF | XF | Unc | BU |
|---|---|---|---|---|---|---|
| 1980 | 125,000 | 0.25 | 0.50 | 1.00 | 2.00 | — |

**50 LIRE** **KM# 121** **Composition:** Steel

| Date | Mintage | F | VF | XF | Unc | BU |
|---|---|---|---|---|---|---|
| 1981 | 100,000 | 0.15 | 0.25 | 0.50 | 1.00 | — |

**50 LIRE** **KM# 136** **Composition:** Steel **Subject:** Social conquests

| Date | Mintage | F | VF | XF | Unc | BU |
|---|---|---|---|---|---|---|
| 1982R | 78,000 | 0.15 | 0.25 | 0.50 | 1.00 | — |

**50 LIRE** **KM# 150** **Composition:** Steel **Subject:** Nuclear war threat **Reverse:** Beast above woman

| Date | Mintage | F | VF | XF | Unc | BU |
|---|---|---|---|---|---|---|
| 1983R | 72,000 | 0.20 | 0.40 | 0.80 | 1.50 | — |

**50 LIRE** **KM# 164** **Composition:** Steel **Reverse:** Pierre and Marie Curie

| Date | Mintage | F | VF | XF | Unc | BU |
|---|---|---|---|---|---|---|
| 1984R | 65,000 | 0.20 | 0.40 | 0.80 | 1.50 | — |

**50 LIRE** **KM# 178** **Composition:** Steel **Subject:** War on drugs **Reverse:** Stylized figures

| Date | Mintage | F | VF | XF | Unc | BU |
|---|---|---|---|---|---|---|
| 1985R | 110,000 | — | 0.10 | 0.20 | 0.85 | — |

**50 LIRE** **KM# 192** **Composition:** Steel **Subject:** Revolution of technology

| Date | Mintage | F | VF | XF | Unc | BU |
|---|---|---|---|---|---|---|
| 1986R | 50,000 | — | 0.10 | 0.20 | 0.85 | — |

**50 LIRE** **KM# 206** **Composition:** Steel **Subject:** 15th anniversary - resumption of coinage

| Date | Mintage | F | VF | XF | Unc | BU |
|---|---|---|---|---|---|---|
| 1987R | 93,000 | — | 0.10 | 0.20 | 0.85 | — |

**50 LIRE** **KM# 223** **Composition:** Steel **Subject:** Fortifications **Reverse:** Ramp leading to gate house

| Date | Mintage | F | VF | XF | Unc | BU |
|---|---|---|---|---|---|---|
| 1988R | 38,000 | — | 0.10 | 0.20 | 0.85 | — |

**50 LIRE** **KM# 236** **Composition:** Steel **Subject:** History **Reverse:** Cross bow

| Date | Mintage | VG | F | VF | XF | Unc |
|---|---|---|---|---|---|---|
| 1989R | 87,000 | — | — | 0.10 | 0.20 | 0.85 |

**50 LIRE** **KM# 253** **Composition:** Steel **Subject:** 1,600 years of history **Reverse:** Bird

| Date | Mintage | F | VF | XF | Unc | BU |
|---|---|---|---|---|---|---|
| 1990R | 52,000 | — | 0.10 | 0.20 | 0.85 | — |

**50 LIRE** **KM# 266** **Composition:** Steel **Reverse:** Hand holding cannon barrels and wheat stalks

| Date | Mintage | F | VF | XF | Unc | BU |
|---|---|---|---|---|---|---|
| 1991R | — | — | 0.10 | 0.20 | 0.85 | — |

**50 LIRE** **KM# 283** **Composition:** Steel **Subject:** Columbus **Reverse:** Seagulls flying over radiant seascape

| Date | Mintage | F | VF | XF | Unc | BU |
|---|---|---|---|---|---|---|
| 1992R | — | — | 0.10 | 0.20 | 0.85 | — |

**50 LIRE** **KM# 298** **Composition:** Steel **Reverse:** Wheat growing through barbed wire

| Date | Mintage | F | VF | XF | Unc | BU |
|---|---|---|---|---|---|---|
| 1993R | — | — | 0.10 | 0.20 | 0.85 | — |

**50 LIRE** **KM# 311** **Composition:** Stainless Steel **Reverse:** Two stonecutters

| Date | Mintage | F | VF | XF | Unc | BU |
|---|---|---|---|---|---|---|
| 1994R | 40,000 | — | 0.10 | 0.20 | 0.85 | — |

**50 LIRE** **KM# 327** **Composition:** Stainless Steel **Reverse:** Child hugging bird

| Date | Mintage | F | VF | XF | Unc | BU |
|---|---|---|---|---|---|---|
| 1995R | — | — | 0.10 | 0.20 | 0.85 | — |

**50 LIRE** **KM# 354** **Composition:** Stainless Steel **Reverse:** Descartes

| Date | Mintage | F | VF | XF | Unc | BU |
|---|---|---|---|---|---|---|
| 1996 | 32,000 | — | 0.10 | 0.20 | 0.85 | — |

**50 LIRE** **KM# 364** **Composition:** Stainless Steel **Subject:** The arts - sculpture **Reverse:** Han Dynasty horse statue

| Date | Mintage | F | VF | XF | Unc | BU |
|---|---|---|---|---|---|---|
| 1997 | 28,000 | — | 0.10 | 0.20 | 0.85 | — |

**50 LIRE** **KM# 380** **Composition:** Copper-Nickel **Subject:** Engineering **Reverse:** Cogwheel mind

| Date | Mintage | F | VF | XF | Unc | BU |
|---|---|---|---|---|---|---|
| 1998 | — | — | 0.10 | 0.20 | 0.85 | — |

**50 LIRE** **KM# 391** **Composition:** Copper-Nickel **Subject:** Exploration **Obverse:** Crowned arms **Reverse:** Ship sail, sun and waves

| Date | Mintage | F | VF | XF | Unc | BU |
|---|---|---|---|---|---|---|
| 1999 | — | — | 0.10 | 0.20 | 0.85 | — |

**50 LIRE** **KM# 401** **Weight:** 4.5000 g. **Composition:** Copper-Nickel **Subject:** Equality **Obverse:** Child of the Universe **Reverse:** 5 different plant leaves on 1 stem **Edge:** Plain **Size:** 19.2 mm. **Note:** Struck at Rome.

| Date | Mintage | F | VF | XF | Unc | BU |
|---|---|---|---|---|---|---|
| 2000 | — | — | 0.10 | 0.20 | 0.85 | — |

**50 LIRE** **KM# 426** **Weight:** 4.5000 g. **Composition:** Stainless Steel **Obverse:** Three towers. **Reverse:** Tree. **Edge:** Plain. **Size:** 19.2 mm.

| Date | Mintage | F | VF | XF | Unc | BU |
|---|---|---|---|---|---|---|
| 2001 | — | — | — | — | 0.85 | — |

**100 LIRE** **KM# 20** **Composition:** Steel

| Date | Mintage | F | VF | XF | Unc | BU |
|---|---|---|---|---|---|---|
| 1972 | 291,000 | 0.15 | 0.30 | 0.60 | 1.50 | — |

**100 LIRE** **KM# 28** **Composition:** Steel

| Date | Mintage | F | VF | XF | Unc | BU |
|---|---|---|---|---|---|---|
| 1973 | 291,000 | 0.15 | 0.30 | 0.60 | 1.50 | — |

**100 LIRE** **KM# 36** **Composition:** Steel

| Date | Mintage | F | VF | XF | Unc | BU |
|---|---|---|---|---|---|---|
| 1974 | 276,000 | 0.15 | 0.30 | 0.65 | 1.65 | — |

**100 LIRE** **KM# 46** **Composition:** Steel

| Date | Mintage | F | VF | XF | Unc | BU |
|---|---|---|---|---|---|---|
| 1975 | 821,000 | 0.15 | 0.30 | 0.65 | 1.85 | — |

**100 LIRE** **KM# 57** **Composition:** Steel

| Date | Mintage | F | VF | XF | Unc | BU |
|---|---|---|---|---|---|---|
| 1976 | 1,853,000 | 0.15 | 0.30 | 0.60 | 1.50 | — |

**100 LIRE** **KM# 69** **Composition:** Steel

| Date | Mintage | F | VF | XF | Unc | BU |
|---|---|---|---|---|---|---|
| 1977 | 565,000 | 0.15 | 0.30 | 0.60 | 1.50 | — |

**100 LIRE** **KM# 70** **Composition:** Steel

| Date | Mintage | F | VF | XF | Unc | BU |
|---|---|---|---|---|---|---|
| 1977 | 565,000 | 0.15 | 0.30 | 0.60 | 1.50 | — |

**100 LIRE** **KM# 82** **Composition:** Steel **Series:** F.A.O.

| Date | Mintage | F | VF | XF | Unc | BU |
|---|---|---|---|---|---|---|
| 1978 | 875,000 | 0.15 | 0.30 | 0.60 | 1.50 | — |

**100 LIRE** **KM# 95** **Composition:** Steel

| Date | Mintage | F | VF | XF | Unc | BU |
|---|---|---|---|---|---|---|
| 1979 | 665,000 | 0.15 | 0.30 | 0.60 | 1.50 | — |

**100 LIRE** **KM# 108** **Composition:** Steel **Series:** 1980 Olympics **Subject:** Archery

| Date | Mintage | F | VF | XF | Unc | BU |
|---|---|---|---|---|---|---|
| 1980 | 350,000 | 0.25 | 0.50 | 1.00 | 2.00 | — |

**100 LIRE** **KM# 122** **Composition:** Steel

| Date | Mintage | F | VF | XF | Unc | BU |
|---|---|---|---|---|---|---|
| 1981 | 512,000 | 0.15 | 0.30 | 0.60 | 1.50 | — |

**100 LIRE** **KM# 137** **Composition:** Steel **Subject:** Social conquests

| Date | Mintage | F | VF | XF | Unc | BU |
|---|---|---|---|---|---|---|
| 1982R | 178,000 | 0.15 | 0.30 | 0.60 | 1.50 | — |

**100 LIRE KM# 151 Composition:** Steel **Subject:** Nuclear war threat **Reverse:** Beast above man and woman

| Date | Mintage | F | VF | XF | Unc | BU |
|---|---|---|---|---|---|---|
| 1983R | 172,000 | 0.15 | 0.30 | 0.60 | 1.50 | — |

**100 LIRE KM# 165 Composition:** Steel **Reverse:** Guglielmo Marconi

| Date | Mintage | F | VF | XF | Unc | BU |
|---|---|---|---|---|---|---|
| 1984R | 165,000 | 0.15 | 0.30 | 0.60 | 1.50 | — |

**100 LIRE KM# 179 Composition:** Steel **Subject:** War on drugs **Reverse:** 3 figures in discussion

| Date | Mintage | F | VF | XF | Unc | BU |
|---|---|---|---|---|---|---|
| 1985R | 210,000 | — | — | 0.35 | 1.25 | — |

**100 LIRE KM# 193 Composition:** Steel **Subject:** Revolution of technology

| Date | Mintage | F | VF | XF | Unc | BU |
|---|---|---|---|---|---|---|
| 1986R | 150,000 | — | — | 0.35 | 1.25 | — |

**100 LIRE KM# 207 Composition:** Steel **Subject:** 15th anniversary - resumption of coinage

| Date | Mintage | F | VF | XF | Unc | BU |
|---|---|---|---|---|---|---|
| 1987R | 143,000 | — | — | 0.35 | 1.25 | — |

**100 LIRE KM# 224 Composition:** Steel **Subject:** Fortifications **Reverse:** Gate tower

| Date | Mintage | F | VF | XF | Unc | BU |
|---|---|---|---|---|---|---|
| 1988R | 38,000 | — | — | 0.35 | 1.25 | — |

**100 LIRE KM# 237 Composition:** Steel **Subject:** History **Reverse:** Teacher and student

| Date | Mintage | F | VF | XF | Unc | BU |
|---|---|---|---|---|---|---|
| 1989R | 37,000 | — | — | 0.35 | 1.25 | — |

**100 LIRE KM# 254 Composition:** Steel **Subject:** 1,600 years of history **Reverse:** Balance scale

| Date | Mintage | F | VF | XF | Unc | BU |
|---|---|---|---|---|---|---|
| 1990R | 1,086,000 | — | — | 0.35 | 1.25 | — |

**100 LIRE KM# 267 Composition:** Steel **Reverse:** Clasped hands

| Date | Mintage | F | VF | XF | Unc | BU |
|---|---|---|---|---|---|---|
| 1991R | — | — | — | 0.35 | 1.25 | — |

**100 LIRE KM# 284 Composition:** Steel **Subject:** Columbus **Reverse:** Sailing ship

| Date | Mintage | F | VF | XF | Unc | BU |
|---|---|---|---|---|---|---|
| 1992R | — | — | — | 0.35 | 1.25 | — |

**100 LIRE KM# 299 Composition:** Copper-Nickel **Reverse:** Pan swallow above western Europe

| Date | Mintage | F | VF | XF | Unc | BU |
|---|---|---|---|---|---|---|
| 1993R | — | — | — | 0.35 | 1.25 | — |

**100 LIRE KM# 312 Composition:** Copper-Nickel **Reverse:** 2 stonecutters

| Date | Mintage | F | VF | XF | Unc | BU |
|---|---|---|---|---|---|---|
| 1994R | 40,000 | — | — | 0.35 | 1.25 | — |

**100 LIRE KM# 328 Composition:** Copper-Nickel **Reverse:** 3 children

| Date | Mintage | F | VF | XF | Unc | BU |
|---|---|---|---|---|---|---|
| 1995R | — | — | — | 0.35 | 1.25 | — |

**100 LIRE KM# 355 Composition:** Copper-Nickel **Reverse:** Rousseau

| Date | Mintage | F | VF | XF | Unc | BU |
|---|---|---|---|---|---|---|
| 1996 | 32,000 | — | — | 0.35 | 1.25 | — |

**100 LIRE KM# 365 Composition:** Copper-Nickel **Subject:** The arts - dance **Reverse:** Ballet

| Date | Mintage | F | VF | XF | Unc | BU |
|---|---|---|---|---|---|---|
| 1997 | 28,000 | — | — | 0.35 | 1.25 | — |

**100 LIRE KM# 381 Composition:** Copper-Nickel **Subject:** Physics **Reverse:** Human, crossbow

| Date | Mintage | F | VF | XF | Unc | BU |
|---|---|---|---|---|---|---|
| 1998 | — | — | — | 0.35 | 1.25 | — |

**100 LIRE KM# A352 Composition:** Copper-Nickel **Subject:** Exploration **Obverse:** Crowned arms **Reverse:** Submarine below Arctic ice-cap

| Date | Mintage | F | VF | XF | Unc | BU |
|---|---|---|---|---|---|---|
| 1999 | — | — | — | 0.35 | 1.25 | — |

**100 LIRE KM# 402 Weight:** 4.5000 g. **Composition:** Copper-Nickel **Subject:** Ecology **Obverse:** Child of the Universe **Reverse:** Leaf on house on leaf **Edge:** Reeded and plain sectioned **Size:** 22 mm.

| Date | Mintage | F | VF | XF | Unc | BU |
|---|---|---|---|---|---|---|
| 2000 | — | — | — | 0.35 | 1.25 | — |

**100 LIRE KM# 427 Weight:** 4.5000 g. **Composition:** Copper-Nickel **Obverse:** Three towers. **Reverse:** Two hands. **Edge:** Plain and reeded sections. **Size:** 22 mm.

| Date | Mintage | F | VF | XF | Unc | BU |
|---|---|---|---|---|---|---|
| 2001 | — | — | — | — | 1.25 | — |

**200 LIRE** **KM# 83** **Composition:** Aluminum-Bronze

| Date | Mintage | F | VF | XF | Unc | BU |
|---|---|---|---|---|---|---|
| 1978 | 530,000 | — | 0.25 | 0.75 | 1.75 | — |

**200 LIRE** **KM# 96** **Composition:** Aluminum-Bronze **Series:** F.A.O.

| Date | Mintage | F | VF | XF | Unc | BU |
|---|---|---|---|---|---|---|
| 1979 | 675,000 | — | 0.25 | 0.75 | 1.75 | — |

**200 LIRE** **KM# 109** **Composition:** Aluminum-Bronze **Series:** 1980 Olympics **Reverse:** Wrestling

| Date | Mintage | F | VF | XF | Unc | BU |
|---|---|---|---|---|---|---|
| 1980 | 675,000 | — | 0.50 | 1.00 | 2.50 | — |

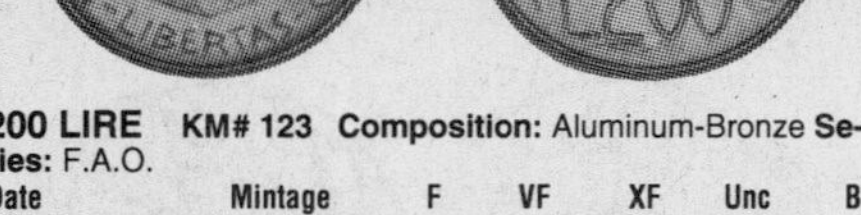

**200 LIRE** **KM# 123** **Composition:** Aluminum-Bronze **Series:** F.A.O.

| Date | Mintage | F | VF | XF | Unc | BU |
|---|---|---|---|---|---|---|
| 1981 | 700,000 | — | 0.25 | 0.75 | 1.75 | — |

**200 LIRE** **KM# 138** **Composition:** Aluminum-Bronze **Subject:** Social conquests

| Date | Mintage | F | VF | XF | Unc | BU |
|---|---|---|---|---|---|---|
| 1982R | 178,000 | — | 0.25 | 0.75 | 1.75 | — |

**200 LIRE** **KM# 152** **Composition:** Aluminum-Bronze **Subject:** Nuclear war threat **Reverse:** Rider spreading victim

| Date | Mintage | F | VF | XF | Unc | BU |
|---|---|---|---|---|---|---|
| 1983 | 172,000 | — | 0.25 | 0.75 | 1.75 | — |

**200 LIRE** **KM# 166** **Composition:** Aluminum-Bronze **Reverse:** Enrico Fermi

| Date | Mintage | F | VF | XF | Unc | BU |
|---|---|---|---|---|---|---|
| 1984R | 165,000 | — | 0.25 | 0.75 | 1.75 | — |

**200 LIRE** **KM# 180** **Composition:** Aluminum-Bronze **Subject:** War on drugs **Reverse:** Family group

| Date | Mintage | F | VF | XF | Unc | BU |
|---|---|---|---|---|---|---|
| 1985R | 210,000 | — | — | 0.40 | 1.50 | — |

**200 LIRE** **KM# 194** **Composition:** Aluminum-Bronze **Subject:** Revolution of technology

| Date | Mintage | F | VF | XF | Unc | BU |
|---|---|---|---|---|---|---|
| 1986R | 150,000 | — | — | 0.40 | 1.50 | — |

**200 LIRE** **KM# 208** **Composition:** Aluminum-Bronze **Subject:** 15th anniversary - resumption of coinage

| Date | Mintage | F | VF | XF | Unc | BU |
|---|---|---|---|---|---|---|
| 1987R | 143,000 | — | — | 0.40 | 1.50 | — |

**200 LIRE** **KM# 225** **Composition:** Aluminum-Bronze **Subject:** Fortifications **Reverse:** Tower

| Date | Mintage | F | VF | XF | Unc | BU |
|---|---|---|---|---|---|---|
| 1988R | 38,000 | — | — | 0.40 | 1.50 | — |

**200 LIRE** **KM# 238** **Composition:** Aluminum-Bronze **Subject:** History **Reverse:** Stylized view of San Marino

| Date | Mintage | F | VF | XF | Unc | BU |
|---|---|---|---|---|---|---|
| 1989R | 1,037,000 | — | — | 0.40 | 1.50 | — |

**200 LIRE** **KM# 255** **Composition:** Aluminum-Bronze **Subject:** 1,600 years of history **Reverse:** Female portrait

| Date | Mintage | F | VF | XF | Unc | BU |
|---|---|---|---|---|---|---|
| 1990R | 36,000 | — | — | 0.40 | 1.50 | — |

**200 LIRE** **KM# 268** **Composition:** Aluminum-Bronze **Reverse:** Hand holding coin die

| Date | Mintage | F | VF | XF | Unc | BU |
|---|---|---|---|---|---|---|
| 1991R | — | — | — | 0.40 | 1.50 | — |

**200 LIRE** **KM# 285** **Composition:** Aluminum-Bronze **Reverse:** Columbus navigating by the stars

| Date | Mintage | F | VF | XF | Unc | BU |
|---|---|---|---|---|---|---|
| ND(1992)R | — | — | — | 0.40 | 1.50 | — |

**200 LIRE** **KM# 300** **Composition:** Aluminum-Bronze **Reverse:** Door and arches

| Date | Mintage | F | VF | XF | Unc | BU |
|---|---|---|---|---|---|---|
| 1993R | — | — | — | 0.40 | 1.50 | — |

**200 LIRE** **KM# 313** **Composition:** Aluminum-Bronze **Reverse:** Man and tame bear

| Date | Mintage | F | VF | XF | Unc | BU |
|---|---|---|---|---|---|---|
| 1994R | 40,000 | — | — | 0.40 | 1.50 | — |

**200 LIRE** **KM# 329** **Composition:** Aluminum-Bronze **Reverse:** 2 children

| Date | Mintage | F | VF | XF | Unc | BU |
|---|---|---|---|---|---|---|
| 1995R | — | — | — | 0.40 | 1.50 | — |

**200 LIRE** **KM# 356** **Composition:** Aluminum-Bronze **Subject:** Kant

| Date | Mintage | F | VF | XF | Unc | BU |
|---|---|---|---|---|---|---|
| 1996 | 32,000 | — | — | 0.40 | 1.50 | — |

**200 LIRE** **KM# 366** **Composition:** Aluminum-Bronze **Subject:** The arts - painting

| Date | Mintage | F | VF | XF | Unc | BU |
|---|---|---|---|---|---|---|
| 1997 | 28,000 | — | — | 0.40 | 1.50 | — |

**200 LIRE** **KM# 382** **Composition:** Aluminum-Bronze **Subject:** Zoology **Reverse:** 2 dolphins

| Date | Mintage | F | VF | XF | Unc | BU |
|---|---|---|---|---|---|---|
| 1998 | — | — | — | 0.40 | 1.50 | — |

**200 LIRE** **KM# 393** **Composition:** Aluminum-Bronze **Subject:** Exploration **Obverse:** Crowned arms **Reverse:** Stonehenge beneath the sun and stars

| Date | Mintage | F | VF | XF | Unc | BU |
|---|---|---|---|---|---|---|
| 1999 | — | — | — | 0.40 | 1.50 | — |

**200 LIRE** **KM# 403** **Weight:** 5.0000 g. **Composition:** Aluminum-Bronze **Subject:** Knowledge **Obverse:** Child of the Universe **Reverse:** Allegorical female portrait **Edge:** Reeded **Size:** 24 mm. **Note:** Struck at Rome.

| Date | Mintage | VG | F | VF | XF | Unc |
|---|---|---|---|---|---|---|
| 2000 | — | — | — | — | 0.40 | 1.50 |

**200 LIRE** **KM# 428** **Weight:** 5.0000 g. **Composition:** Aluminum-Bronze **Obverse:** Three towers. **Reverse:** Broken chain, leaves and vines. **Edge:** Reeded. **Size:** 24 mm.

| Date | Mintage | F | VF | XF | Unc | BU |
|---|---|---|---|---|---|---|
| 2001 | — | — | — | — | 1.50 | — |

**500 LIRE** **KM# 21** **Weight:** 11.0000 g. **Composition:** 0.8350 Silver .2953 oz. ASW **Note:** 22,374 coins melted at the mint.

| Date | Mintage | F | VF | XF | Unc | BU |
|---|---|---|---|---|---|---|
| 1972 | 291,000 | — | — | 6.00 | 10.00 | — |

**500 LIRE** **KM# 29** **Weight:** 11.0000 g. **Composition:** 0.8350 Silver .2953 oz. ASW **Note:** 6,544 coins melted at the mint.

| Date | Mintage | F | VF | XF | Unc | BU |
|---|---|---|---|---|---|---|
| 1973 | 291,000 | — | — | 6.00 | 10.00 | — |

**500 LIRE** **KM# 37** **Weight:** 11.0000 g. **Composition:** 0.8350 Silver .2953 oz. ASW **Reverse:** Two pigeons **Note:** 6,295 coins melted at the mint.

| Date | Mintage | F | VF | XF | Unc | BU |
|---|---|---|---|---|---|---|
| 1974 | 276,000 | — | — | 6.50 | 11.50 | — |

**500 LIRE** **KM# 47** **Weight:** 11.0000 g. **Composition:** 0.8350 Silver .2953 oz. ASW **Note:** 119,743 coins melted at the mint.

| Date | Mintage | F | VF | XF | Unc | BU |
|---|---|---|---|---|---|---|
| 1975 | 291,000 | — | — | 7.00 | 12.50 | — |

**500 LIRE** **KM# 48** **Weight:** 11.0000 g. **Composition:** 0.8350 Silver .2953 oz. ASW **Subject:** Numismatic Agency opening **Note:** 47,495 coins melted at the mint.

| Date | Mintage | F | VF | XF | Unc | BU |
|---|---|---|---|---|---|---|
| 1975 | 200,000 | — | — | 6.50 | 11.50 | — |

**500 LIRE** **KM# 58** **Weight:** 11.0000 g. **Composition:** 0.8350 Silver .2953 oz. ASW **Note:** 40,509 coins melted at the mint.

| Date | Mintage | F | VF | XF | Unc | BU |
|---|---|---|---|---|---|---|
| 1976 | 195,000 | — | — | 6.50 | 11.50 | — |

**500 LIRE** **KM# 59** **Weight:** 11.0000 g. **Composition:** 0.8350 Silver .2953 oz. ASW **Subject:** Social Security **Note:** 106,604 coins melted at the mint.

| Date | Mintage | F | VF | XF | Unc | BU |
|---|---|---|---|---|---|---|
| 1976 | 195,000 | — | — | 6.50 | 11.50 | — |

**500 LIRE** **KM# 71** **Weight:** 11.0000 g. **Composition:** 0.8350 Silver .2953 oz. ASW **Note:** 45,483 coins melted at the mint.

| Date | Mintage | F | VF | XF | Unc | BU |
|---|---|---|---|---|---|---|
| 1977 | 180,000 | — | — | 6.50 | 11.50 | — |

**500 LIRE** **KM# 84** **Weight:** 11.0000 g. **Composition:** 0.8350 Silver .2953 oz. ASW **Note:** 16,297 coins melted at the mint.

| Date | Mintage | F | VF | XF | Unc | BU |
|---|---|---|---|---|---|---|
| 1978 | 130,000 | — | — | 6.50 | 11.50 | — |

**500 LIRE** **KM# 97** **Weight:** 11.0000 g. **Composition:** 0.8350 Silver .2953 oz. ASW **Note:** 33,278 coins melted at the mint.

| Date | Mintage | F | VF | XF | Unc | BU |
|---|---|---|---|---|---|---|
| 1979 | 125,000 | — | — | 7.00 | 12.50 | — |

**500 LIRE** **KM# 110** **Weight:** 11.0000 g. **Composition:** 0.8350 Silver .2953 oz. ASW **Series:** 1980 Olympics **Note:** 47,724 coins melted at the mint.

| Date | Mintage | F | VF | XF | Unc | BU |
|---|---|---|---|---|---|---|
| 1980 | 125,000 | — | — | 7.00 | 12.50 | — |

**500 LIRE** **KM# 124** **Weight:** 11.0000 g. **Composition:** 0.8350 Silver .2953 oz. ASW **Subject:** 2,000th anniversary - Virgil's death **Note:** 9,122 coins melted at the mint.

| Date | Mintage | F | VF | XF | Unc | BU |
|---|---|---|---|---|---|---|
| 1981 | 75,000 | — | — | 7.00 | 12.50 | — |

**500 LIRE** **KM# 125** **Weight:** 11.0000 g. **Composition:** 0.8350 Silver .2953 oz. ASW **Subject:** 2,000th anniversary - Virgil's death **Note:** 9,122 coins melted at the mint.

| Date | Mintage | F | VF | XF | Unc | BU |
|---|---|---|---|---|---|---|
| 1981 | 75,000 | — | — | 7.00 | 12.50 | — |

**500 LIRE** **KM# 126** **Weight:** 11.0000 g. **Composition:** 0.8350 Silver .2953 oz. ASW **Note:** 21,124 coins melted at the mint.

| Date | Mintage | F | VF | XF | Unc | BU |
|---|---|---|---|---|---|---|
| 1981 | 100,000 | — | — | 7.00 | 12.50 | — |

**500 LIRE** **KM# 139** **Weight:** 11.0000 g. **Composition:** 0.8350 Silver .2953 oz. ASW **Subject:** Centennial - death of Garibaldi **Note:** 112 uncirculated and 369 proof coins melted at the mint.

| Date | Mintage | F | VF | XF | Unc | BU |
|---|---|---|---|---|---|---|
| ND(1982)R | 48,000 | — | — | 7.00 | 12.50 | — |
| ND(1982)R Proof | 13,000 | Value: 22.50 | | | | |

**500 LIRE** **KM# 140** **Ring Composition:** Steel **Center Composition:** Aluminum-Bronze **Subject:** Social conquests

| Date | Mintage | F | VF | XF | Unc | BU |
|---|---|---|---|---|---|---|
| 1982R | 1,900,000 | — | — | 1.00 | 3.00 | — |

**500 LIRE** **KM# 153** **Ring Composition:** Steel **Center Composition:** Aluminum-Bronze **Subject:** Nuclear war threat **Reverse:** 3 horses above 2 people

| Date | Mintage | F | VF | XF | Unc | BU |
|---|---|---|---|---|---|---|
| 1983R | 1,922,000 | — | — | 1.00 | 3.00 | — |

**500 LIRE** **KM# 154** **Weight:** 11.0000 g. **Composition:** 0.8350 Silver .2953 oz. ASW **Subject:** 500th anniversary - birth of artist Raphael **Note:** 80 uncirculated and 1,939 proof coins melted at the mint.

| Date | Mintage | F | VF | XF | Unc | BU |
|---|---|---|---|---|---|---|
| 1983R | 42,000 | — | — | 7.00 | 12.50 | — |
| 1983R Proof | 12,000 | Value: 22.50 | | | | |

**500 LIRE** **KM# 167** **Ring Composition:** Steel **Center Composition:** Aluminum-Bronze **Reverse:** Albert Einstein

| Date | Mintage | F | VF | XF | Unc | BU |
|---|---|---|---|---|---|---|
| 1984R | 2,633,000 | — | — | 1.00 | 3.00 | — |

**500 LIRE** **KM# 168** **Weight:** 11.0000 g. **Composition:** 0.8350 Silver .2953 oz. ASW **Series:** 1984 Summer Olympics **Note:** 2,920 uncirculated and 20 proof coins melted at the mint.

| Date | Mintage | F | VF | XF | Unc | BU |
|---|---|---|---|---|---|---|
| 1984 | 52,000 | — | — | 6.50 | 10.00 | — |
| 1984 Proof | 15,000 | Value: 12.50 | | | | |

**500 LIRE** **KM# 181** **Ring Composition:** Steel **Center Composition:** Aluminum-Bronze **Subject:** War on drugs **Reverse:** Cured addict

| Date | Mintage | F | VF | XF | Unc | BU |
|---|---|---|---|---|---|---|
| 1985R | 2,647,000 | — | — | 1.00 | 3.00 | — |

**500 LIRE** **KM# 182** **Weight:** 11.0000 g. **Composition:** 0.8350 Silver .2953 oz. ASW **Subject:** European Music Year **Note:** 6,704 uncirculated and 122 proof coins melted at the mint.

| Date | Mintage | F | VF | XF | Unc | BU |
|---|---|---|---|---|---|---|
| 1985 | 40,000 | — | — | 7.00 | 12.50 | — |
| 1985 Proof | 12,000 | Value: 15.00 | | | | |

**500 LIRE** **KM# 195** **Ring Composition:** Steel **Center Composition:** Aluminum-Bronze **Subject:** Revolution of technology

| Date | Mintage | F | VF | XF | Unc | BU |
|---|---|---|---|---|---|---|
| 1986R | 3,111,000 | — | — | 1.00 | 3.00 | — |

**500 LIRE** **KM# 196** **Weight:** 11.0000 g. **Composition:** 0.8350 Silver .2953 oz. ASW **Subject:** Soccer **Reverse:** Field **Note:** 5,212 uncirculated and 60 proof coins melted at the mint.

| Date | Mintage | F | VF | XF | Unc | BU |
|---|---|---|---|---|---|---|
| 1986R | 45,000 | — | — | — | 12.50 | — |
| 1986R Proof | 12,000 | Value: 15.00 | | | | |

**500 LIRE** **KM# 209** **Ring Composition:** Steel **Center Composition:** Aluminum-Bronze **Subject:** 15th anniversary - resumption of coinage

| Date | Mintage | F | VF | XF | Unc | BU |
|---|---|---|---|---|---|---|
| 1987R | 3,063,000 | — | — | 1.00 | 3.00 | — |

**500 LIRE** **KM# 213** **Weight:** 11.0000 g. **Composition:** 0.8350 Silver .2953 oz. ASW **Subject:** Zagreb University Games **Reverse:** Runner **Note:** 9,208 uncirculated and 1,206 proof coins melted at the mint.

| Date | Mintage | F | VF | XF | Unc | BU |
|---|---|---|---|---|---|---|
| 1987R | 35,000 | — | — | — | 12.50 | — |
| 1987R Proof | 10,000 | Value: 15.00 | | | | |

**500 LIRE** **KM# 216** **Weight:** 11.0000 g. **Composition:** 0.8350 Silver .2953 oz. ASW **Series:** Winter Olympics **Reverse:** Downhill skier **Note:** 146 uncirculated and 3 proof coins melted at the mint.

| Date | Mintage | F | VF | XF | Unc | BU |
|---|---|---|---|---|---|---|
| 1988R | 32,000 | — | — | — | 9.00 | — |
| 1988R Proof | 9,600 | Value: 15.00 | | | | |

**500 LIRE** **KM# 226** **Ring Composition:** Steel **Center Composition:** Aluminum-Bronze **Subject:** Fortifications **Reverse:** Hilltop fortification

| Date | Mintage | F | VF | XF | Unc | BU |
|---|---|---|---|---|---|---|
| 1988R | 3,526,000 | — | — | 1.00 | 3.00 | — |

**500 LIRE** **KM# 239** **Ring Composition:** Steel **Center Composition:** Aluminum-Bronze **Subject:** History **Reverse:** Stone carver

| Date | Mintage | F | VF | XF | Unc | BU |
|---|---|---|---|---|---|---|
| 1989R | 3,145,000 | — | — | 1.00 | 3.00 | — |

**500 LIRE** **KM# 243** **Weight:** 11.0000 g. **Composition:** 0.8350 Silver .2953 oz. ASW **Subject:** San Marino Grand Prix **Note:** 5,180 coins melted at the mint.

| Date | Mintage | F | VF | XF | Unc | BU |
|---|---|---|---|---|---|---|
| 1989R | 30,000 | — | — | — | 10.00 | — |
| 1989R Proof | 8,000 | Value: 25.00 | | | | |

**500 LIRE** **KM# 246** **Weight:** 11.0000 g. **Composition:** 0.8350 Silver .2953 oz. ASW **Subject:** World Cup soccer championship game

| Date | Mintage | F | VF | XF | Unc | BU |
|---|---|---|---|---|---|---|
| 1990R | 40,000 | — | — | — | 10.00 | — |
| 1990R Proof | 19,000 | Value: 20.00 | | | | |

**500 LIRE** **KM# 256** **Ring Composition:** Steel **Center Composition:** Aluminum-Bronze **Subject:** 1,600 years of history **Reverse:** Birds and stamp

| Date | Mintage | F | VF | XF | Unc | BU |
|---|---|---|---|---|---|---|
| 1990R | Est. 60,000 | — | — | 1.00 | 3.00 | — |

**500 LIRE** **KM# 269** **Ring Composition:** Steel **Center Composition:** Aluminum-Bronze **Reverse:** Hand holding flowers

| Date | Mintage | F | VF | XF | Unc | BU |
|---|---|---|---|---|---|---|
| 1991R | — | — | — | 1.00 | 3.00 | — |

**500 LIRE** **KM# 271** **Weight:** 11.0000 g. **Composition:** 0.8350 Silver .2953 oz. ASW **Series:** Barcelona Olympics **Reverse:** Priestess lighting fire with sun beam

| Date | Mintage | F | VF | XF | Unc | BU |
|---|---|---|---|---|---|---|
| 1991R | Est. 60,000 | — | — | — | 9.00 | — |
| 1991R Proof | Est. 8,000 | Value: 20.00 | | | | |

**500 LIRE** **KM# 276** **Weight:** 11.0000 g. **Composition:** 0.8350 Silver .2953 oz. ASW **Series:** Olympics **Reverse:** Chariot

| Date | Mintage | F | VF | XF | Unc | BU |
|---|---|---|---|---|---|---|
| 1992R | Est. 70,000 | — | — | — | 10.00 | — |
| 1992R Proof | — | Value: 20.00 | | | | |

**500 LIRE** **KM# 286** **Ring Composition:** Steel **Center Composition:** Aluminum-Bronze **Subject:** Columbus **Reverse:** Winds blowing ship

| Date | Mintage | F | VF | XF | Unc | BU |
|---|---|---|---|---|---|---|
| 1992R | — | — | — | — | 3.00 | — |

**500 LIRE** **KM# 291** **Weight:** 11.0000 g. **Composition:** 0.8350 Silver .2953 oz. ASW **Subject:** Wildlife protection **Reverse:** 2 European polecats

| Date | Mintage | F | VF | XF | Unc | BU |
|---|---|---|---|---|---|---|
| 1993R | Est. 35,000 | — | — | — | 12.00 | — |
| 1993R Proof | — | Value: 20.00 | | | | |

**500 LIRE** **KM# 301** **Ring Composition:** Steel **Center Composition:** Aluminum-Bronze **Reverse:** Growth from a tree stump

| Date | Mintage | F | VF | XF | Unc | BU |
|---|---|---|---|---|---|---|
| 1993R | — | — | — | — | 3.00 | — |

**500 LIRE** **KM# 314** **Ring Composition:** Steel **Center Composition:** Aluminum-Bronze **Reverse:** St. Marino receiving Mount Titano

| Date | Mintage | F | VF | XF | Unc | BU |
|---|---|---|---|---|---|---|
| 1994R | 40,000 | — | — | — | 3.00 | — |

**500 LIRE** **KM# 317** **Weight:** 11.0000 g. **Composition:** 0.8350 Silver .2953 oz. ASW **Subject:** World Cup soccer

| Date | Mintage | F | VF | XF | Unc | BU |
|---|---|---|---|---|---|---|
| 1994R Proof | — | Value: 15.00 | | | | |

**500 LIRE** **KM# 330** **Weight:** 11.0000 g. **Composition:** 0.8350 Silver .2953 oz. ASW **Series:** F.A.O. **Subject:** 50th anniversary - F.A.O.

| Date | Mintage | F | VF | XF | Unc | BU |
|---|---|---|---|---|---|---|
| 1995R | 3,000,000 | — | — | — | 3.00 | — |

**500 LIRE** **KM# 357** **Ring Composition:** Stainless Steel **Center Composition:** Aluminum-Bronze **Reverse:** Hegel

| Date | Mintage | F | VF | XF | Unc | BU |
|---|---|---|---|---|---|---|
| 1996 | — | — | — | — | 3.00 | — |

**500 LIRE** **KM# 367** **Ring Composition:** Stainless Steel **Center Composition:** Aluminum-Bronze **Subject:** The arts - music **Reverse:** Woman playing pipes

| Date | Mintage | F | VF | XF | Unc | BU |
|---|---|---|---|---|---|---|
| 1997 | 28,000 | — | — | — | 3.00 | — |

**500 LIRE** **KM# 383** **Ring Composition:** Stainless Steel **Center Composition:** Aluminum-Bronze **Subject:** Chemistry **Reverse:** Laboratory

| Date | Mintage | F | VF | XF | Unc | BU |
|---|---|---|---|---|---|---|
| 1998 | — | — | — | — | 3.00 | — |

**500 LIRE** **KM# 394** **Ring Composition:** Stainless Steel **Center Composition:** Aluminum-Bronze **Subject:** Exploration **Obverse:** Crowned arms **Reverse:** Moon's surface, radio waves and Saturn

| Date | Mintage | F | VF | XF | Unc | BU |
|---|---|---|---|---|---|---|
| 1999 | — | — | — | — | 3.00 | — |

**500 LIRE** **KM# 404** **Ring Composition:** Stainless Steel **Center Composition:** Aluminum-Bronze **Subject:** Work **Obverse:** Child of the Universe **Reverse:** Spinning wheel **Edge:** Reeded and plain sections **Size:** 25.8 mm. **Note:** 6.8 grams

| Date | Mintage | VG | F | VF | XF | Unc |
|---|---|---|---|---|---|---|
| 2000 | — | — | — | — | — | 3.00 |

**500 LIRE** **KM# 429** **Ring Composition:** Stainless Steel **Center Composition:** Aluminum-Bronze **Obverse:** Three towers. **Reverse:** Three different plant stalks. **Edge:** Reeded and plain sections. **Size:** 25.8 mm. **Note:** 6.8 grams.

| Date | Mintage | F | VF | XF | Unc | BU |
|---|---|---|---|---|---|---|
| 2001 | — | — | — | — | 2.00 | — |

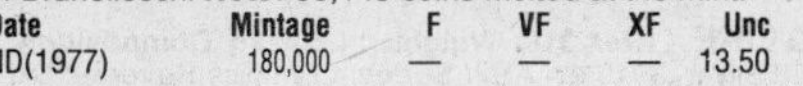

**1000 LIRE** **KM# 72** **Weight:** 14.6000 g. **Composition:** 0.8350 Silver .3919 oz. ASW **Subject:** 600th anniversary - birth of Brunelleschi **Note:** 38,145 coins melted at the mint.

| Date | Mintage | F | VF | XF | Unc | BU |
|---|---|---|---|---|---|---|
| ND(1977) | 180,000 | — | — | — | 13.50 | — |

**1000 LIRE** **KM# 85** **Weight:** 14.6000 g. **Composition:** 0.8350 Silver .3919 oz. ASW **Subject:** 150th anniversary - birth of Tolstoy **Note:** 17,892 coins melted at the mint.

| Date | Mintage | F | VF | XF | Unc | BU |
|---|---|---|---|---|---|---|
| ND(1978) | 130,000 | — | — | — | 13.50 | — |

**1000 LIRE** **KM# 98** **Weight:** 14.6000 g. **Composition:** 0.8350 Silver .3919 oz. ASW **Subject:** European unity **Note:** 14,945 coins melted at the mint.

| Date | Mintage | F | VF | XF | Unc | BU |
|---|---|---|---|---|---|---|
| 1979 | 125,000 | — | — | — | 15.00 | — |

**1000 LIRE** **KM# 112** **Weight:** 14.6000 g. **Composition:** 0.8350 Silver .3919 oz. ASW **Subject:** 1,500th anniversary - birth of St. Benedict **Note:** 49,095 coins melted at the mint.

| Date | Mintage | F | VF | XF | Unc | BU |
|---|---|---|---|---|---|---|
| 1980 | 125,000 | — | — | — | 15.00 | — |

**1000 LIRE** **KM# 127** **Weight:** 14.6000 g. **Composition:** 0.8350 Silver .3919 oz. ASW **Subject:** 200th anniversary - Virgil's death **Note:** 9,122 coins melted at the mint.

| Date | Mintage | F | VF | XF | Unc | BU |
|---|---|---|---|---|---|---|
| 1981 | 75,000 | — | — | — | 15.00 | — |

**1000 LIRE** **KM# 141** **Weight:** 14.6000 g. **Composition:** 0.8350 Silver .3919 oz. ASW **Subject:** Centennial - Garibaldi's death **Note:** 112 uncirculated and 369 proof coins melted at the mint.

| Date | Mintage | F | VF | XF | Unc | BU |
|---|---|---|---|---|---|---|
| ND(1982)R | 48,000 | — | — | — | 15.00 | — |
| ND(1982)R Proof | 13,000 | Value: 25.00 | | | | |

**1000 LIRE** **KM# 155** **Weight:** 14.6000 g. **Composition:** 0.8350 Silver .3919 oz. ASW **Subject:** 500th anniversary - birth of artist Raphael **Note:** 80 uncirculated and 1,939 proof coins melted at the mint.

| Date | Mintage | F | VF | XF | Unc | BU |
|---|---|---|---|---|---|---|
| 1983R | 42,000 | — | — | — | 15.00 | — |
| 1983R Proof | 12,000 | Value: 25.00 | | | | |

**1000 LIRE** **KM# 169** **Weight:** 14.6000 g. **Composition:** 0.8350 Silver .3919 oz. ASW **Series:** 1984 Summer Olympics **Note:** 2,920 uncirculated and 20 proof coins melted at the mint.

| Date | Mintage | F | VF | XF | Unc | BU |
|---|---|---|---|---|---|---|
| 1984R | 52,000 | — | — | — | 12.50 | — |
| 1984R Proof | 15,000 | Value: 25.00 | | | | |

**1000 LIRE** **KM# 183** **Weight:** 14.6000 g. **Composition:** 0.8350 Silver .3919 oz. ASW **Subject:** European Music Year **Reverse:** J.S. Bach **Note:** 6,704 uncirculated and 122 proof coins melted at the mint.

| Date | Mintage | F | VF | XF | Unc | BU |
|---|---|---|---|---|---|---|
| 1985R | 40,000 | — | — | — | 15.00 | — |
| 1985R Proof | 12,000 | Value: 25.00 | | | | |

**1000 LIRE** **KM# 197** **Weight:** 14.6000 g. **Composition:** 0.8350 Silver .3919 oz. ASW **Subject:** Soccer **Reverse:** Flags **Note:** 5,212 uncirculated and 60 proof coins melted at the mint.

| Date | Mintage | F | VF | XF | Unc | BU |
|---|---|---|---|---|---|---|
| 1986R | 45,000 | — | — | — | 16.00 | — |
| 1986R Proof | 12,000 | Value: 30.00 | | | | |

**1000 LIRE** **KM# 210** **Weight:** 14.6000 g. **Composition:** 0.8350 Silver .3919 oz. ASW **Subject:** 15th anniversary - resumption of coinage **Note:** 13 coins melted at the mint.

| Date | Mintage | F | VF | XF | Unc | BU |
|---|---|---|---|---|---|---|
| 1987R | 43,000 | — | — | — | 18.00 | — |

**1000 LIRE** **KM# 214** **Weight:** 14.6000 g. **Composition:** 0.8350 Silver .3919 oz. ASW **Subject:** Zagreb University Games **Reverse:** Pole vaulter **Note:** 9,207 uncirculated and 1,206 proof coins melted at the mint.

| Date | Mintage | F | VF | XF | Unc | BU |
|---|---|---|---|---|---|---|
| 1987R | 35,000 | — | — | — | 16.00 | — |
| 1987R Proof | 10,000 | Value: 30.00 | | | | |

**1000 LIRE** **KM# 217** **Weight:** 14.6000 g. **Composition:** 0.8350 Silver .3919 oz. ASW **Series:** Summer Olympics **Reverse:** Diver **Note:** 146 uncirculated and 3 proof coins melted at the mint.

| Date | Mintage | F | VF | XF | Unc | BU |
|---|---|---|---|---|---|---|
| 1988R | 32,000 | — | — | — | 17.50 | — |
| 1988R Proof | 9,600 | Value: 30.00 | | | | |

**1000 LIRE** **KM# 227** **Weight:** 14.6000 g. **Composition:** 0.8350 Silver .3919 oz. ASW **Subject:** Fortifications **Reverse:** Walls and towers

| Date | Mintage | F | VF | XF | Unc | BU |
|---|---|---|---|---|---|---|
| 1988R | 38,000 | — | — | — | 20.00 | — |

**1000 LIRE** **KM# 240** **Weight:** 14.6000 g. **Composition:** 0.8350 Silver .3919 oz. ASW **Subject:** History **Reverse:** 2 men in boat

| Date | Mintage | F | VF | XF | Unc | BU |
|---|---|---|---|---|---|---|
| 1989R | 32,000 | — | — | — | 20.00 | — |

**1000 LIRE** **KM# 244** **Weight:** 14.6000 g. **Composition:** 0.8350 Silver .3919 oz. ASW **Subject:** San Marino Grand Prix **Note:** 5,180 coins melted at the mint.

| Date | Mintage | F | VF | XF | Unc | BU |
|---|---|---|---|---|---|---|
| 1989R | 30,000 | — | — | — | 20.00 | — |
| 1989R Proof | 8,000 | Value: 35.00 | | | | |

**1000 LIRE** **KM# 247** **Weight:** 14.6000 g. **Composition:** 0.8350 Silver .3919 oz. ASW **Subject:** World Cup soccer championship games

| Date | Mintage | F | VF | XF | Unc | BU |
|---|---|---|---|---|---|---|
| 1990R | 40,000 | — | — | — | 20.00 | — |
| 1990R Proof | 19,000 | Value: 30.00 | | | | |

**1000 LIRE** **KM# 257** **Weight:** 14.6000 g. **Composition:** 0.8350 Silver .3919 oz. ASW **Subject:** 1,600 years of history **Reverse:** Hand and 2 figures

| Date | Mintage | F | VF | XF | Unc | BU |
|---|---|---|---|---|---|---|
| 1990R | 36,000 | — | — | — | 20.00 | — |

**1000 LIRE** **KM# 270** **Weight:** 14.6000 g. **Composition:** 0.8350 Silver .3919 oz. ASW **Reverse:** Hand holding dove

| Date | Mintage | F | VF | XF | Unc | BU |
|---|---|---|---|---|---|---|
| 1991R | — | — | — | — | 20.00 | — |

**1000 LIRE** **KM# 272** **Weight:** 14.6000 g. **Composition:** 0.8350 Silver .3919 oz. ASW **Series:** Barcelona Olympics

| Date | Mintage | F | VF | XF | Unc | BU |
|---|---|---|---|---|---|---|
| 1991R | Est. 60,000 | — | — | — | 20.00 | — |
| 1991R Proof | Est. 8,000 | Value: 32.50 | | | | |

**1000 LIRE** **KM# 277** **Weight:** 14.6000 g. **Composition:** 0.8350 Silver .3919 oz. ASW **Series:** Olympics **Reverse:** 3 athletes

| Date | Mintage | F | VF | XF | Unc | BU |
|---|---|---|---|---|---|---|
| 1992R | Est. 70,000 | — | — | — | 20.00 | — |
| 1992R Proof | — | Value: 32.50 | | | | |

**1000 LIRE** **KM# 287** **Weight:** 14.6000 g. **Composition:** 0.8350 Silver .3919 oz. ASW **Reverse:** Columbus studying chart

| Date | Mintage | F | VF | XF | Unc | BU |
|---|---|---|---|---|---|---|
| ND(1992)R | — | — | — | — | 22.50 | — |

**1000 LIRE** **KM# 292** **Weight:** 14.6000 g. **Composition:** 0.8350 Silver .3919 oz. ASW **Series:** Wildlife Protection **Reverse:** Falcon and woodpecker

| Date | Mintage | F | VF | XF | Unc | BU |
|---|---|---|---|---|---|---|
| 1993R | Est. 35,000 | — | — | — | 20.00 | — |
| 1993R Proof | — | Value: 30.00 | | | | |

**1000 LIRE** **KM# 302** **Weight:** 14.6000 g. **Composition:** 0.8350 Silver .3919 oz. ASW **Reverse:** Wing above globe

| Date | Mintage | F | VF | XF | Unc | BU |
|---|---|---|---|---|---|---|
| 1993R | — | — | — | — | 22.50 | — |

**1000 LIRE** **KM# 315** **Weight:** 14.6000 g. **Composition:** 0.8350 Silver .3919 oz. ASW **Subject:** Founder building first San Marino church

| Date | Mintage | F | VF | XF | Unc | BU |
|---|---|---|---|---|---|---|
| 1994R | 40,000 | — | — | — | 22.50 | — |

**1000 LIRE** **KM# 316** **Weight:** 14.6000 g. **Composition:** 0.8350 Silver .3919 oz. ASW **Series:** Olympics **Reverse:** Ski jumper

| Date | Mintage | F | VF | XF | Unc | BU |
|---|---|---|---|---|---|---|
| 1994R Proof | — | Value: 20.00 | | | | |

**1000 LIRE** **KM# 318** **Weight:** 14.6000 g. **Composition:** 0.8350 Silver .3919 oz. ASW **Subject:** World Cup soccer

| Date | Mintage | F | VF | XF | Unc | BU |
|---|---|---|---|---|---|---|
| 1994R Proof | — | Value: 27.50 | | | | |

**1000 LIRE** **KM# 331** **Weight:** 14.6000 g. **Composition:** 0.8350 Silver .3919 oz. ASW **Subject:** Pyramid of children

| Date | Mintage | F | VF | XF | Unc | BU |
|---|---|---|---|---|---|---|
| 1995R | — | — | — | — | 22.50 | — |

**1000 LIRE** **KM# 332** **Weight:** 14.6000 g. **Composition:** 0.8350 Silver .3919 oz. ASW **Series:** 1996 Olympics **Reverse:** Pole vaulting and discus

| Date | Mintage | F | VF | XF | Unc | BU |
|---|---|---|---|---|---|---|
| 1995R Proof | 50,000 | Value: 22.50 | | | | |

**1000 LIRE** **KM# 358** **Weight:** 14.6000 g. **Composition:** 0.8350 Silver .3919 oz. ASW **Reverse:** Popper

| Date | Mintage | F | VF | XF | Unc | BU |
|---|---|---|---|---|---|---|
| 1996 | 32,000 | — | — | — | 22.50 | — |

**1000 LIRE** **KM# 368** **Ring Composition:** Aluminum-Bronze **Center Composition:** Copper-Nickel **Obverse:** Heraldic lion **Reverse:** Statue, building and denomination

| Date | Mintage | F | VF | XF | Unc | BU |
|---|---|---|---|---|---|---|
| 1997 | — | — | — | — | 8.00 | — |

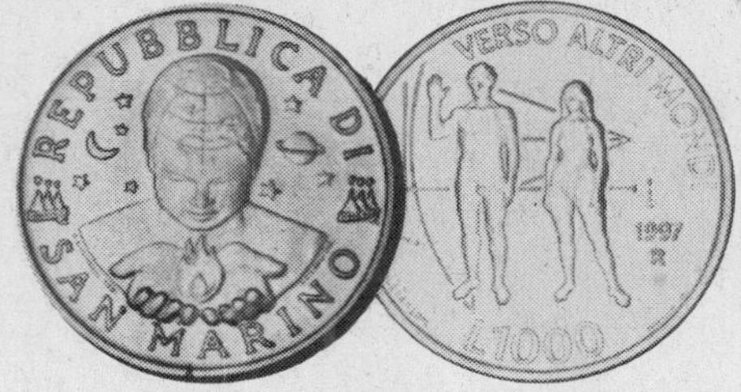


**1000 LIRE** **KM# 369** **Weight:** 14.6000 g. **Composition:** 0.8350 Silver .3919 oz. ASW **Subject:** The arts - interplanetary communication **Reverse:** Nude couple from Pioneer 10 space probe plaque

| Date | Mintage | F | VF | XF | Unc | BU |
|---|---|---|---|---|---|---|
| 1997 | 28,000 | — | — | — | 25.00 | — |

**1000 LIRE** **KM# 384** **Ring Composition:** Aluminum-Bronze **Center Composition:** Copper-Nickel **Subject:** Geology **Reverse:** Family standing on earth

| Date | Mintage | F | VF | XF | Unc | BU |
|---|---|---|---|---|---|---|
| 1998 | — | — | — | — | 8.00 | — |

**1000 LIRE** **KM# 395** **Ring Composition:** Aluminum-Bronze **Center Composition:** Copper-Nickel **Subject:** Exploration **Obverse:** Crowned arms **Reverse:** Radiant north star design

| Date | Mintage | F | VF | XF | Unc | BU |
|---|---|---|---|---|---|---|
| 1999 | — | — | — | — | 8.00 | — |

**1000 LIRE** **KM# 405** **Ring Composition:** Aluminum-Bronze **Center Composition:** Stainless Steel **Subject:** Liberty **Obverse:** Child of the Universe **Reverse:** Dove flying over world globe **Edge:** Reeded and plain sectioned **Size:** 27 mm. **Note:** 8.8 grams. Struck at Rome.

| Date | Mintage | VG | F | VF | XF | Unc |
|---|---|---|---|---|---|---|
| 2000 | — | — | — | — | — | 9.00 |

**1000 LIRE** **KM# 430** **Ring Composition:** Aluminum-Bronze **Center Composition:** Stainless Steel **Obverse:** Three towers. **Reverse:** Circle of birds. **Edge:** Reeded and plain sections. **Size:** 27 mm. **Note:** 8.8 grams.

| Date | Mintage | F | VF | XF | Unc | BU |
|---|---|---|---|---|---|---|
| 2001 | — | — | — | — | 7.50 | — |

**5000 LIRE** **KM# 333** **Weight:** 18.0000 g. **Composition:** 0.8350 Silver .4832 oz. ASW **Subject:** Sail training ship "Amerigo Vespucci"

| Date | Mintage | F | VF | XF | Unc | BU |
|---|---|---|---|---|---|---|
| 1995R Proof | Est. 35,000 | Value: 17.50 | | | | |

**5000 LIRE** **KM# 340** **Weight:** 18.0000 g. **Composition:** 0.8350 Silver .4832 oz. ASW **Series:** Wildlife Protection **Reverse:** Falcons

| Date | Mintage | F | VF | XF | Unc | BU |
|---|---|---|---|---|---|---|
| 1996 Proof | Est. 35,000 | Value: 22.50 | | | | |

**5000 LIRE** **KM# 370** **Weight:** 18.0000 g. **Composition:** 0.8350 Silver .4832 oz. ASW **Reverse:** Sailing ship "Vasco de Gama" and African map

| Date | Mintage | F | VF | XF | Unc | BU |
|---|---|---|---|---|---|---|
| 1997 Proof | — | Value: 17.50 | | | | |

**5000 LIRE** **KM# 385** **Weight:** 18.0000 g. **Composition:** 0.8350 Silver .4832 oz. ASW **Subject:** Medicine **Reverse:** Emblem

| Date | Mintage | F | VF | XF | Unc | BU |
|---|---|---|---|---|---|---|
| 1998 | — | — | — | — | 18.00 | — |

**5000 LIRE** **KM# 386** **Weight:** 18.0000 g. **Composition:** 0.8350 Silver .4832 oz. ASW **Subject:** Europe in the new millennium **Reverse:** Euro bridge with ivy, olive and oak trees **Edge:** Lettered **Edge Lettering:** RELINQUO VOS LIBEROS **Size:** 32 mm. **Note:** Struck at Rome.

| Date | Mintage | VG | F | VF | XF | Unc |
|---|---|---|---|---|---|---|
| 1998 Proof | — | Value: 20.00 | | | | |

**5000 LIRE** **KM# 396** **Weight:** 18.0000 g. **Composition:** 0.8350 Silver .4832 oz. ASW **Subject:** Exploration **Obverse:** Crowned arms **Reverse:** Solar system, European map and dish in human mind

| Date | Mintage | F | VF | XF | Unc | BU |
|---|---|---|---|---|---|---|
| 1999 | — | — | — | — | 18.00 | — |

**5000 LIRE** **KM# 410** **Weight:** 18.0000 g. **Composition:** 0.8350 Silver .4832 oz. ASW **Subject:** European Union **Reverse:** Denomination above flags **Edge:** Lettered **Edge Lettering:** RELINQUO VOS LIBEROS

| Date | Mintage | VG | F | VF | XF | Unc |
|---|---|---|---|---|---|---|
| 1999 Proof | — | Value: 30.00 | | | | |

**5000 LIRE** **KM# 406** **Weight:** 18.0000 g. **Composition:** 0.8350 Silver .4832 oz. ASW **Subject:** Peace **Obverse:** Child of the Universe **Reverse:** Hawk and dove with same olive branch in their beaks **Edge:** Reeded and plain sectioned **Size:** 32 mm. **Note:** Struck at Rome.

| Date | Mintage | VG | F | VF | XF | Unc |
|---|---|---|---|---|---|---|
| 2000 | — | — | — | — | — | 18.00 |

**5000 LIRE** **KM# 421** **Weight:** 18.0000 g. **Composition:** 0.8350 Silver .4832 oz. ASW **Subject:** First holy year jubilee **Reverse:** Pope Boniface VIII with 2 aides **Edge:** Lettered **Edge Lettering:** RELINQUO VOS LIBEROS

| Date | Mintage | VG | F | VF | XF | Unc |
|---|---|---|---|---|---|---|
| 2000 Proof | — | Value: 20.00 | | | | |

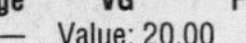

**5000 LIRE** **KM# 436** **Weight:** 18.0000 g. **Composition:** 0.8350 Silver .4832 oz. ASW **Subject:** Last Lire Coinage **Obverse:** National arms. **Reverse:** Six old coin designs. **Edge:** Lettered. **Size:** 32 mm.

| Date | Mintage | VG | F | VF | XF | Unc |
|---|---|---|---|---|---|---|
| 2001 Proof | 20,000 | Value: 20.00 | | | | |

**5000 LIRE** **KM# 431** **Weight:** 18.0000 g. **Composition:** 0.8350 Silver .4832 oz. ASW **Obverse:** Three towers. **Reverse:** Dove on laurel branch. **Edge:** Reeded and plain sections. **Size:** 32 mm.

| Date | Mintage | F | VF | XF | Unc | BU |
|---|---|---|---|---|---|---|
| 2001 | — | — | — | — | 15.00 | — |

**10000 LIRE** **KM# 334** **Weight:** 22.0000 g. **Composition:** 0.8350 Silver .5907 oz. ASW **Subject:** Amerigo Vespucci

| Date | Mintage | F | VF | XF | Unc | BU |
|---|---|---|---|---|---|---|
| 1995R Proof | Est. 35,000 | Value: 22.50 | | | | |

**10000 LIRE** **KM# 341** **Weight:** 22.0000 g. **Composition:** 0.8350 Silver .5907 oz. ASW **Series:** Wildlife Protection **Reverse:** Wolves

| Date | Mintage | F | VF | XF | Unc | BU |
|---|---|---|---|---|---|---|
| 1996 Proof | Est. 35,000 | Value: 35.00 | | | | |

**10000 LIRE** **KM# 342** **Weight:** 22.0000 g. **Composition:** 0.8350 Silver .5907 oz. ASW **Subject:** Euro **Reverse:** Parliament building and map

| Date | Mintage | F | VF | XF | Unc | BU |
|---|---|---|---|---|---|---|
| 1996 Proof | — | Value: 30.00 | | | | |

**10000 LIRE** **KM# 371** **Weight:** 22.0000 g. **Composition:** 0.8350 Silver .5907 oz. ASW **Subject:** Giovanni Caboto 1497 **Reverse:** Ship, Atlantic map

| Date | Mintage | F | VF | XF | Unc | BU |
|---|---|---|---|---|---|---|
| 1997 Proof | — | Value: 30.00 | | | | |

**10000 LIRE** **KM# 372** **Weight:** 22.0000 g. **Composition:** 0.8350 Silver .5907 oz. ASW **Subject:** Euro - "Libertas" **Obverse:** National arms above the 9 Casteli arms

| Date | Mintage | F | VF | XF | Unc | BU |
|---|---|---|---|---|---|---|
| 1997 Proof | — | Value: 32.00 | | | | |

**10000 LIRE** **KM# 376** **Weight:** 22.0000 g. **Composition:** 0.8350 Silver .5907 oz. ASW **Subject:** Soccer World Championship **Reverse:** 3 soccer players

| Date | Mintage | F | VF | XF | Unc | BU |
|---|---|---|---|---|---|---|
| 1998 Proof | — | Value: 30.00 | | | | |

**10000 LIRE** **KM# 377** **Weight:** 22.0000 g. **Composition:** 0.8350 Silver .5907 oz. ASW **Subject:** 50th anniversary - Ferrari **Obverse:** Crowned arms **Reverse:** 2 racing Ferraris above denomination **Edge:** Reeded and plain sectioned **Size:** 34 mm. **Note:** Struck at Rome.

| Date | Mintage | VG | F | VF | XF | Unc |
|---|---|---|---|---|---|---|
| 1998 Proof | 30,000 | Value: 27.50 | | | | |

**10000 LIRE** **KM# 387** **Weight:** 22.0000 g. **Composition:** 0.8350 Silver .5907 oz. ASW **Subject:** Europe in the new millennium **Obverse:** Crowned arms **Reverse:** Child with flags

| Date | Mintage | F | VF | XF | Unc | BU |
|---|---|---|---|---|---|---|
| 1998 Proof | — | Value: 27.50 | | | | |

**10000 LIRE** **KM# 397** **Weight:** 22.0000 g. **Composition:** 0.8350 Silver .5907 oz. ASW **Subject:** III millennium **Obverse:**

Crowned arms **Reverse:** Allegorical portrait of DNA unraveling from human mind

| Date | Mintage | F | VF | XF | Unc | BU |
|---|---|---|---|---|---|---|
| 1999 Proof | Est. 25,000 | Value: 30.00 | | | | |

**10000 LIRE** **KM# 398** **Weight:** 22.0000 g. **Composition:** 0.8350 Silver .5907 oz. ASW **Series:** 2000 Olympics **Obverse:** Crowned arms **Reverse:** Prone shooter

| Date | Mintage | F | VF | XF | Unc | BU |
|---|---|---|---|---|---|---|
| 1999 Proof | Est. 35,000 | Value: 27.50 | | | | |

**10000 LIRE** **KM# 411** **Weight:** 22.0000 g. **Composition:** 0.8350 Silver .5907 oz. ASW **Subject:** European Union **Reverse:** Circle of paper dolls above denomination

| Date | Mintage | VG | F | VF | XF | Unc |
|---|---|---|---|---|---|---|
| 1999 Proof | — | Value: 35.00 | | | | |

**10000 LIRE** **KM# 419** **Weight:** 22.0000 g. **Composition:** 0.8350 Silver .5907 oz. ASW **Subject:** 17th centennial of the republic **Reverse:** St. Marino's portrait

| Date | Mintage | VG | F | VF | XF | Unc |
|---|---|---|---|---|---|---|
| 2000 Proof | 18,000 | Value: 22.50 | | | | |

**10000 LIRE** **KM# 422** **Weight:** 22.0000 g. **Composition:** 0.8350 Silver .5907 oz. ASW **Subject:** Holy Year **Obverse:** Crowned arms **Reverse:** Pope kneeling before an open door **Edge:** Reeded and plain sections **Size:** 34 mm.

| Date | Mintage | VG | F | VF | XF | Unc |
|---|---|---|---|---|---|---|
| 2000 Proof | — | Value: 30.00 | | | | |

**10000 LIRE** **KM# 423** **Weight:** 22.0000 g. **Composition:** 0.8350 Silver .5907 oz. ASW **Subject:** Michelangelo's Sacred Family painting **Obverse:** Crowned arms **Reverse:** Painting detail **Edge:** Reeded and plain sections **Size:** 34 mm.

| Date | Mintage | VG | F | VF | XF | Unc |
|---|---|---|---|---|---|---|
| 2000 Proof | — | Value: 30.00 | | | | |

**10000 LIRE** **KM# 437** **Weight:** 22.0000 g. **Composition:** 0.8350 Silver .5907 oz. ASW **Subject:** Last Lire Coinage **Obverse:** National arms. **Reverse:** Six old coin designs. **Edge:** Reeded and plain sections. **Size:** 34 mm.

| Date | Mintage | VG | F | VF | XF | Unc |
|---|---|---|---|---|---|---|
| 2001 Proof | 20,000 | Value: 30.00 | | | | |

**10000 LIRE** **KM# 438** **Weight:** 22.0000 g. **Composition:** 0.8350 Silver .5906 oz. ASW **Subject:** 2nd International Chambers of Commerce Convention **Obverse:** National arms. **Reverse:** Mercury running by a computer. **Edge:** Reeded and plain sections. **Size:** 34 mm.

| Date | Mintage | VG | F | VF | XF | Unc |
|---|---|---|---|---|---|---|
| 2001 Proof | 20,000 | Value: 20.00 | | | | |

**10000 LIRE** **KM# 432** **Weight:** 22.0000 g. **Composition:** 0.8350 Silver .5906 oz. ASW **Subject:** Ferrari **Obverse:** Three towers. **Reverse:** Race car with "FERRARI" background. **Edge:** Reeded and plain sections. **Size:** 34 mm.

| Date | Mintage | F | VF | XF | Unc | BU |
|---|---|---|---|---|---|---|
| 2001 Proof | 20,000 | Value: 25.00 | | | | |

**1/2 SCUDO** **KM# 416** **Weight:** 1.6100 g. **Composition:** 0.9000 Gold .0466 oz. AGW **Subject:** Ilcenacolo **Obverse:** Crowned arms **Reverse:** Bearded portrait **Edge:** Reeded **Size:** 14 mm. **Note:** Struck at Rome. 1,915 coins melted at the mint.

| Date | Mintage | F | VF | XF | Unc | BU |
|---|---|---|---|---|---|---|
| 1998 | 8,000 | — | — | — | 37.50 | — |

**1/2 SCUDO** **KM# 413** **Weight:** 1.6100 g. **Composition:** 0.9000 Gold .0466 oz. AGW **Subject:** Ritratto di Agnolo Doni **Obverse:** Crowned arms **Reverse:** Portrait

| Date | Mintage | VG | F | VF | XF | Unc |
|---|---|---|---|---|---|---|
| 1999 Proof | 8,000 | Value: 35.00 | | | | |

**1/2 SCUDO** **KM# 407** **Weight:** 1.6100 g. **Composition:** 0.9000 Gold .0466 oz. AGW **Subject:** Ritratto di Agnolo Doni **Obverse:** Crowned arms **Reverse:** Portrait

| Date | Mintage | F | VF | XF | Unc | BU |
|---|---|---|---|---|---|---|
| 2000 Proof | 6,000 | — | — | — | 35.00 | — |

**1/2 SCUDO** **KM# 433** **Weight:** 1.6100 g. **Composition:** 0.9000 Gold .0466 oz. AGW **Subject:** Cavaliere **Obverse:** National arms. **Reverse:** Horse and rider. **Edge:** Reeded. **Size:** 13.8 mm.

| Date | Mintage | F | VF | XF | Unc | BU |
|---|---|---|---|---|---|---|
| 2001 Proof | 4,500 | Value: 26.00 | | | | |

**SCUDO** **KM# 38** **Weight:** 3.0000 g. **Composition:** 0.9170 Gold .0883 oz. AGW **Note:** 2,491 coins melted at the mint.

| Date | Mintage | F | VF | XF | Unc | BU |
|---|---|---|---|---|---|---|
| 1974 | 87,000 | — | — | — | 55.00 | — |

**SCUDO** **KM# 49** **Weight:** 3.0000 g. **Composition:** 0.9170 Gold .0883 oz. AGW **Note:** 37,668 coins melted at the mint.

| Date | Mintage | F | VF | XF | Unc | BU |
|---|---|---|---|---|---|---|
| 1975 | 90,000 | — | — | — | 65.00 | — |

**SCUDO** **KM# 60** **Weight:** 3.0000 g. **Composition:** 0.9170 Gold .0883 oz. AGW **Note:** 30,026 coins melted at the mint.

| Date | Mintage | F | VF | XF | Unc | BU |
|---|---|---|---|---|---|---|
| 1976 | 65,000 | — | — | — | 55.00 | — |

**SCUDO** **KM# 73** **Weight:** 3.0000 g. **Composition:** 0.9170 Gold .0883 oz. AGW **Subject:** Democrazia **Note:** 1,839 coins melted at the mint.

| Date | Mintage | F | VF | XF | Unc | BU |
|---|---|---|---|---|---|---|
| 1977 | 35,000 | — | — | — | 60.00 | — |

**SCUDO** **KM# 86** **Weight:** 3.0000 g. **Composition:** 0.9170 Gold .0883 oz. AGW **Subject:** Miss Liberta **Note:** 9,021 coins melted at the mint.

| Date | Mintage | F | VF | XF | Unc | BU |
|---|---|---|---|---|---|---|
| 1978 | 38,000 | — | — | — | 60.00 | — |

**SCUDO** **KM# 99** **Weight:** 3.0000 g. **Composition:** 0.9170 Gold .0883 oz. AGW **Subject:** Peace **Note:** 4,152 coins melted at the mint.

| Date | Mintage | F | VF | XF | Unc | BU |
|---|---|---|---|---|---|---|
| 1979 | 38,000 | — | — | — | 60.00 | — |

**SCUDO** **KM# 113** **Weight:** 3.0000 g. **Composition:** 0.9170 Gold .0883 oz. AGW **Note:** 10,309 coins melted at the mint.

| Date | Mintage | F | VF | XF | Unc | BU |
|---|---|---|---|---|---|---|
| 1980 | 38,000 | — | — | — | 60.00 | — |

**SCUDO** **KM# 128** **Weight:** 3.0000 g. **Composition:** 0.9170 Gold .0883 oz. AGW **Series:** World Food Day **Note:** 196 coins melted at the mint.

| Date | Mintage | F | VF | XF | Unc | BU |
|---|---|---|---|---|---|---|
| 1981 | 31,000 | — | — | — | 60.00 | — |

**SCUDO** **KM# 142** **Weight:** 3.0000 g. **Composition:** 0.9170 Gold .0883 oz. AGW **Note:** 1,192 coins melted at the mint.

| Date | Mintage | F | VF | XF | Unc | BU |
|---|---|---|---|---|---|---|
| 1982R | 17,000 | — | — | — | 60.00 | — |

**SCUDO** **KM# 156** **Weight:** 2.0000 g. **Composition:** 0.9170 Gold .059 oz. AGW **Subject:** Perpetual liberty **Note:** 917 coins melted at the mint.

| Date | Mintage | F | VF | XF | Unc | BU |
|---|---|---|---|---|---|---|
| 1983R | 14,000 | — | — | — | 65.00 | — |

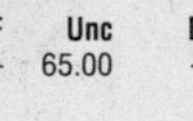

**SCUDO** **KM# 170** **Weight:** 2.0000 g. **Composition:** 0.9170 Gold .059 oz. AGW **Subject:** Peace **Obverse:** Similar to 2 Scudi, KM#171 **Note:** 979 coins melted at the mint.

| Date | Mintage | F | VF | XF | Unc | BU |
|---|---|---|---|---|---|---|
| 1984R | 11,000 | — | — | — | 65.00 | — |

**SCUDO** **KM# 184** **Weight:** 2.0000 g. **Composition:** 0.9170 Gold .059 oz. AGW **Subject:** International Year for Youth **Note:** 1,162 coins melted at the mint.

| Date | Mintage | F | VF | XF | Unc | BU |
|---|---|---|---|---|---|---|
| 1985R | 10,000 | — | — | — | 90.00 | — |

**SCUDO** **KM# 198** **Weight:** 3.3920 g. **Composition:** 0.9170 Gold .1 oz. AGW **Subject:** Insects at work **Note:** 1,308 coins melted at the mint.

| Date | Mintage | F | VF | XF | Unc | BU |
|---|---|---|---|---|---|---|
| 1986R | 9,000 | — | — | — | 70.00 | — |

**SCUDO** **KM# 211** **Weight:** 3.3920 g. **Composition:** 0.9170 Gold .1 oz. AGW **Subject:** European Year for Environment **Note:** 962 coins melted at the mint.

| Date | Mintage | F | VF | XF | Unc | BU |
|---|---|---|---|---|---|---|
| 1987R | 8,000 | — | — | — | 70.00 | — |

**SCUDO** **KM# 228** **Weight:** 3.3920 g. **Composition:** 0.9170 Gold .1 oz. AGW **Subject:** Disarmament **Note:** 873 coins melted at the mint.

| Date | Mintage | F | VF | XF | Unc | BU |
|---|---|---|---|---|---|---|
| 1988R | 7,000 | — | — | — | 70.00 | — |

**SCUDO** **KM# 241** **Weight:** 3.2258 g. **Composition:** 0.9000 Gold .0933 oz. AGW **Subject:** French Revolution **Note:** 731 coins melted at the mint.

| Date | Mintage | F | VF | XF | Unc | BU |
|---|---|---|---|---|---|---|
| 1989R | 7,500 | — | — | — | 65.00 | — |

**SCUDO** **KM# 258** **Weight:** 3.2258 g. **Composition:** 0.9000 Gold .0933 oz. AGW **Subject:** San Marino's presidency of the European Council

| Date | Mintage | F | VF | XF | Unc | BU |
|---|---|---|---|---|---|---|
| 1990R | 7,300 | — | — | — | 65.00 | — |

**SCUDO** **KM# 273** **Weight:** 3.2258 g. **Composition:** 0.9000 Gold .0933 oz. AGW **Subject:** Peace **Reverse:** Child fleeing

| Date | Mintage | F | VF | XF | Unc | BU |
|---|---|---|---|---|---|---|
| 1991R Proof | Est. 7,500 | Value: 65.00 | | | | |

**SCUDO** **KM# 288** **Weight:** 3.2258 g. **Composition:** 0.9000 Gold .0933 oz. AGW **Subject:** San Marino's entry into the United Nations

| Date | Mintage | F | VF | XF | Unc | BU |
|---|---|---|---|---|---|---|
| 1992R | 8,500 | Value: 65.00 | | | | |

**SCUDO** **KM# 303** **Weight:** 3.2258 g. **Composition:** 0.9000 Gold .0933 oz. AGW **Series:** International Monetary Fund **Reverse:** 3 figures **Note:** 455 coins melted at the mint.

| Date | Mintage | F | VF | XF | Unc | BU |
|---|---|---|---|---|---|---|
| 1993R | 7,500 | — | — | — | 60.00 | — |
| 1993R Proof | — | Value: 70.00 | | | | |

**SCUDO** **KM# 319** **Weight:** 3.2258 g. **Composition:** 0.9000 Gold .0933 oz. AGW **Series:** International Year of the Family **Note:** Sets only. 648 coins melted at the mint.

| Date | Mintage | F | VF | XF | Unc | BU |
|---|---|---|---|---|---|---|
| 1994R Proof | 7,500 | Value: 75.00 | | | | |

**SCUDO** **KM# 335** **Weight:** 3.2258 g. **Composition:** 0.9000 Gold .0933 oz. AGW **Series:** 50th anniversary - United Nations **Note:** Sets only. 494 coins melted at the mint.

| Date | Mintage | F | VF | XF | Unc | BU |
|---|---|---|---|---|---|---|
| 1995R Proof | 6,500 | Value: 65.00 | | | | |

**SCUDO** **KM# 338** **Weight:** 3.2258 g. **Composition:** 0.9000 Gold .0933 oz. AGW **Series:** 1996 Olympics **Reverse:** Boxers **Note:** 664 coins melted at the mint.

| Date | Mintage | F | VF | XF | Unc | BU |
|---|---|---|---|---|---|---|
| 1996 Proof | 7,000 | Value: 65.00 | | | | |

**SCUDO** **KM# 373** **Weight:** 3.2258 g. **Composition:** 0.9000 Gold .0933 oz. AGW **Subject:** Michelangelo's "Kneeling Angel" **Note:** 412 coins melted at the mint.

| Date | Mintage | F | VF | XF | Unc | BU |
|---|---|---|---|---|---|---|
| 1997 Proof | 6,500 | Value: 65.00 | | | | |

**SCUDO** **KM# 417** **Weight:** 3.2258 g. **Composition:** 0.9000 Gold .0933 oz. AGW **Subject:** Canone Delle Proporzioni **Obverse:** Crowned arms **Reverse:** Anatomical drawing **Edge:** Reeded **Size:** 15.9 mm. **Note:** Struck at Rome. 312 coins melted at the mint.

| Date | Mintage | F | VF | XF | Unc | BU |
|---|---|---|---|---|---|---|
| 1998 Proof | 6,000 | Value: 65.00 | | | | |

**SCUDO** **KM# 414** **Weight:** 3.2258 g. **Composition:** 0.9000 Gold .0933 oz. AGW **Subject:** La Velata **Obverse:** Crowned arms **Reverse:** Woman's portrait

| Date | Mintage | VG | F | VF | XF | Unc |
|---|---|---|---|---|---|---|
| 1999 Proof | 8,000 | Value: 60.00 | | | | |

**SCUDO** **KM# 408** **Weight:** 3.2258 g. **Composition:** 0.9000 Gold .0933 oz. AGW **Subject:** La Primavera **Obverse:** Crowned arms **Reverse:** 3 allegorical female figures

| Date | Mintage | VG | F | VF | XF | Unc |
|---|---|---|---|---|---|---|
| 2000 Proof | — | Value: 60.00 | | | | |

**SCUDO** **KM# 434** **Weight:** 3.2200 g. **Composition:** 0.9000 Gold .0932 oz. AGW **Subject:** Tiziano **Obverse:** National arms. **Reverse:** Bearded male portrait. **Edge:** Reeded. **Size:** 16 mm.

| Date | Mintage | F | VF | XF | Unc | BU |
|---|---|---|---|---|---|---|
| 2001 Proof | 4,500 | Value: 51.00 | | | | |

**2 SCUDI** **KM# 39** **Weight:** 6.0000 g. **Composition:** 0.9170 Gold .1769 oz. AGW **Note:** 1,637 coins melted at the mint.

| Date | Mintage | F | VF | XF | Unc | BU |
|---|---|---|---|---|---|---|
| 1974 | 77,000 | — | — | — | 90.00 | — |

**2 SCUDI** **KM#50** **Weight:** 6.0000 g. **Composition:** 0.9170 Gold .1769 oz. AGW **Note:** 3,373 coins melted at the mint.

| Date | Mintage | F | VF | XF | Unc | BU |
|---|---|---|---|---|---|---|
| 1975 | 80,000 | — | — | — | 90.00 | — |

**2 SCUDI** **KM#61** **Weight:** 6.0000 g. **Composition:** 0.9170 Gold .1769 oz. AGW **Note:** 20,246 coins melted at the mint.

| Date | Mintage | F | VF | XF | Unc | BU |
|---|---|---|---|---|---|---|
| 1976 | 55,000 | — | — | — | 90.00 | — |

**2 SCUDI** **KM#74** **Weight:** 6.0000 g. **Composition:** 0.9170 Gold .1769 oz. AGW **Subject:** Democrazia **Note:** 912 coins melted at the mint.

| Date | Mintage | F | VF | XF | Unc | BU |
|---|---|---|---|---|---|---|
| 1977 | 34,000 | — | — | — | 100 | — |

**2 SCUDI** **KM#87** **Weight:** 6.0000 g. **Composition:** 0.9170 Gold .1769 oz. AGW **Subject:** Libertas **Note:** 8,120 coins melted at the mint.

| Date | Mintage | F | VF | XF | Unc | BU |
|---|---|---|---|---|---|---|
| 1978 | 37,000 | — | — | — | 100 | — |

**2 SCUDI** **KM#100** **Weight:** 6.0000 g. **Composition:** 0.9170 Gold .1769 oz. AGW **Subject:** Peace **Note:** 3,238 coins melted at the mint.

| Date | Mintage | F | VF | XF | Unc | BU |
|---|---|---|---|---|---|---|
| 1979 | 37,000 | — | — | — | 100 | — |

**2 SCUDI** **KM#114** **Weight:** 6.0000 g. **Composition:** 0.9170 Gold .1769 oz. AGW **Subject:** Justice **Note:** 9,340 coins melted at the mint.

| Date | Mintage | F | VF | XF | Unc | BU |
|---|---|---|---|---|---|---|
| 1980 | 37,000 | — | — | — | 100 | — |

**2 SCUDI** **KM#129** **Weight:** 6.0000 g. **Composition:** 0.9170 Gold .1769 oz. AGW **Series:** World Food Day **Note:** 196 coins melted at the mint.

| Date | Mintage | F | VF | XF | Unc | BU |
|---|---|---|---|---|---|---|
| 1981 | 30,000 | — | — | — | 100 | — |

**2 SCUDI** **KM#143** **Weight:** 6.0000 g. **Composition:** 0.9170 Gold .1769 oz. AGW **Note:** 244 coins melted at the mint.

| Date | Mintage | F | VF | XF | Unc | BU |
|---|---|---|---|---|---|---|
| 1982R | 16,000 | — | — | — | 110 | — |

**2 SCUDI** **KM#157** **Weight:** 4.0000 g. **Composition:** 0.9170 Gold .1179 oz. AGW **Subject:** Perpetual liberty **Note:** 17 coins melted at the mint.

| Date | Mintage | F | VF | XF | Unc | BU |
|---|---|---|---|---|---|---|
| 1983R | 13,000 | — | — | — | 110 | — |

**2 SCUDI** **KM#171** **Weight:** 4.0000 g. **Composition:** 0.9170 Gold .1179 oz. AGW **Subject:** Liberty **Note:** 12 coins melted at the mint.

| Date | Mintage | F | VF | XF | Unc | BU |
|---|---|---|---|---|---|---|
| 1984R | 10,000 | — | — | — | 110 | — |

**2 SCUDI** **KM#185** **Weight:** 4.0000 g. **Composition:** 0.9170 Gold .1179 oz. AGW **Series:** International Year for Youth **Note:** 200 coins melted at the mint.

| Date | Mintage | F | VF | XF | Unc | BU |
|---|---|---|---|---|---|---|
| 1985R | 9,000 | — | — | — | 110 | — |

**2 SCUDI** **KM#199** **Weight:** 6.7840 g. **Composition:** 0.9170 Gold .2 oz. AGW **Subject:** Spider at work **Note:** 329 coins melted at the mint.

| Date | Mintage | F | VF | XF | Unc | BU |
|---|---|---|---|---|---|---|
| 1986R | 8,000 | — | — | — | 150 | — |

**2 SCUDI** **KM#212** **Weight:** 6.7840 g. **Composition:** 0.9170 Gold .2 oz. AGW **Subject:** European Year for Envrionment **Note:** 14 coins melted at the mint.

| Date | Mintage | F | VF | XF | Unc | BU |
|---|---|---|---|---|---|---|
| 1987R | 7,000 | — | — | — | 120 | — |

**2 SCUDI** **KM#229** **Weight:** 6.7840 g. **Composition:** 0.9170 Gold .2 oz. AGW **Subject:** Disarmament **Note:** 7 coins melted at the mint.

| Date | Mintage | F | VF | XF | Unc | BU |
|---|---|---|---|---|---|---|
| 1988R | 6,000 | — | — | — | 120 | — |

**2 SCUDI** **KM#242** **Weight:** 6.4516 g. **Composition:** 0.9000 Gold .1867 oz. AGW **Subject:** French Revolution

| Date | Mintage | F | VF | XF | Unc | BU |
|---|---|---|---|---|---|---|
| 1989R | 6,500 | — | — | — | 110 | — |

**2 SCUDI** **KM#259** **Weight:** 6.4516 g. **Composition:** 0.9000 Gold .1867 oz. AGW **Subject:** San Marino's presidency of the European Council

| Date | Mintage | F | VF | XF | Unc | BU |
|---|---|---|---|---|---|---|
| 1990R | 6,800 | — | — | — | 110 | — |

**2 SCUDI** **KM#274** **Weight:** 6.4516 g. **Composition:** 0.9000 Gold .1867 oz. AGW **Subject:** Peace **Reverse:** New shoots growing from stump

| Date | Mintage | F | VF | XF | Unc | BU |
|---|---|---|---|---|---|---|
| 1991R Proof | Est. 6,500 | Value: 110 | | | | |

**2 SCUDI** **KM#289** **Weight:** 6.4516 g. **Composition:** 0.9000 Gold .1867 oz. AGW **Subject:** San Marino's entry into the United Nations

| Date | Mintage | F | VF | XF | Unc | BU |
|---|---|---|---|---|---|---|
| 1992R Proof | 7,500 | Value: 110 | | | | |

**2 SCUDI** **KM#304** **Weight:** 6.4516 g. **Composition:** 0.9000 Gold .1867 oz. AGW **Series:** International Monetary Fund **Reverse:** 2 figures **Note:** 106 coins melted at the mint.

| Date | Mintage | F | VF | XF | Unc | BU |
|---|---|---|---|---|---|---|
| 1993R | 6,500 | — | — | — | 100 | — |
| 1993R Proof | — | Value: 120 | | | | |

**2 SCUDI** **KM#320** **Weight:** 6.4516 g. **Composition:** 0.9000 Gold .1867 oz. AGW **Series:** International Year of the Family **Note:** Sets only. 252 coins melted at the mint.

| Date | Mintage | F | VF | XF | Unc | BU |
|---|---|---|---|---|---|---|
| 1994R Proof | 6,500 | Value: 125 | | | | |

**2 SCUDI** **KM# 336** **Weight:** 6.4516 g. **Composition:** 0.9000 Gold .1867 oz. AGW **Series:** 50th Anniversary - United Nations **Note:** Sets only.

| Date | Mintage | F | VF | XF | Unc | BU |
|---|---|---|---|---|---|---|
| 1995R Proof | Est. 7,000 | Value: 125 | | | | |

**2 SCUDI** **KM# 339** **Weight:** 6.4516 g. **Composition:** 0.9000 Gold .1867 oz. AGW **Series:** 1996 Olympics **Subject:** Track and field **Note:** 1 coin melted at the mint.

| Date | Mintage | F | VF | XF | Unc | BU |
|---|---|---|---|---|---|---|
| 1996 Proof | 6,000 | Value: 125 | | | | |

**2 SCUDI** **KM# 374** **Weight:** 6.4516 g. **Composition:** 0.9000 Gold .1867 oz. AGW **Subject:** Michelangelo's "David" **Note:** 124 coins melted at the mint.

| Date | Mintage | F | VF | XF | Unc | BU |
|---|---|---|---|---|---|---|
| 1997 Proof | 5,800 | Value: 125 | | | | |

**2 SCUDI** **KM# 418** **Weight:** 6.4516 g. **Composition:** 0.9000 Gold .1867 oz. AGW **Subject:** Vergine Delle Rocce **Obverse:** Crowned arms **Reverse:** Hallowed portrait **Edge:** Reeded **Size:** 21 mm. **Note:** Struck at Rome. 334 coins melted at the mint.

| Date | Mintage | F | VF | XF | Unc | BU |
|---|---|---|---|---|---|---|
| 1998 Proof | 5,500 | Value: 125 | | | | |

**2 SCUDI** **KM# 415** **Weight:** 6.4516 g. **Composition:** 0.9000 Gold .1867 oz. AGW **Subject:** Sposalizio Della Vergine **Obverse:** Crowned arms **Reverse:** Wedding scene

| Date | Mintage | VG | F | VF | XF | Unc |
|---|---|---|---|---|---|---|
| 1999 Proof | 8,000 | Value: 115 | | | | |

**2 SCUDI** **KM# 409** **Weight:** 6.4516 g. **Composition:** 0.9000 Gold .1867 oz. AGW **Subject:** Madonna Della Melagrna **Obverse:** Crowned arms **Reverse:** Madonna and child

| Date | Mintage | VG | F | VF | XF | Unc |
|---|---|---|---|---|---|---|
| 2000 Proof | 6,000 | Value: 115 | | | | |

**2 SCUDI** **KM# 435** **Weight:** 6.4400 g. **Composition:** 0.9000 Gold .1863 oz. AGW **Subject:** "Flora" **Obverse:** National arms. **Reverse:** Portrait. **Edge:** Reeded. **Size:** 21 mm.

| Date | Mintage | F | VF | XF | Unc | BU |
|---|---|---|---|---|---|---|
| 2001 Proof | 4,500 | Value: 102 | | | | |

**5 SCUDI** **KM# 62** **Weight:** 15.0000 g. **Composition:** 0.9170 Gold .4422 oz. AGW **Note:** 25 coins melted at mint.

| Date | Mintage | F | VF | XF | Unc | BU |
|---|---|---|---|---|---|---|
| 1976 | 8,000 | — | — | — | 625 | — |

**5 SCUDI** **KM# 75** **Weight:** 15.0000 g. **Composition:** 0.9170 Gold .4422 oz. AGW **Subject:** Democrazia **Note:** 29 coins melted at mint.

| Date | Mintage | F | VF | XF | Unc | BU |
|---|---|---|---|---|---|---|
| 1977 | 16,000 | — | — | — | 240 | — |

**5 SCUDI** **KM# 101** **Weight:** 15.0000 g. **Composition:** 0.9170 Gold .4422 oz. AGW **Subject:** Peace **Note:** 161 coins melted at mint.

| Date | Mintage | F | VF | XF | Unc | BU |
|---|---|---|---|---|---|---|
| 1979 | 24,000 | — | — | — | 240 | — |

**5 SCUDI** **KM# 115** **Weight:** 15.0000 g. **Composition:** 0.9170 Gold .4422 oz. AGW **Subject:** Justice **Note:** 1,428 coins melted at mint.

| Date | Mintage | F | VF | XF | Unc | BU |
|---|---|---|---|---|---|---|
| 1980 | 24,000 | — | — | — | 240 | — |

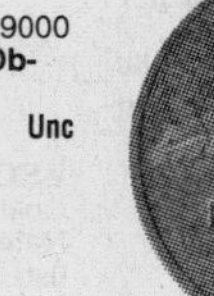

**5 SCUDI** **KM# 130** **Weight:** 15.0000 g. **Composition:** 0.9170 Gold .4422 oz. AGW **Series:** World Food Day **Note:** 33 coins melted at mint.

| Date | Mintage | F | VF | XF | Unc | BU |
|---|---|---|---|---|---|---|
| 1981 | 24,000 | — | — | — | 240 | — |

**5 SCUDI** **KM# 144** **Weight:** 15.0000 g. **Composition:** 0.9170 Gold .4422 oz. AGW **Subject:** Defense of liberty **Note:** 19 coins melted at mint.

| Date | Mintage | F | VF | XF | Unc | BU |
|---|---|---|---|---|---|---|
| 1982R | 15,000 | — | — | — | 240 | — |

**5 SCUDI** **KM# 158** **Weight:** 10.0000 g. **Composition:** 0.9170 Gold .2949 oz. AGW **Subject:** Perpetual liberty **Note:** 25 coins melted at mint.

| Date | Mintage | F | VF | XF | Unc | BU |
|---|---|---|---|---|---|---|
| 1983R | 11,000 | — | — | — | 250 | — |

**5 SCUDI** **KM# 172** **Weight:** 10.0000 g. **Composition:** 0.9170 Gold .2949 oz. AGW **Subject:** Justice **Note:** 28 coins melted at mint.

| Date | Mintage | F | VF | XF | Unc | BU |
|---|---|---|---|---|---|---|
| 1984R | 9,000 | — | — | — | 300 | — |

**5 SCUDI** **KM# 186** **Weight:** 10.0000 g. **Composition:** 0.9170 Gold .2949 oz. AGW **Subject:** Libertas **Note:** 13 coins melted at mint.

| Date | Mintage | F | VF | XF | Unc | BU |
|---|---|---|---|---|---|---|
| 1985R | 7,400 | — | — | — | 400 | — |

**5 SCUDI** **KM# 200** **Weight:** 16.9500 g. **Composition:** 0.9170 Gold .5 oz. AGW **Subject:** Work **Reverse:** Bees **Note:** 14 coins melted at mint.

| Date | Mintage | F | VF | XF | Unc | BU |
|---|---|---|---|---|---|---|
| 1986R | 7,000 | — | — | — | 320 | — |

**5 SCUDI KM# 215 Weight:** 16.9500 g. **Composition:** 0.9170 Gold .5 oz. AGW **Subject:** United Nations **Note:** 49 coins melted at mint.

| Date | Mintage | F | VF | XF | Unc | BU |
|---|---|---|---|---|---|---|
| 1987R | 6,000 | — | — | — | 320 | — |

**5 SCUDI KM# 230 Weight:** 16.9500 g. **Composition:** 0.9170 Gold .5 oz. AGW **Subject:** Human rights **Note:** 11 coins melted at mint.

| Date | Mintage | F | VF | XF | Unc | BU |
|---|---|---|---|---|---|---|
| 1988R | 5,000 | — | — | — | 320 | — |

**5 SCUDI KM# 245 Weight:** 16.9500 g. **Composition:** 0.9170 Gold .5 oz. AGW **Subject:** Entrance of San Marino in Common Market

| Date | Mintage | F | VF | XF | Unc | BU |
|---|---|---|---|---|---|---|
| 1989R | 6,000 | — | — | — | 320 | — |

**5 SCUDI KM# 260 Weight:** 16.9500 g. **Composition:** 0.9170 Gold .5 oz. AGW **Subject:** Founding of the republic

| Date | Mintage | F | VF | XF | Unc | BU |
|---|---|---|---|---|---|---|
| 1990R Proof | 6,500 | Value: 300 | | | | |

**5 SCUDI KM# 275 Weight:** 16.9500 g. **Composition:** 0.9170 Gold .5 oz. AGW **Subject:** Peace and freedom **Reverse:** Family

| Date | Mintage | F | VF | XF | Unc | BU |
|---|---|---|---|---|---|---|
| 1991R Proof | 7,000 | Value: 300 | | | | |

**5 SCUDI KM# 290 Weight:** 16.9500 g. **Composition:** 0.9170 Gold .5 oz. AGW **Subject:** Customer agreement with European Economic Community

| Date | Mintage | F | VF | XF | Unc | BU |
|---|---|---|---|---|---|---|
| 1992R Proof | Est. 6,500 | Value: 300 | | | | |

**5 SCUDI KM# 305 Weight:** 16.9500 g. **Composition:** 0.9170 Gold .5 oz. AGW **Series:** International Monetary Fund **Reverse:** Figure holding scale **Note:** 68 coins melted at the mint.

| Date | Mintage | F | VF | XF | Unc | BU |
|---|---|---|---|---|---|---|
| 1993R Proof | 5,500 | Value: 300 | | | | |

**5 SCUDI KM# 321 Weight:** 16.9500 g. **Composition:** 0.9170 Gold .5 oz. AGW **Series:** International Year of the Family **Note:** 207 coins melted at the mint.

| Date | Mintage | F | VF | XF | Unc | BU |
|---|---|---|---|---|---|---|
| 1994R Proof | 5,500 | Value: 300 | | | | |

**5 SCUDI KM# 337 Weight:** 16.9500 g. **Composition:** 0.9170 Gold .5 oz. AGW **Series:** 50th Anniversary - United Nations **Note:** 65 coins melted at the mint.

| Date | Mintage | F | VF | XF | Unc | BU |
|---|---|---|---|---|---|---|
| 1995R Proof | 5,000 | Value: 300 | | | | |

**5 SCUDI KM# 343 Weight:** 16.9500 g. **Composition:** 0.9170 Gold .5 oz. AGW **Subject:** Pieta **Reverse:** Mary receives Jesus' body **Note:** 19 coins melted at the mint.

| Date | Mintage | F | VF | XF | Unc | BU |
|---|---|---|---|---|---|---|
| 1996 Proof | 5,840 | Value: 300 | | | | |

**5 SCUDI KM# 375 Weight:** 16.9500 g. **Composition:** 0.9170 Gold .5 oz. AGW **Subject:** The Annunciation **Reverse:** Angel **Note:** 469 coins melted at the mint.

| Date | Mintage | F | VF | XF | Unc | BU |
|---|---|---|---|---|---|---|
| 1997 Proof | 5,500 | Value: 300 | | | | |

**5 SCUDI KM# 412 Weight:** 16.9590 g. **Composition:** 0.9170 Gold .5 oz. AGW **Subject:** Madonna Della Seggiola **Reverse:** Woman with 2 children **Note:** 1,151 coins melted at the mint.

| Date | Mintage | F | VF | XF | Unc | BU |
|---|---|---|---|---|---|---|
| 1998 Proof | 5,000 | Value: 300 | | | | |

**5 SCUDI KM# 388 Weight:** 16.9590 g. **Composition:** 0.9170 Gold .5 oz. AGW **Subject:** Birth of Venus **Obverse:** Crowned arms **Reverse:** Venus standing in shell

| Date | Mintage | F | VF | XF | Unc | BU |
|---|---|---|---|---|---|---|
| 1999 Proof | Est. 5,500 | Value: 300 | | | | |

**5 SCUDI KM# 420 Weight:** 16.9590 g. **Composition:** 0.9170 Gold .5 oz. AGW **Subject:** Tiziano's painting "Rape of Europa" **Reverse:** Europa on a bull's (Zeus) back

| Date | Mintage | VG | F | VF | XF | Unc |
|---|---|---|---|---|---|---|
| 2000 Proof | 4,500 | — | — | — | — | 285 |

**5 SCUDI KM# 439 Weight:** 16.9655 g. **Composition:** 0.9166 Gold .5000 oz. AGW **Subject:** San Marino's World Bank Membership **Obverse:** National arms. **Reverse:** Orchid and bee. **Edge:** Reeded. **Size:** 28 mm.

| Date | Mintage | VG | F | VF | XF | Unc |
|---|---|---|---|---|---|---|
| 2001 Proof | 4,000 | Value: 226 | | | | |

**10 SCUDI KM# 88 Weight:** 30.0000 g. **Composition:** 0.9170 Gold .8844 oz. AGW **Note:** 54 coins melted at the mint.

| Date | Mintage | F | VF | XF | Unc | BU |
|---|---|---|---|---|---|---|
| 1978 | 20,000 | — | — | — | 450 | — |

## PROVAS

| KM# | Date | Mintage | Identification | Mkt Val |
|---|---|---|---|---|
| Pr1 | 1925R | 75 | 20 Lire. KM8. | 3,200 |
| Pr2 | 1931R | — | 5 Lire. KM9. | 250 |
| Pr3 | 1931R | — | 10 Lire. KM10. | 225 |
| Pr4 | 1931R | — | 20 Lire. KM11. | 500 |
| Pr5 | 1932R | — | 5 Lire. KM9. | 850 |
| Pr6 | 1932R | — | 10 Lire. KM10. | 500 |
| Pr7 | 1933 | — | 5 Lire. KM9. | 175 |
| Pr8 | 1933 | — | 10 Lire. KM10. | 185 |
| Pr9 | 1933 | — | 20 Lire. KM11. | 200 |
| Pr10 | 1935R | — | 5 Lire. KM9. | 500 |
| Pr11 | 1935R | — | 20 Lire. KM11. | 550 |
| Pr12 | 1937R | — | 10 Lire. KM10. | 400 |

## MINT SETS

| KM# | Date | Mintage | Identification | Issue Price | Mkt Val |
|---|---|---|---|---|---|
| MS1 | 1972 (8) | — | KM14-21 | 5.00 | 12.50 |
| MS2 | 1973 (8) | — | KM22-29 | 6.00 | 12.50 |
| MS3 | 1974 (8) | 60,000 | KM30-37 | 9.00 | 15.00 |
| MS4 | 1974 (2) | 60,000 | KM38-39 | — | 175 |
| MS5 | 1975 (8) | — | KM40-47 | 6.50 | 15.00 |
| MS6 | 1975 (5) | — | KM40-44 | — | — |
| MS7 | 1975 (2) | 90,000 | KM49-50 | — | 175 |
| MS8 | 1976 (8) | — | KM51-58 | 6.00 | 12.50 |
| MS9 | 1976 (2) | 40,000 | KM60-61 | — | 175 |
| MS10 | 1977 (9) | — | KM63-71 | — | 15.00 |
| MS11 | 1977 (2) | 30,000 | KM73-74 | — | 175 |
| MS12 | 1978 (9) | — | KM76-84 | — | 15.00 |
| MS13 | 1978 (2) | — | KM86-87 | — | 160 |
| MS14 | 1979 (9) | — | KM89-98 | — | 15.00 |
| MS15 | 1979 (2) | — | KM99-100 | — | 160 |
| MS16 | 1980 (9) | — | KM102-110 | — | 15.00 |
| MS17 | 1980 (2) | — | KM113-114 | — | 160 |
| MS18 | 1981 (9) | — | KM116-123, 126 | — | 15.00 |
| MS19 | 1981 (3) | — | KM124-125, 127 | — | — |
| MS20 | 1981 (2) | — | KM128-129 | — | 160 |
| MS21 | 1982 (9) | — | KM131-138, 140 | 6.00 | 8.50 |
| MS22 | 1982 (2) | — | KM139, 141 | — | 27.50 |
| MS23 | 1982 (2) | — | KM142-143 | — | 170 |
| MS24 | 1983 (9) | — | KM145-153 | 5.50 | 8.50 |
| MS25 | 1983 (2) | — | KM154-155 | — | 27.50 |
| MS26 | 1983 (2) | — | KM156-157 | — | 175 |
| MS27 | 1984 (9) | — | KM159-167 | — | — |
| MS28 | 1984 (2) | — | KM168-169 | — | 22.00 |
| MS29 | 1984 (2) | — | KM170-171 | — | 175 |
| KM30 | 1985 (9) | — | KM173-181 | — | 8.50 |
| KM31 | 1985 (2) | — | KM182-183 | — | 22.00 |
| MS32 | 1985 (2) | — | KM184-185 | — | 200 |
| MS33 | 1986 (9) | — | KM187-195 | 7.00 | 8.50 |
| MS34 | 1986 (2) | — | KM196-197 | — | 30.00 |
| MS35 | 1986 (2) | — | KM198-199 | — | 190 |
| MS36 | 1987 (10) | 43,000 | KM201-210 | — | 25.00 |
| MS37 | 1987 (2) | — | KM213-214 | — | 30.00 |
| MS38 | 1987 (2) | — | KM211-212 | — | 190 |
| MS39 | 1988 (10) | 80,000 | KM218-227 | 22.00 | 26.00 |
| MS40 | 1988 (2) | — | KM216-217 | — | 30.00 |
| MS41 | 1988 (2) | — | KM228-229 | — | 190 |
| MS42 | 1989 (10) | 32,000 | KM231-240 | — | 28.00 |
| MS43 | 1989 (2) | 30,000 | KM243-244 | — | 30.00 |
| MS44 | 1989 (2) | 6,500 | KM241-242 | — | 170 |
| MS45 | 1990 (10) | 36,000 | KM248-257 | — | 35.00 |
| MS46 | 1990 (2) | 40,000 | KM246-247 | — | 175 |
| MS47 | 1990 (2) | 6,800 | KM258-259 | — | 175 |
| MS48 | 1991 (10) | 36,000 | KM261-270 | — | 32.00 |
| MS49 | 1991 (2) | 25,000 | KM271-272 | — | 32.00 |
| MS50 | 1992 (10) | 45,000 | KM278-287 | — | 32.00 |
| MS51 | 1992 (2) | — | KM276-277 | 34.00 | 40.00 |
| MS52 | 1993 (10) | — | KM293-302 | 18.00 | 28.00 |
| MS53 | 1993 (2) | 35,000 | KM291-292 | 26.00 | 30.00 |
| MS54 | 1994 (10) | 40,000 | KM307-315 | 18.00 | 30.00 |
| MS55 | 1995 (10) | — | KM322-331 | — | 30.00 |
| MS56 | 1996 (10) | 32,000 | KM344, 349-357 | 18.00 | 30.00 |
| MS57 | 1997 (10) | 28,000 | KM358-367 | 18.00 | 30.00 |
| MS58 | 1998 (8) | — | KM378-385 | 18.00 | 25.00 |
| MS59 | 1999 (8) | — | KM389-396 | 18.00 | 25.00 |
| MS60 | 2000 (8) | 28,000 | KM399-406 | 18.00 | 25.00 |
| MS61 | 2001 (8) | 2,000 | KM424-431 | 18.00 | 25.00 |

## PROOF SETS

| KM# | Date | Mintage | Identification | Issue Price | Mkt Val |
|---|---|---|---|---|---|
| PS1 | 1989 (2) | 8,000 | KM243-244 | 55.00 | 60.00 |
| PS2 | 1990 (2) | 18,800 | KM246-247 | 55.00 | 60.00 |
| PS4 | 1991 (2) | 6,800 | KM273-274 | — | 175 |
| PS3 | 1991 (2) | 8,000 | KM271-272 | 55.00 | 60.00 |
| PS5 | 1993 (2) | — | KM303-304 | 158 | 160 |
| PS6 | 1994 (2) | 7,500 | KM319-320 | — | 200 |
| PS7 | 1995 (2) | — | KM333-334 | 31.00 | 45.00 |
| PS8 | 1995 (2) | 7,000 | KM335-336 | 160 | 175 |
| PS9 | 1996 (2) | — | KM340-341 | 35.00 | 45.00 |
| PS10 | 1997 (2) | — | KM347-348 | 35.00 | 45.00 |
| PS11 | 1999 (2) | — | KM410-411 | — | 60.00 |
| PS12 | 1999 (3) | 8,000 | KM413-415 | 178 | 180 |
| PS13 | 2000 (3) | 6,000 | KM407-409 | 178 | 180 |
| PS14 | 2001 (3) | 4,500 | KM433-435 | 178 | 180 |

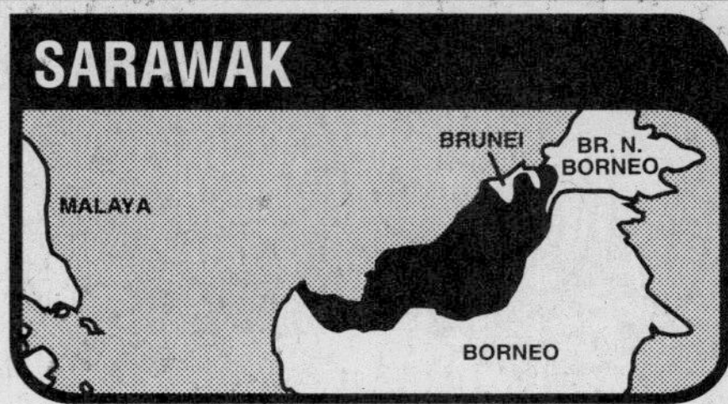


Sarawak is a former British colony located on the north-west coast of Borneo. The Japanese occupation during World War II so thoroughly devastated the economy that Rajah Sir Charles Vyner Brooke ceded it to Great Britain on July 1, 1946. In September, 1963 the colony joined the Federation of Malaysia.

**RULERS**
Charles J. Brooke, Rajah, 1868-1917
Charles V. Brooke, Rajah, 1917-1946

**MINT MARKS**
H - Heaton, Birmingham

**MONETARY SYSTEM**
100 Cents = 1 Dollar

# BRITISH COLONY

## STANDARD COINAGE

100 Cents = 1 Dollar

**1/2 CENT** KM# 20 **Composition:** Bronze **Ruler:** Charles V. Brooke Rajah

| Date | Mintage | F | VF | XF | Unc | BU |
|---|---|---|---|---|---|---|
| 1933H | 2,000,000 | 1.00 | 2.00 | 4.00 | 9.00 | — |
| 1933H Proof | — | Value: 240 | | | | |

**CENT** KM# 12 **Composition:** Copper-Nickel **Ruler:** Charles V. Brooke Rajah

| Date | Mintage | F | VF | XF | Unc | BU |
|---|---|---|---|---|---|---|
| 1920H | 5,000,000 | 3.00 | 7.50 | 18.00 | 55.00 | — |

**CENT** KM# 18 **Composition:** Bronze **Ruler:** Charles V. Brooke Rajah

| Date | Mintage | F | VF | XF | Unc | BU |
|---|---|---|---|---|---|---|
| 1927H | 5,000,000 | 1.25 | 2.25 | 4.50 | 9.00 | — |
| 1927H Proof | — | Value: 210 | | | | |
| 1929H | 2,000,000 | 1.25 | 2.50 | 5.00 | 10.00 | — |
| 1930H | 3,000,000 | 1.25 | 2.50 | 5.00 | 10.00 | — |
| 1930H Proof | — | Value: 210 | | | | |
| 1937H | 3,000,000 | 1.25 | 2.25 | 4.50 | 9.00 | — |
| 1941H | 3,000,000 | 250 | 350 | 525 | 900 | — |

**Note:** Estimate 50 pieces exist.

**5 CENTS** KM# 8 **Weight:** 1.3500 g. **Composition:** 0.8000 Silver .0347 oz. ASW **Ruler:** Charles J. Brooke Rajah

| Date | Mintage | F | VF | XF | Unc | BU |
|---|---|---|---|---|---|---|
| 1908H | 40,000 | 30.00 | 50.00 | 90.00 | 140 | — |
| 1908H Proof | — | Value: 350 | | | | |
| 1911H | 40,000 | 30.00 | 50.00 | 90.00 | 140 | — |
| 1913H | 100,000 | 20.00 | 40.00 | 70.00 | 120 | — |
| 1913H Proof | — | Value: 350 | | | | |

| Date | Mintage | F | VF | XF | Unc | BU |
|---|---|---|---|---|---|---|
| 1915H | 100,000 | 20.00 | 40.00 | 75.00 | 130 | — |
| 1915H Proof | — | Value: 350 | | | | |

**5 CENTS** **KM# 13** **Weight:** 1.3500 g. **Composition:** 0.4000 Silver .0174 oz. ASW **Ruler:** Charles V. Brooke Rajah

| Date | Mintage | F | VF | XF | Unc | BU |
|---|---|---|---|---|---|---|
| 1920H | 100,000 | 40.00 | 60.00 | 100 | 180 | — |
| 1920H Proof | — | Value: 400 | | | | |

**5 CENTS** **KM# 14** **Composition:** Copper-Nickel **Ruler:** Charles V. Brooke Rajah

| Date | Mintage | F | VF | XF | Unc | BU |
|---|---|---|---|---|---|---|
| 1920H | 400,000 | 2.00 | 4.00 | 8.00 | 20.00 | — |
| 1927H | 600,000 | 2.00 | 4.00 | 8.00 | 20.00 | — |
| 1927H Proof | — | Value: 275 | | | | |

**10 CENTS** **KM# 9** **Weight:** 2.7100 g. **Composition:** 0.8000 Silver .0697 oz. ASW **Ruler:** Charles J. Brooke Rajah

| Date | Mintage | F | VF | XF | Unc | BU |
|---|---|---|---|---|---|---|
| 1900H | 150,000 | 15.00 | 22.00 | 45.00 | 95.00 | — |
| 1900H Proof | — | Value: 300 | | | | |
| 1906H | 50,000 | 20.00 | 30.00 | 55.00 | 100 | — |
| 1906H Proof | — | Value: 350 | | | | |
| 1910H | 50,000 | 20.00 | 30.00 | 55.00 | 100 | — |
| 1910H Proof | — | Value: 350 | | | | |
| 1911/10H | 100,000 | 20.00 | 30.00 | 60.00 | 120 | — |
| 1911H | Inc. above | 15.00 | 20.00 | 40.00 | 90.00 | — |
| 1913H | 100,000 | 15.00 | 20.00 | 40.00 | 90.00 | — |
| 1913H Proof | — | Value: 350 | | | | |
| 1915H | 100,000 | 30.00 | 45.00 | 75.00 | 185 | — |
| 1915H Proof | — | Value: 350 | | | | |

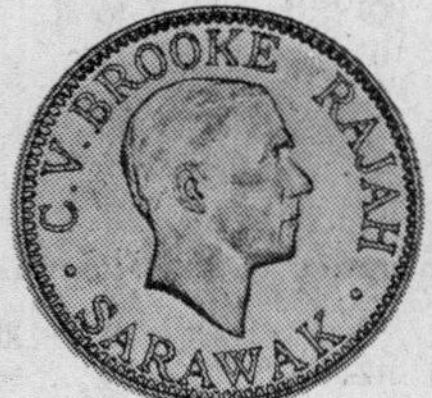

**10 CENTS** **KM# 15** **Weight:** 2.7100 g. **Composition:** 0.4000 Silver .0349 oz. ASW **Ruler:** Charles V. Brooke Rajah

| Date | Mintage | F | VF | XF | Unc | BU |
|---|---|---|---|---|---|---|
| 1920H | 150,000 | 18.00 | 27.50 | 50.00 | 90.00 | — |
| 1920H Proof | — | Value: 350 | | | | |

**10 CENTS** **KM# 16** **Composition:** Copper-Nickel **Ruler:** Charles V. Brooke Rajah

| Date | Mintage | F | VF | XF | Unc | BU |
|---|---|---|---|---|---|---|
| 1920H | 800,000 | 2.00 | 4.00 | 8.00 | 17.50 | — |
| 1927H | 1,000,000 | 2.00 | 3.00 | 6.00 | 17.50 | — |
| 1927H Proof | — | Value: 300 | | | | |
| 1934H | 2,000,000 | 2.00 | 3.00 | 6.00 | 17.50 | — |
| 1934H Proof | — | Value: 300 | | | | |

**20 CENTS** **KM# 10** **Weight:** 5.4300 g. **Composition:** 0.8000 Silver .1396 oz. ASW **Ruler:** Charles J. Brooke Rajah

| Date | Mintage | F | VF | XF | Unc | BU |
|---|---|---|---|---|---|---|
| 1906H | 25,000 | 30.00 | 62.50 | 110 | 220 | — |
| 1906H Proof | — | Value: 550 | | | | |
| 1910H | 25,000 | 30.00 | 62.50 | 110 | 220 | — |
| 1910H Proof | — | Value: 550 | | | | |
| 1911H | 15,000 | 30.00 | 62.50 | 110 | 220 | — |
| 1913H | 25,000 | 30.00 | 62.50 | 110 | 220 | — |
| 1913H Proof | — | Value: 550 | | | | |

| Date | Mintage | F | VF | XF | Unc | BU |
|---|---|---|---|---|---|---|
| 1915H | 25,000 | 125 | 175 | 300 | 500 | — |
| 1915H Proof | — | Value: 725 | | | | |

**20 CENTS** **KM# 17** **Weight:** 5.4300 g. **Composition:** 0.4000 Silver .0699 oz. ASW **Ruler:** Charles V. Brooke Rajah

| Date | Mintage | F | VF | XF | Unc | BU |
|---|---|---|---|---|---|---|
| 1920 | 25,000 | 65.00 | 120 | 220 | 400 | — |
| 1920 Proof | — | Value: 600 | | | | |

**20 CENTS** **KM# 17a** **Weight:** 5.0800 g. **Composition:** 0.4000 Silver .0653 oz. ASW **Ruler:** Charles V. Brooke Rajah

| Date | Mintage | F | VF | XF | Unc | BU |
|---|---|---|---|---|---|---|
| 1927H | 250,000 | 5.00 | 10.00 | 22.50 | 50.00 | — |
| 1927H Proof | — | Value: 400 | | | | |

**50 CENTS** **KM# 11** **Weight:** 13.5700 g. **Composition:** 0.8000 Silver .349 oz. ASW **Ruler:** Charles V. Brooke Rajah

| Date | Mintage | F | VF | XF | Unc | BU |
|---|---|---|---|---|---|---|
| 1906H | 10,000 | 225 | 325 | 500 | 950 | — |
| 1906H Proof | — | Value: 1,350 | | | | |

**50 CENTS** **KM# 19** **Weight:** 10.3000 g. **Composition:** 0.5000 Silver .1656 oz. ASW **Ruler:** Charles V. Brooke Rajah

| Date | Mintage | F | VF | XF | Unc | BU |
|---|---|---|---|---|---|---|
| 1927H | 200,000 | 12.00 | 20.00 | 38.00 | 90.00 | — |
| 1927H Proof | — | Value: 400 | | | | |

# SAUDI ARABIA

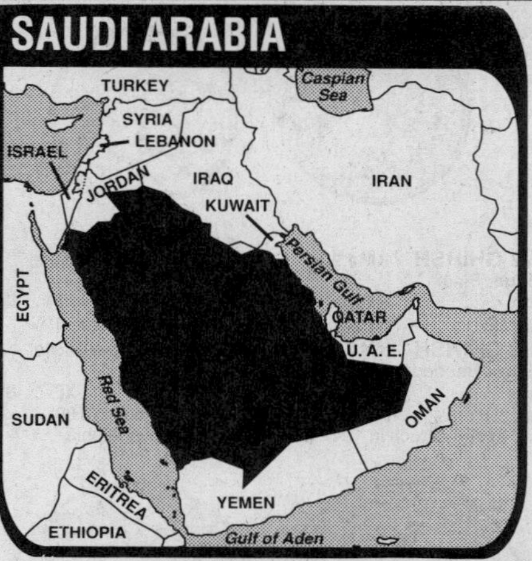


The Kingdom of Saudi Arabia, an independent and absolute hereditary monarchy comprising the former sultanate of Nejd, the old kingdom of Hejaz, Asir and Al Hasa, occupies four-fifths of the Arabian peninsula. The kingdom has an area of 830,000 sq. mi. (2,149,690 sq. km.) and a population of *16.1 million. Capital: Riyadh. The economy is based on oil, which provides 85 percent of Saudi Arabia's revenue.

Mohammed united the Arabs in the 7th century and his followers founded a great empire with its capital at Medina. The Turks established nominal rule over much of Arabia in the 16th and 17th centuries, and in the 18thcentury divided it into principalities.

The Kingdom of Saudi Arabia was created by King Abd Al-Aziz Bin Saud (1882-1953), a descendant of earlier Wahhabi rulers of the Arabian peninsula. In 1901 he seized Riyadh, capital of the Sultanate of Nejd, and in 1905 established himself as Sultan. In 1913 he captured the Turkish province of Al Hasa; took the Hejaz in 1925 and by 1926 most of Asir. In1932 he combined Nejd and Hejaz into the single kingdom of Saudi Arabia. Asir was incorporated into the kingdom a year later.

**TITLES**

العربية السعودية

Al-Arabiya(t) as-Sa'udiya(t)

المملكة العربية السعودية

Al-Mamlaka(t) al-'Arabiya(t) as-Sa'udiya(t)

**RULERS**

**al Sa'ud Dynasty**

Abd Al-Aziz Bin Sa'ud, (Ibn Sa'ud), AH1344-1373/1926-1953AD
Sa'ud Bin Abd Al-Aziz, AH1373-1383/1953-1964AD
Faisal Bin Abd Al-Aziz, AH1383-1395/1964-1975AD
Khalid Bin Abd Al-Aziz, AH1395-1403/1975-1982AD
Fahad Bin Abd Al-Aziz, AH1403-/1982-AD

**MONETARY SYSTEM**

Until 1960

20-22 Ghirsh = 1 Riyal
40 Riyals = 1 Guinea

**NOTE:** Copper-nickel, reeded-edge coins dated AH1356 and silver coins dated AH1354 were struck at the U. S. Mint in Philadelphia between 1944-1949.

## KINGDOM

### STANDARD COINAGE

**1/4 GHIRSH** **KM# 19.1** **Composition:** Copper-Nickel **Edge:** Plain

| Date | Mintage | VG | F | VF | XF | Unc |
|---|---|---|---|---|---|---|
| AH1356 | 1,000,000 | 1.00 | 2.00 | 6.00 | 15.00 | — |

**1/4 GHIRSH** **KM# 19.2** **Composition:** Copper-Nickel **Edge:** Reeded

| Date | Mintage | VG | F | VF | XF | Unc |
|---|---|---|---|---|---|---|
| AH1356 | 21,500,000 | 0.25 | 0.50 | 1.00 | 2.50 | — |

**Note:** Struck in 1947 (AH1366-67) at Philadelphia

**1/2 GHIRSH** **KM# 20.1** **Composition:** Copper-Nickel **Edge:** Plain

| Date | Mintage | VG | F | VF | XF | Unc |
|---|---|---|---|---|---|---|
| AH1356 | 1,000,000 | 1.25 | 3.00 | 8.00 | 20.00 | — |

**1/2 GHIRSH** **KM# 20.2** **Composition:** Copper-Nickel **Edge:** Reeded

| Date | Mintage | VG | F | VF | XF | Unc |
|---|---|---|---|---|---|---|
| AH1356 | 10,850,000 | 0.20 | 0.50 | 1.50 | 3.00 | — |

**Note:** Struck in 1947 (AH1366-67) at Philadelphia

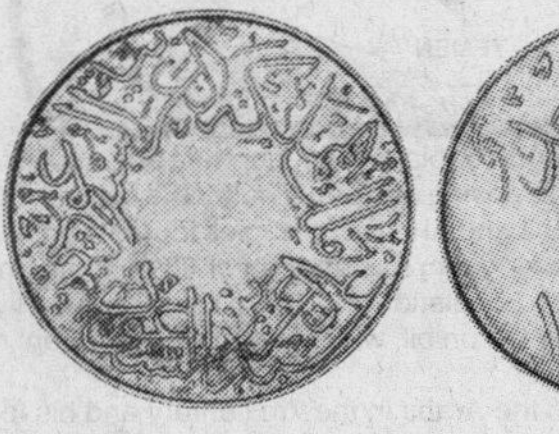

**GHIRSH** **KM# 21.1** **Composition:** Copper-Nickel **Edge:** Plain

| Date | Mintage | VG | F | VF | XF | Unc |
|---|---|---|---|---|---|---|
| AH1356 | 4,000,000 | 1.00 | 2.00 | 6.00 | 15.00 | — |

**GHIRSH** **KM# 21.2** **Composition:** Copper-Nickel **Edge:** Reeded

| Date | Mintage | VG | F | VF | XF | Unc |
|---|---|---|---|---|---|---|
| AH1356 | 7,150,000 | 0.50 | 1.00 | 2.50 | 5.00 | — |

**Note:** Struck in 1947 (AH1366-67) at Philadelphia

**GHIRSH** **KM# 40** **Composition:** Copper-Nickel

| Date | Mintage | F | VF | XF | Unc | BU |
|---|---|---|---|---|---|---|
| AH1376 | 10,000,000 | 0.15 | 0.25 | 0.50 | 3.00 | — |
| AH1378 | 50,000,000 | 0.15 | 0.25 | 0.50 | 2.00 | — |

**2 GHIRSH** **KM# 41** **Composition:** Copper-Nickel

| Date | Mintage | F | VF | XF | Unc | BU |
|---|---|---|---|---|---|---|
| AH1376 | 50,000,000 | 0.10 | 0.35 | 0.75 | 5.00 | — |
| AH1379 | 28,110,000 | 0.10 | 0.35 | 0.70 | 3.50 | — |

**4 GHIRSH** **KM# 42** **Composition:** Copper-Nickel

| Date | Mintage | F | VF | XF | Unc | BU |
|---|---|---|---|---|---|---|
| AH1376 | 49,100,000 | 0.25 | 0.50 | 1.00 | 6.00 | — |
| AH1378 | 10,000,000 | 0.25 | 0.50 | 1.00 | 5.00 | — |

**1/4 RIYAL** **KM# 16** **Weight:** 3.1000 g. **Composition:** 0.9170 Silver .0913 oz. ASW

| Date | Mintage | F | VF | XF | Unc | BU |
|---|---|---|---|---|---|---|
| AH1354 | 900,000 | 1.75 | 2.50 | 3.00 | 5.50 | — |
| AH1354 Proof | — | Value: 150 | | | | |

**1/4 RIYAL** **KM# 37** **Weight:** 2.9500 g. **Composition:** 0.9170 Silver .0869 oz. ASW

| Date | Mintage | F | VF | XF | Unc | BU |
|---|---|---|---|---|---|---|
| AH1374 | 4,000,000 | BV | 1.00 | 3.00 | 5.50 | — |

**1/2 RIYAL** **KM# 17** **Weight:** 5.8500 g. **Composition:** 0.9170 Silver .1724 oz. ASW

| Date | Mintage | F | VF | XF | Unc | BU |
|---|---|---|---|---|---|---|
| AH1354 | 950,000 | 1.50 | 4.00 | 6.00 | 12.50 | — |

**1/2 RIYAL** **KM# 38** **Weight:** 5.9500 g. **Composition:** 0.9170 Silver .1754 oz. ASW

| Date | Mintage | F | VF | XF | Unc | BU |
|---|---|---|---|---|---|---|
| AH1374 | 2,000,000 | 1.50 | 3.00 | 4.50 | 10.00 | — |

**RIYAL** **KM# 18** **Weight:** 11.6000 g. **Composition:** 0.9170 Silver .3419 oz. ASW

| Date | Mintage | F | VF | XF | Unc | BU |
|---|---|---|---|---|---|---|
| AH1354 | 60,000,000 | BV | 2.50 | 5.50 | 12.50 | — |
| AH1354 Proof | 20,000,000 | — | — | — | — | — |
| AH1367 | Inc. above | BV | 2.50 | 5.50 | 15.00 | — |
| AH1370 | — | BV | 2.50 | 5.50 | 17.50 | — |

**RIYAL** **KM# 39** **Weight:** 11.6000 g. **Composition:** 0.9170 Silver .3419 oz. ASW

| Date | Mintage | F | VF | XF | Unc | BU |
|---|---|---|---|---|---|---|
| AH1374 | 48,000,000 | BV | 2.50 | 6.00 | 17.50 | — |

## COUNTERMARKED COINAGE

70 = "65"/Countermark

The following pieces are countermarked examples of earlier types bearing the Arabic numerals "65". They were countermarked in a move to break money changers'monopoly on small coins in AH1365 (1946AD). These countermarks vary in size and are found with the Arabic numbers raised in a circle. Incuse countermarks are considered a recent fabrication.

**1/4 GHIRSH** **KM# 24** **Countermark:** "65" **Note:** Countermark in Arabic numerals on 1/4 Ghirsh, KM#13.

| CM Date | Host Date | Good | VG | F | VF | XF |
|---|---|---|---|---|---|---|
| AH65 | AH1348 | 6.00 | 12.00 | 30.00 | 65.00 | — |

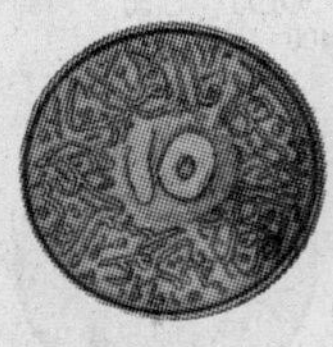

**1/4 GHIRSH** **KM# 25** **Countermark:** "65" **Edge:** Plain **Note:** Countermark in Arabic numerals on 1/4 Ghirsh, KM#19.

| CM Date | Host Date | Good | VG | F | VF | XF |
|---|---|---|---|---|---|---|
| AH65 | AH1356 | 2.50 | 4.00 | 8.00 | 15.00 | — |

**1/4 GHIRSH** **KM# 22** **Countermark:** "65" **Note:** Countermark in Arabic numerals on 1/4 Ghirsh, KM#4.

| CM Date | Host Date | Good | VG | F | VF | XF |
|---|---|---|---|---|---|---|
| AH65 | AH1344 | 6.00 | 12.00 | 30.00 | 65.00 | — |

**1/4 GHIRSH** **KM# 23** **Countermark:** "65" **Note:** Countermark in Arabic numerals on 1/4 Ghirsh, KM#7.

| CM Date | Host Date | Good | VG | F | VF | XF |
|---|---|---|---|---|---|---|
| AH65 | AH1346 | 6.00 | 12.00 | 30.00 | 65.00 | — |

**1/2 GHIRSH** **KM# 28** **Countermark:** "65" **Note:** Countermark in Arabic numerals on 1/2 Ghirsh, KM#14.

| CM Date | Host Date | Good | VG | F | VF | XF |
|---|---|---|---|---|---|---|
| AH65 | AH1348 | 6.00 | 12.00 | 25.00 | 60.00 | — |

**1/2 GHIRSH** **KM# 29** **Countermark:** "65" **Edge:** Plain **Note:** Countermark in Arabic numerals on 1/2 Ghirsh, KM#20.1.

| CM Date | Host Date | Good | VG | F | VF | XF |
|---|---|---|---|---|---|---|
| AH65 | AH1356 | 1.25 | 2.25 | 5.00 | 12.00 | — |

**1/2 GHIRSH** **KM# 26** **Countermark:** "65" **Note:** Countermark in Arabic numerals on 1/2 Ghirsh, KM#5.

| CM Date | Host Date | Good | VG | F | VF | XF |
|---|---|---|---|---|---|---|
| AH65 | AH1344 | 6.00 | 12.00 | 25.00 | 60.00 | — |

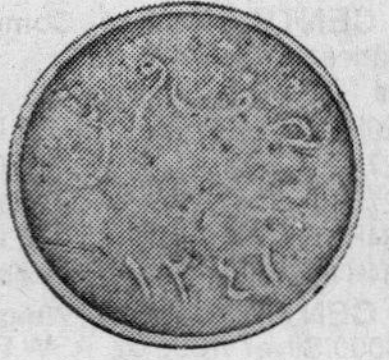

**1/2 GHIRSH** **KM# 27** **Countermark:** "65" **Note:** Countermark in Arabic numerals on 1/2 Ghirsh, KM#8.

| CM Date | Host Date | Good | VG | F | VF | XF |
|---|---|---|---|---|---|---|
| AH65 | AH1346 | 6.00 | 12.00 | 25.00 | 60.00 | — |

**GHIRSH** KM# 32 **Countermark:** "65" **Note:** Countermark in Arabic numerals on 1 Ghirsh, KM#15.

| CM Date | Host Date | Good | VG | F | VF | XF |
|---|---|---|---|---|---|---|
| AH65 | AH1348 | 10.00 | 20.00 | 50.00 | 90.00 | — |

**GHIRSH** KM# 33 **Countermark:** "65" **Edge:** Plain **Note:** Countermark in Arabic numerals on 1 Ghirsh, KM#21.

| CM Date | Host Date | Good | VG | F | VF | XF |
|---|---|---|---|---|---|---|
| AH65 | AH1356 | 2.00 | 3.00 | 8.00 | 20.00 | — |

**GHIRSH** KM# 30 **Countermark:** "65" **Note:** Countermark in Arabic numerals on 1 Ghirsh, KM#6.

| CM Date | Host Date | Good | VG | F | VF | XF |
|---|---|---|---|---|---|---|
| AH65 | AH1344 | 6.00 | 12.00 | 45.00 | 80.00 | — |

**GHIRSH** KM# 31 **Countermark:** "65" **Note:** Countermark in Arabic numerals on 1 Ghirsh, KM#9.

| CM Date | Host Date | Good | VG | F | VF | XF |
|---|---|---|---|---|---|---|
| AH65 | AH1346 | 6.00 | 12.00 | 30.00 | 65.00 | — |

## REFORM COINAGE

5 Halala = 1 Ghirsh; 100 Halala = 1 Riyal

**HALALA** KM# 44 **Composition:** Bronze

| Date | Mintage | F | VF | XF | Unc | BU |
|---|---|---|---|---|---|---|
| AH1383 | 5,000,000 | 0.50 | 0.60 | 0.85 | 3.00 | — |

**HALALA** KM# 60 **Composition:** Bronze **Obverse:** Different inscription

| Date | Mintage | F | VF | XF | Unc | BU |
|---|---|---|---|---|---|---|
| AH1397 Rare | — | — | — | — | — | — |

**Note:** Not released for circulation

**5 HALALA (Ghirsh)** KM# 45 **Composition:** Copper-Nickel

| Date | Mintage | F | VF | XF | Unc | BU |
|---|---|---|---|---|---|---|
| AH1392 | 130,000,000 | 0.10 | 0.15 | 0.30 | 0.50 | — |

**5 HALALA (Ghirsh)** KM# 53 **Composition:** Copper-Nickel

| Date | Mintage | F | VF | XF | Unc | BU |
|---|---|---|---|---|---|---|
| AH1397 | 20,000,000 | 0.15 | 0.25 | 0.60 | 2.00 | — |
| AH1400 | — | 0.15 | 0.25 | 0.60 | 2.00 | — |

**5 HALALA (Ghirsh)** KM# 57 **Composition:** Copper-Nickel **Series:** F.A.O.

| Date | Mintage | F | VF | XF | Unc | BU |
|---|---|---|---|---|---|---|
| AH1398(1977) | 1,500,000 | — | 0.30 | 0.50 | 1.00 | — |

**5 HALALA (Ghirsh)** KM# 61 **Composition:** Copper-Nickel

| Date | Mintage | F | VF | XF | Unc | BU |
|---|---|---|---|---|---|---|
| AH1408 | 80,000,000 | — | 0.30 | 0.50 | 1.00 | — |
| AH1408 Proof | 5,000 | Value: 5.00 | | | | |

**10 HALALA (2 Ghirsh)** KM# 46 **Composition:** Copper-Nickel

| Date | Mintage | F | VF | XF | Unc | BU |
|---|---|---|---|---|---|---|
| AH1392 | 55,000,000 | 0.10 | 0.20 | 0.35 | 0.50 | — |

**10 HALALA (2 Ghirsh)** KM# 54 **Composition:** Copper-Nickel

| Date | Mintage | F | VF | XF | Unc | BU |
|---|---|---|---|---|---|---|
| AH1397 | 50,000,000 | 0.15 | 0.25 | 1.00 | 2.50 | — |
| AH1400 | 29,500,000 | 0.25 | 0.75 | 1.00 | 3.00 | — |

**10 HALALA (2 Ghirsh)** KM# 58 **Composition:** Copper-Nickel **Series:** F.A.O.

| Date | Mintage | F | VF | XF | Unc | BU |
|---|---|---|---|---|---|---|
| AH1398(1977) | 1,000,000 | — | 0.25 | 0.50 | 1.00 | — |

**10 HALALA (2 Ghirsh)** KM# 62 **Composition:** Copper-Nickel

| Date | Mintage | F | VF | XF | Unc | BU |
|---|---|---|---|---|---|---|
| AH1408 | 100,000,000 | — | 0.30 | 0.60 | 1.25 | — |
| AH1408 Proof | 5,000 | Value: 6.00 | | | | |

**25 HALALA (1/4 Riyal)** KM# 48 **Composition:** Copper-Nickel **Note:** Corrected denomination; feminine gender.

| Date | Mintage | F | VF | XF | Unc | BU |
|---|---|---|---|---|---|---|
| AH1392 | Inc. above | 0.25 | 0.50 | 1.00 | 2.00 | — |

**25 HALALA (1/4 Riyal)** KM# 47 **Composition:** Copper-Nickel **Note:** Error. Denomination in masculine gender.

| Date | Mintage | F | VF | XF | Unc | BU |
|---|---|---|---|---|---|---|
| AH1392 | 48,465,000 | 1.00 | 2.00 | 6.00 | 15.00 | — |

**25 HALALA (1/4 Riyal)** KM# 49 **Composition:** Copper-Nickel **Series:** F.A.O.

| Date | Mintage | F | VF | XF | Unc | BU |
|---|---|---|---|---|---|---|
| AH1392(1972) | 200,000 | — | 0.20 | 0.50 | 1.00 | — |

**25 HALALA (1/4 Riyal)** KM# 55 **Composition:** Copper-Nickel

| Date | Mintage | F | VF | XF | Unc | BU |
|---|---|---|---|---|---|---|
| AH1397 | 20,000,000 | 0.35 | 0.50 | 1.00 | 3.00 | — |
| AH1400 | 57,000,000 | 0.35 | 0.50 | 0.85 | 2.50 | — |

**25 HALALA (1/4 Riyal)** KM# 63 **Composition:** Copper-Nickel

| Date | Mintage | F | VF | XF | Unc | BU |
|---|---|---|---|---|---|---|
| AH1408 | 100,000,000 | — | 0.40 | 0.70 | 1.50 | — |
| AH1408 Proof | 5,000 | Value: 7.50 | | | | |

**50 HALALA (1/2 Riyal)** KM# 51 **Composition:** Copper-Nickel

| Date | Mintage | F | VF | XF | Unc | BU |
|---|---|---|---|---|---|---|
| AH1392 | 16,000,000 | 0.20 | 0.35 | 0.60 | 2.00 | — |

**50 HALALA (1/2 Riyal)** KM# 50 **Composition:** Copper-Nickel **Series:** F.A.O.

| Date | Mintage | F | VF | XF | Unc | BU |
|---|---|---|---|---|---|---|
| AH1392(1972) | 500,000 | — | 0.30 | 0.60 | 2.50 | — |

**50 HALALA (1/2 Riyal)** **KM# 56** **Composition:** Copper-Nickel

| Date | Mintage | F | VF | XF | Unc | BU |
|---|---|---|---|---|---|---|
| AH1397 | 20,000,000 | 0.50 | 0.75 | 1.00 | 3.00 | — |
| AH1400 | 21,600,000 | 0.75 | 1.00 | 1.50 | 3.50 | — |

**50 HALALA (1/2 Riyal)** **KM# 64** **Composition:** Copper-Nickel

| Date | Mintage | F | VF | XF | Unc | BU |
|---|---|---|---|---|---|---|
| AH1408 | 70,000,000 | 0.20 | 0.50 | 2.25 | 3.50 | — |
| AH1408 Proof | 5,000 | Value: 15.00 | | | | |

**100 HALALA (1 Riyal)** **KM# 52** **Composition:** Copper-Nickel

| Date | Mintage | F | VF | XF | Unc | BU |
|---|---|---|---|---|---|---|
| AH1396(1976) | 250,000 | — | 0.65 | 1.00 | 3.50 | — |
| AH1400(1980) | 30,000,000 | — | 0.65 | 1.00 | 3.00 | — |

**100 HALALA (1 Riyal)** **KM# 59** **Composition:** Copper-Nickel **Series:** F.A.O.

| Date | Mintage | F | VF | XF | Unc | BU |
|---|---|---|---|---|---|---|
| AH1397(1977) | — | — | — | 125 | 225 | — |
| AH1398(1978) | 10,000,000 | — | 0.75 | 1.50 | 3.50 | — |

**Note:** AH1397 date was struck as samples for the Saudi-Arabia government by the British Royal Mint

**100 HALALA (1 Riyal)** **KM# 65** **Composition:** Copper-Nickel

| Date | Mintage | F | VF | XF | Unc | BU |
|---|---|---|---|---|---|---|
| AH1408(1987) | 40,000,000 | — | 1.00 | 2.00 | 3.00 | — |
| AH1408(1987) Proof | 5,000 | Value: 22.00 | | | | |
| AH1414(1993) | 5,000 | — | 1.00 | 2.00 | 4.00 | — |

**100 HALALA (1 Riyal)** **KM# 66** **Ring Composition:** Copper-Nickel **Center Composition:** Brass **Obverse:** Palm tree above crossed swords **Reverse:** Inscription, denomination, and date

| Date | Mintage | F | VF | XF | Unc | BU |
|---|---|---|---|---|---|---|
| AH1419(1999) | — | — | 1.00 | 2.00 | 3.00 | — |

**100 HALALA (1 Riyal)** **KM# 67** **Ring Composition:** Copper-Nickel **Center Composition:** Brass **Subject:** Centennial of Kingdom **Obverse:** Palm tree design and inscription **Reverse:** Inscription, denomination, and date

| Date | Mintage | F | VF | XF | Unc | BU |
|---|---|---|---|---|---|---|
| AH1419(1999) | — | — | 1.50 | 2.50 | 5.00 | — |
| AH1419(1999) Proof | — | Value: 15.00 | | | | |

## TRADE COINAGE

**GUINEA** **KM# 36** **Weight:** 7.9881 g. **Composition:** 0.9170 Gold .2354 oz. AGW

| Date | Mintage | F | VF | XF | Unc | BU |
|---|---|---|---|---|---|---|
| AH1370 | 2,000,000 | — | BV | 95.00 | 125 | — |

**GUINEA** **KM# 43** **Weight:** 7.9881 g. **Composition:** 0.9170 Gold .2354 oz. AGW

| Date | Mintage | F | VF | XF | Unc | BU |
|---|---|---|---|---|---|---|
| AH1377 | 1,579,000 | — | BV | 100 | 145 | — |

## BULLION COINAGE

**SOVEREIGN (Pound)** **KM# 35** **Weight:** 7.9881 g. **Composition:** 0.9170 Gold .2354 oz. AGW

| Date | Mintage | F | VF | XF | Unc | BU |
|---|---|---|---|---|---|---|
| ND(1947) | 123,000 | — | 300 | 500 | 750 | — |

**4 POUNDS** **KM# 34** **Weight:** 31.9500 g. **Composition:** 0.9170 Gold .9420 oz. AGW

| Date | Mintage | F | VF | XF | Unc | BU |
|---|---|---|---|---|---|---|
| ND(1945-46) | 91,000 | — | — | 600 | 800 | — |

**Note:** KM#35 and KM#34 were struck at the Philadelphia Mint for a concession payment for oil to the Saudi Government; most were melted into bullion

## MINT SETS

| KM# | Date | Mintage | Identification | Issue Price | Mkt Val |
|---|---|---|---|---|---|
| MS1 | AH1408(1988) (5) | — | KM#61-65 | 20.00 | 25.00 |

## PROOF SETS

| KM# | Date | Mintage | Identification | Issue Price | Mkt Val |
|---|---|---|---|---|---|
| PS1 | AH1408(1988) (5) | 5,000 | KM#61-65 | 40.00 | 55.00 |

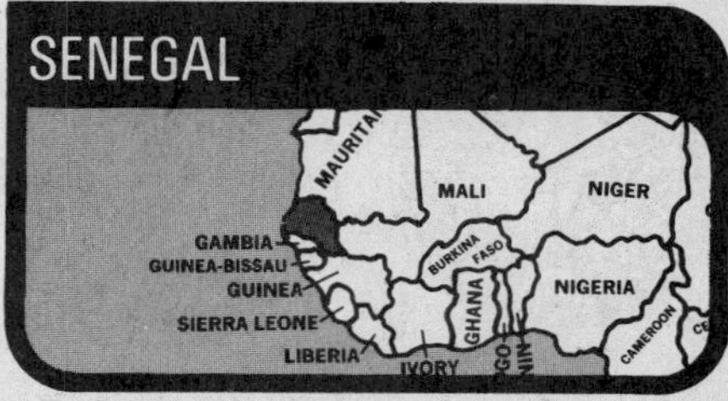


The Republic of Senegal, located on the bulge of West Africa between Mauritania and Guinea-Bissau, has an area of 75,750 sq. mi. (196,190 sq. km.) and a population of *7.5 million. Capital: Dakar. The economy is primarily agricultural. Peanuts and products, phosphates, and canned fish are exported.

An abundance of megalithic remains indicates that Senegal was inhabited in prehistoric times. The Portuguese had some trading stations on the banks of the Senegal River in the 15th century. French commercial establishments date from the 17th century. The French gradually acquired control over the interior regions, which were administered as a protectorate until 1920, and as a colony thereafter. After the 1958 French constitutional referendum, Senegal became a member of the French Community with virtual autonomy. In 1959 Senegal and the French Soudan merged to form the Mali Federation, which became fully independent on June 20, 1960. (April 4, the date the transfer of power agreement was signed with France, is celebrated as Senegal's independence day). The Federation broke up on Aug. 20, 1960, when Senegal seceded and proclaimed the Republic of Senegal. Soudan became the Republic of Mali a month later.

Senegal is a member of a monetary union of autonomous republics called the Monetary Union of West African States (*Union Monetaire Ouest-Africaine*). The other members are Ivory Coast, Benin, Burkina Faso (Upper Volta), Niger, Mauritania and Togo. Mali was a member, but seceded in1962. Some of the member countries have issued coinage in addition to the common currency issued by the Monetary Union of West African States.

# REPUBLIC

## STANDARD COINAGE

**10 FRANCS** **KM# 1** **Weight:** 3.2000 g. **Composition:** 0.9000 Gold .0926 oz. AGW **Subject:** 8th anniversary of independence

| Date | Mintage | F | VF | XF | Unc | BU |
|---|---|---|---|---|---|---|
| 1968 Proof | — | Value: 65.00 | | | | |

**25 FRANCS** **KM# 2** **Weight:** 8.0000 g. **Composition:** 0.9000 Gold .2315 oz. AGW **Subject:** 8th anniversary of independence

| Date | Mintage | F | VF | XF | Unc | BU |
|---|---|---|---|---|---|---|
| 1968 Proof | — | Value: 125 | | | | |

**50 FRANCS** **KM# 3** **Weight:** 16.0000 g. **Composition:** 0.9000 Gold .463 oz. AGW **Subject:** 8th anniversary of independence

| Date | Mintage | F | VF | XF | Unc | BU |
|---|---|---|---|---|---|---|
| 1968 Proof | — | Value: 250 | | | | |

**50 FRANCS** **KM# 5** **Weight:** 28.2800 g. **Composition:** 0.9250 Silver .8411 oz. ASW **Subject:** 25th anniversary of Eurafrique Program

| Date | Mintage | F | VF | XF | Unc | BU |
|---|---|---|---|---|---|---|
| 1975 | 1,968 | — | — | — | 100 | — |
| 1975 Proof | 10,000 | Value: 125 | | | | |

**100 FRANCS** **KM#4** **Weight:** 32.0000 g. **Composition:** 0.9000 Gold .926 oz. AGW **Subject:** 8th anniversary of independence

| Date | Mintage | F | VF | XF | Unc | BU |
|---|---|---|---|---|---|---|
| 1968 Proof | — | Value: 450 | | | | |

**150 FRANCS** **KM# 6** **Weight:** 79.9700 g. **Composition:** 0.9250 Silver 2.3776 oz. ASW **Subject:** 25th anniversary of Eurafrique Program **Reverse:** Similar to 50 Francs, KM#5.

| Date | Mintage | F | VF | XF | Unc | BU |
|---|---|---|---|---|---|---|
| 1975 | 1,075 | — | — | — | 150 | — |
| 1975 Proof | 10,000 | Value: 175 | | | | |

**250 FRANCS** **KM# 7** **Weight:** 3.9800 g. **Composition:** 0.9170 Gold .1172 oz. AGW **Subject:** 25th anniversary of Eurafrique Program

| Date | Mintage | F | VF | XF | Unc | BU |
|---|---|---|---|---|---|---|
| 1975 | 1,000 | — | — | — | 75.00 | — |
| 1975 Proof | 1,250 | Value: 75.00 | | | | |

**500 FRANCS** **KM# 8** **Weight:** 7.9600 g. **Composition:** 0.9170 Gold .2344 oz. AGW **Subject:** 25th anniversary of Eurafrique Program

| Date | Mintage | F | VF | XF | Unc | BU |
|---|---|---|---|---|---|---|
| 1975 | 500 | — | — | — | 150 | — |
| 1975 Proof | 1,250 | Value: 125 | | | | |

**1000 FRANCS** **KM# 9** **Weight:** 15.9500 g. **Composition:** 0.9160 Gold .4697 oz. AGW **Subject:** 25th anniversary of Eurafrique Program

| Date | Mintage | F | VF | XF | Unc | BU |
|---|---|---|---|---|---|---|
| 1975 | 217 | — | — | — | 285 | — |
| 1975 Proof | 1,250 | Value: 250 | | | | |

**2500 FRANCS** **KM#10** **Weight:** 39.9300 g. **Composition:** 0.9160 Gold 1.176 oz. AGW **Subject:** 25th anniversary of Eurafrique Program

| Date | Mintage | F | VF | XF | Unc | BU |
|---|---|---|---|---|---|---|
| 1975 | 195 | — | — | — | 685 | — |
| 1975 Proof | 1,250 | Value: 650 | | | | |

## TOKEN COINAGE

**5 CENTIMES** **KM# Tn2** **Composition:** Aluminum **Issuer:** Dakar, Chamber of Commerce

| Date | Mintage | VG | F | VF | XF | Unc |
|---|---|---|---|---|---|---|
| 1920 | — | 9.00 | 18.00 | 40.00 | 120 | — |

**5 CENTIMES** **KM# Tn7** **Composition:** Aluminum **Issuer:** Kayes, Upper Senegal-Niger Chamber of Commerce

| Date | Mintage | VG | F | VF | XF | Unc |
|---|---|---|---|---|---|---|
| 1920 | — | 12.00 | 22.00 | 45.00 | 125 | — |

**5 CENTIMES** **KM# Tn12** **Composition:** Aluminum **Issuer:** Rufisque, Chamber of Commerce

| Date | Mintage | VG | F | VF | XF | Unc |
|---|---|---|---|---|---|---|
| 1920 | — | 9.00 | 18.00 | 40.00 | 120 | — |

**10 CENTIMES** **KM# Tn3** **Composition:** Aluminum **Issuer:** Dakar, Chamber of Commerce

| Date | Mintage | VG | F | VF | XF | Unc |
|---|---|---|---|---|---|---|
| 1920 | — | 6.00 | 12.00 | 30.00 | 90.00 | — |

**10 CENTIMES** **KM# Tn8** **Composition:** Aluminum **Issuer:** Kayes, Upper Senegal-Niger Chamber of Commerce

| Date | Mintage | VG | F | VF | XF | Unc |
|---|---|---|---|---|---|---|
| 1920 | — | 14.00 | 28.00 | 60.00 | 150 | — |

**10 CENTIMES** **KM# Tn13** **Composition:** Aluminum **Issuer:** Rufisque, Chamber of Commerce

| Date | Mintage | VG | F | VF | XF | Unc |
|---|---|---|---|---|---|---|
| 1920 | — | 6.00 | 12.00 | 30.00 | 100 | — |

**10 CENTIMES** **KM# Tn4** **Composition:** Brass **Issuer:** Dakar, Chamber of Commerce

| Date | Mintage | VG | F | VF | XF | Unc |
|---|---|---|---|---|---|---|
| 1920 | — | 9.00 | 18.00 | 40.00 | 120 | — |

**25 CENTIMES** **KM# Tn5** **Composition:** Aluminum **Issuer:** Dakar, Chamber of Commerce

| Date | Mintage | VG | F | VF | XF | Unc |
|---|---|---|---|---|---|---|
| 1920 | — | 7.00 | 15.00 | 35.00 | 100 | — |

**25 CENTIMES** **KM# Tn9** **Composition:** Aluminum **Issuer:** Kayes, Upper Senegal-Niger Chamber of Commerce

| Date | Mintage | VG | F | VF | XF | Unc |
|---|---|---|---|---|---|---|
| 1920 | — | 15.00 | 30.00 | 65.00 | 180 | — |

**25 CENTIMES** **KM# Tn14** **Composition:** Aluminum **Issuer:** Rufisque, Chamber of Commerce

| Date | Mintage | VG | F | VF | XF | Unc |
|---|---|---|---|---|---|---|
| 1920 | — | 12.00 | 25.00 | 50.00 | 150 | — |

**25 CENTIMES** **KM# Tn10** **Composition:** Copper-Nickel **Issuer:** Kayes, Upper Senegal-Niger Chamber of Commerce

| Date | Mintage | VG | F | VF | XF | Unc |
|---|---|---|---|---|---|---|
| 1920 | — | 18.00 | 35.00 | 75.00 | 220 | — |

**50 CENTIMES** **KM# Tn6** **Composition:** Aluminum **Issuer:** Dakar, Chamber of Commerce

| Date | Mintage | VG | F | VF | XF | Unc |
|---|---|---|---|---|---|---|
| 1920 | — | 12.00 | 25.00 | 50.00 | 150 | — |

**50 CENTIMES** **KM# Tn11** **Composition:** Aluminum **Issuer:** Kayes, Upper Senegal-Niger Chamber of Commerce

| Date | Mintage | VG | F | VF | XF | Unc |
|---|---|---|---|---|---|---|
| 1920 | — | 20.00 | 40.00 | 85.00 | 200 | — |

**50 CENTIMES** **KM# Tn15** **Composition:** Aluminum **Issuer:** Rufisque, Chamber of Commerce

| Date | Mintage | VG | F | VF | XF | Unc |
|---|---|---|---|---|---|---|
| 1920 | — | 18.00 | 30.00 | 60.00 | 160 | — |

**50 CENTIMES** **KM# Tn16** **Composition:** Brass **Issuer:** Rufisque, Chamber of Commerce

| Date | Mintage | VG | F | VF | XF | Unc |
|---|---|---|---|---|---|---|
| 1920 | — | 20.00 | 35.00 | 70.00 | 175 | — |

**50 CENTIMES** **KM# Tn17** **Composition:** Brass **Issuer:** Ziguinchor, Chamber of Commerce

| Date | Mintage | VG | F | VF | XF | Unc |
|---|---|---|---|---|---|---|
| 1921 | — | 22.00 | 40.00 | 80.00 | 180 | — |

**FRANC** **KM# Tn18** **Composition:** Brass **Issuer:** Ziguinchor, Chamber of Commerce

| Date | Mintage | VG | F | VF | XF | Unc |
|---|---|---|---|---|---|---|
| 1921 | — | 30.00 | 45.00 | 90.00 | 200 | — |

**FRANC** **KM# Tn19** **Composition:** Aluminum **Issuer:** Ziguinchor, Chamber of Commerce

| Date | Mintage | VG | F | VF | XF | Unc |
|---|---|---|---|---|---|---|
| 1921 | — | 40.00 | 80.00 | 175 | 350 | — |

## ESSAIS

Standard metals unless otherwise noted

| KM# | Date | Mintage | Identification | Mkt Val |
|---|---|---|---|---|
| E1 | 1920 | — | 25 Centimes. Kayes. KM-Tn10. | 250 |
| E2 | 1921 | — | 50 Centimes. Zinguinchor. KMTn17. | — |
| E3 | 1921 | — | Franc. Zinguinchor. KMTn18. | — |

## MINT SETS

| KM# | Date | Mintage | Identification | Issue Price | Mkt Val |
|---|---|---|---|---|---|
| MS1 | 1975 (4) | 195 | KM7-10 | — | 1,150 |

## PROOF SETS

| KM# | Date | Mintage | Identification | Issue Price | Mkt Val |
|---|---|---|---|---|---|
| PS1 | 1968 (4) | — | KM1-4 | — | 900 |
| PS2 | 1975 (2) | — | KM5-6 | — | 300 |

Serbia, a former inland Balkan kingdom has an area of 34,116 sq. mi. (88,361 sq. km.). Capital: Belgrade.

Serbia emerged as a separate kingdom in the 12th century and attained its greatest expansion and political influence in the mid-14th century. After the Battle of Kosovo, 1389, Serbia became a vassal principality of Turkey and remained under Turkish suzerainty until it was re-established as an independent kingdom by the 1887 Treaty of Berlin. Following World War I, which had its immediate cause in the assassination of Austrian Archduke Francis Ferdinand by a Serbian nationalist, Serbia joined with the Croats and Slovenes to form the new Kingdom of the South Slavs with Peter I of Serbia asking. The name of the kingdom was later changed to Yugoslavia. Invaded by Germany during World War II, Serbia emerged as a constituent republic of the Socialist Federal Republic of Yugoslavia.

**RULERS**

Alexander I, 1889-1902
Peter I, 1903-1918

**MINT MARKS**

A - Paris
(a) - Paris, privy mark only
(g) - Gorham Mfg. Co., Providence, R.I.
H - Birmingham
V - Vienna
зм - (BP) Budapest

**MONETARY SYSTEM**

100 Para = 1 Dinara

**DENOMINATIONS**

мЛГЛ = Para
мЛГЃ = Pare
ЂикЛГ = Dinar
ЂикЛГЛ = Dinara

# KINGDOM

## STANDARD COINAGE

**2 PARE** **KM# 23** **Composition:** Bronze **Ruler:** Peter I **Note:** Medal turn.

| Date | Mintage | F | VF | XF | Unc | BU |
|---|---|---|---|---|---|---|
| 1904 | 12,500,000 | 2.00 | 5.00 | 15.00 | 36.00 | — |

**5 PARA** **KM# 18** **Composition:** Copper-Nickel **Ruler:** Peter I **Note:** Medal turn.

| Date | Mintage | F | VF | XF | Unc | BU |
|---|---|---|---|---|---|---|
| 1904 | 8,000,000 | 1.00 | 2.50 | 6.00 | 15.00 | — |
| 1904 Proof | Inc. above | Value: 200 | | | | |
| 1912 | 10,000,000 | 0.75 | 1.50 | 3.50 | 10.00 | — |
| 1912 Proof | — | Value: 120 | | | | |
| 1917(g) | 5,000,000 | 5.00 | 10.00 | 20.00 | 32.00 | — |

**10 PARA** **KM# 19** **Composition:** Copper-Nickel **Ruler:** Peter I **Note:** Medal turn.

| Date | Mintage | F | VF | XF | Unc | BU |
|---|---|---|---|---|---|---|
| 1904 Proof | — | Value: 350 | | | | |
| 1912 | 7,700,000 | 0.75 | 1.25 | 3.50 | 9.00 | — |
| 1912 Proof | — | Value: 120 | | | | |
| 1917(g) | 5,000,000 | 1.00 | 2.50 | 7.00 | 22.00 | — |
| 1917(g) Proof | — | Value: 200 | | | | |

**20 PARA** **KM# 20** **Composition:** Copper-Nickel **Ruler:** Peter I **Note:** Medal turn.

| Date | Mintage | F | VF | XF | Unc | BU |
|---|---|---|---|---|---|---|
| 1904 Proof | — | Value: 400 | | | | |
| 1912 | 5,650,000 | 0.75 | 2.00 | 4.50 | 10.00 | — |
| 1912 Proof | — | Value: 125 | | | | |
| 1917(g) | 5,000,000 | 1.00 | 3.00 | 9.00 | 25.00 | — |

**50 PARA** **KM# 24.1** **Ruler:** Peter I **Note:** Medal turn.

| Date | Mintage | F | VF | XF | Unc | BU |
|---|---|---|---|---|---|---|
| 1904 | 1,400,000 | 2.00 | 5.00 | 12.50 | 32.00 | — |
| 1904 Proof | — | Value: 200 | | | | |
| 1912 | 800,000 | 2.50 | 6.00 | 15.00 | 34.00 | — |
| 1915(a) | 12,138,000 | 1.00 | 2.00 | 4.50 | 12.00 | — |

**50 PARA** **KM# 24.2** **Weight:** 2.5000 g. **Composition:** 0.8350 Silver .0671 oz. ASW **Ruler:** Peter I **Obverse:** Without designer's signature

| Date | Mintage | F | VF | XF | Unc | BU |
|---|---|---|---|---|---|---|
| 1915(a) | 1,862,000 | 6.00 | 12.00 | 30.00 | 90.00 | — |

**2 DINARA** **KM# 25.1** **Weight:** 5.0000 g. **Composition:** 0.8350 Silver .1342 oz. ASW **Ruler:** Peter I **Obverse:** Designer's signature below neck **Note:** Medal turn.

| Date | Mintage | F | VF | XF | Unc | BU |
|---|---|---|---|---|---|---|
| 1904 | 994,000 | 4.50 | 12.00 | 25.00 | 75.00 | — |
| 1904 Proof | — | Value: 250 | | | | |
| 1912 | 8,000,000 | 3.00 | 6.00 | 15.00 | 35.00 | — |
| 1915(a) | 10,688,000 | 2.00 | 4.00 | 8.00 | 18.00 | — |

**2 DINARA** **KM# 26.1** **Weight:** 10.0000 g. **Composition:** 0.8350 Silver .2684 oz. ASW **Ruler:** Peter I **Obverse:** Designer's signature below neck **Note:** Medal turn.

| Date | Mintage | F | VF | XF | Unc | BU |
|---|---|---|---|---|---|---|
| 1904 | 1,150,000 | 7.50 | 15.00 | 32.00 | 85.00 | — |
| 1904 Proof | — | Value: 325 | | | | |
| 1912 | 800,000 | 8.00 | 16.00 | 35.00 | 85.00 | — |
| 1915(a) | 4,174,000 | 5.00 | 10.00 | 18.00 | 35.00 | — |

**2 DINARA** **KM# 25.2** **Weight:** 5.0000 g. **Composition:** 0.8350 Silver .1342 oz. ASW **Ruler:** Peter I **Obverse:** Without designer's signature **Note:** Metal turn.

| Date | Mintage | F | VF | XF | Unc | BU |
|---|---|---|---|---|---|---|
| 1915(a) | 2,322,000 | 5.00 | 14.00 | 32.00 | 80.00 | — |

**2 DINARA** **KM# 26.2** **Weight:** 10.0000 g. **Composition:** 0.8350 Silver .2684 oz. ASW **Ruler:** Peter I **Obverse:** Without designer's signature **Note:** Metal turn.

| Date | Mintage | F | VF | XF | Unc | BU |
|---|---|---|---|---|---|---|
| 1915(a) | 826,000 | 8.00 | 20.00 | 40.00 | 110 | — |

**2 DINARA** **KM# 26.3** **Weight:** 10.0000 g. **Composition:** 0.8350 Silver .2684 oz. ASW **Ruler:** Peter I **Note:** Coin turn.

| Date | Mintage | VG | F | VF | XF | Unc |
|---|---|---|---|---|---|---|
| 1915(a) | Inc. above | — | 5.00 | 10.00 | 18.00 | 35.00 |

**5 DINARA** **KM# 27** **Weight:** 25.0000 g. **Composition:** 0.9000 Silver .7234 oz. ASW **Ruler:** Peter I **Subject:** 100th anniversary - Karageorgevich Dynasty **Edge:** Lettered, Type I

| Date | Mintage | F | VF | XF | Unc | BU |
|---|---|---|---|---|---|---|
| 1904 | 200,000 | 35.00 | 70.00 | 175 | 650 | — |
| 1904 Proof | — | Value: 2,000 | | | | |

**5 DINARA** **KM# 28** **Weight:** 25.0000 g. **Composition:** 0.9000 Silver .7234 oz. ASW **Ruler:** Peter I **Subject:** 100th anniversary - Karageorgevich Dynasty **Edge:** Lettered, Type II

| Date | Mintage | F | VF | XF | Unc | BU |
|---|---|---|---|---|---|---|
| 1904 | Inc. above | 150 | 250 | 425 | 1,600 | — |

# GERMAN OCCUPATION

## World War II

## OCCUPATION COINAGE

**50 PARA** **KM# 30** **Composition:** Zinc

| Date | Mintage | F | VF | XF | Unc | BU |
|---|---|---|---|---|---|---|
| 1942(BP) | — | 2.00 | 4.50 | 10.00 | 18.00 | — |

**DINAR** **KM# 31** **Composition:** Zinc

| Date | Mintage | F | VF | XF | Unc | BU |
|---|---|---|---|---|---|---|
| 1942(BP) | — | 0.50 | 1.50 | 5.00 | 14.00 | — |

**2 DINARA** **KM# 32** **Composition:** Zinc

| Date | Mintage | F | VF | XF | Unc | BU |
|---|---|---|---|---|---|---|
| 1942(BP) | — | 0.50 | 1.50 | 6.00 | 16.00 | — |

**10 DINARA** **KM# 33** **Composition:** Zinc

| Date | Mintage | F | VF | XF | Unc | BU |
|---|---|---|---|---|---|---|
| 1943(BP) | 1,750,000 | 1.00 | 2.50 | 7.50 | 18.00 | — |

## PATTERNS

| KM# | Date | Mintage | Identification | Mkt Val |
|---|---|---|---|---|
| PnD6 | 1904 | 4 | 5 Dinara. Gold. 44.5000 g. | — |
| PnC6 | 1904 | — | 2 Dinara. Bronze. | 1,500 |
| Pn6 | 1917 | — | 5 Para. Gold. | — |
| Pn7 | 1917 | — | 10 Para. Gold. | — |
| Pn8 | 1917 | — | 20 Para. Gold. | — |
| Pn9 | 1917 | — | 20 Dinara. Gold. | — |

## SEYCHELLES

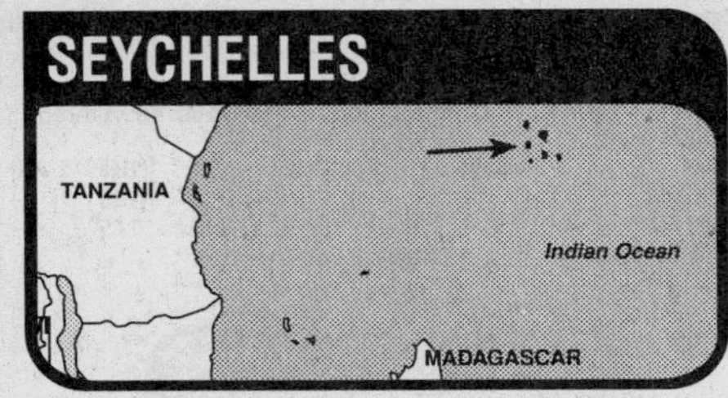


The Republic of Seychelles, an archipelago of 85 granite and coral islands situated in the Indian Ocean 600 miles (965 km.) northeast of Madagascar, has an area of 156sq. mi. (455 sq. km.) and a population of *70,000. Among these islands are the Aldabra Islands, the Farquhar Group, and Ile Desroches, which the United Kingdom ceded to the Seychelles upon its independence. Capital: Victoria, on Mahe. The economy is based on fishing, a plantation system of agriculture, and tourism. Copra, cinnamon and vanilla are exported.

Although the Seychelles is marked on Portuguese charts of the early 16th century, the first recorded visit to the islands, by an English ship, occurred in 1609. The Seychelles were annexed to France by Captain Lazare Picault in 1743 and permanently settled in 1768, with the intention of establishing spice plantations to compete with the Dutch monopoly of the spice trade. British troops seized the islands in 1810, during the Napoleonic Wars; the Treaty of Paris, 1814, formally ceded them to Britain. The Seychelles was a dependency of Mauritius until Aug. 31, 1903, when they became a separate British Crown Colony. The colony was granted limited internal self-government in 1970, and attained independence on June 28, 1976, becoming Britain's last African possession to do so. Seychelles is a member of the Commonwealth of Nations. The president is the Head of State and of Government.

**RULERS**
British, until 1976

**MINT MARKS**
PM - Pobjoy Mint
None - British Royal Mint

**MONETARY SYSTEM**
100 Cents = 1 Rupee

# BRITISH CROWN COLONY

## STANDARD COINAGE

100 Cents = 1 Rupee

**CENT** **KM# 5** **Composition:** Bronze

| Date | Mintage | F | VF | XF | Unc | BU |
|---|---|---|---|---|---|---|
| 1948 | 300,000 | — | 0.25 | 0.50 | 1.25 | — |
| 1948 Proof | — | Value: 50.00 | | | | |

**CENT** **KM# 14** **Composition:** Bronze

| Date | Mintage | F | VF | XF | Unc | BU |
|---|---|---|---|---|---|---|
| 1959 | 30,000 | — | 0.75 | 1.50 | 3.00 | — |
| 1959 Proof | — | — | — | — | — | — |
| 1961 | 30,000 | — | 0.50 | 1.00 | 2.25 | — |
| 1961 Proof | — | — | — | — | — | — |
| 1963 | 40,000 | — | 0.50 | 1.00 | 1.50 | — |
| 1963 Proof | — | — | — | — | — | — |
| 1965 | 20,000 | — | 2.00 | 3.00 | 5.00 | — |
| 1969 | Est. 5,000 | — | 15.00 | 25.00 | 60.00 | — |

**Note:** Latest reports indicate only 5,000 circulation strikes have been releasesd to date in addition to proof issues

| Date | Mintage | F | VF | XF | Unc | BU |
|---|---|---|---|---|---|---|
| 1969 Proof | — | Value: 5.00 | | | | |

**CENT** **KM# 17** **Composition:** Aluminum **Series:** F.A.O. **Reverse:** Cow

| Date | Mintage | F | VF | XF | Unc | BU |
|---|---|---|---|---|---|---|
| 1972 | 2,350,000 | — | — | 0.10 | 0.25 | — |

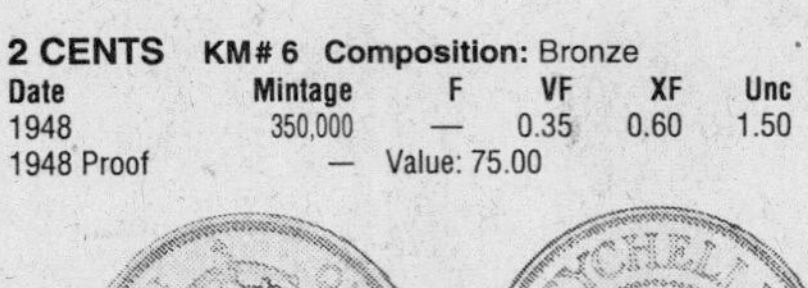

**2 CENTS** **KM# 6** **Composition:** Bronze

| Date | Mintage | F | VF | XF | Unc | BU |
|---|---|---|---|---|---|---|
| 1948 | 350,000 | — | 0.35 | 0.60 | 1.50 | — |
| 1948 Proof | — | Value: 75.00 | | | | |

**2 CENTS** **KM# 15** **Composition:** Bronze

| Date | Mintage | F | VF | XF | Unc | BU |
|---|---|---|---|---|---|---|
| 1959 | 30,000 | — | 0.50 | 1.00 | 2.50 | — |
| 1959 Proof | — | — | — | — | — | — |
| 1961 | 30,000 | — | 0.50 | 1.00 | 2.75 | — |
| 1961 Proof | — | — | — | — | — | — |
| 1963 | 40,000 | — | 0.75 | 1.25 | 2.50 | — |
| 1963 Proof | — | — | — | — | — | — |
| 1965 | 20,000 | — | 2.00 | 3.00 | 4.00 | — |
| 1968 | 20,000 | — | 2.00 | 3.00 | 5.50 | — |
| 1969 Proof | 5,000 | Value: 4.00 | | | | |

**5 CENTS** **KM# 7** **Composition:** Bronze

| Date | Mintage | F | VF | XF | Unc | BU |
|---|---|---|---|---|---|---|
| 1948 | 300,000 | — | 0.40 | 0.80 | 2.00 | — |
| 1948 Proof | — | Value: 100 | | | | |

**5 CENTS** **KM# 16** **Composition:** Bronze

| Date | Mintage | F | VF | XF | Unc | BU |
|---|---|---|---|---|---|---|
| 1964 | 20,000 | — | 1.00 | 2.00 | 4.50 | — |
| 1964 Proof | — | — | — | — | — | — |
| 1965 | 40,000 | — | 1.50 | 2.50 | 5.50 | — |
| 1967 | 20,000 | — | 1.50 | 3.00 | 8.00 | — |
| 1968 | 40,000 | — | 1.00 | 2.00 | 7.00 | — |
| 1969 | 100,000 | — | 0.50 | 1.00 | 5.00 | — |
| 1969 Proof | — | Value: 4.00 | | | | |
| 1971 | 25,000 | — | 0.50 | 1.50 | 2.50 | — |

**5 CENTS** **KM# 18** **Composition:** Aluminum **Series:** F.A.O. **Reverse:** Cabbage

| Date | Mintage | F | VF | XF | Unc | BU |
|---|---|---|---|---|---|---|
| 1972 | 2,200,000 | — | — | 0.10 | 0.25 | — |
| 1975 | 1,200,000 | — | — | 0.10 | 0.25 | — |

**10 CENTS** **KM# 1** **Composition:** Copper-Nickel

| Date | Mintage | F | VF | XF | Unc | BU |
|---|---|---|---|---|---|---|
| 1939 | 36,000 | — | 8.00 | 20.00 | 70.00 | — |
| 1939 Proof | — | Value: 150 | | | | |
| 1943 | 36,000 | — | 6.00 | 12.00 | 40.00 | — |
| 1944 | 36,000 | — | 6.00 | 12.00 | 40.00 | — |
| 1944 Proof | — | Value: 175 | | | | |

**10 CENTS** **KM# 8** **Composition:** Copper-Nickel

| Date | Mintage | F | VF | XF | Unc | BU |
|---|---|---|---|---|---|---|
| 1951 | 36,000 | — | 2.00 | 5.00 | 9.00 | — |
| 1951 Proof | — | Value: 135 | | | | |

**10 CENTS** **KM# 10** **Composition:** Nickel-Brass

| Date | Mintage | F | VF | XF | Unc | BU |
|---|---|---|---|---|---|---|
| 1953 | 130,000 | — | 0.50 | 1.00 | 3.00 | — |
| 1953 Proof | — | Value: 100 | | | | |
| 1965 | 40,000 | — | 1.00 | 1.50 | 5.00 | — |
| 1967 | 20,000 | — | 4.00 | 7.50 | 15.00 | — |
| 1968 | 50,000 | — | 1.00 | 4.00 | 12.50 | — |
| 1969 | 60,000 | — | 1.00 | 2.00 | 7.00 | — |
| 1969 Proof | — | Value: 2.00 | | | | |
| 1970 | 75,000 | — | 0.50 | 1.00 | 4.50 | — |
| 1971 | 100,000 | — | 0.50 | 1.00 | 1.75 | — |
| 1972 | 120,000 | — | 0.30 | 0.50 | 1.00 | — |
| 1973 | 100,000 | — | 0.15 | 0.25 | 1.00 | — |
| 1974 | 100,000 | — | 0.15 | 0.25 | 0.75 | — |

**25 CENTS** **KM# 2** **Weight:** 2.9200 g. **Composition:** 0.5000 Silver .0469 oz. ASW

| Date | Mintage | F | VF | XF | Unc | BU |
|---|---|---|---|---|---|---|
| 1939 | 36,000 | — | 7.50 | 35.00 | 125 | — |
| 1939 Proof | — | Value: 200 | | | | |
| 1943 | 36,000 | — | 5.00 | 25.00 | 100 | — |
| 1944 | 36,000 | — | 3.50 | 20.00 | 85.00 | — |
| 1944 Proof | — | Value: 300 | | | | |

**25 CENTS** **KM# 9** **Composition:** Copper-Nickel

| Date | Mintage | F | VF | XF | Unc | BU |
|---|---|---|---|---|---|---|
| 1951 | 36,000 | — | 2.00 | 7.50 | 35.00 | — |
| 1951 Proof | — | Value: 160 | | | | |

**25 CENTS** **KM# 11** **Composition:** Copper-Nickel

| Date | Mintage | F | VF | XF | Unc | BU |
|---|---|---|---|---|---|---|
| 1954 | 124,000 | — | 0.75 | 1.25 | 4.00 | — |
| 1954 Proof | — | Value: 120 | | | | |
| 1960 | 40,000 | — | 0.75 | 1.25 | 2.00 | — |
| 1960 Proof | — | — | — | — | — | — |
| 1964 | 40,000 | — | 1.00 | 2.00 | 5.00 | — |
| 1965 | 40,000 | — | 1.00 | 2.00 | 5.00 | — |
| 1966 | 10,000 | — | 3.50 | 10.00 | 22.50 | — |
| 1967 | 20,000 | — | 2.50 | 4.00 | 15.00 | — |
| 1968 | 20,000 | — | 2.50 | 4.00 | 15.00 | — |
| 1969 | 100,000 | — | 1.00 | 2.00 | 4.00 | — |
| 1969 Proof | — | Value: 3.00 | | | | |
| 1970 | 40,000 | — | 1.50 | 3.00 | 10.00 | — |
| 1972 | 120,000 | — | 0.50 | 0.75 | 1.50 | — |
| 1973 | 100,000 | — | 0.50 | 0.75 | 1.50 | — |
| 1974 | 100,000 | — | 0.50 | 0.75 | 1.50 | — |

**1/2 RUPEE** KM# 3 **Weight:** 5.8300 g. **Composition:** 0.5000 Silver .0937 oz. ASW

| Date | Mintage | F | VF | XF | Unc | BU |
|---|---|---|---|---|---|---|
| 1939 | 36,000 | — | 12.00 | 50.00 | 175 | — |
| 1939 Proof | — | Value: 250 | | | | |

**1/2 RUPEE** KM# 12 **Composition:** Copper-Nickel

| Date | Mintage | F | VF | XF | Unc | BU |
|---|---|---|---|---|---|---|
| 1954 | 72,000 | — | 0.50 | 1.25 | 3.75 | — |
| 1954 Proof | — | Value: 150 | | | | |
| 1960 | 60,000 | — | 0.50 | 1.00 | 3.00 | — |
| 1960 Proof | — | Value: 150 | | | | |
| 1966 | 15,000 | — | 1.50 | 5.00 | 20.00 | — |
| 1967 | 20,000 | — | 3.00 | 8.00 | 25.00 | — |
| 1968 | 20,000 | — | 3.00 | 8.00 | 30.00 | — |
| 1969 | 60,000 | — | 0.75 | 1.00 | 12.00 | — |
| 1969 Proof | — | Value: 3.00 | | | | |
| 1970 | 50,000 | — | 0.75 | 1.00 | 8.00 | — |
| 1971 | 100,000 | — | 0.75 | 1.00 | 3.00 | — |
| 1972 | 120,000 | — | 0.50 | 0.75 | 1.00 | — |
| 1974 | 100,000 | — | 0.50 | 0.75 | 1.00 | — |

**RUPEE** KM# 4 **Weight:** 11.6600 g. **Composition:** 0.5000 Silver .1874 oz. ASW

| Date | Mintage | F | VF | XF | Unc | BU |
|---|---|---|---|---|---|---|
| 1939 | 90,000 | — | 15.00 | 60.00 | 165 | — |
| 1939 Proof | — | Value: 400 | | | | |

**RUPEE** KM# 13 **Composition:** Copper-Nickel

| Date | Mintage | F | VF | XF | Unc | BU |
|---|---|---|---|---|---|---|
| 1954 | 150,000 | — | 0.50 | 1.00 | 3.00 | — |
| 1954 Proof | — | Value: 200 | | | | |
| 1960 | 60,000 | — | 0.75 | 1.25 | 3.50 | — |
| 1960 Proof | — | — | — | — | — | — |
| 1966 | 45,000 | — | 1.25 | 2.25 | 8.50 | — |
| 1967 | 10,000 | — | 3.50 | 7.50 | 27.50 | — |

| Date | Mintage | F | VF | XF | Unc | BU |
|---|---|---|---|---|---|---|
| 1968 | 40,000 | — | 2.50 | 5.00 | 20.00 | — |
| 1969 | 50,000 | — | 1.50 | 3.00 | 12.50 | — |
| 1969 Proof | — | Value: 5.00 | | | | |
| 1970 | 50,000 | — | 1.50 | 2.50 | 10.00 | — |
| 1971 | 100,000 | — | 0.75 | 1.50 | 5.00 | — |
| 1972 | 120,000 | — | 0.75 | 1.50 | 2.00 | — |
| 1974 | 100,000 | — | — | — | 1.50 | — |

**5 RUPEES** KM# 19 **Composition:** Copper-Nickel

| Date | Mintage | F | VF | XF | Unc | BU |
|---|---|---|---|---|---|---|
| 1972 | 220,000 | — | 1.50 | 2.50 | 5.00 | — |

**5 RUPEES** KM# 19a **Weight:** 15.5000 g. **Composition:** 0.9250 Silver .4609 oz. ASW

| Date | Mintage | F | VF | XF | Unc | BU |
|---|---|---|---|---|---|---|
| 1972 Proof | 2,500 | Value: 16.50 | | | | |
| 1974 Proof | 5,000 | Value: 14.50 | | | | |

**10 RUPEES** KM# 20 **Composition:** Copper-Nickel

| Date | Mintage | F | VF | XF | Unc | BU |
|---|---|---|---|---|---|---|
| 1974 | — | — | 2.00 | 3.50 | 7.00 | — |

**10 RUPEES** KM# 20a **Weight:** 28.2800 g. **Composition:** 0.9250 Silver .8411 oz. ASW

| Date | Mintage | F | VF | XF | Unc | BU |
|---|---|---|---|---|---|---|
| 1974 Proof | 25,000 | Value: 12.50 | | | | |

# REPUBLIC

## STANDARD COINAGE

100 Cents = 1 Rupee

**CENT** KM# 21 **Composition:** Aluminum **Subject:** Declaration of Independence

| Date | Mintage | F | VF | XF | Unc | BU |
|---|---|---|---|---|---|---|
| 1976 | 109,000 | — | 0.10 | 0.20 | 0.50 | — |
| 1976 Proof | 8,500 | Value: 1.50 | | | | |

**CENT** KM# 30 **Composition:** Aluminum **Reverse:** Boueteur Fish

| Date | Mintage | F | VF | XF | Unc | BU |
|---|---|---|---|---|---|---|
| 1977 | — | — | — | 0.15 | 0.50 | — |

**CENT** KM# 46.1 **Composition:** Brass

| Date | Mintage | F | VF | XF | Unc | BU |
|---|---|---|---|---|---|---|
| 1982 | 500,000 | — | — | 0.15 | 0.50 | — |
| 1982 Proof | — | Value: 2.25 | | | | |

**CENT** KM# 46.2 **Composition:** Brass **Obverse:** Altered coat of arms

| Date | Mintage | F | VF | XF | Unc | BU |
|---|---|---|---|---|---|---|
| 1990 PM | — | — | — | 0.15 | 0.45 | — |
| 1992 PM | — | — | — | 0.15 | 0.45 | — |
| 1992 PM Proof | — | Value: 2.25 | | | | |

**5 CENTS** KM# 22 **Composition:** Aluminum **Subject:** Declaration of Independence **Note:** Varieties exist.

| Date | Mintage | F | VF | XF | Unc | BU |
|---|---|---|---|---|---|---|
| 1976 | 209,000 | — | 0.10 | 0.20 | 0.50 | — |
| 1976 Proof | 8,500 | Value: 1.50 | | | | |

**5 CENTS** KM# 31 **Composition:** Aluminum **Series:** F.A.O **Reverse:** Bourgeois Fish

| Date | Mintage | F | VF | XF | Unc | BU |
|---|---|---|---|---|---|---|
| 1977 | 300,000 | — | — | 0.15 | 0.50 | — |

**5 CENTS** KM# 43 **Composition:** Brass **Series:** World Food Day

| Date | Mintage | F | VF | XF | Unc | BU |
|---|---|---|---|---|---|---|
| 1981 | 720,000 | — | — | 0.15 | 0.45 | — |

**5 CENTS** KM# 47.1 **Composition:** Brass

| Date | Mintage | F | VF | XF | Unc | BU |
|---|---|---|---|---|---|---|
| 1982 | 1,500,000 | — | — | 0.10 | 0.30 | — |
| 1982 Proof | Inc. above | Value: 2.50 | | | | |

**5 CENTS** KM# 47.2 **Composition:** Brass **Obverse:** Altered coat of arms

| Date | Mintage | F | VF | XF | Unc | BU |
|---|---|---|---|---|---|---|
| 1990 PM | — | — | — | 0.10 | 0.30 | — |
| 1992 PM | — | — | — | 0.10 | 0.30 | — |
| 1992 PM Proof | — | Value: 2.50 | | | | |
| 1995 PM | — | — | — | 0.10 | 0.30 | — |
| 1997 PM | — | — | — | 0.10 | 0.30 | — |
| 1997 PM Proof | — | Value: 2.50 | | | | |

**10 CENTS** KM# 23 **Composition:** Nickel-Brass **Subject:** Declaration of Independence

| Date | Mintage | F | VF | XF | Unc | BU |
|---|---|---|---|---|---|---|
| 1976 | 209,000 | — | 0.20 | 0.50 | 1.50 | — |
| 1976 Proof | 8,500 | Value: 2.50 | | | | |

**10 CENTS** KM# 32 **Composition:** Nickel-Brass **Series:** F.A.O. **Reverse:** Sailfish

| Date | Mintage | F | VF | XF | Unc | BU |
|---|---|---|---|---|---|---|
| 1977 | 125,000 | — | 0.10 | 0.35 | 1.50 | — |

**10 CENTS** **KM# 44** **Composition:** Brass **Series:** World Food Day

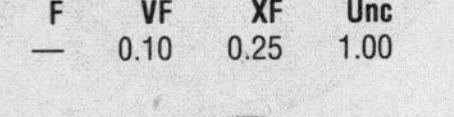

| Date | Mintage | F | VF | XF | Unc | BU |
|---|---|---|---|---|---|---|
| 1981 | 145,000 | — | 0.10 | 0.25 | 1.00 | — |

**10 CENTS** **KM# 48.1** **Composition:** Brass

| Date | Mintage | F | VF | XF | Unc | BU |
|---|---|---|---|---|---|---|
| 1982 | 1,000,000 | — | 0.10 | 0.25 | 1.00 | — |
| 1982 Proof | Inc. above | Value: 2.75 | | | | |

**10 CENTS** **KM# 48.2** **Composition:** Brass **Obverse:** Altered coat of arms

| Date | Mintage | F | VF | XF | Unc | BU |
|---|---|---|---|---|---|---|
| 1990 | — | — | 0.10 | 0.25 | 1.00 | — |
| 1992 | — | — | 0.10 | 0.25 | 1.00 | — |
| 1992 Proof | — | Value: 2.75 | | | | |
| 1994 | — | — | 0.10 | 0.25 | 1.00 | — |
| 1997 | — | — | 0.10 | 0.25 | 1.00 | — |

**25 CENTS** **KM# 24** **Composition:** Copper-Nickel **Subject:** Declaration of Independence

| Date | Mintage | F | VF | XF | Unc | BU |
|---|---|---|---|---|---|---|
| 1976 | 209,000 | — | 0.50 | 1.00 | 3.00 | — |
| 1976 Proof | 8,500 | Value: 3.50 | | | | |

**25 CENTS** **KM# 33** **Composition:** Copper-Nickel **Reverse:** Black Parrot

| Date | Mintage | F | VF | XF | Unc | BU |
|---|---|---|---|---|---|---|
| 1977 | — | — | 0.25 | 0.75 | 2.50 | — |

**25 CENTS** **KM# 49.1** **Composition:** Copper-Nickel

| Date | Mintage | F | VF | XF | Unc | BU |
|---|---|---|---|---|---|---|
| 1982 | 375,000 | — | 0.25 | 0.75 | 2.50 | — |
| 1982 Proof | Inc. above | Value: 3.00 | | | | |

**25 CENTS** **KM# 49.2** **Composition:** Copper-Nickel **Obverse:** Altered coat of arms

| Date | Mintage | F | VF | XF | Unc | BU |
|---|---|---|---|---|---|---|
| 1989 | 1,500,000 | — | 0.25 | 0.75 | 2.50 | — |
| 1992 PM | — | — | 0.25 | 0.75 | 2.50 | — |
| 1992 PM Proof | — | Value: 3.00 | | | | |
| 1997 PM | — | — | 0.25 | 0.75 | 2.50 | — |

**25 CENTS** **KM# 49.3** **Composition:** Nickel Clad Steel

| Date | Mintage | F | VF | XF | Unc | BU |
|---|---|---|---|---|---|---|
| 1993 PM | — | — | 0.25 | 0.75 | 2.50 | — |

**50 CENTS** **KM# 25** **Composition:** Copper-Nickel **Subject:** Declaration of Independence

| Date | Mintage | F | VF | XF | Unc | BU |
|---|---|---|---|---|---|---|
| 1976 | 209,000 | — | 0.50 | 1.00 | 2.50 | — |
| 1976 Proof | 8,500 | Value: 3.50 | | | | |

**50 CENTS** **KM# 34** **Composition:** Copper-Nickel **Reverse:** Vanilla Orchid

| Date | Mintage | F | VF | XF | Unc | BU |
|---|---|---|---|---|---|---|
| 1977 | — | — | 0.20 | 0.45 | 1.00 | — |

**RUPEE** **KM# 26** **Composition:** Copper-Nickel **Subject:** Declaration of Independence

| Date | Mintage | F | VF | XF | Unc | BU |
|---|---|---|---|---|---|---|
| 1976 | 259,000 | — | 0.75 | 1.00 | 1.75 | — |
| 1976 Proof | 8,500 | Value: 2.50 | | | | |

**RUPEE** **KM# 35** **Composition:** Copper-Nickel **Reverse:** Triton Conch Shell

| Date | Mintage | F | VF | XF | Unc | BU |
|---|---|---|---|---|---|---|
| 1977 | — | — | 0.50 | 0.75 | 1.50 | — |

**RUPEE** **KM# 50.1** **Composition:** Copper-Nickel

| Date | Mintage | F | VF | XF | Unc | BU |
|---|---|---|---|---|---|---|
| 1982 | 2,000,000 | — | 0.25 | 0.50 | 1.25 | — |
| 1982 Proof | Inc. above | Value: 5.00 | | | | |
| 1983 | — | — | 0.50 | 1.00 | 2.00 | — |

**RUPEE** **KM# 50.2** **Composition:** Copper-Nickel **Obverse:** Altered coat of arms

| Date | Mintage | F | VF | XF | Unc | BU |
|---|---|---|---|---|---|---|
| 1992 PM | — | — | 0.25 | 0.50 | 1.25 | — |
| 1992 PM Proof | — | Value: 5.00 | | | | |
| 1995 PM | — | — | 0.25 | 0.50 | 1.25 | — |
| 1997 PM | — | — | 0.25 | 0.50 | 1.25 | — |

**RUPEE** **KM# 85** **Composition:** Copper-Nickel **Reverse:** British Queen Mother wedding portrait

| Date | Mintage | F | VF | XF | Unc | BU |
|---|---|---|---|---|---|---|
| 1995 | Est. 30,000 | — | — | — | 10.00 | — |

**5 RUPEES** **KM# 27** **Composition:** Copper-Nickel **Subject:** Declaration of Independence

| Date | Mintage | F | VF | XF | Unc | BU |
|---|---|---|---|---|---|---|
| 1976 | 50,000 | — | 1.25 | 1.75 | 3.00 | — |

**5 RUPEES** **KM# 27a** **Weight:** 15.5000 g. **Composition:** 0.9250 Silver .4609 oz. ASW

| Date | Mintage | F | VF | XF | Unc | BU |
|---|---|---|---|---|---|---|
| 1976 Proof | 8,500 | Value: 10.00 | | | | |

**5 RUPEES** **KM# 36** **Composition:** Copper-Nickel **Reverse:** Coco-de-mer Palm Tree

| Date | Mintage | F | VF | XF | Unc | BU |
|---|---|---|---|---|---|---|
| 1977 | — | — | 1.00 | 1.50 | 2.25 | — |

**5 RUPEES** **KM# 51.1** **Composition:** Copper-Nickel

| Date | Mintage | F | VF | XF | Unc | BU |
|---|---|---|---|---|---|---|
| 1982 | 300,000 | — | 1.00 | 1.50 | 2.00 | — |
| 1982 Proof | Inc. above | Value: 5.00 | | | | |

**5 RUPEES** **KM# 51.2** **Composition:** Copper-Nickel **Obverse:** Altered coat of arms

| Date | Mintage | F | VF | XF | Unc | BU |
|---|---|---|---|---|---|---|
| 1992 PM | — | — | 1.00 | 1.50 | 2.00 | — |
| 1992 PM Proof | — | Value: 5.00 | | | | |
| 1997 PM | — | — | 1.00 | 1.50 | 2.00 | — |

**5 RUPEES** **KM# 89** **Composition:** Copper-Nickel **Series:** 50th Anniversary United Nations

| Date | Mintage | F | VF | XF | Unc | BU |
|---|---|---|---|---|---|---|
| 1995 | — | — | — | — | 10.00 | — |

**5 RUPEES** **KM# 109** **Composition:** Copper-Nickel **Subject:** Marriage of Prince Edward **Obverse:** National arms **Reverse:** Tied initials and birds **Note:** Similar to 25 Rupees, KM#110.

| Date | Mintage | F | VF | XF | Unc | BU |
|---|---|---|---|---|---|---|
| 1999 | — | — | — | — | 10.00 | — |

**5 RUPEES** **KM# 112** **Composition:** Copper-Nickel **Subject:** Millennium **Obverse:** National arms **Reverse:** Latent image 1999-2000 dates **Note:** Similar to 25 Rupees, KM#113.

| Date | Mintage | F | VF | XF | Unc | BU |
|---|---|---|---|---|---|---|
| 2000 | — | — | — | — | 10.00 | — |

**5 RUPEES** **KM# 114** **Composition:** Copper-Nickel **Subject:** British Queen Mother **Obverse:** National arms **Reverse:** Queen Mother's portrait **Edge:** Reeded

| Date | Mintage | F | VF | XF | Unc | BU |
|---|---|---|---|---|---|---|
| 2000 | — | — | — | — | 10.00 | — |

**10 RUPEES** **KM# 28** **Composition:** Copper-Nickel **Subject:** Declaration of Independence

| Date | Mintage | F | VF | XF | Unc | BU |
|---|---|---|---|---|---|---|
| 1976 | 50,000 | — | 2.00 | 2.75 | 5.00 | — |

**10 RUPEES** **KM# 28a** **Weight:** 28.2800 g. **Composition:** 0.9250 Silver .8411 oz. ASW **Subject:** Declaration of Independence

| Date | Mintage | F | VF | XF | Unc | BU |
|---|---|---|---|---|---|---|
| 1976 Proof | 29,000 | Value: 11.50 | | | | |

**10 RUPEES** **KM# 37** **Composition:** Copper-Nickel **Series:** F.A.O **Reverse:** Turtle

| Date | Mintage | F | VF | XF | Unc | BU |
|---|---|---|---|---|---|---|
| 1977 | — | — | 2.00 | 3.00 | 5.00 | — |
| 1977 Proof | — | Value: 7.00 | | | | |

**10 RUPEES** **KM# 64** **Weight:** 10.0000 g. **Composition:** 0.9250 Silver .2974 oz. ASW **Series:** Endagered Wildlife **Reverse:** Magpie Robin **Note:** Similar to 25 Rupees, KM#65.

| Date | Mintage | F | VF | XF | Unc | BU |
|---|---|---|---|---|---|---|
| 1993 Proof | Est. 20,000 | Value: 16.50 | | | | |

**10 RUPEES** **KM# 87** **Weight:** 10.0000 g. **Composition:** 0.5000 Silver .1607 oz. ASW **Series:** 1996 Olympics **Reverse:** Cyclist

| Date | Mintage | F | VF | XF | Unc | BU |
|---|---|---|---|---|---|---|
| 1996 | Est. 10,000 | — | — | — | 30.00 | — |

**20 RUPEES** **KM# 52** **Composition:** Copper-Nickel **Subject:** 5th Anniversary of Central Bank

| Date | Mintage | F | VF | XF | Unc | BU |
|---|---|---|---|---|---|---|
| 1983 | — | — | 4.00 | 5.00 | 6.00 | — |

**20 RUPEES** **KM# 52a** **Weight:** 19.4400 g. **Composition:** 0.9250 Silver .5781 oz. ASW

| Date | Mintage | F | VF | XF | Unc | BU |
|---|---|---|---|---|---|---|
| 1983 Proof | 5,000 | Value: 50.00 | | | | |

**20 RUPEES** **KM# 52b** **Weight:** 33.9000 g. **Composition:** 0.9170 Gold .9994 oz. AGW **Subject:** 5th Anniversary of Central Bank

| Date | Mintage | F | VF | XF | Unc | BU |
|---|---|---|---|---|---|---|
| 1983 Proof | 50 | Value: 950 | | | | |

**25 RUPEES** **KM# 38** **Weight:** 28.2800 g. **Composition:** 0.5000 Silver .4546 oz. ASW **Subject:** Queen's Silver Jubilee

| Date | Mintage | F | VF | XF | Unc | BU |
|---|---|---|---|---|---|---|
| ND(1977) | 17,000 | — | — | — | 8.00 | — |

**25 RUPEES** **KM# 38a** **Weight:** 28.2800 g. **Composition:** 0.9250 Silver .8411 oz. ASW

| Date | Mintage | F | VF | XF | Unc | BU |
|---|---|---|---|---|---|---|
| ND(1977) Proof | 15,000 | Value: 12.50 | | | | |

**25 RUPEES** **KM# 53** **Composition:** Copper-Nickel **Subject:** World Fisheries Conference

| Date | Mintage | F | VF | XF | Unc | BU |
|---|---|---|---|---|---|---|
| 1983 | 100,000 | — | 5.00 | 6.00 | 9.00 | — |

**25 RUPEES** **KM# 53a** **Weight:** 28.2800 g. **Composition:** 0.9250 Silver .8411 oz. ASW

| Date | Mintage | F | VF | XF | Unc | BU |
|---|---|---|---|---|---|---|
| 1983 Proof | 20,000 | Value: 40.00 | | | | |

**25 RUPEES** **KM# 53b** **Weight:** 47.5400 g. **Composition:** 0.9170 Gold 1.4015 oz. AGW **Subject:** World Fisheries Conference

| Date | Mintage | F | VF | XF | Unc | BU |
|---|---|---|---|---|---|---|
| 1983 Proof | 100 | Value: 1,000 | | | | |

**25 RUPEES** **KM# 63** **Weight:** 31.4700 g. **Composition:** 0.9250 Silver .9359 oz. ASW **Subject:** 40th Anniversary of Queen Elizabeth's Coronation

| Date | Mintage | F | VF | XF | Unc | BU |
|---|---|---|---|---|---|---|
| 1993 Proof | Est. 10,000 | Value: 45.00 | | | | |

**25 RUPEES** **KM# 65** **Weight:** 28.2800 g. **Composition:** 0.9250 Silver .8411 oz. ASW **Series:** Endangered Wildlife **Reverse:** Magpie Robin

| Date | Mintage | F | VF | XF | Unc | BU |
|---|---|---|---|---|---|---|
| 1993 Proof | Est. 20,000 | Value: 28.50 | | | | |

**25 RUPEES** **KM# 67** **Weight:** 31.4600 g. **Composition:** 0.9250 Silver .9359 oz. ASW **Subject:** World Cup Soccer **Reverse:** Goalie at net

| Date | Mintage | F | VF | XF | Unc | BU |
|---|---|---|---|---|---|---|
| 1993 Proof | Est. 15,000 | Value: 28.00 | | | | |

**25 RUPEES** **KM# 68** **Weight:** 31.4600 g. **Composition:** 0.9250 Silver .9359 oz. ASW **Obverse:** Coat of arms **Reverse:** Space shuttle

| Date | Mintage | F | VF | XF | Unc | BU |
|---|---|---|---|---|---|---|
| 1993 Proof | Est. 10,000 | Value: 25.00 | | | | |

**25 RUPEES** **KM# 69** **Weight:** 31.4600 g. **Composition:** 0.9250 Silver .9359 oz. ASW **Subject:** First French Landing

| Date | Mintage | F | VF | XF | Unc | BU |
|---|---|---|---|---|---|---|
| 1993 Proof | Est. 10,000 | Value: 22.50 | | | | |

**25 RUPEES** **KM# 70** **Weight:** 31.4600 g. **Composition:** 0.9250 Silver .9359 oz. ASW **Series:** 1992 Olympics **Reverse:** Balance beam gymnasts

| Date | Mintage | F | VF | XF | Unc | BU |
|---|---|---|---|---|---|---|
| 1993 Proof | Est. 40,000 | Value: 13.50 | | | | |

**25 RUPEES** **KM# 71** **Weight:** 31.4600 g. **Composition:** 0.9250 Silver .9359 oz. ASW **Series:** Protect Our World **Reverse:** Fish and coral

| Date | Mintage | F | VF | XF | Unc | BU |
|---|---|---|---|---|---|---|
| 1993 Proof | Est. 10,000 | Value: 35.00 | | | | |

**25 RUPEES** **KM# 72** **Weight:** 19.4400 g. **Composition:** 0.9250 Silver .5782 oz. ASW **Subject:** 15th Anniversary - Central Bank

| Date | Mintage | F | VF | XF | Unc | BU |
|---|---|---|---|---|---|---|
| 1993 Proof | Est. 1,000 | Value: 60.00 | | | | |

**25 RUPEES** **KM# 74** **Weight:** 19.4400 g. **Composition:** 0.9250 Silver .5782 oz. ASW **Series:** Endangered Wildlife **Reverse:** Milkweed Butterfly

| Date | Mintage | F | VF | XF | Unc | BU |
|---|---|---|---|---|---|---|
| 1994PM Proof | 20,000 | Value: 32.50 | | | | |

**25 RUPEES** **KM# 79** **Weight:** 31.4700 g. **Composition:** 0.9250 Silver .9359 oz. ASW **Reverse:** British Queen Mother - wedding portrait

| Date | Mintage | F | VF | XF | Unc | BU |
|---|---|---|---|---|---|---|
| 1994 Proof | 50,000 | Value: 28.00 | | | | |

**25 RUPEES** **KM# 78** **Weight:** 28.2800 g. **Composition:** 0.9250 Silver .8411 oz. ASW **Series:** Endangered Wildlife **Reverse:** Kestrel

| Date | Mintage | F | VF | XF | Unc | BU |
|---|---|---|---|---|---|---|
| 1995 Proof | Est. 20,000 | Value: 30.00 | | | | |

**25 RUPEES** **KM# 80** **Weight:** 28.2800 g. **Composition:** 0.9250 Silver .8411 oz. ASW **Series:** Olympics **Reverse:** Sailing

| Date | Mintage | F | VF | XF | Unc | BU |
|---|---|---|---|---|---|---|
| 1995 Proof | Est. 30,000 | Value: 25.00 | | | | |

**25 RUPEES** **KM# 81** **Weight:** 28.2800 g. **Composition:** 0.9250 Silver .8411 oz. ASW **Subject:** Vasco Da Gama

| Date | Mintage | F | VF | XF | Unc | BU |
|---|---|---|---|---|---|---|
| 1995 Proof | Est. 10,000 | Value: 37.50 | | | | |

**25 RUPEES** **KM# 108** **Weight:** 28.2800 g. **Composition:** 0.9250 Silver .8411 oz. ASW **Series:** 50th Anniversary U.N.

| Date | Mintage | F | VF | XF | Unc | BU |
|---|---|---|---|---|---|---|
| 1995 Proof | — | Value: 37.50 | | | | |

**25 RUPEES** **KM# 97** **Weight:** 31.4700 g. **Composition:** 0.9250 Silver .9359 oz. ASW **Series:** 1996 Olympic Games **Obverse:** National arms **Reverse:** Cyclist

| Date | Mintage | F | VF | XF | Unc | BU |
|---|---|---|---|---|---|---|
| 1995 Proof | — | Value: 25.00 | | | | |

**25 RUPEES** **KM# 88** **Weight:** 31.4700 g. **Composition:** 0.9250 Silver .9359 oz. ASW **Subject:** Foundation of the commonwealth **Reverse:** Crown and flags

| Date | Mintage | F | VF | XF | Unc | BU |
|---|---|---|---|---|---|---|
| 1996 | 40,000 | — | — | — | 42.00 | — |

**25 RUPEES** **KM# 83** **Weight:** 28.2800 g. **Composition:** 0.9250 Silver .8411 oz. ASW **Series:** Endangered Wildlife **Reverse:** Paradise Flycatcher Bird

| Date | Mintage | F | VF | XF | Unc | BU |
|---|---|---|---|---|---|---|
| 1996 Proof | Est. 20,000 | Value: 40.00 | | | | |

**25 RUPEES** **KM# 92** **Weight:** 1.2400 g. **Composition:** 0.9990 Gold .0398 oz. AGW **Subject:** Diana - The People's Princess **Note:** Similar to KM#91.

| Date | Mintage | F | VF | XF | Unc | BU |
|---|---|---|---|---|---|---|
| 1997 Proof | Est. 10,000 | Value: 45.00 | | | | |

**25 RUPEES** **KM# 96** **Weight:** 1.2400 g. **Composition:** 0.9990 Gold .0398 oz. AGW **Subject:** Diana - The People's Princess **Note:** Similar to KM#95.

| Date | Mintage | F | VF | XF | Unc | BU |
|---|---|---|---|---|---|---|
| 1997 Proof | Est. 10,000 | Value: 50.00 | | | | |

**25 RUPEES** **KM# 100** **Weight:** 1.2400 g. **Composition:** 0.9990 Gold .0398 oz. AGW **Subject:** Diana - The People's Princess **Note:** Similar to KM#99.

| Date | Mintage | F | VF | XF | Unc | BU |
|---|---|---|---|---|---|---|
| 1997 Proof | Est. 10,000 | Value: 50.00 | | | | |

**25 RUPEES** **KM# 91** **Weight:** 28.2800 g. **Composition:** 0.9250 Silver .8410 oz. ASW **Subject:** Diana - The People's Princess

| Date | Mintage | F | VF | XF | Unc | BU |
|---|---|---|---|---|---|---|
| 1997 Proof | Est. 10,000 | Value: 40.00 | | | | |

**25 RUPEES** **KM# 95** **Weight:** 28.2800 g. **Composition:** 0.9250 Silver .8410 oz. ASW **Subject:** Diana - The People's Princess **Reverse:** Holding baby William

| Date | Mintage | F | VF | XF | Unc | BU |
|---|---|---|---|---|---|---|
| 1997 Proof | Est. 10,000 | Value: 32.50 | | | | |

**25 RUPEES** **KM# 99** **Weight:** 28.2800 g. **Composition:** 0.9250 Silver .8410 oz. ASW **Subject:** Diana - The People's Princess **Reverse:** Holding young cancer patient

| Date | Mintage | F | VF | XF | Unc | BU |
|---|---|---|---|---|---|---|
| 1997 Proof | Est. 10,000 | Value: 40.00 | | | | |

**25 RUPEES** **KM# 103** **Weight:** 28.2800 g. **Composition:** 0.9250 Silver .8410 oz. ASW **Subject:** Diana - The People's Princess **Reverse:** In summer clothes

| Date | Mintage | F | VF | XF | Unc | BU |
|---|---|---|---|---|---|---|
| 1998 Proof | Est. 10,000 | Value: 42.50 | | | | |

**25 RUPEES** **KM# 104** **Weight:** 1.2441 g. **Composition:** 0.9999 Gold .0400 oz. AGW **Subject:** Diana - The People's Princess **Note:** Similar to KM#103.

| Date | Mintage | F | VF | XF | Unc | BU |
|---|---|---|---|---|---|---|
| 1998 Proof | Est. 10,000 | Value: 55.00 | | | | |

**25 RUPEES** **KM# 110** **Weight:** 28.2800 g. **Composition:** 0.9250 Silver .8410 oz. ASW **Series:** Olympics Games 2000 **Subject:** Marriage of Prince Edward **Obverse:** National arms **Reverse:** Tied letters and birds

| Date | Mintage | F | VF | XF | Unc | BU |
|---|---|---|---|---|---|---|
| 1999 Proof | Est. 10,000 | Value: 47.50 | | | | |

**25 RUPEES** **KM# 113** **Weight:** 1.2441 g. **Composition:** 0.9999 Gold .0400 oz. AGW **Subject:** Millennium **Obverse:** National arms **Reverse:** Latent image of 1999-2000 dates

| Date | Mintage | F | VF | XF | Unc | BU |
|---|---|---|---|---|---|---|
| 2000 Proof | Est. 10,000 | Value: 47.50 | | | | |

**25 RUPEES** **KM# 115** **Weight:** 1.2441 g. **Composition:** 0.9999 Gold .0400 oz. AGW **Subject:** 100th Birthday - British Queen Mother **Obverse:** National arms **Reverse:** Queen Mother's portrait **Edge:** Reeded

| Date | Mintage | F | VF | XF | Unc | BU |
|---|---|---|---|---|---|---|
| 2000 Proof | Est. 10,000 | Value: 47.50 | | | | |

**50 RUPEES** **KM# 39** **Weight:** 28.2800 g. **Composition:** 0.9250 Silver .8411 oz. ASW **Subject:** Conservation **Reverse:** Squirrel Fish

| Date | Mintage | F | VF | XF | Unc | BU |
|---|---|---|---|---|---|---|
| 1978 | 4,453 | — | — | — | 16.50 | — |
| 1978 Proof | 4,281 | Value: 20.00 | | | | |

**50 RUPEES** **KM# 42** **Weight:** 19.4400 g. **Composition:** 0.9250 Silver .5781 oz. ASW **Series:** UNICEF and International Year of the Child

| Date | Mintage | F | VF | XF | Unc | BU |
|---|---|---|---|---|---|---|
| 1980 Proof | 10,000 | Value: 17.50 | | | | |

**50 RUPEES** **KM# 54** **Weight:** 19.4400 g. **Composition:** 0.9250 Silver .5781 oz. ASW **Series:** Decade for Women

| Date | Mintage | F | VF | XF | Unc | BU |
|---|---|---|---|---|---|---|
| 1985 Proof | 500 | Value: 30.00 | | | | |

**50 RUPEES** **KM# 75** **Weight:** 1.2440 g. **Composition:** 0.9999 Gold .0497 oz. AGW **Series:** Endangered Wildlife **Obverse:** Coat of arms **Reverse:** Milkweed Butterfly **Note:** Similar to 25 Rupees, KM#74.

| Date | Mintage | F | VF | XF | Unc | BU |
|---|---|---|---|---|---|---|
| 1994 PM Prooflike | — | — | — | — | — | — |

**50 RUPEES** **KM# 107** **Weight:** 3.1100 g. **Composition:** 0.5833 Gold .0583 oz. AGW **Series:** Olympics Games 2000 **Obverse:** National arms **Reverse:** Two divers

| Date | Mintage | F | VF | XF | Unc | BU |
|---|---|---|---|---|---|---|
| 1997 Proof | 5,000 | Value: 50.00 | | | | |

**100 RUPEES** **KM# 40** **Weight:** 31.6500 g. **Composition:** 0.9250 Silver .9413 oz. ASW **Subject:** Consservation **Reverse:** White-tailed Tropicbird

| Date | Mintage | F | VF | XF | Unc | BU |
|---|---|---|---|---|---|---|
| 1978 | 4,453 | — | — | — | 20.00 | — |
| 1978 Proof | 4,075 | Value: 25.00 | | | | |

**100 RUPEES** **KM# 45** **Weight:** 31.6500 g. **Composition:** 0.9250 Silver .9413 oz. ASW **Series:** World Food Day

| Date | Mintage | F | VF | XF | Unc | BU |
|---|---|---|---|---|---|---|
| 1981 | 6,000 | — | — | — | 22.50 | — |
| 1981 Proof | 5,000 | Value: 37.50 | | | | |

**100 RUPEES** **KM# 45a** **Weight:** 35.0000 g. **Composition:** 0.5000 Silver .5627 oz. ASW

| Date | Mintage | F | VF | XF | Unc | BU |
|---|---|---|---|---|---|---|
| 1981 Proof | 10,000 | Value: 25.00 | | | | |

**100 RUPEES** **KM# 55** **Weight:** 19.4400 g. **Composition:** 0.9250 Silver .5781 oz. ASW **Subject:** 10th Anniversary of Independence

| Date | Mintage | F | VF | XF | Unc | BU |
|---|---|---|---|---|---|---|
| ND(1986) Proof | 1,000 | Value: 45.00 | | | | |

**100 RUPEES** **KM# 57** **Weight:** 19.4400 g. **Composition:** 0.9250 Silver .5781 oz. ASW **Subject:** 10th Anniversary of Liberation

| Date | Mintage | F | VF | XF | Unc | BU |
|---|---|---|---|---|---|---|
| ND(1987) PM Proof | 1,000 | Value: 40.00 | | | | |

**100 RUPEES** **KM# 59** **Weight:** 19.4000 g. **Composition:** 0.9170 Silver .5720 oz. ASW **Subject:** 10th Anniversary of Central Bank

| Date | Mintage | F | VF | XF | Unc | BU |
|---|---|---|---|---|---|---|
| ND(1988) PM Proof | — | Value: 75.00 | | | | |

**100 RUPEES** **KM# 60** **Weight:** 1.7000 g. **Composition:** 0.9170 Gold .0501 oz. AGW **Subject:** 10th Anniversary of Central Bank **Obverse:** Arms **Reverse:** Sea turtle **Note:** Similar to KM#59.

| Date | Mintage | F | VF | XF | Unc | BU |
|---|---|---|---|---|---|---|
| ND(1988) PM Proof | — | Value: 75.00 | | | | |

**100 RUPEES** **KM# 76** **Weight:** 3.1103 g. **Composition:** 0.9999 Gold .1000 oz. AGW **Series:** Endangered Wildlife **Obverse:** Coat of arms **Reverse:** Milkweed Butterfly **Note:** Similar to 25 Rupees, KM#74.

| Date | Mintage | F | VF | XF | Unc | BU |
|---|---|---|---|---|---|---|
| 1994 PM Prooflike | — | — | — | — | — | — |

**100 RUPEES** **KM# 82** **Weight:** 7.7760 g. **Composition:** 0.5830 Gold .1458 oz. AGW **Series:** Olympics **Reverse:** Sailboats

| Date | Mintage | F | VF | XF | Unc | BU |
|---|---|---|---|---|---|---|
| 1995 Proof | Est. 3,000 | Value: 120 | | | | |

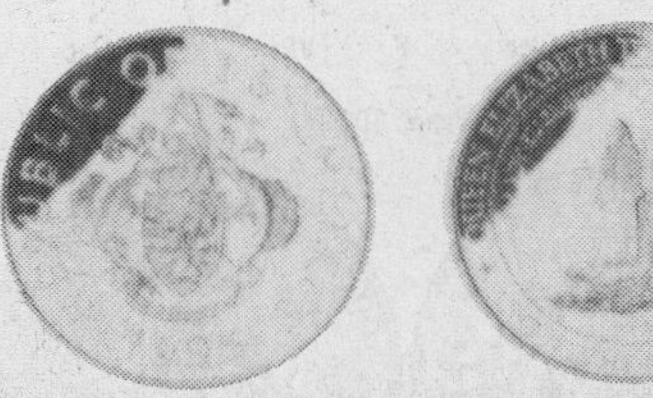

**100 RUPEES** **KM# 86** **Weight:** 7.7760 g. **Composition:** 0.5830 Gold .1458 oz. AGW **Subject:** British Queen Mother

| Date | Mintage | F | VF | XF | Unc | BU |
|---|---|---|---|---|---|---|
| 1995 | Est. 5,000 | — | — | — | 125 | — |

**100 RUPEES** **KM# 93** **Weight:** 7.7760 g. **Composition:** 0.5830 Gold .1458 oz. AGW **Subject:** Diana - The People's Princess **Note:** Similar to 25 Rupees, KM#91.

| Date | Mintage | F | VF | XF | Unc | BU |
|---|---|---|---|---|---|---|
| 1997 Proof | Est. 7,500 | Value: 110 | | | | |

**100 RUPEES** **KM# A97** **Weight:** 7.7760 g. **Composition:** 0.5830 Gold .1458 oz. AGW **Subject:** Diana - The People's Princess **Note:** Similar to 25 Rupees, KM#95.

| Date | Mintage | F | VF | XF | Unc | BU |
|---|---|---|---|---|---|---|
| 1997 | 7,500 | Value: 110 | | | | |

**100 RUPEES** **KM# 101** **Weight:** 7.7760 g. **Composition:** 0.5830 Gold .1458 oz. AGW **Subject:** Diana - The People's Princess **Note:** Similar to 25 Rupees, KM#99.

| Date | Mintage | F | VF | XF | Unc | BU |
|---|---|---|---|---|---|---|
| 1997 Proof | Est. 7,500 | Value: 110 | | | | |

**100 RUPEES** **KM# 105** **Weight:** 7.7760 g. **Composition:** 0.5830 Gold .1458 oz. AGW **Subject:** Diana - The People's Princess **Note:** Similar to 25 Rupees, KM#103.

| Date | Mintage | F | VF | XF | Unc | BU |
|---|---|---|---|---|---|---|
| 1998 Proof | Est. 7,500 | Value: 110 | | | | |

**100 RUPEES** **KM# 111** **Weight:** 6.2200 g. **Composition:** 0.9999 Gold .2000 oz. AGW **Subject:** Marriage of Prince Edward **Obverse:** National arms **Reverse:** Tied initials and birds **Note:** Similar to 25 Rupees, KM#110.

| Date | Mintage | F | VF | XF | Unc | BU |
|---|---|---|---|---|---|---|
| 1999 Proof | Est. 2,000 | Value: 185 | | | | |

**100 RUPEES** **KM# 116** **Weight:** 6.2200 g. **Composition:** 0.9999 Gold .2000 oz. AGW **Subject:** 100th Birthday Queen Mother **Obverse:** National arms **Reverse:** Queen Mother's portrait **Edge:** Reeded **Size:** 22 mm.

| Date | Mintage | F | VF | XF | Unc | BU |
|---|---|---|---|---|---|---|
| 2000 Proof | 2,000 | Value: 175 | | | | |

**250 RUPEES** **KM# 66** **Weight:** 6.2200 g. **Composition:** 0.9990 Gold .2000 oz. AGW **Series:** Endangered Wildlife **Reverse:** Magpie Robin **Note:** Similar to 25 Rupees, KM#65.

| Date | Mintage | F | VF | XF | Unc | BU |
|---|---|---|---|---|---|---|
| 1993 Proof | — | Value: 145 | | | | |

**250 RUPEES** **KM# 77** **Weight:** 6.2200 g. **Composition:** 0.9990 Gold .2000 oz. AGW **Series:** Endangered Wildlife **Obverse:** Coat of arms **Reverse:** Milkweed Butterfly **Note:** Similar to 25 Rupees, KM#74.

| Date | Mintage | F | VF | XF | Unc | BU |
|---|---|---|---|---|---|---|
| 1993 Proof | — | Value: 190 | | | | |
| 1994 PM Prooflike | — | — | — | — | — | — |
| 1996PM Proof | 5,000 | — | — | — | — | — |

**250 RUPEES** **KM# 84** **Weight:** 6.2200 g. **Composition:** 0.9990 Gold .2000 oz. AGW **Series:** Endangered Wildlife **Reverse:** Paradise Flycatcher Bird **Note:** Similar to 25 Rupees, KM#83.

| Date | Mintage | F | VF | XF | Unc | BU |
|---|---|---|---|---|---|---|
| 1996 Proof | Est. 5,000 | Value: 185 | | | | |

**250 RUPEES** **KM# 94** **Weight:** 6.2200 g. **Composition:** 0.9990 Gold .2000 oz. AGW **Subject:** Diana - The People's Princess **Note:** Similar to 25 Rupees, KM#91.

| Date | Mintage | F | VF | XF | Unc | BU |
|---|---|---|---|---|---|---|
| 1997 Proof | Est. 5,000 | Value: 185 | | | | |

**250 RUPEES** **KM# 98** **Weight:** 6.2200 g. **Composition:** 0.9990 Gold .2000 oz. AGW **Subject:** Diana - The People's Princess **Note:** Similar to 25 Rupees, KM#95.

| Date | Mintage | F | VF | XF | Unc | BU |
|---|---|---|---|---|---|---|
| 1997 Proof | Est. 5,000 | Value: 185 | | | | |

**250 RUPEES** **KM# 102** **Weight:** 6.2200 g. **Composition:** 0.9990 Gold .2000 oz. AGW **Subject:** Diana - The People's Princess **Note:** Similar to 25 Rupees, KM#99.

| Date | Mintage | F | VF | XF | Unc | BU |
|---|---|---|---|---|---|---|
| 1997 Proof | Est. 5,000 | Value: 185 | | | | |

**250 RUPEES** **KM# 106** **Weight:** 6.2200 g. **Composition:** 0.9990 Gold .2000 oz. AGW **Subject:** Diana - The People's Princess **Note:** Similar to 25 Rupees, KM#103.

| Date | Mintage | F | VF | XF | Unc | BU |
|---|---|---|---|---|---|---|
| 1998 Proof | Est. 5,000 | Value: 185 | | | | |

**500 RUPEES** KM# 62 **Weight:** 7.1300 g. **Composition:** 0.9000 Gold .2036 oz. AGW **Series:** Decade for Women

| Date | Mintage | F | VF | XF | Unc | BU |
|---|---|---|---|---|---|---|
| 1985 Proof | 500 | Value: 135 | | | | |

**1000 RUPEES** KM#29 **Weight:** 15.9800 g. **Composition:** 0.9170 Gold .4707 oz. AGW **Subject:** Declaration of Independence **Obverse:** President Mancham **Reverse:** Tortoise, date, value

| Date | Mintage | F | VF | XF | Unc | BU |
|---|---|---|---|---|---|---|
| 1976 | 5,000 | — | — | — | 200 | — |
| 1976 Proof | 1,000 | Value: 300 | | | | |

**1000 RUPEES** KM#56 **Weight:** 15.9800 g. **Composition:** 0.9170 Gold .4707 oz. AGW **Subject:** 10th Anniversary of Independence

| Date | Mintage | F | VF | XF | Unc | BU |
|---|---|---|---|---|---|---|
| ND(1986) Proof | 100 | Value: 385 | | | | |

**1000 RUPEES** KM#58 **Weight:** 15.9800 g. **Composition:** 0.9170 Gold .4707 oz. AGW **Subject:** 10th Anniversary of Liberation

| Date | Mintage | F | VF | XF | Unc | BU |
|---|---|---|---|---|---|---|
| ND(1987) PM Proof | 100 | Value: 375 | | | | |

**1000 RUPEES** KM#61 **Weight:** 15.9400 g. **Composition:** 0.9170 Gold .4698 oz. AGW **Subject:** 100th Anniversary of Central Bank **Obverse:** Arms **Reverse:** Sea turtle **Note:** Similar to 100 Rupees, KM#59.

| Date | Mintage | F | VF | XF | Unc | BU |
|---|---|---|---|---|---|---|
| ND(1988) PM Proof | Est. 5,000 | Value: 235 | | | | |

**1000 RUPEES** KM#73 **Weight:** 15.9800 g. **Composition:** 0.9170 Gold .4710 oz. AGW **Subject:** Central Banking

| Date | Mintage | F | VF | XF | Unc | BU |
|---|---|---|---|---|---|---|
| 1993 Proof | Est. 200 | Value: 350 | | | | |

**1500 RUPEES** KM#41 **Weight:** 33.4370 g. **Composition:** 0.9000 Gold .9676 oz. AGW **Subject:** Conservation **Reverse:** Black Paradise Flycatcher

| Date | Mintage | F | VF | XF | Unc | BU |
|---|---|---|---|---|---|---|
| 1978 | 683 | — | — | — | 475 | — |
| 1978 Proof | 201 | Value: 850 | | | | |

## PATTERNS

Including off metal strikes

| KM# | Date | Mintage | Identification | Mkt Val |
|---|---|---|---|---|
| Pn1 | 1974 | — | 10 Rupees. Brass. KM#20. | — |
| Pn2 | 1974 | — | 10 Rupees. Bronze. KM#20. | — |
| Pn3 | 1974 | — | 10 Rupees. Copper-Nickel. KM#20. | — |
| Pn4 | 1974 | — | 10 Rupees. Silver. KM#20. | — |
| Pn6 | 1976 | — | 1000 Rupees. Bronze. KM#29. | — |
| Pn5 | 1976 | — | 10 Cents. Silver. KM#23, thick planchet. | 250 |

## PIEFORTS

| KM# | Date | Mintage | Identification | Mkt Val |
|---|---|---|---|---|
| P1 | 1980 | 78 | 50 Rupees. KM#42. | 85.00 |
| P2 | 1983 | 500 | 50 Rupees. | 65.00 |
| P3 | 1984 | 500 | 50 Rupees. 0.9250 Silver. | 65.00 |
| P4 | 1984 | 100 | 50 Rupees. 0.9000 Gold. | 1,500 |

## MINT SETS

| KM# | Date | Mintage | Identification | Issue Price | Mkt Val |
|---|---|---|---|---|---|
| MS5 | 1982 (6) | — | KM#46-51 | — | 5.00 |
| MS6 | 1992 (6) | — | KM#46-48, 49.2, 50-51 | 12.00 | 12.00 |
| MS1 | 1972 (7) | — | KM#10-13, 17-19 | — | 8.50 |
| MS2 | 1974 (5) | — | KM#10-13, 20 | — | 8.50 |
| MS3 | 1976 (8) | — | KM#21-28 | — | 16.00 |
| MS4 | 1977 (8) | — | KM#30-37 | — | 11.50 |
| MS7 | Mixed dates (6) | — | KM#46.2 (1990), 47.2-51.2 (1997) | — | 8.50 |

## PROOF SETS

| KM# | Date | Mintage | Identification | Issue Price | Mkt Val |
|---|---|---|---|---|---|
| PS1 | 1939 (4) | — | KM#1-4 | — | 1,000 |
| PS2 | 1969 (7) | 5,000 | KM#10-16 | 8.40 | 20.00 |
| PS3 | 1974 (2) | 5,000 | KM#19-a, 20a | 37.00 | 32.50 |
| PS4 | 1976 (9) | 1,000 | KM#21-26 , 27a, 28a, 29 | 375 | 375 |
| PS5 | 1976 (8) | 7,500 | KM#21-26, 27a, 28a | 42.50 | 42.50 |
| PS6 | 1982 (6) | 5,000 | KM#46.1-51.1 | 29.95 | 20.00 |
| PS7 | 1992 (6) | — | KM#46.2-51.2 | — | 20.00 |

# SHARJAH

Sharjah is the only one of the emirates that shares boundaries with all of the others plus Oman. It has an area of 1,000 sq. mi. (2,600 sq. km.) and a population of 40,000. Sharjah was an important pirate base in the 18th and early 19th centuries. Most of the treaties and diplomatic relations were with Great Britain.

**TITLES**

Ash-Sharqa(t) الشارقة

**RULERS**

Saqr Bin Khalid al-Qasimi, 1883-1914
Khalid Bin Ahmad al-Qasimi, 1914-1924
Sultan Bin Saqr al-Qasimi, 1924-1951
Saqr Bin Sultan al-Qasimi, 1951-1965
Khalid Bin Muhammad al-Qasimi, 1965-1972
Sultan Bin Muhammad al-Qasimi,1972-

## UNITED ARAB EMIRATE

### NON-CIRCULATING LEGAL TENDER COINAGE

**5 RUPEE** KM#1 **Weight:** 25.0000 g. **Composition:** 0.7200 Silver .5787 oz. ASW **Ruler:** Khalid bin Muhammad al-Qasimi **Subject:** President John F. Kennedy Memorial

| Date | Mintage | F | VF | XF | Unc | BU |
|---|---|---|---|---|---|---|
| 1964 | — | — | — | — | 15.00 | — |
| 1964 PROOF below flags on obverse | — | Value: 25.00 | | | | |

**Note:** KM#1 was ordered by the Sheik, who according to the British has no authority to issue it

**RIYAL** KM#2 **Weight:** 3.0000 g. **Composition:** 1.0000 Silver .0965 oz. ASW **Ruler:** Khalid bin Muhammad al-Qasimi **Subject:** Mona Lisa

| Date | Mintage | F | VF | XF | Unc | BU |
|---|---|---|---|---|---|---|
| AH1389(1969) Proof | 3,850 | Value: 17.50 | | | | |

**2 RIYALS** KM#3 **Weight:** 6.0000 g. **Composition:** 1.0000 Silver .1929 oz. ASW **Ruler:** Khalid bin Muhammad al-Qasimi **Subject:** Mexico World Soccer Cup

| Date | Mintage | F | VF | XF | Unc | BU |
|---|---|---|---|---|---|---|
| AH1389(1969) Proof | 4,500 | Value: 27.50 | | | | |

**5 RIYALS** KM# 4 **Weight:** 15.0000 g. **Composition:** 1.0000 Silver .4823 oz. ASW **Ruler:** Khalid bin Muhammad al-Qasimi **Subject:** Napoleon

| Date | Mintage | F | VF | XF | Unc | BU |
|---|---|---|---|---|---|---|
| AH1389(1969) Proof | 2,500 | Value: 37.50 | | | | |

**10 RIYALS** KM# 5 **Weight:** 30.0000 g. **Composition:** 1.0000 Silver .9646 oz. ASW **Ruler:** Khalid bin Muhammad al-Qasimi **Subject:** Bolivar **Obverse:** Similar to 1 Riyal, KM#2

| Date | Mintage | F | VF | XF | Unc | BU |
|---|---|---|---|---|---|---|
| AH1389(1969) Proof | 3,200 | Value: 60.00 | | | | |

**25 RIYALS** KM# 7 **Weight:** 5.1800 g. **Composition:** 0.9000 Gold .1499 oz. AGW **Ruler:** Khalid bin Muhammad al-Qasimi **Subject:** Mona Lisa

| Date | Mintage | F | VF | XF | Unc | BU |
|---|---|---|---|---|---|---|
| AH1389(1969) Proof | 6,775 | Value: 175 | | | | |

**50 RIYALS** KM# 8 **Weight:** 10.3600 g. **Composition:** 0.9000 Gold .2998 oz. AGW **Ruler:** Khalid bin Muhammad al-Qasimi **Subject:** Mexico World Soccer Cup **Obverse:** Similar to 25 Riyals, KM#7

| Date | Mintage | F | VF | XF | Unc | BU |
|---|---|---|---|---|---|---|
| AH1389(1969) Proof | 1,815 | Value: 250 | | | | |

**100 RIYALS** KM# 9 **Weight:** 20.7300 g. **Composition:** 0.9000 Gold .5999 oz. AGW **Ruler:** Khalid bin Muhammad al-Qasimi **Subject:** Napoleon

| Date | Mintage | F | VF | XF | Unc | BU |
|---|---|---|---|---|---|---|
| AH1389(1969) Proof | — | Value: 450 | | | | |

**100 RIYALS** KM# 10 **Weight:** 20.7300 g. **Composition:** 0.9000 Gold .5999 oz. AGW **Ruler:** Khalid bin Muhammad al-Qasimi **Subject:** Bolivar

| Date | Mintage | F | VF | XF | Unc | BU |
|---|---|---|---|---|---|---|
| AH1389(1969) Proof | — | Value: 375 | | | | |

**200 RIYALS** KM# 11 **Weight:** 41.4600 g. **Composition:** 0.9000 Gold 1.1998 oz. AGW **Ruler:** Khalid bin Muhammad al-Qasimi **Subject:** Khalid III **Obverse:** Similar to 25 Riyals, KM#7

| Date | Mintage | F | VF | XF | Unc | BU |
|---|---|---|---|---|---|---|
| AH1389(1969) Proof | 435 | Value: 750 | | | | |

## PROOF SETS

| KM# | Date | Mintage | Identification | Issue Price | Mkt Val |
|---|---|---|---|---|---|
| PS1 | 1970 (9) | — | KM#2-5, 7-11 | — | 2,125 |
| PS2 | 1970 (5) | — | KM#7-11 | — | 2,000 |
| PS3 | 1970 (4) | 2,500 | KM#2-5 | 25.30 | 140 |

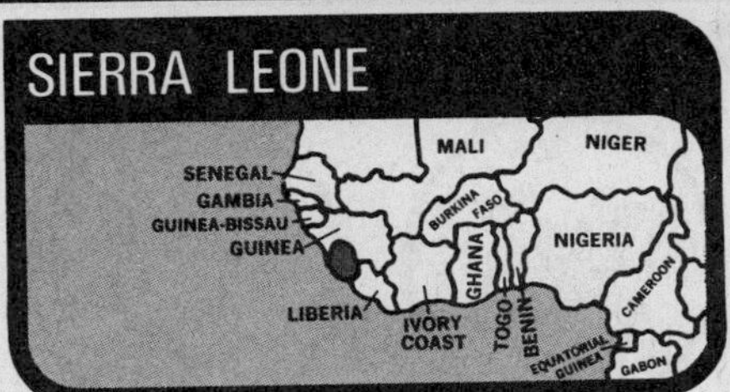


The Republic of Sierra Leone, a British Commonwealth nation located in western Africa between Guinea and Liberia, has an area of 27,699 sq. mi. (71,740 sq. km.) and a population of *4.1 million. Capital: Freetown. The economy is predominantly agricultural but mining contributes significantly to export revenues. Diamonds, iron ore, palm kernels, cocoa, and coffee are exported.

The coast of Sierra Leone was first visited by Portuguese and British slavers in the 15th and 16thcenturies. The first settlement, at Freetown, 1787, was established as a refuge for freed slaves within the British Empire, runaway slaves from the United States and Negroes discharged from the British armed forces. The first settlers were virtually wiped out by tribal attacks and disease. The colony was re-established under the auspices of the Sierra Leone Company and transferred to the British Crown in 1807. The interior region was secured and established as a protectorate in 1896. Sierra Leone became independent within the Commonwealth on April 27, 1961, and adopted a republican constitution ten years later. It is a member of the Commonwealth of Nations. The president is Chief of State and Head of Government.

For similar coinage refer to British West Africa.

**RULERS**

British, until 1971

**MONETARY SYSTEM**

Until 1906

100 Cents = 50 Pence = 1 Dollar

Until 1964

12 Pence = 1 Shilling

Commencing 1964

100 Cents = 1 Leone

**NOTE:** "$" indicates the claim that the coins struck by the Pobjoy Mint are backed by U.S. Dollars. See 1 Leone, KM#71.

# REPUBLIC

## STANDARD COINAGE

**1/2 CENT** KM# 16 **Composition:** Bronze **Obverse:** Bonga Fish

| Date | Mintage | F | VF | XF | Unc | BU |
|---|---|---|---|---|---|---|
| 1964 | 600,000 | — | — | 0.15 | 0.25 | — |
| 1964 Proof | 10,000 | Value: 1.00 | | | | |

**1/2 CENT** KM# 16a **Weight:** 2.8300 g. **Composition:** 0.9250 Silver .0841 oz. ASW

| Date | Mintage | F | VF | XF | Unc | BU |
|---|---|---|---|---|---|---|
| 1964 Proof | 22 | Value: 650 | | | | |

**1/2 CENT** KM# 31 **Composition:** Bronze

| Date | Mintage | F | VF | XF | Unc | BU |
|---|---|---|---|---|---|---|
| 1980 | — | — | 0.15 | 0.30 | 1.00 | — |
| 1980 Proof | 10,000 | Value: 1.50 | | | | |

**CENT** KM# 17 **Composition:** Bronze **Obverse:** Palm branches and fruit stalks

| Date | Mintage | F | VF | XF | Unc | BU |
|---|---|---|---|---|---|---|
| 1964 | 35,000,000 | — | — | 0.15 | 0.25 | — |
| 1964 Proof | 10,000 | Value: 1.25 | | | | |

**CENT** KM# 17a **Weight:** 5.6700 g. **Composition:** 0.9250 Silver .1686 oz. ASW

| Date | Mintage | F | VF | XF | Unc | BU |
|---|---|---|---|---|---|---|
| 1964 Proof | 22 | Value: 650 | | | | |

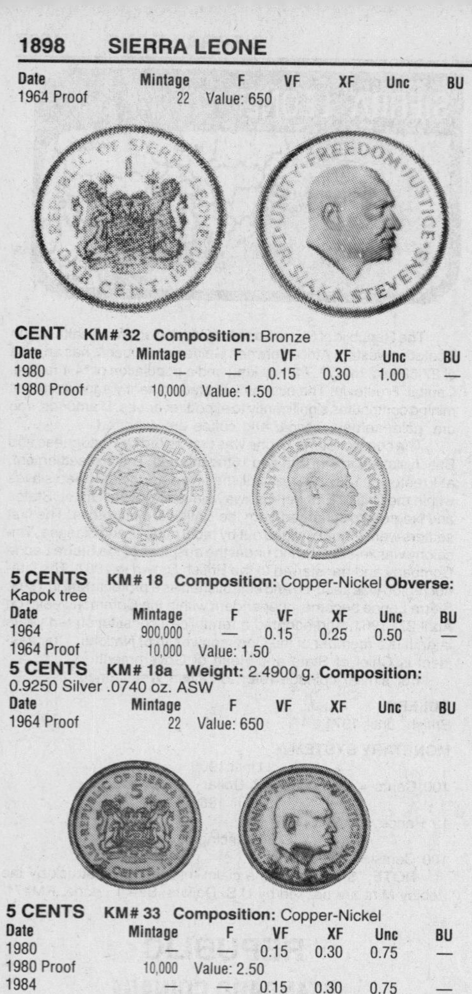

**CENT** **KM# 32** **Composition:** Bronze

| Date | Mintage | F | VF | XF | Unc | BU |
|---|---|---|---|---|---|---|
| 1980 | — | — | 0.15 | 0.30 | 1.00 | — |
| 1980 Proof | 10,000 | Value: 1.50 | | | | |

**5 CENTS** **KM# 18** **Composition:** Copper-Nickel **Obverse:** Kapok tree

| Date | Mintage | F | VF | XF | Unc | BU |
|---|---|---|---|---|---|---|
| 1964 | 900,000 | — | 0.15 | 0.25 | 0.50 | — |
| 1964 Proof | 10,000 | Value: 1.50 | | | | |

**5 CENTS** **KM# 18a** **Weight:** 2.4900 g. **Composition:** 0.9250 Silver .0740 oz. ASW

| Date | Mintage | F | VF | XF | Unc | BU |
|---|---|---|---|---|---|---|
| 1964 Proof | 22 | Value: 650 | | | | |

**5 CENTS** **KM# 33** **Composition:** Copper-Nickel

| Date | Mintage | F | VF | XF | Unc | BU |
|---|---|---|---|---|---|---|
| 1980 | — | — | 0.15 | 0.30 | 0.75 | — |
| 1980 Proof | 10,000 | Value: 2.50 | | | | |
| 1984 | — | — | 0.15 | 0.30 | 0.75 | — |

**10 CENTS** **KM# 19** **Composition:** Copper-Nickel **Obverse:** Cocoa beans

| Date | Mintage | F | VF | XF | Unc | BU |
|---|---|---|---|---|---|---|
| 1964 | 24,000,000 | — | 0.25 | 0.40 | 0.65 | — |
| 1964 Proof | 10,000 | Value: 1.25 | | | | |

**10 CENTS** **KM# 19a** **Weight:** 4.9200 g. **Composition:** 0.9250 Silver .1463 oz. ASW

| Date | Mintage | F | VF | XF | Unc | BU |
|---|---|---|---|---|---|---|
| 1964 Proof | 22 | Value: 650 | | | | |

**10 CENTS** **KM# 34** **Composition:** Copper-Nickel

| Date | Mintage | F | VF | XF | Unc | BU |
|---|---|---|---|---|---|---|
| 1978 | 200,000 | — | 0.25 | 0.50 | 1.00 | — |
| 1980 | — | — | 0.20 | 0.40 | 0.75 | — |
| 1980 Proof | 10,000 | Value: 5.00 | | | | |
| 1984 | — | — | 0.20 | 0.40 | 0.75 | — |

**20 CENTS** **KM# 20** **Composition:** Copper-Nickel

| Date | Mintage | F | VF | XF | Unc | BU |
|---|---|---|---|---|---|---|
| 1964 | 11,000,000 | — | 0.35 | 0.60 | 1.25 | — |
| 1964 Proof | 10,000 | Value: 2.00 | | | | |

**20 CENTS** **KM# 20a** **Weight:** 8.2200 g. **Composition:** 0.9250 Silver .2444 oz. ASW

| Date | Mintage | F | VF | XF | Unc | BU |
|---|---|---|---|---|---|---|
| 1964 Proof | 22 | Value: 650 | | | | |

**20 CENTS** **KM# 30** **Composition:** Copper-Nickel

| Date | Mintage | F | VF | XF | Unc | BU |
|---|---|---|---|---|---|---|
| 1978 | 2,375,000 | — | 0.35 | 0.65 | 1.50 | — |
| 1980 | — | — | 0.35 | 0.60 | 1.25 | — |
| 1980 Proof | 10,000 | Value: 7.00 | | | | |
| 1984 | — | — | 0.35 | 0.60 | 1.25 | — |

**50 CENTS** **KM# 25** **Composition:** Copper-Nickel

| Date | Mintage | F | VF | XF | Unc | BU |
|---|---|---|---|---|---|---|
| 1972 | 1,000,000 | — | 1.00 | 1.75 | 3.00 | — |
| 1972 Proof | 2,000 | Value: 5.00 | | | | |
| 1980 | — | — | 1.00 | 1.50 | 2.75 | — |
| 1980 Proof | 10,000 | Value: 10.00 | | | | |
| 1984 | — | — | 1.00 | 1.50 | 2.75 | — |

**LEONE** **KM#21** **Composition:** Copper-Nickel **Reverse:** Sir Milton Marcai

| Date | Mintage | F | VF | XF | Unc | BU |
|---|---|---|---|---|---|---|
| 1964 Proof | 10,000 | Value: 10.00 | | | | |

**LEONE** **KM# 21a** **Weight:** 22.6220 g. **Composition:** 0.9250 Silver .6738 oz. ASW

| Date | Mintage | F | VF | XF | Unc | BU |
|---|---|---|---|---|---|---|
| 1964 Proof | 12 | Value: 1,000 | | | | |

**LEONE** **KM#21b** **Composition:** 0.9170 Gold **Reverse:** Sir Milton Marcai head facing right

| Date | Mintage | F | VF | XF | Unc | BU |
|---|---|---|---|---|---|---|
| 1964 Proof | 10 | Value: 2,500 | | | | |

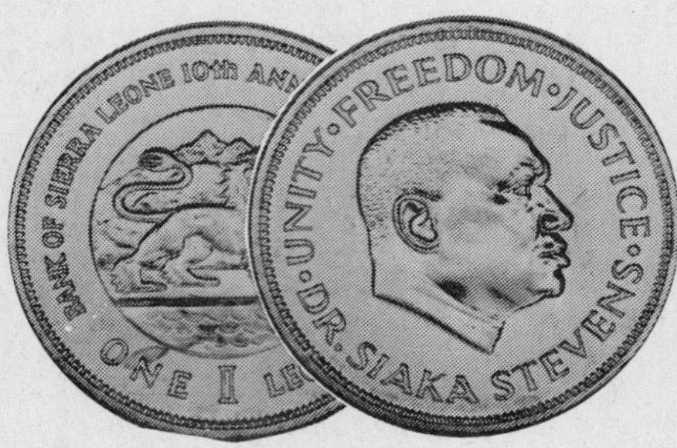

**LEONE** **KM# 26** **Composition:** Copper-Nickel **Subject:** 10 Anniversary of Bank

| Date | Mintage | F | VF | XF | Unc | BU |
|---|---|---|---|---|---|---|
| ND(1974) | 103,000 | — | 1.50 | 2.50 | 5.50 | — |

**LEONE** **KM# 26a** **Weight:** 28.2800 g. **Composition:** 0.9250 Silver .8411 oz. ASW

| Date | Mintage | F | VF | XF | Unc | BU |
|---|---|---|---|---|---|---|
| 1974 Proof | 22,000 | Value: 12.50 | | | | |

**LEONE** **KM# 26b** **Composition:** Gold **Subject:** 10 Anniversary of Bank

| Date | Mintage | F | VF | XF | Unc | BU |
|---|---|---|---|---|---|---|
| 1974 | 100 | — | — | — | 1,200 | — |

**LEONE** **KM# 36** **Composition:** Copper-Nickel **Subject:** O.A.U. Summit Conference

| Date | Mintage | F | VF | XF | Unc | BU |
|---|---|---|---|---|---|---|
| 1980 | 75,000 | — | 1.75 | 2.75 | 6.00 | — |

**LEONE** **KM# 36a** **Weight:** 28.2800 g. **Composition:** 0.9250 Silver .8411 oz. ASW

| Date | Mintage | F | VF | XF | Unc | BU |
|---|---|---|---|---|---|---|
| 1980 Proof | 15,000 | Value: 20.00 | | | | |

**LEONE** **KM# 40** **Weight:** 9.5000 g. **Composition:** 0.9250 Silver .2825 oz. ASW **Subject:** Freetown Bicentennial

| Date | Mintage | F | VF | XF | Unc | BU |
|---|---|---|---|---|---|---|
| 1987 Proof | 3,000 | Value: 25.00 | | | | |

**LEONE** **KM# 40a** **Weight:** 16.0000 g. **Composition:** 0.9170 Gold .4716 oz. AGW **Subject:** Freetown Bicentennial

| Date | Mintage | F | VF | XF | Unc | BU |
|---|---|---|---|---|---|---|
| 1987 Proof | 1,250 | Value: 275 | | | | |

**LEONE** **KM# 43** **Composition:** Nickel-Bronze

| Date | Mintage | F | VF | XF | Unc | BU |
|---|---|---|---|---|---|---|
| 1987 | — | — | 0.50 | 0.75 | 1.50 | — |
| 1988 | — | — | 0.50 | 0.75 | 1.50 | — |

**DOLLAR** **KM# 47** **Composition:** Copper-Nickel **Obverse:** Crowned lion **Note:** Similar to 10 Dollars, KM#49.

| Date | Mintage | F | VF | XF | Unc | BU |
|---|---|---|---|---|---|---|
| 1997 | — | — | — | — | 7.50 | — |

**DOLLAR** **KM# 48** **Composition:** Copper-Nickel **Obverse:** Unicorn **Note:** Similar to 10 Dollars, KM#50.

| Date | Mintage | F | VF | XF | Unc | BU |
|---|---|---|---|---|---|---|
| 1997 | — | — | — | — | 7.50 | — |

**DOLLAR** **KM# 53** **Composition:** Copper-Nickel **Subject:** Golden Wedding Anniversary **Reverse:** E and P monogram **Note:** Similar to 10 Dollars, KM#54.

| Date | Mintage | F | VF | XF | Unc | BU |
|---|---|---|---|---|---|---|
| 1997 | — | — | — | — | 10.00 | — |

**DOLLAR** **KM# 56** **Composition:** Copper-Nickel **Subject:** Golden Wedding Anniversary **Reverse:** Yacht **Note:** Similar to 10 Dollars, KM#57.

| Date | Mintage | F | VF | XF | Unc | BU |
|---|---|---|---|---|---|---|
| 1997 | — | — | — | — | 7.00 | — |

**DOLLAR** **KM# 59** **Composition:** Copper-Nickel **Subject:** Golden Wedding Anniversary **Reverse:** Royal couple **Note:** Similar to 10 Dollars, KM#60.

| Date | Mintage | F | VF | XF | Unc | BU |
|---|---|---|---|---|---|---|
| 1997 | — | — | — | — | 7.00 | — |

**DOLLAR** **KM# 62** **Composition:** Copper-Nickel **Subject:** Golden Wedding Anniversary **Reverse:** Fireworks above palace **Note:** Similar to 10 Dollars, KM#63.

| Date | Mintage | F | VF | XF | Unc | BU |
|---|---|---|---|---|---|---|
| 1997 | — | — | — | — | 7.00 | — |

**DOLLAR** **KM# 65** **Composition:** Copper-Nickel **Subject:** Golden Wedding Anniversary **Reverse:** Queen with two children **Note:** Similar to 10 Dollars, KM#66.

| Date | Mintage | F | VF | XF | Unc | BU |
|---|---|---|---|---|---|---|
| 1997 | — | — | — | — | 7.00 | — |

**DOLLAR** **KM# 68** **Composition:** Copper-Nickel **Subject:** Golden Wedding Anniversary **Reverse:** Royal couple with two children **Note:** Similar to 10 Dollars, KM#69.

| Date | Mintage | F | VF | XF | Unc | BU |
|---|---|---|---|---|---|---|
| 1997 | — | — | — | — | 7.00 | — |

**DOLLAR** **KM# 71** **Composition:** Copper-Nickel **Subject:** Diana - The Peoples' Princess **Reverse:** Portrait of Lady Diana

| Date | Mintage | F | VF | XF | Unc | BU |
|---|---|---|---|---|---|---|
| 1997 | — | — | — | — | 8.00 | — |

**DOLLAR** **KM# 77** **Composition:** Copper-Nickel **Subject:** Diana - The Peoples' Princess **Reverse:** Lady Diana and Mother Theresa

| Date | Mintage | F | VF | XF | Unc | BU |
|---|---|---|---|---|---|---|
| 1997 | — | — | — | — | 8.00 | — |

**DOLLAR** **KM# 83** **Composition:** Copper-Nickel **Subject:** Diana - The Peoples' Princess **Reverse:** Lady Diana and AIDS patient

| Date | Mintage | F | VF | XF | Unc | BU |
|---|---|---|---|---|---|---|
| 1997 | — | — | — | — | 8.00 | — |

**DOLLAR** **KM# 89** **Composition:** Copper-Nickel **Subject:** Diana - The Peoples' Princess **Reverse:** Lady Diana with sons William and Harry

| Date | Mintage | F | VF | XF | Unc | BU |
|---|---|---|---|---|---|---|
| 1997 | — | — | — | — | 8.00 | — |

**DOLLAR** **KM# 95** **Composition:** Copper-Nickel **Subject:** Jurassic Park **Reverse:** Velociraptor **Note:** Similar to 10 Dollars, KM#96.

| Date | Mintage | F | VF | XF | Unc | BU |
|---|---|---|---|---|---|---|
| 1997 | — | — | — | — | 9.00 | — |

**DOLLAR** **KM# 103** **Composition:** Copper-Nickel **Subject:** In Memoriam, Diana - The Peoples' Princess **Note:** Similar to 10 Dollars, KM#104.

| Date | Mintage | F | VF | XF | Unc | BU |
|---|---|---|---|---|---|---|
| 1998 | — | — | — | — | 8.00 | — |

**DOLLAR** **KM#109 (KM110)** **Composition:** Copper-Nickel **Subject:** Dr. Livingston **Note:** Similar to 10 Dollars, KM#110.

| Date | Mintage | F | VF | XF | Unc | BU |
|---|---|---|---|---|---|---|
| 1998 | — | — | — | — | 8.00 | — |

**DOLLAR** **KM# 118** **Composition:** Copper-Nickel **Subject:** China 2000 Series **Obverse:** National arms **Reverse:** Kneeling Terracotta warrior **Note:** Similar to 10 Dollars, KM#119.

| Date | Mintage | F | VF | XF | Unc | BU |
|---|---|---|---|---|---|---|
| 1999 | — | — | — | — | 7.50 | — |

**DOLLAR** **KM# 112** **Composition:** Copper-Nickel **Subject:** Amerigo Vespucci **Obverse:** National arms **Reverse:** Ship and mountainous portrait **Note:** Similar to 10 Dollars, KM#113.

| Date | Mintage | F | VF | XF | Unc | BU |
|---|---|---|---|---|---|---|
| 1999 | — | — | — | — | 8.00 | — |

**DOLLAR** **KM# 115** **Composition:** Copper-Nickel **Subject:** Charles Darwin **Obverse:** National arms **Reverse:** Ship and portrait **Note:** Similar to 10 Dollars, KM#116.

| Date | Mintage | F | VF | XF | Unc | BU |
|---|---|---|---|---|---|---|
| 1999 | — | — | — | — | 8.00 | — |

**DOLLAR** **KM# 121** **Composition:** Copper-Nickel **Subject:** China 2000 Series - Ming Dynasty **Obverse:** National arms **Reverse:** Temple of Heaven **Note:** Similar to 10 Dollars, KM#122.

| Date | Mintage | F | VF | XF | Unc | BU |
|---|---|---|---|---|---|---|
| 1999 | — | — | — | — | 7.50 | — |

**DOLLAR** **KM# 124** **Composition:** Copper-Nickel **Subject:** China 2000 Series **Obverse:** National arms **Reverse:** Portion of the Great Wall **Note:** Similar to 10 Dollars, KM#125.

| Date | Mintage | F | VF | XF | Unc | BU |
|---|---|---|---|---|---|---|
| 1999 | — | — | — | — | 7.50 | — |

**DOLLAR** **KM# 127** **Composition:** Copper-Nickel **Subject:** China 2000 Series **Obverse:** National arms **Reverse:** Bronze chariot **Note:** Similar to 10 Dollars, KM#128.

| Date | Mintage | F | VF | XF | Unc | BU |
|---|---|---|---|---|---|---|
| 1999 | — | — | — | — | 7.50 | — |

**DOLLAR** **KM# 130** **Composition:** Copper-Nickel **Subject:** China 2000 Series **Obverse:** National arms **Reverse:** First century armillary sphere **Note:** Similar to 10 Dollars, KM#131.

| Date | Mintage | F | VF | XF | Unc | BU |
|---|---|---|---|---|---|---|
| 1999 | — | — | — | — | 7.50 | — |

**DOLLAR** **KM# 133** **Composition:** Copper-Nickel **Subject:** China 2000 Series **Obverse:** National arms **Reverse:** Tang Dynasy Royal Horse **Note:** Similar to 10 Dollars, KM#134.

| Date | Mintage | F | VF | XF | Unc | BU |
|---|---|---|---|---|---|---|
| 1999 | — | — | — | — | 7.50 | — |

**DOLLAR** **KM# 136** **Composition:** Copper-Nickel **Subject:** Macau returns to China **Obverse:** National arms **Reverse:** Church, car, roulette wheel, and hands shaking **Note:** Similar to 10 Dollars, KM#137.

| Date | Mintage | F | VF | XF | Unc | BU |
|---|---|---|---|---|---|---|
| 1999 | — | — | — | — | 8.00 | — |

**DOLLAR** **KM# 139** **Composition:** Copper-Nickel **Subject:** Prince Edward's Wedding **Obverse:** National arms **Reverse:** Symbolic wedding design **Note:** Similar to 10 Dollars, KM#140.

| Date | Mintage | F | VF | XF | Unc | BU |
|---|---|---|---|---|---|---|
| 1999 | — | — | — | — | 8.50 | — |

**DOLLAR** **KM# 142** **Composition:** Copper-Nickel **Subject:** Year of the Dragon **Obverse:** National arms **Reverse:** Dragon **Note:** Similar to 10 Dollars, KM#143.

| Date | Mintage | F | VF | XF | Unc | BU |
|---|---|---|---|---|---|---|
| 2000 | — | — | — | — | 8.50 | — |

**DOLLAR** **KM# 150** **Weight:** 28.2800 g. **Composition:** Copper-Nickel **Obverse:** National arms **Reverse:** Two Phoenix birds **Edge:** Reeded **Note:** Struck at Pobjoy Mint.

| Date | Mintage | F | VF | XF | Unc | BU |
|---|---|---|---|---|---|---|
| 2000 | — | — | — | — | 8.50 | — |

**DOLLAR** **KM# 151** **Composition:** Copper-Nickel **Reverse:** Chinese dragon

| Date | Mintage | F | VF | XF | Unc | BU |
|---|---|---|---|---|---|---|
| 2000 | — | — | — | — | 8.50 | — |

**DOLLAR** **KM# 152** **Weight:** 28.4300 g. **Composition:** Copper-Nickel **Obverse:** National arms **Reverse:** Chinese unicorn **Edge:** Reeded **Size:** 38.7 mm.

| Date | Mintage | F | VF | XF | Unc | BU |
|---|---|---|---|---|---|---|
| 2000 | — | — | — | — | 8.50 | — |

**Note:** Reported as an error date resulting from muled dies

**DOLLAR** **KM# 174** **Composition:** Copper-Nickel **Subject:** Buddha **Reverse:** Seated Buddha

| Date | Mintage | F | VF | XF | Unc | BU |
|---|---|---|---|---|---|---|
| 2000 | — | — | — | — | 8.50 | — |

**DOLLAR** **KM# 175** **Composition:** Copper-Nickel **Reverse:** Goddess of Mercy

| Date | Mintage | F | VF | XF | Unc | BU |
|---|---|---|---|---|---|---|
| 2000 | — | — | — | — | 8.50 | — |

**DOLLAR** **KM# 176** **Composition:** Copper-Nickel **Reverse:** Tzai-yen holding scroll

| Date | Mintage | F | VF | XF | Unc | BU |
|---|---|---|---|---|---|---|
| 2000 | — | — | — | — | 10.00 | — |

**DOLLAR** **KM# 198** **Weight:** 28.2800 g. **Composition:** Copper-Nickel **Subject:** Year of the Snake **Obverse:** National arms **Reverse:** Snake **Edge:** Reeded **Size:** 38.6 mm.

| Date | Mintage | F | VF | XF | Unc | BU |
|---|---|---|---|---|---|---|
| 2001 | — | — | — | — | 10.00 | — |

**DOLLAR** **KM# 206** **Composition:** Copper-Nickel **Subject:** P'an Ku **Obverse:** National arms **Reverse:** Dragon

| Date | Mintage | F | VF | XF | Unc | BU |
|---|---|---|---|---|---|---|
| 2001 | — | — | — | — | 10.00 | — |

**DOLLAR** **KM# 214** **Composition:** Copper-Nickel **Subject:** P'an Ku **Obverse:** National arms **Reverse:** Dragon and three animals

| Date | Mintage | F | VF | XF | Unc | BU |
|---|---|---|---|---|---|---|
| 2001 | — | — | — | — | 10.00 | — |

**DOLLAR** **KM# 222** **Weight:** 28.2800 g. **Composition:** Copper-Nickel **Series:** The Big Five **Obverse:** National arms **Reverse:** Rhino **Edge:** Reeded **Size:** 38.6 mm.

| Date | Mintage | F | VF | XF | Unc | BU |
|---|---|---|---|---|---|---|
| 2001 | — | — | — | — | 10.00 | — |

**DOLLAR** **KM# 225** **Weight:** 28.2800 g. **Composition:** Copper-Nickel **Series:** The Big Five **Obverse:** National arms **Reverse:** Lion

| Date | Mintage | F | VF | XF | Unc | BU |
|---|---|---|---|---|---|---|
| 2001 | — | — | — | — | 10.00 | — |

**DOLLAR** **KM# 228** **Weight:** 28.2800 g. **Composition:** Copper-Nickel **Series:** The Big Five **Obverse:** National arms **Reverse:** Leopard

| Date | Mintage | F | VF | XF | Unc | BU |
|---|---|---|---|---|---|---|
| 2001 | — | — | — | — | 10.00 | — |

**DOLLAR** **KM# 231** **Weight:** 28.2800 g. **Composition:** Copper-Nickel **Series:** The Big Five **Obverse:** National arms **Reverse:** Elephants

| Date | Mintage | F | VF | XF | Unc | BU |
|---|---|---|---|---|---|---|
| 2001 | — | — | — | — | 10.00 | — |

**DOLLAR** **KM# 234** **Weight:** 28.2800 g. **Composition:** Copper-Nickel **Series:** The Big Five **Obverse:** National arms **Reverse:** Buffalo

| Date | Mintage | F | VF | XF | Unc | BU |
|---|---|---|---|---|---|---|
| 2001 | — | — | — | — | 10.00 | — |

**DOLLAR** **KM# 237** **Weight:** 28.2800 g. **Composition:** Copper-Nickel **Series:** The Big Five **Obverse:** National arms **Reverse:** All five animals

| Date | Mintage | F | VF | XF | Unc | BU |
|---|---|---|---|---|---|---|
| 2001 | — | — | — | — | 10.00 | — |

**DOLLAR** **KM# 241** **Weight:** 28.2800 g. **Composition:** Copper-Nickel **Series:** Big Cats **Obverse:** National arms **Reverse:** Male and female lions **Edge:** Reeded **Size:** 38.6 mm.

| Date | Mintage | F | VF | XF | Unc | BU |
|---|---|---|---|---|---|---|
| 2001 | — | — | — | — | 10.00 | — |

**DOLLAR** **KM# 241a** **Weight:** 28.2800 g. **Composition:** Copper-Nickel **Series:** Big Cats **Reverse:** Colorized lions **Edge:** Reeded **Size:** 38.6 mm.

| Date | Mintage | F | VF | XF | Unc | BU |
|---|---|---|---|---|---|---|
| 2001 | — | — | — | — | 13.50 | — |

**DOLLAR** **KM# 242** **Weight:** 28.2800 g. **Composition:** Copper-Nickel **Series:** Big Cats **Reverse:** Tiger **Edge:** Reeded **Size:** 38.6 mm.

| Date | Mintage | F | VF | XF | Unc | BU |
|---|---|---|---|---|---|---|
| 2001 | — | — | — | — | 10.00 | — |

**DOLLAR** **KM# 242a** **Weight:** 28.2800 g. **Composition:** Copper-Nickel **Series:** Big Cats **Reverse:** Colorized tiger **Edge:** Reeded **Size:** 38.6 mm.

| Date | Mintage | F | VF | XF | Unc | BU |
|---|---|---|---|---|---|---|
| 2001 | — | — | — | — | 13.50 | — |

**DOLLAR** **KM# 243** **Weight:** 28.2800 g. **Composition:** Copper-Nickel **Series:** Big Cats **Reverse:** Cheetah **Edge:** Reeded **Size:** 38.6 mm.

| Date | Mintage | F | VF | XF | Unc | BU |
|---|---|---|---|---|---|---|
| 2001 | — | — | — | — | 10.00 | — |

**DOLLAR** **KM# 243a** **Weight:** 28.2800 g. **Composition:** Copper-Nickel **Series:** Big Cats **Reverse:** Colorized cheetah **Edge:** Reeded **Size:** 38.6 mm.

| Date | Mintage | F | VF | XF | Unc | BU |
|---|---|---|---|---|---|---|
| 2001 | — | — | — | — | 13.50 | — |

**DOLLAR** **KM# 244** **Weight:** 28.2800 g. **Composition:** Copper-Nickel **Series:** Big Cats **Reverse:** Cougar **Edge:** Reeded **Size:** 38.6 mm.

| Date | Mintage | F | VF | XF | Unc | BU |
|---|---|---|---|---|---|---|
| 2001 | — | — | — | — | 10.00 | — |

**DOLLAR** **KM# 244a** **Weight:** 28.2800 g. **Composition:** Copper-Nickel **Series:** Big Cats **Reverse:** Colorized cougar **Edge:** Reeded **Size:** 38.6 mm.

| Date | Mintage | F | VF | XF | Unc | BU |
|---|---|---|---|---|---|---|
| 2001 | — | — | — | — | 13.50 | — |

**DOLLAR** **KM# 245** **Weight:** 28.2800 g. **Composition:** Copper-Nickel **Series:** Big Cats **Reverse:** Black panther **Edge:** Reeded **Size:** 38.6 mm.

| Date | Mintage | F | VF | XF | Unc | BU |
|---|---|---|---|---|---|---|
| 2001 | — | — | — | — | 10.00 | — |

**DOLLAR** **KM# 245a** **Weight:** 28.2800 g. **Composition:** Copper-Nickel **Series:** Big Cats **Reverse:** Colorized black panther **Edge:** Reeded **Size:** 38.6 mm.

| Date | Mintage | F | VF | XF | Unc | BU |
|---|---|---|---|---|---|---|
| 2001 | — | — | — | — | 13.50 | — |

**DOLLAR** **KM# 256** **Weight:** 28.2800 g. **Composition:** Copper Nickel **Subject:** Year of the Horse **Obverse:** National arms. **Reverse:** Horse. **Edge:** Reeded. **Size:** 38.6 mm.

| Date | Mintage | F | VF | XF | Unc | BU |
|---|---|---|---|---|---|---|
| 2002 | — | — | — | — | 10.00 | — |

**2 LEONES** **KM# 29** **Composition:** Copper-Nickel **Series:** F.A.O **Subject:** Regional Conference for Africa

| Date | Mintage | F | VF | XF | Unc | BU |
|---|---|---|---|---|---|---|
| 1976 | 20,000 | — | 1.00 | 2.50 | 5.50 | — |

**5 DOLLARS** **KM# 98** **Weight:** 15.5517 g. **Composition:** 0.9990 Silver .5000 oz. ASW **Subject:** Shanghai Coin and Stamp Exposition **Obverse:** National arms **Reverse:** Crowned lion

| Date | Mintage | F | VF | XF | Unc | BU |
|---|---|---|---|---|---|---|
| 1997 Proof | Est. 10,000 | Value: 30.00 | | | | |

**5 DOLLARS** **KM# 99** **Weight:** 15.5517 g. **Composition:** 0.9990 Silver .5000 oz. ASW **Subject:** Shanghai Coin and Stamp Exposition **Reverse:** Unicorn

| Date | Mintage | F | VF | XF | Unc | BU |
|---|---|---|---|---|---|---|
| 1997 Proof | Est. 10,000 | Value: 30.00 | | | | |

**5 DOLLARS** **KM# 101** **Weight:** 15.5517 g. **Composition:** 0.9990 Silver .5000 oz. ASW **Subject:** Visit of President Clinton to China

| Date | Mintage | F | VF | XF | Unc | BU |
|---|---|---|---|---|---|---|
| 1998 Proof | Est. 10,000 | Value: 30.00 | | | | |

**5 DOLLARS** **KM# 102** **Weight:** 15.5517 g. **Composition:** 0.9990 Silver .5000 oz. ASW **Subject:** Visit of President Clinton to Beijing **Reverse:** Great Wall

| Date | Mintage | F | VF | XF | Unc | BU |
|---|---|---|---|---|---|---|
| 1998 Proof | Est. 10,000 | Value: 30.00 | | | | |

**10 LEONES** **KM# 38** **Weight:** 28.2800 g. **Composition:** 0.9250 Silver .8411 oz. ASW **Series:** Year of the Scout

| Date | Mintage | F | VF | XF | Unc | BU |
|---|---|---|---|---|---|---|
| ND(1983) | 10,000 | — | — | — | 35.00 | — |
| ND(1983) Proof | 10,000 | Value: 47.50 | | | | |

**10 LEONES** **KM# 41** **Weight:** 28.2800 g. **Composition:** 0.9250 Silver .8411 oz. ASW **Series:** World Wildlife Fund **Subject:** Pygmy Hippopotamus

| Date | Mintage | F | VF | XF | Unc | BU |
|---|---|---|---|---|---|---|
| 1987 Proof | 25,000 | Value: 25.00 | | | | |

**10 LEONES** **KM# 44** **Composition:** Nickel Clad Steel **Obverse:** Denomination **Reverse:** Mammy Yoko portrait

| Date | Mintage | F | VF | XF | Unc | BU |
|---|---|---|---|---|---|---|
| 1996 | — | — | — | — | 0.75 | — |

**10 DOLLARS** **KM# 49** **Weight:** 28.2800 g. **Composition:** 0.9250 Silver .8411 oz. ASW **Obverse:** National arms **Reverse:** Crowned lion

| Date | Mintage | F | VF | XF | Unc | BU |
|---|---|---|---|---|---|---|
| 1997 Proof | Est. 10,000 | Value: 47.50 | | | | |

**10 DOLLARS** **KM# 50** **Weight:** 28.2800 g. **Composition:** 0.9250 Silver .8411 oz. ASW **Reverse:** Unicorn

| Date | Mintage | F | VF | XF | Unc | BU |
|---|---|---|---|---|---|---|
| 1997 Proof | Est. 10,000 | Value: 47.50 | | | | |

**10 DOLLARS** **KM# 54** **Weight:** 28.2800 g. **Composition:** 0.9250 Silver .8411 oz. ASW **Subject:** Golden Wedding Anniversary **Reverse:** E and P monogram

| Date | Mintage | F | VF | XF | Unc | BU |
|---|---|---|---|---|---|---|
| 1997 Proof | Est. 10,000 | Value: 47.50 | | | | |

**10 DOLLARS** **KM# 57** **Weight:** 28.2800 g. **Composition:** 0.9250 Silver .8411 oz. ASW **Subject:** Golden Wedding Anniversary **Reverse:** Royal Yacht "Britannia"

| Date | Mintage | F | VF | XF | Unc | BU |
|---|---|---|---|---|---|---|
| 1997 Proof | Est. 10,000 | Value: 47.50 | | | | |

**10 DOLLARS** **KM# 60** **Weight:** 28.2800 g. **Composition:** 0.9250 Silver .8411 oz. ASW **Subject:** Golden Wedding Anniversary **Reverse:** Royal couple

| Date | Mintage | F | VF | XF | Unc | BU |
|---|---|---|---|---|---|---|
| 1997 Proof | Est. 10,000 | Value: 47.50 | | | | |

**10 DOLLARS** **KM# 63** **Weight:** 28.2800 g. **Composition:** 0.9250 Silver .8411 oz. ASW **Subject:** Golden Wedding Anniversary **Reverse:** Fireworks above palace

| Date | Mintage | F | VF | XF | Unc | BU |
|---|---|---|---|---|---|---|
| 1997 Proof | Est. 10,000 | Value: 47.50 | | | | |

**10 DOLLARS** **KM# 66** **Weight:** 28.2800 g. **Composition:** 0.9250 Silver .8411 oz. ASW **Subject:** Golden Wedding Anniversary **Reverse:** Queen with two children

| Date | Mintage | F | VF | XF | Unc | BU |
|---|---|---|---|---|---|---|
| 1997 Proof | Est. 10,000 | Value: 47.50 | | | | |

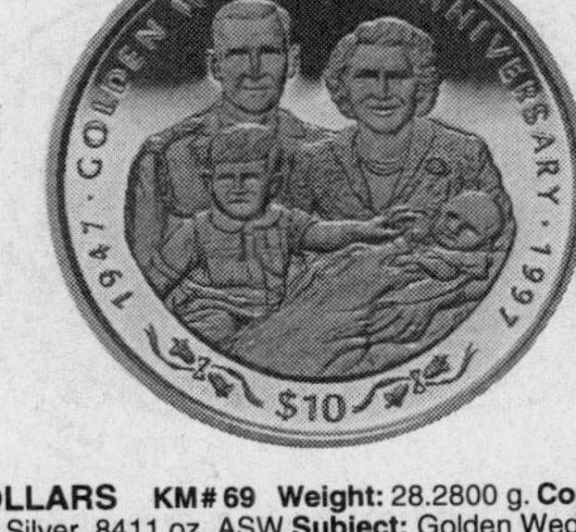


**10 DOLLARS** **KM# 69** **Weight:** 28.2800 g. **Composition:** 0.9250 Silver .8411 oz. ASW **Subject:** Golden Wedding Anniversary **Reverse:** Royal couple with two children

| Date | Mintage | F | VF | XF | Unc | BU |
|---|---|---|---|---|---|---|
| 1997 Proof | Est. 10,000 | Value: 47.50 | | | | |

**10 DOLLARS** **KM# 72** **Weight:** 28.2800 g. **Composition:** 0.9250 Silver .8411 oz. ASW **Subject:** Diana - The Peoples' Princess **Note:** Similar to 1 Dollar, KM#71.

| Date | Mintage | F | VF | XF | Unc | BU |
|---|---|---|---|---|---|---|
| 1997 Proof | Est. 10,000 | Value: 30.00 | | | | |

**10 DOLLARS** **KM# 78** **Weight:** 28.2800 g. **Composition:** 0.9250 Silver .8411 oz. ASW **Subject:** Diana - The Peoples' Princess **Note:** Similar to 1 Dollar, KM#77.

| Date | Mintage | F | VF | XF | Unc | BU |
|---|---|---|---|---|---|---|
| 1997 | Est. 10,000 | Value: 42.50 | | | | |

**10 DOLLARS** **KM# 84** **Weight:** 28.2800 g. **Composition:** 0.9250 Silver .8411 oz. ASW **Subject:** Diana - The Peoples' Princess **Note:** Similar to 1 Dollar, KM#83.

| Date | Mintage | F | VF | XF | Unc | BU |
|---|---|---|---|---|---|---|
| 1997 Proof | Est. 10,000 | Value: 27.50 | | | | |

**10 DOLLARS** **KM# 90** **Weight:** 28.2800 g. **Composition:** 0.9250 Silver .8411 oz. ASW **Subject:** Diana - The Peoples' Princess **Note:** Similar to 1 Dollar, KM#89.

| Date | Mintage | F | VF | XF | Unc | BU |
|---|---|---|---|---|---|---|
| 1997 Proof | Est. 10,000 | Value: 32.50 | | | | |

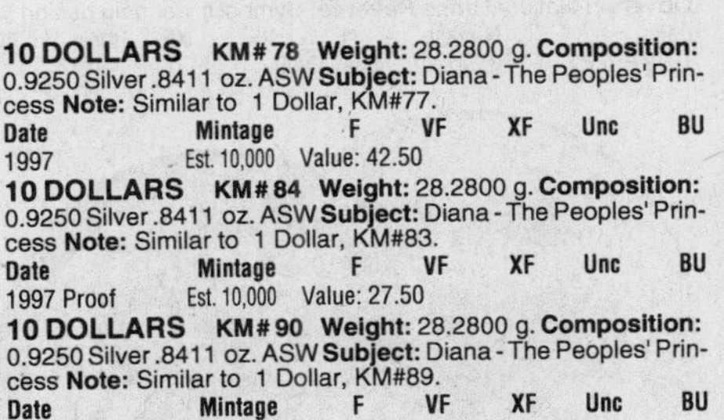

**10 DOLLARS** **KM# 96** **Weight:** 28.2800 g. **Composition:** 0.9250 Silver .8411 oz. ASW **Subject:** Jurassic Park **Reverse:** Velociraptor

| Date | Mintage | F | VF | XF | Unc | BU |
|---|---|---|---|---|---|---|
| 1997 Proof | Est. 10,000 | Value: 47.50 | | | | |

**10 DOLLARS** **KM# 104** **Weight:** 28.2800 g. **Composition:** 0.9250 Silver .8411 oz. ASW **Subject:** In Memoriam, Diana - The Peoples' Princess **Reverse:** Laidy Diana portrait

| Date | Mintage | F | VF | XF | Unc | BU |
|---|---|---|---|---|---|---|
| 1998 Proof | Est. 10,000 | Value: 37.50 | | | | |

**10 DOLLARS** **KM# A110** **Weight:** 28.2800 g. **Composition:** 0.9250 Silver .8411 oz. ASW **Subject:** Dr. Livingstone **Note:** Previously KM#110.

| Date | Mintage | F | VF | XF | Unc | BU |
|---|---|---|---|---|---|---|
| 1998 Proof | Est. 10,000 | Value: 50.00 | | | | |

**10 DOLLARS** **KM# 113** **Weight:** 28.2800 g. **Composition:** 0.9250 Silver .8411 oz. ASW **Subject:** Amerigo Vespucci **Obverse:** National arms **Reverse:** Ship and Vespucci portrait

| Date | Mintage | F | VF | XF | Unc | BU |
|---|---|---|---|---|---|---|
| 1999 Proof | Est. 10,000 | Value: 50.00 | | | | |



**10 DOLLARS** **KM# 116** **Weight:** 28.2800 g. **Composition:** 0.9250 Silver .8411 oz. ASW **Subject:** Charles Darwin **Obverse:** National arms **Reverse:** Ship and portrait

| Date | Mintage | F | VF | XF | Unc | BU |
|---|---|---|---|---|---|---|
| 1999 Proof | Est. 10,000 | Value: 50.00 | | | | |

**10 DOLLARS** **KM# 119** **Weight:** 28.2800 g. **Composition:** 0.9250 Silver .8411 oz. ASW **Subject:** China 2000 Series **Obverse:** National arms **Reverse:** Kneeling Terracotta warrior

| Date | Mintage | F | VF | XF | Unc | BU |
|---|---|---|---|---|---|---|
| 1999 Proof | Est. 10,000 | Value: 47.50 | | | | |

**10 DOLLARS** **KM# 122 Weight:** 28.2800 g. **Composition:** 0.9250 Silver .8411 oz. ASW **Subject:** China 2000 Series - Ming Dynasty **Obverse:** National arms **Reverse:** Temple of Heaven

| Date | Mintage | F | VF | XF | Unc | BU |
|---|---|---|---|---|---|---|
| 1999 Proof | Est. 10,000 | Value: 47.50 | | | | |

**10 DOLLARS** **KM# 134 Weight:** 28.2800 g. **Composition:** 0.9250 Silver .8411 oz. ASW **Subject:** China 2000 Series - Tang Dynasty **Obverse:** National arms **Reverse:** Tang Dynasty royal horse

| Date | Mintage | F | VF | XF | Unc | BU |
|---|---|---|---|---|---|---|
| 1999 Proof | Est. 10,000 | Value: 47.50 | | | | |

**10 DOLLARS** **KM# 153 Weight:** 28.2800 g. **Composition:** 0.9250 Silver .8411 oz. ASW **Obverse:** National arms **Reverse:** Two Phoenix birds **Note:** Struck at Pobjoy Mint.

| Date | Mintage | F | VF | XF | Unc | BU |
|---|---|---|---|---|---|---|
| 2000 Proof | Est. 10,000 | Value: 47.50 | | | | |

**10 DOLLARS** **KM# 125 Weight:** 28.2800 g. **Composition:** 0.9250 Silver .8411 oz. ASW **Subject:** China 2000 Series - The Great Wall **Obverse:** National arms **Reverse:** Portion of the Great Wall

| Date | Mintage | F | VF | XF | Unc | BU |
|---|---|---|---|---|---|---|
| 1999 Proof | Est. 10,000 | Value: 47.50 | | | | |

**10 DOLLARS** **KM# 137 Weight:** 28.2800 g. **Composition:** 0.9250 Silver .8411 oz. ASW **Subject:** Macau return to China **Obverse:** National arms **Reverse:** Church, car, roulette wheel, and hands shaking

| Date | Mintage | F | VF | XF | Unc | BU |
|---|---|---|---|---|---|---|
| 1999 Proof | Est. 10,000 | Value: 50.00 | | | | |

**10 DOLLARS** **KM# 154 Weight:** 28.2800 g. **Composition:** 0.9250 Silver .8411 oz. ASW **Reverse:** Chinese dragon

| Date | Mintage | F | VF | XF | Unc | BU |
|---|---|---|---|---|---|---|
| 2000 Proof | Est. 10,000 | Value: 47.50 | | | | |

**10 DOLLARS** **KM# 128 Weight:** 28.2800 g. **Composition:** 0.9250 Silver .8411 oz. ASW **Subject:** China 2000 Series **Obverse:** National arms **Reverse:** Bronze chariot

| Date | Mintage | F | VF | XF | Unc | BU |
|---|---|---|---|---|---|---|
| 1999 Proof | Est. 10,000 | Value: 47.50 | | | | |

**10 DOLLARS** **KM# 140 Weight:** 28.2800 g. **Composition:** 0.9250 Silver .8411 oz. ASW **Subject:** Prince Edward's Wedding **Obverse:** National arms **Reverse:** Symbolic wedding design

| Date | Mintage | F | VF | XF | Unc | BU |
|---|---|---|---|---|---|---|
| 1999 Proof | Est. 10,000 | Value: 50.00 | | | | |

**10 DOLLARS** **KM# 155 Weight:** 28.2800 g. **Composition:** 0.9250 Silver .8411 oz. ASW **Reverse:** Chinese unicorn

| Date | Mintage | F | VF | XF | Unc | BU |
|---|---|---|---|---|---|---|
| 2000 Proof | Est. 10,000 | Value: 47.50 | | | | |

**10 DOLLARS** **KM# 131 Weight:** 28.2800 g. **Composition:** 0.9250 Silver .8411 oz. ASW **Subject:** China 2000 Series - Armillary Sphere **Obverse:** National arms **Reverse:** First century armillary sphere

| Date | Mintage | F | VF | XF | Unc | BU |
|---|---|---|---|---|---|---|
| 1999 Proof | Est. 10,000 | Value: 47.50 | | | | |

**10 DOLLARS** **KM# 143 Weight:** 28.2800 g. **Composition:** 0.9250 Silver .8411 oz. ASW **Subject:** Year of the Dragon **Obverse:** National arms **Reverse:** Dragon

| Date | Mintage | F | VF | XF | Unc | BU |
|---|---|---|---|---|---|---|
| 2000 Proof | Est. 25,000 | Value: 47.50 | | | | |

**10 DOLLARS** **KM# 177 Weight:** 28.2800 g. **Composition:** 0.9250 Silver .8411 oz. ASW **Reverse:** Seated Buddha

| Date | Mintage | F | VF | XF | Unc | BU |
|---|---|---|---|---|---|---|
| 2000 Proof | Est. 25,000 | Value: 47.50 | | | | |

**10 DOLLARS** **KM#178** **Weight:** 28.2800 g. **Composition:** 0.9250 Silver .8411 oz. ASW **Reverse:** Goddess of Mercy

| Date | Mintage | F | VF | XF | Unc | BU |
|---|---|---|---|---|---|---|
| 2000 Proof | Est. 25,000 | Value: 47.50 | | | | |

**10 DOLLARS** **KM#179** **Weight:** 28.2800 g. **Composition:** 0.9250 Silver .8411 oz. ASW **Reverse:** Tzai-yen holding scroll

| Date | Mintage | F | VF | XF | Unc | BU |
|---|---|---|---|---|---|---|
| 2000 Proof | Est. 25,000 | Value: 47.50 | | | | |

**10 DOLLARS** **KM#199** **Weight:** 28.2800 g. **Composition:** 0.9250 Silver .8410 oz. ASW **Subject:** Year of the Snake **Obverse:** National arms **Reverse:** Snake on bamboo **Edge:** Reeded **Size:** 38.6 mm.

| Date | Mintage | F | VF | XF | Unc | BU |
|---|---|---|---|---|---|---|
| 2001 Proof | Est. 25,000 | Value: 47.50 | | | | |

**10 DOLLARS** **KM#207** **Weight:** 28.2800 g. **Composition:** 0.9250 Silver .8410 oz. ASW **Subject:** P'an Ku **Obverse:** National arms **Reverse:** Dragon

| Date | Mintage | F | VF | XF | Unc | BU |
|---|---|---|---|---|---|---|
| 2001 | Est. 5,000 | Value: 47.50 | | | | |

**10 DOLLARS** **KM#215** **Weight:** 28.2800 g. **Composition:** 0.9250 Silver .8410 oz. ASW **Subject:** P'an Ku **Obverse:** National arms **Reverse:** Dragon and three animals

| Date | Mintage | F | VF | XF | Unc | BU |
|---|---|---|---|---|---|---|
| 2001 Proof | Est. 5,000 | Value: 47.50 | | | | |

**Note:**

**10 DOLLARS** **KM#223** **Weight:** 28.2800 g. **Composition:** 0.9250 Silver .8410 oz. ASW **Series:** The Big Five **Obverse:** National arms **Reverse:** Rhino **Edge:** Reeded **Size:** 38.6 mm.

| Date | Mintage | F | VF | XF | Unc | BU |
|---|---|---|---|---|---|---|
| 2001 | — | — | — | — | 47.50 | — |

**10 DOLLARS** **KM#226** **Weight:** 28.2800 g. **Composition:** 0.9250 Silver .8410 oz. ASW **Series:** The Big Five **Obverse:** National arms **Reverse:** Lion

| Date | Mintage | F | VF | XF | Unc | BU |
|---|---|---|---|---|---|---|
| 2001 Proof | Est. 10,000 | Value: 47.50 | | | | |

**10 DOLLARS** **KM#229** **Weight:** 28.2800 g. **Composition:** 0.9250 Silver .8410 oz. ASW **Series:** The Big Five **Obverse:** National arms **Reverse:** Leopard

| Date | Mintage | F | VF | XF | Unc | BU |
|---|---|---|---|---|---|---|
| 2001 Proof | Est. 10,000 | Value: 47.50 | | | | |

**10 DOLLARS** **KM#232** **Weight:** 28.2800 g. **Composition:** 0.9250 Silver .8410 oz. ASW **Series:** The Big Five **Obverse:** National arms **Reverse:** Elephants

| Date | Mintage | F | VF | XF | Unc | BU |
|---|---|---|---|---|---|---|
| 2001 Proof | Est. 10,000 | Value: 47.50 | | | | |

**10 DOLLARS** **KM#235** **Weight:** 28.2800 g. **Composition:** 0.9250 Silver .8410 oz. ASW **Series:** The Big Five **Obverse:** National arms **Reverse:** Buffalo

| Date | Mintage | F | VF | XF | Unc | BU |
|---|---|---|---|---|---|---|
| 2001 Proof | Est. 10,000 | Value: 47.50 | | | | |

**10 DOLLARS** **KM#238** **Weight:** 28.2800 g. **Composition:** 0.9250 Silver .8410 oz. ASW **Series:** The Big Five **Obverse:** National arms **Reverse:** All five animals

| Date | Mintage | F | VF | XF | Unc | BU |
|---|---|---|---|---|---|---|
| 2001 Proof | Est. 10,000 | Value: 47.50 | | | | |



**10 DOLLARS** **KM#246** **Weight:** 28.2800 g. **Composition:** 0.9250 Silver .8410 oz. ASW **Series:** Big Cats **Obverse:** National arms **Reverse:** Male and female lions **Edge:** Reeded **Size:** 38.6 mm.

| Date | Mintage | F | VF | XF | Unc | BU |
|---|---|---|---|---|---|---|
| 2001 Proof | 10,000 | Value: 47.50 | | | | |

**10 DOLLARS** **KM# 246a** **Weight:** 28.2800 g. **Composition:** 0.9250 Silver .8410 oz. ASW **Series:** Big Cats **Reverse:** Colorized lions **Edge:** Reeded **Size:** 38.6 mm.

| Date | Mintage | F | VF | XF | Unc | BU |
|---|---|---|---|---|---|---|
| 2001 Proof | — | Value: 50.00 | | | | |

**10 DOLLARS** **KM#247** **Weight:** 28.2800 g. **Composition:** 0.9250 Silver .8410 oz. ASW **Series:** Big Cats **Reverse:** Tiger **Edge:** Reeded **Size:** 38.6 mm.

| Date | Mintage | F | VF | XF | Unc | BU |
|---|---|---|---|---|---|---|
| 2001 Proof | — | Value: 47.50 | | | | |

**10 DOLLARS** **KM# 247a** **Weight:** 28.2800 g. **Composition:** 0.9250 Silver .8410 oz. ASW **Series:** Big Cats **Reverse:** Colorized tiger **Edge:** Reeded **Size:** 38.6 mm.

| Date | Mintage | F | VF | XF | Unc | BU |
|---|---|---|---|---|---|---|
| 2001 Proof | — | Value: 50.00 | | | | |

**10 DOLLARS** **KM#248** **Weight:** 28.2800 g. **Composition:** 0.9250 Silver .8410 oz. ASW **Series:** Big Cats **Reverse:** Cheetah **Edge:** Reeded **Size:** 38.6 mm.

| Date | Mintage | F | VF | XF | Unc | BU |
|---|---|---|---|---|---|---|
| 2001 Proof | 10,000 | Value: 47.50 | | | | |

**10 DOLLARS** **KM# 248a** **Weight:** 28.2800 g. **Composition:** 0.9250 Silver .8410 oz. ASW **Series:** Big Cats **Reverse:** Colorized cheetah **Edge:** Reeded **Size:** 38.6 mm.

| Date | Mintage | F | VF | XF | Unc | BU |
|---|---|---|---|---|---|---|
| 2001 Proof | — | Value: 50.00 | | | | |

**10 DOLLARS** **KM#249** **Weight:** 28.2800 g. **Composition:** 0.9250 Silver .8410 oz. ASW **Series:** Big Cats **Reverse:** Cougar **Edge:** Reeded **Size:** 38.6 mm.

| Date | Mintage | F | VF | XF | Unc | BU |
|---|---|---|---|---|---|---|
| 2001 Proof | 10,000 | Value: 47.50 | | | | |

**10 DOLLARS** **KM# 249a** **Weight:** 28.2800 g. **Composition:** 0.9250 Silver .8410 oz. ASW **Series:** Big Cats **Reverse:** Colorized cougar **Edge:** Reeded **Size:** 38.6 mm.

| Date | Mintage | F | VF | XF | Unc | BU |
|---|---|---|---|---|---|---|
| 2001 Proof | — | Value: 50.00 | | | | |

**10 DOLLARS** **KM#250** **Weight:** 28.2800 g. **Composition:** 0.9250 Silver .8410 oz. ASW **Series:** Big Cats **Reverse:** Black panther **Edge:** Reeded **Size:** 38.6 mm.

| Date | Mintage | F | VF | XF | Unc | BU |
|---|---|---|---|---|---|---|
| 2001 Proof | 10,000 | Value: 47.50 | | | | |

**10 DOLLARS** **KM# 250a** **Weight:** 28.2800 g. **Composition:** 0.9250 Silver .8410 oz. ASW **Series:** Big Cats **Reverse:** Colorized black panther **Edge:** Reeded **Size:** 38.6 mm.

| Date | Mintage | F | VF | XF | Unc | BU |
|---|---|---|---|---|---|---|
| 2001 Proof | — | Value: 50.00 | | | | |

**10 DOLLARS** **KM#257** **Weight:** 28.2800 g. **Composition:** 0.9250 Silver .8410 oz. ASW **Subject:** Year of the Horse **Obverse:** National arms. **Reverse:** Horse. **Edge:** Reeded. **Size:** 38.6 mm.

| Date | Mintage | F | VF | XF | Unc | BU |
|---|---|---|---|---|---|---|
| 2002 Proof | 5,000 | Value: 47.50 | | | | |

**20 DOLLARS** **KM# 73** **Weight:** 1.2441 g. **Composition:** 0.9990 Gold .0400 oz. AGW **Subject:** Diana - The Peoples' Princess **Note:** Similar to 1 Dollar, KM#71.

| Date | Mintage | F | VF | XF | Unc | BU |
|---|---|---|---|---|---|---|
| 1997 Proof | Est. 101,000 | Value: 45.00 | | | | |

**20 DOLLARS** **KM# 79** **Weight:** 1.2441 g. **Composition:** 0.9990 Gold .0400 oz. AGW **Subject:** Diana - The Peoples' Princess **Reverse:** Lady Diana and Mother Theresa **Note:** Similar to 1 Dollar, KM#77.

| Date | Mintage | F | VF | XF | Unc | BU |
|---|---|---|---|---|---|---|
| 1997 Proof | Est. 101,000 | Value: 45.00 | | | | |

**20 DOLLARS** **KM# 85** **Weight:** 1.2441 g. **Composition:** 0.9990 Gold .0400 oz. AGW **Subject:** Diana - The Peoples' Princess **Reverse:** Lady Diana and AIDS patient **Note:** Similar to 1 Dollar, KM#83.

| Date | Mintage | F | VF | XF | Unc | BU |
|---|---|---|---|---|---|---|
| 1997 Proof | Est. 101,000 | Value: 45.00 | | | | |

**20 DOLLARS** **KM# 91** **Weight:** 1.2441 g. **Composition:** 0.9990 Gold .0400 oz. AGW **Subject:** Diana - The Peoples' Princess **Reverse:** With sons William and Harry **Note:** Similar to 1 Dollar, KM#89.

| Date | Mintage | F | VF | XF | Unc | BU |
|---|---|---|---|---|---|---|
| 1997 Proof | Est. 101,000 | Value: 45.00 | | | | |

**20 DOLLARS** **KM# 105** **Weight:** 1.2441 g. **Composition:** 0.9990 Gold .0400 oz. AGW **Subject:** In Memorium **Note:** Similar to 1 Dollar, KM#104.

| Date | Mintage | F | VF | XF | Unc | BU |
|---|---|---|---|---|---|---|
| 1998 Proof | Est. 10,000 | Value: 50.00 | | | | |

**20 DOLLARS** **KM# 144** **Weight:** 1.2441 g. **Composition:** 0.9990 Gold .0400 oz. AGW **Subject:** Year of the Dragon **Obverse:** National arms **Reverse:** Dragon **Note:** Similar to 1 Dollar, KM#143.

| Date | Mintage | F | VF | XF | Unc | BU |
|---|---|---|---|---|---|---|
| 2000 Proof | Est. 15,000 | Value: 55.00 | | | | |

**20 DOLLARS** **KM# 180** **Weight:** 1.2400 g. **Composition:** 0.9990 Gold .0399 oz. AGW **Subject:** Buddha **Obverse:** National arms **Reverse:** Seated Buddha **Edge:** Reeded **Note:** Struck at Pobjoy Mint.

| Date | Mintage | F | VF | XF | Unc | BU |
|---|---|---|---|---|---|---|
| 2000 Proof | Est. 5,000 | Value: 55.00 | | | | |

**20 DOLLARS** **KM# 181** **Weight:** 1.2400 g. **Composition:** 0.9990 Gold .0399 oz. AGW **Reverse:** Goddess of Mercy

| Date | Mintage | F | VF | XF | Unc | BU |
|---|---|---|---|---|---|---|
| 2000 Proof | Est. 5,000 | Value: 55.00 | | | | |

**20 DOLLARS** **KM# 182** **Weight:** 1.2400 g. **Composition:** 0.9990 Gold .0399 oz. AGW **Reverse:** Tzai-yen holding scroll

| Date | Mintage | F | VF | XF | Unc | BU |
|---|---|---|---|---|---|---|
| 2000 Proof | Est. 5,000 | Value: 55.00 | | | | |

**20 DOLLARS** **KM# 200** **Weight:** 1.2441 g. **Composition:** 0.9990 Gold .0400 oz. AGW **Subject:** Year of the Snake **Obverse:** National arms **Reverse:** Snake **Edge:** Reeded **Size:** 13.9 mm.

| Date | Mintage | F | VF | XF | Unc | BU |
|---|---|---|---|---|---|---|
| 2001 Proof | Est. 50,000 | Value: 58.00 | | | | |

**20 DOLLARS** **KM# 208** **Weight:** 1.2441 g. **Composition:** 0.9990 Gold .0400 oz. AGW **Subject:** P'an Ku **Obverse:** National arms **Reverse:** Dragon

| Date | Mintage | F | VF | XF | Unc | BU |
|---|---|---|---|---|---|---|
| 2001 Proof | Est. 5,000 | Value: 58.00 | | | | |

**20 DOLLARS** **KM# 216** **Weight:** 1.2441 g. **Composition:** 0.9990 Gold .0400 oz. AGW **Subject:** P'an Ku **Obverse:** National arms **Reverse:** Dragon and three animals

| Date | Mintage | F | VF | XF | Unc | BU |
|---|---|---|---|---|---|---|
| 2001 Proof | Est. 5,000 | Value: 58.00 | | | | |

**20 DOLLARS** **KM# 258** **Weight:** 1.2400 g. **Composition:** 0.9990 Gold .0398 oz. AGW **Subject:** Year of the Horse **Obverse:** National arms. **Reverse:** Horse. **Edge:** Reeded. **Size:** 13.92 mm.

| Date | Mintage | F | VF | XF | Unc | BU |
|---|---|---|---|---|---|---|
| 2002 Proof | 5,000 | Value: 49.50 | | | | |

**50 LEONES** **KM# 45** **Composition:** Nickel Clad Steel **Obverse:** Building above denomination **Reverse:** Sir Henry Lightfoot bust

| Date | Mintage | F | VF | XF | Unc | BU |
|---|---|---|---|---|---|---|
| 1996 | — | — | — | — | 1.25 | — |

**50 DOLLARS** **KM# 74** **Weight:** 3.1100 g. **Composition:** 0.9990 Gold .1000 oz. AGW **Subject:** Diana - The Peoples' Princess **Note:** Similar to 1 Dollar, KM#71.

| Date | Mintage | F | VF | XF | Unc | BU |
|---|---|---|---|---|---|---|
| 1997 Proof | Est. 7,500 | Value: 85.00 | | | | |

**50 DOLLARS** **KM# 80** **Weight:** 3.1100 g. **Composition:** 0.9990 Gold .1000 oz. AGW **Subject:** Diana - The Peoples' Princess **Reverse:** Lady Diana and Mother Theresa **Note:** Similar to 1 Dollar, KM#77.

| Date | Mintage | F | VF | XF | Unc | BU |
|---|---|---|---|---|---|---|
| 1997 Proof | Est. 7,500 | Value: 85.00 | | | | |

**50 DOLLARS** **KM# 86** **Weight:** 3.1100 g. **Composition:** 0.9990 Gold .1000 oz. AGW **Subject:** Diana - The Peoples' Princess **Reverse:** Lady Diana and AIDS patient **Note:** Similar to 1 Dollar, KM#83.

| Date | Mintage | F | VF | XF | Unc | BU |
|---|---|---|---|---|---|---|
| 1997 Proof | Est. 7,500 | Value: 85.00 | | | | |

**50 DOLLARS** **KM# 92** **Weight:** 3.1100 g. **Composition:** 0.9990 Gold .1000 oz. AGW **Subject:** Diana - The Peoples' Princess **Reverse:** With sons William and Harry **Note:** Similar to 1 Dollar, KM#89.

| Date | Mintage | F | VF | XF | Unc | BU |
|---|---|---|---|---|---|---|
| 1997 Proof | Est. 7,500 | Value: 85.00 | | | | |

**50 DOLLARS** **KM# 106** **Weight:** 3.1100 g. **Composition:** 0.9990 Gold .1000 oz. AGW **Subject:** Diana - The Peoples' Princess **Note:** Similar to 1 Dollar, KM#104.

| Date | Mintage | F | VF | XF | Unc | BU |
|---|---|---|---|---|---|---|
| 1998 Proof | Est. 7,500 | Value: 85.00 | | | | |

**50 DOLLARS** **KM# 184** **Weight:** 3.1100 g. **Composition:** 0.9990 Gold .1000 oz. AGW **Reverse:** Goddess of Mercy

| Date | Mintage | F | VF | XF | Unc | BU |
|---|---|---|---|---|---|---|
| 2000 Proof | Est. 5,000 | Value: 95.00 | | | | |

**50 DOLLARS** **KM# 145** **Weight:** 3.1100 g. **Composition:** 0.9990 Gold .1000 oz. AGW **Subject:** Year of the Dragon **Obverse:** National arms **Reverse:** Dragon **Note:** Similar to 1 Dollar, KM#143.

| Date | Mintage | F | VF | XF | Unc | BU |
|---|---|---|---|---|---|---|
| 2000 Proof | Est. 20,000 | Value: 90.00 | | | | |

**50 DOLLARS** **KM# 183** **Weight:** 3.1100 g. **Composition:** 0.9990 Gold .1000 oz. AGW **Subject:** Buddha **Obverse:** National arms **Reverse:** Seated Buddha **Edge:** Reeded **Note:** Similar to 1 Dollar, KM#143. Struck at Pobjoy Mint.

| Date | Mintage | F | VF | XF | Unc | BU |
|---|---|---|---|---|---|---|
| 2000 Proof | Est. 5,000 | Value: 95.00 | | | | |

**50 DOLLARS** **KM# 185** **Weight:** 3.1100 g. **Composition:** 0.9990 Gold .1000 oz. AGW **Reverse:** Tzai-yen holding scroll

| Date | Mintage | F | VF | XF | Unc | BU |
|---|---|---|---|---|---|---|
| 2000 Proof | Est. 5,000 | Value: 95.00 | | | | |

**50 DOLLARS** **KM# 201** **Weight:** 3.1103 g. **Composition:** 0.9990 Gold .1000 oz. AGW **Subject:** Year of the Snake **Obverse:** National arms **Reverse:** Snake **Edge:** Reeded **Size:** 18 mm.

| Date | Mintage | F | VF | XF | Unc | BU |
|---|---|---|---|---|---|---|
| 2001 Proof | Est. 10,000 | Value: 95.00 | | | | |

**50 DOLLARS** **KM# 209** **Weight:** 3.1103 g. **Composition:** 0.9990 Gold .1000 oz. AGW **Subject:** P'an Ku **Obverse:** National arms **Reverse:** Dragon

| Date | Mintage | F | VF | XF | Unc | BU |
|---|---|---|---|---|---|---|
| 2001 Proof | Est. 5,000 | Value: 95.00 | | | | |

**50 DOLLARS** **KM# 217** **Weight:** 3.1103 g. **Composition:** 0.9990 Gold .1000 oz. AGW **Subject:** P'an Ku **Obverse:** National arms **Reverse:** Dragon and three animals

| Date | Mintage | F | VF | XF | Unc | BU |
|---|---|---|---|---|---|---|
| 2001 Proof | Est. 5,000 | Value: 95.00 | | | | |

**50 DOLLARS** **KM# 259** **Weight:** 3.1100 g. **Composition:** 0.9990 Gold .0999 oz. AGW **Subject:** Year of the Horse **Obverse:** National arms. **Reverse:** Horse. **Edge:** Reeded. **Size:** 17.95 mm.

| Date | Mintage | F | VF | XF | Unc | BU |
|---|---|---|---|---|---|---|
| 2002 Proof | 5,000 | Value: 95.00 | | | | |

**100 LEONES** **KM# 39** **Weight:** 15.9800 g. **Composition:** 0.9170 Gold .4711 oz. AGW **Series:** Year of the Scout

| Date | Mintage | F | VF | XF | Unc | BU |
|---|---|---|---|---|---|---|
| ND(1983) | 2,000 | — | — | — | 275 | — |
| ND(1983) Proof | 2,000 | Value: 350 | | | | |

**100 LEONES** **KM# 46** **Composition:** Nickel Clad Steel **Obverse:** Cocoa pods **Reverse:** Naimbana bust

| Date | Mintage | F | VF | XF | Unc | BU |
|---|---|---|---|---|---|---|
| 1996 | — | — | — | — | 1.75 | — |

**100 DOLLARS** **KM# 51** **Weight:** 6.2200 g. **Composition:** 0.9999 Gold .2000 oz. AGW **Subject:** Shanghai Coin and Stamp Expostion **Reverse:** Crowned lion **Note:** Similar to 5 Dollars, KM#98.

| Date | Mintage | F | VF | XF | Unc | BU |
|---|---|---|---|---|---|---|
| 1997 Proof | Est. 5,000 | Value: 175 | | | | |

**100 DOLLARS** **KM# 52** **Weight:** 6.2200 g. **Composition:** 0.9999 Gold .2000 oz. AGW **Subject:** Shanghai Coin and Stamp Exposition **Reverse:** Crowned lion **Note:** Similar to 5 Dollars, KM#99.

| Date | Mintage | F | VF | XF | Unc | BU |
|---|---|---|---|---|---|---|
| 1997 Proof | Est. 5,000 | Value: 175 | | | | |

**100 DOLLARS** **KM# 55** **Weight:** 6.2200 g. **Composition:** 0.9999 Gold .2000 oz. AGW **Subject:** Golden Wedding Anniversary **Reverse:** E and P monogram **Note:** Similar to 10 Dollars, KM#54.

| Date | Mintage | F | VF | XF | Unc | BU |
|---|---|---|---|---|---|---|
| 1997 Proof | Est. 3,500 | Value: 175 | | | | |

**100 DOLLARS** **KM# 58** **Weight:** 6.2200 g. **Composition:** 0.9999 Gold .2000 oz. AGW **Subject:** Golden Wedding Anniversary **Reverse:** Yacht **Note:** Similar to 10 Dollars, KM#57.

| Date | Mintage | F | VF | XF | Unc | BU |
|---|---|---|---|---|---|---|
| 1997 Proof | Est. 3,500 | Value: 175 | | | | |

**100 DOLLARS** **KM# 61** **Weight:** 6.2200 g. **Composition:** 0.9999 Gold .2000 oz. AGW **Subject:** Golden Wedding Anniversary **Reverse:** Royal couple **Note:** Similar to 10 Dollars, KM#60.

| Date | Mintage | F | VF | XF | Unc | BU |
|---|---|---|---|---|---|---|
| 1997 Proof | Est. 10,000 | Value: 175 | | | | |

**100 DOLLARS** **KM# 64** **Weight:** 6.2200 g. **Composition:** 0.9999 Gold .2000 oz. AGW **Subject:** Golden Wedding Anniversary **Reverse:** Fireworks above palace **Note:** Similar to 10 Dollars, KM#63.

| Date | Mintage | F | VF | XF | Unc | BU |
|---|---|---|---|---|---|---|
| 1997 Proof | Est. 3,500 | Value: 175 | | | | |

**100 DOLLARS** **KM# 67** **Weight:** 6.2200 g. **Composition:** 0.9999 Gold .2000 oz. AGW **Subject:** Golden Wedding Anniversary **Reverse:** Queen with two children **Note:** Similar to 10 Dollars, KM#66.

| Date | Mintage | F | VF | XF | Unc | BU |
|---|---|---|---|---|---|---|
| 1997 Proof | Est. 3,500 | Value: 175 | | | | |

**100 DOLLARS** **KM# 70** **Weight:** 6.2200 g. **Composition:** 0.9999 Gold .2000 oz. AGW **Subject:** Golden Wedding Anniversary **Reverse:** Royal couple with two children **Note:** Similar to 10 Dollars, KM#69.

| Date | Mintage | F | VF | XF | Unc | BU |
|---|---|---|---|---|---|---|
| 1997 Proof | Est. 3,500 | Value: 175 | | | | |

**100 DOLLARS** **KM# 75** **Weight:** 6.2200 g. **Composition:** 0.9999 Gold .2000 oz. AGW **Subject:** Diana - The Peoples' Princess **Note:** Similar to 1 Dollar, KM#71.

| Date | Mintage | F | VF | XF | Unc | BU |
|---|---|---|---|---|---|---|
| 1997 Proof | Est. 5,000 | Value: 160 | | | | |

**100 DOLLARS** **KM# 81** **Weight:** 6.2200 g. **Composition:** 0.9999 Gold .2000 oz. AGW **Subject:** Diana - The Peoples' Princess **Reverse:** Lady Diana and Mother Theresa

| Date | Mintage | F | VF | XF | Unc | BU |
|---|---|---|---|---|---|---|
| 1997 Proof | Est. 5,000 | Value: 160 | | | | |

**100 DOLLARS** **KM# 87** **Weight:** 6.2200 g. **Composition:** 0.9999 Gold .2000 oz. AGW **Subject:** Diana - The Peoples' Princess **Reverse:** Lady Diana and AIDS patient **Note:** Similar to 1 Dollar, KM#83.

| Date | Mintage | F | VF | XF | Unc | BU |
|---|---|---|---|---|---|---|
| 1997 Proof | Est. 5,000 | Value: 160 | | | | |

**100 DOLLARS** **KM# 93** **Weight:** 6.2200 g. **Composition:** 0.9999 Gold .2000 oz. AGW **Subject:** Diana - The Peoples' Princess **Reverse:** With two children, sons William and Harry **Note:** Similar to 1 Dollar, KM#89.

| Date | Mintage | F | VF | XF | Unc | BU |
|---|---|---|---|---|---|---|
| 1997 Proof | Est. 5,000 | Value: 160 | | | | |

**100 DOLLARS** **KM# 97** **Weight:** 6.2200 g. **Composition:** 0.9999 Gold .2000 oz. AGW **Subject:** Jurassic Park **Reverse:** Velociraptor **Note:** Similar to 10 Dollars, KM#96.

| Date | Mintage | F | VF | XF | Unc | BU |
|---|---|---|---|---|---|---|
| 1997 Proof | Est. 5,000 | Value: 175 | | | | |

**100 DOLLARS** **KM# 100** **Weight:** 6.2200 g. **Composition:** 0.9999 Gold .2000 oz. AGW **Subject:** Queen Victoria's Diamond Jubilee Centennial **Obverse:** National arms **Reverse:** Youthful portrait of Queen with .06 carat diamond mounted in gown

| Date | Mintage | F | VF | XF | Unc | BU |
|---|---|---|---|---|---|---|
| 1997 Proof | Est. 3,500 | Value: 200 | | | | |

**100 DOLLARS** **KM# 107** **Weight:** 6.2200 g. **Composition:** 0.9999 Gold .2000 oz. AGW **Subject:** Diana - The People's Princess **Note:** Similar to 10 Dollars, KM#104.

| Date | Mintage | F | VF | XF | Unc | BU |
|---|---|---|---|---|---|---|
| 1998 Proof | Est. 5,000 | Value: 160 | | | | |

**100 DOLLARS** **KM# 111** **Weight:** 6.2200 g. **Composition:** 0.9999 Gold .2000 oz. AGW **Subject:** Dr. Livingstone **Obverse:** National arms **Note:** Similar to 10 Dollars, KM#110.

| Date | Mintage | F | VF | XF | Unc | BU |
|---|---|---|---|---|---|---|
| 1998 Proof | Est. 5,000 | Value: 165 | | | | |

**100 DOLLARS** **KM# 114** **Weight:** 6.2200 g. **Composition:** 0.9999 Gold .2000 oz. AGW **Subject:** Amerigo Vespucci **Obverse:** National arms **Reverse:** Ship and mountainous portrait **Note:** Similar to 10 Dollars, KM#113.

| Date | Mintage | F | VF | XF | Unc | BU |
|---|---|---|---|---|---|---|
| 1999 Proof | Est. 5,000 | Value: 175 | | | | |

**100 DOLLARS** **KM# 117** **Weight:** 6.2200 g. **Composition:** 0.9999 Gold .2000 oz. AGW **Subject:** Charles Darwin **Obverse:** National arms **Reverse:** Ship and portrait **Note:** Similar to 10 Dollars, KM#116.

| Date | Mintage | F | VF | XF | Unc | BU |
|---|---|---|---|---|---|---|
| 1999 Proof | Est. 5,000 | Value: 175 | | | | |

**100 DOLLARS** **KM# 120** **Weight:** 6.2200 g. **Composition:** 0.9999 Gold .2000 oz. AGW **Subject:** China 2000 Series **Obverse:** National arms **Reverse:** Kneeling terracotta warrior **Note:** Similar to 10 Dollars, KM#119.

| Date | Mintage | F | VF | XF | Unc | BU |
|---|---|---|---|---|---|---|
| 1999 Proof | Est. 5,000 | Value: 165 | | | | |

**100 DOLLARS** **KM# 123** **Weight:** 6.2200 g. **Composition:** 0.9999 Gold .2000 oz. AGW **Subject:** China 2000 Series - Ming Dynasty **Obverse:** National arms **Reverse:** Temple of Heaven **Note:** Similar to 10 Dollars, KM#122.

| Date | Mintage | F | VF | XF | Unc | BU |
|---|---|---|---|---|---|---|
| 1999 Proof | Est. 5,000 | Value: 165 | | | | |

**100 DOLLARS** **KM# 126** **Weight:** 6.2200 g. **Composition:** 0.9999 Gold .2000 oz. AGW **Subject:** China 2000 Series - The Great Wall **Obverse:** National arms **Reverse:** Portion of the Great Wall **Note:** Similar to 10 Dollars, KM#125.

| Date | Mintage | F | VF | XF | Unc | BU |
|---|---|---|---|---|---|---|
| 1999 Proof | Est. 5,000 | Value: 165 | | | | |

**100 DOLLARS** **KM# 129** **Weight:** 6.2200 g. **Composition:** 0.9999 Gold .2000 oz. AGW **Subject:** China 2000 Series **Obverse:** National arms **Reverse:** Bronze chariot **Note:** Similar to 10 Dollars, KM#128.

| Date | Mintage | F | VF | XF | Unc | BU |
|---|---|---|---|---|---|---|
| 1999 Proof | Est. 5,000 | Value: 165 | | | | |

**100 DOLLARS** **KM# 132** **Weight:** 6.2200 g. **Composition:** 0.9999 Gold .2000 oz. AGW **Subject:** China 2000 Series **Obverse:** National arms **Reverse:** First century armillary sphere **Note:** Similar to 10 Dollars, KM#131.

| Date | Mintage | F | VF | XF | Unc | BU |
|---|---|---|---|---|---|---|
| 1999 Proof | Est. 5,000 | Value: 165 | | | | |

**100 DOLLARS** KM# 135 **Weight:** 6.2200 g. **Composition:** 0.9999 Gold .2000 oz. AGW **Subject:** China 2000 Series **Obverse:** National arms **Reverse:** Tang Dynasty royal horse **Note:** Similar to 10 Dollars, KM#134.

| Date | Mintage | F | VF | XF | Unc | BU |
|---|---|---|---|---|---|---|
| 1999 Proof | Est. 5,000 | Value: 165 | | | | |

**100 DOLLARS** KM# 138 **Weight:** 6.2200 g. **Composition:** 0.9999 Gold .2000 oz. AGW **Subject:** Macau Return to China **Obverse:** National arms **Reverse:** Church, car, roulette wheel, and hands shaking **Note:** Similar to 10 Dollars, KM#137.

| Date | Mintage | F | VF | XF | Unc | BU |
|---|---|---|---|---|---|---|
| 1999 Proof | Est. 5,000 | Value: 175 | | | | |

**100 DOLLARS** KM# 141 **Weight:** 6.2200 g. **Composition:** 0.9999 Gold .2000 oz. AGW **Subject:** Prince Edward's Wedding **Obverse:** National arms **Reverse:** Symbolic wedding design **Note:** Similar to 10 Dollars, KM#140.

| Date | Mintage | F | VF | XF | Unc | BU |
|---|---|---|---|---|---|---|
| 1999 Proof | Est. 5,000 | Value: 175 | | | | |

**100 DOLLARS** KM# 146 **Weight:** 6.2200 g. **Composition:** 0.9999 Gold .2000 oz. AGW **Subject:** Year of the Dragon **Obverse:** National arms **Reverse:** Dragon **Note:** Similar to 10 Dollars, KM#143.

| Date | Mintage | F | VF | XF | Unc | BU |
|---|---|---|---|---|---|---|
| 2000 Proof | Est. 20,000 | Value: 165 | | | | |

**100 DOLLARS** KM# 186 **Weight:** 6.2200 g. **Composition:** 0.9999 Gold .2000 oz. AGW **Subject:** Buddha **Obverse:** National arms **Reverse:** Seated Buddha **Edge:** Reeded **Note:** Struck at Pobjoy Mint.

| Date | Mintage | F | VF | XF | Unc | BU |
|---|---|---|---|---|---|---|
| 2000 | Est. 5,000 | Value: 175 | | | | |

**100 DOLLARS** KM# 187 **Weight:** 6.2200 g. **Composition:** 0.9999 Gold .2000 oz. AGW **Subject:** Buddha **Obverse:** National arms **Reverse:** Goddess of Mercy

| Date | Mintage | F | VF | XF | Unc | BU |
|---|---|---|---|---|---|---|
| 2000 Proof | Est. 5,000 | Value: 175 | | | | |

**100 DOLLARS** KM# 188 **Weight:** 6.2200 g. **Composition:** 0.9999 Gold .2000 oz. AGW **Reverse:** Tzai-yen holding scroll

| Date | Mintage | F | VF | XF | Unc | BU |
|---|---|---|---|---|---|---|
| 2000 Proof | Est. 5,000 | Value: 175 | | | | |

**100 DOLLARS** KM# 251 **Weight:** 6.2200 g. **Composition:** 0.9990 Gold .1998 oz. AGW **Series:** Big Cats **Obverse:** National arms **Reverse:** Male and female lions **Edge:** Reeded **Size:** 22 mm.

| Date | Mintage | F | VF | XF | Unc | BU |
|---|---|---|---|---|---|---|
| 2001 Proof | 5,000 | Value: 175 | | | | |

**100 DOLLARS** KM# 252 **Weight:** 6.2200 g. **Composition:** 0.9990 Gold .1998 oz. AGW **Series:** Big Cats **Reverse:** Tiger **Edge:** Reeded **Size:** 22 mm.

| Date | Mintage | F | VF | XF | Unc | BU |
|---|---|---|---|---|---|---|
| 2001 Proof | 5,000 | Value: 175 | | | | |

**100 DOLLARS** KM# 253 **Weight:** 6.2200 g. **Composition:** 0.9990 Gold .1998 oz. AGW **Series:** Big Cats **Reverse:** Cheetah **Edge:** Reeded **Size:** 22 mm.

| Date | Mintage | F | VF | XF | Unc | BU |
|---|---|---|---|---|---|---|
| 2001 Proof | 5,000 | Value: 175 | | | | |

**100 DOLLARS** KM# 254 **Weight:** 6.2200 g. **Composition:** 0.9990 Gold .1998 oz. AGW **Series:** Big Cats **Reverse:** Cougar **Edge:** Reeded **Size:** 22 mm.

| Date | Mintage | F | VF | XF | Unc | BU |
|---|---|---|---|---|---|---|
| 2001 Proof | 5,000 | Value: 175 | | | | |

**100 DOLLARS** KM# 255 **Weight:** 6.2200 g. **Composition:** 0.9990 Gold .1998 oz. AGW **Series:** Big Cats **Reverse:** Black panther **Edge:** Reeded **Size:** 22 mm.

| Date | Mintage | F | VF | XF | Unc | BU |
|---|---|---|---|---|---|---|
| 2001 Proof | 5,000 | Value: 175 | | | | |

**100 DOLLARS** KM# 202 **Weight:** 6.2200 g. **Composition:** 0.9990 Gold .2000 oz. AGW **Subject:** Year of the Snake **Obverse:** National arms **Reverse:** Snake **Edge:** Reeded **Size:** 22 mm.

| Date | Mintage | F | VF | XF | Unc | BU |
|---|---|---|---|---|---|---|
| 2001 Proof | — | Value: 175 | | | | |

**100 DOLLARS** KM# 210 **Weight:** 6.2200 g. **Composition:** 0.9990 Gold .2000 oz. AGW **Subject:** P'an Ku **Obverse:** National arms **Reverse:** Dragon

| Date | Mintage | F | VF | XF | Unc | BU |
|---|---|---|---|---|---|---|
| 2001 Proof | Est. 10,000 | Value: 175 | | | | |

**100 DOLLARS** KM# 218 **Weight:** 6.2200 g. **Composition:** 0.9990 Gold .2000 oz. AGW **Subject:** P'an Ku **Obverse:** National arms **Reverse:** Dragon and three animals

| Date | Mintage | F | VF | XF | Unc | BU |
|---|---|---|---|---|---|---|
| 2001 Proof | Est. 10,000 | Value: 175 | | | | |

**100 DOLLARS** KM# 224 **Weight:** 6.2200 g. **Composition:** 0.9990 Gold .2000 oz. AGW **Series:** The Big Five **Obverse:** National arms **Reverse:** Rhino **Edge:** Reeded **Size:** 22 mm.

| Date | Mintage | F | VF | XF | Unc | BU |
|---|---|---|---|---|---|---|
| 2001 Proof | Est. 5,000 | Value: 175 | | | | |

**100 DOLLARS** KM# 227 **Weight:** 6.2200 g. **Composition:** 0.9990 Gold .2000 oz. AGW **Series:** The Big Five **Obverse:** National arms **Reverse:** Lion

| Date | Mintage | F | VF | XF | Unc | BU |
|---|---|---|---|---|---|---|
| 2001 Proof | Est. 5,000 | Value: 175 | | | | |

**100 DOLLARS** KM# 230 **Weight:** 6.2200 g. **Composition:** 0.9990 Gold .2000 oz. AGW **Series:** The Big Five **Obverse:** National arms **Reverse:** Leopard

| Date | Mintage | F | VF | XF | Unc | BU |
|---|---|---|---|---|---|---|
| 2001 Proof | Est. 5,000 | Value: 175 | | | | |

**100 DOLLARS** KM# 233 **Weight:** 6.2200 g. **Composition:** 0.9990 Gold .2000 oz. AGW **Series:** The Big Five **Obverse:** National arms **Reverse:** Elephants

| Date | Mintage | F | VF | XF | Unc | BU |
|---|---|---|---|---|---|---|
| 2001 Proof | Est. 5,000 | Value: 175 | | | | |

**100 DOLLARS** KM# 236 **Weight:** 6.2200 g. **Composition:** 0.9990 Gold .2000 oz. AGW **Series:** The Big Five **Obverse:** National arms **Reverse:** Buffalo

| Date | Mintage | F | VF | XF | Unc | BU |
|---|---|---|---|---|---|---|
| 2001 Proof | Est. 5,000 | Value: 175 | | | | |

**100 DOLLARS** KM# 239 **Weight:** 6.2200 g. **Composition:** 0.9990 Gold .2000 oz. AGW **Series:** The Big Five **Obverse:** National arms

**Reverse:** All five animal

| Date | Mintage | F | VF | XF | Unc | BU |
|---|---|---|---|---|---|---|
| 2001 Proof | Est. 5,000 | Value: 175 | | | | |

**100 DOLLARS** KM# 260 **Weight:** 6.2200 g. **Composition:** 0.9990 Gold .1998 oz. AGW **Subject:** Year of the Horse **Obverse:** National arms. **Reverse:** Horse. **Edge:** Reeded. **Size:** 22 mm.

| Date | Mintage | F | VF | XF | Unc | BU |
|---|---|---|---|---|---|---|
| 2002 Proof | 2,000 | Value: 175 | | | | |

**250 DOLLARS** KM# 240 **Weight:** 15.5500 g. **Composition:** 0.9999 Gold .4999 oz. AGW **Subject:** Centennial of Queen Victoria's Diamond Jubilee **Obverse:** National arms **Reverse:** Young portrait of Queen Victoria with a .06 carat diamond mounted on her gown **Edge:** Reeded **Size:** 29.9 mm. **Note:** This denomination was never offered to the public. The entire issue is reported to have been commissioned by and sold to a single purchaser.

| Date | Mintage | F | VF | XF | Unc | BU |
|---|---|---|---|---|---|---|
| 1997 Proof | Est. 1,000 | — | — | — | 300 | — |

**250 DOLLARS** KM# 76 **Weight:** 15.5000 g. **Composition:** 0.9990 Gold .5000 oz. AGW **Subject:** Diana - The Peoples' Princess **Note:** Similar to 1 Dollar, KM#71.

| Date | Mintage | F | VF | XF | Unc | BU |
|---|---|---|---|---|---|---|
| 1997 Proof | Est. 3,000 | Value: 320 | | | | |

**250 DOLLARS** KM# 82 **Weight:** 15.5000 g. **Composition:** 0.9990 Gold .5000 oz. AGW **Subject:** Diana - The Peoples' Princess **Reverse:** Mother Theresa and Lady Diana **Note:** Similar to 1 Dollar, KM#77.

| Date | Mintage | F | VF | XF | Unc | BU |
|---|---|---|---|---|---|---|
| 1997 Proof | Est. 3,000 | Value: 320 | | | | |

**250 DOLLARS** KM# 88 **Weight:** 15.5000 g. **Composition:** 0.9990 Gold .5000 oz. AGW **Subject:** Diana - The Peoples' Princess **Reverse:** Lady Diana with AIDS patient **Note:** Similar to 1 Dollar, KM#83.

| Date | Mintage | F | VF | XF | Unc | BU |
|---|---|---|---|---|---|---|
| 1997 Proof | Est. 3,000 | Value: 320 | | | | |

**250 DOLLARS** KM# 94 **Weight:** 15.5000 g. **Composition:** 0.9990 Gold .5000 oz. AGW **Subject:** Diana - The Peoples' Princess **Reverse:** Lady Diana with sons William and Harry **Note:** Similar to 1 Dollar, KM#89.

| Date | Mintage | F | VF | XF | Unc | BU |
|---|---|---|---|---|---|---|
| 1997 Proof | Est. 3,000 | Value: 320 | | | | |

**250 DOLLARS** KM# 108 **Weight:** 15.5000 g. **Composition:** 0.9990 Gold .5000 oz. AGW **Subject:** Diana - The Peoples' Princess **Note:** Similar to 10 Dollars, KM#104.

| Date | Mintage | F | VF | XF | Unc | BU |
|---|---|---|---|---|---|---|
| 1998 Proof | Est. 3,000 | Value: 320 | | | | |

**250 DOLLARS** KM# 147 **Weight:** 15.5000 g. **Composition:** 0.9990 Gold .5000 oz. AGW **Subject:** Year of the Dragon **Obverse:** National arms **Reverse:** Dragon **Note:** Similar to 10 Dollars, KM#143

| Date | Mintage | F | VF | XF | Unc | BU |
|---|---|---|---|---|---|---|
| 2000 Proof | Est. 5,000 | Value: 300 | | | | |

**250 DOLLARS** KM# 189 **Weight:** 15.5000 g. **Composition:** 0.9990 Gold .5000 oz. AGW **Subject:** Buddha **Obverse:** National arms **Reverse:** Seated Buddha

| Date | Mintage | F | VF | XF | Unc | BU |
|---|---|---|---|---|---|---|
| 2000 Proof | Est. 5,000 | Value: 340 | | | | |

**250 DOLLARS** KM# 190 **Weight:** 15.5500 g. **Composition:** 0.9990 Gold .5000 oz. AGW **Reverse:** Goddess of Mercy

| Date | Mintage | F | VF | XF | Unc | BU |
|---|---|---|---|---|---|---|
| 2000 Proof | Est. 5,000 | Value: 340 | | | | |

**250 DOLLARS** KM# 191 **Weight:** 15.5500 g. **Composition:** 0.9990 Gold .5000 oz. AGW **Reverse:** Tzai-yen holding scroll

| Date | Mintage | F | VF | XF | Unc | BU |
|---|---|---|---|---|---|---|
| 2000 Proof | Est. 5,000 | Value: 340 | | | | |

**250 DOLLARS** KM# 203 **Weight:** 15.5118 g. **Composition:** 0.9990 Gold .5000 oz. AGW **Subject:** Year of the Snake **Obverse:** National arms **Reverse:** Snake **Edge:** Reeded **Size:** 30 mm.

| Date | Mintage | F | VF | XF | Unc | BU |
|---|---|---|---|---|---|---|
| 2001 Proof | Est. 5,000 | Value: 340 | | | | |

**250 DOLLARS** KM# 211 **Weight:** 15.5518 g. **Composition:** 0.9990 Gold .5000 oz. AGW **Subject:** P'an Ku **Obverse:** National arms **Reverse:** Dragon

| Date | Mintage | F | VF | XF | Unc | BU |
|---|---|---|---|---|---|---|
| 2001 Proof | Est. 2,000 | Value: 340 | | | | |

**250 DOLLARS** KM# 219 **Weight:** 15.5518 g. **Composition:** 0.9990 Gold .5000 oz. AGW **Subject:** P'an Ku **Obverse:** National arms **Reverse:** Dragon and three animals

| Date | Mintage | F | VF | XF | Unc | BU |
|---|---|---|---|---|---|---|
| 2001 Proof | Est. 2,000 | Value: 340 | | | | |

**250 DOLLARS** KM# 261 **Weight:** 15.5500 g. **Composition:** 0.9990 Gold .4994 oz. AGW **Subject:** Year of the Horse **Obverse:** National arms. **Reverse:** Horse. **Edge:** Reeded. **Size:** 30 mm.

| Date | Mintage | F | VF | XF | Unc | BU |
|---|---|---|---|---|---|---|
| 2002 Proof | 2,000 | Value: 340 | | | | |

**500 DOLLARS** KM# 148 **Weight:** 31.1035 g. **Composition:** 0.9990 Gold 1.0000 oz. AGW **Subject:** Year of the Dragon **Obverse:** National arms **Reverse:** Dragon **Note:** Similar to 10 Dollars, KM#143.

| Date | Mintage | F | VF | XF | Unc | BU |
|---|---|---|---|---|---|---|
| 2000 Proof | Est. 1,000 | Value: 650 | | | | |

**500 DOLLARS** KM# 192 **Weight:** 31.1035 g. **Composition:** 0.9990 Gold 1.0000 oz. AGW **Subject:** Buddha **Obverse:** National arms **Reverse:** Seated Buddha **Edge:** Reeded **Note:** Struck at Pobjoy Mint.

| Date | Mintage | F | VF | XF | Unc | BU |
|---|---|---|---|---|---|---|
| 2000 Proof | Est. 5,000 | Value: 650 | | | | |

**500 DOLLARS** KM# 193 **Weight:** 31.1035 g. **Composition:** 0.9990 Gold 1.0000 oz. AGW **Reverse:** Goddess of Mercy

| Date | Mintage | F | VF | XF | Unc | BU |
|---|---|---|---|---|---|---|
| 2000 Proof | Est. 5,000 | Value: 650 | | | | |

**500 DOLLARS** KM# 194 **Weight:** 31.1035 g. **Composition:** 0.9990 Gold 1.0000 oz. AGW **Reverse:** Tzai-yen holding scroll

| Date | Mintage | F | VF | XF | Unc | BU |
|---|---|---|---|---|---|---|
| 2000 Proof | Est. 5,000 | Value: 650 | | | | |

**500 DOLLARS** KM# 204 **Weight:** 31.1035 g. **Composition:** 0.9990 Gold 1.000 oz. AGW **Subject:** Year of the Snake **Obverse:** National arms **Reverse:** Snake **Edge:** Reeded **Size:** 32.7 mm.

| Date | Mintage | F | VF | XF | Unc | BU |
|---|---|---|---|---|---|---|
| 2001 Proof | Est. 1,000 | Value: 650 | | | | |

**500 DOLLARS** KM# 212 **Weight:** 31.1035 g. **Composition:** 0.9990 Gold 1.0000 oz. AGW **Subject:** P'an Ku **Obverse:** National arms **Reverse:** Dragon

| Date | Mintage | F | VF | XF | Unc | BU |
|---|---|---|---|---|---|---|
| 2001 Proof | Est. 1,000 | Value: 650 | | | | |

**500 DOLLARS** KM# 220 **Weight:** 31.1035 g. **Composition:** 0.9990 Gold 1.0000 oz. AGW **Subject:** P'an Ku **Obverse:** National arms **Reverse:** Dragon and three animals

| Date | Mintage | F | VF | XF | Unc | BU |
|---|---|---|---|---|---|---|
| 2001 Proof | Est. 1,000 | Value: 650 | | | | |

**500 DOLLARS** KM# 262 **Weight:** 31.1000 g. **Composition:** 0.9990 Gold .9989 oz. AGW **Subject:** Year of the Horse **Obverse:** National arms. **Reverse:** Horse. **Edge:** Reeded. **Size:** 32.7 mm.

| Date | Mintage | F | VF | XF | Unc | BU |
|---|---|---|---|---|---|---|
| 2002 Proof | 1,000 | Value: 650 | | | | |

**2500 DOLLARS** KM# 149 **Weight:** 155.5175 g. **Composition:** 0.9990 Gold 5.0000 oz. AGW **Subject:** Year of the Dragon **Obverse:** National arms **Reverse:** Dragon **Note:** Similar to 10 Dollars, KM#143.

| Date | Mintage | F | VF | XF | Unc | BU |
|---|---|---|---|---|---|---|
| 2000 Proof | 250 | Value: 3,250 | | | | |

**2500 DOLLARS** KM# 195 **Weight:** 155.5175 g. **Composition:** 0.9990 Gold 5.0000 oz. AGW **Subject:** Buddha **Obverse:** National arms **Reverse:** Seated Buddha **Edge:** Reeded **Note:** Struck at Pobjoy Mint.

| Date | Mintage | F | VF | XF | Unc | BU |
|---|---|---|---|---|---|---|
| 2000 Proof | Est. 250 | Value: 3,250 | | | | |

**2500 DOLLARS** KM# 196 **Weight:** 155.5175 g. **Composition:** 0.9990 Gold 5.0000 oz. AGW **Reverse:** Goddess of Mercy

| Date | Mintage | F | VF | XF | Unc | BU |
|---|---|---|---|---|---|---|
| 2000 Proof | Est. 250 | Value: 3,250 | | | | |

**2500 DOLLARS** KM# 197 **Weight:** 155.5175 g. **Composition:** 0.9990 Gold 5.0000 oz. AGW **Reverse:** Tzai-yen holding scroll

| Date | Mintage | F | VF | XF | Unc | BU |
|---|---|---|---|---|---|---|
| 2000 Proof | Est. 250 | Value: 3,250 | | | | |

**2500 DOLLARS** KM# 205 **Weight:** 155.5175 g. **Composition:** 0.9990 Gold 5.0000 oz. AGW **Subject:** Year of the Snake **Obverse:** National arms **Reverse:** Snake **Edge:** Reeded **Size:** 50 mm.

| Date | Mintage | F | VF | XF | Unc | BU |
|---|---|---|---|---|---|---|
| 2001 Proof | Est. 250 | Value: 3,000 | | | | |

**2500 DOLLARS** KM# 213 **Weight:** 155.5175 g. **Composition:** 0.9990 Gold 5.0000 oz. AGW **Subject:** P'an Ku **Obverse:** National arms **Reverse:** Dragon

| Date | Mintage | F | VF | XF | Unc | BU |
|---|---|---|---|---|---|---|
| 2001 Proof | Est. 250 | Value: 3,000 | | | | |

**2500 DOLLARS** KM# 263 **Weight:** 155.5100 g. **Composition:** 0.9990 Gold 4.9948 oz. AGW **Subject:** Year of the Horse **Obverse:** National arms. **Reverse:** Horse. **Edge:** Reeded. **Size:** 50 mm.

| Date | Mintage | F | VF | XF | Unc | BU |
|---|---|---|---|---|---|---|
| 2002 Proof | 250 | Value: 3,000 | | | | |

**1/4 GOLDE** KM# 22 **Weight:** 13.6360 g. **Composition:** 0.9000 Gold .3946 oz. AGW **Subject:** 5th Anniversary of Independence

| Date | Mintage | F | VF | XF | Unc | BU |
|---|---|---|---|---|---|---|
| ND(1966) | 5,000 | — | — | — | 180 | — |

**1/4 GOLDE** **KM# 23** **Weight:** 27.2730 g. **Composition:** 0.9000 Gold .7891 oz. AGW **Subject:** 5th Anniversary of Independence

| Date | Mintage | F | VF | XF | Unc | BU |
|---|---|---|---|---|---|---|
| ND(1966) | 2,500 | — | — | — | 350 | — |

**1/4 GOLDE** **KM# 23a** **Weight:** 30.0000 g. **Composition:** 0.9160 Gold .8836 oz. AGW

| Date | Mintage | F | VF | XF | Unc | BU |
|---|---|---|---|---|---|---|
| ND(1966) Proof | 600 | Value: 450 | | | | |

**1/4 GOLDE** **KM# 22a** **Weight:** 15.0000 g. **Composition:** 0.9160 Gold .4418 oz. AGW

| Date | Mintage | F | VF | XF | Unc | BU |
|---|---|---|---|---|---|---|
| ND(1966) Proof | 600 | Value: 300 | | | | |

**1/4 GOLDE** **KM# 22b** **Weight:** 10.3150 g. **Composition:** Palladium

| Date | Mintage | F | VF | XF | Unc | BU |
|---|---|---|---|---|---|---|
| ND(1966) Proof | 100 | Value: 350 | | | | |

**1/4 GOLDE** **KM# 23b** **Weight:** 20.6290 g. **Composition:** Palladium

| Date | Mintage | F | VF | XF | Unc | BU |
|---|---|---|---|---|---|---|
| ND(1966) Proof | 100 | Value: 550 | | | | |

**GOLDE** **KM# 24** **Weight:** 54.5450 g. **Composition:** 0.9000 Gold 1.5783 oz. AGW **Subject:** 5th Anniversary of Independence

| Date | Mintage | F | VF | XF | Unc | BU |
|---|---|---|---|---|---|---|
| ND(1966) | 1,500 | — | — | — | 800 | — |
| ND(1966) | 1,500 | — | — | — | 800 | — |

**GOLDE** **KM# 24a** **Weight:** 60.0000 g. **Composition:** 0.9160 Gold 1.7672 oz. AGW

| Date | Mintage | F | VF | XF | Unc | BU |
|---|---|---|---|---|---|---|
| ND(1966) Proof | 400 | Value: 1,000 | | | | |

**GOLDE** **KM# 24b** **Weight:** 41.2590 g. **Composition:** Palladium

| Date | Mintage | F | VF | XF | Unc | BU |
|---|---|---|---|---|---|---|
| ND(1966) Proof | 100 | Value: 1,150 | | | | |

**GOLDE** **KM# 24c** **Weight:** 41.2590 g. **Composition:** Platinum APW

| Date | Mintage | F | VF | XF | Unc | BU |
|---|---|---|---|---|---|---|
| ND(1966) Proof | — | Value: 1,000 | | | | |

**5 GOLDE** **KM# 37** **Weight:** 15.9800 g. **Composition:** 0.9170 Gold .4711 oz. AGW **Subject:** O.A.U. Summit Conference

| Date | Mintage | F | VF | XF | Unc | BU |
|---|---|---|---|---|---|---|
| 1980 | 457 | — | — | — | 245 | — |
| 1980 Proof | 325 | Value: 285 | | | | |

**5 GOLDE** **KM# 42** **Weight:** 15.9980 g. **Composition:** 0.9170 Gold .4711 oz. AGW **Series:** World Wildlife Fund **Reverse:** Duiker Zebra

| Date | Mintage | F | VF | XF | Unc | BU |
|---|---|---|---|---|---|---|
| 1987 Proof | 5,000 | Value: 250 | | | | |

**10 GOLDE** **KM# 28** **Weight:** 57.6000 g. **Composition:** 0.9160 Gold 1.6965 oz. AGW **Subject:** 70th Birthday - Dr. Siaka Stevens

| Date | Mintage | F | VF | XF | Unc | BU |
|---|---|---|---|---|---|---|
| ND(1975) | 727 | — | — | — | 850 | — |
| ND(1975) Proof | 307 | Value: 1,000 | | | | |

## TRIAL STRILKES

| KM# | Date | Mintage | Identification | Mkt Val |
|---|---|---|---|---|
| TS1 | ND | — | 5 Centesimos. Steel. Portrait of Milton Margai, Prime Minster (1967-67). Uruguay 5 Centavos design with MBLAT top, HA in number 5,. Reeded edge. | 65.00 |

| KM# | Date | Mintage | Identification | Mkt Val |
|---|---|---|---|---|
| TS2 | ND(1964) | — | 10 Cents. Brass. Reverse of KM#19. Uruguay 10 Centesimos. | 65.00 |

| KM# | Date | Mintage | Identification | Mkt Val |
|---|---|---|---|---|
| TS3 | ND(1964) | — | 10 Cents. Aluminum. Reverse of KM#19. Uruguay 10 Centesimos. | 65.00 |

## MINT SETS

| KM# | Date | Mintage | Identification | Issue Price | Mkt Val |
|---|---|---|---|---|---|
| MS1 | 1966 (3) | — | KM#22-24 | — | 1,400 |

## PROOF SETS

| KM# | Date | Mintage | Identification | Issue Price | Mkt Val |
|---|---|---|---|---|---|
| PS1 | 1964 (6) | 10,000 | KM#16-21 | — | 16.50 |
| PS2 | 1964 (6) | 12 | KM#16a-20a, 21b | — | 5,750 |
| PS3 | 1964 (6) | 10 | KM#16a-21a | — | 4,250 |
| PS4 | 1966 (3) | 400 | KM#22a-24a | — | 1,750 |
| PS5 | 1972 (2) | 1,000 | KM25 (2 pieces with 50 cent bank note (0 serial#) in plush case | — | 20.00 |
| PS6 | 1980 (6) | 10,000 | KM25, 30-34 | 34.00 | 28.00 |

# SINGAPORE

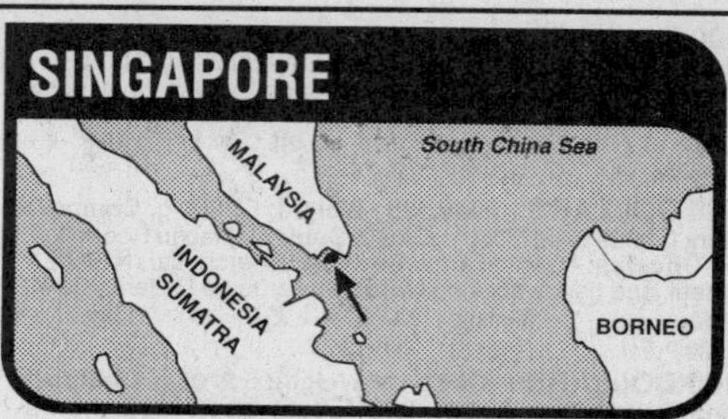


The Republic of Singapore, a British Commonwealth nation situated off the southern tip of the Malay peninsula, has an area of 224 sq. mi. (633 sq. km.) and a population of *2.7 million. Capital: Singapore. The economy is based on entrepot trade, manufacturing and oil. Rubber, petroleum products, machinery and spices are exported.

Singapore's modern history - it was an important shipping center in the 14th century before the rise of Malacca and Penang - began in 1819 when Sir Thomas Stamford Raffles, an agent for the British East India Company, founded the town of Singapore. By 1825 its trade exceeded that of Malacca and Penang combined. The opening of the Suez Canal (1869) and the demand for rubber and tin created by the automobile and packaging industries combined to make Singapore one of the major ports of the world. In 1826 Singapore, Penang and Malacca were combined to form the Straits Settlements, which was made a Crown Colony in 1867. Singapore became a separate Crown Colony in 1946 when the Straits Settlements was dissolved. It joined in the formation of Malaysia in 1963, but broke away on Aug. 9, 1965, to become an independent republic. The President is Chief of State. The prime minister is Head of Government.

For earlier coinage see Straits Settlements, Malaya, Malaya and British Borneo.

**MINT MARKS**

sm = ***"sm"*** - Singapore Mint monogram

**MONETARY SYSTEM**

100 Cents = 1 Dollar

## REPUBLIC

### STANDARD COINAGE

100 Cents = 1 Dollar

**CENT** **KM# 1** **Composition:** Bronze **Reverse:** Apartment Building

| Date | Mintage | F | VF | XF | Unc | BU |
|---|---|---|---|---|---|---|
| 1967 | 7,500,000 | — | — | 0.20 | 0.40 | — |
| 1967 Proof | 2,000 | Value: 2.25 | | | | |
| 1968 | 2,969,000 | — | — | 0.25 | 0.50 | — |
| 1968 Proof | 5,000 | Value: 2.00 | | | | |
| 1969 | 7,220,000 | — | — | 0.20 | 0.30 | — |
| 1969 Proof | 3,000 | Value: 10.00 | | | | |
| 1970 | 1,402,000 | — | — | 0.40 | 0.80 | — |
| 1971 | 9,731,000 | — | — | 0.20 | 0.25 | — |
| 1972 | 1,665,000 | — | — | 0.20 | 0.70 | — |
| 1972 Proof | 749 | Value: 40.00 | | | | |
| 1973 | 6,377,000 | — | — | 0.10 | 0.20 | — |
| 1973 Proof | 1,000 | Value: 5.00 | | | | |
| 1974 | 9,421,000 | — | — | — | 0.20 | — |
| 1974 Proof | 1,500 | Value: 4.00 | | | | |
| 1975 | 24,226,000 | — | — | — | 0.20 | — |
| 1975 Proof | 3,000 | Value: 1.50 | | | | |
| 1976 | 2,500,000 | — | — | 0.10 | 0.60 | — |
| 1976sm Proof | 3,500 | Value: 1.25 | | | | |
| 1977sm Proof | 3,500 | Value: 1.25 | | | | |
| 1978sm Proof | 4,000 | Value: 1.25 | | | | |
| 1979sm Proof | 3,500 | Value: 1.25 | | | | |
| 1980sm Proof | 14,000 | Value: 1.00 | | | | |
| 1982sm Proof | 20,000 | Value: 1.00 | | | | |
| 1983sm Proof | 15,000 | Value: 1.00 | | | | |
| 1984sm Proof | 15,000 | Value: 1.00 | | | | |

**CENT** **KM# 1a** **Composition:** Copper Clad Steel

| Date | Mintage | F | VF | XF | Unc | BU |
|---|---|---|---|---|---|---|
| 1976 | 13,665,000 | — | — | — | 0.25 | — |
| 1977 | 13,940,000 | — | — | — | 0.25 | — |
| 1978 | 5,931,000 | — | — | — | 0.25 | — |
| 1979 | 11,986,000 | — | — | — | 0.15 | — |
| 1980 | 19,922,000 | — | — | — | 0.15 | — |
| 1981 | 38,084,000 | — | — | — | 0.10 | — |
| 1982 | 24,105,000 | — | — | — | 0.10 | — |
| 1983 | 2,204,000 | — | — | — | 0.10 | — |
| 1984 | 5,695,000 | — | — | — | 0.10 | — |
| 1985 | 148,000 | — | — | 0.15 | 0.35 | — |

**CENT** **KM# 1b** **Weight:** 2.9200 g. **Composition:** 0.9250 Silver .0869 oz. ASW

| Date | Mintage | F | VF | XF | Unc | BU |
|---|---|---|---|---|---|---|
| 1981sm Proof | 30,000 | Value: 5.00 | | | | |

**CENT** **KM# 49a** **Weight:** 1.8100 g. **Composition:** 0.9250 Silver .0538 oz. ASW

| Date | Mintage | F | VF | XF | Unc | BU |
|---|---|---|---|---|---|---|
| 1985sm Proof | 20,000 | Value: 2.25 | | | | |
| 1986sm Proof | 15,000 | Value: 2.25 | | | | |
| 1987sm Proof | 15,000 | Value: 2.25 | | | | |
| 1988 Proof | 15,000 | Value: 2.25 | | | | |
| 1989 Proof | 15,000 | Value: 2.25 | | | | |
| 1990 Proof | 15,000 | Value: 2.25 | | | | |
| 1991 Proof | 15,000 | Value: 2.25 | | | | |

**CENT** **KM# 49** **Composition:** Bronze **Reverse:** Vanda Miss Joaquim Plants

| Date | Mintage | F | VF | XF | Unc | BU |
|---|---|---|---|---|---|---|
| 1986 | 20,000,000 | — | — | — | 0.10 | — |
| 1987 | — | — | — | — | 0.10 | — |
| 1988 | — | — | — | — | 0.10 | — |
| 1989 | 20,080,000 | — | — | — | 0.10 | — |
| 1990 | 10,000,000 | — | — | — | 0.10 | — |

**CENT** **KM# 49b** **Composition:** Copper Plated Zinc

| Date | Mintage | F | VF | XF | Unc | BU |
|---|---|---|---|---|---|---|
| 1991 | — | — | — | — | 0.10 | — |

**CENT** **KM# 98a** **Weight:** 1.8100 g. **Composition:** 0.9250 Silver .0538 oz. ASW

| Date | Mintage | F | VF | XF | Unc | BU |
|---|---|---|---|---|---|---|
| 1992 Proof | 15,000 | Value: 2.25 | | | | |
| 1993 Proof | 15,000 | Value: 2.25 | | | | |
| 1994 Proof | 10,000 | Value: 2.25 | | | | |
| 1995 Proof | 10,000 | Value: 2.25 | | | | |
| 1996 Proof | 17,000 | Value: 2.25 | | | | |
| 1997 Proof | 20,000 | Value: 2.25 | | | | |
| 1998 Proof | — | Value: 2.25 | | | | |
| 1999 Proof | — | Value: 2.25 | | | | |
| 2000 Proof | 17,000 | Value: 2.25 | | | | |

**CENT** **KM# 98** **Composition:** Copper Plated Zinc **Note:** Similar to KM#49 but motto ribbon on arms curves down at center.

| Date | Mintage | F | VF | XF | Unc | BU |
|---|---|---|---|---|---|---|
| 1992 | 20,000,000 | — | — | — | 0.10 | — |
| 1993 | 39,920,000 | — | — | — | 0.10 | — |
| 1994 | 130,810,000 | — | — | — | 0.10 | — |
| 1995 | 220,000,000 | — | — | — | 0.10 | — |
| 1996 | — | — | — | — | 0.10 | — |
| 1997 | — | — | — | — | 0.10 | — |
| 1998 | — | — | — | — | 0.10 | — |
| 1999 | — | — | — | — | 0.10 | — |
| 2000 | — | — | — | — | 0.10 | — |

**5 CENTS** **KM# 2** **Composition:** Copper-Nickel **Reverse:** Great White Egret

| Date | Mintage | F | VF | XF | Unc | BU |
|---|---|---|---|---|---|---|
| 1967 | 28,000,000 | — | — | 0.15 | 0.30 | — |
| 1967 Proof | 2,000 | Value: 3.25 | | | | |
| 1968 | 4,217,000 | — | — | 0.20 | 0.40 | — |
| 1968 Proof | 5,000 | Value: 3.00 | | | | |
| 1969 | 14,778,000 | — | — | 0.10 | 0.30 | — |
| 1969 Proof | 3,000 | Value: 15.00 | | | | |
| 1970 | 4,065,000 | — | — | 0.20 | 0.40 | — |
| 1971 | 13,202,000 | — | — | 0.10 | 0.25 | — |
| 1972 | 9,817,000 | — | — | 0.10 | 0.25 | — |
| 1972 Proof | 749 | Value: 50.00 | | | | |
| 1973 | 2,980,000 | — | — | 0.30 | 0.50 | — |
| 1973 Proof | 1,000 | Value: 7.50 | | | | |
| 1974 | 10,868,000 | — | — | 0.10 | 0.25 | — |
| 1974 Proof | 1,500 | Value: 6.50 | | | | |
| 1975 | 1,729,000 | — | — | 0.40 | 1.00 | — |
| 1975 Proof | 3,000 | Value: 2.50 | | | | |
| 1976 | 15,541,000 | — | — | 0.10 | 0.25 | — |
| 1976sm Proof | 3,500 | Value: 2.25 | | | | |
| 1977 | 9,956,000 | — | — | 0.10 | 0.25 | — |
| 1977sm Proof | 3,500 | Value: 2.25 | | | | |
| 1978 | 5,956,000 | — | — | 0.10 | 0.25 | — |
| 1978sm Proof | 4,000 | Value: 2.25 | | | | |
| 1979 | 9,974,000 | — | — | — | 0.25 | — |
| 1979sm Proof | 3,500 | Value: 2.25 | | | | |
| 1980 | 20,534,000 | — | — | — | 0.25 | — |
| 1980sm Proof | 14,000 | Value: 2.00 | | | | |
| 1981 | 110,000 | — | — | — | 0.25 | — |
| 1982 | 160,000 | — | — | — | 0.25 | — |
| 1982sm Proof | 20,000 | Value: 2.00 | | | | |
| 1983 | 40,000 | — | — | — | 0.25 | — |
| 1983sm Proof | 15,000 | Value: 2.00 | | | | |
| 1984 | 18,880,000 | — | — | — | 0.25 | — |
| 1984sm Proof | 15,000 | Value: 2.00 | | | | |
| 1985 | 148,000 | — | — | — | 0.25 | — |

**5 CENTS** **KM# 8** **Composition:** Aluminum **Series:** F.A.O.

| Date | Mintage | F | VF | XF | Unc | BU |
|---|---|---|---|---|---|---|
| 1971 | 3,049,000 | — | — | 0.10 | 0.35 | — |

**5 CENTS** **KM# 2a** **Composition:** Copper-Nickel Clad Steel

| Date | Mintage | F | VF | XF | Unc | BU |
|---|---|---|---|---|---|---|
| 1980 | 12,001,000 | — | — | — | 0.25 | — |
| 1981 | 23,866,000 | — | — | — | 0.25 | — |
| 1982 | 24,413,000 | — | — | — | 0.25 | — |
| 1983 | 4,016,000 | — | — | — | 0.25 | — |
| 1984 | 18,880,000 | — | — | — | 0.25 | — |

**5 CENTS** **KM# 2b** **Weight:** 1.6500 g. **Composition:** 0.9250 Silver .0491 oz. ASW

| Date | Mintage | F | VF | XF | Unc | BU |
|---|---|---|---|---|---|---|
| 1981 Proof | 30,000 | Value: 5.00 | | | | |

**5 CENTS** **KM# 50** **Composition:** Aluminum-Bronze **Reverse:** Fruit Salad Plant

| Date | Mintage | F | VF | XF | Unc | BU |
|---|---|---|---|---|---|---|
| 1985 | 14,840,000 | — | — | — | 0.10 | — |
| 1986 | 15,480,000 | — | — | — | 0.10 | — |
| 1987 | 31,040,000 | — | — | — | 0.10 | — |
| 1988 | 45,180,000 | — | — | — | 0.10 | — |
| 1989 | 69,988,000 | — | — | — | 0.10 | — |
| 1990 | 26,052,000 | — | — | — | 0.10 | — |
| 1991 | — | — | — | — | 0.10 | — |

**5 CENTS** **KM# 50a** **Weight:** 2.0000 g. **Composition:** 0.9250 Silver .0595 oz. ASW

| Date | Mintage | F | VF | XF | Unc | BU |
|---|---|---|---|---|---|---|
| 1985sm Proof | 20,000 | Value: 2.50 | | | | |
| 1986sm Proof | 15,000 | Value: 2.50 | | | | |
| 1987sm Proof | 15,000 | Value: 2.50 | | | | |
| 1988 Proof | 15,000 | Value: 2.50 | | | | |
| 1989 Proof | 15,000 | Value: 2.50 | | | | |
| 1990 Proof | 15,000 | Value: 2.50 | | | | |
| 1991 Proof | 15,000 | Value: 2.50 | | | | |

**5 CENTS** **KM# 99a** **Weight:** 2.0000 g. **Composition:** 0.9250 Silver .0595 oz. ASW

| Date | Mintage | F | VF | XF | Unc | BU |
|---|---|---|---|---|---|---|
| 1992 Proof | 15,000 | Value: 2.50 | | | | |
| 1993 Proof | 15,000 | Value: 2.50 | | | | |
| 1994 Proof | 10,000 | Value: 2.50 | | | | |
| 1995 Proof | 10,000 | Value: 2.50 | | | | |
| 1996 Proof | 17,000 | Value: 2.50 | | | | |
| 1997 Proof | 20,000 | Value: 2.50 | | | | |
| 1998 Proof | — | Value: 2.50 | | | | |
| 1999 Proof | — | Value: 2.50 | | | | |
| 2000 Proof | 17,000 | Value: 2.50 | | | | |

**5 CENTS** **KM# 99** **Composition:** Aluminum-Bronze **Note:** Similar to KM#50 but motto ribbon on arms curves down at center.

| Date | Mintage | F | VF | XF | Unc | BU |
|---|---|---|---|---|---|---|
| 1992 | — | — | — | — | 0.10 | — |
| 1993 | 7,296,000 | — | — | — | 0.10 | — |
| 1994 | — | — | — | — | 0.10 | — |
| 1995 | 90,000,000 | — | — | — | 0.10 | — |
| 1996 | — | — | — | — | 0.10 | — |
| 1997 | — | — | — | — | 0.10 | — |
| 1998 | — | — | — | — | 0.10 | — |
| 1999 | — | — | — | — | 0.10 | — |
| 2000 | — | — | — | — | 0.10 | — |

**10 CENTS** **KM# 3** **Composition:** Copper-Nickel **Reverse:** Stylized Great Crowned Seahorse

| Date | Mintage | F | VF | XF | Unc | BU |
|---|---|---|---|---|---|---|
| 1967 | 40,000,000 | — | — | 0.15 | 0.30 | — |
| 1967 Proof | 2,000 | Value: 4.50 | | | | |
| 1968 | 36,261,000 | — | — | 0.20 | 0.40 | — |
| 1968 Proof | 5,000 | Value: 4.25 | | | | |
| 1969 | 25,000,000 | — | — | 0.10 | 0.50 | — |
| 1969 Proof | 3,000 | Value: 20.00 | | | | |
| 1970 | 21,304,000 | — | — | 0.20 | 0.50 | — |
| 1971 | 33,040,999 | — | — | 0.10 | 0.30 | — |
| 1972 | 2,675,000 | — | — | 0.10 | 0.35 | — |
| 1972 Proof | 749 | Value: 60.00 | | | | |
| 1973 | 14,290,000 | — | — | 0.10 | 0.25 | — |
| 1973 Proof | 1,000 | Value: 10.00 | | | | |
| 1974 | 13,450,000 | — | — | 0.10 | 0.25 | — |
| 1974 Proof | 1,500 | Value: 7.50 | | | | |
| 1975 | 828,000 | — | 0.10 | 0.60 | 1.25 | — |
| 1975 Proof | 3,000 | Value: 4.00 | | | | |
| 1976 | 29,718,000 | — | — | 0.10 | 0.25 | — |
| 1976sm Proof | 3,500 | Value: 3.50 | | | | |
| 1977 | 11,776,000 | — | — | 0.10 | 0.20 | — |
| 1977sm Proof | 3,500 | Value: 3.50 | | | | |
| 1978 | 5,936,000 | — | — | 0.10 | 0.30 | — |
| 1978sm Proof | 4,000 | Value: 3.50 | | | | |
| 1979 | 12,001,000 | — | — | 0.10 | 0.20 | — |
| 1979sm Proof | 3,500 | Value: 3.50 | | | | |
| 1980 | 40,299,000 | — | — | 0.10 | 0.20 | — |
| 1980sm Proof | 14,000 | Value: 3.00 | | | | |
| 1981 | 58,600,000 | — | — | 0.10 | 0.20 | — |
| 1982 | 48,514,000 | — | — | 0.10 | 0.20 | — |
| 1982sm Proof | 20,000 | Value: 3.00 | | | | |
| 1983 | 10,415,000 | — | — | 0.10 | 0.20 | — |
| 1983sm Proof | 15,000 | Value: 3.00 | | | | |
| 1984 | 29,700,000 | — | — | 0.10 | 0.20 | — |
| 1984sm Proof | 15,000 | Value: 3.00 | | | | |
| 1985 | 148,000 | — | — | 0.10 | 0.20 | — |

**10 CENTS** **KM# 3a** **Weight:** 3.3500 g. **Composition:** 0.9250 Silver .0996 oz. ASW

| Date | Mintage | F | VF | XF | Unc | BU |
|---|---|---|---|---|---|---|
| 1981sm Proof | 30,000 | Value: 7.50 | | | | |

**10 CENTS** **KM# 51** **Composition:** Copper-Nickel **Reverse:** Star Jasmine Plant

| Date | Mintage | F | VF | XF | Unc | BU |
|---|---|---|---|---|---|---|
| 1985 | 45,040,000 | — | — | — | 0.20 | — |
| 1986 | 113,000,000 | — | — | — | 0.20 | — |
| 1987 | 90,000,000 | — | — | — | 0.20 | — |
| 1988 | 54,455,000 | — | — | — | 0.20 | — |
| 1989 | 134,190,000 | — | — | — | 0.20 | — |
| 1990 | 51,720,000 | — | — | — | 0.20 | — |
| 1991 | 159,770,000 | — | — | — | 0.20 | — |

**10 CENTS** **KM# 51a** **Weight:** 3.0500 g. **Composition:** 0.9250 Silver .0907 oz. ASW

| Date | Mintage | F | VF | XF | Unc | BU |
|---|---|---|---|---|---|---|
| 1985sm Proof | 20,000 | Value: 4.00 | | | | |
| 1986sm Proof | 15,000 | Value: 4.00 | | | | |
| 1987sm Proof | 15,000 | Value: 4.00 | | | | |
| 1988 Proof | 15,000 | Value: 4.00 | | | | |
| 1989 Proof | 15,000 | Value: 4.00 | | | | |
| 1990 Proof | 15,000 | Value: 4.00 | | | | |
| 1991 Proof | 15,000 | Value: 4.00 | | | | |

**10 CENTS** **KM# 100a** **Weight:** 3.0500 g. **Composition:** 0.9250 Silver .0907 oz. ASW

| Date | Mintage | F | VF | XF | Unc | BU |
|---|---|---|---|---|---|---|
| 1992 Proof | 15,000 | Value: 4.00 | | | | |
| 1993 Proof | 15,000 | Value: 4.00 | | | | |
| 1994 Proof | 10,000 | Value: 4.00 | | | | |
| 1995 Proof | 10,000 | Value: 4.00 | | | | |
| 1996 Proof | 17,000 | Value: 4.00 | | | | |
| 1997 Proof | 20,000 | Value: 4.00 | | | | |
| 1998 Proof | — | Value: 4.00 | | | | |
| 1999 Proof | — | Value: 4.00 | | | | |
| 2000 Proof | 17,000 | Value: 4.00 | | | | |

**10 CENTS** **KM# 100** **Composition:** Copper-Nickel **Note:** Similar to KM#51 but motto ribbon on arms curves down at center.

| Date | Mintage | F | VF | XF | Unc | BU |
|---|---|---|---|---|---|---|
| 1992 | — | — | — | — | 0.20 | — |
| 1993 | 89,855,000 | — | — | — | 0.20 | — |
| 1994 | — | — | — | — | 0.20 | — |
| 1995 | — | — | — | — | 0.20 | — |
| 1996 | — | — | — | — | 0.20 | — |
| 1997 | — | — | — | — | 0.20 | — |
| 1998 | — | — | — | — | 0.20 | — |
| 1999 | — | — | — | — | 0.20 | — |
| 2000 | — | — | — | — | 0.20 | — |

**20 CENTS** **KM# 4** **Composition:** Copper-Nickel **Reverse:** Swordfish

| Date | Mintage | F | VF | XF | Unc | BU |
|---|---|---|---|---|---|---|
| 1967 | 36,500,000 | — | 0.15 | 0.30 | 0.60 | — |
| 1967 Proof | 2,000 | Value: 7.00 | | | | |
| 1968 | 10,934,000 | — | 0.15 | 0.30 | 0.60 | — |
| 1968 Proof | 5,000 | Value: 6.00 | | | | |
| 1969 | 8,460,000 | — | 0.15 | 0.30 | 0.60 | — |
| 1969 Proof | 3,000 | Value: 30.00 | | | | |
| 1970 | 3,250,000 | — | 0.15 | 0.30 | 0.60 | — |
| 1971 | 1,732,000 | — | 0.15 | 0.70 | 2.00 | — |
| 1972 | 9,107,000 | — | 0.15 | 0.30 | 0.60 | — |
| 1972 Proof | 749 | Value: 70.00 | | | | |
| 1973 | 8,838,000 | — | 0.15 | 0.30 | 0.60 | — |
| 1973 Proof | 1,000 | Value: 17.50 | | | | |
| 1974 | 4,567,000 | — | 0.15 | 0.30 | 0.60 | — |
| 1974 Proof | 1,500 | Value: 12.50 | | | | |
| 1975 | 1,546,000 | — | 0.15 | 0.50 | 1.00 | — |
| 1975 Proof | 3,000 | Value: 6.50 | | | | |
| 1976 | 19,760,000 | — | 0.15 | 0.25 | 0.50 | — |
| 1976sm Proof | 3,500 | Value: 6.00 | | | | |
| 1977 | 7,074,000 | — | 0.15 | 0.30 | 0.60 | — |
| 1977sm Proof | 3,500 | Value: 6.00 | | | | |
| 1978 | 4,450,000 | — | 0.15 | 0.30 | 0.60 | — |
| 1978sm Proof | 4,000 | Value: 6.00 | | | | |
| 1979 | 14,865,000 | — | — | 0.15 | 0.30 | — |
| 1979sm Proof | 3,500 | Value: 6.00 | | | | |
| 1980 | 27,903,000 | — | — | 0.15 | 0.30 | — |
| 1980sm Proof | 14,000 | Value: 5.00 | | | | |
| 1981 | 46,997,000 | — | — | 0.15 | 0.30 | — |
| 1982 | 25,234,000 | — | — | 0.15 | 0.30 | — |
| 1982sm Proof | 20,000 | Value: 4.00 | | | | |
| 1983 | 6,424,000 | — | — | 0.15 | 0.30 | — |
| 1983sm Proof | 15,000 | Value: 4.00 | | | | |
| 1984 | 9,290,000 | — | — | 0.15 | 0.30 | — |
| 1984sm Proof | 15,000 | Value: 4.00 | | | | |
| 1985 | 148,000 | — | — | 0.15 | 0.30 | — |

**20 CENTS** KM# 4a **Weight:** 6.5100 g. **Composition:** 0.9250 Silver .1936 oz. ASW

| Date | Mintage | F | VF | XF | Unc | BU |
|---|---|---|---|---|---|---|
| 1981sm Proof | 30,000 | Value: 12.50 | | | | |

**20 CENTS** KM# 52 **Composition:** Copper-Nickel **Reverse:** Powder-puff Plant

| Date | Mintage | F | VF | XF | Unc | BU |
|---|---|---|---|---|---|---|
| 1985 | 25,980,000 | — | — | 0.15 | 0.30 | — |
| 1986 | 47,560,000 | — | — | 0.15 | 0.30 | — |
| 1987 | 80,010,000 | — | — | 0.15 | 0.30 | — |
| 1988 | 35,783,000 | — | — | 0.15 | 0.30 | — |
| 1989 | 51,890,000 | — | — | 0.15 | 0.30 | — |
| 1990 | 49,958,000 | — | — | 0.15 | 0.30 | — |
| 1991 | 60,000,000 | — | — | 0.15 | 0.30 | — |

**20 CENTS** KM# 52a **Weight:** 5.2400 g. **Composition:** 0.9250 Silver .1559 oz. ASW

| Date | Mintage | F | VF | XF | Unc | BU |
|---|---|---|---|---|---|---|
| 1985sm Proof | 20,000 | Value: 6.50 | | | | |
| 1986sm Proof | 15,000 | Value: 6.50 | | | | |
| 1987sm Proof | 15,000 | Value: 6.50 | | | | |
| 1988 Proof | 15,000 | Value: 6.50 | | | | |
| 1989 Proof | 15,000 | Value: 6.50 | | | | |
| 1990 Proof | 15,000 | Value: 6.50 | | | | |
| 1991 Proof | 15,000 | Value: 6.50 | | | | |

**20 CENTS** KM# 101a **Weight:** 5.2400 g. **Composition:** 0.9250 Silver .1936 oz. ASW

| Date | Mintage | F | VF | XF | Unc | BU |
|---|---|---|---|---|---|---|
| 1992 Proof | 15,000 | Value: 6.50 | | | | |
| 1993 Proof | 15,000 | Value: 6.50 | | | | |
| 1994 Proof | 10,000 | Value: 6.50 | | | | |
| 1995 Proof | 10,000 | Value: 6.50 | | | | |
| 1996 Proof | 17,000 | Value: 6.50 | | | | |
| 1997 Proof | 20,000 | Value: 6.50 | | | | |
| 1998 Proof | — | Value: 6.50 | | | | |
| 1999 Proof | — | Value: 6.50 | | | | |
| 2000 Proof | 17,000 | Value: 6.50 | | | | |

**20 CENTS** KM# 101 **Composition:** Copper-Nickel **Note:** Similar to KM#52 but motto ribbon on arms curves down at center.

| Date | Mintage | F | VF | XF | Unc | BU |
|---|---|---|---|---|---|---|
| 1992 | — | — | — | — | 0.30 | — |
| 1993 | 24,998,000 | — | — | — | 0.30 | — |
| 1994 | — | — | — | — | 0.30 | — |
| 1995 | — | — | — | — | 0.30 | — |
| 1996 | — | — | — | — | 0.30 | — |
| 1997 | — | — | — | — | 0.30 | — |
| 1998 | — | — | — | — | 0.30 | — |
| 1999 | — | — | — | — | 0.30 | — |
| 2000 | — | — | — | — | 0.30 | — |

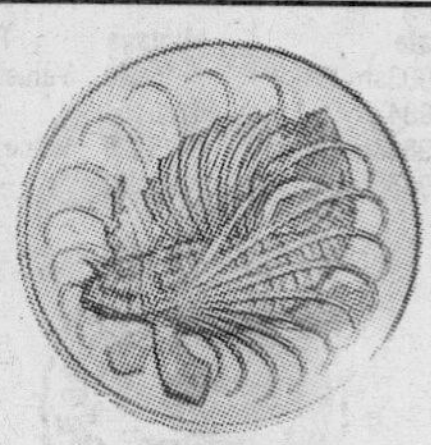

**50 CENTS** KM# 5 **Composition:** Copper-Nickel **Reverse:** Zebra Fish

| Date | Mintage | F | VF | XF | Unc | BU |
|---|---|---|---|---|---|---|
| 1967 | 11,000,000 | | 0.30 | 0.40 | 0.80 | — |
| 1967 Proof | 2,000 | Value: 10.00 | | | | |
| 1968 | 3,189,000 | — | 0.30 | 0.60 | 1.50 | — |
| 1968 Proof | 5,000 | Value: 8.50 | | | | |
| 1969 | 2,008,000 | — | 0.30 | 0.60 | 1.50 | — |
| 1969 Proof | 3,000 | Value: 35.00 | | | | |
| 1970 | 3,102,000 | — | 0.30 | 0.60 | 1.50 | — |
| 1971 | 3,933,000 | — | 0.30 | 0.60 | 1.50 | — |
| 1972 | 5,427,000 | — | 0.30 | 0.50 | 0.90 | — |
| 1972 Proof | 749 | Value: 90.00 | | | | |
| 1973 | 4,474,000 | — | 0.30 | 0.50 | 0.90 | — |
| 1973 Proof | 1,000 | Value: 30.00 | | | | |
| 1974 | 11,550,000 | — | — | 0.40 | 0.75 | — |
| 1974 Proof | 1,500 | Value: 22.50 | | | | |
| 1975 | 1,432,000 | — | 0.35 | 0.75 | 2.00 | — |
| 1975 Proof | 3,000 | Value: 10.00 | | | | |
| 1976 | 5,728,000 | — | 0.30 | 0.50 | 0.90 | — |
| 1976sm Proof | 3,500 | Value: 8.50 | | | | |
| 1977 | 6,953,000 | — | — | 0.40 | 0.75 | — |
| 1977sm Proof | 3,500 | Value: 8.50 | | | | |
| 1978 | 3,934,000 | — | — | 0.40 | 0.75 | — |
| 1978sm Proof | 4,000 | Value: 8.50 | | | | |
| 1979 | 8,461,000 | — | — | 0.40 | 0.75 | — |
| 1979sm Proof | 3,500 | Value: 8.50 | | | | |
| 1980 | 14,717,000 | — | — | 0.35 | 0.60 | — |
| 1980sm Proof | 14,000 | Value: 7.00 | | | | |
| 1981 | 29,542,000 | — | — | 0.35 | 0.60 | — |
| 1982 | 13,756,000 | — | — | 0.35 | 0.60 | — |
| 1982sm Proof | 20,000 | Value: 5.00 | | | | |
| 1983 | 4,482,000 | — | — | 0.35 | 0.60 | — |
| 1983sm Proof | 15,000 | Value: 5.00 | | | | |
| 1984 | 3,658,000 | — | — | 0.35 | 0.60 | — |
| 1984sm Proof | 15,000 | Value: 5.00 | | | | |
| 1985 | 148,000 | — | — | 0.35 | 0.60 | — |

**50 CENTS** KM# 5a **Weight:** 10.8200 g. **Composition:** 0.9250 Silver .3218 oz. ASW

| Date | Mintage | F | VF | XF | Unc | BU |
|---|---|---|---|---|---|---|
| 1981sm Proof | 30,000 | Value: 15.00 | | | | |

**50 CENTS** KM# 53.1 **Composition:** Copper-Nickel **Reverse:** Yellow Allamanda Plant **Edge:** Reeded

| Date | Mintage | F | VF | XF | Unc | BU |
|---|---|---|---|---|---|---|
| 1985 | 14,960,000 | — | — | 0.35 | 0.60 | — |
| 1986 | 15,022,000 | — | — | 0.35 | 0.60 | — |
| 1987 | 30,000,000 | — | — | 0.35 | 0.60 | — |
| 1988 | 25,000,000 | — | — | 0.35 | 0.60 | — |

**50 CENTS** KM# 53.1a **Weight:** 8.5600 g. **Composition:** 0.9250 Silver .2546 oz. ASW

| Date | Mintage | F | VF | XF | Unc | BU |
|---|---|---|---|---|---|---|
| 1985sm Proof | 20,000 | Value: 12.00 | | | | |
| 1986sm Proof | 15,000 | Value: 12.00 | | | | |
| 1987sm Proof | 15,000 | Value: 12.00 | | | | |
| 1988 Proof | 15,000 | Value: 12.00 | | | | |

**50 CENTS** KM# 53.2 **Composition:** Copper-Nickel **Edge:** Lettered

| Date | Mintage | F | VF | XF | Unc | BU |
|---|---|---|---|---|---|---|
| 1989 | 20,046,000 | — | — | 0.35 | 0.60 | — |
| 1990 | 472,000,000 | — | — | 0.35 | 0.60 | — |
| 1991 | 508,000,000 | — | — | 0.35 | 0.60 | — |

**50 CENTS** KM# 53.2a **Weight:** 8.5600 g. **Composition:** 0.9250 Silver .2546 oz. ASW

| Date | Mintage | F | VF | XF | Unc | BU |
|---|---|---|---|---|---|---|
| 1989 Proof | 15,000 | Value: 12.00 | | | | |
| 1990 Proof | — | Value: 12.00 | | | | |
| 1991 Proof | — | Value: 12.00 | | | | |

**50 CENTS** KM# 102a **Weight:** 8.5600 g. **Composition:** 0.9250 Silver .2546 oz. ASW

| Date | Mintage | F | VF | XF | Unc | BU |
|---|---|---|---|---|---|---|
| 1992 Proof | 15,000 | Value: 12.00 | | | | |
| 1993 Proof | 15,000 | Value: 12.00 | | | | |
| 1994 Proof | 10,000 | Value: 12.00 | | | | |
| 1995 Proof | 10,000 | Value: 12.00 | | | | |
| 1996 Proof | 17,000 | Value: 12.00 | | | | |
| 1997 Proof | 20,000 | Value: 12.00 | | | | |
| 1998 Proof | — | Value: 12.00 | | | | |
| 1999 Proof | — | Value: 12.00 | | | | |
| 2000 Proof | 17,000 | Value: 12.00 | | | | |

**50 CENTS** KM# 102 **Composition:** Copper-Nickel **Note:** Similar to KM#53 but motto ribbon on arms curves down at center.

| Date | Mintage | F | VF | XF | Unc | BU |
|---|---|---|---|---|---|---|
| 1992 | — | — | — | — | 0.60 | — |
| 1993 | 4,878,000 | — | — | — | 0.60 | — |
| 1994 | — | — | — | — | 0.60 | — |
| 1995 | 49,440,000 | — | — | — | 0.60 | — |
| 1996 | — | — | — | — | 0.60 | — |
| 1997 | — | — | — | — | 0.60 | — |
| 1998 | — | — | — | — | 0.60 | — |
| 1999 | — | — | — | — | 0.60 | — |
| 2000 | — | — | — | — | 0.60 | — |

**DOLLAR** KM# 6 **Composition:** Copper-Nickel

| Date | Mintage | F | VF | XF | Unc | BU |
|---|---|---|---|---|---|---|
| 1967 | 3,000,000 | — | 0.65 | 1.00 | 2.00 | — |
| 1967 Proof | 2,000 | Value: 22.50 | | | | |
| 1968 | 2,194,000 | — | 0.65 | 1.00 | 2.00 | — |
| 1968 Proof | 5,000 | Value: 20.00 | | | | |
| 1969 | 1,871,000 | — | 0.65 | 1.00 | 2.00 | — |
| 1969 Proof | 3,000 | Value: 75.00 | | | | |
| 1970 | 560,000 | — | 0.65 | 1.25 | 2.50 | — |
| 1971 | 900,000 | — | 0.65 | 1.00 | 2.00 | — |
| 1972 | 458,000 | — | 0.75 | 2.00 | 4.00 | — |
| 1972 Proof | 749 | Value: 150 | | | | |
| 1973 | 341,000 | — | 0.75 | 1.50 | 3.00 | — |
| 1973 Proof | 1,000 | Value: 50.00 | | | | |
| 1974 | 352,000 | — | 0.75 | 1.50 | 3.00 | — |
| 1974 Proof | 1,500 | Value: 40.00 | | | | |
| 1975 | 430,000 | — | 0.75 | 1.50 | 3.00 | — |
| 1975 Proof | 3,000 | Value: 20.00 | | | | |
| 1976 | 165,000 | — | 0.75 | 2.00 | 4.00 | — |
| 1976sm Proof | 3,500 | Value: 13.50 | | | | |
| 1977 | 132,000 | — | 0.75 | 3.00 | 6.00 | — |
| 1977sm Proof | 3,500 | Value: 13.50 | | | | |
| 1978 | 37,000 | — | 1.00 | 6.00 | 12.00 | — |
| 1978sm Proof | 4,000 | Value: 13.50 | | | | |
| 1979 | 100,000 | — | — | 2.00 | 4.00 | — |
| 1979sm Proof | 3,500 | Value: 13.50 | | | | |
| 1980 | 166,000 | — | — | 2.00 | 4.00 | — |
| 1980sm Proof | 14,000 | Value: 10.00 | | | | |
| 1981 | 1,230,000 | — | — | 1.00 | 2.00 | — |
| 1982 | 1,080,000 | — | — | 1.00 | 2.00 | — |
| 1983 | 101,000 | — | — | 1.25 | 3.00 | — |
| 1984 | 170,000 | — | — | 1.00 | 2.00 | — |
| 1985 | 148,000 | — | — | 0.65 | 1.25 | — |

**DOLLAR** KM# 6a **Weight:** 18.0500 g. **Composition:** 0.9250 Silver .5368 oz. ASW

| Date | Mintage | F | VF | XF | Unc | BU |
|---|---|---|---|---|---|---|
| 1975 Proof | 3,000 | Value: 50.00 | | | | |
| 1976sm Proof | 10,000 | Value: 16.50 | | | | |
| 1977sm Proof | 10,000 | Value: 16.50 | | | | |
| 1978sm Proof | 10,000 | Value: 16.50 | | | | |
| 1979sm Proof | 8,000 | Value: 18.50 | | | | |
| 1980sm Proof | 15,000 | Value: 16.50 | | | | |
| 1981sm Proof | 30,000 | Value: 12.50 | | | | |
| 1982sm Proof | 20,000 | Value: 15.00 | | | | |
| 1983sm Proof | 15,000 | Value: 12.50 | | | | |
| 1984sm Proof | 15,000 | Value: 12.50 | | | | |

**DOLLAR** KM# 28 **Weight:** 3.1100 g. **Composition:** 0.9990 Gold .1000 oz. AGW **Reverse:** Carp and lotus flower

| Date | Mintage | F | VF | XF | Unc | BU |
|---|---|---|---|---|---|---|
| 1983 | 20,000 | — | — | — | BV+15% | — |
| 1984 | 10,000 | — | — | — | BV+15% | — |

**DOLLAR** KM# 54 **Composition:** Copper-Nickel **Reverse:** Periwinkle

| Date | Mintage | F | VF | XF | Unc | BU |
|---|---|---|---|---|---|---|
| 1985 | 120,000 | — | — | — | 1.75 | — |
| 1986 | 120,000 | — | — | — | 1.75 | — |
| 1987 | 120,000 | — | — | — | 1.75 | — |

**DOLLAR** KM# 54a **Weight:** 9.9700 g. **Composition:** 0.9250 Silver .2965 oz. ASW

| Date | Mintage | F | VF | XF | Unc | BU |
|---|---|---|---|---|---|---|
| 1985sm Proof | 20,000 | Value: 15.00 | | | | |
| 1986sm Proof | 15,000 | Value: 15.00 | | | | |

**DOLLAR** KM# 54b **Composition:** Aluminum-Bronze

| Date | Mintage | F | VF | XF | Unc | BU |
|---|---|---|---|---|---|---|
| 1987 | 21,772,000 | — | — | 0.75 | 1.50 | — |
| 1988 | 59,332,000 | — | — | 0.75 | 1.50 | — |
| 1989 | 62,586,000 | — | — | 0.75 | 1.50 | — |
| 1990 | 37,608,000 | — | — | 0.75 | 1.50 | — |
| 1991 | — | — | — | 0.75 | 1.50 | — |

**DOLLAR** KM# 54c **Weight:** 8.4273 g. **Composition:** 0.9250 Silver .2507 oz. ASW

| Date | Mintage | F | VF | XF | Unc | BU |
|---|---|---|---|---|---|---|
| 1987sm Proof | 15,000 | Value: 15.00 | | | | |
| 1988 Proof | 15,000 | Value: 15.00 | | | | |
| 1989 Proof | 15,000 | Value: 15.00 | | | | |
| 1990 | 15,000 | — | — | — | — | — |
| 1991 | 15,000 | — | — | — | — | — |

**DOLLAR** KM# 103a **Weight:** 8.4273 g. **Composition:** 0.9250 Silver .2507 oz. ASW

| Date | Mintage | F | VF | XF | Unc | BU |
|---|---|---|---|---|---|---|
| 1992 Proof | 15,000 | Value: 15.00 | | | | |
| 1993 Proof | 15,000 | Value: 15.00 | | | | |
| 1994 Proof | 10,000 | Value: 15.00 | | | | |
| 1995 Proof | 10,000 | Value: 15.00 | | | | |
| 1996 Proof | 17,000 | Value: 15.00 | | | | |
| 1997 Proof | 20,000 | Value: 15.00 | | | | |
| 1998 Proof | — | Value: 15.00 | | | | |
| 1999 Proof | — | Value: 15.00 | | | | |
| 2000 Proof | 17,000 | Value: 15.00 | | | | |

**DOLLAR** KM# 103 **Composition:** Aluminum-Bronze **Note:** Similar to KM#54 but motto ribbon on arms curves down at center.

| Date | Mintage | F | VF | XF | Unc | BU |
|---|---|---|---|---|---|---|
| 1992 | — | — | — | — | 1.50 | — |
| 1993 | — | — | — | — | 1.50 | — |
| 1994 | 5,000 | — | — | — | 1.50 | — |
| 1995 | 65,000,000 | — | — | — | 1.50 | — |
| 1996 | — | — | — | — | 1.50 | — |
| 1997 | — | — | — | — | 1.50 | — |
| 1998 | — | — | — | — | 1.50 | — |
| 1999 | — | — | — | — | 1.50 | — |
| 2000 | — | — | — | — | 1.50 | — |

**DOLLAR** KM# 144 **Weight:** 1.5552 g. **Composition:** 0.9990 Gold .0400 oz. AGW **Subject:** Year of the Rat **Reverse:** Lion

| Date | Mintage | F | VF | XF | Unc | BU |
|---|---|---|---|---|---|---|
| 1996 Proof | 2,688 | Value: 30.00 | | | | |

**DOLLAR** KM# 158 **Weight:** 1.5552 g. **Composition:** 0.9990 Gold .0400 oz. AGW **Subject:** Year of the Ox **Reverse:** Lion **Note:** Similar to 20 DOllars, KM#161.

| Date | Mintage | F | VF | XF | Unc | BU |
|---|---|---|---|---|---|---|
| 1997 Proof | Est. 2,200 | Value: 40.00 | | | | |

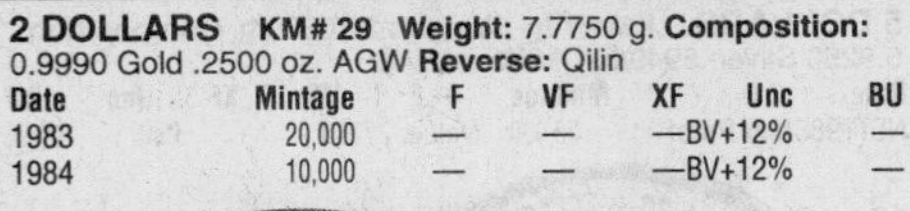

**2 DOLLARS** KM# 29 **Weight:** 7.7750 g. **Composition:** 0.9990 Gold .2500 oz. AGW **Reverse:** Qilin

| Date | Mintage | F | VF | XF | Unc | BU |
|---|---|---|---|---|---|---|
| 1983 | 20,000 | — | — | — | BV+12% | — |
| 1984 | 10,000 | — | — | — | BV+12% | — |

**2 DOLLARS** KM# 156 **Weight:** 20.0000 g. **Composition:** 0.9250 Silver .5948 oz. ASW **Series:** UNICEF **Obverse:** National arms **Reverse:** Children Using Computer

| Date | Mintage | F | VF | XF | Unc | BU |
|---|---|---|---|---|---|---|
| 1997 Proof | 25,000 | Value: 90.00 | | | | |

**5 DOLLARS** KM# 10 **Weight:** 25.0000 g. **Composition:** 0.5000 Silver .4019 oz. ASW **Subject:** 7th Southeast Asia Peninsular Games

| Date | Mintage | F | VF | XF | Unc | BU |
|---|---|---|---|---|---|---|
| 1973 | 250,000 | — | — | — | 8.00 | — |
| 1973 Proof | 5,000 | Value: 40.00 | | | | |

**5 DOLLARS** KM# 19 **Composition:** Copper-Nickel **Reverse:** Changi Airport

| Date | Mintage | F | VF | XF | Unc | BU |
|---|---|---|---|---|---|---|
| 1981 | 220,000 | — | — | 3.50 | 6.50 | — |

**5 DOLLARS** KM# 19a **Weight:** 18.0500 g. **Composition:** 0.9250 Silver .5368 oz. ASW

| Date | Mintage | F | VF | XF | Unc | BU |
|---|---|---|---|---|---|---|
| 1981sm Proof | 20,000 | Value: 18.50 | | | | |

**5 DOLLARS** KM# 22 **Composition:** Copper-Nickel **Reverse:** Benjamin Shears Bridge

| Date | Mintage | F | VF | XF | Unc | BU |
|---|---|---|---|---|---|---|
| 1982 | 260,000 | — | — | 3.50 | 6.50 | — |

**5 DOLLARS** KM# 22a **Weight:** 18.0500 g. **Composition:** 0.9250 Silver .5368 oz. ASW

| Date | Mintage | F | VF | XF | Unc | BU |
|---|---|---|---|---|---|---|
| 1982sm Proof | 20,000 | Value: 18.50 | | | | |

**5 DOLLARS** KM# 25 **Composition:** Copper-Nickel **Subject:** 12th SEA Games

| Date | Mintage | F | VF | XF | Unc | BU |
|---|---|---|---|---|---|---|
| 1983 | 270,000 | — | — | 3.50 | 6.50 | — |

**5 DOLLARS** KM# 25a **Weight:** 20.0000 g. **Composition:** 0.9250 Silver .5949 oz. ASW

| Date | Mintage | F | VF | XF | Unc | BU |
|---|---|---|---|---|---|---|
| 1983sm Proof | 20,000 | Value: 20.00 | | | | |

**5 DOLLARS** KM# 30 **Weight:** 15.5500 g. **Composition:** 0.9990 Gold .5000 oz. AGW **Reverse:** Phoenix

| Date | Mintage | F | VF | XF | Unc | BU |
|---|---|---|---|---|---|---|
| 1983 | 10,000 | — | — | — | BV+9% | — |
| 1984 | 10,000 | — | — | — | BV+9% | — |

**5 DOLLARS** KM# 32 **Composition:** Copper-Nickel **Subject:** 25 Years of Nation Building

| Date | Mintage | F | VF | XF | Unc | BU |
|---|---|---|---|---|---|---|
| ND(1984) | 270,000 | — | — | 3.50 | 6.50 | — |

**5 DOLLARS** **KM# 32a** **Weight:** 20.0000 g. **Composition:** 0.9250 Silver .5949 oz. ASW

| Date | Mintage | F | VF | XF | Unc | BU |
|---|---|---|---|---|---|---|
| ND(1984)sm Proof | 20,000 | Value: 18.50 | | | | |

**5 DOLLARS** **KM# 48** **Composition:** Copper-Nickel **Subject:** 25 Years of Public Housing **Obverse:** Coat of arms and legend

| Date | Mintage | F | VF | XF | Unc | BU |
|---|---|---|---|---|---|---|
| 1985 | 117,000 | — | — | 3.50 | 6.50 | — |

**5 DOLLARS** **KM# 48a** **Weight:** 20.0000 g. **Composition:** 0.9250 Silver .5949 oz. ASW

| Date | Mintage | F | VF | XF | Unc | BU |
|---|---|---|---|---|---|---|
| 1985sm Proof | 20,000 | Value: 18.50 | | | | |

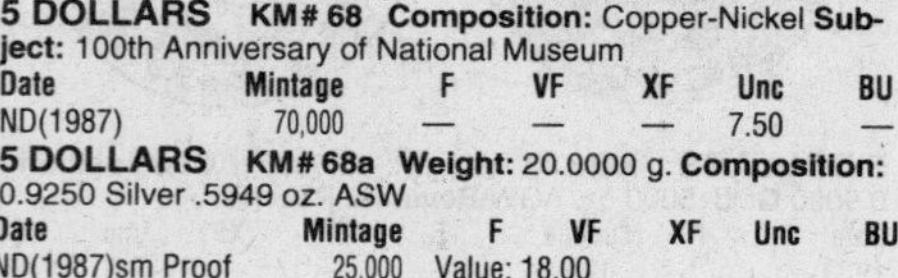

**5 DOLLARS** **KM# 68** **Composition:** Copper-Nickel **Subject:** 100th Anniversary of National Museum

| Date | Mintage | F | VF | XF | Unc | BU |
|---|---|---|---|---|---|---|
| ND(1987) | 70,000 | — | — | — | 7.50 | — |

**5 DOLLARS** **KM# 68a** **Weight:** 20.0000 g. **Composition:** 0.9250 Silver .5949 oz. ASW

| Date | Mintage | F | VF | XF | Unc | BU |
|---|---|---|---|---|---|---|
| ND(1987)sm Proof | 25,000 | Value: 18.00 | | | | |

**5 DOLLARS** **KM# 70** **Composition:** Copper-Nickel **Subject:** 100th Anniversary of Singapore Fire Brigade

| Date | Mintage | F | VF | XF | Unc | BU |
|---|---|---|---|---|---|---|
| ND(1988) | 50,000 | — | — | — | 15.00 | — |

**5 DOLLARS** **KM# 70a** **Weight:** 20.0000 g. **Composition:** 0.9250 Silver .5949 oz. ASW

| Date | Mintage | F | VF | XF | Unc | BU |
|---|---|---|---|---|---|---|
| ND(1988)sm Proof | 25,000 | Value: 27.50 | | | | |

**5 DOLLARS** **KM# 74** **Composition:** Copper-Nickel **Subject:** Rapid Transit System

| Date | Mintage | F | VF | XF | Unc | BU |
|---|---|---|---|---|---|---|
| 1989 | 60,000 | — | — | — | 12.00 | — |

**5 DOLLARS** **KM# 74a** **Weight:** 20.0000 g. **Composition:** 0.9250 Silver .5949 oz. ASW

| Date | Mintage | F | VF | XF | Unc | BU |
|---|---|---|---|---|---|---|
| 1989 Proof | 30,000 | Value: 20.00 | | | | |

**5 DOLLARS** **KM# 77** **Weight:** 20.0000 g. **Composition:** 0.9250 Silver .5949 oz. ASW **Series:** Save the Children Fund

| Date | Mintage | F | VF | XF | Unc | BU |
|---|---|---|---|---|---|---|
| 1989 Proof | 20,000 | Value: 25.00 | | | | |

**5 DOLLARS** **KM# 79** **Weight:** 1.5550 g. **Composition:** 0.9990 Gold .0500 oz. AGW

| Date | Mintage | F | VF | XF | Unc | BU |
|---|---|---|---|---|---|---|
| 1990 | 8,000 | — | — | —BV+20% | | — |
| 1990 Proof | Est. 2,000 | Value: 30.00 | | | | |

**5 DOLLARS** **KM# 94** **Composition:** Copper-Aluminum-Nickel **Subject:** 25th Anniversary of Independence

| Date | Mintage | F | VF | XF | Unc | BU |
|---|---|---|---|---|---|---|
| 1990 | 1,000,000 | — | — | — | 8.00 | — |

**5 DOLLARS** **KM# 86** **Composition:** Copper-Nickel **Subject:** Civil Defense

| Date | Mintage | F | VF | XF | Unc | BU |
|---|---|---|---|---|---|---|
| 1991 | 55,000 | — | — | — | 8.00 | — |
| 1991 Proof | 10,000 | Value: 16.50 | | | | |

**5 DOLLARS** **KM# 86a** **Weight:** 20.0000 g. **Composition:** 0.9250 Silver .4949 oz. ASW

| Date | Mintage | F | VF | XF | Unc | BU |
|---|---|---|---|---|---|---|
| 1991 Proof | 15,000 | Value: 25.00 | | | | |

**5 DOLLARS** **KM# 87** **Weight:** 1.5550 g. **Composition:** 0.9990 Gold .0500 oz. AGW **Subject:** Year of the Goat

| Date | Mintage | F | VF | XF | Unc | BU |
|---|---|---|---|---|---|---|
| 1991 | 8,000 | — | — | —BV+20% | | — |
| 1991 Proof | 2,500 | Value: 30.00 | | | | |

**5 DOLLARS** **KM# 104** **Ring Composition:** Copper-Nickel **Center Composition:** Aluminum-Bronze **Subject:** Vanda Miss Joaquim

| Date | Mintage | F | VF | XF | Unc | BU |
|---|---|---|---|---|---|---|
| 1992 In mint sets only | — | — | — | — | 14.00 | — |
| 1993 In mint sets only | — | — | — | — | 15.00 | — |
| 1994 In mint sets only | — | — | — | — | 15.00 | — |
| 1995 In mint sets only | — | — | — | — | 15.00 | — |
| 1996 In mint sets only | — | — | — | — | 14.00 | — |
| 1997 In mint sets only | — | — | — | — | 14.00 | — |
| 1998 In mint sets only | — | — | — | — | 14.00 | — |
| 1999 In mint sets only | — | — | — | — | 14.00 | — |
| 2000 In mint sets only | — | — | — | — | 14.00 | — |

**5 DOLLARS** **KM# 104a** **Weight:** 20.0000 g. **Composition:** 0.9250 Silver .4949 oz. ASW

| Date | Mintage | F | VF | XF | Unc | BU |
|---|---|---|---|---|---|---|
| 1992 Proof | 15,000 | Value: 25.00 | | | | |
| 1994 Proof | 10,000 | Value: 25.00 | | | | |
| 1995 Proof | 10,000 | Value: 25.00 | | | | |
| 1996 Proof | 17,000 | Value: 25.00 | | | | |
| 1997 Proof | 20,000 | Value: 25.00 | | | | |
| 1998 Proof | — | Value: 25.00 | | | | |
| 1999 Proof | — | Value: 25.00 | | | | |
| 2000 Proof | 17,000 | Value: 25.00 | | | | |

**5 DOLLARS** **KM# 108** **Weight:** 1.5550 g. **Composition:** 0.9990 Gold .0500 oz. AGW **Subject:** Year of the Monkey

| Date | Mintage | F | VF | XF | Unc | BU |
|---|---|---|---|---|---|---|
| 1992 | 6,500 | — | — | —BV+20% | | — |
| 1992 Proof | 2,000 | Value: 30.00 | | | | |

**5 DOLLARS** **KM# 115** **Composition:** Copper-Nickel **Subject:** XVII Sea Games - Martial Arts

| Date | Mintage | F | VF | XF | Unc | BU |
|---|---|---|---|---|---|---|
| 1993 | 23,000 | — | — | — | 9.00 | — |
| 1993 Proof | 2,000 | Value: 30.00 | | | | |

**5 DOLLARS** **KM# 115a** **Weight:** 20.0000 g. **Composition:** 0.9250 Silver .5949 oz. ASW

| Date | Mintage | F | VF | XF | Unc | BU |
|---|---|---|---|---|---|---|
| 1993 Proof | 10,000 | Value: 32.50 | | | | |

**5 DOLLARS** **KM# 117** **Weight:** 1.5550 g. **Composition:** 0.9990 Gold .0500 oz. AGW **Subject:** Year of the Rooster

| Date | Mintage | F | VF | XF | Unc | BU |
|---|---|---|---|---|---|---|
| 1993 | 3,400 | — | — | — | BV+20% | — |
| 1993 In proof sets only | Est. 1,500 | — | — | — | 35.00 | — |

**5 DOLLARS** **KM# 124** **Composition:** Copper-Nickel **Subject:** Year of the Family

| Date | Mintage | F | VF | XF | Unc | BU |
|---|---|---|---|---|---|---|
| 1994 | 20,000 | — | — | — | 8.00 | — |

**5 DOLLARS** **KM# 124a** **Weight:** 20.0000 g. **Composition:** 0.9250 Silver .4949 oz. ASW

| Date | Mintage | F | VF | XF | Unc | BU |
|---|---|---|---|---|---|---|
| 1994 Proof | 8,000 | Value: 30.00 | | | | |

**5 DOLLARS** **KM# 128** **Weight:** 1.5550 g. **Composition:** 0.9990 Gold .0500 oz. AGW **Subject:** Year of the Dog

| Date | Mintage | F | VF | XF | Unc | BU |
|---|---|---|---|---|---|---|
| 1994 | — | — | — | — | BV+20% | — |
| 1994 In proof sets only | Est. 1,500 | — | — | — | 35.00 | — |

**5 DOLLARS** **KM# 133** **Weight:** 1.5550 g. **Composition:** 0.9990 Gold .0500 oz. AGW **Subject:** Year of the Pig

| Date | Mintage | F | VF | XF | Unc | BU |
|---|---|---|---|---|---|---|
| 1995 | — | — | — | — | BV+20% | — |
| 1995 Proof | 1,500 | Value: 35.00 | | | | |

**5 DOLLARS** **KM# 138** **Ring Composition:** Copper-Nickel **Center Composition:** Aluminum-Bronze **Series:** 50th Anniversary - United Nations

| Date | Mintage | F | VF | XF | Unc | BU |
|---|---|---|---|---|---|---|
| 1995 | 500,000 | — | — | — | 10.00 | — |

**5 DOLLARS** **KM# 139** **Weight:** 20.0000 g. **Composition:** 0.9250 Silver .4949 oz. ASW **Series:** 50th Anniversary - United Nations

| Date | Mintage | F | VF | XF | Unc | BU |
|---|---|---|---|---|---|---|
| 1995 Proof | 9,000 | Value: 60.00 | | | | |

**5 DOLLARS** **KM# 150** **Composition:** Copper-Nickel **Subject:** 30th Anniversary - Singapore's Independence

| Date | Mintage | F | VF | XF | Unc | BU |
|---|---|---|---|---|---|---|
| 1995 | 20,000 | — | — | — | 8.00 | — |

**5 DOLLARS** **KM# 150a** **Weight:** 20.0000 g. **Composition:** 0.9250 Silver .4949 oz. ASW

| Date | Mintage | F | VF | XF | Unc | BU |
|---|---|---|---|---|---|---|
| 1995 Proof | 8,000 | Value: 30.00 | | | | |

**5 DOLLARS** **KM# 149** **Composition:** Copper-Nickel **Subject:** World Trade Organization Conference

| Date | Mintage | F | VF | XF | Unc | BU |
|---|---|---|---|---|---|---|
| 1996 | — | — | — | — | 12.00 | — |

**5 DOLLARS** **KM# 149a** **Weight:** 20.0000 g. **Composition:** 0.9250 Silver .4949 oz. ASW **Obverse:** Mintmark

| Date | Mintage | F | VF | XF | Unc | BU |
|---|---|---|---|---|---|---|
| 1996 Proof | 17,000 | Value: 40.00 | | | | |

**5 DOLLARS** **KM# 145** **Weight:** 3.1103 g. **Composition:** 0.9990 Gold .1000 oz. AGW **Subject:** Year of the Rat

| Date | Mintage | F | VF | XF | Unc | BU |
|---|---|---|---|---|---|---|
| 1996 Proof | 2,688 | Value: 55.00 | | | | |

**5 DOLLARS** **KM# 151** **Composition:** Copper-Nickel **Subject:** 50th Anniversary - Singapore Airlines **Obverse:** National arms, no mint mark

| Date | Mintage | F | VF | XF | Unc | BU |
|---|---|---|---|---|---|---|
| 1997 | — | — | — | — | 12.00 | — |

**5 DOLLARS** **KM# 151a** **Weight:** 20.0000 g. **Composition:** 0.9250 Silver .4949 oz. ASW **Obverse:** With mint mark

| Date | Mintage | F | VF | XF | Unc | BU |
|---|---|---|---|---|---|---|
| 1997 Proof | 23,000 | Value: 40.00 | | | | |

**5 DOLLARS** **KM# 157** **Weight:** 7.7760 g. **Composition:** 0.9999 Gold .2500 oz. AGW **Series:** UNICEF **Reverse:** Children Using Computer **Note:** Similar to 2 Dollars, KM#156.

| Date | Mintage | F | VF | XF | Unc | BU |
|---|---|---|---|---|---|---|
| 1997 Proof | 10,000 | Value: 665 | | | | |

**5 DOLLARS** **KM# 159** **Weight:** 3.1103 g. **Composition:** 0.9999 Gold .1000 oz. AGW **Subject:** Year of the Ox **Reverse:** Lion **Note:** Similar to 20 Dollars, KM#161.

| Date | Mintage | F | VF | XF | Unc | BU |
|---|---|---|---|---|---|---|
| 1997 Proof | Est. 2,200 | Value: 65.00 | | | | |

**5 DOLLARS** **KM# 163** **Composition:** Copper-Nickel **Subject:** Charity Work in Singapore **Obverse:** National arms **Reverse:** Two hands holding heart-shaped fruit

| Date | Mintage | F | VF | XF | Unc | BU |
|---|---|---|---|---|---|---|
| 1998 | — | — | — | — | 12.00 | — |

**5 DOLLARS** **KM# 163a** **Weight:** 20.0000 g. **Composition:** 0.9250 Silver .5948 oz. ASW **Subject:** Charity Work in Singapore **Obverse:** National arms **Reverse:** Two hands holding golden heart-shaped fruit

| Date | Mintage | F | VF | XF | Unc | BU |
|---|---|---|---|---|---|---|
| 1998 Proof | 12,000 | Value: 50.00 | | | | |

**5 DOLLARS** **KM# 173** **Weight:** 20.0000 g. **Composition:** Copper-Nickel **Subject:** Parliament **Obverse:** National arms **Reverse:** Parliament building **Edge:** Reeded

| Date | Mintage | F | VF | XF | Unc | BU |
|---|---|---|---|---|---|---|
| 1999 | — | — | — | — | 12.00 | — |

**5 DOLLARS** **KM# 173a** **Weight:** 20.0000 g. **Composition:** 0.9250 Silver .5948 oz. ASW

| Date | Mintage | F | VF | XF | Unc | BU |
|---|---|---|---|---|---|---|
| 1999 Proof | 10,000 | Value: 55.00 | | | | |

**5 DOLLARS** **KM# 171** **Center Weight:** 6.7200 g. **Center Composition:** Brass **Obverse:** Arms above latent date **Reverse:** Symbolic design **Edge:** Scalloped

| Date | Mintage | F | VF | XF | Unc | BU |
|---|---|---|---|---|---|---|
| 2000 | — | — | — | — | 11.50 | — |

**5 DOLLARS** **KM# 172** **Center Weight:** 31.1030 g. **Center Composition:** 0.9990 Gold 1.0000 oz. AGW **Subject:** Millennium **Obverse:** Multicolor holographic national arms **Reverse:** Millennium design **Edge:** Scalloped

| Date | Mintage | F | VF | XF | Unc | BU |
|---|---|---|---|---|---|---|
| 2000 Proof | 3,000 | Value: 1,250 | | | | |

**10 DOLLARS** **KM# 9.1** **Weight:** 31.1000 g. **Composition:** 0.9000 Silver .8999 oz. ASW **Obv. Legend:** SINGAPORE inverted

| Date | Mintage | F | VF | XF | Unc | BU |
|---|---|---|---|---|---|---|
| 1972 | 80,000 | — | — | — | 16.50 | — |
| 1972 Proof | 3,000 | Value: 37.50 | | | | |

**10 DOLLARS** **KM# 9.2** **Weight:** 31.1000 g. **Composition:** 0.9000 Silver .8999 oz. ASW

| Date | Mintage | F | VF | XF | Unc | BU |
|---|---|---|---|---|---|---|
| 1973 | 80,000 | — | — | — | 16.50 | — |
| 1973 Proof | 5,000 | Value: 32.50 | | | | |

**10 DOLLARS** **KM# 9.2a** **Weight:** 31.1000 g. **Composition:** 0.5000 Silver .5000 oz. ASW

| Date | Mintage | F | VF | XF | Unc | BU |
|---|---|---|---|---|---|---|
| 1974 | 100,000 | — | — | — | 12.50 | — |
| 1974 Proof | 6,000 | Value: 22.50 | | | | |

**10 DOLLARS** **KM# 11** **Weight:** 31.1000 g. **Composition:** 0.5000 Silver .5000 oz. ASW **Subject:** 10th Anniversary of Independence

| Date | Mintage | F | VF | XF | Unc | BU |
|---|---|---|---|---|---|---|
| ND(1975) | 200,000 | — | — | — | 6.00 | — |
| ND(1975) Proof | 10,000 | Value: 17.50 | | | | |

**10 DOLLARS** **KM# 15** **Weight:** 31.1000 g. **Composition:** 0.5000 Silver .5000 oz. ASW

| Date | Mintage | F | VF | XF | Unc | BU |
|---|---|---|---|---|---|---|
| 1976 | 150,000 | — | — | — | 6.00 | — |
| 1976sm Proof | 10,000 | Value: 17.50 | | | | |
| 1977 | 150,000 | — | — | — | 6.00 | — |
| 1977sm Proof | 10,000 | Value: 17.50 | | | | |

**10 DOLLARS** **KM# 16** **Weight:** 31.1000 g. **Composition:** 0.5000 Silver .5000 oz. ASW **Subject:** ASEAN 10th Anniversary

| Date | Mintage | F | VF | XF | Unc | BU |
|---|---|---|---|---|---|---|
| ND(1977) | 200,000 | — | — | — | 7.00 | — |
| ND(1977)sm Proof | 10,000 | Value: 20.00 | | | | |

**10 DOLLARS** **KM# 17.1** **Weight:** 31.1000 g. **Composition:** 0.5000 Silver .5000 oz. ASW **Subject:** Communications Satellites

| Date | Mintage | F | VF | XF | Unc | BU |
|---|---|---|---|---|---|---|
| 1978 | 167,000 | — | — | — | 7.50 | — |
| 1978sm Proof | 10,000 | Value: 14.50 | | | | |
| 1979 | 168,000 | — | — | — | 7.50 | — |
| 1979sm Proof | 9,000 | Value: 14.50 | | | | |

**10 DOLLARS** **KM# 17.1a** **Composition:** Copper-Nickel

| Date | Mintage | F | VF | XF | Unc | BU |
|---|---|---|---|---|---|---|
| 1980 | 120,000 | — | — | — | 8.00 | — |

**10 DOLLARS** **KM# 17.2** **Composition:** Copper-Nickel **Obverse:** Raised stars and moon in arms

| Date | Mintage | F | VF | XF | Unc | BU |
|---|---|---|---|---|---|---|
| 1980sm Proof | 15,000 | Value: 15.00 | | | | |

**10 DOLLARS** **KM# 20** **Composition:** Copper-Nickel **Subject:** Year of the Rooster

| Date | Mintage | F | VF | XF | Unc | BU |
|---|---|---|---|---|---|---|
| 1981 | 180,000 | — | — | — | 17.50 | — |

**10 DOLLARS** **KM# 20a** **Weight:** 31.1000 g. **Composition:** 0.5000 Silver .5000 oz. ASW

| Date | Mintage | F | VF | XF | Unc | BU |
|---|---|---|---|---|---|---|
| 1981sm Proof | 20,000 | Value: 65.00 | | | | |

**10 DOLLARS** **KM# 23** **Composition:** Nickel **Subject:** Year of the Dog

| Date | Mintage | F | VF | XF | Unc | BU |
|---|---|---|---|---|---|---|
| 1982 | 210,000 | — | — | — | 20.00 | — |

**10 DOLLARS** **KM# 23a** **Weight:** 31.1000 g. **Composition:** 0.5000 Silver .5000 oz. ASW

| Date | Mintage | F | VF | XF | Unc | BU |
|---|---|---|---|---|---|---|
| 1982sm Proof | 20,000 | Value: 50.00 | | | | |

**10 DOLLARS** **KM# 26** **Composition:** Nickel **Subject:** Year of the Pig

| Date | Mintage | F | VF | XF | Unc | BU |
|---|---|---|---|---|---|---|
| 1983 | 307,000 | — | — | — | 15.00 | — |

**10 DOLLARS** **KM# 26a** **Weight:** 31.1000 g. **Composition:** 0.5000 Silver .5000 oz. ASW

| Date | Mintage | F | VF | XF | Unc | BU |
|---|---|---|---|---|---|---|
| 1983sm Proof | 20,000 | Value: 45.00 | | | | |

**10 DOLLARS** KM# 31 **Weight:** 31.1000 g. **Composition:** 0.9990 Gold 1.0000 oz. AGW **Subject:** Year of the Dragon

| Date | Mintage | F | VF | XF | Unc | BU |
|---|---|---|---|---|---|---|
| 1983 | 10,000 | — | — | — | BV+7% | — |
| 1984 Proof | 10,000 | — | — | — | BV+7% | — |

**10 DOLLARS** KM# 33 **Composition:** Nickel **Subject:** Year of the Rat

| Date | Mintage | F | VF | XF | Unc | BU |
|---|---|---|---|---|---|---|
| 1984 | 300,000 | — | — | — | 15.00 | — |

**10 DOLLARS** KM# 33a **Weight:** 31.1000 g. **Composition:** 0.5000 Silver .5000 oz. ASW

| Date | Mintage | F | VF | XF | Unc | BU |
|---|---|---|---|---|---|---|
| 1984sm Proof | 20,000 | Value: 42.50 | | | | |

**10 DOLLARS** KM# 44 **Composition:** Nickel **Subject:** Year of the Ox

| Date | Mintage | F | VF | XF | Unc | BU |
|---|---|---|---|---|---|---|
| 1985 | 307,000 | — | — | — | 15.00 | — |

**10 DOLLARS** KM# 44a **Weight:** 31.1000 g. **Composition:** 0.5000 Silver .5000 oz. ASW

| Date | Mintage | F | VF | XF | Unc | BU |
|---|---|---|---|---|---|---|
| 1985sm Proof | 20,000 | Value: 55.00 | | | | |

**10 DOLLARS** KM# 59 **Composition:** Nickel **Subject:** Year of the Tiger

| Date | Mintage | F | VF | XF | Unc | BU |
|---|---|---|---|---|---|---|
| 1986 | 300,000 | — | — | — | 15.00 | — |

**10 DOLLARS** KM# 59a **Weight:** 31.1000 g. **Composition:** 0.5000 Silver .5000 oz. ASW

| Date | Mintage | F | VF | XF | Unc | BU |
|---|---|---|---|---|---|---|
| 1986 Proof | 20,000 | Value: 42.50 | | | | |

**10 DOLLARS** KM# 66 **Composition:** Nickel **Subject:** Year of the Rabbit

| Date | Mintage | F | VF | XF | Unc | BU |
|---|---|---|---|---|---|---|
| 1987 | 300,000 | — | — | — | 15.00 | — |

**10 DOLLARS** KM# 66a **Weight:** 31.1000 g. **Composition:** 0.5000 Silver .5000 oz. ASW

| Date | Mintage | F | VF | XF | Unc | BU |
|---|---|---|---|---|---|---|
| 1987sm Proof | 25,000 | Value: 32.50 | | | | |

**10 DOLLARS** KM# 67 **Composition:** Copper-Nickel **Subject:** Association of Southeast Asian Nations **Obverse:** Coat of arms above 1967-1987 **Reverse:** ASEAN logo within legend, value below

| Date | Mintage | F | VF | XF | Unc | BU |
|---|---|---|---|---|---|---|
| 1987 | 80,000 | — | — | — | 8.50 | — |

**10 DOLLARS** KM# 67a **Weight:** 31.1030 g. **Composition:** 0.5000 Silver .5000 oz. ASW

| Date | Mintage | F | VF | XF | Unc | BU |
|---|---|---|---|---|---|---|
| 1987sm Proof | 25,000 | Value: 20.00 | | | | |

**10 DOLLARS** KM# 69 **Composition:** Nickel **Subject:** Year of the Dragon

| Date | Mintage | F | VF | XF | Unc | BU |
|---|---|---|---|---|---|---|
| 1988 | 300,000 | — | — | — | 15.00 | — |

**10 DOLLARS** KM# 69a **Weight:** 31.1030 g. **Composition:** 0.5000 Silver .5000 oz. ASW

| Date | Mintage | F | VF | XF | Unc | BU |
|---|---|---|---|---|---|---|
| 1988 Proof | 25,000 | Value: 42.50 | | | | |

**10 DOLLARS** KM# 71 **Composition:** Nickel **Subject:** Year of the Snake

| Date | Mintage | F | VF | XF | Unc | BU |
|---|---|---|---|---|---|---|
| 1989 | 250,000 | — | — | — | 15.00 | — |

**10 DOLLARS** KM# 71a **Weight:** 31.1030 g. **Composition:** 0.9250 Silver .9250 oz. ASW

| Date | Mintage | F | VF | XF | Unc | BU |
|---|---|---|---|---|---|---|
| 1989 Proof | 25,000 | Value: 37.50 | | | | |

**10 DOLLARS** KM# 75 **Composition:** Nickel **Subject:** Year of the Horse

| Date | Mintage | F | VF | XF | Unc | BU |
|---|---|---|---|---|---|---|
| 1990 | 330,000 | — | — | — | 15.00 | — |

**10 DOLLARS** KM# 75a **Weight:** 31.1030 g. **Composition:** 0.9250 Silver .9250 oz. ASW

| Date | Mintage | F | VF | XF | Unc | BU |
|---|---|---|---|---|---|---|
| 1990sm Proof | 30,000 | Value: 32.50 | | | | |

**10 DOLLARS** KM# 80 **Weight:** 3.1103 g. **Composition:** 0.9990 Gold .1000 oz. AGW

| Date | Mintage | F | VF | XF | Unc | BU |
|---|---|---|---|---|---|---|
| 1990 | Est. 5,000 | — | — | — | BV+15% | — |
| 1990 Proof | Est. 2,000 | Value: 50.00 | | | | |

**10 DOLLARS** KM# 95 **Weight:** 3.1103 g. **Composition:** 0.9990 Gold .1000 oz. AGW **Subject:** 25th Anniversary of Independence

| Date | Mintage | F | VF | XF | Unc | BU |
|---|---|---|---|---|---|---|
| 1990 Proof | 50,000 | Value: 25.00 | | | | |

**10 DOLLARS** KM# 84 **Composition:** Nickel

| Date | Mintage | F | VF | XF | Unc | BU |
|---|---|---|---|---|---|---|
| 1991 | 300,000 | — | — | — | 15.00 | — |

**10 DOLLARS** KM# 84a **Weight:** 31.1030 g. **Composition:** 0.9250 Silver .9250 oz. ASW

| Date | Mintage | F | VF | XF | Unc | BU |
|---|---|---|---|---|---|---|
| 1991sm Proof | 30,000 | Value: 32.50 | | | | |

**10 DOLLARS** KM# 88 **Weight:** 3.1103 g. **Composition:** 0.9990 Gold .1000 oz. AGW **Subject:** Year of the Goat

| Date | Mintage | F | VF | XF | Unc | BU |
|---|---|---|---|---|---|---|
| 1991 | 5,500 | — | — | — | BV+15% | — |
| 1991 Proof | 2,500 | Value: 50.00 | | | | |

**10 DOLLARS** KM# 92a **Weight:** 31.1030 g. **Composition:** 0.9250 Silver .9250 oz. ASW

| Date | Mintage | F | VF | XF | Unc | BU |
|---|---|---|---|---|---|---|
| 1992 Proof | 30,000 | Value: 30.00 | | | | |

**10 DOLLARS** **KM# 105** **Composition:** 0.9250 Silver .0550 oz. ASW **Subject:** 25th Anniversary - Board of Commissioners of Currency

| Date | Mintage | F | VF | XF | Unc | BU |
|---|---|---|---|---|---|---|
| 1992 Proof | 15,000 | Value: 65.00 | | | | |

**10 DOLLARS** **KM#92** **Composition:** Nickel **Subject:** Year of the Monkey **Note:** Similar to 500 Dollars, KM#93.

| Date | Mintage | F | VF | XF | Unc | BU |
|---|---|---|---|---|---|---|
| 1992 | 300,000 | — | — | — | 10.00 | — |

**10 DOLLARS** **KM# 109** **Weight:** 3.1103 g. **Composition:** 0.9990 Gold .1000 oz. AGW **Reverse:** Similar to KM#88 **Note:** Year of the Monkey Privy Mark.

| Date | Mintage | F | VF | XF | Unc | BU |
|---|---|---|---|---|---|---|
| 1992 | 4,000 | — | — | —BV+15% | | — |
| 1992 Proof | 2,000 | Value: 50.00 | | | | |

**10 DOLLARS** **KM# 118** **Weight:** 3.1103 g. **Composition:** 0.9990 Gold .1000 oz. AGW **Note:** Lion/Year of the Rooster Privy Mark.

| Date | Mintage | F | VF | XF | Unc | BU |
|---|---|---|---|---|---|---|
| 1993 | 3,100 | — | — | —BV+15% | | — |
| 1993 In proof sets only | Est. 1,500 | Value: 55.00 | | | | |

**10 DOLLARS** **KM# 113** **Composition:** Copper-Nickel **Subject:** Year of the Rooster **Obverse:** Similar to 250 Dollars, KM#114

| Date | Mintage | F | VF | XF | Unc | BU |
|---|---|---|---|---|---|---|
| 1993 Prooflike | 209,000 | — | — | — | 27.50 | — |

**10 DOLLARS** **KM# 113a** **Weight:** 62.2070 g. **Composition:** 0.9990 Silver 2.0000 oz. ASW

| Date | Mintage | F | VF | XF | Unc | BU |
|---|---|---|---|---|---|---|
| 1993 Proof | 40,000 | Value: 50.00 | | | | |

**10 DOLLARS** **KM# 122** **Composition:** Copper-Nickel **Subject:** Year of the Dog

| Date | Mintage | F | VF | XF | Unc | BU |
|---|---|---|---|---|---|---|
| 1994 Prooflike | 215,000 | — | — | — | 28.00 | — |

**10 DOLLARS** **KM# 122a** **Weight:** 62.2070 g. **Composition:** 0.9990 Silver 2.0000 oz. ASW **Reverse:** Silver content at bottom

| Date | Mintage | F | VF | XF | Unc | BU |
|---|---|---|---|---|---|---|
| 1994 Proof | 35,000 | Value: 55.00 | | | | |

**10 DOLLARS** **KM# 129** **Weight:** 3.1103 g. **Composition:** 0.9990 Gold .1000 oz. AGW **Note:** Lion/Year of the Dog Privy Mark.

| Date | Mintage | F | VF | XF | Unc | BU |
|---|---|---|---|---|---|---|
| 1994 | — | — | — | —BV+15% | | — |
| 1994 In proof sets only | Est. 1,500 | Value: 55.00 | | | | |

**10 DOLLARS** **KM# 134** **Weight:** 3.1103 g. **Composition:** 0.9990 Gold .1000 oz. AGW **Note:** Lion/Year of the Pig Privy Mark.

| Date | Mintage | F | VF | XF | Unc | BU |
|---|---|---|---|---|---|---|
| 1995 | — | — | — | —BV+15% | | — |
| 1995 Proof | — | Value: 55.00 | | | | |

**10 DOLLARS** **KM# 125** **Composition:** Copper-Nickel **Subject:** Year of the Pig

| Date | Mintage | F | VF | XF | Unc | BU |
|---|---|---|---|---|---|---|
| 1995 Prooflike | 210,000 | — | — | — | 17.50 | — |

**10 DOLLARS** **KM# 125a** **Weight:** 62.2070 g. **Composition:** 0.9990 Silver 2.0000 oz. ASW **Reverse:** Silver content at bottom

| Date | Mintage | F | VF | XF | Unc | BU |
|---|---|---|---|---|---|---|
| 1995 Proof | 35,000 | Value: 70.00 | | | | |

**10 DOLLARS** **KM# 141** **Composition:** Copper-Nickel **Subject:** Year of the Rat

| Date | Mintage | F | VF | XF | Unc | BU |
|---|---|---|---|---|---|---|
| 1996 Prooflike | 245,000 | — | — | — | 16.00 | — |

**10 DOLLARS** **KM# 141a** **Weight:** 62.2070 g. **Composition:** 0.9990 Silver 2.0000 oz. ASW **Reverse:** Silver content at bottom

| Date | Mintage | F | VF | XF | Unc | BU |
|---|---|---|---|---|---|---|
| 1996 Proof | 35,000 | Value: 70.00 | | | | |

**10 DOLLARS** **KM# 146** **Weight:** 7.7759 g. **Composition:** 0.9990 Gold .2500 oz. AGW **Note:** Year of the Rat Privy Mark.

| Date | Mintage | F | VF | XF | Unc | BU |
|---|---|---|---|---|---|---|
| 1996 Proof | 2,688 | Value: 115 | | | | |

**10 DOLLARS** **KM# 160** **Weight:** 7.7759 g. **Composition:** 0.9999 Gold .2500 oz. AGW **Note:** Lion/Year of the Ox Privy Mark. Similar to KM#154.

| Date | Mintage | F | VF | XF | Unc | BU |
|---|---|---|---|---|---|---|
| 1997 Proof | Est. 2,200 | Value: 125 | | | | |

**10 DOLLARS** **KM# 153** **Composition:** Copper-Nickel **Subject:** Year of the Ox **Note:** Similar to KM#154.

| Date | Mintage | F | VF | XF | Unc | BU |
|---|---|---|---|---|---|---|
| 1997 Prooflike | — | — | — | — | 15.00 | — |

**10 DOLLARS** **KM#154** **Weight:** 62.2070 g. **Composition:** 0.9990 Silver 2.0000 oz. ASW **Subject:** Year of the Ox

| Date | Mintage | F | VF | XF | Unc | BU |
|---|---|---|---|---|---|---|
| 1997 Proof | 38,000 | Value: 70.00 | | | | |

**10 DOLLARS** **KM#165** **Weight:** 62.2070 g. **Composition:** 0.9990 Silver 1.9980 oz. ASW **Subject:** Year of the Tiger **Obverse:** National arms **Reverse:** Stylized tiger

| Date | Mintage | F | VF | XF | Unc | BU |
|---|---|---|---|---|---|---|
| 1998 Proof | 38,000 | Value: 70.00 | | | | |

**10 DOLLARS** **KM# 164** **Composition:** Copper-Nickel **Subject:** Year of the Tiger **Obverse:** National emblem **Reverse:** Stylized tiger **Note:** Similar to KM#165.

| Date | Mintage | F | VF | XF | Unc | BU |
|---|---|---|---|---|---|---|
| 1998 Prooflike | — | — | — | — | 15.00 | — |

**10 DOLLARS** **KM#167** **Weight:** 28.0000 g. **Composition:** Copper-Nickel **Subject:** Year of the Rabbit **Obverse:** National arms **Reverse:** Stylized rabbit **Edge:** Reeded

| Date | Mintage | F | VF | XF | Unc | BU |
|---|---|---|---|---|---|---|
| 1999 | — | — | — | — | 15.00 | — |

**10 DOLLARS** **KM#168** **Weight:** 62.2070 g. **Composition:** 0.9990 Silver 1.9980 oz. ASW

| Date | Mintage | F | VF | XF | Unc | BU |
|---|---|---|---|---|---|---|
| 1999 Proof | 38,000 | Value: 70.00 | | | | |

**10 DOLLARS** **KM# 174** **Composition:** Copper-Nickel **Subject:** Year of the Dragon **Obverse:** National arms **Reverse:** Dragon **Edge:** Reeded

| Date | Mintage | F | VF | XF | Unc | BU |
|---|---|---|---|---|---|---|
| 2000 Prooflike | — | — | — | — | 15.00 | — |

**10 DOLLARS** **KM#175** **Weight:** 62.2060 g. **Composition:** 0.9990 Silver 1.9980 oz. ASW **Subject:** Year of the Dragon **Obverse:** National arms **Reverse:** Dragon **Edge:** Reeded **Size:** 40.7 mm. **Note:** Size: 40.7 millimeters, piefort thickness.

| Date | Mintage | F | VF | XF | Unc | BU |
|---|---|---|---|---|---|---|
| 2000 Proof | 38,000 | Value: 70.00 | | | | |

**20 DOLLARS** **KM# 147** **Weight:** 15.5517 g. **Composition:** 0.9990 Gold .5000 oz. AGW **Note:** Lion/Year of the Rat Privy Mark.

| Date | Mintage | F | VF | XF | Unc | BU |
|---|---|---|---|---|---|---|
| 1996 Proof | 2,688 | Value: 200 | | | | |

**20 DOLLARS** **KM# 161** **Weight:** 15.5517 g. **Composition:** 0.9999 Gold .5000 oz. AGW **Note:** Lion/Year of the Ox Privy Mark.

| Date | Mintage | F | VF | XF | Unc | BU |
|---|---|---|---|---|---|---|
| 1997 Proof | Est. 2,200 | Value: 220 | | | | |

**25 DOLLARS** **KM# 81** **Weight:** 7.7757 g. **Composition:** 0.9990 Gold .2500 oz. AGW

| Date | Mintage | F | VF | XF | Unc | BU |
|---|---|---|---|---|---|---|
| 1990 | Est. 5,000 | — | — | — | BV+12% | — |
| 1990 Proof | Est. 2,000 | Value: 90.00 | | | | |

**25 DOLLARS** **KM# 89** **Weight:** 7.7757 g. **Composition:** 0.9990 Gold .2500 oz. AGW **Note:** Year of the Goat Privy Mark.

| Date | Mintage | F | VF | XF | Unc | BU |
|---|---|---|---|---|---|---|
| 1991 | 5,500 | — | — | — | BV+12% | — |
| 1991 Proof | 2,500 | Value: 90.00 | | | | |

**25 DOLLARS** **KM# 110** **Weight:** 7.7757 g. **Composition:** 0.9990 Gold .2500 oz. AGW **Note:** Year of the Monkey Privy Mark.

| Date | Mintage | F | VF | XF | Unc | BU |
|---|---|---|---|---|---|---|
| 1992 | 4,000 | — | — | — | BV+12% | — |
| 1992 Proof | 2,000 | Value: 90.00 | | | | |

**25 DOLLARS** **KM# 119** **Weight:** 7.7757 g. **Composition:** 0.9990 Gold .2500 oz. AGW **Note:** Year of the Rooster Privy Mark.

| Date | Mintage | F | VF | XF | Unc | BU |
|---|---|---|---|---|---|---|
| 1993 | 3,000 | — | — | — | BV+12% | — |
| 1993 In proof sets only | Est. 1,500 | Value: 95.00 | | | | |

**25 DOLLARS** **KM# 130** **Weight:** 7.7757 g. **Composition:** 0.9990 Gold .2500 oz. AGW **Note:** Year of the Dog Privy Mark.

| Date | Mintage | F | VF | XF | Unc | BU |
|---|---|---|---|---|---|---|
| 1994 | — | — | — | — | BV+12% | — |
| 1994 In proof sets only | Est. 1,500 | Value: 95.00 | | | | |

**25 DOLLARS** **KM# 135** **Weight:** 7.7757 g. **Composition:** 0.9990 Gold .2500 oz. AGW **Note:** Year of the Pig Privy Mark.

| Date | Mintage | F | VF | XF | Unc | BU |
|---|---|---|---|---|---|---|
| 1995 | — | — | — | — | BV+12% | — |
| 1995 Proof | 1,500 | Value: 95.00 | | | | |

**50 DOLLARS** **KM# 18** **Weight:** 31.1000 g. **Composition:** 0.5000 Silver .5000 oz. ASW **Subject:** International Financial Center

| Date | Mintage | F | VF | XF | Unc | BU |
|---|---|---|---|---|---|---|
| 1980 | 25,000 | — | — | — | 35.00 | — |
| 1980sm Proof | 15,000 | Value: 45.00 | | | | |
| 1981 | 50,000 | — | — | — | 30.00 | — |
| 1981sm Proof | 20,000 | Value: 35.00 | | | | |

**50 DOLLARS** **KM# 78** **Weight:** 10.0000 g. **Composition:** 0.9160 Gold .2945 oz. AGW **Series:** Save the Children Fund

| Date | Mintage | F | VF | XF | Unc | BU |
|---|---|---|---|---|---|---|
| 1989 Proof | 3,000 | Value: 150 | | | | |

**50 DOLLARS** **KM# 82** **Weight:** 15.5500 g. **Composition:** 0.9990 Gold .5000 oz. AGW

| Date | Mintage | F | VF | XF | Unc | BU |
|---|---|---|---|---|---|---|
| 1990 | Est. 5,000 | — | — | — | BV | — |
| 1990 Proof | Est. 2,000 | Value: 185 | | | | |

**50 DOLLARS** **KM# 90** **Weight:** 15.5500 g. **Composition:** 0.9990 Gold .5000 oz. AGW **Note:** Year of the Goat Privy Mark.

| Date | Mintage | F | VF | XF | Unc | BU |
|---|---|---|---|---|---|---|
| 1991 | 5,500 | — | — | — | BV+10% | — |
| 1991 Proof | 2,500 | Value: 185 | | | | |

**50 DOLLARS** **KM# 111** **Weight:** 15.5500 g. **Composition:** 0.9990 Gold .5000 oz. AGW **Note:** Year of the Monkey Privy Mark.

| Date | Mintage | F | VF | XF | Unc | BU |
|---|---|---|---|---|---|---|
| 1992 | 4,000 | — | — | — | BV+10% | — |
| 1992 Proof | 2,000 | Value: 185 | | | | |

**50 DOLLARS** **KM# 120** **Weight:** 15.5500 g. **Composition:** 0.9990 Gold .5000 oz. AGW **Note:** Year of the Rooster Privy Mark.

| Date | Mintage | F | VF | XF | Unc | BU |
|---|---|---|---|---|---|---|
| 1993 | 2,600 | — | — | — | BV+10% | — |
| 1993 In proof sets only | Est. 1,500 | Value: 190 | | | | |

**50 DOLLARS** **KM# 131** **Weight:** 15.5500 g. **Composition:** 0.9990 Gold .5000 oz. AGW **Note:** Year of the Dog Privy Mark.

| Date | Mintage | F | VF | XF | Unc | BU |
|---|---|---|---|---|---|---|
| 1994 | — | — | — | — | BV+10% | — |
| 1994 In proof sets only | Est. 1,500 | Value: 190 | | | | |

**50 DOLLARS** **KM# 136** **Weight:** 15.5500 g. **Composition:** 0.9990 Gold .5000 oz. AGW **Note:** Year of the Pig Privy Mark.

| Date | Mintage | F | VF | XF | Unc | BU |
|---|---|---|---|---|---|---|
| 1995 | — | — | — | — | BV+10% | — |
| 1995 Proof | 1,500 | Value: 190 | | | | |

**50 DOLLARS** **KM# 140** **Weight:** 31.1035 g. **Composition:** 0.9999 Gold 1.0000 oz. AGW **Series:** 50th Anniversary - United Nations

| Date | Mintage | F | VF | XF | Unc | BU |
|---|---|---|---|---|---|---|
| 1995 Proof | 1,000 | Value: 750 | | | | |

**50 DOLLARS** **KM# 148** **Weight:** 31.1035 g. **Composition:** 0.9999 Gold 1.0000 oz. AGW **Note:** Lion/Year of the Rat Privy Mark.

| Date | Mintage | F | VF | XF | Unc | BU |
|---|---|---|---|---|---|---|
| 1996 Proof | 2,688 | Value: 420 | | | | |

**50 DOLLARS** **KM# 162** **Weight:** 31.1035 g. **Composition:** 0.9999 Gold 1.0000 oz. AGW **Note:** Lion/Year of the Ox Privy Mark.

| Date | Mintage | F | VF | XF | Unc | BU |
|---|---|---|---|---|---|---|
| 1997 Proof | Est. 2,200 | Value: 435 | | | | |

**50 DOLLARS** KM# 152 **Weight:** 31.1035 g. **Composition:** 0.9999 Gold 1.0000 oz. AGW **Subject:** 50th Anniversary - Singapore Airlines

| Date | Mintage | F | VF | XF | Unc | BU |
|---|---|---|---|---|---|---|
| 1997 Proof | 3,576 | Value: 500 | | | | |

**50 DOLLARS** KM# 170 **Weight:** 31.1035 g. **Composition:** 0.9999 Gold 1.0000 oz. AGW **Subject:** Parliament **Obverse:** National arms **Reverse:** Parliament House buildings

| Date | Mintage | F | VF | XF | Unc | BU |
|---|---|---|---|---|---|---|
| 1999 Proof | 1,000 | Value: 750 | | | | |

**100 DOLLARS** KM# 12 **Weight:** 6.9119 g. **Composition:** 0.9000 Gold .2000 oz. AGW **Subject:** 10th Anniversary of Independence

| Date | Mintage | F | VF | XF | Unc | BU |
|---|---|---|---|---|---|---|
| 1975 | 100,000 | — | — | — | 75.00 | — |
| 1975 Proof | 3,000 | Value: 125 | | | | |

**100 DOLLARS** KM# 83 **Weight:** 31.1000 g. **Composition:** 0.9990 Gold 1.0000 oz. AGW

| Date | Mintage | F | VF | XF | Unc | BU |
|---|---|---|---|---|---|---|
| 1990 | Est. 5,000 | — | — | — | BV+7% | — |
| 1990 Proof | Est. 2,000 | Value: 375 | | | | |

**100 DOLLARS** KM# 91 **Weight:** 31.1000 g. **Composition:** 0.9990 Gold 1.0000 oz. AGW **Note:** Year of the Goat Privy Mark.

| Date | Mintage | F | VF | XF | Unc | BU |
|---|---|---|---|---|---|---|
| 1991 | 13,000 | — | — | — | BV+7% | — |
| 1991 Proof | 2,500 | Value: 375 | | | | |

**100 DOLLARS** KM# 112 **Weight:** 31.1000 g. **Composition:** 0.9990 Gold 1.0000 oz. AGW **Note:** Year of the Monkey Privy Mark.

| Date | Mintage | F | VF | XF | Unc | BU |
|---|---|---|---|---|---|---|
| 1992 | 4,000 | — | — | — | BV+7% | — |
| 1992 Proof | 2,000 | Value: 375 | | | | |

**100 DOLLARS** KM# 106 **Weight:** 31.1000 g. **Composition:** 0.9990 Gold 1.0000 oz. AGW **Subject:** 25th Anniversary - Board of Commissioners of Currency

| Date | Mintage | F | VF | XF | Unc | BU |
|---|---|---|---|---|---|---|
| 1992 Proof | 800 | Value: 485 | | | | |

**100 DOLLARS** KM# 121 **Weight:** 31.1000 g. **Composition:** 0.9990 Gold 1.0000 oz. AGW **Note:** Year of the Rooster Privy Mark.

| Date | Mintage | F | VF | XF | Unc | BU |
|---|---|---|---|---|---|---|
| 1993 | 3,100 | — | — | — | BV+7% | — |
| 1993 In proof sets only | Est. 1,500 | Value: 385 | | | | |

**100 DOLLARS** KM# 132 **Weight:** 31.1000 g. **Composition:** 0.9990 Gold 1.0000 oz. AGW **Note:** Year of the Dog Privy Mark.

| Date | Mintage | F | VF | XF | Unc | BU |
|---|---|---|---|---|---|---|
| 1994 | — | — | — | — | BV+7% | — |
| 1994 In proof sets only | Est. 1,500 | Value: 385 | | | | |

**100 DOLLARS** KM# 137 **Weight:** 31.1000 g. **Composition:** 0.9990 Gold 1.0000 oz. AGW **Note:** Year of the Pig Privy Mark.

| Date | Mintage | F | VF | XF | Unc | BU |
|---|---|---|---|---|---|---|
| 1995 | — | — | — | — | BV+7% | — |
| 1995 Proof | 1,500 | Value: 385 | | | | |

**150 DOLLARS** KM# 7 **Weight:** 24.8830 g. **Composition:** 0.9160 Gold .7360 oz. AGW **Subject:** 150th Anniversary - Founding of Singapore

| Date | Mintage | F | VF | XF | Unc | BU |
|---|---|---|---|---|---|---|
| ND(1969) | 198,000 | — | — | — | 265 | — |
| ND(1969) Proof | 500 | Value: 1,350 | | | | |

**200 DOLLARS** KM# 107 **Weight:** 31.1035 g. **Composition:** 0.9990 Platinum 1.0000 oz. APW **Subject:** 25th Anniversary - Board of Commissioners of Currency **Note:** Similar to KM#106.

| Date | Mintage | F | VF | XF | Unc | BU |
|---|---|---|---|---|---|---|
| 1992 Proof | 300 | Value: 650 | | | | |

**250 DOLLARS** KM# 13 **Weight:** 17.2797 g. **Composition:** 0.9000 Gold .5000 oz. AGW **Subject:** 10th Anniversary of Independence

| Date | Mintage | F | VF | XF | Unc | BU |
|---|---|---|---|---|---|---|
| ND(1975) | 30,000 | — | — | — | 175 | — |
| ND(1975) Proof | 2,000 | Value: 275 | | | | |

**250 DOLLARS** KM# 96 **Weight:** 31.1040 g. **Composition:** 0.9990 Gold 1.0000 oz. AGW **Subject:** 25th Anniversary of Independence

| Date | Mintage | F | VF | XF | Unc | BU |
|---|---|---|---|---|---|---|
| 1990 Proof | 6,000 | Value: 500 | | | | |

**250 DOLLARS** KM# 114 **Weight:** 31.1035 g. **Composition:** 0.9990 Gold 1.0000 oz. AGW **Subject:** Year of the Rooster

| Date | Mintage | F | VF | XF | Unc | BU |
|---|---|---|---|---|---|---|
| 1993 Proof | 10,000 | Value: 425 | | | | |

**250 DOLLARS** KM# 123 **Weight:** 31.1035 g. **Composition:** 0.9990 Gold 1.0000 oz. AGW **Subject:** Year of the Dog

| Date | Mintage | F | VF | XF | Unc | BU |
|---|---|---|---|---|---|---|
| 1994 Proof | 7,500 | Value: 450 | | | | |

**250 DOLLARS** KM# 127 **Weight:** 31.1035 g. **Composition:** 0.9990 Gold 1.0000 oz. AGW **Subject:** Year of the Pig

| Date | Mintage | F | VF | XF | Unc | BU |
|---|---|---|---|---|---|---|
| 1995 Proof | 7,500 | Value: 485 | | | | |

**250 DOLLARS** KM# 143 **Weight:** 31.1035 g. **Composition:** 0.9990 Gold 1.0000 oz. AGW **Subject:** Year of the Rat

| Date | Mintage | F | VF | XF | Unc | BU |
|---|---|---|---|---|---|---|
| 1996 Proof | 7,500 | Value: 485 | | | | |

**250 DOLLARS** **KM# 155** **Weight:** 31.1035 g. **Composition:** 0.9990 Gold 1.0000 oz. AGW **Subject:** Year of the Ox

| Date | Mintage | F | VF | XF | Unc | BU |
|---|---|---|---|---|---|---|
| 1997 Proof | 7,800 | Value: 520 | | | | |

**250 DOLLARS** **KM# 166** **Weight:** 31.1035 g. **Composition:** 0.9990 Gold 1.0000 oz. AGW **Subject:** Year of the Tiger **Obverse:** National arms **Reverse:** Stylized tiger

| Date | Mintage | F | VF | XF | Unc | BU |
|---|---|---|---|---|---|---|
| 1998 Proof | 7,600 | Value: 520 | | | | |

**250 DOLLARS** **KM# 169** **Weight:** 31.1035 g. **Composition:** 0.9990 Gold 1.0000 oz. AGW **Obverse:** National arms **Reverse:** Stylized rabbit **Edge:** Reeded

| Date | Mintage | F | VF | XF | Unc | BU |
|---|---|---|---|---|---|---|
| 1999 Proof | 7,600 | Value: 520 | | | | |

**250 DOLLARS** **KM# 176** **Weight:** 31.1035 g. **Composition:** 0.9990 Gold 1.0000 oz. AGW **Subject:** Year of the Dragon **Obverse:** National arms **Reverse:** Dragon **Edge:** Reeded **Size:** 32.12 mm.

| Date | Mintage | F | VF | XF | Unc | BU |
|---|---|---|---|---|---|---|
| 2000 Proof | 7,600 | Value: 520 | | | | |

**500 DOLLARS** **KM# 14** **Weight:** 34.5594 g. **Composition:** 0.9000 Gold 1.0000 oz. AGW **Subject:** 10th Anniversary of Independence

| Date | Mintage | F | VF | XF | Unc | BU |
|---|---|---|---|---|---|---|
| ND(1975) | 30,000 | — | — | — | 365 | — |
| ND(1975) Proof | 2,000 | Value: 625 | | | | |

**500 DOLLARS** **KM# 21** **Weight:** 16.9650 g. **Composition:** 0.9160 Gold .5000 oz. AGW **Subject:** Year of the Rooster

| Date | Mintage | F | VF | XF | Unc | BU |
|---|---|---|---|---|---|---|
| 1981sm Proof | 12,000 | Value: 360 | | | | |

**500 DOLLARS** **KM# 24** **Weight:** 16.9650 g. **Composition:** 0.9160 Gold .5000 oz. AGW **Subject:** Year of the Dog

| Date | Mintage | F | VF | XF | Unc | BU |
|---|---|---|---|---|---|---|
| 1982sm Proof | 5,500 | Value: 400 | | | | |

**500 DOLLARS** **KM# 27** **Weight:** 16.9650 g. **Composition:** 0.9160 Gold .5000 oz. AGW **Subject:** Year of the Pig

| Date | Mintage | F | VF | XF | Unc | BU |
|---|---|---|---|---|---|---|
| 1983sm Proof | 5,000 | Value: 400 | | | | |

**500 DOLLARS** **KM# 34** **Weight:** 16.9650 g. **Composition:** 0.9160 Gold .5000 oz. AGW **Subject:** Year of the Rat

| Date | Mintage | F | VF | XF | Unc | BU |
|---|---|---|---|---|---|---|
| 1984sm Proof | 4,000 | Value: 415 | | | | |

**500 DOLLARS** **KM# 45** **Weight:** 16.9650 g. **Composition:** 0.9160 Gold .5000 oz. AGW **Subject:** Year of the Ox

| Date | Mintage | F | VF | XF | Unc | BU |
|---|---|---|---|---|---|---|
| 1985sm Proof | 4,000 | Value: 415 | | | | |

**500 DOLLARS** **KM# 60** **Weight:** 16.9650 g. **Composition:** 0.9160 Gold .5000 oz. AGW **Subject:** Year of the Tiger

| Date | Mintage | F | VF | XF | Unc | BU |
|---|---|---|---|---|---|---|
| 1986sm Proof | 3,000 | Value: 500 | | | | |

**500 DOLLARS** **KM# 64** **Weight:** 16.9650 g. **Composition:** 0.9160 Gold .5000 oz. AGW **Subject:** Year of the Rabbit

| Date | Mintage | F | VF | XF | Unc | BU |
|---|---|---|---|---|---|---|
| 1987sm Proof | 2,400 | Value: 725 | | | | |

**500 DOLLARS** **KM# 73** **Weight:** 16.9650 g. **Composition:** 0.9160 Gold .5000 oz. AGW **Subject:** Year of the Dragon

| Date | Mintage | F | VF | XF | Unc | BU |
|---|---|---|---|---|---|---|
| 1988sm Proof | 4,000 | Value: 420 | | | | |

**500 DOLLARS** **KM# 72** **Weight:** 16.9650 g. **Composition:** 0.9160 Gold .5000 oz. AGW **Subject:** Year of the Snake

| Date | Mintage | F | VF | XF | Unc | BU |
|---|---|---|---|---|---|---|
| 1989sm Proof | 2,500 | Value: 700 | | | | |

**500 DOLLARS** **KM# 76** **Weight:** 16.9650 g. **Composition:** 0.9160 Gold .5000 oz. AGW **Subject:** Year of the Horse

| Date | Mintage | F | VF | XF | Unc | BU |
|---|---|---|---|---|---|---|
| 1990sm Proof | 5,000 | Value: 385 | | | | |

**500 DOLLARS** **KM# 97** **Weight:** 31.1040 g. **Composition:** 0.9990 Platinum 1.0000 oz. APW **Subject:** 25th Anniversary of Independence

| Date | Mintage | F | VF | XF | Unc | BU |
|---|---|---|---|---|---|---|
| 1990 Proof | 2,000 | Value: 650 | | | | |

**500 DOLLARS** **KM# 85** **Weight:** 16.9650 g. **Composition:** 0.9160 Gold .5000 oz. AGW **Subject:** Year of the Goat

| Date | Mintage | F | VF | XF | Unc | BU |
|---|---|---|---|---|---|---|
| 1991sm Proof | 5,000 | Value: 385 | | | | |

**500 DOLLARS** **KM# 93** **Weight:** 16.9650 g. **Composition:** 0.9160 Gold .5000 oz. AGW **Subject:** Year of the Monkey

| Date | Mintage | F | VF | XF | Unc | BU |
|---|---|---|---|---|---|---|
| 1992sm Proof | 5,000 | Value: 385 | | | | |

## MINT SETS

| KM# | Date | Mintage | Identification | Issue Price | Mkt Val |
|---|---|---|---|---|---|
| MS1 | 1967 (6) | 8,000 | KM#1-6 | 1.50 | 20.00 |
| MS2 | 1968 (6) | 16,000 | KM#1-6 | 1.50 | 20.00 |
| MS3 | 1969 (6) | 14,000 | KM#1-6 | 1.50 | 25.00 |
| MS4 | 1970 (6) | 13,000 | KM#1-6 | 1.50 | 60.00 |
| MS5 | 1970 (6) | 27,000 | KM#1-6 | 1.75 | 60.00 |

| KM# | Date | Mintage | Identification | Issue Price | Mkt Val |
|---|---|---|---|---|---|
| MS7 | 1972 (6) | 13,000 | KM#1-6 | 3.00 | 35.00 |
| MS8 | 1973 (6) | 15,000 | KM#1-6 | 2.00 | 18.00 |
| MS9 | 1974 (6) | 20,000 | KM#1-6 | 2.00 | 15.00 |
| MS10 | 1975 (6) | 30,000 | KM#1-6 | 12.00 | 15.00 |
| MS11 | 1975 (3) | 30,000 | KM#12-14 | — | 875 |
| MS12 | 1976 (6) | 35,000 | KM#1-6 | 2.00 | 12.00 |
| MS13 | 1977 (6) | 40,000 | KM#1a, 2-6 | 2.00 | 12.00 |
| MS14 | 1978 (6) | 55,000 | KM#1a, 2-6 | — | 25.00 |
| MS15 | 1979 (6) | 65,000 | KM#1a, 2-6 | — | 10.00 |
| MS16 | 1980 (6) | 70,000 | kM#1a, 2-6 | — | 8.00 |
| MS17 | 1981 (6) | 110,000 | KM#1a, 2-6 | 5.00 | 6.50 |
| MS18 | 1982 (6) | 160,000 | KM#1a, 2-6 | 5.00 | 6.50 |
| MS19 | 1983 (6) | 40,000 | KM#1a, 2-6 with Medallion, I.A.P.N. | — | 9.00 |
| MS20 | 1983 (6) | 150,000 | KM#1a, 2-6 | 5.00 | 8.00 |
| MS21 | 1984 (6) | 160,000 | KM#1a, 2-6 | 3.75 | 7.50 |
| MS22 | 1985 (6) | 148,424 | KM#1a, 2-6 | — | 15.00 |
| MS23 | 1986 (6) | 120,000 | KM#49-52, 53.1, 54 | — | 7.00 |
| MS24 | 1987 (6) | 120,000 | KM#49-52, 53.1, 54 | — | 7.00 |
| MS25 | 1988 (6) | 120,000 | KM#49-52, 53.1, 54b | — | 5.50 |
| MS26 | 1989 (6) | 100,000 | KM#49-52, 53.2, 54b | — | 5.50 |
| MS27 | 1990 (6) | 100,000 | KM#49-52, 53.2, 54b | — | 5.50 |
| MS28 | 1990 (5) | 5,000 | KM#79-83 | — | 700 |
| MS29 | 1991 (7) | 70,000 | KM#49b, 50-52, 53.2, 54b (1991), 94 (1990) | — | 20.00 |
| MS30 | 1992 (7) | 55,000 | KM#98-104 | — | 20.00 |
| MS31 | 1993 (7) | — | KM#98-104 | — | 20.00 |
| MS32 | 1994 (7) | 100,000 | KM#98-104 | — | 20.00 |
| MS33 | 1995 (7) | 124,000 | KM#98-104 | — | 20.00 |
| MS34 | 1996 (7) | 180,000 | KM#98-104 | — | 20.00 |
| MS35 | 1997 (7) | — | KM#98-104 | — | 20.00 |
| MS36 | 1998 (7) | — | KM#98-104 | — | 20.00 |
| MS37 | 1999 (7) | — | KM#98-104 | — | 20.00 |
| MS38 | 2000 (7) | — | KM#98-104 | — | 20.00 |

## PROOF SETS

| KM# | Date | Mintage | Identification | Issue Price | Mkt Val |
|---|---|---|---|---|---|
| PS21 | 1987 (5) | 1,000 | KM-MB28-MB32 | 1,400 | 1,650 |
| PS23 | 1988 (5) | 500 | KM-MB41-45 | — | 1,650 |
| PS25 | 1989 (5) | 200 | KM-MB51-55 | — | 1,975 |
| PS1 | 1967 (6) | 2,000 | KM#1-6 | 25.00 | 60.00 |
| PS2 | 1968 (6) | 5,000 | KM#1-6 | 25.00 | 55.00 |
| PS3 | 1969 (6) | 3,000 | KM#1-6 | 25.00 | 275 |
| PS4 | 1972 (6) | 749 | KM#1-6 | 25.00 | 475 |
| PS5 | 1973 (6) | 1,000 | KM#1-6 | 32.00 | 175 |
| PS6 | 1974 (6) | 1,500 | KM#1-6 | 34.00 | 130 |
| PS7 | 1975 (6) | 3,000 | KM#1-6 | 35.00 | 60.00 |
| PS8 | 1975 (3) | 2,000 | KM#12-14 | — | 1,400 |
| PS9 | 1976 (6) | 3,500 | KM#1-6 | 37.00 | 50.00 |
| PS10 | 1977 (6) | 3,500 | kM#1-6 | — | 50.00 |
| PS11 | 1978 (6) | 4,000 | KM#1-6 | — | 60.00 |
| PS12 | 1979 (7) | 3,500 | KM#1-6, 17.1 | — | 120 |
| PS13 | 1980 (7) | 14,000 | KM#1-6, 17.2 | 64.00 | 90.00 |
| PS14 | 1981 (6) | 30,000 | KM#1b-2b, 3a-6a, .925 Silver | 82.00 | 100 |
| PS15 | 1982 (6) | 20,000 | KM#1-5, 6a | 52.00 | 50.00 |
| PS16 | 1983 (6) | 15,000 | KM#1-5, 6a | 52.00 | 50.00 |
| PS17 | 1984 (6) | 15,000 | KM#1-5, 6a | 52.00 | 50.00 |
| PS18 | 1985 (6) | 20,000 | KM#49a-52a, 53.1a, 54a | 40.00 | 50.00 |
| PS19 | 1986 (6) | 15,000 | KM#49a-52a, 53.1a, 54a | — | 48.00 |
| PS20 | 1987 (6) | 15,000 | KM#49a-52a, 53.1a, 54c | 42.00 | 48.00 |
| PS22 | 1988 (6) | 15,000 | KM#49a-52a, 53.1a, 54c | — | 45.00 |
| PS24 | 1989 (6) | 15,000 | KM#49a-52a, 53.2a, 54c | — | 45.00 |
| PS26 | 1990 (6) | 15,000 | KM#49a-52a, 53.2a, 54c | — | 45.00 |
| PS27 | 1990 (5) | 2,000 | KM#79-83 | — | 750 |
| PSA28 | 1990 (3) | 1,000 | KM#95-97 | — | 1,700 |
| PS28 | 1991 (7) | 15,000 | KM#49a-52a, 53.2a, 54c, 86a | — | 70.00 |
| PS30 | 1991 (2) | 5,000 | KM#86, 86a | — | 40.00 |
| PS29 | 1991 (5) | 2,500 | KM#87-91 | — | 750 |
| PS31 | 1992 (7) | 15,000 | KM#98a-104a | — | 75.00 |
| PS33 | 1992 (3) | 200 | KM#105-107 | — | 1,490 |
| PS32 | 1992 (5) | 2,000 | KM#108-112 Ingot | — | 750 |
| PS34 | 1993 (7) | 15,000 | KM#98a-104a | — | 75.00 |
| PS36 | 1993 (2) | 2,000 | KM#115, 115a | — | 50.00 |
| PS35 | 1993 (5) | 1,500 | KM#117-121 Ingot | — | 775 |
| PS37 | 1994 (7) | 10,000 | KM#98a-104a | — | 75.00 |
| PS38 | 1994 (5) | 1,500 | KM#128-132 Ingot | — | 775 |
| PS39 | 1995 (7) | 10,000 | KM#98a-104a | — | 75.00 |
| PS42 | 1995 (3) | 2,689 | KM#138-140 | 1,052 | 650 |
| PS41 | 1995 (5) | 1,500 | KM#133-137 Ingot | 1,718 | 775 |
| PS43 | 1996 (7) | 17,000 | KM#98a-104a Ingot | — | 75.00 |
| PS44 | 1996 (5) | 2,688 | KM#144-148 Ingot | — | 820 |
| PS45 | 1996 (2) | 2,800 | KM#149, 149a | 66.00 | 66.00 |
| PS46 | 1997 (7) | 20,000 | KM#98a-104a Ingot | 90.00 | 100 |
| PS47 | 1997 (2) | 3,800 | KM#151, 151a Ingot | — | 60.00 |
| PS48 | 1997 (3) | 888 | KM#151, 151a, 152 Ingot | — | 550 |
| PS49 | 1997 (5) | 2,200 | KM#158-162 | — | 885 |
| PS50 | 1998 (3) | 1,998 | KM#164-166 Ingot | — | 600 |
| PS51 | 1998 (7) | — | KM#98a-104a | — | 100 |
| PS52 | 1999 (7) | — | KM#98a-104a | — | 100 |
| PS53 | 2000 (7) | 17,000 | KM#98a-104a | 74.25 | 100 |
| PS54 | 2000 (3) | 2,000 | KM#174-176 Plus Ingot | — | 605 |

The Republic of Slovakia has an area of 18,923 sq. mi. (49,035 sq. km.) and a population of 4.9 million. Capital: Bratislava. Textiles, steel, and wood products are exported.

The Slovak lands were united with the Czechs and the Czechoslovak State came into existence on Oct. 28, 1918 upon the dissolution of Austro-Hungarian Empire at the close of World War I. In March 1939, the German-influenced Slovak government proclaimed Slovakia independent and Germany incorporated the Czech lands into the Third Reich as the "Protectorate of Bohemia and Moravia". A Czechoslovak government-in-exile was setup in London in July 1940. The Soviet and USA forces liberated the area by May, 1945. At the close of World War II, Communist influence increased steadily while pressure for liberalization culminated in the overthrow of the Stalinist leader Antonin Novotn'y and his associates in 1968. The Communist Party then introduced far reaching reforms which received warnings from Moscow, followed by occupation by Warsaw Pact forces resulting in stationing of Soviet forces. Mass civilian demonstrations for reform began in Nov. 1989 and the Federal Assembly abolished the Communist Party's sole right to govern. New governments followed on Dec. 3 and Dec. 10 and the Czech and Slovak Federal Republic was formed. The Movement for Democratic Slovakia was apparent in the June 1992 elections with the Slovak National Council adopting a declaration of sovereignty. Later, a constitution for an independent Slovakia with the Federal Assembly voting for the dissolution of the Republic came into effect on Dec. 31, 1992, and two new republics came into being on Jan. 1, 1993.

**MINT MARK**

Kremnica Mint

# AUTONOMOUS REPUBLIC

## STANDARD COINAGE

100 Halierov = 1 Koruna Slovenska (Ks)

**5 HALIEROV** **KM# 8** **Composition:** Zinc

| Date | Mintage | F | VF | XF | Unc | BU |
|---|---|---|---|---|---|---|
| 1942 | 1,000,000 | 1.50 | 3.00 | 7.50 | 20.00 | — |

**10 HALIEROV** **KM# 1** **Composition:** Bronze

| Date | Mintage | F | VF | XF | Unc | BU |
|---|---|---|---|---|---|---|
| 1939 | 15,000,000 | 1.50 | 2.00 | 4.00 | 8.00 | — |
| 1942 | 7,000,000 | 1.50 | 2.00 | 4.00 | 8.00 | — |

**20 HALIEROV** **KM# 4** **Composition:** Bronze

| Date | Mintage | F | VF | XF | Unc | BU |
|---|---|---|---|---|---|---|
| 1940 | 10,972,000 | 1.25 | 2.00 | 3.00 | 6.00 | — |
| 1941 | 4,028,000 | 1.25 | 2.00 | 3.00 | 6.00 | — |
| 1942 | 6,474,000 | 1.25 | 3.00 | 5.00 | 9.00 | — |

**20 HALIEROV** **KM# 4a** **Composition:** Aluminum **Note:** Varieties exist.

| Date | Mintage | F | VF | XF | Unc | BU |
|---|---|---|---|---|---|---|
| 1942 | Inc. above | 1.00 | 1.50 | 2.00 | 4.50 | — |
| 1943 | 15,000,000 | 1.00 | 1.50 | 2.00 | 4.50 | — |

**50 HALIEROV** **KM# 5** **Composition:** Copper-Nickel

| Date | Mintage | F | VF | XF | Unc | BU |
|---|---|---|---|---|---|---|
| 1940 | Inc. above | 30.00 | 45.00 | 60.00 | 125 | — |
| 1941 | 8,000,000 | 1.00 | 2.00 | 3.00 | 6.00 | — |

**50 HALIEROV** **KM# 5a** **Composition:** Aluminum

| Date | Mintage | F | VF | XF | Unc | BU |
|---|---|---|---|---|---|---|
| 1943 | 4,400,000 | 1.00 | 1.50 | 2.50 | 5.00 | — |
| 1944 | 2,621,000 | 1.25 | 2.00 | 4.00 | 7.00 | — |

**KORUNA** **KM# 6** **Composition:** Copper-Nickel

| Date | Mintage | F | VF | XF | Unc | BU |
|---|---|---|---|---|---|---|
| 1940 | 2,350,000 | 0.75 | 1.25 | 2.25 | 6.00 | — |
| 1941 | 11,650,000 | 0.50 | 1.00 | 2.00 | 5.00 | — |
| 1942 | 6,000,000 | 0.50 | 1.00 | 2.00 | 5.00 | — |
| **Note:** Varieties exist of 1942, in the numeral 4 | | | | | | |
| 1944 | 884,000 | 1.50 | 2.50 | 4.50 | 10.00 | — |
| 1945 | 3,321,000 | 0.75 | 1.25 | 2.25 | 6.00 | — |

**5 KORUN** **KM# 2** **Composition:** Nickel **Note:** Two varieties exist in the letter A in NAROD.

| Date | Mintage | F | VF | XF | Unc | BU |
|---|---|---|---|---|---|---|
| 1939 | 5,101,000 | 1.50 | 2.00 | 3.50 | 12.50 | — |

**Note:** Approximately 2,000,000 pieces were melted down by the Czechoslovak National Bank in 1947

**10 KORUN** **KM# 9.1** **Weight:** 7.0000 g. **Composition:** 0.5000 Silver .1125 oz. ASW **Subject:** Pribina **Reverse:** Variety 1 - Cross atop church held by left figure

| Date | Mintage | F | VF | XF | Unc | BU |
|---|---|---|---|---|---|---|
| 1944 | 1,381,000 | 2.00 | 4.00 | 5.00 | 8.00 | — |

**10 KORUN** **KM# 9.2** **Weight:** 7.0000 g. **Composition:** 0.5000 Silver .1125 oz. ASW **Reverse:** Variety 2 - Without cross atop church held by left figure

| Date | Mintage | F | VF | XF | Unc | BU |
|---|---|---|---|---|---|---|
| 1944 | Inc. above | 2.50 | 5.00 | 7.00 | 10.00 | — |

**20 KORUN** **KM# 3** **Weight:** 15.0000 g. **Composition:** 0.5000 Silver .2411 oz. ASW **Reverse:** Dr. Joseph Tiso bust facing right

| Date | Mintage | F | VF | XF | Unc | BU |
|---|---|---|---|---|---|---|
| 1939 | 200,000 | 5.00 | 10.00 | 15.00 | 30.00 | — |

**20 KORUN** KM# 7.1 **Weight:** 15.0000 g. **Composition:** 0.5000 Silver .2411 oz. ASW **Subject:** St. Kyrill and St. Methodius **Reverse:** Variety 1 - Single bar cross in curch at lower right

| Date | Mintage | F | VF | XF | Unc | BU |
|---|---|---|---|---|---|---|
| 1941 | 2,500,000 | 2.00 | 3.50 | 5.00 | 10.00 | — |

**20 KORUN** KM# 7.2 **Weight:** 15.0000 g. **Composition:** 0.5000 Silver .2411 oz. ASW **Reverse:** Variety 2 - Double bar cross

| Date | Mintage | F | VF | XF | Unc | BU |
|---|---|---|---|---|---|---|
| 1941 | Inc. above | 4.00 | 6.50 | 9.00 | 15.00 | — |

**50 KORUN** KM# 10 **Weight:** 16.5000 g. **Composition:** 0.7000 Silver .3713 oz. ASW **Subject:** 5th anniversary of Independence

| Date | Mintage | F | VF | XF | Unc | BU |
|---|---|---|---|---|---|---|
| 1944 | 2,000,000 | 3.00 | 5.00 | 7.50 | 12.50 | — |

# REPUBLIC

## STANDARD COINAGE

100 Halierov = 1 Slovak Koruna (Sk)

**10 HALIEROV** KM# 17 **Composition:** Aluminum **Reverse:** Church steeple

| Date | Mintage | F | VF | XF | Unc | BU |
|---|---|---|---|---|---|---|
| 1993 | — | — | — | — | 0.35 | — |
| 1994 | — | — | — | — | 0.35 | — |
| 1995 In sets only | — | — | — | — | 1.00 | — |
| 1996 | — | — | — | — | 0.35 | — |
| 1997 | — | — | — | — | 0.35 | — |
| 1998 | — | — | — | — | 0.35 | — |
| 1999 | 31,420,000 | — | — | — | 0.35 | — |
| 2000 | 30,060,000 | — | — | — | 0.35 | — |

**Note:** In 1999 and 2000, 11,500 proofs were struck for mint sets

**20 HALIEROV** KM# 18 **Composition:** Aluminum **Reverse:** Mountain peak

| Date | Mintage | F | VF | XF | Unc | BU |
|---|---|---|---|---|---|---|
| 1993 | — | — | — | — | 0.45 | — |
| 1994 | — | — | — | — | 0.45 | — |
| 1995 In sets only | — | — | — | — | 1.00 | — |
| 1996 | — | — | — | — | 0.45 | — |
| 1997 | — | — | — | — | 0.45 | — |
| 1998 | — | — | — | — | 0.45 | — |
| 1999 | 15,710,000 | — | — | — | 0.45 | — |
| 2000 | 31,120,000 | — | — | — | 0.45 | — |

**Note:** In 1999 (11,500) and in 2000 (12,500) proofs were struck for proof sets

**50 HALIEROV** KM# 15 **Composition:** Aluminum **Reverse:** Watch tower

| Date | Mintage | F | VF | XF | Unc | BU |
|---|---|---|---|---|---|---|
| 1993 | — | — | — | — | 0.55 | — |
| 1994 In sets only | 20,000 | — | — | — | 1.50 | — |
| 1995 In sets only | — | — | — | — | 1.50 | — |

**50 HALIEROV** KM#35 **Composition:** Copper Plated Steel **Reverse:** Watch tower

| Date | Mintage | F | VF | XF | Unc | BU |
|---|---|---|---|---|---|---|
| 1996 | — | — | — | — | 0.60 | — |
| 1997 In sets only | — | — | — | — | 1.50 | — |
| 1998 | — | — | — | — | 0.60 | — |
| 1999 In sets only | 115,000 | — | — | — | 1.50 | — |
| 2000 | 20,212,000 | — | — | — | 0.60 | — |

**Note:** In 2000, 12,500 were struck for sets only

**KORUNA** KM# 12 **Composition:** Bronze Clad Steel

| Date | Mintage | F | VF | XF | Unc | BU |
|---|---|---|---|---|---|---|
| 1993 | — | — | — | — | 0.75 | — |
| 1994 | — | — | — | — | 0.75 | — |
| 1995 | — | — | — | — | 0.75 | — |
| 1996 In sets only | — | — | — | — | 1.50 | — |
| 1997 In sets only | — | — | — | — | 1.50 | — |
| 1998 In sets only | — | — | — | — | 1.50 | — |
| 1999 In sets only | — | — | — | — | 1.50 | — |
| 2000 In sets only | — | — | — | — | 1.50 | — |

**2 KORUNA** KM# 13 **Composition:** Nickel Clad Steel

| Date | Mintage | F | VF | XF | Unc | BU |
|---|---|---|---|---|---|---|
| 1993 | — | — | — | — | 0.85 | — |
| 1994 | — | — | — | — | 0.85 | — |
| 1995 | — | — | — | — | 0.85 | — |
| 1996 In sets only | — | — | — | — | 2.00 | — |
| 1997 In sets only | — | — | — | — | 2.00 | — |
| 1998 In sets only | — | — | — | — | 2.00 | — |
| 1999 In sets only | — | — | — | — | 2.00 | — |
| 2000 In sets only | — | — | — | — | 2.00 | — |

**5 KORUNA** KM# 14 **Composition:** Nickel Clad Steel

| Date | Mintage | F | VF | XF | Unc | BU |
|---|---|---|---|---|---|---|
| 1993 | — | — | — | — | 1.25 | — |
| 1994 | — | — | — | — | 1.25 | — |
| 1995 | — | — | — | — | 1.25 | — |
| 1996 In sets only | — | — | — | — | 2.00 | — |
| 1997 In sets only | — | — | — | — | 2.00 | — |
| 1998 In sets only | — | — | — | — | 2.00 | — |
| 1999 In sets only | — | — | — | — | 2.00 | — |
| 2000 In sets only | — | — | — | — | 2.00 | — |

**10 KORUNA** KM# 11.1 **Composition:** Brass

| Date | Mintage | F | VF | XF | Unc | BU |
|---|---|---|---|---|---|---|
| 1993 | — | — | — | — | 2.50 | — |
| 1994 | — | — | — | — | 2.50 | — |
| 1995 | — | — | — | — | 2.50 | — |
| 1996 In sets only | — | — | — | — | 4.00 | — |
| 1997 In sets only | — | — | — | — | 4.00 | — |
| 1998 In sets only | — | — | — | — | 4.00 | — |
| 1999 In sets only | — | — | — | — | 4.00 | — |
| 2000 In sets only | — | — | — | — | 4.00 | — |

**10 KORUNA** KM# 11.2 **Weight:** 8.5000 g. **Composition:** 0.7500 Silver .2527 oz. ASW

| Date | Mintage | F | VF | XF | Unc | BU |
|---|---|---|---|---|---|---|
| 1993 Proof | 1,000 | Value: 350 | | | | |

**Note:** These coins are numbered and punched with an R

**100 KORUN** KM# 16 **Weight:** 13.0000 g. **Composition:** 0.7500 Silver .3135 oz. ASW **Subject:** National Independence

| Date | Mintage | F | VF | XF | Unc | BU |
|---|---|---|---|---|---|---|
| 1993 | 65,000 | — | — | — | 9.00 | — |
| 1993 Proof | 5,000 | Value: 18.00 | | | | |

**200 KORUN** KM# 19 **Weight:** 20.0000 g. **Composition:** 0.7500 Silver .4823 oz. ASW **Subject:** 150th Anniversary of Slovak Language

| Date | Mintage | F | VF | XF | Unc | BU |
|---|---|---|---|---|---|---|
| 1993 | 35,000 | — | — | — | 15.00 | — |
| 1993 Proof | 2,000 | Value: 30.00 | | | | |

**200 KORUN** KM# 20 **Weight:** 20.0000 g. **Composition:** 0.7500 Silver .4823 oz. ASW **Subject:** 30th Anniversary - Birth of Jan Kollar

| Date | Mintage | F | VF | XF | Unc | BU |
|---|---|---|---|---|---|---|
| 1993 | 35,000 | — | — | — | 15.00 | — |
| 1993 Proof | 2,000 | Value: 35.00 | | | | |

**200 KORUN** **KM# 21** **Weight:** 20.0000 g. **Composition:** 0.7500 Silver .4823 oz. ASW **Subject:** 100th Anniversary - Olympic Committee

| Date | Mintage | F | VF | XF | Unc | BU |
|---|---|---|---|---|---|---|
| 1994 | 45,000 | — | — | — | 15.00 | — |
| 1994 Proof | 3,000 | Value: 32.50 | | | | |

**200 KORUN** **KM# 22** **Weight:** 20.0000 g. **Composition:** 0.7500 Silver .4823 oz. ASW **Subject:** 100th Anniversary - Birth of poet and painter Janko Alexy

| Date | Mintage | F | VF | XF | Unc | BU |
|---|---|---|---|---|---|---|
| 1994 | 32,000 | — | — | — | 15.00 | — |
| 1994 Proof | 2,500 | Value: 35.00 | | | | |

**200 KORUN** **KM# 23** **Weight:** 20.0000 g. **Composition:** 0.7500 Silver .4823 oz. ASW **Subject:** 50th Anniversary - D-Day

| Date | Mintage | F | VF | XF | Unc | BU |
|---|---|---|---|---|---|---|
| 1994 | 35,000 | — | — | — | 20.00 | — |
| 1994 Proof | 2,600 | Value: 45.00 | | | | |

**200 KORUN** **KM# 24** **Weight:** 20.0000 g. **Composition:** 0.7500 Silver .4823 oz. ASW **Subject:** 200th Anniversary - Birth of Pavol Jozef Safarik **Edge Lettering:** ZAKLADATEL VEDECKEJ SLAVISTIKY

| Date | Mintage | F | VF | XF | Unc | BU |
|---|---|---|---|---|---|---|
| 1995 | 24,000 | — | — | — | 15.00 | — |
| 1995 Proof | 1,500 | Value: 37.50 | | | | |

**200 KORUN** **KM# 25** **Weight:** 20.0000 g. **Composition:** 0.7500 Silver .4823 oz. ASW **Subject:** 100th Anniversary - Birth of Mikulas Galanda **Edge Lettering:** MIKULAS GALANDA - MALIAR A GRAFIK

| Date | Mintage | F | VF | XF | Unc | BU |
|---|---|---|---|---|---|---|
| 1995 | 24,000 | — | — | — | 15.00 | — |
| 1995 Proof | 1,500 | Value: 30.00 | | | | |

**200 KORUN** **KM# 26** **Weight:** 20.0000 g. **Composition:** 0.7500 Silver .4823 oz. ASW **Subject:** European Environmental Protection **Reverse:** Stork feeding young **Edge Lettering:** ENCY 1995 (3 fish)

| Date | Mintage | F | VF | XF | Unc | BU |
|---|---|---|---|---|---|---|
| 1995 | 28,000 | — | — | — | 15.00 | — |
| 1995 Proof | 2,000 | Value: 40.00 | | | | |

**200 KORUN** **KM# 27** **Weight:** 20.0000 g. **Composition:** 0.7500 Silver .4823 oz. ASW **Subject:** Centennial of Bratislava Electric Tram

| Date | Mintage | F | VF | XF | Unc | BU |
|---|---|---|---|---|---|---|
| 1995 | 26,000 | — | — | — | 15.00 | — |
| 1995 Proof | 1,600 | Value: 40.00 | | | | |

**200 KORUN** **KM# 30** **Weight:** 20.0000 g. **Composition:** 0.7500 Silver .4823 oz. ASW **Subject:** 200th Anniversary - Birth of Samuel Jurkovic

| Date | Mintage | F | VF | XF | Unc | BU |
|---|---|---|---|---|---|---|
| 1996 | 26,000 | — | — | — | 15.00 | — |
| 1996 Proof | 1,600 | Value: 37.50 | | | | |

**200 KORUN** **KM# 31** **Weight:** 20.0000 g. **Composition:** 0.7500 Silver .4823 oz. ASW **Subject:** Olympic Games **Reverse:** Oval track

| Date | Mintage | F | VF | XF | Unc | BU |
|---|---|---|---|---|---|---|
| 1996 | 23,000 | — | — | — | 16.50 | — |
| 1996 Proof | 1,700 | Value: 35.00 | | | | |

**200 KORUN** **KM# 32** **Weight:** 20.0000 g. **Composition:** 0.7500 Silver .4823 oz. ASW **Subject:** 100th Anniversary - Birth of Jozef Ciger Hronsky **Edge Lettering:** NIET KRAJSICH SLOVAKO SKUTKY

| Date | Mintage | F | VF | XF | Unc | BU |
|---|---|---|---|---|---|---|
| 1996 | 20,000 | — | — | — | 15.00 | — |
| 1996 Proof | 1,500 | Value: 32.50 | | | | |

**200 KORUN** **KM# 33** **Weight:** 20.0000 g. **Composition:** 0.7500 Silver .4823 oz. ASW **Subject:** Centennial - Rack Railway **Edge Lettering:** VYSOKE TATRY VYSOKE TATRY

| Date | Mintage | F | VF | XF | Unc | BU |
|---|---|---|---|---|---|---|
| 1996 | 22,000 | — | — | — | 15.00 | — |
| 1996 Proof | 1,600 | Value: 32.50 | | | | |

**200 KORUN** **KM# 34** **Weight:** 20.0000 g. **Composition:** 0.7500 Silver .4823 oz. ASW **Subject:** 200th Anniversary - Birth of Moric Benovsky **Edge Lettering:** IN ADVERSIS ET PROSPERIS

| Date | Mintage | F | VF | XF | Unc | BU |
|---|---|---|---|---|---|---|
| 1996 | 21,000 | — | — | — | 15.00 | — |
| 1996 Proof | 2,000 | Value: 40.00 | | | | |

**200 KORUN** **KM# 37** **Weight:** 20.0000 g. **Composition:** 0.7500 Silver .4823 oz. ASW **Subject:** 150th Anniversary - Birth of Svetozar Hurban Vajansky 1847-1916 **Edge Lettering:** POLITIK SPISOVATEL KRITIK NOVINAR

| Date | Mintage | F | VF | XF | Unc | BU |
|---|---|---|---|---|---|---|
| 1997 | 19,000 | — | — | — | 15.00 | — |
| 1997 Proof | 1,800 | Value: 35.00 | | | | |

**200 KORUN** **KM# 38** **Weight:** 20.0000 g. **Composition:** 0.7500 Silver .4823 oz. ASW **Subject:** Banska Stiavnica - UNESCO **Edge Lettering:** PATRIMOINE MODIAL

| Date | Mintage | F | VF | XF | Unc | BU |
|---|---|---|---|---|---|---|
| 1997 | 17,000 | — | — | — | 15.00 | — |
| 1997 Proof | 1,700 | Value: 37.50 | | | | |

**200 KORUN** **KM# 40** **Weight:** 20.0000 g. **Composition:** 0.7500 Silver .4823 oz. ASW **Subject:** 200th Anniversary - Birth of Stefan Moyses, 1797-1997 **Obverse:** Stylized national emblem in tree form **Edge Lettering:** PRVY PREDSEDA MATICE SLOVENSKEJ

| Date | Mintage | F | VF | XF | Unc | BU |
|---|---|---|---|---|---|---|
| 1997 | — | — | — | — | 15.00 | — |
| 1997 Proof | — | Value: 35.00 | | | | |

**200 KORUN** **KM# 41** **Weight:** 20.0000 g. **Composition:** 0.7500 Silver .4823 oz. ASW **Subject:** 50th Anniversary - Slovak National Gallery **Obverse:** Madonna and child **Edge Lettering:** GOTIKA A BAROK V ZBIERKACH SNG

| Date | Mintage | F | VF | XF | Unc | BU |
|---|---|---|---|---|---|---|
| 1998 | 15,000 | — | — | — | 15.00 | — |
| 1998 Proof | 1,600 | Value: 30.00 | | | | |

**200 KORUN** **KM# 42** **Weight:** 20.0000 g. **Composition:** 0.7500 Silver .4823 oz. ASW **Subject:** 150th Anniversary - 1st Railroad in Slovakia **Obverse:** Train emerging from tunnel **Edge Lettering:** 150 ROKOV ZELEZNIC NA SLOVENSKU

| Date | Mintage | F | VF | XF | Unc | BU |
|---|---|---|---|---|---|---|
| 1998 | 14,000 | — | — | — | 15.00 | — |
| 1998 Proof | 1,800 | Value: 32.50 | | | | |

**200 KORUN** **KM# 43** **Weight:** 20.0000 g. **Composition:** 0.7500 Silver .4823 oz. ASW **Subject:** 150th Anniversary - Slovak Revolt of 1848 - Standing Revolutionary **Edge Lettering:** ZA NARODNU SLOBODU

| Date | Mintage | F | VF | XF | Unc | BU |
|---|---|---|---|---|---|---|
| 1998 | 13,000 | — | — | — | 15.00 | — |
| 1998 Proof | 1,500 | Value: 37.50 | | | | |

**200 KORUN** **KM# 44** **Weight:** 20.0000 g. **Composition:** 0.7500 Silver .4823 oz. ASW **Subject:** Spis Castle - UNESCO **Obverse:** St. Martin's Cathedral towers **Edge Lettering:** PATRIMONIE MONDIAL WORLD HERITAGE

| Date | Mintage | F | VF | XF | Unc | BU |
|---|---|---|---|---|---|---|
| 1998 | 14,000 | — | — | — | 15.00 | — |
| 1998 Proof | 1,500 | Value: 35.00 | | | | |

**200 KORUN** **KM# 45** **Weight:** 20.0000 g. **Composition:** 0.7500 Silver .4823 oz. ASW **Subject:** Centennial - Birth of Jan Smrek **Obverse:** Seated female figure **Edge Lettering:** BASNIK JAN SMREK 100 VYROCIE NARODENIA

| Date | Mintage | F | VF | XF | Unc | BU |
|---|---|---|---|---|---|---|
| 1998 | 13,000 | — | — | — | 15.00 | — |
| 1998 Proof | 1,500 | Value: 35.00 | | | | |

**200 KORUN** **KM# 48** **Weight:** 20.0000 g. **Composition:** 0.7500 Silver .4823 oz. ASW **Subject:** 150th Anniversary - Birth of Pavol Orszagh Hviezdoslav **Obverse:** Portrait of face made with tree tops **Reverse:** Portrait of the artist **Edge Lettering:** HEROLD SUITAJUCICH CASOV

| Date | Mintage | F | VF | XF | Unc | BU |
|---|---|---|---|---|---|---|
| 1999 | 13,000 | — | — | — | 15.00 | — |
| 1999 Proof | 1,400 | Value: 35.00 | | | | |

**200 KORUN** **KM# 49** **Weight:** 20.0000 g. **Composition:** 0.7500 Silver .4823 oz. ASW **Subject:** 50th Anniversary - Slovac Philharmonic **Obverse:** Pipe organ above national arms **Reverse:** Reduta building bay window **Edge Lettering:** HUDBA-UNIVERZALNA LUSTVA

| Date | Mintage | F | VF | XF | Unc | BU |
|---|---|---|---|---|---|---|
| 1999 | 13,000 | — | — | — | 15.00 | — |
| 1999 Proof | 1,400 | Value: 35.00 | | | | |

**200 KORUN** **KM# 55** **Weight:** 20.0000 g. **Composition:** 0.7500 Silver .4823 oz. ASW **Subject:** Juraj Fandly **Obverse:** Radiant book above arms **Reverse:** Portrait writing **Edge Lettering:** NOE SOLOU ANO MOCOU ALE MOJIM DUCHOM **Size:** 33.9 mm.

| Date | Mintage | F | VF | XF | Unc | BU |
|---|---|---|---|---|---|---|
| 2000 | — | — | — | — | 20.00 | — |
| 2000 Proof | — | Value: 35.00 | | | | |

**200 KORUN** **KM# 59** **Weight:** 20.0000 g. **Composition:** 0.7500 Silver .4823 oz. ASW **Subject:** Alexander Dubeck **Obverse:** National arms and tree **Reverse:** Portrait **Edge Lettering:** "BUDSKOST SLOBODA DEMOKRACIA" **Size:** 34 mm.

| Date | Mintage | F | VF | XF | Unc | BU |
|---|---|---|---|---|---|---|
| 2001 | 12,800 | — | — | — | 15.00 | — |
| 2001 Proof | 3,000 | Value: 30.00 | | | | |

**500 KORUN** **KM# 28** **Weight:** 33.6300 g. **Composition:** 0.9250 Silver 1.0001 oz. ASW **Subject:** Slovensky Raj National Park **Edge Lettering:** OCHRANA PRIRODY A. KRAJINY

| Date | Mintage | F | VF | XF | Unc | BU |
|---|---|---|---|---|---|---|
| 1994 | 28,000 | — | — | — | 35.00 | — |
| 1994 Proof | 2,400 | Value: 45.00 | | | | |

**500 KORUN** **KM# 39** **Weight:** 33.6300 g. **Composition:** 0.9250 Silver 1.0001 oz. ASW **Subject:** Pieninsky National Park **Obverse:** Butterfly **Edge Lettering:** OCHRANA PRIRODY A KRAJINA

| Date | Mintage | F | VF | XF | Unc | BU |
|---|---|---|---|---|---|---|
| 1997 | 15,000 | — | — | — | 45.00 | — |
| 1997 Proof | 1,700 | Value: 65.00 | | | | |

**500 KORUN** **KM# 47** **Weight:** 33.6300 g. **Composition:** 0.9250 Silver 1.0001 oz. ASW **Subject:** Tatransky National Park **Obverse:** Two tatran chamois and Leontopodium flowers **Edge Lettering:** OCHRANA PRIRODY A KRAJINY

| Date | Mintage | F | VF | XF | Unc | BU |
|---|---|---|---|---|---|---|
| 1999 | 12,000 | — | — | — | 42.00 | — |
| 1999 Proof | 1,400 | Value: 60.00 | | | | |

**500 KORUN** **KM# 50** **Weight:** 33.6300 g. **Composition:** 0.9250 Silver 1.0001 oz. ASW **Subject:** 500th Anniversary - First Thalers of Kremnica **Obverse:** Mining scene **Reverse:** Old coin designs and city view **Edge Lettering:** GUILDINER-PRED-CHODCA TOLÁRA

| Date | Mintage | F | VF | XF | Unc | BU |
|---|---|---|---|---|---|---|
| 1999 | 12,000 | — | — | — | 40.00 | — |
| 1999 Proof | 1,400 | Value: 60.00 | | | | |

**500 KORUN** **KM# 53** **Weight:** 33.6300 g. **Composition:** 0.9250 Silver 1.0001 oz. ASW **Subject:** 250th Anniversary - Dealth of Samuel Mikovini **Obverse:** Allegorical scene and map **Reverse:** Portrait and instruments **Edge Lettering:** KARTOGRAF - MATEMATIK - STAVITEL

| Date | Mintage | F | VF | XF | Unc | BU |
|---|---|---|---|---|---|---|
| 2000 | 12,000 | — | — | — | 40.00 | — |
| 2000 Proof | 1,400 | Value: 60.00 | | | | |

**500 KORUN** **KM# 56** **Weight:** 33.6300 g. **Composition:** 0.9250 Silver 1.0001 oz. ASW **Subject:** Mala Fatra National Park **Obverse:** National arms center of insect cross. **Reverse:** Orchid with mountain background. **Edge Lettering:** OCHRANA PRIRODY A KRAJINY. **Size:** 40 mm.

| Date | Mintage | F | VF | XF | Unc | BU |
|---|---|---|---|---|---|---|
| 2001 | 10,200 | — | — | — | 40.00 | — |
| 2001 Proof | 1,800 | Value: 60.00 | | | | |

**500 KORUN** **KM# 57** **Weight:** 31.1035 g. **Composition:** 0.9990 Silver 1.0000 oz. ASW **Subject:** Third Millennium **Obverse:** "The Universe" **Reverse:** Three hands **Edge:** Plain, triangular shape **Size:** 45 mm.

| Date | Mintage | F | VF | XF | Unc | BU |
|---|---|---|---|---|---|---|
| 2001 | 13,000 | — | — | — | 40.00 | — |
| 2001 Proof | 4,000 | Value: 60.00 | | | | |

**500 KORUN** **KM# 58** **Series:** Third Millennium **Obverse:** "The Universe" **Reverse:** Three hands **Edge:** Plain, triangular shape **Size:** 50 mm. **Note:** 31.1035, .999 Silver, 1.0000 oz ASW with 6,2200, .999 Gold, .1998 oz AGW and .3100, .999 Platinum, .0100 oz APW inserts.

| Date | Mintage | F | VF | XF | Unc | BU |
|---|---|---|---|---|---|---|
| 2001 Proof | 8,000 | Value: 400 | | | | |

**2000 KORUN** **KM# 51** **Weight:** 124.4140 g. **Composition:** 0.9990 Silver 3.9960 oz. ASW **Subject:** 2000 Bi-millennium **Obverse:** National arms, denomination, historical scenes **Reverse:** Jesus with churches

| Date | Mintage | F | VF | XF | Unc | BU |
|---|---|---|---|---|---|---|
| MM(2000) Proof | Est. 2,000 | Value: 200 | | | | |

**5000 KORUN** **KM# 29** **Weight:** 7.0000 g. **Composition:** 0.9000 Gold .2025 oz. AGW **Subject:** 1100th Anniversary - Death of Great Moravian King Svatopluk

| Date | Mintage | F | VF | XF | Unc | BU |
|---|---|---|---|---|---|---|
| 1994 Proof | 5,000 | Value: 500 | | | | |

**5000 KORUN** **KM# 36** **Weight:** 9.5000 g. **Composition:** 0.9000 Gold .2749 oz. AGW **Subject:** Banska Stiavnica Historical Mines - UNESCO

| Date | Mintage | F | VF | XF | Unc | BU |
|---|---|---|---|---|---|---|
| 1997 Proof | 8,000 | Value: 325 | | | | |

**5000 KORUN** **KM# 46** **Weight:** 9.5000 g. **Composition:** 0.9000 Gold .2749 oz. AGW **Subject:** Spissky Castle - UNESCO

| Date | Mintage | F | VF | XF | Unc | BU |
|---|---|---|---|---|---|---|
| 1998 Proof | 6,000 | Value: 300 | | | | |

**5000 KORUN** **KM# 54** **Weight:** 9.5000 g. **Composition:** 0.9000 Gold .2749 oz. AGW **Subject:** 500th Anniversary - Kremnica Mint **Obverse:** Hungarian coin design **Reverse:** Hungarian coin design **Edge:** Reeded

| Date | Mintage | F | VF | XF | Unc | BU |
|---|---|---|---|---|---|---|
| ND(1999) Proof | 5,500 | Value: 325 | | | | |

**10000 KORUN** **KM# 52** **Weight:** 19.0000 g. **Composition:** 0.9000 Gold .5498 oz. AGW **Subject:** 2000 Bi-millennium **Obverse:** National arms, denomination, historical scenes **Reverse:** Jesus with churches **Note:** Similar to 2000 Korun, KM#51.

| Date | Mintage | F | VF | XF | Unc | BU |
|---|---|---|---|---|---|---|
| MM(2000) Proof | Est. 3,500 | Value: 600 | | | | |

## ESSAIS

| KM# | Date | Mintage | Identification | Mkt Val |
|---|---|---|---|---|
| E1 | 1939 | — | 20 Korun. 0.5000 Silver. KM#7 | — |
| E2 | 1941 | — | 10 Korun. 0.5000 Silver. KM#9.1 | — |

## MINT SETS

| KM# | Date | Mintage | Identification | Issue Price | Mkt Val |
|---|---|---|---|---|---|
| MS1 | 1993 (7) | — | KM#11.1-15, 17-18, plus medal | — | 12.00 |
| MS2 | 1994 (7) | — | KM#11.1-15, 17-18, plus medal | — | 12.00 |
| MS3 | 1995 (7) | — | KM#11.1-15, 17-18, plus medal | — | 12.00 |
| MS4 | 1996 (7) | — | KM#11.1-15, 17-18, plus medal | — | 12.00 |
| MS5 | 1997 (7) | — | KM#11.1-15, 17-18, plus medal | — | 12.00 |
| MS6 | 1998 (7) | — | KM#11.1-15, 17-18, plus medal | — | 12.00 |
| MS7 | 1999 (7) | — | KM#11.1-15, 17-18, plus medal | — | 12.00 |
| MS8 | 2000 (7) | 13,000 | KM#11.1-15, plus medal | — | 12.00 |

The Republic of Slovenia is located northwest of Yugoslavia in the valleys of the Danube River. It has an area of 7,819 sq. mi. and a population of *1.9 million. Capital: Ljubljana. Agriculture is the main industry with large amounts of hops and fodder crops grown as well as many varieties of fruit trees. Sheep raising, timber production and the mining of mercury from one of the country's oldest mines are also very important to the economy.

Slovenia was important as a land route between Europe and the eastern Mediterranean region. The Roman Catholic Austro-Hungarian Empire gained control of the area during the 14th century and retained its dominance until World War I. The United Kingdom of the Serbs, Croats and Slovenes (Yugoslavia) was founded in 1918 and consisted of various groups of South Slavs.

In 1929, King Alexander declared his assumption of power temporarily, however he was assassinated in 1934.His son Peter's regent, Prince Paul tried to settle internal problems, however, the Slovenes denounced the agreement he made. He resigned in 1941 and Peter assumed the throne. Peter was forced to flee when Yugoslavia was occupied. Slovenia was divided between Germany and Italy. Even though Yugoslavia attempted to remain neutral, the Nazis occupied the country and were resisted by guerilla armies, most notably Marshal Josif Broz Tito.

Under Marshal Tito, the Constitution of 1946 established6 constituent republics which made up Yugoslavia. Each republic was permitted Liberties under supervision of the Communist Party.

In Oct. 1989 the Slovene Assembly voted a constitutional amendment giving it the right to secede from Yugoslavia. A referendum on Dec. 23, 1990 resulted in a majority vote for independence, which was formally declared on Dec. 26.

On June 25 Slovenia declared independence, but agreed to suspend this for3 months at peace talks sponsored by the EC. Federal troops moved into Slovenia on June 27 to secure Yugoslavia's external borders, but after some fighting withdrew by the end of July. The 3-month moratorium agreed at the EC having expired, Slovenia (and Croatia) declared their complete independence of the Yugoslav federation on Oct.8, 1991.

**MINT MARKS**

Based on last digit in date.
(K) - Kremnitz (Slovakia): open 4, upturned 5
(BP) - Budapest (Hungary): closed 4, downturned 5

**MONETARY SYSTEM**

100 Stotinov = 1 Tolar

# REPUBLIC

## STANDARD COINAGE

100 Stotinow = 1 Tolar

**10 STOTINOV** **KM# 7** **Composition:** Aluminum **Reverse:** Salamandar - larval stage **Note:** Varieties exist.

| Date | Mintage | F | VF | XF | Unc | BU |
|---|---|---|---|---|---|---|
| 1992 | 2,515,000 | — | — | — | 0.25 | — |
| 1992 Proof | 1,000 | Value: 3.00 | | | | |
| 1993 | 2,515,000 | — | — | — | 0.25 | — |
| 1993 Proof | 1,000 | Value: 3.00 | | | | |
| 1994 In sets only | 1,000 | — | — | — | — | 3.00 |
| 1994 Proof | 1,000 | Value: 3.00 | | | | |
| 1995 In sets only | 1,000 | — | — | — | — | 3.00 |
| 1995 Proof | 1,000 | Value: 3.00 | | | | |

**20 STOTINOV** **KM# 8** **Composition:** Aluminum **Obverse:** Similar to 10 Stotinov, KM#7 **Reverse:** Long-eared owl **Note:** Minor reverse varieties exist for 1992 and 1993.

| Date | Mintage | F | VF | XF | Unc | BU |
|---|---|---|---|---|---|---|
| 1992 | 2,515,000 | — | — | — | 0.25 | — |
| 1992 Proof | 1,000 | Value: 4.00 | | | | |
| 1993 | 2,515,000 | — | — | — | 0.25 | — |
| 1993 Proof | 1,000 | Value: 4.00 | | | | |
| 1994 In sets only | 1,000 | — | — | — | — | 4.00 |
| 1994 Proof | 1,000 | Value: 4.00 | | | | |
| 1995 In sets only | 1,000 | — | — | — | — | 4.00 |
| 1995 Proof | 1,000 | Value: 4.00 | | | | |

**50 STOTINOV** **KM# 3** **Composition:** Aluminum **Reverse:** Bee **Note:** Minor reverse varieties exist for 1992.

| Date | Mintage | F | VF | XF | Unc | BU |
|---|---|---|---|---|---|---|
| 1992 | 5,015,000 | — | — | 0.10 | 0.35 | — |
| 1992 Proof | 1,000 | Value: 6.00 | | | | |
| 1993 | 18,315,000 | — | — | 0.10 | 0.35 | — |
| 1993 Proof | 1,000 | Value: 6.00 | | | | |
| 1994 In sets only | 1,000 | — | — | — | — | 6.00 |
| 1994 Proof | 1,000 | Value: 6.00 | | | | |
| 1995 | 3,000,000 | — | — | 0.10 | 0.35 | — |
| 1995 In sets only | 1,000 | — | — | — | — | 6.00 |
| 1995 Proof | 1,000 | Value: 6.00 | | | | |
| 1996 | 3,000,000 | — | — | 0.10 | 0.35 | — |
| 1996 Proof | Est. 3,000 | Value: 6.00 | | | | |

**TOLAR** **KM# 4** **Composition:** Brass **Reverse:** 3 brown trout **Note:** Varieties exist.

| Date | Mintage | F | VF | XF | Unc | BU |
|---|---|---|---|---|---|---|
| 1992 | 10,015,000 | — | — | 0.20 | 0.65 | — |
| 1992 Proof | 1,000 | Value: 5.00 | | | | |
| 1993 | 30,015,000 | — | — | 0.20 | 0.65 | — |
| 1993 Proof | 1,000 | Value: 5.00 | | | | |
| 1994 (K) 4 open to the top | 10,000,000 | — | — | — | 0.50 | — |
| 1994 (K) 4 open to right, in sets only | 1,000 | — | — | — | — | 5.00 |
| 1994 (K) 4 open to right, proof | 1,000 | Value: 5.00 | | | | |
| 1994 (BP) | 5,000,000 | — | — | — | 0.50 | — |
| 1995 (K) | 10,000,000 | — | — | — | 0.50 | — |
| 1995 (K) In sets only | 1,000 | — | — | — | — | 5.00 |
| 1995 (K) Proof | 1,000 | Value: 5.00 | | | | |
| 1995 (BP) | 10,000,000 | — | — | — | 0.50 | — |
| 1996 | Est. 21,800,000 | — | — | — | 0.50 | — |
| 1996 Proof | Est. 3,000 | Value: 5.00 | | | | |
| 1997 | 8,000,000 | — | — | — | 0.50 | — |
| 1998 | 12,000,000 | — | — | — | 0.50 | — |
| 1999 | 8,000,000 | — | — | — | 0.50 | — |
| 2000 | Est. 15,000,000 | — | — | — | 0.50 | — |

**2 TOLARJA** **KM# 5** **Composition:** Brass **Reverse:** Barn swallow in flight **Note:** Minor varieties exist for each date after 1998.

| Date | Mintage | F | VF | XF | Unc | BU |
|---|---|---|---|---|---|---|
| 1992 | 5,015,000 | — | — | 0.25 | 0.75 | — |
| 1992 Proof | 1,000 | Value: 7.00 | | | | |
| 1993 | 10,015,000 | — | — | 0.25 | 0.75 | — |
| 1993 Proof | 1,000 | Value: 7.00 | | | | |
| 1994 (K) 4 open to the top | 10,000,000 | — | — | — | 0.65 | — |
| 1994 (K) 4 open to right, in sets only | 1,000 | — | — | — | — | 7.00 |
| 1994 (K) 4 open to right, proof | 1,000 | Value: 7.00 | | | | |
| 1994 (BP) | 5,000,000 | — | — | — | 0.65 | — |
| 1995 (K) | 10,000,000 | — | — | — | 0.65 | — |
| 1995 (K) In sets only | 1,000 | — | — | — | — | 7.00 |
| 1995 (K) Proof | 1,000 | Value: 7.00 | | | | |
| 1995 (BP) | 10,000,000 | — | — | — | 0.65 | — |
| 1996 | Est. 16,600,000 | — | — | — | 0.65 | — |
| 1996 Proof | 1,000 | Value: 7.00 | | | | |
| 1997 | 6,060,000 | — | — | — | 0.65 | — |
| 1998 | 5,000,000 | — | — | — | 0.65 | — |
| 1999 | 5,200,000 | — | — | — | 0.65 | — |
| 2000 | Est. 15,000,000 | — | — | — | 0.65 | — |

**5 TOLARJEV** **KM# 6** **Composition:** Brass **Reverse:** Head and horns of ibex **Note:** Varieties exist.

| Date | Mintage | F | VF | XF | Unc | BU |
|---|---|---|---|---|---|---|
| 1992 | 10,015,000 | — | — | 0.35 | 1.00 | — |
| 1992 Proof | 1,000 | Value: 8.00 | | | | |
| 1993 | 10,015,000 | — | — | 0.35 | 1.00 | — |
| 1993 Proof | 1,000 | Value: 8.00 | | | | |
| 1994 (K) 4 open to the top | 10,000,000 | — | — | — | 0.85 | — |
| 1994 (K) 4 open to right, in sets only | 1,000 | — | — | — | — | 8.00 |
| 1994 (K) 4 open to right, proof | 1,000 | Value: 8.00 | | | | |
| 1994 (BP) | 5,000,000 | — | — | — | 0.85 | — |
| 1995 | 5,000,000 | — | — | — | 0.85 | — |
| 1996 | 6,000,000 | — | — | — | 0.85 | — |
| 1996 Proof | Est. 3,000 | Value: 8.00 | | | | |
| 1997 | 8,000,000 | — | — | — | 0.85 | — |
| 1998 | 10,000,000 | — | — | — | 0.85 | — |
| 1999 | 6,403,000 | — | — | — | 0.85 | — |

**5 TOLARJEV** **KM# 9** **Composition:** Brass **Subject:** Battle of Sisek

| Date | Mintage | F | VF | XF | Unc | BU |
|---|---|---|---|---|---|---|
| 1993 | 100,000 | — | — | — | 1.65 | — |

**5 TOLARJEV** **KM# 12** **Composition:** Brass **Subject:** Operosorum Labacensium Academy

| Date | Mintage | F | VF | XF | Unc | BU |
|---|---|---|---|---|---|---|
| 1993 | 100,000 | — | — | — | 1.65 | — |

**5 TOLARJEV** **KM# 15** **Composition:** Brass **Subject:** 50th anniversary - Slovenian Bank

| Date | Mintage | F | VF | XF | Unc | BU |
|---|---|---|---|---|---|---|
| 1994 | 100,000 | — | — | — | 1.65 | — |

**5 TOLARJEV** **KM# 16** **Composition:** Brass **Subject:** 1,000th anniversary - Glagolitic alphabet

| Date | Mintage | F | VF | XF | Unc | BU |
|---|---|---|---|---|---|---|
| 1994 | 200,000 | — | — | — | 1.65 | — |

**5 TOLARJEV** **KM# 21** **Composition:** Brass **Series:** F.A.O. **Subject:** 50th anniversary - F.A.O.

| Date | Mintage | F | VF | XF | Unc | BU |
|---|---|---|---|---|---|---|
| 1995 | 500,000 | — | — | — | 1.65 | — |

**5 TOLARJEV** **KM# 22** **Composition:** Brass **Subject:** 50th anniversary - defeat of Fascism

| Date | Mintage | F | VF | XF | Unc | BU |
|---|---|---|---|---|---|---|
| 1995 | 200,000 | — | — | — | 1.65 | — |

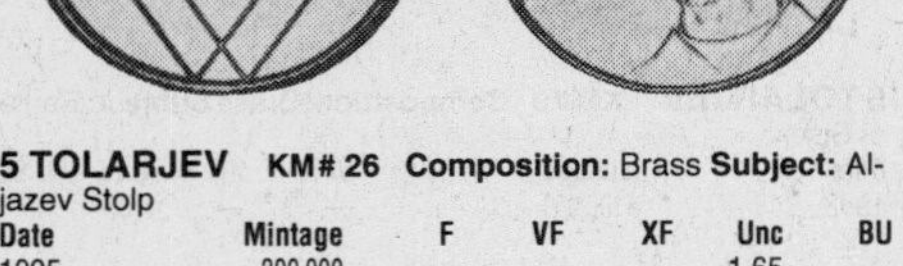


**5 TOLARJEV** **KM# 26** **Composition:** Brass **Subject:** Aljazev Stolp

| Date | Mintage | F | VF | XF | Unc | BU |
|---|---|---|---|---|---|---|
| 1995 | 200,000 | — | — | — | 1.65 | — |

**5 TOLARJEV** **KM# 29** **Composition:** Brass **Subject:** 100th anniversary - first railway in Slovenia

| Date | Mintage | F | VF | XF | Unc | BU |
|---|---|---|---|---|---|---|
| 1996 | Est. 300,000 | — | — | — | 1.65 | — |
| 1996 Proof | Inc. above | Value: 8.00 | | | | |

**5 TOLARJEV** **KM# 32** **Composition:** Brass **Subject:** 5th anniversary of independence **Reverse:** Stylized flower

| Date | Mintage | F | VF | XF | Unc | BU |
|---|---|---|---|---|---|---|
| 1996 | 200,000 | — | — | — | 1.65 | — |
| 1996 Proof | — | Value: 8.00 | | | | |

**5 TOLARJEV** **KM# 33** **Composition:** Brass **Series:** Olympics **Subject:** Olympics centennial **Reverse:** Gymnast

| Date | Mintage | F | VF | XF | Unc | BU |
|---|---|---|---|---|---|---|
| 1996 | 200,000 | — | — | — | 1.65 | — |
| 1996 Proof | Est. 3,000 | Value: 8.00 | | | | |

**5 TOLARJEV** **KM# 38** **Composition:** Brass **Subject:** Ziga Zois **Obverse:** Denomination

| Date | Mintage | F | VF | XF | Unc | BU |
|---|---|---|---|---|---|---|
| 1997 | 200,000 | — | — | — | 1.65 | — |

**500 TOLARJEV** **KM# 1** **Weight:** 15.0000 g. **Composition:** 0.9250 Silver .4461 oz. ASW **Subject:** 1st anniversary of independence **Note:** Eight minor obverse and reverse varieties exist.

| Date | Mintage | F | VF | XF | Unc | BU |
|---|---|---|---|---|---|---|
| 1991 Proof | 50,000 | Value: 35.00 | | | | |

**500 TOLARJEV** **KM# 10** **Weight:** 15.0000 g. **Composition:** 0.9250 Silver .4461 oz. ASW **Subject:** Battle of Sisek

| Date | Mintage | F | VF | XF | Unc | BU |
|---|---|---|---|---|---|---|
| 1993 Proof | Est. 5,000 | Value: 28.50 | | | | |

**500 TOLARJEV** **KM# 13** **Weight:** 15.0000 g. **Composition:** 0.9250 Silver .4461 oz. ASW **Subject:** Operasorum Labacensium Academy

| Date | Mintage | F | VF | XF | Unc | BU |
|---|---|---|---|---|---|---|
| 1993 Proof | 5,000 | Value: 28.50 | | | | |

**500 TOLARJEV** **KM# 17** **Weight:** 15.0000 g. **Composition:** 0.9250 Silver .4461 oz. ASW **Subject:** 50th anniversary - Slovenian Bank

| Date | Mintage | F | VF | XF | Unc | BU |
|---|---|---|---|---|---|---|
| 1994 Proof | 5,000 | Value: 28.50 | | | | |

**500 TOLARJEV** **KM# 19** **Weight:** 15.0000 g. **Composition:** 0.9250 Silver .4461 oz. ASW **Subject:** 1000th Anniversary - Bishop Abraham - Glagolistic alphabet

| Date | Mintage | F | VF | XF | Unc | BU |
|---|---|---|---|---|---|---|
| 1994 Proof | 3,000 | Value: 28.50 | | | | |

**500 TOLARJEV** **KM# 23** **Weight:** 15.0000 g. **Composition:** 0.9250 Silver .4461 oz. ASW **Subject:** 50th anniversary - defeat of Fascism

| Date | Mintage | F | VF | XF | Unc | BU |
|---|---|---|---|---|---|---|
| 1995 Proof | 3,000 | Value: 28.50 | | | | |

**500 TOLARJEV** **KM# 25** **Weight:** 15.0000 g. **Composition:** 0.9250 Silver .4461 oz. ASW **Series:** F.A.O. **Subject:** 50th anniversary - F.A.O.

| Date | Mintage | F | VF | XF | Unc | BU |
|---|---|---|---|---|---|---|
| 1995 Proof | 3,000 | Value: 28.50 | | | | |

**500 TOLARJEV** **KM# 27** **Weight:** 15.0000 g. **Composition:** 0.9250 Silver .4461 oz. ASW **Subject:** 100th anniversary - Aljazev Stolp

| Date | Mintage | F | VF | XF | Unc | BU |
|---|---|---|---|---|---|---|
| 1995 Proof | 3,000 | Value: 28.50 | | | | |

**500 TOLARJEV** **KM# 30** **Weight:** 15.0000 g. **Composition:** 0.9250 Silver .4461 oz. ASW **Subject:** 100th anniversary - first railway in Slovenia

| Date | Mintage | F | VF | XF | Unc | BU |
|---|---|---|---|---|---|---|
| 1996 Proof | 3,000 | Value: 28.50 | | | | |

**500 TOLARJEV** **KM# 34** **Weight:** 15.0000 g. **Composition:** 0.9250 Silver .4461 oz. ASW **Subject:** 5th anniversary of independence **Obverse:** Map of Slovenia **Reverse:** Globe

| Date | Mintage | F | VF | XF | Unc | BU |
|---|---|---|---|---|---|---|
| 1996 Proof | 3,000 | Value: 28.50 | | | | |

**500 TOLARJEV** **KM# 36** **Weight:** 15.0000 g. **Composition:** 0.9250 Silver .4461 oz. ASW **Series:** Olympics **Reverse:** Gymnast

| Date | Mintage | F | VF | XF | Unc | BU |
|---|---|---|---|---|---|---|
| 1996 Proof | 3,000 | Value: 27.50 | | | | |

**500 TOLARJEV** **KM# 39** **Weight:** 15.0000 g. **Composition:** 0.9250 Silver .4461 oz. ASW **Subject:** Zois Ziga

| Date | Mintage | F | VF | XF | Unc | BU |
|---|---|---|---|---|---|---|
| 1997 Proof | 3,000 | Value: 28.50 | | | | |

**5000 TOLARJEV** **KM# 2.1** **Weight:** 7.0000 g. **Composition:** 0.9000 Gold .2025 oz. AGW **Subject:** 1st anniversary of independence **Reverse:** Bird's beak at center of spiral

| Date | Mintage | F | VF | XF | Unc | BU |
|---|---|---|---|---|---|---|
| 1991 Proof | 4,000 | Value: 225 | | | | |

**5000 TOLARJEV** **KM# 2.2** **Weight:** 7.0000 g. **Composition:** 0.9000 Gold .2025 oz. AGW **Reverse:** Bird's beak lower than center of spiral

| Date | Mintage | F | VF | XF | Unc | BU |
|---|---|---|---|---|---|---|
| 1991 Proof | Inc. above | Value: 200 | | | | |

**5000 TOLARJEV** **KM# 11** **Weight:** 7.0000 g. **Composition:** 0.9000 Gold .2025 oz. AGW **Subject:** Battle of Sisek

| Date | Mintage | F | VF | XF | Unc | BU |
|---|---|---|---|---|---|---|
| 1993 Proof | Est. 2,000 | Value: 200 | | | | |

**5000 TOLARJEV** **KM# 14** **Weight:** 7.0000 g. **Composition:** 0.9000 Gold .2025 oz. AGW **Subject:** Operosorum Labacensium Academy

| Date | Mintage | F | VF | XF | Unc | BU |
|---|---|---|---|---|---|---|
| 1993 Proof | 2,000 | Value: 210 | | | | |

**5000 TOLARJEV** **KM# 18** **Weight:** 7.0000 g. **Composition:** 0.9000 Gold .2025 oz. AGW **Subject:** 50th anniversary - Slovenian Bank

| Date | Mintage | F | VF | XF | Unc | BU |
|---|---|---|---|---|---|---|
| 1994 Proof | 2,000 | Value: 200 | | | | |

**5000 TOLARJEV** **KM# 20** **Weight:** 7.0000 g. **Composition:** 0.9000 Gold .2025 oz. AGW **Subject:** 1000th anniversary - Bishop Abraham - Glagolitic alphabet

| Date | Mintage | F | VF | XF | Unc | BU |
|---|---|---|---|---|---|---|
| 1994 Proof | 1,000 | Value: 200 | | | | |

**5000 TOLARJEV** **KM# 24** **Weight:** 7.0000 g. **Composition:** 0.9000 Gold .2025 oz. AGW **Subject:** 50th anniversary - defeat of Fascism

| Date | Mintage | F | VF | XF | Unc | BU |
|---|---|---|---|---|---|---|
| 1995 Proof | 1,000 | Value: 200 | | | | |

**5000 TOLARJEV** **KM# 28** **Weight:** 7.0000 g. **Composition:** 0.9000 Gold .2025 oz. AGW **Subject:** Aljazev Stolp and Mountain Summit

| Date | Mintage | F | VF | XF | Unc | BU |
|---|---|---|---|---|---|---|
| 1995 Proof | 1,000 | Value: 200 | | | | |

**5000 TOLARJEV** **KM# 31** **Weight:** 7.0000 g. **Composition:** 0.9000 Gold .2025 oz. AGW **Subject:** 100th anniversary - first railway in Slovenia

| Date | Mintage | F | VF | XF | Unc | BU |
|---|---|---|---|---|---|---|
| 1996 Proof | 1,000 | Value: 210 | | | | |

**5000 TOLARJEV** **KM# 35** **Weight:** 7.0000 g. **Composition:** 0.9000 Gold .2025 oz. AGW **Subject:** 5th anniversary of independence **Reverse:** 5-petal flower

| Date | Mintage | F | VF | XF | Unc | BU |
|---|---|---|---|---|---|---|
| 1996 Proof | 1,000 | Value: 200 | | | | |

**5000 TOLARJEV** **KM# 37** **Weight:** 7.0000 g. **Composition:** 0.9000 Gold .2025 oz. AGW **Series:** Olympics **Reverse:** Gymnast

| Date | Mintage | F | VF | XF | Unc | BU |
|---|---|---|---|---|---|---|
| 1996 Proof | 1,000 | Value: 225 | | | | |

**5000 TOLARJEV** **KM# 40** **Weight:** 7.0000 g. **Composition:** 0.9000 Gold .2025 oz. AGW **Subject:** Zois Ziga

| Date | Mintage | F | VF | XF | Unc | BU |
|---|---|---|---|---|---|---|
| 1997 Proof | 1,000 | Value: 200 | | | | |

## TOKEN COINAGE

100 Vinar = 1 Lipa

**VINAR** **KM# Tn1** **Composition:** Copper-Zinc

| Date | Mintage | F | VF | XF | Unc | BU |
|---|---|---|---|---|---|---|
| 1990 | 6,000 | — | — | — | 20.00 | — |

**2/1000 LIPE** **KM# Tn4** **Composition:** Copper-Zinc

| Date | Mintage | F | VF | XF | Unc | BU |
|---|---|---|---|---|---|---|
| 1991 Fewer than 5 known | | — | — | — | — | — |

**0.02 LIPE** **KM# Tn5** **Composition:** Brass **Note:** Some examples of KM#Tn5 have been found struck over Yugoslavian 10 Para 1990, KM#139.

| Date | Mintage | F | VF | XF | Unc | BU |
|---|---|---|---|---|---|---|
| 1992 | — | — | — | — | 2.00 | — |

**0.02 LIPE** **KM# Tn11** **Composition:** Brass

| Date | Mintage | F | VF | XF | Unc | BU |
|---|---|---|---|---|---|---|
| 1992 | — | — | — | — | 4.00 | — |

**0.05 LIPE** **KM# Tn6** **Composition:** Brass

| Date | Mintage | F | VF | XF | Unc | BU |
|---|---|---|---|---|---|---|
| 1991 | 5,000 | — | — | — | 4.00 | — |

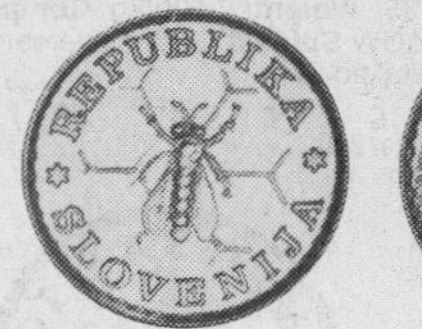

**0.10 LIPE** **KM# Tn7** **Composition:** Brass

| Date | Mintage | F | VF | XF | Unc | BU |
|---|---|---|---|---|---|---|
| 1991 | 5,000 | — | — | — | 5.00 | — |

**0.20 LIPE** **KM# Tn8** **Composition:** Copper-Nickel

| Date | Mintage | F | VF | XF | Unc | BU |
|---|---|---|---|---|---|---|
| 1991 | 5,000 | — | — | — | 7.00 | — |

**0.50 LIPE** **KM# Tn9** **Composition:** Copper-Nickel

| Date | Mintage | F | VF | XF | Unc | BU |
|---|---|---|---|---|---|---|
| 1991 | — | — | — | — | — | — |

**LIPA** **KM# Tn2** **Weight:** 11.0000 g. **Composition:** 0.9250 Silver .3272 oz. ASW **Subject:** Dr. France Preseren

| Date | Mintage | F | VF | XF | Unc | BU |
|---|---|---|---|---|---|---|
| 1990 Proof | 10,000 | Value: 50.00 | | | | |

**10 LIP** **KM# Tn10** **Weight:** 6.7500 g. **Composition:** 0.9000 Gold .1953 oz. AGW **Reverse:** Ivan Cankar bust facing left

| Date | Mintage | F | VF | XF | Unc | BU |
|---|---|---|---|---|---|---|
| 1991 Proof | 273 | Value: 325 | | | | |

**50 LIP** **KM# Tn3** **Weight:** 11.0000 g. **Composition:** 0.9000 Gold .3183 oz. AGW **Reverse:** Ivan Cankar bust facing forward

| Date | Mintage | F | VF | XF | Unc | BU |
|---|---|---|---|---|---|---|
| 1990 Proof | 400 | Value: 400 | | | | |

## MINT SETS

| KM# | Date | Mintage | Identification | Issue Price | Mkt Val |
|---|---|---|---|---|---|
| MS1 | 1992 (6) | — | KM3-8 | — | 8.00 |
| MS2 | 1992 (5) | 15,000 | KM4-8 | — | 7.00 |
| MS3 | 1993 (6) | — | KM3-8 | — | 8.00 |
| MS4 | 1993 (5) | 15,000 | KM4-8 | — | 7.00 |
| MS6 | 1994 | 1,000 | KM3-8 | — | 35.00 |
| MS7 | 1995 | 1,000 | KM3-8 | — | 35.00 |
| MS5 | 1996 (9) | 300 | KM4-6, 29-30, 32-34, 36 | — | 45.00 |

## PROOF SETS

| KM# | Date | Mintage | Identification | Issue Price | Mkt Val |
|---|---|---|---|---|---|
| PS1 | 1991 (2) | — | KM1, 2.2 | — | 325 |
| PS2 | 1992 (6) | 1,000 | KM3-8 | — | 35.00 |
| PS3 | 1992 (5) | 1,000 | KM4-8 | — | 30.00 |
| PS4 | 1993 (6) | 1,000 | KM3-8 | — | 35.00 |
| PS5 | 1993 (5) | 1,000 | KM4-8 | — | 30.00 |
| PS7 | 1994 | 1,000 | KM3-8 | — | 35.00 |
| PS8 | 1995 | 1,000 | KM3-8 | — | 35.00 |
| PS6 | 1996 (9) | 3,000 | KM4-6, 29-30, 32-34, 36 | — | 125 |

# SOLOMON ISLANDS

The Solomon Islands, located in the southwest Pacific east of Papua New Guinea, has an area of 10,983 sq. mi. (28,450 sq. km.) and a population of *324,000. Capital: Honiara. The most important islands of the Solomon chain are Guadalcanal (scene of some of the fiercest fighting of World War II), Malaitia, New Georgia, Florida, Vella Lavella, Choiseul, Rendova, San Cristobal, the Lord Howe group, the Santa Cruz islands, and the Duff group. Copra is the only important cash crop but it is hoped that timber will become an economic factor.

The Solomon Islands were discovered by Spanish navigator Alvaro de Mendana in 1567, and in 1569 he made an unsuccessful attempt to colonize them. European know-ledge of the group would not be completed until the end of the 18th century. Germany declared a protectorate over the northern Solomons in 1885. The British protectorate over the southern Solomons was established in 1893. In1899 Germany transferred its claim to all Solomon Islands except Buka and Bougainville to Great Britain in exchange for recognition of German claims in Western Samoa. Australia occupied the two German islands in 1914, and administered them after1920.

The Japanese invaded the Solomons during 1942-43,but were driven out by an American counteroffensive after a series of bloody clashes.

Following World War II, the islands returned to the status of a British protectorate. In 1976 the protectorate was abolished, and the Solomons became a self-governing dependency. Full independence was achieved on July 7,1978. Solomon Islands is a member of the Common-wealth of Nations. Queen Elizabeth II is Head of State, as Queen of the Solomon Islands.

**RULERS**

British, until 1978

**MINT MARKS**

FM - Franklin Mint, U.S.A.*

**NOTE:** From 1977-1985 the Franklin Mint produced coinage in up to 3 different qualities. Qualities of issue are designated in ( ) after each date and are defined as follows:

**(M) MATTE** - Normal circulation strike or a dull finish produced by sandblasting special uncirculated (polish finish) or proof quality dies.

**(U) - SPECIAL UNCIRCULATED** - Polished or proof-like in appearance without any frosted features.

**(P) PROOF** - The highest quality obtainable having mirror-like fields and frosted features.

**MONETARY SYSTEM**

100 Cents = 1 Dollar

# COMMONWEALTH NATION

## STANDARD COINAGE

100 Cents = 1 Dollar

**CENT** **KM# 1** **Composition:** Bronze **Series:** F.A.O. **Reverse:** Food bowl

| Date | Mintage | F | VF | XF | Unc | BU |
|---|---|---|---|---|---|---|
| 1977 | 1,828,000 | — | — | 0.10 | 0.20 | — |
| 1977FM (M) | 6,000 | — | — | — | 0.50 | — |
| 1977FM (U) | — | — | — | — | 2.00 | — |
| 1977FM (P) | 14,000 | Value: 1.00 | | | | |
| 1978FM (M) | 6,000 | — | — | — | 0.50 | — |
| 1978FM (U) | 544 | — | — | — | 2.00 | — |
| 1978FM (P) | 5,122 | Value: 1.00 | | | | |
| 1979FM (M) | 6,000 | — | — | — | 0.50 | — |
| 1979FM (U) | 677 | — | — | — | 2.00 | — |
| 1979FM (P) | 2,845 | Value: 1.50 | | | | |
| 1980FM (M) | 6,000 | — | — | — | 0.50 | — |
| 1980FM (U) | 624 | — | — | — | 2.00 | — |
| 1980FM (P) | 1,031 | Value: 1.50 | | | | |
| 1981 | — | — | — | — | 0.50 | — |
| 1981FM (M) | 6,000 | — | — | — | 0.50 | — |
| 1981FM (U) | 212 | — | — | — | 2.00 | — |
| 1981FM (P) | 448 | Value: 1.50 | | | | |
| 1982FM (U) | — | — | — | — | 2.00 | — |
| 1982FM (P) | — | Value: 1.50 | | | | |
| 1983FM (M) | — | — | — | — | 0.50 | — |
| 1983FM (U) | 200 | — | — | — | 3.00 | — |
| 1983FM (P) | — | Value: 1.50 | | | | |

**CENT** **KM# 1a** **Composition:** Bronze Plated Steel **Series:** F.A.O. **Reverse:** Food bowl

| Date | Mintage | F | VF | XF | Unc | BU |
|---|---|---|---|---|---|---|
| 1985 | — | — | — | — | 0.35 | — |

**CENT** **KM# 24** **Composition:** Bronze Plated Steel **Series:** F.A.O. **Reverse:** Food bowl

| Date | Mintage | F | VF | XF | Unc | BU |
|---|---|---|---|---|---|---|
| 1987 | — | — | — | — | 0.35 | — |
| 1996 | — | — | — | — | 0.35 | — |

**2 CENTS** **KM# 2** **Composition:** Bronze **Subject:** Eagle Spirit of Malaita

| Date | Mintage | F | VF | XF | Unc | BU |
|---|---|---|---|---|---|---|
| 1977 | 2,400,000 | — | — | 0.10 | 0.25 | — |
| 1977FM (M) | 6,000 | — | — | — | 0.75 | — |
| 1977FM (U) | — | — | — | — | 3.00 | — |
| 1977FM (P) | 14,000 | Value: 1.50 | | | | |
| 1978FM (M) | 6,000 | — | — | — | 0.75 | — |
| 1978FM (U) | 544 | — | — | — | 3.00 | — |
| 1978FM (P) | 5,122 | Value: 1.50 | | | | |
| 1979FM (M) | 6,000 | — | — | — | 0.75 | — |
| 1979FM (U) | 677 | — | — | — | 3.00 | — |
| 1979FM (P) | 2,845 | Value: 2.00 | | | | |
| 1980FM (M) | 6,000 | — | — | — | 0.75 | — |
| 1980FM (U) | 624 | — | — | — | 3.00 | — |
| 1980FM (P) | 1,031 | — | — | — | 2.00 | — |
| 1981FM (M) | 6,000 | — | — | — | 0.75 | — |
| 1981FM (U) | 212 | — | — | — | 3.00 | — |
| 1981FM (P) | 448 | Value: 2.00 | | | | |
| 1982FM (U) | — | — | — | — | 3.00 | — |
| 1982FM (P) | — | Value: 2.00 | | | | |
| 1983FM (M) | — | — | — | — | 0.75 | — |
| 1983FM (U) | 200 | — | — | — | 3.00 | — |
| 1983FM (P) | — | Value: 2.00 | | | | |

**2 CENTS** **KM# 2a** **Composition:** Bronze Plated Steel **Subject:** Eagle Spirit of Malaita

| Date | Mintage | F | VF | XF | Unc | BU |
|---|---|---|---|---|---|---|
| 1985 | — | — | — | — | 0.35 | — |

**2 CENTS** **KM# 25** **Composition:** Bronze Plated Steel **Obverse:** Similar to Cent, KM#24

| Date | Mintage | F | VF | XF | Unc | BU |
|---|---|---|---|---|---|---|
| 1987 | — | — | — | — | 0.35 | — |
| 1996 | — | — | — | — | 0.35 | — |

**5 CENTS** **KM# 3** **Composition:** Copper-Nickel **Subject:** Santa Ysabel - native mask

| Date | Mintage | F | VF | XF | Unc | BU |
|---|---|---|---|---|---|---|
| 1977 | 1,200,000 | — | 0.10 | 0.20 | 0.40 | — |
| 1977FM (U) | — | — | — | — | 3.00 | — |
| 1977FM (M) | 6,000 | — | — | — | 1.50 | — |
| 1977FM (P) | 14,000 | Value: 2.00 | | | | |
| 1978FM (M) | 6,000 | — | — | — | 1.50 | — |
| 1978FM (U) | 544 | — | — | — | 3.00 | — |
| 1978FM (P) | 5,122 | Value: 2.00 | | | | |
| 1979FM (M) | 6,000 | — | — | — | 1.50 | — |
| 1979FM (U) | 677 | — | — | — | 3.00 | — |
| 1979FM (P) | 2,845 | Value: 2.50 | | | | |
| 1980FM (M) | 6,000 | — | — | — | 1.50 | — |
| 1980FM (U) | 624 | — | — | — | 3.00 | — |
| 1980FM (P) | 1,031 | Value: 2.50 | | | | |
| 1981 | — | — | — | — | — | — |
| 1981FM (M) | 6,000 | — | — | — | 1.50 | — |
| 1981FM (U) | 212 | — | — | — | 3.00 | — |
| 1981FM (P) | 448 | Value: 2.50 | | | | |
| 1982FM (U) | — | — | — | — | 3.00 | — |
| 1982FM (P) | — | Value: 2.50 | | | | |
| 1983FM (M) | — | — | — | — | 1.50 | — |
| 1983FM (U) | 200 | — | — | — | 4.00 | — |
| 1983FM (P) | — | Value: 2.50 | | | | |
| 1985 | — | — | — | — | 0.30 | — |

**5 CENTS** **KM# 26** **Composition:** Copper-Nickel **Obverse:** Similar to Cent, KM#24

| Date | Mintage | F | VF | XF | Unc | BU |
|---|---|---|---|---|---|---|
| 1988 | — | — | — | — | 0.40 | — |
| 1993 | — | — | — | — | 0.40 | — |
| 1996 | — | — | — | — | 0.40 | — |

**10 CENTS** **KM# 4** **Composition:** Copper-Nickel **Subject:** Ngorieru - sea spirit

| Date | Mintage | F | VF | XF | Unc | BU |
|---|---|---|---|---|---|---|
| 1977 | 3,600,000 | — | 0.15 | 0.25 | 0.50 | — |
| 1977FM (M) | 6,000 | — | — | — | 2.00 | — |
| 1977FM (U) | — | — | — | — | 5.00 | — |
| 1977FM (P) | 14,000 | Value: 3.00 | | | | |
| 1978FM (M) | 6,000 | — | — | — | 2.00 | — |
| 1978FM (U) | 544 | — | — | — | 5.00 | — |
| 1978FM (P) | 5,122 | Value: 3.00 | | | | |
| 1979FM (M) | 6,000 | — | — | — | 2.00 | — |
| 1979FM (U) | 677 | — | — | — | 5.00 | — |
| 1979FM (P) | 2,845 | Value: 4.00 | | | | |
| 1980FM (M) | 6,000 | — | — | — | 2.00 | — |
| 1980FM (U) | 624 | — | — | — | 5.00 | — |
| 1980FM (P) | 1,031 | Value: 4.00 | | | | |
| 1981FM (M) | 6,000 | — | — | — | 2.00 | — |
| 1981FM (U) | 212 | — | — | — | 5.00 | — |
| 1981FM (P) | 448 | Value: 4.00 | | | | |
| 1982FM (U) | — | — | — | — | 5.00 | — |
| 1982FM (P) | — | Value: 4.00 | | | | |
| 1983FM (M) | — | — | — | — | 2.00 | — |
| 1983FM (U) | 200 | — | — | — | 6.00 | — |
| 1983FM (P) | — | Value: 4.00 | | | | |

**10 CENTS** **KM# 27** **Composition:** Copper-Nickel **Subject:** Ngorieru - sea spirit

| Date | Mintage | F | VF | XF | Unc | BU |
|---|---|---|---|---|---|---|
| 1988 | — | — | — | — | 0.65 | — |

**10 CENTS** **KM# 27a** **Composition:** Nickel-Clad Steel **Subject:** Ngorieru - sea spirit

| Date | Mintage | F | VF | XF | Unc | BU |
|---|---|---|---|---|---|---|
| 1990 | — | — | — | — | 0.65 | — |
| 1996 | — | — | — | — | 0.65 | — |

**20 CENTS** **KM# 28** **Composition:** Nickel-Clad Steel **Subject:** Malaita pendant design

| Date | Mintage | F | VF | XF | Unc | BU |
|---|---|---|---|---|---|---|
| 1989 | — | — | — | — | 0.85 | — |
| 1996 | — | — | — | — | 0.85 | — |

**50 CENTS** **KM# 23** **Composition:** Copper-Nickel **Subject:** 10th anniversary of independence

| Date | Mintage | F | VF | XF | Unc | BU |
|---|---|---|---|---|---|---|
| 1988 | — | — | — | — | 2.50 | — |

**50 CENTS** **KM# 29** **Composition:** Copper-Nickel **Note:** Circulation type.

| Date | Mintage | F | VF | XF | Unc | BU |
|---|---|---|---|---|---|---|
| 1990 | — | — | — | — | 2.50 | — |
| 1996 | — | — | — | — | 2.50 | — |

**DOLLAR** **KM# 6** **Composition:** Copper-Nickel **Subject:** Nusu-Nusu head - sea spirit

| Date | Mintage | F | VF | XF | Unc | BU |
|---|---|---|---|---|---|---|
| 1977 | 1,500,000 | — | 1.00 | 1.50 | 2.50 | — |
| 1977FM (M) | 3,000 | — | — | — | 5.00 | — |
| 1977FM (P) | 14,000 | Value: 6.50 | | | | |
| 1978FM (M) | 3,000 | — | — | — | 5.00 | — |
| 1978FM (U) | 544 | — | — | — | 9.00 | — |
| 1978FM (P) | 5,122 | Value: 6.50 | | | | |
| 1979FM (M) | 3,000 | — | — | — | 5.00 | — |
| 1979FM (U) | 677 | — | — | — | 9.00 | — |
| 1979FM (P) | 2,845 | Value: 7.50 | | | | |
| 1980FM (M) | 3,000 | — | — | — | 5.00 | — |
| 1980FM (U) | 624 | — | — | — | 9.00 | — |
| 1980FM (P) | 1,031 | Value: 8.50 | | | | |
| 1981FM (M) | 3,000 | — | — | — | 5.00 | — |
| 1981FM (U) | 212 | — | — | — | 10.00 | — |
| 1981FM (P) | 448 | Value: 8.50 | | | | |
| 1982FM (U) | — | — | — | — | 10.00 | — |
| 1982FM (P) | — | Value: 8.50 | | | | |
| 1983FM (M) | — | — | — | — | 5.00 | — |
| 1983FM (U) | 200 | — | — | — | 12.00 | — |
| 1983FM (P) | — | Value: 8.50 | | | | |

**DOLLAR** **KM# 19** **Composition:** Copper-Nickel **Series:** 1984 Olympics **Reverse:** Runners

| Date | Mintage | F | VF | XF | Unc | BU |
|---|---|---|---|---|---|---|
| 1984 | 5,000 | — | — | — | 18.00 | — |

**DOLLAR** **KM# 30** **Composition:** Copper-Nickel **Subject:** 50th anniversary of Pearl Harbor

| Date | Mintage | F | VF | XF | Unc | BU |
|---|---|---|---|---|---|---|
| 1991 | — | — | — | — | 7.00 | — |

**DOLLAR** **KM# 30a** **Weight:** 28.2800 g. **Composition:** 0.9250 Silver .8411 oz. ASW **Subject:** 50th anniversary of Pearl Harbor

| Date | Mintage | F | VF | XF | Unc | BU |
|---|---|---|---|---|---|---|
| 1991 Proof | Est. 25,000 | Value: 27.50 | | | | |

**DOLLAR** **KM# 35** **Composition:** Copper-Nickel **Subject:** 50th anniversary - Battle of the Coral Sea

| Date | Mintage | F | VF | XF | Unc | BU |
|---|---|---|---|---|---|---|
| 1992 | — | — | — | — | 7.00 | — |

**DOLLAR** **KM# 35a** **Weight:** 28.2800 g. **Composition:** 0.9250 Silver .8411 oz. ASW **Subject:** 50th anniversary - Battle of the Coral Sea

| Date | Mintage | F | VF | XF | Unc | BU |
|---|---|---|---|---|---|---|
| 1992 Proof | Est. 25,000 | Value: 35.00 | | | | |

**20 CENTS** **KM# 5** **Composition:** Copper-Nickel **Subject:** Malaita pendant design

| Date | Mintage | F | VF | XF | Unc | BU |
|---|---|---|---|---|---|---|
| 1977 | 3,000,000 | — | 0.20 | 0.35 | 0.80 | — |
| 1977FM (M) | 5,000 | — | — | — | 3.00 | — |
| 1977FM (P) | 14,000 | Value: 4.00 | | | | |
| 1978 | 293,000 | — | 0.25 | 0.50 | 1.00 | — |
| 1978FM (M) | 5,000 | — | — | — | 3.00 | — |
| 1978FM (U) | 544 | — | — | — | 5.50 | — |
| 1978FM (P) | 5,122 | Value: 4.00 | | | | |
| 1979FM (M) | 5,000 | — | — | — | 3.00 | — |
| 1979FM (U) | 677 | — | — | — | 5.00 | — |
| 1979FM (P) | 2,845 | Value: 4.00 | | | | |
| 1980FM (M) | 5,000 | — | — | — | 3.00 | — |
| 1980FM (U) | 624 | — | — | — | 5.00 | — |
| 1980FM (P) | 1,031 | Value: 4.00 | | | | |
| 1981FM (M) | 5,000 | — | — | — | 3.00 | — |
| 1981FM (U) | 212 | — | — | — | 6.00 | — |
| 1981FM (P) | 448 | Value: 4.00 | | | | |
| 1982FM (U) | — | — | — | — | 6.00 | — |
| 1982FM (P) | — | Value: 4.00 | | | | |
| 1983FM (M) | — | — | — | — | 3.00 | — |
| 1983FM (U) | 200 | — | — | — | 7.00 | — |
| 1983FM (P) | — | Value: 4.00 | | | | |

**DOLLAR** **KM# 41** **Composition:** Copper-Nickel **Subject:** 50th anniversary - Battle of Guadalcanal

| Date | Mintage | F | VF | XF | Unc | BU |
|---|---|---|---|---|---|---|
| 1992 | — | — | — | — | 7.00 | — |

**DOLLAR** **KM# 41a** **Weight:** 28.2800 g. **Composition:** 0.9250 Silver .8411 oz. ASW **Subject:** 50th anniversary - Battle of Guadalcanal

| Date | Mintage | F | VF | XF | Unc | BU |
|---|---|---|---|---|---|---|
| 1992 Proof | Est. 25,000 | Value: 30.00 | | | | |

**DOLLAR** **KM# 64** **Composition:** Copper-Nickel **Subject:** World Wildlife Fund - conserving nature **Obverse:** Queen's portrait **Reverse:** Fish eagle descending on prey

| Date | Mintage | F | VF | XF | Unc | BU |
|---|---|---|---|---|---|---|
| 1998 | — | — | — | — | 7.00 | — |

**DOLLAR** **KM# 64a** **Weight:** 28.2800 g. **Composition:** 0.9250 Silver .8411 oz. ASW **Subject:** World Wildlife Fund - conserving nature **Obverse:** Queen's portrait **Reverse:** Fish eagle descending on prey

| Date | Mintage | F | VF | XF | Unc | BU |
|---|---|---|---|---|---|---|
| 1998 Proof | — | Value: 35.00 | | | | |

**DOLLAR** **KM#65** **Weight:** 32.3200 g. **Composition:** Silver **Series:** Olympics 2000 **Obverse:** Queen's head right **Reverse:** Multicolored koala swimming **Edge:** Reeded **Size:** 38.6 mm. **Note:** Struck at Valcambi.

| Date | Mintage | F | VF | XF | Unc | BU |
|---|---|---|---|---|---|---|
| 2000 Proof | 50,000 | Value: 15.00 | | | | |

**DOLLAR** **KM#66** **Weight:** 32.3200 g. **Composition:** Silver **Series:** Olympics 2000 **Obverse:** Queen's head right **Reverse:** Multicolored kangaroo sail boarding

| Date | Mintage | F | VF | XF | Unc | BU |
|---|---|---|---|---|---|---|
| 2000 Proof | 50,000 | Value: 15.00 | | | | |

**5 DOLLARS** **KM# 7** **Weight:** 28.2800 g. **Composition:** 0.9250 Silver .8411 oz. ASW **Obverse:** Bokolo - fossilized clam shell

| Date | Mintage | F | VF | XF | Unc | BU |
|---|---|---|---|---|---|---|
| 1977FM (U) | 200 | — | — | — | 50.00 | — |
| 1977FM (P) | 15,000 | Value: 12.50 | | | | |
| 1978FM (P) | 5,148 | Value: 15.00 | | | | |
| 1979FM (P) | 2,845 | Value: 20.00 | | | | |
| 1980FM (P) | 1,031 | Value: 22.50 | | | | |
| 1981FM (P) | 448 | Value: 30.00 | | | | |
| 1983FM (P) | 339 | Value: 30.00 | | | | |

**5 DOLLARS** **KM# 7a** **Composition:** Copper-Nickel **Obverse:** Bokolo - fossilized clam shell

| Date | Mintage | F | VF | XF | Unc | BU |
|---|---|---|---|---|---|---|
| 1978FM (M) | 200 | — | — | — | 40.00 | — |
| 1978FM (U) | 544 | — | — | — | 18.00 | — |
| 1979FM (M) | 200 | — | — | — | 40.00 | — |
| 1979FM (U) | 677 | — | — | — | 18.00 | — |
| 1980FM (M) | 200 | — | — | — | 40.00 | — |
| 1980FM (U) | 624 | — | — | — | 18.00 | — |
| 1981FM (M) | 200 | — | — | — | 40.00 | — |
| 1981FM (U) | 212 | — | — | — | 35.00 | — |
| 1983FM (U) | 202 | — | — | — | 35.00 | — |

**5 DOLLARS** **KM# 8** **Weight:** 28.2800 g. **Composition:** 0.9250 Silver .8411 oz. ASW **Subject:** Coronation jubilee **Obverse:** Similar to 20 Cents, KM#5

| Date | Mintage | F | VF | XF | Unc | BU |
|---|---|---|---|---|---|---|
| 1978 | 8,886 | Value: 15.00 | | | | |

**5 DOLLARS** **KM# 13** **Composition:** Copper-Nickel **Subject:** Battle of Guadalcanal **Obverse:** Similar to 20 Cents, KM#5

| Date | Mintage | F | VF | XF | Unc | BU |
|---|---|---|---|---|---|---|
| 1982FM (U) | — | — | — | — | 25.00 | — |

**5 DOLLARS** **KM# 13a** **Weight:** 28.2800 g. **Composition:** 0.9250 Silver .8411 oz. ASW **Subject:** Battle of Guadalcanal **Obverse:** Similar to 20 Cents, KM#5

| Date | Mintage | F | VF | XF | Unc | BU |
|---|---|---|---|---|---|---|
| 1982FM (P) | 1,368 | Value: 45.00 | | | | |

**5 DOLLARS** **KM# 15** **Weight:** 30.2800 g. **Composition:** 0.5000 Silver .4868 oz. ASW **Subject:** 30th anniversary of coronation

| Date | Mintage | F | VF | XF | Unc | BU |
|---|---|---|---|---|---|---|
| 1983FM (P) | 2,944 | Value: 18.00 | | | | |

**5 DOLLARS** **KM# 16** **Weight:** 28.2800 g. **Composition:** 0.9250 Silver .8411 oz. ASW **Series:** International Year of the Child

| Date | Mintage | F | VF | XF | Unc | BU |
|---|---|---|---|---|---|---|
| 1983 Proof | 5,775 | Value: 18.00 | | | | |

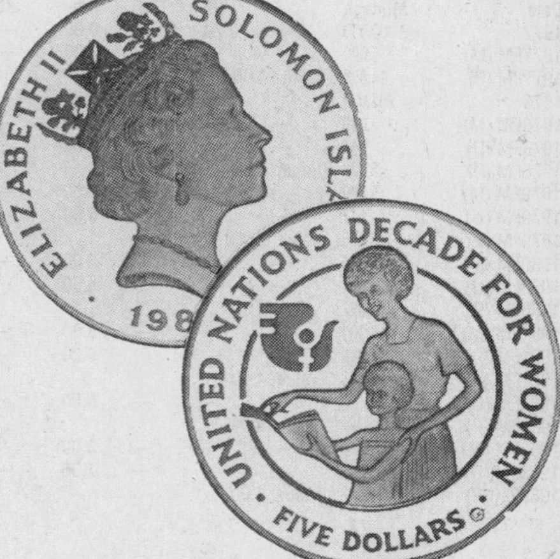


**5 DOLLARS** **KM# 22** **Weight:** 28.2800 g. **Composition:** 0.9250 Silver .8589 oz. ASW **Series:** Decade for Women

| Date | Mintage | F | VF | XF | Unc | BU |
|---|---|---|---|---|---|---|
| 1985 Proof | 1,050 | Value: 28.00 | | | | |

**5 DOLLARS** KM# 63 **Weight:** 10.0000 g. **Composition:** 0.5000 Silver .1607 oz. ASW **Subject:** Alvaro Mendana de Neyra

| Date | Mintage | F | VF | XF | Unc | BU |
|---|---|---|---|---|---|---|
| 1994 Proof | Est. 20,000 | Value: 17.50 | | | | |

**5 DOLLARS** KM# 54 **Composition:** Copper-Nickel **Subject:** MacArthur accepting Japanese surrender

| Date | Mintage | F | VF | XF | Unc | BU |
|---|---|---|---|---|---|---|
| 1995 | — | — | — | — | 8.50 | — |

**5 DOLLARS** KM# 54a **Weight:** 28.2800 g. **Composition:** 0.9250 Silver .8411 oz. ASW **Subject:** MacArthur accepting Japanese surrender **Note:** Similar to 50 Dollars, KM#57.

| Date | Mintage | F | VF | XF | Unc | BU |
|---|---|---|---|---|---|---|
| 1995 Proof | Est. 10,000 | Value: 50.00 | | | | |

**5 DOLLARS** KM# 69 **Weight:** 20.1000 g. **Composition:** 0.8000 Silver .5170 oz. ASW **Subject:** Ship of Death **Obverse:** Portrait of Queen Elizabeth II **Reverse:** Sailing ship circa 1596 **Edge:** Reeded **Size:** 33.9 mm.

| Date | Mintage | F | VF | XF | Unc | BU |
|---|---|---|---|---|---|---|
| 1999 Proof | Est. 20,000 | Value: 30.00 | | | | |

**5 DOLLARS** KM# 67 **Weight:** 24.9100 g. **Composition:** 0.9250 Silver .7408 oz. ASW **Series:** Olympics 2000 **Obverse:** Queen's head right **Reverse:** Multicolored koala tennis player **Edge:** Reeded **Size:** 38.7 mm. **Note:** Struck at Valcambi.

| Date | Mintage | F | VF | XF | Unc | BU |
|---|---|---|---|---|---|---|
| 2000 Proof | 15,000 | Value: 37.50 | | | | |

**5 DOLLARS** KM# 68 **Weight:** 24.9100 g. **Composition:** 0.9250 Silver .7408 oz. ASW **Series:** Olympics 2000 **Obverse:** Queen's head right **Reverse:** Multicolored kangaroo bicyclist

| Date | Mintage | F | VF | XF | Unc | BU |
|---|---|---|---|---|---|---|
| 2000 Proof | 15,000 | Value: 37.50 | | | | |

**10 DOLLARS** KM# 10 **Composition:** Copper-Nickel **Subject:** Frigate bird **Obverse:** Similar to 20 Cents, KM#5

| Date | Mintage | F | VF | XF | Unc | BU |
|---|---|---|---|---|---|---|
| 1979FM (M) | 100 | — | — | — | 65.00 | — |
| 1979FM (U) | 777 | — | — | — | 20.00 | — |
| 1980FM (M) | 100 | — | — | — | 65.00 | — |
| 1980FM (U) | 624 | — | — | — | 20.00 | — |
| 1981FM (M) | 100 | — | — | — | 65.00 | — |
| 1981FM (U) | 212 | — | — | — | 25.00 | — |
| 1982FM (U) | — | — | — | — | 20.00 | — |

**10 DOLLARS** KM# 10a **Weight:** 42.2700 g. **Composition:** 0.9250 Silver 1.2571 oz. ASW **Subject:** Frigate bird **Obverse:** Similar to 20 Cents, KM#5

| Date | Mintage | F | VF | XF | Unc | BU |
|---|---|---|---|---|---|---|
| 1979FM (P) | 4,670 | Value: 20.00 | | | | |
| 1980FM (P) | 1,569 | Value: 27.50 | | | | |
| 1981FM (P) | 593 | Value: 40.00 | | | | |
| 1982FM (P) | 579 | Value: 40.00 | | | | |

**10 DOLLARS** KM# 17 **Composition:** Copper-Nickel **Subject:** 5th anniversary of independence

| Date | Mintage | F | VF | XF | Unc | BU |
|---|---|---|---|---|---|---|
| 1983FM (U) | 202 | — | — | — | 28.00 | — |

**10 DOLLARS** KM# 17a **Weight:** 40.5000 g. **Composition:** 0.9250 Silver 1.2045 oz. ASW **Subject:** 5th anniversary of independence

| Date | Mintage | F | VF | XF | Unc | BU |
|---|---|---|---|---|---|---|
| 1983FM (P) | 425 | Value: 65.00 | | | | |

**10 DOLLARS** KM# 20 **Weight:** 33.4400 g. **Composition:** 0.9250 Silver .9946 oz. ASW **Series:** 1984 Olympics **Reverse:** Runners

| Date | Mintage | F | VF | XF | Unc | BU |
|---|---|---|---|---|---|---|
| 1984 Proof | 2,500 | Value: 40.00 | | | | |

**10 DOLLARS** KM# 47 **Weight:** 31.8000 g. **Composition:** 0.9250 Silver .9457 oz. ASW **Subject:** Alvardo de Neyra

| Date | Mintage | F | VF | XF | Unc | BU |
|---|---|---|---|---|---|---|
| 1991 Proof | — | Value: 22.50 | | | | |

**10 DOLLARS** KM# 31 **Weight:** 3.1300 g. **Composition:** 0.9990 Gold .1006 oz. AGW **Subject:** 50th anniversary of Pearl Harbor

| Date | Mintage | F | VF | XF | Unc | BU |
|---|---|---|---|---|---|---|
| 1991 Proof | Est. 500 | Value: 85.00 | | | | |

**10 DOLLARS** KM# 48 **Weight:** 31.4200 g. **Composition:** 0.9250 Silver .9359 oz. ASW **Series:** 1992 Olympics **Reverse:** Runners

| Date | Mintage | F | VF | XF | Unc | BU |
|---|---|---|---|---|---|---|
| 1991 Proof | Est. 40,000 | Value: 15.00 | | | | |

**10 DOLLARS** KM# 36 **Weight:** 3.1300 g. **Composition:** 0.9990 Gold .1006 oz. AGW **Subject:** 50th anniversary - Battle of the Coral Sea

| Date | Mintage | F | VF | XF | Unc | BU |
|---|---|---|---|---|---|---|
| 1992 Proof | 500 | Value: 85.00 | | | | |

**10 DOLLARS** **KM# 40** **Weight:** 31.4700 g. **Composition:** 0.9250 Silver .9359 oz. ASW **Subject:** First lunar vehicle

| Date | Mintage | F | VF | XF | Unc | BU |
|---|---|---|---|---|---|---|
| 1992 Proof | Est. 10,000 | Value: 28.00 | | | | |

**10 DOLLARS** **KM# 42** **Weight:** 3.1300 g. **Composition:** 0.9990 Gold .1006 oz. AGW **Subject:** 50th anniversary - Battle of Guadalcanal

| Date | Mintage | F | VF | XF | Unc | BU |
|---|---|---|---|---|---|---|
| 1992 Proof | 500 | Value: 85.00 | | | | |

**10 DOLLARS** **KM# 46** **Weight:** 31.4700 g. **Composition:** 0.9250 Silver .9359 oz. ASW **Subject:** 40th anniversary - Queen Elizabeth's coronation

| Date | Mintage | F | VF | XF | Unc | BU |
|---|---|---|---|---|---|---|
| 1992 Proof | Est. 50,000 | Value: 22.50 | | | | |

**10 DOLLARS** **KM# 50** **Weight:** 31.4700 g. **Composition:** 0.9250 Silver .9359 oz. ASW **Series:** 1992 Olympics **Reverse:** Boxer

| Date | Mintage | F | VF | XF | Unc | BU |
|---|---|---|---|---|---|---|
| 1992 Proof | 40,000 | Value: 17.50 | | | | |

**10 DOLLARS** **KM# 51** **Weight:** 31.4700 g. **Composition:** 0.9250 Silver .9359 oz. ASW **Series:** Endangered Wildlife **Reverse:** Crocodile

| Date | Mintage | F | VF | XF | Unc | BU |
|---|---|---|---|---|---|---|
| 1992 Proof | Est. 10,000 | Value: 35.00 | | | | |

**10 DOLLARS** **KM# 49** **Weight:** 28.2800 g. **Composition:** 0.9250 Silver .8411 oz. ASW **Subject:** 100 years as British protectorate

| Date | Mintage | F | VF | XF | Unc | BU |
|---|---|---|---|---|---|---|
| 1993 Proof | 5,000 | Value: 50.00 | | | | |

**10 DOLLARS** **KM# 59** **Weight:** 31.4700 g. **Composition:** 0.9250 Silver .9359 oz. ASW **Subject:** Protect Our World **Reverse:** Orchid and butterfly

| Date | Mintage | F | VF | XF | Unc | BU |
|---|---|---|---|---|---|---|
| 1993 Proof | Est. 10,000 | Value: 37.50 | | | | |

**10 DOLLARS** **KM# 52** **Weight:** 28.2800 g. **Composition:** 0.9250 Silver .8411 oz. ASW **Subject:** Sailing ship "Swallow"

| Date | Mintage | F | VF | XF | Unc | BU |
|---|---|---|---|---|---|---|
| 1994 Proof | Est. 15,000 | Value: 27.50 | | | | |

**10 DOLLARS** **KM# 53** **Weight:** 28.2800 g. **Composition:** 0.9250 Silver .8411 oz. ASW **Series:** 1996 Olympics **Reverse:** Relay runners

| Date | Mintage | F | VF | XF | Unc | BU |
|---|---|---|---|---|---|---|
| 1994 Proof | Est. 30,000 | Value: 20.00 | | | | |

**10 DOLLARS** **KM# 55** **Weight:** 31.1300 g. **Composition:** 0.9990 Gold .1006 oz. AGW **Reverse:** Marine and armored vehicle

| Date | Mintage | F | VF | XF | Unc | BU |
|---|---|---|---|---|---|---|
| 1995 Proof | Est. 500 | Value: 90.00 | | | | |

**25 DOLLARS** **KM# 32** **Weight:** 7.8100 g. **Composition:** 0.9990 Gold .2514 oz. AGW **Subject:** 50th anniversary - Pearl Harbor

| Date | Mintage | F | VF | XF | Unc | BU |
|---|---|---|---|---|---|---|
| 1991 Proof | Est. 3,000 | Value: 175 | | | | |

**25 DOLLARS** **KM# 37** **Weight:** 7.8100 g. **Composition:** 0.9990 Gold .2514 oz. AGW **Subject:** 50th anniversary - Battle of the Coral Sea

| Date | Mintage | F | VF | XF | Unc | BU |
|---|---|---|---|---|---|---|
| 1992 Proof | Est. 3,000 | Value: 175 | | | | |

**25 DOLLARS** **KM# 43** **Weight:** 7.8100 g. **Composition:** 0.9990 Gold .2514 oz. AGW **Subject:** 50th anniversary - Battle of Guadalcanal

| Date | Mintage | F | VF | XF | Unc | BU |
|---|---|---|---|---|---|---|
| 1992 Proof | Est. 3,000 | Value: 175 | | | | |

**25 DOLLARS** **KM# 56** **Weight:** 7.8100 g. **Composition:** 0.9990 Gold .2514 oz. AGW **Subject:** 50th anniversary - Iwo Jima flag raising

| Date | Mintage | F | VF | XF | Unc | BU |
|---|---|---|---|---|---|---|
| 1995 Proof | Est. 2,500 | Value: 220 | | | | |

**50 DOLLARS** **KM# 33** **Weight:** 15.6000 g. **Composition:** 0.9990 Gold .5016 oz. AGW **Subject:** 50th anniversary - Pearl Harbor

| Date | Mintage | F | VF | XF | Unc | BU |
|---|---|---|---|---|---|---|
| 1991 Proof | Est. 500 | Value: 390 | | | | |

**50 DOLLARS** KM# 38 **Weight:** 15.6000 g. **Composition:** 0.9990 Gold .5016 oz. AGW **Subject:** 50th anniversary - Battle of the Coral Sea

| Date | Mintage | F | VF | XF | Unc | BU |
|---|---|---|---|---|---|---|
| 1992 Proof | Est. 500 | Value: 390 | | | | |

**50 DOLLARS** KM# 44 **Weight:** 15.6000 g. **Composition:** 0.9990 Gold .5016 oz. AGW **Subject:** 50th anniversary - Battle of Guadalcanal

| Date | Mintage | F | VF | XF | Unc | BU |
|---|---|---|---|---|---|---|
| 1992 Proof | Est. 500 | Value: 390 | | | | |

**50 DOLLARS** KM# 60 **Weight:** 7.7600 g. **Composition:** 0.5830 Gold .1458 oz. AGW **Series:** Endangered Wildlife **Reverse:** Sanford's eagle

| Date | Mintage | F | VF | XF | Unc | BU |
|---|---|---|---|---|---|---|
| 1993 Proof | Est. 3,000 | Value: 150 | | | | |

**50 DOLLARS** KM# 61 **Weight:** 155.5175 g. **Composition:** 0.9990 Silver 5 oz. ASW **Subject:** Johannes Kepler **Size:** 65 mm. **Note:** Illustration reduced.

| Date | Mintage | F | VF | XF | Unc | BU |
|---|---|---|---|---|---|---|
| 1994 Proof | Est. 2,000 | Value: 200 | | | | |

**50 DOLLARS** KM# 62 **Weight:** 31.4700 g. **Composition:** 0.9250 Silver .9359 oz. ASW **Subject:** MacArthur accepting Japanese surrender **Note:** Similar to 5 Dollars, KM#54.

| Date | Mintage | F | VF | XF | Unc | BU |
|---|---|---|---|---|---|---|
| 1995 Proof | — | Value: 65.00 | | | | |

**50 DOLLARS** KM# 57 **Weight:** 15.6100 g. **Composition:** 0.9990 Gold .5016 oz. AGW **Subject:** MacArthur accepting Japanese surrender **Note:** In proof sets only.

| Date | Mintage | F | VF | XF | Unc | BU |
|---|---|---|---|---|---|---|
| 1995 Proof | 500 | Value: 425 | | | | |

**100 DOLLARS** KM# 9 **Weight:** 9.3700 g. **Composition:** 0.9000 Gold .2711 oz. AGW **Subject:** Attainment of sovereignty

| Date | Mintage | F | VF | XF | Unc | BU |
|---|---|---|---|---|---|---|
| 1978FM (M) | 50 | — | — | — | 275 | — |
| 1978FM (U) | 213 | — | — | — | 225 | — |
| 1978FM (P) | 3,159 | Value: 185 | | | | |

**100 DOLLARS** KM# 11 **Weight:** 7.6400 g. **Composition:** 0.5000 Gold .1228 oz. AGW **Subject:** Native art

| Date | Mintage | F | VF | XF | Unc | BU |
|---|---|---|---|---|---|---|
| 1980FM (U) | 50 | — | — | — | 200 | — |
| 1980FM (P) Proof | 7,500 | Value: 100 | | | | |

**100 DOLLARS** KM# 12 **Weight:** 7.6400 g. **Composition:** 0.5000 Gold .1228 oz. AGW **Reverse:** Shark

| Date | Mintage | F | VF | XF | Unc | BU |
|---|---|---|---|---|---|---|
| 1981 Proof | 675 | Value: 245 | | | | |

**100 DOLLARS** KM# 14 **Weight:** 9.3700 g. **Composition:** 0.9000 Gold .2711 oz. AGW **Subject:** Battle of Guadalcanal

| Date | Mintage | F | VF | XF | Unc | BU |
|---|---|---|---|---|---|---|
| 1982FM (P) | 311 | Value: 325 | | | | |

**100 DOLLARS** KM# 18 **Weight:** 9.3700 g. **Composition:** 0.9000 Gold .2711 oz. AGW **Subject:** 5th anniversary of independence

| Date | Mintage | F | VF | XF | Unc | BU |
|---|---|---|---|---|---|---|
| 1983FM (P) | 268 | Value: 275 | | | | |

**100 DOLLARS** KM# 21 **Weight:** 7.5000 g. **Composition:** 0.9170 Gold .2211 oz. AGW **Series:** 1984 Olympics **Reverse:** Weightlifter

| Date | Mintage | F | VF | XF | Unc | BU |
|---|---|---|---|---|---|---|
| 1984 Proof | 500 | Value: 225 | | | | |

**100 DOLLARS** KM# 34 **Weight:** 31.2100 g. **Composition:** 0.9990 Gold 1.0035 oz. AGW **Subject:** 50th anniversary of Pearl Harbor

| Date | Mintage | F | VF | XF | Unc | BU |
|---|---|---|---|---|---|---|
| 1991 Proof | Est. 500 | Value: 590 | | | | |

**100 DOLLARS** KM# 39 **Weight:** 31.2100 g. **Composition:** 0.9990 Gold 1.0035 oz. AGW **Subject:** 50th anniversary - Battle of Coral Sea

| Date | Mintage | F | VF | XF | Unc | BU |
|---|---|---|---|---|---|---|
| 1992 Proof | Est. 500 | Value: 590 | | | | |

**100 DOLLARS** KM# 45 **Weight:** 31.2100 g. **Composition:** 0.9990 Gold 1.0035 oz. AGW **Subject:** 50th anniversary - Battle of Guadalcanal

| Date | Mintage | F | VF | XF | Unc | BU |
|---|---|---|---|---|---|---|
| 1992 Proof | Est. 500 | Value: 590 | | | | |

**100 DOLLARS** KM# 58 **Weight:** 31.2100 g. **Composition:** 0.9990 Gold 1.0035 oz. AGW **Reverse:** B-25 bomber and mushroom cloud **Note:** In proof sets only.

| Date | Mintage | F | VF | XF | Unc | BU |
|---|---|---|---|---|---|---|
| 1995 Proof | Est. 500 | Value: 850 | | | | |

## PIEFORTS

| KM# | Date | Mintage | Identification | Mkt Val |
|---|---|---|---|---|
| P1 | 1983 | 62 | 5 Dollars. KM16. | 100 |

## MINT SETS

| KM# | Date | Mintage | Identification | Issue Price | Mkt Val |
|---|---|---|---|---|---|
| MS1 | 1978 (7) | 544 | KM1-6, 7a | 22.00 | 32.50 |
| MS2 | 1979 (8) | 677 | KM1-6, 7a, 10 | 31.00 | 42.50 |
| MS3 | 1980 (8) | 624 | KM1-6, 7a, 10 | 35.00 | 50.00 |
| MS4 | 1981 (8) | 212 | KM1-6, 7a, 10 | 36.00 | 60.00 |
| MS5 | 1982 (8) | — | KM1-6, 10, 13 | 36.00 | 65.00 |
| MS6 | 1983 (8) | 192 | KM1-6, 7a, 17 | 36.00 | 72.00 |

## PROOF SETS

| KM# | Date | Mintage | Identification | Issue Price | Mkt Val |
|---|---|---|---|---|---|
| PS1 | 1977 (7) | 72,748 | KM1-7 | 40.00 | 28.00 |
| PSA2 | 1977 (6) | — | KM1-6 | — | 16.50 |
| PS2 | 1978 (7) | 5,122 | KM1-7 | 45.00 | 32.50 |
| PS3 | 1979 (8) | 2,845 | KM1-7, 10a | 77.00 | 65.00 |
| PS4 | 1980 (8) | 1,031 | KM1-7, 10a | 135 | 70.00 |
| PS5 | 1981 (8) | 448 | KM1-7, 10a | 137 | 80.00 |
| PS6 | 1982 (8) | — | KM1-6, 10a, 13a | 87.00 | 100 |
| PS7 | 1983 (8) | 334 | KM1-7, 17a | 137 | 90.00 |
| PS8 | 1991 (4) | 500 | KM31-34 | 1,650 | 1,250 |
| PS9 | 1991 (2) | — | KM30a, 32 | — | 250 |
| PS10 | 1992 (4) | 500 | KM36-39 | 1,595 | 1,250 |
| PS11 | 1992 (4) | 500 | KM42-45 | 1,595 | 1,250 |
| PS12 | 1995 (4) | 500 | KM55-58 | 1,595 | 1,595 |

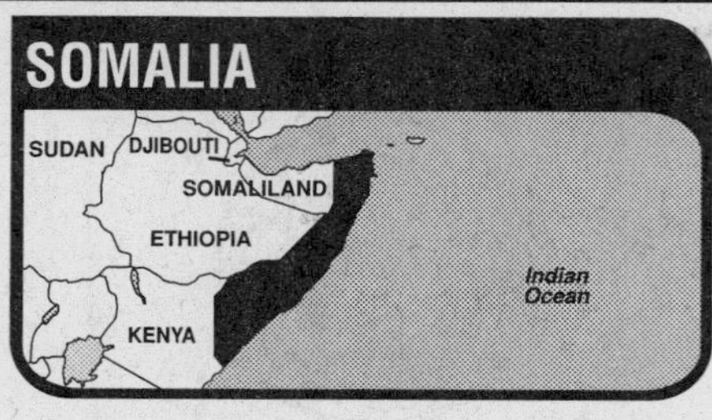


The Somali Democratic Republic, comprised of the former Italian Somaliland, is located on the coast of the eastern projection of the African continent commonly referred to as the "Horn". It has an area of 178,201 sq. mi. (461,657 sq. km.) and a population of *8.2 million. Capital: Mogadishu. The economy is pastoral and agricultural. Livestock, bananas and hides are exported.

The area of the British Somaliland Protectorate was known to the Egyptians at least 1,500 years B.C., and was occupied by the Arabs and Portuguese before British sea captains obtained trading and anchorage rights in 1827. The land of sandy clay and sporadic rainfall acquired a strategic importance with the opening of the Suez Canal in 1869. After negotiating treaties with the tribes, Britain declared the area a protectorate in 1888. Italy acquired Italian Somaliland in 1895 by purchase from the Sultan of Zanzibar. Britain occupied Italian Somaliland in 1941 and administered it until April 1, 1950, when it was returned to Italy as a U.N. trusteeship. The British Somaliland protectorate became independent on June 26, 1960. Five days later it joined with Italian Somaliland to form the Somali Republic. The country was under a revolutionary military regime installed Oct. 21, 1969. After eleven years of civil war rebel forces fought their way into the capital. A.M. Muhammad became president in Aug. 1991, but inter-factional fighting continued. A UN-sponsored truce was signed in March 1992 and a peace plan and pact was signed Jan. 15, 1993.

The Northern Somali National Movement (SNM) declared a secession of the northwestern Somaliland Republic on May 17, 1991, which is not recognized by the Somali Democratic Republic.

**TITLES**

Al-Jumhuriya(t)as - Somaliya(t)

**RULERS**

Italian, until 1941
British, until 1950

**MINT MARKS**

Az - Arezzo (Italy)
R – Rome

**MONETARY SYSTEM**

100 Centesimi = 1 Somalo

# BRITISH ADMINISTRATION

## STANDARD COINAGE

100 Centesimi = 1 Somalo

**CENTESIMO** KM# 1 **Composition:** Copper

| Date | Mintage | F | VF | XF | Unc | BU |
|---|---|---|---|---|---|---|
| AH1369(1950) | 4,000,000 | — | 0.20 | 0.50 | 2.00 | — |

**5 CENTESIMI** KM# 2 **Composition:** Copper

| Date | Mintage | F | VF | XF | Unc | BU |
|---|---|---|---|---|---|---|
| AH1369(1950) | 6,800,000 | — | 0.30 | 1.00 | 3.50 | — |

**10 CENTESIMI** KM# 3 **Composition:** Copper

| Date | Mintage | F | VF | XF | Unc | BU |
|---|---|---|---|---|---|---|
| AH1369(1950) | 7,400,000 | — | 0.50 | 2.00 | 6.00 | — |

**50 CENTESIMI** KM# 4 **Weight:** 3.8000 g. **Composition:** 0.2500 Silver .0305 oz. ASW

| Date | Mintage | F | VF | XF | Unc | BU |
|---|---|---|---|---|---|---|
| AH1369(1950) | 1,800,000 | — | 1.25 | 3.75 | 9.00 | — |

**SOMALO** KM# 5 **Weight:** 7.6000 g. **Composition:** 0.2500 Silver .0610 oz. ASW

| Date | Mintage | F | VF | XF | Unc | BU |
|---|---|---|---|---|---|---|
| AH1369(1950) | 11,480,000 | — | 2.25 | 4.75 | 12.50 | — |

# SOMALI REPUBLIC

## STANDARD COINAGE

100 Centesimi = 1 Somalo

**5 CENTESIMI** KM# 6 **Composition:** Brass

| Date | Mintage | F | VF | XF | Unc | BU |
|---|---|---|---|---|---|---|
| 1967 | 10,000,000 | — | — | 0.20 | 0.60 | — |

**10 CENTESIMI** KM# 7 **Composition:** Brass

| Date | Mintage | F | VF | XF | Unc | BU |
|---|---|---|---|---|---|---|
| 1967 | 15,000,000 | — | 0.15 | 0.25 | 0.70 | — |

**50 CENTESIMI** KM# 8 **Composition:** Copper-Nickel

| Date | Mintage | F | VF | XF | Unc | BU |
|---|---|---|---|---|---|---|
| 1967 | 5,100,000 | — | 0.50 | 1.00 | 2.50 | — |

**SCELLINO (Schilling)** KM# 9 **Composition:** Copper-Nickel

| Date | Mintage | F | VF | XF | Unc | BU |
|---|---|---|---|---|---|---|
| 1967 | 8,150,000 | — | 1.00 | 3.00 | 6.00 | — |

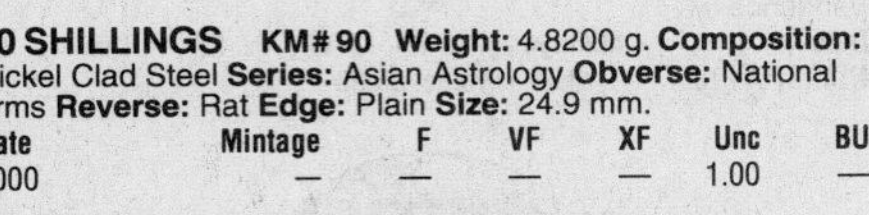

**10 SHILLINGS** **KM# 90** **Weight:** 4.8200 g. **Composition:** Nickel Clad Steel **Series:** Asian Astrology **Obverse:** National arms **Reverse:** Rat **Edge:** Plain **Size:** 24.9 mm.

| Date | Mintage | F | VF | XF | Unc | BU |
|---|---|---|---|---|---|---|
| 2000 | — | — | — | — | 1.00 | — |

**10 SHILLINGS** **KM# 91** **Weight:** 4.8200 g. **Composition:** Nickel Clad Steel **Series:** Asian Astrology **Obverse:** National arms **Reverse:** Ox

| Date | Mintage | F | VF | XF | Unc | BU |
|---|---|---|---|---|---|---|
| 2000 | — | — | — | — | 1.00 | — |

**10 SHILLINGS** **KM# 92** **Weight:** 4.8200 g. **Composition:** Nickel Clad Steel **Series:** Asian Astrology **Obverse:** National arms **Reverse:** Tiger

| Date | Mintage | F | VF | XF | Unc | BU |
|---|---|---|---|---|---|---|
| 2000 | — | — | — | — | 1.00 | — |

**10 SHILLINGS** **KM# 93** **Weight:** 4.8200 g. **Composition:** Nickel Clad Steel **Series:** Asian astrology **Obverse:** National arms **Reverse:** Rabbit

| Date | Mintage | F | VF | XF | Unc | BU |
|---|---|---|---|---|---|---|
| 2000 | — | — | — | — | 1.00 | — |

**10 SHILLINGS** **KM# 94** **Weight:** 4.8200 g. **Composition:** Nickel Clad Steel **Series:** Asian astrology **Obverse:** National arms **Reverse:** Dragon

| Date | Mintage | F | VF | XF | Unc | BU |
|---|---|---|---|---|---|---|
| 2000 | — | — | — | — | 1.00 | — |

**10 SHILLINGS** **KM# 95** **Weight:** 4.8200 g. **Composition:** Nickel Clad Steel **Series:** Asian astrology **Obverse:** National arms **Reverse:** Snake

| Date | Mintage | F | VF | XF | Unc | BU |
|---|---|---|---|---|---|---|
| 2000 | — | — | — | — | 1.00 | — |

**10 SHILLINGS** **KM# 96** **Weight:** 4.8200 g. **Composition:** Nickel Clad Steel **Series:** Asian astrology **Obverse:** National arms **Reverse:** Horse

| Date | Mintage | F | VF | XF | Unc | BU |
|---|---|---|---|---|---|---|
| 2000 | — | — | — | — | 1.00 | — |

**10 SHILLINGS** **KM# 97** **Weight:** 4.8200 g. **Composition:** Nickel Clad Steel **Series:** Asian astrology **Obverse:** National arms **Reverse:** Goat

| Date | Mintage | F | VF | XF | Unc | BU |
|---|---|---|---|---|---|---|
| 2000 | — | — | — | — | 1.00 | — |

**10 SHILLINGS** **KM# 98** **Weight:** 4.8200 g. **Composition:** Nickel Clad Steel **Series:** Asian astrology **Obverse:** National arms **Reverse:** Monkey

| Date | Mintage | F | VF | XF | Unc | BU |
|---|---|---|---|---|---|---|
| 2000 | — | — | — | — | 1.00 | — |

**10 SHILLINGS** **KM# 99** **Weight:** 4.8200 g. **Composition:** Nickel Clad Steel **Series:** Asian astrology **Obverse:** National arms **Reverse:** Rooster

| Date | Mintage | F | VF | XF | Unc | BU |
|---|---|---|---|---|---|---|
| 2000 | — | — | — | — | 1.00 | — |

**10 SHILLINGS** **KM# 100** **Weight:** 4.8200 g. **Composition:** Nickel Clad Steel **Series:** Asian astrology **Obverse:** National arms **Reverse:** Dog

| Date | Mintage | F | VF | XF | Unc | BU |
|---|---|---|---|---|---|---|
| 2000 | — | — | — | — | 1.00 | — |

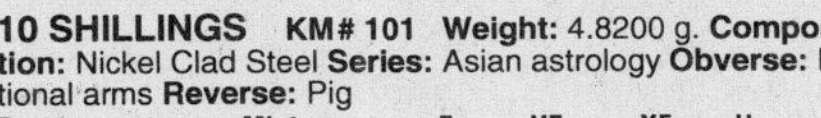

**10 SHILLINGS** **KM# 101** **Weight:** 4.8200 g. **Composition:** Nickel Clad Steel **Series:** Asian astrology **Obverse:** National arms **Reverse:** Pig

| Date | Mintage | F | VF | XF | Unc | BU |
|---|---|---|---|---|---|---|
| 2000 | — | — | — | — | 1.00 | — |

**20 SHILLINGS (Scellini)** **KM# 10** **Weight:** 2.8000 g. **Composition:** 0.9000 Gold .0810 oz. AGW **Subject:** 5th anniversary of independence

| Date | Mintage | F | VF | XF | Unc | BU |
|---|---|---|---|---|---|---|
| 1965Az Proof | 6,325 | Value: 50.00 | | | | |
| 1966Az Proof | — | Value: 50.00 | | | | |

**50 SHILLINGS** **KM# 11** **Weight:** 7.0000 g. **Composition:** 0.9000 Gold .2025 oz. AGW **Subject:** 5th anniversary of independence

| Date | Mintage | F | VF | XF | Unc | BU |
|---|---|---|---|---|---|---|
| 1965Az Proof | 6,325 | Value: 100 | | | | |
| 1966Az Proof | — | Value: 100 | | | | |

**100 SHILLINGS** **KM# 12** **Weight:** 14.0000 g. **Composition:** 0.9000 Gold .4051 oz. AGW **Subject:** 5th anniversary of independence

| Date | Mintage | F | VF | XF | Unc | BU |
|---|---|---|---|---|---|---|
| 1965Az Proof | 6,325 | Value: 185 | | | | |
| 1966Az Proof | — | Value: 185 | | | | |

**200 SHILLINGS** **KM# 13** **Weight:** 28.0000 g. **Composition:** 0.9000 Gold .8102 oz. AGW **Subject:** 5th anniversary of independence

| Date | Mintage | F | VF | XF | Unc | BU |
|---|---|---|---|---|---|---|
| 1965Az Proof | 6,325 | Value: 375 | | | | |
| 1966Az Proof | — | Value: 375 | | | | |

**250 SHILLINGS** **KM# 102** **Weight:** 24.0000 g. **Composition:** 0.9000 Silver .6945 oz. ASW **Subject:** Olympics **Obverse:**

National arms. **Reverse:** Multicolor skier. **Edge:** Reeded. **Size:** 38.1 mm.

| Date | Mintage | F | VF | XF | Unc | BU |
|---|---|---|---|---|---|---|
| 1998 Proof | — | Value: 40.00 | | | | |

**500 SHILLINGS** KM# 14 **Weight:** 70.0000 g. **Composition:** 0.9000 Gold 2.0257 oz. AGW **Subject:** 5th anniversary of independence **Obverse:** Similar to 20 Shillings, KM#10

| Date | Mintage | F | VF | XF | Unc | BU |
|---|---|---|---|---|---|---|
| 1965Az Proof | 6,325 | Value: 875 | | | | |
| 1966Az Proof | — | Value: 875 | | | | |

**5000 SHILLINGS** KM# 84 **Weight:** 7.0600 g. **Composition:** 0.9990 Silver .2268 oz. ASW **Subject:** Tall Ship Series: Amerigo Vespucci **Obverse:** National arms **Reverse:** Sailing ship **Edge:** Plain **Size:** 29.7 mm.

| Date | Mintage | F | VF | XF | Unc | BU |
|---|---|---|---|---|---|---|
| 1998 Proof | — | Value: 25.00 | | | | |

**5000 SHILLINGS** KM# 85 **Weight:** 7.0600 g. **Composition:** 0.9990 Silver .2268 oz. ASW **Subject:** Tall Ships Series: Sedov **Obverse:** National arms **Reverse:** Sailing ship

| Date | Mintage | F | VF | XF | Unc | BU |
|---|---|---|---|---|---|---|
| 1998 Proof | — | Value: 25.00 | | | | |

**5000 SHILLINGS** KM# 86 **Weight:** 7.0600 g. **Composition:** 0.9990 Silver .2268 oz. ASW **Subject:** Tall Ships Series: Gorch Fock **Obverse:** National arms **Reverse:** Sailing ship

| Date | Mintage | F | VF | XF | Unc | BU |
|---|---|---|---|---|---|---|
| 1998 Proof | — | Value: 25.00 | | | | |

**5000 SHILLINGS** KM# 87 **Weight:** 7.0600 g. **Composition:** 0.9990 Silver .2268 oz. ASW **Subject:** Tall Ships Series: Libertad **Obverse:** National arms **Reverse:** Sailing ship

| Date | Mintage | F | VF | XF | Unc | BU |
|---|---|---|---|---|---|---|
| 1998 Proof | — | Value: 25.00 | | | | |

**5000 SHILLINGS** KM# 88 **Weight:** 7.0600 g. **Composition:** 0.9990 Silver .2268 oz. ASW **Subject:** Tall Ships Series: Alexander von Humboldt **Obverse:** National arms **Reverse:** Sailing ship

| Date | Mintage | F | VF | XF | Unc | BU |
|---|---|---|---|---|---|---|
| 1998 Proof | — | Value: 25.00 | | | | |

**5000 SHILLINGS** KM# 89 **Weight:** 7.0600 g. **Composition:** 0.9990 Silver .2268 oz. ASW **Subject:** Tall Ship Series: Eagle **Obverse:** National arms **Reverse:** Sailing ship

| Date | Mintage | F | VF | XF | Unc | BU |
|---|---|---|---|---|---|---|
| 1998 Proof | — | Value: 25.00 | | | | |

# DEMOCRATIC REPUBLIC

## STANDARD COINAGE

100 Centesimi = 1 Somalo

**5 SHILLINGS** KM# 15 **Composition:** Copper-Nickel **Subject:** 2nd F.A.O. Conference

| Date | Mintage | F | VF | XF | Unc | BU |
|---|---|---|---|---|---|---|
| 1970 | 100,000 | — | 1.50 | 2.50 | 5.50 | — |
| 1970 Proof | 1,000 | Value: 16.50 | | | | |

**20 SHILLINGS** KM# 16 **Weight:** 2.8000 g. **Composition:** 0.9000 Gold .0810 oz. AGW **Subject:** 10th anniversary of independence

| Date | Mintage | F | VF | XF | Unc | BU |
|---|---|---|---|---|---|---|
| ND(1970) Proof | 8,000 | Value: 85.00 | | | | |

**50 SHILLINGS** KM# 17 **Weight:** 7.0000 g. **Composition:** 0.9000 Gold .2025 oz. AGW **Subject:** 10th anniversary of independence

| Date | Mintage | F | VF | XF | Unc | BU |
|---|---|---|---|---|---|---|
| ND(1970) Proof | 8,000 | Value: 165 | | | | |

**50 SHILLINGS** KM# 18 **Weight:** 7.0000 g. **Composition:** 0.9000 Gold .2025 oz. AGW **Subject:** 1st anniversary of 1969 revolution

| Date | Mintage | F | VF | XF | Unc | BU |
|---|---|---|---|---|---|---|
| ND(1970) Proof | — | Value: 165 | | | | |

**100 SHILLINGS** KM# 19 **Weight:** 14.0000 g. **Composition:** 0.9000 Gold .4051 oz. AGW **Subject:** 10th anniversary of independence

| Date | Mintage | F | VF | XF | Unc | BU |
|---|---|---|---|---|---|---|
| ND(1970) Proof | 8,000 | Value: 300 | | | | |

**100 SHILLINGS** KM# 20 **Weight:** 14.0000 g. **Composition:** 0.9000 Gold .4051 oz. AGW **Subject:** 1st anniversary of the 1969 revolution

| Date | Mintage | F | VF | XF | Unc | BU |
|---|---|---|---|---|---|---|
| ND(1970) Proof | — | Value: 285 | | | | |

**200 SHILLINGS** KM# 21 **Weight:** 28.0000 g. **Composition:** 0.9000 Gold .8102 oz. AGW **Subject:** 10th anniversary of independence

| Date | Mintage | F | VF | XF | Unc | BU |
|---|---|---|---|---|---|---|
| ND(1970) Proof | 8,000 | Value: 625 | | | | |

**200 SHILLINGS** KM# 22 **Weight:** 28.0000 g. **Composition:** 0.9000 Gold .8102 oz. AGW **Subject:** 1st anniversary of 1969 revolution

| Date | Mintage | F | VF | XF | Unc | BU |
|---|---|---|---|---|---|---|
| ND(1970) Proof | — | Value: 600 | | | | |

**500 SHILLINGS** KM# 23 **Weight:** 70.0000 g. **Composition:** 0.9000 Gold 2.0257 oz. AGW **Subject:** 10th anniversary of independence **Obverse:** Similar to 200 Shillings, KM#22

| Date | Mintage | F | VF | XF | Unc | BU |
|---|---|---|---|---|---|---|
| ND(1970) Proof | 8,000 | Value: 1,100 | | | | |

## REFORM COINAGE

100 Senti = 1 Shilling

**5 SENTI** KM# A24 **Composition:** Aluminum **Series:** F.A.O.

| Date | Mintage | F | VF | XF | Unc | BU |
|---|---|---|---|---|---|---|
| 1976 | — | — | — | — | 200 | — |

**5 SENTI** KM# 24 **Composition:** Aluminum **Series:** F.A.O.

| Date | Mintage | F | VF | XF | Unc | BU |
|---|---|---|---|---|---|---|
| 1976 | 18,500,000 | — | 0.10 | 0.20 | 0.35 | — |

**10 SENTI** KM# 25 **Composition:** Aluminum **Series:** F.A.O.

| Date | Mintage | F | VF | XF | Unc | BU |
|---|---|---|---|---|---|---|
| 1976 | 40,500,000 | — | 0.10 | 0.20 | 0.50 | — |

**50 SENTI** KM# 26 **Composition:** Copper-Nickel **Series:** F.A.O.

| Date | Mintage | F | VF | XF | Unc | BU |
|---|---|---|---|---|---|---|
| 1976 | 10,080,000 | — | 0.15 | 0.25 | 0.75 | — |

**50 SENTI** KM# 26a **Composition:** Nickel Plated Steel **Series:** F.A.O.

| Date | Mintage | F | VF | XF | Unc | BU |
|---|---|---|---|---|---|---|
| 1984 | — | — | 1.00 | 2.00 | 5.00 | — |

**SHILLING** KM# 27 **Composition:** Copper-Nickel **Series:** F.A.O.

| Date | Mintage | F | VF | XF | Unc | BU |
|---|---|---|---|---|---|---|
| 1976 | 20,040,000 | — | 0.35 | 0.65 | 2.25 | — |

**SHILLING** KM# 27a **Composition:** Nickel Plated Steel **Series:** F.A.O.

| Date | Mintage | F | VF | XF | Unc | BU |
|---|---|---|---|---|---|---|
| 1984 | — | — | 2.00 | 4.00 | 10.00 | — |

**10 SHILLINGS** KM# 28 **Composition:** Copper-Nickel **Subject:** 10th anniversary of republic **Reverse:** Workers

| Date | Mintage | F | VF | XF | Unc | BU |
|---|---|---|---|---|---|---|
| ND(1979) | — | — | — | — | 7.00 | — |

**10 SHILLINGS** KM# 28a **Weight:** 28.2800 g. **Composition:** 0.9250 Silver .8411 oz. ASW **Subject:** 10th anniversary of republic **Reverse:** Workers

| Date | Mintage | F | VF | XF | Unc | BU |
|---|---|---|---|---|---|---|
| ND(1979) Proof | Est. 5,000 | Value: 37.50 | | | | |

**10 SHILLINGS** KM# 29 **Composition:** Copper-Nickel **Subject:** 10th anniversary of republic **Reverse:** Camp scene

| Date | Mintage | F | VF | XF | Unc | BU |
|---|---|---|---|---|---|---|
| ND(1979) | — | — | — | — | 7.00 | — |

**10 SHILLINGS** KM# 29a **Weight:** 28.2800 g. **Composition:** 0.9250 Silver .8411 oz. ASW **Subject:** 10th anniversary of republic **Reverse:** Camp scene

| Date | Mintage | F | VF | XF | Unc | BU |
|---|---|---|---|---|---|---|
| ND(1979) Proof | Est. 5,000 | Value: 37.50 | | | | |

**10 SHILLINGS** KM# 30 **Composition:** Copper-Nickel **Subject:** 10th anniversary of republic **Reverse:** Lab workers

| Date | Mintage | F | VF | XF | Unc | BU |
|---|---|---|---|---|---|---|
| ND(1979) | — | — | — | — | 7.00 | — |

**10 SHILLINGS** KM# 30a **Weight:** 28.2800 g. **Composition:** 0.9250 Silver .8411 oz. ASW **Subject:** 10th anniversary of republic **Reverse:** Lab workers

| Date | Mintage | F | VF | XF | Unc | BU |
|---|---|---|---|---|---|---|
| ND(1979) Proof | Est. 5,000 | Value: 37.50 | | | | |

**10 SHILLINGS** KM# 31 **Composition:** Copper-Nickel **Subject:** 10th anniversary of republic **Reverse:** Dancers

| Date | Mintage | F | VF | XF | Unc | BU |
|---|---|---|---|---|---|---|
| ND(1979) | — | — | — | — | 7.00 | — |

**10 SHILLINGS** KM# 31a **Weight:** 28.2800 g. **Composition:** 0.9250 Silver .8411 oz. ASW **Subject:** 10th anniversary of republic **Reverse:** Dancers

| Date | Mintage | F | VF | XF | Unc | BU |
|---|---|---|---|---|---|---|
| ND(1979) Proof | Est. 5,000 | Value: 37.50 | | | | |

**10 SHILLINGS** KM# 32 **Composition:** Copper-Nickel **Subject:** 10th anniversary of republic **Reverse:** Man and woman

| Date | Mintage | F | VF | XF | Unc | BU |
|---|---|---|---|---|---|---|
| ND(1979) | — | — | — | — | 7.00 | — |

**10 SHILLINGS** KM# 32a **Weight:** 28.2800 g. **Composition:** 0.9250 Silver .8411 oz. ASW **Subject:** 10th anniversary of republic **Reverse:** Man and woman

| Date | Mintage | F | VF | XF | Unc | BU |
|---|---|---|---|---|---|---|
| ND(1979) Proof | Est. 5,000 | Value: 37.50 | | | | |

**25 SHILLINGS** KM# 40 **Composition:** Copper-Nickel **Subject:** World Fisheries Conference

| Date | Mintage | F | VF | XF | Unc | BU |
|---|---|---|---|---|---|---|
| ND(1984) | 100,000 | — | — | 12.00 | 30.00 | — |

**25 SHILLINGS** **KM# 40a** **Weight:** 28.2800 g. **Composition:** 0.9250 Silver .8411 oz. ASW **Subject:** World Fisheries Conference

| Date | Mintage | F | VF | XF | Unc | BU |
|---|---|---|---|---|---|---|
| ND(1984) Proof | 20,000 | Value: 65.00 | | | | |

**25 SHILLINGS** **KM# 40b** **Weight:** 47.5400 g. **Composition:** 0.9170 Gold 1.4011 oz. AGW **Subject:** World Fisheries Conference

| Date | Mintage | F | VF | XF | Unc | BU |
|---|---|---|---|---|---|---|
| ND(1984) Proof | 200 | Value: 1,000 | | | | |

**150 SHILLINGS** **KM# 38** **Weight:** 28.2800 g. **Composition:** 0.9250 Silver .8411 oz. ASW **Series:** International Year of Disabled Persons **Obverse:** Cost of arms, date

| Date | Mintage | F | VF | XF | Unc | BU |
|---|---|---|---|---|---|---|
| 1983 | 5,500 | — | — | — | 40.00 | — |
| 1983 Proof | 5,500 | Value: 45.00 | | | | |

**1500 SHILLINGS** **KM# 33** **Weight:** 15.9800 g. **Composition:** 0.9170 Gold .4711 oz. AGW **Subject:** 10th anniversary of republic **Obverse:** Similar to KM#35

| Date | Mintage | F | VF | XF | Unc | BU |
|---|---|---|---|---|---|---|
| ND(1979) | 500 | — | — | — | 225 | — |
| ND(1979) Proof | 500 | Value: 250 | | | | |

**1500 SHILLINGS** **KM# 34** **Weight:** 15.9800 g. **Composition:** 0.9170 Gold .4711 oz. AGW **Subject:** 10th anniversary of republic **Obverse:** Similar to KM#35

| Date | Mintage | F | VF | XF | Unc | BU |
|---|---|---|---|---|---|---|
| ND(1979) | 500 | — | — | — | 225 | — |
| ND(1979) Proof | 500 | Value: 250 | | | | |

**1500 SHILLINGS** **KM# 35** **Weight:** 15.9800 g. **Composition:** 0.9170 Gold .4711 oz. AGW **Subject:** 10th anniversary of republic

| Date | Mintage | F | VF | XF | Unc | BU |
|---|---|---|---|---|---|---|
| ND(1979) | 500 | — | — | — | 225 | — |
| ND(1979) Proof | 500 | Value: 250 | | | | |

**1500 SHILLINGS** **KM# 36** **Weight:** 15.9800 g. **Composition:** 0.9170 Gold .4711 oz. AGW **Subject:** 10th anniversary of republic

| Date | Mintage | F | VF | XF | Unc | BU |
|---|---|---|---|---|---|---|
| ND(1979) | 500 | — | — | — | 225 | — |
| ND(1979) Proof | 500 | Value: 250 | | | | |

**1500 SHILLINGS** **KM# 37** **Weight:** 15.9800 g. **Composition:** 0.9170 Gold .4711 oz. AGW **Subject:** 10th anniversary of republic **Obverse:** Similar to KM#35

| Date | Mintage | F | VF | XF | Unc | BU |
|---|---|---|---|---|---|---|
| 1979 | 500 | — | — | — | 225 | — |
| 1979 Proof | 500 | Value: 250 | | | | |

**1500 SHILLINGS** **KM# 39** **Weight:** 15.9800 g. **Composition:** 0.9170 Gold .4711 oz. AGW **Series:** International Year of Disabled Persons

| Date | Mintage | F | VF | XF | Unc | BU |
|---|---|---|---|---|---|---|
| 1983 | — | — | — | — | 350 | — |
| 1983 Proof | — | Value: 400 | | | | |

## REPUBLIC OF SOMALIA

### STANDARD COINAGE

**5 SHILLING / SCELLINI** **KM# 45** **Composition:** Aluminum **Series:** F.A.O. **Obverse:** National arms **Reverse:** Elephant

| Date | Mintage | F | VF | XF | Unc | BU |
|---|---|---|---|---|---|---|
| 2000(1999) | — | — | — | — | 1.50 | — |

**10 SHILLINGS / SCELLINI** **KM# 46** **Composition:** Aluminum **Series:** F.A.O. **Obverse:** National arms **Reverse:** Camel

| Date | Mintage | F | VF | XF | Unc | BU |
|---|---|---|---|---|---|---|
| 2000(1999) | — | — | — | — | 2.00 | — |

**25 SHILLINGS** **KM# 41** **Composition:** Copper-Nickel **Subject:** History of world shipping - sinking of Titanic **Obverse:** National arms

| Date | Mintage | F | VF | XF | Unc | BU |
|---|---|---|---|---|---|---|
| 1998 Proof | — | Value: 17.50 | | | | |

**25 SHILLINGS** **KM# 50** **Composition:** Copper-Nickel **Subject:** History of world shipping - Cutty Sark **Obverse:** National arms **Reverse:** Multicolor clipper ship "Cutty Sark" **Edge:** Plain **Note:** Weight varies 18.42-20.2g.

| Date | Mintage | F | VF | XF | Unc | BU |
|---|---|---|---|---|---|---|
| 1998 Proof | — | Value: 11.50 | | | | |

**25 SHILLINGS** **KM# 51** **Composition:** Copper-Nickel **Subject:** History of world shipping - Caravel Nina **Obverse:** National arms

| Date | Mintage | F | VF | XF | Unc | BU |
|---|---|---|---|---|---|---|
| 1998 Proof | — | Value: 11.50 | | | | |

**25 SHILLINGS** **KM# 47** **Weight:** 2.0000 g. **Composition:** Copper-Nickel **Subject:** Wildlife of Somalia **Reverse:** Multicolored hippopotamus **Edge:** Plain **Size:** 37.9 mm.

| Date | Mintage | F | VF | XF | Unc | BU |
|---|---|---|---|---|---|---|
| 1998 | — | — | — | — | 18.00 | — |

**25 SHILLINGS** **KM# 52** **Composition:** Copper-Nickel **Subject:** History of world shipping **Reverse:** Greek trireme **Note:** Multicolored. Weight varies 18.42-20.2g.

| Date | Mintage | VG | F | VF | XF | Unc |
|---|---|---|---|---|---|---|
| 1998 | — | — | — | — | — | 11.50 |

**25 SHILLINGS** **KM# 53** **Composition:** Copper-Nickel **Subject:** History of world shipping **Reverse:** Roman merchant ship **Note:** Multicolored. Weight varies 18.42-20.2g.

| Date | Mintage | F | VF | XF | Unc | BU |
|---|---|---|---|---|---|---|
| 1998 | — | — | — | — | 11.50 | — |

**25 SHILLINGS** **KM# 57** **Composition:** Copper-Nickel **Subject:** Wildlife of Somalia **Reverse:** Running Eland **Note:** Multicolored. Weight varies 18.42-20.2g.

| Date | Mintage | F | VF | XF | Unc | BU |
|---|---|---|---|---|---|---|
| 1998 | — | — | — | — | 15.00 | — |

**25 SHILLINGS** **KM# 61** **Composition:** Copper-Nickel **Subject:** Wildlife of Somalia **Reverse:** Variable Sunbird on a thin branch **Note:** Multicolored. Weight varies 18.42-20.2g.

| Date | Mintage | F | VF | XF | Unc | BU |
|---|---|---|---|---|---|---|
| 1998 | — | — | — | — | 15.00 | — |

**25 SHILLINGS** **KM# 54** **Composition:** Copper-Nickel **Subject:** History of world shipping **Reverse:** Hansa trading cog **Note:** Multicolored. Weight varies 18.42-20.2g.

| Date | Mintage | F | VF | XF | Unc | BU |
|---|---|---|---|---|---|---|
| 1998 | — | — | — | — | 11.50 | — |

**25 SHILLINGS** **KM# 58** **Composition:** Copper-Nickel **Subject:** Wildlife of Somalia **Reverse:** Yellow-necked Spurfowl in grass **Note:** Multicolored. Weight varies 18.42-20.2g.

| Date | Mintage | F | VF | XF | Unc | BU |
|---|---|---|---|---|---|---|
| 1998 | — | — | — | — | 15.00 | — |

**25 SHILLINGS** **KM# 62** **Composition:** Copper-Nickel **Subject:** Wildlife of Somalia **Reverse:** Superb Starling on broken branch **Note:** Multicolored. Weight varies 18.42-20.2g.

| Date | Mintage | F | VF | XF | Unc | BU |
|---|---|---|---|---|---|---|
| 1998 | — | — | — | — | 15.00 | — |

**25 SHILLINGS** **KM# 55** **Composition:** Copper-Nickel **Subject:** History of world shipping **Reverse:** Titanic **Note:** Multicolored. Weight varies 18.42-20.2g.

| Date | Mintage | F | VF | XF | Unc | BU |
|---|---|---|---|---|---|---|
| 1998 | — | — | — | — | 11.50 | — |

**25 SHILLINGS** **KM# 59** **Composition:** Copper-Nickel **Subject:** Wildlife of Somalia **Reverse:** Leopard **Note:** Multicolored. Weight varies 18.42-20.2g.

| Date | Mintage | F | VF | XF | Unc | BU |
|---|---|---|---|---|---|---|
| 1998 | — | — | — | — | 15.00 | — |

**25 SHILLINGS** **KM# 70** **Composition:** Copper-Nickel **Subject:** Winston Churchill **Obverse:** National arms **Reverse:** Portrait **Edge:** Plain **Size:** 38 mm.

| Date | Mintage | F | VF | XF | Unc | BU |
|---|---|---|---|---|---|---|
| 2000 | — | — | — | — | 5.00 | — |

**25 SHILLINGS** **KM# 56** **Composition:** Copper-Nickel **Subject:** Wildlife of Somalia **Obverse:** National arms **Reverse:** Ostrich **Note:** Multicolored. Weight varies 18.42-20.2g.

| Date | Mintage | F | VF | XF | Unc | BU |
|---|---|---|---|---|---|---|
| 1998 | — | — | — | — | 15.00 | — |

**25 SHILLINGS** **KM# 60** **Composition:** Copper-Nickel **Subject:** Wildlife of Somalia **Reverse:** Golden Palm Weaver on branch **Note:** Multicolored. Weight varies 18.42-20.2g.

| Date | Mintage | F | VF | XF | Unc | BU |
|---|---|---|---|---|---|---|
| 1998 | — | — | — | — | 15.00 | — |

**25 SHILLINGS** **KM# 71** **Composition:** Copper-Nickel **Subject:** Pope John Paul II **Obverse:** National arms **Reverse:** Portrait **Edge:** Plain **Size:** 38 mm.

| Date | Mintage | F | VF | XF | Unc | BU |
|---|---|---|---|---|---|---|
| 2000 | — | — | — | — | 5.00 | — |

**25 SHILLINGS** **KM# 72** **Weight:** 20.0000 g. **Composition:** Copper-Nickel **Subject:** Nelson Mandela **Obverse:** National arms **Reverse:** Portrait **Edge:** Reeded **Size:** 38 mm.

| Date | Mintage | F | VF | XF | Unc | BU |
|---|---|---|---|---|---|---|
| 2000 | — | — | — | — | 5.00 | — |

**25 SHILLINGS** **KM# 73** **Composition:** Copper-Nickel **Subject:** Che Guevara **Obverse:** National arms **Reverse:** Portrait

| Date | Mintage | F | VF | XF | Unc | BU |
|---|---|---|---|---|---|---|
| 2000 | — | — | — | — | 5.00 | — |

**25 SHILLINGS** **KM# 74** **Composition:** Copper-Nickel **Subject:** Emperor Hirohito **Obverse:** National arms **Reverse:** Portrait **Edge:** Plain **Size:** 37.9 mm.

| Date | Mintage | F | VF | XF | Unc | BU |
|---|---|---|---|---|---|---|
| 2000 Prooflike | — | — | — | — | 7.00 | — |

**25 SHILLINGS** **KM# 75** **Composition:** Copper-Nickel **Subject:** Mao Tse-Tung **Obverse:** National arms **Reverse:** Portrait

| Date | Mintage | F | VF | XF | Unc | BU |
|---|---|---|---|---|---|---|
| 2000 Prooflike | — | — | — | — | 7.00 | — |

**25 SHILLINGS** **KM# 76** **Composition:** Copper-Nickel **Subject:** Berlin **Obverse:** National arms **Reverse:** Berlin wall destruction scene

| Date | Mintage | F | VF | XF | Unc | BU |
|---|---|---|---|---|---|---|
| ND(2000) Prooflike | — | — | — | — | 7.00 | — |

**150 SHILLINGS** **KM# 77** **Weight:** 14.8100 g. **Composition:** 0.9990 Silver .4757 oz. ASW **Subject:** Christopher Columbus **Obverse:** National arms **Reverse:** Cameo above 3 ships **Edge:** Reeded **Size:** 34.25 mm.

| Date | Mintage | F | VF | XF | Unc | BU |
|---|---|---|---|---|---|---|
| 2000 Proof | — | Value: 25.00 | | | | |

**250 SHILLINGS** **KM# 42** **Weight:** 23.5000 g. **Composition:** 0.9250 Silver .6989 oz. ASW **Subject:** History of world shipping - sinking of Titanic **Obverse:** National arms

| Date | Mintage | F | VF | XF | Unc | BU |
|---|---|---|---|---|---|---|
| 1998 Proof | 20,000 | Value: 40.00 | | | | |

**250 SHILLINGS** **KM# 48** **Weight:** 23.7000 g. **Composition:** 0.9250 Silver .7048 oz. ASW **Subject:** Wildlife of Somalia **Reverse:** Hippopotamus **Edge:** Reeded **Size:** 38.1 mm. **Note:** Multicolored.

| Date | Mintage | F | VF | XF | Unc | BU |
|---|---|---|---|---|---|---|
| 1998 Proof | — | Value: 35.00 | | | | |

**250 SHILLINGS** **KM# 42a** **Ring Composition:** Copper-Nickel **Center Composition:** Brass **Subject:** Historic Ships **Obverse:** National arms **Reverse:** Multicolor sinking Titanic **Note:** Copper-nickel ring is within another brass ring.

| Date | Mintage | F | VF | XF | Unc | BU |
|---|---|---|---|---|---|---|
| 1998 | — | — | — | — | 30.00 | — |

**250 SHILLINGS** **KM# 48a** **Ring Composition:** Copper-Nickel **Center Composition:** Brass **Subject:** Wildlife of Somalia **Obverse:** National arms **Reverse:** Hippopotamus **Edge:** Reeded **Note:** Multicolored. Copper-nickel ring is within another brass ring.

| Date | Mintage | F | VF | XF | Unc | BU |
|---|---|---|---|---|---|---|
| 1998 | — | — | — | — | 22.50 | — |

**250 SHILLINGS** **KM# 49** **Weight:** 23.7000 g. **Composition:** 0.9250 Silver .7048 oz. ASW **Subject:** Wildlife of Somalia **Reverse:** Ostrich **Note:** Multicolored.

| Date | Mintage | F | VF | XF | Unc | BU |
|---|---|---|---|---|---|---|
| 1998 Proof | — | Value: 35.00 | | | | |

**250 SHILLINGS** **KM# 49a** **Ring Composition:** Copper-Nickel **Center Composition:** Brass **Subject:** Wildlife of Somalia **Obverse:** National arms **Reverse:** Ostrich **Note:** Multicolored. Copper-nickel ring is within another brass ring.

| Date | Mintage | F | VF | XF | Unc | BU |
|---|---|---|---|---|---|---|
| 1998 | — | — | — | — | 22.50 | — |

**250 SHILLINGS** **KM# 64** **Weight:** 24.8300 g. **Composition:** 0.9000 Silver .7185 oz. ASW **Subject:** Wildlife of Somalia **Obverse:** National arms **Reverse:** Yellow-necked Spurfowl in grass **Edge:** Reeded **Size:** 37.2 mm. **Note:** Multicolored.

| Date | Mintage | F | VF | XF | Unc | BU |
|---|---|---|---|---|---|---|
| 1998 Proof | — | Value: 35.00 | | | | |

**250 SHILLINGS** **KM# 64a** **Ring Composition:** Copper-Nickel **Center Composition:** Brass **Subject:** Wildlife of Somalia **Obverse:** National arms **Reverse:** Yellow-necked Spurfowl in grass **Note:** Multicolored. Copper-nickel ring is within another brass ring.

| Date | Mintage | F | VF | XF | Unc | BU |
|---|---|---|---|---|---|---|
| 1998 | — | — | — | — | 22.50 | — |

**250 SHILLINGS** **KM# 65** **Weight:** 24.8300 g. **Composition:** 0.9000 Silver .7185 oz. ASW **Subject:** Wildlife of Somalia **Reverse:** Running Eland **Note:** Multicolored.

| Date | Mintage | F | VF | XF | Unc | BU |
|---|---|---|---|---|---|---|
| 1998 Proof | — | Value: 35.00 | | | | |

**250 SHILLINGS** **KM# 66** **Weight:** 24.8300 g. **Composition:** 0.9000 Silver .7185 oz. ASW **Subject:** Wildlife of Somalia **Reverse:** Leopard **Note:** Multicolored.

| Date | Mintage | F | VF | XF | Unc | BU |
|---|---|---|---|---|---|---|
| 1998 Proof | — | Value: 35.00 | | | | |

**250 SHILLINGS** **KM# 66a** **Ring Composition:** Copper-Nickel **Center Composition:** Brass **Subject:** Wildlife of Somalia **Obverse:** National arms **Reverse:** Leopard **Note:** Multicolored. Copper-nickel ring is within a brass ring.

| Date | Mintage | F | VF | XF | Unc | BU |
|---|---|---|---|---|---|---|
| 1998 | — | — | — | — | 22.50 | — |

**250 SHILLINGS** **KM# 67** **Weight:** 24.8300 g. **Composition:** 0.9000 Silver .7185 oz. ASW **Subject:** Wildlife of Somalia **Reverse:** Golden Palm Weaver on branch **Note:** Multicolored.

| Date | Mintage | F | VF | XF | Unc | BU |
|---|---|---|---|---|---|---|
| 1998 Proof | — | Value: 35.00 | | | | |

**250 SHILLINGS** **KM# 67a** **Ring Composition:** Copper-Nickel **Center Composition:** Brass **Subject:** Wildlife of Somalia **Obverse:** National arms **Reverse:** Golden Palm Weaver on branch **Note:** Multicolored. Copper-nickel ring is within another brass ring.

| Date | Mintage | F | VF | XF | Unc | BU |
|---|---|---|---|---|---|---|
| 1998 | — | — | — | — | 22.50 | — |

**250 SHILLINGS** **KM# 68** **Weight:** 24.8300 g. **Composition:** 0.9000 Silver .7185 oz. ASW **Subject:** Wildlife of Somalia **Reverse:** Variable Sunbird on branch **Note:** Multicolored.

| Date | Mintage | F | VF | XF | Unc | BU |
|---|---|---|---|---|---|---|
| 1998 Proof | — | Value: 35.00 | | | | |

**250 SHILLINGS** **KM# 68a** **Ring Composition:** Copper-Nickel **Center Composition:** Brass **Subject:** Wildlife of Somalia **Obverse:** National arms **Reverse:** Variable Sunbird on branch **Note:** Multicolored. Copper-nickel ring is within another brass ring.

| Date | Mintage | F | VF | XF | Unc | BU |
|---|---|---|---|---|---|---|
| 1998 | — | — | — | — | 22.50 | — |

**250 SHILLINGS** **KM# 69** **Weight:** 24.8300 g. **Composition:** 0.9000 Silver .7185 oz. ASW **Subject:** Wildlife of Somalia **Reverse:** Superb Starling on broken tree limb **Note:** Multicolored.

| Date | Mintage | F | VF | XF | Unc | BU |
|---|---|---|---|---|---|---|
| 1998 Proof | — | Value: 35.00 | | | | |

**250 SHILLINGS** **KM# 69a** **Ring Composition:** Copper-Nickel **Center Composition:** Brass **Subject:** Wildlife of Somalia **Obverse:** National arms **Reverse:** Superb Starling on broken tree limb **Note:** Multicolored. Copper-nickel ring is within another brass ring.

| Date | Mintage | F | VF | XF | Unc | BU |
|---|---|---|---|---|---|---|
| 1998 | — | — | — | — | 22.50 | — |

**250 SHILLINGS** **KM# 78a** **Ring Composition:** Copper-Nickel **Center Composition:** Brass **Subject:** History of world shipping **Obverse:** National arms **Reverse:** Titanic **Note:** Multicolored. Copper-nickel ring is within another brass ring.

| Date | Mintage | F | VF | XF | Unc | BU |
|---|---|---|---|---|---|---|
| 1998 | — | — | — | — | 30.00 | — |

**250 SHILLINGS** **KM# 79a** **Ring Composition:** Copper-Nickel **Center Composition:** Brass **Subject:** History of world shipping **Obverse:** National arms **Reverse:** Greek trirema **Note:** Multicolored. Copper-nickel ring is within another brass ring.

| Date | Mintage | F | VF | XF | Unc | BU |
|---|---|---|---|---|---|---|
| 1998 | — | — | — | — | 30.00 | — |

**250 SHILLINGS** **KM# 80a** **Ring Composition:** Copper-Nickel **Center Composition:** Brass **Subject:** History of world shipping **Obverse:** National arms **Reverse:** Roman merchant ship **Note:** Multicolored. Copper-nickel ring is within another brass ring.

| Date | Mintage | F | VF | XF | Unc | BU |
|---|---|---|---|---|---|---|
| 1998 | — | — | — | — | 30.00 | — |

**250 SHILLINGS** **KM# 81a** **Ring Composition:** Copper-Nickel **Center Composition:** Brass **Subject:** History of world shipping **Obverse:** National arms **Reverse:** Hanseatic trading cog **Note:** Multicolored. Copper-nickel ring is within another brass ring.

| Date | Mintage | F | VF | XF | Unc | BU |
|---|---|---|---|---|---|---|
| 1998 | — | — | — | — | 30.00 | — |

**250 SHILLINGS** **KM# 82a** **Ring Composition:** Copper-Nickel **Center Composition:** Brass **Subject:** History of world shipping **Obverse:** National arms **Reverse:** Caravel "Nina" **Note:** Multicolored. Copper-nickel ring is within another brass ring.

| Date | Mintage | F | VF | XF | Unc | BU |
|---|---|---|---|---|---|---|
| 1998 | — | — | — | — | 30.00 | — |

**250 SHILLINGS** **KM# 83a** **Ring Composition:** Copper-Nickel **Center Composition:** Brass **Subject:** History of world shipping **Obverse:** National arms **Reverse:** Clipper "Cutty Sark" **Note:** Multicolored. Copper-nickel ring is within another brass ring.

| Date | Mintage | F | VF | XF | Unc | BU |
|---|---|---|---|---|---|---|
| 1998 | — | — | — | — | 30.00 | — |

**250 SHILLINGS** **KM# 63** **Weight:** 24.8300 g. **Composition:** 0.9000 Silver .7185 oz. ASW **Subject:** Marine life protection **Obverse:** National arms **Reverse:** 2 multicolor penguins **Edge:** Reeded **Size:** 37.2 mm. **Note:** Multicolored.

| Date | Mintage | F | VF | XF | Unc | BU |
|---|---|---|---|---|---|---|
| 2000 Proof | — | Value: 45.00 | | | | |

**10000 SHILLINGS** KM# 43 **Weight:** 15.0000 g. **Composition:** 0.9990 Silver .4818 oz. ASW **Subject:** Fauna of Africa **Obverse:** National arms **Reverse:** 2 ostriches

| Date | Mintage | F | VF | XF | Unc | BU |
|---|---|---|---|---|---|---|
| 1998 Proof | — | Value: 40.00 | | | | |

**10000 SHILLINGS** KM# 44 **Weight:** 15.0000 g. **Composition:** 0.9990 Silver .4818 oz. ASW **Subject:** Fauna of Africa **Obverse:** National arms **Reverse:** Scimitar-horned Oryx

| Date | Mintage | F | VF | XF | Unc | BU |
|---|---|---|---|---|---|---|
| 1998 Proof | — | Value: 40.00 | | | | |

## PIEFORTS

| KM# | Date | Mintage | Identification | Mkt Val |
|---|---|---|---|---|
| P1 | 1983 | 500 | 150 Shillings. 0.9250 Silver. | 115 |
| P2 | 1983 | — | 1500 Shillings. KM39. | 850 |
| P3 | (1984) | 500 | 25 Shillings. 0.9250 Silver. | 100 |
| P4 | 1998 | 2,500 | 250 Shillings. 0.9250 Silver. 47.5400 g. Skier. | 135 |
| P6 | 1998 | — | 250 Shillings. 0.9250 Silver. Ostrich. KM49. | 60.00 |
| P5 | 1998 | — | 250 Shillings. Titanic. KM42. | 70.00 |

## PROVAS

| KM# | Date | Mintage | Identification | Mkt Val |
|---|---|---|---|---|
| Pr1 | 1950 | — | Centesimo. | 50.00 |
| Pr2 | 1950 | — | 5 Centesimi. | 50.00 |
| Pr3 | 1950 | — | 10 Centesimi. | 50.00 |
| Pr4 | 1950 | — | 50 Centesimi. | 75.00 |
| Pr5 | 1950 | — | Somalo. | 100 |

## MINT SETS

| KM# | Date | Mintage | Identification | Issue Price | Mkt Val |
|---|---|---|---|---|---|
| MS1 | 1979 (5) | — | KM33-37 | 2,375 | 1,125 |

## PROOF SETS

| KM# | Date | Mintage | Identification | Issue Price | Mkt Val |
|---|---|---|---|---|---|
| PS1 | 1965 (5) | 6,325 | KM10-14 | — | 1,575 |
| PS2 | 1965 (5) | — | KM10-14. Giilt copper nickel. | — | — |
| PS3 | 1970 (5) | 8,000 | KM16, 17, 19, 21, 23 | 334 | 2,500 |
| PS4 | 1970 (3) | 14,500 | KM18, 20, 22 | — | 1,075 |
| PS5 | 1979 (5) | 5,000 | KM28a-32a | 325 | 150 |
| PS6 | 1979 (5) | — | KM33-37 | 3,125 | 1,250 |

# SOMALILAND

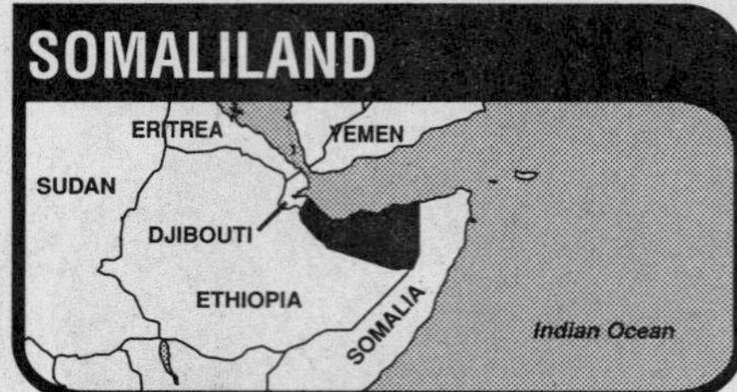


The Somaliland Republic, comprising of the former British Somaliland Protectorate is located on the coast of the northeastern projection of the African continent commonly referred to as the "Horn" on the southwestern end of the Gulf of Aden.

Bordered by Eritrea to the west, Ethiopia to west and south and Somalia to the east. It has an area of 68,000* sq. mi. (176,000* sq. km). Capital: Hargeysa. It is mostly arid and mountainous except for the gulf shoreline.

The Protectorate of British Somaliland was established in 1888 and from 1905 a commissioner under the British Colonial Office administered the territory. Italian Somaliland was administered as a colony from1893 to 1941, when British forces occupied the territory. In 1950 the United Nations allowed Italy to resume control of Italian Somaliland under a trusteeship. In 1960 British and Italian Somaliland were united as Somalia, an independent republic outside the Commonwealth.

Civil war erupted in the late 1970's and continued until the capital of Somalia was taken in 1990. The United Nations provided aid and peacekeeping. A UN sponsored truce was signed in March 1992 and a peace plan and pact was signed Jan. 15, 1993. The northern Somali National Movement (SNM) declared a secession of the Somaliland Republic on May 17, 1991, which is not recognized by the Somali Democratic Republic.

The currency issued by the East African Currency Board was used in British Somaliland from 1945 to 1961; Somali currency was used later until 1995.

## REPUBLIC

### STANDARD COINAGE

**SHILLING** KM# 1 **Composition:** Aluminum **Obverse:** Bird **Reverse:** Denomination

| Date | Mintage | F | VF | XF | Unc | BU |
|---|---|---|---|---|---|---|
| 1994 | — | — | — | 1.50 | 3.00 | — |

# SOUTH AFRICA

The Republic of South Africa, located at the southern tip of Africa, has an area, including the enclave of Walvis Bay, of 472,359 sq. mi. (1,221,040 sq. km.) and a population of *38.5 million. Capitals: Administrative, Pretoria; Legislative, Cape Town; Judicial, Bloemfontein. Manufacturing, mining and agriculture are the principal industries. Exports include wool, diamonds, gold, and metallic ores.

Portuguese navigator Bartholomew Diaz became the first European to sight the region of South Africa when he rounded the Cape of Good Hope in 1488, but throughout the 16th century the only white men to come ashore were the survivors of ships wrecked while attempting the stormy Cape passage. Jan van Riebeeck of the Dutch East India Company established the first permanent settlement in 1652. In subsequent decades additional Dutch, German and Huguenot refugees from France settled in the Cape area to form the Afrikaner segment of today's population.

Great Britain captured the Cape colony in 1795, and again in 1806, receiving permanent title in 1814. To escape British political rule and cultural dominance, many Afrikaner farmers (Boers) migrated northward (the Great Trek) beginning in 1836, and established the independent Boer Republics of the Transvaal (the South African Republic, Zuid Afrikaansche Republic) in 1852, and the Orange Free State in 1854. British political intrigues against the two republics, coupled with the discovery of diamonds and gold in the Boer-settled regions, led to the bitter Boer Wars (1880-81, 1899-1902) and the incorporation of the Boer republics into the British Empire.

On May 31, 1910, the two former Boer Republics (Transvaal and Orange Free State) were joined with the British colonies of Cape of Good Hope and Natal to form the Union of South Africa, a dominion of the British Empire. In 1934 the Union achieved status as a sovereign state within the British Empire.

Political integration of the various colonies did not still the conflict between the Afrikaners and the English-speaking groups, which continued to have a significant impact on political developments. A resurgence of Afrikaner nationalism in the 1940s and 1950s led to a referendum in the white community authorizing the relinquishment of dominion status and the establishment of a republic. The decision took effect on May 31, 1961. The Republic of South Africa withdrew from the British Commonwealth in Oct. 1961.

The apartheid era ended April 27, 1994 with the first democratic election for all people of South Africa. Nelson Mandela was inaugurated President May 10, 1994, and South Africa was readmitted into the Commonwealth of Nations.

South African coins and currency bear inscriptions in tribal languages, Afrikaans and English.

**RULERS**

British, until 1934

**MONETARY SYSTEM**

Until 1961

12 Pence = 1 Shilling
2 Shillings = 1 Florin
20 Shillings = 1 Pound (Pond)

Commencing 1961

100 Cents = 1 Rand

## ZUID-AFRIKAANSCHE REPUBLIEK

### STANDARD COINAGE

12 Pence = 1 Shilling; 20 Shillings = 1 Pond

**1/2 POND** KM# 11 **Composition:** 0.9990 Gold **Subject:** Veld-Boer War Siege Issue

| Date | Mintage | F | VF | XF | Unc | BU |
|---|---|---|---|---|---|---|
| 1902 | 986 | 600 | 1,200 | 2,000 | 3,500 | — |

# UNION OF SOUTH AFRICA

## STANDARD COINAGE

12 Pence = 1 Shilling; 2 Shillings = 1 Florin; 20 Shillings 1 Pound

### 1/4 PENNY (Farthing) KM# 12.1 Composition: Bronze
**Reverse:** Denomination: 1/4 PENNY 1/4

| Date | Mintage | F | VF | XF | Unc | BU |
|---|---|---|---|---|---|---|
| 1923 | 33,000 | 2.00 | 5.00 | 10.00 | 20.00 | — |
| 1923 Proof | 1,402 | Value: 30.00 | | | | |
| 1924 | 95,000 | 1.50 | 2.50 | 5.00 | 10.00 | — |

### 1/4 PENNY (Farthing) KM# 12.2 Composition: Bronze
**Reverse:** Denomination: 1/4 PENNY

| Date | Mintage | F | VF | XF | Unc | BU |
|---|---|---|---|---|---|---|
| 1926 Proof | 16 | Value: 6,000 | | | | |
| 1928 | 64,000 | 1.50 | 3.00 | 5.00 | 12.50 | — |
| 1930 | 6,560 | 30.00 | 60.00 | 120 | 200 | — |
| 1930 Proof | 14 | Value: 1,200 | | | | |
| 1931 | 154,000 | 1.00 | 1.50 | 4.00 | 6.00 | — |

### 1/4 PENNY (Farthing) KM# 12.3 Composition: Bronze
**Reverse:** Denomination: 1/4 D

| Date | Mintage | F | VF | XF | Unc | BU |
|---|---|---|---|---|---|---|
| 1931 | Inc. above | 5.00 | 10.00 | 15.00 | 35.00 | — |
| 1931 Proof | 62 | Value: 200 | | | | |
| 1932 | 105,000 | 1.00 | 1.50 | 3.50 | 7.00 | — |
| 1932 Proof | 12 | Value: 375 | | | | |
| 1933 | 76 | 750 | 1,450 | 2,200 | 3,250 | — |
| 1933 Proof | 20 | Value: 4,000 | | | | |
| 1934 | 52 | 750 | 1,450 | 2,200 | 3,250 | — |
| 1934 Proof | 24 | Value: 3,750 | | | | |
| 1935 | 61,000 | 1.00 | 1.50 | 3.50 | 8.00 | — |
| 1935 Proof | 20 | Value: 3,000 | | | | |
| 1936 | 43 | 350 | 750 | 1,100 | 2,000 | — |
| 1936 Proof | 40 | Value: 3,000 | | | | |

### 1/4 PENNY (Farthing) KM# 23 Composition: Bronze

| Date | Mintage | F | VF | XF | Unc | BU |
|---|---|---|---|---|---|---|
| 1937 | 38,000 | 1.50 | 3.00 | 6.00 | 12.50 | — |
| 1937 Proof | 116 | Value: 40.00 | | | | |
| 1938 | 51,000 | 1.00 | 2.00 | 4.00 | 8.00 | — |
| 1938 Proof | 44 | Value: 100 | | | | |
| 1939 | 102,000 | 0.50 | 1.50 | 3.00 | 7.50 | — |
| 1939 Proof | 30 | Value: 125 | | | | |
| 1941 | 91,000 | 0.50 | 1.50 | 3.00 | 7.50 | — |
| 1942 | 3,756,000 | 0.25 | 0.50 | 1.00 | 2.00 | — |
| 1943 | 9,918,000 | 0.25 | 0.50 | 0.75 | 1.50 | — |
| 1943 Proof | 104 | Value: 40.00 | | | | |
| 1944 | 4,468,000 | 0.25 | 0.50 | 0.75 | 2.00 | — |
| 1944 Proof | 150 | Value: 35.00 | | | | |
| 1945 | 5,297,000 | 0.25 | 0.50 | 1.50 | 3.00 | — |
| 1945 Proof | 150 | Value: 35.00 | | | | |
| 1946 | 4,378,000 | 0.25 | 0.50 | 1.50 | 4.00 | — |
| 1946 Proof | 150 | Value: 35.00 | | | | |
| 1947 | 3,895,000 | 0.25 | 0.50 | 1.50 | 4.00 | — |
| 1947 Proof | 2,600 | Value: 4.00 | | | | |

### 1/4 PENNY (Farthing) KM# 32.1 Composition: Bronze

| Date | Mintage | F | VF | XF | Unc | BU |
|---|---|---|---|---|---|---|
| 1948 | 2,415,000 | 0.25 | 0.50 | 1.00 | 2.00 | — |
| 1948 Proof | 1,120 | Value: 3.00 | | | | |
| 1949 | 3,568,000 | 0.25 | 0.50 | 1.00 | 2.50 | — |
| 1949 Proof | 800 | Value: 5.00 | | | | |
| 1950 | 8,694,000 | 0.25 | 0.50 | 0.75 | 1.50 | — |
| 1950 Proof | 500 | Value: 8.00 | | | | |

### 1/4 PENNY (Farthing) KM# 32.2 Composition: Bronze
**Reverse:** Reversed legend **Rev. Legend:** SUID AFRIKA-SOUTH AFRICA

| Date | Mintage | F | VF | XF | Unc | BU |
|---|---|---|---|---|---|---|
| 1951 | 3,511,000 | 0.15 | 0.35 | 0.75 | 2.50 | — |
| 1951 Proof | 2,000 | Value: 2.00 | | | | |
| 1952 | 2,805,000 | 0.15 | 0.35 | 0.75 | 2.00 | — |
| 1952 Proof | 16,000 | Value: 2.00 | | | | |

### 1/4 PENNY (Farthing) KM# 44 Composition: Bronze

| Date | Mintage | F | VF | XF | Unc | BU |
|---|---|---|---|---|---|---|
| 1953 | 7,193,000 | 0.15 | 0.25 | 0.50 | 1.50 | — |
| 1953 Proof | 5,000 | Value: 2.00 | | | | |
| 1954 | 6,568,000 | 0.15 | 0.25 | 0.50 | 1.50 | — |
| 1954 Proof | 3,150 | Value: 2.00 | | | | |
| 1955 | 11,798,000 | 0.15 | 0.25 | 0.50 | 1.50 | — |
| 1955 Proof | 2,850 | Value: 2.00 | | | | |
| 1956 | 1,287,000 | 0.15 | 0.25 | 0.50 | 2.50 | — |
| 1956 Proof | 1,700 | Value: 3.00 | | | | |
| 1957 | 3,065,000 | 0.15 | 0.25 | 0.50 | 1.50 | — |
| 1957 Proof | 1,130 | Value: 4.00 | | | | |
| 1958 | 5,452,000 | 0.15 | 0.25 | 0.50 | 1.50 | — |
| 1958 Proof | 985 | Value: 5.00 | | | | |
| 1959 | 1,567,000 | 0.15 | 0.25 | 0.50 | 1.50 | — |
| 1959 Proof | 900 | Value: 6.00 | | | | |
| 1960 | 1,022,999 | 0.15 | 0.25 | 0.50 | 2.00 | — |
| 1960 Proof | 3,360 | Value: 1.50 | | | | |

### 1/2 PENNY KM# 13.1 Composition: Bronze Reverse: Denomination: 1/2 PENNY 1/2

| Date | Mintage | F | VF | XF | Unc | BU |
|---|---|---|---|---|---|---|
| 1923 | 12,000 | 25.00 | 40.00 | 70.00 | 100 | — |
| 1923 Proof | 1,402 | Value: 100 | | | | |
| 1924 | 64,000 | 7.50 | 12.50 | 30.00 | 60.00 | — |
| 1925 | 69,000 | 7.50 | 12.50 | 30.00 | 80.00 | — |
| 1926 | 65,000 | 10.00 | 15.00 | 35.00 | 100 | — |

### 1/2 PENNY KM# 13.2 Composition: Bronze Reverse: Denomination: 1/2 PENNY

| Date | Mintage | F | VF | XF | Unc | BU |
|---|---|---|---|---|---|---|
| 1928 | 105,000 | 5.00 | 12.50 | 35.00 | 75.00 | — |
| 1929 | 272,000 | 2.50 | 5.00 | 15.00 | 35.00 | — |
| 1930 | 147,000 | 3.50 | 7.00 | 20.00 | 40.00 | — |
| 1930 Proof | 14 | Value: 400 | | | | |
| 1930 Without star after date | Inc. above | 4.00 | 8.00 | 25.00 | 50.00 | — |
| 1931 | 145,000 | 3.50 | 7.00 | 25.00 | 50.00 | — |

### 1/2 PENNY KM# 13.3 Composition: Bronze Reverse: Denomination: 1/2 D

| Date | Mintage | F | VF | XF | Unc | BU |
|---|---|---|---|---|---|---|
| 1931 Proof | 62 | Value: 1,000 | | | | |
| 1932 | 106,000 | 5.00 | 10.00 | 30.00 | 75.00 | — |
| 1932 Proof | 12 | Value: 1,000 | | | | |
| 1933 | 63,000 | 8.00 | 25.00 | 55.00 | 100 | — |
| 1933 Proof | 20 | Value: 500 | | | | |
| 1934 | 326,000 | 1.50 | 5.00 | 15.00 | 45.00 | — |
| 1934 Proof | 24 | Value: 500 | | | | |
| 1935 | 405,000 | 1.50 | 5.00 | 15.00 | 40.00 | — |
| 1935 Proof | 20 | Value: 500 | | | | |
| 1936 | 407,000 | 1.50 | 5.00 | 15.00 | 30.00 | — |
| 1936 Proof | 40 | Value: 200 | | | | |

### 1/2 PENNY KM# 24 Composition: Bronze

| Date | Mintage | F | VF | XF | Unc | BU |
|---|---|---|---|---|---|---|
| 1937 | 638,000 | 1.00 | 2.00 | 9.00 | 15.00 | — |
| 1937 Proof | 116 | Value: 50.00 | | | | |
| 1938 | 560,000 | 1.00 | 2.00 | 6.00 | 15.00 | — |
| 1938 Proof | 44 | Value: 125 | | | | |
| 1939 | 271,000 | 2.50 | 5.00 | 10.00 | 20.00 | — |
| 1939 Proof | 30 | Value: 175 | | | | |
| 1940 | 1,535,000 | 0.30 | 0.75 | 3.00 | 8.00 | — |
| 1941 | 2,053,000 | 0.30 | 0.75 | 3.00 | 8.00 | — |
| 1942 | 8,382,000 | 0.25 | 0.60 | 2.00 | 6.00 | — |
| 1943 | 5,135,000 | 0.25 | 0.60 | 2.00 | 6.00 | — |
| 1943 Proof | 104 | Value: 45.00 | | | | |
| 1944 | 3,920,000 | 0.25 | 0.75 | 3.00 | 8.00 | — |
| 1944 Proof | 150 | Value: 35.00 | | | | |
| 1945 | 2,357,000 | 0.25 | 0.60 | 2.50 | 7.00 | — |
| 1945 Proof | 150 | Value: 35.00 | | | | |
| 1946 | 1,022,000 | 0.25 | 0.75 | 3.00 | 9.00 | — |
| 1946 Proof | 150 | Value: 35.00 | | | | |
| 1947 | 258,000 | 1.00 | 3.00 | 6.00 | 17.50 | — |
| 1947 Proof | 2,600 | Value: 10.00 | | | | |

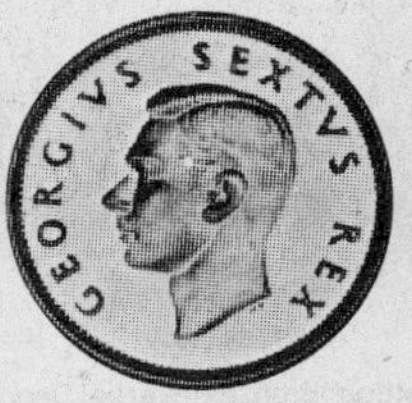

### 1/2 PENNY KM# 33 Composition: Bronze

| Date | Mintage | F | VF | XF | Unc | BU |
|---|---|---|---|---|---|---|
| 1948 | 685,000 | 0.50 | 1.00 | 4.00 | 9.00 | — |
| 1948 Proof | 1,120 | Value: 15.00 | | | | |
| 1949 | 1,850,000 | 0.25 | 0.50 | 1.75 | 4.00 | — |
| 1949 Proof | 800 | Value: 15.00 | | | | |
| 1950 | 2,186,000 | 0.25 | 0.50 | 1.50 | 3.00 | — |
| 1950 Proof | 500 | Value: 6.00 | | | | |
| 1951 | 3,746,000 | 0.25 | 0.50 | 1.25 | 3.00 | — |
| 1951 Proof | 2,000 | Value: 5.00 | | | | |
| 1952 | 4,174,000 | 0.25 | 0.50 | 1.00 | 2.50 | — |
| 1952 Proof | 1,550 | Value: 4.00 | | | | |

**1/2 PENNY** KM# 45 **Composition:** Bronze

| Date | Mintage | F | VF | XF | Unc | BU |
|---|---|---|---|---|---|---|
| 1953 | 5,572,000 | 0.15 | 0.35 | 1.00 | 3.00 | — |
| 1953 Proof | 5,000 | Value: 4.00 | | | | |
| 1954 | 101,000 | 2.00 | 4.00 | 7.50 | 12.50 | — |
| 1954 Proof | 3,150 | Value: 15.00 | | | | |
| 1955 | 3,774,000 | 0.15 | 0.35 | 1.00 | 3.00 | — |
| 1955 Proof | 2,850 | Value: 4.00 | | | | |
| 1956 | 1,305,000 | 0.15 | 0.35 | 1.00 | 3.00 | — |
| 1956 Proof | 1,700 | Value: 4.00 | | | | |
| 1957 | 2,025,000 | 0.15 | 0.35 | 1.00 | 3.00 | — |
| 1957 Proof | 1,130 | Value: 4.00 | | | | |
| 1958 | 2,171,000 | 0.15 | 0.35 | 1.00 | 2.50 | — |
| 1958 Proof | 985 | Value: 5.00 | | | | |
| 1959 | 2,397,000 | 0.15 | 0.25 | 0.75 | 2.00 | — |
| 1959 Proof | 900 | Value: 6.00 | | | | |
| 1960 | 2,552,000 | 0.15 | 0.25 | 0.75 | 2.00 | — |
| 1960 Proof | 3,360 | Value: 1.50 | | | | |

**PENNY** KM# 14.1 **Composition:** Bronze **Reverse:** Denomination: 1 PENNY 1

| Date | Mintage | F | VF | XF | Unc | BU |
|---|---|---|---|---|---|---|
| 1923 | 91,000 | 3.00 | 7.00 | 17.50 | 35.00 | — |
| 1923 Proof | 1,402 | Value: 50.00 | | | | |
| 1924 | 134,000 | 4.00 | 10.00 | 25.00 | 50.00 | — |

**PENNY** KM# 14.2 **Composition:** Bronze **Reverse:** Denomination: PENNY

| Date | Mintage | F | VF | XF | Unc | BU |
|---|---|---|---|---|---|---|
| 1926 | 393,000 | 3.00 | 10.00 | 40.00 | 100 | — |
| 1926 Proof | 16 | Value: 600 | | | | |
| 1927 | 285,000 | 3.00 | 10.00 | 40.00 | 90.00 | — |
| 1928 | 386,000 | 3.00 | 10.00 | 40.00 | 90.00 | — |
| 1929 | 1,093,000 | 1.00 | 5.00 | 15.00 | 35.00 | — |
| 1930 | 754,000 | 1.00 | 5.00 | 20.00 | 40.00 | — |
| 1930 Proof | 14 | Value: 600 | | | | |

**PENNY** KM# 14.3 **Composition:** Bronze **Reverse:** Denomination: 1 D

| Date | Mintage | F | VF | XF | Unc | BU |
|---|---|---|---|---|---|---|
| 1931 | 284,000 | 1.00 | 5.00 | 17.50 | 40.00 | — |
| 1931 Proof | 62 | Value: 400 | | | | |
| 1932 | 260,000 | 1.00 | 5.00 | 20.00 | 50.00 | — |
| 1932 Proof | 12 | Value: 800 | | | | |
| 1933 | 225,000 | 2.00 | 10.00 | 30.00 | 45.00 | — |
| 1933 Proof | 20 | Value: 500 | | | | |
| 1933 Without star after date | Inc. above | 4.00 | 10.00 | 30.00 | 50.00 | — |
| 1934 | 2,089,999 | 0.50 | 1.50 | 8.00 | 22.50 | — |
| 1934 Proof | 24 | Value: 600 | | | | |
| 1935 | 2,295,000 | 0.50 | 1.50 | 8.00 | 22.50 | — |
| 1935 Proof | 20 | Value: 600 | | | | |
| 1936 | 1,819,000 | 0.35 | 1.00 | 5.00 | 20.00 | — |
| 1936 Proof | 40 | Value: 300 | | | | |

**PENNY** KM# 25 **Composition:** Bronze

| Date | Mintage | F | VF | XF | Unc | BU |
|---|---|---|---|---|---|---|
| 1937 | 3,281,000 | 0.50 | 1.50 | 10.00 | 25.00 | — |
| 1937 Proof | 116 | Value: 75.00 | | | | |
| 1938 | 1,840,000 | 0.50 | 1.50 | 8.00 | 30.00 | — |
| 1938 Proof | 44 | Value: 100 | | | | |
| 1939 | 1,506,000 | 0.50 | 1.50 | 10.00 | 25.00 | — |
| 1939 Proof | 30 | Value: 175 | | | | |
| 1940 | 3,592,000 | 0.35 | 1.00 | 4.00 | 10.00 | — |
| 1940 Without star after date | Inc. above | 1.50 | 3.00 | 6.00 | 15.00 | — |
| 1941 | 7,871,000 | 0.25 | 0.75 | 2.50 | 7.00 | — |
| 1942 | 14,428,000 | 0.25 | 0.75 | 2.00 | 6.00 | — |
| 1942 Without star after date | Inc. above | 3.00 | 6.00 | 12.50 | 30.00 | — |
| 1943 | 4,010,000 | 0.25 | 0.75 | 2.50 | 6.00 | — |
| 1943 Proof | 104 | Value: 55.00 | | | | |
| 1944 | 6,425,000 | 0.25 | 0.75 | 2.50 | 7.00 | — |
| 1944 Proof | 150 | Value: 45.00 | | | | |
| 1945 | 4,810,000 | 0.25 | 0.75 | 2.50 | 7.00 | — |
| 1945 Proof | 150 | Value: 45.00 | | | | |
| 1946 | 2,605,000 | 0.25 | 0.75 | 3.00 | 8.00 | — |
| 1946 Proof | 150 | Value: 45.00 | | | | |
| 1947 | 135,000 | 2.50 | 4.00 | 7.50 | 17.50 | — |
| 1947 Proof | 2,600 | Value: 7.00 | | | | |

**PENNY** KM# 34.1 **Composition:** Bronze

| Date | Mintage | F | VF | XF | Unc | BU |
|---|---|---|---|---|---|---|
| 1948 | 2,398,000 | 0.25 | 0.75 | 2.50 | 6.00 | — |
| 1948 Proof | 1,120 | Value: 5.00 | | | | |
| 1948 Without star after date | Inc. above | 1.00 | 2.00 | 5.00 | 10.00 | — |
| 1949 | 3,634,000 | 0.25 | 0.75 | 2.00 | 6.00 | — |
| 1949 Proof | 800 | Value: 12.00 | | | | |
| 1950 | 4,890,000 | 0.25 | 0.75 | 2.00 | 5.00 | — |
| 1950 Proof | 500 | Value: 10.00 | | | | |

**PENNY** KM# 34.2 **Composition:** Bronze **Rev. Legend:** SUID AFRIKA-SOUTH AFRICA

| Date | Mintage | F | VF | XF | Unc | BU |
|---|---|---|---|---|---|---|
| 1951 | 3,787,000 | 0.25 | 0.75 | 1.50 | 4.00 | — |
| 1951 Proof | 2,000 | Value: 5.00 | | | | |
| 1952 | 12,674,000 | 0.25 | 0.50 | 1.00 | 2.50 | — |
| 1952 Proof | 16,000 | Value: 4.00 | | | | |

**PENNY** KM# 46 **Composition:** Bronze

| Date | Mintage | F | VF | XF | Unc | BU |
|---|---|---|---|---|---|---|
| 1953 | 5,491,000 | 0.20 | 0.35 | 0.75 | 2.00 | — |
| 1953 Proof | 5,000 | Value: 2.00 | | | | |
| 1954 | 6,665,000 | 1.00 | 2.00 | 5.00 | 10.00 | — |
| 1954 Proof | 3,150 | Value: 15.00 | | | | |
| 1955 | 6,508,000 | 0.20 | 0.35 | 0.75 | 3.00 | — |
| 1955 Proof | 2,850 | Value: 2.00 | | | | |
| 1956 | 4,390,000 | 0.20 | 0.35 | 1.00 | 4.00 | — |
| 1956 Proof | 1,700 | Value: 3.00 | | | | |
| 1957 | 3,973,000 | 0.20 | 0.35 | 0.75 | 3.00 | — |
| 1957 Proof | 1,130 | Value: 5.00 | | | | |
| 1958 | 5,311,000 | 0.20 | 0.35 | 0.75 | 3.00 | — |
| 1958 Proof | 985 | Value: 6.00 | | | | |
| 1959 | 5,066,000 | 0.20 | 0.35 | 0.75 | 2.00 | — |
| 1959 Proof | 900 | Value: 7.00 | | | | |
| 1960 | 5,106,000 | 0.20 | 0.35 | 0.75 | 2.00 | — |
| 1960 Proof | 3,360 | Value: 2.00 | | | | |

**3 PENCE** KM# 15.1 **Weight:** 1.4100 g. **Composition:** 0.8000 Silver .0362 oz. ASW

| Date | Mintage | F | VF | XF | Unc | BU |
|---|---|---|---|---|---|---|
| 1923 | 302,000 | 4.00 | 8.00 | 20.00 | 45.00 | — |
| 1923 Proof | 1,402 | Value: 50.00 | | | | |
| 1924 | 501,000 | 4.00 | 10.00 | 25.00 | 50.00 | — |
| 1925 | — | 10.00 | 35.00 | 200 | 475 | — |

**3 PENCE** KM# 15.2 **Weight:** 1.4100 g. **Composition:** 0.8000 Silver .0362 oz. ASW **Reverse:** Denomination: 3 PENCE

| Date | Mintage | F | VF | XF | Unc | BU |
|---|---|---|---|---|---|---|
| 1925 | 358,000 | 5.00 | 25.00 | 90.00 | 175 | — |
| 1926 | 1,572,000 | 1.00 | 3.50 | 20.00 | 50.00 | — |
| 1926 Proof | 16 | Value: 2,000 | | | | |
| 1927 | 2,285,000 | 1.00 | 2.50 | 15.00 | 45.00 | — |
| 1928 | 919,000 | 1.50 | 3.50 | 20.00 | 50.00 | — |
| 1929 | 1,948,000 | 1.00 | 2.50 | 15.00 | 45.00 | — |
| 1930 | 981,000 | 1.00 | 3.50 | 20.00 | 50.00 | — |
| 1930 Proof | 14 | Value: 800 | | | | |

**3 PENCE** KM# 15.3 **Weight:** 1.4100 g. **Composition:** 0.8000 Silver .0362 oz. ASW **Reverse:** Denomination: 3D

| Date | Mintage | F | VF | XF | Unc | BU |
|---|---|---|---|---|---|---|
| 1931 | 66 | 750 | 1,000 | 1,750 | 3,500 | — |
| 1931 Proof | 62 | Value: 3,500 | | | | |
| 1932 | 2,622,000 | 1.00 | 2.50 | 15.00 | 30.00 | — |
| 1932 Proof | 12 | Value: 1,000 | | | | |
| 1933 | 5,135,000 | 1.00 | 2.50 | 15.00 | 30.00 | — |
| 1933 Proof | 20 | Value: 1,000 | | | | |
| 1934 | 2,357,000 | 1.00 | 2.50 | 15.00 | 30.00 | — |
| 1934 Proof | 24 | Value: 1,000 | | | | |
| 1935 | 1,655,000 | 1.00 | 2.50 | 15.00 | 30.00 | — |
| 1935 Proof | 20 | Value: 1,000 | | | | |
| 1936 | 1,095,000 | 1.00 | 2.50 | 15.00 | 35.00 | — |
| 1936 Proof | 40 | Value: 250 | | | | |

**3 PENCE** KM# 26 **Weight:** 1.4100 g. **Composition:** 0.8000 Silver .0362 oz. ASW

| Date | Mintage | F | VF | XF | Unc | BU |
|---|---|---|---|---|---|---|
| 1937 | 3,576,000 | 0.50 | 1.00 | 3.00 | 10.00 | — |
| 1937 Proof | 116 | Value: 80.00 | | | | |
| 1938 | 2,394,000 | 0.50 | 1.50 | 7.00 | 20.00 | — |
| 1938 Proof | 44 | Value: 100 | | | | |
| 1939 | 3,224,000 | 0.50 | 1.50 | 5.00 | 12.50 | — |
| 1939 Proof | 30 | Value: 250 | | | | |
| 1940 | 4,887,000 | 0.50 | 1.00 | 3.00 | 12.50 | — |
| 1941 | 8,968,000 | 0.50 | 1.00 | 3.00 | 9.00 | — |
| 1942 | 8,055,999 | 0.50 | 1.00 | 3.00 | 9.00 | — |
| 1943 | 14,827,000 | 0.50 | 1.00 | 2.50 | 6.00 | — |
| 1943 Proof | 104 | Value: 70.00 | | | | |
| 1944 | 3,331,000 | 0.50 | 1.00 | 3.00 | 9.00 | — |
| 1944 Proof | 150 | Value: 60.00 | | | | |
| 1945/3 | 4,094,000 | 1.00 | 3.00 | 10.00 | 20.00 | — |
| 1945 | Inc. above | 0.50 | 1.00 | 3.00 | 9.00 | — |
| 1945 Proof | 150 | Value: 60.00 | | | | |

| Date | Mintage | F | VF | XF | Unc | BU |
|---|---|---|---|---|---|---|
| 1946 | 2,219,000 | 0.50 | 1.00 | 3.00 | 10.00 | — |
| 1946 Proof | 150 | Value: 65.00 | | | | |
| 1947 | 1,127,000 | 0.50 | 1.00 | 2.50 | 8.00 | — |
| 1947 Proof | 2,600 | Value: 8.00 | | | | |

**3 PENCE** **KM# 35.1** **Weight:** 1.4100 g. **Composition:** 0.8000 Silver .0362 oz. ASW

| Date | Mintage | F | VF | XF | Unc | BU |
|---|---|---|---|---|---|---|
| 1948 | 2,720,000 | 0.50 | 1.00 | 3.00 | 7.00 | — |
| 1948 Proof | 1,120 | Value: 5.00 | | | | |
| 1949 | 1,904,000 | 0.50 | 1.00 | 3.00 | 7.00 | — |
| 1949 Proof | 800 | Value: 5.00 | | | | |
| 1950 | 4,096,000 | 0.50 | 1.00 | 2.50 | 5.00 | — |
| 1950 Proof | 500 | Value: 7.00 | | | | |

**3 PENCE** **KM# 35.2** **Weight:** 1.4100 g. **Composition:** 0.5000 Silver .0226 oz. ASW **Reverse:** Modified design **Note:** Many varieties exist of George VI 3 Pence.

| Date | Mintage | F | VF | XF | Unc | BU |
|---|---|---|---|---|---|---|
| 1951 | 6,323,000 | 0.25 | 0.50 | 1.00 | 3.00 | — |
| 1951 Proof | 2,000 | Value: 4.00 | | | | |
| 1952 | 13,057,000 | 0.25 | 0.50 | 1.00 | 2.00 | — |
| 1952 Proof | 16,000 | Value: 2.00 | | | | |

**3 PENCE** **KM# 47** **Weight:** 1.4100 g. **Composition:** 0.5000 Silver .0226 oz. ASW

| Date | Mintage | F | VF | XF | Unc | BU |
|---|---|---|---|---|---|---|
| 1953 | 5,483,000 | 0.25 | 0.50 | 1.00 | 3.00 | — |
| 1953 Proof | 5,000 | Value: 3.00 | | | | |
| 1954 | 3,898,000 | 0.25 | 0.50 | 1.00 | 3.50 | — |
| 1954 Proof | 3,150 | Value: 4.00 | | | | |
| 1955 | 4,720,000 | 0.25 | 0.50 | 1.00 | 3.00 | — |
| 1955 Proof | 2,850 | Value: 3.00 | | | | |
| 1956 | 6,189,000 | 0.25 | 0.50 | 1.00 | 3.00 | — |
| 1956 Proof | 1,700 | Value: 4.00 | | | | |
| 1957 | 1,893,000 | 0.25 | 0.50 | 1.00 | 3.00 | — |
| 1957 Proof | 1,130 | Value: 5.00 | | | | |
| 1958 | 3,227,000 | 0.25 | 0.50 | 1.00 | 3.00 | — |
| 1958 Proof | 985 | Value: 6.00 | | | | |
| 1959 | 2,552,000 | 0.25 | 0.50 | 1.00 | 2.00 | — |
| 1959 No K-G on reverse | Inc. above | 2.00 | 3.00 | 5.00 | 10.00 | — |
| 1959 Proof | 900 | Value: 7.00 | | | | |
| 1960 | 18,000 | 1.00 | 2.50 | 4.00 | 7.00 | — |
| 1960 Proof | 3,360 | Value: 3.00 | | | | |

**6 PENCE** **KM# 16.1** **Weight:** 2.8300 g. **Composition:** 0.8000 Silver .0727 oz. ASW

| Date | Mintage | F | VF | XF | Unc | BU |
|---|---|---|---|---|---|---|
| 1923 | 208,000 | 4.00 | 15.00 | 35.00 | 80.00 | — |
| 1923 Proof | 1,402 | Value: 80.00 | | | | |
| 1924 | 326,000 | 3.50 | 12.50 | 30.00 | 70.00 | — |

**6 PENCE** **KM# 16.2** **Weight:** 2.8300 g. **Composition:** 0.8000 Silver .0727 oz. ASW **Reverse:** Denomination: 6 PENCE

| Date | Mintage | F | VF | XF | Unc | BU |
|---|---|---|---|---|---|---|
| 1925 | 79,000 | 5.00 | 20.00 | 60.00 | 125 | — |
| 1926 | 722,000 | 2.00 | 10.00 | 45.00 | 100 | — |
| 1926 Proof | 16 | Value: 3,000 | | | | |
| 1927 | 1,548,000 | 1.50 | 4.00 | 25.00 | 50.00 | — |
| 1929 | 784,000 | 2.00 | 8.00 | 30.00 | 60.00 | — |
| 1930 | 448,000 | 2.00 | 8.00 | 35.00 | 70.00 | — |
| 1930 Proof | 14 | Value: 1,000 | | | | |

**6 PENCE** **KM# 16.3** **Weight:** 2.8300 g. **Composition:** 0.8000 Silver .0727 oz. ASW **Reverse:** Denomination: 6 D **Rev. Legend:** 6 D

| Date | Mintage | F | VF | XF | Unc | BU |
|---|---|---|---|---|---|---|
| 1931 | 4,743 | 75.00 | 150 | 250 | 550 | — |
| 1931 Proof | 62 | Value: 1,000 | | | | |
| 1932 | 1,525,000 | 1.00 | 5.00 | 17.50 | 35.00 | — |
| 1932 Proof | 12 | Value: 1,200 | | | | |
| 1933 | 2,819,000 | 1.00 | 5.00 | 17.50 | 35.00 | — |
| 1933 Proof | 20 | Value: 1,200 | | | | |
| 1934 | 1,519,000 | 1.00 | 7.00 | 20.00 | 40.00 | — |
| 1934 Proof | 24 | Value: 1,200 | | | | |
| 1935 | 573,000 | 2.00 | 8.00 | 30.00 | 100 | — |
| 1935 Proof | 20 | Value: 1,200 | | | | |
| 1936 | 627,000 | 1.00 | 7.00 | 20.00 | 40.00 | — |
| 1936 Proof | 40 | Value: 275 | | | | |

**6 PENCE** **KM# 27** **Weight:** 2.8300 g. **Composition:** 0.8000 Silver .0727 oz. ASW

| Date | Mintage | F | VF | XF | Unc | BU |
|---|---|---|---|---|---|---|
| 1937 | 1,696,000 | 1.00 | 2.00 | 7.00 | 17.50 | — |
| 1937 Proof | 116 | Value: 90.00 | | | | |
| 1938 | 1,725,000 | 1.00 | 2.00 | 7.00 | 17.50 | — |
| 1938 Proof | 44 | Value: 125 | | | | |
| 1939 Proof | 30 | Value: 3,750 | | | | |
| 1940 | 1,629,000 | 1.00 | 1.50 | 5.00 | 10.00 | — |
| 1941 | 2,263,000 | 1.00 | 1.50 | 5.00 | 10.00 | — |
| 1942 | 4,936,000 | 0.75 | 1.25 | 3.00 | 8.00 | — |
| 1943 | 3,776,000 | 0.75 | 1.25 | 3.00 | 8.00 | — |
| 1943 Proof | 104 | Value: 85.00 | | | | |
| 1944 | 228,000 | 2.00 | 7.00 | 15.00 | 30.00 | — |
| 1944 Proof | 150 | Value: 75.00 | | | | |
| 1945 | 420,000 | 1.00 | 5.00 | 15.00 | 35.00 | — |
| 1945 Proof | 150 | Value: 75.00 | | | | |
| 1946 | 290,000 | 1.00 | 6.00 | 15.00 | 30.00 | — |
| 1946 Proof | 150 | Value: 80.00 | | | | |
| 1947 | 577,000 | 1.00 | 1.50 | 5.00 | 10.00 | — |
| 1947 Proof | 2,600 | Value: 10.00 | | | | |

**6 PENCE** **KM# 36.1** **Weight:** 2.8300 g. **Composition:** 0.8000 Silver .0727 oz. ASW

| Date | Mintage | F | VF | XF | Unc | BU |
|---|---|---|---|---|---|---|
| 1948 | 2,266,000 | 0.75 | 1.25 | 2.50 | 6.00 | — |
| 1948 Proof | 1,120 | Value: 10.00 | | | | |
| 1949 | 196,000 | 3.00 | 7.50 | 15.00 | 30.00 | — |
| 1949 Proof | 800 | Value: 15.00 | | | | |
| 1950 | 2,122,000 | 0.75 | 1.00 | 2.00 | 5.00 | — |
| 1950 Proof | 500 | Value: 15.00 | | | | |

**6 PENCE** **KM# 36.2** **Weight:** 2.8300 g. **Composition:** 0.5000 Silver .0454 oz. ASW

| Date | Mintage | F | VF | XF | Unc | BU |
|---|---|---|---|---|---|---|
| 1951 | 2,602,000 | 0.50 | 1.00 | 2.00 | 4.00 | — |
| 1951 Proof | 2,000 | Value: 4.00 | | | | |
| 1952 | 4,265,000 | 0.50 | 0.75 | 1.25 | 3.00 | — |
| 1952 Proof | 16,000 | Value: 2.00 | | | | |

**6 PENCE** **KM# 48** **Weight:** 2.8300 g. **Composition:** 0.5000 Silver .0454 oz. ASW

| Date | Mintage | F | VF | XF | Unc | BU |
|---|---|---|---|---|---|---|
| 1953 | 2,496,000 | 0.50 | 0.75 | 1.75 | 4.50 | — |
| 1953 Proof | 5,000 | Value: 3.00 | | | | |
| 1954 | 2,196,000 | 0.50 | 1.00 | 2.00 | 4.50 | — |
| 1954 Proof | 3,150 | Value: 4.00 | | | | |
| 1955 | 1,969,000 | 0.50 | 1.00 | 2.00 | 4.50 | — |
| 1955 Proof | 2,850 | Value: 3.00 | | | | |
| 1956 | 1,772,000 | 0.50 | 1.00 | 2.00 | 5.00 | — |
| 1956 Proof | 1,700 | Value: 4.00 | | | | |
| 1957 | 3,288,000 | 0.50 | 0.75 | 1.75 | 4.50 | — |
| 1957 Proof | 1,130 | Value: 6.00 | | | | |
| 1958 | 1,172,000 | 0.50 | 1.00 | 2.00 | 4.50 | — |
| 1958 Proof | 985 | Value: 6.00 | | | | |
| 1959 | 261,000 | 1.00 | 2.00 | 4.00 | 12.00 | — |
| 1959 Proof | 900 | Value: 8.00 | | | | |
| 1960 | 1,587,000 | 0.50 | 0.75 | 1.25 | 2.50 | — |
| 1960 Proof | 3,360 | Value: 2.50 | | | | |

**SHILLING** **KM# 17.1** **Weight:** 5.6600 g. **Composition:** 0.8000 Silver .1455 oz. ASW **Reverse:** Denomination: 1 SHILLING 1

| Date | Mintage | F | VF | XF | Unc | BU |
|---|---|---|---|---|---|---|
| 1923 | 808,000 | 4.00 | 15.00 | 35.00 | 75.00 | — |
| 1923 Proof | 1,402 | Value: 80.00 | | | | |
| 1924 | 1,269,000 | 3.50 | 12.50 | 30.00 | 75.00 | — |

**SHILLING** **KM# 17.2** **Weight:** 5.6600 g. **Composition:** 0.8000 Silver .1455 oz. ASW **Reverse:** Denomination: SHILLING

| Date | Mintage | F | VF | XF | Unc | BU |
|---|---|---|---|---|---|---|
| 1926 | 238,000 | 15.00 | 75.00 | 400 | 1,150 | — |
| 1926 Proof | 16 | Value: 3,000 | | | | |
| 1927 | 488,000 | 10.00 | 25.00 | 150 | 375 | — |
| 1928 | 889,000 | 8.00 | 25.00 | 100 | 250 | — |
| 1929 | 926,000 | 5.00 | 10.00 | 30.00 | 175 | — |
| 1930 | 422,000 | 6.00 | 15.00 | 60.00 | 150 | — |
| 1930 Proof | 14 | Value: 1,000 | | | | |

**SHILLING** **KM# 17.3** **Weight:** 5.6600 g. **Composition:** 0.8000 Silver .1455 oz. ASW

| Date | Mintage | F | VF | XF | Unc | BU |
|---|---|---|---|---|---|---|
| 1931 | 6,541 | 80.00 | 165 | 375 | 600 | — |
| 1931 Proof | 62 | Value: 1,200 | | | | |
| 1932 | 2,537,000 | 2.50 | 5.00 | 15.00 | 50.00 | — |
| 1932 Proof | 12 | Value: 1,400 | | | | |
| 1933 | 1,463,000 | 3.50 | 7.00 | 30.00 | 70.00 | — |
| 1933 Proof | 20 | Value: 1,400 | | | | |
| 1934 | 821,000 | 3.50 | 7.00 | 35.00 | 80.00 | — |
| 1934 Proof | 24 | Value: 1,400 | | | | |
| 1935 | 685,000 | 4.00 | 8.50 | 45.00 | 90.00 | — |
| 1935 Proof | 20 | Value: 1,400 | | | | |
| 1936 | 693,000 | 3.50 | 7.00 | 25.00 | 60.00 | — |
| 1936 Proof | 40 | Value: 500 | | | | |

**SHILLING** **KM# 28** **Weight:** 5.6600 g. **Composition:** 0.8000 Silver .1455 oz. ASW

| Date | Mintage | F | VF | XF | Unc | BU |
|---|---|---|---|---|---|---|
| 1937 | 1,194,000 | 1.50 | 3.00 | 10.00 | 25.00 | — |
| 1937 Proof | 116 | Value: 120 | | | | |
| 1938 | 1,160,000 | 1.50 | 3.00 | 10.00 | 25.00 | — |

| Date | Mintage | F | VF | XF | Unc | BU |
|---|---|---|---|---|---|---|
| 1938 Proof | 44 | Value: 250 | | | | |
| 1939 Proof | 30 | Value: 4,000 | | | | |
| 1940 | 1,365,000 | 1.50 | 2.50 | 7.50 | 17.50 | — |
| 1941 | 1,826,000 | 1.50 | 2.50 | 7.50 | 17.50 | — |
| 1942 | 3,867,000 | 1.50 | 2.50 | 7.50 | 17.50 | — |
| 1943 | 4,187,999 | 1.00 | 2.00 | 5.00 | 10.00 | — |
| 1943 Proof | 104 | Value: 165 | | | | |
| 1944 | 48,000 | 8.00 | 20.00 | 45.00 | 80.00 | — |
| 1944 Proof | 160 | Value: 150 | | | | |
| 1945 | 54,000 | 8.00 | 20.00 | 45.00 | 80.00 | — |
| 1945 Proof | 150 | Value: 150 | | | | |
| 1946 | 27,000 | 10.00 | 30.00 | 60.00 | 120 | — |
| 1946 Proof | 150 | Value: 165 | | | | |
| 1947 | 7,184 | 10.00 | 20.00 | 40.00 | 70.00 | — |
| 1947 Proof | 2,600 | Value: 75.00 | | | | |

**SHILLING** KM# 37.1 **Weight:** 5.6600 g. **Composition:** 0.8000 Silver .1455 oz. ASW

| Date | Mintage | F | VF | XF | Unc | BU |
|---|---|---|---|---|---|---|
| 1948 | 4,974 | 10.00 | 20.00 | 40.00 | 70.00 | — |
| 1948 Proof | 1,120 | Value: 75.00 | | | | |
| 1949 Proof | 800 | Value: 225 | | | | |
| 1950 | 1,704,000 | 1.50 | 2.50 | 4.00 | 8.00 | — |
| 1950 Proof | 500 | Value: 40.00 | | | | |

**SHILLING** KM# 37.2 **Weight:** 5.6600 g. **Composition:** 0.5000 Silver .0909 oz. ASW **Reverse:** Denomination: 1 S

| Date | Mintage | F | VF | XF | Unc | BU |
|---|---|---|---|---|---|---|
| 1951 | 2,405,000 | 1.00 | 1.50 | 4.00 | 8.00 | — |
| 1951 Proof | 2,000 | Value: 4.00 | | | | |
| 1952 | 1,934,000 | 1.00 | 1.50 | 3.50 | 7.00 | — |
| 1952 Proof | 1,550 | Value: 3.00 | | | | |

**SHILLING** KM# 49 **Weight:** 5.6600 g. **Composition:** 0.5000 Silver .0909 oz. ASW

| Date | Mintage | F | VF | XF | Unc | BU |
|---|---|---|---|---|---|---|
| 1953 | 2,672,000 | 0.75 | 1.25 | 2.50 | 5.50 | — |
| 1953 Proof | 5,000 | Value: 4.00 | | | | |
| 1954 | 3,576,000 | 0.75 | 1.25 | 2.00 | 5.50 | — |
| 1954 Proof | 3,150 | Value: 4.00 | | | | |
| 1955 | 2,206,000 | 0.75 | 1.25 | 2.50 | 5.50 | — |
| 1955 Proof | 2,850 | Value: 5.50 | | | | |
| 1956 | 2,142,000 | 0.75 | 1.25 | 2.50 | 6.00 | — |
| 1956 Proof | 1,700 | Value: 6.00 | | | | |
| 1957 | 791,000 | 1.00 | 2.00 | 5.00 | 10.00 | — |
| 1957 Proof | 1,130 | Value: 6.00 | | | | |
| 1958 | 4,067,000 | 0.75 | 1.25 | 2.00 | 5.50 | — |
| 1958 Proof | 985 | Value: 8.00 | | | | |
| 1959 | 205,000 | 1.50 | 3.00 | 5.00 | 10.00 | — |
| 1959 Proof | 900 | Value: 10.00 | | | | |
| 1960 | 2,187,000 | 0.75 | 1.25 | 2.00 | 5.50 | — |
| 1960 Proof | 3,360 | Value: 3.00 | | | | |

**FLORIN** KM# 18 **Weight:** 11.3100 g. **Composition:** 0.8000 Silver .2909 oz. ASW

| Date | Mintage | F | VF | XF | Unc | BU |
|---|---|---|---|---|---|---|
| 1923 | 695,000 | 5.00 | 20.00 | 40.00 | 80.00 | — |
| 1923 Proof | 1,402 | Value: 125 | | | | |
| 1924 | 1,513,000 | 4.00 | 15.00 | 40.00 | 150 | — |
| 1925 | 50,000 | 125 | 350 | 1,000 | 2,200 | — |
| 1926 | 324,000 | 7.50 | 40.00 | 250 | 650 | — |
| 1927 | 399,000 | 7.50 | 35.00 | 200 | 600 | — |
| 1928 | 1,092,000 | 4.00 | 10.00 | 100 | 200 | — |
| 1929 | 648,000 | 5.00 | 15.00 | 120 | 225 | — |
| 1930 | 267,000 | 5.00 | 15.00 | 75.00 | 150 | — |
| 1930 Proof | 14 | Value: 1,200 | | | | |

**2 SHILLINGS** KM# 22 **Weight:** 11.3100 g. **Composition:** 0.8000 Silver .2909 oz. ASW **Reverse:** Denomination: 2 SHILLINGS

| Date | Mintage | F | VF | XF | Unc | BU |
|---|---|---|---|---|---|---|
| 1931 | 383 | 250 | 450 | 700 | 1,200 | — |
| 1931 Proof | 62 | Value: 1,500 | | | | |
| 1932 | 1,315,000 | 3.00 | 6.00 | 18.00 | 75.00 | — |
| 1932 Proof | 12 | Value: 2,000 | | | | |
| 1933 | 891,000 | 4.00 | 8.00 | 25.00 | 85.00 | — |
| 1933 Proof | 20 | Value: 2,000 | | | | |
| 1934 | 559,000 | 4.00 | 8.00 | 25.00 | 60.00 | — |
| 1934 Proof | 24 | Value: 1,650 | | | | |
| 1935 | 554,000 | 5.00 | 9.00 | 25.00 | 90.00 | — |
| 1935 Proof | 20 | Value: 1,650 | | | | |
| 1936 | 669,000 | 4.00 | 8.00 | 25.00 | 65.00 | — |
| 1936 Proof | 40 | Value: 650 | | | | |

**2 SHILLINGS** KM# 29 **Weight:** 11.3100 g. **Composition:** 0.8000 Silver .2909 oz. ASW

| Date | Mintage | F | VF | XF | Unc | BU |
|---|---|---|---|---|---|---|
| 1937 | 1,495,000 | 2.50 | 5.00 | 10.00 | 30.00 | — |
| 1937 Proof | 116 | Value: 150 | | | | |
| 1938 | 214,000 | 5.00 | 10.00 | 20.00 | 50.00 | — |
| 1938 Proof | 44 | Value: 325 | | | | |
| 1939 | 279,000 | 5.00 | 10.00 | 20.00 | 50.00 | — |
| 1939 Proof | 30 | Value: 1,000 | | | | |
| 1940 | 2,600,000 | 2.50 | 3.50 | 8.00 | 20.00 | — |
| 1941 | 1,764,000 | 2.50 | 3.50 | 8.00 | 20.00 | — |
| 1942 | 2,847,000 | 2.00 | 3.00 | 5.00 | 10.00 | — |
| 1943 | 3,125,000 | 2.00 | 3.00 | 5.00 | 10.00 | — |
| 1943 Proof | 104 | Value: 135 | | | | |
| 1944 | 225,000 | 3.50 | 7.00 | 17.50 | 40.00 | — |
| 1945 | 473,000 | 3.00 | 6.00 | 15.00 | 35.00 | — |
| 1945 Proof | 150 | Value: 120 | | | | |
| 1946 | 14,000 | 7.50 | 20.00 | 40.00 | 90.00 | — |
| 1946 Proof | 150 | Value: 135 | | | | |
| 1947 | 2,892 | 15.00 | 25.00 | 40.00 | 85.00 | — |
| 1947 Proof | 2,600 | Value: 75.00 | | | | |

**2 SHILLINGS** KM# 38.1 **Weight:** 11.3100 g. **Composition:** 0.8000 Silver .2909 oz. ASW

| Date | Mintage | F | VF | XF | Unc | BU |
|---|---|---|---|---|---|---|
| 1948 | 6,773 | 15.00 | 20.00 | 40.00 | 85.00 | — |
| 1948 Proof | 1,120 | Value: 75.00 | | | | |
| 1949 | 203,000 | 5.00 | 10.00 | 15.00 | 35.00 | — |
| 1949 Proof | 800 | Value: 65.00 | | | | |
| 1950 | 4,945 | 20.00 | 40.00 | 80.00 | 140 | — |
| 1950 Proof | 500 | Value: 175 | | | | |

**2 SHILLINGS** KM# 38.2 **Weight:** 11.3100 g. **Composition:** 0.5000 Silver .1818 oz. ASW **Reverse:** Denomination: 2 S

| Date | Mintage | F | VF | XF | Unc | BU |
|---|---|---|---|---|---|---|
| 1951 | 730,000 | 2.00 | 3.00 | 5.00 | 10.00 | — |
| 1951 Proof | 2,000 | Value: 15.00 | | | | |
| 1952 | 3,570,000 | 1.50 | 2.00 | 3.00 | 6.50 | — |
| 1952 Proof | 16,000 | Value: 8.00 | | | | |

**2 SHILLINGS** KM# 50 **Weight:** 11.3100 g. **Composition:** 0.5000 Silver .1818 oz. ASW

| Date | Mintage | F | VF | XF | Unc | BU |
|---|---|---|---|---|---|---|
| 1953 | 3,274,000 | 1.50 | 2.25 | 4.00 | 8.50 | — |
| 1953 Proof | 5,000 | Value: 6.50 | | | | |
| 1954 | 5,866,000 | 1.50 | 2.25 | 3.00 | 7.00 | — |
| 1954 Proof | 3,150 | Value: 6.50 | | | | |
| 1955 | 3,745,000 | 1.50 | 2.25 | 3.00 | 7.50 | — |
| 1955 Proof | 2,850 | Value: 6.50 | | | | |
| 1956 | 2,549,000 | 1.50 | 2.25 | 4.00 | 9.00 | — |
| 1956 Proof | 1,700 | Value: 7.50 | | | | |
| 1957 | 2,507,000 | 1.50 | 2.25 | 4.00 | 10.00 | — |
| 1957 Proof | 1,130 | Value: 7.50 | | | | |
| 1958 | 2,821,000 | 1.50 | 2.25 | 4.00 | 10.00 | — |
| 1958 Proof | 985 | Value: 15.00 | | | | |
| 1959 | 1,219,000 | 1.50 | 2.25 | 4.00 | 10.00 | — |
| 1959 Proof | 900 | Value: 20.00 | | | | |
| 1960 | 1,951,000 | 1.50 | 2.25 | 3.00 | 5.00 | — |
| 1960 Proof | 3,360 | Value: 4.00 | | | | |

**2-1/2 SHILLINGS** KM# 19.1 **Weight:** 14.1400 g. **Composition:** 0.8000 Silver .3637 oz. ASW **Reverse:** Denomination: 2-1/2 SHILLINGS 2-1/2 **Rev. Legend:** ZUID-AFRICA

| Date | Mintage | F | VF | XF | Unc | BU |
|---|---|---|---|---|---|---|
| 1923 | 1,227,000 | 4.00 | 15.00 | 35.00 | 70.00 | — |
| 1923 Proof | 1,402 | Value: 125 | | | | |
| 1924 | 2,556,000 | 3.50 | 10.00 | 50.00 | 120 | — |
| 1925 | 460,000 | 8.00 | 30.00 | 180 | 600 | — |

**2-1/2 SHILLINGS** KM# 19.2 **Weight:** 14.1400 g. **Composition:** 0.8000 Silver .3637 oz. ASW **Reverse:** Denomination: 2-1/2 SHILLINGS

| Date | Mintage | F | VF | XF | Unc | BU |
|---|---|---|---|---|---|---|
| 1926 | 205,000 | 10.00 | 40.00 | 250 | 650 | — |
| 1926 Proof | 16 | Value: 4,000 | | | | |
| 1927 | 194,000 | 10.00 | 40.00 | 350 | 850 | — |
| 1928 | 984,000 | 5.00 | 25.00 | 125 | 325 | — |
| 1929 | 617,000 | 5.00 | 25.00 | 175 | 350 | — |
| 1930 | 324,000 | 5.00 | 15.00 | 100 | 250 | — |
| 1930 Proof | 14 | Value: 1,650 | | | | |

**2-1/2 SHILLINGS** **KM# 19.3** **Weight:** 14.1400 g. **Composition:** 0.8000 Silver .3637 oz. ASW **Rev. Legend:** SUID. AFRICA

| Date | Mintage | F | VF | XF | Unc | BU |
|---|---|---|---|---|---|---|
| 1931 | 790 | 225 | 450 | 700 | 1,300 | — |
| 1931 Proof | 62 | Value: 1,800 | | | | |
| 1932 | 1,028,999 | 4.00 | 6.00 | 22.50 | 85.00 | — |
| 1932 Proof | 12 | Value: 2,400 | | | | |
| 1933 | 136,000 | 8.00 | 40.00 | 185 | 300 | — |
| 1933 Proof | 20 | Value: 2,400 | | | | |
| 1934 | 416,000 | 4.00 | 8.00 | 30.00 | 100 | — |
| 1934 Proof | 24 | Value: 1,650 | | | | |
| 1935 | 345,000 | 5.00 | 12.50 | 32.50 | 125 | — |
| 1935 Proof | 20 | Value: 1,650 | | | | |
| 1936 | 553,000 | 4.00 | 8.00 | 25.00 | 90.00 | — |
| 1936 Proof | 40 | Value: 800 | | | | |

**2-1/2 SHILLINGS** **KM# 30** **Weight:** 14.1400 g. **Composition:** 0.8000 Silver .3637 oz. ASW

| Date | Mintage | F | VF | XF | Unc | BU |
|---|---|---|---|---|---|---|
| 1937 | 1,154,000 | 3.00 | 5.00 | 15.00 | 32.50 | — |
| 1937 Proof | 116 | Value: 175 | | | | |
| 1938 | 534,000 | 4.00 | 8.00 | 20.00 | 60.00 | — |
| 1938 Proof | 44 | Value: 400 | | | | |
| 1939 | 133,000 | 6.00 | 15.00 | 40.00 | 80.00 | — |
| 1939 Proof | 30 | Value: 800 | | | | |
| 1940 | 2,976,000 | 3.00 | 4.50 | 8.00 | 20.00 | — |
| 1941 | 1,988,000 | 3.00 | 4.50 | 8.00 | 20.00 | — |
| 1942 | 3,180,000 | 3.00 | 4.50 | 8.00 | 20.00 | — |
| 1943 | 2,098,000 | 3.00 | 4.50 | 8.00 | 20.00 | — |
| 1943 Proof | 104 | Value: 150 | | | | |
| 1944 | 1,360,000 | 3.00 | 5.00 | 10.00 | 25.00 | — |
| 1944 Proof | 150 | Value: 130 | | | | |
| 1945 | 183,000 | 3.50 | 7.00 | 25.00 | 60.00 | — |
| 1945 Proof | 150 | Value: 130 | | | | |
| 1946 | 11,000 | 15.00 | 30.00 | 50.00 | 90.00 | — |
| 1946 Proof | 150 | Value: 150 | | | | |
| 1947 | 3,582 | 20.00 | 35.00 | 60.00 | 100 | — |
| 1947 Proof | 2,600 | Value: 125 | | | | |

**2-1/2 SHILLINGS** **KM# 39.1** **Weight:** 14.1400 g. **Composition:** 0.8000 Silver .3637 oz. ASW

| Date | Mintage | F | VF | XF | Unc | BU |
|---|---|---|---|---|---|---|
| 1948 | 1,600 | 30.00 | 50.00 | 80.00 | 100 | — |
| 1948 Proof | 1,120 | Value: 110 | | | | |
| 1949 | 1,891 | 30.00 | 50.00 | 80.00 | 120 | — |
| 1949 Proof | 800 | Value: 125 | | | | |
| 1950 | 5,076 | 30.00 | 50.00 | 80.00 | 150 | — |
| 1950 Proof | 500 | Value: 200 | | | | |

**2-1/2 SHILLINGS** **KM# 39.2** **Weight:** 14.1400 g. **Composition:** 0.5000 Silver .2273 oz. ASW **Reverse:** Denomination: 2-1/2 S

| Date | Mintage | F | VF | XF | Unc | BU |
|---|---|---|---|---|---|---|
| 1951 | 783,000 | 3.00 | 4.50 | 6.00 | 15.00 | — |
| 1951 Proof | 2,000 | Value: 9.00 | | | | |
| 1952 | 1,996,000 | 2.00 | 3.00 | 4.00 | 8.50 | — |
| 1952 Proof | 16,000 | Value: 5.00 | | | | |

**2-1/2 SHILLINGS** **KM# 51** **Weight:** 14.1400 g. **Composition:** 0.5000 Silver .2273 oz. ASW

| Date | Mintage | F | VF | XF | Unc | BU |
|---|---|---|---|---|---|---|
| 1953 | 2,513,000 | 2.00 | 3.00 | 4.00 | 8.50 | — |
| 1953 Proof | 6,000 | Value: 6.00 | | | | |
| 1954 | 4,249,000 | 2.00 | 3.00 | 4.00 | 8.50 | — |
| 1954 Proof | 3,150 | Value: 7.50 | | | | |
| 1955 | 3,863,000 | 2.00 | 3.00 | 4.00 | 8.50 | — |
| 1955 Proof | 2,850 | Value: 7.50 | | | | |
| 1956 | 2,437,000 | 2.00 | 3.00 | 4.00 | 8.50 | — |
| 1956 Proof | 1,700 | Value: 8.50 | | | | |
| 1957 | 2,137,000 | 2.00 | 3.00 | 4.00 | 8.50 | — |
| 1957 Proof | 1,130 | Value: 8.50 | | | | |
| 1958 | 2,260,000 | 2.00 | 3.00 | 4.50 | 9.00 | — |
| 1958 Proof | 985 | Value: 14.00 | | | | |
| 1959 | 46,000 | 2.50 | 4.00 | 6.00 | 12.00 | — |
| 1959 Proof | 900 | Value: 18.00 | | | | |
| 1960 | 12,000 | 3.00 | 5.00 | 7.50 | 12.50 | — |
| 1960 Proof | 3,360 | Value: 5.00 | | | | |

**5 SHILLINGS** **KM# 31** **Weight:** 28.2800 g. **Composition:** 0.8000 Silver .7274 oz. ASW **Subject:** Royal Visit

| Date | Mintage | F | VF | XF | Unc | BU |
|---|---|---|---|---|---|---|
| 1947 | 300,000 | BV | 7.00 | 7.50 | 15.00 | — |
| 1947 Proof | 5,600 | Value: 45.00 | | | | |

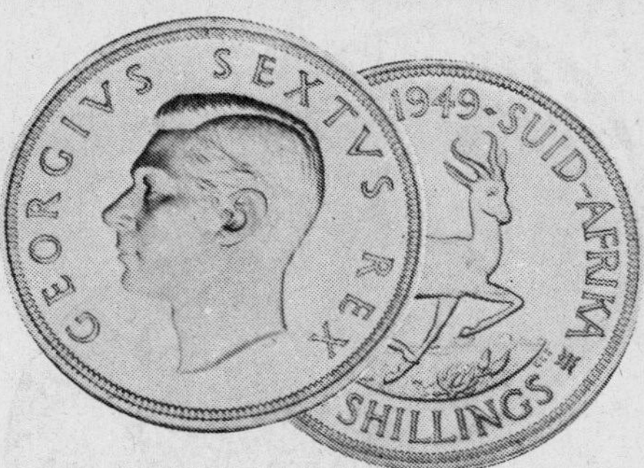

**5 SHILLINGS** **KM# 40.1** **Weight:** 28.2800 g. **Composition:** 0.8000 Silver .7274 oz. ASW

| Date | Mintage | F | VF | XF | Unc | BU |
|---|---|---|---|---|---|---|
| 1948 | 780,000 | BV | 6.00 | 7.50 | 15.00 | — |
| 1948 Prooflike | 1,000 | — | — | — | 20.00 | — |
| 1948 Proof | 1,120 | Value: 25.00 | | | | |
| 1949 | 535,000 | BV | 6.00 | 7.50 | 15.00 | — |
| 1949 Prooflike | 2,000 | — | — | — | 35.00 | — |
| 1949 Proof | 800 | Value: 50.00 | | | | |
| 1950 | 83,000 | BV | 10.00 | 12.50 | 25.00 | — |
| 1950 Prooflike | 1,200 | — | — | — | 60.00 | — |
| 1950 Proof | 500 | Value: 75.00 | | | | |

**5 SHILLINGS** **KM# 40.2** **Weight:** 28.2800 g. **Composition:** 0.5000 Silver .4546 oz. ASW **Reverse:** Denomination: 5 S

| Date | Mintage | F | VF | XF | Unc | BU |
|---|---|---|---|---|---|---|
| ND(1951) | 363,000 | BV | 5.00 | 7.00 | 15.00 | — |
| ND(1951) Prooflike | 1,483 | — | — | — | 25.00 | — |
| ND(1951) Proof | 2,000 | Value: 35.00 | | | | |

**5 SHILLINGS** **KM# 41** **Weight:** 28.2800 g. **Composition:** 0.5000 Silver .4546 oz. ASW **Subject:** 300th Anniversary - Founding of Capetown

| Date | Mintage | F | VF | XF | Unc | BU |
|---|---|---|---|---|---|---|
| 1952 | 1,698,000 | BV | 4.50 | 5.50 | 8.50 | — |
| 1952 Prooflike | 12,000 | — | — | — | 12.50 | — |
| 1952 Proof | 16,000 | Value: 15.00 | | | | |

**5 SHILLINGS** KM# 52 **Weight:** 28.2800 g. **Composition:** 0.5000 Silver .4546 oz. ASW

| Date | Mintage | F | VF | XF | Unc | BU |
|---|---|---|---|---|---|---|
| 1953 | 250,000 | BV | 5.00 | 7.00 | 12.00 | — |
| 1953 Prooflike | 8,000 | — | — | — | 15.00 | — |
| 1953 Proof | 5,000 | Value: 20.00 | | | | |
| 1953 Matte Proof | — | Value: 700 | | | | |
| 1954 | 10,000 | BV | 8.50 | 12.50 | 20.00 | — |
| 1954 Prooflike | 3,890 | — | — | — | 22.00 | — |
| 1954 Proof | 3,150 | Value: 25.00 | | | | |
| 1955 | 40,000 | BV | 7.50 | 10.00 | 15.00 | — |
| 1955 Prooflike | 2,230 | — | — | — | 20.00 | — |
| 1955 Proof | 2,850 | Value: 25.00 | | | | |
| 1956 | 100,000 | BV | 5.00 | 7.00 | 12.00 | — |
| 1956 Prooflike | 2,200 | — | — | — | 20.00 | — |
| 1956 Proof | 1,700 | Value: 25.00 | | | | |
| 1957 | 154,000 | BV | 5.00 | 7.00 | 12.00 | — |
| 1957 Prooflike | 1,600 | — | — | — | 25.00 | — |
| 1957 Proof | 1,130 | Value: 30.00 | | | | |
| 1958 | 233,000 | BV | 5.00 | 7.00 | 12.00 | — |
| 1958 Prooflike | 1,500 | — | — | — | 25.00 | — |
| 1958 Proof | 985 | Value: 30.00 | | | | |
| 1959 | 2,989 | 20.00 | 35.00 | 65.00 | 100 | — |
| 1959 Prooflike | 2,200 | — | — | — | 110 | — |
| 1959 Proof | 950 | Value: 125 | | | | |

**5 SHILLINGS** KM# 55 **Weight:** 28.2800 g. **Composition:** 0.5000 Silver .4546 oz. ASW **Subject:** 50th Anniversary - South African Union **Note:** Many varieties exist of letters HM below building.

| Date | Mintage | F | VF | XF | Unc | BU |
|---|---|---|---|---|---|---|
| 1960 | 396,000 | BV | 4.50 | 5.50 | 7.50 | — |
| 1960 Prooflike | 22,000 | — | — | — | 11.50 | — |
| 1960 Proof | 3,360 | Value: 15.00 | | | | |

**1/2 SOVEREIGN** KM# 20 **Weight:** 3.9940 g. **Composition:** 0.9170 Gold .1177 oz. AGW **Note:** British type with Pretoria mint mark: SA.

| Date | Mintage | F | VF | XF | Unc | BU |
|---|---|---|---|---|---|---|
| 1923 Proof | 655 | Value: 425 | | | | |
| 1925 | 947,000 | 55.00 | 65.00 | 75.00 | 100 | — |
| 1926 | 809,000 | 55.00 | 65.00 | 75.00 | 100 | — |

**1/2 POUND** KM# 42 **Weight:** 3.9940 g. **Composition:** 0.9170 Gold .1177 oz. AGW **Note:** Similar to 1 Pound, KM#43.

| Date | Mintage | F | VF | XF | Unc | BU |
|---|---|---|---|---|---|---|
| 1952 | 4,002 | — | — | — | 65.00 | — |
| 1952 Proof | 12,000 | Value: 80.00 | | | | |

**1/2 POUND** KM# 53 **Weight:** 3.9940 g. **Composition:** 0.9170 Gold .1177 oz. AGW **Obverse:** Elizabeth II

| Date | Mintage | F | VF | XF | Unc | BU |
|---|---|---|---|---|---|---|
| 1953 Proof | 4,000 | Value: 75.00 | | | | |
| 1954 Proof | 1,275 | Value: 85.00 | | | | |
| 1955 Proof | 900 | Value: 100 | | | | |
| 1956 Proof | 508 | Value: 180 | | | | |
| 1957 Proof | 560 | Value: 150 | | | | |
| 1958 Proof | 515 | Value: 175 | | | | |
| 1959 | 500 | — | — | — | 90.00 | — |
| 1959 Proof | 630 | Value: 135 | | | | |
| 1960 | 1,052 | — | — | — | 65.00 | — |
| 1960 Proof | 1,950 | Value: 75.00 | | | | |

**SOVEREIGN** KM# 21 **Weight:** 7.9881 g. **Composition:** 0.9170 Gold .2354 oz. AGW **Note:** British type with Pretoria mint mark: SA.

| Date | Mintage | F | VF | XF | Unc | BU |
|---|---|---|---|---|---|---|
| 1923 | 64 | 200 | 300 | 400 | 500 | — |
| 1923 Proof | 655 | Value: 550 | | | | |
| 1924 | 3,184 | 700 | 1,350 | 2,250 | 4,500 | — |
| 1925 | 6,086,000 | — | BV | 100 | 125 | — |
| 1926 | 11,108,000 | — | BV | 100 | 125 | — |
| 1927 | 16,379,999 | — | BV | 100 | 125 | — |
| 1928 | 18,235,000 | — | BV | 100 | 125 | — |

**SOVEREIGN** KM# A22 **Weight:** 7.9881 g. **Composition:** 0.9170 Gold .2354 oz. AGW **Obverse:** Modifield effigy, slightly smaller bust

| Date | Mintage | F | VF | XF | Unc | BU |
|---|---|---|---|---|---|---|
| 1929 | 12,024,000 | — | BV | 100 | 125 | — |
| 1930 | 10,028,000 | — | BV | 100 | 125 | — |
| 1931 | 8,512,000 | — | BV | 100 | 125 | — |
| 1932 | 1,067,000 | — | BV | 110 | 145 | — |

**POUND** KM# 43 **Weight:** 7.9881 g. **Composition:** 0.9170 Gold .2354 oz. AGW

| Date | Mintage | F | VF | XF | Unc | BU |
|---|---|---|---|---|---|---|
| 1952 | 4,508 | — | — | — | 125 | — |
| 1952 Proof | 12,000 | Value: 135 | | | | |

**POUND** KM# 54 **Weight:** 7.9881 g. **Composition:** 0.9170 Gold .2354 oz. AGW

| Date | Mintage | F | VF | XF | Unc | BU |
|---|---|---|---|---|---|---|
| 1953 Proof | 4,000 | Value: 125 | | | | |
| 1954 Proof | 1,275 | Value: 135 | | | | |
| 1955 Proof | 900 | Value: 150 | | | | |
| 1956 Proof | 508 | Value: 245 | | | | |
| 1957 Proof | 560 | Value: 235 | | | | |
| 1958 Proof | 515 | Value: 235 | | | | |
| 1959 | 502 | — | — | — | 150 | — |
| 1959 Proof | 630 | Value: 200 | | | | |
| 1960 | 1,161 | — | — | — | 125 | — |
| 1960 Proof | 1,950 | Value: 135 | | | | |

# REPUBLIC

## STANDARD COINAGE

100 Cents = 1 Rand

**1/2 CENT** KM# 56 **Composition:** Brass

| Date | Mintage | F | VF | XF | Unc | BU |
|---|---|---|---|---|---|---|
| 1961 | 39,189,000 | — | 0.15 | 0.25 | 1.25 | — |
| 1961 Proof | 7,530 | Value: 1.00 | | | | |
| 1962 | 17,895,000 | — | 0.15 | 0.25 | 1.25 | — |
| 1962 Proof | 3,844 | Value: 1.00 | | | | |
| 1963 | 11,611,000 | — | 0.15 | 0.25 | 2.00 | — |
| 1963 Proof | 4,025 | Value: 1.00 | | | | |
| 1964 | 9,258,000 | — | 0.15 | 0.25 | 1.25 | — |
| 1964 Proof | 16,000 | Value: 1.00 | | | | |

**1/2 CENT** KM# 81 **Composition:** Bronze **Reverse:** Sparrows **Note:** Bilingual.

| Date | Mintage | F | VF | XF | Unc | BU |
|---|---|---|---|---|---|---|
| 1970 | Est. 57,721,000 | — | 0.10 | 0.25 | 0.50 | — |

**Note:** Coins dated 1970 were also struck for circulation in 1971, 1972 and 1973

| Date | Mintage | F | VF | XF | Unc | BU |
|---|---|---|---|---|---|---|
| 1970 Proof | 10,000 | Value: 2.50 | | | | |
| 1971 | 8,000 | — | — | — | 2.50 | — |
| 1971 Proof | 12,000 | Value: 2.50 | | | | |
| 1972 | 8,000 | — | — | — | 2.50 | — |
| 1972 Proof | 12,000 | Value: 2.50 | | | | |
| 1973 | 20,000 | — | 0.10 | 0.20 | 2.50 | — |
| 1973 Proof | 11,000 | Value: 2.50 | | | | |
| 1974 | 20,000 | — | 0.20 | 0.40 | 2.50 | — |
| 1974 Proof | 15,000 | Value: 2.50 | | | | |
| 1975 | 20,000 | — | 0.10 | 0.20 | 2.50 | — |
| 1975 Proof | 18,000 | Value: 2.50 | | | | |
| 1977 | 20,000 | — | 0.10 | 0.20 | 2.50 | — |
| 1977 Proof | 19,000 | Value: 2.50 | | | | |
| 1978 | 18,000 | — | 0.10 | 0.20 | 2.50 | — |
| 1978 Proof | 19,000 | Value: 2.50 | | | | |
| 1980 Proof | 15,000 | Value: 2.50 | | | | |
| 1981 Proof | 10,000 | Value: 2.50 | | | | |
| 1983 Proof | 14,000 | Value: 2.50 | | | | |

**1/2 CENT** KM# 90 **Composition:** Bronze **Subject:** President Fouche **Note:** Similar to 1 Cent, KM#91.

| Date | Mintage | F | VF | XF | Unc | BU |
|---|---|---|---|---|---|---|
| 1976 | 20,000 | — | — | — | 1.00 | — |
| 1976 Proof | 21,000 | Value: 1.50 | | | | |

**1/2 CENT** KM# 97 **Composition:** Bronze **Subject:** President Diederichs

| Date | Mintage | F | VF | XF | Unc | BU |
|---|---|---|---|---|---|---|
| 1979 | 18,000 | — | — | — | 1.00 | — |
| 1979 Proof | 17,000 | Value: 1.50 | | | | |

**1/2 CENT** KM# 108 **Composition:** Bronze **Subject:** President Vorster

| Date | Mintage | F | VF | XF | Unc | BU |
|---|---|---|---|---|---|---|
| 1982 Proof | 12,000 | Value: 1.50 | | | | |

**CENT** **KM# 57** **Composition:** Brass

| Date | Mintage | F | VF | XF | Unc | BU |
|---|---|---|---|---|---|---|
| 1961 | 52,266,000 | — | 0.15 | 0.40 | 1.50 | — |
| 1961 Proof | 7,530 | Value: 0.75 | | | | |
| 1962 | 21,929,000 | — | 0.15 | 0.40 | 1.50 | — |
| 1962 Proof | 3,844 | Value: 1.00 | | | | |
| 1963 | 9,081,000 | — | 0.15 | 0.50 | 3.00 | — |
| 1963 Proof | 4,025 | Value: 1.00 | | | | |
| 1964 | 14,265,000 | — | 0.15 | 0.40 | 1.50 | — |
| 1964 Proof | 16,000 | Value: 2.00 | | | | |

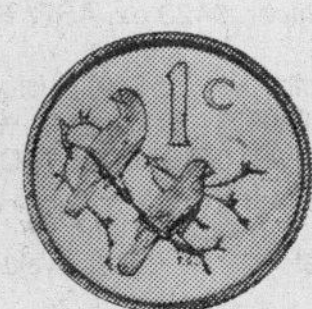

**CENT** **KM# 65.1** **Composition:** Bronze **Obverse:** English legend **Reverse:** Sparrows

| Date | Mintage | F | VF | XF | Unc | BU |
|---|---|---|---|---|---|---|
| 1965 | 26,000 | — | — | — | 2.00 | — |
| 1965 Proof | 25,000 | Value: 2.50 | | | | |
| 1966 | 50,157,000 | — | — | 0.10 | 0.50 | — |
| 1967 | 21,114,000 | — | — | 0.10 | 0.50 | — |
| 1969 | 10,196,000 | — | — | 0.10 | 0.50 | — |

**CENT** **KM# 65.2** **Composition:** Bronze **Obverse:** Afrikaans legend

| Date | Mintage | F | VF | XF | Unc | BU |
|---|---|---|---|---|---|---|
| 1965 | 846 | — | 100 | 200 | 300 | — |
| 1965 Proof | 185 | Value: 350 | | | | |
| 1966 | 50,157,000 | — | — | 0.10 | 0.50 | — |
| 1966 Proof | 25,000 | Value: 1.00 | | | | |
| 1967 | 21,114,000 | — | — | 0.10 | 0.50 | — |
| 1967 Proof | 25,000 | Value: 1.00 | | | | |
| 1969 | 10,196,000 | — | — | 0.10 | 0.50 | — |
| 1969 Proof | 12,000 | Value: 1.50 | | | | |

**CENT** **KM# 74.1** **Composition:** Bronze **Subject:** President Charles Swart **Obverse:** English legend

| Date | Mintage | F | VF | XF | Unc | BU |
|---|---|---|---|---|---|---|
| 1968 | 6,000,000 | — | — | 0.10 | 0.30 | — |
| 1968 Proof | 25,000 | Value: 1.00 | | | | |

**CENT** **KM# 74.2** **Composition:** Bronze **Obverse:** Afrikaans legend

| Date | Mintage | F | VF | XF | Unc | BU |
|---|---|---|---|---|---|---|
| 1968 | 6,000,000 | — | — | 0.10 | 0.30 | — |

**CENT** **KM# 82** **Composition:** Bronze **Obverse:** Bilingual legend

| Date | Mintage | F | VF | XF | Unc | BU |
|---|---|---|---|---|---|---|
| 1970 | 37,072,000 | — | — | — | 0.30 | — |
| 1970 Proof | 10,000 | Value: 1.00 | | | | |
| 1971 | 34,053,000 | — | — | — | 0.30 | — |
| 1971 Proof | 12,000 | Value: 1.00 | | | | |
| 1972 | 35,662,000 | — | — | — | 0.30 | — |
| 1972 Proof | 10,000 | Value: 1.00 | | | | |
| 1973 | 35,898,000 | — | 0.10 | 0.20 | 0.40 | — |
| 1973 Proof | 11,000 | Value: 1.00 | | | | |
| 1974 | 54,940,000 | — | — | — | 0.25 | — |
| 1974 Proof | 15,000 | Value: 1.00 | | | | |
| 1975 | 62,982,000 | — | — | — | 0.25 | — |
| 1975 Proof | 18,000 | Value: 1.00 | | | | |
| 1977 | 72,444,000 | — | — | — | 0.25 | — |
| 1977 Proof | 19,000 | Value: 1.00 | | | | |
| 1978 | 70,152,000 | — | — | — | 0.20 | — |
| 1978 Proof | 17,000 | Value: 0.50 | | | | |
| 1980 | 63,432,000 | — | — | — | 0.20 | — |
| 1980 Proof | 15,000 | Value: 0.50 | | | | |
| 1981 | 63,444,000 | — | — | — | 0.20 | — |
| 1981 Proof | 10,000 | Value: 0.50 | | | | |
| 1983 | 182,131,000 | — | — | — | 0.20 | — |
| 1983 Proof | 14,000 | Value: 0.50 | | | | |
| 1984 | 107,155,000 | — | — | — | 0.20 | — |
| 1984 Proof | 11,000 | Value: 0.50 | | | | |
| 1985 | 186,042,000 | — | — | — | 0.20 | — |
| 1985 Proof | 9,859 | Value: 0.50 | | | | |
| 1986 | 169,734,000 | — | — | — | 0.20 | — |
| 1986 Proof | 7,000 | Value: 0.50 | | | | |
| 1987 | 120,674,000 | — | — | — | 0.20 | — |
| 1987 Proof | 6,781 | Value: 0.50 | | | | |
| 1988 | 240,272,000 | — | — | — | 0.20 | — |
| 1988 Proof | 7,250 | Value: 0.50 | | | | |
| 1989 | — | — | — | — | 0.20 | — |
| 1989 Proof | — | Value: 0.50 | | | | |

**CENT** **KM# 91** **Composition:** Bronze **Subject:** President Fouche

| Date | Mintage | F | VF | XF | Unc | BU |
|---|---|---|---|---|---|---|
| 1976 | 91,860,000 | — | — | 0.30 | 0.50 | — |
| 1976 Proof | 21,000 | Value: 0.75 | | | | |

**CENT** **KM# 98** **Composition:** Bronze **Subject:** President Diederichs

| Date | Mintage | F | VF | XF | Unc | BU |
|---|---|---|---|---|---|---|
| 1979 | 63,432,000 | — | — | 0.30 | 0.50 | — |
| 1979 Proof | 15,000 | Value: 0.75 | | | | |

**CENT** **KM# 109** **Composition:** Bronze **Subject:** President Vorster

| Date | Mintage | F | VF | XF | Unc | BU |
|---|---|---|---|---|---|---|
| 1982 | 145,954,000 | — | — | 0.30 | 0.50 | — |
| 1982 Proof | 12,000 | Value: 0.75 | | | | |

**CENT** **KM# 132** **Composition:** Chrome Plated Steel

| Date | Mintage | F | VF | XF | Unc | BU |
|---|---|---|---|---|---|---|
| 1990 | — | — | — | — | 0.25 | — |
| 1990 Proof | — | Value: 0.50 | | | | |
| 1991 | — | — | — | — | 0.25 | — |
| 1991 Proof | — | Value: 0.50 | | | | |
| 1992 | — | — | — | — | 0.25 | — |
| 1992 Proof | — | Value: 0.50 | | | | |
| 1993 | — | — | — | — | 0.25 | — |
| 1993 Proof | 7,790 | Value: 0.50 | | | | |
| 1994 | — | — | — | — | 0.25 | — |
| 1994 Proof | 5,804 | Value: 0.50 | | | | |
| 1995 | — | — | — | — | 0.25 | — |
| 1995 Proof | — | Value: 0.50 | | | | |

**CENT** **KM# 158** **Composition:** Chrome Plated Steel **Obverse:** Zulu legend

| Date | Mintage | F | VF | XF | Unc | BU |
|---|---|---|---|---|---|---|
| 1996 | — | — | — | — | 0.25 | — |
| 1996 Proof | 10,000 | Value: 0.50 | | | | |

**CENT** **KM# 170** **Composition:** Chrome Plated Steel **Obverse:** Ndebele legend **Reverse:** 2 cape sparrows

| Date | Mintage | F | VF | XF | Unc | BU |
|---|---|---|---|---|---|---|
| 1997 | — | — | — | — | 0.25 | — |
| 1997 Proof | 3,596 | Value: 0.50 | | | | |
| 1998 | — | — | — | — | 0.25 | — |
| 1998 Proof | — | Value: 0.50 | | | | |
| 1999 | — | — | — | — | 0.25 | — |
| 1999 Proof | — | Value: 0.50 | | | | |
| 2000 | — | Value: 0.25 | | | | |

**CENT** **KM# 221** **Weight:** 1.5100 g. **Composition:** Copper Plated Steel **Obverse:** National arms **Reverse:** Two birds **Edge:** Plain **Size:** 14.9 mm.

| Date | Mintage | F | VF | XF | Unc | BU |
|---|---|---|---|---|---|---|
| 2001 | — | — | — | — | 0.35 | — |

**2 CENTS** **KM# 66.1** **Composition:** Bronze **Obverse:** English legend **Reverse:** White-tailed Gnu

| Date | Mintage | F | VF | XF | Unc | BU |
|---|---|---|---|---|---|---|
| 1965 | 29,887,000 | — | — | 0.10 | 0.35 | — |
| 1966 | 9,267,000 | — | — | 0.10 | 0.40 | — |
| 1966 Proof | 25,000 | Value: 0.50 | | | | |
| 1967 | 11,862,000 | — | — | 0.10 | 0.35 | — |
| 1967 Proof | 25,000 | Value: 0.50 | | | | |
| 1969 | 5,817,000 | — | — | 0.10 | 0.40 | — |
| 1969 Proof | 12,000 | Value: 0.50 | | | | |

**2 CENTS** **KM# 66.2** **Composition:** Bronze **Obverse:** Afrikaans legend

| Date | Mintage | F | VF | XF | Unc | BU |
|---|---|---|---|---|---|---|
| 1965 | 29,887,000 | — | — | 0.10 | 0.35 | — |
| 1965 Proof | 25,000 | Value: 0.50 | | | | |
| 1966 | 9,267,000 | — | — | 0.10 | 0.35 | — |
| 1967 | 11,862,000 | — | — | 0.10 | 0.35 | — |
| 1969 | 5,817,000 | — | — | 0.10 | 0.40 | — |

**2 CENTS** **KM# 75.1** **Composition:** Bronze **Subject:** President Charles Swart **Obverse:** English legend

| Date | Mintage | F | VF | XF | Unc | BU |
|---|---|---|---|---|---|---|
| 1968 | 5,500,000 | — | — | 0.20 | 0.50 | — |

**2 CENTS** **KM# 75.2** **Composition:** Bronze **Obverse:** Afrikaans legend

| Date | Mintage | F | VF | XF | Unc | BU |
|---|---|---|---|---|---|---|
| 1968 | 5,525,000 | — | — | 0.20 | 0.50 | — |
| 1968 Proof | 25,000 | Value: 1.00 | | | | |

**2 CENTS** **KM# 83** **Composition:** Bronze **Obverse:** Bilingual legend

| Date | Mintage | F | VF | XF | Unc | BU |
|---|---|---|---|---|---|---|
| 1970 | 35,217,000 | — | — | 0.10 | 0.35 | — |
| 1970 Proof | 10,000 | Value: 0.50 | | | | |
| 1971 | 24,093,000 | — | — | 0.10 | 0.35 | — |
| 1971 Proof | 12,000 | Value: 0.50 | | | | |
| 1972 | 7,304,000 | — | — | 0.10 | 0.35 | — |
| 1972 Proof | 10,000 | Value: 0.50 | | | | |
| 1973 | 18,685,000 | — | — | 0.10 | 0.35 | — |
| 1973 Proof | 11,000 | Value: 0.50 | | | | |
| 1974 | 25,301,000 | — | — | 0.10 | 0.35 | — |
| 1974 Proof | 15,000 | Value: 0.50 | | | | |
| 1975 | 24,982,000 | — | — | 0.10 | 0.35 | — |
| 1975 Proof | 18,000 | Value: 0.50 | | | | |
| 1977 | 45,116,000 | — | — | 0.10 | 0.35 | — |
| 1977 Proof | 19,000 | Value: 0.50 | | | | |
| 1978 | 50,527,000 | — | — | 0.10 | 0.35 | — |
| 1978 Proof | 17,000 | Value: 0.50 | | | | |
| 1980 | 37,795,000 | — | — | 0.10 | 0.35 | — |
| 1980 Proof | 15,000 | Value: 0.50 | | | | |
| 1981 | 79,350,000 | — | — | 0.10 | 0.35 | — |
| 1981 Proof | 10,000 | Value: 0.50 | | | | |
| 1983 | 112,575,000 | — | — | 0.10 | 0.35 | — |
| 1983 Proof | 14,000 | Value: 0.50 | | | | |
| 1984 | 101,497,000 | — | — | 0.10 | 0.35 | — |
| 1984 Proof | 11,000 | Value: 0.50 | | | | |
| 1985 | 102,708,000 | — | — | 0.10 | 0.35 | — |
| 1985 Proof | 9,859 | Value: 0.50 | | | | |
| 1986 | 683,294,000 | — | — | 0.10 | 0.35 | — |
| 1986 Proof | 7,100 | Value: 0.50 | | | | |
| 1987 | 104,981,000 | — | — | 0.10 | 0.35 | — |
| 1987 Proof | 6,781 | Value: 0.50 | | | | |
| 1988 | 182,036,000 | — | — | 0.10 | 0.35 | — |
| 1988 Proof | 7,250 | Value: 0.50 | | | | |
| 1989 | — | — | — | 0.10 | 0.35 | — |
| 1989 Proof | — | Value: 0.50 | | | | |
| 1990 | 215,192,000 | — | — | 0.10 | 0.35 | — |

**2 CENTS** **KM# 92** **Composition:** Bronze **Subject:** President Fouche

| Date | Mintage | F | VF | XF | Unc | BU |
|---|---|---|---|---|---|---|
| 1976 | 51,474,000 | — | — | 0.25 | 0.50 | — |
| 1976 Proof | 21,000 | Value: 0.75 | | | | |

**2 CENTS** **KM# 99** **Composition:** Bronze **Subject:** President Diederichs

| Date | Mintage | F | VF | XF | Unc | BU |
|---|---|---|---|---|---|---|
| 1979 | 40,043,000 | — | — | 0.25 | 0.50 | — |
| 1979 Proof | 15,000 | Value: 0.75 | | | | |

**2 CENTS** **KM# 110** **Composition:** Bronze **Subject:** President Vorster

| Date | Mintage | F | VF | XF | Unc | BU |
|---|---|---|---|---|---|---|
| 1982 | 53,962,000 | — | — | 0.25 | 0.50 | — |
| 1982 Proof | 12,000 | Value: 0.75 | | | | |

**2 CENTS** **KM# 133** **Composition:** Chrome Plated Steel

| Date | Mintage | F | VF | XF | Unc | BU |
|---|---|---|---|---|---|---|
| 1990 | — | — | — | — | 1.50 | — |
| 1990 Proof | — | Value: 2.00 | | | | |
| 1991 | — | — | — | — | 1.50 | — |
| 1991 Proof | 12,000 | Value: 2.00 | | | | |
| 1992 | — | — | — | — | 0.50 | — |
| 1992 Proof | — | Value: 2.00 | | | | |
| 1993 | — | — | — | — | 0.50 | — |
| 1993 Proof | 7,790 | Value: 2.00 | | | | |
| 1994 | — | — | — | — | 0.50 | — |
| 1994 Proof | 5,804 | Value: 2.00 | | | | |
| 1995 | — | — | — | — | 0.50 | — |
| 1995 Proof | — | Value: 2.00 | | | | |

**2 CENTS** **KM# 159** **Composition:** Chrome Plated Steel **Obverse:** Venda legend

| Date | Mintage | F | VF | XF | Unc | BU |
|---|---|---|---|---|---|---|
| 1996 | — | — | — | — | 0.50 | — |
| 1996 Proof | — | Value: 1.00 | | | | |
| 1997 | — | — | — | — | 0.50 | — |
| 1997 Proof | 3,596 | Value: 1.00 | | | | |
| 1998 | — | — | — | — | 0.50 | — |
| 1998 Proof | — | Value: 1.00 | | | | |
| 1999 | — | — | — | — | 0.50 | — |
| 1999 Proof | — | Value: 1.00 | | | | |
| 2000 | — | — | — | — | 0.50 | — |

**2 CENTS** **KM# 222** **Weight:** 3.0000 g. **Composition:** Copper Plated Steel **Obverse:** National arms **Reverse:** Eagle catching fish **Edge:** Plain **Size:** 17.9 mm.

| Date | Mintage | F | VF | XF | Unc | BU |
|---|---|---|---|---|---|---|
| 2001 | — | — | — | — | 0.30 | — |

**2-1/2 CENTS** **KM# 58** **Weight:** 1.4100 g. **Composition:** 0.5000 Silver .0226 oz. ASW

| Date | Mintage | F | VF | XF | Unc | BU |
|---|---|---|---|---|---|---|
| 1961 | 292,000 | — | 0.50 | 1.00 | 2.00 | — |
| 1961 Proof | 7,530 | Value: 4.00 | | | | |
| 1962 | 8,745 | — | 2.00 | 4.00 | 8.00 | — |
| 1962 Proof | 3,844 | Value: 8.00 | | | | |
| 1963 | 33,000 | — | 1.50 | 2.50 | 4.00 | — |
| 1963 Proof | 4,025 | Value: 6.00 | | | | |
| 1964 | 14,000 | — | 2.00 | 4.00 | 6.00 | — |
| 1964 Proof | 16,000 | Value: 4.00 | | | | |

**2-1/2 CENTS** **KM# 174** **Weight:** 1.4140 g. **Composition:** 0.9250 Silver .0420 oz. ASW **Obverse:** Protea flower **Reverse:** Knysa seahorse

| Date | Mintage | F | VF | XF | Unc | BU |
|---|---|---|---|---|---|---|
| 1997 Proof | Est. 2,627 | Value: 18.50 | | | | |

**2-1/2 CENTS** **KM# 176** **Weight:** 1.4140 g. **Composition:** 0.9250 Silver .0420 oz. ASW **Reverse:** Jackass penguin

| Date | Mintage | F | VF | XF | Unc | BU |
|---|---|---|---|---|---|---|
| 1998 Proof | Est. 5,000 | Value: 17.50 | | | | |

**2-1/2 CENTS** **KM# 217** **Weight:** 1.4100 g. **Composition:** 0.9250 Silver .0419 oz. ASW **Obverse:** Protea flower **Reverse:** Great white shark

| Date | Mintage | F | VF | XF | Unc | BU |
|---|---|---|---|---|---|---|
| 1999 Proof | 5,000 | Value: 17.50 | | | | |

**5 CENTS** **KM# 59** **Weight:** 2.8300 g. **Composition:** 0.5000 Silver .0454 oz. ASW

| Date | Mintage | F | VF | XF | Unc | BU |
|---|---|---|---|---|---|---|
| 1961 | 1,479,000 | — | BV | 0.85 | 2.00 | — |
| 1961 Proof | 7,530 | Value: 2.50 | | | | |
| 1962 | 4,187,999 | — | BV | 0.75 | 1.50 | — |
| 1962 Proof | 3,844 | Value: 3.00 | | | | |
| 1963 | 8,054,000 | — | BV | 0.65 | 1.25 | — |
| 1963 Proof | 4,025 | Value: 3.00 | | | | |
| 1964 | 3,567,000 | — | BV | 0.65 | 1.25 | — |
| 1964 Proof | 16,000 | Value: 1.50 | | | | |

**5 CENTS** **KM# 67.1** **Composition:** Nickel **Obverse:** English legend **Reverse:** Blue crane

| Date | Mintage | F | VF | XF | Unc | BU |
|---|---|---|---|---|---|---|
| 1965 | 32,689,999 | — | — | 0.15 | 0.70 | — |
| 1965 Proof | 25,000 | Value: 0.80 | | | | |
| 1966 | 4,101,000 | — | — | 0.15 | 0.75 | — |
| 1967 | 4,590,000 | — | — | 0.15 | 0.75 | — |
| 1969 | 5,020,000 | — | — | 0.15 | 0.75 | — |

**5 CENTS** **KM# 67.2** **Composition:** Nickel **Obverse:** Afrikaans legend

| Date | Mintage | F | VF | XF | Unc | BU |
|---|---|---|---|---|---|---|
| 1965 | 32,689,999 | — | — | 0.15 | 0.75 | — |
| 1966 | 4,101,000 | — | — | 0.15 | 0.75 | — |
| 1966 Proof | 25,000 | Value: 0.80 | | | | |
| 1967 | 4,590,000 | — | — | 0.15 | 0.75 | — |
| 1967 Proof | 25,000 | Value: 0.80 | | | | |
| 1969 | 5,020,000 | — | — | 0.15 | 0.75 | — |
| 1969 Proof | 12,000 | Value: 0.80 | | | | |

**5 CENTS** **KM# 76.1** **Composition:** Nickel **Subject:** President Charles Swart **Obverse:** English legend

| Date | Mintage | F | VF | XF | Unc | BU |
|---|---|---|---|---|---|---|
| 1968 | 6,000,000 | — | — | 0.15 | 0.75 | — |
| 1968 Proof | 25,000 | Value: 0.80 | | | | |

**5 CENTS** **KM# 76.2** **Composition:** Nickel **Obverse:** Afrikaans legend

| Date | Mintage | F | VF | XF | Unc | BU |
|---|---|---|---|---|---|---|
| 1968 | 6,000,000 | — | — | 0.15 | 0.75 | — |

**5 CENTS** **KM# 84** **Composition:** Nickel **Obverse:** Bilingual legend

| Date | Mintage | F | VF | XF | Unc | BU |
|---|---|---|---|---|---|---|
| 1970 | 6,652,000 | — | — | 0.15 | 0.75 | — |
| 1970 Proof | 10,000 | Value: 0.80 | | | | |
| 1971 | 20,329,000 | — | — | 0.15 | 0.75 | — |
| 1971 Proof | 12,000 | Value: 0.80 | | | | |
| 1972 | 3,117,000 | — | — | 0.15 | 0.75 | — |
| 1972 Proof | 9,000 | Value: 0.80 | | | | |
| 1973 | 17,092,000 | — | — | 0.15 | 0.75 | — |
| 1973 Proof | 11,000 | Value: 0.80 | | | | |
| 1974 | 19,978,000 | — | — | 0.15 | 0.75 | — |
| 1974 Proof | 15,000 | Value: 0.80 | | | | |
| 1975 | 21,982,000 | — | — | 0.15 | 0.75 | — |
| 1975 Proof | 18,000 | Value: 0.80 | | | | |
| 1977 | 51,729,000 | — | — | 0.15 | 0.75 | — |
| 1977 Proof | 19,000 | Value: 0.80 | | | | |
| 1978 | 30,050,000 | — | — | 0.15 | 0.75 | — |
| 1978 Proof | 19,000 | Value: 0.80 | | | | |
| 1980 | 46,665,000 | — | — | 0.15 | 0.75 | — |
| 1980 Proof | 15,000 | Value: 0.80 | | | | |
| 1981 | 40,351,000 | — | — | 0.15 | 0.75 | — |
| 1981 Proof | 10,000 | Value: 0.80 | | | | |
| 1983 | 57,487,000 | — | — | 0.15 | 0.75 | — |
| 1983 Proof | 14,000 | Value: 0.80 | | | | |
| 1984 | 67,345,000 | — | — | 0.15 | 0.75 | — |
| 1984 Proof | 11,000 | Value: 0.80 | | | | |
| 1985 | 57,167,000 | — | — | 0.15 | 0.75 | — |
| 1985 Proof | 9,859 | Value: 0.80 | | | | |
| 1986 | 54,226,000 | — | — | 0.15 | 0.75 | — |
| 1986 Proof | 7,100 | Value: 0.80 | | | | |
| 1987 | 42,786,000 | — | — | 0.15 | 0.75 | — |
| 1987 Proof | 5,297 | Value: 0.80 | | | | |
| 1988 | 110,164,000 | — | — | 0.15 | 0.75 | — |
| 1988 Proof | 7,250 | Value: 0.80 | | | | |
| 1989 | 35,540,000 | — | — | 0.15 | 0.75 | — |
| 1989 Proof | Inc. above | Value: 1.50 | | | | |

**5 CENTS** **KM# 93** **Composition:** Nickel **Subject:** President Fouche

| Date | Mintage | F | VF | XF | Unc | BU |
|---|---|---|---|---|---|---|
| 1976 | 48,972,000 | — | — | 0.30 | 0.75 | — |
| 1976 Proof | 19,000 | Value: 1.50 | | | | |

**5 CENTS** **KM# 100** **Composition:** Nickel **Subject:** President Diederichs

| Date | Mintage | F | VF | XF | Unc | BU |
|---|---|---|---|---|---|---|
| 1979 | 17,533,000 | — | — | 0.30 | 0.75 | — |
| 1979 Proof | 17,000 | Value: 1.50 | | | | |

**5 CENTS** **KM# 111** **Composition:** Nickel **Subject:** President Vorster

| Date | Mintage | F | VF | XF | Unc | BU |
|---|---|---|---|---|---|---|
| 1982 | 47,236,000 | — | — | 0.30 | 0.75 | — |
| 1982 Proof | 12,000 | Value: 1.50 | | | | |

**5 CENTS** **KM# 134** **Composition:** Chrome Plated Steel

| Date | Mintage | F | VF | XF | Unc | BU |
|---|---|---|---|---|---|---|
| 1990 | — | — | — | 0.15 | 0.75 | — |
| 1990 Proof | — | Value: 0.80 | | | | |
| 1991 | — | — | — | 0.15 | 0.75 | — |
| 1991 Proof | 12,000 | Value: 0.80 | | | | |
| 1992 | — | — | — | 0.15 | 0.75 | — |
| 1992 Proof | — | Value: 0.80 | | | | |
| 1993 | — | — | — | 0.15 | 0.75 | — |
| 1993 Proof | 7,790 | Value: 0.80 | | | | |
| 1994 | — | — | — | 0.15 | 0.75 | — |
| 1994 Proof | 5,804 | Value: 0.80 | | | | |
| 1995 | — | — | — | 0.15 | 0.75 | — |
| 1995 Proof | — | Value: 0.80 | | | | |

**5 CENTS** **KM# 160** **Composition:** Chrome Plated Steel **Obverse:** Tsonga legend

| Date | Mintage | F | VF | XF | Unc | BU |
|---|---|---|---|---|---|---|
| 1996 | — | — | — | 0.15 | 0.75 | — |
| 1996 Proof | — | Value: 0.80 | | | | |
| 1997 | — | — | — | 0.15 | 0.75 | — |
| 1997 Proof | 3,596 | Value: 0.80 | | | | |
| 1998 | — | — | — | 0.15 | 0.75 | — |
| 1998 Proof | — | Value: 1.25 | | | | |
| 1999 | — | — | — | 0.15 | 0.75 | — |
| 1999 Proof | — | Value: 1.25 | | | | |
| 2000 | — | — | — | 0.15 | 0.75 | — |

**5 CENTS** **KM# 223** **Weight:** 4.4300 g. **Composition:** Copper Plated Steel **Obverse:** National arms **Reverse:** Crane standing on shore

**Edge:** Plain **Size:** 21 mm.

| Date | Mintage | F | VF | XF | Unc | BU |
|---|---|---|---|---|---|---|
| 2001 | — | — | — | — | 0.50 | — |

**10 CENTS** **KM# 60** **Weight:** 5.6600 g. **Composition:** 0.5000 Silver .0909 oz. ASW

| Date | Mintage | F | VF | XF | Unc | BU |
|---|---|---|---|---|---|---|
| 1961 | 1,136,000 | — | BV | 1.25 | 2.50 | — |
| 1961 Proof | 7,530 | Value: 2.50 | | | | |
| 1962 | 2,447,000 | — | BV | 1.25 | 2.50 | — |
| 1962 Proof | 3,844 | Value: 3.50 | | | | |
| 1963 | 3,327,000 | — | BV | 1.25 | 2.50 | — |
| 1963 Proof | 4,025 | Value: 3.50 | | | | |
| 1964 | 4,152,999 | — | BV | 1.25 | 2.00 | — |
| 1964 Proof | 16,000 | Value: 2.50 | | | | |

**10 CENTS** **KM# 68.1** **Composition:** Nickel **Obverse:** English legend **Reverse:** Aloe plant

| Date | Mintage | F | VF | XF | Unc | BU |
|---|---|---|---|---|---|---|
| 1965 | 29,210,000 | — | — | 0.10 | 0.35 | — |
| 1966 | 3,685,000 | — | — | 0.10 | 0.45 | — |
| 1966 Proof | 25,000 | Value: 0.60 | | | | |
| 1967 | 50,000 | — | — | — | 1.00 | — |
| 1967 Proof | 25,000 | Value: 0.60 | | | | |
| 1969 | 558,000 | — | — | 0.10 | 0.50 | — |
| 1969 Proof | 12,000 | Value: 1.00 | | | | |

**10 CENTS** **KM# 68.2** **Composition:** Nickel **Obverse:** Afrikaans legend

| Date | Mintage | F | VF | XF | Unc | BU |
|---|---|---|---|---|---|---|
| 1965 | 29,210,000 | — | — | 0.10 | 0.35 | — |
| 1965 Proof | 25,000 | Value: 0.60 | | | | |
| 1966 | 3,685,000 | — | — | 0.10 | 0.45 | — |
| 1967 | 50,000 | — | — | — | 1.00 | — |
| 1969 | 558,000 | — | 0.10 | 0.20 | 2.50 | — |

**10 CENTS** **KM# 77.1** **Composition:** Nickel **Subject:** President Charles Swart **Obverse:** English legend

| Date | Mintage | F | VF | XF | Unc | BU |
|---|---|---|---|---|---|---|
| 1968 | 50,000 | — | — | — | 2.00 | — |

**10 CENTS** **KM# 77.2** **Composition:** Nickel **Obverse:** Afrikaans legend

| Date | Mintage | F | VF | XF | Unc | BU |
|---|---|---|---|---|---|---|
| 1968 | 50,000 | — | — | — | 1.50 | — |
| 1968 Proof | 25,000 | Value: 0.60 | | | | |

**10 CENTS** **KM# 85** **Composition:** Nickel **Obverse:** Bilingual legend

| Date | Mintage | F | VF | XF | Unc | BU |
|---|---|---|---|---|---|---|
| 1970 | 7,598,000 | — | — | 0.10 | 0.35 | — |
| 1970 Proof | 10,000 | Value: 0.60 | | | | |
| 1971 | 6,440,000 | — | — | 0.10 | 0.35 | — |
| 1971 Proof | 12,000 | Value: 0.60 | | | | |
| 1972 | 10,028,000 | — | — | 0.10 | 0.35 | — |
| 1972 Proof | 10,000 | Value: 0.60 | | | | |
| 1973 | 1,760,000 | — | — | 0.10 | 0.35 | — |
| 1973 Proof | 11,000 | Value: 0.60 | | | | |
| 1974 | 9,897,000 | — | — | 0.10 | 0.35 | — |
| 1974 Proof | 15,000 | Value: 0.60 | | | | |
| 1975 | 12,982,000 | — | — | 0.10 | 0.35 | — |
| 1975 Proof | 18,000 | Value: 0.60 | | | | |
| 1977 | 28,851,000 | — | — | 0.10 | 0.35 | — |
| 1977 Proof | 19,000 | Value: 0.60 | | | | |
| 1978 | 25,008,000 | — | — | 0.10 | 0.35 | — |
| 1978 Proof | 19,000 | Value: 0.60 | | | | |
| 1980 | 5,040,000 | — | — | 0.10 | 0.35 | — |
| 1980 Proof | 15,000 | Value: 0.60 | | | | |
| 1981 | 9,604,000 | — | — | 0.10 | 0.35 | — |
| 1981 Proof | 10,000 | Value: 0.60 | | | | |
| 1983 | 26,495,000 | — | — | 0.10 | 0.35 | — |
| 1983 Proof | 14,000 | Value: 0.60 | | | | |
| 1984 | 35,465,000 | — | — | 0.10 | 0.35 | — |
| 1984 Proof | 11,000 | Value: 0.60 | | | | |
| 1985 | 29,270,000 | — | — | 0.10 | 0.35 | — |
| 1985 Proof | 9,859 | Value: 0.60 | | | | |
| 1986 | 24,480,000 | — | — | 0.10 | 0.35 | — |
| 1986 Proof | 7,100 | Value: 0.60 | | | | |
| 1987 | 43,234,000 | — | — | 0.10 | 0.35 | — |
| 1987 Proof | 6,781 | Value: 0.60 | | | | |
| 1988 | 48,267,000 | — | — | 0.10 | 0.35 | — |
| 1988 Proof | 7,250 | Value: 0.60 | | | | |

| Date | Mintage | F | VF | XF | Unc | BU |
|---|---|---|---|---|---|---|
| 1989 | — | — | — | — | 0.35 | — |
| 1989 Proof | — | Value: 0.60 | | | | |

**10 CENTS** KM# 94 **Composition:** Nickel **Subject:** President Fouche

| Date | Mintage | F | VF | XF | Unc | BU |
|---|---|---|---|---|---|---|
| 1976 | 30,986,000 | — | — | 0.40 | 1.00 | — |
| 1976 Proof | 21,000 | Value: 1.50 | | | | |

**10 CENTS** KM# 101 **Composition:** Nickel **Subject:** President Diederichs

| Date | Mintage | F | VF | XF | Unc | BU |
|---|---|---|---|---|---|---|
| 1979 | 5,042,000 | — | — | 0.40 | 1.00 | — |
| 1979 Proof | 17,000 | Value: 1.50 | | | | |

**10 CENTS** KM# 112 **Composition:** Nickel **Subject:** President Vorster

| Date | Mintage | F | VF | XF | Unc | BU |
|---|---|---|---|---|---|---|
| 1982 | 15,806,000 | — | — | 0.40 | 1.00 | — |
| 1982 Proof | 12,000 | Value: 1.50 | | | | |

**10 CENTS** KM# 135 **Composition:** Brass Plated Steel

| Date | Mintage | F | VF | XF | Unc | BU |
|---|---|---|---|---|---|---|
| 1990 | — | — | — | — | 0.40 | — |
| 1990 Proof | — | Value: 0.60 | | | | |
| 1991 | — | — | — | — | 0.40 | — |
| 1991 Proof | 12,000 | Value: 0.60 | | | | |
| 1992 | — | — | — | — | 0.40 | — |
| 1992 Proof | — | Value: 0.60 | | | | |
| 1993 | — | — | — | — | 0.40 | — |
| 1993 Proof | 7,790 | Value: 0.60 | | | | |
| 1994 | — | — | — | — | 0.40 | — |
| 1994 Proof | 5,804 | Value: 0.60 | | | | |
| 1995 | — | — | — | — | 0.40 | — |
| 1995 Proof | — | Value: 0.60 | | | | |

**10 CENTS** KM# 161 **Composition:** Brass Plated Steel **Obverse:** English legend above arms

| Date | Mintage | F | VF | XF | Unc | BU |
|---|---|---|---|---|---|---|
| 1996 | — | — | — | — | 0.40 | — |
| 1996 Proof | — | Value: 0.75 | | | | |
| 1997 | — | — | — | — | 0.40 | — |
| 1997 Proof | 3,596 | Value: 0.75 | | | | |
| 1998 | — | — | — | — | 0.40 | — |
| 1998 Proof | — | Value: 1.75 | | | | |
| 1999 | — | — | — | — | 0.40 | — |
| 1999 Proof | — | Value: 1.75 | | | | |
| 2000 | — | — | — | — | 0.40 | — |

**10 CENTS** KM# 224 **Weight:** 2.0000 g. **Composition:** Brass Plated Steel **Obverse:** National arms **Reverse:** Flower and denomination **Edge:** Reeded **Size:** 15.9 mm.

| Date | Mintage | F | VF | XF | Unc | BU |
|---|---|---|---|---|---|---|
| 2001 | — | — | — | — | 0.60 | — |

**20 CENTS** KM# 61 **Weight:** 11.3100 g. **Composition:** 0.5000 Silver .1818 oz. ASW

| Date | Mintage | F | VF | XF | Unc | BU |
|---|---|---|---|---|---|---|
| 1961 | 2,954,000 | — | BV | 1.50 | 2.50 | — |
| 1961 Proof | 7,530 | Value: 3.50 | | | | |
| 1962 Small 2 | 3,568,000 | — | BV | 1.50 | 2.50 | — |
| 1962 Large 2 | Inc. above | — | — | — | — | — |
| 1962 Small 2; Proof | 3,844 | Value: 4.00 | | | | |
| 1963 | 4,380,000 | — | BV | 1.50 | 2.50 | — |
| 1963 Proof | 4,025 | Value: 4.00 | | | | |
| 1964 | 4,335,000 | — | BV | 1.50 | 2.50 | — |
| 1964 Proof | 16,000 | Value: 2.50 | | | | |

**20 CENTS** KM# 69.1 **Composition:** Nickel **Subject:** Protea Cynaroides and Protea Repens **Obverse:** English legend

| Date | Mintage | F | VF | XF | Unc | BU |
|---|---|---|---|---|---|---|
| 1965 | 29,210,000 | — | 0.15 | 0.20 | 0.40 | — |
| 1965 Proof | 25,000 | Value: 0.60 | | | | |
| 1966 | 4,049,000 | — | 0.15 | 0.20 | 0.50 | — |
| 1967 | 58,000 | — | — | — | 1.00 | — |
| 1969 | 9,952 | — | — | — | 10.00 | — |

**20 CENTS** KM# 69.2 **Composition:** Nickel **Obverse:** Afrikaans legend

| Date | Mintage | F | VF | XF | Unc | BU |
|---|---|---|---|---|---|---|
| 1965 | 29,210,000 | — | 0.15 | 0.20 | 0.40 | — |
| 1966 | 4,049,000 | — | 0.15 | 0.20 | 0.50 | — |
| 1966 Proof | 25,000 | Value: 0.60 | | | | |
| 1967 | 58,000 | — | — | — | 1.00 | — |
| 1967 Proof | 25,000 | Value: 0.60 | | | | |
| 1969 | 9,952 | — | — | — | 6.00 | — |
| 1969 Proof | 12,000 | Value: 4.00 | | | | |

**20 CENTS** KM# 78.1 **Composition:** Nickel **Subject:** President Charles Swart **Obverse:** English legend

| Date | Mintage | F | VF | XF | Unc | BU |
|---|---|---|---|---|---|---|
| 1968 | 50,000 | — | — | — | 3.00 | — |
| 1968 Proof | 25,000 | Value: 0.60 | | | | |

**20 CENTS** KM# 78.2 **Composition:** Nickel **Obverse:** Afrikaans legend

| Date | Mintage | F | VF | XF | Unc | BU |
|---|---|---|---|---|---|---|
| 1968 | 50,000 | — | — | — | 3.50 | — |

**20 CENTS** KM# 86 **Composition:** Nickel **Obverse:** Bilingual legend **Note:** Varieties exist.

| Date | Mintage | F | VF | XF | Unc | BU |
|---|---|---|---|---|---|---|
| 1970 | 14,000 | — | — | — | 10.00 | — |
| 1970 Proof | 10,000 | Value: 1.50 | | | | |
| 1971 | 5,893,000 | — | 0.15 | 0.25 | 0.60 | — |
| 1971 Proof | 12,000 | Value: 1.50 | | | | |
| 1972 | 9,069,000 | — | 0.15 | 0.25 | 0.60 | — |
| 1972 Proof | 10,000 | Value: 1.50 | | | | |
| 1973 | 20,000 | — | — | — | 5.00 | — |
| 1973 Proof | 11,000 | Value: 1.50 | | | | |
| 1974 | 2,436,000 | — | 0.15 | 0.35 | 0.75 | — |
| 1974 Proof | 15,000 | Value: 1.50 | | | | |
| 1975 | 12,982,000 | — | — | 0.20 | 0.60 | — |
| 1975 Proof | 18,000 | Value: 1.00 | | | | |
| 1977 | 30,650,000 | — | — | 0.20 | 0.60 | — |
| 1977 Proof | 19,000 | Value: 0.75 | | | | |
| 1978 | 10,049,000 | — | — | 0.20 | 0.60 | — |
| 1978 Proof | 19,000 | Value: 0.75 | | | | |
| 1980 | 13,335,000 | — | — | 0.20 | 0.60 | — |
| 1980 Proof | 15,000 | Value: 0.75 | | | | |
| 1981 | 8,534,000 | — | — | 0.20 | 0.60 | — |
| 1981 Proof | 10,000 | Value: 0.75 | | | | |
| 1983 | 25,667,000 | — | — | 0.20 | 0.60 | — |
| 1983 Proof | 14,000 | Value: 0.75 | | | | |
| 1984 | 31,607,000 | — | — | 0.20 | 0.60 | — |
| 1984 Proof | 11,000 | Value: 0.75 | | | | |
| 1985 | 29,329,000 | — | — | 0.20 | 0.60 | — |
| 1985 Proof | 9,859 | Value: 0.75 | | | | |
| 1986 | 11,408,000 | — | — | 0.20 | 0.60 | — |
| 1986 Proof | 7,100 | Value: 0.75 | | | | |
| 1987 | 36,904,000 | — | — | 0.20 | 0.60 | — |
| 1987 Proof | 6,781 | Value: 0.75 | | | | |
| 1988 | 43,115,000 | — | — | 0.20 | 0.60 | — |
| 1988 Proof | 7,250 | Value: 0.75 | | | | |
| 1989 | — | — | — | 0.20 | 0.60 | — |
| 1989 Proof | — | Value: 0.75 | | | | |
| 1990 | 98,512,000 | — | — | 0.20 | 0.60 | — |

**20 CENTS** KM# 95 **Composition:** Nickel **Subject:** President Fouche

| Date | Mintage | F | VF | XF | Unc | BU |
|---|---|---|---|---|---|---|
| 1976 | 18,826,000 | — | — | 0.70 | 1.50 | — |
| 1976 Proof | 21,000 | Value: 2.50 | | | | |

**20 CENTS** KM# 102 **Composition:** Nickel **Subject:** President Diederichs

| Date | Mintage | F | VF | XF | Unc | BU |
|---|---|---|---|---|---|---|
| 1979 | 5,032,000 | — | — | 0.70 | 1.50 | — |
| 1979 Proof | 15,000 | Value: 2.50 | | | | |

**20 CENTS** KM# 113 **Composition:** Nickel **Subject:** President Vorster

| Date | Mintage | F | VF | XF | Unc | BU |
|---|---|---|---|---|---|---|
| 1982 | 18,083,000 | — | — | 0.70 | 1.50 | — |
| 1982 Proof | 12,000 | Value: 2.50 | | | | |

**20 CENTS** **KM# 136** **Composition:** Brass Plated Steel

| Date | Mintage | F | VF | XF | Unc | BU |
|---|---|---|---|---|---|---|
| 1990 | — | — | — | — | 4.00 | — |
| 1990 Proof | — | Value: 8.00 | | | | |
| 1991 | — | — | — | — | 4.00 | — |
| 1991 Proof | 11,800 | Value: 8.00 | | | | |
| 1992 | — | — | — | — | 0.60 | — |
| 1992 Proof | — | Value: 8.00 | | | | |
| 1993 | — | — | — | — | 0.60 | — |
| 1993 Proof | 7,790 | Value: 8.00 | | | | |
| 1994 | — | — | — | — | 0.60 | — |
| 1994 Proof | 5,804 | Value: 8.00 | | | | |
| 1995 | — | — | — | — | 0.60 | — |
| 1995 Proof | — | Value: 8.00 | | | | |

**20 CENTS** **KM# 162** **Composition:** Brass Plated Steel **Obverse:** Tswana legend above arms

| Date | Mintage | F | VF | XF | Unc | BU |
|---|---|---|---|---|---|---|
| 1996 | — | — | — | — | 0.60 | — |
| 1996 Proof | — | Value: 4.00 | | | | |
| 1997 | — | — | — | — | 0.60 | — |
| 1997 Proof | 3,596 | Value: 4.00 | | | | |
| 1998 | — | — | — | — | 0.60 | — |
| 1998 Proof | — | Value: 4.00 | | | | |
| 1999 | — | — | — | — | 0.60 | — |
| 1999 Proof | — | Value: 4.00 | | | | |
| 2000 | — | — | — | — | 0.60 | — |

**20 CENTS** **KM# 225** **Weight:** 3.4500 g. **Composition:** Brass Plated Steel **Obverse:** National arms **Reverse:** Protea flower and denomination **Edge:** Reeded **Size:** 19 mm.

| Date | Mintage | F | VF | XF | Unc | BU |
|---|---|---|---|---|---|---|
| 2001 | — | — | — | — | 0.75 | — |

**50 CENTS** **KM# 62** **Weight:** 28.2800 g. **Composition:** 0.5000 Silver .4546 oz. ASW **Note:** Varieties exist with narrow, high relief and wide, low letters.

| Date | Mintage | F | VF | XF | Unc | BU |
|---|---|---|---|---|---|---|
| 1961 | 26,000 | — | BV | 6.00 | 10.00 | — |
| 1961 Prooflike | 20,000 | — | — | — | 10.00 | — |
| 1961 Proof | 8,530 | Value: 18.00 | | | | |
| 1962 | 15,000 | — | BV | 6.00 | 10.00 | — |
| 1962 Prooflike | 6,024 | — | — | — | 12.50 | — |
| 1962 Proof | 3,844 | Value: 20.00 | | | | |
| 1963 | 143,000 | — | BV | 5.00 | 9.00 | — |
| 1963 Prooflike | 10,000 | — | — | — | 12.50 | — |
| 1963 Proof | 4,025 | Value: 20.00 | | | | |
| 1964 | 86,000 | — | BV | 5.00 | 9.00 | — |
| 1964 Prooflike | 25,000 | — | — | — | 10.00 | — |
| 1964 Proof | 16,000 | Value: 10.00 | | | | |

**50 CENTS** **KM# 70.1** **Composition:** Nickel **Subject:** Zantedeschia Elliottiana **Obverse:** English legend

| Date | Mintage | F | VF | XF | Unc | BU |
|---|---|---|---|---|---|---|
| 1965 Proof | — | Value: 3,500 | | | | |
| 1966 | 8,055,999 | — | — | 0.50 | 2.50 | — |
| 1966 Proof | 25,000 | Value: 4.00 | | | | |
| 1967 In sets only | 52,000 | — | — | — | 1.50 | — |
| 1967 Proof | 25,000 | Value: 4.00 | | | | |
| 1969 In sets only | 7,968 | — | — | — | 10.00 | — |
| 1969 Proof | 12,000 | Value: 10.00 | | | | |

**50 CENTS** **KM# 70.2** **Composition:** Nickel **Obverse:** Afrikaans legend

| Date | Mintage | F | VF | XF | Unc | BU |
|---|---|---|---|---|---|---|
| 1965 | 28,000 | — | — | — | 6.00 | — |
| 1965 Proof | 25,000 | Value: 6.00 | | | | |
| 1966 | 8,055,999 | — | — | 0.50 | 2.50 | — |
| 1967 In sets only | 52,000 | — | — | — | 3.50 | — |
| 1969 In sets only | 7,968 | — | — | — | 15.00 | — |

**50 CENTS** **KM# 79.1** **Composition:** Nickel **Subject:** President Charles Swart **Obverse:** English legend

| Date | Mintage | F | VF | XF | Unc | BU |
|---|---|---|---|---|---|---|
| 1968 | 750,000 | — | — | 0.50 | 1.50 | — |

**50 CENTS** **KM# 79.2** **Composition:** Nickel **Obverse:** Afrikaans legend

| Date | Mintage | F | VF | XF | Unc | BU |
|---|---|---|---|---|---|---|
| 1968 | 750,000 | — | — | 0.50 | 2.00 | — |
| 1968 Proof | 25,000 | Value: 3.50 | | | | |

**50 CENTS** **KM# 87** **Composition:** Nickel **Obverse:** Bilingual legend **Note:** Varieties exist.

| Date | Mintage | F | VF | XF | Unc | BU |
|---|---|---|---|---|---|---|
| 1970 | 4,098,000 | — | — | 0.50 | 1.50 | — |
| 1970 Proof | 10,000 | Value: 2.00 | | | | |
| 1971 | 5,062,000 | — | — | 0.50 | 1.50 | — |
| 1971 Proof | 12,000 | Value: 2.00 | | | | |
| 1972 | 771,000 | — | — | 0.50 | 1.50 | — |
| 1972 Proof | 10,000 | Value: 2.00 | | | | |
| 1973 | 1,042,999 | — | — | 0.50 | 1.50 | — |
| 1973 Proof | 11,000 | Value: 2.00 | | | | |
| 1974 | 1,942,000 | — | — | 0.50 | 1.50 | — |
| 1974 Proof | 15,000 | Value: 2.00 | | | | |
| 1975 | 4,888,000 | — | — | 0.50 | 1.50 | — |
| 1975 Proof | 18,000 | Value: 2.00 | | | | |
| 1977 | 10,196,000 | — | — | 0.50 | 1.50 | — |
| 1977 Proof | 19,000 | Value: 2.00 | | | | |
| 1978 | 5,071,000 | — | — | 0.50 | 1.50 | — |
| 1978 Proof | 17,000 | Value: 2.00 | | | | |
| 1980 | 4,268,000 | — | — | 0.50 | 1.50 | — |
| 1980 Proof | 15,000 | Value: 2.00 | | | | |
| 1981 | 5,681,000 | — | — | 0.50 | 1.50 | — |
| 1981 Proof | 10,000 | Value: 2.00 | | | | |
| 1983 | 5,150,000 | — | — | 0.40 | 1.00 | — |
| 1983 Proof | 14,000 | Value: 1.50 | | | | |
| 1984 | 9,687,000 | — | — | 0.40 | 1.00 | — |
| 1984 Proof | 11,000 | Value: 1.50 | | | | |
| 1985 | 13,339,000 | — | — | 0.40 | 1.00 | — |
| 1985 Proof | 9,859 | Value: 1.50 | | | | |
| 1986 | 2,294,000 | — | — | 0.40 | 1.00 | — |
| 1986 Proof | 7,100 | Value: 1.50 | | | | |
| 1987 | 19,071,000 | — | — | 0.40 | 1.00 | — |
| 1987 Proof | 6,781 | Value: 1.50 | | | | |
| 1988 | 27,698,000 | — | — | 0.40 | 1.00 | — |
| 1988 Proof | 7,250 | Value: 1.50 | | | | |
| 1989 | — | — | — | 0.40 | 1.00 | — |
| 1989 Proof | — | Value: 1.50 | | | | |
| 1990 | 29,442,000 | — | — | 0.40 | 1.00 | — |

**50 CENTS** **KM# 96** **Composition:** Nickel **Subject:** President Fouche

| Date | Mintage | F | VF | XF | Unc | BU |
|---|---|---|---|---|---|---|
| 1976 | 9,632,000 | — | 0.75 | 1.50 | 3.00 | — |
| 1976 Proof | 21,000 | Value: 5.00 | | | | |

**50 CENTS** **KM# 103** **Composition:** Nickel **Subject:** President Diederichs

| Date | Mintage | F | VF | XF | Unc | BU |
|---|---|---|---|---|---|---|
| 1979 | 5,051,000 | — | 0.75 | 1.50 | 3.50 | — |
| 1979 Proof | 15,000 | Value: 5.00 | | | | |

**50 CENTS** **KM# 114** **Composition:** Nickel **Subject:** President Vorster

| Date | Mintage | F | VF | XF | Unc | BU |
|---|---|---|---|---|---|---|
| 1982 | 2,069,999 | — | 0.75 | 1.50 | 3.50 | — |
| 1982 Proof | 12,000 | Value: 5.00 | | | | |

**50 CENTS** **KM# 137** **Composition:** Brass Plated Steel

| Date | Mintage | F | VF | XF | Unc | BU |
|---|---|---|---|---|---|---|
| 1990 | — | — | — | — | 5.00 | — |
| 1990 Proof | — | Value: 10.00 | | | | |

| Date | Mintage | F | VF | XF | Unc | BU |
|---|---|---|---|---|---|---|
| 1991 | — | — | — | — | 5.00 | — |
| 1991 Proof | 12,000 | Value: 10.00 | | | | |
| 1992 | — | — | — | — | 1.00 | — |
| 1992 Proof | — | Value: 10.00 | | | | |
| 1993 | — | — | — | — | 1.00 | — |
| 1993 Proof | 7,790 | Value: 10.00 | | | | |
| 1994 | — | — | — | — | 1.00 | — |
| 1994 Proof | 5,804 | Value: 10.00 | | | | |
| 1995 | — | — | — | — | 1.00 | — |
| 1995 Proof | — | Value: 10.00 | | | | |

**50 CENTS** **KM# 163** **Composition:** Bronze Plated Steel **Obverse:** Sotho legend

| Date | Mintage | F | VF | XF | Unc | BU |
|---|---|---|---|---|---|---|
| 1996 | — | — | — | — | 1.00 | — |
| 1996 Proof | — | Value: 5.00 | | | | |
| 1997 | — | — | — | — | 1.00 | — |
| 1997 Proof | — | Value: 5.00 | | | | |
| 1998 | — | — | — | — | 1.00 | — |
| 1998 Proof | — | Value: 5.00 | | | | |
| 1999 | — | — | — | — | 1.00 | — |
| 1999 Proof | — | Value: 5.00 | | | | |
| 2000 | — | — | — | — | 1.00 | — |

**50 CENTS** **KM# 226** **Weight:** 4.9000 g. **Composition:** Brass Plated Steel **Obverse:** National arms **Reverse:** Grass-like plant and denomination **Edge:** Reeded **Size:** 22 mm.

| Date | Mintage | F | VF | XF | Unc | BU |
|---|---|---|---|---|---|---|
| 2001 | — | — | — | — | 1.00 | — |

**RAND** **KM# 63** **Weight:** 3.9940 g. **Composition:** 0.9170 Gold .1177 oz. AGW

| Date | Mintage | F | VF | XF | Unc | BU |
|---|---|---|---|---|---|---|
| 1961 | 4,246 | — | — | — | BV+15% | — |
| 1961 Proof | 4,932 | — | — | — | BV+20% | — |
| 1962 | 3,955 | — | — | — | BV+15% | — |
| 1962 Proof | 2,344 | — | — | — | BV+20% | — |
| 1963 | 4,023 | — | — | — | BV+15% | — |
| 1963 Proof | 2,508 | — | — | — | BV+20% | — |
| 1964 | 5,866 | — | — | — | BV+15% | — |
| 1964 Proof | 4,000 | — | — | — | BV+20% | — |
| 1965 | 10,000 | — | — | — | BV+15% | — |
| 1965 Proof | 6,024 | — | — | — | BV+20% | — |
| 1966 | 10,000 | — | — | — | BV+15% | — |
| 1966 Proof | 11,000 | — | — | — | BV+20% | — |
| 1967 | 10,000 | — | — | — | BV+15% | — |
| 1967 Proof | 11,000 | — | — | — | BV+20% | — |
| 1968 | 10,000 | — | — | — | BV+15% | — |
| 1968 Proof | 11,000 | — | — | — | BV+20% | — |
| 1969 | 10,000 | — | — | — | BV+15% | — |
| 1969 Proof | 8,000 | — | — | — | BV+20% | — |
| 1970 | 10,000 | — | — | — | BV+15% | — |
| 1970 Proof | 7,000 | — | — | — | BV+20% | — |
| 1971 | 10,000 | — | — | — | BV+15% | — |
| 1971 Proof | 7,650 | — | — | — | BV+20% | — |
| 1972 | 12,000 | — | — | — | BV+15% | — |
| 1972 Proof | 7,500 | — | — | — | BV+20% | — |
| 1973 | 15,000 | — | — | — | BV+15% | — |
| 1973 Proof | 12,000 | — | — | — | BV+20% | — |
| 1974 | 23,000 | — | — | — | BV+15% | — |
| 1974 Proof | 17,000 | — | — | — | BV+20% | — |
| 1975 | 12,000 | — | — | — | BV+15% | — |
| 1975 Proof | 18,000 | — | — | — | BV+20% | — |
| 1976 | 12,000 | — | — | — | BV+15% | — |
| 1976 Proof | 21,000 | — | — | — | BV+20% | — |
| 1977 | 27,000 | — | — | — | BV+15% | — |
| 1977 Proof | 20,000 | — | — | — | BV+20% | — |
| 1978 | 13,000 | — | — | — | BV+15% | — |
| 1978 Proof | 19,000 | — | — | — | BV+20% | — |
| 1979 | 17,000 | — | — | — | BV+15% | — |
| 1979 Proof | 17,000 | — | — | — | BV+20% | — |
| 1980 | 14,000 | — | — | — | BV+15% | — |
| 1980 Proof | 18,000 | — | — | — | BV+20% | — |
| 1981 | 9,274 | — | — | — | BV+15% | — |
| 1981 Proof | 10,000 | — | — | — | BV+20% | — |
| 1982 | 14,000 | — | — | — | BV+20% | — |
| 1983 | 15,000 | — | — | — | BV+20% | — |

**RAND** **KM# 71.1** **Weight:** 15.0000 g. **Composition:** 0.8000 Silver .3858 oz. ASW **Obverse:** English legend

| Date | Mintage | F | VF | XF | Unc | BU |
|---|---|---|---|---|---|---|
| 1965 | — | — | — | BV | 5.00 | — |
| 1965 Proof | 25,000 | Value: 20.00 | | | | |
| 1966 | 1,434,000 | — | — | BV | 4.00 | — |
| 1966 Proof | 20 | Value: 1,250 | | | | |
| 1968 In sets only | 50,000 | — | — | — | 4.00 | — |
| 1968 Proof | 25,000 | Value: 5.00 | | | | |

**RAND** **KM# 71.2** **Weight:** 15.0000 g. **Composition:** 0.8000 Silver .3858 oz. ASW **Obverse:** Afrikaans legend

| Date | Mintage | F | VF | XF | Unc | BU |
|---|---|---|---|---|---|---|
| 1965 V.I.P. Proof | — | — | — | — | 1,000 | — |
| 1966 | 1,434,000 | — | — | BV | 4.50 | — |
| 1966 Proof | 25,000 | Value: 6.00 | | | | |
| 1968 In sets only | 50,000 | — | — | — | 7.50 | — |
| 1968 Proof | Est. 20 | Value: 1,250 | | | | |

**RAND** **KM# 72.1** **Weight:** 15.0000 g. **Composition:** 0.8000 Silver .3858 oz. ASW **Subject:** 1st Anniversary - Death of Dr. Verwoerd **Obverse:** English legend

| Date | Mintage | F | VF | XF | Unc | BU |
|---|---|---|---|---|---|---|
| 1967 | 1,544,000 | — | — | BV | 4.00 | — |
| 1967 Proof | Est. 20 | Value: 1,250 | | | | |

**RAND** **KM# 72.2** **Weight:** 15.0000 g. **Composition:** 0.8000 Silver .3858 oz. ASW **Obverse:** Afrikaans legend

| Date | Mintage | F | VF | XF | Unc | BU |
|---|---|---|---|---|---|---|
| 1967 | 1,544,000 | — | — | BV | 4.50 | — |
| 1967 Proof | 25,000 | Value: 6.00 | | | | |

**RAND** **KM# 80.1** **Weight:** 15.0000 g. **Composition:** 0.8000 Silver .3858 oz. ASW **Subject:** Dr. T.E. Donges **Obverse:** English legend **Note:** The South African mint does not acknowledge the existence of these 1 Rand pieces struck in proof.

| Date | Mintage | F | VF | XF | Unc | BU |
|---|---|---|---|---|---|---|
| 1969 | 506,000 | — | — | BV | 4.50 | — |
| 1969 Proof | Est. 20 | Value: 1,250 | | | | |

**RAND** **KM# 80.2** **Weight:** 15.0000 g. **Composition:** 0.8000 Silver .3858 oz. ASW **Obverse:** Afrikaans legend

| Date | Mintage | F | VF | XF | Unc | BU |
|---|---|---|---|---|---|---|
| 1969 | 506,000 | — | — | BV | 4.50 | — |
| 1969 Proof | 12,000 | Value: 6.00 | | | | |

**RAND** **KM# 88** **Weight:** 15.0000 g. **Composition:** 0.8000 Silver .3858 oz. ASW **Obverse:** Bilingual legend

| Date | Mintage | F | VF | XF | Unc | BU |
|---|---|---|---|---|---|---|
| 1970 | 14,000 | — | — | BV | 6.00 | — |
| 1970 Proof | 10,000 | Value: 8.00 | | | | |
| 1971 | 20,000 | — | — | BV | 6.00 | — |
| 1971 Proof | 12,000 | Value: 8.00 | | | | |
| 1972 | 20,000 | — | — | BV | 6.00 | — |
| 1972 Proof | 10,000 | Value: 8.00 | | | | |
| 1973 | 20,000 | — | — | BV | 6.00 | — |
| 1973 Proof | 11,000 | Value: 8.00 | | | | |
| 1975 | 20,000 | — | — | BV | 6.00 | — |
| 1975 Proof | 18,000 | Value: 8.00 | | | | |
| 1976 | 20,000 | — | — | BV | 6.00 | — |
| 1976 Proof | 21,000 | Value: 8.00 | | | | |
| 1977 Proof | 19,000 | Value: 9.00 | | | | |
| 1978 Proof | 17,000 | Value: 9.00 | | | | |
| 1979 Proof | 15,000 | Value: 9.00 | | | | |
| 1980 Proof | 15,000 | Value: 9.00 | | | | |
| 1981 Proof | 12,000 | Value: 12.50 | | | | |
| 1982 Proof | 10,000 | Value: 12.50 | | | | |
| 1983 Proof | 14,000 | Value: 12.50 | | | | |
| 1984 Proof | 11,000 | Value: 12.50 | | | | |
| 1987 | 4,526 | — | — | BV | 15.00 | — |
| 1987 Proof | 13,000 | Value: 12.50 | | | | |
| 1988 | 21 | — | — | — | — | — |
| 1988 Proof | 7,250 | Value: 15.00 | | | | |
| 1989 | 3,684 | — | — | BV | 15.00 | — |
| 1989 Proof | 15,000 | Value: 12.50 | | | | |

**RAND** KM# 89 **Weight:** 15.0000 g. **Composition:** 0.8000 Silver .3858 oz. ASW **Subject:** 50th Anniversary of Pretoria Mint

| Date | Mintage | F | VF | XF | Unc | BU |
|---|---|---|---|---|---|---|
| 1974 | 20,000 | — | — | — | 12.50 | — |
| 1974 Proof | 15,000 | Value: 15.00 | | | | |

**RAND** KM# 88a **Composition:** Nickel

| Date | Mintage | F | VF | XF | Unc | BU |
|---|---|---|---|---|---|---|
| 1977 | 29,871,000 | — | — | 0.75 | 2.00 | — |
| 1977 Proof | 10 | Value: 1,500 | | | | |
| 1978 | 12,021,000 | — | — | 0.75 | 2.00 | — |
| 1978 Proof | 10 | Value: 1,500 | | | | |
| 1980 | 2,690,000 | — | — | 0.75 | 2.00 | — |
| 1981 | 2,035,000 | — | — | 0.75 | 2.00 | — |
| 1983 | 7,182,000 | — | — | 0.75 | 2.00 | — |
| 1983 Proof | 10 | Value: 1,500 | | | | |
| 1984 | 5,736,000 | — | — | 0.75 | 2.00 | — |
| 1984 Proof | 11,000 | Value: 5.00 | | | | |
| 1986 | 1,570,000 | — | — | 0.75 | 2.00 | — |
| 1986 Proof | 7,000 | Value: 5.00 | | | | |
| 1987 | 12,152,000 | — | — | 0.75 | 2.00 | — |
| 1987 Proof | 6,781 | Value: 5.00 | | | | |
| 1988 | 21,335,000 | — | — | 0.75 | 2.00 | — |
| 1988 Proof | 7,250 | Value: 5.00 | | | | |
| 1989 | — | — | — | — | 2.00 | — |
| 1989 Proof | — | Value: 5.00 | | | | |

**RAND** KM# 104 **Composition:** Nickel **Subject:** President Diederichs

| Date | Mintage | F | VF | XF | Unc | BU |
|---|---|---|---|---|---|---|
| 1979 | 13,466,000 | — | 2.00 | 4.00 | 10.00 | — |
| 1979 Proof | 5 | Value: 2,000 | | | | |

**RAND** KM# 115 **Composition:** Nickel .3858 oz. **Subject:** President Vorster

| Date | Mintage | F | VF | XF | Unc | BU |
|---|---|---|---|---|---|---|
| 1982 | 7,685,000 | — | 2.50 | 5.00 | 10.00 | — |
| 1982 Proof | 15 | Value: 1,500 | | | | |

**RAND** KM# 116 **Weight:** 15.0000 g. **Composition:** 0.8000 Silver .3858 oz. ASW **Subject:** 75th Anniversary of Parliament

| Date | Mintage | F | VF | XF | Unc | BU |
|---|---|---|---|---|---|---|
| 1985 | 8,731 | — | — | — | 11.50 | — |
| 1985 Proof | 26,000 | Value: 18.50 | | | | |

**RAND** KM# 117 **Composition:** Nickel **Subject:** President Marais Viljoen

| Date | Mintage | F | VF | XF | Unc | BU |
|---|---|---|---|---|---|---|
| 1985 | 3,983,000 | — | 2.50 | 5.00 | 10.00 | — |
| 1985 Proof | 9,859 | Value: 5.00 | | | | |

**RAND** KM# 119 **Weight:** 15.0000 g. **Composition:** 0.8000 Silver .3858 oz. ASW **Subject:** 100th Anniversary of Johannesburg

| Date | Mintage | F | VF | XF | Unc | BU |
|---|---|---|---|---|---|---|
| 1986 | 7,501 | — | — | — | 13.50 | — |
| 1986 Proof | 5,683 | Value: 25.00 | | | | |

**RAND** KM# 120 **Weight:** 15.0000 g. **Composition:** 0.8000 Silver .3858 oz. ASW **Series:** Year of the Disabled

| Date | Mintage | F | VF | XF | Unc | BU |
|---|---|---|---|---|---|---|
| 1986 | 1,005 | — | — | — | 40.00 | — |
| 1986 Proof | 5,150 | Value: 27.50 | | | | |

**RAND** KM# 122 **Weight:** 15.0000 g. **Composition:** 0.8000 Silver .3858 oz. ASW **Subject:** Bartolomeu Dias

| Date | Mintage | F | VF | XF | Unc | BU |
|---|---|---|---|---|---|---|
| 1988 | 7,091 | — | — | — | 12.50 | — |
| 1988 Proof | 9,640 | Value: 20.00 | | | | |

**RAND** KM# 125 **Weight:** 15.0000 g. **Composition:** 0.8000 Silver .3858 oz. ASW **Subject:** Huguenots

| Date | Mintage | F | VF | XF | Unc | BU |
|---|---|---|---|---|---|---|
| 1988 | 5,497 | — | — | — | 12.50 | — |
| 1988 Proof | 9,028 | Value: 20.00 | | | | |

**RAND** KM# 128 **Weight:** 15.0000 g. **Composition:** 0.8000 Silver .3858 oz. ASW **Subject:** The Great Trek

| Date | Mintage | F | VF | XF | Unc | BU |
|---|---|---|---|---|---|---|
| 1988 | 6,555 | — | — | — | 12.50 | — |
| 1988 Proof | 7,941 | Value: 20.00 | | | | |

**RAND** KM# 141 **Composition:** Nickel **Subject:** President Botha

| Date | Mintage | F | VF | XF | Unc | BU |
|---|---|---|---|---|---|---|
| 1990 | 25,323,000 | — | — | 1.75 | 3.50 | — |
| 1990 Proof | 15,000 | Value: 10.00 | | | | |

**RAND** KM# 148 **Composition:** Nickel Plated Copper

| Date | Mintage | F | VF | XF | Unc | BU |
|---|---|---|---|---|---|---|
| 1990 | 12,000 | — | — | — | 10.00 | — |
| 1990 Proof | 10,000 | Value: 20.00 | | | | |

**RAND** KM# 138 **Composition:** Nickel Plated Copper

| Date | Mintage | F | VF | XF | Unc | BU |
|---|---|---|---|---|---|---|
| 1991 | 20,765,000 | — | — | — | 2.50 | — |
| 1991 Proof | 12,000 | Value: 20.00 | | | | |
| 1992 | 59,571,000 | — | — | — | 2.50 | — |
| 1992 Proof | 10,000 | Value: 20.00 | | | | |
| 1993 | 37,977,000 | — | — | — | 2.50 | — |
| 1993 Proof | 7,790 | Value: 20.00 | | | | |
| 1994 | 54,633,000 | — | — | — | 2.50 | — |
| 1994 Proof | 5,804 | Value: 20.00 | | | | |
| 1995 | 28,012,000 | — | — | — | 2.50 | — |
| 1995 Proof | 5,816 | Value: 20.00 | | | | |

**RAND** **KM# 142** **Weight:** 14.9700 g. **Composition:** 0.9250 Silver .4452 oz. ASW **Subject:** South African Nursing Schools

| Date | Mintage | F | VF | XF | Unc | BU |
|---|---|---|---|---|---|---|
| 1991 | 4,901 | — | — | — | 12.50 | — |
| 1991 Proof | 8,675 | Value: 11.50 | | | | |

**RAND** **KM# 143** **Weight:** 14.9700 g. **Composition:** 0.9250 Silver .4452 oz. ASW **Subject:** Coinage Centennial

| Date | Mintage | F | VF | XF | Unc | BU |
|---|---|---|---|---|---|---|
| 1992 | 5,826 | — | — | — | 12.50 | — |
| 1992 Proof | 8,094 | Value: 20.00 | | | | |

**RAND** **KM# 168** **Weight:** 14.9700 g. **Composition:** 0.9250 Silver .4452 oz. ASW **Subject:** 200 Years of Banking

| Date | Mintage | F | VF | XF | Unc | BU |
|---|---|---|---|---|---|---|
| 1993 | 3,677 | — | — | — | 15.00 | — |
| 1993 Proof | 3,907 | Value: 22.50 | | | | |

**RAND** **KM# 149** **Weight:** 14.9700 g. **Composition:** 0.8000 Silver .3858 oz. ASW **Subject:** Presidential Inauguration

| Date | Mintage | F | VF | XF | Unc | BU |
|---|---|---|---|---|---|---|
| 1994 Proof | 6,269 | Value: 27.50 | | | | |

**RAND** **KM# 167** **Weight:** 15.0000 g. **Composition:** 0.9250 Silver .4461 oz. ASW **Subject:** Conservation

| Date | Mintage | F | VF | XF | Unc | BU |
|---|---|---|---|---|---|---|
| 1994 | 6,404 | — | — | — | 12.50 | — |
| 1994 Proof | 4,706 | Value: 17.50 | | | | |

**RAND** **KM# 152** **Weight:** 15.0000 g. **Composition:** 0.9250 Silver .4461 oz. ASW **Subject:** Protea/Railway Centennial

| Date | Mintage | F | VF | XF | Unc | BU |
|---|---|---|---|---|---|---|
| 1995 | 3,515 | — | — | — | 15.00 | — |
| 1995 Proof | 4,491 | Value: 25.00 | | | | |

**RAND** **KM# 164** **Composition:** Nickel Plated Copper **Subject:** Afrikaans Legend

| Date | Mintage | F | VF | XF | Unc | BU |
|---|---|---|---|---|---|---|
| 1996 | 12,199,000 | — | — | — | 1.75 | — |
| 1996 Proof | 4,827 | Value: 6.00 | | | | |
| 1997 | 38,876,000 | — | — | — | 1.75 | — |
| 1997 Proof | 3,596 | Value: 6.00 | | | | |
| 1998 | — | — | — | — | 1.75 | — |
| 1998 Proof | — | Value: 6.00 | | | | |
| 1999 | — | — | — | — | 1.75 | — |
| 1999 Proof | — | Value: 6.00 | | | | |
| 2000 | — | — | — | — | 1.75 | — |

**RAND** **KM# 169** **Weight:** 15.0000 g. **Composition:** 0.9250 Silver .4461 oz. ASW **Subject:** Constitution

| Date | Mintage | F | VF | XF | Unc | BU |
|---|---|---|---|---|---|---|
| 1996 | 2,585 | — | — | — | 16.50 | — |
| 1996 Proof | 2,474 | Value: 28.00 | | | | |

**RAND** **KM# 181** **Weight:** 15.0000 g. **Composition:** 0.9250 Silver .4461 oz. ASW **Subject:** Women of South Africa

| Date | Mintage | F | VF | XF | Unc | BU |
|---|---|---|---|---|---|---|
| 1997 | 1,983 | — | — | — | 16.50 | — |
| 1997 Proof | 2,329 | Value: 28.00 | | | | |

**RAND** **KM# 182** **Weight:** 3.1103 g. **Composition:** 0.9999 Gold .1000 oz. AGW **Subject:** 30th Anniversary - First Heart Transplant

| Date | Mintage | F | VF | XF | Unc | BU |
|---|---|---|---|---|---|---|
| 1997 Proof | 1,000 | Value: 100 | | | | |

**RAND** **KM# 177** **Weight:** 15.0000 g. **Composition:** 0.9250 Silver .4461 oz. ASW **Obverse:** Protea flower **Reverse:** Divided into 16 sections

| Date | Mintage | F | VF | XF | Unc | BU |
|---|---|---|---|---|---|---|
| 1998 Proof | — | Value: 27.50 | | | | |

**RAND** **KM# 178** **Weight:** 3.1103 g. **Composition:** 0.9999 Gold .1000 oz. AGW **Subject:** San Tribe **Reverse:** Tribesman Hunting

| Date | Mintage | F | VF | XF | Unc | BU |
|---|---|---|---|---|---|---|
| 1998 | — | — | — | — | 100 | — |

**RAND** **KM# 219** **Weight:** 3.1103 g. **Composition:** 0.9999 Gold .1000 oz. AGW **Obverse:** National arms **Reverse:** Zulu warrior **Edge:** Reeded **Size:** 16.5 mm.

| Date | Mintage | F | VF | XF | Unc | BU |
|---|---|---|---|---|---|---|
| 1999 Proof | 1,000 | Value: 100 | | | | |

**RAND** **KM# 227** **Weight:** 4.0000 g. **Composition:** Nickel Plated Steel **Obverse:** National arms **Reverse:** Spring Bok and denomination **Edge:** Reeded and plain sections **Size:** 20 mm.

| Date | Mintage | F | VF | XF | Unc | BU |
|---|---|---|---|---|---|---|
| 2001 | — | — | — | — | 1.75 | — |

**2 RAND** **KM# 64** **Weight:** 7.9881 g. **Composition:** 0.9170 Gold .2354 oz. AGW

| Date | Mintage | F | VF | XF | Unc | BU |
|---|---|---|---|---|---|---|
| 1961 | 3,014 | — | — | — | BV+10% | — |
| 1961 Proof | 3,932 | — | — | — | BV+15% | — |
| 1962 | 10,000 | — | — | — | BV+10% | — |
| 1962 Proof | 2,344 | — | — | — | BV+15% | — |
| 1963 | 3,179 | — | — | — | BV+10% | — |
| 1963 Proof | 2,508 | — | — | — | BV+15% | — |
| 1964 | 3,994 | — | — | — | BV+10% | — |
| 1964 Proof | 4,000 | — | — | — | BV+15% | — |
| 1965 | 10,000 | — | — | — | BV+10% | — |
| 1965 Proof | 6,024 | — | — | — | BV+15% | — |
| 1966 | 10,000 | — | — | — | BV+10% | — |
| 1966 Proof | 11,000 | — | — | — | BV+15% | — |
| 1967 | 10,000 | — | — | — | BV+10% | — |
| 1967 Proof | 11,000 | — | — | — | BV+15% | — |
| 1968 | 10,000 | — | — | — | BV+10% | — |
| 1968 Proof | 11,000 | — | — | — | BV+15% | — |
| 1969 | 10,000 | — | — | — | BV+10% | — |
| 1969 Proof | 8,000 | — | — | — | BV+15% | — |
| 1970 | 10,000 | — | — | — | BV+10% | — |
| 1970 Proof | 7,000 | — | — | — | BV+15% | — |
| 1971 | 10,000 | — | — | — | BV+10% | — |
| 1971 Proof | 7,650 | — | — | — | BV+15% | — |
| 1972 | 18,000 | — | — | — | BV+10% | — |
| 1972 Proof | 7,500 | — | — | — | BV+15% | — |
| 1973 | 14,000 | — | — | — | BV+10% | — |
| 1973 Proof | 13,000 | — | — | — | BV+15% | — |
| 1974 | 13,000 | — | — | — | BV+10% | — |
| 1974 Proof | 17,000 | — | — | — | BV+15% | — |
| 1975 | 12,000 | — | — | — | BV+10% | — |
| 1975 Proof | 18,000 | — | — | — | BV+15% | — |
| 1976 | 12,000 | — | — | — | BV+10% | — |
| 1976 Proof | 21,000 | — | — | — | BV+15% | — |
| 1977 | 12,000 | — | — | — | BV+10% | — |
| 1977 Proof | 20,000 | — | — | — | BV+15% | — |
| 1978 | 11,000 | — | — | — | BV+10% | — |
| 1978 Proof | 19,000 | — | — | — | BV+15% | — |
| 1979 | 12,000 | — | — | — | BV+10% | — |
| 1979 Proof | 20,000 | — | — | — | BV+15% | — |
| 1980 | 12,000 | — | — | — | BV+10% | — |
| 1980 Proof | 18,000 | — | — | — | BV+15% | — |
| 1981 | 8,538 | — | — | — | BV+10% | — |
| 1981 Proof | 10,000 | — | — | — | BV+15% | — |

| Date | Mintage | F | VF | XF | Unc | BU |
|---|---|---|---|---|---|---|
| 1982 | 2,030 | — | — | — | BV+10% | — |
| 1982 Proof | 12,000 | — | — | — | BV+15% | — |
| 1983 | 15,000 | — | — | — | BV+15% | — |

**2 RAND** **KM# 139** **Composition:** Nickel Plated Copper

| Date | Mintage | F | VF | XF | Unc | BU |
|---|---|---|---|---|---|---|
| 1989 | 65,233,000 | — | — | — | 2.00 | — |
| 1989 Proof | 13,000 | Value: 10.00 | | | | |
| 1990 | 70,655,000 | — | — | — | 2.00 | — |
| 1990 Proof | 10,000 | Value: 7.50 | | | | |
| 1991 | 39,243,000 | — | — | — | 2.00 | — |
| 1991 Proof | 12,000 | Value: 7.50 | | | | |
| 1992 | 2,115,000 | — | — | — | 2.00 | — |
| 1992 Proof | 10,000 | Value: 7.50 | | | | |
| 1993 | 92,000 | — | — | — | 2.00 | — |
| 1993 Proof | 7,790 | Value: 7.50 | | | | |
| 1994 | 994,000 | — | — | — | 2.00 | — |
| 1994 Proof | 5,804 | Value: 7.50 | | | | |
| 1995 | 13,213,000 | — | — | — | 2.00 | — |
| 1995 Proof | 5,816 | Value: 7.50 | | | | |

**2 RAND** **KM# 145** **Weight:** 33.4700 g. **Composition:** 0.9250 Silver .9954 oz. ASW **Subject:** Coin Minting

| Date | Mintage | F | VF | XF | Unc | BU |
|---|---|---|---|---|---|---|
| 1992 | 50 | — | — | — | — | — |
| 1992 Proof | 6,688 | Value: 35.00 | | | | |

**2 RAND** **KM# 147** **Weight:** 33.4700 g. **Composition:** 0.9250 Silver .9954 oz. ASW **Series:** Barcelona Olympics **Reverse:** 3 event athletes

| Date | Mintage | F | VF | XF | Unc | BU |
|---|---|---|---|---|---|---|
| 1992 | 1,670 | — | — | — | — | — |
| 1992 Proof | 15,000 | Value: 27.50 | | | | |

**2 RAND** **KM# 151** **Weight:** 33.4700 g. **Composition:** 0.9250 Silver .9954 oz. ASW **Subject:** Peace

| Date | Mintage | F | VF | XF | Unc | BU |
|---|---|---|---|---|---|---|
| 1993 | 828 | — | — | — | — | — |
| 1993 Proof | 4,800 | Value: 40.00 | | | | |

**2 RAND** **KM# 156** **Weight:** 33.6750 g. **Composition:** 0.9250 Silver 1.0014 oz. ASW **Subject:** World Cup Soccer **Reverse:** Ball and North American Map

| Date | Mintage | F | VF | XF | Unc | BU |
|---|---|---|---|---|---|---|
| 1994 | 288 | — | — | — | — | — |
| 1994 Proof | 3,210 | Value: 40.00 | | | | |

**2 RAND** **KM# 153** **Weight:** 33.6260 g. **Composition:** 0.9250 Silver 1.0000 oz. ASW **Subject:** Rugby World Cup

| Date | Mintage | F | VF | XF | Unc | BU |
|---|---|---|---|---|---|---|
| 1995 Proof | 3,981 | Value: 40.00 | | | | |

**2 RAND** **KM# 154** **Weight:** 33.6260 g. **Composition:** 0.9250 Silver 1.0000 oz. ASW **Series:** 50th Anniversary - F.A.O.

| Date | Mintage | F | VF | XF | Unc | BU |
|---|---|---|---|---|---|---|
| 1995 Proof | 1,743 | Value: 42.00 | | | | |

**2 RAND** **KM# 155** **Weight:** 33.6260 g. **Composition:** 0.9250 Silver 1.0000 oz. ASW **Series:** 50th Anniversary - United Nations

| Date | Mintage | F | VF | XF | Unc | BU |
|---|---|---|---|---|---|---|
| 1995 Proof | 1,412 | Value: 40.00 | | | | |

**2 RAND** **KM# 157** **Weight:** 33.6260 g. **Composition:** 0.9250 Silver 1.0000 oz. ASW **Reverse:** Soccer Player

| Date | Mintage | F | VF | XF | Unc | BU |
|---|---|---|---|---|---|---|
| 1996 Proof | 2,690 | Value: 40.00 | | | | |

**2 RAND** **KM# 165** **Composition:** Nickel Plated Copper **Obverse:** Xhosa legend

| Date | Mintage | F | VF | XF | Unc | BU |
|---|---|---|---|---|---|---|
| 1996 | 123,000 | — | — | — | 2.00 | — |
| 1996 Proof | 4,827 | Value: 8.00 | | | | |
| 1997 | 1,804,000 | — | — | — | 2.00 | — |
| 1997 Proof | 3,596 | Value: 8.00 | | | | |
| 1998 | — | — | — | — | 2.00 | — |
| 1998 Proof | — | Value: 8.00 | | | | |
| 1999 | — | — | — | — | 2.00 | — |
| 1999 Proof | — | Value: 8.00 | | | | |
| 2000 | — | — | — | — | 2.00 | — |

**2 RAND** **KM# 175** **Weight:** 33.6260 g. **Composition:** 0.9250 Silver 1.0000 oz. ASW **Reverse:** Sea horse

| Date | Mintage | F | VF | XF | Unc | BU |
|---|---|---|---|---|---|---|
| 1997 Proof | 3,000 | Value: 45.00 | | | | |

**2 RAND** **KM# 183** **Weight:** 7.7700 g. **Composition:** 0.9999 Gold .2500 oz. AGW **Subject:** Early Man **Reverse:** Australopithecus Africanus

| Date | Mintage | F | VF | XF | Unc | BU |
|---|---|---|---|---|---|---|
| 1997 Proof | 1,000 | Value: 175 | | | | |

**2 RAND** **KM# 179** **Weight:** 33.6200 g. **Composition:** 0.9250 Silver 1.0000 oz. ASW **Reverse:** Jackass penguin

| Date | Mintage | F | VF | XF | Unc | BU |
|---|---|---|---|---|---|---|
| 1998 Proof | Est. 3,000 | Value: 50.00 | | | | |

**2 RAND** **KM# 180** **Weight:** 7.7770 g. **Composition:** 0.9999 Gold .2500 oz. AGW **Reverse:** Coelacanth Fish and Fossil

| Date | Mintage | F | VF | XF | Unc | BU |
|---|---|---|---|---|---|---|
| 1998 Proof | — | Value: 175 | | | | |

**2 RAND** **KM# 220** **Weight:** 7.7759 g. **Composition:** 0.9999 Gold .2500 oz. AGW **Obverse:** National arms **Reverse:** Thrinaxodon dinosaur

| Date | Mintage | F | VF | XF | Unc | BU |
|---|---|---|---|---|---|---|
| 1999 Proof | 1,000 | Value: 200 | | | | |

**2 RAND** **KM# 218** **Weight:** 33.6000 g. **Composition:** 0.9250 Silver .9992 oz. ASW **Obverse:** National arms **Reverse:** Great white shark **Edge:** Reeded **Size:** 38.7 mm. **Note:** Struck at Pretoria.

| Date | Mintage | F | VF | XF | Unc | BU |
|---|---|---|---|---|---|---|
| 1999 Proof | 3,000 | Value: 37.50 | | | | |

**2 RAND** **KM# 228** **Weight:** 5.4300 g. **Composition:** Nickel Plated Steel **Obverse:** National arms **Reverse:** Koodoo and denomination **Edge:** Reeded and plain sections **Size:** 23 mm.

| Date | Mintage | F | VF | XF | Unc | BU |
|---|---|---|---|---|---|---|
| 2001 | — | — | — | — | 2.00 | — |

**5 RAND** **KM# 140** **Composition:** Nickel Plated Copper **Reverse:** Wildebeest

| Date | Mintage | F | VF | XF | Unc | BU |
|---|---|---|---|---|---|---|
| 1994 | 45,212,000 | — | — | — | 4.50 | — |
| 1994 Proof | 5,804 | Value: 10.00 | | | | |
| 1995 | 41,238,000 | — | — | — | 4.50 | — |
| 1995 Proof | 5,816 | Value: 10.00 | | | | |

**5 RAND** **KM# 150** **Composition:** Nickel Plated Copper **Subject:** Presidential Inauguration

| Date | Mintage | F | VF | XF | Unc | BU |
|---|---|---|---|---|---|---|
| 1994 | 10,095,000 | — | — | — | 5.50 | — |
| 1994 Proof | 10,000 | Value: 8.50 | | | | |

**5 RAND** **KM# 166** **Composition:** Nickel Plated Copper **Obverse:** Zulu/Swati legend above arms

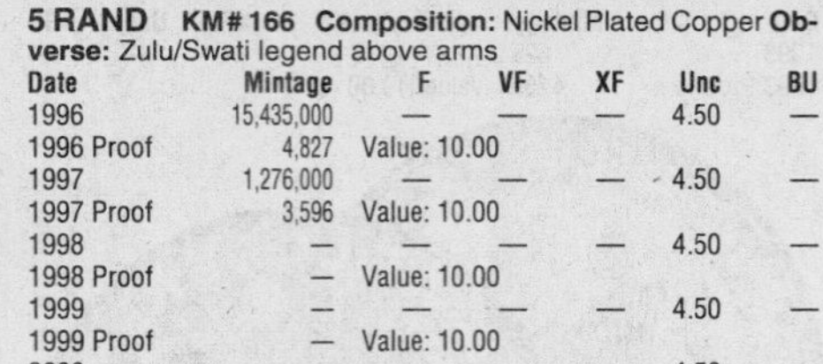

| Date | Mintage | F | VF | XF | Unc | BU |
|---|---|---|---|---|---|---|
| 1996 | 15,435,000 | — | — | — | 4.50 | — |
| 1996 Proof | 4,827 | Value: 10.00 | | | | |
| 1997 | 1,276,000 | — | — | — | 4.50 | — |
| 1997 Proof | 3,596 | Value: 10.00 | | | | |
| 1998 | — | — | — | — | 4.50 | — |
| 1998 Proof | — | Value: 10.00 | | | | |
| 1999 | — | — | — | — | 4.50 | — |
| 1999 Proof | — | Value: 10.00 | | | | |
| 2000 | — | — | — | — | 4.50 | — |

**5 RAND** **KM# 230** **Weight:** 6.9400 g. **Composition:** Nickel Plated Steel **Subject:** Nelson Mandela **Obverse:** Portrait **Reverse:** Wildebeest and denomination **Edge:** Reeded and plain sections **Size:** 25.9 mm.

| Date | Mintage | F | VF | XF | Unc | BU |
|---|---|---|---|---|---|---|
| 2000 | — | — | — | — | 4.50 | — |

**5 RAND** **KM# 229** **Weight:** 6.9400 g. **Composition:** Nickel Plated Steel **Obverse:** National arms **Reverse:** Wildebeest and denomination **Edge:** Reeded and plain sections **Size:** 26 mm.

| Date | Mintage | F | VF | XF | Unc | BU |
|---|---|---|---|---|---|---|
| 2001 | — | — | — | — | 4.50 | — |

## BULLION COINAGE

Mint mark: GRC - Gold Reef City

**1/10 KRUGERRAND** **KM# 105** **Weight:** 3.3900 g. **Composition:** 0.9170 Gold .1000 oz. AGW

| Date | Mintage | F | VF | XF | Unc | BU |
|---|---|---|---|---|---|---|
| 1980 | 857,000 | — | — | — | BV+15% | — |
| 1980 Proof | 60 | Value: 2,500 | | | | |
| 1981 | 1,321,000 | — | — | — | BV+15% | — |
| 1981 Proof | 7,500 | Value: 90.00 | | | | |
| 1982 | 1,065,000 | — | — | — | BV+15% | — |
| 1982 Proof | 11,000 | Value: 85.00 | | | | |
| 1983 | 508,000 | — | — | — | BV+15% | — |
| 1983 Proof | 12,000 | Value: 85.00 | | | | |
| 1984 | 898,000 | — | — | — | BV+15% | — |
| 1984 Proof | 13,000 | Value: 85.00 | | | | |
| 1985 | 282,000 | — | — | — | BV+15% | — |
| 1985 Proof | 6,700 | Value: 85.00 | | | | |
| 1986 | 87,000 | — | — | — | BV+15% | — |
| 1986 Proof | 8,001 | Value: 85.00 | | | | |
| 1987 | 53,000 | — | — | — | BV+15% | — |
| 1987 Proof | 6,065 | Value: 85.00 | | | | |
| 1987 GRC Proof | 1,126 | Value: 400 | | | | |
| 1988 | 87,000 | — | — | — | BV+15% | — |
| 1988 Proof | 2,056 | Value: 90.00 | | | | |
| 1988 GRC Proof | 949 | Value: 400 | | | | |
| 1989 | — | — | — | — | BV+15% | — |
| 1989 Proof | 3,316 | Value: 90.00 | | | | |
| 1989 GRC Proof | 377 | Value: 1,000 | | | | |
| 1990 | — | — | — | — | BV+15% | — |
| 1990 Proof | 3,459 | Value: 90.00 | | | | |
| 1990 GRC Proof | 1,096 | Value: 275 | | | | |
| 1991 Proof | 3,524 | Value: 90.00 | | | | |
| 1991 GRC Proof | 426 | Value: 275 | | | | |
| 1992 Proof | 1,789 | Value: 90.00 | | | | |
| 1993 | 54,000 | — | — | — | BV+15% | — |
| 1993 Proof | 3,811 | Value: 90.00 | | | | |
| 1994 | 86,000 | — | — | — | BV+15% | — |
| 1994 Proof | — | Value: 90.00 | | | | |
| 1995 | 25,000 | — | — | — | BV+15% | — |
| 1995 Proof | 750 | Value: 120 | | | | |
| 1996 Proof | 4,000 | Value: 90.00 | | | | |
| 1997 Proof | 3,410 | Value: 90.00 | | | | |
| 1997 Proof | 30 | Value: 300 | | | | |
| **Note:** 30th Anniversary of Krugerrand privy mark | | | | | | |
| 1998 Proof | — | Value: 90.00 | | | | |
| 1999 Proof | — | Value: 90.00 | | | | |

**1/4 KRUGERRAND** **KM# 106** **Weight:** 8.4800 g. **Composition:** 0.9170 Gold .2500 oz. AGW

| Date | Mintage | F | VF | XF | Unc | BU |
|---|---|---|---|---|---|---|
| 1980 | 534,000 | — | — | — | BV+10% | — |
| 1980 Proof | 60 | Value: 3,000 | | | | |
| 1981 | 726,000 | — | — | — | BV+10% | — |
| 1981 Proof | 7,500 | Value: 165 | | | | |
| 1982 | 1,269,000 | — | — | — | BV+10% | — |
| 1982 Proof | 11,000 | Value: 165 | | | | |
| 1983 | 64,000 | — | — | — | BV+10% | — |
| 1983 Proof | 12,000 | Value: 165 | | | | |
| 1984 | 503,000 | — | — | — | BV+10% | — |
| 1984 Proof | 13,000 | Value: 165 | | | | |
| 1985 | 594,000 | — | — | — | BV+10% | — |
| 1985 Proof | 6,700 | Value: 165 | | | | |
| 1986 Proof | 8,001 | Value: 165 | | | | |
| 1987 Proof | 6,050 | Value: 165 | | | | |
| 1987 GRC Proof | 1,121 | Value: 500 | | | | |
| 1988 | 5,946 | — | — | — | BV+10% | — |
| 1988 Proof | 2,056 | Value: 175 | | | | |
| 1988 GRC Proof | 835 | Value: 500 | | | | |
| 1989 | 5,943 | — | — | — | BV+10% | — |
| 1989 Proof | 3,316 | Value: 175 | | | | |
| 1989 GRC Proof | 318 | Value: 1,400 | | | | |
| 1990 Proof | 2,750 | Value: 175 | | | | |
| 1990 GRC Proof | 1,066 | Value: 400 | | | | |
| 1991 Proof | 1,626 | Value: 175 | | | | |
| 1991 GRC Proof | 426 | Value: 400 | | | | |
| 1992 Proof | 1,629 | Value: 175 | | | | |
| 1993 Proof | 3,061 | Value: 175 | | | | |
| 1994 | 39,000 | — | — | — | BV+10% | — |
| 1994 Proof | 1,874 | Value: 175 | | | | |
| 1995 | 13,000 | — | — | — | BV+10% | — |
| 1995 Proof | 1,095 | Value: 200 | | | | |
| 1996 Proof | 1,853 | Value: 175 | | | | |
| 1997 Proof | 1,440 | Value: 175 | | | | |
| 1997 Proof | 30 | Value: 450 | | | | |
| **Note:** 30th Anniversary of Krugerrand privy mark | | | | | | |
| 1998 Proof | — | Value: 175 | | | | |
| 1999 Proof | — | Value: 175 | | | | |

**1/2 KRUGERRAND** **KM# 107** **Weight:** 16.9700 g. **Composition:** 0.9170 Gold .5000 oz. AGW

| Date | Mintage | F | VF | XF | Unc | BU |
|---|---|---|---|---|---|---|
| 1980 | 374,000 | — | — | — | BV+8% | — |
| 1980 Proof | 60 | Value: 3,500 | | | | |
| 1981 | 178,000 | — | — | — | BV+8% | — |
| 1981 Proof | 9,000 | Value: 285 | | | | |
| 1982 | 429,000 | — | — | — | BV+8% | — |
| 1982 Proof | 13,000 | Value: 285 | | | | |
| 1983 | 60,000 | — | — | — | BV+8% | — |
| 1983 Proof | 14,000 | Value: 285 | | | | |
| 1984 | 187,000 | — | — | — | BV+8% | — |
| 1984 Proof | 9,900 | Value: 285 | | | | |
| 1985 | 104,000 | — | — | — | BV+8% | — |
| 1985 Proof | 5,945 | Value: 285 | | | | |
| 1986 Proof | 8,002 | Value: 285 | | | | |
| 1987 Proof | 5,389 | Value: 285 | | | | |
| 1987 GRC Proof | 1,186 | Value: 800 | | | | |
| 1988 | 5,454 | — | — | — | BV+8% | — |
| 1988 Proof | 2,282 | Value: 300 | | | | |
| 1988 GRC Proof | 1,026 | Value: 800 | | | | |
| 1989 | 4,980 | — | — | — | BV+8% | — |
| 1989 Proof | 3,727 | Value: 300 | | | | |
| 1989 GRC Proof | 399 | Value: 1,500 | | | | |
| 1990 Proof | 2,850 | Value: 300 | | | | |
| 1990 GRC Proof | 1,066 | Value: 500 | | | | |
| 1991 Proof | 3,459 | Value: 300 | | | | |
| 1991 GRC Proof | 426 | Value: 500 | | | | |
| 1992 Proof | 1,501 | Value: 300 | | | | |
| 1993 | 11,000 | — | — | — | BV+8% | — |
| 1993 Proof | 2,439 | Value: 300 | | | | |
| 1994 | 16,000 | — | — | — | BV+8% | — |
| 1994 Proof | 2,146 | Value: 300 | | | | |
| 1995 | 10,000 | — | — | — | BV+8% | — |
| 1995 Proof | 1,012 | Value: 300 | | | | |
| 1996 Proof | 1,788 | Value: 300 | | | | |
| 1997 Proof | 2,000 | Value: 300 | | | | |
| 1997 Proof | 30 | Value: 550 | | | | |
| **Note:** 30th Anniversary of Krugerrand privy mark | | | | | | |

| Date | Mintage | F | VF | XF | Unc | BU |
|---|---|---|---|---|---|---|
| 1998 Proof | — | Value: 275 | | | | |
| 1999 Proof | — | Value: 300 | | | | |

**KRUGERRAND** **KM# 73** **Weight:** 33.9305 g. **Composition:** 0.9170 Gold 1.0000 oz. AGW

| Date | Mintage | F | VF | XF | Unc | BU |
|---|---|---|---|---|---|---|
| 1967 | 40,000 | — | — | — | BV+5% | — |
| 1967 Proof | 10,000 | Value: 525 | | | | |
| 1968 | 20,000 | — | — | — | BV+5% | — |
| 1968 Proof | 5,000 | Value: 1,000 | | | | |
| **Note:** Frosted bust and frosted reverse | | | | | | |
| 1968 Proof | 8,956 | Value: 550 | | | | |
| 1969 | 20,000 | — | — | — | BV+5% | — |
| 1969 Proof | 10,000 | Value: 525 | | | | |
| 1970 | 211,000 | — | — | — | BV+5% | — |
| 1970 Proof | 10,000 | Value: 485 | | | | |
| 1971 | 550,000 | — | — | — | BV+5% | — |
| 1971 Proof | 6,000 | Value: 485 | | | | |
| 1972 | 544,000 | — | — | — | BV+5% | — |
| 1972 Proof | 6,625 | Value: 485 | | | | |
| 1973 | 859,000 | — | — | — | BV+5% | — |
| 1973 Proof | 10,000 | Value: 485 | | | | |
| 1974 | 3,204,000 | — | — | — | BV+5% | — |
| 1974 Proof | 6,352 | Value: 485 | | | | |
| 1975 | 4,804,000 | — | — | — | BV+5% | — |
| 1975 Proof | 5,600 | Value: 485 | | | | |
| 1976 | 3,005,000 | — | — | — | BV+5% | — |
| 1976 Proof | 6,600 | Value: 485 | | | | |
| 1977 | 3,331,000 | — | — | — | BV+5% | — |
| **Note:** 188 serrations on edge | | | | | | |
| 1977 Proof | 8,500 | Value: 485 | | | | |
| **Note:** 188 serrations on edge | | | | | | |
| 1977 | Inc. above | — | — | — | BV+5% | — |
| **Note:** 220 serrations on edge | | | | | | |
| 1977 Proof | Inc. above | Value: 485 | | | | |
| **Note:** 220 serrations on edge | | | | | | |
| 1978 | 6,012,000 | — | — | — | BV+5% | — |
| 1978 Proof | 10,000 | Value: 485 | | | | |
| 1979 | 4,941,000 | — | — | — | BV+5% | — |
| 1979 Proof | 12,000 | Value: 485 | | | | |
| 1980 | 3,143,000 | — | — | — | BV+5% | — |
| 1980 Proof | 12,000 | Value: 485 | | | | |
| 1981 | 3,560,000 | — | — | — | BV+5% | — |
| 1981 Proof | 13,000 | Value: 485 | | | | |
| 1982 | 2,566,000 | — | — | — | BV+5% | — |
| 1982 Proof | 17,000 | Value: 485 | | | | |
| 1983 | 3,368,000 | — | — | — | BV+5% | — |
| 1983 Proof | 19,000 | Value: 485 | | | | |
| 1984 | 2,070,000 | — | — | — | BV+5% | — |
| 1984 Proof | 14,000 | Value: 485 | | | | |
| 1985 | 875,000 | — | — | — | BV+5% | — |
| 1985 Proof | 10,000 | Value: 485 | | | | |
| 1986 Proof | 20,000 | Value: 485 | | | | |
| 1987 | 11,000 | — | — | — | BV+5% | — |
| 1987 Proof | 11,000 | Value: 485 | | | | |
| 1987 GRC Proof | 1,160 | Value: 1,200 | | | | |
| 1988 | 615,000 | — | — | — | BV+5% | — |
| 1988 Proof | 4,268 | Value: 500 | | | | |
| 1988 GRC Proof | 1,220 | Value: 1,200 | | | | |
| 1989 | 194,000 | — | — | — | BV+5% | — |
| 1989 Proof | 5,070 | Value: 500 | | | | |
| 1989 GRC Proof | 987 | Value: 1,600 | | | | |
| 1990 | 391,000 | — | — | — | BV+5% | — |
| 1990 Proof | 3,032 | Value: 500 | | | | |
| 1990 GRC Proof | 1,066 | Value: 1,600 | | | | |
| 1991 | 283,000 | — | — | — | BV+5% | — |
| 1991 Proof | 2,181 | Value: 500 | | | | |
| 1991 GRC Proof | 426 | Value: 1,600 | | | | |
| 1992 | 1,803 | — | — | — | BV+5% | — |
| 1992 Proof | 2,067 | Value: 500 | | | | |
| 1993 | 162,000 | — | — | — | BV+5% | — |
| 1993 Proof | 3,963 | Value: 500 | | | | |
| 1994 | 130,000 | — | — | — | BV+5% | — |
| 1994 Proof | 1,761 | Value: 500 | | | | |
| 1995 | 59,000 | — | — | — | BV+5% | — |
| 1995 Proof | 1,678 | Value: 500 | | | | |
| 1996 Proof | 2,188 | Value: 500 | | | | |
| 1997 Proof | 1,663 | Value: 500 | | | | |
| 1997 SS Proof | 72 | Value: 850 | | | | |
| 1997 Proof | 30 | Value: 1,250 | | | | |
| **Note:** 30th Anniversary of Krugerrand privy mark | | | | | | |
| 1998 Proof | — | Value: 500 | | | | |
| 1999 Proof | — | Value: 500 | | | | |

**OUNCE** **KM# 118** **Weight:** 33.9305 g. **Composition:** 0.9170 Gold 1.0000 oz. AGW **Subject:** 75th Anniversary of Parliament

| Date | Mintage | F | VF | XF | Unc | BU |
|---|---|---|---|---|---|---|
| 1985 Proof | 3,019 | Value: 1,200 | | | | |

**OUNCE** **KM# 184** **Weight:** 31.1070 g. **Composition:** 0.9999 Gold 1.0000 oz. AGW **Subject:** Presidential Inauguration

| Date | Mintage | F | VF | XF | Unc | BU |
|---|---|---|---|---|---|---|
| 1994 Proof | 1,742 | Value: 600 | | | | |

**OUNCE** **KM# 185** **Weight:** 31.1070 g. **Composition:** 0.9999 Gold 1.0000 oz. AGW **Subject:** Rugby

| Date | Mintage | F | VF | XF | Unc | BU |
|---|---|---|---|---|---|---|
| 1995 Proof | 406 | Value: 625 | | | | |

**1/10 PROTEA** **KM# 131** **Weight:** 3.3900 g. **Composition:** 0.9170 Gold .1000 oz. AGW **Subject:** 100th Anniversary of Johannesburg

| Date | Mintage | F | VF | XF | Unc | BU |
|---|---|---|---|---|---|---|
| 1986 Proof | 5,212 | Value: 100 | | | | |

**1/10 PROTEA** **KM# 123** **Weight:** 3.3900 g. **Composition:** 0.9170 Gold .1000 oz. AGW **Subject:** Bartolomew Dias

| Date | Mintage | F | VF | XF | Unc | BU |
|---|---|---|---|---|---|---|
| 1988 Proof | 2,199 | Value: 100 | | | | |

**1/10 PROTEA** **KM# 126** **Weight:** 3.3900 g. **Composition:** 0.9170 Gold .1000 oz. AGW **Subject:** Huguenots

| Date | Mintage | F | VF | XF | Unc | BU |
|---|---|---|---|---|---|---|
| 1988 Proof | 2,060 | Value: 100 | | | | |

**1/10 PROTEA** **KM# 129** **Weight:** 3.3900 g. **Composition:** 0.9170 Gold .1000 oz. AGW **Subject:** The Great Trek

| Date | Mintage | F | VF | XF | Unc | BU |
|---|---|---|---|---|---|---|
| 1988 Proof | 2,999 | Value: 100 | | | | |

**1/10 PROTEA** **KM# 171** **Weight:** 3.3900 g. **Composition:** 0.9170 Gold .1000 oz. AGW **Subject:** South African Nursing Schools **Note:** Similar to 1 Rand, KM#142.

| Date | Mintage | F | VF | XF | Unc | BU |
|---|---|---|---|---|---|---|
| 1991 Proof | 3,950 | Value: 100 | | | | |

**1/10 PROTEA** **KM# 172** **Weight:** 3.3900 g. **Composition:** 0.9170 Gold .1000 oz. AGW **Subject:** 200 Years of Banking **Note:** Similar to 1 Rand, KM#168.

| Date | Mintage | F | VF | XF | Unc | BU |
|---|---|---|---|---|---|---|
| 1991 Proof | 5,064 | Value: 100 | | | | |

**1/10 PROTEA** **KM# 144** **Weight:** 3.3900 g. **Composition:** 0.9170 Gold .1000 oz. AGW **Subject:** Coinage Centennial

| Date | Mintage | F | VF | XF | Unc | BU |
|---|---|---|---|---|---|---|
| 1992 Proof | 2,503 | Value: 100 | | | | |

**1/10 PROTEA** **KM# 187** **Weight:** 3.3900 g. **Composition:** 0.9170 Gold .1000 oz. AGW **Subject:** Conservation

| Date | Mintage | F | VF | XF | Unc | BU |
|---|---|---|---|---|---|---|
| 1994 Proof | 1,485 | Value: 110 | | | | |

**1/10 PROTEA** **KM# 193** **Weight:** 3.3900 g. **Composition:** 0.9170 Gold .1000 oz. AGW **Subject:** Railways

| Date | Mintage | F | VF | XF | Unc | BU |
|---|---|---|---|---|---|---|
| 1995 Proof | 1,217 | Value: 110 | | | | |

**1/10 PROTEA** **KM# 199** **Weight:** 3.3900 g. **Composition:** 0.9170 Gold .1000 oz. AGW **Subject:** Constitution

| Date | Mintage | F | VF | XF | Unc | BU |
|---|---|---|---|---|---|---|
| 1996 Proof | 946 | Value: 110 | | | | |

**1/10 PROTEA** **KM# 205** **Weight:** 3.3900 g. **Composition:** 0.9170 Gold .1000 oz. AGW **Subject:** Women of South Africa

| Date | Mintage | F | VF | XF | Unc | BU |
|---|---|---|---|---|---|---|
| 1997 Proof | 648 | Value: 115 | | | | |

**1/10 PROTEA** **KM# 211** **Weight:** 3.3900 g. **Composition:** 0.9170 Gold .1000 oz. AGW **Subject:** Year of the Child

| Date | Mintage | F | VF | XF | Unc | BU |
|---|---|---|---|---|---|---|
| 1998 Proof | — | Value: 115 | | | | |

**PROTEA** **KM# 121** **Weight:** 33.9300 g. **Composition:** 0.9170 Gold 1.0000 oz. AGW **Subject:** 100th Anniversary of Johannesburg

| Date | Mintage | F | VF | XF | Unc | BU |
|---|---|---|---|---|---|---|
| 1986 Proof | 4,701 | Value: 600 | | | | |

**PROTEA** **KM# 124** **Weight:** 33.9300 g. **Composition:** 0.9170 Gold 1.0000 oz. AGW **Subject:** Bartolomeu Dias

| Date | Mintage | F | VF | XF | Unc | BU |
|---|---|---|---|---|---|---|
| 1988 Proof | 3,776 | Value: 600 | | | | |

**PROTEA** **KM# 127** **Weight:** 33.9300 g. **Composition:** 0.9170 Gold 1.0000 oz. AGW **Subject:** Huguenots

| Date | Mintage | F | VF | XF | Unc | BU |
|---|---|---|---|---|---|---|
| 1988 Proof | 3,391 | Value: 600 | | | | |

**PROTEA** **KM# 130** **Weight:** 33.9300 g. **Composition:** 0.9170 Gold 1.0000 oz. AGW **Subject:** The Great Trek

| Date | Mintage | F | VF | XF | Unc | BU |
|---|---|---|---|---|---|---|
| 1988 Proof | 2,956 | Value: 600 | | | | |

**PROTEA** **KM# 186** **Weight:** 33.9300 g. **Composition:** 0.9170 Gold 1.0000 oz. AGW **Subject:** Nursing

| Date | Mintage | F | VF | XF | Unc | BU |
|---|---|---|---|---|---|---|
| 1991 Proof | 3,004 | Value: 600 | | | | |

**PROTEA** **KM# 146** **Weight:** 33.9300 g. **Composition:** 0.9170 Gold 1.0000 oz. AGW **Subject:** Coinage Centennial

| Date | Mintage | F | VF | XF | Unc | BU |
|---|---|---|---|---|---|---|
| 1992 Proof | 1,752 | Value: 600 | | | | |

**PROTEA** **KM# 173** **Weight:** 33.9300 g. **Composition:** 0.9170 Gold 1.0000 oz. AGW **Subject:** 200 Years of Banking **Note:** Similar to 1 Rand, KM#168.

| Date | Mintage | F | VF | XF | Unc | BU |
|---|---|---|---|---|---|---|
| 1993 Proof | 2,032 | Value: 600 | | | | |
| 1993 GRC Proof | 500 | Value: 620 | | | | |

**PROTEA KM# 188 Weight:** 33.9300 g. **Composition:** 0.9170 Gold 1.0000 oz. AGW **Subject:** Conservation

| Date | Mintage | F | VF | XF | Unc | BU |
|---|---|---|---|---|---|---|
| 1994 Proof | 1,187 | Value: 600 | | | | |
| 1994 Proof | 600 | Value: 620 | | | | |

**Note:** PTA.ZOO

**PROTEA KM# 194 Weight:** 33.9300 g. **Composition:** 0.9170 Gold 1.0000 oz. AGW **Subject:** Railway

| Date | Mintage | F | VF | XF | Unc | BU |
|---|---|---|---|---|---|---|
| 1995 Proof | 694 | Value: 620 | | | | |

**PROTEA KM# 200 Weight:** 33.9300 g. **Composition:** 0.9170 Gold 1.0000 oz. AGW **Subject:** Constitution

| Date | Mintage | F | VF | XF | Unc | BU |
|---|---|---|---|---|---|---|
| 1996 Proof | 641 | Value: 620 | | | | |

**PROTEA KM# 206 Weight:** 33.9300 g. **Composition:** 0.9170 Gold 1.0000 oz. AGW **Subject:** Women of South Africa

| Date | Mintage | F | VF | XF | Unc | BU |
|---|---|---|---|---|---|---|
| 1997 Proof | 207 | Value: 635 | | | | |

**PROTEA KM# 212 Weight:** 33.9300 g. **Composition:** 0.9170 Gold 1.0000 oz. AGW **Subject:** Year of the Child

| Date | Mintage | F | VF | XF | Unc | BU |
|---|---|---|---|---|---|---|
| 1998 Proof | — | Value: 635 | | | | |

## NATURA GOLD BULLION COINAGE

**1/10 OUNCE KM# 189 Weight:** 31.1104 g. **Composition:** 0.9990 Gold .1000 oz. AGW **Reverse:** Lions drinking

| Date | Mintage | F | VF | XF | Unc | BU |
|---|---|---|---|---|---|---|
| 1994 Proof | 6,660 | Value: 100 | | | | |

**1/10 OUNCE KM# 195 Weight:** 31.1104 g. **Composition:** 0.9990 Gold .1000 oz. AGW **Reverse:** Rhinocerous drinking

| Date | Mintage | F | VF | XF | Unc | BU |
|---|---|---|---|---|---|---|
| 1995 Proof | 2,703 | Value: 100 | | | | |

**1/10 OUNCE KM# 201 Weight:** 31.1104 g. **Composition:** 0.9990 Gold .1000 oz. AGW **Reverse:** Elephant

| Date | Mintage | F | VF | XF | Unc | BU |
|---|---|---|---|---|---|---|
| 1996 Proof | 9,014 | Value: 100 | | | | |

**1/10 OUNCE KM# 207 Weight:** 31.1104 g. **Composition:** 0.9990 Gold .1000 oz. AGW **Reverse:** Buffalo

| Date | Mintage | F | VF | XF | Unc | BU |
|---|---|---|---|---|---|---|
| 1997 Proof | 3,590 | Value: 100 | | | | |

**1/10 OUNCE KM# 213 Weight:** 31.1104 g. **Composition:** 0.9990 Gold .1000 oz. AGW **Reverse:** Leopard

| Date | Mintage | F | VF | XF | Unc | BU |
|---|---|---|---|---|---|---|
| 1998 Proof | — | Value: 100 | | | | |

**1/4 OUNCE KM# 190 Weight:** 7.7770 g. **Composition:** 0.9999 Gold .2500 oz. AGW **Reverse:** Lions

| Date | Mintage | F | VF | XF | Unc | BU |
|---|---|---|---|---|---|---|
| 1994 Proof | 4,159 | Value: 185 | | | | |

**1/4 OUNCE KM# 196 Weight:** 7.7770 g. **Composition:** 0.9999 Gold .2500 oz. AGW **Reverse:** Rhinocerous

| Date | Mintage | F | VF | XF | Unc | BU |
|---|---|---|---|---|---|---|
| 1995 Proof | 1,752 | Value: 185 | | | | |

**1/4 OUNCE KM# 202 Weight:** 7.7770 g. **Composition:** 0.9999 Gold .2500 oz. AGW **Reverse:** Elephant

| Date | Mintage | F | VF | XF | Unc | BU |
|---|---|---|---|---|---|---|
| 1996 Proof | 3,740 | Value: 185 | | | | |

**1/4 OUNCE KM# 208 Weight:** 7.7770 g. **Composition:** 0.9999 Gold .2500 oz. AGW **Reverse:** Buffalo

| Date | Mintage | F | VF | XF | Unc | BU |
|---|---|---|---|---|---|---|
| 1997 Proof | 2,164 | Value: 185 | | | | |

**1/4 OUNCE KM# 214 Weight:** 7.7770 g. **Composition:** 0.9999 Gold .2500 oz. AGW **Reverse:** Leopard

| Date | Mintage | F | VF | XF | Unc | BU |
|---|---|---|---|---|---|---|
| 1998 Proof | — | Value: 185 | | | | |

**1/2 OUNCE KM# 191 Weight:** 15.5530 g. **Composition:** 0.9999 Gold .5000 oz. AGW **Reverse:** Lions

| Date | Mintage | F | VF | XF | Unc | BU |
|---|---|---|---|---|---|---|
| 1994 Proof | 3,999 | Value: 300 | | | | |

**1/2 OUNCE KM# 197 Weight:** 15.5530 g. **Composition:** 0.9999 Gold .5000 oz. AGW **Reverse:** Rhinocerous

| Date | Mintage | F | VF | XF | Unc | BU |
|---|---|---|---|---|---|---|
| 1995 Proof | 1,551 | Value: 300 | | | | |

**1/2 OUNCE KM# 203 Weight:** 15.5530 g. **Composition:** 0.9999 Gold .5000 oz. AGW **Reverse:** Elephant

| Date | Mintage | F | VF | XF | Unc | BU |
|---|---|---|---|---|---|---|
| 1996 Proof | 3,457 | Value: 300 | | | | |

**1/2 OUNCE KM# 209 Weight:** 15.5530 g. **Composition:** 0.9999 Gold .5000 oz. AGW **Reverse:** Buffalo

| Date | Mintage | F | VF | XF | Unc | BU |
|---|---|---|---|---|---|---|
| 1997 Proof | 1,912 | Value: 300 | | | | |

**1/2 OUNCE KM# 215 Weight:** 15.5530 g. **Composition:** 0.9999 Gold .5000 oz. AGW **Reverse:** Leopard

| Date | Mintage | F | VF | XF | Unc | BU |
|---|---|---|---|---|---|---|
| 1998 Proof | — | Value: 300 | | | | |

**OUNCE KM# 192 Weight:** 31.1070 g. **Composition:** 0.9999 Gold 1.0000 oz. AGW **Reverse:** Lions

| Date | Mintage | F | VF | XF | Unc | BU |
|---|---|---|---|---|---|---|
| 1994 Proof | 2,902 | Value: 600 | | | | |
| 1994 Proof | 775 | Value: 620 | | | | |

**Note:** Pre.Zoo

**OUNCE KM# 198 Weight:** 31.1070 g. **Composition:** 0.9999 Gold 1.0000 oz. AGW **Reverse:** Rhinocerous

| Date | Mintage | F | VF | XF | Unc | BU |
|---|---|---|---|---|---|---|
| 1995 Proof | 1,800 | Value: 600 | | | | |
| 1995 Proof | 350 | Value: 620 | | | | |

**Note:** Hluhuwe

**OUNCE KM# 204 Weight:** 31.1070 g. **Composition:** 0.9999 Gold 1.0000 oz. AGW **Reverse:** Elephant

| Date | Mintage | F | VF | XF | Unc | BU |
|---|---|---|---|---|---|---|
| 1996 Proof | 4,472 | Value: 600 | | | | |
| 1996 Proof | — | Value: 620 | | | | |

**Note:** Mandleve

**OUNCE KM# 210 Weight:** 31.1070 g. **Composition:** 0.9999 Gold 1.0000 oz. AGW **Reverse:** Buffalo

| Date | Mintage | F | VF | XF | Unc | BU |
|---|---|---|---|---|---|---|
| 1997 Proof | 2,472 | Value: 600 | | | | |
| 1997 SS Proof | 220 | Value: 620 | | | | |

**OUNCE KM# 216 Weight:** 31.1070 g. **Composition:** 0.9999 Gold 1.0000 oz. AGW **Reverse:** Leopard

| Date | Mintage | F | VF | XF | Unc | BU |
|---|---|---|---|---|---|---|
| 1998 Proof | — | Value: 600 | | | | |

## PATTERNS

Including off metal strikes

| KM# | Date | Mintage | Identification | Mkt Val |
|---|---|---|---|---|
| Pn1 | 1925 | — | 1/4 Penny. Lead. | — |
| Pn3 | 1942 | — | 1/4 Penny. Bronze. Smaller head of George VI. | — |

## TRIAL STRIKES

| KM# | Date | Mintage | Identification | Mkt Val |
|---|---|---|---|---|
| TS1 | 1925 | — | (No Denomination). Lead. Uniface. 2s6d. | — |

## MINT SETS

| KM# | Date | Mintage | Identification | Issue Price | Mkt Val |
|---|---|---|---|---|---|
| MS1 | 1967 (7) | 50,000 | KM#65.1-70.1, 72.1 | 7.50 | 10.00 |
| MS2 | 1967 (7) | 50,000 | KM#65.2-70.2, 72.2 | 7.50 | 10.00 |
| MS3 | 1968 (7) | 50,000 | KM#71.1, 74.1-79.1 | 7.50 | 12.00 |
| MS4 | 1968 (7) | 50,000 | KM#71.2, 74.2-79.2 | 7.50 | 12.00 |
| MS5 | 1969 (7) | 7,500 | KM#65.1-70.1, 80.1 | 7.50 | 50.00 |
| MS6 | 1969 (7) | 7,500 | KM#65.2-70.2, 80.2 | 7.50 | 50.00 |
| MS7 | 1970 (8) | 16,000 | KM#81-88 | 7.50 | 12.00 |
| MS8 | 1971 (8) | 20,000 | KM#81-88 | 7.50 | 8.00 |
| MS9 | 1972 (8) | 20,000 | KM#81-88 | 7.50 | 8.00 |
| MS10 | 1973 (8) | 20,000 | KM#81-88 | 7.50 | 8.00 |
| MS11 | 1974 (8) | 20,000 | KM#81-87, 89 | 7.50 | 17.50 |
| MS12 | 1975 (8) | 20,000 | KM#81-88 | 7.50 | 8.00 |
| MS13 | 1976 (8) | 20,000 | KM#88, 90-96 | 5.65 | 8.00 |
| MS14 | 1977 (8) | 20,000 | KM#81-87, 88a | — | 8.00 |
| MS15 | 1978 (8) | 20,000 | KM#81-87, 88a | — | 8.00 |
| MS16 | 1979 (8) | 20,000 | KM#97-104 | — | 25.00 |
| MS17 | 1980 (7) | 20,000 | KM#82-87, 88a | — | 8.00 |
| MS18 | 1981 (7) | 10,000 | KM#82-87, 88a | — | 10.00 |
| MS19 | 1982 (7) | 10,000 | KM#109-115 | — | 25.00 |
| MS20 | 1983 (7) | 23,000 | KM#82-87, 88a | — | 8.00 |
| MS21 | 1984 (7) | 13,875 | KM#82-87, 88a | — | 10.00 |
| MS22 | 1985 (7) | 10,200 | KM#82-87, 117 | — | 17.50 |
| MS23 | 1986 (7) | 9,100 | KM#82-87, 88a | — | 12.00 |
| MS24 | 1987 (7) | 7,642 | KM#82-87, 88a | — | 12.00 |
| MS25 | 1988 (7) | 6,250 | KM#82-87, 88a | — | 25.00 |
| MS26 | 1989 (7) | 13,000 | KM#82-87, 88a | — | 15.00 |
| MS27 | 1990 (8) | 12,000 | KM#132-137, 139, 148 | — | 30.00 |
| MS28 | 1991 (8) | 15,000 | KM#132-139 | — | 30.00 |
| MSA29 | 1992 (8) | 15,000 | KM#132-139 | — | 30.00 |
| MS29 | 1993 (8) | 11,000 | KM#132-139 | — | 30.00 |
| MS30 | 1994 (9) | 6,786 | KM#132-140 | — | 35.00 |
| MS31 | 1995 (9) | 8,477 | KM#132-140 Plastic holder | — | 35.00 |
| MS32 | 1995 (9) | — | KM#132-140 Cardboard holder | — | 30.00 |
| MS33 | 1996 (9) | 12,000 | KM#158-166 | 12.50 | 15.00 |
| MS34 | 1997 (9) | 7,515 | KM#159-166, 170 | — | 30.00 |
| MS35 | 1998 (9) | — | KM#159-166, 170 | — | 30.00 |
| MS36 | 1999 (9) | 10,000 | KM#159-166, 170 | 19.50 | 30.00 |
| MS37 | 2000 (9) | — | KM#159-166, 170 | — | 30.00 |

## PROOF SETS

| KM# | Date | Mintage | Identification | Issue Price | Mkt Val |
|---|---|---|---|---|---|
| PS1 | 1923 (10) | 655 | KM#12.1-17.1, 18, 19.1, 20-21 | — | 1,500 |
| PS2 | 1923 (8) | 747 | KM#12.1-17.1, 18, 19.1 | — | 600 |
| PS3 | 1926 (6) | 3 | KM#12.2, 14-2-17.2, 19.2 | — | 20,000 |
| PS5 | 1930 (8) | — | KM#12.2 (dated 1928), 13.2-17.2, 18, 19.2 | — | 15,000 |
| PS4 | 1930 (8) | 14 | KM#12.2-17.2, 18, 19.2 | — | 7,500 |
| PS6 | 1931 (8) | 62 | KM#12.3-17.3, 19.3, 22 | — | 9,000 |
| PS7 | 1932 (8) | 12 | KM#12.3-17.3, 19.3, 22 | — | 7,500 |
| PS8 | 1933 (8) | 20 | KM#12.3-17.3, 19.3, 22 | — | 9,000 |
| PS9 | 1934 (8) | 24 | KM#12.3-17.3, 19.3, 22 | — | 7,500 |
| PS10 | 1935 (8) | 20 | KM#12.3-17.3, 19.3, 22 | — | 6,500 |
| PS11 | 1936 (8) | 40 | KM#12.3-17.3, 19.3, 22 | — | 3,500 |
| PS12 | 1937 (8) | 116 | KM#23-30 | — | 750 |
| PS13 | 1938 (8) | 44 | KM#23-30 | — | 1,500 |
| PS14 | 1939 (8) | 30 | KM#23-30 | — | 8,000 |
| PS15 | 1943 (8) | 104 | KM#23-30 | — | 700 |
| PS16 | 1944 (8) | 150 | KM#23-30 | — | 600 |
| PS17 | 1945 (8) | 150 | KM#23-30 | — | 600 |
| PS18 | 1946 (8) | 150 | KM#23-30 | — | 700 |
| PS19 | 1947 (8) | 2,600 | KM#23-30 | — | 225 |
| PS20 | 1948 (9) | 1,120 | KM#32.1, 33, 34.1-40.1 | — | 250 |
| PS21 | 1949 (9) | 800 | KM#32.1, 33, 34.1-40.1 | — | 350 |
| PS22 | 1950 (9) | 500 | KM#32.1, 33, 34.1-40.1 | — | 400 |
| PS23 | 1951 (9) | 2,000 | KM#32.2, 33, 34.2-40.2 | — | 60.00 |
| PS24 | 1952 (11) | 12,000 | KM#32.2, 33, 34.2-39.2, 41-43 | — | 210 |
| PS25 | 1952 (9) | 3,500 | KM#32.2, 33, 34.2-39.2, 41 | — | 35.00 |
| PS26 | 1953 (11) | 3,000 | KM#44-54 | 29.40 | 220 |
| PS28 | 1953 (2) | 1,000 | KM#53-54 | 25.20 | 200 |
| PS27 | 1953 (9) | 2,000 | KM#44-52 | 4.35 | 35.00 |
| PS29 | 1954 (11) | 875 | KM#44-54 | 29.40 | 250 |
| PS31 | 1954 (2) | 350 | KM#53-54 | 25.20 | 210 |
| PS30 | 1954 (9) | 2,275 | KM#44-52 | 4.35 | 40.00 |
| PS32 | 1955 (11) | 600 | KM#44-54 | 29.40 | 275 |
| PS34 | 1955 (2) | 300 | KM#53-54 | 25.20 | 240 |
| PS33 | 1955 (9) | 2,250 | KM#44-52 | 4.35 | 30.00 |
| PS35 | 1956 (11) | 350 | KM#44-54 | 29.40 | 350 |
| PS37 | 1956 (2) | 158 | KM#53-54 | 25.20 | 300 |
| PS36 | 1956 (9) | 1,350 | KM#44-52 | 4.35 | 45.00 |
| PS38 | 1957 (11) | 380 | KM#44-54 | 29.40 | 340 |
| PS40 | 1957 (2) | 180 | KM#53-54 | 25.20 | 280 |
| PS39 | 1957 (9) | 750 | KM#44-52 | 4.35 | 75.00 |
| PS41 | 1958 (11) | 360 | KM#44-54 | 29.40 | 350 |
| PS43 | 1958 (2) | 155 | KM#53-54 | 25.20 | 300 |
| PS42 | 1958 (9) | 625 | KM#44-52 | 4.35 | 85.00 |
| PS44 | 1959 (11) | 390 | KM#44-54 | 29.40 | 425 |
| PS45 | 1959 (9) | 560 | KM#44-52 | 4.35 | 175 |
| PS46 | 1959 (2) | 240 | KM#53-54 | 25.20 | 250 |
| PS47 | 1960 (11) | 1,500 | KM#44-51, 53-55 | 29.40 | 220 |
| PS48 | 1960 (9) | 1,860 | KM#44-51, 55 | 4.35 | 20.00 |
| PS49 | 1960 (2) | 450 | KM#53-54 | 25.20 | 180 |
| PS50 | 1961 (9) | 3,139 | KM#56-64 | — | 200 |
| PS51 | 1961 (7) | 4,391 | KM#56-62 | — | 20.00 |
| PS52 | 1961 (2) | 793 | KM#63-64 | — | — |
| PS53 | 1962 (9) | 1,544 | KM#56-64 | — | 210 |
| PS54 | 1962 (7) | 2,300 | KM#56-62 | — | 15.00 |
| PS55 | 1962 (2) | 800 | KM#63-64 | — | — |
| PS56 | 1963 (9) | 1,500 | KM#56-64 | — | 200 |
| PS57 | 1963 (7) | 2,525 | KM#56-62 | — | 12.00 |
| PS58 | 1963 (2) | 1,008 | KM#63-64 | — | — |
| PS59 | 1964 (9) | 3,000 | KM#56-64 | — | 190 |
| PS60 | 1964 (7) | 13,000 | KM#56-62 | — | 10.00 |
| PS61 | 1964 (2) | 1,000 | KM#63-64 | — | — |
| PS63 | 1965 (9) | 85 | KM#63-64, 65.1-66.2, 67.1, 68.2, 69.1, 70.2, 71.2 V.I.P. | — | 1,200 |
| PS62 | 1965 (9) | 5,099 | KM#63-64, 65.1, 66.2, 67.1, 68.2, 69.1, 70.2, 71.1 | 23.50 | 185 |
| PS64 | 1965 (7) | 19,889 | KM#65.1, 66.2, 67.1, 68.2, 69.1, 70.2, 71.1 | 5.00 | 12.00 |
| PS65 | 1965 (2) | 925 | KM#63-64 | 18.15 | — |
| PS66 | 1966 (9) | 10,000 | KM#63-64, 65.2, 66.1, 67.2, 68.1, 69.2, 70.1, 71.2 | 24.10 | 185 |
| PS67 | 1966 (7) | 15,000 | KM#65.2, 66.1, 67.2, 68.1, 69.2, 70.1, 71.2 | 5.00 | 8.00 |
| PS68 | 1966 (2) | 1,000 | KM#63-64 | 18.15 | — |
| PS69 | 1967 (9) | 10,000 | KM#63-64, 65.2, 66.1, 67.2, 68.1, 69.2, 70.1, 72.2 | 24.10 | 185 |
| PS70 | 1967 (7) | 15,000 | KM#65.2, 66.1, 67.2, 68.1, 69.2, 70.1, 72.2 | 5.00 | 8.00 |
| PS71 | 1967 (2) | 1,000 | KM#63-64 | 18.15 | — |
| PS72 | 1968 (9) | 10,000 | KM#63-64, 71.1, 74.1, 75.2, 76.1, 77.2, 78.1, 79.2 | 35.00 | 185 |
| PS73 | 1968 (7) | 15,000 | KM#71.1, 74.1, 75.2, 76.1, 77.2, 78.1, 79.2 | 16.00 | 8.00 |
| PS74 | 1968 (2) | 1,000 | KM#63-64 | 28.00 | — |
| PS75 | 1969 (9) | 7,000 | KM#63-64, 65.2, 66.1, 67.2, 68.1, 69.2, 70.1, 80.2 | 34.85 | 185 |
| PS76 | 1969 (7) | 5,000 | KM#65.2, 66.1, 67.2, 68.1, 69.2, 70.1, 80.2 | 13.95 | 8.00 |
| PS77 | 1969 (2) | 1,000 | KM#63-64 | 27.85 | — |
| PS78 | 1970 (10) | 6,000 | KM#63-64, 81-88 | 35.05 | 185 |
| PS79 | 1970 (8) | 4,000 | KM#81-88 | 14.00 | 9.00 |
| PS80 | 1970 (2) | 1,000 | KM#63-64 | 28.05 | — |
| PS81 | 1971 (10) | 7,000 | KM#63-64, 81-88 | 35.00 | 185 |
| PS82 | 1971 (8) | 5,000 | KM#81-88 | 14.00 | 9.00 |
| PS83 | 1971 (2) | 650 | KM#63-64 | 28.00 | — |
| PS84 | 1972 (10) | 6,000 | KM#63-64, 81-88 | 32.80 | 185 |
| PS85 | 1972 (8) | 4,000 | KM#81-88 | 13.10 | 9.00 |
| PS86 | 1972 (2) | 1,500 | KM#63-64 | 26.25 | — |
| PS87 | 1973 (10) | 6,850 | KM#63-64, 81-88 | 32.00 | 185 |
| PS88 | 1973 (8) | 4,000 | KM#81-88 | 12.80 | 9.00 |
| PS89 | 1973 (2) | 6,088 | KM#63-64 | 25.60 | — |
| PS90 | 1974 (10) | 11,000 | KM#63-64, 81-87, 89 | 52.50 | 185 |
| PS91 | 1974 (8) | 4,000 | KM#81-87, 89 | 15.00 | 9.00 |
| PS92 | 1974 (2) | 5,600 | KM#63-64 | 45.00 | — |
| PS93 | 1975 (10) | 12,500 | KM#63-64, 81-87, 88 | 116 | 185 |
| PS94 | 1975 (8) | 5,500 | KM#81-88 | 14.55 | 9.00 |
| PS95 | 1975 (2) | 7,000 | KM#63-64 | 101 | — |
| PS96 | 1976 (10) | 14,000 | KM#63-64, 88, 90-96 | 92.00 | 185 |
| PS97 | 1976 (8) | 7,000 | KM#88, 90-96 | 11.50 | 9.00 |
| PS98 | 1976 (2) | 8,000 | KM#63-64 | 80.50 | — |
| PS100 | 1977 (8) | 7,000 | KM#81-88 | 11.50 | 12.00 |
| PS99 | 1977 (10) | 12,000 | KM#63-64, 81-88 | 92.00 | 185 |
| PS101 | 1977 (2) | 8,000 | KM#63-64 | 80.50 | — |
| PS102 | 1978 (10) | 10,000 | KM#63-64, 81-88 | — | 185 |
| PS103 | 1978 (8) | 7,000 | KM#81-88 | — | 12.00 |
| PS104 | 1978 (2) | 9,000 | KM#63-64 | — | — |
| PS106 | 1979 (8) | 5,000 | KM#88, 97-103 | — | 22.00 |
| PS105 | 1979 (10) | 10,000 | KM#63-64, 97-103, 104a | — | 185 |
| PS107 | 1979 (2) | 10,000 | KM#63-64 | — | — |
| PS108 | 1980 (10) | 10,000 | KM#63-64, 81-88 | — | 185 |
| PS109 | 1980 (8) | 5,000 | KM#81-88 | — | 22.00 |
| PS110 | 1980 (2) | 8,000 | KM#63-64 | — | — |
| PS111 | 1980 (2) | 8,000 | KM#63-64 | — | — |
| PS112 | 1980 (3) | 60 | KM#105-107 | — | 9,000 |
| PS113 | 1981 (10) | 6,000 | KM#63-64, 81-88 | — | 185 |
| PS114 | 1981 (8) | 4,900 | KM#81-88 | — | 22.00 |
| PS115 | 1981 (2) | 6,238 | KM#63-64 | — | — |
| PS116 | 1982 (10) | 7,100 | KM#63-64, 108-115 | — | 190 |
| PS117 | 1982 (8) | 4,900 | KM#88, 108-114 | — | 22.00 |

| KM# | Date | Mintage | Identification | Issue Price | Mkt Val |
|---|---|---|---|---|---|
| PS118 | 1982 (2) | 6,930 | KM#63-64 | — | — |
| PS119 | 1983 (10) | 7,300 | KM#63-64, 81-88 | — | 185 |
| PS120 | 1983 (8) | 6,835 | KM#81-88 | — | 22.00 |
| PS121 | 1983 (2) | 7,300 | KM#63-64 | — | — |
| PS122 | 1984 (8) | 11,250 | KM#82-88, 88a | — | 15.00 |
| PS123 | 1985 (8) | 9,859 | KM#82-87, 116, 117 | — | 25.00 |
| PS125 | 1986 (2) | 428 | KM#73, 121 Plus large gold plated Silver #1 | — | 1,400 |
| PS126 | 1986 (2) | 750 | KM#121, 131 | — | 700 |
| PS127 | 1986 (3) | 500 | KM#119, 121, 131 | — | 725 |
| PS124 | 1986 (8) | 7,000 | KM#82-87, 88a, 119 | — | 25.00 |
| PS129 | 1987 (4) | 750 | KM#73, 105-107 | — | 1,050 |
| PS130 | 1987 GRC (4) | 1,121 | KM#73, 105-107 | — | 2,900 |
| PS128 | 1987 (8) | 6,781 | KM#82-88, 88a | — | 25.00 |
| PS135 | 1988 (3) | 600 | KM#124, 127, 130 | — | 2,750 |
| PS132 | 1988 (4) | 806 | KM#73, 105-107 | — | 1,050 |
| PS133 | 1988 GRC (4) | 835 | KM#73, 105-107 | — | 2,900 |
| PS131 | 1988 (8) | 7,250 | KM#82-88, 88a | — | 50.00 |
| PS134 | 1988 (3) | 3,388 | KM#122, 125, 128 | — | 70.00 |
| PS136 | 1989 (8) | 9,571 | KM#82-88, 88a | — | 50.00 |
| PS137 | 1989 (4) | — | KM#73, 105-107 | — | 1,050 |
| PS138 | 1989 GRC (4) | 318 | KM#73, 105-107 | — | 5,500 |
| PS139 | 1990 (8) | 10,000 | KM#132-137, 139, 148 | — | 70.00 |
| PS140 | 1990 (4) | — | KM#73, 105-107 | — | 1,050 |
| PS141 | 1990 GRC (4) | 1,066 | KM#73, 105-107 | — | 2,775 |
| PS142 | 1991 (8) | 12,000 | KM#132-139 | — | 70.00 |
| PSA143 | 1991 GRC (4) | 426 | KM#73, 105-107 | — | 2,775 |
| PS143 | 1992 (8) | 10,000 | KM#132-139 | — | 50.00 |
| PS144 | 1993 (8) | — | KM#132-139 | — | 50.00 |
| PS146 | 1994 (4) | 168 | KM#189-192 Wood case | — | 1,200 |
| PS147 | 1994 (4) | 1,750 | KM#189-192 Velvet case | — | 1,175 |
| PS148 | 1994 (3) | 420 | KM#167, 187-188 | — | 750 |
| PS145 | 1994 (9) | 5,804 | KM#132-140 | — | 60.00 |
| PS152 | 1995 (4) | 89 | KM#195-198 Wood case | — | 1,200 |
| PS153 | 1995 (4) | 925 | KM#195-198 Velvet case | — | 1,175 |
| PS154 | 1995 (3) | 210 | KM#152, 193-194 | — | 755 |
| PS150 | 1995 (4) | 750 | KM#73, 105-107 | — | 1,400 |
| PS151 | 1995 | — | KM#73, 105-107 Wooden box | — | 1,425 |
| PS149 | 1995 (9) | 5,816 | KM#132-140 | — | 65.00 |
| PS156 | 1996 (4) | 368 | KM#201-402 Wood case | — | 1,200 |
| PS157 | 1996 (4) | 1,677 | KM#201-204 Velvet case | — | 1,175 |
| PS158 | 1996 (3) | 346 | KM#169, 199-200 | — | 760 |
| PS155 | 1996 (9) | 4,827 | KM#158-166 | 30.00 | 36.00 |
| PS160 | 1997 (4) | 500 | KM#207-210 Wood case | — | 1,200 |
| PS161 | 1997 (4) | 1,015 | KM#207-210 Velvet case | — | 1,175 |
| PS162 | 1997 (3) | 144 | KM#181, 205-206 | — | 780 |
| PS159 | 1997 (4) | 500 | KM#73, 105-107 | — | 1,100 |
| PS163 | 1997 (4) | 30 | KM#73, 105-107, 30 Year Wine set with privy marks | — | 2,550 |
| PS164 | 1997 (9) | 3,596 | KM#159-166, 170 | — | 40.00 |
| PS165 | 1998 (9) | — | KM#159-166, 170 | — | 40.00 |
| PS166 | 1998 (4) | — | KM#213-216 Wood case | — | 1,200 |
| PS167 | 1998 (4) | — | KM#213-216 Velvet case | — | 1,175 |
| PS168 | 1998 (3) | — | KM#177, 211-212 | — | 780 |
| PS169 | 1999 (9) | 6,000 | KM#159-166, 170 | 39.50 | 40.00 |

## SPECIMEN SETS (SS)

| KM# | Date | Mintage | Identification | Issue Price | Mkt Val |
|---|---|---|---|---|---|
| SS1 | 1994 (9) | 5,508 | KM#132-140 | — | 25.00 |
| SS2 | 1995 (9) | 4,956 | KM#132-140 | — | 25.00 |
| SS3 | 1996 (9) | 5,766 | KM#158-166 | 19.50 | 25.00 |
| SS4 | 1997 (9) | 4,236 | KM#159-166, 170 | — | 25.00 |
| SS5 | 1998 (9) | — | KM#159-166, 170 | — | 25.00 |
| SS6 | 1999 (9) | — | KM#159-166, 170 | — | 25.00 |

# SOUTH ARABIA

Fifteen of the sixteen Western Protectorate States, the Wahidi State of the Eastern Protectorate, and Aden Colony joined to form the Federation of South Arabia.

In 1959, Britain agreed to prepare South Arabia for full independence, which was achieved on Nov. 30, 1967, at which time South Arabia, including Aden, changed its name to the Peoples Republic of Southern Yemen. On Dec. 1, 1970, following the overthrow of the new government by the National Liberation Front, Southern Yemen changed its name to the Peoples Democratic Republic of Yemen.

**TITLES**

Al-Junubiya(t) al-Arabiya(t)

**MONETARY SYSTEM**

1000 Fils = 1 Dinar

## FEDERATION

### STANDARD COINAGE

**FILS** **KM# 1** **Composition:** Aluminum

| Date | Mintage | F | VF | XF | Unc | BU |
|---|---|---|---|---|---|---|
| 1964 | 10,000,000 | — | — | 0.10 | 0.15 | — |
| 1964 Proof | — | Value: 1.50 | | | | |

**5 FILS** **KM# 2** **Composition:** Bronze

| Date | Mintage | F | VF | XF | Unc | BU |
|---|---|---|---|---|---|---|
| 1964 | 10,000,000 | — | 0.15 | 0.25 | 0.50 | — |
| 1964 Proof | — | Value: 2.00 | | | | |

**25 FILS** **KM# 3** **Composition:** Copper-Nickel

| Date | Mintage | F | VF | XF | Unc | BU |
|---|---|---|---|---|---|---|
| 1964 | 4,000,000 | — | 0.25 | 0.45 | 0.85 | — |
| 1964 Proof | — | Value: 2.75 | | | | |

**50 FILS** **KM# 4** **Composition:** Copper-Nickel

| Date | Mintage | F | VF | XF | Unc | BU |
|---|---|---|---|---|---|---|
| 1964 | 6,000,000 | — | 0.45 | 0.65 | 1.25 | — |
| 1964 Proof | — | Value: 3.75 | | | | |

## PROOF SETS

| KM# | Date | Mintage | Identification | Issue Price | Mkt Val |
|---|---|---|---|---|---|
| PS1 | 1964 (4) | 10,500 | KM1-4 | 9.90 | 10.00 |

# S. GEORGIA & THE S. SANDWICH IS.

South Georgia and the South Sandwich Islands are a dependency of the Falkland Islands, and located about 800 miles east of them. South Georgia is 1,450 sq. mi. (1,770 sq. km.), South Sandwich Islands is 120 sq. mi. (311 sq. km.) Fishing and Antarctic research are the main industries. The islands were claimed for Great Britain in 1775 by Captain James Cook.

**RULERS**

British since 1775

## BRITISH ADMINISTRATION

### STANDARD COINAGE

**2 POUNDS** **KM# 1** **Weight:** 28.2800 g. **Composition:** Copper-Nickel **Subject:** 100th Birthday - Queen Mother **Obverse:** Queen Elizabeth's head right **Reverse:** Queen Mother's coat of arms **Edge:** Reeded **Size:** 38.7 mm. **Note:** Struck at the Pobjoy Mint.

| Date | Mintage | F | VF | XF | Unc | BU |
|---|---|---|---|---|---|---|
| 2000 | — | — | — | — | 10.00 | — |

**2 POUNDS** **KM# 1a** **Weight:** 28.2800 g. **Composition:** 0.9250 Silver .841 oz. ASW **Subject:** 100th Birthday - Queen Mother **Obverse:** Queen Elizabeth's head right **Reverse:** Queen Mother's coat of arms **Edge:** Reeded **Note:** Struck at the Pobjoy Mint.

| Date | Mintage | F | VF | XF | Unc | BU |
|---|---|---|---|---|---|---|
| 2000 Proof | — | Value: 50.00 | | | | |

**2 POUNDS** **KM# 3** **Weight:** 28.2800 g. **Composition:** Copper-Nickel **Subject:** Antoine de la Roche **Obverse:** Queen Elizabeth's head right **Reverse:** Antoine de la Roche standing on the deck of the ship Discovery **Edge:** Reeded **Size:** 38.6 mm. **Note:** Struck at the Pobjoy Mint.

| Date | Mintage | F | VF | XF | Unc | BU |
|---|---|---|---|---|---|---|
| 2000 | — | — | — | — | 8.50 | — |

**2 POUNDS** **KM# 3a** **Weight:** 28.2800 g. **Composition:** 0.9250 Silver .841 oz. ASW **Subject:** Antoine de la Roche **Obverse:** Queen Elizabeth's head right **Reverse:** Antoine de la Roche standing on the deck of the ship Discovery **Edge:** Reeded **Size:** 38.7 mm. **Note:** Struck at the Pobjoy Mint.

| Date | Mintage | F | VF | XF | Unc | BU |
|---|---|---|---|---|---|---|
| 2000 Proof | — | Value: 47.50 | | | | |

**2 POUNDS** KM# 4 **Weight:** 28.2800 g. **Composition:** Copper-Nickel **Subject:** 225th Anniversary - Possession by Captain Cook **Obverse:** Queen Elizabeth's head right **Reverse:** 1/3-length bust of Captain Cook right **Note:** Struck at the Pobjoy Mint.

| Date | Mintage | F | VF | XF | Unc | BU |
|---|---|---|---|---|---|---|
| 2000 | — | — | — | — | 8.50 | — |

**2 POUNDS** KM# 4a **Weight:** 28.2800 g. **Composition:** 0.9250 Silver .841 oz. ASW **Subject:** 225th Anniversary - Possession by Captain Cook **Obverse:** Queen Elizabeth's head right **Reverse:** 1/3-length bust of Captain Cook right **Note:** Struck at the Pobjoy Mint.

| Date | Mintage | F | VF | XF | Unc | BU |
|---|---|---|---|---|---|---|
| 2000 Proof | — | Value: 47.50 | | | | |

**2 POUNDS** KM# 7 **Weight:** 28.2800 g. **Composition:** Copper-Nickel **Subject:** Sir Ernest H. Shackleton **Obverse:** Queen's portrait **Reverse:** Portrait and ship **Edge:** Reeded **Size:** 38.6 mm.

| Date | Mintage | F | VF | XF | Unc | BU |
|---|---|---|---|---|---|---|
| 2001 | — | — | — | — | 10.00 | — |

**2 POUNDS** KM# 7a **Weight:** 28.2800 g. **Composition:** 0.9250 Silver .8410 oz. ASW

| Date | Mintage | F | VF | XF | Unc | BU |
|---|---|---|---|---|---|---|
| 2001 Proof | Est. 10,000 | — | — | — | 47.50 | — |

**2 POUNDS** KM# 9 **Composition:** Copper-Nickel **Subject:** Sir Joseph Banks **Obverse:** Queen's portrait **Reverse:** Cameo portrait and ship

| Date | Mintage | F | VF | XF | Unc | BU |
|---|---|---|---|---|---|---|
| 2001 | — | — | — | — | 10.00 | — |

**20 POUNDS** KM# 2 **Weight:** 6.2200 g. **Composition:** 0.9999 Gold .2 oz. AGW **Subject:** 100th Birthday - Queen Mother **Obverse:** Queen Elizabeth's head right **Reverse:** Queen Mother's coat of arms **Edge:** Reeded **Note:** Struck at the Pobjoy Mint.

| Date | Mintage | F | VF | XF | Unc | BU |
|---|---|---|---|---|---|---|
| 2000 Proof | — | Value: 185 | | | | |

**20 POUNDS** KM# 5 **Weight:** 6.2200 g. **Composition:** 0.9999 Gold .2 oz. AGW **Subject:** Antoine de la Roche **Obverse:** Queen Elizabeth's head right **Reverse:** Antoine de la Roche standing on the deck of the ship Discovery **Edge:** Reeded **Size:** 22 mm. **Note:** Struck at the Pobjoy Mint.

| Date | Mintage | F | VF | XF | Unc | BU |
|---|---|---|---|---|---|---|
| 2000 Proof | — | Value: 175 | | | | |

**20 POUNDS** KM# 6 **Weight:** 6.2200 g. **Composition:** 0.9999 Gold .2 oz. AGW **Subject:** 225th Anniversary - Possession by Captain Cook **Obverse:** Queen Elizabeth's head right **Reverse:** 1/3-length bust of Captain Cook right **Note:** Struck at the Pobjoy Mint.

| Date | Mintage | F | VF | XF | Unc | BU |
|---|---|---|---|---|---|---|
| 2000 Proof | — | Value: 175 | | | | |

**20 POUNDS** KM# 8 **Weight:** 6.2200 g. **Composition:** 0.9999 Gold .2000 oz. AGW **Subject:** Sir Ernest H. Shackleton **Obverse:** Queen's portrait **Reverse:** Portrait and ship **Edge:** Reeded **Size:** 22 mm.

| Date | Mintage | F | VF | XF | Unc | BU |
|---|---|---|---|---|---|---|
| 2001 Proof | Est. 2,000 | Value: 175 | | | | |

**20 POUNDS** KM# 10 **Weight:** 6.2200 g. **Composition:** 0.9999 Gold .2000 oz. AGW **Subject:** Sir Joseph Banks **Obverse:** Queen's portrait **Reverse:** Cameo portrait and ship

| Date | Mintage | F | VF | XF | Unc | BU |
|---|---|---|---|---|---|---|
| 2001 Proof | Est. 2,000 | Value: 175 | | | | |

# SOUTHERN RHODESIA

**RULERS**
British, until 1966

**MONETARY SYSTEM**
12 Pence = 1 Shilling
2 Shillings = 1 Florin
5 Shillings = 1 Crown
20 Shillings = 1 Pound

## BRITISH COLONY

### POUND COINAGE

**1/2 PENNY** KM# 6 **Composition:** Copper-Nickel

| Date | Mintage | F | VF | XF | Unc | BU |
|---|---|---|---|---|---|---|
| 1934 | 240,000 | 1.00 | 2.00 | 8.00 | 22.50 | — |
| 1934 Proof | — | Value: 125 | | | | |
| 1936 | 240,000 | 4.00 | 8.00 | 25.00 | 150 | — |
| 1936 Proof | — | — | — | — | — | — |

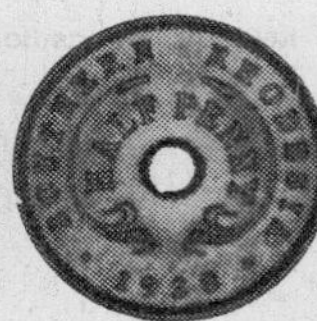

**1/2 PENNY** KM# 14 **Composition:** Copper-Nickel

| Date | Mintage | F | VF | XF | Unc | BU |
|---|---|---|---|---|---|---|
| 1938 | 240,000 | 0.75 | 1.75 | 6.50 | 20.00 | — |
| 1938 Proof | — | — | — | — | — | — |
| 1939 | 480,000 | 1.00 | 2.00 | 9.00 | 60.00 | — |
| 1939 Proof | — | — | — | — | — | — |

**1/2 PENNY** KM# 14a **Composition:** Bronze

| Date | Mintage | F | VF | XF | Unc | BU |
|---|---|---|---|---|---|---|
| 1942 | 480,000 | 0.60 | 1.50 | 3.50 | 25.00 | — |
| 1942 Proof | — | — | — | — | — | — |
| 1943 | 960,000 | 0.35 | 0.75 | 2.25 | 6.50 | — |
| 1944 | 960,000 | 0.35 | 0.75 | 2.50 | 8.00 | — |
| 1944 Proof | — | — | — | — | — | — |

**1/2 PENNY** KM# 26 **Composition:** Bronze **Obv. Legend:** KING GEORGE THE SIXTH

| Date | Mintage | F | VF | XF | Unc | BU |
|---|---|---|---|---|---|---|
| 1951 | 480,000 | 0.75 | 1.25 | 2.25 | 6.50 | — |
| 1951 Proof | — | — | — | — | — | — |
| 1952 | 480,000 | 0.75 | 1.25 | 2.50 | 10.00 | — |
| 1952 Proof | — | — | — | — | — | — |

**1/2 PENNY** KM# 28 **Composition:** Bronze

| Date | Mintage | F | VF | XF | Unc | BU |
|---|---|---|---|---|---|---|
| 1954 | 960,000 | 0.75 | 2.00 | 10.00 | 75.00 | — |
| 1954 Proof | 20 | Value: 350 | | | | |

**PENNY** KM# 7 **Composition:** Copper-Nickel

| Date | Mintage | F | VF | XF | Unc | BU |
|---|---|---|---|---|---|---|
| 1934 | 360,000 | 0.75 | 1.50 | 3.50 | 30.00 | — |
| 1934 Proof | — | Value: 125 | | | | |
| 1935 | 492,000 | 0.75 | 2.50 | 12.00 | 125 | — |
| 1935 Proof | — | — | — | — | — | — |
| 1936 | 1,044,000 | 0.60 | 1.25 | 3.50 | 40.00 | — |
| 1936 Proof | — | — | — | — | — | — |

**PENNY** KM# 8 **Composition:** Copper-Nickel

| Date | Mintage | F | VF | XF | Unc | BU |
|---|---|---|---|---|---|---|
| 1937 | 908,000 | 0.60 | 1.25 | 3.50 | 25.00 | — |
| 1937 Proof | — | Value: 300 | | | | |
| 1938 | 240,000 | 1.50 | 3.00 | 7.50 | 40.00 | — |
| 1938 Proof | — | — | — | — | — | — |
| 1939 | 1,284,000 | 0.45 | 1.00 | 3.50 | 40.00 | — |
| 1939 Proof | — | — | — | — | — | — |
| 1940 | 1,080,000 | 0.45 | 1.00 | 3.50 | 40.00 | — |
| 1940 Proof | — | — | — | — | — | — |
| 1941 | 720,000 | 0.50 | 1.25 | 4.50 | 45.00 | — |
| 1941 Proof | — | — | — | — | — | — |
| 1942 | 960,000 | 0.50 | 1.25 | 4.50 | 70.00 | — |
| 1942 | — | — | — | — | — | — |

**PENNY** KM# 8a **Composition:** Bronze

| Date | Mintage | F | VF | XF | Unc | BU |
|---|---|---|---|---|---|---|
| 1942 | 480,000 | 4.00 | 6.50 | 22.50 | 100 | — |
| 1942 Proof | — | Value: 400 | | | | |
| 1943 | 3,120,000 | 0.50 | 0.80 | 2.50 | 15.00 | — |
| 1944 | 2,400,000 | 0.50 | 0.80 | 2.50 | 20.00 | — |
| 1944 Proof | — | — | — | — | — | — |
| 1947 | 3,600,000 | 0.75 | 1.25 | 3.50 | 20.00 | — |
| 1947 Proof | — | — | — | — | — | — |

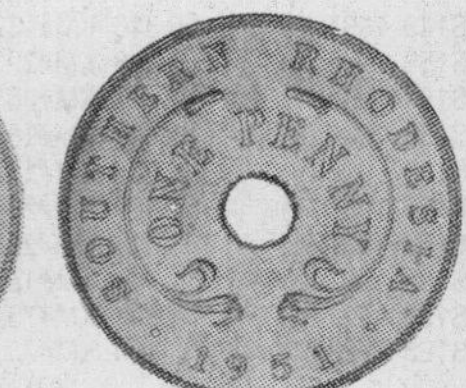


**PENNY** KM# 25 **Composition:** Bronze

| Date | Mintage | F | VF | XF | Unc | BU |
|---|---|---|---|---|---|---|
| 1949 | 1,440,000 | 0.50 | 1.00 | 2.00 | 30.00 | — |
| 1949 Proof | — | Value: 125 | | | | |
| 1950 | 720,000 | 1.00 | 1.75 | 5.00 | 45.00 | — |
| 1950 Proof | — | Value: 125 | | | | |
| 1951 | 4,896,000 | 0.50 | 0.75 | 1.25 | 10.00 | — |
| 1951 Proof | — | Value: 125 | | | | |
| 1952 | 2,400,000 | 0.50 | 0.75 | 1.75 | 15.00 | — |
| 1952 Proof | — | — | — | — | — | — |

**PENNY** KM# 29 **Composition:** Bronze

| Date | Mintage | F | VF | XF | Unc | BU |
|---|---|---|---|---|---|---|
| 1954 | 960,000 | 4.00 | 8.00 | 35.00 | 250 | — |
| 1954 Proof | 20 | Value: 450 | | | | |

**3 PENCE** KM# 1 **Weight:** 1.4100 g. **Composition:** 0.9250 Silver .0419 oz. ASW

| Date | Mintage | F | VF | XF | Unc | BU |
|---|---|---|---|---|---|---|
| 1932 | 688,000 | 0.75 | 1.50 | 6.50 | 32.00 | — |
| 1932 Proof | — | Value: 60.00 | | | | |
| 1934 | 628,000 | 0.75 | 2.00 | 10.00 | 60.00 | — |
| 1934 Proof | — | — | — | — | — | — |
| 1935 | 840,000 | 0.75 | 2.00 | 7.00 | 50.00 | — |
| 1935 Proof | — | — | — | — | — | — |

| Date | Mintage | F | VF | XF | Unc | BU |
|---|---|---|---|---|---|---|
| 1936 | 1,052,000 | 0.75 | 2.00 | 7.00 | 50.00 | — |
| 1936 Proof | — | — | — | — | — | — |

**3 PENCE** KM# 9 **Weight:** 1.4100 g. **Composition:** 0.9250 Silver .0419 oz. ASW

| Date | Mintage | F | VF | XF | Unc | BU |
|---|---|---|---|---|---|---|
| 1937 | 1,228,000 | 0.75 | 2.00 | 6.00 | 30.00 | — |
| 1937 Proof | — | Value: 250 | | | | |

**3 PENCE** KM# 16 **Weight:** 1.4100 g. **Composition:** 0.9250 Silver .0419 oz. ASW **Obverse:** KING moved behind head

| Date | Mintage | F | VF | XF | Unc | BU |
|---|---|---|---|---|---|---|
| 1939 | 160,000 | 6.00 | 10.00 | 22.00 | 150 | — |
| 1939 Proof | — | Value: 300 | | | | |
| 1940 | 1,200,000 | 0.75 | 2.00 | 7.00 | 40.00 | — |
| 1940 Proof | — | — | — | — | — | — |
| 1941 | 600,000 | 2.50 | 5.00 | 10.00 | 50.00 | — |
| 1941 Proof | — | — | — | — | — | — |
| 1942 | 2,000,000 | 0.50 | 1.50 | 6.50 | 30.00 | — |
| 1942 Proof | — | — | — | — | — | — |

**3 PENCE** KM# 16a **Weight:** 1.4100 g. **Composition:** 0.5000 Silver .0226 oz. ASW

| Date | Mintage | F | VF | XF | Unc | BU |
|---|---|---|---|---|---|---|
| 1944 | 1,600,000 | 0.50 | 1.50 | 10.00 | 65.00 | — |
| 1945 | 800,000 | 1.00 | 3.00 | 12.00 | 65.00 | — |
| 1945 Proof | — | — | — | — | — | — |
| 1946 | 2,400,000 | 0.50 | 1.50 | 7.00 | 35.00 | — |
| 1946 Proof | — | — | — | — | — | — |

**3 PENCE** KM# 16b **Composition:** Copper-Nickel

| Date | Mintage | F | VF | XF | Unc | BU |
|---|---|---|---|---|---|---|
| 1947 | 8,000,000 | 0.40 | 0.80 | 2.50 | 20.00 | — |
| 1947 Proof | — | Value: 250 | | | | |

**3 PENCE** KM# 20 **Composition:** Copper-Nickel

| Date | Mintage | F | VF | XF | Unc | BU |
|---|---|---|---|---|---|---|
| 1948 | 2,000,000 | 0.40 | 0.80 | 3.50 | 30.00 | — |
| 1948 Proof | — | — | — | — | — | — |
| 1949 | 4,000,000 | 0.40 | 0.80 | 3.00 | 25.00 | — |
| 1949 Proof | — | Value: 150 | | | | |
| 1951 | 5,600,000 | 0.40 | 0.80 | 2.50 | 20.00 | — |
| 1951 Proof | — | — | — | — | — | — |
| 1952 | 4,800,000 | 0.40 | 0.80 | 2.50 | 30.00 | — |
| 1952 Proof | — | Value: 150 | | | | |

**6 PENCE** KM# 2 **Weight:** 2.8300 g. **Composition:** 0.9250 Silver .0841 oz. ASW

| Date | Mintage | F | VF | XF | Unc | BU |
|---|---|---|---|---|---|---|
| 1932 | 544,000 | 2.00 | 3.50 | 10.00 | 60.00 | — |
| 1932 Proof | — | Value: 75.00 | | | | |
| 1934 | 214,000 | 3.00 | 7.00 | 30.00 | 100 | — |
| 1935 | 380,000 | 2.00 | 6.00 | 30.00 | 100 | — |
| 1935 Proof | — | — | — | — | — | — |
| 1936 | 675,000 | 1.50 | 3.50 | 15.00 | 65.00 | — |
| 1936 Proof | — | — | — | — | — | — |

**6 PENCE** KM# 10 **Weight:** 2.8300 g. **Composition:** 0.9250 Silver .0841 oz. ASW

| Date | Mintage | F | VF | XF | Unc | BU |
|---|---|---|---|---|---|---|
| 1937 | 823,000 | 2.50 | 5.00 | 15.00 | 60.00 | — |
| 1937 Proof | — | Value: 300 | | | | |

**6 PENCE** KM# 17 **Weight:** 2.8300 g. **Composition:** 0.9250 Silver .0841 oz. ASW **Obverse:** KING moved behind head

| Date | Mintage | F | VF | XF | Unc | BU |
|---|---|---|---|---|---|---|
| 1939 | 200,000 | 3.00 | 7.00 | 45.00 | 200 | — |
| 1939 Proof | — | Value: 450 | | | | |
| 1940 | 600,000 | 1.50 | 3.00 | 20.00 | 75.00 | — |
| 1940 Proof | — | — | — | — | — | — |
| 1941 | 300,000 | 2.00 | 4.00 | 15.00 | 65.00 | — |
| 1941 Proof | — | — | — | — | — | — |
| 1942 | 1,200,000 | 1.00 | 2.00 | 7.50 | 55.00 | — |
| 1942 Proof | — | Value: 200 | | | | |

**6 PENCE** KM# 17a **Weight:** 2.8300 g. **Composition:** 0.5000 Silver .0454 oz. ASW

| Date | Mintage | F | VF | XF | Unc | BU |
|---|---|---|---|---|---|---|
| 1944 | 800,000 | 1.25 | 2.50 | 15.00 | 90.00 | — |
| 1945 | 400,000 | 15.00 | 25.00 | 45.00 | 150 | — |
| 1945 Proof | — | — | — | — | — | — |
| 1946 | 1,600,000 | 1.25 | 2.50 | 15.00 | 60.00 | — |
| 1946 Proof | — | — | — | — | — | — |

**6 PENCE** KM# 17b **Composition:** Copper-Nickel

| Date | Mintage | F | VF | XF | Unc | BU |
|---|---|---|---|---|---|---|
| 1947 | 5,000,000 | 0.50 | 1.00 | 4.00 | 20.00 | — |
| 1947 Proof | — | Value: 250 | | | | |

**6 PENCE** KM# 21 **Composition:** Copper-Nickel

| Date | Mintage | F | VF | XF | Unc | BU |
|---|---|---|---|---|---|---|
| 1948 | 1,000,000 | 0.50 | 1.25 | 4.50 | 27.50 | — |
| 1948 Proof | — | — | — | — | — | — |
| 1949 | 2,000,000 | 0.50 | 1.00 | 3.50 | 30.00 | — |
| 1949 Proof | — | Value: 250 | | | | |
| 1950 | 2,000,000 | 0.50 | 1.00 | 4.50 | 45.00 | — |
| 1950 Proof | — | Value: 250 | | | | |
| 1951 | 2,800,000 | 0.50 | 1.00 | 2.50 | 22.50 | — |
| 1951 Proof | — | — | — | — | — | — |
| 1952 | 1,200,000 | 0.50 | 1.50 | 3.50 | 45.00 | — |
| 1952 Proof | — | — | — | — | — | — |

**SHILLING** KM# 3 **Weight:** 5.6600 g. **Composition:** 0.9250 Silver .1683 oz. ASW **Reverse:** Bird sculpture

| Date | Mintage | F | VF | XF | Unc | BU |
|---|---|---|---|---|---|---|
| 1932 | 896,000 | 2.00 | 4.00 | 12.00 | 85.00 | — |
| 1932 Proof | — | Value: 90.00 | | | | |
| 1934 | 333,000 | 4.00 | 8.00 | 35.00 | 175 | — |
| 1935 | 830,000 | 2.00 | 4.00 | 12.00 | 125 | — |
| 1935 Proof | — | Value: 220 | | | | |
| 1936 | 1,663,000 | 1.50 | 3.50 | 10.00 | 125 | — |
| 1936 Proof | — | — | — | — | — | — |

**SHILLING** KM# 11 **Weight:** 5.6600 g. **Composition:** 0.9250 Silver .1683 oz. ASW

| Date | Mintage | F | VF | XF | Unc | BU |
|---|---|---|---|---|---|---|
| 1937 | 1,700,000 | 2.00 | 4.00 | 12.00 | 90.00 | — |
| 1937 Proof | — | Value: 300 | | | | |

**SHILLING** KM# 18 **Weight:** 5.6600 g. **Composition:** 0.9250 Silver .1683 oz. ASW **Obverse:** KING moved behind head

| Date | Mintage | F | VF | XF | Unc | BU |
|---|---|---|---|---|---|---|
| 1939 | 420,000 | 7.00 | 15.00 | 70.00 | 300 | — |
| 1939 Proof | — | Value: 500 | | | | |
| 1940 | 750,000 | 5.50 | 12.00 | 50.00 | 175 | — |
| 1940 Proof | — | — | — | — | — | — |
| 1941 | 800,000 | 6.50 | 12.00 | 45.00 | 150 | — |
| 1941 Proof | — | — | — | — | — | — |
| 1942 | 2,100,000 | 2.00 | 4.00 | 15.00 | 55.00 | — |
| 1942 Proof | — | — | — | — | — | — |

**SHILLING** KM# 18a **Weight:** 5.6600 g. **Composition:** 0.5000 Silver .0909 oz. ASW

| Date | Mintage | F | VF | XF | Unc | BU |
|---|---|---|---|---|---|---|
| 1944 | 1,600,000 | 2.00 | 4.00 | 12.50 | 80.00 | — |
| 1946 | 1,700,000 | 3.50 | 8.00 | 40.00 | 120 | — |
| 1946 Proof | — | — | — | — | — | — |

**SHILLING** KM# 18b **Composition:** Copper-Nickel

| Date | Mintage | F | VF | XF | Unc | BU |
|---|---|---|---|---|---|---|
| 1947 | 8,000,000 | 0.75 | 1.50 | 4.50 | 40.00 | — |
| 1947 Proof | — | Value: 300 | | | | |

**SHILLING** KM# 22 **Composition:** Copper-Nickel

| Date | Mintage | F | VF | XF | Unc | BU |
|---|---|---|---|---|---|---|
| 1948 | 1,500,000 | 0.75 | 1.50 | 6.50 | 30.00 | — |
| 1948 Proof | — | — | — | — | — | — |
| 1949 | 4,000,000 | 0.75 | 1.25 | 4.50 | 35.00 | — |
| 1949 Proof | — | Value: 250 | | | | |
| 1950 | 2,000,000 | 1.00 | 3.00 | 10.00 | 55.00 | — |
| 1950 Proof | — | Value: 225 | | | | |
| 1951 | 3,000,000 | 0.75 | 1.25 | 4.50 | 20.00 | — |
| 1951 Proof | — | — | — | — | — | — |
| 1952 | 2,600,000 | 0.75 | 1.50 | 4.50 | 55.00 | — |
| 1952 Proof | — | — | — | — | — | — |

**2 SHILLINGS** KM# 4 **Weight:** 11.3100 g. **Composition:** 0.9250 Silver .3363 oz. ASW **Reverse:** Sable antelope

| Date | Mintage | F | VF | XF | Unc | BU |
|---|---|---|---|---|---|---|
| 1932 | 498,000 | 4.00 | 10.00 | 30.00 | 110 | — |
| 1932 Proof | — | Value: 125 | | | | |
| 1934 | 154,000 | 12.50 | 20.00 | 60.00 | 225 | — |
| 1935 | 365,000 | 5.00 | 10.00 | 40.00 | 125 | — |
| 1935 Proof | — | — | — | — | — | — |
| 1936 | 683,000 | 5.00 | 10.00 | 40.00 | 125 | — |
| 1936 Proof | — | — | — | — | — | — |

**2 SHILLINGS** KM# 12 **Weight:** 11.3100 g. **Composition:** 0.9250 Silver .3363 oz. ASW

| Date | Mintage | F | VF | XF | Unc | BU |
|---|---|---|---|---|---|---|
| 1937 | 552,000 | 7.50 | 20.00 | 45.00 | 135 | — |
| 1937 Proof | — | Value: 400 | | | | |

**2 SHILLINGS** **KM# 19** **Weight:** 11.3100 g. **Composition:** 0.9250 Silver .3363 oz. ASW **Obverse:** KING moved behind head

| Date | Mintage | F | VF | XF | Unc | BU |
|---|---|---|---|---|---|---|
| 1939 | 120,000 | 50.00 | 125 | 350 | 650 | — |
| 1939 Proof | — | Value: 750 | | | | |
| 1940 | 525,000 | 8.00 | 16.00 | 75.00 | 250 | — |
| 1940 Proof | — | — | — | — | — | — |
| 1941 | 400,000 | 8.00 | 16.00 | 100 | 300 | — |
| 1941 Proof | — | — | — | — | — | — |
| 1942 | 850,000 | 4.00 | 8.00 | 25.00 | 90.00 | — |

**2 SHILLINGS** **KM# 19a** **Weight:** 11.3100 g. **Composition:** 0.5000 Silver .1818 oz. ASW

| Date | Mintage | F | VF | XF | Unc | BU |
|---|---|---|---|---|---|---|
| 1944 | 1,300,000 | 6.00 | 12.00 | 35.00 | 135 | — |
| 1946 | 700,000 | 100 | 200 | 300 | 650 | — |
| 1946 Proof | — | — | — | — | — | — |

**2 SHILLINGS** **KM# 19b** **Composition:** Copper-Nickel

| Date | Mintage | F | VF | XF | Unc | BU |
|---|---|---|---|---|---|---|
| 1947 | 3,750,000 | 1.75 | 4.00 | 12.50 | 55.00 | — |
| 1947 Proof | — | Value: 300 | | | | |

**2 SHILLINGS** **KM# 23** **Composition:** Copper-Nickel

| Date | Mintage | F | VF | XF | Unc | BU |
|---|---|---|---|---|---|---|
| 1948 | 750,000 | 1.00 | 3.00 | 10.00 | 40.00 | — |
| 1948 Proof | — | — | — | — | — | — |
| 1949 | 2,000,000 | 1.00 | 3.00 | 10.00 | 50.00 | — |
| 1949 Proof | — | Value: 350 | | | | |
| 1950 | 1,000,000 | 1.00 | 4.00 | 15.00 | 75.00 | — |
| 1950 Proof | — | Value: 350 | | | | |
| 1951 | 2,600,000 | 1.00 | 3.00 | 6.00 | 27.50 | — |
| 1951 Proof | — | — | — | — | — | — |
| 1952 | 1,800,000 | 1.00 | 3.00 | 10.00 | 75.00 | — |
| 1952 Proof | — | — | — | — | — | — |

**2 SHILLINGS** **KM# 30** **Composition:** Copper-Nickel

| Date | Mintage | F | VF | XF | Unc | BU |
|---|---|---|---|---|---|---|
| 1954 | 300,000 | 30.00 | 75.00 | 225 | 950 | — |
| 1954 Proof | 20 | Value: 1,250 | | | | |

**1/2 CROWN** **KM# 5** **Weight:** 14.1400 g. **Composition:** 0.9250 Silver .4205 oz. ASW

| Date | Mintage | F | VF | XF | Unc | BU |
|---|---|---|---|---|---|---|
| 1932 | 634,000 | 5.00 | 8.00 | 30.00 | 100 | — |
| 1932 Proof | — | Value: 125 | | | | |
| 1934 | 419,000 | 6.00 | 10.00 | 45.00 | 250 | — |
| 1934 Proof | — | — | — | — | — | — |
| 1935 | 512,000 | 5.00 | 8.00 | 32.50 | 175 | — |
| 1935 Proof | — | — | — | — | — | — |
| 1936 | 518,000 | 5.00 | 8.00 | 30.00 | 145 | — |
| 1936 Proof | — | — | — | — | — | — |

**1/2 CROWN** **KM# 13** **Weight:** 14.1400 g. **Composition:** 0.9250 Silver .4205 oz. ASW

| Date | Mintage | F | VF | XF | Unc | BU |
|---|---|---|---|---|---|---|
| 1937 | 1,174,000 | 4.50 | 8.00 | 30.00 | 135 | — |
| 1937 Proof | — | Value: 350 | | | | |

**1/2 CROWN** **KM# 15** **Weight:** 14.1400 g. **Composition:** 0.9250 Silver .4205 oz. ASW

| Date | Mintage | F | VF | XF | Unc | BU |
|---|---|---|---|---|---|---|
| 1938 | 400,000 | 5.00 | 8.50 | 32.00 | 150 | — |
| 1938 Proof | — | — | — | — | — | — |
| 1939 | 224,000 | 10.00 | 20.00 | 65.00 | 300 | — |
| 1939 Proof | — | Value: 500 | | | | |
| 1940 | 800,000 | 5.00 | 8.50 | 27.50 | 80.00 | — |
| 1940 Proof | — | — | — | — | — | — |
| 1941 | 1,240,000 | 3.00 | 6.00 | 15.00 | 65.00 | — |
| 1941 Proof | — | — | — | — | — | — |
| 1942 | 2,008,000 | 3.00 | 6.00 | 15.00 | 70.00 | — |
| 1942 Proof | — | — | — | — | — | — |

**1/2 CROWN** **KM# 15a** **Weight:** 14.1400 g. **Composition:** 0.5000 Silver .2273 oz. ASW

| Date | Mintage | F | VF | XF | Unc | BU |
|---|---|---|---|---|---|---|
| 1944 | 800,000 | 4.00 | 8.00 | 22.50 | 80.00 | — |
| 1946 | 1,400,000 | 4.00 | 10.00 | 27.50 | 150 | — |
| 1946 Proof | — | — | — | — | — | — |

**1/2 CROWN** **KM# 15b** **Composition:** Copper-Nickel

| Date | Mintage | F | VF | XF | Unc | BU |
|---|---|---|---|---|---|---|
| 1947 | 6,000,000 | 1.25 | 2.50 | 5.00 | 20.00 | — |
| 1947 Proof | — | Value: 300 | | | | |

**1/2 CROWN** **KM# 24** **Composition:** Copper-Nickel

| Date | Mintage | F | VF | XF | Unc | BU |
|---|---|---|---|---|---|---|
| 1948 | 800,000 | 1.25 | 2.50 | 10.00 | 50.00 | — |
| 1948 Proof | — | — | — | — | — | — |
| 1949 | 1,600,000 | 1.25 | 2.50 | 9.00 | 45.00 | — |
| 1949 Proof | — | Value: 450 | | | | |
| 1950 | 1,200,000 | 1.25 | 2.50 | 10.00 | 65.00 | — |
| 1950 Proof | — | Value: 450 | | | | |
| 1951 | 3,200,000 | 1.25 | 2.50 | 7.00 | 30.00 | — |
| 1951 Proof | — | Value: 350 | | | | |
| 1952 | 2,800,000 | 1.25 | 2.50 | 8.00 | 60.00 | — |
| 1952 Proof | — | Value: 350 | | | | |

**1/2 CROWN** **KM# 31** **Composition:** Copper-Nickel

| Date | Mintage | F | VF | XF | Unc | BU |
|---|---|---|---|---|---|---|
| 1954 | 1,200,000 | 10.00 | 17.50 | 45.00 | 85.00 | — |
| 1954 Proof | 20 | Value: 450 | | | | |

**CROWN** **KM# 27** **Weight:** 28.2800 g. **Composition:** 0.5000 Silver .4546 oz. ASW **Subject:** Birth of Cecil Rhodes Centennial **Edge Lettering:** 1853 OUT OF VISION CAME REALITY 1953 **Note:** Both upright and inverted edge varieties exist.

| Date | Mintage | F | VF | XF | Unc | BU |
|---|---|---|---|---|---|---|
| 1953 | 124,000 | 4.00 | 5.50 | 8.00 | 15.00 | — |
| 1953 Proof | 1,500 | Value: 85.00 | | | | |
| 1953 Matte Proof | — | Value: 350 | | | | |

## PROOF SETS

| KM# | Date | Mintage | Identification | Issue Price | Mkt Val |
|---|---|---|---|---|---|
| PS1 | 1932 (5) | 496 | KM#1-5 | — | 450 |
| PS2 | 1937 (6) | 40 | KM#8-13 | — | 2,000 |
| PS3 | 1939 (5) | 10 | KM#15-19 | — | 2,500 |
| PS6 | 1947 (5) | 10 | KM#15b-19b | — | 1,500 |
| PS4 | 1953 (2) | 3 | KM#27 Double set; Rare | — | — |
| PS5 | 1954 (4) | 20 | KM#28-31 | — | 2,500 |

The Spanish State, forming the greater part of the Iberian Peninsula of southwest Europe, has an area of 195,988 sq. mi. (504,714 sq. km.) and a population of 39.4 million including the Balearic and the Canary Islands. Capital: Madrid. The economy is based on agriculture, industry and tourism. Machinery, fruit, vegetables and chemicals are exported.

It isn't known when man first came to the Iberian Peninsula - the Altamira caves off the Cantabrian coast approximately 50 miles west of Santander were fashioned in Paleolithic times. Spain was a battleground for centuries before it became a united nation, fought for by Phoenicians, Carthaginians, Greeks, Celts, Romans, Vandals, Visigoths and Moors. Ferdinand and Isabella destroyed the last Moorish stronghold in 1492, freeing the national energy and resources for the era of discovery and colonization that would make Spain the most powerful country in Europe during the 16th century. After the destruction of the Spanish Armada, 1588, Spain never again played a major role in European politics. Forcing Ferdinand to give up his throne and placing him under military guard at Valencay in 1808, Napoleonic France ruled Spain until 1814. When the monarchy was restored in 1814 it continued, only interrupted by the short-lived republic of 1873-74, until the exile of Alfonso XIII in 1931 when the Second Republic was established.

Discontent against the mother country increased after1808 as colonists faced new imperialist policies from Napoleon or Spanish liberals. The revolutionary movement was established which resulted in the eventual independence of the Vice-royalties of New Spain, New Granada and Rio de la Plata within 2 decades.

The doomed republic was trapped in a tug-of-war between the right and left wing forces inevitably resulting in the Spanish Civil War of 1936-38. The leftist Republicans were supported by the U.S.S.R. and the International Brigade, which consisted of mainly communist volunteers from all over the western world. The right wing Nationalists were sup-ported by the Fascist governments of Italy and Germany. Under the leadership of Gen. Francisco Franco, the Nationalists emerged victorious and immediately embarked on a program of reconstruction and neutrality as dictated by the new "Caudillo"(leader) Franco.

The monarchy was reconstituted in 1947 under the regency of General Francisco Franco; the king designate to be crowned after Franco's death. Franco died on Nov.20, 1975. Two days after his passing, Juan Carlos de Borbon, the grandson of Alfonso XIII, was proclaimed King of Spain.

**RULERS**

Alfonso XIII, 1886-1931
2nd Republic and Civil War, 1931-1939
Francisco Franco, caudillo, 1939-1947
as Caudillo and regent, 1947-1975
Juan Carlos I, 1975-

**NOTE**: From 1868 to 1982, two dates may be found on most Spanish coinage. The larger date is the year of authorization and the smaller date incused on the two 6-pointed-stars found on most types is the year of issue. The latter appears in parentheses in these listings.

**MINT MARKS**

**Until 1980**
6-pointed star - Madrid
NOTE: Letters after date are initials of mint officials.

**After 1982**
Crowned M – Madrid

# KINGDOM, PRE-1931

## DECIMAL COINAGE

Peseta System

100 Centimos = 1 Peseta

**CENTIMO** **KM# 726** **Composition:** Bronze **Note:** Mint mark: 6-pointed star.

| Date | Mintage | F | VF | XF | Unc | BU |
|---|---|---|---|---|---|---|
| 1906 (6) SL-V | 7,500,000 | 0.25 | 0.65 | 1.25 | 3.50 | — |
| 1906 (6) SM-V | Inc. above | 100 | 300 | 400 | 600 | — |

**CENTIMO** **KM# 731** **Composition:** Bronze **Note:** Mint mark: 6-pointed star.

| Date | Mintage | F | VF | XF | Unc | BU |
|---|---|---|---|---|---|---|
| 1911 (1) PC-V | 1,462,000 | 20.00 | 40.00 | 60.00 | 85.00 | — |
| 1912 (2) PC-V | 2,109,000 | 1.50 | 2.50 | 4.00 | 9.00 | — |
| 1913 (3) PC-V | 1,429,000 | 2.50 | 5.00 | 10.00 | 20.00 | — |

**2 CENTIMOS** **KM# 722** **Composition:** Copper **Note:** Mint mark: 6-pointed star.

| Date | Mintage | F | VF | XF | Unc | BU |
|---|---|---|---|---|---|---|
| 1904 (04) SM-V | 10,000,000 | 0.35 | 1.50 | 3.50 | 8.00 | — |
| 1905 (05) SM-V | 5,000,000 | 0.35 | 2.00 | 4.50 | 9.00 | — |

**2 CENTIMOS** **KM# 732** **Composition:** Copper **Note:** Mint mark: 6-pointed star.

| Date | Mintage | F | VF | XF | Unc | BU |
|---|---|---|---|---|---|---|
| 1911 (11) PC-V | 2,284,000 | 0.35 | 1.50 | 3.50 | 9.50 | — |
| 1912 (12) PC-V | 5,216,000 | 0.35 | 1.50 | 3.00 | 8.50 | — |

**25 CENTIMOS** **KM# 740** **Composition:** Copper-Nickel

| Date | Mintage | F | VF | XF | Unc | BU |
|---|---|---|---|---|---|---|
| 1925 PC-S | 8,001,000 | 0.35 | 1.50 | 10.00 | 30.00 | — |

**25 CENTIMOS** **KM# 742** **Composition:** Copper-Nickel

| Date | Mintage | F | VF | XF | Unc | BU |
|---|---|---|---|---|---|---|
| 1927 PC-S | 12,000,000 | 0.35 | 1.00 | 8.00 | 30.00 | — |

**50 CENTIMOS** **KM# 723** **Weight:** 2.5000 g. **Composition:** 0.8350 Silver .0671 oz. ASW **Note:** Mint mark: 6-pointed star.

| Date | Mintage | F | VF | XF | Unc | BU |
|---|---|---|---|---|---|---|
| 1904 (04) SM-V | 4,851,000 | 1.25 | 2.25 | 4.00 | 15.00 | — |
| 1904 (10) PC-V | 1,303,000 | 1.25 | 2.50 | 5.00 | 18.00 | — |

**50 CENTIMOS** **KM# 730** **Weight:** 2.5000 g. **Composition:** 0.8350 Silver .0671 oz. ASW **Note:** Mint mark: 6-pointed star.

| Date | Mintage | F | VF | XF | Unc | BU |
|---|---|---|---|---|---|---|
| 1910 (10) PC-V | 4,526,000 | 1.25 | 3.00 | 6.00 | 20.00 | — |

**50 CENTIMOS** **KM# 741** **Weight:** 2.5000 g. **Composition:** 0.8350 Silver .0671 oz. ASW

| Date | Mintage | VG | F | VF | XF | Unc |
|---|---|---|---|---|---|---|
| 1926 PC-S | 4,000,000 | — | 1.25 | 2.25 | 3.25 | 9.00 |

**PESETA** **KM# 721** **Weight:** 5.0000 g. **Composition:** 0.8350 Silver .1342 oz. ASW **Note:** Mint mark 6 pointed star

| Date | Mintage | VG | F | VF | XF | Unc |
|---|---|---|---|---|---|---|
| 1903 (03) SM-V | 10,602,000 | — | 2.00 | 4.50 | 18.00 | 50.00 |
| 1904 (04) SM-V | 5,294,000 | — | 2.00 | 6.50 | 25.00 | 65.00 |
| 1905 (05) SM-V | 492,000 | — | 40.00 | 100 | 375 | 750 |

**2 PESETAS** **KM# 725** **Weight:** 10.0000 g. **Composition:** 0.8350 Silver .2685 oz. ASW **Note:** Mint mark: 6-pointed star.

| Date | Mintage | F | VF | XF | Unc | BU |
|---|---|---|---|---|---|---|
| 1905 (05) SM-V | 3,589,000 | 4.50 | 7.00 | 14.00 | 22.50 | — |

# REPUBLIC

## 1931 - 1939

## DECIMAL COINAGE

Peseta System

100 Centimos = 1 Peseta

**5 CENTIMOS** **KM# 752** **Composition:** Iron

| Date | Mintage | F | VF | XF | Unc | BU |
|---|---|---|---|---|---|---|
| 1937 | 10,000,000 | 0.35 | 1.00 | 3.00 | 6.00 | — |

**10 CENTIMOS** **KM# 756** **Composition:** Iron

| Date | Mintage | F | VF | XF | Unc | BU |
|---|---|---|---|---|---|---|
| 1938 | 1,000 | 350 | 750 | 1,350 | 1,850 | — |

**Note:** This coin was never released into circulation

**25 CENTIMOS** **KM# 751** **Composition:** Copper-Nickel

| Date | Mintage | F | VF | XF | Unc | BU |
|---|---|---|---|---|---|---|
| 1934 | 12,272,000 | 0.20 | 0.50 | 3.50 | 12.00 | — |

**25 CENTIMOS KM# 753 Composition:** Copper-Nickel **Note:** Struck at the Vienna mint

| Date | Mintage | F | VF | XF | Unc | BU |
|---|---|---|---|---|---|---|
| 1937 | 42.000.000 | 0.20 | 0.40 | 1.00 | 3.00 | — |

**Note:** This coin was issued by way of decree April 5, 1938, by Franco and the Nationalist forces that controlled the majority of Spain by this point in time

**25 CENTIMOS KM# 757 Composition:** Copper

| Date | Mintage | F | VF | XF | Unc | BU |
|---|---|---|---|---|---|---|
| 1938 | 45.500.000 | 0.75 | 1.50 | 3.50 | 6.50 | — |

**50 CENTIMOS KM# 754.2 Composition:** Copper **Reverse:** Border of rectangles **Note:** Mint mark: 6-pointed star.

| Date | Mintage | F | VF | XF | Unc | BU |
|---|---|---|---|---|---|---|
| 1937 (36) | Inc. above | 1.00 | 2.50 | 5.00 | 18.00 | — |

**50 CENTIMOS KM# 754.1 Composition:** Copper **Reverse:** Border of dots **Note:** Mint mark: 6-pointed star. Several varieties exist.

| Date | Mintage | F | VF | XF | Unc | BU |
|---|---|---|---|---|---|---|
| 1937 (34) | 50.000.000 | 0.35 | 1.50 | 4.00 | 12.00 | — |
| 1937 (36) | 1.000.000 | 0.35 | 1.25 | 3.00 | 10.00 | — |
| 1937 Without stars | Inc. above | 3.00 | 6.00 | 12.00 | 25.00 | — |

**PESETA KM# 750 Weight:** 5.0000 g. **Composition:** 0.8350 Silver .1342 oz. ASW **Note:** Mint mark: 6-pointed star.

| Date | Mintage | F | VF | XF | Unc | BU |
|---|---|---|---|---|---|---|
| 1933 (3-4) | 2.000.000 | 4.00 | 8.00 | 14.00 | 20.00 | — |

**Note:** Rotated reverse varieties exist, with values increasing by the degree of rotation.

**PESETA KM# 755 Composition:** Brass

| Date | Mintage | F | VF | XF | Unc | BU |
|---|---|---|---|---|---|---|
| 1937 | 50.000.000 | 0.35 | 0.75 | 1.75 | 4.50 | — |

# NATIONALIST GOVERNMENT
## 1939 - 1947

## DECIMAL COINAGE
Peseta System

100 Centimos = 1 Peseta

**5 CENTIMOS KM# 765 Composition:** Aluminum **Note:** Mint mark: 6-pointed star. To realize the values below all Unc. and BU coins must have full strike including letters.

| Date | Mintage | F | VF | XF | Unc | BU |
|---|---|---|---|---|---|---|
| 1940 | 175.000.000 | — | 1.50 | 5.00 | 20.00 | 30.00 |
| 1941 | 202.107.000 | — | 0.50 | 2.00 | 8.00 | 12.00 |
| 1945 | 221.500.000 | — | 0.25 | 1.00 | 4.00 | 8.00 |
| 1953 | 31.573.000 | — | 7.50 | 12.50 | 40.00 | 60.00 |

**10 CENTIMOS KM# 766 Composition:** Aluminum **Note:** Mint mark: 6-pointed star. Varieties exist. To realize the values below all Unc. and BU coins must have full strike including letters.

| Date | Mintage | F | VF | XF | Unc | BU |
|---|---|---|---|---|---|---|
| 1940 | 225.000.000 | — | 2.00 | 6.00 | 25.00 | 35.00 |
| 1941 | 247.981.000 | — | 0.75 | 3.50 | 8.00 | 12.00 |
| 1945 | 250.000.000 | — | 0.50 | 2.00 | 5.00 | 8.00 |
| 1953 | 865.850.000 | — | 0.35 | 1.25 | 3.50 | 4.50 |

**PESETA KM# 767 Composition:** Aluminum-Bronze **Note:** Mint mark: 6-pointed star. To realize the values below all Unc. and BU coins must have full strike including letters.

| Date | Mintage | F | VF | XF | Unc | BU |
|---|---|---|---|---|---|---|
| 1944 | 150.000.000 | — | 0.25 | 6.50 | 15.00 | 25.00 |

# KINGDOM, 1949-PRESENT

## DECIMAL COINAGE
Peseta System

100 Centimos = 1 Peseta

**10 CENTIMOS KM# 790 Composition:** Aluminum **Note:** Mint mark: 6-pointed star.

| Date | Mintage | F | VF | XF | Unc | BU |
|---|---|---|---|---|---|---|
| 1959 | 900.000.000 | — | — | — | 0.10 | 0.15 |
| 1959 Proof | 101.000 | Value: 1.50 | | | | |

**50 CENTIMOS KM# 776 Composition:** Copper-Nickel **Reverse:** Arrows pointing down **Note:** Mint mark: 6-pointed star.

| Date | Mintage | F | VF | XF | Unc | BU |
|---|---|---|---|---|---|---|
| 1949 (51) | 990.000 | — | 5.00 | 8.00 | 18.00 | 30.00 |

**50 CENTIMOS KM# 777 Composition:** Copper-Nickel **Reverse:** Arrows pointing up **Note:** Mint mark: 6-pointed star.

| Date | Mintage | F | VF | XF | Unc | BU |
|---|---|---|---|---|---|---|
| 1949 (51) | 8.010.000 | — | 0.25 | 3.00 | 12.00 | 20.00 |
| 1949 (E51) | Est. 5.000 | — | — | — | 450 | 700 |

**Note:** Issued to commemorate a numismatic exposition December 2, 1951. An E replaces the 19 on the lower star

| Date | Mintage | F | VF | XF | Unc | BU |
|---|---|---|---|---|---|---|
| 1949 (52) | 18.567.000 | — | 0.15 | 1.50 | 9.00 | 16.00 |
| 1949 (53) | 17.500.000 | — | 0.15 | 3.00 | 20.00 | 30.00 |
| 1949 (54) | 37.000.000 | — | 0.15 | 2.50 | 8.00 | 16.00 |
| 1949 (56) | 38.000.000 | — | 0.15 | 2.00 | 7.00 | 15.00 |
| 1949 (62) | 31.000.000 | — | 0.15 | 1.00 | 5.00 | 10.00 |
| 1963 (63) | 4.000.000 | — | 0.15 | 5.00 | 22.00 | 35.00 |

| Date | Mintage | F | VF | XF | Unc | BU |
|---|---|---|---|---|---|---|
| 1963 (64) | 20.000.000 | — | 0.10 | 0.25 | 1.50 | 3.50 |
| 1963 (65) | 14.000.000 | — | 0.10 | 0.25 | 1.50 | 2.50 |

**50 CENTIMOS KM# 795 Composition:** Aluminum **Note:** Mint mark: 6 pointed star

| Date | Mintage | F | VF | XF | Unc | BU |
|---|---|---|---|---|---|---|
| 1966 (67) | 80.000.000 | — | — | 0.10 | 0.50 | 0.75 |
| 1966 (68) | 100.000.000 | — | — | 0.10 | 0.25 | 0.45 |
| 1966 (69) | 50.000.000 | — | — | 0.25 | 1.00 | 2.00 |
| 1966 (70) Prooflike | Est. 6.000 | Value: 100 | | | | |
| 1966 (71) | 99.000.000 | — | — | 0.10 | 0.25 | 0.50 |
| 1966 (72) | 2.283.000 | — | — | 0.25 | 1.25 | 2.00 |
| 1966 (72) Proof | 23.000 | Value: 4.00 | | | | |
| 1966 (73) | 10.000.000 | — | — | 0.10 | 0.25 | 0.50 |
| 1966 (73) Proof | 28.000 | Value: 1.50 | | | | |
| 1966 (74) Proof | 25.000 | Value: 35.00 | | | | |
| 1966 (75) Proof | 75.000 | Value: 5.00 | | | | |

**50 CENTIMOS KM# 805 Composition:** Copper-Nickel **Note:** Mint mark: 6 pointed star

| Date | Mintage | F | VF | XF | Unc | BU |
|---|---|---|---|---|---|---|
| 1975 (76) | 4.060.000 | — | — | 0.10 | 0.25 | 0.45 |
| 1975 (76) | — | Value: 0.85 | | | | |

**50 CENTIMOS KM# 815 Center Composition:** Aluminum **Subject:** World Cup Soccer Games **Note:** Mint mark: 6 pointed star

| Date | Mintage | F | VF | XF | Unc | BU |
|---|---|---|---|---|---|---|
| 1980 (80) | 15.000.000 | — | — | 0.10 | 0.20 | 0.35 |

**PESETA KM# 775 Composition:** Aluminum-Bronze **Note:** Mint mark: 6-pointed star.

| Date | Mintage | F | VF | XF | Unc | BU |
|---|---|---|---|---|---|---|
| 1946 (46) | Est. 5.000 | — | 750 | 1,500 | — | — |
| 1947 (48) | 15.000.000 | — | 1.00 | 15.00 | 75.00 | 125 |
| 1947 (49) | 27.600.000 | — | 0.75 | 15.00 | 65.00 | 100 |
| 1947 (50) | 4.000.000 | — | 5.00 | 20.00 | 140 | 335 |
| 1947 (51) | 9.185.000 | — | 2.50 | 12.00 | 85.00 | 275 |
| 1947 (E51) | Est. 5.000 | — | — | — | 425 | 550 |

**Note:** Issued to commemorate the Second National Numismatic Exposition December 2, 1951. An E replaces the 19 on the lower star.

| Date | Mintage | F | VF | XF | Unc | BU |
|---|---|---|---|---|---|---|
| 1947 (52) | 19.195.000 | — | 1.00 | 5.00 | 45.00 | 75.00 |
| 1947 (53) | 34.000.000 | — | 0.75 | 4.00 | 28.00 | 50.00 |
| 1947 (54) | 50.000.000 | — | 0.75 | 4.00 | 28.00 | 55.00 |
| 1947 (56) | — | — | 15.00 | 45.00 | 225 | 375 |
| 1953 (54) | 40.272.000 | — | 4.00 | 15.00 | 100 | 225 |
| 1953 (56) | 118.000.000 | — | 0.10 | 0.75 | 3.50 | 6.00 |
| 1953 (60) | 45.160.000 | — | 0.75 | 8.00 | 35.00 | 85.00 |
| 1953 (61) | 25.830.000 | — | 0.60 | 6.00 | 25.00 | 55.00 |
| 1953 (62) | 66.252.000 | — | 0.10 | 0.50 | 1.75 | 3.50 |
| 1953 (63) | 37.000.000 | — | 0.25 | 1.50 | 6.00 | 15.00 |
| 1963 (63) | 36.000.000 | — | 0.25 | 1.50 | 8.00 | 15.00 |
| 1963 (64) | 80.000.000 | — | 0.10 | 0.50 | 1.75 | 3.00 |
| 1963 (65) | 70.000.000 | — | 0.10 | 0.50 | 1.75 | 3.00 |
| 1963 (66) | 63.000.000 | — | 0.10 | 0.50 | 2.00 | 4.50 |
| 1963 (67) | 11.300.000 | — | 2.00 | 6.00 | 30.00 | 60.00 |

**PESETA** **KM# 796** **Composition:** Aluminum-Bronze **Note:** Mint mark: 6-pointed star.

| Date | Mintage | F | VF | XF | Unc | BU |
|---|---|---|---|---|---|---|
| 1966 (74) | 25,000 | Value: 1.00 | | | | |
| 1966 (68) | 120,000,000 | — | 0.10 | 0.20 | 1.00 | 1.50 |
| 1966 (69) | 120,000,000 | — | 0.10 | 0.20 | 1.00 | 1.50 |
| 1966 (70) | 75,000,000 | — | 0.10 | 0.20 | 1.75 | 2.50 |
| 1966 (71) | 115,270,000 | — | 0.10 | 0.20 | 1.00 | 1.25 |
| 1966 (72) | 106,000,000 | — | — | 0.10 | 0.50 | 0.75 |
| 1966 (72) | 23,000 | Value: 1.50 | | | | |
| 1966 (73) | 152,000,000 | — | — | 0.10 | 0.35 | 0.65 |
| 1966 (73) | 28,000,000 | Value: 1.00 | | | | |
| 1966 (74) | 181,000,000 | — | — | 0.10 | 0.35 | 0.65 |
| 1966 (75) | 227,580,000 | — | — | 0.10 | 0.25 | 0.35 |
| 1966 (75) | 25,000 | Value: 0.50 | | | | |

**PESETA** **KM# 806** **Composition:** Aluminum-Bronze **Note:** Two varieties of tilde size for the n in Espana exist of this date. Large is Madrid mint, small is Santiago de Chile.

| Date | Mintage | F | VF | XF | Unc | BU |
|---|---|---|---|---|---|---|
| 1975 (76) | 170,380,000 | — | — | 0.10 | 0.25 | 0.35 |
| 1975 (76) | 177,080,000 | Value: 0.75 | | | | |
| 1975 (77) | 243,380,000 | — | — | 0.10 | 0.25 | 0.35 |
| 1975 (77) | Inc. above | Value: 0.75 | | | | |
| 1975 (78) | Est. 603,320,000 | — | — | 0.10 | 0.25 | 0.35 |
| 1975 (79) | 507,000,000 | — | — | 0.10 | 0.25 | 0.35 |
| 1975 (79) | — | Value: 0.75 | | | | |
| 1975 (80) | 590,000,000 | — | — | 0.10 | 0.25 | 0.35 |

**PESETA** **KM# 816** **Composition:** Aluminum-Bronze **Subject:** World Cup Soccer Games

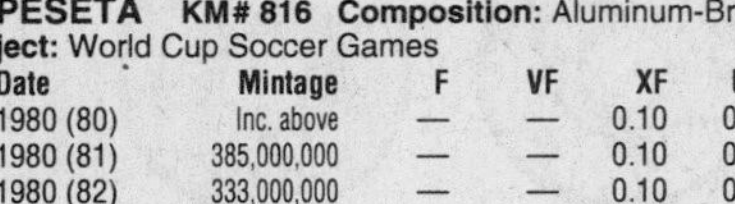

| Date | Mintage | F | VF | XF | Unc | BU |
|---|---|---|---|---|---|---|
| 1980 (80) | Inc. above | — | — | 0.10 | 0.20 | 0.30 |
| 1980 (81) | 385,000,000 | — | — | 0.10 | 0.25 | 0.35 |
| 1980 (82) | 333,000,000 | — | — | 0.10 | 0.25 | 0.35 |

**PESETA** **KM# 821** **Composition:** Aluminum

| Date | Mintage | F | VF | XF | Unc | BU |
|---|---|---|---|---|---|---|
| 1982 | — | — | — | 0.10 | 0.20 | 0.35 |
| **Note:** Mintage included in KM#816, 1980 (82) | | | | | | |
| 1983 | 52,000,000 | — | — | 0.10 | 0.50 | 1.00 |
| 1984 | 131,000,000 | — | — | 0.10 | 0.20 | 0.35 |
| 1985 | 220,065,000 | — | — | 0.10 | 0.20 | 0.35 |
| 1986 | 299,960,000 | — | — | 0.10 | 0.20 | 0.35 |
| 1987 | 299,550,000 | — | — | 0.10 | 0.20 | 0.35 |
| 1988 | 223,460,000 | — | — | 0.10 | 0.20 | 0.35 |
| 1989 | — | — | — | 0.10 | 0.50 | 1.00 |
| **Note:** Mintage included in KM#832, 1989 | | | | | | |

**PESETA** **KM# 832** **Composition:** Aluminum

| Date | Mintage | F | VF | XF | Unc | BU |
|---|---|---|---|---|---|---|
| 1989 | 198,415,000 | — | — | 0.10 | 0.20 | 0.25 |
| 1990 | 197,700,000 | — | — | 0.10 | 0.20 | 0.25 |
| 1991 | 173,780,000 | — | — | 0.10 | 0.30 | 0.50 |
| 1992 | 168,870,000 | — | — | 0.10 | 0.20 | 0.25 |
| 1993 | 300,013,000 | — | — | 0.10 | 0.20 | 0.25 |
| 1994 | 162,860,000 | — | — | 0.10 | 0.20 | 0.25 |
| 1995 | 183,175,000 | — | — | 0.10 | 0.20 | 0.25 |
| 1996 | 101,885,000 | — | — | 0.10 | 0.20 | 0.25 |
| 1997 | — | — | — | 0.10 | 0.20 | 0.25 |
| 1998 | — | — | — | 0.10 | 0.20 | 0.25 |
| 1999 | — | — | — | 0.10 | 0.20 | 0.25 |
| 2000 | — | — | — | 0.10 | 0.20 | 0.25 |
| 2001 | — | — | — | 0.10 | 0.20 | 0.25 |

**2 PESETAS** **KM# 822** **Composition:** Aluminum

| Date | Mintage | F | VF | XF | Unc | BU |
|---|---|---|---|---|---|---|
| 1984 | 47,650,000 | — | — | 0.10 | 0.30 | 0.50 |

**2-1/2 PESETAS** **KM# 785** **Composition:** Aluminum-Bronze

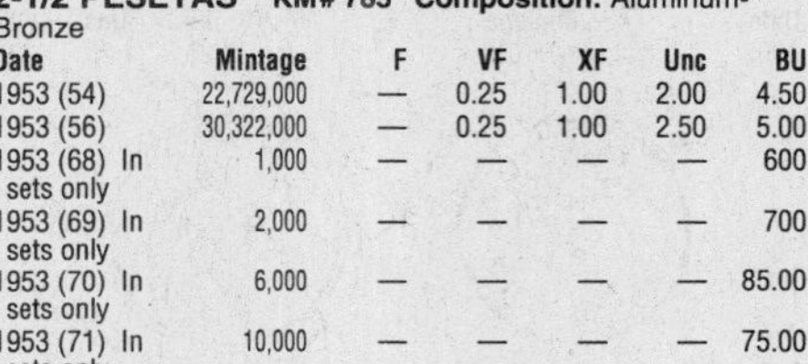

| Date | Mintage | F | VF | XF | Unc | BU |
|---|---|---|---|---|---|---|
| 1953 (54) | 22,729,000 | — | 0.25 | 1.00 | 2.00 | 4.50 |
| 1953 (56) | 30,322,000 | — | 0.25 | 1.00 | 2.50 | 5.00 |
| 1953 (68) In sets only | 1,000 | — | — | — | — | 600 |
| 1953 (69) In sets only | 2,000 | — | — | — | — | 700 |
| 1953 (70) In sets only | 6,000 | — | — | — | — | 85.00 |
| 1953 (71) In sets only | 10,000 | — | — | — | — | 75.00 |

**5 PESETAS** **KM# 778** **Composition:** Nickel

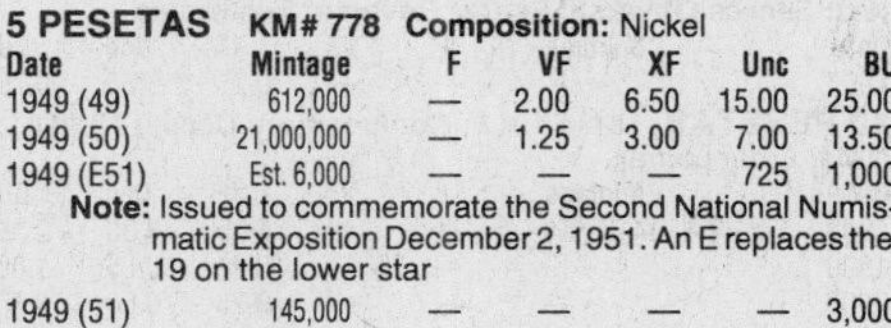

| Date | Mintage | F | VF | XF | Unc | BU |
|---|---|---|---|---|---|---|
| 1949 (49) | 612,000 | — | 2.00 | 6.50 | 15.00 | 25.00 |
| 1949 (50) | 21,000,000 | — | 1.25 | 3.00 | 7.00 | 13.50 |
| 1949 (E51) | Est. 6,000 | — | — | — | 725 | 1,000 |
| **Note:** Issued to commemorate the Second National Numismatic Exposition December 2, 1951. An E replaces the 19 on the lower star | | | | | | |
| 1949 (51) | 145,000 | — | — | — | — | 3,000 |
| 1949 (52) | Est. 200,000 | — | — | — | — | 5,000 |

**5 PESETAS** **KM# 786** **Composition:** Copper-Nickel **Note:** For issues struck from 1958 to 1968 prices in uncirculated drop substantially when the PLUS in legend is not fully struck and readable.

| Date | Mintage | F | VF | XF | Unc | BU |
|---|---|---|---|---|---|---|
| 1957 (58) | 13,000,000 | — | 0.75 | 4.00 | 30.00 | 60.00 |
| 1957 BA | Est. 43,000 | — | 40.00 | 75.00 | 120 | 165 |
| **Note:** Issued to commemorate the 1958 2nd Ibero-American Numismatic Exposition in Barcelona with BA replacing the star on left side of reverse | | | | | | |
| 1957 (59) | 107,000,000 | — | 0.10 | 1.00 | 10.00 | 17.00 |
| 1957 (60) | 26,000,000 | — | 0.10 | 0.75 | 7.50 | 15.00 |
| 1957 (61) | 78,992,000 | — | 0.10 | 2.00 | 12.50 | 22.50 |
| 1957 (62) | 40,963,000 | — | 0.10 | 1.00 | 3.50 | 12.50 |
| 1957 (63) | 50,000,000 | — | 2.00 | 15.00 | 70.00 | 135 |
| 1957 (64) | 51,000,000 | — | 0.10 | 0.75 | 8.00 | 16.00 |
| 1957 (65) | 25,000,000 | — | 0.10 | 0.25 | 4.50 | 7.50 |
| 1957 (66) | 28,000,000 | — | 0.10 | 1.00 | 10.00 | 20.00 |
| 1957 (67) | 30,000,000 | — | 0.10 | 0.25 | 2.00 | 3.50 |
| 1957 (68) | 60,000,000 | — | 0.10 | 0.25 | 1.75 | 3.00 |
| 1957 (69) | 40,000,000 | — | 0.10 | 0.25 | 2.25 | 4.00 |
| 1957 (70) | 43,000,000 | — | 0.10 | 0.25 | 3.00 | 7.00 |
| 1957 (71) | 77,000,000 | — | 0.10 | 0.25 | 1.50 | 3.00 |
| 1957 (72) | 70,000,000 | — | — | 0.10 | 1.50 | 3.00 |
| 1957 (72) | 23,000 | Value: 5.00 | | | | |
| 1957 (73) | 78,000,000 | — | — | 0.10 | 0.75 | 1.00 |
| 1957 (73) | 28,000 | Value: 2.00 | | | | |
| 1957 (74) | 100,000,000 | — | — | 0.10 | 0.45 | 0.75 |
| 1957 (74) | 25,000 | Value: 2.00 | | | | |
| 1957 (75) | 139,047,000 | — | — | 0.10 | 0.25 | 0.45 |
| 1957 (75) | 25,000 | Value: 1.00 | | | | |

**5 PESETAS** **KM# 811** **Composition:** Copper-Nickel **Obverse:** KM#807 **Reverse:** KM#817 with (80) star **Note:** Mule.

| Date | Mintage | F | VF | XF | Unc | BU |
|---|---|---|---|---|---|---|
| 1975 (80) | Est. 30,000 | — | — | 80.00 | 145 | 175 |

**5 PESETAS** **KM# 807** **Composition:** Copper-Nickel

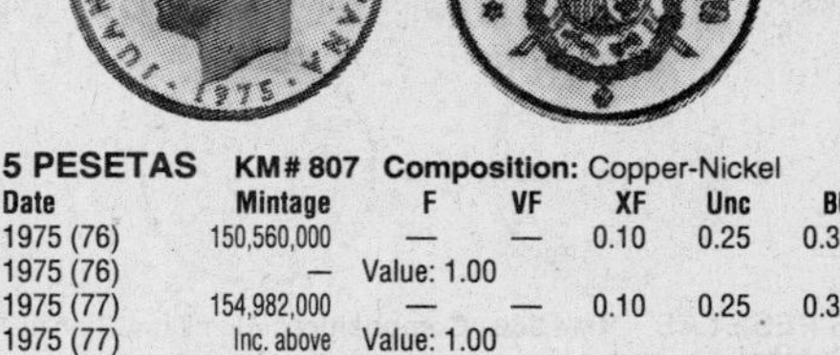

| Date | Mintage | F | VF | XF | Unc | BU |
|---|---|---|---|---|---|---|
| 1975 (76) | 150,560,000 | — | — | 0.10 | 0.25 | 0.35 |
| 1975 (76) | — | Value: 1.00 | | | | |
| 1975 (77) | 154,982,000 | — | — | 0.10 | 0.25 | 0.35 |
| 1975 (77) | Inc. above | Value: 1.00 | | | | |
| 1975 (78) | 412,610,000 | — | — | 0.10 | 0.50 | 1.00 |
| 1975 (79) | 436,000,000 | — | — | 0.10 | 0.25 | 0.35 |
| 1975 (79) | — | Value: 1.00 | | | | |
| 1975 (80) | 322,000,000 | — | — | 0.10 | 0.50 | 1.00 |

**5 PESETAS** **KM# 817** **Composition:** Copper-Nickel **Subject:** World Cup Soccer Games

| Date | Mintage | F | VF | XF | Unc | BU |
|---|---|---|---|---|---|---|
| 1980 (80) | 75,000,000 | — | — | 0.10 | 0.25 | 0.35 |
| 1980 (81) | 294,000,000 | — | — | 0.10 | 0.25 | 0.50 |
| 1980 (82) | 291,000,000 | — | — | 0.10 | 0.25 | 0.50 |

**5 PESETAS** **KM# 823** **Composition:** Copper-Nickel **Note:** Mint mark: Crowned M.

| Date | Mintage | F | VF | XF | Unc | BU |
|---|---|---|---|---|---|---|
| 1982 | — | — | — | 0.10 | 0.75 | 1.50 |
| **Note:** Mintage included in KM#817, 1980 (82) | | | | | | |
| 1983 | 200,000,000 | — | — | 0.10 | 0.25 | 0.50 |
| 1984 | 169,000,000 | — | — | 0.10 | 0.45 | 0.80 |
| 1989 | — | — | — | 0.10 | 0.35 | 0.75 |

**5 PESETAS** **KM# 833** **Composition:** Aluminum-Bronze

| Date | Mintage | F | VF | XF | Unc | BU |
|---|---|---|---|---|---|---|
| 1989 | 109,270,000 | — | — | 0.10 | 0.25 | 0.40 |
| 1990 | 191,740,000 | — | — | 0.10 | 0.25 | 0.50 |
| 1991 | 313,820,000 | — | — | 0.10 | 0.25 | 0.35 |
| 1992 | 493,224,000 | — | — | 0.10 | 0.25 | 0.35 |
| 1998 | — | — | — | 0.10 | 0.25 | 0.35 |
| 2000 | — | — | — | 0.10 | 0.25 | 0.35 |
| 2001 | — | — | — | 0.10 | 0.25 | 0.35 |

**5 PESETAS** **KM# 919** **Composition:** Nickel-Brass **Subject:** Jacobeo **Note:** Coins with extra metal in the denomination 5 sell for a premium.

| Date | Mintage | F | VF | XF | Unc | BU |
|---|---|---|---|---|---|---|
| 1993 | 372,746,000 | — | — | — | 0.20 | 0.35 |

**5 PESETAS** **KM# 931** **Composition:** Nickel-Brass **Subject:** Aragon **Note:** Wide rim variety exists.

| Date | Mintage | F | VF | XF | Unc | BU |
|---|---|---|---|---|---|---|
| 1994 | 199,678,000 | — | — | — | 0.20 | 0.35 |

**5 PESETAS** **KM# 946** **Composition:** Aluminum-Bronze **Subject:** Asturias

| Date | Mintage | F | VF | XF | Unc | BU |
|---|---|---|---|---|---|---|
| 1995 | 301,756,000 | — | — | — | 0.20 | 0.35 |

**5 PESETAS** **KM# 960** **Composition:** Aluminum-Bronze **Subject:** La Rioja

| Date | Mintage | F | VF | XF | Unc | BU |
|---|---|---|---|---|---|---|
| 1996 | 199,091,000 | — | — | — | 0.20 | 0.35 |

**5 PESETAS** **KM# 981** **Composition:** Brass **Subject:** Balearic Islands **Obverse:** Stone monument **Reverse:** Horse and rider

| Date | Mintage | F | VF | XF | Unc | BU |
|---|---|---|---|---|---|---|
| 1997 | — | — | — | — | 0.20 | 0.35 |

**5 PESETAS** **KM# 1008** **Composition:** Brass **Reverse:** Waterwheel

| Date | Mintage | F | VF | XF | Unc | BU |
|---|---|---|---|---|---|---|
| 1999 | — | — | — | — | 0.20 | 0.35 |

**10 PESETAS** **KM# 827** **Composition:** Copper-Nickel **Note:** Denomination DIEZ

| Date | Mintage | F | VF | XF | Unc | BU |
|---|---|---|---|---|---|---|
| 1983 | 149,000,000 | — | — | 0.25 | 0.35 | 0.40 |
| 1984 | 66,000,000 | — | — | 0.25 | 0.50 | 0.75 |
| 1985 | 45,706,000 | — | — | 0.25 | 0.50 | 0.60 |

**10 PESETAS** **KM# 903** **Composition:** Copper-Nickel

| Date | Mintage | F | VF | XF | Unc | BU |
|---|---|---|---|---|---|---|
| 1992 | 51,820,000 | — | — | 0.25 | 0.30 | 0.35 |
| 1998 | — | — | — | 0.25 | 0.30 | 0.35 |
| 1999 | 2,125,000 | — | — | 0.35 | 0.75 | 1.00 |

**10 PESETAS** **KM# 918** **Composition:** Copper-Nickel **Subject:** Juan Miro

| Date | Mintage | F | VF | XF | Unc | BU |
|---|---|---|---|---|---|---|
| 1993 | 53,845,000 | — | — | 0.25 | 0.40 | 0.65 |

**10 PESETAS** **KM# 932** **Composition:** Copper-Nickel **Subject:** Musician P. Sarasate

| Date | Mintage | F | VF | XF | Unc | BU |
|---|---|---|---|---|---|---|
| 1994 | 3,050,000 | — | — | 0.25 | 0.65 | 1.00 |

**10 PESETAS** **KM# 947** **Composition:** Copper-Nickel **Subject:** Don Francisco de Quevedo

| Date | Mintage | F | VF | XF | Unc | BU |
|---|---|---|---|---|---|---|
| 1995 | 1,050,000 | — | — | 0.25 | 1.25 | 2.00 |

**10 PESETAS** **KM# 961** **Composition:** Copper-Nickel **Subject:** Emilia Pardo Bazan

| Date | Mintage | F | VF | XF | Unc | BU |
|---|---|---|---|---|---|---|
| 1996 | 1,060,000 | — | — | 0.25 | 0.85 | 1.25 |

**10 PESETAS** **KM# 982** **Composition:** Copper-Nickel **Subject:** Seneca **Obverse:** Portrait **Reverse:** Castle gate

| Date | Mintage | F | VF | XF | Unc | BU |
|---|---|---|---|---|---|---|
| 1997 | — | — | — | 0.25 | 0.65 | 0.75 |

**10 PESETAS** **KM# 1012** **Composition:** Copper-Nickel **Note:** Older portrait.

| Date | Mintage | F | VF | XF | Unc | BU |
|---|---|---|---|---|---|---|
| 1998 | 14,965,000 | — | — | 0.25 | 0.30 | 0.35 |
| 1999 | — | — | — | 0.25 | 0.65 | 1.00 |
| 2000 | — | — | — | 0.25 | 0.50 | 0.75 |
| 2001 | — | — | — | — | — | — |

**25 PESETAS** **KM# 787** **Composition:** Copper-Nickel

| Date | Mintage | F | VF | XF | Unc | BU |
|---|---|---|---|---|---|---|
| 1957 (58) | 8,635,000 | — | 0.50 | 7.00 | 40.00 | 75.00 |
| 1957 BA | 43,000 | — | 20.00 | 40.00 | 60.00 | 80.00 |

**Note:** Issued to commemorate the 1958 Barcelona Exposition with BA replacing the star on left isde of reverse

| Date | Mintage | F | VF | XF | Unc | BU |
|---|---|---|---|---|---|---|
| 1957 (59) | 42,185,000 | — | 0.20 | 1.00 | 18.00 | 35.00 |
| 1957 (61) | 24,120,000 | — | 3.00 | 15.00 | 75.00 | 115 |
| 1957 (64) | 42,200,000 | — | 0.20 | 1.00 | 12.00 | 20.00 |
| 1957 (65) | 20,000,000 | — | 0.20 | 0.75 | 3.50 | 5.00 |
| 1957 (66) | 15,000,000 | — | 0.20 | 1.00 | 4.50 | 7.00 |
| 1957 (67) | 20,000,000 | — | 0.20 | 1.75 | 10.00 | 15.00 |
| 1957 (68) | 30,000,000 | — | 0.20 | 0.65 | 2.50 | 5.00 |
| 1957 (68) | 24,000,000 | — | 0.20 | 0.50 | 1.50 | 3.00 |
| 1957 (70) | 25,000,000 | — | 0.20 | 0.30 | 3.00 | 5.50 |
| 1957 (71) | 7,800,000 | — | 1.00 | 5.00 | 20.00 | 35.00 |

| Date | Mintage | F | VF | XF | Unc | BU |
|---|---|---|---|---|---|---|
| 1957 (72) | 4,733,000 | — | 0.20 | 0.75 | 3.50 | 5.50 |
| 1957 (72) | 23,000 | Value: 6.50 | | | | |
| 1957 (73) | 28,000 | Value: 65.00 | | | | |
| 1957 (74) | 5,000,000 | — | 0.20 | 0.30 | 4.00 | 5.50 |
| 1957 (74) | 25,000 | Value: 6.00 | | | | |
| 1957 (75) | 10,270,000 | — | 0.20 | 0.30 | 1.50 | 2.00 |
| 1957 (75) | 25,000 | Value: 3.50 | | | | |

**25 PESETAS** **KM# 808** **Composition:** Copper-Nickel

| Date | Mintage | F | VF | XF | Unc | BU |
|---|---|---|---|---|---|---|
| 1975 (76) | 35,707,000 | — | 0.20 | 0.25 | 0.75 | 1.00 |
| 1975 (76) | — | Value: 1.00 | | | | |
| 1975 (77) | 46,690,000 | — | 0.20 | 0.25 | 0.75 | 1.00 |
| 1975 (77) | Inc. above | Value: 1.00 | | | | |
| 1975 (78) | 97,555,000 | — | 0.20 | 0.25 | 2.00 | 3.00 |
| 1975 (79) | 172,000,000 | — | 0.20 | 0.25 | 0.75 | 1.00 |
| 1975 (79) | — | Value: 1.00 | | | | |
| 1975 (80) | 136,000,000 | — | 0.20 | 0.25 | 2.00 | 3.00 |

**25 PESETAS** **KM# 818** **Composition:** Copper-Nickel **Subject:** World Cup Soccer Games

| Date | Mintage | F | VF | XF | Unc | BU |
|---|---|---|---|---|---|---|
| 1980 (80) | 35,000,000 | — | 0.20 | 0.30 | 0.60 | 0.75 |
| 1980 (81) | 117,000,000 | — | 0.20 | 0.30 | 0.75 | 1.00 |
| 1980 (82) | 100,000,000 | — | 0.20 | 0.30 | 1.00 | 2.00 |

**25 PESETAS** **KM# 824** **Composition:** Copper-Nickel **Note:** Mint mark: Crowned M.

| Date | Mintage | F | VF | XF | Unc | BU |
|---|---|---|---|---|---|---|
| 1982 | 146,000,000 | — | 0.20 | 0.30 | 2.00 | 3.00 |
| 1983 | 248,000,000 | — | 0.20 | 0.30 | 1.00 | 1.50 |
| 1984 | 242,000,000 | — | 0.20 | 0.30 | 2.00 | 3.00 |

**25 PESETAS** **KM# 850** **Composition:** Nickel-Bronze **Subject:** 1992 Olympics **Obv. Designer:** Discus thrower

| Date | Mintage | F | VF | XF | Unc | BU |
|---|---|---|---|---|---|---|
| 1990 | 150,000,000 | — | 0.25 | 0.30 | 0.75 | 1.00 |
| 1991 | Inc. above | — | 0.25 | 0.35 | 2.00 | 3.50 |

**25 PESETAS** **KM# 851** **Composition:** Nickel-Bronze **Subject:** 1992 Olympics **Reverse:** High jumper

| Date | Mintage | F | VF | XF | Unc | BU |
|---|---|---|---|---|---|---|
| 1990 | Inc. above | — | — | — | 1.00 | 1.50 |
| 1991 | 87,000,000 | — | — | — | 0.75 | 1.00 |

**25 PESETAS** **KM# 904** **Composition:** Nickel-Bronze **Subject:** Giralda Tower of Sevilla

| Date | Mintage | F | VF | XF | Unc | BU |
|---|---|---|---|---|---|---|
| 1992 | 179,833,000 | — | — | — | 1.50 | 2.00 |

**25 PESETAS** **KM# 905** **Composition:** Nickel-Bronze **Subject:** Tower of Goldin Seville **Obverse:** Globe

| Date | Mintage | F | VF | XF | Unc | BU |
|---|---|---|---|---|---|---|
| 1992 | Inc. above | — | — | — | 0.75 | 1.25 |

**25 PESETAS** **KM# 920** **Composition:** Nickel-Bronze **Subject:** Vasc Country

| Date | Mintage | F | VF | XF | Unc | BU |
|---|---|---|---|---|---|---|
| 1993 | 150,012,000 | — | — | — | 0.60 | 1.00 |

**25 PESETAS** **KM# 933** **Composition:** Nickel-Bronze **Subject:** Canary Islands

| Date | Mintage | F | VF | XF | Unc | BU |
|---|---|---|---|---|---|---|
| 1994 | 242,566,000 | — | — | — | 0.60 | 1.00 |

**25 PESETAS** **KM# 948** **Composition:** Brass **Subject:** Castilla and Leon

| Date | Mintage | F | VF | XF | Unc | BU |
|---|---|---|---|---|---|---|
| 1995 | 221,963,000 | — | — | — | 1.00 | 1.50 |
| 1995 without Y | Inc. above | — | 25.00 | 45.00 | 75.00 | 100 |

**25 PESETAS** **KM# 962** **Composition:** Copper-Zinc-Nickel **Subject:** Don Quixote

| Date | Mintage | F | VF | XF | Unc | BU |
|---|---|---|---|---|---|---|
| 1996 | 37,403,000 | — | — | — | 0.45 | 1.00 |

**25 PESETAS** **KM# 983** **Composition:** Brass **Subject:** Melilla **Obverse:** Two towered buildings **Reverse:** Ancient amphora, dates

| Date | Mintage | F | VF | XF | Unc | BU |
|---|---|---|---|---|---|---|
| 1997 | — | — | — | — | 0.45 | 1.00 |

**25 PESETAS** **KM# 990** **Composition:** Copper-Zinc-Nickel **Subject:** Ceuta **Obverse:** Ornamented building corner **Reverse:** Statue on wall shelf

| Date | Mintage | F | VF | XF | Unc | BU |
|---|---|---|---|---|---|---|
| 1998 | — | — | — | — | 0.45 | 1.00 |

**25 PESETAS** **KM# 1007** **Composition:** Nickel-Brass **Subject:** Navarra **Reverse:** Man running from bull

| Date | Mintage | F | VF | XF | Unc | BU |
|---|---|---|---|---|---|---|
| 1999 | — | — | — | — | 1.00 | 1.50 |

**25 PESETAS** **KM# 1013** **Composition:** Nickel-Brass **Subject:** Navarra **Obverse:** King's portrait **Reverse:** Crown, denomination and order **Edge:** Plain **Size:** 219.5 mm.

| Date | Mintage | F | VF | XF | Unc | BU |
|---|---|---|---|---|---|---|
| 2000 | — | — | — | — | 0.50 | 1.00 |
| 2001 | — | — | — | — | 0.50 | 1.00 |

**50 PESETAS** **KM# 788** **Composition:** Copper-Nickel

| Date | Mintage | F | VF | XF | Unc | BU |
|---|---|---|---|---|---|---|
| 1957 (58) | 21,471,000 | — | 0.50 | 0.75 | 2.50 | 3.50 |
| 1957 (58) BA | Est. 43,000 | — | 18.00 | 35.00 | 55.00 | 75.00 |

**Note:** Issued to commemorate the 1958 Barcelona Exposition with BA replacing the star on left side of reverse

| Date | Mintage | F | VF | XF | Unc | BU |
|---|---|---|---|---|---|---|
| 1957 (59) | 28,000,000 | — | 0.50 | 0.75 | 2.50 | 3.50 |
| 1957 (60) | 24,800,000 | — | 0.50 | 0.75 | 2.50 | 3.50 |
| 1957 (67) | 850,000 | — | 0.75 | 1.50 | 5.00 | 7.00 |
| 1957 (68) In sets only | 1,000 | — | — | — | — | 650 |
| 1957 (69) In sets only | 1,200 | — | — | — | — | 550 |
| 1957 (70) In sets only | 19,000 | — | — | — | — | 125 |
| 1957 (71) | 4,400,000 | — | 1.00 | 2.00 | 10.00 | 20.00 |
| 1957 (72) Proof | 23,000 | Value: 20.00 | | | | |
| 1957 (73) Proof | 28,000 | Value: 35.00 | | | | |
| 1957 (74) Proof | 25,000 | Value: 40.00 | | | | |
| 1957 (75) Proof | 25,000 | Value: 6.00 | | | | |

**Note:** Edge varieties exist

**50 PESETAS** **KM# 809** **Composition:** Copper-Nickel

| Date | Mintage | F | VF | XF | Unc | BU |
|---|---|---|---|---|---|---|
| 1975 (76) | 4,400,000 | — | 0.50 | 0.65 | 1.00 | 1.50 |
| 1975 (76) Proof | — | Value: 2.00 | | | | |
| 1975 (78) | 17,555,000 | — | 0.50 | 0.75 | 2.50 | 3.50 |
| 1975 (79) | 33,000,000 | — | 0.50 | 0.60 | 1.00 | 1.50 |
| 1975 (79) Proof | — | Value: 2.00 | | | | |
| 1975 (80) | 34,000 | — | 0.50 | 0.60 | 3.50 | 4.50 |

**50 PESETAS** **KM# 819** **Composition:** Copper-Nickel **Subject:** World Cup Soccer Games

| Date | Mintage | F | VF | XF | Unc | BU |
|---|---|---|---|---|---|---|
| 1980 (80) | 15,000,000 | — | 0.50 | 0.60 | 0.85 | 1.25 |
| 1980 (81) | 38,300 | — | 0.50 | 0.60 | 1.25 | 2.25 |
| 1980 (82) | 30,950,000 | — | 0.50 | 0.60 | 2.00 | 2.75 |

**50 PESETAS** **KM# 825** **Composition:** Copper-Nickel
**Note:** Mint mark: Crowned M.

| Date | Mintage | F | VF | XF | Unc | BU |
|---|---|---|---|---|---|---|
| 1982 | 27,000,000 | — | 0.50 | 1.00 | 2.50 | 4.50 |
| 1983 | 93,000,000 | — | 0.50 | 1.00 | 2.00 | 2.75 |
| 1984 | 17,500,000 | — | 3.00 | 10.00 | 25.00 | 30.00 |

**50 PESETAS** **KM# 852** **Composition:** Copper-Nickel **Subject:** Expo '92 **Obverse:** Juan Carlos I

| Date | Mintage | F | VF | XF | Unc | BU |
|---|---|---|---|---|---|---|
| 1990 | 25,234,000 | — | — | — | 1.00 | 1.50 |

**50 PESETAS** **KM# 853** **Composition:** Copper-Nickel **Subject:** Expo '92 **Obverse:** City view

| Date | Mintage | F | VF | XF | Unc | BU |
|---|---|---|---|---|---|---|
| 1990 | 7,916,000 | — | — | — | 1.00 | 1.35 |

**50 PESETAS** **KM# 906** **Composition:** Copper-Nickel **Subject:** 1992 Olympics **Obverse:** "La Pedrera" building (Gaudi)

| Date | Mintage | F | VF | XF | Unc | BU |
|---|---|---|---|---|---|---|
| 1992 | 40,370,000 | — | — | — | 0.75 | 1.25 |

**50 PESETAS** **KM# 907** **Composition:** Copper-Nickel **Subject:** 1992 Olympics **Obverse:** Cathedral Sagrada Familia (Gaudi)

| Date | Mintage | F | VF | XF | Unc | BU |
|---|---|---|---|---|---|---|
| 1992 | Inc. above | — | — | — | 1.00 | 1.35 |

**50 PESETAS** **KM# 921** **Composition:** Copper-Nickel **Subject:** Extremadura

| Date | Mintage | F | VF | XF | Unc | BU |
|---|---|---|---|---|---|---|
| 1993 | 24,314,000 | — | — | — | 1.00 | 1.35 |

**50 PESETAS** **KM# 934** **Composition:** Copper-Nickel **Subject:** Altamira Cave Paintings

| Date | Mintage | F | VF | XF | Unc | BU |
|---|---|---|---|---|---|---|
| 1994 | 3,002,000 | — | — | — | 1.50 | 2.00 |

**50 PESETAS** **KM# 949** **Composition:** Copper-Nickel **Subject:** Alcala Gate

| Date | Mintage | F | VF | XF | Unc | BU |
|---|---|---|---|---|---|---|
| 1995 | 1,001,000 | — | — | — | 2.00 | 2.75 |

**50 PESETAS** **KM# 963** **Composition:** Copper-Nickel **Subject:** Philip V

| Date | Mintage | F | VF | XF | Unc | BU |
|---|---|---|---|---|---|---|
| 1996 | 501,000 | — | — | — | 1.50 | 2.00 |

**50 PESETAS** **KM# 985** **Composition:** Copper-Nickel **Obverse:** Juan De Herrera **Reverse:** Escorial Monastery

| Date | Mintage | F | VF | XF | Unc | BU |
|---|---|---|---|---|---|---|
| 1997 | — | — | — | — | 1.25 | 2.00 |

**50 PESETAS** **KM# 991** **Composition:** Copper-Nickel **Obverse:** King Juan Carlos **Reverse:** National arms and denomination

| Date | Mintage | F | VF | XF | Unc | BU |
|---|---|---|---|---|---|---|
| 1998 | — | — | — | — | 1.25 | 2.00 |
| 1999 | — | — | — | — | 1.75 | 2.50 |
| 2000 | — | — | — | — | 1.50 | 2.00 |
| 2001 | — | — | — | — | — | — |

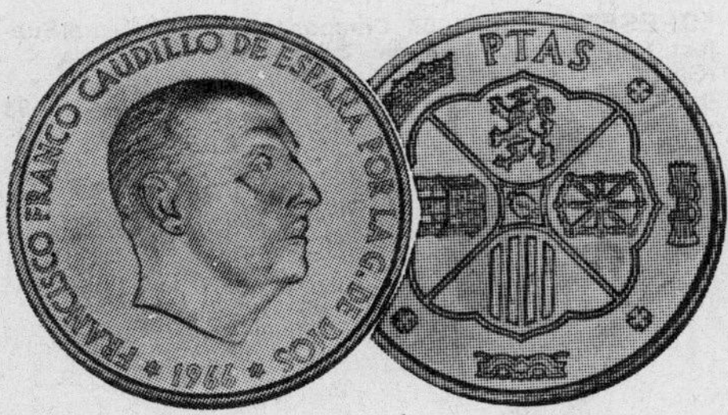


**100 PESETAS** **KM# 797** **Weight:** 19.0000 g. **Composition:** 0.8000 Silver .4887 oz. ASW

| Date | Mintage | F | VF | XF | Unc | BU |
|---|---|---|---|---|---|---|
| 1966 (66) | 35,000,000 | — | — | 3.00 | 5.00 | 6.00 |
| 1966 (67) | 15,000,000 | — | — | 3.00 | 6.00 | 7.00 |
| 1966 (68) | 24,000,000 | — | — | 3.00 | 5.00 | 6.00 |
| 1966 (69) | 1,000,000 | — | — | — | 225 | 275 |
| **Note:** 69 with straight 9 in star | | | | | | |
| 1966 (69) | Inc. above | — | — | — | 80.00 | 100 |
| **Note:** 69 with curved 9 in star | | | | | | |
| 1966 (70) | 995,000 | — | 4.00 | 7.50 | 12.50 | 17.50 |

**Note:** 1966(69) coins heavily altered; authentication recommended

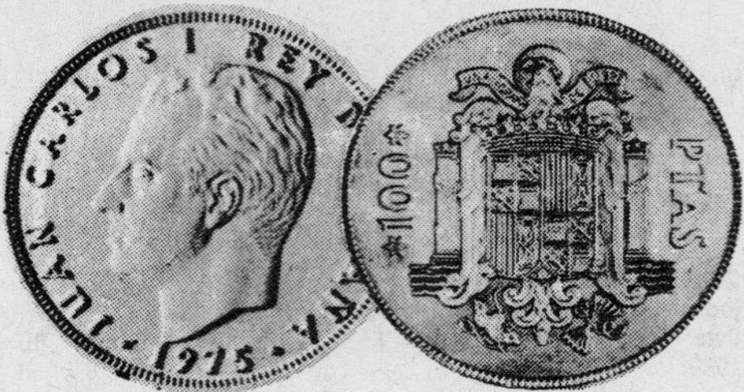


**100 PESETAS** **KM# 810** **Composition:** Copper-Nickel

| Date | Mintage | F | VF | XF | Unc | BU |
|---|---|---|---|---|---|---|
| 1975 (76) | 4,400,000 | — | — | 0.75 | 1.00 | 2.00 |
| 1975 (76) Proof | — | Value: 3.00 | | | | |

**100 PESETAS** **KM# 820** **Composition:** Copper-Nickel **Subject:** World Cup Soccer Games

| Date | Mintage | F | VF | XF | Unc | BU |
|---|---|---|---|---|---|---|
| 1980 (80) | 20,000,000 | — | — | 0.75 | 1.00 | 2.00 |

**100 PESETAS** **KM# 826** **Composition:** Aluminum-Bronze

| Date | Mintage | F | VF | XF | Unc | BU |
|---|---|---|---|---|---|---|
| 1982 | 117,600,000 | — | 0.75 | 1.25 | 2.75 | 4.00 |
| 1982 Proof | — | Value: 5.00 | | | | |
| 1983 | — | — | 0.75 | 1.25 | 12.00 | 30.00 |
| 1984 | 208,000,000 | — | 0.75 | 1.25 | 3.50 | 5.50 |
| 1985 | 118,000,000 | — | 0.75 | 1.25 | 7.50 | 11.50 |
| 1986 | 160,000,000 | — | 0.75 | 1.25 | 2.25 | 2.75 |
| 1988 | 125,674,000 | — | 0.75 | 1.25 | 2.75 | 4.00 |
| 1989 | 80,877,000 | — | 0.75 | 1.25 | 2.25 | 2.75 |
| 1990 | 25,636,000 | — | 0.75 | 1.25 | 2.50 | 3.75 |

**Note:** Varieties exist

**100 PESETAS** **KM# 834** **Weight:** 1.6800 g. **Composition:** 0.9250 Silver .0500 oz. ASW **Subject:** Discovery of America **Reverse:** Mayan pyramid

| Date | Mintage | F | VF | XF | Unc | BU |
|---|---|---|---|---|---|---|
| 1989 | 43,000 | — | — | — | — | 5.00 |
| 1989 Proof | 57,000 | Value: 6.00 | | | | |

**100 PESETAS** **KM# 854** **Weight:** 1.6800 g. **Composition:** 0.9250 Silver .0500 oz. ASW **Obverse:** Brother Juniper Serra **Reverse:** Mission ruins within legend

| Date | Mintage | F | VF | XF | Unc | BU |
|---|---|---|---|---|---|---|
| 1990 | 24,000 | — | — | — | — | 6.00 |
| 1990 Proof | 27,000 | Value: 6.00 | | | | |

**100 PESETAS** **KM# 882** **Weight:** 1.6800 g. **Composition:** 0.9250 Silver .0500 oz. ASW **Obverse:** Celestino Mutis **Reverse:** Flower plant within legend

| Date | Mintage | F | VF | XF | Unc | BU |
|---|---|---|---|---|---|---|
| 1991 | 14,000 | — | — | — | — | 8.00 |
| 1991 Proof | — | Value: 8.50 | | | | |

**100 PESETAS** **KM# 908** **Composition:** Aluminum-Bronze

| Date | Mintage | F | VF | XF | Unc | BU |
|---|---|---|---|---|---|---|
| 1992 | 22,661,000 | — | — | — | 2.00 | 3.00 |

**Note:** Edge varieties exist with positioning of fleur-de-lis

**100 PESETAS** **KM# 993** **Weight:** 1.6800 g. **Composition:** 0.9250 Silver .0500 oz. ASW **Subject:** Seville Expo '92 **Obverse:** Bridge

| Date | Mintage | F | VF | XF | Unc | BU |
|---|---|---|---|---|---|---|
| 1992 | 16,000 | — | — | — | — | 9.50 |
| 1992 Proof | 16,000 | Value: 10.00 | | | | |

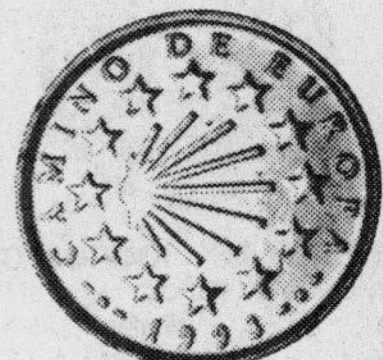


**100 PESETAS** **KM# 922** **Composition:** Nickel-Brass **Subject:** European unity **Obverse:** Jacobean track to Santiago de Compostela

| Date | Mintage | F | VF | XF | Unc | BU |
|---|---|---|---|---|---|---|
| 1993 | 39,723,000 | — | — | — | 1.75 | 2.50 |

**100 PESETAS** **KM# 935** **Composition:** Nickel-Brass **Subject:** Museo del Prado

| Date | Mintage | F | VF | XF | Unc | BU |
|---|---|---|---|---|---|---|
| 1994 | 24,853,000 | — | — | — | 1.50 | 2.25 |

**100 PESETAS** **KM# 950** **Composition:** Copper-Nickel **Series:** F.A.O

| Date | Mintage | F | VF | XF | Unc | BU |
|---|---|---|---|---|---|---|
| 1995 | 71,957,000 | — | — | — | 1.50 | 2.25 |

**100 PESETAS** **KM# 964** **Composition:** Copper-Zinc-Nickel **Reverse:** National Library

| Date | Mintage | F | VF | XF | Unc | BU |
|---|---|---|---|---|---|---|
| 1996 | 21,466,000 | — | — | — | 1.25 | 2.00 |

**100 PESETAS** **KM# 984** **Composition:** Copper-Zinc-Nickel **Subject:** Teatro Real **Obverse:** King Juan Carlos

| Date | Mintage | F | VF | XF | Unc | BU |
|---|---|---|---|---|---|---|
| 1997 | — | — | — | — | 1.25 | 2.00 |

**100 PESETAS** **KM# 989** **Composition:** Aluminum-Bronze **Subject:** King Juan Carlos

| Date | Mintage | F | VF | XF | Unc | BU |
|---|---|---|---|---|---|---|
| 1998 | — | — | — | — | 1.25 | 2.00 |
| 2000 | — | — | — | — | 1.25 | 2.25 |
| 2001 | — | — | — | — | — | — |

**100 PESETAS** **KM# 1006** **Composition:** Brass **Obverse:** King Juan Carlos **Reverse:** Denomination

| Date | Mintage | F | VF | XF | Unc | BU |
|---|---|---|---|---|---|---|
| 1999 | 60,332,000 | — | — | — | 1.25 | 2.25 |

**100 PESETAS** **KM# 1016** **Weight:** 9.8000 g. **Composition:** Aluminum-Bronze **Ruler:** Juan Carlos I **Subject:** 132nd Anniversary of the Peseta **Obverse:** King's portrait **Reverse:** Seated allegorical figure from an old coin design **Edge:** Ornamented **Size:** 24.4 mm.

| Date | Mintage | F | VF | XF | Unc | BU |
|---|---|---|---|---|---|---|
| 2001 | — | — | — | — | 3.50 | — |

**200 PESETAS** **KM# 829** **Composition:** Copper-Nickel

| Date | Mintage | F | VF | XF | Unc | BU |
|---|---|---|---|---|---|---|
| 1986 | 43,576,000 | — | — | 2.00 | 5.50 | 7.50 |
| 1987 | 66,718,000 | — | — | 2.00 | 8.50 | 11.50 |
| 1988 | 37,190,000 | — | — | 2.00 | 9.50 | 12.50 |

**200 PESETAS** **KM# 830** **Composition:** Copper-Nickel **Subject:** Madrid Numismatic Exposition

| Date | Mintage | F | VF | XF | Unc | BU |
|---|---|---|---|---|---|---|
| 1987 (E87) Proof | 60,000 | Value: 28.00 | | | | |

**200 PESETAS** **KM# 835** **Weight:** 3.3700 g. **Composition:** 0.9250 Silver .1000 oz. ASW **Subject:** Discovery of America **Reverse:** Astrolobe

| Date | Mintage | F | VF | XF | Unc | BU |
|---|---|---|---|---|---|---|
| 1989 | 43,000 | — | — | — | — | 7.00 |
| 1989 Proof | 57,000 | Value: 8.00 | | | | |

**200 PESETAS** **KM# 855** **Composition:** Copper-Nickel

| Date | Mintage | F | VF | XF | Unc | BU |
|---|---|---|---|---|---|---|
| 1990 | 8,000,000 | — | — | — | 3.00 | 4.00 |

**200 PESETAS** **KM# 856** **Weight:** 3.3700 g. **Composition:** 0.9250 Silver .1000 oz. ASW **Subject:** Alonso de Frcilla **Reverse:** Hand writing in a book within legend

| Date | Mintage | F | VF | XF | Unc | BU |
|---|---|---|---|---|---|---|
| 1990 | 24,000 | — | — | — | — | 8.00 |
| 1990 Proof | 27,000 | Value: 8.00 | | | | |

**200 PESETAS** **KM# 883** **Weight:** 3.3700 g. **Composition:** 0.9250 Silver .1000 oz. ASW **Subject:** Las Casas **Reverse:** 3 indian figures

| Date | Mintage | F | VF | XF | Unc | BU |
|---|---|---|---|---|---|---|
| 1991 | 14,000 | — | — | — | — | 9.50 |
| 1991 Proof | 14,000 | Value: 10.00 | | | | |

**200 PESETAS** **KM# 884** **Composition:** Copper-Nickel **Subject:** Madrid - European Culture Capital

| Date | Mintage | F | VF | XF | Unc | BU |
|---|---|---|---|---|---|---|
| 1991 | 11,400,000 | — | — | — | 2.00 | 3.00 |

**200 PESETAS** **KM# 884a** **Weight:** 12.2500 g. **Composition:** 0.9250 Silver .3643 oz. ASW **Subject:** Madrid - European Culture Capital

| Date | Mintage | F | VF | XF | Unc | BU |
|---|---|---|---|---|---|---|
| 1992 Proof | 38,000,000 | Value: 85.00 | | | | |

**200 PESETAS** **KM# 909** **Composition:** Copper-Nickel **Subject:** Madrid - European Culture Capital **Reverse:** Equestrian

| Date | Mintage | F | VF | XF | Unc | BU |
|---|---|---|---|---|---|---|
| 1992 | Inc. above | — | — | — | 2.25 | 3.00 |

**200 PESETAS** **KM# 910** **Composition:** Copper-Nickel **Subject:** Madrid - European Culture Capital **Reverse:** Bear by tree

| Date | Mintage | F | VF | XF | Unc | BU |
|---|---|---|---|---|---|---|
| 1992 | Inc. above | — | — | — | 2.00 | 2.50 |

**200 PESETAS** **KM# 994** **Weight:** 3.3700 g. **Composition:** 0.9250 Silver .1000 oz. ASW **Subject:** Seville Expo '92 **Obverse:** Hydro-electric dam **Reverse:** Tower of Seville

| Date | Mintage | F | VF | XF | Unc | BU |
|---|---|---|---|---|---|---|
| 1992 | 17,000 | — | — | — | — | 12.00 |
| 1992 | 16,000 | Value: 12.50 | | | | |

**200 PESETAS** **KM# 923** **Composition:** Copper-Nickel **Subject:** Juan Luis Vives

| Date | Mintage | F | VF | XF | Unc | BU |
|---|---|---|---|---|---|---|
| 1993 | 2,811,000 | — | — | — | 4.00 | 5.00 |

**200 PESETAS** **KM# 936** **Composition:** Copper-Nickel **Subject:** Spanish "Old Masters" Paintings

| Date | Mintage | F | VF | XF | Unc | BU |
|---|---|---|---|---|---|---|
| 1994 | 2,997,000 | — | — | — | 2.50 | 3.50 |

**200 PESETAS** **KM# 951** **Composition:** Copper-Nickel **Subject:** Spanish painters

| Date | Mintage | F | VF | XF | Unc | BU |
|---|---|---|---|---|---|---|
| 1995 | 1,022,000 | — | — | — | 5.00 | 6.00 |

**200 PESETAS** **KM# 965** **Composition:** Copper-Nickel **Subject:** Musicians

| Date | Mintage | F | VF | XF | Unc | BU |
|---|---|---|---|---|---|---|
| 1996 | 9,206,000 | — | — | — | 2.50 | 4.00 |

**200 PESETAS** **KM# 986** **Composition:** Copper-Nickel **Subject:** Jacinto Benavente **Obverse:** Stylized books **Reverse:** Potrait in inner circle

| Date | Mintage | F | VF | XF | Unc | BU |
|---|---|---|---|---|---|---|
| 1997 | 6,845,000 | — | — | — | 2.50 | 4.00 |

**200 PESETAS** **KM# 992** **Composition:** Copper-Nickel **Obverse:** King Juan Carlos and Crown Prince **Reverse:** Denomination

| Date | Mintage | F | VF | XF | Unc | BU |
|---|---|---|---|---|---|---|
| 1998 | 5,008,000 | — | — | — | 2.50 | 4.00 |
| 1999 | — | — | — | — | 2.75 | 4.25 |
| 2000 | — | — | — | — | 3.00 | 5.00 |
| 2001 | — | — | — | — | 3.00 | 5.00 |

**500 PESETAS** **KM# 831** **Composition:** Copper-Aluminum-Nickel **Obverse:** Juan Carlos and Sofia, busts facing left

| Date | Mintage | F | VF | XF | Unc | BU |
|---|---|---|---|---|---|---|
| 1987 | 400,000,000 | — | — | 3.50 | 9.00 | 10.00 |
| 1987 | Inc. above | Value: 10.00 | | | | |
| 1988 | 81,309,000 | — | — | 3.50 | 7.50 | 9.00 |
| 1989 | 103,861,000 | — | — | 3.50 | 5.00 | 6.00 |
| 1990 | 28,372,000 | — | — | 3.50 | 9.00 | 10.00 |

**500 PESETAS** **KM# 836** **Weight:** 6.7500 g. **Composition:** 0.9250 Silver .2008 oz. ASW **Subject:** Discovery of America - Juego De Pelota Game

| Date | Mintage | F | VF | XF | Unc | BU |
|---|---|---|---|---|---|---|
| 1989 | 43,000 | — | — | — | — | 10.00 |
| 1989 Proof | 57,000 | Value: 10.00 | | | | |

**500 PESETAS** **KM# 857** **Weight:** 6.7500 g. **Composition:** 0.9250 Silver .2008 oz. ASW **Obverse:** Juan de la Cosa **Reverse:** Ocean navigation map within legend

| Date | Mintage | F | VF | XF | Unc | BU |
|---|---|---|---|---|---|---|
| 1990 | 24,000 | — | — | — | — | 12.00 |
| 1990 Proof | 27,000 | Value: 12.00 | | | | |

**500 PESETAS** **KM# 885** **Weight:** 6.7500 g. **Composition:** 0.9250 Silver .2008 oz. ASW **Obverse:** Jorge Juan **Reverse:** World globe map within legend

| Date | Mintage | F | VF | XF | Unc | BU |
|---|---|---|---|---|---|---|
| 1991 | 14,000 | — | — | — | — | 16.00 |
| 1991 Proof | 14,000 | Value: 16.00 | | | | |

**500 PESETAS** **KM# 995** **Weight:** 6.7500 g. **Composition:** 0.9250 Silver .2008 oz. ASW **Subject:** Seville Expo '92 **Obverse:** Church **Reverse:** Palace Portal

| Date | Mintage | F | VF | XF | Unc | BU |
|---|---|---|---|---|---|---|
| 1992 | 17,000 | — | — | — | — | 20.00 |
| 1992 Proof | 16,000 | Value: 20.00 | | | | |

**500 PESETAS** **KM# 924** **Composition:** Copper-Aluminum-Nickel

| Date | Mintage | F | VF | XF | Unc | BU |
|---|---|---|---|---|---|---|
| 1993 | 3,059,000 | — | — | — | 8.00 | 10.00 |
| 1994 | 3,041,000 | — | — | — | 9.00 | 11.00 |
| 1995 | 1,015,000 | — | — | — | 8.00 | 10.00 |
| 1996 | 1,031,000 | — | — | — | 8.00 | 10.00 |
| 1997 | 4,881,000 | — | — | — | 6.00 | 8.00 |
| 1998 | 5,161,000 | — | — | — | 6.00 | 8.00 |
| 1999 | 2,030,000 | — | — | — | 8.00 | 9.50 |
| 2000 | — | — | — | — | 8.00 | 9.50 |
| 2001 | — | — | — | — | — | — |

**1000 PESETAS** **KM# 837** **Weight:** 13.5000 g. **Composition:** 0.9250 Silver .4015 oz. ASW **Subject:** Discovery of America - Capture of Granada

| Date | Mintage | F | VF | XF | Unc | BU |
|---|---|---|---|---|---|---|
| 1989 | 43,000 | — | — | — | — | 12.50 |
| 1989 Proof | 57,000 | Value: 12.50 | | | | |

**1000 PESETAS** **KM# 858** **Weight:** 13.5000 g. **Composition:** 0.9250 Silver .4015 oz. ASW **Subject:** Magallanes and Elcano **Reverse:** Primitive global world map within legend

| Date | Mintage | F | VF | XF | Unc | BU |
|---|---|---|---|---|---|---|
| 1990 | 24,000 | — | — | — | — | 15.00 |
| 1990 Proof | 27,000 | Value: 15.00 | | | | |

**1000 PESETAS** **KM# 886** **Weight:** 13.5000 g. **Composition:** 0.9250 Silver .4015 oz. ASW **Subject:** Simon Bolivar and San Martin **Reverse:** Portrait within legend

| Date | Mintage | F | VF | XF | Unc | BU |
|---|---|---|---|---|---|---|
| 1991 | 14,000 | — | — | — | — | 20.00 |
| 1991 Proof | 14,000 | Value: 20.00 | | | | |

**1000 PESETAS** **KM# 996** **Weight:** 13.5000 g. **Composition:** 0.9250 Silver .4015 oz. ASW **Subject:** Seville Expo '92 **Obverse:** Expo buildings **Reverse:** India's Archives Building

| Date | Mintage | F | VF | XF | Unc | BU |
|---|---|---|---|---|---|---|
| 1992 | 17,000 | — | — | — | — | 25.00 |
| 1992 Proof | 16,000 | Value: 25.00 | | | | |

**1000 PESETAS** **KM# 952** **Weight:** 13.6600 g. **Composition:** 0.9250 Silver .4062 oz. ASW **Subject:** 1996 Olympics

| Date | Mintage | F | VF | XF | Unc | BU |
|---|---|---|---|---|---|---|
| 1995 Proof | 75,000 | Value: 22.50 | | | | |

**1000 PESETAS** **KM# 973** **Weight:** 13.6600 g. **Composition:** 0.9250 Silver .4062 oz. ASW **Subject:** Olympics **Reverse:** 3 divers

| Date | Mintage | F | VF | XF | Unc | BU |
|---|---|---|---|---|---|---|
| 1996 Proof | 75,000 | Value: 25.00 | | | | |

**1000 PESETAS** **KM# 988** **Weight:** 13.5000 g. **Composition:** 0.9250 Silver .4015 oz. ASW **Subject:** Soccer **Obverse:** King Juan Carlos **Reverse:** 2 soccer players

| Date | Mintage | F | VF | XF | Unc | BU |
|---|---|---|---|---|---|---|
| 1998 Proof | Est. 30,000 | Value: 40.00 | | | | |

**1000 PESETAS** **KM# 1000** **Weight:** 13.5000 g. **Composition:** 0.9250 Silver .4015 oz. ASW **Subject:** Expo '98 Lisbon **Reverse:** Sailing ship

| Date | Mintage | F | VF | XF | Unc | BU |
|---|---|---|---|---|---|---|
| 1998 Proof | 50,000 | Value: 25.00 | | | | |

**1000 PESETAS** **KM# 1009** **Weight:** 13.5000 g. **Composition:** 0.9250 Silver .4015 oz. ASW **Subject:** Olympics **Reverse:** Water polo players

| Date | Mintage | F | VF | XF | Unc | BU |
|---|---|---|---|---|---|---|
| 1999 Proof | Est. 50,000 | Value: 25.00 | | | | |

**1500 PESETAS** **KM# 1010** **Weight:** 19.8300 g. **Composition:** 0.9250 Silver .5897 oz. ASW **Subject:** Millennium **Reverse:** Space walking astronaut above Columbus' ships

| Date | Mintage | F | VF | XF | Unc | BU |
|---|---|---|---|---|---|---|
| 1999 Proof | Est. 50,000 | Value: 27.50 | | | | |

**2000 PESETAS** **KM# 838** **Weight:** 27.0000 g. **Composition:** 0.9250 Silver .8031 oz. ASW **Subject:** Discovery of America **Reverse:** Columbus

| Date | Mintage | F | VF | XF | Unc | BU |
|---|---|---|---|---|---|---|
| 1989 | 43,000 | — | — | — | — | 18.50 |
| 1989 Proof | 57,000 | Value: 18.50 | | | | |

**2000 PESETAS** **KM# 859** **Weight:** 27.0000 g. **Composition:** 0.9250 Silver .8031 oz. ASW **Subject:** 1992 Olympics **Obverse:** Similar to KM#861 **Reverse:** Symbols

| Date | Mintage | F | VF | XF | Unc | BU |
|---|---|---|---|---|---|---|
| 1990 | 135,000 | — | — | — | — | 21.50 |
| 1990 Proof | 235,000 | Value: 21.50 | | | | |

**Note:** See note below KM#914

**2000 PESETAS** **KM# 861** **Weight:** 26.7000 g. **Composition:** 0.9250 Silver .7940 oz. ASW **Subject:** 1992 Olympics **Reverse:** Archer

| Date | Mintage | F | VF | XF | Unc | BU |
|---|---|---|---|---|---|---|
| 1990 | 135,000 | — | — | — | — | 21.50 |
| 1990 Proof | 235,000 | Value: 21.50 | | | | |

**Note:** Unc strikes have medallic die alignment and edges w/reeded and plain sections; Proof strikes have coin die alignment and reeded edges

**2000 PESETAS** **KM# 862** **Weight:** 26.7000 g. **Composition:** 0.9250 Silver .7940 oz. ASW **Subject:** 1992 Olympics **Reverse:** Soccer player

| Date | Mintage | F | VF | XF | Unc | BU |
|---|---|---|---|---|---|---|
| 1990 | Est. 135,000 | — | — | — | — | 21.50 |
| 1990 Proof | Est. 235,000 | Value: 21.50 | | | | |

**Note:** Unc strikes have medallic die alignment and edges w/reeded and plain sections; Proof strikes have coin die alignment and reeded edges

**2000 PESETAS** **KM# 863** **Weight:** 26.7000 g. **Composition:** 0.9250 Silver .7940 oz. ASW **Subject:** 1992 Olympics **Reverse:** Human pyramid

| Date | Mintage | F | VF | XF | Unc | BU |
|---|---|---|---|---|---|---|
| 1990 | Est. 135,000 | — | — | — | — | 24.50 |
| 1990 Proof | Est. 235,000 | Value: 24.50 | | | | |

**Note:** Unc strikes have medallic die alignment and edges w/reeded and plain sections; Proof strikes have coin die alignment and reeded edges

**2000 PESETAS** **KM# 864** **Weight:** 26.7000 g. **Composition:** 0.9250 Silver .7940 oz. ASW **Subject:** 1992 Olympics **Obverse:** Similar to KM#859 **Reverse:** Greek runner

| Date | Mintage | F | VF | XF | Unc | BU |
|---|---|---|---|---|---|---|
| 1990 | Est. 80,000 | — | — | — | — | 24.50 |
| 1990 Proof | Est. 180,000 | Value: 24.50 | | | | |

**Note:** Unc strikes have medallic die alignment and edges w/reeded and plain sections; Proof strikes have coin die alignment and reeded edges

**2000 PESETAS** **KM# 865** **Weight:** 26.7000 g. **Composition:** 0.9250 Silver .7940 oz. ASW **Subject:** 1992 Olympics **Obverse:** Similar to KM#859 **Reverse:** Ancient boat

| Date | Mintage | F | VF | XF | Unc | BU |
|---|---|---|---|---|---|---|
| 1990 | Est. 80,000 | — | — | — | — | 27.50 |
| 1990 Proof | Est. 180,000 | Value: 27.50 | | | | |

**Note:** Unc strikes have medallic die alignment and edges w/reeded and plain sections; Proof strikes have coin die alignment and reeded edges

**2000 PESETAS** **KM# 866** **Weight:** 26.7000 g. **Composition:** 0.9250 Silver .7940 oz. ASW **Subject:** 1992 Olympics **Obverse:** Similar to KM#859 **Reverse:** Basketball players

| Date | Mintage | F | VF | XF | Unc | BU |
|---|---|---|---|---|---|---|
| 1990 | Est. 80,000 | — | — | — | — | 28.50 |
| 1990 Proof | Est. 180,000 | Value: 28.50 | | | | |

**Note:** Unc strikes have medallic die alignment and edges w/reeded and plain sections; Proof strikes have coin die alignment and reeded edges

**2000 PESETAS** **KM# 867** **Weight:** 26.7000 g. **Composition:** 0.9250 Silver .7940 oz. ASW **Subject:** 1992 Olympics **Obverse:** Similar to KM#859 **Reverse:** Pelota player

| Date | Mintage | F | VF | XF | Unc | BU |
|---|---|---|---|---|---|---|
| 1990 | Est. 80,000 | — | — | — | — | 27.50 |
| 1990 Proof | Est. 180,000 | Value: 27.50 | | | | |

**Note:** Unc strikes have medallic die alignment and edges w/reeded and plain sections; Proof strikes have coin die alignment and reeded edges

**2000 PESETAS** **KM# 868** **Weight:** 26.7000 g. **Composition:** 0.9250 Silver .7940 oz. ASW **Subject:** Hidalgo, Morelos and Juarez **Reverse:** Aztec pictorial design within legend

| Date | Mintage | F | VF | XF | Unc | BU |
|---|---|---|---|---|---|---|
| 1990 | 24,000 | — | — | — | — | 20.00 |
| 1990 Proof | 27,000 | Value: 20.00 | | | | |

**2000 PESETAS** **KM# 860** **Weight:** 26.7000 g. **Composition:** 0.9250 Silver .7940 oz. ASW **Counterstamp:** INUTILIZACION/OCTOBRE 1992 **Note:** Counterstamp on reverse below Olympic rings

| Date | Mintage | F | VF | XF | Unc | BU |
|---|---|---|---|---|---|---|
| 1990 1992; Proof | — | Value: 35.00 | | | | |

**Note:** Unc strikes have medallic die alignment and edges w/reeded and plain sections; Proof strikes have coin die alignment and reeded edges

**2000 PESETAS** **KM# 887** **Weight:** 26.7000 g. **Composition:** 0.9250 Silver .7940 oz. ASW **Subject:** Olympics **Reverse:** Torch and flag

| Date | Mintage | F | VF | XF | Unc | BU |
|---|---|---|---|---|---|---|
| 1991 | — | — | — | — | — | 24.50 |
| 1991 Proof | — | Value: 24.50 | | | | |

**2000 PESETAS** **KM# 888** **Weight:** 26.7000 g. **Composition:** 0.9250 Silver .7940 oz. ASW **Subject:** Olympics **Obverse:** Similar to KM#887 **Reverse:** Tennis player

| Date | Mintage | F | VF | XF | Unc | BU |
|---|---|---|---|---|---|---|
| 1991 | — | — | — | — | — | 40.00 |
| 1991 Proof | — | Value: 40.00 | | | | |

**Note:** Medal rotation

**2000 PESETAS** **KM# 889** **Weight:** 26.7000 g. **Composition:** 0.9250 Silver .7940 oz. ASW **Subject:** Olympics **Obverse:** Similar to KM#887 **Reverse:** Medieval rider

| Date | Mintage | F | VF | XF | Unc | BU |
|---|---|---|---|---|---|---|
| 1991 | — | — | — | — | — | 42.50 |
| 1991 Proof | — | Value: 42.50 | | | | |

**Note:** Medal rotation

**2000 PESETAS** **KM# 890** **Weight:** 26.7000 g. **Composition:** 0.9250 Silver .7940 oz. ASW **Subject:** Olympics **Obverse:** Similar to KM#887 **Reverse:** Bowling

| Date | Mintage | F | VF | XF | Unc | BU |
|---|---|---|---|---|---|---|
| 1991 | — | — | — | — | — | 47.50 |
| 1991 Proof | — | Value: 47.50 | | | | |

**Note:** Medal rotation

**2000 PESETAS** **KM# 891** **Weight:** 26.7000 g. **Composition:** 0.9250 Silver .7940 oz. ASW **Subject:** Ibero - American Series

| Date | Mintage | F | VF | XF | Unc | BU |
|---|---|---|---|---|---|---|
| (19)91 Proof | Est. 50,000 | Value: 75.00 | | | | |

**2000 PESETAS** **KM# 892** **Weight:** 26.7000 g. **Composition:** 0.9250 Silver .7940 oz. ASW **Subject:** Federman, Quesada and Benalcazar

| Date | Mintage | F | VF | XF | Unc | BU |
|---|---|---|---|---|---|---|
| 1991 | 14,000 | — | — | — | — | 25.00 |
| 1991 Proof | 14,000 | Value: 25.00 | | | | |

**2000 PESETAS** **KM# 911** **Weight:** 26.7000 g. **Composition:** 0.9250 Silver .7940 oz. ASW **Subject:** Olympics **Reverse:** Tug-of-war

| Date | Mintage | F | VF | XF | Unc | BU |
|---|---|---|---|---|---|---|
| 1992 | Est. 34,000 | — | — | — | — | 45.00 |
| 1992 Proof | 9,043 | Value: 52.50 | | | | |

**Note:** Unc strikes have medallic die alignment and edges w/reeded and plain sections; Proof strikes have coin die alignment and reeded edges

**2000 PESETAS** **KM# 912** **Weight:** 26.7000 g. **Composition:** 0.9250 Silver .7940 oz. ASW **Subject:** Olympics **Reverse:** Wheelchair basketball

| Date | Mintage | F | VF | XF | Unc | BU |
|---|---|---|---|---|---|---|
| 1992 | Est. 28,000 | — | — | — | — | 47.50 |
| 1992 Proof | 8,997 | Value: 52.50 | | | | |

**Note:** Unc strikes have medallic die alignment and edges w/reeded and plain sections; Proof strikes have coin die alignment and reeded edges

**2000 PESETAS** **KM# 913** **Weight:** 26.7000 g. **Composition:** 0.9250 Silver .7940 oz. ASW **Subject:** Olympics **Reverse:** Sprinters

| Date | Mintage | F | VF | XF | Unc | BU |
|---|---|---|---|---|---|---|
| 1992 | 16,000 | — | — | — | — | 40.00 |
| 1992 Proof | 42,000 | Value: 40.00 | | | | |

**Note:** Unc strikes have medallic die alignment and edges w/reeded and plain sections; Proof strikes have coin die alignment and reeded edges

**2000 PESETAS** **KM# 914** **Weight:** 26.7000 g. **Composition:** 0.9250 Silver .7940 oz. ASW **Subject:** Olympics **Reverse:** Chariot racing

| Date | Mintage | F | VF | XF | Unc | BU |
|---|---|---|---|---|---|---|
| 1992 | 13,000 | — | — | — | — | 50.00 |
| 1992 Proof | 37,000 | Value: 50.00 | | | | |

**Note:** Unc strikes have medallic die alignment and edges w/reeded and plain sections; Proof strikes have coin die alignment and reeded edges

**2000 PESETAS** **KM# 980** **Weight:** 26.7000 g. **Composition:** 0.9250 Silver .7940 oz. ASW **Subject:** Seville Expo '92 **Obverse:** Exposition Building, date **Reverse:** Tower of Seville

| Date | Mintage | F | VF | XF | Unc | BU |
|---|---|---|---|---|---|---|
| 1992 | 17,000 | — | — | — | — | 35.00 |
| 1992 Proof | 16,000 | Value: 35.00 | | | | |

**2000 PESETAS** **KM# 925** **Weight:** 26.7000 g. **Composition:** 0.9250 Silver .7940 oz. ASW **Subject:** Holy Jacobean Year **Reverse:** German Jacobean Pilgrims

| Date | Mintage | F | VF | XF | Unc | BU |
|---|---|---|---|---|---|---|
| 1993 Proof | 10,000 | Value: 75.00 | | | | |

**2000 PESETAS** **KM# 926** **Weight:** 26.7000 g. **Composition:** 0.9250 Silver .7940 oz. ASW **Subject:** Holy Jacobean Year **Reverse:** Santiago cross and scallop shell

| Date | Mintage | F | VF | XF | Unc | BU |
|---|---|---|---|---|---|---|
| 1993 Proof | 17,000 | Value: 75.00 | | | | |

**2000 PESETAS** **KM# 937** **Weight:** 18.0000 g. **Composition:** 0.9250 Silver .5353 oz. ASW **Subject:** International Monetary Fund and Bank

| Date | Mintage | F | VF | XF | Unc | BU |
|---|---|---|---|---|---|---|
| 1994 | 8,669,000 | — | — | — | 12.50 | 20.00 |

**2000 PESETAS** **KM# 938** **Weight:** 27.0000 g. **Composition:** 0.9250 Silver .8031 oz. ASW **Subject:** Courtyard of the lions

| Date | Mintage | F | VF | XF | Unc | BU |
|---|---|---|---|---|---|---|
| 1994 Proof | 50,000 | Value: 40.00 | | | | |

**2000 PESETAS** **KM# 939** **Weight:** 27.0000 g. **Composition:** 0.9250 Silver .8031 oz. ASW **Subject:** Environmental Protection **Reverse:** Spanish lynx

| Date | Mintage | F | VF | XF | Unc | BU |
|---|---|---|---|---|---|---|
| 1994 Proof | 20,000 | Value: 75.00 | | | | |

**2000 PESETAS** **KM# 940** **Weight:** 27.0000 g. **Composition:** 0.9250 Silver .8031 oz. ASW **Subject:** Purple Herons in swamp

| Date | Mintage | F | VF | XF | Unc | BU |
|---|---|---|---|---|---|---|
| 1994 Proof | 75,000 | Value: 37.50 | | | | |

**2000 PESETAS** **KM# 941** **Weight:** 27.0000 g. **Composition:** 0.9250 Silver .8031 oz. ASW **Subject:** 2 bulls

| Date | Mintage | F | VF | XF | Unc | BU |
|---|---|---|---|---|---|---|
| 1994 Proof | 75,000 | Value: 45.00 | | | | |

**2000 PESETAS** **KM# 953** **Weight:** 27.0000 g. **Composition:** 0.9250 Silver .8031 oz. ASW **Reverse:** Capercaillie bird

| Date | Mintage | F | VF | XF | Unc | BU |
|---|---|---|---|---|---|---|
| 1995 Proof | 50,000 | Value: 45.00 | | | | |

**2000 PESETAS** **KM# 954** **Weight:** 27.0000 g. **Composition:** 0.9250 Silver .8031 oz. ASW **Subject:** Presidential Council - V.E

| Date | Mintage | F | VF | XF | Unc | BU |
|---|---|---|---|---|---|---|
| 1995 | — | — | — | — | 12.50 | 20.00 |

**2000 PESETAS** **KM# 955** **Weight:** 27.0000 g. **Composition:** 0.9250 Silver .8031 oz. ASW **Subject:** 50th Anniversary United Nations

| Date | Mintage | F | VF | XF | Unc | BU |
|---|---|---|---|---|---|---|
| 1995 Proof | 120,000 | Value: 65.00 | | | | |

**2000 PESETAS** **KM# 966** **Weight:** 27.0000 g. **Composition:** 0.9250 Silver .8031 oz. ASW **Subject:** Wolves

| Date | Mintage | F | VF | XF | Unc | BU |
|---|---|---|---|---|---|---|
| 1996 Proof | Est. 35,000 | Value: 60.00 | | | | |

**2000 PESETAS** **KM# 967** **Weight:** 27.0000 g. **Composition:** 0.9250 Silver .8031 oz. ASW **Subject:** Bears

| Date | Mintage | F | VF | XF | Unc | BU |
|---|---|---|---|---|---|---|
| 1996 Proof | Est. 35,000 | Value: 47.50 | | | | |

**2000 PESETAS** **KM# 968** **Weight:** 18.0000 g. **Composition:** 0.9250 Silver .5353 oz. ASW **Subject:** Francisco de Goya

| Date | Mintage | F | VF | XF | Unc | BU |
|---|---|---|---|---|---|---|
| 1996 | — | — | — | — | 12.50 | 20.00 |

**2000 PESETAS** **KM# 974** **Weight:** 27.0000 g. **Composition:** 0.9250 Silver .8031 oz. ASW **Subject:** Patrimonio de la Humanidad - Taj Mahal, India **Obverse:** UNESCO logo

| Date | Mintage | F | VF | XF | Unc | BU |
|---|---|---|---|---|---|---|
| 1996 Proof | 30,000 | Value: 32.50 | | | | |

**2000 PESETAS** **KM# 975** **Weight:** 27.0000 g. **Composition:** 0.9250 Silver .8031 oz. ASW **Subject:** Patrimonio de la Humanidad - Djenne, Mali **Obverse:** Similar to KM#293

| Date | Mintage | F | VF | XF | Unc | BU |
|---|---|---|---|---|---|---|
| 1996 Proof | 30,000 | Value: 30.00 | | | | |

**2000 PESETAS** **KM# 976** **Weight:** 27.0000 g. **Composition:** 0.9250 Silver .8031 oz. ASW **Subject:** Patrimonio de la Humanidad - Abu Simbel, Egypt **Obverse:** Similar to KM#293

| Date | Mintage | F | VF | XF | Unc | BU |
|---|---|---|---|---|---|---|
| 1996 Proof | 30,000 | Value: 35.00 | | | | |

**2000 PESETAS** **KM# 977** **Weight:** 27.0000 g. **Composition:** 0.9250 Silver .8031 oz. ASW **Subject:** Patrimonio de la Humanidad - Palenque, Mexico **Obverse:** Similar to KM#293

| Date | Mintage | F | VF | XF | Unc | BU |
|---|---|---|---|---|---|---|
| 1996 Proof | 30,000 | Value: 37.50 | | | | |

**2000 PESETAS** **KM# 978** **Weight:** 27.0000 g. **Composition:** 0.9250 Silver .8031 oz. ASW **Subject:** Patrimonio de la Humanidad - Merida, Spain **Obverse:** Similar to KM#293

| Date | Mintage | F | VF | XF | Unc | BU |
|---|---|---|---|---|---|---|
| 1996 Proof | 30,000 | Value: 30.00 | | | | |

**2000 PESETAS** **KM# 999** **Weight:** 18.0000 g. **Composition:** 0.9250 Silver .5353 oz. ASW **Subject:** Don Quixote **Obverse:** King Juan Carlos **Reverse:** Quixote and friend plus cameo of Cervantes

| Date | Mintage | F | VF | XF | Unc | BU |
|---|---|---|---|---|---|---|
| 1997 | — | — | — | — | 12.50 | 20.00 |

**2000 PESETAS** **KM# 1018** **Weight:** 27.0000 g. **Composition:** 0.9250 Silver .8031 oz. ASW **Ruler:** Juan Carlos I **Series:** "Patrimono de la Humanidad UNESCO **Obverse:** UNESCO logo **Reverse:** Abomey lion **Edge:** Reeded **Size:** 40 mm.

| Date | Mintage | F | VF | XF | Unc | BU |
|---|---|---|---|---|---|---|
| 1997 Proof | 30,000 | Value: 30.00 | | | | |

**2000 PESETAS** **KM# 1019** **Weight:** 27.0000 g. **Composition:** 0.9250 Silver .8031 oz. ASW **Ruler:** Juan Carlos I **Series:** "Patrimono de la Humanidad" UNESCO **Obverse:** UNESCO logo **Reverse:** Easter Island statues

| Date | Mintage | F | VF | XF | Unc | BU |
|---|---|---|---|---|---|---|
| 1997 Proof | 30,000 | Value: 30.00 | | | | |

**2000 PESETAS** **KM# 1020** **Weight:** 27.0000 g. **Composition:** 0.9250 Silver .8031 oz. ASW **Ruler:** Juan Carlos I **Series:** "Patrimono de la Humanidad" UNESCO **Obverse:** UNESCO logo **Reverse:** Temple at Petra

| Date | Mintage | F | VF | XF | Unc | BU |
|---|---|---|---|---|---|---|
| 1997 Proof | 30,000 | Value: 30.00 | | | | |

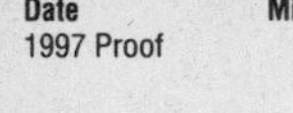

**2000 PESETAS** **KM# 1021** **Weight:** 27.0000 g. **Composition:** 0.9250 Silver .8031 oz. ASW **Ruler:** Juan Carlos I **Series:** "Patrimono de la Humanidad" UNESCO **Obverse:** UNESCO logo **Reverse:** Acropolis

| Date | Mintage | F | VF | XF | Unc | BU |
|---|---|---|---|---|---|---|
| 1997 Proof | 30,000 | Value: 30.00 | | | | |

**2000 PESETAS** **KM# 1022** **Weight:** 27.0000 g. **Composition:** 0.9250 Silver .8031 oz. ASW **Ruler:** Juan Carlos I **Series:** "Patrimono de la Humanidad" UNESCO **Obverse:** UNESCO logo **Reverse:** Horyu-Ji pagoda

| Date | Mintage | F | VF | XF | Unc | BU |
|---|---|---|---|---|---|---|
| 1997 Proof | 30,000 | Value: 30.00 | | | | |

**2000 PESETAS** **KM# 1024** **Weight:** 27.0000 g. **Composition:** 0.9250 Silver .0831 oz. ASW **Ruler:** Juan Carlos I **Subject:** House of Borbon - Philip V **Obverse:** Portrait of Philip V **Reverse:** Figural sculpture **Edge:** Reeded **Size:** 40 mm.

| Date | Mintage | F | VF | XF | Unc | BU |
|---|---|---|---|---|---|---|
| 1997 Proof | — | Value: 30.00 | | | | |

**2000 PESETAS** **KM# 1025** **Weight:** 27.0000 g. **Composition:** 0.9250 Silver .8031 oz. ASW **Ruler:** Juan Carlos I **Subject:** House of Borbon - Louis I **Obverse:** Portrait of Louis I **Reverse:** Crowned arms in order chain

| Date | Mintage | F | VF | XF | Unc | BU |
|---|---|---|---|---|---|---|
| 1997 Proof | — | Value: 30.00 | | | | |

**2000 PESETAS** **KM# 1026** **Weight:** 27.0000 g. **Composition:** 0.9250 Silver .8031 oz. ASW **Ruler:** Juan Carlos I **Subject:** House of Borbon - Ferdinand VI **Obverse:** Portrait of Ferdinand VI **Reverse:** Spanish galleon

| Date | Mintage | F | VF | XF | Unc | BU |
|---|---|---|---|---|---|---|
| 1997 Proof | — | Value: 30.00 | | | | |

**2000 PESETAS** **KM# 987** **Weight:** 18.0000 g. **Composition:** 0.9250 Silver **Subject:** Philip II **Obverse:** King Juan Carlos

| Date | Mintage | F | VF | XF | Unc | BU |
|---|---|---|---|---|---|---|
| 1998 | — | — | — | — | 12.50 | 20.00 |

**2000 PESETAS** **KM# 1011** **Weight:** 18.0000 g. **Composition:** 0.9250 Silver **Subject:** St. Jacob **Obverse:** King Juan Carlos **Reverse:** St. Jacob, denomination and dagger

| Date | Mintage | F | VF | XF | Unc | BU |
|---|---|---|---|---|---|---|
| 1999 Proof | — | Value: 30.00 | | | | |

**2000 PESETAS** **KM# 1029** **Weight:** 27.0000 g. **Composition:** 0.9250 Silver .8031 oz. ASW **Ruler:** Juan Carlos I **Subject:** Barcelona City Government 750 Years **Obverse:** Portrait of the King **Reverse:** Stylized city arms

| Date | Mintage | F | VF | XF | Unc | BU |
|---|---|---|---|---|---|---|
| 1999 Proof | 30,000 | Value: 30.00 | | | | |

**2000 PESETAS** **KM# 1030** **Weight:** 27.0000 g. **Composition:** 0.9250 Silver .8031 oz. ASW **Ruler:** Juan Carlos I **Subject:** House of Borbon - Isabel II **Obverse:** Portrait of Isabel II

| Date | Mintage | F | VF | XF | Unc | BU |
|---|---|---|---|---|---|---|
| 1999 Proof | — | Value: 30.00 | | | | |

**2000 PESETAS** **KM# 1031** **Weight:** 27.0000 g. **Composition:** 0.9250 Silver .8031 oz. ASW **Ruler:** Juan Carlos I **Subject:** House of Borbon - Alfonso XII **Obverse:** Portrait of Alfonso XII

| Date | Mintage | F | VF | XF | Unc | BU |
|---|---|---|---|---|---|---|
| 1999 Proof | — | Value: 30.00 | | | | |

**2000 PESETAS** **KM# 1032** **Weight:** 27.0000 g. **Composition:** 0.9250 Silver .8031 oz. ASW **Ruler:** Juan Carlos I **Subject:** House of Borbon - Alfonso XIII **Obverse:** Childhood portrait of Alfonso XIII

| Date | Mintage | F | VF | XF | Unc | BU |
|---|---|---|---|---|---|---|
| 1999 Proof | — | Value: 30.00 | | | | |

**2000 PESETAS** **KM# 1033** **Weight:** 27.0000 g. **Composition:** 0.9250 Silver .8031 oz. ASW **Ruler:** Juan Carlos I **Subject:** House of Borbon - Alfonso XIII **Obverse:** Adult portrait of Alfonso XIII

| Date | Mintage | F | VF | XF | Unc | BU |
|---|---|---|---|---|---|---|
| 1999 Proof | — | Value: 30.00 | | | | |

**2000 PESETAS** **KM# 1015** **Weight:** 18.0000 g. **Composition:** 0.9250 Silver .5353 oz. ASW **Subject:** Charles V **Obverse:** King's portrait **Reverse:** Portrait of Charles V **Edge:** Plain **Size:** 33 mm.

| Date | Mintage | F | VF | XF | Unc | BU |
|---|---|---|---|---|---|---|
| 2000 | 2,000 | — | — | — | 25.00 | — |

**2000 PESETAS** KM# 1017 **Weight:** 18.0000 g. **Composition:** 0.9250 Silver .5353 oz. ASW **Subject:** 132nd Anniversary of the Peseta **Obverse:** Portraits of King and Queen. **Reverse:** Seated allegorical design from the 1869 Spanish coin series. **Edge:** Plain. **Size:** 32.9 mm.

| Date | Mintage | F | VF | XF | Unc | BU |
|---|---|---|---|---|---|---|
| 2001 | — | — | — | — | 30.00 | — |

**5000 PESETAS** KM# 839 **Weight:** 54.0000 g. **Composition:** 0.9250 Silver 1.6059 oz. ASW **Subject:** Discovery of America **Reverse:** Santa Maria

| Date | Mintage | F | VF | XF | Unc | BU |
|---|---|---|---|---|---|---|
| 1989 | 24,000 | — | — | — | — | 45.00 |
| 1989 Proof | 33,000 | Value: 45.00 | | | | |

**5000 PESETAS** KM# 840 **Weight:** 1.6800 g. **Composition:** 0.9990 Gold .0540 oz. AGW **Subject:** Discovery of America **Reverse:** Compass face

| Date | Mintage | F | VF | XF | Unc | BU |
|---|---|---|---|---|---|---|
| 1989 | 6,000 | — | — | — | — | 60.00 |
| 1989 Proof | 8,000 | Value: 60.00 | | | | |

**5000 PESETAS** KM# 869 **Weight:** 54.0000 g. **Composition:** 0.9250 Silver 1.6059 oz. ASW **Subject:** Cortes, Montezuma, and Marina **Reverse:** Scene from Aztec mythology within legend

| Date | Mintage | F | VF | XF | Unc | BU |
|---|---|---|---|---|---|---|
| 1990 | 11,000 | — | — | — | — | 60.00 |
| 1990 Proof | 13,000 | Value: 60.00 | | | | |

**5000 PESETAS** KM# 870 **Weight:** 1.6800 g. **Composition:** 0.9990 Gold .0540 oz. AGW **Subject:** Philip V **Reverse:** Similar to KM#840

| Date | Mintage | F | VF | XF | Unc | BU |
|---|---|---|---|---|---|---|
| 1990 | 3,000 | — | — | — | — | 65.00 |
| 1990 Proof | 4,000 | Value: 65.00 | | | | |

**5000 PESETAS** KM# 893 **Weight:** 54.0000 g. **Composition:** 0.9250 Silver 1.6059 oz. ASW **Subject:** Pizarro and Atahualpa **Reverse:** Incan ruins in mountains within legend

| Date | Mintage | F | VF | XF | Unc | BU |
|---|---|---|---|---|---|---|
| 1991 | 8,000 | — | — | — | — | 85.00 |
| 1991 Proof | 8,145 | Value: 85.00 | | | | |

**5000 PESETAS** KM# 894 **Weight:** 1.6800 g. **Composition:** 0.9990 Gold .0540 oz. AGW **Subject:** Ferdinando VI **Reverse:** Similar to KM#840

| Date | Mintage | F | VF | XF | Unc | BU |
|---|---|---|---|---|---|---|
| 1991 | 1,000 | — | — | — | — | 90.00 |
| 1991 Proof | 2,000 | Value: 90.00 | | | | |

**5000 PESETAS** KM# 997 **Weight:** 54.0000 g. **Composition:** 0.9250 Silver 1.6059 oz. ASW **Subject:** Seville Expo '92 **Obverse:** Mint building **Reverse:** Old coin press

| Date | Mintage | F | VF | XF | Unc | BU |
|---|---|---|---|---|---|---|
| 1992 | 8,000 | — | — | — | — | 100 |
| 1992 Proof | 7,000 | Value: 100 | | | | |

**5000 PESETAS** KM# 1001 **Weight:** 54.0000 g. **Composition:** 0.9250 Silver 1.6059 oz. ASW **Obverse:** Similar to KM#840 **Reverse:** Screw press

| Date | Mintage | F | VF | XF | Unc | BU |
|---|---|---|---|---|---|---|
| 1992 | 1,000 | — | — | — | — | 110 |
| 1992 Proof | — | Value: 110 | | | | |

**5000 PESETAS** KM# 942 **Weight:** 54.0000 g. **Composition:** 0.9250 Silver 1.6059 oz. ASW **Subject:** Imperial Eagle

| Date | Mintage | F | VF | XF | Unc | BU |
|---|---|---|---|---|---|---|
| 1994 Proof | 30,000 | Value: 70.00 | | | | |

**5000 PESETAS** KM# 956 **Weight:** 54.0000 g. **Composition:** 0.9250 Silver 1.6059 oz. ASW **Subject:** Spanish Ibex

| Date | Mintage | F | VF | XF | Unc | BU |
|---|---|---|---|---|---|---|
| 1995 Proof | 25,000 | Value: 70.00 | | | | |

**5000 PESETAS** KM# 969 **Weight:** 54.0000 g. **Composition:** 0.9250 Silver 1.6059 oz. ASW **Subject:** Gaudi Sculpture

| Date | Mintage | F | VF | XF | Unc | BU |
|---|---|---|---|---|---|---|
| 1996 Proof | Est. 20,000 | Value: 65.00 | | | | |

**10000 PESETAS** KM# 842 **Weight:** 3.3700 g. **Composition:** 0.9990 Gold .1084 oz. AGW **Subject:** Discovery of America **Reverse:** Armillary sphere

| Date | Mintage | F | VF | XF | Unc | BU |
|---|---|---|---|---|---|---|
| 1989 | 5,000 | — | — | — | — | 90.00 |
| 1989 Proof | 7,000 | Value: 90.00 | | | | |

**10000 PESETAS** **KM# 841** **Weight:** 168.7500 g. **Composition:** 0.9250 Silver 5.0191 oz. ASW **Subject:** Regional Autonomy **Reverse:** Crowned Provincial arms **Note:** Illustration reduced, actual size 73mm

| Date | Mintage | F | VF | XF | Unc | BU |
|---|---|---|---|---|---|---|
| 1989 | 47,000 | — | — | — | — | 120 |
| 1989 Proof | — | Value: 120 | | | | |

**10000 PESETAS** **KM# 873** **Weight:** 168.7500 g. **Composition:** 0.9250 Silver 5.0191 oz. ASW **Subject:** Spanish Royal Family **Reverse:** Similar to KM#896 **Note:** Illustration reduced, actual size 73mm

| Date | Mintage | F | VF | XF | Unc | BU |
|---|---|---|---|---|---|---|
| 1990 | 26,000 | — | — | — | — | 140 |
| 1990 Proof | — | Value: 140 | | | | |

**10000 PESETAS** **KM# 871** **Weight:** 3.3700 g. **Composition:** 0.9990 Gold .1084 oz. AGW **Subject:** 1992 Olympics **Reverse:** Stylized field hockey player

| Date | Mintage | F | VF | XF | Unc | BU |
|---|---|---|---|---|---|---|
| 1990 | 3,000 | — | — | — | — | 90.00 |
| 1990 Proof | 5,000 | Value: 90.00 | | | | |

**Note:** Unc strikes have medallic die alignment and edges with reeded and plain sections. Proof strikes have coin die alignment and reeded edges

**10000 PESETAS** **KM# 872** **Weight:** 3.3700 g. **Composition:** 0.9990 Gold .1084 oz. AGW **Subject:** 1992 Olympics **Reverse:** Stylized gymnast

| Date | Mintage | F | VF | XF | Unc | BU |
|---|---|---|---|---|---|---|
| 1990 | 2,000 | — | — | — | — | 95.00 |
| 1990 Proof | 3,000 | Value: 95.00 | | | | |

**Note:** Unc strikes have medallic die alignment and edges with reeded and plain sections. Proof strikes have coin die alignment and reeded edges

**10000 PESETAS** **KM# 874** **Weight:** 3.3700 g. **Composition:** 0.9990 Gold .1084 oz. AGW **Subject:** Quauchtemoc **Reverse:** Similar to 5,000 Pesetas, KM#840

| Date | Mintage | F | VF | XF | Unc | BU |
|---|---|---|---|---|---|---|
| 1990 | 9,000 | — | — | — | — | 95.00 |
| 1990 Proof | 2,000 | Value: 95.00 | | | | |

**10000 PESETAS** **KM# 895** **Weight:** 3.3700 g. **Composition:** 0.9990 Gold .1084 oz. AGW **Subject:** Olympics **Reverse:** Karate participant

| Date | Mintage | F | VF | XF | Unc | BU |
|---|---|---|---|---|---|---|
| 1991 | 2,000 | — | — | — | — | 180 |
| 1991 Proof | 3,000 | Value: 180 | | | | |

**Note:** See note below KM#915

**10000 PESETAS** **KM# 897** **Weight:** 3.3700 g. **Composition:** 0.9990 Gold .1084 oz. AGW **Subject:** Tupac Amaru II **Reverse:** Similar to KM#842

| Date | Mintage | F | VF | XF | Unc | BU |
|---|---|---|---|---|---|---|
| 1991 | 1,000 | — | — | — | — | 150 |
| 1991 Proof | 2,000 | Value: 150 | | | | |

**10000 PESETAS** **KM# 896** **Weight:** 168.7500 g. **Composition:** 0.9250 Silver 5.0191 oz. ASW **Subject:** Discoverers and Liberators **Reverse:** Similar to KM#873 **Note:** Illustration reduced, actual size 73mm

| Date | Mintage | F | VF | XF | Unc | BU |
|---|---|---|---|---|---|---|
| 1991 | 17,000 | — | — | — | — | 175 |
| 1991 Proof | — | Value: 175 | | | | |

**10000 PESETAS** **KM# 1002** **Weight:** 3.3700 g. **Composition:** 0.9990 Gold .1084 oz. AGW **Ruler:** Juan Carlos I **Obverse:** Similar to KM#842 **Reverse:** Worker operating screw press

| Date | Mintage | F | VF | XF | Unc | BU |
|---|---|---|---|---|---|---|
| 1992 | 1,000 | — | — | — | — | 180 |
| 1992 Proof | — | Value: 180 | | | | |

**10000 PESETAS** **KM# 915** **Weight:** 3.3700 g. **Composition:** 0.9990 Gold .1084 oz. AGW **Subject:** Olympics **Reverse:** Baseball player

| Date | Mintage | F | VF | XF | Unc | BU |
|---|---|---|---|---|---|---|
| 1992 | 1,000 | — | — | — | — | 180 |
| 1992 Proof | 6,000 | Value: 180 | | | | |

**Note:** Unc strikes have medallic die alignment and edges with reeded and plain sections. Proof strikes have coin die alignment and reeded edges

**10000 PESETAS** **KM# 998** **Weight:** 168.7500 g. **Composition:** 0.9250 Silver 5.0191 oz. ASW **Subject:** Seville Expo '92 - Nobel Prize winners **Reverse:** Royal Family portraits

| Date | Mintage | F | VF | XF | Unc | BU |
|---|---|---|---|---|---|---|
| 1992 Proof | 14,000 | Value: 235 | | | | |

**10000 PESETAS** **KM# 928** **Weight:** 168.7500 g. **Composition:** 0.9250 Silver 5.0191 oz. ASW **Subject:** Holy Jacobean Year **Reverse:** Cathedral and Pilgrims of the Middle Ages **Note:** Illustration reduced, actual size 75mm

| Date | Mintage | F | VF | XF | Unc | BU |
|---|---|---|---|---|---|---|
| 1993 Proof | 7,000 | Value: 265 | | | | |

**10000 PESETAS** **KM# 943** **Weight:** 167.7500 g. **Composition:** 0.9250 Silver 4.9888 oz. ASW **Subject:** Goya's paintings **Reverse:** Bull fighting scene **Note:** Illustration reduced, actual size 73mm

| Date | Mintage | F | VF | XF | Unc | BU |
|---|---|---|---|---|---|---|
| 1994 Proof | Est. 30,000 | Value: 150 | | | | |

**10000 PESETAS** **KM# 957** **Weight:** 168.7500 g. **Composition:** 0.9250 Silver 5.0018 oz. ASW **Subject:** Velaguez's paintings **Note:** Illustration reduced, actual size 73mm

| Date | Mintage | F | VF | XF | Unc | BU |
|---|---|---|---|---|---|---|
| 1995 Proof | Est. 25,000 | Value: 150 | | | | |

**10000 PESETAS** **KM# 970** **Weight:** 168.7500 g. **Composition:** 0.9250 Silver 5.0018 oz. ASW **Subject:** Velaguez's paintings **Reverse:** Family picking flowers

| Date | Mintage | F | VF | XF | Unc | BU |
|---|---|---|---|---|---|---|
| 1996 Proof | Est. 15,000 | Value: 150 | | | | |

**10000 PESETAS** **KM# 1027** **Weight:** 168.7500 g. **Composition:** 0.9250 Silver 5.0185 oz. ASW **Ruler:** Juan Carlos I **Subject:** House of Borbon - Juan Carlos I **Obverse:** King standing and Queen seated **Reverse:** Spanish arms in circle of portraits **Edge:** Reeded **Size:** 73 mm.

| Date | Mintage | F | VF | XF | Unc | BU |
|---|---|---|---|---|---|---|
| 1997 Proof | — | Value: 150 | | | | |

**20000 PESETAS** **KM# 843** **Weight:** 6.7500 g. **Composition:** 0.9990 Gold .2170 oz. AGW **Subject:** Discovery of America **Reverse:** Pinzon Brother

| Date | Mintage | F | VF | XF | Unc | BU |
|---|---|---|---|---|---|---|
| 1989 | 5,000 | — | — | — | — | 150 |
| 1989 Proof | 6,500 | Value: 150 | | | | |

**20000 PESETAS** **KM# 875** **Weight:** 6.7500 g. **Composition:** 0.9990 Gold .2170 oz. AGW **Subject:** 1992 Olympics - La Sagrada Familia **Reverse:** Cathedral towers

| Date | Mintage | F | VF | XF | Unc | BU |
|---|---|---|---|---|---|---|
| 1990 | 4,000 | — | — | — | — | 180 |
| 1990 Proof | 10,000 | Value: 180 | | | | |

**Note:** Unc strikes have medallic die alignment and edges with reeded and plain sections. Proof strikes have coin die alignment and reeded edges

**20000 PESETAS** **KM# 876** **Weight:** 6.7500 g. **Composition:** 0.9990 Gold .2170 oz. AGW **Subject:** 1992 Olympics **Reverse:** Ruins of Empuries

| Date | Mintage | F | VF | XF | Unc | BU |
|---|---|---|---|---|---|---|
| 1990 | 2,000 | — | — | — | — | 180 |
| 1990 Proof | 4,000 | Value: 180 | | | | |

**Note:** Unc strikes have medallic die alignment and edges with reeded and plain sections; Proof strikes have coin die alignment and reeded edges.

**20000 PESETAS** **KM# 877** **Weight:** 6.7500 g. **Composition:** 0.9990 Gold .2170 oz. AGW **Subject:** Tupac Amaru I **Obverse:** Similar to KM#843

| Date | Mintage | F | VF | XF | Unc | BU |
|---|---|---|---|---|---|---|
| 1990 | 2,000 | — | — | — | — | 180 |
| 1990 Proof | 3,000 | Value: 180 | | | | |

**20000 PESETAS** **KM# 898** **Weight:** 6.7500 g. **Composition:** 0.9990 Gold .2170 oz. AGW **Subject:** Olympics **Reverse:** Montjuic Stadium

| Date | Mintage | F | VF | XF | Unc | BU |
|---|---|---|---|---|---|---|
| 1991 | 2,000 | — | — | — | — | 270 |
| 1991 Proof | 3,000 | Value: 270 | | | | |

**Note:** Unc strikes have medallic die alignment and edges with reeded and plain sections; Proof strikes have coin die alignment and reeded edges.

**20000 PESETAS** **KM# 899** **Weight:** 6.7500 g. **Composition:** 0.9990 Gold .2170 oz. AGW **Subject:** Huascar **Obverse:** Portrait of Juan Carlos

| Date | Mintage | F | VF | XF | Unc | BU |
|---|---|---|---|---|---|---|
| 1991 | 1,000 | — | — | — | — | 240 |
| 1991 Proof | 2,000 | Value: 240 | | | | |

**20000 PESETAS** **KM# 916** **Weight:** 6.7500 g. **Composition:** 0.9990 Gold .2170 oz. AGW **Subject:** Olympics **Reverse:** Dome building

| Date | Mintage | F | VF | XF | Unc | BU |
|---|---|---|---|---|---|---|
| 1992 | 1,000 | — | — | — | — | 270 |
| 1992 Proof | 3,000 | Value: 270 | | | | |

**Note:** Unc strikes have medallic die alignment and edges with reeded and plain sections; Proof strikes have coin die alignment and reeded edges.

**20000 PESETAS** **KM# 1003** **Weight:** 6.7500 g. **Composition:** 0.9990 Gold .2170 oz. AGW **Obverse:** Similar to KM#843 **Reverse:** Worker feeding screw press

| Date | Mintage | F | VF | XF | Unc | BU |
|---|---|---|---|---|---|---|
| 1992 | 1,000 | — | — | — | — | 270 |
| 1992 Proof | — | Value: 270 | | | | |

**20000 PESETAS** **KM# 929** **Weight:** 6.7500 g. **Composition:** 0.9990 Gold .2170 oz. AGW **Subject:** Holy Jacobean Year - Conveyance of Santiago's body

| Date | Mintage | F | VF | XF | Unc | BU |
|---|---|---|---|---|---|---|
| 1993 Proof | 2,000 | Value: 240 | | | | |

**20000 PESETAS** KM# 944 **Weight:** 6.7500 g. **Composition:** 0.9990 Gold .2170 oz. AGW **Subject:** Paleolithic Cave Painting

| Date | Mintage | F | VF | XF | Unc | BU |
|---|---|---|---|---|---|---|
| 1994 Proof | 8,000 | Value: 260 | | | | |

**20000 PESETAS** KM# 958 **Weight:** 6.7500 g. **Composition:** 0.9990 Gold .2170 oz. AGW **Subject:** Ancient Sculpture - Dama de Elche

| Date | Mintage | F | VF | XF | Unc | BU |
|---|---|---|---|---|---|---|
| 1995 Proof | 8,000 | Value: 220 | | | | |

**20000 PESETAS** KM# 971 **Weight:** 6.7500 g. **Composition:** 0.9990 Gold .2170 oz. AGW **Reverse:** Pillars and arches

| Date | Mintage | F | VF | XF | Unc | BU |
|---|---|---|---|---|---|---|
| 1996 Proof | Est. 6,000 | Value: 220 | | | | |

**40000 PESETAS** KM# 844 **Weight:** 13.5000 g. **Composition:** 0.9990 Gold .4341 oz. AGW **Subject:** Discovery of America **Reverse:** Sea monster attacking ship

| Date | Mintage | F | VF | XF | Unc | BU |
|---|---|---|---|---|---|---|
| 1989 | 4,500 | — | — | — | — | 320 |
| 1989 Proof | 6,000 | Value: 320 | | | | |

**40000 PESETAS** KM# 878 **Weight:** 13.5000 g. **Composition:** 0.9990 Gold .4341 oz. AGW **Subject:** Felipe II **Obverse:** Similar to KM#844

| Date | Mintage | F | VF | XF | Unc | BU |
|---|---|---|---|---|---|---|
| 1990 | 2,000 | — | — | — | — | 350 |
| 1990 Proof | 3,000 | Value: 350 | | | | |

**40000 PESETAS** KM# 900 **Weight:** 13.5000 g. **Composition:** 0.9990 Gold .4341 oz. AGW **Obverse:** Similar to KM#844 **Reverse:** Imperial double eagle

| Date | Mintage | F | VF | XF | Unc | BU |
|---|---|---|---|---|---|---|
| 1991 | 1,000 | — | — | — | — | 450 |
| 1991 Proof | 2,000 | Value: 450 | | | | |

**40000 PESETAS** KM# 1004 **Weight:** 13.5000 g. **Composition:** 0.9990 Gold .4341 oz. AGW **Obverse:** Similar to KM#844 **Reverse:** Horse-powered coin press

| Date | Mintage | F | VF | XF | Unc | BU |
|---|---|---|---|---|---|---|
| 1992 | 1,000 | — | — | — | — | 500 |
| 1992 Proof | — | Value: 500 | | | | |

**40000 PESETAS** KM# 979 **Weight:** 13.5000 g. **Composition:** 0.9990 Gold .4341 oz. AGW **Subject:** Patrimonio de la Humanidad **Obverse:** UNESCO logo **Reverse:** Statues at Abu Simbel

| Date | Mintage | F | VF | XF | Unc | BU |
|---|---|---|---|---|---|---|
| 1996 Proof | 4,000 | Value: 425 | | | | |

**40000 PESETAS** KM# 1023 **Weight:** 13.5000 g. **Composition:** 0.9990 Gold .4341 oz. AGW **Ruler:** Juan Carlos I **Series:** "Patrimonio de la Humanidad - UNESCO" **Obverse:** UNESCO logo **Reverse:** Horyu-Ji pagoda **Edge:** Reeded **Size:** 30 mm.

| Date | Mintage | F | VF | XF | Unc | BU |
|---|---|---|---|---|---|---|
| 1997 Proof | 4,000 | Value: 425 | | | | |

**80000 PESETAS** KM# 845 **Weight:** 27.0000 g. **Composition:** 0.9990 Gold .8682 oz. AGW **Subject:** Discovery of America **Reverse:** Ferdinand and Isabella

| Date | Mintage | F | VF | XF | Unc | BU |
|---|---|---|---|---|---|---|
| 1989 | 6,000 | — | — | — | — | 625 |
| 1989 Proof | 7,000 | Value: 625 | | | | |

**80000 PESETAS** KM# 879 **Weight:** 27.0000 g. **Composition:** 0.9990 Gold .8682 oz. AGW **Subject:** 1992 Olympics **Reverse:** Discus thrower

| Date | Mintage | F | VF | XF | Unc | BU |
|---|---|---|---|---|---|---|
| 1990 | 3,000 | — | — | — | — | 625 |
| 1990 Proof | 5,000 | Value: 625 | | | | |

**Note:** Unc strikes have medallic die alignment and edges with reeded and plain sections; Proof strikes have coin die alignment and reeded edges

**80000 PESETAS** KM# 880 **Weight:** 27.0000 g. **Composition:** 0.9990 Gold .8682 oz. AGW **Subject:** 1992 Olympics **Reverse:** Prince Balthasar Carlos on horseback

| Date | Mintage | F | VF | XF | Unc | BU |
|---|---|---|---|---|---|---|
| 1990 | 1,000 | — | — | — | — | 675 |
| 1990 Proof | 4,000 | Value: 675 | | | | |

**Note:** Unc strikes have medallic die alignment and edges with reeded and plain sections; Proof strikes have coin die alignment and reeded edges

**80000 PESETAS** KM# 881 **Weight:** 27.0000 g. **Composition:** 0.9990 Gold .8682 oz. AGW **Subject:** Carlos V **Obverse:** Similar to KM#845

| Date | Mintage | F | VF | XF | Unc | BU |
|---|---|---|---|---|---|---|
| 1990 | 2,000 | — | — | — | — | 675 |
| 1990 Proof | 3,000 | Value: 675 | | | | |

**80000 PESETAS** KM# 901 **Weight:** 27.0000 g. **Composition:** 0.9990 Gold .8682 oz. AGW **Subject:** Olympics **Reverse:** Women tossing man

| Date | Mintage | F | VF | XF | Unc | BU |
|---|---|---|---|---|---|---|
| 1991 | 1,000 | — | — | — | — | 1,000 |
| 1991 Proof | 2,000 | Value: 1,000 | | | | |

**Note:** Unc strikes have medallic die alignment and edges with reeded and plain sections; Proof strikes have coin die alignment and reeded edges

**80000 PESETAS** **KM# 902** **Weight:** 27.0000 g. **Composition:** 0.9990 Gold .8682 oz. AGW **Subject:** Carlos III **Obverse:** Similar to KM#845

| Date | Mintage | F | VF | XF | Unc | BU |
|---|---|---|---|---|---|---|
| 1991 | 1,000 | — | — | — | — | 925 |
| 1991 Proof | 2,000 | Value: 925 | | | | |

**80000 PESETAS** **KM# 917** **Weight:** 27.0000 g. **Composition:** 0.9990 Gold .8682 oz. AGW **Subject:** Olympics **Reverse:** Two children playing

| Date | Mintage | F | VF | XF | Unc | BU |
|---|---|---|---|---|---|---|
| 1992 | 1,000 | — | — | — | — | 1,000 |
| 1992 Proof | 2,000 | Value: 1,000 | | | | |

**Note:** Unc strikes have medallic die alignment and edges with reeded and plain sections; Proof strikes have coin die alignment and reeded edges

**80000 PESETAS** **KM# 1005** **Weight:** 27.0000 g. **Composition:** 0.9990 Gold .8682 oz. AGW **Obverse:** Similar to KM#845 **Reverse:** Hammer minting scene

| Date | Mintage | F | VF | XF | Unc | BU |
|---|---|---|---|---|---|---|
| 1992 | 1,000 | — | — | — | — | 1,000 |
| 1992 Proof | — | Value: 1,000 | | | | |

**80000 PESETAS** **KM# 930** **Weight:** 27.0000 g. **Composition:** 0.9990 Gold .8682 oz. AGW **Subject:** Holy Jacobean Year **Reverse:** French Fraternity of Santiago Medallion

| Date | Mintage | F | VF | XF | Unc | BU |
|---|---|---|---|---|---|---|
| 1993 Proof | 1,500 | Value: 850 | | | | |

**80000 PESETAS** **KM# 945** **Weight:** 27.0000 g. **Composition:** 0.9990 Gold .8682 oz. AGW **Reverse:** Iberian Lynx

| Date | Mintage | F | VF | XF | Unc | BU |
|---|---|---|---|---|---|---|
| 1994 Proof | 5,000 | Value: 750 | | | | |

**80000 PESETAS** **KM# 959** **Weight:** 27.0000 g. **Composition:** 0.9990 Gold .8682 oz. AGW **Subject:** Leda and the swan

| Date | Mintage | F | VF | XF | Unc | BU |
|---|---|---|---|---|---|---|
| 1995 Proof | 5,000 | Value: 800 | | | | |

**80000 PESETAS** **KM# 972** **Weight:** 27.0000 g. **Composition:** 0.9990 Gold .8682 oz. AGW **Reverse:** Folk dancers

| Date | Mintage | F | VF | XF | Unc | BU |
|---|---|---|---|---|---|---|
| 1996 Proof | Est. 3,500 | Value: 800 | | | | |

**80000 PESETAS** **KM# 1028** **Weight:** 27.0000 g. **Composition:** 0.9990 Gold .8672 oz. AGW **Ruler:** Juan Carlos I **Subject:** House of Borbon **Obverse:** 8 Escudo obverse design of 1752 within legend **Reverse:** 8 Escudo reverse design of 1752 within legend **Edge:** Reeded **Size:** 38 mm.

| Date | Mintage | F | VF | XF | Unc | BU |
|---|---|---|---|---|---|---|
| 1997 Proof | 4,000 | Value: 800 | | | | |

## MEDALLIC COINAGE

### European Currency Unit

**ECU** **KM# M1** **Weight:** 6.2200 g. **Composition:** 0.9250 Silver .1850 oz. ASW **Reverse:** Europa on back of bull (Zeus)

| Date | Mintage | F | VF | XF | Unc | BU |
|---|---|---|---|---|---|---|
| 1989 Proof | 500,000 | Value: 15.00 | | | | |

**ECU** **KM# M8** **Weight:** 6.2200 g. **Composition:** 0.9250 Silver .1850 oz. ASW **Subject:** Madrid as European cuture capital

| Date | Mintage | F | VF | XF | Unc | BU |
|---|---|---|---|---|---|---|
| 1992 Proof | — | Value: 16.50 | | | | |

**ECU** **KM# M12** **Weight:** 6.2200 g. **Composition:** 0.9250 Silver .1850 oz. ASW **Subject:** Don Quixote

| Date | Mintage | F | VF | XF | Unc | BU |
|---|---|---|---|---|---|---|
| 1994 Proof | — | Value: 17.50 | | | | |

**ECU** **KM# M16** **Weight:** 6.2200 g. **Composition:** 0.9250 Silver .1850 oz. ASW **Subject:** Nautilus **Reverse:** Ship

| Date | Mintage | F | VF | XF | Unc | BU |
|---|---|---|---|---|---|---|
| 1996 Proof | — | Value: 17.50 | | | | |

**5 ECU** **KM# M2** **Weight:** 31.1000 g. **Composition:** 0.9250 Silver .9250 oz. ASW **Subject:** Charles V

| Date | Mintage | F | VF | XF | Unc | BU |
|---|---|---|---|---|---|---|
| 1989 Proof | 250,000 | Value: 22.00 | | | | |

**5 ECU** **KM# M6** **Weight:** 31.1000 g. **Composition:** 0.9250 Silver .9250 oz. ASW **Subject:** Alphonso X of Castile

| Date | Mintage | F | VF | XF | Unc | BU |
|---|---|---|---|---|---|---|
| 1990 Proof | 50,000 | Value: 32.50 | | | | |

**5 ECU** **KM# M7** **Weight:** 33.6200 g. **Composition:** 0.9250 Silver .9998 oz. ASW **Subject:** Averroes - Moorish Philosopher

| Date | Mintage | F | VF | XF | Unc | BU |
|---|---|---|---|---|---|---|
| 1991 Proof | 50,000 | Value: 32.50 | | | | |

**5 ECU** **KM# M11** **Weight:** 33.6200 g. **Composition:** 0.9250 Silver .9998 oz. ASW **Subject:** Madrid as European culture capital **Reverse:** Carlos III

| Date | Mintage | F | VF | XF | Unc | BU |
|---|---|---|---|---|---|---|
| 1992 Proof | Est. 100,000 | Value: 65.00 | | | | |

**5 ECU** **KM# M9** **Weight:** 33.6200 g. **Composition:** 0.9250 Silver .9998 oz. ASW **Reverse:** Don Juan

| Date | Mintage | F | VF | XF | Unc | BU |
|---|---|---|---|---|---|---|
| 1993 Proof | 36,000 | Value: 35.00 | | | | |

**5 ECU** **KM# M13** **Weight:** 33.6200 g. **Composition:** 0.9250 Silver .9998 oz. ASW **Reverse:** Don Quixote

| Date | Mintage | F | VF | XF | Unc | BU |
|---|---|---|---|---|---|---|
| 1994 Proof | Est. 75,000 | Value: 37.50 | | | | |

**5 ECU** **KM# M17** **Weight:** 33.6200 g. **Composition:** 0.9250 Silver .9998 oz. ASW **Reverse:** Coca de Mataro

| Date | Mintage | F | VF | XF | Unc | BU |
|---|---|---|---|---|---|---|
| 1996 Proof | — | Value: 32.50 | | | | |

**10 ECU** **KM# M3** **Weight:** 3.1100 g. **Composition:** 0.9000 Gold .0900 oz. AGW **Subject:** Crowned pillars of Hercules

| Date | Mintage | F | VF | XF | Unc | BU |
|---|---|---|---|---|---|---|
| 1989 Proof | 28,000 | Value: 75.00 | | | | |

**50 ECU** **KM# M4** **Weight:** 15.5500 g. **Composition:** 0.9000 Gold .4500 oz. AGW **Subject:** Philip II

| Date | Mintage | F | VF | XF | Unc | BU |
|---|---|---|---|---|---|---|
| 1989 Proof | 15,000 | Value: 250 | | | | |

**25 ECU** **KM# M18** **Weight:** 168.6200 g. **Composition:** 0.9250 Silver 5.0147 oz. ASW **Subject:** Madrid: European cultural capital **Obverse:** Denomination and city list **Reverse:** Portrait above palace **Edge:** Plain **Size:** 73.2 mm. **Note:** Illustration reduced

| Date | Mintage | F | VF | XF | Unc | BU |
|---|---|---|---|---|---|---|
| 1992 Proof | — | Value: 125 | | | | |

**25 ECU** **KM# M19** **Weight:** 168.7500 g. **Composition:** 0.9250 Silver 5.0185 oz. ASW **Obverse:** Three portraits. **Reverse:** Large sailing ships. **Edge:** Plain. **Size:** 73 mm.

| Date | Mintage | F | VF | XF | Unc | BU |
|---|---|---|---|---|---|---|
| 1995 Proof | 75,000 | Value: 17.50 | | | | |

**100 ECU** **KM# M5** **Weight:** 31.1000 g. **Composition:** 0.9000 Gold .9000 oz. AGW

| Date | Mintage | F | VF | XF | Unc | BU |
|---|---|---|---|---|---|---|
| 1989 Proof | 10,000 | Value: 500 | | | | |

**100 ECU** **KM# M14** **Weight:** 34.5500 g. **Composition:** 0.9000 Gold .9998 oz. AGW **Subject:** Madrid as European culture capital **Reverse:** Carlos III

| Date | Mintage | F | VF | XF | Unc | BU |
|---|---|---|---|---|---|---|
| 1992 Proof | Est. 10,000 | Value: 550 | | | | |

**100 ECU** **KM# M10** **Weight:** 34.5500 g. **Composition:** 0.9000 Gold .9998 oz. AGW **Subject:** Don Juan de Borbon

| Date | Mintage | F | VF | XF | Unc | BU |
|---|---|---|---|---|---|---|
| ND(1993) Proof | 2,020 | Value: 775 | | | | |

**100 ECU** **KM# M15** **Weight:** 34.5500 g. **Composition:** 0.9000 Gold .9998 oz. AGW **Subject:** Don Quixote

| Date | Mintage | F | VF | XF | Unc | BU |
|---|---|---|---|---|---|---|
| 1994 Proof | Est. 3,500 | Value: 650 | | | | |

## TRIAL STRIKES

| KM# | Date | Mintage | Identification | Mkt Val |
|---|---|---|---|---|
| TS1 | 1987 | — | 500 Pesetas. Silver. | 10.00 |
| TS2 | 1987 | — | 500 Pesetas. Stainless Steel. | 7.50 |
| TS3 | 1987 | — | 500 Pesetas. Silver. | 10.00 |

| KM# | Date | Mintage | Identification | Mkt Val |
|---|---|---|---|---|
| TS4 | 1987 | — | 500 Pesetas. Stainless Steel. | 7.50 |

| KM# | Date | Mintage | Identification | Mkt Val |
|---|---|---|---|---|
| TS5 | | — | 2000 Pesetas. Mint mark. Same as KM#859. | — |

## PATTERNS

Including off metal strikes

| KM# | Date | Mintage | Identification | Mkt Val |
|---|---|---|---|---|
| Pn16 | 1937 | — | 10 Centimos. Zinc. | — |

## MINT SETS

| KM# | Date | Mintage | Identification | Issue Price | Mkt Val |
|---|---|---|---|---|---|
| MS1 | 1949 (E51) (3) | 5,000 | KM#776, 777-778 | — | 2,250 |
| MS2 | 1958Ba (3) | — | KM#786-788 | — | 300 |
| MS3 | 1964 (7) | — | KM#777, 785-788, 790, 797. Note: Set contains KM#790, dated 1959 with added 'strike date' to match the set | 3.60 | 65.00 |
| MS4 | 1965 (7) | — | KM#777, 785-788, 790, 797. Note: Set contains KM#790, dated 1959 with added 'strike date' to match the set | 3.60 | 60.00 |
| MS5 | 1966 (8) | — | KM#775, 777, 785-788, 790, 797. Note: Set contains KM#790, dated 1959 with added 'strike date' to match the set | — | 200 |
| MS6 | 1966 (8) | — | KM#775, 777, 785-788, 790, 797. Note: Set contains KM#790, dated 1959 with added 'strike date' to match the set | — | 175 |

| KM# | Date | Mintage | Identification | Issue Price | Mkt Val |
|---|---|---|---|---|---|
| MS7 | 1968 (8) | 1,000 | KM#785-788, 790, 795-797. Note: Set contains KM#790, dated 1959 with added 'strike date' to match the set | 3.60 | 1,800 |
| MS8 | 1969 (8) | 1,200 | KM#785-788, 790, 795-797. Note: Set contains KM#790, dated 1959 with added 'strike date' to match the set | 3.60 | 1,150 |
| MS9 | 1970 (8) | 6,000 | KM#785-788, 790, 795-797. Note: Set contains KM#790, dated 1959 with added 'strike date' to match the set | 3.60 | 350 |
| MS10 | 1971 (8) | 10,000 | KM#785-788, 790, 795-797. Note: Set contains KM#790, dated 1959 with added 'strike date' to match the set | 3.60 | 175 |
| MS11 | 1980(80) (6) | — | KM#815-820 | — | 5.00 |
| MS13 | 1990 (U) (5) | — | KM#854, 856-858, 868 | — | 60.00 |
| MS15 | 1991 (U) (5) | — | KM#882-883, 885-886, 892 | — | 85.00 |
| MS18 | 1992 (10) | — | KM#832-833, 903-910 | — | 30.00 |
| MS19 | 1993 (8) | — | KM#832, 918-919, 920-924 | — | 25.00 |
| MS20 | 1994 (8) | — | KM#832, 924, 931-936 | — | 35.00 |
| MS21 | 1995 (8) | — | KM#832, 924, 946-951 | — | 65.00 |
| MS22 | 1996 (8) | — | KM#832, 924, 960-965 | — | 35.00 |
| MS23 | 1997 (8) | — | KM#832, 924, 981-986 | — | 15.00 |
| MS24 | 1998 (8) | — | KM#832-833, 924, 989-992, 1012 | — | 20.00 |
| MS25 | 1999 (8) | — | KM#832, 924, 991-992, 1006-1008, 1012 | — | 20.00 |
| MS26 | 2000 (8) | — | KM#832-833, 924, 989, 991-992, 1012-1013 | — | 20.00 |
| MS27 | 2000-2001 (8) | — | KM#832-833, 924, 991-992 (both dated 2000), 1012-1013, 1016 | — | 20.00 |

## PROOF SETS

| KM# | Date | Mintage | Identification | Issue Price | Mkt Val |
|---|---|---|---|---|---|
| PS8 | 1987 (6) | — | KM#831, Pn4, Pn4a, Pn5-6 | 55.00 | 35.00 |
| PS3 | 1974 (6) | 23,000 | KM#786-788, 790, 795-796 | 10.00 | 90.00 |
| PS1 | 1972 (6) | 30,000 | KM#786-788, 790, 795-796 | 10.00 | 35.00 |
| PS2 | 1973 (6) | 25,000 | KM#786-788, 790, 795-796 | 10.00 | 90.00 |
| PS4 | 1975 (6) | 75,000 | KM#786-788, 790, 795-796 | 10.00 | 15.00 |
| PS5 | 1976 (6) | 400,000 | KM#805-810 | 7.50 | 5.00 |
| PS6 | 1977 (3) | 300,000 | KM#806-808 | — | 2.00 |
| PS7 | 1979 (4) | 300,000 | KM#806-809 | — | 3.00 |
| PS9 | 1987 (2) | — | KM#828, 830 | — | 50.00 |
| PS10 | 1989 (7) | — | KM#834-839, 841 | — | 250 |
| PS11 | 1989 (5) | — | KM#M1-M5 | — | 950 |
| PS12 | 1989 (5) | — | KM#840, 842-845 | 3,177 | 1,775 |
| PS13 | 1990 (7) | — | KM#854, 856-858, 868-869, 873 | — | 250 |
| PS14 | 1991 (7) | — | KM#882-883, 885-886, 892-893, 896 | — | 375 |
| PS15 | 1992 (7) | — | KM#980, 993-998 | — | 450 |
| PS16 | 1995 (6) | I.A. | KM#938, 953, 956-959 | — | 1,350 |
| PS17 | 1995 (4) | 25,000 | KM#938, 953, 956-959 | — | 300 |
| PS18 | 1996 (6) | — | KM#966-967, 969-972 | 1,675 | 1,300 |
| PS19 | 1996 (6) | — | KM#966-967, 969-972 | 1,650 | 1,300 |
| PS20 | 1996 (4) | — | KM#966-967, 969-972 | — | 240 |
| PS21 | 1996 (4) | — | KM#966-967, 969-970 | — | 240 |
| PS22 | 1996 (5) | — | KM#973-978 | 198 | 160 |
| PS23 | 1996 (6) | — | KM#973-979 | 702 | 600 |

With the loss of her American empire, Spain drifted into chaotic times. Stung by their defeats in Cuba, the army blamed the Socialists for what they considered to be mismanagement at home. Additional political complications were derived from the successful Russian Revolution which gave impetus to an already thriving Socialist party and trade union movement. Finally, King Alphonso XIII committed the fatal mistake of encouraging a reckless general to start a campaign in Morocco that ended in the virtual extermination of the Spanish army. Fearing that the inevitable parliamentary investigation would incriminate the crown, he offered no objection when General Primo de Rivera seized the government and established himself as dictator in 1926. Rivera fell from power in 1930, and the government was taken over by an alliance of Liberals and Socialists who tried to separate the Church and State, take the army out of politics, and introduce effective labor and agrarian reforms despite numerous strikes and street riots. The election of 1936 brought to power a coalition of Socialists, Liberals and Communists, to the dismay of the traditionalists and landowners.

A number of right-wing generals, including the young and clever Francisco Franco, began preparations for a military coup which erupted into a civil war in July of 1936.The destructive conflict, in which more than a million died, lasted three years. During the struggle, areas under control of both the Nationalist (rebels) and the Republican (Loyalists) issued coinages that circulated to whatever extent the political and military situation permitted. The war ended defeat for the Loyalists when Madrid fell to Franco on March 28, 1939.

During the Spanish Civil War (1936-1939) a great many coins and tokens were minted in the provincial districts. The coins are grouped here under the heading of the district in which they most commonly circulated.

**CAUTIONARY NOTE**: Many counterfeits of the Civil War coinage exist. Authentication has been recommended by leading experts in this field.

## ARENYS DE MAR

A resort village on the Mediterranean shore that is 20 miles north of Barcelona. One of the villages in the area of operations of General Mola at the beginning of the war.

### REPUBLICAN ZONE

#### DECIMAL COINAGE

**50 CENTIMOS** **KM#1** **Composition:** Aluminum **Note:** Uniface.

| Date | Mintage | F | VF | XF | Unc | BU |
|---|---|---|---|---|---|---|
| ND(1937) | 6,000 | 50.00 | 75.00 | 90.00 | — | — |

**PESETA** **KM#2** **Composition:** Aluminum **Note:** Uniface.

| Date | Mintage | F | VF | XF | Unc | BU |
|---|---|---|---|---|---|---|
| ND(1937) | 3,500 | 55.00 | 80.00 | 100 | — | — |

## ASTURIAS AND LEON

Asturias is a province on the northern coast of Spain with the province of Leon just to its south. The councils of these adjoining provinces decided to mint coins in1937 for use in the area due to lack of other circulating coins in the north.

### REPUBLICAN ZONE

#### DECIMAL COINAGE

**50 CENTIMOS** **KM#1** **Composition:** Copper-Nickel **Note:** Struck at Gijon.

| Date | Mintage | F | VF | XF | Unc | BU |
|---|---|---|---|---|---|---|
| 1937 | 200,000 | 15.00 | 20.00 | 25.00 | 32.00 | — |

**PESETA** **KM#2** **Composition:** Copper **Note:** Struck at Guernica.

| Date | Mintage | F | VF | XF | Unc | BU |
|---|---|---|---|---|---|---|
| 1937 | 100,000 | 15.00 | 20.00 | 30.00 | 50.00 | — |

**2 PESETAS** **KM#3** **Composition:** Copper-Nickel **Note:** Struck at Gijon. Varieties exist with differences in the leaves.

| Date | Mintage | F | VF | XF | Unc | BU |
|---|---|---|---|---|---|---|
| 1937 | 400,000 | 5.00 | 7.50 | 10.00 | 15.00 | — |

**Note:** Varieties exist with differences in the leaves

## CAZALLA DE SIERRA

A town 43 miles north of Seville that issued a 10 Centimos in brass in 1936 (undated).

### NATIONALIST ZONE

#### DECIMAL COINAGE

**10 CENTIMOS** **KM#1** **Composition:** Brass

| Date | Mintage | F | VF | XF | Unc | BU |
|---|---|---|---|---|---|---|
| ND(1936) | 10,000 | 22.00 | 30.00 | 40.00 | — | — |

## EL ARAHAL

A town 30 miles east of Seville. Issued 3 undated types of coins in 1936.

### NATIONALIST ZONE

#### DECIMAL COINAGE

**50 CENTIMOS** KM# 1 **Composition:** Brass **Note:** Uniface.

| Date | Mintage | F | VF | XF | Unc | BU |
|---|---|---|---|---|---|---|
| ND(1936) | 3,000 | 50.00 | 100 | 150 | 200 | — |

**PESETA** KM# 2 **Composition:** Brass **Note:** Uniface.

| Date | Mintage | F | VF | XF | Unc | BU |
|---|---|---|---|---|---|---|
| ND(1936) | 10,000 | 20.00 | 30.00 | 50.00 | 75.00 | — |

**2 PESETAS** KM# 3 **Composition:** Brass **Note:** Uniface.

| Date | Mintage | F | VF | XF | Unc | BU |
|---|---|---|---|---|---|---|
| ND(1936) | 10,000 | 20.00 | 30.00 | 50.00 | 75.00 | — |

## EUZKADI

Euzkadi or the Viscayan Republic was located in north central Spain adjoining the southeast corner of France. It was made up of 4 provinces - Bilbao, Guipuzcoa, Navarre, and Victoria. These Basque provinces declared autonomy on October 8, 1936. The 2 nickel coins were made in Brussels, Belgium and saw some circulation before the end of the Republic on June 18, 1937.

### REPUBLICAN ZONE
### Viscayan Republic
### DECIMAL COINAGE

**PESETA** KM# 1 **Composition:** Nickel **Note:** Struck at Brussels.

| Date | Mintage | F | VF | XF | Unc | BU |
|---|---|---|---|---|---|---|
| 1937 | 7,000,000 | 2.00 | 3.00 | 4.00 | 6.00 | — |

**2 PESETAS** KM# 2 **Composition:** Nickel **Note:** Struck at Brussels.

| Date | Mintage | F | VF | XF | Unc | BU |
|---|---|---|---|---|---|---|
| 1937 | 6,000,000 | 2.00 | 3.00 | 4.00 | 7.00 | — |

## IBI

A village north and west of Alicante on the east coast of Spain. The isolation of the area in comparison with other contending areas made the maintaining of this area during the war very difficult.

### REPUBLICAN ZONE
### DECIMAL COINAGE

**25 CENTIMOS** KM# 1.1 **Composition:** Copper **Note:** Varieties exist.

| Date | Mintage | F | VF | XF | Unc | BU |
|---|---|---|---|---|---|---|
| 1937 | 30,000 | 15.00 | 25.00 | 35.00 | 50.00 | — |

**25 CENTIMOS** KM# 1.2 **Composition:** Copper **Obverse:** Map in field

| Date | Mintage | F | VF | XF | Unc | BU |
|---|---|---|---|---|---|---|
| 1937 | 7,000 | 50.00 | 100 | 125 | 150 | — |

**PESETA** KM# 2 **Composition:** Nickel-Brass

| Date | Mintage | F | VF | XF | Unc | BU |
|---|---|---|---|---|---|---|
| 1937 | 5,000 | 50.00 | 75.00 | 125 | 200 | — |

## L'AMETLLA DEL VALLES

A town in the province of Tarragona in northeastern Spain. The town adopted the name L'Ametlla del Valles in 1933. Before that the name was La Ametlla.

### REPUBLICAN ZONE
### DECIMAL COINAGE

**25 CENTIMOS** KM# 1 **Composition:** Brass

| Date | Mintage | F | VF | XF | Unc | BU |
|---|---|---|---|---|---|---|
| ND(1937) | 50,000 | 10.00 | 15.00 | 20.00 | 35.00 | — |

**50 CENTIMOS** KM# 2.1 **Composition:** Aluminum

| Date | Mintage | F | VF | XF | Unc | BU |
|---|---|---|---|---|---|---|
| ND(1937) | 3,000 | 100 | 150 | 200 | 250 | — |

**50 CENTIMOS** KM# 2.2 **Composition:** Aluminum **Obverse:** Without legend

| Date | Mintage | F | VF | XF | Unc | BU |
|---|---|---|---|---|---|---|
| ND(1937) | 30,000 | 25.00 | 50.00 | 70.00 | 100 | — |

**PESETA** KM# 3.1 **Composition:** Aluminum

| Date | Mintage | F | VF | XF | Unc | BU |
|---|---|---|---|---|---|---|
| ND(1937) | 3,000 | 50.00 | 75.00 | 100 | 150 | — |

**PESETA** KM# 3.2 **Composition:** Aluminum **Obverse:** Without legend

| Date | Mintage | F | VF | XF | Unc | BU |
|---|---|---|---|---|---|---|
| ND(1937) | 30,000 | 15.00 | 25.00 | 30.00 | 50.00 | — |

## LA PUEBLA DE CAZALLA

A village only a few miles east of El Arahal and some 40 miles from Sevilla. Undated coins of 2 values were issued in 1936.

### NATIONALIST ZONE
### DECIMAL COINAGE

**10 CENTIMOS** KM# 1 **Composition:** Brass **Size:** 23 mm. **Note:** Counterstamped varieties exist.

| Date | Mintage | F | VF | XF | Unc | BU |
|---|---|---|---|---|---|---|
| ND(1936) | 1,500 | 75.00 | 100 | 150 | 200 | — |

**25 CENTIMOS** KM# 2 **Composition:** Brass **Note:** Counterstamped varieties exist.

| Date | Mintage | F | VF | XF | Unc | BU |
|---|---|---|---|---|---|---|
| ND(1936) | 5,000 | 50.00 | 75.00 | 100 | 150 | — |

## LORA DEL RIO

A town 35 miles northeast of Seville. Issued an undated 25 Centimos in 1936.

### NATIONALIST ZONE
### DECIMAL COINAGE

**25 CENTIMOS** KM# 1 **Composition:** Brass **Obverse:** Crowned arms of Lora del rio on cross **Reverse:** 5-line inscription, wheat ear right

| Date | Mintage | F | VF | XF | Unc | BU |
|---|---|---|---|---|---|---|
| ND(1936) | 1,500 | 200 | 250 | 300 | 350 | — |

## MARCHENA

A village 30 miles east of Seville. It was the last issuer in Seville province. Two varieties of undated coins were produced in 1936.

# NATIONALIST ZONE

## DECIMAL COINAGE

**25 CENTIMOS** **KM# 1.1** **Composition:** Brass **Note:** Uniface; denomination: 25C.

| Date | Mintage | F | VF | XF | Unc | BU |
|---|---|---|---|---|---|---|
| ND(1936) | 5,000 | 30.00 | 75.00 | 100 | — | — |

**25 CENTIMOS** **KM# 1.2** **Composition:** Brass **Note:** Uniface; denomination: 025C.

| Date | Mintage | F | VF | XF | Unc | BU |
|---|---|---|---|---|---|---|
| ND(1936) | 500 | 300 | 400 | 500 | — | — |

## MENORCA

Menorca is the smaller of the 2 major islands in the Balearic Islands. A serious coin and supply shortage developed during the war because of the isolation of the island from the mainland.

# REPUBLICAN ZONE

## DECIMAL COINAGE

**5 CENTIMOS** **KM# 1** **Composition:** Brass **Note:** Varieties exist.

| Date | Mintage | F | VF | XF | Unc | BU |
|---|---|---|---|---|---|---|
| 1937 | 42,000 | — | 25.00 | 30.00 | 50.00 | — |

**10 CENTIMOS** **KM# 2** **Composition:** Brass **Note:** Varieties exist.

| Date | Mintage | F | VF | XF | Unc | BU |
|---|---|---|---|---|---|---|
| 1937 | 32,000 | — | 18.00 | 20.00 | 25.00 | — |

**Note:**

**25 CENTIMOS** **KM# 3** **Composition:** Brass

| Date | Mintage | F | VF | XF | Unc | BU |
|---|---|---|---|---|---|---|
| 1937 | 38,000 | — | 12.50 | 15.00 | 20.00 | — |

**PESETA** **KM# 4** **Composition:** Brass

| Date | Mintage | F | VF | XF | Unc | BU |
|---|---|---|---|---|---|---|
| 1937 | 37,000 | — | 12.50 | 15.00 | 20.00 | — |

**2-1/2 PESETAS** **KM# 5** **Composition:** Brass

| Date | Mintage | F | VF | XF | Unc | BU |
|---|---|---|---|---|---|---|
| 1937 | 24,000 | — | 25.00 | 30.00 | 50.00 | — |

## NULLES

Nulles is a mountain village in the province of Tarragona. The mountainous terrain of the area isolated the village from friendly forces and normal commerce. Therefore, in 1937, an undated series of 5 denominations were issued.

# REPUBLICAN ZONE

## DECIMAL COINAGE

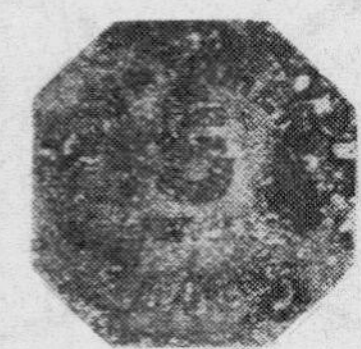

**5 CENTIMOS** **KM# 1** **Composition:** Zinc **Note:** Uniface, legends similar to 10 Centimos, KM#2. Octagonal.

| Date | Mintage | F | VF | XF | Unc | BU |
|---|---|---|---|---|---|---|
| ND(1937) | 5,000 | 75.00 | 200 | 300 | — | — |

**10 CENTIMOS** **KM# 2** **Composition:** Zinc **Note:** Uniface.

| Date | Mintage | F | VF | XF | Unc | BU |
|---|---|---|---|---|---|---|
| ND(1937) | 3,000 | 100 | 250 | 325 | — | — |

**25 CENTIMOS** **KM# 3** **Composition:** Brass **Note:** Square, uniface. Legends similar to 10 Centimos, KM#2.

| Date | Mintage | F | VF | XF | Unc | BU |
|---|---|---|---|---|---|---|
| ND(1937) | 5,000 | 75.00 | 200 | 300 | — | — |

**50 CENTIMOS** **KM# 4** **Composition:** Brass **Note:** Octagonal. Uniface, legends similar to 10 Centimos, KM#2.

| Date | Mintage | F | VF | XF | Unc | BU |
|---|---|---|---|---|---|---|
| ND(1937) | 1,000 | 100 | 250 | 325 | — | — |

**PESETA** **KM# 5** **Composition:** Brass **Note:** Uniface.

| Date | Mintage | F | VF | XF | Unc | BU |
|---|---|---|---|---|---|---|
| ND(1937) | 5,000 | 75.00 | 125 | 175 | — | — |

## OLOT

A village in the province of Gerona in northeastern Spain near the French border. The village council authorized 2 denominations of coins on September 24, 1937.

# REPUBLICAN ZONE

## DECIMAL COINAGE

**10 CENTIMOS** **KM# 1** **Composition:** Iron

| Date | Mintage | F | VF | XF | Unc | BU |
|---|---|---|---|---|---|---|
| 1937 | 25,000 | 40.00 | 60.00 | 125 | — | — |

**15 CENTIMOS** **KM# 2** **Composition:** Iron

| Date | Mintage | F | VF | XF | Unc | BU |
|---|---|---|---|---|---|---|
| 1937 | 100 | 1500 | 1800 | 2000 | — | — |

**Note:** The above is considered a pattern.

## SANTANDER, PALENCIA & BURGOS

# REPUBLICAN ZONE

## DECIMAL COINAGE

**50 CENTIMOS** **KM# 1.1** **Composition:** Copper-Nickel **Size:** 20 mm.

| Date | Mintage | F | VF | XF | Unc | BU |
|---|---|---|---|---|---|---|
| 1937 | 100,000 | — | 15.00 | 25.00 | 40.00 | — |

**50 CENTIMOS** **KM# 1.2** **Composition:** Copper-Nickel **Reverse:** Letters PR or PJR below CTS

| Date | Mintage | F | VF | XF | Unc | BU |
|---|---|---|---|---|---|---|
| 1937 | 10,000 | 12.00 | 22.00 | 30.00 | 45.00 | — |

**PESETA** **KM# 2** **Composition:** Copper-Nickel

| Date | Mintage | F | VF | XF | Unc | BU |
|---|---|---|---|---|---|---|
| 1937 | 300,000 | — | 9.00 | 12.00 | 20.00 | — |

# SEGARRA DE GAIA

A village in the southern part of the province of Tarragona. A single denomination of coin was authorized in 1937.

## REPUBLICAN ZONE

### DECIMAL COINAGE

**PESETA** **KM# 1** **Composition:** Copper-Nickel

| Date | Mintage | F | VF | XF | Unc | BU |
|---|---|---|---|---|---|---|
| ND(1937) | 5,000 | 14.50 | 17.50 | 20.00 | 35.00 | — |

**PESETA** **KM# 1a** **Composition:** Copper **Size:** 23 mm. **Note:** Uniface. Value over bars of Aragon in circle.

| Date | Mintage | F | VF | XF | Unc | BU |
|---|---|---|---|---|---|---|
| ND(1937) | 20,000 | 30.00 | 75.00 | 100 | 125 | — |

**PESETA** **KM# 2** **Composition:** Aluminum

| Date | Mintage | F | VF | XF | Unc | BU |
|---|---|---|---|---|---|---|
| ND(1937) | 30,000 | — | — | — | — | — |

**Note:** Reported, not confirmed

**PESETA** **KM# 2a** **Composition:** Brass **Note:** Numbered, uniface, 5-line inscription.

| Date | Mintage | F | VF | XF | Unc | BU |
|---|---|---|---|---|---|---|
| ND(1937) | — | 30.00 | 75.00 | 100 | 125 | — |

# SPITZBERGEN

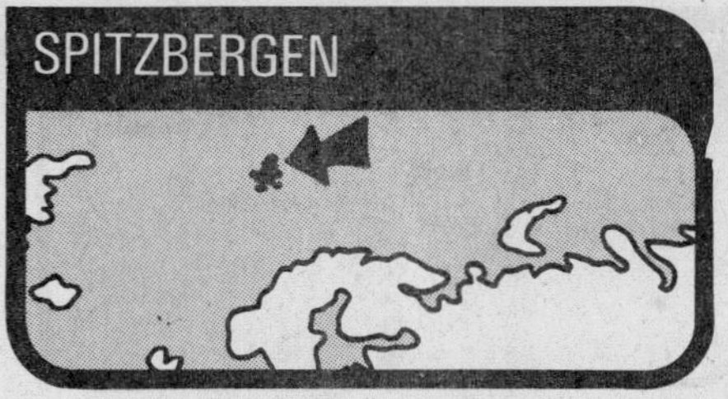

Spitzbergen (Svalbard), a Norwegian territory, is a group of mountainous islands in the Arctic Ocean 360miles (579 km.) north of Norway. The islands have an area of 23,957 sq. mi. (62,050 sq. km.) and a population of about 4,000. West Spitzbergen, the largest island, is the seat of administration. Sealing and fishing are economically important. Despite rich carboniferous and tertiary coal deposits, coal mining, which was started on a commercial scale by the Arctic Coal Co. of Boston, Mass. in 1904,produces only small quantities.

Spitzbergen was probably discovered in 1194, but modern knowledge of it dates from its discovery by William Barents in 1596. Quarrels among the various nationalities involved in the whaling industry, which was set up in 1611, resulted in a de facto division of the coast, but despite diverse interests in, and claims to the islands by British, Dutch, Norwegians, Swedes, Danes, Russians and Americans, the question of sovereignty was not resolved until 1920, when a treaty agreed to by the claimants awarded the islands to Norway.

In 1932, the Russian mining company Arktikugol' began operations in the islands. The tokens listed here were minted in Leningrad for use by the company in Spitzbergen.

**RULERS**

Norwegian, 1920-

## NORWEGIAN TERRITORY

### TOKEN COINAGE

Arktikugol

**10 KOPEKS** **KM# Tn1** **Composition:** Aluminum-Bronze

| Date | Mintage | F | VF | XF | Unc | BU |
|---|---|---|---|---|---|---|
| 1946 | — | 15.00 | 25.00 | 45.00 | 115 | — |

**15 KOPEKS** **KM# Tn2** **Composition:** Aluminum-Bronze

| Date | Mintage | F | VF | XF | Unc | BU |
|---|---|---|---|---|---|---|
| 1946 | — | 20.00 | 30.00 | 50.00 | 120 | — |

**20 KOPEKS** **KM# Tn3** **Composition:** Copper-Nickel

| Date | Mintage | F | VF | XF | Unc | BU |
|---|---|---|---|---|---|---|
| 1946 | — | 22.00 | 38.00 | 60.00 | 135 | — |

**50 KOPEKS** **KM# Tn4.1** **Composition:** Copper-Nickel **Obverse:** Large star

| Date | Mintage | F | VF | XF | Unc | BU |
|---|---|---|---|---|---|---|
| 1946 | — | 25.00 | 40.00 | 65.00 | 140 | — |

**50 KOPEKS** **KM# Tn4.2** **Composition:** Copper-Nickel **Obverse:** Small star

| Date | Mintage | F | VF | XF | Unc | BU |
|---|---|---|---|---|---|---|
| 1946 | — | 25.00 | 40.00 | 65.00 | 140 | — |

**10 ROUBLES** **KM# Tn5** **Composition:** Copper-Nickel Clad Steel

| Date | Mintage | F | VF | XF | Unc | BU |
|---|---|---|---|---|---|---|
| 1993 | — | — | — | — | 3.50 | — |

**25 ROUBLES** **KM# Tn6** **Composition:** Copper-Nickel Clad Steel

| Date | Mintage | F | VF | XF | Unc | BU |
|---|---|---|---|---|---|---|
| 1993 | — | — | — | — | 4.50 | — |

**50 ROUBLES** **KM# Tn7** **Composition:** Copper-Nickel Clad Steel

| Date | Mintage | F | VF | XF | Unc | BU |
|---|---|---|---|---|---|---|
| 1993 | — | — | — | — | 6.50 | — |

**100 ROUBLES** **KM# Tn8** **Composition:** Aluminum-Bronze

| Date | Mintage | F | VF | XF | Unc | BU |
|---|---|---|---|---|---|---|
| 1993 | — | — | — | — | 9.00 | — |

### REFORM COINAGE

**10 KOPEKS (0.1 Rouble)** **KM# 9** **Composition:** Aluminum **Obverse:** 2 walruses above world globe **Reverse:** Numeric value

| Date | Mintage | F | VF | XF | Unc | BU |
|---|---|---|---|---|---|---|
| 1998 | 6,000 | — | — | — | 3.00 | — |

**25 KOPEKS (0.25 Rouble)** **KM# 10** **Composition:** Aluminum **Obverse:** 2 walruses above world globe **Reverse:** Numeric value

| Date | Mintage | F | VF | XF | Unc | BU |
|---|---|---|---|---|---|---|
| 1998 | 6,000 | — | — | — | 3.50 | — |

**50 KOPEKS (0.5 Rouble)** **KM# 11** **Composition:** Aluminum **Obverse:** 2 walruses above world globe **Reverse:** Numeric value

| Date | Mintage | F | VF | XF | Unc | BU |
|---|---|---|---|---|---|---|
| 1998 | 6,000 | — | — | — | 4.00 | — |

**ROUBLE** **KM# 12** **Composition:** Brass **Obverse:** Polar bear above world globe **Reverse:** Numeric value

| Date | Mintage | F | VF | XF | Unc | BU |
|---|---|---|---|---|---|---|
| 1998 | 4,000 | — | — | — | 5.00 | — |

**2 ROUBLES** **KM# 13** **Composition:** Brass **Obverse:** Polar bear above world globe **Reverse:** Numeric value

| Date | Mintage | F | VF | XF | Unc | BU |
|---|---|---|---|---|---|---|
| 1998 | 4,000 | — | — | — | 5.50 | — |

**5 ROUBLES** **KM# 14** **Composition:** Copper-Nickel **Obverse:** Whale above world globe **Reverse:** Numeric value

| Date | Mintage | F | VF | XF | Unc | BU |
|---|---|---|---|---|---|---|
| 1998 | 4,000 | — | — | — | 6.50 | — |

# SRI (SHRI) LANKA

The Democratic Socialist Republic of Sri (Shri) Lanka (formerly Ceylon) situated in the Indian Ocean 18 miles (29 km.) southeast of India, has an area of 25,332 sq. mi.(65,610 sq. km.) and a population of *16.9 million. Capital: Colombo. The economy is chiefly agricultural. Tea, coconut products and rubber are exported.

The earliest known inhabitants of Ceylon, the Veddahs, were subjugated by the Sinhalese from northern India in the 6th century B.C. Sinhalese rule was maintained until 1408, after which the island was controlled by China for30 years. The Portuguese came to Ceylon in 1505 and maintained control of the coastal area for 150 years. The Dutch supplanted them in 1658, which were in turn supplanted by the British who seized the Dutch colonies in 1796, and made them a Crown Colony in 1802. In 1815,the British conquered the independent Kingdom of Kandy in the central part of the island. Constitutional changes in 1931 and 1946 granted the Ceylonese a measure of autonomy and a parliamentary form of government. Britain granted Ceylon independence as a self-governing republic within the British Commonwealth on Feb. 4, 1948. On May 22, 1972, the Ceylonese adopted a new Constitution, which declared Ceylon to be the Republic of Sri Lanka –'Resplendent Island'. Sri Lanka is a member of the Commonwealth of Nations. The president is Chief of State. The prime minister is Head of Government. The present leaders of the country have reverted the country name back to Sri Lanka.

**RULERS**
British, 1796-1972

# CEYLON
## BRITISH COLONIAL
### DECIMAL COINAGE

100 Cents = 1 Rupee

**1/4 CENT** **KM# 90** **Composition:** Copper

| Date | Mintage | F | VF | XF | Unc | BU |
|---|---|---|---|---|---|---|
| 1901 | 216,000 | 1.50 | 3.00 | 5.00 | 12.00 | — |
| 1901 Proof | — | Value: 100 | | | | |

**1/4 CENT** **KM# 100** **Composition:** Gold

| Date | Mintage | F | VF | XF | Unc | BU |
|---|---|---|---|---|---|---|
| 1904 | 103,000 | 2.50 | 5.00 | 10.00 | 22.00 | — |
| 1904 Proof | — | Value: 150 | | | | |

**1/2 CENT** **KM# 91** **Composition:** Copper

| Date | Mintage | F | VF | XF | Unc | BU |
|---|---|---|---|---|---|---|
| 1901 | 2,020,000 | 1.25 | 2.50 | 4.00 | 10.00 | — |

**1/2 CENT** **KM# 101** **Composition:** Copper

| Date | Mintage | F | VF | XF | Unc | BU |
|---|---|---|---|---|---|---|
| 1904 | 2,012,000 | 1.00 | 2.00 | 5.00 | 12.00 | — |
| 1904 Proof | — | Value: 120 | | | | |
| 1905 | 1,000,000 | 1.50 | 3.00 | 6.00 | 15.00 | — |
| 1905 Proof | — | Value: 120 | | | | |
| 1906 | 3,056,000 | 1.00 | 2.00 | 5.00 | 12.00 | — |
| 1906 Proof | — | Value: 120 | | | | |
| 1908 | 1,000,000 | 1.50 | 3.00 | 6.00 | 15.00 | — |
| 1908 Proof | — | Value: 200 | | | | |
| 1909 | 3,000,000 | 1.00 | 2.00 | 5.00 | 12.00 | — |
| 1909 Proof | — | Value: 120 | | | | |

**1/2 CENT** **KM# 106** **Composition:** Gold

| Date | Mintage | F | VF | XF | Unc | BU |
|---|---|---|---|---|---|---|
| 1912 | 5,008,000 | 1.25 | 2.75 | 4.00 | 10.00 | — |
| 1912 Proof | — | Value: 120 | | | | |
| 1914 | 2,000,000 | 1.25 | 2.75 | 6.00 | 12.00 | — |
| 1914 Proof | — | Value: 120 | | | | |
| 1917 | 2,000,000 | 1.50 | 3.00 | 6.00 | 12.00 | — |
| 1917 Proof | — | Value: 120 | | | | |
| 1926 | 5,000,000 | 0.50 | 1.00 | 2.00 | 5.00 | — |
| 1926 Proof | — | Value: 120 | | | | |

**1/2 CENT** **KM# 110** **Composition:** Gold

| Date | Mintage | F | VF | XF | Unc | BU |
|---|---|---|---|---|---|---|
| 1937 | 3,026,000 | 0.30 | 0.85 | 1.50 | 3.50 | — |
| 1937 Proof | — | Value: 175 | | | | |
| 1940 | 5,080,000 | 0.25 | 0.65 | 1.25 | 3.00 | — |

**CENT** **KM# 92** **Composition:** Copper

| Date | Mintage | F | VF | XF | Unc | BU |
|---|---|---|---|---|---|---|
| 1901 | 1,014,000 | 2.50 | 5.00 | 10.00 | 22.00 | — |

**CENT** **KM# 102** **Composition:** Copper

| Date | Mintage | F | VF | XF | Unc | BU |
|---|---|---|---|---|---|---|
| 1904 | 2,529,000 | 1.00 | 2.00 | 4.00 | 8.00 | — |
| 1904 Proof | — | Value: 125 | | | | |
| 1905 | 1,509,000 | 1.25 | 2.25 | 5.00 | 10.00 | — |
| 1905 Proof | — | Value: 125 | | | | |
| 1906 | 1,751,000 | 1.25 | 2.25 | 5.00 | 10.00 | — |
| 1906 Proof | — | Value: 125 | | | | |
| 1908 | — | 1.00 | 2.00 | 4.00 | 8.00 | — |
| 1908 Proof | — | Value: 225 | | | | |
| 1909 | 2,500,000 | 1.00 | 2.00 | 4.00 | 8.00 | — |
| 1909 Proof | — | Value: 125 | | | | |
| 1910 | 8,236,000 | 0.50 | 1.00 | 2.50 | 5.00 | — |
| 1910 Proof | — | Value: 125 | | | | |

**CENT** **KM# 107** **Composition:** Copper

| Date | Mintage | F | VF | XF | Unc | BU |
|---|---|---|---|---|---|---|
| 1912 | 5,855,000 | 0.50 | 1.00 | 2.00 | 4.00 | — |
| 1912 Proof | — | Value: 115 | | | | |
| 1914 | 6,000,000 | 0.50 | 1.00 | 2.25 | 5.00 | — |
| 1914 Proof | — | Value: 115 | | | | |
| 1917 | 1,000,000 | 1.00 | 1.75 | 3.00 | 8.00 | — |
| 1917 Proof | — | Value: 115 | | | | |
| 1920 | 2,000,000 | 0.50 | 1.00 | 2.25 | 5.00 | — |
| 1920 Proof | — | Value: 115 | | | | |
| 1922 | 2,930,000 | 0.50 | 1.00 | 2.25 | 5.00 | — |
| 1922 Proof | — | Value: 115 | | | | |
| 1923 | 2,500,000 | 0.50 | 1.00 | 2.25 | 5.00 | — |
| 1923 Proof | — | Value: 115 | | | | |
| 1925 | 7,490,000 | 0.35 | 0.75 | 1.50 | 3.50 | — |
| 1925 Proof | — | Value: 115 | | | | |
| 1926 | 3,750,000 | 0.35 | 0.75 | 1.50 | 3.50 | — |
| 1926 Proof | — | Value: 115 | | | | |
| 1928 | 2,500,000 | 0.35 | 0.75 | 1.50 | 4.00 | — |
| 1928 Proof | — | Value: 115 | | | | |
| 1929 | 5,000,000 | 0.35 | 0.75 | 1.50 | 3.50 | — |
| 1929 Proof | — | Value: 115 | | | | |

**CENT** **KM# 111** **Composition:** Copper **Obverse:** PM below bust of George VI **Note:** High relief.

| Date | Mintage | F | VF | XF | Unc | BU |
|---|---|---|---|---|---|---|
| 1937 | 4,538,000 | 0.25 | 0.50 | 1.25 | 3.00 | — |
| 1937 Proof | — | Value: 100 | | | | |
| 1940 | 10,190,000 | 0.15 | 0.30 | 1.00 | 2.00 | — |
| 1940 Proof | — | Value: 75.00 | | | | |
| 1942 | 20,780,000 | 0.15 | 0.30 | 1.00 | 2.00 | — |

**CENT** **KM# 111a** **Composition:** Bronze **Obverse:** Without initials PM below bust of George VI **Note:** Low relief. Thin planchet.

| Date | Mintage | F | VF | XF | Unc | BU |
|---|---|---|---|---|---|---|
| 1942 | Inc. above | 0.15 | 0.30 | 0.75 | 1.75 | — |
| 1942 Proof | — | Value: 75.00 | | | | |
| 1943 | 43,705,000 | 0.15 | 0.30 | 0.50 | 1.00 | — |
| 1945 | 34,100,000 | 0.15 | 0.35 | 0.60 | 1.20 | — |
| 1945 Proof | — | Value: 20.00 | | | | |

**Note:** Restruck in quantity.

**2 CENTS** **KM# 117** **Composition:** Nickel-Brass

| Date | Mintage | F | VF | XF | Unc | BU |
|---|---|---|---|---|---|---|
| 1944 | 30,165,000 | 0.10 | 0.25 | 0.50 | 1.25 | — |

**2 CENTS** **Composition:** Brass

| Date | Mintage | F | VF | XF | Unc | BU |
|---|---|---|---|---|---|---|
| 1944 Proof | — | — | — | — | — | — |

**2 CENTS** **KM# 119** **Composition:** Brass **Obv. Legend:** Without EMPEROR OF INDIA

| Date | Mintage | F | VF | XF | Unc | BU |
|---|---|---|---|---|---|---|
| 1951 | 15,000,000 | 0.10 | 0.25 | 0.75 | 1.75 | — |
| 1951 Proof | — | Value: 20.00 | | | | |

**2 CENTS** **KM# 124** **Composition:** Brass

| Date | Mintage | F | VF | XF | Unc | BU |
|---|---|---|---|---|---|---|
| 1955 | 37,131,000 | 0.10 | 0.15 | 0.25 | 0.65 | — |
| 1957 | 38,200,000 | 0.10 | 0.15 | 0.25 | 0.65 | — |
| 1957 Proof | — | Value: 75.00 | | | | |

**5 CENTS** **KM# 103** **Composition:** Copper-Nickel

| Date | Mintage | F | VF | XF | Unc | BU |
|---|---|---|---|---|---|---|
| 1909 | 2,000,000 | 1.50 | 3.00 | 5.00 | 17.00 | — |
| 1910 | 4,000,000 | 1.00 | 2.00 | 3.50 | 12.00 | — |

**5 CENTS** **KM# 108** **Composition:** Copper-Nickel

| Date | Mintage | F | VF | XF | Unc | BU |
|---|---|---|---|---|---|---|
| 1912 H | 4,000,000 | 0.75 | 1.50 | 3.00 | 10.00 | — |
| 1920 | 6,000,000 | 0.50 | 1.00 | 2.00 | 7.00 | — |
| 1926 | 3,000,000 | 0.75 | 1.50 | 4.00 | 12.50 | — |

**5 CENTS** **KM# 113.1** **Composition:** Nickel-Brass

| Date | Mintage | F | VF | XF | Unc | BU |
|---|---|---|---|---|---|---|
| 1942 | 12,752,000 | 0.35 | 0.75 | 1.50 | 4.50 | — |
| 1942 Proof | — | Value: 50.00 | | | | |
| 1943 | Inc. above | 0.35 | 0.75 | 1.50 | 4.50 | — |
| 1943 Proof | — | Value: 50.00 | | | | |

**5 CENTS** **KM# 113.2** **Composition:** Nickel-Brass **Note:** Thin planchet.

| Date | Mintage | F | VF | XF | Unc | BU |
|---|---|---|---|---|---|---|
| 1944 | 18,064,000 | 0.20 | 0.35 | 0.70 | 2.00 | — |
| 1945 | 31,192,000 | 0.15 | 0.30 | 0.60 | 1.75 | — |
| 1945 Proof | — | Value: 60.00 | | | | |

**Note:** Varieties exist in bust, denomination and legend placement for 1945.

**5 CENTS** **KM# 120** **Composition:** Nickel-Brass **Obv. Legend:** Without EMPEROR OF INDIA

| Date | Mintage | F | VF | XF | Unc | BU |
|---|---|---|---|---|---|---|
| 1951 Proof | — | Value: 20.00 | | | | |

**10 CENTS** **KM# 97** **Weight:** 1.1664 g. **Composition:** 0.8000 Silver .03 oz. ASW

| Date | Mintage | F | VF | XF | Unc | BU |
|---|---|---|---|---|---|---|
| 1902 | 1,000,000 | 1.00 | 2.75 | 6.00 | 20.00 | — |
| 1902 Proof | — | Value: 150 | | | | |
| 1903 | 1,000,000 | 1.00 | 2.75 | 6.00 | 20.00 | — |
| 1903 Proof | — | Value: 150 | | | | |
| 1907 | 500,000 | 2.50 | 5.00 | 15.00 | 25.00 | — |
| 1908 | 1,500,000 | 1.00 | 2.75 | 6.00 | 15.00 | — |
| 1909 | 1,000,000 | 1.00 | 2.75 | 6.00 | 15.00 | — |
| 1910 | 2,000,000 | 1.00 | 2.75 | 6.00 | 15.00 | — |

**10 CENTS** **KM# 104** **Weight:** 1.1664 g. **Composition:** 0.8000 Silver .03 oz. ASW

| Date | Mintage | F | VF | XF | Unc | BU |
|---|---|---|---|---|---|---|
| 1911 | 1,000,000 | 1.00 | 1.75 | 5.00 | 12.00 | — |
| 1912 | 1,000,000 | 1.25 | 2.00 | 6.00 | 15.00 | — |
| 1913 | 2,000,000 | 1.00 | 1.50 | 4.00 | 10.00 | — |
| 1914 | 2,000,000 | 1.00 | 1.50 | 4.00 | 10.00 | — |
| 1914 Proof | — | Value: 150 | | | | |
| 1917 | 879,000 | 1.00 | 2.50 | 7.50 | 17.50 | — |
| 1917 Proof | — | Value: 150 | | | | |

**10 CENTS** **KM# 104a** **Weight:** 1.1664 g. **Composition:** 0.5500 Silver .0206 oz. ASW

| Date | Mintage | F | VF | XF | Unc | BU |
|---|---|---|---|---|---|---|
| 1919 B | 750,000 | 1.50 | 3.50 | 10.00 | 20.00 | — |
| 1919 B Proof | — | Value: 150 | | | | |
| 1920 B | 3,059,000 | 1.00 | 2.50 | 6.00 | 15.00 | — |
| 1920 B Proof | — | Value: 150 | | | | |
| 1921 B | 1,583,000 | 0.75 | 1.75 | 5.00 | 10.00 | — |
| 1921 Proof | — | Value: 150 | | | | |
| 1922 | 282,000 | 1.75 | 3.50 | 10.00 | 25.00 | — |
| 1922 Proof | — | Value: 150 | | | | |
| 1924 | 1,508,000 | 0.75 | 1.75 | 4.00 | 10.00 | — |
| 1924 Proof | — | Value: 150 | | | | |
| 1925 | 1,500,000 | 0.75 | 1.75 | 4.00 | 10.00 | — |
| 1925 Proof | — | Value: 150 | | | | |
| 1926 | 1,500,000 | 0.75 | 1.75 | 4.00 | 10.00 | — |
| 1926 Proof | — | Value: 150 | | | | |
| 1927 | 1,500,000 | 0.75 | 1.75 | 4.00 | 10.00 | — |
| 1927 Proof | — | Value: 150 | | | | |
| 1928 | 1,500,000 | 0.75 | 1.75 | 4.00 | 10.00 | — |
| 1928 Proof | — | Value: 150 | | | | |

**10 CENTS** **KM# 112** **Weight:** 1.1664 g. **Composition:** 0.8000 Silver .03 oz. ASW

| Date | Mintage | F | VF | XF | Unc | BU |
|---|---|---|---|---|---|---|
| 1941 | 16,271,000 | 0.65 | 1.00 | 2.50 | 6.00 | — |

**10 CENTS** **KM# 118** **Composition:** Nickel-Brass

| Date | Mintage | F | VF | XF | Unc | BU |
|---|---|---|---|---|---|---|
| 1944 | 30,500,000 | 0.25 | 0.50 | 1.00 | 3.00 | — |
| 1944 Proof | — | Value: 90.00 | | | | |

**10 CENTS** **KM# 121** **Composition:** Nickel-Brass **Obv. Legend:** Without EMPEROR OF INDIA

| Date | Mintage | F | VF | XF | Unc | BU |
|---|---|---|---|---|---|---|
| 1951 | 34,760,000 | 0.10 | 0.20 | 0.40 | 1.25 | — |
| 1951 Proof | — | Value: 15.00 | | | | |
| 1951 Proof, restrike | Est. 3,000,000 | Value: 4.00 | | | | |

**Note:** Restrikes differ in the formation of native characters.

**25 CENTS** **KM# 98** **Weight:** 2.9160 g. **Composition:** 0.8000 Silver .075 oz. ASW

| Date | Mintage | F | VF | XF | Unc | BU |
|---|---|---|---|---|---|---|
| 1902 | 400,000 | 4.00 | 8.00 | 20.00 | 40.00 | — |
| 1902 Proof | — | Value: 150 | | | | |
| 1903 | 400,000 | 4.00 | 8.00 | 20.00 | 40.00 | — |
| 1903 Proof | — | Value: 150 | | | | |
| 1907 | 120,000 | 7.50 | 20.00 | 30.00 | 50.00 | — |
| 1908 | 400,000 | 4.00 | 8.00 | 15.00 | 35.00 | — |
| 1909 | 400,000 | 4.00 | 8.00 | 15.00 | 35.00 | — |
| 1910 | 800,000 | 2.00 | 5.00 | 10.00 | 20.00 | — |

**25 CENTS** **KM# 105** **Weight:** 2.9160 g. **Composition:** 0.8000 Silver .075 oz. ASW

| Date | Mintage | F | VF | XF | Unc | BU |
|---|---|---|---|---|---|---|
| 1911 | 400,000 | 3.00 | 6.00 | 12.00 | 30.00 | — |
| 1911 Proof | — | Value: 175 | | | | |
| 1913 | 1,200,000 | 1.50 | 2.50 | 7.50 | 17.50 | — |
| 1913 Proof | — | Value: 175 | | | | |
| 1914 | 400,000 | 3.00 | 6.00 | 12.00 | 25.00 | — |
| 1914 Proof | — | Value: 175 | | | | |
| 1917 | 300,000 | 4.00 | 8.00 | 15.00 | 35.00 | — |
| 1917 Proof | — | Value: 175 | | | | |

**25 CENTS** **KM# 105a** **Weight:** 2.9160 g. **Composition:** 0.5500 Silver .0516 oz. ASW

| Date | Mintage | F | VF | XF | Unc | BU |
|---|---|---|---|---|---|---|
| 1919 B | 1,400,000 | 1.25 | 3.00 | 7.50 | 15.00 | — |
| 1919 B Proof | — | Value: 150 | | | | |
| 1920 B | 1,600,000 | 1.25 | 3.00 | 7.50 | 15.00 | — |
| 1920 B Proof | — | Value: 150 | | | | |
| 1921 B | 600,000 | 3.50 | 7.50 | 15.00 | 30.00 | — |
| 1921 B Proof | — | Value: 150 | | | | |
| 1922 | 1,211,000 | 1.25 | 3.25 | 7.50 | 15.00 | — |
| 1922 Proof | — | Value: 150 | | | | |
| 1925 | 1,004,000 | 1.25 | 3.50 | 7.50 | 15.00 | — |
| 1925 Proof | — | Value: 150 | | | | |
| 1926 | 1,000,000 | 1.25 | 3.50 | 7.50 | 15.00 | — |
| 1926 Proof | — | Value: 150 | | | | |

**25 CENTS** **KM# 115** **Composition:** Nickel-Brass

| Date | Mintage | F | VF | XF | Unc | BU |
|---|---|---|---|---|---|---|
| 1943 | 13,920,000 | 0.25 | 0.50 | 1.00 | 2.50 | — |

**25 CENTS** **KM# 122** **Composition:** Nickel-Brass
**Obv. Legend:** Without EMPEROR OF INDIA

| Date | Mintage | F | VF | XF | Unc | BU |
|---|---|---|---|---|---|---|
| 1951 | 25,940,000 | 0.10 | 0.30 | 0.60 | 1.75 | — |
| 1951 Proof | — | Value: 20.00 | | | | |
| 1951 Proof, restrike | Est. 2,500,000 | Value: 4.00 | | | | |

**Note:** Numerals 9 and 5 differ on restrikes.

**50 CENTS** **KM# 99** **Weight:** 5.8319 g. **Composition:** 0.8000 Silver .15 oz. ASW

| Date | Mintage | F | VF | XF | Unc | BU |
|---|---|---|---|---|---|---|
| 1902 | 200,000 | 5.00 | 10.00 | 30.00 | 70.00 | — |
| 1902 Proof | — | Value: 175 | | | | |
| 1903 | 800,000 | 3.00 | 8.00 | 18.00 | 35.00 | — |
| 1903 Proof | — | Value: 175 | | | | |
| 1910 | 200,000 | 7.00 | 13.00 | 30.00 | 60.00 | — |

**50 CENTS** **KM# 109** **Weight:** 5.8319 g. **Composition:** 0.8000 Silver .15 oz. ASW

| Date | Mintage | F | VF | XF | Unc | BU |
|---|---|---|---|---|---|---|
| 1913 | 400,000 | 7.00 | 13.00 | 30.00 | 60.00 | — |
| 1913 Proof | — | Value: 175 | | | | |
| 1914 | 200,000 | 5.00 | 15.00 | 30.00 | 60.00 | — |
| 1914 Proof | — | Value: 175 | | | | |
| 1917 | 1,073,000 | 2.50 | 5.00 | 10.00 | 20.00 | — |
| 1917 Proof | — | Value: 175 | | | | |

**50 CENTS** **KM# 109a** **Weight:** 5.8319 g. **Composition:** 0.5500 Silver .1031 oz. ASW

| Date | Mintage | F | VF | XF | Unc | BU |
|---|---|---|---|---|---|---|
| 1919 B | 750,000 | 1.00 | 3.00 | 7.00 | 16.00 | — |
| 1919 B Proof | — | Value: 120 | | | | |
| 1920 B | 800,000 | 1.00 | 3.00 | 7.00 | 16.00 | — |
| 1920 B Proof | — | Value: 120 | | | | |
| 1921 B | 800,000 | 1.00 | 3.00 | 7.00 | 16.00 | — |
| 1921 B Proof | — | Value: 120 | | | | |
| 1922 | 1,040,000 | 1.00 | 3.00 | 7.00 | 16.00 | — |
| 1922 Proof | — | Value: 120 | | | | |
| 1924 | 1,010,000 | 1.00 | 3.00 | 7.00 | 16.00 | — |
| 1924 Proof | — | Value: 120 | | | | |
| 1925 | 500,000 | 2.00 | 5.00 | 10.00 | 20.00 | — |
| 1925 Proof | — | Value: 120 | | | | |
| 1926 | 500,000 | 2.00 | 5.00 | 10.00 | 20.00 | — |
| 1926 Proof | — | Value: 120 | | | | |
| 1927 | 500,000 | 2.00 | 5.00 | 10.00 | 20.00 | — |
| 1927 Proof | — | Value: 120 | | | | |
| 1928 | 500,000 | 2.00 | 5.00 | 10.00 | 20.00 | — |
| 1928 Proof | — | Value: 120 | | | | |
| 1929 | 500,000 | 2.00 | 5.00 | 10.00 | 20.00 | — |
| 1929 Proof | — | Value: 120 | | | | |

**50 CENTS** **KM# 114** **Weight:** 5.8319 g. **Composition:** 0.8000 Silver .15 oz. ASW

| Date | Mintage | F | VF | XF | Unc | BU |
|---|---|---|---|---|---|---|
| 1942 | 662,000 | 2.00 | 4.00 | 8.00 | 17.50 | — |

**50 CENTS** **Composition:** Brass

| Date | Mintage | F | VF | XF | Unc | BU |
|---|---|---|---|---|---|---|
| 1943 Proof, 6 known | — | Value: 500 | | | | |

**50 CENTS** **KM# 116** **Composition:** Nickel-Brass

| Date | Mintage | F | VF | XF | Unc | BU |
|---|---|---|---|---|---|---|
| 1943 | 8,600,000 | 0.35 | 0.75 | 1.50 | 3.50 | — |

**50 CENTS** **KM# 123** **Composition:** Nickel-Brass
**Obv. Legend:** Without EMPEROR OF INDIA

| Date | Mintage | F | VF | XF | Unc | BU |
|---|---|---|---|---|---|---|
| 1951 | 19,980,000 | 0.20 | 0.35 | 0.75 | 1.75 | — |
| 1951 Proof | — | Value: 20.00 | | | | |
| 1951 Proof, restrike | Est. 1,500,000 | Value: 5.00 | | | | |

**Note:** Restrikes differ slightly in the formation of native inscriptions.

**RUPEE** **KM# 125** **Composition:** Copper-Nickel **Subject:** 2,500 years of Buddhism

| Date | Mintage | F | VF | XF | Unc | BU |
|---|---|---|---|---|---|---|
| 1957 | 2,000,000 | 0.50 | 1.00 | 2.00 | 3.00 | — |
| 1957 Proof | 1,800 | Value: 12.00 | | | | |

**5 RUPEES** **KM# 126** **Weight:** 28.2757 g. **Composition:** 0.9250 Silver .8409 oz. ASW **Subject:** 2,500 years of Buddhism

| Date | Mintage | F | VF | XF | Unc | BU |
|---|---|---|---|---|---|---|
| 1957 | 500,000 | 8.00 | 12.50 | 17.50 | 30.00 | — |
| 1957 Proof | 1,800 | Value: 65.00 | | | | |

## REPUBLIC

### DECIMAL COINAGE

**CENT** **KM# 127** **Composition:** Aluminum

| Date | Mintage | F | VF | XF | Unc | BU |
|---|---|---|---|---|---|---|
| 1963 | 33,000,000 | — | — | — | 0.10 | — |
| 1965 | 12,000,000 | — | — | 0.10 | 0.15 | — |
| 1967 | 10,000,000 | — | — | 0.10 | 0.15 | — |
| 1968 | 22,505,000 | — | — | — | 0.10 | — |
| 1969 | 10,000,000 | — | — | — | 0.10 | — |
| 1970 | 15,000,000 | — | — | — | 0.10 | — |
| 1971 | 55,000,000 | — | — | — | 0.10 | — |
| 1971 Proof | 20,000 | Value: 0.50 | | | | |

**2 CENTS** **KM# 128** **Composition:** Aluminum

| Date | Mintage | F | VF | XF | Unc | BU |
|---|---|---|---|---|---|---|
| 1963 | 26,000,000 | — | — | 0.10 | 0.15 | — |
| 1965 | 7,000,000 | — | — | 0.10 | 0.15 | — |
| 1967 | 15,000,000 | — | — | 0.10 | 0.15 | — |
| 1968 | 15,000,000 | — | — | 0.10 | 0.15 | — |
| 1970 | 13,000,000 | — | — | 0.10 | 0.15 | — |
| 1971 | 45,000,000 | — | — | 0.10 | 0.15 | — |
| 1971 Proof | 20,000 | Value: 1.00 | | | | |

**5 CENTS** **KM# 129** **Composition:** Nickel-Brass

| Date | Mintage | F | VF | XF | Unc | BU |
|---|---|---|---|---|---|---|
| 1963 | 16,000,000 | — | 0.10 | 0.15 | 0.25 | — |
| 1965 | 9,000,000 | — | 0.10 | 0.15 | 0.25 | — |
| 1968 | 12,000,000 | — | 0.10 | 0.15 | 0.25 | — |
| 1968 Proof | — | Value: 3.00 | | | | |
| 1969 | 2,500,000 | — | 0.10 | 0.20 | 0.40 | — |
| 1970 | 7,000,000 | — | 0.10 | 0.15 | 0.25 | — |
| 1971 | 32,000,000 | — | 0.10 | 0.15 | 0.25 | — |
| 1971 Proof | 20,000 | Value: 1.50 | | | | |

**10 CENTS** **KM# 130** **Composition:** Nickel-Brass

| Date | Mintage | F | VF | XF | Unc | BU |
|---|---|---|---|---|---|---|
| 1963 | 14,000,000 | — | 0.10 | 0.15 | 0.25 | — |
| 1965 | 3,000,000 | — | 0.10 | 0.15 | 0.35 | — |
| 1969 | 6,000,000 | — | 0.10 | 0.15 | 0.25 | — |
| 1971 | 29,000,000 | — | 0.10 | 0.15 | 0.20 | — |
| 1971 Proof | 20,000 | Value: 1.25 | | | | |

**25 CENTS** **KM# 131** **Composition:** Copper-Nickel

| Date | Mintage | F | VF | XF | Unc | BU |
|---|---|---|---|---|---|---|
| 1963 | 30,000,000 | — | 0.10 | 0.20 | 0.40 | — |
| 1965 | 8,000,000 | — | 0.10 | 0.25 | 0.50 | — |
| 1971 | 24,000,000 | — | 0.10 | 0.15 | 0.30 | — |
| 1971 Proof | 20,000 | Value: 1.50 | | | | |

**50 CENTS** **KM# 132** **Composition:** Copper-Nickel

| Date | Mintage | F | VF | XF | Unc | BU |
|---|---|---|---|---|---|---|
| 1963 | 15,000,000 | 0.10 | 0.20 | 0.35 | 0.75 | — |
| 1965 | 7,000,000 | 0.10 | 0.20 | 0.35 | 0.75 | — |
| 1971 | 4,000,000 | 0.25 | 0.50 | 0.75 | 1.50 | — |
| 1971 Proof | 20,000 | Value: 2.00 | | | | |

**RUPEE** **KM# 133** **Composition:** Copper-Nickel

| Date | Mintage | F | VF | XF | Unc | BU |
|---|---|---|---|---|---|---|
| 1963 | 20,000,000 | 0.10 | 0.20 | 0.40 | 1.00 | — |
| 1965 | 5,000,000 | 0.15 | 0.25 | 0.50 | 1.25 | — |
| 1969 | 2,500,000 | 0.15 | 0.25 | 0.50 | 1.75 | — |
| 1971 | 5,000,000 | 0.15 | 0.25 | 0.50 | 1.50 | — |
| 1971 Proof | 20,000 | Value: 4.00 | | | | |

**2 RUPEES** KM# 134 **Composition:** Copper-Nickel **Series:** F.A.O.

| Date | Mintage | F | VF | XF | Unc | BU |
|---|---|---|---|---|---|---|
| 1968 | 500,000 | 0.50 | 1.50 | 2.25 | 3.00 | — |

## PATTERNS

Including off metal strikes

| KM# | Date | Mintage | Identification | Mkt Val |
|---|---|---|---|---|
| Pn8 | 1904 | — | 5 Cents. Gold. | 3,500 |
| Pn9 | 1943 | — | 50 Cents. | — |

## PROOF SETS

| KM# | Date | Mintage | Identification | Issue Price | Mkt Val |
|---|---|---|---|---|---|
| PS1 | 1951 (6) | 150 | KM111a (1945), 119-123 (1951). Restrikes exist. | — | 40.00 |
| PS2 | 1957 (2) | 400 | KM125-126 | — | 90.00 |
| PS3 | 1957 (4) | 700 | KM125-126, 2 each | — | 160 |
| PS4 | 1971 (7) | 20,000 | KM127-133 | — | 10.00 |

# DEMOCRATIC SOCIALIST REPUBLIC

## DECIMAL COINAGE

100 Cents = 1 Rupee

**CENT** KM# 137 **Composition:** Aluminum

| Date | Mintage | F | VF | XF | Unc | BU |
|---|---|---|---|---|---|---|
| 1975 | 52,778,000 | — | — | 0.10 | 0.25 | — |
| 1975 Proof | 1,431 | Value: 2.50 | | | | |
| 1978 | 34,006,000 | — | — | 0.10 | 0.25 | — |
| 1978 Proof | 20,000 | Value: 2.50 | | | | |
| 1989 | — | — | — | 0.10 | 0.25 | — |
| 1994 | — | — | — | 0.10 | 0.25 | — |

**2 CENTS** KM# 138 **Composition:** Aluminum

| Date | Mintage | F | VF | XF | Unc | BU |
|---|---|---|---|---|---|---|
| 1975 | 62,503,000 | — | — | 0.10 | 0.25 | — |
| 1975 Proof | 1,431 | Value: 2.50 | | | | |
| 1978 | 23,425,000 | — | — | 0.10 | 0.25 | — |
| 1978 Proof | 20,000 | Value: 3.00 | | | | |

**5 CENTS** KM# 139 **Composition:** Nickel-Brass

| Date | Mintage | F | VF | XF | Unc | BU |
|---|---|---|---|---|---|---|
| 1975 | 19,584,000 | — | — | 0.10 | 0.25 | — |
| 1975 Proof | 1,431 | Value: 2.50 | | | | |

**5 CENTS** KM# 139a **Composition:** Aluminum

| Date | Mintage | F | VF | XF | Unc | BU |
|---|---|---|---|---|---|---|
| 1978 | 272,308,000 | — | — | 0.10 | 0.25 | — |
| 1978 Proof | 20,000 | Value: 3.00 | | | | |
| 1988 | 40,000,000 | — | — | 0.10 | 0.25 | — |
| 1991 | — | — | — | 0.10 | 0.25 | — |

**10 CENTS** KM# 140 **Composition:** Nickel-Brass

| Date | Mintage | F | VF | XF | Unc | BU |
|---|---|---|---|---|---|---|
| 1975 | 10,800,000 | — | — | 0.10 | 0.25 | — |
| 1975 Proof | 1,431 | Value: 4.25 | | | | |

**10 CENTS** KM# 140a **Composition:** Aluminum

| Date | Mintage | F | VF | XF | Unc | BU |
|---|---|---|---|---|---|---|
| 1978 | 188,820,000 | — | — | 0.10 | 0.25 | — |
| 1978 Proof | 20,000 | Value: 3.50 | | | | |
| 1988 | 40,000,000 | — | — | 0.10 | 0.25 | — |
| 1991 | — | — | — | 0.10 | 0.25 | — |

**25 CENTS** KM# 141.1 **Composition:** Copper-Nickel **Edge:** Security

| Date | Mintage | F | VF | XF | Unc | BU |
|---|---|---|---|---|---|---|
| 1975 | 39,600,000 | — | — | 0.10 | 0.25 | — |
| 1975 Proof | 1,431 | Value: 4.00 | | | | |
| 1978 | 65,009,000 | — | — | 0.10 | 0.25 | — |
| 1978 Proof | 20,000 | Value: 3.50 | | | | |

**25 CENTS** KM# 141.2 **Composition:** Copper-Nickel **Edge:** Reeded

| Date | Mintage | F | VF | XF | Unc | BU |
|---|---|---|---|---|---|---|
| 1982 | 90,000,000 | — | — | 0.10 | 0.25 | — |
| 1989 | — | — | — | 0.10 | 0.25 | — |
| 1991 | — | — | — | 0.10 | 0.25 | — |
| 1994 | — | — | — | 0.10 | 0.25 | — |

**25 CENTS** KM# 141.2a **Composition:** Nickel Clad Steel **Edge:** Reeded

| Date | Mintage | VG | F | VF | XF | Unc |
|---|---|---|---|---|---|---|
| 1996 | 50,000,000 | — | — | — | 0.10 | 0.25 |
| 2001 | 10,000,000 | — | — | — | 0.10 | 0.25 |

**50 CENTS** KM# 135.1 **Composition:** Copper-Nickel **Edge:** Security

| Date | Mintage | F | VF | XF | Unc | BU |
|---|---|---|---|---|---|---|
| 1972 | 11,014,000 | — | 0.15 | 0.30 | 0.75 | — |
| 1975 | 34,000,000 | — | 0.15 | 0.30 | 0.75 | — |
| 1975 Proof | 1,431 | Value: 5.00 | | | | |
| 1978 | 66,010,000 | — | 0.15 | 0.30 | 0.75 | — |
| 1978 Proof | 20,000 | Value: 4.50 | | | | |

**50 CENTS** KM# 135.2 **Composition:** Copper-Nickel **Edge:** Reeded

| Date | Mintage | F | VF | XF | Unc | BU |
|---|---|---|---|---|---|---|
| 1982 | 65,000,000 | — | 0.10 | 0.25 | 0.65 | — |
| 1991 | — | — | 0.10 | 0.25 | 0.65 | — |
| 1994 | — | — | 0.10 | 0.25 | 0.65 | — |

**50 CENTS** KM# 135.2a **Composition:** Nickel Clad Steel **Edge:** Reeded

| Date | Mintage | VG | F | VF | XF | Unc |
|---|---|---|---|---|---|---|
| 1996 | 50,000,000 | — | — | 0.10 | 0.25 | 0.65 |
| 2001 | 30,000,000 | — | — | 0.10 | 0.25 | 0.65 |

**RUPEE** KM# 136.1 **Composition:** Copper-Nickel **Edge:** Security

| Date | Mintage | F | VF | XF | Unc | BU |
|---|---|---|---|---|---|---|
| 1972 | 6,149,000 | — | 0.30 | 0.60 | 1.25 | — |
| 1975 | 31,500,000 | — | 0.25 | 0.50 | 1.00 | — |
| 1975 Proof | 1,431 | Value: 6.50 | | | | |
| 1978 | 37,018,000 | — | 0.25 | 0.50 | 1.00 | — |
| 1978 Proof | 20,000 | Value: 6.50 | | | | |

**RUPEE** KM# 144.1 **Composition:** Copper Nickel **Obverse:** Portrait with truncation line.

| Date | Mintage | F | VF | XF | Unc | BU |
|---|---|---|---|---|---|---|
| 1978 | 2,600 | — | — | — | — | — |

**RUPEE** KM# 144 **Composition:** Copper-Nickel **Subject:** Inauguration of President Jayewardene **Note:** Right shoulder curves upward

| Date | Mintage | F | VF | XF | Unc | BU |
|---|---|---|---|---|---|---|
| 1978 | 1,997,400 | — | 0.30 | 0.60 | 1.25 | — |
| 1978 Right shoulder straight | 2,600 | — | — | — | — | 50.00 |
| 1978 Proof | 20,000 | Value: 6.50 | | | | |

**Note:** In sets only.

**RUPEE** KM# 144a **Composition:** Gold **Subject:** Inauguration of President Jayawardene

| Date | Mintage | F | VF | XF | Unc | BU |
|---|---|---|---|---|---|---|
| 1978 Proof | 40 | — | — | — | — | — |

**RUPEE** KM# 136.2 **Composition:** Copper-Nickel **Edge:** Reeded

| Date | Mintage | F | VF | XF | Unc | BU |
|---|---|---|---|---|---|---|
| 1982 | 75,000,000 | — | 0.25 | 0.50 | 1.00 | — |
| 1994 | — | — | 0.25 | 0.50 | 1.00 | — |

**RUPEE** KM# 151a **Composition:** 0.9250 Silver **Subject:** 3rd anniversary - induction of president

| Date | Mintage | VG | F | VF | XF | Unc |
|---|---|---|---|---|---|---|
| 1992 Brilliant Proof | 2,000 | — | — | — | — | — |
| 1992 Frosted Proof | 2,500 | — | — | — | — | — |

**RUPEE** KM# 151 **Composition:** Copper-Nickel **Subject:** 2nd Executive President Premadusa

| Date | Mintage | F | VF | XF | Unc | BU |
|---|---|---|---|---|---|---|
| 1992 | 25,000,000 | — | 0.30 | 0.65 | 1.75 | — |
| 1992 Proof | — | Value: 6.50 | | | | |

**RUPEE** KM# 151b **Composition:** 0.9167 Gold **Subject:** 3rd anniversary - induction of president

| Date | Mintage | VG | F | VF | XF | Unc |
|---|---|---|---|---|---|---|
| 1992 Proof | 100 | — | — | — | — | — |

**RUPEE** KM# 136.2a **Composition:** Nickel Clad Steel **Edge:** Reeded

| Date | Mintage | VG | F | VF | XF | Unc |
|---|---|---|---|---|---|---|
| 1996 | 50,000,000 | — | — | 0.25 | 0.50 | 1.00 |
| 2000 | 30,000,000 | — | — | 0.25 | 0.50 | 1.00 |

**RUPEE** KM# 157 **Composition:** Gold **Series:** UNICEF **Subject:** UNICEF 50th anniversary **Obverse:** Denomination

| Date | Mintage | F | VF | XF | Unc | BU |
|---|---|---|---|---|---|---|
| 1996 | 5,000,000 | — | — | — | 1.75 | — |

**RUPEE** KM# 162 **Weight:** 7.1300 g. **Composition:** Nickel Plated Steel **Subject:** Army's 50th Anniversary **Obverse:** National arms on crossed swords above dates. **Reverse:** Soldier giving dove to boy. **Edge:** Reeded. **Size:** 25.4 mm.

| Date | Mintage | F | VF | XF | Unc | BU |
|---|---|---|---|---|---|---|
| 1999 | 127,000 | — | — | — | 2.00 | — |
| 1999 Proof | 8,000 | Value: 6.00 | | | | |

**RUPEE** KM# 164 **Weight:** 7.1300 g. **Composition:** Nickel Plated Steel **Subject:** Sri Lankan Navy 50 Years **Obverse:** Patrol

boat. **Reverse:** Navy emblem. **Edge:** Reeded. **Size:** 25.4 mm. **Note:** Struck at Paris Mint.

| Date | Mintage | F | VF | XF | Unc | BU |
|---|---|---|---|---|---|---|
| 2000 | 20,000 | — | — | — | 2.00 | — |

**RUPEE** **KM# 164a** **Composition:** Copper Nickel **Subject:** Sri Lankan Navy 50 Years **Obverse:** Patrol boat. **Reverse:** Navy emblem. **Edge:** Reeded. **Size:** 25.4 mm.

| Date | Mintage | F | VF | XF | Unc | BU |
|---|---|---|---|---|---|---|
| 2000 Proof | 2,000 | Value: 6.00 | | | | |

**RUPEE** **KM# 166** **Weight:** 7.1300 g. **Composition:** Copper Nickel **Subject:** Air Force's 50th Anniversary **Obverse:** National arms on air force insignia. **Reverse:** Two jets above propeller plane. **Edge:** Reeded. **Size:** 25.4 mm. **Note:** Struck at British Royal Mint.

| Date | Mintage | F | VF | XF | Unc | BU |
|---|---|---|---|---|---|---|
| 2001 Proof | 2,000 | Value: 8.00 | | | | |

**2 RUPEES** **KM# 142** **Composition:** Copper-Nickel **Subject:** Non-Aligned Nations Conference

| Date | Mintage | F | VF | XF | Unc | BU |
|---|---|---|---|---|---|---|
| 1976 | 2,000,000 | — | 0.50 | 1.50 | 2.25 | — |
| 1976 Proof | 500 | Value: 10.00 | | | | |

**2 RUPEES** **KM# 145** **Composition:** Copper-Nickel **Subject:** Mahaweli Dam

| Date | Mintage | F | VF | XF | Unc | BU |
|---|---|---|---|---|---|---|
| 1981 | 45,000,000 | — | 0.35 | 0.75 | 2.50 | — |

**2 RUPEES** **KM# 147** **Composition:** Copper-Nickel

| Date | Mintage | F | VF | XF | Unc | BU |
|---|---|---|---|---|---|---|
| 1984 | 25,000,000 | — | 0.25 | 0.50 | 1.00 | — |
| 1993 | — | — | 0.30 | 0.60 | 1.35 | — |
| 1996 | — | — | 0.30 | 0.60 | 1.35 | — |
| 2001 | 10,000,000 | — | 0.30 | 0.60 | 1.35 | — |

**2 RUPEES** **KM# 155** **Composition:** Copper-Nickel **Series:** F.A.O. **Subject:** F.A.O. 50th anniversary

| Date | Mintage | F | VF | XF | Unc | BU |
|---|---|---|---|---|---|---|
| 1995 | 40,000,000 | — | — | — | 2.25 | — |

**2 RUPEES** **KM# 167** **Weight:** 8.2500 g. **Composition:** Copper Nickel **Subject:** Colombo Plan's 50th Anniversary **Obverse:** Denomination. **Reverse:** Gear wheel. **Edge:** Reeded. **Size:** 28.5 mm. **Note:** Struck at British Royal Mint.

| Date | Mintage | F | VF | XF | Unc | BU |
|---|---|---|---|---|---|---|
| 2001 | 10,000,000 | — | — | — | 2.00 | — |

**5 RUPEES** **KM# 143** **Composition:** Nickel **Subject:** Non-Aligned Nations Conference

| Date | Mintage | F | VF | XF | Unc | BU |
|---|---|---|---|---|---|---|
| 1976 | 1,000,000 | — | 0.75 | 1.50 | 3.50 | — |
| 1976 Proof | 500 | Value: 12.00 | | | | |

**5 RUPEES** **KM# 146** **Composition:** Copper-Nickel **Subject:** 50th anniversary - Universal Adult Franchise

| Date | Mintage | F | VF | XF | Unc | BU |
|---|---|---|---|---|---|---|
| 1981 | 2,000,000 | — | 0.75 | 1.50 | 3.50 | — |

**5 RUPEES** **KM# 148.1** **Composition:** Aluminum-Bronze **Edge:** Lettered **Edge Lettering:** CBC - Currency Board of Ceylon

| Date | Mintage | F | VF | XF | Unc | BU |
|---|---|---|---|---|---|---|
| 1984 | 25,000,000 | — | 0.35 | 0.75 | 2.50 | — |

**5 RUPEES** **KM# 148.2** **Composition:** Aluminum-Bronze **Edge:** Lettered **Edge Lettering:** CBSL - Currency Board of Sri Lanka

| Date | Mintage | F | VF | XF | Unc | BU |
|---|---|---|---|---|---|---|
| 1986 | — | — | 0.35 | 0.75 | 2.50 | — |
| 1991 | — | — | 0.35 | 0.75 | 2.50 | — |
| 1994 | — | — | 0.35 | 0.65 | 2.25 | — |

**5 RUPEES** **KM# 156** **Composition:** Aluminum-Bronze **Subject:** 50th anniversary - United Nations **Obverse:** Denomination

| Date | Mintage | F | VF | XF | Unc | BU |
|---|---|---|---|---|---|---|
| 1995 Proof | 5,000 | — | — | — | — | — |
| 1995 | 50,000,000 | — | — | — | 3.00 | — |

**5 RUPEES** **KM# 161** **Composition:** Aluminum-Bronze **Subject:** World cricket champions **Obverse:** Trophy **Reverse:** Batsman

| Date | Mintage | F | VF | XF | Unc | BU |
|---|---|---|---|---|---|---|
| 1999 | 50,000,000 | — | — | — | 3.50 | — |

**10 RUPEES** **KM# 149** **Composition:** Copper-Nickel **Subject:** International Year of Shelter for Homeless

| Date | Mintage | F | VF | XF | Unc | BU |
|---|---|---|---|---|---|---|
| 1987 Proof | 200 | — | — | — | — | — |
| 1987 | 2,000,000 | — | — | — | 4.00 | — |

**10 RUPEES** **KM# 158** **Ring Composition:** Copper-Nickel **Center Composition:** Brass **Subject:** 50th anniversary of independence **Edge:** CBSL, (4 times) reeded

| Date | Mintage | F | VF | XF | Unc | BU |
|---|---|---|---|---|---|---|
| 1998 | 50,000,000 | — | — | — | 4.50 | — |

**100 RUPEES** **KM# 152** **Weight:** 10.2000 g. **Composition:** 0.9250 Silver .3033 oz. ASW **Subject:** 5th South Asian Federation Games

| Date | Mintage | F | VF | XF | Unc | BU |
|---|---|---|---|---|---|---|
| 1991 Proof | 20,000 | Value: 32.00 | | | | |

**500 RUPEES** **KM# 150** **Weight:** 28.2800 g. **Composition:** 0.9250 Silver .8411 oz. ASW **Subject:** 40th anniversary of central bank

| Date | Mintage | F | VF | XF | Unc | BU |
|---|---|---|---|---|---|---|
| 1990 Proof | 10,000 | Value: 60.00 | | | | |

**500 RUPEES** **KM# 153** **Weight:** 1.6000 g. **Composition:** 0.5000 Gold .0257 oz. AGW **Subject:** 5th South Asian Federation Games

| Date | Mintage | F | VF | XF | Unc | BU |
|---|---|---|---|---|---|---|
| 1991 Proof | 8,000 | Value: 30.00 | | | | |

**500 RUPEES** **KM# 154** **Weight:** 28.2800 g. **Composition:** 0.9250 Silver .8411 oz. ASW **Subject:** 2,300th anniversary - Buddha's teachings in Sri Lanka **Note:** This is the only coin on which the country name SHRI LANKA appears. Shri Lanka was used only from June 1992 to December 1993, without constitutional authority, by decision of President Premadasa.

| Date | Mintage | F | VF | XF | Unc | BU |
|---|---|---|---|---|---|---|
| 1993 Proof | 30,000 | Value: 55.00 | | | | |

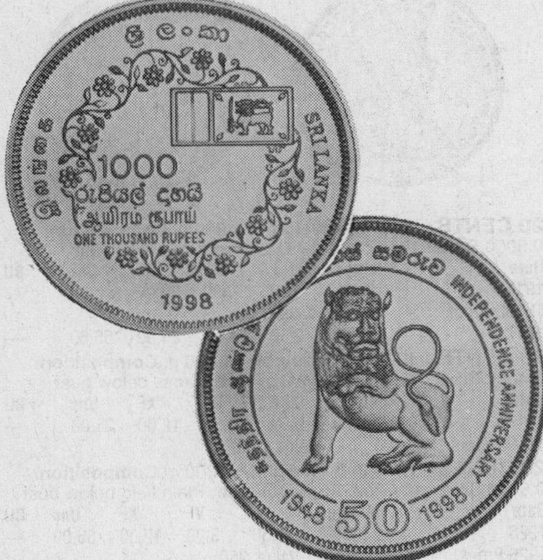

**1000 RUPEES** **KM# 159** **Weight:** 28.2800 g. **Composition:** 0.9250 Silver .841 oz. ASW **Subject:** 50 years of independence **Obverse:** Flag and denomination in wreath **Reverse:** Lion statue

| Date | Mintage | F | VF | XF | Unc | BU |
|---|---|---|---|---|---|---|
| 1998 Proof | 25,000 | Value: 55.00 | | | | |

**1000 RUPEES** **KM# 163** **Weight:** 28.2800 g. **Composition:** 0.9250 Silver 8410 oz. ASW **Subject:** 1996 Cricket Champions **Obverse:** Trophy. **Reverse:** Two players. **Edge:** Reeded. **Size:** 38.6 mm. **Note:** Struck at British Royal Mint.

| Date | Mintage | F | VF | XF | Unc | BU |
|---|---|---|---|---|---|---|
| 1999 Proof | 25,000 | Value: 45.00 | | | | |

**1000 RUPEES** **KM# 165** **Weight:** 28.2800 g. **Composition:** 0.9250 Silver .8410 oz. ASW **Subject:** Central Bank 50 Years **Obverse:** Sun face. **Reverse:** Building. **Edge:** Milled. **Size:** 38.6 mm. **Note:** Struck at British Royal Mint.

| Date | Mintage | F | VF | XF | Unc | BU |
|---|---|---|---|---|---|---|
| 2000 Proof | 10,000 | Value: 50.00 | | | | |

**5000 RUPEES** **KM# 160** **Weight:** 7.9800 g. **Composition:** 0.9167 Gold .2352 oz. AGW **Subject:** 50 years of independence **Obverse:** Flag and denomination in wreath **Reverse:** Dancer statue

| Date | Mintage | F | VF | XF | Unc | BU |
|---|---|---|---|---|---|---|
| 1998 Proof | 5,000 | Value: 235 | | | | |

## PATTERNS

Including off metal strikes

| KM# | Date | Mintage | Identification | Mkt Val |
|---|---|---|---|---|
| pn1 | 1975 | — | 5 Cents. Aluminum. KM#139a | — |
| pn2 | 1975 | — | 10 Cents. Aluminum. KM#140a | — |
| | 1978 | — | Cent. Aluminum. 1.8300 g. 24.9 mm. National arms. Denomination. Plain edge. KM137. | 80.00 |

**Note:** Probable fantasy piece

## PROOF SETS

| KM# | Date | Mintage | Identification | Issue Price | Mkt Val |
|---|---|---|---|---|---|
| PS1 | 1978 (8) | 20,000 | KM135.1, 136.1, 137, 138, 139a, 140a, 141.1, 144 | 26.00 | 35.00 |

# STRAITS SETTLEMENTS

Straits Settlements, a former British crown colony situated on the Malay Peninsula of Asia, was formed in 1826 by combining the territories of Singapore, Penang and Malacca. The colony was administered by the East India Company until its abolition in 1853. Straits Settlements was a part of British India from 1858 to 1867 at which time it became a Crown Colony. This name was changed to Malaya in 1939.

**RULERS**
British

**MINT MARKS**
H - Heaton, Birmingham
W - Soho Mint
B - Bombay

**MONETARY SYSTEM**
100 Cents = 1 Dollar

## BRITISH COLONY
### 1867-1939
### STANDARD COINAGE

**1/4 CENT** **KM# 14** **Composition:** Bronze **Edge:** Reeded

| Date | Mintage | F | VF | XF | Unc | BU |
|---|---|---|---|---|---|---|
| 1901 | 2,000,000 | 2.00 | 4.00 | 20.00 | 50.00 | — |

**1/4 CENT** **KM# 17** **Composition:** Bronze

| Date | Mintage | F | VF | XF | Unc | BU |
|---|---|---|---|---|---|---|
| 1904 Proof, plain edge | — | Value: 500 | | | | |
| 1904 Proof, milled edge | — | Value: 500 | | | | |
| 1905 | 2,008,000 | 1.25 | 6.00 | 15.00 | 40.00 | — |
| 1905 Proof | — | Value: 250 | | | | |
| 1908 | 1,200,000 | 1.25 | 6.00 | 17.50 | 45.00 | — |

**1/4 CENT** **KM# 27** **Composition:** Bronze

| Date | Mintage | F | VF | XF | Unc | BU |
|---|---|---|---|---|---|---|
| 1916 | 4,000,000 | 1.00 | 2.00 | 4.50 | 12.00 | — |
| 1916 Proof | — | Value: 220 | | | | |

**1/2 CENT** **KM# 18** **Composition:** Bronze

| Date | Mintage | F | VF | XF | Unc | BU |
|---|---|---|---|---|---|---|
| 1904 Proof | — | Value: 350 | | | | |
| 1908 | 2,000,000 | 2.50 | 5.00 | 15.00 | 45.00 | — |

**1/2 CENT** **KM# 28** **Composition:** Bronze

| Date | Mintage | F | VF | XF | Unc | BU |
|---|---|---|---|---|---|---|
| 1916 | 3,000,000 | 1.00 | 2.50 | 7.50 | 17.50 | — |
| 1916 Proof | — | Value: 300 | | | | |

**1/2 CENT** KM# 37 **Composition:** Bronze

| Date | Mintage | F | VF | XF | Unc | BU |
|---|---|---|---|---|---|---|
| 1932 | 5,000,000 | 0.75 | 1.00 | 3.00 | 12.50 | — |
| 1932 Proof | — | Value: 240 | | | | |

**CENT** KM# 16 **Composition:** Bronze **Edge:** Reeded

| Date | Mintage | F | VF | XF | Unc | BU |
|---|---|---|---|---|---|---|
| 1901 | 15,230,000 | 1.25 | 4.00 | 13.50 | 42.00 | — |

**CENT** KM# 19 **Composition:** Bronze

| Date | Mintage | F | VF | XF | Unc | BU |
|---|---|---|---|---|---|---|
| 1903 | 7,053,000 | 1.50 | 4.50 | 13.50 | 37.50 | — |
| 1903 Proof | — | Value: 200 | | | | |
| 1904 | 6,647,000 | 1.50 | 4.50 | 13.50 | 37.50 | — |
| 1904 Proof | — | Value: 200 | | | | |
| 1906 | 7,504,000 | 3.50 | 8.00 | 22.50 | 60.00 | — |
| 1907 | 5,015,000 | 1.00 | 4.00 | 15.00 | 40.00 | — |
| 1908 | Inc. above | 1.00 | 2.50 | 10.00 | 30.00 | — |
| 1908 Proof | — | Value: 200 | | | | |

**CENT** KM# 32 **Composition:** Bronze

| Date | Mintage | F | VF | XF | Unc | BU |
|---|---|---|---|---|---|---|
| 1919 | 20,165,000 | 0.50 | 0.75 | 6.00 | 20.00 | — |
| 1919 Proof | — | Value: 175 | | | | |
| 1920 | 55,000,000 | 0.50 | 0.75 | 3.00 | 12.50 | — |
| 1920 Proof | — | Value: 150 | | | | |
| 1926/0 | 5,000,000 | 2.00 | 5.00 | 10.00 | 25.00 | — |
| 1926 | Inc. above | 0.50 | 0.75 | 7.50 | 25.00 | — |

**5 CENTS** KM# 10 **Weight:** 1.3600 g. **Composition:** 0.8000 Silver .0349 oz. ASW

| Date | Mintage | F | VF | XF | Unc | BU |
|---|---|---|---|---|---|---|
| 1901 | 3,000,000 | 1.50 | 2.50 | 12.50 | 45.00 | — |

**5 CENTS** KM# 20 **Weight:** 1.3600 g. **Composition:** 0.8000 Silver .0349 oz. ASW

| Date | Mintage | F | VF | XF | Unc | BU |
|---|---|---|---|---|---|---|
| 1902 | 1,920,000 | 5.00 | 12.00 | 50.00 | 90.00 | — |
| 1902 Proof | — | Value: 350 | | | | |
| 1903 | 2,270,000 | 5.00 | 12.00 | 50.00 | 90.00 | — |
| 1903 Proof | — | Value: 350 | | | | |

**5 CENTS** KM# 20a **Weight:** 1.3600 g. **Composition:** 0.6000 Silver .0262 oz. ASW

| Date | Mintage | F | VF | XF | Unc | BU |
|---|---|---|---|---|---|---|
| 1910B | 13,012,000 | 1.25 | 2.25 | 5.50 | 12.00 | — |
| 1910B Proof | — | Value: 350 | | | | |

**5 CENTS** KM# 31 **Weight:** 1.3600 g. **Composition:** 0.4000 Silver .0174 oz. ASW

| Date | Mintage | F | VF | XF | Unc | BU |
|---|---|---|---|---|---|---|
| 1918 | 3,100,000 | 0.50 | 1.25 | 5.00 | 12.00 | — |
| 1919 | 6,900,000 | 0.50 | 1.25 | 5.00 | 12.00 | — |
| 1920 | 4,000,000 | 120 | 250 | 600 | 1,200 | — |

**5 CENTS** KM# 34 **Composition:** Copper-Nickel

| Date | Mintage | F | VF | XF | Unc | BU |
|---|---|---|---|---|---|---|
| 1920 | 20,000,000 | 1.00 | 12.00 | 50.00 | 100 | — |
| 1920 Proof | — | Value: 525 | | | | |

**5 CENTS** KM# 36 **Weight:** 1.3600 g. **Composition:** 0.6000 Silver .0262 oz. ASW **Note:** Similar to KM#31, smaller bust, broader rim.

| Date | Mintage | F | VF | XF | Unc | BU |
|---|---|---|---|---|---|---|
| 1926 Proof | — | Value: 240 | | | | |
| 1926 | 10,000,000 | 0.50 | 0.75 | 4.00 | 12.00 | — |
| 1935 | 3,000,000 | 0.50 | 0.75 | 4.00 | 9.00 | — |
| 1935 Proof | — | Value: 240 | | | | |

**10 CENTS** KM# 11 **Weight:** 2.7100 g. **Composition:** 0.8000 Silver .0697 oz. ASW

| Date | Mintage | F | VF | XF | Unc | BU |
|---|---|---|---|---|---|---|
| 1901 | 2,700,000 | 1.75 | 2.75 | 7.00 | 25.00 | — |

**10 CENTS** KM# 21 **Weight:** 2.7100 g. **Composition:** 0.8000 Silver .0697 oz. ASW

| Date | Mintage | F | VF | XF | Unc | BU |
|---|---|---|---|---|---|---|
| 1902 | 6,118,000 | 2.50 | 10.00 | 25.00 | 60.00 | — |
| 1902 Proof | — | Value: 250 | | | | |
| 1903 | 1,401,000 | 3.00 | 12.00 | 32.50 | 80.00 | — |
| 1903 Proof | — | Value: 250 | | | | |

**10 CENTS** KM# 21a **Weight:** 2.7100 g. **Composition:** 0.6000 Silver .0522 oz. ASW

| Date | Mintage | F | VF | XF | Unc | BU |
|---|---|---|---|---|---|---|
| 1909B | 11,088,000 | 5.00 | 20.00 | 40.00 | 90.00 | — |
| 1910B | 1,657,000 | 1.00 | 2.00 | 3.00 | 10.00 | — |
| 1910B Proof | — | Value: 250 | | | | |

**10 CENTS** KM# 29 **Weight:** 2.7100 g. **Composition:** 0.6000 Silver .0522 oz. ASW **Obverse:** Dot below bust

| Date | Mintage | F | VF | XF | Unc | BU |
|---|---|---|---|---|---|---|
| 1916 | 600,000 | 3.00 | 7.00 | 20.00 | 35.00 | — |
| 1917 | 5,600,000 | 1.00 | 2.00 | 7.00 | 22.00 | — |

**10 CENTS** KM# 29a **Weight:** 2.7100 g. **Composition:** 0.4000 Silver .0348 oz. ASW **Obverse:** Cross below bust

| Date | Mintage | F | VF | XF | Unc | BU |
|---|---|---|---|---|---|---|
| 1918 | 7,500,000 | 1.00 | 2.50 | 8.00 | 22.00 | — |
| 1919 | 11,500,000 | 1.00 | 2.50 | 8.00 | 22.00 | — |
| 1920 | 4,000,000 | 5.00 | 15.00 | 40.00 | 115 | — |

**10 CENTS** KM# 29b **Weight:** 2.7100 g. **Composition:** 0.6000 Silver .0522 oz. ASW **Obverse:** Plain field below bust

| Date | Mintage | F | VF | XF | Unc | BU |
|---|---|---|---|---|---|---|
| 1926 | 20,000,000 | 1.00 | 1.50 | 5.00 | 15.00 | — |
| 1926 Proof | — | Value: 225 | | | | |
| 1927 | 23,000,000 | 0.50 | 0.75 | 1.00 | 3.25 | — |
| 1927 Proof | — | Value: 225 | | | | |

**20 CENTS** KM# 12 **Weight:** 5.4300 g. **Composition:** 0.8000 Silver .1396 oz. ASW

| Date | Mintage | F | VF | XF | Unc | BU |
|---|---|---|---|---|---|---|
| 1901 | 600,000 | 3.00 | 4.50 | 12.50 | 40.00 | — |

**20 CENTS** KM# 22 **Weight:** 5.4300 g. **Composition:** 0.8000 Silver .1396 oz. ASW

| Date | Mintage | F | VF | XF | Unc | BU |
|---|---|---|---|---|---|---|
| 1902 | 1,105,000 | 6.00 | 15.00 | 50.00 | 120 | — |
| 1902 Proof | — | Value: 300 | | | | |
| 1903 | 1,150,000 | 6.00 | 15.00 | 50.00 | 120 | — |
| 1903 Proof | — | Value: 300 | | | | |

**20 CENTS** KM# 22a **Weight:** 5.4300 g. **Composition:** 0.6000 Silver .1047 oz. ASW

| Date | Mintage | F | VF | XF | Unc | BU |
|---|---|---|---|---|---|---|
| 1910B | 3,276,000 | 2.00 | 3.50 | 10.00 | 25.00 | — |
| 1910B Proof | — | Value: 300 | | | | |

**20 CENTS** KM# 30 **Weight:** 5.4300 g. **Composition:** 0.6000 Silver .1047 oz. ASW **Obverse:** Dot below bust

| Date | Mintage | F | VF | XF | Unc | BU |
|---|---|---|---|---|---|---|
| 1916B | 545,000 | 4.00 | 10.00 | 30.00 | 70.00 | — |
| 1916B Proof | — | Value: 250 | | | | |
| 1917B | 652,000 | 2.50 | 4.50 | 25.00 | 55.00 | — |

**20 CENTS** KM# 30a **Weight:** 5.4300 g. **Composition:** 0.4000 Silver .0698 oz. ASW **Obverse:** Cross below bust

| Date | Mintage | F | VF | XF | Unc | BU |
|---|---|---|---|---|---|---|
| 1919B | 2,500,000 | 2.50 | 4.50 | 12.00 | 35.00 | — |
| 1919B Proof | — | Value: 250 | | | | |

**20 CENTS** KM# 30b **Weight:** 5.4300 g. **Composition:** 0.6000 Silver .1047 oz. ASW **Obverse:** Plain field below bust

| Date | Mintage | F | VF | XF | Unc | BU |
|---|---|---|---|---|---|---|
| 1926 | 2,500,000 | 1.50 | 3.00 | 12.00 | 35.00 | — |
| 1926 Proof | — | Value: 250 | | | | |
| 1927 | 3,000,000 | 1.50 | 2.50 | 6.00 | 12.00 | — |
| 1927 Proof | — | Value: 250 | | | | |
| 1935 Round-top 3 | 1,000,000 | 1.50 | 2.50 | 3.50 | 7.00 | — |
| 1935 Flat-top 3 | Inc. above | 1.50 | 2.50 | 3.50 | 7.00 | — |

**50 CENTS** KM# 13 **Weight:** 13.5769 g. **Composition:** 0.8000 Silver .3492 oz. ASW

| Date | Mintage | F | VF | XF | Unc | BU |
|---|---|---|---|---|---|---|
| 1901 | 120,000 | 25.00 | 50.00 | 120 | 280 | — |

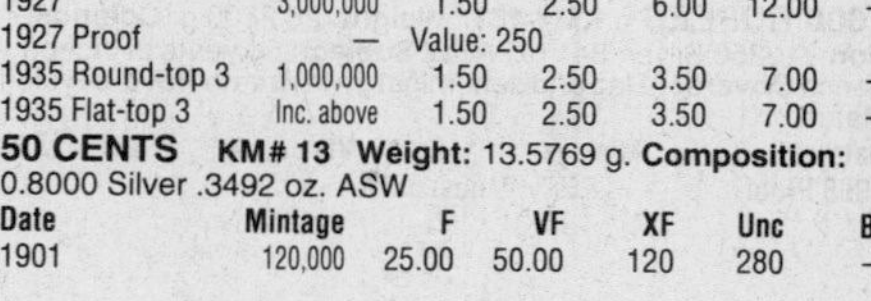

**50 CENTS** KM# 23 **Weight:** 13.5769 g. **Composition:** 0.8000 Silver .3492 oz. ASW

| Date | Mintage | F | VF | XF | Unc | BU |
|---|---|---|---|---|---|---|
| 1902 | 148,000 | 50.00 | 80.00 | 175 | 280 | — |
| 1902 Proof | — | Value: 900 | | | | |
| 1903 | 193,000 | 50.00 | 80.00 | 175 | 280 | — |
| 1903 Proof | — | Value: 900 | | | | |
| 1904 Proof | — | Value: 1,000 | | | | |

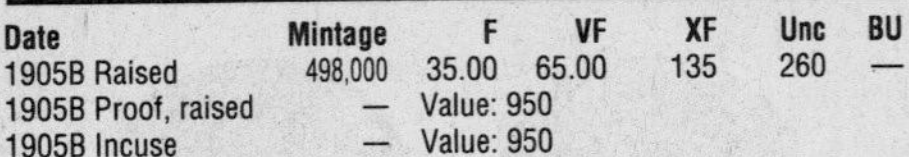

| Date | Mintage | F | VF | XF | Unc | BU |
|---|---|---|---|---|---|---|
| 1905B Raised | 498,000 | 35.00 | 65.00 | 135 | 260 | — |
| 1905B Proof, raised | — | Value: 950 | | | | |
| 1905B Incuse | — | Value: 950 | | | | |

**50 CENTS** **KM# 24** **Weight:** 10.1000 g. **Composition:** 0.9000 Silver .2922 oz. ASW

| Date | Mintage | F | VF | XF | Unc | BU |
|---|---|---|---|---|---|---|
| 1907 | 464,000 | 5.50 | 10.00 | 22.00 | 60.00 | — |
| 1907H | 2,667,000 | 5.50 | 10.00 | 22.00 | 60.00 | — |
| 1907H Proof | — | Value: 200 | | | | |
| 1908 | 2,869,000 | 7.00 | 12.50 | 27.50 | 80.00 | — |
| 1908H | Inc. above | 7.00 | 10.00 | 22.00 | 60.00 | — |

**Note:** Mintage included with 1907H

**50 CENTS** **KM# 35.1** **Weight:** 8.4200 g. **Composition:** 0.5000 Silver .1353 oz. ASW **Obverse:** Cross below bust

| Date | Mintage | F | VF | XF | Unc | BU |
|---|---|---|---|---|---|---|
| 1920 | 3,900,000 | 2.00 | 3.50 | 7.00 | 15.00 | — |
| 1920 Proof | — | Value: 250 | | | | |
| 1921 | 2,579,000 | 2.50 | 4.50 | 9.00 | 18.00 | — |
| 1921 Proof | — | Value: 250 | | | | |

**50 CENTS** **KM# 35.2** **Weight:** 8.4200 g. **Composition:** 0.5000 Silver .1353 oz. ASW **Obverse:** Dot below bust

| Date | Mintage | F | VF | XF | Unc | BU |
|---|---|---|---|---|---|---|
| 1920 | Inc. above | 120 | 185 | 300 | 550 | — |

**DOLLAR** **KM# 25** **Weight:** 26.9500 g. **Composition:** 0.9000 Silver .7799 oz. ASW

| Date | Mintage | F | VF | XF | Unc | BU |
|---|---|---|---|---|---|---|
| 1903 Proof | — | Value: 1,000 | | | | |
| 1903B Incuse | 15,010,000 | 15.00 | 25.00 | 50.00 | 100 | — |
| 1903B Raised | Inc. above | 70.00 | 120 | 250 | 600 | — |
| 1903B Proof, raised | — | Value: 1,100 | | | | |
| 1904B | 20,365,000 | 12.50 | 20.00 | 35.00 | 85.00 | — |
| 1904B Proof | — | Value: 1,000 | | | | |

**DOLLAR** **KM# 26** **Weight:** 20.2100 g. **Composition:** 0.9000 Silver .5848 oz. ASW **Size:** 34.5 mm. **Note:** Reduced size.

| Date | Mintage | F | VF | XF | Unc | BU |
|---|---|---|---|---|---|---|
| 1907 | 6,842,000 | 7.50 | 10.00 | 20.00 | 60.00 | — |
| 1907H | 4,000,000 | 7.50 | 10.00 | 20.00 | 60.00 | — |
| 1907H Proof | — | Value: 550 | | | | |
| 1908 | 4,152,000 | 7.50 | 10.00 | 20.00 | 60.00 | — |
| 1908 Proof | — | Value: 550 | | | | |
| 1909 | 1,014,000 | 10.00 | 15.00 | 25.00 | 80.00 | — |
| 1909 Proof | — | Value: 550 | | | | |

**DOLLAR** **KM# 33** **Weight:** 16.8500 g. **Composition:** 0.5000 Silver .2709 oz. ASW

| Date | Mintage | F | VF | XF | Unc | BU |
|---|---|---|---|---|---|---|
| 1919 | 6,000,000 | 15.00 | 30.00 | 90.00 | 140 | — |
| 1919 Proof, restrike | — | Value: 75.00 | | | | |
| 1920 | 8,164,000 | 10.00 | 20.00 | 30.00 | 70.00 | — |
| 1920 Proof, restrike | — | Value: 75.00 | | | | |
| 1925 | — | 450 | 850 | 1,250 | — | — |
| 1925 Proof | — | Value: 3,500 | | | | |
| 1925 Proof, restrike | — | Value: 600 | | | | |
| 1926 | — | 450 | 850 | 1,250 | — | — |
| 1926 Proof | — | Value: 3,500 | | | | |
| 1926 Proof | — | Value: 600 | | | | |

# SUDAN

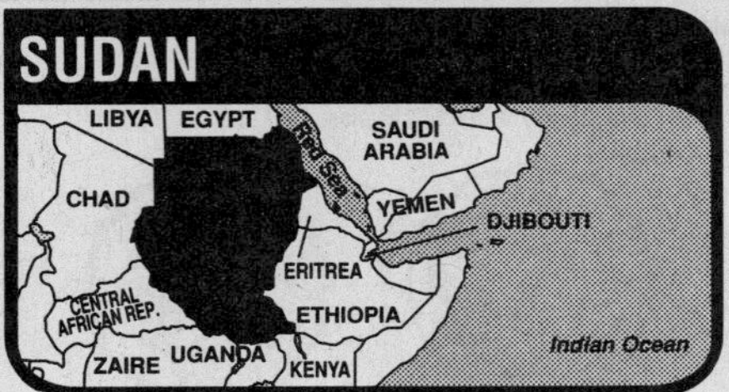


The Democratic Republic of the Sudan, located in northeast Africa on the Red Sea between Egypt and Ethiopia, has an area of 967,500 sq. mi. (2,505,810 sq. km.) and a population of *24.5 million. Capital: Khartoum. Agriculture and livestock raising are the chief occupations. Cotton, gum arabic and peanuts are exported.

The Sudan, site of the powerful Nubian kingdom of Roman times, was a collection of small independent states from the 14th century until 1820-22 when it was conquered and united by Mohammed Ali, Pasha of Egypt. Egyptian forces were driven from the area during the Mahdist revolt, 1881-98, but the Sudan was retaken by Anglo-Egyptian expeditions, 1896-98, and established as an Anglo-Egyptian condominium in 1899. Britain supplied the administrative apparatus and personnel, but the appearance of joint Anglo-Egyptian administration was continued until Jan. 9, 1954, when the first Sudanese self-government parliament was inaugurated. The Sudan achieved independence on Jan. 1, 1956 with the consent of the British and Egyptian government.

**TITLES**

جمهورية السودان

Jumhuriya(t) as-Sudan

الجمهورية السودان الديمقراطية

al-Jumhuriya(t) as-Sudan ad-Dimiqratiya(t)

**MINTNAME**

Omdurman ام درمان

## REPUBLIC

### STANDARD COINAGE

**MILLIM** **KM# 29.1** **Composition:** Bronze **Obverse:** Large legend and written denomination

| Date | Mintage | F | VF | XF | Unc | BU |
|---|---|---|---|---|---|---|
| AH1376(1956) | 5,000,000 | — | — | 0.15 | 0.30 | — |
| AH1379(1960) | 1,300,000 | — | — | 0.15 | 0.35 | — |
| AH1386(1966) Proof | — | — | — | — | — | — |
| AH1387(1967) | — | — | — | 0.15 | 0.30 | — |
| AH1388(1968) | — | — | — | 0.15 | 0.30 | — |
| AH1389(1969) | — | — | — | 0.15 | 0.30 | — |

**MILLIM** **KM# 29.2** **Composition:** Bronze **Obverse:** Small legend and written denomination **Note:** Except for proof sets, mintage figures have generally not been released since 1967.

| Date | Mintage | F | VF | XF | Unc | BU |
|---|---|---|---|---|---|---|
| AH1387(1967) Proof | 7,834 | Value: 0.25 | | | | |
| AH1388(1968) Proof | 5,251 | Value: 0.50 | | | | |
| AH1389(1969) Proof | 2,149 | Value: 0.75 | | | | |

**MILLIM** **KM# 39** **Composition:** Bronze **Obverse:** New Arabic legend

| Date | Mintage | F | VF | XF | Unc | BU |
|---|---|---|---|---|---|---|
| AH1390(1970) | — | — | — | — | — | — |
| AH1390(1970) Proof | 1,646 | Value: 1.00 | | | | |
| AH1391(1971) Proof | 1,772 | Value: 1.00 | | | | |

**2 MILLIM** **KM# 30.1** **Composition:** Bronze **Obverse:** Large written denomination

| Date | Mintage | F | VF | XF | Unc | BU |
|---|---|---|---|---|---|---|
| AH1376(1956) | 5,000,000 | — | — | 0.15 | 0.45 | — |
| AH1386(1966) Proof | — | Value: 1.00 | | | | |
| AH1387(1967) | — | — | — | 0.15 | 0.45 | — |
| AH1388(1968) | — | — | — | 0.15 | 0.45 | — |
| AH1389(1969) | — | — | — | 0.15 | 0.45 | — |

**2 MILLIM** **KM# 30.2** **Composition:** Bronze **Obverse:** Small written denomination

| Date | Mintage | F | VF | XF | Unc | BU |
|---|---|---|---|---|---|---|
| AH1387(1967) Proof | 7,834 | Value: 0.50 | | | | |
| AH1388(1968) Proof | 5,251 | Value: 0.75 | | | | |
| AH1389(1969) Proof | 2,149 | Value: 1.00 | | | | |

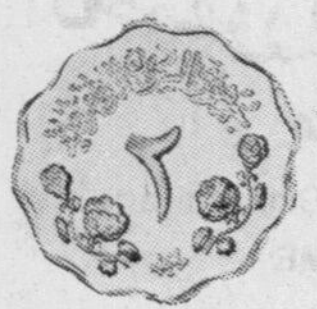

**2 MILLIM** **KM# 40** **Composition:** Bronze **Obverse:** New Arabic legend **Note:** Existence of circulation strikes is uncertain.

| Date | Mintage | F | VF | XF | Unc | BU |
|---|---|---|---|---|---|---|
| AH1390(1970) Proof | 1,646 | Value: 1.25 | | | | |
| AH1391(1971) Proof | 1,772 | Value: 1.25 | | | | |

**5 MILLIM** **KM# 31.1** **Composition:** Bronze **Obverse:** Thin legend and large denomination **Note:** Camel and rider size varieties exist.

| Date | Mintage | F | VF | XF | Unc | BU |
|---|---|---|---|---|---|---|
| AH1376(1956) | 30,000,000 | — | 0.10 | 0.20 | 0.45 | — |
| AH1382(1962) | 6,000,000 | — | 0.10 | 0.20 | 0.50 | — |
| AH1386(1966) | 4,000,000 | — | 0.10 | 0.15 | 0.35 | — |
| AH1386(1966) Proof | — | — | — | — | — | — |
| AH1387(1967) | 4,000,000 | — | 0.10 | 0.15 | 0.35 | — |
| AH1388(1968) | — | — | 0.10 | 0.15 | 0.35 | — |
| AH1389(1969) | — | — | 0.10 | 0.15 | 0.35 | — |

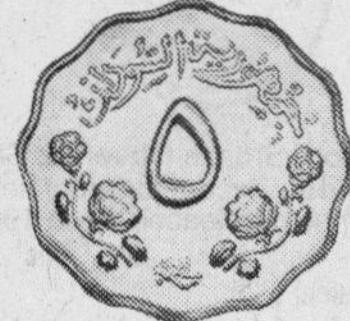

**5 MILLIM** **KM# 31.2** **Composition:** Bronze **Obverse:** Thick legend and small denomination

| Date | Mintage | F | VF | XF | Unc | BU |
|---|---|---|---|---|---|---|
| AH1387(1967) Proof | 7,834 | Value: 0.75 | | | | |
| AH1388(1968) Proof | 5,251 | Value: 1.00 | | | | |
| AH1389(1969) Proof | 2,149 | Value: 1.25 | | | | |

**5 MILLIM** **KM# 41.1** **Composition:** Bronze **Obverse:** New large Arabic legend and denomination

| Date | Mintage | F | VF | XF | Unc | BU |
|---|---|---|---|---|---|---|
| AH1390(1970) | — | — | 0.20 | 0.45 | 1.25 | — |
| AH1391(1971) | 3,000,000 | — | 0.20 | 0.45 | 1.25 | — |

**5 MILLIM** **KM# 41.2** **Composition:** Bronze **Obverse:** Small legend and denomination

| Date | Mintage | F | VF | XF | Unc | BU |
|---|---|---|---|---|---|---|
| AH1390(1970) Proof | 1,646 | Value: 1.25 | | | | |
| AH1391(1971) Proof | 1,772 | Value: 1.25 | | | | |

**5 MILLIM** **KM# 47** **Composition:** Bronze **Subject:** 2nd anniversary of revolution

| Date | Mintage | F | VF | XF | Unc | BU |
|---|---|---|---|---|---|---|
| AH1391(1971) | 500,000 | — | 0.15 | 0.25 | 0.50 | — |

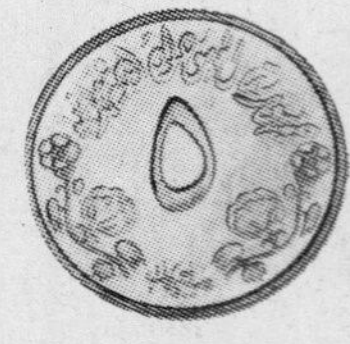

**5 MILLIM** **KM# 53** **Composition:** Bronze **Series:** F.A.O.

| Date | Mintage | F | VF | XF | Unc | BU |
|---|---|---|---|---|---|---|
| AH1392(1972) | 6,000,000 | — | — | 0.15 | 0.35 | — |
| AH1393(1973) | 9,000,000 | — | — | 0.15 | 0.35 | — |

**5 MILLIM** **KM# 54** **Composition:** Bronze **Note:** Similar to 10 Millim, KM#55, but round.

| Date | Mintage | F | VF | XF | Unc | BU |
|---|---|---|---|---|---|---|
| AH1392(1972) | — | — | — | 0.20 | 0.45 | — |

**5 MILLIM** **KM# 54a.1** **Composition:** Brass **Obverse:** Thick legend and written denomination **Reverse:** Ribbon with 3 equal sections

| Date | Mintage | F | VF | XF | Unc | BU |
|---|---|---|---|---|---|---|
| AH1395(1975) | 4,132,000 | — | — | 0.20 | 0.40 | — |
| AH1398(1978) | — | — | — | 0.20 | 0.40 | — |

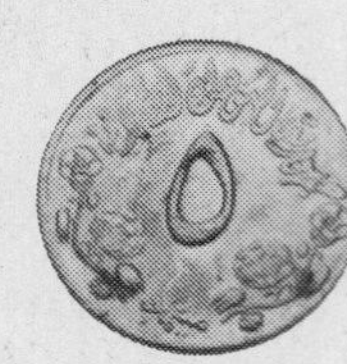

**5 MILLIM** **KM# 60** **Composition:** Brass **Series:** F.A.O.

| Date | Mintage | F | VF | XF | Unc | BU |
|---|---|---|---|---|---|---|
| AH1396(1976) | 7,868,000 | — | — | 0.10 | 0.20 | — |
| AH1398(1978) | 7,000,000 | — | — | 0.10 | 0.20 | — |

**5 MILLIM** **KM# 94** **Composition:** Brass **Subject:** 20th anniversary of independence

| Date | Mintage | F | VF | XF | Unc | BU |
|---|---|---|---|---|---|---|
| AH1396(1976) | — | — | 0.15 | 0.20 | 0.25 | — |

**5 MILLIM** **KM# 54a.2** **Composition:** Brass **Reverse:** Ribbon with long center section

| Date | Mintage | F | VF | XF | Unc | BU |
|---|---|---|---|---|---|---|
| AH1398(1978) | — | — | — | 0.20 | 0.40 | — |

**5 MILLIM** **KM# 54a.3** **Composition:** Brass **Obverse:** Thin legend and written denomination, different style **Reverse:** Ribbon with 3 equal sections

| Date | Mintage | F | VF | XF | Unc | BU |
|---|---|---|---|---|---|---|
| AH1400(1980) Proof | — | Value: 1.00 | | | | |

**5 MILLIM** **KM# 54a.4** **Composition:** Brass **Obverse:** Small 5, crude lettering **Reverse:** Large eagle, ribbon with long center section

| Date | Mintage | F | VF | XF | Unc | BU |
|---|---|---|---|---|---|---|
| AH1403(1983) | — | — | — | — | — | — |

**10 MILLIM** **KM# 32.1** **Composition:** Bronze **Obverse:** Large written denomination **Note:** Camel and rider size varieties exist.

| Date | Mintage | F | VF | XF | Unc | BU |
|---|---|---|---|---|---|---|
| AH1376(1956) | 15,000,000 | — | 0.15 | 0.25 | 0.60 | — |
| AH1380(1960) | 12,250,000 | — | 0.15 | 0.20 | 0.50 | — |
| AH1381(1962) High date | — | — | 0.15 | 0.20 | 0.50 | — |
| AH1381(1962) Low date | — | — | 0.15 | 0.20 | 0.50 | — |
| AH1386(1966) | 1,000,000 | — | 0.15 | 0.25 | 0.60 | — |
| AH1386(1966) Proof | — | — | — | — | — | — |
| AH1387(1967) | 1,000,000 | — | 0.15 | 0.20 | 0.50 | — |
| AH1388(1968) | — | — | 0.15 | 0.20 | 0.50 | — |
| AH1389(1969) | — | — | 0.15 | 0.20 | 0.50 | — |

**10 MILLIM** **KM# 32.2** **Composition:** Bronze **Obverse:** Small written denomination

| Date | Mintage | F | VF | XF | Unc | BU |
|---|---|---|---|---|---|---|
| AH1387(1967) Proof | 7,834 | Value: 1.00 | | | | |
| AH1388(1968) Proof | 5,251 | Value: 1.25 | | | | |
| AH1389(1969) Proof | 2,149 | Value: 1.50 | | | | |

**10 MILLIM** **KM# 42.1** **Composition:** Bronze **Obverse:** New large Arabic legend and written denomination

| Date | Mintage | F | VF | XF | Unc | BU |
|---|---|---|---|---|---|---|
| AH1390(1970) | — | — | 0.20 | 0.40 | 0.90 | — |
| AH1391(1971) | 3,000,000 | — | 0.20 | 0.40 | 0.90 | — |

**10 MILLIM** **KM# 42.2** **Composition:** Bronze **Obverse:** Small legend and written denomination

| Date | Mintage | F | VF | XF | Unc | BU |
|---|---|---|---|---|---|---|
| AH1390(1970) Proof | 1,646 | Value: 1.25 | | | | |
| AH1391(1971) Proof | 1,772 | Value: 1.25 | | | | |

**10 MILLIM** **KM# 48** **Composition:** Bronze **Subject:** 2nd anniversary of revolution

| Date | Mintage | F | VF | XF | Unc | BU |
|---|---|---|---|---|---|---|
| AH1391(1971) | 500,000 | — | 10.00 | 15.00 | 25.00 | — |

**10 MILLIM** **KM# 55** **Composition:** Bronze

| Date | Mintage | F | VF | XF | Unc | BU |
|---|---|---|---|---|---|---|
| AH1392(1972) | 6,500,000 | — | 0.15 | 0.25 | 0.50 | — |

**10 MILLIM** **KM# 55a.1** **Composition:** Brass **Obverse:** Thick legend and written denomination **Reverse:** Ribbon with 3 equal sections

| Date | Mintage | F | VF | XF | Unc | BU |
|---|---|---|---|---|---|---|
| AH1395(1975) | 12,000,000 | — | 0.25 | 0.35 | 0.75 | — |
| AH1398(1978) | 9,410,000 | — | 0.25 | 0.45 | 1.00 | — |

**10 MILLIM** **KM# 61** **Composition:** Brass **Series:** F.A.O.

| Date | Mintage | F | VF | XF | Unc | BU |
|---|---|---|---|---|---|---|
| AH1396(1976) | 3,000,000 | — | 0.10 | 0.15 | 0.25 | — |
| AH1398(1978) | — | — | 0.10 | 0.15 | 0.25 | — |

**10 MILLIM** **KM# 62** **Composition:** Brass **Subject:** 20th anniversary of independence

| Date | Mintage | F | VF | XF | Unc | BU |
|---|---|---|---|---|---|---|
| AH1396(1976) | 3,610,000 | — | 0.10 | 0.20 | 0.40 | — |

**10 MILLIM** **KM# 55a.2** **Composition:** Brass **Reverse:** Ribbon with long center section

| Date | Mintage | F | VF | XF | Unc | BU |
|---|---|---|---|---|---|---|
| AH1398(1978) | — | — | 0.75 | 1.75 | 4.25 | — |

**10 MILLIM** **KM# 55a.3** **Composition:** Brass **Obverse:** Thin legend and written denomination, different style **Reverse:** Ribbon with 3 equal sections

| Date | Mintage | F | VF | XF | Unc | BU |
|---|---|---|---|---|---|---|
| AH1400(1980) | 2,490,000 | — | 0.25 | 0.45 | 1.00 | — |
| AH1400(1980) Proof | — | Value: 2.50 | | | | |

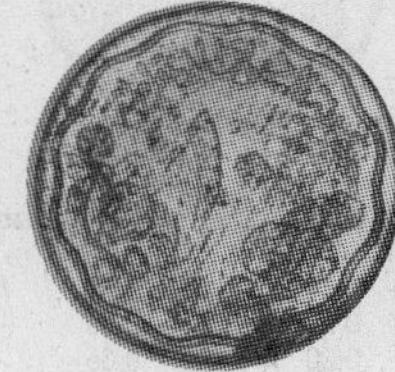

**10 MILLIM** **KM# 111** **Composition:** Brass **Reverse:** Ribbon with long center section

| Date | Mintage | F | VF | XF | Unc | BU |
|---|---|---|---|---|---|---|
| AH1400(1980) | — | — | 1.25 | 3.75 | 7.50 | — |

**GHIRSH** **KM# 97** **Composition:** Brass **Reverse:** Ribbon with 3 equal sections

| Date | Mintage | F | VF | XF | Unc | BU |
|---|---|---|---|---|---|---|
| AH1403(1983) | 1,140,000 | — | 0.25 | 0.65 | 2.00 | — |

**GHIRSH** **KM# 99** **Composition:** Aluminum-Bronze

| Date | Mintage | F | VF | XF | Unc | BU |
|---|---|---|---|---|---|---|
| AH1408(1987) | — | — | 0.30 | 0.80 | 3.00 | — |

**2 GHIRSH** **KM# 33** **Composition:** Copper-Nickel

| Date | Mintage | F | VF | XF | Unc | BU |
|---|---|---|---|---|---|---|
| AH1376(1956) | 5,000,000 | — | 0.15 | 0.35 | 0.50 | — |
| AH1381(1962) | — | — | 0.15 | 0.35 | 0.50 | — |

**2 GHIRSH** **KM# 36** **Composition:** Copper-Nickel

| Date | Mintage | F | VF | XF | Unc | BU |
|---|---|---|---|---|---|---|
| AH1382(1963) | 1,250,000 | — | 0.15 | 0.35 | 0.75 | — |
| AH1386(1966) Proof | — | — | — | — | — | — |
| AH1387(1967) | 7,834 | — | 0.15 | 0.35 | 0.75 | — |
| AH1387(1967) Proof | 7,834 | Value: 1.50 | | | | |
| AH1388(1968) | 5,251 | — | 0.15 | 0.35 | 0.75 | — |
| AH1388(1968) Proof | 5,251 | Value: 1.50 | | | | |
| AH1389(1969) | 2,149 | — | 0.15 | 0.35 | 0.75 | — |
| AH1389(1969) Proof | 2,149 | Value: 1.75 | | | | |

**2 GHIRSH** **KM# 43.1** **Composition:** Copper-Nickel **Obverse:** New large Arabic legend and written denomination

| Date | Mintage | F | VF | XF | Unc | BU |
|---|---|---|---|---|---|---|
| AH1390(1970) | — | — | 0.30 | 0.60 | 1.25 | — |

**2 GHIRSH** **KM# 43.2** **Composition:** Copper-Nickel **Obverse:** Small legend and written denomination

| Date | Mintage | F | VF | XF | Unc | BU |
|---|---|---|---|---|---|---|
| AH1390(1970) Proof | 1,646 | Value: 1.25 | | | | |
| AH1391(1971) Proof | 1,772 | Value: 1.25 | | | | |

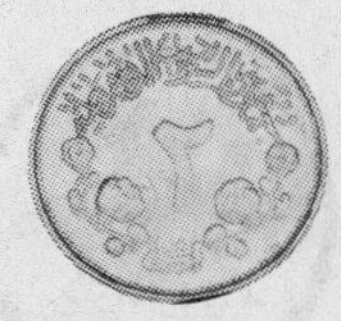

**2 GHIRSH** **KM# 49** **Composition:** Copper-Nickel **Subject:** 2nd anniversary of revolution

| Date | Mintage | F | VF | XF | Unc | BU |
|---|---|---|---|---|---|---|
| AH1391(1971) | 500,000 | — | 0.25 | 0.45 | 0.80 | — |

**2 GHIRSH** **KM# 57.1** **Composition:** Copper-Nickel **Obverse:** Thick legend and denomination **Reverse:** Ribbon with 3 equal sections

| Date | Mintage | F | VF | XF | Unc | BU |
|---|---|---|---|---|---|---|
| AH1395(1975) | 1,000,000 | — | 0.20 | 0.35 | 0.75 | — |
| AH1398(1978) | 1,250,000 | — | 0.20 | 0.35 | 0.75 | — |

**2 GHIRSH** **KM# 63.1** **Composition:** Copper-Nickel **Series:** F.A.O. **Obverse:** Thick denomination

| Date | Mintage | F | VF | XF | Unc | BU |
|---|---|---|---|---|---|---|
| AH1396(1976) | 500,000 | — | 0.20 | 0.35 | 0.75 | — |
| AH1398(1978) | Inc. above | — | 0.20 | 0.35 | 0.75 | — |

**2 GHIRSH** **KM# 64** **Composition:** Copper-Nickel **Subject:** 20th anniversary of independence

| Date | Mintage | F | VF | XF | Unc | BU |
|---|---|---|---|---|---|---|
| AH1396(1976) | 1,750,000 | — | 0.20 | 0.30 | 0.60 | — |

**2 GHIRSH** **KM# 57.2** **Composition:** Copper-Nickel **Reverse:** Ribbon with long center section

| Date | Mintage | F | VF | XF | Unc | BU |
|---|---|---|---|---|---|---|
| AH1398(1978) | — | — | 0.20 | 0.35 | 0.75 | — |
| AH1400(1980) | — | — | 0.20 | 0.35 | 0.75 | — |

**2 GHIRSH** **KM# 63.2** **Composition:** Copper-Nickel **Series:** F.A.O. **Obverse:** Thin denomination

| Date | Mintage | F | VF | XF | Unc | BU |
|---|---|---|---|---|---|---|
| AH1398(1978) | Inc. above | — | 5.00 | 7.00 | 10.00 | — |

**2 GHIRSH** **KM# 57.3** **Composition:** Copper-Nickel **Obverse:** Thin legend and denomination **Reverse:** Ribbon with 3 equal sections

| Date | Mintage | F | VF | XF | Unc | BU |
|---|---|---|---|---|---|---|
| AH1399(1979) | 2,000,000 | — | 0.20 | 0.35 | 0.75 | — |
| AH1400(1980) | 6,825,000 | — | 0.20 | 0.35 | 0.75 | — |
| AH1400(1980) Proof | Inc. above | Value: 2.00 | | | | |

**2 GHIRSH** **KM# 57.2a** **Composition:** Brass **Obverse:** Legend with different style

| Date | Mintage | F | VF | XF | Unc | BU |
|---|---|---|---|---|---|---|
| AH1403(1983) | 100,000 | — | 0.75 | 1.50 | 3.50 | — |

**5 GHIRSH** **KM# 34.1** **Composition:** Copper-Nickel **Obverse:** Large written denomination

| Date | Mintage | F | VF | XF | Unc | BU |
|---|---|---|---|---|---|---|
| AH1376(1956) | 40,000,000 | — | 0.20 | 0.40 | 1.00 | — |
| AH1386(1966) Proof | — | Value: 1.50 | | | | |
| AH1387(1967) | — | — | 0.20 | 0.30 | 0.70 | — |
| AH1388(1968) | — | — | 0.20 | 0.30 | 0.70 | — |
| AH1389(1969) | — | — | 0.20 | 0.30 | 0.70 | — |

**5 GHIRSH** **KM# 34.2** **Composition:** Copper-Nickel **Obverse:** Small written denomination

| Date | Mintage | F | VF | XF | Unc | BU |
|---|---|---|---|---|---|---|
| AH1387(1967) Proof | 7,834 | Value: 1.50 | | | | |
| AH1388(1968) Proof | 5,251 | Value: 1.75 | | | | |
| AH1389(1969) Proof | 2,149 | Value: 2.50 | | | | |

**5 GHIRSH** **KM# 44** **Composition:** Copper-Nickel **Obverse:** New Arabic legend **Note:** Existence of circulation strikes is uncertain.

| Date | Mintage | F | VF | XF | Unc | BU |
|---|---|---|---|---|---|---|
| AH1390(1970) Proof | 1,646 | Value: 2.50 | | | | |
| AH1391(1971) Proof | 1,772 | Value: 2.50 | | | | |

**5 GHIRSH** **KM# 51** **Composition:** Copper-Nickel **Subject:** 2nd anniversary of revolution

| Date | Mintage | F | VF | XF | Unc | BU |
|---|---|---|---|---|---|---|
| AH1391(1971) | 500,000 | — | 0.30 | 0.60 | 1.20 | — |

**5 GHIRSH** **KM# 58.1** **Composition:** Copper-Nickel **Obverse:** Large legend and denomination **Reverse:** Ribbon with 3 equal sections

| Date | Mintage | F | VF | XF | Unc | BU |
|---|---|---|---|---|---|---|
| AH1395(1975) | 1,600,000 | — | 0.25 | 0.45 | 0.85 | — |

**5 GHIRSH** **KM# 65** **Composition:** Copper-Nickel **Series:** F.A.O.

| Date | Mintage | F | VF | XF | Unc | BU |
|---|---|---|---|---|---|---|
| AH1396(1976) | 500,000 | — | 0.20 | 0.30 | 0.65 | — |
| AH1398(1978) | — | — | 0.20 | 0.30 | 0.65 | — |

**5 GHIRSH** **KM# 66** **Composition:** Copper-Nickel **Subject:** 20th anniversary of independence

| Date | Mintage | F | VF | XF | Unc | BU |
|---|---|---|---|---|---|---|
| AH1396(1976) | 3,940,000 | — | 0.25 | 0.50 | 1.00 | — |

**5 GHIRSH** **KM# 58.3** **Composition:** Copper-Nickel **Obverse:** Small legend, different style

| Date | Mintage | F | VF | XF | Unc | BU |
|---|---|---|---|---|---|---|
| AH1397(1977) | 2,000,000 | — | 0.25 | 0.45 | 0.85 | — |
| AH1398(1978) | 1,000,000 | — | 0.25 | 0.45 | 0.85 | — |
| AH1400(1980) | 1,000,000 | — | 0.25 | 0.45 | 0.85 | — |
| AH1400(1980) Proof | Inc. above | Value: 3.00 | | | | |

**5 GHIRSH** **KM# 74** **Composition:** Copper-Nickel **Subject:** Council of Arab Economic Unity **Note:** Edge varieties exist.

| Date | Mintage | F | VF | XF | Unc | BU |
|---|---|---|---|---|---|---|
| AH1398(1978) | 5,040,000 | — | 0.15 | 0.25 | 0.50 | — |

**5 GHIRSH** **KM# 58.2** **Composition:** Copper-Nickel **Obverse:** Large legend style change, small denomination **Reverse:** Ribbon with long center section **Note:** Edge varieties exist.

| Date | Mintage | F | VF | XF | Unc | BU |
|---|---|---|---|---|---|---|
| AH1400(1980) | — | — | 0.25 | 0.45 | 0.85 | — |

**Note:** Mintage included with KM#58.1.

**5 GHIRSH** **KM# 58.4** **Composition:** Copper-Nickel **Obverse:** Large legend and small denomination, style similar to KM#58.1 **Note:** Edge varieties exist.

| Date | Mintage | F | VF | XF | Unc | BU |
|---|---|---|---|---|---|---|
| AH1400(1980) | — | — | 0.25 | 0.45 | 0.85 | — |

**Note:** Mintage included with KM#58.1.

**5 GHIRSH** **KM# 84** **Composition:** Copper-Nickel **Series:** F.A.O. **Note:** Edge varieties exist.

| Date | Mintage | F | VF | XF | Unc | BU |
|---|---|---|---|---|---|---|
| AH1401(1981) | 1,000,000 | — | 0.20 | 0.40 | 0.75 | — |

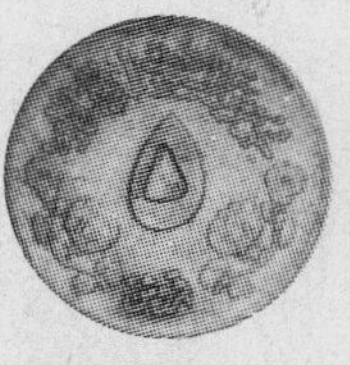

**5 GHIRSH** **KM# 110.1** **Composition:** Brass **Obverse:** Large denomination **Reverse:** Ribbon with 3 equal sections

| Date | Mintage | F | VF | XF | Unc | BU |
|---|---|---|---|---|---|---|
| AH1403(1983) | — | — | 0.25 | 0.60 | 1.55 | — |

**5 GHIRSH** **KM# 110.3** **Composition:** Brass **Obverse:** Small denomination, legend different style

| Date | Mintage | F | VF | XF | Unc | BU |
|---|---|---|---|---|---|---|
| AH1403(1983) | — | — | 5.00 | 7.00 | 10.00 | — |

**5 GHIRSH** **KM# 110.2** **Composition:** Brass **Reverse:** Ribbon with long center section

| Date | Mintage | F | VF | XF | Unc | BU |
|---|---|---|---|---|---|---|
| AH1403(1983) | — | — | 0.50 | 1.25 | 2.25 | — |

**5 GHIRSH** **KM# 110.4** **Composition:** Brass **Obverse:** Large denomination and legend, similar to KM#110.1

| Date | Mintage | F | VF | XF | Unc | BU |
|---|---|---|---|---|---|---|
| AH1403(1983) | — | — | 1.50 | 4.50 | 7.50 | — |

**5 GHIRSH** **KM# 100** **Composition:** Aluminum-Bronze **Obverse:** Denomination **Reverse:** Central bank building

| Date | Mintage | F | VF | XF | Unc | BU |
|---|---|---|---|---|---|---|
| AH1408(1987) | — | — | 0.40 | 1.00 | 2.00 | — |

**10 GHIRSH** **KM# 35.1** **Composition:** Copper-Nickel **Obverse:** Large written denomination

| Date | Mintage | F | VF | XF | Unc | BU |
|---|---|---|---|---|---|---|
| AH1376(1956) | 15,000,000 | — | 0.35 | 0.75 | 2.00 | — |
| AH1386(1966) Proof | — | — | — | — | — | — |
| AH1387(1967) | — | — | 0.30 | 0.60 | 1.50 | — |
| AH1388(1968) | — | — | 0.30 | 0.60 | 1.50 | — |
| AH1389(1969) | — | — | 0.30 | 0.60 | 1.50 | — |

**10 GHIRSH** **KM# 35.2** **Composition:** Copper-Nickel **Obverse:** Small written denomination

| Date | | Mintage | F | VF | XF | Unc | BU |
|---|---|---|---|---|---|---|---|
| AH1387(1967) | Proof | 7,834 | Value: 1.75 | | | | |
| AH1388(1968) | Proof | 5,251 | Value: 2.00 | | | | |
| AH1389(1969) | Proof | 2,149 | Value: 2.25 | | | | |

**10 GHIRSH** **KM# 45.1** **Composition:** Copper-Nickel **Obverse:** New large Arabic legend and written denomination

| Date | Mintage | F | VF | XF | Unc | BU |
|---|---|---|---|---|---|---|
| AH1390(1970) | — | — | 0.60 | 1.25 | 2.50 | — |
| AH1391(1971) | 385,000 | — | 0.60 | 1.25 | 2.50 | — |

**10 GHIRSH** **KM# 45.2** **Composition:** Copper-Nickel **Obverse:** Small legend and written denomination

| Date | | Mintage | F | VF | XF | Unc | BU |
|---|---|---|---|---|---|---|---|
| AH1390(1970) | Proof | 1,646 | Value: 3.00 | | | | |
| AH1391(1971) | Proof | 1,772 | Value: 3.00 | | | | |

**10 GHIRSH** **KM# 52** **Composition:** Copper-Nickel **Subject:** 2nd anniversary of revolution

| Date | Mintage | F | VF | XF | Unc | BU |
|---|---|---|---|---|---|---|
| AH1391(1971) | 500,000 | — | 0.60 | 1.25 | 3.00 | — |

**10 GHIRSH** **KM# 59.1** **Composition:** Copper-Nickel **Obverse:** Thick legend **Reverse:** Ribbon with equal sections

| Date | Mintage | F | VF | XF | Unc | BU |
|---|---|---|---|---|---|---|
| AH1395(1975) | 1,000,000 | — | 0.50 | 1.00 | 2.50 | — |

**10 GHIRSH** **KM# 67** **Composition:** Copper-Nickel **Series:** F.A.O.

| Date | Mintage | F | VF | XF | Unc | BU |
|---|---|---|---|---|---|---|
| AH1396(1976) | 500,000 | — | 0.30 | 0.65 | 1.50 | — |
| AH1398(1978) | — | — | 0.30 | 0.65 | 1.50 | — |

**10 GHIRSH** **KM# 68** **Composition:** Copper-Nickel **Subject:** 20th anniversary of independence **Note:** Edge varieties exist.

| Date | Mintage | F | VF | XF | Unc | BU |
|---|---|---|---|---|---|---|
| AH1396(1976) | 5,540,000 | — | 0.25 | 0.60 | 1.25 | — |

**10 GHIRSH** **KM# 59.5** **Composition:** Copper-Nickel **Obverse:** Thin legend, different style

| Date | | Mintage | F | VF | XF | Unc | BU |
|---|---|---|---|---|---|---|---|
| AH1397(1977) | | 1,000,000 | — | 0.50 | 1.00 | 2.75 | — |
| AH1400(1980) | | 2,965,000 | — | 0.50 | 1.00 | 2.75 | — |
| AH1400(1980) | Proof | — | Value: 4.50 | | | | |

**10 GHIRSH** **KM# 95** **Composition:** Copper-Nickel **Subject:** Council of Arab Economic Unity **Note:** Edge varieties exist.

| Date | Mintage | F | VF | XF | Unc | BU |
|---|---|---|---|---|---|---|
| AH1398(1978) | 1,000,000 | — | 0.60 | 1.25 | 2.50 | — |

**10 GHIRSH** **KM# 59.2** **Composition:** Copper-Nickel **Reverse:** Ribbon with long center section **Note:** Edge varieties exist.

| Date | Mintage | F | VF | XF | Unc | BU |
|---|---|---|---|---|---|---|
| AH1400(1980) | — | — | 0.50 | 1.00 | 2.50 | — |

**10 GHIRSH** **KM# 85** **Composition:** Copper-Nickel **Series:** F.A.O. **Note:** Edge varieties exist.

| Date | Mintage | F | VF | XF | Unc | BU |
|---|---|---|---|---|---|---|
| AH1401(1981) | 1,000,000 | — | 0.60 | 1.25 | 2.50 | — |

**10 GHIRSH** **KM# 59.3** **Composition:** Copper-Nickel **Note:** Reduced size. Edge varieties exist.

| Date | Mintage | F | VF | XF | Unc | BU |
|---|---|---|---|---|---|---|
| AH1403(1983) | — | — | 0.50 | 1.00 | 2.50 | — |

**10 GHIRSH** **KM# 59.4** **Composition:** Copper-Nickel **Obverse:** Similar to KM#59.3 **Reverse:** Ribbon with 3 equal sections

| Date | Mintage | F | VF | XF | Unc | BU |
|---|---|---|---|---|---|---|
| AH1403(1983) | 1,100,000 | — | 7.00 | 10.00 | 20.00 | — |

**10 GHIRSH** **KM# 107** **Composition:** Aluminum-Bronze **Obverse:** Denomination **Reverse:** Central bank building

| Date | Mintage | F | VF | XF | Unc | BU |
|---|---|---|---|---|---|---|
| AH1408(1987) | — | — | 0.75 | 1.50 | 3.00 | — |

**20 GHIRSH** **KM# 37** **Composition:** Copper-Nickel

| Date | | Mintage | F | VF | XF | Unc | BU |
|---|---|---|---|---|---|---|---|
| AH1387(1967) | Proof | 7,834 | Value: 2.50 | | | | |
| AH1388(1968) | Proof | 5,251 | Value: 3.00 | | | | |
| AH1389(1969) | Proof | 2,149 | Value: 6.00 | | | | |

**20 GHIRSH** **KM# 46** **Composition:** Copper-Nickel **Obverse:** New Arabic legend

| Date | | Mintage | F | VF | XF | Unc | BU |
|---|---|---|---|---|---|---|---|
| AH1390(1970) | Proof | 1,646 | Value: 8.50 | | | | |
| AH1391(1971) | Proof | 1,772 | Value: 8.50 | | | | |

**20 GHIRSH** **KM# 98** **Composition:** Copper-Nickel

| Date | Mintage | F | VF | XF | Unc | BU |
|---|---|---|---|---|---|---|
| AH1403(1983) | 72,000 | — | — | — | 5.00 | — |

**20 GHIRSH** **KM# 96** **Composition:** Copper-Nickel **Series:** F.A.O.

| Date | Mintage | F | VF | XF | Unc | BU |
|---|---|---|---|---|---|---|
| AH1405(1985) | — | — | — | — | 3.00 | — |

**20 GHIRSH** **KM# 101.1** **Composition:** Aluminum-Bronze **Obverse:** Small denomination **Reverse:** Central bank building

| Date | Mintage | F | VF | XF | Unc | BU |
|---|---|---|---|---|---|---|
| AH1408(1987) | — | — | 0.60 | 1.25 | 2.50 | — |

**20 GHIRSH** **KM# 101.2** **Composition:** Aluminum-Bronze **Obverse:** Large denomination

| Date | Mintage | F | VF | XF | Unc | BU |
|---|---|---|---|---|---|---|
| AH1408(1987) | — | — | 0.60 | 1.25 | 2.50 | — |

**25 GHIRSH** KM# 38 **Composition:** Copper-Nickel **Series:** F.A.O.

| Date | Mintage | F | VF | XF | Unc | BU |
|---|---|---|---|---|---|---|
| AH1388(1968) | 224,000 | — | — | — | 15.00 | — |
| Prooflike | | | | | | |

**25 GHIRSH** KM# 102 **Composition:** Aluminum-Bronze **Obverse:** Denomination **Reverse:** Central bank building

| Date | Mintage | F | VF | XF | Unc | BU |
|---|---|---|---|---|---|---|
| AH1408(1987) | — | — | 0.85 | 1.75 | 3.50 | — |

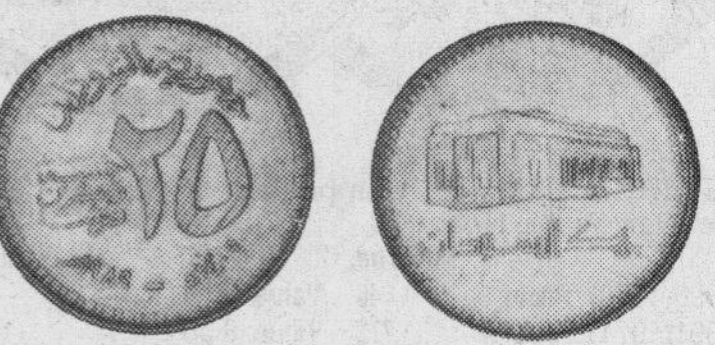

**25 GHIRSH** KM# 108 **Composition:** Stainless Steel **Obverse:** Denomination **Reverse:** Central bank building

| Date | Mintage | F | VF | XF | Unc | BU |
|---|---|---|---|---|---|---|
| AH1409(1989) | — | — | 0.50 | 1.00 | 2.25 | — |

**50 GHIRSH** KM# 56.1 **Composition:** Copper-Nickel **Series:** F.A.O. **Reverse:** Large design

| Date | Mintage | F | VF | XF | Unc | BU |
|---|---|---|---|---|---|---|
| AH1392(1972) | 1,000,000 | — | 1.50 | 3.00 | 7.50 | — |

**50 GHIRSH** KM# 56.2 **Composition:** Copper-Nickel **Series:** F.A.O. **Reverse:** Small design **Note:** Struck in 1976.

| Date | Mintage | F | VF | XF | Unc | BU |
|---|---|---|---|---|---|---|
| AH1392(1972) | 30,000 | — | 5.00 | 10.00 | 20.00 | — |

**50 GHIRSH** KM# 69 **Composition:** Copper-Nickel **Subject:** Establishment of Arab Cooperative

| Date | Mintage | F | VF | XF | Unc | BU |
|---|---|---|---|---|---|---|
| AH1396(1976) | — | — | 1.00 | 2.25 | 4.50 | — |

**50 GHIRSH** KM# 73 **Composition:** Copper-Nickel **Subject:** 8th anniversary of 1969 revolt

| Date | Mintage | F | VF | XF | Unc | BU |
|---|---|---|---|---|---|---|
| AH1397(1977) | 100,000 | — | 1.00 | 2.25 | 4.50 | — |

**50 GHIRSH** KM# 103 **Composition:** Aluminum-Bronze **Obverse:** Denomination **Reverse:** Central bank building

| Date | Mintage | F | VF | XF | Unc | BU |
|---|---|---|---|---|---|---|
| AH1408(1987) | — | — | 0.75 | 1.75 | 3.75 | — |

**50 GHIRSH** KM# 105 **Composition:** Aluminum-Bronze **Subject:** 33rd anniversary of independence

| Date | Mintage | F | VF | XF | Unc | BU |
|---|---|---|---|---|---|---|
| AH1409(1989) | — | — | 0.75 | 1.75 | 3.75 | — |

**50 GHIRSH** KM# 109 **Composition:** Stainless Steel **Obverse:** Denomination **Reverse:** Central Bank building

| Date | Mintage | F | VF | XF | Unc | BU |
|---|---|---|---|---|---|---|
| AH1409(1989) | — | — | 0.65 | 1.25 | 2.75 | — |

**POUND** KM# 75 **Composition:** Copper-Nickel **Series:** F.A.O., Rural Women

| Date | Mintage | F | VF | XF | Unc | BU |
|---|---|---|---|---|---|---|
| AH1398(1978) | 456,000 | — | 2.50 | 4.00 | 8.00 | — |

**POUND** KM# 104 **Composition:** Aluminum-Bronze **Obverse:** Denomination **Reverse:** Central Bank building

| Date | Mintage | F | VF | XF | Unc | BU |
|---|---|---|---|---|---|---|
| AH1408(1987) | — | — | 2.00 | 3.00 | 7.00 | — |

**POUND** KM# 106 **Composition:** Stainless Steel **Obverse:** Denomination **Reverse:** Central Bank building

| Date | Mintage | F | VF | XF | Unc | BU |
|---|---|---|---|---|---|---|
| AH1409(1989) | — | — | 0.75 | 1.50 | 3.75 | — |

**2-1/2 POUNDS** KM# 70 **Weight:** 28.2800 g. **Composition:** 0.9250 Silver .841 oz. ASW **Subject:** Conservation **Reverse:** Shoebill stork

| Date | Mintage | F | VF | XF | Unc | BU |
|---|---|---|---|---|---|---|
| AH1396(1976) | 5,183 | — | — | — | 16.50 | — |
| AH1396(1976) Proof | 5,590 | Value: 20.00 | | | | |

**5 POUNDS** KM# 71 **Weight:** 35.0000 g. **Composition:** 0.9250 Silver 1.0409 oz. ASW **Subject:** Conservation **Reverse:** Hippopotamus

| Date | Mintage | F | VF | XF | Unc | BU |
|---|---|---|---|---|---|---|
| AH1396(1976) | 5,087 | — | — | — | 22.50 | — |
| AH1396(1976) Proof | 5,393 | Value: 30.00 | | | | |

**5 POUNDS** **KM# 76** **Weight:** 17.5000 g. **Composition:** 0.9250 Silver .5205 oz. ASW **Subject:** Khartoum meeting of O.A.U.

| Date | Mintage | F | VF | XF | Unc | BU |
|---|---|---|---|---|---|---|
| AH1398(1978) | 21 | — | — | — | — | — |
| AH1398(1978) Proof without countermarks | 1,423 | Value: 22.50 | | | | |
| AH1398(1978) Proof | 2,000 | Value: 15.00 | | | | |

**Note:** AH1398 with countermarks of B23 in hexagon and bell between dates.

**5 POUNDS** **KM# 80** **Weight:** 17.5000 g. **Composition:** 0.9250 Silver .5205 oz. ASW **Subject:** 1,400th anniversary of Islam

| Date | Mintage | F | VF | XF | Unc | BU |
|---|---|---|---|---|---|---|
| AH1400(1980) | 7,500 | — | — | — | 17.50 | — |
| AH1400(1980) Proof | 5,500 | Value: 22.50 | | | | |

**5 POUNDS** **KM# 86** **Weight:** 28.2800 g. **Composition:** 0.9250 Silver .841 oz. ASW **Subject:** 25th anniversary of independence

| Date | Mintage | F | VF | XF | Unc | BU |
|---|---|---|---|---|---|---|
| AH1401(1981) | 20,000 | — | — | — | 40.00 | — |
| AH1401(1981) Proof | 20,000 | Value: 50.00 | | | | |

**5 POUNDS** **KM# 87** **Weight:** 19.4400 g. **Composition:** 0.9250 Silver .5781 oz. ASW **Series:** UNICEF, International Year of the Child

| Date | Mintage | F | VF | XF | Unc | BU |
|---|---|---|---|---|---|---|
| AH1401(1981) Proof | 35,000 | Value: 13.50 | | | | |

**5 POUNDS** **KM# 92** **Weight:** 19.4400 g. **Composition:** 0.9250 Silver .5781 oz. ASW **Series:** Decade for Women

| Date | Mintage | F | VF | XF | Unc | BU |
|---|---|---|---|---|---|---|
| AH1404(1984) Proof | 20,000 | Value: 22.50 | | | | |

**10 POUNDS** **KM# 77** **Weight:** 35.0000 g. **Composition:** 0.9250 Silver 1.0409 oz. ASW **Subject:** Khartoum meeting of O.A.U.

| Date | Mintage | F | VF | XF | Unc | BU |
|---|---|---|---|---|---|---|
| AH1398(1978) | 21 | — | — | — | — | — |
| AH1398(1978) Proof without countermarks | 1,417 | Value: 40.00 | | | | |
| AH1398(1978) Proof | 2,000 | Value: 35.00 | | | | |

**Note:** AH1398 with countermarks of B23 in hexagon and bell between dates.

**10 POUNDS** **KM# 81** **Weight:** 35.0000 g. **Composition:** 0.9250 Silver 1.0409 oz. ASW **Subject:** 1,400th anniversary of Islam

| Date | Mintage | F | VF | XF | Unc | BU |
|---|---|---|---|---|---|---|
| AH1400(1980) | 3,000 | — | — | — | 32.50 | — |
| AH1400(1980) Proof | 2,000 | Value: 40.00 | | | | |

**10 POUNDS** **KM# 88** **Weight:** 28.2800 g. **Composition:** 0.9250 Silver .8411 oz. ASW **Series:** Year of the Disabled Person

| Date | Mintage | F | VF | XF | Unc | BU |
|---|---|---|---|---|---|---|
| AH1401(1981) | Est. 10,000 | — | — | — | 37.50 | — |
| AH1401(1981) Proof | 10,000 | Value: 42.50 | | | | |

**25 POUNDS** **KM# 78** **Weight:** 8.2500 g. **Composition:** 0.9170 Gold .2432 oz. AGW **Subject:** Khartoum meeting of O.A.U.

| Date | Mintage | F | VF | XF | Unc | BU |
|---|---|---|---|---|---|---|
| AH1398(1978) | 15 | — | — | — | 600 | — |
| AH1398(1978) Proof without countermarks | 467 | Value: 200 | | | | |
| AH1398(1978) Proof | 350 | Value: 150 | | | | |

**Note:** With countermarks of B23 in hexagon and bell between dates.

**25 POUNDS** **KM# 82** **Weight:** 8.2500 g. **Composition:** 0.9170 Gold .2432 oz. AGW **Subject:** 1,400th anniversary of Islam

| Date | Mintage | F | VF | XF | Unc | BU |
|---|---|---|---|---|---|---|
| AH1400(1980) | 7,500 | — | — | — | 120 | — |
| AH1400(1980) Proof | 5,500 | Value: 135 | | | | |

**50 POUNDS** **KM# 79** **Weight:** 17.5000 g. **Composition:** 0.9170 Gold .5160 oz. AGW **Subject:** Khartoum meeting of O.A.U.

| Date | Mintage | F | VF | XF | Unc | BU |
|---|---|---|---|---|---|---|
| AH1398(1978) | 11 | — | — | — | 1,500 | — |
| AH1398(1978) Proof without countermarks | 211 | Value: 300 | | | | |
| AH1398(1978) Proof | 350 | Value: 265 | | | | |

**Note:** With countermarks of B23 in hexagon and bell between dates.

**50 POUNDS** KM# 83 **Weight:** 17.5000 g. **Composition:** 0.9170 Gold .5160 oz. AGW **Subject:** 1,400th anniversary of Islam

| Date | Mintage | F | VF | XF | Unc | BU |
|---|---|---|---|---|---|---|
| AH1400(1979) | 3,000 | — | — | — | 240 | — |
| AH1400(1979) Proof | 2,000 | Value: 260 | | | | |

**50 POUNDS** KM# 89 **Weight:** 7.9900 g. **Composition:** 0.9170 Gold .2353 oz. AGW **Subject:** 25th anniversary of independence

| Date | Mintage | F | VF | XF | Unc | BU |
|---|---|---|---|---|---|---|
| AH1401(1981) | 5,000 | — | — | — | 115 | — |
| AH1401(1981) Proof | 5,000 | Value: 125 | | | | |

**100 POUNDS** KM# 72 **Weight:** 33.4370 g. **Composition:** 0.9000 Gold .9676 oz. AGW **Subject:** Conservation **Reverse:** Scimitar-horned oryx

| Date | Mintage | F | VF | XF | Unc | BU |
|---|---|---|---|---|---|---|
| AH1396(1976) | 872 | — | — | — | 500 | — |
| AH1396(1976) Proof | 251 | Value: 725 | | | | |

**100 POUNDS** KM# 90 **Weight:** 15.9800 g. **Composition:** 0.9170 Gold .4706 oz. AGW **Subject:** 25th anniversary of independence

| Date | Mintage | F | VF | XF | Unc | BU |
|---|---|---|---|---|---|---|
| AH1401(1981) | 2,500 | — | — | — | 250 | — |
| AH1401(1981) Proof | 2,500 | Value: 275 | | | | |

**100 POUNDS** KM# 91 **Weight:** 15.9800 g. **Composition:** 0.9170 Gold .4706 oz. AGW **Series:** Year of the Disabled Person

| Date | Mintage | F | VF | XF | Unc | BU |
|---|---|---|---|---|---|---|
| AH1401(1981) | 2,000 | — | — | — | 325 | — |
| AH1401(1981) Proof | 2,000 | Value: 425 | | | | |

**100 POUNDS** KM# 93 **Weight:** 8.1000 g. **Composition:** 0.9170 Gold .2388 oz. AGW **Series:** Decade for Women

| Date | Mintage | F | VF | XF | Unc | BU |
|---|---|---|---|---|---|---|
| AH1404(1984) Proof | 513 | Value: 200 | | | | |

## REFORM COINAGE

100 Dirhams = 1 Dinar

10 Pounds = 1 Dinar

**DINAR** KM# 112 **Composition:** Brass **Obverse:** Denomination **Reverse:** Central Bank building

| Date | Mintage | F | VF | XF | Unc | BU |
|---|---|---|---|---|---|---|
| AH1415(1994) | — | — | 0.35 | 0.75 | 1.50 | — |

**2 DINAR** KM# 113 **Composition:** Brass Plated Steel **Obverse:** Denomination **Reverse:** Central bank building

| Date | Mintage | F | VF | XF | Unc | BU |
|---|---|---|---|---|---|---|
| AH1415(1994) | — | — | 0.75 | 1.50 | 3.00 | — |

**5 DINARS** KM# 114 **Composition:** Brass **Obverse:** Denomination **Reverse:** Central bank building

| Date | Mintage | F | VF | XF | Unc | BU |
|---|---|---|---|---|---|---|
| AH1417(1996) | — | — | 1.00 | 2.00 | 4.50 | — |

**10 DINARS** KM# 115 **Composition:** Brass **Reverse:** Central bank building

| Date | Mintage | VG | F | VF | XF | Unc |
|---|---|---|---|---|---|---|
| AH1417 | — | — | — | 1.50 | 3.00 | 6.50 |

**20 DINARS** KM# 116 **Composition:** Copper-Nickel **Reverse:** Central Bank building

| Date | Mintage | VG | F | VF | XF | Unc |
|---|---|---|---|---|---|---|
| AH1417 | — | — | — | 1.75 | 3.50 | 7.50 |

## ESSAIS

| KM# | Date | Mintage | Identification | Mkt Val |
|---|---|---|---|---|
| E1 | AH1978 | 25 | 5 Pounds. Aluminum. | 40.00 |
| E3 | AH1978 | 25 | 10 Pounds. Aluminum. | 40.00 |
| E7 | AH1978 | 25 | 50 Pounds. Aluminum. | 40.00 |
| E5 | AH1978 | 25 | 25 Pounds. Aluminum. | 40.00 |
| E6 | AH1978 | 21 | 25 Pounds. Copper. | 75.00 |
| E8 | AH1978 | 21 | 50 Pounds. Copper. | 85.00 |
| E4 | AH1978 | 21 | 10 Pounds. Copper. KM77. | 125 |
| E2 | AH1978 | 15 | 5 Pounds. Copper. | 85.00 |
| E9 | AH1979 | 15 | 5 Pounds. Copper. KM817. | 85.00 |
| E10 | AH1979 | 40 | 10 Pounds. Aluminum. KM81. | 40.00 |
| E12 | AH1979 | 21 | 50 Pounds. Copper. KM83. | 85.00 |
| E11 | AH1979 | 21 | 10 Pounds. Copper. KM81. | 125 |
| E13 | AH1980 | 25 | 5 Pounds. Aluminum. | 40.00 |
| E15 | AH1980 | 25 | 10 Pounds. Aluminum. | 40.00 |
| E17 | AH1980 | 25 | 25 Pounds. Aluminum. | 40.00 |
| E19 | AH1980 | 25 | 50 Pounds. Aluminum. | 40.00 |
| E20 | AH1980 | 21 | 50 Pounds. Copper. | 85.00 |
| E18 | AH1980 | 20 | 25 Pounds. Copper. | 75.00 |
| E14 | AH1980 | 15 | 5 Pounds. Copper. | 85.00 |
| E16 | AH1980 | 21 | 10 Pounds. Copper. | 125 |

## PIEFORTS

| KM# | Date | Mintage | Identification | Mkt Val |
|---|---|---|---|---|
| P1 | AH1978 | 5 | 5 Pounds. Copper. KM76. | 185 |
| P3 | AH1978 | 5 | 10 Pounds. Copper. | 225 |
| P5 | AH1978 | 5 | 25 Pounds. Copper. | 185 |
| P2 | AH1978 | 10 | 5 Pounds. 0.9250 Silver. KM76. | — |
| P4 | AH1978 | 10 | 10 Pounds. 0.9250 Silver. KM77. | — |
| P12 | AH1979 | — | 50 Pounds. Copper. KM83. Gold plated. | — |
| P16 | AH1979 | — | 50 Pounds. Gold. KM83. | — |
| P6 | AH1979 | 5 | 5 Pounds. Copper. KM80. | 185 |
| P8 | AH1979 | 5 | 10 Pounds. Copper. KM81. | 225 |
| P10 | AH1979 | — | 25 Pounds. Brass. KM83. | 185 |
| P11 | AH1979 | 10 | 25 Pounds. Silver. KM83. | 185 |
| P7 | AH1979 | 10 | 5 Pounds. 0.9250 Silver. KM80. | — |
| P9 | AH1979 | 10 | 10 Pounds. 0.9250 Silver. KM81. | — |
| P13 | AH1980 | 5 | 5 Pounds. Copper. | 185 |
| P14 | AH1980 | 5 | 10 Pounds. Copper. | 225 |
| P15 | AH1980 | 5 | 25 Pounds. Copper. | 185 |
| P17 | AH1981 | 2,587 | 5 Pounds. KM87. | 40.00 |
| P18 | AH1981 | 1,000 | 10 Pounds. KM88. | 85.00 |
| P19 | AH1981 | — | 100 Pounds. KM91. | 1,250 |

## PIEFORTS

| KM# | Date | Mintage | Identification | Mkt Val |
|---|---|---|---|---|
| P1 | AH1978 | 5 | 5 Pounds. Copper. KM76. | 185 |
| P3 | AH1978 | 5 | 10 Pounds. Copper. | 225 |
| P5 | AH1978 | 5 | 25 Pounds. Copper. | 185 |
| P2 | AH1978 | 10 | 5 Pounds. 0.9250 Silver. KM76. | — |
| P4 | AH1978 | 10 | 10 Pounds. 0.9250 Silver. KM77. | — |
| P12 | AH1979 | — | 50 Pounds. Copper. KM83. Gold plated. | — |
| P16 | AH1979 | — | 50 Pounds. Gold. KM83. | — |
| P6 | AH1979 | 5 | 5 Pounds. Copper. KM80. | 185 |
| P8 | AH1979 | 5 | 10 Pounds. Copper. KM81. | 225 |
| P10 | AH1979 | — | 25 Pounds. Brass. KM83. | 185 |
| P11 | AH1979 | 10 | 25 Pounds. Silver. KM83. | 185 |
| P7 | AH1979 | 10 | 5 Pounds. 0.9250 Silver. KM80. | — |
| P9 | AH1979 | 10 | 10 Pounds. 0.9250 Silver. KM81. | — |
| P13 | AH1980 | 5 | 5 Pounds. Copper. | 185 |
| P14 | AH1980 | 5 | 10 Pounds. Copper. | 225 |
| P15 | AH1980 | 5 | 25 Pounds. Copper. | 185 |
| P17 | AH1981 | 2,587 | 5 Pounds. KM87. | 40.00 |
| P18 | AH1981 | 1,000 | 10 Pounds. KM88. | 85.00 |
| P19 | AH1981 | — | 100 Pounds. KM91. | 1,250 |

## MINT SETS

| KM# | Date | Mintage | Identification | Issue Price | Mkt Val |
|---|---|---|---|---|---|
| MS1 | 1976 (2) | — | KM70-71 | — | 40.00 |

## PROOF SETS

| KM# | Date | Mintage | Identification | Issue Price | Mkt Val |
|---|---|---|---|---|---|
| PS1 | 1967 (8) | 7,834 | KM29-32, 34-37 | 12.25 | 7.50 |
| PS2 | 1968 (8) | 5,251 | KM29-32, 34-37 | 15.25 | 8.00 |
| PS3 | 1969 (8) | 2,149 | KM29-32, 34-37 | 15.25 | 10.00 |
| PS4 | 1970 (8) | 1,646 | KM39-46 | 15.25 | 15.00 |
| PS5 | 1971 (8) | 1,772 | KM39-46 | 15.25 | 15.00 |
| PS6 | 1976 (2) | — | KM70-71 | — | 50.00 |
| PS7 | 1978 (4) | — | KM76-79 | — | 600 |
| PS9 | 1980 (4) | — | KM80-83 | — | 535 |
| PS8 | 1980 (5) | — | KM54, 55a, 57-59 | 12.00 | — |

# DARFUR

The province of Darfur makes up most of the western border of the Republic of Sudan. Darfur had been an independent kingdom until taken over by Egypt in 1874.While the British were involved in subduing the eastern Sudan, Ali Dinar established the sultanate of Darfur in1898. His coins copied the Ottoman coins of Egypt. The mint was located at Al Fasher (the capital of the province) and was active from 1909 to 1914.

**TITLES**

الفشير

al-Fasher

**RULERS**

Ali Dinar, AH1316-1335/1898-1916AD

## KINGDOM

### HAMMERED COINAGE

**1/2 PIASTRE** KM# 4 **Composition:** Billon **Obverse:** Toughra **Note:** Struck at al-Fasher mint.

| Date | Mintage | Good | VG | F | VF | XF |
|---|---|---|---|---|---|---|
| AH1328/8 Rare | — | — | — | — | — | — |

**Note:** Due to the low denomination and little demand, this coin was only struck for a very short time, though varieties do exist

**PIASTRE** **KM# 1** **Composition:** Copper-Nickel-Zinc **Note:** Struck at al-Fasher mint.

| Date | Mintage | Good | VG | F | VF | XF |
|---|---|---|---|---|---|---|
| AH1213 (sic)/13 Rare | — | — | — | — | — | — |
| AH1223 (sic)/13 Rare | — | — | — | — | — | — |

**Note:** Due to a shortage of small change, thin, unmilled imitations of Egyptian Qirsh (Piastre) KM#181, which had been produced outside of Sudan were brought into circulation in Darfur from AH1323-1325/1905-1907AD in agreement with the Sultan

**PIASTRE** **KM# 2** **Composition:** Billon **Obverse:** Toughra **Note:** Struck at al-Fasher mint. Struck from 1908-1914. Most are crudely struck and flan size varies and usually bear the date AH1327, regnal year 71, probably the sultan's approved type. Other year and date couplings may exist. All Hejira years and some regnal years are thought to have been copied from specimens of the Egyptian prototypes.

| Date | Mintage | Good | VG | F | VF | XF |
|---|---|---|---|---|---|---|
| AH1227(sic)/5 | — | — | — | — | — | — |
| AH1237(sic)/71 | — | — | — | — | — | — |
| **Note:** With retrograde 3 | | | | | | |
| AH1321(sic)/71 | — | — | — | — | — | — |
| AH1323(sic)/65 | — | — | — | — | — | — |
| AH1327(sic)/17 | — | 30.00 | 80.00 | 160 | 190 | — |
| AH1327(sic)/26 | — | — | — | — | — | — |
| AH1327(sic)/71 | — | 15.00 | 30.00 | 45.00 | 60.00 | — |
| AH1327(sic)/71 | — | — | — | — | — | — |
| **Note:** Retrograde 3 | | | | | | |
| AH1327(sic)/76 | — | — | — | — | — | — |
| AHx321(sic)/17 | — | — | — | — | — | — |
| AH1387(sic)/17 | — | — | — | — | — | — |
| AH7132(sic)/x | — | — | — | — | — | — |

**5 PIASTRES (1/4 Rial)** **KM# 5** **Composition:** Copper-Nickel-Zinc **Obverse:** Toughra **Note:** Struck at al-Fasher mint.

| Date | Mintage | Good | VG | F | VF | XF |
|---|---|---|---|---|---|---|
| AH1328 Rare | — | — | — | — | — | — |

**Note:** Copied from Ottoman Mejidiye coinage; about 800 are reported having been put into circulation; further striking was discontinued as the coin was unpopular due to low silver content and uncommon denomination

## COUNTERMARKED COINAGE

**PIASTRE** **KM# 3** **Composition:** Copper-Nickel-Zinc **Countermark:** "Ali" 1312 **Note:** Countermark on KM#1.

| CM Date | Host Date | Good | VG | F | VF | XF |
|---|---|---|---|---|---|---|
| AH | AH1213/13 Rare | — | — | — | — | — |
| AH | AH1223/13 Rare | — | — | — | — | — |

**Note:** In a move to control import and circulation of KM#1, the Sultan ordered the countermarking; AH1312 is probably an error for AH1316/1898AD, the year of Ali Dinar's accession

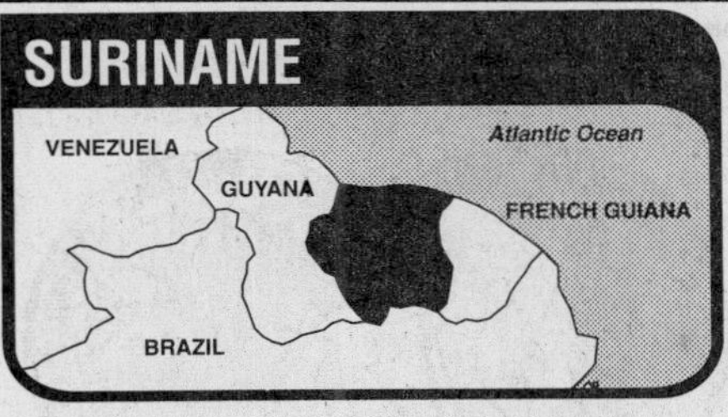


The Republic of Suriname also known as Dutch Guiana, located on the north central coast of South America between Guyana and French Guiana has an area of 63,037 sq. mi. (163,270 sq. km.) and a population of *433,000.Capital: Paramaribo. The country is rich in minerals and forests, and self-sufficient in rice, the staple food crop. The mining, processing and exporting of bauxite is the principal economic activity.

Lieutenants of Amerigo Vespucci sighted the Guiana coast in 1499. Spanish explorers of the 16th century, disappointed at finding no gold, departed leaving the area to be settled by the British in 1652. The colony prospered and the Netherlands acquired it in 1667 in exchange for the Dutch rights in Nieuw Nederland (state of New York). During the European wars of the 18th and 19th centuries, which were fought in part in the new world, Suriname was occupied by the British from 1781-1784 and 1796-1814.Suriname became an autonomous part of the Kingdom of the Netherlands on Dec. 15, 1954. Full independence was achieved on Nov. 25, 1975. In 1980, a coup installed a military government, which has since been dissolved.

**RULERS**

Dutch, until 1975

**MINT MARKS**

(B) - British Royal Mint, no mint mark
FM - Franklin Mint, U.S.A.**
P - Philadelphia, U.S.A.
S - Sydney
(u) - Utrecht (privy marks only)

****NOTE**: From 1975-1985 the Franklin Mint produced coinage in up to 3 different qualities. Qualities of issue are designated in () after each date and are defined as follows:

**(M) MATTE** - Normal circulation strike or a dull finish produced by sandblasting special uncirculated (polish finish) or proof quality dies.
**(U) SPECIAL UNCIRCULATED** - Polished or proof-like in appearance without any frosted features.
**(P) PROOF** - The highest quality obtainable having mirror-like fields and frosted features.

**MONETARY SYSTEM**

100 Cents = 1 Gulden (Guilders)

# REPUBLIC

## WORLD WAR II COINAGE

The 1942-1943 issues that follow are homeland coinage types of the Netherlands. KM#152, KM#163 and KM#164 were executed expressly for use in Suriname. Related issues produced for use in Curacao and Suriname are listed under Curacao. They are distinguished by a palm tree (acorn on homeland issues) and a mint mark (P-Philadelphia, D-Denver, S-San Francisco) flanking the date. See the Netherlands for similar issues. See Curacao for similar coins dated 1941-P, 1942-P and 1943-P.

**CENT** **KM# 10** **Composition:** Brass

| Date | Mintage | F | VF | XF | Unc | BU |
|---|---|---|---|---|---|---|
| 1943P Palm | 4,000,000 | 1.25 | 3.00 | 6.00 | 12.00 | — |

**CENT** **KM# 10a** **Composition:** Bronze

| Date | Mintage | F | VF | XF | Unc | BU |
|---|---|---|---|---|---|---|
| 1957(u) | 1,200,000 | — | 0.40 | 1.75 | 4.00 | — |
| 1957(u) Proof | — | Value: 25.00 | | | | |
| 1959(u) | 1,800,000 | — | 0.40 | 1.75 | 4.00 | — |
| 1959(u) Proof | — | Value: 25.00 | | | | |
| 1960(u) | 1,200,000 | — | 0.40 | 1.75 | 4.00 | — |
| 1960(u) Proof | — | Value: 25.00 | | | | |

**10 CENTS** **KM# 9** **Weight:** 1.4000 g. **Composition:** 0.6400 Silver .0288 oz. ASW

| Date | Mintage | F | VF | XF | Unc | BU |
|---|---|---|---|---|---|---|
| 1942P Palm | 1,500,000 | 3.00 | 6.00 | 12.00 | 25.00 | — |

## MODERN COINAGE

**CENT** **KM# 11** **Composition:** Bronze

| Date | Mintage | F | VF | XF | Unc | BU |
|---|---|---|---|---|---|---|
| 1962(u) Fish | 6,000,000 | — | 0.25 | 0.50 | 1.00 | — |
| 1962(u) S Proof | 650 | Value: 28.00 | | | | |
| 1966(u) | 6,500,000 | — | 0.25 | 0.50 | 1.00 | — |
| 1966(u) Proof | — | Value: 40.00 | | | | |
| 1970(u) Cock | 5,000,000 | — | 0.25 | 0.50 | 1.00 | — |
| 1972(u) | 6,000,000 | — | 0.25 | 0.50 | 1.00 | — |

**CENT** **KM# 11a** **Composition:** Aluminum

| Date | Mintage | F | VF | XF | Unc | BU |
|---|---|---|---|---|---|---|
| 1972 Proof | — | Value: 450 | | | | |
| 1974(u) | 1,000,000 | — | 0.10 | 0.25 | 0.45 | — |
| 1975(u) | 1,000,000 | — | 0.10 | 0.25 | 0.45 | — |
| 1976(u) | 3,000,000 | — | 0.10 | 0.25 | 0.45 | — |
| 1976 Proof | Est. 10 | Value: 50.00 | | | | |
| 1977(u) | 10,000,000 | — | — | 0.25 | 0.45 | — |
| 1978(u) | 6,000,000 | — | — | 0.25 | 0.45 | — |
| 1979(u) | 10,000,000 | — | — | 0.25 | 0.45 | — |
| 1980(u) | 8,000,000 | — | — | 0.25 | 0.45 | — |
| **Note:** Cock and star privy marks. | | | | | | |
| 1982(u) Anvil | 8,000,000 | — | — | 0.25 | 0.45 | — |
| 1984 | 5,000,000 | — | — | 0.25 | 0.45 | — |
| 1985 | 2,000,000 | — | — | 0.25 | 0.45 | — |
| 1986 | 3,000,000 | — | — | 0.25 | 0.45 | — |

**CENT** **KM# 11b** **Composition:** Copper Plated Steel

| Date | Mintage | F | VF | XF | Unc | BU |
|---|---|---|---|---|---|---|
| 1987(B) | — | — | — | — | 0.45 | — |
| 1988(B) Proof | Est. 1,500 | Value: 2.00 | | | | |
| 1989(B) | — | — | — | — | 0.45 | — |

**5 CENTS** **KM# 12.1** **Composition:** Nickel-Brass

| Date | Mintage | F | VF | XF | Unc | BU |
|---|---|---|---|---|---|---|
| 1962(u) Fish | 2,200,000 | — | 0.35 | 0.70 | 1.25 | — |
| 1962(u) S Proof | 650 | Value: 22.00 | | | | |
| 1966(u) | 2,300,000 | — | 0.35 | 0.70 | 1.25 | — |
| **Note:** Privy marks. | | | | | | |
| 1966(u) Proof | — | Value: 50.00 | | | | |
| 1966 | 400,000 | — | 1.25 | 2.50 | 5.00 | — |
| **Note:** Without privy marks. | | | | | | |
| 1971(u) Cock | 500,000 | — | 1.25 | 2.50 | 5.00 | — |
| 1972(u) | 1,500,000 | — | 0.35 | 0.70 | 1.25 | — |

**5 CENTS** **KM# 12.1a** **Composition:** Aluminum

| Date | Mintage | F | VF | XF | Unc | BU |
|---|---|---|---|---|---|---|
| 1966(u) Proof | — | Value: 450 | | | | |
| 1976(u) | 5,500,000 | — | 0.10 | 0.20 | 0.50 | — |
| 1976 Proof | Est. 10 | Value: 75.00 | | | | |
| 1978(u) | 3,000,000 | — | 0.10 | 0.20 | 0.50 | — |
| 1979(u) | 2,000,000 | — | 0.10 | 0.20 | 0.50 | — |
| 1980(u) | 1,000,000 | — | 0.10 | 0.20 | 0.50 | — |
| **Note:** Cock and star privy marks. | | | | | | |
| 1982(u) Anvil | 1,000,000 | — | 0.10 | 0.20 | 0.50 | — |
| 1985(u) | 1,000,000 | — | 0.10 | 0.20 | 0.50 | — |
| 1986(u) | 1,500,000 | — | 0.10 | 0.20 | 0.50 | — |

**5 CENTS** **KM# 12.2** **Composition:** Nickel-Brass **Note:** Medal struck.

| Date | Mintage | F | VF | XF | Unc | BU |
|---|---|---|---|---|---|---|
| 1966(u) | — | — | 5.00 | 10.00 | 20.00 | — |

**5 CENTS** **KM# 12.1b** **Composition:** Copper Plated Steel

| Date | Mintage | F | VF | XF | Unc | BU |
|---|---|---|---|---|---|---|
| 1987(B) | — | — | — | 0.20 | 0.50 | — |
| 1988(B) | — | — | — | 0.20 | 0.50 | — |
| 1988(B) Proof | Est. 1,500 | Value: 2.00 | | | | |
| 1989(B) | — | — | — | 0.20 | 0.50 | — |

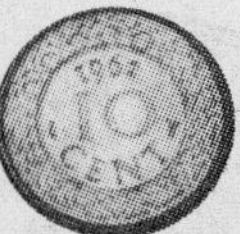

**10 CENTS** **KM# 13** **Composition:** Copper-Nickel

| Date | Mintage | F | VF | XF | Unc | BU |
|---|---|---|---|---|---|---|
| 1962(u) Fish | 3,000,000 | — | 0.35 | 0.70 | 1.25 | — |
| 1962(u) S Proof | 650 | Value: 22.00 | | | | |
| 1966(u) | 2,500,000 | — | 0.35 | 0.75 | 1.25 | — |
| 1966(u) Proof | — | Value: 50.00 | | | | |
| 1971(u) Cock | 500,000 | 0.40 | 0.80 | 1.75 | 3.00 | — |
| 1972(u) | 1,500,000 | — | 0.35 | 0.70 | 1.25 | — |
| 1974(u) | 1,500,000 | — | 0.35 | 0.70 | 1.25 | — |
| 1976(u) | 5,000,000 | — | 0.10 | 0.25 | 0.50 | — |
| 1976 Proof | Est. 10 | Value: 100 | | | | |

| Date | Mintage | F | VF | XF | Unc | BU |
|---|---|---|---|---|---|---|
| 1978(u) | 2,000,000 | — | 0.10 | 0.25 | 0.50 | — |
| 1979(u) | 2,000,000 | — | 0.10 | 0.25 | 0.50 | — |
| 1982(u) Anvil | 1,000,000 | — | 0.10 | 0.25 | 0.50 | — |
| 1985(u) | 1,000,000 | — | 0.10 | 0.25 | 0.50 | — |
| 1986(u) | 1,500,000 | — | 0.10 | 0.25 | 0.50 | — |

**10 CENTS** **KM# 13a** **Composition:** Nickel Plated Steel

| Date | Mintage | F | VF | XF | Unc | BU |
|---|---|---|---|---|---|---|
| 1987(B) | — | — | 0.20 | 0.35 | 0.75 | — |
| 1988(B) Proof | Est. 1,500 | Value: 3.00 | | | | |
| 1989(B) | — | — | 0.20 | 0.35 | 0.75 | — |

**25 CENTS** **KM# 14** **Composition:** Copper-Nickel

| Date | Mintage | F | VF | XF | Unc | BU |
|---|---|---|---|---|---|---|
| 1962(u) Fish | 2,300,000 | 0.25 | 0.35 | 0.65 | 1.25 | — |
| 1962(u) S Proof | 650 | Value: 22.00 | | | | |
| 1966(u) | 2,300,000 | 0.25 | 0.35 | 0.65 | 1.25 | — |
| 1966(u) Proof | — | Value: 50.00 | | | | |
| 1972(u) Cock | 1,800,000 | 0.25 | 0.35 | 0.65 | 1.25 | — |
| 1974(u) | 1,500,000 | 0.30 | 0.35 | 0.65 | 1.25 | — |
| 1976(u) | 5,000,000 | 0.20 | 0.35 | 0.65 | 1.25 | — |
| 1976 Proof | Est. 10 | Value: 125 | | | | |
| 1979(u) | 2,000,000 | 0.20 | 0.35 | 0.65 | 1.25 | — |
| 1982(u) Anvil | 2,000,000 | 0.20 | 0.35 | 0.65 | 1.25 | — |
| 1985(u) | 1,000,000 | 0.20 | 0.35 | 0.65 | 1.25 | — |
| 1986(u) | 1,500,000 | 0.20 | 0.35 | 0.65 | 1.25 | — |

**25 CENTS** **KM# 14a** **Composition:** Nickel Plated Steel

| Date | Mintage | F | VF | XF | Unc | BU |
|---|---|---|---|---|---|---|
| 1987(B) | — | 0.20 | 0.30 | 0.60 | 1.20 | — |
| 1988(B) | — | 0.20 | 0.30 | 0.60 | 1.20 | — |
| 1988(B) Proof | Est. 1,500 | Value: 5.00 | | | | |
| **Note:** Never officially released to circulation. | | | | | | |
| 1989(B) | — | 0.20 | 0.30 | 0.60 | 1.20 | — |

**100 CENTS** **KM# 23** **Composition:** Copper-Nickel

| Date | Mintage | F | VF | XF | Unc | BU |
|---|---|---|---|---|---|---|
| 1987(B) | — | — | 0.50 | 0.85 | 1.75 | — |
| 1988(B) | — | — | 0.50 | 0.85 | 1.75 | — |
| 1988(B) Proof | Est. 1,500 | Value: 12.00 | | | | |
| **Note:** Never officially released to circulation. | | | | | | |
| 1989(B) | — | — | 0.50 | 0.85 | 1.75 | — |

**250 CENTS** **KM# 24** **Composition:** Copper-Nickel

| Date | Mintage | F | VF | XF | Unc | BU |
|---|---|---|---|---|---|---|
| 1987(B) | — | — | 0.75 | 1.50 | 3.00 | — |
| 1988(B) | — | — | 0.75 | 1.50 | 3.00 | — |
| 1988(B) Proof | Est. 1,500 | Value: 17.50 | | | | |
| **Note:** Never officially released to circulation. | | | | | | |
| 1989(B) | — | — | 0.75 | 1.50 | 3.00 | — |

**GULDEN** **KM# 15** **Weight:** 10.0000 g. **Composition:** 0.7200 Silver .2315 oz. ASW

| Date | Mintage | F | VF | XF | Unc | BU |
|---|---|---|---|---|---|---|
| 1962(u) | 150,000 | — | 2.50 | 5.00 | 10.00 | — |
| 1962(u) S Proof | 650 | Value: 40.00 | | | | |
| 1966(u) | Est. 100,000 | — | — | 50.00 | 100 | — |
| **Note:** Never officially released to circulation. | | | | | | |
| 1966(u) Proof | — | Value: 150 | | | | |

**10 GULDEN** **KM# 16** **Weight:** 15.9500 g. **Composition:** 0.9250 Silver .4743 oz. ASW **Subject:** 1st anniversary of independence

| Date | Mintage | F | VF | XF | Unc | BU |
|---|---|---|---|---|---|---|
| 1976(u) | 100,000 | — | — | 7.50 | 10.00 | — |
| 1976(u) Proof | 5,711 | Value: 13.50 | | | | |

**25 GULDEN** **KM# 17** **Weight:** 25.8500 g. **Composition:** 0.9250 Silver .7687 oz. ASW **Subject:** 1st anniversary of independence **Reverse:** Similar to 10 Gulden, KM#8

| Date | Mintage | F | VF | XF | Unc | BU |
|---|---|---|---|---|---|---|
| 1976(u) | 75,000 | — | — | — | 20.00 | — |
| 1976(u) F Proof | 5,503 | Value: 25.00 | | | | |

**25 GULDEN** **KM# 19** **Weight:** 15.5000 g. **Composition:** 0.9250 Silver .461 oz. ASW **Subject:** 1st anniversary of independence

| Date | Mintage | F | VF | XF | Unc | BU |
|---|---|---|---|---|---|---|
| 1981FM (U) | 10,000 | — | — | 18.00 | 30.00 | — |
| 1981FM (P) | 800 | Value: 70.00 | | | | |

**25 GULDEN** **KM# 21** **Weight:** 25.1000 g. **Composition:** 0.9250 Silver .7435 oz. ASW **Subject:** 5th anniversary of revolution

| Date | Mintage | F | VF | XF | Unc | BU |
|---|---|---|---|---|---|---|
| ND(1985)(u) | 4,800 | — | — | — | 55.00 | — |
| ND(1985)(u) Proof | 200 | Value: 90.00 | | | | |

**25 GUILDER** **KM# 32** **Weight:** 28.2800 g. **Composition:** 0.9250 Silver .8411 oz. ASW **Subject:** World Cup soccer

| Date | Mintage | F | VF | XF | Unc | BU |
|---|---|---|---|---|---|---|
| 1990(B) Proof | 50,000 | Value: 30.00 | | | | |

**25 GUILDER** **KM# 36** **Weight:** 28.2800 g. **Composition:** 0.9250 Silver .8411 oz. ASW **Series:** Save the Children

| Date | Mintage | F | VF | XF | Unc | BU |
|---|---|---|---|---|---|---|
| 1991(B) Proof | 30,000 | Value: 40.00 | | | | |

**30 GULDEN** **KM# 27** **Weight:** 14.0200 g. **Composition:** 0.9250 Silver .417 oz. ASW **Subject:** 30th anniversary of central bank

| Date | Mintage | F | VF | XF | Unc | BU |
|---|---|---|---|---|---|---|
| 1987(u) | 7,000 | — | — | — | 35.00 | — |

**50 GUILDER** **KM# 28** **Weight:** 28.2800 g. **Composition:** 0.9250 Silver .8411 oz. ASW **Series:** Seoul Olympics **Subject:** Swimming

| Date | Mintage | F | VF | XF | Unc | BU |
|---|---|---|---|---|---|---|
| 1988(B) Proof | Est. 25,000 | Value: 30.00 | | | | |

**50 GUILDER** **KM# 30** **Weight:** 28.2800 g. **Composition:** 0.9250 Silver .8411 oz. ASW **Subject:** 125th anniversary of the Suriname Bank

| Date | Mintage | F | VF | XF | Unc | BU |
|---|---|---|---|---|---|---|
| ND(1990)(B) Proof | Est. 7,500 | Value: 45.00 | | | | |

**50 GUILDER** **KM# 34** **Weight:** 26.0000 g. **Composition:** 0.9250 Silver .7733 oz. ASW **Subject:** 15th anniversary of independence **Note:** Similar to 500 Guilders, KM#27.

| Date | Mintage | F | VF | XF | Unc | BU |
|---|---|---|---|---|---|---|
| ND(1990)(B) Proof | Est. 5,000 | Value: 40.00 | | | | |

**50 GUILDER** **KM# 38** **Weight:** 26.0000 g. **Composition:** 0.9250 Silver .7733 oz. ASW **Subject:** 35th anniversary of central bank

| Date | Mintage | F | VF | XF | Unc | BU |
|---|---|---|---|---|---|---|
| ND(1992) Proof | Est. 1,500 | Value: 55.00 | | | | |

**100 GULDEN** **KM# 18** **Weight:** 6.7200 g. **Composition:** 0.9000 Gold .1945 oz. AGW **Subject:** 1st anniversary of independence **Note:** Uncirculated pieces struck in "rose" gold have been reported. They are valued at $150-$200.

| Date | Mintage | F | VF | XF | Unc | BU |
|---|---|---|---|---|---|---|
| 1976(u) | 20,000 | — | — | — | 80.00 | — |
| 1976(u) Proof | 4,749 | Value: 90.00 | | | | |

**100 GUILDER** **KM# 40** **Weight:** 20.1200 g. **Composition:** 0.9990 Silver .6468 oz. ASW **Series:** Barcelona Olympics **Subject:** Basketball **Note:** Struck at Barcelona.

| Date | Mintage | F | VF | XF | Unc | BU |
|---|---|---|---|---|---|---|
| 1992 Proof | Est. 15,000 | Value: 32.50 | | | | |

**100 GUILDER** **KM# 41** **Weight:** 20.1200 g. **Composition:** 0.9990 Silver .6468 oz. ASW **Series:** Barcelona Olympics **Subject:** Cyclists **Note:** Struck at Barcelona.

| Date | Mintage | F | VF | XF | Unc | BU |
|---|---|---|---|---|---|---|
| 1992 Proof | Est. 15,000 | Value: 35.00 | | | | |

**100 GUILDER** **KM# 42.1** **Weight:** 20.1200 g. **Composition:** 0.9990 Silver .6468 oz. ASW **Series:** Barcelona Olympics **Reverse:** A. Nesty - swimming **Note:** Struck at Kaapstad (Capetown, South Africa).

| Date | Mintage | F | VF | XF | Unc | BU |
|---|---|---|---|---|---|---|
| ND(1992) Proof | 2,500 | Value: 50.00 | | | | |

**100 GUILDER** **KM# 42.2** **Weight:** 20.1200 g. **Composition:** 0.9990 Silver .6468 oz. ASW **Series:** Barcelona Olympics **Reverse:** A. Nesty - swimming, "200 M" above swimmer **Note:** Struck at Kaapstad (Capetown, South Africa).

| Date | Mintage | F | VF | XF | Unc | BU |
|---|---|---|---|---|---|---|
| ND(1992) Proof | — | Value: 65.00 | | | | |

**100 GUILDER** **KM# 43.1** **Weight:** 19.7000 g. **Composition:** 0.9990 Silver .6330 oz. ASW **Subject:** World Cup soccer **Reverse:** 2 players, "999 E.P." at right

| Date | Mintage | F | VF | XF | Unc | BU |
|---|---|---|---|---|---|---|
| ND(1994) Proof | — | Value: 37.50 | | | | |

**100 GUILDER** **KM# 43.2** **Weight:** 19.7000 g. **Composition:** 0.9990 Silver .6330 oz. ASW **Subject:** World Cup soccer **Reverse:** 2 players, "999 E.P." at left

| Date | Mintage | F | VF | XF | Unc | BU |
|---|---|---|---|---|---|---|
| ND(1994) Proof | — | Value: 55.00 | | | | |

**100 GUILDER** **KM# 44** **Weight:** 20.0000 g. **Composition:** 0.9990 Silver .6430 oz. ASW **Subject:** World Cup soccer **Reverse:** Brazil winner **Note:** Struck at Capetown.

| Date | Mintage | F | VF | XF | Unc | BU |
|---|---|---|---|---|---|---|
| ND(1994) Proof | — | Value: 37.50 | | | | |

**100 GUILDER** **KM# 46** **Composition:** Copper-Nickel **Reverse:** 1956 Ford Thunderbird

| Date | Mintage | F | VF | XF | Unc | BU |
|---|---|---|---|---|---|---|
| 1996 Proof | 500 | Value: 42.50 | | | | |

**100 GUILDER** **KM# 47** **Composition:** Copper-Nickel **Reverse:** 1957 Ford Thunderbird

| Date | Mintage | F | VF | XF | Unc | BU |
|---|---|---|---|---|---|---|
| 1996 Proof | 500 | Value: 42.50 | | | | |

**100 GUILDER** **KM# 49** **Composition:** Copper-Nickel **Series:** Olympics **Reverse:** Discus thrower

| Date | Mintage | F | VF | XF | Unc | BU |
|---|---|---|---|---|---|---|
| 1996 Proof | — | Value: 125 | | | | |

**200 GULDEN** KM# 20 **Weight:** 7.1200 g. **Composition:** 0.5000 Gold .1144 oz. AGW **Subject:** 1st anniversary of revolution

| Date | Mintage | F | VF | XF | Unc | BU |
|---|---|---|---|---|---|---|
| 1981FM (U) | 11,000 | — | — | — | 110 | — |
| 1981FM (P) Proof | 1,363 | Value: 175 | | | | |

**250 GULDEN** KM# 22 **Weight:** 6.7200 g. **Composition:** 0.9000 Gold .1945 oz. AGW **Subject:** 5th anniversary of revolution **Obverse:** Dove and 10 on map-shaped flag **Reverse:** Stylized fist on star design **Note:** Similar to 25 Gulden, KM#13.

| Date | Mintage | F | VF | XF | Unc | BU |
|---|---|---|---|---|---|---|
| 1985(u) | 5,000 | — | — | — | 135 | — |
| 1985(u) Proof | 200 | Value: 225 | | | | |

**250 GULDEN** KM# 33 **Weight:** 7.9800 g. **Composition:** 0.9170 Gold .2353 oz. AGW **Subject:** World Cup soccer

| Date | Mintage | F | VF | XF | Unc | BU |
|---|---|---|---|---|---|---|
| 1990(B) Proof | 1,000 | Value: 200 | | | | |

**250 GULDER** KM# 37 **Weight:** 7.9800 g. **Composition:** 0.9170 Gold .2353 oz. AGW **Series:** Save the Children

| Date | Mintage | F | VF | XF | Unc | BU |
|---|---|---|---|---|---|---|
| 1991 Proof | 3,000 | — | — | — | 150 | — |
| 1992 | — | — | — | — | 150 | — |

**500 GULDEN** KM# 25 **Weight:** 7.9800 g. **Composition:** 0.9170 Gold .2353 oz. AGW **Subject:** 40th anniversary - Military Sports Organization **Obverse:** Similar to 1,000 Guilders, KM#18

| Date | Mintage | F | VF | XF | Unc | BU |
|---|---|---|---|---|---|---|
| ND(1988)(B) Proof | 2,500 | Value: 225 | | | | |

**500 GULDER** KM# 29 **Weight:** 7.9800 g. **Composition:** 0.9170 Gold .2353 oz. AGW **Series:** Seoul Olympics **Subject:** Swimming

| Date | Mintage | F | VF | XF | Unc | BU |
|---|---|---|---|---|---|---|
| 1988(B) Proof | Est. 2,000 | Value: 225 | | | | |

**500 GULDER** KM# 31 **Weight:** 7.9800 g. **Composition:** 0.9170 Gold .2353 oz. AGW **Subject:** 125th anniversary - Suriname Bank **Note:** Similar to 50 Guilders, KM#22.

| Date | Mintage | F | VF | XF | Unc | BU |
|---|---|---|---|---|---|---|
| 1990(B) Proof | Est. 2,000 | Value: 300 | | | | |

**500 GULDER** KM# 35 **Weight:** 7.9800 g. **Composition:** 0.9170 Gold .2353 oz. AGW **Subject:** 15th anniversary of independence

| Date | Mintage | F | VF | XF | Unc | BU |
|---|---|---|---|---|---|---|
| ND(1990)(B) Proof | Est. 1,250 | Value: 325 | | | | |

**500 GULDER** KM# 39 **Weight:** 7.9800 g. **Composition:** 0.9170 Gold .2353 oz. AGW **Subject:** 35th anniversary of central bank **Reverse:** Bank symbol and dates within circle and legend **Note:** Similar to 50 Guilders, KM#30.

| Date | Mintage | F | VF | XF | Unc | BU |
|---|---|---|---|---|---|---|
| 1992(B) Proof | Est. 300 | Value: 300 | | | | |

**1000 GUILDER** KM# 26 **Weight:** 15.9800 g. **Composition:** 0.9170 Gold .4708 oz. AGW **Subject:** 40th anniversary - Military Sports Organization **Note:** Similar to 500 Guilders, KM#25.

| Date | Mintage | F | VF | XF | Unc | BU |
|---|---|---|---|---|---|---|
| ND(1988)(B) Proof | 1,250 | Value: 425 | | | | |

**1000 GUILDER** KM# 48 **Weight:** 4.8000 g. **Composition:** Gold Plated Brass .4708 oz. **Series:** Olympics **Reverse:** Cyclists **Edge:** Plain **Note:** Similar to 100 Guilders, KM#41. Struck at Capetown.

| Date | Mintage | F | VF | XF | Unc | BU |
|---|---|---|---|---|---|---|
| 1992 | — | — | — | — | — | — |

**1000 GUILDER** KM# 48a **Weight:** 7.9800 g. **Composition:** 0.9160 Gold .2355 oz. AGW **Series:** Olympics **Reverse:** Cyclists **Edge:** Reeded **Note:** Similar to 100 Guilders, KM#41. Struck at Capetown.

| Date | Mintage | F | VF | XF | Unc | BU |
|---|---|---|---|---|---|---|
| 1992 Proof | 400 | Value: 275 | | | | |

**12500 GULDEN** KM# 50 **Weight:** 28.2800 g. **Composition:** 0.9250 Silver .8410 oz. ASW **Subject:** Hindu immigration **Obverse:** National arms **Reverse:** Hindu couple with ship in background

| Date | Mintage | F | VF | XF | Unc | BU |
|---|---|---|---|---|---|---|
| ND(1999) Proof | Est. 1,000 | Value: 60.00 | | | | |

**50000 GULDEN** KM# 51 **Weight:** 7.9800 g. **Composition:** 0.9170 Gold .2353 oz. AGW **Subject:** Hindu immigration **Obverse:** National arms **Reverse:** Hindu couple with ship in background **Note:** Similar to 12,500 Gulden, KM#50.

| Date | Mintage | F | VF | XF | Unc | BU |
|---|---|---|---|---|---|---|
| ND(1999) Proof | Est. 1,000 | Value: 250 | | | | |

**75000 GULDEN** KM# 53 **Weight:** 7.9800 g. **Composition:** 0.9170 Gold .2353 oz. AGW **Subject:** Coppename Bridge

| Date | Mintage | F | VF | XF | Unc | BU |
|---|---|---|---|---|---|---|
| 1999 Proof | — | Value: 700 | | | | |

## PATTERNS

Including off metal strikes

| KM# | Date | Mintage | Identification | Mkt Val |
|---|---|---|---|---|
| Pn1 | 1962 | — | Gulden. Bronze. KM#15. Nickel coated. | 4,000 |
| Pn2 | (1994) | — | 100 Guilder. Copper-Nickel. KM#44. | 45.00 |
| Pn3 | (1994) | — | 100 Guilder. Silver. KM#44. | — |

## TRIAL COINAGE

| KM# | Date | Mintage | Identification | Mkt Val |
|---|---|---|---|---|
| TS1 | 1984 | — | 10 Guilders. Silver. | — |

## PROOF SETS

| KM# | Date | Mintage | Identification | Issue Price | Mkt Val |
|---|---|---|---|---|---|
| PS1 | 1962 (5) | 650 | KM11-15 | — | 100 |
| PS2 | 1966 (5) | — | KM11-15 | — | 225 |
| PS3 | 1976 (4) | 10 | KM11a, 12.1a, 13, 14 | — | 300 |
| PS4 | 1976 (3) | — | KM16-18 | 145 | 115 |
| PS5 | 1976 (2) | — | KM16-17 | 50.00 | 50.00 |
| PS6 | 1988 (6) | 1,500 | KM11b, 12.1b, 13a, 14a, 23, 24 | 42.00 | 50.00 |

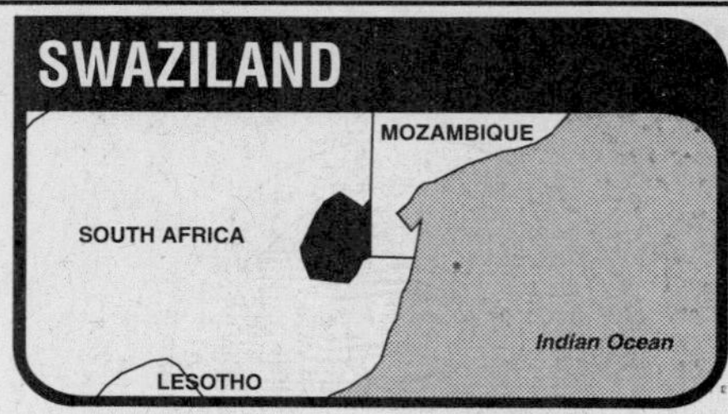


The Kingdom of Swaziland, located in southeastern Africa, has an area of 6,704 sq. mi. (17,360 sq. km.) and a population of *756,000. Capital: Mbabane (administrative); Lobamba (legislative). The diversified economy includes mining, agriculture, and light industry. Asbestos, iron ore, wood pulp, and sugar are exported.

The people of the present Swazi nation established themselves in an area including what is now Swaziland in the early 1800s. The first Swazi contact with the British came early in the reign of the extremely able Swazi leader Mswati when he asked the British for aid against Zulu raids into Swaziland. The British and Transvaal responded by guaranteeing the independence of Swaziland, 1881. South Africa assumed the power of protection and administration in 1894 and Swaziland continued under this administration until the conquest of the Transvaal during the Anglo-Boer War, when administration was transferred to the British government. After World War II, Britain began to prepare Swaziland for independence, which was achieved on Sept. 6, 1968. The Kingdom is a member of the Commonwealth of Nations. King Mswati III is Head of State. The prime minister is Head of Government.

**RULERS**

Sobhuza II, 1968-1982
Queen Dzeliwe, Regent for
Prince Makhosetive, 1982-1986
King Msawati III, 1986-

**MONETARY SYSTEM**

100 Cents = 1 Luhlanga
25 Luhlanga = 1 Lilangeni
(plural - Emalangeni)

# KINGDOM

## STANDARD COINAGE

**CENT** KM# 7 **Composition:** Bronze **Subject:** Ananas

| Date | Mintage | F | VF | XF | Unc | BU |
|---|---|---|---|---|---|---|
| 1974 | 6,002,000 | — | — | 0.10 | 0.20 | — |
| 1974 Proof | 13,000 | Value: 0.75 | | | | |
| 1975 | — | — | — | 0.10 | 0.25 | — |
| 1979 | 500,000 | — | — | 0.10 | 0.25 | — |
| 1979 Proof | 10,000 | Value: 0.75 | | | | |
| 1982 | — | — | — | 0.10 | 0.25 | — |
| 1983 | 1,100,000 | — | — | 0.10 | 0.25 | — |

**CENT** KM# 21 **Composition:** Bronze **Series:** F.A.O.

| Date | Mintage | F | VF | XF | Unc | BU |
|---|---|---|---|---|---|---|
| 1975 | 2,500,000 | — | — | 0.10 | 0.25 | — |

**CENT** KM# 39 **Composition:** Copper Plated Steel

| Date | Mintage | F | VF | XF | Unc | BU |
|---|---|---|---|---|---|---|
| 1986 | 2,000,000 | — | — | 0.10 | 0.25 | — |
| 1987 | 10,000,000 | — | — | 0.10 | 0.25 | — |

**CENT** KM# 39a **Composition:** Bronze

| Date | Mintage | F | VF | XF | Unc | BU |
|---|---|---|---|---|---|---|
| 1986 | — | — | — | — | — | — |

**CENT** **KM# 51** **Composition:** Bronze **Obverse:** King's bust **Reverse:** Pineapple

| Date | Mintage | F | VF | XF | Unc | BU |
|---|---|---|---|---|---|---|
| 1995 | — | — | — | — | 0.25 | — |

**2 CENTS** **KM# 8** **Composition:** Bronze

| Date | Mintage | F | VF | XF | Unc | BU |
|---|---|---|---|---|---|---|
| 1974 | 2,252,000 | — | — | 0.15 | 0.30 | — |
| 1974 Proof | 13,000 | Value: 0.75 | | | | |
| 1975 | — | — | — | 0.15 | 0.30 | — |
| 1979 | 1,000,000 | — | — | 0.15 | 0.30 | — |
| 1979 Proof | 10,000 | Value: 1.00 | | | | |
| 1982 | 500,000 | — | — | 0.15 | 0.30 | — |

**2 CENTS** **KM# 22** **Composition:** Bronze **Series:** F.A.O.

| Date | Mintage | F | VF | XF | Unc | BU |
|---|---|---|---|---|---|---|
| 1975 | 1,500,000 | — | — | 0.15 | 0.30 | — |

**5 CENTS** **KM# 1** **Weight:** 2.7500 g. **Composition:** 0.8000 Silver .0707 oz. ASW **Subject:** Independence commemorative

| Date | Mintage | F | VF | XF | Unc | BU |
|---|---|---|---|---|---|---|
| 1968 Proof | 10,000 | Value: 5.00 | | | | |

**5 CENTS** **KM# 9** **Composition:** Copper-Nickel **Reverse:** Arum lily

| Date | Mintage | F | VF | XF | Unc | BU |
|---|---|---|---|---|---|---|
| 1974 | 1,252,000 | — | 0.10 | 0.20 | 0.40 | — |
| 1974 Proof | 13,000 | Value: 1.00 | | | | |
| 1975 | 1,500,000 | — | 0.10 | 0.20 | 0.40 | — |
| 1979 | 1,680,000 | — | 0.10 | 0.20 | 0.40 | — |
| 1979 Proof | 10,000 | Value: 1.75 | | | | |

**5 CENTS** **KM# 40.1** **Composition:** Copper-Nickel **Reverse:** Arum lily

| Date | Mintage | F | VF | XF | Unc | BU |
|---|---|---|---|---|---|---|
| 1986 | — | — | 0.15 | 0.25 | 0.50 | — |

**5 CENTS** **KM# 40.2** **Composition:** Nickel Plated Steel **Reverse:** Arum lily

| Date | Mintage | F | VF | XF | Unc | BU |
|---|---|---|---|---|---|---|
| 1992 | — | — | 0.15 | 0.25 | 0.50 | — |

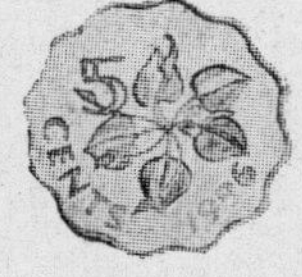

**5 CENTS** **KM# 48** **Composition:** Nickel Plated Steel **Obverse:** King Msawati III

| Date | Mintage | F | VF | XF | Unc | BU |
|---|---|---|---|---|---|---|
| 1995 | — | — | — | — | 0.50 | — |
| 1996 | — | — | — | — | 0.50 | — |
| 1998 | — | — | — | — | 0.50 | — |

**10 CENTS** **KM# 2** **Weight:** 4.3800 g. **Composition:** 0.8000 Silver .1126 oz. ASW **Subject:** Independence commemorative

| Date | Mintage | F | VF | XF | Unc | BU |
|---|---|---|---|---|---|---|
| 1968 Proof | 10,000 | Value: 7.00 | | | | |

**10 CENTS** **KM# 10** **Composition:** Copper-Nickel **Reverse:** Sugar cane

| Date | Mintage | F | VF | XF | Unc | BU |
|---|---|---|---|---|---|---|
| 1974 | 752,000 | — | 0.15 | 0.25 | 0.50 | — |
| 1974 Proof | 13,000 | Value: 1.00 | | | | |
| 1979 | 500,000 | — | 0.15 | 0.25 | 0.50 | — |
| 1979 Proof | 4,231 | Value: 2.50 | | | | |

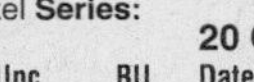

**10 CENTS** **KM# 23** **Composition:** Copper-Nickel **Series:** F.A.O. **Reverse:** Sugar cane

| Date | Mintage | F | VF | XF | Unc | BU |
|---|---|---|---|---|---|---|
| 1975 | 1,500,000 | — | 0.15 | 0.25 | 0.50 | — |

**10 CENTS** **KM# 41 (KM41.1)** **Composition:** Copper-Nickel **Reverse:** Sugar cane

| Date | Mintage | F | VF | XF | Unc | BU |
|---|---|---|---|---|---|---|
| 1986 | — | — | 0.15 | 0.25 | 0.50 | — |
| 1992 | — | — | 0.15 | 0.25 | 0.50 | — |

**10 CENTS** **KM# 49** **Composition:** Copper-Nickel **Obverse:** King Msawati III **Reverse:** Sugar cane

| Date | Mintage | F | VF | XF | Unc | BU |
|---|---|---|---|---|---|---|
| 1995 | — | — | — | — | 0.50 | — |
| 1996 | — | — | — | — | 0.50 | — |
| 1998 | — | — | — | — | 0.50 | — |

**20 CENTS** **KM# 3** **Weight:** 6.6300 g. **Composition:** 0.8000 Silver .1705 oz. ASW **Subject:** Independence commemorative

| Date | Mintage | F | VF | XF | Unc | BU |
|---|---|---|---|---|---|---|
| 1968 Proof | 10,000 | Value: 8.00 | | | | |

**20 CENTS** **KM# 11** **Composition:** Copper-Nickel

| Date | Mintage | F | VF | XF | Unc | BU |
|---|---|---|---|---|---|---|
| 1974 | 502,000 | — | 0.35 | 0.75 | 2.00 | — |
| 1974 Proof | 13,000 | Value: 3.00 | | | | |
| 1975 | 1,000,000 | — | 0.35 | 0.75 | 2.00 | — |
| 1979 | — | — | 0.35 | 0.75 | 2.00 | — |
| 1979 Proof | — | Value: 4.00 | | | | |
| 1984 | — | — | 0.35 | 0.75 | 2.00 | — |

**20 CENTS** **KM# 31** **Composition:** Copper-Nickel **Series:** F.A.O.

| Date | Mintage | F | VF | XF | Unc | BU |
|---|---|---|---|---|---|---|
| 1981 | 150,000 | — | 0.40 | 0.80 | 1.75 | — |

**20 CENTS** **KM# 42** **Composition:** Copper-Nickel

| Date | Mintage | F | VF | XF | Unc | BU |
|---|---|---|---|---|---|---|
| 1986 | — | — | 0.40 | 0.80 | 2.00 | — |

**20 CENTS** **KM# 50** **Composition:** Copper-Nickel **Obverse:** King Msawati III

| Date | Mintage | F | VF | XF | Unc | BU |
|---|---|---|---|---|---|---|
| 1996 | — | — | 0.40 | 0.80 | 2.00 | — |
| 1998 | — | — | 0.40 | 0.80 | 2.00 | — |

**50 CENTS** **KM# 4** **Weight:** 10.3900 g. **Composition:** 0.8000 Silver .2672 oz. ASW **Subject:** Independence commemorative

| Date | Mintage | F | VF | XF | Unc | BU |
|---|---|---|---|---|---|---|
| 1968 Proof | 10,000 | Value: 9.00 | | | | |

**50 CENTS** **KM# 12** **Composition:** Copper-Nickel

| Date | Mintage | F | VF | XF | Unc | BU |
|---|---|---|---|---|---|---|
| 1974 | 252,000 | — | 1.00 | 1.50 | 2.75 | — |
| 1974 Proof | 13,000 | Value: 3.00 | | | | |
| 1975 | 500,000 | — | 1.00 | 1.50 | 2.75 | — |
| 1979 | — | — | 0.50 | 1.00 | 2.50 | — |
| 1979 Proof | 10,000 | Value: 5.00 | | | | |
| 1981 | 1,150,000 | — | 0.50 | 1.00 | 2.50 | — |

**50 CENTS** **KM# 43** **Composition:** Copper-Nickel

| Date | Mintage | F | VF | XF | Unc | BU |
|---|---|---|---|---|---|---|
| 1986 | 1,000,000 | — | 0.50 | 1.50 | 3.50 | — |
| 1993 | — | — | 0.50 | 1.50 | 3.50 | — |

**50 CENTS** **KM# 52** **Composition:** Copper-Nickel **Obverse:** King Msawati III

| Date | Mintage | F | VF | XF | Unc | BU |
|---|---|---|---|---|---|---|
| 1996 | — | — | — | — | 3.75 | — |
| 1998 | — | — | — | — | 3.75 | — |

**LUHLANGA** **KM# 5** **Weight:** 15.0000 g. **Composition:** 0.8000 Silver .3858 oz. ASW **Subject:** Independence commemorative

| Date | Mintage | VG | F | VF | XF | Unc |
|---|---|---|---|---|---|---|
| 1968 Proof | 10,000 | Value: 12.00 | | | | |

**LILANGENI** **KM# 6** **Weight:** 33.9305 g. **Composition:** 0.9170 Gold 1 oz. AGW **Subject:** Independence commemorative **Note:** Approximately 1,450 melted.

| Date | Mintage | F | VF | XF | Unc | BU |
|---|---|---|---|---|---|---|
| 1968 Proof | 2,000 | Value: 550 | | | | |

**LILANGENI** **KM# 13** **Composition:** Copper-Nickel

| Date | Mintage | F | VF | XF | Unc | BU |
|---|---|---|---|---|---|---|
| 1974 | 127,000 | — | 1.50 | 2.50 | 4.50 | — |
| 1974 Proof | 13,000 | Value: 6.00 | | | | |
| 1979 | — | — | 1.00 | 2.00 | 4.50 | — |
| 1979 Proof | 110,000 | Value: 7.50 | | | | |

**LILANGENI** **KM# 24** **Composition:** Copper-Nickel **Series:** F.A.O., International Women's Year

| Date | Mintage | F | VF | XF | Unc | BU |
|---|---|---|---|---|---|---|
| 1975 | 100,000 | — | 1.50 | 2.75 | 6.50 | — |

**LILANGENI** **KM# 28** **Composition:** Copper-Nickel **Series:** F.A.O.

| Date | Mintage | F | VF | XF | Unc | BU |
|---|---|---|---|---|---|---|
| 1976 | 100,000 | — | 1.50 | 2.75 | 6.50 | — |

**LILANGENI** **KM# 29.1** **Weight:** 15.5500 g. **Composition:** 0.9990 Gold .5 oz. AGW **Subject:** 80th anniversary - birth of King Sobhuza II **Reverse:** Dates 1921-1979 above arms

| Date | Mintage | F | VF | XF | Unc | BU |
|---|---|---|---|---|---|---|
| ND(1979) | 1,250 | — | — | — | 250 | — |
| ND(1979) Proof | Inc. above | Value: 275 | | | | |

**LILANGENI** **KM# 29.2** **Weight:** 15.5500 g. **Composition:** 0.9990 Gold .5 oz. AGW **Subject:** 80th anniversary - birth of King Sobhuza II **Reverse:** Dates 1923-1979 above arms

| Date | Mintage | F | VF | XF | Unc | BU |
|---|---|---|---|---|---|---|
| ND(1979) | — | — | — | — | 300 | — |

**LILANGENI** **KM# 32** **Composition:** Copper-Nickel **Series:** F.A.O.

| Date | Mintage | F | VF | XF | Unc | BU |
|---|---|---|---|---|---|---|
| 1981 | 871,000 | — | 1.50 | 3.00 | 7.00 | — |

**LILANGENI** **KM# 32a** **Weight:** 11.6600 g. **Composition:** 0.9250 Silver .3468 oz. ASW

| Date | Mintage | F | VF | XF | Unc | BU |
|---|---|---|---|---|---|---|
| 1981 | 5,000 | — | — | — | 22.50 | — |
| 1981 Proof | 5,000 | Value: 32.50 | | | | |

**LILANGENI** **KM# 44.1** **Composition:** Nickel-Brass

| Date | Mintage | F | VF | XF | Unc | BU |
|---|---|---|---|---|---|---|
| 1986 | 1,025,000 | — | — | 2.00 | 4.00 | — |

**LILANGENI** **KM# 44.2** **Composition:** Nickel-Brass Plated Steel

| Date | Mintage | F | VF | XF | Unc | BU |
|---|---|---|---|---|---|---|
| 1992 | — | — | — | 1.50 | 3.50 | — |

**LILANGENI** **KM# 45** **Composition:** Brass

| Date | Mintage | F | VF | XF | Unc | BU |
|---|---|---|---|---|---|---|
| 1995 | — | — | — | 1.50 | 3.50 | — |
| 1998 | — | — | — | 1.50 | 3.50 | — |

**2 EMALANGENI** **KM# 33** **Weight:** 17.0000 g. **Composition:** 0.9250 Silver .5056 oz. ASW **Subject:** Diamond jubilee of King Sobhuza II

| Date | Mintage | F | VF | XF | Unc | BU |
|---|---|---|---|---|---|---|
| 1981 Proof | — | Value: 27.50 | | | | |

**2 EMALANGENI** **KM# 33a** **Composition:** Copper-Nickel **Subject:** Diamond jubilee of King Sobhuza II

| Date | Mintage | F | VF | XF | Unc | BU |
|---|---|---|---|---|---|---|
| 1981 | 50,000 | — | 2.00 | 3.50 | 7.50 | — |

**2 EMALANGENI** **KM# 46** **Composition:** Brass

| Date | Mintage | F | VF | XF | Unc | BU |
|---|---|---|---|---|---|---|
| 1995 | — | — | — | — | 3.75 | — |

**5 EMALANGENI** **KM# 14** **Weight:** 10.3000 g. **Composition:** 0.9250 Silver .3063 oz. ASW **Subject:** 75th anniversary - birth of King Sobhuza II

| Date | Mintage | F | VF | XF | Unc | BU |
|---|---|---|---|---|---|---|
| 1974 Proof | — | Value: 50.00 | | | | |

**5 EMALANGENI** **KM# 15** **Weight:** 5.5600 g. **Composition:** 0.9000 Gold .1609 oz. AGW **Subject:** 75th anniversary - birth of King Sobhuza II

| Date | Mintage | F | VF | XF | Unc | BU |
|---|---|---|---|---|---|---|
| 1974 Proof | 60,000 | Value: 85.00 | | | | |

**5 EMALANGENI** KM# 47 **Composition:** Brass

| Date | Mintage | F | VF | XF | Unc | BU |
|---|---|---|---|---|---|---|
| 1996 | — | — | — | — | 6.00 | — |
| 1998 | — | — | — | — | 6.00 | — |

**5 EMALANGENI** KM# 53 **Composition:** Brass **Subject:** Central bank's 25th anniversary **Obverse:** King's portrait **Reverse:** Bank seal

| Date | Mintage | F | VF | XF | Unc | BU |
|---|---|---|---|---|---|---|
| ND(1999) | — | — | — | — | 5.50 | — |

**7-1/2 EMALANGENI** KM# 16 **Weight:** 16.2000 g. **Composition:** 0.9250 Silver .4818 oz. ASW **Subject:** 75th anniversary - birth of King Sobhuza II

| Date | Mintage | F | VF | XF | Unc | BU |
|---|---|---|---|---|---|---|
| 1974 Proof | — | Value: 65.00 | | | | |

**10 EMALANGENI** KM# 17 **Weight:** 11.1200 g. **Composition:** 0.9000 Gold .3218 oz. AGW **Subject:** 75th anniversary - birth of King Sobhuza II

| Date | Mintage | F | VF | XF | Unc | BU |
|---|---|---|---|---|---|---|
| 1974 Proof | Est. 40,000 | Value: 250 | | | | |

**10 EMALANGENI** KM# 25 **Weight:** 25.5000 g. **Composition:** 0.9250 Silver .7584 oz. ASW **Subject:** 75th anniversary - birth of King Sobhuza II

| Date | Mintage | F | VF | XF | Unc | BU |
|---|---|---|---|---|---|---|
| 1975 | Est. 1,000 | — | — | — | 40.00 | — |
| 1975 Proof | Est. 1,500 | Value: 55.00 | | | | |

**15 EMALANGENI** KM# 18 **Weight:** 32.6000 g. **Composition:** 0.9250 Silver .9696 oz. ASW **Subject:** 75th anniversary - birth of King Sobhuza II **Obverse:** Similar to 25 Emalangeni, KM#20 **Reverse:** Stamped serial number

| Date | Mintage | F | VF | XF | Unc | BU |
|---|---|---|---|---|---|---|
| 1974 Proof | — | Value: 85.00 | | | | |

**20 EMALANGENI** KM# 19 **Weight:** 22.2300 g. **Composition:** 0.9000 Gold .6433 oz. AGW **Subject:** 75th anniversary - birth of King Sobhuza II

| Date | Mintage | F | VF | XF | Unc | BU |
|---|---|---|---|---|---|---|
| 1974 Proof | Est. 25,000 | Value: 350 | | | | |

**25 EMALANGENI** KM# 20 **Weight:** 27.7800 g. **Composition:** 0.9000 Gold .8039 oz. AGW **Subject:** 75th anniversary - birth of King Sobhuza II

| Date | Mintage | F | VF | XF | Unc | BU |
|---|---|---|---|---|---|---|
| 1974 | Est. 15,000 | — | — | — | 375 | — |

**25 EMALANGENI** KM# 34 **Weight:** 28.2800 g. **Composition:** 0.9250 Silver .8411 oz. ASW **Subject:** Diamond jubilee of King Sobhuza II

| Date | Mintage | F | VF | XF | Unc | BU |
|---|---|---|---|---|---|---|
| 1981 | Est. 10,000 | — | — | — | 37.50 | — |
| 1981 Proof | Est. 10,000 | Value: 55.00 | | | | |

**25 EMALANGENI** KM# 37 **Weight:** 28.2800 g. **Composition:** 0.9250 Silver .8411 oz. ASW **Subject:** Accession of King Makhosetive

| Date | Mintage | F | VF | XF | Unc | BU |
|---|---|---|---|---|---|---|
| 1986 Proof | Est. 2,500 | Value: 45.00 | | | | |

**50 EMALANGENI** KM# 26 **Weight:** 4.3100 g. **Composition:** 0.9000 Gold .1247 oz. AGW **Subject:** 75th anniversary - birth of King Sobhuza II

| Date | Mintage | F | VF | XF | Unc | BU |
|---|---|---|---|---|---|---|
| 1975 | 3,510 | — | — | — | 70.00 | — |
| 1975 Proof | 3,262 | Value: 85.00 | | | | |

**100 EMALANGENI** KM# 27 **Weight:** 8.6400 g. **Composition:** 0.9000 Gold .25 oz. AGW **Subject:** 75th anniversary - birth of King Sobhuza II

| Date | Mintage | F | VF | XF | Unc | BU |
|---|---|---|---|---|---|---|
| 1975 | 1,000 | — | — | — | 165 | — |
| 1975 Proof | 1,000 | Value: 200 | | | | |

**250 EMALANGENI** **KM# 35** **Weight:** 15.9800 g. **Composition:** 0.9170 Gold .4711 oz. AGW **Subject:** Diamond jubilee of King Sobhuza II

| Date | Mintage | F | VF | XF | Unc | BU |
|---|---|---|---|---|---|---|
| 1981 | 2,000 | — | — | — | 225 | — |
| 1981 Proof | 2,000 | Value: 325 | | | | |

**250 EMALANGENI** **KM# 38** **Weight:** 15.9800 g. **Composition:** 0.9170 Gold .4711 oz. AGW **Subject:** Accession of King Makhosetive

| Date | Mintage | F | VF | XF | Unc | BU |
|---|---|---|---|---|---|---|
| ND(1986) | 250 | — | — | — | 275 | — |
| ND(1986) Proof | 250 | Value: 375 | | | | |

## GOLD BULLION COINAGE

**2 EMALANGENI** **KM# 30** **Weight:** 31.1000 g. **Composition:** 0.9990 Gold 1 oz. AGW **Subject:** 80th anniversary - birth of King Sobhuza II

| Date | Mintage | F | VF | XF | Unc | BU |
|---|---|---|---|---|---|---|
| ND(1979) | 1,250 | — | — | — | 450 | — |
| ND(1979) Proof | Inc. above | Value: 550 | | | | |

**5 EMALANGENI** **KM# 36** **Weight:** 31.1000 g. **Composition:** 0.9990 Gold 1 oz. AGW **Subject:** Queen Elizabeth II's silver jubilee

| Date | Mintage | F | VF | XF | Unc | BU |
|---|---|---|---|---|---|---|
| ND(1978) Proof | — | Value: 550 | | | | |

## MINT SETS

| KM# | Date | Mintage | Identification | Issue Price | Mkt Val |
|---|---|---|---|---|---|
| MS1 | 1974 (7) | — | KM7-13 | 10.00 | 10.00 |
| MS2 | 1975 (3) | 1,000 | KM25-27 | — | 280 |
| MS3 | 1986 (6) | — | KM39-44 | — | 8.00 |

## PROOF SETS

| KM# | Date | Mintage | Identification | Issue Price | Mkt Val |
|---|---|---|---|---|---|
| PS1 | 1968 (5) | 10,000 | KM1-5 | 25.80 | 40.00 |
| PS3 | 1974 (4) | — | KM15, 17, 19, 20 | 745 | 965 |
| PS4 | 1974 (3) | — | KM14, 16, 17 | 70.00 | 335 |
| PS2 | 1974 (7) | 20,000 | KM7-13 | 18.00 | 15.00 |
| PS5 | 1975 (3) | — | KM25-27 | — | 340 |
| PS6 | 1975 (2) | — | KM26-27 | 252 | 285 |
| PS7 | 1979 (7) | 3,231 | KM7-13 | 34.00 | 22.50 |
| PS8 | 1979 (2) | — | KM29.1, 30 | 1,172 | 825 |

# SWEDEN

The Kingdom of Sweden, a limited constitutional monarchy located in northern Europe between Norway and Finland, has an area of 173,732 sq. mi. (449,960 sq. km.) and a population of *8.5 million. Capital: Stockholm. Mining, lumbering and a specialized machine industry dominate the economy. Machinery, paper, iron and steel, motor vehicles and wood pulp are exported.

Sweden was founded as a Christian stronghold by Olaf Skottkonung late in the 10th century. After conquering Finland late in the 13th century, Sweden, together with Norway, came under the rule of Denmark, 1397-1523, in an association known as the Union of Kalmar. Modern Sweden had its beginning in 1523 when Gustaf Vasa drove the Danes out of Sweden and was himself chosen king. Under Gustaf Adolphus II and Charles XII, Sweden was one of the great powers of 17th century Europe – until Charles invaded Russia in 1708, and was defeated at the Battle of Pultowa in June, 1709. Early in the 18th century, a coalition of Russia, Poland and Denmark took away Sweden's Baltic empire and in 1809 Sweden was forced to cede Finland to Russia. Norway was ceded to Sweden by the Treaty of Kiel in January, 1814. The Norwegians resisted for a time but later signed the Act of Union at the Convention of Moss in August, 1814,The Union was dissolved in 1905 and Norway became independent. A new constitution which took effect on Jan. 1, 1975, restricts the function of the king largely to a ceremonial role.

**RULERS**

Oscar II, 1872-1907
Gustaf V, 1907-1950
Gustaf VI, 1950-1973
Carl XVI Gustaf, 1973-

**MINT OFFICIALS INITIALS**

| Letter | Date | Name |
|---|---|---|
| AL | 1898-1916 | Adolf Lindberg, engraver |
| D | 1986- | Bengt Dennis |
| EB | 1876-1908 | Emil Brusewitz |
| EL | 1916-1944 | Erik Lindberg, engraver |
| G | 1927-1945 | Alf Grabe |
| LH | 1944-1974 | Leo Holmberg, engraver |
| TS | 1945-1961 | Torsten Swensson |
| U | 1961-1986 | Benkt Ulvfot |
| W | 1908-1927 | Karl-August Wallroth |

**MONETARY SYSTEM**

100 Ore = 1 Krona

# KINGDOM

## REFORM COINAGE

100 Ore = 1 Krona

**ORE** **KM# 750** **Composition:** Bronze **Obverse:** Legend lengthened

| Date | Mintage | F | VF | XF | Unc | BU |
|---|---|---|---|---|---|---|
| 1901 | 3,075,000 | 1.00 | 3.00 | 7.50 | 20.00 | — |
| 1902 | 2,685,000 | 1.00 | 3.00 | 7.50 | 25.00 | — |
| 1903 | 2,696,000 | 1.00 | 3.00 | 7.50 | 25.00 | — |
| 1904 | 2,033,000 | 1.00 | 2.50 | 7.50 | 17.50 | — |
| 1905 | 3,556,000 | 1.00 | 2.50 | 5.00 | 25.00 | — |

**ORE** **KM# 768** **Composition:** Bronze

| Date | Mintage | F | VF | XF | Unc | BU |
|---|---|---|---|---|---|---|
| 1906 | 1,783,000 | 3.00 | 7.50 | 12.50 | 65.00 | — |
| 1907 | 8,251,000 | 0.20 | 0.50 | 2.00 | 14.50 | — |

**ORE** **KM# 777.1** **Composition:** Bronze **Obverse:** Small cross

| Date | Mintage | F | VF | XF | Unc | BU |
|---|---|---|---|---|---|---|
| 1909 | 3,810,000 | 6.00 | 8.00 | 17.50 | 85.00 | — |

**ORE** **KM# 777.2** **Composition:** Bronze **Obverse:** Large cross

| Date | Mintage | F | VF | XF | Unc | BU |
|---|---|---|---|---|---|---|
| 1909 | Inc. above | 2.00 | 3.00 | 7.50 | 25.00 | — |
| 1910 | 1,583,000 | 3.00 | 6.00 | 10.00 | 40.00 | — |
| 1911 | 3,150,000 | 0.75 | 1.50 | 3.00 | 12.50 | — |
| 1912/1 | 3,170,000 | 7.50 | 20.00 | 40.00 | 200 | — |
| 1912 | Inc. above | 0.75 | 1.50 | 3.00 | 12.50 | — |
| 1913/12 | 3,197,000 | 3.50 | 10.00 | 20.00 | 100 | — |
| 1913 | Inc. above | 0.75 | 1.50 | 3.00 | 12.50 | — |
| 1914 Open 4 | 2,214,000 | 35.00 | 60.00 | 110 | 350 | — |
| 1914 Closed 4 | Inc. above | 0.75 | 1.50 | 4.50 | 25.00 | — |
| 1915/3 | 4,471,000 | 2.00 | 6.00 | 10.00 | 30.00 | — |
| 1915 | Inc. above | 0.25 | 0.50 | 1.50 | 6.00 | — |

| Date | Mintage | F | VF | XF | Unc | BU |
|---|---|---|---|---|---|---|
| 1916 Short 6 | 7,620,000 | 0.25 | 0.50 | 1.50 | 6.00 | — |

| Date | Mintage | F | VF | XF | Unc | BU |
|---|---|---|---|---|---|---|
| 1916 Long 6 | Inc. above | 0.30 | 0.75 | 2.00 | 9.00 | — |
| 1920 | 5,548,000 | 0.25 | 0.50 | 1.00 | 4.50 | — |
| 1921 | 7,442,000 | 0.25 | 0.50 | 1.00 | 4.50 | — |
| 1922 | 1,166,000 | 2.00 | 4.00 | 6.00 | 25.00 | — |
| 1923 | 4,512,000 | 0.35 | 0.75 | 1.50 | 6.00 | — |
| 1924 | 2,579,000 | 0.25 | 0.75 | 1.50 | 7.00 | — |
| 1925 | 4,715,000 | 0.15 | 0.35 | 0.50 | 3.00 | — |
| 1926 | 6,739,000 | 0.15 | 0.35 | 0.50 | 3.00 | — |
| 1927 | 3,601,000 | 0.15 | 0.35 | 0.50 | 3.00 | — |
| 1928 | 2,381,000 | 0.25 | 0.75 | 2.00 | 9.00 | — |
| 1929 Curved 2 | 6,091,000 | 0.20 | 0.35 | 0.75 | 3.50 | — |
| 1929 Straight 2 | Inc. above | 0.40 | 0.60 | 2.00 | 7.50 | — |
| 1930 | 5,477,000 | 0.20 | 0.35 | 0.75 | 3.50 | — |
| 1931 | 5,680,000 | 0.20 | 0.35 | 0.75 | 3.50 | — |
| 1932 | 3,339,000 | — | 0.45 | 1.50 | 6.00 | — |
| 1933 | 3,427,000 | — | 0.45 | 0.75 | 5.00 | — |
| 1934 | 6,121,000 | — | 0.30 | 0.50 | 3.00 | — |
| 1935 | 4,600,000 | — | 0.30 | 0.50 | 3.00 | — |

| Date | Mintage | F | VF | XF | Unc | BU |
|---|---|---|---|---|---|---|
| 1936 Long 6 | 6,116,000 | 0.20 | 0.45 | 1.00 | 3.50 | — |

| Date | Mintage | F | VF | XF | Unc | BU |
|---|---|---|---|---|---|---|
| 1936 Short 6 | Inc. above | — | 0.25 | 0.50 | 2.50 | — |
| 1937 | 7,738,000 | — | 0.20 | 0.50 | 1.50 | — |
| 1938 | 6,993,000 | — | 0.20 | 0.50 | 1.50 | — |
| 1939 | 6,562,000 | — | 0.20 | 0.50 | 1.50 | — |
| 1940 | 4,060,000 | — | 0.20 | 0.35 | 1.25 | — |
| 1941 | 11,599,000 | — | 0.20 | 0.35 | 1.25 | — |
| 1942 | 3,992,000 | — | 0.20 | 0.50 | 1.50 | — |
| 1950 | 22,421,000 | — | 0.20 | 0.30 | 1.25 | — |

**ORE** **KM# 789** **Composition:** Iron **Note:** World War I issues.

| Date | Mintage | F | VF | XF | Unc | BU |
|---|---|---|---|---|---|---|
| 1917 | 8,128,000 | 0.75 | 1.50 | 4.00 | 25.00 | — |
| 1918 | 9,706,000 | 1.00 | 2.25 | 6.00 | 35.00 | — |
| 1919 | 7,170,000 | 1.50 | 3.00 | 7.00 | 45.00 | — |

**ORE** **KM# 810** **Composition:** Iron **Note:** World War II issues. Similar to KM#777.

| Date | Mintage | F | VF | XF | Unc | BU |
|---|---|---|---|---|---|---|
| 1942 | 10,053,000 | — | 0.20 | 0.60 | 3.00 | — |
| 1943 | 10,714,000 | — | 0.20 | 0.75 | 4.00 | — |
| 1944 | 8,699,000 | — | 0.20 | 0.60 | 4.00 | — |
| 1945 | 9,527,000 | — | 0.20 | 0.60 | 4.00 | — |
| 1945 Serif 4 | Inc. above | 3.00 | 6.00 | 12.50 | 22.50 | — |

| Date | Mintage | F | VF | XF | Unc | BU |
|---|---|---|---|---|---|---|
| 1946 | 6,611,000 | — | 0.25 | 1.00 | 5.00 | — |
| 1947 | 14,245,000 | — | 0.20 | 0.40 | 2.00 | — |
| 1948 | 15,442,000 | — | 0.20 | 0.40 | 2.00 | — |
| 1949 | 11,779,000 | — | 0.20 | 0.40 | 2.00 | — |
| 1950 | 14,432,000 | — | 0.20 | 0.40 | 2.00 | — |

**ORE** **KM# 820** **Composition:** Bronze **Note:** Varieties exist.

| Date | Mintage | F | VF | XF | Unc | BU |
|---|---|---|---|---|---|---|
| 1952 TS | 3,819,000 | — | 0.20 | 0.75 | 3.00 | — |
| 1953 TS | 22,636,000 | — | — | 0.25 | 2.00 | — |
| 1954 TS | 15,492,000 | — | — | 0.25 | 2.00 | — |
| 1955 TS | 24,008,000 | — | — | 0.25 | 2.00 | — |
| 1956 TS | 20,792,000 | — | — | 0.25 | 2.00 | — |
| 1957 TS | 21,019,000 | — | — | 0.25 | 2.00 | — |
| 1958 TS | 20,220,000 | — | — | 0.25 | 2.00 | — |
| 1959 TS | 14,028,000 | — | — | 0.25 | 2.00 | — |
| 1960 TS | 21,840,000 | — | — | 0.20 | 2.00 | — |
| 1961 TS | 11,458,000 | — | — | 0.30 | 2.25 | — |
| 1961 U | 4,928,000 | — | 0.20 | 0.50 | 4.00 | — |
| 1962 U | 19,698,000 | — | — | 0.25 | 2.00 | — |
| 1963 U | 26,070,000 | — | — | 0.10 | 0.30 | — |
| 1964 U | 19,290,000 | — | — | 0.10 | 0.30 | — |
| 1965 U | 22,335,000 | — | — | 0.10 | 0.30 | — |
| 1966 U | 24,093,000 | — | — | 0.10 | 0.20 | — |
| 1967 U | 30,420,000 | — | — | 0.10 | 0.20 | — |
| 1968 U | 20,760,000 | — | — | 0.10 | 0.20 | — |
| 1969 U | 20,198,000 | — | — | 0.10 | 0.20 | — |
| 1970 U | 44,400,000 | — | — | 0.10 | 0.20 | — |
| 1971 U | 16,490,000 | — | — | 0.10 | 0.20 | — |

**2 ORE** **KM# 746** **Composition:** Bronze **Obverse:** Large lettering

| Date | Mintage | F | VF | XF | Unc | BU |
|---|---|---|---|---|---|---|
| 1901 | 1,420,000 | 0.50 | 1.00 | 3.00 | 20.00 | — |
| 1902 | 2,040,000 | 0.50 | 1.00 | 3.00 | 20.00 | — |
| 1904 | 698,000 | 0.50 | 1.00 | 4.00 | 25.00 | — |
| 1905 | 1,430,000 | 0.50 | 1.00 | 3.00 | 20.00 | — |

**2 ORE** **KM# 769** **Composition:** Bronze

| Date | Mintage | F | VF | XF | Unc | BU |
|---|---|---|---|---|---|---|
| 1906/5 | 994,000 | 150 | 250 | 450 | 900 | — |
| 1906 | Inc. above | 4.00 | 7.00 | 22.50 | 80.00 | — |
| 1907 | 3,810,000 | 0.25 | 0.50 | 2.00 | 12.50 | — |

**2 ORE** **KM# 778** **Composition:** Bronze

| Date | Mintage | F | VF | XF | Unc | BU |
|---|---|---|---|---|---|---|
| 1909 | 1,580,000 | 0.50 | 2.00 | 8.00 | 40.00 | — |
| 1910 | 809,000 | 2.25 | 11.00 | 20.00 | 75.00 | — |
| 1912 | 446,000 | 4.75 | 16.00 | 30.00 | 85.00 | — |
| 1913 | 806,000 | 0.25 | 2.00 | 10.00 | 40.00 | — |
| 1914 | 1,200,000 | 0.25 | 2.00 | 10.00 | 40.00 | — |
| 1915/4 | 814,000 | 4.00 | 12.50 | 35.00 | 85.00 | — |
| 1915 | Inc. above | 0.25 | 2.00 | 10.00 | 40.00 | — |
| 1916/5 | 2,820,000 | 3.00 | 9.00 | 25.00 | 75.00 | — |
| 1916 Short 6 | Inc. above | 0.25 | 0.50 | 5.00 | 25.00 | — |
| 1916 Long 6 | Inc. above | 0.25 | 0.50 | 5.00 | 25.00 | — |
| 1919 | 1,203,000 | 0.25 | 0.50 | 4.00 | 20.00 | — |
| 1920 | 3,465,000 | 0.30 | 0.50 | 2.00 | 10.00 | — |
| 1921 | 2,958,000 | 0.30 | 0.50 | 2.00 | 10.00 | — |
| 1922 | 932,000 | 0.80 | 1.50 | 6.00 | 30.00 | — |
| 1923 | 769,000 | 1.00 | 2.50 | 6.00 | 40.00 | — |
| 1924 | 1,283,000 | 0.25 | 0.75 | 3.00 | 22.50 | — |
| 1925 | 3,903,000 | 0.20 | 0.50 | 1.50 | 12.50 | — |
| 1926 | 3,579,000 | 0.20 | 0.50 | 1.50 | 12.50 | — |
| 1927 | 2,190,000 | 0.20 | 0.50 | 1.50 | 12.50 | — |
| 1928 | 832,000 | 0.40 | 1.00 | 4.00 | 25.00 | — |
| 1929 | 2,384,000 | 0.20 | 0.30 | 1.50 | 10.00 | — |
| 1930 | 2,590,000 | 0.20 | 0.30 | 1.50 | 10.00 | — |
| 1931 | 2,296,000 | 0.20 | 0.30 | 1.50 | 10.00 | — |
| 1932 | 1,179,000 | 0.30 | 0.75 | 4.00 | 25.00 | — |
| 1933 | 1,721,000 | 0.20 | 0.35 | 1.50 | 10.00 | — |
| 1934 | 1,795,000 | 0.20 | 0.35 | 1.50 | 10.00 | — |
| 1935 | 3,678,000 | 0.20 | 0.30 | 1.00 | 6.00 | — |
| 1936 Short 6 | 2,244,000 | 0.10 | 0.25 | 0.75 | 5.00 | — |
| 1936 Long 6 | Inc. above | 0.75 | 1.25 | 3.00 | 15.00 | — |
| 1937 | 2,981,000 | 0.10 | 0.25 | 1.00 | 5.00 | — |
| 1938 | 3,225,000 | 0.10 | 0.25 | 0.50 | 5.00 | — |
| 1939 | 4,014,000 | 0.10 | 0.25 | 0.50 | 4.00 | — |
| 1940 | 3,305,000 | 0.10 | 0.25 | 0.50 | 4.00 | — |
| 1941 | 7,337,000 | 0.10 | 0.25 | 0.50 | 4.00 | — |
| 1942 | 1,614,000 | 0.30 | 0.75 | 1.25 | 10.00 | — |
| 1950 | 5,823,000 | 0.10 | 0.25 | 0.50 | 4.00 | — |

**2 ORE** **KM# 790** **Composition:** Iron **Note:** World War I Issues. Similar to KM#553.

| Date | Mintage | F | VF | XF | Unc | BU |
|---|---|---|---|---|---|---|
| 1917 | 4,576,000 | 2.00 | 3.50 | 8.00 | 40.00 | — |
| 1918 | 4,982,000 | 2.50 | 5.50 | 12.50 | 50.00 | — |
| 1919 | 2,923,000 | 8.00 | 12.50 | 25.00 | 80.00 | — |
| 1920 | 1 | — | — | — | — | — |

**2 ORE** **KM# 811** **Composition:** Iron **Note:** World War II Issues.

| Date | Mintage | F | VF | XF | Unc | BU |
|---|---|---|---|---|---|---|
| 1942 | 9,344,000 | 0.15 | 0.30 | 1.50 | 9.00 | — |
| 1943 | 6,999,000 | 0.15 | 0.30 | 1.50 | 9.00 | — |
| 1944 | 6,126,000 | 0.15 | 0.30 | 1.50 | 9.00 | — |
| 1945 | 4,773,000 | 0.20 | 0.40 | 1.50 | 10.00 | — |
| 1946 | 5,854,000 | 0.15 | 0.30 | 1.50 | 9.00 | — |
| 1947 | 9,536,000 | 0.15 | 0.30 | 0.75 | 6.00 | — |
| 1948 | 11,424,000 | 0.15 | 0.30 | 0.75 | 6.00 | — |
| 1949 Long 9 | 10,600,000 | 0.15 | 0.30 | 0.75 | 6.00 | — |
| 1949 Short 9 | Inc. above | 0.15 | 0.30 | 0.75 | 6.00 | — |
| 1950 | 13,323,000 | 0.15 | 0.30 | 0.75 | 6.00 | — |

**2 ORE** **KM# 821** **Composition:** Bronze **Note:** Varieties exist.

| Date | Mintage | F | VF | XF | Unc | BU |
|---|---|---|---|---|---|---|
| 1952 TS | 3,011,000 | 0.20 | 0.50 | 0.75 | 5.00 | — |
| 1953 TS | 15,620,000 | 0.10 | 0.20 | 0.75 | 4.00 | — |
| 1954 TS | 10,086,000 | 0.10 | 0.20 | 0.75 | 4.00 | — |
| 1955 TS | 12,963,000 | 0.10 | 0.20 | 0.75 | 4.00 | — |
| 1956 TS | 13,890,000 | 0.10 | 0.20 | 0.75 | 4.00 | — |
| 1957 TS | 9,997,000 | 0.10 | 0.20 | 0.75 | 4.00 | — |
| 1958 TS | 10,106,000 | 0.10 | 0.20 | 0.75 | 4.00 | — |
| 1959 TS | 11,572,000 | 0.10 | 0.20 | 0.75 | 4.00 | — |
| 1960 TS | 11,093,000 | 0.10 | 0.20 | 0.75 | 4.00 | — |
| 1961 TS | 9,673,000 | 0.10 | 0.20 | 0.75 | 4.00 | — |
| 1961 U | 1,075,000 | 0.75 | 1.50 | 3.00 | 12.50 | — |
| 1962 U | 9,569,000 | — | 0.10 | 0.50 | 1.75 | — |
| 1963 U | 13,338,000 | — | 0.10 | 0.50 | 1.75 | — |
| 1964 U | 19,346,000 | — | 0.10 | 0.20 | 1.75 | — |
| 1965 U | 23,356,000 | — | 0.10 | 0.20 | 0.75 | — |
| 1966 U | 18,278,000 | — | 0.10 | 0.20 | 0.75 | — |
| 1967 U | 23,931,000 | — | — | 0.10 | 0.45 | — |
| 1968 U | 26,238,000 | — | — | 0.10 | 0.45 | — |
| 1969 U | 16,843,000 | — | — | 0.10 | 0.45 | — |
| 1970 U | 31,254,000 | — | — | 0.10 | 0.45 | — |
| 1971 U | 19,179,000 | — | — | 0.10 | 0.45 | — |

**5 ORE** **KM# 757** **Composition:** Bronze **Obverse:** Large lettering

| Date | Mintage | F | VF | XF | Unc | BU |
|---|---|---|---|---|---|---|
| 1901 | 442,000 | 1.00 | 4.50 | 11.50 | 50.00 | — |
| 1902 | 652,000 | 1.00 | 4.50 | 11.50 | 50.00 | — |
| 1903 | 243,000 | 1.75 | 5.50 | 17.50 | 60.00 | — |
| 1904 | 414,000 | 1.00 | 4.50 | 11.50 | 42.00 | — |
| 1905 | 545,000 | 1.00 | 4.50 | 13.50 | 45.00 | — |

**5 ORE** **KM# 770** **Composition:** Bronze

| Date | Mintage | F | VF | XF | Unc | BU |
|---|---|---|---|---|---|---|
| 1906 | 565,000 | 0.75 | 3.50 | 11.50 | 40.00 | — |
| 1907 | 1,953,000 | 0.50 | 2.00 | 6.00 | 22.00 | — |

**5 ORE** **KM# 779.1** **Composition:** Bronze **Obverse:** Small cross

| Date | Mintage | F | VF | XF | Unc | BU |
|---|---|---|---|---|---|---|
| 1909 | 917,000 | 2.00 | 6.50 | 32.00 | 175 | — |

**5 ORE** **KM# 779.2** **Composition:** Bronze **Obverse:** Large cross **Note:** Varieties exist.

| Date | Mintage | F | VF | XF | Unc | BU |
|---|---|---|---|---|---|---|
| 1909 | Inc. above | 6.00 | 40.00 | 250 | 900 | — |
| 1910 | 31,000 | 100 | 250 | 450 | 1,150 | — |
| 1911 | 778,000 | 0.75 | 3.50 | 22.00 | 115 | — |
| 1912 | 547,000 | 1.00 | 3.50 | 32.00 | 160 | — |
| 1913 | 762,000 | 0.75 | 2.25 | 22.00 | 110 | — |
| 1914 | 400,000 | 2.25 | 5.50 | 40.00 | 190 | — |
| 1915 | 1,222,000 | 0.50 | 2.75 | 17.50 | 55.00 | — |
| 1916/5 | 955,000 | 10.00 | 20.00 | 35.00 | 135 | — |
| 1916 Short 6 | Inc. above | 0.50 | 2.75 | 14.50 | 60.00 | — |
| 1916 Long 6 | Inc. above | 0.50 | 2.75 | 14.50 | 60.00 | — |
| 1917 | 1 | — | — | — | — | — |
| 1919 | 1,129,000 | 0.25 | 1.00 | 12.50 | 55.00 | — |
| 1920 | 2,361,000 | 0.25 | 1.00 | 8.00 | 32.00 | — |
| 1921 | 1,879,000 | 0.20 | 0.75 | 10.00 | 45.00 | — |
| 1922 | 763,000 | 0.20 | 2.50 | 25.00 | 100 | — |
| 1923 | 506,000 | 0.75 | 4.50 | 60.00 | 200 | — |
| 1924 | 900,000 | 0.25 | 1.50 | 17.50 | 75.00 | — |
| 1925 | 1,944,000 | 0.20 | 0.75 | 9.00 | 45.00 | — |
| 1926 | 1,742,000 | 0.20 | 0.75 | 9.00 | 45.00 | — |
| 1927 | 36,000 | 75.00 | 175 | 600 | 1,250 | — |
| 1928 | 987,000 | 0.20 | 1.00 | 10.00 | 55.00 | — |
| 1929 | 1,670,000 | 0.20 | 0.50 | 9.00 | 45.00 | — |
| 1930 | 1,716,000 | 0.20 | 0.50 | 9.00 | 45.00 | — |
| 1931 | 1,131,000 | — | 0.50 | 9.00 | 45.00 | — |
| 1932 | 1,165,000 | — | 0.50 | 9.00 | 45.00 | — |
| 1933 | 574,000 | 0.65 | 2.50 | 25.00 | 110 | — |
| 1934 | 1,710,000 | — | 0.35 | 5.00 | 32.00 | — |
| 1935 | 1,682,000 | — | 0.35 | 5.00 | 32.00 | — |
| 1936 Short 6 | 1,626,000 | — | 0.35 | 6.00 | 32.00 | — |
| 1936 | Inc. above | 0.25 | 0.75 | 7.00 | 37.50 | — |
| 1937 | 2,637,000 | — | 0.30 | 4.00 | 22.00 | — |
| 1938 | 2,354,000 | — | 0.30 | 4.00 | 22.00 | — |
| 1939 | 2,592,000 | — | 0.45 | 6.00 | 27.50 | — |
| 1940 | 2,730,000 | — | 0.35 | 3.00 | 16.50 | — |
| 1940 Serif 4 | Inc. above | — | 0.35 | 3.00 | 16.50 | — |
| 1941 | 2,055,000 | — | 0.35 | 3.00 | 16.50 | — |
| 1942 | 395,000 | 2.25 | 4.75 | 25.00 | 100 | — |
| 1950 | 12,559,000 | — | 0.25 | 0.75 | 5.50 | — |

**5 ORE** **KM# 791** **Composition:** Iron **Note:** World War I Issues. Similar to KM#554.

| Date | Mintage | F | VF | XF | Unc | BU |
|---|---|---|---|---|---|---|
| 1917 | 2,953,000 | 4.00 | 8.00 | 17.50 | 60.00 | — |
| 1918 | 2,458,000 | 9.00 | 20.00 | 30.00 | 125 | — |
| 1919 | 2,302,000 | 9.00 | 20.00 | 30.00 | 100 | — |

**5 ORE** **KM# 812** **Composition:** Iron **Note:** World War II Issues.

| Date | Mintage | F | VF | XF | Unc | BU |
|---|---|---|---|---|---|---|
| 1942 | 4,343,000 | 0.20 | 0.75 | 4.00 | 25.00 | — |
| 1943 | 5,570,000 | 0.20 | 0.75 | 4.00 | 25.00 | — |
| 1944 | 4,562,000 | 0.20 | 0.75 | 4.00 | 25.00 | — |
| 1945 | 3,771,000 | 0.20 | 0.75 | 4.00 | 25.00 | — |
| 1946 | 2,375,000 | — | 0.50 | 3.00 | 16.50 | — |

| Date | Mintage | F | VF | XF | Unc | BU |
|---|---|---|---|---|---|---|
| 1947 | 6,035,000 | — | 0.50 | 3.00 | 16.50 | — |
| 1948 | 6,250,000 | — | 0.50 | 3.00 | 16.50 | — |
| 1949 | 7,840,000 | — | 0.50 | 2.00 | 14.50 | — |
| 1950 | 5,290,000 | — | 0.50 | 2.00 | 14.50 | — |

**5 ORE** KM# 822 **Composition:** Bronze

| Date | Mintage | F | VF | XF | Unc | BU |
|---|---|---|---|---|---|---|
| 1952 TS | 3,065,000 | 0.20 | 0.50 | 1.50 | 7.50 | — |
| 1953 TS | 12,329,000 | 0.20 | 0.50 | 1.75 | 7.50 | — |
| 1954 TS | 7,232,000 | 0.20 | 0.50 | 1.75 | 7.50 | — |
| 1955 TS | 8,465,000 | 0.20 | 0.50 | 1.50 | 7.50 | — |
| 1956 TS | 7,997,000 | 0.20 | 0.50 | 1.75 | 7.50 | — |
| 1957 TS | 6,276,000 | 0.20 | 0.50 | 1.75 | 7.50 | — |
| 1958 TS | 9,498,000 | 0.20 | 0.50 | 1.75 | 7.50 | — |
| 1959 TS | 8,370,000 | 0.20 | 0.50 | 1.75 | 7.50 | — |
| 1960 TS | 10,542,000 | 0.20 | 0.40 | 1.25 | 6.50 | — |
| 1961 TS | 3,909,000 | 0.20 | 0.40 | 1.25 | 6.50 | — |
| 1961 U | 2,452,000 | 0.20 | 0.50 | 1.25 | 7.50 | — |
| 1962 U | 22,306,000 | — | 0.10 | 0.50 | 3.00 | — |
| 1963 U | 17,156,000 | — | 0.10 | 0.50 | 3.00 | — |
| 1964 U | 10,923,000 | — | 0.10 | 0.75 | 6.00 | — |
| 1964 U 50 in crown | Inc. above | 2.50 | 5.00 | 10.00 | 25.00 | — |
| 1965 U | 22,635,000 | — | 0.10 | 0.20 | 1.00 | — |
| 1966 U | 18,213,000 | — | 0.10 | 0.20 | 1.00 | — |
| 1967 U | 20,776,000 | — | 0.10 | 0.20 | 1.00 | — |
| 1968 U | 27,094,000 | — | 0.10 | 0.20 | 1.00 | — |
| 1969 U | 26,887,000 | — | 0.10 | 0.20 | 1.00 | — |
| 1970 U | 29,420,000 | — | 0.10 | 0.20 | 1.00 | — |
| 1971 U | 15,749,000 | — | 0.10 | 0.20 | 1.00 | — |

**5 ORE** KM# 845 **Composition:** Bronze

| Date | Mintage | F | VF | XF | Unc | BU |
|---|---|---|---|---|---|---|
| 1972 U | 107,894,000 | — | — | 0.10 | 0.20 | — |
| 1973 U | 193,038,000 | — | — | 0.10 | 0.20 | — |

**5 ORE** KM# 849 **Composition:** Copper-Tin-Zinc

| Date | Mintage | F | VF | XF | Unc | BU |
|---|---|---|---|---|---|---|
| 1976 U | 4,672,000 | — | — | 0.10 | 0.35 | — |
| 1977 U | 31,037,000 | — | — | 0.10 | 0.25 | — |
| 1978 U | 46,022,000 | — | — | 0.10 | 0.25 | — |
| 1979 U | 65,833,000 | — | — | 0.10 | 0.25 | — |
| 1980 U | 60,997,000 | — | — | 0.10 | 0.20 | — |
| 1981 U | 19,791,000 | — | — | 0.10 | 0.20 | — |

**5 ORE** KM# 849a **Composition:** Copper-Zinc

| Date | Mintage | F | VF | XF | Unc | BU |
|---|---|---|---|---|---|---|
| 1981 | 35,170,000 | — | — | 0.10 | 0.15 | — |
| 1982 | 40,471,000 | — | — | 0.10 | 0.15 | — |
| 1983 | 36,471,000 | — | — | 0.10 | 0.15 | — |
| 1984 | 13,455,000 | — | — | 0.10 | 0.15 | — |

**10 ORE** KM# 755 **Weight:** 1.4500 g. **Composition:** 0.4000 Silver .0186 oz. ASW **Obverse:** Large lettering **Note:** Varieties exist.

| Date | Mintage | F | VF | XF | Unc | BU |
|---|---|---|---|---|---|---|
| 1902 EB | 1,946,000 | 1.00 | 3.50 | 11.50 | 27.50 | — |
| 1903 EB | 1,509,000 | 1.00 | 3.50 | 11.50 | 27.50 | — |
| 1904 EB | 3,280,000 | 0.75 | 1.50 | 8.00 | 18.50 | — |

**10 ORE** KM# 774 **Weight:** 1.4500 g. **Composition:** 0.4000 Silver .0186 oz. ASW

| Date | Mintage | F | VF | XF | Unc | BU |
|---|---|---|---|---|---|---|
| 1907 EB | 7,320,000 | 0.40 | 1.00 | 4.50 | 16.50 | — |

**10 ORE** KM# 780 **Weight:** 1.4500 g. **Composition:** 0.4000 Silver .0186 oz. ASW

| Date | Mintage | F | VF | XF | Unc | BU |
|---|---|---|---|---|---|---|
| 1909 W | 1,610,000 | 1.25 | 4.00 | 12.50 | 55.00 | — |
| 1911 W | 3,180,000 | 0.35 | 2.00 | 7.50 | 25.00 | — |
| 1913 W | 1,581,000 | 1.00 | 2.50 | 10.00 | 40.00 | — |
| 1914 W | 1,571,000 | 0.75 | 3.00 | 7.50 | 25.00 | — |
| 1914 Serif 4 | Inc. above | 0.75 | 2.50 | 10.00 | 40.00 | — |
| 1915 W | 1,547,000 | 0.50 | 2.50 | 7.50 | 37.50 | — |
| 1916/5 W | 3,035,000 | 2.50 | 7.50 | 20.00 | 85.00 | — |
| 1916 W | Inc. above | 0.75 | 1.75 | 6.00 | 25.00 | — |
| 1917 W | 4,996,000 | 0.35 | 0.75 | 2.50 | 14.50 | — |
| 1918 W | 4,114,000 | 0.35 | 0.75 | 2.50 | 14.50 | — |
| 1919 W | 5,740,000 | 0.35 | 0.75 | 2.50 | 14.50 | — |
| 1927 W | 2,510,000 | 0.25 | 0.60 | 2.50 | 17.50 | — |
| 1928 G | 2,901,000 | 0.25 | 0.60 | 2.50 | 17.50 | — |
| 1929 G | 5,505,000 | 0.25 | 0.60 | 1.75 | 8.50 | — |
| 1930 G | 3,223,000 | 0.25 | 0.60 | 1.75 | 8.50 | — |
| 1931 G | 4,272,000 | 0.25 | 0.60 | 1.75 | 8.50 | — |
| 1933 G | 1,948,000 | 0.85 | 1.75 | 3.00 | 20.00 | — |
| 1934 G | 4,059,000 | 0.25 | 0.50 | 1.00 | 6.00 | — |
| 1935 G | 2,426,000 | 0.25 | 0.50 | 1.00 | 6.00 | — |
| 1936 G Short 6 | 5,097,000 | 1.75 | 4.00 | 16.00 | 48.00 | — |
| 1936 G Long 6 | Inc. above | 0.25 | 0.45 | 1.25 | 7.50 | — |
| 1937 G | 5,117,000 | 0.25 | 0.40 | 0.80 | 6.00 | — |
| 1938 G | 7,428,000 | 0.25 | 0.40 | 0.80 | 6.00 | — |
| 1938 G Proof | — | Value: 12.50 | | | | |
| 1939/29 G | 2,021,000 | 3.50 | 7.50 | 18.50 | 45.00 | — |
| 1939 G | Inc. above | 0.25 | 0.60 | 2.00 | 11.50 | — |
| 1939 G Proof | — | Value: 17.50 | | | | |
| 1940 G | 3,017,000 | 0.25 | 0.50 | 1.00 | 6.00 | — |
| 1941 G | 9,106,000 | 0.25 | 0.50 | 1.00 | 6.00 | — |
| 1942 G | 3,692,000 | 0.25 | 0.50 | 1.00 | 6.00 | — |

**10 ORE** KM# 795 **Composition:** Nickel-Bronze

| Date | Mintage | F | VF | XF | Unc | BU |
|---|---|---|---|---|---|---|
| 1920 W | 3,612,000 | 0.50 | 1.25 | 5.00 | 32.00 | — |
| 1920 W Large W | Inc. above | 12.50 | 25.00 | 50.00 | 235 | — |
| 1921 W | 2,270,000 | 0.50 | 1.50 | 6.50 | 32.00 | — |
| 1923 W | 2,144,000 | 0.50 | 1.50 | 7.50 | 40.00 | — |
| 1924 W | 1,600,000 | 0.50 | 2.00 | 8.00 | 55.00 | — |
| 1925 W | 1,472,000 | 0.75 | 3.50 | 15.00 | 70.00 | — |
| 1940 G | 3,374,000 | 0.20 | 0.50 | 2.00 | 14.00 | — |
| 1941 | 816,000 | 0.75 | 1.50 | 4.00 | 25.00 | — |
| 1946 TS | 4,117,000 | 0.10 | 0.30 | 0.75 | 5.50 | — |
| 1947 TS | 4,133,000 | 0.10 | 0.30 | 0.75 | 5.50 | — |

**10 ORE** KM# 813 **Weight:** 1.4400 g. **Composition:** 0.4000 Silver .0185 oz. ASW **Note:** Varieties exist.

| Date | Mintage | F | VF | XF | Unc | BU |
|---|---|---|---|---|---|---|
| 1942 G | 1,600,000 | 0.25 | 0.40 | 1.00 | 5.50 | — |
| 1942 G Proof | — | Value: 35.00 | | | | |
| 1943 G | 7,661,000 | 0.25 | 0.40 | 1.00 | 5.50 | — |
| 1944 G | 12,277,000 | 0.20 | 0.35 | 0.75 | 4.50 | — |
| 1945 G | 11,703,000 | 0.20 | 0.35 | 0.75 | 4.50 | — |
| 1945 TS | Inc. above | 0.20 | 0.35 | 0.75 | 4.50 | — |
| 1945 TS/G | Inc. above | 0.20 | 0.35 | 1.00 | 5.50 | — |
| 1946/5 TS Open 6 | 3,576,000 | 8.00 | 16.00 | 32.00 | 90.00 | — |
| 1946 TS Open 6 | Inc. above | 0.25 | 0.75 | 2.50 | 25.00 | — |
| 1946 TS Closed 6 | Inc. above | 0.20 | 0.35 | 1.50 | 12.00 | — |
| 1947 TS | 7,293,000 | 0.20 | 0.30 | 0.75 | 4.50 | — |
| 1948 TS | 10,419,000 | 0.20 | 0.30 | 0.60 | 4.50 | — |
| 1949 TS | 12,044,000 | 0.20 | 0.30 | 0.60 | 4.50 | — |
| 1950 TS | 31,824,000 | 0.20 | 0.30 | 0.60 | 3.50 | — |

**10 ORE** KM# 823 **Weight:** 1.4400 g. **Composition:** 0.4000 Silver .0185 oz. ASW

| Date | Mintage | F | VF | XF | Unc | BU |
|---|---|---|---|---|---|---|
| 1952 TS | 4,660,000 | BV | 0.40 | 0.75 | 4.00 | — |
| 1953 TS | 28,484,000 | BV | 0.15 | 0.75 | 4.00 | — |
| 1954 TS | 15,913,000 | BV | 0.15 | 0.75 | 4.00 | — |
| 1955 TS | 16,687,000 | BV | 0.15 | 0.75 | 4.00 | — |
| 1956 TS | 21,986,000 | BV | 0.15 | 0.50 | 3.00 | — |
| 1957 TS | 21,294,000 | BV | 0.15 | 0.50 | 3.00 | — |
| 1958 TS | 19,605,000 | BV | 0.15 | 0.50 | 3.00 | — |
| 1959 TS | 18,523,000 | BV | 0.15 | 0.50 | 3.00 | — |
| 1960 TS | 16,605,000 | BV | 0.15 | 0.50 | 3.00 | — |
| 1961 TS | 8,284,000 | BV | 0.15 | 0.50 | 3.00 | — |
| 1961 U | 7,843,000 | BV | 0.15 | 0.50 | 3.00 | — |
| 1962 U | 8,619,000 | BV | 0.15 | 0.50 | 3.00 | — |

**10 ORE** KM# 835 **Composition:** Copper-Nickel

| Date | Mintage | F | VF | XF | Unc | BU |
|---|---|---|---|---|---|---|
| 1962 U | 8,814,000 | 0.10 | 0.25 | 0.50 | 3.00 | — |
| 1963 U | 28,170,000 | — | — | 0.10 | 0.50 | — |
| 1964 U | 36,895,000 | — | — | 0.10 | 0.50 | — |
| 1965 U | 29,870,000 | — | — | 0.10 | 0.50 | — |
| 1966 U | 20,435,000 | — | — | 0.10 | 0.50 | — |
| 1967 U | 18,245,000 | — | — | 0.10 | 0.50 | — |
| 1968 U | 51,490,000 | — | — | 0.10 | 0.40 | — |
| 1969 U | 55,880,000 | — | — | 0.10 | 0.40 | — |
| 1970 U | 60,910,000 | — | — | 0.10 | 0.40 | — |
| 1971 U | 27,075,000 | — | — | 0.10 | 0.40 | — |
| 1972 U | 36,750,000 | — | — | 0.10 | 0.20 | — |
| 1973 U | 160,740,000 | — | — | 0.10 | 0.20 | — |

**10 ORE** KM# 850 **Composition:** Copper-Nickel

| Date | Mintage | F | VF | XF | Unc | BU |
|---|---|---|---|---|---|---|
| 1976 U | 4,173,000 | — | — | 0.15 | 0.40 | — |
| 1977 U | 44,517,000 | — | — | 0.10 | 0.30 | — |
| 1978 U | 74,342,000 | — | — | 0.10 | 0.30 | — |
| 1979 U | 75,306,000 | — | — | 0.10 | 0.15 | — |
| 1980 U | 108,294,000 | — | — | 0.10 | 0.15 | — |
| 1981 U | 102,454,000 | — | — | 0.10 | 0.15 | — |
| 1982 U | 103,906,000 | — | — | 0.10 | 0.15 | — |
| 1983 U | 77,315,000 | — | — | 0.10 | 0.15 | — |
| 1984 U | 122,100,000 | — | — | 0.10 | 0.15 | — |
| 1985 U | 74,222,000 | — | — | 0.10 | 0.15 | — |
| 1986 U | 83,193,000 | — | — | 0.10 | 0.15 | — |
| 1986 D | 17,205,000 | — | — | 0.10 | 0.15 | — |
| 1987 D | 146,877,000 | — | — | 0.10 | 0.15 | — |
| 1988 D | 194,986,000 | — | — | 0.10 | 0.15 | — |
| 1989 D | 245,181,000 | — | — | 0.10 | 0.15 | — |
| 1990 D | 139,238,000 | — | — | 0.10 | 0.15 | — |
| 1991 D | 5,177,000 | — | — | 0.15 | 0.35 | — |

**25 ORE** KM# 739 **Weight:** 2.4200 g. **Composition:** 0.6000 Silver 0.0467 oz. ASW **Obverse:** Large lettering

| Date | Mintage | F | VF | XF | Unc | BU |
|---|---|---|---|---|---|---|
| 1902 EB | 1,259,000 | 2.50 | 7.50 | 25.00 | 80.00 | — |
| 1904 EB | 692,000 | 2.50 | 7.50 | 20.00 | 80.00 | — |
| 1905 EB | 732,000 | 2.50 | 7.50 | 15.00 | 70.00 | — |

**25 ORE** KM# 775 **Weight:** 2.4200 g. **Composition:** 0.6000 Silver 0.0467 oz. ASW

| Date | Mintage | F | VF | XF | Unc | BU |
|---|---|---|---|---|---|---|
| 1907 EB | 3,223,000 | 0.75 | 2.00 | 5.50 | 35.00 | — |

**25 ORE** KM# 785 **Weight:** 2.4200 g. **Composition:** 0.6000 Silver 0.0467 oz. ASW

| Date | Mintage | F | VF | XF | Unc | BU |
|---|---|---|---|---|---|---|
| 1910 W Large cross | 2,044,000 | 0.65 | 1.75 | 5.00 | 40.00 | — |
| 1910 W Small cross | Inc. above | 6.50 | 25.00 | 65.00 | 370 | — |
| 1912 W | 1,014,000 | 0.65 | 2.50 | 12.50 | 55.00 | — |
| 1914 W | 3,719,000 | 0.65 | 2.50 | 12.50 | 32.00 | — |
| 1916 W | 1,270,000 | 0.65 | 2.50 | 12.50 | 55.00 | — |
| 1917 W | 1,657,000 | 0.65 | 2.00 | 4.50 | 32.00 | — |
| 1918 W Small 8 | 2,365,000 | 0.65 | 2.00 | 6.50 | 40.00 | — |
| 1918 W Wide 8 | Inc. above | 0.65 | 2.00 | 8.00 | 45.00 | — |
| 1919 W | 3,205,000 | 0.65 | 1.50 | 4.00 | 28.00 | — |
| 1927 W | 1,688,000 | 0.65 | 1.75 | 4.00 | 28.00 | — |
| 1928 G | 837,000 | 0.65 | 2.00 | 8.00 | 45.00 | — |
| 1929 G | 1,125,000 | 0.65 | 1.75 | 5.00 | 32.00 | — |

| Date | Mintage | F | VF | XF | Unc | BU |
|---|---|---|---|---|---|---|
| 1930 G | 3,490,000 | 0.50 | 1.50 | 2.50 | 14.50 | — |
| 1931 G | 1,392,000 | 0.50 | 1.50 | 2.50 | 14.50 | — |
| 1932 G | 1,133,000 | 0.50 | 1.50 | 2.50 | 14.50 | — |
| 1933 G | 964,000 | 0.50 | 1.50 | 6.50 | 28.00 | — |
| 1934 G | 1,404,000 | 0.50 | 1.50 | 2.50 | 10.00 | — |
| 1936 G | 1,852,000 | 0.50 | 1.50 | 2.50 | 10.00 | — |
| 1937 G Small G | — | 0.50 | 1.75 | 3.50 | 14.50 | — |
| 1937 G Proof | — | Value: 20.00 | | | | |
| 1937 G Large G | — | 0.75 | 1.75 | 3.50 | 20.00 | — |
| 1938 | 3,679,000 | 0.50 | 1.50 | 2.50 | 6.50 | — |
| 1939 | 2,137,000 | 0.30 | 1.25 | 2.50 | 6.50 | — |
| 1940 | 2,302,000 | 0.30 | 1.25 | 2.50 | 6.50 | — |
| 1941 | 1,960,000 | 0.30 | 1.25 | 2.50 | 6.50 | — |

**25 ORE** KM# 798 **Composition:** Nickel-Bronze

| Date | Mintage | F | VF | XF | Unc | BU |
|---|---|---|---|---|---|---|
| 1921 W | 1,355,000 | 2.00 | 3.50 | 12.50 | 70.00 | — |
| 1940 G | 2,333,000 | 0.15 | 0.50 | 3.00 | 18.00 | — |
| 1941 G | 1,057,000 | 0.15 | 0.50 | 3.00 | 22.00 | — |
| 1946 TS | 2,066,000 | 0.15 | 0.25 | 1.00 | 7.50 | — |
| 1947 TS | 1,594,000 | 0.15 | 0.25 | 1.00 | 7.50 | — |

**25 ORE** KM# 816 **Weight:** 2.3200 g. **Composition:** 0.4000 Silver .0298 oz. ASW

| Date | Mintage | F | VF | XF | Unc | BU |
|---|---|---|---|---|---|---|
| 1943 G | 9,855,000 | BV | 0.50 | 1.00 | 6.50 | — |
| 1944 G | 9,532,000 | BV | 0.50 | 1.00 | 6.50 | — |
| 1945 G | 5,363,000 | BV | 0.50 | 1.00 | 6.50 | — |
| 1945 TS | Inc. above | 0.35 | 0.75 | 2.00 | 10.00 | — |
| 1945 G/TS | Inc. above | BV | 0.60 | 3.00 | 13.50 | — |
| 1946 TS | 2,250,000 | BV | 0.35 | 2.00 | 10.00 | — |
| 1947 TS | 5,633,000 | BV | 0.35 | 1.00 | 4.50 | — |
| 1948 TS | 3,191,000 | BV | 0.35 | 1.00 | 4.50 | — |
| 1949 TS | 5,812,000 | BV | 0.35 | 1.00 | 4.50 | — |
| 1950 TS | 12,059,000 | BV | 0.35 | 1.00 | 3.50 | — |

**25 ORE** KM# 824 **Weight:** 2.3200 g. **Composition:** 0.4000 Silver .0298 oz. ASW

| Date | Mintage | F | VF | XF | Unc | BU |
|---|---|---|---|---|---|---|
| 1952 TS | 2,114,000 | BV | 0.35 | 1.00 | 4.00 | — |
| 1953 TS | 18,177,000 | BV | 0.35 | 1.00 | 2.50 | — |
| 1954 TS | 9,492,000 | BV | 0.35 | 1.00 | 2.50 | — |
| 1955 TS | 7,663,000 | BV | 0.35 | 1.00 | 3.50 | — |
| 1956 TS | 10,931,000 | BV | 0.35 | 1.00 | 3.00 | — |
| 1957 TS | 12,498,000 | BV | 0.35 | 1.00 | 3.00 | — |
| 1958 TS | 6,884,000 | BV | 0.35 | 1.00 | 3.00 | — |
| 1959 TS | 4,772,000 | BV | 0.35 | 1.00 | 3.00 | — |
| 1960 TS | 4,374,000 | BV | 0.50 | 2.00 | 9.00 | — |
| 1961 TS | 8,380,000 | BV | 0.35 | 0.75 | 3.00 | — |

**25 ORE** KM# 836 **Composition:** Copper-Nickel

| Date | Mintage | F | VF | XF | Unc | BU |
|---|---|---|---|---|---|---|
| 1962 U | 4,426,000 | — | 0.25 | 0.75 | 3.00 | — |
| 1963 U | 26,710,000 | — | 0.20 | 0.40 | 2.00 | — |
| 1964 U | 17,300,000 | — | 0.20 | 0.40 | 2.00 | — |
| 1965 U | 6,884,000 | — | 0.20 | 0.40 | 2.00 | — |
| 1966 U | 12,932,000 | — | — | 0.20 | 1.00 | — |
| 1967 U | 28,038,000 | — | — | 0.15 | 0.50 | — |
| 1968 U | 14,366,000 | — | — | 0.15 | 0.50 | — |
| 1969 U | 20,214,000 | — | — | 0.15 | 0.50 | — |
| 1970 U | 23,780,000 | — | — | 0.15 | 0.50 | — |
| 1971 U | 8,606,000 | — | — | 0.15 | 0.50 | — |
| 1972 U | 13,270,000 | — | — | 0.15 | 0.50 | — |
| 1973 U | 76,993,000 | — | — | 0.15 | 0.35 | — |

**25 ORE** KM# 851 **Composition:** Copper-Nickel

| Date | Mintage | F | VF | XF | Unc | BU |
|---|---|---|---|---|---|---|
| 1976 U | 2,815,000 | — | — | 0.15 | 0.50 | — |
| 1977 U | 5,509,000 | — | — | 0.15 | 0.40 | — |
| 1978 U | 54,593,000 | — | — | 0.10 | 0.25 | — |
| 1979 U | 48,423,000 | — | — | 0.10 | 0.25 | — |
| 1980 U | 38,889,000 | — | — | 0.10 | 0.25 | — |
| 1981 U | 46,371,000 | — | — | 0.10 | 0.25 | — |
| 1982 U | 43,218,000 | — | — | 0.10 | 0.25 | — |
| 1983 U | 28,954,000 | — | — | 0.10 | 0.25 | — |
| 1984 U | 7,302,000 | — | — | 0.10 | 0.25 | — |

**50 ORE** KM# 771 **Weight:** 5.0000 g. **Composition:** 0.6000 Silver .0965 oz. ASW

| Date | Mintage | F | VF | XF | Unc | BU |
|---|---|---|---|---|---|---|
| 1906 EB | 319,000 | 2.50 | 8.50 | 32.00 | 150 | — |
| 1907 EB | 803,000 | 2.00 | 5.50 | 28.00 | 100 | — |

**50 ORE** KM# 788 **Weight:** 5.0000 g. **Composition:** 0.6000 Silver .0965 oz. ASW

| Date | Mintage | F | VF | XF | Unc | BU |
|---|---|---|---|---|---|---|
| 1911 W | 472,000 | 3.00 | 7.50 | 25.00 | 110 | — |
| 1912 W | 482,000 | 4.00 | 8.50 | 27.50 | 130 | — |
| 1914 W | 378,000 | 4.00 | 8.50 | 27.50 | 130 | — |
| 1916 W | 537,000 | 3.00 | 7.50 | 22.00 | 110 | — |
| 1919 W | 458,000 | 3.00 | 7.50 | 25.00 | 95.00 | — |
| 1927 W | 672,000 | 1.50 | 3.00 | 13.50 | 65.00 | — |
| 1928 G | 1,135,000 | 1.25 | 2.00 | 6.50 | 40.00 | — |
| 1929 G | 471,000 | 1.50 | 3.00 | 13.50 | 65.00 | — |
| 1930 G | 548,000 | 1.50 | 3.00 | 13.50 | 60.00 | — |
| 1931 G | 671,000 | BV | 2.00 | 11.50 | 45.00 | — |
| 1933 G | 548,000 | BV | 2.00 | 11.50 | 45.00 | — |
| 1934 G | 613,000 | BV | 2.00 | 6.50 | 32.00 | — |
| 1935 G | 691,000 | BV | 2.00 | 6.50 | 32.00 | — |
| 1936 G Short 6 | 823,000 | BV | 2.00 | 6.50 | 32.00 | — |
| 1936 G Long 6 | Inc. above | BV | 3.50 | 11.50 | 55.00 | — |
| 1938 G | 442,000 | BV | 1.25 | 4.50 | 22.00 | — |
| 1939 G | 922,000 | BV | 1.00 | 3.00 | 14.50 | — |
| 1939 G Proof | — | Value: 35.00 | | | | |

**50 ORE** KM# 796 **Composition:** Nickel-Bronze **Note:** Varieties exist.

| Date | Mintage | F | VF | XF | Unc | BU |
|---|---|---|---|---|---|---|
| 1920 W Oval 0 | 480,000 | 1.75 | 10.00 | 38.00 | 160 | — |
| 1920 W Round 0 | Inc. above | 35.00 | 80.00 | 235 | 765 | — |
| 1921 W | 215,000 | 4.00 | 35.00 | 125 | 500 | — |
| 1924 W | 645,000 | 1.50 | 12.50 | 42.00 | 335 | — |
| 1940 G | 1,341,000 | 0.25 | 1.00 | 4.50 | 30.00 | — |
| 1946 TS | 1,426,000 | 0.25 | 1.00 | 3.50 | 20.00 | — |
| 1947 TS | 1,032,000 | 0.25 | 1.00 | 3.50 | 20.00 | — |

**50 ORE** KM# 817 **Weight:** 4.8000 g. **Composition:** 0.4000 Silver .0617 oz. ASW

| Date | Mintage | F | VF | XF | Unc | BU |
|---|---|---|---|---|---|---|
| 1943 G | 785,000 | 1.50 | 3.25 | 9.00 | 45.00 | — |
| 1944 G | 1,540,000 | BV | 1.00 | 2.00 | 11.50 | — |
| 1945 G | 2,585,000 | BV | 1.00 | 2.00 | 11.50 | — |
| 1946 TS | 1,091,000 | BV | 1.00 | 2.00 | 11.50 | — |
| 1947 TS | 1,771,000 | BV | 1.00 | 2.00 | 11.50 | — |
| 1948 TS | 1,731,000 | BV | 1.00 | 2.00 | 11.50 | — |
| 1949 TS | 1,883,000 | BV | 1.00 | 2.00 | 11.50 | — |
| 1950 TS | 3,354,000 | BV | 1.00 | 1.50 | 10.00 | — |

**50 ORE** KM# 825 **Weight:** 4.8000 g. **Composition:** 0.4000 Silver .0617 oz. ASW

| Date | Mintage | F | VF | XF | Unc | BU |
|---|---|---|---|---|---|---|
| 1952 TS | 1,198,000 | BV | 0.75 | 3.00 | 18.00 | — |
| 1953 TS | 4,396,000 | BV | 0.75 | 2.50 | 16.50 | — |
| 1954 TS | 5,779,000 | BV | 0.75 | 2.50 | 16.50 | — |
| 1955 TS | 2,700,000 | BV | 0.75 | 3.50 | 15.00 | — |
| 1956 TS | 7,057,000 | BV | 0.75 | 2.00 | 8.00 | — |
| 1957 TS | 2,405,000 | BV | 0.75 | 2.50 | 15.00 | — |
| 1958 TS | 1,660,000 | BV | 0.75 | 2.50 | 15.00 | — |
| 1961 TS | 2,775,000 | BV | 0.75 | 2.00 | 10.00 | — |

**50 ORE** KM# 837 **Composition:** Copper-Nickel

| Date | Mintage | F | VF | XF | Unc | BU |
|---|---|---|---|---|---|---|
| 1962 U | 1,400,000 | 0.50 | 0.80 | 3.00 | 17.50 | — |
| 1963 U | 5,808,000 | 0.15 | 0.25 | 1.00 | 10.00 | — |
| 1964 U | 5,325,000 | 0.15 | 0.25 | 1.00 | 10.00 | — |
| 1965 U | 6,453,000 | 0.15 | 0.25 | 0.50 | 6.00 | — |
| 1966 U | 6,309,000 | 0.15 | 0.25 | 0.40 | 5.00 | — |
| 1967 U | 7,890,000 | 0.15 | 0.25 | 0.40 | 5.00 | — |
| 1968 U | 9,198,000 | — | 0.15 | 0.25 | 1.00 | — |
| 1969 U | 7,265,000 | — | 0.15 | 0.25 | 1.00 | — |
| 1970 U | 9,426,000 | — | 0.15 | 0.25 | 1.00 | — |
| 1971 U | 7,218,000 | — | 0.15 | 0.25 | 1.00 | — |
| 1972 U | 7,388,000 | — | 0.15 | 0.25 | 1.00 | — |
| 1973 U | 52,467,000 | — | 0.15 | 0.20 | 0.60 | — |

**50 ORE** KM# 855 **Composition:** Copper-Nickel

| Date | Mintage | F | VF | XF | Unc | BU |
|---|---|---|---|---|---|---|
| 1976 U | 2,589,000 | — | 0.15 | 0.25 | 0.70 | — |
| 1977 U | 10,360,000 | — | — | 0.15 | 0.30 | — |
| 1978 U | 33,282,000 | — | — | 0.15 | 0.30 | — |
| 1979 U | 30,274,000 | — | — | 0.15 | 0.30 | — |
| 1980 U | 28,666,000 | — | — | 0.15 | 0.30 | — |
| 1981 U | 15,516,000 | — | — | 0.15 | 0.30 | — |
| 1982 U | 14,778,000 | — | — | 0.15 | 0.30 | — |
| 1983 U | 17,530,000 | — | — | 0.15 | 0.30 | — |
| 1984 U | 27,541,000 | — | — | 0.15 | 0.30 | — |
| 1985 U | 14,062,000 | — | — | 0.15 | 0.30 | — |
| 1986 U | 937,000 | — | — | 0.20 | 0.50 | — |
| 1987 D | 1,077,000 | — | — | 0.20 | 0.50 | — |
| 1988 D | 532,000 | — | — | 0.20 | 0.50 | — |
| 1989 D | 606,000 | — | — | 0.20 | 0.50 | — |
| 1990 D | 31,935,000 | — | — | 0.10 | 0.15 | — |
| 1991 D | 16,315,000 | — | — | 0.10 | 0.15 | — |

**50 ORE** KM# 878 **Composition:** Bronze

| Date | Mintage | F | VF | XF | Unc | BU |
|---|---|---|---|---|---|---|
| 1992 B | 39,531,000 | — | — | 0.15 | 0.30 | — |
| 1992 B | — | — | — | 0.15 | 0.30 | — |
| 1993 B | 644,000 | — | — | 0.20 | 0.50 | — |
| 1994 B | 518,000 | — | — | 0.20 | 0.50 | — |
| 1995 B | 487,000 | — | — | 0.10 | 0.20 | — |
| 1996 B | 248,000 | — | — | 0.10 | 0.20 | — |

| Date | Mintage | F | VF | XF | Unc | BU |
|---|---|---|---|---|---|---|
| 1997 B | 70,000 | — | — | 0.10 | 0.20 | — |
| 1998 B | — | — | — | 0.10 | 0.20 | — |
| 1999 B | 5,065,000 | — | — | 0.10 | 0.20 | — |
| 2000 B | 33,060,252 | — | — | 0.10 | 0.20 | — |

**KRONA** KM# 760 **Weight:** 7.5000 g. **Composition:** 0.8000 Silver .1929 oz. ASW **Obverse:** Without initials below bust

| Date | Mintage | F | VF | XF | Unc | BU |
|---|---|---|---|---|---|---|
| 1901/898 EB | 271,000 | 8.00 | 32.00 | 135 | 550 | — |
| 1901 EB | Inc. above | 6.50 | 30.00 | 120 | 450 | — |
| 1903 EB | 473,000 | 5.50 | 27.50 | 85.00 | 325 | — |
| 1904 EB | 564,000 | 8.00 | 17.50 | 85.00 | 375 | — |

**KRONA** KM# 772 **Weight:** 7.5000 g. **Composition:** 0.8000 Silver .1929 oz. ASW

| Date | Mintage | F | VF | XF | Unc | BU |
|---|---|---|---|---|---|---|
| 1906 EB | 427,000 | 5.00 | 20.00 | 75.00 | 345 | — |
| 1907 EB | 1,058,000 | 3.75 | 14.50 | 55.00 | 225 | — |

**KRONA** KM# 786.1 **Weight:** 7.5000 g. **Composition:** 0.8000 Silver .1929 oz. ASW **Obverse:** With dots in date

| Date | Mintage | F | VF | XF | Unc | BU |
|---|---|---|---|---|---|---|
| 1.9.1.0 W | 643,000 | 3.00 | 12.50 | 40.00 | 140 | — |
| 1.9.1.2 W | 303,000 | 8.00 | 22.50 | 90.00 | 360 | — |
| 1.9.1.3 W | 353,000 | 3.50 | 12.50 | 40.00 | 150 | — |
| 1.9.1.4 W | 622,000 | 3.00 | 12.50 | 35.00 | 140 | — |
| 1.9.1.5 W | 1,416,000 | 3.00 | 7.50 | 25.00 | 120 | — |
| 1.9.1.6/5 W | 1,139,000 | 4.00 | 14.00 | 50.00 | 180 | — |
| 1.9.1.6 W | Inc. above | 3.00 | 12.00 | 35.00 | 150 | — |
| 1.9.1.8 W | 258,000 | 3.00 | 6.00 | 27.00 | 160 | — |
| 1.9.2.3 W | 746,000 | 2.00 | 8.00 | 25.00 | 120 | — |
| 1.9.2.4 W | 2,066,000 | 2.00 | 6.00 | 17.00 | 85.00 | — |

**KRONA** KM# 786.2 **Weight:** 7.5000 g. **Composition:** 0.8000 Silver .1929 oz. ASW **Obverse:** Without dots in date

| Date | Mintage | F | VF | XF | Unc | BU |
|---|---|---|---|---|---|---|
| 1924 W | Inc. above | 1.50 | 5.00 | 20.00 | 80.00 | — |
| 1925 W | 370,000 | 3.00 | 8.50 | 40.00 | 160 | — |
| 1926 W | 465,000 | 2.50 | 7.50 | 25.00 | 110 | — |
| 1927 G | 401,000 | 3.00 | 8.50 | 35.00 | 145 | — |
| 1928 G | 739,000 | 1.50 | 4.00 | 20.00 | 70.00 | — |
| 1929 G | 1,346,000 | 1.25 | 3.00 | 12.00 | 40.00 | — |
| 1930 G | 1,744,000 | 1.25 | 2.50 | 6.50 | 30.00 | — |
| 1931 G | 1,008,000 | 1.25 | 2.50 | 6.50 | 30.00 | — |
| 1932 G | 1,036,000 | 1.25 | 2.50 | 6.50 | 30.00 | — |
| 1933 G | 1,045,000 | 1.25 | 2.50 | 6.50 | 30.00 | — |
| 1934 G | 586,000 | 1.25 | 2.50 | 12.00 | 50.00 | — |
| 1935 G | 1,604,000 | 1.00 | 2.00 | 3.00 | 12.00 | — |
| 1936 G | 3,223,000 | 1.00 | 2.00 | 3.00 | 10.00 | — |
| 1937 G | 2,667,000 | 1.00 | 2.00 | 3.00 | 10.00 | — |
| 1938 G | 1,911,000 | 1.00 | 2.00 | 3.00 | 10.00 | — |
| 1938 G Proof | — | Value: 25.00 | | | | |
| 1939 G | 7,589,000 | 1.00 | 2.00 | 3.00 | 5.00 | — |
| 1940 G | 6,917,000 | 1.00 | 2.00 | 3.00 | 5.00 | — |
| 1941/4 G | 2,183,000 | 4.00 | 8.00 | 17.50 | 45.00 | — |
| 1941 G | Inc. above | 1.00 | 2.00 | 3.50 | 10.00 | — |
| 1942 G | 240,000 | 35.00 | 65.00 | 150 | 400 | — |

**KRONA** KM# 814 **Weight:** 7.0000 g. **Composition:** 0.4000 Silver .0900 oz. ASW

| Date | Mintage | F | VF | XF | Unc | BU |
|---|---|---|---|---|---|---|
| 1942 G | 5,650,000 | BV | 1.00 | 3.00 | 15.00 | — |
| 1943 G Plain 4 | 7,916,000 | BV | 1.00 | 3.00 | 15.00 | — |
| 1943 G Crosslet 4 | Inc. above | BV | 1.00 | 3.00 | 15.00 | — |
| 1944 G | 7,423,000 | BV | 1.00 | 2.00 | 7.00 | — |
| 1945 G | 7,359,000 | BV | 1.00 | 2.00 | 7.00 | — |
| 1945 TS | Inc. above | BV | 1.25 | 2.75 | 12.50 | — |
| 1945 TS/G | Inc. above | BV | 1.50 | 3.00 | 17.50 | — |
| 1946 TS | 19,170,000 | BV | 1.00 | 1.75 | 5.00 | — |
| 1947 TS | 9,124,000 | BV | 1.00 | 1.75 | 5.00 | — |
| 1948 TS | 10,447,000 | BV | 1.00 | 1.75 | 5.00 | — |
| 1949 TS | 7,981,000 | BV | 1.00 | 1.75 | 5.00 | — |
| 1950 TS | 5,310,000 | BV | 1.00 | 1.50 | 7.00 | — |

**KRONA** KM# 826 **Weight:** 7.0000 g. **Composition:** 0.4000 Silver .0900 oz. ASW

| Date | Mintage | F | VF | XF | Unc | BU |
|---|---|---|---|---|---|---|
| 1952 TS | 1,102,000 | BV | 1.00 | 2.50 | 20.00 | — |
| 1953/2 TS | Inc. above | BV | 1.50 | 5.00 | 25.00 | — |
| 1953 TS | 3,306,000 | BV | 1.00 | 2.50 | 17.50 | — |
| 1954 TS | 6,461,000 | BV | 1.00 | 2.50 | 12.50 | — |
| 1955 TS | 4,141,000 | BV | 1.00 | 2.50 | 12.50 | — |
| 1956 TS | 6,227,000 | BV | 1.00 | 2.50 | 7.00 | — |
| 1957 TS | 3,544,000 | BV | 1.00 | 2.50 | 8.00 | — |
| 1958 TS | 1,439,000 | BV | 1.50 | 3.50 | 17.50 | — |
| 1959 TS | 1,187,000 | 1.25 | 2.50 | 6.00 | 30.00 | — |
| 1960 TS | 4,085,000 | BV | 1.00 | 1.75 | 5.00 | — |
| 1961 TS | 4,283,000 | BV | 1.00 | 1.75 | 5.00 | — |
| 1961 U | 2,973,000 | BV | 1.25 | 2.50 | 17.50 | — |
| 1962 U | 6,839,000 | BV | 1.00 | 1.75 | 5.00 | — |
| 1963 U | 14,228,000 | BV | BV | 1.25 | 3.00 | — |
| 1964 U | 15,973,000 | BV | BV | 1.00 | 2.75 | — |
| 1965 U | 18,639,000 | BV | BV | 1.00 | 2.75 | — |
| 1966 U | 22,396,000 | BV | BV | 1.00 | 2.00 | — |
| 1967 U | 17,235,000 | BV | BV | 1.00 | 2.00 | — |
| 1968 U | 12,326,000 | BV | BV | 1.00 | 2.00 | — |

**KRONA** KM# 826a **Composition:** Copper-Nickel Clad Copper

| Date | Mintage | F | VF | XF | Unc | BU |
|---|---|---|---|---|---|---|
| 1968 U | 5,177,000 | — | 0.30 | 1.00 | 3.00 | — |
| 1969 U | 30,856,000 | — | 0.30 | 0.40 | 1.25 | — |
| 1970 U | 25,315,000 | — | 0.30 | 0.40 | 1.25 | — |
| 1971 U | 18,342,000 | — | 0.30 | 0.40 | 1.25 | — |
| 1972 U | 21,941,000 | — | 0.30 | 0.40 | 1.25 | — |
| 1973 U | 142,000,000 | — | 0.30 | 0.40 | 1.25 | — |

**KRONA** KM# 852 **Composition:** Copper-Nickel Clad Copper

| Date | Mintage | F | VF | XF | Unc | BU |
|---|---|---|---|---|---|---|
| 1976 U | 4,321,000 | — | 0.30 | 0.50 | 1.25 | — |
| 1977 U | 80,478,000 | — | 0.30 | 0.40 | 0.60 | — |
| 1978 U | 81,408,000 | — | 0.30 | 0.40 | 0.60 | — |
| 1979 U | 47,450,000 | — | 0.30 | 0.40 | 0.60 | — |
| 1980 U | 51,694,000 | — | 0.30 | 0.40 | 0.60 | — |
| 1981 U | 62,079,000 | — | 0.30 | 0.40 | 0.60 | — |

**KRONA** KM# 852a **Composition:** Copper-Nickel

| Date | Mintage | F | VF | XF | Unc | BU |
|---|---|---|---|---|---|---|
| 1982 U | 24,837,000 | — | — | 0.30 | 0.50 | — |
| 1983 U | 23,530,000 | — | — | 0.30 | 0.50 | — |
| 1984 U | 37,805,000 | — | — | 0.30 | 0.50 | — |
| 1985 U | 4,893,000 | — | — | 0.30 | 0.55 | — |
| 1986 U | 901,000 | — | — | 0.40 | 0.60 | — |
| 1987 B | 21,543,000 | — | — | 0.30 | 0.50 | — |
| 1988 B | 30,342,000 | — | — | 0.30 | 0.45 | — |
| 1989 B | 55,963,000 | — | — | — | 0.25 | — |
| 1990 B | 54,470,000 | — | — | — | 0.25 | — |

| Date | Mintage | F | VF | XF | Unc | BU |
|---|---|---|---|---|---|---|
| 1991 B | 34,250,000 | — | — | — | 0.25 | — |
| 1992 B | 16,771,000 | — | — | — | 0.25 | — |
| 1993 B | 407,000 | — | 0.30 | 0.50 | 0.80 | — |
| 1994 B | 547,000 | — | 0.30 | 0.50 | 0.80 | — |
| 1995 B | 500,000 | — | 0.30 | 0.50 | 0.80 | — |
| 1996 B | 324,000 | — | — | — | 0.20 | — |
| 1997 B | 25,042,000 | — | — | — | 0.20 | — |
| 1998 B | 39,748,000 | — | — | — | 0.20 | — |
| 1999 B | 55,019,000 | — | — | — | 0.20 | — |
| 2000 B | 104,213,074 | — | — | — | 0.20 | — |

**KRONA** KM# 894 **Weight:** 6.9800 g. **Composition:** Copper-Nickel **Ruler:** Carl XVI Gustaf **Obverse:** King's new portrait **Reverse:** Crown and denomination **Edge:** Reeded **Size:** 24.9 mm.

| Date | Mintage | F | VF | XF | Unc | BU |
|---|---|---|---|---|---|---|
| 2001B | 2,978,113 | — | — | — | 0.50 | — |

**2 KRONOR** KM# 807 **Weight:** 15.0000 g. **Composition:** 0.8000 Silver .3858 oz. ASW **Subject:** 300th Anniversary - Settlement of Delaware

| Date | Mintage | F | VF | XF | Unc | BU |
|---|---|---|---|---|---|---|
| ND(1938) G | 509,000 | 3.00 | 5.50 | 10.00 | 20.00 | — |

**2 KRONOR** KM# 761 **Weight:** 15.0000 g. **Composition:** 0.8000 Silver .3858 oz. ASW **Obverse:** Without initials below bust

| Date | Mintage | F | VF | XF | Unc | BU |
|---|---|---|---|---|---|---|
| 1903 EB | 64,000 | 30.00 | 85.00 | 210 | 765 | — |
| 1904 EB | 175,000 | 10.00 | 40.00 | 130 | 385 | — |

**2 KRONOR** KM# 773 **Weight:** 15.0000 g. **Composition:** 0.8000 Silver .3858 oz. ASW

| Date | Mintage | F | VF | XF | Unc | BU |
|---|---|---|---|---|---|---|
| 1906 EB | 112,000 | 8.00 | 22.00 | 85.00 | 325 | — |
| 1907 EB | 301,000 | 6.00 | 18.00 | 70.00 | 300 | — |

**2 KRONOR** KM# 776 **Weight:** 15.0000 g. **Composition:** 0.8000 Silver .3858 oz. ASW **Subject:** Golden Wedding Anniversary

| Date | Mintage | F | VF | XF | Unc | BU |
|---|---|---|---|---|---|---|
| 1907 | 251,000 | 4.00 | 6.00 | 9.00 | 18.00 | — |

**2 KRONOR** **KM# 787** **Weight:** 15.0000 g. **Composition:** 0.8000 Silver .3858 oz. ASW

| Date | Mintage | F | VF | XF | Unc | BU |
|---|---|---|---|---|---|---|
| 1910 W Initial far from date | 375,000 | 6.00 | 15.00 | 60.00 | 175 | — |
| 1910 W | Inc. above | 35.00 | 100 | 325 | 800 | — |
| 1912 W | 157,000 | 8.00 | 25.00 | 85.00 | 250 | — |
| 1913 W | 305,000 | 5.00 | 12.00 | 50.00 | 175 | — |
| 1914 W | 192,000 | 5.00 | 15.00 | 60.00 | 185 | — |
| 1915 W | 156,000 | 7.00 | 17.50 | 65.00 | 200 | — |
| 1922 W | 202,000 | 5.00 | 8.00 | 30.00 | 90.00 | — |
| 1924 W | 199,000 | 5.00 | 8.00 | 30.00 | 95.00 | — |
| 1926 W | 222,000 | 5.00 | 7.00 | 25.00 | 85.00 | — |
| 1928 G | 160,000 | 5.00 | 8.00 | 30.00 | 140 | — |
| 1929 G | 184,000 | 4.75 | 7.00 | 25.00 | 90.00 | — |
| 1930 G | 178,000 | 4.75 | 7.00 | 25.00 | 80.00 | — |
| 1931 G | 211,000 | 4.00 | 5.00 | 10.00 | 25.00 | — |
| 1934 G | 273,000 | 3.00 | 5.00 | 10.00 | 25.00 | — |
| 1935 G | 211,000 | 3.00 | 5.00 | 10.00 | 25.00 | — |
| 1936 G | 491,000 | 2.25 | 5.00 | 8.00 | 16.00 | — |
| 1937 G | 130,000 | 5.50 | 8.00 | 15.00 | 60.00 | — |
| 1937 G Proof | — | Value: 200 | | | | |
| 1938 G | 639,000 | BV | 4.00 | 7.00 | 15.00 | — |
| 1938 G Proof | — | Value: 30.00 | | | | |
| 1939 G | 1,200,000 | BV | 4.00 | 7.00 | 12.00 | — |
| 1939 G Proof | — | Value: 30.00 | | | | |
| 1940 G | 518,000 | BV | 4.00 | 7.00 | 12.00 | — |
| 1940 G Serif 4 | Inc. above | 3.00 | 4.50 | 8.50 | 25.00 | — |

**2 KRONOR** **KM# 799** **Weight:** 15.0000 g. **Composition:** 0.8000 Silver .3858 oz. ASW **Subject:** 400th Anniversary of Political Liberty

| Date | Mintage | F | VF | XF | Unc | BU |
|---|---|---|---|---|---|---|
| 1921 W | 265,000 | 3.00 | 5.00 | 8.00 | 18.00 | — |

**2 KRONOR** **KM# 805** **Weight:** 15.0000 g. **Composition:** 0.8000 Silver .3858 oz. ASW **Subject:** 300th Anniversary - Death of Gustaf II Adolf

| Date | Mintage | F | VF | XF | Unc | BU |
|---|---|---|---|---|---|---|
| 1932 G | 254,000 | 4.00 | 6.00 | 12.50 | 25.00 | — |

**2 KRONOR** **KM# 815** **Weight:** 14.0000 g. **Composition:** 0.4000 Silver .1800 oz. ASW

| Date | Mintage | F | VF | XF | Unc | BU |
|---|---|---|---|---|---|---|
| 1942 G | 200,000 | 2.00 | 3.50 | 6.00 | 27.50 | — |
| 1943 G | 272,000 | 3.00 | 6.00 | 12.50 | 60.00 | — |
| 1944 G | 627,000 | BV | 2.00 | 4.00 | 16.00 | — |
| 1945 G | 970,000 | BV | 2.00 | 4.00 | 16.00 | — |
| 1945 G Without dots in motto | Inc. above | 6.00 | 12.00 | 26.00 | 75.00 | — |
| 1945 TS | Inc. above | BV | 2.00 | 4.00 | 16.00 | — |
| 1945 TS/G | Inc. above | 2.00 | 4.00 | 8.00 | 30.00 | — |
| 1946 TS | 978,000 | BV | 1.50 | 3.00 | 12.00 | — |
| 1947 TS | 1,466,000 | BV | 1.50 | 3.00 | 12.00 | — |
| 1948 TS | 282,000 | BV | 2.00 | 4.00 | 16.00 | — |
| 1949 TS | 332,000 | BV | 2.00 | 4.00 | 16.00 | — |
| 1950/1 TS | 3,727,000 | BV | 1.50 | 3.00 | 12.00 | — |
| 1950 TS | Inc. above | BV | 1.50 | 3.00 | 9.00 | — |

**2 KRONOR** **KM# 827** **Weight:** 14.0000 g. **Composition:** 0.4000 Silver .1800 oz. ASW

| Date | Mintage | F | VF | XF | Unc | BU |
|---|---|---|---|---|---|---|
| 1952 TS | 315,000 | 1.50 | 2.50 | 5.00 | 18.00 | — |
| 1953 TS | 1,009,000 | BV | 1.25 | 2.50 | 8.00 | — |
| 1954 TS | 2,301,000 | BV | 1.25 | 2.50 | 8.00 | — |
| 1955 TS | 1,138,000 | BV | 1.25 | 2.50 | 8.00 | — |
| 1956 TS | 1,708,000 | BV | 1.25 | 2.50 | 8.00 | — |
| 1957 TS | 689,000 | BV | 1.25 | 4.50 | 17.50 | — |
| 1958 TS | 1,104,000 | BV | 1.25 | 2.00 | 7.00 | — |
| 1959 TS | 581,000 | BV | 1.50 | 4.75 | 18.00 | — |
| 1961 TS | 534,000 | BV | 1.50 | 3.50 | 13.00 | — |
| 1963 U | 1,469,000 | BV | BV | 2.00 | 4.50 | — |
| 1964 U | 1,213,000 | BV | BV | 2.00 | 4.00 | — |
| 1965 U | 1,190,000 | BV | BV | 2.00 | 4.00 | — |
| 1966 U | 989,000 | BV | BV | 2.00 | 4.50 | — |

**2 KRONOR** **KM# 827a** **Composition:** Copper-Nickel

| Date | Mintage | F | VF | XF | Unc | BU |
|---|---|---|---|---|---|---|
| 1968 U | 1,171,000 | 0.50 | 0.65 | 1.50 | 3.50 | — |
| 1969 U | 1,148,000 | 0.50 | 0.65 | 0.85 | 2.25 | — |
| 1970 U | 1,159,000 | 0.50 | 0.65 | 0.85 | 2.25 | — |
| 1971 U | 1,213,000 | 0.50 | 0.65 | 1.00 | 2.75 | — |

**5 KRONOR** **KM# 766** **Weight:** 2.2402 g. **Composition:** 0.9000 Gold .0648 oz. AGW

| Date | Mintage | F | VF | XF | Unc | BU |
|---|---|---|---|---|---|---|
| 1901 EB | 109,000 | 35.00 | 50.00 | 65.00 | 100 | — |

**5 KRONOR** **KM# 797** **Weight:** 2.2402 g. **Composition:** 0.9000 Gold .0648 oz. AGW

| Date | Mintage | F | VF | XF | Unc | BU |
|---|---|---|---|---|---|---|
| 1920 W | 103,000 | 30.00 | 45.00 | 60.00 | 90.00 | — |

**5 KRONOR** **KM# 828** **Weight:** 22.7000 g. **Composition:** 0.4000 Silver .2920 oz. ASW **Subject:** 70th Birthday of Gustaf VI Adolf

| Date | Mintage | F | VF | XF | Unc | BU |
|---|---|---|---|---|---|---|
| ND(1925) TS | 219,000 | 5.00 | 10.00 | 15.00 | 25.00 | — |

**5 KRONOR** **KM# 806** **Weight:** 25.0000 g. **Composition:** 0.9000 Silver .7234 oz. ASW **Subject:** 500th Anniversary of Riksdag

| Date | Mintage | F | VF | XF | Unc | BU |
|---|---|---|---|---|---|---|
| ND(1935) G | 664,000 | 5.00 | 7.50 | 12.50 | 20.00 | — |

**5 KRONOR** **KM# 829** **Weight:** 18.0000 g. **Composition:** 0.4000 Silver .2315 oz. ASW **Note:** Regular issue.

| Date | Mintage | F | VF | XF | Unc | BU |
|---|---|---|---|---|---|---|
| 1954 TS | 1,510,000 | — | BV | 3.00 | 6.00 | — |
| 1955 TS | 3,569,000 | — | BV | 2.50 | 5.00 | — |
| 1971 U | 713,000 | — | BV | 2.50 | 5.00 | — |

**5 KRONOR** **KM# 830** **Weight:** 18.0000 g. **Composition:** 0.4000 Silver .2315 oz. ASW **Subject:** Constitution Sesquicentennial

| Date | Mintage | F | VF | XF | Unc | BU |
|---|---|---|---|---|---|---|
| 1959 TS | 504,000 | — | BV | 4.00 | 7.00 | — |

**5 KRONOR** **KM# 838** **Weight:** 18.0000 g. **Composition:** 0.4000 Silver .2315 oz. ASW **Subject:** 80th Birthday of Gustaf VI Adolf

| Date | Mintage | F | VF | XF | Unc | BU |
|---|---|---|---|---|---|---|
| ND(1962) U | 256,000 | — | 7.50 | 12.50 | 27.50 | — |

**Note:** 596,525 melted

**5 KRONOR** KM# 839 **Weight:** 18.0000 g. **Composition:** 0.4000 Silver .2315 oz. ASW **Subject:** 100th Anniversary of Constitution Reform

| Date | Mintage | F | VF | XF | Unc | BU |
|---|---|---|---|---|---|---|
| 1966 U | 1,024,000 | — | BV | 2.75 | 5.00 | — |

**5 KRONOR** KM# 846 **Composition:** Copper-Nickel Clad Nickel

| Date | Mintage | F | VF | XF | Unc | BU |
|---|---|---|---|---|---|---|
| 1972 U | 21,736,000 | — | 1.25 | 1.50 | 2.25 | — |
| 1973 U | 1,139,000 | — | 1.25 | 1.50 | 4.00 | — |

**5 KRONOR** KM# 853 **Composition:** Copper-Nickel

| Date | Mintage | F | VF | XF | Unc | BU |
|---|---|---|---|---|---|---|
| 1976 U | 2,253,000 | — | — | 1.25 | 3.50 | — |
| 1977 U | 3,985,000 | — | — | 1.25 | 2.00 | — |
| 1978 U | 3,952,000 | — | — | 1.25 | 2.00 | — |
| 1979 U | 3,164,000 | — | — | 1.25 | 2.00 | — |
| 1980 U | 2,222,000 | — | — | 1.25 | 2.50 | — |
| 1981 U | 5,507,000 | — | — | 1.25 | 2.00 | — |
| 1982 U | 36,604,000 | — | — | 1.25 | 1.50 | — |
| 1983 U | 31,364,000 | — | — | 1.25 | 1.50 | — |
| 1984 U | 27,687,000 | — | — | 1.25 | 1.50 | — |
| 1985 U | 10,375,000 | — | — | 1.25 | 1.50 | — |
| 1986 U | 714,000 | — | — | 1.25 | 4.00 | — |
| 1987 D | 15,117,000 | — | — | 1.25 | 1.50 | — |
| 1988 D | 18,644,000 | — | — | 1.25 | 1.50 | — |
| 1989 D | 961,000 | — | — | 1.25 | 3.00 | — |
| 1990 D | 10,558,000 | — | — | 1.25 | 1.50 | — |
| 1991 D | 15,793,000 | — | — | 1.25 | 1.50 | — |
| 1991 U | 800 | — | 80.00 | 120 | 175 | — |
| 1992 D | 5,351,000 | — | — | 1.25 | 1.50 | — |

**5 KRONOR** KM# 853a **Composition:** Copper-Nickel Clad Nickel

| Date | Mintage | F | VF | XF | Unc | BU |
|---|---|---|---|---|---|---|
| 1993 B | 275,000 | — | — | — | 1.50 | — |
| 1994 B | 173,000 | — | — | — | 2.25 | — |
| 1995 B | 187,000 | — | — | — | 0.80 | — |
| 1996 B | 180,000 | — | — | — | 0.80 | — |
| 1997 B | 174,000 | — | — | — | 0.80 | — |
| 1998 B | 85,000 | — | — | — | 0.80 | — |
| 1999 B | 96,000 | — | — | — | 0.80 | — |
| 2000 B | 3,851,326 | — | — | — | 0.80 | — |

**5 KRONOR** KM# 885 **Composition:** Copper-Nickel Clad Nickel **Subject:** 50th Anniversary - United Nations

| Date | Mintage | F | VF | XF | Unc | BU |
|---|---|---|---|---|---|---|
| ND(1995) B | 300,000 | — | — | — | 4.00 | — |

**10 KRONOR** KM# 767 **Weight:** 4.4803 g. **Composition:** 0.9000 Gold .1296 oz. AGW **Obverse:** Large head

| Date | Mintage | F | VF | XF | Unc | BU |
|---|---|---|---|---|---|---|
| 1901 EB | 213,000 | 40.00 | 60.00 | 90.00 | 125 | — |
| 1901 EB Proof | Inc. above | Value: 525 | | | | |

**10 KRONOR** KM# 800 **Weight:** 8.9606 g. **Composition:** 0.9000 Gold .2593 oz. AGW

| Date | Mintage | F | VF | XF | Unc | BU |
|---|---|---|---|---|---|---|
| 1925 W | 387,000 | 175 | 300 | 400 | 600 | — |

**10 KRONOR** KM# 847 **Weight:** 18.0000 g. **Composition:** 0.8300 Silver .4803 oz. ASW **Subject:** 90th Birthday of Gustaf VI Adolf

| Date | Mintage | F | VF | XF | Unc | BU |
|---|---|---|---|---|---|---|
| 1972 U | 2,000,000 | — | BV | 4.00 | 7.00 | — |

**10 KRONOR** KM# 877 **Composition:** Copper-Aluminum-Zinc

| Date | Mintage | F | VF | XF | Unc | BU |
|---|---|---|---|---|---|---|
| 1991 B Medal | 106,548,000 | — | — | 2.25 | 3.25 | — |
| 1991 B Coin | Inc. above | 22.50 | 40.00 | 55.00 | 100 | — |
| 1992 B | 42,507,000 | — | — | — | 1.75 | — |
| 1993 B | 201,107,000 | — | — | — | 1.75 | — |
| 1994 B | 573,000 | — | — | — | 1.75 | — |
| 1995 B | 524,000 | — | — | — | 1.75 | — |
| 1996 B | 295,000 | — | — | — | 1.75 | — |
| 1997 B | 332,000 | — | — | — | 1.75 | — |
| 1999 B | 81,000 | — | — | — | 1.75 | — |
| 2000 B | 8,520,983 | — | — | — | 1.75 | — |

**10 KRONOR** KM# 895 **Weight:** 6.5700 g. **Composition:** Copper-Aluminum-Zinc **Ruler:** Carl XVI Gustaf **Obverse:** King's new portrait **Reverse:** Three crowns and denomination **Edge:** Reeded and plain sections **Size:** 20.4 mm.

| Date | Mintage | F | VF | XF | Unc | BU |
|---|---|---|---|---|---|---|
| 2001B | — | — | — | — | 1.75 | — |

**20 KRONOR** KM# 765 **Weight:** 8.9606 g. **Composition:** 0.9000 Gold .2593 oz. AGW **Obverse:** Large head

| Date | Mintage | F | VF | XF | Unc | BU |
|---|---|---|---|---|---|---|
| 1901 EB | 227,000 | 90.00 | 110 | 135 | 225 | — |
| 1902 EB | 114,000 | 90.00 | 110 | 145 | 235 | — |

**50 KRONOR** KM# 848 **Weight:** 27.0000 g. **Composition:** 0.9250 Silver .8029 oz. ASW **Subject:** Constitutional Reform

| Date | Mintage | F | VF | XF | Unc | BU |
|---|---|---|---|---|---|---|
| 1975 U | 500,000 | — | — | 11.50 | 15.00 | — |

**50 KRONOR** KM# 854 **Weight:** 27.0000 g. **Composition:** 0.9250 Silver .8029 oz. ASW **Subject:** Wedding of King Carl XVI Gustaf and Queen Silvia

| Date | Mintage | F | VF | XF | Unc | BU |
|---|---|---|---|---|---|---|
| ND(1976) U | 2,000,000 | — | — | 12.00 | 14.50 | — |

**100 KRONOR** KM# 861 **Weight:** 16.0000 g. **Composition:** 0.9250 Silver .4759 oz. ASW **Subject:** Parliament

| Date | Mintage | F | VF | XF | Unc | BU |
|---|---|---|---|---|---|---|
| 1983 | 400,000 | — | — | — | 22.50 | — |

**100 KRONOR** KM# 863 **Weight:** 16.0000 g. **Composition:** 0.9250 Silver .4759 oz. ASW **Subject:** Stockholm Conference

| Date | Mintage | F | VF | XF | Unc | BU |
|---|---|---|---|---|---|---|
| 1984 | 300,000 | — | — | — | 22.50 | — |

**100 KRONOR** KM# 864 **Weight:** 16.0000 g. **Composition:** 0.9250 Silver .4759 oz. ASW **Subject:** International Youth Year

| Date | Mintage | F | VF | XF | Unc | BU |
|---|---|---|---|---|---|---|
| 1985 | 120,000 | — | — | — | 22.50 | — |

**100 KRONOR** KM# 865 **Weight:** 16.0000 g. **Composition:** 0.9250 Silver .4759 oz. ASW **Subject:** European Music Year

| Date | Mintage | F | VF | XF | Unc | BU |
|---|---|---|---|---|---|---|
| 1985 | 120,000 | — | — | — | 22.50 | — |

**100 KRONOR** **KM# 866** **Weight:** 16.0000 g. **Composition:** 0.9250 Silver .4759 oz. ASW **Subject:** International Year of the Forest

| Date | Mintage | F | VF | XF | Unc | BU |
|---|---|---|---|---|---|---|
| 1985 | 120,000 | — | — | — | 30.00 | — |

**100 KRONOR** **KM# 867.1** **Weight:** 16.0000 g. **Composition:** 0.9250 Silver .4759 oz. ASW **Subject:** 350th Anniversary of Swedigh Colony in Delaware **Obverse:** Large head

| Date | Mintage | F | VF | XF | Unc | BU |
|---|---|---|---|---|---|---|
| ND(1988) | 32,000 | — | — | — | 32.50 | — |

**100 KRONOR** **KM# 867.2** **Weight:** 16.0000 g. **Composition:** 0.9250 Silver .4759 oz. ASW **Obverse:** Small head

| Date | Mintage | F | VF | XF | Unc | BU |
|---|---|---|---|---|---|---|
| ND(1988) | 118,000 | — | — | — | — | — |

**200 KRONOR** **KM# 860** **Weight:** 27.0000 g. **Composition:** 0.9250 Silver .8029 oz. ASW **Subject:** Swedish Royal Succession Law

| Date | Mintage | F | VF | XF | Unc | BU |
|---|---|---|---|---|---|---|
| 1980 U Prooflike | 500,000 | — | — | — | 37.50 | — |

**200 KRONOR** **KM# 862** **Weight:** 27.0000 g. **Composition:** 0.9250 Silver .8029 oz. ASW **Subject:** 10th Anniversary of Reign

| Date | Mintage | F | VF | XF | Unc | BU |
|---|---|---|---|---|---|---|
| 1983 | 100,000 | — | — | — | 42.50 | — |

**200 KRONOR** **KM# 869** **Weight:** 27.0000 g. **Composition:** 0.9250 Silver .8029 oz. ASW **Subject:** Ice Hockey

| Date | Mintage | F | VF | XF | Unc | BU |
|---|---|---|---|---|---|---|
| 1989 | Est. 80,000 | — | — | — | 40.00 | — |

**200 KRONOR** **KM# 875** **Weight:** 27.0000 g. **Composition:** 0.9250 Silver .8029 oz. ASW **Subject:** War Ship - Vasa

| Date | Mintage | F | VF | XF | Unc | BU |
|---|---|---|---|---|---|---|
| 1990 | 50,000 | — | — | — | 40.00 | — |

**200 KRONOR** **KM# 879** **Weight:** 27.0000 g. **Composition:** 0.9250 Silver .8029 oz. ASW **Subject:** 200th Anniversary - Death of Gustaf III

| Date | Mintage | F | VF | XF | Unc | BU |
|---|---|---|---|---|---|---|
| ND(1992) | 50,000 | — | — | — | 40.00 | — |

**200 KRONOR** **KM# 881** **Weight:** 27.0000 g. **Composition:** 0.9250 Silver .8029 oz. ASW **Subject:** 20th Anniversary of Reign

| Date | Mintage | F | VF | XF | Unc | BU |
|---|---|---|---|---|---|---|
| 1993 | 50,000 | — | — | — | 40.00 | — |

**200 KRONOR** **KM# 882** **Weight:** 27.0000 g. **Composition:** 0.9250 Silver .8029 oz. ASW **Subject:** 50th Birthday of Queen Silvia

| Date | Mintage | F | VF | XF | Unc | BU |
|---|---|---|---|---|---|---|
| ND(1993) | 49,000 | — | — | — | 40.00 | — |
| ND(1993) Prooflike | 1,000 | — | — | — | 75.00 | — |

**200 KRONOR** **KM# 886** **Weight:** 27.0000 g. **Composition:** 0.9250 Silver .8029 oz. ASW **Subject:** 1000th Anniversary - Swedish Mint

| Date | Mintage | F | VF | XF | Unc | BU |
|---|---|---|---|---|---|---|
| ND(1995) | 49,000 | — | — | — | 40.00 | — |
| ND(1995) Prooflike | 1,000 | — | — | — | 75.00 | — |

**200 KRONOR** **KM# 888** **Weight:** 27.0000 g. **Composition:** 0.9250 Silver .8029 oz. ASW **Subject:** 50th Birthday - King Carl XVI Gustaf

| Date | Mintage | F | VF | XF | Unc | BU |
|---|---|---|---|---|---|---|
| ND(1996) | 49,000 | — | — | — | 45.00 | — |
| ND(1996) Prooflike | 1,000 | — | — | — | 75.00 | — |

**200 KRONOR** **KM# 890** **Weight:** 27.0000 g. **Composition:** 0.9250 Silver .8029 oz. ASW **Subject:** Kelmer Union **Obverse:** King's portrait **Reverse:** Queen Margareta's portrait and castle

| Date | Mintage | F | VF | XF | Unc | BU |
|---|---|---|---|---|---|---|
| 1997 | Est. 50,000 | — | — | — | 45.00 | — |

**200 KRONOR** **KM# 892** **Weight:** 27.0000 g. **Composition:** 0.9250 Silver .8029 oz. ASW **Subject:** 25th Anniversary - Reign of Carl XVI **Obverse:** King Carl XVI Gustaf

| Date | Mintage | F | VF | XF | Unc | BU |
|---|---|---|---|---|---|---|
| 1998 Proof | 50,000 | Value: 40.00 | | | | |

**200 KRONOR** **KM# 896** **Weight:** 27.2500 g. **Composition:** 0.9250 Silver .8104 oz. ASW **Ruler:** Carl XVI Gustaf **Subject:** 25th Wedding Anniversary **Obverse:** King and Queen's portraits **Reverse:** National arms **Edge:** Plain **Size:** 36 mm.

| Date | Mintage | F | VF | XF | Unc | BU |
|---|---|---|---|---|---|---|
| ND(2001) Proof | 50,000 | Value: 45.00 | | | | |

**1000 KRONOR** **KM# 868** **Weight:** 5.8000 g. **Composition:** 0.9000 Gold .1678 oz. AGW **Subject:** 350th anniversary of Swedish Colony in Delaware

| Date | Mintage | F | VF | XF | Unc | BU |
|---|---|---|---|---|---|---|
| ND(1988) | 10,000 | — | — | 270 | 400 | — |

**1000 KRONOR** **KM# 870** **Weight:** 5.8000 g. **Composition:** 0.9000 Gold .1678 oz. AGW **Subject:** Ice Hockey

| Date | Mintage | F | VF | XF | Unc | BU |
|---|---|---|---|---|---|---|
| 1989 | 20,000 | — | — | 180 | 220 | — |

**1000 KRONOR** **KM# 876** **Weight:** 5.8000 g. **Composition:** 0.9000 Gold .1678 oz. AGW **Subject:** The Vasa - Arms

| Date | Mintage | F | VF | XF | Unc | BU |
|---|---|---|---|---|---|---|
| 1990 | 15,000 | — | — | 200 | 245 | — |

**1000 KRONOR** **KM# 880** **Weight:** 5.8000 g. **Composition:** 0.9000 Gold .1678 oz. AGW **Subject:** 200th Anniversary - Death of Gustaf III

| Date | Mintage | F | VF | XF | Unc | BU |
|---|---|---|---|---|---|---|
| ND(1992) | 15,000 | — | — | 200 | 245 | — |

**1000 KRONOR** **KM# 883** **Weight:** 5.8000 g. **Composition:** 0.9000 Gold .1678 oz. AGW **Subject:** 20th Anniversary of Reign **Obverse:** King's bust

| Date | Mintage | F | VF | XF | Unc | BU |
|---|---|---|---|---|---|---|
| 1993 | 15,000 | — | — | 170 | 210 | — |

**1000 KRONOR** **KM# 884** **Weight:** 5.8000 g. **Composition:** 0.9000 Gold .1678 oz. AGW **Subject:** 50th Birthday of Queen Silvia

| Date | Mintage | F | VF | XF | Unc | BU |
|---|---|---|---|---|---|---|
| ND(1993) | 14,000 | — | — | 170 | 210 | — |
| ND(1993) Prooflike | 1,000 | — | — | — | 385 | — |

**1000 KRONOR** **KM# 887** **Weight:** 5.8000 g. **Composition:** 0.9000 Gold .1678 oz. AGW **Subject:** 100th Anniversary - Swedish Mint

| Date | Mintage | F | VF | XF | Unc | BU |
|---|---|---|---|---|---|---|
| ND(1995) | 14,000 | — | — | — | 210 | — |
| ND(1995) Prooflike | 1,000 | — | — | — | 350 | — |

**1000 KRONOR** **KM# 889** **Weight:** 5.8000 g. **Composition:** 0.9000 Gold .1678 oz. AGW **Subject:** 50th Birthday - King Carl XVI Gustaf

| Date | Mintage | F | VF | XF | Unc | BU |
|---|---|---|---|---|---|---|
| ND(1996) | 14,000 | — | — | — | 210 | — |
| ND(1996) Prooflike | 1,000 | — | — | — | 350 | — |

**1000 KRONOR** **KM# 891** **Weight:** 5.8000 g. **Composition:** 0.9000 Gold .1678 oz. AGW **Subject:** Kalmar Union - Queen Margareta **Obverse:** King's bust

| Date | Mintage | F | VF | XF | Unc | BU |
|---|---|---|---|---|---|---|
| 1997 | Est. 15,000 | — | — | — | 185 | — |

**1000 KRONOR** **KM# 893** **Weight:** 5.8000 g. **Composition:** 0.9000 Gold .1678 oz. AGW **Subject:** 25th Anniversary - Reign of King Carl XVI **Obverse:** King Carl XVI Gustaf

| Date | Mintage | F | VF | XF | Unc | BU |
|---|---|---|---|---|---|---|
| 1998 Proof | 15,000 | Value: 190 | | | | |

## PATTERNS

Including off metal strikes

| KM# | Date | Mintage | Identification | Mkt Val |
|---|---|---|---|---|
| Pn99 | 1901 | — | 2 Ore. Iron. KM#716 | — |
| Pn100 | 1901 | — | 5 Kronor. Bronze. KM#766 | — |
| Pn101 | 1909 | — | 2 Ore. Bronze. Flat-based 2 | — |
| Pn102 | 1909 | — | 5 Ore. Bronze. Flat-based 5 | — |
| Pn103 | 1913 | — | 2 Kronor. Bronze. KM#787 | — |
| Pn104 | 1916 | — | Ore. Iron. KM#777.2 | — |
| Pn105 | 1916 | — | 2 Ore. Iron. KM#778 | — |
| Pn106 | 1916 | — | 5 Ore. Iron. KM#779.2 | — |
| Pn107 | 1918 W | — | 10 Ore. Iron. Center hole | — |
| Pn108 | 1918 W | — | 25 Ore. Iron. Center hole | — |
| Pn109 | 1918 W | — | 25 Ore. Silver. Center hole | — |
| Pn110 | 1918 W | — | 50 Ore. Iron. Center hole | — |
| Pn111 | 1918 W | — | 50 Ore. Silver. Center hole | — |
| Pn112 | 1918 W | — | Krona. Iron. Center hole | — |
| Pn113 | 1918 W | — | Krona. Nickel. Center hole | — |
| Pn114 | 1918 W | — | Krona. Silver. Center hole | — |
| Pn115 | 1918 | — | 5 Kronor. Nickel. KM#797 | — |
| Pn116 | 1919 | — | Ore. Bronze. Center hole | — |
| Pn117 | 1919 | — | 5 Ore. Iron. Center hole | — |
| Pn118 | 1919 | — | 5 Ore. Bronze. Center hole | — |
| Pn119 | 1919 | — | 10 Ore. Nickel. KM#780 | — |
| Pn120 | 1919 | — | 2 Kronor. Bronze. KM#787 | — |
| Pn121 | 1920 | — | 2 Ore. Bronze. Copper hole | — |
| Pn122 | 1920 | — | 5 Ore. Bronze. Center hole | — |
| Pn123 | 1920 W | — | 50 Ore. Silver. | — |
| Pn124 | 1921 | — | 2 Kronor. Bronze. KM#787 | — |
| Pn125 | 1949 | — | 5 Ore. Bronze. "PROV" | — |
| PnA126 | 1949 | — | 50 Ore. Aluminum. "PROV" | — |
| Pn126 | 1950 | — | Ore. Copper Plated Iron. KM#810 | — |
| Pn127 | 1950 | — | Ore. Copper Plated Iron. "PROV" | — |
| Pn128 | 1950 | — | 2 Ore. Copper Plated Iron. KM#811 | — |
| Pn129 | 1950 | — | 2 Ore. Copper Plated Iron. "PROV" | — |
| Pn130 | 1950 | — | 5 Ore. Tombac Plated Iron. KM#812 | — |
| Pn131 | 1950 | — | 5 Ore. Copper Plated Iron. "PROV" | — |
| Pn132 | 1950 | — | 10 Ore. Nickel Plated Iron. "PROV" | — |
| Pn133 | 1950 | — | 25 Ore. Nickel Plated Iron. "PROV" | — |
| Pn134 | 1951 | — | 2 Ore. Bronze. "PROV" | — |
| Pn135 | 1951 | — | 2 Ore. Iron. "PROV" | — |
| Pn136 | 1951 | — | 50 Ore. Silver. "PROV" | — |
| Pn137 | 1951 | — | Krona. Silver. Plain edge. "PROV" | — |
| Pn138 | 1951 | — | Krona. Silver. Reeded edge. "PROV" | — |
| Pn139 | 1951 TS | — | Krona. Silver. "PROV" | — |
| Pn140 | 1951 TS | — | 5 Kronor. Silver. "PROV" | — |
| Pn141 | 1952 TS | — | 5 Ore. Bronze. "PROV" | — |
| Pn142 | 1952 TS | — | 10 Ore. Silver. "PROV" | — |
| Pn143 | 1952 TS | — | 10 Ore. Copper-Nickel. "PROV" | — |
| Pn144 | 1952 TS | — | 10 Ore. Silver. "PROV" | — |
| Pn145 | 1952 TS | — | 25 Ore. Silver. "PROV" | — |
| Pn146 | 1952 TS | — | 50 Ore. Silver. "PROV", high relief | — |
| Pn147 | 1952 TS | — | 50 Ore. Silver. "PROV", low relief | — |
| Pn148 | 1952 TS | — | Krona. Silver. "PROV" | — |
| Pn149 | 1952 TS | — | Krona. Silver. "PROV"; different head | — |
| Pn150 | 1952 TS | — | 5 Kronor. Silver. Plain edge. "PROV" | — |
| Pn151 | 1952 TS | — | 5 Kronor. Silver. Reeded edge. "PROV" | — |
| Pn152 | 1953 TS | — | 5 Kronor. Silver. Plain edge. "PROV" | — |
| Pn153 | 1953 TS | — | 5 Kronor. Silver. Reeded edge. "PROV" | — |
| Pn154 | 1953 TS | — | 5 Kronor. Silver. "PROV"; small value | — |
| Pn155 | 1953 TS | — | 5 Kronor. Silver. "PROV"; large value | — |
| Pn156 | 1954 TS | — | 5 Kronor. Silver. "PROV" | — |
| Pn157 | 1970 U | — | Ore. Iron. 1.5000 g. KM#820 | 175 |

## MINT SETS

| KM# | Date | Mintage | Identification | Issue Price | Mkt Val |
|---|---|---|---|---|---|
| MSA1 | 1955, 1964, 1965 (9) | — | KM#820-822, 826-827, 829, 835-837 | — | 25.00 |
| MS1 | 1973 (6) | 20,000 | KM#826A, 835-837, 845-846 | 5.00 | 22.50 |
| MS2 | 1976 (6) | 61,234 | KM#849-853, 855 | 5.00 | 12.00 |
| MS3 | 1976 (6) | 10,000 | KM#849-853, 855 | 5.00 | 12.00 |
| MS4 | 1977 (6) | 43,346 | KM#849-853, 855 | 5.00 | 15.00 |
| MS5 | 1977 (6) | 5,800 | KM#849-853, 855 | 5.00 | 17.50 |
| MS6 | 1978 (6) | 20,115 | KM#849-853, 855 | 5.00 | 15.00 |
| MS7 | 1978 (6) | 1,500 | KM#849-853, 855 | 5.00 | 30.00 |
| MS8 | 1978 (6) | 31,245 | KM#849-853, 855 | 5.00 | 20.00 |
| MS9 | 1979 (6) | 10,200 | KM#849-853, 855 | 5.00 | 13.00 |
| MS10 | 1979 (6) | 1,900 | KM#849-853, 855 | 5.00 | 25.00 |
| MS11 | 1979 (6) | 38,957 | KM#849-853, 855 | 5.00 | 17.50 |
| MS12 | 1979 (6) | 9,871 | KM#849-853, 855 | 5.00 | 25.00 |
| MS13 | 1980 (6) | 10,140 | KM#849-853, 855 | 5.00 | 10.00 |
| MS14 | 1980 (6) | 2,000 | KM#849-853, 855 | 5.00 | 25.00 |
| MS15 | 1980 (6) | 45,495 | KM#849-853, 855 | 5.50 | 12.50 |
| MS16 | 1980 (6) | 9,880 | KM#849-853, 855 | 5.50 | 25.00 |
| MS17 | 1981 (6) | 11,927 | KM#849a, 850-853, 855 | 5.50 | 7.50 |
| MS18 | 1981 (6) | 2,000 | KM#849a, 850-853, 855 | 5.50 | 25.00 |
| MS19 | 1981 (6) | 65,338 | KM#849a, 850-853, 855 | 5.50 | 7.50 |
| MS20 | 1981 (6) | 5,000 | KM#849a, 850-853, 855 | 5.50 | 30.00 |
| MS21 | 1982 (6) | 9,463 | KM#849a, 850-851, 852a, 853 | 5.50 | 7.50 |
| MS22 | 1982 (6) | 2,300 | KM#849a, 850-851, 852a, 853 | 5.50 | 15.00 |
| MS23 | 1982 (6) | 58,772 | KM#849a, 850-851, 852a, 853 | 5.50 | 8.50 |
| MS24 | 1982 (6) | 4,978 | KM#849a, 850-851, 852a, 853 | 5.50 | 30.00 |
| MS25 | 1983 (6) | 10,300 | KM#849a, 850-851, 852a, 853 | 6.00 | 7.50 |
| MS26 | 1983 (6) | 2,750 | KM#849a, 850-851, 852a, 853 | 6.00 | 17.50 |

| KM# | Date | Mintage | Identification | Issue Price | Mkt Val |
|---|---|---|---|---|---|
| MS27 | 1983 (6) | 57,205 | KM#849a, 850-851, 852a, 853 | 6.00 | 8.50 |
| MS28 | 1983 (6) | 5,017 | KM#849a, 850-851, 852a, 853 | 6.00 | 32.50 |
| MS29 | 1984 (6) | 10,100 | KM#849a, 850-851, 852a, 853 | 6.00 | 7.50 |
| MS30 | 1984 (6) | 1,600 | KM#849a, 850-851, 852a, 853 | 6.00 | 30.00 |
| MS31 | 1984 (6) | 70,849 | KM#849a, 850-851, 852a, 853 | 6.00 | 7.50 |
| MS32 | 1984 (6) | 4,271 | KM#849a, 850-851, 852a, 853 | 6.00 | 32.50 |
| MS33 | 1985 (4) | 8,000 | KM#850, 852a, 853, 855 | 6.50 | 9.00 |
| MS34 | 1985 (4) | 1,445 | KM#850, 852a, 853, 855 | 6.50 | 30.00 |
| MS35 | 1985 (4) | 52,462 | KM#850, 852a, 853, 855 | 6.50 | 8.00 |
| MS36 | 1985 (4) | 2,717 | KM#850, 852a, 853, 855 | 6.50 | 42.50 |
| MS37 | 1986 (4) | 16,265 | KM#850, 852a, 853, 855 | 6.50 | 17.50 |
| MS38 | 1986 (4) | 1,880 | KM#850, 852a, 853, 855 | 6.50 | 30.00 |
| MS39 | 1986 (4) | 54,890 | KM#850, 852a, 853, 855 | 6.50 | 20.00 |
| MS40 | 1986 (4) | 967 | KM#850, 852a, 853, 855 | 6.50 | 100 |
| MS41 | 1987 (4) | 5,600 | KM#850, 852a, 853, 855 | 6.50 | 8.50 |
| MS42 | 1987 (4) | 1,100 | KM#850, 852a, 853, 855 | 6.55 | 30.00 |
| MS43 | 1987 (4) | 70,060 | KM#850, 852a, 853, 855 | 6.50 | 7.50 |
| MS44 | 1987 (4) | 557 | KM#850, 852a, 853, 855 | 6.50 | 200 |
| MS45 | 1988 (4) | 4,815 | KM#850, 852a, 853, 855 | 6.50 | 10.00 |
| MS46 | 1988 (4) | 2,456 | KM#850, 852a, 853, 855 | 6.50 | 17.50 |
| MS47 | 1988 (4) | 56,753 | KM#850, 852a, 853, 855 | 6.50 | 14.50 |
| MS48 | 1988 (4) | 1,777 | KM#850, 852a, 853, 855 | 6.50 | 50.00 |
| MS49 | 1989 (4) | 7,170 | KM#850, 852a, 853, 855 | 6.50 | 2.50 |
| MS50 | 1989 (4) | 56,895 | KM#850, 852a, 853, 855 | 6.50 | 10.00 |
| MS51 | 1989 (4) | 2,780 | KM#850, 852a, 853, 855 | — | 18.50 |
| MS52 | 1989 (4) | 1,000 | KM#850, 852a, 853, 855 | — | 30.00 |
| MS53 | 1990 (4) | 6,503 | KM#850, 852a, 853, 855 | 6.50 | 80.00 |
| MS54 | 1990 (4) | 55,265 | KM#850, 852a, 853, 855 | 6.50 | 80.00 |
| MS55 | 1990 (4) | 1,000 | KM#850, 852a, 853, 855 | — | 15.50 |
| MS56 | 1990 (4) | 2,492 | KM#850, 852a, 853, 855 | — | 12.00 |
| MS57 | 1991 (5) | 8,079 | KM#850, 852a, 853, 855, 877 | — | 22.50 |
| MS58 | 1991 (5) | 1,680 | KM#850, 852a, 853, 855, 877 | — | 22.50 |
| MS59 | 1991 (5) | 62,517 | KM#850, 852a, 853, 855, 877 | — | 25.00 |
| MS60 | 1991 (5) | 2,884 | KM#850, 852a, 853, 855, 877 | — | 27.50 |
| MS61 | 1991 (5) | 5,000 | KM#850 (3), 855 (2), medal | — | 12.00 |
| MS62 | 1992 (4) | 5,600 | KM#852a, 853, 877-878 | 6.50 | 10.00 |
| MS63 | 1992 (4) | 1,840 | KM#852a, 853, 877-878 | 6.50 | 10.00 |
| MS64 | 1992 (4) | 61,183 | KM#852a, 853, 877-878 | 6.50 | 11.00 |
| MS65 | 1992 (4) | 2,187 | KM#852a, 853, 877-878 | 6.50 | 12.50 |
| MS66 | 1993 (4) | 4,784 | KM#852a, 853a, 877, 878 | 6.50 | 12.50 |
| MS67 | 1993 (4) | 2,016 | KM#852a, 853a, 877, 878 | 6.50 | 11.00 |
| MS68 | 1993 (4) | 57,700 | KM#852a, 853a, 877, 878 | 6.50 | 12.50 |
| MS69 | 1993 (4) | 2,164 | KM#852a, 853a, 877, 878 | 6.50 | 15.00 |
| MS70 | 1993 (4) | 4,956 | KM#852a, 853a, 877, 878 | — | 17.50 |
| MS71 | 1994 (4) | 5,360 | KM#852a, 853a, 877, 878 | — | 12.50 |
| MS72 | 1994 (4) | 2,240 | KM#852a, 853a, 877, 878 | — | 16.00 |
| MS73 | 1994 (4) | 48,881 | KM#852a, 853a, 877, 878, mint medal | — | 10.00 |
| MS74 | 1994 (4) | 1,966 | KM#852a, 853a, 877, 878, mint medal | — | 17.50 |
| MS75 | 1994 (4) | 9,950 | KM#852a, 853a, 877, 878, mint medal | — | 10.00 |
| MS76 | 1995 (5) | 5,350 | KM#852a, 853a, 877, 878, 885 | 14.00 | 18,350 |
| MS77 | 1995 (4) | 45,836 | KM#852a, 877, 878, 885, medal | 20.00 | 15.00 |
| MS78 | 1995 (5) | 4,650 | KM#852a, 853a, 877, 878, 885 | — | 25.00 |
| MS79 | 1995 (4) | 2,479 | KM#852a, 853a, 877, 878, 885, medal | — | 25.00 |
| MS80 | 1995 (4) | 5,350 | KM#852a, 877, 878, 885, medal | — | 10.00 |
| MS81 | 1996 (4) | 42,729 | KM#852a, 853a, 877, 878 | 11.05 | 12.50 |
| MS82 | 1996 (4) | 2,000 | KM#852a, 853a, 877, 878 | 11.05 | 17.50 |
| MS83 | 1996 (4) | 7,100 | KM#852a, 853a, 877, 878 | 7.55 | 10.00 |
| MS84 | 1996 (4) | 2,500 | KM#852a, 853a, 877, 878 | 7.55 | 14.50 |
| MS85 | 1996 (4) | 5,481 | KM#852a, 853a, 877, 878 | 11.05 | 12.50 |
| MS86 | 1997 (4) | 39,470 | KM#852a, 853a, 877, 878 | 11.05 | 12.50 |
| MS87 | 1997 (4) | 1,997 | KM#852a, 853a, 877, 878 | 11.05 | 17.50 |
| MS88 | 1997 (4) | 5,100 | KM#852a, 853a, 877, 878 | 7.55 | 10.00 |
| MS89 | 1997 (4) | 2,200 | KM#852a, 853a, 877, 878 | 7.55 | 12.50 |
| MS90 | 1997 (4) | 4,954 | KM#852a, 853a, 877, 878 | 11.05 | 12.50 |
| MS91 | 1998 (4) | 7,067 | KM#852a, 853a, 877, 878 | 13.34 | 15.00 |
| MS92 | 1998 (4) | 5,170 | KM#852A-853A, 877-878 | — | 9.75 |
| MS93 | 1998 (4) | 2,000 | KM#852A-853A, 877-878 | — | 9.75 |
| MS94 | 1998 (4) | 34,750 | KM#852A-853A, 877-878 | — | 15.00 |
| MS95 | 1998 (4) | 1,980 | KM#852A-853A, 877-878 | — | 15.00 |
| MS96 | 1999 (4) | 4,480 | KM#852A-853A, 877-878 | — | 9.75 |
| MS97 | 1999 (4) | 2,080 | KM#852A-853A, 877-878 | — | 9.75 |
| MS98 | 1999 (4) | 33,334 | KM#852A-853A, 877-878 | — | 15.00 |
| MS99 | 1999 (4) | 1,970 | KM#852A-853A, 877-878 | — | 15.00 |
| MS100 | 1999 (4) | 8,045 | KM#852A-853A, 877-878 | — | 12.50 |
| MS101 | 2000 (4) | 5,000 | KM#852A-853A, 877-878 | — | 8.00 |
| MS102 | 2000 (4) | 1,000 | KM#852A-853A, 877-878 | — | 8.00 |
| MS103 | 2000 (4) | 30,912 | KM#852A-853A, 877-878 | — | 12.50 |
| MS104 | 2000 (4) | 1,801 | KM#852A-853A, 877-878 | — | 12.50 |
| MS105 | 2000 (4) | 7,209 | KM#852A-853A, 877-878 | — | 12.50 |
| MS106 | 2000 (4) | 14,300 | KM#852A-853A, 877-878 | — | 20.00 |

## PROOF-LIKE SETS (PL)

| KM# | Date | Mintage | Identification | Issue Price | Mkt Val |
|---|---|---|---|---|---|
| PL1 | 1993 (2) | 1,000 | KM#882, 884 | — | 460 |
| PL2 | 1995 (2) | 1,000 | KM#886, 887 | — | 425 |
| PL3 | ND(1996) (2) | 1,000 | KM#888, 889 | — | 425 |

# SWITZERLAND

The Swiss Confederation, located in central Europe north of Italy and south of Germany, has an area of 15,941 sq. mi. (41,290 sq. km.) and a population of *6.6 million. Capital: Bern. The economy centers about a well developed manufacturing industry. Machinery, chemicals, watches and clocks, and textiles are exported.

Switzerland, the habitat of lake dwellers in prehistoric times, was peopled by the Celtic Helvetians when Julius Caesar made it a part of the Roman Empire in 58 B.C. After the decline of Rome, Switzerland was invaded by Teutonic tribes, who established small temporal holdings which in the Middle Ages, became a federation of fiefs of the Holy Roman Empire. As a nation, Switzerland originated in 1291 when the districts of Nidwalden, Schwyz and Uri united to defeat Austria and attain independence as the Swiss Confederation. After acquiring new cantons in the 14th century, Switzerland was made independent from the Holy Roman Empire by the 1648 Treaty of Westphalia. The revolutionary armies of Napoleonic France occupied Switzerland and set up the Helvetian Republic, 1798-1803. After the fall of Napoleon, the Congress of Vienna, 1815, recognized the independence of Switzerland and guaranteed its neutrality. The Swiss Constitutions of 1848 and 1874 established a union modeled upon that of the United States.

**MINT MARKS**

B - Bern
BA - Basel
BB - Strasbourg
S – Solothurn

**NOTE**: The coinage of Switzerland has been struck at the Bern Mint since 1853 with but a few exceptions. All coins minted there carry a B' mint mark through 1969, except for the 2-Centime and 2-Franc values where the mintmark was discontinued after 1968. In 1968 and 1969 some issues were struck at both Bern (B) and in London (no mint mark).

**MONETARY SYSTEM**

100 Rappen (Centimes) = 1 Franc

# CONFEDERATION

## DECIMAL COINAGE

100 Rappen (Centimes) = 1 Franc

**RAPPEN** **KM# 3.2** **Composition:** Bronze **Obverse:** Thin cross in shield

| Date | Mintage | F | VF | XF | Unc | BU |
|---|---|---|---|---|---|---|
| 1902B | 950,000 | — | 50.00 | 80.00 | 150 | 200 |
| 1903B | 1,000,000 | — | 25.00 | 35.00 | 65.00 | 90.00 |
| 1904B | 1,000,000 | — | 25.00 | 35.00 | 60.00 | 85.00 |
| 1905B | 2,000,000 | — | 8.00 | 12.00 | 16.00 | 24.00 |
| 1906B | 1,000,000 | — | 17.50 | 30.00 | 40.00 | 54.00 |
| 1907B | 2,000,000 | — | 8.00 | 15.00 | 18.00 | 25.00 |
| 1908B | 3,000,000 | — | 2.50 | 6.00 | 12.00 | 18.00 |
| 1909B | 1,000,000 | — | 15.00 | 20.00 | 35.00 | 54.00 |
| 1910B | 500,000 | — | 8.00 | 14.00 | 18.00 | 25.00 |
| 1911B | 500,000 | — | 8.00 | 14.00 | 20.00 | 25.00 |
| 1912B | 2,000,000 | — | 2.50 | 5.00 | 14.00 | 21.50 |
| 1913B | 3,000,000 | — | 1.00 | 2.00 | 4.00 | 7.00 |
| 1914B | 3,500,000 | — | 1.50 | 3.50 | 7.00 | 12.00 |
| 1915B | 3,000,000 | — | 1.50 | 3.50 | 7.00 | 12.00 |
| 1917B | 2,000,000 | — | 3.50 | 6.00 | 18.00 | 30.00 |
| 1918B | 3,000,000 | — | 1.50 | 3.00 | 6.00 | 10.00 |
| 1919B | 3,000,000 | — | 1.50 | 3.00 | 6.00 | 110 |
| 1920B | 1,000,000 | — | 3.00 | 7.00 | 10.00 | 15.00 |
| 1921B | 3,000,000 | — | 1.50 | 3.00 | 5.00 | 8.00 |
| 1924B | 2,000,000 | — | 4.00 | 8.00 | 15.00 | 20.00 |
| 1925/4B | 2,500,000 | — | 4.50 | 10.00 | 20.00 | 30.00 |
| 1925B | Inc. above | — | 2.00 | 4.00 | 6.00 | 10.00 |
| 1926B | 2,000,000 | — | 2.00 | 4.00 | 6.50 | 10.00 |
| 1927B | 1,500,000 | — | 3.00 | 6.00 | 11.00 | 15.00 |
| 1928B | 2,000,000 | — | 1.50 | 3.00 | 8.50 | 13.00 |
| 1929B | 4,000,000 | — | 0.50 | 1.00 | 3.00 | 5.00 |
| 1930B | 2,500,000 | — | 1.50 | 3.50 | 5.00 | 8.00 |
| 1931B | 5,000,000 | — | 0.50 | 1.25 | 3.00 | 6.00 |
| 1932B | 5,000,000 | — | 0.50 | 1.00 | 3.00 | 6.00 |
| 1933B | 3,000,000 | — | 0.75 | 1.50 | 3.00 | 6.00 |
| 1934B | 3,000,000 | — | 0.50 | 1.00 | 3.00 | 6.00 |
| 1936B | 2,000,000 | — | 1.50 | 2.50 | 6.00 | 12.00 |
| 1937B | 2,400,000 | — | 0.50 | 1.00 | 3.00 | 5.00 |
| 1938B | 5,300,000 | — | 0.50 | 1.00 | 3.00 | 5.00 |
| 1939B | 10,000 | — | 35.00 | 50.00 | 70.00 | 110 |
| 1940B | 3,027,000 | — | 1.00 | 1.50 | 6.00 | 9.00 |
| 1941B | 12,794,000 | — | 0.25 | 0.50 | 1.50 | 2.50 |

**RAPPEN** **KM# 3a** **Composition:** Zinc

| Date | Mintage | F | VF | XF | Unc | BU |
|---|---|---|---|---|---|---|
| 1942B | 17,969,000 | — | 0.50 | 1.00 | 3.50 | 6.00 |
| 1943B | 8,647,000 | — | 0.75 | 1.25 | 3.50 | 6.00 |
| 1944B | 11,825,000 | — | 0.50 | 1.00 | 3.50 | 6.00 |
| 1945B | 2,800,000 | — | 6.00 | 9.00 | 17.50 | 27.50 |
| 1946B | 12,063,000 | — | 0.50 | 1.00 | 3.50 | 6.00 |

**RAPPEN** **KM# 46** **Composition:** Bronze

| Date | Mintage | F | VF | XF | Unc | BU |
|---|---|---|---|---|---|---|
| 1948B | 10,500,000 | — | 0.10 | 0.50 | 2.00 | 5.00 |
| 1949B | 11,100,000 | — | 0.10 | 0.50 | 2.00 | 5.00 |
| 1950B | 3,610,000 | — | 1.00 | 2.50 | 4.00 | 7.00 |
| 1951B | 22,624,000 | — | 0.10 | 0.30 | 2.00 | 4.00 |
| 1952B | 11,520,000 | — | 0.10 | 0.30 | 2.00 | 4.00 |
| 1953B | 5,947,000 | — | 0.10 | 0.30 | 2.00 | 4.00 |
| 1954B | 5,175,000 | — | 0.10 | 0.30 | 2.00 | 4.00 |
| 1955B | 5,282,000 | — | 0.10 | 0.60 | 2.00 | 4.00 |
| 1956B | 4,960,000 | — | 0.10 | 0.30 | 2.00 | 4.00 |
| 1957B | 15,226,000 | — | 0.10 | 0.15 | 0.35 | 0.50 |
| 1958B | 20,142,000 | — | 0.10 | 0.15 | 0.35 | 0.50 |
| 1959B | 5,582,000 | — | 0.10 | 0.15 | 0.35 | 0.50 |
| 1962B | 5,010,000 | — | 0.10 | 0.15 | 0.35 | 0.50 |
| 1963B | 15,920,000 | — | — | 0.10 | 0.25 | 0.35 |
| 1966B | 5,030,000 | — | — | 0.10 | 0.25 | 0.35 |
| 1967B | 3,020,000 | — | — | 0.10 | 0.25 | 0.35 |
| 1968B | 4,920,000 | — | — | 0.10 | 0.25 | 0.35 |
| 1969B | 4,810,000 | — | — | 0.10 | 0.25 | 0.35 |
| 1970 | 7,810,000 | — | — | 0.10 | 0.25 | 0.35 |
| 1971 | 5,030,000 | — | — | 0.10 | 0.25 | 0.35 |
| 1973 | 3,000,000 | — | — | 0.10 | 0.25 | 0.35 |
| 1974 | 3,007,000 | — | — | 0.10 | 0.25 | 0.35 |
| 1974 Proof | 2,400 | Value: 10.00 | | | | |
| 1975 | 3,010,000 | — | — | 0.10 | 0.25 | 0.35 |
| 1975 Proof | 10,000 | Value: 1.25 | | | | |
| 1976 | 3,005,000 | — | — | 0.10 | 0.25 | 0.35 |
| 1976 Proof | 5,130 | Value: 1.50 | | | | |
| 1977 | 2,007,000 | — | — | 0.10 | 0.25 | 0.35 |
| 1977 Proof | 7,030 | Value: 1.00 | | | | |
| 1978 | 2,009,999 | — | — | 0.10 | 0.25 | 0.35 |
| 1978 Proof | 10,000 | Value: 1.00 | | | | |
| 1979 | 1,030,000 | — | — | 0.10 | 0.35 | 0.50 |
| 1979 Proof | 10,000 | Value: 1.00 | | | | |
| 1980 | 1,030,000 | — | — | 0.10 | 0.35 | 0.50 |
| 1980 Proof | 10,000 | Value: 1.00 | | | | |
| 1981 | 4,935,000 | — | — | 0.10 | 0.25 | 0.35 |
| 1981 Proof | 10,000 | Value: 1.00 | | | | |
| 1982 | 6,655,000 | — | — | 0.10 | 0.20 | 0.30 |
| 1982 Proof | 10,000 | Value: 2.00 | | | | |
| 1983 | 4,030,999 | — | — | 0.10 | 0.25 | 0.35 |
| 1983 Proof | 11,000 | Value: 1.00 | | | | |
| 1984 | 3,995,000 | — | — | 0.10 | 0.25 | 0.35 |
| 1984 Proof | 14,000 | Value: 1.00 | | | | |
| 1985 | 3,027,000 | — | — | 0.10 | 0.25 | 0.35 |
| 1985 Proof | 12,000 | Value: 1.00 | | | | |
| 1986B | 2,031,000 | — | — | 0.10 | 0.50 | 1.00 |
| 1986B Proof | 10,000 | Value: 1.00 | | | | |
| 1987B | 1,028,000 | — | — | 0.10 | 0.50 | 1.00 |
| 1987B Proof | 8,800 | Value: 1.25 | | | | |
| 1988B | 2,029,000 | — | — | 0.10 | 0.35 | 0.50 |
| 1988B Proof | 9,000 | Value: 1.25 | | | | |
| 1989B | 2,032,000 | — | — | 0.10 | 0.35 | 0.50 |
| 1989B Proof | 8,800 | Value: 1.25 | | | | |
| 1990B | 1,032,000 | — | — | — | 0.50 | 1.00 |
| 1990B Proof | 8,900 | Value: 1.25 | | | | |
| 1991B | 536,000 | — | — | — | 1.50 | 2.50 |
| 1991B Proof | 9,900 | Value: 5.00 | | | | |
| 1992B | 527,000 | — | — | — | 1.50 | 2.50 |
| 1992B Proof | 7,450 | Value: 3.50 | | | | |
| 1993B | 522,000 | — | — | — | 3.00 | 4.00 |
| 1993B Proof | 6,200 | Value: 5.00 | | | | |
| 1994B | 2,023,000 | — | — | — | 0.25 | 0.50 |
| 1994B Proof | 6,100 | Value: 1.00 | | | | |
| 1995B | 6,024,000 | — | — | — | 0.25 | 0.50 |
| 1995B Proof | 6,100 | Value: 1.00 | | | | |
| 1996B | 1,022,999 | — | — | — | 0.50 | 1.00 |
| 1996B Proof | 6,100 | Value: 2.00 | | | | |
| 1997B | 1,022,999 | — | — | — | 0.50 | 1.00 |
| 1997B Proof | 5,500 | Value: 2.00 | | | | |
| 1998B | 1,020,999 | — | — | — | 0.50 | 1.00 |
| 1998B Proof | 4,800 | Value: 2.00 | | | | |
| 1999B | 1,020,999 | — | — | — | 0.50 | 1.00 |
| 1999B Proof | 5,000 | Value: 2.00 | | | | |
| 2000B | 1,026,000 | — | — | — | 0.50 | 1.00 |
| 2000B Proof | 5,500 | Value: 2.00 | | | | |
| 2001B | — | — | — | — | 0.50 | 1.00 |
| 2001B Proof | 6,000 | Value: 2.00 | | | | |

**2 RAPPEN** **KM# 4** **Composition:** Bronze

| Date | Mintage | F | VF | XF | Unc | BU |
|---|---|---|---|---|---|---|
| 1902B | 500,000 | — | 24.00 | 35.00 | 60.00 | 100 |
| 1903B | 500,000 | — | 24.00 | 30.00 | 50.00 | 75.00 |
| 1904B | 500,000 | — | 22.00 | 30.00 | 50.00 | 75.00 |
| 1906B | 500,000 | — | 22.00 | 30.00 | 50.00 | 75.00 |
| 1907B | 1,000,000 | — | 4.00 | 8.00 | 20.00 | 30.00 |
| 1908B | 100,000 | — | 3.00 | 5.00 | 12.00 | 18.00 |
| 1909B | 100,000 | — | 4.00 | 8.00 | 12.00 | 18.00 |
| 1910B | 500,000 | — | 20.00 | 27.50 | 45.00 | 60.00 |
| 1912B | 100,000 | — | 4.50 | 7.00 | 17.50 | 30.00 |
| 1913B | 1,000,000 | — | 5.50 | 8.00 | 20.00 | 30.00 |
| 1914B | 1,000,000 | — | 5.50 | 8.00 | 20.00 | 30.00 |
| 1915B | 1,000,000 | — | 4.50 | 8.00 | 20.00 | 30.00 |
| 1918B | 1,000,000 | — | 4.00 | 5.00 | 12.50 | 20.00 |
| 1919B | 2,000,000 | — | 1.50 | 3.00 | 8.00 | 12.00 |
| 1920B | 500,000 | — | 25.00 | 40.00 | 70.00 | 90.00 |
| 1925B | 1,250,000 | — | 1.00 | 3.00 | 8.00 | 12.00 |
| 1926B | 750,000 | — | 17.50 | 30.00 | 40.00 | 60.00 |
| 1927B | 500,000 | — | 25.00 | 35.00 | 50.00 | 75.00 |
| 1928B | 500,000 | — | 25.00 | 35.00 | 50.00 | 75.00 |
| 1929B | 750,000 | — | 7.50 | 12.00 | 18.00 | 25.00 |
| 1930B | 1,000,000 | — | 2.00 | 4.00 | 10.00 | 15.00 |
| 1931B | 1,288,000 | — | 3.00 | 6.00 | 10.00 | 15.00 |
| 1932B | 1,500,000 | — | 1.00 | 2.00 | 6.00 | 9.00 |
| 1933B | 1,000,000 | — | 3.00 | 6.00 | 10.00 | 15.00 |
| 1934B | 500,000 | — | 12.50 | 22.50 | 40.00 | 55.00 |
| 1936B | 500,000 | — | 5.00 | 9.00 | 15.00 | 24.00 |
| 1937B | 1,200,000 | — | 2.00 | 3.00 | 5.00 | 8.00 |
| 1938B | 1,369,000 | — | 2.00 | 4.00 | 8.00 | 12.00 |
| 1941B | 3,448,000 | — | 0.75 | 1.50 | 3.00 | 6.00 |

**2 RAPPEN** **KM# 4a** **Composition:** Zinc

| Date | Mintage | F | VF | XF | Unc | BU |
|---|---|---|---|---|---|---|
| 1942B | 8,954,000 | — | 0.50 | 1.50 | 4.00 | 7.00 |
| 1943B | 4,499,000 | — | 0.75 | 3.00 | 8.00 | 12.00 |
| 1944B | 8,086,000 | — | 0.50 | 1.50 | 4.00 | 7.00 |
| 1945B | 3,640,000 | — | 2.00 | 6.00 | 16.00 | 22.50 |
| 1946B | 1,393,000 | — | 10.00 | 20.00 | 30.00 | 45.00 |

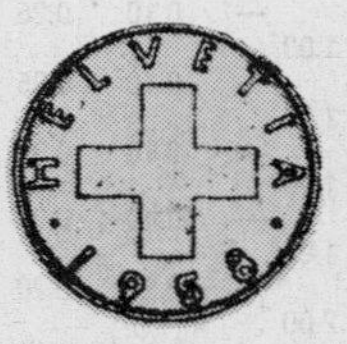

**2 RAPPEN** **KM# 47** **Composition:** Bronze

| Date | Mintage | F | VF | XF | Unc | BU |
|---|---|---|---|---|---|---|
| 1948B | 10,197,000 | — | 0.25 | 0.50 | 4.00 | 6.00 |
| 1951B | 9,622,000 | — | 0.25 | 0.50 | 3.00 | 5.00 |
| 1952B | 1,915,000 | — | 0.50 | 1.00 | 2.50 | 5.00 |
| 1953B | 2,006,000 | — | 0.50 | 1.00 | 2.50 | 4.00 |
| 1954B | 2,539,000 | — | 0.50 | 1.00 | 2.50 | 4.00 |
| 1955B | 2,493,000 | — | 0.25 | 1.00 | 2.50 | 3.50 |
| 1957B | 8,099,000 | — | 0.15 | 0.25 | 1.25 | 2.00 |
| 1958B | 6,078,000 | — | 0.15 | 0.25 | 1.25 | 2.00 |
| 1963B | 10,065,000 | — | 0.10 | 0.15 | 0.45 | 0.75 |
| 1966B | 2,510,000 | — | 0.10 | 0.20 | 0.45 | 0.75 |
| 1967B | 1,510,000 | — | 0.10 | 0.20 | 0.50 | 0.75 |
| 1968B | 2,860,000 | — | 0.10 | 0.20 | 0.45 | 0.75 |
| 1969 | 6,200,000 | — | 0.10 | 0.15 | 0.45 | 0.75 |
| 1970 | 3,115,000 | — | 0.10 | 0.15 | 0.45 | 0.75 |
| 1974 | 3,540,000 | — | 0.10 | 0.15 | 0.45 | 0.75 |
| 1974 Proof | 2,400 | Value: 25.00 | | | | |

**5 RAPPEN** **KM# 26** **Composition:** Copper-Nickel

| Date | Mintage | F | VF | XF | Unc | BU |
|---|---|---|---|---|---|---|
| 1901B | 3,000,000 | — | 1.50 | 10.00 | 27.50 | 42.00 |
| 1902B | 1,000,000 | — | 15.00 | 50.00 | 90.00 | 130 |
| 1903B | 2,000,000 | — | 2.50 | 15.00 | 40.00 | 60.00 |
| 1904B | 1,000,000 | — | 14.00 | 40.00 | 95.00 | 140 |
| 1905B | 1,000,000 | — | 12.00 | 22.50 | 75.00 | 110 |
| 1906B | 3,000,000 | — | 1.50 | 7.00 | 20.00 | 30.00 |
| 1907B | 5,000,000 | — | 1.00 | 4.00 | 10.00 | 15.00 |
| 1908B | 3,000,000 | — | 1.25 | 7.00 | 15.00 | 22.00 |
| 1909B | 2,000,000 | — | 1.50 | 8.00 | 20.00 | 27.00 |
| 1910B | 1,000,000 | — | 8.00 | 15.00 | 45.00 | 65.00 |
| 1911B | 2,000,000 | — | 1.50 | 6.00 | 12.50 | 18.00 |
| 1912B | 3,000,000 | — | 1.00 | 6.00 | 12.50 | 18.00 |
| 1913B | 3,000,000 | — | 1.00 | 6.00 | 14.00 | 20.00 |
| 1914B | 3,000,000 | — | 1.00 | 6.00 | 48.00 | 70.00 |
| 1915B | 3,000,000 | — | 1.00 | 10.00 | 120 | 175 |
| 1917B | 1,000,000 | — | 4.00 | 10.00 | 60.00 | 100 |
| 1919B | 6,000,000 | — | 0.25 | 5.00 | 16.00 | 24.00 |
| 1920B | 5,000,000 | — | 0.25 | 5.00 | 16.00 | 24.00 |
| 1921B | 3,000,000 | — | 0.25 | 5.00 | 16.00 | 24.00 |
| 1922B | 4,000,000 | — | 0.25 | 4.00 | 12.50 | 20.00 |
| 1925B | 3,000,000 | — | 0.25 | 4.00 | 12.50 | 20.00 |
| 1926B | 3,000,000 | — | 0.25 | 4.00 | 12.50 | 20.00 |
| 1927B | 2,000,000 | — | 0.25 | 4.00 | 17.50 | 25.00 |
| 1928B | 2,000,000 | — | 0.25 | 4.00 | 15.00 | 22.50 |
| 1929B | 2,000,000 | — | 0.25 | 2.50 | 12.50 | 20.00 |
| 1930B | 3,000,000 | — | 0.25 | 2.50 | 12.00 | 17.50 |
| 1931B | 5,037,000 | — | 0.25 | 2.00 | 8.00 | 12.50 |
| 1940B | 1,416,000 | — | 0.40 | 1.50 | 50.00 | 75.00 |
| 1942B | 5,078,000 | — | 0.25 | 1.00 | 10.00 | 17.50 |
| 1943B | 6,591,000 | — | 0.25 | 1.00 | 10.00 | 17.50 |
| 1944B | 9,981,000 | — | 0.25 | 1.00 | 10.00 | 17.50 |
| 1945B | 985,000 | — | 1.00 | 9.00 | 75.00 | 110 |
| 1946B | 6,179,000 | — | 0.25 | 1.00 | 5.00 | 8.00 |
| 1947B | 5,125,000 | — | 0.25 | 1.00 | 8.00 | 12.00 |
| 1948B | 4,710,000 | — | 0.25 | 1.00 | 3.00 | 4.50 |
| 1949B | 4,589,000 | — | 0.25 | 1.00 | 3.00 | 4.00 |
| 1950B | 920,000 | — | 0.50 | 1.00 | 2.00 | 3.00 |
| 1951B | 2,141,000 | — | 0.50 | 1.00 | 16.00 | 24.00 |
| 1952B | 4,690,000 | — | 0.20 | 0.35 | 3.00 | 4.00 |
| 1953B | 9,131,000 | — | 0.20 | 0.35 | 2.00 | 3.00 |
| 1954B | 8,038,000 | — | 0.20 | 0.35 | 2.00 | 3.00 |
| 1955B | 19,943,000 | — | 0.20 | 0.35 | 1.50 | 2.25 |
| 1957B | 10,147,000 | — | 0.20 | 0.35 | 1.50 | 2.25 |
| 1958B | 10,217,000 | — | 0.20 | 0.35 | 1.50 | 2.25 |
| 1959B | 11,086,000 | — | 0.20 | 0.35 | 1.50 | 2.25 |
| 1962B | 23,840,000 | — | 0.10 | 0.20 | 50.00 | 2.00 |
| 1963B | 29,730,000 | — | 0.10 | 0.20 | 50.00 | 1.50 |
| 1964B | 17,080,000 | — | 0.10 | 0.20 | 50.00 | 1.00 |
| 1965B | 1,430,000 | — | 0.10 | 0.20 | 0.75 | 1.25 |
| 1966B | 10,010,000 | — | — | 0.15 | 0.35 | 0.50 |
| 1967B | 13,010,000 | — | — | 0.15 | 0.35 | 0.50 |
| 1968B | 10,020,000 | — | — | 0.15 | 0.40 | 0.65 |
| 1969B | 32,990,000 | — | — | 0.10 | 0.35 | 0.50 |
| 1970 | 34,800,000 | — | — | 0.10 | 0.30 | 0.50 |
| 1971 | 40,020,000 | — | — | 0.10 | 0.30 | 0.50 |
| 1974 | 30,002,000 | — | — | 0.10 | 0.30 | 0.50 |
| 1974 Proof | 2,400 | Value: 20.00 | | | | |
| 1975 | 34,005,000 | — | — | 0.10 | 0.30 | 0.50 |
| 1975 Proof | 10,000 | Value: 2.00 | | | | |
| 1976 | 12,005,000 | — | — | 0.10 | 0.30 | 0.50 |
| 1976 Proof | 5,130 | Value: 2.25 | | | | |
| 1977 | 14,012,000 | — | — | 0.10 | 0.30 | 0.40 |
| 1977 Proof | 7,030 | Value: 1.75 | | | | |
| 1978 | 16,415,000 | — | — | 0.10 | 0.30 | 0.40 |
| 1978 Proof | 10,000 | Value: 1.00 | | | | |
| 1979 | 27,010,000 | — | — | 0.10 | 0.30 | 0.40 |
| 1979 Proof | 10,000 | Value: 1.00 | | | | |
| 1980 | 15,500,000 | — | — | 0.10 | 0.30 | 0.40 |
| 1980 Proof | 10,000 | Value: 1.00 | | | | |

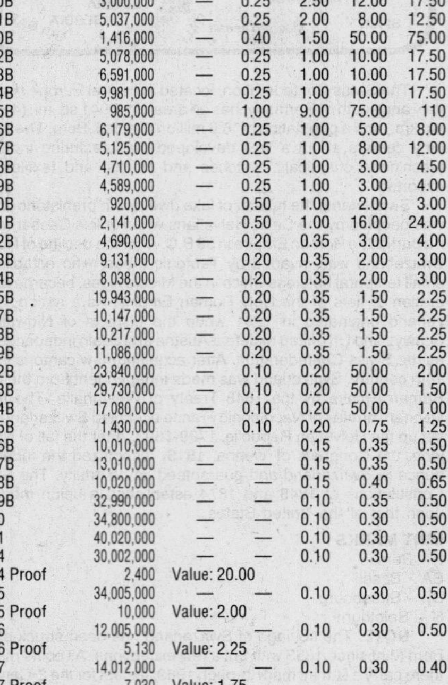

**5 RAPPEN** **KM# 26a** **Composition:** Brass

| Date | Mintage | F | VF | XF | Unc | BU |
|---|---|---|---|---|---|---|
| 1918B | 6,000,000 | | 12.50 | 20.00 | 25.00 | 40.00 |

**5 RAPPEN** **KM# 26b** **Composition:** Nickel

| Date | Mintage | F | VF | XF | Unc | BU |
|---|---|---|---|---|---|---|
| 1932B | 6,000,000 | — | 0.25 | 1.00 | 3.50 | 6.00 |
| 1933B | 3,000,000 | — | 0.25 | 1.00 | 6.00 | 9.00 |
| 1934B | 4,000,000 | — | 0.25 | 1.00 | 5.00 | 7.00 |
| 1936B | 1,000,000 | — | 0.25 | 1.50 | 7.00 | 11.00 |
| 1937B | 2,000,000 | — | 0.25 | 1.25 | 8.00 | 12.00 |
| 1938B | 1,000,000 | — | 0.25 | 1.50 | 6.00 | 9.00 |
| 1939B | 10,048,000 | — | 0.25 | 1.00 | 3.00 | 5.00 |
| 1941B | 3,030,000 | — | 2.00 | 4.00 | 25.00 | 35.00 |

**5 RAPPEN** **KM# 26c** **Composition:** Aluminum-Brass

| Date | Mintage | F | VF | XF | Unc | BU |
|---|---|---|---|---|---|---|
| 1981 | 79,020,000 | — | — | — | 0.20 | 0.30 |
| 1981 Proof | 10,000 | Value: 1.00 | | | | |
| 1982 | 75,340,000 | — | — | — | 0.20 | 0.30 |
| 1982 Proof | 10,000 | Value: 1.50 | | | | |
| 1983 | 92,746,000 | — | — | — | 0.20 | 0.30 |
| 1983 Proof | 11,000 | Value: 1.00 | | | | |
| 1984 | 69,960,000 | — | — | — | 0.20 | 0.30 |
| 1984 Proof | 14,000 | Value: 1.00 | | | | |
| 1985 | 60,032,000 | — | — | — | 0.20 | 0.30 |
| 1985 Proof | 12,000 | Value: 1.00 | | | | |
| 1986B | 55,041,000 | — | — | — | 0.20 | 0.30 |
| 1986B Proof | 10,000 | Value: 1.00 | | | | |
| 1987B | 39,828,000 | — | — | — | 0.20 | 0.50 |
| 1987B Proof | 8,800 | Value: 1.25 | | | | |
| 1988B | 5,044,000 | — | — | — | 0.20 | 0.30 |
| 1988B Proof | 9,000 | Value: 1.25 | | | | |
| 1989B | 45,031,000 | — | — | — | 0.20 | 0.30 |
| 1989B Proof | 8,800 | Value: 1.25 | | | | |
| 1990B | 16,042,000 | — | — | — | 0.20 | 0.30 |
| 1990B Proof | 8,900 | Value: 1.25 | | | | |
| 1991B | 35,036,000 | — | — | — | 0.20 | 0.30 |
| 1991B Proof | 9,900 | Value: 1.25 | | | | |
| 1992B | 35,027,000 | — | — | — | 0.20 | 0.30 |
| 1992B Proof | 7,450 | Value: 1.00 | | | | |
| 1993B | 38,022,000 | — | — | — | 0.20 | 0.30 |
| 1993B Proof | 6,200 | Value: 1.25 | | | | |
| 1994B | 35,023,000 | — | — | — | 0.20 | 0.30 |
| 1994B Proof | 6,100 | Value: 1.25 | | | | |
| 1995B | 20,024,000 | — | — | — | 0.20 | 0.30 |
| 1995B Proof | 6,100 | Value: 1.25 | | | | |
| 1996B | 25,023,000 | — | — | — | 0.20 | 0.30 |
| 1996B Proof | 6,100 | Value: 1.25 | | | | |
| 1997B | 25,022,000 | — | — | — | 0.20 | 0.30 |
| 1997B Proof | 5,500 | Value: 1.25 | | | | |
| 1998B | 10,021,000 | — | — | — | 0.20 | 0.30 |
| 1998B Proof | 4,800 | Value: 1.25 | | | | |
| 1999B | 8,021,000 | — | — | — | 0.20 | 0.30 |
| 1999B Proof | 5,000 | Value: 1.25 | | | | |
| 2000B | 5,026,000 | — | — | — | 0.20 | 0.30 |
| 2000B Proof | 5,500 | Value: 1.25 | | | | |
| 2001B | | — | — | — | 0.20 | 0.30 |
| 2001B Proof | 6,000 | Value: 1.25 | | | | |

**10 RAPPEN** **KM# 27** **Composition:** Copper-Nickel

| Date | Mintage | F | VF | XF | Unc | BU |
|---|---|---|---|---|---|---|
| 1901B | 1,000,000 | — | 3.50 | 15.00 | 50.00 | 75.00 |
| 1902B | 1,000,000 | — | 3.50 | 12.00 | 50.00 | 72.00 |
| 1903B | 1,000,000 | — | 3.50 | 12.00 | 60.00 | 85.00 |
| 1904B | 1,000,000 | — | 3.50 | 10.00 | 125 | 200 |
| 1906B | 1,000,000 | — | 3.50 | 15.00 | 45.00 | 65.00 |
| 1907B | 2,000,000 | — | 1.50 | 7.00 | 25.00 | 36.00 |
| 1908B | 2,000,000 | — | 1.50 | 6.00 | 20.00 | 30.00 |
| 1909B | 2,000,000 | — | 1.50 | 7.00 | 20.00 | 30.00 |
| 1911B | 1,000,000 | — | 3.00 | 12.00 | 30.00 | 42.00 |
| 1912B | 1,500,000 | — | 1.00 | 5.00 | 40.00 | 55.00 |
| 1913B | 2,000,000 | — | 1.00 | 5.00 | 40.00 | 60.00 |
| 1914B | 2,000,000 | — | 1.00 | 7.00 | 50.00 | 70.00 |
| 1915B | 1,200,000 | — | 2.00 | 12.00 | 160 | 250 |
| 1919B | 3,000,000 | — | 0.25 | 5.00 | 17.50 | 24.00 |
| 1920B | 3,500,000 | — | 0.25 | 3.00 | 17.50 | 24.00 |
| 1921B | 3,000,000 | — | 0.25 | 3.00 | 12.50 | 18.00 |
| 1922B | 2,000,000 | — | 0.25 | 3.00 | 22.50 | 35.00 |
| 1924B | 2,000,000 | — | 0.25 | 3.00 | 22.50 | 35.00 |
| 1925B | 3,000,000 | — | 0.25 | 2.00 | 18.00 | 24.00 |
| 1926B | 3,000,000 | — | 0.25 | 2.00 | 16.00 | 22.50 |
| 1927B | 2,000,000 | — | 0.25 | 2.00 | 14.00 | 21.00 |
| 1928B | 2,000,000 | — | 0.25 | 2.00 | 14.00 | 21.00 |
| 1929B | 2,000,000 | — | 0.25 | 2.00 | 14.00 | 21.00 |
| 1930B | 2,000,000 | — | 0.25 | 1.50 | 27.50 | 40.00 |
| 1931B | 2,244,000 | — | 0.25 | 1.50 | 25.00 | 36.00 |
| 1940B | 2,000,000 | — | 0.25 | 5.00 | 55.00 | 90.00 |
| 1942B | 2,110,000 | — | 0.25 | 5.00 | 32.00 | 47.50 |
| 1943B | 3,176,000 | — | 0.25 | 5.00 | 30.00 | 40.00 |
| 1944B | 6,133,000 | — | 0.25 | 1.50 | 6.00 | 9.00 |
| 1945B | 993,000 | — | 0.75 | 5.00 | 60.00 | 85.00 |
| 1946B | 4,010,000 | — | 0.25 | 1.50 | 25.00 | 36.00 |
| 1947B | 3,152,000 | — | 0.25 | 1.50 | 19.00 | 27.00 |
| 1948B | 1,000,000 | — | 0.50 | 3.00 | 80.00 | 125 |
| 1949B | 2,269,000 | — | 0.25 | 1.00 | 20.00 | 30.00 |
| 1950B | 3,200,000 | — | 0.25 | 1.00 | 2.50 | 4.00 |
| 1951B | 3,430,000 | — | 0.25 | 0.75 | 6.00 | 9.00 |
| 1952B | 4,452,000 | — | 0.25 | 0.75 | 6.00 | 9.00 |
| 1953B | 6,149,000 | — | 0.25 | 0.75 | 4.00 | 6.00 |
| 1954B | 3,200,000 | — | 0.25 | 1.00 | 15.00 | 22.50 |
| 1955B | 11,795,000 | — | 0.20 | 0.50 | 4.00 | 6.00 |
| 1957B | 10,092,000 | — | 0.20 | 0.50 | 4.00 | 6.00 |
| 1958B | 10,040,000 | — | 0.20 | 0.50 | 4.00 | 6.00 |
| 1959B | 13,053,000 | — | 0.20 | 0.50 | 6.00 | 10.00 |
| 1960B | 4,040,000 | — | 0.20 | 0.50 | 2.00 | 3.00 |
| 1961B | 7,949,000 | — | 0.20 | 0.35 | 1.25 | 2.00 |
| 1962B | 34,965,000 | — | — | 0.20 | 0.75 | 1.50 |
| 1964B | 16,340,000 | — | — | 0.20 | 0.75 | 1.50 |
| 1965B | 14,190,000 | — | — | 0.20 | 0.75 | 1.50 |
| 1966B | 4,025,000 | — | — | 0.20 | 0.75 | 1.50 |
| 1967B | 10,000,000 | — | — | 0.20 | 0.75 | 1.50 |
| 1968B | 14,065,000 | — | — | 0.15 | 0.50 | 0.75 |
| 1969B | 28,855,000 | — | — | 0.15 | 0.50 | 0.75 |
| 1970 | 40,020,000 | — | — | 0.15 | 0.40 | 0.75 |
| 1972 | 7,877,000 | — | — | 0.15 | 0.30 | 0.50 |
| 1973 | 30,350,000 | — | — | 0.15 | 0.30 | 0.50 |
| 1974 | 30,007,000 | — | — | 0.15 | 0.30 | 0.50 |
| 1974 Proof | 2,400 | Value: 20.00 | | | | |
| 1975 | 25,003,000 | — | — | — | 0.30 | 0.50 |
| 1975 Proof | 10,000 | Value: 2.00 | | | | |
| 1976 | 19,013,000 | — | — | — | 0.30 | 0.50 |
| 1976 Proof | 5,130 | Value: 2.50 | | | | |
| 1977 | 10,007,000 | — | — | — | 0.30 | 0.50 |
| 1977 Proof | 7,030 | Value: 1.50 | | | | |
| 1978 | 19,958,000 | — | — | — | 0.30 | 0.50 |
| 1978 Proof | 10,000 | Value: 1.25 | | | | |
| 1979 | 18,010,000 | — | — | — | 0.30 | 0.50 |
| 1979 Proof | 10,000 | Value: 1.25 | | | | |
| 1980 | 18,005,000 | — | — | — | 0.30 | 0.50 |
| 1980 Proof | 10,000 | Value: 1.50 | | | | |
| 1981 | 30,140,000 | — | — | — | 0.30 | 0.50 |
| 1981 Proof | 10,000 | Value: 1.50 | | | | |
| 1982 | 50,110,000 | — | — | — | 0.30 | 0.50 |
| 1982 Proof | 10,000 | Value: 2.50 | | | | |
| 1983 | 40,033,000 | — | — | — | 0.30 | 0.50 |
| 1983 Proof | 11,000 | Value: 1.50 | | | | |
| 1984 | 22,022,000 | — | — | — | 0.30 | 0.50 |
| 1984 Proof | 14,000 | Value: 1.50 | | | | |
| 1985 | 3,032,000 | — | — | — | 0.50 | 0.75 |
| 1985 Proof | 12,000 | Value: 1.50 | | | | |
| 1986B | 2,324,000 | — | — | — | 0.50 | 0.75 |
| 1986B Proof | 10,000 | Value: 1.65 | | | | |
| 1987B | 5,028,000 | — | — | — | 0.50 | 0.75 |
| 1987B Proof | 8,800 | Value: 2.00 | | | | |
| 1988B | 5,029,000 | — | — | — | 0.50 | 0.75 |
| 1988B Proof | 9,000 | Value: 2.00 | | | | |
| 1989B | 41,031,000 | — | — | — | 0.30 | 0.50 |
| 1989B Proof | 8,800 | Value: 2.25 | | | | |
| 1990B | 40,032,000 | — | — | — | 0.20 | 0.50 |

| Date | Mintage | F | VF | XF | Unc | BU |
|---|---|---|---|---|---|---|
| 1990B Proof | 8,900 | Value: 2.00 | | | | |
| 1991B | 35,046,000 | — | — | — | 0.20 | 0.40 |
| 1991B Proof | 9,900 | Value: 2.00 | | | | |
| 1992B | 18,027,000 | — | — | — | 0.20 | 0.40 |
| 1992B Proof | 7,450 | Value: 1.50 | | | | |
| 1993B | 27,022,000 | — | — | — | 0.20 | 0.40 |
| 1993B Proof | 6,200 | Value: 1.50 | | | | |
| 1994B | 18,023,000 | — | — | — | 0.20 | 0.40 |
| 1994B Proof | 6,100 | Value: 1.50 | | | | |
| 1995B | 5,024,000 | — | — | — | 0.20 | 0.40 |
| 1995B Proof | 6,100 | Value: 1.50 | | | | |
| 1996B | 18,023,000 | — | — | — | 0.20 | 0.40 |
| 1996B Proof | 6,100 | Value: 1.50 | | | | |
| 1997B | 15,022,000 | — | — | — | 0.20 | 0.40 |
| 1997B Proof | 5,500 | Value: 1.50 | | | | |
| 1998B | 10,021,000 | — | — | — | 0.20 | 0.40 |
| 1998B Proof | 4,800 | Value: 1.50 | | | | |
| 1999B | 7,021,000 | — | — | — | 0.20 | 0.40 |
| 1999B Proof | 5,000 | Value: 1.50 | | | | |
| 2000B | 5,026,000 | — | — | — | 0.20 | 0.40 |
| 2000B Proof | 5,500 | Value: 1.50 | | | | |
| 2001B | — | — | — | — | 0.20 | 0.40 |
| 2001B Proof | 6,000 | Value: 1.50 | | | | |

### 10 RAPPEN
**KM# 27a Composition:** Brass

| Date | Mintage | F | VF | XF | Unc | BU |
|---|---|---|---|---|---|---|
| 1918B | 6,000,000 | — | 15.00 | 25.00 | 35.00 | 50.00 |
| 1919B | 3,000,000 | — | 60.00 | 45.00 | 130 | 175 |

### 10 RAPPEN
**KM# 27b Composition:** Nickel

| Date | Mintage | F | VF | XF | Unc | BU |
|---|---|---|---|---|---|---|
| 1932B | 3,500,000 | — | 0.25 | 1.00 | 6.00 | 9.00 |
| 1933B | 2,000,000 | — | 0.25 | 1.00 | 8.00 | 12.00 |
| 1934B | 3,000,000 | — | 0.25 | 1.00 | 10.00 | 15.00 |
| 1936B | 1,500,000 | — | 0.25 | 1.00 | 10.00 | 15.00 |
| 1937B | 1,000,000 | — | 0.35 | 1.50 | 10.00 | 15.00 |
| 1938B | 1,000,000 | — | 0.25 | 1.50 | 8.00 | 12.00 |
| 1939B | 10,022,000 | — | 0.25 | 1.00 | 6.00 | 9.00 |

### 20 RAPPEN
**KM# 29 Composition:** Nickel

| Date | Mintage | F | VF | XF | Unc | BU |
|---|---|---|---|---|---|---|
| 1901B | 1,000,000 | — | 1.50 | 10.00 | 100 | 150 |
| 1902B | 1,000,000 | — | 1.50 | 10.00 | 45.00 | 75.00 |
| 1903B | 1,000,000 | — | 1.50 | 10.00 | 45.00 | 75.00 |
| 1906B | 1,000,000 | — | 1.50 | 10.00 | 45.00 | 75.00 |
| 1907B | 1,000,000 | — | 1.50 | 10.00 | 30.00 | 50.00 |
| 1908B | 1,500,000 | — | 0.50 | 8.00 | 27.50 | 40.00 |
| 1909B | 2,000,000 | — | 0.50 | 8.00 | 27.50 | 40.00 |
| 1911B | 1,000,000 | — | 1.00 | 8.00 | 60.00 | 90.00 |
| 1912B | 2,000,000 | — | 0.50 | 8.00 | 30.00 | 60.00 |
| 1913B | 1,500,000 | — | 0.50 | 8.00 | 30.00 | 60.00 |
| 1919B | 1,500,000 | — | 0.50 | 6.00 | 27.50 | 50.00 |
| 1920B | 3,100,000 | — | 0.35 | 4.00 | 16.00 | 25.00 |
| 1921B | 2,500,000 | — | 0.35 | 4.00 | 16.00 | 25.00 |
| 1924B | 1,100,000 | — | 1.00 | 4.00 | 32.00 | 55.00 |
| 1925B | 1,500,000 | — | 0.35 | 3.00 | 12.50 | 25.00 |
| 1926B | 1,500,000 | — | 0.35 | 3.00 | 12.50 | 25.00 |
| 1927B | 500,000 | — | 3.00 | 15.00 | 100 | 150 |
| 1929B | 2,000,000 | — | 0.30 | 1.00 | 13.00 | 20.00 |
| 1930B | 2,000,000 | — | 0.30 | 1.00 | 13.00 | 20.00 |
| 1931B | 2,250,000 | — | 0.30 | 1.00 | 13.00 | 20.00 |
| 1932B | 2,000,000 | — | 0.30 | 1.00 | 13.00 | 20.00 |
| 1933B | 1,500,000 | — | 0.30 | 1.00 | 13.00 | 20.00 |
| 1934B | 2,000,000 | — | 0.30 | 0.50 | 13.00 | 20.00 |
| 1936B | 1,000,000 | — | 1.00 | 1.60 | 31.00 | 45.00 |
| 1938B | 2,805,000 | — | 0.30 | 0.60 | 28.00 | 40.00 |

### 20 RAPPEN
**KM# 29a Composition:** Copper-Nickel

| Date | Mintage | F | VF | XF | Unc | BU |
|---|---|---|---|---|---|---|
| 1939B | 8,100,000 | — | 0.25 | 3.00 | 125 | 175 |
| 1943B | 10,173,000 | — | 0.25 | 1.00 | 20.00 | 30.00 |
| 1944B | 7,139,000 | — | 0.25 | 1.00 | 8.00 | 12.00 |
| 1945B | 1,992,000 | — | 0.50 | 2.50 | 32.50 | 47.50 |
| 1947B | 5,131,000 | — | 0.25 | 0.50 | 17.00 | 24.00 |
| 1950B | 5,970,000 | — | 0.25 | 0.50 | 2.50 | 4.00 |
| 1951B | 3,640,000 | — | 0.25 | 0.50 | 7.00 | 12.00 |
| 1952B | 3,070,000 | — | 0.25 | 0.50 | 7.00 | 12.00 |
| 1953B | 6,958,000 | — | 0.25 | 0.50 | 4.00 | 6.00 |
| 1954B | 1,504,000 | — | 0.50 | 1.00 | 40.00 | 75.00 |
| 1955B | 9,104,000 | — | 0.25 | 0.50 | 4.00 | 6.00 |
| 1956B | 5,111,000 | — | 0.25 | 0.50 | 4.00 | 6.00 |
| 1957B | 2,535,000 | — | 0.35 | 2.50 | 35.00 | 90.00 |
| 1958B | 5,037,000 | — | 0.25 | 0.50 | 4.00 | 5.50 |
| 1959B | 10,136,000 | — | — | 0.35 | 3.00 | 4.00 |
| 1960B | 15,467,000 | — | — | 0.35 | 3.00 | 4.00 |
| 1961B | 8,234,000 | — | — | 0.35 | 2.00 | 3.00 |
| 1962B | 30,145,000 | — | — | 0.35 | 2.00 | 3.00 |
| 1963B | 9,020,000 | — | — | 0.35 | 2.00 | 3.00 |
| 1964B | 14,370,000 | — | — | 0.25 | 2.00 | 3.00 |
| 1965B | 15,005,000 | — | — | 0.25 | 2.00 | 3.00 |
| 1966B | 10,785,000 | — | — | 0.25 | 1.00 | 1.50 |
| 1967B | 8,995,000 | — | — | 0.30 | 1.25 | 1.75 |
| 1968B | 10,540,000 | — | — | 0.25 | 0.50 | 1.00 |
| 1969B | 39,875,000 | — | — | — | 0.40 | 0.60 |
| 1970 | 45,605,000 | — | — | — | 0.40 | 0.60 |
| 1971 | 25,160,000 | — | — | — | 0.40 | 0.60 |
| 1974 | 30,025,000 | — | — | — | 0.40 | 0.60 |
| 1974 Proof | 2,400 | Value: 25.00 | | | | |
| 1975 | 50,060,000 | — | — | — | 0.40 | 0.60 |
| 1975 Proof | 10,000 | Value: 2.50 | | | | |
| 1976 | 23,150,000 | — | — | — | 0.40 | 0.60 |
| 1976 Proof | 5,130 | Value: 3.50 | | | | |
| 1977 | 14,012,000 | — | — | — | 0.40 | 0.60 |
| 1977 Proof | 7,030 | Value: 2.25 | | | | |
| 1978 | 14,815,000 | — | — | — | 0.40 | 0.60 |
| 1978 Proof | 10,000 | Value: 2.00 | | | | |
| 1979 | 18,380,000 | — | — | — | 0.40 | 0.60 |
| 1979 Proof | 10,000 | Value: 2.00 | | | | |
| 1980 | 24,560,000 | — | — | — | 0.40 | 0.60 |
| 1980 Proof | 10,000 | Value: 2.50 | | | | |
| 1981 | 22,020,000 | — | — | — | 0.40 | 0.60 |
| 1981 Proof | 10,000 | Value: 2.50 | | | | |
| 1982 | 25,035,000 | — | — | — | 0.40 | 0.60 |
| 1982 Proof | 10,000 | Value: 3.00 | | | | |
| 1983 | 10,026,000 | — | — | — | 0.40 | 0.60 |
| 1983 Proof | 11,000 | Value: 2.00 | | | | |
| 1984 | 22,055,000 | — | — | — | 0.40 | 0.60 |
| 1984 Proof | 14,000 | Value: 2.00 | | | | |
| 1985 | 40,027,000 | — | — | — | 0.40 | 0.60 |
| 1985 Proof | 12,000 | Value: 2.00 | | | | |
| 1986B | 10,299,000 | — | — | — | 0.40 | 0.60 |
| 1986B Proof | 10,000 | Value: 2.00 | | | | |
| 1987B | 10,028,000 | — | — | — | 0.40 | 0.60 |
| 1987B Proof | 8,800 | Value: 2.25 | | | | |
| 1988B | 25,029,000 | — | — | — | 0.40 | 0.60 |
| 1988B Proof | 9,000 | Value: 2.50 | | | | |
| 1989B | 20,031,000 | — | — | — | 0.40 | 0.60 |
| 1989B Proof | 8,800 | Value: 2.50 | | | | |
| 1990B | 6,534,000 | — | — | — | 0.35 | 0.50 |
| 1990B Proof | 8,900 | Value: 2.50 | | | | |
| 1991B | 48,076,000 | — | — | — | 0.35 | 0.50 |
| 1991B Proof | 9,900 | Value: 2.50 | | | | |
| 1992B | 12,627,000 | — | — | — | 0.35 | 0.50 |
| 1992B Proof | 7,450 | Value: 2.25 | | | | |
| 1993B | 32,522,000 | — | — | — | 0.35 | 0.50 |
| 1993B Proof | 6,200 | Value: 3.50 | | | | |
| 1994B | 20,023,000 | — | — | — | 0.30 | 0.40 |
| 1994B Proof | 6,100 | Value: 2.25 | | | | |
| 1995B | 8,023,999 | — | — | — | 0.30 | 0.40 |
| 1995B Proof | 6,100 | Value: 2.25 | | | | |
| 1996B | 4,022,999 | — | — | — | 0.30 | 0.40 |
| 1996B Proof | 6,100 | Value: 2.25 | | | | |
| 1997B | 6,022,000 | — | — | — | 0.30 | 0.40 |
| 1997B Proof | 5,500 | Value: 2.25 | | | | |
| 1998B | 7,020,000 | — | — | — | 0.30 | 0.40 |
| 1998B Proof | 4,800 | Value: 2.25 | | | | |
| 1999B | 4,021,000 | — | — | — | 0.30 | 0.40 |
| 1999B Proof | 5,000 | Value: 2.25 | | | | |
| 2000B | 3,026,000 | — | — | — | 0.30 | 0.40 |
| 2000B Proof | 5,500 | Value: 2.25 | | | | |
| 2001B | — | — | — | — | 0.30 | 0.40 |
| 2001B Proof | 6,000 | Value: 2.25 | | | | |

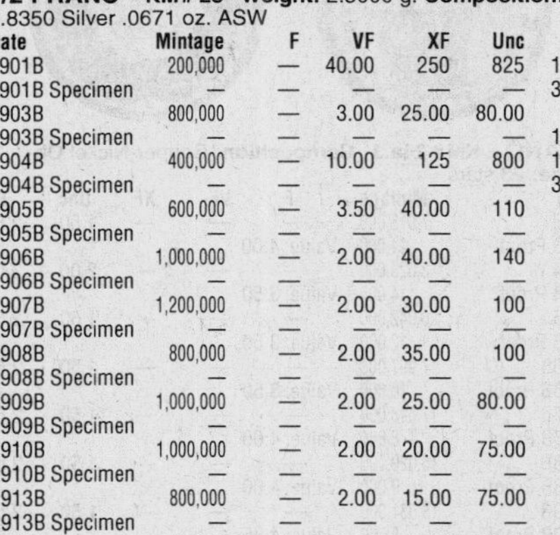

### 1/2 FRANC
**KM# 23 Weight:** 2.5000 g. **Composition:** 0.8350 Silver .0671 oz. ASW

| Date | Mintage | F | VF | XF | Unc | BU |
|---|---|---|---|---|---|---|
| 1901B | 200,000 | — | 40.00 | 250 | 825 | 1,250 |
| 1901B Specimen | — | — | — | — | — | 3,000 |
| 1903B | 800,000 | — | 3.00 | 25.00 | 80.00 | 125 |
| 1903B Specimen | — | — | — | — | — | 1,000 |
| 1904B | 400,000 | — | 10.00 | 125 | 800 | 1,250 |
| 1904B Specimen | — | — | — | — | — | 3,000 |
| 1905B | 600,000 | — | 3.50 | 40.00 | 110 | 165 |
| 1905B Specimen | — | — | — | — | — | 900 |
| 1906B | 1,000,000 | — | 2.00 | 40.00 | 140 | 210 |
| 1906B Specimen | — | — | — | — | — | 900 |
| 1907B | 1,200,000 | — | 2.00 | 30.00 | 100 | 150 |
| 1907B Specimen | — | — | — | — | — | 750 |
| 1908B | 800,000 | — | 2.00 | 35.00 | 100 | 155 |
| 1908B Specimen | — | — | — | — | — | 750 |
| 1909B | 1,000,000 | — | 2.00 | 25.00 | 80.00 | 120 |
| 1909B Specimen | — | — | — | — | — | 750 |
| 1910B | 1,000,000 | — | 2.00 | 20.00 | 75.00 | 110 |
| 1910B Specimen | — | — | — | — | — | 750 |
| 1913B | 800,000 | — | 2.00 | 15.00 | 75.00 | 110 |
| 1913B Specimen | — | — | — | — | — | 600 |
| 1914B | 2,000,000 | — | 2.00 | 7.50 | 30.00 | 45.00 |
| 1914B Specimen | — | — | — | — | — | 360 |
| 1916B | 800,000 | — | 2.00 | 8.00 | 75.00 | 110 |
| 1916B Specimen | — | — | — | — | — | 450 |
| 1920B | 5,400,000 | — | 1.50 | 7.00 | 14.00 | 21.00 |
| 1920B Specimen | — | — | — | — | — | 150 |
| 1921B | 6,000,000 | — | 1.50 | 7.00 | 14.00 | 21.00 |
| 1921B Specimen | — | — | — | — | — | 150 |
| 1928B | 1,000,000 | — | 2.00 | 12.50 | 80.00 | 120 |
| 1928B Specimen | — | — | — | — | — | 300 |
| 1929B | 2,000,000 | — | 1.50 | 7.00 | 16.00 | 24.00 |
| 1929B Specimen | — | — | — | — | — | 180 |
| 1931B | 1,000,000 | — | 1.50 | 10.00 | 40.00 | 65.00 |
| 1931B Specimen | — | — | — | — | — | 240 |
| 1932B | 1,000,000 | — | 1.50 | 8.00 | 20.00 | 30.00 |
| 1932B Specimen | — | — | — | — | — | 240 |
| 1934B | 2,000,000 | — | 1.50 | 5.00 | 14.00 | 21.00 |
| 1934B Specimen | — | — | — | — | — | 120 |
| 1936B | 400,000 | — | 2.00 | 10.00 | 40.00 | 100 |
| 1936B Specimen | — | — | — | — | — | 240 |
| 1937B | 1,000,000 | — | 1.25 | 5.00 | 14.00 | 21.00 |
| 1937B Specimen | — | — | — | — | — | 180 |
| 1939B | 1,000,999 | — | 1.25 | 5.00 | 14.00 | 21.00 |
| 1939B Specimen | — | — | — | — | — | 120 |
| 1940B | 2,001,999 | — | 1.25 | 4.00 | 12.00 | 18.00 |
| 1940B Specimen | — | — | — | — | — | 120 |
| 1941B | 200,000 | — | 1.50 | 5.00 | 16.00 | 22.00 |
| 1941B Specimen | — | — | — | — | — | 90.00 |
| 1942B | 2,969,000 | — | 1.25 | 3.00 | 6.00 | 9.00 |
| 1942B Specimen | — | — | — | — | — | 90.00 |
| 1943B | 4,572,000 | — | 1.00 | 3.00 | 6.00 | 9.00 |
| 1943B Specimen | — | — | — | — | — | 90.00 |
| 1944B | 7,456,000 | — | 1.00 | 2.50 | 4.00 | 6.00 |
| 1944B Specimen | — | — | — | — | — | 90.00 |
| 1945B | 4,928,000 | — | 1.00 | 2.50 | 4.00 | 6.00 |
| 1945B Specimen | — | — | — | — | — | 90.00 |
| 1946B | 6,817,000 | — | 1.00 | 2.50 | 4.00 | 6.00 |
| 1946B Specimen | — | — | — | — | — | 90.00 |
| 1948B | 6,113,000 | — | 0.75 | 1.50 | 2.50 | 4.00 |
| 1948B Specimen | — | — | — | — | — | 90.00 |
| 1950B | 7,148,000 | — | 0.75 | 1.50 | 2.25 | 3.50 |
| 1950B Specimen | — | — | — | — | — | 90.00 |
| 1951B | 8,530,000 | — | 0.65 | 1.50 | 2.25 | 3.50 |
| 1951B Specimen | — | — | — | — | — | 90.00 |
| 1952B | 14,023,000 | — | 0.60 | 1.25 | 2.00 | 3.00 |
| 1952B Specimen | — | — | — | — | — | 75.00 |
| 1953B | 3,567,000 | — | 0.65 | 1.25 | 3.00 | 4.25 |
| 1953B Specimen | — | — | — | — | — | 90.00 |
| 1955B | 1,320,000 | — | 0.71 | 1.50 | 6.00 | 9.00 |
| 1955B Specimen | — | — | — | — | — | 110 |
| 1956B | 4,250,000 | — | 0.60 | 1.00 | 2.25 | 3.25 |
| 1956B Specimen | — | — | — | — | — | 60.00 |
| 1957B | 12,085,000 | — | 0.50 | 0.85 | 2.00 | 3.00 |
| 1957B Specimen | — | — | — | — | — | 30.00 |
| 1958B | 11,558,000 | — | 0.50 | 0.85 | 2.00 | 3.00 |
| 1958B Specimen | — | — | — | — | — | 30.00 |
| 1959B | 12,581,000 | — | 0.50 | 0.85 | 2.00 | 3.00 |
| 1959B Specimen | — | — | — | — | — | 30.00 |
| 1960B | 14,528,000 | — | 0.50 | 0.85 | 2.00 | 3.00 |
| 1960B Specimen | — | — | — | — | — | 30.00 |
| 1961B | 6,906,000 | — | 0.50 | 0.85 | 2.00 | 3.00 |
| 1961B Specimen | — | — | — | — | — | 30.00 |
| 1962B | 18,272,000 | — | 0.50 | 0.75 | 1.50 | 2.25 |
| 1962B Specimen | — | — | — | — | — | 30.00 |
| 1963B | 25,168,000 | — | 0.50 | 0.75 | 1.50 | 2.25 |
| 1963B Specimen | — | — | — | — | — | 30.00 |
| 1964B | 22,720,000 | — | 0.50 | 0.75 | 1.50 | 2.25 |
| 1964B Specimen | — | — | — | — | — | 30.00 |
| 1965B | 17,920,000 | — | 0.50 | 0.75 | 1.50 | 2.25 |
| 1965B Specimen | — | — | — | — | — | 30.00 |
| 1966B | 10,008,000 | — | 0.50 | 0.75 | 1.50 | 2.25 |
| 1966B Specimen | — | — | — | — | — | 30.00 |
| 1967B | 16,096,000 | — | 0.50 | 0.75 | 1.50 | 2.25 |
| 1967B Specimen | — | — | — | — | — | 30.00 |

### 1/2 FRANC
**KM# 23a.1 Composition:** Copper-Nickel

| Date | Mintage | F | VF | XF | Unc | BU |
|---|---|---|---|---|---|---|
| 1968 | 20,000,000 | — | — | — | 1.00 | 1.50 |
| 1968B | 44,920,000 | — | — | — | 1.00 | 1.50 |
| 1969 | 31,400,000 | — | — | — | 0.75 | 1.25 |
| 1969B | 51,704,000 | — | — | — | 0.75 | 1.25 |
| 1970 | 52,620,000 | — | — | — | 0.75 | 1.25 |
| 1971 | 34,472,000 | — | — | — | 0.75 | 1.25 |
| 1972 | 9,996,000 | — | — | — | 0.75 | 1.25 |
| 1973 | 5,000,000 | — | — | — | 0.75 | 1.25 |
| 1974 | 45,006,000 | — | — | — | 0.75 | 1.25 |
| 1974 Proof | 2,400 | Value: 35.00 | | | | |
| 1975 | 27,234,000 | — | — | — | 0.75 | 1.25 |
| 1975 Proof | 10,000 | Value: 3.50 | | | | |
| 1976 | 10,009,000 | — | — | — | 0.75 | 1.25 |
| 1976 Proof | 5,130 | Value: 4.00 | | | | |
| 1977 | 19,011,000 | — | — | — | 0.75 | 1.25 |
| 1977 Proof | 7,030 | Value: 3.00 | | | | |
| 1978 | 20,818,000 | — | — | — | 0.75 | 1.25 |
| 1978 Proof | 10,000 | Value: 2.50 | | | | |
| 1979 | 27,010,000 | — | — | — | 0.75 | 1.25 |
| 1979 Proof | 10,000 | Value: 2.50 | | | | |
| 1980 | 31,064,000 | — | — | — | 0.75 | 1.25 |
| 1980 Proof | 10,000 | Value: 3.00 | | | | |
| 1981 | 30,155,000 | — | — | — | 0.75 | 1.25 |
| 1981 Proof | 10,000 | Value: 3.00 | | | | |

### 1/2 FRANC
**KM# 23a.2 Composition:** Copper-Nickel **Obverse:** 22 stars around figure **Note:** Medal alignment.

| Date | Mintage | F | VF | XF | Unc | BU |
|---|---|---|---|---|---|---|
| 1982 | 30,151,000 | — | — | — | 0.75 | 1.25 |
| 1982 Proof | 10,000 | Value: 6.00 | | | | |

### 1/2 FRANC
**KM# 23a.3 Composition:** Copper-Nickel **Obverse:** 23 stars

| Date | Mintage | F | VF | XF | Unc | BU |
|---|---|---|---|---|---|---|
| 1983 | 22,020,000 | — | — | — | 0.75 | 1.25 |
| 1983 Proof | 11,000 | Value: 3.00 | | | | |
| 1984 | 22,036,000 | — | — | — | 0.75 | 1.25 |
| 1984 Proof | 14,000 | Value: 2.75 | | | | |
| 1985 | 6,026,000 | — | — | — | 0.75 | 1.25 |
| 1985 Proof | 12,000 | Value: 2.75 | | | | |

| Date | Mintage | F | VF | XF | Unc | BU |
|---|---|---|---|---|---|---|
| 1986B | 5,031,000 | — | — | — | 0.75 | 1.25 |
| 1986B Proof | 10,000 | Value: 3.00 | | | | |
| 1987B | 10,028,000 | — | — | — | 0.75 | 1.25 |
| 1987B Proof | 8,800 | Value: 3.25 | | | | |
| 1988B | 5,029,000 | — | — | — | 0.75 | 1.25 |
| 1988B Proof | 9,000 | Value: 3.25 | | | | |
| 1989B | 10,031,000 | — | — | — | 0.75 | 1.25 |
| 1989B Proof | 8,800 | Value: 3.25 | | | | |
| 1990B | 20,032,000 | — | — | — | 0.60 | 1.00 |
| 1990B Proof | 8,900 | Value: 3.25 | | | | |
| 1991B | 10,036,000 | — | — | — | 0.60 | 1.00 |
| 1991B Proof | 9,900 | Value: 3.25 | | | | |
| 1992B | 30,027,000 | — | — | — | 0.60 | 1.00 |
| 1992B Proof | 7,450 | Value: 3.00 | | | | |
| 1993B | 13,022,000 | — | — | — | 0.60 | 1.00 |
| 1993B Proof | 6,200 | Value: 3.00 | | | | |
| 1994B | 15,023,000 | — | — | — | 0.60 | 1.00 |
| 1994B Proof | 6,100 | Value: 3.50 | | | | |
| 1995B | 10,024,000 | — | — | — | 0.60 | 1.00 |
| 1995B Proof | 6,000 | Value: 3.50 | | | | |
| 1996B | 8,023,000 | — | — | — | 0.60 | 1.00 |
| 1996B Proof | 6,100 | Value: 3.50 | | | | |
| 1997B | 6,022,000 | — | — | — | 0.60 | 1.00 |
| 1997B Proof | 5,500 | Value: 3.50 | | | | |
| 1998B | 6,021,000 | — | — | — | 0.60 | 1.00 |
| 1998B Proof | 4,800 | Value: 3.50 | | | | |
| 1999B | 5,021,000 | — | — | — | 0.60 | 1.00 |
| 1999B Proof | 5,000 | Value: 3.50 | | | | |
| 2000B | 4,026,000 | — | — | — | 0.60 | 1.00 |
| 2000B Proof | 5,500 | Value: 3.50 | | | | |
| 2001B | — | — | — | — | 0.60 | 1.00 |
| 2001B Proof | 6,000 | Value: 3.50 | | | | |

**FRANC** **KM# 24** **Weight:** 5.0000 g. **Composition:** 0.8350 Silver .1342 oz. ASW

| Date | Mintage | F | VF | XF | Unc | BU |
|---|---|---|---|---|---|---|
| 1901B | 400,000 | — | 12.00 | 250 | 575 | 850 |
| 1901B Specimen | — | — | — | — | — | 2,400 |
| 1903B | 1,000,000 | — | 5.00 | 40.00 | 140 | 210 |
| 1903B Specimen | — | — | — | — | — | 1,200 |
| 1904B | 400,000 | — | 15.00 | 300 | 1,000 | 1,500 |
| 1904B Specimen | — | — | — | — | — | 4,800 |
| 1905B | 700,000 | — | 5.00 | 45.00 | 200 | 275 |
| 1905B Specimen | — | — | — | — | — | 1,200 |
| 1906B | 700,000 | — | 5.00 | 75.00 | 325 | 475 |
| 1906B Specimen | — | — | — | — | — | 1,200 |
| 1907B | 800,000 | — | 5.00 | 75.00 | 300 | 425 |
| 1907B Specimen | — | — | — | — | — | 1,200 |
| 1908B | 1,200,000 | — | 5.00 | 40.00 | 125 | 200 |
| 1908B Specimen | — | — | — | — | — | 1,200 |
| 1909B | 900,000 | — | 5.00 | 25.00 | 125 | 200 |
| 1909B Specimen | — | — | — | — | — | 1,200 |
| 1910B | 1,000,000 | — | 5.00 | 30.00 | 100 | 150 |
| 1910B Specimen | — | — | — | — | — | 1,200 |
| 1911B | 1,200,000 | — | 5.00 | 25.00 | 100 | 150 |
| 1911B Specimen | — | — | — | — | — | 900 |
| 1912B | 1,200,000 | — | 5.00 | 20.00 | 70.00 | 100 |
| 1912B Specimen | — | — | — | — | — | 750 |
| 1913B | 1,200,000 | — | 5.00 | 20.00 | 75.00 | 110 |
| 1913B Specimen | — | — | — | — | — | 900 |
| 1914B | 4,200,000 | — | 4.00 | 10.00 | 35.00 | 55.00 |
| 1914B Specimen | — | — | — | — | — | 600 |
| 1916B | 1,000,000 | — | 5.00 | 15.00 | 85.00 | 120 |
| 1916B Specimen | — | — | — | — | — | 1,050 |
| 1920B | 3,300,000 | — | 3.00 | 6.00 | 25.00 | 35.00 |
| 1920B Specimen | — | — | — | — | — | 180 |
| 1921B | 3,800,000 | — | 3.00 | 6.00 | 25.00 | 35.00 |
| 1921B Specimen | — | — | — | — | — | 180 |
| 1928B | 1,500,000 | — | 3.00 | 7.50 | 22.50 | 35.00 |
| 1928B Specimen | — | — | — | — | — | 240 |
| 1931B | 1,000,000 | — | 3.50 | 7.50 | 32.50 | 48.00 |
| 1931B Specimen | — | — | — | — | — | 240 |
| 1932B | 500,000 | — | 4.00 | 15.00 | 75.00 | 110 |
| 1932B Specimen | — | — | — | — | — | 480 |
| 1934B | 500,000 | — | 4.00 | 20.00 | 65.00 | 100 |
| 1934B Specimen | — | — | — | — | — | 480 |
| 1936B | 500,000 | — | 4.00 | 15.00 | 60.00 | 100 |
| 1936B Specimen | — | — | — | — | — | 360 |
| 1937B | 1,000,000 | — | 3.00 | 5.00 | 25.00 | 36.00 |
| 1937B Specimen | — | — | — | — | — | 240 |
| 1939B | 2,106,000 | — | 2.00 | 3.00 | 10.00 | 15.00 |
| 1939B Specimen | — | — | — | — | — | 150 |
| 1940B | 2,003,000 | — | 2.00 | 3.00 | 9.00 | 12.50 |
| 1940B Specimen | — | — | — | — | — | 150 |
| 1943B | 3,526,000 | — | 1.50 | 3.00 | 6.00 | 9.00 |
| 1943B Specimen | — | — | — | — | — | 150 |
| 1944B | 6,225,000 | — | 1.50 | 3.00 | 4.50 | 6.50 |
| 1944B Specimen | — | — | — | — | — | 150 |
| 1945B | 7,794,000 | — | 1.50 | 3.00 | 5.00 | 7.50 |
| 1945B Specimen | — | — | — | — | — | 150 |
| 1946B | 2,539,000 | — | 1.50 | 3.00 | 7.00 | 10.00 |
| 1946B Specimen | — | — | — | — | — | 150 |
| 1947B | 624,000 | — | 2.50 | 5.00 | 16.00 | 22.00 |
| 1947B Specimen | — | — | — | — | — | 150 |
| 1952B | 2,853,000 | — | 1.50 | 2.50 | 4.50 | 6.50 |
| 1952B Specimen | — | — | — | — | — | 120 |
| 1953B | 786,000 | — | 3.00 | 5.00 | 17.50 | 24.00 |
| 1953B Specimen | — | — | — | — | — | 120 |
| 1955B | 194,000 | — | 5.00 | 8.00 | 22.00 | 32.00 |
| 1955B Specimen | — | — | — | — | — | 120 |
| 1956B | 2,500,000 | — | 1.50 | 2.50 | 5.00 | 7.50 |
| 1956B Specimen | — | — | — | — | — | 90.00 |
| 1957B | 6,420,000 | — | 1.25 | 2.00 | 4.50 | 6.00 |
| 1957B Specimen | — | — | — | — | — | 45.00 |
| 1958B | 3,580,000 | — | 1.25 | 2.00 | 4.50 | 6.50 |
| 1958B Specimen | — | — | — | — | — | 45.00 |
| 1959B | 1,859,000 | — | 1.25 | 2.00 | 4.50 | 6.50 |
| 1959B Specimen | — | — | — | — | — | 45.00 |
| 1960B | 3,523,000 | — | — | 1.50 | 3.00 | 5.00 |
| 1960B Specimen | — | — | — | — | — | 45.00 |
| 1961B | 6,549,000 | — | — | 1.50 | 3.00 | 5.00 |
| 1961B Specimen | — | — | — | — | — | 45.00 |
| 1962B | 6,220,000 | — | — | 1.50 | 3.00 | 5.00 |
| 1962B Specimen | — | — | — | — | — | 45.00 |
| 1963B | 13,476,000 | — | — | 1.25 | 3.00 | 4.50 |
| 1963B Specimen | — | — | — | — | — | 45.00 |
| 1964B | 12,560,000 | — | — | 1.25 | 3.00 | 4.50 |
| 1964B Specimen | — | — | — | — | — | 45.00 |
| 1965B | 5,032,000 | — | — | 1.25 | 3.00 | 5.00 |
| 1965B Specimen | — | — | — | — | — | 45.00 |
| 1966B | 3,032,000 | — | — | 1.25 | 3.50 | 5.50 |
| 1966B Specimen | — | — | — | — | — | 45.00 |
| 1967B | 2,088,000 | — | — | 1.00 | 3.50 | 5.50 |
| 1967B Specimen | — | — | — | — | — | 45.00 |

**FRANC** **KM# 24a.1** **Composition:** Copper-Nickel

| Date | Mintage | F | VF | XF | Unc | BU |
|---|---|---|---|---|---|---|
| 1968 | 15,000,000 | — | — | — | 2.00 | 3.00 |
| 1968B | 40,864,000 | — | — | — | 2.00 | 3.00 |
| 1969B | 37,598,000 | — | — | — | 2.00 | 3.00 |
| 1970 | 24,240,000 | — | — | — | 2.00 | 3.00 |
| 1971 | 11,496,000 | — | — | — | 2.00 | 3.00 |
| 1973 | 5,000,000 | — | — | — | 2.00 | 3.00 |
| 1974 | 15,012,000 | — | — | — | 1.50 | 2.50 |
| 1974 Proof | 2,400 | Value: 65.00 | | | | |
| 1975 | 13,012,000 | — | — | — | 1.50 | 2.50 |
| 1975 Proof | 10,000 | Value: 5.00 | | | | |
| 1976 | 5,009,000 | — | — | — | 2.00 | 3.00 |
| 1976 Proof | 5,130 | Value: 6.50 | | | | |
| 1977 | 6,019,000 | — | — | — | 2.00 | 3.00 |
| 1977 Proof | 7,030 | Value: 4.00 | | | | |
| 1978 | 13,548,000 | — | — | — | 1.50 | 2.50 |
| 1978 Proof | 10,000 | Value: 3.50 | | | | |
| 1979 | 10,800,000 | — | — | — | 1.50 | 2.50 |
| 1979 Proof | 10,000 | Value: 3.50 | | | | |
| 1980 | 11,002,000 | — | — | — | 1.50 | 2.50 |
| 1980 Proof | 10,000 | Value: 4.00 | | | | |
| 1981 | 18,013,000 | — | — | — | 1.50 | 2.50 |
| 1981 Proof | 10,000 | Value: 4.00 | | | | |

**FRANC** **KM# 24a.2** **Composition:** Copper-Nickel **Obverse:** 22 stars around figure **Note:** Medal alignment.

| Date | Mintage | F | VF | XF | Unc | BU |
|---|---|---|---|---|---|---|
| 1982 | 15,039,000 | — | — | — | 2.00 | 3.00 |
| 1982 Proof | 10,000 | Value: 12.00 | | | | |

**FRANC** **KM# 24a.3** **Composition:** Copper-Nickel **Obverse:** 23 stars

| Date | Mintage | F | VF | XF | Unc | BU |
|---|---|---|---|---|---|---|
| 1983 | 7,018,000 | — | — | — | 1.50 | 2.50 |
| 1983 Proof | 11,000 | Value: 4.00 | | | | |
| 1984 | 3,028,000 | — | — | — | 2.00 | 3.00 |
| 1984 Proof | 14,000 | Value: 3.50 | | | | |
| 1985 | 20,042,000 | — | — | — | 1.50 | 2.50 |
| 1985 Proof | 12,000 | Value: 3.50 | | | | |
| 1986B | 17,997,000 | — | — | — | 1.50 | 2.50 |
| 1986B Proof | 10,000 | Value: 3.50 | | | | |
| 1987B | 17,028,000 | — | — | — | 1.50 | 2.50 |
| 1987B Proof | 8,800 | Value: 4.00 | | | | |
| 1988B | 18,029,000 | — | — | — | 1.50 | 2.50 |
| 1988B Proof | 9,000 | Value: 4.00 | | | | |
| 1989B | 15,031,000 | — | — | — | 1.50 | 2.50 |
| 1989B Proof | 8,800 | Value: 4.25 | | | | |
| 1990B | 2,032,000 | — | — | — | 1.50 | 2.50 |
| 1990B Proof | 8,900 | Value: 4.00 | | | | |
| 1991B | 9,036,000 | — | — | — | 1.00 | 1.50 |
| 1991B Proof | 9,900 | Value: 4.00 | | | | |
| 1992B | 12,028,000 | — | — | — | 1.00 | 1.50 |
| 1992B Proof | 7,450 | Value: 3.50 | | | | |
| 1993B | 12,023,000 | — | — | — | 1.00 | 1.50 |
| 1993B Proof | 6,200 | Value: 3.50 | | | | |
| 1994B | 10,023,000 | — | — | — | 1.00 | 1.50 |
| 1994B Proof | 6,100 | Value: 4.00 | | | | |
| 1995B | 13,024 | — | — | — | 1.00 | 1.50 |
| 1995B Proof | 6,100 | Value: 4.00 | | | | |
| 1996B | 3,023,000 | — | — | — | 1.00 | 1.50 |
| 1996B Proof | 6,100 | Value: 4.00 | | | | |
| 1997B | 3,022,000 | — | — | — | 1.00 | 1.50 |
| 1997B Proof | 5,500 | Value: 4.00 | | | | |
| 1998B | 3,021,000 | — | — | — | 1.00 | 1.50 |
| 1998B Proof | 4,800 | Value: 4.00 | | | | |
| 1999B | 3,021,000 | — | — | — | 1.00 | 1.50 |
| 1999B Proof | 5,000 | Value: 4.00 | | | | |
| 2000B | 4,026,000 | — | — | — | 1.00 | 1.50 |
| 2000B Proof | 5,500 | Value: 4.00 | | | | |
| 2001B | — | — | — | — | 1.00 | 1.50 |
| 2001B Proof | 6,000 | Value: 4.00 | | | | |

**2 FRANCS** **KM# 21** **Weight:** 10.0000 g. **Composition:** 0.8350 Silver .2685 oz. ASW

| Date | Mintage | F | VF | XF | Unc | BU |
|---|---|---|---|---|---|---|
| 1901B | 50,000 | — | 200 | 1,250 | 6,500 | 9,000 |
| 1901B Specimen; Rare | — | — | — | — | — | — |
| 1903B | 300,000 | — | 10.00 | 80.00 | 600 | 1,000 |
| 1903B Specimen | — | — | — | — | — | 2,700 |
| 1904B | 200,000 | — | 20.00 | 350 | 1,200 | 2,000 |
| 1904B Specimen | — | — | — | — | — | 5,700 |
| 1905B | 300,000 | — | 10.00 | 75.00 | 475 | 750 |
| 1905B Specimen | — | — | — | — | — | 2,700 |
| 1906B | 400,000 | — | 10.00 | 85.00 | 500 | 850 |
| 1906B Specimen | — | — | — | — | — | 3,000 |
| 1907B | 300,000 | — | 12.50 | 145 | 725 | 1,200 |
| 1907B Specimen | — | — | — | — | — | 3,000 |
| 1908B | 200,000 | — | 20.00 | 350 | 1,500 | 2,200 |
| 1908B Specimen | — | — | — | — | — | 5,400 |
| 1909B | 300,000 | — | 9.00 | 75.00 | 350 | 700 |
| 1909B Specimen | — | — | — | — | — | 3,900 |
| 1910B | 250,000 | — | 9.00 | 175 | 800 | 1,250 |
| 1910B Specimen | — | — | — | — | — | 4,200 |
| 1911B | 400,000 | — | 7.50 | 40.00 | 180 | 300 |
| 1911B Specimen | — | — | — | — | — | 1,800 |
| 1912B | 400,000 | — | 7.50 | 40.00 | 125 | 200 |
| 1912B Specimen | — | — | — | — | — | 1,500 |
| 1913B | 300,000 | — | 7.50 | 40.00 | 160 | 275 |
| 1913B Specimen | — | — | — | — | — | 2,100 |
| 1914B | 1,000,000 | — | 5.00 | 25.00 | 100 | 175 |
| 1914B Specimen | — | — | — | — | — | 1,200 |
| 1916B | 250,000 | — | 7.50 | 130 | 500 | 800 |
| 1916B Specimen | — | — | — | — | — | 2,400 |
| 1920B | 2,300,000 | — | 3.00 | 10.00 | 27.50 | 50.00 |
| 1920B Specimen | — | — | — | — | — | 450 |
| 1921B | 2,000,000 | — | 3.00 | 10.00 | 25.00 | 50.00 |
| 1921B Specimen | — | — | — | — | — | 450 |
| 1922B | 400,000 | — | 3.00 | 35.00 | 160 | 225 |
| 1922B Specimen | — | — | — | — | — | 1,200 |
| 1928B | 750,000 | — | 3.00 | 12.50 | 30.00 | 50.00 |
| 1928B Specimen | — | — | — | — | — | 450 |
| 1931B | 500,000 | — | 3.00 | 12.50 | 40.00 | 70.00 |
| 1931B Specimen | — | — | — | — | — | 450 |
| 1932B | 250,000 | — | 4.00 | 40.00 | 220 | 300 |
| 1932B Specimen | — | — | — | — | — | 1,050 |
| 1936B | 250,000 | — | 4.00 | 35.00 | 110 | 165 |
| 1936B Specimen | — | — | — | — | — | 600 |
| 1937B | 250,000 | — | 4.00 | 22.50 | 70.00 | 100 |
| 1937B Specimen | — | — | — | — | — | 450 |
| 1939B | 1,455,000 | — | 2.25 | 5.00 | 8.00 | 12.00 |
| 1939B Specimen | — | — | — | — | — | 600 |
| 1940B | 2,502,000 | — | 2.25 | 5.00 | 8.00 | 12.00 |
| 1940B Specimen | — | — | — | — | — | 180 |
| 1941B | 1,192,000 | — | 2.25 | 5.00 | 8.00 | 12.00 |
| 1941B Specimen | — | — | — | — | — | 180 |
| 1943B | 2,089,000 | — | 2.25 | 4.00 | 8.00 | 12.00 |
| 1943B Specimen | — | — | — | — | — | 180 |
| 1944B | 6,276,000 | — | 2.25 | 4.00 | 8.00 | 12.00 |
| 1944B Specimen | — | — | — | — | — | 180 |
| 1945B | 1,134,000 | — | 2.50 | 7.00 | 15.00 | 22.50 |
| 1945B Specimen | — | — | — | — | — | 180 |
| 1946B | 1,629,000 | — | 2.50 | 4.00 | 10.00 | 15.00 |
| 1946B Specimen | — | — | — | — | — | 180 |
| 1947B | 500,000 | — | 4.00 | 8.00 | 22.00 | 32.00 |
| 1947B Specimen | — | — | — | — | — | 180 |
| 1948B | 920,000 | — | 2.50 | 4.00 | 10.00 | 15.00 |
| 1948B Specimen | — | — | — | — | — | 180 |
| 1953B | 438,000 | — | 3.00 | 6.00 | 20.00 | 30.00 |
| 1953B Specimen | — | — | — | — | — | 180 |
| 1955B | 1,032,000 | — | 2.50 | 3.50 | 6.00 | 9.00 |
| 1955B Specimen | — | — | — | — | — | 150 |
| 1957B | 2,298,000 | — | 2.00 | 3.00 | 4.00 | 6.00 |
| 1957B Specimen | — | — | — | — | — | 60.00 |
| 1958B | 650,000 | — | 2.50 | 3.50 | 5.00 | 7.00 |
| 1958B Specimen | — | — | — | — | — | 60.00 |
| 1959B | 2,905,000 | — | 2.00 | 3.00 | 4.00 | 6.00 |
| 1959B Specimen | — | — | — | — | — | 60.00 |
| 1960B | 1,980,000 | — | 2.00 | 3.00 | 4.00 | 6.00 |
| 1960B Specimen | — | — | — | — | — | 60.00 |
| 1961B | 4,653,000 | — | — | 2.50 | 4.00 | 7.00 |
| 1961B Specimen | — | — | — | — | — | 60.00 |
| 1963B | 8,029,999 | — | — | 2.00 | 4.00 | 7.00 |
| 1963B Specimen | — | — | — | — | — | 60.00 |
| 1964B | 4,558,000 | — | — | 2.00 | 4.00 | 7.00 |
| 1964B Specimen | — | — | — | — | — | 60.00 |
| 1965B | 8,526,000 | — | — | 2.00 | 4.00 | 7.00 |
| 1965B Specimen | — | — | — | — | — | 60.00 |
| 1967B | 4,131,999 | — | — | 2.00 | 4.00 | 7.00 |
| 1967B Specimen | — | — | — | — | — | 60.00 |

**2 FRANCS** **KM# 21a.1** **Composition:** Copper-Nickel

| Date | Mintage | F | VF | XF | Unc | BU |
|---|---|---|---|---|---|---|
| 1968 | 10,000,000 | — | — | — | 4.00 | 6.00 |
| 1968B | 31,588,000 | — | — | — | 4.00 | 6.00 |
| 1969B | 17,296,000 | — | — | — | 4.00 | 6.00 |
| 1970 | 10,350,000 | — | — | — | 4.00 | 6.00 |
| 1972 | 5,003,000 | — | — | — | 4.00 | 6.00 |
| 1973 | 5,996,000 | — | — | — | 4.00 | 6.00 |
| 1974 | 15,009,000 | — | — | — | 4.00 | 6.00 |
| 1974 Proof | 2,400 | Value: 65.00 | | | | |
| 1975 | 7,061,000 | — | — | — | 4.00 | 6.00 |

| Date | Mintage | F | VF | XF | Unc | BU |
|---|---|---|---|---|---|---|
| 1975 Proof | 10,000 | Value: 9.00 | | | | |
| 1976 | 5,011,000 | — | — | — | 4.00 | 6.00 |
| 1976 Proof | 5,130 | Value: 10.00 | | | | |
| 1977 | 2,009,999 | — | — | — | 4.00 | 6.00 |
| 1977 Proof | 7,030 | Value: 9.00 | | | | |
| 1978 | 12,812,000 | — | — | — | 3.00 | 4.00 |
| 1978 Proof | 10,000 | Value: 7.00 | | | | |
| 1979 | 10,990,000 | — | — | — | 3.00 | 4.00 |
| 1979 Proof | 10,000 | Value: 7.00 | | | | |
| 1980 | 10,001,000 | — | — | — | 3.00 | 4.00 |
| 1980 Proof | 10,000 | Value: 7.00 | | | | |
| 1981 | 13,852,000 | — | — | — | 3.00 | 4.00 |
| 1981 Proof | 10,000 | Value: 7.00 | | | | |

**2 FRANCS** **KM# 21a.2** **Composition:** Copper-Nickel **Obverse:** 22 stars around figure **Note:** Medal alignment.

| Date | Mintage | F | VF | XF | Unc | BU |
|---|---|---|---|---|---|---|
| 1982 | 5,912,000 | — | — | — | 4.00 | 6.00 |
| 1982 Proof | 10,000 | Value: 15.00 | | | | |

**2 FRANCS** **KM# 21a.3** **Composition:** Copper-Nickel **Obverse:** 23 stars

| Date | Mintage | F | VF | XF | Unc | BU |
|---|---|---|---|---|---|---|
| 1983 | 3,023,000 | — | — | — | 3.00 | 4.00 |
| 1983 Proof | 11,000 | Value: 8.00 | | | | |
| 1984 | 2,029,000 | — | — | — | 3.00 | 4.00 |
| 1984 Proof | 14,000 | Value: 8.00 | | | | |
| 1985 | 3,022,000 | — | — | — | 3.00 | 4.00 |
| 1985 Proof | 12,000 | Value: 8.00 | | | | |
| 1986B | 3,032,000 | — | — | — | 3.00 | 4.00 |
| 1986B Proof | 10,000 | Value: 8.00 | | | | |
| 1987B | 8,028,000 | — | — | — | 2.50 | 3.50 |
| 1987B Proof | 8,800 | Value: 7.50 | | | | |
| 1988B | 10,029,000 | — | — | — | 2.50 | 3.50 |
| 1988B Proof | 9,000 | Value: 7.50 | | | | |
| 1989B | 8,031,000 | — | — | — | 2.50 | 3.50 |
| 1989B Proof | 8,800 | Value: 7.50 | | | | |
| 1990B | 5,045,000 | — | — | — | 2.50 | 3.50 |
| 1990B Proof | 8,900 | Value: 7.50 | | | | |
| 1991B | 12,036,000 | — | — | — | 2.00 | 3.00 |
| 1991B Proof | 9,900 | Value: 7.50 | | | | |
| 1992B | 10,027,000 | — | — | — | 2.00 | 3.00 |
| 1992B Proof | 7,450 | Value: 7.00 | | | | |
| 1993B | 13,049,000 | — | — | — | 2.00 | 3.00 |
| 1993B Proof | 6,200 | Value: 7.00 | | | | |
| 1994B | 16,023,000 | — | — | — | 2.00 | 3.00 |
| 1994B Proof | 6,100 | Value: 7.00 | | | | |
| 1995B | 7,024,000 | — | — | — | 2.00 | 3.00 |
| 1995B Proof | 6,100 | Value: 7.00 | | | | |
| 1996B | 5,023,000 | — | — | — | 2.00 | 3.00 |
| 1996B Proof | 6,100 | Value: 7.00 | | | | |
| 1997B | 5,022,000 | — | — | — | 2.00 | 3.00 |
| 1997B Proof | 5,500 | Value: 7.00 | | | | |
| 1998B | 4,021,000 | — | — | — | 2.00 | 3.00 |
| 1998B Proof | 4,800 | Value: 7.00 | | | | |
| 1999B | 3,021,000 | — | — | — | 2.00 | 3.00 |
| 1999B Proof | 5,000 | Value: 7.00 | | | | |
| 2000B | 3,026,000 | — | — | — | 2.00 | 3.00 |
| 2000B Proof | 5,500 | Value: 7.00 | | | | |
| 2001B | — | — | — | — | 2.00 | 3.00 |
| 2001B Proof | 6,000 | Value: 7.00 | | | | |

**5 FRANCS** **KM# 34** **Weight:** 25.0000 g. **Composition:** 0.9000 Silver .7234 oz. ASW

| Date | Mintage | F | VF | XF | Unc | BU |
|---|---|---|---|---|---|---|
| 1904B | 40,000 | — | 600 | 1,000 | 2,000 | 3,500 |
| 1904B Specimen | — | — | — | — | — | 7,800 |
| 1907B | 277,000 | — | 125 | 300 | 600 | 1,100 |
| 1907B Specimen | — | — | — | — | — | 3,600 |
| 1908B | 200,000 | — | 135 | 325 | 650 | 1,100 |
| 1908B Specimen | — | — | — | — | — | 3,600 |
| 1909B | 120,000 | — | 175 | 350 | 650 | 1,100 |
| 1909B Specimen | — | — | — | — | — | 3,600 |
| 1912B | 11,000 | — | 2,750 | 3,500 | 4,500 | 7,000 |
| 1912B Specimen | — | — | — | — | — | 12,000 |
| 1916B | 22,000 | — | 1,000 | 1,500 | 2,000 | 3,000 |
| 1916B Specimen | — | — | — | — | — | 6,000 |

**5 FRANCS** **KM# 37** **Weight:** 25.0000 g. **Composition:** 0.9000 Silver .7234 oz. ASW

| Date | Mintage | F | VF | XF | Unc | BU |
|---|---|---|---|---|---|---|
| 1922B | 2,400,000 | — | 50.00 | 125 | 200 | 300 |
| 1922B Specimen | — | — | — | — | — | 1,800 |
| 1923B | 11,300,000 | — | 40.00 | 70.00 | 175 | 250 |
| 1923B Specimen | — | — | — | — | — | 3,000 |

**5 FRANCS** **KM# 38** **Weight:** 25.0000 g. **Composition:** 0.9000 Silver .7234 oz. ASW

| Date | Mintage | F | VF | XF | Unc | BU |
|---|---|---|---|---|---|---|
| 1924B | 182,000 | — | 375 | 550 | 850 | 1,250 |
| 1924B Specimen | — | — | — | — | — | 2,400 |
| 1925B | 2,830,000 | — | 75.00 | 150 | 225 | 325 |
| 1925B Specimen | — | — | — | — | — | 1,500 |
| 1926B | 2,000,000 | — | 80.00 | 150 | 250 | 350 |
| 1926B Specimen | — | — | — | — | — | 1,500 |
| 1928B | 24,000 | — | 7,000 | 9,000 | 12,500 | 16,000 |
| 1928B Specimen; Rare | — | — | — | — | — | — |

**5 FRANCS** **KM# 40** **Weight:** 15.0000 g. **Composition:** 0.8350 Silver .7234 oz. ASW **Note:** Raised edge lettering.

| Date | Mintage | F | VF | XF | Unc | BU |
|---|---|---|---|---|---|---|
| 1931B | 3,520,000 | — | 5.00 | 12.00 | 40.00 | 80.00 |
| **Note:** Edge lettering PROVIDEBIT ********** *** DOMINUS | | | | | | |
| 1931B Specimen | Inc. above | — | — | — | — | 900 |
| **Note:** Edge lettering PROVIDEBIT ********** *** DOMINUS | | | | | | |
| 1931B | Inc. above | — | 12.50 | 25.00 | 75.00 | 110 |
| **Note:** Common variety edge lettering ********** *** DOMINUS PROVIDEBIT | | | | | | |
| 1931B | Inc. above | — | 35.00 | 90.00 | 200 | 300 |
| **Note:** Somewhat rarer ********** PROVIDEBIT *** DOMINUS | | | | | | |
| 1931B | Inc. above | — | 600 | 1,000 | 1,400 | 2,100 |
| **Note:** *** DOMINUS ********** PROVIDEBIT | | | | | | |
| 1932B | 10,580,000 | — | 4.00 | 7.50 | 12.00 | 20.00 |
| 1932B Specimen | — | — | — | — | — | 450 |
| 1933B | 5,900,000 | — | 6.00 | 10.00 | 17.50 | 27.50 |
| 1933B Specimen | — | — | — | — | — | 450 |
| 1935B | 3,000,000 | — | 6.00 | 10.00 | 17.50 | 27.50 |
| 1935B Specimen | — | — | — | — | — | 450 |
| 1937B | 645,000 | — | 6.50 | 12.50 | 32.50 | 50.00 |
| 1937B Specimen | — | — | — | — | — | 900 |
| 1939B | 2,197,000 | — | 5.00 | 7.50 | 12.50 | 20.00 |
| 1939B Specimen | — | — | — | — | — | 450 |
| 1940B | 1,601,000 | — | 6.00 | 10.00 | 20.00 | 30.00 |
| 1940B Specimen | — | — | — | — | — | 600 |
| 1948B | 416,000 | — | 6.50 | 13.00 | 30.00 | 45.00 |
| 1948B Specimen | — | — | — | — | — | 600 |
| 1949B | 407,000 | — | 6.50 | 15.00 | 35.00 | 47.50 |
| 1949B Specimen | — | — | — | — | — | 600 |
| 1950B | 482,000 | — | 6.50 | 10.00 | 30.00 | 45.00 |
| 1950B Specimen | — | — | — | — | — | 600 |
| 1951B | 1,196,000 | — | 5.00 | 10.00 | 20.00 | 30.00 |
| 1951B Specimen | — | — | — | — | — | 300 |
| 1952B | 155,000 | — | 30.00 | 60.00 | 150 | 225 |
| 1952B Specimen | — | — | — | — | — | 750 |
| 1953B | 3,403,000 | — | — | 6.00 | 8.00 | 12.00 |
| 1953B Specimen | — | — | — | — | — | 150 |
| 1954B | 6,600,000 | — | — | 6.00 | 8.00 | 11.00 |
| 1954B Specimen | — | — | — | — | — | 150 |
| 1965B | 5,021,000 | — | — | 4.00 | 7.00 | 10.00 |
| 1965B Specimen | — | — | — | — | — | 120 |
| 1966B | 9,016,000 | — | — | 4.00 | 7.00 | 10.00 |
| 1966B Specimen | — | — | — | — | — | 120 |
| 1967B | 13,817,000 | — | — | 4.00 | 7.00 | 10.00 |
| **Note:** Edge lettering PROVIDEBIT ********** *** DOMINUS | | | | | | |
| 1967B Specimen | — | — | — | — | — | 120 |
| **Note:** Edge lettering PROVIDEBIT ********** *** DOMINUS | | | | | | |
| 1967B | — | — | 50.00 | 80.00 | 110 | 155 |
| **Note:** Common variety edge lettering ********** *** DOMINUS PROVIDEBIT | | | | | | |
| 1967B | — | — | 400 | 750 | 1,100 | 1,550 |
| **Note:** *** DOMINUS ********** PROVIDEBIT | | | | | | |
| 1969B | 8,637,000 | — | — | 4.00 | 7.00 | 10.00 |
| 1969B Specimen | — | — | — | — | — | 120 |

**5 FRANCS** **KM# 40a.1** **Composition:** Copper-Nickel

| Date | Mintage | F | VF | XF | Unc | BU |
|---|---|---|---|---|---|---|
| 1968B | 33,871,000 | — | — | — | 5.00 | 7.00 |
| 1970 | 6,306,000 | — | — | — | 5.00 | 7.00 |
| 1973 | 5,002,000 | — | — | — | 5.00 | 7.00 |
| 1974 | 6,007,000 | — | — | — | 5.00 | 7.00 |
| 1974 Proof | 2,400 | Value: 125 | | | | |
| 1975 | 4,015,000 | — | — | — | 5.00 | 7.00 |
| 1975 Proof | 10,000 | Value: 12.00 | | | | |
| 1976 | 3,007,000 | — | — | — | 5.00 | 7.00 |
| 1976 Proof | 5,130 | Value: 14.00 | | | | |
| 1977 | 2,009,000 | — | — | — | 5.00 | 7.00 |
| 1977 Proof | 7,030 | Value: 12.00 | | | | |
| 1978 | 4,411,000 | — | — | — | 5.00 | 7.00 |
| 1978 Proof | 10,000 | Value: 12.00 | | | | |
| 1979 | 4,011,000 | — | — | — | 5.00 | 7.00 |
| 1979 Proof | 10,000 | Value: 12.00 | | | | |
| 1980 | 4,026,000 | — | — | — | 5.00 | 7.00 |
| 1980 Proof | 10,000 | Value: 12.00 | | | | |
| 1981 | 6,018,000 | — | — | — | 5.00 | 7.00 |
| 1981 Proof | 10,000 | Value: 12.00 | | | | |

**5 FRANCS** **KM# 40a.2** **Composition:** Copper-Nickel **Note:** Medal alignment.

| Date | Mintage | F | VF | XF | Unc | BU |
|---|---|---|---|---|---|---|
| 1982 | 5,050,000 | — | — | — | 6.00 | 8.00 |
| 1982 Proof | 10,000 | Value: 18.00 | | | | |
| 1983 | 4,033,000 | — | — | — | 6.00 | 8.00 |
| 1983 Proof | 11,000 | Value: 12.00 | | | | |
| 1984 | 3,953,000 | — | — | — | 6.00 | 8.00 |
| 1984 Proof | 14,000 | Value: 11.00 | | | | |

**5 FRANCS** **KM# 40a.3** **Composition:** Copper-Nickel **Note:** Incuse edge lettering.

| Date | Mintage | F | VF | XF | Unc | BU |
|---|---|---|---|---|---|---|
| 1985 | 4,050,000 | — | — | — | 5.50 | 7.50 |
| 1985 Proof | 12,000 | Value: 10.00 | | | | |
| 1986B | 7,083,000 | — | — | — | 5.50 | 7.50 |
| 1986B Proof | 10,000 | Value: 11.00 | | | | |
| 1987B | 7,028,000 | — | — | — | 5.50 | 7.50 |
| 1987B Proof | 8,800 | Value: 12.00 | | | | |
| 1988B | 7,029,000 | — | — | — | 5.50 | 7.50 |
| 1988B Proof | 9,000 | Value: 12.00 | | | | |
| 1989B | 5,031,000 | — | — | — | 5.50 | 7.50 |
| 1989B Proof | 8,800 | Value: 12.00 | | | | |
| 1990B | 1,049,000 | — | — | — | 6.00 | 8.00 |
| 1990B Proof | 8,900 | Value: 12.00 | | | | |
| 1991B Mint sets only | 26,000 | — | — | — | — | 110 |
| 1991B Proof | 9,900 | Value: 120 | | | | |
| 1992B | 5,034,000 | — | — | — | 5.00 | 6.50 |
| 1992B Proof | 7,450 | Value: 12.00 | | | | |
| 1993B Mint sets only | 16,000 | — | — | — | — | 110 |
| 1993B Proof | 6,200 | Value: 125 | | | | |

**5 FRANCS** **KM# 40a.4** **Composition:** Copper-Nickel **Note:** Raised edge lettering.

| Date | Mintage | F | VF | XF | Unc | BU |
|---|---|---|---|---|---|---|
| 1994B | 12,023,000 | — | — | — | 5.00 | 6.50 |
| 1994B Proof | 6,100 | Value: 15.00 | | | | |
| 1995B | 12,024,000 | — | — | — | 5.00 | 6.50 |
| 1995B Proof | 6,100 | Value: 15.00 | | | | |
| 1996B | 12,023,000 | — | — | — | 5.00 | 6.50 |
| 1996B Proof | 6,100 | Value: 12.00 | | | | |
| 1997B | 9,022,000 | — | — | — | 5.00 | 6.50 |
| 1997B Proof | 5,500 | Value: 12.00 | | | | |
| 1998B | 9,021,000 | — | — | — | 5.00 | 6.50 |
| 1998B Proof | 4,800 | Value: 12.00 | | | | |
| 1999B | 9,021,000 | — | — | — | 5.00 | 6.50 |
| 1999B Proof | 5,000 | Value: 12.00 | | | | |
| 2000B | 7,026,000 | — | — | — | 5.00 | 6.50 |
| 2000B Proof | 5,500 | Value: 12.00 | | | | |
| 2001B | — | — | — | — | 5.00 | 6.50 |
| 2001B Proof | 6,000 | Value: 12.00 | | | | |

## COMMEMORATIVE COINAGE

**5 FRANCS** **KM# 41** **Weight:** 15.0000 g. **Composition:** 0.8350 Silver .4027 oz. ASW **Subject:** Confederation Armament Fund

| Date | Mintage | F | VF | XF | Unc | BU |
|---|---|---|---|---|---|---|
| 1936B | 200,000 | — | 12.50 | 20.00 | 40.00 | 70.00 |
| 1936B Specimen | — | — | — | — | — | 300 |

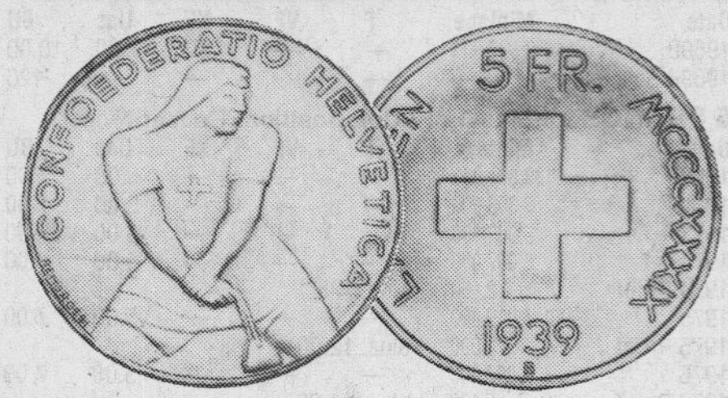


**5 FRANCS** **KM# 42** **Weight:** 15.0000 g. **Composition:** 0.8350 Silver .4027 oz. ASW **Subject:** 600th Anniversary - Battle of Laupen

| Date | Mintage | F | VF | XF | Unc | BU |
|---|---|---|---|---|---|---|
| 1939B | 31,000 | — | 250 | 375 | 500 | 700 |

**5 FRANCS** **KM# 43** **Weight:** 15.0000 g. **Composition:** 0.8350 Silver .4027 oz. ASW **Subject:** Zurich Exposition

| Date | Mintage | F | VF | XF | Unc | BU |
|---|---|---|---|---|---|---|
| 1939 | 60,000 | — | 50.00 | 75.00 | 110 | 150 |
| **Note:** Minted at Huguenin, Le Locle | | | | | | |
| 1939 Specimen | — | — | — | — | — | 900 |
| 1939 Matte | — | — | — | — | — | 1,500 |

**5 FRANCS** **KM# 44** **Weight:** 15.0000 g. **Composition:** 0.8350 Silver .4027 oz. ASW **Subject:** 650th Anniversary of Confederation

| Date | Mintage | F | VF | XF | Unc | BU |
|---|---|---|---|---|---|---|
| ND(1941)B | 100,000 | — | 25.00 | 40.00 | 60.00 | 90.00 |
| ND(1941)B Specimen | — | — | — | — | — | 360 |

**5 FRANCS** **KM# 45** **Weight:** 15.0000 g. **Composition:** 0.8350 Silver .4027 oz. ASW **Subject:** 500th Anniversary - Battle of St. Jakob An Der Birs

| Date | Mintage | F | VF | XF | Unc | BU |
|---|---|---|---|---|---|---|
| 1944B | 102,000 | — | 20.00 | 40.00 | 60.00 | 85.00 |
| 1944B Specimen | — | — | — | — | — | 360 |

**5 FRANCS** **KM# 48** **Weight:** 15.0000 g. **Composition:** 0.8350 Silver .4027 oz. ASW **Subject:** Swiss Constitution Centennial

| Date | Mintage | F | VF | XF | Unc | BU |
|---|---|---|---|---|---|---|
| 1948B | 500,000 | — | 6.00 | 9.00 | 14.00 | 20.00 |
| 1948B Specimen | — | — | — | — | — | 150 |

**5 FRANCS** **KM# A48** **Composition:** Gold

| Date | Mintage | F | VF | XF | Unc | BU |
|---|---|---|---|---|---|---|
| 1948B Rare | Est. 50 | — | — | — | — | — |

**5 FRANCS** **KM# 51** **Composition:** Gold **Subject:** Red Cross Centennial

| Date | Mintage | F | VF | XF | Unc | BU |
|---|---|---|---|---|---|---|
| ND(1963)B | 623,000 | — | 5.00 | 6.50 | 10.00 | 18.00 |
| ND(1963)B Specimen | — | — | — | — | — | 120 |

**5 FRANCS** **KM#52** **Composition:** Copper-Nickel **Subject:** 100th Anniversary - Revision of Constitution

| Date | Mintage | F | VF | XF | Unc | BU |
|---|---|---|---|---|---|---|
| ND(1974) | 3,700,000 | — | — | — | 5.00 | 7.00 |
| ND(1974) Proof | 130,000 | Value: 12.00 | | | | |

**5 FRANCS** **KM#53** **Composition:** Copper-Nickel **Subject:** European Monument Protection Year

| Date | Mintage | F | VF | XF | Unc | BU |
|---|---|---|---|---|---|---|
| 1975 | 2,500,000 | — | — | — | 5.00 | 7.00 |
| 1975 Proof | 60,000 | Value: 20.00 | | | | |

**5 FRANCS** **KM#54** **Composition:** Copper-Nickel **Subject:** 500th Anniversary - Battle of Murten

| Date | Mintage | F | VF | XF | Unc | BU |
|---|---|---|---|---|---|---|
| 1976 | 1,500,000 | — | — | — | 6.00 | 8.00 |
| 1976 Proof | 100,000 | Value: 12.00 | | | | |

**5 FRANCS** **KM#55** **Composition:** Copper-Nickel **Subject:** 150th Anniversary - Death of Johann Pestalozzi

| Date | Mintage | F | VF | XF | Unc | BU |
|---|---|---|---|---|---|---|
| 1977 | 800,000 | — | — | — | 8.00 | 10.00 |
| 1977 Proof | 50,000 | Value: 20.00 | | | | |

**5 FRANCS** **KM#56** **Composition:** Copper-Nickel **Subject:** 150th Anniversary - Birth of Henry Dunant

| Date | Mintage | F | VF | XF | Unc | BU |
|---|---|---|---|---|---|---|
| 1978 | 900,000 | — | — | — | 8.00 | 10.00 |
| 1978 Proof | 60,000 | Value: 16.00 | | | | |

**5 FRANCS** **KM#57** **Composition:** Copper-Nickel **Subject:** Centennial - Birth of Albert Einstein

| Date | Mintage | F | VF | XF | Unc | BU |
|---|---|---|---|---|---|---|
| 1979 | 900,000 | — | — | — | 9.00 | 12.00 |
| 1979 Proof | 35,000 | Value: 50.00 | | | | |

**5 FRANCS** **KM#58** **Composition:** Copper-Nickel **Subject:** Centennial - Birth of Albert Einstein

| Date | Mintage | F | VF | XF | Unc | BU |
|---|---|---|---|---|---|---|
| 1979 | 900,000 | — | — | — | 9.00 | 12.00 |
| 1979 Proof | 35,000 | Value: 50.00 | | | | |

**5 FRANCS** **KM#59** **Composition:** Copper-Nickel **Subject:** Ferdinand Hodler - Painter

| Date | Mintage | F | VF | XF | Unc | BU |
|---|---|---|---|---|---|---|
| 1980 | 950,000 | — | — | — | 6.00 | 8.00 |
| 1980 Proof | 50,000 | Value: 22.00 | | | | |

**5 FRANCS** **KM#60** **Composition:** Copper-Nickel **Subject:** 500th Anniversary - Stans Convention of 1481

| Date | Mintage | F | VF | XF | Unc | BU |
|---|---|---|---|---|---|---|
| 1981 | 900,000 | — | — | — | 6.00 | 8.00 |
| 1981 Proof | 50,000 | Value: 18.00 | | | | |

**5 FRANCS** **KM# 61** **Composition:** Copper-Nickel **Subject:** 100th Anniversary - Gotthard Railway

| Date | Mintage | F | VF | XF | Unc | BU |
|---|---|---|---|---|---|---|
| 1982 | 1,100,000 | — | — | — | 9.00 | 12.00 |
| 1982 Proof | 65,000 | Value: 20.00 | | | | |

**5 FRANCS** **KM# 62** **Composition:** Copper-Nickel **Subject:** 100th Anniversary - Birth of Ernest Ansermet

| Date | Mintage | F | VF | XF | Unc | BU |
|---|---|---|---|---|---|---|
| 1983 | 951,000 | — | — | — | 6.00 | 8.00 |
| 1983 Proof | 60,000 | Value: 20.00 | | | | |

**5 FRANCS** **KM# 63** **Composition:** Copper-Nickel **Subject:** Centennial - Birth of Auguste Piccard

| Date | Mintage | F | VF | XF | Unc | BU |
|---|---|---|---|---|---|---|
| 1984 | 1,000,000 | — | — | — | 6.00 | 8.00 |
| 1984 Proof | 75,000 | Value: 15.00 | | | | |

**5 FRANCS** **KM# 64** **Composition:** Copper-Nickel **Subject:** European Year of Music

| Date | Mintage | F | VF | XF | Unc | BU |
|---|---|---|---|---|---|---|
| 1985 | 1,156,000 | — | — | — | 6.00 | 8.00 |
| 1985 Proof | 84,000 | Value: 12.00 | | | | |

**5 FRANCS** **KM# 65** **Composition:** Copper-Nickel **Subject:** 500th Anniversary - Battle of Sempach

| Date | Mintage | F | VF | XF | Unc | BU |
|---|---|---|---|---|---|---|
| 1986B | 1,080,000 | — | — | — | 6.00 | 8.00 |
| 1986B Proof | 76,000 | Value: 12.00 | | | | |

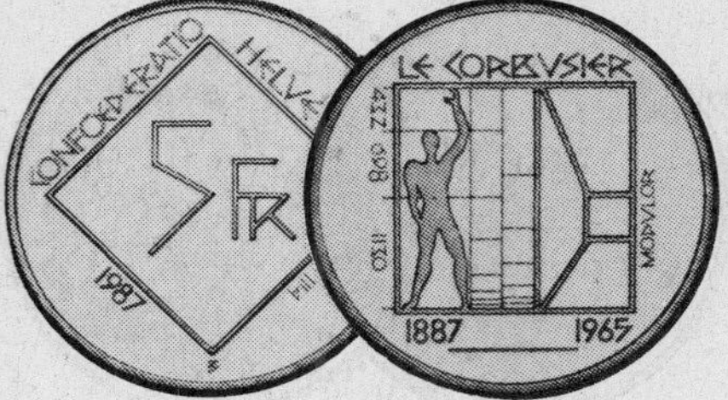


**5 FRANCS** **KM# 66** **Composition:** Copper-Nickel **Subject:** 100th Anniversary - Birth of Le Corbusier

| Date | Mintage | F | VF | XF | Unc | BU |
|---|---|---|---|---|---|---|
| 1987B | 960,000 | — | — | — | 6.00 | 8.00 |
| 1987B Proof | 62,000 | Value: 18.00 | | | | |

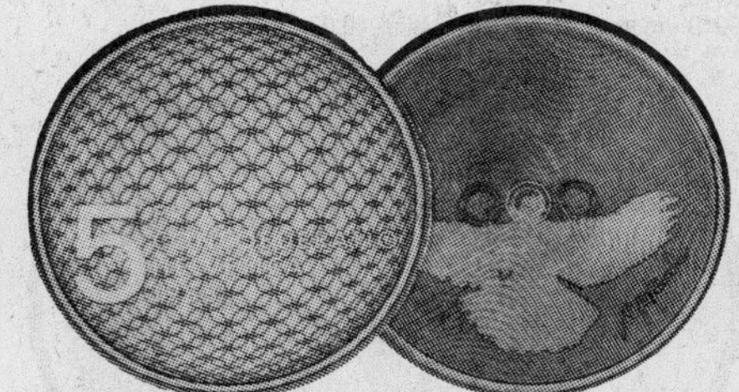

**5 FRANCS** **KM# 67** **Composition:** Copper-Nickel **Subject:** Olympics - Dove and Rings

| Date | Mintage | F | VF | XF | Unc | BU |
|---|---|---|---|---|---|---|
| 1988B | 1,026,000 | — | — | — | 6.00 | 8.00 |
| 1988B Proof | 69,000 | Value: 25.00 | | | | |

**5 FRANCS** **KM# 68** **Composition:** Copper-Nickel **Subject:** General Guisan - 1939 Mobilization

| Date | Mintage | F | VF | XF | Unc | BU |
|---|---|---|---|---|---|---|
| 1989B | 1,270,000 | — | — | — | 6.00 | 8.00 |
| 1989B Proof | 69,000 | Value: 18.00 | | | | |

**5 FRANCS** **KM# 69** **Composition:** Copper-Nickel **Subject:** Gottfried Keller

| Date | Mintage | F | VF | XF | Unc | BU |
|---|---|---|---|---|---|---|
| 1990B | 1,100,000 | — | — | — | 6.00 | 8.00 |
| 1990B Proof | 69,000 | Value: 12.00 | | | | |

**5 FRANCS** **KM# 86** **Ring Composition:** Copper-Nickel **Center Composition:** Brass **Subject:** Wine Festival **Obverse:** Denomination **Reverse:** Grapes

| Date | Mintage | F | VF | XF | Unc | BU |
|---|---|---|---|---|---|---|
| 1999 | 160,000 | — | — | — | — | 6.50 |
| 1999 Proof | 16,000 | Value: 20.00 | | | | |

**5 FRANCS** **KM# 89** **Ring Weight:** 14.9100 g. **Ring Composition:** Copper-Nickel **Center Composition:** Brass **Subject:** Basler Fasnacht **Obverse:** Denomination **Reverse:** Costumed flutists **Edge:** Reeded **Size:** 32.9 mm.

| Date | Mintage | F | VF | XF | Unc | BU |
|---|---|---|---|---|---|---|
| 2000 | 170,000 | — | — | — | — | 6.50 |
| 2000 Proof | 20,000 | Value: 20.00 | | | | |

**5 FRANCS** **KM# 91** **Ring Weight:** 15.0000 g. **Ring Composition:** Copper-Nickel **Center Composition:** Brass **Subject:** Swiss National Coinage, 150 Years **Obverse:** Detailed leaf surface showing vein structure **Reverse:** Honeycomb design **Edge:** Reeded **Size:** 32.9 mm.

| Date | Mintage | F | VF | XF | Unc | BU |
|---|---|---|---|---|---|---|
| 2000 | 150,000 | — | — | — | 6.50 | — |

**5 FRANCS** **KM# 92** **Ring Weight:** 14.8000 g. **Ring Composition:** Copper-Nickel **Center Composition:** Brass **Subject:** Zurcher Sechselauten **Obverse:** Denomination **Reverse:** Burning strawman **Edge:** Reeded **Size:** 32.9 mm.

| Date | Mintage | F | VF | XF | Unc | BU |
|---|---|---|---|---|---|---|
| 2001 | 170,000 | — | — | — | 6.50 | — |

**10 FRANCS** **KM# 36** **Weight:** 3.2258 g. **Composition:** 0.9000 Gold .0933 oz. AGW

| Date | Mintage | F | VF | XF | Unc | BU |
|---|---|---|---|---|---|---|
| 1911B | 100,000 | — | 125 | 200 | 300 | 500 |
| 1912B | 200,000 | — | 50.00 | 90.00 | 125 | 200 |
| 1913B | 600,000 | — | 40.00 | 75.00 | 90.00 | 125 |
| 1914B | 200,000 | — | 45.00 | 75.00 | 100 | 135 |
| 1915B | 400,000 | — | 40.00 | 75.00 | 100 | 135 |
| 1916B | 130,000 | — | 50.00 | 85.00 | 115 | 175 |
| 1922B | 1,020,000 | — | 40.00 | 50.00 | 65.00 | 90.00 |

**20 FRANCS** **KM# 35.1** **Weight:** 6.4516 g. **Composition:** 0.9000 Gold .1867 oz. AGW

| Date | Mintage | F | VF | XF | Unc | BU |
|---|---|---|---|---|---|---|
| 1901B | 500,000 | — | BV | 65.00 | 85.00 | 110 |
| 1901B | 500,000 | — | BV | 70.00 | 90.00 | 115 |
| 1902B | 600,000 | — | BV | 70.00 | 90.00 | 115 |
| 1903B | 200,000 | — | 80.00 | 95.00 | 120 | 145 |

| Date | Mintage | F | VF | XF | Unc | BU |
|---|---|---|---|---|---|---|
| 1904B | 100,000 | — | 90.00 | 110 | 135 | 175 |
| 1905B | 100,000 | — | 90.00 | 110 | 135 | 175 |
| 1906B | 100,000 | — | 90.00 | 110 | 130 | 170 |
| 1907B | 150,000 | — | 80.00 | 95.00 | 115 | 140 |
| 1908B | 355,000 | — | BV | 75.00 | 95.00 | 120 |
| 1909B | 400,000 | — | BV | 75.00 | 95.00 | 120 |
| 1910B | 375,000 | — | BV | 75.00 | 95.00 | 120 |
| 1911B | 350,000 | — | BV | 75.00 | 95.00 | 120 |
| 1912B | 450,000 | — | BV | 75.00 | 95.00 | 120 |
| 1913B | 700,000 | — | BV | 75.00 | 95.00 | 115 |
| 1914B | 700,000 | — | BV | 75.00 | 95.00 | 115 |
| 1915B | 750,000 | — | BV | 75.00 | 95.00 | 115 |
| 1916B | 300,000 | — | BV | 75.00 | 95.00 | 115 |
| 1922B | 2,784,000 | — | BV | 65.00 | 80.00 | 100 |
| 1925B | 400,000 | — | BV | 75.00 | 95.00 | 115 |
| 1926B | 50,000 | — | 125 | 175 | 225 | 300 |
| 1927B | 5,015,000 | — | BV | 65.00 | 75.00 | 100 |
| 1930B | 3,372,000 | — | BV | 65.00 | 75.00 | 100 |
| 1935B | 175,000 | — | BV | 80.00 | 95.00 | 115 |
| 1935L-B | 20,009,000 | — | — | BV | 70.00 | 85.00 |

**Note:** The 1935L-B issue was struck in 1945, 1946 and 1947

**20 FRANCS** **KM# 35.2** **Weight:** 6.4516 g. **Composition:** 0.9000 Gold .1867 oz. AGW **Edge Lettering:** AD LEGEM ANNI MCMXXXI

| Date | Mintage | F | VF | XF | Unc | BU |
|---|---|---|---|---|---|---|
| 1947B | 9,200,000 | — | BV | 65.00 | 75.00 | 95.00 |
| 1949B | 10,000,000 | — | BV | 65.00 | 75.00 | 95.00 |

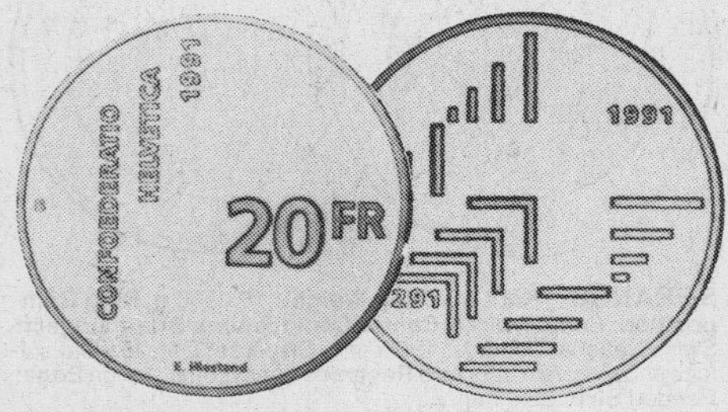


**20 FRANCS** **KM# 70** **Weight:** 20.0000 g. **Composition:** 0.8350 Silver .5369 oz. ASW **Subject:** 700 Years of Confederation

| Date | Mintage | F | VF | XF | Unc | BU |
|---|---|---|---|---|---|---|
| 1991B | 2,440,000 | — | — | — | 20.00 | 22.50 |
| 1991B Proof | 100,000 | Value: 25.00 | | | | |

**20 FRANCS** **KM# 72** **Weight:** 20.0000 g. **Composition:** 0.8350 Silver .5369 oz. ASW **Subject:** Gertrud Kurz

| Date | Mintage | F | VF | XF | Unc | BU |
|---|---|---|---|---|---|---|
| 1992B | 325,000 | — | — | — | 22.00 | 25.00 |
| 1992B Proof | 36,000 | Value: 30.00 | | | | |

**20 FRANCS** **KM# 73** **Weight:** 20.0000 g. **Composition:** 0.8350 Silver .5369 oz. ASW **Subject:** 500th Anniversary - Birth of Paracelsus

| Date | Mintage | F | VF | XF | Unc | BU |
|---|---|---|---|---|---|---|
| 1993B | 260,000 | — | — | — | 22.00 | 25.00 |
| 1993B Proof | 30,000 | Value: 40.00 | | | | |

**20 FRANCS** **KM# 74** **Weight:** 20.0000 g. **Composition:** 0.8350 Silver .5369 oz. ASW **Subject:** Devil's Bridge - Teufelsbrucke **Edge Lettering:** DOMINUS PROVIDEBEIT

| Date | Mintage | F | VF | XF | Unc | BU |
|---|---|---|---|---|---|---|
| 1994B | 240,000 | — | — | — | 22.00 | 25.00 |
| 1994B Proof | 32,000 | Value: 40.00 | | | | |

**20 FRANCS** **KM# 75** **Weight:** 20.0000 g. **Composition:** 0.8350 Silver .5369 oz. ASW **Subject:** Mythological White Snake Queen **Edge Lettering:** DOMINUS PROVIDEBIT (13 stars)

| Date | Mintage | F | VF | XF | Unc | BU |
|---|---|---|---|---|---|---|
| 1995B | 235,000 | — | — | — | 22.00 | 25.00 |
| 1995B Proof | 26,000 | Value: 40.00 | | | | |

**20 FRANCS** **KM# 76** **Weight:** 20.0000 g. **Composition:** 0.8350 Silver .5369 oz. ASW **Subject:** Mythological Giant Boy

| Date | Mintage | F | VF | XF | Unc | BU |
|---|---|---|---|---|---|---|
| 1996B | 206,000 | — | — | — | 22.00 | 25.00 |
| 1996B Proof | 30,000 | Value: 50.00 | | | | |

**20 FRANCS** **KM# 77** **Weight:** 20.0000 g. **Composition:** 0.8350 Silver .5369 oz. ASW **Subject:** Mythological Dragon of Breno

| Date | Mintage | F | VF | XF | Unc | BU |
|---|---|---|---|---|---|---|
| 1996B | 190,000 | — | — | — | 22.00 | 25.00 |
| 1996B Proof | 27,000 | Value: 50.00 | | | | |

**20 FRANCS** **KM# 78** **Weight:** 20.0000 g. **Composition:** 0.8350 Silver .5369 oz. ASW **Subject:** 150 Anniversary - Swiss Railway

| Date | Mintage | F | VF | XF | Unc | BU |
|---|---|---|---|---|---|---|
| 1997 | 215,000 | — | — | — | 22.00 | 25.00 |
| 1997 Proof | 19,000 | Value: 55.00 | | | | |

**20 FRANCS** **KM# 79** **Weight:** 20.0000 g. **Composition:** 0.8350 Silver .5369 oz. ASW **Subject:** 200th Anniversary - Birth of Jeremias Gotthelf

| Date | Mintage | F | VF | XF | Unc | BU |
|---|---|---|---|---|---|---|
| 1997 | 160,000 | — | — | — | 25.00 | 30.00 |
| 1997 Proof | 20,000 | Value: 50.00 | | | | |

**20 FRANCS** **KM# 80** **Weight:** 20.0000 g. **Composition:** 0.8350 Silver .5369 oz. ASW **Subject:** 200th Anniversary - Helvetian Republic **Obverse:** Denomination and boxed crosses design **Reverse:** 1798 coin design

| Date | Mintage | F | VF | XF | Unc | BU |
|---|---|---|---|---|---|---|
| 1998 | 108,000 | — | — | — | 25.00 | 30.00 |
| 1998 Proof | 16,000 | Value: 50.00 | | | | |

**20 FRANCS** **KM# 82** **Weight:** 20.0000 g. **Composition:** 0.8350 Silver .5369 oz. ASW **Subject:** 150th Anniversary - Confederation **Obverse:** Similar to KM#80 **Reverse:** 1848 coin design

| Date | Mintage | F | VF | XF | Unc | BU |
|---|---|---|---|---|---|---|
| 1998 | 109,000 | — | — | — | 25.00 | 30.00 |
| 1998 Proof | 16,000 | Value: 50.00 | | | | |

**20 FRANCS** **KM# 84** **Weight:** 20.0000 g. **Composition:** 0.8350 Silver .5369 oz. ASW **Subject:** Death of C.F. Meyer **Obverse:** Denomination, date and "Helvetia" **Reverse:** Portrait, signature

| Date | Mintage | F | VF | XF | Unc | BU |
|---|---|---|---|---|---|---|
| 1998 | 108,000 | — | — | — | 25.00 | 30.00 |
| 1998 Proof | 15,000 | Value: 45.00 | | | | |

**20 FRANCS** **KM# 85** **Weight:** 20.0000 g. **Composition:** 0.8350 Silver .5369 oz. ASW **Subject:** 150th Anniversary Swiss Postal Service **Obverse:** Denomination, date, country name in wreath **Reverse:** Cartoon-like postal carrier

| Date | Mintage | F | VF | XF | Unc | BU |
|---|---|---|---|---|---|---|
| 1999 | 91,000 | — | — | — | 22.00 | 25.00 |
| 1999 Proof | 12,000 | Value: 50.00 | | | | |

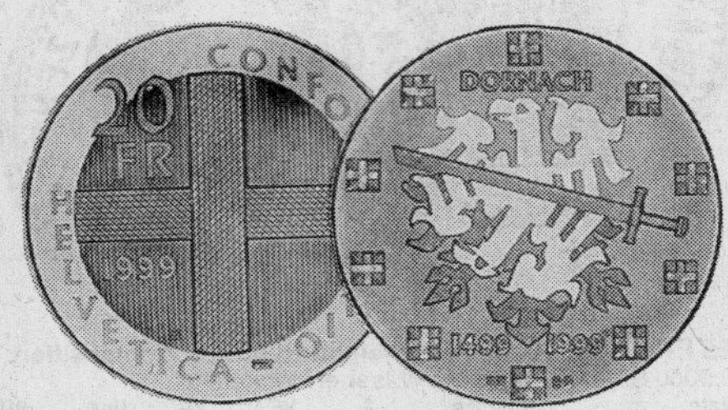

**20 FRANCS** **KM# 87** **Weight:** 20.0000 g. **Composition:** 0.8350 Silver .5369 oz. ASW **Subject:** Battle of Dornach **Obverse:** Denomination and cross design **Reverse:** Sword splitting and eagle **Edge Lettering:** DOMINUS PROVIDEBIT (13 stars)

| Date | Mintage | F | VF | XF | Unc | BU |
|---|---|---|---|---|---|---|
| 1999 | 85,000 | — | — | — | 22.00 | 25.00 |
| 1999 Proof | 11,000 | Value: 50.00 | | | | |

**20 FRANCS** **KM# 90** **Weight:** 20.0000 g. **Composition:** 0.8350 Silver .5369 oz. ASW **Subject:** Year 2000 - Peace on Earth **Obverse:** Olive branch **Reverse:** Angel floating above people **Size:** 32.7 mm.

| Date | Mintage | F | VF | XF | Unc | BU |
|---|---|---|---|---|---|---|
| 2000 | 100,000 | — | — | — | 22.00 | 25.00 |
| 2000 Proof | 15,000 | Value: 45.00 | | | | |

**20 FRANCS** **KM# 97** **Weight:** 20.0000 g. **Composition:** 0.8350 Silver .5369 oz. ASW **Subject:** Lumen Christi **Obverse:** Six line inscription above denomination **Reverse:** Jesus preaching **Size:** 32.7 mm.

| Date | Mintage | F | VF | XF | Unc | BU |
|---|---|---|---|---|---|---|
| 2000 | 85,000 | — | — | — | 22.00 | 25.00 |
| 2000 Proof | 14,000 | Value: 45.00 | | | | |

**20 FRANCS** **KM# 93** **Weight:** 20.0000 g. **Composition:** 0.9250 Silver .5369 oz. ASW **Subject:** Mustair Cloister **Obverse:** Church floor plan

**Reverse:** Walled cloister **Edge:** "DOMINUS PROVIDEBIT" and 13 stars **Size:** 32.6 mm.

| Date | Mintage | F | VF | XF | Unc | BU |
|---|---|---|---|---|---|---|
| 2001 | 100,000 | — | — | — | 22.00 | 25.00 |

**20 FRANCS** **KM# 94** **Weight:** 20.0000 g. **Composition:** 0.8350 Silver .5369 oz. ASW **Subject:** Johanna Spyri **Obverse:** Denomination and handwritten background **Reverse:** Portrait

| Date | Mintage | F | VF | XF | Unc | BU |
|---|---|---|---|---|---|---|
| 2001 | 100,000 | — | — | — | 20.00 | 22.50 |

**25 FRANCS** **KM# 49** **Weight:** 5.6450 g. **Composition:** 0.9000 Gold .1634 oz. AGW **Note:** Not available in commercial channels.

| Date | Mintage | F | VF | XF | Unc | BU |
|---|---|---|---|---|---|---|
| 1955B | 5,000,000 | — | — | — | — | — |
| 1958B | 5,000,000 | — | — | — | — | — |
| 1959B | 5,000,000 | — | — | — | — | — |

**50 FRANCS** **KM# 50** **Weight:** 11.2900 g. **Composition:** 0.9000 Gold .3267 oz. AGW **Note:** Not available in commercial channels.

| Date | Mintage | F | VF | XF | Unc | BU |
|---|---|---|---|---|---|---|
| 1955B | 2,000,000 | — | — | — | — | — |
| 1958B | 2,000,000 | — | — | — | — | — |
| 1959B | 2,000,000 | — | — | — | — | — |

**50 FRANCS** **KM# 95** **Weight:** 11.2900 g. **Composition:** 0.9000 Gold .3267 oz. AGW **Subject:** Heidi **Obverse:** Landscape and denomination **Reverse:** Girl and goat running **Edge:** Lettered **Size:** 25 mm.

| Date | Mintage | F | VF | XF | Unc | BU |
|---|---|---|---|---|---|---|
| 2001 | 7,000 | Value: 200 | | | | |

**100 FRANCS** **KM# 39** **Weight:** 32.2581 g. **Composition:** 0.9000 Gold .9334 oz. AGW

| Date | Mintage | F | VF | XF | Unc | BU |
|---|---|---|---|---|---|---|
| 1925B | 5,000 | — | 4,000 | 5,000 | 6,500 | 8,000 |

**100 FRANCS** **KM# 81** **Weight:** 22.5800 g. **Composition:** 0.9000 Gold .6534 oz. AGW **Subject:** 200th Anniversary of Helvetian Republic **Obverse:** Denomination and boxed crosses design **Reverse:** 1798 coin design

| Date | Mintage | F | VF | XF | Unc | BU |
|---|---|---|---|---|---|---|
| 1998 Proof | 2,500 | Value: 600 | | | | |

**100 FRANCS** **KM# 83** **Weight:** 22.5800 g. **Composition:** 0.9000 Gold .6534 oz. AGW **Subject:** 150th Anniversary of Swiss Confederation **Obverse:** Denomination and boxed crosses design **Reverse:** 1848 coin design

| Date | Mintage | F | VF | XF | Unc | BU |
|---|---|---|---|---|---|---|
| 1998 Proof | 2,500 | Value: 650 | | | | |

**100 FRANCS** **KM# 88** **Weight:** 22.5800 g. **Composition:** 0.9000 Gold .6534 oz. AGW **Subject:** Wine Festival **Obverse:** Denomination, fox looking at grapes **Reverse:** Fox with grapes

| Date | Mintage | F | VF | XF | Unc | BU |
|---|---|---|---|---|---|---|
| 1999 | 3,000 | Value: 400 | | | | |

**250 FRANCS** **KM# 71.1** **Weight:** 8.0000 g. **Composition:** 0.9000 Gold .2315 oz. AGW **Subject:** 700 Years of Confederation **Edge:** Plus sign between dates

| Date | Mintage | F | VF | XF | Unc | BU |
|---|---|---|---|---|---|---|
| 1991B | 297,000 | — | — | — | — | 225 |

**Note:** 200,000 recalled and melted due to poor quality

**250 FRANCS** **KM# 71.2** **Weight:** 8.0000 g. **Composition:** 0.9000 Gold .2315 oz. AGW **Subject:** 700 Years of Confederation **Edge:** Elongated plus sign between dates

| Date | Mintage | F | VF | XF | Unc | BU |
|---|---|---|---|---|---|---|
| 1991B | 193,000 | — | — | — | — | 235 |

## COMMEMORATIVE COINAGE

### Shooting Festival

**5 FRANCS** **KM# S18** **Composition:** 0.8350 Silver **Issuer:** Fribourg

| Date | Mintage | F | VF | XF | Unc | BU |
|---|---|---|---|---|---|---|
| 1934B | 40,000 | — | 15.00 | 35.00 | 55.00 | 80.00 |
| 1934B Specimen | — | — | — | — | — | 180 |
| 1934B Matte | 650 | — | — | — | — | 600 |

**5 FRANCS** **KM# S20** **Composition:** 0.8350 Silver **Issuer:** Lucerne

| Date | Mintage | F | VF | XF | Unc | BU |
|---|---|---|---|---|---|---|
| 1939B | 40,000 | — | 15.00 | 30.00 | 50.00 | 75.00 |
| 1939B Specimen | — | — | — | — | — | 180 |

**5 FRANCS** **KM# S54** **Composition:** Copper-Nickel **Issuer:** Albisgutli

| Date | Mintage | F | VF | XF | Unc | BU |
|---|---|---|---|---|---|---|
| 1998 Proof | 2,500 | Value: 30.00 | | | | |

**20 FRANCS** **KM# S55** **Weight:** 25.0000 g. **Composition:** 0.9990 Silver .0803 oz. ASW **Issuer:** Albisgutli

| Date | Mintage | F | VF | XF | Unc | BU |
|---|---|---|---|---|---|---|
| 1998 Proof | 1,000 | Value: 115 | | | | |

**25 FRANCS** **KM# S22** **Weight:** 25.0000 g. **Composition:** 0.9000 Silver .7235 oz. ASW **Issuer:** Oberhasli

| Date | Mintage | F | VF | XF | Unc | BU |
|---|---|---|---|---|---|---|
| 1984 | 6,000 | — | — | — | 40.00 | 50.00 |
| 1984 Proof | 200 | Value: 600 | | | | |

**25 FRANCS** **KM# S24** **Weight:** 25.0000 g. **Composition:** 0.9000 Silver .7235 oz. ASW **Issuer:** Altdorf

| Date | Mintage | F | VF | XF | Unc | BU |
|---|---|---|---|---|---|---|
| 1985 Proof | 3,500 | Value: 150 | | | | |

**25 FRANCS** **KM# S26** **Weight:** 25.0000 g. **Composition:** 0.9000 Silver .7235 oz. ASW **Issuer:** Appenzell

| Date | Mintage | F | VF | XF | Unc | BU |
|---|---|---|---|---|---|---|
| 1986 Proof | 3,700 | Value: 85.00 | | | | |

**25 FRANCS** **KM# S28** **Weight:** 25.0000 g. **Composition:** 0.9000 Silver .7235 oz. ASW **Issuer:** Glarus

| Date | Mintage | F | VF | XF | Unc | BU |
|---|---|---|---|---|---|---|
| 1987 Proof | 3,200 | Value: 85.00 | | | | |

**25 FRANCS** **KM# S30** **Weight:** 25.0000 g. **Composition:** 0.9000 Silver .7235 oz. ASW **Issuer:** Aargau

| Date | Mintage | F | VF | XF | Unc | BU |
|---|---|---|---|---|---|---|
| 1988 Proof | 3,000 | Value: 145 | | | | |

**25 FRANCS** **KM# S32** **Weight:** 25.0000 g. **Composition:** 0.9000 Silver .7235 oz. ASW **Issuer:** Zug

| Date | Mintage | F | VF | XF | Unc | BU |
|---|---|---|---|---|---|---|
| 1989 Proof | 2,200 | Value: 155 | | | | |

**25 FRANCS** **KM# S34** **Weight:** 25.0000 g. **Composition:** 0.9000 Silver .7235 oz. ASW **Issuer:** Winterthur

| Date | Mintage | F | VF | XF | Unc | BU |
|---|---|---|---|---|---|---|
| 1990 Proof | 5,000 | Value: 70.00 | | | | |

**50 FRANCS** **KM# S38** **Weight:** 25.0000 g. **Composition:** 0.9000 Silver .7235 oz. ASW **Issuer:** Bern **Reverse:** William Tell with rifle and flag

| Date | Mintage | F | VF | XF | Unc | BU |
|---|---|---|---|---|---|---|
| 1991 Proof | 4,000 | Value: 95.00 | | | | |

**50 FRANCS** **KM# S40** **Weight:** 25.0000 g. **Composition:** 0.9000 Silver .7235 oz. ASW **Issuer:** Zurich

| Date | Mintage | F | VF | XF | Unc | BU |
|---|---|---|---|---|---|---|
| 1992 Proof | 1,750 | Value: 120 | | | | |

**50 FRANCS** **KM# S42** **Weight:** 25.0000 g. **Composition:** 0.9000 Silver .7235 oz. ASW **Issuer:** Thurgau

| Date | Mintage | F | VF | XF | Unc | BU |
|---|---|---|---|---|---|---|
| 1993 Proof | 2,000 | Value: 100 | | | | |

**50 FRANCS** **KM# S44** **Weight:** 25.0000 g. **Composition:** 0.9000 Silver .7235 oz. ASW **Issuer:** St. Gall

| Date | Mintage | F | VF | XF | Unc | BU |
|---|---|---|---|---|---|---|
| 1994 Proof | 2,200 | Value: 70.00 | | | | |

**50 FRANCS** **KM# S46** **Weight:** 25.0000 g. **Composition:** 0.9000 Silver .7235 oz. ASW **Issuer:** Thun in Bern

| Date | Mintage | F | VF | XF | Unc | BU |
|---|---|---|---|---|---|---|
| 1995 Proof | Est. 5,000 | Value: 90.00 | | | | |

**50 FRANCS** **KM# S48** **Weight:** 25.0000 g. **Composition:** 0.9000 Silver .7235 oz. ASW **Issuer:** Sempach

| Date | Mintage | F | VF | XF | Unc | BU |
|---|---|---|---|---|---|---|
| 1996 Proof | 1,500 | Value: 80.00 | | | | |

**50 FRANCS** **KM# S50** **Weight:** 25.0000 g. **Composition:** 0.9000 Silver .7235 oz. ASW **Issuer:** Schaffhausen

| Date | Mintage | F | VF | XF | Unc | BU |
|---|---|---|---|---|---|---|
| 1997 Proof | 1,500 | Value: 80.00 | | | | |

**50 FRANCS** **KM# S52** **Weight:** 25.0000 g. **Composition:** 0.9000 Silver .7235 oz. ASW **Issuer:** Schwyz

| Date | Mintage | F | VF | XF | Unc | BU |
|---|---|---|---|---|---|---|
| 1998 Proof | 1,500 | Value: 100 | | | | |

**50 FRANCS** **KM# S57** **Weight:** 25.0000 g. **Composition:** 0.9000 Silver .7235 oz. ASW **Issuer:** Sion

| Date | Mintage | F | VF | XF | Unc | BU |
|---|---|---|---|---|---|---|
| 1999 Proof | 1,500 | Value: 75.00 | | | | |

**50 FRANCS** **KM# S59** **Weight:** 25.0000 g. **Composition:** 0.9000 Silver .7235 oz. ASW **Issuer:** Biere

| Date | Mintage | F | VF | XF | Unc | BU |
|---|---|---|---|---|---|---|
| 2000 Proof | 3,000 | Value: 65.00 | | | | |

**50 FRANCS** **KM# S61** **Weight:** 25.0000 g. **Composition:** 0.9000 Silver .7235 oz. ASW **Issuer:** Uri

| Date | Mintage | F | VF | XF | Unc | BU |
|---|---|---|---|---|---|---|
| 2001 Proof | 1,500 | Value: 65.00 | | | | |

**50 FRANCS** **KM# S63** **Weight:** 25.0000 g. **Composition:** 0.9000 Silver .7235 oz. ASW **Issuer:** Zurich

| Date | Mintage | F | VF | XF | Unc | BU |
|---|---|---|---|---|---|---|
| 2002 Proof | 1,500 | Value: 65.00 | | | | |

**100 FRANCS** **KM# S19** **Weight:** 25.9000 g. **Composition:** 0.9000 Gold .7494 oz. AGW **Issuer:** Fribourg

| Date | Mintage | F | VF | XF | Unc | BU |
|---|---|---|---|---|---|---|
| 1934B | 2,000 | — | 1,250 | 1,750 | 2,250 | 2,750 |

**100 FRANCS** **KM# S21** **Weight:** 17.5000 g. **Composition:** 0.9000 Gold .5064 oz. AGW **Issuer:** Lucerne

| Date | Mintage | F | VF | XF | Unc | BU |
|---|---|---|---|---|---|---|
| 1939B | 6,000 | — | 400 | 475 | 550 | 650 |

**100 FRANCS** **KM# S36** **Weight:** 31.1030 g. **Composition:** 0.9990 Platinum 1.0000 oz. APW **Subject:** William Tell and Son

| Date | Mintage | F | VF | XF | Unc | BU |
|---|---|---|---|---|---|---|
| 1986HF | 60,000 | — | — | — | — | — |
| 1986HF Proof | 10,000 | Value: 650 | | | | |
| 1987HF | — | — | — | — | — | — |
| 1987HF Proof | 15,000 | Value: 650 | | | | |

**100 FRANCS** **KM# S37** **Weight:** 31.1030 g. **Composition:** 0.9990 Platinum 1.0000 oz. APW **Subject:** William Tell

| Date | Mintage | F | VF | XF | Unc | BU |
|---|---|---|---|---|---|---|
| 1988HF Proof | 10,000 | Value: 650 | | | | |

**100 FRANCS** **KM# S37a** **Composition:** Brass

| Date | Mintage | F | VF | XF | Unc | BU |
|---|---|---|---|---|---|---|
| 1988HF Proof | 1,000 | Value: 50.00 | | | | |

**200 FRANCS** **KM# S56** **Weight:** 13.9600 g. **Composition:** 0.9860 Gold .4426 oz. AGW **Issuer:** Albisgutli

| Date | Mintage | F | VF | XF | Unc | BU |
|---|---|---|---|---|---|---|
| 1998 Matte Proof | 100 | Value: 850 | | | | |

**500 FRANCS** **KM# S47** **Weight:** 13.0000 g. **Composition:** 0.9000 Gold .3762 oz. AGW **Issuer:** Thun in Bern

| Date | Mintage | F | VF | XF | Unc | BU |
|---|---|---|---|---|---|---|
| 1995 Proof | 500 | Value: 600 | | | | |

**500 FRANCS** **KM# S49** **Weight:** 13.0000 g. **Composition:** 0.9000 Gold .3762 oz. AGW **Issuer:** Sempach

| Date | Mintage | F | VF | XF | Unc | BU |
|---|---|---|---|---|---|---|
| 1996 Proof | 96 | Value: 800 | | | | |

**500 FRANCS** **KM# S51** **Weight:** 13.0000 g. **Composition:** 0.9000 Gold .3762 oz. AGW **Issuer:** Schaffhausen

| Date | Mintage | F | VF | XF | Unc | BU |
|---|---|---|---|---|---|---|
| 1997 Proof | 97 | Value: 800 | | | | |

**500 FRANCS** **KM# S53** **Weight:** 13.0000 g. **Composition:** 0.9000 Gold .3762 oz. AGW **Issuer:** Schwyz

| Date | Mintage | F | VF | XF | Unc | BU |
|---|---|---|---|---|---|---|
| 1998 Proof | 98 | Value: 700 | | | | |

**500 FRANCS** **KM# S58** **Composition:** Gold **Issuer:** Sion

| Date | Mintage | F | VF | XF | Unc | BU |
|---|---|---|---|---|---|---|
| 1999 Proof | 99 | Value: 700 | | | | |

**500 FRANCS** **KM# S60** **Composition:** Gold **Issuer:** Biere

| Date | Mintage | F | VF | XF | Unc | BU |
|---|---|---|---|---|---|---|
| 2000 Proof | 300 | Value: 600 | | | | |

**500 FRANCS** **KM# S64** **Weight:** 13.0000 g. **Composition:** 0.9000 Gold .3762 oz. AGW **Issuer:** Zurich

| Date | Mintage | F | VF | XF | Unc | BU |
|---|---|---|---|---|---|---|
| 2002 Proof | 125 | Value: 600 | | | | |

**1000 FRANCS** **KM# S35** **Weight:** 26.0000 g. **Composition:** 0.9000 Gold .7524 oz. AGW **Issuer:** Winterthur

| Date | Mintage | F | VF | XF | Unc | BU |
|---|---|---|---|---|---|---|
| 1990 Proof | 400 | Value: 1,100 | | | | |

**1000 FRANCS** **KM# S39** **Weight:** 26.0000 g. **Composition:** 0.9000 Gold .7524 oz. AGW **Issuer:** Bern **Reverse:** William Tell with rifle and flag

| Date | Mintage | F | VF | XF | Unc | BU |
|---|---|---|---|---|---|---|
| 1991 Proof | 400 | Value: 900 | | | | |

**1000 FRANCS** **KM# S41** **Weight:** 26.0000 g. **Composition:** 0.9000 Gold .7524 oz. AGW **Issuer:** Zurich **Note:** Similar to 50 Francs, KM#S40.

| Date | Mintage | F | VF | XF | Unc | BU |
|---|---|---|---|---|---|---|
| 1992 Proof | 175 | Value: 1,100 | | | | |

**1000 FRANCS** **KM# S43** **Weight:** 26.0000 g. **Composition:** 0.9000 Gold .7524 oz. AGW **Issuer:** Thurgau **Note:** Similar to 50 Francs, KM#S42.

| Date | Mintage | F | VF | XF | Unc | BU |
|---|---|---|---|---|---|---|
| 1993 Proof | 200 | Value: 950 | | | | |

**1000 FRANCS** **KM# S45** **Weight:** 26.0000 g. **Composition:** 0.9000 Gold .7524 oz. AGW **Issuer:** St. Gall **Note:** Similar to 50 Francs, KM#S44.

| Date | Mintage | F | VF | XF | Unc | BU |
|---|---|---|---|---|---|---|
| 1994 Proof | 200 | Value: 950 | | | | |

## ESSAIS

| KM# | Date | Mintage | Identification | Mkt Val |
|---|---|---|---|---|
| E4 | 1911 | — | 10 Francs. Gold. | 22,500 |
| E5 | 1928B | — | 100 Francs. Brass. Plain edge. | 6,200 |
| E6 | 1930B | — | 100 Francs. Brass. Lettered edge. | 7,500 |
| E8 | 1930 | — | Franc. Nickel. | 5,000 |

| KM# | Date | Mintage | Identification | Mkt Val |
|---|---|---|---|---|
| E9 | 1998 | 250 | 20 Francs. Silver. KM#80. | 425 |
| E10 | 1998 | 250 | 20 Francs. Silver. KM#82. | 425 |

| KM# | Date | Mintage | Identification | Mkt Val |
|---|---|---|---|---|
| E11 | 1998 | 500 | 20 Francs. Silver. KM#84. | 320 |
| E7 | 1998 | 250 | 5 Francs. Silver. | 5,500 |
| e12 | 2000 | — | 20 Francs. Silver. KM#97 | 185 |

## PATTERNS

| KM# | Date | Mintage | Identification | Mkt Val |
|---|---|---|---|---|
| Pn40 | 1910 | 56 | 10 Francs. Gold. Reeded edge. | 22,500 |
| Pn41 | 1910 | I.A. | 10 Francs. Gold. Plain edge. | 22,500 |
| Pn42 | 1917 | 6 | 5 Rappen. Brass. | 3,000 |
| Pn43 | 1918 | — | 10 Rappen. Nickel. | — |
| Pn44 | 1922B | — | 5 Francs. Silver. | 3,500 |
| Pn45 | 1924B | — | 5 Francs. | 20,000 |
| Pn46 | 1925B | — | 10 Francs. Silver. | 6,000 |
| Pn47 | 1925B | — | 100 Francs. Copper. | 5,000 |
| Pn48 | 1927B | — | 20 Rappen. Nickel. | 4,500 |
| Pn49 | 1928B | — | 20 Rappen. Nickel. | 4,500 |
| Pn50 | 1928B | — | Franc. Nickel. | 3,200 |
| Pn51 | 1928B | — | 2 Francs. Nickel. | 3,200 |
| Pn52 | 1928B | — | 5 Francs. Silver. | 10,000 |
| Pn53 | 1928B | — | 5 Francs. Nickel. | 10,000 |
| Pn55 | 1929B | — | 50 Rappen. Nickel. | 3,500 |
| Pn56 | 1929 | — | 5 Francs. Silver. | 20,000 |
| Pn54 | 1929B | — | 5 Rappen. Bronze. | — |
| Pn61 | 19xxB | — | Franc. Nickel. | — |
| Pn57 | 1930B | — | 10 Rappen. Nickel. | 2,500 |
| Pn58 | 1930B | — | 20 Rappen. Nickel. | 2,500 |
| Pn59 | 1930B | — | 50 Rappen. Nickel. | 2,500 |
| Pn60 | 1930 | — | 50 Rappen. Nickel. Triangle. | 3,000 |
| Pn62 | 19xxB | — | 5 Francs. Silver. | 20,000 |
| Pn63 | 1930B | — | 5 Francs. Silver. | 12,000 |
| Pn65 | 1931 | — | 50 Rappen. Nickel. | 2,000 |
| Pn64 | 1931 | — | 5 Rappen. Copper-Nickel. | — |
| Pn66 | 1935 | — | 20 Francs. Copper. | — |
| Pn67 | 1937B | — | Franc. Copper-Nickel. | 5,000 |
| Pn68 | 1937B | — | 2 Francs. Copper-Nickel. | 5,000 |
| Pn69 | 1937 | — | 5 Francs. Aluminum. | 4,000 |
| Pn70 | 1938B | — | 20 Rappen. Zinc. | 2,500 |
| Pn71 | 1938B | — | Franc. Copper-Nickel. | 2,150 |
| Pn72 | 1938B | — | 2 Francs. Copper-Nickel. | 3,350 |
| Pn73 | 1939B | — | 5 Rappen. Zinc. KM#26. | 1,600 |
| Pn74 | 1939 | — | 5 Francs. Silver. | 6,000 |
| Pn75 | 1940B | — | 5 Rappen. Aluminum. KM#26. | 3,500 |
| Pn76 | 1940B | — | 10 Rappen. Zinc. KM#27. | 2,000 |
| PnA76 | 1940B | — | 20 Rappen. KM#29a. | 2,850 |
| Pn77 | 1940B | — | 10 Rappen. Aluminum. KM#27. | 4,200 |
| Pn78 | 1941B | — | 2 Francs. Silver-Zinc. | 2,500 |
| Pn79 | 1941B | — | Rappen. Aluminum. KM#3. | 2,500 |
| Pn80 | 1941B | — | 2 Rappen. Aluminum. KM#4. | 3,000 |
| Pn81 | 1947 | — | 20 Francs. Gold. | — |
| Pn82 | 1948B | — | 5 Francs. Copper Gilt. | 3,500 |
| Pn83 | 1955B | — | 25 Francs. Silver. KM#49. | 14,000 |
| Pn84 | 1955B | — | 50 Francs. Silver. KM#50. | 14,000 |
| Pn85 | 1979 | — | 5 Rappen. Aluminum-Bronze. | 2,000 |

## TRIAL STRIKES

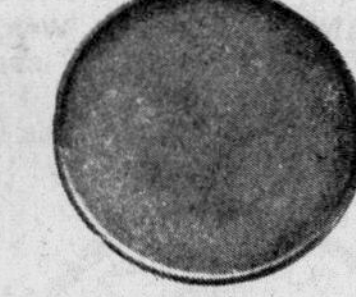

| KM# | Date | Mintage | Identification | Mkt Val |
|---|---|---|---|---|
| TS1 | | 3 | 20 Francs. Nickel. Uniface. | — |

## MINT SETS

| KM# | Date | Mintage | Identification | Issue Price | Mkt Val |
|---|---|---|---|---|---|
| MS10 | 1978 (8) | 10,000 | KM#21a, 23a-24a, 26-27, 29a, 40a, 46 | 9.00 | 21.00 |
| MS11 | 1979 (8) | 10,000 | KM#21a, 23a-24a, 26-27, 29a, 40a, 46 | 9.00 | 21.00 |
| MS12 | 1980 (8) | 15,000 | KM#21a, 23a-24a, 26-27, 29a, 40a, 46 | 9.00 | 35.00 |
| MS13 | 1981 (8) | 15,000 | KM#21a, 23a-24a, 26c, 27, 29a, 40, 46 | 9.00 | 35.00 |
| MS14 | 1982 (8) | 15,000 | KM#21a, 23a-24a, 26c, 27, 29a, 40, 46 | 9.00 | 42.00 |
| MS15 | 1983 (8) | 15,740 | KM#21a, 23a-24a, 26c, 27, 29a, 40, 46 | 9.00 | 35.00 |
| MS16 | 1984 (8) | 20,000 | KM#21a, 3, 23a.3-24a.3, 26c, 27, 29a, 40a.2, 46 | 9.00 | 24.00 |
| MS17 | 1985 (8) | 22,140 | KM#21a.3, 23a.3-24a.3, 26c, 27, 29a, 40a.3, 46 | 9.00 | 24.00 |
| MS18 | 1986 (8) | 21,400 | KM#21a.3, 23a.3-24a.3, 26c, 27, 29a, 40a.3, 46 | 9.00 | 24.00 |
| MS19 | 1987 (8) | 19,100 | KM#21a.3, 23a.3-24a.3, 26c, 27, 29a, 40a.3, 46 | 9.00 | 42.00 |
| MS2 | 1970 (9) | 10,000 | KM#21a, 23a-24a, 26-27, 29a, 40a, 46-47 | 6.40 | 55.00 |
| MS20 | 1988 (8) | 20,700 | KM#21a.3, 23a.3-24a.3, 26c, 27, 29a, 40a.3, 46 | — | 28.00 |
| MS21 | 1989 (8) | 22,700 | KM#21a.3, 23a.3-24a.3, 26c, 27, 29a, 40a.3, 46 | 11.00 | 24.00 |
| MS22 | 1990 (8) | 23,100 | KM#21a.3, 23a.3-24a.3, 26c, 27, 29a, 40a 3, 46 | — | 24.00 |
| MS23 | 1991 (8) | 26,100 | KM#21a.3, 23a.3-24a.3, 26c, 27, 29a, 40a.3, 46 | — | 160 |
| MS24 | 1991 (2) | 110,000 | KM#70-71 | 210 | 250 |
| MS25 | 1992 (8) | 20,300 | KM#21a.3, 23a.3-24a.3, 26c, 27, 29a, 40a.3, 46 | — | 24.00 |
| MS26 | 1993 (8) | 16,200 | KM#21a.3, 23a.3-24a.3, 26c, 27, 29a, 40a.3, 46 | — | 160 |
| MS27 | 1994 (8) | 17,300 | KM#21a.3, 23a.3-24a.3, 26c, 27, 29a, 40a.3, 46 | — | 28.00 |
| MS28 | 1995 (8) | 18,000 | KM#21a.3, 23a.3-24a.3, 26c, 27, 29a, 40a.3, 46 | — | 25.00 |
| MS29 | 1996 (8) | 17,300 | KM#21a.3, 23a.3-24a.3, 26c, 27, 29a, 40a.3, 46 | — | 25.00 |
| MS3 | 1971 (5) | 5,000 | KM#23a-24a, 26, 29a, 40 | 2.40 | 28.00 |
| MS30 | 1997 (8) | 16,500 | KM#21a.3, 23a.3, 24a.3, 26c, 27, 29a, 40a.3, 46 | — | 28.00 |
| MS31 | 1998 (8) | 16,000 | KM#21a.3, 23a.5, 24a.3, 26c, 27, 29a, 40a.3, 46 | — | 28.00 |
| MS32 | 1999 (8) | 16,000 | KM#21a.3, 23a.3, 24a.3, 26c, 27, 29a, 40a.3, 46 | — | 56.00 |
| MS33 | 2000 (9) | 18,000 | KM#21a.3, 23a.3, 24a.3, 26c, 27, 29a, 40a.3, 46, 89 | — | 38.00 |
| MS34 | 2000 | 2,000 | KM#21a.3, 23a.3, 24a.3, 26c, 27, 29a, 40a.3, 46, 91 | — | 155 |
| MS35 | 2001 | 22,000 | KM#21a.3, 23a.3, 24a.3, 26c, 27, 29a, 40a.3, 46, 92 | — | 28.00 |
| MS4 | 1972 (3) | 5,000 | KM#21a, 23a, 27 | 2.40 | 20.00 |
| MS5 | 1973 (6) | 10,000 | KM#21a, 23a-24a, 27, 40a, 46 | 6.40 | 30.00 |
| MS6 | 1974 (9) | 10,000 | KM#21a, 23a-24a, 26-27, 29a, 40a, 46-47 | 6.40 | 55.00 |
| MS7 | 1975 (8) | 10,000 | KM#21a, 23a-24a, 26-27, 29a, 40a, 46 | 6.40 | 40.00 |
| MS8 | 1976 (8) | 10,000 | KM#21a, 23a-24a, 26-27, 29a, 40a, 46 | 9.00 | 40.00 |
| MS9 | 1977 (8) | 10,000 | KM#21a, 23a-24a, 26-27, 29a, 40a, 46 | 9.00 | 31.00 |
| MS1 | 1896 (9) | — | KM3.1,4.2, 21, 23-24, 26-27,29, 34 | — | — |

## PROOF SETS

| KM# | Date | Mintage | Identification | Issue Price | Mkt Val |
|---|---|---|---|---|---|
| PS1 | 1974 (9) | 2,400 | KM#21a.1, 23a.1, 24a.1, 26, 27, 29a, 40a.1, 46-47 | 12.80 | 475 |
| PS10 | 1983 (8) | 11,390 | KM#21a.3, 23a.3, 24a.3, 26c, 27a, 29a, 40a.2, 46 | 30.00 | 22.00 |
| PS11 | 1984 (8) | 14,100 | KM#21a.3, 23a.3, 24a.3, 26c, 27a, 29a, 40a.2, 46 | 30.00 | 22.00 |
| PS12 | 1985 (8) | 12,060 | KM#21a.3, 23a.3-24a.3, 26c, 27, 29a, 40a.3, 46 | 30.00 | 22.00 |
| PS13 | 1986 (8) | 10,000 | KM#21a.3, 23a.3, 24a.3, 26c, 27, 29a, 40a.3, 46 | 30.00 | 22.00 |
| PS14 | 1987 (8) | 8,800 | KM#21a.3, 23a.3, 24a.3, 26c, 27, 29a, 40a.3, 46 | 30.00 | 42.00 |
| PS15 | 1988 (8) | 9,150 | KM#21a.3, 23a.3, 24a.3, 26c, 27, 29a, 40a.3, 46 | — | 42.00 |
| PS16 | 1989 (8) | 8,800 | KM#21a.3, 23a.3, 24a.3, 26c, 27, 29a, 40a.3, 46 | 36.50 | 42.00 |
| PS17 | 1990 (8) | 8,900 | KM#21a.3, 23a.3, 24a.3, 26c, 27, 29a, 40a.3, 46 | — | 52.00 |
| PS18 | 1991 (8) | 9,900 | KM#21a.3, 23a.3, 24a.3, 26c, 27, 29a, 40a.3, 46 | — | 160 |
| PS19 | 1992 (8) | 7,450 | KM#21a.3, 23a.3, 24a.3, 26c, 27, 29a, 40a.3, 46 | — | 42.00 |

| KM# | Date | Mintage | Identification | Issue Price | Mkt Val |
|---|---|---|---|---|---|
| PS2 | 1975 (8) | 10,000 | KM#21a.1, 23a.1, 24a.1, 26, 27, 29a, 40a.1, 46-47 | 16.75 | 25.00 |
| PS20 | 1993 (8) | 6,200 | KM#21a.3, 23a.3, 24a.3, 26c, 27, 29a, 40a.3, 46 | — | 145 |
| PS21 | 1994 (8) | 6,100 | KM#21a.3, 23a.3, 24a.3, 26c, 27, 29a, 40a.4, 46 | — | 56.00 |
| PS22 | 1995 (8) | 6,100 | KM#21a.3, 23a.3, 24a.3, 26c, 27, 29a, 40a.4, 46 | 42.50 | 50.00 |
| PS23 | 1994-1996 (4) | 6,000 | KM#74-77 | 170 | 150 |
| PS24 | 1996 (8) | 6,100 | KM#21a.3, 23a.3, 24a.3, 26c, 27, 29a, 40a.4, 46 | — | 50.00 |
| PS25 | 1997 (8) | 5,500 | KM#21a.3, 23a.3, 24a.3, 26c, 27, 29a, 40a.4, 46 | — | 50.00 |
| PS26 | 1998 (8) | 4,800 | KM#21a.3, 23a.3, 24a.3, 26c, 27, 29a, 40a.4, 46 | — | 50.00 |
| PS27 | 1999 (9) | 5,000 | KM#21a.3, 23a.3, 24a.3, 26c, 27, 29a, 40a.4, 46, 69 | — | 70.00 |
| PS28 | 2000 (9) | 5,500 | KM#21a.3, 23a.3, 24a.3, 26c, 27, 29a, 40a.4, 46, 89 | — | 60.00 |
| PS29 | 2000 (9) | 500 | KM#21a.3, 23a.3, 24a.3, 26c, 27, 29a, 40a.4, 46, 91 | — | 450 |
| PS3 | 1976 (8) | 5,130 | KM#21a.1, 23a.1, 24a.1, 26, 27, 29a, 40a.1, 46-47 | 16.75 | 35.00 |
| PS30 | 2001 (9) | 6,000 | KM#21a.3, 23a.3, 24a.3, 26c, 27, 29a, 40a.4, 46, 92 | — | 45.00 |
| PS4 | 1977 (8) | 7,030 | KM#21a.1, 23a.1, 24a.1, 26, 27, 29a, 40a.1, 46-47 | 16.75 | 25.00 |
| PS5 | 1978 (8) | 10,090 | KM#21a.1, 23a.1, 24a.1, 26, 27, 29a, 40a.1, 46-47 | 28.00 | 25.00 |
| PS6 | 1979 (8) | 10,150 | KM#21a.1, 23a.1, 24a.1, 26, 27, 29a, 40a.1, 46-47 | 28.00 | 25.00 |
| PS7 | 1980 (8) | 10,010 | KM#21a.1, 23a.1, 24a.1, 26, 27, 29a, 40a.1, 46-47 | 30.00 | 28.00 |
| PS8 | 1981 (8) | 10,280 | KM#21a.1, 23a.1, 24a.1, 26c, 27, 29a, 40a.1, 46 | 30.00 | 25.00 |
| PS9 | 1982 (8) | 10,090 | KM#21a.2, 23a.2, 24a.2, 26c, 27, 29a, 40a.2, 46 | 30.00 | 50.00 |

# SYRIA

The Syrian Arab Republic, located in the Near East at the eastern end of the Mediterranean Sea, has an area of 71,498 sq. mi. (185,180 sq. km.) and a population of *12million. Capital: Greater Damascus. Agriculture and animal breeding are the chief industries. Cotton, crude oil and livestock are exported.

Ancient Syria, a land bridge connecting Europe, Africa and Asia, has spent much of its history in thrall to the conqueror's whim. Its subjection by Egypt about 1500 B.C. was followed by successive conquests by the Hebrews, Phoenicians, Babylonians, Assyrians, Persians, Macedonians, Romans, Byzantines and finally, in 636 A.D., by the Moslems. The Arabs made Damascus, one of the oldest continuously inhabited cities of the world, the trade center and capital of an empire stretching from India to Spain. In 1516, following the total destruction of Damascus by the Mongols of Tamerlane, Syria fell to the Ottoman Turks and remained a part of Turkey until the end of World War I. The League of Nations gave France a mandate to the Levant states of Syria and Lebanon in 1920. In 1930, following a series of uprisings, France recognized Syria as an independent republic, but still subject to the mandate. Lebanon became fully independent on Nov. 22, 1943, and Syria on Jan. 1,1944.

**TITLES**

الجمهورية السورية

al-Jumhuriya(t) al-Suriya(t)

الجمهورية لعربية السورية

al-Jumhuriya(t) al-Arabiya(t) as-Suriya(t)

**RULERS**
Ottoman, until 1918
Faysal, 1918-1920

**MINT MARKS**
(a)- Paris, privy marks only

**MINTNAME**

Damascus (Dimask) دمشق

Haleb (Aleppo) حلب

# KINGDOM

## STANDARD COINAGE

**DINAR** KM# 67 **Weight:** 6.7000 g. **Composition:** Gold

| Date | Mintage | F | VF | XF | Unc | BU |
|---|---|---|---|---|---|---|
| AH1338 | Est. 12 | — | — | — | 8,000 | — |

# FRENCH PROTECTORATE

## STANDARD COINAGE

**1/2 PIASTRE** KM# 68 **Composition:** Copper-Nickel

| Date | Mintage | F | VF | XF | Unc | BU |
|---|---|---|---|---|---|---|
| 1921(a) | 4,000,000 | 0.50 | 2.00 | 5.00 | 15.00 | — |

**1/2 PIASTRE** KM# 75 **Composition:** Nickel-Brass

| Date | Mintage | F | VF | XF | Unc | BU |
|---|---|---|---|---|---|---|
| 1935(a) | 600,000 | 1.00 | 4.00 | 12.00 | 42.50 | — |
| 1936(a) | 800,000 | 1.00 | 4.00 | 9.00 | 30.00 | — |

**PIASTRE** KM# 71 **Composition:** Nickel-Brass

| Date | Mintage | F | VF | XF | Unc | BU |
|---|---|---|---|---|---|---|
| 1929(a) | 750,000 | 1.00 | 3.00 | 7.00 | 32.50 | — |
| 1933(a) | 600,000 | 1.50 | 4.00 | 10.00 | 40.00 | — |
| 1935(a) | 1,950,000 | 0.80 | 2.50 | 5.00 | 22.50 | — |
| 1936(a) | 1,400,000 | 0.80 | 2.50 | 7.00 | 25.00 | — |

**PIASTRE** KM# 71a **Composition:** Zinc

| Date | Mintage | F | VF | XF | Unc | BU |
|---|---|---|---|---|---|---|
| 1940(a) | 2,060,000 | 2.00 | 5.00 | 15.00 | 60.00 | — |

**2 PIASTRES** KM# 69 **Composition:** Aluminum-Bronze

| Date | Mintage | F | VF | XF | Unc | BU |
|---|---|---|---|---|---|---|
| 1926(a) | 600,000 | 5.00 | 10.00 | 25.00 | 75.00 | — |
| 1926 without privy marks by date | Inc. above | 5.00 | 10.00 | 25.00 | 75.00 | — |

**2-1/2 PIASTRES** KM# 76 **Composition:** Aluminum-Bronze

| Date | Mintage | F | VF | XF | Unc | BU |
|---|---|---|---|---|---|---|
| 1940(a) | 2,000,000 | 1.25 | 4.00 | 8.00 | 27.50 | — |

**5 PIASTRES** KM# 70 **Composition:** Aluminum-Bronze

| Date | Mintage | F | VF | XF | Unc | BU |
|---|---|---|---|---|---|---|
| 1926(a) | 300,000 | 0.75 | 2.00 | 8.00 | 25.00 | — |
| 1926 | 400,000 | 0.75 | 3.00 | 12.00 | 35.00 | — |
| 1933(a) | 1,200,000 | 0.40 | 2.00 | 12.50 | 40.00 | — |
| 1935(a) | 2,000,000 | 0.30 | 1.50 | 8.00 | 25.00 | — |
| 1936(a) | 900,000 | 0.50 | 2.00 | 10.00 | 30.00 | — |
| 1940(a) | 500,000 | 0.50 | 1.50 | 4.00 | 15.00 | — |

**10 PIASTRES** KM# 72 **Weight:** 2.0000 g. **Composition:** 0.6800 Silver .0437 oz. ASW

| Date | Mintage | F | VF | XF | Unc | BU |
|---|---|---|---|---|---|---|
| 1929 | 1,000,000 | 4.00 | 12.00 | 28.00 | 90.00 | — |

**25 PIASTRES** KM# 73 **Weight:** 5.0000 g. **Composition:** 0.6800 Silver .1093 oz. ASW

| Date | Mintage | F | VF | XF | Unc | BU |
|---|---|---|---|---|---|---|
| 1929 | 1,000,000 | 3.00 | 5.00 | 27.50 | 85.00 | — |
| 1933(a) | 500,000 | 4.00 | 12.00 | 40.00 | 160 | — |
| 1936(a) | 897,000 | 3.50 | 7.00 | 30.00 | 100 | — |
| 1937(a) | 393,000 | 5.00 | 10.00 | 35.00 | 140 | — |

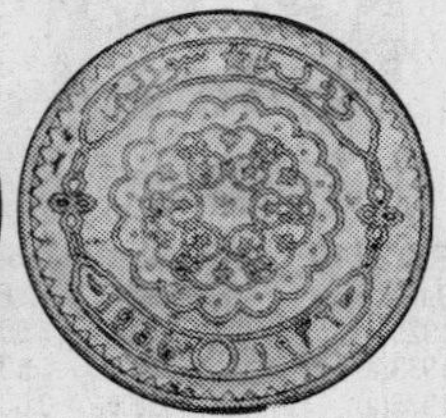

**50 PIASTRES** KM# 74 **Weight:** 10.0000 g. **Composition:** 0.6800 Silver .2186 oz. ASW

| Date | Mintage | F | VF | XF | Unc | BU |
|---|---|---|---|---|---|---|
| 1929 | 880,000 | 4.00 | 8.00 | 35.00 | 140 | — |
| 1933(a) | 250,000 | 6.00 | 10.00 | 45.00 | 190 | — |
| 1936(a) | 400,000 | 5.00 | 10.00 | 40.00 | 160 | — |
| 1937(a) | Inc. above | 7.00 | 12.00 | 50.00 | 200 | — |

## WORLD WAR II EMERGENCY COINAGE

**PIASTRE** KM# 77 **Composition:** Brass

| Date | Mintage | F | VF | XF | Unc | BU |
|---|---|---|---|---|---|---|
| ND | — | 2.50 | 5.00 | 10.00 | 20.00 | — |

**2-1/2 PIASTRES** KM# 78 **Composition:** Aluminum

| Date | Mintage | F | VF | XF | Unc | BU |
|---|---|---|---|---|---|---|
| ND | — | 10.00 | 20.00 | 35.00 | 65.00 | — |

# REPUBLIC

## STANDARD COINAGE

**2-1/2 PIASTRES** KM# 81 **Composition:** Copper-Nickel

| Date | Mintage | F | VF | XF | Unc | BU |
|---|---|---|---|---|---|---|
| AH1367(1948) | 2,500,000 | 0.75 | 1.50 | 3.00 | 6.00 | — |
| AH1375(1956) | 5,000,000 | 0.75 | 1.50 | 3.00 | 6.00 | — |

**5 PIASTRES** KM# 82 **Composition:** Copper-Nickel

| Date | Mintage | F | VF | XF | Unc | BU |
|---|---|---|---|---|---|---|
| AH1367(1948) | 8,000,000 | 0.75 | 1.50 | 3.00 | 6.00 | — |
| AH1375(1956) | 4,000,000 | 0.75 | 1.50 | 3.00 | 6.00 | — |

**10 PIASTRES** KM# 83 **Composition:** Copper-Nickel

| Date | Mintage | F | VF | XF | Unc | BU |
|---|---|---|---|---|---|---|
| AH1367(1948) | — | 0.75 | 1.50 | 3.00 | 6.00 | — |
| AH1375(1956) | 4,000,000 | 0.75 | 1.50 | 3.00 | 6.00 | — |

**25 PIASTRES** KM# 79 **Weight:** 2.5000 g. **Composition:** 0.6000 Silver .0482 oz. ASW

| Date | Mintage | F | VF | XF | Unc | BU |
|---|---|---|---|---|---|---|
| AH1366(1947) | 6,300,000 | 1.50 | 2.50 | 6.00 | 20.00 | — |

**50 PIASTRES** KM# 80 **Weight:** 5.0000 g. **Composition:** 0.6000 Silver .0965 oz. ASW

| Date | Mintage | F | VF | XF | Unc | BU |
|---|---|---|---|---|---|---|
| AH1366(1947) | 4,500,000 | 2.50 | 5.00 | 10.00 | 25.00 | — |

**1/2 POUND** KM# 84 **Weight:** 3.3793 g. **Composition:** 0.9000 Gold .0978 oz. AGW

| Date | Mintage | F | VF | XF | Unc | BU |
|---|---|---|---|---|---|---|
| AH1369(1950) | 100,000 | 45.00 | 55.00 | 65.00 | 100 | — |

**LIRA** KM# 85 **Weight:** 10.0000 g. **Composition:** 0.6800 Silver .2186 oz. ASW

| Date | Mintage | F | VF | XF | Unc | BU |
|---|---|---|---|---|---|---|
| AH1369(1950) | 7,000,000 | 2.50 | 5.00 | 10.00 | 25.00 | — |

**POUND** KM# 86 **Weight:** 6.7586 g. **Composition:** 0.9000 Gold .1956 oz. AGW

| Date | Mintage | F | VF | XF | Unc | BU |
|---|---|---|---|---|---|---|
| AH1369(1950) | 250,000 | 70.00 | 90.00 | 110 | 160 | — |

# UNITED ARAB REPUBLIC

## STANDARD COINAGE

**2-1/2 PIASTRES** KM# 90 **Composition:** Aluminum-Bronze

| Date | Mintage | F | VF | XF | Unc | BU |
|---|---|---|---|---|---|---|
| AH1380(1960) | 1,100,000 | 0.10 | 0.20 | 0.35 | 0.75 | — |

**5 PIASTRES** KM# 91 **Composition:** Aluminum-Bronze

| Date | Mintage | F | VF | XF | Unc | BU |
|---|---|---|---|---|---|---|
| AH1380(1960) | 4,240,000 | 0.10 | 0.20 | 0.35 | 0.75 | — |

**10 PIASTRES** KM# 92 **Composition:** Aluminum-Bronze

| Date | Mintage | F | VF | XF | Unc | BU |
|---|---|---|---|---|---|---|
| AH1380(1960) | 2,800,000 | 0.10 | 0.20 | 0.40 | 1.00 | — |

**25 PIASTRES** KM# 87 **Weight:** 2.5000 g. **Composition:** 0.6000 Silver .0482 oz. ASW

| Date | Mintage | F | VF | XF | Unc | BU |
|---|---|---|---|---|---|---|
| AH1377(1958) | 2,300,000 | 0.75 | 1.50 | 2.00 | 6.00 | — |

**50 PIASTRES** KM# 88 **Weight:** 5.0000 g. **Composition:** 0.6000 Silver .0965 oz. ASW

| Date | Mintage | F | VF | XF | Unc | BU |
|---|---|---|---|---|---|---|
| AH1377(1958) | 120,000 | 2.00 | 3.00 | 6.50 | 18.00 | — |

**50 PIASTRES** KM# 89 **Weight:** 5.0000 g. **Composition:** 0.6000 Silver .0965 oz. ASW **Subject:** 1st anniversary - founding of United Arab Republic

| Date | Mintage | F | VF | XF | Unc | BU |
|---|---|---|---|---|---|---|
| AH1378(1959) | 1,500,000 | 1.50 | 2.50 | 4.50 | 12.00 | — |

# SYRIAN ARAB REPUBLIC

## STANDARD COINAGE

**2-1/2 PIASTRES** **KM# 93** **Composition:** Aluminum-Bronze

| Date | Mintage | F | VF | XF | Unc | BU |
|---|---|---|---|---|---|---|
| AH1382/1962 | 8,000,000 | — | 0.10 | 0.20 | 0.50 | — |
| AH1385/1965 | 8,000,000 | — | 0.10 | 0.20 | 0.50 | — |

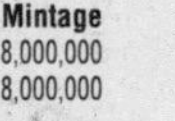
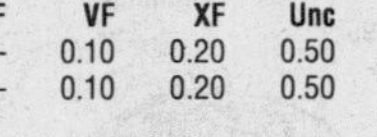

**2-1/2 PIASTRES** **KM# 104** **Composition:** Aluminum-Bronze

| Date | Mintage | F | VF | XF | Unc | BU |
|---|---|---|---|---|---|---|
| AH1393/1973 | 10,000,000 | — | 0.10 | 0.15 | 0.25 | — |

**5 PIASTRES** **KM# 94** **Composition:** Aluminum-Bronze

| Date | Mintage | F | VF | XF | Unc | BU |
|---|---|---|---|---|---|---|
| AH1382/1962 | 7,000,000 | — | 0.10 | 0.15 | 0.35 | — |
| AH1385/1965 | 18,000,000 | — | 0.10 | 0.15 | 0.35 | — |

**5 PIASTRES** **KM# 100** **Composition:** Aluminum-Bronze **Series:** F.A.O.

| Date | Mintage | F | VF | XF | Unc | BU |
|---|---|---|---|---|---|---|
| AH1391/1971 | 15,000,000 | — | 0.10 | 0.15 | 0.25 | — |

**5 PIASTRES** **KM# 105** **Composition:** Aluminum-Bronze

| Date | Mintage | F | VF | XF | Unc | BU |
|---|---|---|---|---|---|---|
| AH1394/1974 | — | — | 0.10 | 0.15 | 0.25 | — |

**5 PIASTRES** **KM# 110** **Composition:** Aluminum-Bronze **Series:** F.A.O.

| Date | Mintage | F | VF | XF | Unc | BU |
|---|---|---|---|---|---|---|
| AH1396/1976 | 2,000,000 | — | 0.10 | 0.15 | 0.25 | — |

**5 PIASTRES** **KM# 116** **Composition:** Aluminum-Bronze **Note:** Similar to KM#94 but heavier neck feathers.

| Date | Mintage | F | VF | XF | Unc | BU |
|---|---|---|---|---|---|---|
| AH1399(1979) | — | — | 0.10 | 0.15 | 0.25 | — |

**10 PIASTRES** **KM# 95** **Composition:** Aluminum-Bronze

| Date | Mintage | F | VF | XF | Unc | BU |
|---|---|---|---|---|---|---|
| AH1382/1962 | 6,000,000 | — | 0.10 | 0.20 | 0.45 | — |
| AH1385/1965 | 22,000,000 | — | 0.10 | 0.20 | 0.45 | — |

**10 PIASTRES** **KM# 106** **Composition:** Aluminum-Bronze

| Date | Mintage | F | VF | XF | Unc | BU |
|---|---|---|---|---|---|---|
| AH1394/1974 | — | — | 0.10 | 0.15 | 0.30 | — |

**10 PIASTRES** **KM# 111** **Composition:** Brass **Series:** F.A.O. **Note:** Similar to 5 Piastres, KM#110.

| Date | Mintage | F | VF | XF | Unc | BU |
|---|---|---|---|---|---|---|
| AH1396/1976 | 500,000 | — | 0.10 | 0.15 | 0.25 | — |

**10 PIASTRES** **KM# 117** **Composition:** Aluminum-Bronze

| Date | Mintage | F | VF | XF | Unc | BU |
|---|---|---|---|---|---|---|
| AH1399/1979 | — | — | 0.10 | 0.15 | 0.30 | — |

**25 PIASTRES** **KM# 96** **Composition:** Nickel

| Date | Mintage | F | VF | XF | Unc | BU |
|---|---|---|---|---|---|---|
| AH1387/1968 | 15,000,000 | — | 0.20 | 0.30 | 0.60 | — |

**25 PIASTRES** **KM# 101** **Composition:** Nickel **Subject:** 25th anniversary - Al-Ba'ath Party

| Date | Mintage | F | VF | XF | Unc | BU |
|---|---|---|---|---|---|---|
| AH1392/1972 | — | — | 0.15 | 0.25 | 0.60 | — |

**25 PIASTRES** **KM# 107** **Composition:** Nickel

| Date | Mintage | F | VF | XF | Unc | BU |
|---|---|---|---|---|---|---|
| AH1394/1974 | — | — | 0.10 | 0.25 | 0.50 | — |

**25 PIASTRES** **KM# 112** **Composition:** Nickel **Series:** F.A.O.

| Date | Mintage | F | VF | XF | Unc | BU |
|---|---|---|---|---|---|---|
| AH1396/1976 | 1,000,000 | — | 0.10 | 0.25 | 0.50 | — |

**25 PIASTRES** **KM# 118** **Composition:** Copper-Nickel

| Date | Mintage | F | VF | XF | Unc | BU |
|---|---|---|---|---|---|---|
| AH1399/1979 | — | — | 0.10 | 0.25 | 0.50 | — |

**50 PIASTRES** **KM# 97** **Composition:** Nickel

| Date | Mintage | F | VF | XF | Unc | BU |
|---|---|---|---|---|---|---|
| AH1387/1968 | 10,000,000 | — | 0.25 | 0.50 | 0.85 | — |

**50 PIASTRES** **KM# 102** **Composition:** Nickel **Subject:** 25th anniversary - Al-Ba'ath Party

| Date | Mintage | F | VF | XF | Unc | BU |
|---|---|---|---|---|---|---|
| AH1392/1972 | — | — | 0.50 | 1.00 | 2.00 | — |

**50 PIASTRES** **KM# 108** **Composition:** Nickel

| Date | Mintage | F | VF | XF | Unc | BU |
|---|---|---|---|---|---|---|
| AH1394/1974 | — | — | 0.20 | 0.30 | 0.75 | — |

**50 PIASTRES** **KM# 113** **Composition:** Nickel **Series:** F.A.O.

| Date | Mintage | F | VF | XF | Unc | BU |
|---|---|---|---|---|---|---|
| AH1396/1976 | 1,000,000 | — | 0.20 | 0.50 | 1.00 | — |

**50 PIASTRES** **KM# 119** **Composition:** Copper-Nickel

| Date | Mintage | F | VF | XF | Unc | BU |
|---|---|---|---|---|---|---|
| AH1399/1979 | — | — | 0.20 | 0.30 | 0.75 | — |

**POUND** **KM# 98** **Composition:** Nickel

| Date | Mintage | F | VF | XF | Unc | BU |
|---|---|---|---|---|---|---|
| AH1387/1968 | 10,000,000 | — | 0.30 | 0.75 | 1.25 | — |
| AH1391/1971 | 10,000,000 | — | 0.30 | 0.75 | 1.25 | — |

**POUND** **KM# 99** **Composition:** Nickel **Series:** F.A.O.

| Date | Mintage | F | VF | XF | Unc | BU |
|---|---|---|---|---|---|---|
| AH1388/1968 | 500,000 | — | 1.00 | 2.00 | 3.00 | — |

**POUND** **KM# 103** **Composition:** Nickel **Subject:** 25th anniversary - Al-Ba'ath Party

| Date | Mintage | F | VF | XF | Unc | BU |
|---|---|---|---|---|---|---|
| AH1392/1972 | 10,000,000 | — | 0.50 | 1.00 | 2.50 | — |

**POUND** **KM# 109** **Composition:** Nickel

| Date | Mintage | F | VF | XF | Unc | BU |
|---|---|---|---|---|---|---|
| AH1394/1974 | — | — | 0.30 | 0.75 | 2.00 | — |

**POUND** **KM# 114** **Composition:** Nickel **Series:** F.A.O.

| Date | Mintage | F | VF | XF | Unc | BU |
|---|---|---|---|---|---|---|
| AH1396/1976 | 500,000 | — | 1.00 | 2.00 | 3.00 | — |

**POUND** **KM# 115** **Composition:** Nickel **Subject:** Re-election of president

| Date | Mintage | F | VF | XF | Unc | BU |
|---|---|---|---|---|---|---|
| AH1398/1978 | — | — | 1.50 | 2.50 | 5.00 | — |

**POUND** **KM# 120.1** **Composition:** Copper-Nickel

| Date | Mintage | F | VF | XF | Unc | BU |
|---|---|---|---|---|---|---|
| AH1399/1979 | — | — | 0.30 | 0.70 | 1.50 | — |

**POUND** **KM# 120.2** **Composition:** Stainless Steel

| Date | Mintage | F | VF | XF | Unc | BU |
|---|---|---|---|---|---|---|
| AH1412/1991 | — | — | 0.30 | 0.70 | 1.50 | — |

**POUND** **KM# 121** **Composition:** Stainless Steel

| Date | Mintage | F | VF | XF | Unc | BU |
|---|---|---|---|---|---|---|
| AH1414/1994 | — | — | 0.30 | 0.70 | 1.50 | — |

**2 POUNDS** **KM# 125** **Composition:** Stainless Steel **Obverse:** National emblem **Reverse:** Ancient ruins

| Date | Mintage | F | VF | XF | Unc | BU |
|---|---|---|---|---|---|---|
| AH1416/1996 | — | — | — | 0.75 | 1.65 | — |

**5 POUNDS** **KM# 123** **Composition:** Copper-Nickel **Reverse:** Palace

| Date | Mintage | F | VF | XF | Unc | BU |
|---|---|---|---|---|---|---|
| AH1416/1996 | — | — | — | 1.00 | 2.00 | — |

**10 POUNDS** **KM# 124** **Composition:** Copper-Nickel **Reverse:** Ancient ruins

| Date | Mintage | F | VF | XF | Unc | BU |
|---|---|---|---|---|---|---|
| AH1416/1996 | — | — | — | 1.25 | 2.50 | — |
| AH1417/1997(a) | — | — | — | 1.25 | 2.50 | — |

**10 POUNDS** **KM# 128** **Weight:** 7.0000 g. **Composition:** Copper-Nickel **Subject:** 50th Anniversary of Al Baath Party **Obverse:** National arms **Reverse:** Map and flag **Edge:** Reeded **Size:** 26.5 mm.

| Date | Mintage | F | VF | XF | Unc | BU |
|---|---|---|---|---|---|---|
| AH1417/1997 | 100,000 | — | — | 1.25 | 2.50 | — |

**25 POUNDS** **KM# 122** **Ring Composition:** Bronze **Center Composition:** Stainless Steel **Obverse:** Heraldic eagle **Reverse:** President

| Date | Mintage | F | VF | XF | Unc | BU |
|---|---|---|---|---|---|---|
| ND(1995) | — | — | — | 2.50 | 7.00 | — |

**25 POUNDS** **KM# 126** **Ring Composition:** Bronze **Center Composition:** Stainless Steel **Obverse:** National emblem **Reverse:** Large modern building

| Date | Mintage | F | VF | XF | Unc | BU |
|---|---|---|---|---|---|---|
| AH1416/1996 | — | — | — | 2.00 | 6.00 | — |

## MEDALLIC COINAGE

**POUND** **KM# M1** **Weight:** 8.0000 g. **Composition:** 0.9000 Gold .2315 oz. AGW

| Date | Mintage | F | VF | XF | Unc | BU |
|---|---|---|---|---|---|---|
| AH1398/1978 | 20,000 | — | — | — | 175 | — |

**5 POUNDS** **KM# M2** **Weight:** 40.0000 g. **Composition:** 0.9000 Gold 1.1574 oz. AGW **Obverse:** Eagle arms, ornaments below **Reverse:** Bust of Hafez al-Assad **Note:** Similar to M1.

| Date | Mintage | F | VF | XF | Unc | BU |
|---|---|---|---|---|---|---|
| AH1398/1978 | 5,000 | — | — | — | — | — |

## ESSAIS

| KM# | Date | Mintage | Identification | Issue Price | Mkt Val |
|---|---|---|---|---|---|
| E1 | 1926(a) | — | 2 Piastres. KM69. | — | 200 |
| E2 | 1926(a) | — | 5 Piastres. KM70. | — | 220 |

| KM# | Date | Mintage | Identification | Issue Price | Mkt Val |
|---|---|---|---|---|---|
| E3 | 1929(a) | — | Piastre. KM71. | — | 115 |
| E4 | 1929(a) | — | 10 Piastres. KM72 | — | 200 |
| E5 | 1929(a) | — | 25 Piastres. KM73. | — | 250 |

| KM# | Date | Mintage | Identification | Issue Price | Mkt Val |
|---|---|---|---|---|---|
| E6 | 1929(a) | — | 50 Piastres. KM74. | — | 265 |
| E7 | AH1350(a) | — | 50 Piastres. | — | 350 |
| E8 | 1935(a) | — | 1/2 Piastre. KM75. | — | 60.00 |

## MINT SETS

| KM# | Date | Mintage | Identification | Issue Price | Mkt Val |
|---|---|---|---|---|---|
| MS1 | 1968 (3) | — | KM96-98 | — | 5.50 |
| MS2 | 1978-79 (6) | — | KM115 (1978), 116-120.1 (1979) | — | 8.50 |

# TAJIKISTAN

The Republic of Tajikistan (Tadjiquistan), was formed from those regions of Bukhara and Turkestan where the population consisted mainly of Tajiks. Is bordered in the north and west by Uzbekistan and Kyrgyzstan, in the east by China and in the south by Afghanistan. It has an area of 55,240 sq. miles (143,100 sq. km.) and a population of 5.95 million. It includes 2 provinces of Khudzand and Khatlon together with the Gorno-Badakhshan Autonomous Region with a population of 5,092,603. Capital: Dushanbe. Tajikistan was admitted as a constituent republic of the Soviet Union on Dec. 5, 1929. In August 1990 the Tajik Supreme Soviet adopted a declaration of republican sovereignty, and in Dec. 1991 the republic became a member of the CIS.

After demonstrations and fighting, the Communist government was replaced by a Revolutionary Coalition Council on May 7, 1992. Following further demonstrations President Nabiev was ousted on Sept. 7, 1992. Civil war broke out, and the government resigned on Nov. 10, 1992. On Nov. 30, 1992 it was announced that a CIS peacekeeping force would be sent to Tajikistan. A state of emergency was imposed in Jan. 1993. A ceasefire was signed in 1996 and a peace agreement signed in June 1997.

**MONETARY SYSTEM**

1 Ruble = 100 Tanga

## REPUBLIC

### DECIMAL COINAGE

**5 DRAMS** KM# 2 **Weight:** 2.0500 g. **Composition:** Brass Clad Steel **Obverse:** Crown **Reverse:** Denomination **Edge:** Plain **Size:** 16.5 mm.

| Date | Mintage | F | VF | XF | Unc | BU |
|---|---|---|---|---|---|---|
| 2001 | — | — | — | — | 0.50 | — |

**10 DRAMS** KM# 3 **Weight:** 2.4700 g. **Composition:** Brass Clad Steel **Obverse:** Crown **Reverse:** Denomination **Edge:** Plain **Size:** 17.5 mm.

| Date | Mintage | F | VF | XF | Unc | BU |
|---|---|---|---|---|---|---|
| 2001 | — | — | — | — | 0.75 | — |

**20 DRAMS** KM# 4 **Weight:** 2.7300 g. **Composition:** Brass Clad Steel **Obverse:** Crown **Reverse:** Denomination **Edge:** Plain **Size:** 18.5 mm.

| Date | Mintage | F | VF | XF | Unc | BU |
|---|---|---|---|---|---|---|
| 2001 | — | — | — | — | 1.00 | — |

**25 DRAMS** KM# 5 **Weight:** 2.8000 g. **Composition:** Brass **Obverse:** Crown **Reverse:** Denomination **Edge:** Plain **Size:** 19.1 mm.

| Date | Mintage | F | VF | XF | Unc | BU |
|---|---|---|---|---|---|---|
| 2001 | — | — | — | — | 1.25 | — |

**50 DRAMS** KM# 6 **Weight:** 3.5500 g. **Composition:** Brass **Obverse:** Crown **Reverse:** Denomination **Edge:** Plain **Size:** 21 mm.

| Date | Mintage | F | VF | XF | Unc | BU |
|---|---|---|---|---|---|---|
| 2001 | — | — | — | — | 1.75 | — |

**20 ROUBLES** KM# 1 **Weight:** 20.0000 g. **Composition:** 0.9250 Silver .5948 oz. ASW **Obverse:** Royal device. **Reverse:** Crowned portrait. **Edge:** Reeded. **Size:** 35.1 mm.

| Date | Mintage | F | VF | XF | Unc | BU |
|---|---|---|---|---|---|---|
| 1999 Proof | — | Value: 65.00 | | | | |

# TANNU TUVA

The Tannu-Tuva Peoples Republic (Tuva), an autonomous part of Russia located in central Asia on the northwest border of Outer Mongolia, has an area of 64,000 sq. mi. (165,760 sq. km.) and a population of about 175,000. Capital: Kyzyl. The economy is based on herding, forestry and mining.

As Urianghi, Tuva was part of Outer Mongolia of the Chinese Empire when tsarist Russia, after fomenting a separatist movement, extended its protection to the mountainous country in 1914. Tuva declared its independence as the Tannu-Tuva Peoples Republic in 1921 under the auspices of the Tuva Peoples Revolutionary Party. In 1926, following Russia's successful mediation of the resultant Tuvinian-Mongolian territorial dispute, Tannu-Tuva and Outer Mongolia formally recognized each other's independence. The Tannu-Tuva Peoples Republic became an autonomous region of the U.S.S.R. on Oct. 13, 1944.

**MONETARY SYSTEM**

100 Kopejek (Kopeks) = 1 Aksha

## REPUBLIC

### STANDARD COINAGE

**KOPEJEK** KM# 1 **Composition:** Aluminum-Bronze

| Date | Mintage | VG | F | VF | XF | Unc |
|---|---|---|---|---|---|---|
| 1934 | — | 20.00 | 30.00 | 45.00 | 75.00 | — |

**2 KOPEJEK** KM# 2 **Composition:** Aluminum-Bronze

| Date | Mintage | VG | F | VF | XF | Unc |
|---|---|---|---|---|---|---|
| 1933 | — | — | — | — | — | — |
| 1934 | — | 22.50 | 32.50 | 55.00 | 85.00 | — |

**3 KOPEJEK** KM# 3 **Composition:** Aluminum-Bronze

| Date | Mintage | VG | F | VF | XF | Unc |
|---|---|---|---|---|---|---|
| 1933 | — | — | — | — | — | — |
| 1934 | — | 20.00 | 30.00 | 45.00 | 75.00 | — |

**5 KOPEJEK** KM# 4 **Composition:** Aluminum-Bronze

| Date | Mintage | VG | F | VF | XF | Unc |
|---|---|---|---|---|---|---|
| 1934 | — | 22.50 | 32.50 | 55.00 | 85.00 | — |

**10 KOPEJEK** KM# 5 **Composition:** Copper-Nickel

| Date | Mintage | VG | F | VF | XF | Unc |
|---|---|---|---|---|---|---|
| 1934 | — | 22.50 | 32.50 | 55.00 | 85.00 | — |

**15 KOPEJEK** KM# 6 **Composition:** Copper-Nickel

| Date | Mintage | VG | F | VF | XF | Unc |
|---|---|---|---|---|---|---|
| 1934 | — | 22.50 | 32.50 | 55.00 | 85.00 | — |

**20 KOPEJEK** KM# 7 **Composition:** Copper-Nickel

| Date | Mintage | VG | F | VF | XF | Unc |
|---|---|---|---|---|---|---|
| 1934 | — | 22.50 | 32.50 | 55.00 | 85.00 | — |

# TANZANIA

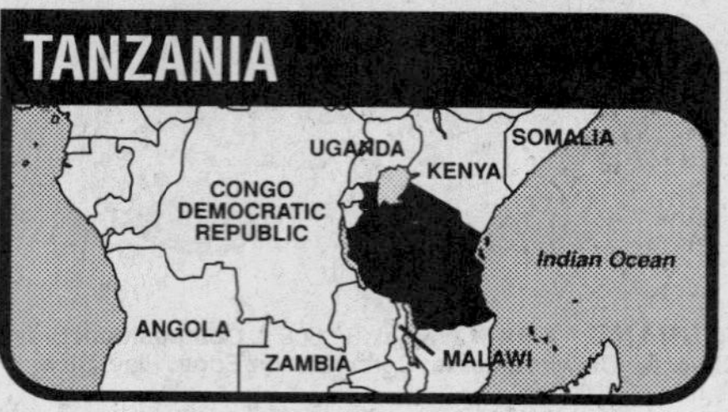


The United Republic of Tanzania, located on the east coast of Africa between Kenya and Mozambique, consists of Tanganyika and the islands of Zanzibar and Pemba. It has an area of 364,900 sq. mi. (945,090 sq. km.) and a population of *25.2 million. Capital: Dar es Salaam (Haven of Peace). The chief exports are cotton, coffee, diamonds, sisal, cloves, petroleum products, and cashew nuts.

Tanzania is a member of the Commonwealth of Nations. The President is Chief of State.

## REPUBLIC

### STANDARD COINAGE

100 Senti = 1 Shilingi

**5 SENTI** KM# 1 **Composition:** Bronze

| Date | Mintage | F | VF | XF | Unc | BU |
|---|---|---|---|---|---|---|
| 1966 | 55,250,000 | — | 0.10 | 0.20 | 0.50 | — |
| 1966 Proof | 5,500 | Value: 1.00 | | | | |
| 1971 | 5,000,000 | — | 0.10 | 0.20 | 0.50 | — |
| 1972 | — | — | 0.10 | 0.20 | 0.50 | — |
| 1973 | 20,000,000 | — | 0.10 | 0.20 | 0.50 | — |
| 1974 | 12,500,000 | — | 0.10 | 0.20 | 0.50 | — |
| 1975 | — | — | 0.10 | 0.20 | 0.50 | — |
| 1976 | 37,500,000 | — | 0.10 | 0.20 | 0.50 | — |
| 1977 | 10,000,000 | — | 0.10 | 0.20 | 0.50 | — |
| 1979 | 7,200,000 | — | 0.10 | 0.20 | 0.50 | — |
| 1980 | 10,000,000 | — | 0.10 | 0.20 | 0.50 | — |
| 1981 | 13,650,000 | — | 0.10 | 0.20 | 0.50 | — |
| 1982 | — | — | 0.10 | 0.20 | 0.50 | — |
| 1983 | 18,000 | — | 0.10 | 0.20 | 0.50 | — |
| 1984 | — | — | 0.10 | 0.20 | 0.50 | — |

**10 SENTI** KM# 11 **Composition:** Nickel-Brass

| Date | Mintage | F | VF | XF | Unc | BU |
|---|---|---|---|---|---|---|
| 1977 | 19,505,000 | — | 1.00 | 2.00 | 5.00 | — |
| 1979 | 8,000,000 | — | 1.00 | 2.00 | 5.00 | — |
| 1980 | 10,000,000 | — | 1.00 | 2.00 | 5.00 | — |
| 1981 | 10,000,000 | — | 1.00 | 2.00 | 5.00 | — |
| 1984 | — | — | 1.00 | 2.00 | 5.00 | — |

**20 SENTI** KM# 2 **Composition:** Nickel-Brass

| Date | Mintage | F | VF | XF | Unc | BU |
|---|---|---|---|---|---|---|
| 1966 | 26,500,000 | — | 0.20 | 0.40 | 1.50 | — |
| 1966 Proof | 5,500 | Value: 1.50 | | | | |
| 1970 | 5,000,000 | — | 0.20 | 0.40 | 1.50 | — |
| 1973 | 20,100,000 | — | 0.20 | 0.40 | 1.50 | — |
| 1975 | — | — | 0.20 | 0.40 | 1.50 | — |
| 1976 | 10,000,000 | — | 0.20 | 0.40 | 1.50 | — |
| 1977 | 10,000,000 | — | 0.20 | 0.40 | 1.50 | — |
| 1979 | 10,000,000 | — | 0.20 | 0.40 | 1.50 | — |
| 1980 | 10,000,000 | — | 0.20 | 0.40 | 1.50 | — |
| 1981 | 10,000,000 | — | 0.20 | 0.40 | 1.50 | — |
| 1982 | — | — | 0.20 | 0.40 | 1.50 | — |
| 1983 | 50,000 | — | 0.20 | 0.40 | 1.50 | — |
| 1984 | — | — | 0.20 | 0.40 | 1.50 | — |

**50 SENTI** KM# 3 **Composition:** Copper-Nickel

| Date | Mintage | F | VF | XF | Unc | BU |
|---|---|---|---|---|---|---|
| 1966 | 6,250,000 | — | 0.20 | 0.40 | 2.00 | — |
| 1966 Proof | 5,500 | Value: 3.00 | | | | |
| 1970 | 10,000,000 | — | 0.20 | 0.40 | 2.00 | — |
| 1973 | 10,000,000 | — | 0.25 | 0.50 | 2.00 | — |
| 1980 | 10,000,000 | — | 0.25 | 0.50 | 2.00 | — |
| 1981 | — | — | 0.25 | 0.50 | 2.00 | — |
| 1982 | 10,000,000 | — | 0.25 | 0.50 | 2.00 | — |
| 1983 | — | — | 0.25 | 0.50 | 2.00 | — |
| 1984 | 10,000,000 | — | 0.25 | 0.50 | 2.00 | — |

**50 SENTI** KM# 26 **Composition:** Nickel Clad Steel **Reverse:** Rabbit

| Date | Mintage | F | VF | XF | Unc | BU |
|---|---|---|---|---|---|---|
| 1988 | 10,000,000 | — | 0.25 | 0.75 | 1.50 | — |
| 1989 | — | — | 0.25 | 0.75 | 1.50 | — |
| 1990 | — | — | 0.25 | 0.75 | 1.50 | — |

**SHILINGI** KM# 4 **Composition:** Copper-Nickel

| Date | Mintage | F | VF | XF | Unc | BU |
|---|---|---|---|---|---|---|
| 1966 | 48,000,000 | — | 0.25 | 0.50 | 1.50 | — |
| 1966 Proof | 5,500 | Value: 5.00 | | | | |
| 1972 | 10,000,000 | — | 0.25 | 0.50 | 1.50 | — |
| 1974 | 15,000,000 | — | 0.30 | 0.60 | 1.75 | — |
| 1975 | — | — | 0.30 | 0.60 | 1.75 | — |
| 1977 | 5,000,000 | — | 0.30 | 0.60 | 1.75 | — |
| 1980 | 10,000,000 | — | 0.25 | 0.50 | 1.50 | — |
| 1981 | — | — | 0.30 | 0.60 | 1.75 | — |
| 1982 | 10,000,000 | — | 0.30 | 0.60 | 1.75 | — |
| 1983 | 10,000,000 | — | 0.30 | 0.60 | 1.75 | — |
| 1984 | 10,000,000 | — | 0.30 | 0.60 | 1.75 | — |

**SHILINGI** KM# 22 **Composition:** Nickel Clad Steel

| Date | Mintage | F | VF | XF | Unc | BU |
|---|---|---|---|---|---|---|
| 1987 | 5,000,000 | — | 0.40 | 0.80 | 1.85 | — |
| 1988 | 10,000,000 | — | 0.40 | 0.80 | 1.85 | — |
| 1989 | — | — | 0.40 | 0.80 | 1.85 | — |
| 1990 | — | — | 0.20 | 0.40 | 1.00 | — |
| 1991 | — | — | 0.20 | 0.40 | 1.00 | — |
| 1992 | — | — | 0.20 | 0.40 | 1.00 | — |

**5 SHILINGI** **KM# 5** **Composition:** Copper-Nickel **Series:** F.A.O. **Subject:** 10th Anniversary of Independence

| Date | Mintage | F | VF | XF | Unc | BU |
|---|---|---|---|---|---|---|
| ND(1971) | 1,000,000 | — | 0.75 | 1.50 | 3.50 | — |

**5 SHILINGI** **KM# 6** **Composition:** Copper-Nickel **Series:** F.A.O.

| Date | Mintage | F | VF | XF | Unc | BU |
|---|---|---|---|---|---|---|
| 1972 | 8,000,000 | — | 0.75 | 1.50 | 3.50 | — |
| 1973 | 5,000,000 | — | 0.75 | 1.75 | 4.00 | — |
| 1980 | 5,000,000 | — | 0.75 | 1.75 | 4.00 | — |

**5 SHILINGI** **KM# 10** **Composition:** Copper-Nickel **Subject:** 10th Anniversary - Bank of Tanzania

| Date | Mintage | F | VF | XF | Unc | BU |
|---|---|---|---|---|---|---|
| ND(1976) | 1,000,000 | — | 0.75 | 1.50 | 3.50 | — |
| ND(1976) Proof | 200 | Value: 40.00 | | | | |

**5 SHILINGI** **KM# 12** **Composition:** Copper-Nickel **Series:** F.A.O. **Subject:** Regional Conference for Africa

| Date | Mintage | F | VF | XF | Unc | BU |
|---|---|---|---|---|---|---|
| 1978 | 50,000 | — | 0.75 | 1.50 | 2.75 | — |
| 1978 Proof | 2,000 | Value: 11.50 | | | | |

**5 SHILINGI** **KM# 23** **Composition:** Copper-Nickel

| Date | Mintage | F | VF | XF | Unc | BU |
|---|---|---|---|---|---|---|
| 1987 | 5,000,000 | — | 0.75 | 1.50 | 3.00 | — |
| 1988 | 10,000,000 | — | 0.75 | 1.50 | 3.00 | — |
| 1989 | — | — | 0.75 | 1.50 | 3.00 | — |

**5 SHILINGI** **KM# 23a** **Composition:** Nickel Clad Steel

| Date | Mintage | F | VF | XF | Unc | BU |
|---|---|---|---|---|---|---|
| 1990 | — | — | 0.60 | 1.20 | 1.85 | — |
| 1991 | — | — | 0.60 | 1.20 | 1.85 | — |
| 1992 | — | — | 0.50 | 1.00 | 1.50 | — |
| 1993 | — | — | 0.50 | 1.00 | 1.50 | — |

**10 SHILINGI** **KM# 20** **Composition:** Copper-Nickel

| Date | Mintage | F | VF | XF | Unc | BU |
|---|---|---|---|---|---|---|
| 1987 | 10,000,000 | — | 1.00 | 1.50 | 3.25 | — |
| 1988 | 10,000,000 | — | 1.00 | 1.50 | 3.25 | — |
| 1989 | — | — | 1.00 | 1.50 | 3.25 | — |

**10 SHILINGI** **KM# 20a** **Composition:** Nickel Clad Steel

| Date | Mintage | F | VF | XF | Unc | BU |
|---|---|---|---|---|---|---|
| 1990 | — | — | 1.00 | 1.50 | 2.25 | — |
| 1991 | — | — | 1.00 | 1.50 | 2.25 | — |
| 1992 | — | — | 0.85 | 1.25 | 2.00 | — |
| 1993 | — | — | 0.85 | 1.25 | 2.00 | — |

**20 SHILINGI** **KM# 13** **Composition:** Copper-Nickel **Subject:** 20th Anniversary of Independence

| Date | Mintage | F | VF | XF | Unc | BU |
|---|---|---|---|---|---|---|
| ND(1981) | 997,000 | — | 3.00 | 6.00 | 12.00 | — |

**20 SHILINGI** **KM# 13a** **Weight:** 16.0000 g. **Composition:** 0.9250 Silver .4759 oz. ASW

| Date | Mintage | F | VF | XF | Unc | BU |
|---|---|---|---|---|---|---|
| ND(1981) Proof | 20,000 | Value: 42.50 | | | | |

**20 SHILINGI** **KM# 21** **Composition:** Copper-Nickel **Subject:** 20th Anniversary of Central Bank

| Date | Mintage | F | VF | XF | Unc | BU |
|---|---|---|---|---|---|---|
| ND(1986) | — | — | 4.00 | 10.00 | 20.00 | — |

**20 SHILINGI** **KM# 21a** **Weight:** 16.0000 g. **Composition:** 0.9250 Silver .4759 oz. ASW

| Date | Mintage | F | VF | XF | Unc | BU |
|---|---|---|---|---|---|---|
| ND(1986) Proof | 5,000 | Value: 110 | | | | |

**20 SHILINGI** **KM# 27.1** **Composition:** Nickel Bonded Steel **Reverse:** Elephants

| Date | Mintage | F | VF | XF | Unc | BU |
|---|---|---|---|---|---|---|
| 1990 | — | — | 1.50 | 2.00 | 3.50 | — |
| 1991 | — | — | 1.50 | 2.00 | 3.50 | — |

**20 SHILINGI** **KM# 27.2** **Composition:** Nickel Bonded Steel **Note:** Reduced size.

| Date | Mintage | F | VF | XF | Unc | BU |
|---|---|---|---|---|---|---|
| 1992 | — | — | 1.25 | 1.75 | 3.25 | — |

**25 SHILINGI** **KM# 7** **Weight:** 25.4000 g. **Composition:** 0.5000 Silver .4083 oz. ASW **Subject:** Conservation **Obverse:** Similar to 1500 Shilingi, KM#9 **Reverse:** Southern Giraffe

| Date | Mintage | F | VF | XF | Unc | BU |
|---|---|---|---|---|---|---|
| 1974 | 8,848 | — | — | — | 18.00 | — |

**25 SHILINGI** **KM# 7a** **Weight:** 28.2800 g. **Composition:** 0.9250 Silver .8411 oz. ASW

| Date | Mintage | F | VF | XF | Unc | BU |
|---|---|---|---|---|---|---|
| 1974 Proof | 13,000 | Value: 22.50 | | | | |

**25 SHILINGI** **KM# 30** **Composition:** Copper-Nickel **Subject:** 25 Years of Independence

| Date | Mintage | F | VF | XF | Unc | BU |
|---|---|---|---|---|---|---|
| ND(1985) Proof | — | Value: 100 | | | | |

**25 SHILINGI** **KM# 28** **Composition:** Nickel Bonded Steel **Subject:** 25th Anniversary of Central Bank

| Date | Mintage | F | VF | XF | Unc | BU |
|---|---|---|---|---|---|---|
| ND(1991) | — | — | — | — | 3.00 | — |

**25 SHILINGI** **KM# 28a** **Weight:** 13.0400 g. **Composition:** 0.9250 Silver .3878 oz. ASW

| Date | Mintage | F | VF | XF | Unc | BU |
|---|---|---|---|---|---|---|
| ND(1991) Proof | Est. 2,000 | Value: 65.00 | | | | |

**50 SHILINGI** **KM# 8** **Weight:** 31.8500 g. **Composition:** 0.5000 Silver .5120 oz. ASW **Subject:** Conservation **Obverse:** Similar to 1500 Shilingi, KM#9 **Reverse:** Black Rhinoceros

| Date | Mintage | F | VF | XF | Unc | BU |
|---|---|---|---|---|---|---|
| 1974 | 8,826 | — | — | — | 21.50 | — |

**50 SHILINGI** **KM# 8a** **Weight:** 35.0000 g. **Composition:** 0.9250 Silver 1.0409 oz. ASW

| Date | Mintage | F | VF | XF | Unc | BU |
|---|---|---|---|---|---|---|
| 1974 Proof | 12,000 | Value: 27.50 | | | | |

**50 SHILINGI** **KM# 33** **Composition:** Brass Plated Steel **Subject:** Conservation **Reverse:** Mother rhino and calf

| Date | Mintage | F | VF | XF | Unc | BU |
|---|---|---|---|---|---|---|
| 1996 | — | — | — | — | 3.25 | — |

**100 SHILINGI** **KM# 16** **Weight:** 23.3300 g. **Composition:** 0.9250 Silver .6938 oz. ASW **Series:** Decade for Women

| Date | Mintage | F | VF | XF | Unc | BU |
|---|---|---|---|---|---|---|
| 1984 Proof | 1,000 | Value: 42.50 | | | | |

**100 SHILINGI** **KM# 18** **Composition:** Copper-Nickel **Subject:** Conservation **Reverse:** Elephant mother and calf

| Date | Mintage | F | VF | XF | Unc | BU |
|---|---|---|---|---|---|---|
| 1986 | — | — | — | — | 6.50 | — |

**100 SHILINGI** **KM# 18a** **Weight:** 19.4400 g. **Composition:** 0.9250 Silver .5782 oz. ASW

| Date | Mintage | F | VF | XF | Unc | BU |
|---|---|---|---|---|---|---|
| 1986 Proof | 25,000 | Value: 27.50 | | | | |

**100 SHILINGI** **KM# 24** **Weight:** 19.4400 g. **Composition:** 0.9250 Silver .5782 oz. ASW **Series:** Save the Children Fund

| Date | Mintage | F | VF | XF | Unc | BU |
|---|---|---|---|---|---|---|
| 1990 Proof | Est. 20,000 | Value: 22.50 | | | | |

**100 SHILINGI** **KM# 32** **Composition:** Brass **Subject:** Conservation **Reverse:** Four Impalas

| Date | Mintage | F | VF | XF | Unc | BU |
|---|---|---|---|---|---|---|
| 1993 | — | — | — | — | 4.00 | |
| 1994 | — | — | — | — | 4.00 | |

**200 SHILINGI** **KM# 14** **Weight:** 28.2800 g. **Composition:** 0.9250 Silver .8411 oz. ASW **Subject:** 20th Anniversary of Independence **Obverse:** Similar to 20 Shilingi, KM#13

| Date | Mintage | F | VF | XF | Unc | BU |
|---|---|---|---|---|---|---|
| ND(1981) | 110 | — | — | — | 135 | — |
| ND(1981) Proof | Inc. above | Value: 150 | | | | |

**200 SHILINGI** **KM# 41** **Weight:** 20.0000 g. **Composition:** 0.5000 Silver .3214 oz. ASW **Subject:** Wildlife of Africa **Obverse:** National arms **Reverse:** Adult and juvenile rhinos **Edge:** Reeded **Size:** 34 mm.

| Date | Mintage | F | VF | XF | Unc | BU |
|---|---|---|---|---|---|---|
| 1997 Proof | — | Value: 22.50 | | | | |

**200 SHILINGI** **KM# 34** **Composition:** Copper-Nickel-Zinc **Obverse:** Portrait of Sheikh Karume **Reverse:** Two lions **Edge:** Plain and reeded sections

| Date | Mintage | F | VF | XF | Unc | BU |
|---|---|---|---|---|---|---|
| 1998 | — | — | — | — | 5.00 | — |

**200 SHILINGI** **KM# 40** **Weight:** 15.4000 g. **Composition:** 0.9250 Silver .4580 oz. ASW **Subject:** Pan Troglodytes **Obverse:** National arms **Reverse:** Chimpanzee family **Edge:** Reeded **Size:** 33.9 mm.

| Date | Mintage | F | VF | XF | Unc | BU |
|---|---|---|---|---|---|---|
| 1999 Proof | — | Value: 30.00 | | | | |

**250 SHILINGI** **KM# 29** **Weight:** 28.1600 g. **Composition:** 0.9250 Silver .8374 oz. ASW **Subject:** 25th Anniversary of Independence

| Date | Mintage | F | VF | XF | Unc | BU |
|---|---|---|---|---|---|---|
| ND(1985) Proof | — | Value: 250 | | | | |

**500 SHILINGI** **KM# 44** **Weight:** 20.0000 g. **Composition:** 0.9990 Silver .6424 oz. ASW **Subject:** Visit of Richard von Weizsacker **Obverse:** Arms **Reverse:** Weizsacker and Elephant

| Date | Mintage | F | VF | XF | Unc | BU |
|---|---|---|---|---|---|---|
| 1992 Proof | Est. 20,000 | Value: 35.00 | | | | |

**500 SHILINGI** **KM# 43** **Weight:** 33.8000 g. **Composition:** 0.9250 Silver 1.0052 oz. ASW **Subject:** Serengeti Wildlife **Obverse:** National arms. **Reverse:** Lions. **Edge:** Reeded. **Size:** 38.5 mm.

| Date | Mintage | F | VF | XF | Unc | BU |
|---|---|---|---|---|---|---|
| 1998 Proof | — | Value: 40.00 | | | | |

**1000 SHILINGI** **KM# 17** **Weight:** 8.1000 g. **Composition:** 0.9000 Gold .2344 oz. AGW **Series:** Decade for Women

| Date | Mintage | F | VF | XF | Unc | BU |
|---|---|---|---|---|---|---|
| 1984 Proof | 500 | Value: 185 | | | | |

**1000 SHILINGI** **KM# 45** **Weight:** 6.0000 g. **Composition:** 0.9990 Gold .1927 oz. AGW **Subject:** Visit of Richard von Weizsacker **Obverse:** Arms **Reverse:** Weizsacker and Elephant

| Date | Mintage | F | VF | XF | Unc | BU |
|---|---|---|---|---|---|---|
| 1992 Proof | Est. 8,000 | Value: 125 | | | | |

**1500 SHILINGI** **KM# 9** **Weight:** 33.4370 g. **Composition:** 0.9000 Gold .9676 oz. AGW **Subject:** Conservation **Reverse:** Cheetah

| Date | Mintage | F | VF | XF | Unc | BU |
|---|---|---|---|---|---|---|
| 1974 | 2,779 | — | — | — | 420 | — |
| 1974 Proof | 866 | Value: 650 | | | | |

**2000 SHILINGI** **KM# 15** **Weight:** 15.9800 g. **Composition:** 0.9170 Gold .4712 oz. AGW **Subject:** 20th Anniversary of Independence **Reverse:** Two figures supporting large shield

| Date | Mintage | F | VF | XF | Unc | BU |
|---|---|---|---|---|---|---|
| ND(1981) | 110 | — | — | — | 375 | — |
| ND(1981) Proof | Inc. above | Value: 425 | | | | |

**2000 SHILINGI** **KM# 19** **Weight:** 15.9800 g. **Composition:** 0.9170 Gold .4712 oz. AGW **Subject:** Conservation **Reverse:** Banded Green Sunbird

| Date | Mintage | F | VF | XF | Unc | BU |
|---|---|---|---|---|---|---|
| 1986 Proof | 5,000 | Value: 275 | | | | |

**2000 SHILINGI** **KM# 25** **Weight:** 10.0000 g. **Composition:** 0.9170 Gold .2948 oz. AGW **Series:** Save the Children Fund

| Date | Mintage | F | VF | XF | Unc | BU |
|---|---|---|---|---|---|---|
| 1990 Proof | Est. 3,000 | Value: 225 | | | | |

**2000 SHILINGI** **KM# 46** **Weight:** 10.0000 g. **Composition:** 0.9990 Gold .3212 oz. AGW **Subject:** Visit of Richard von Weizsacker **Obverse:** Arms **Reverse:** Weizsacker and Elephant

| Date | Mintage | F | VF | XF | Unc | BU |
|---|---|---|---|---|---|---|
| 1992 Proof | Est. 5,000 | Value: 200 | | | | |

**2500 SHILINGI** **KM# 31** **Weight:** 46.8500 g. **Composition:** 0.9170 Gold 1.3808 oz. AGW **Subject:** 25 Years of Independence

| Date | Mintage | F | VF | XF | Unc | BU |
|---|---|---|---|---|---|---|
| ND(1985) Proof | — | Value: 850 | | | | |

**2500 SHILINGI** **KM# 39** **Weight:** 155.3600 g. **Composition:** 0.9990 Silver 4.9899 oz. ASW **Subject:** Serengeti Wildlife **Reverse:** Gazelle

| Date | Mintage | F | VF | XF | Unc | BU |
|---|---|---|---|---|---|---|
| 1998 Proof | — | Value: 85.00 | | | | |

**2500 SHILINGI** **KM# 35** **Weight:** 155.3600 g. **Composition:** 0.9990 Silver 4.9899 oz. ASW **Subject:** Serengeti Wildlife **Obverse:** National arms **Reverse:** Zebra head and full body portraits **Edge:** Reeded **Size:** 65 mm. **Note:** Illustration reduced.

| Date | Mintage | F | VF | XF | Unc | BU |
|---|---|---|---|---|---|---|
| 1998 Proof | — | Value: 95.00 | | | | |

**2500 SHILINGI** **KM# 36** **Weight:** 155.3600 g. **Composition:** 0.9990 Silver 4.9899 oz. ASW **Subject:** Serengeti Wildlife **Reverse:** Giraffe head and full body portrait **Size:** 65 mm. **Note:** Illustration reduced.

| Date | Mintage | F | VF | XF | Unc | BU |
|---|---|---|---|---|---|---|
| 1998 Proof | — | Value: 95.00 | | | | |

**2500 SHILINGI** **KM# 37** **Weight:** 155.3600 g. **Composition:** 0.9990 Silver 4.9899 oz. ASW **Subject:** Serengeti Wildlife **Reverse:** Cheetah head and full body portrait **Size:** 65 mm. **Note:** Illustration reduced.

| Date | Mintage | F | VF | XF | Unc | BU |
|---|---|---|---|---|---|---|
| 1998 Proof | — | Value: 115 | | | | |

**2500 SHILINGI** **KM# 38** **Weight:** 155.3600 g. **Composition:** 0.9990 Silver 4.9899 oz. ASW **Subject:** Serengeti Wildlife **Reverse:** Wildebeest **Size:** 65 mm. **Note:** Illustration reduced.

| Date | Mintage | F | VF | XF | Unc | BU |
|---|---|---|---|---|---|---|
| 1998 Proof | — | Value: 85.00 | | | | |

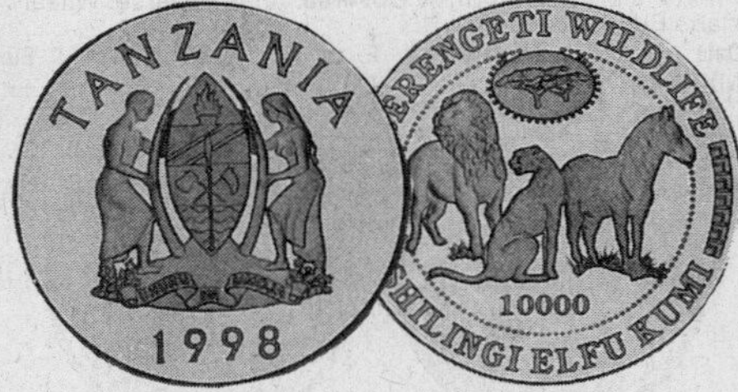


**10000 SHILINGI** **KM# 42** **Weight:** 31.1035 g. **Composition:** 0.9999 Gold 1.0000 oz. AGW **Subject:** Serengeti Wildlife **Obverse:** National arms **Reverse:** Lion, cheetah, and zebra **Edge:** Reeded **Size:** 32.5 mm.

| Date | Mintage | F | VF | XF | Unc | BU |
|---|---|---|---|---|---|---|
| 1998 Proof | Est. 1,000 | Value: 600 | | | | |

## PROOF SETS

| KM# | Date | Mintage | Identification | Issue Price | Mkt Val |
|---|---|---|---|---|---|
| PS1 | 1966 (4) | 5,500 | KM#1-4 | 10.20 | 10.00 |
| PS2 | 1974 (2) | 30,000 | KM#7a-8a | 50.00 | 50.00 |
| PS3 | 1985 (3) | — | KM#29-31 | — | 12.00 |

# TATARSTAN

Tatarstan, an autonomous republic in the Russian Federation, is situated between the middle of the Volga river and its tributary Kama, extends east to the Ural mountains, covering 26,500 sq. mi. (68,000 sq. km.) and as of the 1970 census, has a population of 3,743,600. Capital: Kazan. Tatarstan's economy combines its ancient traditions in the craftmanship of wood, leather, cloth, and ceramics with modern engineering, chemical, and food industries.

Colonized by the Bulgars in the 5th century, the territory of the Volga-Kama Bulgar State was inhabited by Turks. In the 13th century, Ghengis Khan conquered the area and established control until the 15th century, when residual Mongol influence left Tatarstan as the Tatar Khanate, seat of the Kazan (Tatar) Khans. In 1552, under Ivan IV (The Terrible), Russia conquered, absorbed and controlled Tatarstan until the dissolution of the U.S.S.R. in the late 20th century.

Constituted as an autonomous republic on May 27,1990, and as a sovereign state equal with Russia April, 1992, Tatarstan, with Russia's president, signed a treaty in Feb. 1994 defining Tatarstan as a state united with Russia (Commonwealth of Independent States).

**RULERS**

President Mintimir Shaimiev

## RUSSIAN STATE

### TOKEN COINAGE

**KILO (Bread)** **KM# Tn1** **Composition:** Bronze **Ruler:** President Mintimir Shaimiev **Obverse:** Arms **Reverse:** Wheat stalks **Edge:** Reeded

| Date | Mintage | F | VF | XF | Unc | BU |
|---|---|---|---|---|---|---|
| ND(1993) | — | 1.25 | 2.50 | 4.00 | 6.50 | — |

**10 LITRES (Petrol)** **KM# Tn2** **Composition:** Bronze **Ruler:** President Mintimir Shaimiev **Obverse:** Arms **Reverse:** Oil well pump **Edge:** Reeded **Note:** The bronze 10 Litres token was withdrawn from circulation because it was nickel plated in large numbers and passed off as the higher valued copper-nickel version KM-Tn3.

| Date | Mintage | F | VF | XF | Unc | BU |
|---|---|---|---|---|---|---|
| ND(1993) | — | 2.00 | 3.50 | 6.50 | 10.00 | — |

**20 LITRES (Petrol)** **KM# Tn3** **Composition:** Copper Nickel **Ruler:** President Mintimir Shaimiev **Obverse:** Arms **Reverse:** Oil well pump **Edge:** Reeded **Note:** The copper-nickel Tn3 are often found with test file notches, because of the nickel plating problems of the bronze Tn2.

| Date | Mintage | F | VF | XF | Unc | BU |
|---|---|---|---|---|---|---|
| ND(1993) | — | 2.50 | 4.00 | 7.50 | 11.50 | — |

# THAILAND

The Kingdom of Thailand (formerly Siam), a constitutional monarchy located in the center of mainland Southeast Asia between Burma and Laos, has an area of 198,457mi. (514,000 sq. km.) and a population of *55.5 million. Capital: Bangkok. The economy is based on agriculture and mining. Rubber, rice, teakwood, tin and tungsten are exported.

The history of The Kingdom of Siam, the only country in south and Southeast Asia that was never colonized by an European power, dates from the 6th century A.D. when Thai people started to migrate into the area a process that accelerated with the Mongol invasion of China in the 13th century. After 400 years of sporadic warfare with the neighboring Burmese, King Taskin won the last battle in 1767. He founded a new capital, Dhonburi, on the west bank of the Chao Praya River. King Rama I moved the capital to Bangkok in 1782,thus initiating the so-called Bangkok Period of Siamese coinage characterized by Pot Duang money (bullet coins) stamped with regal symbols.

The Portuguese, who were followed by the Dutch, British and French, introduced the Thai to the Western world. Rama III of the present ruling dynasty negotiated a treaty of friendship and commerce with Britain in 1826,and in 1896 the independence of the kingdom was guaranteed by an Anglo-French accord.

In 1909 Siam ceded to Great Britain its suzerain rights over the dependencies of Kedah, Kelantan, Trengganu and Perlis, Malay states situated in southern Siam just north of British Malaya, which eliminated any British jurisdiction in Siam proper.

The absolute monarchy was changed into a constitutional monarchy in 1932.

On Dec. 8, 1941, after five hours of fighting, Thailand agreed to permit Japanese troops passage through the country to invade Northern British Malaysia. This eventually led to increased Japanese intervention and finally occupation of the country. On Jan. 25, 1942, Thailand declared war on Great Britain and the United States. A free Thai guerilla movement was soon organized to counteract the Japanese. In July 1943 Japan transferred the four northern Malay States back to Thailand. These were returned to Great Britain after peace treaties were signed in 1946.

**RULERS**

Rama V (Phra Maha Chulalongkorn), 1868-1910
Rama VI (Phra Maha Vajiravudh), 1910-1925
Rama VII (Phra Maha Prajadhipok), 1925-1935
Rama VIII (Phra Maha Ananda Mahidol), 1935-1946
Rama IX (Phra Maha Bhumifhol Adulyadej), 1946-

**MONETARY SYSTEM**

Old currency system

2 Solos = 1 Att
2 Att = 1 Sio (Pai)
2 Sio = 1 Sik
2 Sik = 1 Fuang
2 Fuang = 1 Salung (not Sal'ung)
4 Salung = 1 Baht
4 Baht = 1 Tamlung
20 Tamlung = 1 Chang

UNITS OF OLD THAI CURRENCY

| | | | |
|---|---|---|---|
| Chang - | ชั่ง | Sik - | ซีก |
| Tamlung - | ตำลึง | Sio (Pai) - | เสี้ยว |
| Baht - | บาท | Att - | อัฐ |
| Salung - | สลึง | Solos - | โสพส |
| Fuang - | เฟื้อง | | |

**MINT MARKS**

H-Heaton Birmingham

DATING

Typical BE Dating

1 2 3 8 1244

Typical CS Dating

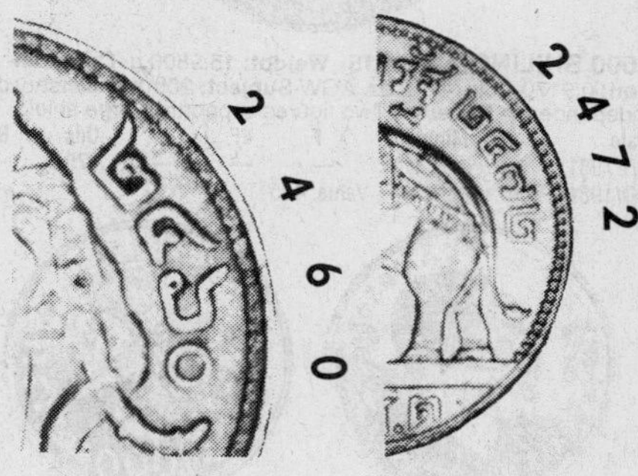


**NOTE**: Sometimes the era designator *BE* or *CS* will actually appear on the coin itself.

**Denomination**

2-1/2 (Satang) RS Dating

**DATE CONVERSION TABLES**

B.E. date - 543 = A.D. date
Ex: 2516 - 543 = 1973
R.S. date + 1781 = A.D. date
Ex: 127 + 1781 = 1908
C.S. date + 638 = A.D. date
Ex 1238 + 638 = 1876

Primary denominations used were 1 Baht, 1/4 and 1/8 Baht up to the reign of Rama IV. Other denominations are much scarcer.

## KINGDOM

### STANDARD COINAGE

**1/2 ATT (1 Solot)** **Y# 21** **Composition:** Bronze **Ruler:** Rama V Phra Maha Chulalongkorn

| Date | Mintage | F | VF | XF | Unc | BU |
|---|---|---|---|---|---|---|
| RS124 | — | 1.50 | 3.00 | 15.00 | 85.00 | — |

**Note:** These coins were also minted in RS114, RS115, RS121 ad RS122. The last year had a mintage of 5,120,000. Coins with these dates have not been observed and were probably additional mintings of coins dated RS109 and RS118. A nickel pattern dated RS114 does exist. Varieties in numeral size and rotated dies exist

**ATT (1/64 Baht)** **Y# 22** **Composition:** Bronze **Ruler:** Rama V Phra Maha Chulalongkorn **Note:** Full red uncirculated coins of this type carry a substantial premium.

| Date | Mintage | F | VF | XF | Unc | BU |
|---|---|---|---|---|---|---|
| RS121 | 11,251,000 | 1.50 | 2.50 | 8.50 | 80.00 | — |
| RS122 | 4,109,000 | 1.50 | 3.00 | 10.00 | 90.00 | — |

**Note:** Exists with large (greater than 1mm) and small (less than 1mm) numerals

| Date | Mintage | F | VF | XF | Unc | BU |
|---|---|---|---|---|---|---|
| RS124 | — | 1.50 | 3.00 | 10.00 | 90.00 | — |

**2 ATT** **Y# 23** **Composition:** Bronze **Ruler:** Rama V Phra Maha Chulalongkorn **Note:** Varieties in numeral size and rotated dies exist. Full red uncirculated coins of this type carry a substantial premium.

| Date | Mintage | F | VF | XF | Unc | BU |
|---|---|---|---|---|---|---|
| RS121 | 2,797,000 | 1.50 | 3.00 | 12.00 | 125 | — |
| RS122 | 2,323,000 | 1.50 | 3.00 | 12.00 | 125 | — |
| RS124 | — | 1.50 | 3.00 | 12.00 | 125 | — |

**FUANG (1/8 Baht)** **Y# 32a** **Weight:** 1.8900 g. **Composition:** Silver **Ruler:** Rama V Phra Maha Chulalongkorn

| Date | Mintage | F | VF | XF | Unc | BU |
|---|---|---|---|---|---|---|
| RS120 | — | 3.00 | 7.00 | 20.00 | 100 | — |
| RS121 | 380,000 | 3.00 | 7.00 | 20.00 | 100 | — |
| RS122 | 460,000 | 3.00 | 7.00 | 20.00 | 100 | — |
| RS123 | 310,000 | 3.00 | 7.00 | 20.00 | 100 | — |
| RS124 | 410,000 | 3.00 | 7.00 | 20.00 | 100 | — |
| RS125 | — | 3.00 | 7.00 | 20.00 | 100 | — |
| RS126 | — | 3.00 | 7.00 | 20.00 | 100 | — |
| RS127 | 480,000 | 3.00 | 7.00 | 20.00 | 100 | — |

**FUANG (1/8 Baht)** **Y# 32c** **Composition:** Gold **Ruler:** Rama V Phra Maha Chulalongkorn

| Date | Mintage | F | VF | XF | Unc | BU |
|---|---|---|---|---|---|---|
| RS122 | — | 300 | 600 | 1,250 | 2,000 | — |
| RS123 | — | 300 | 600 | 1,250 | 2,000 | — |
| RS124 | — | 300 | 600 | 1,250 | 2,000 | — |
| RS125 | — | 300 | 600 | 1,250 | 2,000 | — |
| RS126 | — | 300 | 600 | 1,250 | 2,000 | — |
| RS127 | — | 300 | 600 | 1,250 | 2,000 | — |
| RS128 | — | 300 | 600 | 1,250 | 2,000 | — |
| RS129 | — | 300 | 600 | 1,250 | 2,000 | — |

**SALUNG (1/4 Baht)** **Y# 33a** **Weight:** 3.8200 g. **Composition:** Silver **Ruler:** Rama V Phra Maha Chulalongkorn

| Date | Mintage | F | VF | XF | Unc | BU |
|---|---|---|---|---|---|---|
| RS120 | — | 5.00 | 12.00 | 35.00 | 275 | — |
| RS121 | 560,000 | 3.50 | 9.00 | 27.50 | 170 | — |
| RS122 | 340,000 | 3.50 | 9.00 | 27.50 | 170 | — |
| RS123 | 190,000 | 3.50 | 9.00 | 27.50 | 170 | — |
| RS125 | — | 3.50 | 9.00 | 27.50 | 170 | — |
| RS126 | — | 3.50 | 9.00 | 27.50 | 170 | — |
| RS127 | 270,000 | 3.50 | 9.00 | 27.50 | 200 | — |

**BAHT** **Y# 34a** **Composition:** Silver **Ruler:** Rama V Phra Maha Chulalongkorn

| Date | Mintage | F | VF | XF | Unc | BU |
|---|---|---|---|---|---|---|
| RS120 | — | 75.00 | 165 | 350 | 1,400 | — |
| RS121 | 4,070,000 | 7.50 | 25.00 | 80.00 | 300 | — |

**Note:** Because of a faulty die used the second 1 appears to be a 0 in some examples of this date

| Date | Mintage | F | VF | XF | Unc | BU |
|---|---|---|---|---|---|---|
| RS122 | 19,150,000 | 6.50 | 22.00 | 65.00 | 275 | — |
| RS123 | 4,790,000 | 6.50 | 22.00 | 55.00 | 275 | — |
| RS124 | 6,770,000 | 6.50 | 22.00 | 55.00 | 275 | — |
| RS125 | — | 6.50 | 22.00 | 55.00 | 275 | — |
| RS126 | — | 15.00 | 35.00 | 100 | 375 | — |

## DECIMAL COINAGE

25 Satang = 1 Salung; 100 Satang = 1 Baht

**1/2 SATANG** **Y# 50** **Composition:** Bronze **Ruler:** Rama VIII Phra Maha Ananda Mahidol

| Date | Mintage | F | VF | XF | Unc | BU |
|---|---|---|---|---|---|---|
| BE2480(1937) | — | — | 0.75 | 1.75 | 3.50 | — |

**SATANG** **Y# 35** **Composition:** Bronze **Note:** Variations in lettering exist.

| Date | Mintage | F | VF | XF | Unc | BU |
|---|---|---|---|---|---|---|
| RS127(1908) | 17,000,000 | — | 2.50 | 5.00 | 18.00 | — |
| RS128(1909) | 150,000 | — | 3.50 | 10.00 | 28.00 | — |
| RS129(1910) | 9,000,000 | — | 1.50 | 3.50 | 18.00 | — |
| RS130(1911) | 30,000,000 | — | 1.50 | 3.50 | 12.50 | — |
| BE2456(1913) | 10,000,000 | — | 1.00 | 1.50 | 4.00 | — |
| RS132(1913) Rare | | — | — | — | — | — |
| BE2457(1914) | 1,000,000 | — | 2.00 | 4.00 | 12.50 | — |
| BE2458(1915) | 5,000,000 | — | 0.75 | 1.00 | 2.75 | — |
| BE2461(1918) | 18,880,000 | — | 0.65 | 1.25 | 3.00 | — |
| BE2462(1919) | 6,400,000 | — | 0.65 | 1.00 | 2.75 | — |
| BE2463(1920) | 17,240,000 | — | 1.00 | 1.50 | 3.50 | — |
| BE2464(1921) | 6,360,000 | — | 15.00 | 25.00 | 40.00 | — |
| BE2466(1923) | 14,000,000 | — | 0.75 | 1.00 | 2.75 | — |
| BE2467(1924) | Inc. above | — | 1.00 | 1.50 | 3.50 | — |
| BE2469(1926) | 20,000,000 | — | 0.50 | 0.75 | 2.50 | — |
| BE2470(1927) | — | — | 0.50 | 0.75 | 2.50 | — |
| BE2472(1929) | — | — | 0.50 | 1.00 | 2.75 | — |
| BE2478(1935) | — | — | 0.50 | 0.70 | 2.00 | — |
| BE2480(1937) | — | — | 0.50 | 0.70 | 2.00 | — |

**SATANG** **Y# 51** **Composition:** Bronze

| Date | Mintage | F | VF | XF | Unc | BU |
|---|---|---|---|---|---|---|
| BE2482(1939) | 24,400,000 | — | 1.50 | 3.00 | 6.00 | — |

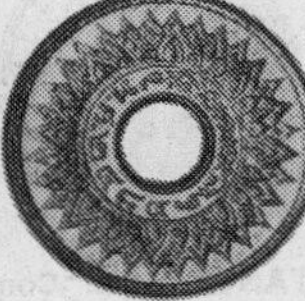

**SATANG** **Y# 54** **Composition:** Bronze **Ruler:** Rama VIII Phra Maha Ananda Mahidol

| Date | Mintage | F | VF | XF | Unc | BU |
|---|---|---|---|---|---|---|
| BE2484(1941) | — | — | 0.50 | 1.50 | 3.00 | — |

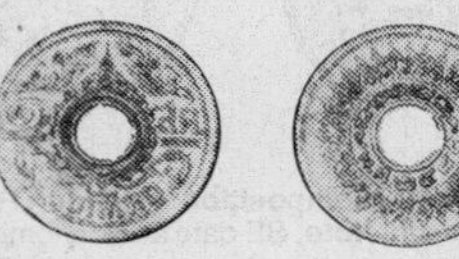

**SATANG** **Y# 57** **Composition:** Tin **Ruler:** Rama VIII Phra Maha Ananda Mahidol **Note:** BE date and denomination in Thai numberals, without hole.

| Date | Mintage | F | VF | XF | Unc | BU |
|---|---|---|---|---|---|---|
| BE2485(1942) | 20,700,000 | — | 0.30 | 0.50 | 1.00 | — |

**Note:** Approximately 790,000 coins were struck for circulation 1967-73

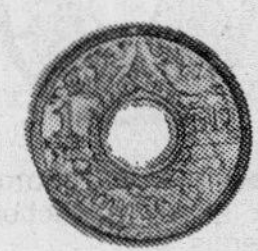
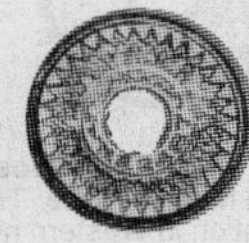

**SATANG** **Y# 60** **Composition:** Tin **Ruler:** Rama VIII Phra Maha Ananda Mahidol **Note:** BE date and denomination in Western numerals.

| Date | Mintage | F | VF | XF | Unc | BU |
|---|---|---|---|---|---|---|
| BE2487(1944) | 500,000 | — | 0.10 | 0.20 | 0.50 | — |

**SATANG** **Y# 186** **Composition:** Aluminum **Ruler:** Rama IX Phra Maha Bhumithol Adulyadej

| Date | Mintage | F | VF | XF | Unc | BU |
|---|---|---|---|---|---|---|
| BE2530(1987) | 93,000 | — | — | — | 0.10 | — |
| BE2531(1988) | 200,000 | — | — | — | 0.10 | — |
| BE2533(1990) | — | — | — | — | 0.10 | — |
| BE2534(1991) | — | — | — | — | 0.10 | — |
| BE2535(1992) | — | — | — | — | 0.10 | — |
| BE2536(1993) | — | — | — | — | 0.10 | — |
| BE2537(1994) | — | — | — | — | 0.10 | — |

**SATANG** **Y# 342** **Composition:** Aluminum **Ruler:** Rama IX Phra Maha Bhumithol Adulyadej **Subject:** 50th Anniversary - Reign of King Rama IX **Obverse:** King Rama IX

| Date | Mintage | F | VF | XF | Unc | BU |
|---|---|---|---|---|---|---|
| BE2539(1996) | — | — | — | — | 0.15 | — |

**5 SATANG** **Y# 36** **Composition:** Nickel

| Date | Mintage | F | VF | XF | Unc | BU |
|---|---|---|---|---|---|---|
| RS127(1908) | 7,000,000 | — | 3.00 | 4.00 | 8.00 | — |
| RS128(1909) | 4,000,000 | — | 3.50 | 4.50 | 10.00 | — |
| RS129(1910) | 4,000,000 | — | 1.50 | 2.00 | 7.00 | — |
| RS131(1912) | 2,000,000 | — | 1.50 | 2.50 | 8.00 | — |
| RS132(1913) Rare | — | — | — | — | — | — |
| BE2456(1913) | 2,000,000 | — | 1.50 | 2.50 | 6.00 | — |
| BE2457(1914) | 2,000,000 | — | 1.50 | 2.50 | 6.00 | — |
| BE2461(1918) | 2,000,000 | — | 1.50 | 2.50 | 6.00 | — |
| BE2462(1919) | 2,000,000 | — | 1.00 | 2.00 | 6.00 | — |
| BE2463(1920) | 9,900,000 | — | 1.00 | 1.50 | 4.50 | — |
| BE2464(1921) | 13,000,000 | — | 0.60 | 1.25 | 3.00 | — |
| BE2469(1926) | 20,000,000 | — | 0.60 | 1.25 | 3.00 | — |
| BE2478(1935) | 10,000,000 | — | 0.60 | 1.25 | 3.00 | — |
| BE2480(1937) | 20,000,000 | — | 0.60 | 1.25 | 3.00 | — |

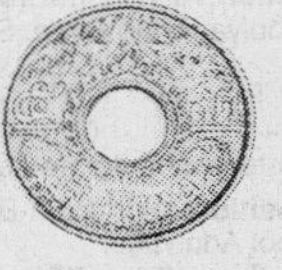
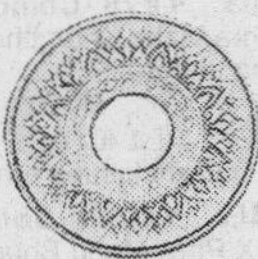

**5 SATANG** **Y# 55** **Weight:** 1.5000 g. **Composition:** 0.6500 Silver .0313 oz. ASW **Ruler:** Rama VIII Phra Maha Ananda Mahidol

| Date | Mintage | F | VF | XF | Unc | BU |
|---|---|---|---|---|---|---|
| BE2484(1941) | — | — | 1.50 | 3.00 | 4.50 | — |

**5 SATANG** **Y#58** **Composition:** Tin **Ruler:** Rama VIII Phra Maha Ananda Mahidol **Note:** BE date and denomination in Thai numerals.

| Date | Mintage | F | VF | XF | Unc | BU |
|---|---|---|---|---|---|---|
| BE2485(1942) | — | — | 0.50 | 1.50 | 3.00 | — |

**5 SATANG** **Y#61** **Composition:** Tin **Ruler:** Rama VIII Phra Maha Ananda Mahidol **Note:** Thick (2.2mm) planchet. BE date and denomination in Western numerals.

| Date | Mintage | F | VF | XF | Unc | BU |
|---|---|---|---|---|---|---|
| BE2487(1944) | — | — | 0.50 | 1.25 | 3.00 | — |
| BE2488(1945) | — | — | 0.50 | 1.25 | 3.00 | — |

**5 SATANG** **Y#61a** **Composition:** Tin **Ruler:** Rama VIII Phra Maha Ananda Mahidol **Note:** Thin (2.0mm) planchet.

| Date | Mintage | F | VF | XF | Unc | BU |
|---|---|---|---|---|---|---|
| BE2488(1945) | — | — | 0.50 | 1.25 | 3.00 | — |

**5 SATANG** **Y#61b** **Composition:** Tin **Ruler:** Rama VIII Phra Maha Ananda Mahidol **Note:** Medium planchet.

| Date | Mintage | F | VF | XF | Unc | BU |
|---|---|---|---|---|---|---|
| BE2488(1945) | — | — | 0.50 | 1.25 | 3.00 | — |

**5 SATANG** **Y#64** **Composition:** Tin **Ruler:** Rama VIII Phra Maha Ananda Mahidol **Obverse:** King Ananda, child head

| Date | Mintage | F | VF | XF | Unc | BU |
|---|---|---|---|---|---|---|
| BE2489(1946) | — | — | 0.50 | 1.00 | 2.00 | — |

**5 SATANG** **Y#68** **Composition:** Tin **Ruler:** Rama VIII Phra Maha Ananda Mahidol **Obverse:** King Ananda, youth head

| Date | Mintage | F | VF | XF | Unc | BU |
|---|---|---|---|---|---|---|
| BE2489(1946) | 24,480,000 | — | 0.15 | 0.50 | 1.00 | — |

**5 SATANG** **Y#72** **Composition:** Tin **Ruler:** Rama IX Phra Maha Bhumithol Adulyadej **Obverse:** King Rama IX, 1 medal on uniform

| Date | Mintage | F | VF | XF | Unc | BU |
|---|---|---|---|---|---|---|
| BE2493(1950) | Est. 6,480,000 | — | 0.50 | 0.75 | 1.25 | — |

**Note:** Coins bearing this date were also struck in 1954, 58, 59, and 73. Mintages are included here

**5 SATANG** **Y#72a** **Composition:** Aluminum-Bronze **Ruler:** Rama IX Phra Maha Bhumithol Adulyadej

| Date | Mintage | F | VF | XF | Unc | BU |
|---|---|---|---|---|---|---|
| BE2493(1950) | 15,500,000 | — | 0.25 | 1.00 | 2.00 | — |

**5 SATANG** **Y#78** **Composition:** Aluminum-Bronze **Ruler:** Rama IX Phra Maha Bhumithol Adulyadej **Obverse:** Small head, 3 medals on uniform

| Date | Mintage | F | VF | XF | Unc | BU |
|---|---|---|---|---|---|---|
| BE2500(1957) | Est. 46,440,000 | — | — | 0.10 | 0.25 | — |

**Note:** Current issues are minted without date change

**5 SATANG** **Y#78a** **Composition:** Aluminum-Bronze **Ruler:** Rama IX Phra Maha Bhumithol Adulyadej

| Date | Mintage | F | VF | XF | Unc | BU |
|---|---|---|---|---|---|---|
| BE2500(1957) | Est. 6,240,000 | — | 0.50 | 1.50 | 2.00 | — |

**5 SATANG** **Y#78b** **Composition:** Tin **Ruler:** Rama IX Phra Maha Bhumithol Adulyadej

| Date | Mintage | F | VF | XF | Unc | BU |
|---|---|---|---|---|---|---|
| BE2500(1957) | — | — | 1.75 | 3.00 | 5.00 | — |

**Note:** The above coins were struck to replace Y#72 in mint sets

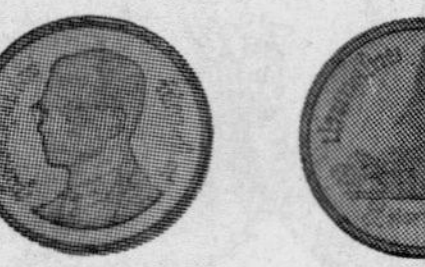

**5 SATANG** **Y#208** **Composition:** Aluminum **Ruler:** Rama IX Phra Maha Bhumithol Adulyadej

| Date | Mintage | F | VF | XF | Unc | BU |
|---|---|---|---|---|---|---|
| BE2530(1987) | — | — | — | — | 20.00 | — |
| BE2531(1988) | 704,000 | — | — | — | 0.10 | — |
| BE2533(1990) | — | — | — | — | 0.10 | — |
| BE2534(1991) | — | — | — | — | 0.10 | — |
| BE2535(1992) | — | — | — | — | 0.10 | — |
| BE2536(1993) | — | — | — | — | 0.10 | — |
| BE2537(1994) | — | — | — | — | 0.10 | — |

**5 SATANG** **Y#343** **Composition:** Aluminum **Ruler:** Rama IX Phra Maha Bhumithol Adulyadej **Subject:** 50th Anniversary - Reign of King Rama IX **Obverse:** King Rama IX

| Date | Mintage | F | VF | XF | Unc | BU |
|---|---|---|---|---|---|---|
| BE2539(1996) | — | — | — | — | 0.25 | — |

**10 SATANG** **Y#37** **Composition:** Nickel **Note:** Variations in lettering exist.

| Date | Mintage | F | VF | XF | Unc | BU |
|---|---|---|---|---|---|---|
| RS127(1908) | 7,000,000 | — | 1.50 | 3.00 | 8.50 | — |
| RS129(1910) | 5,000,000 | — | 1.50 | 3.00 | 8.50 | — |
| RS130(1911) | 500,000 | — | 2.00 | 5.00 | 12.00 | — |
| RS131(1912) | 1,500,000 | — | 1.50 | 3.00 | 10.00 | — |
| BE2456(1913) | 1,000,000 | — | 1.25 | 2.00 | 6.00 | — |
| BE2457(1914) | 1,000,000 | — | 1.25 | 2.00 | 6.00 | — |
| BE2461(1918) | 770,000 | — | 2.50 | 3.50 | 9.00 | — |
| BE2462(1919) | 774,000 | — | 1.25 | 1.50 | 3.50 | — |
| BE2463(1920) | Inc. above | — | 1.25 | 1.50 | 3.50 | — |
| BE2464(1921) | 21,727,000 | — | 1.00 | 1.25 | 3.00 | — |
| BE2478(1935) | 5,000,000 | — | 1.00 | 1.25 | 3.00 | — |
| BE2480(1937) | 5,000,000 | — | 0.75 | 1.00 | 2.50 | — |

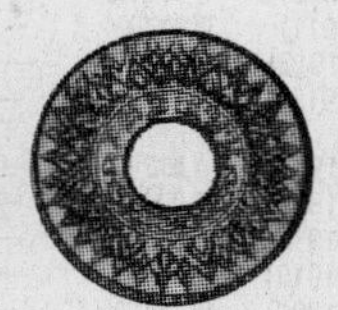

**10 SATANG** **Y#56** **Weight:** 2.5000 g. **Composition:** 0.6500 Silver .0522 oz. ASW **Ruler:** Rama VIII Phra Maha Ananda Mahidol

| Date | Mintage | F | VF | XF | Unc | BU |
|---|---|---|---|---|---|---|
| BE2484(1941) | — | — | 2.00 | 4.00 | 8.00 | — |

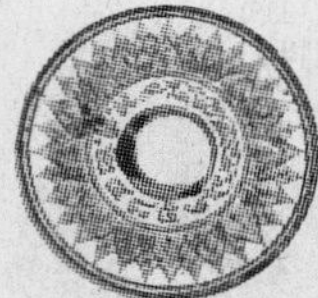

**10 SATANG** **Y#59** **Composition:** Tin **Ruler:** Rama VIII Phra Maha Ananda Mahidol **Note:** BE date and denomination in Thai numberals.

| Date | Mintage | F | VF | XF | Unc | BU |
|---|---|---|---|---|---|---|
| BE2485(1942) | 230,000 | — | 1.00 | 2.00 | 3.50 | — |

**10 SATANG** **Y#62** **Composition:** Tin **Ruler:** Rama VIII Phra Maha Ananda Mahidol **Note:** Thick (2.5mm) planchet. BE date and denomination in Western numerals.

| Date | Mintage | F | VF | XF | Unc | BU |
|---|---|---|---|---|---|---|
| BE2487(1944) | — | — | 1.00 | 2.00 | 3.50 | — |
| BE2488(1945) | — | — | 3.50 | 7.00 | 15.00 | — |

**10 SATANG** **Y#62a** **Composition:** Tin **Ruler:** Rama IX Phra Maha Bhumithol Adulyadej **Note:** Thin (2.0mm) planchet.

| Date | Mintage | F | VF | XF | Unc | BU |
|---|---|---|---|---|---|---|
| BE2488(1945) | — | — | 1.00 | 2.50 | 4.00 | — |

**10 SATANG** **Y#65** **Composition:** Tin **Ruler:** Rama IX Phra Maha Bhumithol Adulyadej **Obverse:** King Ananda, child head

| Date | Mintage | F | VF | XF | Unc | BU |
|---|---|---|---|---|---|---|
| BE2489(1946) | — | — | 0.50 | 1.25 | 2.25 | — |

**10 SATANG** **Y#69** **Composition:** Tin **Ruler:** Rama IX Phra Maha Bhumithol Adulyadej **Obverse:** Youth head

| Date | Mintage | F | VF | XF | Unc | BU |
|---|---|---|---|---|---|---|
| BE2489(1946) | 40,470,000 | — | 0.50 | 1.25 | 2.00 | — |

**10 SATANG** **Y#73** **Composition:** Tin **Ruler:** Rama IX Phra Maha Bhumithol Adulyadej **Obverse:** King Bhumiphol, 1 medal on uniform

| Date | Mintage | F | VF | XF | Unc | BU |
|---|---|---|---|---|---|---|
| BE2493(1950) | 139,695,000 | — | 0.40 | 1.00 | 1.50 | — |

**Note:** These coins were also struck in 1954-1973 and the mintages are also included here

**10 SATANG** **Y#73a** **Composition:** Aluminum-Bronze **Ruler:** Rama IX Phra Maha Bhumithol Adulyadej

| Date | Mintage | F | VF | XF | Unc | BU |
|---|---|---|---|---|---|---|
| BE2493(1950) | 4,060,000 | — | 0.75 | 1.50 | 2.50 | — |

**10 SATANG** **Y#79** **Composition:** Aluminum-Bronze **Ruler:** Rama IX Phra Maha Bhumithol Adulyadej **Obverse:** Smaller head. 3 medals on uniform **Rev. Legend:** THIN STYLE

| Date | Mintage | F | VF | XF | Unc | BU |
|---|---|---|---|---|---|---|
| BE2500(1957) | Est. 55,410,000 | — | 0.10 | 0.25 | 0.50 | — |

**Note:** Current issues are melted without date change

**10 SATANG** **Y#79d** **Composition:** Aluminum-Bronze **Ruler:** Rama IX Phra Maha Bhumithol Adulyadej **Rev. Legend:** THICK STYLE

| Date | Mintage | F | VF | XF | Unc | BU |
|---|---|---|---|---|---|---|
| BE2500(1957) | — | — | 0.10 | 0.25 | 0.50 | — |

**10 SATANG** **Y#79a** **Composition:** Bronze **Ruler:** Rama IX Phra Maha Bhumithol Adulyadej **Rev. Legend:** THICK STYLE

| Date | Mintage | F | VF | XF | Unc | BU |
|---|---|---|---|---|---|---|
| BE2500(1957) | 13,365,000 | — | 0.25 | 0.75 | 1.25 | — |
| BE2501(1958) | — | — | 0.25 | 0.75 | 1.25 | — |

**10 SATANG** **Y#79c** **Composition:** Bronze **Ruler:** Rama IX Phra Maha Bhumithol Adulyadej **Rev. Legend:** THIN STYLE

| Date | Mintage | F | VF | XF | Unc | BU |
|---|---|---|---|---|---|---|
| BE2500(1957) | Inc. above | — | 2.50 | 5.00 | 10.00 | — |

**10 SATANG** **Y# 79b** **Composition:** Tin **Ruler:** Rama IX Phra Maha Bhumithol Adulyadej

| Date | Mintage | F | VF | XF | Unc | BU |
|---|---|---|---|---|---|---|
| BE2500(1957) | — | — | 7.00 | 15.00 | 45.00 | — |

**10 SATANG** **Y# 209** **Composition:** Aluminum **Ruler:** Rama IX Phra Maha Bhumithol Adulyadej

| Date | Mintage | F | VF | XF | Unc | BU |
|---|---|---|---|---|---|---|
| BE2530(1987) | — | — | — | — | 20.00 | — |
| BE2531(1988) | 900,000 | — | — | — | 0.10 | — |
| BE2533(1990) | — | — | — | — | 0.10 | — |
| BE2534(1991) | — | — | — | — | 0.10 | — |
| BE2535(1992) | — | — | — | — | 0.10 | — |
| BE2536(1993) | — | — | — | — | 0.10 | — |
| BE2537(1994) | — | — | — | — | 0.10 | — |

**10 SATANG** **Y# 344** **Composition:** Aluminum **Ruler:** Rama IX Phra Maha Bhumithol Adulyadej **Subject:** 50th Anniversary - Reign of King Rama IX

| Date | Mintage | F | VF | XF | Unc | BU |
|---|---|---|---|---|---|---|
| BE2539(1996) | — | — | — | — | 0.35 | — |

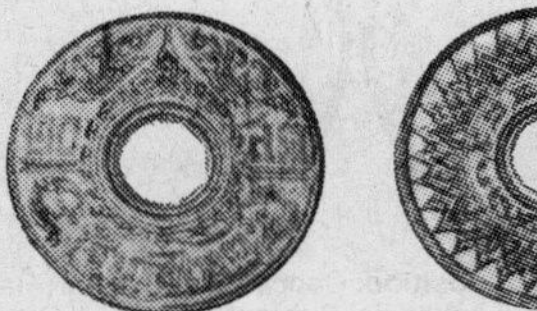

**20 SATANG** **Y# A56** **Weight:** 3.0000 g. **Composition:** 0.6500 Silver .0627 oz. ASW **Ruler:** Rama VIII Phra Maha Ananda Mahidol **Note:** BE date and denomination in Thai numerals

| Date | Mintage | F | VF | XF | Unc | BU |
|---|---|---|---|---|---|---|
| BE2485(1942) | — | — | 3.00 | 6.00 | 12.00 | — |

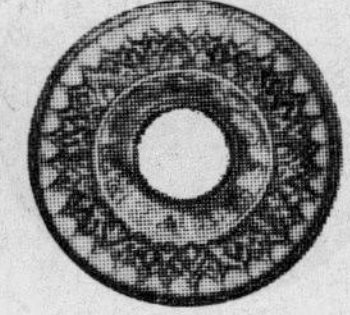

**20 SATANG** **Y# 63** **Composition:** Tin **Ruler:** Rama VIII Phra Maha Ananda Mahidol **Note:** BE date and denomination in Western numerals.

| Date | Mintage | F | VF | XF | Unc | BU |
|---|---|---|---|---|---|---|
| BE2488(1945) | — | — | 1.00 | 2.50 | 4.00 | — |

**25 SATANG = 1/4 BAHT** **Y# 48** **Weight:** 3.7500 g. **Composition:** 0.6500 Silver .0784 oz. ASW **Ruler:** Rama VII Phra Maha Prajadhipok

| Date | Mintage | F | VF | XF | Unc | BU |
|---|---|---|---|---|---|---|
| BE2472(1929) | — | — | 4.50 | 9.00 | 22.50 | — |

**25 SATANG = 1/4 BAHT** **Y# 66** **Composition:** Tin **Ruler:** Rama VIII Phra Maha Ananda Mahidol **Obverse:** King Ananda, child's head

| Date | Mintage | F | VF | XF | Unc | BU |
|---|---|---|---|---|---|---|
| BE2489(1946) | — | — | 2.50 | 4.50 | 12.50 | — |

**25 SATANG = 1/4 BAHT** **Y# 70** **Composition:** Tin **Ruler:** Rama VIII Phra Maha Ananda Mahidol **Obverse:** Youth's head

| Date | Mintage | F | VF | XF | Unc | BU |
|---|---|---|---|---|---|---|
| BE2489(1946) | Est. 226,348,000 | — | 0.20 | 0.40 | 0.75 | — |

**Note:** These coins were also struck 1954-64 and mintage figure is a total

**25 SATANG = 1/4 BAHT** **Y# 76** **Composition:** Aluminum-Bronze **Ruler:** Rama IX Phra Maha Bhumithol Adulyadej **Obverse:** King Rama IX, 1 medal on uniform

| Date | Mintage | F | VF | XF | Unc | BU |
|---|---|---|---|---|---|---|
| BE2493(1950) | 23,170,000 | — | 0.75 | 1.75 | 4.00 | — |

**25 SATANG = 1/4 BAHT** **Y# 80** **Composition:** Aluminum-Bronze **Ruler:** Rama IX Phra Maha Bhumithol Adulyadej **Obverse:** Smaller head; 3 medals on uniform

| Date | Mintage | F | VF | XF | Unc | BU |
|---|---|---|---|---|---|---|
| BE2500(1957) | 620,480,000 | — | 0.10 | 0.15 | 0.25 | — |

**Note:** Current issues are minted without date change and with and without reeded edges

**25 SATANG = 1/4 BAHT** **Y# 109** **Composition:** Brass **Ruler:** Rama IX Phra Maha Bhumithol Adulyadej **Note:** Date varieties exist.

| Date | Mintage | F | VF | XF | Unc | BU |
|---|---|---|---|---|---|---|
| BE2520(1977) | 183,356,000 | — | — | 0.10 | 0.15 | — |

**25 SATANG = 1/4 BAHT** **Y# 187** **Composition:** Aluminum-Bronze **Ruler:** Rama IX Phra Maha Bhumithol Adulyadej

| Date | Mintage | F | VF | XF | Unc | BU |
|---|---|---|---|---|---|---|
| BE2530(1987) | 5,108,000 | — | — | — | 0.20 | — |
| BE2531(1988) | 42,096,000 | — | — | — | 0.10 | — |
| BE2532(1989) | — | — | — | — | 0.10 | — |
| BE2533(1990) | — | — | — | — | 0.10 | — |
| BE2534(1991) | — | — | — | — | 0.10 | — |
| BE2535(1992) | — | — | — | — | 0.10 | — |
| BE2536(1993) | — | — | — | — | 0.10 | — |
| BE2537(1994) | — | — | — | — | 0.10 | — |
| BE2538(1995) | — | — | — | — | 0.10 | — |

**25 SATANG = 1/4 BAHT** **Y# 345** **Composition:** Brass **Ruler:** Rama IX Phra Maha Bhumithol Adulyadej **Subject:** Golden Jubilee - Reign of King Rama IX

| Date | Mintage | F | VF | XF | Unc | BU |
|---|---|---|---|---|---|---|
| BE2539(1996) | — | — | — | — | 0.50 | — |

**SALUNG (1/4 Baht)** **Y# 43b** **Weight:** 3.7500 g. **Composition:** 0.5000 Silver .0603 oz. ASW **Ruler:** Rama VI Phra Maha Vajirajudh

| Date | Mintage | F | VF | XF | Unc | BU |
|---|---|---|---|---|---|---|
| BE2462(1919) Dot after legend | Inc. above | — | 40.00 | 65.00 | 120 | — |

**SALUNG = 1/4 BAHT** **Y# 43** **Weight:** 3.7500 g. **Composition:** 0.8000 Silver .0965 oz. ASW **Ruler:** Rama VI Phra Maha Vajirajudh

| Date | Mintage | F | VF | XF | Unc | BU |
|---|---|---|---|---|---|---|
| BE2458(1915) | 2,040,000 | — | 5.00 | 10.00 | 20.00 | — |

**SALUNG = 1/4 BAHT** **Y# 43a** **Weight:** 3.7500 g. **Composition:** 0.6500 Silver .0784 oz. ASW **Ruler:** Rama VI Phra Maha Vajirajudh

| Date | Mintage | F | VF | XF | Unc | BU |
|---|---|---|---|---|---|---|
| BE2460(1917) | 1,100,000 | — | 4.00 | 8.00 | 18.50 | — |
| BE2461(1918) | 2,170,000 | — | 4.00 | 8.00 | 18.50 | — |
| BE2462(1919) | 7,860,000 | — | 3.00 | 6.50 | 15.00 | — |
| BE2467(1924) | 2,100,000 | — | 4.00 | 8.00 | 18.50 | — |
| BE2468(1925) | — | — | 4.00 | 8.00 | 18.50 | — |

**50 SATANG = 1/2 BAHT** **Y# 49** **Weight:** 7.5000 g. **Composition:** 0.6500 Silver .1567 oz. ASW **Ruler:** Rama VII Phra Maha Prajadhipok

| Date | Mintage | F | VF | XF | Unc | BU |
|---|---|---|---|---|---|---|
| BE2472(1929) | 17,008,000 | — | 7.00 | 16.50 | 35.00 | — |

**50 SATANG = 1/2 BAHT** **Y# 67** **Composition:** Tin **Ruler:** Rama VIII Phra Maha Ananda Mahidol **Obverse:** King Ananda, child's head

| Date | Mintage | F | VF | XF | Unc | BU |
|---|---|---|---|---|---|---|
| BE2489(1946) | — | — | 40.00 | 75.00 | 180 | — |

**50 SATANG = 1/2 BAHT** **Y# 71** **Composition:** Tin **Ruler:** Rama VIII Phra Maha Ananda Mahidol **Obverse:** Youth's head

| Date | Mintage | F | VF | XF | Unc | BU |
|---|---|---|---|---|---|---|
| BE2489(1946) | 17,008,000 | — | 0.75 | 1.50 | 3.00 | — |

**Note:** These coins were minted from 1954-1957 and mintage figure is a total

**50 SATANG = 1/2 BAHT** **Y# 77** **Composition:** Aluminum-Bronze **Ruler:** Rama IX Phra Maha Bhumithol Adulyadej **Obverse:** King Rama IX, 1 medal on uniform

| Date | Mintage | F | VF | XF | Unc | BU |
|---|---|---|---|---|---|---|
| BE2493(1950) | 20,710,000 | — | 0.75 | 1.75 | 5.00 | — |

**50 SATANG = 1/2 BAHT** **Y# 81** **Composition:** Aluminum-Bronze **Ruler:** Rama IX Phra Maha Bhumithol Adulyadej **Obverse:** Smaller head; 3 medals on uniform

| Date | Mintage | F | VF | XF | Unc | BU |
|---|---|---|---|---|---|---|
| BE2500(1957) | 439,874,000 | — | 0.10 | 0.15 | 0.25 | — |

**Note:** Current issues are minted without date change

**50 SATANG = 1/2 BAHT** **Y# 168** **Composition:** Aluminum-Bronze **Ruler:** Rama IX Phra Maha Bhumithol Adulyadej

| Date | Mintage | F | VF | XF | Unc | BU |
|---|---|---|---|---|---|---|
| BE2523(1980) | 122,260,000 | — | 0.10 | 0.15 | 0.25 | — |

**50 SATANG = 1/2 BAHT** **Y# 203** **Composition:** Brass **Ruler:** Rama IX Phra Maha Bhumithol Adulyadej

| Date | Mintage | F | VF | XF | Unc | BU |
|---|---|---|---|---|---|---|
| BE2530(1987) | — | — | — | — | 0.10 | — |
| BE2531(1988) | 23,776,000 | — | — | — | 0.10 | — |
| BE2532(1989) | — | — | 0.20 | 0.30 | 1.00 | — |
| BE2533(1990) | — | — | — | — | 0.10 | — |
| BE2534(1991) | — | — | — | — | 0.10 | — |
| BE2535(1992) | — | — | — | — | 0.10 | — |
| BE2536(1993) | — | — | — | — | 0.10 | — |
| BE2537(1994) | — | — | — | — | 0.10 | — |
| BE2538(1995) | — | — | — | — | 0.10 | — |
| BE2539(1996) | — | — | — | — | 0.10 | — |

**50 SATANG = 1/2 BAHT** **Y# 329** **Composition:** Aluminum-Bronze **Ruler:** Rama IX Phra Maha Bhumithol Adulyadej **Subject:** 50th Year of Reign - King Rama IX

| Date | Mintage | F | VF | XF | Unc | BU |
|---|---|---|---|---|---|---|
| BE2539(1996) | — | — | — | — | 0.35 | — |

**2 SALUNG = 1/2 BAHT** **Y# 44** **Weight:** 7.5000 g. **Composition:** 0.8000 Silver .1929 oz. ASW **Ruler:** Rama VI Phra Maha Vajirajudh

| Date | Mintage | F | VF | XF | Unc | BU |
|---|---|---|---|---|---|---|
| BE2458(1915) | 2,740,000 | — | 7.50 | 18.50 | 40.00 | — |

**2 SALUNG = 1/2 BAHT** **Y# 44b** **Weight:** 7.5000 g. **Composition:** 0.5000 Silver .1206 oz. ASW **Ruler:** Rama VI Phra Maha Vajirajudh

| Date | Mintage | F | VF | XF | Unc | BU |
|---|---|---|---|---|---|---|
| AH2462(1919) Large dot after legend | Inc. above | — | 7.50 | 16.50 | 32.50 | — |
| AH2462(1919) Small dot after legend | Inc. above | — | 7.50 | 16.50 | 32.50 | — |

**2 SALUNG = 1/2 BAHT** **Y# 44a** **Weight:** 7.5000 g. **Composition:** 0.6500 Silver .1568 oz. ASW **Ruler:** Rama VI Phra Maha Vajirajudh **Note:** Date varieties exist.

| Date | Mintage | F | VF | XF | Unc | BU |
|---|---|---|---|---|---|---|
| AH2462(1919) | 3,230,000 | — | 6.00 | 14.00 | 30.00 | — |
| AH2463(1920) | 4,970,000 | — | 6.00 | 14.00 | 30.00 | — |
| AH2464(1921) | — | — | 6.00 | 14.00 | 30.00 | — |

**BAHT** **Y# 39** **Weight:** 15.0000 g. **Composition:** 0.9000 Silver .4340 oz. ASW **Ruler:** Rama V Phra Maha Chulalongkorn

| Date | Mintage | F | VF | XF | Unc | BU |
|---|---|---|---|---|---|---|
| RS127(1908) | 1,037,000 | — | 2,500 | 3,750 | 7,000 | — |

**BAHT** **Y# 45** **Weight:** 15.0000 g. **Composition:** 0.9000 Silver .4340 oz. ASW **Ruler:** Rama VI Phra Maha Vajirajudh

| Date | Mintage | F | VF | XF | Unc | BU |
|---|---|---|---|---|---|---|
| BE2456(1913) | 2,690,000 | — | 10.00 | 17.50 | 40.00 | — |

**Note:** BE2456 is often found weakly struck so it does appear similar to a counterfeit

| Date | Mintage | F | VF | XF | Unc | BU |
|---|---|---|---|---|---|---|
| BE2457(1914) | 490,000 | — | 12.50 | 25.00 | 50.00 | — |
| BE2458(1915) | 5,000,000 | — | 10.00 | 17.50 | 40.00 | — |
| BE2459(1916) | 9,080,000 | — | 10.00 | 17.50 | 32.00 | — |
| BE2460(1917) | 14,340,000 | — | 10.00 | 17.50 | 32.00 | — |
| BE2461(1918) | 3,840,000 | — | 10.00 | 17.50 | 45.00 | — |

**BAHT** **Y# 82.2** **Composition:** Copper-Nickel **Ruler:** Rama IX Phra Maha Bhumithol Adulyadej **Obverse:** King Rama IX, 1 medal on uniform. **Reverse:** National arms.

| Date | Mintage | F | VF | XF | Unc | BU |
|---|---|---|---|---|---|---|
| BE2493(1950) | — | — | 0.75 | 1.50 | 6.00 | — |

**BAHT** **Y# 82.1 (Y82)** **Composition:** Copper-Nickel-Silver-Zinc **Ruler:** Rama IX Phra Maha Bhumithol Adulyadej **Obverse:** King Rama IX, 3 medals on uniform. **Reverse:** National arms.

| Date | Mintage | F | VF | XF | Unc | BU |
|---|---|---|---|---|---|---|
| BE2500(1957) | 3,143,000 | — | 0.75 | 1.50 | 6.00 | — |

**Note:** These coins were minted from 1958-60 and mintage figure is a total

**BAHT** **Y# 82a** **Composition:** Silver **Ruler:** Rama IX Phra Maha Bhumithol Adulyadej

| Date | Mintage | F | VF | XF | Unc | BU |
|---|---|---|---|---|---|---|
| BE2500(1957) | — | — | — | — | 30.00 | — |

**BAHT** **Y# 83** **Composition:** Copper-Nickel **Ruler:** Rama IX Phra Maha Bhumithol Adulyadej **Subject:** King Rama IX and Queen Sirikit

| Date | Mintage | F | VF | XF | Unc | BU |
|---|---|---|---|---|---|---|
| BE2504(1961) | 4,430,000 | — | 0.40 | 0.75 | 2.00 | — |

**BAHT** **Y# 84** **Composition:** Copper-Nickel **Ruler:** Rama IX Phra Maha Bhumithol Adulyadej

| Date | Mintage | F | VF | XF | Unc | BU |
|---|---|---|---|---|---|---|
| BE2505(1962) | 883,086,000 | — | 0.10 | 0.15 | 0.50 | — |

**Note:** These coins were minted from 1962-82 and mintage figure is a total

**BAHT** **Y# 85** **Composition:** Copper-Nickel **Ruler:** Rama IX Phra Maha Bhumithol Adulyadej **Subject:** 36th Birthday - King Rama IX

| Date | Mintage | F | VF | XF | Unc | BU |
|---|---|---|---|---|---|---|
| ND(1963) | 3,000,000 | — | 0.25 | 0.75 | 2.00 | — |

**BAHT** **Y# 87** **Composition:** Copper-Nickel **Ruler:** Rama IX Phra Maha Bhumithol Adulyadej **Subject:** 5th Asian Games

| Date | Mintage | F | VF | XF | Unc | BU |
|---|---|---|---|---|---|---|
| BE2509(1966) | 9,000,000 | — | 0.25 | 0.75 | 3.00 | — |

**BAHT** **Y# 91** **Composition:** Copper-Nickel **Ruler:** Rama IX Phra Maha Bhumithol Adulyadej **Subject:** 6th Asian Games

| Date | Mintage | F | VF | XF | Unc | BU |
|---|---|---|---|---|---|---|
| BE2513(1970) | 9,000,000 | — | 0.25 | 0.75 | 1.50 | — |

**BAHT** **Y# 96** **Composition:** Copper-Nickel **Ruler:** Rama IX Phra Maha Bhumithol Adulyadej **Series:** F.A.O.

| Date | Mintage | F | VF | XF | Unc | BU |
|---|---|---|---|---|---|---|
| BE2515(1972) | 9,000,000 | — | 0.10 | 0.25 | 0.75 | — |

**BAHT** **Y# 97** **Composition:** Copper-Nickel **Ruler:** Rama IX Phra Maha Bhumithol Adulyadej **Subject:** Prince Vajiralongkorn Investiture

| Date | Mintage | F | VF | XF | Unc | BU |
|---|---|---|---|---|---|---|
| BE2515(1972) | 9,000,000 | — | 0.15 | 0.40 | 1.00 | — |

**BAHT** **Y# 99** **Composition:** Copper-Nickel **Ruler:** Rama IX Phra Maha Bhumithol Adulyadej **Subject:** 25th Anniversary - World Health Organization

| Date | Mintage | F | VF | XF | Unc | BU |
|---|---|---|---|---|---|---|
| BE2516(1973) | 1,000,000 | — | 0.25 | 0.65 | 1.25 | — |

**BAHT** **Y# 100** **Composition:** Copper-Nickel **Ruler:** Rama IX Phra Maha Bhumithol Adulyadej

| Date | Mintage | F | VF | XF | Unc | BU |
|---|---|---|---|---|---|---|
| BE2517(1974) | 248,978,000 | — | 0.15 | 0.40 | 1.00 | — |

**BAHT** **Y# 105** **Composition:** Copper-Nickel **Ruler:** Rama IX Phra Maha Bhumithol Adulyadej **Subject:** 8th SEAP Games

| Date | Mintage | F | VF | XF | Unc | BU |
|---|---|---|---|---|---|---|
| BE2518(1975) | 3,000,000 | — | 0.25 | 0.65 | 1.25 | — |

**BAHT** **Y# 107** **Composition:** Copper-Nickel **Ruler:** Rama IX Phra Maha Bhumithol Adulyadej **Subject:** 75th Birthday of Princess Mother

| Date | Mintage | F | VF | XF | Unc | BU |
|---|---|---|---|---|---|---|
| BE2518(1975) | 9,000,000 | — | 0.15 | 0.40 | 1.00 | — |

**BAHT** **Y# 110** **Composition:** Copper-Nickel **Ruler:** Rama IX Phra Maha Bhumithol Adulyadej

| Date | Mintage | F | VF | XF | Unc | BU |
|---|---|---|---|---|---|---|
| BE2520(1977) | 506,460,000 | — | 0.10 | 0.20 | 0.50 | — |

**BAHT** **Y# 112** **Composition:** Copper-Nickel **Ruler:** Rama IX Phra Maha Bhumithol Adulyadej **Series:** F.A.O.

| Date | Mintage | F | VF | XF | Unc | BU |
|---|---|---|---|---|---|---|
| BE2520(1977) | 2,000,000 | — | 0.15 | 0.40 | 1.00 | — |

**BAHT** **Y# 114** **Composition:** Copper-Nickel **Ruler:** Rama IX Phra Maha Bhumithol Adulyadej **Subject:** Graduation of Princess Sirindhorn

| Date | Mintage | F | VF | XF | Unc | BU |
|---|---|---|---|---|---|---|
| BE2520(1977) | 8,998,000 | — | 0.15 | 0.40 | 1.00 | — |

**BAHT** **Y# 114a** **Composition:** Bronze **Ruler:** Rama IX Phra Maha Bhumithol Adulyadej

| Date | Mintage | F | VF | XF | Unc | BU |
|---|---|---|---|---|---|---|
| BE2520(1977) | — | — | — | — | — | — |

**BAHT** **Y# 124** **Composition:** Copper-Nickel **Ruler:** Rama IX Phra Maha Bhumithol Adulyadej **Subject:** Investiture of Princess Sirindhorn

| Date | Mintage | F | VF | XF | Unc | BU |
|---|---|---|---|---|---|---|
| BE2520(1977) | 5,000,000 | — | 0.15 | 0.40 | 1.00 | — |

**BAHT** **Y# 127** **Composition:** Copper-Nickel **Ruler:** Rama IX Phra Maha Bhumithol Adulyadej **Subject:** Graduation of Crown Prince Vijiralongkorn

| Date | Mintage | F | VF | XF | Unc | BU |
|---|---|---|---|---|---|---|
| BE2521(1978) | 5,000,000 | — | 0.10 | 0.20 | 0.50 | — |

**BAHT** **Y# 130** **Composition:** Copper-Nickel **Ruler:** Rama IX Phra Maha Bhumithol Adulyadej **Subject:** 8th Asian Games

| Date | Mintage | F | VF | XF | Unc | BU |
|---|---|---|---|---|---|---|
| BE2521(1978) | 5,000,000 | — | 0.10 | 0.20 | 0.50 | — |

**BAHT** **Y# 157** **Composition:** Copper-Nickel **Ruler:** Rama IX Phra Maha Bhumithol Adulyadej **Series:** World Food Day

| Date | Mintage | F | VF | XF | Unc | BU |
|---|---|---|---|---|---|---|
| BE2525(1982) | 1,500,000 | — | 0.10 | 0.20 | 0.50 | — |

**BAHT** **Y# 159.2** **Composition:** Copper-Nickel **Ruler:** Rama IX Phra Maha Bhumithol Adulyadej **Obverse:** Small portrait with space between collar and lower hairline

| Date | Mintage | F | VF | XF | Unc | BU |
|---|---|---|---|---|---|---|
| BE2525(1982) | Inc. above | — | 2.50 | 5.00 | 10.00 | — |

**BAHT** **Y# 159.1** **Composition:** Copper-Nickel **Ruler:** Rama IX Phra Maha Bhumithol Adulyadej **Obverse:** Large portrait with collar touching hairline **Note:** 2527 and 2528 are frozen dates, with the Thai numerals for 27 and 28 in the Finance Ministry decal at the bottom of the reverse.

| Date | Mintage | F | VF | XF | Unc | BU |
|---|---|---|---|---|---|---|
| BE2525(1982) | 123,585,000 | — | 0.10 | 0.20 | 0.50 | — |
| BE2525(1984) | — | — | 0.10 | 0.20 | 0.50 | — |
| BE2525(1985) | — | — | 0.10 | 0.20 | 0.50 | — |

**BAHT** **Y# 183** **Composition:** Copper-Nickel **Ruler:** Rama IX Phra Maha Bhumithol Adulyadej **Note:** Circulation coinage. Varieties exist.

| Date | Mintage | F | VF | XF | Unc | BU |
|---|---|---|---|---|---|---|
| BE2529(1986) | — | — | 0.20 | 0.30 | 1.00 | — |
| BE2530(1987) | 325,271,000 | — | — | — | 0.10 | — |
| BE2531(1988) | 391,442,000 | — | — | — | 0.10 | — |
| BE2532(1989) | — | — | — | — | 0.10 | — |
| BE2533(1990) | — | — | — | — | 0.10 | — |
| BE2534(1991) | — | — | — | — | 0.10 | — |
| BE2535(1992) | — | — | — | — | 0.10 | — |
| BE2536(1993) | — | — | — | — | 0.10 | — |
| BE2537(1994) | — | — | — | — | 0.10 | — |
| BE2538(1995) | — | — | — | — | 0.10 | — |
| BE2539(1996) | — | — | — | — | 0.10 | — |
| BE2540(1997) | — | — | — | — | 0.10 | — |

**BAHT** **Y# 330** **Composition:** Copper-Nickel **Ruler:** Rama IX Phra Maha Bhumithol Adulyadej **Subject:** 50th Anniversary - Reign of King Rama IX

| Date | Mintage | F | VF | XF | Unc | BU |
|---|---|---|---|---|---|---|
| BE2539(1996) | — | — | — | — | 0.35 | — |

**2 BAHT** **Y# 134** **Composition:** Copper-Nickel **Ruler:** Rama IX Phra Maha Bhumithol Adulyadej **Subject:** Graduation of Princess Chulabhorn

| Date | Mintage | F | VF | XF | Unc | BU |
|---|---|---|---|---|---|---|
| BE2522(1979) | 5,000,000 | — | 0.20 | 0.40 | 1.00 | — |

**2 BAHT** **Y# 176** **Composition:** Copper-Nickel Clad Copper **Ruler:** Rama IX Phra Maha Bhumithol Adulyadej **Subject:** International Youth Year

| Date | Mintage | F | VF | XF | Unc | BU |
|---|---|---|---|---|---|---|
| BE2528(1985) | 10,000,000 | — | 0.20 | 0.40 | 1.00 | — |

**2 BAHT** **Y# 177** **Composition:** Copper-Nickel Clad Copper **Ruler:** Rama IX Phra Maha Bhumithol Adulyadej **Subject:** XII SEA Games

| Date | Mintage | F | VF | XF | Unc | BU |
|---|---|---|---|---|---|---|
| BE2528(1985) | 5,000,000 | — | 0.20 | 0.40 | 1.00 | — |

**2 BAHT** **Y# 178** **Composition:** Copper-Nickel Clad Copper **Ruler:** Rama IX Phra Maha Bhumithol Adulyadej **Subject:** National YEars of the Trees

| Date | Mintage | F | VF | XF | Unc | BU |
|---|---|---|---|---|---|---|
| ND(1986)(1986) | 3,000,000 | — | 0.50 | 1.00 | 3.50 | — |

**2 BAHT** **Y# 180** **Composition:** Copper-Nickel Clad Copper **Ruler:** Rama IX Phra Maha Bhumithol Adulyadej **Subject:** Year of Peace

| Date | Mintage | F | VF | XF | Unc | BU |
|---|---|---|---|---|---|---|
| BE2529(1986) | 5,000,000 | — | — | — | 0.50 | — |

**2 BAHT** **Y# 191** **Composition:** Copper-Nickel Clad Copper **Ruler:** Rama IX Phra Maha Bhumithol Adulyadej **Subject:** Princess Chulabhorn Awarded Einstein Medal

| Date | Mintage | F | VF | XF | Unc | BU |
|---|---|---|---|---|---|---|
| BE2529(1986) | 3,000,000 | — | — | — | 0.50 | — |

**2 BAHT** **Y# 194** **Composition:** Copper-Nickel Clad Copper **Ruler:** Rama IX Phra Maha Bhumithol Adulyadej **Subject:** 60th Birthday - King Rama IX

| Date | Mintage | F | VF | XF | Unc | BU |
|---|---|---|---|---|---|---|
| BE2530(1987) | 10,000 | — | — | — | 0.50 | — |

**2 BAHT** **Y# 188** **Composition:** Copper-Nickel Clad Copper **Ruler:** Rama IX Phra Maha Bhumithol Adulyadej **Subject:** Chulachomklao Royal Military Academy

| Date | Mintage | F | VF | XF | Unc | BU |
|---|---|---|---|---|---|---|
| BE2530(1987) | 3,000,000 | — | — | — | 0.50 | — |

**2 BAHT** **Y# 204** **Composition:** Copper-Nickel Clad Copper **Ruler:** Rama IX Phra Maha Bhumithol Adulyadej **Subject:** 72nd Anniversary of Thai Cooperatives

| Date | Mintage | F | VF | XF | Unc | BU |
|---|---|---|---|---|---|---|
| BE2531(1988) | 3,000,000 | — | — | — | 0.50 | — |

**2 BAHT** **Y# 210** **Composition:** Copper-Nickel Clad Copper **Ruler:** Rama IX Phra Maha Bhumithol Adulyadej **Subject:** 42nd Anniversary - Reign of King Rama IX

| Date | Mintage | F | VF | XF | Unc | BU |
|---|---|---|---|---|---|---|
| BE2531(1988) | 5,000,000 | — | — | — | 0.50 | — |

**2 BAHT** **Y# 220** **Composition:** Copper-Nickel Clad Copper **Ruler:** Rama IX Phra Maha Bhumithol Adulyadej **Subject:** 100th Anniversary of Siriraj Hospital

| Date | Mintage | F | VF | XF | Unc | BU |
|---|---|---|---|---|---|---|
| BE2531(1988) | 3,412,000 | — | — | — | 0.50 | — |

**2 BAHT** **Y# 222** **Composition:** Copper-Nickel Clad Copper **Ruler:** Rama IX Phra Maha Bhumithol Adulyadej **Subject:** Crown Prince's Birthday

| Date | Mintage | F | VF | XF | Unc | BU |
|---|---|---|---|---|---|---|
| BE2531(1988) | 2,000,000 | — | — | — | 0.50 | — |

**2 BAHT** **Y# 225** **Composition:** Copper-Nickel Clad Copper **Ruler:** Rama IX Phra Maha Bhumithol Adulyadej **Subject:** 72nd Anniversary of Chulalongkorn University

| Date | Mintage | F | VF | XF | Unc | BU |
|---|---|---|---|---|---|---|
| BE2532(1989) | 3,000,000 | — | — | — | 0.50 | — |

**2 BAHT** **Y# 230** **Composition:** Copper-Nickel Clad Copper **Ruler:** Rama IX Phra Maha Bhumithol Adulyadej **Subject:** Centennial of First Medical College

| Date | Mintage | F | VF | XF | Unc | BU |
|---|---|---|---|---|---|---|
| BE2533(1990) | 1,000,000 | — | — | — | 0.50 | — |

**2 BAHT** **Y# 232** **Composition:** Copper-Nickel Clad Copper **Ruler:** Rama IX Phra Maha Bhumithol Adulyadej **Subject:** 90th Birthday of Queen Mother

| Date | Mintage | F | VF | XF | Unc | BU |
|---|---|---|---|---|---|---|
| BE2533(1990) | 2,000,000 | — | — | — | 0.50 | — |

**2 BAHT** **Y# 235** **Composition:** Copper-Nickel Clad Copper **Ruler:** Rama IX Phra Maha Bhumithol Adulyadej **Subject:** 100th Anniversary - Office of the Comptroller General

| Date | Mintage | F | VF | XF | Unc | BU |
|---|---|---|---|---|---|---|
| BE2533(1990) | 1,000,000 | — | — | — | 0.50 | — |

**2 BAHT** **Y# 243** **Composition:** Copper-Nickel Clad Copper **Ruler:** Rama IX Phra Maha Bhumithol Adulyadej **Subject:** World Health Organization

| Date | Mintage | F | VF | XF | Unc | BU |
|---|---|---|---|---|---|---|
| BE2533(1990) | 2,000,000 | — | — | — | 1.00 | — |

**2 BAHT** **Y# 237** **Composition:** Copper-Nickel Clad Copper **Ruler:** Rama IX Phra Maha Bhumithol Adulyadej **Subject:** 36th Birthday of Princess Sirindhorn

| Date | Mintage | F | VF | XF | Unc | BU |
|---|---|---|---|---|---|---|
| BE2534(1991) | 2,300,000 | — | — | — | 0.50 | — |

**2 BAHT** **Y# 240** **Composition:** Copper-Nickel Clad Copper **Ruler:** Rama IX Phra Maha Bhumithol Adulyadej **Subject:** 80th Anniversary of Thai Boy Scouts

| Date | Mintage | F | VF | XF | Unc | BU |
|---|---|---|---|---|---|---|
| BE2534(1991) | 2,000,000 | — | — | — | 1.50 | — |

**2 BAHT** **Y# 255** **Composition:** Copper-Nickel Clad Copper **Ruler:** Rama IX Phra Maha Bhumithol Adulyadej **Subject:** Princess Sirindhorn's Magsaysay Foundation Award

| Date | Mintage | F | VF | XF | Unc | BU |
|---|---|---|---|---|---|---|
| BE2534(1991) | 12,000,000 | — | — | — | 0.50 | — |

**2 BAHT** **Y# 248** **Composition:** Copper-Nickel Clad Copper **Ruler:** Rama IX Phra Maha Bhumithol Adulyadej **Subject:** Centenary Celebration - Father of King Rama IX

| Date | Mintage | F | VF | XF | Unc | BU |
|---|---|---|---|---|---|---|
| BE2535(1992) | 2,308,000 | — | — | — | 0.50 | — |

**2 BAHT** **Y# 251** **Composition:** Copper-Nickel Clad Copper **Ruler:** Rama IX Phra Maha Bhumithol Adulyadej **Subject:** Ministry of Justice Centennial

| Date | Mintage | F | VF | XF | Unc | BU |
|---|---|---|---|---|---|---|
| BE2535(1992) | 1,500,000 | — | — | — | 0.50 | — |

**2 BAHT** **Y# 253** **Composition:** Copper-Nickel Clad Copper **Ruler:** Rama IX Phra Maha Bhumithol Adulyadej **Subject:** Ministry of Interior Centennial

| Date | Mintage | F | VF | XF | Unc | BU |
|---|---|---|---|---|---|---|
| 1992(1992) | 1,500,000 | — | — | — | 0.50 | — |

**2 BAHT** **Y# 259** **Composition:** Copper-Nickel Clad Copper **Ruler:** Rama IX Phra Maha Bhumithol Adulyadej **Subject:** Queen's 60th Birthday

| Date | Mintage | F | VF | XF | Unc | BU |
|---|---|---|---|---|---|---|
| BE2535(1992) | 1,700,000 | — | — | — | 0.50 | — |

**2 BAHT** **Y# 268** **Composition:** Copper-Nickel Clad Copper **Ruler:** Rama IX Phra Maha Bhumithol Adulyadej **Subject:** 60th Anniversary of the National Assembly - Anatasamakhom Throne Hall

| Date | Mintage | F | VF | XF | Unc | BU |
|---|---|---|---|---|---|---|
| BE2535(1992) | 1,000,000 | — | — | — | 0.50 | — |

**2 BAHT** **Y# 270** **Composition:** Copper-Nickel Clad Copper **Ruler:** Rama IX Phra Maha Bhumithol Adulyadej **Subject:** Ministry of Agriculture

| Date | Mintage | F | VF | XF | Unc | BU |
|---|---|---|---|---|---|---|
| BE2535(1992) | 1,000,000 | — | — | — | 0.50 | — |

**2 BAHT** **Y# 272** **Composition:** Copper-Nickel Clad Copper **Ruler:** Rama IX Phra Maha Bhumithol Adulyadej **Subject:** King's 64th Birthday

| Date | Mintage | F | VF | XF | Unc | BU |
|---|---|---|---|---|---|---|
| BE2535(1992) | 1,000,000 | — | — | — | 0.50 | — |

**2 BAHT** **Y# 276** **Composition:** Copper-Nickel Clad Copper **Ruler:** Rama IX Phra Maha Bhumithol Adulyadej **Subject:** Centennial of Thai Teacher Training - Emblem

| Date | Mintage | F | VF | XF | Unc | BU |
|---|---|---|---|---|---|---|
| BE2535(1992) | 1,200,000 | — | — | — | 0.50 | — |

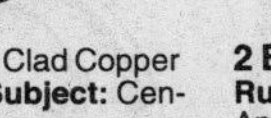

**2 BAHT** **Y# 277** **Composition:** Copper-Nickel Clad Copper **Ruler:** Rama IX Phra Maha Bhumithol Adulyadej **Subject:** Centennial of Thai National Bank - Seated Figure

| Date | Mintage | F | VF | XF | Unc | BU |
|---|---|---|---|---|---|---|
| BE2535(1992) | 1,000,000 | — | — | — | 0.50 | — |

**2 BAHT** **Y# 278** **Composition:** Copper-Nickel Clad Copper **Ruler:** Rama IX Phra Maha Bhumithol Adulyadej **Subject:** Centennial of Attorney General's Office - Scale

| Date | Mintage | F | VF | XF | Unc | BU |
|---|---|---|---|---|---|---|
| BE2536(1993) | 1,000,000 | — | — | — | 0.50 | — |

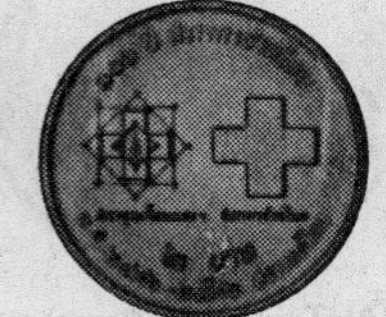

**2 BAHT** **Y# 279** **Composition:** Copper-Nickel Clad Copper **Ruler:** Rama IX Phra Maha Bhumithol Adulyadej **Subject:** Centennial of Thai Red Cross **Reverse:** Symbols

| Date | Mintage | F | VF | XF | Unc | BU |
|---|---|---|---|---|---|---|
| BE2536(1993) | 1,200,000 | — | — | — | 0.50 | — |

**2 BAHT** **Y# 282** **Composition:** Copper-Nickel Clad Copper **Ruler:** Rama IX Phra Maha Bhumithol Adulyadej **Subject:** Treasury Department

| Date | Mintage | F | VF | XF | Unc | BU |
|---|---|---|---|---|---|---|
| BE2536(1993) | 1,200,000 | — | — | — | 0.50 | — |

**2 BAHT** **Y# 288** **Composition:** Copper-Nickel Clad Copper **Ruler:** Rama IX Phra Maha Bhumithol Adulyadej **Subject:** 100th Anniversary of Rama VII

| Date | Mintage | F | VF | XF | Unc | BU |
|---|---|---|---|---|---|---|
| BE2536(1993) | 1,500,000 | — | — | — | 0.50 | — |

**2 BAHT** **Y# 292** **Composition:** Copper-Nickel Clad Copper **Ruler:** Rama IX Phra Maha Bhumithol Adulyadej **Subject:** 60th Anniversary - Royal Institute

| Date | Mintage | F | VF | XF | Unc | BU |
|---|---|---|---|---|---|---|
| BE2537(1994) | 1,200,000 | — | — | — | 0.50 | — |

**2 BAHT** **Y# 294** **Composition:** Copper-Nickel Clad Copper **Ruler:** Rama IX Phra Maha Bhumithol Adulyadej **Subject:** 120th Anniversary - Juridical Council

| Date | Mintage | F | VF | XF | Unc | BU |
|---|---|---|---|---|---|---|
| BE2537(1994) | 1,200,000 | — | — | — | 0.50 | — |

**2 BAHT** **Y# 296** **Composition:** Copper-Nickel Clad Copper **Ruler:** Rama IX Phra Maha Bhumithol Adulyadej **Subject:** 60th Anniversary - Thammasat University

| Date | Mintage | F | VF | XF | Unc | BU |
|---|---|---|---|---|---|---|
| BE2537(1994) | 1,250,000 | — | — | — | 0.50 | — |

**2 BAHT** **Y# 307** **Composition:** Copper-Nickel Clad Copper **Ruler:** Rama IX Phra Maha Bhumithol Adulyadej **Series:** F.A.O.

| Date | Mintage | F | VF | XF | Unc | BU |
|---|---|---|---|---|---|---|
| BE2538(1995) | — | — | — | — | 0.65 | — |

**2 BAHT** **Y# 313** **Composition:** Copper-Nickel Clad Copper **Ruler:** Rama IX Phra Maha Bhumithol Adulyadej **Subject:** Information Technology Year

| Date | Mintage | F | VF | XF | Unc | BU |
|---|---|---|---|---|---|---|
| BE2538(1995) | — | — | — | — | 0.50 | — |

**2 BAHT** **Y# 315** **Composition:** Copper-Nickel Clad Copper **Ruler:** Rama IX Phra Maha Bhumithol Adulyadej **Subject:** Asian Environment Year

| Date | Mintage | F | VF | XF | Unc | BU |
|---|---|---|---|---|---|---|
| BE2538(1995) | — | — | — | — | 0.50 | — |

**2 BAHT** **Y# 317** **Composition:** Copper-Nickel Clad Copper **Ruler:** Rama IX Phra Maha Bhumithol Adulyadej **Subject:** Siriraj Nursing and Midwifery School Centennial

| Date | Mintage | F | VF | XF | Unc | BU |
|---|---|---|---|---|---|---|
| BE2539(1996) | — | — | — | — | 0.65 | — |

**2 BAHT** **Y# 319** **Composition:** Copper-Nickel Clad Copper **Ruler:** Rama IX Phra Maha Bhumithol Adulyadej **Subject:** King's 50th Year of Reign

| Date | Mintage | F | VF | XF | Unc | BU |
|---|---|---|---|---|---|---|
| BE2539(1996) | — | — | — | — | 1.25 | — |

**5 BAHT** **Y# 98** **Composition:** Copper-Nickel **Ruler:** Rama IX Phra Maha Bhumithol Adulyadej

| Date | Mintage | F | VF | XF | Unc | BU |
|---|---|---|---|---|---|---|
| BE2515(1972) | 30,016,000 | — | 0.30 | 0.60 | 1.20 | — |

**5 BAHT** **Y# 111** **Composition:** Copper-Nickel Clad Copper **Ruler:** Rama IX Phra Maha Bhumithol Adulyadej

| Date | Mintage | F | VF | XF | Unc | BU |
|---|---|---|---|---|---|---|
| BE2520(1977) | 27,257,000 | — | 0.30 | 0.60 | 1.20 | — |
| BE2522(1979) | 72,740,000 | — | 0.30 | 0.60 | 1.20 | — |

**5 BAHT** **Y# 120** **Composition:** Copper-Nickel Clad Copper **Ruler:** Rama IX Phra Maha Bhumithol Adulyadej **Subject:** 50th Birthday - King Rama IX **Obv. Legend:** PRATHET THAI

| Date | Mintage | F | VF | XF | Unc | BU |
|---|---|---|---|---|---|---|
| BE2520(1977) | 500,000 | — | 0.35 | 0.75 | 1.50 | — |

**5 BAHT** **Y# 121** **Composition:** Copper-Nickel Clad Copper **Ruler:** Rama IX Phra Maha Bhumithol Adulyadej **Obverse:** Error **Obv. Legend:** "SIAM MINTA"

| Date | Mintage | F | VF | XF | Unc | BU |
|---|---|---|---|---|---|---|
| BE2520(1977) | — | — | 7.00 | 15.00 | 30.00 | — |

**5 BAHT** **Y# 131** **Composition:** Copper-Nickel Clad Copper **Ruler:** Rama IX Phra Maha Bhumithol Adulyadej **Subject:** 8th Asian Games

| Date | Mintage | F | VF | XF | Unc | BU |
|---|---|---|---|---|---|---|
| BE2521(1978) | 500,000 | — | 1.50 | 3.50 | 6.50 | — |

**5 BAHT** **Y# 132** **Composition:** Copper-Nickel Clad Copper **Ruler:** Rama IX Phra Maha Bhumithol Adulyadej **Subject:** Royal Cradle Ceremony

| Date | Mintage | F | VF | XF | Unc | BU |
|---|---|---|---|---|---|---|
| BE2522(1979) | 1,000,000 | — | 0.50 | 1.00 | 2.00 | — |

**5 BAHT** **Y# 137** **Composition:** Copper-Nickel Clad Copper **Ruler:** Rama IX Phra Maha Bhumithol Adulyadej **Subject:** Queen's Anniversary and F.A.O. Ceres Medal

| Date | Mintage | F | VF | XF | Unc | BU |
|---|---|---|---|---|---|---|
| BE2523(1980) | 9,000,000 | — | 0.25 | 0.50 | 1.50 | — |

**5 BAHT** **Y# 140** **Composition:** Copper-Nickel Clad Copper **Ruler:** Rama IX Phra Maha Bhumithol Adulyadej **Subject:** 80th Birthday of King's Mother

| Date | Mintage | F | VF | XF | Unc | BU |
|---|---|---|---|---|---|---|
| BE2523(1980) | 3,504,000 | — | 0.25 | 0.50 | 1.50 | — |

**5 BAHT** **Y# 144** **Composition:** Copper-Nickel Clad Copper **Ruler:** Rama IX Phra Maha Bhumithol Adulyadej **Subject:** Rama VII Constitutional Monarchy

| Date | Mintage | F | VF | XF | Unc | BU |
|---|---|---|---|---|---|---|
| BE2523(1980) | 2,113,000 | — | 0.25 | 0.50 | 1.50 | — |

**5 BAHT** **Y# 142** **Composition:** Copper-Nickel Clad Copper **Ruler:** Rama IX Phra Maha Bhumithol Adulyadej **Subject:** Centennial - Birth of King Rama VI

| Date | Mintage | F | VF | XF | Unc | BU |
|---|---|---|---|---|---|---|
| BE2524(1981) | 2,222,000 | — | 0.25 | 0.50 | 1.50 | — |

**5 BAHT** **Y# 149** **Composition:** Copper-Nickel Clad Copper **Ruler:** Rama IX Phra Maha Bhumithol Adulyadej **Subject:** Bicentennial of Bangkok

| Date | Mintage | F | VF | XF | Unc | BU |
|---|---|---|---|---|---|---|
| BE2525(1982) | 5,000,000 | — | 0.25 | 0.50 | 1.50 | — |

**5 BAHT** **Y# 158** **Composition:** Copper-Nickel Clad Copper **Ruler:** Rama IX Phra Maha Bhumithol Adulyadej **Series:** World Food Day

| Date | Mintage | F | VF | XF | Unc | BU |
|---|---|---|---|---|---|---|
| BE2525(1982) | 400,000 | — | 0.35 | 0.75 | 1.50 | — |

**5 BAHT** **Y# 161** **Composition:** Copper-Nickel Clad Copper **Ruler:** Rama IX Phra Maha Bhumithol Adulyadej **Subject:** 75th Anniversary of Boy Scouts

| Date | Mintage | F | VF | XF | Unc | BU |
|---|---|---|---|---|---|---|
| BE2525(1982) | 206,000 | — | 1.50 | 3.50 | 6.50 | — |

**5 BAHT** **Y# 160** **Composition:** Copper-Nickel Clad Copper **Ruler:** Rama IX Phra Maha Bhumithol Adulyadej **Note:** 2525 is a frozen date, with the Thai numerals for the first 2 digits of the actual year (25, 28, 29) in the Finance Minstry decal at the bottom of the reverse.

| Date | Mintage | F | VF | XF | Unc | BU |
|---|---|---|---|---|---|---|
| BE2525 (25)(1982) | 200,000 | — | 0.50 | 1.00 | 2.00 | — |
| BE2526(1983) | — | — | 0.60 | 1.25 | 2.25 | — |
| BE2527(1984) | — | — | 0.60 | 1.25 | 2.25 | — |
| BE2525(1985) | — | — | 5.00 | 10.00 | 25.00 | — |
| BE2528(1985) | — | — | 1.00 | 2.00 | 5.00 | — |
| BE2525(1986) | — | — | 0.20 | 0.50 | 1.00 | — |
| BE2529(1986) | — | — | 0.20 | 0.50 | 1.00 | — |

**5 BAHT** **Y# 171** **Composition:** Copper-Nickel Clad Copper **Ruler:** Rama IX Phra Maha Bhumithol Adulyadej **Subject:** 84th Birthday of Princess Mother

| Date | Mintage | F | VF | XF | Unc | BU |
|---|---|---|---|---|---|---|
| BE2527(1984) | 600,000 | — | 1.00 | 2.00 | 4.50 | — |

**5 BAHT** **Y# 184** **Composition:** Copper-Nickel Clad Copper **Ruler:** Rama IX Phra Maha Bhumithol Adulyadej **Subject:** 200th Anniversary - Birth of Rama III

| Date | Mintage | F | VF | XF | Unc | BU |
|---|---|---|---|---|---|---|
| BE2530(1987) | 2,000,000 | — | — | — | 0.75 | — |

**5 BAHT** **Y# 195** **Composition:** Copper-Nickel Clad Copper **Ruler:** Rama IX Phra Maha Bhumithol Adulyadej **Subject:** 60th Birthday - King Rama IX

| Date | Mintage | F | VF | XF | Unc | BU |
|---|---|---|---|---|---|---|
| BE2530(1987) | 1,500,000 | — | — | — | 2.00 | — |

**5 BAHT** **Y# 185** **Composition:** Copper-Nickel Clad Copper **Ruler:** Rama IX Phra Maha Bhumithol Adulyadej **Note:** Circulation coinage.

| Date | Mintage | F | VF | XF | Unc | BU |
|---|---|---|---|---|---|---|
| BE2530(1987) | 14,000,000 | — | — | — | 0.75 | — |
| BE2531(1988) | — | — | — | — | 0.75 | — |

**5 BAHT** **Y# 219** **Composition:** Copper-Nickel Clad Copper **Ruler:** Rama IX Phra Maha Bhumithol Adulyadej **Note:** Circulation coinage.

| Date | Mintage | F | VF | XF | Unc | BU |
|---|---|---|---|---|---|---|
| BE2531(1988) | — | — | — | — | 0.50 | — |
| BE2532(1989) | — | — | — | — | 0.50 | — |
| BE2533(1990) | — | — | — | — | 0.50 | — |
| BE2534(1991) | — | — | — | — | 0.50 | — |
| BE2535(1992) | — | — | — | — | 0.50 | — |
| BE2536(1993) | — | — | — | — | 0.50 | — |
| BE2537(1994) | — | — | — | — | 0.50 | — |
| BE2538(1995) | — | — | — | — | 0.50 | — |

**5 BAHT** **Y# 211** **Composition:** Copper-Nickel Clad Copper **Ruler:** Rama IX Phra Maha Bhumithol Adulyadej **Subject:** 42nd Anniversary - Reign of King Rama IX

| Date | Mintage | F | VF | XF | Unc | BU |
|---|---|---|---|---|---|---|
| BE2531(1988) | 1,500,000 | — | — | — | 2.00 | — |

**5 BAHT** **Y# 260** **Composition:** Copper-Nickel Clad Copper **Ruler:** Rama IX Phra Maha Bhumithol Adulyadej **Subject:** Queen's 60th Birthday

| Date | Mintage | F | VF | XF | Unc | BU |
|---|---|---|---|---|---|---|
| BE2535(1992) | 1,000,000 | — | — | — | 1.25 | — |

**5 BAHT** **Y# 306** **Composition:** Copper-Nickel Clad Copper **Ruler:** Rama IX Phra Maha Bhumithol Adulyadej **Subject:** 18th SEA Games

| Date | Mintage | F | VF | XF | Unc | BU |
|---|---|---|---|---|---|---|
| BE2538(1995) | — | — | — | — | 1.25 | — |

**5 BAHT** **Y# 320** **Composition:** Copper-Nickel Clad Copper **Ruler:** Rama IX Phra Maha Bhumithol Adulyadej **Subject:** King's 50th Year of Reign

| Date | Mintage | F | VF | XF | Unc | BU |
|---|---|---|---|---|---|---|
| BE2539(1996) | — | — | — | — | 1.50 | — |

**10 BAHT** **Y# 92** **Weight:** 5.0000 g. **Composition:** 0.8000 Silver .1286 oz. ASW **Ruler:** Rama IX Phra Maha Bhumithol Adulyadej **Subject:** 25th Anniversary - Reign of King Rama IX

| Date | Mintage | F | VF | XF | Unc | BU |
|---|---|---|---|---|---|---|
| BE2514(1971) | 2,000,000 | — | BV | 2.00 | 4.50 | — |

**10 BAHT** **Y# 117** **Composition:** Nickel **Ruler:** Rama IX Phra Maha Bhumithol Adulyadej **Subject:** Crown Prince Vajiralongkorn and Princess Soamsawali Wedding

| Date | Mintage | F | VF | XF | Unc | BU |
|---|---|---|---|---|---|---|
| BE2520(1977) | 1,890,000 | — | 0.50 | 1.00 | 2.50 | — |

**10 BAHT** **Y# 115** **Composition:** Nickel **Ruler:** Rama IX Phra Maha Bhumithol Adulyadej **Subject:** Graduation of Princess Sirindhorn

| Date | Mintage | F | VF | XF | Unc | BU |
|---|---|---|---|---|---|---|
| BE2520(1977) | 2,097,000 | — | 0.50 | 1.00 | 2.50 | — |

**10 BAHT** **Y# 115a** **Composition:** Bronze **Ruler:** Rama IX Phra Maha Bhumithol Adulyadej

| Date | Mintage | F | VF | XF | Unc | BU |
|---|---|---|---|---|---|---|
| BE2520(1977) | — | — | — | — | 20.00 | — |

**10 BAHT** **Y# 135** **Composition:** Nickel **Ruler:** Rama IX Phra Maha Bhumithol Adulyadej **Subject:** Graduation of Princess Chulabhorn

| Date | Mintage | F | VF | XF | Unc | BU |
|---|---|---|---|---|---|---|
| BE2522(1979) | 1,196,000 | — | 0.50 | 1.00 | 2.50 | — |

**10 BAHT** **Y# 141** **Composition:** Nickel **Ruler:** Rama IX Phra Maha Bhumithol Adulyadej **Subject:** 80th Birthday of King's Mother

| Date | Mintage | F | VF | XF | Unc | BU |
|---|---|---|---|---|---|---|
| BE2523(1980) | 1,288,000 | — | 0.50 | 1.00 | 2.50 | — |

**10 BAHT** **Y# 145** **Composition:** Nickel **Ruler:** Rama IX Phra Maha Bhumithol Adulyadej **Subject:** 30th Anniversary of Buddhist Fellowship

| Date | Mintage | F | VF | XF | Unc | BU |
|---|---|---|---|---|---|---|
| BE2523(1980) | 1,035,000 | — | 0.50 | 1.00 | 2.50 | — |

**10 BAHT** **Y# 146** **Composition:** Nickel **Ruler:** Rama IX Phra Maha Bhumithol Adulyadej **Subject:** King Rama IX Anniversary of Reign

| Date | Mintage | F | VF | XF | Unc | BU |
|---|---|---|---|---|---|---|
| BE2524(1981) | 2,039,000 | — | 0.50 | 1.00 | 2.50 | — |

**10 BAHT** **Y# 154** **Composition:** Nickel **Ruler:** Rama IX Phra Maha Bhumithol Adulyadej **Subject:** 50th Birthday of Queen Sirikit

| Date | Mintage | F | VF | XF | Unc | BU |
|---|---|---|---|---|---|---|
| BE2525(1982) | 500,000 | — | 0.75 | 1.50 | 3.50 | — |
| BE2525(1982) Proof | 9,999 | Value: 22.50 | | | | |

**10 BAHT** **Y# 162** **Composition:** Nickel **Ruler:** Rama IX Phra Maha Bhumithol Adulyadej **Subject:** 75th Anniversary of Boy Scouts **Note:** Similar to 5 Baht, Y#161.

| Date | Mintage | F | VF | XF | Unc | BU |
|---|---|---|---|---|---|---|
| BE2525(1982) | 100,000 | — | 1.25 | 2.50 | 5.00 | — |
| BE2525(1982) Proof | 1,500 | Value: 45.00 | | | | |

**10 BAHT** **Y# 163** **Composition:** Nickel **Ruler:** Rama IX Phra Maha Bhumithol Adulyadej **Subject:** 100th Anniversary of Postal Service

| Date | Mintage | F | VF | XF | Unc | BU |
|---|---|---|---|---|---|---|
| BE2526(1983) | 300,000 | — | 0.75 | 1.50 | 3.50 | — |
| BE2526(1983) Proof | 5,000 | Value: 25.00 | | | | |

**10 BAHT** **Y# 165** **Composition:** Nickel **Ruler:** Rama IX Phra Maha Bhumithol Adulyadej **Subject:** 700th Anniversary of Thai Alphabet

| Date | Mintage | F | VF | XF | Unc | BU |
|---|---|---|---|---|---|---|
| BE2526(1983) | 500,000 | — | 0.75 | 1.50 | 3.50 | — |
| BE2526(1983) Proof | 5,167 | Value: 22.50 | | | | |

**10 BAHT** **Y# 172** **Composition:** Nickel **Ruler:** Rama IX Phra Maha Bhumithol Adulyadej **Subject:** 84th Birthday of Princess Mother **Note:** Similar to 5 Baht, Y#171.

| Date | Mintage | F | VF | XF | Unc | BU |
|---|---|---|---|---|---|---|
| BE2527(1984) | 200,000 | — | 1.25 | 2.50 | 5.50 | — |
| BE2527(1984) Proof | 3,492 | Value: 37.50 | | | | |

**10 BAHT** **Y# 175** **Composition:** Nickel **Ruler:** Rama IX Phra Maha Bhumithol Adulyadej **Subject:** 72nd Anniversary of Government Savings Bank

| Date | Mintage | F | VF | XF | Unc | BU |
|---|---|---|---|---|---|---|
| BE2528(1985) | 500,000 | — | 0.50 | 1.00 | 2.50 | — |
| BE2528(1985) Proof | 3,000 | Value: 37.50 | | | | |

**10 BAHT** **Y# 179** **Composition:** Nickel **Ruler:** Rama IX Phra Maha Bhumithol Adulyadej **Subject:** National Years of the Trees

| Date | Mintage | F | VF | XF | Unc | BU |
|---|---|---|---|---|---|---|
| ND(1986)(1986) | 100,000 | — | 1.50 | 3.00 | 6.50 | — |
| ND(1986)(1986) Proof | 2,100 | Value: 45.00 | | | | |

**10 BAHT** **Y# 181** **Composition:** Nickel **Ruler:** Rama IX Phra Maha Bhumithol Adulyadej **Subject:** 6th ASEAN Orchid Congress

| Date | Mintage | F | VF | XF | Unc | BU |
|---|---|---|---|---|---|---|
| BE2529(1986) | 200,000 | — | — | — | 2.50 | — |
| BE2529(1986) Proof | 3,000 | Value: 37.50 | | | | |

**10 BAHT** **Y# 192** **Composition:** Nickel **Ruler:** Rama IX Phra Maha Bhumithol Adulyadej **Subject:** Princess Chulabhorn Awarded Einstein Medal

| Date | Mintage | F | VF | XF | Unc | BU |
|---|---|---|---|---|---|---|
| BE2529(1986) | 200,000 | — | — | — | 2.50 | — |
| BE2529(1986) Proof | 1,080 | Value: 50.00 | | | | |

**10 BAHT** **Y# 196** **Composition:** Nickel **Ruler:** Rama IX Phra Maha Bhumithol Adulyadej **Subject:** 60th Birthday of King Rama IX

| Date | Mintage | F | VF | XF | Unc | BU |
|---|---|---|---|---|---|---|
| BE2530(1987) | 500,000 | — | — | — | 2.50 | — |
| BE2530(1987) Proof | 5,000 | Value: 27.50 | | | | |

**10 BAHT** **Y# 189** **Composition:** Nickel **Ruler:** Rama IX Phra Maha Bhumithol Adulyadej **Subject:** Chulachomklao Royal Military Academy

| Date | Mintage | F | VF | XF | Unc | BU |
|---|---|---|---|---|---|---|
| BE2530(1987) | 300,000 | — | — | — | 2.50 | — |
| BE2530(1987) Proof | 2,060 | Value: 45.00 | | | | |

**10 BAHT** **Y# 190** **Composition:** Nickel **Ruler:** Rama IX Phra Maha Bhumithol Adulyadej **Subject:** Asian Institute of Technology

| Date | Mintage | F | VF | XF | Unc | BU |
|---|---|---|---|---|---|---|
| BE2530(1987) | 300,000 | — | — | — | 2.50 | — |
| BE2530(1987) Proof | 2,100 | Value: 45.00 | | | | |

**10 BAHT** **Y# 227** **Ring Composition:** Stainless Steel **Center Composition:** Aluminum-Bronze **Ruler:** Rama IX Phra Maha Bhumithol Adulyadej **Note:** Varieties exist.

| Date | Mintage | F | VF | XF | Unc | BU |
|---|---|---|---|---|---|---|
| BE2531(1988) Prooflike; Rare | 100,000 | — | — | — | — | — |

**Note:** The BE2531 (1988) pieces were not released to general circulation and are very scarce in the numismatic community

| Date | Mintage | F | VF | XF | Unc | BU |
|---|---|---|---|---|---|---|
| BE2532(1989) | 200,000,000 | — | — | — | 2.50 | — |
| BE2534(1991) | — | — | — | — | 2.50 | — |
| BE2535(1992) | — | — | — | — | 2.50 | — |
| BE2536(1993) | — | — | — | — | 2.50 | — |
| BE2537(1994) | — | — | — | — | 3.00 | — |
| BE2538(1995) | — | — | — | — | 3.00 | — |
| BE2539(1996) | — | — | — | — | 3.00 | — |

**10 BAHT Y# 205 Composition:** Nickel **Ruler:** Rama IX Phra Maha Bhumithol Adulyadej **Subject:** 72nd Anniversary of Thai Cooperatives

| Date | Mintage | F | VF | XF | Unc | BU |
|---|---|---|---|---|---|---|
| BE2531(1988) | 143,000 | — | — | — | 2.50 | — |
| BE2530(1988) Proof | 3,000 | Value: 27.50 | | | | |

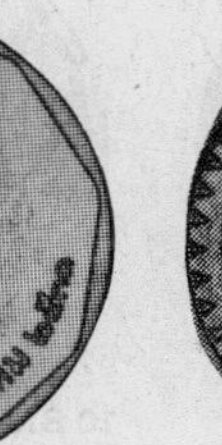

**10 BAHT Y# 212 Composition:** Nickel **Ruler:** Rama IX Phra Maha Bhumithol Adulyadej **Subject:** 42nd Anniversary - Reign of King Rama IX

| Date | Mintage | F | VF | XF | Unc | BU |
|---|---|---|---|---|---|---|
| BE2531(1988) | 500,000 | — | — | — | 2.50 | — |
| BE2531(1988) Proof | 8,110 | Value: 18.50 | | | | |

**10 BAHT Y# 221 Composition:** Nickel **Ruler:** Rama IX Phra Maha Bhumithol Adulyadej **Subject:** 100th Anniversary of Siriraj Hospital

| Date | Mintage | F | VF | XF | Unc | BU |
|---|---|---|---|---|---|---|
| BE2531(1988) | 290,000 | — | — | — | 2.50 | — |
| BE2531(1988) Proof | 5,000 | Value: 18.50 | | | | |

**10 BAHT Y# 223 Composition:** Nickel **Ruler:** Rama IX Phra Maha Bhumithol Adulyadej **Subject:** Crown Prince's Birthday

| Date | Mintage | F | VF | XF | Unc | BU |
|---|---|---|---|---|---|---|
| BE2531(1988) | 200,000 | — | — | — | 2.50 | — |
| BE2531(1988) Proof | 3,000 | Value: 18.50 | | | | |

**10 BAHT Y# 228 Composition:** Nickel **Ruler:** Rama IX Phra Maha Bhumithol Adulyadej **Subject:** Chulalongkorn University

| Date | Mintage | F | VF | XF | Unc | BU |
|---|---|---|---|---|---|---|
| BE2532(1989) | 500,000 | — | — | — | 2.50 | — |

**10 BAHT Y# 231 Composition:** Copper-Nickel **Ruler:** Rama IX Phra Maha Bhumithol Adulyadej **Subject:** Centennial of First Medical College

| Date | Mintage | F | VF | XF | Unc | BU |
|---|---|---|---|---|---|---|
| BE2533(1990) | 300,000 | — | — | — | 2.50 | — |
| BE2533(1990) Proof | 3,772 | Value: 32.50 | | | | |

**10 BAHT Y# 233 Composition:** Copper-Nickel **Ruler:** Rama IX Phra Maha Bhumithol Adulyadej **Subject:** 90th Birthday of the Princess Mother

| Date | Mintage | F | VF | XF | Unc | BU |
|---|---|---|---|---|---|---|
| BE2533(1990) | 500,000 | — | — | — | 2.50 | — |
| BE2533(1991) Proof | 6,076 | Value: 32.50 | | | | |

**10 BAHT Y# 236 Composition:** Copper-Nickel **Ruler:** Rama IX Phra Maha Bhumithol Adulyadej **Subject:** 100th Anniversary - OFfice of Comptroller General

| Date | Mintage | F | VF | XF | Unc | BU |
|---|---|---|---|---|---|---|
| BE2533(1990) | 300,000 | — | — | — | 2.50 | — |

**10 BAHT Y# 244 Composition:** Copper-Nickel **Ruler:** Rama IX Phra Maha Bhumithol Adulyadej **Subject:** World Health Organization

| Date | Mintage | F | VF | XF | Unc | BU |
|---|---|---|---|---|---|---|
| BE2533(1990) | 800,000 | — | — | — | 3.00 | — |
| BE2533(1990) Proof | 34,000 | Value: 18.50 | | | | |

**10 BAHT Y# 238 Composition:** Copper-Nickel **Ruler:** Rama IX Phra Maha Bhumithol Adulyadej **Subject:** 36th Birthday of Princess Sirindhorn

| Date | Mintage | F | VF | XF | Unc | BU |
|---|---|---|---|---|---|---|
| BE2534(1991) | 1,100,000 | — | — | — | 2.50 | — |
| BE2534(1991) Proof | 3,300 | Value: 30.00 | | | | |

**10 BAHT Y# 241 Composition:** Copper-Nickel **Ruler:** Rama IX Phra Maha Bhumithol Adulyadej **Subject:** 80th Anniversary of Thai Boy Scouts

| Date | Mintage | F | VF | XF | Unc | BU |
|---|---|---|---|---|---|---|
| BE2534(1991) | 650,000 | — | — | — | 3.00 | — |
| BE2534(1991) Proof | 3,237 | Value: 30.00 | | | | |

**10 BAHT Y# 256 Composition:** Copper-Nickel **Ruler:** Rama IX Phra Maha Bhumithol Adulyadej **Subject:** Princess Sirindhorn's Magsaysay Foundation Award

| Date | Mintage | F | VF | XF | Unc | BU |
|---|---|---|---|---|---|---|
| BE2534(1991) | 800,000 | — | — | — | 2.50 | — |
| BE2534(1991) Proof | 2,111 | Value: 37.50 | | | | |

**10 BAHT Y# 249 Composition:** Copper-Nickel **Ruler:** Rama IX Phra Maha Bhumithol Adulyadej **Subject:** Centenary Celebration - Father of King Rama IX

| Date | Mintage | F | VF | XF | Unc | BU |
|---|---|---|---|---|---|---|
| BE2535(1992) | 800,000 | — | — | — | 2.50 | — |
| BE2535(1992) Proof | 5,314 | Value: 22.50 | | | | |

**10 BAHT Y# 252 Composition:** Copper-Nickel **Ruler:** Rama IX Phra Maha Bhumithol Adulyadej **Subject:** Ministry of Justice Centennial

| Date | Mintage | F | VF | XF | Unc | BU |
|---|---|---|---|---|---|---|
| BE2535(1992) | 800,000 | — | — | — | 2.50 | — |
| BE2535(1992) Proof | — | Value: 18.50 | | | | |

**10 BAHT Y# 254 Composition:** Copper-Nickel **Ruler:** Rama IX Phra Maha Bhumithol Adulyadej **Subject:** Ministry of Interior Centennial

| Date | Mintage | F | VF | XF | Unc | BU |
|---|---|---|---|---|---|---|
| BE2535(1992) | 800,000 | — | — | — | 2.50 | — |
| BE2535(1992) Proof | 10,000 | Value: 17.50 | | | | |

**10 BAHT** **Y# 261** **Composition:** Copper-Nickel **Ruler:** Rama IX Phra Maha Bhumithol Adulyadej **Subject:** Queen's 60th Birthday

| Date | Mintage | F | VF | XF | Unc | BU |
|---|---|---|---|---|---|---|
| BE2535(1992) | 1,100,000 | — | — | — | 3.00 | — |
| BE2535(1992) Proof | 18,000 | Value: 17.50 | | | | |

**10 BAHT** **Y# 269** **Composition:** Copper-Nickel **Ruler:** Rama IX Phra Maha Bhumithol Adulyadej **Subject:** 60th Anniversary of National Assembly

| Date | Mintage | F | VF | XF | Unc | BU |
|---|---|---|---|---|---|---|
| BE2535(1992) | 44,000 | — | — | — | 2.50 | — |

**10 BAHT** **Y# 271** **Composition:** Copper-Nickel **Ruler:** Rama IX Phra Maha Bhumithol Adulyadej **Subject:** Ministry of Agriculture

| Date | Mintage | F | VF | XF | Unc | BU |
|---|---|---|---|---|---|---|
| BE2535(1992) | 550,000 | — | — | — | 2.50 | — |
| BE2535(1992) Proof | — | Value: 22.50 | | | | |

**10 BAHT** **Y# 273** **Composition:** Copper-Nickel **Ruler:** Rama IX Phra Maha Bhumithol Adulyadej **Subject:** King's 64th Birthday

| Date | Mintage | F | VF | XF | Unc | BU |
|---|---|---|---|---|---|---|
| BE2535(1992) | 550,000 | — | — | — | 2.50 | — |
| BE2535(1992) Proof | 3,711 | Value: 25.00 | | | | |

**10 BAHT** **Y# 284** **Composition:** Copper-Nickel **Ruler:** Rama IX Phra Maha Bhumithol Adulyadej **Subject:** Centennial of Thai Teacher Training **Reverse:** Emblem

| Date | Mintage | F | VF | XF | Unc | BU |
|---|---|---|---|---|---|---|
| BE2535(1992) | 700,000 | — | — | — | 2.50 | — |

**10 BAHT** **Y# 285** **Composition:** Copper-Nickel **Ruler:** Rama IX Phra Maha Bhumithol Adulyadej **Subject:** Centennial of Thai National Bank **Reverse:** Seated figure

| Date | Mintage | F | VF | XF | Unc | BU |
|---|---|---|---|---|---|---|
| BE2535(1992) | 700,000 | — | — | — | 2.50 | — |
| BE2535(1992) Proof | 6,927 | Value: 18.50 | | | | |

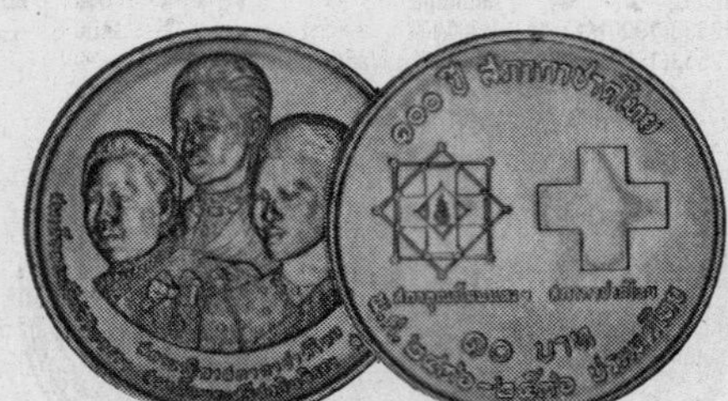

**10 BAHT** **Y# 280** **Composition:** Copper-Nickel **Ruler:** Rama IX Phra Maha Bhumithol Adulyadej **Subject:** Centennial of Thai Red Cross **Reverse:** Symbols

| Date | Mintage | F | VF | XF | Unc | BU |
|---|---|---|---|---|---|---|
| BE2536(1993) | 700,000 | — | — | — | 2.50 | — |
| BE2535(1993) Proof | 14,000 | Value: 17.50 | | | | |

**10 BAHT** **Y# 283** **Composition:** Copper-Nickel **Ruler:** Rama IX Phra Maha Bhumithol Adulyadej **Subject:** Treasury Department

| Date | Mintage | F | VF | XF | Unc | BU |
|---|---|---|---|---|---|---|
| BE2536(1993) | 600,000 | — | — | — | 2.50 | — |
| BE2535(1993) Proof | 10,000 | Value: 17.50 | | | | |

**10 BAHT** **Y# 286** **Composition:** Copper-Nickel **Ruler:** Rama IX Phra Maha Bhumithol Adulyadej **Subject:** Centennial of Attorney General's Office

| Date | Mintage | F | VF | XF | Unc | BU |
|---|---|---|---|---|---|---|
| BE2536(1993) | 700,000 | — | — | — | 2.50 | — |

**10 BAHT** **Y# 289** **Composition:** Copper-Nickel **Ruler:** Rama IX Phra Maha Bhumithol Adulyadej **Subject:** 100th Anniversary of Rama VII

| Date | Mintage | F | VF | XF | Unc | BU |
|---|---|---|---|---|---|---|
| BE2536(1993) | 800,000 | — | — | — | 2.50 | — |
| BE2536(1993) Proof | 10,000 | Value: 17.50 | | | | |

**10 BAHT** **Y# 293** **Composition:** Copper-Nickel **Ruler:** Rama IX Phra Maha Bhumithol Adulyadej **Subject:** 60th Anniversary - Royal Institute

| Date | Mintage | F | VF | XF | Unc | BU |
|---|---|---|---|---|---|---|
| BE2537(1994) | 700,000 | — | — | — | 2.50 | — |
| BE2537(1994) Proof | 10,000 | Value: 17.50 | | | | |

**10 BAHT** **Y# 295** **Composition:** Copper-Nickel **Ruler:** Rama IX Phra Maha Bhumithol Adulyadej **Subject:** 120th Anniversary - Juridical Council

| Date | Mintage | F | VF | XF | Unc | BU |
|---|---|---|---|---|---|---|
| BE2537(1994) | 800,000 | — | — | — | 2.50 | — |
| BE2537(1994) Proof | 12,000 | Value: 17.50 | | | | |

**10 BAHT** **Y# 297** **Composition:** Copper-Nickel **Ruler:** Rama IX Phra Maha Bhumithol Adulyadej **Subject:** 60th Anniversary - Thammasat University

| Date | Mintage | F | VF | XF | Unc | BU |
|---|---|---|---|---|---|---|
| BE2537(1994) | 800,000 | — | — | — | 2.50 | — |
| BE2537(1994) Proof | 12,000 | Value: 17.50 | | | | |

**10 BAHT** **Y# 334** **Composition:** Copper-Nickel **Ruler:** Rama IX Phra Maha Bhumithol Adulyadej **Subject:** 50th Anniversary - Reign of King Rama IX and F.A.O. World Summit

| Date | Mintage | F | VF | XF | Unc | BU |
|---|---|---|---|---|---|---|
| BE2539(1996) | — | — | — | — | 3.50 | — |

**10 BAHT** **Y# 339** **Composition:** Copper-Nickel **Ruler:** Rama IX Phra Maha Bhumithol Adulyadej **Subject:** International Rice Award **Obverse:** King with camera **Reverse:** Rice plant

| Date | Mintage | F | VF | XF | Unc | BU |
|---|---|---|---|---|---|---|
| BE2535(1996) | — | — | — | — | 3.50 | — |

**10 BAHT** **Y# 328.1** **Composition:** Copper-Nickel **Ruler:** Rama IX Phra Maha Bhumithol Adulyadej **Subject:** 50th Anniversary - Reign of King Rama IX **Obverse:** Small portrait does not contact inner ring

| Date | Mintage | F | VF | XF | Unc | BU |
|---|---|---|---|---|---|---|
| BE2539(1996) | — | — | — | — | 3.00 | — |

**10 BAHT** **Y# 328.2** **Composition:** Copper-Nickel **Ruler:** Rama IX Phra Maha Bhumithol Adulyadej **Subject:** 50th Anniversary - Reign of King Rama IX **Obverse:** Large portrait contacts inner ring

| Date | Mintage | F | VF | XF | Unc | BU |
|---|---|---|---|---|---|---|
| BE2539(1996) | — | — | — | — | 3.00 | — |

**10 BAHT** **Y# 347** **Composition:** Copper-Nickel **Ruler:** Rama IX Phra Maha Bhumithol Adulyadej **Subject:** 100th Anniversary of Chulalongkorn's European Tour

| Date | Mintage | F | VF | XF | Unc | BU |
|---|---|---|---|---|---|---|
| BE2540(1997) | — | — | — | — | 2.50 | — |

**10 BAHT** **Y# 346** **Composition:** Copper-Nickel **Ruler:** Rama IX Phra Maha Bhumithol Adulyadej **Subject:** 100th Anniversary - Central General Hospital - Medication Office

| Date | Mintage | F | VF | XF | Unc | BU |
|---|---|---|---|---|---|---|
| BE2541(1998) | — | — | — | — | 2.50 | — |

**10 BAHT** **Y# 348** **Composition:** Copper-Nickel **Ruler:** Rama IX Phra Maha Bhumithol Adulyadej **Subject:** 13th Asian Games **Reverse:** Symbols

| Date | Mintage | F | VF | XF | Unc | BU |
|---|---|---|---|---|---|---|
| BE2541(1998) | 10,000,000 | — | — | — | 2.50 | — |

**10 BAHT** **Y# 352** **Composition:** Bi-Metallic **Ruler:** Rama IX Phra Maha Bhumithol Adulyadej **Edge:** Plain. **Size:** 26 mm.

| Date | Mintage | F | VF | XF | Unc | BU |
|---|---|---|---|---|---|---|
| BE2541(1998) | — | — | — | — | — | — |

**10 BAHT** **Y# 349** **Composition:** Bi-Metallic **Ruler:** Rama IX Phra Maha Bhumithol Adulyadej **Edge:** Reeded and plain sections. **Size:** 26 mm.

| Date | Mintage | F | VF | XF | Unc | BU |
|---|---|---|---|---|---|---|
| BE2542(1999) | — | — | — | — | — | — |

**10 BAHT** **Y# 350** **Composition:** Bi-Metallic **Ruler:** Rama IX Phra Maha Bhumithol Adulyadej **Edge:** Reeded and plain sections. **Size:** 26 mm.

| Date | Mintage | F | VF | XF | Unc | BU |
|---|---|---|---|---|---|---|
| BE2542(1999) | 10,000,000 | — | — | — | 0.50 | — |

**10 BAHT** **Y# 371** **Ring Weight:** 8.4500 g. **Ring Composition:** Copper-Nickel **Center Composition:** Brass **Ruler:** Rama IX Phra Maha Bhumithol Adulyadej **Subject:** National Economic and Social Development Board **Obverse:** King's portrait **Reverse:** Three seated figures **Edge:** Plain and reeded sections **Size:** 25.9 mm.

| Date | Mintage | F | VF | XF | Unc | BU |
|---|---|---|---|---|---|---|
| BE2543(2000) | — | — | — | — | 2.00 | — |

**10 BAHT** **Y# 354** **Ring Composition:** Copper-Nickel **Center Composition:** Brass **Ruler:** Rama IX Phra Maha Bhumithol Adulyadej **Subject:** 100th Anniversary Army Medical Department **Obverse:** Two portraits **Reverse:** Departmental emblem

| Date | Mintage | F | VF | XF | Unc | BU |
|---|---|---|---|---|---|---|
| ND(2000)(2000) | — | — | — | — | 1.75 | — |

**10 BAHT** **Y# 358** **Ring Composition:** Copper-Nickel **Center Composition:** Brass **Ruler:** Rama IX Phra Maha Bhumithol Adulyadej **Subject:** 80th Anniversary - Commerce Ministry **Obverse:** King's portrait **Reverse:** Ministry logo **Edge:** Reeded and plain sections **Size:** 25.9 mm.

| Date | Mintage | F | VF | XF | Unc | BU |
|---|---|---|---|---|---|---|
| BE2543(2000) | — | — | — | — | 1.75 | — |

**10 BAHT** **Y# 361** **Ring Composition:** Copper-Nickel **Center Composition:** Brass **Ruler:** Rama IX Phra Maha Bhumithol Adulyadej **Subject:** 100th Birthday - Princess Mother **Obverse:** Princess Mother's portrait **Reverse:** Emblem divides date **Edge:** Reeded and plain sections **Size:** 26 mm.

| Date | Mintage | F | VF | XF | Unc | BU |
|---|---|---|---|---|---|---|
| BE2543(2000) | — | — | — | — | 1.75 | — |

**10 BAHT** **Y# 373** **Ring Weight:** 8.5000 g. **Ring Composition:** Copper-Nickel **Center Composition:** Brass **Ruler:** Rama IX Phra Maha Bhumithol Adulyadej **Subject:** Department of Lands Centennial **Obverse:** Portraits of Kings Chulalongkorn and Bhumibol Adulyadej **Reverse:** Department seal **Edge:** Reeded and plain sections **Size:** 25.6 mm.

| Date | Mintage | F | VF | XF | Unc | BU |
|---|---|---|---|---|---|---|
| BE2544(2001) | — | — | — | — | 2.50 | — |

**20 BAHT** **Y# 86** **Weight:** 19.6000 g. **Composition:** 0.7500 Silver .4726 oz. ASW **Ruler:** Rama IX Phra Maha Bhumithol Adulyadej **Subject:** 36th Birthday - King Rama IX

| Date | Mintage | F | VF | XF | Unc | BU |
|---|---|---|---|---|---|---|
| ND(1963)(1963) | 1,000,000 | — | — | 4.50 | 9.00 | 12.50 |

**20 BAHT** **Y# 298** **Composition:** Copper-Nickel **Ruler:** Rama IX Phra Maha Bhumithol Adulyadej **Subject:** 120th Anniversary - Ministry of Finance

| Date | Mintage | F | VF | XF | Unc | BU |
|---|---|---|---|---|---|---|
| BE2538(1994) | 800,000 | — | — | — | 3.50 | — |
| BE2538(1994) Proof | 1,920 | Value: 28.00 | | | | |

**20 BAHT** **Y# 300** **Composition:** Copper-Nickel **Ruler:** Rama IX Phra Maha Bhumithol Adulyadej **Subject:** 108th Anniversary - Minstry of Defense

| Date | Mintage | F | VF | XF | Unc | BU |
|---|---|---|---|---|---|---|
| BE2538(1994) | 800,000 | — | — | — | 3.50 | — |
| BE2538(1994) Proof | 2,000 | Value: 28.00 | | | | |

**20 BAHT** **Y# 302** **Composition:** Copper-Nickel **Ruler:** Rama IX Phra Maha Bhumithol Adulyadej **Subject:** 120th Anniversary - Ministry of Foreign Affairs

| Date | Mintage | F | VF | XF | Unc | BU |
|---|---|---|---|---|---|---|
| BE2538(1994) | 800,000 | — | — | — | 3.50 | — |
| BE2538(1994) Proof | 740 | Value: 55.00 | | | | |

**20 BAHT** Y# 308 **Composition:** Copper-Nickel **Ruler:** Rama IX Phra Maha Bhumithol Adulyadej **Series:** F.A.O.

| Date | Mintage | F | VF | XF | Unc | BU |
|---|---|---|---|---|---|---|
| BE2538(1995) | 400,000 | — | — | — | 3.50 | — |
| BE2538(1995) Proof | — | Value: 18.50 | | | | |

**20 BAHT** Y# 309 **Composition:** Copper-Nickel **Ruler:** Rama IX Phra Maha Bhumithol Adulyadej **Subject:** 80th Anniversary - Department of Revenue

| Date | Mintage | F | VF | XF | Unc | BU |
|---|---|---|---|---|---|---|
| BE2538(1995) | 800,000 | — | — | — | 3.50 | — |
| BE2538(1995) Proof | — | Value: 18.50 | | | | |

**20 BAHT** Y# 311 **Composition:** Copper-Nickel **Ruler:** Rama IX Phra Maha Bhumithol Adulyadej **Subject:** 120th Anniversary - Audit Council

| Date | Mintage | F | VF | XF | Unc | BU |
|---|---|---|---|---|---|---|
| BE2538(1995) | 800,000 | — | — | — | 3.50 | — |
| BE2538(1995) Proof | — | Value: 18.50 | | | | |

**20 BAHT** Y# 314 **Composition:** Copper-Nickel **Ruler:** Rama IX Phra Maha Bhumithol Adulyadej **Subject:** Information Technology Year

| Date | Mintage | F | VF | XF | Unc | BU |
|---|---|---|---|---|---|---|
| BE2538(1995) | — | — | — | — | 3.50 | — |
| BE2538(1995) Proof | — | Value: 18.50 | | | | |

**20 BAHT** Y# 316 **Composition:** Copper-Nickel **Ruler:** Rama IX Phra Maha Bhumithol Adulyadej **Subject:** Asean Environment Year

| Date | Mintage | F | VF | XF | Unc | BU |
|---|---|---|---|---|---|---|
| BE2538(1995) | — | — | — | — | 3.50 | — |
| BE2538(1995) Proof | — | Value: 18.50 | | | | |

**20 BAHT** Y# 331 **Composition:** Copper-Nickel **Ruler:** Rama IX Phra Maha Bhumithol Adulyadej **Subject:** Ministry of Commerce **Reverse:** Seal

| Date | Mintage | F | VF | XF | Unc | BU |
|---|---|---|---|---|---|---|
| BE2538(1995) | — | — | — | — | 4.00 | — |

**20 BAHT** Y# 338 **Composition:** Copper-Nickel **Ruler:** Rama IX Phra Maha Bhumithol Adulyadej **Subject:** 50 Years of Peace

| Date | Mintage | F | VF | XF | Unc | BU |
|---|---|---|---|---|---|---|
| ND(BE2538)(1995) | — | — | — | — | 3.50 | — |

**20 BAHT** Y# 304 **Composition:** Copper-Nickel **Ruler:** Rama IX Phra Maha Bhumithol Adulyadej **Subject:** 72nd Birthday of Princess **Note:** Similar to 600 Baht, Y#305.

| Date | Mintage | F | VF | XF | Unc | BU |
|---|---|---|---|---|---|---|
| BE2538(1995) | 800,000 | — | — | — | 3.50 | — |
| BE2538(1995) Proof | 1,560 | Value: 22.50 | | | | |

**20 BAHT** Y# 318 **Composition:** Copper-Nickel **Ruler:** Rama IX Phra Maha Bhumithol Adulyadej **Subject:** Siriraj Nursing and Midwife School Centennial

| Date | Mintage | F | VF | XF | Unc | BU |
|---|---|---|---|---|---|---|
| BE2539(1996) | — | — | — | — | 3.50 | — |

**20 BAHT** Y# 321.1 **Composition:** Copper-Nickel **Ruler:** Rama IX Phra Maha Bhumithol Adulyadej **Subject:** 50th Anniversary - Reign of King Rama IX

| Date | Mintage | F | VF | XF | Unc | BU |
|---|---|---|---|---|---|---|
| BE2539(1996) | — | — | — | — | 4.00 | — |
| BE2539(1996) Proof | — | Value: 25.00 | | | | |

**20 BAHT** Y# 321.2 **Composition:** Copper-Nickel **Ruler:** Rama IX Phra Maha Bhumithol Adulyadej **Reverse:** Incomplete - missing the "Unalom" in center

| Date | Mintage | F | VF | XF | Unc | BU |
|---|---|---|---|---|---|---|
| BE2539(1996) | — | — | — | — | 4.00 | — |
| BE2539(1996) Proof | — | Value: 25.00 | | | | |

**20 BAHT** Y# 335 **Composition:** Copper-Nickel **Ruler:** Rama IX Phra Maha Bhumithol Adulyadej **Subject:** 50th Anniversary - Reign of King Rama IX and F.A.O. World Food Summit

| Date | Mintage | F | VF | XF | Unc | BU |
|---|---|---|---|---|---|---|
| BE2539(1996) | — | — | — | — | 3.50 | — |

**20 BAHT** Y# 340 **Composition:** Copper-Nickel **Ruler:** Rama IX Phra Maha Bhumithol Adulyadej **Subject:** International Rice Award

| Date | Mintage | F | VF | XF | Unc | BU |
|---|---|---|---|---|---|---|
| BE2539(1996) | — | — | — | — | 3.50 | — |

**20 BAHT** Y# 332 **Composition:** Copper-Nickel **Ruler:** Rama IX Phra Maha Bhumithol Adulyadej **Subject:** 100th Anniversary - Thai Railway

| Date | Mintage | F | VF | XF | Unc | BU |
|---|---|---|---|---|---|---|
| BE2540(1997) | — | — | — | — | 3.50 | — |
| BE2540(1997) Proof | — | Value: 30.00 | | | | |

**20 BAHT** Y# 333 **Composition:** Copper-Nickel **Ruler:** Rama IX Phra Maha Bhumithol Adulyadej **Subject:** 84th Anniversary - Thai Savings Bank

| Date | Mintage | F | VF | XF | Unc | BU |
|---|---|---|---|---|---|---|
| BE2540(1997) | — | — | — | — | 3.50 | — |
| BE2540(1997) Proof | — | Value: 28.00 | | | | |

**20 BAHT** Y# 341 **Composition:** Copper-Nickel **Ruler:** Rama IX Phra Maha Bhumithol Adulyadej **Subject:** 50th Anniversary - Thai Veterans Organization

| Date | Mintage | F | VF | XF | Unc | BU |
|---|---|---|---|---|---|---|
| BE2541(1998) | — | — | — | — | 3.50 | — |
| BE2541(1998) Proof | — | Value: 12.50 | | | | |

**20 BAHT** **Y# 351** **Composition:** Bi-Metallic **Ruler:** Rama IX Phra Maha Bhumithol Adulyadej **Edge:** Reeded. **Size:** 32 mm.

| Date | Mintage | F | VF | XF | Unc | BU |
|---|---|---|---|---|---|---|
| BE2542(1999) | — | — | — | — | 1.00 | — |
| BE2542(1999) Proof | 5,000 | Value: 5.00 | | | | |

**20 BAHT** **Y# 355** **Weight:** 14.9100 g. **Composition:** Copper Nickel **Ruler:** Rama IX Phra Maha Bhumithol Adulyadej **Subject:** 84th Anniversary - Audit Council Bureau **Obverse:** King's portrait. **Reverse:** Balance scale. **Edge:** Reeded. **Size:** 31.9 mm.

| Date | Mintage | F | VF | XF | Unc | BU |
|---|---|---|---|---|---|---|
| BE2542(1999) | — | — | — | — | 3.50 | — |

**20 BAHT** **Y# 357** **Composition:** Copper-Nickel **Ruler:** Rama IX Phra Maha Bhumithol Adulyadej **Subject:** Asian Development Bank Board Meeting **Obverse:** King's portrait **Reverse:** Chieng money illustration **Edge:** Reeded **Size:** 32 mm.

| Date | Mintage | F | VF | XF | Unc | BU |
|---|---|---|---|---|---|---|
| ND(2000)(2000) | — | — | — | — | 3.50 | — |

**20 BAHT** **Y# 362** **Composition:** Copper-Nickel **Ruler:** Rama IX Phra Maha Bhumithol Adulyadej **Subject:** 100th Birthday - Princess Mother **Obverse:** Princess Mother's portrait **Reverse:** Emblem divides date **Edge:** Reeded **Size:** 32 mm.

| Date | Mintage | F | VF | XF | Unc | BU |
|---|---|---|---|---|---|---|
| BE2543(2000) | — | — | — | — | 3.50 | — |
| BE2543(2000) Proof | — | Value: 12.50 | | | | |

**20 BAHT** **Y# 376** **Weight:** 15.0000 g. **Composition:** Copper-Nickel **Ruler:** Rama IX Phra Maha Bhumithol Adulyadej **Subject:** King's 72nd Birthday **Obverse:** King and Rama I portraits **Reverse:** Two royal symbols **Edge:** Reeded **Size:** 31.9 mm.

| Date | Mintage | F | VF | XF | Unc | BU |
|---|---|---|---|---|---|---|
| BE2543(2000) | — | — | — | — | 3.50 | — |

**20 BAHT** **Y# 374** **Weight:** 15.1000 g. **Composition:** Copper-Nickel **Ruler:** Rama IX Phra Maha Bhumithol Adulyadej **Subject:** Chulalongkorn University 84th Anniversary **Obverse:** Portraits of Kings Chulalongkorn, Vjiravudh, and Bhumibol Adulyadej **Reverse:** University emblem dividing denomination **Edge:** Reeded **Size:** 31.9 mm.

| Date | Mintage | F | VF | XF | Unc | BU |
|---|---|---|---|---|---|---|
| BE2544(2001) | — | — | — | — | 3.50 | — |

**20 BAHT** **Y# 375** **Weight:** 15.1000 g. **Composition:** Copper-Nickel **Ruler:** Rama IX Phra Maha Bhumithol Adulyadej **Subject:** Civil Service Comission 72nd Anniversary **Obverse:** Portrait of Kings Prajadhipok and Bhumibol Adulyadej **Reverse:** Civil service emblem dividing denomination

| Date | Mintage | F | VF | XF | Unc | BU |
|---|---|---|---|---|---|---|
| BE2544(2001) | — | — | — | — | 3.50 | — |

**50 BAHT** **Y# 95** **Weight:** 24.7000 g. **Composition:** 0.9000 Silver .7147 oz. ASW **Ruler:** Rama IX Phra Maha Bhumithol Adulyadej **Subject:** 20th Year Buddhist Fellowship

| Date | Mintage | F | VF | XF | Unc | BU |
|---|---|---|---|---|---|---|
| BE2514(1971) | 200,000 | — | — | 8.00 | 14.00 | — |
| BE2514(1971) Prooflike | 60,000 | — | — | — | 20.00 | — |

**50 BAHT** **Y# 101** **Weight:** 24.8500 g. **Composition:** 0.4000 Silver .3195 oz. ASW **Ruler:** Rama IX Phra Maha Bhumithol Adulyadej **Subject:** National Museum Centennial

| Date | Mintage | F | VF | XF | Unc | BU |
|---|---|---|---|---|---|---|
| BE2517(1974) | 200,000 | — | — | 6.50 | 13.50 | — |

**50 BAHT** **Y# 102** **Weight:** 25.5500 g. **Composition:** 0.5000 Silver .4173 oz. ASW **Ruler:** Rama IX Phra Maha Bhumithol Adulyadej **Series:** Conservation **Reverse:** Sumatran Rhinoceros

| Date | Mintage | F | VF | XF | Unc | BU |
|---|---|---|---|---|---|---|
| BE2517(1974) | 20,000 | — | — | — | 30.00 | — |

**50 BAHT** **Y# 102a** **Weight:** 28.2800 g. **Composition:** 0.9250 Silver .8411 oz. ASW **Ruler:** Rama IX Phra Maha Bhumithol Adulyadej **Series:** Conservation

| Date | Mintage | F | VF | XF | Unc | BU |
|---|---|---|---|---|---|---|
| BE2517(1974) Proof | 9,885 | Value: 65.00 | | | | |

**50 BAHT** **Y# 336** **Composition:** Nickel **Ruler:** Rama IX Phra Maha Bhumithol Adulyadej **Subject:** 50th Anniversary - Reign of King Rama IX and F.A.O. Wrld Food Summit **Note:** Similar to 20 Baht, Y#335.

| Date | Mintage | F | VF | XF | Unc | BU |
|---|---|---|---|---|---|---|
| BE2538(1995) | — | — | — | — | 10.00 | — |

**50 BAHT** **Y# 363** **Weight:** 20.0000 g. **Composition:** 0.9250 Silver .5948 oz. ASW **Ruler:** Rama IX Phra Maha Bhumithol Adulyadej **Subject:** Year of the Dragon **Obverse:** King's portrait **Reverse:** Dragon and latent image date pearl **Edge:** Reeded **Size:** 38.7 mm.

| Date | Mintage | F | VF | XF | Unc | BU |
|---|---|---|---|---|---|---|
| BE2543(2000) Proof | 8,500 | Value: 50.00 | | | | |

**50 BAHT** **Y# 364** **Weight:** 20.0000 g. **Composition:** 0.9250 Silver .5948 oz. ASW **Ruler:** Rama IX Phra Maha Bhumithol Adulyadej **Subject:** Year of the Dragon **Obverse:** King's portrait **Reverse:** 2 dragons with pearl hologram

| Date | Mintage | F | VF | XF | Unc | BU |
|---|---|---|---|---|---|---|
| BE2543(2000) Proof | 8,500 | Value: 150 | | | | |

**50 BAHT** **Y#365** **Weight:** 20.0000 g. **Composition:** 0.9250 Silver .5948 oz. ASW **Ruler:** Rama IX Phra Maha Bhumithol Adulyadej **Subject:** Year of the Dragon **Obverse:** King's portrait **Reverse:** Dragon with gold plated pearl

| Date | Mintage | F | VF | XF | Unc | BU |
|---|---|---|---|---|---|---|
| BE2543(2000) Proof | 8,500 | Value: 50.00 | | | | |

**100 BAHT** **Y# 103** **Weight:** 31.9000 g. **Composition:** 0.5000 Silver .5128 oz. ASW **Ruler:** Rama IX Phra Maha Bhumithol Adulyadej **Series:** Conservation **Reverse:** Brown-antlered deer

| Date | Mintage | F | VF | XF | Unc | BU |
|---|---|---|---|---|---|---|
| BE2517(1974) | 20,000 | — | — | — | 37.50 | — |

**100 BAHT** **Y# 103a** **Weight:** 35.0000 g. **Composition:** 0.9250 Silver 1.0409 oz. ASW **Ruler:** Rama IX Phra Maha Bhumithol Adulyadej

| Date | Mintage | F | VF | XF | Unc | BU |
|---|---|---|---|---|---|---|
| BE2517(1974) Proof | 9,294 | Value: 75.00 | | | | |

**100 BAHT** **Y# 106** **Weight:** 25.0000 g. **Composition:** 0.9000 Silver .7234 oz. ASW **Ruler:** Rama IX Phra Maha Bhumithol Adulyadej **Subject:** 100th Anniversary - Ministry of Finance

| Date | Mintage | F | VF | XF | Unc | BU |
|---|---|---|---|---|---|---|
| BE2518(1975) | 30,000 | — | — | 9.00 | 18.50 | — |

**100 BAHT** **Y# 242** **Composition:** Copper-Nickel **Ruler:** Rama IX Phra Maha Bhumithol Adulyadej **Subject:** World Bank - International Monetary Fund

| Date | Mintage | F | VF | XF | Unc | BU |
|---|---|---|---|---|---|---|
| BE2534(1991) | 500,000 | — | — | — | 12.50 | — |
| BE2534(1991) Proof | 60,000 | Value: 32.50 | | | | |

**100 BAHT** **Y# 287** **Composition:** Copper-Nickel **Ruler:** Rama IX Phra Maha Bhumithol Adulyadej **Subject:** King and Prince in Scouting **Reverse:** Emblem

| Date | Mintage | F | VF | XF | Unc | BU |
|---|---|---|---|---|---|---|
| BE2536(1993) | 200,000 | — | — | — | 17.50 | — |
| BE2536(1993) Proof | 30,000 | Value: 37.50 | | | | |

**100 BAHT** **Y# 359** **Weight:** 15.0000 g. **Composition:** 0.9250 Silver .4461 oz. ASW **Ruler:** Rama IX Phra Maha Bhumithol Adulyadej **Series:** World Wildlife Fund **Obverse:** King's portrait **Reverse:** Tiger head, denomination **Size:** 30mm mm. **Note:** Thickness of coin is 4.7mm.

| Date | Mintage | F | VF | XF | Unc | BU |
|---|---|---|---|---|---|---|
| BE2540(1997) Proof | 50,000 | Value: 32.50 | | | | |

**100 BAHT** **Y#366** **Weight:** 7.7759 g. **Composition:** 0.9999 Gold .2500 oz. AGW **Ruler:** Rama IX Phra Maha Bhumithol Adulyadej **Subject:** Year of the Dragon **Obverse:** King's portrait **Reverse:** Dragon with Golden Pearl **Edge:** Reeded **Size:** 22 mm.

| Date | Mintage | F | VF | XF | Unc | BU |
|---|---|---|---|---|---|---|
| BE2543(2000) Proof | 1,800 | Value: 150 | | | | |

**150 BAHT** **Y# 88** **Weight:** 3.7500 g. **Composition:** 0.9000 Gold .1085 oz. AGW **Ruler:** Rama IX Phra Maha Bhumithol Adulyadej **Subject:** Queen Sirikit 36th Birthday

| Date | Mintage | F | VF | XF | Unc | BU |
|---|---|---|---|---|---|---|
| BE2511(1968) | 202,000 | — | — | — | 55.00 | — |

**150 BAHT** **Y# 108** **Weight:** 22.0000 g. **Composition:** 0.9250 Silver .6543 oz. ASW **Ruler:** Rama IX Phra Maha Bhumithol Adulyadej **Subject:** 75th Birthday of Princess Mother

| Date | Mintage | F | VF | XF | Unc | BU |
|---|---|---|---|---|---|---|
| BE2518(1975) | 200,000 | — | — | 9.00 | 17.50 | — |

**150 BAHT** **Y# 113** **Weight:** 22.0000 g. **Composition:** 0.9250 Silver .6543 oz. ASW **Ruler:** Rama IX Phra Maha Bhumithol Adulyadej **Series:** F.A.O.

| Date | Mintage | F | VF | XF | Unc | BU |
|---|---|---|---|---|---|---|
| BE2520(1977) | 50,000 | — | — | 9.00 | 17.50 | — |

**150 BAHT** **Y# 118** **Weight:** 22.0000 g. **Composition:** 0.9250 Silver .6543 oz. ASW **Ruler:** Rama IX Phra Maha Bhumithol Adulyadej **Subject:** Crown Prince Vajiralongkorn and Princess Soamsawali Wedding

| Date | Mintage | F | VF | XF | Unc | BU |
|---|---|---|---|---|---|---|
| BE2520(1977) | 200,000 | — | — | 8.50 | 14.50 | — |

**150 BAHT** **Y# 116** **Weight:** 22.0000 g. **Composition:** 0.9250 Silver .6543 oz. ASW **Ruler:** Rama IX Phra Maha Bhumithol Adulyadej **Subject:** Graduation of Princess Sirindhorn

| Date | Mintage | F | VF | XF | Unc | BU |
|---|---|---|---|---|---|---|
| BE2520(1977) | 100,000 | — | — | 8.50 | 14.50 | — |

**150 BAHT** **Y# 125** **Weight:** 22.0000 g. **Composition:** 0.9250 Silver .6543 oz. ASW **Ruler:** Rama IX Phra Maha Bhumithol Adulyadej **Subject:** Investiture of Princess Sirindhorn

| Date | Mintage | F | VF | XF | Unc | BU |
|---|---|---|---|---|---|---|
| BE2520(1977) | 50,000 | — | — | 12.50 | 27.50 | — |

**150 BAHT** **Y# 123** **Weight:** 22.0000 g. **Composition:** 0.9250 Silver .6543 oz. ASW **Ruler:** Rama IX Phra Maha Bhumithol Adulyadej **Subject:** 9th World Orchid Conference

| Date | Mintage | F | VF | XF | Unc | BU |
|---|---|---|---|---|---|---|
| BE2521(1978) | 30,000 | — | — | 11.50 | 25.00 | — |

**150 BAHT** **Y# 128** **Weight:** 22.0000 g. **Composition:** 0.9250 Silver .6543 oz. ASW **Ruler:** Rama IX Phra Maha Bhumithol Adulyadej **Subject:** Graduation of Crown Prince Vijiralongkorn

| Date | Mintage | F | VF | XF | Unc | BU |
|---|---|---|---|---|---|---|
| BE2521(1978) | 50,000 | — | — | 9.00 | 17.50 | — |

**150 BAHT** **Y# 197** **Weight:** 7.5000 g. **Composition:** 0.9250 Silver .2230 oz. ASW **Ruler:** Rama IX Phra Maha Bhumithol Adulyadej **Subject:** 60th Birthday - King Rama IX **Note:** Similar to 6000 Baht, Y#202.

| Date | Mintage | F | VF | XF | Unc | BU |
|---|---|---|---|---|---|---|
| BE2530(1987) | 12,000 | — | — | — | 25.00 | — |
| BE2530(1987) Proof | 1,100 | Value: 125 | | | | |

**150 BAHT** **Y# 213** **Weight:** 7.5000 g. **Composition:** 0.9250 Silver .2230 oz. ASW **Ruler:** Rama IX Phra Maha Bhumithol Adulyadej **Subject:** 42nd Anniversary - Reign of King Rama IX **Note:** Similar to 10 Baht, Y#212.

| Date | Mintage | F | VF | XF | Unc | BU |
|---|---|---|---|---|---|---|
| BE2531(1988) | 20,000 | — | — | — | 25.00 | — |
| BE2531(1988) Proof | 2,454 | Value: 135 | | | | |

**150 BAHT** **Y# 262** **Weight:** 7.5000 g. **Composition:** 0.9250 Silver .2230 oz. ASW **Ruler:** Rama IX Phra Maha Bhumithol Adulyadej **Subject:** Queen's 60th Birthday **Note:** Similar to 10 Baht, Y#261.

| Date | Mintage | F | VF | XF | Unc | BU |
|---|---|---|---|---|---|---|
| BE2535(1992) | 25,000 | — | — | — | 25.00 | — |
| BE2535(1992) Proof | 5,600 | Value: 45.00 | | | | |

**150 BAHT** **Y# 322** **Weight:** 7.5000 g. **Composition:** 0.9250 Silver .2230 oz. ASW **Ruler:** Rama IX Phra Maha Bhumithol Adulyadej **Subject:** 50th Anniversary - Reign of King Rama IX **Note:** Similar to 20 Baht, Y#321.1.

| Date | Mintage | F | VF | XF | Unc | BU |
|---|---|---|---|---|---|---|
| BE2539(1996) | — | — | — | — | 17.50 | — |
| BE2539(1996) Proof | — | Value: 45.00 | | | | |

**200 BAHT** **Y# 133** **Weight:** 22.0000 g. **Composition:** 0.9250 Silver .6544 oz. ASW **Ruler:** Rama IX Phra Maha Bhumithol Adulyadej **Subject:** Royal Cradle Ceremony

| Date | Mintage | F | VF | XF | Unc | BU |
|---|---|---|---|---|---|---|
| BE2522(1979) | 50,000 | — | — | 9.00 | 16.50 | — |

**200 BAHT** **Y# 152** **Weight:** 23.3200 g. **Composition:** 0.9250 Silver .6935 oz. ASW **Ruler:** Rama IX Phra Maha Bhumithol Adulyadej **Series:** International Year of the Child

| Date | Mintage | F | VF | XF | Unc | BU |
|---|---|---|---|---|---|---|
| BE2524(1981) Proof | 9,525 | Value: 70.00 | | | | |

**200 BAHT** **Y# 206** **Weight:** 23.1800 g. **Composition:** 0.9250 Silver .6894 oz. ASW **Ruler:** Rama IX Phra Maha Bhumithol Adulyadej **Series:** 25th Anniversary of World Wildlife Fund **Reverse:** Siamese Fireback Pheasant

| Date | Mintage | F | VF | XF | Unc | BU |
|---|---|---|---|---|---|---|
| BE2530(1987) Proof | 25,000 | Value: 40.00 | | | | |

**200 BAHT** **Y# 360** **Weight:** 23.1800 g. **Composition:** 0.9250 Silver .6894 oz. ASW **Ruler:** Rama IX Phra Maha Bhumithol Adulyadej **Series:** World Wildlife Fund **Obverse:** King's portrait **Reverse:** Two tigers above denomination **Edge:** Reeded **Size:** 38.5 mm. **Note:** Thickness of coin is 4.7mm.

| Date | Mintage | F | VF | XF | Unc | BU |
|---|---|---|---|---|---|---|
| BE2541(1998) Proof | 15,000 | Value: 50.00 | | | | |

**200 BAHT** **Y# 367** **Weight:** 155.5175 g. **Composition:** 0.9250 Silver 4.625 oz. ASW **Ruler:** Rama IX Phra Maha Bhumithol Adulyadej **Subject:** Year of the Dragon **Obverse:** King's portrait **Reverse:** 2 dragons around silver pearl in orange circle **Edge:** Reeded **Size:** 65 mm.

| Date | Mintage | F | VF | XF | Unc | BU |
|---|---|---|---|---|---|---|
| BE2543(2000) Proof | 2,000 | Value: 175 | | | | |

**250 BAHT** **Y# 169** **Weight:** 28.2800 g. **Composition:** 0.9250 Silver .8411 oz. ASW **Ruler:** Rama IX Phra Maha Bhumithol Adulyadej **Series:** International Year of Disabled Persons

| Date | Mintage | F | VF | XF | Unc | BU |
|---|---|---|---|---|---|---|
| BE2526(1983) | 307 | — | — | — | 250 | — |
| BE2526(1983) Proof | 233 | Value: 550 | | | | |

**250 BAHT** **Y# 368** **Weight:** 15.5510 g. **Composition:** 0.9999 Gold .5000 oz. AGW **Ruler:** Rama IX Phra Maha Bhumithol Adulyadej **Subject:** Year of the Dragon **Obverse:** King's portrait **Reverse:** Dragon with latent image pearl **Edge:** Reeded **Size:** 27 mm.

| Date | Mintage | F | VF | XF | Unc | BU |
|---|---|---|---|---|---|---|
| BE2543(2000) Proof | 2,800 | Value: 350 | | | | |

**300 BAHT** **Y# 89** **Weight:** 7.5000 g. **Composition:** 0.9000 Gold .2170 oz. AGW **Ruler:** Rama IX Phra Maha Bhumithol Adulyadej **Subject:** Queen Sirikit 36th Birthday

| Date | Mintage | F | VF | XF | Unc | BU |
|---|---|---|---|---|---|---|
| BE2511(1968) | 101,000 | — | — | — | 110 | — |

**300 BAHT** **Y# 136** **Weight:** 22.0000 g. **Composition:** 0.9250 Silver .6543 oz. ASW **Ruler:** Rama IX Phra Maha Bhumithol Adulyadej **Subject:** Graduation of Princess Chulabhorn **Note:** Similar to 10 Baht, Y#135.

| Date | Mintage | F | VF | XF | Unc | BU |
|---|---|---|---|---|---|---|
| BE2522(1979) | 20,000 | — | — | 15.00 | 20.00 | — |

**300 BAHT** **Y# 198** **Weight:** 15.0000 g. **Composition:** 0.9250 Silver .4461 oz. ASW **Ruler:** Rama IX Phra Maha Bhumithol Adulyadej **Subject:** 60th Birthday - King Rama IX **Note:** Similar to 6000 Baht, Y#202.

| Date | Mintage | F | VF | XF | Unc | BU |
|---|---|---|---|---|---|---|
| BE2530(1987) | 6,680 | — | — | — | 25.00 | — |
| BE2530(1987) Proof | 800 | Value: 50.00 | | | | |

**300 BAHT** **Y# 214** **Weight:** 15.0000 g. **Composition:** 0.9250 Silver .4461 oz. ASW **Ruler:** Rama IX Phra Maha Bhumithol Adulyadej **Subject:** 42nd Anniversary - Reign of King Rama IX **Note:** Similar to 10 Baht, Y#212.

| Date | Mintage | F | VF | XF | Unc | BU |
|---|---|---|---|---|---|---|
| BE2531(1988) | 11,000 | — | — | — | 20.00 | — |
| BE2531(1988) Proof | 2,391 | Value: 50.00 | | | | |

**300 BAHT** **Y# 263** **Weight:** 15.0000 g. **Composition:** 0.9250 Silver .4461 oz. ASW **Ruler:** Rama IX Phra Maha Bhumithol Adulyadej **Subject:** Queen's 60th Birthday **Note:** Similar to 10 Baht, Y#261.

| Date | Mintage | F | VF | XF | Unc | BU |
|---|---|---|---|---|---|---|
| BE2535(1992) | 25,000 | — | — | — | 35.00 | — |
| BE2535(1992) Proof | 4,000 | Value: 45.00 | | | | |

**300 BAHT** **Y# 323** **Weight:** 15.0000 g. **Composition:** 0.9250 Silver .4461 oz. ASW **Ruler:** Rama IX Phra Maha Bhumithol Adulyadej **Subject:** 50th Anniversary - Reign of King Rama IX **Note:** Similar to 20 Baht, Y#321.1.

| Date | Mintage | F | VF | XF | Unc | BU |
|---|---|---|---|---|---|---|
| BE2539(1996) | — | — | — | — | 22.50 | — |
| BE2539(1996) Proof | — | Value: 50.00 | | | | |

**400 BAHT** **Y# 93** **Weight:** 10.0000 g. **Composition:** 0.9000 Gold .2893 oz. AGW **Ruler:** Rama IX Phra Maha Bhumithol Adulyadej **Subject:** 25th Anniversary - Reign of King Rama IX

| Date | Mintage | F | VF | XF | Unc | BU |
|---|---|---|---|---|---|---|
| BE2514(1971) | 47,000 | — | — | — | 125 | — |

**600 BAHT** **Y#90** **Weight:** 15.0000 g. **Composition:** 0.9000 Gold .4340 oz. AGW **Ruler:** Rama IX Phra Maha Bhumithol Adulyadej **Subject:** Queen Sirikit 36th Birthday

| Date | Mintage | F | VF | XF | Unc | BU |
|---|---|---|---|---|---|---|
| BE2511(1968) | 46,000 | — | — | — | 190 | — |

**600 BAHT** **Y# 138** **Weight:** 14.9000 g. **Composition:** 0.9250 Silver .4432 oz. ASW **Ruler:** Rama IX Phra Maha Bhumithol Adulyadej **Subject:** Queen's Anniversary and F.A.O. Ceres Medal

| Date | Mintage | F | VF | XF | Unc | BU |
|---|---|---|---|---|---|---|
| BE2523(1980) | 23,000 | — | — | 18.00 | 28.00 | — |

**600 BAHT** **Y# 143** **Weight:** 14.9000 g. **Composition:** 0.9250 Silver .4432 oz. ASW **Ruler:** Rama IX Phra Maha Bhumithol Adulyadej **Subject:** Centennial - Birth of Rama VI

| Date | Mintage | F | VF | XF | Unc | BU |
|---|---|---|---|---|---|---|
| BE2524(1981) | 19,000 | — | — | 20.00 | 30.00 | — |

**600 BAHT** **Y# 147** **Weight:** 22.0000 g. **Composition:** 0.9250 Silver .6543 oz. ASW **Ruler:** Rama IX Phra Maha Bhumithol Adulyadej **Subject:** 35th Anniversary - Reign of King Rama IX

| Date | Mintage | F | VF | XF | Unc | BU |
|---|---|---|---|---|---|---|
| BE2524(1981) | 15,000 | — | — | 20.00 | 30.00 | — |

**600 BAHT** **Y# 150** **Weight:** 22.0000 g. **Composition:** 0.9250 Silver .6543 oz. ASW **Ruler:** Rama IX Phra Maha Bhumithol Adulyadej **Subject:** Bicentennial of Bangkok

| Date | Mintage | F | VF | XF | Unc | BU |
|---|---|---|---|---|---|---|
| BE2525(1982) | 15,000 | — | — | 20.00 | 30.00 | — |

**600 BAHT** **Y# 155** **Weight:** 22.0000 g. **Composition:** 0.9250 Silver .6543 oz. ASW **Ruler:** Rama IX Phra Maha Bhumithol Adulyadej **Subject:** 50th Birthday of Queen Sirikit

| Date | Mintage | F | VF | XF | Unc | BU |
|---|---|---|---|---|---|---|
| BE2525(1982) | 3,895 | — | — | 28.00 | 55.00 | — |
| BE2525(1982) Proof | 1,011 | Value: 225 | | | | |

**600 BAHT** **Y# 164** **Weight:** 22.0000 g. **Composition:** 0.9250 Silver .6543 oz. ASW **Ruler:** Rama IX Phra Maha Bhumithol Adulyadej **Subject:** 100th Anniversary of Postage Stamps

| Date | Mintage | F | VF | XF | Unc | BU |
|---|---|---|---|---|---|---|
| BE2526(1983) | 5,000 | — | — | 28.00 | 55.00 | — |
| BE2526(1983) Proof | 1,400 | Value: 165 | | | | |

**600 BAHT** **Y# 166** **Weight:** 22.0000 g. **Composition:** 0.9250 Silver .6543 oz. ASW **Ruler:** Rama IX Phra Maha Bhumithol Adulyadej **Subject:** 700th Anniversary of Thai Alphabet

| Date | Mintage | F | VF | XF | Unc | BU |
|---|---|---|---|---|---|---|
| BE2526(1983) | 4,300 | — | — | 28.00 | 55.00 | — |
| BE2526(1983) Proof | 1,000 | Value: 200 | | | | |

**600 BAHT** **Y# 173** **Weight:** 22.0000 g. **Composition:** 0.9250 Silver .6543 oz. ASW **Ruler:** Rama IX Phra Maha Bhumithol Adulyadej **Subject:** 84th Birthday of Princess Mother

| Date | Mintage | F | VF | XF | Unc | BU |
|---|---|---|---|---|---|---|
| BE2527(1984) | 3,530 | — | — | 28.00 | 45.00 | — |
| BE2527(1984) Proof | 520 | Value: 260 | | | | |

**600 BAHT** **Y# 193** **Weight:** 22.0000 g. **Composition:** 0.9250 Silver .6543 oz. ASW **Ruler:** Rama IX Phra Maha Bhumithol Adulyadej **Subject:** Princess Chulabhorn Awarded Einstein Medal **Note:** Similar to 10 Baht, Y#192.

| Date | Mintage | F | VF | XF | Unc | BU |
|---|---|---|---|---|---|---|
| BE2529(1986) | 2,400 | — | — | — | 55.00 | — |
| BE2529(1986) Proof | 212 | Value: 225 | | | | |

**600 BAHT** **Y# 182** **Weight:** 22.0000 g. **Composition:** 0.9250 Silver .6543 oz. ASW **Ruler:** Rama IX Phra Maha Bhumithol Adulyadej **Subject:** 6th ASEAN Orchid Congress **Note:** Similar to 10 Baht, Y#181.

| Date | Mintage | F | VF | XF | Unc | BU |
|---|---|---|---|---|---|---|
| BE2529(1986) | 5,000 | — | — | — | 45.00 | — |
| BE2529(1986) Proof | 300 | Value: 200 | | | | |

**600 BAHT** **Y# 229** **Weight:** 30.0000 g. **Composition:** 0.9250 Silver .8922 oz. ASW **Ruler:** Rama IX Phra Maha Bhumithol Adulyadej **Subject:** Asian Institute of Technology **Note:** Similar to 10 Baht, Y#190.

| Date | Mintage | F | VF | XF | Unc | BU |
|---|---|---|---|---|---|---|
| BE2530(1987) | 2,700 | — | — | — | 40.00 | — |
| BE2530(1987) Proof | 400 | Value: 175 | | | | |

**600 BAHT** **Y# 199** **Weight:** 30.0000 g. **Composition:** 0.9250 Silver .8922 oz. ASW **Ruler:** Rama IX Phra Maha Bhumithol Adulyadej **Subject:** 60th Birthday - King Rama IX **Note:** Similar to 6000 Baht, Y#202.

| Date | Mintage | F | VF | XF | Unc | BU |
|---|---|---|---|---|---|---|
| BE2530(1987) | 5,000 | — | — | — | 100 | — |
| BE2530(1987) Proof | 750 | Value: 350 | | | | |

**600 BAHT** **Y# 215** **Weight:** 30.0000 g. **Composition:** 0.9250 Silver .8922 oz. ASW **Ruler:** Rama IX Phra Maha Bhumithol Adulyadej **Subject:** 42nd Anniversary - Reign of King Rama IX **Note:** Similar to 10 Baht, Y#212.

| Date | Mintage | F | VF | XF | Unc | BU |
|---|---|---|---|---|---|---|
| BE2531(1988) | 8,840 | — | — | — | 45.00 | — |
| BE2531(1988) Proof | 1,110 | Value: 175 | | | | |

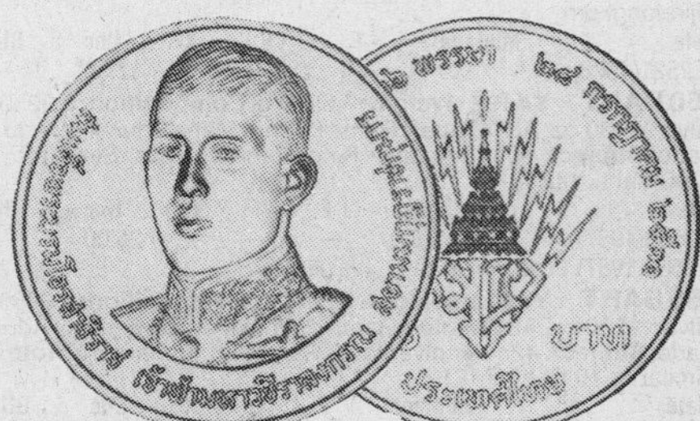

**600 BAHT** **Y# 224** **Weight:** 30.0000 g. **Composition:** 0.9250 Silver .8922 oz. ASW **Ruler:** Rama IX Phra Maha Bhumithol Adulyadej **Subject:** Crown Prince's Birthday

| Date | Mintage | F | VF | XF | Unc | BU |
|---|---|---|---|---|---|---|
| BE2531(1988) | 5,000 | — | — | — | 45.00 | — |
| BE2531(1988) Proof | 1,000 | Value: 180 | | | | |

**600 BAHT** **Y# 226** **Weight:** 30.0000 g. **Composition:** 0.9000 Silver .8682 oz. ASW **Ruler:** Rama IX Phra Maha Bhumithol Adulyadej **Subject:** 72nd Anniversary of Chulalongkorn University

| Date | Mintage | F | VF | XF | Unc | BU |
|---|---|---|---|---|---|---|
| BE2532(1989) | 10,000 | — | — | — | 50.00 | — |

**600 BAHT** **Y# 234** **Weight:** 30.0000 g. **Composition:** 0.9250 Silver .8922 oz. ASW **Ruler:** Rama IX Phra Maha Bhumithol Adulyadej **Subject:** 90th Birthdayof Princess Mother

| Date | Mintage | F | VF | XF | Unc | BU |
|---|---|---|---|---|---|---|
| BE2533(1990) | 20,000 | — | — | — | 32.50 | — |
| BE2533(1990) Proof | 2,000 | Value: 150 | | | | |

**600 BAHT** **Y# 245** **Weight:** 30.0000 g. **Composition:** 0.9250 Silver .8922 oz. ASW **Ruler:** Rama IX Phra Maha Bhumithol Adulyadej **Subject:** World Health Organization **Note:** Similar to 10 Baht, Y#244.

| Date | Mintage | F | VF | XF | Unc | BU |
|---|---|---|---|---|---|---|
| BE2533(1990) | 25,000 | — | — | — | 32.50 | — |
| BE2533(1990) Proof | 596 | Value: 275 | | | | |

**600 BAHT** **Y# 239** **Weight:** 30.0000 g. **Composition:** 0.9000 Silver .8682 oz. ASW **Ruler:** Rama IX Phra Maha Bhumithol Adulyadej **Subject:** 36th Birthday of Princess Sirindhorn

| Date | Mintage | F | VF | XF | Unc | BU |
|---|---|---|---|---|---|---|
| BE2534(1991) | 30,000 | — | — | — | 32.50 | — |
| BE2534(1991) Proof | 2,583 | Value: 135 | | | | |

**600 BAHT** **Y# 257** **Weight:** 30.0000 g. **Composition:** 0.9250 Silver .8922 oz. ASW **Ruler:** Rama IX Phra Maha Bhumithol Adulyadej **Subject:** Princess Sirindhorn's Magsaysay Foundation Award

| Date | Mintage | F | VF | XF | Unc | BU |
|---|---|---|---|---|---|---|
| BE2534(1991) | 15,000 | — | — | — | 32.50 | — |
| BE2534(1991) Proof | 10,000 | Value: 130 | | | | |

**600 BAHT** **Y# 250** **Weight:** 30.0000 g. **Composition:** 0.9250 Silver .8922 oz. ASW **Ruler:** Rama IX Phra Maha Bhumithol Adulyadej **Subject:** Centenary Celebration - Father of King Rama IX **Note:** Similar to 10 Baht, Y#249.

| Date | Mintage | F | VF | XF | Unc | BU |
|---|---|---|---|---|---|---|
| BE2535(1992) | 19,000 | — | — | — | 32.50 | — |
| BE2535(1992) Proof | 11,000 | Value: 130 | | | | |

**600 BAHT** **Y# 264** **Weight:** 30.0000 g. **Composition:** 0.9250 Silver .8922 oz. ASW **Ruler:** Rama IX Phra Maha Bhumithol Adulyadej **Subject:** Queen's 60th Birthday **Note:** Similar to 10 Baht, Y#261.

| Date | Mintage | F | VF | XF | Unc | BU |
|---|---|---|---|---|---|---|
| BE2535(1992) | 25,000 | — | — | — | 32.50 | — |
| BE2535(1992) Proof | 3,500 | Value: 125 | | | | |

**600 BAHT** **Y# 274** **Weight:** 30.0000 g. **Composition:** 0.9250 Silver .8922 oz. ASW **Ruler:** Rama IX Phra Maha Bhumithol Adulyadej **Subject:** 64th Birthday - King Rama IX **Note:** Similar to 10 Baht, Y#273.

| Date | Mintage | F | VF | XF | Unc | BU |
|---|---|---|---|---|---|---|
| BE2535(1992) | 10,000 | — | — | — | 35.00 | — |
| BE2535(1992) Proof | 511 | Value: 320 | | | | |

**600 BAHT** **Y# 290** **Weight:** 30.0000 g. **Composition:** 0.9250 Silver .8922 oz. ASW **Ruler:** Rama IX Phra Maha Bhumithol Adulyadej **Subject:** 100th Anniversary of Rama VII **Note:** Similar to 10 Baht, Y#289.

| Date | Mintage | F | VF | XF | Unc | BU |
|---|---|---|---|---|---|---|
| BE2536(1993) | 12,000 | — | — | — | 35.00 | — |
| BE2536(1993) Proof | 1,000 | Value: 185 | | | | |

**600 BAHT** **Y# 281** **Weight:** 30.0000 g. **Composition:** 0.9250 Silver .8922 oz. ASW **Ruler:** Rama IX Phra Maha Bhumithol Adulyadej **Subject:** Centennial of Thai Red Cross **Reverse:** Emblems

| Date | Mintage | F | VF | XF | Unc | BU |
|---|---|---|---|---|---|---|
| BE2536(1993) | 13,000 | — | — | — | 32.50 | — |

**600 BAHT** **Y# 299** **Weight:** 22.1500 g. **Composition:** 0.9250 Silver .6587 oz. ASW **Ruler:** Rama IX Phra Maha Bhumithol Adulyadej **Subject:** 120th Anniversary - Ministry of Finance

| Date | Mintage | F | VF | XF | Unc | BU |
|---|---|---|---|---|---|---|
| BE2538(1995) | 17,000 | — | — | — | 32.50 | — |
| BE2538(1995) Proof | 480 | Value: 170 | | | | |

**600 BAHT** **Y# 301** **Weight:** 22.1500 g. **Composition:** 0.9250 Silver .6587 oz. ASW **Ruler:** Rama IX Phra Maha Bhumithol Adulyadej **Subject:** Ministry of Defense

| Date | Mintage | F | VF | XF | Unc | BU |
|---|---|---|---|---|---|---|
| BE2538(1995) | 18,000 | — | — | — | 32.50 | — |
| BE2538(1995) Proof | 2,960 | Value: 125 | | | | |

**600 BAHT** **Y# 303** **Weight:** 22.1500 g. **Composition:** 0.9250 Silver .6587 oz. ASW **Ruler:** Rama IX Phra Maha Bhumithol Adulyadej **Subject:** Ministry of Foreign Affairs

| Date | Mintage | F | VF | XF | Unc | BU |
|---|---|---|---|---|---|---|
| BE2538(1995) | 14,000 | — | — | — | 32.50 | — |
| BE2538(1995) Proof | 16 | — | — | — | — | — |

**600 BAHT** **Y# 305** **Weight:** 22.1500 g. **Composition:** 0.9250 Silver .6587 oz. ASW **Ruler:** Rama IX Phra Maha Bhumithol Adulyadej **Subject:** 72nd Birthday of Princess

| Date | Mintage | F | VF | XF | Unc | BU |
|---|---|---|---|---|---|---|
| BE2538(1995) | 12,000 | — | — | — | 35.00 | — |
| BE2538(1995) Proof | 600 | Value: 165 | | | | |

**600 BAHT** **Y# 310** **Weight:** 22.0000 g. **Composition:** 0.9250 Silver .6543 oz. ASW **Ruler:** Rama IX Phra Maha Bhumithol Adulyadej **Subject:** 80th Anniversary - Department of Revenue

| Date | Mintage | F | VF | XF | Unc | BU |
|---|---|---|---|---|---|---|
| BE2538(1995) | — | — | — | — | 32.50 | — |

**600 BAHT** **Y# 312** **Weight:** 22.0000 g. **Composition:** 0.9250 Silver .6543 oz. ASW **Ruler:** Rama IX Phra Maha Bhumithol Adulyadej **Subject:** 120th Anniversary - Audit Council

| Date | Mintage | F | VF | XF | Unc | BU |
|---|---|---|---|---|---|---|
| BE2538(1995) | — | — | — | — | 32.50 | — |

**600 BAHT** **Y# 324** **Weight:** 30.0000 g. **Composition:** 0.9250 Silver .8922 oz. ASW **Ruler:** Rama IX Phra Maha Bhumithol Adulyadej **Subject:** 50th Anniversary - Reign of King Rama IX **Note:** Similar to 20 Baht, Y#321.1.

| Date | Mintage | F | VF | XF | Unc | BU |
|---|---|---|---|---|---|---|
| BE2539(1996) | — | — | — | — | 32.50 | — |
| BE2539(1996) Proof | — | Value: 125 | | | | |

**600 BAHT** **Y# 356** **Weight:** 22.1500 g. **Composition:** 0.9250 Silver .6587 oz. ASW **Ruler:** Rama IX Phra Maha Bhumithol Adulyadej **Subject:** King's 6th Cycle Birthday Anniversary **Obverse:** Portrait. **Reverse:** Radiant arms. **Edge:** Reeded. **Size:** 35 mm.

| Date | Mintage | F | VF | XF | Unc | BU |
|---|---|---|---|---|---|---|
| BE2542(1999) | 100,000 | — | — | — | 15.00 | — |
| BE2542(1999) Proof | 30,000 | Value: 30.00 | | | | |

**600 BAHT** **Y# 377** **Weight:** 22.1500 g. **Composition:** 0.9250 Silver .6587 oz. ASW **Ruler:** Rama IX Phra Maha Bhumithol Adulyadej **Subject:** King's 72nd Birthday **Obverse:** King and Rama I portraits **Reverse:** Two royal symbols **Edge:** Reeded **Size:** 35 mm.

| Date | Mintage | F | VF | XF | Unc | BU |
|---|---|---|---|---|---|---|
| BE2543(2000) Proof | — | Value: 125 | | | | |

**800 BAHT** **Y# 94** **Weight:** 20.0000 g. **Composition:** 0.9000 Gold .5787 oz. AGW **Ruler:** Rama IX Phra Maha Bhumithol Adulyadej **Subject:** 25th Anniversary - Reign of King Rama IX

| Date | Mintage | F | VF | XF | Unc | BU |
|---|---|---|---|---|---|---|
| BE2514(1971) | 22,000 | — | — | — | 250 | — |

**1500 BAHT** **Y# 200** **Weight:** 3.7500 g. **Composition:** 0.9000 Gold .1085 oz. AGW **Ruler:** Rama IX Phra Maha Bhumithol Adulyadej **Subject:** 60th Birthday - King Rama IX

| Date | Mintage | F | VF | XF | Unc | BU |
|---|---|---|---|---|---|---|
| BE2530(1987) | 5,000 | — | — | — | 80.00 | — |
| BE2530(1987) Proof | 400 | Value: 170 | | | | |

**1500 BAHT** **Y# 216** **Weight:** 3.7500 g. **Composition:** 0.9000 Gold .1085 oz. AGW **Ruler:** Rama IX Phra Maha Bhumithol Adulyadej **Subject:** 42nd Anniversary - Reign of King Rama IX

| Date | Mintage | F | VF | XF | Unc | BU |
|---|---|---|---|---|---|---|
| BE2531(1988) | 11,000 | — | — | — | 75.00 | — |
| BE2531(1988) Proof | 995 | Value: 150 | | | | |

**1500 BAHT** **Y# 265** **Weight:** 3.7500 g. **Composition:** 0.9000 Gold .1085 oz. AGW **Ruler:** Rama IX Phra Maha

Bhumithol Adulyadej **Subject:** Queen's 60th Birthday **Obverse:** Queen's portrait **Reverse:** Crowned monogram **Note:** Similar to 10 Baht, Y#261.

| Date | Mintage | F | VF | XF | Unc | BU |
|---|---|---|---|---|---|---|
| BE2535(1992) | 10,000 | — | — | — | 75.00 | — |
| BE2535(1992) Proof | 1,500 | Value: 140 | | | | |

**2500 BAHT** **Y# 119** **Weight:** 15.0000 g. **Composition:** 0.9000 Gold .4340 oz. AGW **Ruler:** Rama IX Phra Maha Bhumithol Adulyadej **Subject:** Crown Prince Vajiralongkorn and Princess Soamsawali Wedding

| Date | Mintage | F | VF | XF | Unc | BU |
|---|---|---|---|---|---|---|
| BE2520(1977) | 20,000 | — | — | — | 225 | — |

**2500 BAHT** **Y# 126** **Weight:** 15.0000 g. **Composition:** 0.9000 Gold .4340 oz. AGW **Ruler:** Rama IX Phra Maha Bhumithol Adulyadej **Subject:** Investiture of Princess Sirindhorn

| Date | Mintage | F | VF | XF | Unc | BU |
|---|---|---|---|---|---|---|
| BE2520(1977) | 5,000 | — | — | — | 300 | — |

**2500 BAHT** **Y# 170** **Weight:** 15.0000 g. **Composition:** 0.9000 Gold .4340 oz. AGW **Ruler:** Rama IX Phra Maha Bhumithol Adulyadej **Series:** International Year of Disabled Persons

| Date | Mintage | F | VF | XF | Unc | BU |
|---|---|---|---|---|---|---|
| BE2526(1983) | 92 | — | — | — | 1,400 | — |
| BE2526(1983) Proof | 793 | Value: 1,250 | | | | |

**2500 BAHT** **Y# 207** **Weight:** 15.9800 g. **Composition:** 0.9000 Gold .4625 oz. AGW **Ruler:** Rama IX Phra Maha Bhumithol Adulyadej **Series:** 25th Anniversary of World Wildlife Fund **Reverse:** Asian Elephant

| Date | Mintage | F | VF | XF | Unc | BU |
|---|---|---|---|---|---|---|
| BE2530(1987) Proof | Est. 5,000 | Value: 350 | | | | |

**2500 BAHT** **Y# 325** **Weight:** 3.7500 g. **Composition:** 0.9000 Gold .1085 oz. AGW **Ruler:** Rama IX Phra Maha Bhumithol Adulyadej **Subject:** 50th Anniversary - Reign of King Rama IX **Obverse:** King's portrait **Reverse:** King's emblem supported by elephants **Note:** Similar to 20 Baht, Y#321.1.

| Date | Mintage | F | VF | XF | Unc | BU |
|---|---|---|---|---|---|---|
| BE2539(1996) | — | — | — | — | 75.00 | — |
| BE2539(1996) Proof | — | Value: 135 | | | | |

**2500 BAHT** **Y# 369** **Weight:** 155.5175 g. **Composition:** 0.9999 Gold 5.0000 oz. AGW **Ruler:** Rama IX Phra Maha Bhumithol Adulyadej **Subject:** Year of the Dragon **Obverse:** King's portrait **Reverse:** 2 dragons with multicolor hologram pearl **Edge:** Reeded **Size:** 55 mm.

| Date | Mintage | F | VF | XF | Unc | BU |
|---|---|---|---|---|---|---|
| BE2543(2000) | 500 | — | — | — | 3,300 | — |
| In sets only | | | | | | |

**3000 BAHT** **Y# 129** **Weight:** 15.0000 g. **Composition:** 0.9000 Gold .4340 oz. AGW **Ruler:** Rama IX Phra Maha Bhumithol Adulyadej **Subject:** Graduation of Crown Prince Vijiralongkorn

| Date | Mintage | F | VF | XF | Unc | BU |
|---|---|---|---|---|---|---|
| BE2521(1978) | 10,000 | — | — | — | 200 | — |

**3000 BAHT** **Y# 201** **Weight:** 7.5000 g. **Composition:** 0.9000 Gold .2170 oz. AGW **Ruler:** Rama IX Phra Maha Bhumithol Adulyadej **Subject:** 60th Birthday - King Rama IX

| Date | Mintage | F | VF | XF | Unc | BU |
|---|---|---|---|---|---|---|
| BE2530(1987) | 3,000 | — | — | — | 150 | — |
| BE2530(1987) Proof | 400 | Value: 260 | | | | |

**3000 BAHT** **Y# 217** **Weight:** 7.5000 g. **Composition:** 0.9000 Gold .2170 oz. AGW **Ruler:** Rama IX Phra Maha Bhumithol Adulyadej **Subject:** 42nd Anniversary - Reign of King Rama IX

| Date | Mintage | F | VF | XF | Unc | BU |
|---|---|---|---|---|---|---|
| BE2531(1988) | 7,904 | — | — | — | 175 | — |
| BE2531(1988) Proof | 780 | Value: 320 | | | | |

**3000 BAHT** **Y# 266** **Weight:** 7.5000 g. **Composition:** 0.9000 Gold .2170 oz. AGW **Ruler:** Rama IX Phra Maha Bhumithol Adulyadej **Subject:** Queen's 60th Birthday **Obverse:** Queen's portrait **Reverse:** Crowned monogram **Note:** Similar to 10 Baht, Y#261.

| Date | Mintage | F | VF | XF | Unc | BU |
|---|---|---|---|---|---|---|
| BE2535(1992) | 7,000 | — | — | — | 175 | — |
| BE2535(1992) Proof | 1,100 | Value: 330 | | | | |

**3000 BAHT** **Y# 326** **Weight:** 7.5000 g. **Composition:** 0.9000 Gold .2170 oz. AGW **Ruler:** Rama IX Phra Maha Bhumithol Adulyadej **Subject:** 50th Anniversary - Reign of King Rama IX **Obverse:** King's portrait **Reverse:** King's emblem supported by elephants **Note:** Similar to 20 Baht, Y#321.1.

| Date | Mintage | F | VF | XF | Unc | BU |
|---|---|---|---|---|---|---|
| BE2539(1996) | — | — | — | — | 185 | — |
| BE2539(1996) Proof | — | Value: 325 | | | | |

**4000 BAHT** **Y# 153** **Weight:** 17.1700 g. **Composition:** 0.9000 Gold .4969 oz. AGW **Ruler:** Rama IX Phra Maha Bhumithol Adulyadej **Series:** Internatioanl Year of the Child

| Date | Mintage | F | VF | XF | Unc | BU |
|---|---|---|---|---|---|---|
| BE2524(1981) Proof | 3,963 | Value: 325 | | | | |

**5000 BAHT** **Y# 104** **Weight:** 33.4370 g. **Composition:** 0.9000 Gold .9676 oz. AGW **Ruler:** Rama IX Phra Maha Bhumithol Adulyadej **Series:** Conservation **Subject:** White-eyed River Martin

| Date | Mintage | F | VF | XF | Unc | BU |
|---|---|---|---|---|---|---|
| BE2517(1974) | 2,602 | — | — | — | 650 | — |
| BE2517(1974) Proof | 623 | Value: 1,600 | | | | |

**5000 BAHT** **Y# 122** **Weight:** 30.0000 g. **Composition:** 0.9000 Gold .8681 oz. AGW **Ruler:** Rama IX Phra Maha Bhumithol Adulyadej **Subject:** 50th Birthday - King Rama IX

| Date | Mintage | F | VF | XF | Unc | BU |
|---|---|---|---|---|---|---|
| BE2520(1977) | 6,400 | — | — | — | 400 | — |

**6000 BAHT** **Y# 156** **Weight:** 15.0000 g. **Composition:** 0.9000 Gold .4341 oz. AGW **Ruler:** Rama IX Phra Maha Bhumithol Adulyadej **Subject:** 50th Birthday - Queen Sirikit

| Date | Mintage | F | VF | XF | Unc | BU |
|---|---|---|---|---|---|---|
| BE2525(1982) | 1,471 | — | — | — | 425 | — |
| BE2525(1982) Proof | 99 | Value: 4,000 | | | | |

**6000 BAHT** **Y# 167** **Weight:** 15.0000 g. **Composition:** 0.9000 Gold .4341 oz. AGW **Ruler:** Rama IX Phra Maha Bhumithol Adulyadej **Subject:** 700th Anniversary - Thai Alphabet

| Date | Mintage | F | VF | XF | Unc | BU |
|---|---|---|---|---|---|---|
| BE2526(1983) | 700 | — | — | — | 325 | — |
| BE2526(1983) Proof | 235 | Value: 600 | | | | |

**6000 BAHT** **Y# 174** **Weight:** 15.0000 g. **Composition:** 0.9000 Gold .4341 oz. AGW **Ruler:** Rama IX Phra Maha Bhumithol Adulyadej **Subject:** 84th Birthday - Princess Mother

| Date | Mintage | F | VF | XF | Unc | BU |
|---|---|---|---|---|---|---|
| BE2527(1984) | 835 | — | — | — | 350 | — |
| BE2527(1984) Proof | 246 | Value: 650 | | | | |

**6000 BAHT** **Y# 202** **Weight:** 15.0000 g. **Composition:** 0.9000 Gold .4341 oz. AGW **Ruler:** Rama IX Phra Maha Bhumithol Adulyadej **Subject:** 60th Birthday - King Rama IX

| Date | Mintage | F | VF | XF | Unc | BU |
|---|---|---|---|---|---|---|
| BE2530(1987) | 2,000 | — | — | — | 275 | — |
| BE2530(1987) Proof | 350 | Value: 425 | | | | |

**6000 BAHT** **Y# 247** **Weight:** 15.0000 g. **Composition:** 0.9000 Gold .4341 oz. AGW **Ruler:** Rama IX Phra Maha Bhumithol Adulyadej **Subject:** Asian Institute of Technology

| Date | Mintage | F | VF | XF | Unc | BU |
|---|---|---|---|---|---|---|
| BE2530(1987) | 700 | — | — | — | 350 | — |
| BE2530(1987) Proof | 100 | Value: 650 | | | | |

**6000 BAHT** **Y# 218** **Weight:** 15.0000 g. **Composition:** 0.9000 Gold .4341 oz. AGW **Ruler:** Rama IX Phra Maha Bhumithol Adulyadej **Subject:** 42nd Anniversary - Reign of King Rama IX

| Date | Mintage | F | VF | XF | Unc | BU |
|---|---|---|---|---|---|---|
| BE2531(1988) | 6,067 | — | — | — | 300 | — |
| BE2531(1988) Proof | 670 | Value: 500 | | | | |

**6000 BAHT** **Y# 246** **Weight:** 15.0000 g. **Composition:** 0.9000 Gold .4341 oz. AGW **Ruler:** Rama IX Phra Maha Bhumithol Adulyadej **Subject:** World Health Organization

| Date | Mintage | F | VF | XF | Unc | BU |
|---|---|---|---|---|---|---|
| BE2534(1991) | 5,000 | — | — | — | 350 | — |
| BE2534(1991) Proof | 591 | Value: 600 | | | | |

**6000 BAHT** **Y# 258** **Weight:** 15.0000 g. **Composition:** 0.9000 Gold .4341 oz. AGW **Ruler:** Rama IX Phra Maha Bhumithol Adulyadej **Subject:** Princess Sirindhorn's Magsaysay Foundation Award **Obverse:** Princess seated with children **Reverse:** Obverse of medal above larger reverse with inscription

| Date | Mintage | F | VF | XF | Unc | BU |
|---|---|---|---|---|---|---|
| BE2535(1992) | 1,600 | — | — | — | 300 | — |
| BE2535(1992) Proof | 500 | Value: 600 | | | | |

**6000 BAHT** **Y# 267** **Weight:** 15.0000 g. **Composition:** 0.9000 Gold .4341 oz. AGW **Ruler:** Rama IX Phra Maha Bhumithol Adulyadej **Subject:** Queen's 60th Birthday **Obverse:** Queen's portrait **Reverse:** Crowned monogram **Note:** Similar to 10 Baht, Y#261.

| Date | Mintage | F | VF | XF | Unc | BU |
|---|---|---|---|---|---|---|
| BE2535(1992) | 7,000 | — | — | — | 300 | — |
| BE2535(1992) Proof | 1,200 | Value: 450 | | | | |

**6000 BAHT** **Y# 275** **Weight:** 15.0000 g. **Composition:** 0.9000 Gold .4341 oz. AGW **Ruler:** Rama IX Phra Maha Bhumithol Adulyadej **Subject:** 64th Birthday - King Rama IX **Obverse:** Portrait of Rama IX and Rama IV left **Reverse:** Crowned monograms of Rama IX and Rama IV **Note:** Similar to 10 Baht, Y#273.

| Date | Mintage | F | VF | XF | Unc | BU |
|---|---|---|---|---|---|---|
| BE2535(1992) | 3,000 | — | — | — | 300 | — |
| BE2535(1992) Proof | 500 | Value: 600 | | | | |

**6000 BAHT** **Y# 291** **Weight:** 15.0000 g. **Composition:** 0.9000 Gold .4341 oz. AGW **Ruler:** Rama IX Phra Maha Bhumithol Adulyadej **Subject:** 100th Anniversary of Rama VII **Obverse:** Portrait left **Reverse:** Royal crown and accouterments

| Date | Mintage | F | VF | XF | Unc | BU |
|---|---|---|---|---|---|---|
| BE2536(1993) | 2,484 | — | — | — | 300 | — |
| BE2536(1993) Proof | 300 | Value: 600 | | | | |

**6000 BAHT** **Y# 327** **Weight:** 15.0000 g. **Composition:** 0.9000 Gold .4341 oz. AGW **Ruler:** Rama IX Phra Maha Bhumithol Adulyadej **Subject:** King's 50th Year of Reign **Obverse:** King's portrait **Reverse:** King's emblem supported by elephants **Note:** Similar to 20 Baht, Y#321.1.

| Date | Mintage | F | VF | XF | Unc | BU |
|---|---|---|---|---|---|---|
| BE2539(1996) | — | — | — | — | 300 | — |
| BE2539(1996) Proof | — | Value: 550 | | | | |

**6000 BAHT** **Y# 337** **Weight:** 15.0000 g. **Composition:** 0.9000 Gold .4341 oz. AGW **Ruler:** Rama IX Phra Maha Bhumithol Adulyadej **Series:** F.A.O. **Subject:** 50th Anniversary - Reign of King Rama IX and World Food Summit **Obverse:** King's portrait **Reverse:** King planting seedlings before adoring crowd **Note:** Similar to 20 Baht, Y#335.

| Date | Mintage | F | VF | XF | Unc | BU |
|---|---|---|---|---|---|---|
| BE2539(1996) | — | — | — | — | 300 | — |
| BE2539(1996) Proof | — | Value: 550 | | | | |

**6000 BAHT** **Y# 370** **Weight:** 15.0000 g. **Composition:** 0.9000 Gold .4341 oz. AGW **Ruler:** Rama IX Phra Maha Bhumithol Adulyadej **Subject:** King's 72nd Birthday **Obverse:** King's portrait **Reverse:** Crowned emblem

| Date | Mintage | F | VF | XF | Unc | BU |
|---|---|---|---|---|---|---|
| BE2542(1999) | 20,000 | — | — | — | 150 | — |
| BE2542(1999) Proof | 10,000 | Value: 300 | | | | |

**6000 BAHT** **Y# 378** **Weight:** 15.0000 g. **Composition:** 0.9000 Gold .4340 oz. AGW **Ruler:** Rama IX Phra Maha Bhumithol Adulyadej **Subject:** King's 72nd Birthday **Obverse:** King and Rama I portraits **Reverse:** Two royal symbols **Edge:** Reeded **Size:** 26 mm.

| Date | Mintage | F | VF | XF | Unc | BU |
|---|---|---|---|---|---|---|
| BE2543(2000) Proof | — | Value: 300 | | | | |

**9000 BAHT** **Y# 139** **Weight:** 12.0000 g. **Composition:** 0.9000 Gold .3472 oz. AGW **Ruler:** Rama IX Phra Maha Bhumithol Adulyadej **Series:** F.A.O. Ceres Medal **Subject:** Queen's Anniversary **Note:** Similar to 5 Baht, Y#137.

| Date | Mintage | F | VF | XF | Unc | BU |
|---|---|---|---|---|---|---|
| BE2523(1980) | 3,900 | — | — | — | 375 | — |

**9000 BAHT** **Y# A143** **Weight:** 12.0000 g. **Composition:** 0.9000 Gold .3472 oz. AGW **Ruler:** Rama IX Phra Maha Bhumithol Adulyadej **Subject:** Centennial - Birth of King Rama VI

| Date | Mintage | F | VF | XF | Unc | BU |
|---|---|---|---|---|---|---|
| BE2524(1981) | 2,600 | — | — | — | 375 | — |

**9000 BAHT** **Y# 148** **Weight:** 15.0000 g. **Composition:** 0.9000 Gold .4340 oz. AGW **Ruler:** Rama IX Phra Maha Bhumithol Adulyadej **Subject:** King Rama IX Anniversary of Reign

| Date | Mintage | F | VF | XF | Unc | BU |
|---|---|---|---|---|---|---|
| BE2524(1981) | 4,000 | — | — | — | 375 | — |

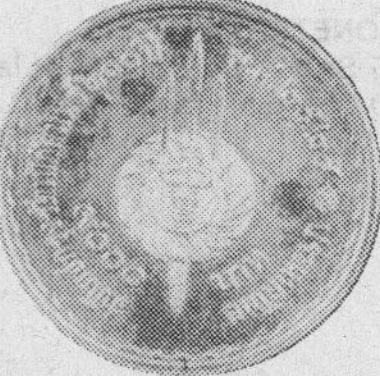

**9000 BAHT** **Y# 151** **Weight:** 15.0000 g. **Composition:** 0.9000 Gold .4340 oz. AGW **Ruler:** Rama IX Phra Maha Bhumithol Adulyadej **Subject:** Bicentennial of Bangkok

| Date | Mintage | F | VF | XF | Unc | BU |
|---|---|---|---|---|---|---|
| BE2525(1982) | 3,290 | — | — | — | 375 | — |

## OCCUPATION COINAGE

These coins were to be circulated in the four occupied provinces of Malaya during World War II. They were not put into circulation there but were later used in Japanese military service clubs in Bangkok before Japan's surrender in 1945.

**SEN** **KM# 5** **Composition:** Tin **Ruler:** Rama IX Phra Maha Bhumithol Adulyadej

| Date | Mintage | F | VF | XF | Unc | BU |
|---|---|---|---|---|---|---|
| BE2486 | — | — | — | — | 2,250 | — |

**5 SEN** **KM# 10** **Composition:** Tin **Ruler:** Rama IX Phra Maha Bhumithol Adulyadej

| Date | Mintage | F | VF | XF | Unc | BU |
|---|---|---|---|---|---|---|
| BE2486 | — | — | — | — | 2,250 | — |

**10 SEN** **KM# 15** **Composition:** Tin **Ruler:** Rama IX Phra Maha Bhumithol Adulyadej

| Date | Mintage | F | VF | XF | Unc | BU |
|---|---|---|---|---|---|---|
| BE2486 | — | — | — | 1,000 | 1,500 | — |

## BULLION COINAGE

In 1943, the government of Thailand made an internal loan by virtue of the Royal Act of Internal Loan related regulation of the Ministry of Finance, both dated 17th May, 1943.

Eight years later another Regulation of the Ministry of Finance dated 11th June, 1951 related to the actual redemption of the loan above mentioned was proclaimed with the following effect: Bond holders have the choice to be paid either in gold coins or gold bars or in other forms, all of which should bear the Garuda emblem and the specific inscription as to its weight and gold purity.

**50 BAHT** **KM# 1** **Weight:** 8.6930 g. **Composition:** 0.9950 Gold .2781 oz. AGW **Ruler:** Rama IX Phra Maha Bhumithol Adulyadej

| Date | Mintage | F | VF | XF | Unc | BU |
|---|---|---|---|---|---|---|
| ND(1951) | — | — | 175 | 210 | 275 | — |

**100 BAHT** **KM# 2** **Weight:** 17.3870 g. **Composition:** 0.9950 Gold .5562 oz. AGW **Ruler:** Rama IX Phra Maha Bhumithol Adulyadej

| Date | Mintage | F | VF | XF | Unc | BU |
|---|---|---|---|---|---|---|
| ND(1951) | — | — | 350 | 420 | 575 | — |

**1000 BAHT** **KM# 3** **Weight:** 173.8790 g. **Composition:** 0.9950 Gold 5.5620 oz. AGW **Ruler:** Rama IX Phra Maha Bhumithol Adulyadej

| Date | Mintage | F | VF | XF | Unc | BU |
|---|---|---|---|---|---|---|
| ND(1951) | — | — | 6,000 | 9,000 | 14,000 | — |

## ESSAIS

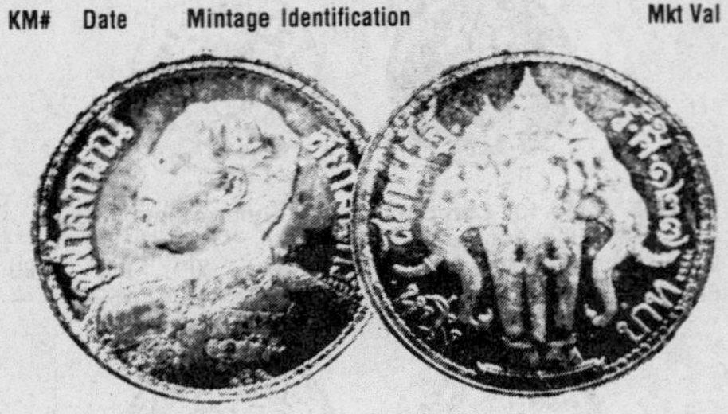

| KM# | Date | Mintage | Identification | Mkt Val |
|---|---|---|---|---|
| E1 | RS127 | — | Baht. Silver. Y#39. | 23,000 |

| KM# | Date | Mintage | Identification | Mkt Val |
|---|---|---|---|---|
| E2 | RS128 | — | 1/4 Baht. Silver. | 10,000 |
| E3 | RS129 | — | 1/2 Baht. Silver. | — |

**Note:** Struck at the Paris MInt. Taisei-Baldwin-Gillio Hong Kong sale 25 9-97 BU realized $23,000. Spink-Taisei Singapore Auction 14 3-93 Unc set of E 1, 2 and 2 realized $190,000

## PATTERNS

Including off metal strikes

| KM# | Date | Mintage | Identification | Mkt Val |
|---|---|---|---|---|
| Pn47 | RS124 | — | 2 Att. Copper. Facing bust. | 300 |
| Pn48 | RS126 | — | Baht. Silver. Y#39. Vishnu and Garuda. | 6,000 |
| Pn50 | RS127 | — | Satang. Gold. Y#35a. | 6,000 |
| Pn51 | RS127 | — | 5 Satang. Gold. Y#36a. | 7,000 |
| Pn52 | RS127 | — | 10 Satang. Gold. Y#37a. | 8,000 |
| Pn49 | RS127 | — | Satang. Nickel. Y#35. | — |
| Pn53 | RS129 | — | Baht. Silver. Y#39. | — |
| Pn54 | BE2489 | — | Baht. Tin. Y#67. | — |
| Pn55 | BE2505 | — | Baht. Copper-Nickel. Y#84. | — |
| Pn56 | BE2515 | — | 5 Baht. Copper-Nickel. Small bust, Y#28. | — |
| Pn57 | BE2515 | — | 5 Baht. Copper-Nickel. Royal parasol. | — |
| Pn58 | BE2515 | — | 5 Baht. Copper-Nickel. Different bust. | — |

## PIEFORTS

| KM# | Date | Mintage | Identification | Mkt Val |
|---|---|---|---|---|
| P1 | BE2524 | 126 | 200 Baht. I.Y.O.C. | 850 |
| P2 | BE2524 | 61 | 4000 Baht. I.Y.O.C. | 2,200 |
| P3 | BE2526 | 500 | 250 Baht. 0.9250 Silver. I.Y.D.P. | 1,250 |
| P4 | BE2526 | — | 2500 Baht. Gold. I.Y.D.P. | 6,500 |
| P5 | BE2540 | — | 100 Baht. 0.9250 Silver. 30.0000 g. WWF Tiger. | 75.00 |
| P6 | BE2541 | — | 200 Baht. 0.9250 Silver. 46.3600 g. WWF Tigers. | 115 |
| P7 | BE2541 | — | 200 Baht. 0.9250 Silver. 46.3600 g. WWF Elephants. | 120 |

## MINT SETS

| KM# | Date | Mintage | Identification | Issue Price | Mkt Val |
|---|---|---|---|---|---|
| MS2 | Mixed (32) | — | Two each Y#57, 70, 72, 73, 78a, 78-87, 91 | 22.00 | 45.00 |
| MS3 | Mixed (30) | 100,000 | Two each Y#60, 70, 72, 73, 78, 78a, 79, 79a, 80-86 | 20.00 | 30.00 |
| MS4 | Mixed (10) | — | Y#70, 72, 73, 78, 78a, 79, 79a, 80-82 | — | 12.00 |
| MS5 | Mixed (10) | — | Y#70, 78, 78a, 78b, 79a, 79b, 79d, 80, 81, 82 | — | 12.00 |
| MS6 | Mixed (8) | — | Y#83, 85-87, 91, 92, 95, 97 | 11.00 | 35.00 |
| MS7 | 1975 (2) | — | Y#102-103 | 32.50 | 70.00 |
| MS8 | 1988 (7) | — | Y#183, 185-187, 203, 208-209 | — | 3.50 |
| MS9 | 1991 (8) | — | Y#183, 186-187, 203, 208-209, 219, 227 | 4.00 | 10.00 |
| MS10 | 1992 (8) | — | Y#183, 186-187, 203, 208-209, 219, 227 | — | 10.00 |
| MS11 | 1993 (8) | — | Y#183, 186-187, 203, 208-209, 219, 227 | — | 10.00 |
| MS12 | 1994 (8) | — | Y#183, 186-187, 203, 208-209, 219, 227 | — | 10.00 |
| MS13 | Mixed (34) | — | Two each Y#57, 70, 72-73, 78, 78a, 79, 79a, 80-87, 91 | — | 60.00 |
| MS14 | Mixed (29) | — | Y#86 plus two each Y#57, 68, 73, 78, 78a, 79, 79a, 80-85, 87 | — | 35.00 |

## PROOF SETS

| KM# | Date | Mintage | Identification | Issue Price | Mkt Val |
|---|---|---|---|---|---|
| PS1 | 1974 (2) | — | Y#102a-103a | 50.00 | 160 |
| PS2 | 2000 (3) | 3,500 | Y#363-365 | 115 | 115 |
| PS3 | 2000 (5) | 500 | Y#363-365, 367, 369 | 3,480 | 3,650 |
| PS4 | 2000 (2) | 1,800 | Y#366, 368 | 446 | 450 |

# TIBET

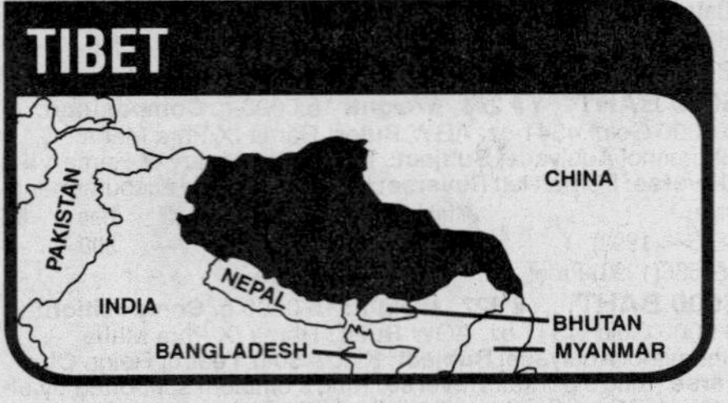
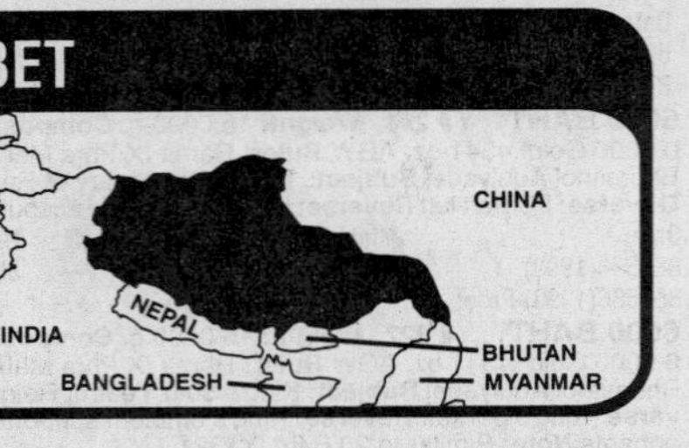


Tibet, an autonomous region of China located in central Asia between the Himalayan and Kunlun Mts. has an area of 471,660 sq. mi. (1,221,599 sq. km.) and a population of*1.9 million. Capital: Lhasa. The economy is based on agriculture and livestock raising. Wool, livestock, salt and hides are exported.

Lamaism, a form of Buddhism, developed in Tibet in the 8th century. From that time until the 1900s, the Tibetan rulers virtually isolated the country from the outside world. The British in India achieved some influence in the early 20th century. British troops were sent with the Young husband mission to extend trade in the north of India in December 1903; leaving during September 1904. The 13th dalai lama had fled to Urga where he remained until 1907. In April 1905 a revolt broke out and spread through southwestern Szechuan and northwestern Yunnan. Chao Erh-feng was appointed to subdue this rebellion and entered Lhasa in January 1910 with 2,000 troops. The dalai lama fled to India until he returned in June 1912., The British encouraged Tibet to declare its independence from China in 1913. The Communist revolution in China marked a new era in Tibetan history. Chinese Communist troops invaded Tibet in Oct., 1950. After a token resistance, Tibet signed an agreement with China in which China recognized the spiritual and temporal leadership of the dalai lama, and Tibet recognized the suzerainty of China. In 1959, a nationwide revolt triggered by Communist-initiated land reform broke out. The revolt was ruthlessly crushed. The dalai lama fled to India, and on Sept. 1,1965, the Chinese made Tibet an autonomous region of China.

The first coins to circulate in Tibet were those of neighboring Nepal from about 1570. Shortly after 1720, the Nepalese government began striking specific issues for use in Tibet. These coins had a lower silver content than those struck for use in Nepal and were exchanged with the Tibetans for an equal weight in silver bullion. Around 1763 the Tibetans struck their own coins for the first time in history. The number of coins struck at that time must have been very small. Larger quantities of coins were struck by the Tibetan government mint, which opened in 1791 with the permission of the Chinese. Operations of this mint however were suspended two years later. The Chinese opened a second mint in Lhasa in 1792. It produced a coinage until 1836. Shortly thereafter, the Tibetan mint was reopened and the government of Tibet continued to strike coins until 1953.

**DATING**

Based on the Tibetan calendar, Tibetan coins are dated by the cycle which contains 60 years. To calculate the western date use the following formula: Number of cycles -1, x 60 + number of years + 1026.Example 15th cycle 25th year = 1891 AD. Example: 15th cycle, 25th year 15 - 1 x 60 + 25 + 1026 = 1891AD.

| | | |
|---|---|---|
| 13/30 = 1776 | 14/30 = 1836 | 15/30 = 1896 |
| 13/40 = 1786 | 14/40 = 1846 | 15/40 = 1906 |
| 13/50 = 1796 | 14/50 = 1856 | 15/50 = 1916 |
| 13/60 = 1806 | 14/60 = 1866 | 15/60 = 1926 |
| 14/10 = 1816 | 15/10 = 1876 | 16/10 = 1936 |
| 14/20 = 1826 | 15/20 = 1886 | 16/20 = 1946 |

Certain Sino-Tibetan issues are dated in the year of reign of the Emperor of China.

**MONETARY SYSTEM**

15 Skar = 1-1/2 Sho = 1 Tangka
10 Sho = 1 Srang

**TANGKA**

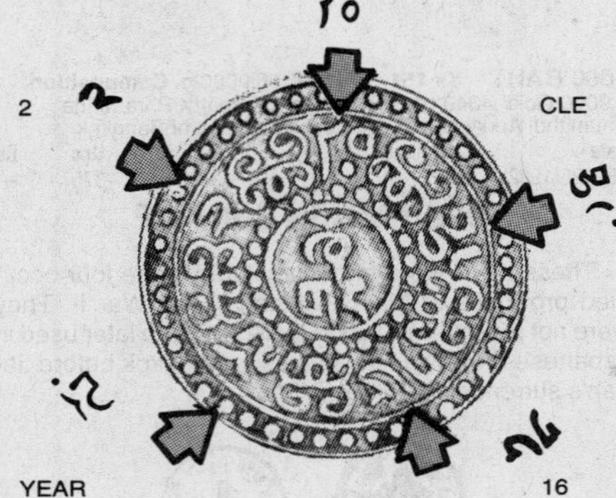


16(th)CYCLE 2(nd)YEAR = 1928AD

16(th) CYCLE 7(th) YEAR = 1933AD

**NUMERALS**

| | | | | |
|---|---|---|---|---|
| 1 | ༡ | གཅིག | | |
| 2 | ༢ | གཉིས | | |
| 3 | ༣ | གསུམ | | |
| 4 | ༤ | བཞི | | |
| 5 | ༥ | ལྔ | | |
| 6 | ༦ | དྲུག | | |
| 7 | ༧ | བདུན | | |
| 8 | ༨ | བརྒྱད | | |
| 9 | ༩ | དགུ | | |
| 10 | ༡༠ | བཅུ | or | བཅུ་ཐམ་པ |
| 11 | ༡༡ | བཅུག | or | བཅུ་གཅིག |
| 12 | ༡༢ | བཅུས | or | བཅུ་གཉིས |
| 13 | ༡༣ | བཅུ ས | or | བཅུ་གསུམ |
| 14 | ༡༤ | བཅུ་བཞི | | |
| 15 | ༡༥ | བཅོ་ལྔ | | |
| 16 | ༡༦ | བཅུ་དྲུག | | |
| 17 | ༡༧ | བཅུ་བདུན | | |
| 18 | ༡༨ | བཅོ་བརྒྱད | | |
| 19 | ༡༩ | བཅུ་དགུ | | |
| 20 | ༢༠ | ཉི་ཤུ | | |
| 21 | ༢༡ | ཉི་ཤུ་རྩ་གཅིག | or | ཉེར་གཅིག |
| 22 | ༢༢ | ཉེར་གཉིས | | |
| 23 | ༢༣ | ཉེར་གསུམ | | |
| 24 | ༢༤ | ཉེར་ བཞི | | |
| 25 | ༢༥ | ཉེར་ལྔ | | |
| 26 | ༢༦ | ཉེར་དྲུག | | |
| 27 | ༢༧ | ཉེར་བདུན | | |
| 28 | ༢༨ | ཉེར་བརྒྱད | | |

# KINGDOM

## SINO-TIBETAN COINAGE

**1/2 SKAR** **Y# A4** **Composition:** Copper **Ruler:** Hsüan-tung **Reverse:** Inscription: Hsüan-tung.... **Note:** 3.10-3.60 grams.

| Date | Mintage | Good | VG | F | VF | XF |
|---|---|---|---|---|---|---|
| ND(1910) | — | 300 | 400 | 500 | 600 | — |

**SKAR** **Y# 4** **Composition:** Copper **Ruler:** Hsüan-tung **Reverse:** Inscription: Hsüan-tung.... **Note:** 5.40-6.60 grams. Varieties exist. Modern counterfeits exist.

| Date | Mintage | Good | VG | F | VF | XF |
|---|---|---|---|---|---|---|
| ND(1910) | — | 90.00 | 150 | 250 | 400 | — |

**SHO** **Y# 5** **Composition:** Silver **Ruler:** Hsüan-tung **Reverse:** Inscription: Hsüan-tung.... **Note:** 3.30-4.10 grams. Vvarieties exist, one having the inner circle of dots, on the Chinese side, connected by lines. Modern counterfeits exist.

| Date | Mintage | Good | VG | F | VF | XF |
|---|---|---|---|---|---|---|
| ND(1910) | — | 20.00 | 30.00 | 50.00 | 80.00 | — |

**2 SHO** **Y# 6** **Composition:** Silver **Ruler:** Hsüan-tung **Reverse:** Inscription: Hsüan-tung.... **Note:** 5.20-8.40 grams. Varieties with different dragon claws and lotus exist. Modern counterfeits exist.

| Date | Mintage | Good | VG | F | VF | XF |
|---|---|---|---|---|---|---|
| ND(1910) | — | 25.00 | 40.00 | 80.00 | 125 | — |

## TANGKA COINAGE

Size of Kong-par Tangka

**TANGKA** **C# 27** **Composition:** Silver **Note:** Ca. 5.40 grams. In addition to the meaningful (probably) dated, the following meaningless ones exist: 13-16, 13-31, 13-92, 16-16, 16-61, 16-64, 16-69, 16-92, 16-93, 92-34, 92-39, 96-61 (sixes may be reversed threes and nines reversed ones). These are of billon, varying from 3.9 to 4.7 grams.

| Date | Mintage | Good | VG | F | VF | XF |
|---|---|---|---|---|---|---|
| BE15-40(1906) | — | 8.00 | 15.00 | 25.00 | 40.00 | — |
| BE15-46(1912) | — | 28.00 | 40.00 | 60.00 | 90.00 | — |

**Note:** The legend of this Rajana Tangka appears to be in ornamental Lansa script and has yet to be deciphered. The type is a copy of the Nepalese debased Tangka of Pretop Simha. Struck unofficially by Nepalese traders in Tibet between 1880 and 1912, it was legal tender, due to an edict issued in 1881 ordering that no distinction be made between false and genuine coins. The Tangka, C#27 was cut in parts of 3, 4, and 5 petals to make change and the resulting fractions are occasionally encountered.

**TANGKA (Ga-den)** **Y# 13.2** **Composition:** Silver **Obverse:** Three elongated dots on either side of lotus center and new arrangement of 8 symbols **Note:** 3.90-5.20 grams. Struck at Tip Arsenal Mint. Five major varieties exist.

| Date | Mintage | VG | F | VF | XF | Unc |
|---|---|---|---|---|---|---|
| ND(ca.1895-1901) | — | 4.00 | 6.00 | 9.00 | 13.50 | — |

**TANGKA (Ga-den)** **Y# 13.4** **Composition:** Silver **Note:** 3.80-5.70 grams. Similar to Y#13.3, but not uniform. Eight major varieties exist, including an error having the 8 symbols rotated one position clockwise.

| Date | Mintage | VG | F | VF | XF | Unc |
|---|---|---|---|---|---|---|
| ND(ca.1901-06) | — | 3.00 | 4.50 | 6.00 | 9.50 | — |

**TANGKA (Ga-den)** **Y# 13.5** **Composition:** Silver **Obverse:** 8 milimeter circle around lotus, north and west sybols are similar **Note:** 3.80 grams.

| Date | Mintage | VG | F | VF | XF | Unc |
|---|---|---|---|---|---|---|
| ND(ca.1905) | — | 20.00 | 30.00 | 50.00 | 100 | — |

**TANGKA (Ga-den)** **Y# 13.6** **Composition:** Silver **Obverse:** Nine dots within lotus circle **Note:** 3.00-5.60 grams. Struck at Dote Mint. Eight major varieties exist. See Y#13.9 13.10, and 13.11 for other types, having nne dots within lotus circle.

| Date | Mintage | VG | F | VF | XF | Unc |
|---|---|---|---|---|---|---|
| ND(ca.1906-12) | — | 3.00 | 4.50 | 6.00 | 9.50 | — |

**TANGKA (Ga-den)** **Y# 14** **Composition:** Silver **Obv. Legend:** "Gaden Palace, victorious in all directions" **Reverse:** Eight Buddhist lucky symbols surround encircled symbols of sensuality **Note:** 2.70-5.00 grams. Obverse varieties exist without or up to two dots inside trapezes enclosing the legend. Struck for presentation to monks.

| Date | Mintage | VG | F | VF | XF | Unc |
|---|---|---|---|---|---|---|
| ND(ca.1909) | — | 6.00 | 9.00 | 13.50 | 20.00 | — |

**TANGKA (Ga-den)** **Y# 13.7** **Composition:** Billon **Obverse:** 11 dots within lotus circle **Note:** 3.30-5.88 grams. Four major varieties and numerous minor ones exist (40-78 dots compose outer circles).

| Date | Mintage | VG | F | VF | XF | Unc |
|---|---|---|---|---|---|---|
| ND(ca.1912-23) | — | 3.00 | 4.50 | 6.00 | 9.50 | — |

**TANGKA (Ga-den)** **Y# 13.8** **Composition:** Billon **Obverse:** Nine dots within lotus circle **Note:** 3.00-5.00 grams. Five major varieties and numerous minor ones exist (35-68 dots compose outer circles).

| Date | Mintage | VG | F | VF | XF | Unc |
|---|---|---|---|---|---|---|
| ND(ca.1914-23) | — | 3.00 | 4.00 | 5.50 | 8.50 | — |

**TANGKA (Ga-den)** **Y# 13.9** **Composition:** Billon **Note:** 3.30-4.60 grams. Struck at Ser-khang Mint. Several other features are unique to this type.

| Date | Mintage | VG | F | VF | XF | Unc |
|---|---|---|---|---|---|---|
| ND(ca.1921) | — | 4.00 | 6.00 | 9.00 | 15.00 | — |

**TANGKA (Ga-den)** **Y# 13.10** **Composition:** Billon **Obverse:** Nine dots within lotus circle, uniform thickness (1mm) **Note:** 3.80-4.30 grams. Struck at Dote Mint. 2 minor die varieties exist.

| Date | Mintage | VG | F | VF | XF | Unc |
|---|---|---|---|---|---|---|
| ND(1929) | — | 10.00 | 14.00 | 19.00 | 26.00 | — |

**TANGKA (Ga-den)** **Y# 31** **Composition:** Silver **Note:** 3.10-5.30 grams. Struck at Tapchi Mint. This type was struck for presentation to monks.

| Date | Mintage | VG | F | VF | XF | Unc |
|---|---|---|---|---|---|---|
| ND(1953) | — | 7.00 | 9.00 | 14.00 | 20.00 | — |
| ND (1947) | — | 7.00 | 9.00 | 14.00 | 20.00 | — |

**2 TANGKA** Y# 15 **Composition:** Billon **Note:** 7.80-10.50 grams. Struck at Dode Mint. Struck in a collar. Two varieties exist.

| Date | Mintage | VG | F | VF | XF | Unc |
|---|---|---|---|---|---|---|
| ND(ca.1912) | — | 125 | 175 | 300 | 450 | — |

## SHO-SRANG COINAGE

Size same as Kong-par Tangka. All coins of the first 1909 series as well as Y18, A18, A18.1, A19 (dated 15-55), 22, 27, 32 and trade coinage Y1-3 exist as counterfeits.

**1/8 SHO** Y# A7 **Composition:** Copper **Note:** Struck at Dode Mint. A silver striking of this type exists (rare), possibly a pattern. Varieties exist.

| Date | Mintage | Good | VG | F | VF | XF |
|---|---|---|---|---|---|---|
| BE1(1909) | — | 85.00 | 150 | 225 | 350 | — |

**1/4 SHO** Y# B7 **Composition:** Copper **Note:** This coin struck in silver is a forgery. Modern forgeries struck in copper and copper-nickel exist.

| Date | Mintage | Good | VG | F | VF | XF |
|---|---|---|---|---|---|---|
| BE1(1909) | — | 85.00 | 150 | 225 | 350 | — |

**2-1/2 SKAR** Y# 10 **Composition:** Copper **Note:** Struck at Dode Mint. Lion varieties exist.

| Date | Mintage | Good | VG | F | VF | XF |
|---|---|---|---|---|---|---|
| BE15-43(1909) | — | 150 | 250 | 350 | 500 | — |

**2-1/2 SKAR** Y# 16.1 (Y16) **Composition:** Copper **Obverse:** Lion crouching and looking upwards **Size:** 23.5 mm. **Note:** 4.0-7.5 g. Varieties exist.

| Date | Mintage | Good | VG | F | VF | XF |
|---|---|---|---|---|---|---|
| BE15-47(1913) | — | 5.00 | 12.00 | 20.00 | 50.00 | — |
| BE15-48(1914) | — | 5.00 | 12.00 | 20.00 | 50.00 | — |
| BE15-49(1915) | — | 8.00 | 16.00 | 30.00 | 70.00 | — |
| BE15-50(1916) | — | 8.00 | 16.00 | 30.00 | 70.00 | — |
| BE15-51(1917) | — | 8.00 | 16.00 | 30.00 | 70.00 | — |
| BE15-52(1918) | — | 6.50 | 14.00 | 25.00 | 60.00 | — |

**2-1/2 SKAR** Y# 16.2 (Y16.1) **Composition:** Copper **Obverse:** Lion standing and looking backwards **Note:** Struck at Mekyi Mint. 2.80-4.00 grams. Varieties exist, one with retrograde syllables on reverse top (error).

| Date | Mintage | Good | VG | F | VF | XF |
|---|---|---|---|---|---|---|
| BE15-48(1914) | — | 8.00 | 16.00 | 30.00 | 70.00 | — |

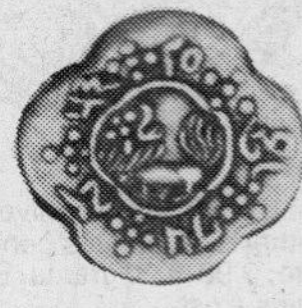 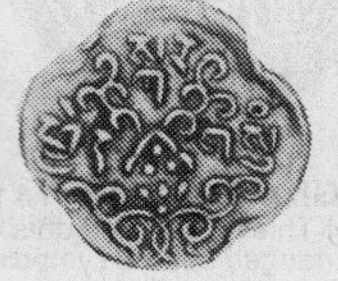

**2-1/2 SKAR** Y# A19 **Composition:** Copper **Ruler:** Hsüan-tung **Note:** Struck at Dode Mint.

| Date | Mintage | Good | VG | F | VF | XF |
|---|---|---|---|---|---|---|
| BE15-52(1918) | — | 35.00 | 55.00 | 75.00 | 100 | — |
| BE15-53(1918) | — | 35.00 | 60.00 | 80.00 | 110 | — |
| BE15-55(1921) | — | 35.00 | 60.00 | 80.00 | 110 | — |

**Note:** Counterfeits dated 15-53 and 15-55 exist.

**5 SKAR** Y# A10 **Composition:** Copper **Note:** Struck at Dode Mint.

| Date | Mintage | Good | VG | F | VF | XF |
|---|---|---|---|---|---|---|
| BE15-43(1909) | — | 150 | 250 | 350 | 500 | — |

**5 SKAR** Y# 17 **Composition:** Copper **Obverse:** Lion looking upwards **Size:** 27 mm.

| Date | Mintage | Good | VG | F | VF | XF |
|---|---|---|---|---|---|---|
| BE15-47(1913) | — | 5.00 | 8.00 | 18.00 | 40.00 | — |
| BE15-48(1914) | — | 4.00 | 7.00 | 15.00 | 35.00 | — |
| BE15-49(1915) | — | 5.00 | 8.00 | 18.00 | 40.00 | — |
| BE15-50(1916) | — | 5.00 | 8.00 | 18.00 | 40.00 | — |
| BE15-51(1917) | — | 3.50 | 6.00 | 12.00 | 30.00 | — |
| BE15-52(1918) | — | 5.00 | 8.00 | 18.00 | 40.00 | — |

**5 SKAR** Y# 17.2 **Composition:** Copper **Obverse:** Lion looking backwards and upwards

| Date | Mintage | Good | VG | F | VF | XF |
|---|---|---|---|---|---|---|
| BE15-48(1914) | — | 5.00 | 9.00 | 20.00 | 45.00 | — |
| BE15-49(1915) | — | 8.00 | 14.00 | 35.00 | 70.00 | — |

**5 SKAR** Y# 17.3 **Composition:** Copper **Reverse:** Flower with eight petals rather than wheel with eight spokes

| Date | Mintage | Good | VG | F | VF | XF |
|---|---|---|---|---|---|---|
| BE15-48(1914) | — | 6.00 | 10.00 | 25.00 | 55.00 | — |

**5 SKAR** Y# 17.1 **Composition:** Copper **Obverse:** Lion looking backwards **Note:** Struck at Mekyi Mint. Varieties exist with rotated reverse symbols. Size of obverse circle and weight of coin vary considerably.

| Date | Mintage | Good | VG | F | VF | XF |
|---|---|---|---|---|---|---|
| BE15-49(1915) | — | 4.00 | 7.00 | 15.00 | 32.00 | — |
| BE15-50(1916) | — | 4.00 | 7.00 | 15.00 | 32.00 | — |
| BE15-51(1917) | — | 4.00 | 7.00 | 15.00 | 32.00 | — |
| BE15-52(1918) | — | 5.00 | 8.00 | 18.00 | 40.00 | — |

**5 SKAR** Y# 19 **Composition:** Copper **Note:** Struck at Lower Dode Mint. Varieties exist.

| Date | Mintage | Good | VG | F | VF | XF |
|---|---|---|---|---|---|---|
| BE15-52(1918) | — | 2.25 | 3.50 | 6.00 | 12.00 | — |
| BE15-53(1919) | — | 2.00 | 3.00 | 5.50 | 11.00 | — |
| BE15-54(1920) | — | 1.50 | 2.50 | 5.00 | 10.00 | — |
| BE15-55(1921) | — | 1.50 | 2.50 | 5.00 | 10.00 | — |
| BE15-56(1922) | — | 1.50 | 2.50 | 5.00 | 10.00 | — |
| BE56-15(1922) Error | — | 25.00 | 40.00 | 70.00 | 110 | — |

**Note:** Reverse inscription reads counterclockwise on error date coin

**5 SKAR** Y# 19.1 **Composition:** Copper **Reverse:** Dot added above center **Note:** Struck at Upper Dode Mint.

| Date | Mintage | Good | VG | F | VF | XF |
|---|---|---|---|---|---|---|
| BE15-55(1921) | — | 10.00 | 20.00 | 35.00 | 65.00 | — |
| BE15-56(1922) | — | 4.00 | 8.00 | 15.00 | 25.00 | — |

**7-1/2 SKAR** Y# 11 **Composition:** Copper **Note:** Struck at Dode Mint.

| Date | Mintage | Good | VG | F | VF | XF |
|---|---|---|---|---|---|---|
| BE15-43(1909) | — | 150 | 250 | 350 | 500 | — |

**7-1/2 SKAR** Y# 20 **Composition:** Copper **Note:** Some 15-52, 15-53, and 15-55 specimens have the reverse central "whirlwind" in a counterclockwise direction. Many varieties exist, with five die varieties reported for 15-60 specimens.

| Date | Mintage | Good | VG | F | VF | XF |
|---|---|---|---|---|---|---|
| BE15-52(1918) | — | 2.00 | 3.00 | 5.00 | 8.50 | — |
| BE15-53(1919) | — | 1.50 | 2.50 | 4.00 | 7.00 | — |
| BE15-54(1920) | — | 1.50 | 2.50 | 4.00 | 7.00 | — |
| BE15-55(1921) | — | 1.50 | 2.50 | 4.00 | 7.00 | — |
| BE15-56(1922) | — | 1.50 | 2.50 | 4.00 | 7.00 | — |
| BE15-60(1926) | — | 15.00 | 25.00 | 40.00 | 75.00 | — |

**SHO** **Y# 21.1** **Composition:** Copper **Obverse:** Lion looking upwards, without dot in reverse (NE), arabesque. **Size:** 24 mm. **Note:** 3.95-7.13 grams. Struck at Mekyi Mint. Varieties exist.

| Date | Mintage | Good | VG | F | VF | XF |
|---|---|---|---|---|---|---|
| BE15-52(1918) | — | 1.50 | 2.00 | 3.25 | 7.00 | — |
| BE15-53/52(1919) | — | — | — | — | — | — |
| BE15-53(1919) | — | 1.00 | 1.50 | 2.50 | 5.00 | — |
| BE15-54(1920) | — | 1.00 | 1.50 | 2.50 | 5.00 | — |
| BE15-55(1921) | — | 1.00 | 1.50 | 2.50 | 5.00 | — |
| BE15-56(1922) | — | 1.00 | 1.50 | 2.50 | 5.00 | — |
| BE15-57(1923) | — | 1.50 | 2.00 | 3.25 | 7.00 | — |
| BE15-57(1923) W/o dots (obv.) | — | — | — | — | — | — |
| BE58-15(1924) (error) year and cycle transposed | — | — | — | — | — | — |
| BE15-58(1924) | — | 1.00 | 1.50 | 2.50 | 5.00 | — |
| BE15-59(1925) | — | 1.00 | 1.50 | 2.50 | 5.00 | — |
| BE15-59(1925) W/o dots (obv.) | — | — | — | — | — | — |
| BE15-6(1926) (error) for 15-60 | — | — | — | — | — | — |
| BE15-60(1926) | — | 1.00 | 1.50 | 2.50 | 5.00 | — |
| BE16-1(1927) | — | 1.00 | 1.50 | 2.50 | 5.00 | — |
| BE16-2(1928) | — | 1.00 | 1.50 | 2.50 | 5.00 | — |

**SHO** **Y# 21** **Composition:** Copper **Obverse:** Lion looking upwards **Reverse:** Central legend horizontal **Note:** Struck at Dode Mint.

| Date | Mintage | Good | VG | F | VF | XF |
|---|---|---|---|---|---|---|
| BE15-52(1918) | — | 30.00 | 45.00 | 75.00 | 120 | — |

**SHO** **Y# 21b** **Composition:** Copper **Obverse:** Lion looking backwards

| Date | Mintage | Good | VG | F | VF | XF |
|---|---|---|---|---|---|---|
| BE15-52(1918) | — | 30.00 | 45.00 | 75.00 | 120 | — |

**SHO** **Y# 21.2** **Composition:** Copper **Obverse:** Lion looking upwards, with dot in reverse (NE) arabesque. **Note:** 3.01-7.27 grams. Struck at Ser-Khang Mint. Varieties of lion's head, size of circle, overstrikes exist, also position of cycle and year are known.

| Date | Mintage | Good | VG | F | VF | XF |
|---|---|---|---|---|---|---|
| BE15-54(1920) | — | 2.00 | 3.00 | 5.00 | 9.00 | — |

**Note:** Specimens dated 15-54 may all be contemporary forgeries

| Date | Mintage | Good | VG | F | VF | XF |
|---|---|---|---|---|---|---|
| BE54-15(1920) (Error) year and cycle transposed | — | 25.00 | 40.00 | 65.00 | 100 | — |
| BE15/51-54(1920) (error) cycle transposed | — | 25.00 | 40.00 | 65.00 | 100 | — |
| BE15-55(1921) | — | 1.50 | 2.50 | 4.50 | 7.00 | — |
| BE55-15(1921) Error; "year" and "cycle" transposed | — | 25.00 | 40.00 | 65.00 | 100 | — |
| BE15-56/5(1921) | — | 1.00 | 1.50 | 2.50 | 5.00 | — |
| BE15-56(1922) | — | 1.00 | 1.50 | 2.50 | 5.00 | — |
| BE15-57(1923) | — | 1.25 | 1.75 | 3.25 | 7.00 | — |
| BE15-58(1924) | — | 1.00 | 1.50 | 2.50 | 5.00 | — |
| BE15-59(1925) | — | 1.00 | 1.50 | 2.50 | 5.00 | — |
| BE15-60(1926) | — | 1.00 | 1.50 | 2.50 | 5.00 | — |
| BE16-1/15-60(1927) | — | 15.00 | 25.00 | 40.00 | 65.00 | — |
| BE16-1(1927) | — | 1.00 | 1.50 | 2.50 | 5.00 | — |
| BE16-2/1(1928) | — | 1.00 | 1.50 | 2.50 | 5.00 | — |
| BE16-2(1928) | — | 1.00 | 1.50 | 2.50 | 5.00 | — |

**SHO** **Y# 21a** **Composition:** Copper **Reverse:** Central legend vertical **Note:** 3.43-4.73 grams. Struck at Dode Mint. Two varieties (lion) exist for each of the following dates: 15-56, 15-57, 15-58, and 16-2. Overstrikes on 5 Skar, Y#17 exist.

| Date | Mintage | VG | F | VF | XF | Unc |
|---|---|---|---|---|---|---|
| BE15-56(1922) | — | 8.00 | 13.50 | 20.00 | 30.00 | — |
| BE15-57(1923) | — | 2.00 | 3.50 | 6.00 | 10.00 | — |
| BE57-15(1923) Error; year and cycle transposed | — | 25.00 | 40.00 | 65.00 | 100 | — |
| BE15-58(1924) | — | 2.00 | 3.50 | 6.00 | 10.00 | — |
| BE15-59/8(1925) | — | 1.25 | 2.25 | 4.00 | 8.00 | — |
| BE15-59(1925) | — | 1.25 | 2.25 | 4.00 | 8.00 | — |
| BE15-60(1925) | — | 1.25 | 2.25 | 4.00 | 8.00 | — |
| BE15-60/59(1926) | — | 1.25 | 2.25 | 4.00 | 8.00 | — |
| BE16-1(1927) | — | 1.25 | 2.25 | 4.00 | 8.00 | — |
| BE16-1(1927) Dot below 0 above denomination | — | 1.25 | 2.25 | 4.00 | 8.00 | — |
| BE16-2(1928) | — | 2.00 | 3.50 | 6.00 | 10.00 | — |

**Note:** A scarce 16-2 variety features a reversed 2

| Date | Mintage | VG | F | VF | XF | Unc |
|---|---|---|---|---|---|---|
| BE16-2(1928) dot below rab | — | — | — | — | — | — |

**SHO** **Y# 23** **Composition:** Copper **Note:** 4.02-6.09 grams. Struck at Tapchi Mint. Exists with thick and thin planchets and many obverse varieties. Barieties of 8 and 9 in dates 16-8 and 16-9 exist.

| Date | Mintage | VG | F | VF | XF | Unc |
|---|---|---|---|---|---|---|
| BE16-6(1932) (a) | — | 2.00 | 3.00 | 6.00 | 10.00 | — |
| BE16-7(1933) (a) | — | 2.25 | 3.50 | 6.50 | 11.00 | — |
| BE16-8(1934) (a) | — | 2.50 | 4.00 | 9.00 | 15.00 | — |
| BE16-9(1935) (a) | — | 2.00 | 3.50 | 6.00 | 11.00 | — |
| BE16-9(1935) (b) | — | 1.50 | 3.00 | 5.00 | 10.00 | — |

**Note:** A scarce 16-9 variety features a "bird" on the Sengi's (lion's) back

| Date | Mintage | VG | F | VF | XF | Unc |
|---|---|---|---|---|---|---|
| BE16-10(1936) (a) | — | 5.00 | 10.00 | 15.00 | 25.00 | — |
| BE16-10(1936) (b) | — | 5.00 | 10.00 | 15.00 | 25.00 | — |
| BE16-10(1936) (c) | — | 1.50 | 3.00 | 5.00 | 10.00 | — |
| BE16-11(1937) (a) | — | 2.50 | 4.00 | 9.00 | 15.00 | — |
| BE16-11(1937) (b) | — | 5.00 | 10.00 | 15.00 | 25.00 | — |
| BE16-11(1937) (c) | — | 2.50 | 4.00 | 9.00 | 15.00 | — |
| BE16-11(1937) (d) | — | 2.50 | 4.00 | 9.00 | 15.00 | — |
| BE16-11(1937) (e) | — | 1.50 | 3.00 | 5.00 | 10.00 | — |
| BE16-11(1937) (f) | — | 5.00 | 10.00 | 15.00 | 25.00 | — |
| BE16-11(1937) (g) | — | 5.00 | 10.00 | 15.00 | 25.00 | — |
| BE16-12(1938) (d) | — | 5.00 | 10.00 | 15.00 | 25.00 | — |
| BE16-12(1938) (f) | — | 4.00 | 8.00 | 12.00 | 20.00 | — |
| BE16-12(1938) (g) | — | 4.00 | 8.00 | 12.00 | 20.00 | — |
| BE16-16(1942) (f) Rare | — | — | — | — | — | — |

**3 SHO** **Y# 27.1 (Y27)** **Composition:** Copper **Note:** Single cloud line. Four varieties of conch shell on reverse.

| Date | Mintage | VG | F | VF | XF | Unc |
|---|---|---|---|---|---|---|
| BE16-20(1946) | — | 8.00 | 15.00 | 25.00 | 40.00 | — |

**3 SHO** **Y# 27.2 (Y27.1)** **Composition:** Copper **Note:** Double cloud line.

| Date | Mintage | VG | F | VF | XF | Unc |
|---|---|---|---|---|---|---|
| BE16-20(1946) | — | 15.00 | 30.00 | 50.00 | 85.00 | — |

**5 SHO** **Y# 8** **Composition:** Silver **Ruler:** Hsüan-tung **Note:** 9.4 - 9.7 grams

| Date | Mintage | VG | F | VF | XF | Unc |
|---|---|---|---|---|---|---|
| BE1(1909) | — | 600 | 1,200 | 2,000 | 2,500 | — |

**Note:** A forgery exists with some of the stars blundered and letters inaccurate

**5 SHO** **Y# 18** **Composition:** Silver **Obverse:** Lion looking upwards **Note:** Struck at Dode Mint. 8.4 - 11.4 grams.

| Date | Mintage | VG | F | VF | XF | Unc |
|---|---|---|---|---|---|---|
| BE15-47(1913) | — | 50.00 | 70.00 | 100 | 150 | — |
| BE15-48(1914) | — | 35.00 | 50.00 | 80.00 | 125 | — |
| BE15-49(1915) | — | 35.00 | 50.00 | 80.00 | 125 | — |
| BE15-50(1916) | — | 35.00 | 50.00 | 80.00 | 125 | — |

**Note:** Two 15-50 varieties exist; small and large lions, or 13.5mm vs. 14.5mm obverse circle

| Date | Mintage | VG | F | VF | XF | Unc |
|---|---|---|---|---|---|---|
| BE15-58(1924) | — | 500 | 650 | 800 | 1,000 | — |
| BE15-59(1925) | — | 85.00 | 140 | 200 | 300 | — |
| BE15-60(1926) | — | 100 | 175 | 250 | 350 | — |

**5 SHO** **Y# 18.1** **Composition:** Silver **Obverse:** Lion looking backwards **Note:** Struck at Mekyi Mint. 7.4 - 9.8 grams. Varieties exist.

| Date | Mintage | VG | F | VF | XF | Unc |
|---|---|---|---|---|---|---|
| BE15-49(1915) | — | 35.00 | 50.00 | 80.00 | 125 | — |
| BE15-50(1916) | — | 35.00 | 50.00 | 80.00 | 125 | — |
| BE15-51(1917) | — | 35.00 | 50.00 | 80.00 | 125 | — |
| BE15-52(1918) | — | 35.00 | 50.00 | 80.00 | 125 | — |
| BE15-53(1919) | — | 85.00 | 125 | 180 | 275 | — |
| BE15-56(1922) | — | 85.00 | 125 | 180 | 275 | — |
| BE15-59(1925) | — | 500 | 650 | 800 | 1,000 | — |
| BE15-60(1926) | — | 250 | 325 | 400 | 500 | — |
| BE16-1(1927) | — | 100 | 135 | 200 | 300 | — |

**5 SHO** **Y# 18.2** **Composition:** Silver **Note:** Struck at Dode Mint. 8.0 - 9.7 grams.

| Date | Mintage | VG | F | VF | XF | Unc |
|---|---|---|---|---|---|---|
| BE15-52(1918) | — | 125 | 175 | 250 | 350 | — |

**5 SHO Y# 18.1a Composition:** Copper

| Date | Mintage | VG | F | VF | XF | Unc |
|---|---|---|---|---|---|---|
| BE15-53(1919) | — | 225 | 300 | 400 | 500 | — |

**5 SHO Y# 32 Composition:** Silver **Note:** 5.43 - 6.55 grams. Considered a pattern by some authorities.

| Date | Mintage | VG | F | VF | XF | Unc |
|---|---|---|---|---|---|---|
| ND(1928-29)(1928) | — | 375 | 500 | 650 | 800 | — |

a. "CYCLE"

b. "YEAR"

c. "16"

**5 SHO Y# 28 Composition:** Copper **Obverse:** Two mountains with two suns **Size:** 29 mm. **Note:** Struck at Tapchi Mint. 3 die varieties exist.

| Date | Mintage | VG | F | VF | XF | Unc |
|---|---|---|---|---|---|---|
| BE16-21(1947) | — | 4.00 | 7.50 | 10.00 | 20.00 | — |

**5 SHO Y# 28.1 Composition:** Copper **Obverse:** Three mountains with two suns **Note:** Die varieties involving tail hairs (5 to 8), leg hairs (2 to 5) and yin-yang features (S, reversed S or the incuse of either) include 5 of 16-21, 38 of 16-22 and 30 of 16-23. A modern medallic series dated 16-21 (1947) exists struck in copper, silver, and gold which were authorized by the Dalai Lama while in exile. Refer to "Unusual World Coins", 3rd edition, Krause Publications, 1992.

| Date | Mintage | VG | F | VF | XF | Unc |
|---|---|---|---|---|---|---|
| BE16-21(1947) | — | 2.00 | 3.50 | 6.00 | 10.00 | — |
| BE16-22(1948) dots a & c | — | 2.50 | 4.00 | 7.50 | 12.50 | — |
| BE16-22(1948) without dot a | — | 23.00 | 30.00 | 40.00 | 50.00 | — |
| BE16-22(1948) without dot c | — | 1.50 | 3.00 | 5.00 | 8.50 | — |
| BE16-22(1948) without dots a & c | — | 15.00 | 23.00 | 30.00 | 40.00 | — |
| BE16-23(1949) dots a & c | — | 5.00 | 8.00 | 14.00 | 25.00 | — |
| BE16-23(1949) without dot c | — | 1.50 | 3.00 | 5.00 | 8.50 | — |
| BE16-24(1950) | — | 30.00 | 40.00 | 50.00 | 65.00 | — |
| BE16-24/23(1950) | — | 30.00 | 40.00 | 50.00 | 65.00 | — |

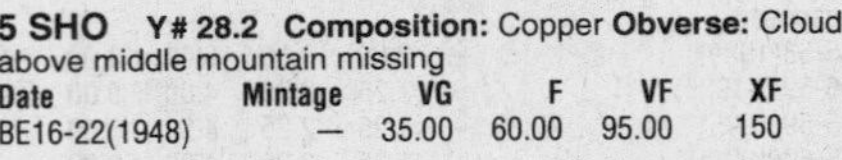

**5 SHO Y# 28.2 Composition:** Copper **Obverse:** Cloud above middle mountain missing

| Date | Mintage | VG | F | VF | XF | Unc |
|---|---|---|---|---|---|---|
| BE16-22(1948) | — | 35.00 | 60.00 | 95.00 | 150 | — |

**5 SHO Y# 28a Composition:** Copper **Obverse:** Moon and sun above 3 mountains **Note:** Edge varieties exist.

| Date | Mintage | VG | F | VF | XF | Unc |
|---|---|---|---|---|---|---|
| BE16-23(1949) | — | 20.00 | 28.00 | 38.00 | 50.00 | — |
| BE16-24(1950) dots a & b | — | 2.00 | 3.50 | 6.50 | 11.00 | — |
| BE16-24(1950) mountain as in illustration | — | 10.00 | 15.00 | 22.00 | 30.00 | — |
| BE16-24(1950) without dot a | — | 35.00 | 50.00 | 75.00 | 120 | — |
| BE16-24(1950) Moon engraved over sun | — | 15.00 | 22.00 | 30.00 | 40.00 | — |
| BE16-25/24(1951) | — | 4.00 | 7.00 | 12.50 | 20.00 | — |
| BE16-25(1951) dot b is tiny | — | 15.00 | 25.00 | 30.00 | 40.00 | — |
| BE16-25(1951) moon over engraved sun | — | 2.00 | 3.50 | 6.50 | 11.00 | — |
| BE16-26(1952) without dot b | — | 4.00 | 7.00 | 12.00 | 20.00 | — |
| BE16-26(1952) with dot b | — | 4.00 | 7.00 | 12.00 | 20.00 | — |
| BE16-27(1953) with dots a & b | — | 6.00 | 10.00 | 18.00 | 30.00 | — |
| BE16-27(1953) without dot a | — | 23.00 | 30.00 | 40.00 | 50.00 | — |
| BE16-27(1953) without dot b | — | 6.00 | 10.00 | 18.00 | 30.00 | — |
| BE16-27(1953) without a & b | — | 6.00 | 10.00 | 18.00 | 30.00 | — |

**SRANG Y# 9 Composition:** Silver **Note:** 17.2-19.9 g. Obverse varieties exist. Struck at Dode Mint.

| Date | Mintage | VG | F | VF | XF | Unc |
|---|---|---|---|---|---|---|
| BE1(1909) | — | 125 | 185 | 275 | 400 | — |

**SRANG Y# 12 Composition:** Silver **Edge:** Plain **Note:** 18.0 - 18.3 grams. Varieties exist.

| Date | Mintage | VG | F | VF | XF | Unc |
|---|---|---|---|---|---|---|
| BE15-43(1909) | — | 140 | 225 | 325 | 450 | — |

**SRANG Y# A18 Weight:** 18.1000 g. **Composition:** Silver **Obverse:** Lion looking upwards **Edge:** Reeded **Note:** Varieties exist.

| Date | Mintage | VG | F | VF | XF | Unc |
|---|---|---|---|---|---|---|
| BE15-48(1914) | — | 400 | 700 | 1,200 | 1,750 | — |

**SRANG Y# A18.1 Composition:** Silver **Obverse:** Lion looking backwards **Note:** 17.8 - 18.3 grams. Struck at Mekyi mint.

| Date | Mintage | VG | F | VF | XF | Unc |
|---|---|---|---|---|---|---|
| BE15-52(1918) | — | 275 | 450 | 700 | 1,000 | — |
| BE15-53(1919) | — | 275 | 450 | 700 | 1,000 | — |

**1-1/2 SRANG Y# 24 Weight:** 5.0000 g. **Composition:** Silver **Note:** Struck at Tapchi Mint. Dates are written in words, not numerals. Obverse varieties exist.

| Date | Mintage | F | VF | XF | Unc | BU |
|---|---|---|---|---|---|---|
| BE16-10(1936) | — | 3.00 | 6.00 | 10.00 | 20.00 | — |
| BE16-11(1937) | — | 2.50 | 5.00 | 9.00 | 17.00 | — |
| BE16-12(1938) | — | 3.00 | 6.00 | 10.00 | 20.00 | — |
| BE16-20(1946) | — | 11.00 | 20.00 | 30.00 | 40.00 | — |

**3 SRANG Y# 25 Weight:** 11.3000 g. **Composition:** Silver **Note:** Struck at Tapchi Mint. Dates are written in words, not numerals. Varieties exist in lion.

| Date | Mintage | F | VF | XF | Unc | BU |
|---|---|---|---|---|---|---|
| BE16-7(1933) | — | 8.00 | 12.00 | 20.00 | 35.00 | — |
| BE16-8(1934) | — | 8.00 | 12.00 | 20.00 | 35.00 | — |

**3 SRANG** Y# 26 **Composition:** Silver **Note:** Dates are written in words, not numerals. Varieties in circular obverse and reverse inscriptions exist.

| Date | Mintage | F | VF | XF | Unc | BU |
|---|---|---|---|---|---|---|
| BE16-9(1935) | — | 7.00 | 10.00 | 18.00 | 30.00 | — |
| BE16-10(1936) | — | 6.00 | 9.00 | 15.00 | 25.00 | — |
| BE16-10/9(1936) | — | — | — | — | — | — |
| BE16-11(1937) | — | 6.00 | 9.00 | 15.00 | 25.00 | — |
| BE16-12(1938) | — | 6.00 | 9.00 | 15.00 | 25.00 | — |
| BE16-20(1946) | — | 20.00 | 25.00 | 30.00 | 40.00 | — |

**10 SRANG** Y# 29 **Composition:** Billon **Obverse:** Two suns **Reverse:** Numerals for denomination at center right **Note:** Struck at Tapchi Mint.

| Date | Mintage | F | VF | XF | Unc | BU |
|---|---|---|---|---|---|---|
| BE16-22(1948) | — | 4.50 | 9.00 | 18.00 | 40.00 | — |

**10 SRANG** Y# 29a **Composition:** Billon **Obverse:** Moon and sun **Note:** The "dot" is after the denomination. A modern medallic series dated 16-24 (1950) exists struck in copper-nickel, silver, and gold which were authorized by the Dalai Lama while in exile. Refer to "Unusual World Coins", 3rd edition, Krause Publications, 1992.

| Date | Mintage | F | VF | XF | Unc | BU |
|---|---|---|---|---|---|---|
| BE16-23(1949) With dot | — | 20.00 | 45.00 | 100 | 175 | — |
| BE16-24/23(1950) With dot | — | 7.00 | 15.00 | 30.00 | 60.00 | — |
| BE16-24/23(1950) with dot and moon cut over sun | — | 20.00 | 40.00 | 80.00 | 140 | — |
| BE16-24/22(1950) | — | 9.00 | 18.00 | 35.00 | 70.00 | — |
| BE16-24(1950) Moon cut over sun, denomination in words | — | 10.00 | 20.00 | 40.00 | 70.00 | — |
| BE16-24(1950) With dot | — | 12.00 | 22.00 | 50.00 | 90.00 | — |
| BE16-25/24(1951) With dot | — | 7.00 | 15.00 | 30.00 | 60.00 | — |
| BE16-25/24(1951) Without dot | — | 10.00 | 20.00 | 40.00 | 70.00 | — |
| BE16-25(1951) With dot | — | 7.00 | 15.00 | 30.00 | 60.00 | — |
| BE16-26/25(1952) Without dot | — | 7.00 | 15.00 | 30.00 | 60.00 | — |
| BE16-26(1952) With dot | — | 7.00 | 15.00 | 30.00 | 60.00 | — |

**10 SRANG** Y# 29.1 **Composition:** Billon **Reverse:** Words for denomination at center right

| Date | Mintage | F | VF | XF | Unc | BU |
|---|---|---|---|---|---|---|
| BE16-23/22(1949) | — | 12.00 | 20.00 | 35.00 | 70.00 | — |
| BE16-23(1949) With dot before and after ten | — | 6.00 | 10.00 | 20.00 | 40.00 | — |
| BE16-23(1949) Without dot after ten | — | 6.00 | 10.00 | 20.00 | 40.00 | — |

**10 SRANG** Y# 30 **Composition:** Billon **Note:** Struck at Dogu Mint. With dot after year.

| Date | Mintage | F | VF | XF | Unc | BU |
|---|---|---|---|---|---|---|
| BE16-24(1950) | — | 6.00 | 12.00 | 25.00 | 55.00 | — |
| BE16-24(1950) | — | 7.00 | 15.00 | 30.00 | 65.00 | — |
| BE16-25(1951) | — | 5.00 | 10.00 | 20.00 | 45.00 | — |

**20 SRANG** Y# 22 **Composition:** Gold **Obverse:** Eight Buddhist lucky symbols in outer circle **Note:** Struck at Ser-Khang Mint.

| Date | Mintage | F | VF | XF | Unc | BU |
|---|---|---|---|---|---|---|
| BE15-52(1918) with dot in reverse center | — | 425 | 575 | 800 | 1,100 | — |
| BE15-53(1919) with large circle in reverse center | — | 425 | 575 | 800 | 1,100 | — |
| **Note:** Silver and copper strikings for 15-53 exist and are believed to be forgeries | | | | | | |
| BE15-54(1920) without dot in reverse center | — | 425 | 575 | 800 | 1,100 | — |
| **Note:** Silver and copper strikings for 15-54 exist and are believed to be forgeries | | | | | | |
| BE15-55(1921) | — | 700 | 1,000 | 1,500 | 2,000 | — |

## TRADE COINAGE

1 Rupee = 3 Tangka

Total mintage of the 1 Rupee between 1902 and 1942 was between 25.5 and 27.5 million according to Chinese sources. In addition to the types illustrated above, large quantities of the following coins also circulated in Tibet: China Dollars, Y#318a, 329, and 345 plus Szechuan issues Y#449 and 459, and Indian Rupees, KM#473, 492, and 508. Similar crown-size pieces struck in silver and gold are fantasies.

Rupees exist with local merchant countermarks in Chinese, Tibetan, and other scripts.

**1/4 RUPEE** **Weight:** 2.8000 g. **Composition:** 0.9350 Silver **Ruler:** Hsüan-tung **Note:** Struck at Chengdu (Szechuan) Mint. Varieties exist.

| Date | Mintage | F | VF | XF | Unc | BU |
|---|---|---|---|---|---|---|
| ND(1904-05, 1912) | 120,000 | 40.00 | 60.00 | 90.00 | 150 | — |

**1/4 RUPEE** Y# 1 **Weight:** 2.8000 g. **Composition:** 0.9350 Silver **Note:** Struck at Chengdu (Szechuan) Mint. Varieties exist.

| Date | Mintage | F | VF | XF | Unc | BU |
|---|---|---|---|---|---|---|
| ND(1904-05) | 120,000 | 40.00 | 60.00 | 90.00 | 150 | — |
| ND(1904-05) | 120,000 | 40.00 | 60.00 | 90.00 | 150 | — |
| ND(1912) | Inc. above | 40.00 | 60.00 | 90.00 | 150 | — |

**1/4 RUPEE** Y# 1a **Weight:** 5.4500 g. **Composition:** Gold **Note:** Struck at Chengdu (Szechuan) Mint.

| Date | Mintage | F | VF | XF | Unc | BU |
|---|---|---|---|---|---|---|
| ND(1905) | — | 1,150 | 1,900 | 2,650 | 3,450 | — |

**1/4 RUPEE** Y# 2a **Weight:** 9.3800 g. **Composition:** Gold **Note:** Struck at Chengdu (Szechuan) Mint.

| Date | Mintage | F | VF | XF | Unc | BU |
|---|---|---|---|---|---|---|
| ND(1905) | — | 1,250 | 2,000 | 2,750 | 3,500 | — |

**1/2 RUPEE** Y# 2 **Weight:** 5.6000 g. **Composition:** 0.9350 Silver **Note:** Struck at Chengdu (Szechuan) Mint. Varieties exist.

| Date | Mintage | F | VF | XF | Unc | BU |
|---|---|---|---|---|---|---|
| ND(1904-05, 1907, 1912) | 130,000 | 50.00 | 75.00 | 125 | 200 | — |

**RUPEE** C# 20 **Composition:** Silver **Ruler:** Hsüan-tung

| Date | Mintage | Good | VG | F | VF | XF |
|---|---|---|---|---|---|---|
| ND(1902) | — | 750 | 1,000 | 1,500 | 2,250 | — |

**Note:** Struck in or near Tachienlu (today Kang Ting) and known as Lu Kuan Rupee. It was meant to replace the Indian Rupee which was used in eastern Tibet and western Szechuan (Sichuan) in the 19th century and is considered the forerunner of the Szechuan Rupee (Y#3). Varieties exist.

**RUPEE** Y# 3 **Weight:** 11.4000 g. **Composition:** 0.9350 Silver **Obverse:** Small bust without collar **Reverse:** Vertical rosette **Note:** Struck at Chengdu (Szechuan) Mint. Two reverse varieties exist.

| Date | Mintage | F | VF | XF | Unc | BU |
|---|---|---|---|---|---|---|
| ND(1902-11) | — | 25.00 | 45.00 | 70.00 | 110 | — |

**RUPEE** Y# 3.1 **Weight:** 11.4000 g. **Composition:** 0.9350 Silver **Reverse:** Horizontal rosette **Note:** Two reverse varieties exist.

| Date | Mintage | F | VF | XF | Unc | BU |
|---|---|---|---|---|---|---|
| ND(1902-11) | — | 20.00 | 35.00 | 50.00 | 85.00 | — |

**RUPEE** Y# 3b **Weight:** 20.6700 g. **Composition:** Gold **Note:** A strike with two obverses exists (20.40 grams)

| Date | Mintage | F | VF | XF | Unc | BU |
|---|---|---|---|---|---|---|
| ND(ca. 1903-05) | — | 900 | 1,200 | 1,750 | — | — |

**RUPEE** Y# 3.2 **Composition:** Silver **Obverse:** Small bust with collar **Reverse:** Vertical rosette **Note:** .0935-.800 silver. Struck at Kangding (Tachienlu) Mint after 1930. Two reverse varieties exist.

| Date | Mintage | F | VF | XF | Unc | BU |
|---|---|---|---|---|---|---|
| ND(1911-16, 1930-33) | — | 12.00 | 20.00 | 35.00 | 60.00 | — |

**RUPEE** Y# 3.3 **Composition:** 0.5000 Silver **Obverse:** Large bust **Note:** Struck at Kangding (Tachienlu) Mint. Varieties exist.

| Date | Mintage | F | VF | XF | Unc | BU |
|---|---|---|---|---|---|---|
| ND(1939-42) | — | 20.00 | 32.50 | 50.00 | 90.00 | — |

**RUPEE** Y# 3.4 **Composition:** Silver **Obverse:** Older bust, revised non-floral gown. **Reverse:** Vertical rosette **Note:** .650-.500 silver

| Date | Mintage | F | VF | XF | Unc | BU |
|---|---|---|---|---|---|---|
| ND(1933-39) | — | 20.00 | 32.50 | 50.00 | 90.00 | — |

**RUPEE** Y# 3.5 **Composition:** Silver **Reverse:** Horizontal rosette **Note:** .650-.500 silver.

| Date | Mintage | F | VF | XF | Unc | BU |
|---|---|---|---|---|---|---|
| ND(1933-39) | — | 30.00 | 50.00 | 80.00 | 150 | — |

**RUPEE** Y# 3a **Composition:** Debased Silver/Billon

| Date | Mintage | F | VF | XF | Unc | BU |
|---|---|---|---|---|---|---|
| ND(1939-42) | — | 8.00 | 15.00 | 30.00 | 60.00 | — |

**Note:** Coins with copper base and silver wash exist

## CUT COINAGE

Tibetan Rupees (Y3) due to their inscriptions also called Szechuan Rupees, have been cut in half and quarter for use as small change. The process of cutting the rupee frequently allowed customers to chip away from the coin's middle. In 1934 the treasury made cutting of the rupee illegal. To enforce this decree, all official payments had to be made with uncut coins; payment of smaller values was to be made with copper coins. However, the shortage of coinage made this decree impractical.

**1/4 RUPEE** Y# A5 **Note:** 1/4 segment of 1 Rupee, Y#3.

| Date | Mintage | VG | F | VF | XF | Unc |
|---|---|---|---|---|---|---|
| ND (1902-42) Rare | — | — | — | — | — | — |

**1/2 RUPEE** Y# B5 **Note:** 1/2 segment of 1 Rupee, Y#3.

| Date | Mintage | VG | F | VF | XF | Unc |
|---|---|---|---|---|---|---|
| ND (1902-42) Rare | — | — | — | — | — | — |

## TOKEN COINAGE

**4 SHO** KM# Tn1 **Composition:** Copper **Note:** 8.23-8.98 grams. Struck over 3 Sho, Y#27.

| Date | Mintage | VG | F | VF | XF | Unc |
|---|---|---|---|---|---|---|
| ND Rare | — | — | — | — | — | — |

**4 SHO** KM# Tn2 (KMtn2) **Composition:** Copper **Note:** Struck over 5 Sho, Y#28a and Y#28.1

| Date | Mintage | VG | F | VF | XF | Unc |
|---|---|---|---|---|---|---|
| ND | — | 75.00 | 100 | 130 | 160 | 220 |

## PATTERNS

Including off metal strikes

| KM# | Date | Mintage | Identification | Mkt Val |
|---|---|---|---|---|
| Pn1 | ND (1908) | — | 1/2 Sho. Silver. Hsien Feng | — |
| Pn2 | ND (1908) | — | Sho. Silver. Hsien Feng | — |
| Pn3 | ND (1909) | — | 10 Tam. Silver. 27.6700 g. | — |
| Pn4 | ND (1910) | — | Shokang. Silver. 3.6000 g. Y5 | — |
| Pn5 | BE15-57 (1923) | — | Sho. Copper. | — |
| Pn6 | BE15-57 (1923) | — | Sho. Brass. | — |
| | BE15-17 (1923) | — | 20 Tam. Brass. 7.2300 g. | — |
| Pn8 | BE15-57 (1923) | — | 20 Srang. Brass. 7.2300 g. | — |
| Pn9 | BE16-1 (1928) | — | Sho. Brass. 5.2600 g. | — |
| Pn10 | ND (1928) | — | Srang. Silver. | — |
| Pn11 | ND (1928) | — | 10 Tam. Silver. 12.6100 g. | — |
| Pn10 | ND (1928) | — | Srang. Silver. | — |
| Pn12 | ND (1929-30) | — | 10 Tam. Silver. 8.3000 g. | — |
| Pn13 | BE16-4 (1931) | — | 5 Sho. Silver. 5.0000 g. | — |
| Pn14 | Yr.925 (1951) | — | 25 Srang. Silver. 13.5200 g. | — |
| Pn15 | Yr.925 (1951) | — | 50 Srang. Copper. 17.3000 g. | — |
| Pn16 | Yr.925 (1951) | — | 50 Srang. Silver. 26.0000 g. | — |
| Pn17 | Yr.925 (1951) | — | 50 Srang. Silver. 26.0000 g. | — |
| Pn18 | ND (1951) | — | 50 Srang. Silver. 25.1000 g. | — |
| Pn17 | Yr.925 (1951) | — | 50 Srang. Silver. 26.0000 g. | — |
| | Yr.925 (1953) | — | 50 Srang. Silver. 26.4000 g. | — |
| Pn20 | Yr.927 (1953) | — | 5 Srang. Copper. 6.2000 g. | — |
| Pn21 | Yr. 927 (1953) | — | 5 Srang. Silver. 5.0000 g. | — |

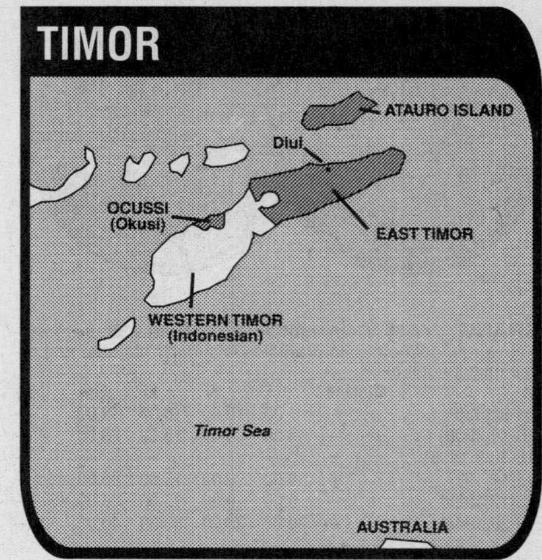


An island in the Lesser Sunda group, presently part of Indonesia but a treaty of 1859 fixed the division between Portugal and the Netherlands. Portugal discovered and owned the eastern half of the island including the Island of Atauro, located to its north, and the enclave of Ocussi situated on the northeastern portion of the island since 1524 and made coins for this colony. From 1865-1896, Timor was under the jurisdiction of Macao but was made a province in 1896 and became a colony in 1926. All of Timor fell under Japanese occupation from 1942-1945. In 1951 they became an overseas province.

**MONETARY SYSTEM**

100 Avos = 1 Pataca

# INDONESIAN PROVINCE

## COLONIAL COINAGE

100 Avos = 1 Pataca

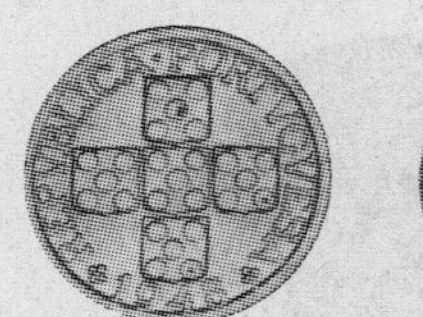

**10 AVOS** KM# 5 **Composition:** Bronze

| Date | Mintage | F | VF | XF | Unc | BU |
|---|---|---|---|---|---|---|
| 1945 | 50,000 | 120 | 220 | 400 | 1,000 | — |
| 1948 | 500,000 | 3.50 | 8.00 | 17.00 | 35.00 | — |
| 1951 | 6,250,000 | 1.50 | 3.50 | 7.50 | 15.00 | — |

**20 AVOS** KM# 6 **Composition:** Nickel-Bronze

| Date | Mintage | F | VF | XF | Unc | BU |
|---|---|---|---|---|---|---|
| 1945 | 50,000 | 16.00 | 35.00 | 70.00 | 175 | — |

**50 AVOS** KM# 7 **Weight:** 3.5000 g. **Composition:** 0.6500 Silver .0731 oz. ASW

| Date | Mintage | F | VF | XF | Unc | BU |
|---|---|---|---|---|---|---|
| 1945 | 100,000 | 45.00 | 90.00 | 135 | 275 | — |
| 1948 | 500,000 | 3.00 | 5.50 | 12.00 | 30.00 | — |
| 1951 | 6,250,000 | 2.00 | 3.75 | 8.50 | 18.00 | — |

## REFORM COINAGE

100 Centavos = 1 Escudo

**10 CENTAVOS** KM# 10 **Composition:** Bronze

| Date | Mintage | F | VF | XF | Unc | BU |
|---|---|---|---|---|---|---|
| 1958 | 1,000,000 | 1.00 | 3.00 | 15.00 | 35.00 | — |

**20 CENTAVOS** KM# 17 **Composition:** Bronze

| Date | Mintage | F | VF | XF | Unc | BU |
|---|---|---|---|---|---|---|
| 1970 | 1,000,000 | 0.45 | 1.00 | 2.50 | 5.00 | — |

**30 CENTAVOS** KM# 11 **Composition:** Bronze

| Date | Mintage | F | VF | XF | Unc | BU |
|---|---|---|---|---|---|---|
| 1958 | 2,000,000 | 0.75 | 1.50 | 12.00 | 30.00 | — |

**50 CENTAVOS** KM# 18 **Composition:** Bronze

| Date | Mintage | F | VF | XF | Unc | BU |
|---|---|---|---|---|---|---|
| 1970 | 1,000,000 | 0.45 | 1.00 | 2.75 | 6.00 | — |

**60 CENTAVOS** KM# 12 **Composition:** Copper-Nickel-Zinc

| Date | Mintage | F | VF | XF | Unc | BU |
|---|---|---|---|---|---|---|
| 1958 | 1,000,000 | 1.25 | 2.75 | 12.00 | 30.00 | — |

**ESCUDO** KM# 13 **Composition:** Copper-Nickel-Zinc

| Date | Mintage | F | VF | XF | Unc | BU |
|---|---|---|---|---|---|---|
| 1958 | 1,200,000 | 2.00 | 4.00 | 40.00 | 80.00 | — |

**ESCUDO** KM# 19 **Composition:** Bronze

| Date | Mintage | F | VF | XF | Unc | BU |
|---|---|---|---|---|---|---|
| 1970 | 1,200,000 | 1.50 | 3.50 | 9.00 | 18.00 | — |

**2-1/2 ESCUDOS** KM# 20 **Composition:** Copper-Nickel

| Date | Mintage | F | VF | XF | Unc | BU |
|---|---|---|---|---|---|---|
| 1970 | 1,000,000 | 0.75 | 1.50 | 3.50 | 7.50 | — |

**3 ESCUDOS** KM# 14 **Weight:** 3.5000 g. **Composition:** 0.6500 Silver .0731 oz. ASW

| Date | Mintage | F | VF | XF | Unc | BU |
|---|---|---|---|---|---|---|
| 1958 | 1,000,000 | 3.00 | 5.00 | 10.00 | 25.00 | — |

**5 ESCUDOS** KM# 21 **Composition:** Copper-Nickel

| Date | Mintage | F | VF | XF | Unc | BU |
|---|---|---|---|---|---|---|
| 1970 | 1,200,000 | 1.50 | 3.50 | 8.00 | 16.00 | — |

**6 ESCUDOS** KM# 15 **Weight:** 7.0000 g. **Composition:** 0.6500 Silver .1463 oz. ASW

| Date | Mintage | F | VF | XF | Unc | BU |
|---|---|---|---|---|---|---|
| 1958 | 1,000,000 | 3.50 | 6.00 | 12.50 | 25.00 | — |

**10 ESCUDOS** KM# 16 **Weight:** 7.0000 g. **Composition:** 0.6500 Silver .1463 oz. ASW

| Date | Mintage | F | VF | XF | Unc | BU |
|---|---|---|---|---|---|---|
| 1964 | 600,000 | 3.50 | 6.00 | 12.50 | 25.00 | — |

**10 ESCUDOS** KM# 22 **Composition:** Copper-Nickel

| Date | Mintage | F | VF | XF | Unc | BU |
|---|---|---|---|---|---|---|
| 1970 | 700,000 | 3.00 | 5.50 | 12.00 | 24.00 | — |

# TOGO

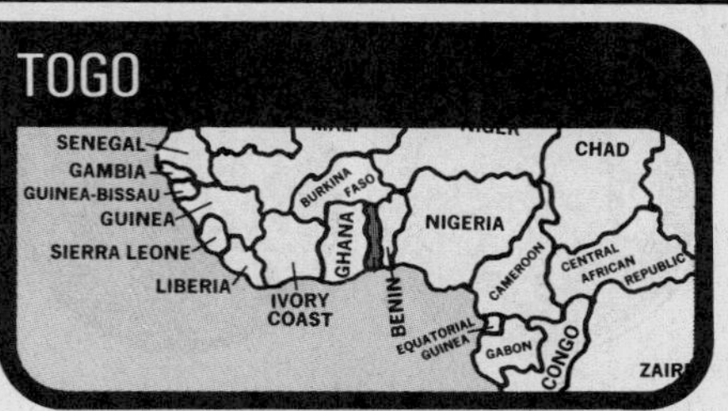


The Republic of Togo (formerly part of German Togoland), situated on the Gulf of Guinea in West Africa between Ghana and Dahomey, has an area of 21,622 sq.mi. (56,790 sq. km.) and a population of *3.4 million. Capital: Lome. Agriculture and herding, the production of dyewoods, and the mining of phosphates and iron ore are the chief industries. Copra, phosphates and coffee are exported.

Although Brazilians were the first traders to settle in Togo, Germany achieved possession, in 1884, by inducing coastal chiefs to place their territories under German protection. The German protectorate was extended international recognition at the Berlin conference of 1885 and its ultimate boundaries delimited by treaties with France in 1897 and with Britain in 1904. Anglo-French forces occupied Togoland in 1914, subsequently becoming a League of Nations mandate and a U.N. trusteeship divided, for administrative purpose, between Great Britain and France. The British portion voted in 1957 for incorporation with Ghana. The French portion became the independent Republic of Togo on April 27, 1960.

**RULERS**
German, 1884-1914
Anglo - French, 1914-1957
French, 1957-1960

**MINT MARKS**
(a) - Paris, privy marks only

**MONETARY SYSTEM**
100 Centimes = 1 Franc

## FRENCH COLONIAL

### U.N. Trusteeship

## STANDARD COINAGE

100 Centimes = 1 Franc

**50 CENTIMES** KM# 1 **Composition:** Aluminum-Bronze

| Date | Mintage | F | VF | XF | Unc | BU |
|---|---|---|---|---|---|---|
| 1924(a) | 3,691,000 | 2.50 | 7.00 | 20.00 | 80.00 | — |
| 1925(a) | 2,064,000 | 3.00 | 8.00 | 22.00 | 90.00 | — |
| 1926(a) | 445,000 | 9.00 | 25.00 | 85.00 | 250 | — |

**FRANC** KM# 2 **Composition:** Aluminum-Bronze

| Date | Mintage | F | VF | XF | Unc | BU |
|---|---|---|---|---|---|---|
| 1924(a) | 3,472,000 | 3.50 | 7.50 | 40.00 | 125 | — |
| 1925(a) | 2,768,000 | 4.00 | 9.00 | 45.00 | 140 | — |

**FRANC** KM# 4 **Composition:** Aluminum

| Date | Mintage | F | VF | XF | Unc | BU |
|---|---|---|---|---|---|---|
| 1948(a) | 5,000,000 | 2.50 | 7.00 | 22.00 | 55.00 | — |

**2 FRANCS** KM# 3 **Composition:** Aluminum-Bronze

| Date | Mintage | F | VF | XF | Unc | BU |
|---|---|---|---|---|---|---|
| 1924(a) | 750,000 | 6.00 | 15.00 | 60.00 | 250 | — |
| 1925(a) | 580,000 | 7.00 | 18.00 | 80.00 | 300 | — |

**2 FRANCS** KM# 5 **Composition:** Aluminum **Note:** Similar to 1 Franc, KM#4.

| Date | Mintage | F | VF | XF | Unc | BU |
|---|---|---|---|---|---|---|
| 1948(a) | 5,000,000 | 3.50 | 9.00 | 28.00 | 60.00 | — |

**5 FRANCS** KM# 6 **Composition:** Aluminum-Bronze

| Date | Mintage | F | VF | XF | Unc | BU |
|---|---|---|---|---|---|---|
| 1956(a) | 10,000,000 | 1.50 | 3.00 | 6.00 | 12.50 | — |

# REPUBLIC

## STANDARD COINAGE

100 Centimes = 1 Franc

**5000 FRANCS** KM# 8 **Weight:** 24.3600 g. **Composition:** 0.9250 Silver .7245 oz. ASW **Subject:** 10th Year of General Eyadema as President

| Date | Mintage | F | VF | XF | Unc | BU |
|---|---|---|---|---|---|---|
| 1977 Proof | — | Value: 60.00 | | | | |

**10000 FRANCS** KM# 9 **Weight:** 49.3200 g. **Composition:** 0.9250 Silver 1.4669 oz. ASW **Subject:** 10th Year of General Eyadema as President

| Date | Mintage | F | VF | XF | Unc | BU |
|---|---|---|---|---|---|---|
| 1977 Proof | — | Value: 75.00 | | | | |

**15000 FRANCS** KM# 10 **Weight:** 4.4800 g. **Composition:** 0.9170 Gold .1320 oz. AGW **Subject:** 10th Year of General Eyadema as President

| Date | Mintage | F | VF | XF | Unc | BU |
|---|---|---|---|---|---|---|
| 1977 Proof | — | Value: 125 | | | | |

**25000 FRANCS** KM# 11 **Weight:** 9.0000 g. **Composition:** 0.9170 Gold .2653 oz. AGW **Subject:** 10th Year of General Eyadema as President

| Date | Mintage | F | VF | XF | Unc | BU |
|---|---|---|---|---|---|---|
| 1977 Proof | — | Value: 245 | | | | |

**50000 FRANCS** KM# 12 **Weight:** 18.0000 g. **Composition:** 0.9170 Gold .5306 oz. AGW **Subject:** 10th Year of General Eyadema as President **Note:** Similar to 25,000 Francs, KM#11.

| Date | Mintage | F | VF | XF | Unc | BU |
|---|---|---|---|---|---|---|
| 1977 Proof | — | Value: 485 | | | | |

## ESSAIS

| KM# | Date | Mintage | Identification | Mkt Val |
|---|---|---|---|---|
| E1 | 1924(a) | — | 50 Centimes. KM#1. | 100 |
| E2 | 1924(a) | — | Franc. KM#2. | 150 |
| E3 | 1924(a) | — | 2 Francs. KM#3. | 200 |
| E4 | 1948(a) | 2,000 | Franc. Copper-Nickel. KM#4. | 30.00 |
| E5 | 1948(a) | 2,000 | 2 Francs. Copper-Nickel. KM#5. | 37.50 |
| E6 | 1956(a) | 2,300 | 5 Francs. KM#6. | 15.00 |
| E7 | 1956(a) | 2,300 | 10 Francs. KM#7. | 35.00 |
| E8 | 1956(a) | 2,300 | 25 Francs. | 45.00 |
| E9 | 1977 | 25 | 5000 Francs. Aluminum. KM#8. | 35.00 |
| E10 | 1977 | 20 | 5000 Francs. Copper. KM#8. | 80.00 |
| E11 | 1977 | 25 | 10000 Francs. Aluminum. KM#9. | 35.00 |
| E12 | 1977 | 20 | 10000 Francs. Copper. KM#9. | 100 |
| E13 | 1977 | 25 | 15000 Francs. Aluminum. KM#10. | 35.00 |
| E14 | 1977 | 20 | 15000 Francs. Copper. KM#10. | 70.00 |
| E15 | 1977 | 25 | 25000 Francs. Aluminum. KM#11. | 35.00 |
| E16 | 1977 | 20 | 25000 Francs. Copper. KM#11. | 90.00 |

## PIEFORTS

| KM# | Date | Mintage | Identification | Mkt Val |
|---|---|---|---|---|
| P1 | 1977 | 5 | 5000 Francs. Copper. KM#8. | 130 |
| P2 | 1977 | 5 | 5000 Francs. Silver. 48.7200 g. KM#8. | 250 |
| P3 | 1977 | 5 | 10000 Francs. Copper. KM#9. | 160 |
| P3a | 1977 | 5 | 10000 Francs. Silver. KM#9. | 275 |
| P4 | 1977 | 5 | 15000 Francs. Copper. KM#10. | 110 |
| P5 | 1977 | 5 | 25000 Francs. Copper. KM#11. | 140 |
| P6 | 1977 | — | 25000 Francs. Gold. KM#11. | 1,000 |

## PIEFORTS WITH ESSAIS

| KM# | Date | Mintage | Identification | Mkt Val |
|---|---|---|---|---|
| PE1 | 1948(a) | 104 | Franc. KM#4. | 70.00 |
| PE2 | 1948(a) | 104 | 2 Francs. KM#5. | 100 |

# TOKELAU ISLANDS

Tokelau or Union Islands, a New Zealand Territory located in the South Pacific 2,100 miles (3,379 km.) northeast of New Zealand and 300 miles (483 km.) north of Samoa, has an area of 4 sq. mi. (10 sq. km.) and a population of *2,000. Geographically, the group consists of four atolls - Atafu, Nukunono, Fakaofo and Swains – but the last belongs to American Samoa (and the United States claims the other three). The people are of Polynesian origin; Samoan is the official language. The New Zealand Minister for Foreign Affairs governs the islands; councils of family elders handle local government at the village level. The chief settlement is Fenuafala, on Fakaofo. It is connected by wireless with the offices of the New Zealand Administrative Center, located at Apia, Western Samoa. Subsistence farming and the production of copra for export are the main occupations. Revenue is also derived from the sale of postage stamps and, since 1978,coins.

Great Britain annexed the group of islands in 1889. They were added to the Gilbert and Ellice Islands colony in1916. In 1926, they were brought under the jurisdiction of Western Samoa, which was held as a mandate of the League of Nations by New Zealand. They were declared a part of New Zealand in 1948.

Tokelau Islands issued its first coin in 1978, a "$1 TahiTala," Tokelauan for "One Dollar." The coin has a number of unusual features. The edge is inscribed, "Tokelau's First Coin." The obverse portrait of Queen Elizabeth II is identified by neither name nor title. The three dots of each such group comprising the obverse border symbolize the three principal atolls.

**RULERS**
British

**MINT MARKS**
PM - Pobjoy

# NEW ZEALAND TERRITORY

## STANDARD COINAGE

**TALA** KM# 1 **Composition:** Copper-Nickel

| Date | Mintage | F | VF | XF | Unc | BU |
|---|---|---|---|---|---|---|
| 1978 | 10,000 | — | 1.00 | 2.00 | 7.50 | — |

**TALA** KM# 1a **Weight:** 27.2500 g. **Composition:** 0.9250 Silver .8104 oz. ASW

| Date | Mintage | F | VF | XF | Unc | BU |
|---|---|---|---|---|---|---|
| 1978 Proof | 5,000 | Value: 22.50 | | | | |

**TALA** KM# 2 **Composition:** Copper-Nickel

| Date | Mintage | F | VF | XF | Unc | BU |
|---|---|---|---|---|---|---|
| 1979 | — | — | 1.00 | 2.00 | 6.50 | — |

**TALA** **KM# 2a** **Weight:** 27.2500 g. **Composition:** 0.9250 Silver .8104 oz. ASW

| Date | Mintage | F | VF | XF | Unc | BU |
|---|---|---|---|---|---|---|
| 1979 Proof | — | Value: 20.00 | | | | |

**TALA** **KM# 3** **Composition:** Copper-Nickel **Reverse:** Coconut Crab

| Date | Mintage | F | VF | XF | Unc | BU |
|---|---|---|---|---|---|---|
| 1980 | 10,000 | — | 1.00 | 2.00 | 5.00 | — |

**TALA** **KM# 3a** **Weight:** 27.2500 g. **Composition:** 0.9250 Silver .8104 oz. ASW

| Date | Mintage | F | VF | XF | Unc | BU |
|---|---|---|---|---|---|---|
| 1980 Proof | 6,004 | Value: 22.50 | | | | |

**TALA** **KM# 4** **Composition:** Copper-Nickel **Reverse:** Frigate Bird

| Date | Mintage | F | VF | XF | Unc | BU |
|---|---|---|---|---|---|---|
| 1981 | 6,500 | — | 1.00 | 2.00 | 5.00 | — |

**TALA** **KM# 4a** **Weight:** 27.2500 g. **Composition:** 0.9250 Silver .8104 oz. ASW

| Date | Mintage | F | VF | XF | Unc | BU |
|---|---|---|---|---|---|---|
| 1981 Proof | 6,500 | Value: 22.50 | | | | |

**TALA** **KM# 5** **Composition:** Copper-Nickel **Reverse:** Outrigger Canoe

| Date | Mintage | F | VF | XF | Unc | BU |
|---|---|---|---|---|---|---|
| 1982 | 10,000 | — | 1.00 | 2.00 | 3.50 | — |

**TALA** **KM# 5a** **Weight:** 27.2500 g. **Composition:** 0.9250 Silver .8104 oz. ASW

| Date | Mintage | F | VF | XF | Unc | BU |
|---|---|---|---|---|---|---|
| 1982 Proof | 5,000 | Value: 25.00 | | | | |

**TALA** **KM# 6** **Composition:** Copper-Nickel

| Date | Mintage | F | VF | XF | Unc | BU |
|---|---|---|---|---|---|---|
| 1983 | 2,000 | — | 1.00 | 2.50 | 6.00 | — |

**5 TALA** **KM# 7** **Weight:** 28.2800 g. **Composition:** 0.9250 Silver .8411 oz. ASW **Subject:** Water Conservation **Note:** Similar to 1 Tala, KM#6.

| Date | Mintage | F | VF | XF | Unc | BU |
|---|---|---|---|---|---|---|
| 1983 Proof | 1,000 | Value: 45.00 | | | | |

**5 TALA** **KM# 8.1** **Weight:** 27.0500 g. **Composition:** 0.9250 Silver .8045 oz. ASW **Reverse:** Fisherman in Sailboat **Edge:** Plain

| Date | Mintage | F | VF | XF | Unc | BU |
|---|---|---|---|---|---|---|
| 1984 | 1,500 | — | — | — | 28.50 | — |

**5 TALA** **KM# 8.2** **Weight:** 27.0500 g. **Composition:** 0.9250 Silver .8045 oz. ASW **Edge:** Reeded

| Date | Mintage | F | VF | XF | Unc | BU |
|---|---|---|---|---|---|---|
| 1984 Proof | 500 | Value: 45.00 | | | | |

**5 TALA** **KM# 10** **Weight:** 27.0500 g. **Composition:** 0.9250 Silver .8045 oz. ASW **Series:** Olympics **Reverse:** Javelin Thrower

| Date | Mintage | F | VF | XF | Unc | BU |
|---|---|---|---|---|---|---|
| 1988 | 20,000 | — | — | — | 20.00 | — |

**5 TALA** **KM# 9** **Weight:** 27.2100 g. **Composition:** 0.9250 Silver .8093 oz. ASW **Subject:** Captain John Byron and HMS Dolphin **Edge:** Reeded

| Date | Mintage | F | VF | XF | Unc | BU |
|---|---|---|---|---|---|---|
| 1989 Proof | 500 | Value: 35.00 | | | | |

**5 TALA** **KM# 11** **Composition:** Copper-Nickel **Subject:** 50th Anniversary of Attack on Pearl Harbor

| Date | Mintage | F | VF | XF | Unc | BU |
|---|---|---|---|---|---|---|
| 1991 Proof-like | — | — | — | — | 8.50 | — |

**5 TALA** **KM# 13** **Composition:** Copper-Nickel **Subject:** Battle of Guadalcanal

| Date | Mintage | F | VF | XF | Unc | BU |
|---|---|---|---|---|---|---|
| 1991 Proof-like | — | — | — | — | 8.00 | — |

**5 TALA** **KM# 14** **Composition:** Copper-Nickel **Subject:** General Dwight Eisenhower

| Date | Mintage | F | VF | XF | Unc | BU |
|---|---|---|---|---|---|---|
| 1991 Proof-like | — | — | — | — | 8.00 | — |

**5 TALA** **KM# 15** **Composition:** Copper-Nickel **Subject:** Raising the Flag on Iwo Jima

| Date | Mintage | F | VF | XF | Unc | BU |
|---|---|---|---|---|---|---|
| 1991 Proof-like | — | — | — | — | 8.00 | — |

**5 TALA** **KM# 16** **Weight:** 31.4700 g. **Composition:** 0.9250 Silver .9359 oz. ASW **Subject:** First Lunar Orbit

| Date | Mintage | F | VF | XF | Unc | BU |
|---|---|---|---|---|---|---|
| 1993 Proof | 10,000 | Value: 35.00 | | | | |

**5 TALA** **KM# 17** **Weight:** 31.4700 g. **Composition:** 0.9250 Silver .9359 oz. ASW **Series:** Endangered Wildlife **Reverse:** Iguana

| Date | Mintage | F | VF | XF | Unc | BU |
|---|---|---|---|---|---|---|
| 1993 Proof | 15,000 | Value: 37.50 | | | | |

**5 TALA** **KM# 18** **Weight:** 31.4700 g. **Composition:** 0.9250 Silver .9359 oz. ASW **Subject:** H.M.S. Pandora

| Date | Mintage | F | VF | XF | Unc | BU |
|---|---|---|---|---|---|---|
| 1993 Proof | 15,000 | Value: 35.00 | | | | |

**5 TALA** **KM# 19** **Weight:** 31.4700 g. **Composition:** 0.9250 Silver .9359 oz. ASW **Series:** Olympics **Subject:** Swimming

| Date | Mintage | F | VF | XF | Unc | BU |
|---|---|---|---|---|---|---|
| 1994 Proof | 40,000 | Value: 25.00 | | | | |

**5 TALA** **KM# 20** **Weight:** 31.4700 g. **Composition:** 0.9250 Silver .9359 oz. ASW **Subject:** World Cup Soccer

| Date | Mintage | F | VF | XF | Unc | BU |
|---|---|---|---|---|---|---|
| 1994 Proof | 25,000 | Value: 28.00 | | | | |

**5 TALA** **KM# 21** **Weight:** 31.4700 g. **Composition:** 0.9250 Silver .9359 oz. ASW **Series:** Protect Our World **Subject:** Swamp Scene

| Date | Mintage | F | VF | XF | Unc | BU |
|---|---|---|---|---|---|---|
| 1994 Proof | 10,000 | Value: 37.50 | | | | |

**5 TALA** **KM# 22** **Weight:** 31.4700 g. **Composition:** 0.9250 Silver .9359 oz. ASW **Series:** Olympics **Subject:** Sailboarding

| Date | Mintage | F | VF | XF | Unc | BU |
|---|---|---|---|---|---|---|
| 1994 Proof | 50,000 | Value: 35.00 | | | | |

**5 TALA** **KM# 23** **Weight:** 31.4700 g. **Composition:** 0.9250 Silver .9359 oz. ASW **Reverse:** Queen Mother & Daughter seated, holding Son

| Date | Mintage | F | VF | XF | Unc | BU |
|---|---|---|---|---|---|---|
| 1995 Proof | 30,000 | Value: 40.00 | | | | |

**5 TALA** **KM# 25** **Weight:** 31.4700 g. **Composition:** 0.9250 Silver .9359 oz. ASW **Subject:** H.M.S. Dolphin **Obverse:** Queen's portrait **Reverse:** Sailing ship **Edge:** Reeded **Size:** 38.5 mm.

| Date | Mintage | F | VF | XF | Unc | BU |
|---|---|---|---|---|---|---|
| 1998 Proof | — | Value: 40.00 | | | | |

**50 TALA** **KM# 12** **Weight:** 31.1030 g. **Composition:** 0.9990 Silver 1 oz. ASW **Subject:** 50th Anniversary of Attack on Pearl Harbor **Note:** Similar to 5 Tala, KM#11.

| Date | Mintage | F | VF | XF | Unc | BU |
|---|---|---|---|---|---|---|
| 1991 Proof | 50,000 | Value: 55.00 | | | | |

**100 TALA** **KM# 24** **Weight:** 32.1480 g. **Composition:** 0.9990 Silver 1 oz. ASW **Reverse:** Three War Ships **Note:** Illustration reduced - actual size = 100 millimeters.

| Date | Mintage | F | VF | XF | Unc | BU |
|---|---|---|---|---|---|---|
| 1996 Proof | 1,500 | Value: 375 | | | | |

## TONGA

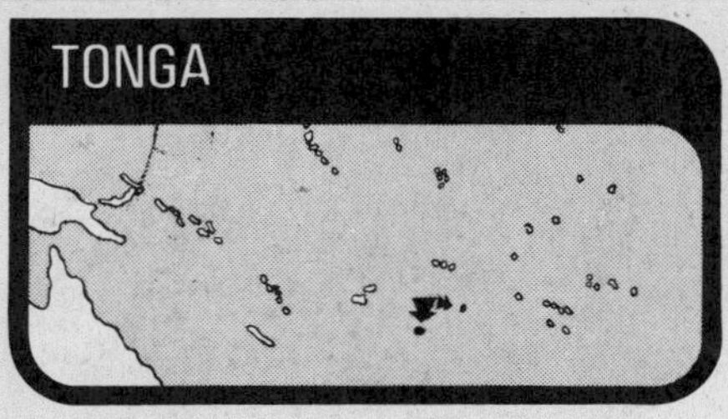

The Kingdom of Tonga (or Friendly Islands), a member of the British Commonwealth, is an archipelago situated in the southern Pacific Ocean south of Western Samoa and east of Fiji comprising 150 islands. Tonga has an area of270 sq. mi. (748 sq. km.) and a population of *100,000.Capital: Nuku'alofa. Primarily agricultural, the kingdom exports bananas and copra.

Dutch navigators Willem Schouten and Jacob Lemaire were the first Europeans to visit Tonga in 1616. They were followed by the noted Dutch explorer Abel Tasman who visited the Tongatapu group in 1643. No further European contact was made until 1773 when British navigator Capt. James Cook arrived and, impressed by the peaceful deportment of the natives, named the islands the Friendly Islands. Within a few years of Cook's visit, Tonga was embroiled in a civil war that lasted until the great chief Taufa'ahau, who reigned as Siasoi Tupou I (1845-93), was converted to Christianity and brought unity and peace to the islands. Tonga became a self-governing protectorate of Great Britain in 1900 and a fully independent state on June 4, 1970. The monarchy is a member of the Commonwealth of Nations. King Taufa'ahau is Head of State and Government.

**RULERS**

Queen Salote, 1918-1965
King Taufa'ahau IV, 1967—

**MONETARY SYSTEM**

16 Pounds = 1 Koula

# KINGDOM

## STANDARD COINAGE

16 Pounds = 1 Koula

**1/4 KOULA** **KM# 1** **Weight:** 8.1250 g. **Composition:** 0.9160 Gold .2395 oz. AGW

| Date | Mintage | F | VF | XF | Unc | BU |
|---|---|---|---|---|---|---|
| 1962 | — | — | — | — | 110 | — |
| 1962 Proof | 6,300 | Value: 125 | | | | |

**1/4 KOULA** **KM# 1a** **Composition:** Platinum APW

| Date | Mintage | F | VF | XF | Unc | BU |
|---|---|---|---|---|---|---|
| 1962 Proof | — | Value: 500 | | | | |

**1/2 KOULA** **KM# 2** **Weight:** 16.2500 g. **Composition:** 0.9160 Gold .4789 oz. AGW

| Date | Mintage | F | VF | XF | Unc | BU |
|---|---|---|---|---|---|---|
| 1962 | — | — | — | — | 210 | — |
| 1962 Proof | 3,000 | Value: 240 | | | | |

**1/2 KOULA** **KM# 2a** **Composition:** Platinum APW

| Date | Mintage | F | VF | XF | Unc | BU |
|---|---|---|---|---|---|---|
| 1962 Proof | — | Value: 750 | | | | |

**KOULA** **KM# 3** **Weight:** 32.5000 g. **Composition:** 0.9160 Gold .9278 oz. AGW

| Date | Mintage | F | VF | XF | Unc | BU |
|---|---|---|---|---|---|---|
| 1962 | — | — | — | — | 435 | — |
| 1962 Proof | — | Value: 575 | | | | |

**KOULA** **KM# 3a** **Composition:** Platinum APW

| Date | Mintage | F | VF | XF | Unc | BU |
|---|---|---|---|---|---|---|
| 1962 Proof | — | Value: 1,000 | | | | |

## DECIMAL COINAGE

100 Senti = 1 Pa'anga; 100 Pa'anga = 1 Hau

**SENITI** **KM# 4** **Composition:** Bronze **Reverse:** Giant Tortoise

| Date | Mintage | F | VF | XF | Unc | BU |
|---|---|---|---|---|---|---|
| 1967 | 500,000 | — | 0.10 | 0.15 | 1.50 | — |
| 1967 Proof | — | Value: 2.00 | | | | |

**SENITI** **KM# 27** **Composition:** Bronze

| Date | Mintage | F | VF | XF | Unc | BU |
|---|---|---|---|---|---|---|
| 1968 | 500,000 | — | 0.10 | 0.15 | 1.50 | — |
| 1968 Proof | — | Value: 2.00 | | | | |

**SENITI** **KM# 27a** **Composition:** Brass

| Date | Mintage | F | VF | XF | Unc | BU |
|---|---|---|---|---|---|---|
| 1974 | 500,000 | — | 0.10 | 0.15 | 1.00 | — |

**SENITI** **KM# 42** **Composition:** Bronze **Series:** F.A.O.

| Date | Mintage | F | VF | XF | Unc | BU |
|---|---|---|---|---|---|---|
| 1975 | 1,000,000 | — | — | 0.10 | 0.50 | — |
| 1979 | 1,000,000 | — | — | 0.10 | 0.50 | — |

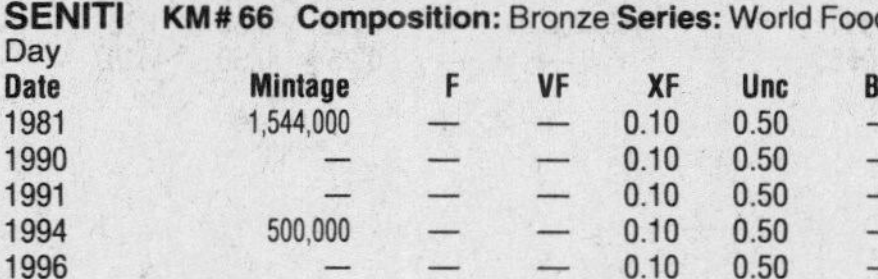


**SENITI** **KM# 66** **Composition:** Bronze **Series:** World Food Day

| Date | Mintage | F | VF | XF | Unc | BU |
|---|---|---|---|---|---|---|
| 1981 | 1,544,000 | — | — | 0.10 | 0.50 | — |
| 1990 | — | — | — | 0.10 | 0.50 | — |
| 1991 | — | — | — | 0.10 | 0.50 | — |
| 1994 | 500,000 | — | — | 0.10 | 0.50 | — |
| 1996 | — | — | — | 0.10 | 0.50 | — |

**2 SENITI** **KM# 5** **Composition:** Bronze **Reverse:** Giant Tortoise

| Date | Mintage | F | VF | XF | Unc | BU |
|---|---|---|---|---|---|---|
| 1967 | 500,000 | — | 0.10 | 0.20 | 2.00 | — |
| 1967 Proof | — | Value: 2.50 | | | | |

**2 SENITI** **KM# 28** **Composition:** Bronze

| Date | Mintage | F | VF | XF | Unc | BU |
|---|---|---|---|---|---|---|
| 1968 | 200,000 | — | 0.10 | 0.20 | 2.50 | — |
| 1968 Proof | — | Value: 2.00 | | | | |
| 1974 | 25,000 | — | 0.10 | 0.20 | 2.50 | — |

**2 SENITI** **KM# 43** **Composition:** Bronze **Series:** F.A.O.

| Date | Mintage | F | VF | XF | Unc | BU |
|---|---|---|---|---|---|---|
| 1975 | 400,000 | — | — | 0.15 | 0.65 | — |
| 1979 | 500,000 | — | — | 0.15 | 0.65 | — |

**2 SENITI** **KM# 67** **Composition:** Bronze **Series:** World Food Day

| Date | Mintage | F | VF | XF | Unc | BU |
|---|---|---|---|---|---|---|
| 1981 | 1,102,000 | — | — | 0.15 | 0.65 | — |
| 1990 | — | — | — | 0.15 | 0.65 | — |
| 1991 | — | — | — | 0.15 | 0.65 | — |
| 1994 | 250,000 | — | — | 0.15 | 0.65 | — |
| 1996 | — | — | — | 0.15 | 0.65 | — |

**5 SENITI** **KM# 6** **Composition:** Copper-Nickel

| Date | Mintage | F | VF | XF | Unc | BU |
|---|---|---|---|---|---|---|
| 1967 | 300,000 | — | 0.10 | 0.25 | 1.25 | — |
| 1967 Proof | — | Value: 2.50 | | | | |

**5 SENITI** **KM# 29** **Composition:** Copper-Nickel

| Date | Mintage | F | VF | XF | Unc | BU |
|---|---|---|---|---|---|---|
| 1968 | 100,000 | — | 0.10 | 0.25 | 1.25 | — |
| 1968 Proof | — | Value: 2.50 | | | | |
| 1974 | 75,000 | — | 0.10 | 0.25 | 1.25 | — |

**5 SENITI** **KM# 44** **Composition:** Copper-Nickel **Series:** F.A.O.

| Date | Mintage | F | VF | XF | Unc | BU |
|---|---|---|---|---|---|---|
| 1975 | 100,000 | — | 0.10 | 0.25 | 1.00 | — |
| 1977 | 110,000 | — | 0.10 | 0.25 | 1.00 | — |
| 1979 | 100,000 | — | 0.10 | 0.25 | 1.00 | — |

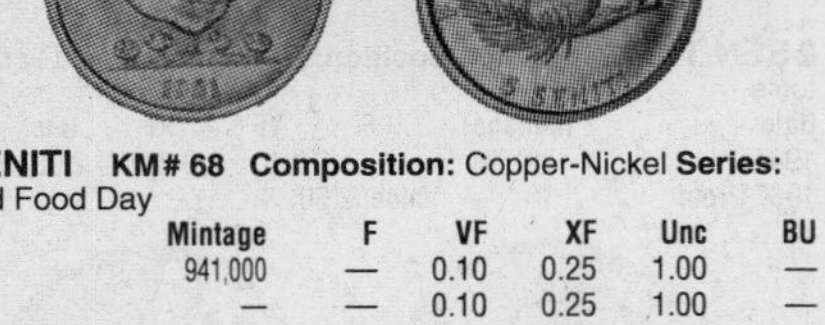

**5 SENITI** **KM# 68** **Composition:** Copper-Nickel **Series:** World Food Day

| Date | Mintage | F | VF | XF | Unc | BU |
|---|---|---|---|---|---|---|
| 1981 | 941,000 | — | 0.10 | 0.25 | 1.00 | — |
| 1990 | — | — | 0.10 | 0.25 | 1.00 | — |
| 1991 | — | — | — | 0.25 | 1.00 | — |
| 1994 | 200,000 | — | 0.10 | 0.25 | 1.00 | — |
| 1996 | — | — | 0.10 | 0.25 | 1.00 | — |

**10 SENITI** **KM# 7** **Composition:** Copper-Nickel

| Date | Mintage | F | VF | XF | Unc | BU |
|---|---|---|---|---|---|---|
| 1967 | 300,000 | — | 0.20 | 0.35 | 1.50 | — |
| 1967 Proof | — | Value: 3.00 | | | | |

**10 SENITI** **KM# 30** **Composition:** Copper-Nickel

| Date | Mintage | F | VF | XF | Unc | BU |
|---|---|---|---|---|---|---|
| 1968 | 100,000 | — | 0.20 | 0.40 | 1.50 | — |
| 1968 Proof | — | Value: 3.00 | | | | |
| 1974 | 50,000 | — | 0.25 | 0.50 | 1.50 | — |

**10 SENITI** **KM# 45** **Composition:** Copper-Nickel **Series:** F.A.O.

| Date | Mintage | F | VF | XF | Unc | BU |
|---|---|---|---|---|---|---|
| 1975 | 75,000 | — | 0.20 | 0.30 | 1.25 | — |
| 1977 | 25,000 | — | 0.20 | 0.30 | 1.25 | — |
| 1979 | 100,000 | — | 0.20 | 0.30 | 1.25 | — |

**10 SENITI** **KM# 69** **Composition:** Copper-Nickel **Series:** World Food Day

| Date | Mintage | F | VF | XF | Unc | BU |
|---|---|---|---|---|---|---|
| 1981 | 712,000 | — | 0.20 | 0.30 | 1.25 | — |
| 1990 | — | — | 0.20 | 0.30 | 1.00 | — |
| 1991 | — | — | 0.20 | 0.30 | 1.00 | — |
| 1994 | 140,000 | — | 0.20 | 0.30 | 1.00 | — |
| 1996 | — | — | 0.20 | 0.30 | 1.00 | — |

**20 SENITI** **KM# 8** **Composition:** Copper-Nickel

| Date | Mintage | F | VF | XF | Unc | BU |
|---|---|---|---|---|---|---|
| 1967 | 150,000 | — | 0.25 | 0.50 | 1.75 | — |
| 1967 Proof | — | Value: 3.50 | | | | |

**20 SENITI** **KM# 13** **Composition:** Copper-Nickel **Subject:** Coronation of Taufa'ahau Tupou IV

| Date | Mintage | F | VF | XF | Unc | BU |
|---|---|---|---|---|---|---|
| ND(1967) | 15,000 | — | 0.75 | 1.25 | 2.50 | — |
| ND(1967) Proof | — | Value: 3.50 | | | | |

**20 SENITI** **KM# 31** **Composition:** Copper-Nickel

| Date | Mintage | F | VF | XF | Unc | BU |
|---|---|---|---|---|---|---|
| 1968 | 35,000 | — | 0.25 | 0.50 | 1.75 | — |
| 1968 Proof | — | Value: 3.00 | | | | |
| 1974 | 50,000 | — | 0.25 | 0.50 | 1.50 | — |

**20 SENITI** **KM# 46** **Composition:** Copper-Nickel **Series:** F.A.O.

| Date | Mintage | F | VF | XF | Unc | BU |
|---|---|---|---|---|---|---|
| 1975 | 75,000 | — | 0.25 | 0.60 | 2.00 | — |
| 1977 | 25,000 | — | 0.25 | 0.60 | 2.00 | — |
| 1979 | 50,000 | — | 0.25 | 0.60 | 2.00 | — |

**20 SENITI** **KM# 70** **Composition:** Copper-Nickel **Series:** World Food Day

| Date | Mintage | F | VF | XF | Unc | BU |
|---|---|---|---|---|---|---|
| 1981 | 610,000 | — | 0.25 | 0.50 | 1.50 | — |
| 1990 | 610,000 | — | 0.25 | 0.50 | 1.25 | — |
| 1991 | — | — | 0.25 | 0.50 | 1.25 | — |
| 1994 | 680,000 | — | 0.25 | 0.50 | 1.25 | — |
| 1996 | — | — | 0.25 | 0.50 | 1.25 | — |

**50 SENITI** **KM# 9** **Composition:** Copper-Nickel

| Date | Mintage | F | VF | XF | Unc | BU |
|---|---|---|---|---|---|---|
| 1967 | 75,000 | — | 0.75 | 1.25 | 2.50 | — |
| 1967 Proof | — | Value: 4.00 | | | | |

**50 SENITI** **KM# 15** **Composition:** Copper-Nickel **Subject:** Coronation of Taufa'ahau Tupou IV

| Date | Mintage | F | VF | XF | Unc | BU |
|---|---|---|---|---|---|---|
| ND(1967) | 15,000 | — | 1.00 | 2.00 | 4.00 | — |
| ND(1967) Proof | — | Value: 6.00 | | | | |

**50 SENITI** **KM# 32** **Composition:** Copper-Nickel

| Date | Mintage | F | VF | XF | Unc | BU |
|---|---|---|---|---|---|---|
| 1968 | 25,000 | — | 0.75 | 1.25 | 2.50 | — |
| 1968 Proof | — | Value: 4.00 | | | | |

**50 SENITI** **KM# 41** **Composition:** Copper-Nickel

| Date | Mintage | F | VF | XF | Unc | BU |
|---|---|---|---|---|---|---|
| 1974 | 50,000 | — | 0.75 | 1.25 | 2.00 | — |

**50 SENITI** **KM# 47** **Composition:** Copper-Nickel **Series:** F.A.O.

| Date | Mintage | F | VF | XF | Unc | BU |
|---|---|---|---|---|---|---|
| 1975 | 40,000 | — | 0.50 | 1.00 | 3.00 | — |

| Date | Mintage | F | VF | XF | Unc | BU |
|---|---|---|---|---|---|---|
| 1977 | 20,000 | — | 0.75 | 1.25 | 3.50 | — |
| 1978 | 60,000 | — | 0.50 | 1.00 | 3.00 | — |

**50 SENITI** **KM# 71** **Composition:** Copper-Nickel **Series:** World Food Day

| Date | Mintage | F | VF | XF | Unc | BU |
|---|---|---|---|---|---|---|
| 1981 | 555,000 | — | 0.45 | 0.75 | 1.75 | — |
| 1990 | — | — | 0.45 | 0.75 | 1.50 | — |
| 1991 | — | — | 0.45 | 0.75 | 1.50 | — |
| 1994 | 41,000 | — | 0.45 | 0.75 | 1.50 | — |
| 1996 | — | — | 0.45 | 0.75 | 1.50 | — |

**50 SENITI** **KM# 82** **Composition:** Copper-Nickel **Subject:** 100th Anniversary of Automobile Industry **Reverse:** Rolls-Royce and Silver Ghost

| Date | Mintage | F | VF | XF | Unc | BU |
|---|---|---|---|---|---|---|
| 1985 | Est. 20,000 | — | — | — | 6.00 | — |

**50 SENITI** **KM# 83** **Composition:** Copper-Nickel **Subject:** 100th Anniversary of Automobile Industry **Reverse:** Range Rover and Land Rover

| Date | Mintage | F | VF | XF | Unc | BU |
|---|---|---|---|---|---|---|
| 1985 | Est. 20,000 | — | — | — | 7.00 | — |

**50 SENITI** **KM# 84** **Composition:** Copper-Nickel **Subject:** 100th Anniversary of Automobile Industry **Reverse:** Mini Morris Cowley and Touring Car

| Date | Mintage | F | VF | XF | Unc | BU |
|---|---|---|---|---|---|---|
| 1985 | Est. 20,000 | — | — | — | 6.00 | — |

**50 SENITI** **KM# 85** **Composition:** Copper-Nickel **Subject:** 100th Anniversary of Automobile Industry **Reverse:** MGB GT and MGTA

| Date | Mintage | F | VF | XF | Unc | BU |
|---|---|---|---|---|---|---|
| 1985 | Est. 20,000 | — | — | — | 6.00 | — |

**50 SENITI** **KM# 98** **Composition:** Copper-Nickel **Subject:** 85th Birthday of Queen Mother **Reverse:** Queen Mother as a young girl

| Date | Mintage | F | VF | XF | Unc | BU |
|---|---|---|---|---|---|---|
| 1985 | Est. 20,000 | — | — | — | 4.50 | — |

**50 SENITI** **KM# 99** **Composition:** Copper-Nickel **Subject:** 85th Birthday of Queen Mother **Reverse:** Wedding of King George VI and Elizabeth

| Date | Mintage | F | VF | XF | Unc | BU |
|---|---|---|---|---|---|---|
| 1985 | Est. 20,000 | — | — | — | 4.50 | — |

**50 SENITI** **KM# 100** **Composition:** Copper-Nickel **Subject:** 85th Birthday of Queen Mother **Reverse:** King George VI and Elizabeth

| Date | Mintage | F | VF | XF | Unc | BU |
|---|---|---|---|---|---|---|
| 1985 | Est. 20,000 | — | — | — | 4.50 | — |

**50 SENITI** **KM# 101** **Composition:** Copper-Nickel **Subject:** 85th Birthday of Queen Mother **Reverse:** Queen Mother holding Queen Elizabeth

| Date | Mintage | F | VF | XF | Unc | BU |
|---|---|---|---|---|---|---|
| 1985 | Est. 20,000 | — | — | — | 4.50 | — |

**50 SENITI** **KM# 102** **Composition:** Copper-Nickel **Subject:** 85th Birthday of Queen Mother **Reverse:** Queen Mother

| Date | Mintage | F | VF | XF | Unc | BU |
|---|---|---|---|---|---|---|
| 1985 | Est. 20,000 | — | — | — | 4.50 | — |

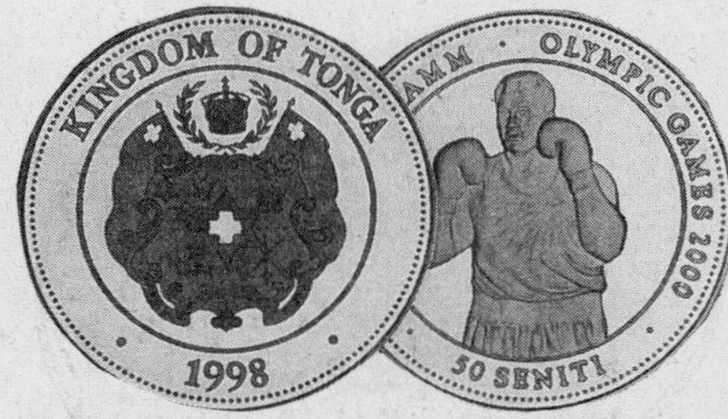


**50 SENITI** **KM# 171** **Weight:** 20.0000 g. **Composition:** 0.9250 Silver .5948 oz. ASW **Subject:** Olympics - Boxing **Obverse:** National arms. **Reverse:** Boxer. **Edge:** Reeded. **Size:** 34 mm.

| Date | Mintage | F | VF | XF | Unc | BU |
|---|---|---|---|---|---|---|
| 1998 Proof | 50,000 | Value: 40.00 | | | | |

**PA'ANGA** **KM# 11** **Composition:** Copper-Nickel

| Date | Mintage | F | VF | XF | Unc | BU |
|---|---|---|---|---|---|---|
| 1967 | 78,000 | — | 1.00 | 2.00 | 4.50 | — |
| 1967 Proof | — | Value: 6.00 | | | | |

**PA'ANGA** KM# 17 **Composition:** Copper-Nickel **Subject:** Coronation of Taufa'ahau Tupou IV

| Date | Mintage | F | VF | XF | Unc | BU |
|---|---|---|---|---|---|---|
| ND(1967) | 13,000 | — | 1.00 | 2.50 | 5.00 | — |
| ND(1967) Proof | 1,923 | Value: 6.50 | | | | |

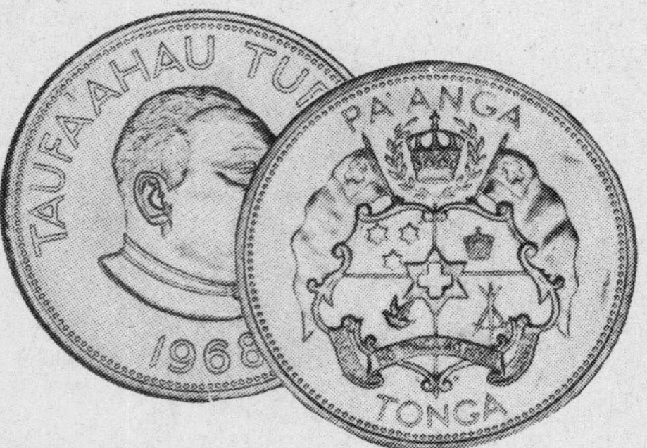


**PA'ANGA** KM# 33 **Composition:** Copper-Nickel

| Date | Mintage | F | VF | XF | Unc | BU |
|---|---|---|---|---|---|---|
| 1968 | 14,000 | — | 1.00 | 2.50 | 5.00 | — |
| 1968 Proof | — | Value: 7.00 | | | | |
| 1974 | 10,000 | — | 1.00 | 2.50 | 6.00 | — |

**PA'ANGA** KM# 48 **Composition:** Copper-Nickel **Series:** F.A.O.

| Date | Mintage | F | VF | XF | Unc | BU |
|---|---|---|---|---|---|---|
| 1975 | 13,000 | — | 1.25 | 3.00 | 7.00 | — |

**PA'ANGA** KM# 57 **Composition:** Copper-Nickel **Series:** F.A.O

| Date | Mintage | F | VF | XF | Unc | BU |
|---|---|---|---|---|---|---|
| 1977 | 25,000 | — | 1.50 | 4.00 | 10.00 | — |

**PA'ANGA** KM# 58 **Composition:** Copper-Nickel **Series:** F.A.O. **Subject:** 60th Birthday **Reverse:** Similar to KM#57

| Date | Mintage | F | VF | XF | Unc | BU |
|---|---|---|---|---|---|---|
| 1978 | 10,000 | — | 1.50 | 4.00 | 10.00 | — |

**PA'ANGA** KM# 58a **Weight:** 24.5000 g. **Composition:** 0.9990 Silver .7869 oz. ASW

| Date | Mintage | F | VF | XF | Unc | BU |
|---|---|---|---|---|---|---|
| 1978 Proof | 750 | Value: 47.50 | | | | |

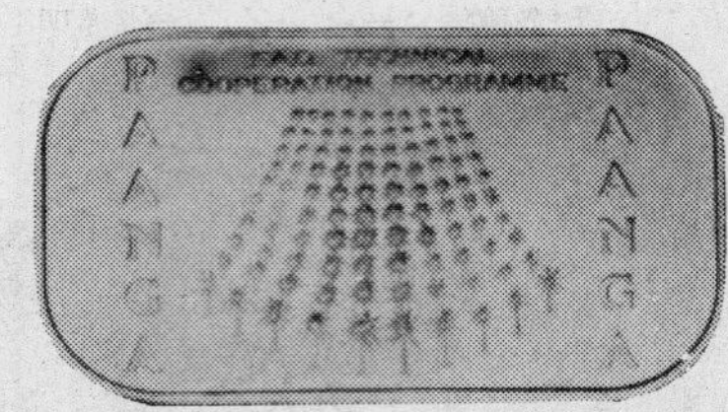


**PA'ANGA** KM# 60 **Composition:** Copper-Nickel **Series:** F.A.O. **Subject:** Technical Cooperation Program

| Date | Mintage | F | VF | XF | Unc | BU |
|---|---|---|---|---|---|---|
| 1979 | 26,000 | — | 1.50 | 4.00 | 10.00 | — |

**PA'ANGA** KM# 60a **Weight:** 24.5000 g. **Composition:** 0.9990 Silver .7869 oz. ASW

| Date | Mintage | F | VF | XF | Unc | BU |
|---|---|---|---|---|---|---|
| 1979 Proof | 850 | Value: 45.00 | | | | |

**PA'ANGA** KM# 62 **Composition:** Copper-Nickel **Series:** F.A.O. **Subject:** Rural Women's Advancement

| Date | Mintage | F | VF | XF | Unc | BU |
|---|---|---|---|---|---|---|
| 1980 | 8,000 | — | 1.50 | 4.00 | 10.00 | — |

**PA'ANGA** KM# 62a **Weight:** 24.5000 g. **Composition:** 0.9990 Silver .7869 oz. ASW

| Date | Mintage | F | VF | XF | Unc | BU |
|---|---|---|---|---|---|---|
| 1980 Proof | 2,200 | Value: 37.50 | | | | |

**PA'ANGA** KM# 72 **Composition:** Copper-Nickel **Series:** World Food Day **Obverse:** Similar to KM#57

| Date | Mintage | F | VF | XF | Unc | BU |
|---|---|---|---|---|---|---|
| 1981 | 485,000 | — | 1.50 | 4.00 | 10.00 | — |

**PA'ANGA** KM# 72a **Weight:** 24.5000 g. **Composition:** 0.9990 Silver .7869 oz. ASW

| Date | Mintage | F | VF | XF | Unc | BU |
|---|---|---|---|---|---|---|
| 1981 Proof | 3,500 | Value: 37.50 | | | | |

**PA'ANGA** KM# 77 **Composition:** Copper-Nickel **Subject:** Christmas

| Date | Mintage | F | VF | XF | Unc | BU |
|---|---|---|---|---|---|---|
| 1982 | 5,000 | — | 0.75 | 1.00 | 3.50 | — |
| 1982 Proof | — | Value: 6.00 | | | | |

**PA'ANGA** KM# 77a **Weight:** 15.5000 g. **Composition:** 0.9250 Silver .4610 oz. ASW

| Date | Mintage | F | VF | XF | Unc | BU |
|---|---|---|---|---|---|---|
| 1982 Proof | 2,500 | Value: 11.50 | | | | |

**PA'ANGA** KM# 77b **Weight:** 26.0000 g. **Composition:** 0.9170 Gold .7666 oz. AGW **Subject:** Christmas

| Date | Mintage | F | VF | XF | Unc | BU |
|---|---|---|---|---|---|---|
| 1982 Proof | 250 | Value: 500 | | | | |

**PA'ANGA** KM# 77c **Weight:** 30.4000 g. **Composition:** 0.9500 Platinum .9286 oz. APW

| Date | Mintage | F | VF | XF | Unc | BU |
|---|---|---|---|---|---|---|
| 1982 Proof | 25 | Value: 800 | | | | |

**PA'ANGA** KM# 80 **Composition:** Copper-Nickel **Subject:** Christmas

| Date | Mintage | F | VF | XF | Unc | BU |
|---|---|---|---|---|---|---|
| 1983 | 5,000 | — | 0.75 | 1.00 | 3.50 | — |

**PA'ANGA** KM# 80a **Weight:** 15.5000 g. **Composition:** 0.9250 Silver .4610 oz. ASW

| Date | Mintage | F | VF | XF | Unc | BU |
|---|---|---|---|---|---|---|
| 1983 Proof | 2,500 | Value: 11.50 | | | | |

**PA'ANGA** KM# 80b **Weight:** 26.0000 g. **Composition:** 0.9170 Gold .7666 oz. AGW **Subject:** Christmas

| Date | Mintage | F | VF | XF | Unc | BU |
|---|---|---|---|---|---|---|
| 1983 Proof | 250 | Value: 500 | | | | |

**PA'ANGA** KM# 80c **Weight:** 30.4000 g. **Composition:** 0.9500 Platinum .9286 oz. APW

| Date | Mintage | F | VF | XF | Unc | BU |
|---|---|---|---|---|---|---|
| 1983 Proof | 25 | Value: 800 | | | | |

**PA'ANGA** KM# 81 **Composition:** Copper-Nickel **Subject:** Christmas

| Date | Mintage | F | VF | XF | Unc | BU |
|---|---|---|---|---|---|---|
| 1984 | 5,000 | — | 0.75 | 1.00 | 3.50 | — |

**PA'ANGA** KM# 81a **Weight:** 15.5000 g. **Composition:** 0.9250 Silver .4610 oz. ASW

| Date | Mintage | F | VF | XF | Unc | BU |
|---|---|---|---|---|---|---|
| 1984 Proof | 2,500 | Value: 11.50 | | | | |

**PA'ANGA** KM# 81b **Weight:** 26.0000 g. **Composition:** 0.9170 Gold .7666 oz. AGW **Subject:** Christmas

| Date | Mintage | F | VF | XF | Unc | BU |
|---|---|---|---|---|---|---|
| 1984 Proof | 250 | Value: 500 | | | | |

**PA'ANGA** KM# 81c **Weight:** 30.4000 g. **Composition:** 0.9500 Platinum .9286 oz. APW

| Date | Mintage | F | VF | XF | Unc | BU |
|---|---|---|---|---|---|---|
| 1984 Proof | 25 | Value: 800 | | | | |

**PA'ANGA** KM# 86 **Composition:** Silver Clad Copper-Nickel **Subject:** 100th Anniversary of Automobile Industry **Reverse:** Rolls-Royce and Silver Ghost

| Date | Mintage | F | VF | XF | Unc | BU |
|---|---|---|---|---|---|---|
| 1985 Proof | — | Value: 7.50 | | | | |

**PA'ANGA** KM# 86a **Weight:** 28.2800 g. **Composition:** 0.9250 Silver .8411 oz. ASW

| Date | Mintage | F | VF | XF | Unc | BU |
|---|---|---|---|---|---|---|
| 1985 Proof | 5,000 | Value: 37.50 | | | | |

**PA'ANGA** **KM# 87** **Composition:** Silver Clad Copper-Nickel **Subject:** 100th Anniversary of Automobile Industry **Reverse:** Range Rover and Land Rover

| Date | Mintage | F | VF | XF | Unc | BU |
|---|---|---|---|---|---|---|
| 1985 Proof | — | Value: 7.50 | | | | |

**PA'ANGA** **KM# 87a** **Weight:** 28.2800 g. **Composition:** 0.9250 Silver .8411 oz. ASW

| Date | Mintage | F | VF | XF | Unc | BU |
|---|---|---|---|---|---|---|
| 1985 Proof | 5,000 | Value: 37.50 | | | | |

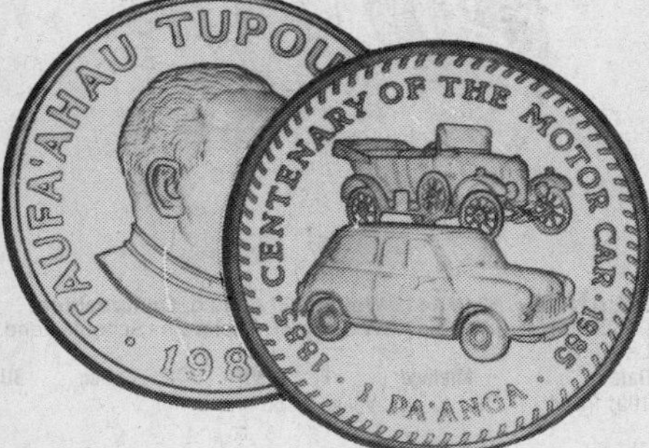


**PA'ANGA** **KM# 88** **Composition:** Silver Clad Copper-Nickel **Subject:** 100th Anniversary of Automobile Industry **Reverse:** Mini Morris Cowley and Touring Car

| Date | Mintage | F | VF | XF | Unc | BU |
|---|---|---|---|---|---|---|
| 1985 Proof | — | Value: 7.50 | | | | |

**PA'ANGA** **KM# 88a** **Weight:** 28.2800 g. **Composition:** 0.9250 Silver .8411 oz. ASW

| Date | Mintage | F | VF | XF | Unc | BU |
|---|---|---|---|---|---|---|
| 1985 Proof | 5,000 | Value: 37.50 | | | | |

**PA'ANGA** **KM# 89** **Composition:** Silver Clad Copper-Nickel **Subject:** 100th Anniversary of Automobile Industry **Reverse:** MGB GT and MG TA **Note:** Similar to 50 Seniti, KM#85.

| Date | Mintage | F | VF | XF | Unc | BU |
|---|---|---|---|---|---|---|
| 1985 Proof | — | Value: 7.50 | | | | |

**PA'ANGA** **KM# 89a** **Weight:** 28.2800 g. **Composition:** 0.9250 Silver .8411 oz. ASW

| Date | Mintage | F | VF | XF | Unc | BU |
|---|---|---|---|---|---|---|
| 1985 Proof | 5,000 | Value: 37.50 | | | | |

**PA'ANGA** **KM# 103** **Composition:** Silver Clad Copper-Nickel **Subject:** 85th Birthday of Queen Mother **Reverse:** Queen Mother as a young girl **Note:** Similar to 50 Seniti, KM#98.

| Date | Mintage | F | VF | XF | Unc | BU |
|---|---|---|---|---|---|---|
| 1985 Proof | — | Value: 5.50 | | | | |

**PA'ANGA** **KM# 103a** **Weight:** 28.2800 g. **Composition:** 0.9250 Silver .8411 oz. ASW

| Date | Mintage | F | VF | XF | Unc | BU |
|---|---|---|---|---|---|---|
| 1985 Proof | 5,000 | Value: 30.00 | | | | |

**PA'ANGA** **KM# 104** **Composition:** Silver Clad Copper-Nickel **Subject:** 85th Birthday of Queen Mother **Reverse:** Wedding of King George VI and Ellizabeth **Note:** Similar to 50 Seniti, KM#99.

| Date | Mintage | F | VF | XF | Unc | BU |
|---|---|---|---|---|---|---|
| 1985 Proof | — | Value: 5.50 | | | | |

**PA'ANGA** **KM# 104a** **Weight:** 28.2800 g. **Composition:** 0.9250 Silver .8411 oz. ASW

| Date | Mintage | F | VF | XF | Unc | BU |
|---|---|---|---|---|---|---|
| 1985 Proof | 5,000 | Value: 30.00 | | | | |

**PA'ANGA** **KM# 105** **Composition:** Silver Clad Copper-Nickel **Subject:** 85th Birthday of Queen Mother **Reverse:** King George VI and Ellizabeth **Note:** Similar to 50 Seniti, KM#100.

| Date | Mintage | F | VF | XF | Unc | BU |
|---|---|---|---|---|---|---|
| 1985 Proof | — | Value: 5.50 | | | | |

**PA'ANGA** **KM# 105a** **Weight:** 28.2800 g. **Composition:** 0.9250 Silver .8411 oz. ASW

| Date | Mintage | F | VF | XF | Unc | BU |
|---|---|---|---|---|---|---|
| 1985 Proof | 5,000 | Value: 30.00 | | | | |

**PA'ANGA** **KM# 106** **Composition:** Silver Clad Copper-Nickel **Subject:** 85th Birthday of Queen Mother **Reverse:** Queen Mother holding Queen Elizabeth **Note:** Similar to 50 Seniti, KM#101.

| Date | Mintage | F | VF | XF | Unc | BU |
|---|---|---|---|---|---|---|
| 1985 Proof | — | Value: 5.50 | | | | |

**PA'ANGA** **KM# 106a** **Weight:** 28.2800 g. **Composition:** 0.9250 Silver .8411 oz. ASW

| Date | Mintage | F | VF | XF | Unc | BU |
|---|---|---|---|---|---|---|
| 1985 Proof | 5,000 | Value: 30.00 | | | | |

**PA'ANGA** **KM# 107** **Composition:** Silver Clad Copper-Nickel **Subject:** 85th Birthday of Queen Mother **Note:** Similar to 50 Seniti, KM#102.

| Date | Mintage | F | VF | XF | Unc | BU |
|---|---|---|---|---|---|---|
| 1985 Proof | — | Value: 5.50 | | | | |

**PA'ANGA** **KM# 107a** **Weight:** 28.2800 g. **Composition:** 0.9250 Silver .8411 oz. ASW

| Date | Mintage | F | VF | XF | Unc | BU |
|---|---|---|---|---|---|---|
| 1985 Proof | 5,000 | Value: 30.00 | | | | |

**PA'ANGA** **KM# 118** **Composition:** Copper-Nickel **Subject:** Christmas

| Date | Mintage | F | VF | XF | Unc | BU |
|---|---|---|---|---|---|---|
| 1985 | — | — | — | 1.00 | 3.00 | — |

**PA'ANGA** **KM# 118a** **Weight:** 15.5000 g. **Composition:** 0.9250 Silver .4610 oz. ASW

| Date | Mintage | F | VF | XF | Unc | BU |
|---|---|---|---|---|---|---|
| 1985 Proof | 250 | Value: 35.00 | | | | |

**PA'ANGA** **KM# 118b** **Weight:** 26.0000 g. **Composition:** 0.9170 Gold .7666 oz. AGW **Subject:** Christmas

| Date | Mintage | F | VF | XF | Unc | BU |
|---|---|---|---|---|---|---|
| 1985 Proof | 250 | Value: 500 | | | | |

**PA'ANGA** **KM# 118c** **Weight:** 30.4000 g. **Composition:** 0.9500 Platinum .9286 oz. APW

| Date | Mintage | F | VF | XF | Unc | BU |
|---|---|---|---|---|---|---|
| 1985 Proof | — | Value: 800 | | | | |

**PA'ANGA** **KM# 123** **Composition:** Copper-Nickel **Subject:** Christmas **Reverse:** Three Wise Men

| Date | Mintage | F | VF | XF | Unc | BU |
|---|---|---|---|---|---|---|
| 1986 | — | — | — | 1.00 | 3.00 | — |

**PA'ANGA** **KM# 123a** **Weight:** 15.5000 g. **Composition:** 0.9250 Silver .4610 oz. ASW

| Date | Mintage | F | VF | XF | Unc | BU |
|---|---|---|---|---|---|---|
| 1986 | — | — | — | — | 35.00 | — |

**PA'ANGA** **KM# 123b** **Weight:** 26.0000 g. **Composition:** 0.9170 Gold .7666 oz. AGW **Subject:** Christmas

| Date | Mintage | F | VF | XF | Unc | BU |
|---|---|---|---|---|---|---|
| 1986 | — | — | — | — | 500 | — |

**PA'ANGA** **KM# 123c** **Weight:** 30.4000 g. **Composition:** 0.9500 Platinum .9286 oz. APW

| Date | Mintage | F | VF | XF | Unc | BU |
|---|---|---|---|---|---|---|
| 1986 | — | — | — | — | 800 | — |

**PA'ANGA** **KM# 128** **Composition:** Copper-Nickel **Series:** 25th Anniversary of World Wildlife Fund

| Date | Mintage | F | VF | XF | Unc | BU |
|---|---|---|---|---|---|---|
| 1986 | — | — | — | — | 4.50 | — |

**PA'ANGA** **KM# 139** **Composition:** Copper-Nickel **Subject:** Christmas **Reverse:** Madonna and child

| Date | Mintage | F | VF | XF | Unc | BU |
|---|---|---|---|---|---|---|
| 1987 | — | — | — | — | 3.00 | — |
| 1987 Proof | — | Value: 5.00 | | | | |

**PA'ANGA** **KM# 127** **Composition:** Copper-Nickel **Subject:** Christmas

| Date | Mintage | F | VF | XF | Unc | BU |
|---|---|---|---|---|---|---|
| 1988 | — | — | — | — | 3.00 | — |
| 1988 Proof | — | Value: 5.00 | | | | |

**PA'ANGA** **KM# 127a** **Weight:** 15.5000 g. **Composition:** 0.9250 Silver .4610 oz. ASW

| Date | Mintage | F | VF | XF | Unc | BU |
|---|---|---|---|---|---|---|
| 1988 Proof | — | Value: 32.50 | | | | |

**PA'ANGA** **KM# 127b** **Weight:** 26.0000 g. **Composition:** 0.9170 Gold .7666 oz. AGW **Subject:** Christmas

| Date | Mintage | F | VF | XF | Unc | BU |
|---|---|---|---|---|---|---|
| 1988 Proof | — | Value: 500 | | | | |

**PA'ANGA** **KM# 127c** **Weight:** 30.4000 g. **Composition:** 0.9500 Platinum .9286 oz. APW

| Date | Mintage | F | VF | XF | Unc | BU |
|---|---|---|---|---|---|---|
| 1988 Proof | — | Value: 800 | | | | |

**PA'ANGA** **KM# 133** **Weight:** 31.7300 g. **Composition:** 0.9250 Silver .9437 oz. ASW **Series:** Olympics **Reverse:** Javelin thrower

| Date | Mintage | F | VF | XF | Unc | BU |
|---|---|---|---|---|---|---|
| 1988 Proof | — | Value: 30.00 | | | | |

**PA'ANGA** **KM# 134** **Weight:** 31.7300 g. **Composition:** 0.9250 Silver .9437 oz. ASW **Series:** Olympics **Reverse:** Swimmers

| Date | Mintage | F | VF | XF | Unc | BU |
|---|---|---|---|---|---|---|
| 1988 Proof | — | Value: 30.00 | | | | |

**PA'ANGA** **KM# 135** **Weight:** 31.7300 g. **Composition:** 0.9250 Silver .9437 oz. ASW **Series:** Olympics **Reverse:** Boxers

| Date | Mintage | F | VF | XF | Unc | BU |
|---|---|---|---|---|---|---|
| 1988 Proof | — | Value: 30.00 | | | | |

**PA'ANGA** **KM# 136** **Weight:** 31.7300 g. **Composition:** 0.9250 Silver .9437 oz. ASW **Series:** Olympics **Reverse:** Discus thrower

| Date | Mintage | F | VF | XF | Unc | BU |
|---|---|---|---|---|---|---|
| 1988 Proof | — | Value: 30.00 | | | | |

**PA'ANGA** **KM# 137** **Weight:** 31.7300 g. **Composition:** 0.9250 Silver .9437 oz. ASW **Series:** Olympics **Reverse:** Shot-put thrower

| Date | Mintage | F | VF | XF | Unc | BU |
|---|---|---|---|---|---|---|
| 1988 Proof | — | Value: 30.00 | | | | |

**PA'ANGA** **KM# 138** **Weight:** 31.7300 g. **Composition:** 0.9250 Silver .9437 oz. ASW **Series:** Olympics **Reverse:** Runners

| Date | Mintage | F | VF | XF | Unc | BU |
|---|---|---|---|---|---|---|
| 1988 Proof | — | Value: 30.00 | | | | |

**PA'ANGA** **KM# 145** **Weight:** 31.7300 g. **Composition:** 0.9250 Silver .9437 oz. ASW **Series:** Olympics **Reverse:** Bicycling

| Date | Mintage | F | VF | XF | Unc | BU |
|---|---|---|---|---|---|---|
| 1988 Proof | — | Value: 30.00 | | | | |

**PA'ANGA** **KM# 146** **Weight:** 31.7300 g. **Composition:** 0.9250 Silver .9437 oz. ASW **Series:** Olympics **Reverse:** Gymnast on rings

| Date | Mintage | F | VF | XF | Unc | BU |
|---|---|---|---|---|---|---|
| 1988 Proof | — | Value: 30.00 | | | | |

**PA'ANGA** **KM# 147** **Weight:** 31.7300 g. **Composition:** 0.9250 Silver .9437 oz. ASW **Series:** Olympics **Reverse:** Diver

| Date | Mintage | F | VF | XF | Unc | BU |
|---|---|---|---|---|---|---|
| 1988 Proof | — | Value: 30.00 | | | | |

**PA'ANGA** **KM# 148** **Weight:** 31.7300 g. **Composition:** 0.9250 Silver .9437 oz. ASW **Series:** Olympics **Reverse:** Judo

| Date | Mintage | F | VF | XF | Unc | BU |
|---|---|---|---|---|---|---|
| 1988 Proof | — | Value: 30.00 | | | | |

**PA'ANGA** **KM# 149** **Weight:** 31.7300 g. **Composition:** 0.9250 Silver .9437 oz. ASW **Series:** Olympics **Reverse:** Broad jump

| Date | Mintage | F | VF | XF | Unc | BU |
|---|---|---|---|---|---|---|
| 1988 Proof | — | Value: 30.00 | | | | |

**PA'ANGA** **KM# 150** **Weight:** 31.7300 g. **Composition:** 0.9250 Silver .9437 oz. ASW **Series:** Olympics **Reverse:** Weight lifter

| Date | Mintage | F | VF | XF | Unc | BU |
|---|---|---|---|---|---|---|
| 1988 Proof | — | Value: 30.00 | | | | |

**PA'ANGA** **KM# 175** **Weight:** 31.8000 g. **Composition:** 0.9250 Silver .9457 oz. ASW **Subject:** 25th Anniversary of Reign **Obverse:** National arms **Reverse:** Sun rising through stone structure

| Date | Mintage | F | VF | XF | Unc | BU |
|---|---|---|---|---|---|---|
| ND(1990) Proof | — | Value: 32.50 | | | | |

**PA'ANGA** **KM# 140** **Weight:** 31.6000 g. **Composition:** 0.9250 Silver .9398 oz. ASW **Series:** Olympics **Reverse:** Diver

| Date | Mintage | F | VF | XF | Unc | BU |
|---|---|---|---|---|---|---|
| 1991 Proof | Est. 40,000 | Value: 16.50 | | | | |

**PA'ANGA** **KM# 141** **Weight:** 31.6000 g. **Composition:** 0.9250 Silver .9398 oz. ASW **Subject:** Explorers - Schouten and LeMaire

| Date | Mintage | F | VF | XF | Unc | BU |
|---|---|---|---|---|---|---|
| 1991 Proof | Est. 10,000 | Value: 22.50 | | | | |

**PA'ANGA** **KM# 143** **Weight:** 31.6000 g. **Composition:** 0.9250 Silver .9398 oz. ASW **Subject:** Endagered Wildlife **Reverse:** Birds

| Date | Mintage | F | VF | XF | Unc | BU |
|---|---|---|---|---|---|---|
| 1991 Proof | — | Value: 22.50 | | | | |

**PA'ANGA** **KM# 156** **Weight:** 31.6000 g. **Composition:** 0.9250 Silver .9398 oz. ASW **Series:** 1996 Olympics **Reverse:** Sailing

| Date | Mintage | F | VF | XF | Unc | BU |
|---|---|---|---|---|---|---|
| 1992 Proof | 40,000 | Value: 18.50 | | | | |

**PA'ANGA** **KM# 157** **Weight:** 31.6000 g. **Composition:** 0.9250 Silver .9398 oz. ASW **Subject:** Soccer **Reverse:** Players

| Date | Mintage | F | VF | XF | Unc | BU |
|---|---|---|---|---|---|---|
| 1992 Proof | 10,000 | Value: 20.00 | | | | |

**PA'ANGA** **KM# 158** **Weight:** 31.6000 g. **Composition:** 0.9250 Silver .9398 oz. ASW **Subject:** Space Flight **Reverse:** Saturn

| Date | Mintage | F | VF | XF | Unc | BU |
|---|---|---|---|---|---|---|
| 1992 Proof | 10,000 | Value: 22.50 | | | | |

**PA'ANGA** **KM# 168** **Weight:** 31.6000 g. **Composition:** 0.9250 Silver .9398 oz. ASW **Subject:** 25th Anniversary - Coronation of Tupou IV

| Date | Mintage | F | VF | XF | Unc | BU |
|---|---|---|---|---|---|---|
| 1992 Proof | Est. 5,000 | Value: 35.00 | | | | |

**PA'ANGA** **KM# 144** **Weight:** 31.4700 g. **Composition:** 0.9250 Silver .9359 oz. ASW **Subject:** 40th Anniversary of Queen Elizabeth's Coronation

| Date | Mintage | F | VF | XF | Unc | BU |
|---|---|---|---|---|---|---|
| 1993 Proof | Est. 10,000 | Value: 17.50 | | | | |

**PA'ANGA** **KM# 151** **Weight:** 31.4700 g. **Composition:** 0.9250 Silver .9359 oz. ASW **Subject:** Herman Orbeth

| Date | Mintage | F | VF | XF | Unc | BU |
|---|---|---|---|---|---|---|
| 1993 Proof | Est. 10,000 | Value: 22.50 | | | | |

**PA'ANGA** **KM# 152** **Weight:** 31.4700 g. **Composition:** 0.9250 Silver .9359 oz. ASW **Subject:** Johannes Gutenberg

| Date | Mintage | F | VF | XF | Unc | BU |
|---|---|---|---|---|---|---|
| 1993 Proof | Est. 10,000 | Value: 25.00 | | | | |

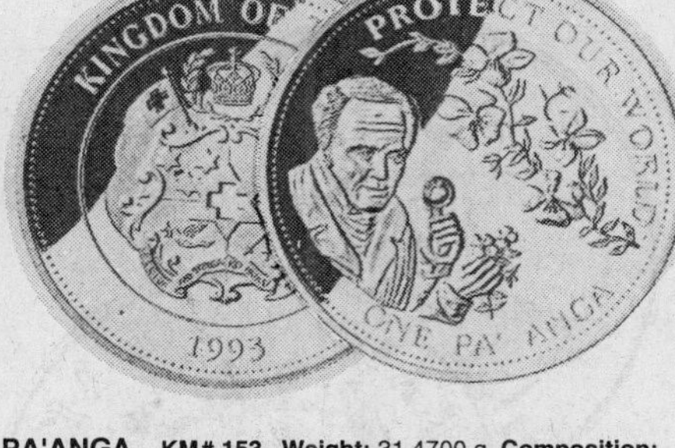


**PA'ANGA** **KM# 153** **Weight:** 31.4700 g. **Composition:** 0.9250 Silver .9359 oz. ASW **Subject:** Protect Our World - Alexander von Humboldt

| Date | Mintage | F | VF | XF | Unc | BU |
|---|---|---|---|---|---|---|
| 1993 Proof | Est. 10,000 | Value: 20.00 | | | | |

**PA'ANGA** **KM# 154** **Weight:** 31.4700 g. **Composition:** 0.9250 Silver .9359 oz. ASW **Subject:** Sailing ship - "La Princesa"

| Date | Mintage | F | VF | XF | Unc | BU |
|---|---|---|---|---|---|---|
| 1993 Proof | Est. 15,000 | Value: 20.00 | | | | |

**PA'ANGA** **KM# 160** **Weight:** 31.4700 g. **Composition:** 0.9250 Silver .9359 oz. ASW **Subject:** Richard Wagner

| Date | Mintage | F | VF | XF | Unc | BU |
|---|---|---|---|---|---|---|
| 1993 Proof | Est. 10,000 | Value: 20.00 | | | | |

**PA'ANGA** **KM# 169** **Weight:** 31.4700 g. **Composition:** 0.9250 Silver .9359 oz. ASW **Subject:** 75th Birthday **Obverse:** King Tupou IV **Reverse:** Siu'a'alo rowers

| Date | Mintage | F | VF | XF | Unc | BU |
|---|---|---|---|---|---|---|
| 1993 Proof | Est. 2,000 | Value: 35.00 | | | | |

**PA'ANGA** **KM# 159** **Weight:** 31.5500 g. **Composition:** 0.9250 Silver .9383 oz. ASW **Series:** 1996 Olympics **Reverse:** Javelin thrower

| Date | Mintage | F | VF | XF | Unc | BU |
|---|---|---|---|---|---|---|
| 1994 Proof | 40,000 | Value: 15.00 | | | | |

**PA'ANGA** **KM# 161** **Weight:** 31.4700 g. **Composition:** 0.9250 Silver .9359 oz. ASW **Subject:** World Cup Soccer **Reverse:** Two players

| Date | Mintage | F | VF | XF | Unc | BU |
|---|---|---|---|---|---|---|
| 1994 Proof | Est. 10,000 | Value: 18.00 | | | | |

**PA'ANGA** **KM# 162** **Weight:** 31.4700 g. **Composition:** 0.9250 Silver .9359 oz. ASW **Series:** Endangered Wildlife **Reverse:** Whales

| Date | Mintage | F | VF | XF | Unc | BU |
|---|---|---|---|---|---|---|
| 1994 Proof | Est. 10,000 | Value: 30.00 | | | | |

**PA'ANGA** **KM# 166** **Weight:** 31.4700 g. **Composition:** 0.9250 Silver .9359 oz. ASW **Subject:** Queen Mothers's Crown

| Date | Mintage | F | VF | XF | Unc | BU |
|---|---|---|---|---|---|---|
| 1996 | Est. 40,000 | — | — | — | 15.00 | — |

**PA'ANGA** **KM# 170** **Weight:** 31.4700 g. **Composition:** 0.9250 Silver .9359 oz. ASW **Subject:** 70th Birthday - Queen Mata'aho

| Date | Mintage | F | VF | XF | Unc | BU |
|---|---|---|---|---|---|---|
| 1996 Proof | Est. 5,000 | Value: 30.00 | | | | |

**PA'ANGA** **KM# 174** **Weight:** 31.4700 g. **Composition:** 0.9250 Silver .9359 oz. ASW **Obverse:** National arms **Reverse:** Polynesian sailing catamaran

| Date | Mintage | F | VF | XF | Unc | BU |
|---|---|---|---|---|---|---|
| 1998 Proof | 20,000 | Value: 20.00 | | | | |

**PA'ANGA** **KM# 176** **Weight:** 31.1100 g. **Composition:** 0.9250 Silver .9252 oz. ASW **Subject:** Millennium 2000 **Obverse:** National arms. **Reverse:** Stone archway. **Edge:** Reeded, scalloped. **Size:** 35.5 mm.

| Date | Mintage | F | VF | XF | Unc | BU |
|---|---|---|---|---|---|---|
| 1999 Proof | — | Value: 45.00 | | | | |

**2 PA'ANGA** **KM# 19** **Composition:** Copper-Nickel **Subject:** Coronation of Taufa'ahau Tupou IV **Reverse:** Similar to KM#37

| Date | Mintage | F | VF | XF | Unc | BU |
|---|---|---|---|---|---|---|
| ND(1967) | 10,000 | — | 1.25 | 3.00 | 6.00 | — |
| ND(1967) Proof | — | Value: 12.00 | | | | |

**2 PA'ANGA** **KM# 37** **Composition:** Copper-Nickel **Reverse:** Similar to KM#19

| Date | Mintage | F | VF | XF | Unc | BU |
|---|---|---|---|---|---|---|
| 1968 | 14,000 | — | 1.25 | 2.25 | 4.50 | — |
| 1968 Proof | — | Value: 9.00 | | | | |
| 1974 | 10,000 | — | 1.25 | 3.50 | 7.50 | — |

**2 PA'ANGA** **KM# 49** **Composition:** Copper-Nickel **Series:** F.A.O.

| Date | Mintage | F | VF | XF | Unc | BU |
|---|---|---|---|---|---|---|
| 1975 | 13,000 | — | 1.25 | 3.50 | 10.00 | — |
| 1977 | 12,000 | — | 1.25 | 3.50 | 10.00 | — |

**2 PA'ANGA** **KM# 59** **Composition:** Copper-Nickel **Series:** F.A.O. **Subject:** 60th Birthday **Reverse:** Similar to KM#49

| Date | Mintage | F | VF | XF | Unc | BU |
|---|---|---|---|---|---|---|
| 1978 | 10,000 | — | 2.50 | 5.00 | 11.00 | — |

**2 PA'ANGA** **KM# 59a** **Weight:** 42.1000 g. **Composition:** 0.9990 Silver 1.3523 oz. ASW

| Date | Mintage | F | VF | XF | Unc | BU |
|---|---|---|---|---|---|---|
| 1978 Proof | 750 | Value: 35.00 | | | | |

**2 PA'ANGA** **KM# 61** **Composition:** Copper-Nickel **Series:** F.A.O. **Subject:** SEA Resource Management

| Date | Mintage | F | VF | XF | Unc | BU |
|---|---|---|---|---|---|---|
| 1979 | 8,000 | — | 1.25 | 3.50 | 10.00 | — |

**2 PA'ANGA** **KM# 61a** **Weight:** 42.1000 g. **Composition:** 0.9990 Silver 1.3523 oz. ASW

| Date | Mintage | F | VF | XF | Unc | BU |
|---|---|---|---|---|---|---|
| 1979 Proof | 850 | Value: 45.00 | | | | |

**2 PA'ANGA** **KM# 63** **Composition:** Copper-Nickel **Series:** F.A.O. **Subject:** SEA Resource Management **Reverse:** Similar to KM#61

| Date | Mintage | F | VF | XF | Unc | BU |
|---|---|---|---|---|---|---|
| 1980 | 8,000 | — | 1.25 | 3.50 | 10.00 | — |

**2 PA'ANGA** **KM# 63a** **Weight:** 42.1000 g. **Composition:** 0.9990 Silver 1.3523 oz. ASW

| Date | Mintage | F | VF | XF | Unc | BU |
|---|---|---|---|---|---|---|
| 1980 Proof | 2,200 | Value: 30.00 | | | | |

**2 PA'ANGA** **KM# 73** **Composition:** Copper-Nickel **Series:** World Food Day **Obverse:** Similar to KM#63

| Date | Mintage | F | VF | XF | Unc | BU |
|---|---|---|---|---|---|---|
| 1981 | 485,000 | — | — | 2.50 | 7.50 | — |

**2 PA'ANGA** **KM# 73a** **Weight:** 42.1000 g. **Composition:** 0.9990 Silver 1.3523 oz. ASW

| Date | Mintage | F | VF | XF | Unc | BU |
|---|---|---|---|---|---|---|
| 1981 Proof | 3,500 | Value: 25.00 | | | | |

**2 PA'ANGA** **KM# 120** **Weight:** 28.2800 g. **Composition:** 0.5000 Silver .4546 oz. ASW **Subject:** Commonwealth Games

| Date | Mintage | F | VF | XF | Unc | BU |
|---|---|---|---|---|---|---|
| 1986 | 50,000 | — | — | — | 12.00 | — |

**2 PA'ANGA** **KM# 120a** **Weight:** 28.2800 g. **Composition:** 0.9250 Silver .8411 oz. ASW

| Date | Mintage | F | VF | XF | Unc | BU |
|---|---|---|---|---|---|---|
| 1986 Proof | 20,000 | Value: 25.00 | | | | |

**2 PA'ANGA** **KM# 121** **Weight:** 28.2800 g. **Composition:** 0.9250 Silver .8411 oz. ASW **Subject:** Wildlife **Reverse:** Whales

| Date | Mintage | F | VF | XF | Unc | BU |
|---|---|---|---|---|---|---|
| 1986 Proof | 25,000 | Value: 22.50 | | | | |

**2 PA'ANGA** **KM# 124** **Weight:** 155.5200 g. **Composition:** 0.9990 Silver 5.0000 oz. ASW **Subject:** America's Cup **Size:** 65 mm. **Note:** Illustration reduced

| Date | Mintage | F | VF | XF | Unc | BU |
|---|---|---|---|---|---|---|
| 1987 Proof | 7,500 | Value: 55.00 | | | | |

**2 PA'ANGA** **KM# 129** **Weight:** 155.5200 g. **Composition:** 0.9990 Silver 5.0000 oz. ASW **Series:** Olympics **Obverse:** Similar to 10 Pa'anga, KM#130 **Reverse:** Swimmers **Size:** 65 mm. **Note:** Illustration reduced.

| Date | Mintage | F | VF | XF | Unc | BU |
|---|---|---|---|---|---|---|
| 1988 Proof | 2,000 | Value: 50.00 | | | | |

**5 PA'ANGA** **KM# 50** **Weight:** 31.0000 g. **Composition:** 0.9990 Silver .9957 oz. ASW **Subject:** Constitution Centennial

| Date | Mintage | F | VF | XF | Unc | BU |
|---|---|---|---|---|---|---|
| ND(1975) | 2,118 | — | — | — | 16.00 | — |
| ND(1975) Proof | 418 | Value: 30.00 | | | | |

**10 PA'ANGA** **KM# 51** **Weight:** 62.0000 g. **Composition:** 0.9990 Silver 1.9915 oz. ASW **Subject:** Constitution Centennial **Reverse:** Similar to 5 Pa'anga, KM#50

| Date | Mintage | F | VF | XF | Unc | BU |
|---|---|---|---|---|---|---|
| ND(1975) | 1,116 | — | — | — | 22.50 | — |
| ND(1975) Proof | 420 | Value: 35.00 | | | | |

**10 PA'ANGA** **KM# 64** **Weight:** 4.0000 g. **Composition:** 0.9170 Gold .0117 oz. AGW **Series:** F.A.O. **Subject:** Rural Women's Advancement **Obverse:** Queen Salote **Reverse:** Female symbol on dove

| Date | Mintage | F | VF | XF | Unc | BU |
|---|---|---|---|---|---|---|
| 1980 | 750 | — | — | — | 20.00 | — |
| 1980 Proof | 2,000 | Value: 20.00 | | | | |

**10 PA'ANGA** **KM# 78** **Weight:** 28.2800 g. **Composition:** 0.9250 Silver .8411 oz. ASW **Subject:** Commonwealth Games

| Date | Mintage | F | VF | XF | Unc | BU |
|---|---|---|---|---|---|---|
| 1982 | 500 | — | — | — | 20.00 | — |
| 1982 Proof | 1,000 | Value: 25.00 | | | | |

**10 PA'ANGA** **KM# 90** **Weight:** 5.1000 g. **Composition:** 0.3750 Gold .0615 oz. AGW **Subject:** 100th Anniversary of Automobile Industry **Reverse:** Rolls-Royce and Silver Ghost **Note:** Similar to 50 Seniti, KM#82

| Date | Mintage | F | VF | XF | Unc | BU |
|---|---|---|---|---|---|---|
| 1985 Proof | 1,000 | Value: 35.00 | | | | |

**10 PA'ANGA** **KM# 90a** **Weight:** 7.9600 g. **Composition:** 0.9170 Gold .2347 oz. AGW

| Date | Mintage | F | VF | XF | Unc | BU |
|---|---|---|---|---|---|---|
| 1985 Proof | 500 | Value: 100 | | | | |

**10 PA'ANGA** **KM# 91** **Weight:** 5.1000 g. **Composition:** 0.3750 Gold .0615 oz. AGW **Subject:** 100th Anniversary of Automobile Industry **Reverse:** Range Rover and Land Rover **Note:** Similar to 50 Seniti, KM#83.2

| Date | Mintage | F | VF | XF | Unc | BU |
|---|---|---|---|---|---|---|
| 1985 Proof | 1,000 | Value: 35.00 | | | | |

**10 PA'ANGA** **KM# 91a** **Weight:** 7.9600 g. **Composition:** 0.9170 Gold .2347 oz. AGW

| Date | Mintage | F | VF | XF | Unc | BU |
|---|---|---|---|---|---|---|
| 1985 Proof | 500 | Value: 100 | | | | |

**10 PA'ANGA** **KM# 92** **Weight:** 5.1000 g. **Composition:** 0.3750 Gold .0615 oz. AGW **Subject:** 100th Anniversary of Automobile Industry **Reverse:** Mini Morris Cowley and Touring Car **Note:** Similar to 50 Seniti, KM#84.

| Date | Mintage | F | VF | XF | Unc | BU |
|---|---|---|---|---|---|---|
| 1985 Proof | 1,000 | Value: 35.00 | | | | |

**10 PA'ANGA** **KM# 92a** **Weight:** 7.9600 g. **Composition:** 0.9170 Gold .2347 oz. AGW

| Date | Mintage | F | VF | XF | Unc | BU |
|---|---|---|---|---|---|---|
| 1985 Proof | 500 | Value: 100 | | | | |

**10 PA'ANGA** **KM# 93** **Weight:** 5.1000 g. **Composition:** 0.3750 Gold .0615 oz. AGW **Subject:** 100th Anniversary of Automobile Industry **Reverse:** MGB GT and MG TA **Note:** Similar to 50 Seniti, KM#85.

| Date | Mintage | F | VF | XF | Unc | BU |
|---|---|---|---|---|---|---|
| 1985 Proof | 1,000 | Value: 35.00 | | | | |

**10 PA'ANGA** **KM# 93a** **Weight:** 7.9600 g. **Composition:** 0.9170 Gold .2347 oz. AGW

| Date | Mintage | F | VF | XF | Unc | BU |
|---|---|---|---|---|---|---|
| 1985 Proof | 500 | Value: 100 | | | | |

**10 PA'ANGA** **KM# 108** **Weight:** 5.1000 g. **Composition:** 0.3750 Gold .0615 oz. AGW **Subject:** 85th Birthday of Queen Mother **Reverse:** Queen Mother as a young girl **Note:** Similar to 50 Seniti, KM#98.

| Date | Mintage | F | VF | XF | Unc | BU |
|---|---|---|---|---|---|---|
| 1985 Proof | 1,000 | Value: 35.00 | | | | |

**10 PA'ANGA** **KM# 108a** **Weight:** 7.9600 g. **Composition:** 0.9170 Gold .2347 oz. AGW

| Date | Mintage | F | VF | XF | Unc | BU |
|---|---|---|---|---|---|---|
| 1985 Proof | 500 | Value: 100 | | | | |

**10 PA'ANGA** **KM# 109** **Weight:** 5.1000 g. **Composition:** 0.3750 Gold .0615 oz. AGW **Subject:** 85th Birthday of Queen Mother **Reverse:** Wedding of King George VI and Elizabeth **Note:** Similar to 50 Seniti, KM#99.

| Date | Mintage | F | VF | XF | Unc | BU |
|---|---|---|---|---|---|---|
| 1985 Proof | 1,000 | Value: 35.00 | | | | |

**10 PA'ANGA** **KM# 109a** **Weight:** 7.9600 g. **Composition:** 0.9170 Gold .2347 oz. AGW

| Date | Mintage | F | VF | XF | Unc | BU |
|---|---|---|---|---|---|---|
| 1985 Proof | 500 | Value: 100 | | | | |

**10 PA'ANGA** **KM# 110** **Weight:** 5.1000 g. **Composition:** 0.3750 Gold .0615 oz. AGW **Subject:** 85th Birthday of Queen Mother **Reverse:** King George VI and Elizabeth **Note:** Similar to 50 Seniti, KM#100.

| Date | Mintage | F | VF | XF | Unc | BU |
|---|---|---|---|---|---|---|
| 1985 Proof | 1,000 | Value: 35.00 | | | | |

**10 PA'ANGA** **KM# 110a** **Weight:** 7.9600 g. **Composition:** 0.9170 Gold .2347 oz. AGW

| Date | Mintage | F | VF | XF | Unc | BU |
|---|---|---|---|---|---|---|
| 1985 Proof | 500 | Value: 100 | | | | |

**10 PA'ANGA** **KM# 111** **Weight:** 5.1000 g. **Composition:** 0.3750 Gold .0615 oz. AGW **Subject:** 85th Birthday of Queen Mother **Reverse:** Queen Mother holding Queen Elizabeth II **Note:** Similar to 50 Seniti, KM#101.

| Date | Mintage | F | VF | XF | Unc | BU |
|---|---|---|---|---|---|---|
| 1985 Proof | 1,000 | Value: 35.00 | | | | |

**10 PA'ANGA** **KM# 111a** **Weight:** 7.9600 g. **Composition:** 0.9170 Gold .2347 oz. AGW

| Date | Mintage | F | VF | XF | Unc | BU |
|---|---|---|---|---|---|---|
| 1985 Proof | 500 | Value: 100 | | | | |

**10 PA'ANGA** **KM# 112** **Weight:** 5.1000 g. **Composition:** 0.3750 Gold .0615 oz. AGW **Subject:** 85th Birthday of Queen Mother **Note:** Similar to 50 Seniti, KM#102.

| Date | Mintage | F | VF | XF | Unc | BU |
|---|---|---|---|---|---|---|
| 1985 Proof | 1,000 | Value: 35.00 | | | | |

**10 PA'ANGA** **KM# 112a** **Weight:** 7.9600 g. **Composition:** 0.9170 Gold .2347 oz. AGW

| Date | Mintage | F | VF | XF | Unc | BU |
|---|---|---|---|---|---|---|
| 1985 Proof | 500 | Value: 100 | | | | |

**10 PA'ANGA** **KM# 126** **Composition:** Copper-Nickel **Subject:** America's Cup **Obverse:** Taufa'ahau Tupou IV **Reverse:** National flags

| Date | Mintage | F | VF | XF | Unc | BU |
|---|---|---|---|---|---|---|
| 1987 | — | — | — | — | 6.00 | — |

**10 PA'ANGA** **KM# 126a** **Weight:** 31.1030 g. **Composition:** 0.9990 Palladium 1.0000 oz. **Subject:** America's Cup **Obverse:** Taufa'ahau Tupou IV **Reverse:** National flags

| Date | Mintage | F | VF | XF | Unc | BU |
|---|---|---|---|---|---|---|
| 1987 Proof | 25,000 | Value: 575 | | | | |

**10 PA'ANGA** **KM# 125** **Weight:** 311.0400 g. **Composition:** 0.9990 Silver 10.0000 oz. ASW **Subject:** America's Cup **Obverse:** Taufa'ahau Tupou IV **Reverse:** Sailboat and map **Size:** 75 mm. **Note:** Illustration reduced.

| Date | Mintage | F | VF | XF | Unc | BU |
|---|---|---|---|---|---|---|
| 1987 Proof | 5,000 | Value: 210 | | | | |

**10 PA'ANGA** **KM# 130** **Weight:** 15.5500 g. **Composition:** 0.9990 Gold .5000 oz. AGW **Series:** Summer Olympics **Subject:** Boxing

| Date | Mintage | F | VF | XF | Unc | BU |
|---|---|---|---|---|---|---|
| 1988 Proof | Est. 2,000 | Value: 175 | | | | |

**10 PA'ANGA** **KM# 131** **Weight:** 31.1000 g. **Composition:** 0.9990 Palladium 1.0000 oz. **Series:** Summer Olympics **Reverse:** Shot putter

| Date | Mintage | F | VF | XF | Unc | BU |
|---|---|---|---|---|---|---|
| 1988 Proof | Est. 2,000 | Value: 850 | | | | |

**10 PA'ANGA** **KM# 132** **Weight:** 15.6300 g. **Composition:** 0.9500 Palladium .5000 oz. **Series:** Summer Olympics **Reverse:** Discus thrower

| Date | Mintage | F | VF | XF | Unc | BU |
|---|---|---|---|---|---|---|
| 1988 Proof | Est. 2,000 | Value: 325 | | | | |

**10 PA'ANGA KM# 173 Weight:** 1.2441 g. **Composition:** 0.9999 Gold .0400 oz. AGW **Subject:** Destruction of the English Privateer "Post-au-Prince" **Obverse:** National arms. **Reverse:** Looted shipwreck and native. **Edge:** Reeded. **Size:** 13.92 mm.

| Date | Mintage | F | VF | XF | Unc | BU |
|---|---|---|---|---|---|---|
| 1998 Proof | — | Value: 50.00 | | | | |

**10 PA'ANGA KM# 172 Weight:** 1.2441 g. **Composition:** 0.9999 Gold .0400 oz. AGW **Subject:** King's 80th Birthday **Obverse:** National arms. **Reverse:** King's portrait. **Edge:** Reeded. **Size:** 13.92 mm. **Note:** Struck at Valcambi Mint.

| Date | Mintage | F | VF | XF | Unc | BU |
|---|---|---|---|---|---|---|
| 1998 Proof | — | Value: 50.00 | | | | |

**20 PA'ANGA KM# 52 Weight:** 140.0000 g. **Composition:** 0.9990 Silver 4.4971 oz. ASW **Subject:** Constitution Centennial **Reverse:** Similar to 5 Pa'anga, KM#50

| Date | Mintage | F | VF | XF | Unc | BU |
|---|---|---|---|---|---|---|
| 1975 | 1,170 | — | — | — | 35.00 | — |
| 1975 Proof | 800 | Value: 55.00 | | | | |

**20 PA'ANGA KM# 65 Weight:** 0.8000 g. **Composition:** 0.9170 Gold .0235 oz. AGW **Series:** F.A.O. **Subject:** Rural Women's Advancement **Obverse:** Queen Salote **Reverse:** Female figure on dove

| Date | Mintage | F | VF | XF | Unc | BU |
|---|---|---|---|---|---|---|
| 1980 | 750 | — | — | — | 30.00 | — |
| 1980 Proof | 2,000 | Value: 30.00 | | | | |

**25 PA'ANGA KM# 53 Weight:** 5.0000 g. **Composition:** 0.9170 Gold .1474 oz. AGW **Subject:** Constitution Centennial **Obverse:** King George Tupou I **Reverse:** Arms

| Date | Mintage | F | VF | XF | Unc | BU |
|---|---|---|---|---|---|---|
| 1975 | 405 | — | — | — | 55.00 | — |
| 1975 Proof | 105 | Value: 70.00 | | | | |

**50 PA'ANGA KM# 54 Weight:** 10.0000 g. **Composition:** 0.9170 Gold .2948 oz. AGW **Subject:** Constitution Centennial **Obverse:** King George Tupou II **Reverse:** Arms

| Date | Mintage | F | VF | XF | Unc | BU |
|---|---|---|---|---|---|---|
| 1975 | 205 | — | — | — | 110 | — |
| 1975 Proof | 105 | Value: 125 | | | | |

**75 PA'ANGA KM# 55 Weight:** 15.0000 g. **Composition:** 0.9170 Gold .4423 oz. AGW **Subject:** Constitution Centennial **Obverse:** Queen Salote Tupou III **Reverse:** Arms

| Date | Mintage | F | VF | XF | Unc | BU |
|---|---|---|---|---|---|---|
| 1975 | 204 | — | — | — | 160 | — |
| 1975 Proof | 105 | Value: 175 | | | | |

**100 PA'ANGA KM#56 Weight:** 20.0000 g. **Composition:** 0.9170 Gold .5897 oz. AGW **Subject:** Constitution Centennial

| Date | Mintage | F | VF | XF | Unc | BU |
|---|---|---|---|---|---|---|
| ND(1975) | 205 | — | — | — | 210 | — |
| ND(1975) Proof | 105 | Value: 225 | | | | |

**100 PA'ANGA KM# 167 Weight:** 17.7000 g. **Composition:** 0.5833 Gold .3319 oz. AGW **Subject:** 25th Jubilee of Accession

| Date | Mintage | F | VF | XF | Unc | BU |
|---|---|---|---|---|---|---|
| ND(1990) Proof | Est. 5,000 | Value: 165 | | | | |

**100 PA'ANGA KM# 155 Weight:** 17.7000 g. **Composition:** 0.5833 Gold .3319 oz. AGW **Series:** Olympics **Reverse:** Gymnast on rings

| Date | Mintage | F | VF | XF | Unc | BU |
|---|---|---|---|---|---|---|
| 1993 Proof | 3,000 | Value: 120 | | | | |

**100 PA'ANGA KM# 163 Weight:** 17.7000 g. **Composition:** 0.5833 Gold .3319 oz. AGW **Subject:** World Cup Soccer **Reverse:** Goalie

| Date | Mintage | F | VF | XF | Unc | BU |
|---|---|---|---|---|---|---|
| 1994 Proof | Est. 3,000 | Value: 120 | | | | |

**100 PA'ANGA KM# 164 Weight:** 17.7000 g. **Composition:** 0.5833 Gold .3319 oz. AGW **Series:** 1996 Olympic Games **Reverse:** High jumper

| Date | Mintage | F | VF | XF | Unc | BU |
|---|---|---|---|---|---|---|
| 1994 Proof | Est. 3,000 | Value: 120 | | | | |

**100 PA'ANGA KM# 165 Weight:** 17.7000 g. **Composition:** 0.5833 Gold .3319 oz. AGW **Series:** Endangered Wildlife **Reverse:** Leguan Lizard

| Date | Mintage | F | VF | XF | Unc | BU |
|---|---|---|---|---|---|---|
| 1994 Proof | Est. 2,000 | Value: 120 | | | | |

**1/4 HAU KM#21 Weight:** 16.0000 g. **Composition:** 0.9800 Palladium .5041 oz. **Subject:** Coronation of Taufa'ahau Tupou IV

| Date | Mintage | F | VF | XF | Unc | BU |
|---|---|---|---|---|---|---|
| 1967 | 1,700 | — | — | — | 425 | — |

**1/2 HAU KM# 23 Weight:** 32.0000 g. **Composition:** 0.9800 Palladium 1.0082 oz. **Subject:** Coronation of Taufa'ahau Tupou IV

| Date | Mintage | F | VF | XF | Unc | BU |
|---|---|---|---|---|---|---|
| 1967 | 1,650 | — | — | — | 875 | — |

**1/2 HAU KM#74 Weight:** 28.2800 g. **Composition:** 0.9250 Silver .8411 oz. ASW **Subject:** Wedding and Treaty of Friendship

| Date | Mintage | F | VF | XF | Unc | BU |
|---|---|---|---|---|---|---|
| 1981 | 1,000 | — | — | — | 35.00 | — |
| 1981 Proof | 15,000 | Value: 30.00 | | | | |

**1/2 HAU KM# 122 Weight:** 10.0000 g. **Composition:** 0.9170 Gold .2948 oz. AGW **Subject:** Wildlife **Reverse:** Ground-dwelling birds

| Date | Mintage | F | VF | XF | Unc | BU |
|---|---|---|---|---|---|---|
| 1986 Proof | 5,000 | Value: 150 | | | | |

**HAU KM#25 Weight:** 64.0000 g. **Composition:** 0.9800 Palladium 2.0164 oz. **Subject:** Coronation of Taufa'ahau Tupou IV

| Date | Mintage | F | VF | XF | Unc | BU |
|---|---|---|---|---|---|---|
| 1967 | 1,500 | — | — | — | 1,750 | — |

**HAU KM#75 Weight:** 7.9900 g. **Composition:** 0.9170 Gold .2356 oz. AGW **Subject:** Wedding and Treaty of Friendship

| Date | Mintage | F | VF | XF | Unc | BU |
|---|---|---|---|---|---|---|
| 1981 | 500 | — | — | — | 125 | — |
| 1981 Proof | 2,500 | Value: 110 | | | | |

**HAU KM#79 Weight:** 7.9900 g. **Composition:** 0.9170 Gold .2356 oz. AGW **Subject:** Commonwealth Games **Obverse:** King Taufa'ahau Tupou IV **Reverse:** Runners

| Date | Mintage | F | VF | XF | Unc | BU |
|---|---|---|---|---|---|---|
| 1982 | 500 | — | — | — | 120 | — |
| 1982 Proof | 500 | Value: 120 | | | | |

**HAU KM# 94 Weight:** 52.0000 g. **Composition:** 0.9500 Platinum 1.5884 oz. APW **Subject:** 100th Anniversary of Automobile Industry **Reverse:** Rolls-Royce and Silver Ghost **Note:** Similar to 50 Seniti, KM#82.

| Date | Mintage | F | VF | XF | Unc | BU |
|---|---|---|---|---|---|---|
| 1985 Proof | — | Value: 975 | | | | |

**HAU KM# 95 Weight:** 52.0000 g. **Composition:** 0.9500 Platinum 1.5884 oz. APW **Subject:** 100th Anniversary of Automobile Industry **Reverse:** Range Rover and Land Rover **Note:** Similar to 50 Seniti, KM#83.

| Date | Mintage | F | VF | XF | Unc | BU |
|---|---|---|---|---|---|---|
| 1985 Proof | — | Value: 975 | | | | |

**HAU KM# 96 Weight:** 52.0000 g. **Composition:** 0.9500 Platinum 1.5884 oz. APW **Subject:** 100th Anniversary of Automobile Industry **Reverse:** Mini Morris Cowley and Touring Car **Note:** Similar to 50 Seniti, KM#84.

| Date | Mintage | F | VF | XF | Unc | BU |
|---|---|---|---|---|---|---|
| 1985 Proof | — | Value: 975 | | | | |

**HAU KM# 97 Weight:** 52.0000 g. **Composition:** 0.9500 Platinum 1.5884 oz. APW **Subject:** 100th Anniversary of Automobile Industry **Reverse:** MGB GT and MG TA **Note:** Similar to 50 Seniti, KM#85.

| Date | Mintage | F | VF | XF | Unc | BU |
|---|---|---|---|---|---|---|
| 1985 Proof | — | Value: 975 | | | | |

**HAU KM# 113 Weight:** 52.0000 g. **Composition:** 0.9500 Platinum 1.5884 oz. APW **Subject:** 85th Birthday of Queen Mother **Reverse:** Queen Mother as a young girl **Note:** Similar to 50 Seniti, KM#98.

| Date | Mintage | F | VF | XF | Unc | BU |
|---|---|---|---|---|---|---|
| 1985 Proof | — | Value: 975 | | | | |

**HAU KM# 114 Weight:** 52.0000 g. **Composition:** 0.9500 Platinum 1.5884 oz. APW **Subject:** 85th Birthday of Queen Mother **Reverse:** Wedding of King George VI and Elizabeth **Note:** Similar to 50 Seniti, KM#99.

| Date | Mintage | F | VF | XF | Unc | BU |
|---|---|---|---|---|---|---|
| 1985 Proof | — | Value: 975 | | | | |

**HAU KM# 115 Weight:** 52.0000 g. **Composition:** 0.9500 Platinum 1.5884 oz. APW **Subject:** 85th Birthday of Queen Mother **Reverse:** King George VI and Elizabeth **Note:** Similar to 50 Seniti, KM#100.

| Date | Mintage | F | VF | XF | Unc | BU |
|---|---|---|---|---|---|---|
| 1985 Proof | — | Value: 975 | | | | |

**HAU KM# 116 Weight:** 52.0000 g. **Composition:** 0.9500 Platinum 1.5884 oz. APW **Subject:** 85th Birthday of Queen Mother **Reverse:** Queen Mother holding Queen Elizabeth **Note:** Similar to 50 Seniti, KM#101.

| Date | Mintage | F | VF | XF | Unc | BU |
|---|---|---|---|---|---|---|
| 1985 Proof | — | Value: 975 | | | | |

**HAU KM# 117 Weight:** 52.0000 g. **Composition:** 0.9500 Platinum 1.5884 oz. APW **Subject:** 85th Birthday of Queen Mother **Note:** Similar to 50 Seniti, KM#102.

| Date | Mintage | F | VF | XF | Unc | BU |
|---|---|---|---|---|---|---|
| 1985 Proof | — | Value: 975 | | | | |

**5 HAU KM# 76 Weight:** 15.9800 g. **Composition:** 0.9170 Gold .4711 oz. AGW **Subject:** Wedding and Treaty of Friendship

| Date | Mintage | F | VF | XF | Unc | BU |
|---|---|---|---|---|---|---|
| 1981 | 250 | — | — | — | 250 | — |
| 1981 Proof | 1,000 | Value: 245 | | | | |

## COUNTERMARKED COMMEMORATIVE COINAGE

Commemorative coins which contain a countermark creating a new commemorative representation. The "Date" listed refers to the original date the coin was struck.

**20 SENITI KM# 10 Composition:** Gilt Copper-Nickel **Countermark:** IN MEMORIAM/1965 +1970 **Note:** Countermark on KM#9.

| Date | Mintage | F | VF | XF | Unc | BU |
|---|---|---|---|---|---|---|
| 1967 | Inc. above | — | — | — | 6.50 | — |

**20 SENITI KM# 14 Composition:** Copper-Nickel **Countermark:** 1918/TTIV/1968 **Note:** Countermark on KM#13.

| Date | Mintage | F | VF | XF | Unc | BU |
|---|---|---|---|---|---|---|
| ND(1967) Proof | 1,577 | Value: 7.50 | | | | |

**20 SENITI KM# 16 Composition:** Copper-Nickel **Countermark:** 1918/TTIV/1968 **Note:** Countermark on KM#15.

| Date | Mintage | F | VF | XF | Unc | BU |
|---|---|---|---|---|---|---|
| ND(1967) Proof | 1,577 | Value: 8.50 | | | | |

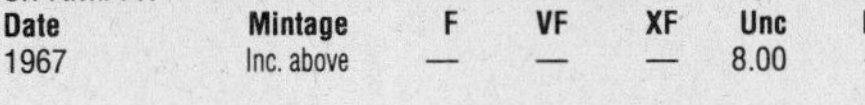

**PA'ANGA KM# 12 Composition:** Gilt Copper-Nickel **Countermark:** IN MEMORIAM/1965 + 1970 **Note:** Countermark on KM#11.

| Date | Mintage | F | VF | XF | Unc | BU |
|---|---|---|---|---|---|---|
| 1967 | Inc. above | — | — | — | 8.00 | — |

**PA'ANGA KM# 18 Composition:** Copper-Nickel **Countermark:** 1918/TTIV/1968 **Note:** Countermark on KM#17.

| Date | Mintage | F | VF | XF | Unc | BU |
|---|---|---|---|---|---|---|
| 1967 Proof | 1,577 | Value: 8.50 | | | | |

**PA'ANGA KM# 34 Composition:** Gilt Copper-Nickel **Countermark:** Oil rig 1969 OIL SEARCH **Note:** Countermark on KM#17.

| Date | Mintage | F | VF | XF | Unc | BU |
|---|---|---|---|---|---|---|
| 1968 | 5,017 | — | 1.50 | 3.50 | 7.00 | — |

**PA'ANGA KM# 35 Composition:** Gilt Copper-Nickel **Countermark:** COMMONWEALTH MEMBER/1970 **Note:** Countermark on KM#17.

| Date | Mintage | F | VF | XF | Unc | BU |
|---|---|---|---|---|---|---|
| 1968 | 3,000 | — | 2.00 | 3.00 | 7.50 | — |

**PA'ANGA KM# 36 Composition:** Gilt Copper-Nickel **Countermark:** INVESTITURE/1971 **Note:** Countermark on KM#17.

| Date | Mintage | F | VF | XF | Unc | BU |
|---|---|---|---|---|---|---|
| 1968 | 3,000 | — | 2.00 | 3.00 | 7.50 | — |
| 1968 Proof | 1,000 | Value: 10.00 | | | | |

**2 PA'ANGA KM# 20 Composition:** Copper-Nickel **Countermark:** 1918/TTIV/1968 **Note:** Countermark on KM#19.

| Date | Mintage | F | VF | XF | Unc | BU |
|---|---|---|---|---|---|---|
| ND(1967) Proof | 1,577 | Value: 12.50 | | | | |

**2 PA'ANGA KM# 38 Composition:** Gilt Copper-Nickel **Countermark:** Oil rig 1969 OIL SEARCH **Note:** Countermark on KM#37.

| Date | Mintage | F | VF | XF | Unc | BU |
|---|---|---|---|---|---|---|
| 1968 | 5,039 | — | 2.50 | 5.50 | 10.00 | — |

**2 PA'ANGA KM# 39 Composition:** Gilt Copper-Nickel **Countermark:** COMMONWEALTH MEMBER/1970 **Note:** Countermark on KM#37.

| Date | Mintage | F | VF | XF | Unc | BU |
|---|---|---|---|---|---|---|
| 1968 | 3,006 | — | 3.00 | 6.00 | 12.00 | — |

**2 PA'ANGA KM# 40 Composition:** Gilt Copper-Nickel **Countermark:** INVESTITURE/1971 **Note:** Countermark on KM#37.

| Date | Mintage | F | VF | XF | Unc | BU |
|---|---|---|---|---|---|---|
| 1968 | 3,000 | — | 3.00 | 6.00 | 12.00 | — |
| 1968 Proof | 1,000 | Value: 15.00 | | | | |

**1/4 HAU KM# 22 Weight:** 16.0000 g. **Composition:** 0.9800 Palladium .5040 oz. **Countermark:** 1918/TTIV/1968 **Note:** Countermark on KM#21.

| Date | Mintage | F | VF | XF | Unc | BU |
|---|---|---|---|---|---|---|
| 1967 | 400 | — | — | — | 475 | — |

**1/2 HAU** KM# 24 **Weight:** 32.0000 g. **Composition:** 0.9800 Palladium 1.0082 oz. **Countermark:** 1918/TTIV/1968 **Note:** Countermark on KM#23.

| Date | Mintage | F | VF | XF | Unc | BU |
|---|---|---|---|---|---|---|
| ND(1967) | 513 | — | — | — | 950 | — |

**HAU** KM# 26 **Weight:** 64.0000 g. **Composition:** 0.9800 Palladium 2.0164 oz. **Countermark:** 1918/TTIV/1968 **Note:** Countermark on KM#25.

| Date | Mintage | F | VF | XF | Unc | BU |
|---|---|---|---|---|---|---|
| ND(1967) | 400 | — | — | — | 1,850 | — |

## MEDALLIC COINAGE

**5 PA'ANGA** KM# M1 **Composition:** Copper-Nickel **Subject:** International Games - Judo

| Date | Mintage | F | VF | XF | Unc | BU |
|---|---|---|---|---|---|---|
| 1984 Proof | — | Value: 17.50 | | | | |

**5 PA'ANGA** KM# M2 **Composition:** Copper-Nickel **Subject:** International Games - Relay **Obverse:** King's portrait **Reverse:** Relay runners

| Date | Mintage | F | VF | XF | Unc | BU |
|---|---|---|---|---|---|---|
| 1984 Proof | — | Value: 17.50 | | | | |

## MINT SETS

| KM# | Date | Mintage | Identification | Issue Price | Mkt Val |
|---|---|---|---|---|---|
| MS15 | 1978 (5) | — | KM#42-46 | — | 5.50 |
| MS8 | 1974 (8) | 10,000 | KM#27-33, 37 | 7.60 | 22.50 |
| MS1 | 1962 (3) | — | KM#1-3 | — | 750 |
| MS2 | 1967 (3) | 1,500 | KM#21, 23, 25 | 207 | 3,050 |
| MS3 | 1968 (3) | 400 | KM#22, 24, 26 | — | 3,275 |
| MS4 | 1970 (2) | 10,000 | KM#10, 12 | 2.30 | 14.50 |
| MS5 | 1969 (2) | 10,000 | KM#34, 38 | 13.68 | 16.50 |
| MS6 | 1970 (2) | 3,000 | KM#35, 39 | 13.68 | 20.00 |
| MS7 | 1971 (2) | 3,000 | KM#36, 40 | 4.80 | 20.00 |
| MS10 | 1975 (4) | — | KM#53-56 | 384 | 535 |
| MS11 | 1975 (3) | — | KM#50-52 | 59.60 | 75.00 |
| MS9 | 1975 (8) | — | KM#42-49 | 7.75 | 25.00 |
| MS12 | 1977 (5) | — | KM#44-47 | 0.85 | 8.00 |
| MS13 | 1977 (2) | — | KM#49, 57 | 3.00 | 20.00 |
| MS14 | 1978 (2) | — | KM#58-59 | 3.00 | 21.50 |
| MS16 | 1979 (2) | 8,008 | KM#60-61 | 3.00 | 20.00 |
| MS17 | 1980 (2) | 8,000 | KM#62-63 | 3.00 | 20.00 |
| MS18 | 1980 (2) | 750 | KM#64-65, Gold | 30.00 | 50.00 |
| MS19 | 1981 (8) | 15,000 | KM#66-73 | 5.38 | 25.00 |
| MS20 | 1985 (5) | 20,000 | KM#98-102 | 25.25 | 22.50 |
| MS21 | 1985 (4) | 20,000 | KM#82-85. Auto Industry. | 21.00 | 25.00 |
| MS22 | 1991 (6) | — | KM#66-71 | — | 6.00 |

## PROOF SETS

| KM# | Date | Mintage | Identification | Issue Price | Mkt Val |
|---|---|---|---|---|---|
| PS16 | 1985 (5) | 20,000 | KM#98-102, Copper-nickel | 26.25 | 20.00 |
| PS2 | 1962 (3) | 25 | KM#1a-3a. Platinum. | — | 2,250 |
| PS1 | 1962 (3) | 250 | KM#1-3 | — | 950 |
| PS6 | 1968 (4) | 1,577 | KM#14, 16, 18, 20 | 22.80 | 37.50 |
| PS3 | 1967 (7) | 5,000 | KM#4-9, 11 | 15.00 | 22.50 |
| PS4 | 1967 (4) | 1,923 | KM#13, 15, 17, 19 | 17.25 | 27.50 |
| PS5 | 1968 (8) | 2,500 | KM#27-33, 37 | 22.50 | 32.00 |
| PS8 | 1971 (2) | 1,000 | KM#36, 40 | 13.40 | 25.00 |
| PS10 | 1975 (4) | 105 | KM#53-56 | 538 | 600 |
| PS9 | 1975 (3) | 418 | KM#50-52 | 82.00 | 120 |
| PS11 | 1978 (2) | 750 | KM#58a-59a | — | 82.50 |
| PS12 | 1979 (2) | 854 | KM#60a-61a | 45.00 | 90.00 |
| PS13 | 1980 (2) | 400 | KM#62a-63a | 80.00 | 70.00 |
| PS14 | 1980 (2) | 200 | KM#64-65 | 60.00 | 55.00 |
| PS15 | 1981 (2) | 3,500 | KM#72a-73a | 88.00 | 62.50 |
| PSA15 | 1981 (3) | — | KM#74-76 | — | 385 |
| PS22 | 1985 (4) | 10,000 | KM#86-89 | 44.00 | 30.00 |
| PS26 | 1985 (4) | 50 | KM#94-97, .950 Platinum. BV+15%. | 4,680 | — |
| PS23 | 1985 (4) | 5,000 | KM#86a-89a, .925 Silver | 144 | 185 |
| PS24 | 1985 (4) | 1,000 | KM#90-93, .374 Gold | 252 | 140 |
| PS25 | 1985 (4) | 500 | KM#90a-93a, .917 Gold | 620 | 400 |
| PS21 | 1985 (5) | 50 | KM#113-117, .950 Platinum. BV+15%. | 5,850 | — |
| PS17 | 1985 (5) | 10,000 | KM#103-107, Silver clad copper-nickel | 55.00 | 30.00 |
| PS18 | 1985 (5) | 5,000 | KM#103a-107a, .925 Silver | 180 | 150 |
| PS19 | 1985 (5) | 1,000 | KM#108-112, .374 Gold | 315 | 175 |
| PS20 | 1985 (5) | 500 | KM#108a-112a, .917 Gold | 775 | 500 |
| PS28 | 1988 (4) | 2,000 | KM#129-132 | — | 1,400 |

# TRANSNISTRIA

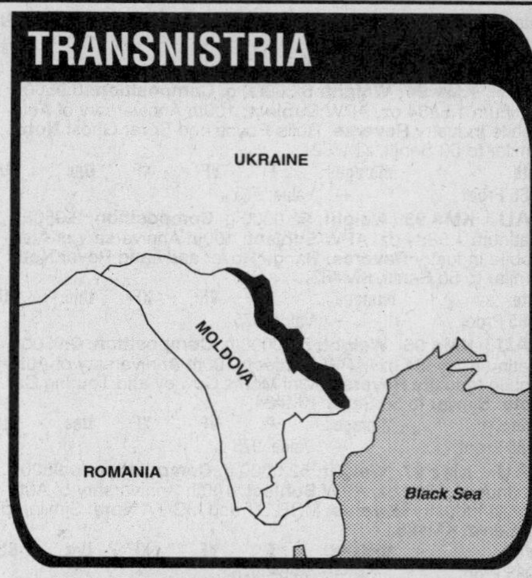


The Transnistria Moldavian Republic was formed in 1990, even before the separation of Moldavia from Russia. It has an area of 11,544 sq. mi. (29,900 sq. km.) and a population of 700,000. Capital: Tiraspol.

The area was conquered from the Turks in the last half of the 18th century, and in 1792 the capital city of Bessarabia (present Moldova and part of the Ukraine) became part of the Russian Empire. During the Russian Revolution, in 1918, the area was taken by Romanian troops, and in 1924 the Moldavian Autonomous SSR was formed on the left bank of the Dniester River. On June 22, 1941, Romania declared war on the U.S.S.R. and Romanian troops fought alongside the Germans up to Stalingrad. A Romanian occupation area between the Dniester and Bug Rivers called Transnistria was established in October 1941. Its center was the port of Odessa.

Once the Moldavian SSR declared independence in August 1991, Transnistria did not want to be part of Moldavia. In 1992, Moldova tried to solve the issue militarily with battles in Bendery and Doubossary. The conflict was ended with Russian mediation and Russian peacekeeping forces were stationed there.

Transnistria has a president, parliament, army and police forces, but as yet it is lacking international recognition.

# MOLDAVIAN REPUBLIC

## STANDARD COINAGE

**KOPEEK** KM# 1 **Weight:** 0.6200 g. **Composition:** Aluminum **Obverse:** State arms **Reverse:** Denomination between wheat stalks **Edge:** Plain **Size:** 15.9 mm.

| Date | Mintage | F | VF | XF | Unc | BU |
|---|---|---|---|---|---|---|
| 2000 | — | — | — | — | 0.50 | — |

**5 KOPEEK** KM# 2 **Weight:** 0.7000 g. **Composition:** Aluminum **Obverse:** State arms **Reverse:** Denomination between wheat stalks **Edge:** Plain **Size:** 17.9 mm.

| Date | Mintage | F | VF | XF | Unc | BU |
|---|---|---|---|---|---|---|
| 2000 | — | — | — | — | 0.75 | — |

**10 KOPEEK** KM# 3 **Weight:** 1.0000 g. **Composition:** Aluminum **Obverse:** State arms **Reverse:** Denomination between wheat stalks **Edge:** Plain **Size:** 20 mm.

| Date | Mintage | F | VF | XF | Unc | BU |
|---|---|---|---|---|---|---|
| 2000 | — | — | — | — | 1.00 | — |

**50 KOPEEK** KM# 4 **Weight:** 2.7500 g. **Composition:** Aluminum **Obverse:** State arms **Reverse:** Denomination between wheat stalks **Edge:** Plain **Size:** 19 mm.

| Date | Mintage | F | VF | XF | Unc | BU |
|---|---|---|---|---|---|---|
| 2000 | — | — | — | — | 1.25 | — |

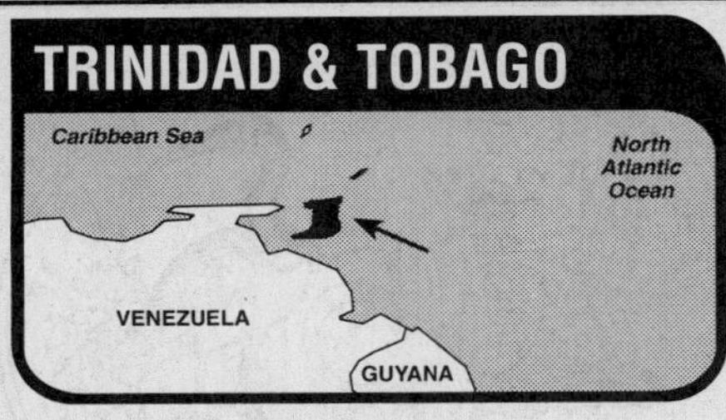


The Republic of Trinidad and Tobago, a member of the British Commonwealth situated 7 miles (11 km.) off the coast of Venezuela, has an area of 1,981 sq. mi. (5,130 sq. km.) and a population of *1.2 million. Capital: Port-of-Spain. The island of Trinidad contains the world's largest natural asphalt bog. Birds of Paradise live on little Tobago, the only place outside of their native New Guinea where they can be found in a wild state. Petroleum and petroleum products are the mainstay of the economy. Petroleum products, crude oil and sugar are exported.

Columbus discovered Trinidad and Tobago in 1498. Trinidad remained under Spanish rule from the time of its settlement in 1592 until its capture by the British in 1797. It was ceded to the British in 1802. Tobago was occupied at various times by the French, Dutch and English before being ceded to Britain in 1814. Trinidad and Tobago were merged into a single colony in 1888. The colony was part of the Federation of the West Indies until Aug. 31, 1962, when it became an independent member of the Commonwealth of Nations. A new constitution establishing a republican form of government was adopted on Aug. 1, 1976. Trinidad and Tobago is a member of the Commonwealth of Nations. The President is Chief of State. The Prime Minister is Head of Government.

**RULERS**

British, until 1976

**MINT MARKS**

FM - Franklin Mint, U.S.A.*

***NOTE**: From 1975-1985 the Franklin Mint produced coinage in up to 3 different qualities. Qualities of issue are designated in ( ) after each date and are defined as follows:

**(M) MATTE** - Normal circulation strike or a dull finish produced by sandblasting special uncirculated (polish finish) or proof quality dies.

**(U) SPECIAL UNCIRCULATED** - Polished or proof-like in appearance without any frosted features.

**(P) PROOF** - The highest quality obtainable having mirror-like fields and frosted features.

**MONETARY SYSTEM**

100 Cents = 1 Dollar

# COLONIAL

## STANDARD COINAGE

100 Cents = 1 Dollar

**CENT KM# 1 Composition:** Bronze

| Date | Mintage | F | VF | XF | Unc | BU |
|---|---|---|---|---|---|---|
| 1966 | 24,500,000 | — | — | — | 0.15 | — |
| 1966 Proof | 8,000 | Value: 1.00 | | | | |
| 1967 | 4,000,000 | — | — | — | 0.15 | — |
| 1968 | 5,000,000 | — | — | — | 0.15 | — |
| 1970 | 5,000,000 | — | — | — | 0.15 | — |
| 1970 Proof | 2,104 | Value: 1.50 | | | | |
| 1971 | 10,600,000 | — | — | — | 0.15 | — |
| 1971FM (M) | 286,000 | — | — | — | 0.20 | — |
| 1971FM (P) | 12,000 | Value: 0.50 | | | | |
| 1972 | 16,500,000 | — | — | — | 0.15 | — |
| 1973 | 10,000,000 | — | — | — | 0.15 | — |

**CENT KM# 9 Composition:** Bronze **Subject:** 10th Anniversary of Independence

| Date | Mintage | F | VF | XF | Unc | BU |
|---|---|---|---|---|---|---|
| 1972 | 5,000,000 | — | — | 0.10 | 0.15 | — |
| 1972FM (M) | 125,000 | — | — | — | 0.25 | — |
| 1972FM (P) | 16,000 | Value: 0.50 | | | | |

**CENT KM# 17 Composition:** Bronze

| Date | Mintage | F | VF | XF | Unc | BU |
|---|---|---|---|---|---|---|
| 1973FM (M) | 127,000 | — | — | — | 0.50 | — |
| 1973FM (P) | 20,000 | Value: 1.50 | | | | |

**CENT KM# 25 Composition:** Bronze **Reverse:** Balisier Hummingbird

| Date | Mintage | F | VF | XF | Unc | BU |
|---|---|---|---|---|---|---|
| 1974FM (M) | 128,000 | — | — | — | 0.25 | — |
| 1974FM (P) | 14,000 | Value: 0.50 | | | | |
| 1975 | 10,000,000 | — | — | — | 0.15 | — |
| 1975FM (M) | 125,000 | — | — | — | 0.15 | — |
| 1975FM (U) | 1,111 | — | — | — | 1.25 | — |
| 1975FM (P) | 24,000 | Value: 0.50 | | | | |
| 1976 | 15,050,000 | — | — | — | 0.15 | — |

**5 CENTS KM# 2 Composition:** Bronze

| Date | Mintage | F | VF | XF | Unc | BU |
|---|---|---|---|---|---|---|
| 1966 | 7,500,000 | — | — | 0.10 | 0.25 | — |
| 1966 Proof | 8,000 | Value: 1.25 | | | | |
| 1967 | 3,000,000 | — | — | 0.10 | 0.25 | — |
| 1970 Proof | 2,104 | Value: 1.75 | | | | |
| 1971 | 2,400,000 | — | — | 0.10 | 0.25 | — |
| 1971FM (M) | 57,000 | — | — | — | 0.15 | — |
| 1971FM (P) | 12,000 | Value: 0.75 | | | | |
| 1972 | 2,250,000 | — | — | 0.10 | 0.20 | — |

**5 CENTS KM# 10 Composition:** Bronze **Subject:** 10th Anniversary of Independence

| Date | Mintage | F | VF | XF | Unc | BU |
|---|---|---|---|---|---|---|
| 1972 | 15,000 | — | — | — | 0.35 | — |
| 1972FM (M) | 25,000 | — | — | — | 0.25 | — |
| 1972FM (P) | 16,000 | Value: 0.75 | | | | |

**5 CENTS KM# 57 Composition:** Bronze

| Date | Mintage | F | VF | XF | Unc | BU |
|---|---|---|---|---|---|---|
| 1973FM (M) | 27,000 | — | — | — | 0.50 | — |
| 1973FM (P) | 20,000 | Value: 1.50 | | | | |

**5 CENTS KM# 26 Composition:** Bronze **Reverse:** Bird of Paradise

| Date | Mintage | F | VF | XF | Unc | BU |
|---|---|---|---|---|---|---|
| 1974FM (M) | 28,000 | — | — | — | 0.50 | — |
| 1974FM (P) | 14,000 | Value: 0.75 | | | | |
| 1975 | 1,500,000 | — | — | 0.10 | 0.20 | — |
| 1975FM (M) | 25,000 | — | — | — | 0.20 | — |
| 1975FM (U) | 1,111 | — | — | — | 1.50 | — |
| 1975FM (P) | 24,000 | Value: 0.75 | | | | |
| 1976 | 7,500,000 | — | — | 0.10 | 0.20 | — |

**10 CENTS KM# 3 Composition:** Copper-Nickel

| Date | Mintage | F | VF | XF | Unc | BU |
|---|---|---|---|---|---|---|
| 1966 | 7,800,000 | — | — | 0.10 | 0.30 | |
| 1966 Proof | 8,000 | Value: 1.50 | | | | |
| 1967 | 4,000,000 | — | — | 0.10 | 0.30 | — |
| 1970 Proof | 2,104 | Value: 2.00 | | | | |
| 1971 | — | — | — | 0.10 | 0.30 | — |
| 1971FM (M) | 29,000 | — | — | — | 0.35 | — |
| 1971FM (P) | 12,000 | Value: 1.00 | | | | |
| 1972 | 4,000,000 | — | — | 0.10 | 0.30 | — |

**10 CENTS KM# 11 Composition:** Copper-Nickel **Subject:** 10th Anniversary of Independence

| Date | Mintage | F | VF | XF | Unc | BU |
|---|---|---|---|---|---|---|
| 1972 | 41,000 | — | — | — | 0.40 | — |
| 1972FM (M) | 13,000 | — | — | — | 0.60 | — |
| 1972FM (P) | 16,000 | Value: 1.00 | | | | |

**10 CENTS KM# 58 Composition:** Copper-Nickel

| Date | Mintage | F | VF | XF | Unc | BU |
|---|---|---|---|---|---|---|
| 1973FM (M) | 14,000 | — | — | — | 1.00 | — |
| 1973FM (P) | 20,000 | Value: 2.50 | | | | |

**10 CENTS KM# 27 Composition:** Copper-Nickel **Reverse:** Flaming Hibiscus

| Date | Mintage | F | VF | XF | Unc | BU |
|---|---|---|---|---|---|---|
| 1974FM (M) | 16,000 | — | — | — | 1.00 | — |
| 1974FM (P) | 14,000 | Value: 1.00 | | | | |
| 1975 | 4,000,000 | — | — | 0.10 | 0.25 | — |
| 1975FM (M) | 13,000 | — | — | — | 0.50 | — |
| 1975FM (U) | 1,111 | — | — | — | 1.75 | — |
| 1975FM (P) | 24,000 | Value: 1.00 | | | | |
| 1976 | 14,720,000 | — | — | 0.10 | 0.20 | |

**25 CENTS KM# 4 Composition:** Copper-Nickel

| Date | Mintage | F | VF | XF | Unc | BU |
|---|---|---|---|---|---|---|
| 1966 | 7,200,000 | — | 0.10 | 0.15 | 0.35 | — |
| 1966 Proof | 8,000 | Value: 1.75 | | | | |
| 1967 | 1,800,000 | — | 0.10 | 0.15 | 0.50 | — |
| 1970 Proof | 2,014 | Value: 2.25 | | | | |
| 1971 | 1,500,000 | — | 0.10 | 0.15 | 0.50 | — |
| 1971FM (M) | 11,000 | — | — | — | 0.65 | — |
| 1971FM (P) | 12,000 | Value: 1.25 | | | | |
| 1972 | 3,000,000 | — | 0.10 | 0.15 | 0.35 | |

**25 CENTS KM# 12 Composition:** Copper-Nickel **Subject:** 10th Anniversary of Independence

| Date | Mintage | F | VF | XF | Unc | BU |
|---|---|---|---|---|---|---|
| 1972 | 14,000 | — | — | — | 0.60 | — |
| 1972FM (M) | 5,000 | — | — | — | 1.50 | — |
| 1972FM (P) | 16,000 | Value: 1.25 | | | | |

**25 CENTS** **KM# 59** **Composition:** Copper-Nickel

| Date | Mintage | F | VF | XF | Unc | BU |
|---|---|---|---|---|---|---|
| 1973FM (M) | 6,575 | — | — | — | 2.25 | — |
| 1973FM (P) | 20,000 | Value: 3.00 | | | | |

**25 CENTS** **KM# 28** **Composition:** Copper-Nickel **Reverse:** Chaconia

| Date | Mintage | F | VF | XF | Unc | BU |
|---|---|---|---|---|---|---|
| 1974FM (M) | 8,258 | — | — | — | 1.75 | — |
| 1974FM (P) | 14,000 | Value: 1.25 | | | | |
| 1975 | 3,000,000 | — | 0.10 | 0.15 | 0.30 | — |
| 1975FM (M) | 5,000 | — | — | — | 1.50 | — |
| 1975FM (U) | 1,111 | — | — | — | 2.00 | — |
| 1975FM (P) | 24,000 | Value: 1.25 | | | | |
| 1976 | 9,000,000 | — | 0.10 | 0.15 | 0.30 | — |

**50 CENTS** **KM# 5** **Composition:** Copper-Nickel

| Date | Mintage | F | VF | XF | Unc | BU |
|---|---|---|---|---|---|---|
| 1966 | 975,000 | — | 0.25 | 0.50 | 1.25 | — |
| 1966 Proof | 8,000 | Value: 2.50 | | | | |
| 1967 | 750,000 | — | 0.25 | 0.50 | 1.25 | — |
| 1970 Proof | 2,104 | Value: 3.00 | | | | |
| 1971FM (M) | 5,714 | — | — | — | 2.00 | — |
| 1971FM (P) | 12,000 | Value: 1.75 | | | | |

**50 CENTS** **KM# 13** **Composition:** Copper-Nickel **Subject:** 10th Anniversary of Independence

| Date | Mintage | F | VF | XF | Unc | BU |
|---|---|---|---|---|---|---|
| 1972 | 375,000 | — | 0.50 | 0.75 | 1.50 | — |
| 1972FM (M) | 2,500 | — | — | — | 5.00 | — |
| 1972FM (P) | 16,000 | Value: 1.75 | | | | |

**50 CENTS** **KM# 22** **Composition:** Copper-Nickel **Reverse:** Steel drum with hands of player

| Date | Mintage | F | VF | XF | Unc | BU |
|---|---|---|---|---|---|---|
| 1973FM (M) | 4,075 | — | — | — | 2.50 | — |
| 1973FM (P) | 20,000 | Value: 2.25 | | | | |
| 1974FM (M) | 5,758 | — | — | — | 2.00 | — |
| 1974FM (P) | 14,000 | Value: 2.25 | | | | |
| 1975FM (M) | 2,500 | — | — | — | 3.75 | — |
| 1975FM (U) | 1,111 | — | — | — | 2.25 | — |
| 1975FM (P) | 24,000 | Value: 2.00 | | | | |
| 1976 | 750,000 | — | 0.50 | 0.75 | 1.50 | — |

**DOLLAR** **KM# 6** **Composition:** Nickel **Series:** F.A.O

| Date | Mintage | F | VF | XF | Unc | BU |
|---|---|---|---|---|---|---|
| 1969 | 250,000 | — | 0.75 | 1.50 | 3.50 | — |

**DOLLAR** **KM# 7** **Composition:** Nickel

| Date | Mintage | F | VF | XF | Unc | BU |
|---|---|---|---|---|---|---|
| 1970 Proof | 2,014 | Value: 5.00 | | | | |

**DOLLAR** **KM# 7a** **Composition:** Copper-Nickel

| Date | Mintage | F | VF | XF | Unc | BU |
|---|---|---|---|---|---|---|
| 1971FM (M) | 2,857 | — | — | — | 4.00 | — |
| 1971FM (P) | 12,000 | Value: 2.00 | | | | |

**DOLLAR** **KM# 14** **Composition:** Copper-Nickel **Subject:** 10th Anniversary of Independence

| Date | Mintage | F | VF | XF | Unc | BU |
|---|---|---|---|---|---|---|
| 1972 | 9,700 | — | — | — | 4.00 | — |
| 1972FM (M) | 1,250 | — | — | — | 12.50 | — |
| 1972FM (P) | 16,000 | Value: 3.00 | | | | |

**DOLLAR** **KM# 23** **Composition:** Copper-Nickel **Reverse:** Coerico

| Date | Mintage | F | VF | XF | Unc | BU |
|---|---|---|---|---|---|---|
| 1973FM (M) | 2,825 | — | — | — | 4.00 | — |
| 1973FM (P) | 20,000 | Value: 3.00 | | | | |
| 1974FM (M) | 4,508 | — | — | — | 4.00 | — |
| 1974FM (P) | 14,000 | Value: 3.00 | | | | |
| 1975FM (M) | 1,250 | — | — | — | 6.00 | — |
| 1975FM (U) | 1,111 | — | — | — | 5.00 | — |
| 1975FM (P) | 24,000 | Value: 3.00 | | | | |

**5 DOLLARS** **KM# 8** **Weight:** 29.7000 g. **Composition:** 0.9250 Silver .8833 oz. ASW **Reverse:** Scarlet Ibis

| Date | Mintage | F | VF | XF | Unc | BU |
|---|---|---|---|---|---|---|
| 1971FM (M) | 571 | — | — | — | 25.00 | — |
| 1971FM (P) | 11,000 | Value: 10.00 | | | | |
| 1973FM (M) | 1,825 | — | — | — | 20.00 | — |
| 1973FM (P) | 25,000 | Value: 9.00 | | | | |
| 1974FM (P) | 16,000 | Value: 12.00 | | | | |
| 1975FM (P) | 26,000 | Value: 9.00 | | | | |

**5 DOLLARS** **KM# 15** **Weight:** 29.7000 g. **Composition:** 0.9250 Silver .8833 oz. ASW **Subject:** 10th Anniversary of Independence

| Date | Mintage | F | VF | XF | Unc | BU |
|---|---|---|---|---|---|---|
| 1972 | 10,000 | — | — | — | 10.00 | — |
| 1972FM | 250 | — | — | — | 40.00 | — |
| 1972FM Proof | 19,000 | Value: 10.00 | | | | |

**5 DOLLARS** **KM# 8a** **Composition:** Copper-Nickel

| Date | Mintage | F | VF | XF | Unc | BU |
|---|---|---|---|---|---|---|
| 1974FM (M) | 3,508 | — | — | — | 6.00 | — |
| 1975FM (M) | 250 | — | — | — | 15.00 | — |
| 1975FM (U) | 1,111 | — | — | — | 8.00 | — |

**10 DOLLARS** **KM# 16** **Weight:** 35.0000 g. **Composition:** 0.9250 Silver 1.0409 oz. ASW **Subject:** 10th Anniversary of Independence

| Date | Mintage | F | VF | XF | Unc | BU |
|---|---|---|---|---|---|---|
| 1972 | — | — | — | — | 11.00 | — |
| 1972FM (M) | 125 | — | — | — | 125 | — |
| 1972FM (P) | 26,000 | Value: 11.00 | | | | |

**10 DOLLARS** KM# 24 **Weight:** 35.0000 g. **Composition:** 0.9250 Silver 1.0409 oz. ASW **Reverse:** Antique mariner's map

| Date | Mintage | F | VF | XF | Unc | BU |
|---|---|---|---|---|---|---|
| 1973FM (M) | 1,700 | — | — | — | 17.50 | — |
| 1973FM (U) | — | — | — | — | 16.50 | — |
| 1973FM (P) | 24,000 | Value: 12.50 | | | | |
| 1974FM (P) | 21,000 | Value: 12.50 | | | | |
| 1975FM (P) | 28,000 | Value: 13.50 | | | | |

**10 DOLLARS** KM# 24a **Composition:** Copper-Nickel

| Date | Mintage | F | VF | XF | Unc | BU |
|---|---|---|---|---|---|---|
| 1974FM (M) | 3,632 | — | — | — | 10.00 | — |
| 1975FM (M) | 125 | — | — | — | 50.00 | — |
| 1975FM (U) | 1,111 | — | — | — | 12.00 | — |

# REPUBLIC

## STANDARD COINAGE

100 Cents = 1 Dollar

**CENT** KM# 29 **Composition:** Bronze

| Date | Mintage | F | VF | XF | Unc | BU |
|---|---|---|---|---|---|---|
| 1976FM (M) | 150,000 | — | — | — | 0.25 | — |
| 1976FM (U) | 582 | — | — | — | 1.50 | — |
| 1976FM (P) | 10,000 | Value: 0.50 | | | | |
| 1977 | 25,000,000 | — | — | — | 0.25 | — |
| 1977FM (M) | 150,000 | — | — | — | 0.25 | — |
| 1977FM (U) | 633 | — | — | — | 1.50 | — |
| 1977FM (P) | 5,337 | Value: 0.50 | | | | |
| 1978 | 12,500,000 | — | — | — | 0.25 | — |
| 1978FM (M) | 150,000 | — | — | — | 0.25 | — |
| 1978FM (U) | 472 | — | — | — | 1.50 | — |
| 1978FM (P) | 4,845 | Value: 1.00 | | | | |
| 1979 | 30,200,000 | — | — | — | 0.25 | — |
| 1979FM (M) | 150,000 | — | — | — | 0.25 | — |
| 1979FM (U) | 518 | — | — | — | 1.50 | — |
| 1979FM (P) | 3,270 | Value: 1.00 | | | | |
| 1980 | 12,500,000 | — | — | — | 0.25 | — |
| 1980FM (M) | 75,000 | — | — | — | 0.25 | — |
| 1980FM (U) | 796 | — | — | — | 1.50 | — |
| 1980FM (P) | 2,393 | Value: 1.00 | | | | |
| 1981 | — | — | — | — | 0.25 | — |
| 1981FM (M) | — | — | — | — | 0.25 | — |
| 1981FM (U) | — | — | — | — | 1.50 | — |
| 1981FM (P) | — | Value: 1.00 | | | | |
| 1982 | — | — | — | — | 0.25 | — |
| 1983 | — | — | — | — | 0.25 | — |
| 1984 | — | — | — | — | 0.25 | — |
| 1985 | 25,400,000 | — | — | — | 0.25 | — |
| 1986 | 10,000,000 | — | — | — | 0.25 | — |
| 1987 | 10,000,000 | — | — | — | 0.25 | — |
| 1988 | 5,000,000 | — | — | — | 0.25 | — |
| 1989 | — | — | — | — | 0.25 | — |
| 1990 | — | — | — | — | 0.25 | — |
| 1991 | — | — | — | — | 0.25 | — |
| 1993 | — | — | — | — | 0.25 | — |
| 1994 | — | — | — | — | 0.25 | — |
| 1995 | — | — | — | — | 0.25 | — |
| 1996 | — | — | — | — | 0.25 | — |
| 1997 | — | — | — | — | 0.25 | — |

**CENT** KM# 29a **Weight:** 2.0000 g. **Composition:** 0.9250 Silver .0594 oz. ASW

| Date | Mintage | F | VF | XF | Unc | BU |
|---|---|---|---|---|---|---|
| 1981FM (P) | 898 | Value: 10.00 | | | | |

**CENT** KM# 42 **Composition:** Bronze **Subject:** 20th Anniversary of Independence

| Date | Mintage | F | VF | XF | Unc | BU |
|---|---|---|---|---|---|---|
| 1982FM (M) | — | — | — | — | 0.15 | — |
| 1982FM (U) | — | — | — | — | 1.50 | — |
| 1982FM (P) | — | Value: 1.00 | | | | |

**CENT** KM# 42a **Weight:** 2.0000 g. **Composition:** 0.9250 Silver .0594 oz. ASW

| Date | Mintage | F | VF | XF | Unc | BU |
|---|---|---|---|---|---|---|
| 1982FM (P) | 699 | Value: 10.00 | | | | |

**CENT** KM# 51 **Composition:** Bronze

| Date | Mintage | F | VF | XF | Unc | BU |
|---|---|---|---|---|---|---|
| 1983FM (M) | — | — | — | — | 1.50 | — |
| 1983FM (P) | — | Value: 1.00 | | | | |
| 1984FM (P) | — | Value: 1.00 | | | | |

**CENT** KM# 51a **Weight:** 2.0000 g. **Composition:** 0.9250 Silver .0594 oz. ASW

| Date | Mintage | F | VF | XF | Unc | BU |
|---|---|---|---|---|---|---|
| 1983FM (P) | 1,344 | Value: 10.00 | | | | |
| 1984FM (P) | — | Value: 10.00 | | | | |

**5 CENTS** KM# 30 **Composition:** Bronze

| Date | Mintage | F | VF | XF | Unc | BU |
|---|---|---|---|---|---|---|
| 1976FM (M) | 30,000 | — | — | — | 0.25 | — |
| 1976FM (U) | 582 | — | — | — | 1.75 | — |
| 1976FM (P) | 10,000 | Value: 0.75 | | | | |
| 1977 | 12,000,000 | — | — | 0.10 | 0.25 | — |
| 1977FM (M) | 30,000 | — | — | — | 0.25 | — |
| 1977FM (U) | 633 | — | — | — | 1.75 | — |
| 1977FM (P) | 5,337 | Value: 0.75 | | | | |
| 1978 | 1,500,000 | — | — | 0.10 | 0.25 | — |
| 1978FM (M) | 30,000 | — | — | — | 0.25 | — |
| 1978FM (U) | 472 | — | — | — | 1.75 | — |
| 1978FM (P) | 4,845 | Value: 1.25 | | | | |
| 1979 | — | — | — | 0.10 | 0.25 | — |
| 1979FM (M) | 30,000 | — | — | — | 0.25 | — |
| 1979FM (U) | 518 | — | — | — | 1.75 | — |
| 1979FM (P) | 3,270 | Value: 1.25 | | | | |
| 1980 | 15,000,000 | — | — | 0.10 | 0.25 | — |
| 1980FM (M) | 15,000 | — | — | — | 0.25 | — |
| 1980FM (U) | 796 | — | — | — | 5.00 | — |
| 1980FM (P) | 2,393 | Value: 1.25 | | | | |
| 1981 | — | — | — | 0.10 | 0.25 | — |
| 1981FM (M) | — | — | — | — | 0.25 | — |
| 1981FM (U) | — | — | — | — | 1.75 | — |
| 1981FM (P) | — | Value: 1.25 | | | | |
| 1983 | — | — | — | 0.10 | 0.25 | — |
| 1984 | 4,094,999 | — | — | 0.10 | 1.00 | — |
| 1988 | 20,000,000 | — | — | 0.10 | 0.25 | — |
| 1990 | — | — | — | 0.10 | 0.25 | — |
| 1992 | — | — | — | 0.10 | 0.25 | — |
| 1995 | — | — | — | 0.10 | 0.25 | — |
| 1996 | — | — | — | 0.10 | 0.25 | — |
| 1997 | — | — | — | 0.10 | 0.25 | — |

**5 CENTS** KM# 30a **Weight:** 3.5000 g. **Composition:** 0.9250 Silver .1040 oz. ASW

| Date | Mintage | F | VF | XF | Unc | BU |
|---|---|---|---|---|---|---|
| 1981FM (P) | 898 | Value: 15.00 | | | | |

**5 CENTS** KM# 43 **Composition:** Bronze **Subject:** 20th Anniversary of Independence **Obverse:** Coat of arms

| Date | Mintage | F | VF | XF | Unc | BU |
|---|---|---|---|---|---|---|
| 1982FM (M) | — | — | — | — | 0.75 | — |
| 1982FM (U) | — | — | — | — | 2.00 | — |
| 1982FM (P) | — | Value: 1.50 | | | | |

**5 CENTS** KM# 43a **Weight:** 3.5000 g. **Composition:** 0.9250 Silver .1040 oz. ASW

| Date | Mintage | F | VF | XF | Unc | BU |
|---|---|---|---|---|---|---|
| 1982FM (P) | 699 | Value: 15.00 | | | | |

**5 CENTS** KM# 52 **Composition:** Bronze **Obverse:** Coat of arms

| Date | Mintage | F | VF | XF | Unc | BU |
|---|---|---|---|---|---|---|
| 1983FM (M) | — | — | — | — | 2.50 | — |
| 1983FM (P) | — | Value: 1.75 | | | | |
| 1984FM (P) | — | Value: 1.75 | | | | |

**5 CENTS** KM# 52a **Weight:** 3.5000 g. **Composition:** 0.9250 Silver .1040 oz. ASW

| Date | Mintage | F | VF | XF | Unc | BU |
|---|---|---|---|---|---|---|
| 1983FM (P) | 1,324 | Value: 15.00 | | | | |
| 1984FM (P) | — | Value: 15.00 | | | | |

**10 CENTS** KM# 31 **Composition:** Copper-Nickel

| Date | Mintage | F | VF | XF | Unc | BU |
|---|---|---|---|---|---|---|
| 1976FM (M) | 15,000 | — | — | — | 0.50 | — |
| 1976FM (U) | 582 | — | — | — | 5.00 | — |
| 1976FM (P) | 10,000 | Value: 1.00 | | | | |
| 1977 | 17,280,000 | — | — | 0.10 | 0.20 | — |
| 1977FM (M) | 15,000 | — | — | — | 0.50 | — |
| 1977FM (U) | 633 | — | — | — | 5.00 | — |
| 1977FM (P) | 5,337 | Value: 1.00 | | | | |
| 1978 | 10,000,000 | — | — | 0.10 | 0.20 | — |
| 1978FM (M) | 15,000 | — | — | — | 0.50 | — |
| 1978FM (U) | 472 | — | — | — | 5.00 | — |
| 1978FM (P) | 4,845 | Value: 1.50 | | | | |
| 1979 | 1,970,000 | — | — | 0.10 | 0.30 | — |
| 1979FM (M) | 15,000 | — | — | — | 0.50 | — |
| 1979FM (U) | 518 | — | — | — | 5.00 | — |
| 1979FM (P) | 3,270 | Value: 1.50 | | | | |
| 1980 | 20,000,000 | — | — | 0.10 | 0.30 | — |
| 1980FM (M) | 7,500 | — | — | — | 0.50 | — |
| 1980FM (U) | 796 | — | — | — | 5.00 | — |
| 1980FM (P) | 2,393 | Value: 1.50 | | | | |
| 1981 | — | — | — | 0.10 | 0.30 | — |
| 1981FM (M) | — | — | — | — | 0.50 | — |
| 1981FM (U) | — | — | — | — | 5.00 | — |
| 1981FM (P) | — | Value: 1.50 | | | | |
| 1990 | — | — | — | 0.10 | 0.30 | — |
| 1997 | — | — | — | — | 0.50 | — |

**10 CENTS** KM# 31a **Weight:** 1.5000 g. **Composition:** 0.9250 Silver .0446 oz. ASW

| Date | Mintage | F | VF | XF | Unc | BU |
|---|---|---|---|---|---|---|
| 1981FM (P) | 898 | Value: 15.00 | | | | |

**10 CENTS** KM# 44 **Composition:** Copper-Nickel **Subject:** 20th Anniversary of Independence **Obverse:** Coat of arms

| Date | Mintage | F | VF | XF | Unc | BU |
|---|---|---|---|---|---|---|
| 1982FM (M) | — | — | — | — | 0.75 | — |
| 1982FM (U) | — | — | — | — | 2.50 | — |
| 1982FM (P) | — | Value: 2.00 | | | | |

**10 CENTS** KM# 44a **Weight:** 1.5000 g. **Composition:** 0.9250 Silver .0446 oz. ASW

| Date | Mintage | F | VF | XF | Unc | BU |
|---|---|---|---|---|---|---|
| 1982FM (P) | 699 | Value: 15.00 | | | | |

**10 CENTS** KM# 53 **Composition:** Copper-Nickel **Obverse:** Coat of arms

| Date | Mintage | F | VF | XF | Unc | BU |
|---|---|---|---|---|---|---|
| 1983FM (M) | — | — | — | — | 2.00 | — |
| 1983FM (P) | — | Value: 1.75 | | | | |
| 1984FM (P) | — | Value: 1.75 | | | | |

**10 CENTS** KM# 53a **Weight:** 1.5000 g. **Composition:** 0.9250 Silver .0446 oz. ASW

| Date | Mintage | F | VF | XF | Unc | BU |
|---|---|---|---|---|---|---|
| 1983FM (P) | — | Value: 10.00 | | | | |
| 1984FM (P) | — | Value: 10.00 | | | | |

**25 CENTS** KM# 32 **Composition:** Copper-Nickel

| Date | Mintage | F | VF | XF | Unc | BU |
|---|---|---|---|---|---|---|
| 1976FM (M) | 6,000 | — | — | — | 1.00 | — |
| 1976FM (U) | 582 | — | — | — | 5.00 | — |
| 1976FM (P) | 10,000 | Value: 1.25 | | | | |
| 1977 | 9,000,000 | — | 0.10 | 0.15 | 0.30 | — |
| 1977FM (M) | 6,000 | — | — | — | 1.00 | — |
| 1977FM (U) | 633 | — | — | — | 5.00 | — |
| 1977FM (P) | 5,337 | Value: 1.25 | | | | |
| 1978 | 5,470,000 | — | 0.10 | 0.15 | 0.30 | — |
| 1978FM (M) | 6,000 | — | — | — | 1.00 | — |
| 1978FM (U) | 472 | — | — | — | 5.00 | — |
| 1978FM (P) | 4,845 | Value: 1.75 | | | | |
| 1979 | — | — | 0.10 | 0.15 | 0.40 | — |
| 1979FM (M) | 6,000 | — | — | — | 1.00 | — |
| 1979FM (U) | 518 | — | — | — | 5.00 | — |
| 1979FM (P) | 3,270 | Value: 1.75 | | | | |
| 1980 | 15,000,000 | — | 0.10 | 0.15 | 0.40 | — |
| 1980FM (M) | 3,000 | — | — | — | 1.00 | — |
| 1980FM (U) | 796 | — | — | — | 5.00 | — |
| 1980FM (P) | 2,393 | Value: 1.75 | | | | |
| 1981 | — | — | 0.10 | 0.15 | 0.40 | — |
| 1981FM (M) | — | — | — | — | 1.00 | — |
| 1981FM (U) | — | — | — | — | 5.00 | — |
| 1981FM (P) | — | Value: 1.75 | | | | |
| 1983 | — | — | 0.10 | 0.15 | 0.40 | — |
| 1983FM (M) | — | — | — | — | 2.00 | — |
| 1983FM (P) | — | Value: 1.75 | | | | |
| 1984 | — | — | 0.10 | 0.15 | 0.40 | — |
| 1984 | — | Value: 1.75 | | | | |
| 1993 | — | — | — | 0.15 | 0.40 | — |
| 1997 | — | — | — | 0.15 | 0.40 | — |

**25 CENTS** KM# 32a **Weight:** 3.6000 g. **Composition:** 0.9250 Silver .1070 oz. ASW

| Date | Mintage | F | VF | XF | Unc | BU |
|---|---|---|---|---|---|---|
| 1981FM (P) | 898 | Value: 10.00 | | | | |
| 1983FM (P) | — | Value: 10.00 | | | | |
| 1984FM (P) | — | Value: 10.00 | | | | |

**25 CENTS** KM# 45 **Composition:** Copper-Nickel **Subject:** 20th Anniversary of Independence **Obverse:** Coat of arms

| Date | Mintage | F | VF | XF | Unc | BU |
|---|---|---|---|---|---|---|
| 1982FM (M) | — | — | — | — | 1.00 | — |
| 1982FM (U) | — | — | — | — | 2.25 | — |
| 1982FM (P) | — | Value: 1.75 | | | | |

**25 CENTS** KM# 45a **Weight:** 3.6000 g. **Composition:** 0.9250 Silver .1070 oz. ASW

| Date | Mintage | F | VF | XF | Unc | BU |
|---|---|---|---|---|---|---|
| 1982FM (P) | 699 | Value: 15.00 | | | | |

**50 CENTS** KM# 33 **Composition:** Copper-Nickel

| Date | Mintage | F | VF | XF | Unc | BU |
|---|---|---|---|---|---|---|
| 1976FM (M) | 3,000 | — | — | — | 3.25 | — |
| 1976FM (U) | 582 | — | — | — | 5.00 | — |
| 1976FM (P) | 10,000 | Value: 1.50 | | | | |
| 1977 | 1,500,000 | — | 0.25 | 0.50 | 1.00 | — |
| 1977FM (M) | 3,000 | — | — | — | 3.00 | — |
| 1977FM (U) | 633 | — | — | — | 5.00 | — |
| 1977FM (P) | 5,337 | Value: 1.50 | | | | |
| 1978 | 563,000 | — | 0.50 | 0.75 | 1.50 | — |
| 1978FM (M) | 3,000 | — | — | — | 3.00 | — |
| 1978FM (U) | 472 | — | — | — | 5.00 | — |
| 1978FM (P) | 4,845 | Value: 2.00 | | | | |
| 1979 | 750,000 | — | 0.50 | 0.75 | 1.50 | — |
| 1979FM (M) | 3,000 | — | — | — | 3.25 | — |
| 1979FM (U) | 518 | — | — | — | 5.00 | — |
| 1979FM (P) | 3,270 | Value: 2.00 | | | | |
| 1980 | 3,750,000 | — | 0.25 | 0.50 | 1.00 | — |
| 1980FM (M) | 1,500 | — | — | — | 3.00 | — |
| 1980FM (U) | 796 | — | — | — | 5.00 | — |
| 1980FM (P) | 2,393 | Value: 2.00 | | | | |
| 1981FM (M) | — | — | — | — | 3.00 | — |
| 1981FM (U) | — | — | — | — | 5.00 | — |
| 1981FM (P) | — | Value: 2.00 | | | | |

**50 CENTS** KM# 33a **Weight:** 7.2500 g. **Composition:** 0.9250 Silver .2156 oz. ASW

| Date | Mintage | F | VF | XF | Unc | BU |
|---|---|---|---|---|---|---|
| 1981FM (P) | 898 | Value: 15.00 | | | | |

**50 CENTS** KM# 46 **Composition:** Copper-Nickel **Subject:** 20th Anniversary of Independence **Obverse:** Coat of arms

| Date | Mintage | F | VF | XF | Unc | BU |
|---|---|---|---|---|---|---|
| 1982FM (M) | — | — | — | — | 3.00 | — |
| 1982FM (U) | — | — | — | — | 2.50 | — |
| 1982FM (P) | — | Value: 2.00 | | | | |

**50 CENTS** KM# 46a **Weight:** 7.2500 g. **Composition:** 0.9250 Silver .2156 oz. ASW

| Date | Mintage | F | VF | XF | Unc | BU |
|---|---|---|---|---|---|---|
| 1982FM (P) | 699 | Value: 20.00 | | | | |

**50 CENTS** KM# 54 **Composition:** Copper-Nickel **Obverse:** Coat of arms

| Date | Mintage | F | VF | XF | Unc | BU |
|---|---|---|---|---|---|---|
| 1983FM (M) | — | — | — | — | 4.00 | — |
| 1983FM (P) | — | Value: 2.00 | | | | |
| 1984FM (P) | — | Value: 2.00 | | | | |

**50 CENTS** KM# 54a **Weight:** 7.2500 g. **Composition:** 0.9250 Silver .2156 oz. ASW

| Date | Mintage | F | VF | XF | Unc | BU |
|---|---|---|---|---|---|---|
| 1983FM (P) | 1,325 | Value: 15.00 | | | | |
| 1984FM (P) | — | Value: 15.00 | | | | |

**DOLLAR** KM# 34 **Composition:** Copper-Nickel

| Date | Mintage | F | VF | XF | Unc | BU |
|---|---|---|---|---|---|---|
| 1976FM (M) | 1,500 | — | — | — | 5.00 | — |
| 1976FM (U) | 582 | — | — | — | 8.00 | — |
| 1976FM (P) | 10,000 | Value: 2.00 | | | | |
| 1977FM (M) | 1,500 | — | — | — | 6.00 | — |
| 1977FM (U) | 633 | — | — | — | 8.00 | — |
| 1977FM (P) | 5,337 | Value: 2.00 | | | | |
| 1978FM (M) | 1,500 | — | — | — | 6.00 | — |
| 1978FM (U) | 472 | — | — | — | 8.00 | — |
| 1978FM (P) | 4,845 | Value: 3.00 | | | | |
| 1979FM (M) | 1,500 | — | — | — | 6.00 | — |
| 1979FM (U) | 518 | — | — | — | 8.00 | — |
| 1979FM (P) | 3,270 | Value: 3.00 | | | | |
| 1980FM (M) | 750 | — | — | — | 8.00 | — |
| 1980FM (U) | 796 | — | — | — | 8.00 | — |
| 1980FM (P) | 2,393 | Value: 5.00 | | | | |
| 1981FM (M) | — | — | — | — | 5.00 | — |
| 1981FM (U) | — | — | — | — | 3.00 | — |
| 1981FM (P) | — | Value: 2.50 | | | | |
| 1983FM (M) | — | — | — | — | 5.00 | — |
| 1983FM (P) | — | Value: 2.50 | | | | |
| 1984FM (P) | — | Value: 2.50 | | | | |

**DOLLAR** KM# 38 **Weight:** 18.6000 g. **Composition:** 0.9250 Silver .5532 oz. ASW **Series:** F.A.O.

| Date | Mintage | F | VF | XF | Unc | BU |
|---|---|---|---|---|---|---|
| 1979 | — | — | 0.75 | 1.50 | 3.50 | — |

**DOLLAR** KM# 34a **Weight:** 18.6000 g. **Composition:** 0.9250 Silver .5532 oz. ASW

| Date | Mintage | F | VF | XF | Unc | BU |
|---|---|---|---|---|---|---|
| 1981FM (P) | 898 | Value: 20.00 | | | | |
| 1983FM (P) | 2,544 | Value: 16.50 | | | | |
| 1984FM (P) | — | Value: 16.50 | | | | |

**DOLLAR** KM# 47 **Composition:** Copper-Nickel **Subject:** 20th Anniversary of Independence **Obverse:** Coat of arms

| Date | Mintage | F | VF | XF | Unc | BU |
|---|---|---|---|---|---|---|
| 1982FM (M) | — | — | — | — | 8.00 | — |
| 1982FM (U) | — | — | — | — | 5.00 | — |
| 1982FM (P) | — | Value: 5.00 | | | | |

**DOLLAR** KM# 47a **Weight:** 18.6000 g. **Composition:** 0.9250 Silver .5532 oz. ASW

| Date | Mintage | F | VF | XF | Unc | BU |
|---|---|---|---|---|---|---|
| 1982FM (P) | 699 | Value: 20.00 | | | | |

**DOLLAR** KM# 61 **Composition:** Copper-Nickel **Subject:** 50th Anniversary - F.A.O.

| Date | Mintage | F | VF | XF | Unc | BU |
|---|---|---|---|---|---|---|
| 1995 | — | — | — | — | 1.75 | — |

**5 DOLLARS** KM# 35 **Weight:** 29.7000 g. **Composition:** 0.9250 Silver .8833 oz. ASW

| Date | Mintage | F | VF | XF | Unc | BU |
|---|---|---|---|---|---|---|
| 1976FM (P) | 11,000 | Value: 10.00 | | | | |
| 1977FM (P) | 6,107 | Value: 12.00 | | | | |
| 1978FM (P) | 5,460 | Value: 12.00 | | | | |
| 1979FM (P) | 3,755 | Value: 15.00 | | | | |
| 1980FM (P) | 2,393 | Value: 20.00 | | | | |
| 1981FM (P) | — | Value: 30.00 | | | | |
| 1983FM (P) | — | Value: 30.00 | | | | |
| 1984FM (P) | — | Value: 30.00 | | | | |

**5 DOLLARS** KM# 35a **Composition:** Copper-Nickel

| Date | Mintage | F | VF | XF | Unc | BU |
|---|---|---|---|---|---|---|
| 1976FM (M) | 300 | — | — | — | 20.00 | — |
| 1976FM (U) | 582 | — | — | — | 25.00 | — |
| 1977FM (M) | 300 | — | — | — | 20.00 | — |
| 1977FM (U) | 633 | — | — | — | 17.00 | — |
| 1978FM (M) | 300 | — | — | — | 20.00 | — |
| 1978FM (U) | 472 | — | — | — | 17.00 | — |
| 1979FM (M) | 300 | — | — | — | 20.00 | — |
| 1979FM (U) | 518 | — | — | — | 17.00 | — |
| 1980FM (M) | 150 | — | — | — | 20.00 | — |
| 1980FM (U) | 796 | — | — | — | 17.00 | — |
| 1981FM (M) | — | — | — | — | 20.00 | — |
| 1981FM (U) | — | — | — | — | 17.00 | — |
| 1981FM (P) | — | Value: 20.00 | | | | |
| 1983FM (U) | — | — | — | — | 20.00 | — |
| 1983FM (P) | 1,312 | Value: 20.00 | | | | |
| 1984FM (P) | — | Value: 20.00 | | | | |

**5 DOLLARS** **KM# 48** **Composition:** Copper-Nickel **Subject:** 20th Anniversary of Independence

| Date | Mintage | F | VF | XF | Unc | BU |
|---|---|---|---|---|---|---|
| 1982FM (M) | — | — | — | — | 20.00 | — |
| 1982FM (U) | — | — | — | — | 12.50 | — |
| 1982FM (P) | — | Value: 17.00 | | | | |

**5 DOLLARS** **KM# 48a** **Weight:** 30.0000 g. **Composition:** 0.9250 Silver .8922 oz. ASW

| Date | Mintage | F | VF | XF | Unc | BU |
|---|---|---|---|---|---|---|
| 1982FM (P) | 699 | Value: 30.00 | | | | |

**10 DOLLARS** **KM# 36** **Weight:** 35.0000 g. **Composition:** 0.9250 Silver 1.0409 oz. ASW **Reverse:** Similar to KM#16

| Date | Mintage | F | VF | XF | Unc | BU |
|---|---|---|---|---|---|---|
| 1976FM (P) | 13,000 | Value: 10.00 | | | | |
| 1977FM (P) | 6,643 | Value: 15.00 | | | | |
| 1978FM (P) | 7,449 | Value: 15.00 | | | | |
| 1979FM (P) | 4,994 | Value: 20.00 | | | | |
| 1980FM (P) | 3,726 | Value: 25.00 | | | | |

**10 DOLLARS** **KM# 36a** **Composition:** Copper-Nickel

| Date | Mintage | F | VF | XF | Unc | BU |
|---|---|---|---|---|---|---|
| 1976FM (M) | 150 | — | — | — | 40.00 | — |
| 1976FM (U) | 582 | — | — | — | 30.00 | — |
| 1977FM (M) | 150 | — | — | — | 40.00 | — |
| 1977FM (U) | 633 | — | — | — | 30.00 | — |
| 1978FM (M) | 150 | — | — | — | 40.00 | — |
| 1978FM (U) | 472 | — | — | — | 30.00 | — |
| 1979FM (M) | 150 | — | — | — | 40.00 | — |
| 1979FM (U) | 796 | — | — | — | 30.00 | — |
| 1980FM (M) | — | — | — | — | 40.00 | — |
| 1980FM (U) | — | — | — | — | 30.00 | — |

**10 DOLLARS** **KM# 40** **Composition:** Copper-Nickel **Subject:** 5th Anniversary of the Republic **Obverse:** Coat of arms

| Date | Mintage | F | VF | XF | Unc | BU |
|---|---|---|---|---|---|---|
| 1981FM (U) | — | — | — | — | 20.00 | — |

**10 DOLLARS** **KM# 40a** **Weight:** 35.0000 g. **Composition:** 0.9250 Silver 1.0409 oz. ASW

| Date | Mintage | F | VF | XF | Unc | BU |
|---|---|---|---|---|---|---|
| 1981FM (P) | 2,374 | Value: 25.00 | | | | |

**10 DOLLARS** **KM# 49** **Composition:** Copper-Nickel **Subject:** 20th Anniversary of Independence **Obverse:** Coat of arms

| Date | Mintage | F | VF | XF | Unc | BU |
|---|---|---|---|---|---|---|
| 1982FM (M) | — | — | — | — | 20.00 | — |
| 1982FM (U) | — | — | — | — | 20.00 | — |
| 1982FM (P) | — | Value: 20.00 | | | | |

**10 DOLLARS** **KM# 49a** **Weight:** 35.0000 g. **Composition:** 0.9250 Silver 1.0409 oz. ASW

| Date | Mintage | F | VF | XF | Unc | BU |
|---|---|---|---|---|---|---|
| 1982FM (P) | 1,682 | Value: 27.50 | | | | |

**10 DOLLARS** **KM# 55** **Composition:** Copper-Nickel **Obverse:** Coat of arms

| Date | Mintage | F | VF | XF | Unc | BU |
|---|---|---|---|---|---|---|
| 1983FM (U) | 288 | — | — | — | 50.00 | — |

**10 DOLLARS** **KM# 55a** **Weight:** 35.0000 g. **Composition:** 0.9250 Silver 1.0409 oz. ASW

| Date | Mintage | F | VF | XF | Unc | BU |
|---|---|---|---|---|---|---|
| 1983FM (P) | 1,565 | Value: 30.00 | | | | |
| 1984FM (P) | — | Value: 30.00 | | | | |

**10 DOLLARS** **KM# 60** **Weight:** 28.2800 g. **Composition:** 0.9250 Silver .8411 oz. ASW **Subject:** 30th Anniversary - Central Bank

| Date | Mintage | F | VF | XF | Unc | BU |
|---|---|---|---|---|---|---|
| 1994 Proof | Est. 5,000 | Value: 47.50 | | | | |

**10 DOLLARS** **KM# 62** **Ring Composition:** Gold Plated **Center Weight:** 12.0000 g. **Center Composition:** 0.9250 Silver .3569 oz. ASW **Subject:** Central Bank 35 Years **Obverse:** National arms **Reverse:** Bank building **Edge:** Reeded **Shape:** Octagonal **Size:** 28.4 mm.

| Date | Mintage | F | VF | XF | Unc | BU |
|---|---|---|---|---|---|---|
| 1999 Proof | 6,500 | Value: 55.00 | | | | |

**Note:** Plus $5.95 per order

**25 DOLLARS** **KM# 39** **Weight:** 30.2800 g. **Composition:** 0.5000 Silver .4868 oz. ASW **Subject:** 10th Anniversary of Caribbean Development Bank

| Date | Mintage | F | VF | XF | Unc | BU |
|---|---|---|---|---|---|---|
| 1980FM (P) | 3,039 | Value: 20.00 | | | | |

**100 DOLLARS** **KM# 37** **Weight:** 6.2100 g. **Composition:** 0.5000 Gold .0998 oz. AGW

| Date | Mintage | F | VF | XF | Unc | BU |
|---|---|---|---|---|---|---|
| 1976FM (M) | 200 | — | — | — | 100 | — |
| 1976FM (P) | 29,000 | Value: 55.00 | | | | |

**100 DOLLARS** **KM# 41** **Weight:** 6.2100 g. **Composition:** 0.5000 Gold .0998 oz. AGW **Subject:** 5th Anniversary of the Republic

| Date | Mintage | F | VF | XF | Unc | BU |
|---|---|---|---|---|---|---|
| 1981FM (U) | 100 | — | — | — | 175 | — |
| 1981FM (P) | 400 | Value: 150 | | | | |

**100 DOLLARS** **KM# 50** **Weight:** 6.2100 g. **Composition:** 0.5000 Gold .0998 oz. AGW **Subject:** 20th Anniversary of Independence

| Date | Mintage | F | VF | XF | Unc | BU |
|---|---|---|---|---|---|---|
| 1982FM (P) | 1,380 | Value: 90.00 | | | | |

**200 DOLLARS** **KM# 56** **Weight:** 11.1700 g. **Composition:** 0.5000 Gold .1796 oz. AGW **Subject:** 20th Anniversary of Central Bank

| Date | Mintage | F | VF | XF | Unc | BU |
|---|---|---|---|---|---|---|
| 1984FM (P) | 1,200 | Value: 100 | | | | |

## MINT SETS

| KM# | Date | Mintage | Identification | Issue Price | Mkt Val |
|---|---|---|---|---|---|
| MS1 | 1973 (8) | 1,575 | KM#8, 18-24 | 24.00 | 22.00 |
| MS12 | 1999 (6) | — | KM#29-33, 61 | 25.00 | 30.00 |
| MS2 | 1974 (8) | 3,258 | KM#8a, 22-23, 24a, 25-28 | 25.00 | 15.00 |
| MS3 | 1975 (8) | 1,111 | KM#8a, 22-23, 24a, 25-28 | 27.50 | 20.00 |
| MS4 | 1976 (8) | 582 | KM#29-34, 35a-36a | 27.50 | 30.00 |
| MS5 | 1977 (8) | 632 | KM#29-34, 35a-36a | 27.50 | 30.00 |
| MS6 | 1978 (8) | 472 | KM#29-34, 35a-36a | 27.50 | 30.00 |
| MS7 | 1979 (8) | 518 | KM#29-34, 35a-36a | 28.50 | 30.00 |
| MS8 | 1980 (8) | 796 | KM#29-34, 35a-36a | 28.50 | 30.00 |
| MS9 | 1981 (8) | — | KM#29-34, 35a, 40 | 28.50 | 40.00 |
| MS10 | 1982 (8) | — | KM#42-49 | 28.50 | 40.00 |
| MS11 | 1983 (8) | 281 | KM#32, 34, 35a, 51-55 | 37.00 | 90.00 |

## PROOF SETS

| KM# | Date | Mintage | Identification | Issue Price | Mkt Val |
|---|---|---|---|---|---|
| PS24 | 1999 (8) | 3,000 | KM#29-33, 35a, 61-62 | 90.00 | 95.00 |
| PS4 | 1971 (6) | 488 | KM#1-6 | 15.00 | 12.50 |
| PS7 | 1973 (8) | 14,615 | KM#8, 17, 19-24 | 35.00 | 20.00 |
| PS8 | 1973 (7) | 5,050 | KM#8, 17, 19-23 | 22.00 | 15.00 |
| PS1 | 1966 (5) | 8,000 | KM#1-5 | 12.50 | 10.00 |
| PS2 | 1970 (6) | 2,104 | KM#1-5, 7 | 15.25 | 12.50 |
| PS3 | 1971 (7) | 11,039 | KM#1-5, 7a, 8 | 21.00 | 15.00 |
| PS5 | 1972 (8) | 13,874 | KM#9-16 | 35.00 | 20.00 |
| PS6 | 1972 (7) | 15,957 | KM#9-15 | 22.00 | 12.50 |
| PS9 | 1974 (8) | 13,991 | KM#8, 22-28 | 50.00 | 20.00 |
| PS10 | 1975 (8) | 24,472 | KM#8, 22-28 | 55.00 | 22.00 |
| PS11 | 1976 (8) | 10,099 | KM#29-36 | 55.00 | 25.00 |
| PS12 | 1977 (8) | 5,337 | KM#29-36 | 55.00 | 35.00 |
| PS13 | 1978 (8) | 4,845 | KM#29-36 | 55.00 | 35.00 |
| PS14 | 1979 (8) | 3,270 | KM#29-36 | 57.00 | 40.00 |
| PS15 | 1980 (8) | 2,393 | KM#29-36 | 66.00 | 55.00 |
| PS16 | 1981 (8) | — | KM#29-34, 35a, 40a | 87.00 | 65.00 |
| PS17 | 1981 (8) | — | KM#29a-34a, 35, 40a | 222 | 125 |
| PS19 | 1982 (8) | — | KM#42a-49a | 222 | 135 |
| PS18 | 1982 (8) | — | KM#42-49 | 87.00 | 65.00 |
| PS20 | 1983 (8) | 461 | KM#32, 34, 35a, 51-54, 55a | 87.00 | 75.00 |
| PS21 | 1983 (8) | 753 | KM#32a, 34a, 35, 51a-55a | 197 | 100 |
| PS22 | 1984 (8) | — | KM#32, 34, 35a, 51-54, 55a | 87.00 | 75.00 |
| PS23 | 1984 (8) | — | KM#32a, 34a, 35, 51a-55a | 197 | 100 |

Tristan da Cunha is the principal island and group name of a small cluster of volcanic islands located in the South Atlantic midway between the Cape of Good Hope and South America, and 1,500 miles (2,414 km.) south-southwest of the British colony of St. Helena. The other islands are Inaccessible, Gough, and the three Nightingale Islands. The group, which comprises a dependency of St. Helena, has a total area of 40 sq. mi. (104 sq. km.) and a population of less than 300. There is a village of 60 houses called Edinburgh. Potatoes are the staple subsistence crop.

Portuguese admiral Tristao da Cunha discovered Tristan da Cunha in 1506. Unsuccessful attempts to colonize the islands were made by the Dutch in 1656, but the first permanent inhabitant didn't arrive until 1810.During the exile of Napoleon on St. Helena, Britain placed a temporary garrison on Tristan da Cunha to prevent any attempt to rescue Napoleon from his island prison. The islands were formally annexed to Britain in 1816 and became a dependency of St. Helena in 1938.

**RULERS**
British

**MINT MARKS**
PM - Pobjoy Mint

**MONETARY SYSTEM**
25 Pence = 1 Crown
4 Crowns = 1 Pound

# ST. HELENA DEPENDENCY

## STANDARD COINAGE

25 Pence = 1 Crown; 4 Crowns = 1 Pound

**25 PENCE** **KM# 1** **Composition:** Copper-Nickel **Subject:** Queen's Silver Jubilee

| Date | Mintage | F | VF | XF | Unc | BU |
|---|---|---|---|---|---|---|
| ND(1977) | 50,000 | — | 1.00 | 2.00 | 5.00 | — |

**25 PENCE** **KM# 1a** **Weight:** 28.2800 g. **Composition:** 0.9250 Silver .8411 oz. ASW

| Date | Mintage | F | VF | XF | Unc | BU |
|---|---|---|---|---|---|---|
| ND(1977) Proof | 25,000 | Value: 15.00 | | | | |

**25 PENCE** **KM# 3** **Composition:** Copper-Nickel **Subject:** 80th Birthday of Queen Mother

| Date | Mintage | F | VF | XF | Unc | BU |
|---|---|---|---|---|---|---|
| ND(1980) | 65,000 | — | 1.00 | 1.75 | 3.50 | — |

**25 PENCE** **KM# 3a** **Weight:** 28.2800 g. **Composition:** 0.9250 Silver .8411 oz. ASW

| Date | Mintage | F | VF | XF | Unc | BU |
|---|---|---|---|---|---|---|
| ND(1980) Proof | 25,000 | Value: 15.00 | | | | |

**25 PENCE** **KM# 4** **Composition:** Copper-Nickel **Subject:** Wedding of Prince Charles and Lady Diana

| Date | Mintage | F | VF | XF | Unc | BU |
|---|---|---|---|---|---|---|
| ND(1981)PM | — | — | 1.00 | 1.75 | 3.50 | — |

**25 PENCE** **KM# 4a** **Weight:** 28.2800 g. **Composition:** 0.9250 Silver .8411 oz. ASW

| Date | Mintage | F | VF | XF | Unc | BU |
|---|---|---|---|---|---|---|
| ND(1981)PM Proof | 30,000 | Value: 20.00 | | | | |

**50 PENCE** **KM# 7** **Weight:** 28.2800 g. **Composition:** 0.9250 Silver .8411 oz. ASW **Subject:** 40th Wedding Anniversary of Queen Elizabeth and Prince Philip

| Date | Mintage | F | VF | XF | Unc | BU |
|---|---|---|---|---|---|---|
| ND(1987) Proof | 2,000 | Value: 25.00 | | | | |

**50 PENCE** **KM# 7a** **Weight:** 47.5400 g. **Composition:** 0.9170 Gold 1.4001 oz. AGW **Subject:** 40th Wedding Anniversary of Queen Elizabeth and Prince Philip

| Date | Mintage | F | VF | XF | Unc | BU |
|---|---|---|---|---|---|---|
| ND(1987) Proof | 75 | Value: 950 | | | | |

**50 PENCE** **KM# 7b** **Composition:** Copper-Nickel

| Date | Mintage | F | VF | XF | Unc | BU |
|---|---|---|---|---|---|---|
| ND(1987) | — | — | — | — | 4.50 | — |

**50 PENCE** **KM# 9a** **Weight:** 28.2800 g. **Composition:** 0.9250 Silver .8411 oz. ASW **Subject:** Winston Churchill

| Date | Mintage | F | VF | XF | Unc | BU |
|---|---|---|---|---|---|---|
| 1999 Proof | 2,500 | Value: 42.50 | | | | |

**50 PENCE** **KM# 9b** **Weight:** 47.5400 g. **Composition:** 0.9170 Gold 1.4001 oz. AGW **Subject:** Winston Churchill

| Date | Mintage | F | VF | XF | Unc | BU |
|---|---|---|---|---|---|---|
| 1999 | Est. 100 | Value: 950 | | | | |

**50 PENCE** **KM# 9** **Weight:** 28.2800 g. **Composition:** Copper-Nickel **Subject:** Winston Churchill **Obverse:** Queen's portrait **Reverse:** Churchill and two fighter planes **Edge:** Reeded **Size:** 38.6 mm. **Note:** Struck at British Royal Mint.

| Date | Mintage | F | VF | XF | Unc | BU |
|---|---|---|---|---|---|---|
| 1999 | — | — | — | — | 6.50 | — |

50 PENCE KM# 11 Weight: 28.6400 g. Composition: Copper-Nickel Subject: Princess Anne's 50th Birthday Obverse: Queen Elizabeth's portrait Reverse: Anne's portrait Edge: Reeded Size: 38.6 mm.

| Date | Mintage | F | VF | XF | Unc | BU |
|---|---|---|---|---|---|---|
| ND(2000) | — | — | — | — | 6.50 | — |

50 PENCE KM# 12 Weight: 29.1000 g. Composition: Copper-Nickel Subject: Queen Elizabeth's 75th Birthday Obverse: Queen's portrait in profile Reverse: Queen's portrait facing viewer Edge: Reeded Size: 38.6 mm.

| Date | Mintage | F | VF | XF | Unc | BU |
|---|---|---|---|---|---|---|
| 2001 | — | — | — | — | 7.00 | — |

50 PENCE KM# 10 Weight: 28.6400 g. Composition: Copper-Nickel Subject: Queen Mother's Centennial Birthday Obverse: Queen Elizabeth's portrait Reverse: Queen Mother's portrait Edge: Reeded Size: 38.6 mm.

| Date | Mintage | F | VF | XF | Unc | BU |
|---|---|---|---|---|---|---|
| ND(2001) | — | — | — | — | 6.50 | — |

50 PENCE KM# 13 Weight: 29.6000 g. Composition: Copper-Nickel Subject: Centennial of Queen Victoria's Death Obverse: Queen Elizabeth's portrait. Reverse: Queen Victoria's portrait. Edge: Reeded. Size: 38.7 mm.

| Date | Mintage | F | VF | XF | Unc | BU |
|---|---|---|---|---|---|---|
| 2001 | — | — | — | — | 8.00 | — |

CROWN KM# 2 Composition: Copper-Nickel Subject: 25th Anniversary of Coronation

| Date | Mintage | F | VF | XF | Unc | BU |
|---|---|---|---|---|---|---|
| 1978PM | — | — | 1.00 | 1.75 | 3.50 | — |

CROWN KM# 2a Weight: 28.2800 g. Composition: 0.9250 Silver .8411 oz. ASW

| Date | Mintage | F | VF | XF | Unc | BU |
|---|---|---|---|---|---|---|
| 1978PM | 70,000 | — | — | — | 12.50 | — |
| 1978PM Proof | 25,000 | Value: 18.50 | | | | |

CROWN KM# 5 Weight: 28.2800 g. Composition: 0.9250 Silver .8411 oz. ASW Series: International Year of the Scout Obverse: Queen Elizabeth II

| Date | Mintage | F | VF | XF | Unc | BU |
|---|---|---|---|---|---|---|
| ND(1983) | 10,000 | — | — | — | 32.50 | — |
| ND(1983) Proof | 10,000 | Value: 47.50 | | | | |

2 POUNDS KM# 6 Weight: 15.9800 g. Composition: 0.9170 Gold .4712 oz. AGW Series: International Year of the Scout Obverse: Queen Elizabeth II Reverse: Sail boat

| Date | Mintage | F | VF | XF | Unc | BU |
|---|---|---|---|---|---|---|
| 1983 | 2,000 | — | — | — | 350 | — |
| 1983 Proof | 2,000 | Value: 500 | | | | |

2 POUNDS KM# 8 Composition: Copper-Nickel Subject: 90th Anniversary of Queen Mother

| Date | Mintage | F | VF | XF | Unc | BU |
|---|---|---|---|---|---|---|
| ND(1990) | — | — | — | — | 12.50 | — |

2 POUNDS KM# 8a Weight: 28.2800 g. Composition: 0.9250 Silver .8411 oz. ASW

| Date | Mintage | F | VF | XF | Unc | BU |
|---|---|---|---|---|---|---|
| ND(1990) Proof | Est. 10,000 | Value: 55.00 | | | | |

# TUNISIA

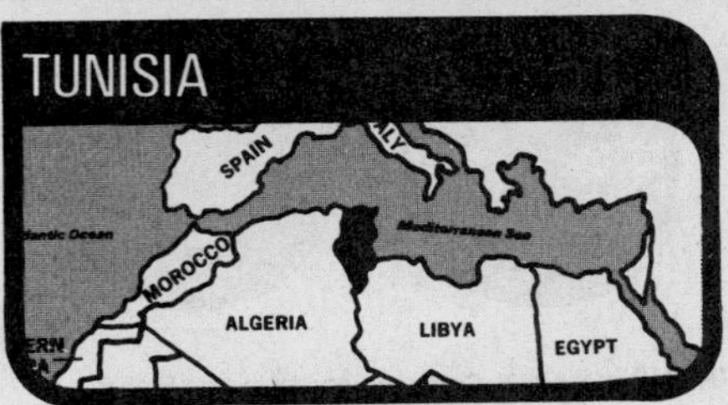


The Republic of Tunisia, located on the northern coast of Africa between Algeria and Libya, has an area of 63,170sq. mi. (163,610 sq. km.) and a population of *7.9 million. Capital: Tunis. Agriculture is the backbone of the economy. Crude oil, phosphates, olive oil, and wine are exported.

Tunisia, settled by the Phoenicians in the 12th century B.C., was the center of the seafaring Carthaginian Empire. After the total destruction of Carthage, Tunisia became part of Rome's African province. It remained a part of the Roman Empire (except for the 439-533 interval of Vandal conquest) until taken by the Arabs, 648, who administered it until the Turkish invasion of 1570. Under Turkish control, the public revenue was heavily dependent upon the piracy of Mediterranean shipping, an endeavor that wasn't abandoned until 1819 when a coalition of powers threatened appropriate reprisal. Deprived of its major source of income, Tunisia underwent a financial regression that ended in bankruptcy, enabling France to establish a protectorate over the country in 1881. National agitation and guerrilla fighting forced France to grant Tunisia internal autonomy in 1955 and to recognize Tunisian independence on March20, 1956. Tunisia abolished the monarchy and established a republic on July 25, 1957.

**TITLES**

المملكة التونسية

al-Mamlaka(t) al-Tunisiya(t)

الجمهورية التونسية

al-Jumhuriya(t) al-Tunisiya(t)

**MINT MARKS**

A - Paris, AH1308/1891-AH1348/1928
(a) - Paris, privy marks, AH1349/1929-AH1376/1957
FM - Franklin Mint, Franklin Center, PA
Numismatic Italiana, Arezzo, Italy

**TUNIS**

Tunis, the capital and major seaport of Tunisia, existed in the Carthaginian era, but its importance dates only from the Moslem conquest, following which it became a major center of Arab power and prosperity. Spain seized it in 1535, lost it in 1564, retook it in 1573 and ceded it to the Turks in 1574. Thereafter the history of Tunis merged with that of Tunisia.

**Local Rulers**

Ali Bey, AH1299-1320/1882-1902AD
Muhammad Al-Hadi Bey, AH1320-1324/1902-1906AD
Muhammad Al-Nasir Bey, AH1324-1340/1906-1922AD
Muhammad Al-Habib Bey, AH1340-1348/1922-1929AD
Ahmad Pasha Bey, AH1348-1361/1929-1942AD
Muhammad Al-Munsif Bey, AH1361-1362/1942-1943AD
Muhammad Al-Amin Bey, AH1362-1376/1943-1957AD

**NOTE:** All coins struck until AH1298/1881AD bear the name of the Ottoman Sultan; the name of the Bey of Tunis was added in AH1272/1855AD. After AH1298, when the French established their protectorate, only the Bey's name appears on the coin until AH1376/1956AD.

TUNISIA

## FRENCH PROTECTORATE

### ANONYMOUS COINAGE

AH1340-64/1921-45AD

Struck in the name of the Tunisian Bey.

50 CENTIMES KM# 246 Composition: Aluminum-Bronze

| Date | Mintage | F | VF | XF | Unc |
|---|---|---|---|---|---|
| AH1340/1921(a) | 4,000,000 | — | 1.00 | 7.00 | 20.00 |
| AH1345/1926(a) | 1,000,000 | — | 3.00 | 10.00 | 25.00 |
| AH1352/1933(a) | 500,000 | — | 6.00 | 17.00 | 50.00 |
| AH1360/1941(a) | 4,646,000 | — | 0.35 | 1.50 | 10.00 |
| AH1364/1945(a) | 11,180,000 | — | 0.25 | 1.00 | 10.00 |

**FRANC** KM# 247 **Composition:** Aluminum-Bronze

| Date | Mintage | F | VF | XF | Unc |
|---|---|---|---|---|---|
| AH1340/1921(a) | 5,000,000 | — | 1.00 | 7.00 | 20.00 |
| AH1344/1926(a) | 1,000,000 | — | 2.00 | 15.00 | 35.00 |
| AH1345/1926(a) | 1,000,000 | — | 4.00 | 17.00 | 40.00 |
| AH1360/1941(a) | 6,612,000 | — | 0.50 | 2.00 | 10.00 |
| AH1364/1945(a) | 10,699,000 | — | 0.35 | 1.75 | 10.00 |

**2 FRANCS** KM# 248 **Composition:** Aluminum-Bronze

| Date | Mintage | F | VF | XF | Unc |
|---|---|---|---|---|---|
| AH1340/1921(a) | 1,500,000 | — | 3.00 | 15.00 | 35.00 |
| AH1343/1924(a) | 500,000 | — | 8.00 | 20.00 | 50.00 |
| AH1345/1926(a) | 500,000 | — | 8.00 | 20.00 | 50.00 |
| AH1360/1941(a) | 1,976,000 | — | 1.50 | 6.00 | 15.00 |
| AH1364/1945(a) | 6,464,000 | — | 1.00 | 5.00 | 15.00 |

## Ali Bey

### AH1299-1320/1882-1902AD

### DECIMAL COINAGE

100 Centimes = 1 Franc

The following coins all bear French inscriptions on one side, Arabic on the other, and usually have both AH and AD dates. Except for KM#246-48, they are struck in the name of the Tunisian Bey.

**50 CENTIMES** KM# 223 **Weight:** 2.5000 g. **Composition:** 0.8350 Silver .0671 oz. ASW **Obv. Legend:** ALI

| Date | Mintage | F | VF | XF | Unc |
|---|---|---|---|---|---|
| AH1319/1901A | 1,000 | — | — | 100 | 175 |
| AH1320/1902A | 1,000 | — | — | 100 | 175 |

**FRANC** KM# 224 **Weight:** 5.0000 g. **Composition:** 0.8350 Silver .1342 oz. ASW **Obv. Legend:** ALI

| Date | Mintage | F | VF | XF | Unc |
|---|---|---|---|---|---|
| AH1319/1901A | 700 | — | — | 135 | 225 |
| AH1320/1902A | 703 | — | — | 135 | 225 |

**2 FRANCS** KM# 225 **Weight:** 10.0000 g. **Composition:** 0.8350 Silver .2685 oz. ASW **Obv. Legend:** ALI

| Date | Mintage | F | VF | XF | Unc |
|---|---|---|---|---|---|
| AH1319/1901A | 300 | — | — | 150 | 250 |
| AH1320/1902A | 300 | — | — | 150 | 250 |

**10 FRANCS** KM# 226 **Weight:** 3.2258 g. **Composition:** 0.9000 Gold .0933 oz. AGW **Obv. Legend:** ALI

| Date | Mintage | F | VF | XF | Unc |
|---|---|---|---|---|---|
| AH1319/1901A | 80 | — | — | 450 | 850 |
| AH1319/1901A | 80 | — | — | 450 | 850 |
| AH1320/1902A | 83 | — | — | 450 | 850 |

**10 FRANCS** KM# 233 **Weight:** 3.2258 g. **Composition:** 0.9000 Gold .0933 oz. AGW **Obv. Legend:** MUHAMMAD AL-HADI

| Date | Mintage | F | VF | XF | Unc |
|---|---|---|---|---|---|
| AH1321/1903A | 83 | — | — | 450 | 900 |
| AH1322/1904A | 83 | — | — | 450 | 900 |
| AH1323/1905A | 83 | — | — | 450 | 900 |
| AH1324/1906A | 83 | — | — | 450 | 900 |

**20 FRANCS** KM# 227 **Weight:** 6.4516 g. **Composition:** 0.9000 Gold .1867 oz. AGW **Obv. Legend:** ALI

| Date | Mintage | F | VF | XF | Unc |
|---|---|---|---|---|---|
| AH1319/1901A | 150,000 | — | BV | 75.00 | 110 |
| AH1319/1901A | 150,000 | — | BV | 75.00 | 110 |
| AH1320/1902A | 20 | — | — | 550 | 1,000 |

## Muhammad al-Hadi Bey

### AH1320-24/1902-1906AD

### DECIMAL COINAGE

100 Centimes = 1 Franc

The following coins all bear French inscriptions on one side, Arabic on the other, and usually have both AH and AD dates. Except for KM#246-48, they are struck in the name of the Tunisian Bey.

**5 CENTIMES** KM# 228 **Composition:** Bronze **Obv. Legend:** MUHAMMAD AL-HADI

| Date | Mintage | F | VF | XF | Unc |
|---|---|---|---|---|---|
| AH1321/1903A | 500,000 | — | 8.00 | 12.00 | 25.00 |
| AH1322/1904A | 1,000,000 | — | 8.00 | 12.00 | 25.00 |

**5 CENTIMES** KM# 235 **Composition:** Bronze **Obv. Legend:** MUHAMMAD AL-NASIR

| Date | Mintage | F | VF | XF | Unc |
|---|---|---|---|---|---|
| AH1325/1907A | 1,000,000 | — | 2.00 | 4.00 | 17.00 |
| AH1326/1908A | 1,000,000 | — | 2.00 | 4.00 | 17.00 |
| AH1330/1912A | 1,000,000 | — | 2.00 | 4.00 | 17.00 |
| AH1332/1914A | 1,000,000 | — | 2.00 | 4.00 | 17.00 |
| AH1334/1916A | 2,000,000 | — | 2.00 | 4.00 | 12.00 |
| AH1336/1917A | 2,021,000 | — | 2.00 | 4.00 | 12.00 |

**10 CENTIMES** KM# 229 **Composition:** Bronze **Obv. Legend:** MUHAMMAD AL-HADI

| Date | Mintage | F | VF | XF | Unc |
|---|---|---|---|---|---|
| AH1321/1903A | 250,000 | — | 10.00 | 20.00 | 30.00 |
| AH1322/1904A | 500,000 | — | 10.00 | 20.00 | 30.00 |

**50 CENTIMES** KM# 230 **Weight:** 2.5000 g. **Composition:** 0.8350 Silver .0671 oz. ASW **Obv. Legend:** MUHAMMAD AL-HADI

| Date | Mintage | F | VF | XF | Unc |
|---|---|---|---|---|---|
| AH1321/1903A | 1,002,999 | — | — | 150 | 250 |
| AH1322/1904A | 1,003 | — | — | 150 | 250 |
| AH1323/1905A | 1,003 | — | — | 150 | 250 |
| AH1324/1906A | 1,003 | — | — | 150 | 250 |

**FRANC** KM# 231 **Weight:** 5.0000 g. **Composition:** 0.8350 Silver .1342 oz. ASW **Obv. Legend:** MUHAMMAD AL-HADI

| Date | Mintage | F | VF | XF | Unc |
|---|---|---|---|---|---|
| AH1321/1903A | 703 | — | — | 135 | 225 |
| AH1322/1904A | 500,000 | — | 50.00 | 80.00 | 150 |
| AH1323/1905A | 703 | — | — | 135 | 225 |
| AH1324/1906A | 703 | — | — | 135 | 225 |

**2 FRANCS** KM# 232 **Weight:** 10.0000 g. **Composition:** 0.8350 Silver .2685 oz. ASW **Obv. Legend:** MUHAMMAD AL-HADI

| Date | Mintage | F | VF | XF | Unc |
|---|---|---|---|---|---|
| AH1321/1903A | 303 | — | — | 150 | 250 |
| AH1322/1904A | 150,000 | — | 70.00 | 110 | 200 |
| AH1323/1905A | 303 | — | — | 150 | 250 |
| AH1324/1906A | 303 | — | — | 150 | 250 |

**20 FRANCS** KM# 234 **Weight:** 6.4516 g. **Composition:** 0.9000 Gold .1867 oz. AGW **Obv. Legend:** MUHAMMAD AL-HADI

| Date | Mintage | F | VF | XF | Unc |
|---|---|---|---|---|---|
| AH1321/1903A | 300,000 | — | BV | 80.00 | 120 |
| AH1321/1904A | 600,000 | — | BV | 80.00 | 120 |
| AH1322/1904A | Inc. above | — | BV | 80.00 | 120 |
| AH1323/1905A | 23 | — | — | 550 | 1,000 |
| AH1324/1906A | 23 | — | — | 550 | 1,000 |

## Muhammad al-Nasir Bey

### AH1324-40/1906-1922AD

### DECIMAL COINAGE

100 Centimes = 1 Franc

The following coins all bear French inscriptions on one side, Arabic on the other, and usually have both AH and AD dates. Except for KM#246-48, they are struck in the name of the Tunisian Bey.

**5 CENTIMES** KM# 242 **Composition:** Nickel-Bronze **Obv. Legend:** MOHAMMED AL-NASIR

| Date | Mintage | F | VF | XF | Unc |
|---|---|---|---|---|---|
| AH1337/1918(a) | 1,549,000 | — | 4.00 | 10.00 | 25.00 |
| AH1337/1919(a) | 4,451,000 | — | 3.00 | 8.00 | 20.00 |
| AH1338/6/1920(a) | 2,206,000 | — | 4.00 | 10.00 | 25.00 |
| AH1338/7/1920(a) | Inc. above | — | 4.00 | 10.00 | 25.00 |
| AH1338/1920(a) | Inc. above | — | 3.00 | 8.00 | 20.00 |
| AH1339/1920(a) | Inc. above | — | 3.00 | 8.00 | 20.00 |

**5 CENTIMES** KM# 245 **Composition:** Nickel-Bronze **Note:** Reduced size.

| Date | Mintage | F | VF | XF | Unc |
|---|---|---|---|---|---|
| AH1339/1920(a) | 1,794,000 | — | 20.00 | 40.00 | 75.00 |

**10 CENTIMES** KM# 236 **Composition:** Bronze **Obv. Legend:** MUHAMMAD AL-NASIR

| Date | Mintage | F | VF | XF | Unc |
|---|---|---|---|---|---|
| AH1325/1907A | 500,000 | — | 3.00 | 6.00 | 20.00 |
| AH1326/1908A | 500,000 | — | 3.00 | 6.00 | 20.00 |
| AH1329/1911A | 500,000 | — | 3.00 | 6.00 | 20.00 |
| AH1330/1912A | 500,000 | — | 3.00 | 6.00 | 20.00 |
| AH1332/1914A | 500,000 | — | 3.00 | 6.00 | 20.00 |
| AH1334/1916A | 1,000,000 | — | 3.00 | 6.00 | 20.00 |
| AH1336/1917A | 1,050,000 | — | 3.00 | 6.00 | 20.00 |

**10 CENTIMES** KM# 243 **Composition:** Nickel-Bronze **Obv. Legend:** MUHAMMAD AL-NASIR

| Date | Mintage | F | VF | XF | Unc |
|---|---|---|---|---|---|
| AH1337/1918(a) | 1,288,000 | — | 3.00 | 8.00 | 25.00 |
| AH1337/1919(a) | 2,712,000 | — | 3.00 | 8.00 | 20.00 |
| AH1338/1920(a) | 3,000,000 | — | 3.00 | 8.00 | 20.00 |

**25 CENTIMES** KM# 244 **Composition:** Nickel-Bronze **Obv. Legend:** MUHAMMAD AL-NASIR

| Date | Mintage | F | VF | XF | Unc |
|---|---|---|---|---|---|
| AH1337/1918(a) | — | — | 4.00 | 12.00 | 35.00 |
| AH1337/1919(a) | 2,000,000 | — | 3.00 | 10.00 | 25.00 |
| AH1338/1920(a) | 2,000,000 | — | 3.00 | 10.00 | 25.00 |

**50 CENTIMES** KM# 237 **Weight:** 2.5000 g. **Composition:** 0.8350 Silver .0671 oz. ASW **Obv. Legend:** MUHAMMAD AL-NASIR

| Date | Mintage | F | VF | XF | Unc |
|---|---|---|---|---|---|
| AH1325/1907A | 201,000 | — | 10.00 | 20.00 | 40.00 |
| AH1326/1908A | 2,006 | — | — | 75.00 | 135 |
| AH1327/1909A | 1,003 | — | — | 100 | 175 |
| AH1328/1910A | 1,003 | — | — | 100 | 175 |
| AH1329/1911A | 1,003 | — | — | 100 | 175 |
| AH1330/1912A | 201,000 | — | 10.00 | 20.00 | 40.00 |
| AH1331/1913A | 1,003 | — | — | 100 | 175 |
| AH1332/1914A | 201,000 | — | 10.00 | 20.00 | 40.00 |
| AH1334/1915A | 707,000 | — | 8.00 | 15.00 | 30.00 |
| AH1334/1916A | 3,614,000 | — | 7.00 | 12.00 | 25.00 |
| AH1335/1916A | Inc. above | — | 7.00 | 12.00 | 25.00 |
| AH1335/1917A | 2,139,000 | — | 7.00 | 12.00 | 25.00 |
| AH1336/1917A | Inc. above | — | 7.00 | 12.00 | 25.00 |
| AH1337/1918A | 1,003 | — | — | 100 | 175 |
| AH1338/1919A | 1,003 | — | — | 100 | 175 |
| AH1339/1920A | 1,003 | — | — | 100 | 175 |
| AH1340/1921A | 1,003 | — | — | 100 | 175 |

**FRANC** KM# 238 **Weight:** 5.0000 g. **Composition:** 0.8350 Silver .1342 oz. ASW **Obv. Legend:** MUHAMMAD AL-NASIR

| Date | Mintage | F | VF | XF | Unc |
|---|---|---|---|---|---|
| AH1325/1907A | 301,000 | — | 10.00 | 20.00 | 35.00 |
| AH1326/1908A | 401,000 | — | 10.00 | 15.00 | 35.00 |
| AH1327/1909A | 703 | — | — | 135 | 225 |
| AH1328/1910A | 703 | — | — | 135 | 225 |
| AH1329/1911A | 1,051,000 | — | 7.00 | 12.00 | 30.00 |
| AH1330/1912A | 501,000 | — | 8.00 | 15.00 | 30.00 |
| AH1331/1913A | 703 | — | — | 135 | 225 |
| AH1332/1914A | 201,000 | — | 8.00 | 15.00 | 25.00 |
| AH1333/1914A | Inc. above | — | 8.00 | 15.00 | 25.00 |
| AH1334/1915A | 1,060,000 | — | 7.00 | 12.00 | 20.00 |
| AH1334/1916A | 3,270,000 | — | 7.00 | 12.00 | 20.00 |
| AH1335/1916A | Inc. above | — | 7.00 | 12.00 | 20.00 |
| AH1335/1917A | 1,628,000 | — | 7.00 | 12.00 | 20.00 |
| AH1336/1918A | 804,000 | — | 7.00 | 12.00 | 18.00 |
| AH1337/1918A | Inc. above | — | 7.00 | 12.00 | 18.00 |
| AH1338/1919A | 703 | — | — | 135 | 225 |
| AH1339/1920A | 703 | — | — | 135 | 225 |
| AH1340/1921A | 703 | — | — | 135 | 225 |

**2 FRANCS** KM# 239 **Weight:** 10.0000 g. **Composition:** 0.8350 Silver .2685 oz. ASW **Obv. Legend:** MUHAMMAD AL-NASIR

| Date | Mintage | F | VF | XF | Unc |
|---|---|---|---|---|---|
| AH1325/1907A | 306 | — | — | 150 | 250 |
| AH1326/1908A | 101,000 | — | 20.00 | 40.00 | 85.00 |
| AH1327/1909A | 303 | — | — | 150 | 250 |
| AH1328/1910A | 303 | — | — | 150 | 250 |
| AH1329/1911A | 475,000 | — | 15.00 | 25.00 | 40.00 |
| AH1330/1912A | 200,000 | — | 15.00 | 25.00 | 45.00 |
| AH1331/1913A | 303 | — | — | 150 | 250 |
| AH1332/1914A | 100,000 | — | 15.00 | 25.00 | 35.00 |
| AH1333/1914A | Inc. above | — | 15.00 | 25.00 | 35.00 |
| AH1334/1915A | 408,000 | — | 15.00 | 25.00 | 35.00 |
| AH1334/1916A | 1,000,000 | — | 15.00 | 25.00 | 35.00 |
| AH1335/1916A | Inc. above | — | 15.00 | 25.00 | 35.00 |
| AH1336/1917A | 303 | — | — | 150 | 250 |
| AH1337/1918A | 303 | — | — | 150 | 250 |
| AH1338/1919A | 303 | — | — | 150 | 250 |
| AH1339/1920A | 303 | — | — | 150 | 250 |
| AH1340/1921A | 303 | — | — | 150 | 250 |

**10 FRANCS** KM# 240 **Weight:** 3.2258 g. **Composition:** 0.9000 Gold .0933 oz. AGW **Obv. Legend:** MUHAMMAD AL-NASIR

| Date | Mintage | F | VF | XF | Unc |
|---|---|---|---|---|---|
| AH1325/1907A | 36 | — | — | 500 | 900 |
| AH1326/1908A | 166 | — | — | 300 | 500 |
| AH1327/1909A | 83 | — | — | 450 | 850 |
| AH1328/1910A | 83 | — | — | 450 | 850 |
| AH1329/1911A | 83 | — | — | 450 | 850 |
| AH1330/1912A | 83 | — | — | 450 | 850 |
| AH1331/1913A | 83 | — | — | 450 | 850 |
| AH1332/1914A | 83 | — | — | 450 | 850 |
| AH1334/1915A | 83 | — | — | 450 | 850 |
| AH1334/1916A | 83 | — | — | 450 | 850 |
| AH1336/1917A | 83 | — | — | 450 | 850 |
| AH1337/1918A | 83 | — | — | 450 | 850 |
| AH1338/1919A | 83 | — | — | 450 | 850 |
| AH1339/1920A | 83 | — | — | 450 | 850 |
| AH1340/1921A | 83 | — | — | 450 | 850 |

**20 FRANCS** KM# 241 **Weight:** 6.4516 g. **Composition:** 0.9000 Gold .1867 oz. AGW **Obv. Legend:** MUHAMMAD AL-NASIR

| Date | Mintage | F | VF | XF | Unc |
|---|---|---|---|---|---|
| AH1325/1907A | 26 | — | — | 550 | 1,000 |
| AH1326/1908A | 46 | — | — | 450 | 850 |
| AH1327/1909A | 23 | — | — | 550 | 1,000 |
| AH1328/1910A | 23 | — | — | 550 | 1,000 |
| AH1329/1911A | 23 | — | — | 550 | 1,000 |
| AH1330/1912A | 23 | — | — | 550 | 1,000 |
| AH1331/1913A | 23 | — | — | 550 | 1,000 |
| AH1332/1914A | 23 | — | — | 550 | 1,000 |
| AH1334/1915A | 23 | — | — | 550 | 1,000 |
| AH1334/1916A | 23 | — | — | 550 | 1,000 |
| AH1336/1917A | 23 | — | — | 550 | 1,000 |
| AH1337/1918A | 23 | — | — | 550 | 1,000 |
| AH1338/1919A | 23 | — | — | 550 | 1,000 |
| AH1339/1920A | 23 | — | — | 550 | 1,000 |
| AH1340/1921A | 23 | — | — | 550 | 1,000 |

## Muhammad al-Habib Bey

### AH1340-48/1922-1929AD

### DECIMAL COINAGE

100 Centimes = 1 Franc

The following coins all bear French inscriptions on one side, Arabic on the other, and usually have both AH and AD dates. Except for KM#246-48, they are struck in the name of the Tunisian Bey.

**10 CENTIMES** KM# 254 **Composition:** Nickel-Bronze **Obv. Legend:** MUHAMMAD AL-HABIB

| Date | Mintage | F | VF | XF | Unc |
|---|---|---|---|---|---|
| AH1345/1926(a) | 1,000,000 | — | 20.00 | 50.00 | 100 |

**50 CENTIMES** KM# 249 **Weight:** 2.5000 g. **Composition:** 0.8350 Silver .0671 oz. ASW **Obv. Legend:** MUHAMMAD AL-HABIB

| Date | Mintage | F | VF | XF | Unc |
|---|---|---|---|---|---|
| AH1341/1922A | 1,003 | — | — | 100 | 200 |
| AH1342/1923A | 2,009 | — | — | 100 | 200 |
| AH1343/1924A | 1,003 | — | — | 100 | 200 |
| AH1344/1925A | 1,003 | — | — | 100 | 200 |
| AH1345/1926A | 1,003 | — | — | 100 | 200 |
| AH1346/1927A | 1,003 | — | — | 100 | 200 |
| AH1347/1928A | 1,003 | — | — | 100 | 200 |

**FRANC** KM# 250 **Weight:** 5.0000 g. **Composition:** 0.8350 Silver .1342 oz. ASW **Obv. Legend:** MUHAMMAD AL-HABIB

| Date | Mintage | F | VF | XF | Unc |
|---|---|---|---|---|---|
| AH1341/1922A | 703 | — | — | 135 | 275 |
| AH1342/1923A | 1,409 | — | — | 100 | 250 |
| AH1343/1924A | 703 | — | — | 135 | 275 |
| AH1344/1925A | 703 | — | — | 135 | 275 |
| AH1345/1926A | 703 | — | — | 135 | 275 |
| AH1346/1927A | 703 | — | — | 135 | 275 |

**FRANC** KM# 250a **Weight:** 5.5000 g. **Composition:** 0.8350 Silver .1476 oz. ASW

| Date | Mintage | F | VF | XF | Unc |
|---|---|---|---|---|---|
| AH1347/1928A | 703 | — | — | 135 | 275 |

**2 FRANCS** KM# 251 **Weight:** 10.0000 g. **Composition:** 0.8350 Silver .2685 oz. ASW **Obv. Legend:** MUHAMMAD AL-HABIB

| Date | Mintage | F | VF | XF | Unc |
|---|---|---|---|---|---|
| AH1341/1922A | 303 | — | — | 150 | 325 |
| AH1342/1923A | 690 | — | — | 135 | 275 |
| AH1343/1924A | 303 | — | — | 150 | 325 |
| AH1344/1925A | 303 | — | — | 150 | 325 |
| AH1345/1926A | 303 | — | — | 150 | 325 |
| AH1346/1927A | 303 | — | — | 150 | 325 |
| AH1347/1928A | 303 | — | — | 150 | 325 |

**10 FRANCS** KM# 252 **Weight:** 3.2258 g. **Composition:** 0.9000 Gold .0933 oz. AGW **Obv. Legend:** MUHAMMAD AL-HABIB BEY

| Date | Mintage | F | VF | XF | Unc |
|---|---|---|---|---|---|
| AH1341/1922A | 83 | — | — | 450 | 850 |
| AH1342/1923A | 169 | — | — | 300 | 500 |
| AH1343/1924A | 83 | — | — | 450 | 850 |
| AH1344/1925A | 83 | — | — | 450 | 850 |
| AH1345/1926A | 83 | — | — | 450 | 850 |
| AH1346/1927A | 83 | — | — | 450 | 850 |
| AH1347/1928A | 83 | — | — | 450 | 850 |

**20 FRANCS** KM# 253 **Weight:** 6.4516 g. **Composition:** 0.9000 Gold .1867 oz. AGW **Obv. Legend:** MUHAMMAD AL-HABIB

| Date | Mintage | F | VF | XF | Unc |
|---|---|---|---|---|---|
| AH1341/1922A | 23 | — | — | 550 | 1,000 |
| AH1342/1923A | 49 | — | — | 450 | 850 |
| AH1343/1924A | 23 | — | — | 550 | 1,000 |
| AH1344/1925A | 23 | — | — | 550 | 1,000 |
| AH1345/1926A | 23 | — | — | 550 | 1,000 |
| AH1346/1927A | 23 | — | — | 550 | 1,000 |
| AH1347/1928A | 23 | — | — | 550 | 1,000 |

## Ahmad Pasha Bey

### AH1348-61/1929-1942AD

### DECIMAL COINAGE

100 Centimes = 1 Franc

The following coins all bear French inscriptions on one side, Arabic on the other, and usually have both AH and AD dates. Except for KM#246-48, they are struck in the name of the Tunisian Bey.

**5 CENTIMES** KM# 258 **Composition:** Nickel-Bronze **Obv. Legend:** AHMAD

| Date | Mintage | F | VF | XF | Unc |
|---|---|---|---|---|---|
| AH1350/1931(a) | 2,000,000 | — | 4.00 | 10.00 | 25.00 |
| AH1352/1933(a) | 1,000,000 | — | 5.00 | 12.00 | 30.00 |
| AH1357/1938(a) | 1,200,000 | — | 4.00 | 10.00 | 25.00 |

**10 CENTIMES** KM# 259 **Composition:** Nickel-Bronze **Obv. Legend:** AHMAD

| Date | Mintage | F | VF | XF | Unc |
|---|---|---|---|---|---|
| AH1350/1931(a) | 750,000 | — | 6.00 | 15.00 | 35.00 |
| AH1352/1933(a) | 1,000,000 | — | 6.00 | 15.00 | 35.00 |
| AH1357/1938(a) | 1,200,000 | — | 5.00 | 12.00 | 25.00 |

**10 CENTIMES** KM# 267 **Composition:** Zinc **Obv. Legend:** AHMAD

| Date | Mintage | F | VF | XF | Unc |
|---|---|---|---|---|---|
| AH1360/1941(a) | 5,000,000 | — | 2.50 | 6.00 | 25.00 |
| AH1361/1942(a) | 10,000,000 | — | 1.50 | 4.00 | 20.00 |

**20 CENTIMES** KM# 268 **Composition:** Zinc **Obv. Legend:** AHMAD

| Date | Mintage | F | VF | XF | Unc |
|---|---|---|---|---|---|
| AH1361/1942A | 5,000,000 | — | 20.00 | 35.00 | 50.00 |

**25 CENTIMES** **KM# 260** **Composition:** Nickel-Aluminum-Bronze **Obv. Legend:** AHMAD

| Date | Mintage | F | VF | XF | Unc |
|---|---|---|---|---|---|
| AH1350/1931(a) | 300,000 | — | 8.00 | 15.00 | 35.00 |
| AH1352/1933(a) | 400,000 | — | 8.00 | 15.00 | 35.00 |
| AH1357/1938(a) | 480,000 | — | 4.00 | 10.00 | 25.00 |

**5 FRANCS** **KM# 261** **Weight:** 5.0000 g. **Composition:** 0.6800 Silver .1093 oz. ASW **Obv. Legend:** AHMAD

| Date | Mintage | F | VF | XF | Unc |
|---|---|---|---|---|---|
| AH1353/1934(a) | 2,000,000 | — | 10.00 | 18.00 | 25.00 |
| AH1355/1936(a) | 2,000,000 | — | 10.00 | 18.00 | 25.00 |

**5 FRANCS** **KM# 264** **Weight:** 5.0000 g. **Composition:** 0.6800 Silver .1093 oz. ASW **Obv. Legend:** AHMAD

| Date | Mintage | F | VF | XF | Unc |
|---|---|---|---|---|---|
| AH1358/1939(a) | 1,600,000 | — | 15.00 | 25.00 | 40.00 |

**10 FRANCS** **KM# 255** **Weight:** 10.0000 g. **Composition:** 0.6800 Silver .2186 oz. ASW **Obv. Legend:** AHMAD

| Date | Mintage | F | VF | XF | Unc |
|---|---|---|---|---|---|
| AH1349/1930(a) | 60,000 | — | 45.00 | 70.00 | 110 |
| AH1350/1931(a) | 1,103 | — | 150 | 250 | 350 |
| AH1351/1932(a) | 60,000 | — | 60.00 | 100 | 200 |
| AH1352/1933(a) | 1,103 | — | 150 | 250 | 350 |
| AH1353/1934(a) | 30,000 | — | 45.00 | 70.00 | 110 |

**10 FRANCS** **KM# 262** **Weight:** 10.0000 g. **Composition:** 0.6800 Silver .2186 oz. ASW

| Date | Mintage | F | VF | XF | Unc |
|---|---|---|---|---|---|
| AH1353/1934(a) | 1,501,000 | — | 10.00 | 20.00 | 35.00 |
| AH1354/1935(a) | 1,103 | — | — | 225 | 350 |
| AH1355/1936(a) | 2,006 | — | — | 225 | 350 |
| AH1356/1937(a) | 1,103 | — | — | 225 | 350 |
| AH1357/1938 | — | — | — | 400 | 600 |
| AH1358/1939 | — | — | — | 400 | 600 |

**10 FRANCS** **KM# 265** **Weight:** 10.0000 g. **Composition:** 0.6800 Silver .2186 oz. ASW

| Date | Mintage | F | VF | XF | Unc |
|---|---|---|---|---|---|
| AH1358/1939(a) | 501,000 | — | 6.00 | 15.00 | 35.00 |
| AH1359/1940(a) | — | — | — | 225 | 350 |
| AH1360/1941(a) | 1,103 | — | — | 225 | 350 |
| AH1361/1942(a) | 1,103 | — | — | 225 | 350 |

**20 FRANCS** **KM# 256** **Weight:** 20.0000 g. **Composition:** 0.6800 Silver .4372 oz. ASW **Obv. Legend:** AHMAD

| Date | Mintage | F | VF | XF | Unc |
|---|---|---|---|---|---|
| AH1349/1930(a) | 20,000 | — | 60.00 | 100 | 175 |
| AH1350/1931(a) | 53 | — | 200 | 300 | 500 |
| AH1351/1932(a) | 20,000 | — | 75.00 | 150 | 275 |
| AH1352/1933(a) | 53 | — | 200 | 300 | 500 |
| AH1353/1934(a) | 9,500 | — | 60.00 | 100 | 175 |

**Note:** It is believed that an additional number of coins dated AH1353/1934(a) were struck and included in mintage figures of KM#263 of the same date

**20 FRANCS** **KM# 263** **Weight:** 20.0000 g. **Composition:** 0.6800 Silver .4372 oz. ASW

| Date | Mintage | F | VF | XF | Unc |
|---|---|---|---|---|---|
| AH1353/1934(a) | 1,250,000 | — | 12.00 | 25.00 | 60.00 |
| AH1354/1935(a) | 53 | — | — | 275 | 450 |
| AH1355/1936(a) | 106 | — | — | 225 | 375 |
| AH1356/1937(a) | 53 | — | — | 275 | 450 |

**20 FRANCS** **KM# 266** **Weight:** 20.0000 g. **Composition:** 0.6800 Silver .4372 oz. ASW

| Date | Mintage | F | VF | XF | Unc |
|---|---|---|---|---|---|
| AH1358/1939(a) | 100,000 | — | 20.00 | 40.00 | 90.00 |
| AH1359/1940(a) | — | — | — | — | — |

**Note:** Reported, not confirmed.

| Date | Mintage | F | VF | XF | Unc |
|---|---|---|---|---|---|
| AH1360/1941(a) | 53 | — | — | 275 | 450 |
| AH1361/1942(a) | 53 | — | — | 275 | 450 |

**100 FRANCS** **KM# 257** **Weight:** 6.5500 g. **Composition:** 0.9000 Gold .1895 oz. AGW **Obv. Legend:** AHMAD

| Date | Mintage | F | VF | XF | Unc |
|---|---|---|---|---|---|
| AH1349/1930(a) | 3,000 | — | 80.00 | 100 | 135 |
| AH1350/1931(a) | 33 | — | — | 500 | 900 |
| AH1351/1932(a) | 3,000 | — | 80.00 | 100 | 135 |
| AH1352/1933(a) | 33 | — | — | 500 | 900 |
| AH1353/1934(a) | 133 | — | — | 300 | 400 |
| AH1354/1935(a) | 3,000 | — | 80.00 | 100 | 135 |
| AH1355/1936(a) | 33 | — | — | 500 | 900 |
| AH1356/1937(a) | 33 | — | — | 500 | 900 |

## MEDALLIC COINAGE

**100 FRANCS** **KM# M1.1** **Weight:** 6.5500 g. **Composition:** 0.9000 Gold .1895 oz. AGW **Obv. Legend:** AHMED BEY **Edge:** Lettered

| Date | Mintage | F | VF | XF | Unc |
|---|---|---|---|---|---|
| AH1357/1938(a) | 66 | — | — | 475 | 600 |
| AH1358/1939(a) | 33 | — | — | 550 | 700 |
| AH1359/1940(a) | 33 | — | — | 550 | 700 |

**100 FRANCS** **KM# M1.2** **Weight:** 6.5500 g. **Composition:** 0.9000 Gold .1895 oz. AGW **Obv. Legend:** AHMED BEY **Edge:** Milled

| Date | Mintage | F | VF | XF | Unc |
|---|---|---|---|---|---|
| AH1360/1941(a) | 33 | — | — | 550 | 700 |
| AH1361/1942(a) | 33 | — | — | 550 | 700 |

# Muhammad al-Munsif Bey

### AH1361-62/1942-1943AD

## MEDALLIC COINAGE

**100 FRANCS** **KM# M2** **Weight:** 6.5500 g. **Composition:** 0.9000 Gold .1895 oz. AGW **Obv. Legend:** MUHAMMAD AL-MUNSIF BEY

| Date | Mintage | F | VF | XF | Unc |
|---|---|---|---|---|---|
| AH1362/1943(a) | 33 | — | — | 750 | 1,000 |

# Muhammad al-Amin Bey

### AH1362-76/1943-1957AD

## DECIMAL COINAGE

100 Centimes = 1 Franc

The following coins all bear French inscriptions on one side, Arabic on the other, and usually have both AH and AD dates. Except for KM#246-48, they are struck in the name of the Tunisian Bey.

**10 CENTIMES** **KM# 271** **Composition:** Nickel-Aluminum-Bronze **Obv. Legend:** MUHAMMAD AL AMIN

| Date | Mintage | F | VF | XF | Unc |
|---|---|---|---|---|---|
| AH1364/1945(a) | 10,000,000 | — | 20.00 | 40.00 | 70.00 |

**Note:** Most were probably melted

**20 CENTIMES** **KM# 272** **Composition:** Zinc **Obv. Legend:** MUHAMMAD AL-AMIN

| Date | Mintage | F | VF | XF | Unc |
|---|---|---|---|---|---|
| AH1364/1945(a) | 5,205,000 | — | 40.00 | 70.00 | 100 |

**Note:** A large quantity was remelted

**5 FRANCS** KM# 273 **Composition:** Aluminum-Bronze **Obv. Legend:** MUHAMMAD AL-AMIN

| Date | Mintage | F | VF | XF | Unc |
|---|---|---|---|---|---|
| AH1365/1946(a) | 10,000,000 | — | 1.50 | 5.00 | 10.00 |

**5 FRANCS** KM# 277 **Composition:** Copper-Nickel

| Date | Mintage | F | VF | XF | Unc |
|---|---|---|---|---|---|
| AH1373/1954(a) | 18,000,000 | — | 1.00 | 2.50 | 5.00 |
| AH1376/1957(a) | 4,000,000 | — | 2.00 | 4.00 | 7.00 |

**10 FRANCS** KM# 269 **Weight:** 10.0000 g. **Composition:** 0.6800 Silver .2186 oz. ASW

| Date | Mintage | F | VF | XF | Unc |
|---|---|---|---|---|---|
| AH1363/1943(a) | 1,503 | — | — | 225 | 350 |
| AH1364/1944(a) | 2,206 | — | — | 200 | 300 |

**20 FRANCS** KM# 270 **Weight:** 20.0000 g. **Composition:** 0.6800 Silver .4372 oz. ASW **Obv. Legend:** MUHAMMAD AL-AMIN

| Date | Mintage | F | VF | XF | Unc |
|---|---|---|---|---|---|
| AH1363/1943(a) | 103 | — | — | 300 | 500 |
| AH1364/1944(a) | 106 | — | — | 300 | 500 |

**20 FRANCS** KM# 274 **Composition:** Copper-Nickel

| Date | Mintage | F | VF | XF | Unc |
|---|---|---|---|---|---|
| AH1370/1950(a) | 10,000,000 | — | 0.60 | 2.25 | 6.50 |
| AH1376/1957(a) | 4,000,000 | — | 0.45 | 1.25 | 4.50 |

**50 FRANCS** KM# 275 **Composition:** Copper-Nickel **Obv. Legend:** MUHAMMAD AL-AMIN

| Date | Mintage | F | VF | XF | Unc |
|---|---|---|---|---|---|
| AH1370/1950(a) | 5,000,000 | — | 0.60 | 2.25 | 6.50 |
| AH1376/1957(a) | 600,000 | — | 1.25 | 2.75 | 6.50 |

**100 FRANCS** KM# 276 **Composition:** Copper-Nickel **Obv. Legend:** MUHAMMAD AL-AMIN

| Date | Mintage | F | VF | XF | Unc |
|---|---|---|---|---|---|
| AH1370/1950(a) | 8,000,000 | — | 2.25 | 5.50 | 11.50 |
| AH1376/1957(a) | 1,000,000 | — | 2.25 | 4.50 | 10.00 |

## MEDALLIC COINAGE

**10 FRANCS** KM# M4 **Weight:** 10.0000 g. **Composition:** 0.6800 Silver .2186 oz. ASW **Obv. Legend:** MUHAMMAD AL-AMIN BEY

| Date | Mintage | F | VF | XF | Unc |
|---|---|---|---|---|---|
| AH1365/1945(a) | 2,606 | — | — | 75.00 | 125 |
| AH1366/1946(a) | 1,103 | — | — | 75.00 | 125 |
| AH1367/1947(a) | 1,103 | — | — | 75.00 | 125 |
| AH1368/1948(a) | 1,103 | — | — | 75.00 | 125 |
| AH1369/1949(a) | 1,103 | — | — | 75.00 | 125 |
| AH1370/1950(a) | 1,103 | — | — | 75.00 | 125 |
| AH1371/1951(a) | 1,703 | — | — | 75.00 | 125 |
| AH1372/1952(a) | 1,703 | — | — | 75.00 | 125 |
| AH1373/1953(a) | 1,703 | — | — | 75.00 | 125 |
| AH1374/1954(a) | 1,703 | — | — | 75.00 | 125 |
| AH1375/1955(a) | 1,703 | — | — | 75.00 | 125 |

**20 FRANCS** KM# M5 **Weight:** 20.0000 g. **Composition:** 0.6800 Silver .4372 oz. ASW **Obv. Legend:** MUHAMMAD AL-AMIN BEY

| Date | Mintage | F | VF | XF | Unc |
|---|---|---|---|---|---|
| AH1365/1945(a) | 156 | — | — | 200 | 400 |
| AH1366/1946(a) | 53 | — | — | 200 | 450 |
| AH1367/1947(a) | 53 | — | — | 200 | 450 |
| AH1368/1948(a) | 53 | — | — | 200 | 450 |
| AH1369/1949(a) | 53 | — | — | 200 | 450 |
| AH1370/1950(a) | 53 | — | — | 200 | 450 |
| AH1371/1951(a) | 303 | — | — | 200 | 400 |
| AH1372/1952(a) | 303 | — | — | 200 | 400 |
| AH1373/1953(a) | 303 | — | — | 200 | 400 |
| AH1374/1954(a) | 303 | — | — | 200 | 400 |
| AH1375/1955(a) | 303 | — | — | 200 | 400 |

**100 FRANCS** KM# M3 **Weight:** 6.5500 g. **Composition:** 0.9000 Gold .1895 oz. AGW **Obv. Legend:** MUHAMMAD AL-AMIN BEY

| Date | Mintage | F | VF | XF | Unc |
|---|---|---|---|---|---|
| AH1363/1943(a) | 66 | — | — | 475 | 600 |
| AH1364/1944(a) | 68 | — | — | 475 | 600 |
| AH1365/1945(a) | 33 | — | — | 550 | 700 |
| AH1366/1946(a) | 33 | — | — | 550 | 700 |
| AH1367/1947(a) | 33 | — | — | 550 | 700 |
| AH1368/1948(a) | 33 | — | — | 550 | 700 |
| AH1369/1949(a) | 33 | — | — | 550 | 700 |
| AH1370/1950(a) | 33 | — | — | 550 | 700 |
| AH1371/1951(a) | 63 | — | — | 475 | 600 |
| AH1372/1952(a) | 63 | — | — | 475 | 600 |
| AH1373/1953(a) | 63 | — | — | 475 | 600 |
| AH1374/1954(a) | 63 | — | — | 475 | 600 |
| AH1375/1955(a) | 63 | — | — | 475 | 600 |

# KINGDOM

## Muhammad al-Amin Bey as Premier.

## MEDALLIC COINAGE

**10 FRANCS** KM# M6 **Weight:** 10.0000 g. **Composition:** 0.6800 Silver .2186 oz. ASW **Obv. Legend:** MUHAMMAD AL-AMIN, PREMIER

| Date | Mintage | F | VF | XF | Unc |
|---|---|---|---|---|---|
| AH1376/1956(a) | 1,703 | — | — | 150 | 275 |

**20 FRANCS** KM# M7 **Weight:** 20.0000 g. **Composition:** 0.6800 Silver .4372 oz. ASW **Obv. Legend:** MUHAMMAD AL-AMIN, PREMIER

| Date | Mintage | F | VF | XF | Unc |
|---|---|---|---|---|---|
| AH1376/1956(a) | 303 | — | — | 250 | 450 |

**100 FRANCS** KM# M8 **Weight:** 6.5500 g. **Composition:** 0.9000 Gold .1895 oz. AGW **Obv. Legend:** MUHAMMAD AL-AMIN, PREMIER

| Date | Mintage | F | VF | XF | Unc |
|---|---|---|---|---|---|
| AH1376/1956(a) | 63 | — | — | 550 | 700 |

# REPUBLIC

## DECIMAL COINAGE

1000 Millim = 1 Dinar

**MILLIM** KM# 280 **Composition:** Aluminum

| Date | Mintage | F | VF | XF | Unc |
|---|---|---|---|---|---|
| 1960 | — | — | — | 0.10 | 0.25 |
| 1983 | — | — | — | 0.10 | 0.25 |

**MILLIM** KM# 349 **Composition:** Aluminum **Series:** F.A.O. **Obverse:** Tree, date **Reverse:** Denomination

| Date | Mintage | F | VF | XF | Unc |
|---|---|---|---|---|---|
| 2000(1999) | — | — | — | — | 1.00 |

**2 MILLIM KM# 281 Composition:** Aluminum

| Date | Mintage | F | VF | XF | Unc |
|---|---|---|---|---|---|
| 1960 | — | — | — | 0.10 | 0.25 |
| 1983 | — | — | — | 0.10 | 0.25 |

**5 MILLIM KM# 282 Composition:** Aluminum

| Date | Mintage | F | VF | XF | Unc |
|---|---|---|---|---|---|
| 1960 | — | — | — | 0.10 | 0.25 |
| 1983 | — | — | — | 0.10 | 0.25 |
| 1993 | — | — | — | 0.10 | 0.25 |
| 1996 | — | — | — | 0.10 | 0.25 |

**5 MILLIM KM# 348 Composition:** Aluminum **Obverse:** Tree above dates **Reverse:** Denomination

| Date | Mintage | F | VF | XF | Unc |
|---|---|---|---|---|---|
| AH1418-1997 | — | — | — | — | 0.50 |

**10 MILLIM KM# 306 Composition:** Brass

| Date | Mintage | F | VF | XF | Unc |
|---|---|---|---|---|---|
| AH1380-1960 | — | — | 0.15 | 0.25 | 0.50 |
| AH1403-1983 | — | — | 0.15 | 0.25 | 0.50 |
| AH1414-1993 | — | — | 0.15 | 0.25 | 0.50 |
| AH1416-1996 | — | — | 0.15 | 0.25 | 0.50 |

**20 MILLIM KM# 307 Composition:** Brass

| Date | Mintage | F | VF | XF | Unc |
|---|---|---|---|---|---|
| AH1380-1960 | — | — | 0.30 | 0.50 | 0.80 |
| AH1403-1983 | — | — | 0.30 | 0.50 | 0.80 |
| AH1414-1993 | — | — | 0.30 | 0.50 | 0.80 |
| AH1416-1996 | — | — | 0.30 | 0.50 | 0.80 |

**50 MILLIM KM# 308 Composition:** Brass

| Date | Mintage | F | VF | XF | Unc |
|---|---|---|---|---|---|
| AH1380-1960 | — | — | 0.65 | 0.85 | 1.25 |
| AH1403-1983 | — | — | 0.65 | 0.85 | 1.25 |
| AH1414-1993 | — | — | 0.65 | 0.85 | 1.25 |
| AH1416-1996 | — | — | 0.65 | 0.85 | 1.25 |

**100 MILLIM KM# 309 Composition:** Brass

| Date | Mintage | F | VF | XF | Unc |
|---|---|---|---|---|---|
| AH1380-1960 | — | — | 1.25 | 1.50 | 2.00 |
| AH1403-1983 | — | — | 1.25 | 1.50 | 2.00 |
| AH1414-1993 | — | — | 1.25 | 1.50 | 2.00 |
| AH1416-1996 | — | — | 1.25 | 1.50 | 2.00 |
| AH1418-1997 | — | — | — | — | — |

**1/2 DINAR KM# 291 Composition:** Nickel

| Date | Mintage | F | VF | XF | Unc |
|---|---|---|---|---|---|
| 1968(a) | 500,000 | — | 1.00 | 2.00 | 4.50 |

**1/2 DINAR KM# 303 Composition:** Copper-Nickel **Series:** F.A.O. **Note:** Varieties exist.

| Date | Mintage | F | VF | XF | Unc |
|---|---|---|---|---|---|
| 1976 | — | — | 1.50 | 3.50 | 6.50 |
| 1983 | — | — | 1.50 | 3.50 | 6.50 |

**1/2 DINAR KM# 318 Composition:** Copper-Nickel **Series:** F.A.O.

| Date | Mintage | F | VF | XF | Unc |
|---|---|---|---|---|---|
| 1988 | — | — | 1.00 | 3.00 | 5.50 |
| 1990 | — | — | 1.00 | 3.00 | 5.50 |

**1/2 DINAR KM# 346 Composition:** Copper-Nickel **Obverse:** National arms **Reverse:** 2 hands with fruit and wheat stalk

| Date | Mintage | F | VF | XF | Unc |
|---|---|---|---|---|---|
| AH1416-1996 | — | — | 1.00 | 2.50 | 4.50 |

**DINAR KM# 292 Weight:** 20.0000 g. **Composition:** 0.9250 Silver .5949 oz. ASW **Reverse:** Hannibal

| Date | Mintage | F | VF | XF | Unc |
|---|---|---|---|---|---|
| 1969FM NI Proof | 15,000 | Value: 12.50 | | | |
| 1969 NI Proof | 5,000 | Value: 47.50 | | | |

**DINAR KM# 293 Weight:** 20.0000 g. **Composition:** 0.9250 Silver .5949 oz. ASW **Obverse:** Similar to KM#292 **Reverse:** Masinissa

| Date | Mintage | F | VF | XF | Unc |
|---|---|---|---|---|---|
| 1969FM NI Proof | 15,000 | Value: 10.00 | | | |
| 1969 NI Proof | 5,000 | Value: 45.00 | | | |

**DINAR KM# 294 Weight:** 20.0000 g. **Composition:** 0.9250 Silver .5949 oz. ASW **Obverse:** Similar to KM#292 **Reverse:** Jugurtha

| Date | Mintage | F | VF | XF | Unc |
|---|---|---|---|---|---|
| 1969FM NI Proof | 15,000 | Value: 10.00 | | | |
| 1969 NI Proof | 5,000 | Value: 45.00 | | | |

**DINAR KM# 295 Weight:** 20.0000 g. **Composition:** 0.9250 Silver .5949 oz. ASW **Obverse:** Similar to KM#292 **Reverse:** Virgil

| Date | Mintage | F | VF | XF | Unc |
|---|---|---|---|---|---|
| 1969FM NI Proof | 15,000 | Value: 10.00 | | | |
| 1969 NI Proof | 5,000 | Value: 45.00 | | | |

**DINAR** **KM# 296** **Weight:** 20.0000 g. **Composition:** 0.9250 Silver .5949 oz. ASW **Obverse:** Similar to KM#292 **Reverse:** St. Augustine

| Date | Mintage | F | VF | XF | Unc |
|---|---|---|---|---|---|
| 1969FM NI Proof | 15,000 | Value: 10.00 | | | |
| 1969 NI Proof | 5,000 | Value: 45.00 | | | |

**DINAR** **KM# 297** **Weight:** 20.0000 g. **Composition:** 0.9250 Silver .5949 oz. ASW **Obverse:** Similar to KM#292 **Reverse:** Phoenician Ship

| Date | Mintage | F | VF | XF | Unc |
|---|---|---|---|---|---|
| 1969FM NI Proof | 15,000 | Value: 18.50 | | | |
| 1969 NI Proof | 5,000 | Value: 55.00 | | | |

**DINAR** **KM# 298** **Weight:** 20.0000 g. **Composition:** 0.9250 Silver .5949 oz. ASW **Obverse:** Similar to KM#292 **Reverse:** Neptune

| Date | Mintage | F | VF | XF | Unc |
|---|---|---|---|---|---|
| 1969FM NI Proof | 15,000 | Value: 10.00 | | | |
| 1969 NI Proof | 5,000 | Value: 45.00 | | | |

**DINAR** **KM# 299** **Weight:** 20.0000 g. **Composition:** 0.9250 Silver .5949 oz. ASW **Obverse:** Similar to KM#292 **Reverse:** Venus

| Date | Mintage | F | VF | XF | Unc |
|---|---|---|---|---|---|
| 1969FM NI Proof | 15,000 | Value: 18.50 | | | |
| 1969 NI Proof | 5,000 | Value: 55.00 | | | |

**DINAR** **KM# 300** **Weight:** 20.0000 g. **Composition:** 0.9250 Silver .5949 oz. ASW **Obverse:** Similar to KM#292 **Reverse:** Thysdrus-El Djem

| Date | Mintage | F | VF | XF | Unc |
|---|---|---|---|---|---|
| 1969FM NI Proof | 15,000 | Value: 10.00 | | | |
| 1969 NI Proof | 5,000 | Value: 45.00 | | | |

**DINAR** **KM# 301** **Weight:** 20.0000 g. **Composition:** 0.9250 Silver .5949 oz. ASW **Obverse:** Similar to KM#292 **Reverse:** Sbeitla-Sufetula

| Date | Mintage | F | VF | XF | Unc |
|---|---|---|---|---|---|
| 1969FM NI Proof | 15,000 | Value: 10.00 | | | |
| 1969 NI Proof | 5,000 | Value: 45.00 | | | |

**DINAR** **KM# 302** **Weight:** 18.0000 g. **Composition:** 0.6800 Silver .3935 oz. ASW **Series:** F.A.O.

| Date | Mintage | F | VF | XF | Unc |
|---|---|---|---|---|---|
| 1970(a) | 100,000 | — | 3.00 | 5.50 | 10.00 |
| 1970(a) Proof | 1,250 | Value: 40.00 | | | |

**DINAR** **KM# 304** **Composition:** Copper-Nickel **Series:** F.A.O. **Note:** Varieties exist. Coins dated 1976 exist with or without dots (error) below iy of Tunisiya.

| Date | Mintage | F | VF | XF | Unc |
|---|---|---|---|---|---|
| 1976 | — | — | 2.00 | 5.00 | 9.00 |
| 1983 | — | — | 2.00 | 5.00 | 9.00 |

**DINAR** **KM# 319** **Composition:** Copper-Nickel **Series:** F.A.O.

| Date | Mintage | F | VF | XF | Unc |
|---|---|---|---|---|---|
| 1988 | — | — | 2.00 | 4.50 | 8.50 |
| 1989 | — | — | 2.00 | 4.50 | 8.50 |
| 1990 | — | — | 2.00 | 4.50 | 8.50 |

**DINAR** **KM# 347** **Composition:** Copper-Nickel **Series:** F.A.O.

| Date | Mintage | F | VF | XF | Unc |
|---|---|---|---|---|---|
| AH1416-1996 | — | — | 2.00 | 4.00 | 7.50 |

**2 DINARS** **KM# 286** **Weight:** 3.8000 g. **Composition:** 0.9000 Gold .1099 oz. AGW **Subject:** 10th Anniversary of Republic

| Date | Mintage | F | VF | XF | Unc |
|---|---|---|---|---|---|
| ND(1967) NI Proof | 7,259 | Value: 60.00 | | | |

**5 DINARS** **KM# 283** **Weight:** 11.7900 g. **Composition:** 0.9000 Gold .3412 oz. AGW **Obverse:** French legends **Reverse:** French legends

| Date | Mintage | F | VF | XF | Unc |
|---|---|---|---|---|---|
| 1962 Proof | — | Value: 550 | | | |

**5 DINARS** **KM# 320** **Weight:** 11.7900 g. **Composition:** 0.9000 Gold .3412 oz. AGW **Obverse:** Arabic legends **Reverse:** Arabic legends

| Date | Mintage | F | VF | XF | Unc |
|---|---|---|---|---|---|
| 1962 Proof | — | Value: 550 | | | |

**5 DINARS** **KM# 284** **Weight:** 11.7900 g. **Composition:** 0.9000 Gold .3412 oz. AGW **Obverse:** French legends **Reverse:** French legends

| Date | Mintage | F | VF | XF | Unc |
|---|---|---|---|---|---|
| 1963 Proof | — | Value: 550 | | | |

**5 DINARS** **KM# 321** **Weight:** 9.3600 g. **Composition:** 0.9000 Gold .2708 oz. AGW **Obverse:** Arabic legends **Reverse:** Arabic legends

| Date | Mintage | F | VF | XF | Unc |
|---|---|---|---|---|---|
| 1963 Proof | — | Value: 550 | | | |

**5 DINARS** **KM# 287** **Weight:** 9.5000 g. **Composition:** 0.9000 Gold .2749 oz. AGW **Subject:** 10th Anniversary of Republic

| Date | Mintage | F | VF | XF | Unc |
|---|---|---|---|---|---|
| ND(1967) NI Proof | 7,259 | Value: 125 | | | |

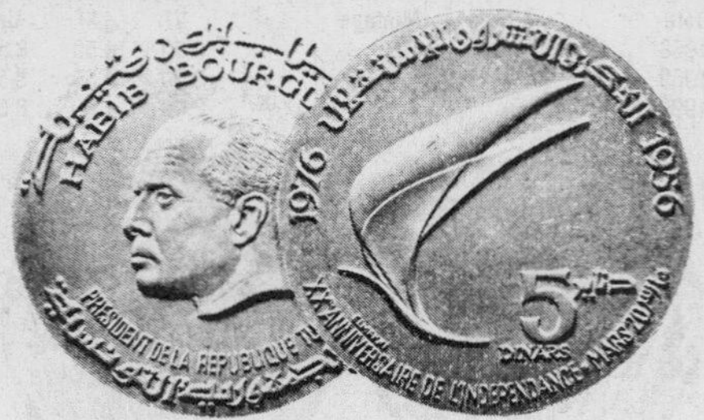


**5 DINARS** KM# 305 **Weight:** 24.0000 g. **Composition:** 0.6800 Silver .5247 oz. ASW **Subject:** 20th Anniversary of Independence

| Date | Mintage | F | VF | XF | Unc |
|---|---|---|---|---|---|
| 1976 | 200,000 | — | — | — | 16.50 |
| 1976 Proof | 1,000 | Value: 40.00 | | | |

**5 DINARS** KM# 284a **Weight:** 9.3600 g. **Composition:** 0.9000 Gold .2708 oz. AGW

| Date | Mintage | F | VF | XF | Unc |
|---|---|---|---|---|---|
| 1976 Proof | — | Value: 500 | | | |

**5 DINARS** KM# 344 **Weight:** 38.0000 g. **Composition:** 0.9000 Silver 1.0995 oz. ASW **Subject:** 20th Anniversary - Central Bank

| Date | Mintage | F | VF | XF | Unc |
|---|---|---|---|---|---|
| 1978 | — | — | — | — | 35.00 |

**5 DINARS** KM# 310 **Weight:** 9.4120 g. **Composition:** 0.9000 Gold .2723 oz. AGW **Obverse:** Habib Bourguiba **Reverse:** President's return

| Date | Mintage | F | VF | XF | Unc |
|---|---|---|---|---|---|
| 1981 Proof | 1,450 | Value: 175 | | | |

**5 DINARS** KM# 313 **Weight:** 27.2200 g. **Composition:** 0.9250 Silver .8096 oz. ASW **Series:** International Year of the Child **Obverse:** Similar to 1 Dinar, KM#302

| Date | Mintage | F | VF | XF | Unc |
|---|---|---|---|---|---|
| 1982 | 7,575 | — | — | — | 15.00 |
| 1982 Proof | 1,108 | Value: 25.00 | | | |

**5 DINARS** KM# 326 **Weight:** 9.4120 g. **Composition:** 0.9000 Gold .2723 oz. AGW **Reverse:** Arabic legends

| Date | Mintage | F | VF | XF | Unc |
|---|---|---|---|---|---|
| AH1402 Proof | 725 | Value: 220 | | | |

**5 DINARS** KM# 325 **Weight:** 9.4120 g. **Composition:** 0.9000 Gold .2723 oz. AGW **Obverse:** President **Reverse:** Coat of arms **Note:** French legends.

| Date | Mintage | F | VF | XF | Unc |
|---|---|---|---|---|---|
| 1982 Proof | 725 | Value: 220 | | | |

**5 DINARS** KM# 327 **Weight:** 9.4120 g. **Composition:** 0.9000 Gold .2723 oz. AGW **Subject:** 25th Anniversary of Republic **Note:** French legends.

| Date | Mintage | F | VF | XF | Unc |
|---|---|---|---|---|---|
| 1983-85 Proof | — | Value: 220 | | | |

**5 DINARS** KM# 328 **Weight:** 9.4120 g. **Composition:** 0.9000 Gold .2723 oz. AGW **Note:** Arabic legends.

| Date | Mintage | F | VF | XF | Unc |
|---|---|---|---|---|---|
| AH1403-05 Proof | — | Value: 220 | | | |

**5 DINARS** KM# 330 **Weight:** 9.4120 g. **Composition:** 0.9000 Gold .2723 oz. AGW **Note:** Arabic legends.

| Date | Mintage | F | VF | XF | Unc |
|---|---|---|---|---|---|
| AH1408 | 375 | — | — | — | 250 |
| AH1409 | Inc. above | — | — | — | 250 |

**5 DINARS** KM# 329 **Weight:** 9.4120 g. **Composition:** 0.9000 Gold .2723 oz. AGW **Obverse:** Map **Reverse:** Allegorical design **Note:** French legends.

| Date | Mintage | F | VF | XF | Unc |
|---|---|---|---|---|---|
| 1988 | 375 | — | — | — | 250 |
| 1989 | Inc. above | — | — | — | 250 |

**10 DINARS** KM# 322 **Weight:** 23.4800 g. **Composition:** 0.9000 Gold .6795 oz. AGW **Obverse:** French legends **Reverse:** French legends

| Date | Mintage | F | VF | XF | Unc |
|---|---|---|---|---|---|
| 1962 Proof | — | Value: 850 | | | |

**10 DINARS** KM# 285 **Weight:** 23.4800 g. **Composition:** 0.9000 Gold .6795 oz. AGW **Obverse:** Arabic legends **Reverse:** Arabic legends

| Date | Mintage | F | VF | XF | Unc |
|---|---|---|---|---|---|
| AH1382-1962 Proof | — | Value: 850 | | | |
| AH1384-1964 Proof | — | Value: 850 | | | |

**10 DINARS** KM# 288 **Weight:** 19.0000 g. **Composition:** 0.9000 Gold .5498 oz. AGW **Subject:** 10th Anniversary of Republic

| Date | Mintage | F | VF | XF | Unc |
|---|---|---|---|---|---|
| ND(1967) NI Proof | 6,480 | Value: 245 | | | |

**10 DINARS** KM# 324 **Composition:** 0.9000 Gold **Subject:** 20th Anniversary of Independence

| Date | Mintage | F | VF | XF | Unc |
|---|---|---|---|---|---|
| 1976 | Est. 2,000 | — | — | — | 750 |

**10 DINARS** KM# 345 **Weight:** 18.8080 g. **Composition:** 0.9000 Gold .5442 oz. AGW **Subject:** 20th Anniversary - Central Bank

| Date | Mintage | F | VF | XF | Unc |
|---|---|---|---|---|---|
| 1978 | 2,000 | — | — | — | 700 |

**10 DINARS** KM# 342 **Weight:** 18.7700 g. **Composition:** 0.9000 Gold .5431 oz. AGW **Obverse:** French legends **Reverse:** French legends

| Date | Mintage | F | VF | XF | Unc |
|---|---|---|---|---|---|
| 1979 | — | — | — | — | 900 |

**10 DINARS** KM# 343 **Weight:** 18.7700 g. **Composition:** 0.9000 Gold .5431 oz. AGW **Obverse:** Arabic legends **Reverse:** Arabic legends

| Date | Mintage | F | VF | XF | Unc |
|---|---|---|---|---|---|
| AH1399-1979 | — | — | — | — | 900 |

**10 DINARS** KM# 311 **Weight:** 18.8240 g. **Composition:** 0.9000 Gold .5447 oz. AGW **Obverse:** Habib Bourguiba **Reverse:** President's return

| Date | Mintage | F | VF | XF | Unc |
|---|---|---|---|---|---|
| 1981 Proof | 2,000 | Value: 550 | | | |

**10 DINARS** KM# 312 **Weight:** 18.8080 g. **Composition:** 0.9000 Gold .5442 oz. AGW **Subject:** 25th Anniversary of Independence **Obverse:** Habib Bourguiba **Reverse:** Silhouette of girl

| Date | Mintage | F | VF | XF | Unc |
|---|---|---|---|---|---|
| 1981 Proof | 2,000 | Value: 550 | | | |

**10 DINARS** KM# 314 **Weight:** 38.0000 g. **Composition:** 0.9000 Silver 1.0995 oz. ASW **Subject:** Gabes Bank

| Date | Mintage | F | VF | XF | Unc |
|---|---|---|---|---|---|
| 1982 Proof | 2,500 | Value: 35.00 | | | |

**10 DINARS** KM# 315 **Weight:** 38.0000 g. **Composition:** 0.9000 Silver 1.0995 oz. ASW **Subject:** Central Bank of Nabeul

| Date | Mintage | F | VF | XF | Unc |
|---|---|---|---|---|---|
| 1982 Proof | 1,000 | Value: 45.00 | | | |

**10 DINARS** KM# 316 **Weight:** 38.0000 g. **Composition:** 0.9000 Silver 1.0995 oz. ASW **Subject:** Sfax Branch Office

| Date | Mintage | F | VF | XF | Unc |
|---|---|---|---|---|---|
| 1982 Proof | 1,000 | Value: 45.00 | | | |

**10 DINARS** KM# 333 **Weight:** 38.0000 g. **Composition:** 0.9000 Silver 1.0995 oz. ASW **Note:** Tunisian girl.

| Date | Mintage | F | VF | XF | Unc |
|---|---|---|---|---|---|
| 1982 Proof | 2,000 | Value: 40.00 | | | |

**10 DINARS** KM# 332 **Weight:** 38.0000 g. **Composition:** 0.9000 Silver 1.0995 oz. ASW **Note:** Arabic legends.

| Date | Mintage | F | VF | XF | Unc |
|---|---|---|---|---|---|
| AH1402 Proof | 700 | Value: 55.00 | | | |

**10 DINARS** KM# 331 **Weight:** 38.0000 g. **Composition:** 0.9000 Silver 1.0995 oz. ASW **Obverse:** President **Reverse:** Coat of arms **Note:** French legends.

| Date | Mintage | F | VF | XF | Unc |
|---|---|---|---|---|---|
| 1982 Proof | 700 | Value: 55.00 | | | |

**10 DINARS** KM# 334 **Weight:** 38.0000 g. **Composition:** 0.9000 Silver 1.0995 oz. ASW **Subject:** 25th Anniversary of Republic **Note:** French legends.

| Date | Mintage | F | VF | XF | Unc |
|---|---|---|---|---|---|
| 1983-85 Proof | — | Value: 45.00 | | | |

**10 DINARS** KM# 335 **Weight:** 38.0000 g. **Composition:** 0.9000 Silver 1.0995 oz. ASW **Note:** Arabic legends.

| Date | Mintage | F | VF | XF | Unc |
|---|---|---|---|---|---|
| AH1403-05 Proof | — | Value: 45.00 | | | |

**10 DINARS** KM# 336 **Weight:** 38.0000 g. **Composition:** 0.9000 Silver 1.0995 oz. ASW **Subject:** 50th Anniversary of the Socialist Party

| Date | Mintage | F | VF | XF | Unc |
|---|---|---|---|---|---|
| 1984 Proof | — | Value: 45.00 | | | |

**10 DINARS** KM# 323 **Weight:** 18.8080 g. **Composition:** 0.9000 Gold .5442 oz. AGW **Obverse:** Portrait left **Reverse:** Statue of Burgiba

| Date | Mintage | F | VF | XF | Unc |
|---|---|---|---|---|---|
| AH1405(1985) Proof | 2,000 | Value: 550 | | | |

**10 DINARS** KM# 337 **Weight:** 18.8080 g. **Composition:** 0.9000 Gold .5442 oz. AGW **Subject:** 30th Anniversary of Independence

| Date | Mintage | F | VF | XF | Unc |
|---|---|---|---|---|---|
| 1986 Proof | — | Value: 550 | | | |

**10 DINARS** KM# 338 **Weight:** 18.8080 g. **Composition:** 0.9000 Gold .5442 oz. AGW **Subject:** 30th Anniversary of Republic

| Date | Mintage | F | VF | XF | Unc |
|---|---|---|---|---|---|
| 1987 Proof | 2,000 | Value: 550 | | | |

**10 DINARS** KM# 339 **Weight:** 38.0000 g. **Composition:** 0.9000 Silver 1.0995 oz. ASW

| Date | Mintage | F | VF | XF | Unc |
|---|---|---|---|---|---|
| 1988 Proof | 4,000 | Value: 35.00 | | | |

**10 DINARS** KM# 341 **Weight:** 18.8080 g. **Composition:** 0.9000 Gold .5442 oz. AGW **Note:** Arabic legends.

| Date | Mintage | F | VF | XF | Unc |
|---|---|---|---|---|---|
| AH1408 | 375 | — | — | — | 650 |
| AH1409 | Inc. above | — | — | — | 650 |

**10 DINARS** KM# 340 **Weight:** 18.8080 g. **Composition:** 0.9000 Gold .5442 oz. AGW **Obverse:** Map **Reverse:** Allegorical design **Note:** French legends.

| Date | Mintage | F | VF | XF | Unc |
|---|---|---|---|---|---|
| 1988 | 375 | — | — | — | 650 |
| 1989 | Inc. above | — | — | — | 650 |

**20 DINARS** KM# 289 **Weight:** 38.0000 g. **Composition:** 0.9000 Gold 1.0996 oz. AGW **Subject:** 10th Anniversary of Republic

| Date | Mintage | F | VF | XF | Unc |
|---|---|---|---|---|---|
| ND(1967) NI | 3,536 | — | — | — | 475 |

**40 DINARS** KM# 290 **Weight:** 76.0000 g. **Composition:** 0.9000 Gold 2.1991 oz. AGW **Subject:** 10th Anniversary of Republic **Obverse:** Similar to 10 Dinars, KM#288

| Date | Mintage | F | VF | XF | Unc |
|---|---|---|---|---|---|
| ND(1967) NI Proof | 3,031 | Value: 950 | | | |

**75 DINARS** KM# 317 **Weight:** 15.5500 g. **Composition:** 0.9000 Gold .4500 oz. AGW **Series:** International Year of the Child

| Date | Mintage | F | VF | XF | Unc |
|---|---|---|---|---|---|
| 1982 Proof | 4,518 | Value: 225 | | | |

## ESSAIS

Standard metals unless otherwise noted

| KM# | Date | Mintage | Identification | Mkt Val |
|---|---|---|---|---|
| E1 | 1918 | — | 5 Centimes. KM#242. | 75.00 |
| E2 | 1918 | — | 10 Centimes. KM#243. | 80.00 |
| E3 | 1918 | — | 25 Centimes. KM#244. | 85.00 |
| E4 | 1920 | — | 5 Centimes. KM#245. | 125 |
| E5 | 1921 | — | 50 Centimes. KM#246. | 90.00 |
| E6 | 1921 | — | Franc. KM#247. | 120 |
| E7 | 1921 | — | Franc. Aluminum. KM#247. | 130 |
| E8 | 1928 | — | Franc. Nickel-Bronze. KM#250a. | 260 |
| E9 | 1928 | — | 2 Francs. Silver-Bronze. KM#251. | 260 |
| E10 | 1930 | — | 10 Francs. KM#255, uniface. | 170 |
| E11 | 1930 | — | 20 Francs. KM#256, uniface. | 350 |
| E12 | 1930 | — | 100 Francs. KM#257, uniface. | 350 |
| E13 | 1931 | — | 5 Centimes. KM#258. | 75.00 |
| E14 | 1931 | — | 10 Centimes. KM#259. | 80.00 |
| E15 | 1931 | — | 25 Centimes. KM#260. | 85.00 |
| E16 | 1353 | — | 5 Francs. KM#261. | 90.00 |
| E17 | 1353 | — | 10 Francs. KM#255. | 100 |
| E18 | 1353 | — | 20 Francs. KM#256. | 175 |

| KM# | Date | Mintage | Identification | Mkt Val |
|---|---|---|---|---|
| E-A19 | 1354 | — | 100 Francs. Gilt Bronze. KM#257. | — |
| E19 | 1938 | — | 100 Francs. Gilt Bronze. KM-M1. | 110 |
| E20 | 1938 | — | 100 Francs. Gold. KM-M1. | 875 |
| E21 | 1939 | — | 5 Francs. KM#264. | 60.00 |
| E22 | 1939 | — | 10 Francs. KM#265. | 80.00 |
| E23 | 1939 | — | 20 Francs. KM#266. | 150 |
| E24 | 1942 | — | 20 Centimes. KM#268. | 50.00 |
| E25 | 1945 | 1,100 | 10 Centimes. KM#271. | 50.00 |
| E26 | 1945 | 1,100 | 20 Centimes. KM#272. | 60.00 |

| KM# | Date | Mintage | Identification | Mkt Val |
|---|---|---|---|---|
| E27 | 1946 | 1,100 | 5 Francs. KM#273. | 35.00 |
| E28 | 1950 | 1,100 | 20 Francs. KM#274. | 35.00 |
| E29 | 1950 | 1,100 | 50 Francs. KM#275. | 35.00 |
| E30 | 1950 | 1,100 | 100 Francs. KM#276. | 35.00 |
| E31 | 1954 | 1,100 | 5 Francs. KM#277. | 20.00 |
| E32 | 1968 | 1,260 | 1/2 Dinar. KM#291. | 35.00 |
| E33 | 1968 | 70 | 1/2 Dinar. Gold. | — |

| KM# | Date | Mintage | Identification | Mkt Val |
|---|---|---|---|---|
| E34 | 1970 | 1,250 | Dinar. KM#302. | 45.00 |
| E35 | 1976 | 2,050 | 1/2 Dinar. KM#303. | 30.00 |
| E36 | 1976 | 2,050 | Dinar. KM#304. | 40.00 |

## MINT SETS

| KM# | Date | Mintage | Identification | Issue Price | Mkt Val |
|---|---|---|---|---|---|
| MS1 | 1960 (7) | — | KM#280-282, 306-309 | — | 5.50 |
| MS2 | 1996 (7) | — | KM#282, 306-309, 346-347 | — | 16.50 |

## PROOF SETS

| KM# | Date | Mintage | Identification | Issue Price | Mkt Val |
|---|---|---|---|---|---|
| PS2 | 1967 (5) | 3,031 | KM#286-290 | — | 1,850 |
| PS3 | 1969FM-NI (10) | 15,202 | KM#292-301 | 77.00 | 120 |
| PS4 | 1969NI (10) | 5,000 | KM#292-301 | — | 475 |

## PIEFORTS

Double thickness; standard metals unless otherwise noted

| KM# | Date | Mintage | Identification | Issue Price | Mkt Val |
|---|---|---|---|---|---|
| P1 | 1968 | 500 | 1/2 Dinar. KM#291 | — | 35.00 |
| P2 | 1982 | 96 | 5 Dinars. KM#313. | — | 165 |
| P3 | 1982 | 55 | 75 Dinars. KM#317. | — | 1,250 |

## PIEFORTS WITH ESSAI

Double thickness

| KM# | Date | Mintage | Identification | Mkt Val |
|---|---|---|---|---|
| PE1 | 1945 | 104 | 20 Centimes. KM#272. | 100 |

| KM# | Date | Mintage | Identification | Mkt Val |
|---|---|---|---|---|
| PE2 | 1945 | 104 | 50 Centimes. KM#246. | 100 |
| PE3 | 1945 | 104 | Franc. KM#247. | 100 |

| KM# | Date | Mintage | Identification | Mkt Val |
|---|---|---|---|---|
| PE4 | 1945 | 104 | 2 Francs. KM#248. | 100 |
| PE5 | 1946 | 104 | 5 Francs. KM#273. | 120 |
| PE6 | 1954 | 104 | 5 Francs. KM#277. | 90.00 |

# TURKEY

a map of The Mints of the Ottoman Empire

The Republic of Turkey, a parliamentary democracy of the Near East located partially in Europe and partially in Asia between the Black and the Mediterranean Seas, has an area of 301,382 sq. mi. (780,580 sq. km.) and a population of *55.4 million. Capital: Ankara. Turkey exports cotton, hazelnuts, and tobacco, and enjoys a virtual monopoly in meerschaum.

The Ottoman Turks, a tribe from Central Asia, first appeared in the early 13th century, and by the 17th century had established the Ottoman Empire which stretched from the Persian Gulf to the southern frontier of Poland, and from the Caspian Sea to the Algerian plateau. The defeat of the Turkish navy by the Holy League in 1571, and of the Turkish forces besieging Vienna in 1683, began the steady decline of the Ottoman Empire which, accelerated by the rise of nationalism, contracted its European border, and by the end of World War I deprived it of its Arab lands. The present Turkish boundaries were largely fixed by the Treaty of Lausanne in 1923. The sultanate and caliphate, the political and spiritual ruling institutions of the old empire, were separated and the sultanate abolished in 1922. On Oct. 29, 1923, Turkey formally became a republic.

**RULERS**

Abdul Hamid II, AH1293-1327/1876-1909AD
Muhammad V, AH1327-1336/1909-1918AD
Muhammad VI, AH1336-1341/1918-1923AD
Republic, AH1341/AD1923-

**MINTNAMES**

Baghdad
See Iraq-Mesopotamia
بغداد

Bursa
(Brusah)
بروسة

Constantine (Constaniyah, Qusantinah) See Algeria-Algiers
قسطنتنيه

Constantinople
(Qustantiniyah)
قسطنطنية

Damascus
(Dimashk) See Syria
دمشق

Edirne
(Adrianople)
ادرنة

Halab
(Aleppo)
See Syria
حلب

Islambul
Istanbul
الاسلامبول or اسلامبول

Jaza'Ir
(See Algeria-Algiers)
Kara Amid
(Amid)
الجزاير

Manistir
مناستر

al-Mascara
See Algeria-Algiers
المعسكر

Medea
See Algeria-Algiers
مديه or مديى

Makkah (Mecca)
See Saudi Arabia
مكه

Misr
See Egypt
مصر

Revan
(Erevan, now Yerevan)
See Armenia
روان

Salonika
(Selanik, Saloniki)
سلانيك

Taqidemt
See Algeria-Algiers
تاقدمت

Tarabalus
See Libya-Tripoli
طرابلس

Tarabalus Gharb
See Libya-Tripoli
طرابلس غرب

Tiflis
See Georgia
تفليس

Tunis
See Tunisia-Tunis
تونس

Van
(Wan) - Until AH1032. AH1133-34
وان

**MONETARY EQUIVALENTS**

3 Akche = 1 Para
5 Para = Beshlik (Beshparalik)
10 Para = Onluk
20 Para = Yirmilik
30 Para = Zolota
40 Para = Kurush (Piastre)
1-1/2 Kurush (Piastres) = Altmishlik

**MONETARY SYSTEM**

Silver Coinage

40 Para = 1 Kurush (Piastre)
2 Kurush (Piastres) = 1 Ikilik
2-1/2 Kurush (Piastres) = Yuzluk
3 Kurush (Piastres) = Uechlik
5 Kurush (Piastres) = Beshlik
6 Kurush (Piastres) = Altilik

Gold Coinage

100 Kurush (Piastres) = 1 Turkish Pound (Lira)

This system has remained essentially unchanged since its introduction by Ahmad III in 1688, except that the Asper and Para have long since ceased to be coined. The Piastre, established as a crown-sized silver coin approximately equal to the French Ecu of Louis XIV, has shrunk to a tiny copper coin, worth about 1/15 of a U.S. cent. Since the establishment of the Republic in 1923, the Turkish terms, Kurus and Lira, have replaced the European names Piastres and Turkish Pounds.

**MINT VISIT ISSUES**

From time to time, certain cities of the Ottoman Empire, such as Bursa, Edirne, Kosova, Manistir and Salonikawere honored by having special coins struck at Istanbul, but with inscriptions stating that they were struck in the city of honor. These were produced on the occasion of the Sultan's visit to that city. The coins were struck in limited, but not small quantities, and were probably intended for distribution to the notables of the city and the Sultan's own followers. Because they were of the same size and type as the regular circulation issues struck at Istanbul, many specimens found their way into circulation and worn or mounted specimens are found today, although some have been preserved in XF or better condition. Mintage statistics are not known.

**MONNAIE DE LUXE**

In the 23rd year of the reign of Abdul Hamid II, two parallel series of gold coins were produced, regular mint issues and monnaies de luxe', which were intended primarily for presentation and jewelry purposes. The Monnaie de Luxe' were struck to a slightly less weight and the same fineness as regular issues, but were broader and thinner, and from more ornate dies.

Coins are listed by type, followed by a list of reported years. Most of the reported years have never been confirmed and other years may also exist. Mintage figures are known for the AH1293 and 1327 series, but are unreliable and of little utility.

Although some years are undoubtedly much rarer than others, there is at present no date collecting of Ottoman gold and therefore little justification for higher prices for rare dates.

There is no change in design in the regular series. Only the toughra, accessional date and regnal year vary. The deluxe series show ornamental changes. The standard coins generally do not bear the denomination.

**HONORIFIC TITLES**

El Ghazi

Reshat

The first coinage of Abdul Hamid II has a flower right of the toughra while the second coinage has *el Ghazi* (The Victorious). The first coinage of Mohammad Reshat Vhas *Reshat* right of the toughra while his second coinage has *el Ghazi*.

# SULTANATE

## Abdul Hamid II

### AH1293-1327/1876-1909AD

### STANDARD COINAGE

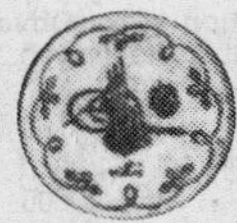

**5 PARA KM# 743 Weight:** 1.0023 g. **Composition:** 0.1000 Silver .0032 oz. ASW **Obverse:** Toughra; "el-Ghazi" to right **Note:** Struck at Qustantiniyah.

| Date | Mintage | VG | F | VF | XF | Unc |
|---|---|---|---|---|---|---|
| AH1293//26(1900) | — | 0.25 | 0.50 | 1.25 | 4.00 | — |
| AH1293//27(1901) | — | 0.25 | 0.50 | 1.25 | 4.00 | — |
| AH1293//28(1902) | — | 0.50 | 1.00 | 3.00 | 12.00 | — |
| AH1293//30(1904) | — | 6.00 | 12.00 | 20.00 | 40.00 | — |

**10 PARA KM# 744 Weight:** 2.0046 g. **Composition:** 0.1000 Silver .0064 oz. ASW **Obverse:** Toughra; "el-Ghazi" to right **Note:** Struck at Qustantiniyah.

| Date | Mintage | VG | F | VF | XF | Unc |
|---|---|---|---|---|---|---|
| AH1293//26(1900) | — | 0.25 | 0.50 | 1.00 | 4.00 | — |
| AH1293//27(1901) | — | 0.25 | 0.50 | 1.00 | 4.00 | — |
| **Note:** Varieties exist in size of regnal year 27 | | | | | | |
| AH1293//28(1902) | — | 0.25 | 0.50 | 1.50 | 6.00 | — |
| AH1293//30(1904) | | 1.00 | 2.00 | 5.00 | 15.00 | — |

**KURUSH KM# 735 Weight:** 1.2027 g. **Composition:** 0.8300 Silver .0321 oz. ASW **Obverse:** Toughra; "el-Ghazi" to right **Note:** Varieties exist in the size of year and inscription. Struck at Qustantiniyah.

| Date | Mintage | VG | F | VF | XF | Unc |
|---|---|---|---|---|---|---|
| AH1293//26(1900) | 55,000 | 3.00 | 7.50 | 15.00 | 30.00 | — |
| AH1293//27(1901) | 9,945,000 | 1.00 | 2.00 | 3.00 | 5.00 | — |
| AH1293//28(1902) | 16,139,000 | 1.00 | 2.00 | 3.00 | 5.00 | — |
| AH1293//29(1903) | 7,076,000 | 1.00 | 2.00 | 3.00 | 5.00 | — |
| AH1293//30(1904) | 707,000 | 2.00 | 4.00 | 8.00 | 15.00 | — |
| AH1293//31(1905) | 1,366,000 | 1.00 | 2.00 | 3.00 | 5.00 | — |
| AH1293//32(1906) | 1,140,000 | 1.00 | 2.00 | 3.00 | 5.00 | — |
| AH1293//33(1907) | 1,700,000 | 1.00 | 2.00 | 3.00 | 5.00 | — |
| AH1293//34(1908) | — | 40.00 | 60.00 | 115 | 225 | — |

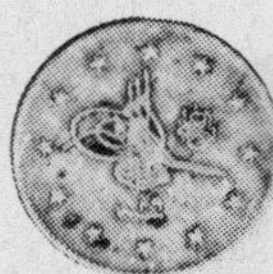

**2 KURUSH KM# 736 Weight:** 2.4055 g. **Composition:** 0.8300 Silver .0642 oz. ASW **Obverse:** Toughra; "el-Ghazi" to right **Note:** Varieties exist in the size of toughra and year. Struck at Qustantiniyah.

| Date | Mintage | VG | F | VF | XF | Unc |
|---|---|---|---|---|---|---|
| AH1293//26(1900) | 17,000 | 15.00 | 25.00 | 35.00 | 75.00 | — |
| AH1293//27(1901) | 4,689,000 | 1.50 | 2.00 | 4.00 | 7.00 | — |
| AH1293//28(1902) | 7,567,000 | 1.50 | 2.00 | 4.00 | 7.00 | — |
| AH1293//29(1903) | 7,775,000 | 1.50 | 2.00 | 4.00 | 7.00 | — |
| AH1293//30(1904) | 1,366,000 | 1.50 | 2.00 | 4.00 | 7.00 | — |
| AH1293//31(1905) | 3,014,000 | 1.50 | 2.00 | 4.00 | 7.00 | — |
| AH1293//32(1906) | 1,625,000 | 1.50 | 2.00 | 4.00 | 7.00 | — |
| AH1293//33(1907) | 2,173,000 | 1.50 | 2.00 | 4.00 | 7.00 | — |
| AH1293//34(1908) | — | 45.00 | 90.00 | 140 | 200 | — |

**5 KURUSH KM# 737 Weight:** 6.0130 g. **Composition:** 0.8300 Silver .1605 oz. ASW **Obverse:** Toughra; "el-Ghazi" to right **Note:** Varieties exist in the size of toughra, inscription, and date. Struck at Qustantiniyah.

| Date | Mintage | VG | F | VF | XF | Unc |
|---|---|---|---|---|---|---|
| AH1293//26(1900) | 8,000 | 15.00 | 30.00 | 45.00 | 75.00 | — |
| AH1293//27(1901) | 16,000 | 15.00 | 30.00 | 45.00 | 75.00 | — |
| AH1293//28(1902) | 6,000 | 15.00 | 30.00 | 45.00 | 75.00 | — |
| AH1293//29(1903) | 7,000 | 15.00 | 30.00 | 45.00 | 75.00 | — |
| AH1293//30(1904) | 38,000 | 5.00 | 10.00 | 15.00 | 30.00 | — |
| AH1293//31(1905) | Inc. above | 3.50 | 4.50 | 7.00 | 15.00 | — |
| AH1293//31/0(1905) | 3,175,000 | 6.00 | 13.00 | 25.00 | 35.00 | — |
| AH1293//32(1906) | 3,334,000 | 2.00 | 3.25 | 4.50 | 9.50 | — |
| AH1293//33(1907) | 907,000 | 3.00 | 5.00 | 9.00 | 16.00 | — |
| AH1293//34(1908) | — | 50.00 | 80.00 | 110 | 200 | — |

**10 KURUSH KM# 738 Weight:** 12.0270 g. **Composition:** 0.8300 Silver .3210 oz. ASW **Obverse:** Toughra; "el-Ghazi" to right **Note:** Struck at Qustantiniyah.

| Date | Mintage | VG | F | VF | XF | Unc |
|---|---|---|---|---|---|---|
| AH1293//31(1905) | 51,000 | 20.00 | 40.00 | 75.00 | 125 | — |
| AH1293//32(1906) | 575,000 | 7.50 | 12.50 | 18.00 | 30.00 | — |
| AH1293//33(1907) | 273,000 | 6.00 | 10.00 | 20.00 | 35.00 | — |

**12-1/2 KURUSH KM# 745 Weight:** 0.8770 g. **Composition:** 0.9170 Gold .0258 oz. AGW **Series:** Monnaie de Luxe **Obverse:** Toughra **Note:** Struck at Qustantiniyah.

| Date | Mintage | VG | F | VF | XF | Unc |
|---|---|---|---|---|---|---|
| AH1293//28(1902) | 800 | 40.00 | 70.00 | 100 | 180 | — |
| AH1293//29(1903) | 12,000 | 20.00 | 30.00 | 45.00 | 75.00 | — |
| AH1293//30(1904) | 13,000 | 20.00 | 30.00 | 45.00 | 75.00 | — |
| AH1293//31(1905) | 24,000 | 20.00 | 30.00 | 45.00 | 75.00 | — |
| AH1293//32(1906) | 14,000 | 20.00 | 30.00 | 45.00 | 75.00 | — |
| AH1293//33(1907) | 13,000 | 20.00 | 30.00 | 45.00 | 75.00 | — |
| AH1293//34(1908) | — | 20.00 | 30.00 | 45.00 | 75.00 | — |

**25 KURUSH KM# 729 Weight:** 1.8040 g. **Composition:** 0.9170 Gold .0532 oz. AGW **Obverse:** Toughra; "el-Ghazi" to right **Note:** Struck at Qustantiniyah.

| Date | Mintage | VG | F | VF | XF | Unc |
|---|---|---|---|---|---|---|
| AH1293//26(1900) | 48,000 | BV | 25.00 | 32.00 | 45.00 | — |
| AH1293//27(1901) | 99,000 | BV | 25.00 | 32.00 | 45.00 | — |
| AH1293//28(1902) | 77,000 | BV | 25.00 | 32.00 | 45.00 | — |
| AH1293//29(1903) | 102,000 | BV | 25.00 | 32.00 | 45.00 | — |
| AH1293//30(1904) | 156,000 | BV | 25.00 | 32.00 | 45.00 | — |
| AH1293//31(1905) | 58,000 | BV | 25.00 | 32.00 | 45.00 | — |
| AH1293//32(1906) | 112,000 | BV | 25.00 | 32.00 | 45.00 | — |
| AH1293//33(1907) | 16,000 | BV | 25.00 | 32.00 | 45.00 | — |
| AH1293//34(1908) | — | BV | 25.00 | 32.00 | 45.00 | — |

**25 KURUSH KM# 739 Weight:** 1.7540 g. **Composition:** 0.9170 Gold .0517 oz. AGW **Series:** Monnaie de Luxe **Obverse:** Toughra; "el-Ghazi" to right **Note:** Struck at Qustantiniyah.

| Date | Mintage | VG | F | VF | XF | Unc |
|---|---|---|---|---|---|---|
| AH1293//26(1900) | — | 50.00 | 65.00 | 75.00 | 95.00 | — |
| AH1293//27(1901) | — | 50.00 | 65.00 | 75.00 | 95.00 | — |
| AH1293//28(1902) | — | 50.00 | 65.00 | 75.00 | 95.00 | — |
| AH1293//29(1903) | — | 50.00 | 65.00 | 75.00 | 95.00 | — |
| AH1293//30(1904) | — | 50.00 | 65.00 | 75.00 | 95.00 | — |
| AH1293//31(1905) | — | 50.00 | 65.00 | 75.00 | 95.00 | — |
| AH1293//32(1906) | — | 50.00 | 65.00 | 75.00 | 95.00 | — |
| AH1293//33(1907) | — | 50.00 | 65.00 | 75.00 | 95.00 | — |
| AH1293//34(1908) | — | 50.00 | 65.00 | 75.00 | 95.00 | — |

**50 KURUSH KM# 731 Weight:** 3.6080 g. **Composition:** 0.9170 Gold .1064 oz. AGW **Obverse:** Toughra; "el-Ghazi" to right **Note:** Struck at Qustantiniyah.

| Date | Mintage | VG | F | VF | XF | Unc |
|---|---|---|---|---|---|---|
| AH1293//26(1900) | 14,000 | BV | 50.00 | 60.00 | 90.00 | — |
| AH1293//27(1901) | 14,000 | BV | 50.00 | 60.00 | 90.00 | — |
| AH1293//28(1902) | 33,000 | BV | 50.00 | 60.00 | 90.00 | — |
| AH1293//29(1903) | 24,000 | BV | 50.00 | 60.00 | 90.00 | — |
| AH1293//30(1904) | 66,000 | BV | 50.00 | 60.00 | 90.00 | — |
| AH1293//31(1905) | 59,000 | BV | 50.00 | 60.00 | 90.00 | — |
| AH1293//32(1906) | 48,000 | BV | 50.00 | 60.00 | 90.00 | — |
| AH1293//33(1907) | 16,000 | BV | 50.00 | 60.00 | 90.00 | — |
| AH1293//34(1908) | — | BV | 50.00 | 60.00 | 90.00 | — |

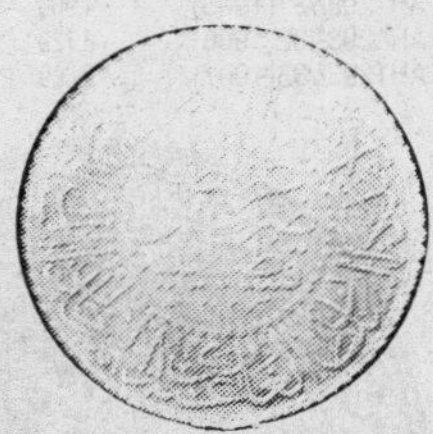

**50 KURUSH KM# 740 Weight:** 3.5080 g. **Composition:** 0.9170 Gold .1034 oz. AGW **Series:** Monnaie de Luxe **Obverse:** Toughra; "el-Ghazi" to right **Note:** Struck at Qustantiniyah.

| Date | Mintage | VG | F | VF | XF | Unc |
|---|---|---|---|---|---|---|
| AH1293//26(1900) | — | 50.00 | 75.00 | 90.00 | 140 | — |
| AH1293//27(1901) | — | 50.00 | 75.00 | 90.00 | 140 | — |
| AH1293//28(1902) | — | 50.00 | 75.00 | 90.00 | 140 | — |
| AH1293//29(1903) | — | 50.00 | 75.00 | 90.00 | 140 | — |
| AH1293//30(1904) | — | 50.00 | 75.00 | 90.00 | 140 | — |
| AH1293//31(1905) | — | 50.00 | 75.00 | 90.00 | 140 | — |
| AH1293//32(1906) | — | 50.00 | 75.00 | 90.00 | 140 | — |
| AH1293//33(1907) | — | 50.00 | 75.00 | 90.00 | 140 | — |
| AH1293//34(1908) | — | 50.00 | 75.00 | 90.00 | 140 | — |

**100 KURUSH KM# 730 Weight:** 7.2160 g. **Composition:** 0.9170 Gold .2128 oz. AGW **Obverse:** Toughra; "el-Ghazi" to right **Note:** Struck at Qustantiniyah.

| Date | Mintage | VG | F | VF | XF | Unc |
|---|---|---|---|---|---|---|
| AH1293//26(1900) | 2,000 | — | BV | 100 | 115 | — |
| AH1293//27(1901) | 48,000 | — | BV | 100 | 115 | — |
| AH1293//28(1902) | 865,000 | — | BV | 100 | 115 | — |
| AH1293//29(1903) | 1,026,000 | — | BV | 100 | 115 | — |
| AH1293//30(1904) | 1,644,000 | — | BV | 100 | 115 | — |

| Date | Mintage | VG | F | VF | XF | Unc |
|---|---|---|---|---|---|---|
| AH1293//31(1905) | 2,748,000 | — | BV | 100 | 115 | — |
| AH1293//32(1906) | 1,952,000 | — | BV | 100 | 115 | — |
| AH1293//33(1907) | 963,000 | — | BV | 100 | 115 | — |
| AH1293//34(1908) | — | — | BV | 100 | 115 | — |

**100 KURUSH** KM# 741 **Weight:** 7.0160 g. **Composition:** 0.9170 Gold .2068 oz. AGW **Series:** Monnaie de Luxe **Obverse:** Toughra; "el-Ghazi" to right **Note:** Struck at Qustantiniyah.

| Date | Mintage | VG | F | VF | XF | Unc |
|---|---|---|---|---|---|---|
| AH1293//26(1900) | — | BV | 100 | 135 | 190 | — |
| AH1293//27(1901) | — | BV | 100 | 135 | 190 | — |
| AH1293//28(1902) | — | BV | 100 | 135 | 190 | — |
| AH1293//29(1903) | — | BV | 100 | 135 | 190 | — |
| AH1293//30(1904) | — | BV | 100 | 135 | 190 | — |
| AH1293//31(1905) | — | BV | 100 | 135 | 190 | — |
| AH1293//32(1906) | — | BV | 100 | 135 | 190 | — |
| AH1293//33(1907) | — | BV | 100 | 135 | 190 | — |
| AH1293//34(1908) | — | BV | 100 | 135 | 190 | — |

**250 KURUSH** KM# 732 **Weight:** 18.0400 g. **Composition:** 0.9170 Gold .5319 oz. AGW **Obverse:** Toughra; "el-Ghazi" to right **Note:** Struck at Qustantiniyah.

| Date | Mintage | VG | F | VF | XF | Unc |
|---|---|---|---|---|---|---|
| AH1293//26(1900) | 1,428 | BV | 250 | 300 | 450 | — |
| AH1293//27(1901) | 1,450 | BV | 250 | 300 | 450 | — |
| AH1293//28(1902) | 7,027 | BV | 250 | 300 | 450 | — |
| AH1293//29(1903) | 7,522 | BV | 250 | 300 | 450 | — |
| AH1293//30(1904) | 7,522 | BV | 250 | 300 | 450 | — |
| AH1293//31(1905) | 4,900 | BV | 250 | 300 | 450 | — |
| AH1293//32(1906) | 8,729 | BV | 250 | 300 | 450 | — |
| AH1293//33(1907) | 2,669 | BV | 225 | 275 | 450 | — |

**250 KURUSH** KM# 742 **Weight:** 17.5400 g. **Composition:** 0.9170 Gold .5169 oz. AGW **Series:** Monnaie de Luxe **Obverse:** Toughra; "el-Ghazi" to right **Note:** Struck at Qustantiniyah.

| Date | Mintage | VG | F | VF | XF | Unc |
|---|---|---|---|---|---|---|
| AH1293//26(1900) | — | BV | 275 | 400 | 600 | — |
| AH1293//27(1901) | — | BV | 275 | 400 | 600 | — |
| AH1293//28(1902) | — | BV | 275 | 400 | 600 | — |
| AH1293//29(1903) | — | BV | 275 | 400 | 600 | — |
| AH1293//30(1904) | — | BV | 275 | 400 | 600 | — |
| AH1293//31(1905) | — | BV | 275 | 400 | 600 | — |
| AH1293//32(1906) | — | BV | 275 | 400 | 600 | — |
| AH1293//33(1907) | — | BV | 275 | 400 | 600 | — |
| AH1293//34(1908) Rare | — | — | — | — | — | — |

**500 KURUSH** KM# 746 **Weight:** 35.0800 g. **Composition:** 0.9170 Gold 1.0338 oz. AGW **Series:** Monnaie de Luxe **Obverse:** Toughra above crossed flags, ornamental base **Note:** Struck at Qustantiniyah.

| Date | Mintage | Good | VG | F | VF | XF |
|---|---|---|---|---|---|---|
| AH1293//26 | — | — | 600 | 750 | 900 | 1,200 |
| AH1293//27 | — | — | 600 | 750 | 900 | 1,200 |
| AH1293//28 | — | — | 600 | 750 | 900 | 1,200 |
| AH1293//29 | — | — | 600 | 750 | 900 | 1,200 |
| AH1293//30 | — | — | 600 | 750 | 900 | 1,200 |
| AH1293//31 | — | — | 600 | 750 | 900 | 1,200 |
| AH1293//32 | — | — | 600 | 750 | 900 | 1,200 |
| AH1293//33 | — | — | 600 | 750 | 900 | 1,200 |
| AH1293//34 | — | — | 600 | 750 | 900 | 1,200 |

**500 KURUSH** KM# 733 **Weight:** 36.0800 g. **Composition:** 0.9170 Gold 1.0638 oz. AGW **Obverse:** Toughra; "el-Ghazi" to right **Note:** Struck at Qustantiniyah.

| Date | Mintage | VG | F | VF | XF | Unc |
|---|---|---|---|---|---|---|
| AH1293//26(1900) | 8,765 | BV | 500 | 550 | 750 | — |
| AH1293//27(1901) | 22,000 | BV | 500 | 550 | 750 | — |
| AH1293//28(1902) | 36,000 | BV | 500 | 550 | 750 | — |
| AH1293//29(1903) | 17,000 | BV | 500 | 550 | 750 | — |
| AH1293//30(1904) | 33,000 | BV | 500 | 550 | 750 | — |
| AH1293//31(1905) | 41,000 | BV | 500 | 550 | 750 | — |
| AH1293//32(1906) | 33,000 | BV | 500 | 550 | 750 | — |
| AH1293//33(1907) | 16,000 | BV | 500 | 550 | 750 | — |
| AH1293//34(1908) | — | BV | 500 | 550 | 750 | — |

## Muhammad V
### AH1327-36/1909-18AD

### STANDARD COINAGE

**5 PARA** KM# 759 **Composition:** Nickel **Obverse:** Toughra; "Reshat" to right **Note:** Struck at Qustantiniyah.

| Date | Mintage | Good | VG | F | VF | XF |
|---|---|---|---|---|---|---|
| AH1327//2 | 1,664,000 | — | 1.00 | 2.00 | 4.00 | 8.00 |
| AH1327//3 | 21,760,000 | — | 0.50 | 1.00 | 2.00 | 4.00 |
| AH1327//4 | 21,392,000 | — | 0.50 | 1.00 | 2.00 | 4.00 |
| AH1327//5 | 30,579,000 | — | 0.50 | 1.00 | 2.00 | 4.00 |
| AH1327//6 | 15,751,000 | — | 0.50 | 1.00 | 2.00 | 4.00 |
| AH1327//7 | 2,512,000 | — | 15.00 | 35.00 | 60.00 | 100 |

**5 PARA** KM# 767 **Composition:** Nickel **Obverse:** Toughra; "el-Ghazi" to right **Note:** Struck at Qustantiniyah.

| Date | Mintage | Good | VG | F | VF | XF |
|---|---|---|---|---|---|---|
| AH1327//7 | 740,000 | — | 15.00 | 30.00 | 45.00 | 70.00 |

**10 PARA** KM# 760 **Composition:** Nickel **Obverse:** Toughra; "el-Ghazi" to right **Note:** Struck at Qustantiniyah.

| Date | Mintage | Good | VG | F | VF | XF |
|---|---|---|---|---|---|---|
| AH1327//2 | 2,576,000 | — | 0.25 | 0.50 | 2.00 | 5.00 |
| AH1327//3 | 18,992,000 | — | 0.15 | 0.25 | 1.00 | 3.00 |
| AH1327//4 | 18,576,000 | — | 0.15 | 0.25 | 1.00 | 3.00 |
| AH1327//5 | 31,799,000 | — | 0.15 | 0.25 | 1.00 | 3.00 |
| AH1327//6 | 17,024,000 | — | 0.15 | 0.25 | 1.00 | 3.00 |
| AH1327//7 | 21,680,000 | — | 0.30 | 0.65 | 1.50 | 4.00 |

**10 PARA** KM# 768 **Composition:** Nickel **Obverse:** Toughra; "el-Ghazi" to right **Note:** Struck at Qustantiniyah.

| Date | Mintage | Good | VG | F | VF | XF |
|---|---|---|---|---|---|---|
| AH1327//7 | — | — | 0.30 | 0.60 | 1.50 | 4.00 |
| **Note:** Mintage included in KM760 | | | | | | |
| AH1327//8 | 7,590,000 | — | 0.50 | 1.00 | 4.00 | 10.00 |

**20 PARA** KM# 761 **Composition:** Nickel **Obverse:** Toughra; "Reshat" to right **Note:** Struck at Qustantiniyah.

| Date | Mintage | Good | VG | F | VF | XF |
|---|---|---|---|---|---|---|
| AH1327 No regnal year | — | — | 5.00 | 8.50 | 15.00 | 25.00 |
| AH1327//2 | 1,524,000 | — | 0.25 | 0.50 | 2.00 | 8.00 |
| AH1327//3 | 11,418,000 | — | 0.15 | 0.35 | 1.50 | 6.00 |
| AH1327//4 | 10,848,000 | — | 0.15 | 0.25 | 1.00 | 5.00 |
| AH1327//5 | 24,350,000 | — | 0.15 | 0.25 | 1.00 | 5.00 |
| AH1327//6 | 20,663,000 | — | 0.15 | 0.25 | 1.00 | 5.00 |
| AH1327//7 Rare | — | — | — | — | — | — |

**20 PARA** KM# 769 **Composition:** Nickel **Obverse:** Toughra; "el-Ghazi" to right **Note:** Struck at Qustantiniyah.

| Date | Mintage | Good | VG | F | VF | XF |
|---|---|---|---|---|---|---|
| AH1327//7 Rare | — | — | — | — | — | — |

**40 PARA** KM# 766 **Composition:** Nickel **Obverse:** Toughra; "el-Ghazi" to right **Note:** Struck at Qustantiniyah.

| Date | Mintage | Good | VG | F | VF | XF |
|---|---|---|---|---|---|---|
| AH1327//3 | 1,992,000 | — | 0.50 | 1.00 | 3.00 | 10.00 |
| AH1327//4 | 8,716,000 | — | 0.15 | 0.30 | 2.00 | 5.00 |
| AH1327//5 | 9,248,000 | — | 0.15 | 0.30 | 2.00 | 5.00 |

**40 PARA** KM# 779 **Composition:** Copper-Nickel **Obverse:** Toughra; "el-Ghazi" to right **Note:** Struck at Qustantiniyah.

| Date | Mintage | Good | VG | F | VF | XF |
|---|---|---|---|---|---|---|
| AH1327//8 | 16,339,000 | — | 0.15 | 0.30 | 2.00 | 5.00 |
| AH1327//9 | 3,034,000 | — | 1.00 | 2.00 | 10.00 | 25.00 |

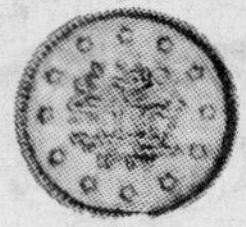

**KURUSH** **KM# 748** **Weight:** 1.2027 g. **Composition:** 0.8300 Silver .0321 oz. ASW **Obverse:** Toughra **Note:** Struck at Qustantiniyah.

| Date | Mintage | Good | VG | F | VF | XF |
|---|---|---|---|---|---|---|
| AH1327//1 | 1,270,000 | — | 1.25 | 2.50 | 3.50 | 6.00 |
| AH1327//2 | 8,770,000 | — | 1.00 | 2.00 | 3.00 | 5.00 |
| AH1327//3 | 840,000 | — | 1.50 | 3.00 | 6.00 | 12.50 |

**2 KURUSH** **KM# 749** **Weight:** 2.4055 g. **Composition:** 0.8300 Silver .0642 oz. ASW **Obverse:** Toughra; "Reshat" to right **Note:** Struck at Qustantiniyah. Varieties exist in the size of date.

| Date | Mintage | Good | VG | F | VF | XF |
|---|---|---|---|---|---|---|
| AH1327//1 | 5,157,000 | — | 1.75 | 2.25 | 3.50 | 7.50 |
| AH1327//2 | 11,120,000 | — | 1.50 | 2.00 | 3.00 | 6.50 |
| AH1327//3 | 6,110,000 | — | 1.50 | 2.00 | 3.00 | 6.50 |
| AH1327//4 | 4,031,000 | — | 1.50 | 2.00 | 3.00 | 6.50 |
| AH1327//5 | 301,000 | — | 2.50 | 5.00 | 10.00 | 20.00 |
| AH1327//6 | 1,884,000 | — | 2.00 | 2.50 | 4.00 | 8.00 |
| AH1327//6/2 | Inc. above | — | 2.00 | 2.50 | 4.00 | 8.00 |

**2 KURUSH** **KM# 770** **Weight:** 2.4055 g. **Composition:** 0.8300 Silver .0642 oz. ASW **Obverse:** Toughra; "el-Ghazi" to right **Note:** Struck at Qustantiniyah. Varieties exist in the size of date.

| Date | Mintage | Good | VG | F | VF | XF |
|---|---|---|---|---|---|---|
| AH1327//7 | 17,000 | — | 12.50 | 25.00 | 40.00 | 75.00 |
| AH1327//8 | 398,000 | — | 20.00 | 30.00 | 50.00 | 100 |
| AH1327//9 | 8,000 | — | 60.00 | 100 | 200 | 350 |

**5 KURUSH** **KM# 750** **Weight:** 6.0130 g. **Composition:** 0.8300 Silver 1605 oz. ASW **Obverse:** Toughra; "Reshat" to right **Note:** Struck at Qustantiniyah.

| Date | Mintage | Good | VG | F | VF | XF |
|---|---|---|---|---|---|---|
| AH1327//1 | 1,558,000 | — | BV | 3.50 | 6.00 | 10.00 |
| AH1327//2 | 1,886,000 | — | BV | 3.50 | 6.00 | 10.00 |
| AH1327//3 | 1,273,000 | — | BV | 3.50 | 6.00 | 10.00 |
| AH1327//4 | 1,635,000 | — | BV | 3.50 | 6.00 | 10.00 |
| AH1327//5 | 194,000 | — | 6.00 | 9.00 | 15.00 | 28.00 |
| AH1327//6 | 664,000 | — | 3.25 | 3.50 | 5.00 | 9.00 |
| AH1327//7 | 834,000 | — | 3.25 | 3.50 | 5.00 | 9.00 |

**5 KURUSH** **KM# 771** **Weight:** 6.0130 g. **Composition:** 0.8300 Silver 1605 oz. ASW **Obverse:** Toughra; "el-Ghazi" to right **Note:** Struck at Qustantiniyah.

| Date | Mintage | Good | VG | F | VF | XF |
|---|---|---|---|---|---|---|
| AH1327//7 Mintage included in KM750 | — | — | 3.50 | 4.50 | 7.00 | 10.00 |
| AH1327//8 | 648,000 | — | 4.00 | 7.00 | 10.00 | 20.00 |
| AH1327//9 | 3,938 | — | 50.00 | 100 | 200 | 350 |

**10 KURUSH** **KM# 751** **Weight:** 12.0270 g. **Composition:** 0.8300 Silver .3210 oz. ASW **Obverse:** Toughra; "Reshat" to right **Note:** Struck at Qustantiniyah.

| Date | Mintage | Good | VG | F | VF | XF |
|---|---|---|---|---|---|---|
| AH1327//1 | 110,000 | — | 12.50 | 25.00 | 50.00 | 100 |
| AH1327//2 | Inc. above | — | 10.00 | 20.00 | 50.00 | 100 |
| AH1327//3 | 8,000 | — | 150 | 250 | 500 | 1,000 |
| AH1327//4 | 96,000 | — | 3.50 | 7.50 | 15.00 | 25.00 |
| AH1327//5 | 34,000 | — | 10.00 | 20.00 | 50.00 | 100 |
| AH1327//6 | 81,000 | — | 7.50 | 12.50 | 17.50 | 30.00 |
| AH1327//7 | 582,000 | — | 5.00 | 10.00 | 16.50 | 32.00 |

**10 KURUSH** **KM# 772** **Weight:** 12.0270 g. **Composition:** 0.8300 Silver .3210 oz. ASW **Obverse:** Toughra; "el-Ghazi" to right **Note:** Struck at Qustantiniyah.

| Date | Mintage | Good | VG | F | VF | XF |
|---|---|---|---|---|---|---|
| AH1327//7 | — | — | 3.50 | 7.50 | 15.00 | 28.00 |
| **Note:** Mintage included in KM751 | | | | | | |
| AH1327//8 | 408,000 | — | 7.00 | 9.00 | 17.50 | 32.00 |
| AH1327//9 | 299,000 | — | 10.00 | 20.00 | 35.00 | 50.00 |
| AH1327//10 | 666,000 | — | 12.50 | 25.00 | 50.00 | 85.00 |

**12-1/2 KURUSH** **KM# 762** **Weight:** 0.9020 g. **Composition:** 0.9170 Gold .0266 oz. AGW **Series:** Monnaie de Luxe **Obverse:** Toughra; "Reshat" right of toughra **Note:** Struck at Qustantiniyah.

| Date | Mintage | Good | VG | F | VF | XF |
|---|---|---|---|---|---|---|
| AH1327//2 | — | — | 20.00 | 30.00 | 50.00 | 90.00 |
| AH1327//3 | — | — | 20.00 | 30.00 | 50.00 | 90.00 |
| AH1327//4 | — | — | 20.00 | 30.00 | 50.00 | 90.00 |
| AH1327//5 | — | — | 20.00 | 30.00 | 50.00 | 90.00 |
| AH1327//6 | — | — | 20.00 | 30.00 | 50.00 | 90.00 |

**20 KURUSH** **KM# 780** **Weight:** 24.0550 g. **Composition:** 0.8300 Silver .6419 oz. ASW **Obverse:** Toughra **Note:** Struck at Qustantiniyah.

| Date | Mintage | Good | VG | F | VF | XF |
|---|---|---|---|---|---|---|
| AH1327//8 | 713,000 | — | 9.00 | 12.00 | 20.00 | 35.00 |
| AH1327//9 | 5,962,000 | — | 8.00 | 10.00 | 15.00 | 30.00 |
| AH1327//10 | 11,025,000 | — | 9.00 | 12.00 | 20.00 | 35.00 |

**25 KURUSH** **KM# 752** **Weight:** 1.8040 g. **Composition:** 0.9170 Gold .0532 oz. AGW **Obverse:** Toughra; "Reshat" to right **Note:** Struck at Qustantiniyah.

| Date | Mintage | Good | VG | F | VF | XF |
|---|---|---|---|---|---|---|
| AH1327//1 | — | — | BV | 30.00 | 40.00 | 50.00 |
| AH1327//2 | — | — | BV | 30.00 | 40.00 | 50.00 |
| AH1327//3 | — | — | BV | 30.00 | 40.00 | 50.00 |
| AH1327//4 | — | — | BV | 30.00 | 40.00 | 50.00 |
| AH1327//5 | — | — | BV | 30.00 | 40.00 | 50.00 |
| AH1327//6 | — | — | BV | 30.00 | 40.00 | 50.00 |

**25 KURUSH** **KM# 763** **Weight:** 1.7540 g. **Composition:** 0.9170 Gold .0517 oz. AGW **Series:** Monnaie de Luxe **Obverse:** Toughra **Note:** Struck at Qustantiniyah.

| Date | Mintage | Good | VG | F | VF | XF |
|---|---|---|---|---|---|---|
| AH1327//2 | — | — | 35.00 | 50.00 | 60.00 | 70.00 |
| AH1327//3 | — | — | 35.00 | 50.00 | 60.00 | 70.00 |
| AH1327//4 | — | — | 35.00 | 50.00 | 60.00 | 70.00 |
| AH1327//5 | — | — | 50.00 | 60.00 | 75.00 | 100 |
| AH1327//6 | — | — | 50.00 | 60.00 | 75.00 | 100 |

**25 KURUSH** **KM# 773** **Weight:** 1.8040 g. **Composition:** 0.9170 Gold .0532 oz. AGW **Obverse:** Toughra; "el-Ghazi" to right **Note:** Struck at Qustantiniyah.

| Date | Mintage | Good | VG | F | VF | XF |
|---|---|---|---|---|---|---|
| AH1327//7 | — | — | BV | 35.00 | 45.00 | 55.00 |
| AH1327//8 | — | — | BV | 35.00 | 45.00 | 55.00 |
| AH1327//9 | — | — | BV | 35.00 | 45.00 | 55.00 |
| AH1327//10 | — | — | 1,000 | 1,500 | 2,000 | 3,000 |

**25 KURUSH** **KM# 774** **Weight:** 1.7540 g. **Composition:** 0.9170 Gold .0517 oz. AGW **Series:** Monnaie de Luxe **Obverse:** Toughra **Note:** Struck at Qustantiniyah.

| Date | Mintage | Good | VG | F | VF | XF |
|---|---|---|---|---|---|---|
| AH1327//8 | — | — | 1,750 | 2,500 | 3,500 | 5,000 |

**50 KURUSH** **KM# 753** **Weight:** 3.6080 g. **Composition:** 0.9170 Gold .1064 oz. AGW **Obverse:** Toughra; "Reshat" to right **Note:** Struck at Qustantiniyah.

| Date | Mintage | Good | VG | F | VF | XF |
|---|---|---|---|---|---|---|
| AH1327//1 | — | — | 1,000 | 1,500 | 2,000 | 3,000 |
| AH1327//2 | — | — | BV | 55.00 | 65.00 | 80.00 |
| AH1327//3 | — | — | BV | 55.00 | 65.00 | 80.00 |
| AH1327//4 | — | — | BV | 55.00 | 65.00 | 80.00 |
| AH1327//5 | — | — | BV | 55.00 | 65.00 | 80.00 |
| AH1327//6 | — | — | BV | 55.00 | 65.00 | 80.00 |

**50 KURUSH** **KM# 764** **Weight:** 3.5080 g. **Composition:** 0.9170 Gold .1034 oz. AGW **Series:** Monnaie de Luxe **Obverse:** Toughra **Note:** Struck at Qustantiniyah.

| Date | Mintage | Good | VG | F | VF | XF |
|---|---|---|---|---|---|---|
| AH1327//2 | — | — | 60.00 | 70.00 | 90.00 | 120 |
| AH1327//3 | — | — | 60.00 | 70.00 | 90.00 | 120 |
| AH1327//4 | — | — | 60.00 | 70.00 | 90.00 | 120 |
| AH1327//5 | — | — | 60.00 | 70.00 | 90.00 | 120 |
| AH1327//6 | — | — | 60.00 | 70.00 | 90.00 | 120 |

**50 KURUSH** **KM# 775** **Weight:** 3.6080 g. **Composition:** 0.9170 Gold .1064 oz. AGW **Obverse:** Toughra; "el-Ghazi" to right **Note:** Struck at Qustantiniyah.

| Date | Mintage | Good | VG | F | VF | XF |
|---|---|---|---|---|---|---|
| AH1327//7 | — | — | 60.00 | 75.00 | 150 | 250 |
| AH1327//8 | — | — | 60.00 | 75.00 | 150 | 250 |
| AH1327//9 | — | — | 60.00 | 75.00 | 150 | 250 |
| AH1327//10 | — | — | 1,000 | 1,500 | 2,000 | 3,000 |

**50 KURUSH** **KM# 781** **Weight:** 3.5080 g. **Composition:** 0.9170 Gold .1034 oz. AGW **Series:** Monnaie de Luxe **Obverse:** Toughra **Note:** Struck at Qustantiniyah.

| Date | Mintage | Good | VG | F | VF | XF |
|---|---|---|---|---|---|---|
| AH1327//8 | — | — | 250 | 400 | 600 | 1,000 |

**100 KURUSH** **KM# 755** **Weight:** 7.0160 g. **Composition:** 0.9170 Gold .2068 oz. AGW **Series:** Monnaie de Luxe **Obverse:** Toughra

| Date | Mintage | Good | VG | F | VF | XF |
|---|---|---|---|---|---|---|
| AH1327//1 | — | — | BV | 100 | 135 | 200 |
| AH1327//2 | — | — | BV | 100 | 135 | 200 |
| AH1327//3 | — | — | BV | 100 | 135 | 200 |
| AH1327//4 | — | — | BV | 100 | 135 | 200 |
| AH1327//5 | — | — | BV | 100 | 135 | 200 |
| AH1327//6 | — | — | BV | 100 | 135 | 200 |

**100 KURUSH** **KM# 754** **Weight:** 7.2160 g. **Composition:** 0.9170 Gold .2125 oz. AGW **Obverse:** Toughra; "Reshat" to right **Note:** Struck at Qustantiniyah.

| Date | Mintage | Good | VG | F | VF | XF |
|---|---|---|---|---|---|---|
| AH1327//1 | — | — | — | BV | 100 | 135 |
| AH1327//2 | — | — | — | BV | 100 | 135 |
| AH1327//3 | — | — | — | BV | 100 | 135 |
| AH1327//4 | — | — | — | BV | 100 | 135 |
| AH1327//5 | — | — | — | BV | 100 | 135 |
| AH1327//6 | — | — | — | BV | 100 | 135 |
| AH1327//7 | — | — | — | BV | 100 | 135 |

**100 KURUSH** **KM# 776** **Weight:** 7.2160 g. **Composition:** 0.9170 Gold .2128 oz. AGW **Obverse:** Toughra; "el-Ghazi" to right **Note:** Struck at Qustantiniyah.

| Date | Mintage | Good | VG | F | VF | XF |
|---|---|---|---|---|---|---|
| AH1327//7 | — | — | — | BV | 110 | 150 |
| AH1327//8 | — | — | — | BV | 110 | 150 |
| AH1327//9 | — | — | — | BV | 110 | 150 |
| AH1327//10 | — | — | — | BV | 110 | 150 |

**100 KURUSH** **KM# 782** **Weight:** 7.0160 g. **Composition:** 0.9170 Gold .2068 oz. AGW **Series:** Monnaie de Luxe **Obverse:** Toughra **Note:** Struck at Qustantiniyah.

| Date | Mintage | Good | VG | F | VF | XF |
|---|---|---|---|---|---|---|
| AH1327//8 | — | — | 250 | 400 | 600 | 1,000 |

**250 KURUSH** **KM# 756** **Weight:** 18.0400 g. **Composition:** 0.9170 Gold .5319 oz. AGW **Obverse:** Toughra; "Reshat" to right **Note:** Struck at Qustantiniyah.

| Date | Mintage | Good | VG | F | VF | XF |
|---|---|---|---|---|---|---|
| AH1327//1 | — | — | — | BV | 350 | 425 |
| AH1327//2 | — | — | — | BV | 350 | 425 |
| AH1327//3 | — | — | — | BV | 350 | 425 |
| AH1327//4 | — | — | — | BV | 350 | 425 |
| AH1327//5 | — | — | — | BV | 350 | 425 |
| AH1327//6 | — | — | — | BV | 350 | 425 |

**250 KURUSH** **KM# 757** **Weight:** 17.5400 g. **Composition:** 0.9170 Gold .5619 oz. AGW **Series:** Monnaie de Luxe **Obverse:** Toughra **Note:** Struck at Qustantiniyah.

| Date | Mintage | Good | VG | F | VF | XF |
|---|---|---|---|---|---|---|
| AH1327//1 | — | — | BV | 350 | 450 | 625 |
| AH1327//2 | — | — | BV | 350 | 450 | 625 |
| AH1327//3 | — | — | BV | 350 | 450 | 625 |
| AH1327//4 | — | — | BV | 350 | 450 | 625 |
| AH1327//5 | — | — | BV | 350 | 450 | 625 |
| AH1327//6 | — | — | BV | 350 | 450 | 625 |

**250 KURUSH** **KM# 777** **Weight:** 18.0400 g. **Composition:** 0.9170 Gold .5319 oz. AGW **Obverse:** Toughra; "el-Ghazi" to right **Note:** Struck at Qustantiniyah.

| Date | Mintage | Good | VG | F | VF | XF |
|---|---|---|---|---|---|---|
| AH1327//7 | 30 | — | 1,250 | 1,750 | 2,800 | 4,000 |
| AH1327//8 | 21 | — | 1,750 | 2,500 | 3,500 | 5,000 |
| AH1327//9 | 28 | — | 1,750 | 2,500 | 3,500 | 5,000 |

**250 KURUSH** **KM# 783** **Weight:** 17.5400 g. **Composition:** 0.9170 Gold .5619 oz. AGW **Series:** Monnaie de Luxe **Obverse:** Toughra **Note:** Struck at Qustantiniyah.

| Date | Mintage | Good | VG | F | VF | XF |
|---|---|---|---|---|---|---|
| AH1327//8 | — | — | 1,250 | 1,750 | 2,500 | 3,500 |

**500 KURUSH** **KM# 758** **Weight:** 17.5400 g. **Composition:** 0.9170 Gold .5619 oz. AGW **Obverse:** Toughra; "Reshat" to right **Note:** Struck at Qustantiniyah.

| Date | Mintage | Good | VG | F | VF | XF |
|---|---|---|---|---|---|---|
| AH1327//1 | — | — | — | BV | 525 | 650 |
| AH1327//2 | — | — | — | BV | 525 | 650 |
| AH1327//3 | — | — | — | BV | 525 | 650 |
| AH1327//4 | — | — | — | BV | 525 | 650 |
| AH1327//5 | — | — | — | BV | 525 | 650 |
| AH1327//6 | — | — | — | BV | 525 | 650 |

**500 KURUSH** **KM# 765** **Weight:** 35.0800 g. **Composition:** 0.9170 Gold 1.0338 oz. AGW **Series:** Monnaie de Luxe **Obverse:** Toughra above crossed flags, ornamental base **Note:** Struck at Qustantiniyah.

| Date | Mintage | Good | VG | F | VF | XF |
|---|---|---|---|---|---|---|
| AH1327//2 | — | — | 600 | 750 | 900 | 1,350 |
| AH1327//3 | — | — | 600 | 750 | 900 | 1,350 |
| AH1327//4 | — | — | 600 | 750 | 900 | 1,350 |
| AH1327//5 | — | — | 600 | 750 | 900 | 1,350 |
| AH1327//6 | — | — | 600 | 750 | 900 | 1,350 |

**500 KURUSH** **KM# 784** **Weight:** 36.0800 g. **Composition:** 0.9170 Gold 1.0638 oz. AGW **Obverse:** Toughra; "el-Ghazi" to right **Note:** Struck at Qustantiniyah.

| Date | Mintage | Good | VG | F | VF | XF |
|---|---|---|---|---|---|---|
| AH1327//7 | 484 | — | 1,750 | 2,500 | 3,500 | 5,000 |
| AH1327//8 | 19 | — | 1,750 | 2,750 | 4,250 | 6,000 |
| AH1327//9 | 22 | — | 1,750 | 2,750 | 4,250 | 6,000 |
| AH1327//10 | — | — | 1,750 | 2,500 | 3,500 | 5,000 |

**500 KURUSH** **KM# 778** **Weight:** 35.0800 g. **Composition:** 0.9170 Gold 1.0338 oz. AGW **Series:** Monnaie de Luxe **Obverse:** Toughra above crossed flags, ornamental base **Note:** Struck at Qustantiniyah.

| Date | Mintage | Good | VG | F | VF | XF |
|---|---|---|---|---|---|---|
| AH1327//7 | 295 | — | 1,200 | 1,750 | 2,500 | 3,500 |
| AH1327//8 | 1,216 | — | 1,000 | 1,500 | 2,200 | 3,000 |

## MINT VISIT COINAGE

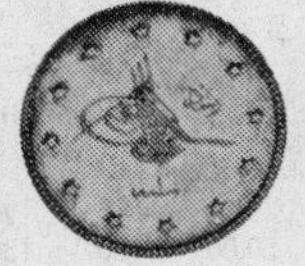

**2 KURUSH** **KM# 785** **Weight:** 2.4055 g. **Composition:** 0.8300 Silver .0642 oz. ASW **Obverse:** Toughra **Note:** Struck at Bursa.

| Date | Mintage | F | VF | XF | Unc |
|---|---|---|---|---|---|
| AH1327//1(1909) | — | 15.00 | 30.00 | 75.00 | 125 |

**2 KURUSH** **KM# 790** **Weight:** 2.4055 g. **Composition:** 0.8300 Silver .0642 oz. ASW **Obverse:** Toughra **Note:** Struck at Edirne.

| Date | Mintage | F | VF | XF | Unc |
|---|---|---|---|---|---|
| AH1327//2(1910) | — | 15.00 | 30.00 | 75.00 | 125 |

**2 KURUSH** **KM# 796** **Weight:** 2.4055 g. **Composition:** 0.8300 Silver .0642 oz. ASW **Obverse:** Toughra **Note:** Struck at Kosova.

| Date | Mintage | F | VF | XF | Unc |
|---|---|---|---|---|---|
| AH1327//3(1911) | 13,000 | 15.00 | 30.00 | 100 | 150 |

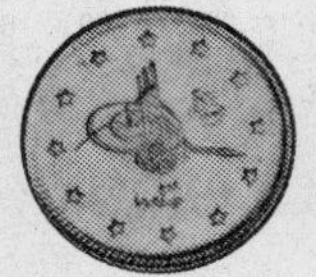

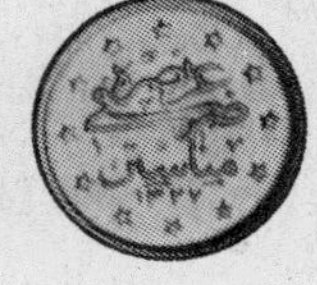

**2 KURUSH** **KM# 802** **Weight:** 2.4055 g. **Composition:** 0.8300 Silver .0642 oz. ASW **Obverse:** Toughra **Note:** Struck at Manastir.

| Date | Mintage | F | VF | XF | Unc |
|---|---|---|---|---|---|
| AH1327//3(1911) | 13,000 | 15.00 | 30.00 | 100 | 150 |

**2 KURUSH** **KM# 808** **Weight:** 2.4055 g. **Composition:** 0.8300 Silver .0642 oz. ASW **Obverse:** Toughra **Note:** Struck at Salonika.

| Date | Mintage | F | VF | XF | Unc |
|---|---|---|---|---|---|
| AH1327//3(1911) | 13,000 | 15.00 | 30.00 | 100 | 150 |

**5 KURUSH** **KM# 786** **Weight:** 6.0130 g. **Composition:** 0.8300 Silver .1605 oz. ASW **Obverse:** Toughra **Note:** Struck at Bursa.

| Date | Mintage | F | VF | XF | Unc |
|---|---|---|---|---|---|
| AH1327//1(1909) | — | 20.00 | 40.00 | 90.00 | 165 |

**5 KURUSH** **KM# 791** **Weight:** 6.0130 g. **Composition:** 0.8300 Silver .1605 oz. ASW **Obverse:** Toughra **Note:** Struck at Edirne.

| Date | Mintage | F | VF | XF | Unc |
|---|---|---|---|---|---|
| AH1327//2(1910) | — | 20.00 | 40.00 | 90.00 | 165 |

**5 KURUSH** **KM# 797** **Weight:** 6.0130 g. **Composition:** 0.8300 Silver .1605 oz. ASW **Obverse:** Toughra **Note:** Struck at Kosova.

| Date | Mintage | F | VF | XF | Unc |
|---|---|---|---|---|---|
| AH1327//3(1911) | 3,000 | 20.00 | 40.00 | 125 | 185 |

**5 KURUSH** **KM# 803** **Weight:** 6.0130 g. **Composition:** 0.8300 Silver .1605 oz. ASW **Obverse:** Toughra **Note:** Struck at Manastir.

| Date | Mintage | F | VF | XF | Unc |
|---|---|---|---|---|---|
| AH1327//3(1911) | 3,000 | 20.00 | 40.00 | 125 | 185 |

**5 KURUSH** **KM# 809** **Weight:** 6.0130 g. **Composition:** 0.8300 Silver .1605 oz. ASW **Obverse:** Toughra **Note:** Struck at Salonika.

| Date | Mintage | F | VF | XF | Unc |
|---|---|---|---|---|---|
| AH1327//3(1911) | 3,000 | 20.00 | 40.00 | 125 | 185 |

**10 KURUSH** **KM# 792** **Weight:** 12.0270 g. **Composition:** 0.8300 Silver .3210 oz. ASW **Obverse:** Toughra **Note:** Struck at Edirne.

| Date | Mintage | F | VF | XF | Unc |
|---|---|---|---|---|---|
| AH1327//2(1910) | — | 90.00 | 150 | 250 | 455 |

**10 KURUSH** **KM# 798** **Weight:** 12.0270 g. **Composition:** 0.8300 Silver .3210 oz. ASW **Obverse:** Toughra **Note:** Struck at Kosova.

| Date | Mintage | F | VF | XF | Unc |
|---|---|---|---|---|---|
| AH1327//3(1911) | 1,500 | 100 | 175 | 300 | 525 |

**10 KURUSH** **KM# 804** **Weight:** 12.0270 g. **Composition:** 0.8300 Silver .3210 oz. ASW **Obverse:** Toughra **Note:** Struck at Manastir.

| Date | Mintage | F | VF | XF | Unc |
|---|---|---|---|---|---|
| AH1327//3(1911) | 1,500 | 100 | 200 | 350 | 550 |

**10 KURUSH** **KM# 810** **Weight:** 12.0270 g. **Composition:** 0.8300 Silver .3210 oz. ASW **Obverse:** Toughra **Note:** Struck at Salonika.

| Date | Mintage | F | VF | XF | Unc |
|---|---|---|---|---|---|
| AH1327//3(1911) | 1,500 | 100 | 200 | 350 | 550 |

**25 KURUSH** **KM# 787** **Weight:** 1.8040 g. **Composition:** 0.9170 Gold .0532 oz. AGW **Obverse:** Toughra **Note:** Struck at Bursa.

| Date | Mintage | F | VF | XF | Unc |
|---|---|---|---|---|---|
| AH1327//1(1909) | — | 185 | 275 | 400 | 800 |

**50 KURUSH** **KM# 788** **Weight:** 3.6080 g. **Composition:** 0.9170 Gold .1064 oz. AGW **Obverse:** Toughra **Note:** Struck at Bursa.

| Date | Mintage | F | VF | XF | Unc |
|---|---|---|---|---|---|
| AH1327//1 | — | 165 | 275 | 350 | 650 |

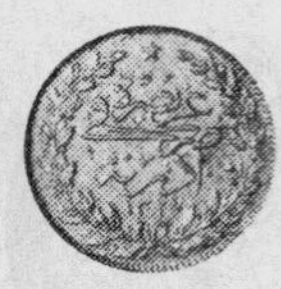

**50 KURUSH** **KM# 793** **Weight:** 3.6080 g. **Composition:** 0.9170 Gold .1064 oz. AGW **Obverse:** Toughra **Note:** Struck at Edirne.

| Date | Mintage | F | VF | XF | Unc |
|---|---|---|---|---|---|
| AH1327//2 | — | 200 | 275 | 350 | 600 |

**50 KURUSH** **KM# 799** **Weight:** 3.6080 g. **Composition:** 0.9170 Gold .1064 oz. AGW **Obverse:** Toughra **Note:** Struck at Kosova.

| Date | Mintage | F | VF | XF | Unc |
|---|---|---|---|---|---|
| AH1327//3 | 1,200 | 225 | 275 | 400 | 700 |

**50 KURUSH** **KM# 805** **Weight:** 3.6080 g. **Composition:** 0.9170 Gold .1064 oz. AGW **Obverse:** Toughra **Note:** Struck at Manastir.

| Date | Mintage | F | VF | XF | Unc |
|---|---|---|---|---|---|
| AH1327//3 | 1,200 | 200 | 325 | 450 | 700 |

**50 KURUSH** **KM# 811** **Weight:** 3.6080 g. **Composition:** 0.9170 Gold .1064 oz. AGW **Obverse:** Toughra **Note:** Struck at Salonika.

| Date | Mintage | F | VF | XF | Unc |
|---|---|---|---|---|---|
| AH1327//3 | 1,200 | 200 | 325 | 400 | 700 |

**100 KURUSH** **KM# 789** **Weight:** 7.2160 g. **Composition:** 0.9170 Gold .2128 oz. AGW **Obverse:** Toughra **Note:** Struck at Bursa.

| Date | Mintage | F | VF | XF | Unc |
|---|---|---|---|---|---|
| AH1327//1(1909) | — | 215 | 325 | 400 | 700 |

**100 KURUSH** **KM# 794** **Weight:** 7.2160 g. **Composition:** 0.9170 Gold .2128 oz. AGW **Obverse:** Toughra **Note:** Struck at Edirne.

| Date | Mintage | F | VF | XF | Unc |
|---|---|---|---|---|---|
| AH1327//2(1910) | — | 250 | 350 | 475 | 700 |

**100 KURUSH** **KM# 800** **Weight:** 7.2160 g. **Composition:** 0.9170 Gold .2128 oz. AGW **Obverse:** Toughra **Note:** Struck at Kosova.

| Date | Mintage | F | VF | XF | Unc |
|---|---|---|---|---|---|
| AH1327//3(1911) | 750 | 250 | 300 | 450 | 750 |

**100 KURUSH** **KM# 806** **Weight:** 7.2160 g. **Composition:** 0.9170 Gold .2128 oz. AGW **Obverse:** Toughra **Note:** Struck at Manastir.

| Date | Mintage | F | VF | XF | Unc |
|---|---|---|---|---|---|
| AH1327//3(1911) | 750 | 225 | 350 | 450 | 750 |

**100 KURUSH** **KM# 812** **Weight:** 7.2160 g. **Composition:** 0.9170 Gold .2128 oz. AGW **Obverse:** Toughra **Note:** Struck at Salonika.

| Date | Mintage | F | VF | XF | Unc |
|---|---|---|---|---|---|
| AH1327//3(1911) | 750 | 225 | 350 | 450 | 750 |

**500 KURUSH** **KM# 795** **Weight:** 36.0800 g. **Composition:** 0.9170 Gold 1.0638 oz. AGW **Obverse:** Toughra **Note:** Struck at Edirne.

| Date | Mintage | F | VF | XF | Unc |
|---|---|---|---|---|---|
| AH1327//2 | — | 1,500 | 2,500 | 3,500 | 4,000 |

**500 KURUSH** **KM# 801** **Weight:** 36.0800 g. **Composition:** 0.9170 Gold 1.0638 oz. AGW **Obverse:** Toughra **Note:** Struck at Kosova.

| Date | Mintage | F | VF | XF | Unc |
|---|---|---|---|---|---|
| AH1327//3 | 20 | 3,000 | 4,000 | 5,000 | 6,000 |

**500 KURUSH** **KM# 807** **Weight:** 36.0800 g. **Composition:** 0.9170 Gold 1.0638 oz. AGW **Obverse:** Toughra **Note:** Struck at Manastir.

| Date | Mintage | F | VF | XF | Unc |
|---|---|---|---|---|---|
| AH1327//3 | 20 | 2,500 | 4,000 | 5,000 | 6,250 |

**500 KURUSH** **KM# 813** **Weight:** 36.0800 g. **Composition:** 0.9170 Gold 1.0638 oz. AGW **Obverse:** Toughra **Note:** Struck at Salonika.

| Date | Mintage | F | VF | XF | Unc |
|---|---|---|---|---|---|
| AH1327//3 | 20 | 2,500 | 4,000 | 5,250 | 6,750 |

# Muhammad VI

## AH1336-41/1918-23AD

## STANDARD COINAGE

**40 PARA** **KM# 828** **Composition:** Copper-Nickel **Obverse:** Toughra **Note:** Struck at Qustantiniyah.

| Date | Mintage | Good | VG | F | VF | XF |
|---|---|---|---|---|---|---|
| AH1336//4 | 6,520,000 | — | 1.75 | 2.50 | 4.00 | 10.00 |

**2 KURUSH** **KM# 815** **Weight:** 2.4055 g. **Composition:** 0.8300 Silver .0642 oz. ASW **Obverse:** Toughra **Note:** Struck at Qustantiniyah.

| Date | Mintage | Good | VG | F | VF | XF |
|---|---|---|---|---|---|---|
| AH1336//1 | 25,000 | — | 50.00 | 100 | 150 | 220 |
| AH1336//2 | 3,000 | — | 75.00 | 125 | 200 | 350 |

**5 KURUSH** **KM# 816** **Weight:** 6.0130 g. **Composition:** 0.8300 Silver .1605 oz. ASW **Obverse:** Toughra **Note:** Struck at Qustantiniyah.

| Date | Mintage | Good | VG | F | VF | XF |
|---|---|---|---|---|---|---|
| AH1336//1 | 10,000 | — | 50.00 | 125 | 175 | 265 |
| AH1336//2 | 2,000 | — | 75.00 | 150 | 225 | 385 |

**10 KURUSH** **KM# 817** **Weight:** 12.0270 g. **Composition:** 0.8300 Silver .3210 oz. ASW **Obverse:** Toughra **Note:** Struck at Qustantiniyah.

| Date | Mintage | Good | VG | F | VF | XF |
|---|---|---|---|---|---|---|
| AH1336//1 | — | — | 120 | 250 | 400 | 600 |
| AH1336//2 | 1,000 | — | 200 | 400 | 600 | 1,000 |

**20 KURUSH** **KM# 818** **Weight:** 24.0550 g. **Composition:** 0.8300 Silver .6419 oz. ASW **Obverse:** Toughra **Note:** Struck at Qustantiniyah.

| Date | Mintage | Good | VG | F | VF | XF |
|---|---|---|---|---|---|---|
| AH1336//1 | — | — | 30.00 | 60.00 | 125 | 185 |
| AH1336//2 | 1,530 | — | 350 | 525 | 650 | 925 |

**25 KURUSH** **KM# 819** **Weight:** 1.8040 g. **Composition:** 0.9170 Gold .0532 oz. AGW **Obverse:** Toughra **Note:** Struck at Qustantiniyah.

| Date | Mintage | Good | VG | F | VF | XF |
|---|---|---|---|---|---|---|
| AH1336//1 | — | — | 30.00 | 40.00 | 50.00 | 100 |
| AH1336//2 | — | — | 30.00 | 40.00 | 50.00 | 100 |
| AH1336//3 | — | — | 40.00 | 75.00 | 150 | 200 |
| AH1336//4 | — | — | 50.00 | 90.00 | 200 | 300 |
| AH1336//5 | — | — | 80.00 | 140 | 240 | 375 |

**25 KURUSH** **KM# 825** **Weight:** 1.7540 g. **Composition:** 0.9170 Gold .0517 oz. AGW **Series:** Monnaie de Luxe **Obverse:** Toughra **Note:** Struck at Qustantiniyah.

| Date | Mintage | Good | VG | F | VF | XF |
|---|---|---|---|---|---|---|
| AH1336//2 | — | — | 60.00 | 80.00 | 100 | 150 |
| AH1336//3 | — | — | 60.00 | 80.00 | 100 | 150 |

**50 KURUSH** **KM# 820** **Weight:** 3.6080 g. **Composition:** 0.9170 Gold .1064 oz. AGW **Obverse:** Toughra **Note:** Struck at Qustantiniyah.

| Date | Mintage | Good | VG | F | VF | XF |
|---|---|---|---|---|---|---|
| AH1336//1 | — | — | 100 | 125 | 150 | 300 |
| AH1336//2 | — | — | 100 | 125 | 150 | 300 |
| AH1336//3 | — | — | 150 | 200 | 250 | 500 |
| AH1336//4 | — | — | 250 | 450 | 750 | 1,500 |
| AH1336//5 | — | — | 200 | 300 | 450 | 1,000 |

**100 KURUSH** **KM# 821** **Weight:** 7.2160 g. **Composition:** 0.9170 Gold .2128 oz. AGW **Obverse:** Toughra **Note:** Struck at Qustantiniyah.

| Date | Mintage | Good | VG | F | VF | XF |
|---|---|---|---|---|---|---|
| AH1336//1 | — | — | BV | 110 | 140 | 180 |
| AH1336//2 | — | — | BV | 110 | 140 | 180 |
| AH1336//3 | — | — | 150 | 180 | 225 | 450 |
| AH1336//5 | — | — | 400 | 600 | 800 | 1,000 |

**100 KURUSH** **KM# 826** **Weight:** 7.0160 g. **Composition:** 0.9170 Gold .2068 oz. AGW **Series:** Monnaie de Luxe **Obverse:** Toughra **Note:** Struck at Qustantiniyah.

| Date | Mintage | Good | VG | F | VF | XF |
|---|---|---|---|---|---|---|
| AH1336//2 | — | — | 250 | 300 | 325 | 375 |
| AH1336//3 | — | — | 250 | 300 | 325 | 375 |

**250 KURUSH** **KM# 822** **Weight:** 18.0400 g. **Composition:** 0.9170 Gold .5319 oz. AGW **Obverse:** Toughra **Note:** Struck at Qustantiniyah.

| Date | Mintage | Good | VG | F | VF | XF |
|---|---|---|---|---|---|---|
| AH1336//1 | — | — | 1,750 | 3,000 | 4,500 | 6,500 |
| AH1336//2 | 26 | — | 1,750 | 3,000 | 4,500 | 6,500 |
| AH1336//3 | 31 | — | 1,750 | 3,000 | 4,500 | 6,500 |

**250 KURUSH** **KM# 827** **Weight:** 17.5400 g. **Composition:** 0.9170 Gold .5169 oz. AGW **Series:** Monnaie de Luxe **Obverse:** Toughra **Note:** Struck at Qustantiniyah.

| Date | Mintage | Good | VG | F | VF | XF |
|---|---|---|---|---|---|---|
| AH1336//2 | 19,000 | — | 300 | 500 | 700 | 900 |
| AH1336//3 | Inc. above | — | 250 | 425 | 600 | 800 |

**500 KURUSH** **KM# 823** **Weight:** 36.0800 g. **Composition:** 0.9170 Gold 1.0638 oz. AGW **Obverse:** Toughra **Note:** Struck at Qustantiniyah.

| Date | Mintage | Good | VG | F | VF | XF |
|---|---|---|---|---|---|---|
| AH1336//1 | — | — | 1,000 | 1,200 | 1,450 | 1,800 |
| AH1336//2 | — | — | 1,000 | 1,200 | 1,450 | 1,800 |
| AH1336//3 | — | — | 1,000 | 1,200 | 1,450 | 1,800 |
| AH1336//4 | 23 | — | 2,000 | 4,000 | 6,000 | 8,000 |
| AH1336//5 | 22 | — | 2,000 | 4,000 | 6,000 | 8,000 |

**500 KURUSH** **KM# 824** **Weight:** 35.0800 g. **Composition:** 0.9170 Gold 1.0338 oz. AGW **Series:** Monnaie de Luxe **Obverse:** Toughra above crossed flage, ornamental base **Note:** Struck at Qustantiniyah.

| Date | Mintage | Good | VG | F | VF | XF |
|---|---|---|---|---|---|---|
| AH1336//1 | — | — | 1,000 | 1,250 | 1,750 | 2,400 |
| AH1336//2 | 5,207 | — | 600 | 750 | 950 | 1,300 |
| AH1336//3 | Inc. above | — | 600 | 750 | 950 | 1,300 |
| AH1336//4 | 88 | — | 1,500 | 2,000 | 2,500 | 3,200 |

# REPUBLIC

## STANDARD COINAGE

### Old Monetary System

**100 PARA** **KM# 830** **Composition:** Aluminum-Bronze

| Date | Mintage | F | VF | XF | Unc |
|---|---|---|---|---|---|
| AH1340 | 1,798,000 | 3.00 | 5.00 | 10.00 | 60.00 |
| AH1341 | 5,583,000 | 1.00 | 2.50 | 5.00 | 30.00 |

**100 PARA** **KM# 834** **Composition:** Aluminum-Bronze

| Date | Mintage | F | VF | XF | Unc |
|---|---|---|---|---|---|
| 1926 | 4,388,000 | 1.00 | 2.50 | 6.00 | 32.00 |
| 1928 | — | 150 | 225 | 400 | 600 |

**5 KURUS** **KM# 831** **Composition:** Aluminum-Bronze

| Date | Mintage | F | VF | XF | Unc |
|---|---|---|---|---|---|
| AH1340 | 5,023,000 | 1.00 | 2.50 | 7.00 | 32.00 |
| AH1341 | 23,545,000 | 1.00 | 2.50 | 7.00 | 32.00 |

**5 KURUS** **KM# 835** **Composition:** Aluminum-Bronze

| Date | Mintage | F | VF | XF | Unc |
|---|---|---|---|---|---|
| 1926 | 356,000 | 1.00 | 2.50 | 7.00 | 32.00 |
| 1928 | — | 175 | 250 | 500 | 700 |

**10 KURUS** **KM# 832** **Composition:** Aluminum-Bronze **Note:** Varieties exist.

| Date | Mintage | F | VF | XF | Unc |
|---|---|---|---|---|---|
| AH1340 | 4,836,000 | 1.50 | 3.00 | 8.00 | 35.00 |
| AH1341 | 14,223,000 | 1.50 | 3.00 | 8.00 | 35.00 |

**10 KURUS** **KM# 836** **Composition:** Aluminum-Bronze

| Date | Mintage | F | VF | XF | Unc |
|---|---|---|---|---|---|
| 1926 | 856,000 | 1.50 | 3.00 | 8.00 | 35.00 |
| 1928 | — | 125 | 200 | 375 | 575 |

**25 KURUS** **KM# 833** **Composition:** Nickel

| Date | Mintage | F | VF | XF | Unc |
|---|---|---|---|---|---|
| AH1341 | 4,973,000 | 2.00 | 4.00 | 10.00 | 30.00 |

**25 KURUS** **KM# 837** **Composition:** Nickel **Note:** Varieties exist.

| Date | Mintage | F | VF | XF | Unc |
|---|---|---|---|---|---|
| 1926 | 27,000 | 175 | 275 | 475 | 675 |
| 1928 | 5,794,000 | 1.50 | 3.00 | 8.00 | 30.00 |

**25 KURUSH** **KM# 840** **Weight:** 1.8040 g. **Composition:** 0.9170 Gold .0532 oz. AGW **Reverse:** AH date: "23 Nisan 1336"

| Date | Mintage | F | VF | XF | Unc |
|---|---|---|---|---|---|
| 1926 | 4,539 | 40.00 | 75.00 | 140 | 175 |
| 1927 | 14,000 | 40.00 | 75.00 | 120 | 150 |
| 1928 | 8,424 | 40.00 | 75.00 | 130 | 165 |
| 1929 | — | 40.00 | 75.00 | 120 | 150 |

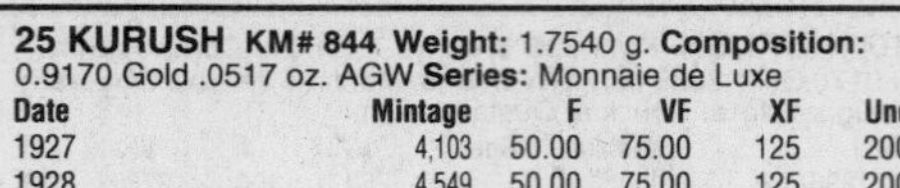

**25 KURUSH** **KM# 844** **Weight:** 1.7540 g. **Composition:** 0.9170 Gold .0517 oz. AGW **Series:** Monnaie de Luxe

| Date | Mintage | F | VF | XF | Unc |
|---|---|---|---|---|---|
| 1927 | 4,103 | 50.00 | 75.00 | 125 | 200 |
| 1928 | 4,549 | 50.00 | 75.00 | 125 | 200 |

**50 KURUSH** **KM# 841** **Weight:** 3.6080 g. **Composition:** 0.9170 Gold .1064 oz. AGW **Reverse:** AH date: "23 Nisan 1336"

| Date | Mintage | F | VF | XF | Unc |
|---|---|---|---|---|---|
| 1926 | 2,168 | 100 | 150 | 200 | 275 |
| 1927 | 2,116 | 100 | 150 | 200 | 275 |
| 1928 | 2,431 | 100 | 150 | 200 | 275 |
| 1929 | — | 100 | 150 | 200 | 275 |

**50 KURUSH** **KM# 845** **Weight:** 3.5080 g. **Composition:** 0.9170 Gold .1034 oz. AGW **Series:** Monnaie de Luxe

| Date | Mintage | F | VF | XF | Unc |
|---|---|---|---|---|---|
| 1927 | 3,903 | 75.00 | 150 | 250 | 375 |
| 1928 | 3,620 | 75.00 | 150 | 250 | 375 |

**100 KURUSH** **KM# 842** **Weight:** 7.2160 g. **Composition:** 0.9170 Gold .2128 oz. AGW **Reverse:** AH date: "23 Nisan 1336"

| Date | Mintage | F | VF | XF | Unc |
|---|---|---|---|---|---|
| 1926 | 1,073 | 120 | 175 | 250 | 350 |
| 1927 | — | 120 | 175 | 250 | 350 |
| 1928 | 920 | 120 | 175 | 250 | 350 |
| 1929 | — | 120 | 175 | 250 | 350 |

**100 KURUSH** **KM# 846** **Weight:** 7.0160 g. **Composition:** 0.9170 Gold .2069 oz. AGW **Series:** Monnaie de Luxe

| Date | Mintage | F | VF | XF | Unc |
|---|---|---|---|---|---|
| 1927 | 8,676 | 125 | 150 | 250 | 350 |
| 1928 | 6,092 | 125 | 150 | 250 | 350 |

**250 KURUSH** **KM# 843** **Weight:** 18.0400 g. **Composition:** 0.9170 Gold .5319 oz. AGW **Reverse:** AH date: "23 Nisan 1336"

| Date | Mintage | F | VF | XF | Unc |
|---|---|---|---|---|---|
| 1926 | 604 | 350 | 450 | 600 | 750 |
| 1927 | 886 | 350 | 450 | 600 | 750 |
| 1928 | 110 | 350 | 450 | 600 | 750 |
| 1929 | — | 350 | 450 | 600 | 750 |

**250 KURUSH** **KM# 847** **Weight:** 17.5400 g. **Composition:** 0.9170 Gold .5169 oz. AGW **Series:** Monnaie de Luxe

| Date | Mintage | F | VF | XF | Unc |
|---|---|---|---|---|---|
| 1927 | 7,411 | BV | 300 | 450 | 600 |
| 1928 | 5,045 | BV | 300 | 450 | 600 |

**500 KURUSH** **KM# 839** **Weight:** 36.0800 g. **Composition:** 0.9170 Gold 1.0638 oz. AGW **Reverse:** AH date: "23 Nisan 1336"

| Date | Mintage | F | VF | XF | Unc |
|---|---|---|---|---|---|
| 1925 | 226 | BV | 700 | 1,000 | 1,500 |
| 1926 | 2,268 | | 500 | 600 | 800 |
| 1927 | 4,011 | BV | 500 | 600 | 800 |
| 1928 | 375 | BV | 700 | 1,000 | 1,500 |
| 1929 | — | BV | 700 | 1,000 | 1,500 |

**500 KURUSH** **KM# 848** **Weight:** 35.0800 g. **Composition:** 0.9170 Gold 1.0344 oz. AGW **Series:** Monnaie de Luxe

| Date | Mintage | F | VF | XF | Unc |
|---|---|---|---|---|---|
| 1927 | 5,097 | BV | 500 | 600 | 800 |
| 1928 | 2,242 | BV | 500 | 600 | 800 |

## DECIMAL COINAGE

Western numerals and Latin alphabet

40 Para = 1 Kurus; 100 Kurus = 1 Lira

Mintage figures of the 1930's and early 1940's may not be exact. It is suspected that in some cases, figures for a particular year may include quantities struck with the previous year's date.

**10 PARA (1/4 Kurus)** **KM# 868** **Composition:** Aluminum-Bronze

| Date | Mintage | VG | F | VF | XF | Unc |
|---|---|---|---|---|---|---|
| 1940 | 30,800,000 | 0.25 | 0.75 | 2.50 | 5.00 | — |
| 1941 | 22,400,000 | 0.25 | 0.75 | 2.50 | 5.00 | — |
| 1942 | 26,800,000 | 0.25 | 0.75 | 2.50 | 5.00 | — |

**1/2 KURUS (20 Para)** **KM# 884** **Composition:** Brass

| Date | Mintage | F | VF | XF | Unc |
|---|---|---|---|---|---|
| 1948 | 150 | — | — | 300 | 550 |

**Note:** Not released to circulation

**1/2 KURUS (20 Para)** **KM# 884a** **Weight:** 3.9000 g. **Composition:** 0.9160 Gold .1149 oz. AGW **Series:** Nostalgia **Obverse:** Same as KM#884 **Reverse:** Same as KM#884 **Edge:** Plain **Size:** 16 mm.

| Date | Mintage | F | VF | XF | Unc |
|---|---|---|---|---|---|
| 1948 | 25,000 | — | — | — | 80.00 |

**KURUS** **KM# 861** **Composition:** Copper-Nickel

| Date | Mintage | VG | F | VF | XF | Unc |
|---|---|---|---|---|---|---|
| 1935 | 784,000 | 2.00 | 4.00 | 6.00 | 15.00 | — |
| 1936 | 5,300,000 | 0.25 | 1.00 | 2.50 | 7.00 | — |
| 1937 | 4,500,000 | 0.25 | 1.00 | 2.50 | 7.00 | — |

**KURUS** **KM# 867** **Composition:** Copper-Nickel

| Date | Mintage | VG | F | VF | XF | Unc |
|---|---|---|---|---|---|---|
| 1938 | 16,400,000 | 0.25 | 0.50 | 1.50 | 4.00 | — |
| 1939 | 21,600,000 | 0.25 | 0.50 | 1.50 | 4.00 | — |
| 1940 | 8,800,000 | 0.50 | 1.00 | 2.00 | 8.00 | — |
| 1941 | 6,700,000 | 0.25 | 0.75 | 1.75 | 5.00 | — |
| 1942 | 10,800,000 | 0.25 | 0.50 | 1.50 | 4.00 | — |
| 1943 | 4,000,000 | 0.25 | 0.75 | 1.75 | 5.00 | — |
| 1944 | 6,000,000 | 0.25 | 0.75 | 1.75 | 5.00 | — |

**KURUS** **KM# 881** **Composition:** Brass

| Date | Mintage | F | VF | XF | Unc |
|---|---|---|---|---|---|
| 1947 | 890,000 | 1.00 | 1.50 | 2.50 | 5.00 |
| 1948 | 35,470,000 | 0.15 | 0.25 | 0.50 | 1.50 |
| 1949 | 29,530,000 | 0.15 | 0.25 | 0.50 | 1.25 |
| 1950 | 32,800,000 | 0.15 | 0.25 | 0.50 | 1.25 |
| 1951 | 6,310,000 | 0.15 | 0.30 | 0.75 | 2.25 |

**KURUS** **KM# 881a** **Weight:** 4.9000 g. **Composition:** 0.9160 Gold .1443 oz. AGW **Series:** Nostalgia **Obverse:** Same as KM#881 **Reverse:** Same as KM#881 **Edge:** Plain **Size:** 18 mm.

| Date | Mintage | F | VF | XF | Unc |
|---|---|---|---|---|---|
| 1949 | 25,000 | — | — | — | 80.00 |

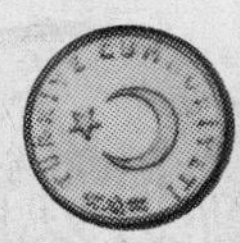

**KURUS** **KM# 895** **Composition:** Brass **Reverse:** Olive branch

| Date | Mintage | F | VF | XF | Unc |
|---|---|---|---|---|---|
| 1961 | 1,180,000 | — | — | 0.10 | 0.30 |
| 1962 | 3,620,000 | — | — | 0.10 | 0.25 |
| 1963 | 1,085,000 | — | — | 0.10 | 0.30 |

**KURUS** **KM# 895a** **Composition:** Bronze

| Date | Mintage | F | VF | XF | Unc |
|---|---|---|---|---|---|
| 1963 | 1,180,000 | — | — | 0.10 | 0.30 |
| 1964 | 2,520,000 | — | — | 0.10 | 0.20 |
| 1965 | 1,860,000 | — | — | 0.10 | 0.20 |
| 1966 | 1,820,000 | — | — | 0.10 | 0.20 |
| 1967 | 2,410,000 | — | — | 0.10 | 0.20 |
| 1968 | 1,040,000 | — | — | 0.10 | 0.20 |
| 1969 | 900,000 | — | — | 0.10 | 0.20 |
| 1970 | 1,960,000 | — | — | 0.10 | 0.20 |
| 1971 | 2,940,000 | — | — | 0.10 | 0.20 |
| 1972 | 720,000 | — | — | 0.10 | 0.30 |
| 1973 | 540,000 | — | — | 0.10 | 0.30 |
| 1374 | 510,000 | — | — | 0.10 | 0.30 |

**KURUS** **KM# 895b** **Composition:** Aluminum

| Date | Mintage | F | VF | XF | Unc |
|---|---|---|---|---|---|
| 1975 | 690,000 | — | 0.10 | 0.25 | 1.00 |
| 1976 | 200,000 | — | 0.10 | 0.25 | 1.50 |
| 1977 | 108,000 | — | 0.10 | 0.25 | 1.75 |

**KURUS** **KM# 924** **Composition:** Bronze **Series:** F.A.O.

| Date | Mintage | F | VF | XF | Unc |
|---|---|---|---|---|---|
| 1979 | 15,000 | — | 0.25 | 1.00 | 3.00 |

**KURUS** **KM# 924a** **Composition:** Aluminum

| Date | Mintage | F | VF | XF | Unc |
|---|---|---|---|---|---|
| 1979 | 15,000 | — | 0.25 | 1.00 | 3.00 |

**2-1/2 KURUS** **KM# 885** **Composition:** Brass

| Date | Mintage | F | VF | XF | Unc |
|---|---|---|---|---|---|
| 1948 | 24,720,000 | 0.25 | 0.50 | 1.00 | 3.00 |
| 1949 | 23,720,000 | 0.25 | 0.50 | 1.00 | 3.00 |
| 1950 | 11,560,000 | 0.35 | 0.65 | 1.25 | 4.00 |
| 1951 | 2,000,000 | 2.00 | 5.00 | 12.00 | 40.00 |

**2-1/2 KURUS** **KM# 885a** **Weight:** 6.9000 g. **Composition:** 0.9160 Gold .2032 oz. AGW **Series:** Nostalgia **Obverse:** Same as KM#885 **Reverse:** Same as KM#885 **Edge:** Plain **Size:** 21 mm.

| Date | Mintage | F | VF | XF | Unc |
|---|---|---|---|---|---|
| 1950 | 25,000 | — | — | — | 85.00 |

**5 KURUS** **KM# 862** **Composition:** Copper-Nickel

| Date | Mintage | VG | F | VF | XF | Unc |
|---|---|---|---|---|---|---|
| 1935 | 100,000 | 2.00 | 5.00 | 8.00 | 20.00 | — |
| 1936 | 2,900,000 | 0.50 | 1.00 | 2.00 | 8.00 | — |
| 1937 | 4,060,000 | 0.30 | 0.75 | 1.50 | 8.00 | — |
| 1938 | 13,380,000 | 0.25 | 0.50 | 1.00 | 5.00 | — |
| 1939 | 12,520,000 | 0.25 | 0.50 | 1.00 | 5.00 | — |
| 1940 | 4,340,000 | 0.30 | 0.75 | 1.50 | 5.00 | — |
| 1942 | 10,160,000 | 0.20 | 0.40 | 1.00 | 5.00 | — |
| 1943 | 15,360,000 | 0.20 | 0.40 | 1.00 | 5.00 | — |

**5 KURUS** **KM# 887** **Composition:** Brass

| Date | Mintage | F | VF | XF | Unc |
|---|---|---|---|---|---|
| 1949 | 4,500,000 | 0.25 | 0.50 | 1.00 | 4.00 |
| 1950 | 45,900,000 | 0.15 | 0.35 | 0.75 | 3.00 |
| 1951 | 29,600,000 | 0.15 | 0.35 | 0.75 | 3.00 |
| 1955 | 15,300,000 | 0.15 | 0.35 | 0.75 | 3.00 |
| 1956 | 21,380,000 | 0.15 | 0.35 | 0.75 | 3.00 |
| 1957 | 3,320,000 | 0.25 | 0.50 | 1.00 | 4.00 |

**5 KURUS** **KM# 890.1** **Weight:** 2.5000 g. **Composition:** Bronze

| Date | Mintage | F | VF | XF | Unc |
|---|---|---|---|---|---|
| 1958 | 25,870,000 | 0.10 | 0.25 | 0.50 | 1.50 |
| 1959 | 21,580,000 | — | — | 0.10 | 0.30 |
| 1960 | 17,150,000 | — | — | 0.10 | 0.30 |
| 1961 | 11,110,000 | — | — | 0.10 | 0.20 |
| 1962 | 15,280,000 | — | — | 0.10 | 0.30 |
| 1963 | 17,680,000 | — | — | 0.10 | 0.20 |
| 1964 | 18,190,000 | — | — | 0.10 | 0.30 |
| 1965 | 19,170,000 | — | — | 0.10 | 0.20 |
| 1966 | 19,840,000 | — | — | 0.10 | 0.30 |
| 1967 | 16,170,000 | — | — | 0.10 | 0.30 |
| 1968 | 26,050,000 | — | — | 0.10 | 0.30 |

**5 KURUS** **KM# 890.2** **Weight:** 2.0000 g. **Composition:** Bronze **Note:** Reduced weight.

| Date | Mintage | F | VF | XF | Unc |
|---|---|---|---|---|---|
| 1969 | 33,630,000 | — | — | 0.10 | 0.30 |
| 1970 | 29,360,000 | — | — | 0.10 | 0.30 |
| 1971 | 17,440,000 | — | — | 0.10 | 0.30 |
| 1972 | 22,670,000 | — | — | 0.10 | 0.20 |
| 1973 | 17,370,000 | — | — | 0.10 | 0.20 |

**5 KURUS** **KM# 890.3** **Weight:** 1.3500 g. **Composition:** Bronze **Note:** Varieties exist.

| Date | Mintage | F | VF | XF | Unc |
|---|---|---|---|---|---|
| 1974 | 13,540,000 | — | — | 0.10 | 0.20 |

**5 KURUS** **KM# 890a** **Composition:** Aluminum

| Date | Mintage | F | VF | XF | Unc |
|---|---|---|---|---|---|
| 1975 | 1,560,000 | — | — | 0.10 | 0.30 |
| 1976 | 1,321,000 | — | — | 0.10 | 0.30 |
| 1977 | 190,000 | — | 0.10 | 0.20 | 1.00 |

**5 KURUS** **KM# 906** **Composition:** Aluminum **Series:** F.A.O.

| Date | Mintage | F | VF | XF | Unc |
|---|---|---|---|---|---|
| 1975 | 1,019,000 | — | — | 0.50 | 1.50 |

**5 KURUS** **KM# 907** **Composition:** Aluminum **Series:** F.A.O.

| Date | Mintage | F | VF | XF | Unc |
|---|---|---|---|---|---|
| 1976 | 17,000 | — | 0.50 | 1.50 | 4.00 |

**5 KURUS** **KM# 934** **Composition:** Bronze **Series:** F.A.O.

| Date | Mintage | F | VF | XF | Unc |
|---|---|---|---|---|---|
| 1980 | 13,000 | — | 0.25 | 0.75 | 2.50 |

**10 KURUS** **KM# 863** **Composition:** Copper-Nickel

| Date | Mintage | VG | F | VF | XF | Unc |
|---|---|---|---|---|---|---|
| 1935 | 60,000 | 2.00 | 5.00 | 8.00 | 20.00 | — |
| 1936 | 3,580,000 | 0.75 | 2.00 | 5.00 | 12.50 | — |
| 1937 | 3,020,000 | 0.50 | 1.00 | 4.00 | 8.00 | — |
| 1938 | 6,610,000 | 0.50 | 1.00 | 4.00 | 8.00 | — |
| 1939 | 4,610,000 | 0.50 | 1.00 | 2.50 | 5.00 | — |
| 1940 | 6,960,000 | 0.50 | 1.00 | 2.50 | 5.00 | — |

**10 KURUS** **KM# 888** **Composition:** Brass

| Date | Mintage | F | VF | XF | Unc |
|---|---|---|---|---|---|
| 1949 | 27,000,000 | 0.10 | 0.25 | 0.75 | 3.00 |
| 1951 | 6,200,000 | 0.10 | 0.25 | 0.75 | 3.00 |

| Date | Mintage | F | VF | XF | Unc |
|---|---|---|---|---|---|
| 1955 | 10,090,000 | 0.10 | 0.25 | 0.75 | 3.00 |
| 1956 | 9,910,000 | 0.10 | 0.25 | 0.75 | 3.00 |

**10 KURUS** **KM# 891.1** **Weight:** 4.0000 g. **Composition:** Bronze

| Date | Mintage | F | VF | XF | Unc |
|---|---|---|---|---|---|
| 1958 | 14,770,000 | — | 0.10 | 0.25 | 1.50 |
| 1959 | 11,160,000 | — | — | 0.10 | 0.40 |
| 1960 | 9,450,000 | — | — | 0.10 | 0.40 |
| 1961 | 5,370,000 | — | — | 0.10 | 0.40 |
| 1962 | 9,250,000 | — | — | 0.10 | 0.40 |
| 1963 | 10,390,000 | — | — | 0.10 | 0.40 |
| 1964 | 9,890,000 | — | — | 0.10 | 0.40 |
| 1965 | 10,480,000 | — | — | 0.10 | 0.40 |
| 1966 | 12,200,000 | — | — | 0.10 | 0.40 |
| 1967 | 11,410,000 | — | — | 0.10 | 0.40 |
| 1968 | 1,862,000 | — | — | 0.10 | 0.40 |

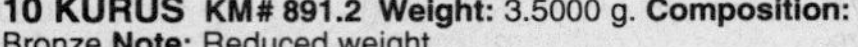

**10 KURUS** **KM# 891.2** **Weight:** 3.5000 g. **Composition:** Bronze **Note:** Reduced weight.

| Date | Mintage | F | VF | XF | Unc |
|---|---|---|---|---|---|
| 1969 | 21,190,000 | — | — | 0.10 | 0.20 |
| 1970 | 19,930,000 | — | — | 0.10 | 0.20 |
| 1971 | 14,780,000 | — | — | 0.10 | 0.20 |
| 1972 | 17,960,000 | — | — | 0.10 | 0.20 |
| 1973 | 11,930,000 | — | — | 0.10 | 0.20 |

**10 KURUS** **KM# 898.1** **Weight:** 3.5000 g. **Composition:** Bronze **Series:** F.A.O.

| Date | Mintage | F | VF | XF | Unc |
|---|---|---|---|---|---|
| 1971 | 630,000 | — | 0.10 | 0.15 | 0.75 |
| 1972 | 500,000 | — | 0.10 | 0.50 | 2.00 |
| 1973 | 10,000 | — | 4.00 | 10.00 | 30.00 |

**10 KURUS** **KM# 898.2** **Weight:** 2.5000 g. **Composition:** Bronze

| Date | Mintage | F | VF | XF | Unc |
|---|---|---|---|---|---|
| 1974 | 605,000 | — | 0.10 | 0.50 | 1.00 |

**10 KURUS** **KM# 891.3** **Weight:** 2.5000 g. **Composition:** Bronze **Note:** Varieties exist.

| Date | Mintage | F | VF | XF | Unc |
|---|---|---|---|---|---|
| 1974 | 9,280,000 | — | — | 0.10 | 0.20 |

**10 KURUS** **KM# 898a** **Composition:** Aluminum

| Date | Mintage | F | VF | XF | Unc |
|---|---|---|---|---|---|
| 1975 | 517,000 | — | 0.10 | 0.25 | 0.75 |

**10 KURUS** **KM# 891a** **Composition:** Aluminum

| Date | Mintage | F | VF | XF | Unc |
|---|---|---|---|---|---|
| 1975 | 2,165,000 | — | — | 0.10 | 0.30 |
| 1976 | 559,000 | — | 0.10 | 0.20 | 0.60 |
| 1977 | 106,000 | — | 0.10 | 0.50 | 1.00 |

**10 KURUS** **KM# 908** **Composition:** Aluminum **Series:** F.A.O.

| Date | Mintage | F | VF | XF | Unc |
|---|---|---|---|---|---|
| 1976 | 17,000 | — | 0.50 | 2.00 | 5.00 |

**10 KURUS** **KM# 935** **Composition:** Bronze **Series:** F.A.O.

| Date | Mintage | F | VF | XF | Unc |
|---|---|---|---|---|---|
| 1980 | 13,000 | — | 0.25 | 1.00 | 2.50 |

**25 KURUS** **KM# 864** **Weight:** 3.0000 g. **Composition:** 0.8300 Silver .0801 oz. ASW

| Date | Mintage | VG | F | VF | XF | Unc |
|---|---|---|---|---|---|---|
| 1935 | 888,000 | 1.00 | 2.00 | 6.00 | 15.00 | — |
| 1936 | 10,576,000 | 1.00 | 2.00 | 10.00 | 20.00 | — |
| 1937 | 8,536,000 | 1.00 | 2.00 | 10.00 | 20.00 | — |

**25 KURUS** **KM# 880** **Composition:** Nickel-Bronze

| Date | Mintage | VG | F | VF | XF | Unc |
|---|---|---|---|---|---|---|
| 1944 | 20,000,000 | 0.25 | 0.50 | 1.00 | 2.50 | — |
| 1945 | 5,328,000 | 0.50 | 1.00 | 1.50 | 3.00 | — |
| 1946 | 2,672,000 | 0.50 | 1.25 | 2.00 | 4.00 | — |

**25 KURUS** **KM# 886** **Composition:** Brass

| Date | Mintage | F | VF | XF | Unc |
|---|---|---|---|---|---|
| 1948 | 18,000,000 | 0.10 | 0.20 | 0.40 | 1.25 |
| 1949 | 21,000,000 | 0.10 | 0.20 | 0.40 | 1.25 |
| 1951 | 2,000,000 | 0.25 | 0.50 | 2.50 | 10.00 |
| 1955 | 9,624,000 | 0.10 | 0.20 | 0.40 | 1.25 |
| 1956 | 14,376,000 | 0.10 | 0.20 | 0.40 | 1.25 |

**25 KURUS** **KM# 886a** **Weight:** 10.0000 g. **Composition:** 0.9160 Gold .2945 oz. AGW **Series:** Nostalgia **Obverse:** Same as KM#886 **Reverse:** Same as KM#886 **Edge:** Plain **Size:** 22.6 mm.

| Date | Mintage | F | VF | XF | Unc |
|---|---|---|---|---|---|
| 1951 | 25,000 | — | — | — | 85.00 |

**25 KURUS** **KM# 892.1** **Weight:** 5.0000 g. **Composition:** Stainless Steel **Obverse:** Smooth ground under woman's feet

| Date | Mintage | F | VF | XF | Unc |
|---|---|---|---|---|---|
| 1959 | 21,864,000 | 0.10 | 0.15 | 0.30 | 0.75 |

**25 KURUS** **KM# 892.2** **Weight:** 5.0000 g. **Composition:** Stainless Steel **Obverse:** Rough ground under woman's feet

| Date | Mintage | F | VF | XF | Unc |
|---|---|---|---|---|---|
| 1960 | 14,778,000 | — | 0.10 | 0.15 | 0.70 |
| 1961 | 7,248,000 | — | 0.10 | 0.15 | 1.00 |
| 1962 | 10,722,000 | — | 0.10 | 0.15 | 0.80 |
| 1963 | 11,016,000 | — | 0.10 | 0.15 | 0.80 |
| 1964 | 13,962,000 | — | 0.10 | 0.15 | 0.70 |
| 1965 | 9,816,000 | — | 0.10 | 0.15 | 0.70 |
| 1966 | 2,424,000 | — | 0.10 | 0.15 | 0.80 |

**25 KURUS** **KM# 892.3** **Weight:** 4.0000 g. **Composition:** Stainless Steel **Note:** Reduced weight

| Date | Mintage | F | VF | XF | Unc |
|---|---|---|---|---|---|
| 1966 | 7,596,000 | — | — | 0.10 | 0.50 |
| 1967 | 17,022,000 | — | — | 0.10 | 0.25 |
| 1968 | 31,482,000 | — | — | 0.10 | 0.25 |
| 1969 | 34,566,000 | — | — | 0.10 | 0.25 |
| 1970 | 32,960,000 | — | — | 0.10 | 0.25 |
| 1973 | 20,496,000 | — | — | 0.10 | 0.25 |
| 1974 | 16,602,000 | — | — | 0.10 | 0.25 |
| 1977 | 10,204,000 | — | — | 0.10 | 0.25 |
| 1978 | 185,000 | 0.35 | 0.75 | 1.25 | 2.00 |

**50 KURUS** **KM# 865** **Weight:** 6.0000 g. **Composition:** 0.8300 Silver .1601 oz. ASW **Obverse:** Head of Kemal Atatürk left

| Date | Mintage | VG | F | VF | XF | Unc |
|---|---|---|---|---|---|---|
| 1935 | 630,000 | 3.00 | 6.00 | 10.00 | 25.00 | — |
| 1936 | 5,082,000 | 2.00 | 5.00 | 8.00 | 17.00 | — |
| 1937 | 4,270,000 | 12.00 | 30.00 | 50.00 | 100 | — |

**50 KURUS** **KM# 882** **Weight:** 4.0000 g. **Composition:** 0.6000 Silver .0772 oz. ASW **Note:** Edge varieties exist.

| Date | Mintage | F | VF | XF | Unc |
|---|---|---|---|---|---|
| 1947 | 9,296,000 | 1.00 | 2.50 | 3.50 | 6.00 |
| 1948 | 12,704,000 | 1.00 | 2.50 | 3.50 | 6.00 |

**50 KURUS** **KM# 899** **Composition:** Stainless Steel

| Date | Mintage | F | VF | XF | Unc |
|---|---|---|---|---|---|
| 1971 | 16,756,000 | — | 0.10 | 0.15 | 0.25 |
| 1972 | 22,152,000 | — | 0.10 | 0.15 | 0.25 |
| 1973 | 18,928,000 | — | 0.10 | 0.15 | 0.25 |
| 1974 | 14,480,000 | — | 0.10 | 0.15 | 0.25 |
| 1975 | 27,714,000 | — | 0.10 | 0.15 | 0.25 |
| 1976 | 27,476,000 | — | 0.10 | 0.15 | 0.25 |
| 1977 | 5,062,000 | — | 0.10 | 0.15 | 0.30 |
| 1979 | 3,714,000 | — | 0.10 | 0.15 | 0.30 |

**50 KURUS** **KM# 913** **Composition:** Stainless Steel **Series:** F.A.O.

| Date | Mintage | F | VF | XF | Unc |
|---|---|---|---|---|---|
| 1978 | 10,000 | — | 0.20 | 0.50 | 1.75 |

**50 KURUS** **KM# 925** **Composition:** Stainless Steel **Series:** F.A.O.

| Date | Mintage | F | VF | XF | Unc |
|---|---|---|---|---|---|
| 1979 | 20,000 | — | 0.20 | 0.50 | 1.75 |

**50 KURUS** **KM# 936** **Composition:** Stainless Steel **Series:** F.A.O.

| Date | Mintage | F | VF | XF | Unc |
|---|---|---|---|---|---|
| 1980 | 13,000 | — | 0.10 | 0.20 | 1.00 |

**100 KURUS (1 Lira)** KM# 860.1 **Weight:** 12.0000 g. **Composition:** 0.8300 Silver .3203 oz. ASW **Obverse:** Head of Kemal Atatürk left **Reverse:** High star

| Date | Mintage | VG | F | VF | XF | Unc |
|---|---|---|---|---|---|---|
| 1934 | 718,000 | 15.00 | 30.00 | 40.00 | 75.00 | — |

**100 KURUS (1 Lira)** KM# 860.2 **Weight:** 12.0000 g. **Composition:** 0.8300 Silver .3203 oz. ASW **Obverse:** Head of Kemal Atatürk left **Reverse:** Low star

| Date | Mintage | VG | F | VF | XF | Unc |
|---|---|---|---|---|---|---|
| 1934 | Inc. above | 10.00 | 20.00 | 30.00 | 50.00 | — |

**100 KURUS (1 Lira)** KM# 860.1a **Weight:** 13.5000 g. **Composition:** 0.9250 Silver .4015 oz. ASW **Series:** Nostalgia **Obverse:** Same as KM#860.1 **Reverse:** Same as KM#860.1 **Edge:** Plain **Size:** 29.5 mm.

| Date | Mintage | F | VF | XF | Unc |
|---|---|---|---|---|---|
| 1934 Matte | 10,000 | — | — | — | 20.00 |

**1/2 LIRA** KM# 941 **Weight:** 7.8600 g. **Composition:** 0.9250 Silver .2337 oz. ASW **Subject:** 100th Anniversary of Ataturk's Birth

| Date | Mintage | F | VF | XF | Unc |
|---|---|---|---|---|---|
| 1981 | 25,000 | — | — | — | 12.50 |

**1/2 LIRA** KM# 941a **Weight:** 8.0000 g. **Composition:** 0.9170 Gold .2358 oz. AGW **Subject:** 100th Anniversary of Ataturk's Birth

| Date | Mintage | F | VF | XF | Unc |
|---|---|---|---|---|---|
| 1981 | 25,000 | — | — | — | 125 |

**LIRA** KM# 866 **Weight:** 12.0000 g. **Composition:** 0.8300 Silver .3203 oz. ASW **Subject:** Head of Kemal Atatürk left

| Date | Mintage | VG | F | VF | XF | Unc |
|---|---|---|---|---|---|---|
| 1937 | 1,624,000 | 5.00 | 10.00 | 15.00 | 32.00 | — |
| 1938 | 8,282,000 | 25.00 | 50.00 | 75.00 | 150 | — |
| 1939 | 376,000 | 5.00 | 10.00 | 15.00 | 32.00 | — |

**LIRA** KM# 869 **Weight:** 12.0000 g. **Composition:** 0.8300 Silver .3203 oz. ASW **Subject:** Head of Ismet Inonu left

| Date | Mintage | VG | F | VF | XF | Unc |
|---|---|---|---|---|---|---|
| 1940 | 253,000 | 7.50 | 12.50 | 15.00 | 25.00 | — |
| 1941 | 6,167,000 | 4.50 | 10.00 | 12.50 | 22.50 | — |

**LIRA** KM# 883 **Weight:** 7.5000 g. **Composition:** 0.6000 Silver .1447 oz. ASW **Note:** Edge varieties exist.

| Date | Mintage | F | VF | XF | Unc |
|---|---|---|---|---|---|
| 1947 | 11,104,000 | 1.50 | 3.50 | 5.00 | 8.50 |
| 1948 | 16,896,000 | 1.50 | 3.00 | 4.00 | 7.50 |

**LIRA** KM# 889 **Composition:** Copper-Nickel

| Date | Mintage | F | VF | XF | Unc |
|---|---|---|---|---|---|
| 1957 | 25,000,000 | 0.25 | 0.50 | 1.00 | 2.50 |

**LIRA** KM# 889a.1 **Weight:** 8.0000 g. **Composition:** Stainless Steel **Obverse:** Head of Kemal Atatürk left

| Date | Mintage | F | VF | XF | Unc |
|---|---|---|---|---|---|
| 1959 | 7,452,000 | — | 0.10 | 0.20 | 0.50 |
| 1960 | 11,436,000 | — | 0.10 | 0.20 | 0.50 |
| 1961 | 2,100,000 | — | 0.10 | 0.20 | 1.00 |
| 1962 | 4,228,000 | — | 0.10 | 0.20 | 0.50 |
| 1963 | 4,316,000 | — | 0.10 | 0.20 | 0.50 |
| 1964 | 4,976,000 | — | 0.10 | 0.20 | 0.50 |
| 1965 | 5,348,000 | — | 0.10 | 0.20 | 0.50 |
| 1966 | 8,040,000 | — | 0.10 | 0.20 | 0.50 |
| 1967 | — | — | 0.10 | 0.20 | 0.50 |

**LIRA** KM# 889a.2 **Weight:** 7.0000 g. **Composition:** Stainless Steel **Obverse:** Head of Kemal Atatürk left **Note:** Reduced weight.

| Date | Mintage | F | VF | XF | Unc |
|---|---|---|---|---|---|
| 1967 | 10,444,000 | — | 0.10 | 0.20 | 0.50 |
| 1968 | 12,728,000 | — | 0.10 | 0.20 | 0.50 |
| 1969 | 6,612,000 | — | 0.10 | 0.20 | 0.50 |
| 1970 | 8,652,000 | — | 0.10 | 0.20 | 0.50 |
| 1971 | 10,504,000 | — | 0.10 | 0.20 | 0.50 |
| 1972 | 26,512,000 | — | 0.10 | 0.20 | 0.50 |
| 1973 | 12,596,000 | — | 0.10 | 0.20 | 0.50 |
| 1974 | 11,596,000 | — | 0.10 | 0.20 | 0.50 |
| 1975 | 20,348,000 | — | 0.10 | 0.20 | 0.50 |
| 1976 | 23,144,000 | — | 0.10 | 0.20 | 0.50 |
| 1977 | 30,244,000 | — | 0.10 | 0.20 | 0.50 |
| 1978 | 22,156,000 | — | 0.10 | 0.20 | 0.50 |
| 1979 | 9,289,000 | — | 0.10 | 0.20 | 0.50 |
| 1980 | 3,585,000 | — | 0.10 | 0.20 | 0.50 |

**LIRA** KM# 914 **Weight:** 8.0000 g. **Composition:** Stainless Steel **Series:** F.A.O.

| Date | Mintage | F | VF | XF | Unc |
|---|---|---|---|---|---|
| 1978 | 20,000 | — | 0.50 | 1.00 | 2.50 |

**LIRA** KM# 926 **Weight:** 8.0000 g. **Composition:** Stainless Steel **Series:** F.A.O. **Note:** Similar to 50 Kurus, KM#925.

| Date | Mintage | F | VF | XF | Unc |
|---|---|---|---|---|---|
| 1979 | 20,000 | — | 0.50 | 1.00 | 2.50 |

**LIRA** KM# 937 **Weight:** 8.0000 g. **Composition:** Stainless Steel **Series:** F.A.O.

| Date | Mintage | F | VF | XF | Unc |
|---|---|---|---|---|---|
| 1980 | 13,000 | — | 0.40 | 0.75 | 2.00 |

**LIRA** KM# 942 **Weight:** 16.0000 g. **Composition:** 0.9250 Silver **Subject:** 100th Anniversary of Ataturk's Birth **Obverse:** Head of Kemal Atatürk 3/4 right

| Date | Mintage | F | VF | XF | Unc |
|---|---|---|---|---|---|
| 1981 | — | — | — | — | 22.50 |

**LIRA** KM# 942a **Weight:** 16.0000 g. **Composition:** 0.9170 Gold .4716 oz. AGW **Subject:** 100th Anniversary of Ataturk's Birth **Obverse:** Head of Kemal Atatürk 3/4 right

| Date | Mintage | F | VF | XF | Unc |
|---|---|---|---|---|---|
| 1981 | 25,000 | — | — | — | 250 |

**LIRA** KM# 943 **Composition:** Aluminum **Obverse:** Head of Kemal Atatürk left **Reverse:** Crescent opens left

| Date | Mintage | F | VF | XF | Unc |
|---|---|---|---|---|---|
| 1981 | 14,432,000 | — | — | 0.10 | 0.25 |

**LIRA** KM# 990 **Composition:** Aluminum **Obverse:** Similar to KM#943 **Reverse:** Crescent opens right with thin "1"

| Date | Mintage | F | VF | XF | Unc |
|---|---|---|---|---|---|
| 1982 | 799,000 | — | — | 0.10 | 0.25 |

**LIRA** KM# 962.1 **Composition:** Aluminum **Obverse:** Head of Kemal Atatürk left **Reverse:** Large (5mm) "1"

| Date | Mintage | F | VF | XF | Unc |
|---|---|---|---|---|---|
| 1984 | 498,000 | — | — | 0.10 | 0.20 |

**LIRA** KM# 962.2 **Composition:** Aluminum **Reverse:** Small (3.5mm) "1" **Note:** Varieties exist.

| Date | Mintage | F | VF | XF | Unc |
|---|---|---|---|---|---|
| 1985 | 712,000 | — | — | 0.10 | 0.20 |
| 1986 | 504,000 | — | — | 0.10 | 0.20 |
| 1987 | 500,000 | — | — | 0.10 | 0.20 |
| 1988 | 75,000 | — | — | 0.10 | 0.20 |
| 1989 | 10,000 | — | — | 0.10 | 0.20 |

**2-1/2 LIRA** KM# 893.1 **Weight:** 12.0000 g. **Composition:** Stainless Steel

| Date | Mintage | F | VF | XF | Unc |
|---|---|---|---|---|---|
| 1960 | 4,015,000 | — | 0.25 | 1.00 | 3.00 |
| 1961 | 1,222,000 | — | 0.25 | 1.00 | 6.00 |
| 1962 | 3,636,000 | — | 0.25 | 1.00 | 3.00 |
| 1963 | 3,108,000 | — | 0.25 | 1.00 | 3.00 |
| 1964 | 2,710,000 | — | 0.25 | 1.00 | 3.00 |
| 1965 | 1,246,000 | — | 0.25 | 1.00 | 4.00 |
| 1966 | 1,788,000 | — | 0.25 | 1.00 | 3.00 |
| 1967 | 5,333,000 | — | 0.25 | 1.00 | 3.00 |
| 1968 | 2,707,000 | — | 0.25 | 1.00 | 3.00 |

**2-1/2 LIRA** KM# 893.1a **Weight:** 11.8000 g. **Composition:** 0.9250 Silver .3509 oz. ASW **Series:** Nostalgia **Obverse:** Same as KM#893.1 **Reverse:** Same as KM#893.1 **Edge:** Plain **Size:** 30 mm.

| Date | Mintage | F | VF | XF | Unc |
|---|---|---|---|---|---|
| 1965 | 10,000 | — | — | — | 20.00 |

**2-1/2 LIRA** KM# 893.2 **Weight:** 9.0000 g. **Composition:** Stainless Steel **Note:** Reduced weight. Varieties exist.

| Date | Mintage | F | VF | XF | Unc |
|---|---|---|---|---|---|
| 1969 | 1,378,000 | — | 0.15 | 0.75 | 2.00 |
| 1970 | 3,777,000 | — | 0.15 | 0.75 | 2.00 |
| 1971 | 2,170,000 | — | 0.15 | 0.75 | 2.00 |
| 1972 | 9,147,000 | — | 0.15 | 0.50 | 2.00 |
| 1973 | 4,348,000 | — | 0.15 | 0.50 | 3.00 |
| 1974 | 3,816,000 | — | 0.15 | 0.50 | 3.00 |

| Date | Mintage | F | VF | XF | Unc |
|---|---|---|---|---|---|
| 1975 | 9,811,000 | — | 0.15 | 0.50 | 2.50 |
| 1976 | 3,952,000 | — | 0.15 | 0.50 | 2.50 |
| 1977 | 21,473,000 | — | 0.10 | 0.25 | 0.50 |
| 1978 | 15,738,000 | — | 0.10 | 0.25 | 0.50 |
| 1979 | 6,074,000 | — | 0.10 | 0.25 | 0.50 |
| 1980 | 2,621,000 | — | 0.10 | 0.25 | 0.75 |

**2-1/2 LIRA KM# 896 Composition:** Stainless Steel **Series:** F.A.O.

| Date | Mintage | F | VF | XF | Unc |
|---|---|---|---|---|---|
| 1970 | 200,000 | — | 0.10 | 0.35 | 1.50 |

**2-1/2 LIRA KM# 910 Composition:** Stainless Steel **Series:** F.A.O.

| Date | Mintage | F | VF | XF | Unc |
|---|---|---|---|---|---|
| 1977 | 25,000 | — | 0.25 | 0.50 | 1.75 |

**2-1/2 LIRA KM# 915 Composition:** Stainless Steel **Series:** F.A.O.

| Date | Mintage | F | VF | XF | Unc |
|---|---|---|---|---|---|
| 1978 | 10,000 | — | 1.00 | 2.00 | 4.00 |

**2-1/2 LIRA KM# 927 Composition:** Stainless Steel **Series:** F.A.O.

| Date | Mintage | F | VF | XF | Unc |
|---|---|---|---|---|---|
| 1979 | 20,000 | — | 1.00 | 2.00 | 4.00 |

**2-1/2 LIRA KM# 938 Composition:** Stainless Steel **Series:** F.A.O.

| Date | Mintage | F | VF | XF | Unc |
|---|---|---|---|---|---|
| 1980 | 13,000 | — | 0.50 | 1.50 | 4.00 |

**5 LIRA KM# 905 Composition:** Stainless Steel

| Date | Mintage | F | VF | XF | Unc |
|---|---|---|---|---|---|
| 1974 | 2,842,000 | — | 0.15 | 0.75 | 3.00 |
| 1975 | 10,855,000 | — | 0.15 | 0.25 | 2.00 |
| 1976 | 17,532,000 | — | 0.15 | 0.25 | 2.00 |
| 1977 | 6,172,000 | — | 0.15 | 0.75 | 3.00 |
| 1978 | 76,000 | 1.50 | 2.50 | 3.50 | 6.00 |
| 1979 | 6,054,000 | — | 0.15 | 0.30 | 1.00 |

**5 LIRA KM# 905a Weight:** 14.7000 g. **Composition:** 0.9250 Silver .4372 oz. ASW **Series:** Nostalgia **Obverse:** Same as KM#905 **Reverse:** Same as KM#905 **Edge:** Plain **Size:** 32.5 mm.

| Date | Mintage | F | VF | XF | Unc |
|---|---|---|---|---|---|
| 1975 | 10,000 | — | — | — | 20.00 |

**5 LIRA KM# 909 Composition:** Stainless Steel **Series:** International Women's Year; F.A.O.

| Date | Mintage | F | VF | XF | Unc |
|---|---|---|---|---|---|
| 1976 | 17,000 | — | 1.50 | 2.50 | 6.50 |

**5 LIRA KM# 911 Composition:** Stainless Steel **Series:** F.A.O.

| Date | Mintage | F | VF | XF | Unc |
|---|---|---|---|---|---|
| 1977 | 25,000 | — | 0.75 | 1.50 | 3.50 |

**5 LIRA KM# 916 Composition:** Stainless Steel **Series:** F.A.O.

| Date | Mintage | F | VF | XF | Unc |
|---|---|---|---|---|---|
| 1978 | 10,000 | — | 1.25 | 3.00 | 7.00 |

**5 LIRA KM# 928 Composition:** Stainless Steel **Series:** F.A.O.

| Date | Mintage | F | VF | XF | Unc |
|---|---|---|---|---|---|
| 1979 | 20,000 | — | 1.25 | 3.00 | 7.00 |

**5 LIRA KM# 939 Composition:** Stainless Steel **Series:** F.A.O.

| Date | Mintage | F | VF | XF | Unc |
|---|---|---|---|---|---|
| 1980 | 13,000 | — | 1.25 | 3.00 | 7.50 |

**5 LIRA KM# 944 Composition:** Aluminum **Reverse:** Crescent opens left

| Date | Mintage | F | VF | XF | Unc |
|---|---|---|---|---|---|
| 1981 | 61,605,000 | — | — | 0.15 | 0.35 |

**5 LIRA KM# 949.1 Composition:** Aluminum **Reverse:** Crescent opens right

| Date | Mintage | F | VF | XF | Unc |
|---|---|---|---|---|---|
| 1982 | 69,975,000 | — | — | 0.15 | 0.35 |

**5 LIRA KM# 949.2 Composition:** Aluminum **Reverse:** Bolder, larger "5"

| Date | Mintage | F | VF | XF | Unc |
|---|---|---|---|---|---|
| 1983 | 90,310,000 | — | — | 0.15 | 0.35 |

**5 LIRA KM# 963 Composition:** Aluminum **Obverse:** Head of Kemal Atatürk left **Note:** Varieties exist.

| Date | Mintage | F | VF | XF | Unc |
|---|---|---|---|---|---|
| 1984 | 17,316,000 | — | — | 0.15 | 0.35 |
| 1985 | 9,405,000 | — | — | 0.15 | 0.35 |
| 1986 | 9,575,000 | — | — | 0.20 | 0.50 |
| 1987 | 500,000 | — | — | 0.20 | 0.50 |
| 1988 | 100,000 | — | — | 0.20 | 0.50 |
| 1989 | 10,000 | — | — | 0.20 | 0.50 |

**10 LIRA KM# 894 Weight:** 15.0000 g. **Composition:** 0.8300 Silver .4003 oz. ASW. **Subject:** 27th May Revolution **Obverse:** Head of Kemal Atatürk left

| Date | Mintage | F | VF | XF | Unc |
|---|---|---|---|---|---|
| ND(1960) | 4,000,000 | — | 3.00 | 4.00 | 8.00 |
| ND(1960) Prooflike | — | — | — | — | 12.00 |

**10 LIRA** **KM# 945** **Composition:** Aluminum **Reverse:** Crescent opens left

| Date | Mintage | F | VF | XF | Unc |
|---|---|---|---|---|---|
| 1981 | 25,520,000 | — | 0.10 | 0.25 | 0.75 |

**10 LIRA** **KM# 950.1** **Composition:** Aluminum **Reverse:** Crescent opens right

| Date | Mintage | F | VF | XF | Unc |
|---|---|---|---|---|---|
| 1982 | 17,092,000 | — | 0.10 | 0.25 | 0.75 |

**10 LIRA** **KM# 950.2** **Composition:** Aluminum

| Date | Mintage | F | VF | XF | Unc |
|---|---|---|---|---|---|
| 1983 | 2,228,000 | — | 0.10 | 0.25 | 0.60 |

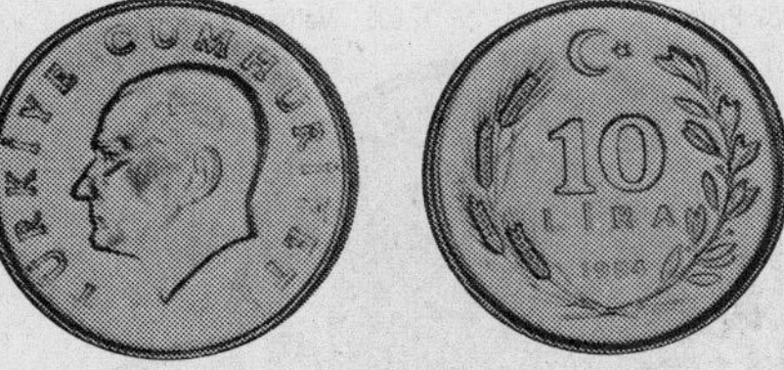

**10 LIRA** **KM# 964** **Composition:** Aluminum **Obverse:** Head of Kemal Atatürk left **Note:** Varieties exist.

| Date | Mintage | F | VF | XF | Unc |
|---|---|---|---|---|---|
| 1984 | 23,360,000 | — | 0.10 | 0.25 | 0.50 |
| 1985 | 41,736,000 | — | — | 0.15 | 0.30 |
| 1986 | 78,224,000 | — | — | 0.15 | 0.30 |
| 1987 | 62,340,000 | — | — | 0.15 | 0.30 |
| 1988 | 17,620,000 | — | — | 0.15 | 0.30 |
| 1989 | 10,000 | — | — | 0.15 | 0.30 |

**20 LIRA** **KM# 946** **Composition:** Aluminum **Series:** World Food Day

| Date | Mintage | F | VF | XF | Unc |
|---|---|---|---|---|---|
| 1981 | 10,000 | — | — | 1.25 | 3.00 |

**20 LIRA** **KM# 965** **Composition:** Copper-Nickel

| Date | Mintage | F | VF | XF | Unc |
|---|---|---|---|---|---|
| 1984 | 1,644,000 | — | 0.10 | 0.25 | 1.00 |
| 1989 | — | — | 0.10 | 0.25 | 1.00 |

**25 LIRA** **KM# 897** **Weight:** 14.6000 g. **Composition:** 0.8300 Silver .3896 oz. ASW **Subject:** 50th Anniversary of National Assembly

| Date | Mintage | F | VF | XF | Unc |
|---|---|---|---|---|---|
| ND(1970) | 23,000 | — | — | 6.00 | 8.00 |
| ND(1970) Proof | Inc. above | Value: 14.00 | | | |

**25 LIRA** **KM# 975** **Composition:** Aluminum **Note:** Varieties exist.

| Date | Mintage | F | VF | XF | Unc |
|---|---|---|---|---|---|
| 1985 | 37,014,000 | — | — | 0.15 | 0.40 |
| 1986 | 49,611,000 | — | — | 0.15 | 0.40 |
| 1987 | 61,335,000 | — | — | 0.15 | 0.40 |
| 1988 | 39,540,000 | — | — | 0.15 | 0.40 |
| 1989 | 10,000 | — | — | 0.15 | 0.40 |

**50 LIRA** **KM# 900** **Weight:** 19.0000 g. **Composition:** 0.8300 Silver .5070 oz. ASW **Subject:** 900th Anniversary - Battle of Malazgirt

| Date | Mintage | F | VF | XF | Unc |
|---|---|---|---|---|---|
| ND(1971) | 33,000 | — | — | 7.00 | 10.00 |
| ND(1971) Proof | Inc. above | Value: 15.00 | | | |

**50 LIRA** **KM# 901** **Weight:** 20.1000 g. **Composition:** 0.8300 Silver .5363 oz. ASW

| Date | Mintage | F | VF | XF | Unc |
|---|---|---|---|---|---|
| ND(1972) | 172,000 | — | — | 6.00 | 9.00 |
| ND(1972) Proof | — | Value: 12.50 | | | |

**50 LIRA** **KM# 902** **Weight:** 13.0000 g. **Composition:** 0.9000 Silver .3761 oz. ASW **Subject:** 50th Anniversary of Republic

| Date | Mintage | F | VF | XF | Unc |
|---|---|---|---|---|---|
| ND(1973) | 70,000 | — | — | 5.00 | 8.00 |
| ND(1973) Proof | Inc. above | Value: 11.50 | | | |

**50 LIRA** **KM# 912** **Weight:** 8.8500 g. **Composition:** 0.8300 Silver .2361 oz. ASW **Series:** F.A.O.

| Date | Mintage | F | VF | XF | Unc |
|---|---|---|---|---|---|
| 1977 | 25,000 | — | — | 7.00 | 10.00 |

**50 LIRA** **KM# 966** **Composition:** Copper-Nickel-Zinc **Obverse:** Head of Kemal Atatürk left **Note:** Varieties exist.

| Date | Mintage | F | VF | XF | Unc |
|---|---|---|---|---|---|
| 1984 | 14,731,000 | — | 0.10 | 0.25 | 0.60 |
| 1985 | 52,658,000 | — | 0.10 | 0.20 | 0.50 |
| 1986 | 80,656,000 | — | 0.10 | 0.20 | 0.50 |
| 1987 | 32,078,000 | — | 0.10 | 0.20 | 0.50 |

**50 LIRA** **KM# 987** **Composition:** Aluminum-Bronze **Obverse:** Head of Kemal Atatürk left **Note:** Varieties exist.

| Date | Mintage | F | VF | XF | Unc |
|---|---|---|---|---|---|
| 1988 | 3,396,000 | — | — | — | 0.15 |
| 1989 | 25,463,000 | — | — | — | 0.15 |
| 1990 | 500,000 | — | — | — | 0.15 |
| 1991 | 10,000 | — | — | — | 0.15 |
| 1992 | 10,000 | — | — | — | 0.15 |
| 1993 | 5,000 | — | — | — | 0.35 |
| 1994 | 2,500 | — | — | — | 0.50 |

**100 LIRA** **KM# 903** **Weight:** 22.0000 g. **Composition:** 0.9000 Silver .6367 oz. ASW **Subject:** 50th Anniversary of Republic

| Date | Mintage | F | VF | XF | Unc |
|---|---|---|---|---|---|
| 1973 | 65,000 | — | — | 8.00 | 15.00 |

**100 LIRA** **KM# 951** **Composition:** Copper-Nickel **Subject:** World Championship Soccer - Madrid

| Date | Mintage | F | VF | XF | Unc |
|---|---|---|---|---|---|
| 1982 | 100,000 | 0.75 | 1.50 | 3.00 | 6.00 |

**100 LIRA** **KM# 967** **Composition:** Copper-Nickel-Zinc **Obverse:** Head of Kemal Atatürk left **Note:** Varieties exist.

| Date | Mintage | F | VF | XF | Unc |
|---|---|---|---|---|---|
| 1984 | 758,000 | — | 0.20 | 0.40 | 0.85 |
| 1985 | 866,000 | — | 0.20 | 0.40 | 0.85 |
| 1986 | 12,064,000 | — | 0.20 | 0.40 | 0.85 |
| 1987 | 91,400,000 | — | 0.15 | 0.25 | 0.65 |
| 1988 | 16,184,000 | — | 0.15 | 0.25 | 0.65 |

**100 LIRA** **KM# 988** **Composition:** Aluminum-Bronze **Obverse:** Head of Kemal Atatürk left **Note:** Varieties exist.

| Date | Mintage | F | VF | XF | Unc |
|---|---|---|---|---|---|
| 1988 | 10,000,000 | — | — | — | 0.20 |
| 1989 | 233,750,000 | — | — | — | 0.20 |
| 1990 | 152,230,000 | — | — | — | 0.20 |
| 1991 | 49,160,000 | — | — | — | 0.20 |
| 1992 | 22,930,000 | — | — | — | 0.20 |
| 1993 | 3,700,000 | — | — | — | 0.20 |
| 1994 | 2,500 | — | — | — | 0.50 |

**150 LIRA** **KM# 917** **Weight:** 9.0000 g. **Composition:** 0.8000 Silver .2314 oz. ASW **Subject:** World Cup Soccer Championship

| Date | Mintage | F | VF | XF | Unc |
|---|---|---|---|---|---|
| 1978 | 5,000 | — | — | — | 22.50 |

**150 LIRA** **KM# 918.1** **Weight:** 9.0000 g. **Composition:** 0.8000 Silver .2314 oz. ASW **Series:** F.A.O. **Edge:** Reeded

| Date | Mintage | F | VF | XF | Unc |
|---|---|---|---|---|---|
| 1978 | 10,000 | — | — | — | 6.50 |

**150 LIRA** **KM# 918.2** **Weight:** 9.0000 g. **Composition:** 0.8000 Silver .2314 oz. ASW **Series:** F.A.O. **Edge:** Lettered

| Date | Mintage | F | VF | XF | Unc |
|---|---|---|---|---|---|
| 1978 Proof | 2,500 | Value: 22.50 | | | |

**150 LIRA** **KM# 929.1** **Weight:** 9.0000 g. **Composition:** 0.8000 Silver .2314 oz. ASW **Series:** F.A.O. **Edge:** Reeded

| Date | Mintage | F | VF | XF | Unc |
|---|---|---|---|---|---|
| 1979 | 10,000 | — | — | — | 6.50 |

**150 LIRA** **KM# 929.2** **Weight:** 9.0000 g. **Composition:** 0.8000 Silver .2314 oz. ASW **Series:** F.A.O. **Edge:** Lettered

| Date | Mintage | F | VF | XF | Unc |
|---|---|---|---|---|---|
| 1979 Proof | 2,500 | Value: 22.50 | | | |

**200 LIRA** **KM# 919** **Weight:** 9.0000 g. **Composition:** 0.8300 Silver .2402 oz. ASW **Subject:** 705th Anniversary - Death of Jalaladdin Rumi

| Date | Mintage | F | VF | XF | Unc |
|---|---|---|---|---|---|
| 1978 | 10,000 | — | — | — | 12.00 |
| 1978 Proof | 1,000 | Value: 25.00 | | | |

**500 LIRA** **KM# 904** **Weight:** 6.0000 g. **Composition:** 0.9170 Gold .1769 oz. AGW **Subject:** 50th Anniversary of Republic

| Date | Mintage | F | VF | XF | Unc |
|---|---|---|---|---|---|
| 1973 | 30,000 | — | — | — | 100 |

**500 LIRA** **KM# 920** **Weight:** 8.0000 g. **Composition:** 0.9170 Gold .2358 oz. AGW **Series:** F.A.O.

| Date | Mintage | F | VF | XF | Unc |
|---|---|---|---|---|---|
| 1978 Proof | 650 | Value: 200 | | | |

**500 LIRA** **KM# 921** **Weight:** 8.0000 g. **Composition:** 0.9170 Gold .2358 oz. AGW **Subject:** 705th Anniversary - Death of Jalaladdin Rumi

| Date | Mintage | F | VF | XF | Unc |
|---|---|---|---|---|---|
| 1978 Proof | 900 | Value: 200 | | | |

**500 LIRA** **KM# 930** **Weight:** 8.0000 g. **Composition:** 0.9170 Gold .2358 oz. AGW **Series:** F.A.O.

| Date | Mintage | F | VF | XF | Unc |
|---|---|---|---|---|---|
| 1979 Proof | 783 | Value: 200 | | | |

**500 LIRA** **KM# 931** **Weight:** 23.3300 g. **Composition:** 0.9250 Silver .6938 oz. ASW **Subject:** UNICEF and I.Y.C.

| Date | Mintage | F | VF | XF | Unc |
|---|---|---|---|---|---|
| 1979(1981) Proof | 10,000 | Value: 20.00 | | | |

**500 LIRA** **KM# 940.1** **Weight:** 9.0000 g. **Composition:** 0.9000 Silver .2604 oz. ASW **Series:** F.A.O. **Edge:** Reeded

| Date | Mintage | F | VF | XF | Unc |
|---|---|---|---|---|---|
| 1980 | 13,000 | — | — | — | 7.50 |

**500 LIRA** **KM# 940.2** **Weight:** 9.0000 g. **Composition:** 0.9000 Silver .2604 oz. ASW **Edge:** Lettered

| Date | Mintage | F | VF | XF | Unc |
|---|---|---|---|---|---|
| 1980 Proof | 4,000 | Value: 20.00 | | | |

**500 LIRA** **KM# 952** **Weight:** 23.3300 g. **Composition:** 0.9250 Silver .6938 oz. ASW **Subject:** World Championship Soccer - Madrid

| Date | Mintage | F | VF | XF | Unc |
|---|---|---|---|---|---|
| 1982 Proof | 12,000 | Value: 18.00 | | | |

**500 LIRA** **KM# 953** **Weight:** 23.3300 g. **Composition:** 0.9250 Silver .6938 oz. ASW **Subject:** World Championship Soccer - Madrid

| Date | Mintage | F | VF | XF | Unc |
|---|---|---|---|---|---|
| 1982 Proof | 12,000 | Value: 18.00 | | | |

**500 LIRA** KM# 957 **Composition:** Copper-Nickel **Subject:** Lydia - First Coin in the World

| Date | Mintage | F | VF | XF | Unc |
|---|---|---|---|---|---|
| 1983 | 3,542 | — | — | 6.50 | 12.50 |

**500 LIRA** KM# 968 **Composition:** Copper-Nickel **Subject:** World Fisheries Conference

| Date | Mintage | F | VF | XF | Unc |
|---|---|---|---|---|---|
| ND (1984) | 3,000 | — | — | 6.50 | 15.00 |

**500 LIRA** KM# 968a **Weight:** 28.2800 g. **Composition:** 0.9250 Silver .8411 oz. ASW **Series:** World Fisheries Conference

| Date | Mintage | F | VF | XF | Unc |
|---|---|---|---|---|---|
| ND(1984) Proof | 763,000 | Value: 75.00 | | | |

**500 LIRA** KM# 968b **Weight:** 47.5400 g. **Composition:** 0.9170 Gold 1.4009 oz. AGW **Subject:** World Fisheries Conference

| Date | Mintage | F | VF | XF | Unc |
|---|---|---|---|---|---|
| ND(1984) Proof | 74 | Value: 1,250 | | | |

**500 LIRA** KM# 979 **Composition:** Copper-Nickel **Subject:** 40th Anniversary of F.A.O.

| Date | Mintage | F | VF | XF | Unc |
|---|---|---|---|---|---|
| ND(1986) Proof | 3,000 | Value: 10.00 | | | |

**500 LIRA** KM# 989 **Composition:** Aluminum-Bronze **Obverse:** Head of Kemal Atatürk left **Note:** Varieties exist.

| Date | Mintage | F | VF | XF | Unc |
|---|---|---|---|---|---|
| 1989 | 141,813,000 | — | — | — | 0.60 |
| 1990 | 100,114,000 | — | — | — | 0.60 |
| 1991 | 30,006,000 | — | — | — | 0.60 |
| 1992 | 10,000 | — | — | — | 0.60 |
| 1993 | 5,000 | — | — | — | 0.75 |
| 1994 | 2,500 | — | — | — | 0.85 |
| 1995 | 2,500 | — | — | — | 0.85 |
| 1996 | 10,000 | — | — | — | 0.60 |
| 1997 | — | — | — | — | 0.60 |

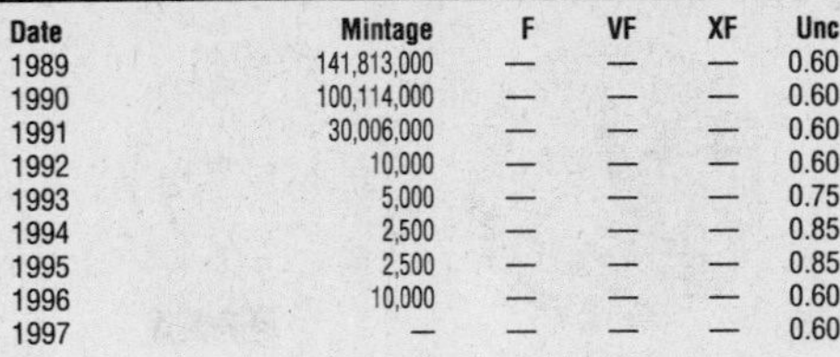

**1000 LIRA** KM# 922 **Weight:** 16.0000 g. **Composition:** 0.9170 Gold .4717 oz. AGW **Series:** F.A.O.

| Date | Mintage | F | VF | XF | Unc |
|---|---|---|---|---|---|
| 1978 Proof | 650 | Value: 375 | | | |

**1000 LIRA** KM# 923 **Weight:** 16.0000 g. **Composition:** 0.9170 Gold .4717 oz. AGW **Subject:** 705th Anniversary - Death of Rumi

| Date | Mintage | F | VF | XF | Unc |
|---|---|---|---|---|---|
| 1978 Proof | 450 | Value: 375 | | | |

**1000 LIRA** KM# 932 **Weight:** 16.0000 g. **Composition:** 0.9170 Gold .4717 oz. AGW **Series:** F.A.O.

| Date | Mintage | F | VF | XF | Unc |
|---|---|---|---|---|---|
| 1979 Proof | 900 | Value: 375 | | | |

**1000 LIRA** KM# 985 **Composition:** Nickel-Bronze **Subject:** Peace

| Date | Mintage | F | VF | XF | Unc |
|---|---|---|---|---|---|
| 1986 Proof | — | Value: 12.00 | | | |

**1000 LIRA** KM# 980 **Composition:** Copper-Nickel **Subject:** Shelter for the Homeless

| Date | Mintage | F | VF | XF | Unc |
|---|---|---|---|---|---|
| ND(1987) Proof | — | Value: 10.00 | | | |

**1000 LIRA** KM# 991 **Composition:** Copper-Nickel **Subject:** 400th Anniversary - Death of Architect Sinan

| Date | Mintage | F | VF | XF | Unc |
|---|---|---|---|---|---|
| ND(1988) Proof | — | Value: 10.00 | | | |

**1000 LIRA** KM# 996 **Composition:** Copper-Zinc-Nickel **Subject:** Environmental Protection

| Date | Mintage | F | VF | XF | Unc |
|---|---|---|---|---|---|
| 1990 | 500,000 | — | — | — | 8.50 |

**1000 LIRA** KM# 997 **Composition:** Copper-Zinc-Nickel **Obverse:** Head of Kemal Atatürk left

| Date | Mintage | F | VF | XF | Unc |
|---|---|---|---|---|---|
| 1990 | 136,480,000 | — | 0.15 | 0.25 | 2.00 |
| 1991 | 110,245,000 | — | 0.15 | 0.25 | 2.00 |
| 1992 | 15,820,000 | — | 0.15 | 0.25 | 2.00 |
| 1993 | 11,675,000 | — | 0.15 | 0.25 | 2.00 |
| 1994 | 61,515,000 | — | 0.15 | 0.25 | 2.00 |

**1000 LIRA** KM# 1028 **Composition:** Bronze Clad Brass **Obverse:** Head of Kemal Atatürk left

| Date | Mintage | F | VF | XF | Unc |
|---|---|---|---|---|---|
| 1995 | 36,820,000 | — | — | — | 1.00 |
| 1996 | 3,900,000 | — | — | — | 1.00 |
| 1997 | — | — | — | — | 1.00 |

**1500 LIRA** KM# 947 **Weight:** 16.0000 g. **Composition:** 0.9250 Silver .4758 oz. ASW **Series:** F.A.O.

| Date | Mintage | F | VF | XF | Unc |
|---|---|---|---|---|---|
| 1981 | 6,000 | — | — | — | 18.50 |
| 1982 | 500 | — | — | — | 37.50 |

**1500 LIRA** KM# 958 **Weight:** 16.0000 g. **Composition:** 0.9250 Silver .4758 oz. ASW **Series:** World Food Day

| Date | Mintage | F | VF | XF | Unc |
|---|---|---|---|---|---|
| 1983 Proof | 1,552 | Value: 40.00 | | | |

**2500 LIRA** **KM# 1015** **Composition:** Nickel-Bronze **Obverse:** Head of Kemal Atatürk left

| Date | Mintage | F | VF | XF | Unc |
|---|---|---|---|---|---|
| 1991 | 22,938,000 | 0.10 | 0.25 | 0.50 | 3.00 |
| 1992 | 48,784,000 | 0.10 | 0.25 | 0.50 | 3.00 |
| 1993 | 2,310,000 | 0.10 | 0.25 | 0.50 | 3.00 |
| 1994 | 2,500 | 0.10 | 0.25 | 0.50 | 4.50 |
| 1995 | 2,500 | 0.10 | 0.25 | 0.50 | 4.50 |
| 1996 | 10,000 | 0.10 | 0.25 | 0.50 | 3.00 |
| 1997 | — | 0.10 | 0.25 | 0.50 | 3.00 |

**3000 LIRA** **KM# 948** **Weight:** 28.2800 g. **Composition:** 0.9250 Silver .8411 oz. ASW **Series:** International Year of Disabled Persons

| Date | Mintage | F | VF | XF | Unc |
|---|---|---|---|---|---|
| 1981 | 14,000 | — | — | — | 45.00 |
| 1981 Proof | 16,000 | Value: 55.00 | | | |

**3000 LIRA** **KM# 959** **Weight:** 28.2800 g. **Composition:** 0.9250 Silver .8411 oz. ASW **Series:** International Year of the Scout

| Date | Mintage | F | VF | XF | Unc |
|---|---|---|---|---|---|
| ND(1982) | 12,000 | — | — | — | 45.00 |
| ND(1982) Proof | 14,000 | Value: 55.00 | | | |

**3000 LIRA** **KM# 960** **Weight:** 16.0000 g. **Composition:** 0.9250 Silver .4758 oz. ASW **Subject:** 60th Anniversary of the Republic **Obverse:** Head of Kemal Atatürk left

| Date | Mintage | F | VF | XF | Unc |
|---|---|---|---|---|---|
| ND(1983) Proof | 4,000 | Value: 35.00 | | | |

**5000 LIRA** **KM# 954** **Weight:** 7.1300 g. **Composition:** 0.5000 Gold .1146 oz. AGW **Subject:** World Championship Soccer - Madrid

| Date | Mintage | F | VF | XF | Unc |
|---|---|---|---|---|---|
| (1982) Proof | 2,400 | Value: 135 | | | |

**5000 LIRA** **KM# 969** **Weight:** 23.3300 g. **Composition:** 0.9250 Silver .6939 oz. ASW **Subject:** Decade for Women

| Date | Mintage | F | VF | XF | Unc |
|---|---|---|---|---|---|
| 1984 Proof | 20,000 | Value: 35.00 | | | |

**5000 LIRA** **KM# 970** **Weight:** 23.3300 g. **Composition:** 0.9250 Silver .6939 oz. ASW **Series:** 1984 Summer Olympics

| Date | Mintage | F | VF | XF | Unc |
|---|---|---|---|---|---|
| ND(1984) Proof | 5,343 | Value: 27.50 | | | |

**5000 LIRA** **KM# 971** **Weight:** 23.3300 g. **Composition:** 0.9250 Silver .6939 oz. ASW **Series:** 1984 Winter Olympics

| Date | Mintage | F | VF | XF | Unc |
|---|---|---|---|---|---|
| 1984 Proof | 4,657 | Value: 50.00 | | | |

**5000 LIRA** **KM# 972** **Weight:** 23.3300 g. **Composition:** 0.9250 Silver .6939 oz. ASW **Subject:** 50th Anniversary of Women's Suffrage

| Date | Mintage | F | VF | XF | Unc |
|---|---|---|---|---|---|
| ND(1984) Proof | 1,000 | Value: 65.00 | | | |

**5000 LIRA** **KM# 976** **Weight:** 23.3300 g. **Composition:** 0.9250 Silver .6939 oz. ASW **Subject:** 500th Anniversary of Turkish Navy

| Date | Mintage | F | VF | XF | Unc |
|---|---|---|---|---|---|
| ND(1985) Proof | 1,000 | Value: 80.00 | | | |

**5000 LIRA** **KM# 977** **Weight:** 23.3300 g. **Composition:** 0.9250 Silver .6939 oz. ASW **Subject:** Forestry Conference - Mexico

| Date | Mintage | F | VF | XF | Unc |
|---|---|---|---|---|---|
| 1985 Proof | 2,000 | Value: 25.00 | | | |

**5000 LIRA** **KM# 978** **Weight:** 23.3300 g. **Composition:** 0.9250 Silver .6939 oz. ASW **Subject:** Youth Year

| Date | Mintage | F | VF | XF | Unc |
|---|---|---|---|---|---|
| 1985 Proof | 2,000 | Value: 25.00 | | | |

**5000 LIRA** **KM# 1011** **Weight:** 23.3300 g. **Composition:** 0.9250 Silver .6939 oz. ASW **Subject:** Architect - Sinan

| Date | Mintage | F | VF | XF | Unc |
|---|---|---|---|---|---|
| ND(1988) Proof | — | Value: 35.00 | | | |

**5000 LIRA** **KM# 1005** **Composition:** Copper-Nickel **Subject:** Yunus Emre Sevgi Yili

| Date | Mintage | F | VF | XF | Unc |
|---|---|---|---|---|---|
| 1991 Proof | — | Value: 7.50 | | | |

**5000 LIRA** **KM# 1018** **Composition:** Copper-Nickel **Subject:** Turkish Jews

| Date | Mintage | F | VF | XF | Unc |
|---|---|---|---|---|---|
| ND(1992) Proof | — | Value: 8.50 | | | |

**5000 LIRA** **KM# 1025** **Composition:** Nickel-Bronze **Obverse:** Head of Kemal Atatürk left

| Date | Mintage | F | VF | XF | Unc |
|---|---|---|---|---|---|
| 1992 | 24,904,000 | 0.10 | 0.25 | 0.50 | 3.00 |
| 1992 Proof | — | Value: 6.50 | | | |
| 1993 | 15,872,000 | 0.10 | 0.25 | 0.50 | 3.00 |
| 1994 | 69,504,000 | 0.10 | 0.25 | 0.50 | 3.00 |

**5000 LIRA** **KM# 1029** **Composition:** Brass **Obverse:** Head of Kemal Atatürk left

| Date | Mintage | F | VF | XF | Unc |
|---|---|---|---|---|---|
| 1995 Large date | 69,550,000 | — | — | — | 1.50 |
| 1995 Small date | Inc. above | — | — | — | 0.75 |
| 1996 | 80,506,000 | — | — | — | 0.75 |
| 1997 | — | — | — | — | 0.75 |
| 1999 | — | — | — | — | 0.75 |

**10000 LIRA (10 Bin Lira)** **KM# 933** **Weight:** 17.1700 g. **Composition:** 0.9000 Gold .4900 oz. AGW **Subject:** UNICEF and I.Y.C. **Note:** Similar to 500 Lira, KM#931

| Date | Mintage | F | VF | XF | Unc |
|---|---|---|---|---|---|
| 1979(1981) Proof | 4,450 | Value: 225 | | | |

**10000 LIRA (10 Bin Lira)** **KM# 986** **Weight:** 23.3300 g. **Composition:** 0.9250 Silver .6939 oz. ASW **Subject:** 1986 World Cup Soccer - Mexico

| Date | Mintage | F | VF | XF | Unc |
|---|---|---|---|---|---|
| 1986 Proof | 5,000 | Value: 18.50 | | | |

**10000 LIRA (10 Bin Lira)** **KM# 1009** **Weight:** 23.3300 g. **Composition:** 0.9250 Silver .6939 oz. ASW **Subject:** 1986 World Cup Soccer **Reverse:** Cactus

| Date | Mintage | F | VF | XF | Unc |
|---|---|---|---|---|---|
| 1986 Proof | 7,000 | Value: 16.50 | | | |

**10000 LIRA (10 Bin Lira)** **KM# 1010** **Weight:** 23.3300 g. **Composition:** 0.9250 Silver .6939 oz. ASW **Subject:** A. Ersoy - Poet

| Date | Mintage | F | VF | XF | Unc |
|---|---|---|---|---|---|
| 1986 Proof | — | Value: 35.00 | | | |

**10000 LIRA (10 Bin Lira)** **KM# 1022** **Weight:** 23.3300 g. **Composition:** 0.9250 Silver .6939 oz. ASW **Subject:** World Peace

| Date | Mintage | F | VF | XF | Unc |
|---|---|---|---|---|---|
| 1986 Proof | Est. 1,200 | Value: 60.00 | | | |

**10000 LIRA (10 Bin Lira)** **KM# 981** **Weight:** 22.9700 g. **Composition:** 0.9250 Silver .6832 oz. ASW **Subject:** Shelter for the Homeless

| Date | Mintage | F | VF | XF | Unc |
|---|---|---|---|---|---|
| ND(1987) Proof | — | Value: 35.00 | | | |

**10000 LIRA (10 Bin Lira)** **KM# 982** **Weight:** 22.9700 g. **Composition:** 0.9250 Silver .6832 oz. ASW **Subject:** 130 Years of Turkish Forestry

| Date | Mintage | F | VF | XF | Unc |
|---|---|---|---|---|---|
| ND(1987) Proof | 5,000 | Value: 40.00 | | | |

**10000 LIRA (10 Bin Lira)** **KM# 983** **Weight:** 23.3300 g. **Composition:** 0.9250 Silver .6939 oz. ASW **Series:** Winter Olympics **Reverse:** Bear holding torch

| Date | Mintage | F | VF | XF | Unc |
|---|---|---|---|---|---|
| 1988 Proof | Est. 10,000 | Value: 35.00 | | | |

**10000 LIRA (10 Bin Lira)** **KM# 984** **Weight:** 23.3300 g. **Composition:** 0.9250 Silver .6939 oz. ASW **Series:** 1988 Summer Olympics **Reverse:** Torch

| Date | Mintage | F | VF | XF | Unc |
|---|---|---|---|---|---|
| 1988 | 1,000 | — | — | — | 50.00 |
| 1988 Proof | Est. 10,000 | Value: 28.00 | | | |

**10000 LIRA (10 Bin Lira)** **KM# 1027.1** **Weight:** 9.7500 g. **Composition:** Copper-Nickel-Zinc **Obverse:** Head of Kemal Atatürk left **Edge:** Reeded with legend **Edge Lettering:** TURKIYE CUMHURIYETI

| Date | Mintage | F | VF | XF | Unc |
|---|---|---|---|---|---|
| 1994 | 17,319,000 | — | 0.10 | 0.25 | 3.00 |
| 1995 | 56,584,000 | — | 0.10 | 0.25 | 3.00 |
| 1996 | 119,572,000 | — | 0.10 | 0.25 | 3.00 |
| 1997 | — | — | 0.10 | 0.25 | 3.00 |

**10000 LIRA (10 Bin Lira)** **KM# 1042** **Composition:** Copper-Nickel-Zinc **Series:** 1994 Olympics

| Date | Mintage | F | VF | XF | Unc |
|---|---|---|---|---|---|
| 1994 | 500,000 | — | — | — | 3.75 |

**10000 LIRA (10 Bin Lira)** **KM# 1027.2** **Weight:** 6.7500 g. **Composition:** Copper-Nickel-Zinc **Edge:** "TC" six times between reeded sections **Note:** Thin planceht

| Date | Mintage | F | VF | XF | Unc |
|---|---|---|---|---|---|
| 1997 | — | — | 0.10 | 0.25 | 3.00 |
| 1998 | — | — | 0.10 | 0.25 | 3.00 |

**20000 LIRA (20 Bin Lira)** **KM# 998** **Weight:** 23.3200 g. **Composition:** 0.9250 Silver .6938 oz. ASW **Subject:** Environmental Protection

| Date | Mintage | F | VF | XF | Unc |
|---|---|---|---|---|---|
| 1988 Proof | Est. 5,000 | Value: 40.00 | | | |

**20000 LIRA (20 Bin Lira)** **KM# 1001** **Weight:** 23.3200 g. **Composition:** 0.9250 Silver .6938 oz. ASW **Subject:** 400th Anniversary - Death of Architect Sinan **Note:** Similar to 1000 Lira, KM#991.

| Date | Mintage | F | VF | XF | Unc |
|---|---|---|---|---|---|
| ND(1988) Proof | Est. 5,000 | Value: 37.50 | | | |

**20000 LIRA (20 Bin Lira)** **KM# 1003** **Weight:** 23.3200 g. **Composition:** 0.9250 Silver .6938 oz. ASW **Subject:** Teacher's Day **Note:** Similar to 200,000 Lira, KM#1004.

| Date | Mintage | F | VF | XF | Unc |
|---|---|---|---|---|---|
| 1989 Proof | 1,013 | Value: 37.50 | | | |

**20000 LIRA (20 Bin Lira)** **KM# 1013** **Weight:** 23.3200 g. **Composition:** 0.9250 Silver .6938 oz. ASW **Subject:** Istanbul Metro

| Date | Mintage | F | VF | XF | Unc |
|---|---|---|---|---|---|
| ND(1989) Proof | Est. 5,000 | Value: 75.00 | | | |

**20000 LIRA (20 Bin Lira)** **KM# 992** **Weight:** 23.3200 g. **Composition:** 0.9250 Silver .6938 oz. ASW **Subject:** 1990 World Cup Soccer

| Date | Mintage | F | VF | XF | Unc |
|---|---|---|---|---|---|
| 1990 Proof | 14,000 | Value: 25.00 | | | |

**20000 LIRA (20 Bin Lira)** **KM# 993** **Weight:** 23.3200 g. **Composition:** 0.9250 Silver .6938 oz. ASW **Subject:** 75th Anniversary - Battle of Gallipoli

| Date | Mintage | F | VF | XF | Unc |
|---|---|---|---|---|---|
| ND(1990) Proof | Est. 5,000 | Value: 30.00 | | | |

**20000 LIRA (20 Bin Lira)** **KM# 995** **Weight:** 23.3200 g. **Composition:** 0.9250 Silver .6938 oz. ASW **Subject:** Soccer

| Date | Mintage | F | VF | XF | Unc |
|---|---|---|---|---|---|
| 1990 Proof | 14,000 | Value: 25.00 | | | |

**20000 LIRA (20 Bin Lira)** **KM# 1014** **Weight:** 23.3200 g. **Composition:** 0.9250 Silver .6938 oz. ASW **Subject:** 70th Anniversary of Parliament

| Date | Mintage | F | VF | XF | Unc |
|---|---|---|---|---|---|
| 1990 Proof | Est. 5,000 | Value: 27.50 | | | |

**20000 LIRA (20 Bin Lira)** **KM# 1057** **Weight:** 23.3200 g. **Composition:** 0.9250 Silver .6938 oz. ASW **Series:** Summer Olympics **Obverse:** National emblem **Reverse:** Bicyclist

| Date | Mintage | F | VF | XF | Unc |
|---|---|---|---|---|---|
| ND (1990) Proof | — | Value: 30.00 | | | |

**20000 LIRA (20 Bin Lira)** **KM# 1077** **Weight:** 23.4200 g. **Composition:** 0.9250 Silver .6965 oz. ASW **Series:** Olympics **Subject:** Speed Skating **Obverse:** Denomination in wreath **Reverse:** Speed skater

| Date | Mintage | F | VF | XF | Unc |
|---|---|---|---|---|---|
| ND(1990) Proof | — | Value: 30.00 | | | |

**25000 LIRA (25 Bin Lira)** **KM# 1041** **Composition:** Copper-Nickel-Zinc **Edge:** Lettered TC and flower five times

| Date | Mintage | F | VF | XF | Unc |
|---|---|---|---|---|---|
| 1995 | 13,740,000 | 0.20 | 0.30 | 0.50 | 3.00 |
| 1996 | 59,742,000 | 0.20 | 0.30 | 0.50 | 3.00 |
| 1997 | — | 0.20 | 0.30 | 0.50 | 3.00 |
| 1998 | — | 0.20 | 0.30 | 0.50 | 3.00 |

**25000 LIRA (25 Bin Lira)** **KM# 1043** **Composition:** Copper-Nickel-Zinc **Series:** Environmental Protection **Reverse:** Three human heads

| Date | Mintage | F | VF | XF | Unc |
|---|---|---|---|---|---|
| 1995 | 500,000 | — | — | — | 5.00 |

**25000 LIRA (25 Bin Lira)** **KM# 1104** **Weight:** 2.7000 g. **Composition:** Copper-Zinc **Obverse:** Bust of Kemal Atatürk **Reverse:** Denomination **Edge:** Plain **Size:** 17 mm.

| Date | Mintage | F | VF | XF | Unc |
|---|---|---|---|---|---|
| 2001 | — | — | — | — | 2.50 |

**30000 LIRA** **KM# 955** **Weight:** 15.9800 g. **Composition:** 0.9170 Gold .4712 oz. AGW **Series:** International Year of Disabled Persons

| Date | Mintage | F | VF | XF | Unc |
|---|---|---|---|---|---|
| 1981 | 4,000 | — | — | — | 400 |
| 1981 Proof | 3,000 | Value: 450 | | | |

**30000 LIRA** **KM# 961** **Weight:** 15.9800 g. **Composition:** 0.9170 Gold .4712 oz. AGW **Series:** International Year of the Scout **Obverse:** Denomination within sprays

| Date | Mintage | F | VF | XF | Unc |
|---|---|---|---|---|---|
| ND(1983) | 2,000 | — | — | — | 450 |
| ND(1983) Proof | 2,000 | Value: 500 | | | |

**50000 LIRA** **KM# 973** **Weight:** 7.1300 g. **Composition:** 0.9000 Gold .2063 oz. AGW **Series:** Decade for Women

| Date | Mintage | F | VF | XF | Unc |
|---|---|---|---|---|---|
| 1984 Proof | 800 | Value: 135 | | | |

**50000 LIRA** **KM# 999** **Weight:** 28.2800 g. **Composition:** 0.9250 Silver .8411 oz. ASW **Series:** Winter Olympics **Reverse:** Speed skater

| Date | Mintage | F | VF | XF | Unc |
|---|---|---|---|---|---|
| ND(1990) Proof | 15,000 | Value: 30.00 | | | |

**50000 LIRA** **KM# 1000** **Weight:** 28.2800 g. **Composition:** 0.9250 Silver .8411 oz. ASW **Series:** 1990 Summer Olympics **Reverse:** Bicyclist

| Date | Mintage | F | VF | XF | Unc |
|---|---|---|---|---|---|
| ND(1990) Proof | 15,000 | Value: 30.00 | | | |

**50000 LIRA** **KM# 1006** **Weight:** 22.8700 g. **Composition:** 0.9250 Silver .6801 oz. ASW **Subject:** Yunus Emre Sevgi Yili

| Date | Mintage | F | VF | XF | Unc |
|---|---|---|---|---|---|
| 1991 Proof | 5,000 | Value: 28.00 | | | |

**50000 LIRA** **KM# 1007** **Weight:** 22.8700 g. **Composition:** 0.9250 Silver .6801 oz. ASW **Subject:** Mozart Opera

| Date | Mintage | F | VF | XF | Unc |
|---|---|---|---|---|---|
| ND(1991) Proof | 5,000 | Value: 30.00 | | | |

**50000 LIRA** **KM# 1019** **Weight:** 22.7700 g. **Composition:** 0.9250 Silver .6772 oz. ASW **Subject:** Hmet Adnan Saygun - Musician

| Date | Mintage | F | VF | XF | Unc |
|---|---|---|---|---|---|
| ND(1991) Proof | — | Value: 30.00 | | | |

**50000 LIRA** **KM# 1016** **Weight:** 23.3300 g. **Composition:** 0.9250 Silver .6858 oz. ASW **Subject:** Turkish Jews

| Date | Mintage | F | VF | XF | Unc |
|---|---|---|---|---|---|
| ND(1992) Proof | Est. 5,000 | Value: 25.00 | | | |

**50000 LIRA** **KM# 1023** **Weight:** 23.0800 g. **Composition:** 0.9250 Silver .6184 oz. ASW **Subject:** 200th Birthday of Rossini

| Date | Mintage | F | VF | XF | Unc |
|---|---|---|---|---|---|
| ND(1992) Proof | — | Value: 25.00 | | | |

**50000 LIRA** **KM# 1020** **Weight:** 23.0800 g. **Composition:** 0.9250 Silver .6184 oz. ASW **Subject:** 1994 World Cup Soccer **Reverse:** Torch with ball

| Date | Mintage | F | VF | XF | Unc |
|---|---|---|---|---|---|
| ND(1993) Proof | Est. 20,000 | Value: 28.00 | | | |

**50000 LIRA** **KM# 1021.1** **Weight:** 23.0800 g. **Composition:** 0.9250 Silver .6184 oz. ASW **Subject:** 1994 World Cup Soccer **Reverse:** Bridge behind player, fuzzy looking rock under bridge

| Date | Mintage | F | VF | XF | Unc |
|---|---|---|---|---|---|
| ND(1993) | 400 | — | — | — | 75.00 |
| ND(1993) Proof | Est. 20,000 | Value: 25.00 | | | |

**50000 LIRA** **KM# 1021.2** **Weight:** 23.0800 g. **Composition:** 0.9250 Silver .6184 oz. ASW **Subject:** 1994 World Cup Soccer **Reverse:** Bridge behind player, sharp looking rock under bridge

| Date | Mintage | F | VF | XF | Unc |
|---|---|---|---|---|---|
| ND(1993) Proof | 1,000 | Value: 40.00 | | | |

**50000 LIRA** **KM# 1044** **Weight:** 23.0800 g. **Composition:** 0.9250 Silver .6184 oz. ASW **Subject:** 125 Years - Turkish Supreme Court

| Date | Mintage | F | VF | XF | Unc |
|---|---|---|---|---|---|
| ND(1993) Proof | — | Value: 30.00 | | | |

**50000 LIRA** **KM# 1024** **Weight:** 23.0800 g. **Composition:** 0.9250 Silver .6184 oz. ASW **Subject:** 25th Anniversary of Turkish Red Crescent

| Date | Mintage | F | VF | XF | Unc |
|---|---|---|---|---|---|
| ND(1993) Proof | — | Value: 25.00 | | | |

**50000 LIRA** **KM# 1026** **Weight:** 22.8400 g. **Composition:** 0.9250 Silver .6793 oz. ASW **Series:** Olympics **Reverse:** Flag and rings

| Date | Mintage | F | VF | XF | Unc |
|---|---|---|---|---|---|
| ND(1994) Proof | 5,000 | Value: 25.00 | | | |

**50000 LIRA** **KM# 1030** **Weight:** 31.4700 g. **Composition:** 0.9250 Silver .9359 oz. ASW **Series:** Endagered Wildlife **Reverse:** Ibis

| Date | Mintage | F | VF | XF | Unc |
|---|---|---|---|---|---|
| ND(1994) Proof | 10,000 | Value: 20.00 | | | |

**50000 LIRA** **KM# 1031** **Weight:** 23.3300 g. **Composition:** 0.9250 Silver .6938 oz. ASW **Subject:** Tschaikovsky

| Date | Mintage | F | VF | XF | Unc |
|---|---|---|---|---|---|
| ND(1994) Proof | 5,000 | Value: 27.50 | | | |

**50000 LIRA** **KM# 1033** **Weight:** 23.3300 g. **Composition:** 0.9250 Silver .6938 oz. ASW **Subject:** 75th Anniversary - Turkish National Assembly

| Date | Mintage | F | VF | XF | Unc |
|---|---|---|---|---|---|
| 1995 Proof | 10,000 | Value: 25.00 | | | |

**50000 LIRA** **KM# 1035** **Weight:** 23.3300 g. **Composition:** 0.9250 Silver .6938 oz. ASW **Subject:** 150th Anniversary - National Police

| Date | Mintage | F | VF | XF | Unc |
|---|---|---|---|---|---|
| 1995 Proof | 10,000 | Value: 22.50 | | | |

**50000 LIRA** **KM# 1037** **Composition:** Brass **Reverse:** Sea turtle **Note:** Oxidized finish

| Date | Mintage | F | VF | XF | Unc |
|---|---|---|---|---|---|
| 1995 | 10,000 | — | — | — | 16.50 |

**50000 LIRA** **KM# 1037a** **Weight:** 23.3300 g. **Composition:** 0.9250 Silver .6938 oz. ASW

| Date | Mintage | F | VF | XF | Unc |
|---|---|---|---|---|---|
| 1995 Proof | 15,000 | Value: 22.50 | | | |

**50000 LIRA** **KM# 1038** **Weight:** 23.3300 g. **Composition:** 0.9250 Silver .6938 oz. ASW **Subject:** Sailing ship - "Piri Reis"

| Date | Mintage | F | VF | XF | Unc |
|---|---|---|---|---|---|
| 1995 Proof | 15,000 | Value: 25.00 | | | |

**50000 LIRA** **KM# 1040** **Weight:** 23.3300 g. **Composition:** 0.9250 Silver .6938 oz. ASW **Series:** 50th Anniversary - F.A.O.

| Date | Mintage | F | VF | XF | Unc |
|---|---|---|---|---|---|
| 1995 Proof | 15,000 | Value: 25.00 | | | |

**50000 LIRA** **KM# 1045** **Weight:** 31.4700 g. **Composition:** 0.9250 Silver .9359 oz. ASW **Series:** Summer Olympics **Reverse:** Wrestlers

| Date | Mintage | F | VF | XF | Unc |
|---|---|---|---|---|---|
| 1995 Proof | Est. 30,000 | Value: 30.00 | | | |

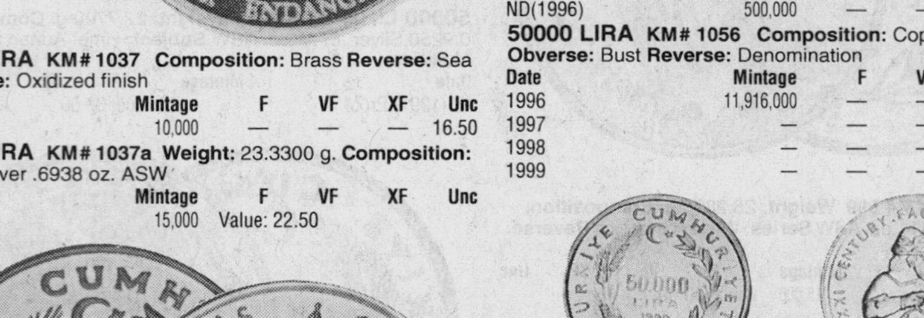


**50000 LIRA** **KM# 1050** **Composition:** Copper-Nickel-Zinc **Series:** F.A.O. **Edge:** "T.C." and four fleur-de-lis repeated four times

| Date | Mintage | F | VF | XF | Unc |
|---|---|---|---|---|---|
| ND(1996) | 500,000 | — | — | — | 4.50 |

**50000 LIRA** **KM# 1056** **Composition:** Copper-Nickel-Zinc **Obverse:** Bust **Reverse:** Denomination

| Date | Mintage | F | VF | XF | Unc |
|---|---|---|---|---|---|
| 1996 | 11,916,000 | — | — | — | 3.50 |
| 1997 | — | — | — | — | 3.50 |
| 1998 | — | — | — | — | 3.50 |
| 1999 | — | — | — | — | 3.50 |

**50000 LIRA** **KM# 1103** **Composition:** Aluminum **Series:** F.A.O **Obverse:** Denomination **Reverse:** Ancient vintner **Edge:** Plain **Size:** 20 mm.

| Date | Mintage | F | VF | XF | Unc |
|---|---|---|---|---|---|
| 1999 | — | — | — | — | 0.75 |

**50000 LIRA** **KM# 1105** **Weight:** 3.2000 g. **Composition:** Copper-Nickel-Zinc **Obverse:** Ataturk's portrait **Reverse:** Denomination **Edge:** Plain **Size:** 17.75 mm.

| Date | Mintage | F | VF | XF | Unc |
|---|---|---|---|---|---|
| 2001 | — | — | — | — | 3.00 |

**100000 LIRA** **KM# 956** **Weight:** 33.8200 g. **Composition:** 0.9170 Gold .9972 oz. AGW **Subject:** Islamic World 15th Century

| Date | Mintage | F | VF | XF | Unc |
|---|---|---|---|---|---|
| 1982 Proof | 12,000 | Value: 650 | | | |

**100000 LIRA** **KM# 1078** **Composition:** Copper-Nickel-Zinc **Subject:** 75th Anniversary of Republic **Obverse:** Denomination **Reverse:** Bust of Kemal Atatürk right

| Date | Mintage | F | VF | XF | Unc |
|---|---|---|---|---|---|
| 1999 | — | — | — | — | 3.00 |

**100000 LIRA** **KM# 1079** **Composition:** Copper-Nickel-Zinc **Subject:** 75th Anniversary of Republic **Obverse:** Denomination **Reverse:** Anniversary logo and dates

| Date | Mintage | F | VF | XF | Unc |
|---|---|---|---|---|---|
| 1999 | — | — | — | — | 4.00 |

**100000 LIRA** **KM# 1106** **Weight:** 4.6000 g. **Composition:** Copper-Nickel-Zinc **Obverse:** Ataturk wearing hat **Reverse:** Denomination **Edge:** Plain **Size:** 21 mm.

| Date | Mintage | F | VF | XF | Unc |
|---|---|---|---|---|---|
| 2001 | — | — | — | — | 3.50 |

**200000 LIRA** **KM# 974** **Weight:** 33.8200 g. **Composition:** 0.9170 Gold .9972 oz. AGW **Subject:** 50th Anniversary of Women's Suffrage

| Date | Mintage | F | VF | XF | Unc |
|---|---|---|---|---|---|
| ND(1984) Proof | 58 | Value: 1,850 | | | |

**200000 LIRA** **KM# 1002** **Weight:** 7.2160 g. **Composition:** 0.9170 Gold .2126 oz. AGW **Subject:** 400th Anniversary - Death of Architect Sinan **Note:** Similar to 1000 Lira, KM#991

| Date | Mintage | F | VF | XF | Unc |
|---|---|---|---|---|---|
| ND(1988) Proof | 500 | Value: 325 | | | |

**200000 LIRA** **KM# 1004** **Weight:** 7.2160 g. **Composition:** 0.9170 Gold .2126 oz. AGW **Subject:** Teacher's Day

| Date | Mintage | F | VF | XF | Unc |
|---|---|---|---|---|---|
| 1989 Proof | 197 | Value: 350 | | | |

**200000 LIRA** **KM# 994** **Weight:** 7.2160 g. **Composition:** 0.9170 Gold .2126 oz. AGW **Subject:** 75th Anniversary - Battle of Gallipoli

| Date | Mintage | F | VF | XF | Unc |
|---|---|---|---|---|---|
| ND(1990) Proof | Est. 500 | Value: 325 | | | |

**400000 LIRA** **KM# 1051** **Composition:** Bronze **Subject:** Habitat II **Obverse:** City view **Reverse:** Conference logo

| Date | Mintage | F | VF | XF | Unc |
|---|---|---|---|---|---|
| 1996 | 5,000 | — | — | — | 12.50 |

**500000 LIRA** **KM# 1008** **Weight:** 7.1300 g. **Composition:** 0.9000 Gold .2063 oz. AGW **Subject:** Yunus Emre

| Date | Mintage | F | VF | XF | Unc |
|---|---|---|---|---|---|
| 1991 Proof | 500 | Value: 320 | | | |

**500000 LIRA** **KM# 1017** **Weight:** 7.1400 g. **Composition:** 0.9000 Gold .2066 oz. AGW **Subject:** 100 Years of Peace and Harmony - Turkish Jews

| Date | Mintage | F | VF | XF | Unc |
|---|---|---|---|---|---|
| ND(1992) Proof | — | Value: 320 | | | |

**500000 LIRA** **KM# 1032** **Weight:** 7.2160 g. **Composition:** 0.9166 Gold .2126 oz. AGW **Subject:** Southeast Anatolian Project

| Date | Mintage | F | VF | XF | Unc |
|---|---|---|---|---|---|
| ND(1994) Proof | 1,500 | Value: 300 | | | |

**500000 LIRA** **KM# 1034** **Weight:** 7.2160 g. **Composition:** 0.9166 Gold .2126 oz. AGW **Subject:** 75th Anniversary - Turkish National Assembly

| Date | Mintage | F | VF | XF | Unc |
|---|---|---|---|---|---|
| 1995 Proof | 1,000 | Value: 300 | | | |

**500000 LIRA** **KM# 1036** **Weight:** 7.2160 g. **Composition:** 0.9166 Gold .2126 oz. AGW **Subject:** Istanbul Gold Exchange

| Date | Mintage | F | VF | XF | Unc |
|---|---|---|---|---|---|
| 1995 Proof | 1,000 | Value: 300 | | | |

**500000 LIRA** **KM# 1039** **Weight:** 7.2160 g. **Composition:** 0.9166 Gold .2126 oz. AGW **Subject:** Sailing Ship - "Piri Reis"

| Date | Mintage | F | VF | XF | Unc |
|---|---|---|---|---|---|
| 1995 Proof | 1,000 | Value: 300 | | | |

**EURO (500000 Lira)** **KM# 1081** **Weight:** 11.9100 g. **Composition:** Copper-Nickel **Subject:** Trojan Horse **Obverse:** Denomination **Reverse:** Ancient Greek soldier and wooden horse **Edge:** Reeded **Note:** Struck at Istanbul.

| Date | Mintage | F | VF | XF | Unc |
|---|---|---|---|---|---|
| 1999 | — | — | — | — | 15.00 |

**750000 LIRA** **KM# 1046** **Weight:** 31.4700 g. **Composition:** 0.9250 Silver .9359 oz. ASW **Subject:** Europa - Various Landmarks

| Date | Mintage | F | VF | XF | Unc |
|---|---|---|---|---|---|
| 1996 Proof | Est. 35,000 | Value: 22.50 | | | |

**750000 LIRA** **KM# 1048.1** **Weight:** 23.2000 g. **Composition:** 0.9250 Silver .6899 oz. ASW **Series:** F.A.O.

| Date | Mintage | F | VF | XF | Unc |
|---|---|---|---|---|---|
| 1996 Proof | — | Value: 18.50 | | | |

**750000 LIRA** **KM# 1048.2** **Weight:** 23.2000 g. **Composition:** 0.9250 Silver .6899 oz. ASW **Reverse:** World globe with corn stalks at right

| Date | Mintage | F | VF | XF | Unc |
|---|---|---|---|---|---|
| 1996 Proof | — | Value: 22.50 | | | |

**750000 LIRA** **KM# 1049** **Weight:** 23.4100 g. **Composition:** 0.9250 Silver .6962 oz. ASW **Subject:** Turkish European Customs Union

| Date | Mintage | F | VF | XF | Unc |
|---|---|---|---|---|---|
| 1996 Proof | — | Value: 22.50 | | | |

**750000 LIRA KM# 1052 Weight:** 23.3700 g. **Composition:** 0.9250 Silver .6950 oz. ASW **Subject:** Nasreddin Hoca

| Date | Mintage | F | VF | XF | Unc |
|---|---|---|---|---|---|
| 1996 Proof | 5,000 | Value: 22.50 | | | |

**750000 LIRA KM# 1063 Weight:** 31.4700 g. **Composition:** 0.9250 Silver .9359 oz. ASW **Subject:** World Cup Soccer **Obverse:** Denomination **Reverse:** Goalie catching ball

| Date | Mintage | F | VF | XF | Unc |
|---|---|---|---|---|---|
| 1996 Proof | 15,000 | Value: 30.00 | | | |

**750000 LIRA KM# 1058 Composition:** Bronze **Subject:** First World Air Games - Manned Flight

| Date | Mintage | F | VF | XF | Unc |
|---|---|---|---|---|---|
| 1997 | — | — | — | — | 10.00 |

**750000 LIRA KM# 1059 Composition:** Bronze **Subject:** XI World Forestry Congress **Reverse:** Stylized bird and tree

| Date | Mintage | F | VF | XF | Unc |
|---|---|---|---|---|---|
| 1997 | — | — | — | — | 12.50 |

**750000 LIRA KM# 1068 Composition:** Bronze **Subject:** Forestry - "TEMA"

| Date | Mintage | F | VF | XF | Unc |
|---|---|---|---|---|---|
| 1998 | — | — | — | — | 15.00 |

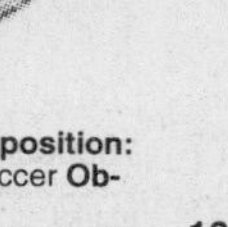

**1000000 LIRA KM# 1047 Weight:** 31.7200 g. **Composition:** 0.9250 Silver .9433 oz. ASW **Series:** Endangered Wildlife **Reverse:** Mediterranean seal

| Date | Mintage | F | VF | XF | Unc |
|---|---|---|---|---|---|
| 1996 Proof | — | Value: 25.00 | | | |

**1000000 LIRA KM# 1053 Weight:** 31.4600 g. **Composition:** 0.9250 Silver .9356 oz. ASW **Series:** Endangered Wildlife **Reverse:** Galathus Elwesii flowers

| Date | Mintage | F | VF | XF | Unc |
|---|---|---|---|---|---|
| 1996 Proof | 5,000 | Value: 22.50 | | | |

**1000000 LIRA KM# 1054 Weight:** 31.4600 g. **Composition:** 0.9250 Silver .9356 oz. ASW **Subject:** Habitat II

| Date | Mintage | F | VF | XF | Unc |
|---|---|---|---|---|---|
| 1996 Proof | 5,000 | Value: 25.00 | | | |

**1000000 LIRA KM# 1055 Weight:** 31.7700 g. **Composition:** 0.9250 Silver .9448 oz. ASW **Subject:** Bust of Hulusi Behcet facing

| Date | Mintage | F | VF | XF | Unc |
|---|---|---|---|---|---|
| 1996 Proof | 5,000 | Value: 22.50 | | | |

**1000000 LIRA KM# 1060 Weight:** 31.5700 g. **Composition:** 0.9250 Silver .9389 oz. ASW **Subject:** Chinese History - Excavation of the Terra Cotta Army **Obverse:** Great Wall of China

| Date | Mintage | F | VF | XF | Unc |
|---|---|---|---|---|---|
| 1997 | 5,000 | — | — | — | 22.50 |

**Note:** This coin does not have any national identification other than the mintmark and denomination

**1000000 LIRA KM# 1066 Weight:** 1.2441 g. **Composition:** 0.9990 Gold .0400 oz. AGW **Obverse:** Denomination in wreath **Reverse:** Head of King Croesus of Lydia right **Edge:** Reeded **Note:** Struck at Istanbul.

| Date | Mintage | F | VF | XF | Unc |
|---|---|---|---|---|---|
| 1997 Proof | — | Value: 50.00 | | | |

**1000000 LIRA KM# 1067 Weight:** 1.2441 g. **Composition:** 0.9990 Gold **Reverse:** Ancient Lydian coin portraying lion

| Date | Mintage | F | VF | XF | Unc |
|---|---|---|---|---|---|
| 1997 Proof | — | Value: 50.00 | | | |

**1000000 LIRA KM# 1069 Weight:** 31.4400 g. **Composition:** 0.9250 Silver .9350 oz. ASW **Subject:** Mehmed Akif Ersoy **Obverse:** Spiral inscription

| Date | Mintage | F | VF | XF | Unc |
|---|---|---|---|---|---|
| 1997 Proof | Est. 5,000 | Value: 22.50 | | | |

**1500000 LIRA** **KM# 1061** **Weight:** 31.4400 g. **Composition:** 0.9250 Silver .9350 oz. ASW **Subject:** First World Air Games - Manned Flight

| Date | Mintage | F | VF | XF | Unc |
|---|---|---|---|---|---|
| 1997 Proof | 5,000 | Value: 25.00 | | | |

**1500000 LIRA** **KM# 1062** **Weight:** 31.4400 g. **Composition:** 0.9250 Silver .9350 oz. ASW **Subject:** XI World Forestry Conference **Reverse:** Stylized bird and tree

| Date | Mintage | F | VF | XF | Unc |
|---|---|---|---|---|---|
| 1997 Proof | 5,000 | Value: 25.00 | | | |

**1500000 LIRA** **KM# 1082** **Weight:** 31.3300 g. **Composition:** 0.9250 Silver .9317 oz. ASW **Subject:** Barbaros Mayreddin **Obverse:** Denomination in wreath **Reverse:** Two war ships c.1533 **Edge:** Reeded **Note:** Struck at Istanbul.

| Date | Mintage | F | VF | XF | Unc |
|---|---|---|---|---|---|
| 1997 Proof | 3,000 | Value: 30.00 | | | |

**1500000 LIRA** **KM# 1100** **Weight:** 31.3700 g. **Composition:** 0.9250 Silver .9329 oz. ASW **Subject:** Myra'li Aziz Noel Baba and Euro **Obverse:** Denomination **Reverse:** Statue and tower **Edge:** Reeded **Size:** 38.6 mm.

| Date | Mintage | F | VF | XF | Unc |
|---|---|---|---|---|---|
| 1997 Proof | — | Value: 25.00 | | | |

**2500000 LIRA** **KM# 1064** **Weight:** 31.1500 g. **Composition:** 0.9250 Silver .9264 oz. ASW **Subject:** Hasan-Sali Yucel

| Date | Mintage | F | VF | XF | Unc |
|---|---|---|---|---|---|
| 1998 Proof | Est. 5,000 | Value: 22.50 | | | |

**2500000 LIRA** **KM# 1065** **Weight:** 31.5800 g. **Composition:** 0.9250 Silver .9392 oz. ASW **Subject:** Forestry - "TEMA" **Reverse:** Wheel of trees design

| Date | Mintage | F | VF | XF | Unc |
|---|---|---|---|---|---|
| 1998 Proof | Est. 5,000 | Value: 22.50 | | | |

**2500000 LIRA** **KM# 1070** **Weight:** 31.4400 g. **Composition:** 0.9250 Silver .9350 oz. ASW **Subject:** 75 Years of Peace **Reverse:** Doves, treaty, and radiant sun

| Date | Mintage | F | VF | XF | Unc |
|---|---|---|---|---|---|
| 1998 Proof | Est. 5,000 | Value: 25.00 | | | |

**2500000 LIRA** **KM# 1083** **Weight:** 31.3500 g. **Composition:** 0.9250 Silver .9323 oz. ASW **Series:** 2000 Olympics **Obverse:** Denomination in wreath **Reverse:** Weight lifter and mosque **Edge:** Reeded **Note:** Struck at Istanbul.

| Date | Mintage | F | VF | XF | Unc |
|---|---|---|---|---|---|
| 1998 Proof | 3,000 | Value: 25.00 | | | |

**10 EURO (2500000 Lira)** **KM# 1084** **Weight:** 23.3000 g. **Composition:** 0.9250 Silver .6929 oz. ASW **Subject:** Ataturk **Obverse:** Denomination in wreath **Reverse:** Head of Kemal Atatürk left **Edge:** Reeded **Note:** Struck at Istanbul.

| Date | Mintage | F | VF | XF | Unc |
|---|---|---|---|---|---|
| 1998 Proof | 3,000 | Value: 35.00 | | | |

**3000000 LIRA** **KM# 1071** **Weight:** 31.3233 g. **Composition:** 0.9250 Silver .9315 oz. ASW **Subject:** 75 Years of Peace **Obverse:** 75th Anniversary logo **Reverse:** Doves, treaty, and radiant sun

| Date | Mintage | F | VF | XF | Unc |
|---|---|---|---|---|---|
| ND(1998) Proof | Est. 5,000 | Value: 30.00 | | | |

**3000000 LIRA** **KM# 1072** **Weight:** 31.3233 g. **Composition:** 0.9250 Silver .9315 oz. ASW **Subject:** 75th Anniversary Republic **Obverse:** 75th Anniversary logo **Reverse:** Two revolutionaries, head of Kemal Atatürk behind

| Date | Mintage | F | VF | XF | Unc |
|---|---|---|---|---|---|
| ND(1998) Proof | Est. 5,000 | Value: 30.00 | | | |

**3000000 LIRA** **KM# 1073** **Weight:** 31.3233 g. **Composition:** 0.9250 Silver .9315 oz. ASW **Subject:** 75th Anniversary of Republic **Obverse:** 75th Anniversary logo

| Date | Mintage | F | VF | XF | Unc |
|---|---|---|---|---|---|
| ND(1998) Proof | Est. 5,000 | Value: 30.00 | | | |

**3000000 LIRA** **KM# 1074** **Weight:** 31.3233 g. **Composition:** 0.9250 Silver .9315 oz. ASW **Obverse:** 75th Anniversary logo **Reverse:** Ataturk with children

| Date | Mintage | F | VF | XF | Unc |
|---|---|---|---|---|---|
| ND(1998) Proof | Est. 5,000 | Value: 30.00 | | | |

**3000000 LIRA** **KM# 1075** **Weight:** 31.3233 g. **Composition:** 0.9250 Silver .9315 oz. ASW **Obverse:** 75th Anniversary logo **Reverse:** Ataturk with cane before crowd

| Date | Mintage | F | VF | XF | Unc |
|---|---|---|---|---|---|
| ND(1998) Proof | Est. 5,000 | Value: 30.00 | | | |

**3000000 LIRA** **KM# 1076** **Weight:** 31.3233 g. **Composition:** 0.9250 Silver .9315 oz. ASW **Obverse:** 75th Anniversary logo **Reverse:** Depictions of arts and sciences in Turkey

| Date | Mintage | F | VF | XF | Unc |
|---|---|---|---|---|---|
| ND(1998) Proof | Est. 5,000 | Value: 30.00 | | | |

**3000000 LIRA** **KM# 1107** **Weight:** 31.4700 g. **Composition:** 0.9250 Silver .9359 oz. ASW **Series:** Olympics **Obverse:** Denomination **Reverse:** Long jumper and logo **Edge:** Reeded **Size:** 38.6 mm.

| Date | Mintage | F | VF | XF | Unc |
|---|---|---|---|---|---|
| 1999 Proof | 31,000 | Value: 35.00 | | | |

**EURO (3000000 Lira)** **KM# 1080** **Weight:** 31.4700 g. **Composition:** 0.9250 Silver .9359 oz. ASW **Obverse:** Denomination in wreath **Reverse:** Dolmababce Palace

| Date | Mintage | F | VF | XF | Unc |
|---|---|---|---|---|---|
| 1998 Proof | — | Value: 30.00 | | | |

**EURO (3000000 Lira)** **KM# 1086** **Weight:** 31.3600 g. **Composition:** 0.9250 Silver .9326 oz. ASW **Subject:** Galata Kulesi **Reverse:** Tower and city view above "EURO"

| Date | Mintage | F | VF | XF | Unc |
|---|---|---|---|---|---|
| 1998 Proof | 3,000 | Value: 32.50 | | | |

**EURO (3000000 Lira)** **KM# 1085** **Weight:** 31.3600 g. **Composition:** 0.9250 Silver .9326 oz. ASW **Subject:** Dolmabance Sarayi Palace **Obverse:** Denomination in wreath **Reverse:** Building above "EURO" **Edge:** Reeded **Note:** Struck at Istanbul.

| Date | Mintage | F | VF | XF | Unc |
|---|---|---|---|---|---|
| 1998 Proof | 3,000 | Value: 32.50 | | | |

**4000000 LIRA** **KM# 1108** **Weight:** 31.4700 g. **Composition:** 0.9250 Silver .9359 oz. ASW **Subject:** Ataturk **Obverse:** Denomination **Reverse:** Atatruk's portrait below "EURO" **Edge:** Reeded **Size:** 38.6 mm.

| Date | Mintage | F | VF | XF | Unc |
|---|---|---|---|---|---|
| 1999 Proof | — | Value: 35.00 | | | |

**4000000 LIRA** **KM# 1087** **Weight:** 31.4000 g. **Composition:** 0.9250 Silver .9338 oz. ASW **Subject:** Fethiye **Obverse:** Denomination in wreath **Reverse:** Two sailing ships **Edge:** Reeded **Note:** Struck at Istanbul.

| Date | Mintage | F | VF | XF | Unc |
|---|---|---|---|---|---|
| 1999 Proof | 13,000 | Value: 30.00 | | | |

**4000000 LIRA** **KM# 1088** **Weight:** 31.4000 g. **Composition:** 0.9250 Silver .9338 oz. ASW **Subject:** 80th Anniversary - Atatürk's Landing at Samsun **Reverse:** Atatürk's bust above steam ship

| Date | Mintage | F | VF | XF | Unc |
|---|---|---|---|---|---|
| 1999 Proof | 27 | Value: 27.50 | | | |

**4000000 LIRA** **KM# 1089** **Weight:** 31.4000 g. **Composition:** 0.9250 Silver .9338 oz. ASW **Subject:** Istanbul Culture Capital **Reverse:** Topkane Cesmesi

| Date | Mintage | F | VF | XF | Unc |
|---|---|---|---|---|---|
| 1999 Proof | 5,000 | Value: 32.50 | | | |

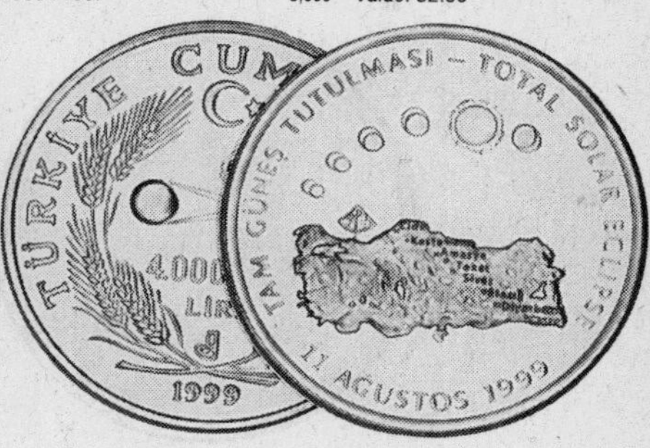


**4000000 LIRA** **KM# 1090** **Weight:** 31.4000 g. **Composition:** 0.9250 Silver .9338 oz. ASW **Subject:** Solar Eclipse **Reverse:** Eclipse stages above map

| Date | Mintage | F | VF | XF | Unc |
|---|---|---|---|---|---|
| 1999 Proof | 35 | Value: 35.00 | | | |

**4000000 LIRA** **KM# 1091** **Weight:** 31.4000 g. **Composition:** 0.9250 Silver .9338 oz. ASW **Subject:** Solar Eclipse **Reverse:** People watching eclipse

| Date | Mintage | F | VF | XF | Unc |
|---|---|---|---|---|---|
| 1999 Proof | 5,000 | Value: 35.00 | | | |

**4000000 LIRA** **KM# 1092** **Weight:** 31.4000 g. **Composition:** 0.9250 Silver .9338 oz. ASW **Subject:** Silk Road **Obverse:** Scroll design with landmarks **Reverse:** Mounted archer hunting lion **Note:** Antiqued finish.

| Date | Mintage | F | VF | XF | Unc |
|---|---|---|---|---|---|
| 1999 Proof | 5,000 | Value: 35.00 | | | |

**4000000 LIRA** **KM# 1093** **Weight:** 31.4000 g. **Composition:** 0.9250 Silver .9338 oz. ASW **Subject:** Osman Gazi **Reverse:** Turbaned 1/2-length bust of Osman Gazi facing half left

| Date | Mintage | F | VF | XF | Unc |
|---|---|---|---|---|---|
| 1999 Proof | 5,000 | Value: 32.50 | | | |

**4000000 LIRA** **KM# 1094** **Weight:** 31.4000 g. **Composition:** 0.9250 Silver .9338 oz. ASW **Reverse:** Gazi leading mounted troops

| Date | Mintage | F | VF | XF | Unc |
|---|---|---|---|---|---|
| 1999 Proof | 5,000 | Value: 32.50 | | | |

**4000000 LIRA** **KM# 1095** **Weight:** 31.4000 g. **Composition:** 0.9250 Silver .9338 oz. ASW **Reverse:** Mounted archers and prey

| Date | Mintage | F | VF | XF | Unc |
|---|---|---|---|---|---|
| 1999 Proof | 5,000 | Value: 32.50 | | | |

**4000000 LIRA** **KM# 1099** **Weight:** 31.4100 g. **Composition:** 0.9250 Silver .9341 oz. ASW **Subject:** Lacerta Clarkorum **Obverse:** Denomination **Reverse:** Two lizards **Edge:** Reeded **Size:** 38.6 mm.

| Date | Mintage | F | VF | XF | Unc |
|---|---|---|---|---|---|
| 1999 Proof | — | Value: 35.00 | | | |

**4000000 LIRA** **KM# 1096** **Weight:** 31.4000 g. **Composition:** 0.9250 Silver .9338 oz. ASW **Reverse:** 700-year-old Islamic coin design

| Date | Mintage | F | VF | XF | Unc |
|---|---|---|---|---|---|
| 1999 Proof | 32 | Value: 32.50 | | | |

**4000000 LIRA** **KM# 1109** **Weight:** 31.4700 g. **Composition:** 0.9250 Silver .9359 oz. ASW **Subject:** "Bogazici" (Bosphorus) **Obverse:** Denomination **Reverse:** Water front mosque above "EURO" **Edge:** Reeded **Size:** 38.6 mm.

| Date | Mintage | F | VF | XF | Unc |
|---|---|---|---|---|---|
| 1999 Proof | 23,000 | Value: 35.00 | | | |

**5000000 LIRA** **KM# 1110** **Weight:** 67.0000 g. **Composition:** Bronze **Subject:** Children's Day **Obverse:** Legend and inscription **Reverse:** Dancing children **Edge:** Plain **Size:** 50 mm.

| Date | Mintage | F | VF | XF | Unc |
|---|---|---|---|---|---|
| 2001 Matte | 15,000 | — | — | — | 10.00 |

**60000000 LIRA** **KM# 1097** **Weight:** 15.0000 g. **Composition:** 0.9167 Gold .4921 oz. AGW **Subject:** 700th Anniversary - The Ottoman Empire **Obverse:** Denomination in wreath **Reverse:** Ottoman coat of arms **Edge:** Reeded **Note:** Struck at Istanbul.

| Date | Mintage | F | VF | XF | Unc |
|---|---|---|---|---|---|
| 1999 Proof | 5,000 | Value: 300 | | | |

**7500000 LIRA** **KM# 1101** **Weight:** 31.4000 g. **Composition:** 0.7500 Silver .7571 oz. ASW **Subject:** 34th World Chess Olympiad **Obverse:** World globe with chess pieces **Reverse:** Logo and horse head **Edge:** Reeded **Size:** 38.6 mm.

| Date | Mintage | F | VF | XF | Unc |
|---|---|---|---|---|---|
| 2000 Proof | Est. 1,000 | Value: 40.00 | | | |

**7500000 LIRA** **KM# 1102** **Weight:** 23.3300 g. **Composition:** 0.9250 Silver .6938 oz. ASW **Subject:** UNICEF **Obverse:** Denomination **Reverse:** Two children candle dancing **Edge:** Reeded **Size:** 38.6 mm.

| Date | Mintage | F | VF | XF | Unc |
|---|---|---|---|---|---|
| 2000 Proof | — | Value: 50.00 | | | |

**7500000 LIRA** **KM# 1111** **Weight:** 31.4700 g. **Composition:** 0.9250 Silver .9359 oz. ASW **Subject:** Ephesus' Celcius Library **Obverse:** Mint logo and denomination **Reverse:** Building **Edge:** Reeded **Size:** 38.6 mm.

| Date | Mintage | F | VF | XF | Unc |
|---|---|---|---|---|---|
| 2000 Matte | 15,000 | — | — | — | 35.00 |
| 2000 Proof | 15,000 | Value: 35.00 | | | |

**7500000 LIRA** **KM# 1112** **Weight:** 31.4700 g. **Composition:** 0.9250 Silver .9359 oz. ASW **Subject:** Traditional Turkish Theater **Obverse:** Mint logo and denomination **Reverse:** Marionette theater scene

| Date | Mintage | F | VF | XF | Unc |
|---|---|---|---|---|---|
| 2000 Proof | 15,000 | Value: 35.00 | | | |

**7500000 LIRA** **KM# 1113** **Weight:** 31.4700 g. **Composition:** 0.9250 Silver .9359 oz. ASW **Subject:** United Nations Summit **Obverse:** Coiled rope design **Reverse:** UN logo and stylized 2000

| Date | Mintage | F | VF | XF | Unc |
|---|---|---|---|---|---|
| 2000 Proof | 15,000 | Value: 35.00 | | | |

**7500000 LIRA** KM# 1114 **Weight:** 31.4700 g. **Composition:** 0.9250 Silver .9359 oz. ASW **Subject:** Turkish European Union Candidacy **Obverse:** Circular design **Reverse:** Cluster of flags behind star and crescent

| Date | Mintage | F | VF | XF | Unc |
|---|---|---|---|---|---|
| 2000 Proof | 15,000 | Value: 35.00 | | | |

**7500000 LIRA** KM# 1115 **Weight:** 31.4700 g. **Composition:** 0.9250 Silver .9359 oz. ASW **Subject:** First Female Pilots **Obverse:** Turkish pilot's badge **Reverse:** Early female pilot saluting

| Date | Mintage | F | VF | XF | Unc |
|---|---|---|---|---|---|
| 2000 Proof | 15,000 | Value: 40.00 | | | |

**7500000 LIRA** KM# 1116 **Weight:** 31.4700 g. **Composition:** 0.9990 Silver 1.0108 oz. ASW **Subject:** President Clinton's Turkish Visit **Obverse:** Mint logo **Reverse:** Clinton holding baby

| Date | Mintage | F | VF | XF | Unc |
|---|---|---|---|---|---|
| 2000 Proof | 100,000 | Value: 40.00 | | | |

**7500000 LIRA** KM# 1117 **Weight:** 31.4700 g. **Composition:** 0.9250 Silver .9359 oz. ASW **Subject:** Iznik Tabak **Obverse:** Two peacocks **Reverse:** Circle of flowers

| Date | Mintage | F | VF | XF | Unc |
|---|---|---|---|---|---|
| 2001 Proof | 15,000 | Value: 35.00 | | | |

**150000000 LIRA** KM# 1119 **Ring Weight:** 17.0000 g. **Ring Composition:** 0.9250 Silver .5056 oz. ASW**Center Weight:** 24.0000 g. **Center Composition:** 0.9160 Gold .7068 oz. AGW **Subject:** President Clinton's Turkish Visit **Obverse:** Mint logo **Reverse:** Clinton holding baby **Edge:** Reeded **Size:** 38.6 mm.

| Date | Mintage | F | VF | XF | Unc |
|---|---|---|---|---|---|
| 2000 Proof | 10,000 | Value: 300 | | | |

**10000000 LIRA** KM# 1118 **Weight:** 31.4700 g. **Composition:** 0.9250 Silver .9359 oz. ASW **Subject:** Divrigi Ulu Camii **Obverse:** Art work in center **Reverse:** Ornate door **Edge:** Reeded **Size:** 38.6 mm.

| Date | Mintage | F | VF | XF | Unc |
|---|---|---|---|---|---|
| 2001 Matte | 15,000 | — | — | — | 40.00 |

## GOLD BULLION COINAGE

Since 1943, the Turkish government has issued regular and deluxe gold coins in five denominations corresponding to the old traditional 25, 50, 100, 250, and 500 Kurush of the Ottoman period. The regular coins are all dated 1923, plus the year of the republic (e.g. 1923/40 = 1963), de Luxe coins bear actual AD dates. For a few years, 1944-1950, the bust of Ismet Inonu replaced that of Kemal Ataturk.

**25 KURUSH** KM# 850 **Weight:** 1.8041 g. **Composition:** 0.9170 Gold .0532 oz. AGW **Obverse:** Head of Ismet Inonu left

| Date | Mintage | F | VF | XF | Unc |
|---|---|---|---|---|---|
| 1923/20 | — | BV | 50.00 | 65.00 | 90.00 |
| 1923/22 | 3,228 | BV | 50.00 | 75.00 | 120 |
| 1923/23 | 2,757 | BV | 50.00 | 75.00 | 120 |
| 1923/24 | 46,000 | BV | 50.00 | 65.00 | 90.00 |
| 1923/25 | 20,000 | BV | 50.00 | 70.00 | 110 |
| 1923/26 | 11,000 | BV | 50.00 | 70.00 | 110 |

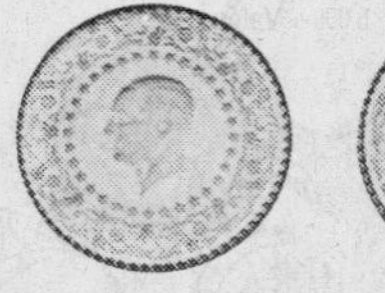

**25 KURUSH** KM# 870 **Weight:** 1.7540 g. **Composition:** 0.9170 Gold .0517 oz. AGW **Series:** Monnaie de Luxe **Obverse:** Head of Kemal Ataturk left

| Date | Mintage | F | VF | XF | Unc |
|---|---|---|---|---|---|
| 1942 | 138 | — | 50.00 | 75.00 | 150 |
| 1943 | 386 | — | 50.00 | 75.00 | 125 |
| 1944 | 811 | — | 50.00 | 75.00 | 125 |
| 1946 | 235 | — | 50.00 | 75.00 | 150 |
| 1950 | 2,053 | — | 22.50 | 32.50 | 55.00 |
| 1951 | 2,035 | — | 22.50 | 32.50 | 55.00 |
| 1952 | 3,374 | — | 22.50 | 32.50 | 55.00 |
| 1953 | 1,944 | — | 22.50 | 32.50 | 55.00 |
| 1954 | 2,244 | — | 22.50 | 32.50 | 55.00 |
| 1955 | 2,573 | — | 22.50 | 32.50 | 55.00 |
| 1956 | 4,004 | — | 22.50 | 32.50 | 55.00 |
| 1957 | 8,842 | — | 22.50 | 32.50 | 55.00 |
| 1958 | 9,546 | — | 22.50 | 32.50 | 55.00 |
| 1959 | 17,000 | — | 20.00 | 28.00 | 45.00 |
| 1960 | 19,000 | — | 20.00 | 28.00 | 45.00 |
| 1961 | 35,000 | — | 20.00 | 28.00 | 45.00 |
| 1962 | 31,000 | — | 20.00 | 28.00 | 45.00 |
| 1963 | 47,000 | — | 20.00 | 28.00 | 45.00 |
| 1964 | 57,000 | — | 20.00 | 28.00 | 45.00 |
| 1965 | 78,000 | — | 20.00 | 28.00 | 45.00 |
| 1966 | 106,000 | — | 20.00 | 28.00 | 45.00 |
| 1967 | 114,000 | — | 20.00 | 28.00 | 45.00 |
| 1968 | 152,000 | — | 20.00 | 28.00 | 45.00 |
| 1969 | 163,000 | — | 20.00 | 28.00 | 45.00 |
| 1970 | 224,000 | — | 20.00 | 28.00 | 45.00 |
| 1971 | 306,000 | — | 20.00 | 28.00 | 45.00 |
| 1972 | 271,000 | — | 20.00 | 28.00 | 45.00 |
| 1973 | 162,000 | — | 20.00 | 28.00 | 45.00 |
| 1974 | 141,000 | — | 20.00 | 28.00 | 45.00 |
| 1975 | 202,000 | — | 20.00 | 28.00 | 45.00 |
| 1976 | 583,000 | — | 20.00 | 28.00 | 45.00 |
| 1977 | 1,089,000 | — | 20.00 | 28.00 | 45.00 |
| 1978 | 238,000 | — | 20.00 | 28.00 | 45.00 |
| 1980 | — | — | 20.00 | 28.00 | 45.00 |

**25 KURUSH** KM# 875 **Weight:** 1.7540 g. **Composition:** 0.9170 Gold .0517 oz. AGW **Series:** Monnaie de Luxe **Obverse:** Head of Ismet Inonu left

| Date | Mintage | F | VF | XF | Unc |
|---|---|---|---|---|---|
| 1943 | — | 70.00 | 90.00 | 140 | 200 |
| **Note:** Mintage included in KM#870 | | | | | |
| 1944 | — | 70.00 | 90.00 | 140 | 200 |
| **Note:** Mintage included in KM#870 | | | | | |
| 1945 | 592 | 70.00 | 90.00 | 140 | 200 |
| 1946 | — | 70.00 | 90.00 | 140 | 200 |
| **Note:** Mintage included in KM#870 | | | | | |
| 1947 | 3,443 | 70.00 | 90.00 | 125 | 185 |
| 1948 | 714 | 70.00 | 90.00 | 140 | 200 |
| 1949 | 552 | 70.00 | 90.00 | 140 | 200 |

**25 KURUSH** KM# 851 **Weight:** 1.8041 g. **Composition:** 0.9170 Gold .0532 oz. AGW **Obverse:** Head of Kemal Ataturk left

| Date | Mintage | F | VF | XF | Unc |
|---|---|---|---|---|---|
| 1923/20 | 14,000 | BV | 20.00 | 25.00 | 40.00 |
| 1923/27 | 18,000 | BV | 20.00 | 25.00 | 40.00 |
| 1923/28 | 15,000 | BV | 20.00 | 25.00 | 40.00 |
| 1923/29 | 15,000 | BV | 20.00 | 25.00 | 40.00 |
| 1923/30 | 17,000 | BV | 20.00 | 25.00 | 40.00 |
| 1923/31 | 19,000 | BV | 20.00 | 25.00 | 40.00 |
| 1923/32 | 5,455 | BV | 20.00 | 25.00 | 40.00 |
| 1923/33 | 11,000 | BV | 20.00 | 25.00 | 40.00 |
| 1923/34 | 20,000 | BV | 20.00 | 25.00 | 40.00 |
| 1923/35 | 25,000 | BV | 20.00 | 25.00 | 40.00 |
| 1923/36 | 34,000 | BV | 20.00 | 25.00 | 40.00 |
| 1923/37 | 31,000 | BV | 20.00 | 25.00 | 40.00 |
| 1923/38 | 35,000 | BV | 20.00 | 25.00 | 40.00 |
| 1923/39 | 46,000 | BV | 20.00 | 25.00 | 40.00 |
| 1923/40 | 49,000 | BV | 20.00 | 25.00 | 40.00 |
| 1923/41 | 59,000 | BV | 20.00 | 25.00 | 40.00 |
| 1923/42 | 74,000 | BV | 20.00 | 25.00 | 40.00 |
| 1923/43 | 90,000 | BV | 20.00 | 25.00 | 40.00 |
| 1923/44 | 85,000 | BV | 20.00 | 25.00 | 40.00 |
| 1923/45 | 73,000 | BV | 20.00 | 25.00 | 40.00 |
| 1923/46 | 89,000 | BV | 20.00 | 25.00 | 40.00 |
| 1923/47 | 119,000 | BV | 20.00 | 25.00 | 40.00 |
| 1923/48 | 112,000 | BV | 20.00 | 25.00 | 40.00 |
| 1923/49 | 112,000 | BV | 20.00 | 25.00 | 40.00 |
| 1923/50 | 67,000 | BV | 20.00 | 25.00 | 40.00 |
| 1923/51 | 40,000 | BV | 20.00 | 25.00 | 40.00 |
| 1923/52 | 71,000 | BV | 20.00 | 25.00 | 40.00 |
| 1923/53 | 124,000 | BV | 20.00 | 25.00 | 40.00 |
| 1923/54 | 196 | BV | 20.00 | 25.00 | 40.00 |
| 1923/55 | 112,000 | BV | 20.00 | 25.00 | 40.00 |
| 1923/56 | — | BV | 20.00 | 25.00 | 40.00 |
| 1923/57 | — | BV | 20.00 | 25.00 | 40.00 |

**50 KURUSH** KM# 853 **Weight:** 3.6083 g. **Composition:** 0.9170 Gold .0517 oz. AGW **Obverse:** Head of Kemal Ataturk left

| Date | Mintage | F | VF | XF | Unc |
|---|---|---|---|---|---|
| 1923/20 | 12,000 | BV | 40.00 | 50.00 | 65.00 |
| 1923/27 | Inc. above | BV | 40.00 | 50.00 | 65.00 |
| 1923/28 | 3,300 | BV | 40.00 | 50.00 | 65.00 |
| 1923/29 | 6,384 | BV | 40.00 | 50.00 | 65.00 |
| 1923/30 | 4,590 | BV | 40.00 | 50.00 | 65.00 |
| 1923/31 | 9,068 | BV | 40.00 | 50.00 | 65.00 |
| 1923/32 | 4,344 | BV | 40.00 | 50.00 | 65.00 |
| 1923/33 | 3,958 | BV | 40.00 | 50.00 | 65.00 |
| 1923/34 | 9,499 | BV | 40.00 | 50.00 | 65.00 |
| 1923/35 | 9,307 | BV | 40.00 | 50.00 | 65.00 |
| 1923/36 | 12,000 | BV | 40.00 | 50.00 | 65.00 |
| 1923/37 | 9,049 | BV | 40.00 | 50.00 | 65.00 |
| 1923/38 | 9,854 | BV | 40.00 | 50.00 | 65.00 |
| 1923/39 | 11,000 | BV | 40.00 | 50.00 | 65.00 |
| 1923/40 | 13,000 | BV | 40.00 | 50.00 | 65.00 |
| 1923/41 | 13,000 | BV | 40.00 | 50.00 | 65.00 |
| 1923/42 | 18,000 | BV | 40.00 | 50.00 | 65.00 |

| Date | Mintage | F | VF | XF | Unc |
|---|---|---|---|---|---|
| 1923/43 | 26,000 | BV | 40.00 | 50.00 | 65.00 |
| 1923/44 | 26,000 | BV | 40.00 | 50.00 | 65.00 |
| 1923/45 | 25,000 | BV | 40.00 | 50.00 | 65.00 |
| 1923/46 | 28,000 | BV | 40.00 | 50.00 | 65.00 |
| 1923/47 | 38,000 | BV | 40.00 | 50.00 | 65.00 |
| 1923/48 | 35,000 | BV | 40.00 | 50.00 | 65.00 |
| 1923/49 | 28,000 | BV | 40.00 | 50.00 | 65.00 |
| 1923/50 | 16,000 | BV | 40.00 | 50.00 | 65.00 |
| 1923/51 | 8,000 | BV | 40.00 | 50.00 | 65.00 |
| 1923/52 | 14,000 | BV | 40.00 | 50.00 | 65.00 |
| 1923/53 | 28,000 | BV | 40.00 | 50.00 | 65.00 |
| 1923/54 | 54,000 | BV | 40.00 | 50.00 | 65.00 |
| 1923/55 | 16,000 | BV | 40.00 | 50.00 | 65.00 |
| 1923/57 | — | BV | 40.00 | 50.00 | 65.00 |

**50 KURUSH** KM# 871 **Weight:** 3.5080 g. **Composition:** 0.9170 Gold .1034 oz. AGW **Series:** Monnaie de Luxe **Obverse:** Head of Kemal Ataturk left

| Date | Mintage | F | VF | XF | Unc |
|---|---|---|---|---|---|
| 1942 | 115 | 100 | 150 | 200 | 250 |
| 1943 | 91 | 100 | 150 | 200 | 250 |
| 1944 | 950 | 70.00 | 120 | 140 | 175 |
| 1946 | 565 | 70.00 | 120 | 140 | 175 |
| 1950 | 1,971 | — | 40.00 | 70.00 | 140 |
| 1951 | 1,780 | — | 40.00 | 70.00 | 140 |
| 1952 | 2,557 | — | 40.00 | 70.00 | 140 |
| 1953 | 2,392 | — | 40.00 | 70.00 | 140 |
| 1954 | 1,714 | — | 40.00 | 70.00 | 140 |
| 1955 | 4,143 | — | 40.00 | 60.00 | 110 |
| 1956 | 2,956 | — | 40.00 | 60.00 | 110 |
| 1957 | 6,855 | — | 40.00 | 60.00 | 110 |
| 1958 | 6,381 | — | 40.00 | 60.00 | 110 |
| 1959 | 12,000 | — | 40.00 | 50.00 | 65.00 |
| 1960 | 12,000 | — | 40.00 | 50.00 | 65.00 |
| 1961 | 15,000 | — | 40.00 | 50.00 | 65.00 |
| 1962 | 22,000 | — | 40.00 | 50.00 | 65.00 |
| 1963 | 29,000 | — | 40.00 | 50.00 | 65.00 |
| 1964 | 34,000 | — | 40.00 | 50.00 | 65.00 |
| 1965 | 44,000 | — | 40.00 | 50.00 | 65.00 |
| 1966 | 58,000 | — | 40.00 | 50.00 | 65.00 |
| 1967 | 64,000 | — | 40.00 | 50.00 | 65.00 |
| 1968 | 82,000 | — | 40.00 | 50.00 | 65.00 |
| 1969 | 79,000 | — | 40.00 | 50.00 | 65.00 |
| 1970 | 109,000 | — | 40.00 | 50.00 | 65.00 |
| 1971 | 154,000 | — | 40.00 | 50.00 | 65.00 |
| 1972 | 110,000 | — | 40.00 | 50.00 | 65.00 |
| 1973 | 73,000 | — | 40.00 | 50.00 | 65.00 |
| 1974 | 45,000 | — | 40.00 | 50.00 | 65.00 |
| 1975 | 72,000 | — | 40.00 | 50.00 | 65.00 |
| 1976 | 196,000 | — | 40.00 | 50.00 | 65.00 |
| 1977 | 361,000 | — | 40.00 | 50.00 | 65.00 |
| 1978 | 161,000 | — | 40.00 | 50.00 | 65.00 |
| 1980 | — | — | 40.00 | 50.00 | 65.00 |

**50 KURUSH** KM# 876 **Weight:** 3.5080 g. **Composition:** 0.9170 Gold .1034 oz. AGW **Series:** Monnaie de Luxe **Obverse:** Head of Ismet Inonu left

| Date | Mintage | F | VF | XF | Unc |
|---|---|---|---|---|---|
| 1943 | — | — | 150 | 200 | 250 |
| **Note:** Mintage included in KM#871 | | | | | |
| 1944 | — | — | 120 | 170 | 220 |
| **Note:** Mintage included in KM#871 | | | | | |
| 1946 | — | — | 90.00 | 140 | 190 |
| **Note:** Mintage included in KM#871 | | | | | |
| 1947 | 3,481 | — | 90.00 | 140 | 190 |
| 1948 | 773 | — | 90.00 | 140 | 190 |
| 1949 | 582 | — | 90.00 | 140 | 190 |

**50 KURUSH** KM# 852 **Weight:** 3.6083 g. **Composition:** 0.9170 Gold .0517 oz. AGW **Obverse:** Head of Ismet Inonu left

| Date | Mintage | F | VF | XF | Unc |
|---|---|---|---|---|---|
| 1923/20 | — | 50.00 | 90.00 | 120 | 175 |
| 1923/22 | 1,093 | 50.00 | 90.00 | 120 | 175 |
| 1923/23 | 897 | 50.00 | 120 | 140 | 200 |
| 1923/24 | 11,000 | 50.00 | 90.00 | 120 | 175 |
| 1923/25 | 3,004 | 50.00 | 90.00 | 120 | 175 |
| 1923/26 | 817 | 50.00 | 120 | 140 | 200 |
| 1923/27 | 5,228 | 50.00 | 90.00 | 120 | 175 |

**100 KURUSH** KM# 872 **Weight:** 7.0160 g. **Composition:** 0.9170 Gold .2069 oz. AGW **Series:** Monnaie de Luxe **Obverse:** Head of Kemal Ataturk left

| Date | Mintage | F | VF | XF | Unc |
|---|---|---|---|---|---|
| 1942 | 8,659 | — | 110 | 140 | 225 |
| 1943 | 6,594 | — | 110 | 140 | 225 |
| 1944 | 7,160 | — | 110 | 140 | 225 |
| 1948 | 14,000 | — | 110 | 140 | 200 |
| 1950 | 25,000 | — | 110 | 140 | 200 |
| 1951 | 35,000 | — | 110 | 140 | 175 |
| 1952 | 41,000 | — | 110 | 140 | 175 |
| 1953 | 32,000 | — | 110 | 140 | 175 |
| 1954 | 24,000 | — | 110 | 140 | 175 |
| 1955 | 4,881 | — | 110 | 140 | 200 |
| 1956 | 11,000 | — | 80.00 | 100 | 130 |
| 1957 | 49,000 | — | 80.00 | 100 | 130 |
| 1958 | 67,000 | — | 80.00 | 100 | 130 |
| 1959 | 89,000 | — | 80.00 | 100 | 130 |
| 1960 | 57,000 | — | 80.00 | 100 | 130 |
| 1961 | 77,000 | — | 80.00 | 100 | 130 |
| 1962 | 108,000 | — | 80.00 | 100 | 130 |
| 1963 | 146,000 | — | 80.00 | 100 | 130 |
| 1964 | 128,000 | — | 80.00 | 100 | 130 |
| 1965 | 157,000 | — | 80.00 | 100 | 130 |
| 1966 | 190,000 | — | 80.00 | 100 | 130 |
| 1967 | 177,000 | — | 80.00 | 100 | 130 |
| 1968 | 143,000 | — | 80.00 | 100 | 130 |
| 1969 | 206,000 | — | 80.00 | 100 | 130 |
| 1970 | 253,000 | — | 80.00 | 100 | 130 |
| 1971 | 293,000 | — | 80.00 | 100 | 130 |
| 1972 | 222,000 | — | 80.00 | 100 | 130 |
| 1973 | 140,000 | — | 80.00 | 100 | 130 |
| 1974 | 82,000 | — | 80.00 | 100 | 130 |
| 1975 | 142,000 | — | 80.00 | 100 | 130 |
| 1976 | 265,000 | — | 80.00 | 100 | 130 |
| 1977 | 277,000 | — | 80.00 | 100 | 130 |
| 1978 | 86,000 | — | 80.00 | 100 | 130 |
| 1980 | — | — | 80.00 | 100 | 130 |

**100 KURUSH** KM# 877 **Weight:** 7.0160 g. **Composition:** 0.9170 Gold .2069 oz. AGW **Series:** Monnaie de Luxe **Obverse:** Head of Ismet Inonu left

| Date | Mintage | F | VF | XF | Unc |
|---|---|---|---|---|---|
| 1943 | — | 140 | 190 | 265 | 325 |
| **Note:** Mintage included in KM#872 | | | | | |
| 1944 | — | 140 | 190 | 265 | 375 |
| **Note:** Mintage included in KM#872 | | | | | |
| 1945 | 2,202 | 140 | 190 | 265 | 400 |
| 1946 | 8,863 | 140 | 190 | 265 | 325 |
| 1947 | 28,000 | 140 | 190 | 265 | 325 |
| 1948 | — | 140 | 190 | 265 | 325 |
| **Note:** Mintage included in KM#872 | | | | | |
| 1949 | 6,578 | 140 | 190 | 265 | 325 |
| 1950 | — | 140 | 190 | 265 | 325 |
| **Note:** Mintage included in KM#872 | | | | | |

**100 KURUSH** KM# 854 **Weight:** 7.2160 g. **Composition:** 0.9170 Gold .2126 oz. AGW **Obverse:** Head of Ismet Inonu left

| Date | Mintage | F | VF | XF | Unc |
|---|---|---|---|---|---|
| 1923/20 | — | — | BV | 80.00 | 140 |
| 1923/22 Rare | 3 | — | — | — | — |
| 1923/23 | 381,000 | — | BV | 80.00 | 140 |
| 1923/24 | 2,274 | — | BV | 80.00 | 150 |
| 1923/25 | 28,000 | — | BV | 80.00 | 150 |
| 1923/26 | 2,097 | — | BV | 80.00 | 150 |
| 1923/27 | 17,000 | — | BV | 80.00 | 150 |

**100 KURUSH** KM# 855 **Weight:** 7.2160 g. **Composition:** 0.9170 Gold .2126 oz. AGW **Obverse:** Head of Kemal Ataturk left

| Date | Mintage | F | VF | XF | Unc |
|---|---|---|---|---|---|
| 1923/20 | 29,000 | — | BV | 80.00 | 100 |
| 1923/27 | Inc. above | — | BV | 80.00 | 100 |
| 1923/28 Rare | 3 | — | — | — | — |
| 1923/29 | 2,111 | — | BV | 80.00 | 100 |
| 1923/30 | 13,000 | — | BV | 80.00 | 100 |
| 1923/31 | 109,000 | — | BV | 80.00 | 100 |
| 1923/32 | 134,000 | — | BV | 80.00 | 100 |
| 1923/33 | 216,000 | — | BV | 80.00 | 100 |
| 1923/34 | 463,000 | — | BV | 80.00 | 100 |
| 1923/35 | 405,000 | — | BV | 80.00 | 100 |
| 1923/36 | 25,000 | — | BV | 80.00 | 100 |
| 1923/37 | 131,000 | — | BV | 80.00 | 100 |
| 1923/38 | 159,000 | — | BV | 80.00 | 100 |
| 1923/39 | 85,000 | — | BV | 80.00 | 100 |
| 1923/40 | 10,000 | — | BV | 80.00 | 100 |
| 1923/41 | 164,000 | — | BV | 80.00 | 100 |
| 1923/42 | 63,000 | — | BV | 80.00 | 100 |
| 1923/43 | 56,000 | — | BV | 80.00 | 100 |
| 1923/44 | 198,000 | — | BV | 80.00 | 100 |
| 1923/45 | 176,000 | — | BV | 80.00 | 100 |
| 1923/46 | 1,290,000 | — | BV | 80.00 | 100 |
| 1923/47 | 513,000 | — | BV | 80.00 | 100 |
| 1923/48 | 600 | 90.00 | 120 | 145 | 200 |
| 1923/49 | 1,300 | — | 90.00 | 115 | 140 |
| 1923/50 | 47,000 | — | BV | 80.00 | 100 |
| 1923/51 | 240,000 | — | BV | 80.00 | 100 |
| 1923/52 | 1,046,999 | — | BV | 80.00 | 100 |
| 1923/53 | 550,000 | — | BV | 80.00 | 100 |
| 1923/54 | 18,000 | — | BV | 80.00 | 100 |
| 1923/55 | 309,000 | — | BV | 80.00 | 100 |
| 1923/57 | — | — | BV | 80.00 | 100 |
| 1923/58 | — | — | BV | 80.00 | 100 |

**250 KURUSH** KM# 873 **Weight:** 17.5400 g. **Composition:** 0.9170 Gold .5169 oz. AGW **Series:** Monnaie de Luxe **Obverse:** Head of Kemal Ataturk left

| Date | Mintage | F | VF | XF | Unc |
|---|---|---|---|---|---|
| 1942 | 10,000 | — | 250 | 425 | 600 |
| 1943 | 11,000 | — | 250 | 425 | 600 |
| 1944 | 15,000 | — | 300 | 650 | 900 |
| 1946 | 16,000 | — | 300 | 650 | 900 |
| 1947 | 42,000 | — | 250 | 425 | 600 |
| 1948 | 13,000 | — | 250 | 425 | 600 |
| 1950 | 45,000 | — | 250 | 425 | 600 |
| 1951 | 41,000 | — | 175 | 200 | 275 |
| 1952 | 59,000 | — | 175 | 200 | 275 |
| 1953 | 45,000 | — | 175 | 200 | 275 |
| 1954 | 40,000 | — | 175 | 200 | 275 |
| 1955 | 7,067 | — | 175 | 200 | 275 |
| 1956 | 14,000 | — | 175 | 200 | 275 |
| 1957 | 47,000 | — | 175 | 200 | 275 |
| 1958 | 75,000 | — | 175 | 200 | 275 |
| 1959 | 93,000 | — | 175 | 200 | 275 |
| 1960 | 50,000 | — | 175 | 200 | 275 |
| 1961 | 65,000 | — | 175 | 200 | 275 |
| 1962 | 99,000 | — | 175 | 200 | 275 |
| 1963 | 137,000 | — | 175 | 200 | 275 |
| 1964 | 152,000 | — | 175 | 200 | 275 |
| 1965 | 194,000 | — | 175 | 200 | 275 |
| 1966 | 218,000 | — | 175 | 200 | 275 |
| 1967 | 201,000 | — | 175 | 200 | 275 |
| 1968 | 150,000 | — | 175 | 200 | 275 |
| 1969 | 262,000 | — | 175 | 200 | 275 |
| 1970 | 301,000 | — | 175 | 200 | 275 |
| 1971 | 356,000 | — | 175 | 200 | 275 |
| 1972 | 305,000 | — | 175 | 200 | 275 |
| 1973 | 198,000 | — | 175 | 200 | 275 |
| 1974 | 142,000 | — | 175 | 200 | 275 |
| 1975 | 223,000 | — | 175 | 200 | 275 |
| 1976 | 345,000 | — | 175 | 200 | 275 |
| 1977 | 227,000 | — | 175 | 200 | 275 |
| 1978 | 311,000 | — | 175 | 200 | 275 |
| 1980 | — | — | 175 | 200 | 275 |

**250 KURUSH** KM# 878 **Weight:** 17.5400 g. **Composition:** 0.9170 Gold .5169 oz. AGW **Series:** Monnaie de Luxe **Obverse:** Head of Ismet Inonu left

| Date | Mintage | F | VF | XF | Unc |
|---|---|---|---|---|---|
| 1943 | — | — | 175 | 200 | 250 |
| **Note:** Mintage included in KM#873 | | | | | |
| 1944 | — | — | 175 | 200 | 250 |
| **Note:** Mintage included in KM#873 | | | | | |
| 1945 | 4,135 | — | 250 | 375 | 550 |
| 1946 | — | — | 175 | 200 | 250 |
| **Note:** Mintage included in KM#873 | | | | | |
| 1947 | — | — | 175 | 200 | 250 |
| **Note:** Mintage included in KM#873 | | | | | |
| 1948 | — | — | 175 | 200 | 250 |
| **Note:** Mintage included in KM#873 | | | | | |

| Date | Mintage | F | VF | XF | Unc |
|---|---|---|---|---|---|
| 1949 | 11,000 | — | 175 | 200 | 250 |
| 1950 | — | — | 175 | 200 | 250 |

**Note:** Mintage included in KM#873

**250 KURUSH** **KM# 856** **Weight:** 18.0400 g. **Composition:** 0.9170 Gold .5319 oz. AGW **Obverse:** Head of Ismet Inonu left

| Date | Mintage | F | VF | XF | Unc |
|---|---|---|---|---|---|
| 1923/20 | — | — | 220 | 270 | 375 |
| 1923/23 | 14,000 | — | 220 | 270 | 375 |
| 1923/24 | 60 | — | 300 | 400 | 500 |

**250 KURUSH** **KM# 857** **Weight:** 18.0400 g. **Composition:** 0.9170 Gold .5319 oz. AGW **Obverse:** Head of Kemal Ataturk left

| Date | Mintage | F | VF | XF | Unc |
|---|---|---|---|---|---|
| 1923/20 | 10,000 | — | BV | 250 | 350 |
| 1923/29 Rare | 3 | — | — | — | — |
| 1923/30 | 130 | — | 450 | 700 | 900 |
| 1923/31 | — | — | 450 | 700 | 900 |
| 1923/38 | 245 | — | 325 | 375 | 600 |
| 1923/39 | 389 | — | 325 | 375 | 600 |
| 1923/40 | 435 | — | 325 | 375 | 600 |
| 1923/41 | 349 | — | 325 | 375 | 600 |
| 1923/42 | 460 | — | 325 | 375 | 600 |
| 1923/43 | 1,008 | — | 200 | 275 | 375 |
| 1923/44 | 712 | — | 200 | 275 | 375 |
| 1923/45 | 1,034 | — | 200 | 275 | 375 |
| 1923/46 | 1,035 | — | 200 | 275 | 375 |
| 1923/47 | 1,408 | — | 200 | 275 | 375 |
| 1923/48 | 904 | — | 200 | 275 | 375 |
| 1923/49 | 1,066 | — | 200 | 275 | 375 |
| 1923/50 | 975 | — | 200 | 275 | 375 |
| 1923/51 | 298 | — | 200 | 275 | 375 |
| 1923/52 | 610 | — | 200 | 275 | 375 |
| 1923/53 | 586 | — | 200 | 275 | 375 |
| 1923/54 | 289 | — | 200 | 275 | 375 |
| 1923/55 | 267 | — | 200 | 275 | 375 |
| 1923/57 | — | — | 200 | 275 | 375 |

**500 KURUSH** **KM# 874** **Weight:** 35.0800 g. **Composition:** 0.9170 Gold 1.0338 oz. AGW **Series:** Monnaie de Luxe **Obverse:** Head of Kemal Ataturk left

| Date | Mintage | F | VF | XF | Unc |
|---|---|---|---|---|---|
| 1942 | 2,949 | — | 385 | 435 | 520 |
| 1943 | 1,210 | — | 385 | 435 | 520 |
| 1944 | 1,254 | — | 385 | 435 | 520 |
| 1947 | 3,699 | — | 385 | 435 | 520 |
| 1950 | 59 | — | 500 | 550 | 650 |
| 1951 | 21 | — | 500 | 550 | 650 |
| 1952 | 26 | — | 500 | 550 | 650 |
| 1953 | 35 | — | 500 | 550 | 650 |
| 1954 | 182 | — | 500 | 550 | 650 |
| 1955 | 14 | — | 500 | 550 | 650 |
| 1956 | 13 | — | 500 | 550 | 650 |
| 1957 | 68 | — | 500 | 550 | 650 |
| 1958 | 121 | — | 500 | 550 | 650 |
| 1959 | 294 | — | 500 | 550 | 650 |
| 1960 | 208 | — | 500 | 550 | 650 |
| 1961 | 619 | — | 385 | 435 | 520 |
| 1962 | 1,228 | — | 385 | 435 | 520 |
| 1963 | 1,985 | — | 385 | 435 | 520 |
| 1964 | 2,787 | — | 370 | 400 | 485 |
| 1965 | 4,631 | — | 370 | 400 | 485 |
| 1966 | 5,572 | — | 370 | 400 | 485 |
| 1967 | 6,637 | — | 370 | 400 | 485 |
| 1968 | 5,983 | — | 370 | 400 | 485 |
| 1969 | 7,152 | — | 370 | 400 | 485 |
| 1970 | 11,000 | — | 370 | 400 | 485 |
| 1971 | 15,000 | — | 370 | 400 | 485 |
| 1972 | 15,000 | — | 370 | 400 | 485 |
| 1973 | 7,939 | — | 370 | 400 | 485 |
| 1974 | 5,412 | — | 370 | 400 | 485 |
| 1975 | 6,205 | — | 370 | 400 | 485 |
| 1976 | 11,000 | — | 370 | 400 | 485 |
| 1977 | 6,931 | — | 370 | 400 | 485 |
| 1978 | 5,740 | — | 370 | 400 | 485 |
| 1980 | — | — | 370 | 400 | 485 |

**500 KURUSH** **KM# 879** **Weight:** 35.0800 g. **Composition:** 0.9170 Gold 1.0338 oz. AGW **Series:** Monnaie de Luxe **Obverse:** Head of Ismet Inonu left

| Date | Mintage | F | VF | XF | Unc |
|---|---|---|---|---|---|
| 1943 | — | — | 385 | 435 | 520 |
| **Note:** Mintage included in KM#874 | | | | | |
| 1944 | — | — | 385 | 435 | 520 |
| **Note:** Mintage included in KM#874 | | | | | |
| 1945 | 115 | — | 500 | 530 | 575 |
| 1946 | 298 | — | 500 | 530 | 575 |
| 1947 | — | — | 385 | 435 | 520 |
| **Note:** Mintage included in KM#874 | | | | | |
| 1948 | 40 | — | 500 | 530 | 575 |

**500 KURUSH** **KM# 858** **Weight:** 36.0800 g. **Composition:** 0.9170 Gold 1.0638 oz. AGW **Obverse:** Head of Ismet Inonu left

| Date | Mintage | F | VF | XF | Unc |
|---|---|---|---|---|---|
| 1923/20 | — | — | BV | 550 | 700 |
| 1923/23 | 9,006 | — | BV | 550 | 700 |
| 1923/24 | 7,923 | — | 650 | 800 | 900 |
| 1923/25 | 272 | — | 750 | 900 | 1,000 |

**500 KURUSH** **KM# 859** **Weight:** 36.0800 g. **Composition:** 0.9170 Gold 1.0638 oz. AGW **Obverse:** Head of Kemal Ataturk left

| Date | Mintage | F | VF | XF | Unc |
|---|---|---|---|---|---|
| 1923/20 | 12,000 | — | BV | 550 | 700 |
| 1923/27 | 615 | — | 650 | 800 | 1,000 |
| 1923/28 | 34 | — | 650 | 800 | 1,000 |
| 1923/29 | 137 | — | 575 | 700 | 900 |
| 1923/30 | 45 | — | 575 | 700 | 900 |
| 1923/31 | 100 | — | 575 | 700 | 900 |
| 1923/32 | 74 | — | 575 | 700 | 900 |
| 1923/33 | 268 | — | 550 | 650 | 800 |
| 1923/34 | 758 | — | 550 | 650 | 800 |
| 1923/35 | 1,586 | — | BV | 375 | 465 |
| 1923/36 | 765 | — | BV | 375 | 465 |
| 1923/37 | 983 | — | BV | 375 | 465 |
| 1923/38 | 1,738 | — | BV | 375 | 465 |
| 1923/39 | 2,629 | — | BV | 375 | 465 |
| 1923/40 | 2,763 | — | BV | 375 | 465 |
| 1923/41 | 3,440 | — | BV | 375 | 465 |
| 1923/42 | 3,335 | — | BV | 375 | 465 |
| 1923/43 | 4,914 | — | BV | 375 | 465 |
| 1923/44 | 4,308 | — | BV | 375 | 465 |
| 1923/45 | 3,488 | — | BV | 375 | 465 |
| 1923/46 | 5,636 | — | BV | 375 | 465 |
| 1923/47 | 7,588 | — | BV | 375 | 465 |
| 1923/48 | 6,060 | — | BV | 375 | 465 |
| 1923/49 | 4,235 | — | BV | 375 | 465 |
| 1923/50 | 4,733 | — | BV | 375 | 465 |
| 1923/51 | 2,757 | — | BV | 375 | 465 |
| 1923/52 | 2,041 | — | BV | 375 | 465 |
| 1923/53 | 4,819 | — | BV | 375 | 465 |
| 1923/54 | 1,401 | — | BV | 375 | 465 |
| 1923/55 | 1,484 | — | BV | 375 | 465 |
| 1923/57 | — | — | BV | 375 | 465 |

## PATTERNS

Including off metal strikes

| KM# | Date | Mintage | Identification | Mkt Val |
|---|---|---|---|---|
| Pn2 | 1948 | — | 5 Kurus. Brass. KM#887 | 500 |
| Pn3 | 1948 | — | 10 Kurus. Brass. KM#888 | 500 |

## PIEFORTS

| KM# | Date | Mintage | Identification | Mkt Val |
|---|---|---|---|---|
| P1 | 1981 | 2,500 | 500 Lira. 0.9250 Silver. KM#931 | 165 |
| P2 | 1981 | 1,200 | 3000 Lira. 0.9250 Silver. KM#948 | 180 |
| P3 | 1981 | — | 30000 Lira. Gold. KM#955 | 1,350 |
| P4 | 1982 | 600 | 3000 Lira. 0.9250 Silver. KM#959 | 125 |

## MINT SETS

| KM# | Date | Mintage | Identification | Issue Price | Mkt Val |
|---|---|---|---|---|---|
| MSA1 | 1949 (8) | — | KM#881-888 | — | — |
| MS1 | 1962 (7) | — | KM#889a.1, 890.1, 891.1, 892.2, 893.1, 894 (1960), 895 | — | — |
| MSA2 | 1963 (6) | — | KM#889a.1, 890.1, 891.1, 892.2, 893.1, 895a | — | — |
| MS2 | 1964 (6) | — | KM#889a.1, 890.1, 891.1, 892.2, 893.1, 895a | — | 4.50 |
| MS3 | 1965 (6) | — | KM#889a.1, 890.1, 891.1, 892.2, 893.1, 895a | — | 4.50 |
| MS4 | 1966 (6) | — | KM#889a.1, 890.1, 891.1, 892.2, 893.1, 895a | — | 4.50 |
| MSA5 | 1967 (6) | — | KM#889a.2, 890.1, 891.1, 892.3, 893.1, 895a | — | — |
| MS5 | 1968 (6) | — | KM#889a.2, 890.1, 891.1, 892.3, 893.1, 895a | — | 4.50 |
| MS6 | 1969 (6) | — | KM#889a.2, 890.2, 891.2, 892.3, 893.2, 895a | — | 3.50 |
| MS7 | 1970 (6) | — | KM#889a.2, 890.2, 891.2, 892.3, 893.2, 895a | — | 3.50 |
| MS8 | 1971 (6) | — | KM#889a.2, 890.2, 891.2, 893.2, 895a, 899 | — | 3.50 |
| MS9 | 1972 (6) | — | KM#889a.2, 890.2, 891.2, 893.2, 895a, 899 | — | 3.50 |
| MS10 | 1973 (7) | — | KM#889a.2, 890.2, 891.2, 892.3, 893.2, 895a, 899 | — | 3.00 |
| MS11 | 1974 (7) | — | KM#889a.2, 890.3-892.3, 893.2, 895a, 899 | — | 3.00 |
| MS12 | 1975 (7) | — | KM#889a.2, 890a, 891a, 893.2, 895c, 899, 905 | — | 3.00 |
| MS13 | 1976 (7) | — | KM#889a.2, 890a, 891a, 893.2, 895c, 899, 905 | — | 3.00 |
| MS14 | 1977 (8) | — | KM#889a.2, 890a, 891a, 892.3, 893.2, 895c, 899, 905 | — | 3.50 |
| MS15 | 1978 (4) | — | KM#889a.2, 892.3, 893.2, 905 | — | 3.00 |
| MS16 | 1979 (4) | — | KM#889a.2, 893.2, 899, 905 | — | 3.00 |
| MS17 | 1980 (2) | — | KM#889a.2, 893.2 | — | 2.00 |
| MS18 | 1981 (3) | — | KM#943-945 | — | 3.00 |
| MS19 | 1982 (3) | — | KM#943, 949.1, 950.1 | — | 3.00 |
| MS20 | 1983 (2) | — | KM#949.2, 950.2 | — | 3.00 |
| MS21 | 1984 (6) | — | KM#962-967 | — | 5.50 |
| MS22 | 1985 (6) | — | KM#962-964, 966, 967, 975 | — | 5.00 |
| MS23 | 1986 (5) | — | KM#963-967 | — | 4.00 |
| MS24 | 1989 (7) | 9,350 | KM#962-964, 975, 987, 988, and medal | 2.00 | 2.00 |
| MS25 | 1990 (5) | 5,300 | KM#987-989, 996, 997, and medal | 4.00 | 8.50 |
| MS26 | 1991 (5) | 2,250 | KM#987-989, 997, 1015, and mint medal | — | 20.00 |
| MS27 | 1992 (6) | 2,240 | KM#987-989, 997, 1015, 1025, and mint medal | — | 20.00 |
| MS28 | 1993 (6) | 1,750 | KM#987-989, 997, 1015, 1025, and mint medal | — | 20.00 |
| MS29 | 1994 (8) | 2,500 | KM#987-989, 997, 1015, 1025, 1027, 1042, plus mint medal | — | 20.00 |
| MS30 | 1995 (7) | 2,500 | KM#989, 1015, 1027-1029, 1041, 1043, plus mint medal | — | 15.00 |
| MS31 | 1996 (8) | 10,000 | KM#989, 1015, 1027-1029, 1041, 1050, 1056, plus mint medal | — | 8.00 |
| MS32 | 1997 (7) | — | KM#989, 1015, 1027.2, 1028, 1029, 1041, 1056, plus silver mint medal | — | 20.00 |
| MS33 | 2000 (3) | 10,000 | KM#860.1a, 893.1a, 905a Mixed dates | 60.00 | — |
| MS34 | 2000 (4) | 25,000 | KM#881a, 884a, 885a, 886a Mixed dates | 325 | — |
| MS35 | 2000 (7) | 10,000 | KM#860.1a, 881a, 884a, 885a, 886a, 893.1a, 905a Mixed dates | 350 | — |

# TURKMENISTAN

The Turkmenistan Republic (formerly the Turkmen Soviet Socialist Republic) covers the territory of the Trans-Caspian Region of Turkestan, the Charjiui Vilayet of Bukhara and the part of Khiva located on the right bank of the Oxus. Bordered on the north by the Autonomous Kara-Kalpak Republic (a constituent of Uzbekistan), by Iran and Afghanistan on the south, by the Usbek Republic on the east and the Caspian Sea on the west. It has an area of 186,400 sq. mi. (488,100 sq. km.) and a population of 3.5 million. Capital: Ashkhabad(formerly Poltoratsk). Main occupation is agricultural products including cotton and maize. It is rich in minerals, oil, coal, sulphur and salt and is also famous for its carpets, Turkoman horses and Karakui sheep.

The Turkomans arrived in Trancaspia as nomadic Seluk Turks in the 11th century. It often became subjected to one of the neighboring states. Late in the 19th century the Czarist Russians invaded with their first victory at Kyzyl Arvat in 1877, arriving in Ashkhabad in 1882 resulting in submission of the Turkmen tribes. By March 18,1884 the Transcaspian province of Russian Turkestan was formed. During WW I the Czarist government tried to conscript the Turkmen; this led to a revolt in Oct. 1916 under the leadership of Aziz Chapykov. In 1918 the Turks captured Baku from the Red army and the British sent a contingent to Merv to prevent a German-Turkish offensive toward Afghanistan and India. In mid-1919 a Bureau of Turkestan Moslem Communist Organization was formed in Moscow hoping to develop one large republic including all surrounding Turkic areas within a Soviet federation. A Turkestan Autonomous Soviet Socialist Republic was formed and plans to partition Turkestan into five republics according to the principle of nationalities was quickly implemented by Joseph Stalin. On Oct. 27, 1924 Turkmenistan became a Soviet Socialist Republic and was accepted as a member of the U.S.S.R. on Jan. 29, 1925. The Bureau of T.M.C.O. was disbanded in 1934. In Aug. 1990 the Turkmen Supreme Soviet adopted a declaration of sovereignty followed by a declaration of independence in Oct. 1991 joining the Commonwealth of Independent States in Dec. A new constitution was adopted in 1992 providing for an executive presidency.

**MONETARY SYSTEM**

100 Tennesi = 1 Manat

## REPUBLIC

### STANDARD COINAGE

100 Tennesi = 1 Manat

**TENNESI** **KM# 1** **Composition:** Copper Plated Steel **Reverse:** President Saparmyrat Nyyazow bust left

| Date | Mintage | F | VF | XF | Unc | BU |
|---|---|---|---|---|---|---|
| 1993 | — | — | — | — | 0.25 | — |

**5 TENNESI** **KM# 2** **Composition:** Copper Plated Steel **Reverse:** President Saparmyrat Nyyazow bust left

| Date | Mintage | F | VF | XF | Unc | BU |
|---|---|---|---|---|---|---|
| 1993 | — | — | — | — | 0.35 | — |

**10 TENNESI** **KM# 3** **Composition:** Copper Plated Steel **Reverse:** President Saparmyrat Nyyazow bust left

| Date | Mintage | F | VF | XF | Unc | BU |
|---|---|---|---|---|---|---|
| 1993 | — | — | — | — | 0.60 | — |

**20 TENNESI** **KM# 4** **Composition:** Nickel Plated Steel **Reverse:** President Saparmyrat Nyyazow bust left

| Date | Mintage | F | VF | XF | Unc | BU |
|---|---|---|---|---|---|---|
| 1993 | — | — | — | — | 1.00 | — |

**50 TENNESI** **KM# 5** **Composition:** Nickel Plated Steel **Reverse:** President Saparmyrat Nyyazow bust left

| Date | Mintage | F | VF | XF | Unc | BU |
|---|---|---|---|---|---|---|
| 1993 | — | — | — | — | 2.00 | — |

**500 MANAT** **KM# 6** **Weight:** 28.2800 g. **Composition:** 0.9250 Silver .8410 oz. ASW **Series:** Endangered Wildlife **Obverse:** Portrait of President Nyyakow **Reverse:** Goitered gazelle

| Date | Mintage | F | VF | XF | Unc | BU |
|---|---|---|---|---|---|---|
| 1996 Proof | Est. 5,000 | Value: 35.00 | | | | |

**500 MANAT** **KM# 7** **Weight:** 28.2800 g. **Composition:** 0.9250 Silver .8410 oz. ASW **Series:** Endangered Wildlife **Obverse:** Portrait of President Nyyakow **Reverse:** Purple Swamphen walking right

| Date | Mintage | F | VF | XF | Unc | BU |
|---|---|---|---|---|---|---|
| 1996 Proof | Est. 5,000 | Value: 35.00 | | | | |

**500 MANAT** **KM# 8** **Weight:** 28.2800 g. **Composition:** 0.9250 Silver .8410 oz. ASW **Series:** Endangered Wildlife **Subject:** Kaspi Ular **Obverse:** Portrait of President Nyyakow **Reverse:** Pair of Caspian Ular snowcock

| Date | Mintage | F | VF | XF | Unc | BU |
|---|---|---|---|---|---|---|
| 1996 Proof | Est. 5,000 | Value: 35.00 | | | | |

**500 MANAT** **KM# 9** **Weight:** 28.2800 g. **Composition:** 0.9250 Silver .8410 oz. ASW **Series:** Endangered Wildlife **Subject:** Manui **Obverse:** Portrait of President Nyyakow **Reverse:** Pallas' cat

| Date | Mintage | F | VF | XF | Unc | BU |
|---|---|---|---|---|---|---|
| 1996 Proof | Est. 5,000 | Value: 35.00 | | | | |

**500 MANAT** **KM# 10** **Weight:** 28.2800 g. **Composition:** 0.9250 Silver .8410 oz. ASW **Series:** Endangered Wildlife **Subject:** Gulan **Obverse:** Portrait of President Nyyakow **Reverse:** Asian wild ass

| Date | Mintage | F | VF | XF | Unc | BU |
|---|---|---|---|---|---|---|
| 1996 Proof | Est. 5,000 | Value: 35.00 | | | | |

**500 MANAT** **KM# 11** **Weight:** 28.2800 g. **Composition:** 0.9250 Silver .8410 oz. ASW **Series:** Endangered Wildlife **Subject:** Turkmen Eublefary **Obverse:** Portrait of President Nyyakow **Reverse:** Turkmenic gecko

| Date | Mintage | F | VF | XF | Unc | BU |
|---|---|---|---|---|---|---|
| 1996 Proof | Est. 5,000 | Value: 35.00 | | | | |

**500 MANAT** **KM# 12** **Composition:** Nickel Clad Steel **Obverse:** Denomination **Reverse:** President Nyyazow head left **Edge:** Reeded

| Date | Mintage | F | VF | XF | Unc | BU |
|---|---|---|---|---|---|---|
| 1999 | Est. 5,000 | — | — | — | 1.25 | — |

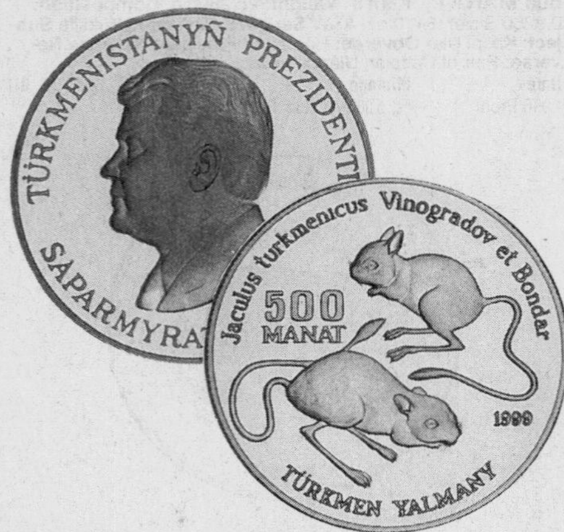

**500 MANAT** KM# 14 **Weight:** 28.2800 g. **Composition:** 0.9250 Silver .8410 oz. ASW **Series:** Wildlife Series **Subject:** Jaculus Turkmenicus **Obverse:** President Nyyazow head left **Reverse:** 2 Turkmenic Jerboa **Edge:** Reeded

| Date | Mintage | F | VF | XF | Unc | BU |
|---|---|---|---|---|---|---|
| 1999 Proof | Est. 5,000 | Value: 35.00 | | | | |

**500 MANAT** KM# 15 **Weight:** 28.2800 g. **Composition:** 0.9250 Silver .8410 oz. ASW **Series:** Wildlife Series **Subject:** Chlamydotis Undulata **Reverse:** 2 Houbara Bustards

| Date | Mintage | F | VF | XF | Unc | BU |
|---|---|---|---|---|---|---|
| 1999 Proof | Est. 5,000 | Value: 35.00 | | | | |

**500 MANAT** KM# 16 **Weight:** 28.2800 g. **Composition:** 0.9250 Silver .8410 oz. ASW **Series:** Wildlife Series **Subject:** Falco cherrug **Reverse:** Saker falcon on branch, falconer in back

| Date | Mintage | F | VF | XF | Unc | BU |
|---|---|---|---|---|---|---|
| 1999 Proof | Est. 5,000 | Value: 35.00 | | | | |

**500 MANAT** KM# 17 **Weight:** 28.2800 g. **Composition:** 0.9250 Silver .8410 oz. ASW **Series:** Wildlife Series **Subject:** Naja Oxiana **Reverse:** Cobra with hood open

| Date | Mintage | F | VF | XF | Unc | BU |
|---|---|---|---|---|---|---|
| 1999 Proof | Est. 5,000 | Value: 35.00 | | | | |

**500 MANAT** KM# 18 **Weight:** 28.2800 g. **Composition:** 0.9250 Silver .8410 oz. ASW **Series:** Wildlife Series **Subject:** Felis Caracal **Reverse:** Caracal seated

| Date | Mintage | F | VF | XF | Unc | BU |
|---|---|---|---|---|---|---|
| 1999 Proof | Est. 5,000 | Value: 35.00 | | | | |

**500 MANAT** KM# 19 **Weight:** 28.2800 g. **Composition:** 0.9250 Silver .8410 oz. ASW **Series:** Wildlife Series **Subject:** Panthera tigris

| Date | Mintage | F | VF | XF | Unc | BU |
|---|---|---|---|---|---|---|
| 1999 Proof | Est. 5,000 | Value: 35.00 | | | | |

**1000 MANAT** KM# 13 **Composition:** Nickel Clad Steel **Obverse:** Denomination **Reverse:** President Nyyazow head left **Edge:** Reeded

| Date | Mintage | F | VF | XF | Unc | BU |
|---|---|---|---|---|---|---|
| 1999 Proof | — | — | — | — | 2.50 | — |

## PROOF SETS

| KM# | Date | Mintage | Identification | Issue Price | Mkt Val |
|---|---|---|---|---|---|
| PS1 | 1996 (6) | 5,000 | KM#6-11 | — | 210 |

The Colony of the Turks and Caicos Islands, a British colony situated in the West Indies at the eastern end of the Bahama Islands, has an area of 166 sq. mi. (430 sq.km.) and a population of *10,000. Capital: Cockburn Town, on Grand Turk. The principal industry of the colony is the production of salt, which is gathered by raking. Salt, crayfish, and conch shells are exported.

The Turks and Caicos Islands were discovered by Juan Ponce de Leon in 1512, but were not settled until 1678when Bermudians arrived to rake salt from the salt ponds. The British settlers were driven from the island by the Spanish in 1710, during the long War of the Spanish Succession. They returned and throughout the remaining years of the war repulsed repeated attacks by France and Spain. In 1799 the islands were granted representation in the Bahamian assembly, but in 1848, on petition of the inhabitants, they were made a separate colony under Jamaica. They were annexed by Jamaica in 1873 and remained a dependency until 1959 when they became a unit territory of the Federation of the West Indies. When the Federation was dissolved in 1962, the Turks and Caicos Islands became a separate Crown Colony.

**RULERS**
British

**MONETARY SYSTEM**
1 Crown = 1 Dollar U.S.A.

# CROWN COLONY

## STANDARD COINAGE

1 Crown = 1 Dollar U.S.A.

**1/4 CROWN** KM# 51 **Composition:** Copper-Nickel

| Date | Mintage | F | VF | XF | Unc | BU |
|---|---|---|---|---|---|---|
| 1981 | — | — | — | — | 1.50 | — |

**1/2 CROWN** KM# 52 **Composition:** Copper-Nickel

| Date | Mintage | F | VF | XF | Unc | BU |
|---|---|---|---|---|---|---|
| 1981 | — | — | — | — | 2.00 | — |

**CROWN** **KM# 1** **Composition:** Copper-Nickel

| Date | Mintage | F | VF | XF | Unc | BU |
|---|---|---|---|---|---|---|
| 1969 | 50,000 | — | — | 2.00 | 4.50 | — |
| 1969 Proof | 6,000 | Value: 6.00 | | | | |

**CROWN** **KM# 5** **Composition:** Copper-Nickel

| Date | Mintage | F | VF | XF | Unc | BU |
|---|---|---|---|---|---|---|
| 1975 Matte | 590 | — | — | — | 10.00 | — |
| 1975 Proof | 1,370 | Value: 7.00 | | | | |
| 1976 | 1,960 | — | — | — | 6.00 | — |
| 1976 Proof | 2,270 | Value: 7.00 | | | | |
| 1977 Proof | 1,420 | Value: 7.00 | | | | |

**CROWN** **KM# 60** **Composition:** Copper-Nickel **Subject:** Prince Andrew's marriage

| Date | Mintage | F | VF | XF | Unc | BU |
|---|---|---|---|---|---|---|
| 1986 | 20,000 | — | — | — | 4.50 | — |

**CROWN** **KM# 60a** **Weight:** 28.2800 g. **Composition:** 0.9250 Silver .8411 oz. ASW **Subject:** Prince Andrew's marriage

| Date | Mintage | F | VF | XF | Unc | BU |
|---|---|---|---|---|---|---|
| 1986 Proof | 5,000 | Value: 12.50 | | | | |

**CROWN** **KM# 122** **Composition:** Copper-Nickel

| Date | Mintage | F | VF | XF | Unc | BU |
|---|---|---|---|---|---|---|
| 1986 | — | — | — | — | 4.00 | — |

**CROWN** **KM# 64** **Composition:** Copper-Nickel **Series:** World Wildlife Fund **Reverse:** Iguana

| Date | Mintage | F | VF | XF | Unc | BU |
|---|---|---|---|---|---|---|
| 1988 | — | — | — | — | 6.50 | — |

**CROWN** **KM# 64a** **Weight:** 28.2800 g. **Composition:** 0.9250 Silver .8411 oz. ASW **Series:** World Wildlife Fund **Reverse:** Iguana

| Date | Mintage | F | VF | XF | Unc | BU |
|---|---|---|---|---|---|---|
| 1988 Proof | Est. 25,000 | Value: 20.00 | | | | |

**CROWN** **KM# 66** **Composition:** Copper-Nickel **Subject:** Queen Mother's 90th birthday

| Date | Mintage | F | VF | XF | Unc | BU |
|---|---|---|---|---|---|---|
| ND(1990) | — | — | — | — | 5.50 | — |

**CROWN** **KM# 66a** **Weight:** 28.2800 g. **Composition:** 0.9250 Silver .8411 oz. ASW **Subject:** Queen Mother's 90th birthday

| Date | Mintage | F | VF | XF | Unc | BU |
|---|---|---|---|---|---|---|
| ND(1990) Proof | Est. 10,000 | Value: 22.50 | | | | |

**CROWN** **KM# 74** **Composition:** Copper-Nickel **Subject:** Royal birthdays

| Date | Mintage | F | VF | XF | Unc | BU |
|---|---|---|---|---|---|---|
| 1991 | — | — | — | — | 4.50 | — |

**CROWN** **KM# 76** **Composition:** Copper-Nickel **Subject:** 10th wedding anniversary - prince and princess of Wales

| Date | Mintage | F | VF | XF | Unc | BU |
|---|---|---|---|---|---|---|
| 1991 | — | — | — | — | 4.00 | — |

**CROWN** **KM# 121** **Composition:** Copper-Nickel **Subject:** 10th wedding anniversary - prince and princess of Wales **Reverse:** Prince Charles

| Date | Mintage | F | VF | XF | Unc | BU |
|---|---|---|---|---|---|---|
| 1991 | — | — | — | — | 4.00 | — |

**DOLLAR** **KM# 143** **Composition:** Copper-Nickel **Series:** Steam Locomotive **Subject:** City of Truro **Note:** Similar to 20 Dollars, KM#145.

| Date | Mintage | F | VF | XF | Unc | BU |
|---|---|---|---|---|---|---|
| 1996 | — | — | — | — | 5.00 | — |

**DOLLAR** **KM# 146** **Composition:** Copper-Nickel **Series:** Steam Locomotive **Subject:** Flying Scotsman **Note:** Similar to 20 Dollars, KM#148.

| Date | Mintage | F | VF | XF | Unc | BU |
|---|---|---|---|---|---|---|
| 1996 | — | — | — | — | 5.00 | — |

**DOLLAR** **KM# 149** **Composition:** Copper-Nickel **Series:** Steam Locomotive **Subject:** Rocket **Note:** Similar to 20 Dollars, KM#151.

| Date | Mintage | F | VF | XF | Unc | BU |
|---|---|---|---|---|---|---|
| 1996 | — | — | — | — | 5.00 | — |

**DOLLAR** **KM# 152** **Composition:** Copper-Nickel **Series:** Steam Locomotive **Subject:** Evening Star **Note:** Similar to 20 Dollars, KM#154.

| Date | Mintage | F | VF | XF | Unc | BU |
|---|---|---|---|---|---|---|
| 1996 | — | — | — | — | 5.00 | — |

**DOLLAR** **KM# 155** **Composition:** Copper-Nickel **Series:** Steam Locomotive **Subject:** Mallard **Note:** Similar to 20 Dollars, KM#157.

| Date | Mintage | F | VF | XF | Unc | BU |
|---|---|---|---|---|---|---|
| 1996 | — | — | — | — | 5.00 | — |

**DOLLAR** **KM# 158** **Composition:** Copper-Nickel **Series:** Steam Locomotive **Subject:** Princess Elizabeth **Note:** Similar to 20 Dollars, KM#160.

| Date | Mintage | F | VF | XF | Unc | BU |
|---|---|---|---|---|---|---|
| 1996 | — | — | — | — | 5.00 | — |

**DOLLAR** **KM# 161** **Composition:** Copper-Nickel **Series:** Steam Locomotive **Subject:** Southern Pacific Lines - Class GS4 **Note:** Similar to 20 Dollars, KM#163.

| Date | Mintage | F | VF | XF | Unc | BU |
|---|---|---|---|---|---|---|
| 1996 | — | — | — | — | 5.00 | — |

**DOLLAR** **KM# 164** **Composition:** Copper-Nickel **Series:** Steam Locomotive **Subject:** German States Railway Class 05 **Note:** Similar to 20 Dollars, KM#166.

| Date | Mintage | F | VF | XF | Unc | BU |
|---|---|---|---|---|---|---|
| 1996 | — | — | — | — | 5.00 | — |

**DOLLAR** **KM# 167** **Composition:** Copper-Nickel **Series:** Steam Locomotive **Subject:** Japanese National Railways Class 62 **Note:** Similar to 20 Dollars, KM#169.

| Date | Mintage | F | VF | XF | Unc | BU |
|---|---|---|---|---|---|---|
| 1996 | — | — | — | — | 5.00 | — |

**DOLLAR** **KM# 170** **Composition:** Copper-Nickel **Series:** Steam Locomotive **Subject:** Chinese State Railways Class RM **Note:** Similar to 20 Dollars, KM#171.

| Date | Mintage | F | VF | XF | Unc | BU |
|---|---|---|---|---|---|---|
| 1996 | — | — | — | — | 5.00 | — |

**5 CROWNS** **KM# 6** **Weight:** 24.2400 g. **Composition:** 0.5000 Silver .3897 oz. ASW

| Date | Mintage | F | VF | XF | Unc | BU |
|---|---|---|---|---|---|---|
| 1975 Matte | 440 | — | — | — | 18.00 | — |
| 1975 Proof | 1,320 | Value: 13.50 | | | | |
| 1976 | 1,760 | — | — | — | 11.50 | — |
| 1976 Proof | 2,220 | Value: 11.50 | | | | |
| 1977 Proof | 1,370 | Value: 13.50 | | | | |

**5 CROWNS** **KM# 47** **Weight:** 14.5800 g. **Composition:** 0.5000 Silver .2344 oz. ASW **Subject:** Lord Mountbatten **Obverse:** Similar to 10 Crowns, KM#45

| Date | Mintage | F | VF | XF | Unc | BU |
|---|---|---|---|---|---|---|
| 1980 Proof | — | Value: 9.50 | | | | |

**5 CROWNS** **KM# 75** **Composition:** Copper-Nickel **Subject:** Discovery of America **Reverse:** Columbus before Ferdinand and Isabella

| Date | Mintage | F | VF | XF | Unc | BU |
|---|---|---|---|---|---|---|
| 1991 | — | — | — | — | 7.50 | — |

**5CROWNS** **KM#68** **Composition:** Copper-Nickel **Series:** Olympics **Reverse:** Equestrian and 3 events

| Date | Mintage | F | VF | XF | Unc | BU |
|---|---|---|---|---|---|---|
| 1992 | — | — | — | — | 4.50 | — |

**5 CROWNS** **KM#69** **Composition:** Copper-Nickel **Series:** Olympics **Reverse:** Gymnast on rings and 5 events

| Date | Mintage | F | VF | XF | Unc | BU |
|---|---|---|---|---|---|---|
| 1992 | — | — | — | — | 4.50 | — |

**5 CROWNS** **KM#70** **Composition:** Copper-Nickel **Series:** Olympics **Reverse:** Weighlifting and 3 events

| Date | Mintage | F | VF | XF | Unc | BU |
|---|---|---|---|---|---|---|
| 1992 | — | — | — | — | 4.50 | — |

**5 CROWNS** **KM#71** **Composition:** Copper-Nickel **Series:** Olympics **Reverse:** Rifle shooting and 3 events

| Date | Mintage | F | VF | XF | Unc | BU |
|---|---|---|---|---|---|---|
| 1992 | — | — | — | — | 4.50 | — |

**5 CROWNS** **KM#72** **Composition:** Copper-Nickel **Series:** Olympics **Reverse:** Sail boarding and 3 events

| Date | Mintage | F | VF | XF | Unc | BU |
|---|---|---|---|---|---|---|
| 1992 | — | — | — | — | 4.50 | — |

**5 CROWNS** **KM#73** **Composition:** Copper-Nickel **Series:** Olympics **Reverse:** Ski jumper and 4 events

| Date | Mintage | F | VF | XF | Unc | BU |
|---|---|---|---|---|---|---|
| 1992 | — | — | — | — | 4.50 | — |

**5 CROWNS** **KM# 77** **Composition:** Copper-Nickel **Subject:** 40th anniversary - reign of Elizabeth II

| Date | Mintage | F | VF | XF | Unc | BU |
|---|---|---|---|---|---|---|
| 1992 | — | — | — | — | 6.75 | — |

**5 CROWNS** **KM# 77a** **Weight:** 28.0400 g. **Composition:** 0.9250 Silver .8339 oz. ASW **Subject:** 40th anniversary - reign of Elizabeth II

| Date | Mintage | F | VF | XF | Unc | BU |
|---|---|---|---|---|---|---|
| 1992 Proof | — | Value: 40.00 | | | | |

**5 CROWNS** **KM# 84** **Composition:** Copper-Nickel **Subject:** 40th anniversary - reign of Elizabeth II

| Date | Mintage | F | VF | XF | Unc | BU |
|---|---|---|---|---|---|---|
| 1992 | — | — | — | — | 6.75 | — |

**5 CROWNS** **KM# 84a** **Weight:** 28.0400 g. **Composition:** 0.9250 Silver .8339 oz. ASW **Subject:** 40th anniversary - reign of Elizabeth II

| Date | Mintage | F | VF | XF | Unc | BU |
|---|---|---|---|---|---|---|
| 1992 Proof | — | Value: 40.00 | | | | |

**5 CROWNS** **KM# 85** **Composition:** Copper-Nickel **Subject:** 40th anniversary - reign of Elizabeth II **Reverse:** King George VI

| Date | Mintage | F | VF | XF | Unc | BU |
|---|---|---|---|---|---|---|
| 1992 | — | — | — | — | 6.75 | — |

**5 CROWNS** **KM# 85a** **Weight:** 28.0400 g. **Composition:** 0.9250 Silver .8339 oz. ASW **Subject:** 40th anniversary - reign of Elizabeth II **Reverse:** King George VI

| Date | Mintage | F | VF | XF | Unc | BU |
|---|---|---|---|---|---|---|
| 1992 Proof | — | Value: 40.00 | | | | |

**5 CROWNS** **KM# 86** **Composition:** Copper-Nickel **Subject:** 40th anniversary - reign of Elizabeth II **Reverse:** Windsor Castle

| Date | Mintage | F | VF | XF | Unc | BU |
|---|---|---|---|---|---|---|
| 1992 | — | — | — | — | 6.75 | — |

**5 CROWNS** **KM# 86a** **Weight:** 28.2800 g. **Composition:** 0.9250 Silver .8339 oz. ASW **Subject:** 40th anniversary - reign of Elizabeth II **Reverse:** Windsor Castle

| Date | Mintage | F | VF | XF | Unc | BU |
|---|---|---|---|---|---|---|
| 1992 Proof | — | Value: 40.00 | | | | |

**5 CROWNS** **KM# 87** **Composition:** Copper-Nickel **Subject:** World Cup '94 **Reverse:** Jules Rimet and trophy

| Date | Mintage | F | VF | XF | Unc | BU |
|---|---|---|---|---|---|---|
| ND(1993) | — | — | — | — | 7.50 | — |

**5 CROWNS** **KM# 88** **Composition:** Copper-Nickel **Subject:** World Cup '94 **Reverse:** Uruguay winners and 2 players

| Date | Mintage | F | VF | XF | Unc | BU |
|---|---|---|---|---|---|---|
| ND(1993) | — | — | — | — | 7.50 | — |

**5 CROWNS** **KM# 89** **Composition:** Copper-Nickel **Subject:** World Cup '94 **Reverse:** Italy winners - Dino Zoff

| Date | Mintage | F | VF | XF | Unc | BU |
|---|---|---|---|---|---|---|
| ND(1993) | — | — | — | — | 7.50 | — |

**5 CROWNS** **KM# 90** **Composition:** Copper-Nickel **Subject:** World Cup '94 **Reverse:** West Germany winners - Franz Beckenbauer

| Date | Mintage | F | VF | XF | Unc | BU |
|---|---|---|---|---|---|---|
| ND(1993) | — | — | — | — | 7.50 | — |

**5 CROWNS** **KM# 91** **Composition:** Copper-Nickel **Subject:** World Cup '94 **Reverse:** Brazil winners - Pele

| Date | Mintage | F | VF | XF | Unc | BU |
|---|---|---|---|---|---|---|
| ND(1993) | — | — | — | — | 7.50 | — |

**5 CROWNS** **KM# 92** **Composition:** Copper-Nickel **Subject:** World Cup '94 **Reverse:** England winners - Bobby Moore

| Date | Mintage | F | VF | XF | Unc | BU |
|---|---|---|---|---|---|---|
| ND(1993) | — | — | — | — | 7.50 | — |

**5 CROWNS** **KM# 93** **Composition:** Copper-Nickel **Subject:** World Cup '94 **Reverse:** Argentina winners - Mario Kempes

| Date | Mintage | F | VF | XF | Unc | BU |
|---|---|---|---|---|---|---|
| ND(1993) | — | — | — | — | 7.50 | — |

**5 CROWNS** **KM# 94** **Composition:** Copper-Nickel **Subject:** World Cup '94 **Reverse:** USA host - trophy and flag

| Date | Mintage | F | VF | XF | Unc | BU |
|---|---|---|---|---|---|---|
| ND(1993) | — | — | — | — | 7.50 | — |

**5 CROWNS** **KM# 103** **Composition:** Copper-Nickel **Subject:** 40th anniversary of coronation **Reverse:** Westminster Abbey

| Date | Mintage | F | VF | XF | Unc | BU |
|---|---|---|---|---|---|---|
| ND(1993) | — | — | — | — | 6.00 | — |

**5 CROWNS** **KM# 104** **Composition:** Copper-Nickel **Subject:** 40th anniversary of coronation **Reverse:** Crown jewels

| Date | Mintage | F | VF | XF | Unc | BU |
|---|---|---|---|---|---|---|
| ND(1993) | — | — | — | — | 6.00 | — |

**5 CROWNS** **KM# 105** **Composition:** Copper-Nickel **Subject:** 40th anniversary of coronation **Reverse:** Queen, clergy and maids of honor

| Date | Mintage | F | VF | XF | Unc | BU |
|---|---|---|---|---|---|---|
| ND(1993) | — | — | — | — | 6.00 | — |

**5 CROWNS** **KM# 106** **Composition:** Copper-Nickel **Subject:** 40th anniversary of coronation **Reverse:** Consort's homage

| Date | Mintage | F | VF | XF | Unc | BU |
|---|---|---|---|---|---|---|
| ND(1993) | — | — | — | — | 6.00 | — |

**5 CROWNS** **KM# 107** **Composition:** Copper-Nickel **Subject:** 40th anniversary of coronation **Reverse:** Enthroned queen

| Date | Mintage | F | VF | XF | Unc | BU |
|---|---|---|---|---|---|---|
| ND(1993) | — | — | — | — | 6.00 | — |

**5 CROWNS** **KM# 108** **Composition:** Copper-Nickel **Subject:** 40th anniversary of coronation **Reverse:** Queen in coach

| Date | Mintage | F | VF | XF | Unc | BU |
|---|---|---|---|---|---|---|
| ND(1993) | — | — | — | — | 6.00 | — |

**5 CROWNS** **KM# 123** **Composition:** Copper-Nickel **Series:** 1994 Winter Olympics **Subject:** Speed skating

| Date | Mintage | F | VF | XF | Unc | BU |
|---|---|---|---|---|---|---|
| 1993 Prooflike | — | — | — | — | 4.75 | — |

**5 CROWNS** **KM# 124** **Composition:** Copper-Nickel **Series:** 1994 Winter Olympics **Subject:** Figure skating

| Date | Mintage | F | VF | XF | Unc | BU |
|---|---|---|---|---|---|---|
| 1993 Prooflike | — | — | — | — | 4.75 | — |

**5 CROWNS** **KM# 125** **Composition:** Copper-Nickel **Series:** 1994 Winter Olympics **Subject:** Ice hockey

| Date | Mintage | F | VF | XF | Unc | BU |
|---|---|---|---|---|---|---|
| 1993 Prooflike | — | — | — | — | 4.75 | — |

**5 CROWNS** **KM# 126** **Composition:** Copper-Nickel **Series:** 1994 Winter Olympics **Subject:** Slalom skiing

| Date | Mintage | F | VF | XF | Unc | BU |
|---|---|---|---|---|---|---|
| 1993 Prooflike | — | — | — | — | 4.75 | — |

**5 CROWNS** **KM# 127** **Composition:** Copper-Nickel **Series:** 1994 Winter Olympics **Subject:** Ski jumping

| Date | Mintage | F | VF | XF | Unc | BU |
|---|---|---|---|---|---|---|
| 1993 Prooflike | — | — | — | — | 4.75 | — |

**5 CROWNS** **KM# 128** **Composition:** Copper-Nickel **Series:** 1994 Winter Olympics **Reverse:** Bob sled and team

| Date | Mintage | F | VF | XF | Unc | BU |
|---|---|---|---|---|---|---|
| 1993 Prooflike | — | — | — | — | 4.75 | — |

**5 CROWNS** **KM# 177** **Composition:** Copper-Nickel **Subject:** 25th anniversary 1969-1994 - Apollo 11

| Date | Mintage | F | VF | XF | Unc | BU |
|---|---|---|---|---|---|---|
| 1993 | — | — | — | — | 6.75 | — |

**5 CROWNS** **KM# 178** **Composition:** Copper-Nickel **Subject:** 25th anniversary 1969-1994 - Apollo 11 **Reverse:** Lunar landing

| Date | Mintage | F | VF | XF | Unc | BU |
|---|---|---|---|---|---|---|
| 1993 | — | — | — | — | 6.75 | — |

**5 CROWNS** **KM# 179** **Composition:** Copper-Nickel **Subject:** 25th anniversary 1969-1994 - Apollo 11 **Reverse:** Astronaut descending ladder

| Date | Mintage | F | VF | XF | Unc | BU |
|---|---|---|---|---|---|---|
| 1993 | — | — | — | — | 6.75 | — |

**5 CROWNS** **KM# 181** **Composition:** Copper-Nickel **Subject:** 25th anniversary 1969-1994 - Apollo 11 **Reverse:** Astronaut walking on the moon

| Date | Mintage | F | VF | XF | Unc | BU |
|---|---|---|---|---|---|---|
| 1993 | — | — | — | — | 6.75 | — |

**5 CROWNS** **KM# 182** **Composition:** Copper-Nickel **Subject:** 25th anniversary 1969-1994 - Apollo 11 **Reverse:** Ocean recovery

| Date | Mintage | F | VF | XF | Unc | BU |
|---|---|---|---|---|---|---|
| 1993 | — | — | — | — | 6.75 | — |

**5 CROWNS** **KM# 180** **Composition:** Copper-Nickel **Subject:** 25th anniversary 1969-1994 - Apollo 11 **Reverse:** Astronauts raising flag on moon

| Date | Mintage | F | VF | XF | Unc | BU |
|---|---|---|---|---|---|---|
| 1994 | — | — | — | — | 6.75 | — |

**5 CROWNS** **KM# 132** **Composition:** Copper-Nickel **Subject:** 25th anniversary 1969-1994 - Apollo 11 **Reverse:** First lunar landing, salute to American Numismatic Association and coin collecting

| Date | Mintage | F | VF | XF | Unc | BU |
|---|---|---|---|---|---|---|
| 1994 Prooflike | 10,000 | — | — | — | 10.00 | — |

**5 CROWNS KM# 173 Composition:** Copper-Nickel **Subject:** 50th anniversary - Normandy landing **Reverse:** Sir Bertram II Ramsay

| Date | Mintage | F | VF | XF | Unc | BU |
|---|---|---|---|---|---|---|
| 1994 | — | — | — | — | 9.50 | — |

**5 CROWNS KM# 174 Composition:** Copper-Nickel **Subject:** 50th anniversary - Normandy landing **Reverse:** Bernard L. Montgomery

| Date | Mintage | F | VF | XF | Unc | BU |
|---|---|---|---|---|---|---|
| 1994 | — | — | — | — | 9.50 | — |

**5 CROWNS KM# 175 Composition:** Copper-Nickel **Subject:** 50th anniversary - Normandy landing **Reverse:** Omar N. Bradley

| Date | Mintage | F | VF | XF | Unc | BU |
|---|---|---|---|---|---|---|
| 1994 | — | — | — | — | 9.50 | — |

**5 CROWNS KM# 176 Composition:** Copper-Nickel **Subject:** 50th anniversary - Normandy landing **Reverse:** Dwight D. Eisenhower

| Date | Mintage | F | VF | XF | Unc | BU |
|---|---|---|---|---|---|---|
| 1994 | — | — | — | — | 9.50 | — |

**5 CROWNS KM# 133 Composition:** Copper-Nickel **Subject:** 50th anniversary - VE Day **Reverse:** Roosevelt, Churchill, and Stalin

| Date | Mintage | F | VF | XF | Unc | BU |
|---|---|---|---|---|---|---|
| 1995 | — | — | — | — | 9.50 | — |

**5 CROWNS KM# 134 Composition:** Copper-Nickel **Subject:** 50th anniversary - VE Day **Obverse:** Similar to KM#133 **Reverse:** Planes

| Date | Mintage | F | VF | XF | Unc | BU |
|---|---|---|---|---|---|---|
| 1995 | — | — | — | — | 7.50 | — |

**5 CROWNS KM# 135 Composition:** Copper-Nickel **Subject:** 50th anniversary - VE Day **Obverse:** Similar to KM#133 **Reverse:** U.S. and Soviet troops meet

| Date | Mintage | F | VF | XF | Unc | BU |
|---|---|---|---|---|---|---|
| 1995 | — | — | — | — | 7.50 | — |

**5 CROWNS KM# 136 Composition:** Copper-Nickel **Subject:** 50th anniversary - VE Day **Obverse:** Similar to KM#133 **Reverse:** London, Washington and Paris

| Date | Mintage | F | VF | XF | Unc | BU |
|---|---|---|---|---|---|---|
| 1995 | — | — | — | — | 7.50 | — |

**5 CROWNS KM# 188 Weight:** 10.0000 g. **Composition:** 0.9990 Silver .3212 oz. ASW **Series:** XXVI Summer Olympics **Reverse:** Hurdlers **Note:** Similar to 20 Crowns, KM#189.

| Date | Mintage | F | VF | XF | Unc | BU |
|---|---|---|---|---|---|---|
| 1995 Proof | — | Value: 15.00 | | | | |

**5 CROWNS KM# 190 Weight:** 10.0000 g. **Composition:** 0.9990 Silver .3212 oz. ASW **Series:** XXVI Summer Olympics **Reverse:** Cyclist **Note:** Similar to 20 Crowns, KM#191.

| Date | Mintage | F | VF | XF | Unc | BU |
|---|---|---|---|---|---|---|
| 1995 Proof | — | Value: 15.00 | | | | |

**5 CROWNS KM# 192 Weight:** 10.0000 g. **Composition:** 0.9990 Silver .3212 oz. ASW **Series:** XXVI Summer Olympics **Reverse:** Fencers **Note:** Similar to 20 Crowns, KM#193.

| Date | Mintage | F | VF | XF | Unc | BU |
|---|---|---|---|---|---|---|
| 1995 Proof | — | Value: 15.00 | | | | |

**5 CROWNS KM# 194 Weight:** 10.0000 g. **Composition:** 0.9990 Silver .3212 oz. ASW **Series:** XXVI Summer Olympics **Reverse:** Equestrian **Note:** Similar to 20 Crowns, KM#195.

| Date | Mintage | F | VF | XF | Unc | BU |
|---|---|---|---|---|---|---|
| 1995 Proof | — | Value: 15.00 | | | | |

**5 CROWNS KM# 196 Weight:** 10.0000 g. **Composition:** 0.9990 Silver .3212 oz. ASW **Series:** XXVI Summer Olympics **Reverse:** Pole vaulter **Note:** Similar to 20 Crowns, KM#197.

| Date | Mintage | F | VF | XF | Unc | BU |
|---|---|---|---|---|---|---|
| 1995 Proof | — | Value: 15.00 | | | | |

**5 CROWNS KM# 198 Weight:** 10.0000 g. **Composition:** 0.9990 Silver .3212 oz. ASW **Series:** XXVI Summer Olympics **Reverse:** Runners **Note:** Similar to 20 Crowns, KM#199.

| Date | Mintage | F | VF | XF | Unc | BU |
|---|---|---|---|---|---|---|
| 1995 Proof | — | Value: 15.00 | | | | |

**5 CROWNS KM# 200 Weight:** 10.0000 g. **Composition:** 0.9990 Silver .3212 oz. ASW **Series:** XXVI Summer Olympics **Reverse:** Gymnast **Note:** Similar to 20 Crowns, KM#201.

| Date | Mintage | F | VF | XF | Unc | BU |
|---|---|---|---|---|---|---|
| 1995 Proof | — | Value: 15.00 | | | | |

**5 CROWNS KM# 202 Weight:** 10.0000 g. **Composition:** 0.9990 Silver .3212 oz. ASW **Series:** XXVI Summer Olympics **Reverse:** Swimmer **Note:** Similar to 20 Crowns, KM#203.

| Date | Mintage | F | VF | XF | Unc | BU |
|---|---|---|---|---|---|---|
| 1995 Proof | — | Value: 15.00 | | | | |

**5 CROWNS KM# 204 Weight:** 10.0000 g. **Composition:** 0.9990 Silver .3212 oz. ASW **Series:** XXVI Summer Olympics **Reverse:** Diver **Note:** Similar to 20 Crowns, KM#205.

| Date | Mintage | F | VF | XF | Unc | BU |
|---|---|---|---|---|---|---|
| 1995 Proof | — | Value: 15.00 | | | | |

**5 CROWNS KM# 206 Weight:** 10.0000 g. **Composition:** 0.9990 Silver .3212 oz. ASW **Series:** XXVI Summer Olympics **Reverse:** Sprinter

| Date | Mintage | F | VF | XF | Unc | BU |
|---|---|---|---|---|---|---|
| 1995 Proof | — | Value: 15.00 | | | | |

**5 CROWNS KM# 225 Weight:** 26.2000 g. **Composition:** Brass **Subject:** Mother Theresa **Obverse:** National arms **Reverse:** Portrait **Edge:** Reeded **Size:** 39.1 mm.

| Date | Mintage | F | VF | XF | Unc | BU |
|---|---|---|---|---|---|---|
| 1997 | — | — | — | — | 10.00 | — |

**5 DOLLARS KM# 144 Weight:** 10.0000 g. **Composition:** 0.9990 Silver .3212 oz. ASW **Series:** Steam Locomotive **Subject:** City of Truro **Note:** Similar to 20 Dollars, KM#145.

| Date | Mintage | F | VF | XF | Unc | BU |
|---|---|---|---|---|---|---|
| 1996 Proof | Est. 25,000 | Value: 22.00 | | | | |

**5 DOLLARS KM# 147 Weight:** 10.0000 g. **Composition:** 0.9990 Silver .3212 oz. ASW **Series:** Steam Locomotive **Subject:** Flying Scotsman **Note:** Similar to 20 Dollars, KM#148.

| Date | Mintage | F | VF | XF | Unc | BU |
|---|---|---|---|---|---|---|
| 1996 Proof | Est. 25,000 | Value: 22.00 | | | | |

**5 DOLLARS KM# 150 Weight:** 10.0000 g. **Composition:** 0.9990 Silver .3212 oz. ASW **Series:** Steam Locomotive **Subject:** Rocket **Note:** Similar to 20 Dollars, KM#151.

| Date | Mintage | F | VF | XF | Unc | BU |
|---|---|---|---|---|---|---|
| 1996 Proof | Est. 25,000 | Value: 22.00 | | | | |

**5 DOLLARS KM# 153 Weight:** 10.0000 g. **Composition:** 0.9990 Silver .3212 oz. ASW **Series:** Steam Locomotive **Subject:** Evening Star **Note:** Similar to 20 Dollars, KM#154.

| Date | Mintage | F | VF | XF | Unc | BU |
|---|---|---|---|---|---|---|
| 1996 Proof | Est. 25,000 | Value: 22.00 | | | | |

**5 DOLLARS KM# 156 Weight:** 10.0000 g. **Composition:** 0.9990 Silver .3212 oz. ASW **Series:** Steam Locomotive **Subject:** Mallard **Note:** Similar to 20 Dollars, KM#157.

| Date | Mintage | F | VF | XF | Unc | BU |
|---|---|---|---|---|---|---|
| 1996 Proof | Est. 25,000 | Value: 22.00 | | | | |

**5 DOLLARS KM# 159 Weight:** 10.0000 g. **Composition:** 0.9990 Silver .3212 oz. ASW **Series:** Steam Locomotive **Subject:** Princess Elizabeth **Note:** Similar to 20 Dollars, KM#160.

| Date | Mintage | F | VF | XF | Unc | BU |
|---|---|---|---|---|---|---|
| 1996 Proof | Est. 25,000 | Value: 22.00 | | | | |

**5 DOLLARS KM# 162 Weight:** 10.0000 g. **Composition:** 0.9990 Silver .3212 oz. ASW **Series:** Steam Locomotive **Subject:** Southern Pacific Lines - Class GS4 **Note:** Similar to 20 Dollars, KM#163.

| Date | Mintage | F | VF | XF | Unc | BU |
|---|---|---|---|---|---|---|
| 1996 Proof | Est. 25,000 | Value: 22.00 | | | | |

**5 DOLLARS KM# 165 Weight:** 10.0000 g. **Composition:** 0.9990 Silver .3212 oz. ASW **Series:** Steam Locomotive **Subject:** German States Railway - Class 05 **Note:** Similar to 20 Dollars, KM#166.

| Date | Mintage | F | VF | XF | Unc | BU |
|---|---|---|---|---|---|---|
| 1996 Proof | Est. 25,000 | Value: 22.00 | | | | |

**5 DOLLARS KM# 168 Weight:** 10.0000 g. **Composition:** 0.9990 Silver .3212 oz. ASW **Series:** Steam Locomotive **Sub-**

ject: Japanese National Railways - Class 62 **Note:** Similar to 20 Dollars, KM#169.

| Date | Mintage | F | VF | XF | Unc | BU |
|---|---|---|---|---|---|---|
| 1996 Proof | Est. 25,000 | Value: 22.00 | | | | |

**5 DOLLARS** **KM# 171** **Weight:** 10.0000 g. **Composition:** 0.9990 Silver .3212 oz. ASW **Series:** Steam Locomotive **Subject:** Chinese State Railways - Class RM **Note:** Similar to 20 Dollars, KM#172.

| Date | Mintage | F | VF | XF | Unc | BU |
|---|---|---|---|---|---|---|
| 1996 Proof | Est. 25,000 | Value: 22.00 | | | | |

**10 CROWNS** **KM# 7** **Weight:** 29.9800 g. **Composition:** 0.9250 Silver .8916 oz. ASW **Subject:** Age of exploration **Reverse:** Spacecraft

| Date | Mintage | F | VF | XF | Unc | BU |
|---|---|---|---|---|---|---|
| 1975 Matte | 1,250 | — | — | — | 16.50 | — |
| 1975 Proof | 2,935 | Value: 14.50 | | | | |

**10 CROWNS** **KM# 12** **Weight:** 29.9800 g. **Composition:** 0.9250 Silver .8916 oz. ASW **Obverse:** Similar to KM#7

| Date | Mintage | F | VF | XF | Unc | BU |
|---|---|---|---|---|---|---|
| 1976 | 4,185 | — | — | — | 12.50 | — |
| 1976 Proof | 2,220 | Value: 16.50 | | | | |
| 1977 Proof | 1,370 | Value: 18.50 | | | | |

**10 CROWNS** **KM# 45** **Weight:** 29.7000 g. **Composition:** 0.9250 Silver .8832 oz. ASW **Subject:** 10th anniversary - Prince Charles' investiture

| Date | Mintage | F | VF | XF | Unc | BU |
|---|---|---|---|---|---|---|
| 1979 Proof | 25,000 | Value: 10.00 | | | | |

**10 CROWNS** **KM# 48** **Weight:** 23.3300 g. **Composition:** 0.5000 Silver .3750 oz. ASW **Subject:** Lord Mountbatten **Obverse:** Similar to KM#45

| Date | Mintage | F | VF | XF | Unc | BU |
|---|---|---|---|---|---|---|
| 1980 Proof | — | Value: 12.50 | | | | |

**10 CROWNS** **KM# 53** **Weight:** 29.7000 g. **Composition:** 0.9250 Silver .8832 oz. ASW **Subject:** Wedding of Prince Charles and Lady Diana **Note:** Similar to 100 Crowns, KM#54.

| Date | Mintage | F | VF | XF | Unc | BU |
|---|---|---|---|---|---|---|
| 1981 Proof | 40,000 | Value: 21.50 | | | | |

**10 CROWNS** **KM# 55** **Weight:** 23.2800 g. **Composition:** 0.9250 Silver .6923 oz. ASW **Series:** International Year of the Child

| Date | Mintage | F | VF | XF | Unc | BU |
|---|---|---|---|---|---|---|
| 1982 Proof | 7,928 | Value: 20.00 | | | | |

**10 CROWNS** **KM# 56** **Weight:** 23.2800 g. **Composition:** 0.9250 Silver .6923 oz. ASW **Subject:** World Football Chmpionship **Reverse:** 1 player

| Date | Mintage | F | VF | XF | Unc | BU |
|---|---|---|---|---|---|---|
| 1982 Proof | 7,865 | Value: 18.50 | | | | |

**10 CROWNS** **KM# 57** **Weight:** 23.2800 g. **Composition:** 0.9250 Silver .6923 oz. ASW **Subject:** World Football Championship **Reverse:** 2 players

| Date | Mintage | F | VF | XF | Unc | BU |
|---|---|---|---|---|---|---|
| 1982 Proof | 7,165 | Value: 18.50 | | | | |

**10 CROWNS** **KM# 58** **Weight:** 23.2800 g. **Composition:** 0.9250 Silver .6923 oz. ASW **Series:** Summer Olympics **Reverse:** Javelin thrower

| Date | Mintage | F | VF | XF | Unc | BU |
|---|---|---|---|---|---|---|
| 1984 Proof | 2,160 | Value: 21.50 | | | | |

**10 CROWNS** **KM# 63** **Weight:** 23.2800 g. **Composition:** 0.9250 Silver .6923 oz. ASW **Series:** Decade for Women

| Date | Mintage | F | VF | XF | Unc | BU |
|---|---|---|---|---|---|---|
| 1985 Proof | 1,001 | Value: 35.00 | | | | |

**20 CROWNS** **KM# 2** **Weight:** 38.7000 g. **Composition:** 0.9250 Silver 1.1509 oz. ASW **Subject:** Centenary - birth of Churchill

| Date | Mintage | F | VF | XF | Unc | BU |
|---|---|---|---|---|---|---|
| 1974 Matte | 268,000 | — | — | — | 17.50 | — |
| 1974 Proof | 8,400 | Value: 25.00 | | | | |

**Note:** 4,100 issued individually; 4,300 issued in binational sets with Cayman Islands 25 Dollars, KM#10.

**20 CROWNS** **KM# 8** **Weight:** 38.7000 g. **Composition:** 0.9250 Silver 1.1509 oz. ASW **Subject:** Age of Exploration **Obverse:** Similar to 10 Crowns, KM#7 **Reverse:** Christopher Columbus

| Date | Mintage | F | VF | XF | Unc | BU |
|---|---|---|---|---|---|---|
| 1975 Matte | 1,037 | — | — | — | 22.50 | — |
| 1975 Proof | 2,769 | Value: 22.50 | | | | |

**20 CROWNS** KM# 13 **Weight:** 38.7000 g. **Composition:** 0.9250 Silver 1.1509 oz. ASW **Subject:** U.S. Bicentennial **Obverse:** Similar to 10 Crowns, KM#7

| Date | Mintage | F | VF | XF | Unc | BU |
|---|---|---|---|---|---|---|
| 1976 Matte | 5,022 | — | — | — | 20.00 | — |
| 1976 Proof | 4,474 | Value: 22.50 | | | | |

**20 CROWNS** KM# 14 **Weight:** 38.7000 g. **Composition:** 0.9250 Silver 1.1509 oz. ASW **Obverse:** Similar to 10 Crowns, KM#7 **Reverse:** 4 Victoria cameos

| Date | Mintage | F | VF | XF | Unc | BU |
|---|---|---|---|---|---|---|
| 1976 | 25,000 | — | — | — | 17.50 | — |
| 1976 Proof | 22,000 | Value: 22.50 | | | | |
| 1977 Proof | 1,934 | Value: 27.50 | | | | |

**20 CROWNS** KM# 18 **Weight:** 38.7000 g. **Composition:** 0.9250 Silver 1.1509 oz. ASW **Obverse:** Similar to 1/2 Crown, KM#52 **Reverse:** 4 George III cameos

| Date | Mintage | F | VF | XF | Unc | BU |
|---|---|---|---|---|---|---|
| 1977 | — | — | — | — | 27.50 | — |
| 1977 Proof | 1,973 | Value: 30.00 | | | | |

**20 CROWNS** KM# 23 **Weight:** 38.7000 g. **Composition:** 0.9250 Silver 1.1509 oz. ASW **Subject:** XI Commonwealth Games **Obverse:** Similar to 10 Crowns, KM#55

| Date | Mintage | F | VF | XF | Unc | BU |
|---|---|---|---|---|---|---|
| 1978 Proof | 10,000 | Value: 20.00 | | | | |

**20 CROWNS** KM# 49 **Weight:** 29.8100 g. **Composition:** 0.5000 Silver .4792 oz. ASW **Subject:** Lord Mountbatten **Obverse:** Similar to 10 Crowns, KM#45

| Date | Mintage | F | VF | XF | Unc | BU |
|---|---|---|---|---|---|---|
| 1980 Proof | — | Value: 22.50 | | | | |

**20 CROWNS** KM# 131.1 **Weight:** 28.0400 g. **Composition:** 0.9250 Silver .8339 oz. ASW **Subject:** Discovery of America **Obverse:** Crude portrait **Reverse:** Columbus and Indians exchange gifts

| Date | Mintage | F | VF | XF | Unc | BU |
|---|---|---|---|---|---|---|
| 1981 Proof | — | Value: 27.50 | | | | |

**20 CROWNS** KM# 67.1 **Weight:** 28.0400 g. **Composition:** 0.9250 Silver .8339 oz. ASW **Subject:** Discovery of America **Obverse:** Crude portrait **Reverse:** Santa Maria

| Date | Mintage | F | VF | XF | Unc | BU |
|---|---|---|---|---|---|---|
| 1989 Proof | — | Value: 27.50 | | | | |

**20 CROWNS** KM# 129.1 **Weight:** 28.0400 g. **Composition:** 0.9250 Silver .8339 oz. ASW **Subject:** Discovery of America **Obverse:** Crude portrait **Reverse:** Columbus sights new world

| Date | Mintage | F | VF | XF | Unc | BU |
|---|---|---|---|---|---|---|
| 1989 Proof | — | Value: 27.50 | | | | |

**20 CROWNS** KM# 115.1 **Weight:** 28.0400 g. **Composition:** 0.9250 Silver .8339 oz. ASW **Subject:** Discovery of America **Obverse:** Crude portrait **Reverse:** The Nina

| Date | Mintage | F | VF | XF | Unc | BU |
|---|---|---|---|---|---|---|
| 1989 Proof | — | Value: 27.50 | | | | |

**20 CROWNS** KM# 116.1 **Weight:** 28.0400 g. **Composition:** 0.9250 Silver .8339 oz. ASW **Subject:** Discovery of America **Obverse:** Crude portrait **Reverse:** The Pinta

| Date | Mintage | F | VF | XF | Unc | BU |
|---|---|---|---|---|---|---|
| 1989 Proof | — | Value: 27.50 | | | | |

**20 CROWNS** KM# 117.1 **Weight:** 28.0400 g. **Composition:** 0.9250 Silver .8339 oz. ASW **Subject:** Discovery of America **Obverse:** Crude portrait **Reverse:** Ships set sail

| Date | Mintage | F | VF | XF | Unc | BU |
|---|---|---|---|---|---|---|
| 1989 Proof | — | Value: 27.50 | | | | |

**20 CROWNS** **KM# 118.1** **Weight:** 28.0400 g. **Composition:** 0.9250 Silver .8339 oz. ASW **Subject:** Discovery of America **Obverse:** Crude portrait **Reverse:** Ships crossing the Atlantic

| Date | Mintage | F | VF | XF | Unc | BU |
|---|---|---|---|---|---|---|
| 1989 Proof | — | Value: 27.50 | | | | |

**20 CROWNS** **KM# 119.1** **Weight:** 28.0400 g. **Composition:** 0.9250 Silver .8339 oz. ASW **Subject:** Discovery of America **Obverse:** Crude portrait **Reverse:** Siting land

| Date | Mintage | F | VF | XF | Unc | BU |
|---|---|---|---|---|---|---|
| 1989 Proof | — | Value: 27.50 | | | | |

**20 CROWNS** **KM# 120.1** **Weight:** 28.0400 g. **Composition:** 0.9250 Silver .8339 oz. ASW **Subject:** Discovery of America **Obverse:** Crude portrait **Reverse:** Columbus explores the Caribbean

| Date | Mintage | F | VF | XF | Unc | BU |
|---|---|---|---|---|---|---|
| 1989 Proof | — | Value: 27.50 | | | | |

**20 CROWNS** **KM# 130.1** **Weight:** 28.0400 g. **Composition:** 0.9250 Silver .8339 oz. ASW **Subject:** Discovery of America **Obverse:** Crude portrait **Reverse:** Columbus claims land for Spain

| Date | Mintage | F | VF | XF | Unc | BU |
|---|---|---|---|---|---|---|
| 1989 Proof | — | Value: 27.50 | | | | |

**20 CROWNS** **KM# 67.2** **Weight:** 28.0400 g. **Composition:** 0.9250 Silver .8339 oz. ASW **Subject:** Discovery of America **Obverse:** Refined portrait **Reverse:** Santa Maria

| Date | Mintage | F | VF | XF | Unc | BU |
|---|---|---|---|---|---|---|
| 1991 Proof | — | Value: 32.50 | | | | |

**20 CROWNS** **KM# 129.2** **Weight:** 28.0400 g. **Composition:** 0.9250 Silver .8339 oz. ASW **Subject:** Discovery of America **Obverse:** Refined portrait **Reverse:** Columbus sights new world

| Date | Mintage | F | VF | XF | Unc | BU |
|---|---|---|---|---|---|---|
| 1991 Proof | — | Value: 32.50 | | | | |

**20 CROWNS** **KM# 115.2** **Weight:** 28.0400 g. **Composition:** 0.9250 Silver .8339 oz. ASW **Subject:** Discovery of America **Obverse:** Refined portrait **Reverse:** The Nina

| Date | Mintage | F | VF | XF | Unc | BU |
|---|---|---|---|---|---|---|
| 1991 Proof | — | Value: 32.50 | | | | |

**20 CROWNS** **KM# 116.2** **Weight:** 28.0400 g. **Composition:** 0.9250 Silver .8339 oz. ASW **Subject:** Discovery of America **Obverse:** Refined portrait **Reverse:** The Pinta

| Date | Mintage | F | VF | XF | Unc | BU |
|---|---|---|---|---|---|---|
| 1991 Proof | — | Value: 32.50 | | | | |

**20 CROWNS** **KM# 117.2** **Weight:** 28.0400 g. **Composition:** 0.9250 Silver .8339 oz. ASW **Subject:** Discovery of America **Obverse:** Refined portrait **Reverse:** Ships set sail

| Date | Mintage | F | VF | XF | Unc | BU |
|---|---|---|---|---|---|---|
| 1991 Proof | — | Value: 32.50 | | | | |

**20 CROWNS** **KM# 118.2** **Weight:** 28.0400 g. **Composition:** 0.9250 Silver .8339 oz. ASW **Subject:** Discovery of America **Obverse:** Refined portrait **Reverse:** Ships crossing the Atlantic

| Date | Mintage | F | VF | XF | Unc | BU |
|---|---|---|---|---|---|---|
| 1991 Proof | — | Value: 32.50 | | | | |

**20 CROWNS** **KM# 119.2** **Weight:** 28.0400 g. **Composition:** 0.9250 Silver .8339 oz. ASW **Subject:** Discovery of America **Obverse:** Refined portrait **Reverse:** Siting land

| Date | Mintage | F | VF | XF | Unc | BU |
|---|---|---|---|---|---|---|
| 1991 Proof | — | Value: 32.50 | | | | |

**20 CROWNS** **KM# 120.2** **Weight:** 28.0400 g. **Composition:** 0.9250 Silver .8339 oz. ASW **Subject:** Discovery of America **Obverse:** Refined portrait **Reverse:** Columbus explores the Caribbean

| Date | Mintage | F | VF | XF | Unc | BU |
|---|---|---|---|---|---|---|
| 1991 Proof | — | Value: 32.50 | | | | |

**20 CROWNS** **KM# 130.2** **Weight:** 28.0400 g. **Composition:** 0.9250 Silver .8339 oz. ASW **Subject:** Discovery of America **Obverse:** Refined portrait **Reverse:** Columbus claims land for Spain

| Date | Mintage | F | VF | XF | Unc | BU |
|---|---|---|---|---|---|---|
| 1991 Proof | — | Value: 32.50 | | | | |

**20 CROWNS** **KM# 131.2** **Weight:** 28.0400 g. **Composition:** 0.9250 Silver .8339 oz. ASW **Subject:** Discovery of America **Obverse:** Refined portrait **Reverse:** Columbus and Indians exchange gifts

| Date | Mintage | F | VF | XF | Unc | BU |
|---|---|---|---|---|---|---|
| 1991 Proof | — | Value: 32.50 | | | | |

**20 CROWNS** **KM# 116.3** **Weight:** 28.0400 g. **Composition:** 0.9250 Silver .8339 oz. ASW **Subject:** Discovery of America **Obverse:** Refined portrait #2, similar to KM#67.3 **Reverse:** The Pinta

| Date | Mintage | F | VF | XF | Unc | BU |
|---|---|---|---|---|---|---|
| 1992 Proof | — | Value: 30.00 | | | | |

**20 CROWNS** **KM# 67.3** **Weight:** 28.0400 g. **Composition:** 0.9250 Silver .8339 oz. ASW **Subject:** Discovery of America **Obverse:** Refined portrait #2 **Reverse:** Santa Maria

| Date | Mintage | F | VF | XF | Unc | BU |
|---|---|---|---|---|---|---|
| 1992 Proof | — | Value: 30.00 | | | | |

**20 CROWNS** **KM# 115.3** **Weight:** 28.0400 g. **Composition:** 0.9250 Silver .8339 oz. ASW **Subject:** Discovery of America **Obverse:** Refined portrait #2, similar to KM#67.3 **Reverse:** The Nina

| Date | Mintage | F | VF | XF | Unc | BU |
|---|---|---|---|---|---|---|
| 1992 Proof | — | Value: 30.00 | | | | |

**20 CROWNS** **KM# 117.3** **Weight:** 28.0400 g. **Composition:** 0.9250 Silver .8339 oz. ASW **Subject:** Discovery of America **Obverse:** Refined portrait #2, similar to KM#67.3 **Reverse:** Ships set sail

| Date | Mintage | F | VF | XF | Unc | BU |
|---|---|---|---|---|---|---|
| 1992 Proof | — | Value: 30.00 | | | | |

**20 CROWNS** **KM# 118.3** **Weight:** 28.0400 g. **Composition:** 0.9250 Silver .8339 oz. ASW **Subject:** Discovery of America **Obverse:** Refined portrait #2, similar to KM#67.3 **Reverse:** Ships crossing the Atlantic

| Date | Mintage | F | VF | XF | Unc | BU |
|---|---|---|---|---|---|---|
| 1992 Proof | — | Value: 30.00 | | | | |

**20 CROWNS** **KM# 119.3** **Weight:** 28.0400 g. **Composition:** 0.9250 Silver .8339 oz. ASW **Subject:** Discovery of America **Obverse:** Refined portrait #2, similar to KM#67.3 **Reverse:** Siting land

| Date | Mintage | F | VF | XF | Unc | BU |
|---|---|---|---|---|---|---|
| 1992 Proof | — | Value: 30.00 | | | | |

**20 CROWNS** **KM# 120.3** **Weight:** 28.0400 g. **Composition:** 0.9250 Silver .8339 oz. ASW **Subject:** Discovery of America **Obverse:** Refined portrait #2, similar to KM#67.3 **Reverse:** Columbus explores the Caribbean

| Date | Mintage | F | VF | XF | Unc | BU |
|---|---|---|---|---|---|---|
| 1992 Proof | — | Value: 30.00 | | | | |

**20 CROWNS** **KM# 129.3** **Weight:** 28.0400 g. **Composition:** 0.9250 Silver .8339 oz. ASW **Subject:** Discovery of America **Obverse:** Refined portrait #2, similar to KM#67.3 **Reverse:** Columbus sights new world

| Date | Mintage | F | VF | XF | Unc | BU |
|---|---|---|---|---|---|---|
| 1992 Proof | — | Value: 30.00 | | | | |

**20 CROWNS** **KM# 130.3** **Weight:** 28.0400 g. **Composition:** 0.9250 Silver .8339 oz. ASW **Subject:** Discovery of America **Obverse:** Refined portrait #2, similar to KM#67.3 **Reverse:** Columbus claims land for Spain

| Date | Mintage | F | VF | XF | Unc | BU |
|---|---|---|---|---|---|---|
| 1992 Proof | — | Value: 30.00 | | | | |

**20 CROWNS** **KM# 131.3** **Weight:** 28.0400 g. **Composition:** 0.9250 Silver .8339 oz. ASW **Subject:** Discovery of America **Obverse:** Refined portrait #2, similar to KM#67.3 **Reverse:** Columbus and Indians exchange gifts

| Date | Mintage | F | VF | XF | Unc | BU |
|---|---|---|---|---|---|---|
| 1992 Proof | — | Value: 30.00 | | | | |

**20 CROWNS** **KM# 78** **Weight:** 31.1000 g. **Composition:** 0.9990 Silver 1 oz. ASW **Series:** Olympics **Obverse:** Similar to KM#2 reverse **Reverse:** Equestrian and 3 events

| Date | Mintage | F | VF | XF | Unc | BU |
|---|---|---|---|---|---|---|
| 1992 Proof | 20,000 | Value: 21.50 | | | | |

**20 CROWNS** **KM# 79** **Weight:** 31.1000 g. **Composition:** 0.9990 Silver 1 oz. ASW **Series:** Olympics **Reverse:** Gymnast on rings and 5 events

| Date | Mintage | F | VF | XF | Unc | BU |
|---|---|---|---|---|---|---|
| 1992 Proof | Est. 20,000 | Value: 21.50 | | | | |

**20 CROWNS** **KM# 80** **Weight:** 31.1000 g. **Composition:** 0.9990 Silver 1 oz. ASW **Series:** Olympics **Reverse:** Weightlifting and 3 events

| Date | Mintage | F | VF | XF | Unc | BU |
|---|---|---|---|---|---|---|
| 1992 Proof | Est. 20,000 | Value: 21.50 | | | | |

**20 CROWNS** **KM# 81** **Weight:** 31.1000 g. **Composition:** 0.9990 Silver 1 oz. ASW **Series:** Olympics **Reverse:** Rifle shooting and 3 events

| Date | Mintage | F | VF | XF | Unc | BU |
|---|---|---|---|---|---|---|
| 1992 Proof | Est. 20,000 | Value: 21.50 | | | | |

**20 CROWNS** **KM# 82** **Weight:** 31.1000 g. **Composition:** 0.9990 Silver 1 oz. ASW **Series:** Olympics **Reverse:** Sail boarding and 3 events

| Date | Mintage | F | VF | XF | Unc | BU |
|---|---|---|---|---|---|---|
| 1992 Proof | Est. 20,000 | Value: 21.50 | | | | |

**20 CROWNS** **KM# 83** **Weight:** 31.1000 g. **Composition:** 0.9990 Silver 1 oz. ASW **Series:** Olympics **Reverse:** Ski jumper and 4 events

| Date | Mintage | F | VF | XF | Unc | BU |
|---|---|---|---|---|---|---|
| 1992 Proof | Est. 20,000 | Value: 21.50 | | | | |

**20 CROWNS** **KM# 95** **Weight:** 31.1000 g. **Composition:** 0.9990 Silver 1 oz. ASW **Subject:** World Cup '94 - Jules Rimet **Note:** Similar to 5 Crowns, KM#87.

| Date | Mintage | F | VF | XF | Unc | BU |
|---|---|---|---|---|---|---|
| ND(1993) Proof | Est. 10,000 | Value: 27.50 | | | | |

**20 CROWNS** **KM# 96** **Weight:** 31.1000 g. **Composition:** 0.9990 Silver 1 oz. ASW **Subject:** World Cup '94 - Uruguay winners **Reverse:** 2 players **Note:** Similar to 5 Crowns, KM#88.

| Date | Mintage | F | VF | XF | Unc | BU |
|---|---|---|---|---|---|---|
| ND(1993) Proof | Est. 10,000 | Value: 30.00 | | | | |

**20 CROWNS** **KM# 97** **Weight:** 31.1000 g. **Composition:** 0.9990 Silver 1 oz. ASW **Subject:** World Cup '94 - Italy winners **Reverse:** Dino Zoff **Note:** Similar to 5 Crowns, KM#89.

| Date | Mintage | F | VF | XF | Unc | BU |
|---|---|---|---|---|---|---|
| ND(1993) Proof | Est. 10,000 | Value: 30.00 | | | | |

**20 CROWNS** **KM# 98** **Weight:** 31.1000 g. **Composition:** 0.9990 Silver 1 oz. ASW **Subject:** World Cup '94 - West German winners **Reverse:** Franz Breckenbauer **Note:** Similar to 5 Crowns, KM#90.

| Date | Mintage | F | VF | XF | Unc | BU |
|---|---|---|---|---|---|---|
| ND(1993) Proof | Est. 10,000 | Value: 30.00 | | | | |

**20 CROWNS** **KM# 99** **Weight:** 31.1000 g. **Composition:** 0.9990 Silver 1 oz. ASW **Subject:** World Cup '94 - Brazil winners **Reverse:** Pele **Note:** Similar to 5 Crowns, KM#91.

| Date | Mintage | F | VF | XF | Unc | BU |
|---|---|---|---|---|---|---|
| ND(1993) Proof | Est. 10,000 | Value: 27.50 | | | | |

**20 CROWNS** **KM# 100** **Weight:** 31.1000 g. **Composition:** 0.9990 Silver 1 oz. ASW **Subject:** World Cup '94 - England winners **Reverse:** Bobby Moore **Note:** Similar to 5 Crowns, KM#92.

| Date | Mintage | F | VF | XF | Unc | BU |
|---|---|---|---|---|---|---|
| ND(1993) Proof | Est. 10,000 | Value: 30.00 | | | | |

**20 CROWNS** **KM# 101** **Weight:** 31.1000 g. **Composition:** 0.9990 Silver 1 oz. ASW **Subject:** World Cup '94 - Argentina winners **Reverse:** Mario Kempes **Note:** Similar to 5 Crowns, KM#93.

| Date | Mintage | F | VF | XF | Unc | BU |
|---|---|---|---|---|---|---|
| ND(1993) Proof | Est. 10,000 | Value: 30.00 | | | | |

**20 CROWNS** **KM# 102** **Weight:** 31.1000 g. **Composition:** 0.9990 Silver 1 oz. ASW **Subject:** World Cup '94 - USA host **Reverse:** Trophy and flag

| Date | Mintage | F | VF | XF | Unc | BU |
|---|---|---|---|---|---|---|
| ND(1993) Proof | Est. 10,000 | Value: 27.50 | | | | |

**20 CROWNS** **KM# 109** **Weight:** 31.1000 g. **Composition:** 0.9990 Silver 1 oz. ASW **Subject:** 40th anniversary of coronation **Reverse:** Westminster Abbey **Note:** Similar to 5 Crowns, KM#103.

| Date | Mintage | F | VF | XF | Unc | BU |
|---|---|---|---|---|---|---|
| ND(1993) Proof | Est. 10,000 | Value: 42.50 | | | | |

**20 CROWNS** **KM# 110** **Weight:** 31.1000 g. **Composition:** 0.9990 Silver 1 oz. ASW **Subject:** 40th anniversary of coronation **Reverse:** Crown jewels **Note:** Similar to 5 Crowns, KM#104.

| Date | Mintage | F | VF | XF | Unc | BU |
|---|---|---|---|---|---|---|
| ND(1993) Proof | Est. 10,000 | Value: 42.50 | | | | |

**20 CROWNS** **KM# 111** **Weight:** 31.1000 g. **Composition:** 0.9990 Silver 1 oz. ASW **Subject:** 40th anniversary of coronation **Reverse:** Queen, clergy and maids of honor **Note:** Similar to 5 Crowns, KM#105.

| Date | Mintage | F | VF | XF | Unc | BU |
|---|---|---|---|---|---|---|
| ND(1993) Proof | Est. 10,000 | Value: 42.50 | | | | |

**20 CROWNS** **KM# 112** **Weight:** 31.1000 g. **Composition:** 0.9990 Silver 1 oz. ASW **Subject:** 40th anniversary of coronation **Reverse:** Consort's homage **Note:** Similar to 5 Crowns, KM#106.

| Date | Mintage | F | VF | XF | Unc | BU |
|---|---|---|---|---|---|---|
| ND(1993) Proof | Est. 10,000 | Value: 42.50 | | | | |

**20 CROWNS** **KM# 113** **Weight:** 31.1000 g. **Composition:** 0.9990 Silver 1 oz. ASW **Subject:** 40th anniversary of coronation **Reverse:** Queen on throne **Note:** Similar to 5 Crowns, KM#107.

| Date | Mintage | F | VF | XF | Unc | BU |
|---|---|---|---|---|---|---|
| ND(1993) Proof | Est. 10,000 | Value: 42.50 | | | | |

**20 CROWNS** **KM# 114** **Weight:** 31.1000 g. **Composition:** 0.9990 Silver 1 oz. ASW **Subject:** 40th anniversary of coronation **Reverse:** Queen in coach **Note:** Similar to 5 Crowns, KM#108.

| Date | Mintage | F | VF | XF | Unc | BU |
|---|---|---|---|---|---|---|
| ND(1993) Proof | Est. 10,000 | Value: 42.50 | | | | |

**20 CROWNS** **KM# 141** **Weight:** 31.1000 g. **Composition:** 0.9990 Silver 1 oz. ASW **Series:** 1994 Olympics **Reverse:** Bobsled

| Date | Mintage | F | VF | XF | Unc | BU |
|---|---|---|---|---|---|---|
| 1993 Proof | — | Value: 27.50 | | | | |

**20 CROWNS** **KM# 142** **Weight:** 31.1000 g. **Composition:** 0.9990 Silver 1 oz. ASW **Subject:** 25th anniversary - Apollo 11 moon landing

| Date | Mintage | F | VF | XF | Unc | BU |
|---|---|---|---|---|---|---|
| 1993 Proof | — | Value: 32.50 | | | | |

**20 CROWNS** **KM# 183** **Weight:** 28.0400 g. **Composition:** 0.9250 Silver .8339 oz. ASW **Subject:** Apollo 11 series - rocket launch **Obverse:** Queen's portrait **Reverse:** Rocket launch scene **Note:** Similar to 5 Crowns, KM#177.

| Date | Mintage | F | VF | XF | Unc | BU |
|---|---|---|---|---|---|---|
| 1993 Proof | — | Value: 35.00 | | | | |

**20 CROWNS** **KM# 184** **Weight:** 28.0400 g. **Composition:** 0.9250 Silver .8339 oz. ASW **Subject:** Apollo 11 series - lunar landing **Obverse:** Queen's portrait **Reverse:** Lunar landing scene **Note:** Similar to 5 Crowns, KM#178.

| Date | Mintage | F | VF | XF | Unc | BU |
|---|---|---|---|---|---|---|
| 1993 Proof | — | Value: 32.50 | | | | |

**20 CROWNS** **KM# 185** **Weight:** 28.0400 g. **Composition:** 0.9250 Silver .8339 oz. ASW **Subject:** Apollo 11 series - leaving lunar lander **Obverse:** Queen's portrait **Reverse:** Astronaut descending ladder **Note:** Similar to 5 Crowns, KM#179.

| Date | Mintage | F | VF | XF | Unc | BU |
|---|---|---|---|---|---|---|
| 1993 Proof | — | Value: 35.00 | | | | |

**20 CROWNS** **KM# 186** **Weight:** 28.0400 g. **Composition:** 0.9250 Silver .8339 oz. ASW **Subject:** Apollo 11 series - planting American flag **Obverse:** Queen's portrait **Reverse:** Astronauts planting flag on moon **Note:** Similar to 5 Crowns, KM#180.

| Date | Mintage | F | VF | XF | Unc | BU |
|---|---|---|---|---|---|---|
| 1993 Proof | — | Value: 32.50 | | | | |

**20 CROWNS** **KM# 187** **Weight:** 28.0400 g. **Composition:** 0.9250 Silver .8339 oz. ASW **Subject:** Apollo 11 series - moon walk **Obverse:** Queen's portrait **Reverse:** Astronaut walking on the moon **Note:** Similar to 5 Crowns, KM#181.

| Date | Mintage | F | VF | XF | Unc | BU |
|---|---|---|---|---|---|---|
| 1993 Proof | — | Value: 32.50 | | | | |

**20 CROWNS** **KM# 208** **Weight:** 21.1300 g. **Composition:** 0.9990 Silver .9999 oz. ASW **Series:** XVII Winter Olympics **Obverse:** Queen's portrait and date **Reverse:** Figure skater **Note:** Reportedly a mule or pattern.

| Date | Mintage | F | VF | XF | Unc | BU |
|---|---|---|---|---|---|---|
| 1994 Proof | — | Value: 125 | | | | |

**20 CROWNS** **KM# 218** **Weight:** 31.1035 g. **Composition:** 0.9990 Silver 1.0000 oz. ASW **Series:** D-Day **Subject:** General Omar Bradley **Obverse:** Queen Elizabeth's portrait **Reverse:** Bradley's portrait **Edge:** Reeded **Size:** 39.1 mm.

| Date | Mintage | F | VF | XF | Unc | BU |
|---|---|---|---|---|---|---|
| 1994 Proof | — | Value: 35.00 | | | | |

**20 CROWNS** **KM# 219** **Weight:** 31.1035 g. **Composition:** 0.9990 Silver 1.0000 oz. ASW **Series:** D-Day **Subject:** General Montgomery **Obverse:** Queen Elizabeth's portrait **Reverse:** General Montgomery's portrait **Edge:** Reeded **Size:** 39.1 mm.

| Date | Mintage | F | VF | XF | Unc | BU |
|---|---|---|---|---|---|---|
| 1994 Proof | — | Value: 35.00 | | | | |

**20 CROWNS** **KM# 220** **Weight:** 31.1035 g. **Composition:** 0.9990 Silver 1.0000 oz. ASW **Series:** D-Day **Subject:** Sir Bertram Ramsay **Obverse:** Queen Elizabeth's portrait **Reverse:** Sir Bertram Ramsay's portrait **Edge:** Reeded **Size:** 39.1 mm.

| Date | Mintage | F | VF | XF | Unc | BU |
|---|---|---|---|---|---|---|
| 1994 Proof | — | Value: 35.00 | | | | |

**20 CROWNS** **KM# 221** **Weight:** 31.1035 g. **Composition:** 0.9990 Silver 1.0000 oz. ASW **Series:** D-Day **Subject:** General Dwight Eisenhower **Obverse:** Queen Elizabeth's portrait **Reverse:** Genreal Dwight Eisenhower's portrait **Edge:** Reeded **Size:** 39.1 mm.

| Date | Mintage | F | VF | XF | Unc | BU |
|---|---|---|---|---|---|---|
| 1994 Proof | — | Value: 35.00 | | | | |

**20 CROWNS** **KM# 137** **Weight:** 31.1035 g. **Composition:** 0.9990 Silver 1 oz. ASW **Subject:** 50th anniversary - VE Day **Reverse:** Churchill, Roosevelt and Stalin

| Date | Mintage | F | VF | XF | Unc | BU |
|---|---|---|---|---|---|---|
| 1995 Proof | 15,000 | Value: 32.50 | | | | |

**20 CROWNS** **KM# 138** **Weight:** 31.1035 g. **Composition:** 0.9990 Silver 1 oz. ASW **Subject:** 50th anniversary - VE Day **Reverse:** 3 planes

| Date | Mintage | F | VF | XF | Unc | BU |
|---|---|---|---|---|---|---|
| 1995 Proof | 15,000 | Value: 32.50 | | | | |

**20 CROWNS** **KM# 139** **Weight:** 31.1035 g. **Composition:** 0.9990 Silver 1 oz. ASW **Subject:** 50th anniversary - VE Day **Reverse:** U.S. and Soviet troops meet

| Date | Mintage | F | VF | XF | Unc | BU |
|---|---|---|---|---|---|---|
| 1995 Proof | 15,000 | Value: 32.50 | | | | |

**20 CROWNS** **KM# 140** **Weight:** 31.1035 g. **Composition:** 0.9990 Silver 1 oz. ASW **Subject:** 50th anniversary - VE Day **Reverse:** London, Washington, Moscow and Paris

| Date | Mintage | F | VF | XF | Unc | BU |
|---|---|---|---|---|---|---|
| 1995 Proof | 15,000 | Value: 40.00 | | | | |

**20 CROWNS** **KM# 189** **Weight:** 31.1035 g. **Composition:** 0.9990 Silver 1 oz. ASW **Series:** XXVI Summer Olympics **Reverse:** Hurdlers

| Date | Mintage | F | VF | XF | Unc | BU |
|---|---|---|---|---|---|---|
| 1995 Proof | — | Value: 28.50 | | | | |

**20 CROWNS** **KM# 191** **Weight:** 31.1035 g. **Composition:** 0.9990 Silver 1 oz. ASW **Series:** XXVI Summer Olympics **Reverse:** Cyclist

| Date | Mintage | F | VF | XF | Unc | BU |
|---|---|---|---|---|---|---|
| 1995 Proof | — | Value: 28.50 | | | | |

**20 CROWNS** **KM# 193** **Weight:** 31.1035 g. **Composition:** 0.9990 Silver 1 oz. ASW **Series:** XXVI Summer Olympics **Reverse:** Fencers

| Date | Mintage | F | VF | XF | Unc | BU |
|---|---|---|---|---|---|---|
| 1995 Proof | — | Value: 27.50 | | | | |

**20 CROWNS** **KM# 195** **Weight:** 31.1035 g. **Composition:** 0.9990 Silver 1 oz. ASW **Series:** XXVI Summer Olympics **Reverse:** Equestrian

| Date | Mintage | F | VF | XF | Unc | BU |
|---|---|---|---|---|---|---|
| 1995 Proof | — | Value: 28.50 | | | | |

**20 CROWNS** **KM# 197** **Weight:** 31.1035 g. **Composition:** 0.9990 Silver 1 oz. ASW **Series:** XXVI Summer Olympics **Reverse:** Pole vaulter

| Date | Mintage | F | VF | XF | Unc | BU |
|---|---|---|---|---|---|---|
| 1995 Proof | — | Value: 28.50 | | | | |

**20 CROWNS** **KM# 199** **Weight:** 31.1035 g. **Composition:** 0.9990 Silver 1 oz. ASW **Series:** XXVI Summer Olympics **Reverse:** Runners

| Date | Mintage | F | VF | XF | Unc | BU |
|---|---|---|---|---|---|---|
| 1995 Proof | — | Value: 27.50 | | | | |

**20 CROWNS** **KM# 201** **Weight:** 31.1035 g. **Composition:** 0.9990 Silver 1 oz. ASW **Series:** XXVI Summer Olympics **Reverse:** Gymnast

| Date | Mintage | F | VF | XF | Unc | BU |
|---|---|---|---|---|---|---|
| 1995 Proof | — | Value: 28.50 | | | | |

**20 CROWNS** **KM# 203** **Weight:** 31.1035 g. **Composition:** 0.9990 Silver 1 oz. ASW **Series:** XXVI Summer Olympics **Reverse:** Swimmer

| Date | Mintage | F | VF | XF | Unc | BU |
|---|---|---|---|---|---|---|
| 1995 Proof | — | Value: 27.50 | | | | |

**20 CROWNS** **KM# 205** **Weight:** 31.1035 g. **Composition:** 0.9990 Silver 1 oz. ASW **Series:** XXVI Summer Olympics **Reverse:** Diver

| Date | Mintage | F | VF | XF | Unc | BU |
|---|---|---|---|---|---|---|
| 1995 Proof | — | Value: 28.50 | | | | |

**20 CROWNS** **KM# 207** **Weight:** 31.1035 g. **Composition:** 0.9990 Silver 1 oz. ASW **Series:** XXVI Summer Olympics **Reverse:** Sprinter

| Date | Mintage | F | VF | XF | Unc | BU |
|---|---|---|---|---|---|---|
| 1995 Proof | — | Value: 28.50 | | | | |

**20 CROWNS** **KM# 222** **Weight:** 31.1035 g. **Composition:** 0.9990 Silver 1.0000 oz. ASW **Subject:** Hong Kong's Return to China **Obverse:** Queen's portrait. **Reverse:** City view. **Edge:** Reeded. **Size:** 38.9 mm. **Note:** Struck at North American Mint, Inc.

| Date | Mintage | F | VF | XF | Unc | BU |
|---|---|---|---|---|---|---|
| 1997 Proof | — | Value: 28.50 | | | | |

**20 CROWNS** **KM# 217** **Weight:** 31.2400 g. **Composition:** 0.9990 Silver 1.0034 oz. ASW **Obverse:** Portrait of Queen Elizabeth **Reverse:** Two bottle-nosed dolphins **Edge:** Reeded **Size:** 39 mm.

| Date | Mintage | F | VF | XF | Unc | BU |
|---|---|---|---|---|---|---|
| 1998 Proof | — | Value: 30.00 | | | | |

**20 CROWNS** **KM# 223** **Weight:** 31.1035 g. **Composition:** 0.9990 Silver 1.0000 oz. ASW **Subject:** Apollo 11 **Obverse:** Queen's portrait. **Reverse:** Spacecraft in flight. **Edge:** Reeded. **Size:** 38.9 mm.

| Date | Mintage | F | VF | XF | Unc | BU |
|---|---|---|---|---|---|---|
| 1999 Proof | — | Value: 30.00 | | | | |

**20 CROWNS** **KM# 224** **Weight:** 31.1035 g. **Composition:** 0.9990 Silver 1.0000 oz. ASW **Subject:** Apollo 11 **Obverse:** Queen's portrait. **Reverse:** Portraits of three astronauts. **Edge:** Reeded. **Size:** 38.9 mm.

| Date | Mintage | F | VF | XF | Unc | BU |
|---|---|---|---|---|---|---|
| 1999 Proof | — | Value: 30.00 | | | | |

**20 DOLLARS** **KM# 145** **Weight:** 31.1035 g. **Composition:** 0.9990 Silver 1 oz. ASW **Series:** Steam Locomotive **Subject:** City of Truro

| Date | Mintage | F | VF | XF | Unc | BU |
|---|---|---|---|---|---|---|
| 1996 Proof | Est. 20,000 | Value: 35.00 | | | | |

**20 DOLLARS** **KM# 148** **Weight:** 31.1035 g. **Composition:** 0.9990 Silver 1 oz. ASW **Series:** Steam Locomotive **Subject:** Flying Scotsman **Obverse:** Similar to KM#145

| Date | Mintage | F | VF | XF | Unc | BU |
|---|---|---|---|---|---|---|
| 1996 Proof | Est. 20,000 | Value: 35.00 | | | | |

**20 DOLLARS** **KM# 151** **Weight:** 31.1035 g. **Composition:** 0.9990 Silver 1 oz. ASW **Series:** Steam Locomotive **Subject:** Rocket **Obverse:** Similar to KM#145

| Date | Mintage | F | VF | XF | Unc | BU |
|---|---|---|---|---|---|---|
| 1996 Proof | Est. 20,000 | Value: 35.00 | | | | |

**20 DOLLARS** **KM# 154** **Weight:** 31.1035 g. **Composition:** 0.9990 Silver 1 oz. ASW **Series:** Steam Locomotive **Subject:** Evening Star **Obverse:** Similar to KM#145

| Date | Mintage | F | VF | XF | Unc | BU |
|---|---|---|---|---|---|---|
| 1996 Proof | Est. 20,000 | Value: 35.00 | | | | |

**20 DOLLARS** **KM# 157** **Weight:** 31.1035 g. **Composition:** 0.9990 Silver 1 oz. ASW **Series:** Steam Locomotive **Subject:** Mallard **Obverse:** Similar to KM#145

| Date | Mintage | F | VF | XF | Unc | BU |
|---|---|---|---|---|---|---|
| 1996 Proof | Est. 20,000 | Value: 35.00 | | | | |

**20 DOLLARS** **KM# 160** **Weight:** 31.1035 g. **Composition:** 0.9990 Silver 1 oz. ASW **Series:** Steam Locomotive **Subject:** Princess Elizabeth **Obverse:** Similar to KM#145

| Date | Mintage | F | VF | XF | Unc | BU |
|---|---|---|---|---|---|---|
| 1996 Proof | Est. 20,000 | Value: 35.00 | | | | |

**20 DOLLARS** **KM# 163** **Weight:** 31.1035 g. **Composition:** 0.9990 Silver 1 oz. ASW **Series:** Steam Locomotive **Subject:** South Pacific Line - Class GS4 **Obverse:** Similar to KM#145

| Date | Mintage | F | VF | XF | Unc | BU |
|---|---|---|---|---|---|---|
| 1996 Proof | Est. 20,000 | Value: 35.00 | | | | |

**20 DOLLARS** **KM# 166** **Weight:** 31.1035 g. **Composition:** 0.9990 Silver 1 oz. ASW **Series:** Steam Locomotive **Subject:** German State Railway - Class 05 **Obverse:** Similar to KM#145

| Date | Mintage | F | VF | XF | Unc | BU |
|---|---|---|---|---|---|---|
| 1996 Proof | Est. 20,000 | Value: 35.00 | | | | |

**20 DOLLARS** **KM# 169** **Weight:** 31.1035 g. **Composition:** 0.9990 Silver 1 oz. ASW **Series:** Steam Locomotive **Subject:** Japanese Railway - Class 62 **Obverse:** Similar to KM#145

| Date | Mintage | F | VF | XF | Unc | BU |
|---|---|---|---|---|---|---|
| 1996 Proof | Est. 20,000 | Value: 35.00 | | | | |

**20 DOLLARS** **KM# 172** **Weight:** 31.1035 g. **Composition:** 0.9990 Silver 1 oz. ASW **Series:** Steam Locomotive **Subject:** Chinese State Railway Class RM **Obverse:** Similar to KM#145

| Date | Mintage | F | VF | XF | Unc | BU |
|---|---|---|---|---|---|---|
| 1996 Proof | Est. 20,000 | Value: 35.00 | | | | |

**25 CROWNS** **KM# 9.1** **Weight:** 4.5000 g. **Composition:** 0.5000 Gold .0723 oz. AGW

| Date | Mintage | F | VF | XF | Unc | BU |
|---|---|---|---|---|---|---|
| 1975 | 1,272 | — | — | — | 35.00 | — |
| 1975 Proof | 2,096 | Value: 40.00 | | | | |

**25 CROWNS** **KM# 9.2** **Weight:** 4.5000 g. **Composition:** 0.5000 Gold .0723 oz. AGW **Size:** 19 mm.

| Date | Mintage | F | VF | XF | Unc | BU |
|---|---|---|---|---|---|---|
| 1976 | — | — | — | — | 35.00 | — |
| 1976 Proof | 2,185 | Value: 40.00 | | | | |
| 1977 Proof | 2,125 | Value: 40.00 | | | | |

**25 CROWNS** **KM# 19** **Weight:** 43.7500 g. **Composition:** 0.9250 Silver 1.3012 oz. ASW **Subject:** Queen's silver jubilee **Obverse:** Similar to 10 Crowns, KM#7

| Date | Mintage | F | VF | XF | Unc | BU |
|---|---|---|---|---|---|---|
| 1977 Matte | — | — | — | — | 22.50 | — |
| 1977 Proof | 13,000 | Value: 25.00 | | | | |

**25 CROWNS** **KM# 24** **Weight:** 43.7500 g. **Composition:** 0.9250 Silver 1.3012 oz. ASW **Subject:** 25th anniversary of coronation **Obverse:** Similar to 50 Crowns, KM#39 **Reverse:** Lion of England

| Date | Mintage | F | VF | XF | Unc | BU |
|---|---|---|---|---|---|---|
| 1978 Proof | — | Value: 30.00 | | | | |

**25 CROWNS** **KM# 25** **Weight:** 43.7500 g. **Composition:** 0.9250 Silver 1.3012 oz. ASW **Subject:** Griffin of Edward III **Obverse:** Similar to 50 Crowns, KM#39

| Date | Mintage | F | VF | XF | Unc | BU |
|---|---|---|---|---|---|---|
| 1978 Proof | — | Value: 30.00 | | | | |

**25 CROWNS** **KM# 26** **Weight:** 43.7500 g. **Composition:** 0.9250 Silver 1.3012 oz. ASW **Subject:** Red dragon of Wales **Obverse:** Similar to 50 Crowns, KM#39

| Date | Mintage | F | VF | XF | Unc | BU |
|---|---|---|---|---|---|---|
| 1978 Proof | — | Value: 30.00 | | | | |

**25 CROWNS** **KM# 27** **Weight:** 43.7500 g. **Composition:** 0.9250 Silver 1.3012 oz. ASW **Subject:** White greyhound of Richmond **Obverse:** Similar to 50 Crowns, KM#39

| Date | Mintage | F | VF | XF | Unc | BU |
|---|---|---|---|---|---|---|
| 1978 Proof | — | Value: 30.00 | | | | |

**25 CROWNS** **KM# 28** **Weight:** 43.7500 g. **Composition:** 0.9250 Silver 1.3012 oz. ASW **Subject:** Unicorn of Scotland **Obverse:** Similar to 50 Crowns, KM#39

| Date | Mintage | F | VF | XF | Unc | BU |
|---|---|---|---|---|---|---|
| 1978 Proof | — | Value: 37.50 | | | | |

**25 CROWNS** **KM# 29** **Weight:** 43.7500 g. **Composition:** 0.9250 Silver 1.3012 oz. ASW **Subject:** White horse of Hannover **Obverse:** Similar to 50 Crowns, KM#39

| Date | Mintage | F | VF | XF | Unc | BU |
|---|---|---|---|---|---|---|
| 1978 Proof | — | Value: 30.00 | | | | |

**25 CROWNS** **KM# 30** **Weight:** 43.7500 g. **Composition:** 0.9250 Silver 1.3012 oz. ASW **Subject:** Black bull of Clarence **Obverse:** Similar to 50 Crowns, KM#39

| Date | Mintage | F | VF | XF | Unc | BU |
|---|---|---|---|---|---|---|
| 1978 Proof | — | Value: 30.00 | | | | |

**25 CROWNS** **KM# 31** **Weight:** 43.7500 g. **Composition:** 0.9250 Silver 1.3012 oz. ASW **Subject:** Yale of Beaufort **Obverse:** Similar to 50 Crowns, KM#41

| Date | Mintage | F | VF | XF | Unc | BU |
|---|---|---|---|---|---|---|
| 1978 Proof | — | Value: 30.00 | | | | |

**25 CROWNS** **KM# 32** **Weight:** 43.7500 g. **Composition:** 0.9250 Silver 1.3012 oz. ASW **Subject:** Falcon of Plantagenets **Obverse:** Similar to 50 Crowns, KM#42

| Date | Mintage | F | VF | XF | Unc | BU |
|---|---|---|---|---|---|---|
| 1978 Proof | — | Value: 30.00 | | | | |

**25 CROWNS** **KM# 33** **Weight:** 43.7500 g. **Composition:** 0.9250 Silver 1.3012 oz. ASW **Subject:** White lion of Mortimer **Obverse:** Similar to 50 Crowns, KM#43

| Date | Mintage | F | VF | XF | Unc | BU |
|---|---|---|---|---|---|---|
| 1978 Proof | — | Value: 30.00 | | | | |

**25 CROWNS** **KM# 209** **Weight:** 155.4400 g. **Composition:** 0.9990 Silver 4.9925 oz. ASW **Subject:** Purple-throated carib **Obverse:** Queen's portrait **Reverse:** Multicolored purple-throated carib bird **Size:** 63 mm. **Note:** Illustration reduced.

| Date | Mintage | F | VF | XF | Unc | BU |
|---|---|---|---|---|---|---|
| 1995 Matte | — | — | — | — | 100 | — |
| 1995 Proof | — | Value: 75.00 | | | | |

**25 CROWNS** **KM# 210** **Weight:** 155.4400 g. **Composition:** 0.9990 Silver 4.9925 oz. ASW **Subject:** Streamertail **Obverse:** Queen's portrait **Reverse:** Multicolored streamertail bird **Size:** 63 mm. **Note:** Illustration reduced.

| Date | Mintage | F | VF | XF | Unc | BU |
|---|---|---|---|---|---|---|
| 1995 Matte | — | — | — | — | 100 | — |
| 1995 Proof | — | Value: 75.00 | | | | |

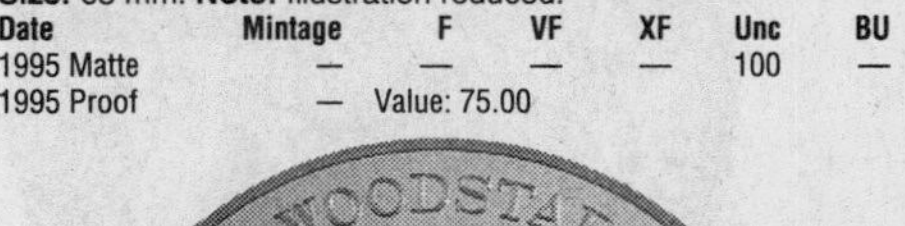

**25 CROWNS** **KM# 211** **Weight:** 155.4400 g. **Composition:** 0.9990 Silver 4.9925 oz. ASW **Subject:** Woodstar **Obverse:** Queen's portrait **Reverse:** Multicolored woodstar bird **Size:** 63 mm. **Note:** Illustration reduced.

| Date | Mintage | F | VF | XF | Unc | BU |
|---|---|---|---|---|---|---|
| 1995 | — | — | — | — | 100 | — |
| 1995 Proof | — | Value: 75.00 | | | | |

**50 CROWNS** **KM# 3** **Weight:** 9.0000 g. **Composition:** 0.5000 Gold .1447 oz. AGW **Subject:** Centenary - birth of Churchill

| Date | Mintage | F | VF | XF | Unc | BU |
|---|---|---|---|---|---|---|
| 1974 Matte | 30,000 | — | — | — | 60.00 | — |
| 1974 Proof | 4,000 | Value: 80.00 | | | | |

**50 CROWNS** **KM# 10** **Weight:** 6.2200 g. **Composition:** 0.5000 Gold .1 oz. AGW **Subject:** Age of Exploration **Reverse:** Christopher Columbus

| Date | Mintage | F | VF | XF | Unc | BU |
|---|---|---|---|---|---|---|
| 1975 | 2,863 | — | — | — | 75.00 | — |
| 1975 Proof | 1,577 | Value: 90.00 | | | | |

**50 CROWNS** **KM# 15** **Weight:** 6.2200 g. **Composition:** 0.5000 Gold .1 oz. AGW **Subject:** U.S. Bicentennial

| Date | Mintage | F | VF | XF | Unc | BU |
|---|---|---|---|---|---|---|
| 1976 | 905 | — | — | — | 100 | — |
| 1976 Proof | 2,421 | Value: 85.00 | | | | |

**50 CROWNS** **KM# 16** **Weight:** 55.1800 g. **Composition:** 0.9250 Silver 1.6412 oz. ASW **Reverse:** 4 Victoria cameos **Note:** Similar to 100 Crowns, KM#17.

| Date | Mintage | F | VF | XF | Unc | BU |
|---|---|---|---|---|---|---|
| 1976 Matte | 3,500 | — | — | — | 40.00 | — |
| 1976 Proof | 2,908 | Value: 45.00 | | | | |
| 1977 Proof | 940 | Value: 50.00 | | | | |

**50 CROWNS** **KM# 20** **Weight:** 9.0000 g. **Composition:** 0.5000 Gold .1447 oz. AGW **Subject:** Queen's silver jubilee

| Date | Mintage | F | VF | XF | Unc | BU |
|---|---|---|---|---|---|---|
| 1977 | — | — | — | — | 65.00 | — |
| 1977 Proof | 2,903 | Value: 85.00 | | | | |

**50 CROWNS** **KM# 21** **Weight:** 55.1800 g. **Composition:** 0.9250 Silver 1.6412 oz. ASW **Reverse:** 4 George III cameos **Note:** Similar to 100 Crowns, KM#22.

| Date | Mintage | F | VF | XF | Unc | BU |
|---|---|---|---|---|---|---|
| 1977 | — | — | — | — | 50.00 | — |
| 1977 Proof | 958 | Value: 55.00 | | | | |

**50 CROWNS** **KM# 34** **Weight:** 9.0000 g. **Composition:** 0.5000 Gold .1447 oz. AGW **Subject:** 25th anniversary of coronation **Reverse:** Lion of England

| Date | Mintage | F | VF | XF | Unc | BU |
|---|---|---|---|---|---|---|
| 1978 Proof | 261 | Value: 165 | | | | |

**50 CROWNS** **KM# 35** **Weight:** 9.0000 g. **Composition:** 0.5000 Gold .1447 oz. AGW **Subject:** Griffin of Edward III

| Date | Mintage | F | VF | XF | Unc | BU |
|---|---|---|---|---|---|---|
| 1978 Proof | 266 | Value: 165 | | | | |

**50 CROWNS** **KM# 36** **Weight:** 9.0000 g. **Composition:** 0.5000 Gold .1447 oz. AGW **Subject:** Red dragon of Wales

| Date | Mintage | F | VF | XF | Unc | BU |
|---|---|---|---|---|---|---|
| 1978 Proof | 266 | Value: 165 | | | | |

**50 CROWNS** **KM# 37** **Weight:** 9.0000 g. **Composition:** 0.5000 Gold .1447 oz. AGW **Subject:** White greyhound of Richmond

| Date | Mintage | F | VF | XF | Unc | BU |
|---|---|---|---|---|---|---|
| 1978 Proof | 270 | Value: 165 | | | | |

**50 CROWNS** **KM# 38** **Weight:** 9.0000 g. **Composition:** 0.5000 Gold .1447 oz. AGW **Subject:** Unicorn of Scotland

| Date | Mintage | F | VF | XF | Unc | BU |
|---|---|---|---|---|---|---|
| 1978 Proof | 268 | Value: 165 | | | | |

**50 CROWNS** **KM# 39** **Weight:** 9.0000 g. **Composition:** 0.5000 Gold .1447 oz. AGW **Subject:** White horse of Hannover

| Date | Mintage | F | VF | XF | Unc | BU |
|---|---|---|---|---|---|---|
| 1978 Proof | 266 | Value: 165 | | | | |

**50 CROWNS** **KM# 40** **Weight:** 9.0000 g. **Composition:** 0.5000 Gold .1447 oz. AGW **Subject:** Black bull of Clarence

| Date | Mintage | F | VF | XF | Unc | BU |
|---|---|---|---|---|---|---|
| 1978 Proof | 269 | Value: 165 | | | | |

**50 CROWNS** **KM# 41** **Weight:** 9.0000 g. **Composition:** 0.5000 Gold .1447 oz. AGW **Subject:** Yale of Beaufort

| Date | Mintage | F | VF | XF | Unc | BU |
|---|---|---|---|---|---|---|
| 1978 Proof | 254 | Value: 165 | | | | |

**50 CROWNS** **KM# 42** **Weight:** 9.0000 g. **Composition:** 0.5000 Gold .1447 oz. AGW **Subject:** Falcon of the Plantagenets

| Date | Mintage | F | VF | XF | Unc | BU |
|---|---|---|---|---|---|---|
| 1978 Proof | 265 | Value: 165 | | | | |

**50 CROWNS** **KM# 43** **Weight:** 9.0000 g. **Composition:** 0.5000 Gold .1447 oz. AGW **Subject:** White lion of Mortimer

| Date | Mintage | F | VF | XF | Unc | BU |
|---|---|---|---|---|---|---|
| 1978 Proof | 265 | Value: 165 | | | | |

**50 CROWNS** **KM# 61** **Weight:** 136.0800 g. **Composition:** 0.9250 Silver 4.0699 oz. ASW **Subject:** Columbus proposes Atlantic voyage to Ferdinand and Isabella **Obverse:** Similar to 5 Crowns, KM#123 **Size:** 63 mm. **Note:** Illustration reduced.

| Date | Mintage | F | VF | XF | Unc | BU |
|---|---|---|---|---|---|---|
| 1986 Proof | 20,000 | Value: 85.00 | | | | |

**100 CROWNS** KM# 4 **Weight:** 18.0150 g. **Composition:** 0.5000 Gold .2896 oz. AGW **Subject:** Birth of Churchill centenary

| Date | Mintage | F | VF | XF | Unc | BU |
|---|---|---|---|---|---|---|
| 1974 | 4,500 | — | — | — | 165 | — |
| 1974 Proof | 5,100 | Value: 165 | | | | |

**100 CROWNS** KM# 11 **Weight:** 12.4400 g. **Composition:** 0.5000 Gold .2000 oz. AGW **Subject:** Age of Exploration **Reverse:** Spacecraft

| Date | Mintage | F | VF | XF | Unc | BU |
|---|---|---|---|---|---|---|
| 1975 | 756 | — | — | — | 135 | — |
| 1975 Proof | 1,508 | Value: 120 | | | | |

**100 CROWNS** KM# 17 **Weight:** 18.0150 g. **Composition:** 0.5000 Gold .2896 oz. AGW **Reverse:** 4 Victoria cameos

| Date | Mintage | F | VF | XF | Unc | BU |
|---|---|---|---|---|---|---|
| 1976 | 250 | — | — | — | 160 | — |
| 1976 Proof | 350 | Value: 175 | | | | |
| 1977 | 1,655 | — | — | — | 150 | — |
| 1977 Proof | 2,648 | Value: 165 | | | | |

**100 CROWNS** KM# 22 **Weight:** 18.0150 g. **Composition:** 0.5000 Gold .2896 oz. AGW **Reverse:** 4 George III cameos

| Date | Mintage | F | VF | XF | Unc | BU |
|---|---|---|---|---|---|---|
| 1977 | — | — | — | — | 165 | — |
| 1977 Proof | 844 | Value: 185 | | | | |

**100 CROWNS** KM# 44 **Weight:** 18.0150 g. **Composition:** 0.5000 Gold .2896 oz. AGW **Subject:** XI Commonwealth Games

| Date | Mintage | F | VF | XF | Unc | BU |
|---|---|---|---|---|---|---|
| 1978 Proof | 540 | Value: 250 | | | | |

**100 CROWNS** KM# 46 **Weight:** 18.0150 g. **Composition:** 0.5000 Gold .2896 oz. AGW **Subject:** 10th anniversary - Prince Charles' investiture

| Date | Mintage | F | VF | XF | Unc | BU |
|---|---|---|---|---|---|---|
| 1979 | 10,000 | — | — | — | 140 | — |

**100 CROWNS** KM# 50 **Weight:** 12.9600 g. **Composition:** 0.5000 Gold .2083 oz. AGW **Subject:** Lord Mountbatten **Obverse:** Similar to 10 Crowns, KM#45

| Date | Mintage | F | VF | XF | Unc | BU |
|---|---|---|---|---|---|---|
| 1980 Proof | — | Value: 140 | | | | |

**100 CROWNS** KM# 54 **Weight:** 6.4800 g. **Composition:** 0.9000 Gold .1875 oz. AGW **Subject:** Wedding of Princes Charles and Lady Diana

| Date | Mintage | F | VF | XF | Unc | BU |
|---|---|---|---|---|---|---|
| 1981 Proof | 1,205 | Value: 115 | | | | |

**100 CROWNS** KM# 59 **Weight:** 6.4800 g. **Composition:** 0.9000 Gold .1875 oz. AGW **Subject:** World Football Championship **Reverse:** 2 players

| Date | Mintage | F | VF | XF | Unc | BU |
|---|---|---|---|---|---|---|
| 1982 Proof | 565 | Value: 225 | | | | |

**100 CROWNS** KM# 62 **Weight:** 7.1300 g. **Composition:** 0.9000 Gold .2063 oz. AGW **Series:** Decade for Women

| Date | Mintage | F | VF | XF | Unc | BU |
|---|---|---|---|---|---|---|
| 1985 Proof | 313 | Value: 275 | | | | |

**100 CROWNS** KM# 65 **Weight:** 10.0000 g. **Composition:** 0.9170 Gold .2949 oz. AGW **Series:** World Wildlife Fund **Subject:** Jumbo shrimp

| Date | Mintage | F | VF | XF | Unc | BU |
|---|---|---|---|---|---|---|
| 1988 Proof | Est. 5,000 | Value: 200 | | | | |

## PATTERNS

Standard metals unless noted otherwise

| KM# | Date | Mintage | Identification | Issue Price | Mkt Val |
|---|---|---|---|---|---|
| Pn1 | (1993) | 50 | 20 Crowns. Silver. Bobsledders. | — | 75.00 |
| Pn2 | (1993) | 50 | 20 Crowns. Silver. Skier. | — | 75.00 |
| Pn3 | (1993) | 50 | 20 Crowns. Silver. Ski jumper. | — | 75.00 |
| Pn4 | (1993) | 50 | 20 Crowns. Silver. Figure skater. | — | 75.00 |
| Pn5 | (1993) | 50 | 20 Crowns. Silver. Hockey player. | — | 75.00 |
| Pn6 | (1993) | 50 | 20 Crowns. Silver. Speed skater. | — | 75.00 |

## PIEFORTS

| KM# | Date | Mintage | Identification | Issue Price | Mkt Val |
|---|---|---|---|---|---|
| P1 | 1980 | 500 | 5 Crowns. KM47. | 79.50 | 32.00 |
| P2 | 1980 | 400 | 10 Crowns. KM48. | 95.00 | 38.00 |
| P3 | 1980 | 300 | 20 Crowns. KM49. | 115 | 40.00 |
| P4 | 1980 | 250 | 100 Crowns. KM50. | 825 | 275 |
| P5 | 1982 | 80 | 10 Crowns. KM55. | — | 135 |
| P6 | 1991 | — | Crown. Silver. KM76. | — | 50.00 |
| P7 | 1991 | 400 | Crown. Silver. KM121. | — | 32.00 |

## MINT SETS

| KM# | Date | Mintage | Identification | Issue Price | Mkt Val |
|---|---|---|---|---|---|
| MS1 | 1975 (7) | 440 | KM5-11 | 214 | 350 |
| MS2 | ND(1993) (8) | — | KM87-94 | 67.20 | 45.00 |
| MS3 | ND(1993) (6) | — | KM103-108 | 49.95 | 35.00 |
| MS4 | 1995 (4) | — | KM133-136 | 33.50 | 33.50 |
| MS5 | 1996 (10) | — | KM143, 146, 149, 152, 155, 158, 161, 164, 167, 170 | 33.50 | 33.50 |

## PROOF SETS

| KM# | Date | Mintage | Identification | Issue Price | Mkt Val |
|---|---|---|---|---|---|
| PS1 | 1974 (2) | 1,600 | KM2, 4 | — | 170 |
| PS2 | 1975 (7) | 1,270 | KM5-8, 9.1, 10-11 | 313 | 385 |
| PS3 | 1976 (4) | 2,185 | KM5, 6, 9.2, 12 | 78.00 | 85.00 |
| PS4 | 1976 (3) | — | KM14, 16, 17 | 280 | 270 |
| PS5 | 1976 (2) | 1,951 | KM13, 15 | 108 | 115 |
| PS6 | 1977 (4) | 1,370 | KM5, 6, 9.2, 12 | 87.50 | 100 |
| PS8 | 1977 (2) | — | KM14, 18 | 62.00 | 115 |
| PS7 | 1977 (3) | — | KM18, 21, 22 | 280 | 380 |
| PS10 | 1978 (10) | — | KM34-43 | 1,120 | 1,650 |
| PS9 | 1978 (10) | — | KM24-33 | 560 | 320 |
| PS11 | 1979 (2) | — | KM45, 46 | 227 | 160 |
| PS12 | 1980 (4) | — | KM47-50 | 457 | 195 |
| PS13 | 1980 (3) | — | KM47-49 | 107 | 45.00 |
| PS15 | ND(1993) (8) | — | KM95-102 | 319 | 325 |
| PS17 | ND(1993) (6) | — | KM109-114 | 234 | 255 |
| PS18 | 1995 (4) | 15,000 | KM137-140 | 160 | 160 |
| PS19 | 1996 (10) | 20,000 | KM144, 147, 150, 153, 156, 159, 162, 165, 168, 171 | 220 | 220 |
| PS20 | 1996 (10) | 20,000 | KM145, 148, 151, 154, 157, 160, 163, 166, 169, 172 | 350 | 350 |

# TUVALU

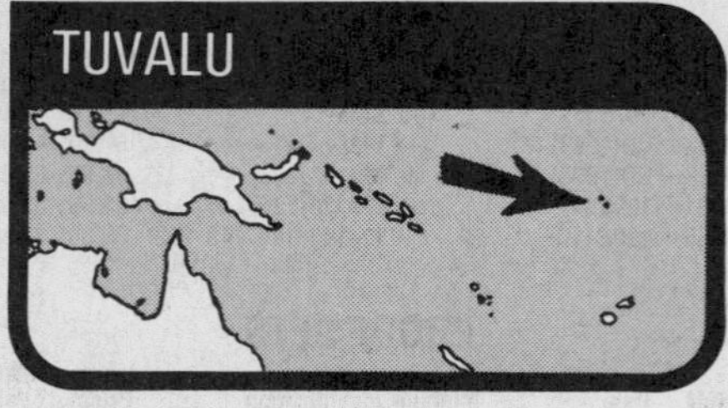

Tuvalu (formerly the Ellice or Lagoon Islands of the Gilbert and Ellice Islands), located in the South Pacific north of the Fiji Islands, has an area of 10 sq. mi. (26 sq.km.) and a population of *9,000. Capital: Funafuti. The independent state includes the islands of Nanumanga, Nanumea, Nui, Niutao, Viatupa, Funafuti, Nukufetau, Nukulailai and Nurakita. The latter four islands were claimed by the United States until relinquished by the Feb.7, 1979, Treaty of Friendship signed by the United States and Tuvalu. The principal industries are copra production and phosphate mining.

The islands were discovered in 1764 by John Byron, a British navigator, and annexed by Britain in 1892. In 1915 they became part of the crown colony of the Gilbert and Ellice Islands. In 1974 the islanders voted to separate from the Gilberts, becoming on Jan. 1, 1976, the separate constitutional dependency of Tuvalu. Full independence was attained on Oct. 1, 1978. Tuvalu is a member of the Commonwealth of Nations. Elizabeth II is Head of State as Queen of Tuvalu.

**RULERS**
British, until 1978

**MONETARY SYSTEM**
100 Cents = 1 Dollar

## BRITISH ADMINISTRATION

### STANDARD COINAGE

100 Cents = 1 Dollar

**CENT KM# 1 Composition:** Bronze **Reverse:** Sea shell

| Date | Mintage | F | VF | XF | Unc | BU |
|---|---|---|---|---|---|---|
| 1976 | 93,000 | — | — | 0.10 | 0.25 | — |
| 1976 Proof | 20,000 | Value: 1.00 | | | | |
| 1981 | — | — | — | 0.10 | 0.25 | — |
| 1981 Proof | — | Value: 1.00 | | | | |
| 1985 | — | — | — | 0.10 | 0.25 | — |

**CENT KM# 26 Composition:** Bronze **Obverse:** Queen's portrait by Maklouf

| Date | Mintage | F | VF | XF | Unc | BU |
|---|---|---|---|---|---|---|
| 1994 | — | — | — | — | 0.35 | — |

**2 CENTS KM# 2 Composition:** Bronze **Reverse:** Stingray

| Date | Mintage | F | VF | XF | Unc | BU |
|---|---|---|---|---|---|---|
| 1976 | 51,000 | — | 0.10 | 0.15 | 0.50 | — |
| 1976 Proof | 20,000 | Value: 1.00 | | | | |
| 1981 | — | — | 0.10 | 0.15 | 0.50 | — |
| 1981 Proof | — | Value: 1.00 | | | | |
| 1985 | — | — | 0.10 | 0.15 | 0.50 | — |

**2 CENTS KM# 30 Composition:** Bronze **Obverse:** Queen's portrait by Maklouf

| Date | Mintage | F | VF | XF | Unc | BU |
|---|---|---|---|---|---|---|
| 1994 | — | — | — | — | 0.50 | — |

**5 CENTS KM# 3 Composition:** Copper-Nickel **Reverse:** Tiger shark

| Date | Mintage | F | VF | XF | Unc | BU |
|---|---|---|---|---|---|---|
| 1976 | 26,000 | — | 0.10 | 0.25 | 1.25 | — |
| 1976 Proof | 20,000 | Value: 1.50 | | | | |
| 1981 | — | — | 0.10 | 0.25 | 1.25 | — |
| 1981 Proof | — | Value: 1.50 | | | | |
| 1985 | — | — | 0.10 | 0.25 | 1.25 | — |

**5 CENTS KM# 31 Composition:** Copper-Nickel **Obverse:** Queen's portrait by Maklouf

| Date | Mintage | F | VF | XF | Unc | BU |
|---|---|---|---|---|---|---|
| 1994 | — | — | — | — | 1.25 | — |

**10 CENTS KM# 4 Composition:** Copper-Nickel **Reverse:** Red-eyed crab

| Date | Mintage | F | VF | XF | Unc | BU |
|---|---|---|---|---|---|---|
| 1976 | 26,000 | 0.15 | 0.20 | 0.30 | 0.75 | — |
| 1976 Proof | 20,000 | Value: 2.00 | | | | |
| 1981 | — | 0.15 | 0.20 | 0.30 | 0.75 | — |
| 1981 Proof | — | Value: 2.00 | | | | |
| 1985 | — | 0.15 | 0.20 | 0.30 | 0.75 | — |

**10 CENTS KM# 32 Composition:** Copper-Nickel **Obverse:** Queen's portrait by Maklouf

| Date | Mintage | F | VF | XF | Unc | BU |
|---|---|---|---|---|---|---|
| 1994 | — | — | — | — | 0.75 | — |

**20 CENTS KM# 5 Composition:** Copper-Nickel **Reverse:** Flying fish

| Date | Mintage | F | VF | XF | Unc | BU |
|---|---|---|---|---|---|---|
| 1976 | 36,000 | 0.30 | 0.40 | 0.50 | 1.00 | — |
| 1976 Proof | 20,000 | Value: 2.50 | | | | |
| 1981 | — | 0.30 | 0.40 | 0.50 | 1.00 | — |
| 1981 Proof | — | Value: 2.50 | | | | |
| 1985 | — | 0.30 | 0.40 | 0.50 | 1.00 | — |

**20 CENTS KM# 33 Composition:** Copper-Nickel **Obverse:** Queen's portrait by Maklouf

| Date | Mintage | F | VF | XF | Unc | BU |
|---|---|---|---|---|---|---|
| 1994 | — | — | — | — | 1.00 | — |

**50 CENTS KM# 6 Composition:** Copper-Nickel **Reverse:** Octopus

| Date | Mintage | F | VF | XF | Unc | BU |
|---|---|---|---|---|---|---|
| 1976 | 19,000 | 0.50 | 0.75 | 1.00 | 4.00 | — |
| 1976 Proof | 20,000 | Value: 5.00 | | | | |
| 1981 | — | 0.50 | 0.75 | 1.00 | 4.00 | — |
| 1981 Proof | — | Value: 5.00 | | | | |
| 1985 | — | 0.50 | 0.75 | 1.00 | 4.00 | — |

**50 CENTS KM# 34 Composition:** Copper-Nickel **Obverse:** Queen's portrait by Maklouf

| Date | Mintage | F | VF | XF | Unc | BU |
|---|---|---|---|---|---|---|
| 1994 | — | — | — | — | 3.00 | — |

**DOLLAR KM# 7 Composition:** Copper-Nickel **Reverse:** Sea turtle

| Date | Mintage | F | VF | XF | Unc | BU |
|---|---|---|---|---|---|---|
| 1976 | 21,000 | 1.00 | 1.50 | 2.00 | 5.00 | — |
| 1976 Proof | 20,000 | Value: 7.00 | | | | |
| 1981 | — | 1.00 | 1.50 | 2.00 | 5.00 | — |
| 1981 Proof | — | Value: 7.00 | | | | |
| 1985 | — | 1.00 | 1.50 | 2.00 | 5.00 | — |

**DOLLAR KM# 35 Composition:** Copper-Nickel **Obverse:** Queen's portrait by Maklouf

| Date | Mintage | F | VF | XF | Unc | BU |
|---|---|---|---|---|---|---|
| 1994 | — | — | — | — | 4.00 | — |

**2 DOLLARS KM# 37 Weight:** 10.0000 g. **Composition:** 0.5000 Silver .1608 oz. ASW **Series:** Olympics **Obverse:** Queen Elizabeth's portrait **Reverse:** Swimmer **Edge:** Reeded **Size:** 30 mm.

| Date | Mintage | F | VF | XF | Unc | BU |
|---|---|---|---|---|---|---|
| 1996 Proof | — | Value: 15.00 | | | | |

**5 DOLLARS KM# 8 Weight:** 28.2800 g. **Composition:** 0.9250 Silver .8411 oz. ASW **Reverse:** Outrigger canoe

| Date | Mintage | F | VF | XF | Unc | BU |
|---|---|---|---|---|---|---|
| 1976 Proof | 20,000 | Value: 20.00 | | | | |

**5 DOLLARS KM# 12 Composition:** Copper-Nickel **Subject:** Wedding of Prince Charles and Lady Diana

| Date | Mintage | F | VF | XF | Unc | BU |
|---|---|---|---|---|---|---|
| 1981 | — | — | — | — | 8.50 | — |

**5 DOLLARS KM# 12a Weight:** 28.2800 g. **Composition:** 0.9250 Silver .8411 oz. ASW

| Date | Mintage | F | VF | XF | Unc | BU |
|---|---|---|---|---|---|---|
| 1981 Proof | 35,000 | Value: 18.50 | | | | |

**10 DOLLARS KM# 10 Weight:** 35.0000 g. **Composition:** 0.5000 Silver .5627 oz. ASW **Subject:** 1st Anniversary of Independence **Obverse:** Similar to 5 Dollars, KM#8 **Reverse:** Brigantine "Rebecca"

| Date | Mintage | F | VF | XF | Unc | BU |
|---|---|---|---|---|---|---|
| 1979 | 5,000 | — | — | — | 25.00 | — |

**10 DOLLARS** **KM# 10a** **Weight:** 35.0000 g. **Composition:** 0.9250 Silver 1.0409 oz. ASW

| Date | Mintage | F | VF | XF | Unc | BU |
|---|---|---|---|---|---|---|
| 1979 Proof | 2,500 | Value: 35.00 | | | | |

**10 DOLLARS** **KM# 11** **Weight:** 35.0000 g. **Composition:** 0.5000 Silver .5627 oz. ASW **Subject:** 80th Birthday of Queen Mother **Obverse:** Similar to 5 Dollars, KM#8

| Date | Mintage | F | VF | XF | Unc | BU |
|---|---|---|---|---|---|---|
| 1980 | — | — | — | — | 15.00 | — |

**10 DOLLARS** **KM# 11a** **Weight:** 35.0000 g. **Composition:** 0.9250 Silver 1.0409 oz. ASW

| Date | Mintage | F | VF | XF | Unc | BU |
|---|---|---|---|---|---|---|
| 1980 Proof | — | Value: 23.50 | | | | |

**10 DOLLARS** **KM# 13** **Weight:** 35.0000 g. **Composition:** 0.5000 Silver .5627 oz. ASW **Subject:** Duke of Edinburgh Award **Obverse:** Similar to 5 Dollars, KM#8

| Date | Mintage | F | VF | XF | Unc | BU |
|---|---|---|---|---|---|---|
| 1981 | 5,000 | — | — | — | 14.50 | — |

**10 DOLLARS** **KM# 13a** **Weight:** 35.0000 g. **Composition:** 0.9250 Silver 1.0409 oz. ASW

| Date | Mintage | F | VF | XF | Unc | BU |
|---|---|---|---|---|---|---|
| 1981 Proof | 3,000 | Value: 22.50 | | | | |

**10 DOLLARS** **KM# 15** **Weight:** 35.0000 g. **Composition:** 0.5000 Silver .5627 oz. ASW **Subject:** Royal Visit **Obverse:** Similar to 5 Dollars, KM#8

| Date | Mintage | F | VF | XF | Unc | BU |
|---|---|---|---|---|---|---|
| 1982 | 2,500 | — | — | — | 20.00 | — |

**10 DOLLARS** **KM# 15a** **Weight:** 35.0000 g. **Composition:** 0.9250 Silver 1.0409 oz. ASW

| Date | Mintage | F | VF | XF | Unc | BU |
|---|---|---|---|---|---|---|
| 1982 Proof | 2,500 | Value: 27.50 | | | | |

**20 DOLLARS** **KM# 16** **Weight:** 31.4700 g. **Composition:** 0.9250 Silver .9359 oz. ASW **Subject:** 40th Anniversary of Coronation

| Date | Mintage | F | VF | XF | Unc | BU |
|---|---|---|---|---|---|---|
| 1993 Proof | Est. 10,000 | Value: 27.50 | | | | |

**20 DOLLARS** **KM# 17** **Weight:** 31.4700 g. **Composition:** 0.9250 Silver .9359 oz. ASW **Subject:** Sir Isaac Newton

| Date | Mintage | F | VF | XF | Unc | BU |
|---|---|---|---|---|---|---|
| 1993 Proof | Est. 10,000 | Value: 27.50 | | | | |

**20 DOLLARS** **KM# 18** **Weight:** 31.4700 g. **Composition:** 0.9250 Silver .9359 oz. ASW **Subject:** HMS Royalist

| Date | Mintage | F | VF | XF | Unc | BU |
|---|---|---|---|---|---|---|
| 1993 Proof | Est. 15,000 | Value: 27.50 | | | | |

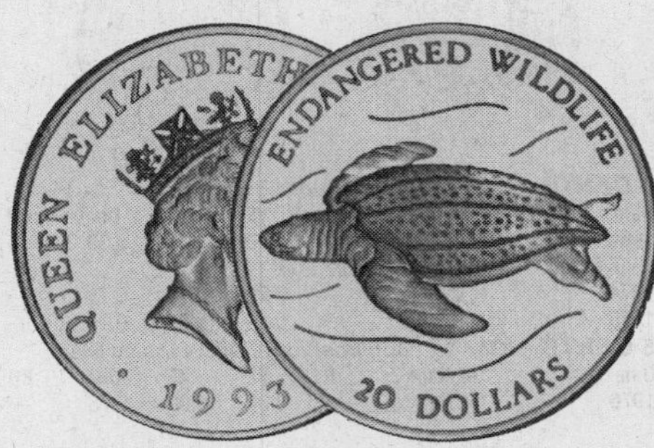


**20 DOLLARS** **KM# 19** **Weight:** 31.4700 g. **Composition:** 0.9250 Silver .9359 oz. ASW **Reverse:** Leatherback turtle

| Date | Mintage | F | VF | XF | Unc | BU |
|---|---|---|---|---|---|---|
| 1993 Proof | Est. 10,000 | Value: 30.00 | | | | |

**20 DOLLARS** **KM# 20** **Weight:** 31.4700 g. **Composition:** 0.9250 Silver .9359 oz. ASW **Reverse:** Dugong - Manatee-like animal

| Date | Mintage | F | VF | XF | Unc | BU |
|---|---|---|---|---|---|---|
| 1994 Proof | Est. 10,000 | Value: 30.00 | | | | |

**20 DOLLARS** **KM# 22** **Weight:** 31.4700 g. **Composition:** 0.9250 Silver .9359 oz. ASW **Subject:** 1994 World Cup Soccer

| Date | Mintage | F | VF | XF | Unc | BU |
|---|---|---|---|---|---|---|
| 1994 Proof | Est. 30,000 | Value: 32.50 | | | | |

**20 DOLLARS** **KM# 24** **Weight:** 31.4700 g. **Composition:** 0.9250 Silver .9359 oz. ASW **Series:** Olympics **Subject:** Swimming

| Date | Mintage | F | VF | XF | Unc | BU |
|---|---|---|---|---|---|---|
| 1994 Proof | Est. 50,000 | Value: 23.50 | | | | |

**20 DOLLARS** **KM# 25** **Weight:** 31.4700 g. **Composition:** 0.9250 Silver .9359 oz. ASW **Series:** Olympics **Subject:** Javelin throwing

| Date | Mintage | F | VF | XF | Unc | BU |
|---|---|---|---|---|---|---|
| 1994 Proof | Est. 50,000 | Value: 22.50 | | | | |

**20 DOLLARS** **KM# 27** **Weight:** 31.7000 g. **Composition:** 0.9250 Silver .9427 oz. ASW **Series:** Protect Our World **Reverse:** Blue coral seascape

| Date | Mintage | F | VF | XF | Unc | BU |
|---|---|---|---|---|---|---|
| 1994 Proof | — | Value: 35.00 | | | | |

**50 DOLLARS** KM# 9 **Weight:** 15.9800 g. **Composition:** 0.9170 Gold Clad Silver .4710 oz. **Reverse:** Native meeting hut

| Date | Mintage | F | VF | XF | Unc | BU |
|---|---|---|---|---|---|---|
| 1976 Proof | 2,074 | Value: 245 | | | | |

**50 DOLLARS** KM# 14 **Weight:** 15.9800 g. **Composition:** 0.9170 Gold .4710 oz. AGW **Subject:** Wedding of Prince Charles and Lady Diana

| Date | Mintage | F | VF | XF | Unc | BU |
|---|---|---|---|---|---|---|
| 1981 Proof | 5,000 | Value: 235 | | | | |

**100 DOLLARS** KM# 29 **Weight:** 7.7760 g. **Composition:** 0.5833 Gold .1458 oz. AGW **Subject:** 40th Anniversary of Coronation **Obverse:** Similar to 20 Dollars, KM#16

| Date | Mintage | F | VF | XF | Unc | BU |
|---|---|---|---|---|---|---|
| 1993 Proof | — | Value: 125 | | | | |

**100 DOLLARS** KM# 21 **Weight:** 7.7760 g. **Composition:** 0.5833 Gold .1458 oz. AGW **Subject:** Todos Los Santos

| Date | Mintage | F | VF | XF | Unc | BU |
|---|---|---|---|---|---|---|
| 1994 Proof | 3,000 | Value: 135 | | | | |

**100 DOLLARS** KM# 23 **Weight:** 7.7760 g. **Composition:** 0.5833 Gold .1458 oz. AGW **Subject:** 1994 World Cup Soccer

| Date | Mintage | F | VF | XF | Unc | BU |
|---|---|---|---|---|---|---|
| 1994 Proof | 3,000 | Value: 145 | | | | |

## MINT SETS

| KM# | Date | Mintage | Identification | Issue Price | Mkt Val |
|---|---|---|---|---|---|
| MS1 | 1985 (7) | — | KM#1-7 | 10.00 | 10.00 |

## PROOF SETS

| KM# | Date | Mintage | Identification | Issue Price | Mkt Val |
|---|---|---|---|---|---|
| PS1 | 1976 (7) | 20,000 | KM#1-7 | 13.00 | 16.00 |
| PS2 | 1981 (7) | — | KM#1-7 | — | 16.00 |

# UGANDA

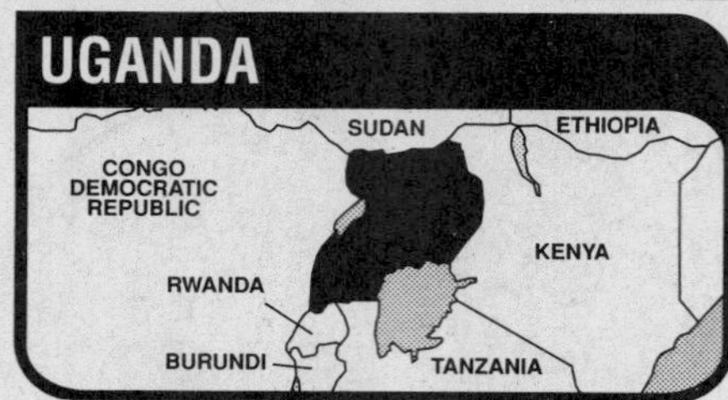


The Republic of Uganda, a former British protectorate located astride the equator in east-central Africa, has an area of 91,134 sq. mi. (236,040 sq. km.) and a population of *17 million. Capital: Kampala. Agriculture, including livestock, is the basis of the economy; there is some mining of copper, tin, gold and lead. Coffee, cotton, copper and tea are exported.

Uganda was first visited by Arab slavers in the 1830s.They were followed in the 1860s by British explorers searching for the headwaters of the Nile. The explorers, and the missionaries who followed them into the Lake Victoria region of south central Africa in 1877-79, found well-developed African kingdoms dating back several centuries. In 1894 the local native Kingdom of Buganda was established as a British protectorate that was extended in 1896 to encompass an area substantially the same as the present Republic of Uganda. The protectorate was given a ministerial form of government in 1955, full internal self-government on March 1, 1962, and complete independence on Oct. 9, 1962. Uganda is a member of the Commonwealth of Nations. The president is Chief of State and Head of Government.

For earlier coinage refer to East Africa.

**RULERS**

British, until 1962

**MONETARY SYSTEM**

100 Cents = 1 Shilling

## REPUBLIC

### STANDARD COINAGE

100 Cents = 1 Shilling

**5 CENTS** KM# 1 **Composition:** Bronze

| Date | Mintage | F | VF | XF | Unc | BU |
|---|---|---|---|---|---|---|
| 1966 | 41,000,000 | — | 0.10 | 0.15 | 0.30 | — |
| 1966 Proof | — | Value: 1.00 | | | | |
| 1974 | 10,000,000 | — | 0.20 | 0.30 | 0.75 | — |
| 1975 | 14,784,000 | — | 0.20 | 0.30 | 0.75 | — |

**5 CENTS** KM# 1a **Composition:** Copper Plated Steel

| Date | Mintage | F | VF | XF | Unc | BU |
|---|---|---|---|---|---|---|
| 1976 | 10,000,000 | — | 0.20 | 0.30 | 0.75 | — |

**10 CENTS** KM# 2 **Composition:** Bronze

| Date | Mintage | F | VF | XF | Unc | BU |
|---|---|---|---|---|---|---|
| 1966 | 19,100,000 | — | 0.10 | 0.15 | 0.35 | — |
| 1966 Proof | — | Value: 1.00 | | | | |
| 1968 | 20,000,000 | — | 0.10 | 0.15 | 0.35 | — |
| 1970 | 6,000,000 | — | 0.20 | 0.30 | 0.75 | — |
| 1972 | 5,000,000 | — | 0.20 | 0.30 | 0.75 | — |
| 1974 | 5,000,000 | — | 0.20 | 0.30 | 0.75 | — |
| 1975 | 14,110,000 | — | 0.20 | 0.30 | 0.75 | — |

**10 CENTS** KM# 2a **Composition:** Copper-Plated-Steel

| Date | Mintage | F | VF | XF | Unc | BU |
|---|---|---|---|---|---|---|
| 1976 | 10,000,000 | — | 0.20 | 0.30 | 0.75 | — |

**20 CENTS** KM# 3 **Composition:** Bronze

| Date | Mintage | F | VF | XF | Unc | BU |
|---|---|---|---|---|---|---|
| 1966 | 7,000,000 | — | 0.30 | 0.70 | 1.65 | — |
| 1966 Proof | — | Value: 2.00 | | | | |
| 1974 | 2,000,000 | — | 0.50 | 1.00 | 2.25 | — |

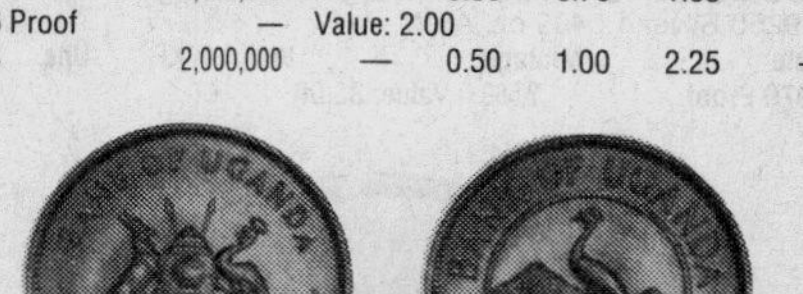

**50 CENTS** KM# 4 **Composition:** Copper-Nickel

| Date | Mintage | F | VF | XF | Unc | BU |
|---|---|---|---|---|---|---|
| 1966 | 16,000,000 | — | 0.20 | 0.40 | 1.85 | — |
| 1966 Proof | — | Value: 2.00 | | | | |
| 1970 | 3,000,000 | — | 0.25 | 0.65 | 2.00 | — |
| 1974 | 10,000,000 | — | 0.25 | 0.65 | 2.00 | — |

**50 CENTS** KM# 4a **Composition:** Copper-Nickel Plated Steel

| Date | Mintage | F | VF | XF | Unc | BU |
|---|---|---|---|---|---|---|
| 1976 | 10,000,000 | — | 0.25 | 0.65 | 2.00 | — |

**SHILLING** KM# 5 **Composition:** Copper-Nickel

| Date | Mintage | F | VF | XF | Unc | BU |
|---|---|---|---|---|---|---|
| 1966 | 24,500,000 | — | 0.25 | 0.50 | 2.25 | — |
| 1966 Proof | — | Value: 3.00 | | | | |
| 1968 | 10,000,000 | — | 0.35 | 0.85 | 2.50 | — |
| 1972 | — | — | 0.35 | 0.85 | 2.50 | — |
| 1975 | 15,540,000 | — | 0.35 | 0.85 | 2.50 | — |

**SHILLING** KM# 5a **Composition:** Copper-Nickel Plated Steel

| Date | Mintage | F | VF | XF | Unc | BU |
|---|---|---|---|---|---|---|
| 1976 | 10,000,000 | — | 0.35 | 0.85 | 2.50 | — |
| 1978 | — | — | 0.35 | 0.85 | 2.50 | — |

**SHILLING** KM# 27 **Composition:** Copper Plated Steel

| Date | Mintage | F | VF | XF | Unc | BU |
|---|---|---|---|---|---|---|
| 1987 | — | — | — | — | 0.25 | — |
| 1987 Proof | — | Value: 2.50 | | | | |

**2 SHILLINGS** KM# 6 **Composition:** Copper-Nickel

| Date | Mintage | F | VF | XF | Unc | BU |
|---|---|---|---|---|---|---|
| 1966 | 4,000,000 | — | 1.00 | 2.00 | 5.00 | — |
| 1966 Proof | — | Value: 6.00 | | | | |

**2 SHILLINGS** KM# 8 **Weight:** 4.0000 g. **Composition:** 0.9990 Silver .1284 oz. ASW **Subject:** Visit of Pope Paul VI

| Date | Mintage | F | VF | XF | Unc | BU |
|---|---|---|---|---|---|---|
| 1969 Proof | 8,170 | Value: 10.00 | | | | |
| 1970 Proof | Inc. above | Value: 10.00 | | | | |

**2 SHILLINGS** KM# 28 **Composition:** Copper Plated Steel

| Date | Mintage | F | VF | XF | Unc | BU |
|---|---|---|---|---|---|---|
| 1987 | — | — | — | — | 1.00 | — |
| 1987 Proof | — | Value: 4.00 | | | | |

**5 SHILLINGS** KM# 7 **Composition:** Copper-Nickel **Series:** F.A.O.

| Date | Mintage | F | VF | XF | Unc | BU |
|---|---|---|---|---|---|---|
| ND(1968) | 100,000 | — | 1.50 | 2.50 | 6.50 | — |
| ND(1968) Proof | 5,000 | Value: 7.50 | | | | |

**5 SHILLINGS** KM# 9 **Weight:** 10.0000 g. **Composition:** 0.9990 Silver .3212 oz. ASW **Subject:** Visit of Pope Paul VI **Reverse:** Crested cranes

| Date | Mintage | F | VF | XF | Unc | BU |
|---|---|---|---|---|---|---|
| 1969 Proof | 7,670 | Value: 17.50 | | | | |
| 1970 Proof | Inc. above | Value: 17.50 | | | | |

**5 SHILLINGS** KM# 18 **Composition:** Copper-Nickel **Note:** Withdrawn from circulation. Almost entire mintage was melted.

| Date | Mintage | F | VF | XF | Unc | BU |
|---|---|---|---|---|---|---|
| 1972 | Est. 8,000,000 | — | 55.00 | 75.00 | 135 | — |

**5 SHILLINGS** KM# 29 **Composition:** Stainless Steel

| Date | Mintage | F | VF | XF | Unc | BU |
|---|---|---|---|---|---|---|
| 1987 | — | — | — | — | 2.50 | — |
| 1987 Proof | — | Value: 6.50 | | | | |

**10 SHILLINGS** KM# 10 **Weight:** 20.0000 g. **Composition:** 0.9990 Silver .6424 oz. ASW **Subject:** Visit of Pope Paul VI **Reverse:** Martyrs' Shrine

| Date | Mintage | F | VF | XF | Unc | BU |
|---|---|---|---|---|---|---|
| 1969 Proof | 6,720 | Value: 22.50 | | | | |
| 1970 Proof | Inc. above | Value: 22.50 | | | | |

**10 SHILLINGS** KM# 21 **Composition:** Copper-Nickel **Subject:** Wedding of Prince Charles and Lady Diana

| Date | Mintage | F | VF | XF | Unc | BU |
|---|---|---|---|---|---|---|
| 1981 | 10,000 | — | — | — | 7.00 | — |

**10 SHILLINGS** KM# 30 **Composition:** Stainless Steel

| Date | Mintage | F | VF | XF | Unc | BU |
|---|---|---|---|---|---|---|
| 1987 | — | — | — | — | 3.50 | — |
| 1987 Proof | — | Value: 12.50 | | | | |

**20 SHILLINGS** KM# 11 **Weight:** 40.0000 g. **Composition:** 0.9990 Silver 1.2848 oz. ASW **Subject:** Visit of Pope Paul VI **Obverse:** Arms **Reverse:** Map

| Date | Mintage | F | VF | XF | Unc | BU |
|---|---|---|---|---|---|---|
| 1969 Proof | 6,670 | Value: 30.00 | | | | |
| 1970 Proof | Inc. above | Value: 32.50 | | | | |

**25 SHILLINGS** KM# 12 **Weight:** 50.0000 g. **Composition:** 0.9990 Silver 1.6061 oz. ASW **Subject:** Visit of Pope Paul VI **Obverse:** Arms **Reverse:** Globe

| Date | Mintage | F | VF | XF | Unc | BU |
|---|---|---|---|---|---|---|
| 1969 Proof | 6,070 | Value: 35.00 | | | | |
| 1970 Proof | Inc. above | Value: 37.50 | | | | |

**30 SHILLINGS** KM# 13 **Weight:** 60.0000 g. **Composition:** 0.9990 Silver 1.9273 oz. ASW **Subject:** Visit of Pope Paul VI **Obverse:** Arms **Size:** 60 mm. **Note:** Illustration reduced.

| Date | Mintage | F | VF | XF | Unc | BU |
|---|---|---|---|---|---|---|
| 1969 Proof | 6,720 | Value: 40.00 | | | | |
| 1970 Proof | Inc. above | Value: 42.50 | | | | |

**50 SHILLINGS** **KM# 14** **Weight:** 6.9100 g. **Composition:** 0.9000 Gold .1999 oz. AGW **Subject:** Visit of Pope Paul VI **Reverse:** Martyrs' Shrine

| Date | Mintage | F | VF | XF | Unc | BU |
|---|---|---|---|---|---|---|
| 1969 Proof | 4,390 | Value: 100 | | | | |
| 1970 Proof | Inc. above | Value: 100 | | | | |

**50 SHILLINGS** **KM# 66** **Composition:** Nickel Plated Steel **Reverse:** Antelope

| Date | Mintage | F | VF | XF | Unc | BU |
|---|---|---|---|---|---|---|
| 1998 | — | — | — | — | 1.00 | — |

**100 SHILLINGS** **KM# 15** **Weight:** 13.8200 g. **Composition:** 0.9000 Gold .3999 oz. AGW **Subject:** Visit of Pope Paul VI **Reverse:** Map

| Date | Mintage | F | VF | XF | Unc | BU |
|---|---|---|---|---|---|---|
| 1969 Proof | 4,190 | Value: 200 | | | | |
| 1970 Proof | Inc. above | Value: 200 | | | | |

**100 SHILLINGS** **KM# 22** **Weight:** 31.4700 g. **Composition:** 0.9250 Silver .9360 oz. ASW **Subject:** Wedding of Prince Charles and Lady Diana

| Date | Mintage | F | VF | XF | Unc | BU |
|---|---|---|---|---|---|---|
| 1981 Proof | 5,000 | Value: 40.00 | | | | |

**100 SHILLINGS** **KM# 67** **Composition:** Copper-Nickel **Reverse:** African bull

| Date | Mintage | F | VF | XF | Unc | BU |
|---|---|---|---|---|---|---|
| 1998 | — | — | — | — | 1.50 | — |

**200 SHILLINGS** **KM# 26** **Weight:** 28.2800 g. **Composition:** 0.9250 Silver .8411 oz. ASW **Series:** International Year of Disabled Persons

| Date | Mintage | F | VF | XF | Unc | BU |
|---|---|---|---|---|---|---|
| 1981 | 10,000 | — | — | — | 27.50 | — |
| 1981 Proof | 10,000 | Value: 37.50 | | | | |

**200 SHILLINGS** **KM# 68** **Composition:** Copper-Nickel **Reverse:** Fish

| Date | Mintage | F | VF | XF | Unc | BU |
|---|---|---|---|---|---|---|
| 1998 | — | — | — | — | 1.75 | — |

**500 SHILLINGS** **KM# 16** **Weight:** 69.1200 g. **Composition:** 0.9000 Gold 2.0002 oz. AGW **Subject:** Visit of Pope Paul VI **Obverse:** Arms **Reverse:** Globe

| Date | Mintage | F | VF | XF | Unc | BU |
|---|---|---|---|---|---|---|
| 1969 Proof | 1,680 | Value: 1,000 | | | | |
| 1970 Proof | Inc. above | Value: 1,000 | | | | |

**500 SHILLINGS** **KM# 23** **Weight:** 136.0000 g. **Composition:** 0.5000 Silver 2.1864 oz. ASW **Series:** Wildlife **Reverse:** Elephants

| Date | Mintage | F | VF | XF | Unc | BU |
|---|---|---|---|---|---|---|
| 1981 | 700 | — | — | — | 115 | — |

**500 SHILLINGS** **KM# 23a** **Weight:** 136.0000 g. **Composition:** 9.2500 Silver 4.045 oz. ASW **Series:** Wildlife **Reverse:** Elephants

| Date | Mintage | F | VF | XF | Unc | BU |
|---|---|---|---|---|---|---|
| 1981 Proof | 700 | Value: 200 | | | | |

**500 SHILLINGS** **KM# 69** **Composition:** Nickel-Brass **Reverse:** Crested crane

| Date | Mintage | F | VF | XF | Unc | BU |
|---|---|---|---|---|---|---|
| 1998 | — | — | — | — | 2.50 | — |

**1000 SHILLINGS** **KM# 17** **Weight:** 138.2400 g. **Composition:** 0.9000 Gold 4.0005 oz. AGW **Subject:** Visit of Pope John Paul VI

| Date | Mintage | F | VF | XF | Unc | BU |
|---|---|---|---|---|---|---|
| 1969 Proof | 1,390 | Value: 2,000 | | | | |
| 1970 Proof | Inc. above | Value: 2,000 | | | | |

**1000 SHILLINGS** **KM# 24** **Weight:** 10.0000 g. **Composition:** 0.5000 Gold .1607 oz. AGW **Subject:** Wedding of Prince Charles and Lady Diana **Reverse:** Busts of Charles and Diana right

| Date | Mintage | F | VF | XF | Unc | BU |
|---|---|---|---|---|---|---|
| 1981 Proof | 1,500 | Value: 125 | | | | |

**1000 SHILLINGS** **KM# 35** **Composition:** Copper-Nickel **Series:** Famous Places **Subject:** Matterhorn Mountain **Reverse:** Multicolored plastic applique

| Date | Mintage | F | VF | XF | Unc | BU |
|---|---|---|---|---|---|---|
| 1993 Proof | 15,000 | Value: 16.50 | | | | |

**1000 SHILLINGS** **KM# 49** **Composition:** Copper-Nickel **Series:** Famous Places **Subject:** Munich

| Date | Mintage | F | VF | XF | Unc | BU |
|---|---|---|---|---|---|---|
| 1994 Proof | — | Value: 16.50 | | | | |

**1000 SHILLINGS** **KM# 40** **Composition:** Copper-Nickel **Series:** 50th Anniversary - United Nations

| Date | Mintage | F | VF | XF | Unc | BU |
|---|---|---|---|---|---|---|
| 1995 Proof | — | Value: 20.00 | | | | |

**1000 SHILLINGS** **KM# 50** **Composition:** Copper-Nickel **Subject:** Year of the Pig **Reverse:** Stylized pig

| Date | Mintage | F | VF | XF | Unc | BU |
|---|---|---|---|---|---|---|
| 1995 Proof | — | Value: 17.50 | | | | |

**1000 SHILLINGS** **KM# 41** **Composition:** Copper-Nickel **Series:** Endangered Wildlife **Reverse:** Multicolored zebra applique

| Date | Mintage | F | VF | XF | Unc | BU |
|---|---|---|---|---|---|---|
| 1996 Proof | — | Value: 17.50 | | | | |

**1000 SHILLINGS** **KM# 44** **Composition:** Copper-Nickel **Series:** Endangered Wildlife **Reverse:** Rhinoceros

| Date | Mintage | F | VF | XF | Unc | BU |
|---|---|---|---|---|---|---|
| 1996 Proof | 15,000 | Value: 22.50 | | | | |

**1000 SHILLINGS** **KM# 45** **Composition:** Copper-Nickel **Series:** Endangered Wildlife **Reverse:** Lion

| Date | Mintage | F | VF | XF | Unc | BU |
|---|---|---|---|---|---|---|
| 1996 Proof | 15,000 | Value: 18.50 | | | | |

**1000 SHILLINGS** **KM# 52** **Composition:** Copper-Nickel **Subject:** Hong Kong's return to China **Obverse:** National arms **Reverse:** City view

| Date | Mintage | F | VF | XF | Unc | BU |
|---|---|---|---|---|---|---|
| 1996 | — | — | — | — | 18.00 | — |

**1000 SHILLINGS** **KM# 54** **Composition:** Copper-Nickel **Subject:** Year of the rat **Obverse:** Pair of rats flanking Chinese symbol **Reverse:** Multicolored rat applique

| Date | Mintage | F | VF | XF | Unc | BU |
|---|---|---|---|---|---|---|
| 1996 | — | — | — | — | 20.00 | — |

**1000 SHILLINGS** **KM# 55** **Composition:** Copper-Nickel **Subject:** Africa - protection of endangered wildlife **Obverse:** National arms **Reverse:** Multicolored elephant applique

| Date | Mintage | F | VF | XF | Unc | BU |
|---|---|---|---|---|---|---|
| 1996 Proof | — | Value: 22.50 | | | | |

**1000 SHILLINGS** **KM# 56** **Composition:** Copper-Nickel **Subject:** Michael Schumacher **Obverse:** National arms **Reverse:** Multicolored applique of Michael Schumacher, car and flag

| Date | Mintage | F | VF | XF | Unc | BU |
|---|---|---|---|---|---|---|
| 1996 Proof | — | Value: 28.00 | | | | |

**1000 SHILLINGS** **KM# 74** **Weight:** 28.5200 g. **Composition:** Copper-Nickel **Subject:** Birth of Jesus and the Modern Dating System **Obverse:** Jesus' portrait **Reverse:** National arms **Edge:** Reeded **Size:** 38.15 mm.

| Date | Mintage | F | VF | XF | Unc | BU |
|---|---|---|---|---|---|---|
| 1996 Proof | — | Value: 20.00 | | | | |

**1000 SHILLINGS** **KM# 57** **Composition:** Copper-Nickel **Subject:** Princess Diana - Queen of Hearts **Obverse:** National arms **Reverse:** Multicolored applique of Princess Diana

| Date | Mintage | F | VF | XF | Unc | BU |
|---|---|---|---|---|---|---|
| 1997 Proof | — | Value: 28.00 | | | | |

**1000 SHILLINGS** **KM# 70** **Weight:** 14.9700 g. **Composition:** 0.9990 Silver .4808 oz. ASW **Series:** XXVII Olympic Games **Obverse:** National arms **Reverse:** Javelin thrower

| Date | Mintage | F | VF | XF | Unc | BU |
|---|---|---|---|---|---|---|
| 1999 Proof | — | Value: 25.00 | | | | |

**2000 SHILLINGS** **KM# 31** **Weight:** 15.9800 g. **Composition:** 0.9170 Gold .4710 oz. AGW **Series:** International Year of Disabled Persons

| Date | Mintage | F | VF | XF | Unc | BU |
|---|---|---|---|---|---|---|
| 1981 | 2,005 | — | — | — | 550 | — |
| 1981 Proof | 2,005 | Value: 700 | | | | |

**2000 SHILLINGS** **KM# 38** **Weight:** 19.8000 g. **Composition:** 0.9990 Silver .6359 oz. ASW **Subject:** World Cup soccer **Reverse:** Player kicking ball

| Date | Mintage | F | VF | XF | Unc | BU |
|---|---|---|---|---|---|---|
| 1993 Proof | — | Value: 50.00 | | | | |

**2000 SHILLINGS** **KM# 39** **Weight:** 19.8000 g. **Composition:** 0.9990 Silver .6359 oz. ASW **Subject:** World Cup soccer **Reverse:** Player kicking ball down field

| Date | Mintage | F | VF | XF | Unc | BU |
|---|---|---|---|---|---|---|
| 1993 Proof | — | Value: 50.00 | | | | |

**2000 SHILLINGS** **KM# 42** **Weight:** 19.9200 g. **Composition:** 0.9990 Silver .6398 oz. ASW **Series:** Famous Places **Subject:** Matterhorn Mountain **Note:** With multicolored applique.

| Date | Mintage | F | VF | XF | Unc | BU |
|---|---|---|---|---|---|---|
| 1993 Proof | 10,000 | Value: 32.50 | | | | |

**2000 SHILLINGS** **KM# 64** **Weight:** 30.4600 g. **Composition:** 0.9990 Silver .9783 oz. ASW **Subject:** Protection of the African elephant **Obverse:** National arms

| Date | Mintage | F | VF | XF | Unc | BU |
|---|---|---|---|---|---|---|
| 1993 Proof | — | Value: 50.00 | | | | |

**2000 SHILLINGS** **KM# 43** **Weight:** 19.9200 g. **Composition:** 0.9990 Silver .6398 oz. ASW **Series:** Famous Places **Subject:** Munich's Frauen Kirche

| Date | Mintage | F | VF | XF | Unc | BU |
|---|---|---|---|---|---|---|
| 1994 Proof | 10,000 | Value: 32.50 | | | | |

**2000 SHILLINGS** **KM# 53** **Composition:** Copper-Nickel **Subject:** Nations United for Peace **Obverse:** National arms **Reverse:** United Nations building

| Date | Mintage | F | VF | XF | Unc | BU |
|---|---|---|---|---|---|---|
| ND(1995) | — | — | — | — | 8.50 | — |

**2000 SHILLINGS** **KM# 58** **Weight:** 30.8400 g. **Composition:** 0.9990 Silver .9904 oz. ASW **Obverse:** Sow and piglets **Reverse:** Multicolored pig applique

| Date | Mintage | F | VF | XF | Unc | BU |
|---|---|---|---|---|---|---|
| 1995 Proof | — | Value: 32.50 | | | | |

**2000 SHILLINGS** **KM# 46** **Weight:** 19.9200 g. **Composition:** 0.9990 Silver .6398 oz. ASW **Series:** Endangered Wildlife **Reverse:** Zebra

| Date | Mintage | F | VF | XF | Unc | BU |
|---|---|---|---|---|---|---|
| 1996 Proof | 10,000 | Value: 37.50 | | | | |

**2000 SHILLINGS** **KM# 47** **Weight:** 19.9200 g. **Composition:** 0.9990 Silver .6398 oz. ASW **Series:** Endangered Wildlife **Reverse:** Rhinocerous

| Date | Mintage | F | VF | XF | Unc | BU |
|---|---|---|---|---|---|---|
| 1996 Proof | 10,000 | Value: 47.50 | | | | |

**2000 SHILLINGS** **KM# 48** **Weight:** 19.9200 g. **Composition:** 0.9990 Silver .6398 oz. ASW **Series:** Endangered Wildlife **Reverse:** Lion

| Date | Mintage | F | VF | XF | Unc | BU |
|---|---|---|---|---|---|---|
| 1996 Proof | 10,000 | Value: 47.50 | | | | |

**2000 SHILLINGS** **KM# 59** **Weight:** 30.8400 g. **Composition:** 0.9990 Silver .9904 oz. ASW **Obverse:** Pair of rats flanking Chinese symbols **Reverse:** Multicolored rat applique

| Date | Mintage | F | VF | XF | Unc | BU |
|---|---|---|---|---|---|---|
| 1996 Proof | — | Value: 40.00 | | | | |

**2000 SHILLINGS** **KM# 60** **Weight:** 7.1000 g. **Composition:** 0.9990 Silver .228 oz. ASW **Subject:** 1998 World Championship Football **Obverse:** National arms **Reverse:** Soccer player and Eiffel Tower

| Date | Mintage | F | VF | XF | Unc | BU |
|---|---|---|---|---|---|---|
| 1996 Proof | — | Value: 20.00 | | | | |

**2000 SHILLINGS** **KM# 61** **Composition:** Copper-Nickel **Series:** XXVI Summer Olympic Games **Obverse:** National arms **Reverse:** 1936 German Olympic stamp

| Date | Mintage | F | VF | XF | Unc | BU |
|---|---|---|---|---|---|---|
| 1996 Proof | — | Value: 20.00 | | | | |

**2000 SHILLINGS** **KM# 62** **Composition:** Copper-Nickel **Series:** Olympics **Obverse:** National arms **Reverse:** Spanish postal stamp design

| Date | Mintage | F | VF | XF | Unc | BU |
|---|---|---|---|---|---|---|
| 1996 Proof | — | Value: 20.00 | | | | |

**2000 SHILLINGS** **KM# 65** **Weight:** 20.2600 g. **Composition:** 0.9990 Silver .6507 oz. ASW **Series:** Endangered Wildlife **Obverse:** National arms **Reverse:** Multicolored elephant

| Date | Mintage | F | VF | XF | Unc | BU |
|---|---|---|---|---|---|---|
| 1996 Proof | — | Value: 45.00 | | | | |

**2000 SHILLINGS** **KM# 63** **Composition:** Copper-Nickel **Subject:** Queen's golden wedding anniversary **Obverse:** National arms **Reverse:** Queen Elizabeth and Prince Philip on horseback

| Date | Mintage | F | VF | XF | Unc | BU |
|---|---|---|---|---|---|---|
| ND(1997) | — | — | — | — | 9.00 | — |

**2000 SHILLINGS** **KM# 51** **Weight:** 19.7400 g. **Composition:** 0.9990 Silver .6346 oz. ASW **Subject:** Hong Kong's return to China **Obverse:** National arms **Reverse:** City view

| Date | Mintage | F | VF | XF | Unc | BU |
|---|---|---|---|---|---|---|
| 1997 Proof | — | Value: 35.00 | | | | |

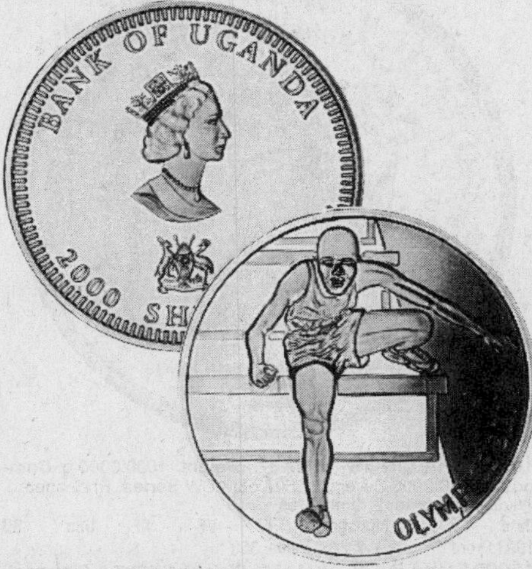


**2000 SHILLINGS** **KM# 71** **Weight:** 26.0000 g. **Composition:** 0.9990 Silver .8351 oz. ASW **Series:** Olympics 2000 **Obverse:** Queen Elizabeth II above arms **Reverse:** Hurdler **Edge:** Reeded **Size:** 40.1 mm.

| Date | Mintage | F | VF | XF | Unc | BU |
|---|---|---|---|---|---|---|
| 2000 Proof | 5,000 | Value: 35.00 | | | | |

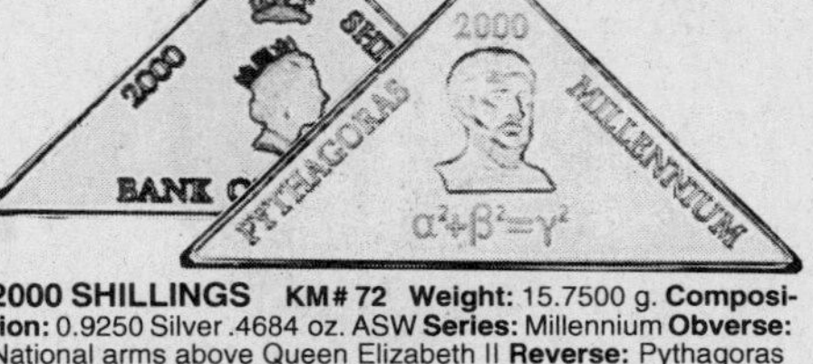


**2000 SHILLINGS** **KM# 72** **Weight:** 15.7500 g. **Composition:** 0.9250 Silver .4684 oz. ASW **Series:** Millennium **Obverse:** National arms above Queen Elizabeth II **Reverse:** Pythagoras **Edge:** Plain, 3 sided **Size:** 45.2x23.2 mm.

| Date | Mintage | F | VF | XF | Unc | BU |
|---|---|---|---|---|---|---|
| 2000 Proof | 10,000 | Value: 30.00 | | | | |

**2000 SHILLINGS** **KM# 73** **Weight:** 25.0000 g. **Composition:** 0.9250 Silver .7435 oz. ASW **Subject:** Wildlife protection **Obverse:** Queen Elizabeth's portrait above Ugandan arms **Reverse:** Three zebras drinking in reflective water **Edge:** Reeded **Size:** 37.9 mm.

| Date | Mintage | F | VF | XF | Unc | BU |
|---|---|---|---|---|---|---|
| 2000 Proof | 5,000 | Value: 32.50 | | | | |

**2000 SHILLINGS** **KM# 75** **Weight:** 49.9000 g. **Composition:** 0.9990 Silver 1.4840 oz. ASW **Subject:** Illusion: "Spirit of the Mountain" **Obverse:** Ugandan arms above Queen Elizabeth's portrait **Reverse:** Landscape that looks like a male portrait **Edge:** Reeded **Size:** 50 mm.

| Date | Mintage | F | VF | XF | Unc | BU |
|---|---|---|---|---|---|---|
| 2001 Proof | — | Value: 40.00 | | | | |

**5000 SHILLINGS** KM# 25 **Weight:** 33.9300 g. **Composition:** 0.9170 Gold 1 oz. AGW **Subject:** Wildlife **Obverse:** Facing bust of Dr. Milton Obote **Reverse:** Crested crane

| Date | Mintage | F | VF | XF | Unc | BU |
|---|---|---|---|---|---|---|
| 1981 | 100 | — | — | — | 550 | — |
| 1981 Proof | 100 | Value: 650 | | | | |

**5000 SHILLINGS** KM# 32 **Weight:** 12.0000 g. **Composition:** 0.9990 Silver .3858 oz. ASW **Subject:** Soccer **Reverse:** Ball and net

| Date | Mintage | F | VF | XF | Unc | BU |
|---|---|---|---|---|---|---|
| 1992 | Est. 10,000 | — | — | — | 25.00 | — |

**5000 SHILLINGS** KM# 36 **Weight:** 500.0000 g. **Composition:** 0.9990 Silver 16.0753 oz. ASW **Series:** Endangered Wildlife **Reverse:** 2 leopards

| Date | Mintage | F | VF | XF | Unc | BU |
|---|---|---|---|---|---|---|
| 1993 Proof | 2,500 | Value: 275 | | | | |

**10000 SHILLINGS** KM# 33 **Weight:** 20.0000 g. **Composition:** 0.9990 Silver .6430 oz. ASW **Subject:** Soccer **Reverse:** Mount Rushmore behind 2 players

| Date | Mintage | F | VF | XF | Unc | BU |
|---|---|---|---|---|---|---|
| ND(1992) Proof | Est. 10,000 | Value: 45.00 | | | | |

**10000 SHILLINGS** KM# 34 **Weight:** 20.0000 g. **Composition:** 0.9990 Silver .6430 oz. ASW **Subject:** Papal visit

| Date | Mintage | F | VF | XF | Unc | BU |
|---|---|---|---|---|---|---|
| 1993 Proof | — | Value: 37.50 | | | | |

**10000 SHILLINGS** KM# 37 **Weight:** 1000.0000 g. **Composition:** 0.9990 Silver 32.1507 oz. ASW **Series:** Endangered Wildlife **Reverse:** 2 rhinoceros

| Date | Mintage | F | VF | XF | Unc | BU |
|---|---|---|---|---|---|---|
| 1993 Proof | 2,000 | Value: 350 | | | | |

**12000 SHILLINGS** KM# 76 **Weight:** 6.2207 g. **Composition:** 0.9999 Gold .2000 oz. AGW **Subject:** Illusion: "Spirit of the Mountain" **Obverse:** Ugandan arms above Queen Elizabeth's portrait **Reverse:** Landscape that looks like a male portrait **Edge:** Reeded **Size:** 22 mm.

| Date | Mintage | F | VF | XF | Unc | BU |
|---|---|---|---|---|---|---|
| 2001 Proof | — | — | — | — | — | — |

## PATTERNS

Including off metal strikes

| KM# | Date | Mintage | Identification | Mkt Val |
|---|---|---|---|---|
| Pn1 | 1994 | — | 1000 Shillings. Copper-Nickel. Soccer player, 999. | — |
| Pn2 | 1994 | — | 1000 Shillings. Copper-Nickel. 3 soccer players, 999 CuNi. | — |
| Pn3 | 1994 | — | 1000 Shillings. Copper-Nickel. 4 soccer players, 999. | — |
| Pn4 | 1996 | — | 1000 Shillings. Gilt Bronze. Surinam. 100 Guilders. | — |

## PIEFORTS

| KM# | Date | Mintage | Identification | Mkt Val |
|---|---|---|---|---|
| P1 | 1981 | — | 200 Shillings. 0.9250 Silver. KM26. | 85.00 |
| P2 | 1981 | 505 | 2000 Shillings. 0.9170 Gold. KM31. | 1,000 |

## TRIAL STRIKES

| KM# | Date | Mintage | Identification | Mkt Val |
|---|---|---|---|---|
| TS1 | 1969 | — | 500 Shillings. Goldine. KM16. | 100 |

| KM# | Date | Mintage | Identification | Mkt Val |
|---|---|---|---|---|
| TS2 | 1970 | — | 1000 Shillings. Goldine. KM17. | 125 |

## MINT SETS

| KM# | Date | Mintage | Identification | Issue Price | Mkt Val |
|---|---|---|---|---|---|
| MS1 | 1987 (4) | — | KM27-30 | 10.50 | 11.50 |

## PROOF SETS

| KM# | Date | Mintage | Identification | Issue Price | Mkt Val |
|---|---|---|---|---|---|
| PS1 | 1966 (6) | 8,250 | KM1-6 | 7.75 | 14.50 |
| PS2 | 1969 (10) | 1,390 | KM8-17 | 790 | 3,450 |
| PS3 | 1969 (6) | 6,070 | KM8-13 | 78.50 | 160 |
| PS4 | 1970 (10) | — | KM8-17, including KM-PS2 | 790 | 3,300 |
| PS5 | 1970 (6) | — | KM8-13, including KM-PS3 | 78.50 | 170 |
| PS6 | 1987 (4) | 2,500 | KM27-30 | 25.00 | 27.50 |

# UKRAINE

Ukraine (formerly the Ukrainian Soviet Socialist Republic) is bordered by Russia to the east, Russia and Belarus to the north, Poland, Slovakia and Hungary to the west, Romania and Moldova to the southwest and in the south by the Black Sea and the Sea of Azov. It has an area of 233,088 sq. mi. (603,700 sq. km.) and a population of 51.9 million. Capital: Kyiv (Kiev). Coal, grain, vegetables and heavy industrial machinery are major exports.

The territory of Ukraine has been inhabited for over 30,000 years. As the result of its location, Ukraine has served as the gateway to Europe for millennia and its early history has been recorded by Arabic, Greek, Roman, as well as Ukrainian historians.

Ukraine, which was known as *Rus'* until the sixteenth century (and from which the name Russia was derived in the 17th century) became the major political and cultural center of Eastern Europe in the 9th century. The Rus' Kingdom, under a dynasty of Varangian origin, due to its position on the intersection of the north-south Scandinavia to Byzantium and the east-west Orient to Europe trade routes, became a focal point of world trade. At its apex Rus' stretched from the Baltic to the Black Sea and from the upper Volga River in the east, almost to the Vistula River in the west. It has family ties to many European dynasties. In 988 knyaz (king) Volodymyr adopted Christianity from Byzantium. With it came church books written in the Cyrillic alphabet, which originated in Bulgaria. The Mongol invasion in 1240 brought an end to the might of the Rus' Kingdom.

In the seventeenth century, after almost four hundred years of Mongol, Lithuanian, Polish, and Turkish domination, the Cosack State under Hetman Bohdan Khmelnytsky regained Ukrainian independence. The Hetman State lasted until the mid-eighteenth century and was followed by a period of foreign rule. Eastern Ukraine was controlled by Russia, which enforced russification through introduction of the Russian language and prohibiting the use of the Ukrainian language in schools, books and public life. Western Ukraine came under relatively benign Austro-Hungarian rule.

With the disintegration of the Russian and Austro-Hungarian Empires in 1917 and 1918. Eastern Ukraine declared its full independence on January 22,1918 and Western Ukraine followed suit on November 1 of that year. On January 22, 1919 both parts united into one state that had to defend itself on three fronts: from the "Red Bolsheviks"and their puppet Ukrainian Soviet Republic formed in Kharkiv, from the "White" czarist Russian forces, and from Poland. Ukraine lost the war. In 1920 Eastern Ukraine was occupied by the Bolsheviks and in 1922 was incorporated into the Soviet Union. There followed a brief resurgence of Ukrainian language and culture which Stalin suppressed in 1928. The artificial famine-genocide of 1932-33 killed 7-10 million Ukrainians, and Stalinist purges in the mid-1930s took a heavy toll. Western Ukraine was partitioned between Poland, Romania, Hungary and Czechoslovakia.

On August 24, 1991 Ukraine once again declared its independence. On December 1, 1991 over 90% of Ukraine's electorate approved full independence from the Soviet Union. On December 5, 1991 the Ukrainian Parliament abrogated the 1922 treaty which incorporated Ukraine into the Soviet Union. Later, Leonid Kravchuk was elected president by a 65% majority.

Ukraine is a charter member of the United Nations and has inherited the third largest nuclear arsenal in the world.

**Rulers**

Russian (Eastern, Northern, Southern, Central Ukraine), 1654-1917
Austrian (Western Ukraine), 1774-1918

**MINT**

w/o mm - Lugansk; Kiev (1997-1998)

**MONETARY SYSTEM**

(1) Kopiyka
(2) Kopiyky КОмёйКН
(5 and up) Kopiyok КОмійОК
100 Kopiyok = 1 Hrynia МРйВЕН†
100,000 Karbovanetsiv = 1 Hryni or Hryven)

## REPUBLIC

### STANDARD COINAGE

**200000 KARBOVANTSIV KM# 9 Composition:** Copper-Nickel **Subject:** Bohdan Khmelnytsky Monument

| Date | Mintage | F | VF | XF | Unc | BU |
|---|---|---|---|---|---|---|
| 1995 Prooflike | 250,000 | — | — | — | 5.50 | — |

**200000 KARBOVANTSIV KM# 10.1 Composition:** Copper-Nickel **Subject:** 50th anniversary - end of World War II **Obverse:** Ukrainian letter "Y" looks similar to "X" **Reverse:** Ukrainian letter "Y" looks similar to "X"

| Date | Mintage | F | VF | XF | Unc | BU |
|---|---|---|---|---|---|---|
| 1995 Prooflike | 10,000 | — | — | — | 22.50 | — |

**200000 KARBOVANTSIV KM# 10.2 Composition:** Copper-Nickel **Subject:** 50th anniversary - end of World War II **Obverse:** Ukrainian letter "Y" like Y/2 in legends **Reverse:** Ukrainian letter "Y" like Y/2 in legends

| Date | Mintage | F | VF | XF | Unc | BU |
|---|---|---|---|---|---|---|
| 1995 Prooflike | 240,000 | — | — | — | 5.50 | — |

**200000 KARBOVANTSIV KM# 11 Composition:** Copper-Nickel **Subject:** World War II - monument at Kerch

| Date | Mintage | F | VF | XF | Unc | BU |
|---|---|---|---|---|---|---|
| 1995 Prooflike | 50,000 | — | — | — | 9.00 | — |

**200000 KARBOVANTSIV KM# 12 Composition:** Copper-Nickel **Subject:** World War II - monument at Odessa

| Date | Mintage | F | VF | XF | Unc | BU |
|---|---|---|---|---|---|---|
| 1995 Prooflike | 75,000 | — | — | — | 5.50 | — |

**200000 KARBOVANTSIV KM# 13 Composition:** Copper-Nickel **Subject:** World War II - monument at Kiev

| Date | Mintage | F | VF | XF | Unc | BU |
|---|---|---|---|---|---|---|
| 1995 Prooflike | 100,000 | — | — | — | 5.50 | — |

**200000 KARBOVANTSIV KM# 14 Composition:** Copper-Nickel **Subject:** World War II - monument at Sevastopol

| Date | Mintage | F | VF | XF | Unc | BU |
|---|---|---|---|---|---|---|
| 1995 Prooflike | 75,000 | — | — | — | 8.00 | — |

**200000 KARBOVANTSIV KM# 15 Composition:** Copper-Nickel **Series:** 50th Anniversary - United Nations

| Date | Mintage | F | VF | XF | Unc | BU |
|---|---|---|---|---|---|---|
| 1995 | 100,000 | — | — | — | 5.50 | — |

**200000 KARBOVANTSIV KM# 17 Composition:** Copper-Nickel **Subject:** Lesya Ukrainka - poetess

| Date | Mintage | F | VF | XF | Unc | BU |
|---|---|---|---|---|---|---|
| 1996 Prooflike | 100,000 | — | — | — | 5.50 | — |

**200000 KARBOVANTSIV KM# 21 Composition:** Copper-Nickel **Subject:** 10th anniversary - Chernobyl disaster

| Date | Mintage | F | VF | XF | Unc | BU |
|---|---|---|---|---|---|---|
| 1996 Prooflike | 250,000 | — | — | — | 5.50 | — |

**200000 KARBOVANTSIV KM# 23 Composition:** Copper-Nickel **Series:** 1st Participation in Summer Olympics **Reverse:** Athletes around octagon

| Date | Mintage | F | VF | XF | Unc | BU |
|---|---|---|---|---|---|---|
| 1996 Prooflike | 100,000 | — | — | — | 5.50 | — |

**200000 KARBOVANTSIV** **KM# 24** **Composition:** Copper-Nickel **Series:** Centennial of Modern Olympics **Reverse:** Flame and logo

| Date | Mintage | F | VF | XF | Unc | BU |
|---|---|---|---|---|---|---|
| 1996 Prooflike | 100,000 | — | — | — | 5.50 | — |

**200000 KARBOVANTSIV** **KM# 27** **Composition:** Copper-Nickel **Subject:** Mikhailo Hrushevsky - 1866-1934

| Date | Mintage | F | VF | XF | Unc | BU |
|---|---|---|---|---|---|---|
| 1996 Prooflike | 75,000 | — | — | — | 5.50 | — |

**1000000 KARBOVANETS** **KM# 16** **Weight:** 16.8110 g. **Composition:** 0.9250 Silver .5 oz. ASW **Subject:** Bohdan Khmelnytsky Monument

| Date | Mintage | F | VF | XF | Unc | BU |
|---|---|---|---|---|---|---|
| 1996 Proof | 10,000 | Value: 30.00 | | | | |

**1000000 KARBOVANETS** **KM# 18** **Weight:** 16.8110 g. **Composition:** 0.9250 Silver .5 oz. ASW **Subject:** Lesya Ukrainka - poetess

| Date | Mintage | F | VF | XF | Unc | BU |
|---|---|---|---|---|---|---|
| 1996 Proof | 10,000 | Value: 30.00 | | | | |

**1000000 KARBOVANETS** **KM# 20** **Weight:** 16.8110 g. **Composition:** 0.9250 Silver .5 oz. ASW **Subject:** Grygory Skovoroda **Obverse:** Similar to KM#16

| Date | Mintage | F | VF | XF | Unc | BU |
|---|---|---|---|---|---|---|
| 1996 Proof | 10,000 | Value: 28.00 | | | | |

**1000000 KARBOVANETS** **KM# 32** **Weight:** 16.8110 g. **Composition:** 0.9250 Silver .5 oz. ASW **Subject:** Mikhailo Hrushevsky - 1866-1934 **Obverse:** National arms

| Date | Mintage | F | VF | XF | Unc | BU |
|---|---|---|---|---|---|---|
| 1996 Proof | 10,000 | Value: 28.00 | | | | |

**2000000 KARBOVANETS** **KM# 19** **Weight:** 33.6220 g. **Composition:** 0.9250 Silver 1 oz. ASW **Series:** 50 Years - United Nations

| Date | Mintage | F | VF | XF | Unc | BU |
|---|---|---|---|---|---|---|
| 1995 Proof | 10,000 | Value: 37.50 | | | | |

**2000000 KARBOVANETS** **KM# 22** **Weight:** 33.6220 g. **Composition:** 0.9250 Silver 1 oz. ASW **Subject:** 10th anniversary - Chernobyl disaster

| Date | Mintage | F | VF | XF | Unc | BU |
|---|---|---|---|---|---|---|
| 1996 Proof | 10,000 | Value: 40.00 | | | | |

**2000000 KARBOVANETS** **KM# 25** **Weight:** 33.6220 g. **Composition:** 0.9250 Silver 1 oz. ASW **Series:** 1st Participation in Summer Olympics **Reverse:** Athletes around octagon

| Date | Mintage | F | VF | XF | Unc | BU |
|---|---|---|---|---|---|---|
| 1996 Proof | 10,000 | Value: 35.00 | | | | |

**2000000 KARBOVANETS** **KM# 26** **Weight:** 33.6220 g. **Composition:** 0.9250 Silver 1 oz. ASW **Series:** Centennial of Modern Olympics **Reverse:** Flame and logo

| Date | Mintage | F | VF | XF | Unc | BU |
|---|---|---|---|---|---|---|
| 1996 Proof | 10,000 | Value: 35.00 | | | | |

**2000000 KARBOVANETS** **KM# 33** **Weight:** 33.6220 g. **Composition:** 0.9250 Silver 1 oz. ASW **Subject:** Independence **Obverse:** National arms

| Date | Mintage | F | VF | XF | Unc | BU |
|---|---|---|---|---|---|---|
| 1996 Proof | 10,000 | Value: 42.50 | | | | |

## REFORM COINAGE

September 2, 1996

100,000 Karbovanets = 1 Hryvnia; 100 Kopiyok = 1 Hryvnia; The Kopiyok has replaced the Karbovanet

**KOPIYKA** **KM# 6** **Composition:** Steel

| Date | Mintage | F | VF | XF | Unc | BU |
|---|---|---|---|---|---|---|
| 1992 | — | — | — | 0.15 | 0.35 | — |
| 1994 | — | — | — | — | — | — |
| 1996 | — | — | — | 1.00 | 1.35 | — |
| 2000 | — | — | — | — | — | — |
| 2001 | — | — | — | — | — | — |

**2 KOPIYKY** **KM# 4** **Composition:** Aluminum

| Date | Mintage | F | VF | XF | Unc | BU |
|---|---|---|---|---|---|---|
| 1992 | — | — | — | — | — | — |
| 1993 | — | — | 0.20 | 0.50 | 1.00 | — |
| 1994 | — | — | 0.20 | 0.50 | 1.00 | — |
| 1996 | — | — | 0.20 | 1.00 | 2.00 | — |

**5 KOPIYOK** **KM# 7** **Composition:** Steel

| Date | Mintage | F | VF | XF | Unc | BU |
|---|---|---|---|---|---|---|
| 1992 | — | — | — | 0.35 | 0.65 | — |
| 1996 | — | — | 0.50 | 1.50 | 3.00 | — |

**10 KOPIYOK** KM# 1.1 **Composition:** Brass **Reverse:** 5 dots right of final "K" in denomination **Note:** Edge varieties - fine or coarse reeding - exist.

| Date | Mintage | F | VF | XF | Unc | BU |
|---|---|---|---|---|---|---|
| 1992 | — | — | 0.50 | 1.00 | 2.25 | — |
| 1994 | — | — | 0.50 | 1.00 | 2.25 | — |
| 1996 | — | — | 0.60 | 1.25 | 2.50 | — |

**10 KOPIYOK** KM# 1.2 **Composition:** Brass **Reverse:** 6 dots right of "K"

| Date | Mintage | F | VF | XF | Unc | BU |
|---|---|---|---|---|---|---|
| 1992 | — | — | 0.50 | 1.00 | 2.25 | — |

**25 KOPIYOK** KM# 2.1 **Composition:** Brass

| Date | Mintage | F | VF | XF | Unc | BU |
|---|---|---|---|---|---|---|
| 1992 | — | — | 0.60 | 1.25 | 2.50 | — |
| 1994 | — | — | 0.60 | 1.25 | 2.50 | — |
| 1995 | — | — | 0.80 | 2.25 | 3.50 | — |
| 1996 | — | — | 0.80 | 2.25 | 3.50 | — |

**25 KOPIYOK** KM# 2.2 **Composition:** Brass **Reverse:** Berries with dots inside

| Date | Mintage | F | VF | XF | Unc | BU |
|---|---|---|---|---|---|---|
| 1992 | — | — | 0.60 | 1.25 | 2.50 | — |

**50 KOPIYOK** KM# 3.1 **Composition:** Brass **Reverse:** 5 dots grouped in wreath to right of final letter "K" in denomination **Edge:** Reeded sections of 16 grooves each

| Date | Mintage | F | VF | XF | Unc | BU |
|---|---|---|---|---|---|---|
| 1992 | — | — | 0.85 | 1.75 | 3.50 | — |
| 1994 | — | — | 0.85 | 1.75 | 3.50 | — |

**50 KOPIYOK** KM# 3.3 **Composition:** Brass **Reverse:** 5 dots grouped in wreath to right of final letter "K" in denomination

| Date | Mintage | F | VF | XF | Unc | BU |
|---|---|---|---|---|---|---|
| 1992 | — | — | 0.85 | 1.75 | 3.50 | — |
| 1994 | — | — | 0.85 | 1.75 | 3.50 | — |
| 1995 | — | — | 0.85 | 2.25 | 4.00 | — |
| 1996 | — | — | 0.85 | 2.25 | 4.00 | — |

**50 KOPIYOK** KM# 3.2 **Composition:** Brass **Reverse:** 4 dots grouped in wreath to right of final letter "K" in denomination **Edge:** Reeded sections of 7 grooves each

| Date | Mintage | F | VF | XF | Unc | BU |
|---|---|---|---|---|---|---|
| 1992 | — | — | 0.85 | 1.75 | 3.50 | — |

**HRYVNIA** KM# 8 **Composition:** Brass

| Date | Mintage | F | VF | XF | Unc | BU |
|---|---|---|---|---|---|---|
| 1992 | — | — | — | 10.00 | 20.00 | — |
| 1995 | — | — | — | 3.50 | 6.50 | — |
| 1996 | — | — | — | 2.50 | 4.50 | — |

**2 HRYVNI** KM# 28 **Composition:** Copper-Nickel **Subject:** 200th anniversary - Sophiyivka Dendrological Park **Reverse:** Partially overgrown stone face

| Date | Mintage | F | VF | XF | Unc | BU |
|---|---|---|---|---|---|---|
| 1996 Prooflike | 30,000 | — | — | — | 12.50 | — |

**2 HRYVNI** KM# 29 **Composition:** Copper-Nickel **Subject:** Desiatynna Church **Obverse:** National arms above Madonna and child

| Date | Mintage | F | VF | XF | Unc | BU |
|---|---|---|---|---|---|---|
| 1996 Prooflike | 30,000 | — | — | — | 12.50 | — |

**2 HRYVNI** KM# 30 **Composition:** Copper-Nickel **Subject:** Modern Ukrainian coinage **Obverse:** National arms

| Date | Mintage | F | VF | XF | Unc | BU |
|---|---|---|---|---|---|---|
| 1996 | 200,000 | — | — | — | 8.00 | — |

**2 HRYVNI** KM# 39 **Composition:** Copper-Nickel **Subject:** Yuri Kondratiuk **Obverse:** National arms on astrological design **Reverse:** Scientific drawing

| Date | Mintage | F | VF | XF | Unc | BU |
|---|---|---|---|---|---|---|
| 1997 Prooflike | 20,000 | — | — | — | 12.50 | — |

**2 HRYVNI** KM# 40 **Composition:** Copper-Nickel **Subject:** 1st anniversary - constitution **Obverse:** National arms **Reverse:** Scroll

| Date | Mintage | F | VF | XF | Unc | BU |
|---|---|---|---|---|---|---|
| 1997 Prooflike | 20,000 | — | — | — | 12.50 | — |

**2 HRYVNI** KM# 41 **Composition:** Copper-Nickel **Subject:** Solomiya Krushelnytska - 1872-1952 **Obverse:** National arms

| Date | Mintage | F | VF | XF | Unc | BU |
|---|---|---|---|---|---|---|
| 1997 Prooflike | 20,000 | — | — | — | 10.00 | — |

**2 HRYVNI** KM# 42 **Composition:** Copper-Nickel **Subject:** 80 years of nationhood **Obverse:** National arms and people above denomination **Reverse:** Cossacks, soldiers **Note:** 50,000 were encapsulated for numismatists.

| Date | Mintage | F | VF | XF | Unc | BU |
|---|---|---|---|---|---|---|
| ND(1998) Prooflike | 200,000 | — | — | — | 7.50 | — |

**2 HRYVNI** KM# 43 **Composition:** Copper-Nickel **Subject:** Bolodimir Sosura - 1898-1965 **Obverse:** National arms **Note:** 20,000 were encapsulated for numismatists.

| Date | Mintage | F | VF | XF | Unc | BU |
|---|---|---|---|---|---|---|
| 1998 Prooflike | 200,000 | — | — | — | 7.50 | — |

**2 HRYVNI** KM# 47 **Composition:** Copper-Nickel **Subject:** 80 years of nationhood **Obverse:** Family group and national arms **Reverse:** Soldiers on guard **Note:** 50,000 were encapsulated for numismatists.

| Date | Mintage | F | VF | XF | Unc | BU |
|---|---|---|---|---|---|---|
| 1998 Prooflike | 200,000 | — | — | — | 7.50 | — |

**2 HRYVNI** **KM# 48** **Composition:** Copper-Nickel **Subject:** European Bank of Reconstruction & Development **Obverse:** National arms and denomination **Reverse:** Legendary founders at Kiev statue

| Date | Mintage | F | VF | XF | Unc | BU |
|---|---|---|---|---|---|---|
| 1998 | 10,000 | — | — | — | 8.50 | — |

**2 HRYVNI** **KM# 49** **Composition:** Copper-Nickel **Subject:** 100th anniversary - Askania-Nova Wildlife Preserve **Obverse:** National arms, denomination, wild animals and plants **Note:** 50,000 were encapsulated for numismatists.

| Date | Mintage | F | VF | XF | Unc | BU |
|---|---|---|---|---|---|---|
| 1998 | 100,000 | — | — | — | 7.50 | — |

**2 HRYVNI** **KM# 51** **Composition:** Copper-Nickel **Subject:** 100th anniversary - Polytechnical Institute **Obverse:** National arms in circular design **Note:** 10,000 were encapsulated for numismatists.

| Date | Mintage | F | VF | XF | Unc | BU |
|---|---|---|---|---|---|---|
| 1998 Prooflike | 50,000 | — | — | — | 9.00 | — |

**2 HRYVNI** **KM# 72** **Composition:** Copper-Nickel-Zinc **Subject:** 50 years - United Nations Human Rights Declaration **Obverse:** National arms **Reverse:** Logo on globe

| Date | Mintage | F | VF | XF | Unc | BU |
|---|---|---|---|---|---|---|
| 1998 | 100,000 | — | — | — | 7.50 | — |

**2 HRYVNI** **KM# 73** **Composition:** Copper-Nickel **Subject:** Steppe eagle **Obverse:** National arms **Reverse:** Eagle in flight

| Date | Mintage | F | VF | XF | Unc | BU |
|---|---|---|---|---|---|---|
| 1999 | — | — | — | — | 7.50 | — |

**2 HRYVNI** **KM# 75** **Composition:** Copper-Nickel **Subject:** 80th anniversary - Ukranian state **Obverse:** National arms **Reverse:** Seated woman

| Date | Mintage | F | VF | XF | Unc | BU |
|---|---|---|---|---|---|---|
| 1999 | — | — | — | — | 7.50 | — |

**2 HRYVNI** **KM# 76** **Composition:** Copper-Nickel **Subject:** P.Y. Rudchenko (1849-1920) **Obverse:** National arms **Reverse:** Portrait with book and quill

| Date | Mintage | F | VF | XF | Unc | BU |
|---|---|---|---|---|---|---|
| 1999 Prooflike | 50,000 | — | — | — | 8.00 | — |

**2 HRYVNI** **KM# 78** **Composition:** Copper-Nickel **Subject:** Anatolyi Solovianenko **Obverse:** National arms **Reverse:** Portrait

| Date | Mintage | F | VF | XF | Unc | BU |
|---|---|---|---|---|---|---|
| 1999 Prooflike | — | — | — | — | 8.00 | — |

**2 HRYVNI** **KM# 81** **Weight:** 12.5500 g. **Composition:** Copper-Nickel **Subject:** Platanthera Bifolia **Obverse:** National arms above denomination **Reverse:** Flower **Edge:** Reeded **Size:** 31.1 mm.

| Date | Mintage | F | VF | XF | Unc | BU |
|---|---|---|---|---|---|---|
| 1999 | 50,000 | — | — | — | 5.50 | — |

**2 HRYVNI** **KM# 82** **Composition:** Copper-Nickel **Subject:** 100 years - Ukraine's National Mining Academy

| Date | Mintage | F | VF | XF | Unc | BU |
|---|---|---|---|---|---|---|
| 1999 | 20,000 | — | — | — | 5.50 | — |

**2 HRYVNI** **KM# 83** **Composition:** Copper-Nickel **Reverse:** Dormouse

| Date | Mintage | F | VF | XF | Unc | BU |
|---|---|---|---|---|---|---|
| 1999 | 50,000 | — | — | — | 5.50 | — |

**2 HRYVNI** **KM# 79** **Composition:** Copper-Nickel **Subject:** 55th annivesary - freedom from Nazi occupation **Obverse:** National arms **Reverse:** Stylized sword design

| Date | Mintage | F | VF | XF | Unc | BU |
|---|---|---|---|---|---|---|
| 1999 | 50,000 | — | — | — | 8.00 | — |

**2 HRYVNI** **KM# 91** **Weight:** 13.4000 g. **Composition:** Copper-Nickel **Subject:** 55th anniversary - victory in World War II **Obverse:** Arms and denomination **Reverse:** Symboblic "Peace" figure **Edge:** Reeded

| Date | Mintage | F | VF | XF | Unc | BU |
|---|---|---|---|---|---|---|
| 2000 | 50,000 | — | — | — | 7.50 | — |

**2 HRYVNI** **KM# 110** **Weight:** 12.9200 g. **Composition:** Copper-Nickel **Subject:** Kateryna Bilokur (1900-1961) **Obverse:** Flower cluster **Reverse:** Woman artist **Edge:** Reeded **Size:** 31 mm.

| Date | Mintage | F | VF | XF | Unc | BU |
|---|---|---|---|---|---|---|
| 2000 | 50,000 | — | — | — | 7.00 | — |

**2 HRYVNI** **KM# 92** **Weight:** 13.4000 g. **Composition:** Copper-Nickel **Subject:** Archaeologist V. Hvoika **Obverse:** Arms within circles and artifacts **Reverse:** V. Hvoika head facing

| Date | Mintage | F | VF | XF | Unc | BU |
|---|---|---|---|---|---|---|
| 2000 | 20,000 | — | — | — | 7.50 | — |

**2 HRYVNI** **KM# 93** **Weight:** 13.4000 g. **Composition:** Copper-Nickel **Series:** Olympics **Subject:** Sydney 2000 **Obverse:** Arms and denomination **Reverse:** Broad jumper

| Date | Mintage | F | VF | XF | Unc | BU |
|---|---|---|---|---|---|---|
| 2000 | 50,000 | — | — | — | 6.50 | — |

**2 HRYVNI** **KM# 94** **Weight:** 13.4000 g. **Composition:** Copper-Nickel **Series:** Olympics **Subject:** Sydney 2000 **Obverse:** Arms and denomination **Reverse:** Gymnast on parallel bars

| Date | Mintage | F | VF | XF | Unc | BU |
|---|---|---|---|---|---|---|
| 2000 | 50,000 | — | — | — | 6.50 | — |

**2 HRYVNI** **KM# 96** **Composition:** Copper-Nickel **Subject:** Musician Ivan Kozlovsbkye **Obverse:** Flowery lyre **Reverse:** I. Kozlovsbkye head left **Edge:** Reeded **Size:** 31 mm.

| Date | Mintage | F | VF | XF | Unc | BU |
|---|---|---|---|---|---|---|
| 2000 | 20,000 | — | — | — | 6.50 | — |

**2 HRYVNI** **KM# 97** **Composition:** Copper-Nickel **Series:** Olympics **Subject:** Sydney 2000 **Obverse:** National arms, sports figures, and denomination **Reverse:** Stylized sailing scene

| Date | Mintage | F | VF | XF | Unc | BU |
|---|---|---|---|---|---|---|
| 2000 | 50,000 | — | — | — | 6.50 | — |

**2 HRYVNI** **KM# 98** **Composition:** Copper-Nickel **Obverse:** National arms, flowers, and denomination **Reverse:** Male portrait with life dates 1918-1995

| Date | Mintage | F | VF | XF | Unc | BU |
|---|---|---|---|---|---|---|
| 2000 | 20,000 | — | — | — | 6.50 | — |

**2 HRYVNI** **KM# 99** **Composition:** Copper-Nickel **Subject:** Potamon Tauricum **Obverse:** National arms and denomination **Reverse:** Crab

| Date | Mintage | F | VF | XF | Unc | BU |
|---|---|---|---|---|---|---|
| 2000 | 50,000 | — | — | — | 6.50 | — |

**2 HRYVNI** **KM# 100** **Composition:** Copper-Nickel **Subject:** 125th anniversary - Chernivtsy National University **Obverse:** National arms above denomination **Reverse:** University viewed through arch **Edge:** Reeded **Size:** 31 mm.

| Date | Mintage | F | VF | XF | Unc | BU |
|---|---|---|---|---|---|---|
| 2000 | 50,000 | — | — | — | 7.50 | — |

**2 HRYVNI** **KM# 101** **Composition:** Copper-Nickel **Series:** Olympics **Subject:** Sydney 2000 **Obverse:** National arms, athletes, and denomination **Reverse:** Gymnast doing floor exercises

| Date | Mintage | F | VF | XF | Unc | BU |
|---|---|---|---|---|---|---|
| 2000 | 50,000 | — | — | — | 7.50 | — |

**2 HRYVNI** **KM# 111** **Weight:** 12.5300 g. **Composition:** Copper-Nickel **Series:** Flora and Fauna **Subject:** Lynx **Obverse:** Denomination **Reverse:** Lynx and offspring **Edge:** Reeded **Size:** 31 mm.

| Date | Mintage | F | VF | XF | Unc | BU |
|---|---|---|---|---|---|---|
| 2001 | — | — | — | — | 7.50 | — |

**2 HRYVNI** **KM# 106** **Weight:** 12.6200 g. **Composition:** Copper-Nickel **Series:** Olympics **Obverse:** National arms and denomination **Reverse:** Stylized ice dancing couple **Edge:** Reeded **Size:** 31 mm.

| Date | Mintage | F | VF | XF | Unc | BU |
|---|---|---|---|---|---|---|
| 2001 | — | — | — | — | 7.50 | — |

**2 HRYVNI** **KM# 133** **Weight:** 12.8000 g. **Composition:** Copper Nickel **Subject:** Kindness to Children **Obverse:** National arms above denomination. **Reverse:** Two children and fountain of knowledge. **Edge:** Reeded. **Size:** 31 mm. **Note:** Struck at Malyn Mint.

| Date | Mintage | F | VF | XF | Unc | BU |
|---|---|---|---|---|---|---|
| 2001 | 100,000 | — | — | — | 7.50 | — |

**2 HRYVNI** **KM# 134** **Weight:** 12.8000 g. **Composition:** Copper Nickel **Subject:** 5th Anniversary of Constitution **Obverse:** National arms above denomination. **Reverse:** Building above book. **Edge:** Reeded. **Size:** 31 mm. **Note:** Struck at Malyn Mint.

| Date | Mintage | F | VF | XF | Unc | BU |
|---|---|---|---|---|---|---|
| 2001 | 30,000 | — | — | — | 7.50 | — |

**5 HRYVNIA** **KM# 66** **Composition:** Copper-Nickel-Zinc **Subject:** St. Michaels Cathedral **Obverse:** Denomination **Reverse:** Cathedral behind human silhouettes

| Date | Mintage | F | VF | XF | Unc | BU |
|---|---|---|---|---|---|---|
| 1998 | 200,000 | — | — | — | 9.50 | — |

**5 HRYVNIA** **KM# 69** **Composition:** Copper-Nickel-Zinc **Subject:** Kyiv-Pecherski Assumption Cathedral **Obverse:** Denomination **Reverse:** Cathedral behind carved ruins

| Date | Mintage | F | VF | XF | Unc | BU |
|---|---|---|---|---|---|---|
| 1999 | 200,000 | — | — | — | 9.50 | — |

**5 HRYVNIA** **KM# 74** **Composition:** Copper-Nickel **Subject:** Novgorad city charter's 900th anniversary **Obverse:** Denomination **Reverse:** Armed horseman

| Date | Mintage | F | VF | XF | Unc | BU |
|---|---|---|---|---|---|---|
| 1999 | 50,000 | — | — | — | 9.50 | — |

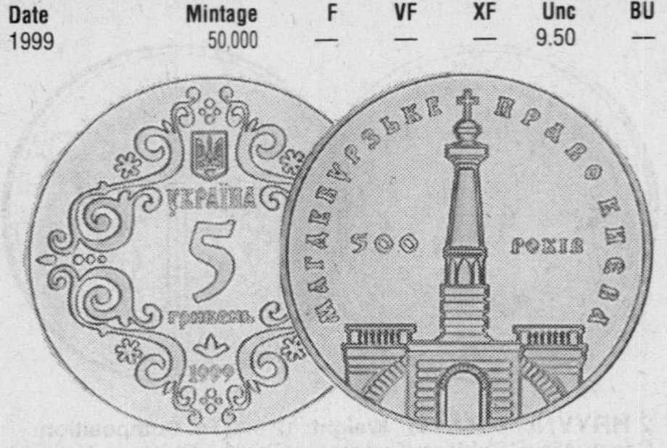


**5 HRYVNIA** **KM# 80** **Composition:** Copper-Nickel **Subject:** Kiev monument to the "Magdeburg Law" of the 13th century **Obverse:** National arms above denomination **Reverse:** Monument

| Date | Mintage | F | VF | XF | Unc | BU |
|---|---|---|---|---|---|---|
| 1999 | 50,000 | — | — | — | 10.00 | — |

**5 HRYVNIA** **KM# 84** **Weight:** 16.3600 g. **Composition:** Copper-Nickel **Subject:** Birth of Jesus **Obverse:** National arms, denomination, and angels **Reverse:** Nativity scene **Edge:** Reeded **Size:** 35.1 mm. **Note:** Struck at Lugansk.

| Date | Mintage | F | VF | XF | Unc | BU |
|---|---|---|---|---|---|---|
| 1999 | 10,000 | — | — | — | 9.00 | — |

**5 HRYVNIA** **KM# 95** **Weight:** 17.0000 g. **Composition:** Copper-Nickel **Subject:** 2,500 years - Bilgorod-Dnestrovski **Obverse:** Arms above denomination **Reverse:** Castle above city arms and ancient coins **Edge:** Reeded

| Date | Mintage | F | VF | XF | Unc | BU |
|---|---|---|---|---|---|---|
| 2000 | 50,000 | — | — | — | 8.00 | — |

**5 HRYVNIA** **KM# 102** **Composition:** Copper-Nickel **Subject:** Russian conversion to Christianity **Obverse:** National arms and angels **Reverse:** Bearded figure and crowd **Edge:** Reeded **Size:** 35 mm.

| Date | Mintage | F | VF | XF | Unc | BU |
|---|---|---|---|---|---|---|
| 2000 | 100,000 | — | — | — | 9.00 | — |

**5 HRYVNIA** **KM# 103** **Composition:** Copper-Nickel **Subject:** Centennial - Lviv's Opera House **Obverse:** National arms and angels **Reverse:** Opera house

| Date | Mintage | F | VF | XF | Unc | BU |
|---|---|---|---|---|---|---|
| 2000 | 50,000 | — | — | — | 8.50 | — |

**5 HRYVNIA** **KM# 105** **Weight:** 16.4500 g. **Composition:** Copper-Nickel-Zinc **Subject:** City of Kerch's 2600th Anniversary **Obverse:** National arms above bracelet and denomination **Reverse:** Ancient coins above pillar **Edge:** Reeded **Size:** 35 mm.

| Date | Mintage | F | VF | XF | Unc | BU |
|---|---|---|---|---|---|---|
| 2000 | 50,000 | — | — | — | 10.00 | — |

**5 HRYVNIA** **KM# 112** **Weight:** 16.2400 g. **Composition:** Copper-Nickel **Subject:** Ostrozbka Academy **Obverse:** Denomination, old writing and printing artifacts **Reverse:** Teaching scene **Edge:** Reeded **Size:** 35 mm.

| Date | Mintage | F | VF | XF | Unc | BU |
|---|---|---|---|---|---|---|
| 2001 | — | — | — | — | 9.50 | — |

**5 HRYVNIA** **KM# 129** **Weight:** 16.2400 g. **Composition:** Copper Nickel **Subject:** National Bank 10th Anniversary **Obverse:** National arms between two arches. **Reverse:** Large building central entrance. **Edge:** Reeded. **Size:** 35 mm. **Note:** Struck at Malyn Mint.

| Date | Mintage | F | VF | XF | Unc | BU |
|---|---|---|---|---|---|---|
| 2001 | 50,000 | — | — | — | 9.50 | — |

**5 HRYVNIA** **KM# 132** **Weight:** 16.2400 g. **Composition:** Copper Nickel **Subject:** National Independence 10th Anniversary **Obverse:** National arms. **Reverse:** Building on map. **Edge:** Reeded. **Size:** 35 mm. **Note:** Struck at Malyn Mint.

| Date | Mintage | F | VF | XF | Unc | BU |
|---|---|---|---|---|---|---|
| 2001 | — | — | — | — | 10.00 | — |

**5 HRYVNIA** **KM# 135** **Weight:** 16.5400 g. **Composition:** Copper Nickel **Subject:** Poltava - 1100th Anniversary **Obverse:** National arms above denomination. **Reverse:** Buildings above arms. **Edge:** Reeded. **Size:** 35 mm. **Note:** Struck at Malyn Mint.

| Date | Mintage | F | VF | XF | Unc | BU |
|---|---|---|---|---|---|---|
| 2001 | 50,000 | — | — | — | 9.00 | — |

**5 HRYVEN** **KM# 104** **Ring Weight:** 9.5000 g. **Ring Composition:** Copper-Nickel **Center Composition:** Brass **Subject:** Third Millennium **Obverse:** National arms **Reverse:** Figure sowing seeds **Edge:** Reeded and plain sections **Size:** 27.9 mm.

| Date | Mintage | F | VF | XF | Unc | BU |
|---|---|---|---|---|---|---|
| 2000 | 50,000 | — | — | — | 7.50 | — |

**5 HRYVEN** **KM# 107** **Ring Weight:** 9.4300 g. **Ring Composition:** Copper-Nickel **Center Composition:** Brass **Subject:** Motherhood **Obverse:** National arms above swirling design **Reverse:** Mother and child **Edge:** Reeded and plain sections **Size:** 27.9 mm.

| Date | Mintage | F | VF | XF | Unc | BU |
|---|---|---|---|---|---|---|
| 2001 | — | — | — | — | 7.50 | — |

**10 HRYVEN** **KM# 34** **Weight:** 16.8110 g. **Composition:** 0.9250 Silver .5 oz. ASW **Subject:** Petro Mohyla - 1596-1647 **Obverse:** National arms, people and building

| Date | Mintage | F | VF | XF | Unc | BU |
|---|---|---|---|---|---|---|
| 1996 Proof | 5,000 | Value: 42.50 | | | | |

**10 HRYVEN** **KM# 44** **Weight:** 33.6220 g. **Composition:** 0.9250 Silver 1 oz. ASW **Series:** Nagano Olympics **Obverse:** National arms **Reverse:** Cross-country skier

| Date | Mintage | F | VF | XF | Unc | BU |
|---|---|---|---|---|---|---|
| 1998 Proof | 7,500 | Value: 40.00 | | | | |

**10 HRYVEN** **KM# 45** **Weight:** 33.6220 g. **Composition:** 0.9250 Silver 1 oz. ASW **Series:** Nagano Olympics **Obverse:** National arms **Reverse:** Biathlon shooter

| Date | Mintage | F | VF | XF | Unc | BU |
|---|---|---|---|---|---|---|
| 1998 Proof | 7,500 | Value: 40.00 | | | | |

**10 HRYVEN** **KM# 50** **Weight:** 33.6220 g. **Composition:** 0.9250 Silver 1 oz. ASW **Subject:** 100th anniversary - Ascania National Park **Obverse:** Plants and animals

| Date | Mintage | F | VF | XF | Unc | BU |
|---|---|---|---|---|---|---|
| 1998 Proof | 10,000 | Value: 42.50 | | | | |

**10 HRYVEN** **KM# 52** **Weight:** 33.6220 g. **Composition:** 0.9250 Silver 1 oz. ASW **Series:** Nagano Olympics **Obverse:** National emblem and denomination **Reverse:** Figure skater

| Date | Mintage | F | VF | XF | Unc | BU |
|---|---|---|---|---|---|---|
| 1998 Proof | 7,500 | Value: 40.00 | | | | |

**10 HRYVEN** **KM# 53** **Weight:** 33.6220 g. **Composition:** 0.9250 Silver 1 oz. ASW **Subject:** Prince Kiy - founder of Kiev **Obverse:** Denomination in ornamental frame **Reverse:** Portrait, riders

| Date | Mintage | F | VF | XF | Unc | BU |
|---|---|---|---|---|---|---|
| 1998 Proof | 10,000 | Value: 42.50 | | | | |

**10 HRYVEN** **KM# 64** **Weight:** 33.6220 g. **Composition:** 0.9250 Silver 1 oz. ASW **Subject:** Prince Danylo of Halych **Obverse:** Denomination **Reverse:** Crowned portrait

| Date | Mintage | F | VF | XF | Unc | BU |
|---|---|---|---|---|---|---|
| 1998 Proof | 10,000 | Value: 42.50 | | | | |

**10 HRYVEN** **KM# 67** **Weight:** 33.6220 g. **Composition:** 0.9250 Silver 1 oz. ASW **Subject:** St. Michael's golden-domed cathedral **Obverse:** National arms in ornamental frame **Reverse:** Cathedral

| Date | Mintage | F | VF | XF | Unc | BU |
|---|---|---|---|---|---|---|
| 1998 Proof | 10,000 | Value: 42.50 | | | | |

**10 HRYVEN** **KM# 70** **Weight:** 33.6220 g. **Composition:** 0.9250 Silver 1 oz. ASW **Subject:** Kiev-Pechersk Assumption Cathedral **Reverse:** Cathedral behind carved ruins

| Date | Mintage | F | VF | XF | Unc | BU |
|---|---|---|---|---|---|---|
| 1998 Proof | 10,000 | Value: 40.00 | | | | |

**10 HRYVEN** **KM# 77** **Weight:** 33.6220 g. **Composition:** 0.9250 Silver 1 oz. ASW **Subject:** Dmitro Vishnevetsbie **Obverse:** National arms **Reverse:** Portrait with bow and arrow

| Date | Mintage | F | VF | XF | Unc | BU |
|---|---|---|---|---|---|---|
| 1999 Proof | 10,000 | Value: 42.50 | | | | |

**10 HRYVEN KM# 85 Weight:** 33.9000 g. **Composition:** 0.9250 Silver 1.0082 oz. ASW **Subject:** Birth of Jesus **Obverse:** National arms, denomination, and angels **Reverse:** Naitivity scene **Edge:** Reeded **Size:** 38.6 mm. **Note:** Struck at Lugansk.

| Date | Mintage | F | VF | XF | Unc | BU |
|---|---|---|---|---|---|---|
| 1999 Proof | 10,000 | Value: 40.00 | | | | |

**10 HRYVEN KM# 86 Weight:** 33.9000 g. **Composition:** 0.9250 Silver 1.0082 oz. ASW **Subject:** Prince Askold **Obverse:** National arms, denomination, and Viking carvings **Reverse:** Prince and Viking ships

| Date | Mintage | F | VF | XF | Unc | BU |
|---|---|---|---|---|---|---|
| 1999 Proof | 10,000 | Value: 40.00 | | | | |

**10 HRYVEN KM# 87 Weight:** 33.9000 g. **Composition:** 0.9250 Silver 1.0082 oz. ASW **Subject:** Magdeburg Rights

| Date | Mintage | F | VF | XF | Unc | BU |
|---|---|---|---|---|---|---|
| 1999 Proof | 5,000 | Value: 40.00 | | | | |

**10 HRYVEN KM# 88 Weight:** 33.9000 g. **Composition:** 0.9250 Silver 1.0082 oz. ASW **Subject:** Petro Doroshenko **Reverse:** P. Doroshenko, Cossack, mounted

| Date | Mintage | F | VF | XF | Unc | BU |
|---|---|---|---|---|---|---|
| 1999 Proof | — | Value: 40.00 | | | | |

**10 HRYVEN KM# 89 Weight:** 33.9000 g. **Composition:** 0.9250 Silver 1.0082 oz. ASW **Reverse:** Dormouse

| Date | Mintage | F | VF | XF | Unc | BU |
|---|---|---|---|---|---|---|
| 1999 Proof | 5,000 | Value: 42.50 | | | | |

**10 HRYVEN KM# 90 Weight:** 33.9000 g. **Composition:** 0.9250 Silver 1.0082 oz. ASW **Subject:** Steppe eagle **Reverse:** Eagle in flight

| Date | Mintage | F | VF | XF | Unc | BU |
|---|---|---|---|---|---|---|
| 1999 Proof | — | Value: 45.00 | | | | |

**10 HRYVEN KM# 116 Weight:** 33.6200 g. **Composition:** 0.9250 Silver .9998 oz. ASW **Series:** Olympics **Obverse:** National arms, denomination and Olympic motto **Reverse:** Broad jumper

| Date | Mintage | F | VF | XF | Unc | BU |
|---|---|---|---|---|---|---|
| 1999 Proof | 15,000 | Value: 40.00 | | | | |

**10 HRYVEN KM# 117 Weight:** 33.6200 g. **Composition:** 0.9250 Silver .9998 oz. ASW **Series:** Olympics **Obverse:** National arms, denomination and Olympic motto **Reverse:** Gymnast on parallel bars

| Date | Mintage | F | VF | XF | Unc | BU |
|---|---|---|---|---|---|---|
| 1999 Proof | 15,000 | Value: 40.00 | | | | |

**10 HRYVEN KM# 118 Weight:** 33.6200 g. **Composition:** 0.9250 Silver .9998 oz. ASW **Subject:** Platanthera Bifolia **Obverse:** National arms, denomination and wreath **Reverse:** Flower

| Date | Mintage | F | VF | XF | Unc | BU |
|---|---|---|---|---|---|---|
| 1999 Proof | 5,000 | Value: 40.00 | | | | |

**10 HRYVEN** **KM# 119** **Weight:** 33.6200 g. **Composition:** 0.9250 Silver .9998 oz. ASW **Subject:** Princess Olga **Obverse:** National arms, denomination in ornamental frame **Reverse:** Portrait and court scene

| Date | Mintage | F | VF | XF | Unc | BU |
|---|---|---|---|---|---|---|
| 2000 Proof | 10,000 | Value: 40.00 | | | | |

**10 HRYVEN** **KM# 120** **Weight:** 33.6200 g. **Composition:** 0.9250 Silver .9998 oz. ASW **Subject:** Petro Sahaydachny **Obverse:** National arms **Reverse:** Ship and cameo portrait

| Date | Mintage | F | VF | XF | Unc | BU |
|---|---|---|---|---|---|---|
| 2000 Proof | 10,000 | Value: 40.00 | | | | |

**10 HRYVEN** **KM# 121** **Weight:** 33.6200 g. **Composition:** 0.9250 Silver .9998 oz. ASW **Subject:** Fresh Water Crab **Obverse:** National arms and denomination in wreath **Reverse:** Crab

| Date | Mintage | F | VF | XF | Unc | BU |
|---|---|---|---|---|---|---|
| 2000 Proof | 5,000 | Value: 40.00 | | | | |

**10 HRYVEN** **KM# 122** **Weight:** 33.6200 g. **Composition:** 0.9250 Silver .9998 oz. ASW **Subject:** Volodymyr the Great **Obverse:** National arms and denomination in ornamental frame **Reverse:** Crowned portrait with raised hands

| Date | Mintage | F | VF | XF | Unc | BU |
|---|---|---|---|---|---|---|
| 2000 Proof | 5,000 | Value: 40.00 | | | | |

**10 HRYVEN** **KM# 123** **Weight:** 33.6200 g. **Composition:** 0.9250 Silver .9998 oz. ASW **Subject:** Lviv Theater and Opera **Obverse:** Two figures on an arch **Reverse:** Large building

| Date | Mintage | F | VF | XF | Unc | BU |
|---|---|---|---|---|---|---|
| 2000 Proof | 3,000 | Value: 40.00 | | | | |

**10 HRYVEN** **KM# 108** **Weight:** 33.6200 g. **Composition:** 0.9250 Silver .9998 oz. ASW **Subject:** End of WWII, 55th Anniversary **Obverse:** National arms and denomination **Reverse:** Figure holding palm branch **Edge:** Reeded **Size:** 38.6 mm.

| Date | Mintage | F | VF | XF | Unc | BU |
|---|---|---|---|---|---|---|
| 2000 Proof | 3,000 | Value: 40.00 | | | | |

**10 HRYVEN** **KM# 109** **Weight:** 33.6200 g. **Composition:** 0.9250 Silver .9998 oz. ASW **Subject:** Conversion of the Russ to Christianity **Obverse:** National arms, denomination and two angels **Reverse:** Mass baptism scene

| Date | Mintage | F | VF | XF | Unc | BU |
|---|---|---|---|---|---|---|
| 2000 Proof | 3,000 | Value: 40.00 | | | | |

**10 HRYVEN** **KM# 113** **Weight:** 33.6200 g. **Composition:** 0.9250 Silver .9998 oz. ASW **Subject:** Ivan Mazepa (1644-1709) **Obverse:** National arms **Reverse:** Portrait of the Cossack leader **Edge:** Reeded **Size:** 38.5 mm.

| Date | Mintage | F | VF | XF | Unc | BU |
|---|---|---|---|---|---|---|
| 2001 Proof | — | Value: 45.00 | | | | |

**10 HRYVEN** **KM# 114** **Weight:** 33.6200 g. **Composition:** 0.9250 Silver .9998 oz. ASW **Subject:** Aroslav Mudriy (1015-1054) **Reverse:** Mosaic portrait and man with scroll

| Date | Mintage | F | VF | XF | Unc | BU |
|---|---|---|---|---|---|---|
| 2001 Proof | — | Value: 45.00 | | | | |

**10 HRYVEN** **KM# 115** **Weight:** 33.6200 g. **Composition:** 0.9250 Silver .998 oz. ASW **Series:** Ukranian Flora and Fauna **Obverse:** Denomination **Reverse:** Lynx with offspring

| Date | Mintage | F | VF | XF | Unc | BU |
|---|---|---|---|---|---|---|
| 2001 Proof | — | Value: 45.00 | | | | |

**10 HRYVEN** **KM# 130** **Weight:** 33.6200 g. **Composition:** 0.9250 Silver .9998 oz. ASW **Subject:** National Bank 10th Anniversary **Obverse:** National arms between arches. **Reverse:** Large building entrance. **Edge:** Reeded. **Size:** 38.6 mm. **Note:** Struck at Malyn Mint.

| Date | Mintage | F | VF | XF | Unc | BU |
|---|---|---|---|---|---|---|
| 2001 Proof | 3,000 | Value: 40.00 | | | | |

**20 HRYVEN** **KM# 35** **Weight:** 33.6220 g. **Composition:** 0.9250 Silver 1 oz. ASW **Subject:** Desyatinna Church **Obverse:** National arms above Madonna and child

| Date | Mintage | F | VF | XF | Unc | BU |
|---|---|---|---|---|---|---|
| 1996 Proof | 5,000 | Value: 45.00 | | | | |

**20 HRYVEN** **KM# 36** **Weight:** 33.6220 g. **Composition:** 0.9250 Silver 1 oz. ASW **Subject:** St. Spassky Cathedral in Chernigiv **Obverse:** National arms above Madonna and child

| Date | Mintage | F | VF | XF | Unc | BU |
|---|---|---|---|---|---|---|
| 1997 Proof | 5,000 | Value: 45.00 | | | | |

**20 HRYVEN** **KM# 46** **Weight:** 33.6220 g. **Composition:** 0.9250 Silver 1 oz. ASW **Subject:** Cossacks in revolt **Obverse:** National arms

| Date | Mintage | F | VF | XF | Unc | BU |
|---|---|---|---|---|---|---|
| 1997 Proof | 5,000 | Value: 45.00 | | | | |

**20 HRYVEN** **KM# 54** **Weight:** 33.6220 g. **Composition:** 0.9250 Silver 1 oz. ASW **Subject:** Cossacks Mamay **Obverse:** National arms supported by St. Michael and lion **Reverse:** Cossack playing a bandre

| Date | Mintage | F | VF | XF | Unc | BU |
|---|---|---|---|---|---|---|
| 1997 Proof | 5,000 | Value: 45.00 | | | | |

**20 HRYVEN** **KM# 57** **Weight:** 33.6220 g. **Composition:** 0.9250 Silver 1 oz. ASW **Subject:** 200th anniversary - Kiev Commodity Futures Market **Obverse:** National arms **Reverse:** Steepled building and sailboat

| Date | Mintage | F | VF | XF | Unc | BU |
|---|---|---|---|---|---|---|
| 1997 Proof | 5,000 | Value: 45.00 | | | | |

**20 HRYVEN** **KM# 58** **Weight:** 33.6220 g. **Composition:** 0.9250 Silver 1 oz. ASW **Subject:** 350th anniversary - Cossack revolt **Obverse:** National arms supported by St. Michael and lion **Reverse:** Cossacks attacking Polish cavalryman

| Date | Mintage | F | VF | XF | Unc | BU |
|---|---|---|---|---|---|---|
| 1998 Proof | 5,000 | Value: 47.50 | | | | |

**10 HRYVEN** **KM# 131** **Weight:** 33.6200 g. **Composition:** 0.9250 Silver .9998 oz. ASW **Subject:** Olympics **Obverse:** National arms and denomination on ice. **Reverse:** Stylized ice dancing couple. **Edge:** Reeded. **Size:** 38.6 mm. **Note:** Struck at Malyn Mint.

| Date | Mintage | F | VF | XF | Unc | BU |
|---|---|---|---|---|---|---|
| 2001 Proof | 3,000 | Value: 40.00 | | | | |

**20 HRYVEN** **KM# 126** **Ring Weight:** 14.7000 g. **Ring Composition:** 0.9250 Silver .2508 oz. ASW **Center Composition:** 0.9160 Gold .1845 oz. AGW **Subject:** Paleolithic Age **Obverse:** Eagle on wheel **Reverse:** Pottery and petroglyphs **Edge:** Reeded and plain sections **Size:** 31 mm.

| Date | Mintage | F | VF | XF | Unc | BU |
|---|---|---|---|---|---|---|
| 2000 Proof | 3,000 | Value: 50.00 | | | | |

**20 HRYVEN** **KM# 127** **Ring Weight:** 14.7000 g. **Ring Composition:** 0.9250 Silver .2508 oz. ASW **Center Composition:** 0.9160 Gold .1845 oz. AGW **Subject:** Trypolean Culture **Obverse:** Eagle on wheel **Reverse:** Ancient sculptures

| Date | Mintage | F | VF | XF | Unc | BU |
|---|---|---|---|---|---|---|
| 2000 Proof | 3,000 | Value: 50.00 | | | | |

**20 HRYVEN** **KM# 128** **Ring Weight:** 14.7000 g. **Ring Composition:** 0.9250 Silver .2508 oz. ASW **Center Composition:** 0.9160 Gold .1845 oz. AGW **Subject:** The Olbian City State **Obverse:** Eagle on wheel **Reverse:** Ancient coin and Greek figures

| Date | Mintage | F | VF | XF | Unc | BU |
|---|---|---|---|---|---|---|
| 2000 Proof | 3,000 | Value: 50.00 | | | | |

**50 HRYVEN** **KM# 59** **Weight:** 3.1104 g. **Composition:** 0.9999 Gold .1 oz. AGW **Subject:** St. Sophia Cathedral in Kiev **Obverse:** Cathedral **Reverse:** Mother of God Mossaic (orante)

| Date | Mintage | F | VF | XF | Unc | BU |
|---|---|---|---|---|---|---|
| 1996 | 2,000 | — | — | — | 175 | — |

**50 HRYVEN** **KM# 124** **Weight:** 17.6300 g. **Composition:** 0.9000 Gold .5101 oz. AGW **Subject:** Birth of Jesus **Obverse:** Two angels, arms and denomination **Reverse:** Nativity scene **Edge:** Plain **Size:** 25 mm.

| Date | Mintage | F | VF | XF | Unc | BU |
|---|---|---|---|---|---|---|
| 1999 Proof | 3,000 | Value: 250 | | | | |

**50 HRYVEN** **KM# 125** **Weight:** 17.6300 g. **Composition:** 0.9000 Gold .5101 oz. AGW **Subject:** Conversion of the Russ to Christianity **Obverse:** Two angels, arms and denomination **Reverse:** Baptism scene

| Date | Mintage | F | VF | XF | Unc | BU |
|---|---|---|---|---|---|---|
| 2000 Proof | 3,000 | Value: 250 | | | | |

**100 HRYVEN** **KM# 63** **Weight:** 17.2797 g. **Composition:** 0.9000 Gold .5 oz. AGW **Subject:** Kyiv Psalm book **Obverse:** Open book **Reverse:** Monk writing book

| Date | Mintage | F | VF | XF | Unc | BU |
|---|---|---|---|---|---|---|
| 1997 Proof | 2,000 | Value: 750 | | | | |

**100 HRYVEN** **KM# 65** **Weight:** 17.2797 g. **Composition:** 0.9000 Gold .5 oz. AGW **Subject:** Poem "Aeneid" by Ivan P. Kotlyarevsky **Obverse:** Helmet and musical instruments **Reverse:** Helmeted figure playing stringed instrument

| Date | Mintage | F | VF | XF | Unc | BU |
|---|---|---|---|---|---|---|
| 1998 Proof | 2,000 | Value: 750 | | | | |

**100 HRYVEN** **KM# 68** **Weight:** 17.2797 g. **Composition:** 0.9000 Gold .5 oz. AGW **Subject:** St. Michael's Cathedral **Obverse:** Denomination **Reverse:** Cathedral behind human silhouettes

| Date | Mintage | F | VF | XF | Unc | BU |
|---|---|---|---|---|---|---|
| 1998 Proof | 3,000 | Value: 700 | | | | |

**100 HRYVEN** **KM# 71** **Weight:** 17.2797 g. **Composition:** 0.9000 Gold .5 oz. AGW **Subject:** Kyiv-Pechersk Assumption Cathedral **Obverse:** Denomination **Reverse:** Cathedral behind carved ruins

| Date | Mintage | F | VF | XF | Unc | BU |
|---|---|---|---|---|---|---|
| 1998 Proof | 3,000 | Value: 700 | | | | |

**125 HRYVEN** **KM# 60** **Weight:** 7.7759 g. **Composition:** 0.9999 Gold .25 oz. AGW **Obverse:** St. Sophia Catheral in Kiev **Reverse:** St. Sophia

| Date | Mintage | F | VF | XF | Unc | BU |
|---|---|---|---|---|---|---|
| 1996 | 4,000 | — | — | — | 350 | — |

**200 HRYVEN** **KM# 37** **Weight:** 17.5000 g. **Composition:** 0.9000 Gold .5 oz. AGW **Subject:** Taras G. Shevchenko **Obverse:** National arms above denomination

| Date | Mintage | F | VF | XF | Unc | BU |
|---|---|---|---|---|---|---|
| 1996 Proof | 10,000 | Value: 400 | | | | |

**200 HRYVEN** **KM# 38** **Weight:** 17.5000 g. **Composition:** 0.9000 Gold .5 oz. AGW **Subject:** Pecherska Lavra **Obverse:** Church above date, denomination

| Date | Mintage | F | VF | XF | Unc | BU |
|---|---|---|---|---|---|---|
| 1996 Proof | 20,000 | Value: 400 | | | | |

**250 HRYVEN** **KM# 61** **Weight:** 15.5518 g. **Composition:** 0.9999 Gold .5 oz. AGW **Obverse:** St. Sophia Cathedral in Kiev **Reverse:** St. Sophia

| Date | Mintage | F | VF | XF | Unc | BU |
|---|---|---|---|---|---|---|
| 1996 | 3,000 | — | — | — | 700 | — |

**500 HRYVEN** **KM# 62** **Weight:** 31.1035 g. **Composition:** 0.9999 Gold 1 oz. AGW **Obverse:** St. Sophia Cathedral in Kiev **Reverse:** St. Sophia

| Date | Mintage | F | VF | XF | Unc | BU |
|---|---|---|---|---|---|---|
| 1996 | 1,000 | — | — | — | 1,400 | — |

## PATTERNS

Including off metal strikes

| KM# | Date | Mintage | Identification | Mkt Val |
|---|---|---|---|---|
| Pn1 | 1992 | — | Kopiyka. Aluminum. | — |
| Pn2 | 1922 | — | 2 Kopiyky. Aluminum. | — |
| Pn3 | 1992 | — | 5 Kopiyok. White Brass. | — |
| Pn4 | 1992 | — | 10 Kopiyok. Brass. Incuse shield. | — |
| Pn5 | 1992 | — | 15 Kopiyok. Brass. | — |
| Pn6 | 1992 | — | 15 Kopiyok. Bronze. | — |
| Pn7 | 1992 | — | 25 Kopiyok. Brass. Incuse shield. | — |
| Pn8 | 1992 | — | 50 Kopiyok. Copper-Nickel. | — |
| Pn9 | 1992 | — | 50 Kopiyok. Brass. Incuse shield. | — |
| Pn10 | 1992 | — | 50 Kopiyok. Brass Clad Steel. | — |
| Pn11 | 1993 | — | 2 Kopiyky. Brass. | — |
| Pn12 | 1993 | — | 2 Kopiyky. Aluminum-Zinc. | — |
| Pn13 | 1993 | — | 15 Kopiyok. Aluminum. | — |
| Pn14 | 1994 | — | Kopiyka. 0.6000 Silver. Specific gravity: 9.8. | — |
| Pn15 | 1994 | — | 2 Kopiyky. Bronze. 3.7500 g. Piefort. | — |
| Pn16 | 1996 | — | Kopiyka. 0.3500 Silver. Specific gravity: 9.43. | — |
| Pn17 | 1996 | — | 25 Kopiyok. Aluminum. | — |
| Pn18 | 1998 | — | 100 Hryvnias. Brass. | — |
| Pn19 | (1998) | — | 100 Hryvnias. Brass. | — |
| Pn20 | 1998 | — | 100 Hryvnias. Brass. | — |
| Pn21 | (1998) | — | 100 Hryvnias. Brass. | — |
| Pn22 | 1998 | — | 100 Hryvnias. Brass. | — |
| Pn23 | (1998) | — | 100 Hryvnias. Brass. | — |

## MINT SETS

| KM# | Date | Mintage | Identification | Issue Price | Mkt Val |
|---|---|---|---|---|---|
| MS1 | 1996 (8) | — | KM1, 2, 3.3, 4, 6A, 7A, 8, 30 | — | — |

# UMM AL QAIWAIN

This emirate, one of the original members of the United Arab Emirates, is the second smallest, least developed and lowest in population. The area is 300 sq. mi. (800 sq. km.) and the population is 5,000. The first recognition by the West was in 1820. Most of the emirate is uninhabited desert. Native boat building is an important activity.

**TITLES**

Umm al Qaiwain

**RULERS**

Ahmad Bin Abdullah al-Mualla, 1872-1904
Rashid Bin Ahmad al-Mualla, 1904-1929
Ahmad Bin Rashid al-Mualla, 1929-1981
Rashid Bin Ahmad al-Mualla, 1981-

## UNITED ARAB EMIRAT

### NON-CIRCULATING LEGAL TENDER COINAGE

**RIYAL** **KM# 1** **Weight:** 3.0000 g. **Composition:** 1.0000 Silver .0965 oz. ASW **Ruler:** Ahmad bin Rashid al-Mualla **Reverse:** Old Cannon

| Date | Mintage | F | VF | XF | Unc | BU |
|---|---|---|---|---|---|---|
| AH1389(1969) Proof | 2,050 | Value: 17.50 | | | | |

**2 RIYALS** **KM# 2** **Weight:** 6.0000 g. **Composition:** 1.0000 Silver .1929 oz. ASW **Ruler:** Ahmad bin Rashid al-Mualla **Reverse:** Fort of the 19th Century

| Date | Mintage | F | VF | XF | Unc | BU |
|---|---|---|---|---|---|---|
| AH1389(1969) Proof | 2,050 | Value: 27.50 | | | | |

**5 RIYALS** **KM# 3** **Weight:** 15.0000 g. **Composition:** 1.0000 Silver .4823 oz. ASW **Ruler:** Ahmad bin Rashid al-Mualla **Reverse:** Gazelles

| Date | Mintage | F | VF | XF | Unc | BU |
|---|---|---|---|---|---|---|
| AH1389(1969) Proof | 2,100 | Value: 37.50 | | | | |

**10 RIYALS** **KM# 4** **Weight:** 30.0000 g. **Composition:** 1.0000 Silver .9646 oz. ASW **Ruler:** Ahmad bin Rashid al-Mualla **Obverse:** Similar to 5 Riyals, KM#3 **Reverse:** Facade of the Great Rock Temple

| Date | Mintage | F | VF | XF | Unc | BU |
|---|---|---|---|---|---|---|
| AH1389(1969) Proof | 2,000 | Value: 65.00 | | | | |

**25 RIYALS** **KM# 6** **Weight:** 5.1800 g. **Composition:** 0.9000 Gold .1499 oz. AGW **Ruler:** Ahmad bin Rashid al-Mualla **Reverse:** Old Cannon

| Date | Mintage | F | VF | XF | Unc | BU |
|---|---|---|---|---|---|---|
| AH1389(1969) Proof | 500 | Value: 150 | | | | |

**50 RIYALS** **KM# 7** **Weight:** 10.3600 g. **Composition:** 0.9000 Gold .2998 oz. AGW **Ruler:** Ahmad bin Rashid al-Mualla **Reverse:** Fort of the 19th Century

| Date | Mintage | F | VF | XF | Unc | BU |
|---|---|---|---|---|---|---|
| AH1389(1969) Proof | 420 | Value: 265 | | | | |

**100 RIYALS** **KM# 8** **Weight:** 20.7300 g. **Composition:** 0.9000 Gold .5999 oz. AGW **Ruler:** Ahmad bin Rashid al-Mualla **Reverse:** Gazelle

| Date | Mintage | F | VF | XF | Unc | BU |
|---|---|---|---|---|---|---|
| AH1389(1969) Proof | 300 | Value: 450 | | | | |

**200 RIYALS** **KM# 9** **Weight:** 41.4600 g. **Composition:** 0.9000 Gold 1.1998 oz. AGW **Ruler:** Ahmad bin Rashid al-Mualla **Obverse:** Similar to 25 Riyals, KM#6 **Reverse:** Sheik Ahmed Ben Rashid al Moalla Bust Left

| Date | Mintage | F | VF | XF | Unc | BU |
|---|---|---|---|---|---|---|
| AH1389(1969) Proof | 230 | Value: 775 | | | | |

### PROOF SETS

| KM# | Date | Mintage | Identification | Issue Price | Mkt Val |
|---|---|---|---|---|---|
| PS1 | 1970 (4) | 2,000 | KM#1-4 | 26.30 | 145 |
| PS2 | 1970 (4) | 230 | KM#6-9 | — | 1,650 |
| PS3 | 1970 (8) | — | KM#1-4, 6-9 | — | 1,800 |

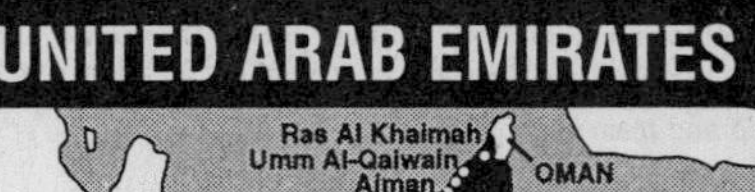


The seven United Arab Emirates (formerly known as the Trucial Sheikhdoms or States), located along the southern shore of the Persian Gulf, are comprised of the Sheikhdoms of Abu Dhabi, Dubai, al-Sharjah, Ajman, Umm al Qaiwain, Ras al-Khaimah and al-Fujairah. They have a combined area of about 32,000 sq. mi. (83,600 sq. km.) and a population of *2.1 million. Capital: Abu Zaby (Abu Dhabi). Since the oil strikes of 1958-60, the economy has centered about petroleum.

The Trucial States came under direct British influence in 1892 when the Maritime Truce Treaty enacted after the supression of pirate activity along the Trucial Coast was enlarged to enjoin the states from disposing of any territory, or entering into any foreign agreements, without British consent in return for British protection from external aggression. In March of 1971 Britain reaffirmed its decision to terminate its treaty relationships with the Trucial Sheikhdoms, whereupon the seven states joined with Bahrain and Qatar in an effort to form a union of Arab Emirates under British protection. When the prospective members failed to agree on terms of union, Bahrain and Qatar declared their respective independence, Aug. and Sept. of 1971. Six of the sheikhdoms united to form the United Arab Emirates on Dec. 2, 1971. Ras al-Khaimah joined a few weeks later.

**TITLES**

الامارات العربية المتحدة

al-Imara(t) al-Arabiya(t) al-Muttahida(t)

**MONETARY SYSTEM**

فلسـاً فلس فلوس

Falus, Fulus — Fals, Fils — Falsan

100 Fils = 1 Dirham

## UNITED SHEIKHDOMS

### STANDARD COINAGE

**FIL** **KM# 1** **Composition:** Bronze **Series:** F.A.O. **Reverse:** Date Palms

| Date | Mintage | F | VF | XF | Unc | BU |
|---|---|---|---|---|---|---|
| AH1393(1973) | 4,000,000 | — | 0.10 | 0.15 | 0.20 | — |
| AH1395(1975) | — | — | 0.10 | 0.15 | 0.20 | — |
| AH1409(1989) | — | — | 0.10 | 0.15 | 0.20 | — |

**5 FILS** **KM# 2.1** **Composition:** Bronze **Series:** F.A.O. **Reverse:** Mata Hari Fish

| Date | Mintage | F | VF | XF | Unc | BU |
|---|---|---|---|---|---|---|
| AH1393(1973) | 11,400,000 | — | 0.10 | 0.15 | 0.25 | — |
| AH1402(1982) | — | — | 0.10 | 0.15 | 0.25 | — |
| AH1407(1987) | — | — | 0.10 | 0.15 | 0.25 | — |
| AH1408(1988) | — | — | 0.10 | 0.15 | 0.25 | — |
| AH1409(1989) | — | — | 0.10 | 0.15 | 0.25 | — |

**5 FILS** **KM# 2.2** **Composition:** Bronze **Series:** F.A.O. **Note:** Reduced size.

| Date | Mintage | F | VF | XF | Unc | BU |
|---|---|---|---|---|---|---|
| AH1416(1996) | — | — | 0.10 | 0.15 | 0.25 | — |

**10 FILS** KM# 3.1 **Composition:** Bronze **Reverse:** Arab Dhow

| Date | Mintage | F | VF | XF | Unc | BU |
|---|---|---|---|---|---|---|
| AH1393(1973) | 6,400,000 | — | 0.25 | 0.40 | 0.90 | — |
| AH1402(1982) | — | — | 0.25 | 0.40 | 0.90 | — |
| AH1404(1984) | — | — | 0.25 | 0.40 | 0.90 | — |
| AH1407(1987) | — | — | 0.25 | 0.40 | 0.90 | — |
| AH1408(1988) | — | — | 0.25 | 0.40 | 0.90 | — |
| AH1409(1989) | — | — | 0.25 | 0.40 | 0.90 | — |

**10 FILS** KM# 3.2 **Composition:** Bronze **Note:** Reduced size.

| Date | Mintage | F | VF | XF | Unc | BU |
|---|---|---|---|---|---|---|
| AH1416(1996) | — | — | 0.20 | 0.30 | 0.70 | — |

**25 FILS** KM# 4 **Composition:** Copper-Nickel **Reverse:** Arab Dune Gazelle

| Date | Mintage | F | VF | XF | Unc | BU |
|---|---|---|---|---|---|---|
| AH1393(1973) | 10,400,000 | — | 0.25 | 0.35 | 0.65 | — |
| AH1402(1982) | — | — | 0.25 | 0.35 | 0.65 | — |
| AH1403(1983) | — | — | 0.25 | 0.35 | 0.65 | — |
| AH1404(1984) | — | — | 0.25 | 0.35 | 0.65 | — |
| AH1406(1986) | — | — | 0.25 | 0.35 | 0.65 | — |
| AH1407(1987) | — | — | 0.25 | 0.35 | 0.65 | — |
| AH1408(1988) | — | — | 0.25 | 0.35 | 0.65 | — |
| AH1409(1989) | — | — | 0.25 | 0.35 | 0.65 | — |
| AH1410(1990) | — | — | 0.25 | 0.35 | 0.65 | — |
| AH1415(1995) | — | — | 0.25 | 0.35 | 0.65 | — |
| AH1416(1996) | — | — | 0.25 | 0.35 | 0.65 | — |

**50 FILS** KM# 5 **Composition:** Copper-Nickel **Reverse:** Oil Derricks

| Date | Mintage | F | VF | XF | Unc | BU |
|---|---|---|---|---|---|---|
| AH1393(1973) | 8,400,000 | — | 0.35 | 0.50 | 1.50 | — |
| AH1402(1982) | — | — | 0.35 | 0.55 | 1.65 | — |
| AH1404(1984) | — | — | 0.35 | 0.55 | 1.65 | — |
| AH1407(1987) | — | — | 0.35 | 0.55 | 1.65 | — |
| AH1408(1988) | — | — | 0.35 | 0.55 | 1.65 | — |
| AH1409(1989) | — | — | 0.35 | 0.55 | 1.65 | — |

**50 FILS** KM# 16 **Composition:** Copper-Nickel **Note:** Reduced size, 7-sided coin.

| Date | Mintage | F | VF | XF | Unc | BU |
|---|---|---|---|---|---|---|
| AH1415(1995) | — | — | 0.25 | 0.45 | 1.35 | — |

**DIRHAM** KM# 6.1 **Composition:** Copper-Nickel **Reverse:** Jug

| Date | Mintage | F | VF | XF | Unc | BU |
|---|---|---|---|---|---|---|
| AH1393(1973) | 13,000,000 | — | 0.50 | 0.75 | 2.00 | — |
| AH1402(1982) | — | — | 0.50 | 0.80 | 2.25 | — |
| AH1404(1984) | — | — | 0.50 | 0.80 | 2.25 | — |
| AH1406(1986) | — | — | 0.50 | 0.80 | 2.25 | — |
| AH1407(1987) | — | — | 0.50 | 0.80 | 2.25 | — |
| AH1408(1988) | — | — | 0.50 | 0.80 | 2.25 | — |
| AH1409(1989) | — | — | 0.50 | 0.80 | 2.25 | — |

**DIRHAM** KM# 10 **Composition:** Copper-Nickel **Subject:** 27th Chess Olympiad in Dubai

| Date | Mintage | F | VF | XF | Unc | BU |
|---|---|---|---|---|---|---|
| 1986 | — | — | 2.00 | 4.50 | 9.00 | — |

**DIRHAM** KM# 11 **Composition:** Copper-Nickel **Subject:** 25th Anniversary - Offshore Oil Drilling

| Date | Mintage | F | VF | XF | Unc | BU |
|---|---|---|---|---|---|---|
| ND(1987) | — | — | 2.00 | 4.50 | 9.00 | — |

**DIRHAM** KM# 14 **Composition:** Copper-Nickel **Subject:** 10th Anniversary - al-Ain University

| Date | Mintage | F | VF | XF | Unc | BU |
|---|---|---|---|---|---|---|
| ND(1987) | — | — | 1.75 | 4.00 | 8.00 | — |

**DIRHAM** KM# 15 **Composition:** Copper-Nickel **Subject:** Soccer

| Date | Mintage | F | VF | XF | Unc | BU |
|---|---|---|---|---|---|---|
| ND(1990) | — | — | 1.50 | 3.00 | 6.50 | — |

**DIRHAM** KM# 6.2a **Composition:** Steel **Note:** Reduced size.

| Date | Mintage | F | VF | XF | Unc | BU |
|---|---|---|---|---|---|---|
| AH1415(1994) | — | — | 0.35 | 0.65 | 1.85 | — |

**DIRHAM** KM# 32 **Composition:** Copper-Nickel **Subject:** Bank of Dubai 35th Anniversary **Obverse:** Denomination **Reverse:** Bank building

| Date | Mintage | F | VF | XF | Unc | BU |
|---|---|---|---|---|---|---|
| ND(1998) | — | — | — | — | 3.50 | — |

**DIRHAM** KM# 35 **Composition:** Copper-Nickel **Subject:** College of Technology: 35 Years **Obverse:** Denomination **Reverse:** Bird viewed through window frame

| Date | Mintage | F | VF | XF | Unc | BU |
|---|---|---|---|---|---|---|
| ND(1998) | — | — | — | — | 3.50 | — |

**DIRHAM** KM# 38 **Composition:** Copper-Nickel **Subject:** 15th Anniversary - Women's Association **Obverse:** Denomination **Reverse:** Logo

| Date | Mintage | F | VF | XF | Unc | BU |
|---|---|---|---|---|---|---|
| ND(1998) | — | — | — | — | 3.50 | — |

**DIRHAM** KM# 39 **Composition:** Copper-Nickel **Subject:** Sharjah Cultural City **Obverse:** Denomination **Reverse:** Stylized flame

| Date | Mintage | F | VF | XF | Unc | BU |
|---|---|---|---|---|---|---|
| ND(1998) | — | — | — | — | 3.50 | — |
| ND(1998) | — | — | — | — | 3.50 | — |

**DIRHAM** KM# 40 **Weight:** 6.3700 g. **Composition:** Copper-Nickel **Subject:** Abu Al Bukhoosh **Obverse:** Denomination **Reverse:** Ocean oil well **Edge:** Reeded **Size:** 24 mm.

| Date | Mintage | F | VF | XF | Unc | BU |
|---|---|---|---|---|---|---|
| ND(1999) | — | — | — | — | 1.00 | — |

**DIRHAM** KM# 41 **Weight:** 6.3700 g. **Composition:** Copper-Nickel **Subject:** Honor Sheik Zayed **Obverse:** Denomination **Reverse:** Square design

| Date | Mintage | F | VF | XF | Unc | BU |
|---|---|---|---|---|---|---|
| AH1420(1999) | — | — | — | — | 1.00 | — |

**DIRHAM** **KM# 43** **Weight:** 6.3700 g. **Composition:** Copper-Nickel **Subject:** Dubai Islamic Bank **Obverse:** Denomination **Reverse:** Bank name

| Date | Mintage | F | VF | XF | Unc | BU |
|---|---|---|---|---|---|---|
| ND(1999) | — | — | — | — | 1.00 | — |

**DIRHAM** **KM# 46** **Weight:** 6.3700 g. **Composition:** Copper-Nickel **Subject:** General Women's Union **Obverse:** Denomination **Reverse:** Stylized gazelle

| Date | Mintage | F | VF | XF | Unc | BU |
|---|---|---|---|---|---|---|
| ND(2000) | — | — | — | — | 1.00 | — |

**5 DIRHAMS** **KM# 9** **Composition:** Copper-Nickel **Subject:** 1500th Anniversary - al-Hegira

| Date | Mintage | F | VF | XF | Unc | BU |
|---|---|---|---|---|---|---|
| AH1401(1981) | — | — | 2.00 | 3.50 | 7.00 | — |

**25 DIRHAMS** **KM# 33** **Weight:** 20.0000 g. **Composition:** 0.9250 Silver .5948 oz. ASW **Subject:** Dubai National Bank: 35 Years **Obverse:** Denomination **Reverse:** Bank building

| Date | Mintage | F | VF | XF | Unc | BU |
|---|---|---|---|---|---|---|
| ND(1998) | — | — | — | — | 30.00 | — |

**25 DIRHAMS** **KM# 44** **Weight:** 20.1000 g. **Composition:** 0.9250 Silver .5978 oz. ASW **Subject:** Dubai Islamic Bank **Obverse:** Denomination **Reverse:** Bank name **Edge:** Reeded **Size:** 27.9 mm.

| Date | Mintage | F | VF | XF | Unc | BU |
|---|---|---|---|---|---|---|
| ND(2000) Proof | 1,000 | Value: 35.00 | | | | |

**50 DIRHAMS** **KM# 7** **Weight:** 27.2200 g. **Composition:** 0.9250 Silver .8095 oz. ASW **Subject:** IYC and UNICEF

| Date | Mintage | F | VF | XF | Unc | BU |
|---|---|---|---|---|---|---|
| AH1400(1980) Proof | 8,031 | Value: 22.50 | | | | |

**50 DIRHAMS** **KM# 17** **Weight:** 40.0000 g. **Composition:** 0.9250 Silver 1.1896 oz. ASW **Subject:** Death of Shaikh Rashid Bin Saeed Al-Maktoum **Obverse:** Portrait **Reverse:** Dubai International Trade Center

| Date | Mintage | F | VF | XF | Unc | BU |
|---|---|---|---|---|---|---|
| AH1410(1990) Proof | — | Value: 65.00 | | | | |

**50 DIRHAMS** **KM# 18** **Weight:** 40.0000 g. **Composition:** 0.9250 Silver 1.1896 oz. ASW **Subject:** 10th Anniversary - UAE Central Bank

| Date | Mintage | F | VF | XF | Unc | BU |
|---|---|---|---|---|---|---|
| AH1410(1990) Proof | — | Value: 65.00 | | | | |

**50 DIRHAMS** **KM# 19** **Weight:** 40.0000 g. **Composition:** 0.9250 Silver 1.1896 oz. ASW **Subject:** 50th Anniversary of the Arab League

| Date | Mintage | F | VF | XF | Unc | BU |
|---|---|---|---|---|---|---|
| AH1415(1995) Proof | — | Value: 60.00 | | | | |

**50 DIRHAMS** **KM# 21** **Weight:** 40.0000 g. **Composition:** 0.9250 Silver 1.1896 oz. ASW **Subject:** 25th Anniversary of the UAE - National Day Issue **Obverse:** Portrait **Reverse:** Heraldic eagle

| Date | Mintage | F | VF | XF | Unc | BU |
|---|---|---|---|---|---|---|
| AH1416(1996) Proof | — | Value: 60.00 | | | | |

**50 DIRHAMS** **KM# 22** **Weight:** 40.0000 g. **Composition:** 0.9250 Silver 1.1896 oz. ASW **Subject:** 30th Anniversary - Reign of Shaikh Zayed **Obverse:** Portrait **Reverse:** Circular design of Arabic lettering

| Date | Mintage | F | VF | XF | Unc | BU |
|---|---|---|---|---|---|---|
| AH1416(1996) Proof | — | Value: 60.00 | | | | |

**50 DIRHAMS** **KM# 34** **Weight:** 40.0000 g. **Composition:** 0.9250 Silver 1.1896 oz. ASW **Subject:** Dubai National Bank: 35 Years **Obverse:** Denomination **Reverse:** Bank building

| Date | Mintage | F | VF | XF | Unc | BU |
|---|---|---|---|---|---|---|
| ND(1998) Proof | — | Value: 60.00 | | | | |

**50 DIRHAMS** **KM# 36** **Weight:** 40.0000 g. **Composition:** 0.9250 Silver 1.1896 oz. ASW **Subject:** Colleges of Technology: 10 Years **Obverse:** Portrait **Reverse:** Bird viewed through window frame

| Date | Mintage | F | VF | XF | Unc | BU |
|---|---|---|---|---|---|---|
| ND(1998) Proof | — | Value: 60.00 | | | | |

**50 DIRHAMS** **KM# 37** **Weight:** 27.5000 g. **Composition:** 0.9250 Silver .8178 oz. ASW **Series:** UNICEF **Obverse:** Denomination **Reverse:** Two children

| Date | Mintage | F | VF | XF | Unc | BU |
|---|---|---|---|---|---|---|
| 1998 Proof | — | Value: 32.50 | | | | |

**50 DIRHAMS** **KM# 42** **Weight:** 40.2200 g. **Composition:** 0.9250 Silver 1.1961 oz. ASW **Subject:** Honor Sheik Zayed **Obverse:** Portrait **Reverse:** Square design **Edge:** Reeded **Size:** 40 mm.

| Date | Mintage | F | VF | XF | Unc | BU |
|---|---|---|---|---|---|---|
| AH1420(1999) Proof | 2,000 | Value: 100 | | | | |

**50 DIRHAMS** **KM# 45** **Weight:** 40.2200 g. **Composition:** 0.9250 Silver 1.1961 oz. ASW **Subject:** Dubai Islamic Bank **Obverse:** Denomination **Reverse:** Bank name

| Date | Mintage | F | VF | XF | Unc | BU |
|---|---|---|---|---|---|---|
| ND(2000) Proof | — | Value: 45.00 | | | | |

**50 DIRHAMS** **KM# 47** **Weight:** 40.2200 g. **Composition:** 0.9250 Silver 1.1961 oz. ASW **Subject:** General Women's Union **Obverse:** Portrait **Reverse:** Stylized gazelle

| Date | Mintage | F | VF | XF | Unc | BU |
|---|---|---|---|---|---|---|
| ND(2000) Proof | 2,000 | Value: 45.00 | | | | |

**500 DIRHAMS** **KM# 12** **Weight:** 19.9700 g. **Composition:** 0.9170 Gold .5886 oz. AGW **Subject:** 5th Anniversary - United Arab Emirates

| Date | Mintage | F | VF | XF | Unc | BU |
|---|---|---|---|---|---|---|
| ND(1976) Proof | 11,000 | Value: 275 | | | | |

**500 DIRHAMS** **KM# 23** **Weight:** 19.9700 g. **Composition:** 0.9170 Gold .5886 oz. AGW **Subject:** Death of Shaikh Rashid **Obverse:** Bust

| Date | Mintage | F | VF | XF | Unc | BU |
|---|---|---|---|---|---|---|
| 1990 Proof | — | Value: 400 | | | | |

**500 DIRHAMS** **KM# 24** **Weight:** 19.9700 g. **Composition:** 0.9170 Gold .5886 oz. AGW **Subject:** 10th Anniversary - Central Bank **Obverse:** Bust

| Date | Mintage | F | VF | XF | Unc | BU |
|---|---|---|---|---|---|---|
| 1990 Proof | — | Value: 400 | | | | |

**500 DIRHAMS** **KM# 25** **Weight:** 19.9700 g. **Composition:** 0.9170 Gold .5886 oz. AGW **Subject:** 10th Anniversary - Women's Association **Obverse:** Heraldic eagle

| Date | Mintage | F | VF | XF | Unc | BU |
|---|---|---|---|---|---|---|
| 1995 Proof | 1,000 | Value: 400 | | | | |

**750 DIRHAMS** **KM# 8** **Weight:** 17.1700 g. **Composition:** 0.9000 Gold .4969 oz. AGW **Subject:** IYC and UNICEF

| Date | Mintage | F | VF | XF | Unc | BU |
|---|---|---|---|---|---|---|
| AH1400(1980) Proof | 3,063 | Value: 245 | | | | |

**1000 DIRHAMS** **KM# 13** **Weight:** 39.9400 g. **Composition:** 0.9170 Gold 1.1771 oz. AGW **Subject:** 5th Anniversary - United Arab Emirates **Note:** Similar to KM#12.

| Date | Mintage | F | VF | XF | Unc | BU |
|---|---|---|---|---|---|---|
| ND(1976) Proof | 10,000 | Value: 625 | | | | |

**1000 DIRHAMS** **KM# 26** **Weight:** 39.9400 g. **Composition:** 0.9170 Gold 1.1771 oz. AGW **Subject:** Death of Shaikh Rashid Bin Saeed al-Maktoum **Obverse:** Portrait **Reverse:** Dubai International Trade Center **Note:** Similar to 50 Dirhams, KM#17.

| Date | Mintage | F | VF | XF | Unc | BU |
|---|---|---|---|---|---|---|
| 1990 Proof | — | Value: 700 | | | | |

**1000 DIRHAMS** **KM# 27** **Weight:** 39.9400 g. **Composition:** 0.9170 Gold 1.1771 oz. AGW **Subject:** 10th Anniversary - UAE Central Bank **Obverse:** Portrait **Reverse:** Bank building **Note:** Similar to 50 Dirhams, KM#18.

| Date | Mintage | F | VF | XF | Unc | BU |
|---|---|---|---|---|---|---|
| 1990 Proof | — | Value: 700 | | | | |

**1000 DIRHAMS** **KM# 28** **Weight:** 39.9400 g. **Composition:** 0.9170 Gold 1.1771 oz. AGW **Subject:** 10th Anniversary - Women's Association **Obverse:** Heraldic eagle **Reverse:** Seal in wreath

| Date | Mintage | F | VF | XF | Unc | BU |
|---|---|---|---|---|---|---|
| 1995 Proof | — | Value: 700 | | | | |

**1000 DIRHAMS** **KM# 29** **Weight:** 39.9400 g. **Composition:** 0.9170 Gold 1.1771 oz. AGW **Subject:** 25th Anniversary of the UAE - National Day Issue **Obverse:** Portrait **Reverse:** Heraldic eagle **Note:** Similar to 50 Dirhams, KM#21.

| Date | Mintage | F | VF | XF | Unc | BU |
|---|---|---|---|---|---|---|
| 1996 Proof | — | Value: 700 | | | | |

**1000 DIRHAMS** **KM# 30** **Weight:** 39.9400 g. **Composition:** 0.9170 Gold 1.1771 oz. AGW **Subject:** 30th Anniversary - Reign of Shaikh Zayed **Obverse:** Portrait **Reverse:** Circular design of Arabic lettering **Note:** Similar to 50 Dirhams, KM#22.

| Date | Mintage | F | VF | XF | Unc | BU |
|---|---|---|---|---|---|---|
| 1996 Proof | — | Value: 700 | | | | |

## MEDALLIC COINAGE

**5000 DIRHAMS** **KM# M1** **Weight:** 2000.0000 g. **Composition:** 0.9167 Gold 5.8945 oz. AGW **Subject:** 25th Anniversary of the UAE - National Day Issue **Obverse:** Bust **Reverse:** Heraldic eagle **Note:** Similar to 50 Dirhams, KM#21.

| Date | Mintage | F | VF | XF | Unc | BU |
|---|---|---|---|---|---|---|
| 1996 Proof; Rare | — | — | — | — | — | — |

**5000 DIRHAMS** **KM# M2** **Weight:** 2000.0000 g. **Composition:** 0.9167 Gold 5.8945 oz. AGW **Subject:** 30th Anniversary - Reign of Shaikh Zayed **Obverse:** Portrait **Reverse:** Circular design of Arabic lettering **Note:** Similar to 50 Dirhams, KM#22.

| Date | Mintage | F | VF | XF | Unc | BU |
|---|---|---|---|---|---|---|
| 1996 Proof; Rare | — | — | — | — | — | — |

## PIEFORTS

| KM# | Date | Mintage | Identification | Mkt Val |
|---|---|---|---|---|
| P1 | 1981 | 75 | 50 Dirhams. KM#7. | 75.00 |
| P2 | 1981 | 100 | 750 Dirhams. KM#8. | 800 |

## MINT SETS

| KM# | Date | Mintage | Identification | Issue Price | Mkt Val |
|---|---|---|---|---|---|
| MS1 | AH1409/1989 (6) | — | KM#1, 2.1-3.1, 4-5, 6.1 | — | 15.00 |

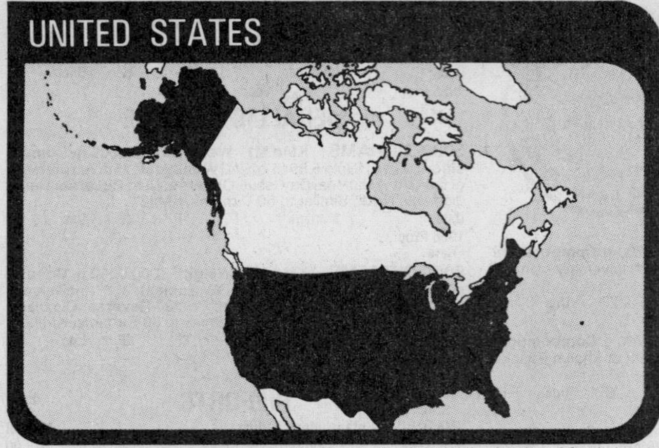


The United States of America as politically organized, under the Articles of Confederation consisted of the 13 original British-American colonies; New Hampshire, Massachusetts, Rhode Island, Connecticut, New York, New Jersey, Pennsylvania, Delaware, Virginia, North Carolina, South Carolina, Georgia and Maryland. Clustered along the eastern seaboard of North American between the forests of Maine and the marshes of Georgia. Under the Article of Confederation, the United States had no national capital: Philadelphia, where the "United States in Congress Assembled", was the "seat of government". The population during this political phase of America's history (1781-1789) was about 3 million, most of whom lived on self-sufficient family farms. Fishing, lumbering and the production of grains for export were major economic endeavors. Rapid strides were also being made in industry and manufacturing by 1775, the (then) colonies were accounting for one-seventh of the world's production of raw iron.

On the basis of the voyage of John Cabot to the North American mainland in 1497, England claimed the entire continent. The first permanent English settlement was established at Jamestown, Virginia, in 1607. France and Spain also claimed extensive territory in North America. At the end of the French and Indian Wars (1763), England acquired all of the territory east of the Mississippi River, including East and West Florida. From 1776 to 1781, the States were governed by the Continental Congress. From 1781 to 1789, they were organized under the Articles of Confederation, during which period the individual States had the right to issue money. Independence from Great Britain was attained by the American Revolution in 1776. The Constitution which organized and governs the present United States was ratified on Nov. 21, 1788.

# CENT

## Indian Head.

1864 "L"

**Designer:** James B. Longacre. **Diameter:** 19 mm. **Weight:** 3.1100 g. **Composition:** Bronze. **Notes:** The 1864 "L" variety has the designer's initial in Liberty's hair to the right of her neck. **KM#** 90a.

| Date | Mintage | G-4 | VG-8 | F-12 | VF-20 | XF-40 | AU-50 | MS-60 | MS-65 | Prf-65 |
|---|---|---|---|---|---|---|---|---|---|---|
| 1901 | 79,611,143 | 1.20 | 1.45 | 2.10 | 3.00 | 8.50 | 18.00 | 26.00 | 145 | 425 |
| 1902 | 87,376,722 | 1.20 | 1.45 | 2.10 | 3.00 | 8.50 | 18.00 | 26.00 | 145 | 425 |
| 1903 | 85,094,493 | 1.20 | 1.45 | 2.10 | 3.00 | 8.50 | 18.00 | 26.00 | 145 | 425 |
| 1904 | 61,328,015 | 1.20 | 1.45 | 2.10 | 3.00 | 8.50 | 18.00 | 26.00 | 145 | 475 |
| 1905 | 80,719,163 | 1.20 | 1.45 | 2.10 | 3.00 | 8.50 | 18.00 | 26.00 | 145 | 475 |
| 1906 | 96,022,255 | 1.15 | 1.40 | 1.95 | 3.00 | 8.00 | 17.00 | 25.00 | 150 | 395 |
| 1907 | 108,138,618 | 1.15 | 1.40 | 1.90 | 3.00 | 8.00 | 17.00 | 25.00 | 150 | 485 |
| 1908 | 32,327,987 | 1.30 | 1.85 | 2.60 | 4.00 | 9.00 | 18.00 | 26.00 | 150 | 395 |
| 1908S | 1,115,000 | 37.00 | 41.00 | 46.00 | 52.50 | 90.00 | 140 | 195 | 650 | — |
| 1909 | 14,370,645 | 2.75 | 3.00 | 4.00 | 6.00 | 17.50 | 26.00 | 35.00 | 155 | 400 |
| 1909S | 309,000 | 240 | 275 | 300 | 345 | 390 | 450 | 485 | 1,400 | — |

## Lincoln. Wheat.

**Designer:** Victor D. Brenner. **Diameter:** 19 mm. **Weight:** 3.1100 g. **Composition:** Bronze. **Notes:** The 1909 "VDB" varieties have the designer's initials inscribed at the 6 o'clock position on the reverse. The initials were removed until 1918, when they were restored on the obverse. **KM#** 132.

| Date | Mintage | G-4 | VG-8 | F-12 | VF-20 | XF-40 | AU-50 | MS-60 | MS-65 | Prf-65 |
|---|---|---|---|---|---|---|---|---|---|---|
| 1909 | 72,702,618 | 1.25 | 1.35 | 1.80 | 2.00 | 3.50 | 8.50 | 14.00 | 75.00 | 520 |
| 1909 VDB | 27,995,000 | 3.30 | 3.40 | 3.55 | 3.85 | 4.85 | 6.50 | 10.00 | 65.00 | 6,000 |
| 1909S | 1,825,000 | 40.00 | 45.00 | 57.00 | 77.00 | 110 | 130 | 150 | 585 | — |
| 1909S VDB | 484,000 | 360 | 420 | 450 | 510 | 570 | 660 | 750 | 3,000 | — |
| 1910 | 146,801,218 | 0.25 | 0.30 | 0.45 | 0.60 | 2.75 | 6.50 | 14.50 | 100.00 | 700 |
| 1910S | 6,045,000 | 7.00 | 8.00 | 9.50 | 12.00 | 26.50 | 54.00 | 60.00 | 365 | — |
| 1911 | 101,177,787 | 0.35 | 0.55 | 1.35 | 1.95 | 4.50 | 8.50 | 18.00 | 175 | 600 |
| 1911D | 12,672,000 | 5.00 | 6.00 | 8.50 | 13.50 | 40.00 | 65.00 | 80.00 | 950 | — |
| 1911S | 4,026,000 | 15.00 | 17.00 | 19.00 | 23.00 | 42.00 | 80.00 | 145 | 1,350 | — |
| 1912 | 68,153,060 | 1.00 | 1.50 | 2.25 | 5.50 | 11.00 | 17.00 | 32.00 | 275 | 950 |
| 1912D | 10,411,000 | 5.75 | 6.25 | 7.50 | 20.00 | 42.00 | 70.00 | 140 | 1,000 | — |
| 1912S | 4,431,000 | 11.00 | 13.00 | 15.00 | 20.00 | 45.00 | 65.00 | 110 | 1,600 | — |
| 1913 | 76,532,352 | 0.65 | 1.00 | 1.75 | 4.00 | 15.00 | 18.50 | 32.00 | 270 | 550 |
| 1913D | 15,804,000 | 2.70 | 3.00 | 3.75 | 8.50 | 28.00 | 55.00 | 85.00 | 1,175 | — |
| 1913S | 6,101,000 | 5.75 | 6.25 | 8.00 | 12.00 | 38.00 | 65.00 | 135 | 2,500 | — |
| 1914 | 75,238,432 | 0.50 | 0.80 | 1.50 | 4.50 | 11.50 | 29.00 | 42.00 | 310 | 600 |
| 1914D | 1,193,000 | 85.00 | 120 | 150 | 235 | 500 | 825 | 1,100 | 8,600 | — |
| 1914S | 4,137,000 | 10.00 | 11.00 | 13.00 | 19.00 | 45.00 | 135 | 235 | 7,500 | — |
| 1915 | 29,092,120 | 1.40 | 1.75 | 4.50 | 12.50 | 48.00 | 68.00 | 80.00 | 575 | 600 |
| 1915D | 22,050,000 | 1.50 | 1.90 | 2.60 | 5.00 | 14.00 | 33.00 | 62.00 | 650 | — |
| 1915S | 4,833,000 | 7.00 | 8.00 | 9.00 | 13.00 | 42.00 | 65.00 | 135 | 3,000 | — |
| 1916 | 131,833,677 | 0.20 | 0.30 | 0.50 | 1.50 | 5.00 | 8.50 | 12.00 | 135 | 1,650 |
| 1916D | 35,956,000 | 0.45 | 0.55 | 1.60 | 3.00 | 10.00 | 20.00 | 52.00 | 1,750 | — |
| 1916S | 22,510,000 | 1.00 | 1.50 | 1.85 | 3.00 | 11.00 | 25.00 | 68.00 | 4,000 | — |
| 1917 | 196,429,785 | 0.20 | 0.30 | 0.45 | 1.60 | 4.00 | 8.00 | 13.00 | 140 | — |
| 1917D | 55,120,000 | 0.30 | 0.40 | 1.00 | 2.50 | 10.00 | 22.00 | 58.00 | 1,275 | — |
| 1917S | 32,620,000 | 0.60 | 0.70 | 1.00 | 2.25 | 8.50 | 19.50 | 58.00 | 4,000 | — |
| 1918 | 288,104,634 | 0.20 | 0.30 | 0.40 | 1.00 | 4.00 | 7.00 | 12.50 | 195 | — |
| 1918D | 47,830,000 | 0.35 | 0.70 | 1.25 | 2.50 | 9.00 | 19.50 | 58.00 | 1,500 | — |
| 1918S | 34,680,000 | 0.40 | 0.75 | 1.00 | 2.25 | 8.00 | 30.00 | 60.00 | 4,600 | — |
| 1919 | 392,021,000 | 0.20 | 0.30 | 0.40 | 0.75 | 2.00 | 5.00 | 9.00 | 120 | — |
| 1919D | 57,154,000 | 0.30 | 0.45 | 0.65 | 2.00 | 7.50 | 29.00 | 50.00 | 1,150 | — |
| 1919S | 139,760,000 | 0.20 | 0.30 | 1.25 | 1.65 | 3.50 | 14.50 | 35.00 | 2,750 | — |
| 1920 | 310,165,000 | 0.20 | 0.25 | 0.40 | 0.75 | 2.50 | 5.50 | 11.00 | 110 | — |
| 1920D | 49,280,000 | 0.30 | 0.45 | 0.95 | 2.50 | 10.00 | 25.00 | 55.00 | 900 | — |
| 1920S | 46,220,000 | 0.25 | 0.35 | 1.25 | 2.00 | 7.00 | 29.00 | 85.00 | 4,400 | — |
| 1921 | 39,157,000 | 0.30 | 0.40 | 0.60 | 1.50 | 5.50 | 17.50 | 35.00 | 195 | — |
| 1921S | 15,274,000 | 1.40 | 1.50 | 2.00 | 4.00 | 17.50 | 65.00 | 85.00 | 4,100 | — |
| 1922D | 7,160,000 | 8.50 | 9.00 | 11.00 | 13.50 | 26.00 | 47.00 | 75.00 | 875 | — |
| 1922 No D-T.2 | Inc. above | 310 | 395 | 460 | 600 | 1,350 | 2,650 | 5,200 | 65,000 | — |
| 1923 | 74,723,000 | 0.20 | 0.30 | 0.40 | 1.25 | 4.50 | 8.50 | 12.00 | 240 | — |
| 1923S | 8,700,000 | 1.60 | 2.00 | 3.50 | 6.00 | 25.00 | 75.00 | 185 | 4,100 | — |
| 1924 | 75,178,000 | 0.20 | 0.30 | 0.50 | 1.25 | 5.00 | 10.00 | 20.00 | 145 | — |
| 1924D | 2,520,000 | 11.00 | 13.00 | 15.00 | 30.00 | 80.00 | 145 | 235 | 4,100 | — |
| 1924S | 11,696,000 | 0.85 | 1.10 | 2.00 | 3.00 | 14.50 | 60.00 | 100.00 | 7,000 | — |
| 1925 | 139,949,000 | 0.20 | 0.30 | 0.40 | 1.00 | 3.50 | 7.50 | 10.00 | 80.00 | — |
| 1925D | 22,580,000 | 0.40 | 0.70 | 1.00 | 2.00 | 9.50 | 27.00 | 50.00 | 1,700 | — |
| 1925S | 26,380,000 | 0.30 | 0.40 | 0.80 | 1.25 | 8.00 | 19.50 | 60.00 | 5,950 | — |
| 1926 | 157,088,000 | 0.15 | 0.20 | 0.30 | 0.80 | 2.00 | 5.50 | 8.00 | 60.00 | — |
| 1926D | 28,020,000 | 0.25 | 0.40 | 0.70 | 1.50 | 7.00 | 25.00 | 60.00 | 1,700 | — |
| 1926S | 4,550,000 | 2.50 | 3.75 | 5.50 | 8.00 | 16.00 | 57.00 | 105 | 30,000 | — |
| 1927 | 144,440,000 | 0.15 | 0.20 | 0.30 | 0.80 | 2.00 | 5.00 | 8.00 | 95.00 | — |
| 1927D | 27,170,000 | 0.20 | 0.30 | 0.60 | 1.25 | 4.00 | 13.50 | 55.00 | 1,250 | — |
| 1927S | 14,276,000 | 0.80 | 1.00 | 1.60 | 3.50 | 13.00 | 28.50 | 68.00 | 3,700 | — |
| 1928 | 134,116,000 | 0.15 | 0.20 | 0.30 | 0.80 | 2.00 | 5.00 | 8.50 | 90.00 | — |
| 1928D | 31,170,000 | 0.20 | 0.30 | 0.50 | 1.00 | 4.00 | 10.00 | 28.00 | 510 | — |
| 1928S | 17,266,000 | 0.65 | 0.75 | 1.20 | 1.75 | 5.00 | 13.50 | 67.50 | 1,700 | — |
| 1929 | 185,262,000 | 0.15 | 0.20 | 0.30 | 0.80 | 1.50 | 5.00 | 6.50 | 90.00 | — |
| 1929D | 41,730,000 | 0.15 | 0.20 | 0.50 | 0.90 | 3.50 | 9.00 | 17.50 | 240 | — |
| 1929S | 50,148,000 | 0.15 | 0.20 | 0.35 | 0.75 | 2.75 | 4.75 | 12.00 | 130 | — |
| 1930 | 157,415,000 | 0.15 | 0.20 | 0.30 | 0.50 | 1.75 | 3.00 | 5.50 | 47.00 | — |
| 1930D | 40,100,000 | 0.15 | 0.20 | 0.45 | 0.75 | 2.50 | 5.50 | 12.00 | 95.00 | — |
| 1930S | 24,286,000 | 0.20 | 0.25 | 0.35 | 0.80 | 1.60 | 5.75 | 10.00 | 47.00 | — |
| 1931 | 19,396,000 | 0.50 | 0.60 | 1.00 | 1.40 | 2.00 | 7.00 | 17.50 | 100.00 | — |
| 1931D | 4,480,000 | 3.25 | 3.40 | 3.75 | 4.75 | 8.50 | 35.50 | 49.00 | 560 | — |
| 1931S | 866,000 | 37.00 | 38.00 | 41.00 | 43.00 | 48.00 | 67.00 | 72.00 | 460 | — |
| 1932 | 9,062,000 | 1.50 | 1.80 | 2.35 | 3.00 | 3.60 | 9.50 | 18.50 | 78.00 | — |
| 1932D | 10,500,000 | 1.00 | 1.35 | 1.45 | 1.75 | 2.75 | 8.00 | 14.50 | 80.00 | — |
| 1933 | 14,360,000 | 1.00 | 1.20 | 1.50 | 1.90 | 3.50 | 9.00 | 16.50 | 67.00 | — |
| 1933D | 6,200,000 | 2.00 | 2.50 | 3.00 | 3.50 | 6.00 | 11.50 | 16.50 | 65.00 | — |
| 1934 | 219,080,000 | — | 0.15 | 0.20 | 0.25 | 0.75 | 1.50 | 4.00 | 27.00 | — |
| 1934D | 28,446,000 | 0.15 | 0.20 | 0.25 | 0.45 | 1.50 | 5.00 | 16.50 | 52.00 | — |
| 1935 | 245,338,000 | — | 0.10 | 0.15 | 0.25 | 0.75 | 1.00 | 2.50 | 13.00 | — |
| 1935D | 11,100,000,000 | — | 0.15 | 0.20 | 0.30 | 0.95 | 2.50 | 5.50 | 9.50 | — |
| 1935S | 38,702,000 | 0.10 | 0.20 | 0.30 | 0.40 | 1.00 | 3.00 | 12.00 | 46.00 | — |
| 1936 | 309,637,569 | — | 0.10 | 0.15 | 0.25 | 0.75 | 1.00 | 2.00 | 6.00 | 1,200 |
| 1936D | 40,620,000 | — | 0.10 | 0.15 | 0.25 | 0.75 | 1.50 | 2.75 | 8.50 | — |
| 1936S | 29,130,000 | 0.10 | 0.15 | 0.25 | 0.35 | 0.85 | 1.75 | 2.75 | 8.50 | — |
| 1937 | 309,179,320 | — | 0.10 | 0.15 | 0.20 | 0.70 | 0.90 | 1.75 | 7.00 | 125 |
| 1937D | 50,430,000 | — | 0.10 | 0.15 | 0.25 | 0.70 | 1.00 | 2.50 | 9.50 | — |
| 1937S | 34,500,000 | — | 0.10 | 0.15 | 0.25 | 0.60 | 1.25 | 3.00 | 8.50 | — |
| 1938 | 156,696,734 | — | 0.10 | 0.15 | 0.20 | 0.50 | 1.00 | 2.00 | 5.75 | 85.00 |
| 1938D | 20,010,000 | 0.20 | 0.25 | 0.35 | 0.45 | 0.75 | 1.50 | 2.70 | 8.50 | — |
| 1938S | 15,180,000 | 0.30 | 0.40 | 0.50 | 0.70 | 0.90 | 1.90 | 2.80 | 8.50 | — |
| 1939 | 316,479,520 | — | 0.10 | 0.15 | 0.20 | 0.30 | 0.50 | 1.00 | 5.75 | 78.00 |
| 1939D | 15,160,000 | 0.30 | 0.30 | 0.35 | 0.60 | 0.85 | 1.90 | 2.25 | 8.50 | — |
| 1939S | 52,070,000 | — | 0.15 | 0.20 | 0.25 | 0.45 | 0.90 | 1.35 | 9.50 | — |
| 1940 | 586,825,872 | — | 0.15 | 0.20 | 0.25 | 0.30 | 0.45 | 0.95 | 5.75 | 70.00 |
| 1940D | 81,390,000 | — | 0.15 | 0.20 | 0.25 | 0.35 | 0.50 | 1.00 | 5.75 | — |
| 1940S | 112,940,000 | — | 0.15 | 0.20 | 0.25 | 0.30 | 0.75 | 1.00 | 5.85 | — |
| 1941 | 887,039,100 | — | — | 0.10 | 0.15 | 0.25 | 0.40 | 0.85 | 5.75 | 65.00 |
| 1941D | 128,700,000 | — | — | 0.15 | 0.20 | 0.25 | 1.00 | 2.00 | 8.50 | — |
| 1941S | 92,360,000 | — | — | 0.15 | 0.20 | 0.25 | 1.25 | 2.25 | 11.00 | — |
| 1942 | 657,828,600 | — | — | 0.10 | 0.15 | 0.20 | 0.25 | 0.50 | 4.60 | 78.00 |
| 1942D | 206,698,000 | — | — | 0.10 | 0.15 | 0.20 | 0.30 | 0.50 | 5.75 | — |
| 1942S | 85,590,000 | — | — | 0.10 | 0.20 | 0.30 | 1.50 | 3.50 | 16.00 | — |

**Designer:** Victor D. Brenner. **Diameter:** 19 mm. **Weight:** 2.7000 g. **Composition:** Zinc Coated Steel. **KM#** 132a.

| Date | Mintage | G-4 | VG-8 | F-12 | VF-20 | XF-40 | AU-50 | MS-60 | MS-65 | Prf-65 |
|---|---|---|---|---|---|---|---|---|---|---|
| 1943 | 684,628,670 | — | — | 0.25 | 0.30 | 0.50 | 0.70 | 0.85 | 4.60 | — |
| 1943D | 217,660,000 | — | — | 0.25 | 0.35 | 0.60 | 0.65 | 1.00 | 6.50 | — |
| 1943S | 191,550,000 | — | 0.30 | 0.35 | 0.40 | 0.70 | 1.00 | 1.75 | 9.50 | — |

**Designer:** Victor D. Brenner. **Diameter:** 19 mm. **Weight:** 3.1100 g. **Composition:** Copper-Zinc. **Notes:** The 1955 "doubled die" has distinct doubling of the date and lettering on the obverse. **KM#** A132.

| Date | Mintage | XF-40 | MS-65 | Prf-65 | Date | Mintage | XF-40 | MS-65 | Prf-65 |
|---|---|---|---|---|---|---|---|---|---|
| 1944 | 1,435,400,000 | 0.20 | 2.00 | — | 1944D | 430,578,000 | 0.20 | 2.00 | — |

| Date | Mintage | XF-40 | MS-65 | Prf-65 |
|---|---|---|---|---|
| 1944D/S | — | 160 | 1,400 | — |
| 1944S | 282,760,000 | 0.20 | 5.50 | — |
| 1945 | 1,040,515,000 | 0.20 | 2.00 | — |
| 1945D | 226,268,000 | 0.20 | 2.00 | — |
| 1945S | 181,770,000 | 0.20 | 5.50 | — |
| 1946 | 991,655,000 | 0.20 | 2.00 | — |
| 1946D | 315,690,000 | 0.20 | 4.50 | — |
| 1946S | 198,100,000 | 0.20 | 4.60 | — |
| 1947 | 190,555,000 | 0.20 | 2.25 | — |
| 1947D | 194,750,000 | 0.20 | 2.00 | — |
| 1947S | 99,000,000 | 0.20 | 5.50 | — |
| 1948 | 317,570,000 | 0.20 | 2.00 | — |
| 1948D | 172,637,000 | 0.20 | 2.25 | — |
| 1948S | 81,735,000 | 0.20 | 5.50 | — |
| 1949 | 217,775,000 | 0.20 | 3.50 | — |
| 1949D | 153,132,000 | 0.20 | 3.50 | — |
| 1949S | 64,290,000 | 0.25 | 5.75 | — |
| 1950 | 272,686,386 | 0.20 | 1.75 | 40.00 |
| 1950D | 334,950,000 | 0.20 | 1.50 | — |
| 1950S | 118,505,000 | 0.20 | 2.50 | — |
| 1951 | 295,633,500 | 0.20 | 2.00 | 40.00 |

| Date | Mintage | XF-40 | MS-65 | Prf-65 |
|---|---|---|---|---|
| 1951D | 625,355,000 | 0.10 | 1.65 | — |
| 1951S | 136,010,000 | 0.15 | 3.00 | — |
| 1952 | 186,856,980 | 0.15 | 2.75 | 34.00 |
| 1952D | 746,130,000 | 0.10 | 1.60 | — |
| 1952S | 137,800,004 | 0.15 | 3.00 | — |
| 1953 | 256,883,800 | 0.10 | 1.25 | 28.00 |
| 1953D | 700,515,000 | 0.10 | 1.25 | — |
| 1953S | 181,835,000 | 0.15 | 1.75 | — |
| 1954 | 71,873,350 | 0.15 | 1.25 | 9.00 |
| 1954D | 251,552,500 | 0.10 | 0.50 | — |
| 1954S | 96,190,000 | 0.15 | 0.75 | — |
| 1955 | 330,958,000 | 0.10 | 0.75 | 13.00 |
| 1955 doubled die | — | 570 | 27,000 | — |
| 1955D | 563,257,500 | 0.10 | 0.75 | — |
| 1955S | 44,610,000 | 0.25 | 1.00 | — |
| 1956 | 421,414,384 | — | 0.50 | 3.00 |
| 1956D | 1,098,201,100 | — | 0.50 | — |
| 1957 | 283,787,952 | — | 0.50 | 2.00 |
| 1957D | 1,051,342,000 | — | 0.50 | — |
| 1958 | 253,400,652 | — | 0.50 | 3.00 |
| 1958D | 800,953,300 | — | 0.50 | — |

## Lincoln. Lincoln Memorial.

**Rev. Designer:** Frank Gasparro. **Weight:** 3.1100 g. **Composition:** Copper-Zinc. **Notes:** The dates were modified in 1960, 1970 and 1982, resulting in large-date and small-date varieties for those years. The 1972 "doubled die" shows doubling of "In God We Trust." The 1979-S and 1981-S Type II proofs have a clearer mint mark than the Type I proofs of those years. Some 1982 cents have the predominantly copper composition; others have the predominantly zinc composition. They can be distinguished by weight. **KM#** 201.

| Date | Mintage | MS-65 | Prf-65 |
|---|---|---|---|
| 1959 | 610,864,291 | 0.50 | 1.50 |
| 1959D | 1,279,760,000 | 0.50 | — |
| 1960 small date | 588,096,602 | 5.00 | 16.00 |
| 1960 large date | Inc. above | 0.30 | 1.25 |
| 1960D small date | 1,580,884,000 | 0.30 | — |
| 1960D large date | Inc. above | 0.30 | — |
| 1961 | 756,373,244 | 0.30 | 1.00 |
| 1961D | 1,753,266,700 | 0.30 | — |
| 1962 | 609,263,019 | 0.30 | 1.00 |
| 1962D | 1,793,148,400 | 0.30 | — |
| 1963 | 757,185,645 | 0.30 | 1.00 |
| 1963D | 1,774,020,400 | 0.30 | — |
| 1964 | 2,652,525,762 | 0.30 | 1.00 |
| 1964D | 3,799,071,500 | 0.30 | — |
| 1965 | 1,497,224,900 | 0.30 | — |
| 1966 | 2,188,147,783 | 0.30 | — |
| 1967 | 3,048,667,100 | 0.30 | — |
| 1968 | 1,707,880,970 | 0.30 | — |
| 1968D | 2,886,269,600 | 0.40 | — |
| 1968S | 261,311,510 | 0.40 | 1.00 |
| 1969 | 1,136,910,000 | 0.60 | — |
| 1969D | 4,002,832,200 | 0.40 | — |
| 1969S | 547,309,631 | 0.40 | 1.10 |
| 1970 | 1,898,315,000 | 0.40 | — |
| 1970D | 2,891,438,900 | 0.40 | — |
| 1970S | 693,192,814 | 0.40 | 1.20 |
| 1970S small date | — | 55.00 | 60.00 |
| 1971 | 1,919,490,000 | 0.35 | — |
| 1971D | 2,911,045,600 | 0.40 | — |
| 1971S | 528,354,192 | 0.25 | 1.20 |
| 1972 | 2,933,255,000 | 0.25 | — |
| 1972 doubled die | — | 410 | — |
| 1972D | 2,665,071,400 | 0.25 | — |
| 1972S | 380,200,104 | 0.25 | 1.15 |
| 1973 | 3,728,245,000 | 0.25 | — |

| Date | Mintage | MS-65 | Prf-65 |
|---|---|---|---|
| 1973D | 3,549,576,588 | 0.25 | — |
| 1973S | 319,937,634 | 0.25 | 0.80 |
| 1974 | 4,232,140,523 | 0.25 | — |
| 1974D | 4,235,098,000 | 0.25 | — |
| 1974S | 412,039,228 | 0.25 | 0.75 |
| 1975 | 5,451,476,142 | 0.25 | — |
| 1975D | 4,505,245,300 | 0.25 | — |
| 1975S | (2,845,450) | — | 5.50 |
| 1976 | 4,674,292,426 | 0.25 | — |
| 1976D | 4,221,592,455 | 0.25 | — |
| 1976S | (4,149,730) | — | 5.00 |
| 1977 | 4,469,930,000 | 0.25 | — |
| 1977D | 4,149,062,300 | 0.25 | — |
| 1977S | (3,251,152) | — | 3.00 |
| 1978 | 5,558,605,000 | 0.25 | — |
| 1978D | 4,280,233,400 | 0.25 | — |
| 1978S | (3,127,781) | — | 3.50 |
| 1979 | 6,018,515,000 | 0.25 | — |
| 1979D | 4,139,357,254 | 0.25 | — |
| 1979S type I, proof only | (3,677,175) | — | 4.00 |
| 1979S type II, proof only | Inc. above | — | 4.25 |
| 1980 | 7,414,705,000 | 0.25 | — |
| 1980D | 5,140,098,660 | 0.25 | — |
| 1980S | (3,554,806) | — | 2.25 |
| 1981 | 7,491,750,000 | 0.25 | — |
| 1981S type II, proof only | Inc. above | — | 60.00 |
| 1981D | 5,373,235,677 | 0.25 | — |
| 1981S type I, proof only | (4,063,083) | — | 3.50 |
| 1982 large date | 10,712,525,000 | 0.25 | — |
| 1982 small date | — | 0.25 | — |
| 1982D large date | 6,012,979,368 | 0.25 | — |

**Diameter:** 19 mm. **Weight:** 2.5000 g. **Composition:** Copper Plated Zinc. **KM#** 201a.

| Date | Mintage | XF-40 | MS-65 | Prf-65 |
|---|---|---|---|---|
| 1982 large date | — | — | 0.50 | — |
| 1982 small date | — | — | 1.00 | — |
| 1982D large date | — | — | 0.30 | — |
| 1982D small date | — | — | 0.25 | — |

**Diameter:** 19 mm **Composition:** Copper Plated Zinc. **Notes:** The 1983 "doubled die reverse" shows doubling of "United States of America." The 1984 "doubled die" shows doubling of Lincoln's ear on the obverse. **KM#** 201b.

| Date | Mintage | MS-65 | Prf-65 |
|---|---|---|---|
| 1982S | (3,857,479) | — | 3.00 |
| 1983 | 7,752,355,000 | 0.25 | — |
| 1983 doubled die | — | 400 | — |
| 1983D | 6,467,199,428 | 0.25 | — |
| 1983S | (3,279,126) | — | 4.00 |
| 1984 | 8,151,079,000 | 0.25 | — |
| 1984 doubled die | — | 275 | — |
| 1984D | 5,569,238,906 | 0.75 | — |
| 1984S | (3,065,110) | — | 4.50 |
| 1985 | 5,648,489,887 | 0.25 | — |
| 1985D | 5,287,399,926 | 0.25 | — |
| 1985S | (3,362,821) | — | 6.00 |
| 1986 | 4,491,395,493 | 1.50 | — |
| 1986D | 4,442,866,698 | 0.75 | — |
| 1986S | (3,010,497) | — | 7.50 |
| 1987 | 4,682,466,931 | 0.25 | — |
| 1987D | 4,879,389,514 | 0.25 | — |
| 1987S | (4,227,728) | — | 5.00 |
| 1988 | 6,092,810,000 | 0.25 | — |
| 1988D | 5,253,740,443 | 0.25 | — |
| 1988S | (3,262,948) | — | 12.50 |
| 1989 | 7,261,535,000 | 0.25 | — |
| 1989D | 5,345,467,111 | 0.25 | — |
| 1989S | (3,220,194) | — | 12.50 |
| 1990 | 6,851,765,000 | 0.25 | — |
| 1990D | 4,922,894,533 | 0.25 | — |
| 1990S | (3,299,559) | — | 5.75 |
| 1990 no S | — | — | 2,750 |
| 1991 | 5,165,940,000 | 0.25 | — |
| 1991D | 4,158,442,076 | 0.25 | — |
| 1991S | (2,867,787) | — | 30.00 |
| 1992 | 4,648,905,000 | 0.25 | — |
| 1992D | 4,448,673,300 | 0.25 | — |
| 1992S | (4,176,560) | — | 5.50 |
| 1993 | 5,684,705,000 | 0.25 | — |
| 1993D | 6,426,650,571 | 0.25 | — |

| Date | Mintage | MS-65 | Prf-65 |
|---|---|---|---|
| 1993S | (3,394,792) | — | 9.50 |
| 1994 | 6,500,850,000 | 0.25 | — |
| 1994D | 7,131,765,000 | 0.25 | — |
| 1994S | (3,269,923) | — | 8.50 |
| 1995 | 6,411,440,000 | 0.25 | — |
| 1995 doubled die | — | 27.00 | — |
| 1995D | 7,128,560,000 | 0.25 | — |
| 1995S | — | — | 9.50 |
| 1996 | 6,612,465,000 | 0.25 | — |
| 1996D | 6,510,795,000 | 0.25 | — |
| 1996S | — | — | 6.50 |
| 1997 | 4,622,800,000 | 0.25 | — |
| 1997D | 4,576,555,000 | 0.25 | — |
| 1997S | (1,975,000) | — | 11.50 |
| 1998 | 5,032,155,000 | 0.25 | — |
| 1998D | 5,255,353,500 | 0.25 | — |
| 1998S | — | — | 9.50 |
| 1999 | 5,237,600,000 | 0.25 | — |
| 1999D | 6,360,065,000 | 0.25 | — |
| 1999S | — | — | 5.00 |
| 2000 | — | 0.25 | — |
| 2000D | — | 0.25 | — |
| 2000S | — | — | 4.00 |
| 2001P | — | 0.25 | — |
| 2001D | — | 0.25 | — |
| 2001S | — | — | 4.00 |
| 2002P | — | — | — |
| 2002D | — | — | — |
| 2002S | — | — | — |

# 5 CENTS

## Liberty. "Cents" below "V".

**Weight:** 5.0000 g. **Composition:** Copper Nickel. **KM#** 112.

| Date | Mintage | G-4 | VG-8 | F-12 | VF-20 | XF-40 | AU-50 | MS-60 | MS-65 | Prf-65 |
|---|---|---|---|---|---|---|---|---|---|---|
| 1901 | 26,480,213 | 1.25 | 3.25 | 6.50 | 11.50 | 27.50 | 48.00 | 60.00 | 500 | 500 |
| 1902 | 31,480,579 | 1.25 | 3.25 | 5.00 | 9.00 | 27.50 | 48.00 | 65.00 | 490 | 500 |
| 1903 | 28,006,725 | 1.25 | 3.25 | 5.00 | 11.50 | 27.50 | 48.00 | 60.00 | 490 | 500 |
| 1904 | 21,404,984 | 1.25 | 3.00 | 5.25 | 11.50 | 28.50 | 48.00 | 60.00 | 490 | 675 |
| 1905 | 29,827,276 | 1.25 | 1.90 | 4.25 | 9.50 | 27.50 | 48.00 | 60.00 | 495 | 520 |
| 1906 | 38,613,725 | 1.25 | 1.90 | 4.00 | 9.00 | 27.50 | 48.00 | 60.00 | 500 | 500 |
| 1907 | 39,214,800 | 1.25 | 1.90 | 4.00 | 8.75 | 27.50 | 48.00 | 60.00 | 700 | 590 |
| 1908 | 22,686,177 | 1.25 | 1.90 | 4.00 | 8.75 | 27.50 | 48.00 | 60.00 | 700 | 500 |
| 1909 | 11,590,526 | 2.50 | 3.00 | 5.00 | 10.00 | 30.00 | 55.00 | 75.00 | 640 | 500 |
| 1910 | 30,169,353 | 1.25 | 1.90 | 4.00 | 8.75 | 25.00 | 45.00 | 60.00 | 590 | 490 |
| 1911 | 39,559,372 | 1.25 | 1.90 | 4.00 | 8.75 | 25.00 | 45.00 | 60.00 | 590 | 490 |
| 1912 | 26,236,714 | 1.25 | 1.90 | 4.00 | 8.75 | 25.00 | 45.00 | 60.00 | 500 | 535 |
| 1912D | 8,474,000 | 1.75 | 2.50 | 6.00 | 22.50 | 55.00 | 135 | 235 | 870 | — |
| 1912S | 238,000 | 52.00 | 65.00 | 95.00 | 250 | 480 | 700 | 850 | 2,500 | — |
| 1913 only 5 known | — | — | — | — | — | — | — | — | — | — |

**Note:** 1913, Superior Sale, March 2001, Proof, $1,840,000.

## Buffalo. Buffalo standing on a mound.

**Designer:** James Earle Fraser. **Diameter:** 21.2 mm. **Weight:** 5.0000 g. **Composition:** Copper-Nickel. **KM#** 133.

| Date | Mintage | G-4 | VG-8 | F-12 | VF-20 | XF-40 | AU-50 | MS-60 | MS-65 | Prf-65 |
|---|---|---|---|---|---|---|---|---|---|---|
| 1913 | 30,993,520 | 5.75 | 6.25 | 6.75 | 9.00 | 14.00 | 21.00 | 32.00 | 110 | 2,350 |
| 1913D | 5,337,000 | 11.00 | 13.00 | 14.50 | 19.00 | 26.00 | 41.50 | 52.00 | 250 | — |
| 1913S | 2,105,000 | 20.00 | 22.00 | 27.50 | 37.00 | 50.00 | 62.00 | 72.00 | 600 | — |

## Buffalo. Buffalo standing on a line.

1937D 3-legged

**Designer:** James Earle Fraser. **Diameter:** 21.2 mm. **Weight:** 5.0000 g. **Composition:** Copper Nickel. **Notes:** In 1913 the reverse design was modified so the ground under the buffalo was represented as a line rather than a mound. On the 1937D 3-legged variety, the buffalo's right front leg is missing, the result of a damaged die. **KM#** 134.

| Date | Mintage | G-4 | VG-8 | F-12 | VF-20 | XF-40 | AU-50 | MS-60 | MS-65 | Prf-65 |
|---|---|---|---|---|---|---|---|---|---|---|
| 1913 | 29,858,700 | 7.50 | 8.50 | 9.50 | 11.00 | 16.00 | 23.00 | 32.50 | 355 | 1,675 |
| 1913D | 4,156,000 | 49.50 | 57.50 | 75.00 | 85.00 | 95.00 | 120 | 162 | 975 | — |
| 1913S | 1,209,000 | 125 | 165 | 185 | 225 | 245 | 290 | 365 | 2,700 | — |
| 1914 | 20,665,738 | 12.00 | 14.00 | 15.00 | 19.50 | 25.00 | 35.00 | 47.00 | 410 | 1,475 |
| 1914D | 3,912,000 | 47.00 | 60.00 | 75.00 | 85.00 | 135 | 170 | 225 | 1,400 | — |
| 1914S | 3,470,000 | 13.50 | 14.50 | 23.00 | 30.00 | 47.00 | 75.00 | 135 | 1,650 | — |
| 1915 | 20,987,270 | 5.00 | 5.50 | 7.00 | 10.50 | 17.50 | 37.00 | 47.00 | 285 | 1,400 |
| 1915D | 7,569,500 | 14.50 | 16.50 | 29.00 | 40.00 | 75.00 | 100.00 | 190 | 1,750 | — |
| 1915S | 1,505,000 | 25.00 | 35.00 | 65.00 | 90.00 | 160 | 310 | 460 | 2,100 | — |
| 1916 | 63,498,066 | 3.50 | 3.75 | 4.00 | 6.00 | 11.00 | 20.00 | 40.00 | 275 | 2,350 |
| 1916/16 | Inc. above | 1,700 | 3,400 | 6,000 | 8,000 | 11,500 | 21,500 | 33,000 | 240,000 | — |
| 1916D | 13,333,000 | 7.00 | 11.00 | 17.50 | 28.50 | 65.00 | 90.00 | 140 | 1,700 | — |
| 1916S | 11,860,000 | 5.00 | 8.00 | 13.50 | 24.50 | 55.00 | 90.00 | 160 | 1,750 | — |
| 1917 | 51,424,029 | 2.00 | 3.25 | 5.00 | 9.00 | 17.50 | 35.00 | 55.00 | 490 | — |
| 1917D | 9,910,800 | 8.00 | 12.00 | 30.00 | 65.00 | 115 | 170 | 280 | 3,250 | — |
| 1917S | 4,193,000 | 12.00 | 17.00 | 37.50 | 70.00 | 135 | 250 | 330 | 3,100 | — |
| 1918 | 32,086,314 | 2.75 | 3.90 | 6.00 | 12.50 | 30.00 | 45.00 | 85.00 | 1,250 | — |
| 1918/17D | 8,362,314 | 400 | 750 | 1,050 | 2,250 | 5,200 | 8,500 | 13,500 | 250,000 | — |
| 1918D | Inc. above | 8.50 | 16.50 | 33.00 | 85.00 | 175 | 275 | 340 | 3,800 | — |
| 1918S | 4,882,000 | 9.00 | 17.50 | 35.00 | 79.00 | 160 | 250 | 390 | 25,000 | — |

| Date | Mintage | G-4 | VG-8 | F-12 | VF-20 | XF-40 | AU-50 | MS-60 | MS-65 | Prf-65 |
|---|---|---|---|---|---|---|---|---|---|---|
| 1919 | 60,868,000 | 1.25 | 1.50 | 2.50 | 6.50 | 15.00 | 35.00 | 50.00 | 485 | — |
| 1919D | 8,006,000 | 8.00 | 12.00 | 38.00 | 89.00 | 195 | 300 | 475 | 5,200 | — |
| 1919S | 7,521,000 | 5.50 | 15.00 | 32.00 | 80.00 | 195 | 310 | 440 | 10,000 | — |
| 1920 | 63,093,000 | 1.00 | 1.50 | 2.50 | 7.00 | 15.00 | 35.00 | 52.00 | 650 | — |
| 1920D | 9,418,000 | 6.50 | 14.00 | 35.00 | 85.00 | 250 | 325 | 450 | 5,000 | — |
| 1920S | 9,689,000 | 3.50 | 6.50 | 18.50 | 80.00 | 175 | 275 | 375 | 15,750 | — |
| 1921 | 10,663,000 | 2.15 | 3.50 | 5.00 | 17.50 | 45.00 | 60.00 | 110 | 700 | — |
| 1921S | 1,557,000 | 36.00 | 55.00 | 90.00 | 400 | 725 | 1,100 | 1,500 | 5,800 | — |
| 1923 | 35,715,000 | 1.50 | 1.75 | 3.00 | 7.50 | 15.00 | 32.50 | 48.00 | 500 | — |
| 1923S | 6,142,000 | 3.00 | 6.00 | 16.50 | 100.00 | 260 | 325 | 385 | 7,500 | — |
| 1924 | 21,620,000 | 1.25 | 1.90 | 3.00 | 8.00 | 20.00 | 35.00 | 62.00 | 660 | — |
| 1924D | 5,258,000 | 3.50 | 6.00 | 17.50 | 65.00 | 185 | 250 | 335 | 3,350 | — |
| 1924S | 1,437,000 | 8.00 | 17.00 | 70.00 | 400 | 1,100 | 1,500 | 2,000 | 8,500 | — |
| 1925 | 35,565,100 | 2.50 | 2.75 | 3.50 | 8.00 | 15.00 | 36.00 | 42.00 | 525 | — |
| 1925D | 4,450,000 | 7.50 | 16.50 | 40.00 | 80.00 | 165 | 245 | 340 | 3,600 | — |
| 1925S | 6,256,000 | 3.50 | 9.00 | 17.50 | 69.00 | 175 | 260 | 375 | 32,000 | — |
| 1926 | 44,693,000 | 1.00 | 1.15 | 1.50 | 6.00 | 14.50 | 25.00 | 35.00 | 175 | — |
| 1926D | 5,638,000 | 4.50 | 10.00 | 29.00 | 85.00 | 160 | 260 | 275 | 3,650 | — |
| 1926S | 970,000 | 11.00 | 21.00 | 60.00 | 335 | 725 | 1,500 | 2,975 | 38,500 | — |
| 1927 | 37,981,000 | 1.00 | 1.15 | 1.50 | 6.00 | 14.50 | 25.00 | 34.00 | 250 | — |
| 1927D | 5,730,000 | 2.00 | 4.00 | 7.00 | 30.00 | 85.00 | 125 | 160 | 4,800 | — |
| 1927S | 3,430,000 | 2.50 | 3.50 | 5.00 | 29.50 | 85.00 | 165 | 450 | 14,500 | — |
| 1928 | 23,411,000 | 1.10 | 1.25 | 1.60 | 7.00 | 15.00 | 30.00 | 35.00 | 300 | — |
| 1928D | 6,436,000 | 1.50 | 2.50 | 6.00 | 17.50 | 39.00 | 55.00 | 59.00 | 675 | — |
| 1928S | 6,936,000 | 1.50 | 1.75 | 2.75 | 12.50 | 30.00 | 125 | 210 | 3,850 | — |
| 1929 | 36,446,000 | 0.90 | 1.05 | 1.50 | 7.00 | 13.00 | 25.00 | 35.00 | 290 | — |
| 1929D | 8,370,000 | 1.10 | 1.45 | 2.00 | 8.00 | 35.00 | 45.00 | 55.00 | 1,550 | — |
| 1929S | 7,754,000 | 1.00 | 1.15 | 1.45 | 4.00 | 14.00 | 30.00 | 45.00 | 375 | — |
| 1930 | 22,849,000 | 0.95 | 1.00 | 1.50 | 4.00 | 9.00 | 20.00 | 29.00 | 135 | — |
| 1930S | 5,435,000 | 1.00 | 1.10 | 2.00 | 5.00 | 12.50 | 30.00 | 43.00 | 460 | — |
| 1931S | 1,200,000 | 6.00 | 6.25 | 7.00 | 8.00 | 19.50 | 38.00 | 45.00 | 235 | — |
| 1934 | 20,213,003 | 0.85 | 0.95 | 1.40 | 4.00 | 10.00 | 19.00 | 28.00 | 335 | — |
| 1934D | 7,480,000 | 1.00 | 1.15 | 2.00 | 8.00 | 18.50 | 42.00 | 52.00 | 875 | — |
| 1935 | 58,264,000 | 0.85 | 0.95 | 1.15 | 2.75 | 4.50 | 9.50 | 18.00 | 100.00 | — |
| 1935D | 12,092,000 | 0.90 | 1.00 | 2.00 | 6.00 | 17.00 | 38.00 | 46.00 | 390 | — |
| 1935S | 10,300,000 | 0.90 | 1.00 | 1.15 | 2.90 | 5.50 | 15.00 | 35.00 | 150 | — |
| 1936 | 119,001,420 | 0.85 | 0.95 | 1.10 | 1.75 | 3.50 | 8.50 | 14.00 | 90.00 | 1,100 |
| 1936D | 24,814,000 | 0.85 | 0.95 | 1.15 | 2.00 | 5.50 | 12.50 | 25.00 | 115 | — |
| 1936S | 14,930,000 | 0.85 | 0.95 | 1.15 | 2.00 | 3.50 | 12.00 | 24.00 | 100.00 | — |
| 1937 | 79,485,769 | 0.85 | 0.95 | 1.15 | 1.75 | 3.50 | 8.50 | 24.00 | 53.00 | 850 |
| 1937D | 17,826,000 | 0.85 | 0.95 | 1.15 | 1.75 | 3.75 | 9.50 | 15.00 | 57.00 | — |
| 1937D 3-legged | Inc. above | 200 | 260 | 280 | 375 | 435 | 650 | 1,200 | 16,500 | — |
| 1937S | 5,635,000 | 0.95 | 1.05 | 1.20 | 1.90 | 3.90 | 9.00 | 18.50 | 55.00 | — |
| 1938D | 7,020,000 | 1.60 | 1.75 | 2.00 | 3.25 | 4.50 | 9.00 | 13.00 | 38.00 | — |
| 1938D/D | — | 2.25 | 4.25 | 5.75 | 10.00 | 14.00 | 17.00 | 19.00 | 60.00 | — |
| 1938D/S | Inc. above | 6.00 | 8.00 | 11.00 | 15.00 | 19.00 | 32.00 | 45.00 | 190 | — |

## Jefferson.

**Designer:** Felix Schlag. **Diameter:** 21.2 mm. **Weight:** 5.0000 g. **Composition:** Copper-Nickel. **Notes:** Some 1939 strikes have doubling of the word "Monticello" on the reverse. **KM#** 192.

| Date | Mintage | VG-8 | F-12 | VF-20 | XF-40 | MS-60 | MS-65 | -65FS | Prf-65 |
|---|---|---|---|---|---|---|---|---|---|
| 1938 | 19,515,365 | 0.25 | 0.40 | 0.80 | 1.25 | 4.00 | 8.00 | 75.00 | 70.00 |
| 1938D | 5,376,000 | 0.90 | 1.00 | 1.25 | 1.75 | 4.25 | 8.00 | 50.00 | — |
| 1938S | 4,105,000 | 1.35 | 1.50 | 1.75 | 2.25 | 4.00 | 8.50 | 100.00 | — |
| 1939 | 120,627,535 | — | 0.20 | 0.25 | 0.30 | 1.75 | 3.50 | 20.00 | 70.00 |
| 1939 doubled Monticello | — | 20.00 | 30.00 | 45.00 | 75.00 | 200 | 550 | — | — |
| 1939D | 3,514,000 | 3.00 | 3.50 | 5.00 | 10.00 | 42.00 | 75.00 | 125 | — |
| 1939S | 6,630,000 | 0.45 | 0.60 | 1.50 | 2.75 | 15.00 | 40.00 | 110 | — |
| 1940 | 176,499,158 | — | — | — | 0.25 | 1.00 | 1.25 | 12.50 | 65.00 |
| 1940D | 43,540,000 | — | 0.20 | 0.30 | 0.40 | 2.50 | 2.75 | 10.00 | — |
| 1940S | 39,690,000 | — | 0.20 | 0.25 | 0.50 | 2.75 | 5.00 | 25.00 | — |
| 1941 | 203,283,720 | — | — | — | 0.20 | 1.00 | 2.00 | 17.50 | 60.00 |
| 1941D | 53,432,000 | — | 0.20 | 0.30 | 0.50 | 2.50 | 5.00 | 10.00 | — |
| 1941S | 43,445,000 | — | 0.20 | 0.30 | 0.50 | 3.75 | 6.75 | 25.00 | — |
| 1942 | 49,818,600 | — | — | — | 0.40 | 5.00 | 8.50 | 35.00 | 55.00 |
| 1942D | 13,938,000 | 0.30 | 0.40 | 0.60 | 2.00 | 27.00 | 50.00 | 50.00 | — |

**Note:** Fully Struck Full Step nickels command higher prices. Bright, Fully Struck coins command even higher prices. 1938 thru 1989 - 5 Full Steps. 1990 to date - 6 Full Steps.

## Jefferson. Mint mark above Monticello.

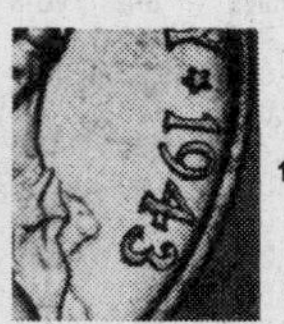

1943/2P

**Designer:** Felix Schlag. **Diameter:** 21.2 mm. **Composition:** 0.3500 Copper-Silver-Manganese, 0.0563 oz. **Notes:** War-time composition nickels have a large mint mark above Monticello on the reverse. **KM#** 192a.

| Date | Mintage | VG-8 | F-12 | VF-20 | XF-40 | MS-60 | MS-65 | -65FS | Prf-65 |
|---|---|---|---|---|---|---|---|---|---|
| 1942P | 57,900,600 | 0.65 | 0.85 | 1.00 | 1.75 | 6.00 | 22.50 | 50.00 | 140 |
| 1942S | 32,900,000 | 0.70 | 1.00 | 1.10 | 1.75 | 6.00 | 20.00 | 50.00 | — |
| 1943P | 271,165,000 | 0.50 | 0.85 | 1.00 | 1.50 | 2.75 | 15.00 | 20.00 | — |
| 1943/2P | Inc. above | 15.00 | 20.00 | 30.00 | 40.00 | 125 | 450 | 1,000 | — |
| 1943D | 15,294,000 | 0.90 | 1.20 | 1.50 | 1.75 | 4.00 | 13.00 | 20.00 | — |
| 1943S | 104,060,000 | 0.55 | 0.70 | 1.00 | 1.50 | 3.00 | 13.00 | 25.00 | — |
| 1944P | 119,150,000 | 0.50 | 0.70 | 1.00 | 1.50 | 4.00 | 17.00 | 50.00 | — |
| 1944D | 32,309,000 | 0.60 | 0.80 | 1.00 | 1.75 | 6.50 | 13.00 | 20.00 | — |
| 1944S | 21,640,000 | 0.70 | 1.00 | 1.25 | 2.00 | 3.50 | 13.00 | 100.00 | — |
| 1945P | 119,408,100 | 0.50 | 0.70 | 1.00 | 1.50 | 3.50 | 12.00 | 70.00 | — |
| 1945D | 37,158,000 | 0.55 | 0.75 | 1.00 | 1.50 | 3.50 | 7.00 | 25.00 | — |
| 1945S | 58,939,000 | 0.50 | 0.70 | 0.80 | 0.90 | 3.00 | 6.50 | 150 | — |

**Note:** Fully Struck Full Step nickels command higher prices. Bright, Fully Struck coins command even higher prices. 1938 thru 1989 - 5 Full Steps. 1990 to date - 6 Full Steps.

## Jefferson. Pre-war design resumed.

**Designer:** Felix Schlag. **Diameter:** 21.2 mm. **Weight:** 5.0000 g. **Composition:** Copper-Nickel. **Notes:** The 1979-S and 1981-S Type II proofs have clearer mint marks than the Type I proofs of those years. **KM#** A192.

| Date | Mintage | VG-8 | F-12 | VF-20 | XF-40 | MS-60 | MS-65 | -65FS | Prf-65 |
|---|---|---|---|---|---|---|---|---|---|
| 1946 | 161,116,000 | — | — | 0.20 | 0.25 | 0.80 | 1.00 | 15.00 | — |
| 1946D | 45,292,200 | — | — | 0.25 | 0.35 | 0.95 | 1.50 | 15.00 | — |
| 1946S | 13,560,000 | — | — | 0.30 | 0.40 | 0.50 | 1.00 | 20.00 | — |
| 1947 | 95,000,000 | — | — | 0.20 | 0.25 | 0.75 | 2.00 | 15.50 | — |
| 1947D | 37,822,000 | — | — | 0.20 | 0.30 | 0.90 | 2.00 | 15.00 | — |
| 1947S | 24,720,000 | — | — | 0.20 | 0.25 | 1.00 | 2.25 | 25.00 | — |
| 1948 | 89,348,000 | — | — | 0.20 | 0.25 | 0.50 | 1.50 | 25.00 | — |
| 1948D | 44,734,000 | — | — | 0.25 | 0.35 | 1.20 | 2.75 | 12.00 | — |
| 1948S | 11,300,000 | — | — | 0.25 | 0.50 | 1.20 | 2.25 | 18.00 | — |
| 1949 | 60,652,000 | — | — | 0.25 | 0.30 | 2.25 | 4.50 | 150 | — |
| 1949D | 36,498,000 | — | — | 0.30 | 0.40 | 1.25 | 3.00 | 20.00 | — |
| 1949D/S | Inc. above | — | 35.00 | 40.00 | 65.00 | 170 | 325 | 500 | — |
| 1949S | 9,716,000 | 0.25 | 0.35 | 0.45 | 0.90 | 1.50 | 3.50 | 105 | — |
| 1950 | 9,847,386 | 0.20 | 0.30 | 0.35 | 0.75 | 1.50 | 3.50 | 60.00 | 45.00 |
| 1950D | 2,630,030 | 5.00 | 5.15 | 5.25 | 5.50 | 6.50 | 10.00 | 16.00 | — |
| 1951 | 28,609,500 | — | — | 0.40 | 0.50 | 1.50 | 2.75 | 40.00 | 30.00 |
| 1951D | 20,460,000 | 0.25 | 0.30 | 0.40 | 0.50 | 3.00 | 6.00 | 20.00 | — |
| 1951S | 7,776,000 | 0.30 | 0.40 | 0.50 | 1.10 | 1.75 | 4.00 | 80.00 | — |
| 1952 | 64,069,980 | — | — | 0.20 | 0.25 | 0.85 | 3.00 | 90.00 | 26.00 |
| 1952D | 30,638,000 | — | — | 0.30 | 0.45 | 2.00 | 4.50 | 32.00 | — |
| 1952S | 20,572,000 | — | — | 0.20 | 0.25 | 0.75 | 3.50 | 110 | — |
| 1953 | 46,772,800 | — | — | 0.20 | 0.25 | 0.40 | 1.50 | 95.00 | 28.00 |
| 1953D | 59,878,600 | — | — | 0.20 | 0.25 | 0.40 | 1.50 | 60.00 | — |
| 1953S | 19,210,900 | — | — | 0.20 | 0.25 | 0.60 | 2.50 | 500 | — |
| 1954 | 47,917,350 | — | — | — | — | 0.60 | 1.50 | 40.00 | 16.00 |
| 1954D | 117,136,560 | — | — | — | — | 0.35 | 1.00 | 110 | — |
| 1954S | 29,384,000 | — | — | — | 0.20 | 0.35 | 2.50 | 350 | — |
| 1954S/D | Inc. above | — | 5.00 | 8.00 | 12.00 | 22.00 | 65.00 | — | — |
| 1955 | 8,266,200 | 0.25 | 0.35 | 0.40 | 0.45 | 0.75 | 2.00 | 60.00 | 16.00 |
| 1955D | 74,464,100 | — | — | — | — | 0.40 | 1.00 | 100.00 | — |
| 1955D/S | Inc. above | — | 5.00 | 8.50 | 13.00 | 33.00 | 75.00 | — | — |
| 1956 | 35,885,384 | — | — | — | — | 0.30 | 0.70 | 14.00 | 2.50 |
| 1956D | 67,222,940 | — | — | — | — | 0.25 | 0.60 | 50.00 | — |
| 1957 | 39,655,952 | — | — | — | — | 0.25 | 0.60 | 25.00 | 1.50 |
| 1957D | 136,828,900 | — | — | — | — | 0.25 | 0.60 | 30.00 | — |
| 1958 | 17,963,652 | — | — | 0.15 | 0.20 | 0.30 | 0.65 | 20.00 | 6.00 |
| 1958D | 168,249,120 | — | — | — | — | 0.25 | 0.60 | 20.00 | — |

**Note:** Fully Struck Full Step nickels command higher prices. Bright, Fully Struck coins command even higher prices. 1938 thru 1989 - 5 Full Steps. 1990 to date - 6 Full Steps.

| Date | Mintage | MS-65 | -65FS | Prf-65 |
|---|---|---|---|---|
| 1959 | 28,397,291 | 0.65 | 15.00 | 1.25 |
| 1959D | 160,738,240 | 0.55 | 24.00 | — |
| 1960 | 57,107,602 | 0.55 | 42.00 | 1.00 |
| 1960D | 192,582,180 | 0.55 | 500 | — |
| 1961 | 76,668,244 | 0.55 | 75.00 | 1.00 |
| 1961D | 229,342,760 | 0.55 | 500 | — |
| 1962 | 100,602,019 | 0.55 | 25.00 | 1.00 |
| 1962D | 280,195,720 | 0.55 | 300 | — |
| 1963 | 178,851,645 | 0.55 | 25.00 | 1.00 |
| 1963D | 276,829,460 | 0.55 | 300 | — |
| 1964 | 1,028,622,762 | 0.55 | 25.00 | 1.00 |
| 1964D | 1,787,297,160 | 0.50 | 200 | — |
| 1965 | 136,131,380 | 0.50 | 150 | — |
| 1966 | 156,208,283 | 0.50 | — | — |
| 1967 | 107,325,800 | 0.50 | — | — |
| 1968 none minted | — | — | — | — |
| 1968D | 91,227,880 | 0.50 | 500 | — |
| 1968S | 103,437,510 | 0.50 | 150 | 0.75 |
| 1969 none minted | — | — | — | — |
| 1969D | 202,807,500 | 0.50 | — | — |
| 1969S | 123,099,631 | 0.50 | 300 | 0.75 |
| 1970 none minted | — | — | — | — |
| 1970D | 515,485,380 | 0.50 | 325 | — |
| 1970S | 241,464,814 | 0.50 | 40.00 | 0.75 |
| 1971 | 106,884,000 | 2.00 | 15.00 | — |
| 1971D | 316,144,800 | 0.50 | 12.00 | — |
| 1971S | (3,220,733) | — | — | 2.00 |
| 1972 | 202,036,000 | 0.50 | 16.00 | — |
| 1972D | 351,694,600 | 0.50 | 15.00 | — |
| 1972S | (3,260,996) | — | — | 2.00 |
| 1973 | 384,396,000 | 0.50 | 11.00 | — |
| 1973D | 261,405,000 | 0.50 | 11.00 | — |
| 1973S | (2,760,339) | — | — | 1.75 |
| 1974 | 601,752,000 | 0.50 | 20.00 | — |
| 1974D | 277,373,000 | 0.50 | 22.50 | — |
| 1974S | (2,612,568) | — | — | 2.00 |
| 1975 | 181,772,000 | 0.75 | 25.00 | — |
| 1975D | 401,875,300 | 0.50 | 20.00 | — |
| 1975S | (2,845,450) | — | — | 2.25 |
| 1976 | 367,124,000 | 0.75 | 125 | — |
| 1976D | 563,964,147 | 0.60 | 25.00 | — |
| 1976S | (4,149,730) | — | — | 2.00 |
| 1977 | 585,376,000 | 0.40 | 40.00 | — |
| 1977D | 297,313,460 | 0.55 | 22.50 | — |
| 1977S | (3,251,152) | — | — | 1.75 |
| 1978 | 391,308,000 | 0.40 | 26.50 | — |
| 1978D | 313,092,780 | 0.40 | 22.50 | — |
| 1978S | (3,127,781) | — | — | 1.75 |
| 1979 | 463,188,000 | 0.40 | 40.00 | — |
| 1979D | 325,867,672 | 0.40 | 25.00 | — |
| 1979S type I, proof only | — | — | — | 1.50 |
| 1979S type II, proof only | — | — | — | 1.75 |
| 1980P | 593,004,000 | 0.40 | 15.00 | — |
| 1980D | 502,323,448 | 0.40 | 12.50 | — |
| 1980S | (3,554,806) | — | — | 1.50 |
| 1981P | 657,504,000 | 0.40 | 37.00 | — |
| 1981D | 364,801,843 | 0.40 | 26.00 | — |
| 1981S type I, proof only | — | — | — | 2.00 |
| 1981S type II, proof only | — | — | — | 2.50 |
| 1982P | 292,355,000 | 3.50 | 15.00 | — |
| 1982D | 373,726,544 | 3.50 | 12.00 | — |
| 1982S | — | — | — | 3.50 |
| 1983P | 561,615,000 | 3.00 | 15.00 | — |
| 1983D | 536,726,276 | 2.00 | 12.00 | — |
| 1983S | (3,279,126) | — | — | 4.00 |
| 1984P | 746,769,000 | 3.00 | 14.00 | — |
| 1984D | 517,675,146 | 0.85 | 17.00 | — |
| 1984S | (3,065,110) | — | — | 5.00 |
| 1985P | 647,114,962 | 0.75 | 36.00 | — |
| 1985D | 459,747,446 | 0.75 | 25.00 | — |
| 1985S | (3,362,821) | — | — | 4.00 |
| 1986P | 536,883,483 | 1.00 | 50.00 | — |
| 1986D | 361,819,140 | 2.00 | 48.00 | — |
| 1986S | (3,010,497) | — | — | 7.00 |
| 1987P | 371,499,481 | 0.75 | 12.00 | — |
| 1987D | 410,590,604 | 0.75 | 11.00 | — |
| 1987S | (4,227,728) | — | — | 3.50 |

| Date | Mintage | MS-65 | -65FS | Prf-65 |
|---|---|---|---|---|
| 1988P | 771,360,000 | 0.75 | — | — |
| 1988D | 663,771,652 | — | 11.00 | — |
| 1988S | (3,262,948) | — | — | 6.50 |
| 1989P | 898,812,000 | 0.75 | 12.00 | — |
| 1989D | 570,842,474 | 0.75 | 11.00 | — |
| 1989S | (3,220,194) | — | — | 5.50 |
| 1990P | 661,636,000 | 0.75 | 15.00 | — |
| 1990D | 663,938,503 | 0.75 | 15.00 | — |
| 1990S | — | — | — | 5.50 |
| 1991P | 614,104,000 | 0.75 | 15.00 | — |
| 1991D | 436,496,678 | 0.75 | 15.00 | — |
| 1991S | (2,867,787) | — | — | 5.00 |
| 1992P | 399,552,000 | 1.50 | 15.00 | — |
| 1992D | 450,565,113 | 0.75 | 15.00 | — |
| 1992S | (4,176,560) | — | — | 4.00 |
| 1993P | 412,076,000 | 0.75 | 15.00 | — |
| 1993D | 406,084,135 | 0.75 | 15.00 | — |
| 1993S | (3,394,792) | — | — | 4.50 |
| 1994P | 722,160,000 | 0.75 | 15.00 | — |
| 1994P matte finish | 167,703 | 75.00 | — | — |
| 1994D | 715,762,110 | 0.75 | 15.00 | — |
| 1994S | (3,269,923) | — | — | 4.00 |
| 1995P | 774,156,000 | 0.75 | 15.00 | — |
| 1995D | 888,112,000 | 0.85 | 15.00 | — |
| 1995S | — | — | — | 7.50 |
| 1996P | 829,332,000 | 0.75 | 15.00 | — |
| 1996D | 817,736,000 | 0.75 | 15.00 | — |
| 1996S | — | — | — | 3.00 |
| 1997P | 470,972,000 | 0.75 | 15.00 | — |
| 1997P matte finish | 25,000 | 250 | — | — |
| 1997D | 466,640,000 | 0.80 | 15.00 | — |
| 1997S | (1,975,000) | — | — | 5.00 |
| 1998P | 688,272,000 | 0.80 | 15.00 | — |
| 1998D | 635,360,000 | 0.80 | 15.00 | — |
| 1998S | — | — | — | 4.50 |
| 1999P | — | 0.80 | 12.00 | — |
| 1999D | — | 0.80 | 12.00 | — |
| 1999S | — | — | — | 3.50 |
| 2000P | — | 0.80 | 12.00 | — |
| 2000D | — | 0.80 | 12.00 | — |
| 2000S | — | — | — | 2.00 |
| 2001P | — | 0.50 | — | — |
| 2001D | — | 0.50 | — | — |
| 2001S | — | — | — | 2.00 |
| 2002P | — | — | — | — |
| 2002D | — | — | — | — |
| 2002S | — | — | — | — |

# DIME

## Barber.

**Designer:** Charles E. Barber. **Diameter:** 17.9 mm. **Weight:** 2.5000 g. **Composition:** 0.9000 Silver, 0.0724 oz. ASW. **Notes:** Commonly called "Barber dime." **KM#** 113.

| Date | Mintage | G-4 | VG-8 | F-12 | VF-20 | XF-40 | AU-50 | MS-60 | MS-65 | Prf-65 |
|---|---|---|---|---|---|---|---|---|---|---|
| 1901 | 18,860,478 | 1.45 | 1.65 | 5.25 | 7.75 | 20.00 | 45.00 | 100.00 | 1,170 | 1,450 |
| 1901O | 5,620,000 | 2.75 | 4.50 | 12.00 | 18.00 | 42.00 | 115 | 360 | 2,900 | — |
| 1901S | 593,022 | 50.00 | 88.00 | 340 | 380 | 450 | 565 | 790 | 5,000 | — |
| 1902 | 21,380,777 | 1.30 | 1.75 | 4.50 | 6.75 | 21.00 | 52.00 | 91.00 | 540 | 1,450 |
| 1902O | 4,500,000 | 2.50 | 6.50 | 13.00 | 20.00 | 41.00 | 105 | 325 | 3,350 | — |
| 1902S | 2,070,000 | 5.50 | 11.00 | 44.00 | 58.00 | 84.00 | 145 | 325 | 3,600 | — |
| 1903 | 19,500,755 | 1.30 | 1.75 | 4.50 | 7.15 | 20.00 | 52.00 | 91.00 | 1,150 | 1,450 |
| 1903O | 8,180,000 | 2.00 | 3.00 | 8.75 | 13.00 | 26.00 | 91.00 | 240 | 5,050 | — |
| 1903S | 613,300 | 44.00 | 85.00 | 320 | 415 | 680 | 855 | 1,050 | 3,800 | — |
| 1904 | 14,601,027 | 1.30 | 1.75 | 5.50 | 9.00 | 20.00 | 52.00 | 105 | 2,100 | 1,450 |
| 1904S | 800,000 | 25.00 | 41.00 | 120 | 155 | 225 | 430 | 565 | 4,700 | — |
| 1905 | 14,552,350 | 1.30 | 1.75 | 4.00 | 6.50 | 19.00 | 52.00 | 91.00 | 540 | 1,450 |
| 1905O | 3,400,000 | 2.50 | 5.75 | 30.00 | 43.00 | 58.00 | 105 | 230 | 2,050 | — |
| 1905S | 6,855,199 | 2.25 | 4.75 | 7.75 | 16.50 | 30.00 | 72.00 | 210 | 725 | — |
| 1906 | 19,958,406 | 1.30 | 1.75 | 3.50 | 6.50 | 21.00 | 52.00 | 91.00 | 540 | 1,450 |
| 1906D | 4,060,000 | 2.25 | 3.75 | 9.00 | 14.00 | 27.00 | 72.00 | 155 | 1,950 | — |
| 1906O | 2,610,000 | 4.00 | 6.00 | 41.00 | 57.00 | 78.00 | 125 | 180 | 1,250 | — |
| 1906S | 3,136,640 | 2.50 | 4.75 | 10.00 | 18.00 | 36.00 | 91.00 | 230 | 1,200 | — |
| 1907 | 22,220,575 | 1.30 | 1.60 | 3.50 | 6.50 | 21.00 | 52.00 | 91.00 | 540 | 1,450 |
| 1907D | 4,080,000 | 2.25 | 4.75 | 9.00 | 15.00 | 32.00 | 91.00 | 260 | 3,550 | — |
| 1907O | 5,058,000 | 1.75 | 3.00 | 25.00 | 37.00 | 52.00 | 72.00 | 200 | 1,100 | — |
| 1907S | 3,178,470 | 2.25 | 5.00 | 9.75 | 18.00 | 41.00 | 100.00 | 325 | 2,300 | — |
| 1908 | 10,600,545 | 1.30 | 1.75 | 3.50 | 6.50 | 18.00 | 52.00 | 91.00 | 540 | 1,450 |
| 1908D | 7,490,000 | 1.75 | 2.25 | 6.50 | 9.50 | 26.00 | 59.00 | 125 | 960 | — |
| 1908O | 1,789,000 | 3.00 | 8.00 | 39.00 | 52.00 | 72.00 | 130 | 260 | 1,860 | — |
| 1908S | 3,220,000 | 2.75 | 4.50 | 9.00 | 14.00 | 32.00 | 145 | 260 | 2,300 | — |
| 1909 | 10,240,650 | 1.75 | 2.25 | 3.50 | 6.50 | 18.00 | 52.00 | 91.00 | 540 | 1,700 |
| 1909D | 954,000 | 4.00 | 11.00 | 58.00 | 85.00 | 105 | 195 | 390 | 2,300 | — |
| 1909O | 2,287,000 | 2.75 | 5.00 | 8.50 | 15.00 | 27.00 | 91.00 | 180 | 1,250 | — |
| 1909S | 1,000,000 | 5.00 | 13.00 | 78.00 | 110 | 145 | 295 | 470 | 3,000 | — |
| 1910 | 11,520,551 | 1.30 | 2.25 | 5.75 | 10.50 | 20.00 | 52.00 | 91.00 | 540 | 1,450 |
| 1910D | 3,490,000 | 2.75 | 4.75 | 7.75 | 15.00 | 34.00 | 91.00 | 195 | 1,800 | — |
| 1910S | 1,240,000 | 4.00 | 10.00 | 45.00 | 62.00 | 88.00 | 150 | 350 | 1,925 | — |
| 1911 | 18,870,543 | 1.30 | 1.75 | 3.00 | 6.50 | 18.00 | 52.00 | 91.00 | 540 | 1,700 |
| 1911D | 11,209,000 | 1.30 | 1.75 | 3.75 | 7.50 | 20.00 | 52.00 | 91.00 | 685 | — |
| 1911S | 3,520,000 | 1.75 | 2.75 | 7.75 | 15.00 | 31.00 | 85.00 | 145 | 725 | — |
| 1912 | 19,350,700 | 1.30 | 1.75 | 2.75 | 6.50 | 20.00 | 52.00 | 91.00 | 540 | 1,700 |
| 1912D | 11,760,000 | 1.30 | 1.75 | 3.75 | 7.50 | 18.00 | 52.00 | 91.00 | 720 | — |
| 1912S | 3,420,000 | 1.75 | 2.75 | 6.50 | 10.00 | 26.00 | 85.00 | 150 | 1,150 | — |
| 1913 | 19,760,622 | 1.50 | 1.75 | 2.75 | 6.50 | 20.00 | 52.00 | 91.00 | 540 | 1,450 |
| 1913S | 510,000 | 9.00 | 14.00 | 67.00 | 100.00 | 175 | 260 | 390 | 1,100 | — |
| 1914 | 17,360,655 | 1.50 | 1.75 | 3.50 | 6.50 | 18.00 | 52.00 | 91.00 | 540 | 1,700 |
| 1914D | 11,908,000 | 1.50 | 1.75 | 3.50 | 6.75 | 18.00 | 52.00 | 91.00 | 540 | — |
| 1914S | 2,100,000 | 2.00 | 2.40 | 6.50 | 10.00 | 31.00 | 72.00 | 145 | 1,250 | — |
| 1915 | 5,620,450 | 1.50 | 1.75 | 3.90 | 7.00 | 20.00 | 52.00 | 91.00 | 540 | 2,000 |
| 1915S | 960,000 | 3.00 | 5.00 | 29.00 | 39.00 | 52.00 | 125 | 235 | 1,775 | — |
| 1916 | 18,490,000 | 1.30 | 1.75 | 3.75 | 6.00 | 18.00 | 50.00 | 91.00 | 540 | — |
| 1916S | 5,820,000 | 1.50 | 2.25 | 4.75 | 6.50 | 20.00 | 52.00 | 91.00 | 780 | — |

## Mercury.

Mint mark

1942/41

**Designer:** Adolph A. Weinman. **Diameter:** 17.9 mm. **Weight:** 2.5000 g. **Composition:** 0.9000 Silver, 0.0724 oz. ASW. **Notes:** All specimens listed as -65FSB are for fully struck MS-65 coins with fully split and rounded horizontal bands on the fasces. **KM#** 140.

| Date | Mintage | G-4 | VG-8 | F-12 | VF-20 | XF-40 | MS-60 | MS-65 | Prf-65 | -65FSB |
|---|---|---|---|---|---|---|---|---|---|---|
| 1916 | 22,180,080 | 2.75 | 4.00 | 5.50 | 6.00 | 7.50 | 30.00 | 90.00 | — | 120 |
| 1916D | 264,000 | 595 | 800 | 1,300 | 1,650 | 2,650 | 4,800 | 19,000 | — | 35,000 |
| 1916S | 10,450,000 | 3.50 | 4.00 | 7.00 | 8.00 | 16.50 | 34.00 | 170 | — | 600 |
| 1917 | 55,230,000 | 1.25 | 1.60 | 2.00 | 4.75 | 7.00 | 28.00 | 155 | — | 375 |
| 1917D | 9,402,000 | 3.50 | 4.75 | 9.50 | 20.00 | 38.00 | 120 | 1,100 | — | 6,500 |
| 1917S | 27,330,000 | 1.35 | 2.00 | 3.00 | 5.50 | 9.50 | 62.00 | 475 | — | 1,150 |
| 1918 | 26,680,000 | 1.80 | 2.00 | 5.00 | 10.00 | 24.00 | 70.00 | 450 | — | 1,200 |
| 1918D | 22,674,800 | 2.50 | 3.00 | 4.00 | 9.50 | 20.00 | 105 | 600 | — | 35,000 |
| 1918S | 19,300,000 | 2.00 | 2.20 | 3.00 | 8.00 | 14.00 | 90.00 | 675 | — | 7,000 |
| 1919 | 35,740,000 | 1.35 | 1.75 | 2.50 | 5.00 | 9.50 | 37.00 | 320 | — | 700 |
| 1919D | 9,939,000 | 2.50 | 5.00 | 10.00 | 20.00 | 32.00 | 175 | 1,400 | — | 35,000 |
| 1919S | 8,850,000 | 2.50 | 2.75 | 7.00 | 13.00 | 30.00 | 175 | 1,000 | — | 12,500 |
| 1920 | 59,030,000 | 1.35 | 1.60 | 2.00 | 3.50 | 6.50 | 27.50 | 240 | — | 550 |
| 1920D | 19,171,000 | 1.75 | 2.50 | 3.50 | 6.50 | 16.00 | 110 | 750 | — | 4,200 |
| 1920S | 13,820,000 | 1.75 | 2.50 | 3.50 | 7.00 | 15.00 | 110 | 1,300 | — | 9,000 |
| 1921 | 1,230,000 | 29.00 | 45.00 | 78.00 | 170 | 450 | 1,000 | 3,000 | — | 3,750 |
| 1921D | 1,080,000 | 41.00 | 80.00 | 120 | 235 | 500 | 1,100 | 2,800 | — | 5,200 |
| 1923 | 50,130,000 | 1.20 | 1.60 | 2.00 | 3.50 | 6.00 | 27.50 | 110 | — | 295 |
| 1923S | 6,440,000 | 1.75 | 2.50 | 6.50 | 12.00 | 53.00 | 160 | 1,200 | — | 6,750 |
| 1924 | 24,010,000 | 1.35 | 1.65 | 2.50 | 4.25 | 12.00 | 42.00 | 175 | — | 520 |
| 1924D | 6,810,000 | 2.00 | 3.50 | 5.50 | 13.00 | 42.00 | 160 | 1,000 | — | 1,400 |
| 1924S | 7,120,000 | 1.65 | 2.75 | 3.50 | 8.00 | 42.00 | 170 | 1,100 | — | 14,000 |
| 1925 | 25,610,000 | 1.15 | 1.50 | 2.00 | 4.00 | 7.50 | 28.00 | 195 | — | 1,000 |
| 1925D | 5,117,000 | 3.50 | 4.00 | 11.00 | 36.00 | 100.00 | 350 | 1,700 | — | 3,500 |
| 1925S | 5,850,000 | 1.75 | 2.25 | 5.75 | 11.50 | 58.00 | 175 | 1,400 | — | 5,000 |
| 1926 | 32,160,000 | 1.00 | 1.50 | 1.70 | 2.75 | 4.50 | 25.00 | 240 | — | 600 |
| 1926D | 6,828,000 | 2.25 | 3.50 | 4.25 | 8.00 | 22.50 | 110 | 550 | — | 2,850 |
| 1926S | 1,520,000 | 5.75 | 7.50 | 20.00 | 45.00 | 200 | 870 | 3,000 | — | 6,500 |
| 1927 | 28,080,000 | 1.00 | 1.50 | 1.75 | 3.50 | 4.50 | 26.00 | 130 | — | 400 |
| 1927D | 4,812,000 | 2.00 | 4.50 | 6.00 | 18.00 | 60.00 | 175 | 1,200 | — | 8,500 |
| 1927S | 4,770,000 | 1.35 | 3.50 | 4.25 | 7.75 | 22.00 | 280 | 1,400 | — | 7,000 |
| 1928 | 19,480,000 | 1.00 | 1.50 | 1.75 | 3.50 | 4.00 | 27.50 | 110 | — | 350 |
| 1928D | 4,161,000 | 2.75 | 3.25 | 8.00 | 17.00 | 41.00 | 170 | 900 | — | 3,000 |
| 1928S | 7,400,000 | 1.35 | 1.75 | 2.50 | 5.50 | 15.50 | 110 | 425 | — | 2,000 |
| 1929 | 25,970,000 | 1.25 | 1.50 | 2.00 | 2.75 | 4.00 | 20.00 | 60.00 | — | 265 |
| 1929D | 5,034,000 | 1.50 | 3.00 | 3.50 | 6.00 | 14.50 | 25.00 | 70.00 | — | 225 |
| 1929S | 4,730,000 | 1.35 | 1.60 | 2.00 | 4.00 | 7.00 | 32.50 | 120 | — | 600 |
| 1930 | 6,770,000 | 1.35 | 1.50 | 2.00 | 3.50 | 7.00 | 26.00 | 115 | — | 600 |
| 1930S | 1,843,000 | 2.50 | 3.50 | 4.50 | 5.50 | 13.50 | 70.00 | 175 | — | 600 |
| 1931 | 3,150,000 | 2.00 | 2.50 | 3.00 | 4.25 | 8.50 | 35.00 | 135 | — | 900 |
| 1931D | 1,260,000 | 5.00 | 7.00 | 9.00 | 15.00 | 27.50 | 84.00 | 210 | — | 400 |
| 1931S | 1,800,000 | 2.00 | 2.50 | 3.50 | 6.00 | 11.00 | 84.00 | 210 | — | 2,000 |
| 1934 | 24,080,000 | 1.00 | 1.45 | 1.75 | 3.00 | 5.00 | 13.00 | 36.00 | — | 150 |
| 1934D | 6,772,000 | 1.60 | 2.10 | 2.75 | 4.00 | 8.00 | 45.00 | 72.00 | — | 375 |
| 1935 | 58,830,000 | 0.80 | 1.00 | 1.50 | 2.15 | 4.25 | 8.00 | 30.00 | — | 75.00 |
| 1935D | 10,477,000 | 1.25 | 1.75 | 2.50 | 3.75 | 7.50 | 35.00 | 72.00 | — | 600 |
| 1935S | 15,840,000 | 1.25 | 1.50 | 1.75 | 3.00 | 5.50 | 24.00 | 31.50 | — | 550 |
| 1936 | 87,504,130 | 0.80 | 1.00 | 1.50 | 2.25 | 3.50 | 8.00 | 25.00 | — | 90.00 |
| 1936D | 16,132,000 | 1.00 | 1.25 | 1.50 | 3.00 | 6.50 | 26.00 | 42.00 | — | 325 |
| 1936S | 9,210,000 | 1.00 | 1.25 | 1.50 | 2.50 | 3.00 | 20.00 | 28.00 | — | 85.00 |
| 1937 | 56,865,756 | 0.80 | 1.00 | 1.50 | 2.00 | 3.25 | 8.00 | 23.00 | — | 45.00 |
| 1937D | 14,146,000 | 1.00 | 1.25 | 1.50 | 3.00 | 5.50 | 21.00 | 43.00 | — | 120 |
| 1937S | 9,740,000 | 1.00 | 1.25 | 1.50 | 3.00 | 5.50 | 24.00 | 34.00 | — | 195 |
| 1938 | 22,198,728 | 0.80 | 1.00 | 1.50 | 2.25 | 3.50 | 13.00 | 23.00 | — | 80.00 |
| 1938D | 5,537,000 | 1.50 | 1.75 | 2.00 | 3.50 | 6.00 | 16.00 | 26.00 | — | 65.00 |
| 1938S | 8,090,000 | 1.35 | 1.55 | 1.75 | 2.35 | 3.75 | 20.00 | 26.00 | — | 140 |
| 1939 | 67,749,321 | 0.80 | 1.00 | 1.50 | 2.00 | 3.25 | 8.50 | 25.00 | — | 160 |
| 1939D | 24,394,000 | 1.00 | 1.25 | 1.50 | 2.00 | 3.50 | 7.50 | 23.00 | — | 45.00 |
| 1939S | 10,540,000 | 1.25 | 1.50 | 2.00 | 2.50 | 4.25 | 21.00 | 35.00 | — | 750 |
| 1940 | 65,361,827 | 0.60 | 0.70 | 0.90 | 1.10 | 2.50 | 5.00 | 27.00 | — | 55.00 |
| 1940D | 21,198,000 | 0.60 | 0.70 | 0.90 | 1.10 | 1.50 | 7.00 | 30.00 | — | 55.00 |
| 1940S | 21,560,000 | 0.60 | 0.70 | 0.90 | 1.10 | 1.50 | 7.00 | 30.00 | — | 110 |
| 1941 | 175,106,557 | 0.60 | 0.70 | 0.90 | 1.10 | 1.50 | 4.00 | 30.00 | — | 45.00 |
| 1941D | 45,634,000 | 0.60 | 0.70 | 0.90 | 1.10 | 1.50 | 6.00 | 23.00 | — | 40.00 |
| 1941S | 43,090,000 | 0.60 | 0.70 | 0.90 | 1.10 | 1.50 | 7.00 | 30.00 | — | 50.00 |
| 1942 | 205,432,329 | 0.60 | 0.70 | 0.90 | 1.10 | 1.50 | 4.00 | 30.00 | — | 50.00 |
| 1942/41 | Inc. above | 275 | 300 | 360 | 370 | 450 | 1,600 | 7,800 | — | 25,000 |
| 1942D | 60,740,000 | 0.60 | 0.70 | 0.90 | 1.10 | 1.50 | 6.00 | 24.00 | — | 40.00 |
| 1942/41D | Inc. above | 290 | 320 | 400 | 420 | 550 | 1,900 | 5,400 | — | 17,500 |
| 1942S | 49,300,000 | 0.60 | 0.70 | 0.90 | 1.10 | 1.50 | 8.00 | 24.00 | — | 140 |
| 1943 | 191,710,000 | 0.60 | 0.70 | 0.90 | 1.10 | 1.50 | 4.00 | 30.00 | — | 60.00 |
| 1943D | 71,949,000 | 0.60 | 0.70 | 0.90 | 1.10 | 1.50 | 5.50 | 27.50 | — | 40.00 |
| 1943S | 60,400,000 | 0.60 | 0.70 | 0.90 | 1.10 | 1.50 | 7.00 | 25.00 | — | 85.00 |
| 1944 | 231,410,000 | 0.60 | 0.70 | 0.90 | 1.10 | 1.50 | 4.00 | 23.00 | — | 95.00 |
| 1944D | 62,224,000 | 0.60 | 0.70 | 0.90 | 1.10 | 1.50 | 5.50 | 23.00 | — | 43.50 |
| 1944S | 49,490,000 | 0.60 | 0.70 | 0.90 | 1.10 | 1.50 | 6.50 | 30.00 | — | 50.00 |
| 1945 | 159,130,000 | 0.60 | 0.70 | 0.90 | 1.10 | 1.50 | 4.00 | 23.00 | — | 7,000 |
| 1945D | 40,245,000 | 0.60 | 0.70 | 0.90 | 1.10 | 1.50 | 4.50 | 23.00 | — | 45.00 |
| 1945S | 41,920,000 | 0.60 | 0.70 | 0.90 | 1.10 | 1.50 | 6.50 | 29.00 | — | 140 |
| 1945S micro | Inc. above | 1.00 | 1.25 | 1.50 | 3.00 | 4.25 | 23.00 | 84.00 | — | 700 |

## Roosevelt.

Mint mark 1946-64

**Designer:** John R. Sinnock. **Diameter:** 17.9 mm. **Weight:** 2.5000 g. **Composition:** 0.9000 Silver, 0.0724 oz. ASW. **KM#** 195.

| Date | Mintage | G-4 | VG-8 | F-12 | VF-20 | XF-40 | AU-50 | MS-60 | MS-65 | Prf-65 |
|---|---|---|---|---|---|---|---|---|---|---|
| 1946 | 225,250,000 | — | — | — | 0.50 | 0.65 | 0.95 | 1.05 | 4.50 | — |
| 1946D | 61,043,500 | — | — | — | 0.50 | 0.65 | 1.10 | 1.25 | 7.00 | — |
| 1946S | 27,900,000 | — | — | — | 0.50 | 0.65 | 0.90 | 1.50 | 10.00 | — |
| 1947 | 121,520,000 | — | — | — | 0.50 | 0.65 | 0.95 | 1.00 | 4.75 | — |
| 1947D | 46,835,000 | — | — | — | 0.50 | 0.95 | 1.50 | 2.25 | 10.00 | — |
| 1947S | 34,840,000 | — | — | — | 0.50 | 0.95 | 1.25 | 1.75 | 12.50 | — |

| Date | Mintage | G-4 | VG-8 | F-12 | VF-20 | XF-40 | AU-50 | MS-60 | MS-65 | Prf-65 |
|---|---|---|---|---|---|---|---|---|---|---|
| 1948 | 74,950,000 | — | — | — | 0.50 | 0.95 | 1.50 | 3.00 | 14.00 | 0.50 |
| 1948D | 52,841,000 | — | — | — | 0.50 | 1.20 | 2.00 | 2.50 | 10.00 | — |
| 1948S | 35,520,000 | — | — | — | 0.50 | 0.95 | 1.10 | 4.00 | 12.00 | — |
| 1949 | 30,940,000 | — | — | — | 1.00 | 1.50 | 4.00 | 15.00 | 35.00 | — |
| 1949D | 26,034,000 | — | — | 0.60 | 0.80 | 1.25 | 2.00 | 5.50 | 20.00 | — |
| 1949S | 13,510,000 | — | 1.00 | 1.25 | 1.50 | 2.75 | 6.00 | 25.00 | 60.00 | — |
| 1950 | 50,181,500 | — | — | — | 0.50 | 0.95 | 1.35 | 2.50 | 12.00 | 37.00 |
| 1950D | 46,803,000 | — | — | — | 0.50 | 0.65 | 1.60 | 2.75 | 8.00 | — |
| 1950S | 20,440,000 | — | 0.85 | 1.00 | 1.10 | 1.25 | 6.00 | 22.00 | 50.00 | — |
| 1951 | 102,937,602 | — | — | — | 0.50 | 0.85 | 1.00 | 1.25 | 3.50 | 26.00 |
| 1951D | 56,529,000 | — | — | — | 0.50 | 0.65 | 0.95 | 1.40 | 4.00 | — |
| 1951S | 31,630,000 | — | — | — | 0.75 | 1.05 | 3.25 | 5.00 | 24.00 | — |
| 1952 | 99,122,073 | — | — | — | 0.50 | 0.90 | 1.15 | 1.65 | 4.00 | 29.00 |
| 1952D | 122,100,000 | — | — | — | 0.50 | 0.65 | 0.95 | 1.00 | 4.00 | — |
| 1952S | 44,419,500 | — | — | — | 0.75 | 1.05 | 1.50 | 3.00 | 11.00 | — |
| 1953 | 53,618,920 | — | — | — | 0.50 | 0.65 | 1.00 | 1.10 | 4.00 | 24.00 |
| 1953D | 136,433,000 | — | — | — | 0.50 | 0.65 | 0.95 | 1.00 | 3.50 | — |
| 1953S | 39,180,000 | — | — | — | 0.50 | 0.65 | 0.75 | 1.00 | 3.25 | — |
| 1954 | 114,243,503 | — | — | — | 0.50 | 0.65 | 0.75 | 1.00 | 3.25 | 11.00 |
| 1954D | 106,397,000 | — | — | — | 0.50 | 0.65 | 0.75 | 1.00 | 3.25 | — |
| 1954S | 22,860,000 | — | — | — | 0.50 | 0.65 | 0.80 | 0.90 | 3.25 | — |
| 1955 | 12,828,381 | — | — | — | 0.70 | 0.80 | 0.85 | 0.95 | 5.00 | 15.00 |
| 1955D | 13,959,000 | — | — | — | 0.65 | 0.75 | 0.80 | 0.90 | 3.50 | — |
| 1955S | 18,510,000 | — | — | — | 0.65 | 0.75 | 0.80 | 0.90 | 4.50 | — |
| 1956 | 109,309,384 | — | — | — | 0.50 | 0.50 | 0.60 | 0.90 | 2.50 | 2.50 |
| 1956D | 108,015,100 | — | — | — | 0.50 | 0.50 | 0.60 | 0.90 | 2.50 | — |
| 1957 | 161,407,952 | — | — | — | 0.50 | 0.50 | 0.60 | 0.90 | 2.60 | 2.00 |
| 1957D | 113,354,330 | — | — | — | 0.50 | 0.50 | 0.60 | 1.00 | 3.50 | — |
| 1958 | 32,785,652 | — | — | — | 0.50 | 0.50 | 0.60 | 0.90 | 3.80 | 2.00 |
| 1958D | 136,564,600 | — | — | — | 0.50 | 0.50 | 0.60 | 0.90 | 3.50 | — |
| 1959 | 86,929,291 | — | — | — | 0.50 | 0.50 | 0.60 | 0.90 | 2.50 | 2.00 |
| 1959D | 164,919,790 | — | — | — | 0.50 | 0.50 | 0.60 | 0.90 | 3.00 | — |
| 1960 | 72,081,602 | — | — | — | 0.50 | 0.50 | 0.60 | 0.90 | 2.50 | 2.00 |
| 1960D | 200,160,400 | — | — | — | 0.50 | 0.50 | 0.60 | 0.90 | 2.50 | — |
| 1961 | 96,758,244 | — | — | — | 0.50 | 0.50 | 0.60 | 0.90 | 2.35 | 2.00 |
| 1961D | 209,146,550 | — | — | — | 0.50 | 0.50 | 0.60 | 0.90 | 2.35 | — |
| 1962 | 75,668,019 | — | — | — | 0.50 | 0.50 | 0.60 | 0.90 | 2.35 | 2.00 |
| 1962D | 334,948,380 | — | — | — | 0.50 | 0.50 | 0.60 | 0.90 | 2.75 | — |
| 1963 | 126,725,645 | — | — | — | 0.50 | 0.50 | 0.60 | 0.90 | 2.35 | 2.00 |
| 1963D | 421,476,530 | — | — | — | 0.50 | 0.50 | 0.60 | 0.90 | 2.35 | — |
| 1964 | 933,310,762 | — | — | — | 0.50 | 0.50 | 0.60 | 0.90 | 2.35 | 2.00 |
| 1964D | 1,357,517,180 | — | — | — | 0.50 | 0.50 | 0.60 | 0.90 | 2.35 | — |

Mint mark 1968 - Present

1982 No mint mark

**Designer:** John R. Sinnock. **Diameter:** 17.9 mm. **Weight:** 2.2700 g. **Composition:** Copper-Nickel Clad Copper. **Notes:** The 1979-S and 1981-S Type II proofs have clearer mint marks than the Type I proofs of those years. On the 1982 no-mint-mark variety, the mint mark was inadvertently left off. **KM#** 195a.

| Date | Mintage | MS-65 | Prf-65 |
|---|---|---|---|
| 1965 | 1,652,140,570 | 0.75 | — |
| 1966 | 1,382,734,540 | 0.65 | — |
| 1967 | 2,244,007,320 | 0.65 | — |
| 1968 | 424,470,000 | 0.60 | — |
| 1968D | 480,748,280 | 0.60 | — |
| 1968S | (3,041,506) | — | 0.75 |
| 1969 | 145,790,000 | 0.75 | — |
| 1969D | 563,323,870 | 0.75 | — |
| 1969S | (2,934,631) | — | 0.65 |
| 1970 | 345,570,000 | 0.60 | — |
| 1970D | 754,942,100 | 0.60 | — |
| 1970S | (2,632,810) | — | 0.65 |
| 1971 | 162,690,000 | 0.75 | — |
| 1971D | 377,914,240 | 0.60 | — |
| 1971S | (3,220,733) | — | 0.60 |
| 1972 | 431,540,000 | 0.60 | — |
| 1972D | 330,290,000 | 0.60 | — |
| 1972S | (3,260,996) | — | 1.00 |
| 1973 | 315,670,000 | 0.60 | — |
| 1973D | 455,032,426 | 0.50 | — |
| 1973S | (2,760,339) | — | 1.00 |
| 1974 | 470,248,000 | 0.50 | — |
| 1974D | 571,083,000 | 0.50 | — |
| 1974S | (2,612,568) | — | 1.00 |
| 1975 | 585,673,900 | 0.60 | — |
| 1975D | 313,705,300 | 0.50 | — |
| 1975S | (2,845,450) | — | 1.25 |
| 1976 | 568,760,000 | 0.60 | — |
| 1976D | 695,222,774 | 0.60 | — |
| 1976S | (4,149,730) | — | 1.00 |
| 1977 | 796,930,000 | 0.50 | — |
| 1977D | 376,607,228 | 0.50 | — |
| 1977S | (3,251,152) | — | 1.00 |
| 1978 | 663,980,000 | 0.50 | — |
| 1978D | 282,847,540 | 0.50 | — |
| 1978S | (3,127,781) | — | 1.00 |
| 1979 | 315,440,000 | 0.50 | — |
| 1979D | 390,921,184 | 0.50 | — |
| 1979 type I | — | — | 1.00 |
| 1979S type I | — | — | 1.00 |
| 1979S type II | — | — | 1.25 |
| 1980P | 735,170,000 | 0.50 | — |
| 1980D | 719,354,321 | 0.50 | — |
| 1980S | (3,554,806) | — | 1.00 |
| 1981P | 676,650,000 | 0.50 | — |
| 1981D | 712,284,143 | 0.50 | — |
| 1981S type I | — | — | 1.00 |
| 1981S type II | — | — | 4.00 |
| 1982P | 519,475,000 | 1.50 | — |
| 1982 no mint mark | — | 200 | — |
| 1982D | 542,713,584 | 2.00 | — |
| 1982S | (3,857,479) | — | 1.20 |
| 1983P | 647,025,000 | 0.75 | — |
| 1983D | 730,129,224 | 0.70 | — |
| 1983S | (3,279,126) | — | 1.10 |
| 1984P | 856,669,000 | 0.50 | — |
| 1984D | 704,803,976 | 0.60 | — |
| 1984S | (3,065,110) | — | 1.60 |
| 1985P | 705,200,962 | 0.60 | — |
| 1985D | 587,979,970 | 0.55 | — |
| 1985S | (3,362,821) | — | 1.10 |
| 1986P | 682,649,693 | 0.70 | — |
| 1986D | 473,326,970 | 0.75 | — |
| 1986S | (3,010,497) | — | 2.50 |
| 1987P | 762,709,481 | 0.50 | — |
| 1987D | 653,203,402 | 0.50 | — |
| 1987S | (4,227,728) | — | 1.50 |
| 1988P | 1,030,550,000 | 0.50 | — |
| 1988D | 962,385,488 | 0.50 | — |
| 1988S | (3,262,948) | — | 3.50 |
| 1989P | 1,298,400,000 | 0.50 | — |
| 1989D | 896,535,597 | 0.50 | — |
| 1989S | (3,220,194) | — | 4.00 |
| 1990P | 1,034,340,000 | 0.50 | — |
| 1990D | 839,995,824 | 0.50 | — |
| 1990S | (3,299,559) | — | 2.75 |
| 1991P | 927,220,000 | 0.50 | — |
| 1991D | 601,241,114 | 0.50 | — |
| 1991S | (2,867,787) | — | 3.25 |
| 1992P | 593,500,000 | 0.50 | — |
| 1992D | 616,273,932 | 0.50 | — |
| 1992S | (2,858,981) | — | 4.00 |
| 1993P | 766,180,000 | 0.50 | — |
| 1993D | 750,110,166 | 0.50 | — |
| 1993S | (2,633,439) | — | 6.00 |
| 1994P | 1,189,000,000 | 0.50 | — |
| 1994D | 1,303,268,110 | 0.50 | — |
| 1994S | (2,484,594) | — | 4.50 |
| 1995P | 1,125,500,000 | 0.50 | — |
| 1995D | 1,274,890,000 | 0.50 | — |
| 1995S | (2,010,384) | — | 20.00 |
| 1996P | 1,421,163,000 | 0.50 | — |
| 1996D | 1,400,300,000 | 0.50 | — |
| 1996W | 1,457,949 | 8.00 | — |
| 1996S | — | — | 2.50 |
| 1997P | 991,640,000 | 0.50 | — |
| 1997D | 979,810,000 | 0.50 | — |
| 1997S | (1,975,000) | — | 6.50 |
| 1998P | 1,163,000,000 | 0.50 | — |
| 1998D | 1,172,250,000 | 0.50 | — |
| 1998S | — | — | 3.50 |
| 1999P | — | 0.50 | — |
| 1999D | — | 0.50 | — |
| 1999S | — | — | 3.00 |
| 2000P | — | 0.50 | — |
| 2000D | — | 0.50 | — |
| 2000S | — | — | 2.00 |
| 2001P | — | 0.50 | — |
| 2001D | — | 0.50 | — |
| 2001S | — | — | 3.00 |
| 2002P | — | — | — |
| 2002D | — | — | — |
| 2002S | — | — | — |

**Composition:** Silver. **KM#** A195.

| Date | Mintage | Prf-65 |
|---|---|---|
| 1992S | (1,317,579) | 4.50 |
| 1993S | (761,353) | 6.00 |
| 1994S | (785,329) | 6.00 |
| 1995S | (838,953) | 18.00 |
| 1996S | — | 6.00 |
| 1997S | — | 3.50 |
| 1998S | — | 5.50 |
| 1999S | — | 5.00 |
| 2000S | — | 4.50 |
| 2001S | — | 4.50 |
| 2002S | — | — |

# QUARTER

## Barber.

**Designer:** Charles E. Barber. **Diameter:** 24.3 mm. **Weight:** 6.2500 g. **Composition:** 0.9000 Silver, 0.1809 oz. ASW. **Notes:** Commonly called "Barber quarter." **KM#** 114.

| Date | Mintage | G-4 | VG-8 | F-12 | VF-20 | XF-40 | AU-50 | MS-60 | MS-65 | Prf-65 |
|---|---|---|---|---|---|---|---|---|---|---|
| 1901 | 8,892,813 | 5.75 | 6.75 | 18.00 | 30.00 | 65.00 | 115 | 170 | 2,350 | 2,200 |
| 1901O | 1,612,000 | 25.00 | 37.50 | 86.00 | 180 | 350 | 625 | 800 | 5,750 | — |
| 1901S | 72,664 | 2,400 | 3,600 | 5,500 | 7,500 | 9,900 | 11,500 | 16,500 | 45,000 | — |
| 1902 | 12,197,744 | 4.00 | 4.50 | 17.00 | 29.00 | 65.00 | 110 | 170 | 1,250 | 2,100 |
| 1902O | 4,748,000 | 5.25 | 11.50 | 35.00 | 54.00 | 100.00 | 180 | 385 | 5,250 | — |
| 1902S | 1,524,612 | 7.75 | 13.50 | 38.00 | 56.00 | 115 | 190 | 500 | 3,500 | — |
| 1903 | 9,670,064 | 4.00 | 5.50 | 17.00 | 29.00 | 65.00 | 110 | 170 | 2,500 | 2,000 |
| 1903O | 3,500,000 | 5.25 | 7.00 | 33.00 | 46.00 | 86.00 | 235 | 400 | 6,500 | — |
| 1903S | 1,036,000 | 9.00 | 17.50 | 37.50 | 60.00 | 100.00 | 260 | 425 | 2,600 | — |
| 1904 | 9,588,813 | 3.75 | 5.50 | 17.50 | 30.00 | 65.00 | 110 | 170 | 1,650 | 2,000 |
| 1904O | 2,456,000 | 6.50 | 11.00 | 45.00 | 72.00 | 175 | 375 | 775 | 3,100 | — |
| 1905 | 4,968,250 | 4.40 | 6.00 | 24.00 | 32.00 | 65.00 | 110 | 175 | 1,950 | 2,000 |
| 1905O | 1,230,000 | 8.00 | 16.00 | 62.00 | 110 | 195 | 340 | 465 | 6,000 | — |
| 1905S | 1,884,000 | 6.00 | 11.00 | 34.00 | 48.00 | 90.00 | 210 | 340 | 4,100 | — |
| 1906 | 3,656,435 | 3.50 | 5.50 | 16.00 | 30.00 | 67.00 | 110 | 170 | 1,300 | 2,000 |
| 1906D | 3,280,000 | 3.75 | 6.00 | 23.00 | 37.50 | 67.00 | 150 | 210 | 2,500 | — |
| 1906O | 2,056,000 | 3.75 | 7.50 | 30.00 | 42.50 | 86.00 | 185 | 285 | 1,400 | — |
| 1907 | 7,192,575 | 3.25 | 4.25 | 17.00 | 30.00 | 65.00 | 110 | 170 | 1,250 | 2,000 |
| 1907D | 2,484,000 | 3.75 | 6.25 | 25.00 | 40.00 | 80.00 | 175 | 240 | 2,500 | — |
| 1907O | 4,560,000 | 3.75 | 5.75 | 17.00 | 32.00 | 67.00 | 135 | 200 | 2,400 | — |
| 1907S | 1,360,000 | 5.00 | 8.75 | 38.00 | 58.00 | 125 | 270 | 440 | 3,600 | — |
| 1908 | 4,232,545 | 3.75 | 5.50 | 19.00 | 30.00 | 67.00 | 110 | 195 | 1,400 | 2,200 |
| 1908D | 5,788,000 | 3.75 | 4.25 | 17.00 | 29.00 | 67.00 | 115 | 215 | 1,750 | — |
| 1908O | 6,244,000 | 3.75 | 4.25 | 17.00 | 29.00 | 72.00 | 125 | 195 | 1,250 | — |
| 1908S | 784,000 | 12.00 | 20.00 | 65.00 | 110 | 240 | 420 | 700 | 5,800 | — |
| 1909 | 9,268,650 | 3.25 | 4.25 | 17.00 | 29.00 | 65.00 | 110 | 170 | 1,250 | 2,000 |
| 1909D | 5,114,000 | 3.75 | 4.25 | 17.00 | 30.00 | 70.00 | 150 | 190 | 2,100 | — |
| 1909O | 712,000 | 12.00 | 25.00 | 67.00 | 160 | 290 | 460 | 750 | 8,500 | — |
| 1909S | 1,348,000 | 3.75 | 6.25 | 27.00 | 40.00 | 68.00 | 185 | 275 | 2,800 | — |
| 1910 | 2,244,551 | 3.75 | 5.00 | 23.00 | 33.00 | 68.00 | 145 | 190 | 1,425 | 2,000 |
| 1910D | 1,500,000 | 5.50 | 6.50 | 36.50 | 55.00 | 98.00 | 220 | 340 | 2,400 | — |
| 1911 | 3,720,543 | 3.50 | 5.50 | 17.00 | 30.00 | 72.00 | 120 | 180 | 1,250 | 2,000 |
| 1911D | 933,600 | 6.50 | 11.00 | 67.00 | 175 | 300 | 450 | 625 | 5,250 | — |
| 1911S | 988,000 | 5.00 | 7.50 | 45.00 | 60.00 | 135 | 300 | 375 | 1,750 | — |
| 1912 | 4,400,700 | 3.75 | 5.25 | 16.00 | 32.00 | 65.00 | 110 | 170 | 1,250 | 2,000 |
| 1912S | 708,000 | 5.25 | 6.50 | 37.50 | 56.00 | 95.00 | 225 | 375 | 3,200 | — |
| 1913 | 484,613 | 8.50 | 15.00 | 60.00 | 139 | 385 | 495 | 900 | 4,250 | 2,200 |
| 1913D | 1,450,800 | 5.50 | 8.50 | 30.00 | 45.00 | 75.00 | 155 | 265 | 1,375 | — |
| 1913S | 40,000 | 525 | 775 | 2,000 | 3,000 | 3,650 | 4,350 | 4,850 | 13,500 | — |
| 1914 | 6,244,610 | 3.60 | 4.75 | 16.00 | 26.50 | 55.00 | 110 | 170 | 1,250 | 2,200 |
| 1914D | 3,046,000 | 3.60 | 4.25 | 15.00 | 26.50 | 58.00 | 110 | 170 | 1,250 | — |
| 1914S | 264,000 | 55.00 | 75.00 | 145 | 180 | 375 | 575 | 875 | 3,250 | — |
| 1915 | 3,480,450 | 3.60 | 4.25 | 15.00 | 26.50 | 65.00 | 110 | 170 | 1,250 | 2,200 |
| 1915D | 3,694,000 | 3.60 | 4.25 | 15.00 | 26.50 | 65.00 | 110 | 170 | 1,250 | — |
| 1915S | 704,000 | 4.00 | 6.00 | 23.50 | 37.50 | 77.00 | 185 | 225 | 1,400 | — |
| 1916 | 1,788,000 | 3.50 | 4.25 | 16.00 | 30.00 | 70.00 | 115 | 170 | 1,250 | — |
| 1916D | 6,540,800 | 3.50 | 4.25 | 15.00 | 27.50 | 55.00 | 110 | 170 | 1,250 | — |

## Standing Liberty. Right breast exposed; Type 1.

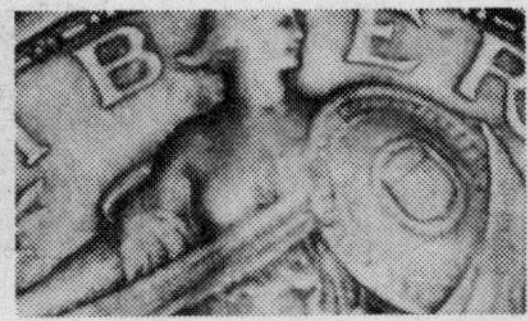

**Designer:** Hermon A. MacNeil. **Diameter:** 24.3 mm. **Weight:** 6.2500 g. **Composition:** 0.9000 Silver, 0.1809 oz. ASW. **KM#** 141.

| Date | Mintage | G-4 | VG-8 | F-12 | VF-20 | XF-40 | AU-50 | MS-60 | MS-65 | -65FH |
|---|---|---|---|---|---|---|---|---|---|---|
| 1916 | 52,000 | 1,500 | 2,100 | 2,750 | 3,250 | 4,150 | 5,500 | 6,000 | 14,500 | 24,000 |
| 1917 | 8,792,000 | 17.50 | 21.00 | 35.00 | 46.00 | 62.00 | 135 | 250 | 750 | 1,450 |
| 1917D | 1,509,200 | 22.50 | 26.00 | 39.00 | 55.00 | 85.00 | 150 | 225 | 850 | 1,900 |
| 1917S | 1,952,000 | 21.50 | 24.00 | 39.00 | 67.00 | 140 | 190 | 250 | 1,600 | 2,675 |

## Standing Liberty. Right breast covered; Type 2. Three stars below eagle.

**Designer:** Hermon A. MacNeil. **Diameter:** 24.3 mm. **Weight:** 6.2500 g. **Composition:** 0.9000 Silver, 0.1809 oz. ASW. **KM#** 145.

| Date | Mintage | G-4 | VG-8 | F-12 | VF-20 | XF-40 | AU-50 | MS-60 | MS-65 | -65FH |
|---|---|---|---|---|---|---|---|---|---|---|
| 1917 | 13,880,000 | 14.00 | 20.00 | 23.00 | 27.50 | 48.00 | 75.00 | 135 | 640 | 925 |
| 1917D | 6,224,400 | 26.00 | 35.00 | 65.00 | 68.00 | 94.00 | 125 | 190 | 1,400 | 3,500 |
| 1917S | 5,522,000 | 24.00 | 35.00 | 47.50 | 55.00 | 75.00 | 105 | 195 | 1,150 | 3,300 |
| 1918 | 14,240,000 | 14.00 | 21.00 | 28.50 | 35.00 | 45.00 | 80.00 | 140 | 625 | 1,700 |
| 1918D | 7,380,000 | 25.00 | 35.00 | 44.00 | 65.00 | 87.00 | 135 | 220 | 1,395 | 5,500 |
| 1918S | 11,072,000 | 15.00 | 21.00 | 39.00 | 42.00 | 49.50 | 85.00 | 175 | 1,300 | 18,000 |
| 1918/17S | Inc. above | 1,400 | 1,500 | 2,100 | 2,900 | 4,900 | 8,900 | 14,500 | 85,000 | 300,000 |
| 1919 | 11,324,000 | 27.00 | 37.00 | 44.00 | 50.00 | 65.50 | 95.00 | 150 | 600 | 1,450 |
| 1919D | 1,944,000 | 65.00 | 85.00 | 135 | 189 | 300 | 495 | 650 | 2,500 | 24,500 |
| 1919S | 1,836,000 | 60.00 | 87.00 | 135 | 225 | 395 | 550 | 925 | 3,300 | 31,000 |
| 1920 | 27,860,000 | 12.50 | 17.50 | 28.00 | 33.00 | 39.00 | 69.00 | 130 | 550 | 1,900 |
| 1920D | 3,586,400 | 37.50 | 49.00 | 70.00 | 90.00 | 120 | 180 | 250 | 2,100 | 6,250 |
| 1920S | 6,380,000 | 15.00 | 22.00 | 28.00 | 38.00 | 57.50 | 98.00 | 250 | 2,400 | 30,000 |
| 1921 | 1,916,000 | 85.00 | 110 | 145 | 210 | 295 | 325 | 450 | 1,650 | 3,975 |
| 1923 | 9,716,000 | 14.00 | 18.00 | 27.00 | 32.50 | 39.00 | 67.00 | 125 | 550 | 3,950 |
| 1923S | 1,360,000 | 225 | 300 | 340 | 380 | 475 | 550 | 660 | 1,800 | 3,500 |
| 1924 | 10,920,000 | 13.50 | 16.50 | 20.00 | 24.00 | 32.00 | 64.00 | 120 | 495 | 1,400 |
| 1924D | 3,112,000 | 45.00 | 52.50 | 65.00 | 75.00 | 95.00 | 130 | 155 | 560 | 4,900 |
| 1924S | 2,860,000 | 25.00 | 29.50 | 37.50 | 42.50 | 87.00 | 175 | 360 | 2,000 | 5,250 |
| 1925 | 12,280,000 | 2.50 | 3.25 | 5.50 | 14.00 | 30.00 | 65.00 | 120 | 550 | 950 |
| 1926 | 11,316,000 | 2.50 | 3.00 | 5.00 | 13.00 | 29.00 | 62.00 | 115 | 500 | 2,250 |
| 1926D | 1,716,000 | 6.50 | 10.00 | 15.00 | 34.00 | 65.00 | 95.00 | 135 | 525 | 26,000 |
| 1926S | 2,700,000 | 3.25 | 4.00 | 12.00 | 25.00 | 99.00 | 295 | 350 | 2,100 | 28,000 |
| 1927 | 11,912,000 | 2.50 | 5.00 | 6.00 | 13.00 | 32.00 | 60.00 | 110 | 490 | 950 |
| 1927D | 976,400 | 7.00 | 12.00 | 16.00 | 39.00 | 90.00 | 135 | 175 | 550 | 3,000 |
| 1927S | 396,000 | 10.00 | 12.50 | 55.00 | 165 | 1,000 | 2,750 | 3,500 | 9,700 | 175,000 |
| 1928 | 6,336,000 | 2.50 | 4.00 | 5.00 | 12.00 | 29.00 | 58.50 | 110 | 525 | 1,500 |
| 1928D | 1,627,600 | 4.50 | 7.00 | 9.50 | 22.00 | 36.00 | 75.00 | 140 | 535 | 5,900 |
| 1928S | 2,644,000 | 3.00 | 3.50 | 6.00 | 13.50 | 32.00 | 70.00 | 135 | 540 | 900 |
| 1929 | 11,140,000 | 2.50 | 5.00 | 6.00 | 13.00 | 29.00 | 60.00 | 110 | 475 | 750 |
| 1929D | 1,358,000 | 4.75 | 6.00 | 9.50 | 18.00 | 32.00 | 70.00 | 140 | 525 | 6,250 |
| 1929S | 1,764,000 | 3.25 | 4.75 | 5.50 | 15.00 | 30.00 | 64.00 | 120 | 490 | 750 |
| 1930 | 5,632,000 | 2.50 | 4.00 | 5.00 | 12.00 | 29.00 | 60.00 | 100.00 | 475 | 725 |
| 1930S | 1,556,000 | 3.50 | 4.00 | 6.50 | 15.50 | 35.00 | 70.00 | 130 | 525 | 900 |

## Washington.

Mint mark 1932-64

**Designer:** John Flanagan. **Diameter:** 24.3 mm. **Weight:** 6.2500 g. **Composition:** 0.9000 Silver, 0.1809 oz. ASW. **KM#** 164.

| Date | Mintage | G-4 | VG-8 | F-12 | VF-20 | XF-40 | AU-50 | MS-60 | MS-65 | Prf-65 |
|---|---|---|---|---|---|---|---|---|---|---|
| 1932 | 5,404,000 | 3.75 | 5.00 | 6.00 | 7.50 | 9.00 | 14.00 | 21.00 | 350 | — |
| 1932D | 436,800 | 55.00 | 70.00 | 80.00 | 95.00 | 160 | 325 | 600 | 9,500 | — |
| 1932S | 408,000 | 60.00 | 70.00 | 75.00 | 85.00 | 110 | 165 | 280 | 3,200 | — |
| 1934 | 31,912,052 | 2.00 | 2.25 | 2.50 | 3.00 | 4.00 | 9.00 | 22.00 | 75.00 | — |
| 1934D | 3,527,200 | 3.75 | 5.75 | 7.00 | 10.00 | 17.00 | 80.00 | 195 | 1,350 | — |
| 1935 | 32,484,000 | 1.75 | 2.00 | 2.50 | 2.75 | 4.00 | 8.00 | 21.00 | 70.00 | — |
| 1935D | 5,780,000 | 2.00 | 3.25 | 4.50 | 10.00 | 19.00 | 95.00 | 220 | 700 | — |
| 1935S | 5,660,000 | 2.00 | 2.75 | 5.00 | 6.00 | 12.50 | 30.00 | 70.00 | 300 | — |
| 1936 | 41,303,837 | 1.75 | 2.00 | 2.25 | 2.75 | 3.50 | 8.50 | 21.00 | 70.00 | 1,050 |
| 1936D | 5,374,000 | 2.25 | 2.75 | 4.75 | 15.00 | 44.00 | 200 | 400 | 850 | — |
| 1936S | 3,828,000 | 2.75 | 3.00 | 3.50 | 5.50 | 11.00 | 45.00 | 74.00 | 225 | — |
| 1937 | 19,701,542 | 1.75 | 2.00 | 3.00 | 3.50 | 3.75 | 16.00 | 22.00 | 90.00 | 380 |
| 1937D | 7,189,600 | 1.90 | 2.50 | 3.00 | 4.50 | 12.00 | 28.00 | 52.00 | 135 | — |
| 1937S | 1,652,000 | 3.50 | 4.50 | 6.00 | 11.50 | 19.00 | 85.00 | 110 | 275 | — |
| 1938 | 9,480,045 | 2.75 | 3.75 | 5.00 | 6.00 | 15.00 | 35.00 | 63.00 | 180 | 225 |
| 1938S | 2,832,000 | 3.00 | 4.00 | 5.50 | 7.00 | 15.00 | 38.00 | 65.00 | 185 | — |
| 1939 | 33,548,795 | 1.75 | 2.00 | 2.25 | 2.50 | 3.50 | 7.00 | 14.00 | 70.00 | 150 |
| 1939D | 7,092,000 | 2.00 | 2.25 | 3.25 | 4.00 | 8.00 | 16.00 | 34.00 | 85.00 | — |
| 1939S | 2,628,000 | 3.00 | 3.25 | 3.75 | 6.50 | 14.00 | 44.00 | 72.00 | 175 | — |
| 1940 | 35,715,246 | 1.75 | 2.00 | 2.25 | 2.50 | 3.00 | 6.50 | 12.50 | 65.00 | 150 |
| 1940D | 2,797,600 | 2.00 | 2.50 | 6.00 | 8.50 | 18.00 | 47.00 | 75.00 | 185 | — |
| 1940S | 8,244,000 | 1.75 | 2.25 | 4.75 | 5.00 | 6.50 | 14.00 | 24.00 | 55.00 | — |
| 1941 | 79,047,287 | — | — | 1.65 | 1.75 | 2.50 | 4.00 | 6.00 | 50.00 | 110 |
| 1941D | 16,714,800 | — | — | 1.75 | 2.25 | 3.50 | 7.50 | 20.00 | 90.00 | — |
| 1941S | 16,080,000 | — | — | 1.75 | 2.25 | 3.25 | 6.50 | 20.00 | 80.00 | — |
| 1942 | 102,117,123 | — | — | 1.65 | 1.75 | 2.50 | 3.00 | 4.00 | 45.00 | 110 |
| 1942D | 17,487,200 | — | — | 1.75 | 2.50 | 3.75 | 7.00 | 13.50 | 50.00 | — |
| 1942S | 19,384,000 | — | — | 2.00 | 3.00 | 5.50 | 16.00 | 55.00 | 140 | — |
| 1943 | 99,700,000 | — | — | 1.50 | 1.75 | 2.10 | 2.75 | 3.50 | 45.00 | — |
| 1943D | 16,095,600 | — | — | 1.75 | 2.25 | 4.00 | 7.00 | 22.00 | 65.00 | — |
| 1943S | 21,700,000 | — | — | 1.75 | 2.25 | 5.50 | 11.00 | 27.00 | 75.00 | — |

| Date | Mintage | G-4 | VG-8 | F-12 | VF-20 | XF-40 | AU-50 | MS-60 | MS-65 | Prf-65 |
|---|---|---|---|---|---|---|---|---|---|---|
| 1944 | 104,956,000 | — | — | 1.50 | 1.75 | 2.10 | 2.85 | 3.75 | 45.00 | — |
| 1944D | 14,600,800 | — | — | 1.75 | 2.50 | 3.75 | 8.00 | 14.00 | 46.00 | — |
| 1944S | 12,560,000 | — | — | 1.85 | 2.75 | 4.00 | 9.00 | 14.00 | 45.00 | — |
| 1945 | 74,372,000 | — | — | 1.50 | 1.75 | 2.10 | 2.85 | 3.75 | 45.00 | — |
| 1945D | 12,341,600 | — | — | 1.75 | 3.00 | 6.00 | 10.50 | 16.00 | 55.00 | — |
| 1945S | 17,004,001 | — | — | 1.65 | 2.50 | 3.75 | 6.00 | 8.00 | 42.00 | — |
| 1946 | 53,436,000 | — | — | 1.50 | 1.85 | 2.25 | 2.75 | 3.75 | 42.00 | — |
| 1946D | 9,072,800 | — | — | 1.50 | 1.85 | 2.25 | 2.75 | 4.00 | 43.00 | — |
| 1946S | 4,204,000 | — | — | 1.65 | 2.00 | 3.00 | 4.00 | 6.00 | 43.00 | — |
| 1947 | 22,556,000 | — | — | 1.65 | 2.25 | 2.75 | 3.50 | 5.00 | 43.00 | — |
| 1947D | 15,338,400 | — | — | 1.65 | 2.25 | 2.50 | 2.75 | 4.50 | 43.00 | — |
| 1947S | 5,532,000 | — | — | 1.65 | 2.25 | 2.75 | 3.00 | 6.00 | 45.00 | — |
| 1948 | 35,196,000 | — | — | 1.65 | 1.85 | 2.25 | 2.75 | 3.50 | 43.00 | — |
| 1948D | 16,766,800 | — | — | 1.65 | 1.85 | 2.25 | 2.75 | 4.00 | 43.00 | — |
| 1948S | 15,960,000 | — | — | 1.75 | 1.95 | 2.50 | 3.00 | 4.50 | 44.00 | — |
| 1949 | 9,312,000 | — | — | 1.65 | 2.50 | 4.50 | 13.00 | 25.00 | 75.00 | — |
| 1949D | 10,068,400 | — | — | 1.60 | 2.25 | 4.00 | 6.00 | 12.00 | 60.00 | — |
| 1950 | 24,971,512 | — | — | 1.50 | 1.65 | 1.75 | 2.10 | 3.00 | 28.00 | 55.00 |
| 1950D | 21,075,600 | — | — | 1.65 | 1.85 | 2.10 | 2.40 | 3.25 | 30.00 | — |
| 1950D/S | Inc. above | 22.00 | 25.00 | 36.00 | 60.00 | 150 | 225 | 275 | 800 | — |
| 1950S | 10,284,004 | — | — | 1.65 | 1.85 | 2.40 | 4.50 | 6.50 | 25.00 | — |
| 1950S/D | Inc. above | 25.00 | 30.00 | 40.00 | 65.00 | 190 | 315 | 400 | 775 | — |
| 1951 | 43,505,602 | — | — | 1.50 | 1.65 | 1.75 | 2.25 | 4.50 | 28.00 | 40.00 |
| 1951D | 35,354,800 | — | — | 1.50 | 1.75 | 2.00 | 2.25 | 3.00 | 35.00 | — |
| 1951S | 9,048,000 | — | — | 1.50 | 1.75 | 3.75 | 7.00 | 17.00 | 55.00 | — |
| 1952 | 38,862,073 | — | — | 1.50 | 1.65 | 1.75 | 2.25 | 3.50 | 28.00 | 37.00 |
| 1952D | 49,795,200 | — | — | 1.50 | 1.65 | 1.75 | 2.25 | 3.25 | 28.00 | — |
| 1952S | 13,707,800 | — | — | 1.50 | 1.75 | 3.25 | 7.00 | 15.00 | 45.00 | — |
| 1953 | 18,664,920 | — | — | 1.50 | 1.65 | 1.75 | 2.10 | 3.25 | 28.00 | 25.00 |
| 1953D | 56,112,400 | — | — | 1.50 | 1.65 | 1.75 | 1.95 | 2.50 | 25.00 | — |
| 1953S | 14,016,000 | — | — | 1.50 | 1.75 | 2.10 | 2.75 | 4.00 | 28.00 | — |
| 1954 | 54,645,503 | — | — | — | 1.50 | 1.65 | 1.75 | 3.00 | 28.00 | 13.00 |
| 1954D | 42,305,500 | — | — | — | 1.50 | 1.65 | 1.75 | 3.00 | 28.00 | — |
| 1954S | 11,834,722 | — | — | — | 1.50 | 1.75 | 2.00 | 2.75 | 25.00 | — |
| 1955 | 18,558,381 | — | — | — | 1.65 | 1.75 | 2.00 | 2.50 | 25.00 | 14.00 |
| 1955D | 3,182,400 | — | — | 1.65 | 2.00 | 2.50 | 2.75 | 3.00 | 25.00 | — |
| 1956 | 44,813,384 | — | — | — | 1.65 | 1.85 | 2.00 | 2.50 | 20.00 | 4.00 |
| 1956D | 32,334,500 | — | — | — | 1.75 | 1.85 | 2.10 | 2.40 | 24.00 | — |
| 1957 | 47,779,952 | — | — | — | 1.65 | 1.75 | 1.95 | 2.25 | 26.00 | 4.00 |
| 1957D | 77,924,160 | — | — | — | 1.65 | 1.75 | 1.95 | 2.50 | 20.00 | — |
| 1958 | 7,235,652 | — | — | — | 1.65 | 1.75 | 2.00 | 2.75 | 20.00 | 6.00 |
| 1958D | 78,124,900 | — | — | — | 1.65 | 1.75 | 1.95 | 2.25 | 20.00 | — |
| 1959 | 25,533,291 | — | — | — | 1.65 | 1.75 | 1.95 | 2.25 | 20.00 | 4.25 |
| 1959D | 62,054,232 | — | — | — | 1.65 | 1.75 | 1.95 | 2.25 | 20.00 | — |
| 1960 | 30,855,602 | — | — | — | 1.65 | 1.75 | 1.95 | 2.25 | 17.00 | 3.75 |
| 1960D | 63,000,324 | — | — | — | 1.65 | 1.75 | 1.95 | 2.25 | 17.00 | — |
| 1961 | 40,064,244 | — | — | — | 1.65 | 1.75 | 1.95 | 2.50 | 18.00 | 3.50 |
| 1961D | 83,656,928 | — | — | — | 1.65 | 1.75 | 1.95 | 2.25 | 16.00 | — |
| 1962 | 39,374,019 | — | — | — | 1.65 | 1.75 | 1.95 | 2.50 | 18.00 | 3.50 |
| 1962D | 127,554,756 | — | — | — | 1.65 | 1.75 | 1.95 | 2.25 | 16.00 | — |
| 1963 | 77,391,645 | — | — | — | 1.50 | 1.60 | 1.75 | 1.95 | 15.00 | 3.50 |
| 1963D | 135,288,184 | — | — | — | 1.50 | 1.60 | 1.75 | 1.95 | 15.00 | — |
| 1964 | 564,341,347 | — | — | — | 1.50 | 1.60 | 1.75 | 1.95 | 15.00 | 3.50 |
| 1964D | 704,135,528 | — | — | — | 1.50 | 1.60 | 1.75 | 1.95 | 15.00 | — |

**Designer:** John Flanagan. **Diameter:** 24.3 mm. **Weight:** 5.6700 g. **Composition:** Copper-Nickel Clad Copper. **KM#** 164a.

| Date | Mintage | MS-65 | Prf-65 | Date | Mintage | MS-65 | Prf-65 |
|---|---|---|---|---|---|---|---|
| 1965 | 1,819,717,540 | 2.75 | — | 1971S | (3,220,733) | — | 1.05 |
| 1966 | 821,101,500 | 2.75 | — | 1972 | 215,048,000 | 2.00 | — |
| 1967 | 1,524,031,848 | 2.75 | — | 1972D | 311,067,732 | 2.00 | — |
| 1968 | 220,731,500 | 2.75 | — | 1972S | (3,260,996) | — | 1.10 |
| 1968D | 101,534,000 | 3.00 | — | 1973 | 346,924,000 | 2.00 | — |
| 1968S | (3,041,506) | — | 1.00 | 1973D | 232,977,400 | 2.25 | — |
| 1969 | 176,212,000 | 4.00 | — | 1973S | (2,760,339) | — | 1.00 |
| 1969D | 114,372,000 | 2.50 | — | 1974 | 801,456,000 | 2.00 | — |
| 1969S | (2,934,631) | — | 1.25 | 1974D | 353,160,300 | 2.25 | — |
| 1970 | 136,420,000 | 2.50 | — | 1974S | (2,612,568) | — | 1.25 |
| 1970D | 417,341,364 | 2.25 | — | 1975 none minted | | — | — |
| 1970S | (2,632,810) | — | 1.00 | 1975D none minted | | — | — |
| 1971 | 109,284,000 | 2.25 | — | 1975S none minted | | — | — |
| 1971D | 258,634,428 | 2.25 | — | | | | |

## Washington. Bicentennial design, drummer boy.

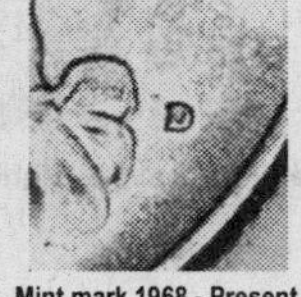

Mint mark 1968 - Present

**Rev. Designer:** Jack L. Ahr. **Diameter:** 24.3 mm. **Weight:** 5.6700 g. **Composition:** Copper-Nickel Clad Copper. **KM#** 204.

| Date | Mintage | G-4 | VG-8 | F-12 | VF-20 | XF-40 | MS-60 | MS-65 | Prf-65 |
|---|---|---|---|---|---|---|---|---|---|
| 1976 | 809,784,016 | — | — | — | — | — | 0.95 | 1.75 | — |
| 1976D | 860,118,839 | — | — | — | — | — | 0.95 | 1.75 | — |
| 1976S | — | — | — | — | — | — | — | — | 1.00 |

## Washington. Bicentennial design, drummer boy.

**Rev. Designer:** Jack L. Ahr. **Diameter:** 24.3 mm. **Weight:** 5.7500 g. **Composition:** Silver Clad, 0.074 oz. **KM#** 204a.

| Date | Mintage | G-4 | VG-8 | F-12 | VF-20 | XF-40 | MS-60 | MS-65 | Prf-65 |
|---|---|---|---|---|---|---|---|---|---|
| 1976S | 11,000,000 | — | — | — | — | — | 1.25 | 1.75 | 2.00 |

## Washington. Regular design resumed.

**Diameter:** 24.3 mm. **Weight:** 5.6700 g. **Composition:** Copper-Nickel Clad Copper. **Notes:** The 1979-S and 1981 Type II proofs have clearer mint marks than the Type I proofs for those years. **KM#** A164a.

| Date | Mintage | MS-65 | Prf-65 |
|---|---|---|---|
| 1977 | 468,556,000 | 1.00 | — |
| 1977D | 256,524,978 | 1.00 | — |
| 1977S | (3,251,152) | — | 1.10 |
| 1978 | 521,452,000 | 1.00 | — |
| 1978D | 287,373,152 | 1.00 | — |
| 1978S | (3,127,781) | — | 1.20 |
| 1979 | 515,708,000 | 1.00 | — |
| 1979D | 489,789,780 | 1.00 | — |
| 1979S T-I | — | — | 1.00 |
| 1979S T-II | — | — | 1.50 |
| 1980P | 635,832,000 | 1.00 | — |
| 1980D | 518,327,487 | 1.00 | — |
| 1980S | (3,554,806) | — | 1.15 |
| 1981P | 601,716,000 | 1.00 | — |
| 1981D | 575,722,833 | 1.00 | — |
| 1981S T-I | — | — | 1.10 |
| 1981S T-II | — | — | 3.00 |
| 1982P | 500,931,000 | 4.50 | — |
| 1982D | 480,042,788 | 3.00 | — |
| 1982S | (3,857,479) | — | 2.00 |
| 1983P | 673,535,000 | 16.00 | — |
| 1983D | 617,806,446 | 9.00 | — |
| 1983S | (3,279,126) | — | 2.25 |
| 1984P | 676,545,000 | 1.75 | — |
| 1984D | 546,483,064 | 2.50 | — |
| 1984S | (3,065,110) | — | 2.40 |
| 1985P | 775,818,962 | 3.50 | — |
| 1985D | 519,962,888 | 5.00 | — |
| 1985S | (3,362,821) | 5.00 | 1.45 |
| 1986P | 551,199,333 | 6.00 | — |
| 1986D | 504,298,660 | 8.50 | — |
| 1986S | (3,010,497) | — | 2.25 |
| 1987P | 582,499,481 | 1.00 | — |
| 1987D | 655,594,696 | 1.00 | — |
| 1987S | (4,227,728) | — | 1.50 |
| 1988P | 562,052,000 | 3.00 | — |
| 1988D | 596,810,688 | 1.50 | — |
| 1988S | (3,262,948) | — | 2.10 |
| 1989P | 512,868,000 | 1.50 | — |
| 1989D | 896,535,597 | 1.50 | — |
| 1989S | (3,220,194) | — | 2.10 |
| 1990P | 613,792,000 | 1.00 | — |
| 1990D | 927,638,181 | 1.00 | — |
| 1990S | (3,299,559) | — | 5.00 |
| 1991P | 570,968,000 | 1.00 | — |
| 1991D | 630,966,693 | 1.00 | — |
| 1991S | (2,867,787) | — | 2.50 |
| 1992P | 384,764,000 | 1.00 | — |
| 1992D | 389,777,107 | 1.35 | — |
| 1992S | (2,858,981) | — | 3.00 |
| 1993P | 639,276,000 | 1.20 | — |
| 1993D | 645,476,128 | 1.50 | — |
| 1993S | (2,633,439) | — | 5.00 |
| 1994P | 825,600,000 | 1.25 | — |
| 1994D | 880,034,110 | 1.25 | — |
| 1994S | (2,484,594) | — | 4.00 |
| 1995P | 1,004,336,000 | 1.20 | — |
| 1995D | 1,103,216,000 | 1.20 | — |
| 1995S | (2,010,384) | — | 20.00 |
| 1996P | 925,040,000 | 1.20 | — |
| 1996S | — | — | 4.00 |
| 1996D | 906,868,000 | 1.20 | — |
| 1997P | 595,740,000 | 1.25 | — |
| 1997D | 599,680,000 | 1.25 | — |
| 1997S | (1,975,000) | — | 10.00 |
| 1998P | 896,268,000 | 1.00 | — |
| 1998D | 821,000,000 | 1.00 | — |
| 1998S | — | — | 10.00 |

**Composition:** Silver. **KM#** A164b.

| Date | Mintage | Prf-65 |
|---|---|---|
| 1992S | (1,317,579) | 7.00 |
| 1993S | (761,353) | 6.00 |
| 1994S | (785,329) | 9.50 |
| 1995S | (838,953) | 18.00 |
| 1996S | — | 18.00 |
| 1997S | — | 7.00 |
| 1998S | — | 9.00 |

# 50 State Quarters

## Connecticut

**Composition:** Copper-Nickel Clad Copper. **KM#** 294.

| Date | Mintage | MS-63 | MS-65 | Prf-65 |
|---|---|---|---|---|
| 1999P | 688,744,000 | 0.75 | 1.00 | — |
| 1999D | 657,480,000 | 0.75 | 1.00 | — |
| 1999S | — | — | — | 6.50 |

**Composition:** 0.9000 Silver. **KM#** 294a.

| Date | Mintage | MS-63 | MS-65 | Prf-65 |
|---|---|---|---|---|
| 1999S | — | — | — | 9.00 |

## Delaware

**Diameter:** 24.3 mm. **Weight:** 5.6700 g. **Composition:** Copper-Nickel Clad Copper. **KM#** 290.

| Date | Mintage | MS-63 | MS-65 | Prf-65 |
|---|---|---|---|---|
| 1999P | 373,400,000 | 1.25 | 1.50 | — |
| 1999D | 401,424,000 | 1.25 | 1.50 | — |
| 1999S | — | — | — | 6.50 |

**Composition:** 0.9000 Silver. **KM#** 290a.

| Date | Mintage | MS-63 | MS-65 | Prf-65 |
|---|---|---|---|---|
| 1999S | — | — | — | 10.00 |

## Georgia

**Composition:** Copper-Nickel Clad Copper. **KM#** 293.

| Date | Mintage | MS-63 | MS-65 | Prf-65 |
|---|---|---|---|---|
| 1999P | 451,188,000 | 0.75 | 1.00 | — |
| 1999D | 488,744,000 | 0.75 | 1.00 | — |
| 1999S | — | — | — | 5.00 |

**Composition:** 0.9000 Silver. **KM#** 293a.

| Date | Mintage | MS-63 | MS-65 | Prf-65 |
|---|---|---|---|---|
| 1999S | — | — | — | 9.50 |

## New Jersey

**Composition:** Copper-Nickel Clad Copper. **KM#** 292.

| Date | Mintage | MS-63 | MS-65 | Prf-65 |
|---|---|---|---|---|
| 1999P | 363,200,000 | 1.00 | 1.50 | — |
| 1999D | 299,028,000 | 1.00 | 1.75 | — |
| 1999S | — | — | — | 5.00 |

**Composition:** 0.9000 Silver. **KM#** 292a.

| Date | Mintage | MS-63 | MS-65 | Prf-65 |
|---|---|---|---|---|
| 1999S | — | — | — | 9.50 |

## Pennsylvania

**Diameter:** 24.3 mm. **Weight:** 5.6700 g. **Composition:** Copper-Nickel Clad Copper. **KM#** 291.

| Date | Mintage | MS-63 | MS-65 | Prf-65 |
|---|---|---|---|---|
| 1999P | 349,000,000 | 1.50 | 2.00 | — |
| 1999D | 358,332,000 | 1.25 | 1.50 | — |
| 1999S | — | — | — | 5.00 |

**Composition:** 0.9000 Silver. **KM#** 291a.

| Date | Mintage | MS-63 | MS-65 | Prf-65 |
|---|---|---|---|---|
| 1999S | — | — | — | 9.00 |

## Maryland

**Composition:** Copper-Nickel Clad Copper. **KM#** 307.

| Date | Mintage | MS-63 | MS-65 | Prf-65 |
|---|---|---|---|---|
| 2000P | 678,200,000 | 0.75 | 1.00 | — |
| 2000D | 556,526,000 | 0.75 | 1.00 | — |
| 2000S | — | — | — | 3.00 |

**Composition:** 0.9000 Silver. **KM#** 307a.

| Date | Mintage | MS-63 | MS-65 | Prf-65 |
|---|---|---|---|---|
| 2000S | — | — | — | 7.50 |

## Massachusetts

**Composition:** Copper-Nickel Clad Copper. **KM#** 306.

| Date | Mintage | MS-63 | MS-65 | Prf-65 |
|---|---|---|---|---|
| 2000P | 629,800,000 | 0.75 | 1.00 | — |
| 2000D | 535,184,000 | 0.75 | 1.00 | — |
| 2000S | — | — | — | 3.00 |

**Composition:** 0.9000 Silver. **KM#** 306a.

| Date | Mintage | MS-63 | MS-65 | Prf-65 |
|---|---|---|---|---|
| 2000S | — | — | — | 7.50 |

## New Hampshire

**Composition:** Copper-Nickel Clad Copper. **KM#** 309.

| Date | Mintage | MS-63 | MS-65 | Prf-65 |
|---|---|---|---|---|
| 2000P | 673,040,000 | 0.75 | 1.00 | — |
| 2000D | 495,976,000 | 0.75 | 1.00 | — |
| 2000S | — | — | — | 3.00 |

**Composition:** 0.9000 Silver. **KM#** 309a.

| Date | Mintage | MS-63 | MS-65 | Prf-65 |
|---|---|---|---|---|
| 2000S | — | — | — | 7.50 |

## South Carolina

**Composition:** Copper-Nickel Clad Copper. **KM#** 308.

| Date | Mintage | MS-63 | MS-65 | Prf-65 |
|---|---|---|---|---|
| 2000P | 742,756,000 | 0.75 | 1.00 | — |
| 2000D | 566,208,000 | 0.75 | 1.00 | — |
| 2000S | — | — | — | 3.00 |

**Composition:** 0.9000 Silver. **KM#** 308a.

| Date | Mintage | MS-63 | MS-65 | Prf-65 |
|---|---|---|---|---|
| 2000S | — | — | — | 7.50 |

## Virginia

**Composition:** Copper-Nickel Clad Copper. **KM#** 310.

| Date | Mintage | MS-63 | MS-65 | Prf-65 |
|---|---|---|---|---|
| 2000P | 943,000,000 | 0.75 | 1.00 | — |
| 2000D | 651,616,000 | 0.75 | 1.00 | — |
| 2000S | — | — | — | 3.00 |

**Composition:** 0.9000 Silver. **KM#** 310a.

| Date | Mintage | MS-63 | MS-65 | Prf-65 |
|---|---|---|---|---|
| 2000S | — | — | — | 7.50 |

## Kentucky

**Composition:** Copper-Nickel Clad Copper. **KM#** 323.

| Date | Mintage | MS-63 | MS-65 | Prf-65 |
|---|---|---|---|---|
| 2001P | — | 0.75 | 1.00 | — |
| 2001D | — | 0.75 | 1.00 | — |
| 2001S | — | — | — | 3.00 |

**Composition:** Silver. **KM#** 323a.

| Date | Mintage | MS-63 | MS-65 | Prf-65 |
|---|---|---|---|---|
| 2001S | — | — | — | 6.00 |

## New York

**Composition:** Copper-Nickel Clad Copper. **KM#** 319.

| Date | Mintage | MS-63 | MS-65 | Prf-65 |
|---|---|---|---|---|
| 2001P | 655,400,000 | 0.75 | 1.00 | — |
| 2001D | 619,640,000 | 0.75 | 1.00 | — |
| 2001S | — | — | — | 3.00 |

**Composition:** Silver. **KM#** 319a.

| Date | Mintage | MS-63 | MS-65 | Prf-65 |
|---|---|---|---|---|
| 2001S | — | — | — | 6.00 |

## North Carolina

**Composition:** Copper-Nickel Clad Copper. **KM#** 320.

| Date | Mintage | MS-63 | MS-65 | Prf-65 |
|---|---|---|---|---|
| 2001P | 627,600,000 | 0.75 | 1.00 | — |
| 2001D | 427,876,000 | 0.75 | 1.00 | — |
| 2001S | — | — | — | 3.00 |

**Composition:** Silver. **KM#** 320a.

| Date | Mintage | MS-63 | MS-65 | Prf-65 |
|---|---|---|---|---|
| 2001S | — | — | — | 6.00 |

## Rhode Island

**Composition:** Copper-Nickel Clad Copper. **KM#** 321.

| Date | Mintage | MS-63 | MS-65 | Prf-65 |
|---|---|---|---|---|
| 2001P | 423,000,000 | 0.75 | 1.00 | — |
| 2001D | 447,100,000 | 0.75 | 1.00 | — |
| 2001S | — | — | — | 3.00 |

**Composition:** Silver. **KM#** 321a.

| Date | Mintage | MS-63 | MS-65 | Prf-65 |
|---|---|---|---|---|
| 2001S | — | — | — | 6.00 |

## Vermont

**Composition:** Copper-Nickel Clad Copper. **KM#** 322.

| Date | Mintage | MS-63 | MS-65 | Prf-65 |
|---|---|---|---|---|
| 2001P | 423,400,000 | 0.75 | 1.00 | — |
| 2001D | 459,404,000 | 0.75 | 1.00 | — |
| 2001S | — | — | — | 3.00 |

**Composition:** Silver. **KM#** 322a.

| Date | Mintage | MS-63 | MS-65 | Prf-65 |
|---|---|---|---|---|
| 2001S | — | — | — | 6.00 |

## Indiana

**Composition:** Copper-Nickel Clad Copper. **KM#** 327.

| Date | Mintage | MS-63 | MS-65 | Prf-65 |
|---|---|---|---|---|
| 2002P | — | — | — | — |
| 2002D | — | — | — | — |
| 2002S | — | — | — | — |

**Composition:** Silver. **KM#** 327a.

| Date | Mintage | MS-63 | MS-65 | Prf-65 |
|---|---|---|---|---|
| 2002S | — | — | — | — |

## Louisiana

**Composition:** Copper-Nickel Clad Copper. **KM#** 326.

| Date | Mintage | MS-63 | MS-65 | Prf-65 |
|---|---|---|---|---|
| 2002P | — | — | — | — |
| 2002D | — | — | — | — |
| 2002S | — | — | — | — |

**Composition:** Silver. **KM#** 326a.

| Date | Mintage | MS-63 | MS-65 | Prf-65 |
|---|---|---|---|---|
| 2002S | — | — | — | — |

## Mississippi

**Composition:** Copper-Nickel Clad Copper. **KM#** 328.

| Date | Mintage | MS-63 | MS-65 | Prf-65 |
|---|---|---|---|---|
| 2002P | — | — | — | — |
| 2002D | — | — | — | — |
| 2002S | — | — | — | — |

**Composition:** Silver. **KM#** 328a.

| Date | Mintage | MS-63 | MS-65 | Prf-65 |
|---|---|---|---|---|
| 2002S | — | — | — | — |

## Ohio

**Composition:** Copper-Nickel Clad Copper. **KM#** 325.

| Date | Mintage | MS-63 | MS-65 | Prf-65 |
|---|---|---|---|---|
| 2002P | — | — | — | — |
| 2002D | — | — | — | — |
| 2002S | — | — | — | — |

**Composition:** Silver. **KM#** 325a.

| Date | Mintage | MS-63 | MS-65 | Prf-65 |
|---|---|---|---|---|
| 2002S | — | — | — | — |

## Tennessee

**Composition:** Copper-Nickel Clad Copper. **KM#** 324.

| Date | Mintage | MS-63 | MS-65 | Prf-65 |
|---|---|---|---|---|
| 2002P | — | 0.75 | 1.00 | — |
| 2002D | — | 0.75 | 1.00 | — |
| 2002S | — | — | — | — |

**Composition:** Silver. **KM#** 324a.

| Date | Mintage | MS-63 | MS-65 | Prf-65 |
|---|---|---|---|---|
| 2002S | — | — | — | — |

# HALF DOLLAR

## Barber.

Mint mark

**Designer:** Charles E. Barber. **Diameter:** 30.6 mm. **Weight:** 12.5000 g. **Composition:** 0.9000 Silver, 0.3618 oz. ASW. **KM#** 116.

| Date | Mintage | G-4 | VG-8 | F-12 | VF-20 | XF-40 | AU-50 | MS-60 | MS-65 | Prf-65 |
|---|---|---|---|---|---|---|---|---|---|---|
| 1901 | 4,268,813 | 8.00 | 10.00 | 24.00 | 65.00 | 135 | 285 | 400 | 4,200 | 3,500 |
| 1901O | 1,124,000 | 9.50 | 15.00 | 50.00 | 115 | 285 | 450 | 1,300 | 14,000 | — |
| 1901S | 847,044 | 16.00 | 31.00 | 110 | 240 | 550 | 920 | 1,500 | 15,000 | — |
| 1902 | 4,922,777 | 7.00 | 10.00 | 24.00 | 65.00 | 135 | 280 | 400 | 4,000 | 3,700 |
| 1902O | 2,526,000 | 8.00 | 13.00 | 38.00 | 80.00 | 190 | 350 | 700 | 7,000 | — |
| 1902S | 1,460,670 | 9.00 | 15.00 | 48.00 | 90.00 | 200 | 360 | 635 | 5,500 | — |
| 1903 | 2,278,755 | 8.00 | 12.50 | 40.00 | 78.00 | 165 | 325 | 450 | 8,400 | 3,825 |
| 1903O | 2,100,000 | 8.00 | 12.00 | 40.00 | 78.00 | 190 | 325 | 650 | 9,500 | — |

| Date | Mintage | G-4 | VG-8 | F-12 | VF-20 | XF-40 | AU-50 | MS-60 | MS-65 | Prf-65 |
|---|---|---|---|---|---|---|---|---|---|---|
| 1903S | 1,920,772 | 8.00 | 12.00 | 40.00 | 78.00 | 210 | 365 | 585 | 4,750 | — |
| 1904 | 2,992,670 | 8.00 | 10.00 | 28.50 | 65.00 | 135 | 300 | 400 | 5,500 | 4,100 |
| 1904O | 1,117,600 | 10.50 | 17.00 | 50.00 | 110 | 300 | 500 | 1,000 | 12,900 | — |
| 1904S | 553,038 | 17.00 | 33.50 | 160 | 420 | 780 | 1,250 | 2,250 | 22,500 | — |
| 1905 | 662,727 | 11.00 | 16.00 | 52.00 | 84.00 | 220 | 330 | 550 | 5,800 | 3,900 |
| 1905O | 505,000 | 14.00 | 26.00 | 80.00 | 150 | 260 | 420 | 730 | 5,000 | — |
| 1905S | 2,494,000 | 8.00 | 10.00 | 38.00 | 78.00 | 190 | 345 | 620 | 9,200 | — |
| 1906 | 2,638,675 | 7.00 | 9.00 | 24.00 | 65.00 | 135 | 285 | 400 | 3,000 | 3,300 |
| 1906D | 4,028,000 | 7.00 | 9.00 | 26.00 | 72.00 | 140 | 300 | 430 | 4,100 | — |
| 1906O | 2,446,000 | 7.00 | 9.00 | 35.00 | 78.00 | 160 | 310 | 600 | 5,400 | — |
| 1906S | 1,740,154 | 8.00 | 13.00 | 42.00 | 80.00 | 190 | 300 | 585 | 5,250 | — |
| 1907 | 2,598,575 | 7.00 | 9.00 | 24.00 | 65.00 | 130 | 300 | 400 | 2,800 | 4,000 |
| 1907D | 3,856,000 | 7.00 | 9.00 | 26.00 | 65.00 | 135 | 300 | 400 | 2,600 | — |
| 1907O | 3,946,000 | 7.00 | 9.00 | 26.00 | 72.00 | 150 | 310 | 570 | 3,000 | — |
| 1907S | 1,250,000 | 7.50 | 12.00 | 60.00 | 100.00 | 310 | 500 | 1,000 | 13,000 | — |
| 1908 | 1,354,545 | 7.00 | 9.00 | 26.00 | 72.00 | 135 | 280 | 400 | 3,600 | 4,000 |
| 1908D | 3,280,000 | 7.00 | 9.00 | 26.00 | 72.00 | 145 | 280 | 400 | 2,800 | — |
| 1908O | 5,360,000 | 7.00 | 9.00 | 26.00 | 72.00 | 145 | 310 | 520 | 2,800 | — |
| 1908S | 1,644,828 | 7.50 | 12.50 | 44.00 | 80.00 | 210 | 340 | 750 | 5,500 | — |
| 1909 | 2,368,650 | 8.00 | 9.00 | 24.00 | 65.00 | 135 | 280 | 400 | 2,800 | 4,000 |
| 1909O | 925,400 | 9.00 | 13.00 | 50.00 | 84.00 | 260 | 480 | 750 | 4,500 | — |
| 1909S | 1,764,000 | 8.00 | 10.00 | 30.00 | 78.00 | 180 | 340 | 570 | 3,500 | — |
| 1910 | 418,551 | 10.00 | 18.50 | 62.50 | 115 | 260 | 400 | 600 | 3,000 | 4,250 |
| 1910S | 1,948,000 | 8.00 | 10.00 | 28.00 | 72.00 | 180 | 330 | 630 | 4,800 | — |
| 1911 | 1,406,543 | 7.00 | 9.00 | 25.00 | 65.00 | 135 | 300 | 410 | 2,800 | 3,300 |
| 1911D | 695,080 | 9.00 | 12.00 | 32.00 | 72.00 | 190 | 280 | 545 | 2,800 | — |
| 1911S | 1,272,000 | 7.00 | 8.50 | 24.00 | 78.00 | 135 | 280 | 400 | 5,400 | — |
| 1912 | 1,550,700 | 7.00 | 8.50 | 24.00 | 65.00 | 135 | 280 | 400 | 3,000 | 4,000 |
| 1912D | 2,300,800 | 7.00 | 8.50 | 24.00 | 65.00 | 135 | 310 | 430 | 3,000 | — |
| 1912S | 1,370,000 | 7.00 | 8.75 | 30.00 | 72.00 | 160 | 320 | 520 | 5,500 | — |
| 1913 | 188,627 | 20.00 | 30.00 | 110 | 185 | 360 | 690 | 925 | 3,600 | 3,800 |
| 1913D | 534,000 | 9.00 | 12.50 | 32.00 | 72.00 | 190 | 295 | 450 | 4,650 | — |
| 1913S | 604,000 | 9.50 | 13.00 | 42.00 | 85.00 | 190 | 350 | 600 | 3,850 | — |
| 1914 | 124,610 | 35.00 | 50.00 | 165 | 330 | 500 | 750 | 950 | 8,000 | 4,300 |
| 1914S | 992,000 | 8.50 | 9.25 | 32.50 | 72.00 | 180 | 345 | 550 | 4,200 | — |
| 1915 | 138,450 | 22.00 | 26.50 | 90.00 | 200 | 375 | 720 | 1,000 | 5,200 | 4,250 |
| 1915D | 1,170,400 | 8.00 | 9.25 | 24.00 | 65.00 | 135 | 280 | 400 | 2,800 | — |
| 1915S | 1,604,000 | 8.00 | 9.25 | 26.00 | 65.00 | 135 | 280 | 420 | 2,800 | — |

## Walking Liberty.

Obverse mint mark

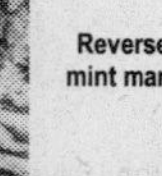

Reverse mint mark

**Designer:** Adolph A. Weinman. **Diameter:** 30.6 mm. **Weight:** 12.5000 g. **Composition:** 0.9000 Silver, 0.3618 oz. ASW. **Notes:** The mint mark appears on the obverse below the word "Trust" on 1916 and some 1917 issues. Starting with some 1917 issues and continuing through the remainder of the series, the mint mark was changed to the reverse, at about the 8 o'clock position near the rim. **KM#** 142.

| Date | Mintage | G-4 | VG-8 | F-12 | VF-20 | XF-40 | AU-50 | MS-60 | MS-65 | Prf-65 |
|---|---|---|---|---|---|---|---|---|---|---|
| 1916 | 608,000 | 27.50 | 32.50 | 55.00 | 110 | 150 | 210 | 270 | 1,425 | — |
| 1916D | 1,014,400 | 21.00 | 27.50 | 40.00 | 70.00 | 135 | 185 | 260 | 1,800 | — |
| 1916S | 508,000 | 85.00 | 90.00 | 130 | 310 | 550 | 700 | 950 | 4,800 | — |
| 1917D obv. mint mark | 765,400 | 14.00 | 21.00 | 40.00 | 84.00 | 140 | 215 | 500 | 6,000 | — |
| 1917S obv. mint mark | 952,000 | 17.00 | 29.00 | 50.00 | 250 | 675 | 1,100 | 1,950 | 16,000 | — |
| 1917 | 12,292,000 | 3.50 | 5.00 | 8.00 | 16.00 | 32.50 | 60.00 | 110 | 800 | — |
| 1917D rev. mint mark | 1,940,000 | 9.00 | 14.00 | 24.00 | 80.00 | 195 | 400 | 700 | 16,000 | — |
| 1917S rev. mint mark | 5,554,000 | 4.00 | 6.50 | 12.00 | 27.50 | 50.00 | 125 | 300 | 9,500 | — |
| 1918 | 6,634,000 | 4.00 | 6.00 | 14.00 | 47.50 | 130 | 245 | 500 | 3,500 | — |
| 1918D | 3,853,040 | 5.50 | 7.50 | 27.50 | 51.00 | 150 | 350 | 825 | 21,000 | — |
| 1918S | 10,282,000 | 4.00 | 6.00 | 14.00 | 27.00 | 55.00 | 145 | 400 | 15,500 | — |
| 1919 | 962,000 | 17.00 | 22.00 | 40.00 | 150 | 400 | 600 | 1,000 | 5,000 | — |
| 1919D | 1,165,000 | 12.00 | 16.00 | 47.50 | 150 | 575 | 875 | 2,700 | 100,000 | — |
| 1919S | 1,552,000 | 14.00 | 18.00 | 32.00 | 150 | 700 | 1,500 | 2,100 | 13,200 | — |
| 1920 | 6,372,000 | 4.00 | 5.00 | 10.00 | 25.00 | 60.00 | 95.00 | 300 | 6,000 | — |
| 1920D | 1,551,000 | 9.00 | 11.00 | 27.50 | 130 | 350 | 665 | 1,075 | 9,800 | — |
| 1920S | 4,624,000 | 5.00 | 7.00 | 14.00 | 47.50 | 195 | 385 | 700 | 10,500 | — |
| 1921 | 246,000 | 100.00 | 135 | 200 | 575 | 1,400 | 2,300 | 3,250 | 12,300 | — |
| 1921D | 208,000 | 145 | 180 | 265 | 690 | 2,000 | 2,700 | 3,200 | 13,800 | — |
| 1921S | 548,000 | 24.00 | 27.00 | 100.00 | 630 | 4,200 | 6,700 | 8,700 | 60,000 | — |
| 1923S | 2,178,000 | 8.00 | 10.00 | 20.00 | 55.00 | 210 | 575 | 1,150 | 12,000 | — |
| 1927S | 2,392,000 | 4.00 | 6.00 | 10.00 | 30.00 | 95.00 | 275 | 720 | 8,200 | — |
| 1928S | 1,940,000 | 4.00 | 6.00 | 11.00 | 35.00 | 100.00 | 300 | 700 | 7,500 | — |
| 1929D | 1,001,200 | 6.00 | 8.00 | 13.00 | 28.00 | 70.00 | 150 | 280 | 2,050 | — |
| 1929S | 1,902,000 | 4.00 | 6.00 | 10.00 | 18.00 | 70.00 | 175 | 325 | 2,200 | — |
| 1933S | 1,786,000 | 5.00 | 7.00 | 9.00 | 11.50 | 45.00 | 215 | 500 | 3,250 | — |

| Date | Mintage | G-4 | VG-8 | F-12 | VF-20 | XF-40 | AU-50 | MS-60 | MS-65 | Prf-65 |
|---|---|---|---|---|---|---|---|---|---|---|
| 1934 | 6,964,000 | 3.25 | 3.50 | 3.75 | 4.00 | 8.00 | 25.00 | 53.00 | 370 | — |
| 1934D | 2,361,400 | 3.50 | 5.00 | 5.50 | 7.50 | 25.00 | 60.00 | 150 | 800 | — |
| 1934S | 3,652,000 | 3.25 | 3.50 | 4.00 | 5.00 | 25.00 | 90.00 | 275 | 3,000 | — |
| 1935 | 9,162,000 | 3.00 | 3.50 | 3.75 | 4.50 | 6.00 | 22.00 | 44.00 | 300 | — |
| 1935D | 3,003,800 | 3.50 | 3.75 | 4.00 | 6.00 | 22.50 | 53.00 | 140 | 1,320 | — |
| 1935S | 3,854,000 | 3.25 | 3.50 | 3.75 | 4.50 | 25.00 | 98.00 | 190 | 2,000 | — |
| 1936 | 12,617,901 | 3.00 | 3.25 | 3.50 | 4.00 | 6.00 | 21.00 | 37.00 | 145 | 3,250 |
| 1936S | 3,884,000 | 3.25 | 3.50 | 4.50 | 5.00 | 19.00 | 60.00 | 125 | 420 | — |
| 1936D | 4,252,400 | 3.25 | 3.50 | 4.00 | 4.50 | 16.00 | 42.00 | 76.00 | 350 | — |
| 1937 | 9,527,728 | 3.00 | 3.25 | 3.50 | 4.50 | 6.00 | 21.00 | 38.00 | 200 | 850 |
| 1937D | 1,676,000 | 5.00 | 6.00 | 8.00 | 11.00 | 28.00 | 80.00 | 150 | 420 | — |
| 1937S | 2,090,000 | 4.00 | 5.00 | 6.00 | 8.00 | 18.00 | 63.00 | 125 | 450 | — |
| 1938 | 4,118,152 | 3.00 | 3.50 | 4.50 | 6.50 | 11.00 | 40.00 | 65.00 | 260 | 580 |
| 1938D | 491,600 | 24.00 | 27.00 | 30.00 | 37.00 | 90.00 | 240 | 400 | 900 | — |
| 1939 | 6,820,808 | 3.00 | 3.25 | 3.50 | 4.50 | 10.00 | 21.00 | 39.00 | 120 | 525 |
| 1939D | 4,267,800 | 3.00 | 3.50 | 4.50 | 5.50 | 10.50 | 22.00 | 39.00 | 130 | — |
| 1939S | 2,552,000 | 4.00 | 5.00 | 6.00 | 9.00 | 13.00 | 49.00 | 100.00 | 180 | — |
| 1940 | 9,167,279 | 3.00 | 3.25 | 3.50 | 5.50 | 9.00 | 11.00 | 29.00 | 125 | 450 |
| 1940S | 4,550,000 | 3.00 | 3.25 | 3.50 | 5.50 | 10.00 | 16.00 | 32.50 | 330 | — |
| 1941 | 24,207,412 | 3.00 | 3.25 | 3.50 | 4.50 | 7.00 | 11.00 | 30.00 | 110 | 375 |
| 1941D | 11,248,400 | 3.00 | 3.25 | 3.50 | 4.50 | 6.00 | 14.00 | 36.00 | 140 | — |
| 1941S | 8,098,000 | 3.00 | 3.25 | 3.50 | 4.75 | 7.00 | 26.00 | 72.00 | 1,000 | — |
| 1942 | 47,839,120 | 3.00 | 3.25 | 3.50 | 4.50 | 5.50 | 11.00 | 30.00 | 105 | 375 |
| 1942D | 10,973,800 | 3.00 | 3.25 | 3.50 | 4.50 | 6.00 | 16.00 | 38.00 | 215 | — |
| 1942S | 12,708,000 | 3.00 | 3.25 | 3.50 | 4.75 | 7.00 | 16.00 | 38.00 | 550 | — |
| 1943 | 53,190,000 | 3.00 | 3.25 | 3.50 | 4.50 | 5.50 | 11.00 | 30.00 | 110 | — |
| 1943D | 11,346,000 | 3.00 | 3.25 | 3.50 | 4.50 | 6.00 | 20.00 | 40.00 | 240 | — |
| 1943S | 13,450,000 | 3.00 | 3.25 | 3.50 | 4.75 | 6.00 | 18.00 | 35.00 | 350 | — |
| 1944 | 28,206,000 | 3.00 | 3.25 | 3.50 | 4.50 | 5.50 | 11.00 | 30.00 | 145 | — |
| 1944D | 9,769,000 | 3.00 | 3.25 | 3.50 | 4.50 | 6.00 | 16.00 | 35.00 | 125 | — |
| 1944S | 8,904,000 | 3.00 | 3.25 | 3.50 | 4.75 | 6.25 | 17.00 | 36.00 | 550 | — |
| 1945 | 31,502,000 | 3.00 | 3.25 | 3.50 | 4.50 | 5.50 | 11.00 | 30.00 | 110 | — |
| 1945D | 9,966,800 | 3.00 | 3.25 | 3.50 | 4.50 | 6.00 | 14.00 | 32.50 | 120 | — |
| 1945S | 10,156,000 | 3.00 | 3.25 | 3.50 | 4.75 | 6.00 | 15.00 | 34.00 | 160 | — |
| 1946 | 12,118,000 | 3.00 | 3.25 | 3.50 | 4.50 | 5.50 | 12.00 | 30.00 | 210 | — |
| 1946D | 2,151,000 | 3.50 | 4.00 | 4.50 | 5.50 | 7.00 | 19.00 | 35.00 | 90.00 | — |
| 1946S | 3,724,000 | 3.00 | 3.50 | 4.00 | 5.00 | 5.50 | 16.00 | 33.00 | 120 | — |
| 1947 | 4,094,000 | 3.00 | 3.50 | 4.00 | 5.00 | 7.00 | 18.00 | 34.00 | 200 | — |
| 1947D | 3,900,600 | 3.00 | 3.50 | 4.00 | 5.00 | 7.00 | 22.00 | 35.00 | 110 | — |

## Franklin.

Mint mark

**Designer:** John R. Sinnock. **Diameter:** 30.6 mm. **Weight:** 12.5000 g. **Composition:** 0.9000 Silver, 0.3618 oz. ASW. **KM#** 199.

| Date | Mintage | G-4 | VG-8 | F-12 | VF-20 | XF-40 | AU-50 | MS-60 | MS-65 | -65FBL | -65CAM |
|---|---|---|---|---|---|---|---|---|---|---|---|
| 1948 | 3,006,814 | — | 3.00 | 4.00 | 4.25 | 4.50 | 6.00 | 13.75 | 90.00 | 315 | — |
| 1948D | 4,028,600 | — | 3.00 | 3.25 | 3.50 | 3.75 | 5.00 | 10.00 | 195 | 325 | — |
| 1949 | 5,614,000 | — | 3.00 | 3.25 | 3.50 | 4.00 | 10.00 | 28.00 | 150 | 290 | — |
| 1949D | 4,120,600 | — | 3.00 | 3.50 | 3.75 | 4.00 | 13.00 | 29.00 | 1,050 | 2,350 | — |
| 1949S | 3,744,000 | — | 3.50 | 4.00 | 6.25 | 8.00 | 21.00 | 48.00 | 210 | 775 | — |
| 1950 | 7,793,509 | — | — | 3.00 | 3.50 | 6.00 | 7.00 | 20.00 | 150 | 350 | 3,700 |
| 1950D | 8,031,600 | — | — | 3.00 | 3.50 | 6.50 | 7.75 | 16.00 | 575 | 1,150 | — |
| 1951 | 16,859,602 | — | — | 3.00 | 3.50 | 4.00 | 4.50 | 9.00 | 95.00 | 375 | 2,200 |
| 1951D | 9,475,200 | — | — | 3.00 | 4.25 | 5.00 | 11.50 | 19.00 | 300 | 550 | — |
| 1951S | 13,696,000 | — | — | 2.75 | 3.00 | 3.50 | 10.00 | 18.00 | 125 | 775 | — |
| 1952 | 21,274,073 | — | — | 2.50 | 2.75 | 3.00 | 4.00 | 7.00 | 90.00 | 325 | 1,100 |
| 1952D | 25,395,600 | — | — | 2.50 | 2.75 | 3.00 | 4.00 | 8.50 | 250 | 450 | — |
| 1952S | 5,526,000 | — | — | 2.50 | 3.25 | 3.75 | 17.00 | 38.00 | 135 | 1,100 | — |
| 1953 | 2,796,920 | 3.00 | 3.00 | 3.25 | 3.50 | 5.00 | 10.00 | 14.00 | 275 | 1,100 | 475 |
| 1953D | 20,900,400 | — | — | 2.25 | 3.50 | 4.00 | 4.25 | 7.00 | 250 | 400 | — |
| 1953S | 4,148,000 | — | — | 2.60 | 4.25 | 4.75 | 8.50 | 17.00 | 70.00 | 9,000 | — |
| 1954 | 13,421,503 | — | — | 2.25 | 3.50 | 3.75 | 4.00 | 5.50 | 85.00 | 275 | 250 |
| 1954D | 25,445,580 | — | — | 2.25 | 3.25 | 3.50 | 4.00 | 5.50 | 165 | 250 | — |
| 1954S | 4,993,400 | — | — | 2.25 | 3.75 | 4.00 | 4.25 | 8.50 | 60.00 | 425 | — |
| 1955 | 2,876,381 | 5.00 | 5.00 | 5.25 | 5.50 | 5.75 | 6.00 | 7.50 | 75.00 | 160 | 195 |
| 1956 | 4,701,384 | — | — | 2.50 | 3.00 | 3.50 | 4.25 | 5.00 | 50.00 | 120 | 75.00 |
| 1957 | 6,361,952 | — | — | 2.50 | 2.75 | 3.00 | 3.75 | 6.00 | 50.00 | 120 | 135 |
| 1957D | 19,966,850 | — | — | — | 2.10 | 2.25 | 2.50 | 5.00 | 50.00 | 105 | — |
| 1958 | 4,917,652 | — | — | 2.25 | 2.50 | 2.75 | 3.00 | 5.00 | 50.00 | 135 | 250 |
| 1958D | 23,962,412 | — | — | — | 2.25 | 2.50 | 2.75 | 4.25 | 50.00 | 105 | — |
| 1959 | 7,349,291 | — | — | — | 2.25 | 2.50 | 2.75 | 4.50 | 150 | 295 | 475 |
| 1959D | 13,053,750 | — | — | — | 2.25 | 2.50 | 2.75 | 5.00 | 150 | 275 | — |
| 1960 | 7,715,602 | — | — | — | 2.25 | 2.50 | 2.75 | 4.25 | 175 | 400 | 75.00 |
| 1960D | 18,215,812 | — | — | — | 2.25 | 2.50 | 2.75 | 4.50 | 750 | 1,450 | — |
| 1961 | 11,318,244 | — | — | — | 2.25 | 2.50 | 2.75 | 4.25 | 275 | 1,900 | 75.00 |
| 1961D | 20,276,442 | — | — | — | 2.25 | 2.50 | 2.75 | 4.50 | 450 | 1,050 | — |
| 1962 | 12,932,019 | — | — | — | 2.25 | 2.50 | 2.75 | 4.25 | 290 | 2,600 | 50.00 |
| 1962D | 35,473,281 | — | — | — | 2.25 | 2.50 | 2.75 | 4.25 | 400 | 1,000 | — |
| 1963 | 25,239,645 | — | — | — | — | 2.50 | 2.75 | 4.00 | 90.00 | 975 | 50.00 |
| 1963D | 67,069,292 | — | — | — | — | 2.50 | 2.75 | 4.00 | 90.00 | 250 | — |

## Kennedy.

Mint mark 1964

1968 - Present

**Obv. Designer:** Gilroy Roberts. **Rev. Designer:** Frank Gasparro. **Diameter:** 30.6 mm. **Weight:** 12.5000 g. **Composition:** 0.9000 Silver, 0.3618 oz. ASW. **KM#** 202.

| Date | Mintage | G-4 | VG-8 | F-12 | VF-20 | XF-40 | MS-60 | MS-65 | Prf-65 |
|---|---|---|---|---|---|---|---|---|---|
| 1964 | 277,254,766 | — | — | — | — | — | 3.00 | 9.00 | 10.00 |
| 1964D | 156,205,446 | — | — | — | — | — | 3.50 | 12.00 | — |

**Obv. Designer:** Gilroy Roberts. **Rev. Designer:** Frank Gasparro. **Diameter:** 30.6 mm. **Weight:** 11.5000 g. **Composition:** 0.4000 Silver, 0.1480 oz. ASW. **KM#** 202a.

| Date | Mintage | G-4 | VG-8 | F-12 | VF-20 | XF-40 | MS-60 | MS-65 | Prf-65 |
|---|---|---|---|---|---|---|---|---|---|
| 1965 | 65,879,366 | — | — | — | — | — | 1.25 | 9.50 | — |
| 1966 | 108,984,932 | — | — | — | — | — | 1.40 | 11.00 | — |
| 1967 | 295,046,978 | — | — | — | — | — | 1.50 | 9.50 | — |
| 1968D | 246,951,930 | — | — | — | — | — | 1.25 | 9.00 | — |
| 1968S | 3,041,506 | — | — | — | — | — | — | — | 5.00 |
| 1969D | 129,881,800 | — | — | — | — | — | 1.25 | 7.50 | — |
| 1969S | 2,934,631 | — | — | — | — | — | — | — | 5.00 |
| 1970D | 2,150,000 | — | — | — | — | — | 9.00 | 32.00 | — |
| 1970S | 2,632,810 | — | — | — | — | — | — | — | 10.00 |

**Obv. Designer:** Gilroy Roberts. **Rev. Designer:** Frank Gasparro. **Diameter:** 30.6 mm. **Weight:** 11.3400 g. **Composition:** Copper-Nickel Clad Copper. **KM#** 202b.

| Date | Mintage | G-4 | VG-8 | F-12 | VF-20 | XF-40 | MS-60 | MS-65 | Prf-65 |
|---|---|---|---|---|---|---|---|---|---|
| 1971 | 155,640,000 | — | — | — | — | — | 1.50 | 12.00 | — |
| 1971D | 302,097,424 | — | — | — | — | — | 1.00 | 5.00 | — |
| 1971S | 3,244,183 | — | — | — | — | — | — | — | 3.00 |
| 1972 | 153,180,000 | — | — | — | — | — | 1.00 | 9.00 | — |
| 1972D | 141,890,000 | — | — | — | — | — | 1.00 | 6.00 | — |
| 1972S | 3,267,667 | — | — | — | — | — | — | — | 2.50 |
| 1973 | 64,964,000 | — | — | — | — | — | 1.00 | 6.00 | — |
| 1973D | 83,171,400 | — | — | — | — | — | — | 5.50 | — |
| 1973S | — | — | — | — | — | — | — | — | 2.50 |
| 1974 | 201,596,000 | — | — | — | — | — | 1.00 | 5.00 | — |
| 1974D | 79,066,300 | — | — | — | — | — | 1.00 | 6.00 | — |
| 1974S | — | — | — | — | — | — | — | — | 3.00 |
| 1975 | — | — | — | — | — | — | — | — | — |
| 1975D none minted | — | — | — | — | — | — | — | — | — |
| 1975S none minted | — | — | — | — | — | — | — | — | — |

## Kennedy. Bicentennial design, Independence Hall.

**Rev. Designer:** Seth Huntington. **Composition:** Copper-Nickel Clad Copper. **KM#** 205.

| Date | Mintage | G-4 | VG-8 | F-12 | VF-20 | XF-40 | MS-60 | MS-65 | Prf-65 |
|---|---|---|---|---|---|---|---|---|---|
| 1976 | 234,308,000 | — | — | — | — | — | 1.00 | 10.00 | — |
| 1976D | 287,565,248 | — | — | — | — | — | 1.00 | 4.50 | — |
| 1976S | — | — | — | — | — | — | — | — | 2.00 |

## Kennedy. Bicentennial design, Independence Hall.

**Rev. Designer:** Seth Huntington. **Weight:** 11.5000 g. **Composition:** 0.4000 Silver, 0.1480 oz. ASW. **KM#** 205a.

| Date | Mintage | G-4 | VG-8 | F-12 | VF-20 | XF-40 | MS-60 | MS-65 | Prf-65 |
|---|---|---|---|---|---|---|---|---|---|
| 1976S | 11,000,000 | — | — | — | — | — | — | 6.50 | 5.00 |

## Kennedy. Regular design resumed.

**Diameter:** 30.6 mm. **Weight:** 11.3400 g. **Composition:** Copper-Nickel Clad Copper. **Notes:** The 1979-S and 1981-S Type II proofs have clearer mint marks than the Type I proofs of those years. **KM#** A202b.

| Date | Mintage | MS-65 | Prf-65 | Date | Mintage | MS-65 | Prf-65 |
|---|---|---|---|---|---|---|---|
| 1977 | 43,598,000 | 6.50 | — | 1983P | 34,139,000 | 5.00 | — |
| 1977D | 31,449,106 | 6.00 | — | 1983D | 32,472,244 | 5.00 | — |
| 1977S | — | — | 2.00 | 1983S | — | — | 3.00 |
| 1978 | 14,350,000 | 6.50 | — | 1984P | 26,029,000 | 5.00 | — |
| 1978D | 13,765,799 | 6.50 | — | 1984D | 26,262,158 | 5.00 | — |
| 1978S | — | — | 2.00 | 1984S | — | — | 4.00 |
| 1979 | 68,312,000 | 5.50 | — | 1985P | 18,706,962 | 5.00 | — |
| 1979D | 15,815,422 | 6.00 | — | 1985D | 19,814,034 | 5.00 | — |
| 1979S type I, proof only | — | — | 2.00 | 1985S | — | — | 4.50 |
| 1979S type II, proof only | — | — | 18.00 | 1986P | 13,107,633 | 16.00 | — |
| 1980P | 44,134,000 | 5.00 | — | 1986D | 15,336,145 | 12.00 | — |
| 1980D | 33,456,449 | 4.50 | — | 1986S | — | — | 7.50 |
| 1980S | — | — | 2.00 | 1987P | 2,890,758 | 9.00 | — |
| 1981P | 29,544,000 | 4.50 | — | 1987D | 2,890,758 | 9.00 | — |
| 1981D | 27,839,533 | 4.50 | — | 1987S | — | — | 3.50 |
| 1981S type I, proof only | — | — | 2.00 | 1988P | 13,626,000 | 6.00 | — |
| 1981S type II, proof only | — | — | 14.50 | 1988D | 12,000,096 | 6.00 | — |
| 1982P | 10,819,000 | 5.00 | — | 1988S | — | — | 7.00 |
| 1982D | 13,140,102 | 5.00 | — | 1989P | 24,542,000 | 8.00 | — |
| 1982S | — | — | 3.50 | 1989S | — | — | 7.00 |
| | | | | 1989D | 23,000,216 | 8.00 | — |

| Date | Mintage | MS-65 | Prf-65 | Date | Mintage | MS-65 | Prf-65 |
|---|---|---|---|---|---|---|---|
| 1990P | 22,780,000 | 15.00 | — | 1997P | 20,882,000 | 7.00 | — |
| 1990D | 20,096,242 | 15.00 | — | 1997D | 19,876,000 | 6.00 | — |
| 1990S | — | — | 5.00 | 1997S | (1,975,000) | — | 25.00 |
| 1991P | 14,874,000 | 7.00 | — | 1998P | 15,646,000 | 9.00 | — |
| 1991D | 15,054,678 | 7.00 | — | 1998D | 15,064,000 | 8.00 | — |
| 1991S | (2,867,787) | — | 11.50 | 1998S | (2,078,494) | — | 14.00 |
| 1992P | 17,628,000 | 7.00 | — | 1998S matte finish | 62,350 | — | 400 |
| 1992D | 17,000,106 | 7.00 | — | 1999P | — | 6.00 | — |
| 1992S | (2,858,981) | — | 10.00 | 1999D | — | 6.00 | — |
| 1993P | 15,510,000 | 1.50 | — | 1999S | (2,543,401) | — | 10.00 |
| 1993D | 15,000,006 | 7.00 | — | 2000P | — | 4.00 | — |
| 1993S | (2,633,439) | — | 14.00 | 2000D | — | 4.00 | — |
| 1994P | 23,718,000 | 6.00 | — | 2000S | — | — | 10.00 |
| 1994D | 23,828,110 | 6.00 | — | 2001P | — | 3.00 | — |
| 1994S | (2,484,594) | — | 8.00 | 2001D | — | 3.00 | — |
| 1995P | 26,496,000 | 6.00 | — | 2001S | — | — | 6.00 |
| 1995D | 26,288,000 | 6.00 | — | 2002P | — | — | — |
| 1995S | (2,010,384) | — | 47.50 | 2002D | — | — | — |
| 1996P | 24,442,000 | 6.00 | — | 2002S | — | — | — |
| 1996D | 24,744,000 | 6.00 | — | | | | |
| 1996S | 2,085,191 | — | 7.50 | | | | |

**Composition:** Silver. **KM#** B202b.

| Date | Mintage | Prf-65 | Date | Mintage | Prf-65 |
|---|---|---|---|---|---|
| 1992S | (1,317,579) | 15.00 | 1998S | — | 30.00 |
| 1993S | (761,353) | 25.00 | 1999S | — | 15.00 |
| 1994S | (785,329) | 35.00 | 2000S | — | 12.50 |
| 1995S | (838,953) | 100.00 | 2001S | — | 12.50 |
| 1996S | — | 50.00 | 2002S | — | — |
| 1997S | — | 100.00 | | | |

# DOLLAR

## Morgan.

**Designer:** George T. Morgan. **Diameter:** 38.1 mm. **Weight:** 26.7300 g. **Composition:** 0.9000 Silver, 0.7736 oz. ASW. **Notes:** "65DMPL" values are for coins grading MS-65 deep-mirror prooflike. The 1878 "8 tail feathers" and "7 tail feathers" varieties are distinguished by the number of feathers in the eagle's tail. On the "reverse of 1878" varieties, the top of the top feather in the arrows held by the eagle is straight across and the eagle's breast is concave. On the "reverse of 1879 varieties," the top feather in the arrows held by the eagle is slanted and the eagle's breast is convex. The 1890-CC "tail-bar variety has a bar extending from the arrow feathers to the wreath on the reverse, the result of a die gouge. **KM#** 110.

| Date | Mintage | VG-8 | F-12 | VF-20 | XF-40 | AU-50 | MS-60 | MS-63 | MS-64 | MS-65 | 65DMPL | Prf-65 |
|---|---|---|---|---|---|---|---|---|---|---|---|---|
| 1901 | 6,962,813 | 15.00 | 22.00 | 33.00 | 60.00 | 230 | 1,500 | 18,000 | 61,000 | 189,000 | 220,000 | 8,100 |
| 1901O | 13,320,000 | 12.00 | 12.50 | 13.00 | 13.50 | 27.00 | 30.00 | 35.00 | 53.00 | 170 | 3,800 | — |
| 1901S | 2,284,000 | 15.00 | 18.00 | 27.00 | 50.00 | 165 | 265 | 525 | 850 | 5,350 | 12,500 | — |
| 1902 | 7,994,777 | 12.00 | 12.50 | 13.00 | 19.00 | 22.00 | 34.00 | 90.00 | 135 | 460 | 15,750 | 5,750 |
| 1902O | 8,636,000 | 12.00 | 12.50 | 13.00 | 13.50 | 23.00 | 25.00 | 35.00 | 51.00 | 140 | 3,600 | — |
| 1902S | 1,530,000 | 27.00 | 37.00 | 80.00 | 105 | 130 | 210 | 310 | 625 | 3,700 | 15,000 | — |
| 1903 | 4,652,755 | 12.50 | 14.00 | 15.00 | 21.00 | 24.00 | 34.00 | 57.00 | 65.00 | 180 | 9,150 | 5,500 |
| 1903O | 4,450,000 | 125 | 150 | 170 | 180 | 200 | 240 | 275 | 275 | 460 | 4,650 | — |
| 1903S | 1,241,000 | 22.00 | 27.00 | 77.00 | 250 | 1,100 | 2,900 | 4,500 | 5,250 | 7,450 | 35,000 | — |
| 1904 | 2,788,650 | 12.00 | 12.50 | 13.00 | 18.00 | 31.00 | 60.00 | 170 | 560 | 4,400 | 38,000 | 5,500 |
| 1904O | 3,720,000 | 12.00 | 12.50 | 13.00 | 14.00 | 21.00 | 24.00 | 35.00 | 51.00 | 105 | 550 | — |
| 1904S | 2,304,000 | 16.00 | 25.00 | 42.00 | 185 | 520 | 950 | 2,100 | 2,750 | 6,550 | 19,000 | — |
| 1921 | 44,690,000 | 11.00 | 11.50 | 12.00 | 13.00 | 14.00 | 18.00 | 23.00 | 35.00 | 150 | 8,800 | — |
| 1921D | 20,345,000 | 11.00 | 11.50 | 12.00 | 13.00 | 15.00 | 32.00 | 37.00 | 70.00 | 300 | 15,000 | — |
| 1921S | 21,695,000 | 11.00 | 11.50 | 12.00 | 13.00 | 16.00 | 26.00 | 53.00 | 150 | 1,850 | 22,000 | — |

## Peace.

Mint mark

**Designer:** Anthony DeFrancisci. **Diameter:** 38.1 mm. **Weight:** 26.7300 g. **Composition:** 0.9000 Silver, 0.7736 oz. ASW. **Notes:** Commonly called Peace dollars. **KM#** 150.

| Date | Mintage | G-4 | VG-8 | F-12 | VF-20 | XF-40 | AU-50 | MS-60 | MS-63 | MS-64 | MS-65 |
|---|---|---|---|---|---|---|---|---|---|---|---|
| 1921 | 1,006,473 | 29.00 | 35.00 | 38.00 | 44.00 | 53.00 | 105 | 145 | 220 | 540 | 2,650 |

| Date | Mintage | G-4 | VG-8 | F-12 | VF-20 | XF-40 | AU-50 | MS-60 | MS-63 | MS-64 | MS-65 |
|---|---|---|---|---|---|---|---|---|---|---|---|
| 1922 | 51,737,000 | 8.00 | 8.25 | 8.50 | 9.00 | 11.00 | 14.00 | 17.00 | 31.00 | 46.00 | 110 |
| 1922D | 15,063,000 | 8.00 | 8.25 | 8.50 | 9.00 | 11.00 | 14.00 | 20.00 | 40.00 | 80.00 | 365 |
| 1922S | 17,475,000 | 8.00 | 8.25 | 8.50 | 9.00 | 11.00 | 14.00 | 20.00 | 60.00 | 230 | 2,150 |
| 1923 | 30,800,000 | 8.00 | 8.25 | 8.50 | 9.00 | 11.00 | 14.00 | 17.00 | 31.00 | 46.00 | 110 |
| 1923D | 6,811,000 | 8.00 | 8.25 | 8.50 | 9.00 | 14.00 | 17.00 | 42.00 | 100.00 | 210 | 1,050 |
| 1923S | 19,020,000 | 8.00 | 8.25 | 8.50 | 9.00 | 12.00 | 16.00 | 20.00 | 60.00 | 210 | 7,000 |
| 1924 | 11,811,000 | 8.00 | 8.25 | 8.50 | 9.00 | 11.00 | 14.00 | 17.00 | 33.00 | 51.00 | 110 |
| 1924S | 1,728,000 | 9.00 | 13.00 | 14.00 | 15.00 | 21.00 | 50.00 | 180 | 350 | 1,300 | 8,500 |
| 1925 | 10,198,000 | 8.00 | 8.25 | 8.50 | 9.00 | 11.00 | 14.00 | 17.00 | 33.00 | 51.00 | 110 |
| 1925S | 1,610,000 | 9.00 | 11.00 | 12.00 | 14.00 | 17.00 | 30.00 | 65.00 | 120 | 600 | 21,000 |
| 1926 | 1,939,000 | 8.00 | 10.00 | 11.00 | 13.00 | 17.00 | 19.00 | 22.00 | 45.00 | 80.00 | 300 |
| 1926D | 2,348,700 | 8.00 | 10.00 | 14.00 | 15.00 | 18.00 | 25.00 | 50.00 | 110 | 240 | 550 |
| 1926S | 6,980,000 | 8.00 | 8.25 | 8.50 | 9.00 | 16.00 | 18.00 | 32.00 | 79.00 | 135 | 850 |
| 1927 | 848,000 | 13.00 | 17.00 | 19.00 | 22.00 | 28.00 | 44.00 | 58.00 | 120 | 250 | 2,350 |
| 1927D | 1,268,900 | 10.00 | 13.00 | 15.00 | 18.00 | 26.00 | 71.00 | 130 | 210 | 580 | 4,900 |
| 1927S | 866,000 | 10.00 | 13.00 | 15.00 | 18.00 | 24.00 | 64.00 | 115 | 270 | 630 | 9,950 |
| 1928 | 360,649 | 100.00 | 125 | 140 | 150 | 165 | 205 | 245 | 320 | 675 | 3,150 |
| 1928S | 1,632,000 | 10.00 | 15.00 | 16.00 | 19.00 | 24.00 | 42.00 | 105 | 285 | 1,050 | 22,000 |
| 1934 | 954,057 | 10.00 | 15.00 | 16.00 | 19.00 | 22.00 | 33.00 | 72.00 | 120 | 265 | 1,150 |
| 1934D | 1,569,500 | 10.00 | 13.00 | 15.00 | 17.00 | 20.00 | 36.00 | 78.00 | 200 | 475 | 2,000 |
| 1934S | 1,011,000 | 13.00 | 16.00 | 21.00 | 55.00 | 135 | 475 | 1,000 | 2,700 | 4,050 | 6,500 |
| 1935 | 1,576,000 | 10.00 | 12.00 | 14.00 | 16.00 | 18.00 | 30.00 | 52.00 | 77.00 | 140 | 600 |
| 1935S | 1,964,000 | 10.00 | 12.00 | 14.00 | 16.00 | 22.00 | 77.00 | 140 | 260 | 450 | 1,050 |

## Eisenhower.

**Designer:** Frank Gasparro. **Diameter:** 38.1 mm. **Weight:** 22.6800 g. **Composition:** Copper-Nickel Clad Copper. **KM#** 203.

| Date | Mintage | (Proof) | MS-63 | Prf-65 |
|---|---|---|---|---|
| 1971 | 47,799,000 | — | 3.75 | — |
| 1971D | 68,587,424 | — | 2.00 | — |
| 1972 | 75,890,000 | — | 2.75 | — |
| 1972D | 92,548,511 | — | 2.25 | — |
| 1973 | 2,000,056 | — | 11.00 | — |
| 1973D | 2,000,000 | — | 11.00 | — |
| 1973S | 2,769,624 | — | — | 11.00 |
| 1974 | 27,366,000 | — | 3.00 | — |
| 1974D | 35,466,000 | — | 2.75 | — |
| 1974S | — | (2,617,350) | — | 6.50 |

**Designer:** Frank Gasparro. **Diameter:** 38.1 mm. **Weight:** 24.5900 g. **Composition:** Silver. **KM#** 203a.

| Date | Mintage | (Proof) | MS-63 | Prf-65 |
|---|---|---|---|---|
| 1971S | 6,868,530 | (4,265,234) | 7.00 | 7.00 |
| 1972S | 2,193,056 | (1,811,631) | 7.50 | 7.00 |
| 1973S | 1,833,140 | (1,005,617) | 8.50 | 30.00 |
| 1974S | 1,720,000 | (1,306,579) | 7.50 | 6.50 |

## Eisenhower. Bicentennial design, moon behind Liberty Bell.

Type I Type II

**Rev. Designer:** Dennis R. Williams. **Diameter:** 38.1mm **Weight:** 22.6800 g. **Composition:** Copper-Nickel Clad Copper. **Notes:** In 1976 the lettering on the reverse on the reverse was changed to thinner letters, resulting in Type I and Type II varieties for that year. **KM#** 206.

| Date | Mintage | (Proof) | MS-63 | Prf-65 |
|---|---|---|---|---|
| 1976 type I | 117,337,000 | — | 4.00 | — |
| 1976 type II | Inc. above | — | 2.00 | — |
| 1976D type I | 103,228,274 | — | 3.25 | — |
| 1976D type II | Inc. above | — | 2.00 | — |
| 1976S type I | — | (2,909,369) | — | 5.75 |
| 1976S type II | — | (4,149,730) | — | 5.75 |
| 1976S type II | — | — | — | 5.75 |

## Eisenhower. Bicentennial design, moon behind Liberty Bell.

**Rev. Designer:** Dennis R. Williams. **Weight:** 24.5900 g. **Composition:** 0.4000 Silver, 0.3162 oz. ASW. **KM#** 206a.

| Date | Mintage | (Proof) | MS-63 | Prf-65 |
|---|---|---|---|---|
| 1976S | 11,000,000 | (4,000,000) | 14.00 | 12.50 |

## Eisenhower. Regular design resumed.

**Diameter:** 38.1 mm. **Composition:** Copper-Nickel Clad Copper. **KM#** A203.

| Date | Mintage | (Proof) | MS-63 | Prf-65 |
|---|---|---|---|---|
| 1977 | 12,596,000 | — | 4.25 | — |
| 1977D | 32,983,006 | — | 3.25 | — |
| 1977S | — | (3,251,152) | — | 8.00 |
| 1978 | 25,702,000 | — | 2.75 | — |
| 1978D | 33,012,890 | — | 3.00 | — |
| 1978S | — | (3,127,788) | — | 10.00 |

## Anthony.

**Designer:** Frank Gasparro. **Diameter:** 26.5 mm. **Weight:** 8.1000 g. **Composition:** Copper-Nickel Clad Copper. **Notes:** The 1979-S and 1981-S Type II coins have a clearer mint mark than the Type I varieties for those years. **KM#** 207.

| Date | Mintage | MS-63 | Date | Mintage | MS-63 |
|---|---|---|---|---|---|
| 1979P | 360,222,000 | 2.00 | 1980S proof | 3,547,030 | 11.00 |
| 1979P near date | Inc. above | 15.00 | 1981P | 3,000,000 | 5.75 |
| 1979D | 288,015,744 | 1.75 | 1981D | 3,250,000 | 5.75 |
| 1979S | 109,576,000 | 2.00 | 1981S | 3,492,000 | 6.00 |
| 1979S proof, type I | 3,677,175 | 12.00 | 1981S proof, type I | 4,063,083 | 10.00 |
| 1979S proof, type II | — | 110 | 1981S proof, type II | — | 185 |
| 1980P | 27,610,000 | 2.00 | 1999P | — | 1.50 |
| 1980D | 41,628,708 | 2.00 | 1999D | — | 1.75 |
| 1980S | 20,422,000 | 2.00 | 1999P | — | 9.50 |

## Sacagawea.

**Diameter:** 26.4 mm. **Weight:** 8.0700 g. **Composition:** Copper-Zinc-Manganese-Nickel Clad Copper. **KM#** 311.

| Date | Mintage | MS-63 | Prf-65 | Date | Mintage | MS-63 | Prf-65 |
|---|---|---|---|---|---|---|---|
| 2000P | — | 1.50 | — | 2001P | — | 1.50 | — |
| 2000D | — | 1.50 | — | 2001D | — | 1.50 | — |
| 2000S | — | — | 7.50 | 2001S | — | — | 7.50 |

# $2.50 (QUARTER EAGLE)

## Coronet Head.

1948 "Cal."

**Designer:** Christian Gobrecht. **Diameter:** 18 mm. **Weight:** 4.1800 g. **Composition:** 0.9000 Gold, 0.121 oz. AGW. **Notes:** Varieties for 1843 are distinguished by the size of the numerals in the date. One 1848 variety has "Cal." inscribed on the reverse, indicating it was made from California gold. The 1873 "closed-3" and "open-3" varieties are distinguished by the amount of space between the upper left and lower left serifs in the 3 in the date. **KM#** 72.

| Date | Mintage | F-12 | VF-20 | XF-40 | AU-50 | MS-60 | Prf-65 |
|---|---|---|---|---|---|---|---|
| 1901 | 91,322 | 110 | 145 | 170 | 180 | 240 | 13,000 |
| 1902 | 133,733 | 110 | 145 | 170 | 180 | 240 | 13,000 |
| 1903 | 201,257 | 110 | 145 | 170 | 180 | 240 | 13,000 |
| 1904 | 160,960 | 110 | 145 | 170 | 180 | 240 | 13,000 |
| 1905 | 217,944 | 110 | 145 | 170 | 180 | 240 | 13,000 |
| 1906 | 176,490 | 110 | 145 | 170 | 180 | 240 | 13,000 |
| 1907 | 336,448 | 110 | 145 | 170 | 180 | 240 | 13,000 |

## Indian Head.

**Designer:** Bela Lyon Pratt. **Diameter:** 18 mm. **Weight:** 4.1800 g. **Composition:** 0.9000 Gold, 0.121 oz. AGW. **KM#** 128.

| Date | Mintage | VF-20 | XF-40 | AU-50 | MS-60 | MS-63 | MS-65 | Prf-65 |
|---|---|---|---|---|---|---|---|---|
| 1908 | 565,057 | 135 | 175 | 185 | 230 | 550 | 2,500 | 15,000 |
| 1909 | 441,899 | 135 | 175 | 185 | 240 | 725 | 3,000 | 29,000 |
| 1910 | 492,682 | 135 | 175 | 185 | 240 | 735 | 5,200 | 16,000 |
| 1911 | 704,191 | 135 | 175 | 185 | 250 | 625 | 3,000 | 15,000 |
| 1911D | 55,680 | 700 | 1,000 | 1,200 | 2,350 | 7,800 | 40,000 | — |
| 1912 | 616,197 | 135 | 175 | 185 | 250 | 900 | 5,200 | 15,500 |
| 1913 | 722,165 | 135 | 175 | 185 | 250 | 600 | 3,300 | 15,800 |
| 1914 | 240,117 | 135 | 175 | 200 | 370 | 2,750 | 10,000 | 16,500 |
| 1914D | 448,000 | 135 | 175 | 185 | 250 | 1,000 | 8,000 | — |
| 1915 | 606,100 | 135 | 175 | 185 | 240 | 560 | 3,200 | 15,250 |
| 1925D | 578,000 | 135 | 175 | 185 | 230 | 500 | 2,000 | — |
| 1926 | 446,000 | 135 | 175 | 185 | 230 | 500 | 2,000 | — |
| 1927 | 388,000 | 135 | 175 | 185 | 230 | 500 | 2,000 | — |
| 1928 | 416,000 | 135 | 175 | 185 | 230 | 500 | 2,000 | — |
| 1929 | 532,000 | 135 | 175 | 185 | 230 | 500 | 3,000 | — |

# $5 (HALF EAGLE)

## Coronet Head. "In God We Trust" above eagle.

**Designer:** Christian Gobrecht. **Diameter:** 21.6 mm. **Weight:** 8.3590 g. **Composition:** 0.9000 Gold, 0.242 oz. AGW. **Notes:** The 1873 "closed-3" and "open-3" varieties are known and are distinguished by the amount of space between the upper left and lower left serifs of the 3 in the date. **KM#** 101.

| Date | Mintage | VF-20 | XF-40 | AU-50 | MS-60 | MS-65 | Prf-65 |
|---|---|---|---|---|---|---|---|
| 1901 | 616,040 | 155 | 165 | 180 | 230 | 3,850 | 12,500 |
| 1901S | 3,648,000 | 150 | 160 | 170 | 230 | 2,900 | — |
| 1902 | 172,562 | 150 | 165 | 180 | 225 | 4,400 | 22,000 |
| 1902S | 939,000 | 150 | 155 | 180 | 215 | 3,100 | — |
| 1903 | 227,024 | 150 | 155 | 180 | 220 | 4,800 | 22,000 |
| 1903S | 1,855,000 | 150 | 155 | 180 | 210 | 3,800 | — |
| 1904 | 392,136 | 150 | 165 | 180 | 215 | 3,900 | 25,000 |
| 1904S | 97,000 | 160 | 170 | 265 | 850 | 16,000 | — |
| 1905 | 302,308 | 150 | 160 | 180 | 215 | 4,500 | 25,000 |
| 1905S | 880,700 | 150 | 160 | 185 | 485 | 11,500 | — |
| 1906 | 348,820 | 150 | 155 | 180 | 220 | 3,800 | 22,000 |
| 1906D | 320,000 | 150 | 160 | 180 | 220 | 4,700 | — |
| 1906S | 598,000 | 150 | 160 | 180 | 220 | 5,750 | — |
| 1907 | 626,192 | 150 | 155 | 175 | 215 | 3,900 | 23,000 |
| 1907D | 888,000 | 150 | 155 | 180 | 215 | 3,200 | — |
| 1908 | 421,874 | 150 | 155 | 180 | 215 | 3,200 | — |

## Indian Head.

**Designer:** Bela Lyon Pratt. **Diameter:** 21.6 mm. **Weight:** 8.3590 g. **Composition:** 0.9000 Gold, .2420 oz. AGW. **KM#** 129.

| Date | Mintage | VF-20 | XF-40 | AU-50 | MS-60 | MS-63 | MS-65 | Prf-65 |
|---|---|---|---|---|---|---|---|---|
| 1908 | 578,012 | 180 | 215 | 225 | 325 | 1,000 | 11,000 | 16,000 |
| 1908D | 148,000 | 180 | 215 | 225 | 325 | 950 | 18,000 | — |
| 1908S | 82,000 | 195 | 415 | 450 | 1,150 | 2,500 | 16,000 | — |
| 1909 | 627,138 | 180 | 215 | 225 | 325 | 1,200 | 14,000 | 29,000 |
| 1909D | 3,423,560 | 175 | 200 | 220 | 310 | 1,150 | 10,000 | — |
| 1909O | 34,200 | 600 | 1,100 | 1,450 | 5,400 | 40,000 | 160,000 | — |
| 1909S | 297,200 | 185 | 240 | 250 | 1,300 | 6,600 | 39,000 | — |
| 1910 | 604,250 | 175 | 200 | 240 | 300 | 1,350 | 14,000 | 32,000 |
| 1910D | 193,600 | 175 | 200 | 240 | 350 | 1,750 | 34,500 | — |
| 1910S | 770,200 | 175 | 220 | 260 | 900 | 5,500 | 36,000 | — |
| 1911 | 915,139 | 175 | 200 | 240 | 300 | 1,200 | 13,000 | 26,000 |
| 1911D | 72,500 | 350 | 440 | 500 | 2,900 | 16,500 | 140,000 | — |
| 1911S | 1,416,000 | 180 | 215 | 250 | 500 | 2,700 | 37,000 | — |
| 1912 | 790,144 | 180 | 210 | 240 | 300 | 1,200 | 14,500 | 26,000 |
| 1912S | 392,000 | 195 | 230 | 270 | 1,450 | 7,500 | 70,000 | — |
| 1913 | 916,099 | 180 | 210 | 230 | 290 | 1,150 | 11,000 | 26,000 |
| 1913S | 408,000 | 200 | 220 | 270 | 1,250 | 9,800 | 100,000 | — |
| 1914 | 247,125 | 180 | 225 | 240 | 335 | 1,400 | 11,500 | 26,000 |
| 1914D | 247,000 | 185 | 225 | 240 | 315 | 2,300 | 29,000 | — |
| 1914S | 263,000 | 200 | 235 | 255 | 1,100 | 8,000 | 72,000 | — |
| 1915 | 588,075 | 190 | 225 | 240 | 300 | 1,200 | 15,000 | 33,000 |
| 1915S | 164,000 | 260 | 300 | 350 | 1,650 | 8,000 | 80,000 | — |
| 1916S | 240,000 | 190 | 250 | 280 | 525 | 2,300 | 18,500 | — |
| 1929 | 662,000 | 2,400 | 4,600 | 4,800 | 5,400 | 7,500 | 23,500 | — |

# $10 (EAGLE)

## Coronet Head. New-style head. "In God We Trust" above eagle.

**Designer:** Christian Gobrecht. **Diameter:** 27 mm. **Weight:** 16.7180 g. **Composition:** 0.9000 Gold, 0.4839 oz. AGW. **Notes:** The 1873 "closed-3" and "open-3" varieties are distinguished by the amount of space between the upper left and lower left serifs of the 3 in the date. **KM#** 102.

| Date | Mintage | VF-20 | XF-40 | AU-50 | MS-60 | MS-65 | Prf-65 |
|---|---|---|---|---|---|---|---|
| 1901 | 1,718,825 | 200 | 210 | 220 | 250 | 2,800 | 30,500 |
| 1901O | 72,041 | 225 | 250 | 300 | 375 | — | — |
| 1901S | 2,812,750 | 200 | 210 | 220 | 250 | 2,500 | — |
| 1902 | 82,513 | 230 | 260 | 295 | 340 | — | 30,500 |
| 1902S | 469,500 | 200 | 210 | 220 | 275 | 2,700 | — |
| 1903 | 125,926 | 210 | 250 | 290 | 315 | — | 30,000 |
| 1903O | 112,771 | 230 | 250 | 290 | 350 | — | — |
| 1903S | 538,000 | 200 | 215 | 230 | 290 | 2,650 | — |
| 1904 | 162,038 | 200 | 215 | 230 | 280 | — | 31,500 |
| 1904O | 108,950 | 230 | 250 | 285 | 340 | — | — |
| 1905 | 201,078 | 200 | 215 | 225 | 265 | 4,800 | 30,000 |
| 1905S | 369,250 | 210 | 230 | 260 | 1,100 | — | — |
| 1906 | 165,497 | 210 | 220 | 230 | 275 | 7,750 | 30,000 |
| 1906D | 981,000 | 230 | 245 | 275 | 325 | 3,850 | — |
| 1906O | 86,895 | 210 | 250 | 310 | 375 | — | — |
| 1906S | 457,000 | 220 | 250 | 300 | 475 | 12,500 | — |
| 1907 | 1,203,973 | 190 | 200 | 220 | 250 | — | 30,000 |
| 1907D | 1,030,000 | 190 | 200 | 240 | 275 | — | — |
| 1907S | 210,500 | 240 | 260 | 300 | 575 | — | — |

## Indian Head. No motto next to eagle.

**Designer:** Augustus Saint-Gaudens. **Diameter:** 27 mm. **Weight:** 16.7180 g. **Composition:** 0.9000 Gold, 0.4839 oz. AGW. **Notes:** 1907 varieties are distinguished by whether the edge is rolled or wired, and whether the legend "E Pluribus Unum" has periods between each word. **KM#** 125.

| Date | Mintage | VF-20 | XF-40 | AU-50 | MS-60 | MS-63 | MS-65 | Prf-65 |
|---|---|---|---|---|---|---|---|---|
| 1907 wire edge, periods before and after legend | 500 | — | 4,500 | 6,000 | 9,500 | 15,500 | 42,000 | — |
| 1907 same, without stars on edge, unique | — | — | — | — | — | — | — | — |
| 1907 rolled edge, periods | 42 | 13,000 | 19,000 | — | 22,000 | 32,500 | 90,000 | — |
| 1907 without periods | 239,406 | 350 | 375 | 400 | 475 | 1,700 | 5,500 | — |
| 1908 without motto | 33,500 | 350 | 375 | 400 | 475 | 1,700 | 5,500 | — |
| 1908D without motto | 210,000 | 320 | 375 | 400 | 675 | 4,500 | 34,000 | — |

## Indian Head. "In God We Trust" left of eagle.

**Designer:** Augustus Saint-Gaudens. **Diameter:** 27 mm. **Weight:** 16.7180 g. **Composition:** 0.9000 Gold, 0.4839 oz. AGW. **KM#** 130.

| Date | Mintage | VF-20 | XF-40 | AU-50 | MS-60 | MS-63 | MS-65 | Prf-65 |
|---|---|---|---|---|---|---|---|---|
| 1908 | 341,486 | 315 | 350 | 365 | 440 | 1,200 | 5,000 | 29,500 |
| 1908D | 836,500 | 320 | 360 | 370 | 625 | 2,950 | 17,500 | — |
| 1908S | 59,850 | 315 | 360 | 400 | 1,400 | 4,900 | 17,000 | — |
| 1909 | 184,863 | 310 | 340 | 360 | 470 | 1,500 | 8,000 | 31,500 |
| 1909D | 121,540 | 310 | 340 | 360 | 515 | 2,150 | 36,000 | — |
| 1909S | 292,350 | 315 | 345 | 370 | 570 | 2,450 | 10,000 | — |
| 1910 | 318,704 | 300 | 325 | 350 | 450 | 850 | 4,500 | 37,000 |
| 1910D | 2,356,640 | 300 | 325 | 350 | 465 | 875 | 5,150 | — |
| 1910S | 811,000 | 300 | 325 | 350 | 685 | 3,100 | 49,000 | — |
| 1911 | 505,595 | 300 | 325 | 350 | 480 | 850 | 5,150 | 32,000 |
| 1911D | 30,100 | 350 | 750 | 800 | 3,500 | 11,000 | 85,000 | — |
| 1911S | 51,000 | 350 | 600 | 675 | 950 | 3,900 | 8,600 | — |
| 1912 | 405,083 | 300 | 325 | 350 | 480 | 750 | 5,900 | 32,000 |
| 1912S | 300,000 | 320 | 340 | 360 | 650 | 2,950 | 43,000 | — |
| 1913 | 442,071 | 300 | 330 | 350 | 440 | 900 | 4,500 | 32,000 |
| 1913S | 66,000 | 350 | 615 | 775 | 3,150 | 9,500 | 85,000 | — |
| 1914 | 151,050 | 300 | 335 | 385 | 525 | 1,350 | 5,850 | 32,000 |

| Date | Mintage | VF-20 | XF-40 | AU-50 | MS-60 | MS-63 | MS-65 | Prf-65 |
|---|---|---|---|---|---|---|---|---|
| 1914D | 343,500 | 300 | 335 | 375 | 515 | 1,250 | 100,000 | — |
| 1914S | 208,000 | 290 | 330 | 360 | 650 | 3,500 | 32,500 | — |
| 1915 | 351,075 | 300 | 340 | 370 | 530 | 1,150 | 5,100 | 40,000 |
| 1915S | 59,000 | 350 | 675 | 735 | 2,600 | 7,800 | 52,500 | — |
| 1916S | 138,500 | 310 | 330 | 350 | 660 | 2,200 | 14,500 | — |
| 1920S | 126,500 | 4,700 | 6,000 | 7,500 | 14,500 | 32,000 | 150,000 | — |
| 1926 | 1,014,000 | 275 | 295 | 315 | 415 | 650 | 3,250 | — |
| 1930S | 96,000 | 3,300 | 6,000 | 7,700 | 8,200 | 110,000 | 24,000 | — |
| 1932 | 4,463,000 | 275 | 295 | 315 | 415 | 640 | 2,950 | — |
| 1933 | 312,500 | 22,500 | 29,000 | 35,000 | 49,000 | 85,000 | 300,000 | — |

# $20 (DOUBLE EAGLE)

## Liberty. "Twenty Dollars" below eagle.

**Weight:** 33.4360 g. **Composition:** 0.9000 Gold, 0.9677 oz. AGW. **KM#** 74.3.

| Date | Mintage | VF-20 | XF-40 | AU-50 | MS-60 | MS-65 | Prf-65 |
|---|---|---|---|---|---|---|---|
| 1901 | 111,526 | 350 | 375 | 400 | 500 | 3,200 | — |
| 1901S | 1,596,000 | 345 | 365 | 380 | 425 | — | — |
| 1902 | 31,254 | 360 | 380 | 415 | 815 | — | — |
| 1902S | 1,753,625 | 345 | 365 | 380 | 425 | — | — |
| 1903 | 287,428 | 340 | 350 | 385 | 450 | 4,250 | 51,500 |
| 1903S | 954,000 | 345 | 365 | 380 | 425 | 10,500 | — |
| 1904 | 6,256,797 | 345 | 365 | 380 | 425 | 2,400 | 50,000 |
| 1904S | 5,134,175 | 345 | 365 | 380 | 425 | 4,700 | — |
| 1905 | 59,011 | 350 | 395 | 475 | 875 | — | — |
| 1905S | 1,813,000 | 345 | 365 | 425 | 550 | — | — |
| 1906 | 69,690 | 345 | 385 | 425 | 515 | 13,500 | 52,500 |
| 1906D | 620,250 | 345 | 365 | 400 | 450 | — | — |
| 1906S | 2,065,750 | 345 | 365 | 400 | 450 | — | — |
| 1907 | 1,451,864 | 340 | 360 | 375 | 415 | 5,800 | — |
| 1907D | 842,250 | 345 | 365 | 395 | 440 | 4,750 | — |
| 1907S | 2,165,800 | 340 | 360 | 375 | 440 | — | — |

## Saint-Gaudens. Roman numerals in date. No motto below eagle.

**Designer:** Augustus Saint-Gaudens. **Diameter:** 34 mm. **Weight:** 33.4360 g. **Composition:** 0.9000 Gold, 0.9677 oz. AGW. **Notes:** The "Roman numerals" varieties for 1907 use Roman numerals for the date instead of Arabic numerals. The lettered-edge varieties have "E Pluribus Unum" on the edge, with stars between the words. **KM#** Pn1874.

| Date | Mintage | VF-20 | XF-40 | AU-50 | MS-60 | MS-63 | MS-65 | Prf-65 |
|---|---|---|---|---|---|---|---|---|
| 1907 extremely high relief, unique | — | — | — | — | — | — | — | — |
| 1907 extremely high relief, lettered edge | — | — | — | — | — | — | — | — |

**Note:** 1907 extremely high relief, lettered edge, Prf-68, private sale, 1990, $1,500,000.

## Saint-Gaudens. Roman numerals in date. No motto below eagle.

**Designer:** Augustus Saint-Gaudens. **Diameter:** 34 mm. **Weight:** 33.4360 g. **Composition:** 0.9000 Gold, 0.9677 oz. AGW. **KM#** 126.

| Date | Mintage | VF-20 | XF-40 | AU-50 | MS-60 | MS-63 | MS-65 | Prf-65 |
|---|---|---|---|---|---|---|---|---|
| 1907 high relief, unique, AU-55, $150,000 | — | — | — | — | — | — | — | — |
| 1907 high relief, wire rim | 11,250 | 3,000 | 4,750 | 5,300 | 8,250 | 12,750 | 28,500 | — |
| 1907 high relief, flat rim | Inc. above | 3,000 | 4,800 | 5,400 | 8,350 | 12,750 | 29,500 | — |

## Saint-Gaudens. Arabic numerals in date. No motto below eagle.

**Designer:** Augustus Saint-Gaudens. **Diameter:** 34 mm. **Weight:** 33.4360 g. **Composition:** 0.9000 Gold, 0.9677 oz. AGW. **KM#** 127.

| Date | Mintage | VF-20 | XF-40 | AU-50 | MS-60 | MS-63 | MS-65 | Prf-65 |
|---|---|---|---|---|---|---|---|---|
| 1907 large letters on edge, unique | — | — | — | — | — | — | — | — |
| 1907 small letters on edge | 361,667 | 430 | 450 | 480 | 500 | 675 | 2,600 | — |
| 1908 | 4,271,551 | 415 | 435 | 465 | 475 | 650 | 900 | — |
| 1908D | 663,750 | 425 | 440 | 460 | 515 | 750 | 10,500 | — |

## Saint-Gaudens. "In God We Trust" below eagle.

**Designer:** Augustus Saint-Gaudens. **Diameter:** 34 mm. **Weight:** 33.4360 g. **Composition:** 0.9000 Gold, 0.9677 oz. AGW. **KM#** 131.

| Date | Mintage | VF-20 | XF-40 | AU-50 | MS-60 | MS-63 | MS-65 | Prf-65 |
|---|---|---|---|---|---|---|---|---|
| 1908 | 156,359 | 375 | 400 | 415 | 430 | 485 | 950 | 38,000 |
| 1908D | 349,500 | 375 | 400 | 415 | 500 | 750 | 4,750 | — |
| 1908S | 22,000 | 650 | 1,100 | 1,400 | 3,900 | 10,000 | 35,000 | — |
| 1909/8 | 161,282 | 525 | 580 | 625 | 1,200 | 4,900 | 24,000 | — |
| 1909 | Inc. above | 450 | 560 | 600 | 700 | 2,700 | 42,000 | 49,000 |
| 1909D | 52,500 | 500 | 690 | 735 | 1,250 | 3,250 | 33,500 | — |
| 1909S | 2,774,925 | 360 | 385 | 400 | 460 | 550 | 4,800 | — |
| 1910 | 482,167 | 365 | 390 | 400 | 440 | 535 | 6,250 | 49,000 |
| 1910D | 429,000 | 365 | 390 | 400 | 440 | 530 | 2,750 | — |
| 1910S | 2,128,250 | 365 | 400 | 425 | 625 | 850 | 7,850 | — |
| 1911 | 197,350 | 365 | 390 | 400 | 490 | 1,475 | 10,500 | 39,500 |
| 1911D | 846,500 | 365 | 385 | 400 | 460 | 495 | 1,350 | — |
| 1911S | 775,750 | 365 | 385 | 400 | 470 | 485 | 4,700 | — |
| 1912 | 149,824 | 385 | 415 | 515 | 560 | 950 | 14,500 | 40,000 |
| 1913 | 168,838 | 365 | 385 | 415 | 465 | 1,675 | 28,000 | 40,000 |
| 1913D | 393,500 | 365 | 385 | 415 | 440 | 675 | 4,500 | — |
| 1913S | 34,000 | 550 | 775 | 750 | 1,150 | 2,900 | 38,000 | — |
| 1914 | 95,320 | 400 | 500 | 520 | 550 | 1,175 | 13,750 | 41,500 |
| 1914D | 453,000 | 360 | 380 | 410 | 450 | 490 | 2,500 | — |
| 1914S | 1,498,000 | 360 | 380 | 400 | 430 | 480 | 1,950 | — |
| 1915 | 152,050 | 390 | 450 | 525 | 600 | 1,450 | 14,000 | 47,500 |
| 1915S | 567,500 | 360 | 380 | 400 | 435 | 550 | 1,950 | — |
| 1916S | 796,000 | 360 | 380 | 410 | 540 | 600 | 1,950 | — |
| 1920 | 228,250 | 365 | 385 | 400 | 450 | 675 | 24,500 | — |
| 1920S | 558,000 | 4,300 | 8,000 | 10,500 | 25,000 | 52,000 | 150,000 | — |
| 1921 | 528,500 | 8,000 | 13,000 | 18,750 | 33,500 | 77,000 | 200,000 | — |
| 1922 | 1,375,500 | 365 | 380 | 400 | 420 | 460 | 3,600 | — |
| 1922S | 2,658,000 | 445 | 650 | 715 | 825 | 1,650 | 36,000 | — |
| 1923 | 566,000 | 360 | 380 | 410 | 440 | 465 | 6,000 | — |
| 1923D | 1,702,250 | 360 | 380 | 400 | 440 | 490 | 1,100 | — |
| 1924 | 4,323,500 | 360 | 375 | 400 | 420 | 460 | 825 | — |
| 1924D | 3,049,500 | 775 | 1,150 | 1,350 | 1,800 | 4,950 | 50,000 | — |
| 1924S | 2,927,500 | 650 | 1,075 | 1,175 | 2,200 | 5,350 | 40,000 | — |
| 1925 | 2,831,750 | 360 | 375 | 400 | 420 | 460 | 825 | — |
| 1925D | 2,938,500 | 1,200 | 1,675 | 1,875 | 3,200 | 7,750 | 50,000 | — |
| 1925S | 3,776,500 | 900 | 1,300 | 1,600 | 5,500 | 18,000 | 72,000 | — |
| 1926 | 816,750 | 365 | 380 | 400 | 425 | 480 | 825 | — |
| 1926D | 481,000 | 1,100 | 2,850 | 3,200 | 7,500 | 19,500 | 85,000 | — |
| 1926S | 2,041,500 | 700 | 1,200 | 1,300 | 1,800 | 2,750 | 32,000 | — |
| 1927 | 2,946,750 | 350 | 375 | 390 | 415 | 475 | 900 | — |
| 1927D | 180,000 | — | — | 150,000 | 265,000 | — | 600,000 | — |
| 1927S | 3,107,000 | 2,000 | 3,900 | 4,550 | 12,500 | 24,000 | 90,000 | — |
| 1928 | 8,816,000 | 350 | 375 | 390 | 415 | 460 | 900 | — |
| 1929 | 1,779,750 | 4,750 | 6,900 | 7,750 | 9,000 | 12,500 | 32,000 | — |
| 1930S | 74,000 | 6,000 | 8,250 | 9,000 | 17,000 | 34,000 | 75,000 | — |
| 1931 | 2,938,250 | 4,250 | 8,000 | 9,250 | 13,500 | 20,000 | 59,000 | — |
| 1931D | 106,500 | 5,500 | 7,750 | 9,000 | 15,000 | 21,000 | 52,000 | — |
| 1932 | 1,101,750 | 7,000 | 10,000 | 11,750 | 16,000 | 22,500 | 33,500 | — |
| 1933 none placed in circulation | 445,500 | — | — | — | — | — | — | — |

## COMMEMORATIVE COINAGE 1901-1954

All commemorative half dollars of 1901-1954 have the following specifications: diameter -- 24.3 millimeters; weight -- 6.2500 grams; composition -- 0.9000 silver, 0.1808 ounces actual silver weight. Values for "PDS sets" contain one example each from the Philadelphia, Denver and San Francisco mints. "Type coin" prices are the most inexpensive single coin available from the date and mint-mark combinations listed.

# HALF DOLLAR

Panama-Pacific Exposition. **Designer:** Charles E. Barber. **KM#** 135

| Date | Mintage | AU-50 | MS-60 | MS-63 | MS-64 | MS-65 |
|---|---|---|---|---|---|---|
| 1915S | 27,134 | 220 | 335 | 680 | 1,250 | 2,700 |

Lincoln-Illinois. **Obv. Designer:** George T. Morgan **Rev. Designer:** John R. Sinnock **KM#** 143

| Date | Mintage | AU-50 | MS-60 | MS-63 | MS-64 | MS-65 |
|---|---|---|---|---|---|---|
| 1918 | 100,058 | 80.00 | 105 | 115 | 185 | 520 |

Maine Centennial. **Designer:** Anthony de Francisci. **KM#** 146

| Date | Mintage | AU-50 | MS-60 | MS-63 | MS-64 | MS-65 |
|---|---|---|---|---|---|---|
| 1920 | 50,028 | 95.00 | 115 | 150 | 260 | 630 |

Pilgrim Tercentenary. **Designer:** Cyrus E. Dallin. **KM#** 147.1

| Date | Mintage | AU-50 | MS-60 | MS-63 | MS-64 | MS-65 |
|---|---|---|---|---|---|---|
| 1920 | 152,112 | 59.00 | 70.00 | 85.00 | 145 | 550 |

Alabama Centennial. **Designer:** Laura G. Fraser. **Obverse:** "2x2" at right above stars **KM#** 148.1

| Date | Mintage | AU-50 | MS-60 | MS-63 | MS-64 | MS-65 |
|---|---|---|---|---|---|---|
| 1921 | 6,006 | 200 | 300 | 525 | 850 | 2,650 |

Alabama Centennial. **Obv. Designer:** Laura G. Fraser **KM#** 148.2

| Date | Mintage | AU-50 | MS-60 | MS-63 | MS-64 | MS-65 |
|---|---|---|---|---|---|---|
| 1921 | 59,038 | 115 | 210 | 450 | 800 | 2,600 |

Missouri Centennial. **Designer:** Robert Aitken. **KM#** 149.1

| Date | Mintage | AU-50 | MS-60 | MS-63 | MS-64 | MS-65 |
|---|---|---|---|---|---|---|
| 1921 | 15,428 | 235 | 430 | 800 | 1,375 | 5,650 |

Missouri Centennial. **Designer:** Robert Aitken. **Obverse:** 2 star 4 in field at left **KM#** 149.2

| Date | Mintage | AU-50 | MS-60 | MS-63 | MS-64 | MS-65 |
|---|---|---|---|---|---|---|
| 1921 | 5,000 | 420 | 500 | 950 | 1,800 | 5,600 |

Pilgrim Tercentenary. **Designer:** Cyrus E. Dallin. **Obverse:** 1921 date next to Pilgrim **KM#** 147.2

| Date | Mintage | AU-50 | MS-60 | MS-63 | MS-64 | MS-65 |
|---|---|---|---|---|---|---|
| 1921 | 20,053 | 110 | 125 | 160 | 240 | 725 |

Grant Memorial. **Designer:** Laura G. Fraser. **KM#** 151.1

| Date | Mintage | AU-50 | MS-60 | MS-63 | MS-64 | MS-65 |
|---|---|---|---|---|---|---|
| 1922 | 67,405 | 80.00 | 85.00 | 160 | 295 | 975 |

Grant Memorial. **Designer:** Laura G. Fraser. **Obverse:** Star above the word "Grant" **KM#** 151.2

| Date | Mintage | AU-50 | MS-60 | MS-63 | MS-64 | MS-65 |
|---|---|---|---|---|---|---|
| 1922 | 4,256 | 690 | 980 | 1,550 | 2,350 | 7,800 |

Monroe Doctrine Centennial. **Designer:** Chester Beach. **KM#** 153

| Date | Mintage | AU-50 | MS-60 | MS-63 | MS-64 | MS-65 |
|---|---|---|---|---|---|---|
| 1923S | 274,077 | 29.00 | 41.00 | 162 | 400 | 2,550 |

Huguenot-Walloon Tercentenary. **Designer:** George T. Morgan. **KM#** 154

| Date | Mintage | AU-50 | MS-60 | MS-63 | MS-64 | MS-65 |
|---|---|---|---|---|---|---|
| 1924 | 142,080 | 95.00 | 110 | 130 | 220 | 530 |

California Diamond Jubilee. **Designer:** Jo Mora. **KM#** 155

| Date | Mintage | AU-50 | MS-60 | MS-63 | MS-64 | MS-65 |
|---|---|---|---|---|---|---|
| 1925S | 86,594 | 110 | 120 | 170 | 275 | 1,050 |

Fort Vancouver Centennial. **Designer:** Laura G. Fraser. **KM#** 158

| Date | Mintage | AU-50 | MS-60 | MS-63 | MS-64 | MS-65 |
|---|---|---|---|---|---|---|
| 1925 | 14,994 | 240 | 300 | 360 | 600 | 1,500 |

Lexington-Concord Sesquicentennial. **Designer:** Chester Beach. **KM#** 156

| Date | Mintage | AU-50 | MS-60 | MS-63 | MS-64 | MS-65 |
|---|---|---|---|---|---|---|
| 1925 | 162,013 | 65.00 | 70.00 | 105 | 185 | 660 |

Stone Mountain Memorial. **Designer:** Gutzon Borglum. **KM#** 157.1

| Date | Mintage | AU-50 | MS-60 | MS-63 | MS-64 | MS-65 |
|---|---|---|---|---|---|---|
| 1925 | 1,314,709 | 35.00 | 40.00 | 66.00 | 90.00 | 210 |

Oregon Trail Memorial. **Designer:** James E. and Laura G. Fraser. **KM#** 159

| Date | Mintage | AU-50 | MS-60 | MS-63 | MS-64 | MS-65 |
|---|---|---|---|---|---|---|
| 1926 | 47,955 | 95.00 | 100.00 | 110 | 145 | 230 |
| 1926S | 83,055 | 95.00 | 100.00 | 115 | 140 | 200 |
| Type coin | — | 95.00 | 100.00 | 110 | 140 | 200 |
| 1928 | 6,028 | 150 | 160 | 170 | 180 | 275 |
| 1933D | 5,008 | 230 | 245 | 270 | 295 | 465 |
| 1934D | 7,006 | 145 | 150 | 160 | 190 | 295 |
| 1936 | 10,006 | 105 | 115 | 125 | 145 | 220 |
| 1936S | 5,006 | 125 | 135 | 170 | 200 | 280 |
| 1937D | 12,008 | 125 | 140 | 150 | 180 | 200 |
| 1938 PDS set | 6,005 | 490 | 540 | 630 | 660 | 670 |
| 1939 PDS Set | 3,004 | 1,170 | 1,200 | 1,350 | 1,450 | 1,750 |

U.S. Sesquicentennial. **Designer:** John R. Sinnock. **KM#** 160

| Date | Mintage | AU-50 | MS-60 | MS-63 | MS-64 | MS-65 |
|---|---|---|---|---|---|---|
| 1926 | 141,120 | 60.00 | 72.00 | 155 | 600 | 5,800 |

Vermont Sesquicentennial. **Obv. Designer:** Charles Keck **KM#** 162

| Date | Mintage | AU-50 | MS-60 | MS-63 | MS-64 | MS-65 |
|---|---|---|---|---|---|---|
| 1927 | 28,142 | 155 | 165 | 190 | 300 | 1,000 |

Hawaiian Sesquicentennial. **Designer:** Juliette M. Fraser. **KM#** 163

| Date | Mintage | AU-50 | MS-60 | MS-63 | MS-64 | MS-65 |
|---|---|---|---|---|---|---|
| 1928 | 10,008 | 1,100 | 1,300 | 1,850 | 2,600 | 5,400 |

Daniel Boone Bicentennial. **Designer:** Augustus Lukeman. **KM#** 165.1

| Date | Mintage | AU-50 | MS-60 | MS-63 | MS-64 | MS-65 |
|---|---|---|---|---|---|---|
| 1934 | 10,007 | 65.00 | 72.00 | 85.00 | 110 | 180 |
| 1935 PDS set | 2,003 | 210 | 225 | 300 | 325 | 565 |

Daniel Boone Bicentennial. **Designer:** Augustus Lukeman. **Reverse:** "1934" added above the word "Pioneer." **KM#** 165.2

| Date | Mintage | AU-50 | MS-60 | MS-63 | MS-64 | MS-65 |
|---|---|---|---|---|---|---|
| 1935 PDS set | 5,005 | 580 | 660 | 820 | 1,100 | 1,850 |
| Type coin | — | 65.00 | 72.00 | 78.00 | 95.00 | 185 |
| 1936 PDS set | 5,005 | 210 | 225 | 280 | 325 | 550 |
| 1937 PDS set | 2,506 | 540 | 630 | 660 | 810 | 1,100 |
| 1938 PDS set | 2,100 | 750 | 820 | 1,000 | 1,150 | 1,500 |

Maryland Tercentenary. **Designer:** Hans Schuler. **KM#** 166

| Date | Mintage | AU-50 | MS-60 | MS-63 | MS-64 | MS-65 |
|---|---|---|---|---|---|---|
| 1934 | 25,015 | 110 | 125 | 160 | 190 | 350 |

Texas Centennial. **Designer:** Pompeo Coppini. **KM#** 167

| Date | Mintage | AU-50 | MS-60 | MS-63 | MS-64 | MS-65 |
|---|---|---|---|---|---|---|
| 1934 | 61,463 | 90.00 | 95.00 | 105 | 110 | 160 |
| Type coin | — | 90.00 | 95.00 | 100.00 | 110 | 160 |
| 1935 PDS set | 9,994 | 270 | 300 | 320 | 340 | 530 |
| 1936 PDS set | 8,911 | 270 | 300 | 310 | 330 | 520 |
| 1937 PDS set | 6,571 | 280 | 300 | 310 | 330 | 510 |
| 1938 PDS set | 3,775 | 550 | 650 | 750 | 810 | 1,150 |

Arkansas Centennial. **Designer:** Edward E. Burr. **KM#** 168

| Date | Mintage | AU-50 | MS-60 | MS-63 | MS-64 | MS-65 |
|---|---|---|---|---|---|---|
| Type coin | — | 62.00 | 70.00 | 78.00 | 90.00 | 230 |
| 1935 PDS set | 5,505 | 200 | 215 | 235 | 320 | 780 |
| 1936 PDS set | 9,600 | 200 | 215 | 235 | 300 | 840 |
| 1937 PDS set | 5,505 | 210 | 225 | 250 | 325 | 1,050 |
| 1938 PDS set | 3,155 | 270 | 360 | 420 | 500 | 1,900 |
| 1939 PDS set | — | 550 | 625 | 900 | 1,100 | 3,200 |

Connecticut Tercentenary. **Designer:** Henry Kreiss. **KM#** 169

| Date | Mintage | AU-50 | MS-60 | MS-63 | MS-64 | MS-65 |
|---|---|---|---|---|---|---|
| 1935 | 25,018 | 175 | 190 | 210 | 290 | 560 |

Hudson, N.Y., Sesquicentennial. **Designer:** Chester Beach. **KM#** 170

| Date | Mintage | AU-50 | MS-60 | MS-63 | MS-64 | MS-65 |
|---|---|---|---|---|---|---|
| 1935 | 10,008 | 445 | 485 | 530 | 730 | 1,500 |

Old Spanish Trail. **Designer:** L.W. Hoffecker. **KM#** 172

| Date | Mintage | AU-50 | MS-60 | MS-63 | MS-64 | MS-65 |
|---|---|---|---|---|---|---|
| 1935 | 10,008 | 800 | 850 | 875 | 1,000 | 1,150 |

San Diego-California-Pacific Exposition. **Designer:** Robert Aitken. **KM#** 171

| Date | Mintage | AU-50 | MS-60 | MS-63 | MS-64 | MS-65 |
|---|---|---|---|---|---|---|
| 1935S | 70,132 | 53.00 | 60.00 | 64.00 | 75.00 | 115 |
| 1936D | 30,092 | 58.00 | 62.00 | 66.00 | 80.00 | 120 |

Albany, N.Y., Charter Anniversary. **Designer:** Gertrude K. Lathrop. **KM#** 173

| Date | Mintage | AU-50 | MS-60 | MS-63 | MS-64 | MS-65 |
|---|---|---|---|---|---|---|
| 1936 | 17,671 | 200 | 210 | 220 | 235 | 340 |

Arkansas Centennial. **Obv. Designer:** Henry Kreiss **Rev. Designer:** Edward E. Burr **Obverse:** Sen. Joseph T. Robinson **KM#** 187

| Date | Mintage | AU-50 | MS-60 | MS-63 | MS-64 | MS-65 |
|---|---|---|---|---|---|---|
| 1936 | 25,265 | 100.00 | 110 | 120 | 130 | 350 |

Battle of Gettysburg 75th Anniversary. **Designer:** Frank Vittor. **KM#** 181

| Date | Mintage | AU-50 | MS-60 | MS-63 | MS-64 | MS-65 |
|---|---|---|---|---|---|---|
| 1936 | 26,928 | 270 | 280 | 300 | 385 | 640 |

Bridgeport, Conn., Centennial. **Designer:** Henry Kreiss. **KM#** 175

| Date | Mintage | AU-50 | MS-60 | MS-63 | MS-64 | MS-65 |
|---|---|---|---|---|---|---|
| 1936 | 25,015 | 110 | 125 | 130 | 140 | 250 |

Cincinnati Music Center. **Designer:** Constance Ortmayer. **KM#** 176

| Date | Mintage | AU-50 | MS-60 | MS-63 | MS-64 | MS-65 |
|---|---|---|---|---|---|---|
| 1936 Type coin | — | 200 | 215 | 225 | 300 | 650 |
| 1936 PDS set | 5,005 | 650 | 720 | 780 | 865 | 2,200 |

Cleveland-Great Lakes Exposition. **Designer:** Brenda Putnam. **KM#** 177

| Date | Mintage | AU-50 | MS-60 | MS-63 | MS-64 | MS-65 |
|---|---|---|---|---|---|---|
| 1936 | 50,030 | 60.00 | 65.00 | 72.00 | 92.50 | 240 |

Columbia, S.C., Sesquicentennial. **Designer:** A. Wolfe Davidson. **KM#** 178

| Date | Mintage | AU-50 | MS-60 | MS-63 | MS-64 | MS-65 |
|---|---|---|---|---|---|---|
| 1936 PDS set | 9,007 | 500 | 540 | 550 | 610 | 740 |
| Type coin | — | 165 | 180 | 190 | 200 | 210 |

Delaware Tercentenary. **Designer:** Carl L. Schmitz. **KM#** 179

| Date | Mintage | AU-50 | MS-60 | MS-63 | MS-64 | MS-65 |
|---|---|---|---|---|---|---|
| 1936 | 20,993 | 215 | 225 | 235 | 240 | 355 |

Elgin, Ill., Centennial. **Designer:** Trygve Rovelstad. **KM#** 180

| Date | Mintage | AU-50 | MS-60 | MS-63 | MS-64 | MS-65 |
|---|---|---|---|---|---|---|
| 1936 | 20,015 | 160 | 175 | 185 | 210 | 275 |

Long Island Tercentenary. **Designer:** Howard K. Weinman. **KM#** 182

| Date | Mintage | AU-50 | MS-60 | MS-63 | MS-64 | MS-65 |
|---|---|---|---|---|---|---|
| 1936 | 81,826 | 60.00 | 65.00 | 75.00 | 120 | 440 |

Lynchburg, Va., Sesquicentennial. **Designer:** Charles Keck. **KM#** 183

| Date | Mintage | AU-50 | MS-60 | MS-63 | MS-64 | MS-65 |
|---|---|---|---|---|---|---|
| 1936 | 20,013 | 145 | 155 | 170 | 215 | 300 |

Norfolk, Va., Bicentennial. **Designer:** William M. and Marjorie E. Simpson. **KM#** 184

| Date | Mintage | AU-50 | MS-60 | MS-63 | MS-64 | MS-65 |
|---|---|---|---|---|---|---|
| 1936 | 16,936 | 395 | 400 | 420 | 440 | 500 |

Rhode Island Tercentenary. **Designer:** Arthur G. Carey and John H. Benson. **KM#** 185

| Date | Mintage | AU-50 | MS-60 | MS-63 | MS-64 | MS-65 |
|---|---|---|---|---|---|---|
| 1936 PDS set | 15,010 | 200 | 215 | 250 | 330 | 700 |
| Type coin | — | 65.00 | 70.00 | 75.00 | 115 | 230 |

San Francisco-Oakland Bay Bridge. **Designer:** Jacques Schnier. **KM#** 174

| Date | Mintage | AU-50 | MS-60 | MS-63 | MS-64 | MS-65 |
|---|---|---|---|---|---|---|
| 1936 | 71,424 | 100.00 | 110 | 120 | 160 | 270 |

Wisconsin Territorial Centennial. **Designer:** David Parsons. **KM#** 188

| Date | Mintage | AU-50 | MS-60 | MS-63 | MS-64 | MS-65 |
|---|---|---|---|---|---|---|
| 1936 | 25,015 | 155 | 170 | 180 | 210 | 245 |

York County, Maine, Tercentenary. **Designer:** Walter H. Rich. **KM#** 189

| Date | Mintage | AU-50 | MS-60 | MS-63 | MS-64 | MS-65 |
|---|---|---|---|---|---|---|
| 1936 | 25,015 | 155 | 160 | 170 | 180 | 190 |

Battle of Antietam 75th Anniversary. **Designer:** William M. Simpson. **KM#** 190

| Date | Mintage | AU-50 | MS-60 | MS-63 | MS-64 | MS-65 |
|---|---|---|---|---|---|---|
| 1937 | 18,028 | 425 | 450 | 460 | 550 | 750 |

Roanoke Island, N.C.. **Designer:** William M. Simpson. **KM#** 186

| Date | Mintage | AU-50 | MS-60 | MS-63 | MS-64 | MS-65 |
|---|---|---|---|---|---|---|
| 1937 | 29,030 | 150 | 230 | 240 | 250 | 260 |

New Rochelle, N.Y.. **Designer:** Gertrude K. Lathrop. **KM#** 191

| Date | Mintage | AU-50 | MS-60 | MS-63 | MS-64 | MS-65 |
|---|---|---|---|---|---|---|
| 1938 | 15,266 | 265 | 280 | 295 | 320 | 430 |

Booker T. Washington. **Designer:** Isaac S. Hathaway. **KM#** 198

| Date | Mintage | AU-50 | MS-60 | MS-63 | MS-64 | MS-65 |
|---|---|---|---|---|---|---|
| 1946 PDS set | 200,113 | — | 43.00 | 54.00 | 67.00 | 120 |
| Type coin | — | 13.00 | 14.50 | 17.00 | 18.00 | 38.50 |
| 1947 PDS set | 100,017 | — | 72.00 | 80.00 | 110 | 250 |
| 1948 PDS set | 8,005 | — | 85.00 | 140 | 160 | 185 |
| 1949 PDS set | 6,004 | — | 215 | 235 | 240 | 320 |
| 1950 PDS set | 6,004 | — | 110 | 115 | 120 | 175 |
| 1951 PDS set | 7,004 | — | 110 | 130 | 140 | 175 |

Iowa Statehood Centennial. **Designer:** Adam Pietz. **KM#** 197

| Date | Mintage | AU-50 | MS-60 | MS-63 | MS-64 | MS-65 |
|---|---|---|---|---|---|---|
| 1946 | 100,057 | 63.00 | 68.00 | 72.00 | 80.00 | 115 |

Booker T. Washington and George Washington Carver. **Designer:** Isaac S. Hathaway. **KM#** 200

| Date | Mintage | AU-50 | MS-60 | MS-63 | MS-64 | MS-65 |
|---|---|---|---|---|---|---|
| 1951 PDS set | 10,004 | — | 85.00 | 100.00 | 120 | 565 |
| Type coin | — | 13.00 | 14.50 | 16.50 | 17.00 | 45.00 |
| 1952 PDS set | 8,006 | — | 80.00 | 110 | 125 | 360 |
| 1953 PDS set | 8,003 | — | 80.00 | 110 | 130 | 540 |
| 1954 PDS set | 12,006 | — | 78.00 | 90.00 | 110 | 390 |

## DOLLAR

Louisiana Purchase Exposition. **Designer:** Charles E. Barber. **Obverse:** Jefferson **Diameter:** 15 mm. **Weight:** 1.6720 g. **Composition:** 0.9000 Gold, 0.0484 oz. AGW. **KM#** 119

| Date | Mintage | AU-50 | MS-60 | MS-63 | MS-64 | MS-65 |
|---|---|---|---|---|---|---|
| 1903 | 17,500 | 350 | 445 | 700 | 1,225 | 2,600 |

Louisiana Purchase Exposition. **Obv. Designer:** Charles E. Barber **Obverse:** McKinley **Diameter:** 15 mm. **Weight:** 1.6720 g. **Composition:** 0.9000 Gold, 0.0484 oz. AGW. **KM#** 120

| Date | Mintage | AU-50 | MS-60 | MS-63 | MS-64 | MS-65 |
|---|---|---|---|---|---|---|
| 1903 | 17,500 | 320 | 395 | 670 | 1,250 | 2,800 |

Lewis and Clark Expo. **Obv. Designer:** Charles E. Barber **Diameter:** 15 mm. **Weight:** 1.6720 g. **Composition:** 0.9000 Gold, 0.7736 oz. AGW. **KM#** 121

| Date | Mintage | AU-50 | MS-60 | MS-63 | MS-64 | MS-65 |
|---|---|---|---|---|---|---|
| 1904 | 10,025 | 550 | 800 | 1,900 | 3,850 | 8,500 |
| 1905 | 10,041 | 535 | 930 | 2,400 | 5,600 | 17,000 |

Panama-Pacific Expo. **Obv. Designer:** Charles Keck **Diameter:** 15 mm. **Weight:** 1.6720 g. **Composition:** 0.9000 Gold, 0.0484 oz. AGW. **KM#** 136

| Date | Mintage | AU-50 | MS-60 | MS-63 | MS-64 | MS-65 |
|---|---|---|---|---|---|---|
| 1915S | 15,000 | 330 | 380 | 500 | 1,000 | 2,600 |

McKinley Memorial. **Obv. Designer:** Charles E. Barber **Rev. Designer:** George T. Morgan **Diameter:** 15 mm. **Weight:** 1.6720 g. **Composition:** 0.9000 Gold, 0.0484 oz. AGW. **KM#** 144

| Date | Mintage | AU-50 | MS-60 | MS-63 | MS-64 | MS-65 |
|---|---|---|---|---|---|---|
| 1916 | 9,977 | 275 | 370 | 510 | 920 | 2,600 |
| 1917 | 10,000 | 360 | 530 | 950 | 1,900 | 3,300 |

Grant Memorial. **Obv. Designer:** Laura G. Fraser **Obverse:** Without a star above the word "Grant" **Diameter:** 15 mm. **Weight:** 1.6720 g. **Composition:** 0.9000 Gold, 0.0484 oz. AGW. **Notes:** The Grant gold-dollar varieties are distinguished by whether a star appears on the obverse above the word 'Grant.' **KM#** 152.1

| Date | Mintage | AU-50 | MS-60 | MS-63 | MS-64 | MS-65 |
|---|---|---|---|---|---|---|
| 1922 | 5,016 | 1,100 | 1,200 | 1,550 | 2,500 | 3,250 |

Grant Memorial. **Obv. Designer:** Laura G. Fraser **Obverse:** With a star above the word "Grant" **Diameter:** 15 mm. **Weight:** 1.6720 g. **Composition:** 0.9000 Gold, 0.0484 oz. AGW. **KM#** 152.3

| Date | Mintage | AU-50 | MS-60 | MS-63 | MS-64 | MS-65 |
|---|---|---|---|---|---|---|
| 1922 | 5,000 | 1,200 | 1,400 | 1,850 | 2,650 | 3,200 |

## $2.50 (QUARTER EAGLE)

Panama Pacific Expo. **Obv. Designer:** Charles E. Barber **Rev. Designer:** George T. Morgan **Diameter:** 18 mm. **Weight:** 4.1800 g. **Composition:** 0.9000 Gold, 0.121 oz. AGW. **KM#** 137

| Date | Mintage | AU-50 | MS-60 | MS-63 | MS-64 | MS-65 |
|---|---|---|---|---|---|---|
| 1915S | 6,749 | 1,225 | 1,450 | 2,950 | 4,250 | 5,500 |

Philadelphia Sesquicentennial. **Obv. Designer:** John R. Sinnock **Diameter:** 18 mm. **Weight:** 4.1800 g. **Composition:** 0.9000 Gold, 0.121 oz. AGW. **KM#** 161

| Date | Mintage | AU-50 | MS-60 | MS-63 | MS-64 | MS-65 |
|---|---|---|---|---|---|---|
| 1926 | 46,019 | 280 | 320 | 510 | 860 | 3,675 |

## $50

Panama Pacific Expo.. **Obv. Designer:** Robert Aitken **Diameter:** 44 mm. **Weight:** 83.5900 g. **Composition:** 0.9000 Gold, 2.419 oz. AGW. **KM#** 138

| Date | Mintage | AU-50 | MS-60 | MS-63 | MS-64 | MS-65 |
|---|---|---|---|---|---|---|
| 1915S | 483 | 25,000 | 28,000 | 41,000 | 51,000 | 129,000 |

Panama Pacific Expo.. **Obv. Designer:** Robert Aitken **Diameter:** 44 mm. **Weight:** 83.5900 g. **Composition:** 0.9000 Gold, 2.419 oz. AGW. **KM#** 139

| Date | Mintage | AU-50 | MS-60 | MS-63 | MS-64 | MS-65 |
|---|---|---|---|---|---|---|
| 1915S | 645 | 22,500 | 26,500 | 37,000 | 51,000 | 110,000 |

**Note:** In 1982, after a hiatus of nearly 20 years, coinage of commemorative half dollars resumed. Those designated with a 'W' were struck at the West Point Mint. Some issues were struck in copper-nickel. Those struck in silver have the same size, weight and composition as the prior commemorative half-dollar series.

## COMMEMORATIVE COINAGE 1982-PRESENT

All commemorative silver dollar coins of 1982-present have the following specifications: diameter -- 38.1 millimeters; weight -- 26.7300 grams; composition -- 0.9000 silver, 0.7736 ounces actual silver weight. All commemorative $5 coins of 1982-present have the following specificiations: diameter -- 21.6 millimeters; weight -- 8.3590 grams; composition: 0.9000 gold, 0.242 ounces actual gold weight.

## HALF DOLLAR

250th Anniversary of George Washington's Birth. **Obv. Designer:** Elizabeth Jones **Diameter:** 30.6 mm. **Weight:** 12.5000 g. **Composition:** 0.9000 Silver, 0.3618 oz. ASW. **KM#** 208

| Date | Mintage | Proof | MS-65 | Prf-65 |
|---|---|---|---|---|
| 1982D | 2,210,458 | — | 5.50 | — |
| 1982S | — | (4,894,044) | — | 6.00 |

Statue of Liberty Centennial. **Weight:** 11.3400 g. **Composition:** Copper-Nickel Clad Copper **KM#** 212

| Date | Mintage | Proof | MS-65 | Prf-65 |
|---|---|---|---|---|
| 1986D | 928,008 | — | 5.50 | — |
| 1986S | — | (6,925,627) | — | 5.75 |

Bicentennial of the Congress. **Weight:** 11.3400 g. **Composition:** Copper-Nickel Clad Copper **KM#** 224

| Date | Mintage | Proof | MS-65 | Prf-65 |
|---|---|---|---|---|
| 1989D | 163,753 | — | 7.00 | — |
| 1989S | — | — | — | 5.50 |

Mount Rushmore Golden Anniversary. **Weight:** 11.3400 g. **Composition:** Copper-Nickel Clad Copper **KM#** 228

| Date | Mintage | Proof | MS-65 | Prf-65 |
|---|---|---|---|---|
| 1991D | 172,754 | — | 11.00 | — |
| 1991S | — | — | — | 11.00 |

500th Anniversary of Columbus Discovery. **Weight:** 11.3400 g. **Composition:** Copper-Nickel Clad Copper **KM#** 237

| Date | Mintage | Proof | MS-65 | Prf-65 |
|---|---|---|---|---|
| 1992D | 135,702 | — | 10.00 | — |
| 1992S | — | (390,154) | — | 12.00 |

Olympics. **Weight:** 11.3400 g. **Composition:** Copper-Nickel Clad Copper **KM#** 233

| Date | Mintage | Proof | MS-65 | Prf-65 |
|---|---|---|---|---|
| 1992P | 161,607 | — | 5.50 | — |
| 1992S | — | (519,645) | — | 8.00 |

James Madison and Bill of Rights. **Weight:** 12.5000 g. **Composition:** 0.9000 Silver, 0.3618 oz. ASW. **KM#** 240

| Date | Mintage | Proof | MS-65 | Prf-65 |
|---|---|---|---|---|
| 1993W | 173,224 | — | 14.00 | — |
| 1993S | — | (559,758) | — | 12.00 |

World War II 50th Anniversary. **Weight:** 11.3400 g. **Composition:** Copper-Nickel Clad Copper **KM#** 243

| Date | Mintage | Proof | MS-65 | Prf-65 |
|---|---|---|---|---|
| 1993P | 192,968 | (290,343) | 12.00 | 12.00 |

1994 World Cup Soccer. **Weight:** 11.3400 g. **Composition:** Copper-Nickel Clad Copper **KM#** 246

| Date | Mintage | Proof | MS-65 | Prf-65 |
|---|---|---|---|---|
| 1994D | 168,208 | — | 9.00 | — |
| 1994P | 122,412 | (609,354) | — | 9.50 |

Atlanta Olympics. **Obverse:** Basketball **Weight:** 11.3400 g. **Composition:** Copper-Nickel Clad Copper **KM#** 257

| Date | Mintage | Proof | MS-65 | Prf-65 |
|---|---|---|---|---|
| 1995S | 171,001 | (169,655) | 24.00 | 17.00 |

Atlanta Olympics. **Obverse:** Baseball **Weight:** 11.3400 g. **Composition:** Copper-Nickel Clad Copper **KM#** 262

| Date | Mintage | Proof | MS-65 | Prf-65 |
|---|---|---|---|---|
| 1995S | 164,605 | (118,087) | 22.00 | 14.00 |

Civil War. **Weight:** 11.3400 g. **Composition:** Copper-Nickel Clad Copper **KM#** 254

| Date | Mintage | Proof | MS-65 | Prf-65 |
|---|---|---|---|---|
| 1995S | 119,510 | (330,099) | 25.00 | 24.00 |

Atlanta Olympics. **Obverse:** Soccer **Weight:** 11.3400 g. **Composition:** Copper-Nickel Clad Copper **KM#** 271

| Date | Mintage | Proof | MS-65 | Prf-65 |
|---|---|---|---|---|
| 1996S | 52,836 | (122,412) | 35.00 | 70.00 |

Atlanta Olympics. **Obverse:** Swimming **Weight:** 11.3400 g. **Composition:** Copper-Nickel Clad Copper **KM#** 267

| Date | Mintage | Proof | MS-65 | Prf-65 |
|---|---|---|---|---|
| 1996S | 49,533 | (114,315) | 60.00 | 12.50 |

Capital Visitor Center. **Weight:** 11.3400 g. **Composition:** Copper-Nickel Clad Copper **KM#** 332

| Date | Mintage | Proof | MS-65 | Prf-65 |
|---|---|---|---|---|
| 2001 | — | — | 12.00 | 13.00 |

## DOLLAR

Los Angeles XXIII Olympiad. **Obv. Designer:** Elizabeth Jones **KM#** 209

| Date | Mintage | Proof | MS-65 | Prf-65 |
|---|---|---|---|---|
| 1983P | 294,543 | — | 11.00 | — |
| 1983D | 174,014 | — | 11.00 | — |
| 1983S | 174,014 | (1,577,025) | 11.00 | 11.00 |

Los Angeles XXIII Olympiad. **Obv. Designer:** Robert Graham **KM#** 210

| Date | Mintage | Proof | MS-65 | Prf-65 |
|---|---|---|---|---|
| 1984P | 217,954 | — | 14.00 | — |
| 1984D | 116,675 | — | 23.00 | — |
| 1984S | 116,675 | (1,801,210) | 24.00 | 12.00 |

Statue of Liberty Centennial. **Obv. Designer:** John Mercanti **KM#** 214

| Date | Mintage | Proof | MS-65 | Prf-65 |
|---|---|---|---|---|
| 1986P | 723,635 | — | 11.50 | — |
| 1986S | — | (6,414,638) | — | 13.00 |

Constitution Bicentennial. **Obv. Designer:** Patricia Lewis Verani **KM#** 220

| Date | Mintage | Proof | MS-65 | Prf-65 |
|---|---|---|---|---|
| 1987P | 451,629 | — | 12.00 | — |
| 1987S | — | (2,747,116) | — | 11.00 |

Olympics. **Obv. Designer:** Patricia Lewis Verani **Rev. Designer:** Sherl Joseph Winter **KM# 222**

| Date | Mintage | Proof | MS-65 | Prf-65 |
|---|---|---|---|---|
| 1988D | 191,368 | — | 11.00 | — |
| 1988S | — | (1,359,366) | — | 11.00 |

Bicentennial of the Congress. **Obv. Designer:** William Woodward **KM# 225**

| Date | Mintage | Proof | MS-65 | Prf-65 |
|---|---|---|---|---|
| 1989D | 135,203 | — | 16.00 | — |
| 1989S | — | (762,198) | — | 16.00 |

Eisenhower Centennial. **Obv. Designer:** John Mercanti **Rev. Designer:** Marcel Jovine **KM# 227**

| Date | Mintage | Proof | MS-65 | Prf-65 |
|---|---|---|---|---|
| 1990W | 241,669 | — | 17.50 | — |
| 1990P | — | (638,335) | — | 18.50 |

Korean War. **Obv. Designer:** John Mercanti **Rev. Designer:** James Ferrell **KM# 231**

| Date | Mintage | Proof | MS-65 | Prf-65 |
|---|---|---|---|---|
| 1991D | 213,049 | — | 14.50 | — |
| 1991P | — | (618,488) | — | 15.00 |

Mount Rushmore Golden Anniversary. **Obv. Designer:** Marika Somogyi **Rev. Designer:** Frank Gasparro **KM# 229**

| Date | Mintage | Proof | MS-65 | Prf-65 |
|---|---|---|---|---|
| 1991P | 133,139 | — | 27.50 | — |
| 1991S | — | (738,419) | — | 31.00 |

USO 50th Anniversary. **Obv. Designer:** Robert Lamb **Rev. Designer:** John Mercanti **KM# 232**

| Date | Mintage | Proof | MS-65 | Prf-65 |
|---|---|---|---|---|
| 1991D | 124,958 | — | 16.00 | — |
| 1991S | — | (321,275) | — | 14.50 |

Columbus Quincentenary. **KM# 238**

| Date | Mintage | Proof | MS-65 | Prf-65 |
|---|---|---|---|---|
| 1992D | 106,949 | — | 26.00 | — |
| 1992P | — | (385,241) | — | 34.00 |

Olympics. **Obv. Designer:** John R. Deecken **Rev. Designer:** Marcel Jovine **KM# 234**

| Date | Mintage | Proof | MS-65 | Prf-65 |
|---|---|---|---|---|
| 1992D | 187,552 | — | 22.00 | — |
| 1992S | — | (504,505) | — | 25.00 |

White House Bicentennial. **KM# 236**

| Date | Mintage | Proof | MS-65 | Prf-65 |
|---|---|---|---|---|
| 1992D | 123,803 | — | 33.50 | — |
| 1992W | — | (375,851) | — | 24.00 |

James Madison and Bill of Rights. **KM# 241**

| Date | Mintage | Proof | MS-65 | Prf-65 |
|---|---|---|---|---|
| 1993D | 98,383 | — | 18.00 | — |
| 1993S | — | (534,001) | — | 19.00 |

Thomas Jefferson 250th Anniversary of Birth. **KM# 249**

| Date | Mintage | Proof | MS-65 | Prf-65 |
|---|---|---|---|---|
| 1993P | 266,927 | — | 26.00 | — |
| 1993S | — | (332,891) | — | 27.50 |

World War II 50th Anniversary. **KM# 244**

| Date | Mintage | Proof | MS-65 | Prf-65 |
|---|---|---|---|---|
| 1993D | 94,708 | — | 24.00 | — |
| 1993W | — | (322,422) | — | 29.00 |

National Prisoner of War Museum. **KM# 251**

| Date | Mintage | Proof | MS-65 | Prf-65 |
|---|---|---|---|---|
| 1994W | 54,790 | — | 55.00 | — |
| 1994P | — | (220,100) | — | 34.00 |

U.S. Capitol Bicentennial. **KM# 253**

| Date | Mintage | Proof | MS-65 | Prf-65 |
|---|---|---|---|---|
| 1994D | 68,352 | — | 21.00 | — |
| 1994S | — | (279,416) | — | 22.00 |

Vietnam Veterans Memorial. **KM# 250**

| Date | Mintage | Proof | MS-65 | Prf-65 |
|---|---|---|---|---|
| 1994W | 57,317 | — | 45.00 | — |
| 1994P | — | (226,262) | — | 55.00 |

Women in Military Service Memorial. **KM# 252**

| Date | Mintage | Proof | MS-65 | Prf-65 |
|---|---|---|---|---|
| 1994W | 53,054 | — | 25.00 | — |
| 1994P | — | (213,201) | — | 24.00 |

World Cup Soccer. **KM# 247**

| Date | Mintage | Proof | MS-65 | Prf-65 |
|---|---|---|---|---|
| 1994D | 81,698 | — | 26.00 | — |
| 1994S | — | (576,978) | — | 29.00 |

Atlanta Olympics. **Obverse:** Gymnastics **KM# 260**

| Date | Mintage | Proof | MS-65 | Prf-65 |
|---|---|---|---|---|
| 1995D | 42,497 | — | 60.00 | — |
| 1995P | — | (182,676) | — | 29.00 |

Atlanta Olympics. **Obverse:** Track and field **KM# 264**

| Date | Mintage | Proof | MS-65 | Prf-65 |
|---|---|---|---|---|
| 1995D | 24,796 | — | 55.00 | — |
| 1995P | — | (136,935) | — | 26.50 |

Atlanta Olympics. **Obverse:** Cycling **KM# 263**

| Date | Mintage | Proof | MS-65 | Prf-65 |
|---|---|---|---|---|
| 1995D | 19,662 | — | 80.00 | — |
| 1995P | — | (118,795) | — | 32.50 |

Atlanta Olympics, Paralympics. **Obverse:** Blind runner **KM# 259**

| Date | Mintage | Proof | MS-65 | Prf-65 |
|---|---|---|---|---|
| 1995D | 28,649 | — | 80.00 | — |
| 1995P | — | (138,337) | — | 32.50 |

Civil War. **KM# 255**

| Date | Mintage | Proof | MS-65 | Prf-65 |
|---|---|---|---|---|
| 1995P | 45,866 | — | 34.00 | — |
| 1995S | — | (55,246) | — | 44.00 |

Special Olympics World Games. **KM# 266**

| Date | Mintage | Proof | MS-65 | Prf-65 |
|---|---|---|---|---|
| 1995W | 89,301 | — | 20.00 | — |
| 1995P | — | (351,764) | — | 16.00 |

Atlanta Olympics. **Obverse:** High jumper **KM# 272A**

| Date | Mintage | Proof | MS-65 | Prf-65 |
|---|---|---|---|---|
| 1996D | 15,697 | — | 210 | — |
| 1996P | — | (124,502) | — | 31.00 |

Atlanta Olympics. **Obverse:** Tennis **KM# 269**

| Date | Mintage | Proof | MS-65 | Prf-65 |
|---|---|---|---|---|
| 1996D | 15,983 | — | 140 | — |
| 1996P | — | (92,016) | — | 49.00 |

Atlanta Olympics. **Obverse:** Rowing **KM# 272**

| Date | Mintage | Proof | MS-65 | Prf-65 |
|---|---|---|---|---|
| 1996D | 16,258 | — | 160 | — |
| 1996P | — | (151,890) | — | 38.00 |

Atlanta Olympics, Paralympics. **Obverse:** Wheelchair racer **KM# 268**

| Date | Mintage | Proof | MS-65 | Prf-65 |
|---|---|---|---|---|
| 1996D | 14,497 | — | 180 | — |
| 1996P | — | (84,280) | — | 49.00 |

National Community Service. **KM#** 275

| Date | Mintage | Proof | MS-65 | Prf-65 |
|---|---|---|---|---|
| 1996S | 23,500 | — | 220 | — |
| 1996S | — | (101,543) | — | 35.00 |

Smithsonian 150th Anniversary. **KM#** 276

| Date | Mintage | Proof | MS-65 | Prf-65 |
|---|---|---|---|---|
| 1996D | 31,230 | — | 85.00 | — |
| 1996P | — | (129,152) | — | 33.50 |

Jackie Robinson 50th Anniversary. **KM#** 279

| Date | Mintage | Proof | MS-65 | Prf-65 |
|---|---|---|---|---|
| 1997S | 30,007 | (110,495) | 53.00 | 37.50 |

National Law Enforcement Officers Memorial. **KM#** 281

| Date | Mintage | Proof | MS-65 | Prf-65 |
|---|---|---|---|---|
| 1997P | 28,575 | (110,428) | 110 | 105 |

U.S. Botanic Gardens 175th Anniversary. **KM#** 278

| Date | Mintage | Proof | MS-65 | Prf-65 |
|---|---|---|---|---|
| 1997P | 57,272 | (264,528) | 36.00 | 44.00 |

Black Patriots. **Obverse:** Crispus Attucks **KM#** 288

| Date | Mintage | Proof | MS-65 | Prf-65 |
|---|---|---|---|---|
| 1998S | 37,210 | (75,070) | 82.50 | 72.00 |

Robert F. Kennedy. **KM#** 287

| Date | Mintage | Proof | MS-65 | Prf-65 |
|---|---|---|---|---|
| 1998S | 106,422 | (99,020) | 31.00 | 38.50 |

Dolley Madison. **KM#** 299

| Date | Mintage | Proof | MS-65 | Prf-65 |
|---|---|---|---|---|
| 1999P | 22,948 | (158,247) | 38.00 | 41.00 |

Yellowstone. **KM#** 300

| Date | Mintage | Proof | MS-65 | Prf-65 |
|---|---|---|---|---|
| 1999P | 23,614 | (128,646) | 37.00 | 38.00 |

Leif Erickson. **KM#** 318

| Date | Mintage | Proof | MS-65 | Prf-65 |
|---|---|---|---|---|
| 2000P | 28,150 | (58,612) | 50.00 | 32.50 |

Library of Congress. **KM#** 316

| Date | Mintage | Proof | MS-65 | Prf-65 |
|---|---|---|---|---|
| 2000P | 52,771 | (196,900) | 36.00 | 40.00 |

American Buffalo. **KM#** 334

| Date | Mintage | Proof | MS-65 | Prf-65 |
|---|---|---|---|---|
| 2001 | — | — | 115 | 115 |

Capital Visitor Center. **KM#** 333

| Date | Mintage | Proof | MS-65 | Prf-65 |
|---|---|---|---|---|
| 2001 | — | — | 39.00 | 39.00 |

## $5 (HALF EAGLE)

Statue of Liberty Centennial. **KM#** 215

| Date | Mintage | Proof | MS-65 | Prf-65 |
|---|---|---|---|---|
| 1986W | 95,248 | (404,013) | 100.00 | 105 |

Constitution Bicentennial. **Obv. Designer:** Marcel Jovine **KM#** 221

| Date | Mintage | Proof | MS-65 | Prf-65 |
|---|---|---|---|---|
| 1987W | 214,225 | (651,659) | 100.00 | 100.00 |

Olympics. **Obv. Designer:** Elizabeth Jones **Rev. Designer:** Marcel Jovine **KM#** 223

| Date | Mintage | Proof | MS-65 | Prf-65 |
|---|---|---|---|---|
| 1988W | 62,913 | (281,456) | 105 | 100.00 |

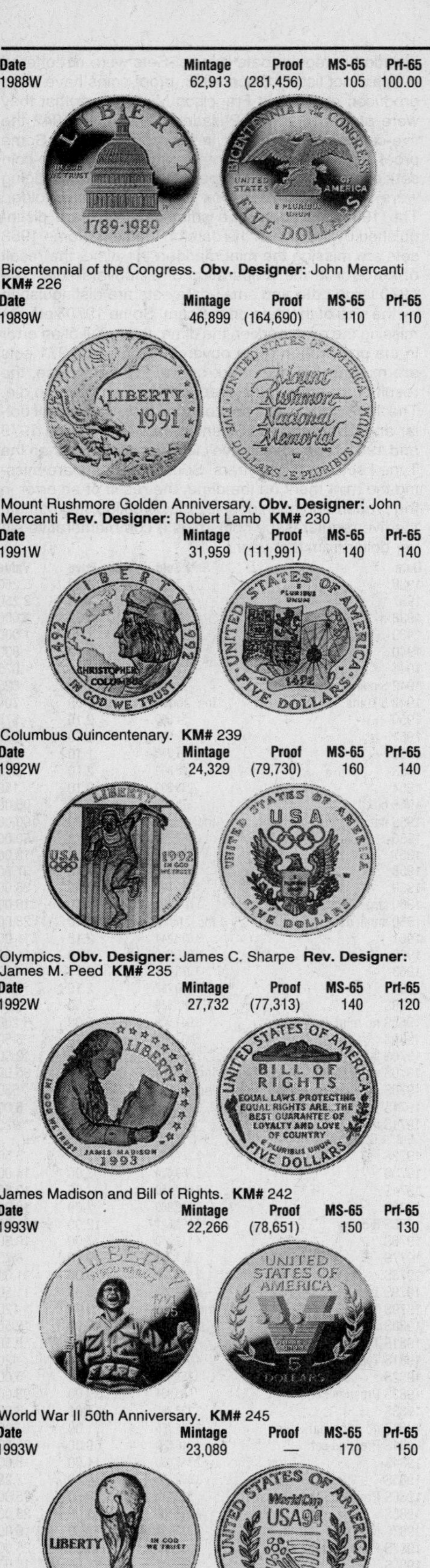

Bicentennial of the Congress. **Obv. Designer:** John Mercanti **KM#** 226

| Date | Mintage | Proof | MS-65 | Prf-65 |
|---|---|---|---|---|
| 1989W | 46,899 | (164,690) | 110 | 110 |

Mount Rushmore Golden Anniversary. **Obv. Designer:** John Mercanti **Rev. Designer:** Robert Lamb **KM#** 230

| Date | Mintage | Proof | MS-65 | Prf-65 |
|---|---|---|---|---|
| 1991W | 31,959 | (111,991) | 140 | 140 |

Columbus Quincentenary. **KM#** 239

| Date | Mintage | Proof | MS-65 | Prf-65 |
|---|---|---|---|---|
| 1992W | 24,329 | (79,730) | 160 | 140 |

Olympics. **Obv. Designer:** James C. Sharpe **Rev. Designer:** James M. Peed **KM#** 235

| Date | Mintage | Proof | MS-65 | Prf-65 |
|---|---|---|---|---|
| 1992W | 27,732 | (77,313) | 140 | 120 |

James Madison and Bill of Rights. **KM#** 242

| Date | Mintage | Proof | MS-65 | Prf-65 |
|---|---|---|---|---|
| 1993W | 22,266 | (78,651) | 150 | 130 |

World War II 50th Anniversary. **KM#** 245

| Date | Mintage | Proof | MS-65 | Prf-65 |
|---|---|---|---|---|
| 1993W | 23,089 | — | 170 | 150 |

World Cup Soccer. **KM#** 248

| Date | Mintage | Proof | MS-65 | Prf-65 |
|---|---|---|---|---|
| 1994W | 22,464 | (89,619) | 150 | 125 |

Civil War. **KM#** 256

| Date | Mintage | Proof | MS-65 | Prf-65 |
|---|---|---|---|---|
| 1995W | 12,735 | (55,246) | 365 | 265 |

Olympics. **Obverse:** Torch runner **KM#** 261

| Date | Mintage | Proof | MS-65 | Prf-65 |
|---|---|---|---|---|
| 1995W | 14,675 | (57,442) | 225 | 160 |

Olympics. **Obverse:** Stadium **KM#** 265

| Date | Mintage | Proof | MS-65 | Prf-65 |
|---|---|---|---|---|
| 1995W | 10,579 | (43,124) | 275 | 180 |

Olympics. **Obverse:** Flag bearer **KM#** 274

| Date | Mintage | Proof | MS-65 | Prf-65 |
|---|---|---|---|---|
| 1996W | 9,174 | (32,886) | 300 | 240 |

Olympics. **Obverse:** Cauldron **KM#** 270

| Date | Mintage | Proof | MS-65 | Prf-65 |
|---|---|---|---|---|
| 1996W | 9,210 | (38,555) | 300 | 245 |

Smithsonian 150th Anniversary. **KM#** 277

| Date | Mintage | Proof | MS-65 | Prf-65 |
|---|---|---|---|---|
| 1996W | 9,068 | (21,772) | 395 | 260 |

Franklin Delano Roosevelt. **KM#** 282

| Date | Mintage | Proof | MS-65 | Prf-65 |
|---|---|---|---|---|
| 1997W | 11,894 | (29,474) | 240 | 230 |

Jackie Robinson 50th Anniversary. **KM#** 280

| Date | Mintage | Proof | MS-65 | Prf-65 |
|---|---|---|---|---|
| 1997W | 5,202 | (24,546) | 1,050 | 325 |

George Washington. **KM#** 301

| Date | Mintage | Proof | MS-65 | Prf-65 |
|---|---|---|---|---|
| 1999W | — | — | 240 | 260 |

Capital Visitor Center. **KM#** 335

| Date | Mintage | Proof | MS-65 | Prf-65 |
|---|---|---|---|---|
| 2001 | — | — | 500 | 225 |

## $10 (EAGLE)

Los Angeles XXIII Olympiad. **Diameter:** 27 mm. **Weight:** 16.7180 g. **Composition:** 0.9000 Gold, 0.4839 oz. AGW. **KM#** 211

| Date | Mintage | Proof | MS-65 | Prf-65 |
|---|---|---|---|---|
| 1984W | 75,886 | (381,085) | 180 | 185 |
| 1984P | 33,309 | — | — | 280 |
| 1984D | 34,533 | — | — | 280 |
| 1984S | 48,551 | — | — | 220 |

Library of Congress. **Weight:** 16.2590 g. **Composition:** Platinum-Gold-Alloy **Notes:** Composition is 48 percent platinum, 48 percent gold, and 4 percent alloy. **KM#** 317

| Date | Mintage | Proof | MS-65 | Prf-65 |
|---|---|---|---|---|
| 2000W | 7,200 | (27,400) | 925 | 540 |

## MODERN COMMEMORATIVE COIN SETS

### Olympic, 1983-1984

| Date | Price |
|---|---|
| 1983 collectors set: 1983 PDS uncirculated dollars; KM209. | 30.00 |
| 1983 & 1984 gold and silver uncirculated set: One 1983 and one 1984 uncirculated dollar and one 1984 uncirculated gold $10; KM209, 210, 211. | 265 |
| 1983 & 1984 gold and silver proof set: One 1983 and one 1984 proof dollar and one 1984 proof gold $10; KM209, 210, 211. | 265 |
| 1983 & 1984 6 coin set: One 1983 and one 1984 uncirculated and proof dollar, one uncirculated and one proof gold $10; KM209, 210, 211. | 500 |
| 1983 & 1984 proof dollars | 20.00 |
| 1984 collectors set: 1984 PDS uncirculated dollars; KM210. | 50.00 |

### Statue of Liberty

| Date | Price |
|---|---|
| 1986 2 coin set: uncirculated silver dollar and clad half dollar; KM212, 214. | 16.00 |
| 1986 2 coin set: proof silver dollar and clad half dollar; KM212, 214. | 16.50 |
| 1986 3 coin set: uncirculated silver dollar, clad half dollar and gold $5; KM212, 214, 215. | 160 |
| 1986 3 coin set: proof silver dollar, clad half dollar and gold $5; KM212, 214, 215. | 160 |
| 1986 6 coin set: 1 each of the proof and uncirculated issues; KM212, 214, 215. | 270 |

## Constitution

| Date | Price |
|---|---|
| 1987 2 coin set: uncirculated silver dollar and gold $5; KM220, 221. | 140 |
| 1987 2 coin set: proof silver dollar and gold $5; KM220, 221. | 130 |
| 1987 4 coin set: 1 each of the proof and uncirculated issues; KM220, 221. | 275 |

## Olympic, 1988

| Date | Price |
|---|---|
| 1988 2 coin set: uncirculated silver dollar and gold $5; KM222, 223. | 145 |
| 1988 2 coin set: Proof silver dollar and gold $5; KM222, 223. | 135 |
| 1988 4 coin set: 1 each of proof and uncirculated issues; KM222, 223. | 290 |

## Congress

| Date | Price |
|---|---|
| 1989 2 coin set: uncirculated silver dollar and clad half dollar; KM224, 225. | 22.00 |
| 1989 2 coin set: proof silver dollar and clad half dollar; KM224, 225. | 17.50 |
| 1989 3 coin set: uncirculated silver dollar, clad half and gold $5; KM224, 225, 226. | 160 |
| 1989 3 coin set: proof silver dollar, clad half and gold $5; KM224, 225, 226. | 160 |
| 1989 6 coin set: 1 each of the proof and uncirculated issues; KM224, 225, 226. | 310 |

## Mt. Rushmore

| Date | Price |
|---|---|
| 1991 2 coin set: uncirculated half dollar and silver dollar; KM228, 229. | 36.00 |
| 1991 2 coin set: proof half dollar and silver dollar; KM228, 229. | 35.00 |
| 1991 3 coin set: uncirculated half dollar, silver dollar and gold $5; KM228, 229, 230. | 170 |
| 1991 3 coin set: proof half dollar, silver dollar and gold $5; KM228, 229, 230. | 165 |
| 1991 6 coin set: 1 each of proof and uncirculated issues; KM228, 229, 230. | 310 |

## Columbus Quincentenary

| Date | Price |
|---|---|
| 1992 2 coin set: uncirculated half dollar and silver dollar; KM237, 238. | 34.00 |
| 1992 2 coin set: proof half dollar and silver dollar; KM237, 238. | 36.00 |
| 1992 3 coin set: uncirculated half dollar, silver dollar and gold $5; KM237, 238, 239. | 180 |
| 1992 3 coin set: proof half dollar, silver dollar and gold $5; KM237, 238, 239. | 165 |
| 1992 6 coin set: 1 each of proof and uncirculated issues; KM237, 238, 239. | 360 |

## Olympic, 1992

| Date | Price |
|---|---|
| 1992 2 coin set: uncirculated half dollar and silver dollar; KM233, 234. | 25.00 |
| 1992 2 coin set: proof half dollar and silver dollar; KM233, 234. | 35.00 |
| 1992 3 coin set: uncirculated half dollar, silver dollar and gold $5; KM233, 234, 235. | 160 |
| 1992 3 coin set: proof half dollar, silver dollar and gold $5; KM233, 234, 235. | 160 |
| 1992 6 coin set: 1 each of proof and uncirculated issues; KM233, 234, 235. | 315 |

## World War II

| Date | Price |
|---|---|
| 1993 2 coin set: uncirculated half dollar and silver dollar; KM243, 244. | 27.50 |
| 1993 2 coin set: proof half dollar and silver dollar; KM243, 244. | 31.00 |
| 1993 3 coin set: uncirculated half dollar, silver dollar and gold $5; KM243, 244, 245. | 180 |
| 1993 3 coin set: proof half dollar, silver dollar and gold $5; KM243, 244, 245. | 175 |
| 1993 6 coin set: 1 each of proof and uncirculated issues; KM243, 244, 245. | 325 |

## Madison / Bill of Rights

| Date | Price |
|---|---|
| 1993 2 coin set: uncirculated half dollar and silver dollar; KM240, 241. | 27.50 |
| 1993 2 coin set: proof half dollar and silver dollar; KM240, 241. | 27.50 |
| 1993 3 coin set: uncirculated half dollar, silver dollar and gold $5; KM240, 241, 242. | 180 |
| 1993 3 coin set: proof half dollar, silver dollar and gold $5; KM240, 241, 242. | 170 |
| 1993 6 coin set: 1 each of proof and uncirculated issues; KM240, 241, 242. | 340 |

## Jefferson

| Date | Price |
|---|---|
| 1993 Jefferson: dollar, nickel and $2 note; KM249, 192. | 80.00 |

## World Cup

| Date | Price |
|---|---|
| 1994 2 coin set: uncirculated half dollar and silver dollar; KM246, 247. | 31.00 |
| 1994 2 coin set: proof half dollar and silver dollar; KM246, 247. | 32.50 |
| 1994 3 coin set: uncirculated half dollar, silver dollar and gold $5; KM246, 247, 248. | 185 |
| 1994 3 coin set: proof half dollar, silver dollar and gold $5; KM246, 247, 248. | 175 |
| 1994 6 coin set: 1 each of proof and uncirculated issues; KM246, 247, 248. | 530 |

## U.S. Veterans

| Date | Price |
|---|---|
| 1994 3 coin set: uncirculated POW, Vietnam, Women dollars; KM250, 251, 252. | 85.00 |
| 1994 3 coin set: proof POW, Vietnam, Women dollars; KM250, 251, 252. | 70.00 |

## Olympic, 1995-96

| Date | Price |
|---|---|
| 1995 4 coin set: uncirculated basketball half, $1 gymnast & blind runner, $5 torch runner; KM257, 259, 260, 261. | 290 |
| 1995 4 coin set: proof basketball half, $1 gymnast & blind runner, $5 torch runner; KM257, 259, 260, 261. | 200 |
| 1995 2 coin set: proof $1 gymnast & blind runner; KM259, 260. | 72.00 |
| 1995 2 coin set: proof $1 track & field, cycling; KM263, 264. | 76.00 |
| 1995-96 4 coin set: proof halves, basketball, baseball, swimming, soccer; KM257, 262, 267, 271. | 58.00 |

## Civil War

| Date | Price |
|---|---|
| 1995 2 coin set: uncirculated half and dollar; KM254, 255. | 40.00 |
| 1995 2 coin set: proof half and dollar; KM254, 255. | 40.00 |
| 1995 3 coin set: uncirculated half, dollar and gold $5; KM254, 255, 256. | 325 |
| 1995 3 coin set: proof half, dollar and gold $5; KM254, 255, 256. | 210 |
| 1995 6 coin set: 1 each of proof and uncirculated issues; KM254, 255, 256. | 530 |

## Smithsonian

| Date | Price |
|---|---|
| 1996 2 coin set: proof dollar and $5 gold; KM276, 277. | 230 |
| 1996 4 coin set: proof and B.U. ; KM276, 277. | 700 |

## Botanic Garden

| Date | Price |
|---|---|
| 1997 2 coin set: dollar, Jefferson nickel and $1 note; KM278, 192. | 180 |

## Jackie Robinson

| Date | Price |
|---|---|
| 1997 2 coin set: proof dollar & $5 gold; KM279, 280. | 240 |
| 1997 4 coin set: proof & BU; KM279, 280. | 1,100 |
| 1997 legacy set. | 400 |

## Kennedy

| Date | Price |
|---|---|
| 1998 2 coin set: proof; KM287. | 80.00 |
| 1998 2 coin collectors set: Robert Kennedy dollar and John Kennedy half dollar; KM287, 202b. Matte finished. | 425 |

## Dolley Madison

| Date | Price |
|---|---|
| 1999 2 coin set: proof and uncirculated silver dollars; KM299. | 80.00 |

## George Washington

| Date | Price |
|---|---|
| 1999 2 coin set: proof and uncirculated gold $5; KM301. | 450 |

## Yellowstone National Park

| Date | Price |
|---|---|
| 1999 2 coin set: proof and uncirculated silver dollars; KM300. | 90.00 |

## Leif Erickson

| Date | Price |
|---|---|
| 2000 2 coin set: proof and uncirculated silver dollars; KM318. | 70.00 |

## Capital Visitor Center

| Date | Price |
|---|---|
| 2001 3 coin set: proof half, silver dollar, gold $5; KM332, 333, 335. | 265 |

## The American Buffalo

| Date | Price |
|---|---|
| 2001 2 coin set: 90% Silver unc. & proof $1.; KM334. | 225 |
| 2001 coin & currency set 90% unc. dollar & replicas of 1899 $5 silver cert.; KM334. | 150 |

# PROOF SETS

Proof coins are produced through a special process involving specially selected, highly polished planchets and dies. They usually receive two strikings from the coin press at increased pressure. The result is a coin with mirrorlike surfaces and, in recent years, a cameo effect on its raised design surfaces. Proof sets have been sold off and on by the U.S. Mint since 1858. Listings here are for sets from what is commonly called the modern era, since 1936. Values for earlier proofs are included in regular date listings. Sets were not offered in years not listed. Since 1968, proof coins have been produced at the San Francisco Mint; before that they were produced at the Philadelphia Mint. In 1942 the five-cent coin was struck in two compositions. Some proof sets for that year contain only one type (five-coin set); others contain both types. Two types of packaging were used in 1955 -- a box and a flat, plastic holder. The 1960 large-date and small-date sets are distinguished by the size of the date on the cent. Some 1968 sets are missing the mint mark on the dime, the result of an error in the preparation of an obverse die. The 1970 large-date and small-date sets are distinguished by the size of the date on the cent. Some 1970 sets are missing the mint mark on the dime, the result of an error in the preparation of an obverse die. Some 1971 sets are missing the mint mark on the five-cent piece, the result of an error in the preparation of an obverse die. The 1976 three-piece set contains the quarter, half dollar and dollar with the Bicentennial designs. The 1979 and 1981 Type II sets have clearer mint marks than the Type I sets for those years. Some 1983 sets are missing the mint mark on the dime, the result of an error in the preparation of an obverse die. Prestige sets contain the five regular-issue coins plus a commemorative silver dollar from that year.

| Date | Sets Sold | Issue Price | Value |
|---|---|---|---|
| 1936 | 3,837 | 1.89 | 5,250 |
| 1937 | 5,542 | 1.89 | 2,250 |
| 1938 | 8,045 | 1.89 | 1,000 |
| 1939 | 8,795 | 1.89 | 1,000 |
| 1940 | 11,246 | 1.89 | 800 |
| 1941 | 15,287 | 1.89 | 675 |
| 1942 6 coins | 21,120 | 1.89 | 825 |
| 1942 5 coins | Inc. above | 1.89 | 700 |
| 1950 | 51,386 | 2.10 | 575 |
| 1951 | 57,500 | 2.10 | 575 |
| 1952 | 81,980 | 2.10 | 290 |
| 1953 | 128,800 | 2.10 | 275 |
| 1954 | 233,300 | 2.10 | 150 |
| 1955 box | 378,200 | 2.10 | 95.00 |
| 1955 flat pack | Inc. above | 2.10 | 100.00 |
| 1956 | 669,384 | 2.10 | 50.00 |
| 1957 | 1,247,952 | 2.10 | 18.00 |
| 1958 | 875,652 | 2.10 | 37.50 |
| 1959 | 1,149,291 | 2.10 | 26.00 |
| 1960 large date | 1,691,602 | 2.10 | 16.00 |
| 1960 small date | Inc. above | 2.10 | 28.00 |
| 1961 | 3,028,244 | 2.10 | 11.00 |
| 1962 | 3,218,019 | 2.10 | 11.00 |
| 1963 | 3,075,645 | 2.10 | 14.00 |
| 1964 | 3,950,762 | 2.10 | 11.00 |
| 1968S | 3,041,509 | 5.00 | 6.50 |
| 1968S no mint mark dime | 3,041,509 | 5.00 | 8,200 |
| 1969S | 2,934,631 | 5.00 | 6.50 |
| 1970S large date | 2,632,810 | 5.00 | 12.50 |
| 1970S small date | Inc. above | 5.00 | 65.00 |
| 1970S no mint mark dime | Inc. above | 5.00 | 630 |
| 1971S | 3,224,138 | 5.00 | 6.00 |
| 1971S no-mint mark nickel Est. 1,655 | 1,655 | 5.00 | 825 |
| 1972S | 3,267,667 | 5.00 | 5.50 |
| 1973S | 2,769,624 | 7.00 | 14.00 |
| 1974S | 2,617,350 | 7.00 | 12.50 |
| 1975S | 2,909,369 | 7.00 | 16.00 |
| 1976S 3 coins | 3,998,621 | 12.00 | 21.00 |
| 1976S | 4,149,730 | 7.00 | 10.50 |
| 1977S | 3,251,152 | 9.00 | 8.75 |
| 1978S | 3,127,788 | 9.00 | 11.00 |
| 1979S Type I | 3,677,175 | 9.00 | 11.50 |
| 1979S Type II | Inc. above | 9.00 | 120 |
| 1980S | 3,547,030 | 10.00 | 12.50 |
| 1981S Type I | 4,063,083 | 11.00 | 9.50 |
| 1981S Type II | 4,063,083 | 11.00 | 420 |
| 1982S | 3,857,479 | 11.00 | 6.00 |
| 1983S Prestige set | 140,361 | 59.00 | 95.00 |
| 1983S | 3,138,765 | 11.00 | 6.50 |
| 1983S no mint mark dime | 3,138,765 | 11.00 | 600 |
| 1984S Prestige set | 316,680 | 59.00 | 25.00 |
| 1984S | 2,748,430 | 11.00 | 8.00 |
| 1985S | 3,362,821 | 11.00 | 7.25 |
| 1986S Prestige set | 599,317 | 48.50 | 25.00 |
| 1986S | 2,411,180 | 11.00 | 28.00 |
| 1987S | 3,972,233 | 11.00 | 6.00 |
| 1987S Prestige set | 435,495 | 45.00 | 25.00 |
| 1988S | 3,031,287 | 11.00 | 15.00 |
| 1988S Prestige set | 231,661 | 45.00 | 40.00 |
| 1989S | 3,009,107 | 11.00 | 14.00 |
| 1989S Prestige set | 211,087 | 45.00 | 43.00 |
| 1990S | 2,793,433 | 11.00 | 20.00 |
| 1990S no S 1¢ | 3,555 | 11.00 | 4,500 |
| 1990S Prestige set | 506,126 | 45.00 | 30.00 |
| 1990S Prestige set, no mint mark cent | 506,126 | 45.00 | 2,300 |
| 1991s | 2,610,833 | 11.00 | 30.00 |
| 1991s Prestige set | 256,954 | 59.00 | 75.00 |
| 1992S | 2,675,618 | 12.50 | 15.00 |
| 1992S Prestige set | 183,285 | 59.00 | 45.00 |
| 1992S Silver | 1,009,585 | 21.00 | 16.50 |

| Date | Sets Sold | Issue Price | Value |
|---|---|---|---|
| 1992S Silver premier | 308,055 | 37.00 | 16.00 |
| 1993S | 2,337,819 | 12.50 | 16.00 |
| 1993S Prestige set | 224,045 | 57.00 | 45.00 |
| 1993S Silver | 570,213 | 21.00 | 33.00 |
| 1993S Silver premier | 191,140 | 37.00 | 30.00 |
| 1994S | 2,308,701 | 13.00 | 14.00 |
| 1994S Prestige Set | 175,893 | 57.00 | 54.00 |
| 1994S Silver | 636,009 | 21.00 | 37.00 |
| 1994S Silver premier | 149,320 | 37.50 | 37.00 |
| 1995S | 2,010,384 | 12.50 | 45.00 |
| 1995S Silver | 549,878 | 21.00 | 105 |
| 1995S Prestige Set | 17,112 | 57.00 | 130 |
| 1995S Silver premier | 130,107 | 37.50 | 110 |
| 1996S | 2,085,191 | 12.50 | 12.00 |
| 1996S Silver | 623,655 | 21.00 | 50.00 |
| 1996S Prestige set | 55,000 | 57.00 | 295 |
| 1996S Silver premier | 151,366 | 37.50 | 70.00 |
| 1997S | 1,975,000 | 12.50 | 65.00 |
| 1997S Silver | 605,473 | 21.00 | 90.00 |
| 1997S Prestige set | 80,000 | 57.00 | 215 |
| 1997S Silver premier | 136,205 | 37.50 | 90.00 |
| 1998S | 2,078,494 | 12.50 | 31.00 |
| 1998S Silver | 638,134 | 21.00 | 34.00 |
| 1998S Silver premier | 240,658 | 37.50 | 44.00 |
| 1999S | 2,543,401 | 19.95 | 53.00 |
| 1999S 5 quarter set | 1,169,958 | 13.95 | 53.00 |
| 1999S Silver | 804,565 | — | 95.00 |
| 2000S | — | 19.95 | 27.00 |
| 2000S 5 quarter set | — | 13.95 | 17.50 |
| 2000S Silver | — | 31.95 | 37.00 |

## MINT SETS

Mint, or uncirculated, sets contain one uncirculated coin of each denomination from each mint produced for circulation that year. Values listed here are only for those sets sold by the U.S. Mint. Sets were not offered in years not listed. In years when the Mint did not offer the sets, some private companies compiled and marketed uncirculated sets. Mint sets from 1947 through 1958 contained two examples of each coin mounted in cardboard holders, which caused the coins to tarnish. Beginning in 1959, the sets have been packaged in sealed Pliofilm packets and include only one specimen of each coin struck for that year. Listings for 1965, 1966 and 1967 are for "special mint sets," which were of higher quality than regular mint sets and were prooflike. They were packaged in plastic cases. The 1970 large-date and small-date varieties are distinguished by the size of the date on the coin. The 1976 three-piece set contains the quarter, half dollar and dollar with the Bicentennial design. The 1971 and 1972 sets do not include a dollar coin; the 1979 set does not include an S-mint-marked dollar.

| Date | Sets Sold | Issue Price | Value |
|---|---|---|---|
| 1947 Est. 5,000 | — | 4.87 | 1,300 |
| 1948 Est. 6,000 | — | 4.92 | 600 |
| 1949 Est. 5,200 | — | 5.45 | 900 |
| 1950 None issued | — | — | — |
| 1951 | 8,654 | 6.75 | 850 |
| 1952 | 11,499 | 6.14 | 750 |
| 1953 | 15,538 | 6.14 | 575 |
| 1954 | 25,599 | 6.19 | 370 |
| 1955 | 49,656 | 3.57 | 180 |
| 1956 | 45,475 | 3.34 | 160 |
| 1957 | 32,324 | 4.40 | 250 |
| 1958 | 50,314 | 4.43 | 170 |
| 1959 | 187,000 | 2.40 | 40.00 |
| 1960 | 260,485 | 2.40 | 22.00 |
| 1961 | 223,704 | 2.40 | 37.00 |
| 1962 | 385,285 | 2.40 | 18.50 |
| 1963 | 606,612 | 2.40 | 15.00 |
| 1964 | 1,008,108 | 2.40 | 10.00 |
| 1965 SMS* | 2,360,000 | 4.00 | 9.00 |
| 1966 SMS* | 2,261,583 | 4.00 | 9.00 |
| 1967 SMS* | 1,863,344 | 4.00 | 10.00 |
| 1968 | 2,105,128 | 2.50 | 4.00 |
| 1969 | 1,817,392 | 2.50 | 6.00 |
| 1970 large date | 2,038,134 | 2.50 | 27.50 |
| 1970 small date | Inc. above | 2.50 | 42.00 |
| 1971 | 2,193,396 | 3.50 | 4.00 |
| 1972 | 2,750,000 | 3.50 | 4.00 |
| 1973 | 1,767,691 | 6.00 | 26.50 |
| 1974 | 1,975,981 | 6.00 | 7.50 |
| 1975 | 1,921,488 | 6.00 | 14.00 |
| 1976 3 coins | 4,908,319 | 9.00 | 17.00 |
| 1976 | 1,892,513 | 6.00 | 14.50 |
| 1977 | 2,006,869 | 7.00 | 9.00 |
| 1978 | 2,162,609 | 7.00 | 8.00 |
| 1979 | 2,526,000 | 8.00 | 7.00 |
| 1980 | 2,815,066 | 9.00 | 7.00 |
| 1981 | 2,908,145 | 11.00 | 19.00 |
| 1982 & 1983 None issued | — | — | — |
| 1984 | 1,832,857 | 7.00 | 7.00 |
| 1985 | 1,710,571 | 7.00 | 8.00 |
| 1986 | 1,153,536 | 7.00 | 26.00 |
| 1987 | 2,890,758 | 7.00 | 9.50 |
| 1988 | 1,646,204 | 7.00 | 9.50 |
| 1989 | 1,987,915 | 7.00 | 9.00 |
| 1990 | 1,809,184 | 7.00 | 9.00 |
| 1991 | 1,352,101 | 7.00 | 14.00 |
| 1992 | 1,500,143 | 7.00 | 9.50 |
| 1993 | 1,297,094 | 8.00 | 10.00 |
| 1994 | 1,234,813 | 8.00 | 12.00 |
| 1995 | 1,038,787 | 8.00 | 20.00 |
| 1996 | 1,457,949 | 8.00 | 24.00 |
| 1997 | 950,473 | 8.00 | 18.00 |
| 1998 | 1,187,325 | 8.00 | 20.00 |
| 1999 | 1,421,625 | 14.95 | 24.00 |
| 2000 | — | — | 19.00 |

## AMERICAN EAGLE BULLION COINS

### GOLD $5

**Obv. Designer:** Augustus Saint-Gaudens. **Rev. Designer:** Miley Busiek. **Diameter:** 16.5 mm. **Weight:** 3.3930 g. **Composition:** 0.9167 GOLD, 0.1 oz. **KM#**216

| Date | Mintage | Unc | Prf. |
|---|---|---|---|
| MCMLXXXVI (1986) | 912,609 | 45.00 | — |
| MCMLXXXVII (1987) | 580,266 | 45.00 | — |
| MCMLXXXVIII (1988) | 159,500 | 85.00 | — |
| MCMLXXXVIIIP (1988)P | 143,881 | — | 56.00 |
| MCMLXXXIX (1989) | 264,790 | 70.00 | — |
| MCMLXXXIXP (1989)P | 82,924 | — | 56.00 |
| MCMXC (1990) | 210,210 | 75.00 | — |
| MCMXCP (1990)P | 99,349 | — | 56.00 |
| MCMXCI (1991) | 165,200 | 80.00 | — |
| MCMXCIP (1991)P | 70,344 | — | 58.00 |
| 1992 | 209,300 | 48.00 | — |
| 1992P | 64,902 | — | 71.00 |
| 1993 | 210,709 | 48.00 | — |
| 1993P | 58,649 | — | 66.00 |
| 1994 | 206,380 | 65.00 | — |
| 1994W | — | — | 60.00 |
| 1995 | 223,025 | 80.00 | — |
| 1995W | — | — | 56.00 |
| 1996 | — | 42.00 | — |
| 1996W | — | — | 74.00 |
| 1997 | 528,515 | 65.00 | — |
| 1997W | — | — | 91.00 |
| 1998 | 1,344,520 | 42.00 | — |
| 1998W | — | — | 58.00 |
| 1999 | — | 42.00 | — |
| 1999W | — | — | 58.00 |
| 2001 | — | — | — |
| 2001W | — | — | — |

### GOLD $10

**Obv. Designer:** Augustus Saint-Gaudens. **Rev. Designer:** Miley Busiek. **Diameter:** 22 mm. **Weight:** 8.4830 g. **Composition:** 0.9167 GOLD, 0.25 oz. **KM#**217

| Date | Mintage | Unc | Prf. |
|---|---|---|---|
| MCMLXXXVI (1986) | 726,031 | 110 | — |
| MCMLXXXVII (1987) | 269,255 | 105 | — |
| MCMLXXXVIII (1988) | 49,000 | 110 | — |
| MCMLXXXVIIIP (1988)P | 98,028 | — | 150 |
| MCMLXXXIX (1989) | 81,789 | 110 | — |
| MCMLXXXIX (1989P) | 53,593 | — | 150 |
| MCMXC (1990) | 41,000 | 185 | — |
| MCMXCP (1990)P | 62,674 | — | 150 |
| MCMXCI (1991) | 36,100 | 230 | — |
| MCMXCIP (1991)P | 50,839 | — | 150 |
| 1992 | 59,546 | 115 | — |
| 1992P | 46,290 | — | 150 |
| 1993 | 71,864 | 120 | — |
| 1993P | 46,271 | — | 150 |
| 1994 | 72,650 | 100.00 | — |
| 1994W | — | — | 150 |
| 1995 | 83,752 | 100.00 | — |
| 1995W | — | — | 150 |
| 1996 | 60,318 | 100.00 | — |
| 1996W | — | — | 150 |
| 1997 | 108,805 | 170 | — |
| 1997W | — | — | 150 |
| 1998 | 309,829 | 100.00 | — |
| 1998W | — | — | 150 |
| 1999 | — | 95.00 | — |
| 1999W | — | — | 150 |
| 2001 | — | — | — |
| 2001W | — | — | — |

### GOLD $25

**Obv. Designer:** Augustus Saint-Gaudens. **Rev. Designer:** Miley Busiek. **Diameter:** 27 mm. **Weight:** 16.9660 g. **Composition:** 0.9167 GOLD, 0.5 oz. **KM#**218

| Date | Mintage | Unc | Prf. |
|---|---|---|---|
| MCMLXXXVI (1986) | 599,566 | 280 | — |
| MCMLXXXVII (1987) | 131,255 | 300 | — |
| MCMLXXXVIIP (1987)P | 143,398 | — | 295 |
| MCMLXXXVIII (1988) | 45,000 | 350 | — |
| MCMLXXXVIIIP (1988)P | 76,528 | — | 280 |
| MCMLXXXIX (1989) | 44,829 | 500 | — |
| MCMLXXXIXP (1989)P | 44,264 | — | 280 |
| MCMXC (1990) | 31,000 | 510 | — |
| MCMXCP (1990)P | 51,636 | — | 280 |
| MCMXCI (1991) | 24,100 | 525 | — |
| MCMXCIP (1991)P | 53,125 | — | 280 |
| 1992 | 54,404 | 280 | — |
| 1992P | 40,982 | — | 280 |
| 1993 | 73,324 | 240 | — |
| 1993P | 43,319 | — | 280 |
| 1994 | 62,400 | 280 | — |
| 1994W | — | — | 280 |
| 1995 | 53,474 | 300 | — |
| 1995W | — | — | 280 |
| 1996 | 39,287 | 400 | — |
| 1996W | — | — | 280 |
| 1997 | 79,605 | 225 | — |
| 1997W | — | — | 280 |
| 1998 | 169,029 | 180 | — |
| 1998W | — | — | 280 |
| 1999 | — | 180 | — |
| 1999W | — | — | 280 |
| 2001 | — | — | — |
| 2001W | — | — | — |

### GOLD $50

**Obv. Designer:** Augustus Saint-Gaudens. **Rev. Designer:** Miley Busiek. **Diameter:** 32.7 mm. **Weight:** 33.9310 g. **Composition:** 0.9167 GOLD, 1 oz. **KM#**219

| Date | Mintage | Unc | Prf. |
|---|---|---|---|
| MCMLXXXVI (1986) | 1,362,650 | 320 | — |
| MCMLXXXVIW (1986)W | 446,290 | — | 570 |
| MCMLXXXVII (1987) | 1,045,500 | 320 | — |
| MCMLXXXVIIW (1987)W | 147,498 | — | 520 |
| MCMLXXXVIII (1988) | 465,000 | 320 | — |
| MCMLXXXVIIIW (1988)W | 87,133 | — | 570 |
| MCMLXXXIX (1989) | 415,790 | 320 | — |
| MCMLXXXIXW (1989)W | 53,960 | — | 570 |
| MCMXC (1990) | 373,210 | 325 | — |
| MCMXCW (1990)W | 62,401 | — | 570 |
| MCMXCI (1991) | 243,100 | 325 | — |
| MCMXCIW (1991)W | 50,411 | — | 570 |
| 1992 | 275,000 | 325 | — |
| 1992W | 44,835 | — | 570 |
| 1993 | 480,192 | 320 | — |
| 1993W | 34,389 | — | 570 |
| 1994 | 221,633 | 325 | — |
| 1994W | — | — | 570 |
| 1995 | 200,636 | 325 | — |
| 1995W | — | — | 570 |
| 1996 | 189,148 | 330 | — |
| 1996W | — | — | 570 |
| 1997 | 664,508 | 320 | — |
| 1997W | — | — | 570 |
| 1998 | 1,468,530 | 320 | — |
| 1998W | — | — | 570 |
| 1999 | — | 320 | — |
| 1999W | — | — | 570 |
| 2001 | — | — | — |
| 2001W | — | — | — |

## SILVER DOLLAR

**Obv. Designer:** Adolph A. Weinman. **Rev. Designer:** John Mercanti. **Diameter:** 40.6 mm. **Weight:** 31.1010 g. **Composition:** 0.9993 SILVER, 1 oz. **Notes:** Prices based on $5.50 spot silver. **KM#273**

| Date | Mintage | Unc | Prf. |
|---|---|---|---|
| 1986 | 5,393,005 | 16.50 | — |
| 1986S | 1,446,778 | — | 25.00 |
| 1987 | 11,442,335 | 8.00 | — |
| 1987S | 904,732 | — | 26.00 |
| 1988 | 5,004,646 | 10.00 | — |
| 1988S | 557,370 | — | 125 |
| 1989 | 5,203,327 | 10.00 | — |
| 1989S | 617,694 | — | 30.00 |
| 1990 | 5,840,210 | 12.00 | — |
| 1990S | 695,510 | — | 30.00 |
| 1991 | 7,191,066 | 8.50 | — |
| 1991S | 511,924 | — | 70.00 |
| 1992 | 5,540,068 | 9.50 | — |
| 1992S | 498,552 | — | 35.00 |
| 1993 | 6,763,762 | 8.50 | — |
| 1993P | 403,625 | — | 125 |
| 1994 | 4,227,319 | 11.00 | — |
| 1994P | 372,168 | — | 125 |
| 1995 | 4,672,051 | 11.00 | — |
| 1995P | 395,400 | — | 125 |
| 1995W 10th Anniversary | 30,125 | — | 2,250 |
| 1996 | 3,603,386 | 18.00 | — |
| 1996P | 473,021 | — | 50.00 |
| 1997 | 4,295,004 | 10.00 | — |
| 1997P | 429,682 | — | 100.00 |
| 1998 | 4,847,549 | 9.00 | — |
| 1998P | 452,319 | — | 57.50 |
| 1999 | — | 9.50 | — |
| 1999P | 549,769 | — | 85.00 |
| 2001W | — | — | 28.00 |

## PLATINUM $10

**Obv. Designer:** John Mercanti. **Rev. Designer:** Thomas D. Rogers Sr.. **Composition:** 0.9990 PLATINUM, 0.1 oz. **KM#283**

| Date | Mintage | Unc | Prf. |
|---|---|---|---|
| 1997 | 56,000 | 80.00 | — |
| 1997W | — | — | 125 |
| 1998 | 39,525 | 80.00 | — |
| 1998W | — | — | 125 |
| 1999 | — | 85.00 | — |
| 1999W | — | — | 125 |
| 2001 | — | — | — |
| 2001W | — | — | — |

## PLATINUM $25

**Obv. Designer:** John Mercanti. **Rev. Designer:** Thomas D. Rogers Sr. **Composition:** 0.9995 PLATINUM, 0.25 oz. **KM#284**

| Date | Mintage | Unc | Prf. |
|---|---|---|---|
| 1997 | 20,500 | 220 | — |
| 1997W | — | — | 210 |
| 1998 | 38,887 | 195 | — |
| 1998W | — | — | 225 |
| 1999 | — | 195 | — |
| 1999W | — | — | 225 |
| 2001 | — | — | — |
| 2001W | — | — | — |

## PLATINUM $50

**Obv. Designer:** John Mercanti. **Rev. Designer:** Thomas D. Rogers Sr. **Composition:** 0.9995 PLATINUM, 0.5 oz. **KM#285**

| Date | Mintage | Unc | Prf. |
|---|---|---|---|
| 1997 | 27,100 | 430 | — |
| 1997W | — | — | 370 |
| 1998 | 32,415 | 350 | — |
| 1998W | — | — | 410 |
| 1999 | — | 300 | — |
| 1999W | — | — | 410 |
| 2001 | — | — | — |
| 2001W | — | — | — |

## PLATINUM $100

**Composition:** 0.9995 PLATINUM, 1 oz. **Notes:** Prices based on $374.00 spot platinum. **KM#286**

| Date | Mintage | Unc | Prf. |
|---|---|---|---|
| 1997 | 70,250 | 630 | — |
| 1997W | — | — | 725 |
| 1998 | 133,002 | 630 | — |
| 1998W | — | — | 715 |
| 1999 | — | 630 | — |
| 1999W | — | — | 715 |
| 2000 | — | 630 | — |
| 2000W | — | — | 715 |
| 2001 | — | — | — |
| 2001W | — | — | — |

The Oriental Republic of Uruguay (so called because of its location on the east bank of the Uruguay River) is situated on the Atlantic coast of South America between Argentina and Brazil. This South American country has an area of 68,536 sq. mi.(176,220 sq. km.) and a population of *3 million. Capital: Montevideo. Uruguay's chief economic asset is its rich, rolling grassy plains. Meat, wool, hides and skins are exported.

Uruguay was discovered in 1516 by Juan Diaz de Solis, a Spaniard, but settled by the Portuguese who founded Colonia in 1680. Spain contested Portuguese possession and, after a long struggle, gained control of the country in 1778. During the general South American struggle for independence, Uruguay 's first attempt was led by Gaucho soldier Jose Gervasio Artigas leading the Banda Oriental which was quelled by Spanish and Portuguese forces in 1811. The armistice was soon broken and Argentine force from Buenos Aires cast off the Spanish bond in the Plata region in 1814 only to be conquered again by the Portuguese from Brazil in the struggle of 1816-20. Revolt flared anew in 1825 and independence was reasserted in 1828 with the help of Argentina. The Uruguayan Republic was established in1830.

**MINT MARKS**

A - Paris, Berlin, Vienna
(a) Paris, privy marks only
D - Lyon (France)
H - Birmingham
Mx, Mo - Mexico City
(p) - Poissy, France
So - Santiago (Small O above S)
(u) – Utrecht

**MONETARY SYSTEM**

100 Centesimo = 1 Peso
1975-1993
1000 Old Pesos = 1 Nuevo (New) Peso
Commencing 1994
1000 Nuevos Pesos = 1 Peso Uruguayo

# REPUBLIC

## DECIMAL COINAGE

**CENTESIMO KM# 19 Weight:** 2.0000 g. **Composition:** Copper Nickel

| Date | Mintage | F | VF | XF | Unc | BU |
|---|---|---|---|---|---|---|
| 1901A | 6,000,000 | 0.45 | 0.75 | 4.00 | 30.00 | — |
| 1901A Proof | — | Value: 225 | | | | |
| 1909A | 5,000,000 | 0.45 | 0.75 | 3.00 | 10.00 | — |
| 1924(p) | 3,000,000 | 0.45 | 0.75 | 2.50 | 12.00 | — |
| 1936A | 2,000,000 | 0.50 | 1.00 | 3.00 | 12.50 | — |

**CENTESIMO KM# 32 Weight:** 1.5000 g. **Composition:** Copper Nickel **Obverse:** Artigas bust right, 'HP' below

| Date | Mintage | F | VF | XF | Unc | BU |
|---|---|---|---|---|---|---|
| 1953 | 5,000,000 | 0.15 | 0.30 | 0.50 | 1.00 | — |
| 1953 Proof | — | Value: 80.00 | | | | |

**2 CENTESIMOS KM# 20 Weight:** 3.5000 g. **Composition:** Copper Nickel

| Date | Mintage | F | VF | XF | Unc | BU |
|---|---|---|---|---|---|---|
| 1901A | 7,500,000 | 0.50 | 1.25 | 3.50 | 16.00 | — |
| 1909A | 10,000,000 | 0.50 | 1.00 | 2.75 | 9.00 | — |
| 1924(p) | 11,000,000 | 0.50 | 1.00 | 2.75 | 7.00 | — |
| 1936A | 6,500,000 | 0.50 | 1.25 | 3.50 | 10.00 | — |
| 1941So | 10,000,000 | 0.50 | 1.00 | 2.75 | 9.00 | — |

**2 CENTESIMOS KM# 20a Weight:** 3.5000 g. **Composition:** Copper

| Date | Mintage | F | VF | XF | Unc | BU |
|---|---|---|---|---|---|---|
| 1943So | 5,000,000 | 0.25 | 0.50 | 2.00 | 6.00 | — |
| 1944So | 3,500,000 | 0.25 | 0.50 | 2.00 | 6.00 | — |
| 1945So | 2,500,000 | 0.25 | 0.50 | 2.00 | 7.00 | — |
| 1946So | 2,500,000 | 0.25 | 0.50 | 2.50 | 7.50 | — |
| 1947So | 5,000,000 | 0.25 | 0.50 | 1.50 | 5.00 | — |
| 1948So | 7,500,000 | 0.25 | 0.50 | 1.00 | 4.00 | — |
| 1949So | 7,400,000 | 0.25 | 0.50 | 1.00 | 4.00 | — |
| 1951So | 12,500,000 | 0.25 | 0.50 | 1.00 | 3.00 | — |

**2 CENTESIMOS KM# 33 Weight:** 2.5000 g. **Composition:** Copper Nickel **Obverse:** Artigas bust right, 'HP' below

| Date | Mintage | F | VF | XF | Unc | BU |
|---|---|---|---|---|---|---|
| 1953 | 50,000,000 | 0.15 | 0.30 | 0.50 | 1.25 | — |
| 1953 Proof | — | Value: 65.00 | | | | |

**2 CENTESIMOS KM# 37 Weight:** 2.0000 g. **Composition:** Nickel-Brass

| Date | Mintage | F | VF | XF | Unc | BU |
|---|---|---|---|---|---|---|
| 1960 | 17,500,000 | — | 0.15 | 0.25 | 0.50 | — |
| 1960 Proof | — | Value: 40.00 | | | | |

**5 CENTESIMOS KM# 21 Weight:** 5.0000 g. **Composition:** Copper Nickel

| Date | Mintage | F | VF | XF | Unc | BU |
|---|---|---|---|---|---|---|
| 1901A | 6,000,000 | 0.25 | 0.75 | 2.50 | 20.00 | — |
| 1901A Proof | — | Value: 325 | | | | |
| 1909A | 5,000,000 | 0.25 | 0.75 | 2.00 | 10.00 | — |
| 1909A Proof | — | Value: 125 | | | | |
| 1924(p) | 5,000,000 | 0.35 | 1.00 | 3.50 | 10.00 | — |
| 1936A | 3,000,000 | 0.35 | 1.00 | 3.00 | 10.00 | — |
| 1941So | 2,400,000 | 0.25 | 0.75 | 2.00 | 6.50 | — |
| 1941So Proof | — | Value: 200 | | | | |

**5 CENTESIMOS KM# 21a Weight:** 5.0000 g. **Composition:** Copper

| Date | Mintage | F | VF | XF | Unc | BU |
|---|---|---|---|---|---|---|
| 1944So | 4,000,000 | 0.20 | 0.65 | 1.50 | 7.50 | — |
| 1946So | 2,000,000 | 0.20 | 0.50 | 2.00 | 8.50 | — |
| 1947So | 2,000,000 | 0.20 | 0.50 | 2.00 | 8.50 | — |
| 1948So | 3,000,000 | 0.20 | 0.50 | 1.50 | 7.50 | — |
| 1949So | 2,800,000 | 0.20 | 0.50 | 1.50 | 7.50 | — |
| 1951So | 15,000,000 | 0.20 | 0.50 | 1.50 | 5.50 | — |

**5 CENTESIMOS KM# 34 Weight:** 3.5000 g. **Composition:** Copper Nickel **Obverse:** Artigas bust right, 'HP' below **Reverse:** Value within wreath

| Date | Mintage | F | VF | XF | Unc | BU |
|---|---|---|---|---|---|---|
| 1953 | 17,500,000 | 0.20 | 0.30 | 0.50 | 1.00 | — |
| 1953 Proof | — | Value: 75.00 | | | | |

**5 CENTESIMOS KM# 38 Weight:** 3.5000 g. **Composition:** Nickel-Brass **Obverse:** Bust right **Reverse:** Value within wreath

| Date | Mintage | F | VF | XF | Unc | BU |
|---|---|---|---|---|---|---|
| 1960 | 88,000,000 | — | 0.15 | 0.25 | 0.50 | — |
| 1960 Proof | — | Value: 40.00 | | | | |

**10 CENTESIMOS KM# 25 Weight:** 8.0000 g. **Composition:** Aluminum-Bronze **Subject:** Constitutional Centennial **Obverse:** MORLON behind neck **Reverse:** Cornucopia and torch flank denomination

| Date | Mintage | F | VF | XF | Unc | BU |
|---|---|---|---|---|---|---|
| 1930(a) | 5,000,000 | 1.00 | 2.50 | 7.50 | 20.00 | — |

**10 CENTESIMOS KM# 28 Weight:** 6.0000 g. **Composition:** Aluminum-Bronze

| Date | Mintage | F | VF | XF | Unc | BU |
|---|---|---|---|---|---|---|
| 1936A | 2,000,000 | 1.50 | 3.50 | 8.50 | 20.00 | — |

**10 CENTESIMOS KM# 35 Weight:** 4.5000 g. **Composition:** Copper Nickel **Obverse:** Artigas bust right, 'HP' below

| Date | Mintage | F | VF | XF | Unc | BU |
|---|---|---|---|---|---|---|
| 1953 | 28,250,000 | 0.15 | 0.20 | 0.30 | 0.75 | — |
| 1953 Proof | — | Value: 75.00 | | | | |
| 1959 | 10,000,000 | 0.20 | 0.30 | 0.50 | 1.50 | — |

**10 CENTESIMOS KM# 39 Weight:** 4.5000 g. **Composition:** Nickel-Brass

| Date | Mintage | F | VF | XF | Unc | BU |
|---|---|---|---|---|---|---|
| 1960 | 72,500,000 | 0.15 | 0.20 | 0.30 | 0.75 | — |
| 1960 Proof | — | Value: 75.00 | | | | |

**20 CENTESIMOS KM# 24 Weight:** 5.0000 g. **Composition:** 0.8000 Silver .1286 oz. ASW **Obverse:** Radiant sun peeks out over shield of arms within wreath **Reverse:** Bust left

| Date | Mintage | F | VF | XF | Unc | BU |
|---|---|---|---|---|---|---|
| 1920 | 2,500,000 | 2.00 | 4.00 | 9.00 | 22.00 | — |

**20 CENTESIMOS** **KM# 26** **Weight:** 5.0000 g. **Composition:** 0.8000 Silver .1286 oz. ASW **Subject:** Constitutional Centennial **Obverse:** Constitution seated left, P. TURIN left of date **Reverse:** Five wheat ears, small cornucopia and torch mintmarks flank stems

| Date | Mintage | F | VF | XF | Unc | BU |
|---|---|---|---|---|---|---|
| 1930(a) | 2,500,000 | 2.00 | 3.50 | 8.00 | 20.00 | — |

**20 CENTESIMOS** **KM# 29** **Weight:** 3.0000 g. **Composition:** 0.7200 Silver .0694 oz. ASW

| Date | Mintage | F | VF | XF | Unc | BU |
|---|---|---|---|---|---|---|
| 1942So | 18,000,000 | 1.25 | 2.50 | 4.50 | 7.00 | — |

**20 CENTESIMOS** **KM# 36** **Weight:** 3.0000 g. **Composition:** 0.7200 Silver .0694 oz. ASW

| Date | Mintage | F | VF | XF | Unc | BU |
|---|---|---|---|---|---|---|
| 1954(u) | 10,000,000 | 0.75 | 1.50 | 2.50 | 4.50 | — |

**20 CENTESIMOS** **KM# 44** **Composition:** Aluminum

| Date | Mintage | F | VF | XF | Unc | BU |
|---|---|---|---|---|---|---|
| 1965So | 40,000,000 | 0.15 | 0.20 | 0.35 | 0.60 | — |

**25 CENTESIMOS** **KM# 40** **Composition:** Copper Nickel **Obverse:** "HP' below bust

| Date | Mintage | F | VF | XF | Unc | BU |
|---|---|---|---|---|---|---|
| 1960 | 48,000,000 | 0.20 | 0.35 | 0.50 | 1.00 | — |
| 1960 Proof | — | Value: 60.00 | | | | |

**50 CENTESIMOS** **KM# 22** **Weight:** 12.5000 g. **Composition:** 0.9000 Silver .3617 oz. ASW

| Date | Mintage | F | VF | XF | Unc | BU |
|---|---|---|---|---|---|---|
| 1916 | 400,000 | 5.00 | 10.00 | 28.00 | 100 | — |
| 1917 | 5,600,000 | 4.00 | 7.00 | 20.00 | 70.00 | — |

**50 CENTESIMOS** **KM# 41** **Composition:** Copper Nickel **Obverse:** Artigas bust right, 'HP' below

| Date | Mintage | F | VF | XF | Unc | BU |
|---|---|---|---|---|---|---|
| 1960 | 18,000,000 | 0.20 | 0.40 | 0.60 | 1.00 | — |
| 1960 Proof | — | Value: 60.00 | | | | |

**50 CENTESIMOS** **KM# 45** **Composition:** Aluminum

| Date | Mintage | F | VF | XF | Unc | BU |
|---|---|---|---|---|---|---|
| 1965So | 50,000,000 | 0.15 | 0.25 | 0.40 | 0.70 | — |

**PESO** **KM# 23** **Weight:** 25.0000 g. **Composition:** 0.9000 Silver .7235 oz. ASW

| Date | Mintage | F | VF | XF | Unc | BU |
|---|---|---|---|---|---|---|
| 1917 | 2,000,000 | 10.00 | 20.00 | 50.00 | 250 | — |

**PESO** **KM# 30** **Weight:** 9.0000 g. **Composition:** 0.7200 Silver .2083 oz. ASW

| Date | Mintage | F | VF | XF | Unc | BU |
|---|---|---|---|---|---|---|
| 1942So | 9,000,000 | BV | 2.25 | 4.50 | 15.00 | — |

**PESO** **KM# 42** **Composition:** Copper Nickel **Obverse:** Artigas bust right, 'HP' below

| Date | Mintage | F | VF | XF | Unc | BU |
|---|---|---|---|---|---|---|
| 1960 | 8,000,000 | 0.25 | 0.50 | 0.75 | 1.25 | — |
| 1960 Proof | — | Value: 75.00 | | | | |

**PESO** **KM# 46** **Composition:** Aluminum-Bronze

| Date | Mintage | F | VF | XF | Unc | BU |
|---|---|---|---|---|---|---|
| 1965So | 60,000,000 | — | 0.15 | 0.35 | 0.60 | — |
| 1965So Proof | 25 | Value: 65.00 | | | | |

**PESO** **KM# 49** **Composition:** Nickel-Brass **Reverse:** Ceibo, national flower

| Date | Mintage | F | VF | XF | Unc | BU |
|---|---|---|---|---|---|---|
| 1968So | 103,200,000 | — | — | 0.15 | 0.30 | — |
| 1968So Proof | 50 | Value: 50.00 | | | | |

**PESO** **KM# 52** **Composition:** Aluminum-Brass

| Date | Mintage | F | VF | XF | Unc | BU |
|---|---|---|---|---|---|---|
| 1969So | 51,800,000 | — | — | 0.15 | 0.30 | — |

**5 PESOS** **KM# 27** **Weight:** 8.4850 g. **Composition:** 0.9170 Gold .2501 oz. AGW **Subject:** Constitution Centennial **Obverse:** Artigas head right, L. BAZOR in left field behind neck

| Date | Mintage | F | VF | XF | Unc | BU |
|---|---|---|---|---|---|---|
| 1930(a) | Est. 100,000 | 100 | 115 | 135 | 175 | — |

**Note:** Only 14,415 were released. Remainder withheld

**5 PESOS** **KM# 47** **Composition:** Aluminum-Bronze

| Date | Mintage | F | VF | XF | Unc | BU |
|---|---|---|---|---|---|---|
| 1965So | 18,000,000 | 0.20 | 0.30 | 0.50 | 1.00 | — |
| 1965So Proof | 25 | Value: 75.00 | | | | |

**5 PESOS** **KM# 50** **Composition:** Nickel-Brass **Reverse:** Ceibo, national flower

| Date | Mintage | F | VF | XF | Unc | BU |
|---|---|---|---|---|---|---|
| 1968So | 42,680,000 | 0.10 | 0.20 | 0.30 | 0.40 | — |
| 1968So Proof | 50 | Value: 65.00 | | | | |

**5 PESOS** **KM# 53** **Composition:** Aluminum-Bronze

| Date | Mintage | F | VF | XF | Unc | BU |
|---|---|---|---|---|---|---|
| 1969So | 42,320,000 | — | — | 0.10 | 0.30 | — |

**10 PESOS** **KM# 43** **Weight:** 12.5000 g. **Composition:** 0.9000 Silver .3617 oz. ASW **Subject:** Sesquicentennial of Revolution Against Spain

| Date | Mintage | F | VF | XF | Unc | BU |
|---|---|---|---|---|---|---|
| 1961 | 3,000,000 | BV | — | 3.50 | 7.00 | — |
| 1961 Proof | — | Value: 600 | | | | |

**10 PESOS** **KM# 48** **Composition:** Aluminum-Bronze

| Date | Mintage | F | VF | XF | Unc | BU |
|---|---|---|---|---|---|---|
| 1965So | 18,000,000 | 0.15 | 0.20 | 0.35 | 1.00 | — |

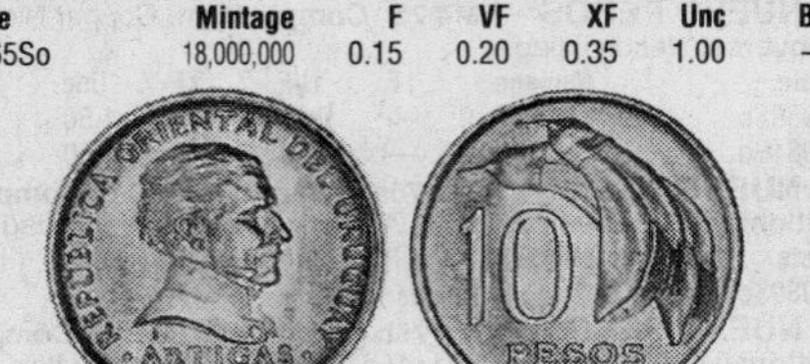


**10 PESOS** **KM# 51** **Composition:** Nickel-Brass **Reverse:** Ceibo, national flower

| Date | Mintage | F | VF | XF | Unc | BU |
|---|---|---|---|---|---|---|
| 1968So | 90,000,000 | 0.15 | 0.20 | 0.35 | 0.65 | — |
| 1968So Proof | 50 | Value: 80.00 | | | | |

**10 PESOS** **KM# 54** **Composition:** Aluminum-Bronze

| Date | Mintage | F | VF | XF | Unc | BU |
|---|---|---|---|---|---|---|
| 1969So | 10,000,000 | 0.15 | 0.20 | 0.35 | 0.65 | — |

**20 PESOS** **KM# 56** **Composition:** Copper Nickel **Reverse:** Spears of wheat

| Date | Mintage | F | VF | XF | Unc | BU |
|---|---|---|---|---|---|---|
| 1970So | 50,000,000 | 0.15 | 0.25 | 0.40 | 0.75 | — |
| 1970So Proof | — | Value: 80.00 | | | | |

**50 PESOS** **KM# 57** **Composition:** Copper Nickel **Reverse:** Spears of wheat

| Date | Mintage | F | VF | XF | Unc | BU |
|---|---|---|---|---|---|---|
| 1970So | 20,000,000 | 0.20 | 0.40 | 0.60 | 1.50 | — |
| 1970So Proof | — | Value: 80.00 | | | | |

**50 PESOS** **KM# 58** **Composition:** Nickel-Brass **Subject:** Centennial - Birth of Rodo

| Date | Mintage | F | VF | XF | Unc | BU |
|---|---|---|---|---|---|---|
| 1971So | 15,000,000 | 0.20 | 0.50 | 1.00 | 2.00 | — |

**50 PESOS** **KM# 58a** **Weight:** 6.0200 g. **Composition:** 0.9000 Silver .1742 oz. ASW **Subject:** Centennial - Birth of Rodo

| Date | Mintage | F | VF | XF | Unc | BU |
|---|---|---|---|---|---|---|
| 1971So Proof | 1,000 | Value: 17.50 | | | | |

**50 PESOS** **KM# 58b** **Composition:** Gold **Subject:** Centennial - Birth of Rodo

| Date | Mintage | F | VF | XF | Unc | BU |
|---|---|---|---|---|---|---|
| 1971So Proof | 100 | Value: 350 | | | | |

**100 PESOS** **KM# 59** **Composition:** Copper Nickel

| Date | Mintage | F | VF | XF | Unc | BU |
|---|---|---|---|---|---|---|
| 1973Mx | 20,000,000 | 0.25 | 0.50 | 1.00 | 2.50 | — |

**Note:** Mx may be designer initials.

**1000 PESOS** **KM# 55** **Weight:** 25.0000 g. **Composition:** 0.9000 Silver .7234 oz. ASW **Series:** F.A.O

| Date | Mintage | F | VF | XF | Unc | BU |
|---|---|---|---|---|---|---|
| 1969So | 500,000 | — | BV | 6.50 | 10.00 | — |
| 1969So Proof | 350 | Value: 150 | | | | |

**1000 PESOS** **KM# 55a** **Composition:** Bronze **Series:** F.A.O.

| Date | Mintage | F | VF | XF | Unc | BU |
|---|---|---|---|---|---|---|
| 1969So | 11,000 | — | — | 16.50 | 30.00 | — |

**1000 PESOS** **KM# 55b** **Composition:** Gold **Series:** F.A.O

| Date | Mintage | F | VF | XF | Unc | BU |
|---|---|---|---|---|---|---|
| 1969So | 450 | — | — | — | 725 | — |

## MEDALLIC COINAGE

**2000 NUEVO PESOS** **KM# M1** **Weight:** 65.0000 g. **Composition:** 0.9000 Silver 1.8810 oz. ASW **Subject:** Royal Visit of Spanish King and Queen

| Date | Mintage | F | VF | XF | Unc | BU |
|---|---|---|---|---|---|---|
| 1983 Proof | 20,000 | Value: 37.50 | | | | |

**2000 NUEVO PESOS** **KM# M1a** **Weight:** 65.0000 g. **Composition:** 0.9000 Gold 1.8810 oz. AGW

| Date | Mintage | F | VF | XF | Unc | BU |
|---|---|---|---|---|---|---|
| 1983 Proof | — | Value: 1,250 | | | | |

**20000 NUEVO PESOS** **KM# M2** **Weight:** 20.0000 g. **Composition:** 0.9000 Gold .5787 oz. AGW **Subject:** Royal Visit of Spanish King and Queen

| Date | Mintage | F | VF | XF | Unc | BU |
|---|---|---|---|---|---|---|
| 1983 Proof | 1,500 | Value: 270 | | | | |

**20000 NUEVO PESOS** **KM# M3** **Weight:** 12.0000 g. **Composition:** 0.9000 Silver .3472 oz. ASW

| Date | Mintage | F | VF | XF | Unc | BU |
|---|---|---|---|---|---|---|
| 1983 Proof | 100 | Value: 75.00 | | | | |

## REFORM COINAGE

1000 Old Pesos = 1 Nuevo (New) Peso

**CENTESIMO** **KM# 71** **Composition:** Aluminum **Obverse:** Radiant sun

| Date | Mintage | F | VF | XF | Unc | BU |
|---|---|---|---|---|---|---|
| 1977So | 10,000,000 | — | — | 0.15 | 0.25 | — |

**CENTESIMO** **KM# 71a** **Weight:** 3.7000 g. **Composition:** 0.9000 Silver .1071 oz. ASW **Obverse:** Radiant sun

| Date | Mintage | F | VF | XF | Unc | BU |
|---|---|---|---|---|---|---|
| 1979So Proof | 202 | Value: 15.00 | | | | |

**CENTESIMO** **KM# 71b** **Weight:** 6.2600 g. **Composition:** 0.9000 Gold .1811 oz. AGW **Obverse:** Radiant sun

| Date | Mintage | F | VF | XF | Unc | BU |
|---|---|---|---|---|---|---|
| 1979So Proof | 50 | Value: 175 | | | | |

**2 CENTESIMOS** **KM# 72** **Composition:** Aluminum **Obverse:** Radiant sun

| Date | Mintage | F | VF | XF | Unc | BU |
|---|---|---|---|---|---|---|
| 1977So | 17,000,000 | — | — | 0.15 | 0.25 | — |
| 1978So | 3,000,000 | — | — | 0.15 | 0.25 | — |

**2 CENTESIMOS** **KM# 72a** **Weight:** 5.2000 g. **Composition:** 0.9000 Silver .1505 oz. ASW **Obverse:** Radiant sun

| Date | Mintage | F | VF | XF | Unc | BU |
|---|---|---|---|---|---|---|
| 1979So Proof | 202 | Value: 20.00 | | | | |

**2 CENTESIMOS** **KM# 72b** **Weight:** 9.2500 g. **Composition:** 0.9000 Gold .2676 oz. AGW **Obverse:** Radiant sun

| Date | Mintage | F | VF | XF | Unc | BU |
|---|---|---|---|---|---|---|
| 1979So Proof | 52 | Value: 275 | | | | |

**5 CENTESIMOS** **KM# 73** **Composition:** Aluminum **Obverse:** Steer left

| Date | Mintage | F | VF | XF | Unc | BU |
|---|---|---|---|---|---|---|
| 1977So | 11,000,000 | — | — | 0.15 | 0.45 | — |
| 1978So | 19,000,000 | — | — | 0.15 | 0.45 | — |

**5 CENTESIMOS** **KM# 73a** **Weight:** 7.4000 g. **Composition:** 0.9000 Silver .2141 oz. ASW **Obverse:** Steer left

| Date | Mintage | F | VF | XF | Unc | BU |
|---|---|---|---|---|---|---|
| 1979So Proof | 202 | Value: 20.00 | | | | |

**5 CENTESIMOS** **KM# 73b** **Weight:** 12.5500 g. **Composition:** 0.9000 Gold .3631 oz. AGW **Obverse:** Steer left

| Date | Mintage | F | VF | XF | Unc | BU |
|---|---|---|---|---|---|---|
| 1979So Proof | 52 | Value: 350 | | | | |

**10 CENTESIMOS** **KM# 66** **Composition:** Aluminum-Bronze **Obverse:** Horse left

| Date | Mintage | F | VF | XF | Unc | BU |
|---|---|---|---|---|---|---|
| 1976So Proof | — | — | — | — | — | — |
| 1976So | 127,400,000 | — | — | 0.20 | 0.70 | — |
| 1977So | 12,700,000 | — | — | 0.25 | 0.75 | — |
| 1978So | 19,900,000 | — | — | 0.25 | 0.75 | — |
| 1981So | — | — | — | 0.25 | 0.75 | — |

**10 CENTESIMOS** **KM# 66a** **Weight:** 3.8000 g. **Composition:** 0.9000 Silver .1100 oz. ASW **Obverse:** Horse left

| Date | Mintage | F | VF | XF | Unc | BU |
|---|---|---|---|---|---|---|
| 1976So Proof | 200 | Value: 20.00 | | | | |
| 1977So Proof | 200 | Value: 20.00 | | | | |

**10 CENTESIMOS** **KM# 66b** **Weight:** 6.0000 g. **Composition:** 0.9000 Gold .1736 oz. AGW **Obverse:** Horse left

| Date | Mintage | F | VF | XF | Unc | BU |
|---|---|---|---|---|---|---|
| 1976So Proof | 50 | Value: 175 | | | | |

**20 CENTESIMOS** **KM# 67** **Composition:** Aluminum-Bronze

| Date | Mintage | F | VF | XF | Unc | BU |
|---|---|---|---|---|---|---|
| 1976So Proof | — | — | — | — | — | — |
| 1976So | 40,000,000 | — | — | 0.20 | 0.45 | — |
| 1977So | 4,700,000 | — | — | 0.20 | 0.60 | — |
| 1978So | 15,300,000 | — | — | 0.20 | 0.45 | — |
| 1981So | — | — | — | 0.20 | 0.45 | — |

**20 CENTESIMOS** **KM# 67a** **Weight:** 6.4000 g. **Composition:** 0.9000 Silver .1852 oz. ASW

| Date | Mintage | F | VF | XF | Unc | BU |
|---|---|---|---|---|---|---|
| 1976So Proof | 200 | Value: 22.50 | | | | |
| 1977So Proof | 200 | Value: 22.50 | | | | |

**20 CENTESIMOS** **KM# 67b** **Weight:** 10.5000 g. **Composition:** 0.9000 Gold .3038 oz. AGW

| Date | Mintage | F | VF | XF | Unc | BU |
|---|---|---|---|---|---|---|
| 1976So Proof | 50 | Value: 350 | | | | |

**50 CENTESIMOS** **KM# 68** **Composition:** Aluminum-Bronze **Obverse:** Scale

| Date | Mintage | F | VF | XF | Unc | BU |
|---|---|---|---|---|---|---|
| 1976So Proof | — | — | — | — | — | — |
| 1976So | 30,000,000 | — | — | 0.20 | 0.50 | — |
| 1977So | 9,800,000 | — | — | 0.20 | 0.50 | — |
| 1978So | 200,000 | — | — | 0.20 | 0.55 | — |
| 1981So | — | — | — | 0.20 | 0.50 | — |

**50 CENTESIMOS** **KM# 68a** **Weight:** 9.0000 g. **Composition:** 0.9000 Silver .2604 oz. ASW **Obverse:** Scale

| Date | Mintage | F | VF | XF | Unc | BU |
|---|---|---|---|---|---|---|
| 1976So Proof | 200 | Value: 35.00 | | | | |
| 1977So Proof | 200 | Value: 35.00 | | | | |

**50 CENTESIMOS** **KM# 68b** **Weight:** 15.0000 g. **Composition:** 0.9000 Gold .4340 oz. AGW **Obverse:** Scale

| Date | Mintage | F | VF | XF | Unc | BU |
|---|---|---|---|---|---|---|
| 1976So Proof | 50 | Value: 500 | | | | |

**NUEVO PESO** **KM# 69** **Composition:** Aluminum-Bronze **Obverse:** Bust of Jose Gervasio Artigas left

| Date | Mintage | F | VF | XF | Unc | BU |
|---|---|---|---|---|---|---|
| 1976So Proof | — | — | — | — | — | — |
| 1976So | 65,540,000 | — | — | 0.30 | 0.60 | — |
| 1977So | 7,360,000 | — | — | 0.30 | 0.65 | — |
| 1978So | 27,100,000 | — | — | 0.30 | 0.65 | — |

**NUEVO PESO** **KM# 69a** **Weight:** 13.5000 g. **Composition:** 0.9000 Silver .3906 oz. ASW **Obverse:** Bust of Jose Gervasio Artigas left

| Date | Mintage | F | VF | XF | Unc | BU |
|---|---|---|---|---|---|---|
| 1976So Proof | 200 | Value: 40.00 | | | | |

**NUEVO PESO** **KM# 69b** **Weight:** 23.0000 g. **Composition:** 0.9000 Gold .6655 oz. AGW **Obverse:** Bust of Jose Gervasio Artigas left

| Date | Mintage | F | VF | XF | Unc | BU |
|---|---|---|---|---|---|---|
| 1976So Proof | 50 | Value: 600 | | | | |

**NUEVO PESO** **KM# 74** **Composition:** Copper Nickel **Obverse:** Radiant sun peeking over shield of arms within wreath

| Date | Mintage | F | VF | XF | Unc | BU |
|---|---|---|---|---|---|---|
| 1980So | 50,000,000 | — | 0.20 | 0.35 | 0.65 | — |
| 1981So | — | — | 0.20 | 0.35 | 0.65 | — |

**NUEVO PESO** **KM# 74a** **Weight:** 7.0000 g. **Composition:** 0.9000 Silver .2026 oz. ASW **Obverse:** Radiant sun peeking over shield of arms within wreath

| Date | Mintage | F | VF | XF | Unc | BU |
|---|---|---|---|---|---|---|
| 1980So Proof | 300 | Value: 25.00 | | | | |

**NUEVO PESO** **KM# 74b** **Weight:** 11.6500 g. **Composition:** 0.9000 Gold .3371 oz. AGW **Obverse:** Radiant sun peeking over shield of arms within wreath

| Date | Mintage | F | VF | XF | Unc | BU |
|---|---|---|---|---|---|---|
| 1980So Proof | 100 | Value: 300 | | | | |

**NUEVO PESO** **KM# 76** **Weight:** 6.9400 g. **Composition:** 0.9000 Silver .2008 oz. ASW **Obverse:** National flag

| Date | Mintage | F | VF | XF | Unc | BU |
|---|---|---|---|---|---|---|
| 1981 Proof | 100 | Value: 30.00 | | | | |

**NUEVO PESO** **KM# 95** **Composition:** Stainless Steel

| Date | Mintage | F | VF | XF | Unc | BU |
|---|---|---|---|---|---|---|
| 1989 | — | — | — | 0.15 | 0.35 | — |

**2 NUEVO PESOS** **KM# 77** **Composition:** Copper-Nickel-Zinc **Subject:** World Food Day

| Date | Mintage | F | VF | XF | Unc | BU |
|---|---|---|---|---|---|---|
| 1981 | 95,000,000 | — | 0.25 | 0.50 | 1.00 | — |

**2 NUEVO PESOS** **KM# 77a** **Weight:** 14.5300 g. **Composition:** 0.9000 Gold .4204 oz. AGW **Subject:** World Food Day

| Date | Mintage | F | VF | XF | Unc | BU |
|---|---|---|---|---|---|---|
| 1981 Proof | 100 | Value: 400 | | | | |

**5 NUEVO PESOS** **KM# 65** **Composition:** Copper-Nickel-Aluminum **Subject:** 150th Anniversary - Revolutionary Movement

| Date | Mintage | F | VF | XF | Unc | BU |
|---|---|---|---|---|---|---|
| ND(1975)So | 3,000,000 | 0.50 | 0.75 | 1.25 | 3.50 | — |

**5 NUEVO PESOS** **KM# 65b** **Composition:** Gold **Subject:** 150th Anniversary - Revolutionary Movement

| Date | Mintage | F | VF | XF | Unc | BU |
|---|---|---|---|---|---|---|
| ND(1975)So Proof | 1,000 | Value: 500 | | | | |

**Note:** 50 pieces each in aluminum, alpaca and copper are reported to have been struck

**5 NUEVO PESOS** **KM# 65a** **Weight:** 18.4300 g. **Composition:** 0.9000 Silver .5332 oz. ASW **Subject:** 150th Anniversary - Revolutionary Movement

| Date | Mintage | F | VF | XF | Unc | BU |
|---|---|---|---|---|---|---|
| ND(1975)So Proof | 2,000 | Value: 15.00 | | | | |

**5 NUEVO PESOS** **KM# 70** **Composition:** Copper-Aluminum **Subject:** 250th Anniversary - Founding of Montevideo

| Date | Mintage | F | VF | XF | Unc | BU |
|---|---|---|---|---|---|---|
| 1976So | 300,000 | 0.75 | 1.00 | 1.50 | 4.00 | — |

**5 NUEVO PESOS** **KM# 70b** **Composition:** Silver **Subject:** 250th Anniversary - Founding of Montevideo

| Date | Mintage | F | VF | XF | Unc | BU |
|---|---|---|---|---|---|---|
| 1976So | — | — | — | — | 175 | — |

**5 NUEVO PESOS** **KM# 70a** **Weight:** 30.0000 g. **Composition:** 0.9000 Gold .8681 oz. AGW **Subject:** 250th Anniversary - Founding of Montevideo

| Date | Mintage | F | VF | XF | Unc | BU |
|---|---|---|---|---|---|---|
| 1976So Proof | 100 | Value: 650 | | | | |

**5 NUEVO PESOS** **KM# 75** **Composition:** Copper Nickel **Obverse:** National flag

| Date | Mintage | F | VF | XF | Unc | BU |
|---|---|---|---|---|---|---|
| 1980So | 50,000,000 | — | 0.20 | 0.40 | 1.50 | — |
| 1981So | — | — | 0.20 | 0.40 | 1.50 | — |

**5 NUEVO PESOS** **KM# 75a** **Weight:** 9.3000 g. **Composition:** 0.9000 Silver .2691 oz. ASW **Obverse:** National flag

| Date | Mintage | F | VF | XF | Unc | BU |
|---|---|---|---|---|---|---|
| 1980So Proof | 300 | Value: 30.00 | | | | |

**5 NUEVO PESOS** **KM# 75b** **Weight:** 15.6000 g. **Composition:** 0.9000 Gold .4514 oz. AGW **Obverse:** National flag

| Date | Mintage | F | VF | XF | Unc | BU |
|---|---|---|---|---|---|---|
| 1980So Proof | 100 | Value: 450 | | | | |

**5 NUEVO PESOS** **KM# 78** **Weight:** 9.3000 g. **Composition:** 0.9000 Silver .2691 oz. ASW **Obverse:** Coat of arms

| Date | Mintage | F | VF | XF | Unc | BU |
|---|---|---|---|---|---|---|
| 1981 Proof | 100 | Value: 30.00 | | | | |

**5 NUEVO PESOS** **KM# 92** **Composition:** Stainless Steel

| Date | Mintage | F | VF | XF | Unc | BU |
|---|---|---|---|---|---|---|
| 1989 | 65,000,000 | — | — | 0.15 | 0.35 | — |

**10 NUEVO PESOS** **KM# 79** **Composition:** Copper Nickel **Obverse:** Bust of Jose Gervasio Artigas half left

| Date | Mintage | F | VF | XF | Unc | BU |
|---|---|---|---|---|---|---|
| 1981So | — | — | 0.20 | 0.50 | 1.75 | — |

**10 NUEVO PESOS** **KM# 79a** **Weight:** 11.6300 g. **Composition:** 0.9000 Silver .3365 oz. ASW **Obverse:** Bust of Jose Gervasio Artigas half left

| Date | Mintage | F | VF | XF | Unc | BU |
|---|---|---|---|---|---|---|
| 1981So Proof | 100 | Value: 35.00 | | | | |

**10 NUEVO PESOS** **KM# 79b** **Weight:** 19.4800 g. **Composition:** 0.9000 Gold .5637 oz. AGW **Obverse:** Bust of Jose Gervasio Artigas half left

| Date | Mintage | F | VF | XF | Unc | BU |
|---|---|---|---|---|---|---|
| 1981So Proof | 100 | Value: 500 | | | | |

**10 NUEVO PESOS** **KM# 93** **Composition:** Stainless Steel

| Date | Mintage | F | VF | XF | Unc | BU |
|---|---|---|---|---|---|---|
| 1989 | 79,000,000 | — | — | 0.20 | 0.50 | — |

**20 NUEVO PESOS** **KM# 86** **Composition:** Copper-Nickel **Subject:** World Fisheries Conference

| Date | Mintage | F | VF | XF | Unc | BU |
|---|---|---|---|---|---|---|
| 1984 | 3,771 | — | — | — | 16.50 | — |

**20 NUEVO PESOS** **KM# 86a** **Weight:** 11.6600 g. **Composition:** 0.9250 Silver .3468 oz. ASW **Subject:** World Fisheries Conference

| Date | Mintage | F | VF | XF | Unc | BU |
|---|---|---|---|---|---|---|
| 1984 Proof | 25,000 | Value: 30.00 | | | | |

**20 NUEVO PESOS** **KM# 86b** **Weight:** 19.6000 g. **Composition:** 0.9170 Gold .5776 oz. AGW **Subject:** World Fisheries Conference

| Date | Mintage | F | VF | XF | Unc | BU |
|---|---|---|---|---|---|---|
| 1984 Proof | 100 | Value: 500 | | | | |

**50 NUEVO PESOS** KM# 94

| Date | Mintage | F | VF | XF | Unc | BU |
|---|---|---|---|---|---|---|
| 1989 | — | — | — | 0.20 | 0.50 | — |

**100 NUEVO PESOS** KM# 80 **Weight:** 12.0000 g. **Composition:** 0.9000 Silver .3472 oz. ASW **Obverse:** Hydroelectric dam

| Date | Mintage | F | VF | XF | Unc | BU |
|---|---|---|---|---|---|---|
| 1981So | 25,000 | — | — | — | 6.50 | — |



**100 NUEVO PESOS** KM# 96 **Composition:** Stainless Steel **Obverse:** Gaucho bust right

| Date | Mintage | F | VF | XF | Unc | BU |
|---|---|---|---|---|---|---|
| 1989 | — | — | — | 0.35 | 0.75 | — |



**200 NUEVO PESOS** KM# 97 **Composition:** Copper Nickel **Obverse:** Unchained Liberty

| Date | Mintage | F | VF | XF | Unc | BU |
|---|---|---|---|---|---|---|
| 1989 | — | — | — | — | 1.50 | — |

**500 NUEVO PESOS** KM# 82 **Weight:** 12.0000 g. **Composition:** 0.9000 Silver .3472 oz. ASW **Obverse:** Hydroelectric dam

| Date | Mintage | F | VF | XF | Unc | BU |
|---|---|---|---|---|---|---|
| 1983So | 15,000 | — | — | — | 6.50 | — |

**500 NUEVO PESOS** KM# 90 **Weight:** 12.0000 g. **Composition:** 0.9000 Silver .3473 oz. ASW **Obverse:** Bust of General Leandro Gomez half left

| Date | Mintage | F | VF | XF | Unc | BU |
|---|---|---|---|---|---|---|
| 1986Mo Proof | 6,000 | Value: 21.50 | | | | |



**500 NUEVO PESOS** KM# 98 **Composition:** Copper Nickel **Obverse:** Bust of Jose Gervasio Artigas half right

| Date | Mintage | F | VF | XF | Unc | BU |
|---|---|---|---|---|---|---|
| 1989 | — | — | — | — | 3.00 | — |

**2000 NUEVO PESOS** KM# 87 **Weight:** 25.0000 g. **Composition:** 0.9000 Silver .7235 oz. ASW **Subject:** 140th Anniversary of Silver Coinage and 25th Meeting of Interamerican Bank Governors **Obverse:** Radiant sun peeking over shield of arms in wreath within inner circle

| Date | Mintage | F | VF | XF | Unc | BU |
|---|---|---|---|---|---|---|
| 1984 Proof | 15,000 | Value: 16.50 | | | | |

**2000 NUEVO PESOS** KM# 88 **Weight:** 25.0000 g. **Composition:** 0.9000 Silver .7235 oz. ASW **Subject:** 25th Meeting of Interamerican Bank Governors **Obverse:** Radiant sun peeking over shield of arms within wreath

| Date | Mintage | F | VF | XF | Unc | BU |
|---|---|---|---|---|---|---|
| 1984 Proof | 15,000 | Value: 16.50 | | | | |

**5000 NUEVO PESOS** KM# 81 **Weight:** 12.0000 g. **Composition:** 0.9000 Silver .3472 oz. ASW **Obverse:** Hydroelectric dam

| Date | Mintage | F | VF | XF | Unc | BU |
|---|---|---|---|---|---|---|
| 1981So Proof | 15,000 | Value: 15.00 | | | | |

**5000 NUEVO PESOS** KM# 91 **Weight:** 35.0000 g. **Composition:** 0.9000 Silver 1.0127 oz. ASW **Subject:** 20th Anniversary of Central Bank

| Date | Mintage | F | VF | XF | Unc | BU |
|---|---|---|---|---|---|---|
| 1987So Proof | 10,000 | Value: 15.00 | | | | |

**5000 NUEVO PESOS** KM# 99 **Weight:** 35.0000 g. **Composition:** 0.9000 Silver 1.0127 oz. ASW **Subject:** Latin America Presidents' Assembly

| Date | Mintage | F | VF | XF | Unc | BU |
|---|---|---|---|---|---|---|
| 1988 Proof | — | Value: 18.50 | | | | |

**20000 NUEVO PESOS** KM# 85 **Weight:** 20.0000 g. **Composition:** 0.9000 Gold .5787 oz. AGW **Obverse:** Hydroelectric dam

| Date | Mintage | F | VF | XF | Unc | BU |
|---|---|---|---|---|---|---|
| 1983So Proof | 2,500 | Value: 275 | | | | |

**20000 NUEVO PESOS** KM# 89 **Subject:** 130th Anniversary of Gold Coinage and 25th Meeting of Interamerican Bank Governors

| Date | Mintage | F | VF | XF | Unc | BU |
|---|---|---|---|---|---|---|
| 1984 Proof | 1,500 | Value: 275 | | | | |

**25000 PESOS** **KM# 101** **Weight:** 12.5000 g. **Composition:** 0.9000 Silver .3617 oz. ASW **Subject:** 25th Anniversary of Central Bank

| Date | Mintage | F | VF | XF | Unc | BU |
|---|---|---|---|---|---|---|
| 1992 | — | — | — | — | 16.50 | — |

**50000 NUEVO PESOS** **KM# 100** **Weight:** 27.0000 g. **Composition:** 0.9250 Silver .8029 oz. ASW **Subject:** Ibero - American Series

| Date | Mintage | F | VF | XF | Unc | BU |
|---|---|---|---|---|---|---|
| 1991 Proof | 70,000 | Value: 32.50 | | | | |

## REFORM COINAGE

March 1993

1,000 Nuevos Pesos = 1 Uruguayan Peso; 100 Centesimos = 1 Uruguayan Peso (UYP)

**10 CENTESIMOS** **KM# 102** **Composition:** Stainless Steel

| Date | Mintage | F | VF | XF | Unc | BU |
|---|---|---|---|---|---|---|
| 1994 | — | — | — | 0.25 | 0.50 | — |

**20 CENTESIMOS** **KM# 105** **Composition:** Stainless Steel

| Date | Mintage | F | VF | XF | Unc | BU |
|---|---|---|---|---|---|---|
| 1994 | — | — | — | 0.30 | 0.60 | — |

**50 CENTESIMOS** **KM# 106** **Composition:** Stainless Steel

| Date | Mintage | F | VF | XF | Unc | BU |
|---|---|---|---|---|---|---|
| 1994 | — | — | — | 0.35 | 0.75 | — |

**PESO** **KM# 103.2** **Weight:** 3.5200 g. **Composition:** Brass **Obverse:** Portrait **Reverse:** Denomination **Edge:** Plain **Size:** 20 mm.

| Date | Mintage | F | VF | XF | Unc | BU |
|---|---|---|---|---|---|---|
| 1998S | — | — | — | — | 0.50 | — |

**2 URUGUAYAN PESOS** **KM# 104** **Composition:** Brass

| Date | Mintage | F | VF | XF | Unc | BU |
|---|---|---|---|---|---|---|
| 1994 | — | — | — | 0.75 | 1.50 | — |

**50 URUGUAYAN PESOS** **Y# 113** **Weight:** 12.5300 g. **Composition:** 0.9000 Silver .3626 oz. ASW **Subject:** Bicentennial - City of Melo **Obverse:** National map **Reverse:** City arms

| Date | Mintage | F | VF | XF | Unc | BU |
|---|---|---|---|---|---|---|
| 1996 Proof | — | Value: 20.00 | | | | |

**50 URUGUAYAN PESOS** **Weight:** 12.5300 g. **Composition:** 0.9000 Silver .3626 oz. ASW **Subject:** Bicentennial - City of Melo **Obverse:** National map **Reverse:** City arms

| Date | Mintage | F | VF | XF | Unc | BU |
|---|---|---|---|---|---|---|
| 1996 Proof | — | Value: 20.00 | | | | |

**100 URUGUAYAN PESOS** **Y# 111** **Weight:** 25.0000 g. **Composition:** 0.9990 Silver .7234 oz. ASW **Subject:** 50th Anniversary - F.A.O **Obverse:** Wheat stalks **Reverse:** F.A.O, logo and dates

| Date | Mintage | F | VF | XF | Unc | BU |
|---|---|---|---|---|---|---|
| ND1995 Proof | — | Value: 21.50 | | | | |

**100 URUGUAYAN PESOS** **Y# 112** **Weight:** 25.0000 g. **Composition:** 0.9990 Silver .7234 oz. ASW **Subject:** Centennial - Central Bank **Obverse:** Radiant sun face **Reverse:** Central Bank building

| Date | Mintage | F | VF | XF | Unc | BU |
|---|---|---|---|---|---|---|
| 1996 Proof | — | Value: 22.50 | | | | |

**200 URUGUAYAN PESOS** **KM# 107** **Weight:** 27.0000 g. **Composition:** 0.9250 Silver .8030 oz. ASW **Subject:** Environmental Protection **Reverse:** Pampas deer right

| Date | Mintage | F | VF | XF | Unc | BU |
|---|---|---|---|---|---|---|
| 1994 MO Proof | 20,000 | Value: 35.00 | | | | |

**200 URUGUAYAN PESOS** **KM# 116** **Weight:** 28.2800 g. **Composition:** 0.9250 Silver .8410 oz. ASW **Subject:** 50th Anniversary - United Nations

| Date | Mintage | F | VF | XF | Unc | BU |
|---|---|---|---|---|---|---|
| 1995 Proof | — | Value: 42.50 | | | | |

**250 URUGUAYAN PESOS** **Y# 114** **Weight:** 26.9500 g. **Composition:** 0.9250 Silver .8015 oz. ASW **Subject:** Ibero - American Series **Reverse:** Gaucho and lady

| Date | Mintage | F | VF | XF | Unc | BU |
|---|---|---|---|---|---|---|
| 1997 Proof | — | Value: 42.50 | | | | |

**250 PESOS** **KM# 117** **Weight:** 27.0000 g. **Composition:** 0.9250 Silver .8030 oz. ASW **Series:** Ibero-American **Obverse:** National arms coin design within circle of arms **Reverse:** Man and woman on horseback **Edge:** Reeded **Size:** 40 mm.

| Date | Mintage | F | VF | XF | Unc | BU |
|---|---|---|---|---|---|---|
| 2000 Proof | — | Value: 42.50 | | | | |

## PATTERNS

Including off metal strikes

| KM# | Date | Mintage | Identification | Mkt Val |
|---|---|---|---|---|
| PnA39 | 1916 | — | 50 Centesimos. Silver. | — |
| Pn39 | 1916 | 45 | 50 Centesimos. Silver. | — |
| Pn40 | 1917 | 20 | Peso. Silver. | — |
| PnA41 | 1920 | — | 20 Centesimos. Copper-Nickel. Similar to KM#24. | — |
| Pn41 | 1942 | 10 | 20 Centesimos. Copper Gilt. | — |
| PnA42 | 1942 | 20 | 20 Centesimos. Silver Gilt. | — |
| Pn42 | 1942 | — | 20 Centesimos. Gold. KM29. | 450 |
| Pn43 | 1942So | — | Peso. Gold. KM30. | 1,000 |
| Pn44 | 1943So | — | 2 Centesimos. Gold. KM20a. | 935 |
| Pn45 | 1943So | — | 50 Centesimos. Gold. KM31 | 1,000 |
| Pn46 | 1953 | 100 | Centesimo. 0.9160 Gold. KM32. | — |
| Pn47 | 1953 | — | 2 Centesimos. Aluminum. KM33. | — |
| Pn48 | 1953 | 100 | 2 Centesimos. 0.9160 Gold. KM33. | — |
| Pn49 | 1953 | 100 | 5 Centesimos. 0.9160 Gold. KM34. | — |
| Pn50 | 1953 | 100 | 10 Centesimos. 0.9160 Gold. KM35. | — |
| PnA51 | 1953 | — | Peso. Aluminum-Bronze. | — |
| PnB51 | 1953 | — | Peso. Brass. Similar to PNA51. | — |
| PnC51 | 1953 | — | Peso. Copper-Nickel. Similar to PNA51. | — |
| PnD51 | 1953 | — | Peso. Silver. Similar to PNA51. | — |
| Pn51 | 1954 | 100 | 20 Centesimos. 0.9830 Gold. KM36. | 500 |
| Pn52 | 1959 | — | 10 Centesimos. 0.9160 Gold. KM35. | — |
| Pn53 | 1960 | 100 | 2 Centesimos. Gold. KM37. | — |
| Pn54 | 1960 | 100 | 5 Centesimos. Gold. KM38. | — |
| Pn55 | 1960 | 100 | 10 Centesimos. Gold. KM39. | — |
| Pn56 | 1960 | 100 | 25 Centesimos. Gold. KM40. | — |
| Pn57 | 1960 | 100 | 50 Centesimos. Gold. KM41. | — |
| Pn58 | 1960 | — | Peso. Gold. KM42. | — |
| PnB54 | ND(1960) | — | 5 Centesimos. Aluminum. Similar to KM#34 and KM#38 reverses. With "HA" in the base of the 5 and "MBL" above the 5. | — |
| Pn59 | 1960 | — | 10 Pesos. Gold. | — |
| PnA60 | 1961 | — | 10 Pesos. Gold. KM43. | — |
| Pn60 | 1965So | 10 | 20 Centesimos. Copper. KM44. | — |
| Pn61 | 1965So | — | 20 Centesimos. Silver. KM44. | — |
| Pn62 | 1965So | — | 20 Centesimos. Gold. KM44. | — |
| Pn63 | 1965So | 25 | 50 Centesimos. Aluminum-Bronze. KM45. | — |
| Pn64 | 1965So | 10 | 50 Centesimos. Copper. KM45. | — |
| Pn65 | 1965So | 25 | 50 Centesimos. Copper-Nickel. KM45. | — |
| Pn66 | 1965So | — | 50 Centesimos. Silver. KM45. | — |
| Pn67 | 1965So | — | 50 Centesimos. Gold. KM45. | — |
| Pn68 | 1965So | 10 | Peso. Copper. KM46. | — |
| Pn69 | 1965So | 25 | Peso. Copper-Nickel. KM46. | — |
| Pn70 | 1965So | — | Peso. Silver. KM46. | — |
| Pn71 | 1965So | — | Peso. Gold. KM46. | — |
| Pn72 | 1965So | 10 | 5 Pesos. Copper. KM47. | — |
| Pn73 | 1965So | 25 | 5 Pesos. Copper-Nickel. KM47. | — |
| Pn74 | 1965So | — | 5 Pesos. Silver. KM47. | — |
| Pn75 | 1965So | — | 5 Pesos. Gold. KM47. | — |
| Pn76 | 1965So | 10 | 10 Pesos. Copper. KM48. | — |
| Pn77 | 1965So | — | 10 Pesos. Silver. KM48. | — |
| PnA69 | 1965 | — | Peso. Aluminum-Bronze. 24 mm. Similar to KM#46. Planchet is 5 Pesos. | — |
| PnA73 | 1965 | — | 5 Pesos. Copper-Nickel. 29 mm. Similar to KM#47. Planchet is 10 Pesos. | — |
| PnB84 | 1968 | — | 20 Pesos. Copper-Nickel. Similar to KM#56; Proof. | — |
| PnC84 | 1968 | — | 20 Pesos. Silver. Star. Similar to KM#56. | — |
| PnB85 | 1968 | — | 50 Pesos. Copper-Nickel. Similar to KM#57; Proof. | — |
| PnC85 | 1968 | — | 50 Pesos. Silver. Star. Similar to KM#57. | — |
| Pn78 | 1968So | 100 | Peso. Copper-Nickel. KM49. | 35.00 |
| Pn79 | 1968So | 1,000 | Peso. Silver. KM49. | 15.00 |
| Pn80 | 1968So | 100 | 5 Pesos. Copper-Nickel. KM50. | 35.00 |
| Pn81 | 1968So | 1,000 | 5 Pesos. Silver. KM50. | 18.00 |
| Pn82 | 1968So | 100 | 10 Pesos. Copper-Nickel. KM51. | 35.00 |
| Pn83 | 1968So | 1,000 | 10 Pesos. Silver. KM51. | 20.00 |
| PnA84 | 1968S | — | 20 Pesos. Yellow Metal. | — |
| Pn84 | 1968So | 1,000 | 20 Pesos. Silver. | 25.00 |
| PnA85 | 1968S | — | 50 Pesos. Yellow Metal. | — |
| Pn85 | 1968So | 1,000 | 50 Pesos. Silver. | 28.00 |
| Pn86 | 1969So | 50 | Peso. Copper-Nickel. KM52. | 30.00 |
| PnA92 | 1969 | — | 10 Pesos. Gold. Similar to KM#54; Proof. | — |
| Pn87 | 1969So | 1,000 | Peso. 0.9000 Silver. KM52. | 15.00 |
| PnA88 | 1969So | — | Peso. Gold. KM52. | 125 |
| Pn88 | 1969So | 50 | 5 Pesos. Copper-Nickel. KM53. | 30.00 |
| Pn89 | 1969So | 1,000 | 5 Pesos. 0.9000 Silver. KM53. | 15.00 |
| PnA90 | 1969So | — | 5 Pesos. Gold. KM53. | 200 |
| Pn90 | 1969So | 50 | 10 Pesos. Copper-Nickel. KM54. | 30.00 |
| Pn91 | 1969So | 1,000 | 10 Pesos. 0.9000 Silver. KM54. | 15.00 |
| Pn92 | 1969 | 20,000 | 1000 Pesos. Copper. | 30.00 |
| Pn93 | 1969 | 250 | 1000 Pesos. Silver. | 45.00 |
| Pn96 | 1970So | — | 20 Pesos. Silver. No star on reverse. KM56. | 15.00 |
| Pn97 | 1970So | 1,000 | 20 Pesos. Gold. KM56. | 200 |
| Pn98 | 1970So | — | 50 Pesos. Silver. KM57. | 15.00 |
| Pn99 | 1970So | 1,000 | 50 Pesos. Gold. KM57. | 275 |
| Pn95 | 1970So | — | 20 Pesos. Silver. Star on reverse. KM56. | — |
| Pn100 | 1971So | — | 50 Pesos. Copper Nickel. KM58. | 55.00 |
| Pn101 | 1971So | 80 | 50 Pesos. Copper Nickel. With F. ORRELLANA, P., KM58 | 55.00 |
| Pn102 | 1971So | 2,000 | 50 Pesos. Silver. KM58. | 25.00 |
| Pn103 | 1971So | 200 | 50 Pesos. Gold. KM58. | 325 |
| Pn104 | 1972So | 3 | 100 Pesos. | — |
| Pn105 | 1972So | 12 | 100 Pesos. Alpaca. | — |
| PnA107 | 1973 | — | 100 Pesos. Gold. Similar to KM#59. | — |
| PnB107 | 1973 | 50 | 100 Pesos. Aluminum. | — |
| Pn106 | 1973 | — | 100 Pesos. Silver. KM59. | 40.00 |
| PnC107 | 1975 | 50 | 5 Pesos. Alpaca. Similar to KM#65. | — |
| PnA108 | 1976 | — | 10 Centesimos. Copper. Similar to KM#66. | — |
| PnB108 | 1976 | — | 10 Centesimos. Aluminum. Similar to KM#66. | — |
| PnC108 | 1976 | — | 20 Centesimos. Copper. Similar to KM#67. | — |
| PnD108 | 1976 | — | 20 Centesimos. Aluminum. Similar to KM#67. | — |
| PnE108 | 1976 | — | 50 Centesimos. Copper. Similar to KM#68. | — |
| PnF108 | 1976 | — | 50 Centesimos. Aluminum. Similar to KM#68. | — |
| PnG108 | 1976 | — | Nuevo Peso. Copper. Similar to KM#69. | — |
| PnH108 | 1976 | — | Nuevo Peso. Aluminum. Similar to KM#69. | — |
| Pn107 | 1976 | — | 5 Nuevo Pesos. Aluminum. KM70. | 75.00 |
| Pn108 | 1976 | — | 5 Nuevo Pesos. Copper-Aluminum. KM70. | 75.00 |
| Pn109 | 1976 | — | 5 Nuevo Pesos. Copper-Nickel. KM70. | 100 |
| Pn110 | 1976 | — | 5 Nuevo Pesos. Silver. KM70. | 150 |
| PnA111 | 1977 | — | Centesimo. Gold. Similar to KM#71. | — |
| PnB111 | 1977 | — | Centesimo. Nickel. Similar to KM#71. | — |
| PnC111 | 1977 | — | Centesimo. Copper. Similar to KM#71. | — |
| PnD111 | 1977 | — | Centesimo. Aluminum-Bronze. Similar to KM#71. | — |
| PnE111 | 1977 | — | 2 Centesimos. Gold. Similar to KM#72. | — |
| PnF111 | 1977 | — | 2 Centesimos. Nickel. Similar to KM#72. | — |
| PnG111 | 1977 | — | 2 Centesimos. Copper. Similar to KM#72. | — |
| PnH111 | 1977 | — | 2 Centesimos. Aluminum-Bronze. Similar to KM#72. | — |
| PnI111 | 1977 | — | 5 Centesimos. Gold. Similar to KM#73. | — |
| PnJ111 | 1977 | — | 5 Centesimos. Nickel. Similar to KM#73. | — |
| PnK111 | 1977 | — | 5 Centesimos. Copper. Similar to KM#73. | — |
| PnL111 | 1977 | — | 5 Centesimos. Aluminum-Bronze. Similar to KM#73. | — |
| PnN111 | 1980 | — | Nuevo Peso. Copper. Similar to KM#74. | — |
| PnM111 | 1980 | — | Nuevo Peso. Aluminum. Similar to KM#74. | — |
| PnB112 | 1980 | — | 5 Nuevo Pesos. Copper. Similar to KM#75. | — |
| PnA112 | 1980 | — | 5 Nuevo Pesos. Aluminum. Similar to KM#75. | — |
| Pn111 | 1980 | — | Peso. Brass. KM74. | — |
| Pn112 | 1980 | — | 5 Pesos. Brass. KM75. | — |
| Pn113 | 1981 | — | 10 Pesos. Brass. KM79. | — |
| PnA113 | 1981 | — | 2 Nuevo Pesos. Silver. Similar to KM#77; Proof. | — |
| PnB113 | 1981 | — | 2 Nuevo Pesos. Aluminum-Bronze. Similar to KM#77; Proof. | — |
| PnC113 | 1981 | — | 10 Nuevo Pesos. Copper. Similar to KM#79. | — |
| PnD113 | 1981 | — | 10 Nuevo Pesos. Aluminum. Similar to KM#79. | — |
| PnA114 | 1981So | — | 100 Nuevo Pesos. 0.9000 Gold. 20.0000 g. KM80. | 375 |
| PnB114 | 1981So | — | 5000 Nuevo Pesos. 0.9000 Gold. 20.0000 g. KM81. | 275 |
| PnC114 | 1983So | — | 500 Nuevo Pesos. 0.9000 Gold. 20.0000 g. KM82. | 500 |
| PnD114 | 1983So | — | 20000 Nuevo Pesos. Silver. KM85. | — |
| PnA118 | 1984 | 40 | 2000 Nuevo Pesos. Silver. Similar to KM#88. Different obverse and reverse; Proof. | — |
| PnA119 | 1984 | — | 20000 Nuevo Pesos. Silver. Similar to KM#89. | — |
| PnB119 | 1984 | — | 20000 Nuevo Pesos. Copper. Similar to KM#89. | — |
| PnC119 | 1984 | — | 20000 Nuevo Pesos. Brass. Similar to KM#89. | — |
| Pn114 | 1984 | — | 2000 Nuevo Pesos. Copper. Thick reeded edge. KM87. | — |
| Pn115 | 1984 | — | 2000 Nuevo Pesos. Aluminum. Thick reeded edge. KM87. | — |
| Pn116 | 1984 | — | 2000 Nuevo Pesos. Aluminum. Thick reeded edge. KM88. | — |
| Pn117 | 1984 | — | 2000 Nuevo Pesos. Aluminum. Thick reeded edge. KM88. | — |
| Pn118 | 1984 | — | 20000 Nuevo Pesos. Aluminum. KM89. | — |
| Pn119 | 1984 | — | 20000 Nuevo Pesos. Gold. KM89. | — |
| Pn120 | 1987 | — | 5000 Pesos. Alpaca. KM91; Alpaca | — |
| Pn121 | 1987 | — | 5000 Pesos. Copper. KM91. | — |
| Pn122 | 1987 | — | 5000 Pesos. Bronze. KM91. | — |
| Pn123 | 1988 | — | 5000 Nuevo Pesos. Copper. Similar to KM#99. | — |
| Pn124 | 1988 | — | 5000 Nuevo Pesos. Alpaca. Similar to KM#99. | — |

## PIEFORTS

Double Thickness

| KM# | Date | Mintage | Identification | Mkt Val |
|---|---|---|---|---|
| P2 | 1983 | 10 | 2000 Nuevo Pesos. Silver. 64.5700 g. Reeded edge. KM#M1. | 300 |
| P3 | 1983 | 10 | 2000 Nuevo Pesos. Copper. Plain edge. KM#M1. | 100 |
| PA4 | 1983 | — | 20000 Nuevo Pesos. Gold. KM#M2. | 950 |
| P4 | 1983 | — | 20000 Nuevo Pesos. Silver. 39.7000 g. KM#M3. | 165 |
| P5 | 1983 | — | 20000 Nuevo Pesos. Copper. Plain edge. KM#M2. | 65.00 |
| P6 | 1984 | 600 | 20 Pesos. Silver. KM86a. | 60.00 |
| P7 | 1984 | — | 2000 Nuevo Pesos. Silver. 50.0000 g. Plain edge. KM87. | 185 |
| P8 | 1984 | — | 2000 Nuevo Pesos. Copper. Thick plain edge. KM87. | 65.00 |
| P9 | 1984 | — | 2000 Nuevo Pesos. Copper Gilt. Thick plain edge. KM87. | 75.00 |
| P10 | 1984 | — | 2000 Nuevo Pesos. Silver. 50.4800 g. Plain edge. KM88. | 185 |
| P11 | 1984 | — | 2000 Nuevo Pesos. Copper. Thick plain edge. KM88. | 65.00 |
| P12 | 1984 | — | 2000 Nuevo Pesos. Copper Gilt. Thick plain edge. KM88. | 75.00 |
| P13 | 1984 | — | 20000 Nuevo Pesos. Silver. 20.7500 g. Reeded edge. KM89. | 135 |
| P14 | 1984 | — | 20000 Nuevo Pesos. Silver. 40.1700 g. Reeded edge. KM89. | 200 |
| P15 | 1984 | — | 20000 Nuevo Pesos. Silver. 40.4400 g. Plain edge. KM89. | 200 |
| P16 | 1984 | — | 20000 Nuevo Pesos. Copper. Thick reeded edge. KM89. | 80.00 |
| P17 | 1984 | — | 20000 Nuevo Pesos. Copper. Reeded edge. KM89. | 80.00 |
| P18 | 1984 | — | 20000 Nuevo Pesos. Copper Gilt. KM89. | 100 |

## MINT SETS

| KM# | Date | Mintage | Identification | Issue Price | Mkt Val |
|---|---|---|---|---|---|
| MS1 | 1969/70 (5) | — | KM52-54, 56-57 | — | 3.50 |
| MS2 | 1969/70 (5) | — | KM52-54, 56-57 | — | 3.50 |
| MS3 | 1976 (4) | — | KM66-69 | — | 2.50 |
| MS4 | 1976 (4) | — | KM#Pn107-110 | — | 400 |

## PROOF SETS

| KM# | Date | Mintage | Identification | Issue Price | Mkt Val |
|---|---|---|---|---|---|
| PS8 | 1976 (4) | — | KM#66a-69a | — | 125 |
| PS1 | 1953 (4) | 100 | KM32-35 | — | 275 |
| PS3 | 1968 (3) | 50 | KM49-51 | — | 200 |
| PS4 | 1968 (3) | 100 | KM#Pn78, 80, 82 | — | 90.00 |
| PS2 | 1968 (5) | 1,000 | KM#Pn79, 81, 83-85 | — | 78.00 |
| PS5 | 1969 (3) | 50 | KM#Pn86, 88, 90 | — | 75.00 |
| PS7 | 1969/70 (5) | 1,000 | KM#Pn87, 89, 91, 96, 98 | — | 50.00 |
| PS6 | 1969 (3) | 1,000 | KM#Pn87, 89, 91 | — | 30.00 |

The Republic of Uzbekistan (formerly the Uzbek S.S.R.), is bordered on the north by Kazakhstan, to the east by Kirghizia and Tajikistan, on the south by Afghanistan and on the west by Turkmenistan. The republic is comprised of the regions of Andizhan, Bukhara, Dzhizak, Ferghana, Kashkadar, Khorezm (Khiva), Namangan, Navoi, Samarkand, Surkhan-.Darya, Syr-Darya, Tashkent and the Karakalpak Autonomous Republic. It has an area of 172,741 sq. mi. (447,400 sq. km.) and a population of 20.3 million. Capital: Tashkent.

Crude oil, natural gas, coal, copper, and gold deposits make up the chief resources, while intensive farming, based on artificial irrigation, provides an abundance of cotton.

On the eve of WW I, Khiva and Bukhara were enclaves within a Russian Turkestan divided into five provinces or oblasti. The czarist government did not attempt to Russify the indigenous Turkic or Tajik populations. The revolution of March 1917 created a confused situation in the area. In Tashkent there was a Turkestan committee of the provisional government; a Communist-controlled council of workers', soldiers' and peasants' deputies; also a Moslem Turkic movement, Shuro-i-Islamiya, and a young Turkestan or Jaddidi (Renovation) party. The last named party claimed full political autonomy for Turkestan and the abolition of the emirate of Bukhara and the khanate of Khiva. After the Communist *coup d'etat* in Petrograd, the council of people's commissars on Nov. 24 (Dec. 7), 1917, published an appeal to "all toiling Moslems in Russia and in the east" proclaiming their right to build their national life "freely and unhindered". In response, the Moslem and Jaddidi organizations in Dec. 1917 convoked a national congress in Khokand which appointed a provisional government headed by Mustafa Chokayev (or Chokaigolu; 1890-1941) and resolved to elect a constituent assembly to decide whether Turkestan should remain within a Russian federal state or proclaim its independence. In the spring of 1919 a Red army group defeated Kolchak and in September its commander, M.V. Frunze, arrived in Tashkent with V.V.Kuibyshev as political commissar. The Communists were still much too weak in Turkestan to proclaim the country part of Soviet Russia. Faizullah Khojayev organized a young Bukhara movement, which on Sept. 14, 1920, proclaimed the dethronement of Emir Mir Alim. Bukhara was then made a S.S.R. In 1920 the Tashkent Communist government declared war on Junaid, who took to flight, and Khiva became another S.S.R. In Oct. 1921, Enver Pasha, the former leader of the young Turks, appeared in Bukhara and assumed command of the Basmachi movement. In Aug. 1922 he was forced to retreat into Tajikistan and died on Aug. 4, in a battle near Baljuvan. Khiva concluded a treaty of alliance with the Russian S.F.S.R. in Sept. 1920, and Bukhara followed suit in March 1921. Theoretically, a Turkestan Autonomous Soviet Socialist Republic had existed since May 1, 1918; in 1920 this "Turk republic", as it was called, was proclaimed part of the R.S.F.S.R. On Sept. 18, 1924, the Uzbek and Turkmen peoples were authorized to form S.S.R.'s of their own, and the Kazakhs, Kirghiz, and Tajiks to form autonomous S.S.R.'s. On Oct.27, 1924, the Uzbek and Turkmen S.S.R. were officially constituted and the former was formally accepted on Jan.15, 1925, as a member of the U.S.S.R. Tajikistan was an autonomous soviet republic within Uzbekistan until Dec.5, 1929, when it became a S.S.R. On Dec. 5, 1936, the Uzbekistan territory was increased by incorporating the Kara-Kalpak A.S.S.R., which had belonged to Kazakhstan until 1930 and afterward had come under direct control of the R.S.F.S.R.

On June 20, 1990 the Uzbek Supreme Soviet adopted a declaration of sovereignty, and in Aug. 1991, following an unsuccessful coup, declared itself independent as the "Republic of Uzbekistan", which was confirmed by referendum in Dec. That same month Uzbekistan became a member of the CIS.

# REPUBLIC

## STANDARD COINAGE

**TIYIN KM# 1.1 Composition:** Brass Clad Steel **Reverse:** Small denomination

| Date | Mintage | F | VF | XF | Unc | BU |
|---|---|---|---|---|---|---|
| 1994 | — | — | — | — | 0.30 | — |

**TIYIN KM# 1.2 Composition:** Brass Clad Steel **Reverse:** Large denomination

| Date | Mintage | F | VF | XF | Unc | BU |
|---|---|---|---|---|---|---|
| 1994 | — | — | — | — | 0.30 | — |

**3 TIYIN KM# 2.1 Composition:** Brass Plated Steel **Reverse:** Small denomination

| Date | Mintage | F | VF | XF | Unc | BU |
|---|---|---|---|---|---|---|
| 1994 | — | — | — | — | 0.40 | — |

**3 TIYIN KM# 2.2 Composition:** Brass Plated Steel **Reverse:** Large denomination

| Date | Mintage | F | VF | XF | Unc | BU |
|---|---|---|---|---|---|---|
| 1994 | — | — | — | — | 0.40 | — |

**5 TIYIN KM# 3.1 Composition:** Brass Plated Steel **Reverse:** Small denomination

| Date | Mintage | F | VF | XF | Unc | BU |
|---|---|---|---|---|---|---|
| 1994 | — | — | — | — | 0.50 | — |

**5 TIYIN KM# 3.2 Composition:** Brass Plated Steel **Reverse:** Large denomination

| Date | Mintage | F | VF | XF | Unc | BU |
|---|---|---|---|---|---|---|
| 1994 | — | — | — | — | 0.50 | — |

**10 TIYIN KM# 4.1 Composition:** Nickel Clad Steel **Reverse:** Small denomination

| Date | Mintage | F | VF | XF | Unc | BU |
|---|---|---|---|---|---|---|
| 1994 | — | — | — | — | 0.60 | — |

**10 TIYIN KM# 4.2 Composition:** Nickel Clad Steel **Reverse:** Large denomination

| Date | Mintage | F | VF | XF | Unc | BU |
|---|---|---|---|---|---|---|
| 1994 | — | — | — | — | 0.60 | — |

**20 TIYIN KM# 5.1 Composition:** Nickel Clad Steel **Reverse:** Small denomination

| Date | Mintage | F | VF | XF | Unc | BU |
|---|---|---|---|---|---|---|
| 1994 | — | — | — | — | 0.75 | — |

**20 TIYIN KM# 5.2 Composition:** Nickel Clad Steel **Reverse:** Large denomination

| Date | Mintage | F | VF | XF | Unc | BU |
|---|---|---|---|---|---|---|
| 1994 | — | — | — | — | 0.75 | — |

**50 TIYIN KM# 6 Composition:** Nickel Clad Steel

| Date | Mintage | F | VF | XF | Unc | BU |
|---|---|---|---|---|---|---|
| 1994 | — | — | — | — | 1.00 | — |

**SOM KM# 8 Composition:** Nickel Clad Steel **Reverse:** Denomination

| Date | Mintage | F | VF | XF | Unc | BU |
|---|---|---|---|---|---|---|
| 1997 | — | — | — | — | 1.35 | — |
| 2000 | — | — | — | — | 1.35 | — |

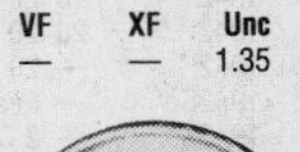

**SOM KM# 12 Weight:** 2.8300 g. **Composition:** Steel **Obverse:** National arms **Reverse:** Denomination and map **Edge:** Reeded **Size:** 18.8 mm.

| Date | Mintage | F | VF | XF | Unc | BU |
|---|---|---|---|---|---|---|
| 2000 | — | — | — | — | 1.35 | — |

**5 SOM KM# 9 Composition:** Nickel Clad Steel **Reverse:** Denomination

| Date | Mintage | F | VF | XF | Unc | BU |
|---|---|---|---|---|---|---|
| 1997 | — | — | — | — | 1.50 | — |

**10 SOM KM# 7 Weight:** 31.1000 g. **Composition:** 0.9990 Silver .9988 oz. ASW **Subject:** 3rd anniversary of independence

| Date | Mintage | F | VF | XF | Unc | BU |
|---|---|---|---|---|---|---|
| 1994 Proof | Est. 1,000 | Value: 60.00 | | | | |

**10 SOM KM# 10 Composition:** Nickel Clad Steel **Reverse:** Denomination

| Date | Mintage | F | VF | XF | Unc | BU |
|---|---|---|---|---|---|---|
| 1997 | — | — | — | — | 2.00 | — |

**25 SOM** KM# 11 **Composition:** Nickel Clad Steel **Subject:** Jaloliddin Manguberdi

| Date | Mintage | F | VF | XF | Unc | BU |
|---|---|---|---|---|---|---|
| 1999 | — | — | — | — | 2.50 | — |

## EMIRATE OF BUKHARA

Bukhara, a city and former emirate in southern Russian Turkestan, formed part (Sogdiana) of the Seleucid empire after the conquest of Alexander the Great and remained an important regional center, sometimes city state, until the 19th century. It became virtually a Russian vassal in1868 as a consequence of the Czarist invasion of 1866,following which it gradually became a part of Russian Turkestan and then part of Uzbekistan S.S.R., now Uzbekistan.

**RULERS**

Russian Vassal, AH1284-1336/1868-1917AD
Independent, AH1336-1338/1917-1920AD

**MINTNAME**

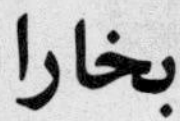

Bukhara

**MONETARY SYSTEM**

10 Falus = 1 Tenga

## KHANATE OF BUKHARA

### ANONYMOUS COINAGE

**FALUS** KM# 87 **Composition:** Copper Or Brass **Note:** In the name of Ma'sum Ibn Danyal. Varieties exist. Previous #Y1.

| Date | Mintage | Good | VG | F | VF | XF |
|---|---|---|---|---|---|---|
| AH1322 | — | 5.00 | 8.50 | 16.50 | 25.00 | — |
| AH1324 | — | 5.00 | 8.50 | 16.50 | 25.00 | — |

**TILLA** KM# 65 **Composition:** Gold **Note:** Previous #Y3 and C#85 and 95.

| Date | Mintage | VG | F | VF | XF | Unc |
|---|---|---|---|---|---|---|
| AH1319 | — | 75.00 | 100 | 135 | 185 | — |
| AH1324/1324 | — | 75.00 | 100 | 135 | 185 | — |
| AH1325 | — | 75.00 | 100 | 135 | 185 | — |
| AH1327 | — | 75.00 | 100 | 135 | 185 | — |
| AH1328 | — | 75.00 | 100 | 135 | 185 | — |
| AH1329 | — | 75.00 | 100 | 135 | 185 | — |

**TENGA** KM# 63 **Weight:** 3.2000 g. **Composition:** Silver **Note:** Varieties exist. Previous #Y2 and C#75, 91.

| Date | Mintage | VG | F | VF | XF | Unc |
|---|---|---|---|---|---|---|
| AH1319//1320 | — | 10.00 | 16.50 | 27.50 | 40.00 | — |
| AH1319 | — | 6.50 | 12.50 | 20.00 | 30.00 | — |
| AH1320 | — | 6.50 | 12.50 | 20.00 | 30.00 | — |
| AH1322 | — | 6.50 | 12.50 | 20.00 | 30.00 | — |
| AH1323//1322 | — | 10.00 | 16.50 | 27.50 | 40.00 | — |
| AH1323 | — | 6.50 | 12.50 | 20.00 | 30.00 | — |

### NAMED COINAGE

10 Falus = 1 Tenga

**FALUS** KM# 85 **Composition:** Copper Or Brass **Ruler:** Alim Ibn Sayyid Mir Amin 1911-1920AD, independent after AH1336 (1917 AD) **Note:** Dates on obverse and reverse. Previous #YA4.

| Date | Mintage | VG | F | VF | XF | Unc |
|---|---|---|---|---|---|---|
| AH132x-1332 | — | — | — | — | — | — |

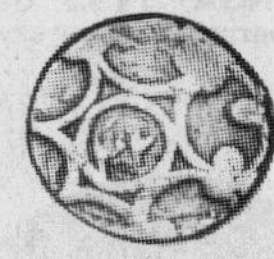

**FALUS** KM# 86 **Composition:** Copper Or Brass **Ruler:** Alim Ibn Sayyid Mir Amin 1911-1920AD, independent after AH1336 (1917 AD) **Reverse:** "32" or "33" or "302" in a circle **Note:** Many varieties exist. Previous #Y4.1.

| Date | Mintage | VG | F | VF | XF | Unc |
|---|---|---|---|---|---|---|
| AH1321 | — | 4.50 | 8.50 | 15.00 | 30.00 | — |
| AH1322 | — | 4.50 | 8.50 | 15.00 | 30.00 | — |
| AH1323 | — | 4.50 | 8.50 | 15.00 | 30.00 | — |
| AH1324 | — | 4.50 | 8.50 | 15.00 | 30.00 | — |
| AH1326 | — | 4.50 | 8.50 | 15.00 | 30.00 | — |
| AH1327 | — | 4.50 | 8.50 | 15.00 | 30.00 | — |
| AH1329 | — | 4.50 | 8.50 | 15.00 | 30.00 | — |
| AH1330 | — | 4.50 | 8.50 | 15.00 | 30.00 | — |
| AH1331 | — | 4.50 | 8.50 | 15.00 | 30.00 | — |
| AH1332 | — | 4.50 | 8.50 | 15.00 | 30.00 | — |
| AH1333 | — | 4.50 | 8.50 | 15.00 | 30.00 | — |
| AH1335 | — | 4.50 | 8.50 | 15.00 | 30.00 | — |
| AH(13)36 | — | 4.50 | 25.00 | 40.00 | 60.00 | — |

**2 FALUS** KM# 42 **Composition:** Copper **Ruler:** Alim Ibn Sayyid Mir Amin 1911-1920AD, independent after AH1336 (1917 AD) **Reverse:** "2" or "4" in a circle **Note:** Date range 1331-1336 reported but not confirmed. Many varieties exist. Previous #Y4.

| Date | Mintage | VG | F | VF | XF | Unc |
|---|---|---|---|---|---|---|
| AH1332 | — | 4.50 | 8.50 | 15.00 | 22.50 | — |
| AH1334 | — | 6.00 | 12.00 | 18.00 | 25.00 | — |

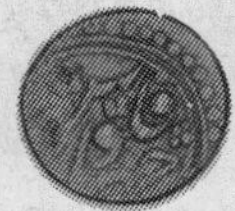

**4 FALUS** KM# 44 **Composition:** Copper **Ruler:** Alim Ibn Sayyid Mir Amin 1911-1920AD, independent after AH1336 (1917 AD) **Note:** Previous #Y5.

| Date | Mintage | VG | F | VF | XF | Unc |
|---|---|---|---|---|---|---|
| AH1334 | — | 6.50 | 12.50 | 20.00 | 35.00 | — |
| AH1335 | — | 6.50 | 12.50 | 20.00 | 35.00 | — |

**8 FALUS** KM# 45 **Composition:** Copper **Ruler:** Alim Ibn Sayyid Mir Amin 1911-1920AD, independent after AH1336 (1917 AD) **Note:** Previous #YA5.

| Date | Mintage | VG | F | VF | XF | Unc |
|---|---|---|---|---|---|---|
| AH1335 | — | 6.50 | 12.50 | 20.00 | 35.00 | — |

**1/2 TENGA** KM# A6 **Composition:** Bronze **Ruler:** Alim Ibn Sayyid Mir Amin 1911-1920AD, independent after AH1336 (1917 AD) **Reverse:** Legend in sextagonal frame **Size:** 14-15 mm. **Note:** Previous #Y6.

| Date | Mintage | VG | F | VF | XF | Unc |
|---|---|---|---|---|---|---|
| AH1336 | — | 15.00 | 30.00 | 50.00 | 100 | — |

**TENGA** KM# 46.2 **Composition:** Bronze **Ruler:** Alim Ibn Sayyid Mir Amin 1911-1920AD, independent after AH1336 (1917 AD) **Reverse:** Stars **Size:** 17-18 mm. **Note:** Large flan, dotted border. Varieties exist. Previous #Y6a.

| Date | Mintage | VG | F | VF | XF | Unc |
|---|---|---|---|---|---|---|
| AH1336 | — | 7.50 | 15.00 | 30.00 | 60.00 | — |
| AH1337 | — | 7.50 | 15.00 | 30.00 | 60.00 | — |

**TENGA** KM# 46.1 **Composition:** Bronze **Ruler:** Alim Ibn Sayyid Mir Amin 1911-1920AD, independent after AH1336 (1917 AD) **Reverse:** No stars **Size:** 14-15 mm. **Note:** Small flan, no border.

| Date | Mintage | VG | F | VF | XF | Unc |
|---|---|---|---|---|---|---|
| AH1336 | — | 1.50 | 15.00 | 30.00 | 60.00 | — |

**2 TENGA** KM# 47 **Composition:** Bronze Or Brass **Ruler:** Alim Ibn Sayyid Mir Amin 1911-1920AD, independent after AH1336 (1917 AD) **Obverse:** Greek meander pattern border **Reverse:** Star with 5 or 6 rays, Greek meander pattern border **Note:** Varieties exist. Previous #Y7.

| Date | Mintage | VG | F | VF | XF | Unc |
|---|---|---|---|---|---|---|
| AH1336 | — | 6.00 | 12.00 | 25.00 | 55.00 | — |
| AH1337 | — | 6.00 | 12.00 | 25.00 | 55.00 | — |

**3 TENGA** KM# 48 **Composition:** Bronze Or Brass **Ruler:** Alim Ibn Sayyid Mir Amin 1911-1920AD, independent after AH1336 (1917 AD) **Reverse:** Star with 5 or 6 rays **Note:** Varieties exist. Previous #Y8.

| Date | Mintage | VG | F | VF | XF | Unc |
|---|---|---|---|---|---|---|
| AH1336 | — | 6.00 | 12.00 | 25.00 | 50.00 | — |
| AH1337 | — | 6.00 | 12.00 | 25.00 | 50.00 | — |

**4 TENGA** KM# 49 **Composition:** Bronze Or Brass **Ruler:** Alim Ibn Sayyid Mir Amin 1911-1920AD, independent after AH1336 (1917 AD) **Note:** Probably a pattern. Previous #Y9.

| Date | Mintage | VG | F | VF | XF | Unc |
|---|---|---|---|---|---|---|
| AH1336 | — | 85.00 | 140 | 200 | 300 | — |

**5 TENGA** KM# 50 **Composition:** Bronze Or Brass **Ruler:** Alim Ibn Sayyid Mir Amin 1911-1920AD, independent after AH1336 (1917 AD) **Note:** Previous #Y10.

| Date | Mintage | VG | F | VF | XF | Unc |
|---|---|---|---|---|---|---|
| AH1336 | — | 22.50 | 35.00 | 50.00 | 80.00 | — |
| AH1337 | — | 22.50 | 35.00 | 50.00 | 80.00 | — |

**10 TENGA** KM# 53 **Composition:** Bronze Or Brass **Ruler:** Alim Ibn Sayyid Mir Amin 1911-1920AD, independent after AH1336 (1917 AD) **Note:** Size of squares vary. Previous #Y11.

| Date | Mintage | VG | F | VF | XF | Unc |
|---|---|---|---|---|---|---|
| AH1337 | — | 10.00 | 17.50 | 35.00 | 65.00 | — |
| AH1338/1337 | — | 10.00 | 17.50 | 35.00 | 65.00 | — |

**20 TENGA** KM# 51 **Composition:** Bronze Or Brass **Ruler:** Alim Ibn Sayyid Mir Amin 1911-1920AD, independent after AH1336 (1917 AD) **Note:** Previous #Y12.

| Date | Mintage | VG | F | VF | XF | Unc |
|---|---|---|---|---|---|---|
| AH1336 | — | 22.50 | 35.00 | 50.00 | 85.00 | — |
| AH1337 | — | 22.50 | 35.00 | 50.00 | 85.00 | — |

# KHANATE OF KHIVA (KHWAREZM)

Khwarezm (Khiva), a present town once a great kingdom under the names of Chorasmia, Khwarezm and Urgenj, is located in Russian Turkestan east of the Caspian Sea and south of the Aral Sea. Russia established relations with Khwarezm (Khiva) in the 17th century, occupied it in 1873, and annexed it in 1875. Revolution concentrated Russia's preoccupation elsewhere during 1917 and Khwarezm (Khiva) seized this opportunity to declare its independence. It was able to sustain this status for a scant two years. By 1919 the Soviet regime had reestablished control over the region and extinguished the independent state. In AH1338/1920AD it became Khwarezm Soviet People's Republic and later became part of the Uzbekistan S.S.R., now Uzbekistan.

**RULERS**

Sayyid Abdullah Khan and Junaid Khan, AH1337-1338/1918-1920AD

**MINTNAME**

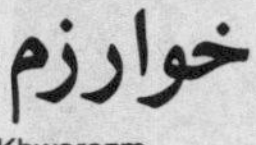


Khwarezm

## INDEPENDANT KHANATE
### AH1337-1338 / 1918-1920AD
### STANDARD COINAGE

**TENGA** Y# 8 **Weight:** 2.3000 g. **Composition:** Silver **Note:** Struck in the name of Sayid Muhammad Rahim. Varieties exist.

| Date | Mintage | VG | F | VF | XF | Unc |
|---|---|---|---|---|---|---|
| AH1337 | — | 100 | 175 | 250 | — | — |

**TENGA** Y# A9 **Composition:** Copper, Bronze Or Brass **Reverse:** Date above or below inscription **Note:** Similar to 5 Tenga, Y#10. Varieties exist.

| Date | Mintage | VG | F | VF | XF | Unc |
|---|---|---|---|---|---|---|
| AH1337 | — | 20.00 | 30.00 | 40.00 | 75.00 | — |

**2-1/2 TENGA** Y# 9.3 **Composition:** Copper, Bronze Or Brass **Obverse:** Full sun in sky, inscription with Falus on left side **Note:** Many die varieties exist. Diameters, ornamentation, die rotation, number of sun rays, and size of circles vary.

| Date | Mintage | VG | F | VF | XF | Unc |
|---|---|---|---|---|---|---|
| AH1337 | — | 27.50 | 37.50 | 50.00 | 90.00 | — |
| AH1338 | — | 27.50 | 37.50 | 50.00 | 90.00 | — |

**2-1/2 TENGA** Y# 9.1 **Composition:** Copper, Bronze Or Brass **Obverse:** Sun rising, inscription with Falus on right side

| Date | Mintage | VG | F | VF | XF | Unc |
|---|---|---|---|---|---|---|
| AH1337 | — | 27.50 | 37.50 | 50.00 | 90.00 | — |

**2-1/2 TENGA** Y# 9.2 **Composition:** Copper, Bronze Or Brass **Obverse:** Full sun in sky, inscription with Falus on right side

| Date | Mintage | VG | F | VF | XF | Unc |
|---|---|---|---|---|---|---|
| AH1337 | — | 27.50 | 37.50 | 50.00 | 90.00 | — |
| AH1338 | — | 27.50 | 37.50 | 50.00 | 90.00 | — |

**5 TENGA** Y# 10.1 **Composition:** Copper, Bronze Or Brass **Obverse:** Full sun in sky, inscription with Falus on right side

| Date | Mintage | VG | F | VF | XF | Unc |
|---|---|---|---|---|---|---|
| AH1337 | — | 37.50 | 52.50 | 70.00 | 110 | — |
| AH1338 | — | 37.50 | 52.50 | 70.00 | 110 | — |

**5 TENGA** Y# 10.2 **Composition:** Copper, Bronze Or Brass **Obverse:** Full sun in sky, inscription with Falus on left side **Note:** Many die varieties exist. Date above or below inscription. Diameters, ornamentation, die rotation, sun rays, and size of circles vary.

| Date | Mintage | VG | F | VF | XF | Unc |
|---|---|---|---|---|---|---|
| AH1337 | — | 37.50 | 52.50 | 70.00 | 110 | — |
| AH1338 | — | 37.50 | 52.50 | 70.00 | 110 | — |

**15 TENGA** Y# 11 **Composition:** Copper, Bronze Or Brass **Note:** Many die varieties exist.

| Date | Mintage | VG | F | VF | XF | Unc |
|---|---|---|---|---|---|---|
| AH1338 | — | 100 | 175 | 250 | — | — |

## PEOPLES REPUBLIC
### AH1338-1343/1920-1924AD
### STANDARD COINAGE

**20 ROUBLES** Y# 5 **Composition:** Bronze Or Brass

| Date | Mintage | VG | F | VF | XF | Unc |
|---|---|---|---|---|---|---|
| AH1338 | — | 20.00 | 30.00 | 40.00 | 75.00 | — |
| AH1339 | — | 20.00 | 30.00 | 40.00 | 75.00 | — |
| AH1340 | — | 20.00 | 30.00 | 40.00 | 75.00 | — |

**25 ROUBLES** Y# 16 **Composition:** Bronze Or Brass **Reverse:** 8-pointed star

| Date | Mintage | VG | F | VF | XF | Unc |
|---|---|---|---|---|---|---|
| AH1339 | — | 17.50 | 30.00 | 40.00 | 75.00 | — |

**25 ROUBLES** Y# 16.1 **Composition:** Bronze Or Brass **Reverse:** 12-pointed star

| Date | Mintage | VG | F | VF | XF | Unc |
|---|---|---|---|---|---|---|
| AH1339 | — | 17.50 | 30.00 | 40.00 | 75.00 | — |

**100 ROUBLES** Y# 17 **Composition:** Bronze Or Brass

| Date | Mintage | VG | F | VF | XF | Unc |
|---|---|---|---|---|---|---|
| AH1339 | — | 17.50 | 25.00 | 32.50 | 60.00 | — |

**500 ROUBLES** Y# 18 **Composition:** Bronze Or Brass

| Date | Mintage | VG | F | VF | XF | Unc |
|---|---|---|---|---|---|---|
| AH1339 | — | 50.00 | 75.00 | 200 | 275 | — |

**500 ROUBLES** Y# 19 **Composition:** Bronze Or Brass **Note:** Varieties exist. Similar 200 and 1,000 Rouble strikes with crude inscriptions are considered fantasies.

| Date | Mintage | VG | F | VF | XF | Unc |
|---|---|---|---|---|---|---|
| AH1339 | — | 20.00 | 30.00 | 40.00 | 75.00 | — |
| AH1340 | — | 20.00 | 30.00 | 40.00 | 75.00 | — |

# VANUATU

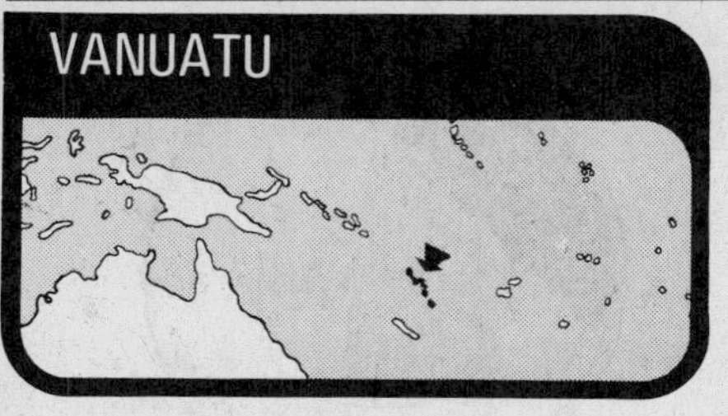

The Republic of Vanuatu, formerly New Hebrides Condominium, a group of islands located in the South Pacific 500 miles (800 km.) west of Fiji, were under the joint sovereignty of Great Britain and France. The islands have an area of 5,700 sq. mi. (14,760 sq. km.) and a population of 165,000, mainly Melanesians of mixed blood. Capital: Port-Vila. The volcanic and coral islands, while malaria land subject to frequent earthquakes, are extremely fertile, and produce copra, coffee, tropical fruits and timber for export.

The New Hebrides were discovered by Portuguese navigator Pedro de Quiros in 1606, visited by French explorer Bougainville in 1768, and named by British navigator Capt. James Cook in 1774. Ships of all nations converged on the islands to trade for sandalwood, prompting France and Britain to relinquish their individual claims and declare the islands a neutral zone in 1878. The New Hebrides were placed under the control of a mixed Anglo-French commission of naval officers during the native uprisings of 1887, and established as a condominium under the joint sovereignty of France and Great Britain in 1906.

Vanuatu became an independent republic within the Commonwealth in July 1980. A president is Head of State and the Prime Minister is Head of Government.

**MINT MARKS**

(a) - Paris, privy marks only

**MONETARY SYSTEM**

100 Centimes = 1 Franc

## REPUBLIC

### STANDARD COINAGE

**VATU** KM# 3 **Composition:** Nickel-Brass

| Date | Mintage | F | VF | XF | Unc | BU |
|---|---|---|---|---|---|---|
| 1983 | — | — | — | 0.10 | 0.35 | — |
| 1983 Proof | — | Value: 1.50 | | | | |
| 1990 | — | — | — | 0.10 | 0.35 | — |
| 1999 | — | — | — | 0.10 | 0.35 | — |

**2 VATU** KM# 4 **Composition:** Nickel-Brass

| Date | Mintage | F | VF | XF | Unc | BU |
|---|---|---|---|---|---|---|
| 1983 | — | — | — | 0.15 | 0.50 | — |
| 1983 Proof | — | Value: 2.00 | | | | |
| 1990 | — | — | — | 0.10 | 0.45 | — |
| 1995 | — | — | — | 0.10 | 0.45 | — |

**5 VATU** KM# 5 **Composition:** Nickel-Brass

| Date | Mintage | F | VF | XF | Unc | BU |
|---|---|---|---|---|---|---|
| 1983 | — | — | — | 0.20 | 0.75 | — |
| 1983 Proof | — | Value: 2.50 | | | | |
| 1990 | — | — | — | 0.15 | 0.60 | — |
| 1995 | — | — | — | 0.15 | 0.60 | — |

**10 VATU** KM# 6 **Composition:** Copper-Nickel **Series:** F.A.O.

| Date | Mintage | F | VF | XF | Unc | BU |
|---|---|---|---|---|---|---|
| 1983 | — | — | — | 0.35 | 1.50 | — |
| 1983 Proof | — | Value: 3.00 | | | | |
| 1990 | — | — | — | 0.35 | 1.50 | — |
| 1995 | — | — | — | 0.35 | 1.50 | — |

**10 VATU** KM# 25 **Composition:** Copper-Nickel **Subject:** End of Victorian Era - Queen Victoria

| Date | Mintage | F | VF | XF | Unc | BU |
|---|---|---|---|---|---|---|
| 1995 | Est. 30,000 | — | — | — | 10.00 | — |

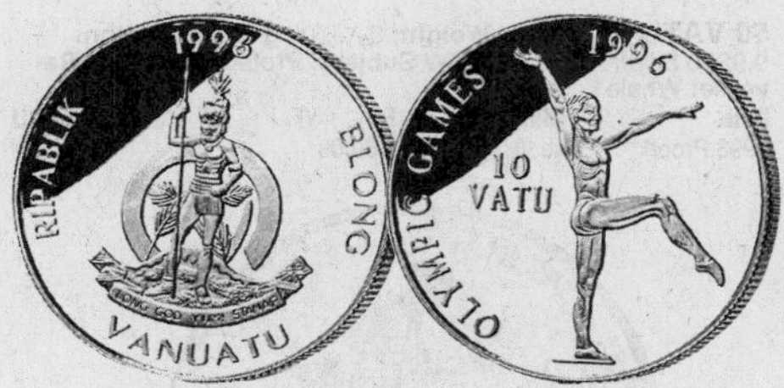


**10 VATU** KM# 28 **Weight:** 10.0000 g. **Composition:** 0.5000 Silver .1607 oz. ASW **Series:** Olympics **Reverse:** Gymnast

| Date | Mintage | F | VF | XF | Unc | BU |
|---|---|---|---|---|---|---|
| 1996 | Est. 10,000 | — | — | — | 14.50 | — |

**20 VATU** KM# 7 **Composition:** Copper-Nickel **Series:** F.A.O

| Date | Mintage | F | VF | XF | Unc | BU |
|---|---|---|---|---|---|---|
| 1983 | — | — | — | 0.35 | 1.50 | — |
| 1983 Proof | — | Value: 4.00 | | | | |
| 1990 | — | — | — | 0.35 | 1.50 | — |
| 1995 | — | — | — | 0.35 | 1.50 | — |

**20 VATU** KM# 19 **Weight:** 20.0000 g. **Composition:** 0.5000 Silver .3215 oz. ASW **Subject:** Captain James Cook

| Date | Mintage | F | VF | XF | Unc | BU |
|---|---|---|---|---|---|---|
| 1994 Proof | Est. 25,000 | Value: 17.50 | | | | |

**20 VATU** KM# 20 **Weight:** 20.0000 g. **Composition:** 0.9250 Silver .5948 oz. ASW **Series:** Endangered Wildlife **Reverse:** Kingfisher

| Date | Mintage | F | VF | XF | Unc | BU |
|---|---|---|---|---|---|---|
| 1994 Proof | Est. 25,000 | Value: 35.00 | | | | |

**50 VATU** KM# 1 **Composition:** Nickel **Subject:** 1st Anniversary of Independence

| Date | Mintage | F | VF | XF | Unc | BU |
|---|---|---|---|---|---|---|
| 1981 | — | — | — | 1.00 | 2.50 | — |

**50 VATU** KM# 1a **Weight:** 15.0000 g. **Composition:** 0.9250 Silver .4461 oz. ASW

| Date | Mintage | F | VF | XF | Unc | BU |
|---|---|---|---|---|---|---|
| 1981 Proof | 846 | Value: 35.00 | | | | |

**50 VATU** KM# 8 **Composition:** Copper-Nickel **Series:** F.A.O.

| Date | Mintage | F | VF | XF | Unc | BU |
|---|---|---|---|---|---|---|
| 1983 | — | — | — | 1.00 | 2.75 | — |
| 1983 Proof | — | Value: 7.00 | | | | |
| 1990 | — | — | — | 1.00 | 2.75 | — |
| 1995 | — | — | — | 1.00 | 2.75 | — |
| 1999 | — | — | — | 1.00 | 2.75 | — |

**50 VATU** KM# 10 **Weight:** 34.0000 g. **Composition:** 0.9250 Silver 1.0111 oz. ASW **Series:** Seoul Olympics **Subject:** Boxing

| Date | Mintage | F | VF | XF | Unc | BU |
|---|---|---|---|---|---|---|
| 1988 Proof | 15,000 | Value: 25.00 | | | | |

**50 VATU** KM# 11 **Weight:** 31.4700 g. **Composition:** 0.9250 Silver .9359 oz. ASW **Subject:** Voyager I

| Date | Mintage | F | VF | XF | Unc | BU |
|---|---|---|---|---|---|---|
| 1992 Proof | 10,000 | Value: 27.50 | | | | |

**50 VATU** **KM# 12** **Weight:** 31.4700 g. **Composition:** 0.9250 Silver .9359 oz. ASW **Subject:** Pedro Fernandez De Quiros

| Date | Mintage | F | VF | XF | Unc | BU |
|---|---|---|---|---|---|---|
| 1992 Proof | — | Value: 26.50 | | | | |

**50 VATU** **KM# 13** **Weight:** 31.4700 g. **Composition:** 0.9250 Silver .9359 oz. ASW **Series:** Endangered Wildlife **Subject:** Earth Pigeons

| Date | Mintage | F | VF | XF | Unc | BU |
|---|---|---|---|---|---|---|
| 1992 Proof | — | Value: 32.50 | | | | |

**50 VATU** **KM# 14** **Weight:** 31.4700 g. **Composition:** 0.9250 Silver .9359 oz. ASW **Series:** Olympics **Subject:** Canoes

| Date | Mintage | F | VF | XF | Unc | BU |
|---|---|---|---|---|---|---|
| 1992 Proof | Est. 40,000 | Value: 17.50 | | | | |

**50 VATU** **KM# 15** **Weight:** 31.4700 g. **Composition:** 0.9250 Silver .9359 oz. ASW **Subject:** 40th Anniversary of Coronation

| Date | Mintage | F | VF | XF | Unc | BU |
|---|---|---|---|---|---|---|
| 1993 Proof | Est. 10,000 | Value: 45.00 | | | | |

**50 VATU** **KM# 16** **Weight:** 31.4700 g. **Composition:** 0.9250 Silver .9359 oz. ASW **Subject:** The Boudeuse **Reverse:** Ship

| Date | Mintage | F | VF | XF | Unc | BU |
|---|---|---|---|---|---|---|
| 1993 Proof | Est. 15,000 | Value: 30.00 | | | | |

**50 VATU** **KM# 17** **Weight:** 31.4700 g. **Composition:** 0.9250 Silver .9359 oz. ASW **Subject:** Protect Our World **Reverse:** Whale

| Date | Mintage | F | VF | XF | Unc | BU |
|---|---|---|---|---|---|---|
| 1993 Proof | Est. 10,000 | Value: 60.00 | | | | |

**50 VATU** **KM# 18** **Weight:** 31.4700 g. **Composition:** 0.9250 Silver .9359 oz. ASW **Subject:** World Cup Soccer

| Date | Mintage | F | VF | XF | Unc | BU |
|---|---|---|---|---|---|---|
| 1994 Proof | Est. 15,000 | Value: 28.00 | | | | |

**50 VATU** **KM# 21** **Weight:** 31.4700 g. **Composition:** 0.9250 Silver .9359 oz. ASW **Subject:** De Bougainville

| Date | Mintage | F | VF | XF | Unc | BU |
|---|---|---|---|---|---|---|
| 1994 Proof | Est. 10,000 | Value: 37.50 | | | | |

**50 VATU** **KM# 22** **Weight:** 31.4700 g. **Composition:** 0.9250 Silver .9359 oz. ASW **Subject:** Queen Victoria

| Date | Mintage | F | VF | XF | Unc | BU |
|---|---|---|---|---|---|---|
| 1994 Proof | Est. 20,000 | Value: 35.00 | | | | |

**50 VATU** **KM# 24** **Weight:** 31.4700 g. **Composition:** 0.9250 Silver .9359 oz. ASW **Series:** Olympics **Reverse:** Swimmers

| Date | Mintage | F | VF | XF | Unc | BU |
|---|---|---|---|---|---|---|
| 1994 Proof | Est. 40,000 | Value: 26.50 | | | | |

**50 VATU** **KM# 30** **Weight:** 31.4700 g. **Composition:** 0.9250 Silver .9359 oz. ASW **Series:** Olympic Games 1996 **Obverse:** National emblem **Reverse:** Gymnast

| Date | Mintage | F | VF | XF | Unc | BU |
|---|---|---|---|---|---|---|
| 1994 Proof | — | Value: 24.50 | | | | |

**50 VATU** **KM# 26** **Weight:** 31.4700 g. **Composition:** 0.9250 Silver .9359 oz. ASW **Subject:** Birth of Great Grandson Prince William

| Date | Mintage | F | VF | XF | Unc | BU |
|---|---|---|---|---|---|---|
| 1995 Proof | Est. 30,000 | Value: 35.00 | | | | |

**50 VATU** KM# 29 **Weight:** 31.4700 g. **Composition:** 0.9250 Silver .9359 oz. ASW **Subject:** Queen Victoria and Prince Albert

| Date | Mintage | F | VF | XF | Unc | BU |
|---|---|---|---|---|---|---|
| 1996 Proof | Est. 10,000 | Value: 42.50 | | | | |

**50 VATU** KM# 31 **Weight:** 1.2441 g. **Composition:** 0.9990 Gold .0400 oz. AGW **Obverse:** National emblem **Reverse:** Spanish 1704 gold coin design

| Date | Mintage | F | VF | XF | Unc | BU |
|---|---|---|---|---|---|---|
| 1998 Proof | — | Value: 45.00 | | | | |

**50 VATU** KM# 32 **Weight:** 1.2441 g. **Composition:** 0.9990 Gold .0400 oz. AGW **Obverse:** National emblem **Reverse:** Boar tusk necklace

| Date | Mintage | F | VF | XF | Unc | BU |
|---|---|---|---|---|---|---|
| 1998 Proof | — | Value: 45.00 | | | | |

**50 VATU** KM# 33 **Weight:** 30.9700 g. **Composition:** 0.9250 Silver .9210 oz. ASW **Subject:** Millennium 2000

| Date | Mintage | F | VF | XF | Unc | BU |
|---|---|---|---|---|---|---|
| 1998 Proof | — | Value: 37.50 | | | | |

**100 VATU** KM# 9 **Composition:** Nickel-Brass

| Date | Mintage | F | VF | XF | Unc | BU |
|---|---|---|---|---|---|---|
| 1988 | — | — | — | — | 3.75 | — |
| 1995 | — | — | — | — | 3.75 | — |

**100 VATU** KM# 23 **Weight:** 7.7760 g. **Composition:** 0.5830 Gold .1458 oz. AGW **Series:** Endangered Wildlife **Reverse:** Kingfisher

| Date | Mintage | F | VF | XF | Unc | BU |
|---|---|---|---|---|---|---|
| 1994 Proof | Est. 2,000 | Value: 150 | | | | |

**100 VATU** KM# 27 **Weight:** 155.5000 g. **Composition:** 0.9250 Silver 4.6245 oz. ASW **Reverse:** Coronation portrait **Size:** 65 mm. **Note:** Illustration reduced.

| Date | Mintage | F | VF | XF | Unc | BU |
|---|---|---|---|---|---|---|
| 1995 Proof | Est. 2,000 | Value: 80.00 | | | | |

**100 VATU** KM# 34 **Weight:** 155.5000 g. **Composition:** 0.9250 Silver 4.6245 oz. ASW **Subject:** H.M.S. Resolution **Obverse:** National arms **Reverse:** Sailing ship and carvings **Edge:** Reeded **Size:** 65.7 mm.

| Date | Mintage | F | VF | XF | Unc | BU |
|---|---|---|---|---|---|---|
| 1996 Proof | 5,000 | Value: 150 | | | | |

**10000 VATU** KM# 2 **Weight:** 15.9800 g. **Composition:** 0.9170 Gold .4712 oz. AGW **Subject:** 1st Anniversary of Independence

| Date | Mintage | F | VF | XF | Unc | BU |
|---|---|---|---|---|---|---|
| 1981 | 538 | — | — | — | 240 | — |
| 1981 Proof | 1,054 | Value: 300 | | | | |

## PROOF SETS

| KM# | Date | Mintage | Identification | Issue Price | Mkt Val |
|---|---|---|---|---|---|
| PS1 | 1983 (6) | — | KM#3-8 | — | 20.00 |

# VATICAN CITY

The State of the Vatican City, a papal state on the right bank of the Tiber River within the boundaries of Rome, has an area of 0.17 sq. mi. (0.44 sq. km.) and a population of *775. Capital: Vatican City.

Vatican City State, comprising the Vatican, St. Peter's and extra territorial right to Castel Gandolfo and 13 buildings in Rome, is all that remains of the extensive papal states over which the Pope exercised temporal power in central Italy. During the struggle for Italian unification, the Papal States, including Rome, were forcibly incorporated into the Kingdom of Italy in 1870. The resultant confrontation of crozier and sword remained unresolved until the signing of the Lateran Treaty, Feb. 11, 1929, between the Vatican and the Kingdom of Italy which recognized the independence and sovereignty of the State of the Vatican City, defined the relationship between the government and the church within Italy, and financially compensated the Holy See for its territorial losses in1870.

Today the Pope exercises supreme legislative, executive and judicial power within the Vatican City, and the State of the Vatican City is recognized by many nations as an independent sovereign state under the temporal jurisdiction of the Pope, even to the extent of ambassadorial exchange.

**PONTIFFS**

Pius XI, 1922-1939
Sede Vacante, Feb. 10 - Mar. 2, 1939
Pius XII, 1939-1958
Sede Vacante, Oct. 9 - 28, 1958
John XXIII, 1958-1963
Sede Vacante, June 3 - 21,1963
Paul VI, 1963-1978
Sede Vacante, Aug. 6 - 26, 1978
John Paul I, Aug. 26 - Sept. 28, 1978
Sede Vacante, Sept. 28 - Oct. 16, 1978
John Paul II, 1978-

**MINT MARKS**

Commencing 1981

R – Rome

**MONETARY SYSTEM**

100 Centesimi = 1 Lira

**DATING**

Most Vatican coins indicate the regnal year of the pope preceded by the word ***Anno*** (or an abbreviation), even if the anno domini date is omitted.

## CITY STATE

### STANDARD COINAGE

100 Centesimi = 1 Lira

**5 CENTESIMI** Y# 1 **Composition:** Bronze **Ruler:** Pope Pius XI

| Date | Mintage | F | VF | XF | Unc | BU |
|---|---|---|---|---|---|---|
| 1929/VIII | 10,000 | — | 5.00 | 7.50 | 16.00 | — |
| 1930/IX | 100,000 | — | 2.50 | 4.00 | 6.00 | — |
| 1931/X | 100,000 | — | 2.50 | 4.00 | 6.00 | — |
| 1932/XI | 100,000 | — | 2.50 | 4.00 | 6.00 | — |
| 1934/XIII | 100,000 | — | 2.50 | 4.00 | 6.00 | — |
| 1935/XIV | 44,000 | — | 5.00 | 10.00 | 20.00 | — |
| 1936/XV | 62,000 | — | 2.50 | 4.00 | 6.50 | — |
| 1937/XVI | 62,000 | — | 2.50 | 4.00 | 6.50 | — |
| 1938/XVII Rare | — | — | — | — | — | — |

**5 CENTESIMI** Y# 11 **Composition:** Bronze **Ruler:** Pope Pius XI **Subject:** Jubilee

| Date | Mintage | F | VF | XF | Unc | BU |
|---|---|---|---|---|---|---|
| 1933-34 | 100,000 | — | 5.00 | 10.00 | 20.00 | — |

**5 CENTESIMI** Y# 22 **Composition:** Aluminum-Bronze **Ruler:** Pope Pius XII

| Date | Mintage | F | VF | XF | Unc | BU |
|---|---|---|---|---|---|---|
| 1939/I | 62,000 | — | 2.50 | 4.00 | 7.50 | — |
| 1940/II | 62,000 | — | 2.50 | 4.00 | 7.50 | — |
| 1941/III | 5,000 | — | 7.50 | 15.00 | 27.00 | — |

**5 CENTESIMI** Y# 31 **Composition:** Brass **Ruler:** Pope Pius XII

| Date | Mintage | F | VF | XF | Unc | BU |
|---|---|---|---|---|---|---|
| 1942/IV | 5,000 | — | 15.00 | 27.50 | 55.00 | — |
| 1943/V | 1,000 | — | 25.00 | 40.00 | 85.00 | — |
| 1944/VI | 1,000 | — | 25.00 | 40.00 | 85.00 | — |
| 1945/VII | 1,000 | — | 25.00 | 40.00 | 85.00 | — |
| 1946/VIII | 1,000 | — | 25.00 | 40.00 | 85.00 | — |

**10 CENTESIMI** Y# 2 **Composition:** Bronze **Ruler:** Pope Pius XII

| Date | Mintage | F | VF | XF | Unc | BU |
|---|---|---|---|---|---|---|
| 1929/VIII | 10,000 | — | 5.00 | 7.50 | 18.00 | — |
| 1930/IX | 90,000 | — | 2.00 | 4.00 | 6.00 | — |
| 1931/X | 90,000 | — | 2.00 | 4.00 | 6.00 | — |
| 1932/XI | 90,000 | — | 2.00 | 4.00 | 6.00 | — |
| 1934/XIII | 90,000 | — | 2.00 | 4.00 | 6.00 | — |
| 1935/XIV | 90,000 | — | 2.00 | 4.00 | 6.00 | — |
| 1936/XV | 81,000 | — | 2.00 | 4.00 | 8.00 | — |
| 1937/XVI | 81,000 | — | 2.00 | 4.00 | 8.00 | — |
| 1938/XVII | — | — | — | — | 950 | — |

**10 CENTESIMI** Y# 12 **Composition:** Bronze **Ruler:** Pope Pius XII **Subject:** Jubilee

| Date | Mintage | F | VF | XF | Unc | BU |
|---|---|---|---|---|---|---|
| 1933-34 | 90,000 | — | 5.00 | 10.00 | 20.00 | — |

**10 CENTESIMI** Y# 23 **Composition:** Aluminum-Bronze **Ruler:** Pope Pius XII

| Date | Mintage | F | VF | XF | Unc | BU |
|---|---|---|---|---|---|---|
| 1939/I | 81,000 | — | 2.50 | 5.00 | 10.00 | — |
| 1940/II | 81,000 | — | 2.50 | 5.00 | 10.00 | — |
| 1941/III | 7,500 | — | 7.50 | 15.00 | 27.00 | — |

**10 CENTESIMI** Y# 32 **Composition:** Brass **Ruler:** Pope Pius XII

| Date | Mintage | F | VF | XF | Unc | BU |
|---|---|---|---|---|---|---|
| 1942/IV | 7,500 | — | 12.50 | 25.00 | 55.00 | — |
| 1943/V | 1,000 | — | 40.00 | 60.00 | 85.00 | — |
| 1944/VI | 1,000 | — | 40.00 | 60.00 | 85.00 | — |
| 1945/VII | 1,000 | — | 40.00 | 60.00 | 85.00 | — |
| 1946/VIII | 1,000 | — | 40.00 | 60.00 | 85.00 | — |

**20 CENTESIMI** Y# 3 **Composition:** Nickel **Ruler:** Pope Pius XI

| Date | Mintage | F | VF | XF | Unc | BU |
|---|---|---|---|---|---|---|
| 1929/VIII | 10,000 | — | 5.00 | 10.00 | 18.00 | — |
| 1930/IX | 80,000 | — | 2.00 | 4.00 | 6.00 | — |
| 1931/X | 80,000 | — | 2.00 | 4.00 | 6.00 | — |
| 1932/XI | 80,000 | — | 2.00 | 4.00 | 6.00 | — |
| 1934/XIII | 80,000 | — | 2.00 | 4.00 | 6.00 | — |
| 1935/XIV | 11,000 | — | 25.00 | 50.00 | 75.00 | — |
| 1936/XV | 64,000 | — | 2.00 | 4.00 | 6.00 | — |
| 1937/XVI | 64,000 | — | 2.00 | 4.00 | 6.00 | — |

**20 CENTESIMI** Y# 13 **Composition:** Nickel **Ruler:** Pope Pius XI **Subject:** Jubilee

| Date | Mintage | F | VF | XF | Unc | BU |
|---|---|---|---|---|---|---|
| 1933-34 | 80,000 | — | 5.00 | 10.00 | 20.00 | — |

**20 CENTESIMI** Y# 24 **Composition:** Nickel **Ruler:** Pope Pius XII

| Date | Mintage | F | VF | XF | Unc | BU |
|---|---|---|---|---|---|---|
| 1939/I | 64,000 | — | 2.00 | 4.00 | 6.00 | — |

**20 CENTESIMI** Y# 24a **Composition:** Stainless Steel **Ruler:** Pope Pius XII

| Date | Mintage | F | VF | XF | Unc | BU |
|---|---|---|---|---|---|---|
| 1940/II | 64,000 | — | 2.00 | 4.00 | 5.50 | — |
| 1941/III | 125,000 | — | 2.00 | 3.00 | 4.50 | — |

**20 CENTESIMI** Y# 33 **Composition:** Stainless Steel **Ruler:** Pope Pius XII

| Date | Mintage | F | VF | XF | Unc | BU |
|---|---|---|---|---|---|---|
| 1942/IV | 125,000 | — | 2.00 | 2.75 | 3.50 | — |
| 1943/V | 1,000 | — | 40.00 | 60.00 | 85.00 | — |
| 1944/VI | 1,000 | — | 40.00 | 60.00 | 85.00 | — |
| 1945/VII | 1,000 | — | 40.00 | 60.00 | 85.00 | — |
| 1946/VIII | 1,000 | — | 40.00 | 60.00 | 85.00 | — |

**50 CENTESIMI** Y# 4 **Composition:** Nickel **Ruler:** Pope Pius XI

| Date | Mintage | F | VF | XF | Unc | BU |
|---|---|---|---|---|---|---|
| 1929/VIII | 10,000 | — | 5.00 | 10.00 | 18.00 | — |
| 1930/IX | 80,000 | — | 2.00 | 4.00 | 6.00 | — |
| 1931/X | 80,000 | — | 2.00 | 4.00 | 6.00 | — |
| 1932/XI | 80,000 | — | 2.00 | 4.00 | 6.00 | — |
| 1934/XIII | 80,000 | — | 2.00 | 4.00 | 6.00 | — |
| 1935/XIV | 14,000 | — | 6.00 | 12.00 | 25.00 | — |
| 1936/XV | 52,000 | — | 2.00 | 4.00 | 6.00 | — |
| 1937/XVI | 52,000 | — | 2.00 | 4.00 | 6.00 | — |

**50 CENTESIMI** Y# 14 **Composition:** Nickel **Ruler:** Pope Pius XI **Subject:** Jubilee

| Date | Mintage | F | VF | XF | Unc | BU |
|---|---|---|---|---|---|---|
| 1933-34 | 80,000 | — | 4.00 | 8.00 | 16.00 | — |

**50 CENTESIMI** Y# 25 **Composition:** Nickel **Ruler:** Pope Pius XII

| Date | Mintage | F | VF | XF | Unc | BU |
|---|---|---|---|---|---|---|
| 1939/I | 52,000 | — | 2.00 | 4.00 | 6.00 | — |

**50 CENTESIMI** Y# 25a **Composition:** Stainless Steel **Ruler:** Pope Pius XII

| Date | Mintage | F | VF | XF | Unc | BU |
|---|---|---|---|---|---|---|
| 1940/II | 52,000 | — | 2.00 | 4.00 | 5.50 | — |
| 1941/III | 180,000 | — | 2.00 | 3.50 | 5.00 | — |

**50 CENTESIMI** Y# 34 **Composition:** Stainless Steel **Ruler:** Pope Pius XII

| Date | Mintage | F | VF | XF | Unc | BU |
|---|---|---|---|---|---|---|
| 1942/IV | 180,000 | — | 2.00 | 3.25 | 4.50 | — |
| 1943/V | 1,000 | — | 40.00 | 60.00 | 85.00 | — |
| 1944/VI | 1,000 | — | 40.00 | 60.00 | 85.00 | — |
| 1945/VII | 1,000 | — | 40.00 | 60.00 | 85.00 | — |
| 1946/VIII | 1,000 | — | 40.00 | 60.00 | 85.00 | — |

**LIRA** Y# 5 **Composition:** Nickel **Ruler:** Pope Pius XI

| Date | Mintage | F | VF | XF | Unc | BU |
|---|---|---|---|---|---|---|
| 1929/VIII | 10,000 | — | 5.00 | 10.00 | 18.00 | — |
| 1930/IX | 80,000 | — | 2.00 | 4.00 | 6.00 | — |
| 1931/X | 80,000 | — | 2.00 | 4.00 | 6.00 | — |
| 1932/XI | 80,000 | — | 2.00 | 4.00 | 6.00 | — |
| 1934/XIII | 80,000 | — | 2.00 | 4.00 | 6.00 | — |
| 1935/XIV | 40,000 | — | 2.00 | 4.00 | 6.00 | — |
| 1936/XV | 40,000 | — | 2.00 | 4.00 | 6.00 | — |
| 1937/XVI | 70,000 | — | 2.00 | 4.00 | 6.00 | — |

**LIRA** **Y# 15** **Composition:** Nickel **Ruler:** Pope Pius XI **Subject:** Jubilee **Note:** Enlargement of date area.

| Date | Mintage | F | VF | XF | Unc | BU |
|---|---|---|---|---|---|---|
| 1933-34 | 80,000 | — | 5.00 | 10.00 | 20.00 | — |

**LIRA** **Y# 26** **Composition:** Nickel **Ruler:** Pope Pius XII

| Date | Mintage | F | VF | XF | Unc | BU |
|---|---|---|---|---|---|---|
| 1939/I | 70,000 | — | 3.00 | 5.00 | 10.00 | — |

**LIRA** **Y# 26a** **Composition:** Stainless Steel **Ruler:** Pope Pius XII

| Date | Mintage | F | VF | XF | Unc | BU |
|---|---|---|---|---|---|---|
| 1940/II | 70,000 | — | 3.00 | 5.00 | 7.50 | — |
| 1941/III | 284,000 | — | 1.00 | 2.00 | 4.50 | — |

**LIRA** **Y# 35** **Composition:** Stainless Steel **Ruler:** Pope Pius XII

| Date | Mintage | F | VF | XF | Unc | BU |
|---|---|---|---|---|---|---|
| 1942/IV | 284,000 | — | 1.00 | 1.75 | 3.50 | — |
| 1943/V | 1,000 | — | 40.00 | 60.00 | 85.00 | — |
| 1944/VI | 1,000 | — | 40.00 | 60.00 | 85.00 | — |
| 1945/VII | 1,000 | — | 40.00 | 60.00 | 85.00 | — |
| 1946/VIII | 1,000 | — | 40.00 | 60.00 | 85.00 | — |

**LIRA** **Y# 40** **Composition:** Aluminum **Ruler:** Pope Pius XII

| Date | Mintage | F | VF | XF | Unc | BU |
|---|---|---|---|---|---|---|
| 1947/IX | 120,000 | — | 1.00 | 2.00 | 4.00 | — |
| 1948/X | 10,000 | — | 2.00 | 4.00 | 7.00 | — |
| 1949/XI | 10,000 | — | 2.00 | 4.00 | 7.00 | — |

**LIRA** **Y# 44** **Composition:** Aluminum **Ruler:** Pope Pius XII **Subject:** Holy Year

| Date | Mintage | F | VF | XF | Unc | BU |
|---|---|---|---|---|---|---|
| 1950 | 50,000 | — | 1.00 | 2.00 | 3.50 | — |

**LIRA** **Y# 49.1** **Composition:** Aluminum **Ruler:** Pope Pius XII **Obv. Legend:** ANNO

| Date | Mintage | F | VF | XF | Unc | BU |
|---|---|---|---|---|---|---|
| 1951/XIII | 400,000 | — | 0.25 | 0.50 | 1.50 | — |
| 1952/XIV | 400,000 | — | 0.25 | 0.50 | 1.50 | — |
| 1953/XV | 400,000 | — | 0.25 | 0.50 | 1.50 | — |
| 1955/XVII | 10,000 | — | 1.50 | 3.00 | 6.00 | — |
| 1957/XIX | 30,000 | — | 0.75 | 2.00 | 3.50 | — |
| 1958/XX | 30,000 | — | 0.75 | 2.00 | 3.50 | — |

**LIRA** **Y# 49.2** **Composition:** Aluminum **Ruler:** Pope Pius XII **Obv. Legend:** A

| Date | Mintage | F | VF | XF | Unc | BU |
|---|---|---|---|---|---|---|
| 1956/XVIII | 10,000 | — | 1.50 | 3.00 | 6.00 | — |

**LIRA** **Y# 58.1** **Composition:** Aluminum **Ruler:** Pope John XXIII **Obv. Legend:** AN

| Date | Mintage | F | VF | XF | Unc | BU |
|---|---|---|---|---|---|---|
| 1959/I | 25,000 | — | 1.00 | 3.50 | 6.00 | — |
| 1960/II | 25,000 | — | 1.00 | 2.00 | 4.00 | — |

**LIRA** **Y# 58.2** **Composition:** Aluminum **Ruler:** Pope John XXIII **Obv. Legend:** A

| Date | Mintage | F | VF | XF | Unc | BU |
|---|---|---|---|---|---|---|
| 1961/III | 25,000 | — | 1.00 | 2.00 | 4.00 | — |
| 1962/IV | 25,000 | — | 1.00 | 2.00 | 4.00 | — |

**LIRA** **Y# 67** **Composition:** Aluminum **Ruler:** Pope John XXIII **Subject:** 2nd Ecumenical Council

| Date | Mintage | F | VF | XF | Unc | BU |
|---|---|---|---|---|---|---|
| 1962/IV | 50,000 | — | 1.00 | 1.50 | 3.00 | — |

**LIRA** **Y# 76.1** **Composition:** Aluminum **Ruler:** Pope Paul VI **Obv. Legend:** AN

| Date | Mintage | F | VF | XF | Unc | BU |
|---|---|---|---|---|---|---|
| 1963/I | 60,000 | — | 0.75 | 2.00 | 4.00 | — |

**LIRA** **Y# 76.2** **Composition:** Aluminum **Ruler:** Pope Paul VI **Obv. Legend:** A

| Date | Mintage | F | VF | XF | Unc | BU |
|---|---|---|---|---|---|---|
| 1964/II | 60,000 | — | 0.50 | 1.00 | 2.00 | — |
| 1965/III | 60,000 | — | 0.50 | 1.00 | 2.00 | — |

**LIRA** **Y# 84** **Composition:** Aluminum **Ruler:** Pope Paul VI

| Date | Mintage | F | VF | XF | Unc | BU |
|---|---|---|---|---|---|---|
| 1966/IV | 90,000 | — | 0.25 | 0.75 | 1.25 | — |

**LIRA** **Y# 92** **Composition:** Aluminum **Ruler:** Pope Paul VI

| Date | Mintage | F | VF | XF | Unc | BU |
|---|---|---|---|---|---|---|
| 1967/V | 100,000 | — | 0.25 | 0.75 | 1.25 | — |

**LIRA** **Y# 100** **Composition:** Aluminum **Ruler:** Pope Paul VI **Series:** F.A.O.

| Date | Mintage | F | VF | XF | Unc | BU |
|---|---|---|---|---|---|---|
| ND(1968)/VI | 100,000 | — | 0.25 | 0.75 | 1.25 | — |

**LIRA** **Y# 108** **Composition:** Aluminum **Ruler:** Pope Paul VI **Series:** F.A.O.

| Date | Mintage | F | VF | XF | Unc | BU |
|---|---|---|---|---|---|---|
| 1969/VII | 100,000 | — | 0.25 | 0.75 | 1.25 | — |

**LIRA** **Y# 116** **Composition:** Aluminum **Ruler:** Pope Paul VI **Series:** F.A.O.

| Date | Mintage | F | VF | XF | Unc | BU |
|---|---|---|---|---|---|---|
| 1970/VIII | 100,000 | — | 0.25 | 0.50 | 1.00 | — |
| 1971/IX | 110,000 | — | 0.25 | 0.50 | 1.00 | — |
| 1972/X | 110,000 | — | 0.25 | 0.50 | 1.00 | — |
| 1973/XI | 132,000 | — | 0.25 | 0.50 | 1.00 | — |
| 1974/XII | 132,000 | — | 0.25 | 0.50 | 1.00 | — |
| 1975/XIII | 150,000 | — | 0.25 | 0.50 | 1.00 | — |
| 1976/XIV | 150,000 | — | 0.25 | 0.50 | 1.00 | — |
| 1977/XV | 135,000 | — | 0.25 | 0.50 | 1.00 | — |

**LIRA** **Y# 124** **Composition:** Aluminum **Ruler:** Pope Paul VI **Subject:** Holy Year

| Date | Mintage | F | VF | XF | Unc | BU |
|---|---|---|---|---|---|---|
| 1975 | 170,000 | — | 0.25 | 0.50 | 1.00 | — |

**2 LIRE** **Y# 6** **Composition:** Nickel **Ruler:** Pope Pius XI

| Date | Mintage | F | VF | XF | Unc | BU |
|---|---|---|---|---|---|---|
| 1929/VIII | 10,000 | — | 5.00 | 10.00 | 18.00 | — |
| 1930/IX | 50,000 | — | 2.00 | 4.00 | 5.50 | — |
| 1931/X | 50,000 | — | 2.00 | 4.00 | 5.50 | — |
| 1932/XI | 50,000 | — | 2.00 | 4.00 | 5.50 | — |
| 1934/XIII | 50,000 | — | 2.00 | 4.00 | 5.50 | — |
| 1935/XIV | 70,000 | — | 2.00 | 4.00 | 5.50 | — |
| 1936/XV | 40,000 | — | 2.00 | 4.00 | 5.50 | — |
| 1937/XVI | 70,000 | — | 2.00 | 4.00 | 5.50 | — |

**2 LIRE** **Y# 16** **Composition:** Nickel **Ruler:** Pope Pius XI **Subject:** Jubilee

| Date | Mintage | F | VF | XF | Unc | BU |
|---|---|---|---|---|---|---|
| 1933-34 | 50,000 | — | 4.00 | 6.00 | 10.00 | — |

**2 LIRE** **Y# 27** **Composition:** Nickel **Ruler:** Pope Pius XII

| Date | Mintage | F | VF | XF | Unc | BU |
|---|---|---|---|---|---|---|
| 1939/I | 40,000 | — | 3.00 | 5.00 | 10.00 | — |

**2 LIRE** **Y# 27a** **Composition:** Stainless Steel **Ruler:** Pope Pius XII

| Date | Mintage | F | VF | XF | Unc | BU |
|---|---|---|---|---|---|---|
| 1940/II | 40,000 | — | 0.75 | 1.50 | 4.00 | — |
| 1941/III | 270,000 | — | 0.50 | 1.00 | 3.00 | — |

**2 LIRE** Y# 36 **Composition:** Stainless Steel **Ruler:** Pope Pius XII

| Date | Mintage | F | VF | XF | Unc | BU |
|---|---|---|---|---|---|---|
| 1942/IV | 270,000 | — | 0.50 | 1.00 | 3.50 | — |
| 1943/V | 1,000 | — | 40.00 | 60.00 | 85.00 | — |
| 1944/VI | 1,000 | — | 40.00 | 60.00 | 85.00 | — |
| 1945/VII | 1,000 | — | 40.00 | 60.00 | 85.00 | — |
| 1946/VIII | 1,000 | — | 40.00 | 60.00 | 85.00 | — |

**2 LIRE** Y# 41 **Composition:** Aluminum **Ruler:** Pope Pius XII

| Date | Mintage | F | VF | XF | Unc | BU |
|---|---|---|---|---|---|---|
| 1947/IX | 65,000 | — | 2.00 | 4.00 | 8.00 | — |
| 1948/X | 110,000 | — | 1.50 | 3.50 | 5.00 | — |
| 1949/XI | 10,000 | — | 4.00 | 6.00 | 10.00 | — |

**2 LIRE** Y# 45 **Composition:** Aluminum **Ruler:** Pope Pius XII **Subject:** Holy Year

| Date | Mintage | F | VF | XF | Unc | BU |
|---|---|---|---|---|---|---|
| 1950 | 50,000 | — | 1.25 | 2.00 | 4.00 | — |

**2 LIRE** Y# 50 **Composition:** Aluminum **Ruler:** Pope Pius XII

| Date | Mintage | F | VF | XF | Unc | BU |
|---|---|---|---|---|---|---|
| 1951/XIII | 400,000 | — | 0.25 | 0.50 | 1.50 | — |
| 1952/XIV | 400,000 | — | 0.25 | 0.50 | 1.50 | — |
| 1953/XV | 400,000 | — | 0.25 | 0.50 | 1.50 | — |
| 1955/XVII | 20,000 | — | 1.00 | 2.00 | 4.00 | — |
| 1956/XVIII | 20,000 | — | 1.00 | 2.00 | 4.00 | — |
| 1957/XIX | 30,000 | — | 0.75 | 1.25 | 2.50 | — |
| 1958/XX | 30,000 | — | 0.75 | 1.25 | 2.50 | — |

**2 LIRE** Y# 59.1 **Composition:** Aluminum **Ruler:** Pope John XXIII **Obv. Legend:** AN

| Date | Mintage | F | VF | XF | Unc | BU |
|---|---|---|---|---|---|---|
| 1959/I | 25,000 | — | 1.50 | 4.00 | 6.00 | — |
| 1960/II | 25,000 | — | 1.50 | 3.00 | 5.00 | — |

**2 LIRE** Y# 59.2 **Composition:** Aluminum **Ruler:** Pope John XXIII **Obv. Legend:** A

| Date | Mintage | F | VF | XF | Unc | BU |
|---|---|---|---|---|---|---|
| 1961/III | 25,000 | — | 1.50 | 3.00 | 5.00 | — |
| 1962/IV | 25,000 | — | 1.50 | 3.00 | 5.00 | — |

**2 LIRE** Y# 68 **Composition:** Aluminum **Ruler:** Pope John XXIII **Subject:** 2nd Ecumenical Council

| Date | Mintage | F | VF | XF | Unc | BU |
|---|---|---|---|---|---|---|
| 1962/IV | 50,000 | — | 1.00 | 1.50 | 3.00 | — |

**2 LIRE** Y# 77.1 **Composition:** Aluminum **Ruler:** Pope Paul VI **Obv. Legend:** AN

| Date | Mintage | F | VF | XF | Unc | BU |
|---|---|---|---|---|---|---|
| 1963/I | 60,000 | — | 0.75 | 2.00 | 3.00 | — |

**2 LIRE** Y# 77.2 **Composition:** Aluminum **Ruler:** Pope Paul VI **Obv. Legend:** A

| Date | Mintage | F | VF | XF | Unc | BU |
|---|---|---|---|---|---|---|
| 1964/II | 60,000 | — | 0.75 | 2.00 | 3.00 | — |
| 1965/III | 60,000 | — | 0.75 | 1.00 | 2.00 | — |

**2 LIRE** Y# 85 **Composition:** Aluminum **Ruler:** Pope Paul VI

| Date | Mintage | F | VF | XF | Unc | BU |
|---|---|---|---|---|---|---|
| 1966/IV | 90,000 | — | 0.25 | 0.75 | 1.25 | — |

**2 LIRE** Y# 93 **Composition:** Aluminum **Ruler:** Pope Paul VI

| Date | Mintage | F | VF | XF | Unc | BU |
|---|---|---|---|---|---|---|
| 1967/V | 100,000 | — | 0.25 | 0.75 | 1.25 | — |

**2 LIRE** Y# 101 **Composition:** Aluminum **Ruler:** Pope Paul VI **Series:** F.A.O.

| Date | Mintage | F | VF | XF | Unc | BU |
|---|---|---|---|---|---|---|
| ND(1968)/VI | 100,000 | — | 0.25 | 0.75 | 1.50 | — |

**2 LIRE** Y# 109 **Composition:** Aluminum **Ruler:** Pope Paul VI

| Date | Mintage | F | VF | XF | Unc | BU |
|---|---|---|---|---|---|---|
| 1969/VII | 100,000 | — | 0.25 | 0.75 | 1.50 | — |

**2 LIRE** Y# 117 **Composition:** Aluminum **Ruler:** Pope Paul VI

| Date | Mintage | F | VF | XF | Unc | BU |
|---|---|---|---|---|---|---|
| 1970/VIII | 100,000 | — | 0.25 | 0.50 | 1.00 | — |
| 1971/IX | 110,000 | — | 0.25 | 0.50 | 1.00 | — |
| 1972/X | 110,000 | — | 0.25 | 0.50 | 1.00 | — |
| 1973/XI | 132,000 | — | 0.25 | 0.50 | 1.00 | — |
| 1974/XII | 132,000 | — | 0.25 | 0.50 | 1.00 | — |
| 1975/XIII | 150,000 | — | 0.25 | 0.50 | 1.00 | — |
| 1976/XIV | 150,000 | — | 0.25 | 0.50 | 1.00 | — |
| 1977/XV | 135,000 | — | 0.25 | 0.50 | 1.00 | — |

**2 LIRE** Y# 125 **Composition:** Aluminum **Ruler:** Pope Paul VI **Subject:** Holy Year

| Date | Mintage | F | VF | XF | Unc | BU |
|---|---|---|---|---|---|---|
| 1975 | 180,000 | — | 0.25 | 0.70 | 1.00 | — |

**5 LIRE** Y# 7 **Weight:** 5.0000 g. **Composition:** 0.8350 Silver .1342 oz. ASW **Ruler:** Pope Pius XI

| Date | Mintage | F | VF | XF | Unc | BU |
|---|---|---|---|---|---|---|
| 1929/VIII | 10,000 | — | 7.50 | 15.00 | 30.00 | — |
| 1930/IX | 50,000 | — | 5.00 | 9.00 | 20.00 | — |
| 1931/X | 50,000 | — | 5.00 | 9.00 | 20.00 | — |
| 1932/XI | 50,000 | — | 5.00 | 9.00 | 20.00 | — |
| 1934/XIII | 30,000 | — | 5.00 | 10.00 | 20.00 | — |
| 1935/XIV | 20,000 | — | 6.00 | 12.00 | 22.50 | — |
| 1936/XV | 40,000 | — | 5.00 | 9.00 | 20.00 | — |
| 1937/XVI | 40,000 | — | 5.00 | 9.00 | 20.00 | — |

**5 LIRE** Y# 17 **Weight:** 5.0000 g. **Composition:** 0.8350 Silver .1342 oz. ASW **Ruler:** Pope Pius XI **Subject:** Jubilee

| Date | Mintage | F | VF | XF | Unc | BU |
|---|---|---|---|---|---|---|
| 1933-34 | 50,000 | — | 5.00 | 10.00 | 20.00 | — |

**5 LIRE** Y# 20 **Weight:** 5.0000 g. **Composition:** 0.8350 Silver .1342 oz. ASW **Ruler:** Pope Pius XI **Subject:** Sede Vacante

| Date | Mintage | F | VF | XF | Unc | BU |
|---|---|---|---|---|---|---|
| 1939 | 40,000 | — | 7.50 | 15.00 | 25.00 | — |

**5 LIRE** Y# 28 **Weight:** 5.0000 g. **Composition:** 0.8350 Silver .1342 oz. ASW **Ruler:** Pope Pius XII

| Date | Mintage | F | VF | XF | Unc | BU |
|---|---|---|---|---|---|---|
| 1939/I | 100,000 | — | 4.00 | 10.00 | 18.00 | — |
| 1940/II | 100,000 | — | 4.00 | 10.00 | 18.00 | — |
| 1941/III | 4,000 | — | 25.00 | 35.00 | 65.00 | — |

**5 LIRE** Y# 37 **Weight:** 5.0000 g. **Composition:** 0.8350 Silver .1342 oz. ASW **Ruler:** Pope Pius XII

| Date | Mintage | F | VF | XF | Unc | BU |
|---|---|---|---|---|---|---|
| 1942/IV | 4,000 | — | 25.00 | 40.00 | 65.00 | — |
| 1943/V | 1,000 | — | 50.00 | 75.00 | 100 | — |
| 1944/VI | 1,000 | — | 50.00 | 75.00 | 100 | — |
| 1945/VII | 1,000 | — | 50.00 | 75.00 | 100 | — |
| 1946/VIII | 1,000 | — | 50.00 | 75.00 | 100 | — |

**5 LIRE** **Y# 42** **Composition:** Aluminum **Ruler:** Pope Pius XII

| Date | Mintage | F | VF | XF | Unc | BU |
|---|---|---|---|---|---|---|
| 1947/IX | 50,000 | — | 2.00 | 4.00 | 7.50 | — |
| 1948/X | 74,000 | — | 2.00 | 4.00 | 7.50 | — |
| 1949/XI | 74,000 | — | 2.00 | 4.00 | 7.50 | — |

**5 LIRE** **Y# 46** **Composition:** Aluminum **Ruler:** Pope Pius XII **Subject:** Holy Year

| Date | Mintage | F | VF | XF | Unc | BU |
|---|---|---|---|---|---|---|
| 1950 | 50,000 | — | 3.00 | 5.00 | 7.50 | — |

**5 LIRE** **Y# 51.1** **Composition:** Aluminum **Ruler:** Pope Pius XII **Obv. Legend:** AN

| Date | Mintage | F | VF | XF | Unc | BU |
|---|---|---|---|---|---|---|
| 1951/XIII | 1,500,000 | — | 0.25 | 0.50 | 1.50 | — |
| 1952/XIV | 1,500,000 | — | 0.25 | 0.50 | 1.50 | — |
| 1953/XV | 1,500,000 | — | 0.25 | 0.50 | 1.50 | — |
| 1955/XVII | 30,000 | — | 0.50 | 0.75 | 2.00 | — |

**5 LIRE** **Y# 51.2** **Composition:** Aluminum **Ruler:** Pope Pius XII **Obv. Legend:** A

| Date | Mintage | F | VF | XF | Unc | BU |
|---|---|---|---|---|---|---|
| 1956/XVIII | 30,000 | — | 0.50 | 0.75 | 2.00 | — |
| 1957/XIX | 30,000 | — | 0.50 | 0.75 | 2.00 | — |
| 1958/XX | 30,000 | — | 0.50 | 0.75 | 2.00 | — |

**5 LIRE** **Y# 60.1** **Composition:** Aluminum **Ruler:** Pope John XXIII **Obv. Legend:** AN

| Date | Mintage | F | VF | XF | Unc | BU |
|---|---|---|---|---|---|---|
| 1959/I | 25,000 | — | 1.50 | 4.00 | 7.00 | — |

**5 LIRE** **Y# 60.2** **Composition:** Aluminum **Ruler:** Pope John XXIII **Obv. Legend:** A

| Date | Mintage | F | VF | XF | Unc | BU |
|---|---|---|---|---|---|---|
| 1960/II | 25,000 | — | 1.50 | 4.00 | 7.00 | — |
| 1961/III | 25,000 | — | 1.50 | 3.00 | 4.50 | — |
| 1962/IV | 25,000 | — | 1.00 | 1.50 | 3.00 | — |

**5 LIRE** **Y# 69** **Composition:** Aluminum **Ruler:** Pope John XXIII **Subject:** 2nd Ecumenical Council

| Date | Mintage | F | VF | XF | Unc | BU |
|---|---|---|---|---|---|---|
| 1962/IV | 50,000 | — | 0.40 | 0.75 | 1.50 | — |

**5 LIRE** **Y# 78.1** **Composition:** Aluminum **Ruler:** Pope Paul VI **Obv. Legend:** AN

| Date | Mintage | F | VF | XF | Unc | BU |
|---|---|---|---|---|---|---|
| 963/I | 60,000 | — | 1.00 | 2.00 | 3.00 | — |

**5 LIRE** **Y# 78.2** **Composition:** Aluminum **Ruler:** Pope Paul VI **Obv. Legend:** A

| Date | Mintage | F | VF | XF | Unc | BU |
|---|---|---|---|---|---|---|
| 964/II | 60,000 | — | 0.50 | 1.00 | 2.00 | — |
| 965/III | 60,000 | — | 0.50 | 1.00 | 2.00 | — |

**5 LIRE** **Y# 86** **Composition:** Aluminum **Ruler:** Pope Paul VI

| Date | Mintage | F | VF | XF | Unc | BU |
|---|---|---|---|---|---|---|
| 1966/IV | 90,000 | — | 0.25 | 0.50 | 1.00 | — |

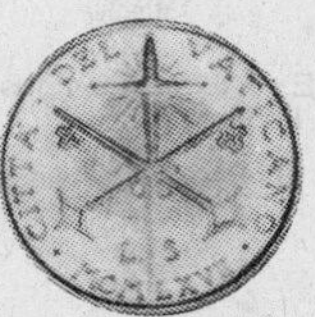

**5 LIRE** **Y# 94** **Composition:** Aluminum **Ruler:** Pope Paul VI

| Date | Mintage | F | VF | XF | Unc | BU |
|---|---|---|---|---|---|---|
| 1967/V | 100,000 | — | 0.25 | 0.50 | 1.00 | — |

**5 LIRE** **Y# 102** **Composition:** Aluminum **Ruler:** Pope Paul VI **Series:** F.A.O.

| Date | Mintage | F | VF | XF | Unc | BU |
|---|---|---|---|---|---|---|
| ND(1968)/VI | 100,000 | — | 0.25 | 0.60 | 1.00 | — |

**5 LIRE** **Y# 110** **Composition:** Aluminum **Ruler:** Pope Paul VI

| Date | Mintage | F | VF | XF | Unc | BU |
|---|---|---|---|---|---|---|
| 1969/VII | 100,000 | — | 0.25 | 0.60 | 1.00 | — |

**5 LIRE** **Y# 118** **Composition:** Aluminum **Ruler:** Pope Paul VI

| Date | Mintage | F | VF | XF | Unc | BU |
|---|---|---|---|---|---|---|
| 1970/VIII | 100,000 | — | 0.25 | 0.60 | 1.25 | — |
| 1971/IX | 110,000 | — | 0.25 | 0.60 | 1.25 | — |
| 1972/X | 110,000 | — | 0.25 | 0.60 | 1.25 | — |
| 1973/XI | 132,000 | — | 0.25 | 0.60 | 1.25 | — |
| 1974/XII | 132,000 | — | 0.25 | 0.60 | 1.25 | — |
| 1975/XIII | 150,000 | — | 0.25 | 0.60 | 1.25 | — |
| 1976/XIV | 150,000 | — | 0.25 | 0.60 | 1.25 | — |
| 1977/XV | 135,000 | — | 0.25 | 0.60 | 1.25 | — |

**5 LIRE** **Y# 126** **Composition:** Aluminum **Ruler:** Pope Paul VI **Subject:** Holy Year

| Date | Mintage | F | VF | XF | Unc | BU |
|---|---|---|---|---|---|---|
| 1975 | 380,000 | — | 0.25 | 0.35 | 1.00 | — |

**5 LIRE** **Y# 133** **Composition:** Aluminum **Ruler:** Pope Paul VI

| Date | Mintage | F | VF | XF | Unc | BU |
|---|---|---|---|---|---|---|
| 1978/XVI | 120,000 | — | 0.25 | 0.40 | 1.00 | — |

**10 LIRE** **Y# 8** **Weight:** 10.0000 g. **Composition:** 0.8350 Silver .2684 oz. ASW **Ruler:** Pope Pius XII

| Date | Mintage | F | VF | XF | Unc | BU |
|---|---|---|---|---|---|---|
| 1929/VIII | 10,000 | — | 7.50 | 15.00 | 32.00 | — |
| 1930/IX | 50,000 | — | 8.00 | 11.50 | 25.00 | — |
| 1931/X | 50,000 | — | 8.00 | 11.50 | 25.00 | — |
| 1932/XI | 50,000 | — | 8.00 | 11.50 | 25.00 | — |
| 1934/XIII | 60,000 | — | 8.00 | 11.50 | 25.00 | — |
| 1935/XIV | 50,000 | — | 8.00 | 11.50 | 25.00 | — |
| 1936/XV | 40,000 | — | 8.00 | 11.50 | 25.00 | — |
| 1937/XVI | 40,000 | — | 8.00 | 11.50 | 25.00 | — |

**10 LIRE** **Y# 18** **Weight:** 10.0000 g. **Composition:** 0.8350 Silver .2684 oz. ASW **Ruler:** Pope Pius XII **Subject:** Jubilee

| Date | Mintage | F | VF | XF | Unc | BU |
|---|---|---|---|---|---|---|
| 1933-34 | 50,000 | — | 8.00 | 15.00 | 30.00 | — |

**10 LIRE** **Y# 21** **Weight:** 10.0000 g. **Composition:** 0.8350 Silver .2684 oz. ASW **Ruler:** Cardinal Eugenio Pacelli **Subject:** Sede Vacante **Obverse:** Arms of Cardinal Pacelli

| Date | Mintage | F | VF | XF | Unc | BU |
|---|---|---|---|---|---|---|
| 1939 | 30,000 | — | 10.00 | 17.50 | 35.00 | — |

**10 LIRE** **Y# 29** **Weight:** 10.0000 g. **Composition:** 0.8350 Silver .2684 oz. ASW **Ruler:** Pope Pius XII

| Date | Mintage | F | VF | XF | Unc | BU |
|---|---|---|---|---|---|---|
| 1939/I | 10,000 | — | 12.00 | 25.00 | 45.00 | — |
| 1940/II | 10,000 | — | 12.00 | 25.00 | 45.00 | — |
| 1941/III | 4,000 | — | 20.00 | 40.00 | 80.00 | — |

**10 LIRE** **Y# 38** **Weight:** 10.0000 g. **Composition:** 0.8350 Silver .2684 oz. ASW **Ruler:** Pope Pius XII

| Date | Mintage | F | VF | XF | Unc | BU |
|---|---|---|---|---|---|---|
| 1942/IV | 4,000 | — | 25.00 | 50.00 | 90.00 | — |
| 1943/V | 1,000 | — | 60.00 | 85.00 | 125 | — |
| 1944/VI | 1,000 | — | 60.00 | 85.00 | 125 | — |
| 1945/VII | 1,000 | — | 60.00 | 85.00 | 125 | — |
| 1946/VIII | 1,000 | — | 60.00 | 85.00 | 125 | — |

**10 LIRE** **Y# 43** **Composition:** Aluminum **Ruler:** Pope Pius XII

| Date | Mintage | F | VF | XF | Unc | BU |
|---|---|---|---|---|---|---|
| 1947/IX | 50,000 | — | 3.00 | 5.00 | 8.00 | — |
| 1948/X | 60,000 | — | 3.00 | 5.00 | 8.00 | — |
| 1949/XI | 60,000 | — | 3.00 | 5.00 | 8.00 | — |

**10 LIRE** **Y# 47** **Composition:** Aluminum **Ruler:** Pope Pius XII **Subject:** Holy Year

| Date | Mintage | F | VF | XF | Unc | BU |
|---|---|---|---|---|---|---|
| 1950 | 60,000 | — | 3.00 | 5.00 | 7.50 | — |

**10 LIRE** **Y# 52.1** **Composition:** Aluminum **Ruler:** Pope Pius XII **Obv. Legend:** AN

| Date | Mintage | F | VF | XF | Unc | BU |
|---|---|---|---|---|---|---|
| 1951/XIII | 1,130,000 | — | 0.50 | 0.75 | 1.50 | — |
| 1952/XIV | 1,130,000 | — | 0.50 | 0.75 | 1.50 | — |
| 1953/XV | 1,130,000 | — | 0.50 | 0.75 | 1.50 | — |
| 1955/XVII | 80,000 | — | 0.75 | 1.50 | 3.00 | — |

**10 LIRE** **Y# 52.2** **Composition:** Aluminum **Ruler:** Pope Pius XII **Obv. Legend:** A

| Date | Mintage | F | VF | XF | Unc | BU |
|---|---|---|---|---|---|---|
| 1956/XVIII | 80,000 | — | 0.75 | 1.50 | 3.00 | — |
| 1957/XIX | 36,000 | — | 0.75 | 1.50 | 3.50 | — |
| 1958/XX | 30,000 | — | 0.75 | 1.50 | 3.50 | — |

**10 LIRE** **Y# 61.1** **Composition:** Aluminum **Ruler:** Pope John XXIII **Obv. Legend:** AN

| Date | Mintage | F | VF | XF | Unc | BU |
|---|---|---|---|---|---|---|
| 1959/I | 50,000 | — | 1.00 | 4.00 | 6.50 | — |

**10 LIRE** **Y# 61.2** **Composition:** Aluminum **Ruler:** Pope John XXIII **Obv. Legend:** A

| Date | Mintage | F | VF | XF | Unc | BU |
|---|---|---|---|---|---|---|
| 1960/II | 50,000 | — | 1.00 | 3.00 | 6.00 | — |
| 1961/III | 50,000 | — | 1.00 | 3.00 | 6.00 | — |
| 1962/IV | 50,000 | — | 1.00 | 2.00 | 4.00 | — |

**10 LIRE** **Y# 70** **Composition:** Aluminum **Ruler:** Pope John XXIII **Subject:** 2nd Ecumenical Council

| Date | Mintage | F | VF | XF | Unc | BU |
|---|---|---|---|---|---|---|
| 1962/IV | 100,000 | — | 1.00 | 1.50 | 3.00 | — |

**10 LIRE** **Y# 79.1** **Composition:** Aluminum **Ruler:** Pope Paul VI **Obv. Legend:** AN

| Date | Mintage | F | VF | XF | Unc | BU |
|---|---|---|---|---|---|---|
| 1963/I | 90,000 | — | 1.00 | 1.50 | 3.00 | — |

**10 LIRE** **Y# 79.2** **Composition:** Aluminum **Ruler:** Pope Paul VI **Obv. Legend:** A

| Date | Mintage | F | VF | XF | Unc | BU |
|---|---|---|---|---|---|---|
| 1964/II | 90,000 | — | 0.75 | 1.00 | 2.00 | — |
| 1965/III | 90,000 | — | 0.75 | 1.00 | 2.00 | — |

**10 LIRE** **Y# 87** **Composition:** Aluminum **Ruler:** Pope Paul VI

| Date | Mintage | F | VF | XF | Unc | BU |
|---|---|---|---|---|---|---|
| 1966/IV | 100,000 | — | 0.25 | 0.75 | 1.25 | — |

**10 LIRE** **Y# 95** **Composition:** Aluminum **Ruler:** Pope Paul VI

| Date | Mintage | F | VF | XF | Unc | BU |
|---|---|---|---|---|---|---|
| ND(1967)/V | 110,000 | — | 0.25 | 0.75 | 1.25 | — |

**10 LIRE** **Y# 103** **Composition:** Aluminum **Ruler:** Pope Paul VI **Series:** F.A.O.

| Date | Mintage | F | VF | XF | Unc | BU |
|---|---|---|---|---|---|---|
| ND(1968)/VI | 110,000 | — | 0.25 | 0.80 | 1.50 | — |

**10 LIRE** **Y# 111** **Composition:** Aluminum **Ruler:** Pope Paul VI

| Date | Mintage | F | VF | XF | Unc | BU |
|---|---|---|---|---|---|---|
| 1969/VII | 110,000 | — | 0.25 | 0.50 | 1.25 | — |

**10 LIRE** **Y# 119** **Composition:** Aluminum **Ruler:** Pope Paul VI

| Date | Mintage | F | VF | XF | Unc | BU |
|---|---|---|---|---|---|---|
| 1970/VIII | 110,000 | — | 0.25 | 0.50 | 1.00 | — |
| 1971/IX | 160,000 | — | 0.25 | 0.50 | 1.00 | — |
| 1972/X | 160,000 | — | 0.25 | 0.50 | 1.00 | — |
| 1973/XI | 170,000 | — | 0.25 | 0.50 | 1.00 | — |
| 1974/XII | 170,000 | — | 0.25 | 0.50 | 1.00 | — |
| 1975/XIII | 200,000 | — | 0.25 | 0.50 | 1.00 | — |
| 1976/XIV | 200,000 | — | 0.25 | 0.50 | 1.00 | — |
| 1977/XV | 200,000 | — | 0.25 | 0.50 | 1.00 | — |

**10 LIRE** **Y# 127** **Composition:** Aluminum **Ruler:** Pope Paul VI **Subject:** Holy Year **Reverse:** Noah's Ark

| Date | Mintage | F | VF | XF | Unc | BU |
|---|---|---|---|---|---|---|
| 1975 | 400,000 | — | 0.25 | 0.75 | 1.50 | — |

**10 LIRE** **Y# 134** **Composition:** Aluminum **Ruler:** Pope Paul VI

| Date | Mintage | F | VF | XF | Unc | BU |
|---|---|---|---|---|---|---|
| 1978/XVI | 250,000 | — | 0.25 | 0.50 | 1.00 | — |

**10 LIRE** **Y# 143** **Composition:** Aluminum **Ruler:** Pope John Paul II

| Date | Mintage | F | VF | XF | Unc | BU |
|---|---|---|---|---|---|---|
| 1979/I | 250,000 | — | 0.25 | 0.50 | 1.00 | — |
| 1980/II | 170,000 | — | 0.25 | 0.50 | 1.00 | — |

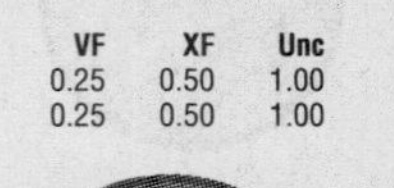

**10 LIRE** **Y# 155** **Composition:** Aluminum **Ruler:** Pope John Paul II **Reverse:** Jesus given water at the well

| Date | Mintage | F | VF | XF | Unc | BU |
|---|---|---|---|---|---|---|
| 1981/III | 170,000 | — | 0.25 | 0.50 | 1.00 | — |

**10 LIRE** **Y# 161** **Composition:** Aluminum **Ruler:** Pope John Paul II **Subject:** Creation of Woman **Obverse:** Similar to 1000 Lire, Y#167

| Date | Mintage | F | VF | XF | Unc | BU |
|---|---|---|---|---|---|---|
| 1982/IV | 220,000 | — | 0.25 | 0.50 | 1.00 | — |

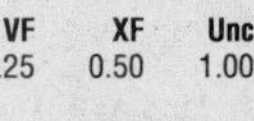

**10 LIRE** **Y# 170** **Composition:** Aluminum **Ruler:** Pope John Paul II **Subject:** Work and Teaching

| Date | Mintage | F | VF | XF | Unc | BU |
|---|---|---|---|---|---|---|
| 1983/V | 110,000 | — | 0.25 | 0.50 | 1.00 | — |

**10 LIRE** **Y#177** **Composition:** Aluminum **Ruler:** Pope John Paul II **Subject:** Year of Peace **Obverse:** Similar to 1000 Lire, Y#183

| Date | Mintage | F | VF | XF | Unc | BU |
|---|---|---|---|---|---|---|
| 1984/VI | 110,000 | — | 0.25 | 0.50 | 1.00 | — |

**10 LIRE** **Y#185** **Composition:** Aluminum **Ruler:** Pope John Paul II

| Date | Mintage | F | VF | XF | Unc | BU |
|---|---|---|---|---|---|---|
| 1985/VII | 90,000 | — | 0.25 | 0.50 | 1.00 | — |

**10 LIRE** **Y#192** **Composition:** Aluminum **Ruler:** Pope John Paul II

| Date | Mintage | F | VF | XF | Unc | BU |
|---|---|---|---|---|---|---|
| 1986/VIII | 90,000 | — | 0.25 | 0.50 | 1.00 | — |

**10 LIRE** **Y#199** **Composition:** Aluminum **Ruler:** Pope John Paul II **Obverse:** Similar to 200 Lire, Y#203 **Reverse:** Basilica behind Pieta Statue

| Date | Mintage | F | VF | XF | Unc | BU |
|---|---|---|---|---|---|---|
| 1987/IX | — | — | 0.25 | 0.50 | 1.00 | — |

**10 LIRE** **Y#206** **Composition:** Aluminum **Ruler:** Pope John Paul II **Subject:** Temptation of Adam and Eve **Obverse:** Similar to 200 Lire, Y#210

| Date | Mintage | F | VF | XF | Unc | BU |
|---|---|---|---|---|---|---|
| 1988/X | — | — | 0.25 | 0.50 | 1.00 | — |

**10 LIRE** **Y#213** **Composition:** Aluminum **Ruler:** Pope John Paul II **Subject:** Jesus the Teacher

| Date | Mintage | F | VF | XF | Unc | BU |
|---|---|---|---|---|---|---|
| 1989/XI | — | — | 0.25 | 0.50 | 1.00 | — |

**10 LIRE** **Y#220** **Composition:** Aluminum **Ruler:** Pope John Paul II **Subject:** Saints Peter and Paul

| Date | Mintage | F | VF | XF | Unc | BU |
|---|---|---|---|---|---|---|
| 1990/XII | — | — | 0.25 | 0.50 | 1.00 | — |

**10 LIRE** **Y#228** **Composition:** Aluminum **Ruler:** Pope John Paul II

| Date | Mintage | F | VF | XF | Unc | BU |
|---|---|---|---|---|---|---|
| 1991/XIII | — | — | 0.25 | 0.50 | 1.00 | — |

**10 LIRE** **Y#236** **Composition:** Aluminum **Ruler:** Pope John Paul II **Reverse:** Bee on flower

| Date | Mintage | F | VF | XF | Unc | BU |
|---|---|---|---|---|---|---|
| 1992/XIV | — | — | 0.25 | 0.50 | 1.00 | — |

**10 LIRE** **Y#244** **Composition:** Aluminum **Ruler:** Pope John Paul II **Reverse:** Sailboat

| Date | Mintage | F | VF | XF | Unc | BU |
|---|---|---|---|---|---|---|
| 1993/XV | — | — | 0.25 | 0.50 | 1.00 | — |

**10 LIRE** **Y#252** **Composition:** Aluminum **Ruler:** Pope John Paul II **Reverse:** Planting trees

| Date | Mintage | F | VF | XF | Unc | BU |
|---|---|---|---|---|---|---|
| 1994/XVI | — | — | 0.25 | 0.50 | 1.00 | — |

**10 LIRE** **Y#262** **Composition:** Aluminum **Ruler:** Pope John Paul II **Reverse:** Preaching

| Date | Mintage | F | VF | XF | Unc | BU |
|---|---|---|---|---|---|---|
| 1995 | — | — | 0.25 | 0.50 | 1.00 | — |

**10 LIRE** **Y#272** **Composition:** Aluminum **Ruler:** Pope John Paul II **Subject:** Child Carried to Peace

| Date | Mintage | F | VF | XF | Unc | BU |
|---|---|---|---|---|---|---|
| 1996 | — | — | 0.25 | 0.50 | 1.00 | — |

**10 LIRE** **Y#280** **Composition:** Aluminum **Ruler:** Pope John Paul II **Reverse:** Angel and man sowing seeds

| Date | Mintage | F | VF | XF | Unc | BU |
|---|---|---|---|---|---|---|
| 1997/XIX | — | — | 0.25 | 0.50 | 1.00 | — |

**10 LIRE** **Y#293** **Composition:** Aluminum **Ruler:** Pope John Paul II **Obverse:** Pope with crucifix **Reverse:** Three figures

| Date | Mintage | F | VF | XF | Unc | BU |
|---|---|---|---|---|---|---|
| 1998 | — | — | 0.25 | 0.50 | 1.00 | — |

**10 LIRE** **Y#305** **Weight:** 1.6000 g. **Composition:** Aluminum **Ruler:** Pope John Paul II **Subject:** Right to Life - Motherhood **Obverse:** Pope John Paul II bust right **Reverse:** Mother with baby and child **Edge:** Plain **Size:** 23.3 mm. **Note:** Struck at Rome.

| Date | Mintage | F | VF | XF | Unc | BU |
|---|---|---|---|---|---|---|
| 1999 | — | — | 0.25 | 0.50 | 1.00 | — |

**10 LIRE** **Y#323** **Weight:** 1.6000 g. **Composition:** Aluminum **Ruler:** Pope John Paul II **Obverse:** Papal arms **Reverse:** Pope lifting child **Edge:** Plain **Size:** 23.2 mm.

| Date | Mintage | F | VF | XF | Unc | BU |
|---|---|---|---|---|---|---|
| XXII(2000) | — | — | — | — | 1.00 | — |

**10 LIRE** **Y#332** **Weight:** 3.5700 g. **Composition:** Brass **Ruler:** Pope John Paul II **Subject:** Pope Pius XI **Obverse:** Portrait **Reverse:** Papal arms **Edge:** Plain **Size:** 21.2 mm.

| Date | Mintage | F | VF | XF | Unc | BU |
|---|---|---|---|---|---|---|
| 2001 | — | — | — | — | 1.00 | — |

**20 LIRE** **Y#A52.1** **Composition:** Aluminum-Bronze **Ruler:** Pope Pius XII **Obv. Legend:** A

| Date | Mintage | F | VF | XF | Unc | BU |
|---|---|---|---|---|---|---|
| 1957/XIX | 20,000 | — | 0.75 | 1.25 | 2.50 | — |

**20 LIRE** **Y#A52.2** **Composition:** Aluminum-Bronze **Ruler:** Pope Pius XII **Obv. Legend:** AN

| Date | Mintage | F | VF | XF | Unc | BU |
|---|---|---|---|---|---|---|
| 1958/XX | 60,000 | — | 0.75 | 1.25 | 2.50 | — |

**20 LIRE** **Y# 62.1** **Composition:** Aluminum-Bronze **Ruler:** Pope John XXIII **Obv. Legend:** AN

| Date | Mintage | F | VF | XF | Unc | BU |
|---|---|---|---|---|---|---|
| 1959/I | 50,000 | — | 0.75 | 1.25 | 2.50 | — |

**20 LIRE** **Y# 62.2** **Composition:** Aluminum-Bronze **Ruler:** Pope John XXIII **Obv. Legend:** A

| Date | Mintage | F | VF | XF | Unc | BU |
|---|---|---|---|---|---|---|
| 1960/II | 50,000 | — | 0.75 | 1.25 | 2.50 | — |
| 1961/III | 50,000 | — | 0.75 | 1.00 | 2.50 | — |
| 1962/IV | 50,000 | — | 0.75 | 1.00 | 2.50 | — |

**20 LIRE** **Y# 71** **Composition:** Aluminum-Bronze **Ruler:** Pope John XXIII **Subject:** 2nd Ecumenical Council

| Date | Mintage | F | VF | XF | Unc | BU |
|---|---|---|---|---|---|---|
| 1962/IV | 100,000 | — | 0.75 | 1.00 | 2.00 | — |

**20 LIRE** **Y# 80.1** **Composition:** Aluminum-Bronze **Ruler:** Pope Paul VI **Obv. Legend:** AN

| Date | Mintage | F | VF | XF | Unc | BU |
|---|---|---|---|---|---|---|
| 1963/I | 90,000 | — | 1.00 | 2.00 | 4.00 | — |
| 1964/II | 90,000 | — | 0.75 | 1.00 | 2.00 | — |

**20 LIRE** **Y# 80.2** **Composition:** Aluminum-Bronze **Ruler:** Pope Paul VI **Obv. Legend:** A

| Date | Mintage | F | VF | XF | Unc | BU |
|---|---|---|---|---|---|---|
| 1965/III | 90,000 | — | 0.75 | 1.00 | 2.00 | — |

**20 LIRE** **Y# 88** **Composition:** Aluminum-Bronze **Ruler:** Pope Paul VI

| Date | Mintage | F | VF | XF | Unc | BU |
|---|---|---|---|---|---|---|
| 1966/IV | 100,000 | — | 0.25 | 0.75 | 1.25 | — |

**20 LIRE** **Y# 96** **Composition:** Aluminum-Bronze **Ruler:** Pope Paul VI **Subject:** Saints Peter and Paul

| Date | Mintage | F | VF | XF | Unc | BU |
|---|---|---|---|---|---|---|
| ND(1967)/V | 105,000 | — | 0.25 | 0.75 | 1.25 | — |

**20 LIRE** **Y# 104** **Composition:** Aluminum-Bronze **Ruler:** Pope Paul VI **Series:** F.A.O.

| Date | Mintage | F | VF | XF | Unc | BU |
|---|---|---|---|---|---|---|
| ND(1968)/VI | 105,000 | — | 0.25 | 0.75 | 1.50 | — |

**20 LIRE** **Y# 112** **Composition:** Aluminum-Bronze **Ruler:** Pope Paul VI

| Date | Mintage | F | VF | XF | Unc | BU |
|---|---|---|---|---|---|---|
| 1969/VII | 105,000 | — | 0.25 | 0.60 | 1.25 | — |

**20 LIRE** **Y# 120** **Composition:** Aluminum-Bronze **Ruler:** Pope Paul VI

| Date | Mintage | F | VF | XF | Unc | BU |
|---|---|---|---|---|---|---|
| 1970/VIII | 105,000 | — | 0.25 | 0.50 | 1.25 | — |
| 1971/IX | 170,000 | — | 0.25 | 0.50 | 1.00 | — |
| 1972/X | 170,000 | — | 0.25 | 0.50 | 1.00 | — |
| 1973/XI | — | — | 0.25 | 0.50 | 1.00 | — |
| 1974/XII | — | — | 0.25 | 0.50 | 1.00 | — |
| 1975/XIII | 250,000 | — | 0.25 | 0.50 | 1.00 | — |
| 1976/XIV | 250,000 | — | 0.25 | 0.50 | 1.00 | — |
| 1977/XV | 250,000 | — | 0.25 | 0.50 | 1.00 | — |

**20 LIRE** **Y# 128** **Composition:** Aluminum-Bronze **Ruler:** Pope Paul VI **Subject:** Holy Year

| Date | Mintage | F | VF | XF | Unc | BU |
|---|---|---|---|---|---|---|
| 1975 | 400,000 | — | 0.25 | 0.50 | 1.25 | — |

**20 LIRE** **Y# 135** **Composition:** Aluminum-Bronze **Ruler:** Pope Paul VI **Subject:** Prodigal Son Parable

| Date | Mintage | F | VF | XF | Unc | BU |
|---|---|---|---|---|---|---|
| 1978/XVI | 120,000 | — | 0.25 | 0.50 | 1.25 | — |

**20 LIRE** **Y# 144** **Composition:** Aluminum-Bronze **Ruler:** Pope John Paul II

| Date | Mintage | F | VF | XF | Unc | BU |
|---|---|---|---|---|---|---|
| 1979/I | 120,000 | — | 0.25 | 0.50 | 1.00 | — |
| 1980/II | 265,000 | — | 0.25 | 0.50 | 1.00 | — |

**20 LIRE** **Y# 156** **Composition:** Aluminum-Bronze **Ruler:** Pope John Paul II

| Date | Mintage | F | VF | XF | Unc | BU |
|---|---|---|---|---|---|---|
| 1981/III | 265,000 | — | 0.25 | 0.50 | 1.00 | — |

**20 LIRE** **Y# 162** **Composition:** Aluminum-Bronze **Ruler:** Pope John Paul II **Subject:** Marriage **Obverse:** Similar to 1000 Lire, Y#167

| Date | Mintage | F | VF | XF | Unc | BU |
|---|---|---|---|---|---|---|
| 1982/IV | 360,000 | — | 0.25 | 0.50 | 1.00 | — |

**20 LIRE** **Y# 171** **Composition:** Aluminum-Bronze **Ruler:** Pope John Paul II **Subject:** Incarnation of the Word

| Date | Mintage | F | VF | XF | Unc | BU |
|---|---|---|---|---|---|---|
| 1983/V | 170,000 | — | 0.25 | 0.50 | 1.00 | — |

**20 LIRE** **Y# 178** **Composition:** Aluminum-Bronze **Ruler:** Pope John Paul II **Subject:** Year of Peace **Obverse:** Similar to 1000 Lire, Y#183

| Date | Mintage | F | VF | XF | Unc | BU |
|---|---|---|---|---|---|---|
| 1984/VI | 170,000 | — | 0.25 | 0.50 | 1.00 | — |

**20 LIRE** **Y# 186** **Composition:** Aluminum-Bronze **Ruler:** Pope John Paul II

| Date | Mintage | F | VF | XF | Unc | BU |
|---|---|---|---|---|---|---|
| 1985/VII | 255,000 | — | 0.25 | 0.50 | 1.00 | — |

**20 LIRE** **Y# 193** **Composition:** Aluminum-Bronze **Ruler:** Pope John Paul II **Obverse:** Similar to 200 Lire, Y#196

| Date | Mintage | F | VF | XF | Unc | BU |
|---|---|---|---|---|---|---|
| 1986/VIII | 100,000 | — | 0.25 | 0.50 | 1.00 | — |

**20 LIRE** **Y# 200** **Composition:** Aluminum-Bronze **Ruler:** Pope John Paul II **Obverse:** Similar to 200 Lire, Y#203 **Reverse:** Assumption of Mother Mary into heaven

| Date | Mintage | F | VF | XF | Unc | BU |
|---|---|---|---|---|---|---|
| 1987/IX | — | — | 0.25 | 0.50 | 1.00 | — |

**20 LIRE** **Y# 207** **Composition:** Aluminum-Bronze **Ruler:** Pope John Paul II **Subject:** Temptation of Adam and Eve **Note:** Similar to 200 Lire, Y#210.

| Date | Mintage | F | VF | XF | Unc | BU |
|---|---|---|---|---|---|---|
| 1988/X | — | — | 0.25 | 0.50 | 1.00 | — |

**20 LIRE** **Y# 214** **Composition:** Aluminum-Bronze **Ruler:** Pope John Paul II **Subject:** The Harvest

| Date | Mintage | F | VF | XF | Unc | BU |
|---|---|---|---|---|---|---|
| 1989/XI | — | — | 0.25 | 0.50 | 1.00 | — |

**20 LIRE** **Y# 221** **Composition:** Aluminum-Bronze **Ruler:** Pope John Paul II **Subject:** Pope John Paul II and Eastern Rite Bishop

| Date | Mintage | F | VF | XF | Unc | BU |
|---|---|---|---|---|---|---|
| 1990/XII | — | — | 0.25 | 0.50 | 1.00 | — |

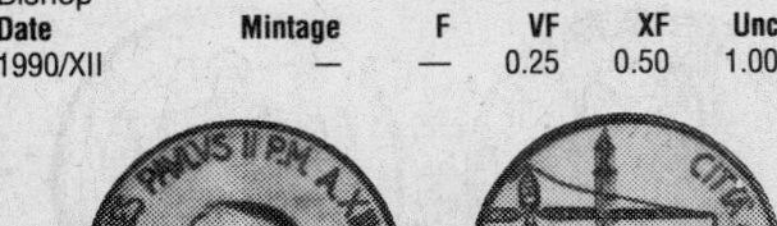

**20 LIRE** **Y# 229** **Composition:** Aluminum-Bronze **Ruler:** Pope John Paul II **Subject:** Crane and Buildings

| Date | Mintage | F | VF | XF | Unc | BU |
|---|---|---|---|---|---|---|
| 1991/XIII | — | — | 0.25 | 0.50 | 1.00 | — |

**20 LIRE** **Y# 237** **Composition:** Aluminum-Bronze **Ruler:** Pope John Paul II **Reverse:** 3 children

| Date | Mintage | F | VF | XF | Unc | BU |
|---|---|---|---|---|---|---|
| 1992/XIV | — | — | 0.25 | 0.50 | 1.00 | — |

**20 LIRE** **Y# 245** **Composition:** Aluminum-Bronze **Ruler:** Pope John Paul II **Reverse:** Crucifix

| Date | Mintage | F | VF | XF | Unc | BU |
|---|---|---|---|---|---|---|
| 1993/XV | — | — | 0.25 | 0.50 | 1.00 | — |

**20 LIRE** **Y# 253** **Composition:** Aluminum-Bronze **Ruler:** Pope John Paul II **Reverse:** Hospital patient with visitors

| Date | Mintage | F | VF | XF | Unc | BU |
|---|---|---|---|---|---|---|
| 1994/XVI | — | — | 0.25 | 0.50 | 1.00 | — |

**20 LIRE** **Y# 263** **Composition:** Aluminum-Bronze **Ruler:** Pope John Paul II **Subject:** Euthanasia

| Date | Mintage | F | VF | XF | Unc | BU |
|---|---|---|---|---|---|---|
| 1995 | — | — | 0.25 | 0.50 | 1.00 | — |

**20 LIRE** **Y# 273** **Composition:** Aluminum-Bronze **Ruler:** Pope John Paul II **Reverse:** Parents praising child

| Date | Mintage | F | VF | XF | Unc | BU |
|---|---|---|---|---|---|---|
| 1996 | — | — | 0.25 | 0.50 | 1.00 | — |

**20 LIRE** **Y# 281** **Composition:** Aluminum-Bronze **Ruler:** Pope John Paul II **Reverse:** Jesus teaching with book

| Date | Mintage | F | VF | XF | Unc | BU |
|---|---|---|---|---|---|---|
| 1997/XIX | — | — | 0.25 | 0.50 | 1.00 | — |

**20 LIRE** **Y# 294** **Composition:** Aluminum-Bronze **Ruler:** Pope John Paul II **Obverse:** Pope with crucifix **Reverse:** Family and sun

| Date | Mintage | F | VF | XF | Unc | BU |
|---|---|---|---|---|---|---|
| 1998 | — | — | 0.25 | 0.50 | 1.00 | — |

**20 LIRE** **Y# 306** **Weight:** 3.6000 g. **Composition:** Aluminum-Bronze **Ruler:** Pope John Paul II **Subject:** Work - The Right to Fulfill One's Potential **Obverse:** Pope John Paul II bust right **Reverse:** Workers **Edge:** Plain **Size:** 21.3 mm. **Note:** Struck at Rome.

| Date | Mintage | F | VF | XF | Unc | BU |
|---|---|---|---|---|---|---|
| 1999 | — | — | 0.25 | 0.50 | 1.00 | — |

**20 LIRE** **Y# 324** **Weight:** 3.5700 g. **Composition:** Brass **Ruler:** Pope John Paul II **Obverse:** Papal arms **Reverse:** Pope star gazing **Edge:** Plain **Size:** 21.2 mm.

| Date | Mintage | F | VF | XF | Unc | BU |
|---|---|---|---|---|---|---|
| XXII(2000) | — | — | — | — | 1.00 | — |

**50 LIRE** **Y# 54.1** **Composition:** Stainless Steel **Ruler:** Pope Pius XII **Obv. Legend:** AN

| Date | Mintage | F | VF | XF | Unc | BU |
|---|---|---|---|---|---|---|
| 1955/XVII | 180,000 | — | 1.00 | 1.50 | 3.00 | — |

**50 LIRE** **Y# 54.2** **Composition:** Stainless Steel **Ruler:** Pope Pius XII **Obv. Legend:** A

| Date | Mintage | F | VF | XF | Unc | BU |
|---|---|---|---|---|---|---|
| 1956/XVIII | 180,000 | — | 1.00 | 1.50 | 3.00 | — |
| 1957/XIX | 180,000 | — | 1.00 | 1.50 | 3.00 | — |
| 1958/XX | 60,000 | — | 1.00 | 1.50 | 3.00 | — |

**50 LIRE** **Y# 63.1** **Composition:** Stainless Steel **Ruler:** Pope John XXIII **Obverse:** Continuous legend

| Date | Mintage | F | VF | XF | Unc | BU |
|---|---|---|---|---|---|---|
| 1959/I | 100,000 | — | 1.00 | 2.50 | 7.00 | — |

**50 LIRE** **Y# 63.2** **Composition:** Stainless Steel **Ruler:** Pope John XXIII **Obverse:** Regnal year under bust

| Date | Mintage | F | VF | XF | Unc | BU |
|---|---|---|---|---|---|---|
| 1960/II | 100,000 | — | 1.00 | 2.50 | 6.50 | — |
| 1961/III | 100,000 | — | 1.00 | 2.00 | 3.50 | — |
| 1962/IV | 100,000 | — | 1.00 | 2.00 | 3.50 | — |

**50 LIRE** **Y# 72** **Composition:** Stainless Steel **Ruler:** Pope John XXIII **Subject:** 2nd Ecumenical Council

| Date | Mintage | F | VF | XF | Unc | BU |
|---|---|---|---|---|---|---|
| 1962/IV | 200,000 | — | 0.50 | 1.25 | 2.50 | — |

**50 LIRE** **Y# 81.1** **Composition:** Stainless Steel **Ruler:** Pope Paul VI **Subject:** Spes - Hope **Obv. Legend:** AN

| Date | Mintage | F | VF | XF | Unc | BU |
|---|---|---|---|---|---|---|
| 1963/I | 120,000 | — | 1.00 | 2.00 | 4.00 | — |
| 1964/II | 120,000 | — | 0.75 | 1.50 | 3.00 | — |

**50 LIRE** **Y# 81.2** **Composition:** Stainless Steel **Ruler:** Pope Paul VI **Obv. Legend:** A

| Date | Mintage | F | VF | XF | Unc | BU |
|---|---|---|---|---|---|---|
| 1965/III | 120,000 | — | 0.50 | 1.00 | 2.00 | — |

**50 LIRE** **Y# 89** **Composition:** Stainless Steel **Ruler:** Pope Paul VI

| Date | Mintage | F | VF | XF | Unc | BU |
|---|---|---|---|---|---|---|
| 1966/IV | 150,000 | — | 0.50 | 1.00 | 2.00 | — |

**50 LIRE** **Y# 97** **Composition:** Stainless Steel **Ruler:** Pope Paul VI **Subject:** Conversion of Saint Paul

| Date | Mintage | F | VF | XF | Unc | BU |
|---|---|---|---|---|---|---|
| 1967/V | 190,000 | — | 0.50 | 1.00 | 2.00 | — |

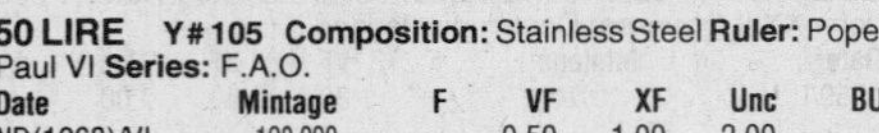

**50 LIRE** **Y# 105** **Composition:** Stainless Steel **Ruler:** Pope Paul VI **Series:** F.A.O.

| Date | Mintage | F | VF | XF | Unc | BU |
|---|---|---|---|---|---|---|
| ND(1968)/VI | 190,000 | — | 0.50 | 1.00 | 2.00 | — |

**50 LIRE** **Y# 113** **Composition:** Stainless Steel **Ruler:** Pope Paul VI **Reverse:** Angel

| Date | Mintage | F | VF | XF | Unc | BU |
|---|---|---|---|---|---|---|
| 1969/VII | 190,000 | — | 0.50 | 1.00 | 2.00 | — |

**50 LIRE** **Y# 121** **Composition:** Stainless Steel **Ruler:** Pope Paul VI

| Date | Mintage | F | VF | XF | Unc | BU |
|---|---|---|---|---|---|---|
| 1970/VIII | 190,000 | — | 0.25 | 0.75 | 1.75 | — |
| 1971/IX | 700,000 | — | 0.25 | 0.75 | 1.50 | — |
| 1972/X | 700,000 | — | 0.25 | 0.75 | 1.50 | — |
| 1973/XI | 750,000 | — | 0.25 | 0.75 | 1.50 | — |
| 1974/XII | 750,000 | — | 0.25 | 0.75 | 1.50 | — |
| 1975/XII | 600,000 | — | 0.25 | 0.75 | 1.50 | — |
| 1976/XIV | 600,000 | — | 0.25 | 0.75 | 1.50 | — |

**50 LIRE** **Y# 129** **Composition:** Stainless Steel **Ruler:** Pope Paul VI **Subject:** Holy Year

| Date | Mintage | F | VF | XF | Unc | BU |
|---|---|---|---|---|---|---|
| 1975 | 500,000 | — | 0.40 | 0.75 | 1.50 | — |

**50 LIRE** **Y# A121** **Composition:** Stainless Steel **Ruler:** Pope Paul VI **Reverse:** Wheat and grapes

| Date | Mintage | F | VF | XF | Unc | BU |
|---|---|---|---|---|---|---|
| 1977/XV | 600,000 | — | 0.25 | 0.35 | 1.25 | — |

**50 LIRE** **Y# 136** **Composition:** Stainless Steel **Ruler:** Pope Paul VI **Subject:** 16th Year

| Date | Mintage | F | VF | XF | Unc | BU |
|---|---|---|---|---|---|---|
| 1978/XVI | 223,000 | — | 0.25 | 0.50 | 1.25 | — |

**50 LIRE** **Y# 145** **Composition:** Stainless Steel **Ruler:** Pope John Paul II

| Date | Mintage | F | VF | XF | Unc | BU |
|---|---|---|---|---|---|---|
| 1979/I | 223,000 | — | 0.25 | 0.50 | 1.25 | — |
| 1980/II | 250,000 | — | 0.25 | 0.50 | 1.25 | — |

**50 LIRE** **Y# 157** **Composition:** Stainless Steel **Ruler:** Pope John Paul II

| Date | Mintage | F | VF | XF | Unc | BU |
|---|---|---|---|---|---|---|
| 1981/III | 240,000 | — | 0.25 | 0.50 | 1.25 | — |

**50 LIRE** **Y# 163** **Composition:** Stainless Steel **Ruler:** Pope John Paul II **Subject:** Maternity **Obverse:** Similar to 1000 Lire, Y#167

| Date | Mintage | F | VF | XF | Unc | BU |
|---|---|---|---|---|---|---|
| 1982/IV | 400,000 | — | 0.25 | 0.50 | 1.25 | — |

**50 LIRE** **Y# 172** **Composition:** Stainless Steel **Ruler:** Pope John Paul II **Subject:** Banishment of Adam and Eve

| Date | Mintage | F | VF | XF | Unc | BU |
|---|---|---|---|---|---|---|
| 1983/V | 300,000 | — | 0.25 | 0.50 | 1.25 | — |

**50 LIRE** **Y# 179** **Composition:** Stainless Steel **Ruler:** Pope John Paul II **Subject:** Year of Peace **Obverse:** Similar to 1000 Lire, Y#183

| Date | Mintage | F | VF | XF | Unc | BU |
|---|---|---|---|---|---|---|
| 1984/VI | 300,000 | — | 0.25 | 0.50 | 1.25 | — |

**50 LIRE** **Y# 187** **Composition:** Stainless Steel **Ruler:** Pope John Paul II

| Date | Mintage | F | VF | XF | Unc | BU |
|---|---|---|---|---|---|---|
| 1985/VII | 360,000 | — | 0.25 | 0.50 | 1.25 | — |

**50 LIRE** **Y# 194** **Composition:** Stainless Steel **Ruler:** Pope John Paul II **Obverse:** Similar to 200 Lire, Y#196

| Date | Mintage | F | VF | XF | Unc | BU |
|---|---|---|---|---|---|---|
| 1986/VIII | 100,000 | — | 0.25 | 0.50 | 1.25 | — |

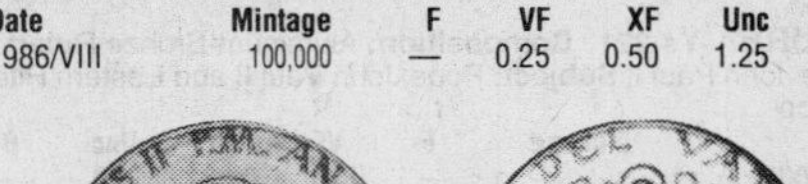

**50 LIRE** **Y# 201** **Composition:** Stainless Steel **Ruler:** Pope John Paul II **Obverse:** Similar to 200 LIre, Y#203 **Reverse:** Mother Mary protecting kneeling sinners

| Date | Mintage | F | VF | XF | Unc | BU |
|---|---|---|---|---|---|---|
| 1987/IX | — | — | 0.25 | 0.50 | 1.25 | — |

**50 LIRE** **Y# 208** **Composition:** Stainless Steel **Ruler:** Pope John Paul II **Subject:** Creation of Eve From Adam's Rib

| Date | Mintage | F | VF | XF | Unc | BU |
|---|---|---|---|---|---|---|
| 1988 | — | — | 0.25 | 0.50 | 1.25 | — |

**50 LIRE** **Y# 215** **Composition:** Stainless Steel **Ruler:** Pope John Paul II **Subject:** Human Solidarity

| Date | Mintage | F | VF | XF | Unc | BU |
|---|---|---|---|---|---|---|
| 1989/XI | — | — | 0.25 | 0.50 | 1.25 | — |

**50 LIRE** **Y# 222** **Composition:** Stainless Steel **Ruler:** Pope John Paul II **Reverse:** Radiant cross in open door

| Date | Mintage | F | VF | XF | Unc | BU |
|---|---|---|---|---|---|---|
| 1990/XII | — | — | 0.25 | 0.50 | 1.25 | — |

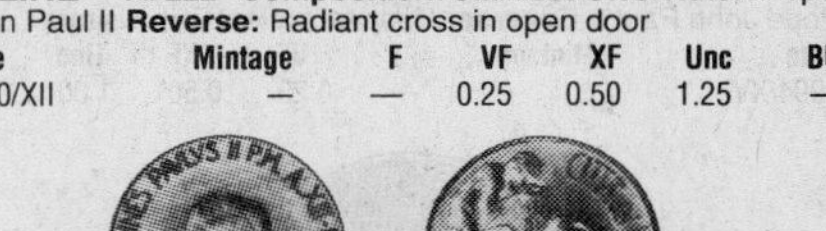

**50 LIRE** **Y# 230** **Composition:** Stainless Steel **Ruler:** Pope John Paul II **Reverse:** Baptism scene

| Date | Mintage | F | VF | XF | Unc | BU |
|---|---|---|---|---|---|---|
| 1991/XIII | — | — | 0.25 | 0.50 | 1.25 | — |

**50 LIRE** **Y# 238** **Composition:** Stainless Steel **Ruler:** Pope John Paul II **Reverse:** Cross as balance scale between agriculture and industry

| Date | Mintage | F | VF | XF | Unc | BU |
|---|---|---|---|---|---|---|
| 1992/XIV | — | — | 0.25 | 0.50 | 1.25 | — |

**50 LIRE** **Y# 246** **Composition:** Stainless Steel **Ruler:** Pope John Paul II **Reverse:** Chalice

| Date | Mintage | F | VF | XF | Unc | BU |
|---|---|---|---|---|---|---|
| 1993/XV | — | — | 0.25 | 0.50 | 1.25 | — |

**50 LIRE** **Y# 254** **Composition:** Stainless Steel **Ruler:** Pope John Paul II **Reverse:** Hands and prison bars

| Date | Mintage | F | VF | XF | Unc | BU |
|---|---|---|---|---|---|---|
| 1994/XVI | — | — | 0.25 | 0.50 | 1.25 | — |

**50 LIRE** **Y# 264** **Composition:** Stainless Steel **Ruler:** Pope John Paul II **Reverse:** Dragon on Prone Woman (Abortion)

| Date | Mintage | F | VF | XF | Unc | BU |
|---|---|---|---|---|---|---|
| 1995 | — | — | 0.25 | 0.50 | 1.25 | — |

**50 LIRE** **Y# 274** **Composition:** Copper-Nickel **Ruler:** Pope John Paul II **Reverse:** Guardian angel protecting child

| Date | Mintage | F | VF | XF | Unc | BU |
|---|---|---|---|---|---|---|
| 1996 | — | — | 0.25 | 0.50 | 1.25 | — |

**50 LIRE** **Y# 282** **Composition:** Copper-Nickel **Ruler:** Pope John Paul II **Reverse:** One man with lowered sword, the other with dove

| Date | Mintage | F | VF | XF | Unc | BU |
|---|---|---|---|---|---|---|
| 1997/XIX | — | — | 0.25 | 0.50 | 1.25 | — |

**50 LIRE** **Y# 295** **Composition:** Copper-Nickel **Ruler:** Pope John Paul II **Obverse:** Pope with crucifix **Reverse:** Two figures and hand

| Date | Mintage | F | VF | XF | Unc | BU |
|---|---|---|---|---|---|---|
| 1998 | — | — | 0.25 | 0.50 | 1.25 | — |

**50 LIRE** **Y# 307** **Weight:** 4.4600 g. **Composition:** Copper-Nickel **Ruler:** Pope John Paul II **Subject:** Ecosystem - Agriculture **Obverse:** Pope John Paul II bust right **Reverse:** Agricultural workers **Edge:** Plain **Size:** 19.2 mm. **Note:** Struck at Rome.

| Date | Mintage | F | VF | XF | Unc | BU |
|---|---|---|---|---|---|---|
| 1999 | — | — | 0.25 | 0.50 | 1.25 | — |

**50 LIRE** **Y# 325** **Weight:** 4.5000 g. **Composition:** Copper-Nickel **Ruler:** Pope John Paul II **Obverse:** Papal arms **Reverse:** Pope about to kiss ground **Edge:** Plain **Size:** 19.2 mm.

| Date | Mintage | F | VF | XF | Unc | BU |
|---|---|---|---|---|---|---|
| XXII(2000) | — | — | — | — | 1.25 | — |

**50 LIRE** **Y# 333** **Weight:** 4.5000 g. **Composition:** Copper-Nickel **Ruler:** Pope John Paul II **Subject:** Pope Pius XI **Obverse:** Portrait **Reverse:** Papal arms **Edge:** Plain **Size:** 19.2 mm.

| Date | Mintage | F | VF | XF | Unc | BU |
|---|---|---|---|---|---|---|
| 2001 | — | — | — | — | 1.25 | — |

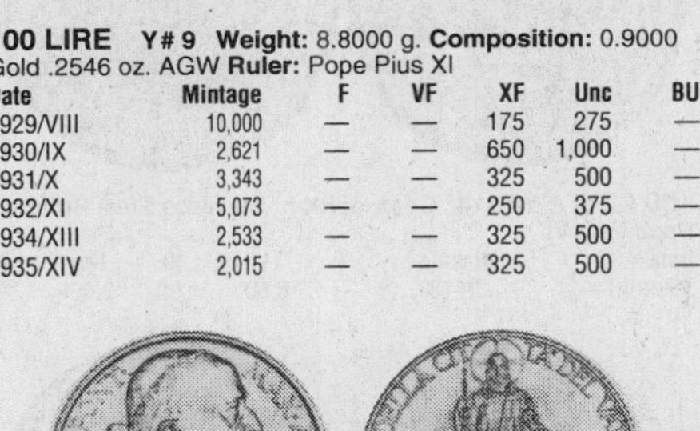

**100 LIRE** **Y# 9** **Weight:** 8.8000 g. **Composition:** 0.9000 Gold .2546 oz. AGW **Ruler:** Pope Pius XI

| Date | Mintage | F | VF | XF | Unc | BU |
|---|---|---|---|---|---|---|
| 1929/VIII | 10,000 | — | — | 175 | 275 | — |
| 1930/IX | 2,621 | — | — | 650 | 1,000 | — |
| 1931/X | 3,343 | — | — | 325 | 500 | — |
| 1932/XI | 5,073 | — | — | 250 | 375 | — |
| 1934/XIII | 2,533 | — | — | 325 | 500 | — |
| 1935/XIV | 2,015 | — | — | 325 | 500 | — |

**100 LIRE** **Y# 19** **Weight:** 8.8000 g. **Composition:** 0.9000 Gold .2546 oz. AGW **Ruler:** Pope Pius XI **Subject:** Jubilee

| Date | Mintage | F | VF | XF | Unc | BU |
|---|---|---|---|---|---|---|
| 1933-34 | 23,000 | — | — | 175 | 245 | — |

**100 LIRE** **Y# 10** **Weight:** 5.1900 g. **Composition:** 0.9000 Gold .1501 oz. AGW **Ruler:** Pope Pius XI

| Date | Mintage | F | VF | XF | Unc | BU |
|---|---|---|---|---|---|---|
| 1936/XV | 8,239 | — | — | 220 | 275 | — |
| 1937/XVI | 2,000 | — | — | 2,000 | 3,000 | — |
| 1938 Rare | 6 | — | — | — | — | — |

**100 LIRE** **Y# 30.1** **Weight:** 5.1900 g. **Composition:** 0.9000 Gold .1501 oz. AGW **Ruler:** Pope Pius XII **Obv. Legend:** AN

| Date | Mintage | F | VF | XF | Unc | BU |
|---|---|---|---|---|---|---|
| 1939/I | 2,700 | — | — | 200 | 350 | — |
| 1940/II | 2,000 | — | — | 250 | 375 | — |

**100 LIRE** **Y# 30.2** **Weight:** 5.1900 g. **Composition:** 0.9000 Gold .1501 oz. AGW **Ruler:** Pope Pius XII **Obv. Legend:** A

| Date | Mintage | F | VF | XF | Unc | BU |
|---|---|---|---|---|---|---|
| 1941/III | 2,000 | — | — | 250 | 375 | — |

**100 LIRE** **Y# 39** **Weight:** 5.1900 g. **Composition:** 0.9000 Gold .1501 oz. AGW **Ruler:** Pope Pius XII

| Date | Mintage | F | VF | XF | Unc | BU |
|---|---|---|---|---|---|---|
| 1942/IV | 2,000 | — | — | 250 | 375 | — |
| 1943/V | 1,000 | — | — | 350 | 600 | — |
| 1944/VI | 1,000 | — | — | 350 | 600 | — |
| 1945/VII | 1,000 | — | — | 350 | 600 | — |
| 1946/VIII | 1,000 | — | — | 350 | 600 | — |
| 1947/IX | 1,000 | — | — | 350 | 600 | — |
| 1948/X | 5,000 | — | — | 200 | 275 | — |
| 1949/XI | 1,000 | — | — | 350 | 600 | — |

**100 LIRE** **Y# 48** **Weight:** 5.1900 g. **Composition:** 0.9000 Gold .1501 oz. AGW **Ruler:** Pope Pius XII **Subject:** Holy Year

| Date | Mintage | F | VF | XF | Unc | BU |
|---|---|---|---|---|---|---|
| 1950 | 20,000 | — | — | 200 | 275 | — |

**100 LIRE** **Y# 53.1** **Weight:** 5.1900 g. **Composition:** 0.9000 Gold .1501 oz. AGW **Ruler:** Pope Pius XII **Obv. Legend:** AN

| Date | Mintage | F | VF | XF | Unc | BU |
|---|---|---|---|---|---|---|
| 1951/XIII | 1,000 | — | — | 350 | 625 | — |
| 1952/XIV | 1,000 | — | — | 350 | 625 | — |
| 1953/XV | 1,000 | — | — | 350 | 625 | — |
| 1954/XVI | 1,000 | — | — | 350 | 625 | — |
| 1955/XVII | 1,000 | — | — | 350 | 625 | — |

**100 LIRE** **Y# 55** **Composition:** Stainless Steel **Ruler:** Pope Pius XII

| Date | Mintage | F | VF | XF | Unc | BU |
|---|---|---|---|---|---|---|
| 1955/XVII | 1,300,000 | — | 0.50 | 1.00 | 2.00 | — |
| 1956/XVII | 1,400,000 | — | 0.50 | 1.00 | 2.00 | — |
| 1957/XIX | 900,000 | — | 0.50 | 1.00 | 2.00 | — |
| 1958/XX | 852,000 | — | 0.50 | 1.00 | 2.00 | — |

**100 LIRE** **Y# 53.2** **Weight:** 5.1900 g. **Composition:** 0.9000 Gold .1501 oz. AGW **Ruler:** Pope Pius XII **Obv. Legend:** A

| Date | Mintage | F | VF | XF | Unc | BU |
|---|---|---|---|---|---|---|
| 1956/XVIII | 1,000 | — | — | 350 | 625 | — |

**100 LIRE** **Y# A53** **Weight:** 5.1900 g. **Composition:** 0.9000 Gold .1501 oz. AGW **Ruler:** Pope Pius XII

| Date | Mintage | F | VF | XF | Unc | BU |
|---|---|---|---|---|---|---|
| 1957/XIX | 2,000 | — | — | 250 | 350 | — |
| 1958/XX | 3,000 | — | — | 250 | 325 | — |

**100 LIRE** **Y# 66** **Weight:** 5.1900 g. **Composition:** 0.9000 Gold .1501 oz. AGW **Ruler:** Pope John XXIII

| Date | Mintage | F | VF | XF | Unc | BU |
|---|---|---|---|---|---|---|
| 1959/I | 3,000 | — | — | 750 | 1,250 | — |

**100 LIRE** **Y# 64.1** **Composition:** Stainless Steel **Ruler:** Pope John XXIII **Obverse:** Continuous legend

| Date | Mintage | F | VF | XF | Unc | BU |
|---|---|---|---|---|---|---|
| 1959/I | 783,000 | — | 1.25 | 2.00 | 4.00 | — |

**100 LIRE** **Y# 64.2** **Composition:** Stainless Steel **Ruler:** Pope John XXIII **Obverse:** Regnal year under bust

| Date | Mintage | F | VF | XF | Unc | BU |
|---|---|---|---|---|---|---|
| 1960/II | 783,000 | — | 1.75 | 3.00 | 6.50 | — |
| 1961/III | 783,000 | — | 0.75 | 1.00 | 2.50 | — |
| 1962/IV | 783,000 | — | 0.75 | 1.00 | 2.50 | — |

**100 LIRE** **Y# 73** **Composition:** Stainless Steel **Ruler:** Pope John XXIII **Subject:** 2nd Ecumenical Council

| Date | Mintage | F | VF | XF | Unc | BU |
|---|---|---|---|---|---|---|
| 1962/IV | 1,566,000 | — | 0.40 | 0.75 | 1.50 | — |

**100 LIRE** **Y# 82.1** **Composition:** Stainless Steel **Ruler:** Pope Paul VI **Obv. Legend:** AN

| Date | Mintage | F | VF | XF | Unc | BU |
|---|---|---|---|---|---|---|
| 1963/I | 558,000 | — | 1.00 | 2.00 | 3.00 | — |

**100 LIRE** **Y# 82.2** **Composition:** Stainless Steel **Ruler:** Pope Paul VI **Obv. Legend:** A

| Date | Mintage | F | VF | XF | Unc | BU |
|---|---|---|---|---|---|---|
| 1964/II | 558,000 | — | 0.50 | 1.00 | 2.00 | — |
| 1965/III | 558,000 | — | 0.50 | 1.00 | 2.00 | — |

**100 LIRE** **Y# 90** **Composition:** Stainless Steel **Ruler:** Pope Paul VI

| Date | Mintage | F | VF | XF | Unc | BU |
|---|---|---|---|---|---|---|
| 1966/IV | 388,000 | — | 0.50 | 1.00 | 2.00 | — |

**100 LIRE** **Y# 98** **Composition:** Stainless Steel **Ruler:** Pope Paul VI

| Date | Mintage | F | VF | XF | Unc | BU |
|---|---|---|---|---|---|---|
| 1967/V | 315,000 | — | 0.50 | 1.00 | 2.00 | — |

**100 LIRE** **Y# 106** **Composition:** Stainless Steel **Ruler:** Pope Paul VI **Series:** F.A.O.

| Date | Mintage | F | VF | XF | Unc | BU |
|---|---|---|---|---|---|---|
| ND(1968)/VI | 315,000 | — | 0.50 | 1.00 | 2.00 | — |

**100 LIRE** **Y# 114** **Composition:** Stainless Steel **Ruler:** Pope Paul VI

| Date | Mintage | F | VF | XF | Unc | BU |
|---|---|---|---|---|---|---|
| 1969/VII | 315,000 | — | 0.50 | 1.00 | 2.00 | — |

**100 LIRE** **Y# 122** **Composition:** Stainless Steel **Ruler:** Pope Paul VI

| Date | Mintage | F | VF | XF | Unc | BU |
|---|---|---|---|---|---|---|
| 1970/VIII | 315,000 | — | 0.50 | 1.00 | 2.00 | — |
| 1971/IX | 966,000 | — | 0.40 | 0.60 | 1.50 | — |
| 1972/X | 966,000 | — | 0.40 | 0.60 | 1.50 | — |
| 1973/XI | 830,000 | — | 0.40 | 0.60 | 1.50 | — |
| 1974/XII | 830,000 | — | 0.40 | 0.60 | 1.50 | — |
| 1975/XIII | 808,000 | — | 0.40 | 0.60 | 1.50 | — |
| 1976/XIV | 808,000 | — | 0.40 | 0.60 | 1.50 | — |
| 1977/XV | 819,000 | — | 0.40 | 0.60 | 1.50 | — |

**100 LIRE** **Y# 130** **Composition:** Stainless Steel **Ruler:** Pope Paul VI **Subject:** Holy Year

| Date | Mintage | F | VF | XF | Unc | BU |
|---|---|---|---|---|---|---|
| 1975 | 605,000 | — | 0.60 | 1.25 | 2.00 | — |

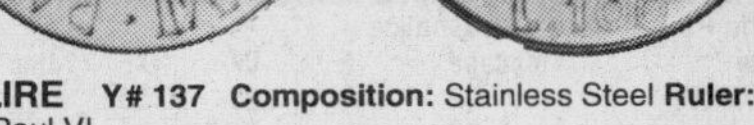

**100 LIRE** **Y# 137** **Composition:** Stainless Steel **Ruler:** Pope Paul VI

| Date | Mintage | F | VF | XF | Unc | BU |
|---|---|---|---|---|---|---|
| 1978/XVI | 399,000 | — | 0.50 | 1.00 | 2.00 | — |

**100 LIRE** **Y# 146** **Composition:** Stainless Steel **Ruler:** Pope John Paul II

| Date | Mintage | F | VF | XF | Unc | BU |
|---|---|---|---|---|---|---|
| 1979/I | 399,000 | — | 0.50 | 1.00 | 2.00 | — |
| 1980/II | 485,000 | — | 0.50 | 1.00 | 2.00 | — |

**100 LIRE** **Y# 158** **Composition:** Stainless Steel **Ruler:** Pope John Paul II

| Date | Mintage | F | VF | XF | Unc | BU |
|---|---|---|---|---|---|---|
| 1981/III | 550,000 | — | 0.50 | 1.00 | 2.00 | — |

**100 LIRE** **Y# 164** **Composition:** Stainless Steel **Ruler:** Pope John Paul II **Subject:** Family **Obverse:** Similar to 1000 Lire, Y#167

| Date | Mintage | F | VF | XF | Unc | BU |
|---|---|---|---|---|---|---|
| 1982/IV | 656,000 | — | 0.40 | 0.60 | 1.50 | — |

**100 LIRE** **Y# 173** **Composition:** Stainless Steel **Ruler:** Pope John Paul II **Subject:** God Gives World to Mankind

| Date | Mintage | F | VF | XF | Unc | BU |
|---|---|---|---|---|---|---|
| 1983/V | 455,000 | — | 0.40 | 0.60 | 1.50 | — |

**100 LIRE** **Y# 180** **Composition:** Stainless Steel **Ruler:** Pope John Paul II **Subject:** Year of Peace **Obverse:** Similar to 1000 Lire, Y#183

| Date | Mintage | F | VF | XF | Unc | BU |
|---|---|---|---|---|---|---|
| 1984/VI | 400,000 | — | 0.40 | 0.60 | 1.50 | — |

**100 LIRE** **Y# 188** **Composition:** Stainless Steel **Ruler:** Pope John Paul II

| Date | Mintage | F | VF | XF | Unc | BU |
|---|---|---|---|---|---|---|
| 1985/VII | 800,000 | — | 0.40 | 0.60 | 1.50 | — |

**100 LIRE** **Y# 195** **Composition:** Stainless Steel **Ruler:** Pope John Paul II **Obverse:** Similar to 200 Lire, Y#196

| Date | Mintage | F | VF | XF | Unc | BU |
|---|---|---|---|---|---|---|
| 1986/VIII | 100,000 | — | 0.40 | 0.60 | 1.50 | — |

**100 LIRE** **Y# 202** **Composition:** Stainless Steel **Ruler:** Pope John Paul II **Subject:** Angel and Mary, The Annunciation

| Date | Mintage | F | VF | XF | Unc | BU |
|---|---|---|---|---|---|---|
| 1987/IX | — | — | 0.40 | 0.60 | 1.50 | — |

**100 LIRE** **Y# 209** **Composition:** Stainless Steel **Ruler:** Pope John Paul II **Subject:** Adam Naming the Animals **Obverse:** Similar to 200 Lire, Y#210

| Date | Mintage | F | VF | XF | Unc | BU |
|---|---|---|---|---|---|---|
| 1988/X | — | — | 0.40 | 0.60 | 1.50 | — |

**100 LIRE** **Y# 216** **Composition:** Stainless Steel **Ruler:** Pope John Paul II **Reverse:** Pelican feeding young

| Date | Mintage | F | VF | XF | Unc | BU |
|---|---|---|---|---|---|---|
| 1989/XI | — | — | 0.40 | 0.60 | 1.50 | — |

**100 LIRE** **Y# 223** **Composition:** Stainless Steel **Ruler:** Pope John Paul II **Subject:** Early Bishop

| Date | Mintage | F | VF | XF | Unc | BU |
|---|---|---|---|---|---|---|
| 1990/XII | — | — | 0.40 | 0.60 | 1.50 | — |

**100 LIRE** **Y# 231** **Composition:** Stainless Steel **Ruler:** Pope John Paul II **Reverse:** Depiction of the Risen Christ

| Date | Mintage | F | VF | XF | Unc | BU |
|---|---|---|---|---|---|---|
| 1991/XIII | — | — | 0.40 | 0.60 | 1.50 | — |

**100 LIRE** **Y# 239** **Composition:** Stainless Steel **Ruler:** Pope John Paul II **Reverse:** Open book

| Date | Mintage | F | VF | XF | Unc | BU |
|---|---|---|---|---|---|---|
| 1992/XIV | — | — | 0.40 | 0.60 | 1.50 | — |

**100 LIRE** **Y# 247** **Composition:** Copper-Nickel **Ruler:** Pope John Paul II **Reverse:** Portrait of Jesus

| Date | Mintage | F | VF | XF | Unc | BU |
|---|---|---|---|---|---|---|
| 1993/XV | — | — | 0.40 | 0.60 | 1.75 | — |

**100 LIRE** **Y# 255** **Composition:** Copper-Nickel **Ruler:** Pope John Paul II **Reverse:** 4 basketball players - 1 in wheelchair

| Date | Mintage | F | VF | XF | Unc | BU |
|---|---|---|---|---|---|---|
| 1994/XVI | — | — | 0.40 | 0.60 | 1.75 | — |

**100 LIRE** **Y# 265** **Composition:** Copper-Nickel **Ruler:** Pope John Paul II **Reverse:** Guard and Prisoners

| Date | Mintage | F | VF | XF | Unc | BU |
|---|---|---|---|---|---|---|
| 1995 | — | — | 0.40 | 0.60 | 1.75 | — |

**100 LIRE** **Y# 275** **Composition:** Copper-Nickel **Ruler:** Pope John Paul II **Reverse:** Women helping children

| Date | Mintage | F | VF | XF | Unc | BU |
|---|---|---|---|---|---|---|
| 1996 | — | — | 0.40 | 0.60 | 1.75 | — |

**100 LIRE** **Y# 283** **Composition:** Copper-Nickel **Ruler:** Pope John Paul II **Reverse:** Woman filling bird bath

| Date | Mintage | F | VF | XF | Unc | BU |
|---|---|---|---|---|---|---|
| 1997/XIX | — | — | 0.40 | 0.60 | 1.75 | — |

**100 LIRE** **Y# 296** **Composition:** Copper-Nickel **Ruler:** Pope John Paul II **Obverse:** Pope with crucifix **Reverse:** Female figure in front of globe

| Date | Mintage | F | VF | XF | Unc | BU |
|---|---|---|---|---|---|---|
| 1998 | — | — | 0.40 | 0.60 | 1.75 | — |

**100 LIRE** **Y# 308** **Weight:** 4.5000 g. **Composition:** Copper-Nickel **Ruler:** Pope John Paul II **Subject:** The Right to Peace **Obverse:** Pope John Paul II bust right **Reverse:** Children of the world gathered in peace **Edge:** Reeded and plain sections **Size:** 22 mm. **Note:** Struck at Rome.

| Date | Mintage | F | VF | XF | Unc | BU |
|---|---|---|---|---|---|---|
| 1999 | — | — | 0.40 | 0.60 | 1.75 | — |

**100 LIRE** **Y# 326** **Weight:** 4.5000 g. **Composition:** Copper-Nickel **Ruler:** Pope John Paul II **Obverse:** Papal arms **Edge:** Plain and reeded sections **Size:** 22 mm.

| Date | Mintage | F | VF | XF | Unc | BU |
|---|---|---|---|---|---|---|
| XXII(2000) | — | — | — | — | 1.75 | — |

**100 LIRE** **Y# 334** **Weight:** 4.5000 g. **Composition:** Copper-Nickel **Ruler:** Pope John Paul II **Subject:** Pope Pius XXIII **Obverse:** Portrait **Reverse:** Papal arms **Edge:** Reeded and plain sections **Size:** 22 mm.

| Date | Mintage | F | VF | XF | Unc | BU |
|---|---|---|---|---|---|---|
| 2001 | — | — | — | — | 1.75 | — |

**200 LIRE** **Y# 138** **Composition:** Aluminum-Bronze **Ruler:** Pope Paul VI

| Date | Mintage | F | VF | XF | Unc | BU |
|---|---|---|---|---|---|---|
| 1978/XVI | 355,000 | — | 0.50 | 1.00 | 2.50 | — |

**200 LIRE** **Y# 147** **Composition:** Aluminum-Bronze **Ruler:** Pope John Paul II

| Date | Mintage | F | VF | XF | Unc | BU |
|---|---|---|---|---|---|---|
| 1979/I | 355,000 | — | 0.50 | 1.00 | 2.50 | — |
| 1980/II | 200,000 | — | 0.50 | 1.00 | 2.50 | — |

**200 LIRE** **Y# 159** **Composition:** Aluminum-Bronze **Ruler:** Pope John Paul II

| Date | Mintage | F | VF | XF | Unc | BU |
|---|---|---|---|---|---|---|
| 1981/III | 170,000 | — | 0.50 | 1.00 | 2.50 | — |

**200 LIRE** **Y# 165** **Composition:** Aluminum-Bronze **Ruler:** Pope John Paul II **Subject:** Labor **Obverse:** Similar to 1000 Lire, Y#167

| Date | Mintage | F | VF | XF | Unc | BU |
|---|---|---|---|---|---|---|
| 1982/IV | 500,000 | — | 0.50 | 1.00 | 2.50 | — |

**200 LIRE** **Y# 174** **Composition:** Aluminum-Bronze **Ruler:** Pope John Paul II **Subject:** Creation of Man

| Date | Mintage | F | VF | XF | Unc | BU |
|---|---|---|---|---|---|---|
| 1983/V | 300,000 | — | 0.40 | 0.75 | 2.25 | — |

**200 LIRE** **Y# 181** **Composition:** Aluminum-Bronze **Ruler:** Pope John Paul II **Subject:** Year of Peace **Obverse:** Similar to 1000 Lire, Y#183

| Date | Mintage | F | VF | XF | Unc | BU |
|---|---|---|---|---|---|---|
| 1984/VI | 250,000 | — | 0.40 | 0.75 | 2.25 | — |

**200 LIRE** **Y# 189** **Composition:** Aluminum-Bronze **Ruler:** Pope John Paul II **Subject:** Winged Ox of St. Luke

| Date | Mintage | F | VF | XF | Unc | BU |
|---|---|---|---|---|---|---|
| 1985/VII | 300,000 | — | 0.40 | 0.75 | 2.25 | — |

**200 LIRE** **Y# 196** **Composition:** Aluminum-Bronze **Ruler:** Pope John Paul II **Subject:** Micheal the Archangel

| Date | Mintage | F | VF | XF | Unc | BU |
|---|---|---|---|---|---|---|
| 1986/VIII | 100,000 | — | 0.40 | 0.75 | 2.25 | — |

**200 LIRE** **Y# 203** **Composition:** Aluminum-Bronze **Ruler:** Pope John Paul II **Subject:** Queen of Peace

| Date | Mintage | F | VF | XF | Unc | BU |
|---|---|---|---|---|---|---|
| 1987/IX | — | — | 0.40 | 0.75 | 2.25 | — |

**200 LIRE** **Y# 210** **Composition:** Aluminum-Bronze **Ruler:** Pope John Paul II **Subject:** Creation of Adam

| Date | Mintage | F | VF | XF | Unc | BU |
|---|---|---|---|---|---|---|
| 1988/X | — | — | 0.40 | 0.75 | 2.25 | — |

**200 LIRE** **Y# 217** **Composition:** Aluminum-Bronze **Ruler:** Pope John Paul II

| Date | Mintage | F | VF | XF | Unc | BU |
|---|---|---|---|---|---|---|
| 1989/XI | — | — | 0.40 | 0.75 | 2.25 | — |

**200 LIRE** **Y# 224** **Composition:** Aluminum-Bronze **Ruler:** Pope John Paul II **Subject:** Blessed Virgin Mary

| Date | Mintage | F | VF | XF | Unc | BU |
|---|---|---|---|---|---|---|
| 1990/XII | — | — | 0.40 | 0.75 | 2.25 | — |

**200 LIRE** **Y# 232** **Composition:** Aluminum-Bronze **Ruler:** Pope John Paul II **Reverse:** Redeemer looking at city views

| Date | Mintage | F | VF | XF | Unc | BU |
|---|---|---|---|---|---|---|
| 1991/XIII | — | — | 0.40 | 0.75 | 2.25 | — |

**200 LIRE** **Y# 240** **Composition:** Aluminum-Bronze **Ruler:** Pope John Paul II **Reverse:** Mother nursing child

| Date | Mintage | F | VF | XF | Unc | BU |
|---|---|---|---|---|---|---|
| 1992/XIV | — | — | 0.40 | 0.75 | 2.25 | — |

**200 LIRE** **Y# 248** **Composition:** Aluminum-Bronze **Ruler:** Pope John Paul II **Subject:** Ten Commandments

| Date | Mintage | F | VF | XF | Unc | BU |
|---|---|---|---|---|---|---|
| 1993/XV | — | — | 0.40 | 0.75 | 2.25 | — |

**200 LIRE** **Y# 256** **Composition:** Aluminum-Bronze **Ruler:** Pope John Paul II **Subject:** Helping Victims of Drug Abuse

| Date | Mintage | F | VF | XF | Unc | BU |
|---|---|---|---|---|---|---|
| 1994/XVI | — | — | 0.40 | 0.75 | 2.25 | — |

**200 LIRE** **Y# 266** **Composition:** Aluminum-Bronze **Ruler:** Pope John Paul II **Reverse:** Family and Farming scene

| Date | Mintage | F | VF | XF | Unc | BU |
|---|---|---|---|---|---|---|
| 1995 | — | — | 0.40 | 0.75 | 2.25 | — |

**200 LIRE** **Y# 276** **Composition:** Aluminum-Bronze **Ruler:** Pope John Paul II **Reverse:** Display of family togetherness

| Date | Mintage | F | VF | XF | Unc | BU |
|---|---|---|---|---|---|---|
| 1996 | — | — | 0.40 | 0.75 | 2.25 | — |

**200 LIRE** **Y# 284** **Composition:** Aluminum-Bronze **Ruler:** Pope John Paul II **Reverse:** Angel guiding 2 people

| Date | Mintage | F | VF | XF | Unc | BU |
|---|---|---|---|---|---|---|
| 1997/XIX | — | — | 0.40 | 0.75 | 2.25 | — |

**200 LIRE** **Y# 297** **Composition:** Aluminum-Bronze **Ruler:** Pope John Paul II **Obverse:** Pope with crucifix **Reverse:** Two figures, one helping the other

| Date | Mintage | F | VF | XF | Unc | BU |
|---|---|---|---|---|---|---|
| 1998 | — | — | 0.40 | 0.75 | 2.25 | — |

**200 LIRE** **Y# 309** **Weight:** 5.0000 g. **Composition:** Aluminum-Bronze **Ruler:** Pope John Paul II **Obverse:** John Paul II bust right **Reverse:** Christ among the poor and outcast **Edge:** Reeded **Size:** 24 mm. **Note:** Struck at Rome.

| Date | Mintage | F | VF | XF | Unc | BU |
|---|---|---|---|---|---|---|
| 1999 | — | — | 0.40 | 0.75 | 2.25 | — |

**200 LIRE** **Y# 327** **Weight:** 5.0000 g. **Composition:** Brass **Ruler:** Pope John Paul II **Obverse:** Papal arms **Reverse:** Pope praying **Edge:** Reeded **Size:** 22 mm.

| Date | Mintage | F | VF | XF | Unc | BU |
|---|---|---|---|---|---|---|
| XXII(2000) | — | — | — | — | 2.25 | — |

**200 LIRE** **Y# 335** **Weight:** 5.0000 g. **Composition:** Brass **Ruler:** Pope John Paul II **Subject:** Pope Paul VI **Obverse:** Portrait **Reverse:** Papal arms **Edge:** Reeded **Size:** 22 mm.

| Date | Mintage | F | VF | XF | Unc | BU |
|---|---|---|---|---|---|---|
| 2001 | — | — | — | — | 2.25 | — |

**500 LIRE** **Y# 56** **Weight:** 11.0000 g. **Composition:** 0.8350 Silver .2953 oz. ASW **Ruler:** Pope Pius XII

| Date | Mintage | F | VF | XF | Unc | BU |
|---|---|---|---|---|---|---|
| 1958/XX | 20,000 | — | 6.00 | 12.50 | 25.00 | — |

**500 LIRE** **Y# 57** **Weight:** 11.0000 g. **Composition:** 0.8350 Silver .2953 oz. ASW **Ruler:** Cardinal Benedetto Aloisi-Masella **Subject:** Sede Vacante **Reverse:** Arms of Cardinal Benedetto Aloisi-Masella

| Date | Mintage | F | VF | XF | Unc | BU |
|---|---|---|---|---|---|---|
| 1958 | 100,000 | — | 4.00 | 6.00 | 10.00 | — |

**500 LIRE** **Y# 65** **Weight:** 11.0000 g. **Composition:** 0.8350 Silver .2953 oz. ASW **Ruler:** Pope John XXIII **Obverse:** Continuous legend

| Date | Mintage | F | VF | XF | Unc | BU |
|---|---|---|---|---|---|---|
| 1959/I | 30,000 | — | 6.00 | 12.50 | 25.00 | — |

**500 LIRE** **Y# 65.1** **Weight:** 11.0000 g. **Composition:** 0.8350 Silver .2953 oz. ASW **Ruler:** Pope John XXIII **Obverse:** Regnal year under bust

| Date | Mintage | F | VF | XF | Unc | BU |
|---|---|---|---|---|---|---|
| 1960/II | 30,000 | — | 7.00 | 15.00 | 30.00 | — |
| 1961/III | 30,000 | — | 6.00 | 12.50 | 25.00 | — |
| 1962/IV | 30,000 | — | 6.00 | 12.50 | 25.00 | — |

**500 LIRE** **Y# 74** **Weight:** 11.0000 g. **Composition:** 0.8350 Silver .2953 oz. ASW **Ruler:** Pope John XXIII **Subject:** 2nd Ecumenical Council

| Date | Mintage | F | VF | XF | Unc | BU |
|---|---|---|---|---|---|---|
| 1962/IV | 60,000 | — | 6.00 | 12.50 | 25.00 | — |

**500 LIRE** **Y# 75** **Weight:** 11.0000 g. **Composition:** 0.8350 Silver .2953 oz. ASW **Ruler:** Cardinal Benedetto Aloisi-Masella **Subject:** Sede Vacante **Reverse:** Arms of Cardinal Benedetto Aloisi-Masella

| Date | Mintage | F | VF | XF | Unc | BU |
|---|---|---|---|---|---|---|
| 1963 | 200,000 | — | 4.00 | 6.00 | 10.00 | — |

**500 LIRE** **Y# 83.1** **Weight:** 11.0000 g. **Composition:** 0.8350 Silver .2953 oz. ASW **Ruler:** Pope Paul VI **Obv. Legend:** AN

| Date | Mintage | F | VF | XF | Unc | BU |
|---|---|---|---|---|---|---|
| 1963/I | 70,000 | — | 8.00 | 16.00 | 32.00 | — |

**500 LIRE** **Y# 83.2** **Weight:** 11.0000 g. **Composition:** 0.8350 Silver .2953 oz. ASW **Ruler:** Pope Paul VI **Obv. Legend:** A

| Date | Mintage | F | VF | XF | Unc | BU |
|---|---|---|---|---|---|---|
| 1964/II | 70,000 | — | 7.00 | 15.00 | 25.00 | — |
| 1965/III | 70,000 | — | 6.00 | 9.00 | 20.00 | — |

**500 LIRE** **Y# 91** **Weight:** 11.0000 g. **Composition:** 0.8350 Silver .2953 oz. ASW **Ruler:** Pope Paul VI

| Date | Mintage | F | VF | XF | Unc | BU |
|---|---|---|---|---|---|---|
| 1966/IV | 100,000 | — | 5.00 | 8.00 | 16.00 | — |

**500 LIRE** **Y# 99** **Weight:** 11.0000 g. **Composition:** 0.8350 Silver .2953 oz. ASW **Ruler:** Pope Paul VI **Subject:** Saint Peter and Paul

| Date | Mintage | F | VF | XF | Unc | BU |
|---|---|---|---|---|---|---|
| ND(1967)/V | 110,000 | — | 4.50 | 7.00 | 14.00 | — |

**500 LIRE** **Y# 107** **Weight:** 11.0000 g. **Composition:** 0.8350 Silver .2953 oz. ASW **Ruler:** Pope Paul VI **Series:** F.A.O.

| Date | Mintage | F | VF | XF | Unc | BU |
|---|---|---|---|---|---|---|
| ND(1968)/VI | 110,000 | — | 4.50 | 7.00 | 14.00 | — |

**500 LIRE** **Y# 115** **Weight:** 11.0000 g. **Composition:** 0.8350 Silver .2953 oz. ASW **Ruler:** Pope Paul VI **Reverse:** Angel

| Date | Mintage | F | VF | XF | Unc | BU |
|---|---|---|---|---|---|---|
| 1969/VII | 110,000 | — | 4.50 | 7.00 | 14.00 | — |

**500 LIRE** **Y# 123** **Weight:** 11.0000 g. **Composition:** 0.8350 Silver .2953 oz. ASW **Ruler:** Pope Paul VI **Reverse:** Wheat and grapes

| Date | Mintage | F | VF | XF | Unc | BU |
|---|---|---|---|---|---|---|
| 1970/VIII | 110,000 | — | — | 5.50 | 11.00 | — |
| 1971/IX | 125,000 | — | — | 5.50 | 11.00 | — |
| 1972/X | 125,000 | — | — | 5.50 | 11.00 | — |
| 1973/XI | 145,000 | — | — | 5.50 | 11.00 | — |
| 1974/XII | 145,000 | — | — | 5.50 | 11.00 | — |
| 1975/XIII | 162,000 | — | — | 5.50 | 11.00 | — |
| 1976/XIV | 162,000 | — | — | 5.50 | 11.00 | — |

**500 LIRE** **Y# 131** **Weight:** 11.0000 g. **Composition:** 0.8350 Silver .2953 oz. ASW **Ruler:** Pope Paul VI **Subject:** Holy Year

| Date | Mintage | F | VF | XF | Unc | BU |
|---|---|---|---|---|---|---|
| 1975 | 200,000 | — | — | 7.00 | 14.00 | — |

**500 LIRE** **Y# 132** **Weight:** 11.0000 g. **Composition:** 0.8350 Silver .2953 oz. ASW **Ruler:** Pope Paul VI **Subject:** Book of the Evengelists

| Date | Mintage | F | VF | XF | Unc | BU |
|---|---|---|---|---|---|---|
| 1977/XV | 160,000 | — | — | 7.00 | 16.50 | — |

**500 LIRE** **Y# 139** **Weight:** 11.0000 g. **Composition:** 0.8350 Silver .2953 oz. ASW **Ruler:** Pope Paul VI **Reverse:** Jesus walking on water

| Date | Mintage | F | VF | XF | Unc | BU |
|---|---|---|---|---|---|---|
| 1978/XVI | 145,000 | — | — | 7.00 | 16.50 | — |

**500 LIRE** **Y# 140** **Weight:** 11.0000 g. **Composition:** 0.8350 Silver .2953 oz. ASW **Ruler:** Cardinal Jean Villot **Subject:** First Sede Vacante **Reverse:** Arms of Cardinal Jean Villot **Rev. Legend:** SEDE VACANTE MCMLXXVIII

| Date | Mintage | F | VF | XF | Unc | BU |
|---|---|---|---|---|---|---|
| 1978 | 500,000 | — | — | 8.00 | 17.50 | — |

**500 LIRE** **Y# 141** **Weight:** 11.0000 g. **Composition:** 0.8350 Silver .2953 oz. ASW **Ruler:** Pope Paul VI **Subject:** Second Sede Vacante **Reverse:** Arms of Cardinal Jean Villot **Rev. Legend:** SEDE VACANTE SEPTEMBER MCMLXXVIII

| Date | Mintage | F | VF | XF | Unc | BU |
|---|---|---|---|---|---|---|
| 1978 | — | — | — | 8.00 | 17.50 | — |

**Note:** Mintage included with Y#140.

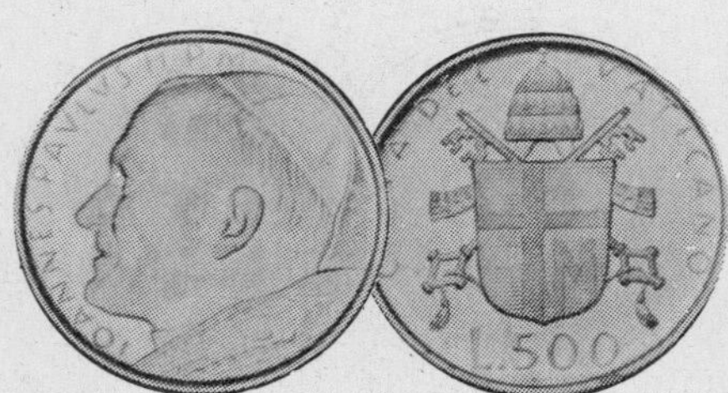

**500 LIRE** **Y# 148** **Weight:** 11.0000 g. **Composition:** 0.8350 Silver .2953 oz. ASW **Ruler:** Pope John Paul II

| Date | Mintage | F | VF | XF | Unc | BU |
|---|---|---|---|---|---|---|
| 1979/I | 145,000 | — | — | 8.00 | 17.50 | — |
| 1980/II | 184,000 | — | — | 8.00 | 17.50 | — |

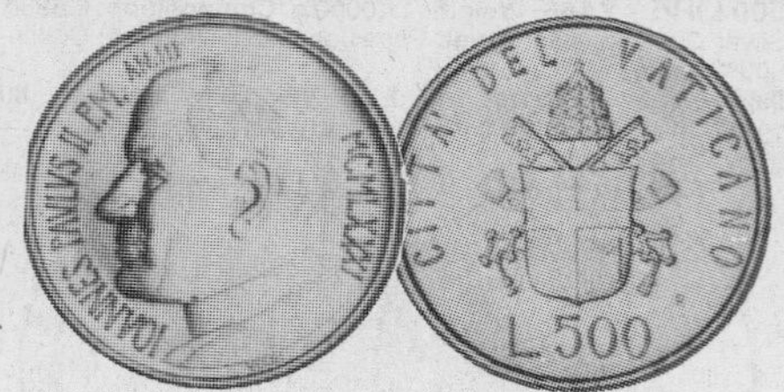

**500 LIRE** **Y# 160** **Weight:** 11.0000 g. **Composition:** 0.8350 Silver .2953 oz. ASW **Ruler:** Pope John Paul II

| Date | Mintage | F | VF | XF | Unc | BU |
|---|---|---|---|---|---|---|
| 1981/III | 184,000 | — | — | 8.00 | 17.50 | — |

**500 LIRE** **Y# 166** **Ring Composition:** Stainless Steel **Center Composition:** Aluminum-Bronze **Ruler:** Pope John Paul II **Subject:** Education **Obverse:** Similar to 1000 Lire, Y#167

| Date | Mintage | F | VF | XF | Unc | BU |
|---|---|---|---|---|---|---|
| 1982/IV | 1,852,000 | — | — | 2.75 | 7.00 | — |

**500 LIRE** **Y# 168** **Weight:** 11.0000 g. **Composition:** 0.8350 Silver .2953 oz. ASW **Ruler:** Pope John Paul II **Subject:** Holy Year

| Date | Mintage | F | VF | XF | Unc | BU |
|---|---|---|---|---|---|---|
| 1983-84 | 130,000 | — | — | 10.00 | 22.50 | — |

**500 LIRE** **Y# 175** **Ring Composition:** Stainless Steel **Center Composition:** Aluminum-Bronze **Ruler:** Pope John Paul II **Subject:** Creation of the Universe

| Date | Mintage | F | VF | XF | Unc | BU |
|---|---|---|---|---|---|---|
| 1983/V | — | — | — | 2.75 | 7.00 | — |

**500 LIRE** **Y# 182** **Ring Composition:** Stainless Steel **Center Composition:** Aluminum-Bronze **Ruler:** Pope John Paul II **Subject:** Year of Peace

| Date | Mintage | F | VF | XF | Unc | BU |
|---|---|---|---|---|---|---|
| 1984/VI | 270,000 | — | — | 2.75 | 7.00 | — |

**500 LIRE** **Y# 184** **Weight:** 11.0000 g. **Composition:** 0.8350 Silver .2953 oz. ASW **Ruler:** Pope John Paul II **Subject:** 2000th Anniversary - Birth of Blessed Virgin Mary

| Date | Mintage | F | VF | XF | Unc | BU |
|---|---|---|---|---|---|---|
| 1984/VI Proof | 105,000 | Value: 22.50 | | | | |

**500 LIRE** **Y# 190** **Ring Composition:** Stainless Steel **Center Composition:** Aluminum-Bronze **Ruler:** Pope John Paul II **Subject:** Saint Peter in boat

| Date | Mintage | F | VF | XF | Unc | BU |
|---|---|---|---|---|---|---|
| 1985/VII | 300,000 | — | — | 2.50 | 6.00 | — |

**500 LIRE** **Y# 197** **Ring Composition:** Stainless Steel **Center Composition:** Aluminum-Bronze **Ruler:** Pope John Paul II **Reverse:** Seated Mary and Jesus

| Date | Mintage | F | VF | XF | Unc | BU |
|---|---|---|---|---|---|---|
| 1986/VIII | 300,000 | — | — | 2.50 | 6.00 | — |

**500 LIRE** **Y# 204** **Ring Composition:** Stainless Steel **Center Composition:** Aluminum-Bronze **Ruler:** Pope John Paul II **Reverse:** Crucified Jesus

| Date | Mintage | F | VF | XF | Unc | BU |
|---|---|---|---|---|---|---|
| 1987/IX | — | — | — | 2.50 | 6.00 | — |

**500 LIRE** **Y# 211** **Ring Composition:** Stainless Steel **Center Composition:** Aluminum-Bronze **Ruler:** Pope John Paul II **Reverse:** Holy Trinity

| Date | Mintage | F | VF | XF | Unc | BU |
|---|---|---|---|---|---|---|
| 1988/X | — | — | — | 2.50 | 6.00 | — |

**500 LIRE** **Y# 218** **Ring Composition:** Stainless Steel **Center Composition:** Aluminum-Bronze **Ruler:** Pope John Paul II **Reverse:** Grape vine

| Date | Mintage | F | VF | XF | Unc | BU |
|---|---|---|---|---|---|---|
| 1989/XI | — | — | — | 2.50 | 6.00 | — |

**500 LIRE** **Y# 225** **Ring Composition:** Stainless Steel **Center Composition:** Aluminum-Bronze **Ruler:** Pope John Paul II **Reverse:** Jesus and 2 kneeling figures

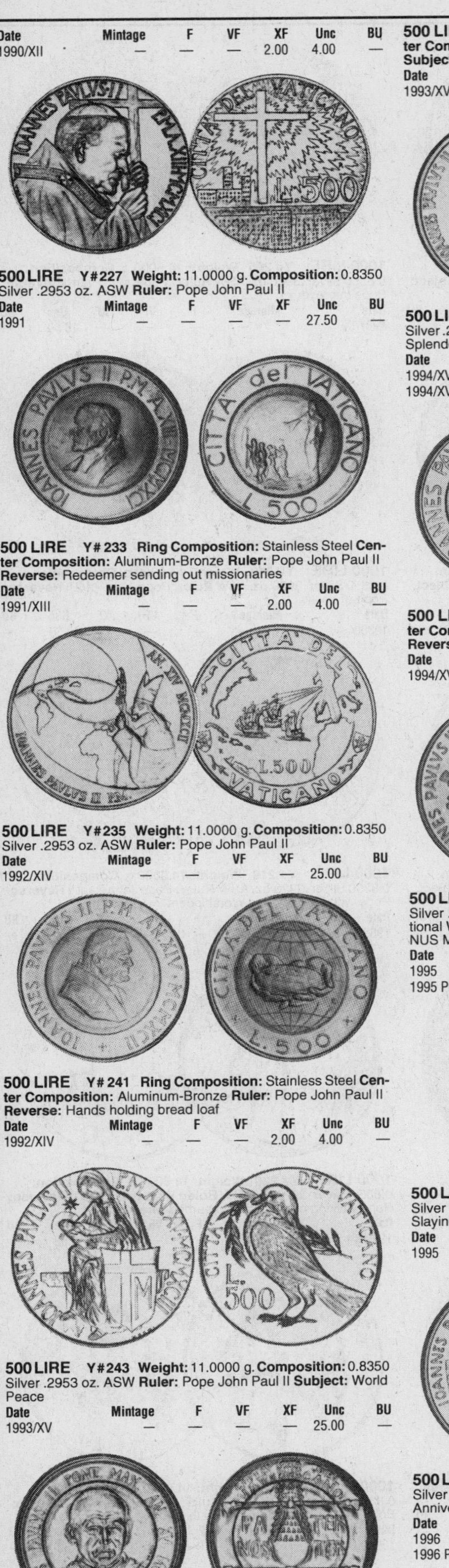

| Date | Mintage | F | VF | XF | Unc | BU |
|---|---|---|---|---|---|---|
| 1990/XII | — | — | — | 2.00 | 4.00 | — |

**500 LIRE** **Y# 227** **Weight:** 11.0000 g. **Composition:** 0.8350 Silver .2953 oz. ASW **Ruler:** Pope John Paul II

| Date | Mintage | F | VF | XF | Unc | BU |
|---|---|---|---|---|---|---|
| 1991 | — | — | — | — | 27.50 | — |

**500 LIRE** **Y# 233** **Ring Composition:** Stainless Steel **Center Composition:** Aluminum-Bronze **Ruler:** Pope John Paul II **Reverse:** Redeemer sending out missionaries

| Date | Mintage | F | VF | XF | Unc | BU |
|---|---|---|---|---|---|---|
| 1991/XIII | — | — | — | 2.00 | 4.00 | — |

**500 LIRE** **Y# 235** **Weight:** 11.0000 g. **Composition:** 0.8350 Silver .2953 oz. ASW **Ruler:** Pope John Paul II

| Date | Mintage | F | VF | XF | Unc | BU |
|---|---|---|---|---|---|---|
| 1992/XIV | — | — | — | — | 25.00 | — |

**500 LIRE** **Y# 241** **Ring Composition:** Stainless Steel **Center Composition:** Aluminum-Bronze **Ruler:** Pope John Paul II **Reverse:** Hands holding bread loaf

| Date | Mintage | F | VF | XF | Unc | BU |
|---|---|---|---|---|---|---|
| 1992/XIV | — | — | — | 2.00 | 4.00 | — |

**500 LIRE** **Y# 243** **Weight:** 11.0000 g. **Composition:** 0.8350 Silver .2953 oz. ASW **Ruler:** Pope John Paul II **Subject:** World Peace

| Date | Mintage | F | VF | XF | Unc | BU |
|---|---|---|---|---|---|---|
| 1993/XV | — | — | — | — | 25.00 | — |

**500 LIRE** **Y# 249** **Ring Composition:** Stainless Steel **Center Composition:** Aluminum-Bronze **Ruler:** Pope John Paul II **Subject:** Thurible

| Date | Mintage | F | VF | XF | Unc | BU |
|---|---|---|---|---|---|---|
| 1993/XV | — | — | — | 2.00 | 4.00 | — |

**500 LIRE** **Y# 251** **Weight:** 11.0000 g. **Composition:** 0.8350 Silver .2953 oz. ASW **Ruler:** Pope John Paul II **Subject:** Veritatis Splendor

| Date | Mintage | F | VF | XF | Unc | BU |
|---|---|---|---|---|---|---|
| 1994/XVI | — | — | — | — | 25.00 | — |
| 1994/XVI Proof | — | Value: 40.00 | | | | |

**500 LIRE** **Y# 257** **Ring Composition:** Stainless Steel **Center Composition:** Aluminum-Bronze **Ruler:** Pope John Paul II **Reverse:** People meeting, Golgotha in background

| Date | Mintage | F | VF | XF | Unc | BU |
|---|---|---|---|---|---|---|
| 1994/XVI | — | — | — | 2.00 | 4.00 | — |

**500 LIRE** **Y# 259** **Weight:** 11.0000 g. **Composition:** 0.8350 Silver .2953 oz. ASW **Ruler:** Pope John Paul II **Series:** International Women Year **Edge Lettering:** INTERNATIONALIS ANNUS MELIEREI DICATUS

| Date | Mintage | F | VF | XF | Unc | BU |
|---|---|---|---|---|---|---|
| 1995 | 20,000 | — | — | — | 35.00 | — |
| 1995 Proof | 7,000 | Value: 55.00 | | | | |

**500 LIRE** **Y# 267** **Weight:** 11.0000 g. **Composition:** 0.8350 Silver .2953 oz. ASW **Ruler:** Pope John Paul II **Subject:** Cain Slaying Abel

| Date | Mintage | F | VF | XF | Unc | BU |
|---|---|---|---|---|---|---|
| 1995 | — | — | — | 2.00 | 4.00 | — |

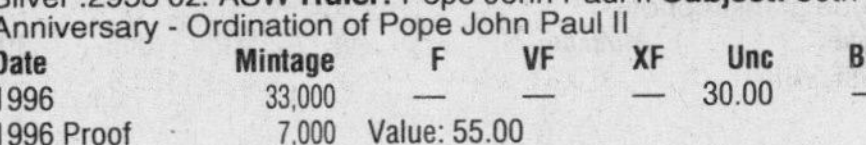

**500 LIRE** **Y# 269** **Weight:** 11.0000 g. **Composition:** 0.8350 Silver .2953 oz. ASW **Ruler:** Pope John Paul II **Subject:** 50th Anniversary - Ordination of Pope John Paul II

| Date | Mintage | F | VF | XF | Unc | BU |
|---|---|---|---|---|---|---|
| 1996 | 33,000 | — | — | — | 30.00 | — |
| 1996 Proof | 7,000 | Value: 55.00 | | | | |

**500 LIRE** **Y# 277** **Ring Composition:** Stainless Steel **Center Composition:** Aluminum-Bronze **Ruler:** Pope John Paul II **Reverse:** Male figure protecting child from serpent

| Date | Mintage | F | VF | XF | Unc | BU |
|---|---|---|---|---|---|---|
| 1996 | — | — | — | 2.00 | 4.00 | — |

**500 LIRE** **Y# 279** **Weight:** 11.0000 g. **Composition:** 0.8350 Silver .2953 oz. ASW **Ruler:** Pope John Paul II **Subject:** XII World Youth Conference **Reverse:** 6 children with Jesus **Edge Lettering:** IUVENTUTIS XII UNIVERSALIS DIES PARISIIS

| Date | Mintage | F | VF | XF | Unc | BU |
|---|---|---|---|---|---|---|
| 1997 | 18,000 | — | — | — | 35.00 | — |
| 1997 Proof | — | Value: 60.00 | | | | |

**500 LIRE** **Y# 285** **Ring Composition:** Stainless Steel **Center Composition:** Aluminum-Bronze **Ruler:** Pope John Paul II **Reverse:** One man freeing another from thorns

| Date | Mintage | F | VF | XF | Unc | BU |
|---|---|---|---|---|---|---|
| 1997/XIX | — | — | — | 2.00 | 4.00 | — |

**500 LIRE** **Y# 292** **Weight:** 11.0000 g. **Composition:** 0.8350 Silver .2953 oz. ASW **Ruler:** Pope John Paul II **Subject:** Shroud of Turin **Edge Lettering:** SACRA SINDON OSTENTATUR AVG. TAVR. MCMXCVIII

| Date | Mintage | F | VF | XF | Unc | BU |
|---|---|---|---|---|---|---|
| 1998/XX | 23,000 | — | — | — | 35.00 | — |

**500 LIRE** **Y# 298** **Ring Composition:** Stainless Steel **Center Composition:** Aluminum-Bronze **Ruler:** Pope John Paul II **Obverse:** Pope's portrait **Reverse:** Two figures

| Date | Mintage | F | VF | XF | Unc | BU |
|---|---|---|---|---|---|---|
| 1998 | — | — | — | 2.00 | 4.00 | — |

**500 LIRE** **Y# 322** **Weight:** 11.0000 g. **Composition:** 0.8350 Silver .2953 oz. ASW **Ruler:** Pope John Paul II **Subject:** 70th Anniversary - Vatican City Arm Arms of Six Popes

| Date | Mintage | F | VF | XF | Unc | BU |
|---|---|---|---|---|---|---|
| 1999 | — | — | — | — | 30.00 | — |
| 1999 Proof | — | Value: 50.00 | | | | |

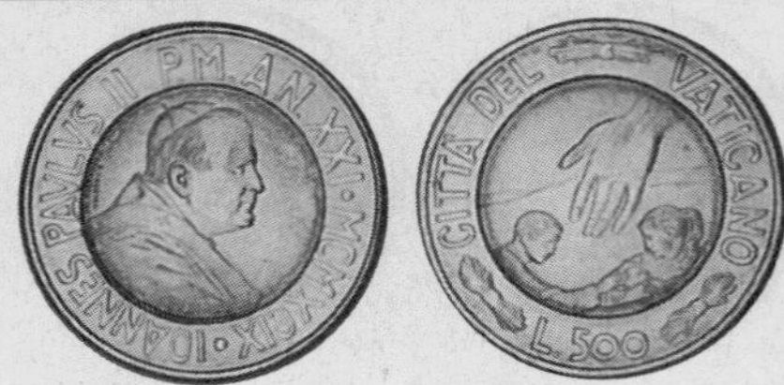

**500 LIRE** **Y# 310** **Ring Composition:** Stainless Steel **Center Weight:** 6.7000 g. **Center Composition:** Aluminum-Bronze **Ruler:** Pope John Paul II **Subject:** Time of Choices, Time of Hope **Obverse:** Pope John Paul II bust right **Reverse:** God's hand above young parent's with baby **Edge:** Reeded **Size:** 25.9 mm. **Note:** Struck at Rome.

| Date | Mintage | F | VF | XF | Unc | BU |
|---|---|---|---|---|---|---|
| 1999 | — | — | — | 2.00 | 4.00 | — |

**500 LIRE** **Y# 328** **Ring Weight:** 6.7700 g. **Ring Composition:** Stainless Steel **Center Composition:** Brass **Ruler:** Pope John Paul II **Obverse:** Papal arms **Reverse:** Pope turning a page **Edge:** Reeded and plain sections **Size:** 25.7 mm.

| Date | Mintage | F | VF | XF | Unc | BU |
|---|---|---|---|---|---|---|
| XXII(2000) | — | — | — | — | 4.00 | — |

**500 LIRE** **Y# 336** **Ring Weight:** 6.7700 g. **Ring Composition:** Stainless Steel **Center Composition:** Brass **Ruler:** Pope John Paul II **Subject:** Pope John Paul I **Obverse:** Portrait **Reverse:** Papal arms **Edge:** Reeded and plain sections **Size:** 25.7 mm.

| Date | Mintage | F | VF | XF | Unc | BU |
|---|---|---|---|---|---|---|
| 2001 | — | — | — | — | 4.00 | — |

**1000 LIRE** **Y# 142** **Weight:** 14.6000 g. **Composition:** 0.8350 Silver .3920 oz. ASW **Ruler:** Pope John Paul I

| Date | Mintage | F | VF | XF | Unc | BU |
|---|---|---|---|---|---|---|
| 1978 | — | — | — | — | 25.00 | — |

**1000 LIRE** **Y# 167** **Weight:** 14.6000 g. **Composition:** 0.8350 Silver .3920 oz. ASW **Ruler:** Pope John Paul II

| Date | Mintage | F | VF | XF | Unc | BU |
|---|---|---|---|---|---|---|
| 1982/IV | 210,000 | — | — | — | 18.50 | — |

**1000 LIRE** **Y# 169** **Weight:** 14.6000 g. **Composition:** 0.8350 Silver .3920 oz. ASW **Ruler:** Pope John Paul II **Subject:** Holy Year

| Date | Mintage | F | VF | XF | Unc | BU |
|---|---|---|---|---|---|---|
| 1983-84 | 130,000 | — | — | — | 18.50 | — |

**1000 LIRE** **Y# 176** **Weight:** 14.6000 g. **Composition:** 0.8350 Silver .3920 oz. ASW **Ruler:** Pope John Paul II **Subject:** Prayer

| Date | Mintage | F | VF | XF | Unc | BU |
|---|---|---|---|---|---|---|
| 1983/V | 110,000 | — | — | — | 20.00 | — |

**1000 LIRE** **Y# 183** **Weight:** 14.6000 g. **Composition:** 0.8350 Silver .3920 oz. ASW **Ruler:** Pope John Paul II **Subject:** Year of Peace

| Date | Mintage | F | VF | XF | Unc | BU |
|---|---|---|---|---|---|---|
| 1984/VI | 105,000 | — | — | — | 20.00 | — |

**1000 LIRE** **Y# 191** **Weight:** 14.6000 g. **Composition:** 0.8350 Silver .3920 oz. ASW **Ruler:** Pope John Paul II

| Date | Mintage | F | VF | XF | Unc | BU |
|---|---|---|---|---|---|---|
| 1985/VII | 86,000 | — | — | — | 22.50 | — |

**1000 LIRE** **Y# 198** **Weight:** 14.6000 g. **Composition:** 0.8350 Silver .3920 oz. ASW **Ruler:** Pope John Paul II **Reverse:** Pope at microphone

| Date | Mintage | F | VF | XF | Unc | BU |
|---|---|---|---|---|---|---|
| 1986/VIII | 80,000 | — | — | — | 18.50 | — |

**1000 LIRE** **Y# 205** **Weight:** 14.6000 g. **Composition:** 0.8350 Silver .3920 oz. ASW **Ruler:** Pope John Paul II **Reverse:** Pope in prayer

| Date | Mintage | F | VF | XF | Unc | BU |
|---|---|---|---|---|---|---|
| 1987/IX | — | — | — | — | 18.50 | — |

**1000 LIRE** **Y# 212** **Weight:** 14.6000 g. **Composition:** 0.8350 Silver .3920 oz. ASW **Ruler:** Pope John Paul II **Reverse:** Pope at desk

| Date | Mintage | F | VF | XF | Unc | BU |
|---|---|---|---|---|---|---|
| 1988/X | — | — | — | — | 18.50 | — |

**1000 LIRE** **Y# 219** **Weight:** 14.6000 g. **Composition:** 0.8350 Silver .3920 oz. ASW **Ruler:** Pope John Paul II **Reverse:** Pope with Prelates and Worshippers

| Date | Mintage | F | VF | XF | Unc | BU |
|---|---|---|---|---|---|---|
| 1989/XI | — | — | — | — | 18.50 | — |

**1000 LIRE** **Y# 226** **Weight:** 14.6000 g. **Composition:** 0.8350 Silver .3920 oz. ASW **Ruler:** Pope John Paul II **Reverse:** Pope walking over destroyed barbed wire fence

| Date | Mintage | F | VF | XF | Unc | BU |
|---|---|---|---|---|---|---|
| 1990/XII | — | — | — | — | 18.50 | — |

**1000 LIRE** **Y# 234** **Weight:** 14.6000 g. **Composition:** 0.8350 Silver .3920 oz. ASW **Ruler:** Pope John Paul II **Reverse:** Pope handing missionary cross to 2 young people

| Date | Mintage | F | VF | XF | Unc | BU |
|---|---|---|---|---|---|---|
| 1991/XIII | — | — | — | — | 18.50 | — |

**1000 LIRE** **Y# 242** **Weight:** 11.0000 g. **Composition:** 0.8350 Silver .2953 oz. ASW **Ruler:** Pope John Paul II **Reverse:** Pope's personal coat of arms

| Date | Mintage | F | VF | XF | Unc | BU |
|---|---|---|---|---|---|---|
| 1992/XIV | — | — | — | — | 18.50 | — |

**1000 LIRE** **Y# 250** **Weight:** 14.6000 g. **Composition:** 0.8350 Silver .3919 oz. ASW **Ruler:** Pope John Paul II **Reverse:** Papal coat of arms

| Date | Mintage | F | VF | XF | Unc | BU |
|---|---|---|---|---|---|---|
| 1993/XV | — | — | — | — | 19.50 | — |

**1000 LIRE** **Y# 258** **Weight:** 14.6000 g. **Composition:** 0.8350 Silver .3919 oz. ASW **Ruler:** Pope John Paul II **Subject:** The Good Samaritan

| Date | Mintage | F | VF | XF | Unc | BU |
|---|---|---|---|---|---|---|
| 1994/XVI | — | — | — | — | 19.50 | — |

**1000 LIRE** **Y# 268** **Weight:** 14.6000 g. **Composition:** 0.8350 Silver .3919 oz. ASW **Ruler:** Pope John Paul II **Subject:** Radiant Virgin Mary

| Date | Mintage | F | VF | XF | Unc | BU |
|---|---|---|---|---|---|---|
| 1995/XVII | — | — | — | — | 20.00 | — |

**1000 LIRE** **Y# 278** **Weight:** 14.6000 g. **Composition:** 0.8350 Silver .3919 oz. ASW **Ruler:** Pope John Paul II **Obverse:** Pope John Paul II releasing doves **Reverse:** Jesus welcomes the little children

| Date | Mintage | F | VF | XF | Unc | BU |
|---|---|---|---|---|---|---|
| 1996 | — | — | — | — | 20.00 | — |

**1000 LIRE** **Y# 287** **Weight:** 14.0000 g. **Composition:** 0.8350 Silver .3919 oz. ASW **Ruler:** Pope John Paul II **Obverse:** John Paul II teaching people **Reverse:** Saint cradling ill man **Edge Lettering:** TOTVS TVVS MCMXCVII

| Date | Mintage | F | VF | XF | Unc | BU |
|---|---|---|---|---|---|---|
| 1997/XIX | — | — | — | — | 20.00 | — |

**1000 LIRE** **Y# 286** **Ring Composition:** Aluminum-Bronze **Center Composition:** Stainless Steel **Ruler:** Pope John Paul II **Obverse:** John Paul II **Reverse:** Papal coat of arms

| Date | Mintage | F | VF | XF | Unc | BU |
|---|---|---|---|---|---|---|
| 1997/XIX | — | — | — | — | 7.00 | — |

**1000 LIRE** **Y# 299** **Ring Composition:** Aluminum-Bronze **Center Composition:** Stainless Steel **Ruler:** Pope John Paul II **Obverse:** Pope's portrait **Reverse:** Papal coat of arms

| Date | Mintage | F | VF | XF | Unc | BU |
|---|---|---|---|---|---|---|
| 1998 | — | — | — | — | 7.00 | — |

**1000 LIRE** **Y# 300** **Weight:** 14.0000 g. **Composition:** 0.8350 Silver .3919 oz. ASW **Ruler:** Pope John Paul II **Obverse:** Pope with crucifix **Reverse:** Jesus on globe **Edge Lettering:** TOTVS TVVS MCMXCVIII

| Date | Mintage | F | VF | XF | Unc | BU |
|---|---|---|---|---|---|---|
| 1998 | — | — | — | — | 20.00 | — |

**1000 LIRE** **Weight:** 14.0000 g. **Composition:** 0.8350 Silver .3919 oz. ASW **Ruler:** Pope John Paul II

| Date | Mintage | F | VF | XF | Unc | BU |
|---|---|---|---|---|---|---|
| 1999 | — | — | — | — | — | — |

**1000 LIRE** **Y# 312** **Weight:** 14.0000 g. **Composition:** 0.8350 Silver .3919 oz. ASW **Ruler:** Pope John Paul II **Subject:** The Right to Religous Freedom **Obverse:** Pope John Paul bust right **Reverse:** Family at altar **Edge:** TOTVS TVVS ++ ++ ++ ++ MCMXCIX ++ ++ ++ ++

| Date | Mintage | F | VF | XF | Unc | BU |
|---|---|---|---|---|---|---|
| 1999 | — | — | — | — | 20.00 | — |

**1000 LIRE** **Y# 311** **Ring Composition:** Aluminum-Bronze **Center Composition:** Stainless Steel **Ruler:** Pope John Paul II **Obverse:** Pope's arms **Reverse:** Couple at base of Christ on cross **Edge:** Reeded and plain sections **Size:** 26.9 mm. **Note:** 8.85 grams. Struck at Rome.

| Date | Mintage | F | VF | XF | Unc | BU |
|---|---|---|---|---|---|---|
| 1999 | — | — | — | — | 7.00 | — |

**1000 LIRE** **Y# 330** **Weight:** 14.6000 g. **Composition:** 0.8350 Silver .3919 oz. ASW **Ruler:** Pope John Paul II **Obverse:** Papal arms **Reverse:** Pope praying between two doors **Edge Lettering:** TOTVS TVVS +++MM+++ **Size:** 31.4 mm.

| Date | Mintage | F | VF | XF | Unc | BU |
|---|---|---|---|---|---|---|
| XXII(2000) | — | — | — | — | 20.00 | — |

**1000 LIRE** **Y# 329** **Ring Composition:** Brass **Center Composition:** Copper-Nickel **Ruler:** Pope John Paul II **Obverse:** Papal arms **Reverse:** Pope and Eastern Orthodox Patriarch **Edge:** Reeded and plain sections **Size:** 26.9 mm. **Note:** 8.85 grams.

| Date | Mintage | F | VF | XF | Unc | BU |
|---|---|---|---|---|---|---|
| XXII(2000) | — | — | — | — | 7.00 | — |

**1000 LIRE** **Y# 338** **Weight:** 14.6000 g. **Composition:** 0.8350 Silver .3919 oz. ASW **Ruler:** Pope John Paul II **Subject:** Peace **Obverse:** Dove over earth **Reverse:** Papal arms **Edge Lettering:** "+++TOTVSTVVS +++ MMI" **Size:** 31.4 mm.

| Date | Mintage | F | VF | XF | Unc | BU |
|---|---|---|---|---|---|---|
| 2001 | — | — | — | — | 20.00 | — |

**1000 LIRE** **Y# 337** **Weight:** 8.8500 g. **Composition:** Copper-Nickel **Ruler:** Pope John Paul II **Subject:** Pope John Paul I **Obverse:** Portrait **Reverse:** Papal arms **Edge:** Reeded and plain sections **Size:** 26.9 mm.

| Date | Mintage | F | VF | XF | Unc | BU |
|---|---|---|---|---|---|---|
| 2001 | — | — | — | — | 7.00 | — |

**2000 LIRE** **Y# 313** **Weight:** 16.0000 g. **Composition:** 0.8350 Silver .4295 oz. ASW **Ruler:** Pope John Paul II **Subject:** Holy Year **Obverse:** Pope standing by open door **Reverse:** 3 hallowed figures **Edge:** Reeded

| Date | Mintage | F | VF | XF | Unc | BU |
|---|---|---|---|---|---|---|
| 2000 | 60,000 | — | — | — | 25.00 | — |
| 2000 Proof | 10,000 | Value: 35.00 | | | | |

**2000 LIRE** **Y# 339** **Weight:** 16.0000 g. **Composition:** 0.8350 Silver .4295 oz. ASW **Ruler:** Pope John Paul II **Subject:** Dialog for Peace **Obverse:** Pope holding staff **Reverse:** Dove above crowd **Edge:** Reeded **Size:** 31.4 mm.

| Date | Mintage | F | VF | XF | Unc | BU |
|---|---|---|---|---|---|---|
| 2001 | 16,000 | — | — | — | 25.00 | — |
| 2001 Proof | 8,000 | Value: 35.00 | | | | |

**5000 LIRE** **Y# 340** **Weight:** 18.0000 g. **Composition:** 0.8350 Silver .4832 oz. ASW **Ruler:** Pope John Paul II **Subject:** Easter **Obverse:** Pope praying **Reverse:** Jesus rising **Edge:** Reeded and plain sections **Size:** 32 mm.

| Date | Mintage | F | VF | XF | Unc | BU |
|---|---|---|---|---|---|---|
| 2001 Proof | 16,000 | Value: 30.00 | | | | |

**10000 LIRE** **Y# 260** **Weight:** 22.0000 g. **Composition:** 0.8350 Silver .5906 oz. ASW **Ruler:** Pope John Paul II **Subject:** The Annunciation **Obverse:** Pope John Paul II

| Date | Mintage | F | VF | XF | Unc | BU |
|---|---|---|---|---|---|---|
| 1995 Proof | 30,000 | Value: 80.00 | | | | |

**Note:** Proof sets only

**10000 LIRE** **Y# 261** **Weight:** 22.0000 g. **Composition:** 0.8350 Silver .5906 oz. ASW **Ruler:** Pope John Paul II **Subject:** The Nativity

| Date | Mintage | F | VF | XF | Unc | BU |
|---|---|---|---|---|---|---|
| 1995 Proof | 30,000 | Value: 80.00 | | | | |

**Note:** Proof sets only

**10000 LIRE** **Y# 270** **Weight:** 22.0000 g. **Composition:** 0.8350 Silver .5906 oz. ASW **Ruler:** Pope John Paul II **Subject:** Holy Year 2000 - Baptism in River Jordan

| Date | Mintage | F | VF | XF | Unc | BU |
|---|---|---|---|---|---|---|
| 1996 Proof | 30,000 | Value: 70.00 | | | | |

**Note:** Proof sets only

**10000 LIRE** **Y# 271** **Weight:** 22.0000 g. **Composition:** 0.8350 Silver .5906 oz. ASW **Ruler:** Pope John Paul II **Subject:** Holy Year 2000 - Jesus Teaching

| Date | Mintage | F | VF | XF | Unc | BU |
|---|---|---|---|---|---|---|
| 1996 Proof | 30,000 | Value: 70.00 | | | | |

**Note:** Proof sets only

**10000 LIRE** **Y# 318** **Weight:** 22.0000 g. **Composition:** 0.8350 Silver .5906 oz. ASW **Ruler:** Pope John Paul II **Subject:** Cure of the Paralytic

| Date | Mintage | F | VF | XF | Unc | BU |
|---|---|---|---|---|---|---|
| 1997 Proof | — | Value: 70.00 | | | | |

**Note:** Proof sets only

**10000 LIRE** **Y# 319** **Weight:** 22.0000 g. **Composition:** 0.8350 Silver .5906 oz. ASW **Ruler:** Pope John Paul II **Subject:** Calming of the Storm

| Date | Mintage | F | VF | XF | Unc | BU |
|---|---|---|---|---|---|---|
| 1997 Proof | — | Value: 70.00 | | | | |

**Note:** Proof sets only

**10000 LIRE** **Y# 290** **Weight:** 22.0000 g. **Composition:** 0.8350 Silver .5906 oz. ASW **Ruler:** Pope John Paul II **Subject:** Last Supper **Obverse:** Pope John Paul II

| Date | Mintage | F | VF | XF | Unc | BU |
|---|---|---|---|---|---|---|
| 1998 Proof | 30,000 | Value: 70.00 | | | | |

**10000 LIRE** **Y# 291** **Weight:** 22.0000 g. **Composition:** 0.8350 Silver .5906 oz. ASW **Ruler:** Pope John Paul II **Subject:** Crucifixion of Jesus **Obverse:** Pope John Paul II

| Date | Mintage | F | VF | XF | Unc | BU |
|---|---|---|---|---|---|---|
| 1998 Proof | 30,000 | Value: 70.00 | | | | |

**10000 LIRE** **Y# 304** **Weight:** 22.0000 g. **Composition:** 0.8350 Silver .5906 oz. ASW **Ruler:** Pope John Paul II **Reverse:** Jesus rising from his tomb

| Date | Mintage | F | VF | XF | Unc | BU |
|---|---|---|---|---|---|---|
| 1999 Proof | 30,000 | Value: 70.00 | | | | |

**10000 LIRE** **Y# 303** **Weight:** 22.0000 g. **Composition:** 0.8350 Silver .5906 oz. ASW **Ruler:** Pope John Paul II **Obverse:** Pope John Paul II bust right **Reverse:** Group with flames above head **Size:** 34 mm. **Note:** Struck at Rome.

| Date | Mintage | F | VF | XF | Unc | BU |
|---|---|---|---|---|---|---|
| 1999 Proof | 30,000 | Value: 70.00 | | | | |

**10000 LIRE** **Y# 314** **Weight:** 22.0000 g. **Composition:** 0.8350 Silver .5906 oz. ASW **Ruler:** Pope John Paul II **Obverse:** Pope John Paul II bust right **Reverse:** Angel holding church above GERUSALEMME

| Date | Mintage | F | VF | XF | Unc | BU |
|---|---|---|---|---|---|---|
| 2000 Proof | 30,000 | Value: 70.00 | | | | |

**10000 LIRE** **Y# 315** **Weight:** 22.0000 g. **Composition:** 0.8350 Silver .5906 oz. ASW **Ruler:** Pope John Paul II **Reverse:** Angel holding church above ROMA

| Date | Mintage | F | VF | XF | Unc | BU |
|---|---|---|---|---|---|---|
| 2000 Proof | 30,000 | Value: 70.00 | | | | |

**50000 LIRE** **Y# 288** **Weight:** 7.5000 g. **Composition:** 0.9170 Gold .2211 oz. AGW **Ruler:** Pope John Paul II **Obverse:** Pope John Paul II and Holy Door **Reverse:** St. Paul

| Date | Mintage | F | VF | XF | Unc | BU |
|---|---|---|---|---|---|---|
| 1997/XIX Proof | 6,000 | Value: 250 | | | | |

**50000 LIRE** Y# 301 **Weight:** 7.5000 g. **Composition:** 0.9170 Gold .2211 oz. AGW **Ruler:** Pope John Paul II **Obverse:** Pope and Holy Door **Reverse:** Madonna and child **Edge:** Reeded **Size:** 23 mm. **Note:** Struck at Rome.

| Date | Mintage | F | VF | XF | Unc | BU |
|---|---|---|---|---|---|---|
| 1998 Proof | 6,000 | Value: 250 | | | | |

**50000 LIRE** Y# 320 **Weight:** 7.5000 g. **Composition:** 0.9170 Gold .2211 oz. AGW **Ruler:** Pope John Paul II **Reverse:** Statue of St. Peter

| Date | Mintage | F | VF | XF | Unc | BU |
|---|---|---|---|---|---|---|
| 1999 Proof | — | Value: 250 | | | | |

**50000 LIRE** Y# 316 **Weight:** 7.5000 g. **Composition:** 0.9170 Gold .2211 oz. AGW **Ruler:** Pope John Paul II **Subject:** Prodigal Son **Obverse:** Pope John Paul II bust right **Reverse:** Father embracing son

| Date | Mintage | F | VF | XF | Unc | BU |
|---|---|---|---|---|---|---|
| 2000 Proof | 6,000 | Value: 250 | | | | |

**100000 LIRE** Y# 289 **Weight:** 15.0000 g. **Composition:** 0.9170 Gold .4422 oz. AGW **Ruler:** Pope John Paul II **Obverse:** Pope John Paul II and Holy Door **Reverse:** Basilica of St. Paul outside the walls

| Date | Mintage | F | VF | XF | Unc | BU |
|---|---|---|---|---|---|---|
| 1997/XIX Proof | 6,000 | Value: 450 | | | | |

**100000 LIRE** Y# 302 **Weight:** 15.0000 g. **Composition:** 0.9170 Gold .4422 oz. AGW **Ruler:** Pope John Paul II **Obverse:** Pope and Holy Door **Reverse:** Basilica of St. Mary Major **Edge:** Reeded **Size:** 28 mm. **Note:** Struck at Rome.

| Date | Mintage | F | VF | XF | Unc | BU |
|---|---|---|---|---|---|---|
| 1998 Proof | 6,000 | Value: 450 | | | | |

**100000 LIRE** Y# 321 **Weight:** 15.0000 g. **Composition:** 0.9170 Gold .4422 oz. AGW **Ruler:** Pope John Paul II **Reverse:** St. Peter's Basilica

| Date | Mintage | F | VF | XF | Unc | BU |
|---|---|---|---|---|---|---|
| 1999 Proof | — | Value: 450 | | | | |

**100000 LIRE** Y# 317 **Weight:** 15.0000 g. **Composition:** 0.9170 Gold .4422 oz. AGW **Ruler:** Pope John Paul II **Subject:** Crucifixion **Obverse:** John Paul II bust right **Reverse:** Crucifixion scene

| Date | Mintage | F | VF | XF | Unc | BU |
|---|---|---|---|---|---|---|
| 2000 Proof | 6,000 | Value: 450 | | | | |

## PROVAS

| KM# | Date | Mintage | Identification | Mkt Val |
|---|---|---|---|---|
| Pr1 | 1951 | 103 | Lira. Silver. Y#49. | 50.00 |
| Pr2 | 1951 | 103 | 2 Lire. Silver. Y#50. | 65.00 |
| Pr3 | 1951 | 103 | 5 Lire. Silver. Y#51. | 85.00 |
| Pr4 | 1951 | 103 | 10 Lire. Silver. Y#52. | 100 |
| Pr5 | 1952 | 103 | Lira. Silver. Y#49. | 50.00 |
| Pr6 | 1952 | 103 | 2 Lire. Silver. Y#50. | 65.00 |
| Pr7 | 1952 | 103 | 5 Lire. Silver. Y#51. | 85.00 |
| Pr8 | 1952 | 103 | 10 Lire. Silver. Y#52. | 100 |
| Pr9 | 1953 | 103 | Lira. Silver. Y#49. | 50.00 |
| Pr10 | 1953 | 103 | 2 Lire. Silver. Y#50. | 65.00 |
| Pr11 | 1953 | 103 | 5 Lire. Silver. Y#51. | 85.00 |
| Pr12 | 1953 | 103 | 10 Lire. Silver. Y#52. | 100 |
| Pr13 | 1955 | 103 | Lira. Silver. Y#49. | 40.00 |
| Pr14 | 1955 | 103 | 2 Lire. Silver. Y#50. | 55.00 |
| Pr15 | 1955 | 103 | 5 Lire. Silver. Y#51. | 65.00 |
| Pr16 | 1955 | 103 | 10 Lire. Silver. Y#52. | 75.00 |
| Pr17 | 1955 | 103 | 50 Lire. Silver. Y#54. | 90.00 |
| Pr18 | 1955 | 103 | 100 Lire. Silver. Y#55. | 100 |
| Pr19 | 1956 | 103 | Lira. Silver. Y#49. | 40.00 |
| Pr20 | 1956 | 103 | 2 Lire. Silver. Y#50. | 55.00 |
| Pr21 | 1956 | 103 | 5 Lire. Silver. Y#51. | 65.00 |
| Pr22 | 1956 | 103 | 10 Lire. Silver. Y#52. | 75.00 |
| Pr23 | 1956 | 103 | 50 Lire. Silver. Y#54. | 90.00 |
| Pr24 | 1956 | 103 | 100 Lire. Silver. Y#55. | 100 |
| Pr25 | 1957 | 103 | Lira. Silver. Y#49. | 40.00 |
| Pr26 | 1957 | 103 | 2 Lire. Silver. Y#50. | 50.00 |
| Pr27 | 1957 | 103 | 5 Lire. Silver. Y#51. | 60.00 |
| Pr28 | 1957 | 103 | 10 Lire. Silver. Y#52. | 70.00 |
| Pr29 | 1957 | 103 | 20 Lire. Silver. Y-A52. | 80.00 |
| Pr30 | 1957 | 103 | 50 Lire. Silver. Y#54. | 90.00 |
| Pr31 | 1957 | 103 | 100 Lire. Silver. Y#55. | 100 |
| Pr32 | 1958 | 103 | Lira. Silver. Y#49. | 40.00 |
| Pr33 | 1958 | 103 | 2 Lire. Silver. Y#50. | 50.00 |
| Pr34 | 1958 | 103 | 5 Lire. Silver. Y#51. | 60.00 |
| Pr35 | 1958 | 103 | 10 Lire. Silver. Y#52. | 70.00 |
| Pr36 | 1958 | 103 | 20 Lire. Silver. Y-A52. | 80.00 |
| Pr37 | 1958 | 103 | 50 Lire. Silver. Y#54. | 90.00 |
| Pr38 | 1958 | 103 | 100 Lire. Silver. Y#55. | 100 |
| Pr39 | 1958 | 103 | 500 Lire. Silver. Y#56. | 125 |
| Pr40 | 1959 | 103 | Lira. Silver. Y#58. | 40.00 |
| Pr41 | 1959 | 103 | 2 Lire. Silver. Y#59. | 50.00 |
| Pr42 | 1959 | 103 | 5 Lire. Silver. Y#60. | 60.00 |
| Pr43 | 1959 | 103 | 10 Lire. Silver. Y#61. | 70.00 |
| Pr44 | 1959 | 103 | 20 Lire. Silver. Y#62. | 80.00 |
| Pr45 | 1959 | 103 | 50 Lire. Silver. Y#63. | 90.00 |
| Pr46 | 1959 | 103 | 100 Lire. Silver. Y#64. | 100 |
| Pr47 | 1959 | 103 | 500 Lire. Silver. Y#65. | 125 |
| Pr48 | 1960 | 103 | Lira. Silver. Y#58. | 40.00 |
| Pr49 | 1960 | 103 | 2 Lire. Silver. Y#59. | 50.00 |
| Pr50 | 1960 | 103 | 5 Lire. Silver. Y#60. | 60.00 |
| Pr51 | 1960 | 103 | 10 Lire. Silver. Y#61. | 70.00 |
| Pr52 | 1960 | 103 | 20 Lire. Silver. Y#62. | 80.00 |
| Pr53 | 1960 | 103 | 50 Lire. Silver. Y#63.1. | 90.00 |
| Pr54 | 1960 | 103 | 100 Lire. Silver. Y#64.1. | 100 |
| Pr55 | 1960 | 103 | 500 Lire. Silver. Y#65.1. | 125 |
| Pr56 | 1961 | 103 | Lira. Silver. Y#58. | 40.00 |
| Pr57 | 1961 | 103 | 2 Lire. Silver. Y#59. | 50.00 |
| Pr58 | 1961 | 103 | 5 Lire. Silver. Y#60. | 60.00 |
| Pr59 | 1961 | 103 | 10 Lire. Silver. Y#61. | 70.00 |
| Pr60 | 1961 | 103 | 20 Lire. Silver. Y#62. | 80.00 |
| Pr61 | 1961 | 103 | 50 Lire. Silver. Y#63.1. | 90.00 |
| Pr62 | 1961 | 103 | 100 Lire. Silver. Y#64.1. | 100 |
| Pr63 | 1961 | 103 | 500 Lire. Silver. Y#65.1. | 125 |
| Pr64 | 1962 | 103 | Lira. Silver. Y#58. | 40.00 |
| Pr65 | 1962 | 103 | 2 Lire. Silver. Y#59. | 50.00 |
| Pr66 | 1962 | 103 | 5 Lire. Silver. Y#60. | 60.00 |
| Pr67 | 1962 | 103 | 10 Lire. Silver. Y#61. | 70.00 |
| Pr68 | 1962 | 103 | 20 Lire. Silver. Y#62. | 80.00 |
| Pr69 | 1962 | 103 | 50 Lire. Silver. Y#63.1. | 90.00 |
| Pr70 | 1962 | 103 | 100 Lire. Silver. Y#64.1. | 100 |
| Pr71 | 1962 | 103 | 500 Lire. Silver. Y#65.1. | 125 |
| Pr72 | 1962 | 103 | Lira. Silver. Y#67. | 40.00 |
| Pr73 | 1962 | 103 | 2 Lire. Silver. Y#68. | 50.00 |
| Pr74 | 1962 | 103 | 5 Lire. Silver. Y#69. | 60.00 |
| Pr75 | 1962 | 103 | 10 Lire. Silver. Y#70. | 70.00 |
| Pr76 | 1962 | 103 | 20 Lire. Silver. Y#71. | 80.00 |
| Pr77 | 1962 | 103 | 50 Lire. Silver. Y#72. | 90.00 |
| Pr78 | 1962 | 103 | 100 Lire. Silver. Y#73. | 100 |
| Pr79 | 1962 | 103 | 500 Lire. Silver. Y#74. | 125 |
| Pr80 | 1963 | 103 | Lira. Silver. Y#76. | 40.00 |
| Pr81 | 1963 | 103 | 2 Lire. Silver. Y#77. | 50.00 |
| Pr82 | 1963 | 103 | 5 Lire. Silver. Y#78. | 60.00 |
| Pr83 | 1963 | 103 | 10 Lire. Silver. Y#79. | 70.00 |
| Pr84 | 1963 | 103 | 20 Lire. Silver. Y#80. | 80.00 |
| Pr85 | 1963 | 103 | 50 Lire. Silver. Y#81. | 90.00 |
| Pr86 | 1963 | 103 | 100 Lire. Silver. Y#82. | 100 |
| Pr87 | 1963 | 103 | 500 Lire. Silver. Y#83. | 125 |
| Pr88 | 1964 | 103 | Lira. Silver. Y#76. | 40.00 |
| Pr89 | 1964 | 103 | 2 Lire. Silver. Y#77. | 50.00 |
| Pr90 | 1964 | 103 | 5 Lire. Silver. Y#78. | 60.00 |
| Pr91 | 1964 | 103 | 10 Lire. Silver. Y#79. | 70.00 |
| Pr92 | 1964 | 103 | 20 Lire. Silver. Y#80. | 80.00 |
| Pr93 | 1964 | 103 | 50 Lire. Silver. Y#81. | 90.00 |
| Pr94 | 1964 | 103 | 100 Lire. Silver. Y#82. | 100 |
| Pr95 | 1964 | 103 | 500 Lire. Silver. Y#83. | 125 |
| Pr96 | 1965 | 103 | Lira. Silver. Y#76. | 40.00 |
| Pr97 | 1965 | 103 | 2 Lire. Silver. Y#77. | 50.00 |
| Pr98 | 1965 | 103 | 5 Lire. Silver. Y#78. | 60.00 |
| Pr99 | 1965 | 103 | 10 Lire. Silver. Y#79. | 70.00 |
| Pr100 | 1965 | 103 | 20 Lire. Silver. Y#80. | 80.00 |
| Pr101 | 1965 | 103 | 50 Lire. Silver. Y#81. | 90.00 |
| Pr102 | 1965 | 103 | 100 Lire. Silver. Y#82. | 100 |
| Pr103 | 1965 | 103 | 500 Lire. Silver. Y#83. | 125 |
| Pr104 | 1966 | 103 | Lira. Silver. Y#84. | 40.00 |
| Pr105 | 1966 | 103 | 2 Lire. Silver. Y#85. | 50.00 |
| Pr106 | 1966 | 103 | 5 Lire. Silver. Y#86. | 60.00 |
| Pr107 | 1966 | 103 | 10 Lire. Silver. Y#87. | 70.00 |
| Pr108 | 1966 | 103 | 20 Lire. Silver. Y#88. | 80.00 |
| Pr109 | 1966 | 103 | 50 Lire. Silver. Y#89. | 90.00 |
| Pr110 | 1966 | 103 | 100 Lire. Silver. Y#90. | 100 |
| Pr111 | 1966 | 103 | 500 Lire. Silver. Y#91. | 125 |
| Pr112 | (1967) | 103 | Lira. Silver. Y#92. | 40.00 |
| Pr113 | (1967) | 103 | 2 Lire. Silver. Y#93. | 50.00 |
| Pr114 | (1967) | 103 | 5 Lire. Silver. Y#94. | 60.00 |
| Pr115 | (1967) | 103 | 10 Lire. Silver. Y#95. | 70.00 |
| Pr116 | (1967) | 103 | 20 Lire. Silver. Y#96. | 80.00 |
| Pr117 | 1967 | 103 | 50 Lire. Silver. Y#97. | 90.00 |
| Pr118 | 1967 | 103 | 100 Lire. Silver. Y#98. | 100 |
| Pr119 | 1967 | 103 | 500 Lire. Silver. Y#99. | 125 |
| Pr120 | (1968) | 103 | Lira. Silver. Y#100. | 40.00 |
| Pr121 | (1968) | 103 | 2 Lire. Silver. Y#101. | 50.00 |
| Pr122 | (1968) | 103 | 5 Lire. Silver. Y#102. | 60.00 |
| Pr123 | (1968) | 103 | 10 Lire. Silver. Y#103. | 70.00 |
| Pr124 | (1968) | 103 | 20 Lire. Silver. Y#104. | 80.00 |
| Pr125 | (1968) | 103 | 50 Lire. Silver. Y#105. | 90.00 |
| Pr126 | (1968) | 103 | 100 Lire. Silver. Y#106. | 100 |
| Pr127 | (1968) | 103 | 500 Lire. Silver. Y#107. | 125 |
| Pr128 | 1969 | 103 | Lira. Silver. Y#108. | 40.00 |
| Pr129 | 1969 | 103 | 2 Lire. Silver. Y#109. | 50.00 |
| Pr130 | 1969 | 103 | 5 Lire. Silver. Y#110. | 60.00 |
| Pr131 | 1969 | 103 | 10 Lire. Silver. Y#111. | 70.00 |
| Pr132 | 1969 | 103 | 20 Lire. Silver. Y#112. | 80.00 |
| Pr133 | 1969 | 103 | 50 Lire. Silver. Y#113. | 90.00 |
| Pr134 | 1969 | 103 | 100 Lire. Silver. Y#114. | 100 |
| Pr135 | 1969 | 103 | 500 Lire. Silver. Y#115. | 125 |
| Pr136 | 1970 | 103 | Lira. Silver. Y#116. | 40.00 |
| Pr137 | 1970 | 103 | 2 Lire. Silver. Y#117. | 50.00 |
| Pr138 | 1970 | 103 | 5 Lire. Silver. Y#118. | 60.00 |
| Pr139 | 1970 | 103 | 10 Lire. Silver. Y#119. | 70.00 |
| Pr140 | 1970 | 103 | 20 Lire. Silver. Y#120. | 80.00 |
| Pr141 | 1970 | 103 | 50 Lire. Silver. Y#121. | 90.00 |
| Pr142 | 1970 | 103 | 100 Lire. Silver. Y#122. | 100 |
| Pr143 | 1970 | 103 | 500 Lire. Silver. Y#123. | 125 |
| Pr144 | 1971 | 103 | Lira. Silver. Y#116. | 40.00 |
| Pr145 | 1971 | 103 | 2 Lire. Silver. Y#117. | 50.00 |
| Pr146 | 1971 | 103 | 5 Lire. Silver. Y#118. | 60.00 |
| Pr147 | 1971 | 103 | 10 Lire. Silver. Y#119. | 70.00 |
| Pr148 | 1971 | 103 | 20 Lire. Silver. Y#120. | 80.00 |
| Pr149 | 1971 | 103 | 50 Lire. Silver. Y#121. | 90.00 |
| Pr150 | 1971 | 103 | 100 Lire. Silver. Y#122. | 100 |
| Pr151 | 1971 | 103 | 500 Lire. Silver. Y#123. | 120 |
| Pr152 | 1972 | 103 | Lira. Silver. Y#116. | 40.00 |
| Pr153 | 1972 | 103 | 2 Lire. Silver. Y#117. | 50.00 |
| Pr154 | 1972 | 103 | 5 Lire. Silver. Y#118. | 60.00 |
| Pr155 | 1972 | 103 | 10 Lire. Silver. Y#119. | 70.00 |
| Pr156 | 1972 | 103 | 20 Lire. Silver. Y#120. | 80.00 |
| Pr157 | 1972 | 103 | 50 Lire. Silver. Y#121. | 90.00 |
| Pr158 | 1972 | 103 | 100 Lire. Silver. Y#122. | 100 |
| Pr159 | 1972 | 103 | 500 Lire. Silver. Y#123. | 125 |
| Pr160 | 1973 | 103 | Lira. Silver. Y#116. | 40.00 |
| Pr161 | 1973 | 103 | 2 Lire. Silver. Y#117. | 50.00 |
| Pr162 | 1973 | 103 | 5 Lire. Silver. Y#118. | 60.00 |
| Pr163 | 1973 | 103 | 10 Lire. Silver. Y#119. | 70.00 |
| Pr164 | 1973 | 103 | 20 Lire. Silver. Y#120. | 80.00 |
| Pr165 | 1973 | 103 | 50 Lire. Silver. Y#121. | 90.00 |
| Pr166 | 1973 | 103 | 100 Lire. Silver. Y#122. | 100 |
| Pr167 | 1973 | 103 | 500 Lire. Silver. Y#123. | 125 |
| Pr168 | 1974 | 103 | Lira. Silver. Y#116. | 40.00 |
| Pr169 | 1974 | 103 | 2 Lire. Silver. Y#117. | 50.00 |
| Pr170 | 1974 | 103 | 5 Lire. Silver. Y#118. | 60.00 |
| Pr171 | 1974 | 103 | 10 Lire. Silver. Y#119. | 70.00 |
| Pr172 | 1974 | 103 | 20 Lire. Silver. Y#120. | 80.00 |
| Pr173 | 1974 | 103 | 50 Lire. Silver. Y#121. | 90.00 |
| Pr174 | 1974 | 103 | 100 Lire. Silver. q edge. Y#122. | 100 |
| Pr175 | 1974 | 103 | 500 Lire. Silver. Y#123. | 125 |
| Pr176 | 1975 | 103 | Lira. Silver. Y#116. | 40.00 |
| Pr177 | 1975 | 103 | 2 Lire. Silver. Y#117. | 50.00 |
| Pr178 | 1975 | 103 | 5 Lire. Silver. Y#118. | 60.00 |
| Pr179 | 1975 | 103 | 10 Lire. Silver. Y#119. | 70.00 |
| Pr180 | 1975 | 103 | 20 Lire. Silver. Y#120. | 80.00 |
| Pr181 | 1975 | 103 | 50 Lire. Silver. Y#121. | 90.00 |
| Pr182 | 1975 | 103 | 100 Lire. Silver. Y#122. | 100 |
| Pr183 | 1975 | 103 | 500 Lire. Silver. Y#123. | 125 |
| Pr184 | 1975 | 103 | Lira. Silver. Y#124. | 40.00 |
| Pr185 | 1975 | 103 | 2 Lire. Silver. Y#125. | 50.00 |
| Pr186 | 1975 | 103 | 5 Lire. Silver. Y#126. | 60.00 |
| Pr187 | 1975 | 103 | 10 Lire. Silver. Y#127. | 70.00 |
| Pr188 | 1975 | 103 | 20 Lire. Silver. Y#128. | 80.00 |
| Pr189 | 1975 | 103 | 50 Lire. Silver. Y#129. | 90.00 |
| Pr190 | 1975 | 103 | 100 Lire. Silver. Y#130. | 100 |
| Pr191 | 1975 | 103 | 500 Lire. Silver. Y#131. | 120 |

## MINT SETS

| KM# | Date | Mintage | Identification | Issue Price | Mkt Val |
|---|---|---|---|---|---|
| MS107 | 2001 (8) | 26,000 | Y#331-338 | 21.25 | 30.00 |
| MS1 | 1929 (9) | 10,000 | Y#1-9 | — | 470 |
| MS2 | 1929 (8) | 10,000 | Y#1-8 | — | 170 |
| MS3 | 1930 (9) | 2,621 | Y#1-9 | — | 825 |
| MS4 | 1930 (8) | 50,000 | Y#1-8 | — | 75.00 |
| MS5 | 1931 (9) | 3,343 | Y#1-9 | — | 575 |
| MS6 | 1931 (8) | 50,000 | Y#1-8 | — | 75.00 |
| MS7 | 1932 (9) | 5,073 | Y#1-9 | — | 475 |
| MS8 | 1932 (8) | 50,000 | Y#1-8 | — | 75.00 |
| MS10 | 1933-34 (8) | 50,000 | Y#11-18 | — | 125 |
| MS9 | 1933-34 (9) | 23,235 | Y#11-19 | — | 400 |
| MS11 | 1934 (9) | 2,533 | Y#1-9 | — | 575 |
| MS12 | 1934 (8) | 30,000 | Y#1-8 | — | 75.00 |
| MS13 | 1935 (9) | 2,105 | Y#1-9 | — | 685 |
| MS14 | 1935 (8) | 9,000 | Y#1-8 | — | 250 |

| KM# | Date | Mintage | Identification | Issue Price | Mkt Val |
|---|---|---|---|---|---|
| MS15 | 1936 (9) | 8,239 | Y#1-8, 10 | — | 350 |
| MS16 | 1936 (8) | 40,000 | Y#1-8 | — | 75.00 |
| MS17 | 1937 (9) | 2,000 | Y#1-8, 10 | — | 3,075 |
| MS18 | 1937 (8) | 20,000 | Y#1-8 | — | 75.00 |
| MS19 | 1938 (3) | — | Y#1-2, 10 Rare | — | — |
| MS20 | 1939 (9) | 2,700 | Y#22-30.1 | — | 435 |
| MS21 | 1939 (8) | 10,000 | Y#22-29 | — | 110 |
| MS22 | 1939 (2) | 30,000 | Y#20, 21 | — | 60.00 |
| MS23 | 1940 (9) | 2,000 | Y#22, 23, 24a-27a, 28-30.1 | — | 470 |
| MS24 | 1940 (8) | 10,000 | Y#22, 23, 24a-27a, 28-29 | — | 100 |
| MS25 | 1941 (9) | 2,000 | Y#22, 23, 24a-27a, 28-30.2 | — | 580 |
| MS26 | 1941 (8) | 4,000 | Y#22, 23, 24a-27a, 28-29 | — | 200 |
| MS27 | 1942 (9) | 2,000 | Y#31-39 | — | 630 |
| MS28 | 1942 (8) | 4,000 | Y#31-38 | — | 230 |
| MSA29 | 1942 (4) | — | Y#33-36 | — | — |
| MS29 | 1943 (9) | 1,000 | Y#31-39 | — | 820 |
| MS30 | 1943 (8) | 1,000 | Y#31-38 | — | 320 |
| MS31 | 1944 (9) | 1,000 | Y#31-39 | — | 820 |
| MS32 | 1944 (8) | 1,000 | Y#31-38 | — | 320 |
| MS33 | 1945 (9) | 1,000 | Y#31-39 | — | 820 |
| MS34 | 1945 (8) | 1,000 | Y#31-38 | — | 320 |
| MS35 | 1946 (9) | 1,000 | Y#31-39 | — | 820 |
| MS36 | 1946 (8) | 1,000 | Y#31-38 | — | 320 |
| MS37 | 1947 (5) | 1,000 | Y#39-43 | — | 530 |
| MS38 | 1947 (4) | 50,000 | Y#40-43 | — | 28.00 |
| MS39 | 1947 (2) | — | Y#42-43 | — | 16.00 |
| MS40 | 1948 (5) | 5,000 | Y#39-43 | — | 280 |
| MS41 | 1948 (4) | 10,000 | Y#40-43 | — | 28.00 |
| MS42 | 1949 (5) | 1,000 | Y#39-43 | — | 535 |
| MS43 | 1949 (4) | 10,000 | Y#40-43 | — | 35.00 |
| MS44 | 1950 (5) | 20,000 | Y#44-48 | — | 265 |
| MS45 | 1950 (4) | 50,000 | Y#44-47 | — | 23.00 |
| MS46 | 1951 (5) | 1,000 | Y#49.1-53.1 | — | 600 |
| MS47 | 1951 (4) | 400,000 | Y#49.1, 50, 51.1-52.1 | — | 5.00 |
| MS48 | 1952 (5) | 1,000 | Y#49.1-52.1, 53.1 | — | 600 |
| MS49 | 1952 (4) | 400,000 | Y#49.1-52.1 | — | 5.00 |
| MS50 | 1953 (5) | 1,000 | Y#49.1-52.1, 53.1 | — | 575 |
| MS51 | 1953 (4) | 400,000 | Y#49.1-52.1 | — | 5.00 |
| MS52 | 1955 (7) | 1,000 | Y#49.1-55 | — | 620 |
| MS53 | 1955 (6) | 10,000 | Y#49.1-52.1, 54.1, 55 | — | 18.00 |
| MS54 | 1956 (7) | 1,000 | Y#49.2-55 | — | 600 |
| MS55 | 1956 (6) | 10,000 | Y#49.2-52.2, 54.2, 55 | — | 18.00 |
| MS56 | 1957 (8) | 2,000 | Y#49.1-A52, A53, 54.2, 55 | — | 300 |
| MS57 | 1957 (6) | 20,000 | Y#49.1-52.2, 54.2, 55 | — | 12.00 |
| MS58 | 1958 (8) | 3,000 | Y#49.1-52.2, 54.2-57 | — | 320 |
| MS59 | 1958 (7) | 20,000 | Y#49.1-52.2, 54.2-56 | — | 35.00 |
| MS60 | 1959 (9) | 3,000 | Y#58.1-64.1, 65-66 | — | 1,300 |
| MS61 | 1959 (8) | 25,000 | Y#58.1-64.1, 65 | — | 75.00 |
| MS62 | 1960 (8) | 25,000 | Y#58.1-59.1, 60.2-64.2, 65.1 | — | 75.00 |
| MS63 | 1961 (8) | 25,000 | Y#58.2-62.2, 63.2-64.2, 65.1 | — | 60.00 |
| MS64 | 1962 (8) | 25,000 | Y#58.2-64.2, 65.1 | — | 55.00 |
| MS65 | 1962 (8) | 50,000 | Y#67-74 | — | 45.00 |
| MS66 | 1963 (8) | 60,000 | Y#76.1-83.1 | — | 65.00 |
| MS68 | 1964 (8) | 60,000 | Y#76.2-79.2, 80.1-81.1, 82.2-83.2 | — | 45.00 |
| MS69 | 1965 (8) | 60,000 | Y#76.2-83.2 | — | 35.00 |
| MS70 | 1966 (8) | 90,000 | Y#84-91 | — | 28.00 |
| MS71 | 1967 (8) | 100,000 | Y#92-99 | 3.25 | 28.00 |
| MS72 | 1968 (8) | 100,000 | Y#100-107 | 4.20 | 28.00 |
| MS73 | 1969 (8) | 100,000 | Y#108-115 | 4.20 | 25.00 |
| MS74 | 1970 (8) | 100,000 | Y#116-123 | 5.00 | 25.00 |
| MS75 | 1971 (8) | 110,000 | Y#116-123 | — | 25.00 |
| MS76 | 1972 (8) | 110,000 | Y#116-123 | 6.00 | 25.00 |
| MS77 | 1973 (8) | 120,000 | Y#116-123 | 6.75 | 25.00 |
| MS78 | 1974 (8) | 120,000 | Y#116-123 | 7.25 | 25.00 |
| MS79 | 1975 (8) | 132,000 | Y#116-123 | 9.00 | 25.00 |
| MS80 | 1975 (8) | 170,000 | Y#124-131 | — | 28.00 |
| MSA80 | 1975 (5) | — | Y#126-130 | — | 7.50 |
| MS81 | 1976 (8) | 180,000 | Y#116-123 | — | 22.00 |
| MS82 | 1977 (7) | 180,000 | Y#116-120, 122, 132 | — | 25.00 |
| MS83 | 1978 (7) | 180,000 | Y#133-139 | — | 25.00 |
| MS84 | 1979 (6) | 156,000 | Y#143-148 | — | 25.00 |
| MS85 | 1980 (6) | — | Y#143-148 | 18.00 | 25.00 |
| MS86 | 1981 (6) | — | Y#155-160 | — | 25.00 |
| MS87 | 1982 (7) | 120,000 | Y#161-167 | — | 30.00 |
| MS88 | 1983 (7) | 120,000 | Y#170-176 | — | 32.00 |
| MS93 | 1983/84 (2) | 130,000 | Y#168-169 | — | 40.00 |
| MS89 | 1984 (7) | — | Y#177-183 | — | 30.00 |
| MS90 | 1985 (7) | — | Y#185-191 | — | 35.00 |
| MS91 | 1986 (7) | — | Y#192-198 | 23.50 | 30.00 |
| MS92 | 1987 (7) | — | Y#199-205 | 27.00 | 30.00 |
| MSA93 | 1987 (5) | — | Y#200-204 | — | 10.00 |
| MS94 | 1988 (7) | — | Y#206-212 | — | 30.00 |
| MS95 | 1989 (7) | — | Y#213-219 | 30.00 | 32.00 |
| MS96 | 1990 (7) | — | Y#220-226 | 33.00 | 35.00 |
| MS97 | 1991 (7) | — | Y#228-234 | 25.00 | 28.00 |
| MS98 | 1992 (7) | — | Y#236-242 | 25.00 | 28.00 |
| MS99 | 1993 (7) | — | Y#244-250 | — | 32.00 |
| MS100 | 1994 (7) | — | Y#252-258 | — | 32.00 |
| MS101 | 1995 (7) | — | Y#262-268 | 32.50 | 35.00 |
| MS102 | 1996 (7) | — | Y#272-278 | 33.00 | 35.00 |
| MS103 | 1997 (8) | — | Y#280-287 | — | 37.50 |
| MS104 | 1998 (8) | — | Y#293-300 | — | 37.50 |
| MS105 | 1999 (8) | — | Y#205-312 | — | 37.50 |
| MS106 | (2000) (8) | — | Y#323-330 | 37.50 | — |

## PROOF SETS

| KM# | Date | Mintage | Identification | Issue Price | Mkt Val |
|---|---|---|---|---|---|
| PS1 | 1995 (2) | 30,000 | Y#260-261 | 75.00 | 100 |
| PS2 | 1996 (2) | 30,000 | Y#270-271 | 75.00 | 140 |
| PS4 | 1997 (2) | 6,000 | Y#288-289 | 547 | 625 |
| PS3 | 1998 (2) | 30,000 | Y#290-291 | — | 140 |

## PROVA SETS

| KM# | Date | Mintage | Identification | Issue Price | Mkt Val |
|---|---|---|---|---|---|
| PrS1 | 1951 (4) | 103 | Pr1-Pr4 | — | 300 |
| PrS2 | 1952 (4) | 103 | Pr5-Pr8 | — | 300 |
| PrS3 | 1953 (4) | 103 | Pr9-Pr12 | — | 300 |
| PrS4 | 1955 (6) | 103 | Pr13-Pr18 | — | 425 |
| PrS5 | 1956 (6) | 103 | Pr19-Pr24 | — | 425 |
| PrS6 | 1957 (7) | 103 | Pr25-31 | — | 425 |
| PrS7 | 1958 (8) | 103 | Pr32-Pr39 | — | 600 |
| PrS8 | 1959 (8) | 103 | Pr40-Pr47 | — | 600 |
| PrS9 | 1960 (8) | 103 | Pr48-Pr55 | — | 600 |
| PrS10 | 1961 (8) | 103 | Pr56-Pr63 | — | 600 |
| PrS11 | 1962 (8) | 103 | Pr64-Pr71 | — | 600 |
| PrS12 | 1962 (8) | 103 | Pr72-Pr79 | — | 600 |
| PrS13 | 1963 (8) | 103 | Pr80-Pr87 | — | 600 |
| PrS14 | 1964 (8) | 103 | Pr88-Pr95 | — | 600 |
| PrS15 | 1965 (8) | 103 | Pr96-103 | — | 600 |
| PrS16 | 1966 (8) | 103 | Pr104-Pr111 | — | 600 |
| PrS17 | 1967 (8) | 103 | Pr112-Pr119 | — | 600 |
| PrS18 | 1968 (8) | 103 | Pr120-Pr127 | — | 600 |
| PrS19 | 1969 (8) | 103 | Pr128-Pr135 | — | 600 |
| PrS20 | 1970 (8) | 103 | Pr136-Pr143 | — | 600 |
| PrS21 | 1971 (8) | 103 | Pr144-Pr151 | — | 600 |
| PrS22 | 1972 (8) | 103 | Pr152-Pr159 | — | 600 |
| PrS23 | 1973 (8) | 103 | Pr160-Pr167 | — | 600 |
| PrS24 | 1974 (8) | 103 | Pr168-Pr175 | — | 600 |
| PrS25 | 1975 (8) | 103 | Pr176-Pr183 | — | 600 |
| PrS26 | 1975 (8) | 103 | Pr184-Pr191 | — | 600 |

The Republic of Venezuela ("Little Venice"), located on the northern coast of South America between Colombia and Guyana, has an area of 352,145 sq. mi.(912,050 sq. km.) and a population of 20 million. Capital: Caracas. Petroleum and mining provide a significant portion of Venezuela's exports. Coffee, grown on 60,000 plantations, is the chief crop. Metalurgy, refining, oil, iron and steel production are the main employment industries.

Columbus discovered Venezuela on his third voyage in 1498. Initial exploration did not reveal Venezuela to be a land of great wealth. An active pearl trade operated on the offshore islands and slavers raided the interior in search of Indians to be sold into slavery, but no significant mainland settlements were made before 1567 when Caracas was founded. Venezuela, the home of Bolivar, was among the first South American colonies to rebel against Spain in 1810. The declaration of Independence of Venezuela was signed by seven provinces which are represented by the seven stars of the Venezuelan flag. Coinage of Caracas and Margarita use the seven stars in their designs. These original provinces were: Barcelona, Barinas, Caracas, Cumana, Margarita, Merida and Trujillo. The Provinces of Coro, Guyana and Maracaibo were added to Venezuela during the Independence War. Independence was attained in 1821 but not recognized by Spain until 1845. Together with Ecuador, Panama and Colombia, Venezuela was part of "Gran Colombia" until 1830, when it became a sovereign and independent state.

**RULERS**

Republic, 1823-present

**MINT MARKS**

A - Paris
(a) - Paris, privy marks only
(aa) - Altena
(b) - Berlin
(bb) - Brussels
(cc) – Canada

(c) - Caracas
(d) - Denver
H, Heaton - Heaton, Birmingham
(l) - London
(m) - Madrid
(mm) - Mexico
(o) - Ontario
(p) - Philadelphia
(s) - San Francisco
(sc) - Schwerte - Vereinigte Deutsche Nickelwerke
(w) - Werdohl - Vereinigte Deutsche Metalwerke

**MONETARY SYSTEM**

100 Centimos = 1 Bolivar

# REPUBLIC OF VENEZUELA

## REFORM COINAGE

1896; 100 Centimos = 1 Bolivar

**5 CENTIMOS** **Y# 27** **Composition:** Copper-Nickel

| Date | Mintage | F | VF | XF | Unc | BU |
|---|---|---|---|---|---|---|
| 1896(b) | 4,000,000 | 0.50 | 2.00 | 17.00 | 75.00 | — |
| 1915(p) | 2,000,000 | 1.00 | 4.00 | 40.00 | 135 | — |
| 1921(p) | 2,000,000 | 0.50 | 2.00 | 50.00 | 150 | — |
| 1925(p) | 2,000,000 | 0.30 | 1.00 | 6.00 | 15.00 | — |
| 1927(p) | 2,000,000 | 0.30 | 1.00 | 6.00 | 15.00 | — |
| 1929(p) | 2,000,000 | 0.25 | 1.00 | 6.00 | 15.00 | — |
| 1936(p) | 5,000,000 | 0.15 | 0.50 | 4.00 | 10.00 | — |
| 1938(p) | 6,000,000 | 0.10 | 0.20 | 3.00 | 8.00 | — |

**5 CENTIMOS** **Y# 29** **Composition:** Brass

| Date | Mintage | F | VF | XF | Unc | BU |
|---|---|---|---|---|---|---|
| 1944(d) | 4,000,000 | 0.50 | 1.00 | 4.50 | 20.00 | — |

**5 CENTIMOS** **Y# 29a** **Composition:** Copper-Nickel

| Date | Mintage | F | VF | XF | Unc | BU |
|---|---|---|---|---|---|---|
| 1945(p) | 12,000,000 | 0.10 | 0.20 | 0.50 | 3.00 | — |
| 1946(p) | 12,000,000 | 0.10 | 0.20 | 0.50 | 3.00 | — |
| 1948(p) | 18,000,000 | 0.10 | 0.20 | 0.50 | 3.00 | — |

**5 CENTIMOS** **Y# 38.1** **Composition:** Copper-Nickel

| Date | Mintage | F | VF | XF | Unc | BU |
|---|---|---|---|---|---|---|
| 1958(p) | 25,000,000 | — | — | — | 0.75 | — |

**5 CENTIMOS** **Y# 38.2** **Composition:** Copper-Nickel

| Date | Mintage | F | VF | XF | Unc | BU |
|---|---|---|---|---|---|---|
| 1964(m) | 40,000,000 | — | — | — | 0.50 | — |
| 1965(m) | 60,000,000 | — | — | — | 0.50 | — |

**5 CENTIMOS** **Y# 38.3** **Composition:** Copper-Nickel

| Date | Mintage | F | VF | XF | Unc | BU |
|---|---|---|---|---|---|---|
| 1971(o) | 40,000,000 | — | — | — | 0.50 | — |

**5 CENTIMOS** **Y# 49** **Composition:** Copper Clad Steel

| Date | Mintage | F | VF | XF | Unc | BU |
|---|---|---|---|---|---|---|
| 1974(w) | 200,000,000 | — | — | — | 0.15 | — |
| 1976(w) | 200,000,000 | — | — | — | 0.15 | — |
| 1977(l) | 600,000,000 | — | — | — | 0.15 | — |

**5 CENTIMOS** **Y# 49a** **Composition:** Nickel Clad Steel

| Date | Mintage | F | VF | XF | Unc | BU |
|---|---|---|---|---|---|---|
| 1983(w) | 600,000,000 | — | — | — | 0.10 | — |

**5 CENTIMOS** **Y# 49b** **Composition:** Copper-Nickel Clad Steel

| Date | Mintage | F | VF | XF | Unc | BU |
|---|---|---|---|---|---|---|
| 1986(w) | 500,000,000 | — | — | — | 0.10 | — |

**10 CENTIMOS** **Y# A40** **Composition:** Copper-Nickel

| Date | Mintage | F | VF | XF | Unc | BU |
|---|---|---|---|---|---|---|
| 1971(o) | 60,000,000 | — | — | 0.10 | 0.25 | — |

**12-1/2 CENTIMOS** **Y# 28** **Composition:** Copper-Nickel
**Note:** Varieties exist.

| Date | Mintage | F | VF | XF | Unc | BU |
|---|---|---|---|---|---|---|
| 1925(p) | 800,000 | 2.50 | 6.50 | 45.00 | 200 | — |
| 1927(p) | 800,000 | 1.00 | 2.00 | 12.00 | 75.00 | — |
| 1929(p) | 800,000 | 0.15 | 0.50 | 5.00 | 45.00 | — |
| 1936(p) | 1,200,000 | 0.15 | 0.30 | 2.00 | 25.00 | — |
| 1938(p) | 1,600,000 | 0.15 | 0.30 | 1.00 | 18.00 | — |

**12-1/2 CENTIMOS** **Y# 30** **Composition:** Brass

| Date | Mintage | F | VF | XF | Unc | BU |
|---|---|---|---|---|---|---|
| 1944(d) | 800,000 | 2.50 | 4.50 | 9.00 | 60.00 | — |

**12-1/2 CENTIMOS** **Y# 30a** **Composition:** Copper-Nickel

| Date | Mintage | F | VF | XF | Unc | BU |
|---|---|---|---|---|---|---|
| 1945(p) | 11,200,000 | 0.10 | 0.20 | 0.35 | 9.00 | — |
| 1946(p) | 9,200,000 | 0.10 | 0.20 | 0.35 | 12.00 | — |
| 1948(s) | 6,000,000 | 0.10 | 0.20 | 0.35 | 8.00 | — |

**12-1/2 CENTIMOS** **Y# 39** **Composition:** Copper-Nickel
**Reverse:** Value within wreath, knobbed 2

| Date | Mintage | F | VF | XF | Unc | BU |
|---|---|---|---|---|---|---|
| 1958(p) | 10,000,000 | — | — | 0.20 | 3.00 | — |

**12-1/2 CENTIMOS** **Y# A39.1** **Composition:** Copper-Nickel **Obverse:** Flat stars **Reverse:** Plain 2

| Date | Mintage | F | VF | XF | Unc | BU |
|---|---|---|---|---|---|---|
| 1969(m) | 2,000,000 | — | — | — | 200 | — |

**12-1/2 CENTIMOS** **Y# A39.2** **Composition:** Copper-Nickel **Obverse:** Raised stars **Reverse:** Outlined stem ends

| Date | Mintage | F | VF | XF | Unc | BU |
|---|---|---|---|---|---|---|
| 1969(m) | Inc. above | — | — | — | 300 | — |

**12-1/2 CENTIMOS** **Y# A39.3** **Composition:** Copper-Nickel **Reverse:** Solid stem ends

| Date | Mintage | F | VF | XF | Unc | BU |
|---|---|---|---|---|---|---|
| 1969(m) | Inc. above | — | — | — | 300 | — |

**Note:** 1969 dated strikes were not released into circulation

**1/4 BOLIVAR** **Y# 20** **Weight:** 1.2500 g. **Composition:** 0.8350 Silver .0336 oz. ASW

| Date | Mintage | F | VF | XF | Unc | BU |
|---|---|---|---|---|---|---|
| 1901(a) | 393,000 | 7.00 | 25.00 | 55.00 | 300 | — |
| 1903(p) | 400,000 | 7.00 | 25.00 | 55.00 | 300 | — |
| 1911(a) | 600,000 | 2.50 | 5.00 | 12.00 | 75.00 | — |
| 1912(a) | 800,000 | 3.00 | 6.00 | 15.00 | 75.00 | — |
| 1919(p) | 400,000 | 2.50 | 5.00 | 12.00 | 75.00 | — |
| 1921(p) High 2 | 800,000 | 2.00 | 4.00 | 10.00 | 50.00 | — |
| 1921(p) Low 2 | Inc. above | 1.00 | 3.00 | 10.00 | 50.00 | — |
| 1924(p) | 400,000 | 1.00 | 3.00 | 10.00 | 35.00 | — |
| 1929(p) | 1,200,000 | — | BV | 1.00 | 6.00 | — |
| 1935(p) | 3,400,000 | — | BV | 1.00 | 3.00 | — |
| 1936(p) | 2,800,000 | — | BV | 1.00 | 3.00 | — |
| 1944(p) | 1,800,000 | — | BV | 1.00 | 2.00 | — |
| 1945(p) | 8,000,000 | — | — | BV | 1.50 | — |
| 1946(p) | 8,000,000 | — | — | BV | 1.00 | — |
| 1948(s) | 8,638,000 | — | — | BV | 1.00 | — |

**25 CENTIMOS** **Y# 35** **Weight:** 1.2500 g. **Composition:** 0.8350 Silver .0336 oz. ASW

| Date | Mintage | F | VF | XF | Unc | BU |
|---|---|---|---|---|---|---|
| 1954(p) | 36,000,000 | — | — | BV | 1.00 | — |

**25 CENTIMOS** **Y# 35a** **Weight:** 1.2500 g. **Composition:** 0.8350 Silver .0336 oz. ASW

| Date | Mintage | F | VF | XF | Unc | BU |
|---|---|---|---|---|---|---|
| 1960(a) | 48,000,000 | — | — | BV | 0.75 | — |

**25 CENTIMOS** **Y# 40** **Composition:** Nickel

| Date | Mintage | F | VF | XF | Unc | BU |
|---|---|---|---|---|---|---|
| 1965(l) | 240,000,000 | — | — | 0.10 | 0.35 | — |

**25 CENTIMOS** **Y# 50.1** **Weight:** 1.7500 g. **Composition:** Nickel **Note:** 1.18 thick

| Date | Mintage | F | VF | XF | Unc | BU |
|---|---|---|---|---|---|---|
| 1977(w) | 240,000,000 | — | — | 0.10 | 0.25 | — |

**25 CENTIMOS** **Y# 50.2** **Weight:** 1.5000 g. **Composition:** Nickel **Note:** Dies vary for each date; thin.

| Date | Mintage | F | VF | XF | Unc | BU |
|---|---|---|---|---|---|---|
| 1977(w) | Inc. above | — | — | 0.10 | 0.25 | — |
| 1978(w) | 200,000,000 | — | — | 0.10 | 0.25 | — |
| 1987 | 150,000,000 | — | — | 0.10 | 0.25 | — |

**25 CENTIMOS** **Y# 50a** **Weight:** 1.5000 g. **Composition:** Nickel Clad Steel **Note:** Varieties exist.

| Date | Mintage | F | VF | XF | Unc | BU |
|---|---|---|---|---|---|---|
| 1989(sc) | 510,000,000 | — | — | 0.10 | 0.25 | — |
| 1990(mm) | 400,000,000 | — | — | 0.10 | 0.25 | — |

**1/2 BOLIVAR** **Y# 21** **Weight:** 2.5000 g. **Composition:** 0.8350 Silver .0671 oz. ASW

| Date | Mintage | F | VF | XF | Unc | BU |
|---|---|---|---|---|---|---|
| 1901(a) | 600,000 | 20.00 | 50.00 | 175 | 1,200 | — |
| 1903(p) | 200,000 | 75.00 | 200 | 600 | 2,000 | — |
| 1911(a) | 300,000 | 30.00 | 60.00 | 200 | 1,600 | — |
| 1912(a) | 1,920,000 | 5.00 | 15.00 | 50.00 | 300 | — |
| 1919(p) | 400,000 | 6.00 | 20.00 | 80.00 | 400 | — |
| 1921(p) Normal date | 600,000 | 2.50 | 7.00 | 16.00 | 100 | — |
| 1921(p) Narrow date | Inc. above | 3.50 | 9.00 | 27.50 | 125 | — |
| 1921(p) Wide date | Inc. above | 3.50 | 9.00 | 27.50 | 125 | — |
| 1924(p) | 800,000 | 2.50 | 7.00 | 16.00 | 85.00 | — |
| 1929(p) | 400,000 | 1.00 | 2.00 | 6.00 | 55.00 | — |
| 1935(p) | 1,000,000 | — | BV | 1.00 | 12.00 | — |
| 1936(p) | 600,000 | BV | 1.00 | 5.00 | 50.00 | — |

**Note:** Privy mark placement varies with 1901 and 1911

**1/2 BOLIVAR** **Y# 21a** **Weight:** 2.5000 g. **Composition:** 0.8350 Silver .0671 oz. ASW

| Date | Mintage | F | VF | XF | Unc | BU |
|---|---|---|---|---|---|---|
| 1944(d) Accent in Bolivar | 500,000 | 1.00 | 3.00 | 5.00 | 15.00 | — |
| 1944(d) Without accent in Bolivar | Inc. above | 1.50 | 5.00 | 10.00 | 25.00 | — |

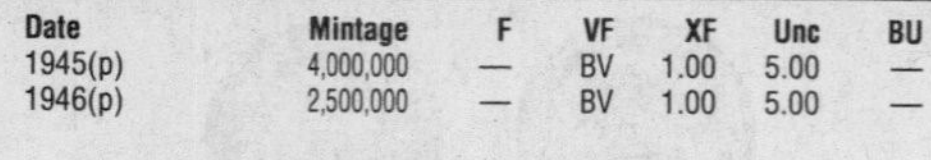

| Date | Mintage | F | VF | XF | Unc | BU |
|---|---|---|---|---|---|---|
| 1945(p) | 4,000,000 | — | BV | 1.00 | 5.00 | — |
| 1946(p) | 2,500,000 | — | BV | 1.00 | 5.00 | — |

**50 CENTIMOS Y# 36 Weight:** 2.5000 g. **Composition:** 0.8350 Silver .0671 oz. ASW

| Date | Mintage | F | VF | XF | Unc | BU |
|---|---|---|---|---|---|---|
| 1954(p) | 15,000,000 | — | — | BV | 3.00 | — |

**50 CENTIMOS Y# 36a Weight:** 2.5000 g. **Composition:** 0.8350 Silver .0671 oz. ASW

| Date | Mintage | F | VF | XF | Unc | BU |
|---|---|---|---|---|---|---|
| 1960(a) | 20,000,000 | — | — | BV | 2.00 | — |

**50 CENTIMOS Y# 41 Composition:** Nickel

| Date | Mintage | F | VF | XF | Unc | BU |
|---|---|---|---|---|---|---|
| 1965(l) | 180,000,000 | — | 0.10 | 0.15 | 0.35 | — |
| 1985(o) | 50,000,000 | — | 0.10 | 0.15 | 0.35 | — |

**50 CENTIMOS Y# 41a Weight:** 3.2000 g. **Composition:** Nickel Clad Steel

| Date | Mintage | F | VF | XF | Unc | BU |
|---|---|---|---|---|---|---|
| 1988(w) | 80,000,000 | — | 0.10 | 0.15 | 0.30 | — |
| 1989(w) | 260,000,000 | — | 0.10 | 0.15 | 0.30 | — |
| 1990(l) | 300,000,000 | — | 0.10 | 0.15 | 0.30 | — |

**Note:** Die varieties exist for 1990 dated strikes

**BOLIVAR Y# 22 Weight:** 5.0000 g. **Composition:** 0.8350 Silver .1342 oz. ASW

| Date | Mintage | F | VF | XF | Unc | BU |
|---|---|---|---|---|---|---|
| 1901(a) | 323,000 | 20.00 | 55.00 | 150 | 450 | — |
| 1903(p) | 800,000 | 5.00 | 15.00 | 90.00 | 260 | — |
| 1911(a) | 1,500,000 | 3.00 | 5.00 | 40.00 | 150 | — |
| 1912(a) Wide date | 820,000 | 6.00 | 16.50 | 75.00 | 250 | — |
| 1912(a) Narrow date | Inc. above | 6.00 | 16.50 | 75.00 | 250 | — |
| 1919(p) | 1,000,000 | 2.00 | 3.00 | 12.00 | 45.00 | — |
| 1921(p) | 1,000,000 | 2.00 | 3.00 | 12.00 | 40.00 | — |
| 1924(p) | 1,500,000 | BV | 2.00 | 6.00 | 30.00 | — |
| 1926(p) | 1,000,000 | BV | 2.00 | 6.00 | 30.00 | — |
| 1929(p) | 2,500,000 | — | BV | 1.50 | 8.00 | — |
| 1935(p) | 5,000,000 | — | BV | 1.50 | 5.00 | — |
| 1936(p) | 5,000,000 | — | BV | 1.50 | 5.00 | — |

**BOLIVAR Y# 22a Weight:** 5.0000 g. **Composition:** 0.8350 Silver .1342 oz. ASW

| Date | Mintage | F | VF | XF | Unc | BU |
|---|---|---|---|---|---|---|
| 1945(p) | 8,000,000 | — | — | BV | 3.50 | — |

**BOLIVAR Y# 37 Weight:** 5.0000 g. **Composition:** 0.8350 Silver .1342 oz. ASW

| Date | Mintage | F | VF | XF | Unc | BU |
|---|---|---|---|---|---|---|
| 1954(p) | 13,500,000 | — | — | BV | 2.50 | — |

**BOLIVAR Y# 37a Weight:** 5.0000 g. **Composition:** 0.8350 Silver .1342 oz. ASW

| Date | Mintage | F | VF | XF | Unc | BU |
|---|---|---|---|---|---|---|
| 1960(a) Thin letters | 30,000,000 | — | — | BV | 1.50 | — |
| 1960(a) Thick letters | Inc. above | — | — | BV | 1.50 | — |
| 1965(l) | 20,000,000 | — | — | BV | 1.50 | — |

**BOLIVAR Y# 42 Composition:** Nickel

| Date | Mintage | F | VF | XF | Unc | BU |
|---|---|---|---|---|---|---|
| 1967(l) | 180,000,000 | — | 0.10 | 0.15 | 0.75 | — |

**BOLIVAR Y# 52 Composition:** Nickel **Note:** Dies vary for each date.

| Date | Mintage | F | VF | XF | Unc | BU |
|---|---|---|---|---|---|---|
| 1977(l) | 200,000,000 | — | 0.10 | 0.15 | 0.65 | — |
| 1986(w) | 200,000,000 | — | 0.10 | 0.15 | 0.50 | — |
| 1986(w) | 50,000,000 | — | — | — | — | — |

**BOLIVAR Y# 52a.2 Composition:** Nickel Clad Steel **Obverse:** Large letters and date **Reverse:** Large letters and date **Note:** Dies vary for each date.

| Date | Mintage | F | VF | XF | Unc | BU |
|---|---|---|---|---|---|---|
| 1989(sc) | 600,000,000 | — | 0.10 | 0.15 | 0.45 | — |
| 1990(mm) | 600,000,000 | — | 0.10 | 0.15 | 0.45 | — |

**BOLIVAR Y# 52a.1 Composition:** Nickel Clad Steel **Obverse:** Small letters and date **Reverse:** Small letters and date

| Date | Mintage | F | VF | XF | Unc | BU |
|---|---|---|---|---|---|---|
| 1989(w) | 370,000,000 | — | 0.10 | 0.15 | 0.45 | — |

**2 BOLIVARES Y# 23 Weight:** 10.0000 g. **Composition:** 0.8350 Silver .2685 oz. ASW

| Date | Mintage | F | VF | XF | Unc | BU |
|---|---|---|---|---|---|---|
| 1902(p) | 500,000 | 11.50 | 45.00 | 200 | 700 | — |
| 1903(p) | 500,000 | 11.50 | 25.00 | 125 | 400 | — |
| 1904(a) Large 0, small 4 | 550,000 | 11.50 | 40.00 | 175 | 50.00 | — |
| 1904(a) Large 0, large 4 | Inc. above | 11.50 | 40.00 | 175 | 650 | — |
| 1904(a) Small 0, large 4 | Inc. above | 11.50 | 45.00 | 200 | 750 | — |
| 1904(a) Small 0, large slant 4 | Inc. above | 11.50 | 45.00 | 200 | 750 | — |
| 1904(a) Small 0, small 4 | 50,000 | 20.00 | 55.00 | 250 | 900 | — |
| 1905(a) Upright 5 | 750,000 | 3.50 | 16.50 | 100 | 400 | — |
| 1905(a) Slant 5 | Inc. above | 3.50 | 16.50 | 120 | 400 | — |
| 1911(a) | 750,000 | 3.50 | 16.50 | 60.00 | 275 | — |
| 1912(a) | 500,000 | 3.50 | 16.50 | 140 | 400 | — |
| 1913(a) Normal date | 210,000 | 40.00 | 250 | 500 | 1,000 | — |
| 1913(a) Raised 3 | Inc. above | 40.00 | 250 | 500 | 1,000 | — |
| 1919(p) | 1,000,000 | BV | 3.50 | 11.50 | 125 | — |
| 1922(p) Narrow date | 1,000,000 | BV | 3.50 | 11.50 | 85.00 | — |
| 1922(p) Wide date | Inc. above | BV | 3.50 | 11.50 | 85.00 | — |
| 1922(p) Low first 2 | Inc. above | BV | 0.50 | 11.50 | 85.00 | — |
| 1924(p) | 1,250,000 | BV | 3.50 | 11.50 | 85.00 | — |
| 1926(p) | 1,000,000 | BV | 3.50 | 11.50 | 85.00 | — |
| 1929(p) | 1,500,000 | BV | 2.75 | 8.00 | 20.00 | — |
| 1930(p) | 425,000 | 2.75 | 7.00 | 25.00 | 130 | — |
| 1935(p) | 3,000,000 | BV | 2.75 | 4.00 | 8.00 | — |
| 1936(p) | 2,500,000 | BV | 2.75 | 4.00 | 8.00 | — |

**2 BOLIVARES Y# 23a Weight:** 10.0000 g. **Composition:** 0.8350 Silver .2685 oz. ASW

| Date | Mintage | F | VF | XF | Unc | BU |
|---|---|---|---|---|---|---|
| 1945(p) | 3,000,000 | — | — | BV | 3.50 | — |

**2 BOLIVARES Y# A37 Weight:** 10.0000 g. **Composition:** 0.8350 Silver .2685 oz. ASW

| Date | Mintage | F | VF | XF | Unc | BU |
|---|---|---|---|---|---|---|
| 1960(a) | 4,000,000 | — | — | BV | 3.50 | — |
| 1965(l) | 7,170,000 | — | — | BV | 3.50 | — |

**2 BOLIVARES Y# 43 Composition:** Nickel **Note:** Dies vary for each date.

| Date | Mintage | F | VF | XF | Unc | BU |
|---|---|---|---|---|---|---|
| 1967(l) | 50,000,000 | — | — | 0.25 | 1.25 | — |
| 1986(w) | 50,000,000 | — | — | 0.25 | 1.25 | — |

**Note:** Die varieites exist for 1986 strikes

| Date | Mintage | F | VF | XF | Unc | BU |
|---|---|---|---|---|---|---|
| 1986(w) | | — | — | — | — | — |

**Note:** Die varieties exist for 1986 strikes

| Date | Mintage | F | VF | XF | Unc | BU |
|---|---|---|---|---|---|---|
| 1988(c) | 80,000,000 | — | — | 0.25 | 1.25 | — |

**2 BOLIVARES Y# 43a.1 Composition:** Nickel Clad Steel **Obverse:** Small letters **Reverse:** Small letters

| Date | Mintage | F | VF | XF | Unc | BU |
|---|---|---|---|---|---|---|
| 1989(sc) | 200,000,000 | — | — | 0.20 | 0.75 | — |
| 1990(c) | 400,000,000 | — | — | 0.20 | 0.75 | — |

**Note:** Two varieties of 1990 exist

**2 BOLIVARES Y# 43a.2 Composition:** Nickel Clad Steel **Obverse:** Large letters **Reverse:** Large letters

| Date | Mintage | F | VF | XF | Unc | BU |
|---|---|---|---|---|---|---|
| 1989(w) | 100,000,000 | — | — | 0.20 | 0.75 | — |
| 1989(c) | 95,000,000 | — | — | 0.20 | 0.75 | — |

**5 BOLIVARES Y# 24.2 (Y24.1) Weight:** 25.0000 g. **Composition:** 0.9000 Silver .7234 oz. ASW **Obverse:** Date on ribbon right of arms 13 DE APRIL DE 1864

| Date | Mintage | F | VF | XF | Unc | BU |
|---|---|---|---|---|---|---|
| 1901(a) | 90,000 | 20.00 | 100 | 375 | 1,500 | — |
| 1902(p) Wide date | 500,000 | 9.00 | 16.00 | 120 | 700 | — |
| 1902(p) Narrow date | Inc. above | 9.00 | 16.00 | 120 | 700 | — |
| 1903(p) | 200,000 | 9.00 | 16.00 | 120 | 700 | — |
| 1904(a) | 200,000 | 9.00 | 16.00 | 150 | 1,000 | — |
| 1905(a) | 300,000 | 9.00 | 16.00 | 120 | 650 | — |
| 1910(a) Oval 0 | 400,000 | 9.00 | 16.00 | 85.00 | 450 | — |
| 1910(a) Round 0 | Inc. above | 12.00 | 25.00 | 130 | 650 | — |
| 1911(a) Normal date | 1,104,000 | 6.50 | 12.50 | 45.00 | 225 | — |
| 1911(a) Wide date | Inc. above | 6.50 | 12.50 | 45.00 | 225 | — |
| 1911(a) Narrow date | Inc. above | 6.50 | 12.50 | 45.00 | 225 | — |
| 1912(a) Normal date | 696,000 | 6.50 | 12.50 | 45.00 | 225 | — |
| 1912(a) Wide date | Inc. above | 6.50 | 12.50 | 45.00 | 225 | — |
| 1912(a) Narrow date | Inc. above | 6.50 | 12.50 | 45.00 | 225 | — |
| 1919(p) | 400,000 | 6.50 | 12.50 | 30.00 | 175 | — |

| Date | Mintage | F | VF | XF | Unc | BU |
|---|---|---|---|---|---|---|
| 1921(p) Wide date | 500,000 | 6.50 | 12.50 | 25.00 | 100 | — |
| 1921(p) Narrow date | Inc. above | 6.50 | 12.50 | 25.00 | 100 | — |
| 1924(p) Wide date | 500,000 | 6.50 | 12.50 | 25.00 | 100 | — |
| 1924(p) Narrow date | Inc. above | 6.50 | 12.50 | 25.00 | 100 | — |
| 1924(p) Low 9 | Inc. above | 6.50 | 12.50 | 25.00 | 100 | — |
| 1926(p) | 800,000 | BV | 8.50 | 22.50 | 80.00 | — |
| 1929(p) High 9 | 800,000 | BV | 8.50 | 22.00 | 60.00 | — |
| 1929(p) Low 9 | Inc. above | BV | 8.50 | 22.00 | 60.00 | — |
| 1935(p) | 1,600,000 | BV | 7.50 | 16.50 | 38.00 | — |
| 1936(p) Normal date | 2,000,000 | BV | 7.50 | 16.50 | 38.00 | — |
| 1936(p) High 3 | Inc. above | BV | 7.50 | 16.50 | 38.00 | — |
| 1936(p) Low 3 | Inc. above | BV | 7.50 | 16.50 | 38.00 | — |

**5 BOLIVARES** **Y# 44** **Composition:** Nickel

| Date | Mintage | F | VF | XF | Unc | BU |
|---|---|---|---|---|---|---|
| 1973(m) | 20,000,000 | — | 0.45 | 0.75 | 1.75 | — |

**5 BOLIVARES** **Y# 53** **Composition:** Nickel

| Date | Mintage | F | VF | XF | Unc | BU |
|---|---|---|---|---|---|---|
| 1977(m) | 60,000,000 | — | — | 0.50 | 1.50 | — |
| 1987(c) | 25,000,000 | — | — | 0.50 | 1.50 | — |
| 1987(c) | — | — | — | — | — | — |
| 1988(w) | 20,000,000 | — | — | 0.50 | 1.50 | — |

**5 BOLIVARES** **Y# 53a.1** **Weight:** 13.3000 g. **Composition:** Nickel Clad Steel **Obverse:** Small letters **Reverse:** Large letters

| Date | Mintage | F | VF | XF | Unc | BU |
|---|---|---|---|---|---|---|
| 1989(w) | 55,000,000 | — | — | 0.50 | 1.50 | — |
| 1989(w) | 26,000,000 | — | — | — | — | — |

**5 BOLIVARES** **Y# 53a.2** **Weight:** 13.3000 g. **Composition:** Nickel Clad Steel **Obverse:** Large letters **Reverse:** Small letters

| Date | Mintage | F | VF | XF | Unc | BU |
|---|---|---|---|---|---|---|
| 1989(sc) | 100,000,000 | — | — | 0.50 | 1.50 | — |
| 1990(c) | 200,000,000 | — | — | 0.50 | 1.50 | — |

**5 BOLIVARES** **Y# 53a.3** **Weight:** 13.3000 g. **Composition:** Nickel Clad Steel **Note:** Large letters in legends.

| Date | Mintage | F | VF | XF | Unc | BU |
|---|---|---|---|---|---|---|
| 1990 | — | — | — | 0.65 | 1.75 | — |

**10 BOLIVARES** **Y# 31** **Weight:** 3.2258 g. **Composition:** 0.9000 Gold .0933 oz. AGW

| Date | Mintage | F | VF | XF | Unc | BU |
|---|---|---|---|---|---|---|
| 1930(p) | Est. 500,000 | — | BV | 40.00 | 75.00 | — |

**Note:** Only 10% of the total mintage was released; the balance remaining as part of the nation's gold reserve

**10 BOLIVARES** **Y# 45** **Weight:** 30.0000 g. **Composition:** 0.9000 Silver .8681 oz. ASW

| Date | Mintage | F | VF | XF | Unc | BU |
|---|---|---|---|---|---|---|
| 1973(o) | 200 | — | — | — | 400 | — |
| 1973(o) Proof | 2,000,000 | Value: 11.50 | | | | |

**10 BOLIVARES** **Y# 75** **Composition:** Nickel Clad Steel **Obverse:** National arms above denomination **Reverse:** Bolivar

| Date | Mintage | F | VF | XF | Unc | BU |
|---|---|---|---|---|---|---|
| 1998 | — | — | — | 0.25 | 0.50 | — |

**10 BOLIVARES** **Y# 80** **Weight:** 2.3300 g. **Composition:** Nickel Clad Steel **Obverse:** National arms and denomination. **Reverse:** Bolivar's portrait with new mint mark at left. **Edge:** Reeded. **Size:** 16.85 mm. **Note:** Struck at Maracay Mint.

| Date | Mintage | F | VF | XF | Unc | BU |
|---|---|---|---|---|---|---|
| 2000 | — | — | — | — | 0.50 | — |

**20 BOLIVARES** **Y# 32** **Weight:** 6.4516 g. **Composition:** 0.9000 Gold .1867 oz. AGW

| Date | Mintage | F | VF | XF | Unc | BU |
|---|---|---|---|---|---|---|
| 1904(a) | 100,000 | BV | 70.00 | 80.00 | 110 | — |
| 1905(a) | 100,000 | BV | 70.00 | 80.00 | 110 | — |
| 1910(a) | 70,000 | BV | 70.00 | 80.00 | 110 | — |

**Note:** Die varieties exist in the placement of dot between date and Lei, Type 1 is evenly space, Type 2 had dot closer to L of Lei

| Date | Mintage | F | VF | XF | Unc | BU |
|---|---|---|---|---|---|---|
| 1911(a) | 80,000 | BV | 70.00 | 80.00 | 110 | — |

**Note:** Die varieties exist in the placement of dot between date and Lei, Type 1 is evenly space, Type 2 had dot closer to L of Lei

| Date | Mintage | F | VF | XF | Unc | BU |
|---|---|---|---|---|---|---|
| 1912(a) | 150,000 | BV | 70.00 | 80.00 | 110 | — |

**Note:** Die varieties exist in the placement of the torch privy mark in relation to bust truncation; Type 1 is well below truncation, Type 2 is slightly below truncation and Type 3 is in line with the truncation

**20 BOLIVARES** **Y# 76** **Composition:** Nickel Clad Steel **Obverse:** National arms above denomination **Reverse:** Bolivar

| Date | Mintage | F | VF | XF | Unc | BU |
|---|---|---|---|---|---|---|
| 1998 | — | — | — | 0.25 | 0.50 | — |

**20 BOLIVARES** **Y# 81** **Weight:** 4.3200 g. **Composition:** Nickel Clad Steel **Obverse:** National arms and denomination. **Reverse:** Bolivar's portrait with new mint mark at left. **Edge:** Plain. **Size:** 20 mm. **Note:** Struck at Maracay Mint.

| Date | Mintage | F | VF | XF | Unc | BU |
|---|---|---|---|---|---|---|
| 2000 | — | — | — | — | 0.65 | — |

**25 BOLIVARES** **Y# 46** **Weight:** 28.2800 g. **Composition:** 0.9250 Silver .8411 oz. ASW **Subject:** Conservation **Reverse:** Jaguar

| Date | Mintage | F | VF | XF | Unc | BU |
|---|---|---|---|---|---|---|
| 1975(l) | 38,000 | — | — | — | 20.00 | — |
| 1975(l) Proof | 8,000,000 | Value: 30.00 | | | | |

**50 BOLIVARES** **Y# 47** **Weight:** 35.0000 g. **Composition:** 0.9250 Silver 1.0409 oz. ASW **Subject:** Conservation **Obverse:** Similar to 25 Bolivares, Y#46 **Reverse:** Giant Armadillo

| Date | Mintage | F | VF | XF | Unc | BU |
|---|---|---|---|---|---|---|
| 1975(l) | 39,000 | — | — | — | 22.50 | — |
| 1975(l) Proof | 8,000,000 | Value: 32.50 | | | | |

**50 BOLIVARES** **Y# 66** **Weight:** 31.1000 g. **Composition:** 0.9000 Silver .9000 oz. ASW **Subject:** 50th Anniversary of Central Bank

| Date | Mintage | F | VF | XF | Unc | BU |
|---|---|---|---|---|---|---|
| 1990(c) Proof | 10,000 | Value: 45.00 | | | | |

**50 BOLIVARES** Y# 67 **Weight:** 15.5500 g. **Composition:** 0.9000 Gold .4500 oz. AGW **Subject:** 50th Anniversary of Central Bank

| Date | Mintage | F | VF | XF | Unc | BU |
|---|---|---|---|---|---|---|
| 1990(c) Proof | 5,000 | Value: 350 | | | | |

**50 BOLIVARES** Y# 77 **Composition:** Nickel Clad Steel **Obverse:** National arms above denomination **Reverse:** Bolivar

| Date | Mintage | F | VF | XF | Unc | BU |
|---|---|---|---|---|---|---|
| 1998 | — | — | — | 0.35 | 0.75 | — |

**50 BOLIVARES** Y# 82 **Weight:** 6.6500 g. **Composition:** Nickel Clad Steel **Obverse:** National arms and denomination. **Reverse:** Bolivar's portrait with new mint mark at left. **Edge:** Reeded. **Size:** 23 mm.

| Date | Mintage | F | VF | XF | Unc | BU |
|---|---|---|---|---|---|---|
| 2000 | — | — | — | — | 0.80 | — |

**75 BOLIVARES** Y# 55 **Weight:** 17.0000 g. **Composition:** 0.9000 Silver .4920 oz. ASW **Subject:** 50th Anniversary - Sucre's Death

| Date | Mintage | F | VF | XF | Unc | BU |
|---|---|---|---|---|---|---|
| 1980(l) | 500,000 | — | — | — | 10.00 | — |
| 1980(l) Proof | 200 | Value: 450 | | | | |

**100 BOLIVARES** Y# 56 **Weight:** 22.0000 g. **Composition:** 0.9000 Silver .6367 oz. ASW **Subject:** 150th Anniversary - Bolivar's Death

| Date | Mintage | F | VF | XF | Unc | BU |
|---|---|---|---|---|---|---|
| 1980(l) | 500,000 | — | — | — | 12.50 | — |
| 1980(l) Proof | 200 | Value: 450 | | | | |

**100 BOLIVARES** Y# 57 **Weight:** 27.0000 g. **Composition:** 0.8350 Silver .7249 oz. ASW **Subject:** 200th Anniversary - Birth of Andres Bello

| Date | Mintage | F | VF | XF | Unc | BU |
|---|---|---|---|---|---|---|
| ND(1981)(w) | 200 | — | — | — | 400 | — |
| ND(1981)(w) Proof | 500,000 | Value: 10.00 | | | | |

**100 BOLIVARES** Y# 58 **Weight:** 31.0000 g. **Composition:** 0.9000 Silver .9000 oz. ASW **Subject:** 200th Anniversary - Birth of Simon Bolivar

| Date | Mintage | F | VF | XF | Unc | BU |
|---|---|---|---|---|---|---|
| ND(1983)(w) Proof | 300,000 | Value: 17.50 | | | | |

**100 BOLIVARES** Y# 60 **Weight:** 31.0000 g. **Composition:** 0.9000 Silver .9000 oz. ASW **Subject:** 200th Anniversary - Birth of Jose M. Vargas

| Date | Mintage | F | VF | XF | Unc | BU |
|---|---|---|---|---|---|---|
| ND(1986)(l) | 500,000 | — | — | — | 8.50 | — |
| ND(1986)(l) Proof | 500 | Value: 250 | | | | |

**Note:** Beware of some altered circulation coins to look like proofs

**100 BOLIVARES** Y# 78 **Composition:** Nickel Clad Steel **Obverse:** National arms above denomination **Reverse:** Bolivar

| Date | Mintage | F | VF | XF | Unc | BU |
|---|---|---|---|---|---|---|
| 1998 | — | — | — | 0.50 | 1.00 | — |

**500 BOLIVARES** Y# 54 **Weight:** 18.0000 g. **Composition:** 0.9000 Gold .5209 oz. AGW **Subject:** Nationalization of Oil Industry

| Date | Mintage | F | VF | XF | Unc | BU |
|---|---|---|---|---|---|---|
| 1975(c) Proof | 100 | Value: 12,000 | | | | |

**500 BOLIVARES** Y# 64 **Weight:** 31.1000 g. **Composition:** 0.9000 Silver .9000 oz. ASW **Reverse:** Jose Antonio Paez

| Date | Mintage | F | VF | XF | Unc | BU |
|---|---|---|---|---|---|---|
| 1990(mm) Proof | 30,000 | Value: 22.50 | | | | |

**500 BOLIVARES** Y# 69 **Weight:** 31.1000 g. **Composition:** 0.9000 Silver .9000 oz. ASW **Subject:** Battle of Matasiete

| Date | Mintage | F | VF | XF | Unc | BU |
|---|---|---|---|---|---|---|
| 1992(w) Proof | 10,000 | Value: 25.00 | | | | |

**500 BOLIVARES** Y# 71 **Weight:** 31.1000 g. **Composition:** 0.9000 Silver .9000 oz. ASW **Subject:** 50th Anniversary - United Nations

| Date | Mintage | F | VF | XF | Unc | BU |
|---|---|---|---|---|---|---|
| 1995(cc) Proof | 10,000 | Value: 25.00 | | | | |

**500 BOLIVARES** Y# 72 **Weight:** 31.1000 g. **Composition:** 0.9000 Silver .9000 oz. ASW **Subject:** 200th Anniversary - Sucre's Birth

| Date | Mintage | F | VF | XF | Unc | BU |
|---|---|---|---|---|---|---|
| 1995(cc) Proof | 15,000 | Value: 25.00 | | | | |

**500 BOLIVARES** Y# 74 **Weight:** 31.1000 g. **Composition:** 0.9000 Silver .9000 oz. ASW **Obverse:** National arms **Reverse:** Two portraits **Note:** Manuel Gual and Jose Maria Espana

| Date | Mintage | F | VF | XF | Unc | BU |
|---|---|---|---|---|---|---|
| 1997A Proof | 10,000 | Value: 25.00 | | | | |

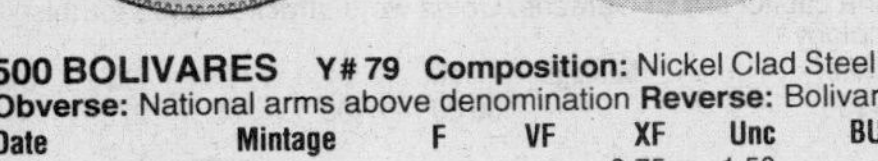

**500 BOLIVARES Y# 79 Composition:** Nickel Clad Steel **Obverse:** National arms above denomination **Reverse:** Bolivar

| Date | Mintage | F | VF | XF | Unc | BU |
|---|---|---|---|---|---|---|
| 1998 | — | — | — | 0.75 | 1.50 | — |

**1000 BOLIVARES Y# 48.1 Weight:** 33.4370 g. **Composition:** 0.9000 Gold .9676 oz. AGW **Subject:** Conservation Series - Cock of the Rocks **Reverse:** Feathered wings

| Date | Mintage | F | VF | XF | Unc | BU |
|---|---|---|---|---|---|---|
| 1975(l) | 5,047 | — | — | — | 475 | — |
| 1975(l) Proof | 483 | Value: 950 | | | | |

**1000 BOLIVARES Y# 48.2 Weight:** 33.4370 g. **Composition:** 0.9000 Gold .9676 oz. AGW **Subject:** Conservation Series - Cock of the Rocks **Reverse:** Smooth wings

| Date | Mintage | F | VF | XF | Unc | BU |
|---|---|---|---|---|---|---|
| 1975(l) | Inc. above | — | — | — | 500 | — |
| 1975(l) Proof reported, not confirmed | Inc. above | — | — | — | — | — |

**1100 BOLIVARES Y# 68 Weight:** 27.0000 g. **Composition:** 0.9250 Silver .8029 oz. ASW **Subject:** Ibero - American Series

| Date | Mintage | F | VF | XF | Unc | BU |
|---|---|---|---|---|---|---|
| 1991(mm) Proof | 30,000 | Value: 50.00 | | | | |

**3000 BOLIVARES Y# 59 Weight:** 31.1000 g. **Composition:** 0.9000 Gold .9000 oz. AGW **Subject:** 200th Anniversary - Birth of Simon Bolivar

| Date | Mintage | F | VF | XF | Unc | BU |
|---|---|---|---|---|---|---|
| ND(1983)(w) Proof | 10,000 | Value: 425 | | | | |

**5000 BOLIVARES Y# 62 Weight:** 15.5500 g. **Composition:** 0.9000 Gold .4500 oz. AGW **Reverse:** Rafael Urdaneta

| Date | Mintage | F | VF | XF | Unc | BU |
|---|---|---|---|---|---|---|
| 1988(cc) Proof | 25,000 | Value: 200 | | | | |

**5000 BOLIVARES Y# 63 Weight:** 15.5500 g. **Composition:** 0.9000 Gold .4500 oz. AGW **Reverse:** Santiago Marino

| Date | Mintage | F | VF | XF | Unc | BU |
|---|---|---|---|---|---|---|
| 1988(cc) Proof | 25,000 | Value: 200 | | | | |

**5000 BOLIVARES Y# 65 Weight:** 15.5500 g. **Composition:** 0.9000 Gold .4500 oz. AGW **Reverse:** Jose Antonio Paez

| Date | Mintage | F | VF | XF | Unc | BU |
|---|---|---|---|---|---|---|
| 1990(mm) Proof | 10,000 | Value: 200 | | | | |

**5000 BOLIVARES Y# 73 Weight:** 15.5500 g. **Composition:** 0.9000 Gold .4500 oz. AGW **Subject:** 200th Anniversary - Sucre's Birth

| Date | Mintage | F | VF | XF | Unc | BU |
|---|---|---|---|---|---|---|
| 1995(cc) Proof | 10,000 | Value: 260 | | | | |

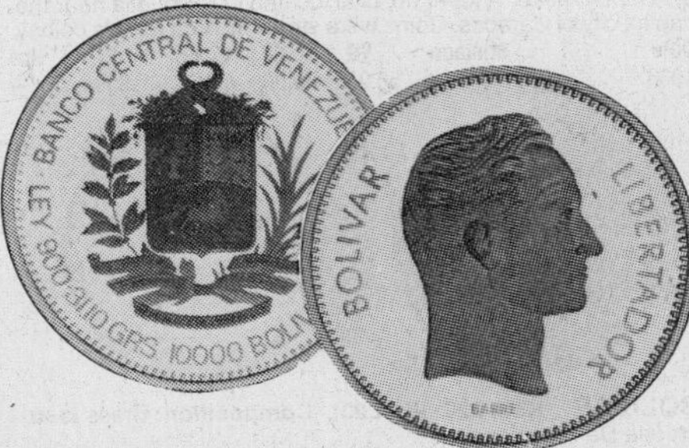

**10000 BOLIVARES Y# 61 Weight:** 31.1000 g. **Composition:** 0.9000 Gold .9000 oz. AGW

| Date | Mintage | F | VF | XF | Unc | BU |
|---|---|---|---|---|---|---|
| 1987(c) Proof | 50,000 | Value: 325 | | | | |

## ESSAIS

| KM# | Date | Mintage | Identification | Mkt Val |
|---|---|---|---|---|
| | 1991(c) | — | 1300 Bolivares. 0.9000 Copper. M1, thin planchet. | — |
| E18 | 1991(c) | — | 1300 Bolivares. 0.9000 Copper. M1, thick planchet. | — |

## PATTERNS

including off metal strikes

| KM# | Date | Mintage | Identification | Mkt Val |
|---|---|---|---|---|
| Pn46-47 | 1973(m) | — | 5 Bolivares. Nickel. | 700 |
| Pn48 | 1977(w) | — | 25 Centimos. Nickel. | 100 |
| Pn49 | 1977(m) | — | 5 Bolivares. Nickel. | 200 |
| Pn50 | 1981(w) | — | 100 Bolivares. Silver. Y57, with LEY. | 400 |
| Pn51 | 1990(c) | — | 50 Bolivares. Lead. | 200 |
| Pn52 | 1990(c) | — | 50 Bolivares. Silver. | 600 |
| Pn53 | 1990(c) | — | 50 Bolivares. Gold. Medal rotation | 600 |
| Pn54 | 1990(c) | — | 50 Bolivares. Gold. Coin rotation. | 600 |
| Pn55 | 1990(c) | — | 50 Bolivares. Gold. | 1,000 |
| Pn56 | 1990 | — | 5000 Bolivares. Copper-Nickel. Y65. | 2,000 |

## TRIAL STRIKES

| KM# | Date | Mintage | Identification | Mkt Val |
|---|---|---|---|---|
| TS10 | 1973(c) | — | 10 Bolivares. Silver. 2 obverses. | 400 |
| TS12 | 1975(c) | — | 500 Bolivares. Gold plated; Uniface reverse. | — |
| TS9 | 1977 | — | 10 Bolivares. 0.9000 Silver. Uniface reverse. | 1,000 |
| TS13 | 1977(m) | — | 5 Bolivares. Nickel. Uniface obverse. | 200 |
| TS14 | 1990(c) | — | 50 Bolivares. Copper. Y66, uniface obverse. | 600 |
| TS15 | 1990(c) | — | 50 Bolivares. Copper. Y66, uniface reverse. | 600 |
| TS16 | 1990(c) | — | 50 Bolivares. Bronze. Y66, uniface obverse. | 600 |
| TS17 | 1990(c) | — | 50 Bolivares. Bronze. Y66, uniface reverse. | 600 |
| TS18 | 1990(c) | — | 50 Bolivares. Silver. Y66, uniface obverse. | 1,000 |
| TS20 | 1990(d) | — | 50 Bolivares. Copper. Y67, uniface obverse. | 600 |
| TS21 | 1990(c) | — | 50 Bolivares. Copper. Y67, uniface reverse. | 600 |
| TS11 | 1975(c) | — | 500 Bolivares. Gold plated; Uniface obverse. | — |
| TS19 | 1990(c) | — | 50 Bolivares. Silver. Y#66. Uniface. | 600 |
| TS24 | 1991(c) | — | 1300 Bolivares. Copper. Y79, uniface obverse. | — |
| TS25 | 1991(c) | — | 1300 Bolivares. Copper. Y79, uniface reverse. | — |
| TS26 | 1991(c) | — | 1300 Bolivares. Silver. Y79, uniface obverse. | — |
| TS27 | 1991(c) | — | 1300 Bolivares. Silver. Y79, uniface reverse. | — |
| TS22 | 1991 | — | 1100 Bolivares. Y68, uniface obverse. | 650 |
| TS23 | ND (1991) | — | 1100 Bolivares. Y68, uniface reverse. | 650 |

## PRIVATE PATTERNS

| KM# | Date | Mintage | Identification | Mkt Val |
|---|---|---|---|---|
| PPn1 | 1930 | — | 5 Bolivares. 0.9000 Silver. Gomez, Bayer Hauptmunzamt, incuse lettered inscription on edge. | 7,000 |

**Note:** Prepared by Karl Goetz. Later strikes and uniface trial strikes with original dies in various metals exist, as do modern fabrications. Mulings with Goetz German patterns exist but are possible modern restrikes or reproductions, refer to Unusual World Coins for detailed listings

| KM# | Date | Mintage | Identification | Mkt Val |
|---|---|---|---|---|
| PPn2 | 1973(c) | — | 10 Bolivares. Silver. Similar to KM45. (Pn5) | 800 |
| PPn3 | 1973(c) | — | 10 Bolivares. Silver. Double obverse similar to KM45. | 600 |

## PRIVATE TRIAL STRIKES

| KM# | Date | Mintage | Identification | Mkt Val |
|---|---|---|---|---|
| PTS1 | 1973 | — | 10 Bolivares. Uniface obverse similar to KM45. (TS2) | 200 |

| KM# | Date | Mintage | Identification | Mkt Val |
|---|---|---|---|---|
| PTS2 | 1973 | — | 10 Bolivares. Uniface reverse similar to KM45. (TS3) | 500 |

## MINT SETS

| KM# | Date | Mintage | Identification | Issue Price | Mkt Val |
|---|---|---|---|---|---|
| MS1 | 1975 (3) | — | Y46-48 | 250 | 500 |

## PROOF SETS

| KM# | Date | Mintage | Identification | Issue Price | Mkt Val |
|---|---|---|---|---|---|
| PS1 | 1975 (3) | — | Y46-48 | — | 1,000 |

## MARACAIBO

The Venezuelan Government maintained a large leper colony on Providencia Island in Lake Maracaibo, where hundreds of people suffering from Hansen's disease were cared for. To provide a monetary system and prevent regular coinage, handled by lepers, to re-circulate in the general population, the Venezuelan Government created a special currency. They had value only on the island until 30 years ago, when the illness was almost fully extinguished in South America and medical research revealed that little risk was involved in handling these coins.

### LEPROSARIUM COINAGE

**0.05 BOLIVAR (5 Centimos)** **KM# L11 (KML10)** **Composition:** Brass **Issuer:** Cabo Blanco, A leper hospital located in Maiquetia near the capitol city of Caracas. Coins were struck in 1936 for this colony.

| Date | Mintage | VG | F | VF | XF | Unc |
|---|---|---|---|---|---|---|
| 1936 | — | 3.00 | 6.00 | 10.00 | 20.00 | — |

**0.05 BOLIVAR (5 Centimos)** **KM# L19 (KML20)** **Composition:** Brass **Issuer:** Isla De Providencia

| Date | Mintage | VG | F | VF | XF | Unc |
|---|---|---|---|---|---|---|
| 1939 | — | 2.00 | 4.00 | 8.00 | 16.00 | — |

**1/8 BOLIVAR** **KM# L3 (KML1)** **Composition:** Brass **Issuer:** Maracaibo Lazareto Nacional

| Date | Mintage | VG | F | VF | XF | Unc |
|---|---|---|---|---|---|---|
| 1913 | — | 3.50 | 7.00 | 12.00 | 25.00 | — |
| 1916 | — | 20.00 | 40.00 | 80.00 | 135 | — |

**1/8 BOLIVAR** **KM# L3a (KML1a)** **Composition:** Copper Nickel **Issuer:** Maracaibo Lazareto Nacional

| Date | Mintage | VG | F | VF | XF | Unc |
|---|---|---|---|---|---|---|
| 1913 Rare | — | — | — | — | — | — |

**0.12-1/2 BOLIVAR (12-1/2 Centimos)** **KM# L12 (KML11)** **Composition:** Brass **Issuer:** Cabo Blanco, A leper hospital located in Maiquetia near the capitol city of Caracas. Coins were struck in 1936 for this colony.

| Date | Mintage | VG | F | VF | XF | Unc |
|---|---|---|---|---|---|---|
| 1936 | — | 25.00 | 50.00 | 85.00 | 135 | — |

**0.12-1/2 BOLIVAR (12-1/2 Centimos)** **KM# L20 (KML21)** **Composition:** Brass **Issuer:** Isla De Providencia

| Date | Mintage | VG | F | VF | XF | Unc |
|---|---|---|---|---|---|---|
| 1939 | — | 2.50 | 5.00 | 9.00 | 18.00 | — |

**0.12-1/2 BOLIVAR (12-1/2 Centimos)** **KM# L20a (KML21a)** **Composition:** Copper-Nickel **Issuer:** Isla De Providencia

| Date | Mintage | VG | F | VF | XF | Unc |
|---|---|---|---|---|---|---|
| 1939 Rare | — | — | — | — | — | — |

**1/2 BOLIVAR** **KM# L4 (KML2)** **Composition:** Brass **Issuer:** Maracaibo Lazareto Nacional **Note:** Similar to 1/8 Bolivar previous KM#L1, now numbered KM#L3.

| Date | Mintage | VG | F | VF | XF | Unc |
|---|---|---|---|---|---|---|
| 1913 | — | 20.00 | 35.00 | 75.00 | 125 | — |
| 1916 | — | 35.00 | 65.00 | 140 | 250 | — |

**0.50 BOLIVAR (50 Centimos)** **KM# L13 (KML12)** **Composition:** Brass **Issuer:** Cabo Blanco, A leper hospital located in Maiquetia near the capitol city of Caracas. Coins were struck in 1936 for this colony.

| Date | Mintage | VG | F | VF | XF | Unc |
|---|---|---|---|---|---|---|
| 1936 | — | 35.00 | 65.00 | 110 | 185 | — |

**0.50 BOLIVAR (50 Centimos)** **KM# L21 (KML22)** **Composition:** Brass **Issuer:** Isla De Providencia

| Date | Mintage | VG | F | VF | XF | Unc |
|---|---|---|---|---|---|---|
| 1939 | — | 20.00 | 40.00 | 75.00 | 125 | — |

**BOLIVAR** **KM# L5 (KML3)** **Composition:** Brass **Issuer:** Maracaibo Lazareto Nacional **Note:** Similar to 1/8 Bolivar, previous KM#L1, now numbered KM#L3.

| Date | Mintage | VG | F | VF | XF | Unc |
|---|---|---|---|---|---|---|
| 1913 | — | 20.00 | 30.00 | 45.00 | 75.00 | — |
| 1916 | — | 25.00 | 40.00 | 55.00 | 85.00 | — |

**BOLIVAR** **KM# L14 (KML13)** **Composition:** Brass **Issuer:** Cabo Blanco, A leper hospital located in Maiquetia near the capitol city of Caracas. Coins were struck in 1936 for this colony.

| Date | Mintage | VG | F | VF | XF | Unc |
|---|---|---|---|---|---|---|
| 1936 | — | 50.00 | 85.00 | 150 | 250 | — |

**BOLIVAR** **KM# L22 (KML23)** **Composition:** Brass **Issuer:** Isla De Providencia

| Date | Mintage | VG | F | VF | XF | Unc |
|---|---|---|---|---|---|---|
| 1939 | — | 25.00 | 50.00 | 90.00 | 150 | — |

**2 BOLIVARES** **KM# L6 (KML4)** **Composition:** Brass **Issuer:** Maracaibo Lazareto Nacional **Obverse:** Similar to 20 Bolivares, previous KM#L7, now numbered KM#L9

| Date | Mintage | VG | F | VF | XF | Unc |
|---|---|---|---|---|---|---|
| 1913 | — | 25.00 | 40.00 | 60.00 | 100 | — |
| 1916 | — | 35.00 | 50.00 | 70.00 | 120 | — |

**2 BOLIVARES** **KM# L15 (KML14)** **Composition:** Brass **Issuer:** Cabo Blanco, A leper hospital located in Maiquetia near the capitol city of Caracas. Coins were struck in 1936 for this colony.

| Date | Mintage | VG | F | VF | XF | Unc |
|---|---|---|---|---|---|---|
| 1936 | — | 60.00 | 100 | 165 | 270 | — |

**2 BOLIVARES** **KM# L23 (KML24)** **Composition:** Brass **Issuer:** Isla De Providencia

| Date | Mintage | VG | F | VF | XF | Unc |
|---|---|---|---|---|---|---|
| 1939 | — | 30.00 | 60.00 | 110 | 185 | — |

**5 BOLIVARES** **KM# L7 (KML5)** **Composition:** Brass **Issuer:** Maracaibo Lazareto Nacional **Note:** Similar to 1/8 Bolivar, prevous KM#L1, now numbered KM#L3.

| Date | Mintage | VG | F | VF | XF | Unc |
|---|---|---|---|---|---|---|
| 1913 | — | 55.00 | 100 | 175 | 275 | — |
| 1916 | — | 85.00 | 120 | 200 | 350 | — |

**5 BOLIVARES** **KM# L16 (KML15)** **Composition:** Brass **Issuer:** Cabo Blanco, A leper hospital located in Maiquetia near the capitol city of Caracas. Coins were struck in 1936 for this colony.

| Date | Mintage | VG | F | VF | XF | Unc |
|---|---|---|---|---|---|---|
| 1936 | — | 80.00 | 140 | 220 | 375 | — |

**5 BOLIVARES** **KM# L24 (KML25)** **Composition:** Brass **Issuer:** Isla De Providencia

| Date | Mintage | VG | F | VF | XF | Unc |
|---|---|---|---|---|---|---|
| 1939 | — | 40.00 | 85.00 | 165 | 275 | — |

**10 BOLIVARES** **KM# L8 (KML6)** **Composition:** Brass **Issuer:** Maracaibo Lazareto Nacional **Note:** Similar to 1/8 Bolivar, previous KM#L1, now numbered KM#L3.

| Date | Mintage | VG | F | VF | XF | Unc |
|---|---|---|---|---|---|---|
| 1913 | — | 60.00 | 120 | 200 | 350 | — |
| 1916 | — | 90.00 | 180 | 300 | 500 | — |

**10 BOLIVARES** **KM# L17 (KML16)** **Composition:** Brass **Issuer:** Cabo Blanco

, A leper hospital located in Maiquetia near the capitol city of Caracas. Coins were struck in 1936 for this colony.

| Date | Mintage | VG | F | VF | XF | Unc |
|---|---|---|---|---|---|---|
| 1936 | — | 120 | 200 | 320 | 500 | — |

**10 BOLIVARES** **KM# L25 (KML26)** **Composition:** Brass **Issuer:** Isla De Providencia

| Date | Mintage | VG | F | VF | XF | Unc |
|---|---|---|---|---|---|---|
| 1939 Reported, not confirmed | — | — | — | — | — | — |

**Note:** According to records, coins with the 10 Bolivares denomination were authorized to be struck, but at present none are known to exist in the numismatic community

**20 BOLIVARES** **KM# L9 (KML7)** **Composition:** Brass **Issuer:** Maracaibo Lazareto Nacional **Reverse:** Similar to 2 Bolivares, previous KM#L4, now numbered KM#L6

| Date | Mintage | VG | F | VF | XF | Unc |
|---|---|---|---|---|---|---|
| 1913 | — | 175 | 275 | 400 | 600 | — |
| 1916 | — | 250 | 350 | 500 | 700 | — |

**20 BOLIVARES** **KM# L18 (KML17)** **Composition:** Brass **Issuer:** Cabo Blanco, A leper hospital located in Maiquetia near the capitol city of Caracas. Coins were struck in 1936 for this colony.

| Date | Mintage | VG | F | VF | XF | Unc |
|---|---|---|---|---|---|---|
| 1936 | — | 175 | 275 | 375 | 650 | — |

# VIET NAM

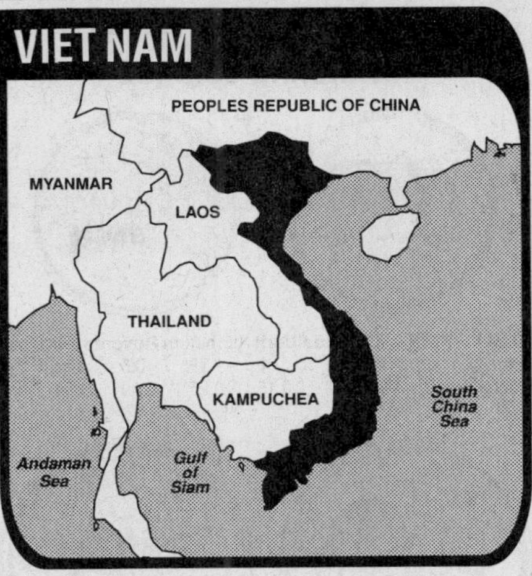


The Socialist Republic of Viet Nam, located in Southeast Asia west of the South China Sea, has an area of 127,300 sq. mi. (329,560 sq. km.) and a population of *66.8 mil-lion. Capital: Hanoi. Agricultural products, coal, and mineral ores are exported.

At the start of World War II, Vietnamese Communists fled to China's Kwangsi provinces where Ho Chi Minh organized the Revolution to free Viet Nam of French rule. The Japanese occupied Viet Nam during World War II. As the end of the war drew near, they ousted the Vichy French administration and granted Viet Nam independence under a puppet government headed by Bao Dai, Emperor of Annam. The Bao Dai government collapsed at the end of the war, and on Sept. 2, 1945, Ho Chi Minh proclaimed the existence of an independent Viet Nam consisting of Cochin-China, Annam, and Tonkin, and set up a Communist government. France recognized the new government as a free state, but reneged and in 1949 reinstalled Bao Dai as Ruler of Viet Nam and extended the regime independence within the French Union. Ho Chi Minh led a guerrilla war, in the first Indochina war, against the French which raged on to the disastrous defeat of the French at Dien Bien Phu on May 7,1954.

An agreement signed at Geneva on July 21, 1954, provided for a temporary division of Viet Nam at the 17th parallel of latitude, between a Communist-supported North and a U.S.-supported South. In Oct. 1955, South Viet Nam deposed Bao Dai by referendum and authorized the establishment of a republic with Ngo Dinh Diem as president. The Republic of South Viet Nam was proclaimed on Oct. 26, 1955, and was immediately recognized by some Western Powers.

The activities of Communists in South Viet Nam led to the second Indochina war which became to a brief halt in 1973 (when a cease-fire was arranged and U.S. forces withdrew), but it didn't end until April 30, 1975 when South Viet Nam surrendered unconditionally. The two Viet Nams were reunited as the Socialist Republic of Viet Nam on July 2, 1976.

For earlier coinage refer to French Indo-China.

**MONETARY SYSTEM**
10 Xu = 1 Hao
10 Hao = 1 Dong

## COMMUNIST

### STANDARD COINAGE

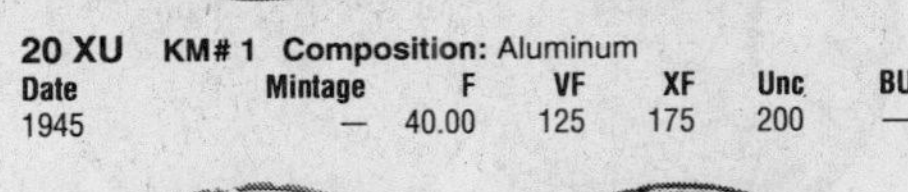

**20 XU** **KM# 1** **Composition:** Aluminum

| Date | Mintage | F | VF | XF | Unc | BU |
|---|---|---|---|---|---|---|
| 1945 | — | 40.00 | 125 | 175 | 200 | — |

**5 HAO** **KM# 2.1** **Composition:** Aluminum **Note:** Value in incuse lettering.

| Date | Mintage | F | VF | XF | Unc | BU |
|---|---|---|---|---|---|---|
| 1946 | — | 3.00 | 9.00 | 18.00 | 40.00 | — |

**Note:** Commonly encountered with rotated dies.

**5 HAO** **KM# 2.2** **Composition:** Aluminum **Note:** Value in raised lettering.

| Date | Mintage | F | VF | XF | Unc | BU |
|---|---|---|---|---|---|---|
| 1946 | — | 20.00 | 40.00 | 100 | 175 | — |

**DONG** **KM# 3** **Composition:** Aluminum

| Date | Mintage | F | VF | XF | Unc | BU |
|---|---|---|---|---|---|---|
| 1946 | — | 30.00 | 75.00 | 165 | 250 | — |

**2 DONG** **KM# 4** **Composition:** Bronze

| Date | Mintage | F | VF | XF | Unc | BU |
|---|---|---|---|---|---|---|
| 1946 | — | 7.50 | 15.00 | 40.00 | 120 | — |

**Note:** Varieties exist.

# NORTH VIET NAM

Tonkin (North Viet Nam), a former French protectorate in North Indo-China, comprises the greater part of present North Viet Nam. It had an area of 44,672 sq. mi. (75,700 sq. km.) and a population of about 4 million. Capital: Hanoi. The initial value of Tonkin to France was contained in the access it afforded to the trade of China's Yunnan province.

France established a protectorate over Annam and Tonkin by the treaties of Tientsin and Hue negotiated in1884. Tonkin was incorporated in the independent state of Viet Nam (within the French Union) and upon the defeat of France by the Viet Minh became the body of ***North Viet Nam.***

**MINT MARKS**
(a) - Paris, privy marks only

## FRENCH PROTECTORATE

### Tonkin

### MILLED COINAGE

**1/600 PIASTRE** **KM# 1** **Weight:** 2.1000 g. **Composition:** Zinc **Obv. Legend:** PROTECTORATE DU TONKIN **Reverse:** Inscription: Value above and below, "Thong-bao" at left and right **Note:** 0.9 millimeter thick planchet.

| Date | Mintage | F | VF | XF | Unc | BU |
|---|---|---|---|---|---|---|
| 1905(a) | 60,000,000 | 3.00 | 7.00 | 15.00 | 40.00 | — |

# COMMUNIST

## MILLED COINAGE

**XU** **KM# 5** **Composition:** Aluminum

| Date | Mintage | F | VF | XF | Unc | BU |
|---|---|---|---|---|---|---|
| 1958 | — | 0.65 | 1.25 | 2.00 | 3.50 | — |

**2 XU** **KM# 6** **Composition:** Aluminum

| Date | Mintage | F | VF | XF | Unc | BU |
|---|---|---|---|---|---|---|
| 1958 | — | 0.65 | 1.25 | 2.00 | 3.50 | — |

**5 XU** **KM# 7** **Composition:** Aluminum

| Date | Mintage | F | VF | XF | Unc | BU |
|---|---|---|---|---|---|---|
| 1958 | — | 0.75 | 1.50 | 2.50 | 4.50 | — |

## ESSAIS

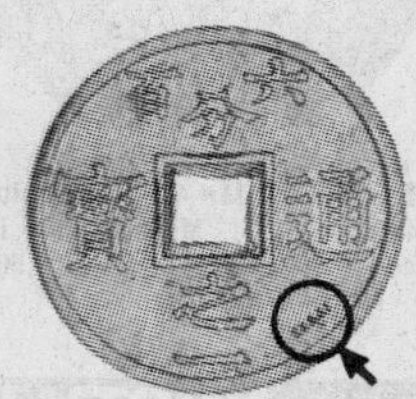

| KM# | Date | Mintage | Identification | Mkt Val |
|---|---|---|---|---|
| E1 | 1905(a) | — | 1/600 Piastre. Zinc. 2.1000 g. PROTECTORATE DU TONKIN. Inscription: Value above and below, "Thong-bao" at left and right. 0.9 millimeter thick planchet. | 300 |

## PIEFORTS

| KM# | Date | Mintage | Identification | Mkt Val |
|---|---|---|---|---|
| P1 | 1905(a) | — | 1/600 Piastre. Zinc. 4.8000 g. PROTECTORATE DU TONKIN. Inscription: Value above and below, "Thong-bao" at left and right. 1.5 millimeter thick planchet. | 700 |

# DEMOCRATIC STATE

## STANDARD COINAGE

**10 SU** **KM# 1** **Composition:** Aluminum **Reverse:** Rice plant

| Date | Mintage | F | VF | XF | Unc | BU |
|---|---|---|---|---|---|---|
| 1953(a) | 20,000,000 | 0.15 | 0.25 | 0.50 | 1.00 | — |

**20 SU** **KM# 2** **Composition:** Aluminum **Reverse:** Rice plant

| Date | Mintage | F | VF | XF | Unc | BU |
|---|---|---|---|---|---|---|
| 1953(a) | 15,000,000 | 0.30 | 0.50 | 0.85 | 1.75 | — |

**50 XU** **KM# 3** **Composition:** Aluminum

| Date | Mintage | F | VF | XF | Unc | BU |
|---|---|---|---|---|---|---|
| 1953(a) | 15,000,000 | 1.50 | 3.00 | 6.00 | 12.50 | — |

# STATE OF SOUTH VIET NAM

South Viet Nam (the former Republic of Viet Nam), located in the Southeast Asia, bounded by North Viet Nam on the north, Laos and Cambodia on the west, and the South China Sea on the east and south, had an area of 66,280 sq. mi. (171,665 sq. km.) and a population of 20 million. Capital: Saigon (now Ho Chi Minh City). The economy of the area is predominantly agricultural.

South Viet Nam, the direct successor of the French--dominated Emperor Bao Dai regime (also known as the State of Viet Nam), was created after the first Indo-China War (between the French and the Viet-Minh) by the Geneva agreement of 1954 which divided Viet Nam at the 17th parallel of latitude. The National Bank of Viet Nam, with headquarters in the old Bank of Indochina building in Saigon, came into being on Dec. 31, 1954. Elections which would have reunified North and South Viet Nam in 1956 never took place, and the North continued the war for unification of Viet Nam under the communist government of the Democratic Republic of Viet Nam begun at the close of World War II. South Viet Nam surrendered unconditionally on April 30, 1975. There followed a short period of coexistence of the two Vietnamese states, but the south was governed by the North through the Peoples' Revolutionary Government (PRG). On July 2, 1976, South and North Viet Nam joined to form the Socialist Republic of Viet Nam.

**MINT MARKS**

(a)- Paris, privy marks only

**MONETARY SYSTEM**

100 Xu (Su) = 1 Dong

# REPUBLIC OF VIET NAM

## STANDARD COINAGE

**50 SU** **KM# 4** **Composition:** Aluminum **Reverse:** Bamboo

| Date | Mintage | F | VF | XF | Unc | BU |
|---|---|---|---|---|---|---|
| 1960 | 10,000,000 | 0.25 | 0.50 | 1.25 | 2.50 | — |
| 1960 Proof | — | Value: 80.00 | | | | |

**50 XU** **KM# 6** **Composition:** Aluminum **Reverse:** Bamboo

| Date | Mintage | F | VF | XF | Unc | BU |
|---|---|---|---|---|---|---|
| 1963 | 20,000,000 | 0.20 | 0.40 | 1.00 | 2.50 | — |
| 1963 Proof | — | Value: 80.00 | | | | |

**DONG** **KM# 5** **Composition:** Copper-Nickel **Reverse:** Bamboo

| Date | Mintage | F | VF | XF | Unc | BU |
|---|---|---|---|---|---|---|
| 1960 | 105,000,000 | 0.15 | 0.50 | 1.25 | 2.50 | — |
| 1960 Proof | — | Value: 80.00 | | | | |

**DONG** **KM# 7** **Composition:** Copper-Nickel **Reverse:** Rice plant

| Date | Mintage | F | VF | XF | Unc | BU |
|---|---|---|---|---|---|---|
| 1964 | 44,000,000 | 0.15 | 0.35 | 0.50 | 1.00 | — |
| 1964 Proof | — | — | — | — | — | — |

**DONG** **KM# 7a** **Composition:** Nickel-Clad Steel

| Date | Mintage | F | VF | XF | Unc | BU |
|---|---|---|---|---|---|---|
| 1971 | — | 0.10 | 0.15 | 0.35 | 1.00 | — |

**DONG** **KM# 12** **Composition:** Aluminum **Series:** F.A.O **Reverse:** Rice plant

| Date | Mintage | F | VF | XF | Unc | BU |
|---|---|---|---|---|---|---|
| 1971 | 30,000,000 | 0.10 | 0.15 | 0.25 | 0.50 | — |

**5 DONG** **KM# 9** **Composition:** Copper-Nickel **Reverse:** Rice plant

| Date | Mintage | F | VF | XF | Unc | BU |
|---|---|---|---|---|---|---|
| 1966 | 100,000,000 | 0.10 | 0.35 | 0.50 | 1.00 | — |

**5 DONG** **KM# 9a** **Composition:** Nickel-Clad Steel

| Date | Mintage | F | VF | XF | Unc | BU |
|---|---|---|---|---|---|---|
| 1971 | 15,000,000 | 0.10 | 0.25 | 0.50 | 1.00 | — |

**10 DONG** **KM# 8** **Composition:** Copper-Nickel **Reverse:** Rice plant

| Date | Mintage | F | VF | XF | Unc | BU |
|---|---|---|---|---|---|---|
| 1964 | 15,000,000 | 0.20 | 0.40 | 0.60 | 1.25 | — |

**10 DONG** **KM# 8a** **Composition:** Nickel-Clad Steel

| Date | Mintage | F | VF | XF | Unc | BU |
|---|---|---|---|---|---|---|
| 1968 | 30,000,000 | 0.10 | 0.20 | 0.35 | 0.75 | — |
| 1970 | 50,000,000 | 0.10 | 0.20 | 0.35 | 0.75 | — |

**10 DONG** **KM# 13** **Composition:** Brass-Clad Steel **Series:** F.A.O

| Date | Mintage | F | VF | XF | Unc | BU |
|---|---|---|---|---|---|---|
| 1974 | 30,000,000 | 0.10 | 0.15 | 0.30 | 0.60 | — |

**20 DONG** KM# 10 **Composition:** Nickel-Clad Steel

| Date | Mintage | F | VF | XF | Unc | BU |
|---|---|---|---|---|---|---|
| 1968 | — | 0.25 | 0.50 | 1.00 | 2.00 | — |

**20 DONG** KM# 11 **Composition:** Nickel-Clad Steel **Series:** F.A.O

| Date | Mintage | F | VF | XF | Unc | BU |
|---|---|---|---|---|---|---|
| 1968 | 500,000 | 0.30 | 0.60 | 1.25 | 3.00 | — |



**50 DONG** KM# 14 **Composition:** Nickel Clad Steel **Series:** F.A.O

| Date | Mintage | F | VF | XF | Unc | BU |
|---|---|---|---|---|---|---|
| 1975 | 1,010,000 | 160 | 250 | 300 | 500 | — |

**Note:** It is reported that all but a few examples were disposed of as scrap metal

# PEOPLE'S REVOLUTIONARY GOVERNMENT

## STANDARD COINAGE

**XU** KM# A8 **Composition:** Aluminum

| Date | Mintage | F | VF | XF | Unc | BU |
|---|---|---|---|---|---|---|
| ND(1975) | — | 0.50 | 1.50 | 2.75 | 7.50 | — |

**2 XU** KM# A9 **Composition:** Aluminum

| Date | Mintage | F | VF | XF | Unc | BU |
|---|---|---|---|---|---|---|
| 1975 | — | 0.50 | 1.50 | 2.75 | 7.50 | — |

**5 XU** KM# A10 **Composition:** Aluminum

| Date | Mintage | F | VF | XF | Unc | BU |
|---|---|---|---|---|---|---|
| ND(1975) | — | 0.50 | 1.50 | 2.75 | 7.50 | — |

## ESSAIS

Standard metals unless otherwise noted

| KM# | Date | Mintage | Identification | Issue Price | Mkt Val |
|---|---|---|---|---|---|
| E1 | 1953 | 1,200 | 10 Su. KM#1 | — | 25.00 |
| E2 | 1953(a) | 1,200 | 20 Su. KM#2 | — | 30.00 |
| E3 | 1953(a) | 1,200 | 50 Su. KM#3 | — | 35.00 |

## PATTERNS

Including off metal strikes

| KM# | Date | Mintage | Identification | Mkt Val |
|---|---|---|---|---|
| Pn1 | 1963 | — | 50 Xu. Aluminum-Bronze. | 300 |
| Pn2 | 1963 | — | 50 Xu. Copper-Nickel. | 300 |

## PIEFORTS WITH ESSAI

Standard metals unless otherwise noted

| KM# | Date | Mintage | Identification | Issue Price | Mkt Val |
|---|---|---|---|---|---|
| PE1 | 1953(a) | 104 | 10 Su. KM#1 | — | 75.00 |
| PE2 | 1953(a) | 104 | 20 Su. KM#2 | — | 85.00 |
| PE3 | 1953(a) | 104 | 50 Xu. KM#3 | — | 95.00 |

# SOCIALIST REPUBLIC

## STANDARD COINAGE

**HAO** KM# 11 **Composition:** Aluminum

| Date | Mintage | F | VF | XF | Unc | BU |
|---|---|---|---|---|---|---|
| 1976 | — | 0.25 | 0.50 | 1.00 | 2.50 | — |

**2 HAO** KM# 12 **Composition:** Aluminum

| Date | Mintage | F | VF | XF | Unc | BU |
|---|---|---|---|---|---|---|
| 1976 | — | 0.35 | 0.65 | 1.50 | 3.50 | — |

**5 HAO** KM# 13 **Composition:** Aluminum

| Date | Mintage | F | VF | XF | Unc | BU |
|---|---|---|---|---|---|---|
| 1976 | — | 0.35 | 0.65 | 1.50 | 3.50 | — |

**DONG** KM# 14 **Composition:** Aluminum

| Date | Mintage | F | VF | XF | Unc | BU |
|---|---|---|---|---|---|---|
| 1976 | — | 0.65 | 1.35 | 3.50 | 7.50 | — |

**5 DONG** KM# 36 **Composition:** Brass **Reverse:** Mythological bird - Phoenix

| Date | Mintage | F | VF | XF | Unc | BU |
|---|---|---|---|---|---|---|
| 1989 Proof | — | Value: 6.00 | | | | |

**5 DONG** KM# 36a **Weight:** 8.7700 g. **Composition:** 0.9000 Silver .2538 oz. ASW

| Date | Mintage | F | VF | XF | Unc | BU |
|---|---|---|---|---|---|---|
| 1989 Proof | — | Value: 12.50 | | | | |

**10 DONG** KM# 15 **Composition:** Copper-Nickel **Subject:** Nature **Reverse:** Water buffalo

| Date | Mintage | F | VF | XF | Unc | BU |
|---|---|---|---|---|---|---|
| 1986(h) | 5,000 | — | — | — | 13.50 | — |

**10 DONG** KM# 16 **Composition:** Copper-Nickel **Subject:** Nature **Reverse:** Peacock

| Date | Mintage | F | VF | XF | Unc | BU |
|---|---|---|---|---|---|---|
| 1986(h) | 5,000 | — | — | — | 14.00 | — |

**10 DONG** KM# 17 **Composition:** Copper-Nickel **Subject:** Nature **Reverse:** Elephant

| Date | Mintage | F | VF | XF | Unc | BU |
|---|---|---|---|---|---|---|
| 1986(h) | 5,000 | — | — | — | 17.50 | — |

**10 DONG** KM# 28 **Composition:** Copper-Nickel **Subject:** Wildlife Preservation **Reverse:** Orangutan

| Date | Mintage | F | VF | XF | Unc | BU |
|---|---|---|---|---|---|---|
| 1987(h) | 22,000 | — | — | — | 17.50 | — |

**10 DONG** KM# 37 **Composition:** Copper-Nickel **Reverse:** Dragon ship

| Date | Mintage | F | VF | XF | Unc | BU |
|---|---|---|---|---|---|---|
| 1988 | — | — | — | — | 8.50 | — |

**10 DONG** **KM# 27** **Composition:** Copper-Nickel **Subject:** Soccer - Italy

| Date | Mintage | F | VF | XF | Unc | BU |
|---|---|---|---|---|---|---|
| 1989(h) | — | — | — | — | 10.00 | — |

**10 DONG** **KM# 38** **Composition:** Brass **Reverse:** Pillar top pagoda above water and legend

| Date | Mintage | F | VF | XF | Unc | BU |
|---|---|---|---|---|---|---|
| 1989 Proof | — | Value: 7.00 | | | | |

**10 DONG** **KM# 38a** **Composition:** 0.9000 Silver

| Date | Mintage | F | VF | XF | Unc | BU |
|---|---|---|---|---|---|---|
| 1989 Proof | — | Value: 20.00 | | | | |

**10 DONG** **KM# 33** **Composition:** Copper-Nickel **Reverse:** Loris

| Date | Mintage | F | VF | XF | Unc | BU |
|---|---|---|---|---|---|---|
| 1990(h) | 20,000 | — | — | — | 40.00 | — |

**10 DONG** **KM# 39** **Composition:** Copper-Nickel **Reverse:** Steam and sail ship - Savannah

| Date | Mintage | F | VF | XF | Unc | BU |
|---|---|---|---|---|---|---|
| 1991 | — | — | — | — | 8.50 | — |

**10 DONG** **KM# 46** **Composition:** Copper **Series:** World Cup Soccer **Reverse:** Player and U.S. Capitol

| Date | Mintage | F | VF | XF | Unc | BU |
|---|---|---|---|---|---|---|
| 1992 | — | — | — | — | 6.50 | 8.50 |

**10 DONG** **KM# 44** **Composition:** Copper-Nickel **Reverse:** Prehistoric animal - Diplodocus

| Date | Mintage | F | VF | XF | Unc | BU |
|---|---|---|---|---|---|---|
| 1993 | — | — | — | — | 22.00 | — |

**10 DONG** **KM# 49** **Composition:** Copper-Nickel **Subject:** World Food Summit **Reverse:** Rice harvesting scene

| Date | Mintage | F | VF | XF | Unc | BU |
|---|---|---|---|---|---|---|
| 1996 | — | — | — | — | 6.00 | 8.00 |

**20 DONG** **KM# 40** **Composition:** Brass **Subject:** 100th Anniversary - Birth of Ho Chi Minh

| Date | Mintage | F | VF | XF | Unc | BU |
|---|---|---|---|---|---|---|
| 1989 Proof | — | Value: 14.50 | | | | |

**20 DONG** **KM# 40a** **Composition:** 0.9000 Silver

| Date | Mintage | F | VF | XF | Unc | BU |
|---|---|---|---|---|---|---|
| 1989 Proof | — | Value: 37.50 | | | | |

**100 DONG** **KM# 18** **Weight:** 12.0000 g. **Composition:** 0.9990 Silver .3855 oz. ASW **Reverse:** Junk under sail

| Date | Mintage | F | VF | XF | Unc | BU |
|---|---|---|---|---|---|---|
| 1986 | 2,000 | — | — | — | 35.00 | — |

**100 DONG** **KM# 19** **Weight:** 12.0000 g. **Composition:** 0.9990 Silver .3855 oz. ASW **Subject:** Wildlife **Reverse:** Water buffalo

| Date | Mintage | F | VF | XF | Unc | BU |
|---|---|---|---|---|---|---|
| 1986 | 5,000 | — | — | — | 32.50 | — |

**100 DONG** **KM# 20** **Weight:** 12.0000 g. **Composition:** 0.9990 Silver .3855 oz. ASW **Subject:** Wildlife **Reverse:** Peacock

| Date | Mintage | F | VF | XF | Unc | BU |
|---|---|---|---|---|---|---|
| 1986 | 5,000 | — | — | — | 27.50 | — |

**100 DONG** **KM# 21** **Weight:** 12.0000 g. **Composition:** 0.9990 Silver .3855 oz. ASW **Subject:** Wildlife **Reverse:** Elephant

| Date | Mintage | F | VF | XF | Unc | BU |
|---|---|---|---|---|---|---|
| 1986 | 5,000 | — | — | — | 45.00 | — |

**100 DONG** **KM# 22** **Weight:** 12.0000 g. **Composition:** 0.9990 Silver .3855 oz. ASW **Subject:** 100 Years of the Automobile

| Date | Mintage | F | VF | XF | Unc | BU |
|---|---|---|---|---|---|---|
| 1986 | 2,000 | — | — | — | 18.00 | — |

**100 DONG** **KM# 23** **Weight:** 6.0000 g. **Composition:** 0.9990 Silver .1927 oz. ASW **Series:** Calgary Olympics **Reverse:** Skier

| Date | Mintage | F | VF | XF | Unc | BU |
|---|---|---|---|---|---|---|
| 1986 | 3,700 | — | — | — | 10.00 | — |

**100 DONG** **KM# 24** **Weight:** 12.0000 g. **Composition:** 0.9990 Silver .3855 oz. ASW **Series:** Seoul Olympics **Reverse:** Fencer

| Date | Mintage | F | VF | XF | Unc | BU |
|---|---|---|---|---|---|---|
| 1986 | 10,000 | — | — | — | 10.00 | — |

**100 DONG** KM# 29 **Weight:** 12.0000 g. **Composition:** 0.9990 Silver .3855 oz. ASW **Subject:** Soccer - Mexico

| Date | Mintage | F | VF | XF | Unc | BU |
|---|---|---|---|---|---|---|
| 1986(h) | 2,000 | — | — | — | 32.50 | — |

**100 DONG** KM# 25.1 **Weight:** 15.9900 g. **Composition:** 0.9800 Silver .5039 oz. ASW

| Date | Mintage | F | VF | XF | Unc | BU |
|---|---|---|---|---|---|---|
| 1988(h) | 3,000 | — | — | — | 20.00 | — |
| 1988(h) Proof | — | Value: 28.50 | | | | |

**100 DONG** KM# 25.2 **Weight:** 15.9900 g. **Composition:** 0.9800 Silver .5039 oz. ASW **Obverse:** State emblem with smaller rice grains; "VIET NAM" on ribbon, smaller denomination

| Date | Mintage | F | VF | XF | Unc | BU |
|---|---|---|---|---|---|---|
| 1988(h) | — | — | — | — | 23.50 | — |

**100 DONG** KM# 26 **Weight:** 12.0000 g. **Composition:** 0.9990 Silver .3855 oz. ASW **Subject:** Soccer - 1988

| Date | Mintage | F | VF | XF | Unc | BU |
|---|---|---|---|---|---|---|
| 1988(h) | 1,500 | — | — | — | 20.00 | — |

**100 DONG** KM# 30 **Weight:** 16.0000 g. **Composition:** 0.9990 Silver .5145 oz. ASW **Subject:** Soccer - Italy

| Date | Mintage | F | VF | XF | Unc | BU |
|---|---|---|---|---|---|---|
| 1989(h) Proof | 10,000 | Value: 27.50 | | | | |

**100 DONG** KM# 31 **Weight:** 16.0000 g. **Composition:** 0.9990 Silver .5145 oz. ASW **Series:** Summer Olympics **Subject:** Rowing

| Date | Mintage | F | VF | XF | Unc | BU |
|---|---|---|---|---|---|---|
| 1989(h) Proof | 10,000 | Value: 25.00 | | | | |

**100 DONG** KM# 32 **Weight:** 16.0000 g. **Composition:** 0.9990 Silver .5145 oz. ASW **Series:** Winter Olympics **Subject:** Hockey

| Date | Mintage | F | VF | XF | Unc | BU |
|---|---|---|---|---|---|---|
| 1990(h) Proof | 10,000 | Value: 40.00 | | | | |

**100 DONG** KM# 34 **Weight:** 12.0000 g. **Composition:** 0.9990 Silver .3858 oz. ASW **Subject:** Soccer

| Date | Mintage | F | VF | XF | Unc | BU |
|---|---|---|---|---|---|---|
| 1991(h) | — | — | — | — | 27.50 | — |

**100 DONG** KM# 35 **Weight:** 16.0000 g. **Composition:** 0.9990 Silver .5145 oz. ASW **Reverse:** Steamship Savannah

| Date | Mintage | F | VF | XF | Unc | BU |
|---|---|---|---|---|---|---|
| 1991(h) Proof | — | Value: 37.50 | | | | |

**100 DONG** KM# 42 **Weight:** 16.0000 g. **Composition:** 0.9990 Silver .5145 oz. ASW **Reverse:** Flying dinosaur - Rhamphorhynchus

| Date | Mintage | F | VF | XF | Unc | BU |
|---|---|---|---|---|---|---|
| 1993 Proof | — | Value: 42.50 | | | | |

**100 DONG** KM# 43 **Weight:** 16.0000 g. **Composition:** 0.9990 Silver .5145 oz. ASW **Reverse:** Elephants

| Date | Mintage | F | VF | XF | Unc | BU |
|---|---|---|---|---|---|---|
| 1993 Proof | — | Value: 40.00 | | | | |

**100 DONG** KM# 45 **Weight:** 16.0000 g. **Composition:** 0.9990 Silver .5145 oz. ASW **Reverse:** Prehistoric animal - Edaphosaurus

| Date | Mintage | F | VF | XF | Unc | BU |
|---|---|---|---|---|---|---|
| 1994 Proof | — | Value: 45.00 | | | | |

**100 DONG** KM# 47 **Weight:** 20.0000 g. **Composition:** 0.9990 Silver .6424 oz. ASW **Series:** Olympics **Reverse:** Gymnast on pummel horse

| Date | Mintage | F | VF | XF | Unc | BU |
|---|---|---|---|---|---|---|
| 1995 Proof | 15,000 | Value: 25.00 | | | | |

**100 DONG** **KM# 48** **Weight:** 20.0000 g. **Composition:** 0.9990 Silver And Enamel .6424 oz. **Reverse:** Caracal

| Date | Mintage | F | VF | XF | Unc | BU |
|---|---|---|---|---|---|---|
| 1996 Proof | — | Value: 60.00 | | | | |

**100 DONG** **KM# 50** **Weight:** 20.0000 g. **Composition:** 0.9990 Silver And Enamel .6430 oz. **Subject:** World Food Summit **Reverse:** Rice harvesting scene

| Date | Mintage | F | VF | XF | Unc | BU |
|---|---|---|---|---|---|---|
| 1996 Proof | — | Value: 40.00 | | | | |

**500 DONG** **KM# 41** **Weight:** 3.1030 g. **Composition:** Gold **Subject:** 100 Anniversary - Birth of Ho Chi Minh

| Date | Mintage | F | VF | XF | Unc | BU |
|---|---|---|---|---|---|---|
| 1989 | — | — | — | — | 165 | — |

**5000 DONG** **KM# 54** **Weight:** 1.2441 g. **Composition:** 0.9999 Gold .0400 oz. AGW **Subject:** Year of the Dragon **Obverse:** National arms **Reverse:** Dragon with radiant sun **Edge:** Reeded **Size:** 13.92 mm.

| Date | Mintage | F | VF | XF | Unc | BU |
|---|---|---|---|---|---|---|
| 2000 | — | Value: 40.00 | | | | |

**10000 DONG** **KM# 51** **Weight:** 20.0000 g. **Composition:** 0.9250 Silver .5948 oz. ASW **Subject:** Year of the Dragon **Obverse:** National arms **Reverse:** Dragon with radiant sun **Edge:** Reeded **Size:** 38.7 mm.

| Date | Mintage | F | VF | XF | Unc | BU |
|---|---|---|---|---|---|---|
| 2000 Proof | 10,000 | Value: 35.00 | | | | |

**10000 DONG** **KM# 52** **Weight:** 20.0000 g. **Composition:** 0.9250 Silver .5948 oz. ASW **Subject:** Year of the Dragon **Obverse:** National arms **Reverse:** Multi-color dragon **Edge:** Reeded **Size:** 38.7 mm.

| Date | Mintage | F | VF | XF | Unc | BU |
|---|---|---|---|---|---|---|
| 2000 Proof | 10,000 | Value: 35.00 | | | | |

**10000 DONG** **KM# 53** **Weight:** 20.0000 g. **Composition:** 0.9250 Silver .5948 oz. ASW **Subject:** Year of the Dragon **Obverse:** National arms **Reverse:** Two dragons **Edge:** Reeded **Size:** 38.7 mm.

| Date | Mintage | F | VF | XF | Unc | BU |
|---|---|---|---|---|---|---|
| 2000 | 10,000 | Value: 35.00 | | | | |

**10000 DONG** **KM# 57** **Weight:** 20.0000 g. **Composition:** 0.9250 Silver .5948 oz. ASW **Subject:** Year of the Snake **Obverse:** State arms **Reverse:** Sea snake **Edge:** Reeded **Size:** 38.7 mm.

| Date | Mintage | F | VF | XF | Unc | BU |
|---|---|---|---|---|---|---|
| 2001 Proof | 3,500 | Value: 40.00 | | | | |

**10000 DONG** **KM# 58** **Weight:** 20.0000 g. **Composition:** 0.9250 Silver .5948 oz. ASW **Subject:** Year of the Snake **Obverse:** State arms **Reverse:** Multi-colored green sea snake

| Date | Mintage | F | VF | XF | Unc | BU |
|---|---|---|---|---|---|---|
| 2001 Proof | 3,500 | Value: 40.00 | | | | |

**10000 DONG** **KM# 59** **Weight:** 20.0000 g. **Composition:** 0.9250 Silver .5948 oz. ASW **Subject:** Year of the Snake **Obverse:** State arms **Reverse:** Multi-colored holographic, cobra in center

| Date | Mintage | F | VF | XF | Unc | BU |
|---|---|---|---|---|---|---|
| 2001 Proof | 3,500 | Value: 40.00 | | | | |

**20000 DONG** **KM# 55** **Weight:** 7.7749 g. **Composition:** 0.9999 Gold .2500 oz. AGW **Subject:** Year of the Dragon **Obverse:** National arms **Reverse:** Dragon and clouds **Edge:** Reeded **Size:** 22 mm.

| Date | Mintage | F | VF | XF | Unc | BU |
|---|---|---|---|---|---|---|
| 2000 Proof | 1,800 | Value: 200 | | | | |

**50000 DONG** **KM# 56** **Weight:** 15.5518 g. **Composition:** 0.9999 Gold .5000 oz. AGW **Subject:** Year of the Dragon **Obverse:** National arms **Reverse:** Dragon before radiant sun **Edge:** Reeded **Size:** 27 mm.

| Date | Mintage | F | VF | XF | Unc | BU |
|---|---|---|---|---|---|---|
| 2000 Proof | 3,800 | Value: 325 | | | | |

## PATTERNS

| KM# | Date | Mintage | Identification | Mkt Val |
|---|---|---|---|---|
| Pn1 | 1976 | — | Hao. Silver. KM#11 | — |
| Pn2 | 1976 | — | Dong. Silver. KM#14 | — |

## PIEFORTS

| KM# | Date | Mintage | Identification | Mkt Val |
|---|---|---|---|---|
| PE1 | 1990(h) | 110 | Dong. KM#32 | 150 |

## MINT SETS

| KM# | Date | Mintage | Identification | Issue Price | Mkt Val |
|---|---|---|---|---|---|
| MS1 | 1958-1976 (7) | — | KM#5-7, Democratic Republic; KM#11-14, Socialist Republic | — | 85.00 |

## PROOF SETS

| KM# | Date | Mintage | Identification | Issue Price | Mkt Val |
|---|---|---|---|---|---|
| PS1 | 2000 (3) | 2,000 | KM#51-53 | — | 100 |
| PS2 | 2000 (2) | 800 | KM#55-56 | — | 525 |
| PS3 | 2001 (3) | 3,500 | KM#57-59 | 120 | — |

# WEST AFRICAN STATES

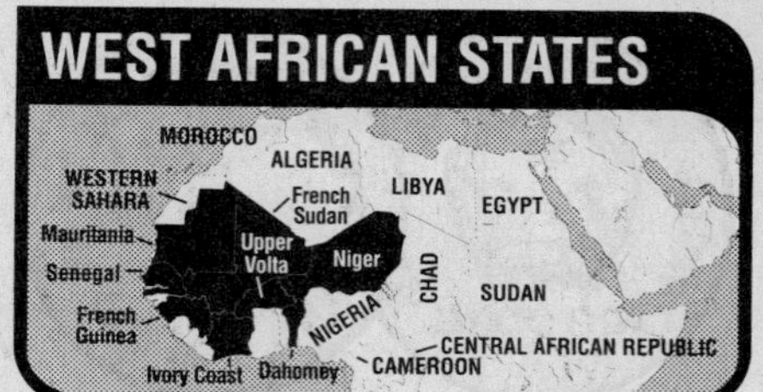


The West African States, a former federation of eight French colonial territories on the northwest coast of Africa, had area of 1,831,079 sq. mi. (4,742,495 sq. km.) and a population of about 17 million. Capital: Dakar. The constituent territories were Mauritania, Senegal, Dahomey, French Sudan, Ivory Coast, Upper Volta, Niger and French Guinea.

The members of the federation were overseas territories within the French Union until Sept. of 1958 when all but French Guinea approved the constitution of the Fifth French Republic, there by electing to become autonomous members of the new French Community. French Guinea voted to become the fully independent Republic of Guinea. The other seven attained independence in 1960. The French West Africa territories were provided with a common currency, a practice which was continued as the monetary union of the West African States which provides a common currency to the autonomous republics of Dahomey (now Benin), Senegal, Upper Volta (now Burkina Faso), Ivory Coast, Mali, Togo and Niger.

For earlier coinage refer to Togo, and French West Africa.

**MINT MARKS**

(a)- Paris, privy marks only

**MONETARY SYSTEM**

100 Centimes = 1 Franc

## FEDERATION

## STANDARD COINAGE

**FRANC** **KM# 3.1** **Composition:** Aluminum

| Date | Mintage | F | VF | XF | Unc | BU |
|---|---|---|---|---|---|---|
| 1961(a) | 3,000,000 | — | 0.15 | 0.30 | 0.60 | — |
| 1964(a) | 5,000,000 | — | 0.15 | 0.30 | 0.60 | — |
| 1965(a) | 6,000,000 | — | 0.15 | 0.30 | 0.60 | — |
| 1967(a) | 2,500,000 | — | 0.15 | 0.30 | 0.60 | — |
| 1971(a) | 4,000,000 | — | 0.15 | 0.30 | 0.60 | — |
| 1972(a) | 4,000,000 | — | 0.15 | 0.30 | 0.60 | — |
| 1973(a) | 4,500,000 | — | 0.15 | 0.30 | 0.60 | — |
| 1974(a) | — | — | 0.15 | 0.30 | 0.60 | — |
| 1975(a) | 10,080,000 | — | 0.15 | 0.30 | 0.60 | — |
| 1976(a) | 8,000,000 | — | 0.15 | 0.30 | 0.60 | — |

**FRANC** **KM# 3.2** **Composition:** Aluminum **Reverse:** Engraver general's name

| Date | Mintage | F | VF | XF | Unc | BU |
|---|---|---|---|---|---|---|
| 1962(a) | 2,000,000 | — | 2.00 | 5.00 | 10.00 | — |
| 1963(a) | 4,500,000 | — | 1.50 | 4.00 | 7.00 | — |

**FRANC** **KM# 8** **Composition:** Steel

| Date | Mintage | F | VF | XF | Unc | BU |
|---|---|---|---|---|---|---|
| 1976(a) | 8,000,000 | — | — | 0.10 | 0.35 | — |
| 1977(a) | 14,700,000 | — | — | 0.10 | 0.35 | — |
| 1978(a) | — | — | — | 0.10 | 0.35 | — |
| 1979(a) | — | — | — | 0.10 | 0.35 | — |
| 1980(a) | — | — | — | 0.10 | 0.35 | — |
| 1981(a) | — | — | — | 0.10 | 0.35 | — |
| 1982(a) | — | — | — | 0.10 | 0.35 | — |
| 1984(a) | — | — | — | 0.10 | 0.35 | — |
| 1985(a) | 26,900,000 | — | — | — | — | — |
| 1990(a) | — | — | — | 0.10 | 0.35 | — |
| 1991(a) | — | — | — | 0.10 | 0.35 | — |
| 1992(a) | — | — | — | 0.10 | 0.35 | — |
| 1995(a) | — | — | — | 0.10 | 0.35 | — |
| 1996(a) | — | — | — | 0.10 | 0.35 | — |

**5 FRANCS** **KM# 2** **Composition:** Aluminum-Bronze

| Date | Mintage | F | VF | XF | Unc | BU |
|---|---|---|---|---|---|---|
| 1960(a) | 5,000,000 | — | 0.20 | 0.40 | 0.70 | — |

**5 FRANCS** **KM# 2a** **Composition:** Aluminum-Nickel-Bronze

| Date | Mintage | F | VF | XF | Unc | BU |
|---|---|---|---|---|---|---|
| 1965(a) | 6,510,000 | — | 0.20 | 0.40 | 0.70 | — |
| 1967(a) | 6,010,000 | — | 0.20 | 0.40 | 0.70 | — |
| 1968(a) | 6,000,000 | — | 0.20 | 0.45 | 0.75 | — |
| 1969(a) | 8,000,000 | — | 0.20 | 0.40 | 0.70 | — |
| 1970(a) | 10,005,000 | — | 0.20 | 0.40 | 0.70 | — |
| 1971(a) | 10,000,000 | — | 0.20 | 0.40 | 0.70 | — |
| 1972(a) | 5,000,000 | — | 0.20 | 0.40 | 0.70 | — |
| 1973(a) | 6,000,000 | — | 0.20 | 0.45 | 0.75 | — |
| 1974(a) | 13,326,000 | — | 0.10 | 0.15 | 0.30 | — |
| 1975(a) | 16,840,000 | — | 0.20 | 0.40 | 0.70 | — |
| 1976(a) | 20,010,000 | — | 0.20 | 0.30 | 0.60 | — |
| 1977(a) | 16,840,000 | — | 0.20 | 0.30 | 0.60 | — |
| 1978(a) | — | — | 0.20 | 0.30 | 0.60 | — |
| 1979(a) | — | — | 0.10 | 0.20 | 0.40 | — |
| 1980(a) | — | — | 0.10 | 0.20 | 0.40 | — |
| 1981(a) | — | — | 0.10 | 0.20 | 0.40 | — |
| 1982(a) | — | — | 0.10 | 0.20 | 0.40 | — |
| 1984(a) | — | — | 0.10 | 0.20 | 0.40 | — |
| 1985(a) | 16,000,000 | — | 0.10 | 0.20 | 0.40 | — |
| 1986(a) | 8,000,000 | — | 0.10 | 0.20 | 0.40 | — |
| 1987(a) | — | — | 0.10 | 0.20 | 0.40 | — |
| 1988(a) | — | — | 0.10 | 0.20 | 0.40 | — |
| 1989(a) | — | — | 0.10 | 0.20 | 0.40 | — |
| 1990(a) | — | — | 0.10 | 0.20 | 0.40 | — |
| 1991(a) | — | — | 0.10 | 0.20 | 0.40 | — |
| 1992(a) | — | — | 0.10 | 0.20 | 0.40 | — |
| 1994(a) | — | — | 0.10 | 0.20 | 0.40 | — |
| 1996(a) | — | — | 0.10 | 0.20 | 0.40 | — |
| 1997(a) | — | — | 0.10 | 0.20 | 0.40 | — |

**10 FRANCS** **KM# 1** **Composition:** Aluminum-Bronze

| Date | Mintage | F | VF | XF | Unc | BU |
|---|---|---|---|---|---|---|
| 1959(a) | 10,000,000 | — | 0.15 | 0.30 | 0.60 | — |
| 1964(a) | 10,000,000 | — | 0.20 | 0.40 | 0.70 | — |

**10 FRANCS** **KM# 1a** **Composition:** Aluminum-Nickel-Bronze

| Date | Mintage | F | VF | XF | Unc | BU |
|---|---|---|---|---|---|---|
| 1966(a) | 6,000,000 | — | 0.20 | 0.40 | 0.70 | — |
| 1967(a) | 3,500,000 | — | 0.25 | 0.50 | 0.90 | — |
| 1968(a) | 6,000,000 | — | 0.20 | 0.40 | 0.70 | — |
| 1969(a) | 7,000,000 | — | 0.25 | 0.50 | 0.90 | — |
| 1970(a) | 7,000,000 | — | 0.15 | 0.30 | 0.60 | — |
| 1971(a) | 8,000,000 | — | 0.15 | 0.30 | 0.60 | — |
| 1972(a) | 5,500,000 | — | 0.20 | 0.40 | 0.70 | — |
| 1973(a) | 3,000,000 | — | 0.20 | 0.40 | 0.70 | — |
| 1974(a) | 10,000,000 | — | 0.15 | 0.30 | 0.60 | — |
| 1975(a) | 17,000,000 | — | 0.15 | 0.30 | 0.60 | — |
| 1976(a) | 18,000,000 | — | 0.15 | 0.30 | 0.60 | — |
| 1977(a) | 9,050,000 | — | 0.15 | 0.25 | 0.50 | — |
| 1978(a) | — | — | 0.15 | 0.25 | 0.50 | — |
| 1979(a) | — | — | 0.15 | 0.25 | 0.50 | — |
| 1980(a) | — | — | 0.15 | 0.25 | 0.50 | — |
| 1981(a) | — | — | 0.15 | 0.25 | 0.50 | — |

**10 FRANCS** **KM# 10** **Composition:** Brass **Series:** F.A.O.

| Date | Mintage | F | VF | XF | Unc | BU |
|---|---|---|---|---|---|---|
| 1981(a) | — | — | 0.25 | 0.50 | 1.25 | — |
| 1982(a) | — | — | 0.25 | 0.50 | 1.25 | — |
| 1983(a) | — | — | 0.25 | 0.50 | 1.25 | — |
| 1984(a) | — | — | 0.25 | 0.50 | 1.25 | — |
| 1985(a) | 5,000,000 | — | 0.25 | 0.50 | 1.25 | — |
| 1986(a) | 7,500,000 | — | 0.25 | 0.50 | 1.25 | — |
| 1987(a) | — | — | 0.25 | 0.50 | 1.25 | — |
| 1989(a) | — | — | 0.25 | 0.50 | 1.25 | — |
| 1990(a) | — | — | 0.25 | 0.50 | 1.25 | — |
| 1991(a) | — | — | 0.25 | 0.50 | 1.25 | — |
| 1992(a) | — | — | 0.25 | 0.50 | 1.25 | — |
| 1994(a) | — | — | 0.25 | 0.50 | 1.25 | — |
| 1995(a) | — | — | 0.25 | 0.50 | 1.25 | — |
| 1996(a) | — | — | 0.25 | 0.50 | 1.25 | — |
| 1997(a) | — | — | 0.25 | 0.50 | 1.25 | — |

**25 FRANCS** **KM# 5** **Composition:** Aluminum-Bronze

| Date | Mintage | F | VF | XF | Unc | BU |
|---|---|---|---|---|---|---|
| 1970(a) | 7,000,000 | — | 0.25 | 0.45 | 0.80 | — |
| 1971(a) | 7,000,000 | — | 0.50 | 0.75 | 1.25 | — |
| 1972(a) | 2,000,000 | — | 1.50 | 2.50 | 4.50 | — |
| 1975(a) | 5,035,000 | — | 0.25 | 0.45 | 0.80 | — |
| 1976(a) | 3,365,000 | — | 0.25 | 0.45 | 0.80 | — |
| 1977(a) | 3,288,000 | — | 0.25 | 0.45 | 0.80 | — |
| 1978(a) | — | — | 0.25 | 0.45 | 0.80 | — |
| 1979(a) | — | — | 0.25 | 0.45 | 0.80 | — |

**25 FRANCS** **KM# 9** **Composition:** Aluminum-Bronze **Series:** F.A.O.

| Date | Mintage | F | VF | XF | Unc | BU |
|---|---|---|---|---|---|---|
| 1980(a) | — | — | 0.25 | 0.75 | 1.75 | — |
| 1981(a) | — | — | 0.25 | 0.75 | 1.75 | — |
| 1982(a) | — | — | 0.25 | 0.75 | 1.75 | — |
| 1984(a) | — | — | 0.25 | 0.75 | 1.75 | — |
| 1985(a) | 8,587,000 | — | — | — | — | — |
| 1987(a) | — | — | 0.25 | 0.75 | 1.75 | — |
| 1989(a) | — | — | 0.25 | 0.75 | 1.75 | — |
| 1990(a) | — | — | 0.25 | 0.75 | 1.75 | — |
| 1994(a) | — | — | 0.25 | 0.75 | 1.75 | — |
| 1996(a) | — | — | 0.25 | 0.75 | 1.75 | — |
| 1997(a) | — | — | 0.25 | 0.75 | 1.75 | — |

**50 FRANCS** **KM# 6** **Composition:** Copper-Nickel **Series:** F.A.O.

| Date | Mintage | F | VF | XF | Unc | BU |
|---|---|---|---|---|---|---|
| 1972(a) | 20,000,000 | — | 0.35 | 0.50 | 1.25 | — |
| 1974(a) | 3,000,000 | — | 0.50 | 0.75 | 1.50 | — |
| 1975(a) | 9,000,000 | — | 0.25 | 0.40 | 1.00 | — |
| 1976(a) | 6,002,000 | — | 0.35 | 0.50 | 1.25 | — |
| 1977(a) | 4,832,000 | — | 0.35 | 0.50 | 1.25 | — |
| 1978(a) | — | — | 0.35 | 0.50 | 1.25 | — |
| 1979(a) | — | — | 0.35 | 0.50 | 1.25 | — |
| 1980(a) | — | — | 0.35 | 0.50 | 1.25 | — |
| 1981(a) | — | — | 0.35 | 0.50 | 1.25 | — |
| 1982(a) | — | — | 0.35 | 0.50 | 1.25 | — |
| 1984(a) | — | — | 0.35 | 0.50 | 1.25 | — |
| 1985(a) | 4,120,000 | — | — | — | — | — |
| 1986(a) | — | — | 0.35 | 0.50 | 1.25 | — |
| 1987(a) | — | — | 0.35 | 0.50 | 1.25 | — |
| 1989(a) | — | — | 0.35 | 0.50 | 1.25 | — |
| 1990(a) | — | — | 0.35 | 0.50 | 1.25 | — |
| 1991(a) | — | — | 0.35 | 0.50 | 1.25 | — |
| 1992(a) | — | — | 0.35 | 0.50 | 1.25 | — |
| 1995(a) | — | — | 0.35 | 0.50 | 1.25 | — |
| 1996(a) | — | — | 0.35 | 0.50 | 1.25 | — |
| 1997(a) | — | — | 0.35 | 0.50 | 1.25 | — |

**100 FRANCS** **KM# 4** **Composition:** Nickel

| Date | Mintage | F | VF | XF | Unc | BU |
|---|---|---|---|---|---|---|
| 1967(a) | — | — | 0.75 | 1.00 | 2.50 | — |
| 1968(a) | 25,000,000 | — | 0.75 | 1.00 | 2.50 | — |
| 1969(a) | 25,000,000 | — | 0.75 | 1.00 | 2.50 | — |
| 1970(a) | 4,510,000 | — | 0.80 | 1.50 | 3.50 | — |
| 1971(a) | 12,000,000 | — | 0.50 | 0.75 | 1.85 | — |
| 1972(a) | 5,000,000 | — | 0.60 | 0.85 | 2.00 | — |
| 1973(a) | 5,000,000 | — | 0.60 | 0.85 | 2.00 | — |
| 1974(a) | 8,500,000 | — | 0.60 | 0.75 | 1.85 | — |
| 1975(a) | 16,000,000 | — | 0.60 | 0.75 | 1.85 | — |
| 1976(a) | 11,575,000 | — | 0.60 | 0.75 | 1.85 | — |
| 1977(a) | 9,355,000 | — | 0.60 | 0.75 | 1.85 | — |
| 1978(a) | — | — | 0.60 | 0.75 | 1.85 | — |
| 1979(a) | — | — | 0.60 | 0.85 | 2.00 | — |
| 1980(a) | — | — | 0.60 | 0.75 | 2.00 | — |
| 1981(a) | — | — | 0.60 | 0.75 | 2.00 | — |
| 1982(a) | — | — | 0.60 | 0.75 | 2.00 | — |
| 1984(a) | — | — | 0.65 | 0.85 | 2.25 | — |
| 1985(a) | 1,460,000 | — | — | — | — | — |
| 1987(a) | — | — | 0.65 | 0.85 | 2.25 | — |
| 1989(a) | — | — | 0.65 | 0.85 | 2.25 | — |
| 1990(a) | — | — | 0.65 | 0.85 | 2.25 | — |
| 1991(a) | — | — | 0.65 | 0.85 | 2.25 | — |
| 1992(a) | — | — | 0.65 | 0.85 | 2.25 | — |
| 1996(a) | — | — | 0.65 | 0.85 | 2.25 | — |
| 1997(a) | — | — | 0.65 | 0.85 | 2.25 | — |

**250 FRANCS** **KM# 13** **Ring Composition:** Copper-Nickel **Center Composition:** Brass

| Date | Mintage | F | VF | XF | Unc | BU |
|---|---|---|---|---|---|---|
| 1992(a) | — | — | 1.75 | 2.75 | 7.00 | — |
| 1993(a) | — | — | 1.75 | 2.75 | 7.00 | — |
| 1996(a) | — | — | 2.00 | 3.00 | 8.00 | — |

**500 FRANCS** **KM# 7** **Weight:** 25.0000 g. **Composition:** 0.9000 Silver .7234 oz. ASW **Subject:** 10th anniversary of monetary union

| Date | Mintage | F | VF | XF | Unc | BU |
|---|---|---|---|---|---|---|
| 1972(a) | 100,000 | — | — | 17.50 | 37.50 | — |

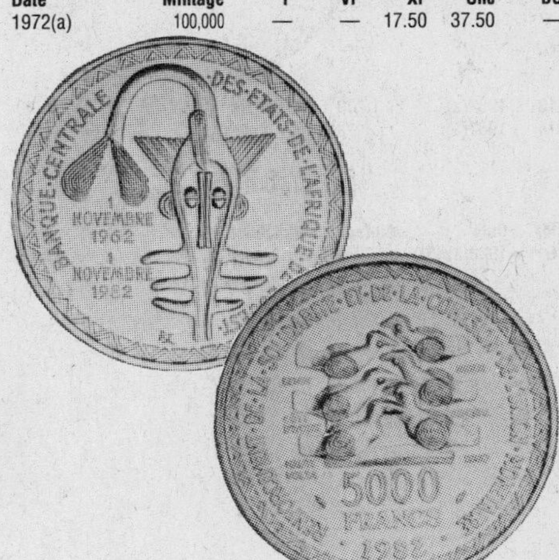


**5000 FRANCS** **KM# 11** **Weight:** 24.9500 g. **Composition:** 0.9000 Silver .7220 oz. ASW **Subject:** 20th anniversary of monetary union

| Date | Mintage | F | VF | XF | Unc | BU |
|---|---|---|---|---|---|---|
| 1982(a) | 200,000 | — | — | 15.00 | 35.00 | — |

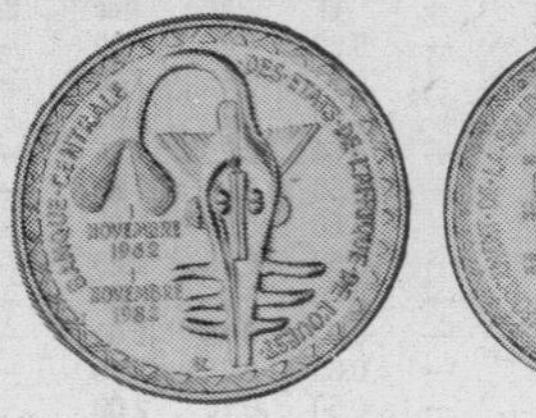

**5000 FRANCS** KM# 12 **Weight:** 14.4900 g. **Composition:** 0.9000 Gold .4193 oz. AGW **Subject:** 20th anniversary of monetary union

| Date | Mintage | F | VF | XF | Unc | BU |
|---|---|---|---|---|---|---|
| 1982(a) | — | — | — | — | 400 | — |

## ESSAIS

| KM# | Date | Mintage | Identification | Issue Price | Mkt Val |
|---|---|---|---|---|---|
| E1 | 1959(a) | — | 10 Francs. KM1. | — | 15.00 |
| E2 | 1960(a) | — | 5 Francs. KM2. | — | 15.00 |
| E3 | 1961(a) | — | Franc. KM3. | — | 12.50 |
| E4 | 1967(a) | 1,600 | 100 Francs. KM4. | — | 17.50 |
| E4a | 1967(a) | 100 | 100 Francs. Silver. KM4. | — | 85.00 |
| E4b | 1967(a) | 21 | 100 Francs. Gold. KM4. | — | 700 |
| E5 | 1970(a) | 1,450 | 25 Francs. KM5. | — | 15.00 |
| E6 | 1972(a) | 1,750 | 50 Francs. KM6. | — | 15.00 |
| E7 | 1972(a) | 2,000 | 500 Francs. KM7. | 5.00 | 50.00 |
| E6a | 1972(a) | 120 | 50 Francs. Silver. KM6. | — | 75.00 |
| E6b | 1972(a) | 17 | 50 Francs. Gold. KM6. | — | 600 |
| E8 | 1976(a) | — | Franc. KM8. | — | 12.50 |

| KM# | Date | Mintage | Identification | Issue Price | Mkt Val |
|---|---|---|---|---|---|
| E9 | 1980(a) | 3,000 | 25 Francs. KM9. | — | 10.00 |
| E10 | 1980(a) | 5 | 25 Francs. Gold. | — | 1,750 |
| E11 | 1980(a) | — | 500 Francs. | — | 40.00 |
| E12 | 1981(a) | 1,950 | 10 Francs. KM10. | — | 12.50 |

| KM# | Date | Mintage | Identification | Issue Price | Mkt Val |
|---|---|---|---|---|---|
| E13 | 1982(a) | 1,700 | 5000 Francs. KM11. | — | 75.00 |
| E14 | 1982(a) | 12 | 5000 Francs. Gold. KM11. | — | 1,500 |

## "FDC" SETS

| KM# | Date | Mintage | Identification | Issue Price | Mkt Val |
|---|---|---|---|---|---|
| SS1 | 1968(a) (3) | — | KM1a, 2a, 4 | — | 9.50 |

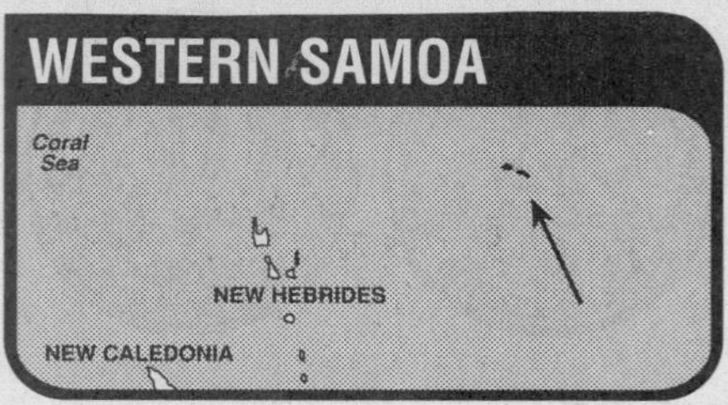


The Territory of American Samoa, with a population of 41,000, consists of seven major islands with a total land area of 76 sq. mi. (199 sq. km.) which are located about 2300 miles south-southwest of Hawaii. American Samoa was settled by the Polynesians around 600 BC. The capital is Pago Pago.

Samoa's long isolation from the western world ended in 1722 when the Dutch explorer, Jacob Roggeveen, came upon the islands. However, it wasn't until 1831 that European influence had any real impact. In that year, John Williams of the London Missionary Society arrived with eight Tahitian missionaries.

By 1900 the Samoan islands were being claimed by both Germany and the United States. Germany annexed several islands, which now comprise Western Samoa; the U.S. took Tutuila to use Pago Pago Bay as a coaling station for naval ships.

As Japan began emerging as an international power in the mid-1930's, the U.S. Naval station on Tutuila began to acquire new strategic importance; and in 1940 the Samoan Islands became a training and staging area for the U.S. Marine Corps.

A. P. Lutali, Governor of American Samoa, signed a historic proclamation on May 23, 1988 that authorized the minting of the first numismatic issue for this unincorporated territory administered by the United States Department of the Interior.

**MONETARY SYSTEM**
100 Cents = 1 Dollar

# BRITISH ADMINISTRATION

## STANDARD COINAGE

**SENE** KM# 1 **Composition:** Bronze

| Date | Mintage | F | VF | XF | Unc | BU |
|---|---|---|---|---|---|---|
| 1967 | 915,000 | — | 0.10 | 0.15 | 0.30 | — |
| 1967 Proof | 15,000 | Value: 0.50 | | | | |

**SENE** KM# 12 **Composition:** Bronze

| Date | Mintage | F | VF | XF | Unc | BU |
|---|---|---|---|---|---|---|
| 1974 | 3,380,000 | — | — | 0.10 | 0.25 | — |
| 1987 | — | — | — | 0.10 | 0.25 | — |
| 1988 | — | — | — | 0.10 | 0.25 | — |
| 1996 | — | — | — | 0.10 | 0.25 | — |

**SENE** KM# 12a **Weight:** 1.9500 g. **Composition:** 0.9250 Silver .0579 oz. ASW

| Date | Mintage | F | VF | XF | Unc | BU |
|---|---|---|---|---|---|---|
| 1974 Proof | 5,578 | Value: 2.50 | | | | |

**2 SENE** KM# 2 **Composition:** Bronze

| Date | Mintage | F | VF | XF | Unc | BU |
|---|---|---|---|---|---|---|
| 1967 | 465,000 | — | 0.10 | 0.20 | 0.40 | — |
| 1967 Proof | 15,000 | Value: 0.50 | | | | |

**2 SENE** KM# 13 **Composition:** Bronze

| Date | Mintage | F | VF | XF | Unc | BU |
|---|---|---|---|---|---|---|
| 1974 | 1,640,000 | — | 0.10 | 0.15 | 0.30 | — |
| 1988 | — | — | 0.10 | 0.15 | 0.30 | — |
| 1996 | — | — | 0.10 | 0.15 | 0.30 | — |

**2 SENE** KM# 13a **Weight:** 3.8000 g. **Composition:** 0.9250 Silver .1130 oz. ASW

| Date | Mintage | F | VF | XF | Unc | BU |
|---|---|---|---|---|---|---|
| 1974 Proof | 5,578 | Value: 3.00 | | | | |

**2 SENE** KM# 122 **Composition:** Bronze **Series:** F.A.O. **Obverse:** King's portrait **Reverse:** Denomination in wreath

| Date | Mintage | F | VF | XF | Unc | BU |
|---|---|---|---|---|---|---|
| 2000(1999) | — | — | — | — | 0.35 | — |

**5 SENE** KM# 3 **Composition:** Copper-Nickel

| Date | Mintage | F | VF | XF | Unc | BU |
|---|---|---|---|---|---|---|
| 1967 | 495,000 | — | 0.15 | 0.25 | 0.50 | — |
| 1967 Proof | 15,000 | Value: 1.00 | | | | |

**5 SENE** KM# 14 **Composition:** Copper-Nickel

| Date | Mintage | F | VF | XF | Unc | BU |
|---|---|---|---|---|---|---|
| 1974 | 1,736,000 | — | 0.10 | 0.20 | 0.40 | — |
| 1987 | — | — | 0.10 | 0.20 | 0.40 | — |
| 1988 | — | — | 0.10 | 0.20 | 0.40 | — |
| 1993 | — | — | 0.10 | 0.20 | 0.40 | — |
| 1996 | — | — | 0.10 | 0.20 | 0.40 | — |

**5 SENE** KM# 14a **Weight:** 3.2500 g. **Composition:** 0.9250 Silver .0966 oz. ASW

| Date | Mintage | F | VF | XF | Unc | BU |
|---|---|---|---|---|---|---|
| 1974 Proof | 5,578 | Value: 3.50 | | | | |

**10 SENE** KM# 4 **Composition:** Copper-Nickel

| Date | Mintage | F | VF | XF | Unc | BU |
|---|---|---|---|---|---|---|
| 1967 | 400,000 | — | 0.20 | 0.35 | 0.70 | — |
| 1967 Proof | 15,000 | Value: 1.00 | | | | |

**10 SENE** KM# 15 **Composition:** Copper-Nickel

| Date | Mintage | F | VF | XF | Unc | BU |
|---|---|---|---|---|---|---|
| 1974 | 1,580,000 | — | 0.15 | 0.30 | 0.60 | — |
| 1987 | — | — | 0.15 | 0.30 | 0.60 | — |
| 1988 | — | — | 0.15 | 0.30 | 0.60 | — |
| 1993 | — | — | 0.15 | 0.30 | 0.60 | — |
| 1996 | — | — | 0.15 | 0.30 | 0.60 | — |

**10 SENE** KM# 15a **Weight:** 6.3700 g. **Composition:** 0.9250 Silver .1894 oz. ASW

| Date | Mintage | F | VF | XF | Unc | BU |
|---|---|---|---|---|---|---|
| 1974 Proof | 5,578 | Value: 4.00 | | | | |

**20 SENE** **KM# 5** **Composition:** Copper-Nickel

| Date | Mintage | F | VF | XF | Unc | BU |
|---|---|---|---|---|---|---|
| 1967 | 400,000 | — | 0.25 | 0.50 | 1.00 | — |
| 1967 Proof | 15,000 | Value: 1.50 | | | | |

**20 SENE** **KM# 16** **Composition:** Copper-Nickel

| Date | Mintage | F | VF | XF | Unc | BU |
|---|---|---|---|---|---|---|
| 1974 | 1,380,000 | — | 0.20 | 0.40 | 0.80 | — |
| 1987 | — | — | 0.20 | 0.40 | 0.80 | — |
| 1988 | — | — | 0.20 | 0.40 | 0.80 | — |
| 1996 | — | — | 0.20 | 0.40 | 0.80 | — |

**20 SENE** **KM# 16a** **Weight:** 12.7000 g. **Composition:** 0.9250 Silver .3776 oz. ASW

| Date | Mintage | F | VF | XF | Unc | BU |
|---|---|---|---|---|---|---|
| 1974 Proof | 5,578 | Value: 5.00 | | | | |

**50 SENE** **KM# 6** **Composition:** Copper-Nickel

| Date | Mintage | F | VF | XF | Unc | BU |
|---|---|---|---|---|---|---|
| 1967 | 80,000 | — | 0.75 | 1.25 | 2.00 | — |
| 1967 Proof | 15,000 | Value: 2.50 | | | | |

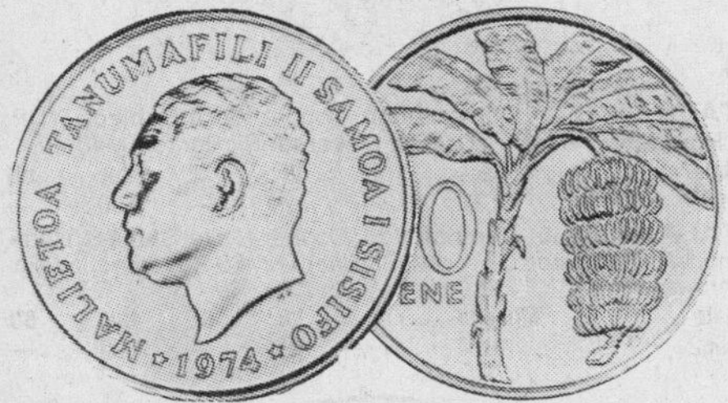


**50 SENE** **KM# 17** **Composition:** Copper-Nickel

| Date | Mintage | F | VF | XF | Unc | BU |
|---|---|---|---|---|---|---|
| 1974 | 50,000 | — | 0.75 | 1.25 | 2.00 | — |
| 1988 | — | — | 0.75 | 1.25 | 2.00 | — |
| 1996 | — | — | 0.75 | 1.25 | 2.00 | — |

**50 SENE** **KM# 17a** **Weight:** 15.4000 g. **Composition:** 0.9250 Silver .4579 oz. ASW

| Date | Mintage | F | VF | XF | Unc | BU |
|---|---|---|---|---|---|---|
| 1974 Proof | 5,578 | Value: 6.00 | | | | |

**50 SENE** **KM# 80** **Composition:** Copper-Nickel **Subject:** 25th anniversary of independence

| Date | Mintage | F | VF | XF | Unc | BU |
|---|---|---|---|---|---|---|
| 1987 | — | — | — | — | 2.50 | — |

**TALA** **KM# 7** **Composition:** Copper-Nickel **Obverse:** Bust left **Reverse:** Similar to 50 Sene, KM#6

| Date | Mintage | F | VF | XF | Unc | BU |
|---|---|---|---|---|---|---|
| 1967 | 20,000 | — | — | — | 3.00 | — |
| 1967 Proof | 15,000 | Value: 6.00 | | | | |

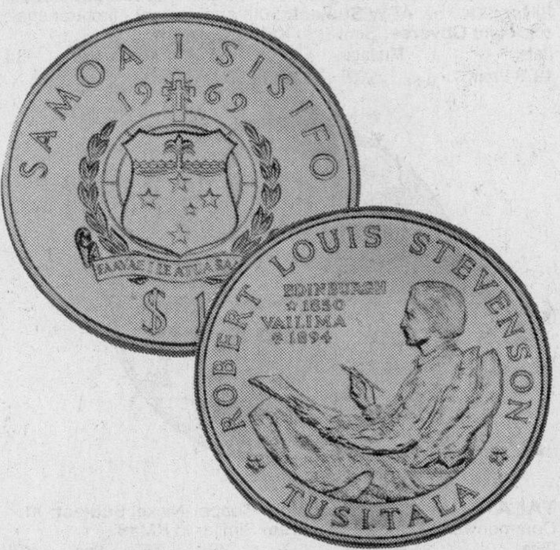


**TALA** **KM# 8** **Composition:** Copper-Nickel **Subject:** 75th anniversary - death of Robert Louis Stevenson

| Date | Mintage | F | VF | XF | Unc | BU |
|---|---|---|---|---|---|---|
| 1969 | 25,000 | — | — | — | 4.00 | — |
| 1969 Proof | 1,500 | Value: 7.50 | | | | |

**TALA** **KM# 9** **Composition:** Copper-Nickel **Subject:** 200th anniversary - Capt. Cook voyages **Obverse:** Similar to KM#8

| Date | Mintage | F | VF | XF | Unc | BU |
|---|---|---|---|---|---|---|
| 1970 | 32,000 | — | — | — | 3.50 | — |
| 1970 Proof | 3,000 | Value: 6.00 | | | | |

**TALA** **KM# 10** **Composition:** Copper-Nickel **Subject:** Visit of Pope Paul VI **Obverse:** Similar to KM#8

| Date | Mintage | F | VF | XF | Unc | BU |
|---|---|---|---|---|---|---|
| 1970 | 35,000 | — | — | — | 3.50 | — |
| 1970 Proof | 3,000 | Value: 7.00 | | | | |

**TALA** **KM# 11** **Composition:** Copper-Nickel **Subject:** Roggeveen's Pacific voyage **Obverse:** Similar to KM#8

| Date | Mintage | F | VF | XF | Unc | BU |
|---|---|---|---|---|---|---|
| 1972 | 35,000 | — | — | — | 3.50 | — |
| 1972 Proof | 3,000 | Value: 8.00 | | | | |

**TALA** **KM# 18** **Composition:** Copper-Nickel **Subject:** 10th British Commonwealth Games **Obverse:** Similar to KM#8

| Date | Mintage | F | VF | XF | Unc | BU |
|---|---|---|---|---|---|---|
| 1974 | 40,000 | — | — | — | 4.50 | — |

**TALA** **KM# 18a** **Weight:** 27.7000 g. **Composition:** 0.9250 Silver .8239 oz. ASW **Subject:** 10th British Commonwealth Games **Obverse:** Similar to KM#8

| Date | Mintage | F | VF | XF | Unc | BU |
|---|---|---|---|---|---|---|
| 1974 Proof | 1,500 | Value: 15.00 | | | | |

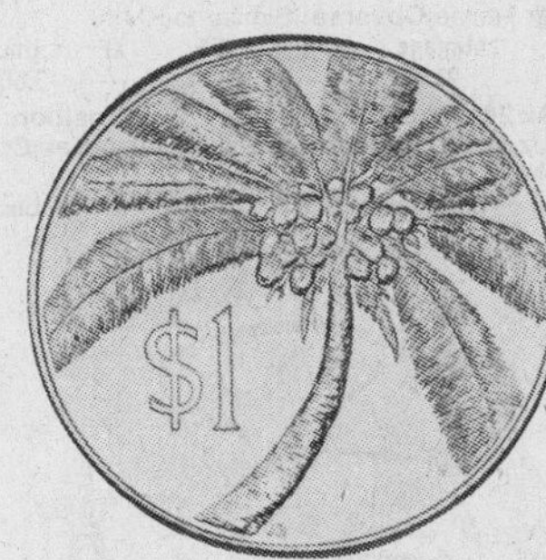


**TALA** **KM# 19** **Composition:** Copper-Nickel **Obverse:** Similar to 50 Sene, KM#17

| Date | Mintage | F | VF | XF | Unc | BU |
|---|---|---|---|---|---|---|
| 1974 | 24,000 | — | — | — | 3.50 | — |

**TALA** **KM# 19a** **Weight:** 31.1500 g. **Composition:** 0.9250 Silver .9263 oz. ASW **Obverse:** Similar to 50 Sene, KM#17

| Date | Mintage | F | VF | XF | Unc | BU |
|---|---|---|---|---|---|---|
| 1974 Proof | 11,000 | Value: 10.00 | | | | |

**TALA** **KM# 20** **Composition:** Copper-Nickel **Subject:** U.S. bicentennial

| Date | Mintage | F | VF | XF | Unc | BU |
|---|---|---|---|---|---|---|
| ND(1976) | 40,000 | — | — | — | 3.50 | — |

**TALA** **KM# 20a** **Weight:** 30.4000 g. **Composition:** 0.9250 Silver .9040 oz. ASW **Subject:** U.S. bicentennial

| Date | Mintage | F | VF | XF | Unc | BU |
|---|---|---|---|---|---|---|
| ND(1976) Proof | 4,127 | Value: 11.50 | | | | |

**TALA** **KM# 22** **Composition:** Copper-Nickel **Series:** Montreal Olympics **Obverse:** Similar to KM#8 **Reverse:** Weight lifter

| Date | Mintage | F | VF | XF | Unc | BU |
|---|---|---|---|---|---|---|
| 1976 | 40,000 | — | — | — | 4.00 | — |

**TALA** **KM# 22a** **Weight:** 30.4000 g. **Composition:** 0.9250 Silver .9040 oz. ASW **Series:** Montreal Olympics **Obverse:** Similar to KM#8 **Reverse:** Weight lifter

| Date | Mintage | F | VF | XF | Unc | BU |
|---|---|---|---|---|---|---|
| 1976 Proof | 6,000 | Value: 15.00 | | | | |

**TALA** **KM# 24** **Composition:** Copper-Nickel **Subject:** Queen's silver jubilee **Obverse:** Similar to KM#8

| Date | Mintage | F | VF | XF | Unc | BU |
|---|---|---|---|---|---|---|
| 1977 | 27,000 | — | — | — | 3.50 | — |

**TALA** **KM# 24a** **Weight:** 30.4000 g. **Composition:** 0.9250 Silver .9040 oz. ASW **Subject:** Queen's silver jubilee **Obverse:** Similar to KM#8

| Date | Mintage | F | VF | XF | Unc | BU |
|---|---|---|---|---|---|---|
| 1977 Proof | 6,171 | Value: 10.00 | | | | |

**TALA** **KM# 26** **Composition:** Copper-Nickel **Subject:** Lindbergh's New York to Paris flight **Obverse:** Similar to KM#8

| Date | Mintage | F | VF | XF | Unc | BU |
|---|---|---|---|---|---|---|
| 1977 | 17,000 | — | — | — | 3.50 | — |

**TALA** **KM# 26a** **Weight:** 30.4000 g. **Composition:** 0.9250 Silver .9040 oz. ASW **Subject:** Lindbergh's New York to Paris flight **Obverse:** Similar to KM#8

| Date | Mintage | F | VF | XF | Unc | BU |
|---|---|---|---|---|---|---|
| 1977 Proof | 4,522 | Value: 11.50 | | | | |

**TALA** **KM# 28** **Composition:** Copper-Nickel **Subject:** 50th anniversary - first transpacific flight **Obverse:** Similar to KM#8

| Date | Mintage | F | VF | XF | Unc | BU |
|---|---|---|---|---|---|---|
| 1978 | 20,000 | — | — | — | 3.50 | — |

**TALA** **KM# 28a** **Weight:** 30.4000 g. **Composition:** 0.9250 Silver .9040 oz. ASW **Subject:** 50th anniversary - first transpacific flight **Obverse:** Similar to KM#8

| Date | Mintage | F | VF | XF | Unc | BU |
|---|---|---|---|---|---|---|
| 1978 Proof | 5,000 | Value: 11.50 | | | | |

**TALA** **KM# 30** **Composition:** Copper-Nickel **Subject:** XI Commonwealth Games **Obverse:** Similar to KM#8

| Date | Mintage | F | VF | XF | Unc | BU |
|---|---|---|---|---|---|---|
| 1978 | 7,710 | — | — | — | 4.50 | — |

**TALA** **KM# 30a** **Weight:** 30.4000 g. **Composition:** 0.9250 Silver .9040 oz. ASW **Subject:** XI Commonwealth Games **Obverse:** Similar to KM#8

| Date | Mintage | F | VF | XF | Unc | BU |
|---|---|---|---|---|---|---|
| 1978 Proof | 5,000 | Value: 11.50 | | | | |

**TALA** **KM# 32** **Composition:** Copper-Nickel **Subject:** Bicentenary - death of Capt. James Cook **Obverse:** Similar to KM#8

| Date | Mintage | F | VF | XF | Unc | BU |
|---|---|---|---|---|---|---|
| 1979 | 5,000 | — | — | — | 3.50 | — |

**TALA** **KM# 35** **Composition:** Copper-Nickel **Series:** 1980 Olympics **Subject:** Hurdles **Obverse:** Similar to KM#8

| Date | Mintage | F | VF | XF | Unc | BU |
|---|---|---|---|---|---|---|
| 1980 | 5,000 | — | — | — | 4.50 | — |

**TALA** **KM# 38** **Composition:** Copper-Nickel **Series:** F.A.O. **Obverse:** Similar to KM#8

| Date | Mintage | F | VF | XF | Unc | BU |
|---|---|---|---|---|---|---|
| 1980 | 10,000 | — | — | — | 3.50 | — |

**TALA** **KM# 40** **Composition:** Copper-Nickel **Subject:** Gov. Wilhelm Solf **Obverse:** Similar to KM#8

| Date | Mintage | F | VF | XF | Unc | BU |
|---|---|---|---|---|---|---|
| 1980 | 5,000 | — | — | — | 4.50 | — |

**TALA** **KM# 43** **Composition:** Copper-Nickel **Subject:** Wedding of Prince Charles and Lady Diana **Obverse:** Similar to KM#8

| Date | Mintage | F | VF | XF | Unc | BU |
|---|---|---|---|---|---|---|
| 1981 | 12,000 | — | — | — | 4.00 | — |

**TALA** **KM# 47** **Composition:** Copper-Nickel **Subject:** IYDP - President Franklin Roosevelt **Obverse:** Similar to KM#8

| Date | Mintage | F | VF | XF | Unc | BU |
|---|---|---|---|---|---|---|
| 1981 | 8,000 | — | — | — | 3.50 | — |

**TALA** **KM# 50** **Composition:** Copper-Nickel **Subject:** Commonwealth Games **Obverse:** Similar to KM#8 **Reverse:** Javelin thrower

| Date | Mintage | F | VF | XF | Unc | BU |
|---|---|---|---|---|---|---|
| 1982 | 6,000 | — | — | — | 4.00 | — |

**TALA** **KM# 53** **Composition:** Copper-Nickel **Subject:** South Pacific Games **Obverse:** Similar to KM#8 **Reverse:** Runner

| Date | Mintage | F | VF | XF | Unc | BU |
|---|---|---|---|---|---|---|
| 1983 | 8,000 | — | — | — | 3.50 | — |

**TALA** **KM# 57** **Composition:** Aluminum-Bronze **Subject:** Circulation coinage

| Date | Mintage | F | VF | XF | Unc | BU |
|---|---|---|---|---|---|---|
| 1984 | 1,000,000 | — | 0.50 | 0.75 | 1.00 | — |

**TALA** **KM# 58** **Composition:** Copper-Nickel **Series:** Summer Olympics **Reverse:** Boxers

| Date | Mintage | F | VF | XF | Unc | BU |
|---|---|---|---|---|---|---|
| 1984 | 5,000 | — | — | — | 6.00 | — |

**TALA** **KM# 63** **Composition:** Copper-Nickel **Subject:** Prince Andrew's marriage

| Date | Mintage | F | VF | XF | Unc | BU |
|---|---|---|---|---|---|---|
| 1986 | 10,000 | — | — | — | 3.00 | — |

**TALA** **KM# 74** **Composition:** Copper-Nickel **Subject:** 25th anniversary of World Wildlife Fund

| Date | Mintage | F | VF | XF | Unc | BU |
|---|---|---|---|---|---|---|
| 1986 | — | — | — | — | 3.00 | — |

**TALA** **KM# 88** **Composition:** Copper-Nickel **Subject:** 40th anniversary - reign of Queen Elizabeth II

| Date | Mintage | F | VF | XF | Unc | BU |
|---|---|---|---|---|---|---|
| ND(1992) | — | — | — | — | 4.50 | — |

**TALA** **KM# 111** **Composition:** Copper-Nickel **Subject:** Queen Mother **Reverse:** Glamis Castle

| Date | Mintage | F | VF | XF | Unc | BU |
|---|---|---|---|---|---|---|
| 1995 | Est. 30,000 | — | — | — | 3.50 | — |

**TALA** **KM# 112** **Weight:** 10.0000 g. **Composition:** 0.5000 Silver .1607 oz. ASW **Series:** Olympics **Reverse:** Gymnast and pummel horse

| Date | Mintage | F | VF | XF | Unc | BU |
|---|---|---|---|---|---|---|
| 1996 | Est. 10,000 | — | — | — | 12.50 | — |

**2 TALA** **KM# 120** **Weight:** 42.4139 g. **Composition:** 0.9250 Silver 1.3636 oz. ASW **Obverse:** National arms **Reverse:** Denomination and 3 scenes **Note:** Part of a tri-national, three-coin matching set with Cook Islands and Fiji.

| Date | Mintage | F | VF | XF | Unc | BU |
|---|---|---|---|---|---|---|
| 1998 Proof | Est. 20,000 | Value: 60.00 | | | | |

**5 TALA** **KM# 115** **Weight:** 15.5518 g. **Composition:** 0.9250 Silver .4625 oz. ASW **Subject:** War and peace **Obverse:** West Samoan arms **Reverse:** Arrows and sword **Note:** Part of a joint matching set with Kiribati.

| Date | Mintage | F | VF | XF | Unc | BU |
|---|---|---|---|---|---|---|
| ND(1997) Proof | Est. 10,000 | Value: 30.00 | | | | |

**5 TALA** **KM# 116** **Weight:** 15.5518 g. **Composition:** 0.9250 Silver .4625 oz. ASW **Subject:** Epoch - making events **Reverse:** Helmet and crowns **Note:** Part of a joint matching set with Kiribati.

| Date | Mintage | F | VF | XF | Unc | BU |
|---|---|---|---|---|---|---|
| ND(1997) Proof | Est. 10,000 | Value: 30.00 | | | | |

**5 TALA** **KM# 117** **Weight:** 15.5518 g. **Composition:** 0.9250 Silver .4625 oz. ASW **Subject:** Tempora mutantur **Reverse:** Man with torch **Note:** Part of a joint matching set with Kiribati.

| Date | Mintage | F | VF | XF | Unc | BU |
|---|---|---|---|---|---|---|
| ND(1997) Proof | Est. 10,000 | Value: 30.00 | | | | |

**5 TALA** **KM# 118** **Weight:** 15.5518 g. **Composition:** 0.9250 Silver .4625 oz. ASW **Subject:** People and buildings **Reverse:** Working hands **Note:** Part of a joint matching set with Kiribati.

| Date | Mintage | F | VF | XF | Unc | BU |
|---|---|---|---|---|---|---|
| ND(1997) Proof | Est. 10,000 | Value: 30.00 | | | | |

**10 TALA** **KM# 33** **Weight:** 31.3300 g. **Composition:** 0.5000 Silver .5036 oz. ASW **Subject:** Bicentenary - death of Capt. James Cook

| Date | Mintage | F | VF | XF | Unc | BU |
|---|---|---|---|---|---|---|
| 1979 | 3,000 | — | — | — | 11.50 | — |

**10 TALA** **KM# 33a** **Weight:** 31.4700 g. **Composition:** 0.9250 Silver .9359 oz. ASW **Subject:** Bicentenary - death of Capt. James Cook

| Date | Mintage | F | VF | XF | Unc | BU |
|---|---|---|---|---|---|---|
| 1979 Proof | 5,000 | Value: 12.50 | | | | |

**10 TALA** **KM# 36** **Weight:** 31.3300 g. **Composition:** 0.5000 Silver .5036 oz. ASW **Series:** 1980 Olympics **Obverse:** Similar to KM#33 **Reverse:** Hurdles

| Date | Mintage | F | VF | XF | Unc | BU |
|---|---|---|---|---|---|---|
| 1980 | 3,000 | — | — | — | 10.00 | — |

**10 TALA** **KM# 36a** **Weight:** 31.4700 g. **Composition:** 0.9250 Silver .9359 oz. ASW **Series:** 1980 Olympics **Obverse:** Similar to KM#33 **Reverse:** Hurdles

| Date | Mintage | F | VF | XF | Unc | BU |
|---|---|---|---|---|---|---|
| 1980 Proof | 4,000 | Value: 12.50 | | | | |

**10 TALA** **KM# 39** **Weight:** 31.3300 g. **Composition:** 0.5000 Silver .5036 oz. ASW **Series:** F.A.O. **Obverse:** Similar to KM#33

| Date | Mintage | F | VF | XF | Unc | BU |
|---|---|---|---|---|---|---|
| 1980 Proof | 3,000 | Value: 10.00 | | | | |

**10 TALA** **KM# 41** **Weight:** 31.3300 g. **Composition:** 0.5000 Silver .5036 oz. ASW **Subject:** Gov. Wilhelm Solf **Obverse:** Similar to KM#33

| Date | Mintage | F | VF | XF | Unc | BU |
|---|---|---|---|---|---|---|
| 1980 | 3,000 | — | — | — | 10.00 | — |

**10 TALA** **KM# 41a** **Weight:** 31.4700 g. **Composition:** 0.9250 Silver .9359 oz. ASW **Subject:** Gov. Wilhelm Solf **Obverse:** Similar to KM#33

| Date | Mintage | F | VF | XF | Unc | BU |
|---|---|---|---|---|---|---|
| 1980 Proof | 4,000 | Value: 13.50 | | | | |

**10 TALA** **KM# 44** **Weight:** 31.4700 g. **Composition:** 0.9250 Silver .9359 oz. ASW **Subject:** Wedding of Prince Charles and Lady Diana

| Date | Mintage | F | VF | XF | Unc | BU |
|---|---|---|---|---|---|---|
| 1981 Proof | 5,000 | Value: 12.50 | | | | |

**10 TALA** KM# 48 **Weight:** 31.4700 g. **Composition:** 0.9250 Silver .9359 oz. ASW **Subject:** IYDP - President Franklin Roosevelt

| Date | Mintage | F | VF | XF | Unc | BU |
|---|---|---|---|---|---|---|
| 1981 Proof | 5,000 | Value: 12.50 | | | | |

**10 TALA** KM# 51 **Weight:** 31.4700 g. **Composition:** 0.9250 Silver .9359 oz. ASW **Subject:** Commonwealth Games **Obverse:** Similar to KM#33 **Reverse:** Javelin thrower

| Date | Mintage | F | VF | XF | Unc | BU |
|---|---|---|---|---|---|---|
| 1982 Proof | 4,000 | Value: 13.50 | | | | |

**10 TALA** KM# 54 **Weight:** 31.4700 g. **Composition:** 0.9250 Silver .9359 oz. ASW **Subject:** South Pacific Games **Obverse:** Similar to KM#33 **Reverse:** Runner

| Date | Mintage | F | VF | XF | Unc | BU |
|---|---|---|---|---|---|---|
| 1983 Proof | 3,000 | Value: 13.50 | | | | |

**10 TALA** KM# 59 **Weight:** 31.4700 g. **Composition:** 0.9250 Silver .9359 oz. ASW **Series:** Summer Olympics **Reverse:** Boxers

| Date | Mintage | F | VF | XF | Unc | BU |
|---|---|---|---|---|---|---|
| 1984 Proof | 2,500 | Value: 35.00 | | | | |

**10 TALA** KM# 64 **Weight:** 31.4700 g. **Composition:** 0.9250 Silver .9359 oz. ASW **Subject:** Prince Andrew's marriage **Note:** Similar to Tala, KM#63.

| Date | Mintage | F | VF | XF | Unc | BU |
|---|---|---|---|---|---|---|
| 1986 Proof | 2,500 | Value: 12.50 | | | | |

**10 TALA** KM# 72 **Weight:** 31.4700 g. **Composition:** 0.9250 Silver .9360 oz. ASW **Subject:** 25th anniversary of World Wildlife Fund

| Date | Mintage | F | VF | XF | Unc | BU |
|---|---|---|---|---|---|---|
| 1986 Proof | Est. 25,000 | Value: 12.50 | | | | |

**10 TALA** KM# 66 **Weight:** 31.1000 g. **Composition:** 0.9990 Silver 1 oz. ASW **Subject:** America's Cup race

| Date | Mintage | F | VF | XF | Unc | BU |
|---|---|---|---|---|---|---|
| 1987 Proof | Est. 50,000 | Value: 11.50 | | | | |

**10 TALA** KM# 70 **Weight:** 31.1000 g. **Composition:** 0.9990 Silver 1 oz. ASW **Series:** 1988 Olympics **Reverse:** 3 torches and athletes

| Date | Mintage | F | VF | XF | Unc | BU |
|---|---|---|---|---|---|---|
| 1988 | 20,000 | — | — | — | 16.50 | — |

**10 TALA** KM# 75 **Weight:** 31.1030 g. **Composition:** 0.9990 Silver 1 oz. ASW **Reverse:** Kon-Tiki raft and map

| Date | Mintage | F | VF | XF | Unc | BU |
|---|---|---|---|---|---|---|
| 1988 Proof | Est. 20,000 | Value: 22.50 | | | | |

**10 TALA** KM# 79 **Weight:** 31.4700 g. **Composition:** 0.9250 Silver .9360 oz. ASW **Series:** Save the Children Fund

| Date | Mintage | F | VF | XF | Unc | BU |
|---|---|---|---|---|---|---|
| 1990 Proof | Est. 20,000 | Value: 18.50 | | | | |

**10 TALA** KM# 82 **Weight:** 31.4700 g. **Composition:** 0.9250 Silver .9360 oz. ASW **Series:** Summer Olympics **Reverse:** Shot putter

| Date | Mintage | F | VF | XF | Unc | BU |
|---|---|---|---|---|---|---|
| 1991 Proof | Est. 70,000 | Value: 11.50 | | | | |

**10 TALA** KM# 83 **Weight:** 31.1030 g. **Composition:** 0.9250 Silver .9250 oz. ASW **Subject:** RA expeditions **Obverse:** Similar to KM#82 **Reverse:** RAI

| Date | Mintage | F | VF | XF | Unc | BU |
|---|---|---|---|---|---|---|
| 1991 Proof | 15,000 | Value: 25.00 | | | | |

**10 TALA** KM# 85 **Weight:** 31.4700 g. **Composition:** 0.9250 Silver .9360 oz. ASW **Series:** Olympics **Reverse:** Javelin thrower

| Date | Mintage | F | VF | XF | Unc | BU |
|---|---|---|---|---|---|---|
| 1991 Proof | Est. 70,000 | Value: 11.50 | | | | |

**10 TALA** KM# 86 **Weight:** 31.4700 g. **Composition:** 0.9250 Silver .9360 oz. ASW **Series:** Olympics **Reverse:** Hammer thrower

| Date | Mintage | F | VF | XF | Unc | BU |
|---|---|---|---|---|---|---|
| 1992 Proof | Est. 70,000 | Value: 12.50 | | | | |

**10 TALA** KM# 89 **Weight:** 31.8600 g. **Composition:** 0.9250 Silver .9476 oz. ASW **Subject:** World Cup soccer **Reverse:** Arena

| Date | Mintage | F | VF | XF | Unc | BU |
|---|---|---|---|---|---|---|
| 1992 Proof | Est. 20,000 | Value: 17.50 | | | | |

**10 TALA** KM# 93 **Weight:** 31.4700 g. **Composition:** 0.9250 Silver .9359 oz. ASW **Subject:** Jakob Roggeveen **Obverse:** Coat of arms

| Date | Mintage | F | VF | XF | Unc | BU |
|---|---|---|---|---|---|---|
| 1992 Proof | 15,000 | Value: 22.50 | | | | |

**10 TALA** KM# 98 **Weight:** 31.3500 g. **Composition:** 0.9250 Silver .9323 oz. ASW **Series:** Endangered Wildlife **Reverse:** Ibis

| Date | Mintage | F | VF | XF | Unc | BU |
|---|---|---|---|---|---|---|
| 1992 Proof | Est. 20,000 | Value: 20.00 | | | | |

**10 TALA** **KM# 99** **Weight:** 31.7700 g. **Composition:** 0.9250 Silver .9448 oz. ASW **Subject:** Roggeveen's fleet

| Date | Mintage | F | VF | XF | Unc | BU |
|---|---|---|---|---|---|---|
| 1992 Proof | Est. 15,000 | Value: 18.00 | | | | |

**10 TALA** **KM# 109** **Weight:** 31.4700 g. **Composition:** 0.9250 Silver .9359 oz. ASW **Subject:** 40th anniversary - reign of Queen Elizabeth II **Obverse:** National arms **Reverse:** Royal carriage and guard around Order of the Garter

| Date | Mintage | F | VF | XF | Unc | BU |
|---|---|---|---|---|---|---|
| 1992 Proof | Est. 5,000 | Value: 25.00 | | | | |

**10 TALA** **KM# 97** **Weight:** 31.8100 g. **Composition:** 0.9250 Silver .9461 oz. ASW **Series:** 1996 Olympics **Reverse:** Gymnast

| Date | Mintage | F | VF | XF | Unc | BU |
|---|---|---|---|---|---|---|
| 1993 Proof | 50,000 | Value: 14.50 | | | | |

**10 TALA** **KM# 91** **Weight:** 31.8100 g. **Composition:** 0.9250 Silver .9461 oz. ASW **Series:** Olympics **Reverse:** Diver

| Date | Mintage | F | VF | XF | Unc | BU |
|---|---|---|---|---|---|---|
| 1994 Proof | Est. 50,000 | Value: 14.50 | | | | |

**10 TALA** **KM# 94** **Weight:** 31.1035 g. **Composition:** 0.9990 Silver 1 oz. ASW **Subject:** Tigris expedition **Reverse:** Building Tigris

| Date | Mintage | F | VF | XF | Unc | BU |
|---|---|---|---|---|---|---|
| 1994 Proof | 500 | Value: 40.00 | | | | |

**10 TALA** **KM# 95** **Weight:** 31.1035 g. **Composition:** 0.9990 Silver 1 oz. ASW **Subject:** Tigris expedition **Reverse:** Burning Tigris

| Date | Mintage | F | VF | XF | Unc | BU |
|---|---|---|---|---|---|---|
| 1994 Proof | 500 | Value: 40.00 | | | | |

**10 TALA** **KM# 100** **Weight:** 31.7700 g. **Composition:** 0.9250 Silver .9448 oz. ASW **Reverse:** Jacob Roggeveen sighting land

| Date | Mintage | F | VF | XF | Unc | BU |
|---|---|---|---|---|---|---|
| 1994 Proof | 10,000 | Value: 22.50 | | | | |

**10 TALA** **KM# 101** **Weight:** 31.2300 g. **Composition:** 0.9250 Silver .9288 oz. ASW **Series:** Endangered Wildlife **Reverse:** Flying fox bat

| Date | Mintage | F | VF | XF | Unc | BU |
|---|---|---|---|---|---|---|
| 1994 Proof | Est. 20,000 | Value: 25.00 | | | | |

**10 TALA** **KM# 102** **Weight:** 31.4700 g. **Composition:** 0.9250 Silver .9359 oz. ASW **Subject:** Comte de la Perouse

| Date | Mintage | F | VF | XF | Unc | BU |
|---|---|---|---|---|---|---|
| 1994 Proof | Est. 20,000 | Value: 20.00 | | | | |

**10 TALA** **KM# 103** **Weight:** 31.4700 g. **Composition:** 0.9250 Silver .9359 oz. ASW **Subject:** Protect our world **Reverse:** Flowers

| Date | Mintage | F | VF | XF | Unc | BU |
|---|---|---|---|---|---|---|
| 1994 Proof | Est. 10,000 | Value: 27.50 | | | | |

**10 TALA** **KM# 104** **Weight:** 31.4700 g. **Composition:** 0.9250 Silver .9359 oz. ASW **Subject:** Queen Mother **Reverse:** Glamis Castle

| Date | Mintage | F | VF | XF | Unc | BU |
|---|---|---|---|---|---|---|
| 1994 Proof | Est. 30,000 | Value: 20.00 | | | | |

**10 TALA** **KM# 105** **Weight:** 31.4700 g. **Composition:** 0.9250 Silver .9359 oz. ASW **Subject:** Edmond Halley

| Date | Mintage | F | VF | XF | Unc | BU |
|---|---|---|---|---|---|---|
| 1995 Proof | 10,000 | Value: 22.50 | | | | |

**10 TALA** **KM# 113** **Weight:** 1.2442 g. **Composition:** 0.9999 Gold .04 oz. AGW **Series:** Olympics **Reverse:** Discus thrower

| Date | Mintage | F | VF | XF | Unc | BU |
|---|---|---|---|---|---|---|
| 1995 | Est. 25,000 | — | — | — | 60.00 | — |

**10 TALA** **KM# 114** **Weight:** 31.7000 g. **Composition:** 0.9250 Silver .9427 oz. ASW **Series:** Olympics **Subject:** Jakob le Maire **Obverse:** National arms **Reverse:** Sailing ship

| Date | Mintage | F | VF | XF | Unc | BU |
|---|---|---|---|---|---|---|
| 1996 Proof | — | Value: 35.00 | | | | |

**10 TALA** **KM# 123** **Weight:** 31.5000 g. **Composition:** 0.9250 Silver .9368 oz. ASW **Subject:** Princess Diana **Obverse:** National arms **Reverse:** Diana holding child **Edge:** Reeded **Size:** 38.6 mm.

| Date | Mintage | F | VF | XF | Unc | BU |
|---|---|---|---|---|---|---|
| 1998 Proof | — | Value: 25.00 | | | | |

**25 TALA** **KM# 62** **Weight:** 155.5000 g. **Composition:** 0.9990 Silver 5 oz. ASW **Subject:** Kon-Tiki **Size:** 65 mm. **Note:** Illustration reduced.

| Date | Mintage | F | VF | XF | Unc | BU |
|---|---|---|---|---|---|---|
| 1986 Proof | Est. 25,000 | Value: 50.00 | | | | |

**25 TALA** **KM# 67** **Weight:** 155.5000 g. **Composition:** 0.9990 Silver 5 oz. ASW **Subject:** America's Cup race **Size:** 65 mm. **Note:** Illustration reduced.

| Date | Mintage | F | VF | XF | Unc | BU |
|---|---|---|---|---|---|---|
| 1987 Proof | Est. 35,000 | Value: 48.00 | | | | |

**50 TALA** **KM# 76** **Weight:** 31.1030 g. **Composition:** 0.9990 Palladium 1 oz. **Subject:** Kon-Tiki **Reverse:** Raft and bamboo poles

| Date | Mintage | F | VF | XF | Unc | BU |
|---|---|---|---|---|---|---|
| 1988 Proof | Est. 10,000 | Value: 775 | | | | |

**50 TALA** **KM# 78** **Weight:** 7.7700 g. **Composition:** 0.9990 Gold .25 oz. AGW **Subject:** Trans-Antarctica expedition

| Date | Mintage | F | VF | XF | Unc | BU |
|---|---|---|---|---|---|---|
| 1988 Proof | Est. 30,000 | Value: 115 | | | | |

**50 TALA** **KM# 90** **Weight:** 7.7760 g. **Composition:** 0.5833 Gold .1458 oz. AGW **Series:** 1996 Olympics **Reverse:** Discus thrower

| Date | Mintage | F | VF | XF | Unc | BU |
|---|---|---|---|---|---|---|
| 1993 Proof | 7,500 | Value: 120 | | | | |

**50 TALA** **KM# 92** **Weight:** 7.7760 g. **Composition:** 0.5833 Gold .1458 oz. AGW **Subject:** World Cup soccer

| Date | Mintage | F | VF | XF | Unc | BU |
|---|---|---|---|---|---|---|
| 1993 Proof | Est. 3,000 | Value: 125 | | | | |

**50 TALA** **KM# 106** **Weight:** 7.7760 g. **Composition:** 0.5833 Gold .1458 oz. AGW **Obverse:** National arms **Reverse:** Portrait

| Date | Mintage | F | VF | XF | Unc | BU |
|---|---|---|---|---|---|---|
| 1993 Proof | Est. 3,000 | Value: 125 | | | | |

**50 TALA** **KM# 107** **Weight:** 7.7760 g. **Composition:** 0.5833 Gold .1458 oz. AGW **Subject:** The Endeavor

| Date | Mintage | F | VF | XF | Unc | BU |
|---|---|---|---|---|---|---|
| 1994 Proof | Est. 2,500 | Value: 125 | | | | |

**50 TALA** **KM# 108** **Weight:** 7.7760 g. **Composition:** 0.5833 Gold .1458 oz. AGW **Series:** Endangered Wildlife **Reverse:** Dolphins

| Date | Mintage | F | VF | XF | Unc | BU |
|---|---|---|---|---|---|---|
| 1995 Proof | Est. 2,500 | Value: 125 | | | | |

**50 TALA** **KM# 119** **Weight:** 7.7750 g. **Composition:** 0.9990 Gold .25 oz. AGW **Subject:** Tempora Mutantur **Obverse:** Western Samoan arms **Reverse:** Man with torch **Note:** Similar to 5 Tala, KM#117. Part of a joint matching set with Kiribati.

| Date | Mintage | F | VF | XF | Unc | BU |
|---|---|---|---|---|---|---|
| ND(1997) Proof | Est. 2,500 | Value: 110 | | | | |

**100 TALA** **KM# 21** **Weight:** 15.5500 g. **Composition:** 0.9170 Gold .4583 oz. AGW **Subject:** U.S. bicentennial

| Date | Mintage | F | VF | XF | Unc | BU |
|---|---|---|---|---|---|---|
| 1976 Proof | 2,000 | Value: 215 | | | | |

**100 TALA** **KM# 23** **Weight:** 15.5500 g. **Composition:** 0.9170 Gold .4583 oz. AGW **Series:** Montreal Olympics **Reverse:** Weight lifter **Note:** Similar to Tala, KM#22.

| Date | Mintage | F | VF | XF | Unc | BU |
|---|---|---|---|---|---|---|
| 1976 Proof | 2,500 | Value: 215 | | | | |

**100 TALA** **KM# 25** **Weight:** 15.5500 g. **Composition:** 0.9170 Gold .4583 oz. AGW **Subject:** Queen's silver jubilee

| Date | Mintage | F | VF | XF | Unc | BU |
|---|---|---|---|---|---|---|
| 1977 Proof | 2,500 | Value: 215 | | | | |

**100 TALA** **KM# 27** **Weight:** 15.5500 g. **Composition:** 0.9170 Gold .4583 oz. AGW **Subject:** Lindbergh's New York to Paris flight

| Date | Mintage | F | VF | XF | Unc | BU |
|---|---|---|---|---|---|---|
| 1977 Proof | 660 | Value: 275 | | | | |

**100 TALA** **KM# 29** **Weight:** 15.5500 g. **Composition:** 0.9170 Gold .4583 oz. AGW **Subject:** 50th anniversary - Trans-pacific flight **Reverse:** Globe with plane flying across Pacific Ocean, portrait of Lindbergh facing left **Note:** Similar to Tala, KM#28.

| Date | Mintage | F | VF | XF | Unc | BU |
|---|---|---|---|---|---|---|
| 1978 Proof | 1,500 | Value: 225 | | | | |

**100 TALA** **KM# 31** **Weight:** 15.5500 g. **Composition:** 0.9170 Gold .4583 oz. AGW **Subject:** XI Commonwealth Games **Reverse:** Runners **Note:** Similar to Tala, KM#30.

| Date | Mintage | F | VF | XF | Unc | BU |
|---|---|---|---|---|---|---|
| 1978 Proof | 1,000 | Value: 225 | | | | |

**100 TALA** **KM# 34** **Weight:** 12.5000 g. **Composition:** 0.9170 Gold .3686 oz. AGW **Subject:** Bicentenary - death of Capt. James Cook **Reverse:** Portrait of Cook at left of sailing ship **Note:** Similar to 10 Tala, KM#33.

| Date | Mintage | F | VF | XF | Unc | BU |
|---|---|---|---|---|---|---|
| 1979 Proof | 1,000 | Value: 225 | | | | |

**100 TALA** **KM# 37** **Weight:** 7.5000 g. **Composition:** 0.9170 Gold .2211 oz. AGW **Series:** 1980 Olympics **Reverse:** Hurdles

| Date | Mintage | F | VF | XF | Unc | BU |
|---|---|---|---|---|---|---|
| 1980 | 250 | — | — | — | 215 | — |
| 1980 Proof | 1,000 | Value: 145 | | | | |

**100 TALA** **KM# 42** **Weight:** 7.5000 g. **Composition:** 0.9170 Gold .2211 oz. AGW **Subject:** Gov. Wilhelm Solf

| Date | Mintage | F | VF | XF | Unc | BU |
|---|---|---|---|---|---|---|
| 1980 | 250 | — | — | — | 120 | — |
| 1980 Proof | 1,000 | Value: 125 | | | | |

**100 TALA** **KM# 45** **Weight:** 7.5000 g. **Composition:** 0.9170 Gold .2211 oz. AGW **Subject:** Wedding of Prince Charles and Lady Diana

| Date | Mintage | F | VF | XF | Unc | BU |
|---|---|---|---|---|---|---|
| 1981 | 250 | — | — | — | 110 | — |
| 1981 Proof | 1,500 | Value: 120 | | | | |

**100 TALA** **KM# 49** **Weight:** 7.5000 g. **Composition:** 0.9170 Gold .2211 oz. AGW **Subject:** IYDP - President Franklin Roosevelt **Reverse:** President Roosevelt in wheel chair **Note:** Similar to Tala, KM#47.

| Date | Mintage | F | VF | XF | Unc | BU |
|---|---|---|---|---|---|---|
| 1981 | 250 | — | — | — | 115 | — |
| 1981 Proof | 1,500 | Value: 125 | | | | |

**100 TALA** **KM# 52** **Weight:** 7.5000 g. **Composition:** 0.9170 Gold .2211 oz. AGW **Subject:** Commonwealth Games **Reverse:** Javelin thrower

| Date | Mintage | F | VF | XF | Unc | BU |
|---|---|---|---|---|---|---|
| 1982 | 250 | — | — | — | 110 | — |
| 1982 Proof | 1,000 | Value: 125 | | | | |

**100 TALA** **KM# 55** **Weight:** 7.5000 g. **Composition:** 0.9170 Gold .2211 oz. AGW **Subject:** South Pacific Games **Reverse:** Runner

| Date | Mintage | F | VF | XF | Unc | BU |
|---|---|---|---|---|---|---|
| 1983 | — | — | — | — | 110 | — |
| 1983 Proof | 1,000 | Value: 125 | | | | |

**100 TALA** **KM# 60** **Weight:** 7.5000 g. **Composition:** 0.9170 Gold .2211 oz. AGW **Series:** Summer Olympics **Reverse:** Boxers, similar to Tala, KM#58

| Date | Mintage | F | VF | XF | Unc | BU |
|---|---|---|---|---|---|---|
| 1984 | 200 | — | — | — | 225 | — |
| 1984 Proof | 500 | Value: 200 | | | | |

**100 TALA** **KM# 68** **Weight:** 7.5000 g. **Composition:** 0.9000 Gold .217 oz. AGW **Subject:** America's Cup race

| Date | Mintage | F | VF | XF | Unc | BU |
|---|---|---|---|---|---|---|
| 1987 Proof | Est. 5,000 | Value: 110 | | | | |

**100 TALA** **KM# 77** **Weight:** 7.5000 g. **Composition:** 0.9000 Gold .217 oz. AGW **Subject:** Kon-Tiki **Reverse:** Raft and inscription

| Date | Mintage | F | VF | XF | Unc | BU |
|---|---|---|---|---|---|---|
| 1988 Proof | Est. 5,000 | Value: 110 | | | | |

**100 TALA** **KM# 81** **Weight:** 7.5000 g. **Composition:** 0.9170 Gold .2211 oz. AGW **Series:** Save the Children

| Date | Mintage | F | VF | XF | Unc | BU |
|---|---|---|---|---|---|---|
| 1990 Proof | 3,000 | Value: 125 | | | | |

**100 TALA** **KM# 84** **Weight:** 7.5000 g. **Composition:** 0.9170 Gold .2211 oz. AGW **Subject:** RA expeditions **Obverse:** Similar to KM#81 **Reverse:** RA II

| Date | Mintage | F | VF | XF | Unc | BU |
|---|---|---|---|---|---|---|
| 1991 Proof | 5,000 | Value: 135 | | | | |

**100 TALA** **KM# 87** **Weight:** 7.5000 g. **Composition:** 0.9000 Gold .217 oz. AGW **Series:** Olympics **Reverse:** Torch runners

| Date | Mintage | F | VF | XF | Unc | BU |
|---|---|---|---|---|---|---|
| 1991 Proof | Est. 6,000 | Value: 110 | | | | |

**100 TALA** **KM# 96** **Weight:** 7.5000 g. **Composition:** 0.9170 Gold .2211 oz. AGW **Subject:** Tigris expedition **Reverse:** Tigris sailing

| Date | Mintage | F | VF | XF | Unc | BU |
|---|---|---|---|---|---|---|
| 1994 Proof | 500 | Value: 265 | | | | |

**1000 TALA** **KM# 46** **Weight:** 33.9500 g. **Composition:** 0.9170 Gold 1.001 oz. AGW **Subject:** Wedding of Prince Charles and Lady Diana **Note:** Similar to 100 Tala, KM#45.

| Date | Mintage | F | VF | XF | Unc | BU |
|---|---|---|---|---|---|---|
| 1981 Proof | 100 | Value: 775 | | | | |

**1000 TALA** **KM# 56** **Weight:** 31.1000 g. **Composition:** 0.9170 Gold .917 oz. AGW **Subject:** South Pacific Games **Reverse:** Runner **Note:** Similar to 10 Tala, KM#54.

| Date | Mintage | F | VF | XF | Unc | BU |
|---|---|---|---|---|---|---|
| 1983 Proof | 100 | Value: 700 | | | | |

**1000 TALA** **KM# 61** **Weight:** 31.1000 g. **Composition:** 0.9170 Gold .917 oz. AGW **Series:** 1984 Olympics **Reverse:** Boxers

| Date | Mintage | F | VF | XF | Unc | BU |
|---|---|---|---|---|---|---|
| 1984 Proof | 100 | Value: 725 | | | | |

**1000 TALA** **KM# 65** **Weight:** 33.9500 g. **Composition:** 0.9170 Gold 1.001 oz. AGW **Subject:** Prince Andrew's marriage **Obverse:** Similar to Tala, KM#8 **Reverse:** Similar to Tala, KM#63

| Date | Mintage | F | VF | XF | Unc | BU |
|---|---|---|---|---|---|---|
| 1986 Proof | 50 | Value: 875 | | | | |

**1000 TALA** **KM# 110** **Weight:** 33.9500 g. **Composition:** 0.9170 Gold 1.001 oz. AGW **Subject:** 40th anniversary - reign of Queen Elizabeth II **Obverse:** National arms **Reverse:** Royal carriage and guard around Order of the Garter

| Date | Mintage | F | VF | XF | Unc | BU |
|---|---|---|---|---|---|---|
| 1992 Proof | Est. 150 | Value: 700 | | | | |

## PIEFORTS

| KM# | Date | Mintage | Identification | Mkt Val |
|---|---|---|---|---|
| P1 | 1984 | 3,000 | Tala. 0.9250 Silver. KM57. | 22.00 |
| P2 | 1992 | — | Tala. 0.9250 Silver. KM109. | 60.00 |

## MINT SETS

| KM# | Date | Mintage | Identification | Issue Price | Mkt Val |
|---|---|---|---|---|---|
| MS1 | 1967 (6) | — | KM1-6 | — | 2.50 |
| MS2 | 1974 (7) | 10,740 | KM12-17, 19 | 5.30 | 5.00 |

## PROOF SETS

| KM# | Date | Mintage | Identification | Issue Price | Mkt Val |
|---|---|---|---|---|---|
| PS1 | 1967 (7) | 15,000 | KM1-7 | 10.00 | 7.00 |
| PS2 | 1974 (7) | 5,578 | KM12a-17a, 19a | 53.00 | 30.00 |
| PS3 | 1988 (3) | — | KM75-77 | — | 910 |
| PS4 | 1991 (2) | 1,000 | KM83-84 | — | 160 |
| PS5 | 1994 (3) | 500 | KM94-96 | — | 345 |

# YEMEN REPUBLIC

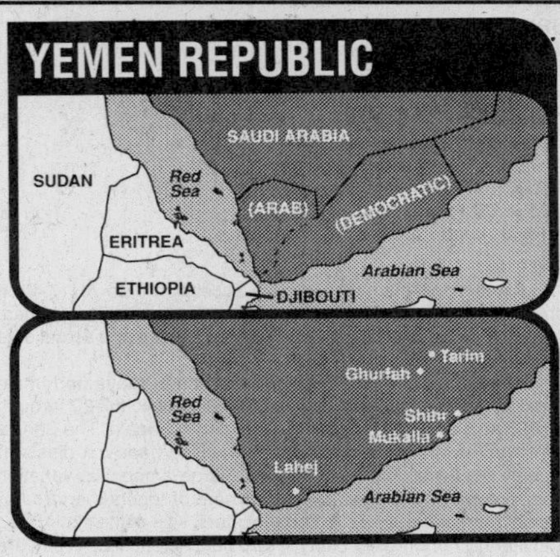


The Republic of Yemen, formerly Yemen Arab Republic and Peoples Republic of Yemen is located on the southern coast of the Arabian Peninsula. It has an area of 205,020sq. mi. (531,000 sq. km.) and a population of 12 million. Capital: San'a. The port of Aden is the main commercial center and the area's most valuable natural resource. Recent oil and gas finds and a developing petroleum industry have improved their economic prospects. Agriculture and local handicrafts are the main industries. Cotton, fish, coffee, rock salt and hides are exported.

On May 22, 1990, the Yemen Arab Republic (North Yemen) and Peoples Democratic Republic of Yemen (South Yemen) merged into a unified Republic of Yemen.

**TITLES**

دار الخلافة

Dar al-Khilafa(t)

## MUTAWAKKILITE

One of the oldest centers of civilization in the Middle East, Yemen was once part of the Minaean Kingdom and of the ancient Kingdom of Sheba, after which it was captured successively by Egyptians, Ethiopians and Romans. It was converted to Islam in 628 A.D. and administered as a caliphate until 1538, when it came under Ottoman occupation in 1849. The second Ottoman occupation which began in 1872 was maintained until 1918 when autonomy was achieved through revolution.

**TITLES**

المملكة المتوكلية اليمنية

al-Mamlaka(t) al-Mutawakkiliya(t) al-Yamaniya(t)

**RULERS**

Ottoman, until 1625

**QASIMID IMAMS**

al-Mansur Muhammad bin Yahya,
(Imam Mansur) AH1307-1322/1890-1904AD
al Hadi al-Hasan bin Yahya
(Counter Imam, in Sa'da) AH1322/1904AD
al-Mutawakkil Yahya bin Muhammad
(Imam Yahya) AH1322-1367/1904-1948AD
al-Nasir Ahmad bin Yahya,
(Imam Ahmad) AH1367-1382/
1948-1962AD
al-Badr Muhammad bin Ahmad,
(Imam Badr) AH1382-1388/
1962-1968AD (mostly in exile)

**MINTNAME**

صنعاء

San'a

**MONETARY SYSTEM**

After Accession of Iman Yahya
AH1322/1904AD
1 Zalat = 1/160 Riyal
2 Zalat = 1 Halala = 1/80 Riyal
2 Halala = 1 Buqsha = 1/40 Riyal
40 Buqsha = 1 Riyal

**NOTE:** The Riyal was called an IMADI (RIYAL) during the reign of Imam Yahya "Imadi" honorific name for Yahyawi and an AHMADI (RIYAL) during the reign of Imam Ahmad. The 1 Zalat, Y#2:1, D1, A3, A4 and all Imam Yahya gold strikes except Y#F10, bear no indication of value. Many of the Mutawakkilite coins after AH1322/1904AD bear the denomination expressed as fraction of the Riyal as follows.

**BRONZE and ALUMINUM**
*Thumn ushr* = 1/80 Riyal = 1/2 Buqsha = 1 Halala
*Rub ushr* = 1/40 Riyal = 1 Buqsha
*Nisf ushr* = 1/20 Riyal = 2 Buqsha = 1/2 Bawlah
*Nisf thumn* = 1/16 Riyal = 2-1/2 Buqsha
*Ushr* = 1/10 Riyal = 4 Buqsha = 1 Bawlah
*Thumn* = 1/8 Riyal = 5 Buqsha
*Rub* = 1/4 Riyal = 10 Buqsha
*Nisf* = 1/2 Riyal = 20 Buqsha
1 Riyal (Imadi, Ahmadi) = 40 Buqsha

**DATING**

All coins of Imam Yahya have accession date AH1322 on obverse and actual date of issue on reverse. All coins of Imam Ahmad bear accession date AH1367 on obverse and actual date on reverse.

If not otherwise noted, all coins of Imam Yahya and Imam Ahad as well as the early issues of the Republic (Y#20 through Y#A25 and Y#32), were struck at the mint in Sana'a. The Sana'a Mint was essentially a medieval mint, using hand-cut dies and crudely machined blanks. There is a large amount of variation from one die to the next in arrangement of legends and ornaments, form of crescents, number of stars, size of the circle, etc., and literally hundreds of subtypes could be identified. Types are divided only when there are changes in the inscriptions, or major variations in the basic type, such as the presence or absence of "Rabb al-Alamin" in the legend or the position of the word *Sana* (= year) in relation to the year.

**NOTE:** All "ZALAT" coins are without mint name or denomination.

# MUTAWAKKILITE KINGDOM

## al-Mansur Muhammad bin Yahya (Imam Mansur)

### AH1307-22/1890-1904AD

### HAMMERED COINAGE

(Imam Mansur)

Coins for this ruler were struck at Qaflat Idhar. Harf and Kabir strikes have similar inscriptions with varieties in position of date, legend arrangements, and ornamentation. No indication of value on coins.

**KABIR KM# 408.1 Composition:** Silver **Obverse:** Ornament below legend **Obv. Legend:** "Bilah/al-Mansu/r" **Reverse:** Legend as circle **Rev. Legend:** "Allah/", date, "Abd" **Note:** 0.40-0.80 grams. 15-17 milimeters. Varieties of shape of ornaments exist.

| Date | Mintage | Good | VG | F | VF | XF |
|---|---|---|---|---|---|---|
| AH1312 | — | — | — | — | — | — |
| AH1316 | — | — | — | — | — | — |
| AH1318 | — | — | — | — | — | — |

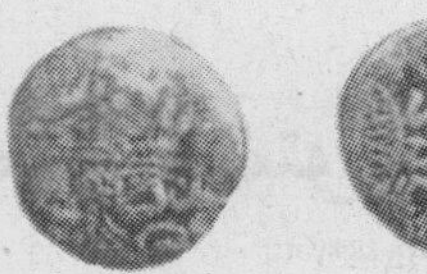

**KABIR KM# 410 Composition:** Silver **Obverse:** Similar to KM#409 **Reverse:** "Allah/Abd/" date, divided by ornament, wtih four circular segments **Note:** 0.60-1.00 gram. 15-16 milimeters. Varieties with three and four stars on reverse exist.

| Date | Mintage | Good | VG | F | VF | XF |
|---|---|---|---|---|---|---|
| AH1316 | — | 15.00 | 30.00 | 50.00 | 85.00 | — |
| AH1319 | — | 15.00 | 30.00 | 50.00 | 85.00 | — |
| AH1320 | — | 15.00 | 30.00 | 50.00 | 85.00 | — |
| AH1321 | — | 15.00 | 30.00 | 50.00 | 85.00 | — |

**KABIR KM# 407.2 Composition:** Silver **Reverse:** Date at bottom **Note:** 0.60-0.70 grams.

| Date | Mintage | Good | VG | F | VF | XF |
|---|---|---|---|---|---|---|
| AH1318 | — | — | — | — | — | — |

**HARF KM# 403 Composition:** Bronze **Note:** Similar to 1 Kabir, KM#410.

| Date | Mintage | Good | VG | F | VF | XF |
|---|---|---|---|---|---|---|
| AH1320 | — | — | — | — | — | — |

## al Hadi al-Hasan

### AH1322/1904AD

### MILLED COINAGE

**HALALA Y# C1 Weight:** 1.9300 g. **Composition:** Bronze **Obverse:** Al-Hasan/bin Yahya/Sana 1322 **Reverse:** Al-Hadi/Li-din Allah

| Date | Mintage | Good | VG | F | VF | XF |
|---|---|---|---|---|---|---|
| AH1322 | — | — | — | — | — | — |

## al-Mutawakkil Yahya bin Muhammad (Imam Yahya)

### AH1322-67/1904-48AD

### MILLED COINAGE

**ZALAT Y# 1.1 Composition:** Bronze **Obverse:** Inscription in three lines above regnal year **Edge:** Plain **Note:** 0.90-1.60 grams. Varieties with two stars. Reverse with eight stars. Size of inner circle varies, various planchet thicknesses.

| Date | Mintage | Good | VG | F | VF | XF |
|---|---|---|---|---|---|---|
| AH1341(1922-23) | — | 15.00 | 30.00 | 100 | 160 | — |
| AH1342(1923-24) | — | 5.00 | 12.00 | 30.00 | 50.00 | — |
| AH1343(1924-25) | — | 4.00 | 10.00 | 20.00 | 40.00 | — |
| **Note:** 1343 also known with seven stars | | | | | | |
| AH1344(1925-26) | — | 5.00 | 12.00 | 30.00 | 50.00 | — |
| **Note:** 1344 also exists with traces of reeded edges | | | | | | |
| AH1345(1926-27) | — | 10.00 | 25.00 | 75.00 | 125 | — |
| AH1346(1927-28) | — | 4.00 | 10.00 | 20.00 | 40.00 | — |

**ZALAT Y# 1.2 Composition:** Bronze **Obverse:** Inscription in two lines above regnal year

| Date | Mintage | Good | VG | F | VF | XF |
|---|---|---|---|---|---|---|
| AH1342(1923-24) | — | 5.00 | 12.00 | 30.00 | 50.00 | — |

**Note:** Obverse: Varieties with 1, 2, and 4 stars, and reverse with 8, 11, 12, 13, 14, 15, 16, 17, 20, and 22 stars exist; Some specimens show traces of reeded edges; Various planchet thicknesses

**ZALAT Y# 1.7 Composition:** Bronze **Reverse:** Date in margin at bottom

| Date | Mintage | Good | VG | F | VF | XF |
|---|---|---|---|---|---|---|
| AH1342(1923-24) Rare | — | — | — | — | — | — |

**Note:** Obverse: Varieties with 1 and 2 stars; Reverse: 11 stars, various planchet thicknesses

**ZALAT Y# 1.4 Composition:** Bronze **Obverse:** Crescent design

| Date | Mintage | Good | VG | F | VF | XF |
|---|---|---|---|---|---|---|
| AH1342(1923-24) | — | 300 | 425 | 650 | 1,000 | — |

**Note:** Varieties exist with 11, 14, 15, 16, and 17 stars on reverse and with 1, 2, and 4 stars on obverse; Various planchet thicknesses

**ZALAT Y# B1 Composition:** Bronze **Note:** Dated accessionally (AH1322) on reverse. Probably struck at Shaharah about 1925. Dies were reportedly prepared in Italy. For silver striked, see Y#A4.

| Date | Mintage | Good | VG | F | VF | XF |
|---|---|---|---|---|---|---|
| NDAH1322(ca.1925) | — | 30.00 | 60.00 | 125 | 200 | — |
| **Note:** This issue is believed to be a pattern | | | | | | |
| NDAH1322(ca.1925) | — | 30.00 | 60.00 | 125 | 200 | — |

**1/80 RIYAL (1/2 Buqsha) Y# 2.1 Composition:** Bronze **Note:** Accession date: AH1322.

| Date | Mintage | Good | VG | F | VF | XF |
|---|---|---|---|---|---|---|
| ND(ca.1911-21) | — | 12.50 | 25.00 | 50.00 | 85.00 | — |

**Note:** Probably struck at Shaharah

**1/80 RIYAL (1/2 Buqsha) Y# D1 Composition:** Bronze **Obverse:** "Rabb al-Alamin" **Reverse:** Toughra design **Note:** Accession date: AH1322. Without denomination or mintname.

| Date | Mintage | Good | VG | F | VF | XF |
|---|---|---|---|---|---|---|
| ND(ca.1911-21) Rare; Accessional date only | — | — | — | — | — | — |

**1/80 RIYAL (1/2 Buqsha) Y# 2.8 Composition:** Bronze **Note:** Mule, two obverses.

| Date | Mintage | Good | VG | F | VF | XF |
|---|---|---|---|---|---|---|
| ND(1911-21) | — | 20.00 | 30.00 | 60.00 | 100 | — |

**1/80 RIYAL (1/2 Buqsha) Y# 2.2 Composition:** Bronze **Note:** Thin flan, 1.50-3.00 grams. The number and arrangement of stars and the size of the circle on the reverse vary as well as the exact arrangement of the legends which sometimes vary within each year. The reverse exists with 10, 12, 14, 20, 22, 24, 28, and 34 stars. Obverse varieties exist with 1, 2, or 3 stars and without stars. Struck at Shaharah.

| Date | Mintage | Good | VG | F | VF | XF |
|---|---|---|---|---|---|---|
| AH1330(1911-12) | — | 20.00 | 35.00 | 60.00 | 100 | — |
| AH1331(1912-13) | — | 20.00 | 35.00 | 75.00 | 150 | — |
| AH1332(1913-14) | — | 10.00 | 15.00 | 25.00 | 40.00 | — |
| AH1333(1914-15) | — | 10.00 | 15.00 | 25.00 | 40.00 | — |
| AH1337(1918-19) | — | 10.00 | 15.00 | 25.00 | 40.00 | — |
| AH1338(1919-20) | — | 10.00 | 15.00 | 25.00 | 40.00 | — |
| AH1339(1920-21) | — | — | — | — | — | — |

**1/80 RIYAL (1/2 Buqsha) Y# 2.7 Composition:** Bronze **Note:** Thick flan. 4.00-4.50 grams. Varieties with 10 and 14 stars on reverse. Obverse with 1, 2, and 3 stars. Varieties of legend distribution. Some coins occur with light silver wash. Struck at Shaharah.

| Date | Mintage | Good | VG | F | VF | XF |
|---|---|---|---|---|---|---|
| AH1332(1913-14) | — | 10.00 | 15.00 | 25.00 | 40.00 | — |
| AH1333(1914-15) | — | 10.00 | 15.00 | 25.00 | 40.00 | — |
| AH1338(1919-20) | — | 10.00 | 15.00 | 25.00 | 40.00 | — |

**1/80 RIYAL (1/2 Buqsha) Y# 2.6 Composition:** Bronze **Reverse:** "Sana" below date **Note:** Thin flan. 3.00 grams. Struck at Shaharah.

| Date | Mintage | Good | VG | F | VF | XF |
|---|---|---|---|---|---|---|
| AH1333(1914-15) | — | 80.00 | 100 | 200 | 300 | — |

**1/80 RIYAL (1/2 Buqsha) Y# 2.5 Composition:** Bronze (Red To Yellow) **Obverse:** "Rabb al-Alamin" **Reverse:** "Sana" above date **Note:** Number and arrangement of stars on reverse (4, 5, 6, 7, or 8) as well as the size of the inner circle vary. Varieties exist in the form of crescent and arrangement of legends and planchet thicknesses.

| Date | Mintage | Good | VG | F | VF | XF |
|---|---|---|---|---|---|---|
| AH1339(1920-21) | — | 7.00 | 12.00 | 25.00 | 40.00 | — |
| AH1341(1922-23) | — | 7.00 | 12.00 | 25.00 | 40.00 | — |
| AH1342(1923-24) | — | 2.00 | 5.00 | 12.00 | 20.00 | — |
| AH1343(1924-25) | — | 2.00 | 5.00 | 12.00 | 20.00 | — |
| AH1344(1925-26) | — | 2.00 | 5.00 | 12.00 | 20.00 | — |
| AH1345(1926-27) | — | 1.50 | 4.00 | 8.00 | 15.00 | — |
| AH1346(1927-28) | — | 1.50 | 3.00 | 6.00 | 12.00 | — |
| **Note:** Some examples of AH1346 show the 6 re-engraved over low I | | | | | | |
| AH1347(1928-29) | — | 1.50 | 4.00 | 8.00 | 15.00 | — |
| AH1348(1929-30) | — | 1.50 | 4.00 | 8.00 | 15.00 | — |
| AH1349(1930-31) | — | 1.50 | 4.00 | 8.00 | 15.00 | — |
| AH1350(1931-32) | — | 1.50 | 4.00 | 8.00 | 15.00 | — |
| AH135x(1932) | — | 1.50 | 4.00 | 8.00 | 15.00 | — |
| AH1351(1932-33) | — | 2.00 | 6.00 | 12.00 | 20.00 | — |
| AH1352(1933-34) | — | 2.00 | 6.00 | 12.00 | 20.00 | — |
| AH1353(1934-35) | — | 2.00 | 6.00 | 12.00 | 20.00 | — |
| AH1359(1940-41) | — | 2.50 | 6.00 | 12.00 | 20.00 | — |
| AH1360(1941-42) | — | 2.50 | 4.00 | 8.00 | 15.00 | — |
| AH1361(1942-43) | — | 4.00 | 8.00 | 15.00 | 25.00 | — |

**1/80 RIYAL (1/2 Buqsha) Y# 2.3 Composition:** Bronze **Reverse:** "Duriba Bi Sana'a" added

| Date | Mintage | Good | VG | F | VF | XF |
|---|---|---|---|---|---|---|
| AH1340(1921-22) | — | 10.00 | 20.00 | 40.00 | 75.00 | — |
| **Note:** AH1340 exists with 4 and 8 stars on reverse | | | | | | |
| AH1341(1922-23) | — | 10.00 | 20.00 | 40.00 | 75.00 | — |

**Note:** AH1341 exists with 4 stars on reverse

**1/80 RIYAL (1/2 Buqsha)** **Y# 2.4** **Composition:** Bronze **Obverse:** Without "Rabb al-Alamin"

| Date | Mintage | Good | VG | F | VF | XF |
|---|---|---|---|---|---|---|
| AH1341(1922-23) | — | 12.00 | 25.00 | 50.00 | 85.00 | — |

**Note:** AH1341 exists with 4 stars on reverse

| Date | Mintage | Good | VG | F | VF | XF |
|---|---|---|---|---|---|---|
| AH1342(1923-24) | — | 12.00 | 25.00 | 50.00 | 85.00 | — |

**Note:** AH1342 coins exist with 4 and 6 stars on reverse

**1/40 RIYAL (1 Buqsha)** **Y# A3** **Composition:** Billon/Silver **Note:** 0.65-1.25 grams. 15-16 milimeters. Accession date: AH1322.

| Date | Mintage | VG | F | VF | XF | Unc |
|---|---|---|---|---|---|---|
| ND(ca.1911-21) | — | 275 | 550 | 1,100 | 1,650 | — |

**Note:** Minted at Qaflat Idhar without mintname or denomination

**1/40 RIYAL (1 Buqsha)** **Y# 3.1** **Composition:** Bronze **Obverse:** Without "Rabb al-Alamin" **Reverse:** "Sana" below date **Note:** Accession date: AH1322.

| Date | Mintage | VG | F | VF | XF | Unc |
|---|---|---|---|---|---|---|
| AH1341(1922-23) | — | 10.00 | 20.00 | 40.00 | 80.00 | — |

**Note:** Varieties of borders, arrangement of legends, and thickness of planchets exist

**1/40 RIYAL (1 Buqsha)** **Y# 3.2** **Composition:** Bronze (Red To Yellow) **Obverse:** "Rabb al-Alamin" **Reverse:** "Sana" above date, small "Sana'a" and three leaf ornaments plus star in border legend

| Date | Mintage | VG | F | VF | XF | Unc |
|---|---|---|---|---|---|---|
| AH1342(1923-24) | — | 4.00 | 10.00 | 20.00 | 60.00 | — |

**Note:** AH1342 exists with 4 leaf ornaments and without star in border legend

| Date | Mintage | VG | F | VF | XF | Unc |
|---|---|---|---|---|---|---|
| AH13442(1923) | — | 65.00 | 125 | — | — | — |
| AH1343(1924-25) | — | 4.00 | 10.00 | 20.00 | 60.00 | — |
| AH1344(1925-26) | — | 15.00 | 30.00 | 50.00 | 75.00 | — |

**1/40 RIYAL (1 Buqsha)** **Y# 3.3** **Composition:** Bronze (Red To Yellow) **Reverse:** Large "Sana'a" in legend **Note:** Varieties in arrangement of legends, ornaments, form of the crescent, and size of the circle on reverse exist.

| Date | Mintage | VG | F | VF | XF | Unc |
|---|---|---|---|---|---|---|
| AH1344(1925-26) | — | 12.00 | 20.00 | 35.00 | 100 | — |
| AH1345(1926-27) | — | 12.00 | 20.00 | 35.00 | 100 | — |
| AH1349(1930-31) | — | 1.50 | 3.50 | 10.00 | 25.00 | — |
| AH1358(1939-40) | — | 2.00 | 4.00 | 10.00 | 25.00 | — |
| AH1359(1940-41) | — | 2.00 | 4.00 | 10.00 | 25.00 | — |
| AH1360(1941-42) | — | 2.00 | 4.00 | 10.00 | 25.00 | — |
| AH1361/0(1942-43) | — | 10.00 | 20.00 | 50.00 | 75.00 | — |
| AH1362/0(1943) | — | 2.50 | 5.00 | 10.00 | 35.00 | — |
| AH1362(1943) | — | 1.50 | 3.50 | 10.00 | 30.00 | — |
| AH1363(1943) | — | 1.50 | 5.00 | 12.00 | 35.00 | — |
| AH1364(1944-45) | — | 1.50 | 5.00 | 12.00 | 35.00 | — |
| AH1365/4(1945) | — | 2.25 | 5.00 | 12.00 | 35.00 | — |
| AH1365(1945-46) | — | 2.50 | 5.00 | 12.00 | 35.00 | — |
| AH1366(1946-47) | — | 1.50 | 3.50 | 12.00 | 30.00 | — |
| AH1366/x(1946) | — | 2.50 | 5.00 | 12.00 | 35.00 | — |
| AH1367(1947-48) | — | 10.00 | 20.00 | 50.00 | 75.00 | — |

**1/20 IMADI RIYAL** **Y# A4** **Composition:** Silver **Note:** Accession date: AH1322.

| Date | Mintage | VG | F | VF | XF | Unc |
|---|---|---|---|---|---|---|
| ND(1911-21) | — | 60.00 | 120 | 250 | 400 | — |

**Note:** Dated accessionally on obverse without mintname or denomination; Probably struck at Shaharah about 1925; Dies were reportedly prepared in Italy; Strikes in nickel reported; See Y#B1; This issue is believed to be a pattern

**1/20 IMADI RIYAL** **Y# B4** **Composition:** Silver **Obverse:** "Rabb al-Alamin" **Reverse:** Without "Sana"

| Date | Mintage | VG | F | VF | XF | Unc |
|---|---|---|---|---|---|---|
| AH1337(1918-19) Rare | — | — | — | — | — | — |

**Note:** Three stars on reverse

**1/20 IMADI RIYAL** **Y# 4.1** **Composition:** Silver **Obverse:** Without "Rabb al-Alamin" **Note:** Varieties in arrangement of legends, size of circle, and with 3 and 4 stars on reverse exist. Variety of Y#4 dated with 2 digits AH(13)22 of the accessional year are considered local contemporary counterfeits by leading authorities. They are reported having been produced by the Zaraing tribe at Bait Al-Faqih. See note below Y#5.5.

| Date | Mintage | VG | F | VF | XF | Unc |
|---|---|---|---|---|---|---|
| AH1337(1918-19) | — | 40.00 | 80.00 | 150 | 250 | — |
| AH1338(1919-20) Rare | — | — | — | — | — | — |
| AH1339(1920-21) | — | 40.00 | 80.00 | 150 | 250 | — |

**Note:** Some strikes show accessional year as 322 only

| Date | Mintage | VG | F | VF | XF | Unc |
|---|---|---|---|---|---|---|
| AH1340(1921-22) | — | 20.00 | 30.00 | 60.00 | 100 | — |

**Note:** Some strikes show accessional year as 322 only

| Date | Mintage | VG | F | VF | XF | Unc |
|---|---|---|---|---|---|---|
| AH1342(1923-24) | — | 5.00 | 12.00 | 30.00 | 60.00 | — |
| AH1343(1924-25) | — | 4.00 | 10.00 | 25.00 | 50.00 | — |
| AH1344(1925-26) | — | 4.00 | 10.00 | 25.00 | 50.00 | — |
| AH1345/2(1926) | — | 4.00 | 10.00 | 25.00 | 50.00 | — |
| AH1345(1926-27) | — | 4.00 | 10.00 | 25.00 | 50.00 | — |
| AH1347(1928-29) | — | 5.00 | 12.00 | 30.00 | 60.00 | — |
| AH1348(1929-30) | — | 4.00 | 10.00 | 25.00 | 50.00 | — |
| AH1349(1930-31) | — | 4.00 | 10.00 | 25.00 | 50.00 | — |
| AH1350(1931-32) | — | 4.00 | 12.00 | 30.00 | 60.00 | — |
| AH1351(1932-33) | — | 5.00 | 15.00 | 35.00 | 75.00 | — |
| AH1352(1933-34) | — | 4.00 | 12.00 | 30.00 | 60.00 | — |
| AH1353(1934-35) | — | 4.00 | 12.00 | 30.00 | 60.00 | — |
| AH1358(1939-40) | — | 3.00 | 8.00 | 20.00 | 40.00 | — |
| AH1359(1940-41) | — | 3.00 | 8.00 | 20.00 | 40.00 | — |
| AH1362/58(1943) | — | 5.00 | 15.00 | 30.00 | 60.00 | — |
| AH1362/59(1943) | — | 5.00 | 15.00 | 30.00 | 60.00 | — |
| AH1363(1943) | — | 4.00 | 10.00 | 30.00 | 60.00 | — |
| AH1364/46(1944) | — | 3.00 | 8.00 | 20.00 | 40.00 | — |
| AH1364(1944-45) | — | 3.00 | 8.00 | 20.00 | 40.00 | — |
| AHx364(1944) | — | 3.00 | 8.00 | 20.00 | 40.00 | — |
| AH1365(1945-46) | — | 3.00 | 10.00 | 25.00 | 50.00 | — |
| AH1366/44(1946) | — | 4.00 | 12.00 | 30.00 | 60.00 | — |
| AH1366(1946-47) | — | 4.00 | 12.00 | 30.00 | 60.00 | — |

**1/20 IMADI RIYAL** **Y# 4.4** **Composition:** Silver **Reverse:** Border legen shifted to left

| Date | Mintage | VG | F | VF | XF | Unc |
|---|---|---|---|---|---|---|
| AH1340(1921-22) Rare | — | — | — | — | — | — |

**Note:** Three stars on reverse

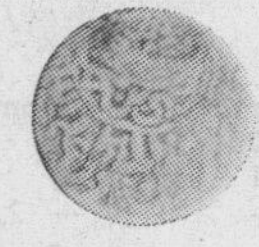

**1/20 IMADI RIYAL** **Y# 4.2** **Composition:** Silver **Reverse:** "Sana" below date, normal legend position **Note:** Four stars on reverse.

| Date | Mintage | VG | F | VF | XF | Unc |
|---|---|---|---|---|---|---|
| AH1341(1922-23) | — | 40.00 | 80.00 | 150 | 250 | — |
| AHx341(1922) | — | 40.00 | 80.00 | 150 | 250 | — |

**1/10 IMADI RIYAL** **Y# 5.1** **Composition:** Silver **Obverse:** "Rabb al-Alamin" **Reverse:** Without "Sana" **Note:** Accession date: AH1322.

| Date | Mintage | VG | F | VF | XF | Unc |
|---|---|---|---|---|---|---|
| AH1337(1918-19) | — | 30.00 | 60.00 | 100 | 175 | — |

**Note:** Reverse varieties with 3, 4, and 5 stars. Size of circle and form of crescent varies

**1/10 IMADI RIYAL** **Y# 5.2** **Composition:** Silver **Obverse:** Without "Rabb al-Alamin"

| Date | Mintage | VG | F | VF | XF | Unc |
|---|---|---|---|---|---|---|
| AH1339(1920-21) | — | 20.00 | 40.00 | 75.00 | 150 | — |

**Note:** Some AH1339 strikes show accession date as 322

| Date | Mintage | VG | F | VF | XF | Unc |
|---|---|---|---|---|---|---|
| AH1340(1921-22) | — | 20.00 | 40.00 | 75.00 | 150 | — |

**Note:** AH1340 also exists with three stars, others with six stars on reverse

| Date | Mintage | VG | F | VF | XF | Unc |
|---|---|---|---|---|---|---|
| AH1341(1922-23) | — | 20.00 | 40.00 | 75.00 | 150 | — |
| AH1348(1929-30) | — | 100 | 150 | 350 | 500 | — |

**1/10 IMADI RIYAL** **Y# 5.3** **Composition:** Silver **Reverse:** "Sana" below date **Note:** Varieties with three and six stars on the reverse exist.

| Date | Mintage | VG | F | VF | XF | Unc |
|---|---|---|---|---|---|---|
| AH1341(1922-23) | — | 20.00 | 40.00 | 75.00 | 150 | — |
| AH1342(1923-24) | — | 20.00 | 40.00 | 75.00 | 150 | — |

**1/10 IMADI RIYAL** **Y# 5.5** **Composition:** Silver **Obverse:** Without "Rabb al-Alamin" **Reverse:** "Sana" above date **Note:** Form of crescent, size of circle on reverse, and arrangement of legends vary. Varieties with 6, 7, 8, 9, 10, and 12 stars on reverse exist. Some earlier dates show traces of reeded edges.

| Date | Mintage | VG | F | VF | XF | Unc |
|---|---|---|---|---|---|---|
| AH1342(1923-24) | — | 4.00 | 10.00 | 25.00 | 50.00 | — |
| AH1343(1924-25) | — | 4.00 | 10.00 | 25.00 | 50.00 | — |
| AH1344(1925-26) | — | 3.00 | 8.00 | 20.00 | 40.00 | — |
| AH1345(1926-27) | — | 3.00 | 8.00 | 20.00 | 40.00 | — |
| AH1347(1928-29) | — | 3.00 | 8.00 | 20.00 | 40.00 | — |
| AH1348(1929-30) | — | 3.00 | 8.00 | 20.00 | 35.00 | — |
| AH1349(1930-31) | — | 3.00 | 6.00 | 15.00 | 30.00 | — |
| AH1351(1932-33) | — | 4.00 | 10.00 | 25.00 | 40.00 | — |
| AH1352(1933-34) | — | 4.00 | 10.00 | 25.00 | 40.00 | — |
| AH1358/49(1939) | — | 3.00 | 8.00 | 15.00 | 30.00 | — |
| AH1358(1939-40) | — | 3.00 | 8.00 | 15.00 | 30.00 | — |
| AH1359/3(1940) | — | 3.00 | 8.00 | 15.00 | 30.00 | — |
| AH1359/49(1940-41) | — | 3.00 | 8.00 | 15.00 | 30.00 | — |
| AH1362/44(1943) | — | 4.00 | 10.00 | 25.00 | 40.00 | — |
| AH1362/59(1943) | — | 4.00 | 10.00 | 25.00 | 40.00 | — |
| AH1363(1943) | — | 3.00 | 8.00 | 25.00 | 45.00 | — |
| AH1364/43(1944) | — | 3.00 | 8.00 | 20.00 | 40.00 | — |
| AH1364/3(1944) | — | 3.00 | 8.00 | 25.00 | 45.00 | — |
| AH1364/52(1944) | — | 3.00 | 8.00 | 25.00 | 45.00 | — |
| AH1364(1944-45) | — | 3.00 | 8.00 | 15.00 | 35.00 | — |
| AH1365(1945-46) | — | 3.00 | 8.00 | 15.00 | 35.00 | — |
| AH1366/5(1945) | — | 3.00 | 10.00 | 20.00 | 50.00 | — |
| AH1366/5x(1945) | — | 3.00 | 10.00 | 20.00 | 50.00 | — |

**1/10 IMADI RIYAL** **Y# 5.4** **Composition:** Silver **Obverse:** "Rabb al-Alamin" **Reverse:** "Sana" above date **Note:** Varieties with 8, 9, and 10 stars on reverse exist.

| Date | Mintage | VG | F | VF | XF | Unc |
|---|---|---|---|---|---|---|
| AH1342(1923-24) | — | 20.00 | 40.00 | 75.00 | 150 | — |

**1/8 IMADI RIYAL** **Y# 8** **Composition:** Silver **Obverse:** One or no stars in crescent **Reverse:** "Thumn" in place of "Ushr" below date, 6 stars

| Date | Mintage | VG | F | VF | XF | Unc |
|---|---|---|---|---|---|---|
| AH1339(1920-21) | — | 325 | 550 | 1,100 | 1,650 | — |

**1/4 IMADI RIYAL** **Y# 6.1** **Composition:** Silver **Obverse:** Without "Rabb al-Alamin" **Reverse:** "Sana" below date

| Date | Mintage | VG | F | VF | XF | Unc |
|---|---|---|---|---|---|---|
| AH1341(1922-23) | — | 20.00 | 45.00 | 75.00 | 150 | — |

**Note:** AH1341 with 4 stars on reverse

| Date | Mintage | VG | F | VF | XF | Unc |
|---|---|---|---|---|---|---|
| AH1342(1923-24) | — | 25.00 | 50.00 | 100 | 175 | — |

**Note:** AH1342 with 6 stars on reverse

**1/4 IMADI RIYAL** **Y# 6.2** **Composition:** Silver **Obverse:** "Rabb al-Alamin" **Reverse:** "Sana" above date, two stars and two ornaments in border

| Date | Mintage | VG | F | VF | XF | Unc |
|---|---|---|---|---|---|---|
| AH1342(1923-24) | — | 70.00 | 100 | 300 | 450 | — |

**1/4 IMADI RIYAL** **Y# 6.3** **Composition:** Silver **Obverse:** Ten crescents and stars in border

| Date | Mintage | VG | F | VF | XF | Unc |
|---|---|---|---|---|---|---|
| AH1342(1923-24) | — | 30.00 | 50.00 | 100 | 175 | — |

**Note:** Plain and traces of reeded edges known

**1/4 IMADI RIYAL Y# 6.5 Composition:** Silver **Reverse:** "Sana" below date, eight stars in border

| Date | Mintage | VG | F | VF | XF | Unc |
|---|---|---|---|---|---|---|
| AH1342(1923-24) | — | 100 | 150 | 300 | 500 | — |

**1/4 IMADI RIYAL Y# 6.6 Composition:** Silver **Reverse:** "Sana" below date, one star in border

| Date | Mintage | VG | F | VF | XF | Unc |
|---|---|---|---|---|---|---|
| AH1342(1923-24) | — | 100 | 150 | 300 | 500 | — |

**Note:** Obverse varieties with one and two stars exist

**1/4 IMADI RIYAL Y# 6.4 Composition:** Silver **Obverse:** With crescents only in border **Note:** Number and form of crescents on obverse vary. 14, 15, and 16 crescents known in border. Plain and traces of reeded edges known.

| Date | Mintage | VG | F | VF | XF | Unc |
|---|---|---|---|---|---|---|
| AH1342(1923-24) | — | 20.00 | 40.00 | 75.00 | 150 | — |
| AH1343(1924-25) | — | 20.00 | 40.00 | 75.00 | 150 | — |

**1/4 IMADI RIYAL Y# 10 Composition:** Silver **Reverse:** Redesigned, date moved to margin **Note:** The size of the reverse inner circle varies, 12 to 16 crescents on obverse. Plain and traces of reeded edges are known.

| Date | Mintage | VG | F | VF | XF | Unc |
|---|---|---|---|---|---|---|
| AH1343(1924-25) | — | 20.00 | 60.00 | 100 | 175 | — |
| AH1344(1925-26) | — | 4.25 | 10.00 | 25.00 | 75.00 | — |
| AH1345(1926-27) | — | 4.25 | 10.00 | 25.00 | 60.00 | — |
| AH1351(1932-33) | — | 20.00 | 30.00 | 50.00 | 100 | — |
| AH1352(1933-34) | — | 5.00 | 12.00 | 20.00 | 40.00 | — |
| AH1358(1939-40) | — | 3.50 | 5.50 | 15.00 | 35.00 | — |
| AH1359(1940-41) | — | 3.50 | 5.50 | 15.00 | 35.00 | — |
| AH1363(1943) | — | 3.50 | 8.00 | 20.00 | 40.00 | — |
| AH1364/3(1944) | — | 4.25 | 8.00 | 20.00 | 40.00 | — |
| AH1364(1944-45) | — | 3.50 | 5.00 | 20.00 | 40.00 | — |
| AH1365/4(1945) | — | 4.25 | 6.00 | 20.00 | 40.00 | — |
| AH1365(1945-46) | — | 3.50 | 5.00 | 20.00 | 40.00 | — |
| AH1366(1946) | — | 3.50 | 5.00 | 20.00 | 40.00 | — |

**IMADI RIYAL Y# 7 Weight:** 28.0700 g. **Composition:** Silver **Note:** Accession date: AH1322. Several die varieties exist, possibly struck over a number of years with frozen date AH1344. Edge varieties exist.

| Date | Mintage | VG | F | VF | XF | Unc |
|---|---|---|---|---|---|---|
| AH1344(1925-26) | — | 7.00 | 12.00 | 18.00 | 28.00 | 40.00 |
| **Note:** Copper trial strikes dated AH1344 reported | | | | | | |
| AH1365(1945-46) Two known | — | — | — | — | 1,000 | — |

## GOLD PRESENTATION COINAGE

All Imam Yahya gold strikes are considered presentation issues which were based on the gold standard of the Turkish Lira.

**1/8 LIRA (1/40 Riyal) Y# A10 Weight:** 0.9200 g. **Composition:** Gold **Note:** Accession date: AH1322.

| Date | Mintage | VG | F | VF | XF | Unc |
|---|---|---|---|---|---|---|
| AH(13)44(1925-26) | — | — | — | — | 1,350 | — |

**1/4 LIRA (1/20 Riyal) Y# B10 Weight:** 1.7000 g. **Composition:** Gold **Note:** Accession date: AH1322.

| Date | Mintage | VG | F | VF | XF | Unc |
|---|---|---|---|---|---|---|
| AH(13)44)1925-26) | — | — | — | — | 1,500 | — |

**1/2 LIRA (1/10 Riyal) Y# C10 Weight:** 3.3100 g. **Composition:** Gold **Note:** Accession date: AH1322.

| Date | Mintage | VG | F | VF | XF | Unc |
|---|---|---|---|---|---|---|
| AH(13)44(1925-26) | — | — | — | — | 1,650 | — |

**LIRA (1/5 Riyal) Y# D10 Weight:** 6.8000 g. **Composition:** Gold **Note:** Accession date: AH1322.

| Date | Mintage | VG | F | VF | XF | Unc |
|---|---|---|---|---|---|---|
| AH(13)44(1925-26) | — | — | — | — | 2,000 | — |

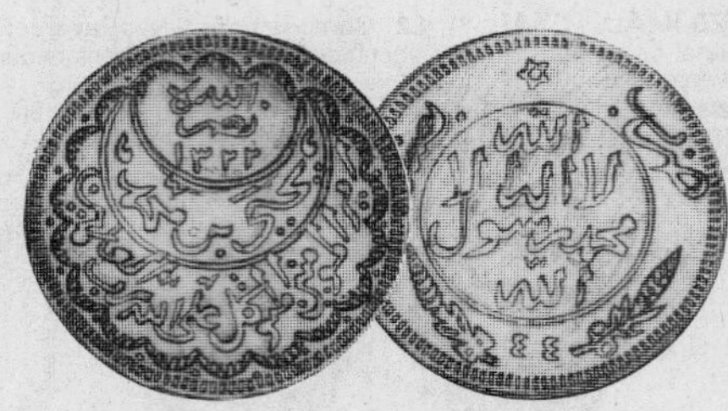

**2-1/2 LIRA (1/2 Riyal) Y# E10 Weight:** 17.7000 g. **Composition:** Gold **Note:** Accession date: AH1322.

| Date | Mintage | VG | F | VF | XF | Unc |
|---|---|---|---|---|---|---|
| AH(13)44(1925-26) | — | — | — | — | 3,500 | — |

**2-1/2 LIRA (1/2 Riyal) Y# K10 Composition:** Gold **Note:** 17.44-17.82 grams. Accession date: AH1322.

| Date | Mintage | VG | F | VF | XF | Unc |
|---|---|---|---|---|---|---|
| AH1352(1933-34) | — | — | — | — | 2,500 | — |

**5 LIRA (1 Riyal) Y# P10 Weight:** 34.2400 g. **Composition:** Gold **Note:** Thin planchet strike of 10 Lira (2 Riyal), Y#N10.

| Date | Mintage | VG | F | VF | XF | Unc |
|---|---|---|---|---|---|---|
| AH1358(1939-40) 2 known | — | — | — | — | 3,250 | — |

**5 LIRA (1 Riyal) Y# F10 Weight:** 35.5000 g. **Composition:** Gold **Note:** Similar to 1 Imadi Riyal, Y#7.

| Date | Mintage | VG | F | VF | XF | Unc |
|---|---|---|---|---|---|---|
| AH1344(1925-26) Rare | — | — | — | — | — | — |

**Note:** Dies of AH1344 Riyal silver and gold strikes are not identical

**10 LIRA (2 Riyal) Y# M10 Weight:** 69.8300 g. **Composition:** Gold **Obverse:** Similar to Gold 2-1/2 Lira, Y#K10 **Note:** Accession date: AH1322.

| Date | Mintage | VG | F | VF | XF | Unc |
|---|---|---|---|---|---|---|
| AH1352(1933-34) | — | — | — | — | 6,500 | — |

**10 LIRA (2 Riyal) Y# N10 Weight:** 69.8300 g. **Composition:** Gold **Reverse:** Two crossed flags in center **Rev. Legend:** "Duriba bi-dar al-khilafa al-mutawakkiliya bi Sana'a 'asimat al-Yamam sana 1358"

| Date | Mintage | VG | F | VF | XF | Unc |
|---|---|---|---|---|---|---|
| AH1358(1939-40) 4 known | — | — | — | — | 5,500 | — |

## al-Nasir Ahmad bin Yahya (Imam Ahmad)

### AH1367-82/1948-62AD

## MILLED COINAGE

**1/80 RIYAL (1 Halala = 1/2 Buqsha) Y# 18 Composition:** Aluminum **Note:** Accession date: AH1367.

| Date | Mintage | VG | F | VF | XF | Unc |
|---|---|---|---|---|---|---|
| ND(1948) | — | 0.15 | 0.25 | 0.50 | 1.00 | — |

**Note:** Struck privately in Lebanon in 1955 and 1956 and released into circulation in 1956

**1/80 RIYAL (1 Halala = 1/2 Buqsha)** **Y# 11.1** **Composition:** Bronze (Red To Yellow) **Reverse:** "Sana" above date **Note:** Accession date: AH1367. There is a variation in the number of stars on reverse, as follows: AH1368 - 8 stars; AH1371-74 and some AH1381 (not overdate) - 7 stars; AH1375-81 including some AH1381, and all AH1381 overdates - 8 stars. Varieties of arrangement of legends, form of crescent, and size of circle on reverse exist. Some earlier dates exist on thinner planchets.

| Date | Mintage | VG | F | VF | XF | Unc |
|---|---|---|---|---|---|---|
| AH1368(1948-49) | — | 1.00 | 2.00 | 5.00 | 10.00 | — |
| AH1371(1951-52) | — | 0.30 | 1.00 | 3.00 | 8.00 | — |
| AH1372(1952-53) | — | 0.30 | 1.00 | 3.00 | 8.00 | — |
| AH1373(1953-54) | — | 0.30 | 0.60 | 1.00 | 3.00 | — |
| AH1374(1954-55) | — | 0.30 | 1.00 | 3.00 | 8.00 | — |
| AH1275(1955) Error for 1375 | — | 1.00 | 2.00 | 6.00 | 12.00 | — |
| AH1375(1955-56) | — | — | — | — | — | — |
| AH1376(1956-57) | — | — | — | — | — | — |
| AH1376/86(1956) Error | — | — | — | — | — | — |
| AH1278(1958) Error for 1378 | — | 1.00 | 2.00 | 6.00 | 12.00 | — |
| AH1378(1958-59) | — | — | — | — | — | — |
| AHx379(1959) | — | 1.00 | 2.00 | 6.00 | 12.00 | — |
| AH1379(1959-60) | — | 0.50 | 1.00 | 2.50 | 5.00 | — |
| AH1380/1(1960) | — | 1.00 | 2.00 | 6.00 | 12.00 | — |
| AH1380/79(1960) | — | 0.50 | 1.00 | 2.50 | 5.00 | — |
| AH1380/9(1960) | — | 0.50 | 1.00 | 2.50 | 5.00 | — |
| AH1380(1960-61) | — | 0.50 | 1.00 | 2.50 | 5.00 | — |
| AH1381/80/79(1961) | — | 0.40 | 0.85 | 1.50 | 2.50 | — |
| AH1381/79(1961) | — | 0.40 | 0.85 | 1.50 | 2.50 | — |
| AH1381(1961-62) | — | 0.20 | 0.40 | 0.75 | 1.25 | — |
| AH1382(1962-63) | — | 5.00 | 10.00 | 15.00 | 20.00 | — |

**1/80 RIYAL (1 Halala = 1/2 Buqsha)** **Y# 11a** **Composition:** Aluminum **Reverse:** "Sana" aboive date **Note:** AH1374 and some AH1380 have 7 stars, the rest have 8 stars on reverse. Dies of 1/80 Riyal, Y#11.1, were used.

| Date | Mintage | VG | F | VF | XF | Unc |
|---|---|---|---|---|---|---|
| AH1374(1954-55) | — | 0.25 | 1.00 | 2.50 | 5.00 | — |
| AH1375(1955-56) | — | 0.75 | 2.50 | 5.50 | 10.00 | — |
| AH1376(1956-57) | — | 0.25 | 1.50 | 4.00 | 8.00 | — |
| AH1377(1957-58) | — | 0.75 | 2.50 | 5.50 | 10.00 | — |
| AH1378(1958-59) | — | 0.25 | 1.00 | 2.50 | 5.00 | — |
| AH1378/6(1958) | — | 0.25 | 1.00 | 2.50 | 5.00 | — |
| AH1379/5(1959) | — | 0.75 | 2.50 | 5.50 | 10.00 | — |
| AH1379/8(1959) | — | 0.75 | 2.50 | 5.50 | 10.00 | — |
| AH1379(1959-60) | — | 0.25 | 1.00 | 2.50 | 5.00 | — |
| AH1380(1960-61) | — | 0.25 | 1.00 | 2.50 | 5.00 | — |

**1/80 RIYAL (1 Halala = 1/2 Buqsha)** **Y# 11.2** **Composition:** Bronze **Reverse:** Without "Sana"

| Date | Mintage | VG | F | VF | XF | Unc |
|---|---|---|---|---|---|---|
| AH1373(1953-54) Rare | — | — | — | — | — | — |

**1/80 RIYAL (1 Halala = 1/2 Buqsha)** **Y# 11.3** **Composition:** Bronze **Note:** Struck with dies of 1/4 Ahmadi Riyal, Y#15 on 1/8 Riyal planchet.

| Date | Mintage | VG | F | VF | XF | Unc |
|---|---|---|---|---|---|---|
| AH(13)80(1960-61) Rare | — | — | — | — | — | — |

**1/40 RIYAL (1 Buqsha)** **Y# 19** **Composition:** Aluminum **Note:** Accession date: AH1367.

| Date | Mintage | VG | F | VF | XF | Unc |
|---|---|---|---|---|---|---|
| ND(1948) | — | 0.15 | 0.25 | 0.40 | 0.75 | — |

**1/40 RIYAL (1 Buqsha)** **Y# 12.1** **Composition:** Bronze (Red To Yellow) **Reverse:** "Sana" above date, large "Sana'a" in border legend **Note:** Accession date: AH1367. Some earlier dates exist on thinner planchets.

| Date | Mintage | VG | F | VF | XF | Unc |
|---|---|---|---|---|---|---|
| AH1368(1948-49) | — | 0.50 | 1.00 | 4.00 | 12.00 | — |
| **Note:** AH1368 also exists with accession date 13776 (error) known | | | | | | |
| AH1369(1949-50) | — | 0.75 | 1.25 | 5.00 | 15.00 | — |
| AH1370(1950-51) | — | 0.35 | 0.75 | 3.00 | 6.00 | — |
| AH1371(1951-52) | — | 0.35 | 0.75 | 3.00 | 6.00 | — |
| AH1372(1952-53) | — | 0.35 | 0.75 | 2.00 | 4.00 | — |
| AH1373/1(1953) | — | — | — | — | — | — |
| AH1373/2(1953) | — | 0.85 | 1.80 | 3.00 | 6.00 | — |
| AH1373(1953-54) | — | 0.35 | 0.75 | 2.00 | 4.00 | — |
| AH1374(1954-55) | — | 0.35 | 0.75 | 2.00 | 4.00 | — |
| AH1375/4(1955-56) | — | 0.50 | 1.00 | 3.00 | 6.00 | — |
| AH1377(1957-58) Reported, not confirmed | — | — | — | — | — | — |

**1/40 RIYAL (1 Buqsha)** **Y# 12a.1** **Composition:** Aluminum **Reverse:** "Sana" above date, large "Sana'a" in border legend **Note:** Dies of 1/40 Riyal, Y#12.1, were used.

| Date | Mintage | VG | F | VF | XF | Unc |
|---|---|---|---|---|---|---|
| AH1371(1951-52) | — | 0.50 | 1.00 | 4.00 | 10.00 | — |
| AH1373(1953-54) | — | 0.50 | 1.00 | 4.00 | 10.00 | — |
| AH1374(1954-55) | — | 0.50 | 1.00 | 4.00 | 10.00 | — |
| AH1375(1955-56) | — | 0.50 | 1.00 | 4.00 | 10.00 | — |
| AH1377(1957-58) | — | 15.00 | 30.00 | 50.00 | 90.00 | — |

**1/40 RIYAL (1 Buqsha)** **Y# 12.3** **Composition:** Bronze (Red To Yellow) **Reverse:** Large "Sana'a" in legend, without "Sana" above date

| Date | Mintage | VG | F | VF | XF | Unc |
|---|---|---|---|---|---|---|
| AH1371(1951-52) | — | 0.50 | 1.00 | 4.00 | 12.00 | — |

**1/40 RIYAL (1 Buqsha)** **Y# 12.2** **Composition:** Bronze (Red To Yellow) **Reverse:** Small "Sana'a" in legend **Note:** Varieties of arrangement of legends, form of crescent, and size of circle exist.

| Date | Mintage | VG | F | VF | XF | Unc |
|---|---|---|---|---|---|---|
| AH1371(1951-52) | — | 0.35 | 0.75 | 3.00 | 6.00 | — |
| AH1374(1954-55) | — | 0.35 | 0.75 | 2.00 | 4.00 | — |
| AH1375(1955-56) | — | 0.35 | 0.75 | 2.00 | 4.00 | — |
| AH1376(1956-57) | — | 0.50 | 1.00 | 5.00 | 12.00 | — |
| **Note:** Exists with accession date 1376 instead of 1367 on obverse | | | | | | |
| AH1377/6(1957-58) | — | 0.85 | 1.75 | 4.00 | 8.00 | — |
| **Note:** Exists with accession date 1376 instead of 1367 on obverse | | | | | | |
| AH1378/5(1958-59) | — | — | — | — | — | — |
| AH1379/7(1959-60) | — | 0.85 | 1.75 | 4.00 | 8.00 | — |
| AH1380/79(1960) | — | 10.00 | 20.00 | 50.00 | 75.00 | — |
| AH1380(1960-61) | — | 0.85 | 1.75 | 4.00 | 8.00 | — |

**1/40 RIYAL (1 Buqsha)** **Y# 12a.2** **Composition:** Aluminum **Reverse:** Small "Sana'a" in legend **Note:** Dies of 1/40 Riyal, Y#12.2, were used. AH1376 and AH1377 plain daates also exist with accession date AH1376 instead of AH1367 on obverse. Varieties exist.

| Date | Mintage | VG | F | VF | XF | Unc |
|---|---|---|---|---|---|---|
| AH1375(1955-56) | — | 0.50 | 1.00 | 4.00 | 10.00 | — |
| AH1376(1956-57) | — | 0.50 | 1.00 | 4.00 | 10.00 | — |
| AH1377/6(1957) | — | 10.00 | 20.00 | 40.00 | 75.00 | — |
| AH1377(1957-58) | — | 15.00 | 30.00 | 50.00 | 90.00 | — |

**1/16 AHMADI RIYAL** **Y# 13** **Composition:** Silver **Obv. Legend:** "Amir al-Mu'minin" **Note:** Accession date: AH1367. Arrangement of legends and size of inner circle on reverse vary.

| Date | Mintage | VG | F | VF | XF | Unc |
|---|---|---|---|---|---|---|
| AH1367(1948) | — | 0.75 | 1.50 | 6.00 | 12.00 | — |
| AH1368(1948-49) | — | 0.75 | 1.50 | 5.00 | 10.00 | — |
| AH1371(1951-52) | — | 0.75 | 1.50 | 5.00 | 10.00 | — |
| AH1374(1954-55) | — | 0.75 | 1.50 | 4.00 | 8.00 | — |

**1/16 AHMADI RIYAL** **Y# 13.1** **Composition:** Silver **Obverse:** 1/8 Ahmadi Riyal, Y#14 **Reverse:** Y#13 **Note:** Mule. Accession date: AH1367. Ends of crescents cut off on reverse.

| Date | Mintage | VG | F | VF | XF | Unc |
|---|---|---|---|---|---|---|
| AH1374(1954-55) | — | 20.00 | 40.00 | 100 | 150 | — |

**1/10 AHMADI RIYAL** **Y# A14** **Composition:** Silver **Note:** Accession date: AH1367.

| Date | Mintage | VG | F | VF | XF | Unc |
|---|---|---|---|---|---|---|
| AH1370(1950-51) | — | 400 | 750 | 1,250 | 1,500 | — |

**1/8 AHMADI RIYAL** **Y# 14** **Composition:** Silver **Note:** Accession date: AH1367. Pentagonal planchet. Arrangement of legends and size of inner circle on reverse vary.

| Date | Mintage | VG | F | VF | XF | Unc |
|---|---|---|---|---|---|---|
| AH1367(1948) | — | 4.00 | 8.00 | 15.00 | 30.00 | — |
| AH1368(1948-49) | — | 2.75 | 3.50 | 8.00 | 20.00 | — |
| AH1370(1950-51) | — | 2.75 | 3.50 | 8.00 | 20.00 | — |
| AH1371(1951-52) | — | 1.75 | 2.50 | 6.00 | 15.00 | — |
| AH1372(1952-53) | — | 1.75 | 2.50 | 4.00 | 10.00 | — |
| AH1373(1953-54) | — | 1.75 | 2.50 | 4.00 | 10.00 | — |
| AH1374(1954-55) | — | 1.75 | 2.50 | 5.00 | 15.00 | — |
| AH1375/1(1955-56) | — | 4.00 | 10.00 | 40.00 | 80.00 | — |
| AH1379/x(1959) | — | 1.75 | 2.50 | 5.00 | 15.00 | — |
| AH1379/5(1959) | — | 1.75 | 2.50 | 5.00 | 15.00 | — |
| AH1379(1959-60) | — | 1.75 | 2.50 | 6.00 | 15.00 | — |
| AH1380(1960-61) | — | 1.75 | 2.50 | 7.00 | 20.00 | — |

**1/8 AHMADI RIYAL** **Y# 14a** **Composition:** Silver **Note:** Hexagonal planchet.

| Date | Mintage | VG | F | VF | XF | Unc |
|---|---|---|---|---|---|---|
| AH1368(1948-49) | — | 350 | 650 | 1,250 | 1,850 | — |

**1/4 AHMADI RIYAL** **Y# 15** **Composition:** Silver **Edge:** Reeded **Note:** Accession date: 1367. The size of inner circle as well as the arrangement of legends on reverse vary. All dates have only the final 2 digits on the coin.

| Date | Mintage | VG | F | VF | XF | Unc |
|---|---|---|---|---|---|---|
| AH(13)67(1948) | — | 3.50 | 5.00 | 7.50 | 15.00 | — |
| AH(13)68(1949-50) | — | 3.50 | 5.00 | 7.50 | 15.00 | — |
| AH(13)70(1950-51) | — | 3.00 | 4.00 | 6.00 | 12.00 | — |
| AH(13)71/68(1951) | — | 6.00 | 8.00 | 12.50 | 20.00 | — |
| AH(13)71/0(1951) | — | 4.50 | 6.00 | 9.00 | 15.00 | — |
| AH(13)71(1951-52) | — | 3.00 | 4.00 | 6.00 | 10.00 | — |
| AH(13)72(1952-53) | — | 3.00 | 4.00 | 6.00 | 10.00 | — |
| AH(13)74(1954-55) | — | 3.00 | 4.00 | 6.00 | 10.00 | — |
| AH(13)75/3(1955) | — | 4.50 | 6.00 | 9.00 | 15.00 | — |
| AH(13)75(1955-56) | — | 3.00 | 4.00 | 6.00 | 10.00 | — |
| AH(13)77/5(1957-58) | — | 4.50 | 6.00 | 9.00 | 15.00 | — |
| AH(13)80(1960-61) | — | 30.00 | 60.00 | 100 | 175 | — |

**1/4 AHMADI RIYAL** **Y# 15a** **Composition:** Copper

| Date | Mintage | VG | F | VF | XF | Unc |
|---|---|---|---|---|---|---|
| AH(13)81(1961-61) Rare | — | — | — | — | — | — |

**Note:** This issue is considered a pattern

**1/2 AHMADI RIYAL** **Y# 16.1** **Composition:** Silver **Reverse:** Full dates; denomination and mint name read inward **Note:** Accession date: 1367.

| Date | Mintage | VG | F | VF | XF | Unc |
|---|---|---|---|---|---|---|
| AH1367(1948) | — | 6.00 | 10.00 | 15.00 | 35.00 | — |
| AH1368(1948-49) | — | 6.00 | 10.00 | 15.00 | 35.00 | — |
| AH1369(1949-50) | — | 5.00 | 8.00 | 12.50 | 20.00 | — |
| AH1370(1950-51) | — | 7.50 | 12.50 | 20.00 | 40.00 | — |
| AH1371(1951/52) | — | 7.50 | 12.50 | 20.00 | 40.00 | — |
| AH1372/68(1952-53) | — | 6.00 | 10.00 | 15.00 | 30.00 | — |
| AH1373(1953-54) | — | 9.00 | 15.00 | 25.00 | 45.00 | — |
| AH(13)75(1955) | — | 30.00 | 50.00 | 80.00 | 100 | — |
| AH1377(1957-58) | — | — | — | — | — | — |

**1/2 AHMADI RIYAL** **Y# 16.2 (prevY16.3)** **Composition:** Silver **Reverse:** Full dates; denomination and mint name read outward **Edge:** Reeded **Note:** Arrangement of legends and size of circle on reverse vary. These coins were struck over blanks punched from Maria Theresa Thalers. The outer rings are reported to have circulated as currency, but this is doubtful, as they are found only counterstamped "Void" in Arabic.

| Date | Mintage | VG | F | VF | XF | Unc |
|---|---|---|---|---|---|---|
| AH1377(1957-58) | — | 5.00 | 8.00 | 12.50 | 20.00 | — |
| AH1378(1958-59) | — | 6.00 | 10.00 | 15.00 | 25.00 | — |
| AH1379(1959-60) | — | 5.00 | 8.00 | 12.50 | 20.00 | — |
| AH1380(1960-61) | — | 17.50 | 30.00 | 40.00 | 75.00 | — |
| AH1381(1961-62) | — | 12.50 | 22.50 | 30.00 | 50.00 | — |
| AH1382(1962-63) | — | 7.50 | 12.50 | 25.00 | 40.00 | — |

**1/2 AHMADI RIYAL** **Y# 16a** **Composition:** Copper

| Date | Mintage | VG | F | VF | XF | Unc |
|---|---|---|---|---|---|---|
| AH1381(1961-62) Rare | — | — | — | — | — | — |

**Note:** This issue is considered a pattern

**AHMADI RIYAL** **Y# 17** **Composition:** Silver **Note:** Accession date: AH1367. These are usually found struck over Austrian Maria Theresa Talers and occasionally over other foreign crowns. All Y-17s have 1367 in the center obverse. The date for each piece is located in the lower left of the reverse. Varieties exist.

| Date | Mintage | F | VF | XF | Unc |
|---|---|---|---|---|---|
| AH1367(1948) | — | 20.00 | 30.00 | 45.00 | 75.00 |
| AH1370(1950-51) | — | 12.50 | 20.00 | 28.50 | 45.00 |
| AH1371(1951-52) | — | 12.50 | 20.00 | 28.50 | 45.00 |
| AH1373(1953-54) | — | 8.50 | 13.50 | 20.00 | 30.00 |

**Note:** Most AH1373 Riyals appear to be weakly struck from recut AH1372 dies, and the dates are easily confused

| Date | Mintage | F | VF | XF | Unc |
|---|---|---|---|---|---|
| AH1374(1954-55) | — | 10.00 | 15.00 | 22.50 | 35.00 |
| AH1375(1955-56) | — | 10.00 | 15.00 | 22.50 | 35.00 |
| AH1378(1958-59) | — | 10.00 | 15.00 | 22.50 | 35.00 |
| AH1380(1960-61) | — | 10.00 | 15.00 | 22.50 | 35.00 |
| AH1381(1961-62) | — | 10.00 | 15.00 | 22.50 | 35.00 |

## GOLD COINAGE

Imam Ahmad gold strikes were based on the gold standard of the Turkish Lira (7.2164 g gold). Strikes on the British Gold Standard can have an additional countermark of an Arabic 1, 2, or 4, probably indicating the equivalence to 1, 2, or 4 British Sovereigns.

**GOLD 1/4 RIYAL (1 Lira - Sovereign)** **Y# G15** **Composition:** Gold **Note:** Accession date: AH1367. 6.30-8.90 grams. Dies of silver 1/4 Ahmadi riyal, (Y#15) were used.

| Date | Mintage | F | VF | XF | Unc |
|---|---|---|---|---|---|
| AH(13)71(1951-52) | — | — | 450 | 850 | 1,500 |
| AH(13)75/3(1955) | — | — | 450 | 850 | 1,500 |
| AH(13)75(1955) | — | — | 450 | 850 | 1,500 |
| AH(13)77/5(1957-58) | — | — | 450 | 850 | 1,500 |

**GOLD 1/2 RIYAL (2-1/2 Lira - 2 Sovereigns)** **Y# G16.1** **Composition:** Gold **Reverse:** Full dates; denomination and mint name read inward **Note:** Accession date: AH1367. 15.57-17.99 grams.

| Date | Mintage | F | VF | XF | Unc |
|---|---|---|---|---|---|
| AH1370(1950-51) | — | 425 | 650 | 1,150 | 2,000 |
| AH1371(1951-52) | — | 425 | 650 | 1,150 | 2,000 |
| AH1375(1955-56) | — | 425 | 650 | 1,150 | 2,000 |
| AH(13)75(1955) | — | 425 | 650 | 1,150 | 2,000 |
| AH1377(1957-58) | — | 425 | 650 | 1,150 | 2,000 |

**GOLD 1/2 RIYAL (2-1/2 Lira - 2 Sovereigns)** **Y# G16.2 (YG16.3)** **Composition:** Gold **Reverse:** Full date; denomination and mint name read outward **Note:** Dies of silver 1/2 Ahmadi Riyal, (Y#16) were used.

| Date | Mintage | F | VF | XF | Unc |
|---|---|---|---|---|---|
| AH1377(1957-58) | — | 425 | 650 | 1,150 | 2,000 |
| AH1378(1958-59) | — | 425 | 650 | 1,150 | 2,000 |
| AH1379(1959-60) | — | 425 | 650 | 1,150 | 2,000 |
| AH1380(1960-61) | — | 425 | 650 | 1,150 | 2,000 |
| AH1381(1961-62) | — | 425 | 650 | 1,150 | 2,000 |

**GOLD RIYAL (5 Lira - 4 Sovereigns)** **Y# G17** **Composition:** Gold **Note:** 30.46-39.06 grams. Accession date: AH1367. Dies of silver Ahmadi Riyal (Y#17) were used.

| Date | Mintage | F | VF | XF | Unc |
|---|---|---|---|---|---|
| AH1371(1951-52) Rare | — | — | — | — | — |
| AH1372(1952-53) Rare | — | — | — | — | — |
| AH1373(1953-54) | — | — | 675 | 1,000 | 1,750 |
| AH1374(1954-55) | — | — | 675 | 1,000 | 1,750 |
| AH1375(1955-56) | — | — | 675 | 1,000 | 1,750 |
| AH1377(1957-58) | — | — | 675 | 1,000 | 1,750 |
| AH1378(1958-59) | — | — | 675 | 1,000 | 1,750 |
| AH1381(1961-62) | — | — | 675 | 1,000 | 1,750 |

# YEMEN ARAB REPUBLIC

## MILLED COINAGE

**1/80 RIYAL (1/2 Buqsha)** **Y# 21.1** **Composition:** Bronze **Reverse:** Full star

| Date | Mintage | F | VF | XF | Unc | BU |
|---|---|---|---|---|---|---|
| AH1382 | — | — | 2.00 | 6.00 | 15.00 | — |

**1/80 RIYAL (1/2 Buqsha)** **Y# 20** **Composition:** Bronze **Note:** Varieties exist.

| Date | Mintage | F | VF | XF | Unc | BU |
|---|---|---|---|---|---|---|
| AH1382 | — | — | 0.50 | 2.00 | 5.00 | — |

**1/80 RIYAL (1/2 Buqsha)** **Y# 21.2** **Composition:** Bronze **Reverse:** Outlined star **Note:** Varieties exist.

| Date | Mintage | F | VF | XF | Unc | BU |
|---|---|---|---|---|---|---|
| AH1382 | — | — | 2.00 | 6.00 | 15.00 | — |
| AH13882 (sic) | — | — | — | — | — | — |

**1/2 BUQSHA** **Y# 32** **Composition:** Bronze **Note:** Varieties exist.

| Date | Mintage | F | VF | XF | Unc | BU |
|---|---|---|---|---|---|---|
| AH1382 | — | — | 3.00 | 5.00 | 9.00 | — |

**1/2 BUQSHA** **Y# 26** **Composition:** Copper-Aluminum **Note:** Varieties exist.Struck at Cairo.

| Date | Mintage | F | VF | XF | Unc | BU |
|---|---|---|---|---|---|---|
| AH1382(1962) | 10,000,000 | — | 0.15 | 0.20 | 0.30 | — |

**1/40 RIYAL (1 Buqsha)** **Y# 22** **Composition:** Brass Or Bronze **Note:** Dated both sides; AH1382, AH1383 and AH1384/3 are dated AH1382 on obverse, actual date on reverse; AH1384 and AH1384/284 dated AH1384 on both sides. There are varieties of date size and design.

| Date | Mintage | F | VF | XF | Unc | BU |
|---|---|---|---|---|---|---|
| AH1382 | — | — | 0.75 | 1.00 | 2.25 | — |
| AH1383/282 | — | — | — | — | — | — |
| AH1383 | — | — | 1.50 | 2.25 | 6.00 | — |
| AH1384/284 | — | — | — | — | — | — |
| AH1384/3 | — | — | — | — | — | — |
| AH1384 | — | — | 4.00 | 7.50 | 20.00 | — |

**BUQSHA** **Y# 27** **Composition:** Copper-Aluminum **Note:** Struck at Cairo.

| Date | Mintage | F | VF | XF | Unc | BU |
|---|---|---|---|---|---|---|
| AH1382(1962) | 10,377,000 | — | 0.20 | 0.30 | 0.50 | — |

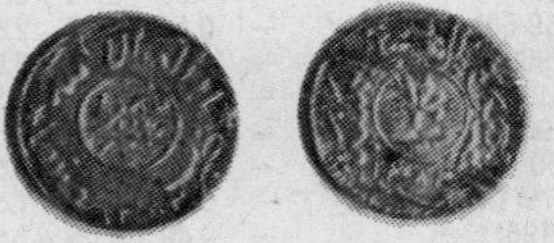

**1/20 RIYAL (2 Buqsha)** **Y# 23.1** **Composition:** 0.7200 Silver **Reverse:** Three stones on top row of wall **Note:** Thick variety, 1.10-1.60 grams

| Date | Mintage | F | VF | XF | Unc | BU |
|---|---|---|---|---|---|---|
| AH1382 | — | — | 6.00 | 10.00 | 30.00 | — |

**1/20 RIYAL (2 Buqsha)** **Y# 23.2** **Composition:** 0.7200 Silver **Reverse:** Two stones on top row of wall **Note:** Thin variety, 0.60-0.90 grams

| Date | Mintage | F | VF | XF | Unc | BU |
|---|---|---|---|---|---|---|
| AH1382 | — | — | 2.00 | 4.00 | 10.00 | — |

**2 BUQSHA** **Y# A27** **Composition:** Copper-Aluminum

| Date | Mintage | F | VF | XF | Unc | BU |
|---|---|---|---|---|---|---|
| AH1382(1962) | — | — | 0.25 | 0.60 | 0.85 | — |

**1/10 RIYAL (4 Buqsha)** **Y# 24.1** **Composition:** 0.7200 Silver **Reverse:** Three or four stones in top row of wall within circle **Note:** Thick variety, 2.40-3.00 grams

| Date | Mintage | F | VF | XF | Unc | BU |
|---|---|---|---|---|---|---|
| AH1382 | — | — | 5.00 | 10.00 | 20.00 | — |

**1/10 RIYAL (4 Buqsha)** **Y# 24.2** **Composition:** 0.7200 Silver **Reverse:** Four stones in top row of wall within circle **Note:** Thin variety, 1.40-1.80 grams. Edge varieties, varying number of stones in wall, exist.

| Date | Mintage | F | VF | XF | Unc | BU |
|---|---|---|---|---|---|---|
| AH1382 | — | — | 2.00 | 4.00 | 10.00 | — |

**5 BUQSHA** **Y# 28** **Composition:** 0.7200 Silver **Note:** Struck at Cairo.

| Date | Mintage | F | VF | XF | Unc | BU |
|---|---|---|---|---|---|---|
| AH1382(1962) | 1,600,000 | — | 1.25 | 1.50 | 2.50 | — |

**2/10 RIYAL (8 Buqsha)** **Y# 25.1** **Composition:** 0.7200 Silver **Note:** Thick variety, 5.80-6.50 grams.

| Date | Mintage | F | VF | XF | Unc | BU |
|---|---|---|---|---|---|---|
| AH1382 | — | — | 8.00 | 15.00 | 25.00 | — |

**2/10 RIYAL (8 Buqsha)** **Y# 25.2** **Composition:** 0.7200 Silver **Note:** Thin variety, 4.90-5.10 grams.

| Date | Mintage | F | VF | XF | Unc | BU |
|---|---|---|---|---|---|---|
| AH1382 | — | — | 60.00 | 100 | 150 | — |

**1/4 RIYAL (10 Buqsha)** **Y# A25.1** **Composition:** 0.7200 Silver **Note:** Thick variety, 6.00-7.30 grams.

| Date | Mintage | F | VF | XF | Unc | BU |
|---|---|---|---|---|---|---|
| AH1382 | — | — | 40.00 | 65.00 | 150 | — |

**1/4 RIYAL (10 Buqsha)** **Y# A25.2** **Composition:** 0.7200 Silver **Note:** Thin variety, 4.00-4.60 grams. Overstrikes over earlier 1/4 Riyal coins exist.

| Date | Mintage | F | VF | XF | Unc | BU |
|---|---|---|---|---|---|---|
| AH1382 | — | — | 40.00 | 65.00 | 150 | — |

**10 BUQSHA** **Y# 29** **Weight:** 5.0000 g. **Composition:** 0.7200 Silver .1157 oz. ASW

| Date | Mintage | F | VF | XF | Unc | BU |
|---|---|---|---|---|---|---|
| AH1382(1962) | 1,024,000 | — | 2.00 | 2.25 | 3.25 | — |

**20 BUQSHA** **Y# 30** **Weight:** 9.8500 g. **Composition:** 0.7200 Silver .2280 oz. ASW

| Date | Mintage | F | VF | XF | Unc | BU |
|---|---|---|---|---|---|---|
| AH1382(1962) | 1,016,000 | — | 4.00 | 5.00 | 7.00 | — |

**RIYAL** **Y# 31** **Weight:** 19.7500 g. **Composition:** 0.7200 Silver .4571 oz. ASW

| Date | Mintage | F | VF | XF | Unc | BU |
|---|---|---|---|---|---|---|
| AH1382(1962) | 4,614,000 | — | 5.00 | 6.00 | 9.50 | — |

## DECIMAL COINAGE

100 Fils = 1 Riyal/Rial

**FILS** **Y# 33** **Composition:** Aluminum

| Date | Mintage | F | VF | XF | Unc | BU |
|---|---|---|---|---|---|---|
| AH1394(1974) | Est. 1,000,000 | — | 3.00 | 5.00 | 10.00 | — |

**Note:** It is doubtful that the entire mintage was released for circulation

| Date | Mintage | F | VF | XF | Unc | BU |
|---|---|---|---|---|---|---|
| AH1394-1974 Proof | 5,024 | Value: 1.50 | | | | |
| AH1400-1980 Proof | 10,000 | Value: 1.50 | | | | |

**FILS** **Y# 43** **Composition:** Aluminum **Series:** F.A.O.

| Date | Mintage | F | VF | XF | Unc | BU |
|---|---|---|---|---|---|---|
| AH1398-1978 | 7,050 | — | — | 1.25 | 3.00 | — |

**5 FILS** **Y# 34** **Composition:** Brass

| Date | Mintage | F | VF | XF | Unc | BU |
|---|---|---|---|---|---|---|
| AH1394-1974 | 10,000,000 | — | 0.50 | 1.00 | 2.50 | — |

**5 FILS** **Y# 38** **Composition:** Brass **Series:** F.A.O.

| Date | Mintage | F | VF | XF | Unc | BU |
|---|---|---|---|---|---|---|
| AH1394-1974 | 500,000 | — | — | 0.10 | 0.25 | — |

**10 FILS** **Y# 35** **Composition:** Brass

| Date | Mintage | F | VF | XF | Unc | BU |
|---|---|---|---|---|---|---|
| AH1394-1974 | 20,000,000 | — | 0.50 | 1.00 | 2.50 | — |
| AH1394-1974 Proof | 5,024 | Value: 2.50 | | | | |
| AH1400-1980 Proof | 10,000 | Value: 2.00 | | | | |

**10 FILS** **Y# 39** **Composition:** Brass **Series:** F.A.O.

| Date | Mintage | F | VF | XF | Unc | BU |
|---|---|---|---|---|---|---|
| AH1394-1974 | 200,000 | — | — | 0.10 | 0.25 | — |

**25 FILS** **Y# 36** **Composition:** Copper-Nickel

| Date | Mintage | F | VF | XF | Unc | BU |
|---|---|---|---|---|---|---|
| AH1394-1974 | 15,000,000 | — | 0.25 | 0.50 | 1.75 | — |
| AH1394-1974 Proof | 5,024 | Value: 3.00 | | | | |
| AH1399-1979 | 11,000,000 | — | 0.25 | 0.50 | 1.75 | — |
| AH1400-1980 Proof | 10,000 | Value: 2.25 | | | | |

**25 FILS** **Y# 40** **Composition:** Copper-Nickel **Series:** F.A.O.

| Date | Mintage | F | VF | XF | Unc | BU |
|---|---|---|---|---|---|---|
| AH1394-1974 | 40,000 | — | 0.20 | 0.40 | 1.00 | — |

**50 FILS** **Y# 37** **Composition:** Copper-Nickel

| Date | Mintage | F | VF | XF | Unc | BU |
|---|---|---|---|---|---|---|
| AH1394-1974 | 10,000,000 | — | 0.35 | 0.75 | 2.50 | — |
| AH1394-1974 Proof | 5,024 | Value: 3.50 | | | | |
| AH1399-1979 | 4,000,000 | — | 0.35 | 0.75 | 2.50 | — |
| AH1400-1980 Proof | 10,000 | Value: 2.50 | | | | |
| AH1405-1985 | — | — | 0.35 | 0.75 | 2.50 | — |

**50 FILS** **Y# 41** **Composition:** Copper-Nickel **Series:** F.A.O.

| Date | Mintage | F | VF | XF | Unc | BU |
|---|---|---|---|---|---|---|
| AH1394-1974 | 25,000 | — | 0.25 | 0.50 | 1.25 | — |

**RIYAL** **KM# 1** **Weight:** 12.0000 g. **Composition:** 0.9250 Silver .3569 oz. ASW **Subject:** Qadhi Mohammed Mahmud Az-zubairi Memorial

| Date | Mintage | F | VF | XF | Unc | BU |
|---|---|---|---|---|---|---|
| 1969 Proof | 3,200 | Value: 15.00 | | | | |

**RIYAL** **KM# 1a** **Weight:** 20.4800 g. **Composition:** 0.9000 Gold .5926 oz. AGW **Subject:** Qadhi Mohammed Mahmud Az-zubairi Memorial

| Date | Mintage | F | VF | XF | Unc | BU |
|---|---|---|---|---|---|---|
| 1969 Proof | 100 | Value: 375 | | | | |

**RIYAL** **Y# 42** **Composition:** Copper-Nickel

| Date | Mintage | F | VF | XF | Unc | BU |
|---|---|---|---|---|---|---|
| AH1396-1976 | 7,800,000 | — | 0.50 | 1.25 | 4.00 | — |
| AH1400-1980 Proof | — | Value: 5.00 | | | | |
| AH1405-1985 | — | — | 0.50 | 1.25 | 4.00 | — |

**RIYAL** Y# 44 **Composition:** Copper-Nickel **Series:** F.A.O.

| Date | Mintage | F | VF | XF | Unc | BU |
|---|---|---|---|---|---|---|
| AH1398-1978 | 7,050 | — | — | 2.00 | 5.00 | — |

**2 RIYALS** KM# 4 **Weight:** 25.0000 g. **Composition:** 0.9250 Silver .7435 oz. ASW **Subject:** Qadhi Mohammed Mahmud Azzubairi Memorial

| Date | Mintage | F | VF | XF | Unc | BU |
|---|---|---|---|---|---|---|
| 1969 Proof | 4,200 | Value: 28.00 | | | | |

**2 RIYALS** KM# 4a **Weight:** 42.2900 g. **Composition:** 0.9000 Gold 1.2238 oz. AGW **Subject:** Qadhi Mohammed Mahmud Azzubairi Memorial

| Date | Mintage | F | VF | XF | Unc | BU |
|---|---|---|---|---|---|---|
| 1969 Proof | 100 | Value: 975 | | | | |

**2 RIYALS** KM# 2.2 **Weight:** 25.0000 g. **Composition:** 0.9250 Silver .7435 oz. ASW **Note:** Border of dots near rim.

| Date | Mintage | F | VF | XF | Unc | BU |
|---|---|---|---|---|---|---|
| 1969 Proof; restrike | 1,000 | Value: 30.00 | | | | |

**2 RIYALS** KM# 3.2 **Weight:** 25.0000 g. **Composition:** 0.9250 Silver .7435 oz. ASW **Note:** Border of dots near rim.

| Date | Mintage | F | VF | XF | Unc | BU |
|---|---|---|---|---|---|---|
| 1969 Proof; restrike | 1,000 | Value: 30.00 | | | | |

**2 RIYALS** KM# 3.1 **Weight:** 25.0000 g. **Composition:** 0.9250 Silver .7435 oz. ASW **Subject:** Apollo II - Moon Landing **Note:** Dotted border.

| Date | Mintage | F | VF | XF | Unc | BU |
|---|---|---|---|---|---|---|
| 1969 | 7,583 | — | — | — | 25.00 | — |
| 1969 Proof | 200 | Value: 50.00 | | | | |

**2 RIYALS** KM# 2.1 **Weight:** 25.0000 g. **Composition:** 0.9250 Silver .7435 oz. ASW **Subject:** Apollo II - Cape Kennedy **Note:** Dotter border.

| Date | Mintage | F | VF | XF | Unc | BU |
|---|---|---|---|---|---|---|
| 1969 | 7,583 | — | — | — | 25.00 | — |
| 1969 Proof | 200 | Value: 50.00 | | | | |

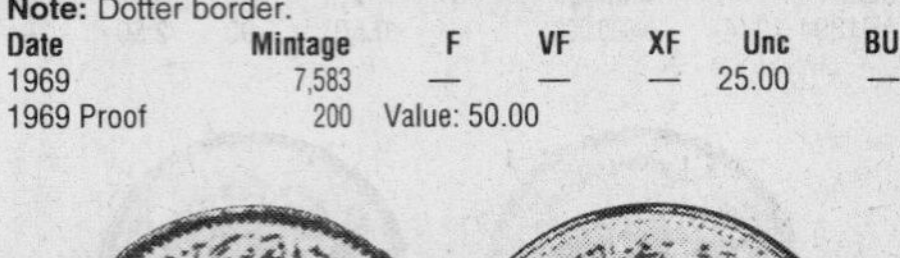

**2-1/2 RIYALS** KM# 14 **Weight:** 9.0000 g. **Composition:** 0.9250 Silver .2676 oz. ASW **Subject:** Oil Exploration

| Date | Mintage | F | VF | XF | Unc | BU |
|---|---|---|---|---|---|---|
| AH1395-1975 | Est. 205,000 | — | — | — | 15.00 | — |
| AH1395-1975 Proof | Est. 5,000 | Value: 35.00 | | | | |

**5 RIYALS/RIALS** KM# 6 **Weight:** 4.9000 g. **Composition:** 0.9000 Gold .1418 oz. AGW **Subject:** Qadhi Mohammed Mahmud Azzubairi Memorial

| Date | Mintage | F | VF | XF | Unc | BU |
|---|---|---|---|---|---|---|
| 1969 Proof | — | Value: 100 | | | | |

**5 RIYALS/RIALS** KM# 15 **Weight:** 18.0000 g. **Composition:** 0.9250 Silver .5353 oz. ASW **Subject:** Mona Lisa

| Date | Mintage | F | VF | XF | Unc | BU |
|---|---|---|---|---|---|---|
| AH1395-1975 | 235,000 | — | — | — | 20.00 | — |
| AH1395-1975 Proof | 5,000 | Value: 50.00 | | | | |

**10 RIYALS/RIALS** KM# 7 **Weight:** 9.8000 g. **Composition:** 0.9000 Gold .2836 oz. AGW **Subject:** Qadhi Mohammed Mahmud Azzubairi Memorial

| Date | Mintage | F | VF | XF | Unc | BU |
|---|---|---|---|---|---|---|
| 1969 Proof | — | Value: 175 | | | | |

**10 RIYALS/RIALS** KM# 23 **Weight:** 12.0800 g. **Composition:** 0.9250 Silver .3569 oz. ASW **Obverse:** KM#7 **Reverse:** KM#1 **Note:** Mule.

| Date | Mintage | F | VF | XF | Unc | BU |
|---|---|---|---|---|---|---|
| 1969 Proof | — | Value: 40.00 | | | | |

**10 RIYALS/RIALS** KM# 16 **Weight:** 36.0000 g. **Composition:** 0.9250 Silver 1.0707 oz. ASW **Series:** Montreal Olympics

| Date | Mintage | F | VF | XF | Unc | BU |
|---|---|---|---|---|---|---|
| AH1395-1975 | 8,000 | — | — | — | 90.00 | — |
| AH1395-1975 Proof | 4,000 | Value: 140 | | | | |

**15 RIALS** KM# 17 **Weight:** 54.0000 g. **Composition:** 0.9250 Silver 1.6061 oz. ASW **Subject:** Jerusalem

| Date | Mintage | F | VF | XF | Unc | BU |
|---|---|---|---|---|---|---|
| AH1395-1975 | 70,000 | — | — | — | 40.00 | — |
| AH1395-1975 Proof | 5,000 | Value: 100 | | | | |

**20 RIYALS/RIALS** KM# 8 **Weight:** 19.6000 g. **Composition:** 0.9000 Gold .5672 oz. AGW **Subject:** Apollo II - Moon Landing

| Date | Mintage | F | VF | XF | Unc | BU |
|---|---|---|---|---|---|---|
| 1969 Proof | — | Value: 350 | | | | |

**20 RIYALS/RIALS** KM# 9 **Weight:** 19.6000 g. **Composition:** 0.9000 Gold .5672 oz. AGW **Subject:** Qadhi Mohammed Mahmud Azzubairi Memorial

| Date | Mintage | F | VF | XF | Unc | BU |
|---|---|---|---|---|---|---|
| 1969 Proof | — | Value: 365 | | | | |

**20 RIYALS/RIALS** KM# 18 **Weight:** 19.6000 g. **Composition:** 0.9000 Gold .5672 oz. AGW **Subject:** Albakiriah Mosque

| Date | Mintage | F | VF | XF | Unc | BU |
|---|---|---|---|---|---|---|
| AH1395-1975 | — | — | — | — | 160 | — |
| AH1395-1975 Proof | 3,500 | Value: 175 | | | | |

**25 RIYALS/RIALS** KM# 19 **Composition:** 0.9000 Gold **Subject:** Oil Exploration

| Date | Mintage | F | VF | XF | Unc | BU |
|---|---|---|---|---|---|---|
| AH1395-1975 | — | — | — | — | 135 | — |
| AH1395-1975 Proof | 3,500 | Value: 150 | | | | |

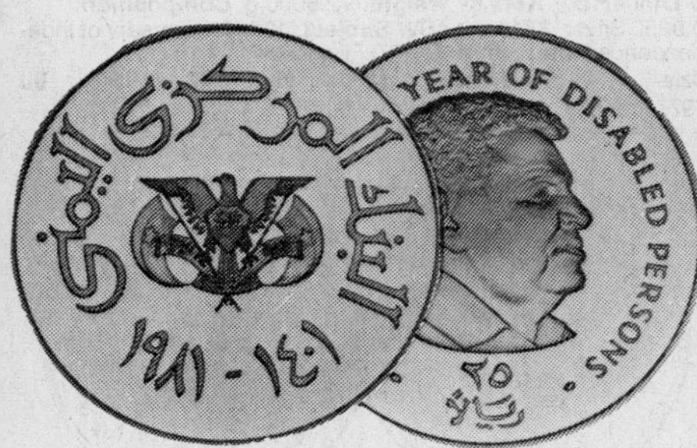

**25 RIYALS/RIALS** Y# 46 **Weight:** 28.2800 g. **Composition:** 0.9250 Silver .8411 oz. ASW **Series:** International Year of the Disabled Person

| Date | Mintage | F | VF | XF | Unc | BU |
|---|---|---|---|---|---|---|
| AH1401-1981 | 10,000 | — | — | — | 32.50 | — |
| AH1401-1981 Proof | Est. 10,000 | Value: 50.00 | | | | |

**25 RIYALS/RIALS** Y# 47 **Weight:** 28.2800 g. **Composition:** 0.9250 Silver .8411 oz. ASW **Subject:** 20th Anniversary of the Revolution

| Date | Mintage | F | VF | XF | Unc | BU |
|---|---|---|---|---|---|---|
| AH1402-1982 Proof | 2,000 | Value: 55.00 | | | | |

**25 RIYALS/RIALS** Y# 45 **Weight:** 28.2500 g. **Composition:** 0.9250 Silver .8402 oz. ASW **Series:** International Year of the Child

| Date | Mintage | F | VF | XF | Unc | BU |
|---|---|---|---|---|---|---|
| AH1403-1983 Proof | 6,604 | Value: 20.00 | | | | |

**25 RIYALS/RIALS** Y# 49 **Weight:** 28.2500 g. **Composition:** 0.9250 Silver .8402 oz. ASW **Series:** Decade for Women

| Date | Mintage | F | VF | XF | Unc | BU |
|---|---|---|---|---|---|---|
| AH1405-1985 Proof | 1,000 | Value: 42.50 | | | | |

**30 RIYALS** KM# 10 **Weight:** 29.4000 g. **Composition:** 0.9000 Gold .8508 oz. AGW **Subject:** Qadhi Mohammed Mahmud Azzubairi Memorial

| Date | Mintage | F | VF | XF | Unc | BU |
|---|---|---|---|---|---|---|
| 1969 Proof | — | Value: 600 | | | | |

**50 RIYALS/RIALS** KM# 11 **Weight:** 49.9700 g. **Composition:** Silver **Subject:** Qadhi Mohammed Mahmud Azzubairi Memorial **Reverse:** Lion

| Date | Mintage | F | VF | XF | Unc | BU |
|---|---|---|---|---|---|---|
| 1969 Proof; restrike | — | Value: 50.00 | | | | |

**50 RIYALS/RIALS** KM# 11a **Weight:** 49.0000 g. **Composition:** 0.9000 Gold 1.4180 oz. AGW **Subject:** Qadhi Mohammed Mahmud Azzubairi Memorial

| Date | Mintage | F | VF | XF | Unc | BU |
|---|---|---|---|---|---|---|
| 1969 Proof | — | Value: 950 | | | | |

**50 RIYALS/RIALS** KM# 20 **Weight:** 9.1000 g. **Composition:** 0.9000 Gold .2633 oz. AGW **Subject:** Mona Lisa

| Date | Mintage | F | VF | XF | Unc | BU |
|---|---|---|---|---|---|---|
| AH1395-1975 | — | — | — | — | 200 | — |
| AH1395-1975 Proof | 3,500 | Value: 350 | | | | |

**75 RIYALS** KM# 21 **Weight:** 13.6500 g. **Composition:** 0.9000 Gold .3950 oz. AGW **Series:** Montreal Olympics **Obverse:** Arms **Reverse:** XXI Olympiad

| Date | Mintage | F | VF | XF | Unc | BU |
|---|---|---|---|---|---|---|
| AH1395-1975 | — | — | — | — | 250 | — |
| AH1395-1975 Proof | 3,500 | Value: 350 | | | | |

**100 RIALS** KM# 22 **Weight:** 18.2000 g. **Composition:** 0.9000 Gold .5266 oz. AGW

| Date | Mintage | F | VF | XF | Unc | BU |
|---|---|---|---|---|---|---|
| AH1395-1975 | — | — | — | — | 325 | — |
| AH1395-1975 Proof | 3,500 | Value: 400 | | | | |

**500 RIYALS/RIALS** KM# 24 **Weight:** 15.9800 g. **Composition:** 0.9170 Gold .4711 oz. AGW **Series:** International Year of the Disabled Person

| Date | Mintage | F | VF | XF | Unc | BU |
|---|---|---|---|---|---|---|
| AH1401-1981 | — | — | — | — | 400 | — |
| AH1401-1981 Proof | — | Value: 500 | | | | |

**500 RIYALS/RIALS** Y# 48 **Weight:** 15.9000 g. **Composition:** 0.9170 Gold .4686 oz. AGW **Subject:** 20th Anniversary of the Revolution

| Date | Mintage | F | VF | XF | Unc | BU |
|---|---|---|---|---|---|---|
| AH1402-1982 Proof | 1,000 | Value: 350 | | | | |

# ROYALIST GOVERNMENT

## MILLED COINAGE

**RIAL KM# 5 Weight:** 24.9200 g. **Composition:** 0.7200 Silver **Subject:** Sir Winston Churchill Memorial

| Date | Mintage | F | VF | XF | Unc | BU |
|---|---|---|---|---|---|---|
| AH1385(1965) | 6,000 | — | — | 8.50 | 14.50 | — |

**Note:** The above coin probably was not intended for circulation, but specimens are known to have been distributed by the exiled monarch to Saudi and other dignitaries

## ESSAIS

| KM# | Date | Mintage | Identification | Mkt Val |
|---|---|---|---|---|
| E1 | AH1385 | 500 | Rial. 0.7200 Silver. | 27.50 |

## PIEFORTS

| KM# | Date | Mintage | Identification | Mkt Val |
|---|---|---|---|---|
| P1 | 1981 | 1,150 | 25 Riyals/Rials. I.Y.D.P.; Y#46 | 115 |
| P2 | 1981 | — | 500 Riyals/Rials. I:Y.P.D.; KM#24 | 1,000 |

## TRIAL STRIKES

| KM# | Date | Mintage | Identification | Mkt Val |
|---|---|---|---|---|

| KM# | Date | Mintage | Identification | Mkt Val |
|---|---|---|---|---|
| TS1 | 1975 | — | 100 Rials. Goldine. Uniface. | — |

## MINT SETS

| KM# | Date | Mintage | Identification | Issue Price | Mkt Val |
|---|---|---|---|---|---|
| MS1 | 1975 (4) | — | KM#14-17 | 50.00 | 175 |
| MS2 | 1975 (5) | — | KM#18-22 | 360 | 1,130 |

## PROOF SETS

| KM# | Date | Mintage | Identification | Issue Price | Mkt Val |
|---|---|---|---|---|---|
| PS1 | 1969 (7) | 2,000 | KM#1, 4, 6, 7, 9-11 | 375 | 1,350 |
| PS2 | 1969 (4) | 1,500 | KM#1-4 | — | 125 |
| PS4 | 1969 (3) | — | KM#2, 3, 6 | 78.00 | 175 |
| PS5 | 1974 (5) | 5,024 | Y#33-37 | 15.00 | 12.50 |
| PS6 | 1975 (5) | 3,500 | KM#18-22 | 485 | 1,450 |
| PS7 | 1975 (4) | 5,000 | KM#14-17 | 75.00 | 335 |
| PS8 | 1980 (6) | 10,000 | Y#33-37, 42 | 31.00 | 16.00 |

# YEMEN REPUBLIC

## MILLED COINAGE

**RIYAL KM# 25 Composition:** Stainless Steel

| Date | Mintage | F | VF | XF | Unc | BU |
|---|---|---|---|---|---|---|
| AH1414(1993) | — | — | — | — | 1.25 | — |

**5 RIYALS KM# 26 Composition:** Stainless Steel

| Date | Mintage | F | VF | XF | Unc | BU |
|---|---|---|---|---|---|---|
| AH1414(1993) | — | — | — | — | 1.75 | — |

**10 RIYALS KM# 27 Composition:** Stainless Steel **Note:** Bridge at Shaharah

| Date | Mintage | F | VF | XF | Unc | BU |
|---|---|---|---|---|---|---|
| AH1416(1995) | — | — | — | — | 2.75 | — |

# PEOPLES DEMOCRATIC REPUBLIC OF YEMEN

**TITLES**

Al-Jumhuriya(t) al-Yamaniya(t)
ad-Dimiqratiya(t) ash-Sha'biya(t)

**MONETARY SYSTEM**

Falus, Fulus — Fals, Fils — Falsan, Filsan

1000 Fils = 1 Dinar

# PEOPLES DEMOCRATIC REPUBLIC

## DECIMAL COINAGE

**2-1/2 FILS KM# 3 Composition:** Aluminum

| Date | Mintage | F | VF | XF | Unc | BU |
|---|---|---|---|---|---|---|
| AH1393-1973 | 20,000,000 | — | 0.25 | 0.65 | 1.50 | — |

**5 FILS KM# 2 Composition:** Bronze

| Date | Mintage | F | VF | XF | Unc | BU |
|---|---|---|---|---|---|---|
| 1971 | 2,000,000 | — | 0.30 | 0.60 | 1.00 | — |

**5 FILS KM# 4 Composition:** Aluminum

| Date | Mintage | F | VF | XF | Unc | BU |
|---|---|---|---|---|---|---|
| AH1393-1973 | 20,000,000 | — | 0.15 | 0.30 | 0.75 | — |
| AH1404-1984 | — | — | 0.15 | 0.30 | 0.75 | — |

**10 FILS KM# 9 Composition:** Aluminum

| Date | Mintage | F | VF | XF | Unc | BU |
|---|---|---|---|---|---|---|
| 1981 | — | — | 0.35 | 0.75 | 2.00 | — |

**25 FILS KM# 5 Composition:** Copper-Nickel

| Date | Mintage | F | VF | XF | Unc | BU |
|---|---|---|---|---|---|---|
| 1976 | 2,000,000 | — | 0.25 | 0.50 | 1.25 | — |
| 1977 | 1,000,000 | — | 0.25 | 0.50 | 1.50 | — |
| 1979 | — | — | 0.25 | 0.50 | 1.50 | — |
| 1982 | — | — | 0.25 | 0.50 | 1.50 | — |
| 1984 | — | — | 0.25 | 0.50 | 1.75 | — |

**50 FILS KM# 6 Composition:** Copper-Nickel

| Date | Mintage | F | VF | XF | Unc | BU |
|---|---|---|---|---|---|---|
| 1976 | 2,000,000 | — | 0.35 | 0.75 | 2.50 | — |
| 1977 | 2,000,000 | — | 0.35 | 0.75 | 2.50 | — |
| 1979 | — | — | 0.35 | 0.75 | 2.50 | — |
| 1984 | — | — | 0.35 | 0.75 | 2.50 | — |

**100 FILS KM# 10 Composition:** Copper-Nickel

| Date | Mintage | F | VF | XF | Unc | BU |
|---|---|---|---|---|---|---|
| 1981 | — | — | 0.50 | 1.00 | 3.00 | — |

**250 FILS KM# 7 Composition:** Copper-Nickel **Subject:** 10th Anniversary of Independence

| Date | Mintage | F | VF | XF | Unc | BU |
|---|---|---|---|---|---|---|
| 1977 | 30,000 | 2.50 | 5.00 | 10.00 | 25.00 | — |

**250 FILS KM# 11 Composition:** Copper-Nickel

| Date | Mintage | F | VF | XF | Unc | BU |
|---|---|---|---|---|---|---|
| 1981 | — | — | 1.50 | 3.00 | 5.50 | — |

**2 DINARS KM# 12 Weight:** 28.2800 g. **Composition:** 0.9250 Silver .8411 oz. ASW **Subject:** lInternational Year of Disabled Persons - Abdulla Baradoni

| Date | Mintage | F | VF | XF | Unc | BU |
|---|---|---|---|---|---|---|
| 1981 | 10,000 | — | — | — | 47.50 | — |
| 1981 Proof | 10,000 | Value: 52.50 | | | | |

**5 DINARS KM# 8 Weight:** 12.5000 g. **Composition:** 0.9250 Silver .3718 oz. ASW **Subject:** 10th Anniversary of Independence **Note:** Similar to 250 Fils, KM#7.

| Date | Mintage | F | VF | XF | Unc | BU |
|---|---|---|---|---|---|---|
| 1977 Proof | 6,000 | Value: 60.00 | | | | |

**50 DINARS KM# 13 Weight:** 15.9800 g. **Composition:** 0.9170 Gold .4712 oz. AGW **Series:** International Year of Disabled Persons

| Date | Mintage | F | VF | XF | Unc | BU |
|---|---|---|---|---|---|---|
| 1981 | 2,100 | — | — | — | 500 | — |
| 1981 Proof | 1,100 | Value: 750 | | | | |

## PIEFORTS

| KM# | Date | Mintage | Identification | Mkt Val |
|---|---|---|---|---|
| P1 | 1981 | 1,050 | 2 Dinars. KM#12. | 200 |
| P2 | 1981 | 500 | 50 Dinars. KM#13. | 1,500 |

# YUGOSLAVIA

The Federal Republic of Yugoslavia, formerly the Socialist Federal Republic of Yugoslavia, a Balkan country located on the east shore of the Adriatic Sea, has an area of 39,450 sq. mi. (102,173 sq. km.) and a population of 10.5 million. Capital: Belgrade. The chief industries area agriculture, mining, manufacturing and tourism. Machinery, nonferrous metals, meat and fabrics are exported.

Yugoslavia was proclaimed on Dec. 1, 1918, after the union of the Kingdom of Serbia, Montenegro and the South Slav territories of Austria-Hungary; and changed its official name from the Kingdom of the Serbs, Croats and Slovenes to the Kingdom of Yugoslavia on Oct. 3, 1929.The republic was composed of six autonomous republics -Serbia, Croatia, Slovenia, Bosnia-Herzegovina, Macedonia and Montenegro - and two autonomous provinces within Serbia: Kosovo-Melohija and Vojvodina. The government of Yugoslavia attempted to remain neutral in World War II but, yielding to German pressure, aligned itself with the Axis powers in March of 1941; a few days later it was overthrown by revolutionary forces and its neutrality reasserted. The Nazis occupied the country on April 6, and throughout the remaining war years were resisted by a number of guerrilla armies, notably that of Marshal Josip Broz Tito. After the defeat of the Axis powers, a leftist coalition headed by Tito abolished the monarchy and, on Jan. 31, 1946, established a "People's Republic". The collapse of the Federal Republic during 1991-1992 has resulted in the autonomous republics of Croatia, Slovenia, Bosnia-Herzegovina and Macedonia declaring their respective independence. Bosnia-Herzegovina is under military contest with the Serbian, Croat and Muslim populace opposing each other. Besides the remainder of the older Serbian sectors, a Serbian enclave in Knin located in southern Croatia has emerged called REPUBLIKE SRPSKEKRAJINE or Serbian Republic - Krajina whose capital is Knin and has also declared its independence in1992 when the former Republics of Serbia and Montenegro became the Federal Republic of Yugoslavia.

The name Yugoslavia appears on the coinage in letters of the Cyrillic alphabet alone until formation of the Federated Peoples Republic of Yugoslavia in 1953, after which both the Cyrillic and Latin alphabets are employed. From 1965, the coin denomination appears in the 4 different languages of the federated republics in letters of both the Cyrillic and Latin alphabets.

**DENOMINATIONS**

Para мЛГЛ
Dinar, ЂйкЛГ, Dinara ЂйкЛГЛ
Dinari ЂйкЛГй, Dinarjev

**RULERS**

Petar I, 1918-1921
Alexander I, 1921-1934
Petar II, 1934-1945

**MINT MARKS**

(a) - Paris, privy marks only
(b) - Brussels
(k) - Клекй…Л,ЙЛ.Ђ. = Kovnica, A.D. (Akcionarno Drustvo) Belgrade
(l) - London
(p) - Poissy (thunderbolt)
(v) – Vienna

**MONETARY SYSTEM**

100 Para = 1 Dinar

# KINGDOM OF THE SERBS, CROATS AND SLOVENES

## STANDARD COINAGE

**5 PARA** **KM# 1** **Composition:** Zinc **Ruler:** Petar I

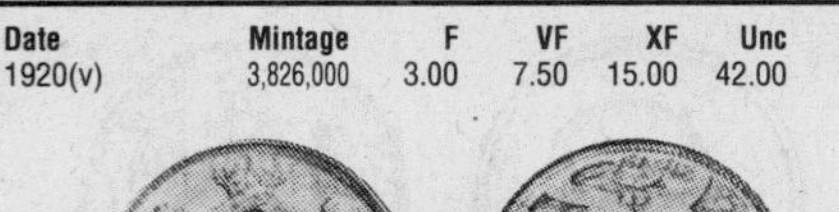

| Date | Mintage | F | VF | XF | Unc | BU |
|---|---|---|---|---|---|---|
| 1920(v) | 3,826,000 | 3.00 | 7.50 | 15.00 | 42.00 | — |

**10 PARA** **KM# 2** **Composition:** Zinc **Ruler:** Petar I

| Date | Mintage | F | VF | XF | Unc | BU |
|---|---|---|---|---|---|---|
| 1920(v) | 58,946,000 | 1.50 | 3.50 | 8.00 | 22.00 | — |

**25 PARA** **KM# 3** **Composition:** Nickel-Bronze **Ruler:** Petar I

| Date | Mintage | F | VF | XF | Unc | BU |
|---|---|---|---|---|---|---|
| 1920(v) | 48,173,000 | 1.50 | 3.00 | 7.50 | 20.00 | — |

**50 PARA** **KM# 4** **Composition:** Nickel-Bronze **Ruler:** Alexander I

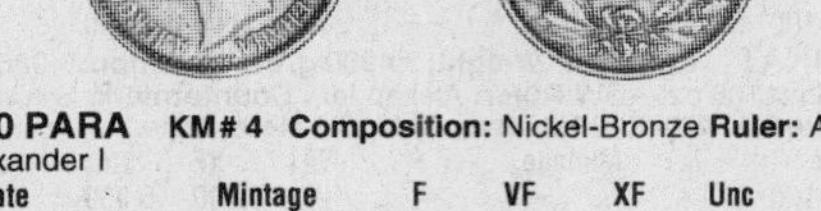

| Date | Mintage | F | VF | XF | Unc | BU |
|---|---|---|---|---|---|---|
| 1925(b) | 24,500,000 | 0.50 | 1.00 | 2.00 | 6.50 | — |
| 1925(p) | 25,000,000 | 0.50 | 1.50 | 3.00 | 7.50 | — |

**DINAR** **KM# 5** **Composition:** Nickel-Bronze **Ruler:** Alexander I

| Date | Mintage | F | VF | XF | Unc | BU |
|---|---|---|---|---|---|---|
| 1925 | 37,500,000 | 0.50 | 1.00 | 2.00 | 6.00 | — |
| 1925 | 37,000,000 | 0.75 | 1.50 | 3.00 | 7.00 | — |

**2 DINARA** **KM# 6** **Composition:** Nickel-Bronze **Ruler:** Alexander I

| Date | Mintage | F | VF | XF | Unc | BU |
|---|---|---|---|---|---|---|
| 1925 | 29,500,000 | 1.00 | 2.00 | 5.00 | 12.00 | — |
| 1925 | 25,004,000 | 1.00 | 2.50 | 5.50 | 14.00 | — |

**20 DINARA** **KM# 7** **Weight:** 6.4516 g. **Composition:** 0.9000 Gold .1867 oz. AGW **Ruler:** Alexander I

| Date | Mintage | F | VF | XF | Unc | BU |
|---|---|---|---|---|---|---|
| 1925 | 1,000 | 125 | 145 | 170 | 225 | — |
| 1925 Proof | — | — | — | — | — | — |

# KINGDOM OF YUGOSLAVIA

## STANDARD COINAGE

**25 PARA** **KM# 17** **Composition:** Bronze **Ruler:** Petar II

| Date | Mintage | F | VF | XF | Unc | BU |
|---|---|---|---|---|---|---|
| 1938 | 40,000,000 | 1.25 | 2.00 | 5.00 | 13.00 | — |
| 1938 Proof | — | — | — | — | — | — |

**50 PARA** **KM# 18** **Composition:** Aluminum-Bronze **Ruler:** Petar II

| Date | Mintage | F | VF | XF | Unc | BU |
|---|---|---|---|---|---|---|
| 1938 | 100,000,000 | 0.50 | 1.00 | 2.50 | 7.50 | — |

**DINAR** **KM# 19** **Composition:** Aluminum-Bronze **Ruler:** Petar II

| Date | Mintage | F | VF | XF | Unc | BU |
|---|---|---|---|---|---|---|
| 1938 | 100,000,000 | 0.50 | 0.75 | 2.00 | 6.00 | — |
| 1938 Proof | — | — | — | — | — | — |

**2 DINARA** **KM# 20** **Composition:** Aluminum-Bronze **Ruler:** Petar II **Obverse:** 14mm Crown

| Date | Mintage | F | VF | XF | Unc | BU |
|---|---|---|---|---|---|---|
| 1938 | 74,250,000 | 0.50 | 1.00 | 3.00 | 8.00 | — |
| 1938 Proof | — | — | — | — | — | — |

**2 DINARA** **KM# 21** **Composition:** Aluminum-Bronze **Ruler:** Petar II **Obverse:** 12mm Crown

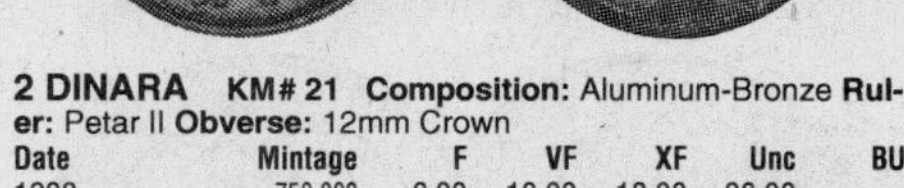

| Date | Mintage | F | VF | XF | Unc | BU |
|---|---|---|---|---|---|---|
| 1938 | 750,000 | 6.00 | 10.00 | 18.00 | 36.00 | — |
| 1938 Proof | — | — | — | — | — | — |

**10 DINARA** **KM# 10** **Weight:** 7.0000 g. **Composition:** 0.5000 Silver .1125 oz. ASW **Ruler:** Petar II

| Date | Mintage | F | VF | XF | Unc | BU |
|---|---|---|---|---|---|---|
| 1931(l) | 16,000,000 | 2.00 | 4.00 | 8.00 | 17.50 | — |
| 1931(l) Proof | — | — | — | — | — | — |
| 1931(a) | 4,000,000 | 3.50 | 7.00 | 15.00 | 32.00 | — |
| 1931(a) Proof | — | — | — | — | — | — |

**10 DINARA** KM# 22 **Composition:** Nickel **Ruler:** Petar II

| Date | Mintage | F | VF | XF | Unc | BU |
|---|---|---|---|---|---|---|
| 1938 | 25,000,000 | 0.50 | 1.00 | 2.00 | 4.00 | — |

**20 DINARA** KM# 11 **Weight:** 14.0000 g. **Composition:** 0.5000 Silver .2250 oz. ASW **Ruler:** Petar II

| Date | Mintage | F | VF | XF | Unc | BU |
|---|---|---|---|---|---|---|
| 1931(k) | 12,500,000 | BV | 6.00 | 12.50 | 33.00 | — |
| 1931(k) Proof | — | — | — | — | — | — |

**20 DINARA** KM# 23 **Weight:** 9.0000 g. **Composition:** 0.7500 Silver .217 oz. ASW **Ruler:** Petar II

| Date | Mintage | F | VF | XF | Unc | BU |
|---|---|---|---|---|---|---|
| 1938 | 15,000,000 | BV | 2.50 | 5.00 | 12.00 | — |

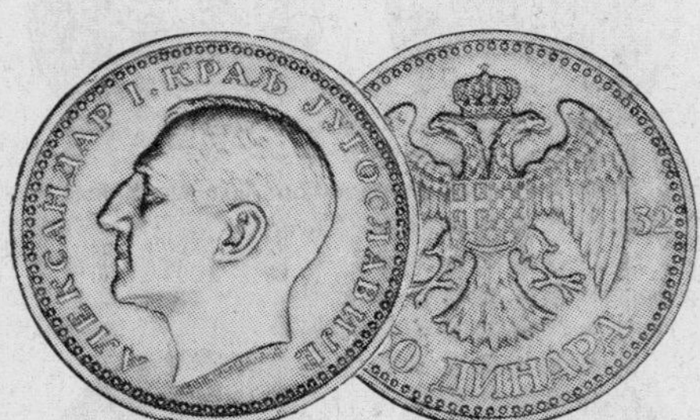

**50 DINARA** KM# 16 **Weight:** 23.3300 g. **Composition:** 0.7500 Silver .5626 oz. ASW **Ruler:** Petar II

| Date | Mintage | F | VF | XF | Unc | BU |
|---|---|---|---|---|---|---|
| 1932(k) | 5,500,000 | 10.00 | 22.00 | 45.00 | 180 | — |
| 1932(l) | 5,500,000 | 10.00 | 25.00 | 50.00 | 200 | — |
| 1932(l) Proof | — | Value: 2,200 | | | | |

**50 DINARA** KM# 24 **Weight:** 15.0000 g. **Composition:** 0.7500 Silver .3617 oz. ASW **Ruler:** Petar II

| Date | Mintage | F | VF | XF | Unc | BU |
|---|---|---|---|---|---|---|
| 1938 | 10,000,000 | 3.00 | 5.00 | 9.00 | 18.00 | — |

## TRADE COINAGE

Trade-coinage countermarks were applied by the Yugoslav Control Office for Noble Metals to confirm gold purity. The initial countermark displayed a sword, but part way through the first production year, this was retired and the second countermark, showing an ear of corn, was used.

**DUKAT** KM# 12.1 **Weight:** 3.4900 g. **Composition:** 0.9860 Gold .1106 oz. AGW **Ruler:** Alexander I **Countermark:** Sword **Obverse:** Small legend with жлекй..., Л.Ђ. below head **Reverse:** Small legend with жлекй..., Л.Ђ. below head

| Date | Mintage | F | VF | XF | Unc | BU |
|---|---|---|---|---|---|---|
| 1931(k) | Est. 50,000 | — | 80.00 | 125 | 185 | — |
| 1932(k) Rare | — | — | — | — | — | — |

**Note:** The 1932(k) examples with sword countermark are believed to be mint sports.

**DUKAT** KM# 12.2 **Weight:** 3.4900 g. **Composition:** 0.9860 Gold .1106 oz. AGW **Ruler:** Alexander I **Countermark:** Ear of corn **Obverse:** Small legend **Reverse:** Small legend **Note:** Forgeries bearing no countermark exist for 1932 and possibly other dates.

| Date | Mintage | F | VF | XF | Unc | BU |
|---|---|---|---|---|---|---|
| 1931(k) | Est. 150,000 | — | 70.00 | 120 | 165 | — |
| 1932(k) | Est. 70,000 | — | 80.00 | 125 | 175 | — |
| 1933(k) | Est. 40,000 | — | 125 | 175 | 285 | — |
| 1934(k) | Est. 2,000 | — | 500 | 800 | 1,200 | — |

**DUKAT** KM# 12.3 **Weight:** 3.4900 g. **Composition:** 0.9860 Gold .1106 oz. AGW **Ruler:** Alexander I **Countermark:** Sword **Obverse:** KM#13.2 **Reverse:** KM#12.1 **Note:** Mule.

| Date | Mintage | F | VF | XF | Unc | BU |
|---|---|---|---|---|---|---|
| 1931(k) | — | — | — | 3,000 | 5,000 | — |

**DUKAT** KM# 13.1 **Weight:** 3.4900 g. **Composition:** 0.9860 Gold .1106 oz. AGW **Ruler:** Petar II **Obverse:** Large legend **Reverse:** Large legend

| Date | Mintage | F | VF | XF | Unc | BU |
|---|---|---|---|---|---|---|
| 1931(k) | 2,869 | — | — | 3,500 | 5,500 | — |

**DUKAT** KM# 13.2 **Weight:** 3.4900 g. **Composition:** 0.9860 Gold .1106 oz. AGW **Ruler:** Alexander I **Countermark:** Sword **Note:** Large-letter varieties bear the Kovnica, A.D. mint mark but were actually struck in Vienna.

| Date | Mintage | F | VF | XF | Unc | BU |
|---|---|---|---|---|---|---|
| 1931(k) | Inc. above | — | — | 4,000 | 6,500 | — |

**4 DUKATA** KM# 14.2 **Weight:** 13.9600 g. **Composition:** 0.9860 Gold .4425 oz. AGW **Ruler:** Alexander I **Countermark:** Ear of corn

| Date | Mintage | F | VF | XF | Unc | BU |
|---|---|---|---|---|---|---|
| 1931(k) | Est. 15,000 | — | 450 | 750 | 950 | — |
| 1932(k) | Est. 10,000 | — | 400 | 725 | 1,000 | — |
| 1933(k) | Est. 2,000 | — | 1,000 | 1,600 | 2,500 | — |
| 1934(k) | — | — | 2,000 | 3,000 | 4,500 | — |

**4 DUKATA** KM# 14.1 **Weight:** 13.9600 g. **Composition:** 0.9860 Gold .4425 oz. AGW **Ruler:** Alexander I **Countermark:** Sword **Obverse:** Small legend **Reverse:** Small legend **Note:** The 1932(k) examples with sword countermark are believed to be mint sports.

| Date | Mintage | F | VF | XF | Unc | BU |
|---|---|---|---|---|---|---|
| 1931(k) | Est. 10,000 | — | 450 | 750 | 950 | — |
| 1932(k) Rare | — | — | — | — | — | — |

**4 DUKATA** KM# 14.3 **Weight:** 13.9600 g. **Composition:** 0.9860 Gold .4425 oz. AGW **Ruler:** Alexander I **Obverse:** Without countermark **Reverse:** Without countermark **Note:** Only one genuine piece has been reported.

| Date | Mintage | F | VF | XF | Unc | BU |
|---|---|---|---|---|---|---|
| 1931(k) Rare | — | — | — | — | — | — |

**4 DUKATA** KM# A15.1 **Weight:** 13.9600 g. **Composition:** 0.9860 Gold .4425 oz. AGW **Ruler:** Alexander I **Obverse:** Large legend **Reverse:** Large legend

| Date | Mintage | F | VF | XF | Unc | BU |
|---|---|---|---|---|---|---|
| 1931(k) Rare | 51 | — | — | — | — | — |

## POST WAR COINAGE

**50 PARA** KM# 25 **Composition:** Zinc

| Date | Mintage | F | VF | XF | Unc | BU |
|---|---|---|---|---|---|---|
| 1945 | 40,000,000 | 0.50 | 1.00 | 3.00 | 9.00 | — |

**DINAR** KM# 26 **Composition:** Zinc

| Date | Mintage | F | VF | XF | Unc | BU |
|---|---|---|---|---|---|---|
| 1945 | 90,000,000 | 0.50 | 1.00 | 2.50 | 7.00 | — |

**2 DINARA** KM# 27 **Composition:** Zinc

| Date | Mintage | F | VF | XF | Unc | BU |
|---|---|---|---|---|---|---|
| 1945 | 70,000,000 | 0.50 | 1.25 | 3.00 | 9.00 | — |

**5 DINARA** KM# 28 **Composition:** Zinc

| Date | Mintage | F | VF | XF | Unc | BU |
|---|---|---|---|---|---|---|
| 1945 | 50,000,000 | 1.00 | 2.00 | 4.00 | 12.00 | — |

# FEDERAL PEOPLE'S REPUBLIC

## STANDARD COINAGE

**50 PARA** KM# 29 **Composition:** Aluminum

| Date | Mintage | F | VF | XF | Unc | BU |
|---|---|---|---|---|---|---|
| 1953 | — | — | — | 0.10 | 0.25 | — |

**DINAR** KM# 30 **Composition:** Aluminum

| Date | Mintage | F | VF | XF | Unc | BU |
|---|---|---|---|---|---|---|
| 1953 | — | — | 0.10 | 0.15 | 0.25 | — |

**2 DINARA** KM# 31 **Composition:** Aluminum

| Date | Mintage | F | VF | XF | Unc | BU |
|---|---|---|---|---|---|---|
| 1953 | — | — | 0.10 | 0.20 | 0.30 | — |

**5 DINARA** KM# 32 **Composition:** Aluminum

| Date | Mintage | F | VF | XF | Unc | BU |
|---|---|---|---|---|---|---|
| 1953 | — | 0.10 | 0.25 | 0.50 | 0.75 | — |

**10 DINARA** KM# 33 **Composition:** Aluminum-Bronze

| Date | Mintage | F | VF | XF | Unc | BU |
|---|---|---|---|---|---|---|
| 1955 | — | 0.15 | 0.30 | 0.75 | 1.50 | — |

**20 DINARA** KM# 34 **Composition:** Aluminum-Bronze

| Date | Mintage | F | VF | XF | Unc | BU |
|---|---|---|---|---|---|---|
| 1955 | — | 0.25 | 0.50 | 1.00 | 2.00 | — |

**50 DINARA** KM# 35 **Composition:** Aluminum-Bronze

| Date | Mintage | F | VF | XF | Unc | BU |
|---|---|---|---|---|---|---|
| 1955 | — | 0.25 | 0.50 | 1.50 | 3.00 | — |

# SOCIALIST FEDERAL REPUBLIC

## STANDARD COINAGE

**5 PARA** KM# 42 **Composition:** Copper-Zinc

| Date | Mintage | F | VF | XF | Unc | BU |
|---|---|---|---|---|---|---|
| 1965 | 23,839,000 | — | 0.10 | 0.20 | 0.40 | — |

**5 PARA** KM# 43 **Composition:** Copper-Zinc

| Date | Mintage | F | VF | XF | Unc | BU |
|---|---|---|---|---|---|---|
| 1965 | 16,200,000 | — | — | 0.10 | 0.20 | — |
| 1973 | 36,384,000 | — | — | 0.10 | 0.15 | — |
| 1974 | 3,628,000 | — | — | 0.10 | 0.25 | — |
| 1975 | 20,272,000 | — | — | 0.10 | 0.15 | — |
| 1976 | 30,490,000 | — | — | 0.10 | 0.15 | — |
| 1977 | 10,270,000 | — | — | 0.10 | 0.15 | — |
| 1978 | 12,000,000 | — | — | 0.10 | 0.15 | — |
| 1979 | 20,414,000 | — | — | 0.10 | 0.15 | — |
| 1980 | 22,412,000 | — | — | 0.10 | 0.15 | — |
| 1981 | 630,000 | — | 0.10 | 0.25 | 0.50 | — |

**10 PARA** KM# 44 **Composition:** Copper-Zinc

| Date | Mintage | F | VF | XF | Unc | BU |
|---|---|---|---|---|---|---|
| 1965 | 15,400,000 | — | — | 0.10 | 0.20 | — |
| 1973 | 16,647,000 | — | — | 0.10 | 0.20 | — |
| 1974 | 60,139,000 | — | — | 0.10 | 0.20 | — |
| 1975 | 36,954,000 | — | — | 0.10 | 0.15 | — |
| 1976 | 36,111,000 | — | — | 0.10 | 0.15 | — |
| 1977 | 40,451,000 | — | — | 0.10 | 0.15 | — |
| 1978 | 50,129,000 | — | — | 0.10 | 0.15 | — |
| 1979 | 89,738,000 | — | — | 0.10 | 0.15 | — |
| 1980 | 90,111,000 | — | — | 0.10 | 0.15 | — |
| 1981 | 14,090,000 | — | — | 0.10 | 0.15 | — |

**10 PARA** KM# 139 **Composition:** Copper-Zinc

| Date | Mintage | F | VF | XF | Unc | BU |
|---|---|---|---|---|---|---|
| 1990 | 174,028,000 | — | — | 0.10 | 0.15 | — |
| 1991 | 60,828,000 | — | — | 0.15 | 0.35 | — |

**20 PARA** KM# 45 **Composition:** Copper-Zinc

| Date | Mintage | F | VF | XF | Unc | BU |
|---|---|---|---|---|---|---|
| 1965 | — | — | — | 0.10 | 0.30 | — |
| 1973 | 30,448,000 | — | — | 0.10 | 0.30 | — |
| 1974 | 31,364,000 | — | — | 0.10 | 0.30 | — |
| 1975 | 44,683,000 | — | — | 0.10 | 0.30 | — |
| 1976 | 33,312,000 | — | — | 0.10 | 0.30 | — |
| 1977 | 40,782,000 | — | — | 0.10 | 0.30 | — |
| 1978 | 39,999,000 | — | — | 0.10 | 0.30 | — |
| 1979 | 49,121,000 | — | — | 0.10 | 0.30 | — |
| 1980 | 73,757,000 | — | — | 0.10 | 0.30 | — |
| 1981 | 96,144,000 | — | — | 0.10 | 0.30 | — |

**20 PARA** KM# 140 **Composition:** Copper-Zinc

| Date | Mintage | VG | F | VF | XF | Unc |
|---|---|---|---|---|---|---|
| 1990 | 41,353,000 | — | — | 0.10 | 0.20 | 0.50 |
| 1991 | 43,118,000 | — | — | 0.10 | 0.20 | 0.50 |

**25 PARA** KM# 84 **Composition:** Bronze

| Date | Mintage | F | VF | XF | Unc | BU |
|---|---|---|---|---|---|---|
| 1982 | 185,316,000 | — | — | 0.10 | 0.25 | — |
| 1983 | 65,290,000 | — | — | 0.15 | 0.30 | — |

**50 PARA** KM# 46.1 **Composition:** Copper-Zinc **Reverse:** Narrow 0 in denomination

| Date | Mintage | F | VF | XF | Unc | BU |
|---|---|---|---|---|---|---|
| 1965 | — | — | 0.10 | 0.20 | 0.65 | — |
| 1973 | 23,739,000 | — | 0.10 | 0.20 | 0.65 | — |
| 1974 | 33,000 | 1.00 | 1.50 | 2.50 | 5.00 | — |
| 1975 | 10,220,000 | — | 0.10 | 0.20 | 0.80 | — |
| 1976 | 8,438,000 | — | 0.10 | 0.20 | 1.00 | — |
| 1977 | 17,864,000 | — | 0.10 | 0.20 | 0.75 | — |
| 1978 | 40,177,000 | — | 0.10 | 0.20 | 0.65 | — |
| 1979 | 3,021,000 | 0.50 | 1.00 | 2.00 | 5.00 | — |

**50 PARA** KM# 46.2 **Composition:** Copper-Zinc **Reverse:** Wide 0 in denomination

| Date | Mintage | F | VF | XF | Unc | BU |
|---|---|---|---|---|---|---|
| 1979 | 12,278,000 | 0.20 | 0.50 | 1.00 | 2.50 | — |
| 1980 | 24,974,000 | — | 0.10 | 0.20 | 0.65 | — |
| 1981 | 40,319,000 | — | 0.10 | 0.20 | 0.65 | — |

**50 PARA** KM# 85 **Composition:** Bronze

| Date | Mintage | F | VF | XF | Unc | BU |
|---|---|---|---|---|---|---|
| 1982 | 79,584,000 | — | — | 0.10 | 0.20 | — |
| 1983 | 72,100,000 | — | — | 0.10 | 0.20 | — |
| 1984 | 59,642,000 | 0.25 | 0.50 | 1.00 | 1.50 | — |

**50 PARA** KM# 141 **Composition:** Copper-Zinc

| Date | Mintage | F | VF | XF | Unc | BU |
|---|---|---|---|---|---|---|
| 1990 | 137,873,000 | — | — | 0.10 | 0.20 | — |
| 1991 | 42,152,000 | — | 0.20 | 0.40 | 1.00 | — |

**DINAR** KM# 36 **Composition:** Aluminum

| Date | Mintage | F | VF | XF | Unc | BU |
|---|---|---|---|---|---|---|
| 1963 | — | — | — | 0.10 | 0.15 | — |

**DINAR** KM# 47 **Composition:** Copper-Nickel

| Date | Mintage | F | VF | XF | Unc | BU |
|---|---|---|---|---|---|---|
| 1965 | 75,822,000 | 0.10 | 0.15 | 0.30 | 0.60 | — |

**DINAR** KM# 48 **Composition:** Copper-Nickel

| Date | Mintage | F | VF | XF | Unc | BU |
|---|---|---|---|---|---|---|
| 1968 | 35,497,000 | 0.10 | 0.20 | 0.40 | 0.80 | — |

**DINAR** KM# 59 **Composition:** Copper-Nickel-Zinc

| Date | Mintage | F | VF | XF | Unc | BU |
|---|---|---|---|---|---|---|
| 1973 | 18,974,000 | — | 0.10 | 0.15 | 0.40 | — |
| 1974 | 42,724,000 | — | 0.10 | 0.15 | 0.35 | — |
| 1975 | 30,260,000 | — | 0.10 | 0.15 | 0.35 | — |
| 1976 | 21,849,000 | — | 0.10 | 0.15 | 0.35 | — |
| 1977 | 30,468,000 | — | 0.10 | 0.15 | 0.35 | — |
| 1978 | 35,032,000 | — | 0.10 | 0.15 | 0.35 | — |
| 1979 | 39,848,000 | — | 0.10 | 0.15 | 0.35 | — |
| 1980 | 60,630,000 | — | 0.10 | 0.15 | 0.35 | — |
| 1981 | 56,650,000 | — | 0.10 | 0.15 | 0.35 | — |

**DINAR** KM# 61 **Composition:** Copper-Nickel-Zinc **Series:** F.A.O.

| Date | Mintage | F | VF | XF | Unc | BU |
|---|---|---|---|---|---|---|
| 1976 | 500,000 | — | 0.10 | 0.30 | 1.00 | — |

**DINAR** KM# 86 **Composition:** Nickel-Brass

| Date | Mintage | F | VF | XF | Unc | BU |
|---|---|---|---|---|---|---|
| 1982 | 70,105,000 | — | — | 0.10 | 0.30 | — |
| 1983 | 114,180,000 | — | — | 0.10 | 0.20 | — |
| 1984 | 172,185,000 | — | — | 0.10 | 0.20 | — |
| 1985 | 34,436,000 | — | — | 0.10 | 0.25 | — |
| 1986 | 122,643,000 | — | — | 0.10 | 0.20 | — |

**DINAR** KM# 142 **Composition:** Copper-Nickel-Zinc

| Date | Mintage | F | VF | XF | Unc | BU |
|---|---|---|---|---|---|---|
| 1990 | 172,105,000 | — | — | 0.10 | 0.25 | — |
| 1991 | 79,549,000 | — | 0.15 | 0.25 | 0.75 | — |

**2 DINARA** KM# 37 **Composition:** Aluminum

| Date | Mintage | F | VF | XF | Unc | BU |
|---|---|---|---|---|---|---|
| 1963 | — | — | 0.10 | 0.15 | 0.25 | — |

**2 DINARA** KM# 55 **Composition:** Copper-Nickel-Zinc **Series:** F.A.O.

| Date | Mintage | F | VF | XF | Unc | BU |
|---|---|---|---|---|---|---|
| 1970 | 500,000 | — | 0.20 | 0.40 | 1.00 | — |

**2 DINARA** KM# 57 **Composition:** Copper-Nickel-Zinc

| Date | Mintage | F | VF | XF | Unc | BU |
|---|---|---|---|---|---|---|
| 1971 | 10,413,000 | — | 0.10 | 0.30 | 0.70 | — |
| 1972 | 18,440,000 | — | 0.10 | 0.20 | 0.50 | — |
| 1973 | 31,848,000 | — | 0.10 | 0.20 | 0.45 | — |
| 1974 | 10,989,000 | — | 0.10 | 0.20 | 0.50 | — |
| 1975 | 92,000 | 2.00 | 4.00 | 7.50 | 15.00 | — |
| 1976 | 6,092,000 | — | 0.10 | 0.20 | 0.50 | — |
| 1977 | 19,335,000 | — | 0.10 | 0.20 | 0.50 | — |
| 1978 | 13,035,000 | — | 0.10 | 0.20 | 0.50 | — |
| 1979 | 20,069,000 | — | 0.10 | 0.20 | 0.45 | — |
| 1980 | 36,088,000 | — | 0.10 | 0.20 | 0.45 | — |
| 1981 | 42,599,000 | — | 0.10 | 0.20 | 0.45 | — |

**2 DINARA** KM# 87 **Composition:** Nickel-Brass

| Date | Mintage | F | VF | XF | Unc | BU |
|---|---|---|---|---|---|---|
| 1982 | 40,632,000 | — | 0.10 | 0.15 | 0.35 | — |
| 1983 | 35,468,000 | — | 0.10 | 0.15 | 0.35 | — |
| 1984 | 51,500,000 | — | 0.10 | 0.15 | 0.35 | — |
| 1985 | 81,100,000 | — | 0.10 | 0.15 | 0.35 | — |
| 1986 | 50,453,000 | — | 0.10 | 0.15 | 0.35 | — |

**2 DINARA** KM# 143 **Composition:** Copper-Nickel-Zinc

| Date | Mintage | F | VF | XF | Unc | BU |
|---|---|---|---|---|---|---|
| 1990 | 15,936,000 | 0.15 | 0.30 | 0.60 | 2.00 | — |
| 1991 | 32,836,000 | — | 0.20 | 0.40 | 1.00 | — |
| 1992 | — | 2.50 | 3.50 | 7.00 | 12.50 | — |

**5 DINARA** KM# 38 **Composition:** Aluminum

| Date | Mintage | F | VF | XF | Unc | BU |
|---|---|---|---|---|---|---|
| 1963 | — | 0.10 | 0.20 | 0.35 | 0.50 | — |

**5 DINARA** KM# 56 **Composition:** Copper-Nickel-Zinc **Series:** F.A.O.

| Date | Mintage | F | VF | XF | Unc | BU |
|---|---|---|---|---|---|---|
| 1970 | 500,000 | 0.20 | 0.50 | 1.00 | 2.50 | — |

**5 DINARA** KM# 58 **Composition:** Copper-Nickel-Zinc **Note:** Regular issue.

| Date | Mintage | F | VF | XF | Unc | BU |
|---|---|---|---|---|---|---|
| 1971 | 10,224,000 | 0.20 | 0.40 | 0.60 | 1.00 | — |
| 1972 | 27,974,000 | 0.10 | 0.20 | 0.35 | 0.60 | — |
| 1973 | 12,705,000 | 0.20 | 0.40 | 0.60 | 1.00 | — |
| 1974 | 6,054,000 | 0.25 | 0.50 | 1.00 | 2.00 | — |
| 1975 | 12,533,000 | 0.10 | 0.20 | 0.35 | 0.60 | — |
| 1976 | 4,965,000 | 0.10 | 0.25 | 0.40 | 0.80 | — |
| 1977 | 922,000 | 0.30 | 0.60 | 1.20 | 2.50 | — |
| 1978 | 1,000,000 | 0.10 | 0.25 | 0.50 | 1.50 | — |
| 1979 | 3,000,000 | 0.10 | 0.25 | 0.40 | 0.80 | — |
| 1980 | 9,977,000 | 0.10 | 0.20 | 0.35 | 0.60 | — |
| 1981 | 15,450,000 | 0.10 | 0.20 | 0.35 | 0.60 | — |

**5 DINARA** KM# 60 **Composition:** Copper-Nickel-Zinc **Subject:** 30th anniversary of Nazi defeat

| Date | Mintage | F | VF | XF | Unc | BU |
|---|---|---|---|---|---|---|
| 1975 | 1,020,000 | 0.25 | 0.50 | 1.00 | 2.50 | — |

**5 DINARA** KM# 88 **Composition:** Nickel-Brass

| Date | Mintage | F | VF | XF | Unc | BU |
|---|---|---|---|---|---|---|
| 1982 | 40,956,000 | — | 0.10 | 0.15 | 0.50 | — |
| 1983 | 40,156,000 | — | 0.10 | 0.15 | 0.50 | — |
| 1984 | 33,023,000 | — | 0.10 | 0.15 | 0.50 | — |
| 1985 | 94,422,000 | — | 0.10 | 0.15 | 0.50 | — |
| 1986 | 37,199,000 | — | 0.10 | 0.15 | 0.50 | — |

**5 DINARA** **KM# 144** **Composition:** Copper-Nickel-Zinc

| Date | Mintage | F | VF | XF | Unc | BU |
|---|---|---|---|---|---|---|
| 1990 | 9,354,000 | 0.25 | 0.45 | 1.00 | 2.50 | — |
| 1991 | 113,420,000 | — | 0.25 | 0.50 | 1.25 | — |
| 1992 | — | 1.50 | 2.50 | 4.00 | 7.00 | — |

**5 DINARA** **KM# 145** **Composition:** Copper-Nickel-Zinc **Subject:** 1990 Chess Olympiad **Reverse:** Logo

| Date | Mintage | F | VF | XF | Unc | BU |
|---|---|---|---|---|---|---|
| 1990 Proof | 20,000 | Value: 7.00 | | | | |

**10 DINARA** **KM# 39** **Composition:** Aluminum-Bronze

| Date | Mintage | F | VF | XF | Unc | BU |
|---|---|---|---|---|---|---|
| 1963 | — | 0.15 | 0.30 | 0.75 | 1.25 | — |

**10 DINARA** **KM# 62** **Composition:** Copper-Nickel

| Date | Mintage | F | VF | XF | Unc | BU |
|---|---|---|---|---|---|---|
| 1976 | 10,550,000 | 0.30 | 0.60 | 0.75 | 1.25 | — |
| 1977 | 39,645,000 | 0.30 | 0.60 | 0.75 | 1.00 | — |
| 1978 | 29,834,000 | 0.30 | 0.60 | 0.75 | 1.00 | — |
| 1979 | 4,969,000 | 0.30 | 0.60 | 0.75 | 1.00 | — |
| 1980 | 10,139,000 | 0.30 | 0.60 | 0.75 | 1.00 | — |
| 1981 | 20,116,000 | 0.30 | 0.60 | 0.75 | 1.00 | — |

**10 DINARA** **KM# 63** **Composition:** Copper-Nickel-Zinc **Series:** F.A.O.

| Date | Mintage | F | VF | XF | Unc | BU |
|---|---|---|---|---|---|---|
| 1976 | 500,000 | 0.50 | 0.75 | 1.00 | 2.50 | — |

**10 DINARA** **KM# 89** **Composition:** Copper-Nickel

| Date | Mintage | F | VF | XF | Unc | BU |
|---|---|---|---|---|---|---|
| 1982 | 8,862,000 | — | 0.10 | 0.20 | 0.80 | — |
| 1983 | 42,400,000 | — | 0.10 | 0.20 | 0.75 | — |
| 1984 | 30,900,000 | — | 0.10 | 0.20 | 0.75 | — |
| 1985 | 31,647,000 | — | 0.10 | 0.20 | 0.75 | — |
| 1986 | 40,739,000 | — | 0.10 | 0.20 | 0.75 | — |
| 1987 | 104,988,000 | — | 0.10 | 0.20 | 0.75 | — |
| 1988 | 27,614,000 | — | 0.10 | 0.20 | 0.75 | — |

**10 DINARA** **KM# 96** **Composition:** Copper-Nickel **Subject:** 40th anniversary - Battle of Neretva River

| Date | Mintage | F | VF | XF | Unc | BU |
|---|---|---|---|---|---|---|
| ND(1983) | 900,000 | — | 1.00 | 2.00 | 4.00 | — |
| ND(1983) Proof | 100,000 | Value: 8.00 | | | | |

**10 DINARA** **KM# 97.1** **Composition:** Copper-Nickel **Subject:** 40th anniversary - Battle of Sutjeska River

| Date | Mintage | F | VF | XF | Unc | BU |
|---|---|---|---|---|---|---|
| ND(1983) | 900,000 | — | 1.00 | 1.50 | 3.00 | — |
| ND(1983) Proof | 100,000 | Value: 7.50 | | | | |

**10 DINARA** **KM# 97.2** **Composition:** Copper-Nickel **Subject:** 40th anniversary - Battle of Sutjeska River **Reverse:** Without pathway in front of monument

| Date | Mintage | F | VF | XF | Unc | BU |
|---|---|---|---|---|---|---|
| ND(1983) | — | — | 3.00 | 6.00 | 10.00 | — |

**10 DINARA** **KM# 131** **Composition:** Brass

| Date | Mintage | F | VF | XF | Unc | BU |
|---|---|---|---|---|---|---|
| 1988 | 35,992,000 | — | — | 0.10 | 0.25 | — |
| 1989 | 75,000,000 | — | — | 0.10 | 0.25 | — |

**20 DINARA** **KM# 40** **Composition:** Aluminum-Bronze

| Date | Mintage | F | VF | XF | Unc | BU |
|---|---|---|---|---|---|---|
| 1963 | — | 0.50 | 1.00 | 1.75 | 3.50 | — |

**20 DINARA** **KM# 49** **Weight:** 9.0000 g. **Composition:** 0.9250 Silver .2676 oz. ASW **Subject:** 25th anniversary of republic **Note:** Similar to 50 Dinara, KM#50.

| Date | Mintage | VG | F | VF | XF | Unc |
|---|---|---|---|---|---|---|
| 1968 Proof | 10,000 | Value: 25.00 | | | | |
| 1968 NI Proof | Inc. above | Value: 25.00 | | | | |

**20 DINARA** **KM# 112** **Composition:** Copper-Zinc-Nickel

| Date | Mintage | F | VF | XF | Unc | BU |
|---|---|---|---|---|---|---|
| 1985 | 5,000,000 | — | 0.10 | 0.15 | 0.50 | — |
| 1986 | 20,932,000 | — | 0.10 | 0.15 | 0.35 | — |
| 1987 | 39,514,000 | — | 0.10 | 0.15 | 0.35 | — |

**20 DINARA** **KM# 132** **Composition:** Brass

| Date | Mintage | F | VF | XF | Unc | BU |
|---|---|---|---|---|---|---|
| 1988 | 29,775,000 | — | — | 0.10 | 0.25 | — |
| 1989 | 12,994,000 | — | — | 0.10 | 0.25 | — |

**50 DINARA** **KM# 41** **Composition:** Aluminum-Bronze **Note:** Exists with filled letter in denomination.

| Date | Mintage | F | VF | XF | Unc | BU |
|---|---|---|---|---|---|---|
| 1963 | — | 1.00 | 2.50 | 6.00 | 16.00 | — |

**50 DINARA** **KM# 50** **Weight:** 20.0000 g. **Composition:** 0.9250 Silver .5948 oz. ASW **Subject:** 25th anniversary of republic

| Date | Mintage | F | VF | XF | Unc | BU |
|---|---|---|---|---|---|---|
| ND(1968) Proof | 10,000 | Value: 42.00 | | | | |
| ND(1968) NI Proof | Inc. above | Value: 42.00 | | | | |

**50 DINARA** **KM# 113** **Composition:** Copper-Zinc-Nickel

| Date | Mintage | F | VF | XF | Unc | BU |
|---|---|---|---|---|---|---|
| 1985 | 25,488,000 | — | 0.10 | 0.25 | 0.75 | — |
| 1986 | 20,353,000 | — | 0.10 | 0.25 | 0.75 | — |
| 1987 | 21,792,000 | — | 0.10 | 0.25 | 0.75 | — |
| 1988 | 28,370,000 | — | 0.10 | 0.25 | 0.75 | — |

**50 DINARA** **KM# 133** **Composition:** Brass

| Date | Mintage | F | VF | XF | Unc | BU |
|---|---|---|---|---|---|---|
| 1988 | 46,973,000 | — | — | 0.10 | 0.25 | — |
| 1989 | 2,999,000 | — | 0.50 | 1.00 | 2.00 | — |

**Note:** Currently not issued.

**100 DINARA** KM# 51 **Weight:** 7.8200 g. **Composition:** 0.9000 Gold .2263 oz. AGW **Subject:** 25th anniversary of republic

| Date | Mintage | F | VF | XF | Unc | BU |
|---|---|---|---|---|---|---|
| ND(1968) Proof | 10,000 | Value: 125 | | | | |
| ND(1968) NI Proof | Inc. above | Value: 125 | | | | |

**100 DINARA** KM# 65 **Weight:** 10.0000 g. **Composition:** 0.9250 Silver .2974 oz. ASW **Subject:** 8th Mediterranean Games at Split

| Date | Mintage | F | VF | XF | Unc | BU |
|---|---|---|---|---|---|---|
| 1978 Proof | 71,000 | Value: 22.50 | | | | |

**100 DINARA** KM# 90 **Weight:** 13.0000 g. **Composition:** 0.9250 Silver .3867 oz. ASW **Series:** 1984 Winter Olympics **Subject:** Ice hockey

| Date | Mintage | F | VF | XF | Unc | BU |
|---|---|---|---|---|---|---|
| 1982 Proof | 110,000 | Value: 10.00 | | | | |

**100 DINARA** KM# 98 **Weight:** 13.0000 g. **Composition:** 0.9250 Silver .3867 oz. ASW **Series:** 1984 Winter Olympics **Subject:** Figure skating

| Date | Mintage | VG | F | VF | XF | Unc |
|---|---|---|---|---|---|---|
| 1983 Proof | — | Value: 10.00 | | | | |

**100 DINARA** KM# 99 **Weight:** 13.0000 g. **Composition:** 0.9250 Silver .3867 oz. ASW **Series:** 1984 Winter Olympics **Subject:** Bobsledding

| Date | Mintage | F | VF | XF | Unc | BU |
|---|---|---|---|---|---|---|
| 1983 Proof | 110,000 | Value: 10.00 | | | | |

**100 DINARA** KM# 105 **Weight:** 13.0000 g. **Composition:** 0.9250 Silver .3867 oz. ASW **Series:** 1984 Winter Olympics **Subject:** Speed skating

| Date | Mintage | F | VF | XF | Unc | BU |
|---|---|---|---|---|---|---|
| 1984 Proof | 110,000 | Value: 10.00 | | | | |

**100 DINARA** KM# 106 **Weight:** 13.0000 g. **Composition:** 0.9250 Silver .3867 oz. ASW **Series:** 1984 Winter Olympics **Subject:** Pairs figure skating

| Date | Mintage | F | VF | XF | Unc | BU |
|---|---|---|---|---|---|---|
| 1984 Proof | 110,000 | Value: 10.00 | | | | |

**100 DINARA** KM# 114 **Composition:** Copper-Zinc-Nickel

| Date | Mintage | F | VF | XF | Unc | BU |
|---|---|---|---|---|---|---|
| 1985 | 18,684,000 | — | 0.25 | 0.65 | 1.50 | — |
| 1986 | 17,905,000 | — | 0.20 | 0.50 | 1.00 | — |
| 1987 | 94,069,000 | — | — | 0.40 | 0.80 | — |
| 1988 | 50,294,000 | — | — | 0.40 | 0.80 | — |

**100 DINARA** KM# 115 **Composition:** Copper-Nickel-Zinc **Subject:** 40th anniversary - liberation from fascism

| Date | Mintage | F | VF | XF | Unc | BU |
|---|---|---|---|---|---|---|
| ND(1985) Proof | 200,000 | Value: 4.00 | | | | |

**100 DINARA** KM# 127.1 **Composition:** Copper-Nickel **Subject:** 200th anniversary - birth of Karajich

| Date | Mintage | F | VF | XF | Unc | BU |
|---|---|---|---|---|---|---|
| 1987 Proof | Est. 200,000 | Value: 4.00 | | | | |

**100 DINARA** KM# 127.2 **Composition:** Copper-Nickel **Subject:** 200th anniversary - birth of Karajich

| Date | Mintage | F | VF | XF | Unc | BU |
|---|---|---|---|---|---|---|
| 1987 Proof | Inc. above | Value: 25.00 | | | | |

**100 DINARA** KM# 134 **Composition:** Brass

| Date | Mintage | F | VF | XF | Unc | BU |
|---|---|---|---|---|---|---|
| 1988 | 12,610,000 | — | — | 0.15 | 0.30 | — |
| 1989 | 124,260,000 | — | — | 0.15 | 0.30 | — |

**100 DINARA** KM# 146 **Weight:** 13.0000 g. **Composition:** 0.9250 Silver .3867 oz. ASW **Subject:** 1990 Chess Olympiad **Reverse:** Petrovaradin clock tower

| Date | Mintage | F | VF | XF | Unc | BU |
|---|---|---|---|---|---|---|
| 1990 Proof | 10,000 | Value: 27.50 | | | | |

**150 DINARA** KM# 66 **Weight:** 12.5000 g. **Composition:** 0.9250 Silver .3717 oz. ASW **Subject:** 8th Mediterranean Games at Split

| Date | Mintage | F | VF | XF | Unc | BU |
|---|---|---|---|---|---|---|
| 1978 Proof | 70,000 | Value: 22.50 | | | | |

**150 DINARA** KM# 147 **Weight:** 17.0000 g. **Composition:** 0.9250 Silver .5056 oz. ASW **Subject:** 1990 Chess Olympiad **Reverse:** Globe

| Date | Mintage | F | VF | XF | Unc | BU |
|---|---|---|---|---|---|---|
| 1990 Proof | 10,000 | Value: 37.50 | | | | |

**200 DINARA** KM# 52 **Weight:** 15.6400 g. **Composition:** 0.9000 Gold .4526 oz. AGW **Subject:** 25th anniversary of republic

| Date | Mintage | F | VF | XF | Unc | BU |
|---|---|---|---|---|---|---|
| ND(1968) Proof | 10,000 | Value: 225 | | | | |
| ND(1968) NI Proof | Inc. above | Value: 225 | | | | |

**200 DINARA** **KM# 64** **Weight:** 15.0000 g. **Composition:** 0.7500 Silver .3617 oz. ASW **Subject:** Tito's 85th birthday

| Date | Mintage | F | VF | XF | Unc | BU |
|---|---|---|---|---|---|---|
| 1977 Proof | 500,000 | Value: 12.50 | | | | |

**200 DINARA** **KM# 64a** **Weight:** 15.0000 g. **Composition:** 0.7500 Silver .2701 oz. ASW **Subject:** Tito's 85th birthday **Note:** Edge varieties with inscription in cyrillic and western exist.

| Date | Mintage | F | VF | XF | Unc | BU |
|---|---|---|---|---|---|---|
| 1977 | 300,000 | — | — | — | 7.50 | — |

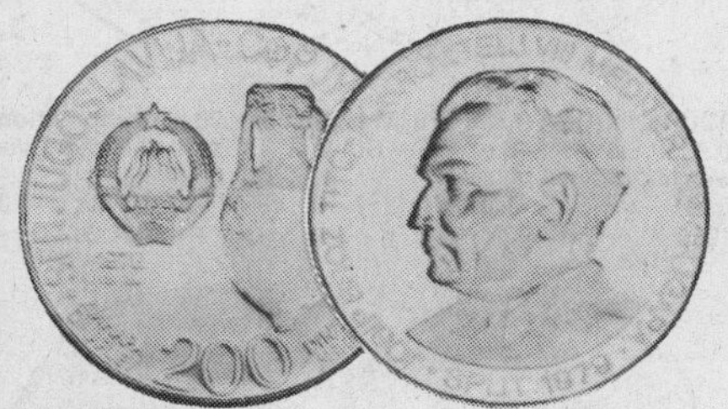

**200 DINARA** **KM# 67** **Weight:** 15.0000 g. **Composition:** .9250 Silver .4461 oz. ASW **Subject:** 8th Mediterranean Games at Split

| Date | Mintage | F | VF | XF | Unc | BU |
|---|---|---|---|---|---|---|
| 1978 Proof | 58,000 | Value: 25.00 | | | | |

**250 DINARA** **KM# 68** **Weight:** 17.5000 g. **Composition:** .9250 Silver .5204 oz. ASW **Subject:** 8th Mediterranean Games at Split

| Date | Mintage | F | VF | XF | Unc | BU |
|---|---|---|---|---|---|---|
| 1978 Proof | 48,000 | Value: 30.00 | | | | |

**ʼ50 DINARA** **KM# 91** **Weight:** 17.0000 g. **Composition:** .9250 Silver .5056 oz. ASW **Series:** 1984 Winter Olympics **Reverse:** Sarajevo view

| Date | Mintage | F | VF | XF | Unc | BU |
|---|---|---|---|---|---|---|
| 1982 Proof | 110,000 | Value: 11.50 | | | | |

**50 DINARA** **KM# 100** **Weight:** 17.0000 g. **Composition:** .9250 Silver .5056 oz. ASW **Series:** 1984 Winter Olympics **Reverse:** Artifact

| Date | Mintage | F | VF | XF | Unc | BU |
|---|---|---|---|---|---|---|
| 1983 Proof | 110,000 | Value: 11.50 | | | | |

**250 DINARA** **KM# 101** **Weight:** 17.0000 g. **Composition:** 0.9250 Silver .5056 oz. ASW **Series:** 1984 Winter Olympics **Reverse:** Radimlja tombs

| Date | Mintage | F | VF | XF | Unc | BU |
|---|---|---|---|---|---|---|
| 1983 Proof | 110,000 | Value: 11.50 | | | | |

**250 DINARA** **KM# 107** **Weight:** 17.0000 g. **Composition:** 0.9250 Silver .5056 oz. ASW **Series:** 1984 Winter Olympics **Reverse:** Jajce village

| Date | Mintage | F | VF | XF | Unc | BU |
|---|---|---|---|---|---|---|
| 1984 Proof | 110,000 | Value: 11.50 | | | | |

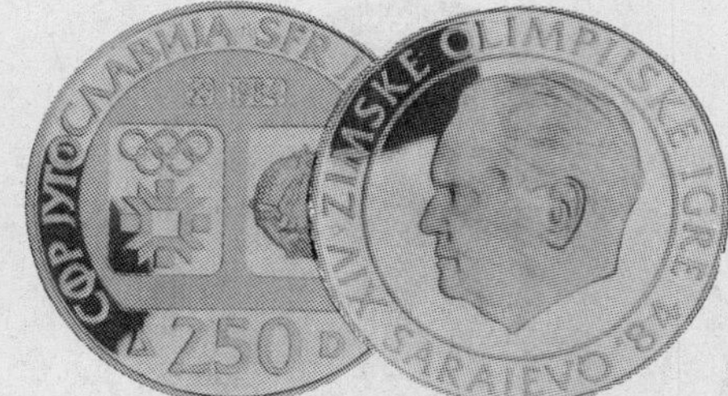

**250 DINARA** **KM# 108** **Weight:** 17.0000 g. **Composition:** 0.9250 Silver .5056 oz. ASW **Series:** 1984 Winter Olympics **Reverse:** Tito

| Date | Mintage | F | VF | XF | Unc | BU |
|---|---|---|---|---|---|---|
| 1984 Proof | 110,000 | Value: 11.50 | | | | |

**300 DINARA** **KM# 69** **Weight:** 20.0000 g. **Composition:** 0.9250 Silver .5948 oz. ASW **Subject:** Eighth Mediterranean Games at Split

| Date | Mintage | F | VF | XF | Unc | BU |
|---|---|---|---|---|---|---|
| 1978 Proof | 36,000 | Value: 35.00 | | | | |

**350 DINARA** **KM# 70** **Weight:** 22.5000 g. **Composition:** 0.9250 Silver .6692 oz. ASW **Subject:** 8th Mediterranean Games at Split

| Date | Mintage | F | VF | XF | Unc | BU |
|---|---|---|---|---|---|---|
| 1978 Proof | 24,000 | Value: 37.50 | | | | |

**400 DINARA** **KM# 71** **Weight:** 25.0000 g. **Composition:** 0.9250 Silver .7435 oz. ASW **Subject:** 8th Mediterranean Games at Split

| Date | Mintage | F | VF | XF | Unc | BU |
|---|---|---|---|---|---|---|
| 1978 Proof | 24,000 | Value: 40.00 | | | | |

**500 DINARA** **KM# 53** **Weight:** 39.1000 g. **Composition:** 0.9000 Gold 1.1315 oz. AGW **Subject:** 25th Anniversary of Republic

| Date | Mintage | F | VF | XF | Unc | BU |
|---|---|---|---|---|---|---|
| ND(1968) Proof | 10,000 | Value: 550 | | | | |
| ND(1968) NI Proof | Inc. above | Value: 550 | | | | |

**500 DINARA** **KM# 76** **Weight:** 8.0000 g. **Composition:** 0.9250 Silver .2379 oz. ASW **Subject:** Vukovar Congress

| Date | Mintage | F | VF | XF | Unc | BU |
|---|---|---|---|---|---|---|
| 1980 Proof | 18,000 | Value: 20.00 | | | | |

**500 DINARA** **KM# 80** **Weight:** 8.0000 g. **Composition:** 0.7500 Silver .1865 oz. ASW **Subject:** World Table Tennis Championship Games

| Date | Mintage | F | VF | XF | Unc | BU |
|---|---|---|---|---|---|---|
| 1981 Proof | 18,000 | Value: 25.00 | | | | |

**500 DINARA** **KM# 92** **Weight:** 23.0000 g. **Composition:** 0.9250 Silver .6841 oz. ASW **Series:** 1984 Winter Olympics **Subject:** Downhill skiing

| Date | Mintage | F | VF | XF | Unc | BU |
|---|---|---|---|---|---|---|
| 1982 Proof | 110,000 | Value: 13.50 | | | | |

**500 DINARA** **KM# 102** **Weight:** 23.0000 g. **Composition:** 0.9250 Silver .6841 oz. ASW **Series:** 1984 Winter Olympics **Subject:** Ski jumping

| Date | Mintage | F | VF | XF | Unc | BU |
|---|---|---|---|---|---|---|
| 1983 Proof | 110,000 | Value: 13.50 | | | | |

**500 DINARA** **KM# 103** **Weight:** 23.0000 g. **Composition:** 0.9250 Silver .6841 oz. ASW **Series:** 1984 Winter Olympics **Subject:** Biathalon

| Date | Mintage | F | VF | XF | Unc | BU |
|---|---|---|---|---|---|---|
| 1983 Proof | 110,000 | Value: 13.50 | | | | |

**500 DINARA** **KM# 109** **Weight:** 23.0000 g. **Composition:** 0.9250 Silver .6841 oz. ASW **Series:** 1984 Winter Olympics **Subject:** Cross country skiing

| Date | Mintage | F | VF | XF | Unc | BU |
|---|---|---|---|---|---|---|
| 1984 Proof | 110,000 | Value: 13.50 | | | | |

**500 DINARA** **KM# 110** **Weight:** 23.0000 g. **Composition:** 0.9250 Silver .6841 oz. ASW **Series:** 1984 Winter Olympics **Subject:** Slalom skiing

| Date | Mintage | F | VF | XF | Unc | BU |
|---|---|---|---|---|---|---|
| 1984 Proof | 110,000 | Value: 13.50 | | | | |

**500 DINARA** **KM# 116** **Weight:** 13.0000 g. **Composition:** 0.9250 Silver .3867 oz. ASW **Subject:** Ski Jumping Championship **Obverse:** Similar to 10,000 Dinara, KM#123 **Reverse:** Herons

| Date | Mintage | F | VF | XF | Unc | BU |
|---|---|---|---|---|---|---|
| 1985 Proof | 50,000 | Value: 15.00 | | | | |

**1000 DINARA** **KM# 54** **Weight:** 78.2000 g. **Composition:** 0.9000 Gold 2.2630 oz. AGW **Subject:** 25th Anniversary of Republic

| Date | Mintage | F | VF | XF | Unc | BU |
|---|---|---|---|---|---|---|
| ND(1968) Proof | 10,000 | Value: 1,150 | | | | |
| ND(1968) NI Proof | Inc. above | Value: 1,150 | | | | |

**1000 DINARA** **KM# 77** **Weight:** 14.0000 g. **Composition:** 0.9250 Silver .4164 oz. ASW **Subject:** Vukovar Congress

| Date | Mintage | F | VF | XF | Unc | BU |
|---|---|---|---|---|---|---|
| 1980 Proof | 16,000 | Value: 27.50 | | | | |

**1000 DINARA** **KM# 78a** **Weight:** 26.0000 g. **Composition:** 0.9250 Silver .7733 oz. ASW **Subject:** Tito's death

| Date | Mintage | F | VF | XF | Unc | BU |
|---|---|---|---|---|---|---|
| 1980 Proof | 200,000 | Value: 32.50 | | | | |
| 1980 ZM Proof | Inc. above | Value: 32.50 | | | | |

**1000 DINARA** **KM# 78** **Weight:** 25.9000 g. **Composition:** 0.7500 Silver .6245 oz. ASW **Subject:** Tito's death **Note:** Eyes with and without pupils.

| Date | Mintage | F | VF | XF | Unc | BU |
|---|---|---|---|---|---|---|
| 1980 | 800,000 | — | — | — | 30.00 | — |

**1000 DINARA** **KM# 81** **Weight:** 14.0000 g. **Composition:** 0.7500 Silver .4164 oz. ASW **Subject:** World Table Tennis Championship Games

| Date | Mintage | F | VF | XF | Unc | BU |
|---|---|---|---|---|---|---|
| 1981 Proof | 16,000 | Value: 27.50 | | | | |

**1000 DINARA** **KM# 82** **Weight:** 14.0000 g. **Composition:** 0.7500 Silver .4164 oz. ASW **Subject:** 40th Anniversary of Uprising and Revolution

| Date | Mintage | F | VF | XF | Unc | BU |
|---|---|---|---|---|---|---|
| 1981 Proof | 100,000 | Value: 22.00 | | | | |

**1000 DINARA** **KM# 93** **Weight:** 18.0000 g. **Composition:** 0.9250 Silver .5354 oz. ASW **Subject:** International Canoeing Championships **Reverse:** City view

| Date | Mintage | F | VF | XF | Unc | BU |
|---|---|---|---|---|---|---|
| 1982 Proof | 46,000 | Value: 30.00 | | | | |

**1000 DINARA** **KM# 117** **Weight:** 23.0000 g. **Composition:** 0.9250 Silver .6841 oz. ASW **Subject:** Ski Jumping Championship **Obverse:** Similar to 10,000 Dinara, KM#123 **Reverse:** Bloudek

| Date | Mintage | F | VF | XF | Unc | BU |
|---|---|---|---|---|---|---|
| 1985 Proof | 20,000 | Value: 30.00 | | | | |

**1000 DINARA** **KM# 118** **Weight:** 23.0000 g. **Composition:** 0.9250 Silver .6841 oz. ASW **Subject:** Ski Jumping Championship **Obverse:** Similar to 10,000 Dinara, KM#123 **Reverse:** Slovenian cradle

| Date | Mintage | F | VF | XF | Unc | BU |
|---|---|---|---|---|---|---|
| 1985 Proof | 20,000 | Value: 30.00 | | | | |

**1000 DINARA** **KM# 119** **Weight:** 6.0000 g. **Composition:** 0.9250 Silver .1784 oz. ASW **Subject:** Sinjska Alka

| Date | Mintage | F | VF | XF | Unc | BU |
|---|---|---|---|---|---|---|
| ND(1985) Proof | 60,000 | Value: 15.00 | | | | |

**1000 DINARA** **KM# 148** **Weight:** 3.5000 g. **Composition:** 0.9000 Gold .1013 oz. AGW **Subject:** 1990 Chess Olympiad **Reverse:** Logo

| Date | Mintage | F | VF | XF | Unc | BU |
|---|---|---|---|---|---|---|
| 1990 Proof | 2,000 | Value: 175 | | | | |

**1500 DINARA** **KM# 72** **Weight:** 8.8000 g. **Composition:** 0.9000 Gold .2546 oz. AGW **Subject:** 8th Mediterranean Games at Split

| Date | Mintage | F | VF | XF | Unc | BU |
|---|---|---|---|---|---|---|
| 1978 Proof | 35,000 | Value: 175 | | | | |

**1500 DINARA** **KM# 79** **Weight:** 22.0000 g. **Composition:** 0.9250 Silver .6542 oz. ASW **Subject:** Vukovar Congress

| Date | Mintage | F | VF | XF | Unc | BU |
|---|---|---|---|---|---|---|
| 1980 Proof | 16,000 | Value: 35.00 | | | | |

**1500 DINARA** **KM# 83** **Weight:** 22.0000 g. **Composition:** 0.7500 Silver .5329 oz. ASW **Subject:** World Table Tennis Championship Games

| Date | Mintage | F | VF | XF | Unc | BU |
|---|---|---|---|---|---|---|
| 1981 Proof | 16,000 | Value: 35.00 | | | | |

**1500 DINARA** **KM# 94** **Weight:** 22.0000 g. **Composition:** 0.9250 Silver .6542 oz. ASW **Subject:** International Canoeing Championships **Reverse:** Tito

| Date | Mintage | F | VF | XF | Unc | BU |
|---|---|---|---|---|---|---|
| 1982 Proof | 36,000 | Value: 32.50 | | | | |

**2000 DINARA** **KM# 73** **Weight:** 11.8000 g. **Composition:** 0.9000 Gold .3414 oz. AGW **Subject:** 8th Mediterranean Games at Split

| Date | Mintage | F | VF | XF | Unc | BU |
|---|---|---|---|---|---|---|
| 1978 Proof | 35,000 | Value: 225 | | | | |

**2000 DINARA** **KM# 120** **Weight:** 14.0000 g. **Composition:** 0.9250 Silver .4164 oz. ASW **Subject:** Sinska Alka

| Date | Mintage | F | VF | XF | Unc | BU |
|---|---|---|---|---|---|---|
| ND(1985) Proof | 20,000 | Value: 22.50 | | | | |

**2500 DINARA** **KM# 74** **Weight:** 14.7000 g. **Composition:** 0.9000 Gold .4254 oz. AGW **Subject:** 8th Mediterranean Games at Split

| Date | Mintage | F | VF | XF | Unc | BU |
|---|---|---|---|---|---|---|
| 1978 Proof | 35,000 | Value: 275 | | | | |

**3000 DINARA** **KM# 121** **Weight:** 26.0000 g. **Composition:** 0.9250 Silver .7733 oz. ASW **Subject:** Sinkska Alka

| Date | Mintage | F | VF | XF | Unc | BU |
|---|---|---|---|---|---|---|
| ND(1985) Proof | 20,000 | Value: 35.00 | | | | |

**3000 DINARA** **KM# 128** **Weight:** 13.0000 g. **Composition:** 0.9250 Silver .3867 oz. ASW **Subject:** 200th Anniversary - Birth of Krajich **Reverse:** Similar to 100 Dinara, KM#127

| Date | Mintage | F | VF | XF | Unc | BU |
|---|---|---|---|---|---|---|
| 1987 Proof | — | Value: 30.00 | | | | |

**5000 DINARA** **KM# 75** **Weight:** 29.5000 g. **Composition:** 0.9000 Gold .8536 oz. AGW **Subject:** 8th Mediterranean Games at Split

| Date | Mintage | F | VF | XF | Unc | BU |
|---|---|---|---|---|---|---|
| 1978 Proof | 12,000 | Value: 450 | | | | |

**5000 DINARA** **KM# 95** **Weight:** 8.0000 g. **Composition:** 0.9000 Gold .2315 oz. AGW **Series:** 1984 Winter Olympics **Reverse:** Emblem

| Date | Mintage | F | VF | XF | Unc | BU |
|---|---|---|---|---|---|---|
| 1982 Proof | 55,000 | Value: 120 | | | | |

**5000 DINARA** **KM# 104** **Weight:** 8.0000 g. **Composition:** 0.9000 Gold .2315 oz. AGW **Series:** 1984 Winter Olympics **Reverse:** Tito

| Date | Mintage | F | VF | XF | Unc | BU |
|---|---|---|---|---|---|---|
| 1983 Proof | 55,000 | Value: 120 | | | | |

**5000 DINARA** **KM# 111** **Weight:** 8.0000 g. **Composition:** 0.9000 Gold .2315 oz. AGW **Series:** 1984 Winter Olympics **Reverse:** Flame

| Date | Mintage | F | VF | XF | Unc | BU |
|---|---|---|---|---|---|---|
| 1984 Proof | 55,000 | Value: 120 | | | | |

**5000 DINARA** **KM# 122** **Weight:** 23.5000 g. **Composition:** 0.9250 Silver .6989 oz. ASW **Subject:** 400th Anniversary - Liberation from Fascism **Note:** Similar to 100 Dinara, KM#115.

| Date | Mintage | F | VF | XF | Unc | BU |
|---|---|---|---|---|---|---|
| 1985 Proof | 100,000 | Value: 40.00 | | | | |

**5000 DINARA** **KM# 129** **Weight:** 17.0000 g. **Composition:** 0.9250 Silver .5056 oz. ASW **Subject:** 200th Anniversary - Birth of Karajich

| Date | Mintage | F | VF | XF | Unc | BU |
|---|---|---|---|---|---|---|
| 1987 Proof | Est. 50,000 | Value: 35.00 | | | | |

**5000 DINARA** **KM# 135** **Composition:** Copper-Zinc-Nickel **Subject:** Non-aligned Summit **Reverse:** Symbol

| Date | Mintage | F | VF | XF | Unc | BU |
|---|---|---|---|---|---|---|
| ND(1989) Proof | 50,000 | Value: 4.50 | | | | |

**10000 DINARA** **KM# 123** **Weight:** 8.0000 g. **Composition:** 0.9000 Gold .2315 oz. AGW **Subject:** World Ski Jumping Championship

| Date | Mintage | F | VF | XF | Unc | BU |
|---|---|---|---|---|---|---|
| 1985 Proof | 10,000 | Value: 165 | | | | |

**10000 DINARA** **KM# 124** **Weight:** 5.0000 g. **Composition:** 0.9000 Gold .1447 oz. AGW **Subject:** Sinjska Alka

| Date | Mintage | F | VF | XF | Unc | BU |
|---|---|---|---|---|---|---|
| ND(1985) Proof | 12,000 | Value: 150 | | | | |

**20000 DINARA** **KM# 125** **Weight:** 8.0000 g. **Composition:** 0.9000 Gold .2315 oz. AGW **Subject:** Sinjska Alka

| Date | Mintage | F | VF | XF | Unc | BU |
|---|---|---|---|---|---|---|
| ND(1985) Proof | 8,000 | Value: 250 | | | | |

**40000 DINARA** **KM# 126** **Weight:** 14.0000 g. **Composition:** 0.9000 Gold .4083 oz. AGW **Subject:** Sinjska Alka

| Date | Mintage | F | VF | XF | Unc | BU |
|---|---|---|---|---|---|---|
| ND(1985) Proof | 5,000 | Value: 475 | | | | |

**50000 DINARA** **KM# 130** **Weight:** 8.0000 g. **Composition:** 0.9000 Gold .2315 oz. AGW **Subject:** 200th Anniversary - Birth of Karajich **Note:** Similar to 5,000 Dinar, KM#129.

| Date | Mintage | F | VF | XF | Unc | BU |
|---|---|---|---|---|---|---|
| 1987 Proof | Est. 10,000 | Value: 175 | | | | |

**50000 DINARA** **KM# 136** **Weight:** 13.0000 g. **Composition:** 0.9250 Silver .3867 oz. ASW **Subject:** Non-aligned Summit **Reverse:** Standing figure

| Date | Mintage | F | VF | XF | Unc | BU |
|---|---|---|---|---|---|---|
| ND(1989) Proof | 15,000 | Value: 25.00 | | | | |

**100000 DINARA** **KM# 137** **Weight:** 17.0000 g. **Composition:** 0.9250 Silver .5056 oz. ASW **Subject:** Non-aligned Summit **Reverse:** Building

| Date | Mintage | F | VF | XF | Unc | BU |
|---|---|---|---|---|---|---|
| ND(1989) Proof | 10,000 | Value: 35.00 | | | | |

**2000000 DINARA** **KM# 138** **Weight:** 8.0000 g. **Composition:** 0.9000 Gold .2315 oz. AGW **Subject:** Non-aligned Summit **Reverse:** Symbol

| Date | Mintage | F | VF | XF | Unc | BU |
|---|---|---|---|---|---|---|
| ND(1989) Proof | 5,000 | Value: 240 | | | | |

# FEDERAL REPUBLIC

## STANDARD COINAGE

**PARA** **KM# 161** **Composition:** Brass

| Date | Mintage | F | VF | XF | Unc | BU |
|---|---|---|---|---|---|---|
| 1994 | 25,350,000 | — | — | — | 0.35 | — |

**5 PARA** **KM# 164.1** **Composition:** Brass

| Date | Mintage | F | VF | XF | Unc | BU |
|---|---|---|---|---|---|---|
| 1994 | 30,408,000 | — | — | — | 0.50 | — |
| 1995 | 3,400,000 | — | — | — | 0.60 | — |

**5 PARA** **KM# 164.2** **Composition:** Brass **Size:** 17 mm. **Note:** Reduced size.

| Date | Mintage | F | VF | XF | Unc | BU |
|---|---|---|---|---|---|---|
| 1996 | — | — | — | — | 0.50 | — |

**10 PARA** **KM# 162.1** **Composition:** Copper-Nickel-Zinc

| Date | Mintage | F | VF | XF | Unc | BU |
|---|---|---|---|---|---|---|
| 1994 | 52,161,000 | — | — | — | 0.50 | — |

**10 PARA** **KM# 162.1a** **Composition:** Brass

| Date | Mintage | F | VF | XF | Unc | BU |
|---|---|---|---|---|---|---|
| 1995 | 31,041,000 | — | — | — | 0.75 | — |

**10 PARA** **KM# 173** **Composition:** Brass **Obverse:** Heraldic double eagle shield **Reverse:** Denomination

| Date | Mintage | F | VF | XF | Unc | BU |
|---|---|---|---|---|---|---|
| 1996 | — | — | — | — | 0.50 | — |
| 1997 | — | — | — | — | 0.50 | — |
| 1998 | — | — | — | — | 0.50 | — |

**10 PARA** **KM# 162.2** **Composition:** Brass **Note:** Reduced size.

| Date | Mintage | F | VF | XF | Unc | BU |
|---|---|---|---|---|---|---|
| 1996 | — | — | — | — | 0.65 | — |

**50 PARA** **KM# 163** **Composition:** Copper-Nickel-Zinc

| Date | Mintage | F | VF | XF | Unc | BU |
|---|---|---|---|---|---|---|
| 1994 | 45,013,000 | — | — | — | 0.75 | — |

**50 PARA** **KM# 163a** **Composition:** Brass

| Date | Mintage | F | VF | XF | Unc | BU |
|---|---|---|---|---|---|---|
| 1995 | 19,193,000 | — | — | — | 1.00 | — |

**50 PARA** KM# 174 **Composition:** Brass **Obverse:** Heraldic double eagle shield

| Date | Mintage | F | VF | XF | Unc | BU |
|---|---|---|---|---|---|---|
| 1996 | — | — | — | — | 1.00 | — |
| 1997 | — | — | — | — | 1.00 | — |
| 1998 | — | — | — | — | 1.00 | — |
| 1999 | — | — | — | — | 1.00 | — |

**50 PARA** KM# 179 **Weight:** 3.3000 g. **Composition:** Brass **Obverse:** Female portrait **Reverse:** National arms above denomination **Edge:** Plain **Size:** 18 mm.

| Date | Mintage | F | VF | XF | Unc | BU |
|---|---|---|---|---|---|---|
| 2000 | — | — | — | — | 0.25 | — |

**DINAR** KM# 149 **Composition:** Copper-Zinc

| Date | Mintage | F | VF | XF | Unc | BU |
|---|---|---|---|---|---|---|
| 1992 | 49,269,000 | — | 0.10 | 0.30 | 0.60 | — |

**DINAR** KM# 154 **Composition:** Copper-Zinc-Nickel

| Date | Mintage | F | VF | XF | Unc | BU |
|---|---|---|---|---|---|---|
| 1993 | 20,249,000 | — | 0.10 | 0.20 | 0.50 | — |

**DINAR** KM# 160 **Composition:** Brass

| Date | Mintage | F | VF | XF | Unc | BU |
|---|---|---|---|---|---|---|
| 1994 | — | — | — | — | 1.00 | — |

**DINAR** KM# 180 **Weight:** 4.4000 g. **Composition:** Copper-Zinc-Nickel **Obverse:** National arms **Reverse:** Large building and denomination **Edge:** Reeded **Size:** 20 mm.

| Date | Mintage | F | VF | XF | Unc | BU |
|---|---|---|---|---|---|---|
| 2000 | — | — | — | — | 0.25 | — |

**NOVI DINAR** KM# 165 **Composition:** Copper-Nickel-Zinc

| Date | Mintage | F | VF | XF | Unc | BU |
|---|---|---|---|---|---|---|
| 1994 | 47,755,000 | — | — | — | 1.00 | — |
| 1995 | 10,359,000 | — | — | — | 1.25 | — |

**NOVI DINAR** KM# 168 **Composition:** Copper-Nickel-Zinc **Note:** Reduced size.

| Date | Mintage | F | VF | XF | Unc | BU |
|---|---|---|---|---|---|---|
| 1996 | — | — | — | — | 1.00 | — |
| 1999 | — | — | — | — | 1.00 | — |

**2 DINARA** KM# 150 **Composition:** Copper-Zinc

| Date | Mintage | F | VF | XF | Unc | BU |
|---|---|---|---|---|---|---|
| 1992 | 10,571,000 | — | 0.20 | 0.40 | 1.00 | — |

**2 DINARA** KM# 155 **Composition:** Copper-Zinc-Nickel

| Date | Mintage | F | VF | XF | Unc | BU |
|---|---|---|---|---|---|---|
| 1993 | 10,263,000 | — | 0.10 | 0.20 | 0.50 | — |

**2 DINARA** KM# 181 **Weight:** 5.2000 g. **Composition:** Copper-Nickel-Zinc **Obverse:** National arms **Reverse:** Church and denomination **Edge:** Reeded **Size:** 21.9 mm.

| Date | Mintage | F | VF | XF | Unc | BU |
|---|---|---|---|---|---|---|
| 2000 | — | — | — | — | 0.25 | — |

**5 DINARA** KM# 151 **Composition:** Copper-Zinc

| Date | Mintage | F | VF | XF | Unc | BU |
|---|---|---|---|---|---|---|
| 1992 | 26,658,000 | — | 0.15 | 0.30 | 0.75 | — |

**5 DINARA** KM# 156 **Composition:** Copper-Zinc-Nickel

| Date | Mintage | F | VF | XF | Unc | BU |
|---|---|---|---|---|---|---|
| 1993 | 10,135,000 | — | 0.10 | 0.20 | 0.50 | — |

**5 DINARA** KM# 182 **Weight:** 6.3000 g. **Composition:** Copper-Nickel-Zinc **Obverse:** National arms **Reverse:** Domed building and denomination **Edge:** Reeded **Size:** 24 mm.

| Date | Mintage | F | VF | XF | Unc | BU |
|---|---|---|---|---|---|---|
| 2000 | — | — | — | — | 1.25 | — |

**10 DINARA** KM# 152 **Composition:** Copper-Zinc-Nickel

| Date | Mintage | F | VF | XF | Unc | BU |
|---|---|---|---|---|---|---|
| 1992 | 76,607,000 | — | 0.10 | 0.25 | 0.60 | — |

**10 DINARA** KM# 157 **Composition:** Copper-Zinc-Nickel

| Date | Mintage | F | VF | XF | Unc | BU |
|---|---|---|---|---|---|---|
| 1993 | — | — | 0.15 | 0.30 | 0.70 | — |

**20 NOVI DINARA** KM# 169 **Composition:** Copper-Zinc-Nickel **Subject:** Nikola Tesla

| Date | Mintage | F | VF | XF | Unc | BU |
|---|---|---|---|---|---|---|
| 1996 Proof | Est. 10,000 | Value: 12.50 | | | | |

**50 DINARA** KM# 153 **Composition:** Copper-Zinc-Nickel

| Date | Mintage | F | VF | XF | Unc | BU |
|---|---|---|---|---|---|---|
| 1992 | 50,571,000 | — | 0.25 | 0.50 | 1.00 | — |

**50 DINARA** KM# 158 **Composition:** Copper-Zinc-Nickel

| Date | Mintage | F | VF | XF | Unc | BU |
|---|---|---|---|---|---|---|
| 1993 | — | — | 0.20 | 0.40 | 0.80 | — |

**100 DINARA** KM# 159 **Composition:** Brass

| Date | Mintage | F | VF | XF | Unc | BU |
|---|---|---|---|---|---|---|
| 1993 | — | — | 0.25 | 0.50 | 1.00 | — |

**150 NOVI DINARA** KM# 166 **Weight:** 7.8000 g. **Composition:** 0.9000 Gold .2257 oz. AGW **Subject:** 110th Anniversary - National Bank

| Date | Mintage | F | VF | XF | Unc | BU |
|---|---|---|---|---|---|---|
| ND(1995) Proof | 100,000 | Value: 175 | | | | |

**200 NOVI DINARA** KM# 170 **Weight:** 13.0000 g. **Composition:** 0.9250 Silver .3867 oz. ASW **Subject:** Nikola Tesla **Note:** Similar to 20 Novi Dinara, KM#169.

| Date | Mintage | F | VF | XF | Unc | BU |
|---|---|---|---|---|---|---|
| 1996 Proof | Est. 10,000 | Value: 32.00 | | | | |

**300 NOVI DINARA** KM# 171 **Weight:** 26.0000 g. **Composition:** 0.9250 Silver .7734 oz. ASW **Subject:** Nikola Tesla **Note:** Similar to 20 Novi Dinara, KM#169.

| Date | Mintage | F | VF | XF | Unc | BU |
|---|---|---|---|---|---|---|
| 1996 Proof | Est. 10,000 | Value: 45.00 | | | | |

**500 DINARA** KM# 167 **Composition:** Brass **Note:** All but 1,000 reported melted. Not released for circulation.

| Date | Mintage | F | VF | XF | Unc | BU |
|---|---|---|---|---|---|---|
| 1993 | — | — | — | — | 6.50 | — |

**600 NOVI DINARA** KM# 175 **Weight:** 3.4550 g. **Composition:** 0.9000 Gold .1 oz. AGW **Subject:** Chilander Monastery **Reverse:** Portraits of SS Simon and Sava

| Date | Mintage | VG | F | VF | XF | Unc |
|---|---|---|---|---|---|---|
| 1998(1999) | 10,000 | — | — | — | — | 125 |

**1000 NOVI DINARA** KM# 172 **Weight:** 8.6400 g. **Composition:** 0.9000 Gold .25 oz. AGW **Subject:** Nikola Tesla **Note:** Similar to 20 Novi Dinara, KM#169.

| Date | Mintage | F | VF | XF | Unc | BU |
|---|---|---|---|---|---|---|
| 1996 Proof | Est. 5,000 | Value: 250 | | | | |

**1500 NOVI DINARA** KM# 176 **Weight:** 8.6400 g. **Composition:** 0.9000 Gold .2500 oz. AGW **Subject:** Chilander Monastery **Reverse:** Portraits of SS Simon and Sava

| Date | Mintage | F | VF | XF | Unc | BU |
|---|---|---|---|---|---|---|
| 1998(1999) | Est. 5,000 | — | — | — | 175 | — |

**3000 NOVI DINARA** KM# 177 **Weight:** 17.2770 g. **Composition:** 0.9000 Gold .4999 oz. AGW **Subject:** Chilander Monastery **Reverse:** Portraits of SS Simon and Sava

| Date | Mintage | F | VF | XF | Unc | BU |
|---|---|---|---|---|---|---|
| 1998(1999) | Est. 500 | — | — | — | 400 | — |

## PATTERNS

Including off metal strikes

Patterns Pn1-Pn8 previously listed here are now listed under Serbia.

| KM# | Date | Mintage | Identification | Mkt Val |
|---|---|---|---|---|
| Pn14 | 1925(a) | — | 10 Dinara. Gold. | — |
| Pn10 | 1925 | — | Dinar. Nickel. KM5. By Pattey. | 400 |
| Pn9 | 1925 | — | 50 Para. Nickel. KM4. By Pattey. | 700 |
| Pn12a | 1925 | — | 2 Dinara. Copper-Nickel. KM6. ESSAI. 3 millimeters thick. | 1,000 |
| Pn12 | 1925 | — | 2 Dinara. Nickel-Bronze. KM6. ESSAI. | 1,000 |
| Pn9a | 1925 | — | 50 Para. Silver. KM4. By Pattey. | 500 |
| Pn10a | 1925 | — | Dinar. Copper. KM5. By Pattey. | 400 |
| PnA11 | 1925 | — | Dinar. Aluminum. By Pattey. | 400 |
| Pn13 | 1925 | — | 2 Dinara. Nickel. KM6. | 600 |
| Pn11 | 1925 | — | Dinar. Nickel. KM5. | 400 |
| Pn15 | 1926(k) | — | Dukat. Gold. | — |
| Pn16 | 1926 | — | 4 Dukata. Silver. River scene. | — |
| Pn17 | 1926(k) | — | 4 Dukata. Gold. River scene. | — |
| Pn19 | 1931 | — | 4 Dukata. Gold. ESSAI. | — |
| Pn20 | ND | — | 4 Dukata. Silver. | — |
| Pn21 | 1932 | — | 50 Dinara. Bronze. Milled edge. | 400 |
| Pn21a | 1932 | — | 50 Dinara. Copper. | 400 |
| Pn22 | 1938 | — | 10 Dinara. Copper. | 200 |
| Pn23 | 1938 | — | 20 Dinara. Copper. | 250 |
| Pn24 | 1938 | — | 50 Dinara. Copper. | 300 |
| Pn25 | 1953 | — | 25 Para. Aluminum. Hole in center. | 400 |
| Pn26 | 1978 | 20 | 25 Para. Aluminum. | — |
| Pn27 | 1978 | 19 | Dinar. Copper-Nickel. | — |
| Pn28 | 1978 | 15 | 10 Dinara. Copper-Nickel. | — |

## PIEFORTS

| KM# | Date | Mintage | Identification | Mkt Val |
|---|---|---|---|---|
| P1 | ND(1931-1934) | — | 4 Dukata. Gold. 46.4500 g. Conjoined busts. | — |

## TRIAL STRIKES

| KM# | Date | Mintage | Identification | Mkt Val |
|---|---|---|---|---|
| TS1 | 1931(a) | — | Dukat. Gold. Uniface. ESSAI Paris/1931. | — |
| TS2 | 1931(a) | — | 4 Dukata. Gold. Uniface. ESSAI Paris/1931. | — |
| TS6 | 1931(k) | — | 8 Dukata. Gold. Uniface. | — |
| TS7 | 1931 | — | 8 Dukata. 0.9000 Gold. 30.6180 g. Uniface. ESSAI/PARIS/1931. | — |
| TS8 | 1931 | 2 | 12 Dukata. 0.9000 Gold. Uniface. ESSAI/PARIS/1931. 45.875-46.45 grams. | — |
| TS3 | 1931 | — | 4 Dukata. Bronze. Uniface. | — |
| TS4 | 1931(k) | — | 4 Dukata. Gold. Uniface. | — |
| TS5 | 1931(k) | — | 4 Dukata. Platinum. Uniface. | — |

## MINT SETS

| KM# | Date | Mintage | Identification | Issue Price | Mkt Val |
|---|---|---|---|---|---|
| MS1 | 1953/1955 (7) | — | KM29-35 | — | 5.00 |
| MS10 | 1986 (7) | — | KM86-89, 112-114 | — | 3.00 |
| MS11 | 1987 (4) | — | KM89, 112-114 | — | 3.00 |
| MS12 | 1988 (7) | — | KM89, 113-114, 131-134 | — | 3.00 |
| MS13 | 1989 (4) | — | KM131-134 | — | 6.50 |
| MS14 | 1990 (6) | — | KM139-144 | — | 4.50 |
| MS15 | 1991 (6) | — | KM139-144 | — | 4.00 |
| MS16 | 1992 (2) | — | KM143-144 | — | 35.00 |
| MS2 | 1963 (6) | — | KM36-41 | — | 8.00 |
| MS3 | 1965 (5) | — | KM42, 44-47 | — | 4.00 |
| MS4 | 1965 (5) | — | KM43-47 | — | 4.00 |
| MS5 | 1982 (6) | — | KM84-89 | — | 3.00 |
| MS6 | 1983 (6) | — | KM84-89 | — | 3.00 |
| MS7 | 1983 (2) | — | KM96-97. Blue plastic wallet. | — | 6.50 |
| MS8 | 1984 (5) | — | KM85-89 | — | 3.00 |
| MS9 | 1985 (7) | — | KM86-89, 112-114 | — | 3.00 |

## PROOF SETS

| KM# | Date | Mintage | Identification | Issue Price | Mkt Val |
|---|---|---|---|---|---|
| PS1 | 1968 (6) | 10,000 | KM49-54 | — | 2,150 |
| PS10 | 1983 (3) | — | KM98, 100, 102 | — | 40.00 |
| PS11 | 1983 (3) | — | KM99, 101, 103 | — | 40.00 |
| PS12 | 1983 (2) | 100,000 | KM96-97 | — | 15.00 |
| PS13 | 1984 (3) | — | KM105, 107, 109 | — | 40.00 |
| PS14 | 1984 (3) | — | KM106, 108, 110 | — | 40.00 |
| PS15 | Mixed dates (3) | — | KM95, 104, 111 | — | 360 |
| PS16 | 1985 (6) | — | KM119-121, 124-126 | — | 935 |
| PS17 | 1985 (4) | — | KM116-118, 123 | — | 240 |
| PS18 | 1985 (3) | — | KM116-118 | — | 75.00 |
| PS19 | 1985 (3) | — | KM119-121 | — | 60.00 |
| PS2 | 1968 (4) | 10,000 | KM51-54 | — | 2,100 |
| PS20 | 1987 (3) | — | KM128-130 | — | 245 |
| PS21 | 1987 (2) | — | KM128-129 | — | 70.00 |
| PS22 | 1989 (3) | — | KM136-138 | — | 300 |
| PS23 | 1989 (2) | — | KM136-137 | — | 60.00 |
| PS24 | 1990 (3) | — | KM146-148 | — | 255 |
| PS25 | 1990 (2) | 10,000 | KM146-147 | — | 80.00 |
| PS3 | 1968 (2) | 10,000 | KM49-50 | 15.00 | 75.00 |
| PS4 | 1978 (7) | 6,000 | KM65-71 | — | 185 |
| PS5 | 1978 (11) | 12,000 | KM65-75 | — | 1,310 |
| PS6 | 1980 (3) | — | KM76-77, 79 | — | 85.00 |
| PS7 | 1981 (3) | — | KM80-81, 83 | — | 95.00 |
| PS8 | 1982 (3) | — | KM90-92 | — | 40.00 |
| PS9 | 1982 (2) | — | KM93-94 | — | 60.00 |

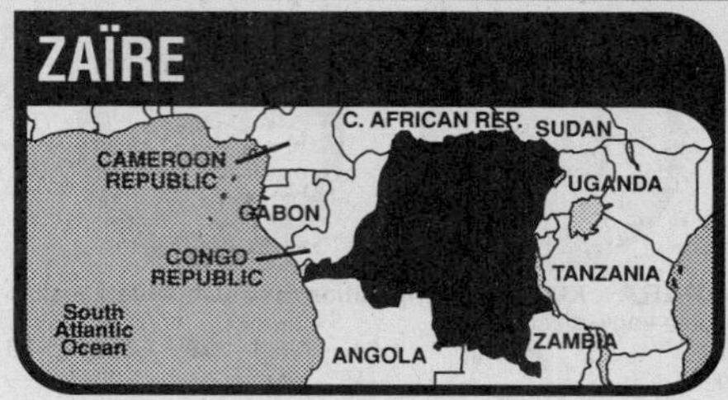


Democratic Republic of the Congo achieved independence on June 30, 1960. It followed the same monetary system as when under the Belgians. Monetary Reform of 1967 introduced new denominations and coins. The name of the country was changed to **Zaire** in 1971.

Under the command of Laurent Kabila, rebel forces overthrew ruler Sese Seko Mobutu in May of 1997. Self appointed President Kabila has officially renamed the country the Democratic Republic of Congo.

**MONETARY SYSTEM**

100 Makuta = 1 Zaire

1993 -

3,000,000 old Zaires = 1 Nouveau Zaire

# REPUBLIC

## DECIMAL COINAGE

**5 MAKUTA** KM# 12 **Composition:** Copper-Nickel

| Date | Mintage | F | VF | XF | Unc | BU |
|---|---|---|---|---|---|---|
| 1977 | 8,000,000 | — | 0.50 | 1.00 | 3.50 | — |

**10 MAKUTA** KM# 7 **Composition:** Copper-Nickel

| Date | Mintage | F | VF | XF | Unc | BU |
|---|---|---|---|---|---|---|
| 1973 | 5,000,000 | — | 2.25 | 4.00 | 8.00 | — |
| 1975 | — | — | 2.25 | 4.00 | 8.00 | — |
| 1976 | — | — | 2.50 | 4.50 | 9.00 | — |
| 1978 | — | — | 2.50 | 4.50 | 9.00 | — |

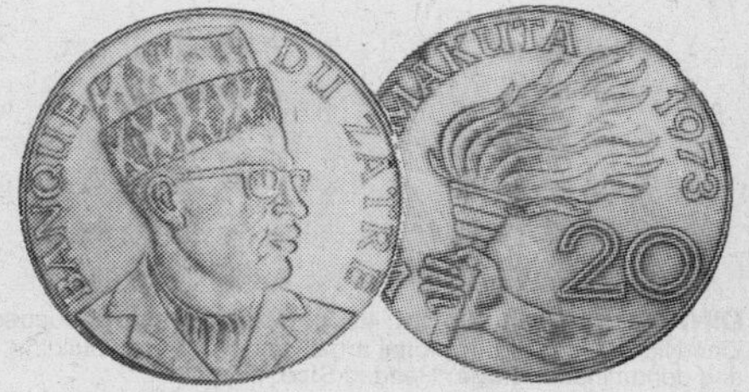

**20 MAKUTA** KM# 8 **Composition:** Copper-Nickel

| Date | Mintage | F | VF | XF | Unc | BU |
|---|---|---|---|---|---|---|
| 1973 | — | — | 3.00 | 5.50 | 10.00 | — |
| 1976 | — | — | 3.50 | 6.50 | 12.00 | — |

**ZAIRE** KM# 13 **Composition:** Brass

| Date | Mintage | F | VF | XF | Unc | BU |
|---|---|---|---|---|---|---|
| 1987 | — | — | 0.50 | 1.00 | 2.00 | — |

**2-1/2 ZAIRES** **KM# 9** **Weight:** 28.2800 g. **Composition:** 0.9250 Silver .8411 oz. ASW **Subject:** Conservation **Reverse:** Mountain gorillas

| Date | Mintage | F | VF | XF | Unc | BU |
|---|---|---|---|---|---|---|
| 1975 | 5,735 | — | — | — | 35.00 | — |
| 1975 Proof | 6,629 | Value: 45.00 | | | | |

**5 ZAIRES** **KM# 1** **Weight:** 27.8401 g. **Composition:** 0.9250 Silver .8280 oz. ASW **Reverse:** Hotel Intercontinental

| Date | Mintage | F | VF | XF | Unc | BU |
|---|---|---|---|---|---|---|
| 1971 Proof | — | Value: 30.00 | | | | |

**5 ZAIRES** **KM# 10** **Weight:** 35.0000 g. **Composition:** 0.9250 Silver 1.0409 oz. ASW **Subject:** Conservation **Reverse:** Okapi

| Date | Mintage | F | VF | XF | Unc | BU |
|---|---|---|---|---|---|---|
| 1975 | 5,734 | — | — | — | 30.00 | — |
| 1975 Proof | 6,431 | Value: 40.00 | | | | |

**5 ZAIRES** **KM# 14** **Composition:** Brass

| Date | Mintage | F | VF | XF | Unc | BU |
|---|---|---|---|---|---|---|
| 1987 | — | — | 0.65 | 1.25 | 2.50 | — |

**10 ZAIRES** **KM# 2** **Weight:** 9.9600 g. **Composition:** 0.9000 Gold .2882 oz. AGW **Reverse:** Hotel Intercontinental

| Date | Mintage | F | VF | XF | Unc | BU |
|---|---|---|---|---|---|---|
| 1971 Proof | — | Value: 140 | | | | |

**10 ZAIRES** **KM# 3** **Weight:** 6.0400 g. **Composition:** 0.9990 Platinum .1940 oz. APW

| Date | Mintage | F | VF | XF | Unc | BU |
|---|---|---|---|---|---|---|
| 1971 Proof | — | Value: 210 | | | | |

**10 ZAIRES** **KM# 19** **Composition:** Brass

| Date | Mintage | F | VF | XF | Unc | BU |
|---|---|---|---|---|---|---|
| 1988 | — | — | 2.00 | 4.50 | 9.00 | — |

**20 ZAIRES** **KM# 4** **Weight:** 20.9000 g. **Composition:** 0.9000 Gold .6048 oz. AGW **Reverse:** Hotel Intercontinental

| Date | Mintage | F | VF | XF | Unc | BU |
|---|---|---|---|---|---|---|
| 1971 Proof | — | Value: 320 | | | | |

**20 ZAIRES** **KM# 5** **Weight:** 3.8900 g. **Composition:** 0.9990 Platinum .1250 oz. APW

| Date | Mintage | F | VF | XF | Unc | BU |
|---|---|---|---|---|---|---|
| 1971 Proof | — | Value: 110 | | | | |

**50 ZAIRES** **KM# 6** **Weight:** 46.9600 g. **Composition:** 0.9000 Gold 1.3590 oz. AGW **Reverse:** Hotel Intercontinental

| Date | Mintage | F | VF | XF | Unc | BU |
|---|---|---|---|---|---|---|
| 1971 Proof | — | Value: 675 | | | | |

**100 ZAIRES** **KM# 11** **Weight:** 33.4370 g. **Composition:** 0.9000 Gold .9676 oz. AGW **Subject:** Conservation **Reverse:** Leopard

| Date | Mintage | F | VF | XF | Unc | BU |
|---|---|---|---|---|---|---|
| 1975 | 1,415 | — | — | — | 465 | — |
| 1975 Proof | 279 | Value: 700 | | | | |

**500 NOUVEAUX ZAIRES** **KM# 20** **Weight:** 20.0000 g. **Composition:** 0.5000 Silver .3215 oz. ASW **Subject:** Wildlife of Africa **Reverse:** Leopard

| Date | Mintage | F | VF | XF | Unc | BU |
|---|---|---|---|---|---|---|
| 1996 Proof | 10,000 | Value: 27.50 | | | | |

**500 NOUVEAUX ZAIRES** **KM# 21** **Weight:** 20.0000 g. **Composition:** 0.5000 Silver .3215 oz. ASW **Subject:** Wildlife of Africa **Reverse:** Gorilla

| Date | Mintage | F | VF | XF | Unc | BU |
|---|---|---|---|---|---|---|
| 1996 Proof | Est. 10,000 | Value: 27.50 | | | | |

**500 NOUVEAUX ZAIRES** **KM# 22** **Weight:** 20.0000 g. **Composition:** 0.5000 Silver .3215 oz. ASW **Subject:** Wildlife of Africa **Reverse:** Two okapi

| Date | Mintage | F | VF | XF | Unc | BU |
|---|---|---|---|---|---|---|
| 1996 Proof | Est. 10,000 | Value: 27.50 | | | | |

**1000 NOUVEAUX ZAIRES** KM# 23 **Weight:** 29.6300 g. **Composition:** 0.9250 Silver .8811 oz. ASW **Subject:** Wildlife of Africa **Obverse:** African map **Reverse:** Hippopotamus

| Date | Mintage | F | VF | XF | Unc | BU |
|---|---|---|---|---|---|---|
| 1997 Proof | Est. 20,000 | Value: 37.50 | | | | |

**1000 NOUVEAUX ZAIRES** KM# 24 **Weight:** 30.0900 g. **Composition:** 0.9250 Silver .8948 oz. ASW **Subject:** Wildlife of Africa **Obverse:** African map **Reverse:** Sailing ship "Portuguese Caravel"

| Date | Mintage | F | VF | XF | Unc | BU |
|---|---|---|---|---|---|---|
| 1997 Proof | Est. 20,000 | Value: 40.00 | | | | |

**5000 NOUVEAUX ZAIRES** KM# 25 **Weight:** 411.4224 g. **Composition:** 0.9990 Silver 13.2143 oz. ASW **Subject:** Wildlife of Africa **Obverse:** Map and national arms **Reverse:** Leopard at rest on branch **Edge:** Reeded

| Date | Mintage | F | VF | XF | Unc | BU |
|---|---|---|---|---|---|---|
| 1996 Proof | — | Value: 225 | | | | |

**10000 NOUVEAUX ZAIRES** KM# 26 **Weight:** 822.8449 g. **Composition:** 0.9990 Silver 26.4286 oz. ASW **Subject:** Wildlife of Africa **Obverse:** Map and national arms **Reverse:** Gorilla **Edge:** Reeded

| Date | Mintage | F | VF | XF | Unc | BU |
|---|---|---|---|---|---|---|
| 1996 Proof | — | Value: 435 | | | | |

## PROOF SETS

| KM# | Date | Mintage | Identification | Issue Price | Mkt Val |
|---|---|---|---|---|---|
| PS1 | 1971 (6) | — | KM1-6 | — | 1,485 |
| PS2 | 1975 (2) | 500 | KM9-10 | 60.00 | 85.00 |

# ZAMBIA

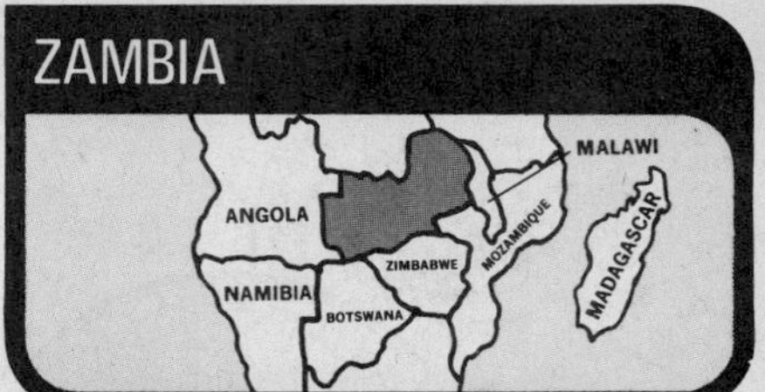


The Republic of Zambia (formerly Northern Rhodesia), a landlocked country in south-central Africa, has an area of 290,586 sq. mi. (752,610 sq. km.) and a population of*7.9 million. Capital: Lusaka. The economy of Zambia is based principally on copper, of which Zambia is the world's third largest producer. Copper, zinc, lead, cobalt and tobacco are exported.

The area that is now Zambia was brought within the British sphere of influence in 1888 by empire builder Cecil Rhodes, who obtained mining concessions in south-central Africa from indigenous chiefs. The territory was ruled by the British South Africa Company, which Rhodes established, until 1924 when its administration was transferred to the British government as a protectorate. In1953, Northern Rhodesia was joined with Nyasaland and the colony of Southern Rhodesia to form the Federation of Rhodesia and Nyasaland. Northern Rhodesia seceded from the Federation on Oct. 24, 1964, and became the independent Republic of Zambia. Zambia is a member of the Commonwealth of Nations. The president is Chief of State.

Zambia converted to a decimal coinage on January 16, 1969.

For earlier coinage refer to Rhodesia and Nyasaland.

**RULERS**

British, until 1964

**MONETARY SYSTEM**

12 Pence = 1 Shilling
20 Shillings = 1 Pound

## REPUBLIC

### STANDARD COINAGE

**PENNY** KM# 5 **Composition:** Bronze

| Date | Mintage | F | VF | XF | Unc | BU |
|---|---|---|---|---|---|---|
| 1966 | 7,200,000 | 0.15 | 0.35 | 0.65 | 1.75 | — |
| 1966 Proof | 60 | — | — | — | — | — |

**SIXPENCE** KM# 1 **Composition:** Copper-Nickel-Zinc **Reverse:** Morning Glory

| Date | Mintage | F | VF | XF | Unc | BU |
|---|---|---|---|---|---|---|
| 1964 | 3,500,000 | 0.15 | 0.30 | 0.60 | 1.20 | — |
| 1964 Proof | 5,000 | Value: 1.50 | | | | |

**SIXPENCE** KM# 6 **Composition:** Copper-Nickel-Zinc

| Date | Mintage | F | VF | XF | Unc | BU |
|---|---|---|---|---|---|---|
| 1966 | 7,200,000 | 0.25 | 0.50 | 1.00 | 2.00 | — |
| 1966 Proof | 60 | — | — | — | — | — |

**SHILLING** KM# 2 **Composition:** Copper-Nickel **Reverse:** Crowned Hornbill

| Date | Mintage | F | VF | XF | Unc | BU |
|---|---|---|---|---|---|---|
| 1964 | 3,510,000 | 0.25 | 0.50 | 1.00 | 2.00 | — |
| 1964 Proof | 5,000 | Value: 3.50 | | | | |

**SHILLING** KM# 7 **Composition:** Copper-Nickel

| Date | Mintage | F | VF | XF | Unc | BU |
|---|---|---|---|---|---|---|
| 1966 | 5,000,000 | 0.35 | 0.75 | 1.50 | 3.25 | — |
| 1966 Proof | 60 | — | — | — | — | — |

**2 SHILLINGS** KM# 3 **Composition:** Copper-Nickel **Note:** Bohor Reedbuck

| Date | Mintage | F | VF | XF | Unc | BU |
|---|---|---|---|---|---|---|
| 1964 | 3,770,000 | 0.35 | 0.75 | 1.50 | 3.00 | — |
| 1964 Proof | 5,000 | Value: 4.50 | | | | |

**2 SHILLINGS** KM# 8 **Composition:** Copper-Nickel

| Date | Mintage | F | VF | XF | Unc | BU |
|---|---|---|---|---|---|---|
| 1966 | 5,000,000 | 0.45 | 1.00 | 2.25 | 4.50 | — |
| 1966 Proof | 60 | — | — | — | — | — |

**5 SHILLINGS** KM# 4 **Composition:** Copper-Nickel **Subject:** 1st Anniversary of Independence

| Date | Mintage | F | VF | XF | Unc | BU |
|---|---|---|---|---|---|---|
| 1965 | 10,000 | — | 2.00 | 3.50 | 6.50 | — |
| 1965 Proof | 20,000 | Value: 7.50 | | | | |

## DECIMAL COINAGE

100 Ngwee = 1 Kwacha

**NGWEE** KM# 9 **Composition:** Bronze **Reverse:** Aardvark

| Date | Mintage | F | VF | XF | Unc | BU |
|---|---|---|---|---|---|---|
| 1968 | 8,000,000 | — | 0.10 | 0.20 | 0.80 | — |
| 1968 Proof | 4,000 | Value: 1.25 | | | | |
| 1969 | 16,000,000 | — | 0.10 | 0.15 | 0.75 | — |
| 1972 | 21,000,000 | — | 0.10 | 0.15 | 0.75 | — |
| 1978 | 23,976,000 | — | 0.10 | 0.15 | 0.75 | — |
| 1978 Proof | 24,000 | Value: 1.50 | | | | |

**NGWEE** KM# 9a **Composition:** Copper-Clad Steel

| Date | Mintage | F | VF | XF | Unc | BU |
|---|---|---|---|---|---|---|
| 1982 | 10,000,000 | — | 0.10 | 0.20 | 0.75 | — |
| 1983 | 60,000,000 | — | 0.10 | 0.15 | 0.65 | — |

**2 NGWEE** KM# 10 **Composition:** Bronze **Reverse:** Martial Eagle

| Date | Mintage | F | VF | XF | Unc | BU |
|---|---|---|---|---|---|---|
| 1968 | 19,000,000 | — | 0.10 | 0.20 | 1.00 | — |
| 1968 Proof | 4,000 | Value: 1.50 | | | | |
| 1978 | — | — | 0.15 | 0.25 | 1.25 | — |
| 1978 Proof | 24,000 | Value: 1.75 | | | | |

**2 NGWEE** KM# 10a **Composition:** Copper-Clad Steel

| Date | Mintage | F | VF | XF | Unc | BU |
|---|---|---|---|---|---|---|
| 1982 | 7,500,000 | — | 0.10 | 0.20 | 1.00 | — |
| 1983 | 60,000,000 | — | 0.10 | 0.15 | 0.50 | — |

**5 NGWEE** KM# 11 **Composition:** Copper-Nickel **Reverse:** Morning Glory

| Date | Mintage | F | VF | XF | Unc | BU |
|---|---|---|---|---|---|---|
| 1968 | 12,000,000 | — | 0.20 | 0.30 | 0.60 | — |
| 1968 Proof | 4,000 | Value: 1.75 | | | | |
| 1972 | 9,000,000 | — | 0.20 | 0.30 | 0.60 | — |
| 1978 | 1,976,000 | — | 0.20 | 0.30 | 0.60 | — |
| 1978 Proof | 24,000 | Value: 2.00 | | | | |
| 1982 | 12,000,000 | — | 0.20 | 0.30 | 0.60 | — |
| 1987 | 10,000,000 | — | 0.20 | 0.30 | 0.60 | — |

**10 NGWEE** KM# 12 **Composition:** Copper-Nickel-Zinc **Reverse:** Crowned Hornbill

| Date | Mintage | F | VF | XF | Unc | BU |
|---|---|---|---|---|---|---|
| 1968 | 1,000,000 | — | 0.40 | 0.85 | 1.75 | — |
| 1968 Proof | 4,000 | Value: 2.00 | | | | |
| 1972 | 1,000,000 | — | 0.30 | 0.50 | 1.00 | — |
| 1978 | 1,976,000 | — | 0.30 | 0.50 | 1.00 | — |
| 1978 Proof | 24,000 | Value: 2.25 | | | | |
| 1982 | 8,000,000 | — | 0.30 | 0.50 | 1.00 | — |
| 1983 | 2,500 | — | 0.30 | 0.50 | 1.00 | — |
| 1987 | 6,000,000 | — | 0.30 | 0.50 | 1.00 | — |

**20 NGWEE** KM# 13 **Composition:** Copper-Nickel **Reverse:** Bohur Reedbuck, similar to KM#3

| Date | Mintage | F | VF | XF | Unc | BU |
|---|---|---|---|---|---|---|
| 1968 | 1,500,000 | — | 0.75 | 1.50 | 2.50 | — |
| 1968 Proof | 4,000 | Value: 2.75 | | | | |
| 1972 | 7,500,000 | — | 0.50 | 1.00 | 2.00 | — |
| 1978 Proof | 24,000 | Value: 3.00 | | | | |
| 1983 | 998,000 | — | 0.75 | 1.50 | 2.50 | — |
| 1987 | — | — | 0.50 | 1.00 | 2.00 | — |
| 1988 | 3,000,000 | — | 0.50 | 1.00 | 2.00 | — |

**20 NGWEE** KM# 22 **Composition:** Copper-Nickel **Series:** F.A.O. - World Food Day

| Date | Mintage | F | VF | XF | Unc | BU |
|---|---|---|---|---|---|---|
| 1981 | 970,000 | — | 0.75 | 1.50 | 2.75 | — |

**20 NGWEE** KM# 23 **Composition:** Copper-Nickel **Subject:** 20th Anniversary - Bank of Zambia

| Date | Mintage | F | VF | XF | Unc | BU |
|---|---|---|---|---|---|---|
| 1985 | — | — | 0.50 | 1.00 | 1.50 | — |

**20 NGWEE** KM# 23a **Weight:** 11.3100 g. **Composition:** 0.9250 Silver .3364 oz. ASW

| Date | Mintage | F | VF | XF | Unc | BU |
|---|---|---|---|---|---|---|
| 1985 | — | Value: 3.50 | | | | |

**25 NGWEE** KM# 29 **Composition:** Nickel Plated Steel **Reverse:** Crowned Hornbill

| Date | Mintage | F | VF | XF | Unc | BU |
|---|---|---|---|---|---|---|
| 1992 | — | — | — | — | 0.75 | — |

**50 NGWEE** KM# 14 **Composition:** Copper-Nickel **Series:** F.A.O.

| Date | Mintage | F | VF | XF | Unc | BU |
|---|---|---|---|---|---|---|
| ND(1969) | 70,000 | — | 2.00 | 3.50 | 5.50 | — |

**50 NGWEE** KM# 15 **Composition:** Copper-Nickel **Series:** F.A.O.

| Date | Mintage | F | VF | XF | Unc | BU |
|---|---|---|---|---|---|---|
| 1972 | 510,000 | — | 1.25 | 2.50 | 4.50 | — |

**50 NGWEE** **KM# 16** **Composition:** Copper-Nickel **Subject:** Second Republic, 13 December 1972

| Date | Mintage | F | VF | XF | Unc | BU |
|---|---|---|---|---|---|---|
| 1972 | 6,000,000 | — | 1.00 | 2.00 | 4.00 | — |
| 1972 Proof | 2,000 | Value: 7.00 | | | | |
| 1978 Proof | 24,000 | Value: 5.00 | | | | |
| 1983 | 998,000 | — | 1.00 | 2.00 | 4.00 | — |

**50 NGWEE** **KM# 24** **Composition:** Copper-Nickel **Subject:** 40th Anniversary of United Nations

| Date | Mintage | F | VF | XF | Unc | BU |
|---|---|---|---|---|---|---|
| 1985 | — | — | 1.00 | 1.25 | 2.50 | — |

**50 NGWEE** **KM# 24a** **Weight:** 11.6600 g. **Composition:** 0.9250 Silver .3468 oz. ASW

| Date | Mintage | F | VF | XF | Unc | BU |
|---|---|---|---|---|---|---|
| 1985 Proof | — | — | — | — | — | — |

**50 NGWEE** **KM# 30** **Composition:** Nickel Plated Steel **Reverse:** Kafue Lechwe

| Date | Mintage | F | VF | XF | Unc | BU |
|---|---|---|---|---|---|---|
| 1992 | — | — | — | — | 1.00 | — |

**KWACHA** **KM# 17** **Composition:** Copper-Nickel **Subject:** 10th Anniverssary of Independence

| Date | Mintage | F | VF | XF | Unc | BU |
|---|---|---|---|---|---|---|
| ND(1974) | 4,000 | — | — | — | 20.00 | — |
| ND(1974) Proof | 1,500 | Value: 35.00 | | | | |

**KWACHA** **KM# 26** **Composition:** Nickel-Brass

| Date | Mintage | F | VF | XF | Unc | BU |
|---|---|---|---|---|---|---|
| 1989 | 8,000,000 | — | 0.75 | 1.50 | 3.50 | — |

**KWACHA** **KM# 38** **Composition:** Brass

| Date | Mintage | F | VF | XF | Unc | BU |
|---|---|---|---|---|---|---|
| 1992 | — | — | — | — | 1.00 | — |

**5 KWACHA** **KM# 18** **Weight:** 25.3100 g. **Composition:** 0.9250 Silver .7527 oz. ASW **Subject:** Conservation **Reverse:** Kafue Lechwe

| Date | Mintage | F | VF | XF | Unc | BU |
|---|---|---|---|---|---|---|
| 1979 | 3,250 | — | — | — | 18.50 | — |

**5 KWACHA** **KM# 18a** **Weight:** 28.2800 g. **Composition:** 0.9250 Silver .8411 oz. ASW

| Date | Mintage | F | VF | XF | Unc | BU |
|---|---|---|---|---|---|---|
| 1979 Proof | 3,407 | Value: 22.50 | | | | |

**5 KWACHA** **KM# 31** **Composition:** Brass **Reverse:** Oryx

| Date | Mintage | F | VF | XF | Unc | BU |
|---|---|---|---|---|---|---|
| 1992 | — | — | — | — | 1.50 | — |

**10 KWACHA** **KM# 19** **Weight:** 31.6500 g. **Composition:** 0.9250 Silver .9398 oz. ASW **Subject:** Conservation **Reverse:** Taita Falcon

| Date | Mintage | F | VF | XF | Unc | BU |
|---|---|---|---|---|---|---|
| 1979 | 3,250 | — | — | — | 22.50 | — |

**10 KWACHA** **KM# 19a** **Weight:** 35.0000 g. **Composition:** 0.9250 Silver 1.0409 oz. ASW

| Date | Mintage | F | VF | XF | Unc | BU |
|---|---|---|---|---|---|---|
| 1979 Proof | 3,256 | Value: 27.50 | | | | |

**10 KWACHA** **KM# 21** **Weight:** 27.2200 g. **Composition:** 0.9250 Silver .8095 oz. ASW **Series:** International Year of the Child **Obverse:** Similar to 20 Ngwee, KM#13 **Reverse:** 3 children on playground equipment

| Date | Mintage | F | VF | XF | Unc | BU |
|---|---|---|---|---|---|---|
| 1980 Proof | 12,000 | Value: 15.00 | | | | |

**10 KWACHA** **KM# 25** **Weight:** 27.2200 g. **Composition:** 0.9250 Silver .8095 oz. ASW **Series:** World Wildlife Fund **Reverse:** White-winged Flufftail

| Date | Mintage | F | VF | XF | Unc | BU |
|---|---|---|---|---|---|---|
| 1986 Proof | 25,000 | Value: 25.00 | | | | |

**10 KWACHA** **KM# 27** **Weight:** 27.2200 g. **Composition:** 0.9250 Silver .8095 oz. ASW **Subject:** 70th Anniversary - Save the Children Fund

| Date | Mintage | F | VF | XF | Unc | BU |
|---|---|---|---|---|---|---|
| 1989 Proof | Est. 20,000 | Value: 23.50 | | | | |

**10 KWACHA** KM# 32 **Composition:** Brass **Reverse:** Rhinoceros

| Date | Mintage | F | VF | XF | Unc | BU |
|---|---|---|---|---|---|---|
| 1992 | — | — | — | — | 2.00 | — |

**10 KWACHA** KM# 39 **Weight:** 20.0000 g. **Composition:** 0.9990 Silver .6430 oz. ASW **Subject:** World Cup Soccer **Reverse:** Player kicking ball; .999 in field

| Date | Mintage | F | VF | XF | Unc | BU |
|---|---|---|---|---|---|---|
| 1994 Proof | — | Value: 50.00 | | | | |

**20 KWACHA** KM# 33 **Weight:** 10.1700 g. **Composition:** 0.9990 Silver .3266 oz. ASW **Series:** 1994 Olympics **Reverse:** Slalom skier

| Date | Mintage | F | VF | XF | Unc | BU |
|---|---|---|---|---|---|---|
| 1994 Proof | 25,000 | Value: 25.00 | | | | |

**75 KWACHA** KM# 51 **Weight:** 5.0000 g. **Composition:** 0.9990 Silver .1606 oz. ASW **Subject:** Diana - The People's Princess **Note:** Similar to 200 Kwacha, KM#52

| Date | Mintage | F | VF | XF | Unc | BU |
|---|---|---|---|---|---|---|
| 1997 Proof | — | — | — | — | — | — |

**100 KWACHA** KM# 28 **Weight:** 28.2800 g. **Composition:** 0.9250 Silver .8411 oz. ASW **Series:** Barcelona Summer Olympics **Subject:** Boxing **Obverse:** National arms **Reverse:** 2 Boxers in ring fighting

| Date | Mintage | F | VF | XF | Unc | BU |
|---|---|---|---|---|---|---|
| 1992 Proof | Est. 50,000 | Value: 27.50 | | | | |

**100 KWACHA** KM# 50 **Composition:** Copper-Nickel **Reverse:** Charging bull elephant

| Date | Mintage | F | VF | XF | Unc | BU |
|---|---|---|---|---|---|---|
| 1997 | — | — | — | — | 15.00 | — |

**100 KWACHA** KM# 56 **Weight:** 28.2800 g. **Composition:** 0.9990 Silver .9083 oz. ASW **Reverse:** Crocodile

| Date | Mintage | F | VF | XF | Unc | BU |
|---|---|---|---|---|---|---|
| 1998 Proof | Est. 25,000 | Value: 50.00 | | | | |

**100 KWACHA** KM# 57 **Weight:** 28.2800 g. **Composition:** 0.9990 Silver .9083 oz. ASW **Reverse:** Leopard

| Date | Mintage | F | VF | XF | Unc | BU |
|---|---|---|---|---|---|---|
| 1998 Proof | Est. 25,000 | Value: 60.00 | | | | |

**100 KWACHA** KM# 58 **Weight:** 28.2800 g. **Composition:** 0.9990 Silver .9083 oz. ASW **Reverse:** Black Rhinoceros

| Date | Mintage | F | VF | XF | Unc | BU |
|---|---|---|---|---|---|---|
| 1998 Proof | Est. 25,000 | Value: 60.00 | | | | |

**100 KWACHA** KM# 59 **Weight:** 28.2800 g. **Composition:** 0.9990 Silver .9083 oz. ASW **Reverse:** Hippopotamus and calf

| Date | Mintage | F | VF | XF | Unc | BU |
|---|---|---|---|---|---|---|
| 1998 Proof | Est. 25,000 | Value: 60.00 | | | | |

**100 KWACHA** KM# 60 **Weight:** 28.2800 g. **Composition:** 0.9990 Silver .9083 oz. ASW **Reverse:** Impala

| Date | Mintage | F | VF | XF | Unc | BU |
|---|---|---|---|---|---|---|
| 1998 Proof | Est. 25,000 | Value: 55.00 | | | | |

**100 KWACHA** KM# 61 **Weight:** 28.2800 g. **Composition:** 0.9990 Silver .9083 oz. ASW **Reverse:** Pelican

| Date | Mintage | F | VF | XF | Unc | BU |
|---|---|---|---|---|---|---|
| 1998 Proof | Est. 25,000 | Value: 55.00 | | | | |

**100 KWACHA** KM# 62 **Weight:** 28.2800 g. **Composition:** 0.9990 Silver .9083 oz. ASW **Reverse:** Stork

| Date | Mintage | F | VF | XF | Unc | BU |
|---|---|---|---|---|---|---|
| 1998 Proof | Est. 25,000 | Value: 55.00 | | | | |

**100 KWACHA** KM# 65 **Weight:** 28.2800 g. **Composition:** 0.9990 Silver .9083 oz. ASW **Reverse:** Giraffes

| Date | Mintage | F | VF | XF | Unc | BU |
|---|---|---|---|---|---|---|
| 1998 Proof | Est. 25,000 | Value: 60.00 | | | | |

**200 KWACHA** KM# 52 **Composition:** Copper-Nickel **Subject:** Diana - The People's Princess **Obverse:** National arms **Reverse:** Diana's portrait, dates 1961 at left, 1997 at right

| Date | Mintage | F | VF | XF | Unc | BU |
|---|---|---|---|---|---|---|
| 1997 Proof | — | Value: 8.00 | | | | |

**100 KWACHA** KM# 63 **Weight:** 28.2800 g. **Composition:** 0.9990 Silver .9083 oz. ASW **Reverse:** Burchell's Zebra

| Date | Mintage | F | VF | XF | Unc | BU |
|---|---|---|---|---|---|---|
| 1998 Proof | Est. 25,000 | Value: 55.00 | | | | |

**100 KWACHA** KM# 66 **Weight:** 28.2800 g. **Composition:** 0.9990 Silver .9083 oz. ASW **Reverse:** Lion

| Date | Mintage | F | VF | XF | Unc | BU |
|---|---|---|---|---|---|---|
| 1998 Proof | Est. 25,000 | Value: 60.00 | | | | |

**250 KWACHA** KM# 20 **Weight:** 33.6300 g. **Composition:** 0.9000 Gold .9371 oz. AGW **Subject:** Conservation **Reverse:** African wild dog

| Date | Mintage | F | VF | XF | Unc | BU |
|---|---|---|---|---|---|---|
| 1979 | 455 | — | — | — | 500 | — |
| 1979 Proof | 245 | Value: 750 | | | | |

**100 KWACHA** KM# 64 **Weight:** 28.2800 g. **Composition:** 0.9990 Silver .9083 oz. ASW **Reverse:** Flamingos

| Date | Mintage | F | VF | XF | Unc | BU |
|---|---|---|---|---|---|---|
| 1998 Proof | Est. 25,000 | Value: 55.00 | | | | |

**100 KWACHA** KM# 67 **Weight:** 28.2800 g. **Composition:** 0.9990 Silver .9083 oz. ASW **Reverse:** Two gazelles

| Date | Mintage | F | VF | XF | Unc | BU |
|---|---|---|---|---|---|---|
| 1998 Proof | Est. 25,000 | Value: 60.00 | | | | |

**250 KWACHA** KM# 34 **Weight:** 136.0800 g. **Composition:** 0.9250 Silver 4.0474 oz. ASW **Reverse:** African fish eagle **Size:** 63 mm. **Note:** Illustration reduced.

**250 KWACHA** **KM# 35** **Weight:** 136.0800 g. **Composition:** 0.9250 Silver 4.0474 oz. ASW **Reverse:** Saddle-billed stork **Size:** 63 mm. **Note:** Illustration reduced.

| Date | Mintage | F | VF | XF | Unc | BU |
|---|---|---|---|---|---|---|
| 1993 | 400 | — | — | — | 125 | — |
| 1993 Proof | 5,000 | Value: 85.00 | | | | |

**250 KWACHA** **KM# 36** **Weight:** 136.0800 g. **Composition:** 0.9250 Silver 4.0474 oz. ASW **Reverse:** Paradise Flycatcher **Size:** 63 mm. **Note:** Illustration reduced.

| Date | Mintage | F | VF | XF | Unc | BU |
|---|---|---|---|---|---|---|
| 1993 | 400 | — | — | — | 125 | — |
| 1993 Proof | 5,000 | Value: 85.00 | | | | |

**250 KWACHA** **KM# 37** **Weight:** 136.0800 g. **Composition:** 0.9250 Silver 4.0474 oz. ASW **Reverse:** Red-breasted Swallow **Size:** 63 mm. **Note:** Illustration reduced.

| Date | Mintage | F | VF | XF | Unc | BU |
|---|---|---|---|---|---|---|
| 1993 | 400 | — | — | — | 145 | — |
| 1993 Proof | 5,000 | Value: 95.00 | | | | |

**500 KWACHA** **KM# 40** **Weight:** 31.7730 g. **Composition:** 0.9990 Silver 1.025 oz. ASW **Subject:** Equality **Reverse:** Black and white face profiles

| Date | Mintage | F | VF | XF | Unc | BU |
|---|---|---|---|---|---|---|
| 1994 Proof | — | Value: 32.50 | | | | |

**500 KWACHA** **KM# 41** **Weight:** 31.7730 g. **Composition:** 0.9990 Silver 1.025 oz. ASW **Subject:** Freedom of Speech **Reverse:** Perched African Fish Eagle

| Date | Mintage | F | VF | XF | Unc | BU |
|---|---|---|---|---|---|---|
| 1994 Proof | — | Value: 30.00 | | | | |

**500 KWACHA** **KM# 42** **Weight:** 31.7730 g. **Composition:** 0.9990 Silver 1.025 oz. ASW **Subject:** Rights of Religion and Culture **Reverse:** Books, scroll, and mask

| Date | Mintage | F | VF | XF | Unc | BU |
|---|---|---|---|---|---|---|
| 1994 Proof | — | Value: 25.00 | | | | |

**500 KWACHA** **KM# 43** **Weight:** 31.7730 g. **Composition:** 0.9990 Silver 1.025 oz. ASW **Subject:** Rights of Association **Reverse:** Lion cub and lamb

| Date | Mintage | F | VF | XF | Unc | BU |
|---|---|---|---|---|---|---|
| 1994 Proof | — | Value: 30.00 | | | | |

**500 KWACHA** **KM# 44** **Weight:** 31.7730 g. **Composition:** 0.9990 Silver 1.025 oz. ASW **Subject:** Rights to Work **Reverse:** African Masked Weaver Bird building nest

| Date | Mintage | F | VF | XF | Unc | BU |
|---|---|---|---|---|---|---|
| 1994 Proof | — | Value: 30.00 | | | | |
| 1993 | 400 | — | — | — | 125 | — |
| 1993 Proof | 5,000 | Value: 85.00 | | | | |

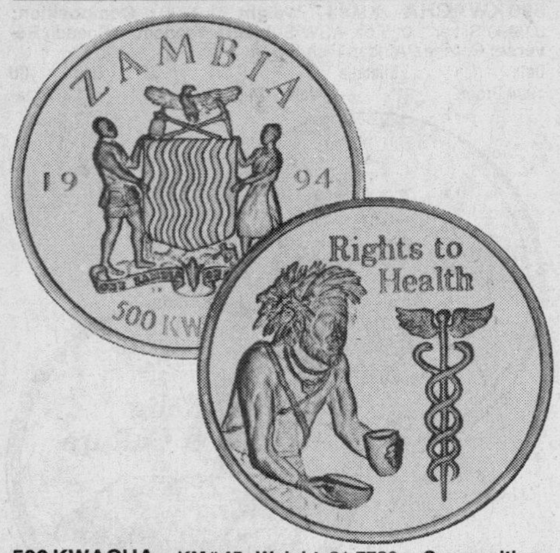


**500 KWACHA** KM# 45 **Weight:** 31.7730 g. **Composition:** 0.9990 Silver 1.025 oz. ASW **Subject:** Rights to Health **Reverse:** Shaman and Caduceus

| Date | Mintage | F | VF | XF | Unc | BU |
|---|---|---|---|---|---|---|
| 1994 Proof | — | Value: 25.00 | | | | |

**500 KWACHA** KM# 46 **Weight:** 31.7730 g. **Composition:** 0.9990 Silver 1.025 oz. ASW **Subject:** Rights of the Disabled **Reverse:** Three elephants

| Date | Mintage | F | VF | XF | Unc | BU |
|---|---|---|---|---|---|---|
| 1994 Proof | — | Value: 32.50 | | | | |

**500 KWACHA** KM# 47 **Weight:** 31.7730 g. **Composition:** 0.9990 Silver 1.025 oz. ASW **Subject:** Rights to a Clean Environment **Reverse:** Two South African Shelducks

| Date | Mintage | F | VF | XF | Unc | BU |
|---|---|---|---|---|---|---|
| 1994 Proof | — | Value: 30.00 | | | | |

**500 KWACHA** KM# 48 **Weight:** 31.7730 g. **Composition:** 0.9990 Silver 1.025 oz. ASW **Subject:** Children's Rights **Reverse:** Fawn

| Date | Mintage | F | VF | XF | Unc | BU |
|---|---|---|---|---|---|---|
| 1994 Proof | — | Value: 30.00 | | | | |

**500 KWACHA** KM# 49 **Weight:** 31.7730 g. **Composition:** 0.9990 Silver 1.025 oz. ASW **Subject:** Women's Rights **Reverse:** Women with firewood

| Date | Mintage | F | VF | XF | Unc | BU |
|---|---|---|---|---|---|---|
| 1994 Proof | — | Value: 22.50 | | | | |

**500 KWACHA** KM# 53 **Weight:** 31.1035 g. **Composition:** 0.9990 Silver 1.0000 oz. ASW **Subject:** Diana - The People's Princess **Note:** Similar to 200 Kwacha, KM#52

| Date | Mintage | F | VF | XF | Unc | BU |
|---|---|---|---|---|---|---|
| 1997 Proof | Est. 13,211 | Value: 27.50 | | | | |

**1000 KWACHA** KM# 91 **Weight:** 28.7200 g. **Composition:** Copper-Nickel **Subject:** European Unity **Obverse:** National arms **Reverse:** Multi-colored 20 euro note **Edge:** Plain **Size:** 38 mm.

| Date | Mintage | F | VF | XF | Unc | BU |
|---|---|---|---|---|---|---|
| 1999 | — | — | — | — | 15.00 | — |

**1000 KWACHA** KM# 109 **Weight:** 20.0000 g. **Composition:** 0.9250 Silver .5948 oz. ASW **Series:** Sydney Olympics **Obverse:** Queen Elizabeth's portrait above Zambian arms **Reverse:** Discus thrower **Edge:** Plain **Size:** 38.6 mm.

| Date | Mintage | F | VF | XF | Unc | BU |
|---|---|---|---|---|---|---|
| 1999 Proof | — | Value: 35.00 | | | | |

**1000 KWACHA** KM# 95 **Composition:** Copper-Nickel **Series:** 1,000 Years of Exploration **Obverse:** Queen Elizabeth's portrait above Zambian arms **Reverse:** Multicolor portrait of Lief Ericksson and Viking ship **Edge:** Reeded **Size:** 48 x 30.1 mm.

| Date | Mintage | F | VF | XF | Unc | BU |
|---|---|---|---|---|---|---|
| 2000 Proof | 15,000 | Value: 10.00 | | | | |

**1000 KWACHA** KM# 96 **Composition:** Copper-Nickel **Series:** 1,000 Years of Exploration **Reverse:** Multicolor portrait of Marco Polo and ship

| Date | Mintage | F | VF | XF | Unc | BU |
|---|---|---|---|---|---|---|
| 2000 Proof | 15,000 | Value: 10.00 | | | | |

**1000 KWACHA** KM# 98 **Composition:** Copper-Nickel **Series:** 1,000 Years of Exploration **Reverse:** Multicolor portrait of Sir Francis Drake and ship

| Date | Mintage | F | VF | XF | Unc | BU |
|---|---|---|---|---|---|---|
| 2000 Proof | 15,000 | Value: 10.00 | | | | |

**1000 KWACHA** KM# 100 **Composition:** Copper-Nickel **Series:** 1,000 Years of Exploration **Reverse:** Multicolor portrait of Amundsen and ship

| Date | Mintage | F | VF | XF | Unc | BU |
|---|---|---|---|---|---|---|
| 2000 Proof | 15,000 | Value: 10.00 | | | | |

**1000 KWACHA** KM# 97 **Composition:** Copper-Nickel **Series:** 1,000 Years of Exploration **Reverse:** Multicolor portrait of Columbus and ship

| Date | Mintage | F | VF | XF | Unc | BU |
|---|---|---|---|---|---|---|
| 2000 Proof | 15,000 | Value: 10.00 | | | | |

**1000 KWACHA** KM# 99 **Composition:** Copper-Nickel **Series:** 1,000 Years of Exploration **Reverse:** Multicolor portrait of Captain Cook and ship

| Date | Mintage | F | VF | XF | Unc | BU |
|---|---|---|---|---|---|---|
| 2000 Proof | 15,000 | Value: 10.00 | | | | |

**1000 KWACHA** KM# 74 **Composition:** Copper-Nickel **Reverse:** 2001 calendar

| Date | Mintage | F | VF | XF | Unc | BU |
|---|---|---|---|---|---|---|
| 2000 Proof | — | Value: 12.50 | | | | |

**1000 KWACHA** KM# 77 **Weight:** 20.0000 g. **Composition:** Copper-Nickel **Subject:** 100th Birthday - Queen Mother **Reverse:** Black and white photo of Queen Mother as an elderly lady **Note:** Size 48x30mm, similar to KM#80.

| Date | Mintage | F | VF | XF | Unc | BU |
|---|---|---|---|---|---|---|
| 2000 Proof | 50,000 | Value: 13.50 | | | | |

**1000 KWACHA** KM# 76 **Weight:** 20.0000 g. **Composition:** Copper-Nickel **Subject:** 100th Birthday - Queen Mother **Reverse:** Black and white photo of Queen Mother seated on throne at 1937 coronation **Note:** Size 48x30mm.

| Date | Mintage | F | VF | XF | Unc | BU |
|---|---|---|---|---|---|---|
| 2000 Proof | 50,000 | Value: 13.50 | | | | |

**1000 KWACHA** KM# 75 **Weight:** 20.0000 g. **Composition:** Copper-Nickel **Subject:** 100th Birthday - Queen Mother **Obverse:** Queen's portrait above Zambian arms **Edge:** Reeded **Note:** Size: 48x30mm, similar to KM#78.

| Date | Mintage | F | VF | XF | Unc | BU |
|---|---|---|---|---|---|---|
| 2000 Proof | — | Value: 13.50 | | | | |

**1000 KWACHA** KM# 87 **Weight:** 28.9100 g. **Composition:** Copper-Nickel **Series:** Patrons of the Ocean **Obverse:** National arms above Queen Elizabeth's portrait **Reverse:** Sea turtle **Edge:** Reeded **Size:** 38 mm.

| Date | Mintage | F | VF | XF | Unc | BU |
|---|---|---|---|---|---|---|
| 2001 Proof | — | Value: 8.00 | | | | |

**1000 KWACHA** KM# 88 **Weight:** 28.9100 g. **Composition:** Copper-Nickel **Series:** Patrons of the Ocean **Reverse:** Coclacanth

| Date | Mintage | F | VF | XF | Unc | BU |
|---|---|---|---|---|---|---|
| 2001 Proof | — | Value: 8.00 | | | | |

**1000 KWACHA** KM# 89 **Weight:** 28.9100 g. **Composition:** Copper-Nickel **Series:** Patrons of the Ocean **Reverse:** Sea horse and fish

| Date | Mintage | F | VF | XF | Unc | BU |
|---|---|---|---|---|---|---|
| 2001 Proof | — | Value: 8.00 | | | | |

**1000 KWACHA** KM# 90 **Weight:** 28.9100 g. **Composition:** Copper-Nickel **Series:** Patrons of the Ocean **Reverse:** Two dolphins

| Date | Mintage | F | VF | XF | Unc | BU |
|---|---|---|---|---|---|---|
| 2001 Proof | — | Value: 8.00 | | | | |

**2000 KWACHA** KM# 54 **Weight:** 3.1103 g. **Composition:** 0.9999 Gold .1000 oz. AGW **Subject:** Diana - The People's Princess **Note:** Similar to 200 Kwacha, KM#52.

| Date | Mintage | F | VF | XF | Unc | BU |
|---|---|---|---|---|---|---|
| 1997 Proof | — | — | — | — | — | — |

**2000 KWACHA** KM# 68 **Weight:** 15.5518 g. **Composition:** 0.9990 Silver .5000 oz. ASW **Subject:** Taipai Subway **Obverse:** National arms **Reverse:** Train with inset diamond headlight **Note:** Struck at Singapore Mint.

| Date | Mintage | F | VF | XF | Unc | BU |
|---|---|---|---|---|---|---|
| 1998 Proof | 9,999 | Value: 40.00 | | | | |

**2000 KWACHA** KM# 118 **Weight:** 31.1035 g. **Composition:** 0.9990 Silver 1.0000 oz. ASW **Subject:** Centennial of the Anglo-Japanese Alliance **Obverse:** Queen Elizabeth **Reverse:** Fantasy Japanese coin design **Edge:** Reeded **Size:** 38.6 mm.

| Date | Mintage | F | VF | XF | Unc | BU |
|---|---|---|---|---|---|---|
| 2002 | 500 | — | — | — | 55.00 | — |

**2500 KWACHA** KM# 55 **Weight:** 155.5175 g. **Composition:** 0.9990 Silver 5.0000 oz. ASW **Subject:** Diana - The People's Princess **Reverse:** With sons, William and Harry **Note:** Similar to 200 Kwacha, KM#52.

| Date | Mintage | F | VF | XF | Unc | BU |
|---|---|---|---|---|---|---|
| 1997 Proof | Est. 1,997 | Value: 115 | | | | |

**2500 KWACHA** KM# 107 **Weight:** 15.5535 g. **Composition:** 0.9250 Silver .4626 oz. ASW **Series:** World Health Organization **Obverse:** Zambian arms **Reverse:** Director Brundtland portrait and logo **Edge:** Reeded **Size:** 36 mm.

| Date | Mintage | F | VF | XF | Unc | BU |
|---|---|---|---|---|---|---|
| 1998 Proof | — | Value: 30.00 | | | | |

**4000 KWACHA** KM# 69 **Weight:** 31.1035 g. **Composition:** 0.9990 Silver 1.0000 oz. ASW **Subject:** Taipai Subway **Obverse:** National arms **Reverse:** Train with inset diamond headlight **Note:** Struck at Singapore Mint.

| Date | Mintage | F | VF | XF | Unc | BU |
|---|---|---|---|---|---|---|
| 1998 Proof | 9,999 | Value: 60.00 | | | | |

**4000 KWACHA** **KM# 106** **Weight:** 20.0000 g. **Composition:** 0.9250 Silver .5948 oz. ASW **Subject:** 1000 Years of Exploration **Reverse:** Multi-colored portrait of Amundsen and ship **Note:** Similar to KM#100.

| Date | Mintage | F | VF | XF | Unc | BU |
|---|---|---|---|---|---|---|
| 2000 Proof | 5,000 | Value: 40.00 | | | | |

**4000 KWACHA** **KM# 103** **Weight:** 20.0000 g. **Composition:** 0.9250 Silver .5948 oz. ASW **Subject:** 1000 Years of Exploration **Reverse:** Multi-colored portrait of Columbus and ship **Note:** Similar to KM#97.

| Date | Mintage | F | VF | XF | Unc | BU |
|---|---|---|---|---|---|---|
| 2000 Proof | 5,000 | Value: 40.00 | | | | |

**4000 KWACHA** **KM# 105** **Weight:** 20.0000 g. **Composition:** 0.9250 Silver .5948 oz. ASW **Subject:** 1000 Years of Exploration **Reverse:** Multi-colored portrait of Captain Cook and ship **Note:** Similar to KM#99.

| Date | Mintage | F | VF | XF | Unc | BU |
|---|---|---|---|---|---|---|
| 2000 Proof | 5,000 | Value: 40.00 | | | | |

**4000 KWACHA** **KM# 102** **Weight:** 20.0000 g. **Composition:** 0.9250 Silver .5948 oz. ASW **Subject:** 1000 Years of Exploration **Reverse:** Multi-colored portrait of Marco Polo and ship **Note:** Similar to KM#96.

| Date | Mintage | F | VF | XF | Unc | BU |
|---|---|---|---|---|---|---|
| 2000 Proof | 5,000 | Value: 40.00 | | | | |

**4000 KWACHA** **KM# 104** **Weight:** 20.0000 g. **Composition:** 0.9250 Silver .5948 oz. ASW **Subject:** 1000 Years of Exploration **Note:** Similar to KM#98.

| Date | Mintage | F | VF | XF | Unc | BU |
|---|---|---|---|---|---|---|
| 2000 Proof | 5,000 | Value: 40.00 | | | | |

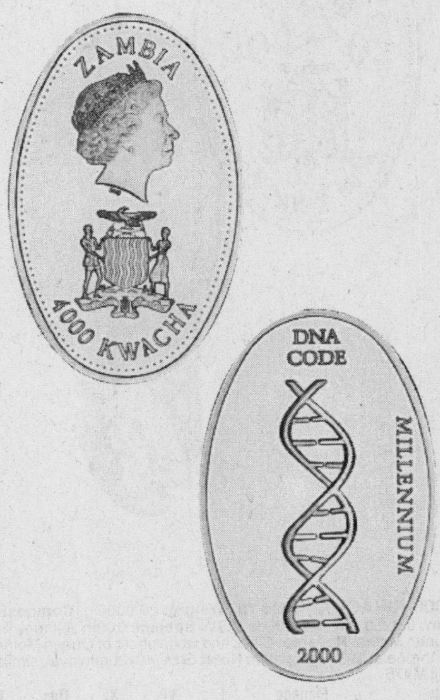


**4000 KWACHA** **KM# 84** **Weight:** 20.0000 g. **Composition:** 0.9250 Silver .5948 oz. ASW **Subject:** Millennium - DNA Code **Obverse:** British Queen's portrait above arms **Reverse:** DNA chain **Edge:** Reeded **Size:** 30.1x48 mm.

| Date | Mintage | F | VF | XF | Unc | BU |
|---|---|---|---|---|---|---|
| 2000 Proof | — | Value: 32.50 | | | | |

**4000 KWACHA** **KM# 85** **Weight:** 25.1000 g. **Composition:** 0.9250 Silver .7465 oz. ASW **Series:** Wildlife Protection **Obverse:** British Queen's portrait below arms **Reverse:** Lion hologram **Edge:** Reeded **Size:** 37.9 mm. **Note:** Lighter weight and smaller diameter than official specifications.

| Date | Mintage | F | VF | XF | Unc | BU |
|---|---|---|---|---|---|---|
| 2000 Proof | 5,000 | Value: 45.00 | | | | |
| 2001 | — | — | — | — | — | — |

**4000 KWACHA** **KM# 79** **Weight:** 20.0000 g. **Composition:** 0.9250 Silver .5948 oz. ASW **Subject:** 100th Birthday - Queen Mother **Reverse:** Black and white photo of Queen Mother on throne at 1937 coronation **Note:** Size: 48x30mm oval, similar to KM#76.

| Date | Mintage | F | VF | XF | Unc | BU |
|---|---|---|---|---|---|---|
| 2000 Proof | 25,000 | Value: 40.00 | | | | |

**4000 KWACHA** **KM# 78** **Weight:** 20.0000 g. **Composition:** 0.9250 Silver .5948 oz. ASW **Subject:** 100th Birthday - Queen Mother **Obverse:** Queen's portrait above Zambian arms **Reverse:** Black and white photo of the Queen Mother as a young lady **Edge:** Reeded **Note:** Size: 48x30mm oval.

| Date | Mintage | F | VF | XF | Unc | BU |
|---|---|---|---|---|---|---|
| 2000 Proof | 25,000 | Value: 40.00 | | | | |

**4000 KWACHA** **KM# 80** **Weight:** 20.0000 g. **Composition:** 0.9250 Silver .5948 oz. ASW **Subject:** 100th Birthday - Queen Mother **Reverse:** Black and white photo of an elderly Queen Mother **Note:** Size: 48x30mm oval.

| Date | Mintage | F | VF | XF | Unc | BU |
|---|---|---|---|---|---|---|
| 2000 Proof | 25,000 | Value: 40.00 | | | | |

**4000 KWACHA** **KM# 110** **Weight:** 20.0000 g. **Composition:** 0.9990 Silver .6424 oz. ASW **Series:** Patrons of the Ocean **Obverse:** Zambian arms above Queen Elizabeth's portrait **Reverse:** Sea turtle **Edge:** Reeded **Size:** 37.9 mm.

| Date | Mintage | F | VF | XF | Unc | BU |
|---|---|---|---|---|---|---|
| 2001 Proof | — | Value: 35.00 | | | | |

**4000 KWACHA** **KM# 111** **Weight:** 20.0000 g. **Composition:** 0.9990 Silver .6424 oz. ASW **Series:** Patrons of the Ocean **Reverse:** Coclacanth fish

| Date | Mintage | F | VF | XF | Unc | BU |
|---|---|---|---|---|---|---|
| 2001 Proof | — | Value: 35.00 | | | | |

**4000 KWACHA** **KM# 112** **Weight:** 20.0000 g. **Composition:** 0.9990 Silver .6424 oz. ASW **Series:** Patrons of the Ocean **Reverse:** Sea horse and fish

| Date | Mintage | F | VF | XF | Unc | BU |
|---|---|---|---|---|---|---|
| 2001 Proof | — | Value: 35.00 | | | | |

**4000 KWACHA** KM# 113 **Weight:** 20.0000 g. **Composition:** 0.9990 Silver .6424 oz. ASW **Series:** Patrons of the Ocean **Reverse:** Two dolphins

| Date | Mintage | F | VF | XF | Unc | BU |
|---|---|---|---|---|---|---|
| 2001 Proof | — | Value: 35.00 | | | | |

**4000 KWACHA** KM# 114 **Weight:** 50.0000 g. **Composition:** 0.9990 Silver 1.6059 oz. ASW **Subject:** Illusion **Obverse:** Zambian arms below Queen Elizabeth's portrait **Reverse:** "Cat in the Window" **Edge:** Plain **Note:** 50x50 milimeters

| Date | Mintage | F | VF | XF | Unc | BU |
|---|---|---|---|---|---|---|
| 2001 Proof | 5,000 | Value: 40.00 | | | | |

**5000 KWACHA** KM# 108 **Weight:** 31.2100 g. **Composition:** 0.9250 Silver .9282 oz. ASW **Subject:** World Health Organization **Obverse:** Zambian arms **Reverse:** Director Brundtland's portrait **Edge:** Reeded **Size:** 40 mm.

| Date | Mintage | F | VF | XF | Unc | BU |
|---|---|---|---|---|---|---|
| 1998 Proof | — | Value: 40.00 | | | | |

**5000 KWACHA** KM# 70 **Weight:** 7.7759 g. **Composition:** 0.9990 Gold .2500 oz. AGW **Subject:** Taipai Subway **Obverse:** National arms **Reverse:** Train with inset diamond headlight **Note:** Struck at Singapore Mint.

| Date | Mintage | F | VF | XF | Unc | BU |
|---|---|---|---|---|---|---|
| 1998 Proof | 999 | Value: 350 | | | | |

**5000 KWACHA** KM# 92 **Weight:** 31.2100 g. **Composition:** 0.9990 Silver 1.0024 oz. ASW **Subject:** African Wildlife **Obverse:** National arms **Reverse:** Elephant mother and calf **Edge:** Reeded **Size:** 38.7 mm.

| Date | Mintage | F | VF | XF | Unc | BU |
|---|---|---|---|---|---|---|
| 1999 Proof | — | Value: 30.00 | | | | |

**5000 KWACHA** KM# 73 **Weight:** 31.1346 g. **Composition:** 0.9990 Silver 1.0000 oz. ASW **Subject:** African Wildlife **Reverse:** Elephant

| Date | Mintage | F | VF | XF | Unc | BU |
|---|---|---|---|---|---|---|
| 1999 | — | — | — | — | 20.00 | — |
| 1999 Matte | — | — | — | — | 30.00 | — |

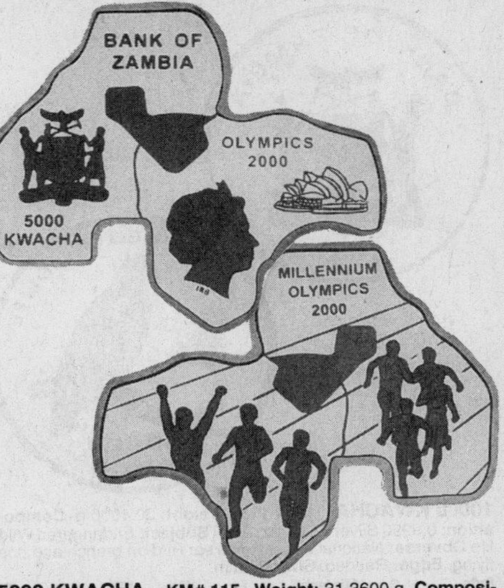


**5000 KWACHA** KM# 115 **Weight:** 31.3600 g. **Composition:** 0.9250 Silver .9326 oz. ASW **Subject:** Olympics **Obverse:** National arms map, Queen Elizabeth's portrait. **Reverse:** Runners and map. **Edge:** Plain. **Size:** 48.7 x 41.75 mm. **Note:** Irregular shape.

| Date | Mintage | F | VF | XF | Unc | BU |
|---|---|---|---|---|---|---|
| 2000 Proof | — | Value: 50.00 | | | | |

**5000 KWACHA** KM# 81 **Weight:** 27.0000 g. **Composition:** 0.9990 Gold .8672 oz. AGW **Subject:** 100th Birthday - Queen Mother **Obverse:** Queen's portrait above Zambian arms **Reverse:** Black and white photo of the Queen Mother as a young lady **Edge:** Reeded **Note:** Size: 48x30mm oval.

| Date | Mintage | F | VF | XF | Unc | BU |
|---|---|---|---|---|---|---|
| 2000 Proof | 100 | Value: 675 | | | | |

**5000 KWACHA** KM# 82 **Weight:** 27.0000 g. **Composition:** 0.9990 Gold .8672 oz. AGW **Subject:** 100th Birthday - Queen Mother **Reverse:** Black ad white photo of Queen Mother on throne at 1937 coronation **Note:** Size: 48x30mm oval.

| Date | Mintage | F | VF | XF | Unc | BU |
|---|---|---|---|---|---|---|
| 2000 Proof | 100 | Value: 675 | | | | |

**5000 KWACHA** KM# 83 **Weight:** 27.0000 g. **Composition:** 0.9990 Gold .8672 oz. AGW **Subject:** 100th Birthday - Queen Mother **Reverse:** Black and white photo of an elderly Queen Mother **Note:** Size: 48x30mm oval.

| Date | Mintage | F | VF | XF | Unc | BU |
|---|---|---|---|---|---|---|
| 2000 Proof | 100 | Value: 675 | | | | |

**5000 KWACHA** KM# 117 **Weight:** 31.3000 g. **Composition:** 0.9990 Silver 1.0053 oz. ASW **Subject:** African Wildlife **Obverse:** National arms. **Reverse:** Elephant mother and calf grazing on grass. **Edge:** Reeded. **Size:** 38.6 mm.

| Date | Mintage | F | VF | XF | Unc | BU |
|---|---|---|---|---|---|---|
| 2001 Proof | — | Value: 50.00 | | | | |

**10000 KWACHA** KM# 116 **Weight:** 30.4000 g. **Composition:** 0.9990 Silver .9764 oz. ASW **Subject:** Endangered Wildlife **Obverse:** National arms. **Reverse:** Bird on branch and one flying. **Edge:** Reeded. **Size:** 34 mm.

| Date | Mintage | F | VF | XF | Unc | BU |
|---|---|---|---|---|---|---|
| 1997 Proof | — | Value: 45.00 | | | | |

**10000 KWACHA** KM# 86 **Weight:** 30.2800 g. **Composition:** 0.9990 Silver .9726 oz. ASW **Series:** Endangered Wildlife **Obverse:** National arms **Reverse:** Lion family **Edge:** Reeded **Note:** Coin size 34mm, thickness is 3.8mm.

| Date | Mintage | F | VF | XF | Unc | BU |
|---|---|---|---|---|---|---|
| 1997 Proof | — | Value: 32.50 | | | | |

**10000 KWACHA** KM# 71 **Weight:** 15.5518 g. **Composition:** 0.9999 Gold .5000 oz. AGW **Subject:** Taipai Subway **Obverse:** National arms **Reverse:** Train with inset diamond headlight **Note:** Struck at Singapore Mint.

| Date | Mintage | F | VF | XF | Unc | BU |
|---|---|---|---|---|---|---|
| 1998 Proof | 99 | Value: 650 | | | | |

**20000 KWACHA** KM# 93 **Weight:** 1000.0000 g. **Composition:** 0.9990 Silver 32.1186 oz. ASW **Subject:** Ko-Imari VOC Plate **Obverse:** Queen Elizabeth's portrait **Reverse:** Multi-colored plate design **Edge:** Reeded **Size:** 101 mm. **Note:** Illustration reduced. Actual size: 100mm. Struck at Perth Mint on behalf of the Fiji International Mint.

| Date | Mintage | F | VF | XF | Unc | BU |
|---|---|---|---|---|---|---|
| 2000FIM Proof | 500 | Value: 690 | | | | |

**40000 KWACHA** KM# 101 **Weight:** 20.0000 g. **Composition:** 0.9250 Silver .5948 oz. ASW **Series:** 1000 Years of Exploration **Obverse:** Queen Elizabeth's portrait and Zambian arms below **Reverse:** Multi-colored portrait of Lief Eriksson and ship **Edge:** Reeded **Note:** 48x30.1 milimeters

| Date | Mintage | F | VF | XF | Unc | BU |
|---|---|---|---|---|---|---|
| 2000 Proof | 5,000 | Value: 40.00 | | | | |

**40000 KWACHA** KM# 94 **Weight:** 31.1035 g. **Composition:** 0.9999 Gold 1.0000 oz. AGW **Series:** Wildlife Protection **Obverse:** Zambian arms above Queen Elizabeth's portrait **Reverse:** Holographic lion picture **Edge:** Reeded **Size:** 37.9 mm.

| Date | Mintage | F | VF | XF | Unc | BU |
|---|---|---|---|---|---|---|
| 2001 Proof | — | Value: 350 | | | | |

**500000 KWACHA** KM# 72 **Weight:** 155.5175 g. **Composition:** 0.9999 Gold 5.0000 oz. AGW **Subject:** Taipai Subway **Obverse:** National arms **Reverse:** Train with inset diamond headlight **Note:** Struck at Singapore Mint.

| Date | Mintage | F | VF | XF | Unc | BU |
|---|---|---|---|---|---|---|
| 1998 Proof | 99 | — | — | — | — | — |

## PATTERNS

| KM# | Date | Mintage | Identification | Mkt Val |
|---|---|---|---|---|
| Pn3 | 1994 | — | 2000 Kwacha. Copper-Nickel. Similar to KM#39 | — |

| KM# | Date | Mintage | Identification | Mkt Val |
|---|---|---|---|---|
| Pn1 | 1994 | — | 10 Kwacha. Copper-Nickel. KM#39 | 80.00 |

| KM# | Date | Mintage | Identification | Mkt Val |
|---|---|---|---|---|
| Pn2 | 1994 | — | 10 Kwacha. Silver. Similar to KM#39, .999 Cu Ni in field. | 80.00 |

| KM# | Date | Mintage | Identification | Mkt Val |
|---|---|---|---|---|

| KM# | Date | Mintage | Identification | Mkt Val |
|---|---|---|---|---|
| Pn4 | 1998 | — | 1000 Kwacha. Copper-Nickel. 28.5000 g. 38.6 mm. National arms. Portrait and memorial. Reeded edge. | 250 |

## PIEFORTS

| KM# | Date | Mintage | Identification | Mkt Val |
|---|---|---|---|---|
| P1 | 1980 | 76 | 10 Kwacha. 54.4400 g. KM#21 | 125 |

## MINT SETS

| KM# | Date | Mintage | Identification | Issue Price | Mkt Val |
|---|---|---|---|---|---|
| MS1 | 1968 (5) | — | KM#9-13 | 2.00 | 7.00 |

## PROOF SETS

| KM# | Date | Mintage | Identification | Issue Price | Mkt Val |
|---|---|---|---|---|---|
| PS1 | 1964 (3) | 5,000 | KM#1-3 | — | 10.00 |
| PS2 | 1965 (2) | 100 | KM#4 (2 pieces) | — | 15.00 |
| PS3 | 1966 (8) | 30 | KM#5-8, double sets | — | — |
| PS4 | 1968 (5) | 4,000 | KM#9-13 | 10.00 | 9.50 |
| PS5 | 1978 (6) | 20,000 | KM#9-13, 16 | 21.00 | 16.50 |
| PS6 | 1994 (10) | — | KM#40-49 | 300 | 285 |
| PS7 | 1998 (12) | 25,000 | KM#56-67 | 672 | 685 |
| PS10 | 2000 (4) | 100 | KM#81-83 | — | 2,025 |
| PS8 | 2000 (3) | 50,000 | KM#75-77 | — | 45.00 |
| PS9 | 2000 (3) | 25,000 | KM#78-80 | — | 120 |

# ZANZIBAR

The British protectorate of Zanzibar and adjacent small islands, located in the Indian Ocean 22 miles (35 km.) off the coast of Tanganyika, comprised a portion of British East Africa. Zanzibar was also the name of a sultanate which included the Zanzibar and Kenya protectorates. Zanzibar has an area of 637 sq. mi. (1,651 sq. km.). Chief city: Zanzibar. The islands are noted for their cloves, of which Zanzibar is the world's foremost producer.

Zanzibar came under Portuguese control in 1503, was conquered by the Omani Arabs in 1698, became independent of Oman in 1860, and (with Pemba) came under British control in 1890. Britain granted the protectorate self-government in 1961, and independence within the British Commonwealth on Dec. 19, 1963. On April 26,1964, Tanganyika and Zanzibar (with Pemba) united to form the United Republic of Tanganyika and Zanzibar. The name of the country, which remained within the British Commonwealth was changed to Tanzania on Oct. 29,1964.

**TITLES**

زنجباراه

Zanjibara

**RULERS**

Sultan Ali Bin Hamud, 1902-1911AD

**MONETARY SYSTEM**

64 Pysa (Pice) = 1 Rupee
136 Pysa = 1 Ryal (to 1908)
100 Cents = 1 Rupee (to 1909)

## BRITISH PROTECTORATE

### DECIMAL COINAGE

100 Cents = 1 Rupee

**CENT** KM# 8 **Composition:** Bronze

| Date | Mintage | F | VF | XF | Unc | BU |
|---|---|---|---|---|---|---|
| 1908 | 1,000,000 | 40.00 | 80.00 | 150 | 350 | — |

**CENT** KM# 9 **Composition:** Bronze

| Date | Mintage | F | VF | XF | Unc | BU |
|---|---|---|---|---|---|---|
| 1908 | 100,000 | 75.00 | 140 | 285 | 550 | — |

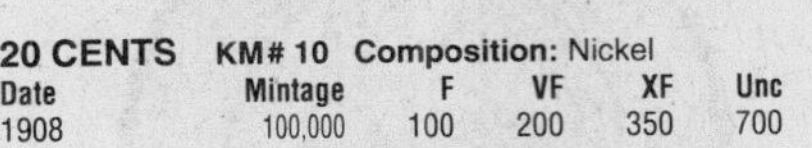

**20 CENTS** KM# 10 **Composition:** Nickel

| Date | Mintage | F | VF | XF | Unc | BU |
|---|---|---|---|---|---|---|
| 1908 | 100,000 | 100 | 200 | 350 | 700 | — |

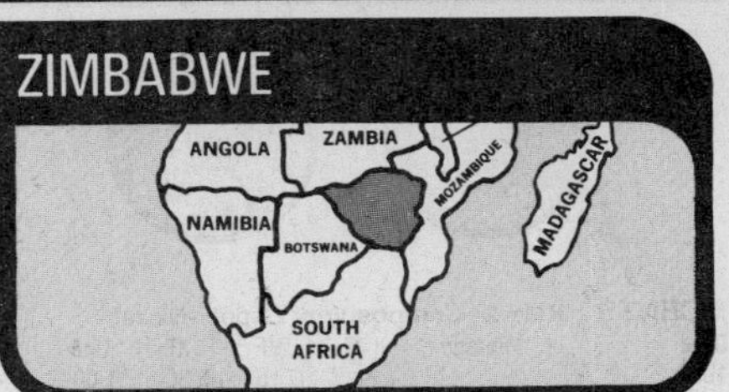


The Republic of Zimbabwe (formerly the Republic of Rhodesia or Southern Rhodesia), located in the east-central part of southern Africa, has an area of 150,804 sq. mi. (390,580sq. km.) and a population of *10.1 million. Capital: Harare (formerly Salisbury). The economy is based on agriculture and mining. Tobacco, sugar, asbestos, copper, chrome, ore and coal are exported.

The Rhodesian area contains extensive evidence of the habitat of paleolithic man and earlier civilizations, notably the world-famous ruins of Zimbabwe, a gold-trading center that flourished about the 14th or 15th century A.D. The Portuguese of the 16th century were the first Europeans to attempt to develop south-central Africa, but it re-mained for Cecil Rhodes and the British South Africa Co. to open the hinterlands. Rhodes obtained a concession for mineral rights from local chiefs in 1888 and administered his African empire (named Southern Rhodesia in 1895) through the British South Africa Co. until 1923, when the British government annexed the area after the white settlers voted for existence as a separate entity, rather than for incorporation into the Union of South Africa. From Sept. of 1953 through 1963 Southern Rhodesia was joined with the British Protectorates of Northern Rhodesia and Nyasaland into a multiracial federation, known as the Federation of Rhodesia and Nyasaland. When the federation was dissolved at the end of 1963, Northern Rhodesia and Nyasaland became the independent states of Zambia and Malawi.

Britain was prepared to grant independence to Southern Rhodesia but declined to do so when the politically dominant white Rhodesians refused to give assurances of representative government. On Nov. 11, 1965, following two years of unsuccessful negotiation with the British government, Prime Minister Ian Smith issued an unilateral declaration of independence. Britain responded with economic sanctions supported by the United Nations. After further futile attempts to effect an accommodation, the Rhodesian Parliament severed all ties with Britain and on March 2, 1970, established the Republic of Rhodesia.

On March 3, 1978, Prime Minister Ian Smith and three moderate black nationalist leaders signed an agreement providing for black majority rule. The name of the country was changed to Zimbabwe Rhodesia. Following a conference in London in December 1979, the opposition government conceded and it was agreed that the British Government should resume control. A British Governor soon returned to Southern Rhodesia. One of his first acts was to affirm the nullification of the purported declaration of independence. On April 18, 1980 pursuant to an act of the British Parliament, the colony of Southern Rhodesia became independent within the Commonwealth as the Republic of Zimbabwe, which remains a member of the British Commonwealth of Nations.

**MONETARY SYSTEM**

100 Cents = 1 Dollar

## REPUBLIC

### DECIMAL COINAGE

**CENT** KM# 1 **Composition:** Bronze

| Date | Mintage | F | VF | XF | Unc | BU |
|---|---|---|---|---|---|---|
| 1980 | 10,000,000 | — | 0.10 | 0.20 | 0.40 | — |
| 1980 Proof | 15,000 | Value: 1.50 | | | | |
| 1982 | — | — | 0.10 | 0.20 | 0.40 | — |
| 1983 | — | — | 0.10 | 0.20 | 0.40 | — |
| 1986 | — | — | 0.10 | 0.20 | 0.40 | — |
| 1988 | — | — | 0.10 | 0.20 | 0.40 | — |

**CENT** KM# 1a **Composition:** Bronze Plated Steel

| Date | Mintage | F | VF | XF | Unc | BU |
|---|---|---|---|---|---|---|
| 1989 | — | — | 0.10 | 0.20 | 0.50 | — |
| 1990 | — | — | 0.10 | 0.20 | 0.50 | — |
| 1991 | — | — | 0.10 | 0.20 | 0.50 | — |
| 1994 | — | — | 0.10 | 0.20 | 0.50 | — |
| 1995 | — | — | 0.10 | 0.20 | 0.50 | — |
| 1997 | — | — | 0.10 | 0.20 | 0.50 | — |
| 1997 Proof | 5,500 | Value: 1.00 | | | | |

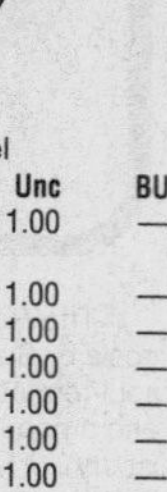

**5 CENTS** **KM# 2** **Composition:** Copper-Nickel

| Date | Mintage | F | VF | XF | Unc | BU |
|---|---|---|---|---|---|---|
| 1980 | — | — | 0.15 | 0.30 | 1.00 | — |
| 1980 Proof | 15,000 | Value: 1.50 | | | | |
| 1982 | — | — | 0.15 | 0.30 | 1.00 | — |
| 1983 | — | — | 0.15 | 0.30 | 1.00 | — |
| 1988 | — | — | 0.15 | 0.30 | 1.00 | — |
| 1989 | — | — | 0.15 | 0.30 | 1.00 | — |
| 1990 | — | — | 0.15 | 0.30 | 1.00 | — |
| 1991 | — | — | 0.15 | 0.30 | 1.00 | — |
| 1995 | — | — | 0.15 | 0.30 | 1.00 | — |
| 1997 | — | — | 0.15 | 0.30 | 1.00 | — |
| 1997 Proof | Est. 5,500 | Value: 2.00 | | | | |

**10 CENTS** **KM# 3** **Composition:** Copper-Nickel

| Date | Mintage | F | VF | XF | Unc | BU |
|---|---|---|---|---|---|---|
| 1980 | — | — | 0.15 | 0.30 | 0.75 | — |
| 1980 Proof | 15,000 | Value: 2.00 | | | | |
| 1983 | — | — | 0.15 | 0.30 | 0.75 | — |
| 1987 | — | — | 0.15 | 0.30 | 0.75 | — |
| 1988 | — | — | 0.15 | 0.30 | 0.75 | — |
| 1989 | — | — | 0.15 | 0.30 | 0.75 | — |
| 1991 | — | — | 0.15 | 0.30 | 0.75 | — |
| 1994 | — | — | 0.15 | 0.30 | 0.75 | — |
| 1997 | — | — | 0.15 | 0.30 | 0.75 | — |
| 1997 Proof | Est. 5,500 | Value: 3.00 | | | | |

**20 CENTS** **KM# 4** **Composition:** Copper-Nickel

| Date | Mintage | F | VF | XF | Unc | BU |
|---|---|---|---|---|---|---|
| 1980 | — | — | 0.25 | 0.50 | 1.50 | — |
| 1980 Proof | 15,000 | Value: 2.50 | | | | |
| 1983 | — | — | 0.25 | 0.50 | 1.50 | — |
| 1987 | — | — | 0.20 | 0.40 | 1.25 | — |
| 1988 | — | — | 0.20 | 0.40 | 1.25 | — |
| 1989 | — | — | 0.20 | 0.40 | 1.25 | — |
| 1990 | — | — | 0.20 | 0.40 | 1.25 | — |
| 1991 | — | — | 0.20 | 0.40 | 1.25 | — |
| 1994 | — | — | 0.20 | 0.40 | 1.25 | — |
| 1996 | — | — | 0.20 | 0.40 | 1.25 | — |
| 1997 | — | — | 0.20 | 0.40 | 1.25 | — |
| 1997 Proof | Est. 5,500 | Value: 4.00 | | | | |

**50 CENTS** **KM# 5** **Composition:** Copper-Nickel

| Date | Mintage | F | VF | XF | Unc | BU |
|---|---|---|---|---|---|---|
| 1980 | — | — | 0.60 | 1.25 | 2.25 | — |
| 1980 Proof | 15,000 | Value: 4.50 | | | | |
| 1988 | — | — | 0.40 | 1.00 | 1.75 | — |
| 1989 | — | — | 0.40 | 1.00 | 1.75 | — |
| 1990 | — | — | 0.40 | 1.00 | 1.75 | — |
| 1993 | — | — | 0.40 | 1.00 | 1.75 | — |
| 1995 | — | — | 0.40 | 1.00 | 1.75 | — |
| 1997 | — | — | 0.40 | 1.00 | 1.75 | — |
| 1997 Proof | Est. 5,500 | Value: 8.00 | | | | |

**DOLLAR** **KM# 6** **Composition:** Copper-Nickel

| Date | Mintage | F | VF | XF | Unc | BU |
|---|---|---|---|---|---|---|
| 1980 | — | — | 1.00 | 1.50 | 3.00 | — |
| 1980 Proof | 15,000 | Value: 6.50 | | | | |
| 1993 | — | — | 1.00 | 1.50 | 3.00 | — |
| 1997 | — | — | 1.00 | 1.50 | 3.00 | — |
| 1997 Proof | Est. 5,500 | Value: 12.00 | | | | |

**2 DOLLARS** **KM# 12** **Composition:** Brass **Reverse:** Pangolin and denomination

| Date | Mintage | F | VF | XF | Unc | BU |
|---|---|---|---|---|---|---|
| 1997 | — | — | — | — | 5.00 | — |
| 1997 Proof | Est. 5,500 | Value: 20.00 | | | | |

**10 DOLLARS** **KM# 7** **Weight:** 31.1035 g. **Composition:** 0.9990 Silver 1.0000 oz. ASW **Series:** Wildlife Landmark **Obverse:** Victoria Falls Bridge **Reverse:** Lions

| Date | Mintage | F | VF | XF | Unc | BU |
|---|---|---|---|---|---|---|
| 1996 Proof | 5,000 | Value: 45.00 | | | | |

**10 DOLLARS** **KM# 8** **Weight:** 31.1035 g. **Composition:** 0.9990 Silver 1.0000 oz. ASW **Series:** Wildlife Landmark **Obverse:** Motopo Hills **Reverse:** Cape buffalo

| Date | Mintage | F | VF | XF | Unc | BU |
|---|---|---|---|---|---|---|
| 1996 Proof | 5,000 | Value: 45.00 | | | | |

**10 DOLLARS** **KM# 9** **Weight:** 31.1035 g. **Composition:** 0.9990 Silver 1.0000 oz. ASW **Series:** Wildlife Landmark **Obverse:** Zimbabwe Ruins **Reverse:** Leopard in a tree

| Date | Mintage | F | VF | XF | Unc | BU |
|---|---|---|---|---|---|---|
| 1996 Proof | 5,000 | Value: 45.00 | | | | |

**10 DOLLARS** **KM# 10** **Weight:** 31.1035 g. **Composition:** 0.9990 Silver 1.0000 oz. ASW **Series:** Wildlife Landmark **Obverse:** Kariba Dam **Reverse:** Two elephants

| Date | Mintage | F | VF | XF | Unc | BU |
|---|---|---|---|---|---|---|
| 1996 Proof | 5,000 | Value: 45.00 | | | | |

**10 DOLLARS** **KM# 11** **Weight:** 31.1035 g. **Composition:** 0.9990 Silver 1.0000 oz. ASW **Series:** Wildlife Landmark **Obverse:** Reserve Bank Building **Reverse:** Rhinoceros

| Date | Mintage | F | VF | XF | Unc | BU |
|---|---|---|---|---|---|---|
| 1996 Proof | 5,000 | Value: 45.00 | | | | |

## PROOF SETS

| KM# | Date | Mintage | Identification | Issue Price | Mkt Val |
|---|---|---|---|---|---|
| PS1 | 1980 (6) | 15,000 | KM#1-6 | 29.00 | 18.50 |
| PS2 | 1997 (7) | 5,500 | KM#1a, 2-6, 12 | 45.00 | 50.00 |

# EUROPE

Compliments of
Evzen Sknovril

### ALBANIA

1 lek = 100 qindarka

### AUSTRIA

1 Euro = 100 cents
1 Schilling = 100 Groschen

### BELARUS

1 rubel = 100 kapeik

### BELGIUM

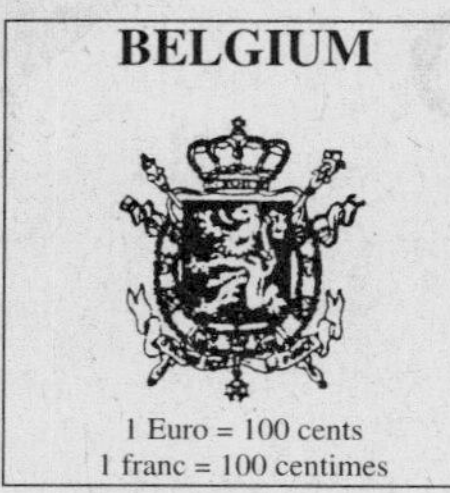

1 Euro = 100 cents
1 franc = 100 centimes

### BOSNIA AND HERZEGOVINA

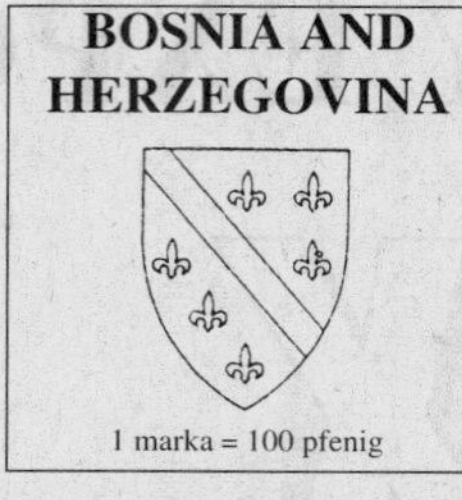

1 marka = 100 pfenig

### BULGARIA

1 lev = 100 stotinki

### CROATIA

1 kuna = 100 lipa

### CZECH REPUBLIC

1 koruna ceska = 100 haleru

### DENMARK

1 krone = 100 ore

### ESTONIA

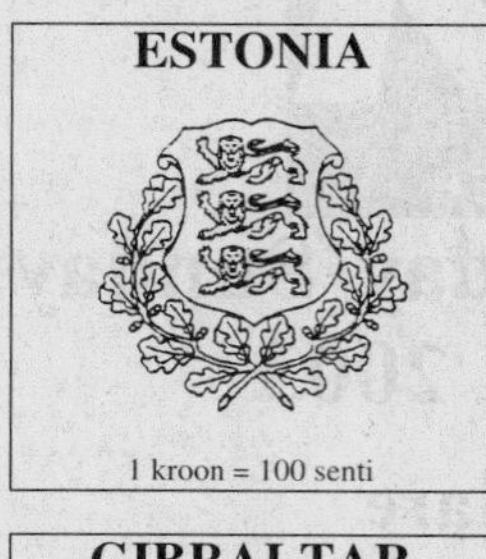

1 kroon = 100 senti

### FAROE ISLANDS

1 krona = 100 ore

### FINLAND

1 Euro = 100 cents
1 markka = 100 pennia

### FRANCE

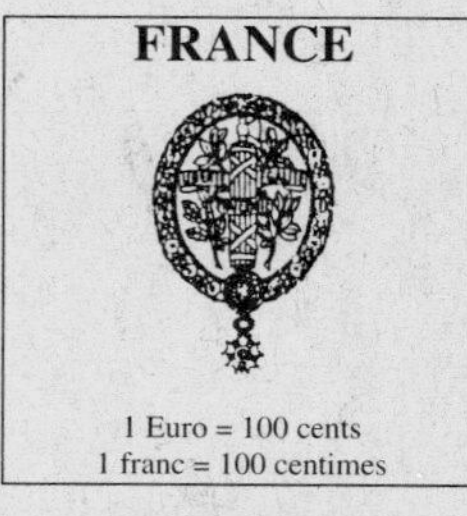

1 Euro = 100 cents
1 franc = 100 centimes

### GERMANY

1 Euro = 100 cents
1 Deutsche Mark = 100 Pfennig

### GIBRALTAR

1 pound = 100 pence

### GREAT BRITAIN

1 pound = 100 pence

### GREECE

1 Euro = 100 cents
1 drachme = 100 lepton

### GUERNSEY

1 pound = 100 pence

### HUNGARY

1 forint = 100 filler

### ICELAND

1 krona = 100 aurar

### IRELAND

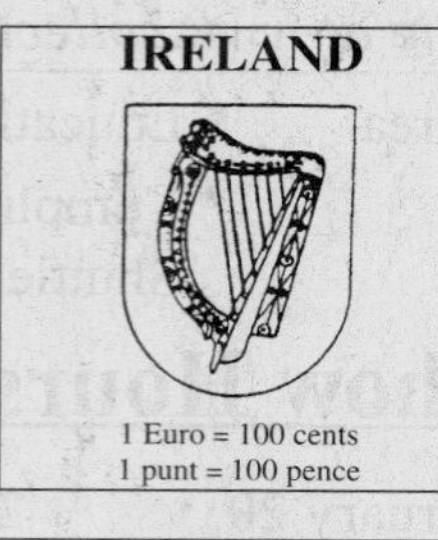

1 Euro = 100 cents
1 punt = 100 pence

### IRELAND NORTHERN

1 pound = 100 pence

### ISLE OF MAN

1 pound = 100 pence

### ITALY

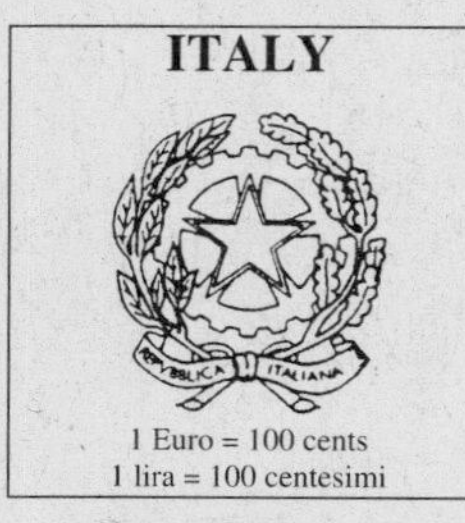

1 Euro = 100 cents
1 lira = 100 centesimi

### JERSEY

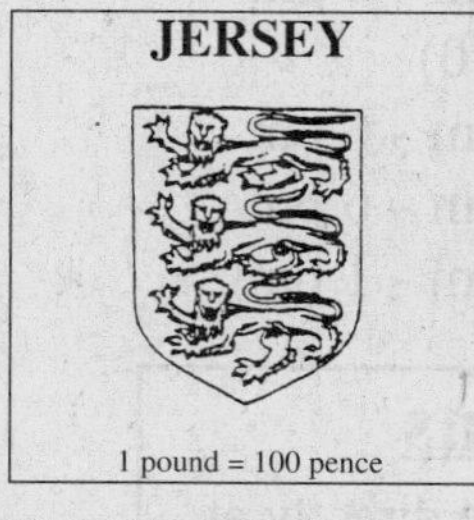

1 pound = 100 pence

### LATVIA

1 lats = 100 santimu

### LITHUANIA

1 litas = 100 centu

### LUXEMBOURG

1 Euro = 100 cents
1 franc = 100 centimes

### MACEDONIA

1 denar = 100 deni

### MALTA

1 lira = 100 cents

### MOLDOVA

1 leu = 100 bani

### NETHERLANDS

1 Euro = 100 cents
1 gulden = 100 cent

### NORWAY

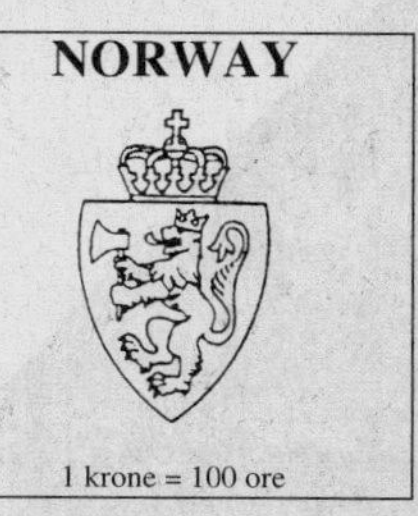

1 krone = 100 ore

# ARMS AND MONETARY SYSTEMS GUIDE

### POLAND

1 zloty = 100 groszy

### PORTUGAL

1 Euro = 100 cents
1 escudo = 100 centavos

### ROMANIA

1 leu = 100 bani

### RUSSIA

1 ruble = 100 kopejek

### SCOTLAND

1 pound = 100 pence

### SLOVAKIA

1 slovenska korun = 100 halierov

### SLOVENIA

1 tolar = stotinov

### SPAIN

1 Euro = 100 cents
1 peseta = 100 centimos

### SWEDEN
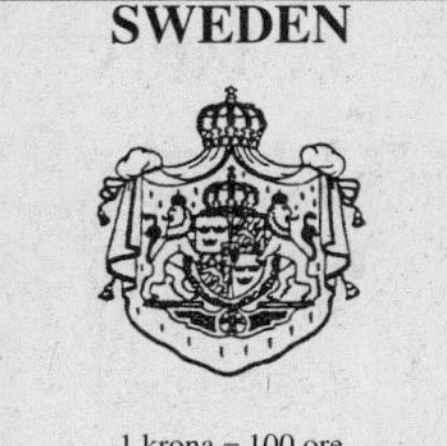
1 krona = 100 ore

### SWITZERLAND
1 frank = 100 rappen

### TRANSNIESTRIA

1 ruble

### UKRAINE
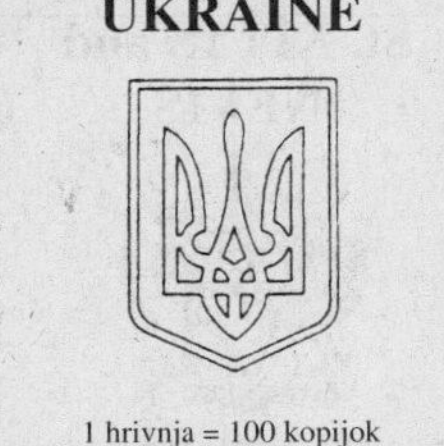
1 hrivnja = 100 kopijok

### YUGOSLAVIA

1 novi dinar = 100 para

## AMERICA

### ANGUILLA

1 (EC) dollar = 100 cents

### ARGENTINA

1 peso (nuevo) = 100 centavos

### ARUBA

1 florin = 100 cent

### BAHAMAS

1 dollar = 100 cent

### BARBADOS

1 dollar = 100 cent

### BELIZE

1 dinar = 100 para

### BERMUDA

1 dollar = 100 cents

### BOLIVIA

1 boliviano = 100 centavos

### BRAZIL
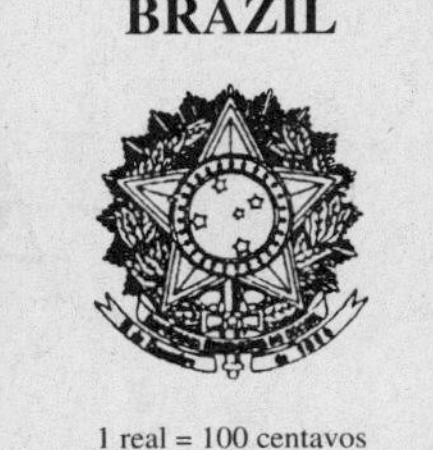
1 real = 100 centavos

### CANADA

1 dollar = 100 cents

### CAYMAN ISLANDS

1 dollar = 100 cents

### CHILE
1 peso = 100 centavos

### COLOMBIA
1 peso = 100 centavos

### COSTA RICA

1 colon = 100 centimos

### CUBA

1 peso = 100 centavos

### DOMINICA

1 (EC) dollar = 100 cents

### DOMINICAN REPUBLIC

1 peso oro = 100 centavos

### ECUADOR

1 sucre = 100 centavos

### EL SALVADOR

1 colon = 100 centavos

### FALKLAND ISLANDS

1 pound = 100 pence

# ARMS AND MONETARY SYSTEMS GUIDE

### FRENCH PACIFIC TERRITORIES
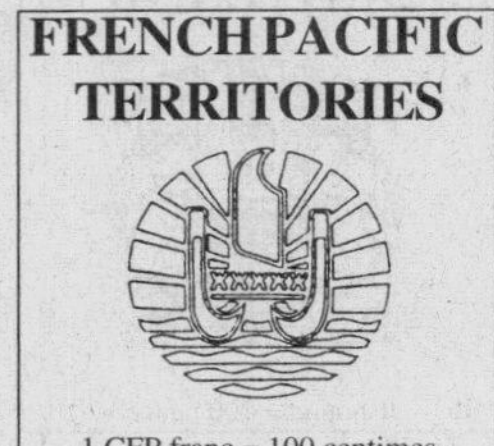
1 CFP franc = 100 centimes

### GRENADA

1 (EC) dollar = 100 cents

### GUATEMALA

1 quetzal = 100 centavos

### GUYANA

1 dollar = 100 cents

### HAITI

1 gourde = 100 centimes

### HONDURAS

1 lempira = 100 centavos

### JAMAICA

1 dollar = 100 cents

### MEXICO

1 nuevo peso = 100 centavos

### MONTSERRAT

1 (EC) dollar = 100 cents

### NETHERLAND ANTILLES

1 gulden = 100 cent

### NICARAGUA

1 cordoba = 100 centavos

### PARAGUAY

1 guarani = 100 centimos

### PERU

1 neuvo sol = 100 dentimos

### St. KITTS and NEVIS
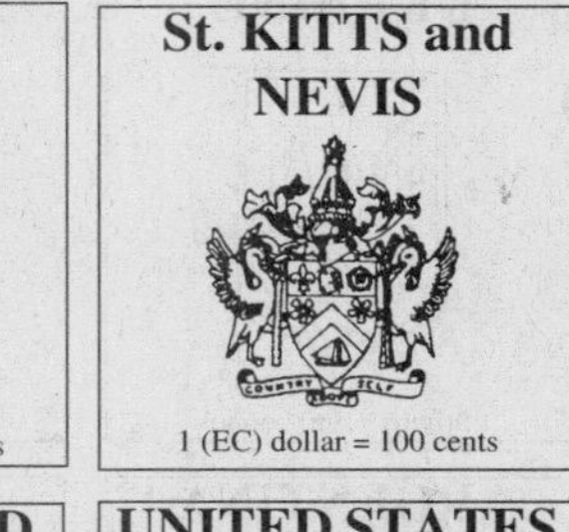
1 (EC) dollar = 100 cents

### St. LUCIA

1 (EC) dollar = 100 cents

### St. VINCENT

1 (EC) dollar = 100 cents

### SURINAM

1 gulden = 100 cent

### TRINIDAD AND TOBAGO
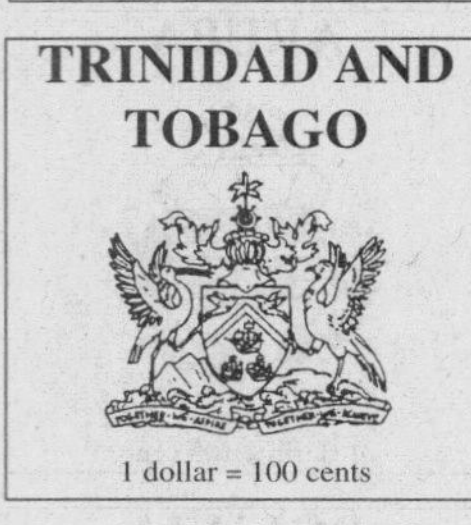
1 dollar = 100 cents

### UNITED STATES OF AMERICA

1 dollar = 100 cents

### URUGUAY

1 Peso = 100 centesimos

### VENEZUELA

1 bolivar = 100 centimos

### AFGHANISTAN

1 afghani = 100 pul

### ARMENIA

1 dram = 100 luma

### AZERBAIJAN

1 manat = 100 qepik

### BAHRAIN
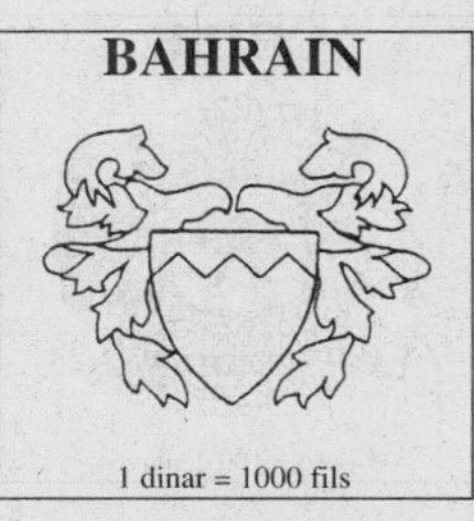
1 dinar = 1000 fils

### BANGLADESH

1 taka = 100 paisa

### BHUTAN

1 ngultrum = 100 chtrum

### BRUNEI

1 ringgit = 100 sen

### CAMBODIA
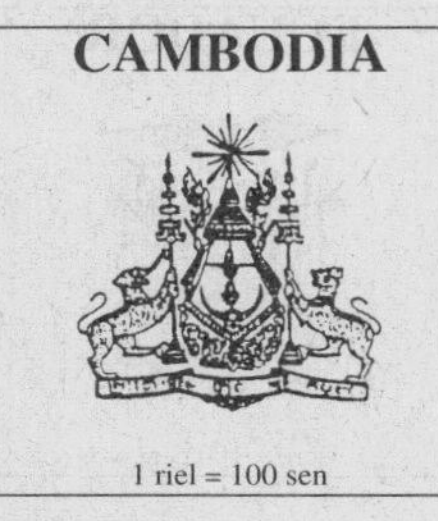
1 riel = 100 sen

### CHINA
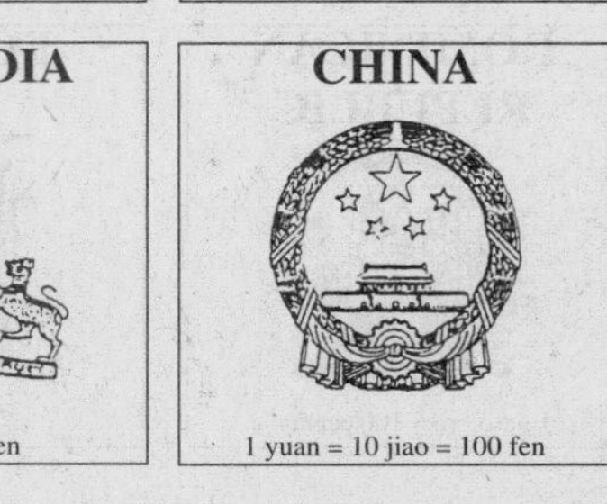
1 yuan = 10 jiao = 100 fen

### CYPRUS
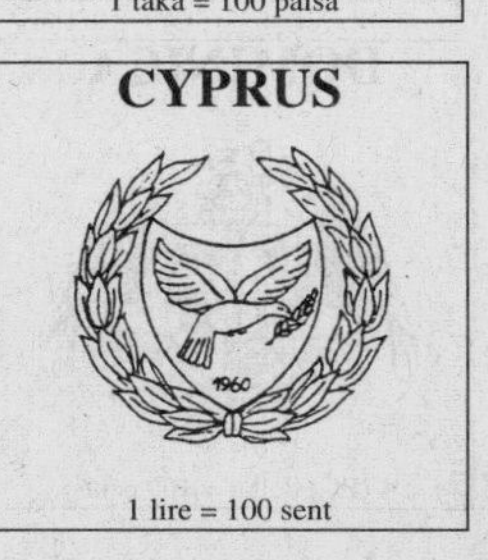

1 lire = 100 sent

# ARMS AND MONETARY SYSTEMS GUIDE

### GEORGIA

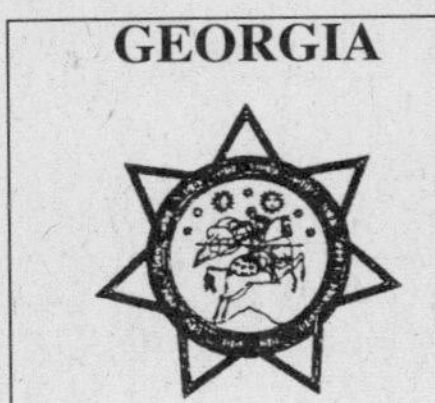

1 lari = 100 tetri

### HONG KONG

1 dollar = 100 cents

### INDIA

1 rupee = 100 paise

### INDONESIA

1 rupiah = 100 sen

### IRAN

1 rijal = 100 dinar

### IRAQ

1 dinar = 1000 fils

### ISRAEL

1 shekel = 100 agorot

### JAPAN

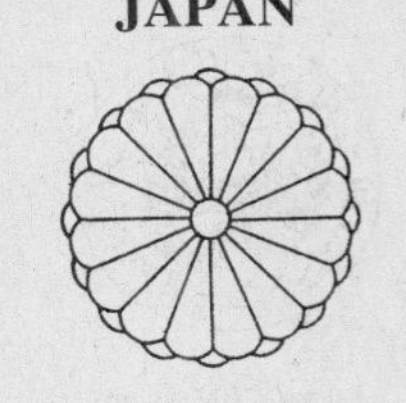

1 jen = 100 sen

### JORDAN

1 dinar = 100 fils

### KAZAKHSTAN

1 tenge = 100 tiyin

### KOREA NORTH

1 won = 100 chon

### KOREA SOUTH

1 won = 100 chon

### KUWAIT

1 dinar = 1000 fils

### KYRGYZSTAN

1 som = 100 tyjin

### LAOS

1 kip = 100 at

### LEBANON

1 livre = 100 pisatres

### MACAO

1 pataca = 100 avos

### MALAYSIA

1 ringgit = 100 sen

### MALDIVE ISLANDS

1 rufiyaa = 100 laari

### MONGOLIA

1 togrog = 100 mongo

### MYANMAR

1 kryat = 100 pya

### NEPAL

1 rupaja = 100 paise

### OMAN

1 rial = 1000 baiza

### PAKISTAN

1 rupaja = 100 pajsa

### PHILIPPINES

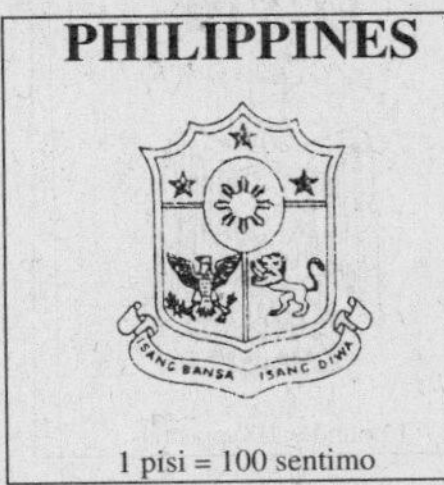

1 pisi = 100 sentimo

### QATAR

1 rijal = 100 dirham

### SAUDI ARABIA

1 rijal = 100 halala

### SINGAPORE

1 dollar = 100 cents

### SRI LANKA

1 rupee = 100 cents

### SYRIA

1 lira = 100 kirs

### TAIWAN

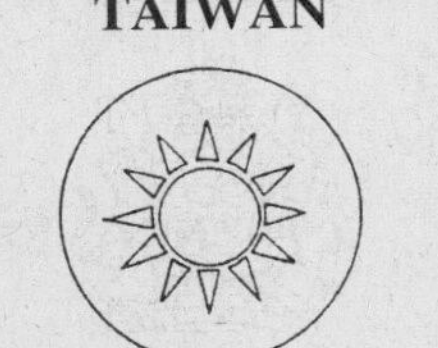

1 juan = 100 fen

### TAJIKISTAN

1 tajik ruble = 100 tanga

### THAILAND

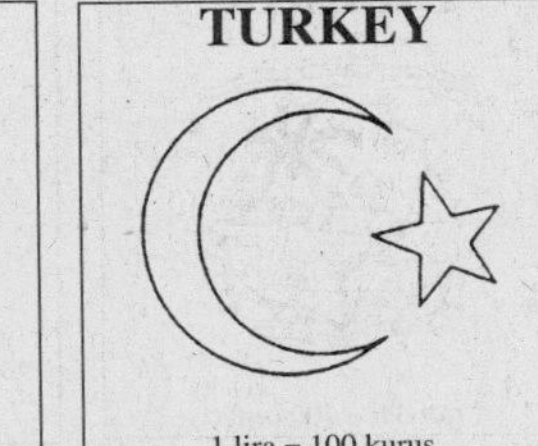

1 bath = 100 satang

### TURKEY

1 lira = 100 kurus

### TURKMENISTAN

1 manat = 100 tenge

# ARMS AND MONETARY SYSTEMS GUIDE

### UNITED ARAB EMIRATES

1 dirham = 100 fils

### UZBEKISTAN

1 sum = 100 tyyn

### VIETNAM

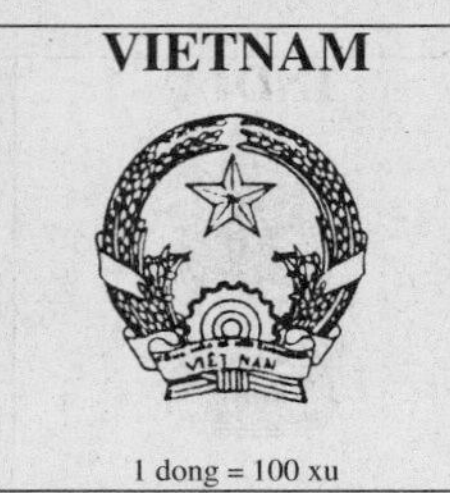


1 dong = 100 xu

### YEMEN

1 rial = 100 fils

# AFRICA

### ALGERIA

1 dinar = 100 santims

### ANGOLA

1 kwanza reajustado = 100 new kwanzas

### BIAFRA

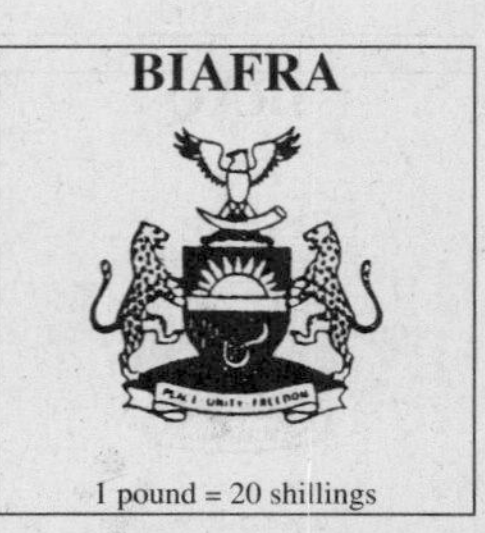

1 pound = 20 shillings

### BOTSWANA

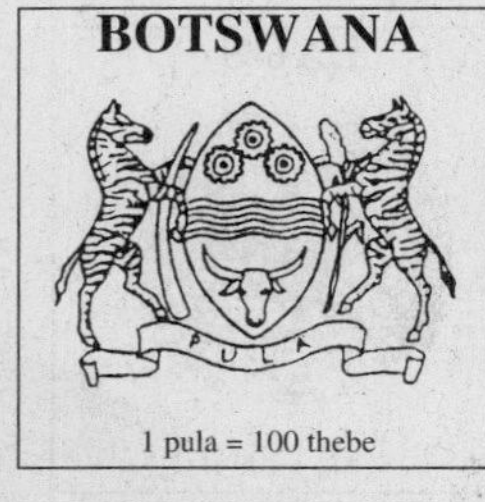


1 pula = 100 thebe

### BURUNDI

1 franc = 100 centimes

### CAMEROON

1 CFA franc = 100 centimes

### CAPE VERDE

1 escudo = 100 centavos

### CENTRAL AFRICAN REPUBLIC

1 CFA franc = 100 centimes

### CHAD

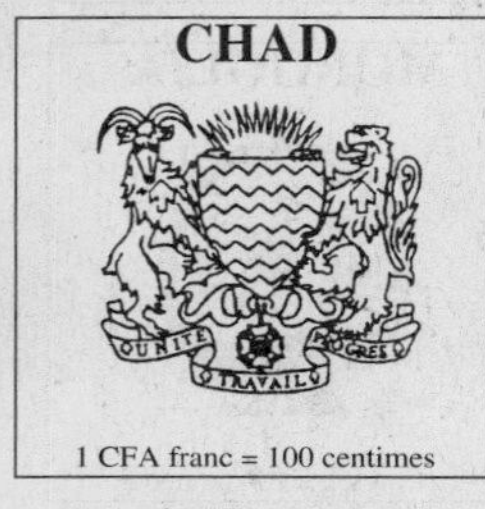

1 CFA franc = 100 centimes

### COMOROS

1 franc = 100 centimos

### CONGO

1 CFA franc = 100 centimes

### CONGO DEMOCRATIC REPUBLIC

1 nouveau zaire = 100 nouveau makuta

### DJIBOUTI

1 djibouti franc = 100 centimes

### EGYPT

1 pound = 100 piastres

### EQUATORIAL GUINEA

1 CFA franc = 100 centimes

### ERITREA

1 nakfa = 100 cents

### ETHIOPIA

1 birr = 100 santeem

### GABON

1 CFA franc = centimes

### GAMBIA

1 dalasi = 100 bututs

### GHANA

1 cedi = 100 pesewas

### GUINEA

1 franc guineen = 100 centimes

### GUINEA-BISSAU

1 peso = 100 centavos

### KENYA

1 shilling = 100 cents

### LESOTHO

1 loti = 100 lisente

### LIBERIA

1 dollar = 100 cents

### LIBYA

1 dinar = 1000 dirham

### MADAGASCAR

1 franc = 100 centimes

### MALAWI

1 kwacha = 100 tambala

# ARMS AND MONETARY SYSTEMS GUIDE

### MAURITANIA

ouguiya

### MAURITIUS

1 rupee = 100 cents

### MOROCCO
1 dirham = 100 santimin

### MOZAMBIQUE

1 metical = 100 centavos

### NAMIBIA

1 dollar = 100 cents

### NIGERIA

1 naira = 100 kobo

### RWANDA
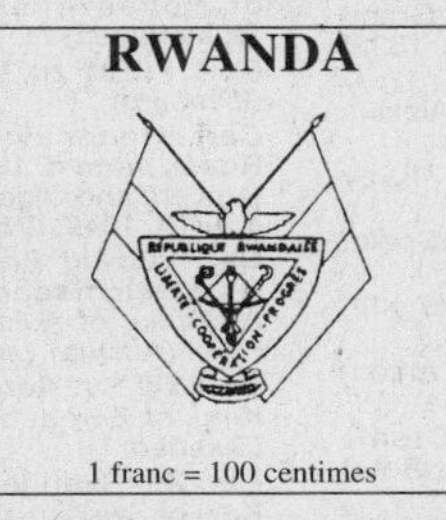
1 franc = 100 centimes

### ST. HELENA

1 pound = 100 pence

### ST. THOMAS & PRINCE

1 dobra = 100 centimos

### SEYCHELLES

1 rupee = 100 cents

### SIERRA LEONE

1 leone = 100 cents

### SOMALIA

1 shilling = 100 cents

### SOMALILAND

shilling

### SOUTH AFRICA

1 rand = 100 cents

### SUDAN

1 dinar = 100 dirham

### SWAZILAND

1 lilangeni = 100 cents

### TANZANIA
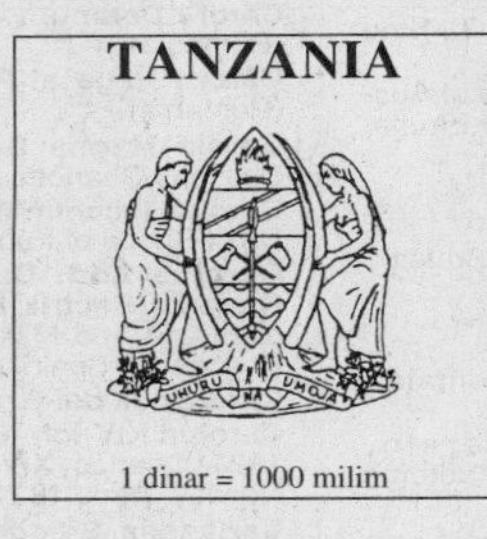
1 dinar = 1000 milim

### TUNISIA

1 dinar = 1000 milim

### UGANDA
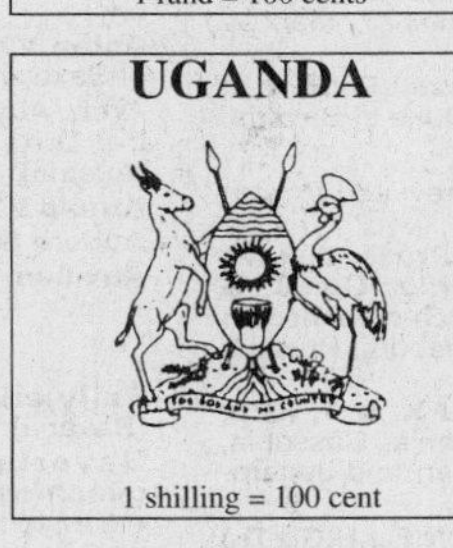
1 shilling = 100 cent

### ZAMBIA

1 kwacha = 100 ngwee

### ZIMBABWE
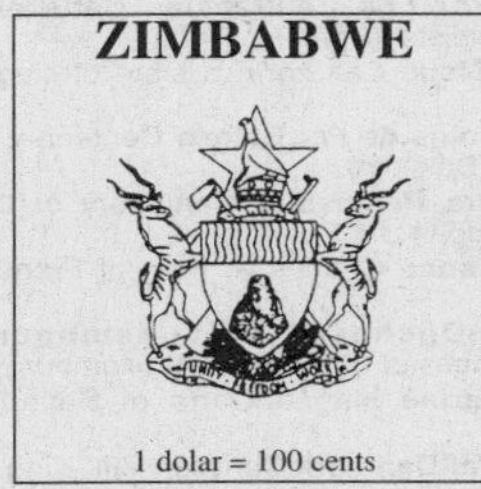
1 dolar = 100 cents

# OCEANIA

### ANTIGUA

1 (EC) dollar = 100 cents

### AUSTRALIA

1 dolar = 100 cents

### COOK ISLAND

1 dollar = 100 cents

### FIJI

1 dollar = 100 cents

### NEW CALEDONIA
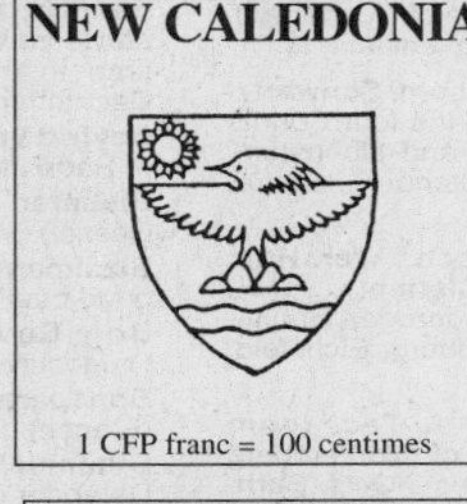
1 CFP franc = 100 centimes

### NEW ZEALAND

1 dollar = 100 cents

### PAPUA NEW GUINEA

1 kina = 100 toea

### SOLOMON ISLANDS

1 dollar = 100 cents

### TONGA

1 pa'anga = 100 seniti

### VANUATU

1 vatu

### WESTERN SAMOA

1 tala = 100 sene

# LEGEND ABBREVIATIONS

Following in alphabetical order is a listing of the Latin legends found on World coins. The legend as it appears on the coin is in bold typeface. The translation is followed by issuer.

## Common Abbreviations

**A.A. - Archidux Austriae.** . . . . Archduke of Austria.

**Arch. Aust. Dux Burg. Mar. Mor. Co. Tyr - Archidux Austriae Dux Burgundiae Marchio Moraviae Comes Tyrolis.** . . . . Archduke of Austria, Duke of Burgundy, Margrave of Moravia, Count of Tyrol.

**D.G. - Dei Gratia.** . . . .By the grace of God.

**Dan. Nor. Van. Got. Rex - Daniae, Norvegiae, Vandalorum Gothorum Rex.** . . . . King of Denmark, Norway, Vandalia, Gotland.

**Dux Sles. Hol. Stor. Ditm. Com. Old. & Delm. - Dux Slesvivi Holsatiae Stormariae et Ditmarsiae Comes in Oldenburg et Delmenhorst.** . . . . Duke of Schleswig-Holstein, Stormarn, and Ditmarsh, Count in Oldenburg and Delmenhorst.

**F.D. - Fidei Defensor.** . . . . Defender of the Faith.

**Ger. Hun. Boh. Rex - Germaniae Hungariae Bohemiae Rex.** . . . . King of Germany, Hungary, Bohemia.

**P.M. - Pontifex Maximus.** . . . . Supreme Pontiff.

**Rex Pol. Ma. Dux Lit. Rus. Prus. Mas. Sam. Liv. nec non Svec. Gotor. Vandal. Haere. Rex - Rex Poloniae Magnus Dux Lithuaniae Russiae Prussiae Masoviae Samgitiae Livoniae nec non Svecorum Gothorum Vandalorum Haereditarius Rex.** . . . . King of Poland, Grand Duke of Lithuania, Russia, Prussia, Masovia, Semgallia, Livonia, as well as hereditary King of Sweden, Gotland, and Vandalia.

## German States Prefaces

Prefaced and numbered below are abbreviations which frequently appear in German States legends. They will be referred to numerous times.

1. **ANHALT - F.A.C.A.D.S.B.I. & K.** . . . . . Prince of Anhalt, Count of Aschersleben, Lord of Zerbst, Bernburg, Jever, and Knyphausen.

2. **BAVARIA - PFALZ - JULICH-BERG - BERG - B.I.C.& M.D.C.V.S.M.R. & M.D.I.R.** . . . . . Bavaria, Julich, Cleves, Berg, Count of Veldenz, Sponheim, Mark & Ravensberg & Moers, Lord in Ravenstein.

**C.P.R.S.R.I. Archit. & El. D.B.** . . . . . Count Palatine of the Rhine, Archtreasurer of the H.R.E., Duke of Bavaria. . . . . (as above)

3. **BRANDENBURG** (Legends are abbreviated in both Latin and German)

**Mar. Brand. S.R.I. Arc. & Elec. Magd. Pruss, dux lvl. (Gu.) Cli. & Mont. (Ber.) (Churf. I. Pr. z. Gu. C. & B.).** . . . . Margrave of Brandenburg, Arch-chamberlain and Elector of the H.R.E., Duke of Magdeburg, Prussia, Julich, Cleves, and Berg.

**Stet. Pomer. Cas. (der C.) W.a.i.S. zu K. u. I. (Cro. Car. Sile.) Hert.** . . . . . Stettin, Pomerania, Cassubia, Vandalia, also Duke in Silesia of Krossen and Jagerndorf.

**B.N.P.R.Co. Ma. & Ra. d.i. Rav. (B.z.N.F.z.R.G.z.D.) P.H.M.C.** . . . . . Burgrave of Nuremberg, Prince of Rugen, Count of Mark & Ravensberg, Lord in Ravenstein, Prince of Halberstadt, Minden, Cammin.

4. **BRUNSWICK - Dux (Hertz.) Bruns. Luneb.** . . . . Duke of Brunswick and Luneburg.

5. **HABSBURG - D.G.R.I.S.A. Germ. Hung. Boh. Rex.** . . . . By the grace of God, Roman Emperor always august, King of Germany, Hungary, Bohemia. . . . . **also S.R.I.** . . . . . Holy Roman Empire.

6. **MANSFELD - Comes & dn. in Mansf. nob. dm. in Held. Seb. et Schrap.** Count and Lord in Mansfeld, noble Lord of Heldrungen, Seeburg, and Schraplau.

7. **SAXONY - Saxo. Iul. Cli. B. (Mon.) A. & W. Lan. Thu. Mar. Mis. Pri. Hen. C.M. & R.D.R.** . . . . . Saxony, Julich, Cleves, Berg, Angria, and Westphalia, Landgrave of Thuringia, Margrave of Meissen, Prince of Henneberg, Count of Mark & Ravensberg, Lord in Ravenstein.

8. **SCHWARZBURG - E. IV. com. imp. com. Schwartz. & Honst. dom. A.S.L.L. et Cl.** . . . . . of the four Counts of the Empire, Count of Schwarzburg and Hohnstein, Lord of Arnstein, Sondershausen, Leutenberg, Lohra, and Klettenberg.

9. **STOLBERG - Stol. Konig. Rut. (Roch.) Wer. Hon. zu Epst. Mintz. Brev. Eich. Lo. u. Cletten.** . . . . . Stolberg, Konigstein, Rochefort, Wernigerode, Hohnstein, Lord of Epstein, Munzenberg, Breuberg, Eichsfeld, Lohra, and Klettenberg.

10. **WURTTEMBERG - Dux Wirt. & Tec. (com Montp.) (in Sil. Ols.) (B.).** . . . . Duke of Wurttemberg and Teck, Count of Mompelgard, in Silesia-Oels, Bernstadt, or Berolstein.

11. **HESSE - Landg. Hass. princ. (admi.) Hersf. C.C.D.Z.E.N.S.Y.B.** . . . . . Landgrave of Hesse, Prince (administrator) of Hersfeld, Katzenellenbogen, Cassel, Diez, Ziegenhayn, Nidda, and Schauenburg, Isenburg, Budingen.

## A

**Ad Norm(am) conv(entionis)** According to the convention standard. (Baden, Furstenberg, Hohenzollern-Hechingen, Wurttemberg)

**Adolph Georg Furst zu Schaumburg-Lippe** Adolph George, Prince of Schaumburg-Lippe. (Schaumburg-Lippe)

**Adolph Herzog zu Nassau** Adolph, Duke of Nassau. (Nassau)

**Agricoltura e Commercio** Agriculture and Commerce. (Italian Republic)

**Albert Furst zu Schwarzburg** Albert, Prince of Schwarzburg. (Schwarzburg)

**Albert Koenig von Sachsen** Albert, King of Saxony. (Saxony)

**Albert Roi des Belges** Albert, King of the Belgians. (Belgium)

**Alex(ander) Carl Herzog zu Anhalt** Alexander Carl, Duke of Anhalt. (Anhalt)

**Alexander I Ces. Ros. Wskrzesiciel Krol Pols.** Alexander I, Tsar of all the Russias, King of Poland. (Poland)

**Alexander I Cesarz Sa. W. Ros. Krol Polski** Alexander I, Tsar of all the Russias, King of Poland. (Poland)

**Alexandrine * Ludwig * Friedrich * Wilhelm und Sophie Grosherzogin von Baden Besuchen die Munzstaette den 29 Febr. 1832. Heil Ihnen** Alexandrina, Ludwig, Frederick, William, and Sophie, Grand Duchess of Baden visit the mint on February 29, 1832. Prosperity to them. (Baden)

**Alexius Friedrich Christian Herzog zu Anhalt** Alexius Frederick Christian, Duke of Anhalt. (Anhalt)

**Alfonso XII Por La G(racia) de Dios** Alfonzo XII, by the grace of God. (Spain)

**Alfonzo XII Rey de Espana** Alfonzo XII, King of Spain. (Spain)

**Alfonzo XIII Por La G(racia) de Dios** Alfonzo XIII, D.G. (Spain)

**Alfred Herzog von Sachsen Coburg und Gotha** Alfred, Duke of Saxe-Coburg-Gotha. (Saxe-Coburg-Gotha)

**Alla Naz(ione) Fran. La Rep(ubblica) Cisal. Riconoscente** To the French nation, the grateful Cisalpine Republic. (Cisalpine Republic)

**Alleanza Dei PopuIi Liberi** Alliance of the free people. (Venice)

**Allgemeine Ausstellung Deutscher Industrie und Gewerbs Erzeugnisse** General Exhibition of German industrial and craft products. (Bavaria)

**Althingi Vas Sett At Rathi Ulfliots Ok Allra Landsmanna** Parliament was established by the Council of Ulfliot and by all the people. (Iceland)

**Amadeo I Rey de Espana** Amadeus I, King of Spain. (Spain)

**Anton Koenig und Friedrich August Mitregent von Sachsen** Anton, King and Frederick August, co-regent of Saxony. (Saxony)

**Anton Koenig von Sachsen (cross) den 6 Iuni 1836** Anton, King of Saxony (died) on June 6, 1836. (Saxony)

**Anton V.G.G. Koenig von Sachsen** Anton, D.G., King of Saxony. (Saxony)

**Arch. Aust. D. Burg. Loth. M. D. Het.** Archduke of Austria, Duke of Burgundy, Lorraine, Grand Duke of Etruria. (Austria)

**Arnold Winkelreid.** (Switzerland)

**Audere Semper** Ever to dare. (Albania)

**Auxilium de Sancto** Aid from the Saint. (Papal States)

## B

**Bai(y)erischer Kronthaler** Bavarian Kronentaler. (Bavaria)

**Bayerisch-Wurtembergischer Zollverein, geschlossen 1827** Bavarian-Wurttemberg customs union, formed 1827. (Bavaria)

**Bayern Errichteten die H. Ottokapelle zu Kiefersfelden zum Andenken an Koen. Otto's Abschied v. seinem Vaterlande** Bavaria, erected the Otto chapel at Kiefersfelden in commemoration of King Otto's departure from his fatherland. (Bavaria)

**Bayerns Treue** Faithfulness of Bavarians. (Bavaria)

**Berathung u. Grundung e. Deutschen Parlaments 31 Marz 1848** Deliberation over the establishment of a German parliament on March 31, 1848. (Frankfurt)

**Berg. und Clevische Land Munz** Legal coin of Berg and Cleves. (Berg)

**Bergische Landmunz** Legal coin of Berg. (Berg)

**Bergsegen des Harzes** Blessings of the Harz mines. (Hannover)

**Bernhard Herzog zu Sachsen Meiningen** Bernhard, Duke of Saxe-Meiningen. (Saxe-Meiningen)

**Besucht zum Erstenmal die von Ihm erbaute Munzstatte zu Wiesbaden den 28 Dec. 1851** Visit for the first time to the mint built by himself at Wiesbaden on December 28, 1851. (Nassau)

**Beytritt von Baden zum Teutschen Zollverein** Joining of Baden to the German Customs Union. (Bavaria)

**Bieberer Silber** Silver of the Bieber (mines). (Hesse-Cassel)

**Bizalmarn Az Osi Erenyben** Affirmed of ancient and good quality. (Hungary)

**Bog Cuva Jugoslaviju** God guard Yugoslavia. (Yugoslavia)

**Bonaparte Premier Consul** Bonaparte, First Consul. (France)

**Britanniarum Regina Fid. Def.** Queen of the Britains, Defender of the Faith. (France)

## C

**Canton Appenzell, Argau, Bern, Freyburg, Graubunden, Luzern, Soloth, Ticino, de Vaud, Zurich. (Swiss Cantons)**

**Capit(ulum) Cath(edrale) Monasterien(se) Sede Vacante** The Cathedral Chapter, Munster. The seat being vacant. (Munster)

**Car. Albertus D.G. Rex Sard. Cyp. et Hier.** Charles Albert, D.G., King of Sardinia, Cyprus, and Jerusalem. (Sardinia)

**Car. Felix D.G. Rex Sar. Cyp. et Hier.** Charles Felix, D.G., King of Sardinia, Cyprus, and Jerusalem. (Sardinia)

**Carl Alexander Grossherzog von Sachsen** Carl Alexander, Grand Duke of Saxony (Weimar). (Saxony)

**Carl Anton Furst zu Hohenzollern Sigmaringen** Carl Anton, Prince of Hohenzollern-Sigmaringen. (Hohenzollern-Sigmaringen)

**Carl August H.Z.S. Weimar u. Eisenach** Carl August, Duke of Saxe-Weimar-Eisenach. (Saxe-Weimar-Eisenach)

**Carl Eduard Herzog V. Sachsen Coburg u. Gotha** Carl Edward, Duke of Saxe-Coburg, and Gotha. (Saxe-Coburg-Gotha)

**Carl Friedr(ich) Grossherzog z(u) Sachsen W(eim.) E(is.)** Carl Frederick, Grand Duke of Saxe-Weimar-Eisenach. (Saxe-Weimar-Eisenach)

**Carl Friedrich Grosherzog von Baden** Carl Frederick, Grand Duke of Baden. (Baden)

**Carl Furst Primas (der Rhein Confoed.)** Carl, Prince Primate of the Rhine Confederation. (Rhine Confederation)

**Carl Furst zu Hohenzollern Sigmaringen** Carl, Prince of Hohenzollern-Sigmaringen. (Hohenzollern-Sigmaringen)

**Carl Furst zu Isenburg** Carl, Prince of Isenburg. (Isenburg)

**Carl Kronpr. v. Wurttemb. u Olga Grosfurstin v. Russl. verm d. 13 Juli 1846** Carl, Crown Prince of Wurttemberg and Olga, Grand Duchess of Russia, married on July 13, 1846. (Wurttemberg)

**Carl Ludwig Erzherzog v. Osterreich Protector D. Osterreichischen Touristen Club** Charles Louis, Archduke of Austria, Sponsor of the Austrian Tourist's Club. (Austria)

**Carl XIII Sv. Norr. Goth. och V. Konung** Charles XIII, King of Sweden, Norway, Gothland, and Vandalia. (Sweden)

**Carl XIII Sveriges Goth. och V. Konung** Charles XIII, King of Sweden, Gothland, and Vandalia. (Sweden)

**Carl XIV Johan, Norges, Sver. G. og V. Konge** Charles XIV, John, King of Norway, Sweden, Gothland, and Vandalia. (Norway)

**Carl XIV Sveriges Norr. Goth. och V. Konung** Charles XIV, King of Sweden, Norway, Gothland, and Vandalia. (Sweden)

**Carl XV Norges Sver. G. V. K9nge** Charles XV, King of Norway, Sweden, Gothland, Vandalia. (Norway)

**Carl XV Sveriges Norr. Goth. och Vend. Konung** Charles XIV, King of Sweden, Gothland, and Vandalia. (Sweden)

**Carlos I Rei de Portugal** Carlos I, King of Portugal. (Portugal)

**Carlos I Rei e Amelia Rainha de Portugal** Carlos I, King and Amelia, Queen of Portugal. (Portugal)

**Carol I Domnul Romaniei** Carol I, Prince of Romania. (Romania)

**Carol I Rege al Romaniei** Carol I, King of Bohemia. (Romania)

**Carola Magna Ducissa Feliciter Regnante** Grand Duchess Charlotte, happily reigning. (Luxembourg)

**Carolus Ioachim D.G. Princ Furstenberg** Carl Ioachim, D.G., Prince of Furstenberg. (Furstenberg)

**Carolus Lud. D.G. Rex Etr(uriae) & M. Aloysia R(egina) Rectrix I. I. H. H.** Charles Louis, D.G., King of Etruria and Maria Luisa, Queen Regent, Prince and Princess of Spain. (Tuscany)

**Carolus IIII dei G.** Charles IV, D.G. (Spain)

**Carolus XIV Ioh. D.G. Rex Svegiae et Norv. An Avril 1821** Charles XIV John, D.G., King of Sweden and Norway, April, 1821. (Sweden)

**Cartagena Sitiada Por Los Centralistas** Cartagena besieged by the Centralists. (Spain)

**Cattaro en Etat de Siege** Cattaro in a state of siege. (Cattaro)

**Centenaire des Chemins de Fer Belges** Centenary of the Belgian railways. (Belgium)

**Centenario da Guerra Peninsular** Centenary of the Peninsular War. (Portugal)

**Charles X Roi de France** Charles X, King of France. (France)

**Charlotte Grande-Duchesse de Luxembourg** Charlotte, Grand Duchess of Luxemburg. (Luxemburg)

**Charta Magna Bavariae** Magna Carta of Bavaria. (Bavaria)

**Christian VIII Konge af Danmark** Christian VIII, King of Denmark. (Denmark)

**Christian IX Konge af Danmark** Christian IX, King of Denmark. (Denmark)

**Christianus VII D.G. Dan. Norv. V.G. Rex** Christian VII, D.G., King of Denmark, Norway, Vandalia, and Gothland. (Denmark)

**Christianus VIII D.G. Daniae V. G. Rex** Christian VIII, D.G., King of Denmark, Vandalia, and Gothland. (Denmark)

**Christianus IX D.G. Daniae V. G. Rex** Christian IX, D.G., King of Denmark, Vandalia, and Gothland. (Denmark)

**Cinque Lire** Five lire. (Tuscany)

**Cinque Lire Italiane Firenze, Marzo 1861** Five Italian lire, Florence, March, 1961. (Italy)

**Civitas Lucemborgensis Millesimum Ovans Expletannum** Completing the celebration of 1000 years of the city of Luxemburg. (Luxemburg)

**Com(es) in Thengen et Sup(remus) Haer(editarius) Prov(inciae) Carn(iolae) Maresch(allus)** Count in Thengen and Supreme Hereditary Marshal in the Province of Carniola. (Auersperg)

**Concordia patriae Nutrix** Peace, the nurse of the fatherland. (Waldeck)

**Concordia Res Parvae Crescunt** Little things grow through concord. (Batavian Republic)

**Confederation Suisse** Swiss Confederation. (Swiss Confederation)

**Confederaz. Svizzera** Swiss Confederation. (Swiss Confederation)

**Confoederatio helvetica** Helvetian Confederation. (Helvetian Confederation)

**Constituirende Versammlung I.D.F. Stadt Frankfurt 18 Mai 1848** Constituting asssembly of the Imperial Diet of Frankfurt, City of Frankfurt, May 18, 1848. (Frankfurt)

**Cum Deo et Iure** With God and Law. (Wurttemberg)

**Custos Regni Deus** God the Guardian of the Realm. (Naples & Sicily)

## D

**D.G. Car. Frid. March. Bad. & H.S.R.I. Elect. C. Pal. Rh. &** D.G., Carl Frederick, Margrave of Baden and Elector of S.R.I., Count Palatine of the Rhine. . . . . (Baden)

**D.G. Henr. XIII S.L. Ruth S.R.I. Princ. Com. E. Dom. Plav.** D.G., Henry XIII, senior line of Reuss, Prince of S.R.I., Count and Lord of Plauen. (Reuss-Greiz)

**D.G. Max(im) Ios(eph) C.P.R.U.B.D. S.R.I.A. & El. (D.I.C. & M.)** D.G., Maximilian Joseph, Count Palatine of the Rhine and also Duke of Bavaria, Archdapifer and Elector of S.R.I., Duke of Julich, Cleves, and Mark. (Bavaria)

**Das Schwert zur Hand in Herzen Gott, So wird D. Schweizer nie z. Spott** The sword in hand and God in the heart, so will the Swiss never become a laughing stock. (Swiss)

**De Namm des Heeren zy Geloofd** The name of the Lord be praised. (Netherlands)

**Decus et Tutamen Anno Regni** Ornament and safeguard in the year of the reign. (Great Britain)

**Dem Bund zum Schutz dem Feind zum Trutz** With the League for offense, against the enemy for defense. (Switzerland)

**Dem Prinzen Albert Ernst Georg und der Prinzessinn Elisabeth v. Sachs. bei Ihrem Besuche in der Munze zu Dresden im Iahre 1839** For Prince Albert Ernest George and the Princess Elizabeth of Saxony on their visit to the mint at Dresden in the year 1839. (Saxony)

**Dem Vaterlande** For the fatherland. (Saxe-Weimar)

**Dem Verdienste seine Kronen, Reichenbach-Fraunhofer** Honor to whom honor is due, Reichenbach and Fraunhofer. (Bavaria)

**Den Benediktinern wieder eine Lehranstalt ubergeben** On the handing over of another school to the Benedictine Order. (Bavaria)

**Den Siegem bei Waterloo gewidmet am 18 Juni 1865** Dedicated to the victors of Waterloo on June 18, 1865. (Hannover)

**Den 29 Ianuar 1869** (Died) on January 29, 1869. (Saxe-Coburg-Gotha)

**Denkm. der Trennung der Koen. Therese von Ihrem Sohne dem Koen. Otto, Errichtet bei Aibling von Bayerischen Frauen** Monument on the separation of Queen Therese from her son, King Otto, erected at Aibling by Bavarian women. (Bavaria)

**Denkmahl der Anhaenglichkeit Bayerns an seinen Herrscherstamm, Errichtet zu Oberwittelsbach** Monument on the devotion of Bavarians to their ruling house, erected at Oberwittelsbach. (Bavaria)

**Denkmahl der Dreyssig Tausend Bayern welche im Russischen Kriege den Tod Fanden** Monument for the 30,000 Bavarians who died in the Russian wars. (Bavaria)

**Denkmahl des Koenigs Maximilian Joseph, Errichtet von der Hauptstadt Munchen** Monument for King Maximilian Joseph, erected by the capital Munich. (Bavaria)

**Denkmahl des Konigs Maximilian II in Lindau, Errichtet v.d. Stadten an der Sud-Nord-Bahn** Monument for King Maximilian II in Lindau, erected by the cities on the South-North railway. (Monaco)

**Deo Juvante** With the aid of God. (Monaco)

**Der Rhein Deutschlands Strom, nicht Deutschlands Grenze** The Rhine, Germany's river, not Germany's frontier. (Germany)

**Der St. Michaels-Orden zum Verdienst-Orden bestimmt** The Order of St. Michael appointed an order of merit. (Bavaria)

**Der Se(e)gen des Bergbaues** The blessings of the mines. (Saxony)

**Des Bergwerks Wohfahrt ist des Harzes Gluck, Die Grube Bergwerks-Wohlfahrt bei Clausthal kam in Ausbeute 1830** The welfare of the mine is the prosperity of Harz, the pits and the prosperity of the mine at Clausthal came into production in 1830. (Hannover)

**Deus et Dies** God and the Day. (Parma)

**Die Eintheilung d. Konigreichs auf Geschichtl Grundlage zuruckgefuhrt 1838** The divisions of the kingdom restored to their historical foundations. (Bavaria)

**Die Koenigin von Bayern Stiftet den Theresien Orden** The Queen of Bavaria founds the Order of Therese. (Bavaria)

**Dieci Lire** Ten lire.

**Dieci Paoli. Quattro Fiorini** Ten paoli, four florins. (Tuscany)

**Dieu Protege La Belgique** God protect Belgium. (Belgium)

**Dieu Protege La France** God protect France. (France)

**Dieus Sveti Latviju** God guard Latvia. (Latvia)

**Dio Benedite L'Italia** God bless Italy. (Italy)

**Dio Premiera La Costanza** God rewards constancy. (Venice)

**Dio Protegge (11 Re e) Il Regno** God protect the king and the realm. (Naples & Sicily)

**Dio Protegge L'Italia** God protect Italy. (Sardinia)

**Dios Es El Rey de Los Reyes** God is the King of Kings. (Spain)

**Dirige Me Domine** Guide me, Lord. (Parma)

**Domine Conserva Nos in Pace** Lord, save us in peace. (Zurich)

**Domine Salvum Fac Regem** Lord, save the king. (France)

**Domine Spes Mea A Iuventute Mea** Lord, my hope in my youth. (Tuscany)

**Dominus Providebit** The Lord will provide. (Bern)

**Drei(y) Ein Halb Gulden XV Ein Pfund Fein** 3-1/2 guldens, 15 to the fine pound. (Bavaria)

**Duodecim Lustris 1848, 1908 Gloriose Peractis** Twelve lustra (60 years) 1848-1908 gloriously completed. (Austria)

**Durch Kampf und Sieg zum Frieden** Through struggle and victory to peace. (Bavaria)

**Dux Sab. Ianvae (or Genvae) et Montisf. Princ. Ped.** Duke of Savoy, Genoa, Montferrat, Prince of Piedmont. (Sardinia)

## E

**Eala Frya Fresena** Frya of all the Frisians. (Hannover)

**Eccl. S. Barbarae Patronae Fodin. Kuttenbergensium Duo Flor. Arg. Puri** The Church of St. Barbara, Patron of the Kuttenberg Mines, two florins of pure silver. (Austria)

**Edwardus VII Dei Gra. Britt. Omn. Rex Fid. Def. Ind. Imp.** Edward VII, D.G., King of all the Britains, Defender of the Faith, Emperor of India. (Britains)

**Eendragt Maakt Magt** Union makes strength. (Netherlands)

**Ehre dem Ehre Gebuhrt** Honor to whom honor is due. (Bavaria)

**Ehre Ist Mein Hoechstes Ziel** Honour is my highest goal. (Switzerland)

**Eidgen Freischiesen Solothiurn** Federal Public Shooting Match in Solothurn. (Switzerland)

**Eidgenossisches Frei(y) schiessen** Federal Public Shooting Match; in Zurich (KM-S5), in Chur; in Bern (KM-S4); in Glarus (KM-20). (Switzerland)

**Eidgenossisches Schutzenfest in Basel** (KM-S14) Federal Shooting Festival in Basel; in Bern (KM-S6); in Nidwalden (KM-S6); in St. Gallen (KM-S12); in Schaffhausen (KM-S8); in Schwyz (KM-S9); in Zug (KM-S10); in Zurich (KM-S11). (Switzerland)

**Ein Gedenkthaler zu Schiller's Hundertjahriger Geburtsfeier** A commemorative thaler on the hundredth anniversary of Schiller's birth. (Frankfurt)

**Ein Gedenkthaler zum Deutschen Schutzenfeste Juli 1862** A commemorative thaler on the German shooting festival July, 1862. (Frankfurt)

**Ein Gott-Ein Recht-Eine Wahrheit** One God, one justice, one truth. (Oldenburg)

**Ein Thaler zu 100 Krzr. - Im Kronen Fuss** One thaler of 100 kreuzer, on the kronen standard. (Baden)

**Ein Vereinsthaler xxx Ein Pfund Fein** One convention thaler, 30 to the fine pound. (Liechtenstein & German States)

**Einigkeit und Recht und Freiheit** Unity and right and freedom. (Germany)

**Eintracht Macht Stark** Union makes strength. (Chur)

**Elizabeth II Dei Gratia Britt. Omn. Regina Fidei Defensor** Elizabeth II, D.G., Queen of Great Britain, Defender of the Faith. (Great Britain)

**Emanuel II Portug. et Algarb. Rex** Manuel II, King of Portugal and Algarve. (Portugal)

**Emma Furstin Regent c. Vormund. zu Waldeck u. P.** Emma, Princess Regent and guardian of Waldeck and Pyrmont. (Waldeck & Pyrmont)

**En Barcelona** In Barcelona. (Spain)

**Entree de Fribourg & Soleure dans La Confederation Suisse** Entry of Fribourg and Solothurn into the Swiss Confederation. (Swiss)

**Er Saete Gerechtigkeit und Erntete Liebe. Hosea X. 12** He sowed justice and harvested love. (Saxony)

**Ernst August Friederike Marie, Marie, Georg** Ernest, August, Frederika, Marie, Marie, George. (Hannover)

**Ernst August - Viktoria Luise Herzog u. Herzogin zu Braunschweig (u. Luneb.)** Ernest August, Victoria Louise, Duke and Duchess of Brunswick-Luneburg. (Brunswick-Luneburg)

**Ernst August V.G.G. Koenig von Hannover** Ernest August, D.G., King of Hannover. (Hannover)

**Ernst August Koenig von Hannover** Ernest August, King of Hannover. (Hannover)

**Ernst Herzog v. Sachsen Coburg u. Gotha** Ernest, Duke of Saxe-Coburg-Gotha. (Saxe-Coburg-Gotha)

**Ernst Herzog von Sachsen Altenburg** Ernest, Duke of Saxe-Altenburg. (Saxe-Altenburg)

**Ernst Herzog z. S. Coburg Saalf. F. z. Lichtenb.** Ernest, Duke of Saxe-Coburg-Saalfeld, Prince of Lichtenburg. (Saxe-Coburg-Saalfeld)

**Ernst Herzog z. S. Coburg u. Gotha F. z. Lichtenb.** Ernest, Duke of Saxe-Coburg and Gotha, Prince of Lichtenburg. (Saxe-Coburg-Gotha)

**Ernst Herzog zu Sachsen Coburg-Gotha** Ernest, Duke of Saxe-Coburg-Gotha. (Saxe-Coburg-Gotha)

**Ernst Herzog zu Sachsen Coburg und Saalfeld** Ernest, Duke of Saxe-Coburg and Saalfeld. (Saxe-Coburg-Saalfeld)

**Ernst Ludwig Grosherzog von Hessen** Ernest Ludwig, Grand Duke of Hesse. (Hesse)

**Eroffnung der Neuen Munze Sept. 1840** Opening of the new mint September, 1840. (Frankfurt)

**Errichtung der Bayerischen Hypotheken-Bank** Establishment of the Bavarian Mortgage Bank. (Bavaria)

**Erste Eisenbahn in Deutschland mit Dampfwagen von Nurnberg nach Furth** First railway in Germany with steam engines from Nuremberg to Furth. (Bavaria)

**Erwahlt zum Kaiser der Deutschen d. 28 Marz 1849** Elected the Emperor of the Germans on March 28, 1849. (Frankfurt)

**Erwahlt zum Reichsverweser uber Deutschland d 29 Iuni 1849** Elected imperial regent over Germany on June 29, 1849. (Frankfurt)

**Erzherzog Johann von Oesterreich** Archduke John of Austria. (Frankfurt)

**Espana** Spain. (Spain)

**Et in Minimus Integer** Faithful even in the smallest things. (Olmutz)

## F

**F. Berhard im Bart** Prince Berhard the bearded. (Germany)

**Feines Silber** Fine silver. (Hannover)

**Feldherrnhalle** Hall of Generals. (Bavaria)

**Felice ed Eliza PP. (Principes) de Lucca e Piombino** Felix and Elisa, Prince and Princess of Lucca and Piombino. (Lucca)

**Ferd(inandus) D.G. H(ungariae) et B(ohemiae) Reg(ius) Pr(inceps) A. A. S(acri) R(omani) I(mperil) Pr(inceps) El(ector) Salisb(urgensis)** Ferdinand, D.G., Royal Prince of Hungary and Bohemia, Archduke of Austria, Prince of S.R.I., Elector of Salzburg. (Salzburg)

**Ferd(inandus) I D. G. Aust(riae) Imp(erator) Hung(ariae) B(ohemiae) Rex H(umus) N(ominis) V R(ex) L(ombardiae) I(llyriae) A.A.** Ferdinand I, D.G., Emperor of Austria, King of Hungary and Bohemia, Fifth of this name, King of Lombardy, Venice, Dalmatia, Galicia, Lodomeria, Illyria, Archduke of Austria. (Hungary)

**Ferd. Hu. et Bo. Reg. Pr. A.A.S.R.I.Pr. El. Salisb.** Ferdinand, Royal Prince of Hungary and Bohemia, Archduke of Austria, Prince of S.R.I., Elector of Salzburg. (Salzburg)

**Ferd. I D.G. Austr. Imp. Hung. Boh. R(ex) H(etruriae) N(eapolis) V(enetiae)** Ferdinand I, D.G., Emperor of Austria, King of Hungary and Bohemia, Fifth of this name, King of Lombardy, Venice, Dalmatia, Galicia, Lodomeria, Illyria, Archduke of Austria. (Austria)

**Ferd. I D.G. Regni Sicilarum et Hier Rex** Ferdinand I, D.G., King of the Sicilies and Jerusalem. (Naples & Sicily)

**Ferd. IV D.G. utr. Sic. et Hier, Rex** Ferdinand IV, D.G., King of the Two Sicilies and Jerusalem. (Naples & Sicily)

**Ferdin. VII Dei G.** Ferdinand VII, D.G. (Spain)

**Ferdinan. III D.G. Sicil. et Hier. Rex** Ferdinand III, D.G., King of Sicily and Jerusalem. (Naples & Sicily)

**Ferdinan. IV D. G. Siciliar, et Hie Rex** Ferdinand IV, D.G., King of the Sicilies and Jerusalem. (Naples & Sicily)

**Ferdinand Souv. Landgraf z. Hessen** Ferdinand, sovereign landgrave of Hesse. (Hesse-Homburg)

**Ferdinandus I D.G. Austriae Imperator** Ferdinand I, D.G., Emperor of Austria. (Austria)

**Ferdinandus II Dei Gratia Rex** Ferdinand II, D.G., King. (Naples & Sicily)

**Ferdinandus III D.G. P(rinceps) R(egius) H(ungariae) et B(ohemiae) A. A. M(agnus) D(ux) Etrur(iae)** Ferdinand III, D.G., Royal Prince of Hungary and Bohemia, Archduke of Austria, Grand Duke of Tuscany. (Tuscany)

**Ferdinandus III D.G. Rex** Ferdinand III, King, D.G. (Naples & Sicily)

**Ferdinandus IV D.G. Rex** Ferdinand IV, King, D.G. (Naples & Sicily)

**Ferdinandus VII Dei G(ratia)** Ferdinand VII, D.G. (Spain)

**Ferencz Jozsef I K.A.Cs. Es. M.H.S.D.O. Ap. Kir** (Hungary)

**Fern. 7 P. La G.D. Dios Y La Const.** Ferdinand VII, D.G. and the Constitution. (Spain)

**Fern. 7 P.L.G.D. Dios Rey de Espan. E Ynd.** Ferdinand VII, D.G., King of Spain and the Indies. (Spain)

**Fernando 7 Por La G. De Dios** Ferdinand VII, D.G. (Spain)

**Fernando 7 Por La Gracia De Dios Y La Constitucion** Ferdinand VII, D.G. and the Constitution. (Spain)

**Fernando VII Rey de Espana** Ferdinand VII, King of Spain. (Spain)

**Fert, Fert, Fert** (A monogram) (Sardinia & Italy)

**Fest Frei Schiessen von Weiner Schutzen Verein** Public Shooting Festival of the Vienna Shooting Association. (Austria)

**Fid. Def. Ind. Imp.** Defender of the Faith, Emperor of India. (Great Britain)

**Fideliter et Constanter** Faithfully and steadfastly. (Saxe-Coburg-Gotha)

**Folkets Karlek Min Beloning** The love of the people is my my compensation. (Sweden)

**Folkets Kjaerlighed Min Styrke, Dod Den 20 Januar 1848** The love of the people is my strength. (Denmark)

**Folkets Val Min Hogsta Lag** The welfare of the people is my strength. (Denmark)

**Fr. Wilh. III K.V. Preuss** Frederick William III, King of Prussia. (Prussia)

**Franc Ios. I D.G. Austr. Imp. et Hung. Rex Ap. Elisabetha Imp. et Reg.** Francis Joseph I, D.G., Emperor of Austria and Apostolic King of Hungary, Elizabeth, Empress and Queen. (Austria)

**Franc Ios. I D.G. Austr. Imp. et Hung. Rex Ap. Elisabetha Imp. et Reg.** Francis Joseph I, D.G., Emperor of Austria, King of Hungary and Bohemia. (Austria)

**Franc. D.G. Ep. Princ Gurc Antiq. Com de Salm Reifferscheid** Francis, D.G., Prince-Bishop of Gurk, Count of Reifferscheid. (Gurk)

**Franc. Ios. I D.G. Austrie Imperator** Francis Joseph I, D.G., Emperor of Austria. (Austria)

**Franc. Ios. I D.G. Imp. Austr. Rex Boh. Gal. Ill. etc. Ap. Rex Hung.** Francis Joseph I, D.G., Emperor of Austria, King of Bohemia, Galicia and Illyria and King of Hungary. (Austria)

**Franc. I D.G. Aust. Imp. Hung. B.L.V.G.L.II. Rex A.A.** Francis I, D.G., Emperor of Austria, King of Hungary and Bohemia, Lombardy, Venice, Galicia, Lodomeria, Illyria, Archduke of Austria. (Hungary)

**Franc. II D.G.R.I.S.A. Conservator Castri** Francis II, D.G., R.I.S.A., Protector of the city. (Frankfurt)

**Francisc. Ios. I D.G. Austriae Imp. et Elisabetha Max. in Bavar. Ducis Fil.** Francis Joseph I, D.G., Emperor of Austria and Elizabeth, daughter of Maximilian, Duke of

Bavaria. (Austria)
**Franciscus I D.G. Austriae Imperator** Francis I, D.G., Emperor of Austria. (Austria)
**Franciscus I Dei Gratia Rex** Francis I, King, D.G. (Naples & Sicily)
**Franciscus II D.G. Rom. et Haer. Aust. Imp.** Francis II, D.G., Emperor of the Romans and Hereditary Emperor of Austria. (Austria)
**Franciscus II D.G. Rom. Imp. Semp. Aug.** Francis II, D.G., R.I.S.A. (Regensburg)
**Franciscus II D.G.R. Imp. S. A. Germ. Hu. Bo. Rex** Francis II, D.G., R.I.S.A., King of Germany, Hungary, Bohemia. (Austria)
**Franciscus II Dei Gratia Rex** Francis II, King, D.G. (Naples & Sicily)
**Franz Herzog zu Sachsen Cob. Saalfeld** Francis, Duke of Saxe-Coburg-Saalfeld. (Saxe-Coburg-Saalfeld)
**Franz Joseph I V.G.G. Kaiser V. Oesterreich** Francis Joseph I, D.G., Kaiser of Austria. (Austria)
**Frederick VII Konge af Danmark** Frederick VII, King of Denmark. (Denmark)
**Fredericus VI D.G. Dan. V.G. Rex** Frederick VI, D.G., King of Denmark, Vendalia, and Gothland. (Denmark)
**Fredericus VII D.G. Daniae V.G. Rex** Frederick VII, D.G., King of Denmark, Vendalia, and Gothland. (Denmark)
**Frederik IX Konge af Danmark** Frede-ik IX, King of Denmark. (Denmark)
**Freie Hansestadt Bremen** Free Hanseatic city of Bremen. (Bremen)
**Freie Stadt Danzig** Free State of Danzig. (Danzig)
**Freie Stadt Frankfurt** Free city of Frankfurt. (Frankfurt)
**Freie und Hansestadt Hamburg** Free Hanseatic city of Hamburg. (Hamburg)
**Freie und Hansestadt Lubeck** Free Hanseatic city of Lubeck. (Lubeck)
**Frid. Aug. Rex Sax(oniae) Dux Varsov** Frederick August, King of Saxony, Duke of Warsaw. (Poland)
**Frid. August D.G. Dux Sax. Elector** Frederick August, D.G., Duke and Elector of Saxony. (Saxony)
**Frid. August D.G. Rex Saxoniae** Frederick August, D.G., King of Saxony. (Saxony)
**Friderich I Koenig von Wurttemberg** Frederick I, King of Wurttemberg. (Wurttemberg)
**Fridericus D.G. Rex Wurt. S.R.I. Ar. Vexill. et Elect** Frederick, D.G., King of Wurttemberg, Archmarshal, Standard Bearer, and Elector of the S.R.I. (Wurttemberg)
**Fridericus D.G. Rex Wurt(t)emberg(iae)** Frederick, D.G., King of Wurttemberg. (Wurttemberg)
**Fridericus Pr. Waldecciae Com. Pyr.** Frederick, Prince of Waldeck, Count of Pyrmont. (Pyrmont)
**Fridericus Wurtembergiae Rex** Frederick, King of Wurttemberg. (Wurttemberg)
**Fridericus II D.G. Dux Wurt. S.R.I. Ar. Vex. et Elector** Frederick II, D.G., Duke of Wurttemberg, Archmarshal, Standard Bearer, and Elector of the S.R.I. (Wurttemberg)
**Friedensschluss zu Frankfurt A.M. 10 Mai 1871** Peace of Frankfurt-on-the-Main May 10, 1871. (Bavaria)
**Friedr(ich) August Koenig v(on) Sachsen** Frederick August, King of Saxony. (Saxony)
**Friedr. Franz. I. 1815 - Friedr. Franz. IV. 1915. Grossherzoge v. Mecklenb. Schw.** Frederick Francis IV, 1915 - Grand Dukes of Mecklenburg-Schwerin. (Mecklenburg-Schwerin)
**Friedr. Gunther Furst zu Schwarzburg** Frederick Gunther, Prince of Schwarzburg. (Schwarzburg-Rudolstadt)
**Friedr. Wilhelm I Kurfurst v. Hessen** Frederick William I, Elector of Hesse. (Hesse-Cassel)
**Friedr. Wilhelm III Koenig v(on) Preussen** Frederick William III, King of Prussia. (Prussia)
**Friedr. Wilhelm IV Koenig v. Preussen** Frederick William IV, King of Prussia. (Prussia)
**Friedrich August Grossherzog v. Oldenburg** Frederick August, Grand Duke of Oldenburg. (Oldenburg)
**Friedrich August Herzog zu Nassau** Frederick August, Duke of Nassau. (Nassau)
**Friedrich August Konig v. Sachsen** Frederick August, King of Saxony. (Saxony)
**Friedrich August V.G.G. Koenig v. Sachsen** Frederick August, D.G., King of Saxony. (Saxony)
**Friedrich August II Koenig von Sachsen d. 9 Aug. 1854** Frederick August II, King of Saxony, (died) on August 9, 1854. (Saxony)
**Friedrich der Streitbare * Friedrich August * 1409 Universitat Leipzig 1909** Frederick the Valiant, Frederick August, 1409, the University of Leipzig 1909. (Saxony)
**Friedrich Deutscher Kaiser Konig v. Preussen** Frederick, Emperor of Germany, King of Prussia. (Prussia)
**Friedrich Franz - Alexandra Grossherzog u. Grossherzogin v. Mecklenb. Schw.** Frederick Francis, Alexandra, Grand Duke and Grand Duchess of Mecklenburg-Schwerin. (Mecklenburg-Schwerin)
**Friedrich Franz Grossh. v. Mecklenb. Schw.** Frederick Francis, Grand Duke of Mecklenburg-Schwerin. (Mecklenburg-Schwerin)
**Friedrich Franz V.G.G. Grossh. v. Mecklenb. Schw.** Frederick Francis, D.G., Grand Duke of Mecklenburg-Schwerin. (Mecklenburg-Schwerin)
**Friedrich Furst zu Waldeck und Pyrmont** Frederick, Prince of Waldeck and Pyrmont. (Waldeck and Pyrmont)
**Friedrich Grosherzog von Vaden** Frederick, Grand Duke of Baden. (Baden)
**Friedrich Gunther Furst zu Schwarzburg Rudolstadt** Frederick Gunther, Prince of Schwarzburg-Rudolstadt. (Schwarzburg-Rudolstadt)
**Friedrich Herzog von Anhalt** Frederick, Duke of Anhalt. (Anhalt)
**Friedrich Prinz und Regent von Baden** Frederick, Prince and Regent of Baden. (Baden)
**Friedrich und Luise von Baden** Frederick and Louise of Baden. (Baden)
**Friedrich W. C. Furst zu Hohenz. Hech.** Frederick William Constantine, Prince of Hohenzollern-Hechingen. (Hohenzollern-Hechingen)
**Friedrich. Wilh. V.G.G. Grossh. v. Mecklenb.** Frederick William, D.G., Grand Duke of Mecklenburg-Strelitz. (Mecklenburg-Strelitz)
**Friedrich Wilhelm Furst zu Nassau** Frederick William, Prince of Nassau. (Nassau)
**Friedrich Wilhelm IV Koenig von Preussen** Frederick William IV, King of Prussia. (Prussia)
**Friedrich I. 1701. Wilhelm II. 1901** Frederick I, 1701, William II, 1901. (Prussia)
**Friedrich II Grossherzog von Baden** Frederick II, Grand Duke of Baden. (Baden)
**Friedrich II. Marie. Herzog und Herzogin von Anhalt** Frederick II, Marie, Duke and Duchess of Anhalt. (Anhalt)
**Fur Freiheit und Vaterland** For freedom and Fatherland. (Switzerland)
**Fur Gott und Vaterland** For God and Fatherland. (Bavaria)
**Furchtlos und Treu** Fearless and true. (Wurttemberg)
**Furstentag zu Frankfurt am Main im August 1863** Assembly of Princes in Frankfurt-on-the-Main in August 1863. (Frankfurt)

## G

**G.N.A. 1808 un Duro** Gerona 1808, one duro. (Spain)
**Garantie National** National Security. (France)
**Gaule Subalpine** Subalpine Gaul. (Subalpine Republic)
**Gedenkthaler zur Eroffnungs Feier der neuen Borse in Bremen am 5 Novemb. 1864** Commemorative thaler on the opening celebration of the new Exchange in Bremen on November 5, 1864. (Bremen)
**Georg Furst zu Schaumburg-Lippe** George, Prince of Schaumburg-Lippe. (Schaumburg-Lippe)
**Georg Furst zu Waldeck und Pyrmont &** George, Prince of Waldeck and Pyrmont, . . . . . (Waldeck and Pyrmont)
**Georg Heinr(ich) Furst z(u) Waldeck u. Pyrmont** George Henry, Prince of Waldeck and Pyrmont. (Waldeck and Pyrmont)
**Georg Herzog zu Sachsen Altenburg** George, Duke of Saxe-Altenburg. (Saxe-Altenburg)
**Georg Herzog zu Sachsen Meiningen** George, Duke of Saxe-Meiningen. (Saxe-Meiningen)
**Georg Koenig von Sachsen** George, King of Saxony. (Saxony)
**Georg Kronprinz von Hannover, Marie Herzoginn v. S. Altenb. Verm. 18 Febr. 1845** George, Crown Prince of Hannover, Marie, Duchess of Saxe-Altenburg, married Feb. 18, 1845. (Hannover)
**Georg Prinz z. Waldeck Furst z. Pyromont** George, Prince of Waldeck, Prince of Pyrmont. (Waldeck and Pyrmont)
**Georg Victor Furst zu Waldeck u Pyrmont** George Victor, Prince of Waldeck and Pyrmont. (Waldeck and Pyrmont)
**Georg Wilhelm Furst zu Schaumburg-Lippe** George William, Prince of Schaumburg-Lippe. (Schaumburg-Lippe)
**Georg II Herzog v(on) Sachsen-Meiningen** George II, Duke of Saxe-Meiningen. (Saxe-Meiningen)
**Georg III V.G.G. Konig und Churfurst** George III, D.G., King and Elector. (Hannover)
**Georg IV Konig v. Grosbritan. u. Hannover** George IV, King of Great Britain and Hannover. (Hannover)
**Georg V V.G.G. Koenig v. Hannover** George V, D.G., King of Hannover. (Hannover)
**Georgius III D.G. Britanniarum Rex F.D.** George III, D.G., King of Great Britain, Defender of the Faith. (Great Britain)
**Georgius III Dei Gratia Rex** George III, King, D.G. (Great Britain)
**Georgius IIII D.G. Britanniar. Rex F.D.** George IV, D.G., King of the Britains, Defender of the Faith. (Great Britain)
**Georgius V D.G. Britt. Omn. Rex F.D. Ind. Imp.** George V, D.G., King of all the Britains, Defender of the Faith, Emperor of India. (Great Britain)
**Georgius V Dei Gra. Britt. Omn. Rex** George V, D.G., King of all the Britains. (Great Britain)
**Georgius VI D.G. Br. Omn. Rex** George VI, D.G., King of all the Britains. (Great Britain)
**Georgius VI D.G. Br. Omn. Rex F.D.** George VI, D.G., King of Great Britain, Defender of the Faith. (Great Britain)
**Gepraegt in Gegenwart S.M. des Koenigs. Dresden d. 24 April 1855** Struck in the presence of His Majesty the King, Dresden on April 24, 1855. (Saxony)
**Gerecht und Beharrlich** Just and firm. (Bavaria)
**Germ. Hun. Boh. Rex A.A.D. Loth. Ven. Sal.** King of Germnay, Hungary, Bohemia, Archduke of Austria, Duke of Lorraine, Venice, Salzburg. (Austria)
**Gerona Ano De 1809** Gerona, Year of 1809. (Spain)
**Gioacchino Napol(eone) (Re Delle Due Sicil(ie)** Joachim Napoleon, King of the Two Sicilies. (Naples & Sicily)
**Glori in Excelsis Deo** Glory to God in the highest. (Sweden)
**Gluckauf! Clausthal in September 1839** Good luck! Clausthal in September 1839. (Hannover)
**God Zy (Zij) Met ons** God be with us. (Netherlands)
**Goethe** Goethe. (Germany)
**Gott Beschirme Uns** God protect us. (Hesse-Cassel)
**Gott Ehre Vaterland** God, Honour, Fatherland. (Hesse-Darmstadt)
**Gott Mit Uns (many)** God with us. (Germany)
**Gott Schirme Mecklenburg** God protect Mecklenburg. (Mecklenburg-Strelitz)
**Gott Schutze Ihn und den Theuren Erben Seines Throns** God protect him and the dear Heir to his Throne. (Prussia)
**Gott Segne Anhalt** God bless Anhalt. (Anhalt-Bernburg)
**Gott Segne Bayern** God bless Bavaria. (Bavaria)
**Gott Segne Handel u. Schiffahrt** God bless business and commerce. (Bremen)
**Gott Segne Sachsen** God bless Saxony. (Saxony)
**Gott und das Vaterland** God and the Fatherland. (Bavaria)
**Gott und Recht** God and right. (Saxe-Weimar)
**Gott war mit Uns** God was with us. (Bremen)
**Gotth. Ephraim Lessing** Gotthold Ephraim Lessing. (Germany)
**Governo Provvisorio di Lombardia** Provisional government of Lombardy. (Lombardy)
**Graf Zeppelin Weltflug** Graf Zeppelin world flight. (Germany)
**Grafl. Schaumburg Lipp. Vormundschaftl. Munze** County Schaumburg-Lippe, guardianship coin. (Schaumburg-Lippe)
**Grand-Duche de Luxembourg** Grand duchy of Luxemburg. (Luxemburg)
**Gregorius XVI (Pon(tifex) M(ax)(imus)** Gregory XVI, Pope. (Papal States)
**Grosherzogthum Baden** Grand duchy of Baden. (Papal States)
**Grosherzogthum Sachsen** Grand duchy of Saxe-Weimar. (Saxe-Weimar)
**Gud och Folket** God and the people. (Sweden)
**Gunth. Fried. Carl Furst z. Schwarzb. Sondersh.** Gunther Frederick Carl, Prince of Schwarzburg-Sonderhausen. (Schwarzburg-Sondershausen)
**Gunther Fr. C. II Furst z. Schwarzb. Sondersh.** Gunther Frederick Carl II, Prince of Schwarzburg-Sondershausen. (Schwarzburg-Sondershausen)
**Gustaf IV Adolph Sv. G. och V. Konung** Gustav IV, Adolph, King of Sweden, Gothland, and Vendalia. (Sweden)
**Gustaf V Sveriges Konung** Gustaf V., King of Sweden. (Sweden)
**Gustaf VI Adolf Sveriges Konung** Gustaf VI, Adolf, King of Sweden. (Sweden)

## H

**Hac Nitimur Hanc Tuemur** With this we strive, this we will defend. (Netherlands)
**Hakimiyet Milletindir** Sovereignty is of the people. (Turkey)
**Handel'sfreiheit durch Eintracht** Free trade through agreement. (Wurttemberg)
**Handelsvertrag zwischen Bayern, Preussen, Wurttemberg und Hessen** Commercial treaty between Bavaria, Prussia, Wurttemberg and Hesse. (Bavaria)
**Hans Landwing Retter das Panner Bei Arbedo** Hans Landwing saves the standard at Arbedo. (Switzerland)
**Harz-Segen** Harz blessings. (Hannover)
**Heinrich d. Li. lung. Linie Furst Reuss von Ebersdorf** Henry of the younger line, line of the princes of Reuss-Ebersdorf. (Reuss-Ebersdorf)
**Heinrich Herzog zu Anhalt** Henry, Duke of Anhalt. (Anhalt-Kothen)
**Heinrich XIV V.G.G. Reg. Furst Reuss I.L.** Henry XIV, D.G., ruling Prince of Reuss, Younger Line. (Reuss-Younger Line)
**Heinrich XX V.G.G. Aelt. L(in) Souv(erain) Furst Reuss** Henry XX, D.G., Older Line, Sovereign Prince of Reuss. (Reuss-Greiz)
**Heinrich XXII V.G.G. Alt. L. Souv. Furst Reuss** Henry XXII, D.G., Older Line, Sovereign Prince of Reuss. (Reuss-Greiz)
**Heinrich LXII lung. Lin. und Stamm. Altest Furst Reuss** Henry LXII, Younger Line and oldest branch, Prince of Reuss. (Reuss-Schleiz)
**Heinrich LXVII V.G.G. Reg. Furst Reuss I.L.** Henry LXVII, D.G., ruling Prince of Reuss, Younger Line. (Reuss-Schleiz)
**Heinrich LXXII Jung. Lin. Furst Reuss** Henry LXXII, Younger Line, Prince of Reuss. (Reuss-Schleiz)
**Helvetia** Switzerland. (Switzerland)
**Helvetische Republik** Swiss Republic. (Swiss Republic)
**Herman Frider. Otto D.G. Princ. de Hohenzollern Heching.** Herman Frederick Otto, D.G., Prince of Hohenzollern-Hechingen. (Hohenzollern-Hechingen)
**Herzogthurn Anhalt, Getheilt 1603 Vereint 1863** Duchy of Anhalt, divided 1603, united 1863. (Anhalt)
**Herzogthurn Nassau** Duchy of Nassau. (Nassau)
**Hieronymus D.G.A. & P.S.A.S.L.N.G. Prim.** Jerome, D.G., Archbishop and Prince of Salzburg. (Salzburg)
**Hieronymus Napoleon** Jerome Napoleon. (Westphalia)
**Hindenburg Reichsprasident** Hindenburg, President of Germany. (Germany)
**Hispaniar(um) Infans** Prince of the Spains. (Spain)
**Hispaniarum et Ind. Rex** King of the Spains and the Indies. (Spain)
**Hispaniarum Rex** King of the Spains. (Spain)
**Honi Soit Qui Mal Y Pense** Evil to him who thinks evil. (Great Britain)
**Honore V Prince de Monaco** Honore V, Prince of Monaco. (Monaco)
**Hun. Boh. Gal. Rex A.A. D. Lo. Sal. Wirc.** King of Hungary, Bohemia, Galicia, Archduke of Austria, Dalmatia, Lodomeria, Salzburg, and Wurzburg. (Austria)
**Hun. Boh. Gal. Rex A.A. Lo Wi. et in Fr. Dux** King of Hungary, Bohemia, Galicia, Archduke of Austria, Lodomeria, Wurzburg, and in Franconia, Duke. (Austria)
**Hundert Jahre Bremerhaven** Centennial of Bremerhaven.

(Germany)
**Hundertjahrige Grundung der Hochschule zu Erlangen durch d. Markgr. Friedr. v. Brandenb. Bayr.** Centenary of the foundation of the University of Erlangen by the Margrave, Frederick of Brandenburg-Bayreuth. (Bavaria)
**Hun(g) Boh. Lomb. et Ven. Gal. Lod. II(I) Rex A.A.** King in Hungary, Bohemia, Lombardy, and Venice, Galicia, Lodomeria, Illyria, Archduke of Austria. (Austria)
**Hungar. Bohem. Gal. Lod. III. Rex. A.A.** King in Hungary, Bohemia, Galicia, Lodomeria, Illyria, Archduke of Austria. (Austria)

## I

**Ich Bau auf Gott** I rely on God. (Reuss-Schleiz)
**Iedem Das Seinige** To each his own. (Appenzell)
**In Hoc Signo Vinces** In this sign you will conquer. (Portugal)
**In Memor. Vindicatae Libert. ac Relig.** In memory of the establishment of liberty and religion. (Sweden)
**In te Domine Speravi** In thee have I hoped, O Lord. (Gurk)
**In Terra Pax** Peace in the land. (Papal States)
**Indipendenza Italiana** Italian Independence. (Italian)
**Ioachim Grosherzog von Berg** Joachim, Grand Duke of Berg. (Berg)
**Ioachim Herzog zu Berg u. Cleve** Joachim, Duke of Berg and Cleves. (Berg)
**Iohann Koenig, Amalie Koenigin v. Sachsen** John, King, Amalie, Queen of Saxony. (Saxony)
**Iohann V.G.G. Koenig v. Sachsen** John, D.G., King of Saxony. (Saxony)
**Ioseph Herzog zu Sachsen Altenburg** Joseph, Duke of Saxe-Altenburg. (Saxe-Altenburg)
**Ioseph Nap. Dei Gratia** Joseph Napoleon, D.G. (Spain)
**Ioseph Napol. D.G. utr. Sicil. Rex** Joseph Napoleon, D.G., King of the Two Sicilies. (Naples & Sicily)
**Isabel 2 Por La Gracia De Dios** Isabel II, D.G. (Spain)
**Isabel 2 Por la Gracia de Dios y La Constitucion** Isabel II, D.G., and the Constitution. (Spain)
**Isti Sunt Patres Tui Verique Pastores** These are your fathers and true shepherds. (Papal States)
**Italia Libera Dio Lo Vuole** A Free Italy, God wills it. (Lombardy)
**Iustitia Regn(orum) Fundamentum** Justice, the Foundation for kingdoms. (Austria)

## J

**Jahrhundertfeier** Centennial. (Mecklenburg-Schwerin)
**Jahrtausend Feier der Rheinlands** Millenary Jubilee of the Rhineland. (Germany)
**Jan de Blannen** John, the Blind. (Luxembourg)
**Joannes D.G. Port. et Alg. P. Regens** John, D.G., Prince Regent of Portugal and Algarve. (Portugal)
**Joannes D.G. P(rinceps) Portugaliae et Alg(arbiae)** John, D.G., Prince of Portugal and Algarve. (Portugal)
**Joannes VI D.G. Portug. Brasil et Algarb. Rex** John VI, D.G., King of Portugal, Brazil, and Algarve. (Portugal)
**Joh. Fried. d. Groszmut Kurf. v. Sachsen, Stifter d. Univ. Jena** John Frederick the magnanimous, Elector of Saxony, Founder of the University of Jena. (Saxony)
**Johann II Furst zu (or von) Liechtenstein** John II, Prince of Liechtenstein. (Liechtenstein)

## K

**Kanton Schwyz** Canton Schwyz. (Schwyz)
**Karl Koenig von Wuerttemberg** Karl, King of Wurttemberg. (Wurttemberg)
**Klar und Fest** Clear and firm. (Liechtenstein)
**Koenig von Westphalen Fr. Pr.** King of Westphalia, Prince of France. (Westphalia)
**Koenigl. Wurttemb. Kronen Thaler** Kingdom of Wurttemberg crown thaler. (Wurttemberg)
**Kong Frederik IX Dronning Ingrid af Danmark** King Frederik IX, Queen Ingrid of Denmark. (Denmark)
**Koningrijk Holland** Kingdom of Holland. (Holland)
**Kon. Wurttemb.** Kingdom of Wurttemberg. (Wurttemberg)
**Kur. Hess. Land Munze** Electorate of Hesse, legal money. (Hesse-Cassel)
**Kurfurstenthurn Hessen** Electorate of Hesse. (Hesse-Cassel)

## L

**L.L. Ph. M.V. Duc de Brabant M.H.A. Duchesse de Brabant 21-22 Aout 1853** Leopold Louis Philippe, Maria Victor, Duke of Brabant, Maria Henrietta, Duchess of Brabant, 21-22 August, 1853. (Belgium)
**Land Skal Med Lov Bygges** The country shall be built by law. (Norway)
**Land Skall Med Lag Byggas** The country shall be built by law. (Sweden)
**Landtag** Provincial legislature. (Bavaria)
**Largiente Numine** Diety bestowing his bounty. (Regensburg)
**Latvijas Republika** Latvian Republic. (Latvia)
**Lege et Fide** By law and faith. (Austria)
**Leo XII Pon(tifex) (Max(imus)** Leo XII, Pope. (Papal States)
**Leopold Friedrich Herzog zu (von) Anhalt** Leopold, Grand Duke of Anhalt. (Anhalt-Dessau)
**Leopold Grosherzog von Baden** Leopold, Grand Duke of Baden. (Baden)
**Leopold Premier Roi des Belges** Leopold I, King of the Belgians. (Belgians)
**Leopold II Roi des Belges** Leopold II, King of the Belgians. (Belgians)
**Leopoldus D.G. P.I.A. P(rinceps) R(egius) H(ungariae) et B(ohemiae) A.A. Magn(us) Dux Etr(uriae)** Leopold II, D.G., Prince of Imperial Austria, Prince Regent of Hungary and Bohemia, Archduke of Austria, Grand Duke of Tuscany. (Tuscany)
**Lerida Ano de 1809** Lerida Year of 1809. (Spain)
**Lex Tua Veritas** Law is your truth. (Tuscany)
**Ley Patria Rey** Law, Fatherland, King. (Spain)
**Ley 900 Milesimas 40 Piezas en Kilog** Law 900/1000, 40 pieces per kilogram. (Spain)
**Liberta Eguaglianza** Liberty, Equality. (Ligurian Republic)
**Libertade Inferme e de' Tiranni Agevol Preda** Weak liberty is the easy prey of tyrants. (Switzerland)
**Liberte, Egalite, Eridania** Liberty, Equality, Eridania. (Subalpine Republic)
**Liberte, Egalite, Fraternite** Liberty, Equality, Fraternity. (France)
**Literatur, Vetenskap, Konst** Literature, Science, Art. (Sweden)
**Lodew. Nap. Kon. Van Holl** Louis Napoleon, King of Holland. (Holland)
**Louis Philippe (I) Roi de France** Louis Philippe I, King of the French. (France)
**Louis XVIII Roi de France** Louis XVIII, King of France. (France)
**Lucilinburhuc** Luxemburg. (Luxemburg)
**Ludewig Grosherzog von Hessen** Ludwig, Grand Duke of Hesse. (Hesse-Darmstadt)
**Ludovicus I D.G. (Hisp(aniarum) Inf(ans) Rex Etruriae Par(mae) Plac(entiae) and Prince** Louis I, D.G., Prince of the Spains, King of Etruria, Prince of Parma and Piacenza. (Tuscany)
**Ludovicus II Bavariae Rex** Ludwig II, King of Bavaria. (Bavaria)
**Ludwig Erbprinz v. B. Geb. 25 August; Ludwig Koen. Prinz v. B. Geb. 7 Januar** Ludwig, Crown Prince of Baden, born August 25; Ludwig, Royal Prince of Baden, born January 7. (Baden)
**Ludwig Grosherzog von Baden** Ludwig, Grand Duke of Baden. (Baden)
**Ludwig Loenig von Bayern** Ludwig, King of Bavaria. (Bavaria)
**Ludwig I Giebt die Krone an seinen Sohn Maximilian am 20 Maerz 1848** Ludwig I, gives his crown to his son Maximilian on March 20, 1848. (Bavaria)
**Ludwig I Koenig von Bayern** Ludwig I, King of Bavaria. (Bavaria)
**Ludwig II Koenig v. Bayern** Ludwig II, King of Bavaria. (Bavaria)
**Ludwig II Grosherzog von Hessen** Ludwig II, Grand Duke of Hesse. (Hesse-Darmstadt)
**Ludwig III Koenig von Bayern** Ludwig III, King of Bavaria. (Bavaria)
**Ludwig III Grosherzog von Hessen** Ludwig III, Grand Duke of Hesse. (Hesse-Darmstadt)
**Ludwig IV Grosherzog von Hessen** Ludwig IV, Grand Duke of Hesse. (Hesse-Darmstadt)
**Ludwigscanal** Ludwig's Canal. (Bavaria)
**Luitpold Prinz-Regent v. Bayern** Leopold, Prince-Regent of Bavaria. (Bavaria)
**Lumen ad Revelationem Gentium** Light and revelation for the peoples. (Papal States)
**L'Union Fait La Force** Union makes strength. (Belgium)

## M

**Magnus ab Integro Saeclorum Nascitur Ordo** The great order of the centuries is born anew. (Bavaria)
**Magyar Kiralysag** Hungarian Kingdom. (Hungarian)
**Magyar Koztarsasag** Hungarian Republic. (Hungarian)
**Manibus Ne Laedar Avris** Lest I be injured by greedy hands. (Sweden)
**Maria Luigia Princ(ipissa) Imp. Arcid. d'Austria** Marie Louise, Imperial Princess Archduchess of Austria. (Parma)
**Maria II D.G. Portug. et Alg. Regina** Maria II, D.G., Queen of Portugal and Algarve. (Portugal)
**Maria II Portug. et Algarb Regina** Maria II, Queen of Portugal and Algarve. (Portugal)
**Matrimonio Coniuncti** Joined in wedlock. (Austria)
**Maximilian Ioseph Churfurst in Baiern** Maximilian Joseph, Elector in Bavaria. (Bavaria)
**Maximilian Ioseph Churfurst zu Pfalzbaiern** Maximilian Joseph, Elector in the Palatinate. (Rhenish Palatinate)
**Maximilian Ioseph Konig von Baiern** Maximilian Joseph, King of Bavaria. (Bavaria)
**Maximilian Kronpr. v. Bayern u. Marie K. Prinz. v. Preuss. verm.d. 12 Octb. 1842** Maximilian, Crown Prince of Bavaria and Marie, Crown Princess of Prussia, married on October 12, 1842. (Bavaria)
**Maximilian II Koenig v. Bayern** Maximilian II, King of Bavaria. (Bavaria)
**Maximilianus Iosephus Bavariae Rex** Maximilian Joseph, King of Bavaria. (Bavaria)
**Med Folket For Fosterlandet** By the people for the fatherland. (Sweden)
**Med Gud for Aere og Ret. Dod Den 15 November 1863** With God, for honor and justice, Died on November 15, 1863. (Denmark)
**Med Logum Skal Land Byggja** By law shall the land be built. (Iceland)
**Megkoronaztatasanak Negyvenedik Evfordulojara** Fortieth anniversary of the coronation. (Hungary)
**Meglio Vivere Un Giorno Da Leone Che Cento Anni Da Pecora** Better to live one day as a lion than a hundred years as a sheep. (Italy)
**Michael I D.G. Portug. et Algarb. Rex** Michael I, D.G., King of Portugal and Algarve. (Portugal)
**Mihai I Regele Romanilor** Michael I, King of Romania. (Romania)
**Mikolay I Ces. Wsz. Rossyi Krol Polski Panuiacy** Nicholas I, Tsar of all the Russians and present King of Poland. (Poland)
**Mit Gott durch Kampf zu Sieg und Einigung** With God through struggle to victory and union. (Wurttemberg)
**Mit Gottes Hulfe** With God's help. (Schaumburg-Lippe)
**Mit Herz und Hand Fuer's Alpenland** With heart and hand for the Alpine land. (Austria)
**Mit Vereinten Kraeften** With united strength. (Austria)
**Mo(neta) Arg(entiae) Ord. Faed. Belg(ii) Holl.** Silver money of the Federated Belgian Union - Holland. (Holland)
**Mo. Arg. Pro Conf(oederatiae) Belg(ii) D(ucatus) Gel(riae). and C(omitatus) Z(utphaniae)** Silver money of the Confederated Belgian Provinces, Duchy of Gelderland and County of Zutphen. (Netherlands)
**Mo. No. Arg. Pro. Confoe. Belg. Trai. . . . .Holl.** New silver money of the confederated Belgian Provinces - Utrecht or Holland. (Netherlands)
**Moldova Lui Stefan in Veci a Romaniei** Moldavia, Stefan the Great, his country of Romania forever. (Romania)
**Mon. Nov. Castri Imp. Friedberg** New money of the free city of Friedberg. (Friedberg)
**Munt van Het Koningryk Der Nederlanden** Money of the Kingdom of the Netherlands. (Netherlands)
**Munzvereinigung Sudteutscher Staaten** Monetary union of the South German States. (Bavaria)

## N

**Nach Funfzig-Jahriger Regierung** For the fiftieth anniversary of the reign. (Schaumburg-Lippe)
**Nap. Lodew. I Kon. Van Holl.** Napoleon Louis I, King of Holland. (Holland)
**Napoleone Imperator E Re** Napoleon, Emperor and King. (Italy)
**Navigare Necesse Est** It is necessary to navigate. (Germany)
**Nec Aspera Terrent** Nor do difficulties terrify. (Brunswick)
**Nec Temere Nec Timide** Neither rashly nor timidly. (Danzig)
**Nicolaus Friedr. Peter Gr. H. v. Oldenburg** Nicholas Frederick Peter, Grand Duke of Oldenburg. (Oldenburg)
**Non Relinquam Vos Orphanos** I shall not leave you as orphans. (Papal States)
**Nulla Dolo Via Sub Bono Principe** There is no path for guile under a good prince. (Naples & Sicily)

## O

**Omnia Cum Deo** Everything with God. (Reuss-Greiz)
**Oscar Norges Sver. G. og V. Konge** Oscar, King of Norway, Sweden, Gothland, and Vendalia. (Norway)
**Oscar Sveriges Norr. Goth. och Vend. Konung** Oscar, King of Sweden, Norway, Gothland, and Vendalia. (Sweden)
**Otto Koenig von Bayern** Otto, King of Bavaria. (Bavaria)
**Otto Prinz v. Bayern Griechenlands Erster Koenig** Otto, Prince of Bavaria, first King of Greece. (Bavaria)

## P

**P.M. Sa. Sc. Cz. nec no. Sv. Go. Va. He. Rex** (4336-41) Prussia, Masovia, Semgallia, Czersk as well as hereditary King of Sweden, Gothland, Vandalia. (Poland)
**Palma Sub Pondere Crescit** The palm grows under its weight. (Waldeck)
**Patria Si Dreptul Meu** The country and my right. (Romania)
**Patrona Bavariae** Patroness of Bavaria. (Bavaria)
**Paul Alexander Leopold Furst zur Lippe.** Paul Alexander Leopold, Prince of hope. (Lippe-Detmold)
**Paul Friedr(ich) August Gr(oss)h(erzog) v(on) Oldenburg** Paul Frederick August, Grand Duke of Oldenburg. (Oldenburg)
**Paul Friedrich Emil Leopold Furst z. Lippe.** Paul Friedrich Emil Leopold, Prince of Lippe. (Lippe-Detmold)
**Per Aspera - Ad Astra** Through difficulties to the stars. (Mecklenburg-Schwerin)
**Per La Gr(acia) Di Dio Duch. di Parma Piac. E. Guast** D.G., Duchess of Parma, Piacenza, and Guastalla. (Parma)
**Peso Grani 1726 Bonta Oncie 10.16** Grain weight 1726, fine ounces 10.16. (Ligurian Republic)
**Petrus IV D.G. Portug. Algarb. Rex** Peter IV, D.G., King of Portugal and Algarve. (Ligurian Republic)
**Philipp Souv. Landgraf zu Hessen** Phillip, Sovereign Landgrave of Hesse. (Hesse-Darmstadt)
**Philipp. Landgraf z. Hessen. Ernst Ludwig Grossherzog v. Hessen u. B. R.** Phillip, Landgrave of Hesse, Ernest Ludwig, Grand Duke of Hesse. (Hesse-Darmstadt)
**Piece de 5 Francs** Piece of 5 francs. (France)
**Pius VII Pon(tifex) M(aximus)** Pius VII, Pope. (Papal States)
**Pius VIII Pont. Max.** Pius VIII, Pope. (Papal States)
**Pius IX Pont. Max.** Pius IX, Pope. (Papal States)
**Post Tenebras Lux** Light after darkness. (Switzerland)
**Pour Etre Forts Soyons Unis** Let us be united to be strong. (Switzerland)
**Primitiae Fodin Kuttenb. ab Aerari. Iterum Susceptarum** First results dug from the Kuttenberg mines in a renewed undertaking. (Austria)
**Prin Statornicie La Izbanda** Through stability to success. (Romania)
**Princ Aichst. Pas. et Ber. S.R.I.P. Elector** Prince of Eichstaedt, Passau, and Berchtesgaden, Prince of S.R.

I., Elector. (Salzburg)

**Princ Aichst. Passau et Berchtolsgad** Prince of Eichstaedt, Passau, and Berchtesgaden. (Salzburg)

**Princ. Gallic Magn. Elect. Imp.** Prince of France, Grand Imperial Elector. (Naples & Sicily)

**Principato di Lucca E Piombino** Principality of Lucca and Piombino. (Naples & Sicily)

**Principe E Grand' Ammiraglio Di Francia** Prince and Grand Admiral of France. (Naples & Sicily)

**Prinz Jean vu Letzeburg** Prince Jean of Luxemburg. (Luxemburg)

**Pro Deo et Populo** For God and the people. (Bavaria)

**Providentia Optimi Principis** With the forethought of the wisest leaders. (Naples & Sicily)

## Q

**Quin Matrimonii Lustrum Celebrant XXIV Aprilis MDCCCLXXIX** They celebrate the 25th wedding anniversary April 24, 1879. (Austria)

**Quinque Coronae** 5 korona. (Austria)

## R

**Ratt och Sanning** Justice and truth. (Sweden)

**Recta Tueri (or Tveri)** Defend the right. (Austria & Hungary)

**Regensburg** Regensburg (Ratisbon). . . . . (Regensburg)

**Regni Vtr. Sic. et Hier.** Of the Kingdom of the Two Sicilies and Jerusalem. (Naples & Sicily)

**Regno D'Italia** Kingdom of Italy. (Italy)

**Regno Delle Due Sicilie** Kingdom of the Two Sicilies. (Naples & Sicily)

**Reitersaule Maximilian's I Churfursten v. Bayern Errichtet v. Konig Ludwig I** Equestrian column of Maximilian I, Elector of Bavaria, erected by King Ludwig I. (Bavaria)

**Relinquo vos Liberos ab Utroque homine** I leave you as children of each man. (San Marino)

**Repubblica de S(an) Marino** Republic of San Marino. (San Marino)

**Repubblica Italiana** Italian Republic. (Italian Republic)

**Repubblica Ligure** Ligurian Republic. (Ligurian Republic)

**Repubblica Veneta** Venetian Republic. (Venetian Republic)

**Republica Bernensis** Republic of Bern. (Republic of Bern)

**Republica Portuguesa** Portugese Republic. (Portugese Republic)

**Republica Portuguesa, 5 de Outubro de 1910** Portugese Republic 5 October, 1910. (Portugese)

**Republik Osterreich, funfzig schilling** Republic of Austria, 50 schilling. (Austria)

**Republika Ceskoslovenska** Republic of Czechoslovakia. (Czechoslovakia)

**Republique et Canton de Geneve** Republic and Canton of Geneva. (Geneve)

**Respublica S. Marini** Republic of San Marino. (San Marino)

**Ret og Sandhed** Justice and truth. (Norway)

**Revolucion - Cinco Pesetas - Cantonal** Revolution, 5 pesetas, Cantonal. (Spain)

**Rex Lomb. et Ven. Dalm. Gal. Lod. Ill. A.A.** King of Lombardy and Venice, Dalmatia, Galicia, Lodomeria, Illyria, Archduke of Austria. (Austria)

**Rey Const. de Espana** Constitutional King of Spain. (Spain)

**Rey de Espana Y de Las Indias** King of Spain and the Indies. (Spain)

**Rey de las Espanas** King of the Spains. (Spain)

**Reyna de Espana Y de Las Indias** Queen of Spain and the Indies. (Spain)

**Rey(i)na de Las Espanas** Queen of the Spains. (Spain)

**Roberto I D. DI PAR. PIAC. Ecc. E Luisa M. Di. Borb. Regg.** Robert I, Duke of Parma, Piacenza, . . . . . and Luisa Maria of Bourbon, Regent. (Parma)

**Royaume de Belgique** Kingdom of Belgium. (Belgium)

**Rudolph Joan D.G. Case. A.R. Hun. Boh. Princ. A.A.** Rudolph John, D.G., Imperial and Royal Prince of Hungary and Bohemia, Archduke of Austria. (Austria)

**Rzeczpospolita Polska** Polish Republic. (Polish)

## S

**S. Carolus Magnus Fundator** St. Charles the Great, Founder. (Munster)

**S. Maria Mater Dei Patrona Hung.** Blessed Mary, Mother of God, Patron of Hungary. (Hungary)

**S.R.E. Tit. S. Petri in Mont. Aur. Card. Archiep. Olom.** Cardinal Archbishop of Olmutz. (Olmutz)

**Salus Populi** The safety of the people. (Spain)

**Salus Reipublicae Suprema Lex** Supreme law is the safety of the state. (Poland)

**Salvam Fac Rempublicam Tuam** Your state safe in union. (San Marino)

**Schweizer(tsche) Eidsgenoss(enschaft)** Swiss Federal

**Scudo di Lire Sei 27 Pratile Anno VIII** Scudo of 6 lire, June 16, 1800. (Cisalpine Republic)

**Sede Vacante** The chair being vacant. (Papal States)

**Segen des Anhalt Bergbaues** Blessings of the Anhalt mines. (Anhalt-Bernburg)

**Segen des Badischer Bergbaues** Blessings of the Baden mines. (Baden)

**Segen des Bergbau** Blessings of the mines. (Saxony)

**Segen des Himmels** Blessings of heaven. (Bavaria)

**Se(e)gen des Mansfelder Bergbaues** Blessings of the Mansfeld mines. (Prussia)

**Seinem Vater Carl Friederich dem Gesegneten** To his father Caarl Frederick the Victorious. (Bavaria)

**Shqipni** Albania. (Albania)

**Sieges Thaler** Victory taler. (Prussia)

**Slovenska Republica** Slovakian Republic. (Slovakian)

**Soberania Nacional** National Sovereignty. (Spain)

**Sous Le Regne du Roi Leopold III** In the reign of King Leopold III. (Belgium)

**Standbild A. Durer's Errichtet zu Nurnberg** Statue of Albrecht Durer, erected at Nuremberg. (Bavaria)

**Standbild des Canzler's Freyherrn v. Kreittmayr, Errichtet in Munchen 1845** Statue of Chancellor Baron von Kreittmayr, erected in Munich, 1845. (Bavaria)

**Standbild des Furstbischof's Julius Echter v. Mespelbrunn, Errichtet zu Wurzburg 1847** Statue of Bishop-Elector Julius Echter of Mespelbrunn, erected at Wurzburg, 1847. (Bavaria)

**Standbild des Johann Christoph Ritter von Gluck, Errichtet in Munchen v. Konig Ludwig I 1848** Statue of John Christopher, Knight von Gluck, erected at Munich by King Ludwig I, 1848. (Bavaria)

**Standbild des Roland de Latre gen. Orlando di Lasso, Errichtet in Munchen v. Konig Ludwig I 1849** Statue of Roland de Latre called Orlando di Lasso, erected in Munich by King Ludwig I, 1849. (Bavaria)

**Standbild Jean Paul Friedrich Richter's, Errichtet zu Bayreuth 1841** Statue of Jean Paul Frederick Richter, erected at Bayreuth, 1841. (Bavaria)

**Stark im Recht** Strong in justice. (Frankfurt)

**Stato Pontificio** The Papal State. (Papal States)

**Stiftung des Ludwigs-Ordens** Founding of the Ludwig Order. (Bavaria)

**Supra Firmam Petram** Upon a firm rock. (Papal States)

**Susceptor Noster Deus** God is our defense. (Tuscany)

**Suum Cuique, Loenungs Thaler** To each his own, coronation thaler. (Prussia)

**Svensk. Odlings Beframjare** Promoter of Swedish culture. (Swedish)

**Svenska Folkets Lagbundna Frihet** Freedom within the law of the Swedish people. (Swedish)

**Sveriges Riksdag** Swedish Parliament. (Swedish)

**Szechenyi, Istvan** Stephen Szechenyi. (Hungary)

**Szt. Istvan** St. Stephen. (Hungary)

**Szuletesenek 75 Evfordulojara** 75th anniversary of his birth. (Hungary)

## T

**Tansics, Mihaly** Michael Tancsics. (Hungary)

**Tausend Jahre Burg und Stadt Meissen** A thousand years of the town and city of Meissen. (Germany)

**(In) Terra Pax** Peace in the land. (Papal States)

**Tir Federal a Fribourg** Federal Shooting Match at Fribourg. (Switzerland)

**Tir Federal a la Chaux-de-Fonds Juillet 1863** Federal Shooting Match at Chaux-de-Fonds, July, 1863. (Switzerland)

**Tir Federal de 1876 a Lausanne** Federal Shooting Match of 1876 at Lausanne. (Switzerland)

**Tiro Federale in Lugano** Federal Shooting Match at Lugano. (Switzerland)

**Tiroler Freiheit** Tyrolean liberty. (Austria)

**Trau - Schau Wem** Trust, look, to whom. (Baden)

**Treu Der Verfassung** Loyal to the constitution. (Germany)

**Tritt die Regierung des Landes an am 13 October 1825** Assumes the government of the country on October 13, 1825. (Bavaria)

**Tueatur Unita Deus, Anno Dom 1847** May God guard these United (Kingdoms) in the year of our Lord 1847. (Great Britain)

**Turkiye Cumhuriyeti** Republic of Turkey. (Turkey)

## U

**Ueb Aug und Hand Fuer's Vaterland** Train eye and hand for the fatherland. (Austria)

**Umberto I Re D'Italia** Humbert I, King of Italy. (Italy)

**Union et Force** Union and strength. (France)

**Unione E Virtu'** Union and strength. (Cisalpine Republic)

**Unione Italiana** Italian Union. (Venice)

**Ut sit suo Pondere Tutus** That he may be safe by his own weight. (Nassau)

**U(V)tr. Sic. Hier. Hisp. Inf(ans)** Of the Two Sicilies and Jerusalem, Prince of Spain. (Naples & Sicily)

## V

**V.G.G. Heinrich d. XIII Aelt. Reuss G.U.H.V.P. Reg. F.z. Greiz** D.G., Henry the XIII, eldest line of Reuss, Count and Lord of Plauen, ruling Prince of Greiz. (Reuss-Greiz)

**Veni Lumen Cordium** Come light of hearts. (Papal States)

**Verbum Dni. Manet in Aeternum** The word of the Lord abides forever. (Hesse-Darmstadt)

**Vereinsmunze (many)** Convention money. (German States)

**Vereinten sich mit den Getreuen Staenden zu neuer Verfassung des Staats** They united themselves with the faithful supporters in the new composition of the state. (Saxony)

**Verfassungssaeule, Errichtet vom Gr. v. Schoenborn, Eingeweiht 1828** Constitution column erected by Count von Schoenborn, dedicated 1828. (Bavaria)

**Veritas Lex Tua** The truth is your law. (Salzburg)

**Verlegung der Ludwig Maximilians Hochschule von Landshut nach Munchen 1826** Removal of the Ludwig Maximilian University from Landshut to Munich, 1826. (Bavaria)

**Verni Sebe-Svorne Napred** Faithful to ourselves, united forward. (Slovakia)

**Vic. Em. D.G. Rex Sar. Cyp. et Ier.** Victor Emmanuel, D.G., King of Sardinia, Cyprus, and Jerusalem. (Sardinia)

**Victoria Dei Gratia** Victoria, D.G. (Great Britain)

**Victoria Dei Gratia Britanniar. Reg. F.D.** Victoria, D.G., Queen of the Britains, Defender of the Faith. (Great Britain)

**Victoria Dei Gra. Britt. Regina Fid. Def. Ind. Imp.** Victoria, D.G., Queen of Britain, Defender of the Faith, Empress of India. (Great Britain)

**Victoria D.G. Britt. Reg. F.D.** Victoria, D.G., Queen of Britain, Defender of the Faith. (Great Britain)

**Victorius Emmanuel II D.G. Rex Sard. Cyp. et Hier.** Victor Emmanuel II, D.G., King of Sardinia, Cyprus, and Jerusalem. (Great Britain)

**Videant Pauperes et Laetentur** Let the poor see and rejoice. (Tuscany)

**Vierzehn Eine Feine Mark** Fourteen to the fine mark. (Prussia)

**Viribus Unitis** With men united. (Austria)

**Virtute et Prudentia** With virtue and prudence. (Austria)

**Virtute Viam Dimetiar** I shall mark the way with valour. (Waldeck)

**Vitez Nagybanyai Horthy Miklos Kormanyzosaganak 10 Evfordulojara** 10th anniversary of the government of the great hero, Nicholas Horthy. (Hungary)

**Vitez Nagybanyai Horthy Miklos Kormanyzorszog Kormanyzoja** Hungarian government of the great hero Nicholas Horthy. (Hungary)

**Vitt. Em. III Re** Victor Emmanuel III, King. (Italy)

**Vittorio Emanuele II** Victor Emmanuel II; . . . . . **Re d'Italia** King of Italy. (Italy)

**Vittorio Emanuele III** Victor Emmanuel III; . . . . . **Re** . . . . . King; **d'Italia** . . . . .of Italy; **E Imperator** . . . . . and Emperor. (Italy)

**Vollendet den 5 Mai 1827, Psalm 91 V. 14-16** Completed on May 5, 1827, Psalm 91, verses 14-16. (Saxony)

**Vollendung der Oesterreichischen Sudbahn** Completion of the Austrian Southern Railways. (Austria)

## W

**W. Setna Rocznice Powstania** 100th anniversary of liberation. (Poland)

**Waldeckischer Kronthaler** Waldeck crown thaler. (Waldeck)

**Walhalla** Valhalla. (Bavaria)

**Wiener Munzvertrag 24 Jan. 1857** Vienna monetary convention January 24, 1857. (Schaumburg-Lippe)

**Wilh. II Kurf. u. Friedr. Wilh. Kurpr. u. Mitregent** William II, Elector, and Frederick William, Elector and Co-Regent. (Hesse-Cassel)

**Wilh. II Kurf. u. Friedr. Wilh. Kurprinz-Mitregent** William II, Elector, and Frederick William, Electoral Prince and Co-Regent. (Hesse-Cassel)

**Wilhalm Ernst - Caroline Groszherzog u. Groszherzogin v. Sachsen** William Ernest, Caroline, Grand Duke and Grand Duchess of Saxony (Weimar). (Saxe-Weimar)

**Wilhelm Deutscher Kaiser Konig v. Preussen** William, Emperor of Germany, King of Prussia. (Prussia)

**Wilhelm Herzog z. Braunschweig u. L(un)** William, Duke of Brunswick and Luneburg. (Brunswick-Luneburg)

**Wilhelm Herzog zu Nassau** William, Duke of Nassau. (Nassau)

**Wilhelm Koenig. Augusta Koenigin v. Preussen** William, King, Augusta, Queen of Prussia. (Prussia)

**Wilhelm Koenig von Preussen** William, King of Prussia. (Prussia)

**Wilhelm Koenig von Wurt(t)em(berg)** William, King of Wurttemberg. (Wurttemberg)

**Wilhelm Konig v. Wurttemberg** William, King of Wurttemberg. (Wurttemberg)

**Wilhelm I Kurf. Souv. Landgr. z. Hessen. Gr. H.v. Fulda** William I, Elector, Sovereign, Landgrave of Hesse, Grand Duke of Fulda. (Hesse-Cassel)

**Wilhelm II Deutscher Kaiser Konig v. Preussen** William II, Emperor of Germany, King of Prussia. (Prussia)

**Wilhelm II Koenig von Wuerttemberg** William II, King of Wurttemberg. (Wurttemberg)

**Wilhelm II Kurf. Souv. Langr. z. Hessen Gr. H. v. Fulda** William II, Elector, Sovereign, Landgrave of Hesse, Grand Duke of Fulda. (Hesse-Cassel)

**Wilhelm IV Koenig v. Gr. Brit. u. Hannover** William IV, King of Great Britain and Hannover. (Hannover)

**Wilhelmina Koningin der Nederlanden** Wilhelmina, Queen of the Netherlands. (Netherlands)

**Wilhelmus S(acri) R(omani) I(mperii) Pr(inceps) Auersperg Dux de Gotshee** William, Prince of S.R.I. and Auersperg, Duke of Gotschee. (Auersperg)

**Wilhelmus I D.G. Elect. Landg. Hass.** William I, D.G., Elector and Landgrave of Hesse. (Hesse-Cassel)

**Wilhelmus IX D.G. Hass. Landg. Com. Han.** William IX, D.G., Landgrave of Hesse, Count of Hanau. (Hesse-Cassel)

**Willem Koning der Ned(erlanden) G(root) H(ertog) V(an) L(uxemburg)** William, King of the Netherlands, Grand Duke of Luxembourg. (Netherlands)

**Willem II Koning der Ned. G.H.V.L.** William II, King of the Netherlands. . . . . (Netherlands)

**Willem III Koning der Ned. G.H.V.L.** William III, King of the Netherlands, . . . . . (Netherlands)

**Wir Wollen Sein Ein Einig Volk von Brudern** We will be a united people of brothers. (Austria)

## Y

**Ylas Baleares** Balearic Islands. (Spain)

## Z

**Z. Sreba Kraiowego** From the nation's silver. (Poland)

**Zehen Eine Feine Mark (many).** 10 to the fine mark. (German States)

**Zehn Eine Feine Mark (many).** 10 to the fine mark. (German States)

**Zehn Eine Mark Feine (many)** 10 to the fine mark. (German States)

**Zollverein mit Preussen, Sachsen, Hessen. U. Thuringen** Customs union with Prussia, Saxony, Hesse, and Thuringia. (Bavaria)

**Zu Gothe's Hundertjahriger Geburtsfeier am 28 August 1849** For the centennial of Goethe's birth on August 28, 1849. (Frankfurt)

**Zu Ihrer Voelker Heil** To the welfare of the peoples. (Bavaria)

**Zur Dritten Sacularfeier desReligions Friedens vom 25 Sept.** For the third centenary of the Religious Peace on September 25. (Frankfurt)

**Zur Erinnerung an d. Wiederherstellung d. Munsters in Ulm** In commemoration of the restoration of the cathedral in Ulm. (Wurttemberg)

**Zur Erinnerung an den Glorreich Erkampften Frieden vom 10 Mai 1871** In commemoration of the gloriously fought for peace of May 10, 1871. (Bremen)

**Zur Erinnerung an die Feier des 13 Dec. 1865** In commemoration of the celebration of December 13, 1865. (Hannover)

**Zur Erinnerung an die Wiederherstellung der Mariensaule in Munchen** In commemoration of the restoration of the Madonna column in Munich. (Bavaria)

**Zur Erinnerung an Sr. Majestat des Konigs und Ihrer Majestat der Konigin allerhochsten Besuch d. Munze** In commemoration of His Majesty the King's and Her Majesty the Queen's most gracious visit to the mint. (Hannover)

**Zur Eroffnung des Carl Ludwig Hauses auf der Raxalpe Im September 1877** On the opening of the Carl Ludwig Inn on the Raxalpe in September, 1877. (Austria)

**Zur Feier der 25 Jaehrigen Regierung** For the of the 25th anniversary of the reign. (Brunswick)

**Zur Feier Funf und Zwanzig Jahriger Regierung** For the celebration of the 25th anniversary of the reign. (Reuss-Ebersdorf)

**Zur Feier 25 Jahriger Regierung am 7 Marz 1867** For the celebration of the 25th anniversary of the reign on March 7, 1867. (Mecklenburg-Schwerin)

**Zur Feier 25 Jaehriger Segensreicher Regierung** For the celebration of the 25th anniversary of the prosperous reign. (Nassau)

**Zur Feier XXV Jaehriger Regierung d. 17 April 1843** For the celebration of the 25th anniversary ofthe reign on April 17, 1843. (Reuss-Schleiz)

**Zur Feier 50 Jaehriger Regierung d. 6 Nov. 1864** For the celebration of the 50th anniversary of the reign on November 6, 1864. (Schwarzburg-Rudolstadt)

**Zurich** Zurich. (Zurich)

**Zur Sicherung des Gewichts** On the guarantee of the weight. (Nassau)

**Zur v. Sacularfeier des Munz-rechts der Stadt Frankfurt A.M.** For the centenary of the minting rights of the city of Frankfurt-on-the-Main. (Frankfurt)

**Zur 50 Jahrigen Jubelfeier der Befreiung Deutschlands** On the 50th anniversary jubilee of the deliverance ofGermany. (Bremen)

**Zur 50 Jahrigen Vereinigung Ostfrieslands mit Hannover** On the 50th anniversary of the union of East Friesland with Hannover. (Hannover)

**Zwei Gulden XLV Ket Forint** Two gulden 45 two florins. (Austria)

**Zwei Vereinsthaler XV Ein Pfund Fein (many)** 2 Vereinstalers, 15 to the fine pound. (German States)

**Zweites Deutsches Bundesschiessen in Bremen 1865** Second German Shooting match in Bremen, 1865. (Bremen)

## RELATIVE VALUES

**75/100 Delar Finsilfver** 75/100 dollar fine silver. (Sweden)

**I Oesterreichisches Bundesschiessen** First Austrian Shooting Match. (Austria)

**I Thaler Hannoverisch Cassen-Geld** One thaler Hannoverian Cassa money. (Hannover)

**III Deutsches Bundes Schiessen Wien1869** Third German Shooting Match at Vienna, 1868. (Austria)

**4 Centenario da Descoberta da India** Fourth centenary of the discovery of India. (Portugal)

**IX Olympische Winterspiele** Ninth Olympic Winter Games. (Austria)

**32 Schillinge Hamburger Courant** 32 schilling current Hamburg. (Hamburg)

**60 Schilling Schlesw. Holst. Courant** 60 schillings current money Schleswig-Holstein. (Schleswig-Holstein)

**450 Jahre Universitat Tubingen** 450th anniversary of Tubingen University. (Germany)

**534 8/9 Troyska Ass Finsilfver**534 8/9 Troy ounces fine silver. (Poland)

**600 Jahre Tirol Osterreich** 600 years Tyrol Austria. (Austria)

**MDCCCLI Civium Industria Floret Civitas** By the industry of the people, the state flourishes 1851. (Great Britain)

# Silver Bullion Chart

| Oz. | $3.00 | 3.50 | 4.00 | 4.50 | 5.00 | 5.50 | 6.50 | 7.00 | 7.50 | 8.00 | 8.50 | 9.00 | 9.50 | 10.00 |
|---|---|---|---|---|---|---|---|---|---|---|---|---|---|---|
| 0.001 | 0.003 | 0.004 | 0.004 | 0.005 | 0.005 | 0.006 | 0.007 | 0.007 | 0.008 | 0.008 | 0.009 | 0.009 | 0.010 | 0.010 |
| 0.002 | 0.006 | 0.007 | 0.008 | 0.009 | 0.010 | 0.011 | 0.013 | 0.014 | 0.015 | 0.016 | 0.017 | 0.018 | 0.019 | 0.020 |
| 0.003 | 0.009 | 0.011 | 0.012 | 0.014 | 0.015 | 0.017 | 0.020 | 0.021 | 0.023 | 0.024 | 0.026 | 0.027 | 0.029 | 0.030 |
| 0.004 | 0.012 | 0.014 | 0.016 | 0.018 | 0.020 | 0.022 | 0.026 | 0.028 | 0.030 | 0.032 | 0.034 | 0.036 | 0.038 | 0.040 |
| 0.005 | 0.015 | 0.018 | 0.020 | 0.023 | 0.025 | 0.028 | 0.033 | 0.035 | 0.038 | 0.040 | 0.043 | 0.045 | 0.048 | 0.050 |
| 0.006 | 0.018 | 0.021 | 0.024 | 0.027 | 0.030 | 0.033 | 0.039 | 0.042 | 0.045 | 0.048 | 0.051 | 0.054 | 0.057 | 0.060 |
| 0.007 | 0.021 | 0.025 | 0.028 | 0.032 | 0.035 | 0.039 | 0.046 | 0.049 | 0.053 | 0.056 | 0.060 | 0.063 | 0.067 | 0.070 |
| 0.008 | 0.024 | 0.028 | 0.032 | 0.036 | 0.040 | 0.044 | 0.052 | 0.056 | 0.060 | 0.064 | 0.068 | 0.072 | 0.076 | 0.080 |
| 0.009 | 0.027 | 0.032 | 0.036 | 0.041 | 0.045 | 0.050 | 0.059 | 0.063 | 0.068 | 0.072 | 0.077 | 0.081 | 0.086 | 0.090 |
| 0.010 | 0.030 | 0.035 | 0.040 | 0.045 | 0.050 | 0.055 | 0.065 | 0.070 | 0.075 | 0.080 | 0.085 | 0.090 | 0.095 | 0.100 |
| 0.020 | 0.060 | 0.070 | 0.080 | 0.090 | 0.100 | 0.110 | 0.130 | 0.140 | 0.150 | 0.160 | 0.170 | 0.180 | 0.190 | 0.200 |
| 0.030 | 0.090 | 0.105 | 0.120 | 0.135 | 0.150 | 0.165 | 0.195 | 0.210 | 0.225 | 0.240 | 0.255 | 0.270 | 0.285 | 0.300 |
| 0.040 | 0.120 | 0.140 | 0.160 | 0.180 | 0.200 | 0.220 | 0.260 | 0.280 | 0.300 | 0.320 | 0.340 | 0.360 | 0.380 | 0.400 |
| 0.050 | 0.150 | 0.175 | 0.200 | 0.225 | 0.250 | 0.275 | 0.325 | 0.350 | 0.375 | 0.400 | 0.425 | 0.450 | 0.475 | 0.500 |
| 0.060 | 0.180 | 0.210 | 0.240 | 0.270 | 0.300 | 0.330 | 0.390 | 0.420 | 0.450 | 0.480 | 0.510 | 0.540 | 0.570 | 0.600 |
| 0.070 | 0.210 | 0.245 | 0.280 | 0.315 | 0.350 | 0.385 | 0.455 | 0.490 | 0.525 | 0.560 | 0.595 | 0.630 | 0.665 | 0.700 |
| 0.080 | 0.240 | 0.280 | 0.320 | 0.360 | 0.400 | 0.440 | 0.520 | 0.560 | 0.600 | 0.640 | 0.680 | 0.720 | 0.760 | 0.800 |
| 0.090 | 0.270 | 0.315 | 0.360 | 0.405 | 0.450 | 0.495 | 0.585 | 0.630 | 0.675 | 0.720 | 0.765 | 0.810 | 0.855 | 0.900 |
| 0.100 | 0.300 | 0.350 | 0.400 | 0.450 | 0.500 | 0.550 | 0.650 | 0.700 | 0.750 | 0.800 | 0.850 | 0.900 | 0.950 | 1.000 |
| 0.110 | 0.330 | 0.385 | 0.440 | 0.495 | 0.550 | 0.605 | 0.715 | 0.770 | 0.825 | 0.880 | 0.935 | 0.990 | 1.045 | 1.100 |
| 0.120 | 0.360 | 0.420 | 0.480 | 0.540 | 0.600 | 0.660 | 0.780 | 0.840 | 0.900 | 0.960 | 1.020 | 1.080 | 1.140 | 1.200 |
| 0.130 | 0.390 | 0.455 | 0.520 | 0.585 | 0.650 | 0.715 | 0.845 | 0.910 | 0.975 | 1.040 | 1.105 | 1.170 | 1.235 | 1.300 |
| 0.140 | 0.420 | 0.490 | 0.560 | 0.630 | 0.700 | 0.770 | 0.910 | 0.980 | 1.050 | 1.120 | 1.190 | 1.260 | 1.330 | 1.400 |
| 0.150 | 0.450 | 0.525 | 0.600 | 0.675 | 0.750 | 0.825 | 0.975 | 1.050 | 1.125 | 1.200 | 1.275 | 1.350 | 1.425 | 1.500 |
| 0.160 | 0.480 | 0.560 | 0.640 | 0.720 | 0.900 | 0.880 | 1.040 | 1.120 | 1.200 | 1.280 | 1.360 | 1.440 | 1.520 | 1.600 |
| 0.170 | 0.510 | 0.595 | 0.680 | 0.765 | 0.850 | 0.935 | 1.105 | 1.190 | 1.275 | 1.360 | 1.445 | 1.530 | 1.615 | 1.700 |
| 0.180 | 0.540 | 0.630 | 0.720 | 0.810 | 0.900 | 0.990 | 1.170 | 1.260 | 1.350 | 1.440 | 1.530 | 1.620 | 1.710 | 1.800 |
| 0.190 | 0.570 | 0.665 | 0.760 | 0.855 | 0.950 | 1.045 | 1.235 | 1.330 | 1.425 | 1.520 | 1.615 | 1.710 | 1.805 | 1.900 |
| 0.200 | 0.600 | 0.700 | 0.800 | 0.900 | 1.000 | 1.100 | 1.300 | 1.400 | 1.500 | 1.600 | 1.700 | 1.800 | 1.900 | 2.000 |
| 0.210 | 0.630 | 0.735 | 0.840 | 0.945 | 1.050 | 1.155 | 1.365 | 1.470 | 1.575 | 1.680 | 1.785 | 1.890 | 1.995 | 2.100 |
| 0.220 | 0.660 | 0.770 | 0.880 | 0.990 | 1.100 | 1.210 | 1.430 | 1.540 | 1.650 | 1.760 | 1.870 | 1.980 | 2.090 | 2.200 |
| 0.230 | 0.690 | 0.805 | 0.920 | 1.035 | 1.150 | 1.265 | 1.495 | 1.610 | 1.725 | 1.840 | 1.955 | 2.070 | 2.185 | 2.300 |
| 0.240 | 0.720 | 0.840 | 0.960 | 1.080 | 1.200 | 1.320 | 1.560 | 1.680 | 1.800 | 1.920 | 2.040 | 2.160 | 2.280 | 2.400 |
| 0.250 | 0.750 | 0.875 | 1.000 | 1.125 | 1.250 | 1.375 | 1.625 | 1.750 | 1.875 | 2.000 | 2.125 | 2.240 | 2.375 | 2.500 |
| 0.260 | 0.780 | 0.910 | 1.040 | 1.170 | 1.300 | 1.430 | 1.690 | 1.820 | 1.950 | 2.080 | 2.210 | 2.340 | 2.470 | 2.600 |
| 0.270 | 0.810 | 0.945 | 1.080 | 1.215 | 1.350 | 1.485 | 1.755 | 1.890 | 2.025 | 2.160 | 2.295 | 2.430 | 2.565 | 2.700 |
| 0.280 | 0.840 | 0.980 | 1.120 | 1.260 | 1.400 | 1.540 | 1.820 | 1.960 | 2.100 | 2.250 | 2.380 | 2.520 | 2.660 | 2.800 |
| 0.290 | 0.870 | 1.015 | 1.160 | 1.305 | 1.450 | 1.595 | 1.885 | 2.030 | 2.175 | 2.320 | 2.465 | 2.610 | 2.755 | 2.900 |
| 0.300 | 0.900 | 1.050 | 1.200 | 1.350 | 1.500 | 1.650 | 1.950 | 2.100 | 2.250 | 2.400 | 2.550 | 2.700 | 2.850 | 3.000 |
| 0.310 | 0.930 | 1.085 | 1.240 | 1.395 | 1.550 | 1.705 | 2.015 | 2.170 | 2.325 | 2.480 | 2.635 | 2.790 | 2.945 | 3.100 |
| 0.320 | 0.960 | 1.120 | 1.280 | 1.440 | 1.600 | 1.760 | 2.080 | 2.240 | 2.400 | 2.560 | 2.720 | 2.880 | 3.040 | 3.200 |
| 0.330 | 0.990 | 1.155 | 1.320 | 1.485 | 1.650 | 1.815 | 2.145 | 2.310 | 2.475 | 2.640 | 2.805 | 2.970 | 3.135 | 3.300 |
| 0.340 | 1.020 | 1.190 | 1.360 | 1.530 | 1.700 | 1.870 | 2.210 | 2.380 | 2.550 | 2.720 | 2.890 | 3.060 | 3.230 | 3.400 |
| 0.350 | 1.050 | 1.225 | 1.400 | 1.575 | 1.750 | 1.925 | 2.275 | 2.450 | 2.625 | 2.800 | 2.975 | 3.150 | 3.325 | 3.500 |
| 0.360 | 1.080 | 1.260 | 1.440 | 1.620 | 1.800 | 1.980 | 2.340 | 2.520 | 2.700 | 2.880 | 2.060 | 3.240 | 3.420 | 3.600 |
| 0.370 | 1.110 | 1.295 | 1.480 | 1.665 | 1.850 | 2.035 | 2.405 | 2.590 | 2.775 | 2.960 | 3.145 | 3.330 | 3.515 | 3.700 |
| 0.380 | 1.140 | 1.330 | 1.520 | 1.710 | 1.900 | 2.090 | 2.470 | 2.660 | 2.850 | 3.040 | 3.230 | 3.420 | 3.610 | 3.800 |
| 0.390 | 1.170 | 1.365 | 1.560 | 1.755 | 1.950 | 2.145 | 2.535 | 2.730 | 2.925 | 3.120 | 3.315 | 3.510 | 3.705 | 3.900 |
| 0.400 | 1.200 | 1.400 | 1.600 | 1.800 | 2.000 | 2.200 | 2.600 | 2.800 | 3.000 | 3.200 | 3.400 | 3.600 | 3.800 | 4.000 |
| 0.410 | 1.230 | 1.435 | 1.640 | 1.845 | 2.050 | 2.255 | 2.665 | 2.870 | 3.075 | 3.280 | 3.485 | 3.690 | 3.895 | 4.100 |
| 0.420 | 1.260 | 1.470 | 1.680 | 1.890 | 2.100 | 2.310 | 2.730 | 2.940 | 3.150 | 3.360 | 3.570 | 3.780 | 3.990 | 4.200 |
| 0.430 | 1.290 | 1.505 | 1.720 | 1.935 | 2.150 | 2.365 | 2.795 | 3.010 | 3.225 | 3.440 | 3.655 | 3.870 | 4.085 | 4.300 |
| 0.440 | 1.320 | 1.540 | 1.760 | 1.980 | 2.200 | 2.420 | 2.860 | 2.080 | 3.300 | 3.520 | 3.740 | 3.960 | 4.180 | 4.400 |
| 0.450 | 1.350 | 1.575 | 1.800 | 2.025 | 2.250 | 2.475 | 2.925 | 3.150 | 3.375 | 3.600 | 3.825 | 4.050 | 4.275 | 4.500 |

| Oz. | $3.00 | 3.50 | 4.00 | 4.50 | 5.00 | 5.50 | 6.50 | 7.00 | 7.50 | 8.00 | 8.50 | 9.00 | 9.50 | 10.00 |
|---|---|---|---|---|---|---|---|---|---|---|---|---|---|---|
| 0.460 | 1.380 | 1.610 | 1.840 | 2.070 | 2.300 | 2.530 | 2.990 | 3.220 | 3.450 | 3.680 | 3.910 | 4.140 | 4.370 | 4.600 |
| 0.470 | 1.410 | 1.645 | 1.880 | 2.115 | 2.350 | 2.585 | 3.055 | 3.290 | 3.525 | 3.760 | 3.995 | 4.230 | 4.465 | 4.700 |
| 0.480 | 1.440 | 1.680 | 1.920 | 2.160 | 2.400 | 2.640 | 3.120 | 3.360 | 3.600 | 3.840 | 4.080 | 4.320 | 4.560 | 4.800 |
| 0.490 | 1.470 | 1.715 | 1.960 | 2.205 | 2.450 | 2.695 | 3.185 | 3.430 | 3.675 | 3.920 | 4.165 | 4.410 | 4.655 | 4.900 |
| 0.500 | 1.500 | 1.750 | 2.000 | 2.250 | 2.500 | 2.750 | 3.250 | 3.500 | 3.750 | 4.000 | 4.250 | 4.500 | 4.750 | 5.000 |
| 0.510 | 1.530 | 1.785 | 2.040 | 2.295 | 2.550 | 2.805 | 3.315 | 3.570 | 3.825 | 4.080 | 4.335 | 4.590 | 4.845 | 5.100 |
| 0.520 | 1.560 | 1.820 | 2.080 | 2.340 | 2.600 | 2.860 | 3.380 | 3.640 | 3.900 | 4.160 | 4.420 | 4.680 | 4.940 | 5.200 |
| 0.530 | 1.590 | 1.855 | 2.120 | 2.385 | 2.650 | 2.915 | 3.445 | 3.710 | 3.975 | 4.240 | 4.505 | 4.770 | 5.035 | 5.300 |
| 0.540 | 1.620 | 1.890 | 2.160 | 2.430 | 2.700 | 2.970 | 3.510 | 3.780 | 4.050 | 4.320 | 4.590 | 4.860 | 5.130 | 5.400 |
| 0.550 | 1.650 | 1.925 | 2.200 | 2.475 | 2.750 | 3.025 | 3.575 | 3.850 | 4.125 | 4.400 | 4.675 | 4.950 | 5.225 | 5.500 |
| 0.560 | 1.680 | 1.960 | 2.240 | 2.520 | 2.800 | 3.080 | 3.640 | 3.920 | 4.200 | 4.480 | 4.760 | 5.040 | 5.320 | 5.600 |
| 0.570 | 1.710 | 1.995 | 2.280 | 2.565 | 2.850 | 3.135 | 3.705 | 3.990 | 4.275 | 4.560 | 4.845 | 5.130 | 5.415 | 5.700 |
| 0.580 | 1.740 | 2.030 | 2.320 | 2.610 | 2.900 | 3.190 | 3.770 | 4.060 | 4.350 | 4.640 | 4.930 | 5.220 | 5.510 | 5.800 |
| 0.590 | 1.770 | 2.065 | 2.360 | 2.655 | 2.950 | 3.245 | 3.835 | 4.130 | 4.425 | 4.720 | 5.015 | 5.310 | 5.605 | 5.900 |
| 0.600 | 1.800 | 2.100 | 2.400 | 2.700 | 3.000 | 3.300 | 3.900 | 4.200 | 4.500 | 4.800 | 5.100 | 5.400 | 5.700 | 6.000 |
| 0.610 | 1.830 | 2.135 | 2.440 | 2.745 | 3.050 | 3.355 | 3.965 | 4.270 | 4.575 | 4.880 | 5.185 | 5.490 | 5.795 | 6.100 |
| 0.620 | 1.860 | 2.170 | 2.480 | 2.790 | 3.100 | 3.410 | 4.030 | 4.340 | 4.650 | 4.960 | 5.270 | 5.580 | 5.890 | 6.200 |
| 0.630 | 1.890 | 2.205 | 2.520 | 2.835 | 3.150 | 3.465 | 4.095 | 4.410 | 4.725 | 5.040 | 5.355 | 5.670 | 5.985 | 6.300 |
| 0.640 | 1.920 | 2.240 | 2.560 | 2.880 | 3.200 | 3.520 | 4.160 | 4.480 | 4.800 | 5.120 | 5.440 | 5.760 | 6.080 | 6.400 |
| 0.650 | 1.950 | 2.275 | 2.600 | 2.925 | 3.250 | 3.575 | 4.225 | 4.550 | 4.875 | 5.200 | 5.525 | 5.850 | 6.175 | 6.500 |
| 0.660 | 1.980 | 2.310 | 2.640 | 2.970 | 3.300 | 3.630 | 4.290 | 4.620 | 4.950 | 5.280 | 5.610 | 5.940 | 6.270 | 6.600 |
| 0.670 | 2.010 | 2.345 | 2.680 | 3.015 | 3.350 | 3.685 | 4.355 | 4.690 | 5.025 | 5.360 | 5.695 | 6.030 | 6.365 | 6.700 |
| 0.680 | 2.040 | 2.380 | 2.720 | 3.060 | 3.400 | 3.740 | 4.420 | 4.760 | 5.100 | 5.440 | 5.780 | 6.120 | 6.460 | 6.800 |
| 0.690 | 2.070 | 2.415 | 2.760 | 3.105 | 3.450 | 3.795 | 4.485 | 4.830 | 5.175 | 5.520 | 5.865 | 6.210 | 6.555 | 6.900 |
| 0.700 | 2.100 | 2.450 | 2.800 | 3.150 | 3.500 | 3.850 | 4.550 | 4.900 | 5.250 | 5.600 | 5.950 | 6.300 | 6.650 | 7.000 |
| 0.710 | 2.130 | 2.485 | 2.840 | 3.195 | 3.550 | 3.905 | 4.615 | 4.970 | 5.325 | 5.680 | 6.035 | 6.390 | 6.745 | 7.100 |
| 0.720 | 2.160 | 2.520 | 2.880 | 3.240 | 3.600 | 3.960 | 4.680 | 5.040 | 5.400 | 5.760 | 6.120 | 6.480 | 6.840 | 7.200 |
| 0.730 | 2.190 | 2.555 | 2.920 | 3.285 | 2.650 | 4.015 | 4.745 | 5.110 | 5.475 | 5.840 | 6.205 | 6.570 | 6.935 | 7.300 |
| 0.740 | 2.220 | 2.590 | 2.960 | 3.330 | 3.700 | 4.070 | 4.810 | 5.180 | 5.550 | 5.920 | 6.290 | 6.660 | 7.030 | 7.400 |
| 0.750 | 2.250 | 2.625 | 3.000 | 3.375 | 2.750 | 4.125 | 4.875 | 5.250 | 5.625 | 6.000 | 6.375 | 6.750 | 7.125 | 7.500 |
| 0.760 | 2.280 | 2.660 | 3.040 | 3.420 | 3.800 | 4.180 | 4.940 | 5.320 | 5.700 | 6.080 | 6.460 | 6.840 | 7.220 | 7.600 |
| 0.770 | 2.310 | 2.695 | 3.080 | 3.465 | 3.850 | 4.235 | 5.005 | 5.390 | 5.775 | 6.160 | 6.545 | 6.930 | 7.315 | 7.700 |
| 0.780 | 2.340 | 2.730 | 3.120 | 3.510 | 3.900 | 4.290 | 5.070 | 5.460 | 5.850 | 6.240 | 6.630 | 7.020 | 7.410 | 7.800 |
| 0.790 | 2.370 | 2.765 | 3.160 | 3.555 | 3.950 | 4.345 | 5.135 | 5.530 | 5.935 | 6.320 | 6.715 | 7.110 | 7.505 | 7.900 |
| 0.800 | 2.400 | 2.800 | 3.200 | 3.600 | 4.000 | 4.400 | 5.200 | 5.600 | 6.000 | 6.400 | 6.800 | 7.200 | 7.600 | 8.000 |
| 0.810 | 2.430 | 2.835 | 3.240 | 3.645 | 4.050 | 4.455 | 5.265 | 5.670 | 6.075 | 6.480 | 6.885 | 7.290 | 7.695 | 8.100 |
| 0.820 | 2.460 | 2.870 | 3.280 | 3.690 | 4.100 | 4.510 | 5.330 | 5.740 | 6.150 | 6.560 | 6.970 | 7.380 | 7.790 | 8.200 |
| 0.830 | 2.490 | 2.905 | 3.320 | 3.735 | 4.150 | 4.565 | 5.395 | 5.810 | 6.225 | 6.640 | 7.055 | 7.470 | 7.885 | 8.300 |
| 0.840 | 2.520 | 2.940 | 3.360 | 3.780 | 4.200 | 4.620 | 5.460 | 5.880 | 6.300 | 6.720 | 7.140 | 7.560 | 7.980 | 8.400 |
| 0.850 | 2.550 | 2.975 | 3.400 | 3.825 | 4.250 | 4.675 | 5.525 | 5.950 | 6.375 | 6.800 | 7.225 | 7.650 | 8.075 | 8.500 |
| 0.860 | 2.580 | 3.010 | 3.440 | 3.870 | 4.300 | 4.730 | 5.590 | 6.020 | 6.450 | 6.880 | 7.310 | 7.740 | 8.170 | 8.600 |
| 0.870 | 2.610 | 3.045 | 3.480 | 3.915 | 4.350 | 4.785 | 5.655 | 6.090 | 6.525 | 6.960 | 7.395 | 7.830 | 8.265 | 8.700 |
| 0.880 | 2.640 | 3.080 | 3.520 | 3.960 | 4.400 | 4.840 | 5.720 | 6.160 | 6.600 | 7.040 | 7.480 | 7.920 | 8.360 | 8.800 |
| 0.890 | 2.670 | 3.115 | 3.560 | 4.005 | 4.450 | 4.895 | 5.785 | 6.230 | 6.675 | 7.120 | 7.565 | 8.010 | 8.455 | 8.900 |
| 0.900 | 2.700 | 3.150 | 3.600 | 4.050 | 4.500 | 4.950 | 5.850 | 6.300 | 6.750 | 7.200 | 7.650 | 8.100 | 8.550 | 9.000 |
| 0.910 | 2.730 | 3.185 | 3.640 | 4.095 | 4.550 | 5.005 | 5.915 | 6.370 | 6.825 | 7.280 | 7.735 | 8.190 | 8.645 | 9.100 |
| 0.920 | 2.760 | 3.220 | 3.680 | 4.140 | 4.600 | 5.060 | 5.980 | 6.440 | 6.900 | 7.360 | 7.820 | 8.280 | 8.740 | 9.200 |
| 0.930 | 2.790 | 3.255 | 3.720 | 4.185 | 4.650 | 5.115 | 6.045 | 6.510 | 6.975 | 7.440 | 7.905 | 8.370 | 8.835 | 9.300 |
| 0.940 | 2.820 | 3.290 | 3.760 | 4.230 | 4.700 | 5.170 | 6.110 | 6.580 | 7.050 | 7.520 | 7.990 | 8.460 | 8.930 | 9.400 |
| 0.950 | 2.850 | 3.325 | 3.800 | 4.275 | 4.750 | 5.225 | 6.175 | 6.650 | 7.125 | 7.600 | 8.075 | 8.550 | 9.025 | 9.500 |
| 0.960 | 2.880 | 3.360 | 3.840 | 4.320 | 4.800 | 5.280 | 6.240 | 6.720 | 7.200 | 7.680 | 8.160 | 8.640 | 9.120 | 9.600 |
| 0.970 | 2.910 | 3.395 | 3.880 | 4.365 | 4.850 | 5.335 | 6.305 | 6.790 | 7.275 | 7.760 | 8.245 | 8.730 | 9.215 | 9.700 |
| 0.980 | 2.940 | 3.430 | 3.920 | 4.410 | 4.900 | 5.390 | 6.370 | 6.860 | 7.350 | 7.840 | 8.330 | 8.820 | 9.310 | 9.800 |
| 0.990 | 2.970 | 3.465 | 3.960 | 4.455 | 4.950 | 5.445 | 6.435 | 6.930 | 7.425 | 7.920 | 8.415 | 8.910 | 9.405 | 9.900 |
| 1.000 | 3.000 | 3.500 | 4.000 | 4.500 | 5.000 | 5.500 | 6.500 | 7.000 | 7.500 | 8.000 | 8.500 | 9.000 | 9.500 | 10.000 |

# Gold Bullion Chart

| Oz. | $270.00 | 280.00 | 290.00 | 300.00 | 310.00 | 320.00 | 330.00 | 340.00 | 350.00 | 360.00 | 370.00 | 380.00 | 390.00 | 400.00 | 410.00 |
|---|---|---|---|---|---|---|---|---|---|---|---|---|---|---|---|
| 0.001 | 0.27 | 0.28 | 0.29 | 0.30 | 0.31 | 0.32 | 0.33 | 0.34 | 0.35 | 0.36 | 0.37 | 0.38 | 0.39 | 0.40 | 0.41 |
| 0.002 | 0.54 | 0.56 | 0.58 | 0.60 | 0.62 | 0.64 | 0.66 | 0.68 | 0.70 | 0.72 | 0.74 | 0.76 | 0.78 | 0.80 | 0.82 |
| 0.003 | 0.81 | 0.84 | 0.87 | 0.90 | 0.93 | 0.96 | 0.99 | 1.02 | 1.05 | 1.08 | 1.11 | 1.14 | 1.17 | 1.20 | 1.23 |
| 0.004 | 1.08 | 1.12 | 1.16 | 1.20 | 1.24 | 1.28 | 1.32 | 1.36 | 1.40 | 1.44 | 1.48 | 1.52 | 1.56 | 1.60 | 1.64 |
| 0.005 | 1.35 | 1.40 | 1.45 | 1.50 | 1.55 | 1.60 | 1.65 | 1.70 | 1.75 | 1.80 | 1.85 | 1.90 | 1.95 | 2.00 | 2.05 |
| 0.006 | 1.62 | 1.68 | 1.74 | 1.80 | 1.86 | 1.92 | 1.98 | 2.04 | 2.10 | 2.16 | 2.22 | 2.28 | 2.34 | 2.40 | 2.46 |
| 0.007 | 1.89 | 1.96 | 2.03 | 2.10 | 2.17 | 2.24 | 2.31 | 2.38 | 2.45 | 2.52 | 2.59 | 2.66 | 2.73 | 2.80 | 2.87 |
| 0.008 | 2.16 | 2.24 | 2.32 | 2.40 | 2.48 | 2.56 | 2.64 | 2.72 | 2.80 | 2.88 | 2.96 | 3.04 | 3.12 | 3.20 | 3.28 |
| 0.009 | 2.43 | 2.52 | 2.61 | 2.70 | 2.79 | 2.88 | 2.97 | 3.06 | 3.15 | 3.24 | 3.33 | 3.42 | 3.51 | 3.60 | 3.69 |
| 0.010 | 2.70 | 2.80 | 2.90 | 3.00 | 3.10 | 3.20 | 3.30 | 3.40 | 3.50 | 3.60 | 3.70 | 3.80 | 3.90 | 4.00 | 4.10 |
| 0.020 | 5.40 | 5.60 | 5.80 | 6.00 | 6.20 | 6.40 | 6.60 | 6.80 | 7.00 | 7.20 | 7.40 | 7.60 | 7.80 | 8.00 | 8.20 |
| 0.030 | 8.10 | 8.40 | 8.70 | 9.00 | 9.30 | 9.60 | 9.90 | 10.20 | 10.50 | 10.80 | 11.10 | 11.40 | 11.70 | 12.00 | 12.30 |
| 0.040 | 10.80 | 11.20 | 11.60 | 12.00 | 12.40 | 12.80 | 13.20 | 13.60 | 14.00 | 14.40 | 14.80 | 15.20 | 15.60 | 16.00 | 16.40 |
| 0.050 | 13.50 | 14.00 | 14.50 | 15.00 | 15.50 | 16.00 | 16.50 | 17.00 | 17.50 | 18.00 | 18.50 | 19.00 | 19.50 | 20.00 | 20.50 |
| 0.060 | 16.20 | 16.80 | 17.40 | 18.00 | 18.60 | 19.20 | 19.80 | 20.40 | 21.00 | 21.60 | 22.20 | 22.80 | 23.40 | 24.00 | 24.60 |
| 0.070 | 18.90 | 19.60 | 20.30 | 21.00 | 21.70 | 22.40 | 23.10 | 23.80 | 24.50 | 25.20 | 25.90 | 26.60 | 27.30 | 28.00 | 28.70 |
| 0.080 | 21.60 | 22.40 | 23.20 | 24.00 | 24.80 | 25.60 | 26.40 | 27.20 | 28.00 | 28.80 | 29.60 | 30.40 | 31.20 | 32.00 | 32.80 |
| 0.090 | 24.30 | 25.20 | 26.10 | 27.00 | 27.90 | 28.80 | 29.70 | 30.60 | 31.50 | 32.40 | 33.30 | 34.20 | 35.10 | 36.00 | 36.90 |
| 0.100 | 27.00 | 28.00 | 29.00 | 30.00 | 31.00 | 32.00 | 33.00 | 34.00 | 35.00 | 36.00 | 37.00 | 38.00 | 39.00 | 40.00 | 41.00 |
| 0.110 | 29.70 | 30.80 | 31.90 | 33.00 | 34.10 | 35.20 | 36.30 | 37.40 | 38.50 | 39.60 | 40.70 | 41.80 | 42.90 | 44.00 | 45.10 |
| 0.120 | 32.40 | 33.60 | 34.80 | 36.00 | 37.20 | 38.40 | 39.60 | 40.80 | 42.00 | 43.20 | 44.40 | 45.60 | 46.80 | 48.00 | 49.20 |
| 0.130 | 35.10 | 36.40 | 37.70 | 39.00 | 40.30 | 41.60 | 42.90 | 44.20 | 45.50 | 46.80 | 48.10 | 49.40 | 50.70 | 52.00 | 53.30 |
| 0.140 | 37.80 | 39.20 | 40.60 | 42.00 | 43.40 | 44.80 | 46.20 | 47.60 | 49.00 | 50.40 | 51.80 | 53.20 | 54.60 | 56.00 | 57.40 |
| 0.150 | 40.50 | 42.00 | 43.50 | 45.00 | 46.50 | 48.00 | 49.50 | 51.00 | 52.50 | 54.00 | 55.50 | 57.00 | 58.50 | 60.00 | 61.50 |
| 0.160 | 43.20 | 44.80 | 46.40 | 48.00 | 49.50 | 51.20 | 52.80 | 54.40 | 56.00 | 57.60 | 59.20 | 60.80 | 62.40 | 64.00 | 65.50 |
| 0.170 | 45.90 | 47.60 | 49.30 | 51.00 | 52.70 | 54.40 | 56.10 | 57.80 | 59.50 | 61.20 | 62.90 | 64.60 | 66.30 | 68.00 | 69.70 |
| 0.180 | 48.60 | 50.40 | 52.20 | 54.00 | 55.80 | 57.60 | 59.40 | 61.20 | 63.00 | 64.80 | 66.60 | 68.40 | 70.20 | 72.00 | 73.80 |
| 0.190 | 51.30 | 53.20 | 55.10 | 57.00 | 58.90 | 60.80 | 62.70 | 64.60 | 66.50 | 68.40 | 70.30 | 72.20 | 74.10 | 76.00 | 77.90 |
| 0.200 | 54.00 | 56.00 | 58.00 | 60.00 | 62.00 | 64.00 | 66.00 | 68.00 | 70.00 | 72.00 | 74.00 | 76.00 | 78.00 | 80.00 | 82.00 |
| 0.210 | 56.70 | 58.80 | 60.90 | 63.00 | 65.10 | 67.20 | 69.30 | 71.40 | 73.50 | 75.60 | 77.70 | 79.80 | 81.90 | 84.00 | 86.10 |
| 0.220 | 59.40 | 61.60 | 63.80 | 66.00 | 68.20 | 70.40 | 72.60 | 74.80 | 77.00 | 79.20 | 81.40 | 83.60 | 85.80 | 88.00 | 90.20 |
| 0.230 | 62.10 | 64.40 | 66.70 | 69.00 | 71.30 | 73.60 | 75.90 | 78.20 | 80.50 | 82.80 | 85.10 | 87.40 | 89.70 | 92.00 | 94.30 |
| 0.240 | 64.80 | 67.20 | 69.60 | 72.00 | 74.40 | 76.80 | 79.20 | 81.60 | 84.00 | 86.40 | 88.80 | 91.20 | 93.60 | 96.00 | 98.40 |
| 0.250 | 67.50 | 70.00 | 72.50 | 75.00 | 77.50 | 80.00 | 82.50 | 85.00 | 87.50 | 90.00 | 92.50 | 95.00 | 97.50 | 100.00 | 102.50 |
| 0.260 | 70.20 | 72.80 | 75.40 | 78.00 | 80.60 | 83.20 | 85.80 | 88.40 | 91.00 | 93.60 | 96.20 | 98.80 | 101.40 | 104.00 | 106.60 |
| 0.270 | 72.90 | 75.60 | 78.30 | 81.00 | 83.70 | 86.40 | 89.10 | 91.80 | 94.50 | 97.20 | 99.90 | 102.60 | 105.30 | 108.00 | 110.70 |
| 0.280 | 75.60 | 78.40 | 81.20 | 84.00 | 86.80 | 89.60 | 92.40 | 95.20 | 98.00 | 100.80 | 103.60 | 106.40 | 109.20 | 112.00 | 114.80 |
| 0.290 | 78.30 | 81.20 | 84.10 | 87.00 | 89.90 | 92.80 | 95.70 | 98.60 | 101.50 | 104.40 | 107.30 | 110.20 | 113.10 | 116.00 | 118.90 |
| 0.300 | 81.00 | 84.00 | 87.00 | 90.00 | 93.00 | 96.00 | 99.00 | 102.00 | 105.00 | 108.00 | 111.00 | 114.00 | 117.00 | 120.00 | 123.00 |
| 0.310 | 83.70 | 86.80 | 89.90 | 93.00 | 96.10 | 99.20 | 102.30 | 105.40 | 108.50 | 111.60 | 114.70 | 117.80 | 120.90 | 124.00 | 127.10 |
| 0.320 | 86.40 | 89.60 | 92.80 | 96.00 | 99.20 | 102.40 | 105.60 | 108.80 | 112.00 | 115.20 | 118.40 | 121.60 | 124.80 | 128.00 | 131.20 |
| 0.330 | 89.10 | 92.40 | 95.70 | 99.00 | 102.30 | 105.60 | 108.90 | 112.20 | 115.50 | 118.80 | 122.10 | 125.40 | 128.70 | 132.00 | 135.30 |
| 0.340 | 91.80 | 95.20 | 98.60 | 102.00 | 105.40 | 108.80 | 112.20 | 115.60 | 119.00 | 122.40 | 125.80 | 129.20 | 132.60 | 136.00 | 139.40 |
| 0.350 | 94.50 | 98.00 | 101.50 | 105.00 | 108.50 | 112.00 | 115.50 | 119.00 | 122.50 | 126.00 | 129.50 | 133.00 | 136.50 | 140.00 | 143.50 |
| 0.360 | 97.20 | 100.80 | 104.40 | 108.00 | 111.60 | 115.20 | 118.80 | 122.40 | 126.00 | 129.60 | 133.20 | 136.80 | 140.40 | 144.00 | 147.60 |
| 0.370 | 99.90 | 103.60 | 107.30 | 111.00 | 114.70 | 118.40 | 122.10 | 125.80 | 129.50 | 133.20 | 136.90 | 140.60 | 144.30 | 148.00 | 151.70 |
| 0.380 | 102.60 | 106.40 | 110.20 | 114.00 | 117.80 | 121.60 | 125.40 | 129.20 | 133.00 | 136.80 | 140.60 | 144.40 | 148.20 | 152.00 | 155.80 |
| 0.390 | 105.30 | 109.20 | 113.10 | 117.00 | 120.90 | 124.80 | 128.70 | 132.60 | 136.50 | 140.40 | 144.30 | 148.20 | 152.10 | 156.00 | 159.90 |
| 0.400 | 108.00 | 112.00 | 116.00 | 120.00 | 124.00 | 128.00 | 132.00 | 136.00 | 140.00 | 144.00 | 148.00 | 152.00 | 156.00 | 160.00 | 164.00 |
| 0.410 | 110.70 | 114.80 | 118.90 | 123.00 | 127.10 | 131.20 | 135.30 | 139.70 | 143.50 | 147.60 | 151.70 | 155.80 | 159.90 | 164.00 | 168.10 |
| 0.420 | 113.40 | 117.60 | 121.80 | 126.00 | 130.20 | 134.40 | 138.60 | 142.80 | 147.00 | 151.20 | 155.40 | 159.60 | 163.80 | 168.00 | 172.20 |
| 0.430 | 116.10 | 120.40 | 124.70 | 129.00 | 133.30 | 137.60 | 141.90 | 146.20 | 150.50 | 154.80 | 159.10 | 163.40 | 167.70 | 172.00 | 176.30 |
| 0.440 | 118.80 | 123.20 | 127.60 | 132.00 | 136.40 | 140.80 | 145.20 | 149.60 | 154.00 | 158.40 | 162.80 | 167.20 | 171.60 | 176.00 | 180.40 |
| 0.450 | 121.50 | 126.00 | 130.50 | 135.00 | 139.50 | 144.00 | 148.50 | 153.00 | 157.50 | 162.00 | 166.50 | 171.00 | 175.50 | 180.00 | 184.50 |

| Oz. | $270.00 | 280.00 | 290.00 | 300.00 | 310.00 | 320.00 | 330.00 | 340.00 | 350.00 | 360.00 | 370.00 | 380.00 | 390.00 | 400.00 | 410.00 |
|---|---|---|---|---|---|---|---|---|---|---|---|---|---|---|---|
| 0.460 | 124.20 | 128.80 | 133.40 | 138.00 | 142.60 | 147.20 | 151.80 | 156.40 | 161.00 | 165.60 | 170.20 | 174.80 | 179.40 | 184.00 | 188.60 |
| 0.470 | 126.90 | 131.60 | 136.30 | 141.00 | 145.70 | 150.40 | 155.10 | 159.80 | 164.50 | 169.20 | 173.90 | 178.60 | 183.30 | 188.00 | 192.70 |
| 0.480 | 129.60 | 134.40 | 139.20 | 144.00 | 148.80 | 153.60 | 158.40 | 163.20 | 168.00 | 172.80 | 177.60 | 182.40 | 187.20 | 192.00 | 196.80 |
| 0.490 | 132.30 | 137.20 | 142.10 | 147.00 | 151.90 | 156.80 | 161.70 | 166.60 | 171.50 | 176.40 | 181.30 | 186.20 | 191.10 | 196.00 | 200.90 |
| 0.500 | 135.00 | 140.00 | 145.00 | 150.00 | 155.00 | 160.00 | 165.00 | 170.00 | 175.00 | 180.00 | 185.00 | 190.00 | 195.00 | 200.00 | 205.00 |
| 0.510 | 137.70 | 142.80 | 147.90 | 153.00 | 158.10 | 163.20 | 168.30 | 173.40 | 178.50 | 183.60 | 188.70 | 193.80 | 198.90 | 204.00 | 209.10 |
| 0.520 | 140.40 | 145.60 | 150.80 | 156.00 | 161.20 | 166.40 | 171.60 | 176.80 | 182.00 | 187.20 | 192.40 | 197.60 | 202.80 | 208.00 | 213.20 |
| 0.530 | 143.10 | 148.40 | 153.70 | 159.00 | 164.30 | 169.60 | 174.90 | 180.20 | 185.50 | 190.80 | 196.10 | 201.40 | 206.70 | 212.00 | 217.30 |
| 0.540 | 145.80 | 151.20 | 156.60 | 162.00 | 167.40 | 172.80 | 178.20 | 183.60 | 189.00 | 194.40 | 199.80 | 205.20 | 210.60 | 216.00 | 221.40 |
| 0.550 | 148.50 | 154.00 | 159.50 | 165.00 | 170.50 | 176.00 | 181.50 | 187.00 | 192.50 | 198.00 | 203.50 | 209.00 | 214.50 | 220.00 | 225.50 |
| 0.560 | 151.20 | 156.80 | 162.40 | 168.00 | 173.60 | 179.20 | 184.80 | 190.40 | 196.00 | 201.60 | 207.20 | 212.80 | 218.40 | 224.00 | 229.60 |
| 0.570 | 153.90 | 159.60 | 165.30 | 171.00 | 176.70 | 182.40 | 188.10 | 193.80 | 199.50 | 205.20 | 210.90 | 216.60 | 222.30 | 228.00 | 233.70 |
| 0.580 | 156.60 | 162.40 | 168.20 | 174.00 | 179.80 | 186.60 | 191.40 | 197.20 | 203.00 | 208.80 | 214.60 | 220.40 | 226.20 | 232.00 | 237.80 |
| 0.590 | 159.30 | 165.20 | 171.10 | 177.00 | 182.90 | 188.80 | 194.70 | 200.60 | 206.50 | 212.40 | 218.30 | 224.20 | 230.10 | 236.00 | 241.90 |
| 0.600 | 162.00 | 158.00 | 174.00 | 180.00 | 186.00 | 192.00 | 198.00 | 204.00 | 210.00 | 216.00 | 222.00 | 228.00 | 234.00 | 240.00 | 246.00 |
| 0.610 | 164.70 | 170.80 | 176.90 | 183.00 | 189.10 | 195.20 | 201.30 | 207.40 | 213.50 | 219.60 | 225.70 | 231.80 | 237.90 | 244.00 | 250.10 |
| 0.620 | 167.40 | 173.60 | 179.80 | 186.00 | 192.20 | 198.40 | 204.60 | 210.80 | 217.00 | 223.20 | 229.40 | 235.60 | 241.80 | 248.00 | 254.20 |
| 0.630 | 170.10 | 176.40 | 182.70 | 189.00 | 195.30 | 201.60 | 207.90 | 214.20 | 220.50 | 226.80 | 233.10 | 239.40 | 245.70 | 252.00 | 258.30 |
| 0.640 | 172.80 | 179.20 | 185.60 | 192.00 | 198.40 | 204.80 | 211.20 | 217.60 | 224.00 | 230.40 | 236.80 | 243.20 | 249.60 | 256.00 | 262.40 |
| 0.650 | 175.50 | 182.00 | 188.50 | 195.00 | 201.50 | 208.00 | 214.50 | 221.00 | 227.50 | 234.00 | 240.50 | 247.00 | 253.50 | 260.00 | 266.50 |
| 0.660 | 178.20 | 184.80 | 191.40 | 198.00 | 204.60 | 211.20 | 217.80 | 224.40 | 231.00 | 237.60 | 244.20 | 250.80 | 257.40 | 264.00 | 270.60 |
| 0.670 | 180.90 | 187.60 | 194.30 | 201.00 | 207.70 | 214.40 | 221.10 | 227.80 | 234.50 | 241.20 | 247.90 | 254.60 | 261.30 | 268.00 | 274.70 |
| 0.680 | 183.60 | 190.40 | 197.20 | 204.00 | 210.80 | 217.60 | 224.40 | 231.20 | 238.00 | 244.80 | 251.60 | 258.40 | 265.20 | 272.00 | 278.80 |
| 0.690 | 186.30 | 193.20 | 200.10 | 207.00 | 213.90 | 220.80 | 227.70 | 234.60 | 241.50 | 248.40 | 255.30 | 262.20 | 269.10 | 276.00 | 282.90 |
| 0.700 | 189.00 | 196.00 | 203.00 | 210.00 | 217.00 | 224.00 | 231.00 | 238.00 | 245.00 | 252.00 | 259.00 | 266.00 | 273.00 | 280.00 | 287.00 |
| 0.710 | 191.70 | 198.80 | 205.90 | 213.00 | 220.10 | 227.20 | 234.30 | 241.40 | 248.50 | 255.60 | 262.70 | 269.80 | 276.90 | 284.00 | 291.10 |
| 0.720 | 194.40 | 201.60 | 208.80 | 216.00 | 223.20 | 230.40 | 237.60 | 244.80 | 252.00 | 259.20 | 266.40 | 273.60 | 280.80 | 288.00 | 295.20 |
| 0.730 | 197.10 | 204.40 | 211.70 | 219.00 | 226.30 | 233.60 | 240.90 | 248.20 | 255.50 | 262.80 | 270.10 | 277.40 | 284.70 | 292.00 | 299.30 |
| 0.740 | 199.80 | 207.20 | 214.60 | 222.00 | 229.40 | 236.80 | 244.20 | 251.60 | 259.00 | 266.40 | 273.80 | 281.20 | 288.60 | 296.00 | 303.40 |
| 0.750 | 202.50 | 210.00 | 217.50 | 225.00 | 232.50 | 240.00 | 247.50 | 255.00 | 262.50 | 270.00 | 277.50 | 285.00 | 292.50 | 300.00 | 307.50 |
| 0.760 | 205.20 | 212.80 | 220.40 | 228.00 | 235.60 | 243.20 | 250.80 | 258.40 | 266.00 | 273.60 | 281.20 | 288.80 | 296.40 | 304.00 | 311.60 |
| 0.770 | 207.90 | 215.60 | 223.30 | 231.00 | 238.70 | 246.40 | 254.10 | 261.80 | 269.50 | 277.20 | 284.90 | 292.60 | 300.30 | 308.00 | 315.70 |
| 0.780 | 210.60 | 218.40 | 226.20 | 234.00 | 241.80 | 249.60 | 257.40 | 265.20 | 273.00 | 280.80 | 288.60 | 296.40 | 304.20 | 312.00 | 319.80 |
| 0.790 | 213.30 | 221.20 | 229.10 | 237.00 | 244.90 | 252.80 | 260.70 | 268.60 | 276.50 | 284.40 | 292.30 | 300.20 | 308.10 | 316.00 | 323.90 |
| 0.800 | 216.00 | 224.00 | 232.00 | 240.00 | 248.00 | 256.00 | 264.00 | 272.00 | 280.00 | 288.00 | 296.00 | 304.00 | 312.00 | 320.00 | 328.00 |
| 0.810 | 218.70 | 226.80 | 234.90 | 243.00 | 251.10 | 259.20 | 267.30 | 276.40 | 283.50 | 291.60 | 299.70 | 307.80 | 315.90 | 324.00 | 332.10 |
| 0.820 | 221.40 | 229.60 | 237.80 | 246.00 | 254.20 | 262.40 | 270.60 | 278.80 | 287.00 | 295.20 | 303.40 | 311.60 | 319.80 | 328.00 | 336.20 |
| 0.830 | 224.10 | 232.40 | 240.70 | 249.00 | 257.30 | 264.60 | 273.90 | 282.20 | 290.50 | 298.80 | 307.10 | 315.40 | 323.70 | 332.00 | 340.30 |
| 0.840 | 226.80 | 235.20 | 243.60 | 252.00 | 260.40 | 268.80 | 277.20 | 285.60 | 294.00 | 302.40 | 310.80 | 319.20 | 327.60 | 336.00 | 344.40 |
| 0.850 | 229.50 | 238.00 | 246.50 | 255.00 | 263.50 | 272.00 | 280.50 | 289.00 | 297.50 | 306.00 | 314.50 | 323.00 | 331.50 | 340.00 | 348.50 |
| 0.860 | 232.20 | 240.80 | 249.40 | 258.00 | 266.60 | 275.20 | 283.80 | 292.40 | 301.00 | 309.60 | 318.20 | 326.80 | 335.40 | 344.00 | 352.60 |
| 0.870 | 234.90 | 243.60 | 252.30 | 261.00 | 269.70 | 278.40 | 287.10 | 295.80 | 304.50 | 313.20 | 321.90 | 330.60 | 339.30 | 348.00 | 356.70 |
| 0.880 | 237.60 | 246.40 | 255.20 | 264.00 | 272.80 | 281.60 | 290.40 | 299.20 | 308.00 | 316.80 | 325.60 | 334.40 | 343.20 | 352.00 | 360.80 |
| 0.890 | 240.30 | 249.20 | 248.10 | 267.00 | 275.90 | 284.80 | 293.70 | 302.60 | 311.50 | 320.40 | 329.30 | 338.20 | 347.10 | 356.00 | 364.90 |
| 0.900 | 243.00 | 252.00 | 261.00 | 270.00 | 279.00 | 288.00 | 297.00 | 306.00 | 315.00 | 324.00 | 333.00 | 342.00 | 351.00 | 360.00 | 369.00 |
| 0.910 | 245.70 | 254.80 | 263.90 | 273.00 | 282.10 | 291.20 | 300.30 | 309.40 | 318.50 | 327.60 | 336.70 | 345.80 | 354.90 | 364.00 | 373.10 |
| 0.920 | 248.40 | 257.60 | 266.80 | 276.00 | 285.20 | 294.40 | 303.60 | 312.80 | 322.00 | 331.20 | 340.40 | 349.60 | 358.80 | 368.00 | 377.20 |
| 0.930 | 251.10 | 260.40 | 269.70 | 279.00 | 288.30 | 297.60 | 306.90 | 316.20 | 325.50 | 334.80 | 344.10 | 353.40 | 362.70 | 372.00 | 381.30 |
| 0.940 | 253.80 | 263.20 | 272.60 | 282.00 | 291.40 | 300.80 | 310.20 | 319.60 | 329.00 | 338.40 | 347.80 | 357.20 | 366.60 | 376.00 | 385.40 |
| 0.950 | 256.50 | 266.00 | 375.50 | 285.00 | 294.50 | 304.00 | 313.50 | 323.00 | 332.50 | 342.00 | 351.50 | 361.00 | 370.50 | 380.00 | 389.50 |
| 0.960 | 259.20 | 268.80 | 278.40 | 288.00 | 297.60 | 307.20 | 316.80 | 326.40 | 336.00 | 345.60 | 355.20 | 364.80 | 374.40 | 384.00 | 393.60 |
| 0.970 | 261.90 | 271.60 | 281.30 | 291.00 | 300.70 | 310.40 | 320.10 | 329.80 | 339.50 | 349.20 | 358.90 | 368.60 | 378.30 | 388.00 | 397.70 |
| 0.980 | 264.60 | 274.40 | 284.20 | 394.00 | 303.80 | 313.60 | 323.40 | 333.20 | 343.00 | 352.80 | 362.60 | 372.40 | 382.20 | 392.00 | 401.80 |
| 0.990 | 267.30 | 277.20 | 287.10 | 397.00 | 306.90 | 316.80 | 326.70 | 336.60 | 346.50 | 356.40 | 366.30 | 376.20 | 385.10 | 396.00 | 405.90 |
| 1.000 | 270.00 | 280.00 | 290.00 | 300.00 | 310.00 | 320.00 | 330.00 | 340.00 | 350.00 | 360.00 | 370.00 | 380.00 | 390.00 | 400.00 | 410.00 |

# CHART OF COIN SIZES BY MILLIMETERS

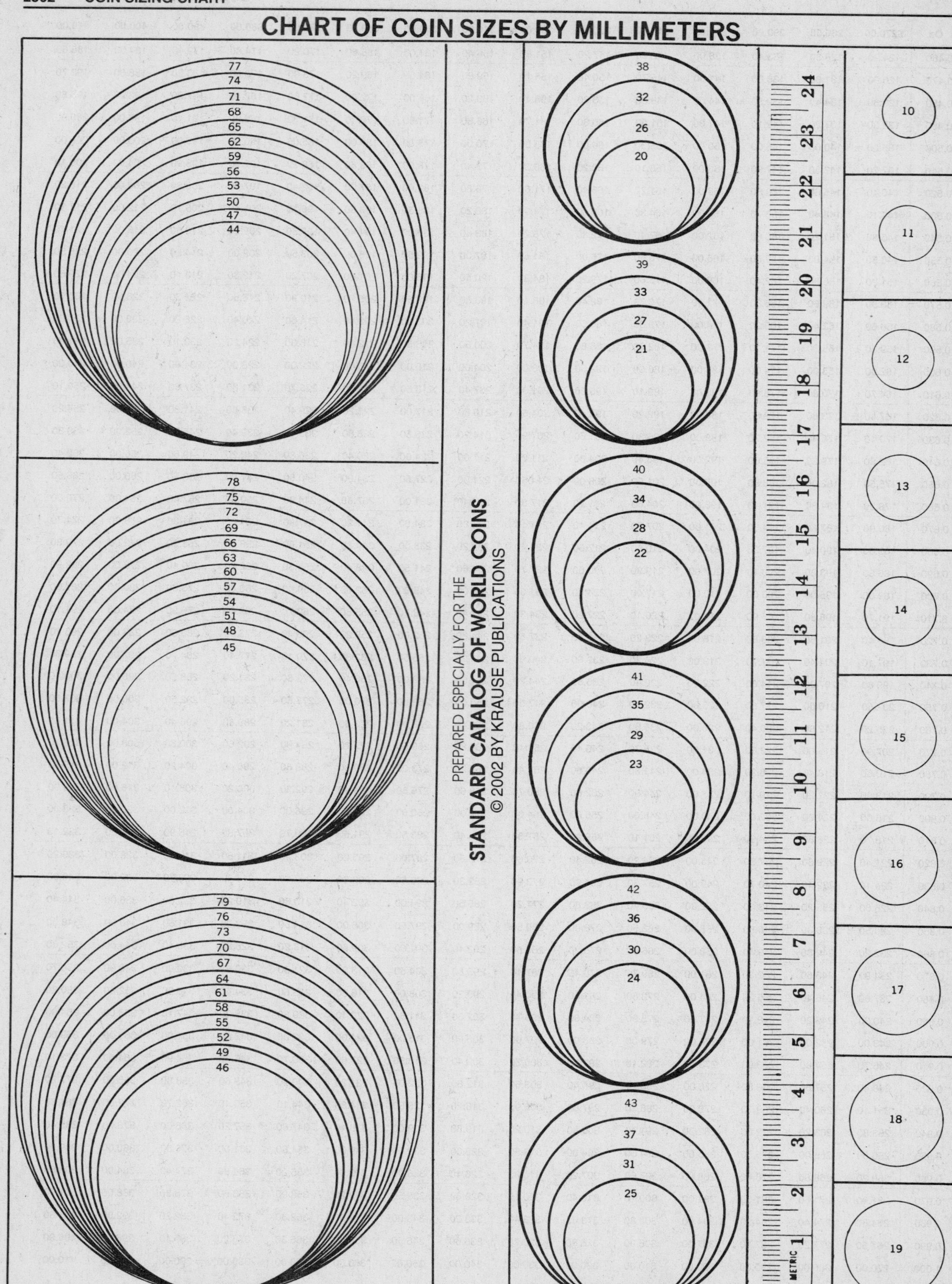

# RECORDS

# RECORDS